BENEZIT

DICTIONARY OF ARTISTS

PUBLISHER'S GUARANTEE

Whilst a great deal of care has gone into the production of this book,
it may contain a printing or manufacturing defect.
In the event of such a defect, the book will be exchanged free of charge.

Simply return the book to the place of purchase or write to us
at the following address, stating the precise nature of the defect.
Your complaint will be dealt with immediately.

Éditions Gründ - 60 Rue Mazarine - 75006 Paris - France

www.grund.fr

ISBN 2 7000 3070 2 (complete set)
ISBN 2 7000 3077 x (vol. 7)
dépôt légal mars 2006

BENEZIT

DICTIONARY OF ARTISTS

VOLUME 7
HERRING - KOORNSTRA

GRÜND
2006

NOTES ON THE AUCTION RECORDS SECTION

Never intended to be an exhaustive directory of sales, these listings provide an invaluable record of the movement in prices of an artist's work. Prices are given in the currency of the country of sale (see abbreviations below) as recorded on the date of sale.

The below tables give an indication of the current value of past sales:

- purchasing power of the US Dollar since 1913
- purchasing power of the British Pound since 1901
- purchasing power of the French Franc/Euro since 1901

CURRENCY ABBREVIATIONS (ISO 4217)

ARS	Argentinian Nuevo Peso	**HKD**	Hong Kong Dollar
ATS	Austrian Schilling	**HUF**	Hungarian Forint
AUD	Australian Dollar	**IEP**	Irish Punt
BEF	Belgian Franc	**ILS**	Israeli Shekel
BRL	Brazilian Real	**ITL**	Italian Lira
CAD	Canadian Dollar	**JPY**	Japanese Yen
CHF	Swiss Franc	**MXN**	Mexican New Peso
CZK	Czech Koruna	**NLG**	Dutch Guilder
DEM	German Mark	**NOK**	Norwegian Krone
DKK	Danish Krone	**NZD**	New Zealand Dollar
EGP	Egyptian Pound	**PLN**	Polish New Zloty
ESP	Spanish Peseta	**PTE**	Portuguese Escudo
EUR	Euro	**SEK**	Swedish Krona
FIM	Finnish Markka	**SGD**	Singapore Dollar
FRF	French Franc	**TWD**	Taiwan Dollar
GBP	British Pound	**USD**	United States Dollar
Gns	Guineas	**UYU**	Uruguayan New Peso
GRD	Greek Drachma	**ZAR**	South African Rand

PURCHASING POWER OF THE US DOLLAR SINCE 1913

1 USD in	in USD in 2002	1 USD in	in USD in 2002	1 USD in	in USD in 2002	1 USD in	in USD in 2002
2002	1.000	1978	2.755	1954	6.685	1930	10.766
2001	1.016	1977	2.966	1953	6.718	1929	10.491
2000	1.045	1976	3.160	1952	6.772	1928	10.491
1999	1.079	1975	3.344	1951	6.917	1927	10.351
1998	1.104	1974	3.649	1950	7.466	1926	10.156
1997	1.121	1973	4.049	1949	7.541	1925	10.254
1996	1.147	1972	4.300	1948	7.466	1924	10.513
1995	1.180	1971	4.435	1947	8.047	1923	10.534
1994	1.214	1970	4.629	1946	9.200	1922	10.723
1993	1.245	1969	4.903	1945	9.986	1921	10.045
1992	1.282	1968	5.167	1944	10.216	1920	8.973
1991	1.320	1967	5.383	1943	10.394	1919	10.394
1990	1.378	1966	5.540	1942	11.029	1918	11.933
1989	1.451	1965	5.694	1941	12.209	1917	14.016
1988	1.522	1964	5.791	1940	12.817	1916	16.460
1987	1.583	1963	5.872	1939	12.941	1915	17.703
1986	1.642	1962	5.942	1938	12.757	1914	17.881
1985	1.669	1961	6.007	1937	12.520	1913	18.124
1984	1.728	1960	6.067	1936	12.973		
1983	1.804	1959	6.164	1935	13.095		
1982	1.862	1958	6.218	1934	13.424		
1981	1.975	1957	6.383	1933	13.871		
1980	2.185	1956	6.615	1932	13.160		
1979	2.482	1955	6.712	1931	11.804		

source: US Bureau of Labor Statistics

PURCHASING POWER OF THE BRITISH POUND SINCE 1901

1 GBP in	in GBP in 2003	1 GBP in	in GBP in 2003	1 GBP in	in GBP in 2003	1 GBP in	in GBP in 2003
2003	1.0000	1976	4.5525	1949	22.3500	1922	35.9397
2002	1.0289	1975	5.3056	1948	22.9968	1921	30.9610
2001	1.0461	1974	6.5917	1947	24.7474	1920	28.2688
2000	1.0646	1973	7.6492	1946	26.4889	1919	32.6575
1999	1.0961	1972	8.3454	1945	27.2977	1918	35.9397
1998	1.1130	1971	8.9400	1944	28.0471	1917	43.8773
1997	1.1511	1970	9.7839	1943	28.8387	1916	55.0154
1996	1.1873	1969	10.4105	1942	29.8000	1915	65.0182
1995	1.2159	1968	10.9693	1941	31.9286	1914	72.9796
1994	1.2580	1967	11.4799	1940	35.4059	1913	72.9796
1993	1.2884	1966	11.7825	1939	41.3410	1912	72.2424
1992	1.3089	1965	12.2466	1938	42.5714	1911	74.5000
1991	1.3579	1964	12.8172	1937	43.0843	1910	74.5000
1990	1.4376	1963	13.2444	1936	44.7000	1909	75.2842
1989	1.5736	1962	13.4943	1935	44.9811	1908	76.0851
1988	1.6960	1961	14.0787	1934	45.2658	1907	76.0851
1987	1.7791	1960	14.5662	1933	45.2658	1906	76.9032
1986	1.8533	1959	14.7160	1932	44.1481	1905	76.9032
1985	1.9164	1958	14.7769	1931	43.0843	1904	76.9032
1984	2.0330	1957	15.2495	1930	41.3410	1903	76.9032
1983	2.1343	1956	15.7881	1929	40.1798	1902	77.7391
1982	2.2322	1955	16.5940	1928	39.7333	1901	77.7391
1981	2.4244	1954	17.3172	1927	39.7333		
1980	2.7122	1953	17.6593	1926	38.6595		
1979	3.2000	1952	18.1985	1925	38.4516		
1978	3.6286	1951	19.8667	1924	38.4516		
1977	3.9297	1950	21.6727	1923	38.2460		

source: British Office for National Statistics

PURCHASING POWER OF THE FRENCH FRANC SINCE 1901 (EURO SINCE 2002)

1 EUR in	in EUR in 2004
2004	1.000
2003	1.021
2002	1.042

1 FRF in	in EUR in 2004
2001	0.16199
2000	0.16468
1999	0.16747
1998	0.16830
1997	0.16947
1996	0.17156
1995	0.17494
1994	0.17796
1993	0.18093
1992	0.18469
1991	0.18907
1990	0.19513
1989	0.20170
1988	0.20899
1987	0.21461
1986	0.22136
1985	0.22724
1984	0.24049
1983	0.25830
1982	0.28315
1981	0.31661
1980	0.35906
1979	0.40772

1 FRF in	in EUR in 2004
1978	0.45158
1977	0.49252
1976	0.53866
1975	0.59046
1974	0.65993
1973	0.75053
1972	0.81968
1971	0.87012
1970	0.91952
1969	0.96747
1968	1.02990
1967	1.07638
1966	1.10572
1965	1.13551
1964	1.16382
1963	1.20384
1962	1.26156
1961	1.32228
1960	1.36597
1959	0.01415
1958	0.01503
1957	0.01729
1956	0.01781
1955	0.01856
1954	0.01874
1953	0.01882
1952	0.01850

1 FRF in	in EUR in 2004
1951	0.02070
1950	0.02406
1949	0.02647
1948	0.02996
1947	0.04755
1946	0.07093
1945	0.10826
1944	0.16078
1943	0.19643
1942	0.24388
1941	0.29331
1940	0.34453
1939	0.40570
1938	0.43410
1937	0.49330
1936	0.62015
1935	0.66785
1934	0.61141
1933	0.58663
1932	0.56377
1931	0.51679
1930	0.49330
1929	0.49897
1928	0.52939
1927	0.52939
1926	0.54950
1925	0.72351

1 FRF in	in EUR in 2004
1924	0.77519
1923	0.88593
1922	0.96468
1921	0.94370
1920	0.81906
1919	1.14238
1918	1.40033
1917	1.80877
1916	2.17052
1915	2.41169
1914	2.89403
1913	2.89403
1912	2.89403
1911	2.89403
1910	3.33926
1909	3.33926
1908	3.33926
1907	3.33926
1906	3.61753
1905	3.33926
1904	3.33926
1903	3.33926
1902	3.33926
1901	3.33926

source: INSEE

GENERAL ABBREVIATIONS

AG Art Gallery
AI Art Institute
AM Art Museum
BNF Bibliothèque nationale de France
CAPC Centre d'Arts Plastiques Contemporains
FAM Fine Art Museum
FMAC Fonds municipal d'Art contemporain
FNAC Fonds national d'Art contemporain
FRAC Fonds régional d'Art contemporain
GA Gallery of Art
Gal. Galerie, Gallery, Galleria, Galeria
GMA Gallery of Modern Art
ICA Institute of Contemporary Art
MA Museum of Art
MAA Museum of Art and Archaeology
MAC Musée d'Art Contemporain, Museo de Arte Contempóraneo, Museu de Arte Contemporânea
MAH Musée d'Art et d'Histoire
MAM Musée d'Art Moderne, Museo de Arte Moderno, Museo d'Arte Moderna
Mamco Musée d'Art moderne et contemporain
MBA Musée des Beaux-Arts, Museo de Bellas Artes, Museo di Belli Arti
MCA Museum of Contemporary Art
MDA Musée des Arts Décoratifs
MFA Museum of Fine Art
MMA Museum of Modern Art
MoCA Museum of Contemporary Art
MoMA Museum of Modern Art
Mus. Musée, Museum, Muséum, Museo, Museu, Museet
Muz. Muzeum, Muzeul, Muzej
NG National Gallery
NGA National Gallery of Art

HERRING, John Frederick (Sr.)
British, 19th century.
Born 1795, in Blackfriars; died 23 September 1865, in Tunbridge Wells.
Painter. Portraits, genre scenes, sporting subjects, horse racing scenes, animals.

John Herring was originally a carriage painter and then a coachman. He dedicated all his free time to art and took some lessons from Abraham Cooper. For many years he painted nothing but racehorses, but towards the end of his career he extended his repertoire to other subjects. His work became very popular and he worked for Queen Victoria, the Duke of Orleans and George IV. His works are highly detailed and powerfully realistic. Few artists have better understood how to depict horses.

He exhibited in London at the Royal Academy, the Suffolk Street Gallery and the British Institution from 1818 to 1865.

Museums and Galleries:

Blackburn (Mus. & AG): *Nanny* (oil on canvas); *William Ward on Horseback* (1839, oil on canvas) - Dublin: *Horse-trough* - Glasgow: *Group of Ducks; Stag Hunting* - Leeds (City AG): *A Frugal Meal* (1857, oil on canvas) - Leeds (Lotherton Hall): *A Happy Family* (oil on canvas); *'Jerry', Winner of the St Leger 1824* (oil on canvas); *Galloping Horse in a Field* (1847, oil on canvas); *Horses by a Farmyard Pond* (oil on canvas) - Leicester: *Halt* - London (Tate Collection): *The Hunting Stud* (1845, oil on canvas); *The Frugal Meal* (exhibited in 1847, oil on canvas) - Melbourne: *Horses and Pigs* - Reading: *Scene in a Farmyard* - Salford (Museum and AG): *Preparing for Market; Returning from Market.*

Auction records:

London, 18 Jan 1908, *Horses and Poultry,* GBP 23. London, 25 Jan 1908, *Farmyard,* GBP 15. London, 22 Feb 1908, *Scene in a Farmyard,* GBP 27. London, 8 May 1908, *Racehorses* (two pendants) GBP 69. London, 10 July 1908, *Farmyard* (1857) GBP 37; *Horses, Pigs and Pigeons,* GBP 52. London, 27 March 1909, *Interior of a Stable* (1850) GBP 189; *Old Pets* (1846) GBP 75. London, 4 June 1909, *Sowing,* GBP 105; *Stirrup Cup,* GBP 120. London, 24 June 1909, *Horses at the Manger* (1846) GBP 336. London, 2 July 1909, *Heads of Horses,* GBP 46. London, 23 July 1909, *Horses Drinking at a Trough, Winter,* GBP 75. London, Nov 1921, *Farm with Horses, Pigs and Cattle,* GBP 13. London, June 1922, *Drinking Trough,* GBP 69. London, May 1923, *Alarm in the Stable,* GBP 84; *Beverley Market,* GBP 105. London, Dec 1923, *After Work,* GBP 60. London, June 1924, *Farm and Outhouses,* GBP 136. London, July 1924, *The Landowner's Horses,* GBP 168. London, 25 Jan 1925, *Frugal Meal,* GBP 262. London, 3 April 1925, *Horses, Pigs and Poultry in a Farmyard,* GBP 94. London, 19 June 1925, *Interior of a Stable with Figures, Horses and Poultry,* GBP 330. London, 3 July 1925, *Fox Hunt,* GBP 525. London, 20 Nov 1925, *Whaletone in a Paddock,* GBP 378. London, 28 Jan 1926, *Series of Four Sporting Scenes,* GBP 850. London, 5 Feb 1926, *Sunday Morning,* GBP 178. London, 23 April 1926, *Midday Meal,* GBP 120. London, 13 April 1927, *Lord Cleveland's Horse Christer with Jockey up,* GBP 131. London, 27 May 1927, *Voltaire, Winner of the Doncaster* (1829) GBP 325; *Coach Horses Waiting for the Arrival of the Coach,* GBP 178. London, 8 July 1927, *Edinburgh-London Mail Coach Descending a Hill,* GBP 577. London, 15 March 1929, *Languish and Pantaloon,* GBP 157. New York, 15 Nov 1929, *Mare and Foal,* USD 370. London, 2 May 1930, *Racehorse with its Owner, Trainer and Stable Boy,* GBP 304. London, 21 June 1930, *John Mylton,* GBP 945. New York, 12 Nov 1931, *Matilda,* USD 1,500. New York, 18 April 1934, *At Bay,* USD 600. London, 23 June 1936, *Sir James Boswell's Horse Constantine,* GBP 42. London, 16 April 1937, *The Kill. Fox Hunt,* GBP 1,365. New York, 3 Feb 1938, *Officer's Horse,* USD 410. London, 31 July 1940, *At Bay,* GBP 150. Paris, 30 March 1942, *Donkey and her Foal,* FRF 4,000. London, 24 June 1942, *Derby,* GBP 60; *Galata,* GBP 150. London, 24 June 1942, *Priam Beating Augustus,* GBP 420; *St Leger,* GBP 260. London, 4 June 1943, *Christus with Jockey up,* GBP 178; *Doncaster Gold Cup,* GBP 945; *London-Edinburgh Coach,* GBP 273; *Fox Hunt,* GBP 325. London, 3 Nov 1944, *Elis in a Landscape,* GBP 46. New York, 28 Feb 1945, *Wanton Beating Theodore and Mandy,* USD 225; *Blue Bonnet,* USD 150; *Six Mile Bottom,* USD 550. London, 27 July 1945, *Baron,* GBP 52. London, 26 Oct 1945, *Farm,* GBP 189. New York, 7 Nov 1945, *Landscape,* USD 325. London, 1 Feb 1946, *Fox Hunt,* GBP 54. London, 22 Feb 1946, *Competition between Acteon and Memnon,* GBP 210. New York, 5 June 1946, *Spaniel,* USD 140; *Thoroughbred,* USD 200; *Horses and Goats in a Stable,* USD 125. New York, 19 Sept 1946, *Lost Horseshoe,* USD 900. London, 5 Feb 1947, *York-London Coach,* GBP 400; *A Litter of Rabbits Eating,* GBP 60. London, 30 May 1947, *The Prior of St Margaret's,* GBP 147; *James Hartley* (sketch) GBP 52. Leeds, 28 July 1947, *Racehorse,* GBP 84. London, 4 Dec 1957, *Steeplechase Horses,* GBP 1,100. London, 1 May 1959, *Start of the Derby,* GBP 3,255. London, 18 Nov 1960, *Flying Dutchman with Charles Marlow up,* GBP 1,732. New York, 20 Jan 1961, *Doncaster Gold Cup* (1826) USD 2,000. London, 19 April 1961, *Leamington Hunt,* GBP 2,800. London, 18 July 1962, *Emilius, a Bay Racehorse,* GBP 1,100. London, 28 June 1963, *The Doncaster Cup,* Gns 4,000. London, 20 Nov 1964, *Portrait of Three Generations of the Sorby Family of Button Hall, Sheffield,* Gns 4,500. London, 13 July 1966, *Hunters Galloping in a Landscape,* GBP 16,000. London, 22 Nov 1968, *Coaching Horses,* Gns 22,000. London, 18 June 1969, *St Gilles with Scott up,* GBP 14,500. London, 18 March 1970, *Start of the Goodwood Cup Race,* GBP 24,500. London, 10 Dec 1971, *Racehorses and Jockeys,* Gns 12,000. London, 23 June 1972, *Three Horses by a River,* Gns 13,000. London, 31 Oct 1973, *Coaching Horses Waiting for the Mail Coach,* GBP 70,000. London, 28 April 1976, *End of the Hunt* (1829, oil on canvas, 22 x 30 1/4 ins / 56 x 77 cm) GBP 12,000. London, 25 Oct 1977, *The Baron's Charger* (oil on canvas, 35 x 44 ins / 89 x 112 cm) GBP 14,000. London, 1 Oct 1979, *Blacksmith Shoeing a White Horse* (1856, oil on canvas, 33 1/2 x 43 1/4 ins / 85 x 110 cm) GBP 31,500. London, 10 July 1980, *A Close Finish* (watercolour and oil/card, 7 3/4 x 11 1/2 ins / 19.5 x 29 cm) GBP 800. London, 16 April 1982, *'Memnon' a Chestnut Racehorse with William Scott up, on Doncaster Racecourse* (1825, oil on canvas, 27 1/2 x 34 ins / 70 x 86.2 cm) GBP 80,000. London, 6 July 1983, *Jerry, a Black Racehorse with Ben Smith up* (1824, oil on canvas, 20 3/4 x 29 1/4 ins / 53 x 74 cm) GBP 41,000. London, 20 Nov 1985, *Vespa, a Bay Racehorse with its Owner Sir Mark Wood* (1833, oil on canvas, 28 x 36 ins / 71 x 91.5 cm) GBP 240,000. London, 24 April 1987, *The Earl of Chesterfield's 'Industry' and 'Caroline' with Jockeys up* (1838, oil on canvas, 27 1/2 x 35 1/2 ins / 69.8 x 90.2 cm) GBP 140,000. London, 15 July 1988, *At the Starting Post, Doncaster Gold Cup 1825* (1825, oil on canvas, 36 1/2 x 50 1/4 ins / 92.7 x 127.7 cm) GBP 440,000. Bern, 26 Oct 1988, *At the Blacksmith's* (oil on canvas, 27 1/2 x 35 3/4 ins / 70 x 91 cm) CHF 16,000. London, 18 Nov 1988, *Confidence Drawing a Cabriolet Driven by a Coachman* (1842, oil on canvas, 38 1/2 x 48 1/2 ins / 97.8 x 123.2 cm) GBP 374,000. London, 14 July 1989, *Farmyard in Winter with Horses, Pigs and Poultry in the Snowy Straw* (1847, oil on canvas, 27 1/2 x 35 1/2 ins / 69.8 x 90.2 cm) GBP 77,000. New York, 25 Oct 1989, *Waiting for the Ferryman* (1841, oil on canvas, 23 1/2 x 32 1/2 ins / 59.7 x 82.5 cm) USD 28,600. London, 15 Nov 1989, *Rustic Scene: Horses Feeding* (1846, oil on canvas, 55 x 43 ins / 140 x 109.5 cm) GBP 231,000. London, 17 Nov 1989, *Leamington Hunt (Mr Harry Bradley's Pack)* (1841, oil on canvas, 30 x 50 ins / 76.2 x 126.9 cm) GBP 660,000. New York, 1 March 1990, *Brown Bay Stallion Jack Spigot* (1824, oil on canvas, 40 x 51 ins / 101.9 x 129.5 cm) USD 143,000. London, 11 July 1990, *Three Ducks by a Pond* (1845, oil on canvas, 21 1/4 x 29 1/2 ins

/ 54 x 75 cm) GBP 15,400. London, 14 Nov 1990, *Drake Guarding Two Ducks and their Broods* (1850, oil on panel, 16 x 13 3/4 ins / 40.5 x 35 cm) GBP 15,950. London, 12 April 1991, *Industry, the Earl of Chesterfield's Filly with W. Scott up* (1838, oil on canvas, 13 1/4 x 17 1/2 ins / 33.7 x 44.5 cm) GBP 17,600. New York, 7 June 1991, *Farmyard* (oil on canvas, 48 ins / 121 cm, 3 1/2 x 78 ins/9 x 198.1 cm) USD 220,000. London, 15 Nov 1991, *Rose* (1853, oil on canvas, 50 x 40 1/4 ins / 127 x 102 cm) GBP 19,800. London, 8 April 1992, *The Stallion Pantaloon in a Meadow* (1846, oil on canvas, 28 x 36 ins / 71 x 91.5 cm) GBP 30,800. New York, 5 June 1992, *Red Fox* (1849, oil on panel, 9 x 12 ins / 22.9 x 30.5 cm) USD 16,500. Rome, 9 June 1992, *Jack Spigot on horseback* (oil on canvas, 20 1/2 x 30 1/4 ins / 52 x 77 cm) ITL 5,000,000. New York, 30 Oct 1992, *Quietude* (1848, oil on canvas, 16 x 16 ins / 40.6 x 40.6 cm) USD 8,800. London, 20 Nov 1992, *London-Edinburgh Mail Coach Descending a Slope* (1833, oil on canvas, 26 1/4 x 35 3/4 ins / 66.7 x 90.8 cm) GBP 30,800. New York, 27 May 1993, *The Baron's Charger* (oil on canvas, 35 x 44 1/4 ins / 88.9 x 112.4 cm) USD 134,500. London, 15 Dec 1993, *Duncan's Horses (Macbeth Act II)* (1842, oil on canvas, 40 1/4 x 52 ins / 102.3 x 132.3 cm) GBP 309,500. New York, 3 June 1994, *Market Day* (1858, oil on canvas, 32 x 72 ins / 81.3 x 182.9 cm) USD 162,000. Perth, 29 Aug 1995, *Cowherds' Meal* (1854, oil on canvas, 24 x 36 ins / 61 x 91.5 cm) GBP 16,100. New York, 12 April 1996, *Start of the Derby at Epsom* (1835, oil on canvas, 43 1/2 x 62 ins / 110.5 x 157.5 cm) USD 2,477,500. London, 10 July 1996, *Scene from Cannock Chase* (oil on canvas, 29 1/2 x 59 1/2 ins / 75 x 151 cm) GBP 496,500. London, 13 Nov 1996, *Mr Gascoigne's Horse Jerry with Ben Smith up at Doncaster* (1824, oil on canvas, 21 1/2 x 28 3/4 ins / 54.5 x 73 cm) GBP 82,900. New York, 26 Feb 1997, *Bay Thoroughbred by a Lake in a Landscape* (oil on canvas, 18 x 24 ins / 45.7 x 61 cm) USD 4,600. London, 9 April 1997, *Two Arab Horses with a Groom* (1851, oil on canvas, 17 1/4 x 23 1/2 ins / 44 x 59.5 cm) GBP 221,500; *Faugh-a-Ballach with its Owner, Jockey, Trainer and Stable Boy* (1844, oil on canvas, 34 x 43 ins / 86.5 x 109 cm) GBP 221,500. New York, 11 April 1997, *Start of the Derby* (1834, oil on canvas, 40 x 60 ins / 101.6 x 152.4 cm) USD 1,487,500; *Attila* (1842, oil on canvas, 13 1/2 x 17 1/2 ins / 34.3 x 44.5 cm) USD 7,475. London, 9 July 1997, *End of the Hunt* (1829, oil on canvas, 22 x 30 ins / 56 x 76 cm) GBP 89,500. London, 12 Nov 1997, *The Bay Thoroughbred Plenipotentiary in a Stable* (oil on canvas, 14 1/4 x 19 1/4 ins / 36 x 49 cm) GBP 19,550. London, 24 Nov 1999, *Mr Thomas Houldsworth's Chestnut Racehorse Vanish with Sam Darling up* (c. 1830, oil on canvas, 22 x 30 ins / 55 x 75 cm) GBP 100,000. New York, 1 Dec 1999, *John Barker of Leighton Hall, Yorkshire and John Batsby with Pointers* (1824, oil on canvas, 40 x 57 ins / 102 x 146 cm) USD 280,000. London, 26 May 2000, *Bay Racehorse with William Scott up on Doncaster Racecourse* (1825, oil on canvas, 24 x 30 ins / 60 x 76 cm) GBP 130,000. London, 26 May 2000, *Racehorse with William Scott up, Hon Edward Petre on a Bay Hack and Groom* (oil on canvas, 28 x 36 ins / 71 x 91 cm) GBP 210,000. New York, 6 June 2001, *Farmyard* (oil on canvas, 48 x 78 ins / 122 x 198 cm) USD 210,000. London, 5 Dec 2001, *Harnessed Plough-horses and Ducks in a Barn* (1848, oil on canvas, 32 x 32 ins / 81 x 81 cm) GBP 130,000. New York, 30 May 2002, *1828 Doncaster Gold Cup* (1829, oil on canvas, 30 x 48 ins / 75 x 122 cm) USD 700,000. London, 28 Aug 2002, *Halt* (1852, oil on canvas, 42 x 72 ins / 107 x 183 cm) GBP 470,000. London, 19 March 2003, *Summer* (oil on canvas, 24 x 36 ins / 61 x 91 cm) GBP 60,000. London, 25 Nov 2003, *Three Horses at a Stable Door with Pigs and Doves* (1848, oil on canvas, 31 x 31 ins / 80 x 80 cm) GBP 80,000. London, 21 May 2004, *Matilda and Mameluke: Finish of the 1827 St Leger* (1827, oil on canvas, 6 x 36 ins / 16 x 91 cm) GBP 460,000. New York, 27 May 2004, *Charles XII, Winner of the St Leger* (1839, oil on canvas, 28 x 36 ins / 71 x 91 cm) USD 270,000.

HERRING, John Frederick (Jr.)

British, 19th - 20th century.

Born 1815 or 1820, in Doncaster; died 6 March 1907, in Cambridge.

Painter. Genre scenes, hunting scenes, landscapes with figures, animals.

Fred, as he was familiarly known, Herring was the son and pupil of John Frederick Herring senior; he married the painter Kate Rolfe, the daughter of A.E. Rolfe, who was also an artist and a friend of J.F. Herring. Fred was the most talented of the three painter brothers and a prolific painter of farm scenes, skilled in both composition and light effects.

He exhibited at the Royal Academy from 1860 to 1875, the British Institution and in Suffolk Street.

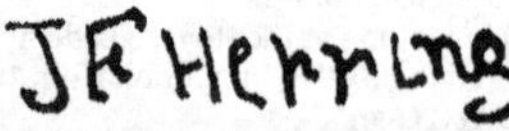

Auction records:

New York, 1 March 1945, *Fox Hunting*, USD 300. London, 28 Feb 1947, *The Race*, GBP 126. London, 15 March 1967, *Hunters and Pack at the Smithy*, GBP 1,500. London, 22 Nov 1968, *Country Scene*, Gns 1,200. London, 4 June 1970, *Stable Interior*, Gns 600. London, 19 Oct 1971, *Horses, Ducks and Pigs in a Landscape*, GBP 1,300. London, 20 June 1972, *The Farmyard*, GBP 2,900. London, 5 Oct 1973, *Country Scenes*, Gns 5,000. London, 19 Nov 1976, *The Farmyard* (oil on canvas, 29 1/2 x 49 1/2 ins / 75 x 125.7 cm) GBP 4,200. London, 29 July 1977, *Landscape with Cart and Hunters* (oil on canvas, 27 1/2 x 35 1/4 ins / 70 x 89.5 cm) GBP 4,000. New York, 25 Jan 1979, *Farm Animals* (oil on canvas, 40 x 50 ins / 101.5 x 127 cm) USD 22,000. New York, 4 June 1982, *The Meet* (oil on canvas, 27 1/4 x 36 1/4 ins / 69.2 x 92.1 cm) USD 18,000. New York, 10 June 1983, *Watering Horses in Woodland* (oil on canvas, 24 x 36 ins / 61 x 91.5 cm) USD 30,000. London, 10 July 1984, *Hunting Scenes* (watercolour heightened with white, four pieces, 7 3/4 x 11 1/2 ins / 19.5 x 29.5 cm) GBP 2,000. London, 1 Oct 1986, *The Farmyard* (oil on canvas, 24 x 36 ins / 61 x 91.5 cm) GBP 20,000. London, 11 March 1987, *The Farmyard in Winter* (oil on canvas, 28 x 36 ins / 71 x 91.5 cm) GBP 60,000. Paris, 22 June 1990, *The Halt* (oil on canvas, 12 x 18 ins / 30.6 x 46 cm) FRF 50,000. New York, 29 Oct 1992, *Sussex Farmyard* (oil on canvas, 14 1/2 x 20 1/2 ins / 37 x 52 cm) USD 4,180. London, 20 Nov 1992, *Carthorses Drinking at a Farmyard Trough* (1862, oil on canvas, 27 x 33 ins / 68.5 x 84 cm) GBP 3,080. London, 3 March 1993, *Horse, Pig and Poultry in a Farmyard* (oil on canvas, 12 x 18 ins / 30.5 x 45.5 cm) GBP 12,880. New York, 4 June 1993, *Horses and Poultry; Horses and Pigs in Winter* (oil on canvas, a pair, each 14 x 20 ins / 35.6 x 50.8 cm) USD 28,750. St Asaph, 2 June 1994, *Farm in Winter* (oil on canvas, 11 1/2 x 17 1/2 ins / 29 x 44.5 cm) GBP 16,675. Ludlow, 29 Sept 1994, *In the Farmyard* (oil on canvas, 29 1/2 x 49 1/2 ins / 75 x 126 cm) GBP 33,350. London, 2 Nov 1994, *Horses and Poultry in a Meadow* (oil on canvas, 24 x 20 ins / 61 x 51 cm) GBP 7,475. London, 29 March 1995, *Horses in a Meadow with a Stable in the Background* (1850, oil on canvas, 15 x 20 ins / 38 x 51 cm) GBP 9,775. New York, 9 June 1995, *Farm Scene* (oil on canvas, 30 x 50 ins / 76.2 x 127 cm) USD 57,500. Montreal, 5 Dec 1995, *Farmyard* (oil on canvas, 16 x 24 ins / 40.6 x 61 cm) CAD 9,750. New York, 12 April 1996, *Horses, Cattle and Pigs Pasturing by a Farm, with a River Landscape in the Background* (oil on canvas, 36 x 60 ins / 91.4 x 152.4 cm) USD 129,000. Montreal, 3 Dec 1996, *Peaceful Corner in the Old Farm* (oil on canvas, 14 1/2 x 19 3/4 ins / 37 x 50 cm) CAD 5,500. New York, 12 Dec 1996, *On the Farm* (oil on canvas, 24 x 36 ins / 61 x 91.4 cm) USD 46,000; *Teams of Horses in a Winter Landscape* (oil on canvas, 18 x 30 ins / 45.7 x 76.2 cm) USD 23,000. London, 12 March 1997, *Home from Market* (oil on canvas, 24 x 36 ins / 61 x 91.5 cm) GBP 22,425. London, 13 March 1997, *Farm*

Workers' Dinner Break (oil on canvas, 20 x 30 ins / 50.8 x 76.3 cm) GBP 13,000. LONDON, 5 Nov 1997, *In a Farmyard* (oil on canvas, 30 x 50 ins / 76 x 127 cm) GBP 41,100.

HERRING, Mabel C.
American, 19th century.
Born 19th century, in Boothlay.
Sculptor.
Mabel C. Herring was a pupil of Merson and Collin in Paris. She showed her works at the Exposition Universelle in Paris in 1900.

HERRLEIN, Andreas
German, 19th century.
Died 1817, in Laibach (now Ljubljana, Slovenia).
Painter.
Andreas Herrlein decorated the churches in the Laibach (Ljubljana) region of Slovenia.

HERRLEIN, Johann Andreas
German, 18th century.
Born 1720 or 1723, in Würzburg; died 1796, in Fulda.
Painter. Genre scenes, landscapes, fruit.
Johann Andreas Herrlein was court painter to the prince bishop of Fulda.
MUSEUMS AND GALLERIES:
BASEL: *Wooded Landscape*; *Hunters and Peasants Cooking* - FRANKFURT AM MAIN: *Evening Party*; *The Players* - KASSEL: *Fruit* - MAINZ: *Peasant Company*.
AUCTION RECORDS:
PARIS, 8 April 1919, *Portrait of M Denis (Landscape Painter)*, FRF 480. COLOGNE, 23 Nov 1977, *Bohemians in a Wooded Landscape* (oil on panel, 11¼ x 14¾ ins / 28.5 x 37.5 cm) DEM 13,000. COLOGNE, 20 May 1985, *Riverscapes with Figures* (oil/copper, a pair, 11½ x 15¼ ins / 29.5 x 38.5 cm) DEM 27,000. COLOGNE, 19 Nov 1987, *The Toilet of Venus* (1794, oil/copper, 16¼ x 22½ ins / 41 x 57 cm) DEM 10,000. MONACO, 2 Dec 1989, *Interior of an Inn* (oil/copper, 11½ x 14¼ ins / 29 x 36.5 cm) FRF 77,700. LONDON, 3 July 1991, *Still-life with Pieces of Meat and Vegetables* (oil on canvas, 20¾ x 26½ ins / 53 x 67 cm) GBP 4,400. STAUFEN, 24 Sept 1999, *Portrait of Nobleman* (oil on canvas, 32 x 26 ins / 81 x 65 cm) DEM 4,700. MUNICH, 1 Dec 1999, *Portrait of Bishop, Possibly Emmerich Josef von Breidbach-Borresheim* (1789, oil on copper, 19 x 13 ins / 48 x 34 cm) DEM 8,000. COLOGNE, 5 April 2001, *Wooded Landscape with Figures* (oil on canvas, 23 x 29 ins / 59 x 73 cm) DEM 13,000.

HERRLEIN, Johann Peter, or Hörlein
German, 18th century.
Active in Egenhausen in 1766.
Painter. Religious subjects.
Johann Peter Herrlein worked in Althausen, Sondheim v. d. Rhön and Geldersheim as well as in the churches of other towns.

HERRLIBERGER, David
Swiss, 18th century.
Born 1697, in Zurich; died 1777, in Zurich.
Engraver. Maps.
Herrliberger was a pupil of Melchior Füssli in Zurich, JD Herz in Augsburg and B Picart in Amsterdam. He engraved some plates on *Swiss Topography*.

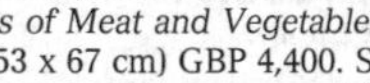

HERRLICH, Philipp
German, 19th century.
Born 25 September 1818, in Solms Laubach; died 17 September 1868.
Painter. Genre scenes.
Herrlich worked in Düsseldorf and exhibited regularly in Berlin.

HERRMANN, Alexander
German, 19th century.
Born 12 May 1814, in Glauchau; died 29 October 1845, in Rome.
Painter. Architectural views, landscapes.
Alexander Herrmann, studied in Dresden and Italy, and first exhibited in 1838. He went on to show his work in Dresden, Hamburg and Leipzig.

HERRMANN, August
German, 18th - 19th century.
Born 1752, in Offenbach; died 1816, in Munich.
Painter.
August Herrmann studied in Düsseldorf and Munich.

HERRMANN, Bernhard Johann
Austrian, 18th century.
Born in Vienna.
Engraver.
Bernard Herrmann engraved mainly religious subjects, but he also engraved some portraits.

HERRMANN, Carl Adalbert
German, 19th century.
Born 25 April 1791, in Oppeln; died 14 April 1845, in Breslau (now Wroclaw, Poland).
Painter. Historical subjects, portraits.
Carl Adalbert Herrmann studied in Italy before 1819. Although he is best known for his *Baptism of Christ*, he mainly made copies after the Italian Old Masters.

HERRMANN, Carl Gustav
German, 19th century.
Born 1857, in Leipzig.
Active in Munich.
Painter. Genre scenes.
Carl Gustav Herrmann first exhibited in Munich in 1889.
MUSEUMS AND GALLERIES:
BUCHAREST (Muz. National de Arta al României): *Still-life*.
AUCTION RECORDS:
LUCERNE, 20 May 1980, *Fisherman's Wife Spreading out the Nets* (1901, oil on card, 16¼ x 20¾ ins / 41.5 x 53 cm) CHF 2,500.

HERRMANN, Charles Henri
French, 20th century.
Born 10 May 1933, in Strasbourg.
Painter. Landscapes.
Charles Henri Herrmann studied at the École des Arts Décoratifs in Strasbourg. He won the Grand Prix in Pont-Aven in 1962. He was a landscape painter, producing at first figurative works and then evolving to Abstract Landscapism. He lived in Rissani and in Chechaouèn in Morocco around 1973, where his discovery of the Moroccan light led him to abandon figuration for a style made up of connections in sombre colours.

Herrmann exhibited in Strasbourg, Paris and Mulhouse and at the Salon d'Automne and Salon des Indépendants in Paris.
MUSEUMS AND GALLERIES:
FRIBOURG (MMA, Graphic Arts Collection).

HERRMANN, Curt
German, 19th - 20th century.
Born 1 February 1854, in Merseburg; died 13 September 1929, in Pretzfeld.
Painter, watercolourist. Portraits, figures, landscapes, still-lifes (flowers/fruit).
Herrmann was a student of Carl Steffek at the academy in Berlin and of Wilhelm von Lindenschmidt at the academy in Munich. He published a book about his theories of Neo-Impressionist painting in 1911, entitled *Der Kampf um den Stil - Probleme der modernen Malerei* (*The Struggle for Style - Problems of Modern Painting*). He exhibited in Berlin and

Munich from 1879 and at the Salon des Indépendants in Paris in 1905 and 1907.
BIBLIOGRAPHY:
Curt Herrmann, exhibition catalogue, Kunsthaus Bühler, Stuttgart, 1990.
MUSEUMS AND GALLERIES:
KASSEL (MFA): *Siesta*.
AUCTION RECORDS:
MUNICH, 31 May 1979, *Landscape* (c. 1925, oil on canvas, 10 x 13 ins / 24.5 x 33 cm) DEM 2,500. COLOGNE, 30 May 1981, *Cabbage Field* (oil on card, 11 3/4 x 16 3/4 ins / 30 x 42.5 cm) DEM 3,800. MUNICH, 6 June 1986, *Landscape with Five Poplars* (1912, oil on canvas, 15 x 18 ins / 38 x 46 cm) DEM 17,000.

HERRMANN, Frank S.
American, 19th - 20th century.
Born 1866, in New York; died 1942.
Painter. Genre scenes, landscapes.
Frank S. Herrmann exhibited in Paris in 1895.
AUCTION RECORDS:
NEW YORK, 25 April 1980, *New York City Lights* (gouache, 20 x 24 1/4 ins / 50.8 x 61.6 cm) USD 1,500. AMSTERDAM, 2 May 1990, *Workers in Bulb Field along River* (1895, oil on canvas, 22 x 36 ins / 55 x 90.5 cm) NLG 9,200. VIENNA, 10 April 2003, *At the Shoemaker's in Venice* (1892, oil on panel, 9 x 14 ins / 24 x 35 cm) EUR 2,600.

HERRMANN, Franz
German, 19th century.
Born 18 May 1864, in Gaudenz.
Painter.
Franz Herrmann studied at the Berlin academy of art.

HERRMANN, Heinrich Gustav
German, 19th century.
Born 8 June 1854, in Colditz.
Painter. Genre scenes.
Heinrich Herrmann studied at the Berlin academy of art and under Jules Schrader. He first exhibited in Berlin in 1877.

HERRMANN, Karl
German, 19th century.
Born 1813, in Koblenz; died 23 August 1881, in Mainz.
Painter. Historical scenes, genre scenes.
Karl Herrmann was a pupil at the Düsseldorf academy of art under Schadow in 1836 and Philipp Veit in 1840. He first exhibited in 1838 and went on to show his works mainly in Mainz.

HERRMANN, Léo
French, 19th century.
Born 2 July 1853, in Paris.
Painter. Figures, portraits.
Léo Herrmann exhibited genre paintings at the Paris Salon from 1875.

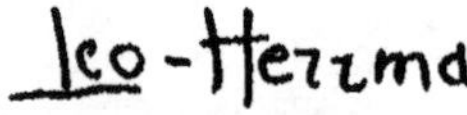

AUCTION RECORDS:
LONDON, 11 Feb 1976, *Cardinal* (oil on canvas, 11 x 8 ins / 27 x 20.5 cm) GBP 400. NEW YORK, 28 Oct 1982, *Breakfast with Le Figaro* (oil on panel, 6 x 4 1/2 ins / 15 x 11.5 cm) USD 8,500. L'ISLE-ADAM, 20 Feb 1983, *Dandy in a Red Suit* (oil on canvas, 12 1/2 x 8 3/4 ins / 32 x 22.5 cm) FRF 31,500. LONDON, 17 June 1994, *Dandy* (oil on panel, 7 3/4 x 5 3/4 ins / 19.7 x 14.6 cm) GBP 1,725.

HERRMANN, Paul
German, 19th century.
Born 4 February 1864, in Munich.
Painter, engraver.
Paul Herrmann, a friend of Paul Heyse, spent several years in Paris, during which time he signed his paintings *Henri Héran*.

HERRMANN, Philipp Ludwig
German, 19th century.
Born 15 February 1841, in Eschau; died 3 June 1894, in Frankfurt am Main.
Painter. Landscapes.
Philipp Herrmann settled in Munich, exhibiting there in 1890. He is best known for his *Environs of Munich*.
AUCTION RECORDS:
NEW YORK, 4 May 1979, *Line Fisherman in a Boat* (1880, oil on panel, 6 1/4 x 8 1/4 ins / 16 x 21 cm) USD 2,200.

HERRMANN, Robert
French, 20th century.
Born in Paris; died 1 October 2000.
Painter, draughtsman, sculptor.
Herrmann studied painting and sculpture in Paris at the École des Arts Appliqués and the École des Arts Décoratifs, and architecture at the École des Beaux-Arts. In 1946, he travelled throughout the Maghreb and was active in Algeria, Tunisia and Morocco, returning to Paris in 1947. He completed his architectural studies in 1952. In 1960, the Ministry of Culture and the City of Paris selected him as one of the people to be responsible for restoring the Marais quarter in Paris. From 1980, he was also one of the experts at UNESCO responsible for the protection and safeguarding of the ancient buildings and historic sites in the Maghreb. His work was inspired by meetings with Brayer, Marquet and Zadkine.

Herrmann took part in group exhibitions in Algiers and Tunis, and in Paris at the Salon d'Automne and UNESCO. His solo exhibitions include: Algiers and the Maghreb, from 1941; Galerie Prouvé-Schlosser, 1984; Centre Culturel Algérien, 1985 and 1991; Maison du Maroc, 1986; and Centre International de Paris Maurice Ravel.

HERRMANN-LÉON, or Hermann-Léon
French, 19th century.
Born 1814, in Lyons; died 1859.
Painter. Landscapes.
Herrmann-Léon was also an opera singer.

HERRMANN-LÉON, Charles
French, 19th century.
Born 22 July 1838, in Le Havre; died 1 January 1908, in Paris.
Painter. Genre scenes, hunting scenes (hunting with hounds), landscapes with figures, still-lifes, animals.
Charles Herrmann-Léon appears to be unrelated to Charles Léon. He studied under Eugène Fromentin and Philippe Rousseau and made his debut at the Paris Salon in 1861. He exhibited at the Société des Artistes Français from 1861 to 1908, and exhibited in Munich in 1879 and in Vienna in 1894. He was awarded a third-class medal in 1873, a second-class medal in 1879 and a silver medal in 1900 at the Exposition Universelle. He was made a member of the Légion d'Honneur in 1897.

Herrmann-Léon started off painting still-lifes and landscapes and then became specialised in hunting scenes and, particularly, hunting with hounds.
MUSEUMS AND GALLERIES:
AMIENS: *Dog from the Vendée* - LE HAVRE: *Wolf!* - PÉRIGUEUX: *St Hubert's Mass*.
AUCTION RECORDS:
PARIS, 26-27 March 1869, *Hunting Dogs*, FRF 160. LONDON, 29 June 1908, *Dandy*, GBP 32. LONDON, 27 May 1910, *Hunter and Dogs*, GBP 9. GRENOBLE, 26 April 1976, *Horses* (oil on canvas, 15 x 18 ins / 38 x 46 cm) FRF 2,100. VERSAILLES, 18 Feb 1979, *Hunting with Hounds* (oil on canvas, 46 x 35 ins / 116 x 89 cm) FRF 15,200. VERSAILLES, 18 Feb 1979, *Hunting*

with Hounds (1906, oil on canvas, 46 x 35 ins / 116 x 89 cm) FRF 15,200. COLOGNE, 23 Oct 1981, *View of Amsterdam* (watercolour, 12¼ x 7¾ ins / 31 x 19.5 cm) DEM 4,200. NEW YORK, 29 Oct 1986, *Fool Surrounded by Three Masked Dogs* (1869, oil on canvas, 27¼ x 32 ins / 69.2 x 81.2 cm) USD 7,000. STOCKHOLM, 15 Nov 1988, *Hilly Landscape with Two Hunting Dogs* (oil on canvas, 18 x 24½ ins / 46 x 62 cm) SEK 14,500. PARIS, 14 Dec 1990, *Portrait of Dogs* (oil on canvas, 24½ x 20 ins / 62 x 50.5 cm) FRF 42,000. PARIS, 25 March 1991, *Terrier* (1861, oil on canvas, 18 x 14¾ ins / 45.5 x 37.5 cm) FRF 6,000. PARIS, 24 April 2002, *Chien Mik* (oil on canvas, 22 x 18 ins / 56 x 46 cm) EUR 2,800.

HERRMANS, H.
German, 19th - 20th century.
Active in Düsseldorf.
Painter, watercolourist. Genre scenes.

Herrmans obtained a bronze medal in 1900 at the Exposition Universelle in Paris.

HERRMANSTÖRFER, Joseph
German, 19th century.
Born 2 February 1817, in Nuremberg; died 22 October 1901, in Munich.
Painter. Genre scenes, landscapes, animals.

Herrmanstörfer, a pupil of Reindel at the Nuremberg school of art, went on to study at the Munich academy of art from 1842. He exhibited in Munich, Bremen, Hanover and London where he was awarded a medal in 1874.

AUCTION RECORDS:
LONDON, 15 June 1979, *Horse Riders in a River Landscape* (1899, oil on panel, 11½ x 20¼ ins / 29.2 x 51.3 cm) GBP 1,200. NEW YORK, 18 June 1982, *Am roten Löwen* (*At the Red Lion*) (1850, oil on canvas, 18½ x 23 ins / 47 x 58.5 cm) USD 3,500.

HERRY, Antoon
Flemish School, 18th century.
Active in Antwerp.
Painter. History painting.

HERRY, Brigitte
French, 20th - 21st century.
Born 27 December 1956, in Sydney.
Painter. Figures, scenes with figures.
Symbolism.

Herry is a self-taught artist; originally a teacher, she concentrated on painting from 1997. She explores themes of life and death and of human and divine relationships in her painting, giving a poetic image of humanity. Her backgrounds are decorative and her figures stylised. She has taken part in collective exhibitions, including: Salon des Indépendants, Paris, 1991; Galerie Everarts, Paris, and 8th Salon d'Été in Mantes-La-Jolie, 1992; Salon du Lyons Club and Château de Plaisir, Yvelines, 1993 and 1994; and the 43rd Salon International d'Art Plastique, Béziers, and Femin'Arts, Pouzolles, 1999.

HERRY, Jean François
French, 18th century.
Active in Paris in 1755.
Painter, sculptor.

HERRY, Rudolf
Swiss, 15th century.
Born in Basel.
Painter.

Rudolf Herry worked for the Solothurn town hall in 1500.

HERSAN, Claude Louis
French, 18th century.
Active in Nantes in 1770.
Painter.

HERSANT, Claude Louis
French, 18th century.
Active in Paris in 1743.
Painter, sculptor.

HERSANT, Louis Étienne
French, 18th century.
Active in Paris in 1772.
Painter, sculptor.

HERSBACH, Hans
German, 16th century.
Active in Cologne.
Painter, draughtsman.

HERSBERGER, Lori
Swiss, 20th - 21st century.
Born 1964, in Basel.
Installation artist, painter.

Hersberger lives in Basel and Zurich. Before devoting himself to the three-dimensional arts after 1990, he was a musician in various groups. From 1991 to 1993 he trained in audiovisual production and sculpture at the Schule für Gestaltung, Basel. Associated with the creation of installations consisting of old, coloured carpets, Hersberger is also a painter. His paintings are inspired by pop and the aesthetics of kitsch, mainly through his use of fluorescent colours, but his style verges on Abstract Expressionism. He creates plays of light on walls, the ground or in mirrors in order to extend the edges of the canvas.

He has participated in group exhibitions, including 1998, *Nonchalance Revisited*, at the art academy, Berlin; 1999, *Apertutto* (*Aperto Over All*), the Venice Biennale. He has held solo shows, the first of which was at the Kleinen Helmhaus, Zurich in 1997, then: 2000, as a consequence of the Prix Manor, Basel; 2001, *Day-glo Blues Conspiracy*, the Museum für Gegenwartskunst (contemporary art), Basel; 2003, the Kunsthaus, Zurich.

BIBLIOGRAPHY:
Lori Hersberger: Day-glo Blues Conspiracy, exhibition catalogue, Museum für Gegenwartskunst, Fondation Emanuel Hoffman, Basel, 2001.

HERSCH, Gotthilf Friedrich. See **HENSCH**

HERSCH, Lee
American, 20th century.
Born 1896, in Cleveland (Ohio); died 1953, in Madrid.
Painter.

Lee Hersch studied at the Cleveland School of Art and the National Academy of Design, New York. In 1918 he went to France with the American Expeditionary Force. After 1943 his painting became abstract, and he later became part of the Tachist movement.

Hersche took part in group exhibitions in the USA, notably in the New York museums, and in France, at the Salon des Réalités Nouvelles in Paris, which devoted a room to his work in 1953. He also had many solo shows in the USA.

AUCTION RECORDS:
NEW YORK, 5 April 1984, *Indian Woman on a White Horse; Two Taos Indian Women* (1920, oil on canvas, a pair, 72 x 37 ins / 183 x 94 cm) USD 4,200. SAN FRANCISCO, 17 June 1999, *Everyday New Mexico* (1918, oil on canvas, 40 x 50 ins / 102 x 127 cm) USD 5,500.

HERSCHEL, Otto
German, 20th century.
Born 31 December 1871, in Teplitz-Schönau (now Teplice, Czech Republic); died 1937.
Painter.

Otto Herschel exhibited in Berlin, Vienna, Munich and Venice.

AUCTION RECORDS:
NEW YORK, 25 June 1985, *Rabbi Studying* (oil on canvas, 19¼ x 15¼ ins / 48.9 x 38.7 cm) USD 2,000. VIENNA, 6 March

2001, *Village in Winter* (1930, oil on canvas, 25 x 28 ins / 63 x 72 cm) ATS 30,000.

HERSCHEND, Oscar
Danish, 19th century.
Born 6 January 1853; died 26 January 1891.
Painter. Landscapes.

Oscar Herschend was a pupil at the Kunstakademi in Copenhagen.

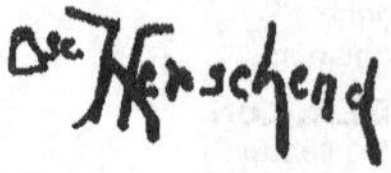

AUCTION RECORDS:
COPENHAGEN, 5 April 1989, *Promenade in a Snow-covered Landscape* (1883, oil on canvas, 11 3/4 x 18 ins / 30 x 46 cm) DKK 4,500. COPENHAGEN, 25 Oct 1989, *Trees Bent by the Wind in Autumn Landscape* (1884, oil on canvas, 15 3/4 x 23 1/2 ins / 40 x 60 cm) DKK 4,000. COPENHAGEN, 21 Feb 1990, *Road in a Fishing Village* (1881, oil on canvas, 11 1/2 x 16 1/4 ins / 29 x 41 cm) DKK 4,400. COPENHAGEN, 2 Feb 1994, *Landscape with Dunes* (1885, oil on canvas, 9 1/2 x 16 1/2 ins / 24 x 42 cm) DKK 5,000. COPENHAGEN, 5 March 2001, *Fishing Boats Going Out* (1887, oil on canvas, 26 x 44 ins / 66 x 111 cm) DKK 12,000. COPENHAGEN, 9 Dec 2003, *The Lifeboat Going Out* (1889, oil on canvas, 20 x 33 ins / 50 x 84 cm) DKK 11,000.

HERSCHER, Ernest Marie
French, 20th century.
Born 20 June 1870, in Paris.
Pastellist, engraver, lithographer, designer. Urban landscapes. Designs for tapestries, designs for stained glass.

Herscher was a member of the Société des Peintres-Graveurs and was on the committee for engraving and decoration at the Salon d'Automne in Paris. He was also an architect. He produced designs for tapestries and stained glass windows and engravings to illustrate *Souvenirs du Paris d'Hier* and *Quelques Images de la Guerre*. Paul Valéry wrote an introduction to a collection of Herscher's lithographs.

MUSEUMS AND GALLERIES:
PARIS (Mus. Carnavalet): *Pont Neuf Seen from Quai des Grands-Augustins.*

HERSCHI, Franz
Swiss, 18th century.
Active in Crostwitz (Lausitz) c. 1700.
Painter.

HERSE, Louise
French, 18th century.
Active in Paris in 1749.
Painter.

HERSECKE, Frans van
Flemish School, 17th - 18th century.
Active in Ghent.
Painter.

HERSECKE, Johannes Baptist van
Flemish School, 17th century.
Painter.

He painted the landscapes in the *Life of St Bernard* by J. van Cleef in the abbey of Baudelo in Ghent.

HERSECKE, Piet Johannis van
Flemish School, 18th century.
Active in Ghent c. 1720.
Painter.

HERSELLE, Adriaen, or Herzeele
Flemish, 15th century.
Active in Bruges in 1468.
Painter.
Flemish School.

HERSEN, Dora
Venezuelan, 20th century.
Born 1924.
Painter.

Dora Hersen studied at the school of plastic and applied arts in Caracas and took part in numerous collective exhibitions. She was awarded a gold medal at the Autumn Exhibition of the Venezuelan-British Institute in 1947 and the José Lorento Arismendi prize at the 9th Venezuelan Art Exhibition in 1948.

HERSENT, Alexandre
French, 19th century.
Born 25 December 1781, in Paris.
Sculptor.

HERSENT, François Étienne
French, 19th century.
Born 9 April 1823, in Paris; died 1880, in Fontaines-Plain-Pied.
Painter. Military subjects.

François Étienne Hersent studied under Couture and exhibited military subjects at the Paris Salon between 1857 and 1868.

MUSEUMS AND GALLERIES:
VERSAILLES (Mus.): *The 5th Zouave Regiment and the 50th Line Regiment Seizing the Mamelon-Vert Fortress.*

HERSENT, Louis
French, 18th - 19th century.
Born 10 March 1777, in Paris; died 2 October 1860, in Paris.
Painter, lithographer. History painting, mythological subjects, portraits, genre scenes.

Louis Hersent studied under Baron Regnault and came second in the Prix de Rome in 1797 with *Death of Cato of Utica*, but his health prevented him from continuing his studies. He exhibited at the Paris Salon from 1802 to 1831 and became a member of the Institut de France in 1822, then professor at the École des Beaux-Arts in Paris in 1825. He was made a member of the Légion d'Honneur in 1819 and promoted to captain in 1824.

Hersent is known for his lithographs, notably his plates for *Voyage dans le Levant* (*Travels in the Levant*) by the Count of Forbin, various subjects drawn from the tales of La Fontaine, *Theocritus*, *Bathers*, and portraits.

MUSEUMS AND GALLERIES:
ANGERS: *Prophet Elysium Raising the Son of Sarephta* - ARRAS: *Narcissus Gazing at Himself in the Water* - AURILLAC: *Portrait of Dr Civiale* - CHANTILLY: *Portrait of Queen Marie-Amélie* - COMPIÈGNE (Mus. national du Château): *The Queen with the Dukes of Aumale and Montpensier* - DIEPPE: *Portrait of Louis-Philippe* - MULHOUSE: *Portrait of an Unknown Man* - NICE: *Masséna* - RUEIL-MALMAISON (Mus. national des châteaux de Malmaison et Bois-Préau): *Fénélon Bringing his Cow to a Peasant* - SENS: *Diana and Endymion; The Graces Visiting a Sleeping Daphnis* - VERSAILLES: *Capture of Landshut; Louis XVI Distributing Alms to the Poor during the Winter of 1788; Duke of Bordeaux and his Sister* - VERSAILLES (Mus. Lambinet): *Portrait of Henry IV.*

AUCTION RECORDS:
PARIS, 10-11 May 1897, *Portrait of the Countess of Rougé*, FRF 190. PARIS, 16-18 March 1898, *Daphnis and Chloe*, FRF 4,240. PARIS, 12 April 1972, *Woman Bathing* (1830, oil on canvas, 59 x 67 ins / 150 x 170 cm) FRF 5,000. LONDON, 5 July 1978, *Portrait of Madame Le Doyen* (1825, oil on canvas, 25 1/2 x 21 1/4 ins / 65 x 54 cm) GBP 1,500. COLOGNE, 12 June 1980, *Portrait of Madame Le Doyen* (1825, oil on canvas, 25 1/2 x 21 1/4 ins / 65 x 54 cm) DEM 6,000. PARIS, 11 Dec 1987,

Charles Bélanger as a Child (oil on canvas, 13 x 10 ins / 33 x 24.5 cm) FRF 6,000. PARIS, 9 July 1992, *Portrait of a Young Woman* (oil on canvas, 25 1/2 x 21 1/2 ins / 65 x 54.5 cm) FRF 62,000. PARIS, 11 Dec 1992, *Daphnis and Chloe* (1817, oil on canvas, 43 3/4 x 35 1/2 ins / 111 x 90 cm) FRF 21,000. NEW YORK, 26 May 1994, *Women Bathing* (1830, oil on canvas, 51 1/2 x 56 ins / 130.8 x 142.2 cm) USD 40,250. PARIS, 30 Nov 1994, *Ottoman Warriors* (oil on canvas, 67 1/4 x 83 1/2 ins / 171 x 212 cm) FRF 135,000. NEW YORK, 23 May 1997, *Daphis and Chloe: The Flute Lesson* (1841, oil on canvas, 24 x 28 3/4 ins / 61 x 73 cm) USD 14,950. PARIS, 5 Feb 1998, *Bust of a Seated Woman* (oil on canvas, 33 x 27 1/4 ins / 84 x 69 cm) FRF 14,000. PARIS, 13 Dec 2000, *Head and Shoulders Portrait, presumed to be of Mme Le Doyen, seen from the front* (1825, oil on canvas, 26 x 22 ins / 65 x 55 cm) FRF 48,000. LONDON, 14 Dec 2000, *Ulysses recognised by his Nurse* (oil on canvas, 13 x 16 ins / 32 x 40 cm) GBP 1,500.

HERSENT, Louise Marie Jeanne
Maiden name: Mauduit
French, 19th century.
Born 7 March 1784, in Paris; died 7 January 1862, in Paris.
Painter. History painting, portraits.

Hersent was a pupil of both Meynier and of her husband, Louis Hersent. She exhibited at the Salon from 1810 to 1824, obtaining first-class medals in 1817 and 1819. Tardieu engraved several of her works.

MUSEUMS AND GALLERIES:
DIEPPE: *La Bonne Mère* - VERSAILLES: *Louis XV Visiting Pierre Legrand at the Hôtel de Lesdiguières.*

HERSHMAN, Lynn, or Hershman Leeson
American, 20th - 21st century.
Born 1941, in Cleveland (Ohio).
Photographer, video artist, digital artist, performance artist.

Lynn Hershman studied at the Case Western Reserve University, graduating with a BA in Education, Museum Administration and Fine Arts in 1963. In 1972 she obtained a Master's degree in Fine Art from San Francisco State University. In the 1970s Hershman created a series of pseudonyms, including the art critics invented for her Master's dissertation, *Prudence Juris, Herbert Goode and Gay Abandon*. Her *Self-portrait as Another Person* (1972), and the fictional character Roberta Breitmore (a series which continued throughout the 1970s and finished in 1978) are examples of Hershman's preoccupation with issues such as identity, reality and gender. Hershman is credited with being the first creator of an interactive laserdisc artwork, *Lorna* (1979-1983). In 1986 she produced a series of prints in black and white showing a woman in black heels and a black dress posing on a white bed and who, instead of a face, has a camera (*Phantom Limb #3*) or a photograph of a face (*Phantom Limb #2*). Hershman developed her interactive work throughout the 1990s, producing *Room of One's Own* (1990-1993) and *America's Finest* (1993-1995). In 1995 she also received a commission from the Seattle Art Museum that lead to the creation of *Paranoid Mirror* (1995-1996).

Hershman experiments with works incorporating the Internet, such as *Difference Engine #3* (1998). In 2002, she produced a film *Teknolust* in which the actress Tilda Swinton plays all four main characters. 2005 saw the first major survey of Hershman's work, *Hershmanlandia: The Art and Films of Lynn Hershman Leeson* at the Henry Art Gallery in Seattle. Hershman has received several awards and recognitions for her work including the Crystal Trophy (1990), the Annie Gerber Award (1996), the Flintridge Foundation Prize (1998), the Cyberstar Award, and the Siemens/ZKM Media Arts Award.

BIBLIOGRAPHY:
Hershmann Leeson, Lynn/Rotzer, Florian/Reneau, Don, *Lyn Hershman: Paranoid Mirror*, Seattle Art Museum, 1995. Leeson, Lynn Hershman, *Clicking in: Hot Links to a Digital Culture*, Bay Press, 1996. Grosenick, Uta, *Women Artists in the 20th and 21st Century*, Taschen, Cologne, 2001.

MUSEUMS AND GALLERIES:
KARLSRUHE (Zentrum für Kunst und Medientechnologie) - MINNEAPOLIS (Walker Art Center) - NEW YORK (MoMA) - OTTAWA (Nat. Gal. of Canada).

HERSON, Émile Antoine François
French, 19th century.
Born 1805, in Paris.
Active in Paris.
Painter, watercolourist, lithographer. Landscapes.
Barbizon School.

Émile Herson was a pupil of Diaz. He first exhibited at the Salon in 1836, showing two watercolours: *View of the Church of St-Médard, in Paris* and *Entrance to the Church of Pierrefonds*. Herson travelled around Normandy, Brittany and the Pyrenées, producing oil paintings, watercolours and lithographs of the religious monuments he saw along the way. He later moved on to painting views of Paris and, in around 1868, took Barbizon and the Forest of Fontainebleau as subjects for many of his paintings. His name appears in the archives for the last time in the catalogue of the 1872 Salon, at which he exhibited two works: *Small Market Square at Vitré (Ille-et-Vilaine)* and *View from Veules (Seine-Maritime)*.

AUCTION RECORDS:
PARIS, 20 and 21 April 1904, *A Street in Vitré*, FRF 205. LONDON, 4 June 1908, *View from Barbizon*, s 15. PARIS, 31 March 1924, *Interior of the Church of St-Séverin* (watercolour) FRF 480. PARIS, 29 June 1927, *Nogent-le-Roi*, FRF 1,600; *Mass in the Church of Nogent-le-Roi*, FRF 1,400. PARIS, 24 March 1947, *People at the Fountain* (1836, watercolour) FRF 650.

HERSON, Simon François
French, 18th century.
Born 1745, in Palaiseau.
Active in Angers between 1778 and 1785.
Sculptor.

HERST, Auguste Clément Joseph
French, 19th century.
Born 28 August 1825, in Rocroy (Ardennes).
Painter, watercolourist. Landscapes, rustic scenes, seascapes, animals, farmyard scenes.

Herst made his début at the Salon of 1861, and continued to participate regularly in the exhibitions held in Paris. In succession, he painted views of landscapes in Boulogne-sur-Mer, Marseilles, La Grande Chartreuse (near Grenoble), Fontainebleau, Savoy and Normandy. He also visited Switzerland, Holland and Algeria.

MUSEUMS AND GALLERIES:
AURILLAC: *The Private Park at St-Cloud* - CHARTRES: *Interior of a Farmyard* - LA ROCHELLE: two watercolours - PARIS (Louvre): *Solitude; Fog Effect.*

AUCTION RECORDS:
PARIS, 14 Nov 1924, *Cows Grazing*, FRF 620. PARIS, 31 March 1943, *Farm Courtyard*, FRF 1,800; *Landscape*, FRF 3,500. CALAIS, 14 March 1999, *Flower Market* (oil on panel, 3 x 7 ins / 8 x 17 cm) FRF 44,000. NEW YORK, 15 Dec 2000, *Park in Bloom* (oil on panel, 13 x 25 ins / 34 x 63 cm) USD 6,000.

HERSTALLE, Balduin de
Flemish School, 18th century.
Engraver.

HERSTEIN, Adolf Eduard
Polish, 19th century.
Born 1869, in Warsaw.

Active mainly in Berlin.
Painter, engraver.

HERTA LEBK, Hélène
German, 20th century.
Born 1934, in Elbing (now Elblag, Poland).
Active in France from 1957.
Painter.

Herta Lebk lived in Turkey from 1954 to 1957. She then settled in Paris, where she met Claude Bellan. She has exhibited in the Salon de la Jeune Peinture in 1963; the Salon d'Automne (of which she is a member) from 1972; in Saarbrücken in 1978 and Bilbao in 1979. She has shown her works in solo exhibitions since 1963 at the Fleuve gallery in Bordeaux and since 1976 in Paris.

HERTEBOUT, Henri. See **ERTEBOUT**

HERTEL
German, 17th century.
Active in Torgau in 1661.
Painter.

HERTEL, Albert
German, 19th - 20th century.
Born 19 April 1843, in Berlin; died 9 December 1912, in Berlin.
Painter. Religious subjects, figures, landscapes.

Hertel was a student at the academy in Berlin and then from 1863 to 1867 a student of Franz-Dreber in Rome. From 1875 to 1877, he was a professor of landscape at the Berlin academy. He received a medal in Munich and Vienna and an honourable mention in Berlin in 1886. He received a diploma in Dresden in 1887 and exhibited in the Exposition Universelle in Paris in 1900.

MUSEUMS AND GALLERIES:
BERLIN: *Coast near Genoa; Young Girls from Capri* - MAINZ: *Landscape* - WROCLAW: *Rest During the Flight to Egypt.*

AUCTION RECORDS:
COLOGNE, 24 March 1972, *Spring Landscape,* DEM 8,000. HEIDELBERG, 9 Oct 1992, *Rocky Coast with Capri in the Background* (1865, oil on canvas, 9 1/4 x 14 3/4 ins / 23.5 x 37.5 cm) DEM 2,550.

HERTEL, Carl Konrad Julius
German, 19th century.
Born 17 October 1837, in Breslau (now Wroclaw, Poland); died 10 October 1895, in Düsseldorf.
Painter. Genre scenes.

Carl Hertel, a pupil of Wilhelm Sohn at the Düsseldorf academy of art, travelled in Germany, the Netherlands and Belgium. He exhibited first in Berlin in 1861 and then in Dresden and Vienna.

MUSEUMS AND GALLERIES:
BERLIN: *Young Germany at School* - LEIPZIG: *The Convalescent; Young Germany.*

AUCTION RECORDS:
LONDON, 24 Nov 1926, *Cottage Interior with Two Young Boys,* GBP 27. MUNICH, 31 May 1990, *Music Disrupting the Fine Arts* (1869, oil on canvas, 26 3/4 x 20 3/4 ins / 68 x 53 cm) DEM 8,800. NEW YORK, 19 Jan 1995, *Mother and Child* (1869, oil on canvas, 26 1/2 x 20 3/4 ins / 67.3 x 52.7 cm) USD 3,450. MUNICH, 1 Dec 1999, *Peasant Woman with Dog at Well in Forest Landscape* (oil on canvas, 21 x 18 ins / 54 x 45 cm) DEM 4,400. STUTTGART, 21 June 2001, *Young Mother with Child Sitting on Steps* (1893, oil on canvas, 43 x 52 ins / 108 x 133 cm) DEM 4,000. COLOGNE, 1 July 2004, *At the Fountain in Kaiserswerth* (oil on canvas, 25 x 31 ins / 63 x 80 cm) EUR 3,800.

HERTEL, Georg Leopold
German, 18th century.
Active in Augsburg at the end of the 18th century.
Engraver.

Georg Hertel, a son of Johann Georg Hertel the Elder, made engravings after Rembrandt, Castiglione, Mazotto and Boucher.

HERTEL, Johann Georg, the Elder
German, 18th century.
Active in Augsburg.
Engraver.

HERTEL, Johann Georg, the Younger
German, 18th century.
Born 18th century, in Augsburg.
Engraver.

Johann Georg Hertel the Younger, brother of Georg Leopold Hertel, made engravings after Oudry, Boucher and Rembrandt.

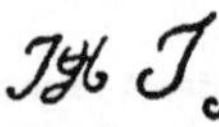

HERTEL, Karl
German, 19th century.
Born 12 August 1843, in Cologne.
Glass painter.

Karl Hertel, a pupil of Janssen, worked in Germany, America, Africa and Asia.

HERTENBERGER, Fernand
French, 20th century.
Born 10 April 1882, in Rheims; died 28 August 1970, in St-Benoit-du-Salut (Indre).
Painter, illustrator.

Fernand Hertenberger was a pupil of Tony Robert-Fleury and Déchenaud. He exhibited at the Salon des Artistes Français in Paris. He illustrated *Là-bas* (*Down There*) by Huysmans and *Colonel Chabert* by Balzac.

HERTENSTEIN, Georg
German, 16th century.
Active in Nuremberg.
Painter.

HERTER, Adele
American, 20th century.
Born 27 February 1869, in New York; died 1946.
Painter.

Adele Herter studied under Bouguereau and Robert-Fleury and was a member of the American Federation of Arts. She received an honourable mention in Buffalo in 1901 and a bronze medal in St Louis in 1904. She was married to the painter Albert Herter.

AUCTION RECORDS:
NEW YORK, 4 April 1984, *Vase of Roses* (oil on card, 16 x 12 ins / 40.5 x 30.5 cm) USD 1,500. NEW YORK, 26 May 1999, *Floral Still-life with Asian Statues* (oil on canvas, 20 x 15 ins / 51 x 38 cm) USD 1,700. NEW YORK, 5 March 2003, *Allium and Queen Anne's Lace* (oil on canvas, 18 x 12 ins / 46 x 30 cm) USD 14,000.

HERTER, Albert
American, 20th century.
Born 2 March 1871, in New York; died 1950.
Painter, watercolourist. Genre scenes. Murals, designs for tapestries.

Herter studied in Paris under Fernand Cormon and Jean-Paul Laurens. Herter specialised in designs for wallpapers and fabrics, and also painted murals, notably at the Metropolitan Museum of Art, New York. He was married to Adele Herter.

Herter exhibited several times at the Salon des Artistes Français in Paris, receiving an honourable mention in 1890.

He also won a bronze medal at the Exposition Universelle in Paris in 1900 and a silver medal in Buffalo in 1901.

AUCTION RECORDS:

NEW YORK, 30 Jan 1980, *Flight of Cinderella* (1894, watercolour/mounted paper/card, 20¼ x 39 ins / 51.4 x 99 cm) USD 4,000. NEW YORK, 2 June 1982, *Ruth St Denis as Kwannon; Ted Shawn in his Indian Eagle Dance* (two oils on canvas, 90¼ x 42¼ ins / 229 x 107 cm) USD 5,500. NEW YORK, 6 Dec 1985, *Lovers' Conversation* (watercolour and pen, 19½ x 14¼ ins / 49.5 x 36.5 cm) USD 6,000. NEW YORK, 30 Sept 1988, *Eastern Blossoms* (1894, watercolour/card, 10 x 13¾ ins / 25.2 x 35.2 cm) USD 4,400. NEW YORK, 24 May 1990, *Just a Song at Twilight* (1908, oil on canvas, 28 x 36 ins / 71.1 x 91.4 cm) USD 57,750. MONACO, 16 June 1990, *Girl in a Kimono* (oil on canvas, 21½ x 19¾ ins / 54.5 x 50 cm) FRF 55,500. NEW YORK, 6 Dec 1991, *Study for a Mural: the Greek Philosophers* (oil and pencil/canvas, 26½ x 98½ ins / 67 x 250 cm) USD 15,400. NEW YORK, 23 Sept 1992, *Beatrice* (oil on canvas, 24 x 20 ins / 61 x 50.8 cm) USD 1,650. NEW YORK, 10 March 1993, *Two Women on Stairs* (watercolour/paper, 15 x 8½ ins / 38.1 x 21.6 cm) USD 11,500. NEW YORK, 27 May 1993, *Portrait of a Young Woman in a Kimono* (1894, oil on canvas, 22 x 20 ins / 55.9 x 50.8 cm) USD 14,950. NEW YORK, 20 March 1996, *Still-life with Flowers* (oil on canvas, 31 x 25 ins / 78.7 x 63.5 cm) USD 4,887. NEW YORK, 1 Dec 1999, *Where Love Abides* (oil on canvas, 24 x 36 ins / 61 x 91 cm) USD 24,000. WASHINGTON, 11 Dec 1999, *Portrait of Editha Macy Lewis* (oil on board, 20 x 14 ins / 51 x 36 cm) USD 4,500. CLEVELAND, 16 Nov 2000, *Amor Rex* (1897, watercolour, 7 x 11 ins / 18 x 28 cm) USD 3,150. LOS ANGELES, 13 Dec 2000, *Judgement of Paris* (oil and pencil on canvasboard, 20 x 14 ins / 51 x 36 cm) USD 4,000. CLEVELAND, 18 June 2001, *Two Ladies in Reverie* (1890, watercolour, 9 x 7 ins / 23 x 18 cm) USD 3,000. PASADENA, 12 Feb 2002, *Circe* (1890, watercolour, 14 x 8 ins / 36 x 20 cm) USD 1,900. MILFORD, 25 April 2002, *Innocence* (1892, Pencil and gouache, 9 x 17 ins / 23 x 43 cm) USD 5,000. PASADENA, 17 June 2003, *Evening Walk* (watercolour and gouache on board, 20 x 16 ins / 51 x 41 cm) USD 5,500. BOSTON, 21 Nov 2003, *Nativity* (watercolour, 13 x 21 ins / 32 x 53 cm) USD 10,000.

HERTER, Ernst Gustav
German, 19th - 20th century.
Born 14 May 1846, in Berlin; died 21 December 1917, in Berlin.
Sculptor.

Herter was a student at the Berlin academy of A. Fisher, Gustav Bläser and A. Wolff. He visited Italy, returned to Germany and was made a professor in 1890 at the Berlin academy, as a successor to F. Schapers. He obtained a silver medal in the 1900 Exposition Universelle in Paris.

MUSEUMS AND GALLERIES:

BERLIN: *Death of Achilles; Alexander Resting.*

HERTER, Wilhelm Friedrich
German, 19th century.
Born 25 November 1865, in New York; died 8 November 1888, in Munich.
Painter.

Herter worked in Stuttgart and Munich, painting genre subjects and portraits.

HERTERICH, Heinrich Joachim
German, 18th - 19th century.
Born 7 June 1772, in Hamburg; died 20 March 1852, in Hamburg.
Painter, engraver (etching), lithographer.

Heinrich Herterich, the son and pupil of Johann Andreas Herterich, set up the first lithographic printing works in Germany with JM Specker. He was also a successful pastellist and miniaturist.

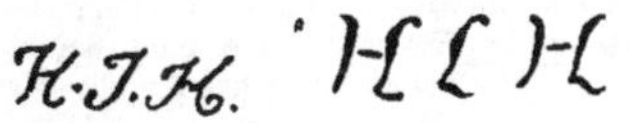

HERTERICH, Johann Andreas
German, 18th century.
Born 1725, in Bayreuth; died 1794, in Hamburg.
Miniaturist, pastellist. Portraits.

Johann Andreas Herterich settled in Hamburg in 1769.

HERTERICH, Johann Caspar
German, 19th century.
Born 23 April 1843, in Ansbach; died 26 October 1905, in Munich.
Painter. Historical scenes, genre scenes.

Johann Caspar Herterich studied under Philipp Foltz and Piloty at the Munich academy of art. He went on to become director there in 1882.

Having first exhibited in Kassel in 1867, he went on to exhibit in Vienna, Berlin and Munich between 1868 and 1888, being awarded a medal in Berlin in 1887.

MUSEUMS AND GALLERIES:

MUNICH (Pinakothek): *Heavenly Farewell.*

AUCTION RECORDS:

LONDON, 11 May 1984, *Verbotene Lektüre (Forbidden Reading)* (oil on canvas, 19¼ x 25 ins / 49 x 63.5 cm) GBP 3,000. LONDON, 30 May 1986, *Milk for the Cat* (oil on panel, 31 x 21 ins / 78.7 x 53.3 cm) GBP 5,500. MUNICH, 29 June 2000, *Crucified Jesus on the Floor, Group of Angels in Clouds* (1900, oil on panel, 31 x 21 ins / 80 x 53 cm) DEM 4,000.

HERTERICH, Ludwig
German, 19th - 20th century.
Born 13 October 1856, in Ansbach; died 1932.
Painter. History painting, genre scenes.

Herterich was the student of his brother Johann Caspar, then of Diez. He settled in Munich and, in 1891, he was a professor at the academy. He first exhibited in 1882; he obtained an honourable mention in Berlin in 1887, a medal in Munich in 1888 and a gold medal in Paris in 1900 at the Exposition Universelle.

MUSEUMS AND GALLERIES:

MUNICH: *St George; Summer Evening; Cavalryman.*

AUCTION RECORDS:

MUNICH, 19 Sept 1979, *Happy Group on a Terrace* (oil on card, 14¼ x 26¾ ins / 36.5 x 68 cm) DEM 2,800.

HERTERVIG, Lars
Norwegian, 19th century.
Born 10 March 1830, in Tysvaer; died 6 January 1902, in Stavanger.
Painter. Landscapes.

Lars Hertervig studied in Norway at the royal school of drawing around 1849 under Johannes Flintoe and Joachim Frich. He went to Düsseldorf from 1852 to 1856, where he studied with fellow Norwegian Hans Gude. On his return to Norway in 1854 he was committed to Gaustad asylum in Christiania (now Oslo). Vivid in colour, his compositions show a solid construction.

HERTH, Francis, or Jean-Marie
French, 20th century.
Born 21 February 1943, in Remiremont (Vosges).
Painter, draughtsman, sculptor, engraver, illustrator.

Herth studied artistic humanities at the Académie St-Luc in Brussels and also for a time at the Accademia Belgica in Rome. When he returned to France at the age of 20, he settled in Paris. He then lived and worked in the Lubéron from 1974 until 1985 before finally returning to La Ruche in Paris in 1987. He has travelled to Italy several times. He won the Prix Victor Choquet for painting in 1974 and was awarded the Prix Charles Oulmont by the Fondation de France in 1987, also for painting. He has illustrated books, including *L'Inexorable* (*Inexorable*) by Charles Juliet and *Hors-saisons* (*Out of Season*) by François Cheng, published by Éditions Fata Morgana. The Belgian state has bought several of his works.

Herth paints with a quill or an oriental brush, using ink and water spread on wet paper. His perfect mastery of this technique can be seen in his washes, which are usually large-scale and sometimes heightened with watercolour or gouache. He draws with great speed, using touches of black or blue ink diluted to varying degrees and covering areas of varying size. Seen from a distance, the picture emerges from these small, rapidly drawn strokes. Having studied the physical aspects of hills and rocks, he moved on to the human form (in the series *Torsos*), and more generally to organic forms, which he draws them in their foetal stage, as seeds or embryos, in formal themes with strokes of his hand.

Herth has taken part in group exhibitions, including: TNP, Brussels, 1965; Galerie Carrefour, Brussels, 1965 and 1971; Galerie Argos, Nantes, 1970; Salon des Réalités Nouvelles, Paris, 1970, 1971 and 1973; Galerie Farber, Brussels, 1973; *Autour de Charles Juliet* (*About Charles Juliet*), Centre d'Arts Plastiques, Villefranche, 1979; *Dessins Français Contemporains* (*Contemporary French Drawings*), Musée de la SEITA, Paris, 1982-1983 (an exhibition touring Europe and the USA); Ghent International Fair, 1987 and 1988; and Centre d'Art Contemporain, Abbaye de Beaulieu, 1990.

His solo exhibitions include: Pinacotheque on the Mont des Arts, Brussels, 1965; Galerie St-André des Arts, Paris, 1969; JWT Art Gallery, Brussels, 1970; Gallery BB, Randers, Denmark, 1972; Galerie Farber, Brussels, 1974; *Turbulences* (*Unrest*) in 1979, 1982 and 1986, and *Aubes* (*Beginnings*) in 1988, at the Galerie Erval in Paris; *Émergences* (*Emergence*), Salon d'Art, Brussels, 1987, 1989 and 1993; Galerie d'Outremont, Belgium, 1984 and 1988; Galerie Alice Chartier, Lyons, 1989; Didier Fetteweis Gallery, Spa, Belgium, 1993; and *Kiyoharu, Japan, Signes du voyage* (*Signs of the Journey*), Galerie Climats, Paris, 1995.

BIBLIOGRAPHY:

Van Hier, Henri (preface), *Francis Herth*, exhibition catalogue, J.W.T. Art Gall., Brussels, 1970. Schulman, Fernande, '*Une cartographie de l'imaginaire*' in *Esprit*, periodical, Paris, 1979. Juliet, Charles (preface), *Francis Herth*, exhibition catalogue, Gal. Erval, Paris, 1982. Brisset, Pierre, '*Francis Herth*' in *L'Œil*, periodical, Paris, May 1982. Meuris, Jacques, '*Les Paysages infinis de Francis Herth*' in *La Libre Belgique*, periodical, Brussels, January 1984. Alquin, Nicolas (preface), *Lavis de l'Oublis*, exhibition catalogue, Gal. Erval, Paris, 1986. Juliet, Charles, *De l'infini à l'immense*, March 1989. Guiraud, Jean, '*Les Dessins de Francis Herth*' in *La Part de l'œil*, periodical, Brussels, 1990.

MUSEUMS AND GALLERIES:

IXELLES (MBA) - PARIS (FNAC).

AUCTION RECORDS:

BRUSSELS, 13 Dec 1990, *Composition* (1968, ink and wash/paper, 18 3/4 x 24 1/2 ins / 47.5 x 62 cm) BEF 27,360; *Composition* (1967, ink and wash/paper, 17 x 21 1/4 ins / 43 x 54 cm) BEF 62,700.

HERTIG, Louis
French, 20th century.
Born in Besançon.
Sculptor.

Louis Hertig was a pupil of Caniez and exhibited at the Salon from 1907.

HERTING, Georg
German, 20th century.
Born 28 September 1872, in Linden.
Sculptor.

Herting was a student of Von Rümann in Munich.

HERTING, Gustav
German, 19th century.
Active in Hamburg.
Painter.

HERTL, Adelina Margarita
French, 19th century.
Born 24 May 1832, in Sedan (Ardennes); died 1872, in Ems (Rhineland-Palatinate, Germany).
Active in Paris.
Painter, pastellist. Flowers.

Adelina Hertl exhibited at the Salon between 1857 and 1870.

HERTL, Paul Antoine
French, 19th century.
Born 9 June 1826, in Sedan (Ardennes).
Painter, watercolourist. Landscapes.

Paul Hertl's Salon début was in 1861.

HERTLING, Wilhelm Jakob
German, 19th century.
Born 16 December 1849, in Katzenelnbogen.
Painter.

Hertling studied under Steinles in Frankfurt am Main.

HERTOCKS, A.
Dutch, 17th century.
Born at the beginning of 17th century, in the Netherlands.
Engraver.

He worked in England between 1626 and 1661. He engraved mostly portraits and frontispieces.

HERTOGHE, Gilles de
Flemish, 16th century.
Active in Antwerp, in 1538.
Sculptor.
Flemish School.

HERTRICH, Michel
French, 19th century.
Born 15 October 1811, in Turckheim; died 1880, in Colmar.
Painter, miniaturist. Portraits.

Hertrich exhibited at the Salon from 1844 to 1848, and won a third-class medal in 1845.

MUSEUMS AND GALLERIES:

COLMAR: *Portrait* (two miniatures).

HERTSEM, Jean de
Flemish School, 17th century.
Active in Ath in 1615.
Sculptor.

HERTVEKS, A.
Dutch, 17th century.
Active in England c. 1660.
Engraver.

HERTWIG, Henry
German, 19th century.
Active in Berlin.
Landscape artist.

Hertwig first exhibited in Berlin in 1870.

HERTZ, Gustav
German, 19th century.
Active in Berlin.
Painter. Historical scenes, portraits.

Hertz studied under Begas.

HERTZ, Lise
French, 20th century.
Born 1943, in Étampes.

Draughtswoman.
Hertz studied geography. She has designed clothes for children and adults. She has taken part in collective exhibitions in La Celle-St-Cloud since 1977, where she won a first prize for drawing in 1984. She took part in the Salon in Taverny in 1986.

HERTZ, Michel
French, 20th century.
Born 20 March 1933, in Strasbourg.
Painter, watercolourist, draughtsman. Landscapes with figures, urban landscapes, seascapes.
Michel Hertz studied in Paris at the École des Beaux-Arts, and the Académie Julian and Académie de la Grande Chaumière. He exhibited at the Salon des Indépendants, the Salon des Artistes Français, the Salon d'Automne, the Salon of Société Nationale des Beaux-Arts and the Salon de la Marine. He was the official painter to the navy.

His subjects are related to the sea: harbours, civil or military ships and fishing boats. Whether in Le Havre, Brest, Toulon, Antwerp, Fécamp, Sète, Dieppe, Paris or Venice, his interest lies in the meeting of water and sky and the urban landscape, and he produces works with a delicate realism in a range of blues, greys and bluish greens.
BIBLIOGRAPHY:
Gauthron, Bernard, '*Michel Hertz*' in *Vision sur les arts*, periodical, Paris. Ginest, Henri, '*Mélodie poétique dans l'œuvre de Hertz*' in *Vision sur les arts*, periodical, Graphisud, Paris, 1988.

HERTZ, Mogens
Danish, 20th century.
Born 26 September 1909, in Copenhagen; died 20 July 1999, in Gudhjem.
Painter. Scenes with figures, rustic scenes, interiors with figures, landscapes, seascapes, still-lifes.
AUCTION RECORDS:
COPENHAGEN, 28 April 1976, *Seashore* (1946, oil on canvas, 28¾ x 36¼ ins / 73 x 92 cm) DKK 3,500. COPENHAGEN, 5 Oct 1977, *Rooftops and Seas* (1951, oil on canvas, 25½ x 39¼ ins / 65 x 100 cm) DKK 10,000. COPENHAGEN, 24 Jan 1979, *Children in an Interior* (1945, oil on canvas, 39¼ x 53¼ ins / 100 x 135 cm) DKK 5,200. COPENHAGEN, 4 May 1988, *Still-life* (23½ x 28¾ ins / 60 x 73 cm) DKK 17,000. COPENHAGEN, 30 Nov 1988, *By the Sea* (oil on canvas, 18 x 22 ins / 46 x 55 cm) DKK 6,000. COPENHAGEN, 20 Sept 1989, *Figures in the Street* (oil on canvas, 21¼ x 25½ ins / 54 x 65 cm) DKK 5,000. COPENHAGEN, 22 Nov 1989, *Street Scene* (1958, oil on canvas, 46 x 38¼ ins / 116 x 97 cm) DKK 21,000. COPENHAGEN, 21-22 March 1990, *Rocks at Ostersøn* (1946, oil on canvas, 25¼ x 36½ ins / 64 x 93 cm) DKK 9,200. COPENHAGEN, 13-14 Feb 1991, *Street with Figures* (1957, oil on canvas, 21¼ x 32 ins / 54 x 81 cm) DKK 6,500. COPENHAGEN, 4 Dec 1991, *Country Landscape in Summer* (1955, oil on canvas, 21¼ x 25½ ins / 54 x 65 cm) DKK 5,000. COPENHAGEN, 1 April 1992, *Street in Gudhjem* (oil on canvas, 15 x 24 ins / 38 x 61 cm) DKK 4,500. COPENHAGEN, 21 Oct 1992, *Interior* (oil on canvas, 46 x 62¼ ins / 116 x 158 cm) DKK 7,000. COPENHAGEN, 21 April 1993, *Street in Gudhjem* (1957, oil on canvas, 21¼ x 32 ins / 54 x 81 cm) DKK 6,800. COPENHAGEN, 26 April 1995, *Harvest Scene in Bornholm* (oil on canvas, 21¼ x 32 ins / 54 x 81 cm) DKK 7,000. COPENHAGEN, 23 March 1999, *Bornholm* (1944, oil on canvas, 24 x 29 ins / 60 x 73 cm) DKK 13,000. COPENHAGEN, 20 June 2000, *Two Nude Women* (1944, oil on canvas, 35 x 42 ins / 90 x 106 cm) DKK 15,000. COPENHAGEN, 2 April 2001, *Fishermen behind Houses by the Sea* (1958, oil on canvas, 21 x 32 ins / 54 x 81 cm) DKK 19,000. COPENHAGEN, 2 April 2001, *Farm with Red Cows* (1955, oil on canvas, 26 x 32 ins / 65 x 81 cm) DKK 20,000. COPENHAGEN, 10 April 2002, *View across Rooftops to the Sea* (oil on canvas, 24 x 32 ins / 60 x 81 cm) DKK 15,000. VEJLE, 11 Nov 2002, *Winter's Day with Figures at Gudhjem, Sea in Background* (oil on canvas, 22 x 29 ins / 55 x 73 cm) DKK 14,500. COPENHAGEN, 12 June 2003, *Street Scene with Figures, Gudhjem* (1958, oil on canvas, 46 x 38 ins / 116 x 97 cm) DKK 18,000. COPENHAGEN, 17 June 2003, *Fishermen Returning Home in Evening, Gudhjem* (1955, oil on canvas, 29 x 46 ins / 73 x 116 cm) DKK 18,000. HAVNEN, 24 April 2004, *From Bornholm's Round Church with Figures* (oil on canvas, 31 x 28 ins / 80 x 70 cm) DKK 18,000. HAVNEN, 24 April 2004, *Street Scene, Bornholm with Figures* (oil on canvas, 24 x 32 ins / 60 x 81 cm) DKK 18,000.

HERTZ, Semmi
German, 19th century.
Died 25 June 1862, in Wandsbek, near Hamburg.
Lithographer.
Hertz primarily executed caricatures.

HERTZ-EYROLLES, Cécile
French, 20th century.
Born in Paris.
Painter.
Hertz-Eyrolles exhibited at the Salon d'Automne in Paris from 1928.

HERTZBERG, Axel Gustaf
Swedish, 19th century.
Born 27 August 1832, in Jämtland; died 2 September 1878, in Düsseldorf.
Painter. Genre scenes.
MUSEUMS AND GALLERIES:
STOCKHOLM: *Confirmation; The Last Drop*.
AUCTION RECORDS:
STOCKHOLM, 4 Nov 1986, *Interior with Mother and Child* (1868, oil on canvas, 21¼ x 24¾ ins / 54 x 63 cm) SEK 45,000. STOCKHOLM, 8 Dec 1987, *Interior with Mother and Sleeping Child* (1868, oil on canvas, 20¾ x 24 ins / 53 x 61 cm) SEK 26,000. LONDON, 11 Oct 1995, *Confirmation* (1871, oil on canvas, 32¼ x 27½ ins / 82 x 70 cm) GBP 2,875. VEJLE, 19 Jan 2000, *Confirmation Candidate* (1872, oil on canvas, 33 x 29 ins / 85 x 73 cm) DKK 18,500. STOCKHOLM, 4 Dec 2001, *Confirmation Candidate* (1872, oil on canvas, 34 x 29 ins / 86 x 74 cm) SEK 20,000.

HERTZBERG, Halfdan
Norwegian, 19th century.
Born 7 February 1857, in Christiania (now Oslo); died 5 July 1890, in Naerstrand, near Stavanger.
Sculptor.
Halfdan Hertzberg's *Child Whistling* is in the museum of Oslo.

HERTZBERG, Rudolf Reinhold
German, 19th century.
Born 1811, in Berlin; died 24 June 1888, in Langenberg Castle.
Painter.
Hertzberg studied at the Berlin academy of art, then went on to live in Scandinavia for many years.

HERTZOG, Anton
Austrian, 18th century.
Born 1692, in Hiltenfingen; died 17 March 1740, in Vienna.
Painter.
Anton Hertzog is best known for a reredos in the Augustinerkirche in Vienna.

HERTZOG, Daniel
German, 17th century.
Active in Augsburg at the beginning of the 17th century.
Painter.
Daniel Hertzog is best known for his paintings of flowers and birds.

HERTZOG, Frederik Gottlieb
Danish, 19th century.
Born 6 January 1821, in Copenhagen; died 13 March 1892, in Copenhagen.
Sculptor.
Frederik Hertzog executed works at the cathedral of Roskilde.
MUSEUMS AND GALLERIES:
COPENHAGEN (Ny Carlsberg Glyptotek): several works.

HERTZOG, Johann
German, 17th century.
Active in Augsburg c. 1600.
Fresco artist.

HERTZOG, Johann Georg
Danish, 18th century.
Born c. 1710, in Copenhagen; died 30 January 1770, in Sorø.
Painter.
Johann Hertzog was known mostly as a portraitist.

HÉRUBEL, Nicolas
French, 20th - 21st century.
Born 1956, in Rouen.
Sculptor, performance artist, installation artist.
Hérubel studied at the École des Beaux-Arts in Rouen. His sculptures are inspired by his previous performances, and were centred on the analysis of the movement of the human body, illustrated and accompanied by the sculptures. Although performance art came to occupy a decreasing place in his work, the body remains just as important, at least symbolically, in the installations he constructs from industrial materials such as steel.

He has taken part in collective exhibitions, including the Salon de la Jeune Sculpture in Paris (1984, 1985, 1989) and the Biennale d'Art Contemporain in Lyons (1997). Solo exhibitions include: Centre d'Action Culturel Jean-Renoir, Dieppe (1988); Galerie Jacqueline Moussion, Paris (1989, 1995); École d'Art Gérard-Jacot, Belfort (1999); and Galerie Duchamp, Yvetot (2001).
BIBLIOGRAPHY:
Cabon, Paul, *Nicolas Hérubel*, exhibition catalogue, École des beaux-arts, Rouen, Écoles nationales d'art décoratif de Limoges et d'Aubusson, École d'art Gérard Jacot de Belfort, centre régional d'Art contemporain Le 19, Montbéliard, 1999.
MUSEUMS AND GALLERIES:
PARIS (FNAC): *Orientation Table No 6* (1988); *Construction Permit No 6 to Do Today and Tomorrow* (1994).

HERUSSE, Jean
French, 16th century.
Active in Dreux c. 1570.
Glass painter, sculptor.

HERVÉ, Abel
French, 19th - 20th century.
Born 22 January 1858, in Vieillevigne.
Painter. Landscapes.
Abel Hervé was a pupil of Léopold Morice. He lived in Nantes and exhibited at the Salon des Artistes Français, notably in 1911.
AUCTION RECORDS:
PARIS, 5 March 1989, *Fisherman on the Banks of the Sèvre* (1902, 23 1/2 x 31 1/2 ins / 60 x 80 cm) FRF 15,000. PARIS, 13 March 1995, *Going Past the Mosque* (1882, oil on canvas, 63 x 47 1/4 ins / 160 x 120 cm) FRF 25,000.

HERVÉ, C.S.
British, 19th century.
Active in London.
Miniaturist. Portraits.
C.S. Hervé exhibited in London at the Royal Academy from 1828 to 1858.

HERVÉ, Charles
British, 19th century.
Born 1833.
Active in London.
Miniaturist.
MUSEUMS AND GALLERIES:
LONDON (Victoria and Albert Mus.): two miniatures.

HERVÉ, F.
British, 19th century.
Active in London.
Miniaturist.
F. Hervé exhibited in London at the Royal Academy from 1818 to 1840.

HERVÉ, Gabriel
French, 19th - 20th century.
Born 5 July 1868, in Bonnes (Charente).
Painter. Genre scenes.
Gabriel Hervé was a pupil of Umbricht. He was a member of the Salon des Artistes Français in Paris from 1907.
AUCTION RECORDS:
LONDON, 30 Jan 1909, *Cicada*, GBP 6.

HERVÉ, Henry
British, 19th century.
Active in London.
Miniaturist.
Henry Hervé occasionally exhibited at the Royal Academy in London between 1813 and 1843.

HERVÉ, Jeannine
French, 20th century.
Born 12 March 1931, in Larmor-Plage (Morbihan).
Painter, watercolourist, draughtswoman, lithographer, engraver (wood/burin), art restorer. Landscapes with figures, landscapes, architectural views, still-lifes.
Designs for tapestries.
From 1936 to 1937, Jeannine Hervé studied drawing and then painting with E. Robert and the engraver Adolphe Beaufrère. She also received lessons from Ernest Guérin. From 1948 she studied at the École des Beaux-Arts in Quimper and then Paris. She also studied engraving with Jean Delpech. From 1962 to 1965 she was an assistant at the Académie Julian, and, from 1963 to 1965, drawing assistant at the École Polytechnique in Fontanarosa. During this period she studied tapestry design with Jean Lurçat. From 1965 to 1970 she restored paintings, drawings and engravings at Versailles with Paulet. This work led to the restoration of paintings in the royal collection in Sweden. From 1973 to 1975 she taught painting and drawing at Bovendren in Germany. From 1975 she produced mainly engravings and wood engravings for the Salon d'Art Sacré.

She has shown her work at many exhibitions, including 1977 Galerie Rue de Berri, Paris; 1979 Galerie Lemoussu in Lorient, and Institut Français, Frankfurt; 1980 Institut Français, Mainz; 1980 Institut Français, Bremen; 1981 Haus-Coburg museum, Delmenhorst-Bremen; 1982 Kunstgalerie Wels, as well as in Switzerland, Belgium, Italy, Spain, Guadeloupe and St-Barthélemy in the French Antilles (Musée Gustavia, 1978). She has won many prizes and distinctions, notably at the Salon des Artistes Français, for painting in 1967 and for engraving in 1975, and the Grand Prix for engraving at the Biennale in Vichy in 1980.

HERVÉ, Jules René
French, 20th century.
Born 14 April 1887, in Langres; died 1981.
Painter. Figures, portraits, local scenes, landscapes.
Jules René Hervé studied with Fernand Cormon and Jules Adler; his compositions reveal his careful observation and

the evocation of delicate feeling. He exhibited in Paris, at the Salon des Artistes Français, and won the silver medal in 1914, and the gold medal in 1925.

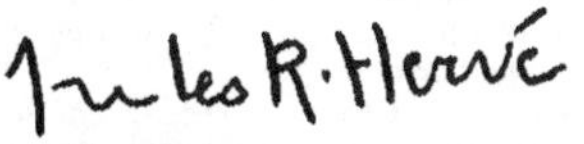

MUSEUMS AND GALLERIES:
LUXEUIL-LES-BAINS (Mus. de la Tour des Échevins): *After the Burial.*
AUCTION RECORDS:
PARIS, 20 Feb 1942, *The Wood Splitter,* FRF 750. PARIS, 24 Feb 1947, *Small Village Scene,* FRF 2,300. PARIS, 19 Nov 1976, *Coming Out of Mass* (oil on canvas, 25 1/2 x 32 ins / 65 x 81 cm) FRF 3,100. NEW YORK, 10 Dec 1982, *Booksellers on the Quays of the Seine* (oil on canvas, 25 3/4 x 32 ins / 65.5 x 81 cm) USD 1,700. BARBIZON, 6 Nov 1983, *The Visit to the Grandparents* (oil on canvas, 15 x 18 ins / 38 x 46 cm) FRF 13,500. PARIS, 13 Nov 1986, *Place du Châtelet* (oil on canvas, 19 3/4 x 39 1/4 ins / 50 x 100 cm) FRF 42,000. SEMUR-EN-AUXOIS, 8 Feb 1987, *Group of Old Men in Front of Posters* (oil on canvas) FRF 24,100. PARIS, 11 Dec 1987, *Scene with Figures* (oil on canvas, 15 x 18 ins / 38 x 46 cm) FRF 17,000. CALAIS, 28 Feb 1988, *St-Germain des Prés Church* (oil on canvas, 9 x 11 ins / 22 x 27 cm) FRF 11,500. PARIS, 18 March 1988, *Children Playing By the River* (oil on canvas, 39 1/4 x 32 ins / 100 x 81 cm) FRF 90,000. NEUILLY, 14 June 1988, *Notre Dame Seen from the Quays,* FRF 42,000. VERSAILLES, 15 June 1988, *Laundresses Near an Animated Village* (oil on canvas, 15 x 18 ins / 38 x 46 cm) FRF 44,000. PARIS, 24 June 1988, *The Seine in Paris* (oil on canvas, 8 x 10 1/4 ins / 20.5 x 26 cm) FRF 12,000. LONDON, 8 Sept 1988, *Notre Dame Seen from City Hall* (oil on canvas, 15 x 18 ins / 38.1 x 46 cm) GBP 3,300. VERSAILLES, 23 Oct 1988, *Ballerinas in the Lounge* (oil on cardboard, 9 x 11 ins / 22 x 27 cm) FRF 19,000. VERSAILLES, 6 Nov 1988, *Animated Scene Near the Village Laundry* (oil on canvas, 9 x 11 ins / 22 x 27 cm) FRF 15,500. VERSAILLES, 18 Dec 1988, *Paris, the Flower Market, Near the Conciergerie* (oil on canvas, 19 3/4 x 24 ins / 50 x 61 cm) FRF 33,500. LA VARENNE-ST-HILAIRE, 12 March 1989, *In the Park of the Tuileries* (oil on canvas, 15 x 18 ins / 38 x 46 cm) FRF 48,000. PARIS, 12 April 1989, *The Quays in Paris* (oil on canvas, 18 x 22 ins / 46 x 55 cm) FRF 46,000. NEW YORK, 3 May 1989, *Children Around the Pool in the Tuileries* (oil on canvas, 8 1/4 x 11 ins / 21 x 27.7 cm) USD 25,530. PARIS, 30 June 1989, *Coming Out of the Church* (oil on canvas, 15 3/4 x 13 ins / 40 x 33 cm) FRF 10,000. PARIS, 11 July 1989, *Place de la Concorde* (oil on canvas, 25 1/2 x 32 ins / 65 x 81 cm) FRF 65,000. LE TOUQUET, 12 Nov 1989, *Children on the Square of Notre Dame* (oil on canvas, 11 x 13 1/2 ins / 27 x 34 cm) FRF 26,000. PARIS, 27 Nov 1989, *Stroll at Notre Dame* (oil on canvas, 18 x 22 ins / 46 x 55 cm) FRF 30,000. STRASBOURG, 29 Nov 1989, *Communicants Coming Out of Church* (oil on canvas, 22 x 18 ins / 55 x 46 cm) FRF 27,000. NEW YORK, 21 Feb 1990, *Children Showing Off by the Edge of the River* (oil on canvas, 39 1/2 x 31 1/2 ins / 100.4 x 80.1 cm) USD 16,500. PARIS, 11 March 1990, *Antique Fair* (oil on canvas, 11 x 13 3/4 ins / 27 x 35 cm) FRF 33,000. LONDON, 11 May 1990, *In the Park at Versailles* (oil on canvas, 18 x 22 ins / 45.8 x 55.9 cm) GBP 3,740. PARIS, 12 June 1990, *The Luxembourg Garden, The Senate* (oil on canvas, 25 1/2 x 17 3/4 ins / 65 x 45 cm) FRF 50,000. PARIS, 20 June 1990, *The Communicants* (oil on canvas, 28 3/4 x 23 1/2 ins / 73 x 60 cm) FRF 88,000. NEW YORK, 10 Oct 1990, *Game of Skittles* (oil on canvas/cardboard, 25 1/4 x 32 ins / 64.1 x 81.4 cm) USD 7,700. AMSTERDAM, 6 Nov 1990, *Children in the Square; Merry Figures Near a Tavern* (oil on canvas, a pair, each 14 1/2 x 17 3/4 ins / 37 x 45 cm) NLG 14,950. NEW YORK, 13 Feb 1991, *The Party* (oil on canvas, 15 x 18 ins / 381 x 45.7 cm) USD 7,150. PARIS, 4 March 1991, *The Champs-Elysees* (oil on canvas, 9 x 11 ins / 22 x 27 cm) FRF 15,000. NEW YORK, 7 May 1991, *Children in a Park* (oil on canvas, 24 x 30 ins / 61 x 76.2 cm) USD 9,350. MONTREAL, 4 June 1991, *Meeting at the Club* (oil on panel, 14 1/2 x 18 ins / 36.8 x 45.8 cm) CAD 2,400. RHEIMS, 20 Oct 1991, *Coming Out of Mass in Brevoines* (oil on canvas, 25 1/2 x 32 ins / 65 x 81 cm) FRF 52,000. MONTREAL, 19 Nov 1991, *The Youngest* (oil on canvas, 8 1/2 x 10 1/2 ins / 21.5 x 26.6 cm) CAD 2,300. AMSTERDAM, 14-15 April 1992, *Nuns Accompanying Schoolchildren in a Street* (oil on canvas, 9 3/4 x 13 ins / 25 x 33 cm) NLG 5,980. NEW YORK, 9 May 1992, *The Tuileries* (oil on canvas, 15 1/4 x 18 ins / 38.8 x 45.7 cm) USD 4,400. PARIS, 26 June 1992, *Childish Curiosity* (oil on canvas, 16 1/4 x 13 ins / 41 x 33 cm) FRF 14,000. AMSTERDAM, 3 Nov 1992, *The Procession* (oil on cardboard, 6 x 7 3/4 ins / 15 x 20 cm) NLG 1,840. NEW YORK, 10 Nov 1992, *The Booksellers* (oil on canvas, 26 x 32 ins / 66 x 81.3 cm) USD 6,600. MONACO, 2 July 1993, *The Tuileries Garden in Paris* (oil on canvas, 29 3/4 x 21 3/4 ins / 75.5 x 55.5 cm) FRF 33, 300. PARIS, 3 Dec 1993, *The Breton Pardon* (oil on canvas, 19 3/4 x 41 1/4 ins / 50 x 105 cm) FRF 32,500. PARIS, 31 March 1994, *The Laundresses* (oil on cardboard, 15 x 18 ins / 38 x 46 cm) FRF 18,500. NEW YORK, 24 Feb 1995, *Flea Market in Paris* (oil on cardboard, 8 1/2 x 11 ins / 21.9 x 27 cm) USD 1,380. CHAUMONT, 10 Dec 1995, *Communicants Coming Out of the Young People's Club in Langres* (oil on canvas, 15 x 18 ins / 38 x 46 cm) FRF 36,000. PARIS, 5 June 1996, *Children in the Jardin du Luxembourg* (oil on canvas, 13 x 16 1/4 ins / 33 x 41 cm) FRF 9,000. NEW YORK, 10 Oct 1996, *Rites of Passage* (oil on canvas, triptych, two 15 x 18 ins / 38.1 x 45.7 cm and one 16 x 13 ins/40.6 x 33 cm) USD 6,900. NEW YORK, 12 Nov 1996, *Mother and Children* (oil on canvas, 13 x 16 ins / 33 x 406 cm) USD 9,775. PARIS, 29 Nov 1996, *Rustic Wedding* (oil on canvas, 18 x 22 ins / 46 x 55 cm) FRF 30,000. PARIS, 12 Dec 1996, *Brittany, Public Auction* (oil on canvas, 15 x 18 ins / 38 x 46 cm) FRF 17,000. PARIS, 16 March 1997, *The Laundresses* (oil on canvas, 18 x 15 ins / 46 x 38 cm) FRF 17,600. PARIS, 28 May 1997, *Place de Paris* (oil on panel, 11 1/2 x 13 ins / 29 x 33 cm) FRF 11,000. PARIS, 27 Oct 1997, *Place de la Concorde* (oil on canvas, 18 x 22 ins / 46 x 55 cm) FRF 24,000. PARIS, 22 March 1998, *Ballerinas* (oil on canvas, 11 x 9 ins / 27 x 22 cm) FRF 14,000. PARIS, 29 Oct 1999, *Beguine Convent, Bruges* (oil on canvas laid on card, 13 x 16 ins / 33 x 41 cm) FRF 40,000. NEW YORK, 7 Dec 1999, *Bassin aux Tuilleries* (oil on canvas, 18 x 21 ins / 46 x 53 cm) USD 7,500. NEW YORK, 8 May 2000, *The Opéra in Paris* (oil on canvas, 18 x 22 ins / 46 x 55 cm) USD 10,000. NEW ORLEANS, 3 June 2000, *Place de L'Opéra, Paris* (1943, oil on canvas, 20 x 24 ins / 51 x 61 cm) USD 7,600. DUBLIN, 28 Feb 2001, *Parisian Scenes* (oil on canvas, a pair, 18 x 22 ins / 46 x 55 cm) IEP 8,000. NEW YORK, 6 Nov 2001, *La Madeleine in Winter* (oil on canvas, 26 x 32 ins / 66 x 81 cm) USD 9,000. EVREUX, 24 March 2002, *Flea Market* (oil on canvas, 20 x 24 ins / 50 x 61 cm) EUR 8,500. CALAIS, 14 April 2002, *Class Walk* (oil on panel, 25 x 31 ins / 64 x 79 cm) EUR 11,000. PARIS, 11 June 2003, *Auction in a Village* (oil on canvas, 26 x 32 ins / 65 x 81 cm) EUR 8,100. LOS ANGELES, 16 Nov 2003, *Lunch Table. Cottage Door. Vegetable Garden* (oil on canvas, set of three, 9 x 11 ins / 22 x 27 cm) USD 8,500. FAIRFIELD, 25 Aug 2004, *Cloudy Day in Langres, France* (oil on canvas, 64 x 51 ins / 163 x 130 cm) USD 23,500. NEW YORK, 29 Sept 2004, *Market Scene with Horses* (oil on canvas, 32 x 39 ins / 81 x 100 cm) USD 9,000.

HERVÉ, Juliane
French, 20th century.
Born 7 July 1921, in Le Mans.
Painter. Figures, interiors, landscapes with figures, landscapes, flowers.

Juliane Hervé is the daughter of Jules Hervé-Mathé Beside the training she received from her father, she studied at the École des Beaux-Arts in Paris in Dupas' studio. Her painting is highly coloured. One of her favourite themes is painting in an almost dreamlike fashion flower bouquets against aquatic backgrounds.

Juliane Hervé began exhibiting in Paris in 1951. She showed at the Salon des Indépendants, the Salon des Artistes Français and the Salon de la Société Coloniale. In 1956 she was awarded the Grand Prix de L'Union des Femmes Peintres et Sculpteurs (Union of Women Painters and Sculptors), and, in 1975, a silver medal at the Salon des Artistes Français.

MUSEUMS AND GALLERIES:

PARIS.

AUCTION RECORDS:

PARIS, 10 Nov 1987, *My Studio in Spring* (oil on canvas, 18 x 22 ins / 46 x 55 cm) FRF 5,100. PARIS, 11 April 1988, *After the Rustic Bath* (oil on cardboard, 11 x 13 3/4 ins / 27 x 35 cm) FRF 2,100.

HERVÉ, Julien
French, 19th century.
Born in the 19th century, in La Basse-Indre (Loire-Atlantique).
Painter. Genre scenes, landscapes.

Hervé was a member of the Société des Artistes Indépendants from 1888 onwards, and regularly participated in the Salon organised by this group.

AUCTION RECORDS:

PARIS, 26 Feb 1945, *Coastal Landscape,* FRF 6,500.

HERVÉ, Loïc
French, 20th - 21st century.
Born 1947, in Rennes.
Sculptor.

Hervé studied at the École des Beaux-Arts in Rennes from 1964 until 1967, then at the Académie Julian in Paris. He worked in marble and stone in Paris. He visited many places around the world between 1967 and 1977 and settled in Africa. He sculpts in granite in an Abstract, geometric style, sometimes painting anthropomorphic motifs on his works in thick bright colours.

He took part in the Salon des Arts Plastiques in Rennes in 1983 and 1984, and the Exposition des Sculpteurs Contemporains de Bretagne in Quimper in 1985. He shows his works in galleries in Quimper (Galerie de l'Épée in 1984) and Paris (Galerie Gérard Laubie in 1985) and at the Galerie Lelia Mordoch.

AUCTION RECORDS:

PARIS, 25 March 1991, *Rhinoceros* (lost-wax bronze, h. 11 1/2 ins / 29 cm) FRF 32,000.

HERVÉ, Margaret
British, 18th - 19th century.
Active in London.
Miniaturist.

Margaret Hervé exhibited in London at the Royal Academy and the Society of British Artists between 1783 and 1816.

HERVÉ, Peter
British, 19th century.
Died 6 June 1827.
Active in London.
Miniaturist.

Peter Hervé exhibited in London at the Royal Academy from 1802 to 1820.

HERVÉ, Simon
Belgian, 20th century.
Born 1888, in Schaerbeek (Brussels).
Painter. Figures, still-lifes.

HERVÉ, Théodore
French, 20th century.
Born 18 November 1879, in Paris.
Sculptor.

Théodore Hervé was a pupil of Verlet. He exhibited at the Salon.

HERVÉ-BARBET, Gilberte, called Gilberte-Hervé
French, 20th century.
Born 1895, in St-Calais (Sarthe); died 1971.
Draughtswoman, watercolourist, pastellist, designer.
Landscapes with figures, landscapes, urban landscapes, flowers. Decorative designs.

Hervé-Barbet was a pupil of Jules Alfred Hervé-Mathé, whom she married in 1920. From 1900 she produced many stencilled dresses, folding screens and hangings with floral designs. Her preferred subject throughout her life was flowers in watercolour and she exhibited at the Salon des Artistes Français in Paris in 1913 and 1914.

She travelled with her husband to Brittany, and lived in Concarneau 1920-1925, Audierne in 1927, Antibes in 1928, Carnaret 1930-1931, and Alsace 1930-1935.

HERVÉ-LACOMBE, Isabelle
Maiden name: Halimbourg
French, 19th century.
Active in Paris.
Painter.

Hervé-Lacombe made her début at the Salon in 1878, and became a member of the Société des Artistes Français in 1891.

HERVÉ-MATHÉ, Jules Alfred, or Mathé, Jules Hervé
French, 19th - 20th century.
Born 8 February 1868, in St-Calais; died 1953, in Paris.
Painter, pastellist, watercolourist. Portraits, scenes with figures, interiors with figures, fishing scenes, landscapes with figures, landscapes, urban landscapes, seascapes.

Hervé-Mathé studied with Jean-Paul Laurens, Benjamin-Constant, Baschet and A. Maignan. A member of the Salon des Artistes Français, he directed the school of applied arts in Le Mans for 30 years. He painted the groves in Normandy, the Breton coastline, and views of Paris and Le Mans with a well-balanced palette and according to the tastes of the academy. In 2001, he was included in the exhibition *Les Peintres et la Sarthe* (*Painters and the Sarthe Region*) at the Musée de la Reine Bérengère, Le Mans (19th century section) and at the Abbaye de l'Épau (20th century section).

BIBLIOGRAPHY:

Arpentinier, Jean, *Sarthe, terre d'artistes*, Éd. de la Reinette, Le Mans, 2001.

MUSEUMS AND GALLERIES:

LE MANS: *Rising Tide in Ploumanach.*

AUCTION RECORDS:

BAYEUX, 3 May 1987, *Wysteria in Spring* (watercolour and gouache, 20 3/4 x 15 ins / 53 x 38 cm) FRF 15,000. PARIS, 8 Nov 1987, *Fishermens' House* (oil on panel, 14 1/2 x 17 3/4 ins / 37 x 45 cm) FRF 13,000. SCEAUX, 11 March 1990, *Flower Market in Dinan* (oil on cardboard, 14 1/2 x 18 ins / 37 x 46 cm) FRF 17,100. VERSAILLES, 22 April 1990, *Les Vosges - Underbrush* (oil on canvas, 10 x 13 3/4 ins / 24.5 x 35 cm) FRF 10,500. PARIS, 30 May 1990, *Departure of the Sardine Fishermen* (oil on canvas, 18 x 24 ins / 46 x 61 cm) FRF 55,000. SCEAUX, 10 June 1990, *Alpine Landscape in Summer* (oil on canvas, 18 x 22 ins / 46 x 55 cm) FRF 15,000. PARIS, 21 Feb 1992, *Luncheon by Lake Annecy* (oil on panel, 13 x 16 1/4 ins / 33 x 41 cm) FRF 12,500. PARIS, 4 March 1992, *Asnières-sur-Vègre (Sarthe)* (oil on canvas, 23 1/2 x 32 ins / 60 x 81 cm) FRF 25,000. PARIS, 1 Oct 1993, *Brittany, Ploumanach* (oil on panel, 7 1/2 x 10 1/2 ins / 18.8 x 26.5 cm) FRF 3,000. CHAUMONT, 17 Sept 1995, *Fishermen on Lake Annecy* (oil on canvas, 15 x 18 ins / 38 x 46 cm) FRF 5,000. LYONS, 6 Feb 2000, *Little Girl in the Salon* (1912, oil on canvas, 45 x 34 ins / 115 x 87 cm) FRF 17,000. Paris, 17 March 2000, *Old Blind Man* (oil on canvas, 15 x 18 ins / 38 x 46 cm) FRF 12,000. Bayeux, 14 July 2002, *Return of the Fishing Fleet, Ville Close de Concarneau* (oil on canvas, 15 x 18 ins / 38 x 46 cm) EUR 2,600. Calais, 29 June 2003, *La Rochelle Harbour* (oil on panel, 18 x 15 ins / 46 x 38 cm) EUR 3,900. Brest, 19 July 2003, *Tuna Boat under Sail, Concarneau* (watercolour, 17 x 12 ins / 44 x 30 cm) EUR 1,800. Paris, 11 June 2004, *Beaulieu-sur-Mer* (1921, oil on canvas, 13 x 16 ins / 33 x 41 cm) EUR 1,800. Brest, 7 July 2004, *Kelp burning* (oil on canvas, 18 x 22 ins / 46 x 55 cm) EUR 1,800.

HERVELIN
French, 18th century.
Active in Paris in 1760.
Sculptor.

HERVENS, Jacques
Belgian, 20th century.
Born 1 December 1890, in St Joost-ten-Node; died 1928, in St-Lambrechts-Woluwe (Brabant).
Painter, engraver. Landscapes, still-lifes.
Hervens was a student of Herman Richir at the Académie des Beaux Arts in Brussels, where he received a number of prizes. He worked a great deal in Italy and North Africa. His highly coloured painting makes wonderful use of the play of light.

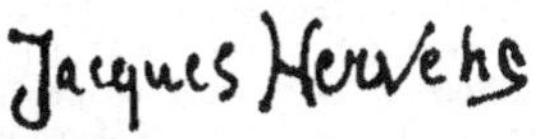

Auction records:
Brussels, 19 Dec 1989, *Flowers* (oil on canvas, 25½ x 19¾ ins / 65 x 50 cm) BEF 42,000. Lokeren, 21 March 1992, *View of Fiesole (Florence)* (oil on paper/canvas, 25¼ x 19¾ ins / 64 x 50 cm) BEF 55,000. Lokeren, 10 Dec 1994, *Winter Landscape* (oil on canvas, 31½ x 46 ins / 80 x 116 cm) BEF 48,000. Amsterdam, 11 April 1995, *Still-life with Roses* (oil on canvas, 27½ x 36¼ ins / 70 x 92 cm) NLG 4,956.

HERVERBAERT, Simon
Flemish, 15th century.
Active in Bruges.
Painter.
Bruges School, Flemish School.
Simon Herverbaert belonged to the Guild of St Luke in 1450.

HERVET, Georges
French, 20th century.
Born 1896; died 1982.
Painter, photographer. Landscapes, seascapes.
Georges Hervet painted in France and especially in Brittany. He exhibited regularly in Paris, at the Salon des Artistes Français, where he won numerous distinctions between 1970 and 1981.
Auction records:
Paris, 13 June 1988, *Trawlers and Boats at Port* (oil on canvas, 25½ x 32 ins / 65 x 81 cm) FRF 3,200.

HERVET, Marie
French, 19th century.
Born in Rueil-Malmaison (Hauts-de-Seine).
Pastellist, painter (glazed earthenware).
Hervet was a pupil of Mademoiselle Dubos. She made her Salon début in 1877.

HERVIAULT, André
French, 20th century.
Born 23 March 1884, in Nantes; died 10 July 1969, in Saintes.
Painter. Local figures.
Orientalism.
André Herviault studied with Fernand Cormon at the École des Beaux-Arts in Paris. He was sent to Togo in western Africa by the French colonial ministry and brought back 18 works which he exhibited at the Salon de la Société Coloniale des Artistes Français in 1929. He exhibited regularly in Paris at the Salon des Artistes Français and received various prizes for his paintings executed in the colonies.
Auction records:
Paris, 11 Dec 1991, *Kuka Warrior (Togo)* (1928, oil on canvas, 36¼ x 22 ins / 92 x 55 cm) FRF 8,000.

HERVIER
French, 18th - 19th century.
Painter, miniaturist. Portraits.
Hervier studied under David and d'Aubry. He exhibited miniatures at the Salon from 1810 to 1817. He also produced some drawings engraved by Girard. He was the father of the great landscapist Louis Hervier.
Auction records:
Paris, 18-22 April 1910, *Napoleon* (miniature allegory) FRF 490.

HERVIER, Aubin
French, 19th century.
Born 11 January 1851, in St-Charmond (Loire); died 1905.
Painter.
Aubin Hervier studied at the École des Beaux-Arts in Lyons from 1872 to 1878, and was also a pupil of Jean-Paul Laurens. His key works are: at the Lyons Salon, *Stream beneath the Woods at Soulages* (charcoal, 1876); and *Banks of the Loire* (1877); at the Paris Salon, *Morning in Rossillon* (1879); *Miracle of St Elizabeth* (1880); *St Margaret of Cortona before the Body of Her Lover* (1881); *Dante and Giotto* (1881); *Charles VI in the Forest of Le Mans* (1882); *Portrait of a Child* (1884); and *Gospel* (charcoal, 1885). He is also known for a series of frescoes he painted in a private chapel in Saint-Galmier (in the Loire Valley, central France).

HERVIER, Louis Adolphe
French, 19th century.
Born 1818, in Paris; died 18 January 1879, in Paris.
Painter, watercolourist, draughtsman, engraver, lithographer. Figures, genre scenes, landscapes.
Barbizon School.
Throughout his life, Louis Adolphe Hervier knew nothing but hardship, and he died before ever achieving recognition. He was the son of Hervier the miniaturist, and a pupil of Léon Cogniet and Eugène Isabey (the latter of whom was his true master). However, Adolphe Hervier was above all an independent artist, and this fact told against him. At the time when his career was just taking off, it was extremely damaging for an artist to express a wish to escape the conventions of the École.

He participated in the Salon of 1849, showing a painting described in the catalogue as 'Belonging to Monsieur Bonvalet', entitled: *Storm: a Study after Nature.* He also exhibited *A Road in Migny* in 1850; *View of the Butte des Moulins* in 1852; and *Return to the Port* and *The Village of Guevilly (Sarthe): Autumn* in 1855. Apart from at these four exhibitions, Hervier's work was not accepted. He first started submitting his works in 1838 and was refused no less than twenty-three times by the official juries.

His early etchings (which date from 1840) and watercolours passed unnoticed. In 1843 he produced an album entitled *Travel Sketches,* containing eight plates engraved on steel, which was published by Alexis Febvre. He lived in extreme poverty, and was often reduced to filling in background landscapes for other painters. This was a meagre source of income, and neither his watercolours, his remarkable lithographs, his paintings, nor his etchings, which are now so sought after, could improve his condition of artist-hireling. Hervier was also regarded as rather a wild figure. Burty was one of his rare contemporary admirers. In 1876, part of Hervier's studio was put up for sale. In the preface to the sale catalogue, Burty described the master as:

'Tall, strong, with a timid gait, faltering speech, a sad face, and long, dark, flashing eyes like an Oriental. He looks like a drowned man who has come back to life. Just like every other original contemporary artist, the public had a horror of him. He lives in a slum on the rue des Martyrs...'

This was his situation less than three years before his death. Although he lacked admirers among the general public, he found invaluable allies in the writer Théophile Gautier, who first praised his talent in 1856, and Champfleury and Burty, who also admired his work. Corot discreetly bought some of his watercolours. His works are now relatively rare: particularly his etchings, which brought him no reward during his lifetime, and which only survive in very small numbers. In 1888, having acquired some of Hervier's works, a bookseller named Monsieur Joly published the *Album Hervier, suite de quarante-trois planches dessinées et gravées de* (*Hervier Album: a Series of Forty-three Plates of Drawings and Engravings*) dating from 1840 to 1860, in a run of 250 copies. These are his best-known works. Hervier also left behind three albums of twelve lithographs, and two larger pieces entitled *Paupers* and *Beggar Woman*, which are every bit as interesting as his etchings.

MUSEUMS AND GALLERIES:

BAGNÈRES-DE-BIGORRE: *View of a Village in Normandy* - DIJON: *Storm Clouds* - MONTPELLIER: *Clearing in a Wood* - THE HAGUE (Mus. Mesdag): *Landscape.*

AUCTION RECORDS:

PARIS, 26 April 1899, *Fishing Boats,* FRF 1,800. PARIS, 21 Feb 1902, *The Fair at Coutances,* FRF 155. PARIS, 3 May 1902, *The Painter,* FRF 530. PARIS, 28 and 29 March 1905, *Village by the River,* FRF 500. LONDON, 3 July 1908, *A Street in a French Town,* GBP 23. LONDON, 28 Nov 1908, *Old Woman Washing,* GBP 23. LONDON, 13 May 1909, *Market in France,* GBP 29. LONDON, 14 May 1909, *Marketplace in Caen* (watercolour) GBP 29. LONDON, 5 March 1910, *Farm in the Woods* (1860) GBP 29. LONDON, 3 June 1910, *Farm,* GBP 44. LONDON, 30 June 1910, *Forest,* GBP 44. PARIS, 5 July 1919, *Windmill at Le Polet,* FRF 940; *The Village of Argillers-sur-Loire,* FRF 760; *The Old Path at Épinay: Morning,* FRF 655; *Farm Courtyard,* FRF 910. PARIS, 1-3 Dec 1919, *Near the Church Gate,* FRF 900. PARIS, 6 and 7 May 1920, *Footbridge,* FRF 3,050. PARIS, 10 Dec 1920, *Path through the Countryside, with Stormy Sun,* FRF 2,550. PARIS, 12 May 1923, *Gorse Pond at the Entrance to the Village: Sunset,* FRF 720. LONDON, June 1923, *Farm Courtyard,* GBP 50. PARIS, 11 June 1924, *Old Houses in Normandy on a Stormy Day* (watercolour) FRF 2,045; *Woman Selling Vegetables* (watercolour) FRF 1,200; *Market,* FRF 2,000. PARIS, 5 and 6 June 1925, *Farm Courtyard,* FRF 1,300; *Women Selling Vegetables,* FRF 1,750. PARIS, 19 April 1926, *Landscape with Windmills and Washerwomen,* FRF 2,310. PARIS, 10 May 1926, *Windmill in a Landscape,* FRF 2,550. PARIS, 3 July 1926, *A Storm Approaching,* FRF 2,700. PARIS, 20 May 1927, *The Egg Market in Paris* (watercolour) FRF 3,400; *Footbridge,* FRF 3,550. PARIS, 23 and 24 May 1927, *The Beach at Étretat,* FRF 2,300; *Port at Rouen* (watercolour) FRF 2,500; *The Essonne at Corbeil,* FRF 4,500. PARIS, 27 Feb 1928, *Small Village* (watercolour) FRF 2,650. PARIS, 13 March 1929, *Fishing Boat on the Beach at Trouville; Fishing Boats at Dieppe* (two watercolours) FRF 2,500. PARIS, 5 and 6 June 1929, *Old Norman Houses and a Bridge over a Stream* (watercolour) FRF 2,150; *The Quai Sainte-Catherine and the Lieutenancy at Honfleur* (watercolour) FRF 3,050. PARIS, 16-18 Feb 1931, *Sartrouville* (drawing with wash) FRF 240. PARIS, 18 March 1931, *Pasture at the Edge of a Pond* (watercolour) FRF 500. PARIS, 21 March 1934, *The Butter and Vegetable Market at Caen* (watercolour) FRF 1,350. PARIS, 4 Nov 1937, *Village Market* (watercolour) FRF 700; *Church (Interior),* FRF 620. PARIS, 8 May 1940, *House in the Country* (watercolour) FRF 400. PARIS, 5 Dec 1940, *The Quai Sainte-Catherine and the Lieutenancy at Honfleur* (watercolour) FRF 2,900. PARIS, 24 June 1942, *Rouen Cathedral* (pencil) FRF 1,600. PARIS, 21 Dec 1942, *Day of the Fair at Coutances* (1864, watercolour) FRF 9,000; *Windmill* (1854, watercolour) FRF 6,500; *Women Selling Fish* (watercolour) FRF 4,300. PARIS, 26 March 1945, *Boat in a Dry Dock* (watercolour) FRF 7,500; *Landscapes* (two watercolours in pairs) FRF 7,800. PARIS, Oct 1945-July 1946, *Path beneath the Woods* (1873) FRF 5,000; *Interior,* FRF 3,300. PARIS, 18 Oct 1946, *Barbary Organ Player, Rue Mouffetard* (1852, watercolour) FRF 3,300; *Amiens, with a Boat on a Canal* (1851, watercolour) FRF 6,100. PARIS, 29 Nov 1976, *Village of St Neuville, near Rouen* (1868, watercolour, 4 x 6 ins / 10 x 15.5 cm) FRF 3,100. PARIS, 8 June 1977, *Farm Courtyard* (oil on canvas, 15 x 22 ins / 38 x 55 cm) FRF 6,500. PARIS, 19 Oct 1979, *Farm Courtyard* (1841, oil on canvas, 12 3/4 x 18 1/2 ins / 32.5 x 47 cm) FRF 12,500. PARIS, 2 March 1981, *Pont-sur-Seine, at the House of Cimon* (1857, drawing in wash and watercolour, 8 3/4 x 12 1/2 ins / 22.5 x 32 cm) FRF 4,200. MONTE CARLO, 27 June 1983, *Market Day in a Town in Normandy* (oil on canvas, 9 1/2 x 12 3/4 ins / 24 x 32.5 cm) FRF 22,000. LONDON, 20 March 1985, *View of a Town at Sunset* (1855, oil on panel, 7 x 14 1/4 ins / 18 x 36 cm) GBP 1,600. PARIS, 27 March 1985, *Children outside a House* (1844, charcoal and graphite, 7 1/4 x 11 ins / 18.3 x 27 cm) FRF 14,000. PARIS, 24 March 1986, *Quai de la Mégisserie, Paris* (1850, watercolour, 11 1/2 x 17 1/4 ins / 29 x 44 cm) FRF 15,000. PARIS, 30 Nov 1987, *Pit Sawyers* (oil on canvas, 29 1/4 x 24 ins / 74 x 61 cm) FRF 6,000. PARIS, 22 Jan 1991, *View of Villeneuve* (1871, watercolour, 5 x 6 3/4 ins / 13 x 17.3 cm) FRF 4,800. AMSTERDAM, 30 Oct 1991, *Birch Trees Lining a Sandy Path* (oil on canvas, 18 x 29 3/4 ins / 45.5 x 75.5 cm) NLG 4,600. CALAIS, 5 July 1992, *Promenade at Barbizon* (1855, oil on canvas, 7 x 9 1/2 ins / 18 x 24 cm) FRF 5,500. PARIS, 18 Nov 1994, *Woman Plucking Poultry* (watercolour, 6 x 4 3/4 ins / 15 x 12 cm) FRF 4,000. PARIS, 12 May 1995, *Church of La Bouille near Rouen* (pencil and watercolour, 5 1/2 x 7 ins / 14 x 18 cm) FRF 5,600. PARIS, 20 Nov 1996, *View of a Port* (lead pencil, brown wash, watercolour, 5 1/2 x 4 1/4 ins / 14 x 10.5 cm) FRF 3,500. PARIS, 11 June 1997, *A Market in Normandy* (1857, watercolour/pen and wash, 5 1/2 x 7 1/4 ins / 13.8 x 18.2 cm) FRF 17,500. PARIS, 30 Oct 1997, *Small Wooden Bridge over a Stream, below a House* (graphite, watercolour and sepia wash/vellum, 10 1/4 x 7 1/2 ins / 26 x 19.3 cm) FRF 5,500. PARIS, 5 Dec 1997, *View of a Courtyard in Caen, after a Study in Oils Made from Nature in 1847* (1864, pen and sepia wash, 4 1/4 x 5 1/4 ins / 10.8 x 13.2 cm) FRF 3,200. FONTAINEBLEAU, 5 Dec 1999, *The Surroundings of Fontainebleau* (oil on canvas/cardboard, 9 x 16 ins / 23 x 40 cm) FRF 21,500. PARIS, 14 April 2000, *Ruined Château* (1856, oil on canvas, 14 x 11 ins / 35 x 28 cm) FRF 13,000. NEW YORK, 1 May 2000, *Man in Boat by Cottage in Wooded River Landscape* (oil on canvas, 24 x 39 ins / 62 x 99 cm) USD 5,000. NEW ORLEANS, 20 Jan 2001, *Sailing and Fishing Boats on Shore at Low Tide* (oil on panel, 13 x 9 ins / 33 x 23 cm) USD 3,600. MELUN, 20 May 2001, *Caulking a Boat near to a Village* (1867, oil on panel, 15 x 11 ins / 37 x 28 cm) FRF 32,000. PARIS, 25 March 2002, *Farm near Ruins* (oil on canvas, 13 x 11 ins / 34 x 28 cm) EUR 2,800. ZURICH, 24 Sept 2002, *Riverside Farmstead* (oil on canvas, 26 x 18 ins / 66 x 45 cm) CHF 4,300. PARIS, 30 March 2004, *Mills along the Road to Migny* (oil on canvas, 17 x 23 ins / 43 x 59 cm) EUR 4,500.

HERVIER, Louis Henri Victor Jules François Adolphe

French, 19th century.

Born in the 19th century, in Paris.

Painter, watercolourist, engraver. Landscapes.

Louis Henri was the son and pupil of Louis Adolphe Hervier, and made his Salon début in 1864. He produced paintings and engravings on similar subjects to those chosen by his father.

Museums and Galleries:

Blois: *Seascape.*

Auction records:

Paris, 26 May 1920, *Village at Sunset,* FRF 1,350; *Interior,* FRF 510. Paris, 12 June 1926, *Farm* (watercolour) FRF 300. Paris, 4 May 1984, *Sartrouville, Oise* (1865, watercolour, 4 1/4 x 6 ins / 10.8 x 15.4 cm) FRF 8,000.

HERVIEU, August

British, 19th century.

Active in London.

Painter. Portraits, genre scenes.

August Hervieu exhibited in London at the Royal Academy, the Suffolk Street Gallery and the British Institution from 1819 to 1858.

HERVIEU, Louise Jeanne Aimée

French, 20th century.

Born 26 October 1878, in Alençon; died 11 September 1954, in Versailles.

Painter, draughtswoman, illustrator. Religious subjects, scenes with figures, figures, nudes, interiors, genre scenes, still-lifes (flowers/fruit).

Louise Hervieu's sufferings nourished her talent and became the basis of her fame. She had inherited chronic meningitis. After studying drawing in Paris, she worked with Lucien Simon, René Menard and André Dauchez. A writer as much as a draughtswoman and a painter, one of her books, *Sangs (Bloods)*, reached a broad audience, propagating the poignant confession of a victim of heredity. A campaigner for the creation of the 'Carnet de Santé' (a record documenting the health of every French child), Louise Hervieu was overcome progressively by her illness and retreated from the world, confined to her room throughout the years. She pursued her limited, but nevertheless considerable, work in solitude. She almost lost her eyesight entirely, which would have brought her drawing, illustrating and writing to a halt.

In 1920, Louise Hervieu illustrated a collective work, *Le livre de Geneviève* (*The Book of Geneviève*), and in 1920 and 1922, *Les Fleurs du Mal* (*The Flowers of Evil*) and *Le Spleen de Paris* (*The Spleen of Paris*) by Charles Baudelaire. In 1924, she introduced *L'Âme du cirque* (*The Soul of the Circus*), illustrated by Bonnard, J.E. Blanche, Bourdelle, Hermann-Paul, Maurice Denis, Daragnès, Dunoyer de Segonzac and others. She illustrated and prefaced Baudelaire's *Poems* in 1946, and Verlaine's *Les Liturgies Intimes* (*The Intimate Liturgies*) in 1948. In the latter, sensual nudes people the shadows of secret interiors.

She published albums of her drawings as well as her own texts which she illustrated including: *Entretiens sur le dessin avec Geneviève* (*Interviews on Drawing with Geneviève*) (1921); *20 Nudes* (1922); *Le bon vouloir* (*Goodwill*) (1927); *Réminiscences* (1946).

No doubt due to her illness, Louise Hervieu gave up painting early and switched to charcoal drawing using a technique somewhat rough but making herself known, despite the falsely 'minor' status of the medium. In her drawings, deep black and white flashes tear through the shadows and evince a strange mixture of emotion, both amorous and morbid. Her figures and still-lifes occupy space in such a way as to reflect the rare rays of light filtered through the closed shutters of a secret universe.

Hervieu made her début as a painter in Paris in 1910, at the Galerie Eugène Blot, but would rarely exhibit her work. In 2003, she was included in the collective exhibition, *Peintres et artistes dans le Perche, 19e - 20e siècles* (*Painters and Artists in the Perche Region, 19th-20th Centuries*), Musée Château St-Jean de Nogent-le-Rotrou. The Galerie Katia Granoff, Paris exhibited an ensemble of her work in 1992.

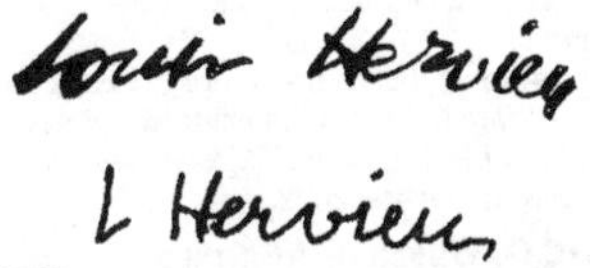

Bibliography:

Monod, Luc, *Manuel de l'amateur de livres illustrés modernes 1875-1975*, Ides et Calendes, Neuchâtel, 1992. Perry, Gillian, *Women artists and the Parisian avant-garde*, Manchester University Press, Manchester, 1995. Arpentinier, Jean, *Peintures et Artistes du Perche 1560-1960*, Editions de la Reinette, Le Mans, 2003.

Auction records:

Paris, 25 June 1923, *The Christ of the Mutilated* (pencil) FRF 67. Paris, 20 and 21 Dec 1926, *The Bohemian* (drawing) FRF 1,600. Paris, 8 Dec 1928, *The Old Servant* (drawing) FRF 5,600. Paris, 8 March 1933, *Still-life* (charcoal) FRF 2,300. Paris, 5 May 1937, *The Decapitated Woman* (lead pencil) FRF 500. Paris, 14 March 1945, *The Fruit Bowl* (pencil) FRF 29,000. Paris, 30 May 1947, *Old France* (charcoal) FRF 15,400. Paris, 9 July 1947, *Lesbians* (two drawings for Les Fleurs du Mal) FRF 12,100. Paris, 15 April 1988, *Nude on the Couch* (drawing in black pencil and charcoal, 21 1/4 x 16 3/4 ins / 54 x 42.5 cm) FRF 2,500. Paris, 6 Oct 1990, *Still-life with Bouquet of Lilacs* (charcoal, 28 x 20 1/2 ins / 71 x 52 cm) FRF 10,100. Paris, 4 April 1991, *Feather with Black Knot* (charcoal, 9 1/2 x 7 ins / 24 x 18 cm) FRF 4,200. Paris, 8 Nov 1993, *Le petit coucher* (*The Privileged Audience*) (charcoal and pencil, 25 x 19 ins / 63.5 x 48.5 cm) FRF 8,500. Paris, 20 March 1995, *At the Piano* (charcoal, 19 3/4 x 15 3/4 ins / 50 x 40 cm) FRF 6,100. Paris, 23 Nov 1997, *Still-life with Books and a Plant* (charcoal, 19 x 25 1/4 ins / 48 x 64 cm) FRF 9,000. Paris, 25 Nov 1997, *Still-life with feathers, Candelabras and Clock* (charcoal, 19 1/4 x 25 ins / 49 x 63.5 cm) FRF 5,600. Stuttgart, 27 Jan 2001, *Mask on the Weak Point* (1952, oil on board, 16 x 12 ins / 40 x 30 cm) DEM 4,500.

HERVIEUX, Jean Georges Louis

French, 20th century.

Born 6 November 1901, in Le Havre; died 1968, in Le Havre.

Painter, draughtsman.

Father of Jean, Jean Georges Louis Hervieux became, from 1905, the business associate of Charles Braque, a painting entrepreneur, and father of the painter Georges Braque. From the age of 15, Jean Hervieux studied with Édouard Courche at the École des Beaux-Arts in Le Havre. Four years later, he pursued his arts studies in Paris, along with his friend Jean Dubuffet, who was of the same age and also came from Le Havre. While fulfilling his military service in Paris, Jean Hervieux took evening courses at the École des Arts Décoratifs, as well as at an art school in Montparnasse. Throughout his life he painted for leisure as he was running a job at the same time. His work was almost entirely destroyed in September 1944, during the bombing of Le Havre by the allies. After the war, he took up painting once again. Louis Hervieux' still-lifes were influenced by his teacher, Édouard Courche, who was a pupil of Charles Lhullier. The latter taught Émile-Othon Friesz and Raoul Dufy, and was at the origin of what is called the École du Havre.

Louis Hervieux exhibited in Honfleur (1958), and in Le Havre (1959). In Le Havre, a street in the painters' quarter is named after him.

HERVIEUX, Nathalie

French, 20th century.

Photographer, mixed media.

In 1996, Nathalie Hervieux participated in the exhibition, *Inside the Visible*, devoted to female artistic creation at the Whitechapel Art Gallery in London.

BIBLIOGRAPHY:

Domino, Christophe, *'Inside the Visible - Venez voir les filles'* in *Beaux-Arts Magazine* n° 150, periodical, Paris, November 1996. Lang, Luc, *Les Invisibles. 12 récits sur l'art contemporain*, Éd. du Regard, Paris, 2002.

HERVIGO, Gustave Adolphe
French, 20th century.
Born 27 October 1896, in Rambouillet; died 1993.
Painter.

Gustave Hervigo received a travel grant from the French government in 1948, which enabled him to travel to equatorial Africa. An official painter in the Navy, he exhibited at the Salon des Indépendants from 1926 and at the Salon de la Société Nationale des Beaux-Arts in Paris from 1930. He featured posthumously in the exhibition, *Les Peintres Officiels de la Marine (Official Naval Painters)*, Galerie St-Hubert, Paris (2003).

HERVILLY, Mélanie Marie, later Mme Hahnemann
French, 19th century.
Born in Brussels, of French parents.
Painter, poet. Portraits, genre scenes.

Hervilly was a pupil of Guillon-Lethière. She exhibited some portraits and genre paintings at the Paris Salon in 1822 and 1824, and won a medal in 1824. She also published a poem in 1825, entitled *The Athenian Swallow*, which was sold in aid of the Greek independence struggle.

HERVO, Erkki
Finnish, 20th century.
Born 1924, in Helsinki.
Engraver.

Erkki Hervo took part in the Tokyo Biennale in 1970.

HERVY, Georges
French, 19th century.
Born in Paris.
Draughtsman, painter (porcelain).

Georges Hervy was a pupil of Houry and H. Lehmann. He first exhibited at the Salon in 1876, and is known for his portrait drawings.

HERVY, Jehan de, the Elder
Flemish, 15th - 16th century.
Born in Valenciennes.
Painter, draughtsman.
Flemish School.

In 1501 Jehan de Hervy the Elder designed the screen for the tomb of Mary of Burgundy in the Liebfrauen church in Bruges. He was a pupil of Pierre Coustain.

HERVY, Jehan de, the Younger
Flemish, 16th century.
Active in Bruges.
Painter.
Flemish School.

Jehan de Hervy the Younger was the son of Jehan de Hervy the Elder.

HERVY, Paul
French, 19th century.
Painter. Portraits, landscapes.

Paul Hervy exhibited at the Salon between 1845 and 1848.

HERVY-VAILLANT, Pierre-Yves
French, 20th - 21st century.
Born 1955.
Painter, installation artist.
Conceptual Art.

Hervy-Vaillant has exhibited his works in public places since 1989, including in Paris, New York and Florence.

AUCTION RECORDS:

PARIS, 29 June 1990, *Information Leaflet - Rembrandt's Night Watch* (engraving and adhesive tape) FRF 5,000.

HERWARTH, Wilhelm
German, 19th - 20th century.
Born 26 July 1853, in Berlin; died December 1916.
Painter, watercolourist. Architectural views.

Herwarth was a student of C. Wilbergs. He exhibited in Berlin from 1883 and was made a professor at the Berlin academy in 1891.

HERWEG, Stephan
German, 19th - 20th century.
Born 11 March 1855, in Elberfeld; died August 1914, in Rapperswil, Switzerland.
Painter.

After studying and working in Munich, Stephan Herweg settled in Rapperswil in 1898.

HERWEGEN, Peter
German, 19th century.
Born 15 February 1814, in Cologne; died 28 December 1893, in Munich.
Painter, draughtsman, lithographer.

Herwegen, a pupil of E Mengelberg from 1826 to 1830, went on to exhibit in Munich and Vienna between 1854 and 1883.

HERWEGEN-MANINI, Veronica Maria
German, 19th century.
Born 30 November 1851, in Munich.
Painter, watercolourist. Architectural views.

Herwegen-Manini, a pupil of W Lendenschmit, worked in Italy and Munich. She exhibited in Munich, Berlin, Vienna and Dresden from 1880.

HERWIG, Ferdinand
German, 19th - 20th century.
Active in Stuttgart.
Painter.

HERWIG, Joseph
German, 19th century.
Painter. Historical scenes.

Herwig worked in Vienna, Düsseldorf and Berlin, exhibiting there and in Munich between 1854 and 1883.

HERWIJCK, Steven Cornelisz. van
Dutch, 16th century.
Born c. 1530, in Utrecht; died perhaps c. 1565, in London.
Sculptor, medallist.

HERWIJNEN, Jan van
Dutch, 20th century.
Born 1889; died 1965.
Painter. Landscapes with figures, still-lifes, flowers.

Van Herwijnen painted some typical Dutch landscapes and some in France, mainly in the Collioure region, but he particularly specialised in painting flowers.

AUCTION RECORDS:

AMSTERDAM, 20 March 1978, *Still-life with Flowers and Fruit* (1951, oil on canvas, 30 x 31 1/4 ins / 76.4 x 79.5 cm) NLG 4,000. AMSTERDAM, 10 April 1989, *Still-life with Flowers* (oil on canvas, 33 1/2 x 30 1/2 ins / 85 x 77.5 cm) NLG 3,220. AMSTERDAM, 5-6 Feb 1991, *Barge on a Canal* (oil on canvas, 32 1/4 x 38 1/2 ins / 82 x 98 cm) NLG 4,025. AMSTERDAM, 23 May 1991, *Still-life with Chrysanthemums* (oil on canvas, 40 x 35 ins / 101.5 x 89 cm) NLG 13,800. AMSTERDAM, 19 May 1992, *Still-life with Chrysanthemums* (oil on canvas, 26 1/2 x 27 1/2 ins / 67 x 70 cm) NLG 1,840. AMSTERDAM, 21 May 1992, *Still-life* (oil on canvas, 24 1/2 x 29 1/4 ins / 62 x 74 cm) NLG 1,150. AMSTERDAM, 10 Dec 1992, *View of the Port at Collioure, France* (oil on canvas, 26 x 28 1/4 ins / 66 x 72 cm) NLG 4,370. AMSTERDAM, 27-28 May 1993, *Provence* (1935, oil on canvas, 24 x 24 1/2 ins / 61 x 62.5

cm) NLG 6,670. AMSTERDAM, 1 June 1994, *View of Collioure* (oil on canvas, 36 1/2 x 38 1/4 ins / 93 x 97 cm) NLG 8,280. AMSTERDAM, 31 May 1995, *Chrysanthemums in a Vase* (oil on canvas, 40 1/4 x 35 ins / 102 x 89 cm) NLG 9,440. AMSTERDAM, 10 Dec 1996, *Yellow Tulips in a Vase* (oil on canvas, 39 3/4 x 35 ins / 101 x 89 cm) NLG 7,495. AMSTERDAM, 2-3 June 1997, *Flowers in a Vase* (1917, oil on canvas, 38 1/4 x 32 ins / 97 x 81 cm) NLG 3,304. AMSTERDAM, 7 June 1999, *Painter's Garden* (1965, oil on board, 25 x 24 ins / 64 x 61 cm) NLG 3,800. AMSTERDAM, 10 June 1999, *Still-life with Plant, Apples and Cherries on a Plate* (oil on canvas, 24 x 20 ins / 60 x 50 cm) NLG 6,000. AMSTERDAM, 2 Dec 2003, *Still-life with Flowers* (1934, oil on canvas, 31 x 30 ins / 79 x 76 cm) EUR 2,700. AMSTERDAM, 9 June 2004, *Landscape at Sunset* (1921, oil on canvas, 32 x 6 ins / 82 x 14 cm) EUR 4,200. AMSTERDAM, 28 June 2004, *Flower Still-life* (oil on canvas, 41 x 32 ins / 103 x 81 cm) EUR 2,400.

HERWORDUS
Austrian, 14th century.
Illuminator.
In 1341 Herwordus painted a number of the illuminations in a Latin Bible now in the imperial museum in Vienna.

HERXHEIMER, Dora
British, 20th century.
Born in London.
Sculptor.
Dora Herxheimer exhibited at the Société Nationale des Beaux-Arts in Paris in 1911 and other years.

HERY, Martin de
French, 17th century.
Active in Paris in 1606.
Painter, sculptor.
Martin de Hery is probably the same artist who was working in Paris in 1629.

HERZ, Benedikt
German, 17th century.
Born 28 August 1594; died 21 October 1635, in Nuremberg.
Sculptor (wood/ivory).
Benedikt Herz was a son of Georg Herz.

HERZ, Emil W.
German, 20th century.
Born 3 December 1877, in Frankfurt am Main.
Painter.
Emil W. Herz worked in Berlin and exhibited in Paris in 1903.

HERZ, Ernesto
Spanish, 20th century.
Born in Barcelona.
Painter. Landscapes, seascapes.
Ernesto Herz studied at the school of fine arts in Barcelona. He took part in various group exhibitions, including the 1920 Barcelona Exhibition of Fine Arts.

HERZ, Georg
German, 17th century.
Born in Nuremberg; died 1634, in Danzig (now Gdansk, Poland).
Painter.
Georg Herz is probably the same artist as the painter and engraver, Johann Daniel Herz the Elder.

HERZ, Jacob
German, 18th century.
Died 6 October 1753, in Munich.
Painter.
MUSEUMS AND GALLERIES:
MUNICH (Mus.): two paintings.

HERZ, Johann
German, 17th century.
Born 18 November 1599, in Nuremberg; died 28 October 1635, in Nuremberg.
Painter.
Johann Herz executed large religious scenes and miniatures.

HERZ, Johann Daniel, the Elder
German, 18th century.
Born 1693, in Augsburg; died 1754, in Augsburg.
Draughtsman, engraver (burin). Historical scenes, figures.
Johann Daniel Herz the Elder, director of the Augsburg academy of art, primarily engraved historical subjects.
AUCTION RECORDS:
PARIS, 24 June 1929, *Old Woman Offering her Gold to a Young Man; Young Man Thanking an Old Woman Giving him her Gold* (two drawings) FRF 430.

HERZ, Johann Daniel, the Younger
German, 18th century.
Born 1720, in Augsburg; died 1793.
Painter, engraver.
Johann Daniel Herz the Younger was the son of Johann Daniel Herz the Elder.

HERZ, Joseph
French, 19th century.
Draughtsman, engraver.

HERZ, Mathias
French, 18th century.
Born 1727; died 1746.
Engraver (burin).
Mathias Herz engraved religious subjects.

HERZ DE HERZBERG, Johann Daniel
German, 18th century.
Active at the end of the 18th century.
Engraver.
Herz de Herzberg made engravings of the figures of saints and should probably be identified as Johann Daniel Herz the Younger.

HERZBERG, Robert
German, 19th century.
Born c. 1824, in Leipzig; died c. 1847.
Painter, lithographer.
Herzberg won the *Prix de Rome* while at the Dresden academy of art, but died before he was able to travel to Italy.

HERZELE, Maximilien
Italian, 20th century.
Born 27 January 1913, in Trieste.
Naturalised in France.
Painter. Designs for mosaics and stained glass windows.
Herzele was a pupil of Fernand Léger, André Lhote and Souverbie. He exhibited in Paris at the Salon des Réalités Nouvelles and the Salon d'Automne. He also made stained glass windows.

HERZGER, Walter
German, 20th century.
Painter.
Herzger is mentioned as a student of the Bauhaus.

HERZIG, August Albert Theodor
German, 19th - 20th century.
Born 3 August 1846, in Hamburg; died 11 July 1919, in Dresden.
Sculptor.

Herzig's most famous work is his *Monument to the War Dead of 1914-1918*, which he produced for the town of Darmstadt.

HERZIG, Édouard, or Edward
French, 19th - 20th century.
Born 1860, in Neuchâtel, Switzerland; died 1926, in Algiers.
Painter (gouache), watercolourist, draughtsman, illustrator, designer. Genre scenes, local scenes, landscapes with figures.
Orientalism.
School of Algiers.

Édouard Herzig arrived in Algeria at a young age, and settled in the Kabyle region. He made Oriental paintings and also numerous designs for carpets, fabrics and furniture, whose motifs derived directly from Arabian art.

He featured in the collective exhibition, *L'École d'Alger* (*The School of Algiers*), Musée des Beaux-Arts, Bordeaux (2003).

BIBLIOGRAPHY:
Barrucand, Victor, *L'Algérie et les Peintres orientalistes*, B. Arthaud éditeur, Grenoble, 1930. Cazenave, Elisabeth/Dalia, Mahammed-Orfali/Vidal-Bué, Marion, *L'École d'Alger*, exhibition catalogue, Musée des Beaux-Arts, Bordeaux, 2003.

MUSEUMS AND GALLERIES:
ALGIERS (Mus. National des Beaux-Arts).

AUCTION RECORDS:
PARIS, 6 April 1990, *Méknès* (gouache, watercolour and charcoal, 18 1/2 x 24 ins / 47 x 61 cm) FRF 12,000. PARIS, 21 June 1993, *Laundresses in the Oued Bou-Sâada* (watercolour, 15 3/4 x 22 1/2 ins / 40 x 57 cm) FRF 6,000. PARIS, 13 March 1995, *Tea at the Fruit Merchant's* (gouache, 17 1/4 x 23 1/2 ins / 44 x 60 cm) FRF 4,500. PARIS, 11 Dec 1995, *The Casbah in Algiers* (gouache, 16 1/4 x 12 1/2 ins / 41 x 32 cm) FRF 14,500. PARIS, 10-11 April 1997, *Tangiers* (1909, watercolour, 16 1/4 x 23 1/4 ins / 41 x 59 cm) FRF 6,500.

HERZIG, Gottfried
Swiss, 20th century.
Born 17 May 1870, in Obersteckholz, near Lotzwil; died in Überlingen (Bavaria).
Painter.

Herzig studied in Munich and then in Paris under the supervision of Constant and Laurens.

AUCTION RECORDS:
BERN, 1 May 1980, *View of the Jungfrau at Dusk* (1902, oil on canvas, 25 1/2 x 32 ins / 65 x 81 cm) CHF 1,900. LUCERNE, 30 Sept 1988, *Landscape from the Emmental Region* (1898, oil on canvas, 15 3/4 x 19 3/4 ins / 40 x 50 cm) CHF 740.

HERZIG, Wolfgang
Austrian, 20th century.
Born 24 October 1941, in Judenburg.
Painter. Figures, figure compositions, scenes with figures.
Wirklichkeiten (Realities) group.

Wolfgang Herzig studied at the Kunstgewerbeschule in Graz from 1955 to 1959. From 1959 to 1965 he completed his training at the Akademie der Bildenden Künste in Vienna under the direction of Sergius Pauser. He was a co-founder of the group Wirklichkeiten (Realities) in 1968 and he became a member of the Vienna Sezession in the same year. He was awarded the City of Vienna Prize for Painting in 1981. He became a member of the Berlin Künstlersonderbund in 1993 and a professor at the Institut für Bildende Kunst (Universität für Angewandte Kunst) in Vienna in 1997.

Together with the other members of the Wirklichkeiten group, Herzig was one of the main representatives of the renaissance of Realist painting in Austria in the late 1960s, even before Pop Art arrived in Vienna. He depicts a world that is reminiscent of that of the Expressionists and the Neue Sachlichkeit (New Objectivity), a world in which men and women become puppets in a vast caricature of a play. He portrays them going about their social business, 'meetings' that seem to be so many meetings missed. He also makes them exist in their unhappy intimacy by emphasising their nudity in a way that is often cruel. It is their physical rather than their amorous relationships that interest him, or perhaps the invincibility of the flesh. His compositions achieve clarity of form allied to an acute sense of colour. Scenes of systematic distortion applied to the figures with a sure sense of decorum, Herzig's paintings have developed in the direction of a synthetic stiffening of form.

Group exhibitions in which he has participated include: *Wirklichkeiten* (*Realities*), the founding exhibition of the group of that name (1968); *Österreichishe Aktzeichnungen von Klimt bis Heute* (*Austrian Nude Drawings from Klimt to the Present Day*) at the Vienna Sezession (1969); *From Austria with Love: Neun Junge Künstler aus Österreich* (*From Austria with Love: Nine Young Artists from Austria*) at the Kulturhaus in Graz (1978); *Wirklichkeiten: Aspekte einer Gruppierung* (*Realities: Aspects of a Grouping*) at the Museum des 20. Jahrhunderts in Vienna (1988); *Wien: Expressionistische Tendenzen nach 1945* (*Vienna: Expressionist Trends after 1945*) at the Salford Museum and Art Gallery in Manchester (1992); and *In Praise of Painting*, a retrospective of the Wirklichkeiten () group at the Kunsthaus Wien in Vienna (2002).

Herzig's solo and retrospective exhibitions include those at the following: the Galerie Synthese in Vienna (1965); the Neue Galerie in Graz (1986); *Wolfgang Herzig* at the Landessammlungen Salzburg Rupertinum in Salzburg (1995); *Wolfgang Herzig: Arbeiten von 1966 bis 1996* (*Wolfgang Herzig: Works from 1966 to 1996*) at the Hochschule für Angewandte Kunst in Vienna (1998).

BIBLIOGRAPHY:
Breicha, Otto von (ed.), *Wirklichkeiten: Aspekte einer Gruppierung*, exhibition catalogue, Museum des 20. Jahrhunderts, Vienna, 1988. Borchhardt-Birbaumer, Brigitte, *Wolfgang Herzig. Arbeiten von 1966 bis 1996*, Hochschule für Angewandte Kunst, Vienna, 1998.

MUSEUMS AND GALLERIES:
PARIS (BNF) - SALZBURG (Rupertinum) - VIENNA (Mus. Moderner Kunst Stiftung Ludwig).

HERZIG, Yvonne, or Kleiss-Herzig
French, 20th century.
Born 1895, in Algeria; died 1968.
Painter.
Orientalism.

Yvonne Herzig was a pupil of Jean-Paul Laurens; she exhibited in Paris at the Salon des Artistes Français.

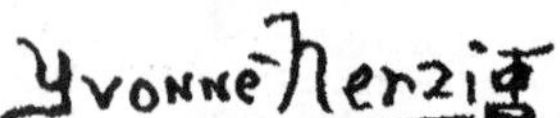

AUCTION RECORDS:
PARIS, 25 March 1977, *Camels* (oil on canvas, 43 1/4 x 31 1/2 ins / 110 x 80 cm) FRf 5,000. PARIS, 13 April 1992, *The Old Mule Driver and the Children* (pastel, 20 x 23 1/2 ins / 51 x 60 cm) FRF 4,600. PARIS, 16 Nov 1992, *Dancer and Musicians* (gouache, diam. 18 ins / 46 cm) FRF 14,500. PARIS, 5 April 1993, *Woman in White* (charcoal, pastel and gouache, 23 1/2 x 16 1/2 ins / 60 x 42 cm) FRF 15,000. PARIS, 10-11 June 1997, *Portrait of a Woman* (pastel/paper, 23 1/4 x 16 1/4 ins / 59 x 41 cm) FRF 8,000. PARIS, 8 Dec 2003, *Fountain* (gouache, 16 x 22 ins / 41 x 55 cm) EUR 3,000.

HERZINGER, Anton, or Hertzinger
Austrian, 18th - 19th century.
Born 18 November 1763, in Fallbach; died possibly 12 December 1826, in Prague.

Painter, engraver.

Herzinger worked at the Akademie der bildenden Künste in Vienna. He painted and engraved mythological subjects, views and animals.

HERZL, Kornel

Hungarian, 19th - 20th century.

Born 4 July 1858, in Budapest; died 6 August 1910, in Paris.

Painter. Genre scenes.

A pupil of Liezen-Mayer in Munich and of Flameng, Roll and Robert-Fleury in Paris, Kornel Herzl settled in France, exhibiting regularly at the Salon de Paris, and from 1888 in Munich, Berlin and Vienna.

AUCTION RECORDS:

London, 6 June 1990, *Flirtation in an Inn* (1893, oil on canvas, 50 3/4 x 38 ins / 129 x 96.5 cm) GBP 6,600.

HERZMANOVSKY-ORLANDO, Fritz von

German (?), 20th century.

Born 1877; died 1954.

Draughtsman.

AUCTION RECORDS:

Munich, 5 June 1981, *Miraculous Mountain* (1919, colouring pencil and graphite, 7 3/4 x 9 1/2 ins / 20 x 24 cm) DEM 2,200. Vienna, 16 March 1982, *Compositions in the Tropics* (1919, lead pencil and colouring pencil, 7 1/2 x 9 3/4 ins / 19 x 25 cm) ATS 18,000. Vienna, 2 Dec 1986, *Bolshevism* (1919, lead pencil and colouring pencil, 7 3/4 x 9 3/4 ins / 20 x 25 cm) ATS 30,000. Vienna, 19 May 1987, *Messenger of Love* (lead pencil and colouring pencil, 7 3/4 x 9 3/4 ins / 20 x 25 cm) ATS 30,000. New York, 2 May 1996, *Tyrolean Dancers* (1919, colouring pencil/paper, 7 3/4 x 10 ins / 20 x 25.1 cm) USD 1,380. Vienna, 29 April 1999, *Sleep-walking Diana with One of Hannibal's Elephants* (1919, pencil, colour pencil and gold, 8 x 7 ins / 20 x 18 cm) ATS 32,000. Vienna, 19 May 1999, *Another Mermaid!* (1920, pencil and colour pencil, 10 x 8 ins / 25 x 20 cm) ATS 32,000. Vienna, 14 May 2002, *Composition* (1919, pencil and colour pen, 8 x 10 ins / 20 x 25 cm) EUR 3,000. Salzburg, 12 June 2002, *Attention - Paris Verdict* (1918, 7 x 9 ins / 18 x 24 cm) EUR 2,200. Vienna, 26 Nov 2003, *Onslaught of the Trinacrie* (1919, pencil and colour pen, 10 x 8 ins / 25 x 20 cm) EUR 3,000. Vienna, 26 Nov 2003, *Two Writers and Two Flying Horses* (1919, 8 x 10 ins / 20 x 25 cm) EUR 3,400. Vienna, 25 May 2004, *Lovesick* (1919, pencil and colour pen, 9 x 7 ins / 23 x 19 cm) EUR 2,000. Vienna, 25 May 2004, *Commedia dell'Arte* (pencil and colour pen, 9 x 11 ins / 22 x 28 cm) EUR 2,600.

HERZOG, Georg

Austrian, 19th century.

Active in Vienna.

Sculptor.

HERZOG, Hermann

German, 19th - 20th century.

Born 15 November 1832, in Bremen; died 1932?.

Painter. Landscapes with figures, landscapes, animals.

Hermann Herzog was a student of W. Schirmer Lessing, Achenbach and Gude at the Düsseldorf academy. He travelled in Switzerland, Italy and Norway, then left for North America, where he settled in Philadelphia. He first exhibited in 1858 and he then exhibited fairly frequently in Berlin, even after his departure from Europe.

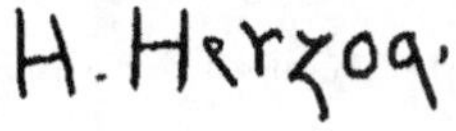

MUSEUMS AND GALLERIES:

Hanover: *Norwegian Fjord*; *Norwegian Waterfall* - Mulhouse: *Waterfall in Norway* - Springfield, MA (MFA): *View of Niagara Falls in Moonlight* (1872, oil on canvas).

AUCTION RECORDS:

Amsterdam, 25 Oct 1904, *In the Black Forest*, FRF 1,108. New York, 19 Jan 1906, *Mill over a Torrent*, USD 376. New York, 27 May 1909, *Torrent in the Alps*, USD 80. New York, 28 Jan 1970, *Arkville, New York*, USD 1,000. New York, 18 Nov 1977, *Lake at Sunset* (1896, oil on canvas, 22 x 36 ins / 56 x 91.5 cm) USD 3,000. New York, 23 May 1979, *View of a Fjord* (oil on canvas, 30 x 42 1/4 ins / 76.5 x 107 cm) USD 6,000. New York, 27 March 1981, *Alpine Landscape* (1869, charcoal and white chalk, 21 1/4 x 15 1/2 ins / 53.8 x 39.3 cm) USD 900. New York, 28 Jan 1982, *Fisherman Returning* (oil on canvas, 24 x 30 ins / 61 x 76.2 cm) USD 8,750. New York, 21 Oct 1983, *Fishing on the Susquehanna River* (oil on canvas, 18 x 27 1/4 ins / 45.8 x 69.2 cm) USD 17,000. New York, 21 Sept 1984, *Alpine Lake* (watercolour and gouache, 8 1/2 x 11 1/2 ins / 21.7 x 29.5 cm) USD 1,400. New York, 5 Dec 1986, *Western Waterfall* (oil on canvas, 33 x 40 1/2 ins / 84 x 103 cm) USD 40,000. New York, 29 May 1987, *Pond in a Wooded Landscape* (oil on canvas, 30 x 40 1/4 ins / 76.2 x 102.2 cm) USD 60,000. New York, 17 March 1988, *Canal in Venice* (oil on canvas, 27 1/2 x 33 1/2 ins / 70 x 85 cm) USD 5,500. New York, 26 May 1988, *The Matterhorn, Switzerland* (oil on canvas, 30 x 40 ins / 76.2 x 101.6 cm) USD 33,000. New York, 30 Sept 1988, *On a Glacier Lake* (oil on canvas, 14 x 19 1/2 ins / 35.7 x 49.8 cm) USD 7,700. New York, 1 Dec 1988, *St John River in Florida* (oil on canvas, 61 x 51 ins / 154.9 x 129.5 cm) USD 41,250. New York, 25 May 1989, *Travellers in the Mountains* (1867, oil on canvas, 37 1/2 x 56 ins / 95.5 x 142.5 cm) USD 33,000. New York, 30 Nov 1989, *Fishing Village by an Alpine Lake* (1859, oil on canvas, 48 x 75 1/2 ins / 122 x 191.8 cm) USD 49,500. London, 6 June 1990, *Fishermen near Boats in a Harbour* (1870, oil on panel, 11 x 14 1/4 ins / 27 x 36.5 cm) GBP 4,070. New York, 26 Sept 1990, *Landscape with a Cabriolet* (oil on canvas, 17 1/4 x 27 ins / 43.8 x 68.6 cm) USD 13,200. New York, 17 Dec 1990, *View over the Hundeck Valley in Switzerland* (oil on canvas, 10 3/4 x 15 1/4 ins / 27.3 x 38.8 cm) USD 3,190. New York, 12 April 1991, *Stag in a Forest Interior in Pike County, Pennsylvania* (1882, oil on canvas, 40 1/2 x 33 ins / 102.9 x 83.8 cm) USD 55,000. New York, 6 Dec 1991, *Fishing* (oil on canvas, 22 x 27 ins / 56 x 68.5 cm) USD 22,000. New York, 27 May 1992, *Waterfall* (oil on canvas, 24 1/2 x 35 ins / 62.2 x 88.9 cm) USD 29,700. New York, 4 Dec 1992, *Break* (oil on canvas, 24 x 28 1/4 ins / 61 x 71.8 cm) USD 24,200. New York, 10 March 1993, *Bear near a Cataract* (1874, oil on card, 17 x 14 ins / 43.2 x 35.6 cm) USD 24,150. New York, 26 May 1993, *Summer Afternoon on a Pond* (oil on canvas, 18 x 24 1/4 ins / 46 x 61.4 cm) USD 46,000. New York, 1 Dec 1994, *Old Watermill* (1872, oil on canvas, 28 x 41 ins / 71.1 x 104.1 cm) USD 54,050. London, 11 Oct 1995, *Mountain Torrent with a Mill* (1858, oil on canvas, 52 x 83 1/2 ins / 132 x 212 cm) GBP 12,650. Amsterdam, 16 April 1996, *Stormy Day* (oil on canvas, 35 3/4 x 48 ins / 91 x 121 cm) NLG 14,160. New York, 23 May 1996, *Deer in a Landscape by Moonlight* (oil on canvas, 20 x 29 ins / 50.8 x 73.6 cm) USD 26,450. New York, 27 Sept 1996, *Relaxation* (oil on canvas, 24 x 28 1/4 ins / 61 x 71.8 cm) USD 9,775. New York, 30 Oct 1996, *Flock of Sheep at Dusk* (oil on canvas, 16 1/4 x 24 1/4 ins / 41 x 61.3 cm) USD 4,312. New York, 25 March 1997, *Evening on an Island, Norway* (oil on canvas, 19 x 27 ins / 48.3 x 68.6 cm) USD 2,875; *Landscape with Raging Torrent and Old Watermill* (1869, oil on canvas, 25 x 37 ins / 63.5 x 94 cm) USD 12,075. New York, 23 April 1997, *Animals Resting in the Woods* (oil on canvas, 18 x 23 ins / 45.7 x 58.4 cm) USD 2,990; *Bridge over the Canal* (oil on canvas, 19 x 16 1/4 ins / 48.5 x 41 cm) USD 5,175; *Heron in the Everglades* (oil on canvas, 22 x 31 ins / 55.9 x 78.7 cm) USD

36,800. NEW YORK, 5 June 1997, *Fishing near the Mill* (1878, oil on canvas, 28 x 40 ins / 71.1 x 101.6 cm) USD 36,800.

HERZOG, Jakob
Swiss, 19th century.
Born 28 May 1867, in Truttikon.
Painter.

Jakob Herzog worked for Winterthur Museum.

HERZOG, Josef
Swiss, 20th century.
Born 1939, in Zoug.
Draughtsman, watercolourist.

Josef Herzog lives in Aarau, where he is a professor of drawing. He mainly produces pencil drawings and watercolours. He creates a kind of landscaped view that consists of forms that are not identifiable or rigorously geometrical and that sometimes contains silhouettes of figures that give the scene a Surrealist dimension. Other series of watercolour drawings are radically abstract. He uses simple colours according to their synaesthetic potential. Herzog took part in the exhibition of artists from Aarau at the town theatre in St Gall in 1971.

HERZOG, Leonhard
German, 19th century.
Born 2 April 1863, in Schweinau.
Sculptor.

Leonhard Herzog worked in Nuremberg.

HERZOG, Lewis
American, 19th century.
Born 15 October 1868, in Philadelphia; died 1943, in Washington DC.
Painter.

Lewis Herzog studied in the great European centres of art. He was a member of the Philadelphia Art Club, the Salmagundi Club and the American Federation of Arts.

HERZOG, Ludwig Edouard
German, 19th - 20th century.
Born 15 October 1871, in Ludenburg (now Breclav, Czech Republic).
Active in the USA.
Painter. Landscapes, seascapes.

Herzog was the student of his father, Hermann Herzog, in Philadelphia, then returned to Germany in 1892 and became a student of Ducker in Düsseldorf. He held his first exhibition in Philadelphia.

MUSEUMS AND GALLERIES:
BERLIN: *Boats on the Rhine* - MUNICH: *Southern Heat.*

HERZOG, Oswald
German, 20th century.
Born 1881; probably died during World War II.
Sculptor.

Herzog, a famous artist in Berlin, associated with the Sturm (Storm) group. In 1919, he joined the Novembergruppe (November Group). He exhibited his works in the same year at the 'Sturm' gallery. He advocated a 'new objectivity' and favoured rhythm, 'proportion of time and space'. His figure sculptures are recumbent, even distorted, to the point of losing any individual form after 1920. His works are rare.

BIBLIOGRAPHY:
Breuer, K., *German Expressionist Sculpture*, exhibition catalogue, Los Angeles County Museum of Art, Los Angeles, 1983.

MUSEUMS AND GALLERIES:
BERLIN (Nationalgal.): *Kneeling Woman* (sculpture).

AUCTION RECORDS:
LONDON, 9 Oct 1996, *Kneeling Female Figure* (c. 1920, painted wood, h. 5 3/4 ins / 14.8 cm) GBP 13,800.

HERZOG, Peter
Swiss, 19th century.
Born 5 May 1794, in Rome; died 13 October 1864, in Rome.
Painter.

Peter Herzog was an officer in the Pope's Swiss Guard.

HESCHLER, David
German, 17th century.
Active in Ulm.
Sculptor.

The Berlin Prints Collection has some drawings by David Heschler.

HESDIN, Jacquemart de. See **JACQUEMART DE HESDIN**

HESDIN, Simon
French, 14th century.
Illuminator.

Simon Hesdin was also a translator.

HESELTINE, Arthur
British, 19th - 20th century.
Born 26 February 1855, near London; died 1930, in Marlotte (now Bourron-Marlotte), near Fontainebleau, France.
Painter, engraver.

Arthur Heseltine was a pupil of Carolus Duran. He produced a series of etchings and oil paintings of Fontainebleau.

HESELTINE, John Postle
British, 19th - 20th century.
Born 6 January 1843, in Dilham (Norfolk); died 2 March 1929.
Engraver.

John Postle Heseltine, who was a friend of Whistler and many other English artists, was a trustee of the National Gallery for which he collected large numbers of pictures, drawings and objets d'art. He was also an amateur etcher, producing prints for various publications, including: *Venice from the Lido* (published in *Art*), *Ramsgate Harbour* and *Willey Churchyard* in *The Etcher*, *Salisbury* in *The Portfolio* and *Grove Park* in the *Art Journal*.

He exhibited at the Royal Academy and at the Salon de Paris from 1869, and was a member of the Royal Society of Painters, Etchers and Gravers and an associate member of the Société Nationale des Beaux-Arts in Paris.

HESELTINE, W.
British, 19th century.
Active in London c. 1800.
Painter, engraver.

W. Heseltine exhibited portraits and genre subjects at the Royal Academy in London.

HESEMAN, Pieter Janzs
Dutch, 17th century.
Active in Amsterdam.
Painter.

A painting by this artist is in the academy in Vienna.

HESEMANN, Heinrich
German, 19th century.
Born 27 June 1814, in Hanover; died 29 May 1856, in Hanover.
Sculptor.

MUSEUMS AND GALLERIES:
HANOVER: *Bust of Leibniz.*

HESKI, Jozef
Polish, 18th - 19th century.
Died at the beginning of 19th century, in Niesvicz.
Painter.

For a time, Jozef Heski worked for the Radzivill gallery in Niesvicz.

HESPEL, Grégoire
French, 20th - 21st century.
Born 3 September 1961, in Paris.
Painter.
Hespel studied at the École des Arts Décoratifs in Paris from 1982 until 1986. Although his subjects are very diverse - a mackerel on a chair, landscapes in the Ardèche, a classic still-life of a lamp and coffee pot, boats, a horse - he nevertheless stamps them with his own personal touch, painting with skill and spontaneity. He has exhibited in Paris, including at the Galerie Claude Bernard in 1994.

HESS, Anton Heinrich
German, 19th century.
Born 20 August 1838, in Munich; died 11 April 1909, in Munich.
Sculptor.
Anton Hess, a pupil of Zumbusch in Munich, travelled for many years in Italy.

HESS, August
German, 19th century.
Born 14 February 1834, in Munich; died 20 October 1893, in Munich.
Painter. Historical scenes.
August Hess first exhibited in 1861.
MUSEUMS AND GALLERIES:
MUNICH: *St Theresa.*

HESS, Benedikt Franz
Swiss, 19th century.
Born 23 June 1817, in Paris.
Painter. Landscapes.
Benedikt Hess, son of Moses Ludwig Hess, studied under Charles Louis Guigon.
AUCTION RECORDS:
NEW YORK, 28 May 1981, *On the Banks of Lake Geneva* (oil on canvas, 25 x 30 ins / 63.5 x 76 cm) USD 2,500. VIENNA, 17 Nov 1982, *View of the Lake of the Four Cantons* (oil on canvas, 25 1/4 x 30 3/4 ins / 64 x 78 cm) ATS 75,000.

HESS, Carl
German, 19th century.
Born 1801, in Düsseldorf; died 10 November 1874, in Reichenhall.
Painter, engraver. Genre scenes, landscapes, animals.
Carl Hess studied engraving with his father, Carl Ernst Christoph Hess. From 1822 he went on to devote himself to painting. He worked at the school of art in Munich under J. Wagenbauer and was particularly successful with his alpine landscapes.

MUSEUMS AND GALLERIES:
MUNICH (NG): *Tyrol Landscape; Cattle Grazing.*
AUCTION RECORDS:
VIENNA, 11 Sept 1985, *Shores of the Lake* (oil on panel, 9 1/4 x 14 1/4 ins / 23.5 x 36 cm) ATS 50,000. DÜSSELDORF, 31 Jan 2000, *Altausee* (oil on panel, 23 x 31 ins / 58 x 78 cm) DEM 7,000.

HESS, Carl Adolph Heinrich
German, 18th - 19th century.
Born 1769, in Dresden; died 3 July 1849, in Wilhemsdorf, near Vienna.
Painter, engraver. Military subjects, horses.
Hess studied with Klass for painting and Krüger for engraving in Dresden. He painted in oil, watercolour and pastel. In addition to his paintings, he left a series of many engravings collated under the title *Riding School.*

HESS, Carl Ernst Christoph
German, 18th - 19th century.
Born 22 January 1755, in Darmstadt; died 25 July 1828, in Munich.
Engraver.
Carl Ernst Hess, originally destined to become a gunsmith, studied metal engraving. A *Hunt* he reproduced on a knife, presented to Maximilian of Bavaria, earned him the patronage of the prince, who provided him with the means to make engravings. His first work was so remarkable that he was elected member of the academy of art in Düsseldorf, where he subsequently became professor. He travelled in Italy and reproduced the paintings of Raphael, Guido and other Old Masters with great accuracy.

HESS, Christian Carl Ludwig
German, 19th century.
Born 8 January 1776, in Weissenfels; died 1853, in Jena.
Engraver.
MUSEUMS AND GALLERIES:
IENA (Stadtmus.): several works.

HESS, David
Swiss, 18th - 19th century.
Born 29 November 1770, in Zurich; died 11 April 1843.
Draughtsman.
David Hess, a Swiss Guard in The Hague, executed caricatures based on the French Revolution.

HESS, Esther, pseudonym of Esther-Hess
Swiss, 20th century.
Born 9 August 1919, in Pforzheim.
Active from 1954 in France.
Sculptor, installation artist, painter. Designs for tapestries.
Esther Hess studied at the school of fine arts in Zurich and then in Berlin. From 1950, she exhibited in Italy, France, Switzerland and Germany. She participated in group exhibitions as a painter, including the 1952 Messina Biennale, the 1956 Salon Comparaisons in Paris and at the museums in St-Étienne and Antibes in 1965. From 1971, she exhibited as a sculptor at the Paris Salons de Mai, Grands et Jeunes d'Aujourd'hui, SAGA and others.

Her abstract sculptures are composed of flat planes stacked one on top of the other, in the manner of architectural models. She also creates colourful tapestries that make use of the effects of different thicknesses of material. Thirdly, she works with the wind, by means of installations made of pieces of fabric, whose movements 'make the invisible visible'. Her work, which is governed by geometry and natural laws, evokes the universe and the forces and energies running through it. It presents space - constellations, compass points, the horizon, imaginary lines of longitude and latitude - in pure, minimalist installations made up of many different materials - crystal, Plexiglas, lead, iron, granite, sulphur and wood.
BIBLIOGRAPHY:
Esther Hess, exhibition leaflet, Centre d'Arts plastiques Albert-Chanot, Clamart, 1992.

HESS, Eugen
German, 19th century.
Born 25 June 1824, in Munich; died 21 November 1862, in Munich.
Painter, engraver. Genre scenes.
Eugen von Hess, having taken lessons with his father, Peter Heinrich Lambert von Hess, went on to work at the Munich academy of art and also in Brussels and Paris. In addition to his paintings, which depict scenes from modern and medieval life, he also executed some etchings, some of which are remarkable in terms of execution. Hess exhibited first in Munich in 1846 and then also in Prague.

Museums and Galleries:
Munich: *Knight as a Guest of the Dominicans; The Swedish General Wrangel on the Hunt Surprised by the Enemy.*
Auction records:
Vienna, 5 Dec 1984, *The Fox Hunt* (1857, oil on canvas, 26½ x 20¾ ins / 67 x 53 cm) ATS 35,000. London, 3 Dec 2002, *Returning from the Hunt* (1855, oil on canvas, 28 x 23 ins / 70 x 59 cm) GBP 1,900.

HESS, Georg
American, 19th century.
Born 29 September 1832, in Pfungstadt, Germany.
Sculptor.
Georg Hess was penniless. He studied in Munich and America and gained something of a reputation for his marble busts, which possess great intensity of expression.

HESS, Heinrich Karl Gottfried
German, 19th century.
Born 7 August 1860, in Frankfurt am Main.
Painter. Portraits, genre scenes.
Heinrich Hess studied under Hasselhorst.

HESS, Heinrich Maria von
German, 19th century.
Born 19 April 1798, in Düsseldorf; died 29 March 1863, in Munich.
Painter, glass painter, draughtsman, fresco artist.
Religious subjects, mythological subjects, genre scenes, landscapes. Designs for stained glass.
Nazarenes group (related to).
Heinrich von Hess, after studying with his father, Carl Ernst Christoph Hess, entered the Munich academy of arts in 1813. Queen Caroline became his patron and bought his first paintings, which appeared in 1817. In 1823, during a stay in Rome, he painted *Parnassus*. A few years later, after returning from Rome, he became a convert to the aesthetic and mystical ideas of the Nazarenes Group, a group founded by a number of artists including the German painter, Friedrich Overbeck, and was appointed professor at the Munich academy of art. His skilfulness at painting on glass earned him the post of director of an establishment set up to promote glass painting.

Hess' works comprise numerous religious paintings, mythological subjects and some genre paintings. Baron Eichtal owns the original of *Christmas Eve*, popularised by the reproduction. Hess executed the cartoon for the stained glass windows in Regensburg Cathedral and the Allerheiligenkirche in Munich.

Museums and Galleries:
Munich: *Countryside; Institution of the Holy Communion; Portrait of Marchioness Florenzi in Ravenna; Altarpiece; Apollo and the Muses; Portrait of the Artist, Thorvaldsen; Peasant on a Pilgrimage to Rome.*
Auction records:
Munich, 29 May 1980, *Woman Reading* (1823, pencil/paper, 9¼ x 5¾ ins / 23.5 x 14.5 cm) DEM 1,800. Berlin, 5 Dec 1986, *Rest during the Flight to Egypt* (pen, 5 x 4 ins / 13 x 10.2 cm) DEM 3,000. London, 19 Nov 1993, *The Flight to Egypt* (1822, oil/metal, 12¼ x 14¼ ins / 31.1 x 36.4 cm) GBP 17,250. New York, 22 Jan 2003, *Allegories of Faith, Hope and Charity* (1819, graphite, pen and ink heightened with white, 13 x 14 ins / 32 x 36 cm) USD 4,200.

HESS, Hieronymus
Swiss, 19th century.
Born 1799, in Basel; died 8 June 1850, in Basel.
Painter, engraver. Historical scenes.
Hieronymus Hess was a pupil of Maximilien Neustuch in Basel and then of JA Kock in Italy, where he lived from 1821 to 1823. He returned to settle in Basel, where he was a teacher at the school of drawing. In addition to his paintings of historial scenes, Hess established a reputation for his extremely witty caricatures. Many of his caricatures were shown at the *Karikaturen von Hogarth bis Daumier* at the Kunsthaus in Zurich in 2001. *Caricatures from Hogarth to Daumier*

Museums and Galleries:
Basel: *The Jews in Rome; The Blacksmiths' Guild; The Battle of St Jacob; The Assassination of King Albrecht.*
Auction records:
Munich, 29 May 1980, *Street Scene, Naples* (1820, watercolour/pen outline, 10¾ x 13¾ ins / 27.5 x 35 cm) DEM 4,800. Bern, 16 May 2002, *Interior of Synagogue in Rome* (pen and watercolour heightened with white, 11 x 18 ins / 29 x 46 cm) CHF 7,100.

HESS, Johann Franz Adam
Swiss, 18th - 19th century.
Born c. 1740, in Fulda; died 25 February 1814, in Geneva.
Engraver.
Johann Franz Adam Hess mainly executed views of Switzerland.

HESS, Johann Friedrich
Bohemian, 17th century.
Died 1693, in Prague.
Painter.
Johann Friedrich Hess painted altarpieces for the churches of St Nicholas and St Giles in Prague.

HESS, Johann Heinrich
German, 18th century.
Born 1746, in Zweibrücken.
Engraver.
Johann Heinrich Hess is best known for his plates copied after Rembrandt.

HESS, Johann Michael. See **HESZ János Mihály**

HESS, Josef Anton
German, 19th century.
Died 28 July 1818, in Cologne.
Active in Cologne.
Painter, decorative designer.
Josef Hess also worked in Würzburg.

HESS, Julius
German, 20th century.
Born 16 April 1878, in Stuttgart; died 1957.
Painter. Still-lifes.
Julius Hess was active mainly in Munich.
Auction records:
Munich, 31 May 1979, *Still-life* (c. 1915, oil on canvas, 22¾ x 29¼ ins / 58 x 74 cm) DEM 3,200. Munich, 27 Feb 1999, *Hofgarten in Munich with Temple of Diana* (oil on canvas, 20 x 26 ins / 52 x 65 cm) DEM 11,500. Stuttgart, 23 Oct 1999, *Girl in Greenhouse* (c. 1920, oil on canvas, 22 x 30 ins / 56 x 76 cm) DEM 6,500. Bremen, 30 March 2001, *Summer Flowers in a White Vase* (oil on canvas, 31 x 28 ins / 79 x 70 cm) DEM 6,000.

HESS, Karl Gotthard
Latvian, 19th century.
Born 1818; died 1867, in Riga.
Lithographer.
Karl Gotthard Hess is known for his views of Riga.

HESS, Leonhard Franz
Swiss, 18th - 19th century.

Born 1772 or 1777, in Presburg; died 1875, in Geneva.
Painter, miniaturist. Frescoes.

MUSEUMS AND GALLERIES:
GENEVA (MAH): *Portrait of a Woman* (after Titian); *Young Man with Crayfish.*

HESS, Ludwig
Swiss, 18th century.
Born 16 October 1760, in Zurich; died 13 April 1800, in Zurich.
Painter, engraver (etching/aquatint).

Ludwig Hess, a pupil of Salomon Gessner, visited Italy around 1794, spending most of his time there in Rome and Florence. He painted mainly views of the Alps and Italian motifs, while his engravings are of landscapes and animals.

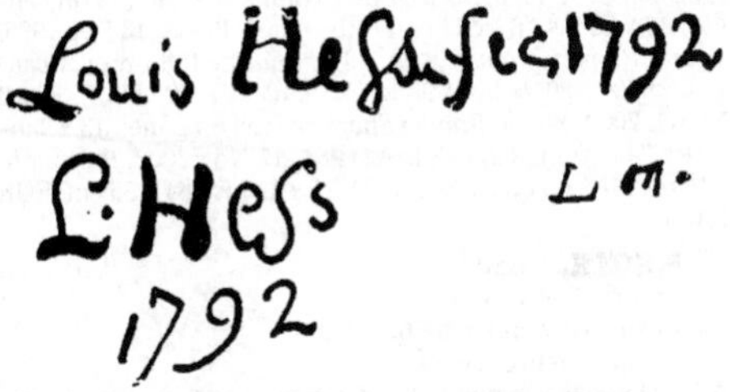

AUCTION RECORDS:
ZURICH, 14 May 1982, *Bernese Oberland Landscape* (1798, oil on panel, 20 1/2 x 25 1/2 ins / 52 x 65 cm) CHF 15,000. LUCERNE, 19 May 1983, *Italian Landscape* (1795, oil on canvas, 20 1/2 x 29 ins / 52 x 73.5 cm) CHF 16,000. ZURICH, 2 June 1994, *Bommerstein Ruins by the Walensee* (1789, watercolour and gouache/paper, 15 1/2 x 21 1/4 ins / 39.5 x 54 cm) CHF 3,680. ZURICH, 8 Dec 1994, *Lake Lugano and the Village of Porlezza* (oil on panel, 13 1/2 x 20 ins / 34 x 50.5 cm) CHF 4,600. ZURICH, 9 June 1999, *Mill on River* (oil on panel, 10 x 14 ins / 26 x 35 cm) CHF 3,500. ZURICH, 4 Nov 2000, *Lower Alpine Landscape with Stream* (1795, oil on panel, 20 x 30 ins / 52 x 75 cm) CHF 8,500. LONDON, 26 April 2001, *Panoramic Landscape with Travellers Resting* (1796, oil on panel, 17 x 29 ins / 42 x 73 cm) GBP 3,300. ZURICH, 3 Dec 2001, *Walensee and Kurfirsten* (1795, oil on canvas, 31 x 46 ins / 80 x 116 cm) CHF 18,000. ZURICH, 24 June 2003, *Landscape with Mountain and Fortress* (oil on panel, 13 x 20 ins / 34 x 50 cm) CHF 3,300. LUCERNE, 19 Nov 2003, *Romantic River Landscape with Ruins* (1782, oil on panel, 11 x 16 ins / 29 x 41 cm) CHF 10,000.

HESS, Ludwig Adolf
Swiss, 19th century.
Born 31 August 1800, in Zurich; died 16 May 1826.
Painter. Landscapes.

Ludwig Adolf Hess was a son of David Hess.

HESS, Marcel
Belgian, 20th century.
Born 1878, in Brussels; died 1948.
Painter, draughtsman. Figures, portraits, flowers.

Marcel Hess studied at the academies in Brussels and Düsseldorf.

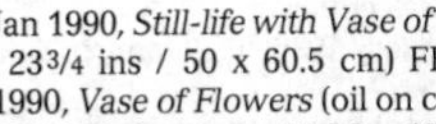

AUCTION RECORDS:
VERSAILLES, 28 Jan 1990, *Still-life with Vase of Flowers* (oil on canvas, 19 3/4 x 23 3/4 ins / 50 x 60.5 cm) FRF 8,000. VERSAILLES, 21 Oct 1990, *Vase of Flowers* (oil on card, 19 x 20 ins / 48 x 51 cm) FRF 5,000. LOKEREN, 23 May 1992, *Seated Girl* (oil on card, 21 x 17 ins / 53.5 x 43 cm) BEF 30,000. AMSTERDAM, 2 Nov 1992, *Feeding Crumbs to the Goldfish* (pastel, 23 3/4 x 13 ins / 60.5 x 33 cm) NLG 3,450. NEW ORLEANS, 8 Dec 2000, *Portrait of a Young Girl in a Pink Dress* (1923, oil on canvas, 40 x 32 ins / 102 x 81 cm) USD 1,500. MAISIERES, 16 May 2004, *Female Nude Looking at Herself, Seen from Behind* (oil on canvas, 53 x 33 ins / 135 x 85 cm) EUR 1,900.

HESS, Mary G.. See **BUEHR Mary G.**

HESS, Max
German, 19th century.
Born 15 October 1825, in Munich; died 19 July 1868, in Lippspringe.
Painter. Historical scenes.

Max Hess, the son of Peter Heinrich Lambert von Hess, taught himself in Paris and in Düsseldorf, where he held the posts of actor, singer and painter decorator at the same time. He first exhibited in 1857.

HESS, Moses Ludwig
Swiss, 19th century.
Born 16 February 1778, in Geneva; died 27 April 1851, in Geneva.
Painter. Still-lifes.

Moses Hess was a son of Johann Franz Adam Hess.

AUCTION RECORDS:
LUCERNE, 30 May 1979, *Still-life with Flowers and Fruit* (oil on canvas, 22 x 18 ins / 56 x 46 cm) CHF 3,500.

HESS, Peter Heinrich Lambert von
German, 19th century.
Born 29 July 1792, in Düsseldorf; died 4 April 1871, in Munich.
Painter, draughtsman, engraver. Historical subjects, battles, military subjects, portraits, genre scenes, landscapes, animals.
Biedermeier.

Peter von Hess, a pupil and son of Carl Ernst Christoph Hess, devoted almost all his attentions to painting historical scenes. He followed the prince of Wrede throughout the 1813-1815 campaign, visited Switzerland and Italy, and accompanied Prince Othon, son of King Max, to Greece. During the course of his travels, he executed many sketches, his last expedition providing him with the subject for the paintings depicting the *Liberation of Greece* that can be seen in the arcades in Munich's Hofgarten. Munich and Berlin Museums preserve many of his works. His *King Othon Entering Nauplia* includes many portraits of his contemporaries. He painted the principal battles of the war of 1812 for the emperor of Russia and was appointed a member of the St Petersburg academy of art, being already a member of the Vienna, Munich and Berlin Academies of Art.

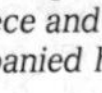

MUSEUMS AND GALLERIES:
BERLIN: *Canteen Scene* - LEIPZIG: *Duck Hunt* - MUNICH: *Battle of Austerlitz; King Othon Entering Nauplia; King Othon Entering Athens; In front of an Italian Inn; Italian Peasant Family in Rivoli; San Marino of Old; Greek Peasants; Capturing Horses in Wallachia; Barbone the Thief Defends Himself against the Soldiers; The Royal Family Residing in Munich; Sketch of Thirty Nine Paintings Depicting Greek Independence; King Othon of Greece and the Twenty Nine Portraits of the People that Accompanied him; Goose Hunt; Cossack Meeting.*

AUCTION RECORDS:
MUNICH, 11 June 1970, *Austrian Patrol in a Mountain Village* (1833) DEM 3,000. MUNICH, 30 Nov 1972, *Patrol in a Mountain Village* (1836) DEM 2,000. NEW YORK, 15 Oct 1976, *Horses in the Stable* (1840, oil on canvas, 10 1/2 x 12 ins / 26.5 x 30.5 cm) USD 1,500. MUNICH, 25 Nov 1982, *Greek Warrior* (1837, pencil heightened with white, 13 x 11 1/2 ins / 33 x 29.5 cm) DEM 2,000. HEIDELBERG, 12 April 1986, *A Soldier* (pencil, 12 x 11 1/4 ins / 30.2 x 28.8 cm) DEM 2,400. MUNICH, 10 May

1989, *View of San Marino* (pencil and oil on paper, 7 1/2 x 11 1/2 ins / 19 x 29 cm) DEM 39,600. MUNICH, 27 Feb 1999, *Greek Landscape with Riders on Spring* (1869, oil on canvas, 24 x 30 ins / 61 x 77 cm) DEM 55,000. MUNICH, 22 June 1999, *Greek Farmers' Wives at Village Fountain* (1839, oil on panel, 12 x 10 ins / 31 x 26 cm) DEM 42,000. PARIS, 12 Oct 2001, *Tartar Horsemen* (oil on panel, 12 x 17 ins / 31 x 42 cm) FRF 28,000. LONDON, 20 Nov 2002, *Don Cossacks with French Captives* (1819, oil on panel, 15 x 19 ins / 38 x 49 cm) GBP 28,000. MUNICH, 2 July 2003, *Farewell Outside the Osteria* (1827, oil on canvas, 21 x 24 ins / 53 x 60 cm) EUR 3,800.

HESS, Richard
German, 20th century.
Born 1937, in Berlin.
Sculptor.

Richard Hess took part in group exhibitions at the Darmstadt Kunsthalle in 1974, the Wiesbaden Kunstverein in 1978, the Staatliche Kunsthalle in Berlin in 1982 and the local museum in Heilbronn in 1991. He also had solo shows in 1980 at the Heilbronn museum and 1983 at the Dominican monastery in Frankfurt am Main.

He is a figurative artist, who prefers to work in stone, creating both sculpture in the round and low reliefs that are sometimes polychrome. His subject is the human form, often women, but also couples. Since 1967, he has received regular public commissions in Germany, particularly for fountains.

BIBLIOGRAPHY:
Richard Hess, Rassegna internazionale di Scultura, Abano Terme (ITA), 1991.

HESS-KIPHING, Emma
American, 19th - 20th century.
Born 18 January 1878, in Chicago.
Miniaturist.

Emma Hess-Kiphing studied in Chicago, where she lived. In 1904 her miniatures were awarded a bronze medal at the St Louis exhibition.

HESSE, Alexandre
French, 19th century.
Born 30 September 1806, in Paris; died 10 August 1879, in Paris.
Painter, watercolourist, pastellist, draughtsman.
Religious subjects, portraits, genre scenes, landscapes with figures. Murals.

Alexandre was the son of Henri Joseph Hesse, and was taught by his father, Victor Bertin and Baron Gros. He entered the École des Beaux-Arts in Paris in 1821. He made regular trips to Italy - in 1833 for example, and from 1842 to 1847 - and had a particular predilection for Venice. His work appeared at the Paris Salon from 1833 to 1861. A retrospective exhibition of his work was held at the Pierre Gaubert Gallery in Paris, in 1979. He became a member of the Institut de Paris in 1867, and won medals in 1833 and 1842. He was made a Chevalier of the Légion d'Honneur in 1842, and an Officer in 1868.

His best-known work is entitled *The Funeral of Titian - as a Chablais Farmer.* He decorated many churches, including: the chapel of Sainte-Geneviève in the church of St-Séverin in Paris; the chapel of St-Gervais and St-Protais in the church of St-Gervais; and the whole of the church of Chevry, in Seine-et-Marne. Two of Hesse's paintings can be seen in the church of Avranches: *Procession of the League* and *The Flight into Egypt.* He also decorated the ceiling of the Bourse du Commerce in Lyons. His work is sometimes rather dry, due to the fresco technique he often employed, and sometimes ebullient, and more like the style of the Baron Gros.

MUSEUMS AND GALLERIES:
NANTES (MBA): *Harvester Holding Her Sickle; Young Girl Carrying Fruit on a Tray; Venetian Concert* - NARBONNE: *Portrait of M. Barthe* - PARIS (Louvre): *Triumph of Pisani* - PÉRIGUEUX: *Holy Family at Rest* - PONTOISE: *Raising of Jairus' Daughter* - VERSAILLES: *Adoption of Godefroy de Bouillon by the Emperor Alexius I Comnenus* - VERSAILLES (Mus. Lambinet): *Henri IV at the Louvre on His Death Bed.*

AUCTION RECORDS:
PARIS, 24 April 1925, *The Two Foscaris,* FRF 220. PARIS, 19-20 Nov 1926, *Bust-length Portrait of a Man,* FRF 230. PARIS, 15 Dec 1943, *Prisoner,* FRF 800. PARIS, July 1946, *Family of Italian Peasants,* FRF 4,100. PARIS, 28 Nov 1986, *Portrait of a Young Girl* (oil on canvas, 26 x 20 1/4 ins / 66 x 51.5 cm) FRF 39,000. PARIS, 15 June 1990, *Roman Woman* (1845, watercolour and gouache, 12 x 7 1/2 ins / 30.3 x 19 cm) FRF 20,500. PARIS, 19 Nov 1992, *Study of a Hand* (red, black chalk heightened with white, 5 3/4 x 9 1/2 ins / 14.8 x 23.9 cm) FRF 3,900. PARIS, 29 Nov 1995, *Portrait of a Young Woman* (oil on canvas, 26 x 20 ins / 66 x 51 cm) FRF 50,000. PARIS, 13 Dec 1996, *Young Roman Woman with a Tambourine* (oil on oval canvas, 38 1/2 x 29 1/4 ins / 98 x 74.5 cm) FRF 32,000. PARIS, 8 March 2002, *Young Roman Shepherd* (oil on panel, 13 x 9 ins / 34 x 24 cm) EUR 2,900. DOULLENS, 17 Nov 2002, *Portrait of a Man* (1877, oil on canvas, oval, 25 x 22 ins / 64 x 55 cm) EUR 2,100.

HESSE, Alice
French, 20th century.
Born 4 November 1876, in Paris.
Painter. Genre scenes.

Alice Hesse was a pupil of A. Cesbron and J. Adler. She exhibited in Paris at the Salon des Artistes Français, notably in 1911. She was a member in Paris of the Salon des Artistes Indépendants from 1905.

HESSE, August
German, 19th century.
Active in Posen (now Poznan, Poland) c. 1840.
Painter, sculptor, lithographer.

August Hesse is best known for his landscapes and views of monuments.

HESSE, Auguste
French, 19th century.
Born 1795, in Paris; died 1868.
Painter. Religious subjects. Murals.

Auguste Hesse studied in the studio of Baron Gros, at the École des Beaux-Arts in Paris, from 1811. He won the Prix de Rome in 1818. In 1863 he became a member of the Institut de Paris. He exhibited at the Paris Salon from 1824 to 1868.

Hesse was an official painter, and received many commissions, including decorations for the churches of St-Eustache and Notre-Dame de Lorette, and the great chamber of the Hôtel de Ville in Paris.

MUSEUMS AND GALLERIES:
LISIEUX: *Freedom.*

AUCTION RECORDS:
PARIS, 24 May 1991, *St Joseph; St David* (oil on canvas, a pair, each 6 1/4 x 4 ins / 16 x 10 cm) FRF 25,000.

HESSE, Eduard
German, 19th century.
Active in Posen (now Poznan, Poland).
Painter, lithographer. Portraits, landscapes.

Eduard Hesse executed views of Posen (now Poznan, Poland).

HESSE, Eva
German, 20th century.
Born 11 January 1936, in Hamburg; died 29 May 1970, in New York.
Painter, draughtswoman, sculptor.
Conceptual Art, Process Art.

Eva Hesse's German Jewish parents emigrated to New York in order to escape the Nazi persecutions in 1939. It was in

New York that she studied, first at the Pratt Institute of Design in 1952-1953, which she left to enter first the Arts Students League and then the Cooper Union until 1957. She accepted a scholarship to attend the Yale Summer School of Music and Art in Norfolk, Connecticut and, in 1957, entered the Yale School of Art and Architecture, where Josef Albers was her professor; she left with a diploma in 1959. In 1960, Hesse met Sol Lewitt, who became one of her closest friends and later an important influence on her work. In 1961, she married the sculptor Tom Doyle. A German textiles industrialist and art collector invited them in 1964 to spend a year working in his disused factories in Kettwig-am-Ruhr, near Düsseldorf. Two years later, through the mediation of Sol Lewitt, she met Dan Graham. Her circle of friends included Mel Bochner, Don Judd, Dan Flavin, Robert Mangold, Robert Ryman, Lucy Lippard, Al Held and Grace Wapner.

Eva Hesse expressed the desire, from adolescence, to acquire 'the strength and some conviction' in order to paint. Her works are specifically inscribed in a context that was fuelled by the emotional and affective stages of a life cut short at the age of 34. However, in the ten years from 1960 to 1970, she developed an entire field of contemporary art. Having emerged from abstract expressionism, she gradually set herself the challenge of discovering how to reconcile this need for expression, which had become a fundamental inner principle, with the formalist rigour of Minimalist art that was tautological in its excess. Her response, more pragmatic than conceptual, was inscribed in the third dimension and led to the series of sculptures in resin and fibreglass, from 1968: *Tori* (1969), a collection of oblong fibreglass forms that she placed on the ground, inflated, lacerated in their context; and *Seven Poles* (1970), long rods sculpted in diaphanous fibreglass that rise from the ground. She also constructed *Right After* (1969), a striking constellation of tangled fibreglass strands that is too fragile to be transported. This sculpture forms a three-year follow-up to *Metronymic Irregularity I* (1966), in which the mass of intersecting threads between two surfaces is reminiscent of Pollock's famous 'dripping'. This is therefore a sculpted work that is inscribed in the history of so-called 'post-Minimalist' forms, described by some as 'abstract expressionism' and by others as originating from 'anti-form' or 'process art' in its choice of non-manufactured materials worked in a tactile relationship with the sculptor and set out accordingly in space (some of her resin works have in fact already disintegrated).

Hesse's paintings of figures and portraits (presumed to be self-portraits), dating from the early 1960s, show a non-mimetic and non-illusionist urge for expression; subsequently, some of her works were influenced by Willem de Kooning and others, more open and spacious, by Achille Gorky. In addition to these oils and gouaches, she never ceased to draw and paint. But she came to see two-dimensional painting as a restriction on constructing 'abstract objects' beyond any possibility of interpretation; it was unable to achieve for her the true confrontation of a face-to-face (body-to-body) encounter in the third dimension.

After two years of work in sculpture, Hesse created *Hang Up* (1966), a work that she considered among her most successful. The large ribboned frame, which changes from hard to fleece-lined, encloses the empty space or, more precisely, the part of the wall to which it is attached. It reveals the hidden part that is usually covered by the work. By reducing the frame to the appearance of its object, she strips the flat space of all its traditional signifying force. This factual situation is reinforced by the presence of the iron wire that, emerging from one of the horizontal frames, falls awkwardly on the ground before penetrating into the other. Such a protuberance breaks any illusionist relationship and alienates any inclination towards identification. Trained as a painter, Eva Hesse remained self-taught as a sculptor; there is therefore no pre-established framework to disrupt her relationship with form. She takes the objects and pieces of material that she needs from around her, then displaces and orientates them at will.

It was in Germany, in the disused factories where she was invited to work with her husband Tom Doyle in 1964, that Hesse began her reliefs. It is primarily in this impulse to give manual expression first to assemblages of objects, then, more directly, to their material that her work gained its full importance and ensures her permanence today. It is an expression that often uses the body as reference, through an anthropomorphic or metaphorical route. She exposes certain characteristics of this body, both exterior and interior: secretions, sexual characteristics, organs in their interconnecting tissues, their imaginary connections. Hesse's collected writings confirm the extent of her concern with Freudianism and theories of sexuality.

The series of reliefs dating from 1965 articulates ends of strings, nozzles and pipes that she trims in the space based on agglomerated plaques fixed to the wall. Almost Surrealist in inspiration, with surprising colours of pale green and broken yellow, these works have some of the humour that characterises her pen and black ink drawings of the same period. Hesse followed on from this in 1965-1966 with the series of surgical cords and tubes painted in black. There, she attains a restraint of line that is absent from her reliefs. In the suspended effect that she places in the foreground, she seeks a new symbolic harmony between form, material and content.

Imprinting her tactile impulse on materials by creating on the scale and in the movement of her own body, this procedure of Eva Hesse's differs radically from that of the minimalists' erasure of themselves behind their materials. She starts from a substance that can be easily manipulated such as plaster, resin, papier-mâché or substrates of material that contain it themselves: balloons, inner tubes, latex and string. Sensitive to an aesthetic of colour - she was a student of Albers - she continued to paint her works, enveloping them under a mask, gathering them together into one. A simultaneity of action, recurrent in her work, fades into a seriality of objects (the reliefs), into a contiguous linkage of repeated forms: work on steel washers in 1967; *Accession II* (1967), thousands of vinyl tubes inserted into the five sides of an open square volume; *Accretion* (1967), 50 fibreglass pipes placed along a wall. Verging on minimalism at times, her sculptures nevertheless avoid any formalism. Hesse provides enough contradictions between interior and exterior, full and empty, hard and soft, organic and geometrical to finally reach a work that she described as 'ordered and yet not ordered: a chaos structured as an anti-chaos'.

She took part in her first collective exhibition in 1961 in New York at the John Heller gallery. Subsequent exhibitions include the 21st international watercolour Biennale at Brooklyn museum and *Drawings* at Wadsworth Athenaeum (1961); *Winterausstellung* (*Winter Exhibition*) at the Kunsthalle, Düsseldorf (1964); *Abstract Inflationism and Stuffed Expressionism*, Graham gallery, and *Eccentric Abstraction*, Fischbach gallery (New York, 1966); *Working Sketches and Other Items Visible on Paper not Necessarily Intended to be Considered as Artworks*, School of Visual Arts; *American Drawing, 1968*, Moore College of Art, Philadelphia, *Directions I: Options* at the Milwaukeee Art Center, *Nine at Leo Castelli*, 'Process' or 'Anti-Form' demonstration (1968); *Sans II*, Whitney art museum annual exhibition, *When Attitudes Become Form*, Bern, *Plastics and New Art* organised by the Institute of Contemporary Art at the university of Pennsylvania, *Anti-Illusion* at the Whitney museum, *557 087*, organised for the Seattle art museum, and *A Plastic Presence*, presented at the Jewish museum in New York (1969); *String and Rope*, Janis gallery, and an exhibition presented at the Owens-Corming Fiberglas Center (New York, 1970). Posthumous exhibitions include: her sculpture *Expanded Expansion* (1969), exhibited at Documenta V, Kassel (1972); Stedelijk museum, Amsterdam (1978); *L'Art Conceptuel: une Perspective* (*Conceptual Art: A Perspective*), Musée d'Art Moderne in Paris (1989-1990); and *Les Années 70: l'Art en Cause* (*The 1970s: Art in Question*), Capc-Musée d'Art Contemporain, Bordeaux (2002).

Eva Hesse had only three solo exhibitions in her lifetime: in 1963 (Allan Stone gallery), 1968 and 1970 (Fischbach gallery). Retrospective exhibitions include: Guggenheim Museum in New York (1972-1973); museums of contemporary art in Chicago and Houston (1973); Yale University Art Gallery, Connecticut, and the Hirschhorn Museum in Washington (1992); national gallery of the Jeu de Paume, Paris (1993); and an exhibition assembling over 150 of the artist's sculptures, paintings and drawings at the Tate Modern in London, the San Francisco museum of modern art and the museum in Wiesbaden (2002).

BIBLIOGRAPHY:

Lippard, Lucy R., *Eva Hesse*, New York University Press, New York, 1976. Krauss, Rosalind, *Eva Hesse (1936-1970)-Sculpture*, exhibition catalogue, Whitechapel Art Gall., London, 1979. Barrett, Bill, *Eva Hesse, sculpture, catalogue raisonné*, Timken Publishers, New York, 1989. Cooper, Helen A./Berger, Maurice, *Eva Hesse: a retrospective*, exhibition catalogue, Yale University Art Gall., New Haven, 1992. David, Catherine/Diserens, Corinne/Norden, Linda/Simon, Joan, *Eva Hesse*, exhibition catalogue, Gal. nationale du Jeu de Paume, Réunion des musées nationaux, Paris, 1993. Reinhardt, Brigitte/Spector, Naomi/Franz, Erich, *Eva Hesse: Bilder und Reliefs (Drawing in Space)*, exhibition catalogue, Ulmer Museum, Cantz, Ostfildern, 1994 (text in German and English). Fer, Briony, et al., *Eva Hesse*, exhibition catalogue, Tate Modern, London, 2002.

MUSEUMS AND GALLERIES:

COLOGNE (Mus. Ludwig): *Accession III* (1967-1968) - PARIS (MNAM-CCI).

AUCTION RECORDS:

NEW YORK, 13 May 1981, *Untitled* (1967, pen and black ink, 11 x 8 1/2 ins / 28 x 21.5 cm) USD 3,400. NEW YORK, 5 May 1986, *Magnet Boards* (1967, sculpted metal with magnets/wood, 24 x 24 x 2 ins / 61 x 61 x 5.2 cm) USD 34,000. NEW YORK, 8 Oct 1986, *Untitled* (1957, oil on canvas, 43 3/4 x 32 ins / 111.2 x 81.3 cm) USD 4,750. NEW YORK, 13 Nov 1986, *Untitled* (1967, pen and black ink, 11 x 9 ins / 28 x 22.6 cm) USD 5,000. NEW YORK, 9 Nov 1989, *Untitled* (1965, ink and pencil/paper, 20 x 26 ins / 51 x 66 cm) USD 16,500. NEW YORK, 9 May 1990, *Untitled* (1967, ink/paper, 8 1/2 x 11 ins / 21.7 x 28 cm) USD 14,300. NEW YORK, 7 Nov 1990, *Tori* (1969, nine bits of fibreglass/metal mesh, variable dimensions from 30 x 12 1/2 x 10 1/4 ins / 76.2 x 31.7 x 26 cm to 47 x 17 x 15 ins/119.4 x 43.2 x 38.1 cm) USD 297,000. NEW YORK, 30 April 1991, *Sans II* (1968, fibreglass and polyester resin, 38 x 86 x 6 ins / 96.5 x 218.5 x 15.5 cm) USD 330,000. NEW YORK, 13 Nov 1991, *Series* (91 latex spheres/sheets of latex, base 30 x 32 ins / 76.2 x 81.4 cm, diam. de each sphère: 2 1/2 ins/6.5 cm) USD 115,500. NEW YORK, 5 May 1992, *Ear in a Sink* (1965, tempera, lacquer, papier mâché, cotton cord and varnish/synthetic resin, 41 1/2 x 17 3/4 ins / 105.7 x 45.1 cm) USD 93,500. NEW YORK, 6 Oct 1992, *Untitled* (1957, oil on canvas, 44 x 32 ins / 111.8 x 81.3 cm) USD 14,300. NEW YORK, 24 Feb 1993, *Untitled* (watercolour, ink, pencil and collage paper/paper, 22 1/2 x 28 1/4 ins / 57.1 x 72 cm) USD 16,500. NEW YORK, 10 Nov 1993, *Several* (1965, papier mâché/balls of rubber and acrylic suspended by elastic, 84 x 11 x 7 ins / 213.4 x 27.9 x 17.8 cm) USD 475,500. NEW YORK, 8 May 1996, *Sans II* (1968, fibreglass and polyester resin, 38 x 86 x 6 1/4 ins / 96.5 x 218.4 x 15.6 cm) USD 662,500. NEW YORK, 19 Nov 1996, *Untitled* (1966, wash, ink and charcoal/paper, 13 3/4 x 13 3/4 ins / 35.2 x 35.2 cm) USD 118,000. NEW YORK, 20 Nov 1996, *Untitled* (1960, oil on canvas, 40 x 30 ins / 101.6 x 75.9 cm) USD 19,550. NEW YORK, 21 Nov 1996, *Untitled* (1959, oil on canvas, 15 x 15 ins / 38.1 x 38.1 cm) USD 12,650. NEW YORK, 10 Nov 1997, *Unfinished, Untitled, or Not Yet* (1966, nine fishing nets, polyethylene, paper, sand and cotton cord, 71 x 15 1/2 x 8 1/4 ins / 180.3 x 39.4 x 21 cm) USD 2,202,500; *Vinculum I* (1969, fibreglass, tubes of rubber, staples and metal plate, 103 x 23 x 31 ins / 261.6 x 58.5 x 78.6 cm) USD 1,212,500. NEW YORK, 14 May 1998, *Self-portrait* (1961, oil on canvas, 36 x 36 ins / 91 x 91 cm) USD 180,000. NEW YORK, 17 Nov 1999, *Untitled, Three Nets* (painted rope net, weights and papier mache, 43 x 11 x 6 ins / 108 x 29 x 15 cm) USD 340,000. NEW YORK, 16 May 2000, *Untitled* (1966, ink wash and pencil, 15 x 11 ins / 39 x 29 cm) USD 195,000. NEW YORK, 17 May 2001, *Untitled, Kardon Glass Case* (plaster, latew resin, cloth, wire mesh and resin tubling, 15 x 10 x 10 ins / 37 x 26 x 26 cm) USD 650,000. NEW YORK, 16 May 2002, *Untitled* (1963, oil on canvas, 72 x 83 ins / 182 x 211 cm) USD 180,000. NEW YORK, 13 Nov 2002, *Untitled* (1967, metal/steel washers/wood) USD 360,000. LONDON, 5 Feb 2003, *Untitled* (1964, oil on canvas, 61 x 41 ins / 155 x 105 cm) GBP 140,000. NEW YORK, 13 May 2004, *Boxes* (1964, acrylic, gouache, pen, ink and collage/paper, 24 x 20 ins / 60 x 50 cm) USD 135,000.

HESSE, Georg Hans

German, 19th - 20th century.
Born 24 September 1845, in Berlin; died 26 March 1920, in Karlsruhe.
Landscape artist.

Georg Hans Hesse was a student of H. Eschke in Berlin from 1864 to 1867 and then of Gude in Karlsruhe until 1871. He first exhibited in Berlin in 1866 and also exhibited in Munich.

HESSE, Hanna

German, 19th century.
Born 1862, in Kavernick.
Painter.

Hanna Hesse worked primarily in Königsberg (now Kaliningrad, Russia).

HESSE, Hans, or Hasse

German, 15th - 16th century.
Active in Zwickau and Annaberg.
Painter.

Hans Hesse executed a number of religious paintings, even working as far afield as Chemnitz and Dittmansdorf.

HESSE, Henri Joseph

French, 19th century.
Born 31 October 1781, in Paris; died 14 August 1849, in Paris.
Painter, watercolourist, miniaturist, draughtsman, lithographer. Portraits.

Henri Joseph was the elder brother of Nicolas Auguste Hesse and the father of Alexandre Hesse. He was taught by David and Isabey the Elder. He made his début at the Salon of 1808 with a painting entitled *Young Woman Watching Her Sleeping Child*. In 1810 he exhibited more portraits in oils, and some miniatures in a frame. He won a second-class medal in 1810 and another in 1833 - his only reappearance after a long absence.

Henri Joseph Hesse appears to have enjoyed most success with his miniatures, although he is well known for some major official portraits: most notably one of the Duchess of Berry, which was exhibited at the Salon of 1819. He also left behind a considerable number of lithographed portraits, of the major figures of the Restoration, and some drawings.

Auction records:
London, 8 March 1910, *Portrait of a Woman* (miniature) FRF 2,800. London, 27 April 1910, *Portrait of a Woman* (miniature) FRF 660; *Portrait of a Young Woman* (miniature) FRF 510. London, 29 Oct 1919, *Portrait of a Woman* (miniature) FRF 850. London, 4 April 1925, *Mid-length Portrait of a Young Girl* (miniature) FRF 605. London, 10 and 11 June 1925, *Presumed Portrait of Honoré de Balzac, Aged Six* (sepia wash) FRF 550. London, 8 and 9 Dec 1933, *Mid-length Portrait of a Woman* (sepia wash) FRF 130. Paris, 3 April 1990, *Bust-length Portrait of Maret, Duke of Bassano* (gouache, oval, 10 1/2 x 7 3/4 ins / 26.5 x 20 cm) FRF 100,000. Paris, 6 June 1990, *Portrait of a Little Girl* (watercolour, oval, 9 1/2 x 7 3/4 ins / 24 x 19.5 cm) FRF 23,500. Paris, 6 Dec 1991, *Portrait of a Young Man* (1812, wash, 7 x 5 3/4 ins / 17.5 x 14.5 cm) FRF 10,000. Paris, 21 May 1992, *Portrait of a Lady of Quality* (watercolour, 7 1/2 x 5 3/4 ins / 19 x 14.5 cm) FRF 4,500. Monaco, 19 June 1994, *Children Crowning a Bust* (1810, watercolour and gouache, 15 x 12 1/4 ins / 38 x 31 cm) FRF 6,660. Paris, 18 Nov 1994, *Portrait of a Gentleman* (1812, watercolour, oval, 7 x 5 1/2 ins / 17.5 x 14 cm) FRF 6,500. New York, 18-19 July 1996, *Portrait of a Lady* (1819, oil on canvas, 33 1/2 x 25 1/2 ins / 85.1 x 64.8 cm) USD 1,840. Paris, 30 June 2000, *Portrait of a Young Mother and Child* (1828, oil on canvas, 40 x 32 ins / 101 x 82 cm) FRF 110,000. London, 6 Nov 2001, *Young Officer in a Scarlet Coat with Silver Embroidered Blue Facings* (1815, miniatures, gilt metal mount, rectangular lemonwood frame, oval, 2 x ? ins / 6 x ? cm) GBP 2,000. Paris, 22 March 2002, *Portrait of a Man with a Beret* (1824, watercolour/gouache, 10 x 8 ins / 26 x 21 cm) EUR 14,500. Paris, 30 March 2004, *Portrait of the Duc d'Orleans, the future Louis-Philippe* (c. 1825, oil on canvas, 9 x 7 ins / 24 x 19 cm) EUR 3,000.

HESSE, Hermann
German, 20th century.
Born 2 July 1877, in Calw; died 1962.
Painter, watercolourist. Landscapes.

Hermann Hesse, the Nobel prize-winning writer who lived in Switzerland for many years, discovered an intimate form of recreation in painting.

Auction records:
Munich, 25 Nov 1977, *View of a Village in Tessin* (1924, watercolour/canvas, 9 1/2 x 10 1/4 ins / 24 x 26 cm) DEM 3,600. Zurich, 1 Nov 1980, *Village Church, Tessin* (1921, watercolour/chalk outline, 10 1/2 x 9 1/2 ins / 26.8 x 24.2 cm) CHF 2,200. Munich, 26 Nov 1982, *Landscape with Red House in Tessin* (1932, watercolour, 9 3/4 x 11 1/4 ins / 25 x 28.5 cm) DEM 8,200. Hamburg, 9 June 1983, *Church Square* (1923, watercolour/pencil outlines, 3 3/4 x 6 ins / 9.4 x 14.3 cm) DEM 7,100. Munich, 2 June 1987, *View of Montagnola* (1933, watercolour, 9 1/2 x 12 1/4 ins / 24 x 31.3 cm) DEM 23,000. Zurich, 2 Dec 1994, *House in Tessin* (1920, watercolour heightened with white/paper, 6 1/4 x 9 ins / 16.1 x 22 cm) CHF 7,500. Bern, 3 Nov 1999, *Village in Evening* (1919, watercolour over pencil, 7 x 6 ins / 18 x 14 cm) CHF 16,000. Munich, 30 Nov 1999, *View from the Window of a Neighbouring House in Tessin* (1924, watercolour over pencil, 9 x 11 ins / 24 x 29 cm) DEM 12,000. Bern, 10 May 2000, *Winter Landscape, Ticino* (1933, watercolour and ink, 4 x 3 ins / 9 x 8 cm) CHF 4,500. Cologne, 11 Nov 2000, *Mountain Landscape* (1927, watercolour over pencil, 7 x 8 ins / 18 x 21 cm) DEM 8,500. New York, 5 Nov 2001, *Tessiner Landschaft* (1922, watercolour, 9 x 12 ins / 23 x 30 cm) USD 22,000. Munich, 15 Nov 2001, *Montagnola. Red House* (1922, watercolour, 12 x 9 ins / 31 x 24 cm) DEM 25,000. Vienna, 27 Nov 2002, *Montagnola Scenes* (pen and watercolour, four, 4 x 5 ins / 11 x 12 cm) EUR 8,500. Vienna, 27 Nov 2002, *Montagnola* (watercolour, 12 x 9 ins / 31 x 24 cm) EUR 11,000. Bern, 20 June 2003, *Pictor's Transformation* (watercolour, fifteen, 9 x 7 ins / 22 x 17 cm) CHF 22,000. Bern, 20 June 2003, *Tessin Villages* (watercolour, twelve, 9 x 7 ins / 22 x 18 cm) CHF 41,000. Zurich, 23 June 2004, *House in Montagnola* (1931, 8 x 10 ins / 20 x 25 cm) CHF 12,000. Zurich, 14 Sept 2004, *Corona, 1924 - Tessin House with Palm Tree* (watercolour on pencil, 9 x 13 ins / 24 x 32 cm) CHF 11,500.

HESSE, Jean, pseudonym of Sainson, Aimé
French, 20th century.
Born 1894; died 1960.
Painter, watercolourist, jeweller. Landscapes.
L'Effort Group.

Jean Hesse participated in all the shows of l'Effort, a group of artists exhibiting at the Salon de Grenoble.

HESSE, Johann Friedrich
German, 19th century.
Born 24 November 1792, in Magdeburg.
Painter, lithographer.

Johann Hesse studied under J. D. Schubert at the Dresden academy of art.

HESSE, Louise
French, 19th century.
Born in the 19th century, in Paris.
Painter, sculptor.

Louise Hesse was a pupil of Gallier, and first exhibited at the Salon in 1869.

HESSE, Ludwig Ferdinand
German, 19th century.
Born 23 January 1795, in Pomerania; died 8 May 1876, in Berlin.
Painter, architect.

Ludwig Hesse worked in Potsdam for Frederick William IV.

HESSE, Nicolas Auguste
French, 19th century.
Born 28 August 1795, in Paris; died 14 June 1869, in Paris.
Painter, draughtsman. Religious subjects, allegorical subjects, mythological subjects, portraits. Murals, designs for stained glass.

This artist, one of the masters of the Classical School, was taught by his brother, Henri Joseph, and by Baron Gros. He entered the École des Beaux-Arts in August 1811 and won the Rome Prize in 1818 with *Philemon and Baucis Receiving Jupiter and Mercury*.

Nicolas Hesse made his début at the Salon of 1824, and from then on occupied a key position among the official painters of the day. He exhibited his *Founding of the Sorbonne College around the Year 1256* at the Salon of 1827; this painting now decorates the church of the Sorbonne. In 1838 he showed *Christ at the Sepulchre* (now in Périgueux Cathedral), and *General Meeting of the Estates-General, 23 June 1789* (now in the Musée d'Amiens). His other famous works are: *Death of Adonis*, a stained-glass window for the church of Chaillot (1843); *The Virgin Swooning* (1845), which was displayed in the Luxembourg Palace; *Jacob Fighting with the Angel* (Avranches Cathedral, 1851); and *Clytie Dying* (Musée d'Amiens, 1853). He won a first-class medal in 1838, was decorated in 1840, and was appointed a member of the Institut, succeeding Delacroix, in 1863.

Other works bought from the painter by the State, and which were exhibited at the Salons mentioned above, include: *Adoration of the Shepherds; Conversion and Martyrdom of St Hippolytus*, in Notre-Dame-de-Lorette; and some major decorative works for monuments. Among these are: decorations for the Chapel of the Catechisms in the church of Sainte-Elisabeth; decorations in the Chapel of the Virgin, in the church of Bonne-Nouvelle; paintings in the church of Les Blancs-Manteaux and in St-Pierre-de-Chaillot, where he painted the cupola of the choir and the subjects for the stained-glass windows, which he executed himself; the cartoons for the stained-glass windows in the Chapel of the Virgin, in the church of St-Eustache; several stained-glass windows for Notre-Dame-de-la-Recouvrance; fifty-five cartoons for the Gothic bay windows in Sainte-Clotilde; decorative paintings for the former Hôtel de Ville in Paris, and the St-Laurent Chapel in the church of St-Gervais; *The Sermon on the Mount* in Sainte-Elisabeth du Temple; and some allegorical figures for the former Conseil d'État (Council of State).

MUSEUMS AND GALLERIES:

AMIENS: *Meeting of the Estates-General; Clytie Dying* - DIJON: *Original Sin* - LISIEUX: *Allegorical Figure of the Republic* - PARIS (Louvre): *The Virgin Swooning* - PONTOISE: *St Barbara; Head of an Old Man* - TROYES: *Portrait of the Sculptor François Girardon.*

AUCTION RECORDS:

PARIS, 30 Nov-2 Dec 1920, *Portrait of a Woman* (sepia) FRF 600. PARIS, 7 March 1923, *Portrait of a Man,* FRF 800. PARIS, 26 Oct 1933, *Portrait of a Man,* FRF 700. PARIS, 11 March 1988, *Untitled* (sepia wash heightened with white/beige paper, 9¾ x 7 ins / 25 x 17.5 cm) FRF 4,200.

HESSE, Richard
German, 19th - 20th century.
Born 13 March 1864, in Dresden; died 8 August 1910, in Dresden.
Painter. Portraits, genre scenes.

From 1882 to 1887, Richard Hesse studied with Pohle and Pauwels at the Dresden academy. He first exhibited in 1886 in Dresden, where he won a silver medal. He also exhibited in Berlin and Munich.

HESSE, Rudolf
German, 20th century.
Born 13 July 1871, in Saarlouis (Saarland).
Painter, draughtsman, engraver, caricaturist.

After studying in Munich and travelling extensively in Europe, Rudolf Hesse worked mainly as a caricaturist.

HESSE, Sophie
Maiden name: von Wyss
Swiss, 20th century.
Born 3 December 1874, in Zurich.
Engraver.

Sophie Hesse painted mainly landscapes.

HESSE-CASSEL, Wilhelm Landgraf von
German, 18th century.
Engraver (etching).

Wilhelm Landgrave of Hesse-Cassel engraved mainly landscapes and portraits.

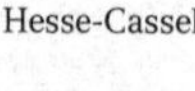

HESSE-CASSEL. See **AUGUSTA OF HESSE-CASSEL (Princess)**

HESSEL, G.
Dutch, 18th century.
Active in Amsterdam.
Engraver (burin).

He is known to have produced *Gathering of Peasants,* after D. Vinkenbooms.

HESSELBACH, Sigmund
German, 19th century.
Active in Würzburg.
Painter, draughtsman, lithographer.

HESSELBARTH, Jean Claude
Swiss, 20th century.
Born 1925, in Lausanne.
Painter.

Jean Claude Hesselbarth studied literature from 1945 to 1947, then painting and sculpture at the École des Beaux-Arts in Lausanne under the supervision of Marcel Poncet. His painting developed fairly rapidly into a delicate form of tachism. He showed his works in several solo exhibitions, mainly in Lausanne. He took part in the exhibition *Le Dessin* (*Drawing*) at the Kunsthalle in Bern in 1957, in *La Peinture Abstraite en Suisse* (*Abstract Painting in Switzerland*) in Neuchâtel in 1957 and in *Troisième Génération, 42 Jeunes Artistes Suisses* (*Third Generation, 42 Young Swiss Artists*) in St Gall in 1960.

HESSELBARTH, Louis
French, 20th century.
Sculptor, painter.

Louis Hesselbarth exhibited painted wooden sculptures inspired by African art at the Salon d'Automne.

HESSELBOM, Otto
Swedish, 19th - 20th century.
Born 13 July 1848, in Ånimskog (Dalsland); died 1913.
Painter, watercolourist. Landscapes.

Otto Hesselbom won a bronze medal at the 1900 Exposition Universelle in Paris.

AUCTION RECORDS:

STOCKHOLM, 23 April 1980, *Summer Landscape* (oil on canvas, 19½ x 27¼ ins / 49.5 x 69 cm) SEK 9,100. GÖTEBORG, 31 March 1982, *The Flat Land* (oil on canvas, 37 x 69 ins / 94 x 175 cm) SEK 35,000. STOCKHOLM, 1 Nov 1983, *Landscape* (1888, oil on canvas, 8¼ x 14¼ ins / 21 x 36 cm) SEK 24,000. STOCKHOLM, 9 April 1985, *Landscape with Lake* (1899, oil on canvas, 13 x 30 ins / 33 x 76 cm) SEK 30,500. STOCKHOLM, 22 April 1986, *Landscape* (watercolour, 11½ x 21¼ ins / 29 x 54 cm) SEK 9,500. LONDON, 25 March 1987, *My Country* (1895, oil on canvas, 46 x 72½ ins / 116 x 184 cm) GBP 22,000. GÖTEBORG, 18 May 1989, *Winter Landscape with a Snow-covered Chalet at Sunset* (1903, oil on canvas, 35½ x 28¼ ins / 90 x 72 cm) SEK 90,000. STOCKHOLM, 15 Nov 1989, *Pale Sun, Landscape in Dalsland* (oil, 17¼ x 28¼ ins / 44 x 72 cm) SEK 75,000. STOCKHOLM, 16 May 1990, *View of Dalsland* (oil on canvas, 31 x 44 ins / 79 x 112 cm) SEK 250,000. STOCKHOLM, 14 Nov 1990, *Birches in Winter* (oil on canvas, 11 x 6 ins / 27 x 15 cm) SEK 9,000. STOCKHOLM, 29 May 1991, *Spring in the Dalsland Region with Lake Ånimmen* (oil on canvas, 25½ x 52 ins / 65 x 132 cm) SEK 50,000. STOCKHOLM, 13 April 1992, *River Mouth in the North* (oil on panel, 15¼ x 23½ ins / 39 x 60 cm) SEK 9,000.

HESSELINCK, Abraham
Dutch, 19th century.
Born 19 July 1862, in Eelde or Paterwolde.
Sculptor. Statues, groups.

He was a pupil at the academy of fine arts in Brussels. He received an honourable mention at the Salon de Paris in 1891.

MUSEUMS AND GALLERIES:

AMSTERDAM (Stedelijk Mus.): *Model for a Statue.*

AUCTION RECORDS:

AMSTERDAM, 24 May 1989, *A Happy Family* (bronze, h. 10¼ ins / 26 cm) NLG 1,725.

HESSELIUS, Gustaf, the Younger
Swedish, 18th century.
Born 1727, in Gagnef (Dalarna); died 1775, in Stockholm.
Painter.

Gustaf Hesselius was probably related to Gustavus the Elder.

HESSELIUS, Gustavus, the Elder
Swedish, 18th century.
Born 1682, in Falun; died 23 May 1755, in Philadelphia.
Painter. Portraits, religious subjects, mythological subjects.

Gustavus Hesselius the Elder, father of portrait painter John Hesselius, studied as a portrait artist, gilder and wood engraver in Sweden, before settling in the USA in 1712. He is said to be the earliest portrait painter of note in the USA, particularly of prominent persons on the east coast and of Native Americans, such as the works *Tishcohan* and *Lapowinsa*, which were painted to commemorate a meeting of representatives of the Penns with the local Natives. Hesselius also painted religious subjects, including altarpieces, and mythological scenes like *Bacchus and Ariadne*. Using his fine technical skill influenced by European Baroque style, he introduced increased realism and painterly style into colonial painting. His later works reflected changing popular taste for brighter colours and elegance in portraits. Hesselius received the first recorded public art commission in the American colonies for *The Last Supper* for St Barnabus Church, Prince George's County, Maryland. Hesselius lived in Wilmington, Delaware from 1711-1717, in Philadelphia from 1717-1721, and in Maryland from 1721, eventually returning to Philadelphia between 1730 and 1735. Hesselius built an organ for the Moravian Church in Bethlehem, Pennsylania and after 1750 concentrated primarily on organ building. His works have been shown in retrospectives at New Jersey State Museum, Trenton (1988); and Delaware Historical Museum, Wilmington (2003).

BIBLIOGRAPHY:

Gustavus Hesselius, 1682-1755, Illustrated book, Philadelphia Museum of Art, Philadelphia, 1938. Keyes, H.E., '*Doubts regarding Hesselius*' in *Antiques*, vol 34, Journal article, 1938. Richardson, E.P., '*Gustavus Hesselius*' in *Art Quarterly*, vol 12, Journal article, 1952. *Gustavus Hesselius: Face Painter to the Middle Colonies*, exhibition catalogue, New Jersey State Museum, Trenton (NJ), 1988.

MUSEUMS AND GALLERIES:

BALTIMORE (Maryland Historical Society): *Thomas Bordley* (c. 1715, oil); *Col. Leonard Hollyday* (c. 1740, oil); *Mary Darnall Carroll (Mrs Charles Carroll, the 'Settler')* (c. 1717-1720, oil); *Man of the Key Family* (c. 1740?, oil); *Sarah Hall Harrison (Mrs Samuel Harrison)* (c. 1740, oil) - DETROIT (IA): *Bacchus and Ariadne* - PHILADELPHIA (MA): *Portrait of an Elderly Woman* (1751, oil) - PHILADELPHIA (Pennsylvania Academy of the Fine Arts): *Bacchanalian Revel* - PHILADELPHIA (Philadelphia Historical Society): *Tishcohan* (1735); *Lapowinsa* (1735); *Lydia Hesselius* (c. 1740); *Self-portrait* (c. 1740).

HESSELIUS, John

American, 18th century.
Born 1728, in Philadelphia; died 9 April 1778, in Anne Arundel County, Maryland.
Painter. Portraits.

John Hesselius was the son and pupil of Gustavus Hesselius the Elder, and also studied with Robert Feke who visited Philadelphia in the 1740s, and with John Wollaston who influenced him in the use of almond-eyed features in portraits. John Hesselius is reputed to have taught the artist Charles Willson Peale. Hesselius was known for his portraits of persons living in Delaware, Maryland and Virginia, and was the most prolific of portrait painters in the region of the pre-Revolutionary era, creating more than 100 paintings. Hesselius used European mezzotint prints for ideas in composition and fashion detail, particularly in his earliest works. His early work had a Baroque style, reflecting his father's influence, but from the 1750s his work became more Rococo in style and showed an unaffected attitude towards his work, increasingly emphasising the character of the sitter. Hesselius was particularly noted for the clarity of his strong colours and his ability to paint the texture of satin clothing, as seen in *Anna Dorothea Finney* (c. 1760), and *Portrait of Elizabeth Chew Smith* (1762).

BIBLIOGRAPHY:

Bolton, T./Groce, G.C., '*John Hesselius: An Account of His Life and the First Catalogue of his Portraits*' in *Art Quarterly*, vol 2, no 1, Journal article, 1939. Fleischer, R.E., '*Three Recently Discovered Portraits by John Hesselius*' in *Antiques*, vol 109, Journal article, 1981.

MUSEUMS AND GALLERIES:

ANNAPOLIS (Peabody Art Collection, Maryland State Archives): *John Paca* (c. 1765, oil) - BALTIMORE (MA): *Elizabeth Calvert* (1761) - BOSTON (MFA): *Jean Dick (Mrs Anthony Stewart)* (1760s, oil) - DETROIT (IA): *Colonel William Allen* (1756-1758, oil) - HAGERSTOWN, MD (Washington County Historical Society Museum): *Mrs Thomas Gough* (1777) - LOS ANGELES (County MA): *Portrait of Elizabeth Chew Smith* (1762, oil) - NEW YORK (Metropolitan Mus. of Art): *Archibald McCall* (c. 1755-1760, watercolour and gold leaf); *Mrs Richard Galloway* (1764, oil) - WASHINGTON DC (National Portrait Gal.): *Daniel of St Thomas Jenifer* (c. 1760-1770, oil).

AUCTION RECORDS:

NEW YORK, 31 Jan 1987, *Portrait of Thomas Clay* (1759, oil on canvas, 28 1/4 x 23 ins / 71.8 x 58.4 cm) USD 40,000. BETHESDA, 20 Sept 2003, *Portraits of Elizabeth Brown and her Husband Robert Seal* (oil on canvas, a pair, 30 x 25 ins / 76 x 64 cm) USD 9,000.

HESSELL, Leonhard Heinrich

Russian, 18th - 19th century.
Born 1757, in St Petersburg; died c. 1830.
Painter, engraver (burin). Portraits.

Leonhard Heinrich Hessell lived in Nuremberg where he worked primarily as a portrait engraver.

HESSELLUND, Hans Andreasen

Danish, 19th century.
Born 15 October 1851, in Dyngby; died 29 July 1907.
Painter. Genre scenes.

Hans Hessellund was a pupil of Oluf August Hermansen in Copenhagen.

AUCTION RECORDS:

COPENHAGEN, 30 Oct 1973, *Rustic Interior with Family*, DKK 6,100. COPENHAGEN, 10 Feb 1976, *The Reading of the Letter* (1893, oil on canvas, 24 1/2 x 21 1/4 ins / 62 x 54 cm) DKK 8,500.

HESSELS, Willem

Flemish, 16th century.
Died c. 1531.
Active in Louvain.
Sculptor.
Flemish School.

In 1524 Willem Hessels delivered an altar of the Passion to the abbey church of Maegdendale.

HESSEN, Heinrich von

German, 20th century.
Painter.

Marcel Brion grouped Heinrich von Hessen with the Surrealists in his *Histoire de la Peinture Allemande* (*History of German Painting*) (Tisné, Paris, 1959).

HESSENS, Arthur

Belgian, 20th century.
Born 1899, in Louvain.
Painter, draughtsman, watercolourist. Portraits, landscapes, seascapes, still-lifes, flowers.

Arthur Hessens studied at the academy of fine arts in Louvain. He painted the countryside of Brabant, the Cevennes and Annecy.

HESSENS, Robert

French, 20th century.
Born 1914.
Painter.

Robert Hessens exhibited in Paris at the first Salon de Mai in 1945.

HESSENSTEIN VON (Count)

German.

Active in Naples.
Engraver (etching).

HESSEUX, L.
Belgian, 20th century.
Born 20th century.
Painter. Figures, landscapes.

Hesseux was a cultural attaché at the Belgian Embassy in Mexico. He painted figures of Mexican Indians and Mexican landscapes.

HESSING, Perle
Polish, 20th century.
Born 12 December 1908, in Zaleszczyki (then part of Poland, now in the Ukraine).
Active and naturalised in Australia.
Painter. Figure compositions, religious subjects.

Perle Hessing was a self-taught artist, who only began to paint seriously from the age of 54 when living in Australia, to which her parents had emigrated in about 1950. Her vividly coloured, highly narrative paintings illustrate her life and childhood memories, as well as deeper themes from philosophy, literature and religious events, drawn from the Old Testament and the Kabbala, told to her by her father. In 1987, in New York she published *A Mirror to my Life*, illustrated with her paintings.

Hessing took part in many collective exhibitions of naive painting in Australia, England and France (at the Musée International d'Art Naïf Anatole Jakovsky, Nice). Solo shows include: 1964, Rudy Kommon Gallery, Sydney; 1966, White Studio Gallery, Adelaide; 1968, Brian Johnson Gallery, Brisbane; 1970, Kim Bonython Gallery, Sydney; 1974, Portal Gallery, London; 1979, Barry Stern Galleries, Sydney; 1980, Hamilton Gallery, London; 1983, Galeria Contini in Caracas, and others.

Bibliography:
Hessing, Perle, *A Mirror to my Life*, Henry Holt and Company Inc., New York, 1988.

Museums and Galleries:
Canberra (Nat. Gal. of Australia) - Jerusalem (Yad Vashem) - Laval (Mus. d'Art naïf) - Prague (Národní Muz.) - Vicq (Mus. International d'Art Naïf).

HESSL, Gustav Auguste
Austrian, 19th - 20th century.
Born 28 May 1849, in Vienna; died 1926.
Painter. Genre scenes.

Gustav Hessl studied with Engerth at the Akademie der Bildenden Künste in Vienna and first exhibited there in 1876. He also exhibited in Munich and Berlin.

Auction records:
New York, 9 Dec 1982, *Mother and Child in a Garden* (oil on canvas, 19 3/4 x 15 1/4 ins / 50 x 39 cm) USD 2,300. London, 15 March 1996, *Le Tricot* (oil on panel, 13 1/4 x 17 1/2 ins / 33.5 x 44.2 cm) GBP 4,600. New York, 18-19 July 1996, *A Teasing Goose* (1883, oil on panel, 10 1/2 x 8 ins / 26.7 x 20.3 cm) USD 5,750.

HESSLER, Otto
German, 19th century.
Born 23 November 1858, in Leipzig.
Painter. Genre scenes.

Hessler, a pupil of E Keller at the Karlsruhe academy of art, exhibited first in Berlin around 1888, and then also in Munich.

Auction records:
London, 26 March 1997, *Allegory of Summer* (oil on canvas, 38 1/2 x 66 1/2 ins / 98 x 169 cm) GBP 6,900.

HESSLOEHL, Wilhelm
German, 19th century.
Born 13 February 1810, in Offenburg.
Engraver.

Hessloehl was a pupil of Oberthür in Strasbourg. He worked there before moving on to work in Karlsruhe.

HESSMERT, Karl
German, 19th - 20th century.
Born 31 March 1869, in Fürstenberg; died 1928.
Painter. Landscapes.

Karl Hessmert worked mainly in Berlin.

Auction records:
New York, 4 Nov 1981, *Farmyard at Dusk* (oil on canvas, 35 3/4 x 58 3/4 ins / 91 x 149.5 cm) USD 3,000. Amsterdam, 8 Dec 1988, *Fortified Farm by a Pond in Winter* (1900, oil on canvas, 32 x 39 1/4 ins / 81 x 100 cm) NLG 2,300. Berlin, 19 June 1999, *Boats at Sunset in Lake Landscape* (oil on canvas, 37 x 49 ins / 95 x 125 cm) DEM 3,200. Berlin, 27 Nov 1999, *Late Summer* (oil on canvas, 22 x 28 ins / 55 x 72 cm) DEM 4,600. Bremen, 30 March 2001, *Small Girl by the Sea* (oil on board, 19 x 26 ins / 49 x 66 cm) DEM 8,500. Ahlden, 28 Nov 2003, *Castle in Schivelbein* (oil on canvas, 24 x 31 ins / 62 x 78 cm) EUR 2,050.

HESTE, Robert van
Belgian, 20th century.
Born 13 July 1913, in Ostend.
Painter, watercolourist. Seascapes.

Robert van Heste was the son of the painter Gustave van Heste. He painted seascapes and the undersea world, mainly in watercolour.

Museums and Galleries:
Ostend (Mus. voor Schone Kunsten).

HESTEAUX, Louis
French, 19th - 20th century.
Born 1858, in Metz; died June 1919.
Active in Nancy.
Painter.

Louis Hesteaux exhibited with the Société Nationale des Beaux-Arts, of which he was a member.

HESTER, Edward Gilbert
British, 19th century.
Died 3 July 1903, in St Albans.
Active in Chiswick.
Engraver.

Edward Hester exhibited in London at the Royal Academy from 1882.

HESTER, Joy
Australian, 20th century.
Born 1920, in Elsternwick (Victoria); died 1960, in Victoria.
Painter. Figures, nudes.

Joy Hester attended classes at the Melbourne Art Gallery School where she met the artist Albert Tucker, whom she married. Little known during her lifetime, her work has increased in value since her death (from Hodgkin's Disease). She exhibited at the Contemporary Art Society and held solo exhibitions in 1950, 1953 and 1956. In 2001, the National Gallery of Australia in Canberra held an exhibition entitled Joy Hester and Friends.

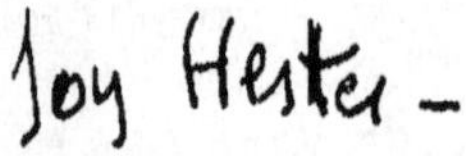

Museums and Galleries:
Adelaide (AG of South Australia): *The Lovers*.

AUCTION RECORDS:
SYDNEY, 23 Sept 1985, *Seated Nude* (1956, mixed media, 13 3/4 x 10 1/4 ins / 35 x 26 cm) ATS 1,400. PADDINGTON, 16 Aug 1999, *Standing Girl* (1957, watercolour, 58 x 20 ins / 148 x 50 cm) AUD 54,000. MELBOURNE, 23 Nov 1999, *Little Girl with Book on Head* (1957, enamel and watercolour on card, 39 x 24 ins / 99 x 62 cm) AUD 210,000. MELBOURNE, 1 May 2000, *Two Figures* (1957, watercolour, 18 x 25 ins / 46 x 63 cm) AUD 26,000. MELBOURNE, 2 May 2000, *Fun-fair* (watercolour and gouache, 9 x 12 ins / 24 x 31 cm) AUD 28,000. MELBOURNE, 8 May 2001, *Figure at a Bar* (watercolour, 7 x 12 ins / 19 x 30 cm) AUD 7,000. MELBOURNE, 20 Aug 2001, *Two Women* (c. 1940, ink and oil on paper, 4 x 6 ins / 10 x 15 cm) AUD 5,000. MELBOURNE, 1 May 2002, *Bouquet* (1955, ink and wash, 28 x 19 ins / 72 x 47 cm) AUD 90,000. MELBOURNE, 4 March 2003, *Lovers* (1955, ink, wash and charcoal, 13 x 10 ins / 33 x 25 cm) AUD 22,000. MELBOURNE, 25 Nov 2003, *Portrait of John and Sunday Reed* (1955, ink, 10 x 6 ins / 25 x 15 cm) AUD 11,000. VICTORIA, 11 Oct 2004, *Untitled* (ink and colour wash, 10 x 7 ins / 25 x 19 cm) AUD 4,250. VICTORIA, 11 Oct 2004, *Portrait of a Woman* (watercolour, 26 x 19 ins / 67 x 49 cm) AUD 5,500.

HESTER, Robert Wallace
British, 19th - 20th century.
Born 1866, in London.
Engraver.

Robert Wallace Hester was the son and pupil of the engraver Edward Gilbert Hester. He exhibited in Paris at the Salon des Artistes Français in 1905 and other years.

HESZ, János Mihály (Johann Michael), or Hess
German, 18th - 19th century.
Born 18 September 1768, in Eger, Hungary; died after 1833, in Vienna.
Painter, engraver. Historical scenes.

Hess, a pupil of Maurer at the Akademie der bildenden Künste in Vienna, was awarded a first-class medal there in 1794. He engraved prints taken from Roman and religious history and taught at the Vienna school of engineering.

HESZELEN
Dutch, 19th century.
Active in Leiden c. 1828.
Painter, engraver.

HET, followed by a second name. See second name

HETEY, Chatherien or Catherine
Hungarian, 20th century.
Born 2 August 1924, in Miskolc.
Active in France from 1947.
Painter.
Groupe Carré.

Chatherien Hetey was a pupil of Szönyi at the school of fine art in Budapest. In 1956 she visited Italy, where she met Alberti Burri and Ignazio Silone.

Denys Chevalier has written of Hetey's work: 'She starts from painting and moves towards space and then form... Used as an alphabet, the industrial packaging that she arranges takes on the presence and the consistency of sculptural volumes. Her actual painting has been not so much modified as a result of these experiments as strengthened and revitalised'.

Chatherien Hetey has featured in collective exhibitions in Budapest and Paris. Solo exhibitions include: Tunis (1961); Paris (1962); Washington and Los Angeles (1963); Stedelijk Museum, Schiedam (Netherlands, 1964); Hamburg (1965); and Rotterdam (1968). She was awarded the young artists' prize in Budapest (1947) and a prize in Scotland for a Bible illustration (1958).

MUSEUMS AND GALLERIES:
BUDAPEST (Magyar Nemzeti Gal.) - HAMBURG (City Coll.).

HETHERINGTON, Ivystan
British, 19th century.
Active in London.
Painter. Portraits, landscapes.

Ivystan Hetherington exhibited in London from 1875, showing works at the Royal Academy between 1877 and 1900.

HETHERINGTON, Walter
British, 20th century.
Born in Liverpool.
Painter.

Walter Hetherington was a pupil of J.-P. Laurens and Benjamin Constant.

HÉTREAU, Rémy
French, 20th century.
Born 31 January 1913, in Patay.
Engraver, designer, illustrator.

Rémy Hétreau studied at the École Boulle, where he became familiar with art techniques. An important name for decoration and imagery, he is known for his murals at the Maison de l'Amérique Latine in Paris and at the École Nationale des Douanes. He was often entrusted with the organisation and decoration of exhibitions on French technique, in Canada as well as in South America. He has a solid reputation as an illustrator.

As an engraver, Rémy Hétreaux executed numerous individual plates as well as illustrations embellished with gracious and solid figures for *L'Hôtel du Nord* by Eugène Dabit; *La Marche des rois* (*The March of Kings*), by Lanza del Vasto; *Le Mouchoir rouge* (*The Red Handkerchief*), by Count Gobineau; *Geneviève* by Jacques Lemarchand; *En arrière* (*Backward*), by Marcel Aymé, and *Aurélia* by Gérard de Nerval.

HETREL, Pierre Charles
French, 18th century.
Active in Paris in 1761.
Painter, sculptor.

HETSCH, Gustav Friedrich
German, 19th century.
Born 28 September 1788, in Stuttgart; died 7 September 1864, in Copenhagen.
Painter, architect.

Gustav Hetsch, the son of Philipp Friedrich von Hetsch, showed remarkable skill in the execution of his architectural paintings. He wrote a *Guide to Perspective* and also executed the plans of many monuments in Copenhagen, where he taught.

HETSCH, Heinrich von
German, 18th century.
Born 1767, in Stuttgart.
Painter. Historical scenes.

Heinrich von Hetsch was director of the Stuttgart Gallery.

HETSCH, Philipp Friedrich von
German, 18th - 19th century.
Born 10 September 1758, in Urach; died 31 December 1838, in Stuttgart.
Painter. Historical scenes, portraits.

Philipp von Hetsch studied with Nicolas Guibal and Adolf Friedrich Harper at the school of art in Stuttgart between 1771 and 1775. In 1780, he was appointed painter to the court of Württemberg. After continuing his studies in Paris with Vien, David and Joseph Vernet between 1781 and 1784, he went to Rome, where he painted *Tullia Riding over the Body of her Father*. He also worked in Dresden, Leipzig and Berlin before being appointed director of the Stuttgart Museum. After various disappointments, he stopped painting in

1819. His painting of *King Frederick and his Entourage at the Summer Palace of Monrepos* was, however, a great success.
MUSEUMS AND GALLERIES:
STUTTGART (Staatsgal.): *Cornelia, Mother of the Gracchi* (1794); *Self-portrait; Portrait of Dorothea van Kahlden.*
AUCTION RECORDS:
HEIDELBERG, 9 Oct 1992, *Two Muses* (gouache, 20 x 16 1/4 ins / 50.5 x 41.4 cm) DEM 3,200. DÜSSELDORF, 31 Jan 2000, *Mars and Venus Seated Beneath Tree* (oil on canvas, 30 x 37 ins / 76 x 93 cm) DEM 22,000. ZURICH, 29 March 2000, *Agrippina* (oil on canvas, 25 x 19 ins / 63 x 47 cm) CHF 24,000.

HETTE, Richard
Romanian, 20th century.
Born in Jossi.
Sculptor.
A pupil of Bourdelle, Richard Hette exhibited work at the Salon.

HETTICH, Eugen
German, 19th century.
Born 18 July 1848, in Besigheim; died 29 March 1888, in Stuttgart.
Painter. Portraits, landscapes.
Hettich, a pupil of Eisenmenger in Vienna, spent an extended period in Florence before moving to Stuttgart where he did most of his work and set up a school of painting.
AUCTION RECORDS:
BERN, 26 Oct 1988, *Landscape at Dusk* (1886, oil on canvas, 13 1/2 x 28 1/4 ins / 34 x 71.5 cm) CHF 1,200. VIENNA, 8 Feb 2000, *Cows Watering* (1878, oil on board, 8 x 15 ins / 21 x 37 cm) ATS 25,000. STUTTGART, 5 Dec 2002, *Rocky River Shore* (1877, oil on canvas, 45 x 56 ins / 114 x 143 cm) EUR 2,500. STUTTGART, 27 March 2003, *River Valley* (1877, oil on canvas, 45 x 56 ins / 114 x 143 cm) EUR 1,700.

HETTINGA, Ype or Epe van
Dutch, 18th century.
Born 15 May 1691 in Bolsward.
Painter.

HETTINGER, Andreas
Austrian, 17th century.
Active in Schwaz in the middle of the 17th century.
Painter.
Andreas Hettinger was a son of Georg Hettinger.

HETTINGER, Dominik
Austrian, 18th century.
Active in Graz in 1704.
Painter.
Dominik Hettinger was a son of Johann Georg Hettinger.

HETTINGER, Franz
Austrian, 17th century.
Active in Schwaz in 1684.
Painter.

HETTINGER, Georg
Austrian, 17th century.
Active in Schwaz c. 1645.
Painter.

HETTINGER, Johann
Austrian, 18th century.
Active in Rosenheim.
Painter.

HETTINGER, Johann Christoph
Austrian, 18th century.
Active in Emsburg in 1708.
Painter.

HETTINGER, Johann Georg
Austrian, 18th century.
Active in Schwaz c. 1700.
Painter.

HETTINGER, Joseph Anton
German, 18th century.
Active in Rosenheim in 1773.
Painter.

HETTINGER, Lorenz
Austrian, 17th century.
Active in Schwaz in 1679.
Painter.

HETTLER, Carl
German, 19th century.
Active in Breslau (now Wroclaw) c. 1820.
Sculptor.
MUSEUMS AND GALLERIES:
WEIMAR (Schlossmus.): bust.

HETTNER, Otto
German, 20th century.
Born 27 January 1875, in Dresden.
Sculptor, painter, engraver, illustrator.
Otto Hettner settled in Paris and became an associate of the Société Nationale des Beaux-Arts in 1903. He illustrated Longus' *Daphnis and Chloe*. He was one of the artists featured in the exhibition of German painters and engravers held in Paris in 1929.

HETTNER, Sabine
Italian, 20th century.
Born 4 October 1907, in Florence; died 1986.
Painter. Landscapes, portraits.
Groupe Réalité Seconde.
The daughter of the German painter, Otto Hettner, Sabine Hettner spent part of her life in Italy. She worked in Paris, in the south of France, as well as in Italy and in Spain. She first became known for her landscapes of Spain, which were unconventional in their treatment of the country, favouring the dramatic qualities in the most humble of villages as well as the outskirts of the large cities of the peninsula. She is also known for her Parisian cityscapes, as well as her robust portraits. Sabine Hettner has participated regularly in collective exhibitions from 1946 particularly in Paris at the Salon Comparaisons. She also had solo exhibitions and was introduced to the Parisian public by André Salmon. She belonged to the group Réalité Seconde which was introduced in Chamalières by the Association Musée de l'Art Contemporain de Chamalières.
AUCTION RECORDS:
VERSAILLES, 29 Oct 1989, *The Odalisque* (oil on canvas, 25 3/4 x 32 ins / 65.5 x 81.5 cm) FRF 11,000. VERSAILLES, 21 Jan 1990, *Interior with Woman* (oil on canvas, 25 1/2 x 32 ins / 65 x 81 cm) FRF 6,800.

HETZ, Eduard
German, 19th century.
Active in Munich.
Painter. Genre scenes.
Eduard Hetz first exhibited in Munich in 1889.

HETZ, Karl
German, 19th century.
Born 11 November 1828, in Kulmbach; died 5 August 1899, in Munich.
Painter. Genre scenes, landscapes.
Karl Hetz worked in Munich and exhibited in Hanover and Bremen from 1880.
AUCTION RECORDS:
COPENHAGEN, 7 Dec 1976, *The New Born Child* (oil on canvas, 22 x 26 1/2 ins / 56 x 67 cm) DKK 20,000. MUNICH, 30 Nov 1978, *The Romantic Meeting* (1871, oil on canvas, 28 3/4 x 34 1/2 ins / 73 x 87.5 cm) FRF 10,000. LONDON, 3 Oct 1979,

Mother and Children in an Interior (oil on canvas, 25 1/2 x 21 1/2 ins / 65 x 54.5 cm) GBP 2,200. NEW YORK, 26 Oct 1983, *Day of the First Communion* (oil on remounted canvas, 27 3/4 x 36 ins / 70.5 x 91.5 cm) USD 5,000. LINDAU (B.), 7 Oct 1987, *Bavarian Landscape* (oil on canvas, 13 1/2 x 20 ins / 34.5 x 51 cm) DEM 6,200. MUNICH, 27 Sept 2000, *Young Peasant Woman with Children in Interior* (1875, oil on canvas, 26 x 20 ins / 67 x 51 cm) DEM 8,000. MUNICH, 27 June 2001, *Easter Feast in Upper Franken Peasant House* (1872, oil on canvas, 12 x 17 ins / 30 x 42 cm) DEM 6,500. PHILADELPHIA, 18 Jan 2002, *Telling his Fortune* (1887, oil on canvas, 30 x 35 ins / 76 x 89 cm) USD 1,600. MUNICH, 11 July 2002, *Young Woman with Fish on Plate* (oil on canvas, 29 x 23 ins / 74 x 59 cm) EUR 2,200. MUNICH, 19 Sept 2003, *Gratefully Received* (oil on panel, 11 x 9 ins / 29 x 22 cm) EUR 3,100.

HETZE, Paul
German, 19th century.
Born 11 September 1866, in Chemnitz; died 27 April 1901, in Munich.
Painter. Genre scenes.
MUSEUMS AND GALLERIES:
MUNICH: *Lonely*.

HETZEL, George
French, 19th century.
Born 1826, in Alsace; died 1899 or 1906.
Painter. Landscapes, still-lifes.
Hetzel went to live in America and worked mostly in Pittsburgh, Pennsylvania.
AUCTION RECORDS:
NEW YORK, 21 Nov 1980, *Still-life with Fruit* (1876, oil on canvas, 20 x 30 ins / 50.8 x 76.2 cm) USD 3,500. NEW YORK, 30 Sept 1982, *Peach* (1873, oil on canvas, 30 1/4 x 50 ins / 76.6 x 126.8 cm) USD 3,000. NEW YORK, 8 Dec 1983, *Still-life with Fruit* (1882, oil on canvas, 22 1/4 x 34 1/4 ins / 56.5 x 87 cm) USD 11,000. SAN FRANCISCO, 27 Feb 1986, *Hudson River Valley* (1873, oil on canvas, 26 x 40 1/4 ins / 66 x 102 cm) USD 4,000. NEW YORK, 3 Dec 1987, *Still-life with Watermelon* (1873, oil on canvas remounted on hardboard, 22 x 30 ins / 55.9 x 76.2 cm) USD 13,000. NEW YORK, 26 Sept 1990, *Still-life with Melons, Pears and Apples* (oil on canvas, 22 1/4 x 34 1/4 ins / 56.5 x 87 cm) USD 12,100. NEW YORK, 14 March 1991, *Stream Running through a Wood* (1882, oil on canvas, 24 x 36 ins / 61 x 91.5 cm) USD 8,800.

HETZELSDÖRFFER, Friedrich
German, 16th century.
Active in Nuremberg c. 1597.
Portrait artist.

HETZER, Johann Christoph
German, 17th century.
Born 1640, in Nuremberg; died 12 September 1665, in Venice.
Painter.
Nicolaus Häublin engraved a self-portrait by Hetzer in 1669.

HEU, Édouard
French, 19th century.
Born 1809, in Dieppe; died 1869.
Ivory worker.
Heu was a pupil of Meugniot.

HEU, Joseph
German, 20th century.
Born 21 February 1876, in Marburg (Hesse).
Painter, sculptor.
Joseph Heu studied with Hellmer at the academy in Vienna and then settled in the city.
AUCTION RECORDS:
VIENNA, 10 Dec 1985, *St Christopher* (1921, bronze, h. 24 3/4 ins / 63 cm) ATS 30,000.

HEUBACH, Walter
German, 19th century.
Born 15 February 1865, in Leicester.
Painter. Historical scenes, genre scenes.
Heubach lived, exhibited and worked in Munich, where he also collaborated with the history painter, F Wagner.
AUCTION RECORDS:
NEW YORK, 3 June 1994, *Feeding Time* (oil on canvas, 27 x 39 1/2 ins / 68.6 x 100.3 cm) USD 14,950.

HEUBEL, Alexander
German, 19th century.
Born 9 April 1813, in Lemsal; died 22 January 1847, in Riga.
Painter. History painting.
Alexander Heubel studied with Schadow at the Düsseldorf academy of art from 1834 to 1840. In 1841, he went to Italy with his friend, the history and portrait painter Ludwig Haach, before settling in Riga in 1844.

HEUBEL, Marcus Joachim
German, 18th - 19th century.
Born 21 March 1773, in Hamburg; died 7 August 1831, in Hamburg.
Painter, engraver.
Marcus Heubel imitated 17th century Flemish and Dutch genre painting.

HEUBES, Jules
Belgian, 19th century.
Painter. Genre scenes, still-lifes.

HEUBNER, Friedrich Leonhard
German, 20th century.
Born 24 December 1886, in Dresden.
Painter, engraver, draughtsman, illustrator. Portraits, landscapes.
Friedrich Heubner was active in Munich, where he rapidly became more famous for his caricatures than for his portraits or his landscapes. He illustrated a German translation of Musset's *Tizianello* in 1920.

HEUBNER, Hermann Ludwig
German, 19th - 20th century.
Born 26 May 1843, in Leipzig; died 25 December 1915, in Leipzig.
Painter. Portraits, genre scenes, landscapes.
Hermann Heubner was a student of Pauwels in Weimar in 1863 and moved to Leipzig in 1869. His works were first shown in Dresden in 1868.

HEUCHER, J. P.
German, 18th century.
Draughtsman.
GF Schmidt engraved a *Portrait of the Clergyman, JF Osterwald*, copied after Heucher.

HEUCQUEVILLE, Christiane d'
French, 20th century.
Born 21 November 1900.
Painter. Portraits.
Christiane d'Heucqueville exhibited in Paris at the Société des Femmes Peintres et Sculpteurs and at the Salon d'Automne.

HEUDE, Nicolas
French, 17th century.
Born in Le Mans; died in London.
Painter, decorative designer.
Nicolas Heude fell foul of the establishment on religious grounds as Catholic advisers pressed Louis XIV to reduce the liberties granted French Protestants by the Edict of Nantes. Heude had been approved by the Académie on 30 April 1672 but, having settled in London without the king's permission, he was struck off the Académie's registers. He

made amends and was readmitted. He became an Académicien on 15 April 1673 with the *Portrait of Condé under the Figure of Hercules, Held Aloft by Valour and Victory* which can be seen at the Versailles museum. On 31 January 1682, on the king's orders, he was excluded from the Académie because of his Protestant faith and went back to England. Mariette asserts that Heude worked in the manner of Verrio, who employed him on a number of his projects. He painted the staircase in Lord Tyrconnel's town house in London and a ceiling at Bulstrode Manor. The sculptor Carpenter studied under him.

MUSEUMS AND GALLERIES:

VERSAILLES (Mus.): *Portrait of Condé under the Figure of Hercules, Held Aloft by Valour and Victory.*

HEUDE, sire

French, 13th century.

Illuminator.

This artist was in Paris in 1292.

HEUDE, Yves

French, 20th century.

Born 23 February 1931, in St-Georges-de-Grehaigne.

Painter, engraver.

Yves Heude has exhibited his work since 1960. His paintings are solidly constructed.

HEUDEBERT, Raymonde

French, 20th century.

Born 16 October 1905, in Paris; died 27 October 1991, in Paris.

Painter, draughtswoman. Portraits, landscapes, urban landscapes, still-lifes.

Raymonde Heudebert was a pupil of Maurice Denis at the Académie Ranson

She painted landscapes of France and Italy in a Post-Cubist style. She executed numerous portraits, including: *Mme Armande de Polignac; Suzanne Lenglen; Mme E. Bourdet; Félix Vallotton; Paul Morand; E. Jaloux; G. Bauer; François Mauriac.*

Raymonde Heudebert also brought back many paintings and drawings from Africa.. She was a member of the Salon d'Automne and the Salon des Tuileries and took part in exhibitions in Geneva, London and New York. Solo exhibitions include: Galerie Bernheim-Jeune, Paris (1931); Galerie Georges Bernheim, Paris (1936); Galerie Bruno Martin Caille, Paris (1969) and Galerie Bernheim, Paris (1974).

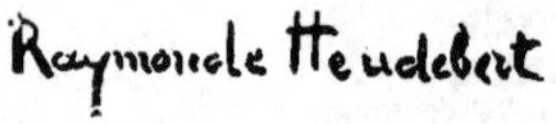

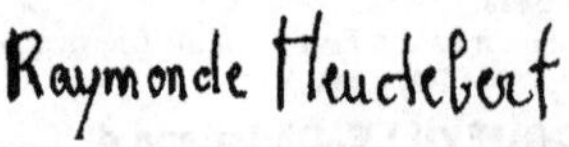

BIBLIOGRAPHY:

Cassou, Jean (preface), *Raymonde Heudebert. Peintures, dessins*, exhibition catalogue, Gal. du Cercle, Paris, 1984.

MUSEUMS AND GALLERIES:

GRENOBLE: *Self-portrait* (1925) - PARIS (Mus. des Arts d'Afrique et d'Océanie): *Crossing the Niger* - ROUEN (MBA): *Paul Morand* (1927).

HEUDELOT, Jean

French, 18th century.

Born 1730, in Montpellier.

Engraver (burin).

Jean Heudelot settled in Paris around 1760. He essentially engraved genre subjects, mostly after A. van Ostade and Lingelbach. He also engraved a few portraits.

HEUER, Barlach

German, 20th century.

Born 1930, in Elmshorn.

Engraver.

Barlach Heuer trained as a cabinetmaker before studying art in Hamburg. He settled in France in 1952. He has exhibited in Hamburg, Paris, Copenhagen, Munich, Toronto and Bremen. His work symbolises reality and the cosmic zones of heaven and earth.

HEUER, Friedrich Carl

German, 19th century.

Active in Hamburg.

Painter.

HEUER, Vilhelm

Danish, 18th - 19th century.

Active in Paris.

Draughtsman, engraver, lithographer.

Vilhelm Heuer engraved *Portraits*. He made lithographs after P. Potter, C. Vernet and H. Vernet.

HEUER, Wilhelm

German, 19th century.

Born 6 November 1813, in Hamburg; died 15 April 1890, in Hamburg.

Lithographer, draughtsman.

Wilhelm Heuer studied in Dresden and then Vienna, then returned to settle in Hamburg in 1842.

HEUERMANN, Magda

American, 19th century.

Born 10 September 1868, in Galesburg, Illinois; died 27 July 1962, in Marshall.

Painter, illustrator.

Magda Heuermann was a pupil at the Art Institute of Chicago and also studied in Munich and Paris. She was a member of the Arts Club of Chicago. She won various prizes and specialised in painting miniatures.

HEUGHE, Patrick

Belgian, 20th century.

Born in Flanders.

Painter. Scenes with figures, urban landscapes.

In 2002, Patrick Heughe featured in the group exhibition *Marcel Aymé et les Peintres* (*Marcel Aymé and the Painters*) at the Galerie Roussard in Paris. He has also exhibited in solo shows, for instance at the Galerie Roussard in 1982. He paints his everyday surroundings using a simple, smooth, meticulous technique, making each picture tell a story by the inclusion of a particular detail.

HEUKLEM, Reynier van, called Wolf

Dutch, 17th century.

Portrait painter, draughtsman.

There exists a portrait by him.

HEULLAND, Georges d'

French, 18th century.

Active in Angers c. 1736.

Engraver.

HEULLAND, Guillaume d'

French, 18th century.

Died c. 1770, in Paris.

Engraver.

Guillaume d'Heulland was the master of P.-P. Choffard.

HEULLANT, Félix Armand

French, 19th century.

Born 23 April 1834, in Paris.

Painter. Mythological subjects, genre scenes.

Heullant began studying at the École des Beaux-Arts in Paris in 1856, in the studios of François Édouard Picot and Giraud. He exhibited at the Salon des Artistes Français in Paris, from 1883 to 1887, and became a member in 1883.

Museums and Galleries:
Bagnères-de-Bigorre: *Idylls* - Nantes (Mus. Dobrée) - Rouen (MBA): *The Flute Lesson*.
Auction records:
Paris, 20-21 April 1904, *The Temple of Love*, FRF 260. London, 27 Nov 1909, *Love Scene*, GBP 3. New York, 16 Feb 1995, *The Meeting* (oil on panel, 27 1/2 x 16 1/2 ins / 69.9 x 41.9 cm) USD 9,200.

HEULLE, Jan van
Flemish, 15th century.
Active in Bruges in 1468.
Painter.
Flemish School.

HEULLUY, Charles
French, 20th century.
Born 1894, in Plombières; died 1975, in Plombières.
Painter, designer. Portraits, landscapes, landscapes with figures, flowers.
Charles Heulluy studied at the École des Beaux-Arts in Nancy in 1911 and 1912 and at the École des Beaux-Arts in Paris in 1913. Wounded in World War I in 1914, he executed several drawings from life. In 1916 and 1917, he took participated in a military mission as a draughtsman in Kiev and witnessed the October Revolution. He was back at the École des Beaux-Arts in Paris, where he studied with Cormon from 1918 to 1920. His body of work mainly consists of landscapes of the Vosges and of the Provence regions, portraits and flowers compositions.
Charles Heulluy participated on several occasions in the Salon des Artistes Français and worked with the Maeght and Romanet galleries. He received the Prix Havard in 1923.
Museums and Galleries:
Paris (Mus. du Petit Palais) - Plombières-les-Bains - Remiremont - St-Dié-des-Vosges.

HEULZ, Henri
19th century.
Lithographer.
Henri Heulz produced views of Biarritz and its neighbourhood.

HEUMANN, Arthur
German, 20th century.
Born 9 May 1883, in Königsee (Thuringia) Germany.
Painter, watercolourist.
Arthur Heumann exhibited in Düsseldorf, Dresden and Munich from 1909.

HEUMANN, Augustin
German, 20th century.
Born 11 November 1885, in Münster; died 1 February 1919, in Cologne.
Painter, sculptor, engraver.
Augustin Heumann studied with Schiemann in Münster. He was mainly active in Munich.

HEUMANN, Georg Daniel
German, 18th century.
Born 1691, in Nuremberg; died 27 June 1759, in Nuremberg.
Engraver.
Georg Heumann made engraved copies of works by other artists including Menkel and Desmarée. He was an engraver at the English court and also at the Göttingen academy of art. His architectural views published in Augsburg in 1724 and his portraits of German figures still exist today. His best known plate is *Peace Banquet*, copied after Joachim van Sandrart.

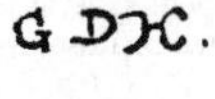

HEUMANN, Joel Paul
German, 18th century.
Born 1690, in Nuremberg; died 1756.
Engraver.
Joel Heumann worked in Göttingen according to Heinecke.

HEUNERT, Friedrich
German, 19th century.
Born 1808, in Soest; died 27 November 1876, in Düsseldorf.
Painter, watercolourist, draughtsman. Landscapes.
Heunert, a pupil of JW Schirmer in Düsseldorf, practised and taught oil and watercolour painting as well as drawing. He gained a certain renown for his small landscapes of Westphalia. He first exhibited in Berlin in 1832, then also in Bremen and Leipzig.

HEUNINCKX, Jan
Belgian, 20th century.
Born 1918, in Mazenzele.
Painter.
Jan Heuninckx was a teacher of fine arts at the Institut Imelda.

HEUNISCH, Johann
German, 17th century.
Active in Kitzingen.
Painter.
Heunisch painted a *Last Supper* signed and dated 1608.

HEUPEL, Ludwig Wilhelm
German, 19th century.
Born 20 June 1864, in Siegen.
Portrait painter.
Heupel worked in Munich, where he was awarded a medal in 1891.

HEUPGEN, Andrée
Belgian, 20th century.
Born 1902, in Lodelinsart (Hainaut).
Painter, draughtsman, collage artist, watercolourist.
Portraits, local scenes, still-lifes, landscapes.
Andrée Heupgen studied under Alfred Delaunois at the Académie des Beaux-Arts in Louvain.

HEUR, Cornelis Joseph de
Flemish School, 18th century.
Born 27 March 1707, in Antwerp; died 12 March 1762, in Antwerp.
Painter. Historical subjects, interiors.
He was the son of Thomas de Heur, a sculptor in Liège, a pupil of Kaspar-Jacob van Opstal in 1716 and, in 1717, of Jan-Jozef Horemans and Peter Snyders. He worked in Paris in 1730. In 1749, he was professor at the Koninklijke Academie voor Schone Kunsten in Antwerp. Several of his works are in Antwerp museum.

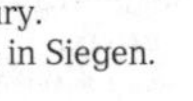

HEUR, Thomas de
Flemish School, 17th - 18th century.
Active in Liège.
Sculptor.

HEURT, Forrest, or Hewit
British, 20th century.
Born at the end of the 19th century, in Salford.
Painter. Figures, landscapes.
Forrest Heurt was a pupil of Walter Sickert. He exhibited in London at the Royal Academy, the New English Art Club and other artistic centres in England, and at the Salon des Artistes Français in Paris.

HEURTAULT, Jacques
French, 18th century.

Active in Paris in 1749.
Painter, sculptor.

HEURTAULT, Marie
French, 20th century.
Born 12 September 1887, in Montargis.
Painter. Portraits.

A pupil of Schommer and Gervais, Marie Heurtault exhibited regularly at the Salon des Artistes Français.

HEURTAULT, Mausse
French, 16th century.
Active in Rouen.
Glass painter.
Rouen School.

Mausse Heurtault worked for the church of St-Ouen in Pont-Audemer.

HEURTAULT, Nicolas
French, 18th century.
Active in Paris.
Sculptor.

Nicolas Heurtault was admitted into the Académie de St-Luc in 1741.

HEURTAUX, André Gaston, Arto
French, 20th century.
Born 25 December 1898, in Paris; died 14 January 1983, in Paris.
Painter, pastellist, draughtsman.
Abstraction-Création group.

André Gaston Heurtaux was a self-taught painter. Initially he drew from life, animating his compositions with figures, portraits and nudes, then his drawing began to move away from reality, first in a Post-Cubist period, and later when was drawn to the possibilities of Abstraction. Through the work of Van Doesbourg, Heurtaux approached Neo-plasticism c. 1933. Closer to the tradition of Russian Suprematism than to Dutch Neo-plasticism, Heurtaux was not satisfied merely with orthogonal contrast or the primary chromatic trinity. His works may be strictly geometric but they are executed using very large, pure surfaces, with delicate colour treatments in muted tones.

He exhibited at the Salon des Indépendants (1925 to 1927 and in 1930), then at the Salon des Surindépendants (1931 to 1971). A member of Abstraction-Création in 1934, and its secretary in 1937, he took part in numerous collective exhibitions including: Réalités Nouvelles group (1939); Galerie Charpentier, Paris and Salon des Réalités Nouvelles (1946, 1947, 1953); Salon Grands et Jeunes d'Aujourd'hui From (1974 to 1980); collective exhibition of Abstract art, Musée de Lille with the Salon des Réalités nouvelles (1947); *Peintures d'aujourd'hui* (*Paintings of Today*), Cannes (1947);, *Découvrir* (*Discover*), Galerie Charpentier, Paris, (1955); *Art Abstrait, Premières Générations 1910-1939* (*Abstract Art: The First Generations 1910-1935*), Musée de St-Étienne (1957); *Esquisse d'un Salon* (*Sketch of a Salon*), Galerie Denise René, Paris (1963); *De Mondrian au cinétisme* (*From Mondrian to Kinetic Art*), Galerie Denise René, Paris (1967); *Paris-Paris 1937-1957. Création en France* (*Paris-Paris 1937-1957: Creation in France*), Centre Beaubourg, Paris (1981); *1960*, Musée de St-Étienne (1983); Venice Biennale (1986). Solo exhibitions include Paris (1972) and Cologne (1972 and 1979). Posthumous retrospectives include: Musée de Cholet and the Musée de La Roche-sur-Yon (1983) and Galerie Denise René, Paris (1985).

Parallel to his career as a painter, André Gaston Heurtaux executed humorous drawings under the pseudonym of Arto for magazines such as *Le Rire* and *Regard*.

BIBLIOGRAPHY:
Lemoine, Serge, *André Heurtaux*, exhibition catalogue, Gal. Denise René, Paris, 1972. Fauchille, B./Lemoine, Serge, *André Heurtaux*, exhibition catalogue, Musée de Cholet, Cholet, 1983.

MUSEUMS AND GALLERIES:
CHOLET (MAH): *Composition on Blue Background* (1932) - GRENOBLE: *Composition N° 115* (1968-1971) - ZURICH (Haus Konstruktiv): *Grey Composition in Degrees*.

AUCTION RECORDS:
PARIS, 24 June 1986, *Composition* (1948-1950, oil on canvas, 30 x 76 3/4 ins / 76 x 195 cm) FRF 18,500. PARIS, 1 Oct 1993, *Still-life with Vase of Flowers* (1928, pastel, 12 3/4 x 9 3/4 ins / 32.5 x 25 cm) FRF 3,800; *Composition with Three Circles* (1953, gouache, 7 1/4 x 25 1/2 ins / 18.6 x 65 cm) FRF 5,500.

HEURTEBISE, Lucien Eugène Olivier
French, 19th century.
Born 12 February 1867, in Le Mans.
Sculptor.

Heurtebise was a pupil of Carlus, and of Théophile Barrau. He became a member of the Société des Artistes Français in 1889.

HEURTELOUP, Henri (Baron)
French, 19th century.
Born c. 1844, in Paris; died 1878.
Painter, watercolourist. Landscapes with figures, landscapes.

Heurteloup made his Salon début in 1876 and mostly painted views of Holland and Belgium. His works are highly regarded.

AUCTION RECORDS:
LONDON, 14 May 1909, *Vlisnugen* (1876) GBP 12; *Scene on a Canal*, GBP 10.

HEURTIER, Jean François
French, 18th - 19th century.
Born 1739, in Paris; died 1822, in Versailles.
Draughtsman.

AUCTION RECORDS:
PARIS, 13 May 1927, *The Terrace of a Palace* (pen and wash) FRF 650. PARIS, 9 Feb 1928, *The Equestrian Statue* (wash) FRF 520. PARIS, 7 June 1979, *The Temple of Love*; *The Fountain of Apollo* (two gouaches with pen, making a pair, each 13 1/4 x 18 ins / 33.5 x 45.5 cm) FRF 10,800.

HEUSCH, Abraham de
Dutch, 17th century.
Died in Utrecht, according to Descamps.
Active in Utrecht in 1638 or in 1650.
Painter, engraver (etching).

He was a pupil of Christian Striep. He engraved landscapes and genre subjects. As a painter, his technique recalls that of Mieris. It is believed he was related to Willelm and Jacob de Heusch.

HEUSCH, Gabriel de
Dutch, 17th century.
Landscape painter.

He may have been father to or a relation of Willelm de Heusch. Jacob de Heusch has sometimes been referred to as Gabriel.

HEUSCH, Jacob de
Dutch, 17th century.
Born 1656 or 1657, in Utrecht; died 9 May 1701, in Amsterdam.
Painter, engraver. Landscapes with figures, seascapes.

He was the pupil of his uncle, Willelm de Heusch. Upon his recommendation, he spent several years in Italy, where he studied the work of Salvator Rosa in particular.

He painted mostly Italian landscapes with figures. He also executed several original engravings.

Museums and Galleries:
Mainz: *Italian Landscape* - St Petersburg (Hermitage): *Two Italian Landscapes; Sea Port in Italy; Landscape with Figures* - Venice (Gal. Reale): *Landscape* - Vienna: *Two Landscapes.*

Auction records:
Paris, 2-3 April 1897, *Landscape,* FRF 515. London, 4 Feb 1911, *Mountain Landscape with Adoration of the Shepherds,* GBP 5. London, 25 Oct 1957, *Wooded Landscape,* GBP 525. London, 4 March 1970, *The Banks of the Tiber with Figures,* GBP 3,100. Scotland, 27 Aug 1971, *Italian Landscape,* GBP 1,600. New York, 18 May 1972, *Port Scenes* (two pendants) USD 8,000. Vienna, 22 May 1973, *The Bay of Naples,* ATS 250,000. London, 26 Oct 1973, *Italian Landscape* (in collaboration with Lingelbach) Gns 6,500. London, 12 July 1978, *Landscape of Ruins with Figures* (oil on canvas, 25 1/4 x 35 ins / 64 x 89 cm) GBP 2,600. London, 30 Nov 1979, *View of the Ponte Rotto, Rome* (oil on canvas, 21 1/4 x 32 ins / 53.9 x 81.3 cm) GBP 16,000. New York, 18 June 1982, *Banks of the Tiber in Rome* (oil on canvas, 26 1/2 x 54 ins / 67.5 x 137 cm) USD 16,000. Monte Carlo, 26 June 1983, *Landscape of the Roman Coast, with the Tomb of Cecilia Mettella* (oil on canvas, 19 1/4 x 25 1/2 ins / 49 x 64.5 cm) FRF 50,000. London, 19 Dec 1985, *Steep Landscape with Fishermen Around a Lake* (oil on canvas, 36 1/2 x 50 1/2 ins / 93 x 128 cm) GBP 5,000. Amsterdam, 1 Dec 1986, *View of the Old City of Lyons* (lead pencil and wash, 9 3/4 x 13 3/4 ins / 24.8 x 35.2 cm) NLG 3,600. New York, 4 June 1987, *Banks of the Tiber with Figures* (oil on canvas, 25 3/4 x 52 3/4 ins / 65.5 x 134 cm) USD 40,000. London, 7 Dec 1987, *Banks of a River* (pen and wash/traces of black chalk, 4 1/4 x 11 ins / 11 x 27 cm) GBP 1,200. Amsterdam, 29 Nov 1988, *Italian Landscape with Woodsmen Resting Under a Tree and a Valley in the Background* (oil on panel, 11 1/2 x 11 ins / 29.4 x 28 cm) NLG 8,625. New York, 10 Jan 1990, *Italian Mountain Landscape with Travellers on a Road Bordering a City* (oil on canvas, 30 x 39 1/4 ins / 76.2 x 99.7 cm) USD 49,500. New York, 1 June 1990, *Port and Figures on the Shore* (oil on canvas, 32 x 53 1/2 ins / 81 x 136 cm) USD 29,700. Amsterdam, 13 Nov 1990, *Italian Landscape with Fishermen at Work on the Shore* (oil on panel, 15 x 19 1/4 ins / 37.8 x 49.2 cm) NLG 59,800. Paris, 28 June 1993, *Walkers on a Mountain Road* (oil on canvas, 25 x 28 1/2 ins / 63.5 x 72.5 cm) FRF 55,000. London, 8 July 1994, *Rocky Islands in the Mediterranean with Brigands* (oil on canvas, 20 x 39 1/2 ins / 50.8 x 100.5 cm) GBP 52,100. Paris, 21 Dec 1994, *Venetian Landscape: View of the Gardens of a Villa* (oil on canvas, 48 1/2 x 76 3/4 ins / 123 x 195 cm) FRF 215,000. New York, 5 Oct 1995, *Classical River Landscape with Travellers on a Path, Fishermen and a Villa in the Distance* (oil on canvas, 24 x 38 3/4 ins / 60.7 x 98.4 cm) USD 23,000. Rome, 14 Nov 1995, *Landscape with Ruins; River Landscape* (oil on canvas, a pair, 22 1/2 x 37 3/4 ins / 57 x 96 cm) ITL 55,200,000. London, 8 Dec 1995, *Italian River Landscape with Peasants on a Rock* (oil on canvas, 19 1/4 x 24 1/2 ins / 49 x 62.5 cm) GBP 7,130. New York, 12 Jan 1996, *Arcadian Landscape with Travellers Talking on a Road and a Peasant Woman with her Child By a Pool* (oil on canvas, 32 3/4 x 35 ins / 83.2 x 89 cm) USD 27,600. London, 3-4 Dec 1997, *Vast Wooded Landscape with a Herdsman and Flock on a Country Road* (1696, oil on canvas, 20 3/4 x 29 1/4 ins / 53 x 74.4 cm) GBP 20,700. Lucerne, 19 May 1999, *The Animals Entering Noah's Ark* (1701, oil on canvas, 35 x 30 ins / 88 x 76 cm) CHF 7,000. Venice, 14 Nov 1999, *View of Rome with the River Tiber and the Church of S Maria del Priorato* (oil on canvas, 18 x 28 ins / 45 x 71 cm) ITL 20,000,000. New York, 27 Jan 2000, *Rocky Landscape with Travellers on a Path with Fishermen by a Waterfall beyond* (oil on canvas, 25 x 28 ins / 63 x 72 cm) USD 20,000. Vienna, 7 June 2000, *River Landscape with Fishermen* (oil on canvas, 19 x 26 ins / 49 x 65 cm) ATS 180,000. Stockholm, 28 May 2002, *Noah's Ark* (1701, oil on canvas, 35 x 30 ins / 88 x 76 cm) SEK 100,000. Cologne, 16 Nov 2002, *Coastal Landscape with Fishermen* (oil on panel, 13 x 18 ins / 33 x 46 cm) EUR 11,000. New York, 4 June 2003, *River Landscape with Travellers on a Path* (oil on canvas, 26 x 35 ins / 66 x 90 cm) USD 8,000. Prato, 27 March 2004, *Landscape in Lazio* (oil on canvas, 52 x 68 ins / 133 x 173 cm) EUR 36,000.

HEUSCH, Lucio de
Canadian, 20th - 21st century.
Born 1946, in Sherbrooke (Quebec).
Painter.

In the early 1970s, Lucio de Heusch's work was characterised by a systematic exploration of the dynamic possibilities of the painted surface. From 1974-1975, he created works using coloured inks, and from 1975-1977, a series of pictures articulating the tension between a 'fictive' space defined by patches of colour, and its inevitable limitation due to the confines of its flat support (the paper or canvas). Works from 1981-1983 comprised large surfaces striped with hatching or fine corrugations, suggestive of architectural forms, columns, doors or archways. Following on from these, the *Container Boxes* are small wall-mounted boxes containing compositions based on a range of materials (fine strips of wood, string, rope). The resulting works combine the physical properties of both sculpture and painting: three-dimensionality and the creation of a flat 'pictorial' surface.

Bibliography:
Les 20 ans du musée à travers sa collection, exhibition catalogue, Musée d'Art contemporain, Montreal, 1985.

Museums and Galleries:
Montreal (MAC): *Box No. 17: Our Homes are Volcanoes* (1983).

HEUSCH, Rolande de
19th - 20th century.
Active in Castau.
Engraver (etching).

Work by Rolande de Heusch was included in the 1910 Exhibition in Brussels.

HEUSCH, Willelm or Guilliam de
Dutch, 17th century.
Born 1625 or 1638, in Utrecht; died 9 March 1692, in Utrecht.
Painter, engraver. Mythological subjects, landscapes, landscapes with figures.

In 1656 at the age of 18, he left for Italy, where he remained for several years. He was a pupil of Jan Both, whose teachings he would always retain.

He returned to Holland an older man, and there he continued to paint landscapes with ruins. He was one of the most acknowledged representatives of the *Dutch Italianates* and preceded the arrival of the great Dutch landscapists.

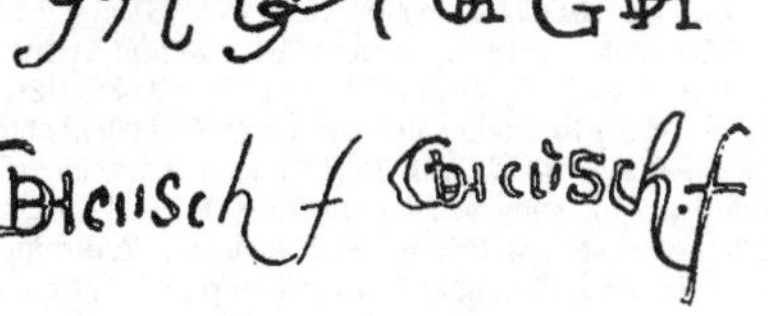

BIBLIOGRAPHY:

De Groot, I., *Landscape Etchings by the Dutch Masters of the Seventeenth Century*, London, 1979 (pp. 188-91).

MUSEUMS AND GALLERIES:

AIX: *The Emigration of Jacob* - AMSTERDAM: *Italian Landscapes; Mountainscape* - ANTWERP: *Italian Landscape* - BUDAPEST: *Italian Landscape* - COPENHAGEN (Statens Mus. for Kunst): *Italian Landscape* - FRANKFURT AM MAIN: *Two Southern Landscapes* - GRENOBLE: *Landscape* - HANOVER: *Italian Landscape* - KASSEL: *Landscape with Hunters* - LA FÈRE: *Landscape* - MILAN (Pinacoteca di Brera): *Rest in the Mountains* - MONTPELLIER: *Two Landscapes* - PARIS (Louvre): *Landscape* - ROTTERDAM: *Italian Landscape* - ROUEN: *Landscape* - STRASBOURG: *Italian Landscape* - STUTTGART: *Diana and Callisto* - THE HAGUE: *Two Italian Landscapes* - VIENNA: *Italian Landscape* - VIENNA (Czernin'sche Gemäldegal.): *Two Landscapes*.

AUCTION RECORDS:

PARIS, 28-29 March 1898, *Landscape*, FRF 3,950. PARIS, 6 March 1901, *Italian Landscape*, FRF 710. LONDON, 29 Feb 1908, *The Garden of a Chateau* (in collaboration with Lingelbach) GBP 23. LONDON, 30 April 1909, *River Scene*, GBP 39. PARIS, 21 April 1910, *Departure for the Hunt* (with Lingelbach) FRF 1,500. LONDON, 18-25 Feb 1911, *Wooded Landscape*, GBP 46. PARIS, 28 Feb 1919, *The Oaks*, FRF 1,900. PARIS, 8-10 June 1920, *Landscape* (pen) FRF 7,100. PARIS, 21-22 Nov 1922, *Landscape* (pen and wash) FRF 4,800. LONDON, 7 May 1926, *Wooded Landscape*, GBP 63. PARIS, 14-15 May 1926, *Hunting Landscape*, FRF 1,580. LONDON, 14 March 1930, *Landscape with Road*, GBP 107. PARIS, 26 Oct 1933, *Landscape* (pen drawing with sepia wash) FRF 2,500. LONDON, 9 March 1934, *Mountain Landscape*, GBP 15. LONDON, 3 Nov 1944, *Landscape* (in collaboration with J. Lingelbach) GBP 37. PARIS, 30 Oct 1968, *Landscape with Shepherdess and Young Boy*, FRF 20,000. COLOGNE, 21 May 1970, *Italian Landscape*, DEM 9,000. VIENNA, 21 Sept 1971, *Mountain Landscape*, ATS 65,000. VIENNA, 6 June 1972, *Italian Landscape*, ATS 110,000. VIENNA, 22 May 1973, *Landscape with Stone Bridge*, ATS 150,000. ROME, 24 May 1973, *The Roman Countryside*, ITL 3,200,000. LONDON, 12 May 1976, *Muledriver with Herd in a Landscape* (oil on panel, 7 1/2 x 9 1/2 ins / 19 x 24 cm) GBP 950. NEW YORK, 15 June 1977, *Wooded River Landscape with Figures* (oil on canvas, 50 1/2 x 61 3/4 ins / 128 x 157 cm) USD 5,500. AMSTERDAM, 15 May 1979, *Travellers in a Sloping Landscape* (oil on canvas, 36 1/4 x 48 ins / 92 x 121 cm) NLG 18,000. LONDON, 10 April 1981, *Wooded River Landscape* (oil on panel, 11 x 17 3/4 ins / 28 x 45 cm) GBP 7,500. NEW YORK, 19 Jan 1984, *Travellers on a Country Road* (oil/copper, 10 x 12 1/2 ins / 24.5 x 31.5 cm) USD 23,000. NEW YORK, 17 Jan 1985, *Sloping Landscape with Figures* (oil on canvas, 6 1/2 x 8 ins / 16.5 x 20.5 cm) USD 15,500. AMSTERDAM, 18 Nov 1985, *Landscape with Dovecote* (pen and wash/outline in black chalk, 6 1/2 x 12 ins / 16.2 x 30.4 cm) NLG 3,000. PARIS, 10 Feb 1992, *Travellers in Landscape with Waterfalls* (oil on canvas, 39 x 50 1/4 ins / 99 x 127.5 cm) FRF 140,000. PARIS, 28 April 1993, *Animated Landscape with Shepherds* (oil on panel, 9 1/2 x 12 1/4 ins / 24 x 31 cm) FRF 40,000. LONDON, 6 July 1994, *Italian Landscape with Fisherman on a Riverbank* (oil on canvas, 12 3/4 x 16 1/4 ins / 32.5 x 41 cm) GBP 2,300. LONDON, 21 Oct 1994, *Pan and Syrinx* (oil on panel, 161 3/4 x 20 ins / 411 x 51.1 cm) GBP 8,625. NEW YORK, 15 May 1996, *Mountain Landscape with Travellers and Loaded Mules on a Road, with Ruins and a River in the Background* (oil on canvas, 37 x 44 ins / 94 x 111.8 cm) USD 17,250. AMSTERDAM, 7 May 1997, *Peasants Returning From the Market on a Mountain Road* (oil on panel, 17 1/4 x 15 ins / 43.9 x 38.2 cm) NLG 13,838. AMSTERDAM, 11 Nov 1997, *Unloading Merchandise from a Sailing Ship Docked Off the Italian Coastline at Sunset* (oil on panel, 19 1/4 x 24 1/2 ins / 48.8 x 62 cm) NLG 25,370. LONDON, 28 Oct 1999, *Wooded Italianate Landscape with Figures and Goats by a Stream* (oil on panel, 9 x 12 ins / 22 x 30 cm) GBP 27,000. LONDON, 26 April 2001, *Southern Landscape with Drovers and their Mules on a Path beside a Lake* (oil on panel, 20 x 20 ins / 51 x 50 cm) GBP 3,500. VIENNA, 3 Oct 2001, *Travellers in Southern River Landscape* (oil on panel, 15 x 22 ins / 39 x 56 cm) ATS 220,000. VIENNA, 5 June 2002, *Travellers in a Wooded Landscape* (oil on wood, 21 x 20 ins / 53 x 51 cm) EUR 8,500. LONDON, 9 July 2002, *Italianate Landscape with a Traveller, a Shepherd and Farm Animals* (oil on panel, 15 x 19 ins / 37 x 48 cm) GBP 2,800. NEW YORK, 23 Jan 2003, *River Landscape with Peasants* (oil on panel, 14 x 19 ins / 36 x 47 cm) USD 20,000. AMSTERDAM, 18 Feb 2003, *Southern Landscape with Travellers beside a Bridge over a River* (oil on panel, 21 x 29 ins / 53 x 74 cm) EUR 6,000.

HEUSDEN, Wout

Dutch, 20th century.
Painter.

Wout Heusden showed three Tachiste abstract landscapes at the Salon des Réalités Nouvelles in Paris in 1950.

HEUSER, Heinrich

German, 20th century.
Born 12 October 1887.
Painter, engraver.

Heinrich Heuser studied in Munich with Walter Thor and Angelo Jank.

AUCTION RECORDS:

SINGAPORE, 27 Sept 1997, *Seated Boy* (oil on canvas/panel, 17 1/4 x 14 1/4 ins / 44 x 36.5 cm) SGD 3,220.

HEUSER, Werner

German, 20th century.
Born 11 November 1880, in Gummersbach.
Painter, engraver.

Werner Heuser studied in Düsseldorf and Dresden, then worked in Paris and Rome.

AUCTION RECORDS:

COLOGNE, 5 Dec 1979, *Juggler* (1922, oil on canvas, 27 1/2 x 23 3/4 ins / 70 x 60.5 cm) DEM 1,800. PHILADELPHIA, 28 Sept 2001, *Laundress* (1929, oil on canvas) USD 3,250.

HEUSINGER, Johann

German, 18th - 19th century.
Born 1769, in Wolfenbüttel; died 1846.
Miniaturist. Portraits.

Heusinger exhibited works in Berlin from 1789, including drawings after Classical Italian and Flemish Old Masters.

HEUSLER, Antonius

German, 16th century.
Born probably in Leipzig.
Painter.

Annaberg museum has three paintings attributed to Antonius Heusler.

HEUSLER, Tobias

German, 16th century.
Active in Leipzig, in 1564.
Painter.

Tobias Heusler lived in Annaberg and was probably the son of Antonius Heusler.

HEUSS, Eduard von

German, 19th century.
Born 5 July 1808, in Oggersheim; died 14 October 1880, in Bodenheim.
Painter. Historical scenes, portraits.

Von Heuss initially embarked on a medical career, but abandoned his medical studies to take up painting. His entire artistic training took place in Italy, with no masters other than the great painters whose works were on show in the museums. He focused on studying Rubens and Rembrandt in particular. On his return to Germany, he exhibited in Munich, Mainz and Berlin from about 1838. He also took part in the Vienna Salons, the Paris Salons from 1846 to 1848 and in the exhibitions of the London Royal Academy from 1842 to 1844.

MUSEUMS AND GALLERIES:

BERLIN: *Portraits of the Artists, Peter van Cornelis and Friedrich Overbeck, and the Landscape Artist, Christian Reinhart* - DARMSTADT: *Rape of Europa* - GENOA: *Marquis Antonio Brignale-Sale; Marchioness Artenusia Brignale-Sale* - LISIEUX: *Portrait of Guizot* - MAINZ: *Thorvaldsen in his Studio; The Councillor, Dr Joh Groser; Mr Jacob Groser; Mr Anton Groser; Portrait of Joh David Ruland; Grand Duke Ludwig II of Hesse* - MUNICH: *Mater Dolorosa; Mater Salvatoris; Mater Amabilis; Mater Gloriosa; Mater Virginium.*

AUCTION RECORDS:

LONDON, 8 Feb 1908, *Portrait of Lady Leverson-Gower* (1862) GBP 3.

HEUSSEN, Nicolaes van, called Claes

Flemish School, 17th century.
Born 1599; died 1672.
Active in Haarlem.
Painter. Still-lifes (fruit).

Kramm cited a *Basket of Grapes*, signed *C. van Heussen* and dated 1626. Ampzig mentioned a painter by the name of Van Heussen in his description of Haarlem. He may be the same artist as a C. van Heussen, whose *Adoration of the Magi* is in the Musée de Rouen.

MUSEUMS AND GALLERIES:

HAARLEM: *Fruit.*

AUCTION RECORDS:

AMSTERDAM, 28 April 1976, *Still-life* (oil on panel, 27 1/4 x 40 1/2 ins / 69.2 x 102.7 cm) NLG 10,000. LONDON, 9 July 1993, *Young Woman in a Workshop with a Display of Fruits and Vegetables and a Wreath of Flowers* (oil on canvas, 59 1/2 x 97 1/2 ins / 151 x 247.5 cm) GBP 54,300.

HEUSSLER, Valéry

Swiss, 20th century.
Born 1920, in Basel.
Painter.

The paintings of Valéry Heussler are allied to fantastic Surrealism.

HEUSSLIN, Simon

German, 17th century.
Active in Frankfurt am Main.
Painter.

Heusslin worked at the Katharinenkirche in Frankfurt am Main.

HEUSTIS, Louise Lyons

American, 19th - 20th century.
Born 1865, in Mobile (Alabama); died 1951.
Active in New York.
Painter, illustrator.

Louise Lyons Heustis studied in New York under William Merritt Chase and in Paris under Charles Lasar and at the Académie Julian. She specialised in portraits.

AUCTION RECORDS:

NEW YORK, 24 June 1988, *Floral Still-life* (oil on canvas, 16 3/4 x 19 3/4 ins / 42.5 x 50 cm) USD 770.

HEUTIER, G.

19th century.
Painter. Genre scenes.

AUCTION RECORDS:

PARIS, 14 April 1891, *Solicitation,* FRF 1,848; *Interior,* FRF 1,155.

HEUVEL, Bernardus van den

Dutch, 20th century.
Born 1899, in Zaandijk.
Painter. Architectural views.

Bernardus van den Heuvel was a metalworker who painted views of public monuments, which are charming in their naively meticulous attention to detail.

BIBLIOGRAPHY:

Gans, Louis, *Meesters der Europese naïven*, exhibition catalogue, Centraal Museum, Utrecht, 1970.

HEUVEL, G. van den

Dutch, 18th century.
Active in The Hague in the second half of the 18th century.
Painter. Genre scenes.

He is believed to be from Amsterdam, although he lived in The Hague and became a member of the painters' guild there in 1768. He specialised in the painting of birds.

HEUVEL, Hendrik van den

Dutch, 18th century.
Portrait painter.

There are no details about this artist. Kramm cited him as being listed in a catalogue in 1773.

HEUVEL, Joachim van den

Dutch, 17th century.
Active in Utrecht c. 1635.
Portrait painter.

He is known to have executed a *Temptation of St Anthony.*

HEUVEL, Théodore Bernard de

Belgian, 19th century.
Born 1817, in Eeklo; died 1906.
Painter. Genre scenes, portraits.

He was a pupil of Josef Geirnaert in Ghent. He was in Paris in 1840, and then settled in Brussels.

He painted mostly genre scenes, favouring subjects of village feasts and children's games.

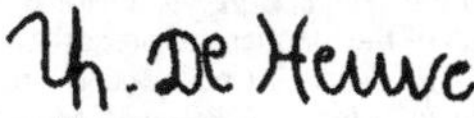

MUSEUMS AND GALLERIES:

MONTREAL: *Colin-Maillard; Village School.*

AUCTION RECORDS:

PARIS, 6-9 March 1872, *Colin-Maillard,* FRF 4,000. LONDON, 12 Feb 1937, *The Meal* (1870) GBP 13. LONDON, 10 Nov 1971, *The Ambush,* GBP 320. LONDON, 23 Feb 1977, *The Market Accounts* (oil on panel, 24 x 19 1/2 ins / 61 x 49.5 cm) GBP 1,200. LONDON, 20 March 1981, *The Dinner* (1838, oil on canvas, 20 x 25 1/4 ins / 50.7 x 64.2 cm) GBP 4,200. PARIS, 28 March 1983, *Interior Scene* (oil on panel, 17 3/4 x 13 1/2 ins / 45 x 34.5 cm) FRF 11,000. LONDON, 8 Oct 1986, *The Classroom* (1859, oil on panel, 13 3/4 x 18 ins / 35 x 46 cm) GBP 6,800. PARIS, 27 June 1989, *The Letter* (oil on panel, 17 3/4 x 13 1/2 ins / 45 x 34 cm) FRF 21,000. LONDON, 4 Oct 1991, *The Nest* (1872, oil on canvas, 12 x 24 ins / 30.5 x 61 cm) GBP 3,080. MONACO, 2 Dec 1994, *The Auction* (1841, oil on canvas, 17 3/4 x 22 1/4 ins / 45 x 56.5 cm) FRF 44,400. LONDON, 16 Sept 1999, *Family Affection* (1859, oil on panel, 13 x 17 ins / 32 x 43 cm) GBP 10,000. COLOGNE, 4 Dec 1999, *Village School* (1861, oil on panel, 25 x 32 ins / 64 x 81 cm) DEM 68,000. LOKEREN, 9 Dec 2000, *Hide and Seek* (oil on panel, 16 x 20 ins / 40 x 50 cm) BEF 135,000. COLOGNE, 15 Nov 2003, *Curious Magpie* (1871, oil on panel, 22 x 26 ins / 55 x 66 cm) EUR 20,000.

HEUVELMANS, Lucienne Antoinette

French, 20th century.

Born 1885, in Paris.
Sculptor.

In Paris, Lucienne Heuvelmanns exhibited at the Salon des Artistes Français, and received an honourable mention in 1907. She won the Prix de Rome in 1911.

AUCTION RECORDS:

PARIS, 16 March 1983, *Young Child with a Cluster of Grapes and a Pigeon* (brown-patinated bronze, h. 16 1/2 ins / 42 cm and l. 17 3/4 ins/45 cm) FRF 5,000. PARIS, 18 May 1989, *Nymph and Putti* (silver-patinated bronze, h. 15 3/4 ins / 40 cm) FRF 8,000.

HEUVICK, Kaspar
Flemish, 16th - 17th century.
Born c. 1550, in Audenarde; died between 1590 and 1611, in Italy.
Painter, draughtsman. History painting.
Flemish School.

Kaspar Heuvick studied in Italy with L. Costa and worked for Bishop Barry in Apulia. Nagler mentions his historical drawings.

HEUZÉ, Edmond Amédée, pseudonym of Letrouvé
French, 20th century.
Born 26 September 1884, in Paris; died 4 March 1967, in Paris.
Painter, engraver. Figures, portraits.

Though Edmond Heuzé was a student at the École Nationale des Beaux-Arts, he liked on numerous occasions to say that he was self-taught. The only traditions to which he laid claim were those of Montmartre, where he was born. He had several jobs none of which ever suggested that he would become a member of the Institut in 1949. He was a tailor, dancer, newspaper vendor and a ringmaster with a travelling circus, where he developed a taste for painting clowns. Later, he painted official portraits from members of the Académie Goncourt to the Army Generals. All his portraits are vividly rendered showing his somewhat cinematic preoccupation: though he sought to convey humanity, Edmond Heuzé began by meditating on and experimenting with geometry at the dawn of Cubism, of which he was one of the first discoverers. He was also a writer and published: *Monsieur Victor* one of the most precious accounts of the 'dangerous classes', to use Mac Orlan's expression. His works include: *Scenes from the Living Dead at the Fratellini, Man with Bouquet, Miss Yelding.* Portraits include: *Porto et Geratto, A. Billy, A. Rouveyre, P. Léautaud* and *General de Lattre de Tassigny*. He illustrated: *The Soul of the Circus* by Louise Hervieu, *La Seigneurie de Thann* (*The Manor of Thann*) and *Une ville d'Alsace au Moyen Âge* (*A City in Alsace in the Middle Ages*). He was named an Officier de la Légion d'Honneur.

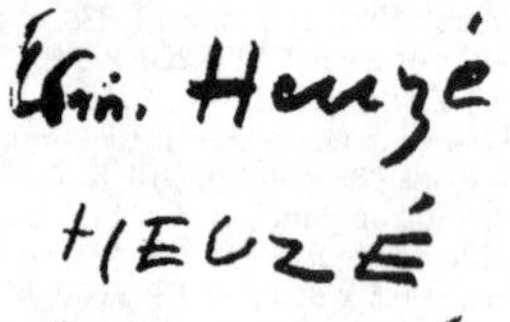

AUCTION RECORDS:

PARIS, 19 May 1930, *The Two Clowns*, FRF 1,100. PARIS, 7 April 1943, *The Model Putting on her Shoes*, FRF 4,600. PARIS, 18 May 1945, *Clown* FRF 5,000. PARIS, 10 Dec 1968, *Rehearsal at the Medrano Circus*, FRF 15,000. PARIS, 13 June 1973, *The Two Bathers*, FRF 4,000. VERSAILLES, 24 Oct 1976, *The Clown Seated with the Guitar* (oil on canvas, 25 1/2 x 21 1/4 ins / 65 x 54 cm) FRF 4,700. VERSAILLES, 16 June 1983, *The Conjurer* (oil on canvas, 51 1/4 x 38 1/4 ins / 130 x 97 cm) FRF 20,000. PARIS, 22 March 1988, *Clown* (oil on canvas, 36 1/4 x 28 3/4 ins / 92 x 73 cm) FRF 16,000. VERSAILLES, 15 May 1988, *Pierrot in the Dressing Room* (oil on cardboard, 25 1/2 x 20 3/4 ins / 64.5 x 53 cm) FRF 6,700. L'ISLE-ADAM, 11 June 1988, *Albert Fratellini and his Brother* (watercolour, 11 3/4 x 7 3/4 ins / 30 x 20 cm) FRF 2,400. PARIS, 17 June 1988, *The Procurer* (1930, lead pencil and red pencil, 7 3/4 x 4 1/2 ins / 20 x 11.5 cm) FRF 2,000. GIEN, 26 June 1988, *Female Nude* (1930, watercolour, 5 1/2 x 16 1/2 ins / 14 x 42 cm) FRF 1,700. LONDON, 21 Oct 1988, *The Beach at Cap Bénat* (oil on canvas, 21 1/4 x 25 1/2 ins / 53.7 x 64.8 cm) GBP 990. RHEIMS, 17 Dec 1989, *The Lawyer in the Courtroom* (oil on panel, 9 1/2 x 7 1/2 ins / 24 x 19 cm) FRF 8,600. PARIS, 19 Jan 1990, *Fisherman on a Barge* (oil on cardboard, 15 x 18 ins / 38 x 46 cm) FRF 11,500. LE TOUQUET, 11 Nov 1990, *Banks of the Seine in Paris* (oil on panel, 26 x 21 1/4 ins / 66 x 54 cm) FRF 15,000. PARIS, 4 March 1991, *The Artist* (oil on cardboard, 16 1/4 x 13 ins / 41 x 33 cm) FRF 8,600. PARIS, 6 July 1992, *Still-life with Melon* (oil on panel, 22 x 18 ins / 55 x 46 cm) FRF 4,000. ST-JEAN-CAP-FERRAT, 16 March 1993, *At the Circus - Dressage* (oil on canvas, 49 1/4 x 35 1/2 ins / 125 x 90 cm) FRF 20,000. DEAUVILLE, 19 Aug 1994, *Entry at the Wings* (watercolour, 25 1/2 x 18 1/2 ins / 65 x 47 cm) FRF 10,000. PARIS, 24 May 1995, *Circus* (1939, oil on canvas, 21 1/4 x 28 3/4 ins / 54 x 73 cm) FRF 14,000. PARIS, 13 June 1996, *The White Clown* (c. 1910, oil on canvas, 35 x 20 1/2 ins / 88 x 52 cm) FRF 50,000. PARIS, 13 Nov 1996, *Woman at her Dressing Table* (c. 1915, oil on canvas, 32 x 23 1/2 ins / 81 x 60 cm) FRF 60,000. PARIS, 12 Dec 1997, *The Fratellini* (oil on canvas, 28 1/4 x 36 1/4 ins / 72 x 92 cm) FRF 7,200.

HEUZE, Fernand
Belgian, 20th century.
Born 1914, in Verviers.
Painter, draughtsman, sculptor.

Fernand Heuze was taught by his father at the Liège academy.

HEUZÉ, Paul
French, 20th century.
Born 4 December 1878, in Le Havre.
Painter, draughtsman, writer.

HEUZÉ, Rosine Victorine
French, 19th century.
Born in Paris.
Painter. Flowers.

Rosine Heuzé was a pupil of Madame T. Voitelhier, and made her Salon début in 1861 with a painting on porcelain.

AUCTION RECORDS:

PARIS, 19 Oct 1997, *Bouquet of Flowers* (1862, oil on canvas, a pair, 24 x 19 3/4 ins / 61 x 50 cm) FRF 62,000. PARIS, 9 March 1998, *Peonies* (oil on canvas, 14 1/4 x 17 3/4 ins / 36 x 45 cm) FRF 9,500.

HEUZEY, Claude
French, 20th century.
Born 17 April 1927, in Paris.
Painter, engraver. Landscapes.

Claude Heuzey studied at the Académie Julian with Cavaillès. A painter of landscapes, she rendered her subjects with delicacy. She was a member of the Salon d'Automne.

HEVELIUS, Johann, or Jan Hewel or Hewelke
German, 17th century.
Born 28 January 1611, in Danzig (now Gdansk, Poland); died 28 January 1687, in Danzig (now Gdansk, Poland).
Active c. 1669.
Engraver.

Hevelius drew and engraved the plates for his *Cometographia*.

HEVERDLE, Ferenc
Hungarian, 19th - 20th century.
Born 10 December 1841, in Budapest; died 27 November 1910.
Painter.
Ferenc Heverdle painted portraits and landscapes in Budapest, Bucharest and Istanbul.

HEVESSY, Pal
Hungarian, 20th century.
Born 1878, in Gomorszollos.
Painter, art critic.
Pal Hevessy was a pupil of Szekeley at the academy in Budapest before going to work in Austria and Italy.

HEVISSEN, Cornelis
16th century.
Active c. 1537.
Painter, engraver (wood).

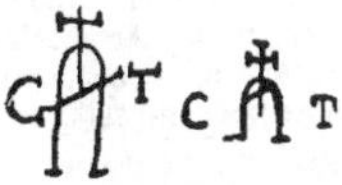

HÉVRARD, Jacques and Pierre
French, 16th century.
Active in Lyons.
Glass painters.
Jacques Hévrard was alive in 1551 and Pierre in 1559-1560. Pierre Hévrard is probably identical with the artist Pierre Evrard.

HEWARD, John
Canadian, 20th century.
Painter.
John Heward exhibited conceptual works in Paris in 1974.

HEWARD, Prudence Efa
Canadian, 20th century.
Born 2 July 1896, in Montreal; died 19 March 1947, in Los Angeles.
Painter. Figures, nudes, portraits, still-lifes.
During World War I Prudence Heward lived in the UK and worked for the Red Cross. On her return to Canada in 1918, she enrolled at the School of the Art Association of Montreal, where her teachers included William Brymner and Randolph Hewton. After receiving the Women's Art Society Prize in 1924, she left for Paris, where she studied at the Académie Colarossi under Charles Guérin and at the École des Beaux-Arts under Bernard Naudin. In this period, 1925-1926, she also travelled to Italy. In 1933 she was a founder member of the Canadian Group of Painters, becoming Vice-President from 1933 to 1939. In 1946 she went to Los Angeles to have treatment for asthma and died there the following year.

Although the Group of Seven invited Heward to participate in some of their exhibitions, they never allowed her to join them, as they systematically excluded women artists, including Emily Carr. Moreover, Heward was primarily a painter of figures and portraits, which were not of great interest to this group. Her art became truly defined during the 1930s, showing the influence of Cubism in its clear outlines and of Expressionism in her choice of colour.

In 1927 Heward participated in the exhibition of Canadian art at the Musée du Jeu de Paume, Paris. Supported by the artists of the Group of Seven, she exhibited for the first time with them in Toronto in 1928, and then again in 1930 and 1931. In 1930 she was selected to take part in an exhibition of contemporary Canadian artists in Washington, in 1936 she was represented at the exhibition at the Carnegie Corporation, New York and in 1938 her work was shown at the Tate Gallery, London, in the context of the exhibition *A Century of Canadian Art*. She was a regular participant in exhibitions of Canadian art, including those at the Yale University Art Gallery, New Haven (Connecticut) and in Rio de Janeiro in 1944. In 1946 she exhibited at the exhibition at the Musée d'Art Moderne, Paris, at the exhibition opened by the United Nations. A retrospective of her work was held in Ottawa in 1948.

BIBLIOGRAPHY:
Expressions of Will: the Art of Prudence Heward, exhibition catalogue, Agnes Etherington Art Gallery, Kingston, 1986 (text in French and English). Reid, Dennis, *A Concise History of Canadian Painting*, Oxford University Press, Toronto, 1988.

MUSEUMS AND GALLERIES:
HAMILTON, NJ (AG): *Girl under a Tree; Farm Window* (1938) - MONTREAL (MBA): *Venice Scene; Rosary* (1935) - OTTAWA (NG. of Canada): *Ann; Girl on the Hill* (1928); *Rollande* (1929); *Girl in a Yellow Cardigan* (1936); *Fruit in the Grass* (1939); *In Bermuda; Portrait of Mrs Zimmerman* (1943); *Farmer's Daughter* (1945) - WINDSOR (Windsor Castle, Royal Collection): *Sisters from Rural Quebec* (1930); *Woman by the Sea* (1930); *Girl at the Window* (1941); *Still-life with Aubergine* (1943).

AUCTION RECORDS:
TORONTO, 12 June 1989, *Eastern Counties Landscape* (oil on card) CAD 1,900. TORONTO, 17 Nov 1999, *Landscape with Bathers* (oil on panel, 12 x 14 ins / 30 x 36 cm) CAD 4,250. VANCOUVER, 10 May 2000, *Spring, Knowlton, Quebec* (1942, oil on canvas, 12 x 14 ins / 30 x 36 cm) CAD 4,250. MONTREAL, 13 June 2000, *Summertime* (oil on board, 12 x 15 ins / 30 x 37 cm) CAD 10,250. TORONTO, 27 May 2003, *Autumn, Knowlton, Quebec* (1940, oil on panel, 12 x 14 ins / 31 x 36 cm) CAD 13,000. TORONTO, 18 Nov 2003, *Bermuda House* (1938-1939, oil on canvas, 22 x 25 ins / 56 x 63 cm) CAD 25,000.

HEWETSON, Christopher
Irish, 18th century.
Born c. 1739.
Active in Rome.
Sculptor.
Christopher Hewetson was born in Ireland, but he spent many years in Rome and then London. He carved a *Bust of the Painter Gavin Hamilton*. He exhibited at the Royal Academy in London in 1786 and 1790.

HEWETT, Prescott Gardiner (Sir)
British, 19th century.
Born 1813; died 1891.
Watercolourist. Landscapes.
Prescott Gardiner Hewett studied in Paris. In London he was a member of the Royal Society and an honorary member of the Society of Painters in Watercolours. In 1876, he became president of the Royal College of Surgeons. He received a knighthood in 1888. He exhibited his paintings at the Society of Painters in Watercolours from 1877 until his death.

MUSEUMS AND GALLERIES:
LONDON (Victoria and Albert Mus.): watercolour.

HEWETT, Sarah F.
British, 19th century.
Active in Leamington.
Painter. Genre scenes.
Sarah Hewett exhibited in London from 1851 to 1883.

AUCTION RECORDS:
LONDON, 14 May 1986, *Hop-Picking* (watercolour, 14 1/2 x 19 1/2 ins / 36.8 x 49.5 cm) GBP 1,000.

HEWIT, Forrest. See **HEURT**

HEWITT, Beatrice
British, 19th - 20th century.
Active in London.
Painter. Portraits.

Beatrice Hewitt exhibited in London at the Royal Academy from 1883.

HEWITT, Clémence
French, 19th century.
Born in Paris.
Watercolourist.

Hewitt was a pupil of Madame Lanjalley. She first exhibited at the Paris Salon in 1877.

HEWITT, H.
British, 19th century.
Born 1818; died 1875 or 1879.
Active in Bristol.
Painter. Landscapes.

H. Hewitt exhibited in London at the Royal Academy, the British Institution and the Suffolk Street Gallery between 1845 and 1870.

AUCTION RECORDS:
LONDON, 10 April 1992, *Wooded Landscape with Palladian House behind a Slope* (1845, oil on canvas, 40 3/4 x 32 ins / 103.5 x 81.5 cm) GBP 3,080. LONDON, 29 Jan 2003, *By the Waterfall* (1848, oil on board, 9 x 15 ins / 23 x 37 cm) GBP 1,100. LONDON, 4 Nov 2003, *Brockley Combe from Backwell Hill, near Bristol* (1855, gouache, 10 x 14 ins / 25 x 35 cm) GBP 1,200.

HEWITT, Helen
British, 20th century.
Born at the end of the 19th century.
Painter. Portraits, landscapes, still-lifes.

Helen Hewitt exhibited in Paris at the Salon des Indépendants.

HEWITT, Henry George
British, 19th century.
Active in London.
Painter. Landscapes.

Henry George Hewitt exhibited at the Royal Academy of Art in London between 1889 and 1903.

HEWITT-BATES, James Samuel
British, 19th century.
Born 20 August 1864, in Leicester.
Illuminator.

James Hewitt-Bates taught on bookbinding and wrote a book on that subject.

HEWLETT
British, 19th century.
Active in England.
Engraver.

Hewlett is mentioned in *Art Prices Current*.

HEWLETT, D.
British, 19th century.
Active in London.
Sculptor.

D. Hewlett exhibited in London at the Royal Academy and the Suffolk Street Gallery between 1847 and 1860.

HEWLETT, James
British, 19th century.
Born 1789; died 1836, in Isleworth.
Painter, watercolourist. Flowers.

James Hewlett specialised in flower painting. His works are remarkable in their accurate detail and attractive use of colour. He lived in Bath and exhibited at the Royal Academy in London between 1799 and 1828.

MUSEUMS AND GALLERIES:
LONDON (Victoria and Albert Mus.): *Flowers* (5 paintings).

HEWLETT, James Monroe
American, 19th century.
Born 1 August 1868, in New York; died 1941, in Lawrence.
Painter, architect. Frescoes, wall decorations.

James Monroe Hewlett was a member of the National Academy of Design in New York and the American Federation of Arts. He produced mural paintings for the Carnegie Technical Schools in Pittsburgh.

HEWSON, Stephen
British, 18th century.
Active in London.
Miniaturist.

Stephen Hewson frequently exhibited in London at the Society of British Artists, the Free Society and the Royal Academy between 1775 and 1805.

HEXAMER, Frédéric
French, 19th century.
Born in the 19th century, in Paris.
Sculptor.

Hexamer was a pupil of Dumont and Lecomte-Vernet, and first exhibited at the Paris Salon in 1869. In 1888 he became a member of the Société des Artistes Français. He won a third-class medal in 1886 and two silver medals at the Expositions Universelles of 1889 and 1900.

HEY, Ans
Dutch, 20th century.
Sculptor.

Ans Hey created seven *Tables of Love*, monumental stone sculptures which she exhibited in 1995 in the quarries at the village of Lacoste.

HEY, Jan
Dutch, 15th century.
Active c. 1480-1500.
Painter. Religious subjects.

Jan Hey's name occurs in the writings of Jean Lemaire. It has been suggested that Jan Hey was also the Master of Moulins in view of the similarities between the Master's known works and Jan Hey's *Ecce Homo* triptych in Brussels.

His work was included in the collective exhibition in 2002, *The Age of Jan Van Eyck: the Mediterranean world of early Netherlandish painting, 1430-1530*, in the Groeningemuseum in Bruges.

BIBLIOGRAPHY:
'*Jean Hey, le Maître de Moulins*' in *Revue de l'Art* n° 1-2, periodical, Flammarion, Paris, 1968. Lorentz, Philippe/Regond, Annie, *Jean Hey: le maître de Moulins*, Imprimerie Pottier, Moulins, 1990. Borchert, T., *The Age of Jan Van Eyck: the Mediterranean world of early Netherlandish painting, 1430 - 1530*, exhibition catalogue, Groeningemuseum, Bruges, Thames and Hudson, London, 2002.

MUSEUMS AND GALLERIES:
BRUSSELS (MBA): *Ecce Homo* (triptych).

HEY, Paul
German, 19th - 20th century.
Born 19 October 1867, in Munich; died 1952.
Painter, watercolourist, illustrator. Genre scenes, landscapes.

Paul Hey studied with Raupp in Munich and spent a long time travelling in Italy, Greece, Egypt and Britain.

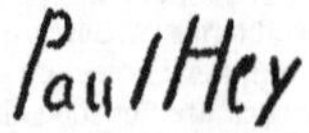

AUCTION RECORDS:
MUNICH, 9 May 1973, *Open-air Café on the Banks of the Moselle*, DEM 12,500. COLOGNE, 25 June 1976, *Stagecoach in a Landscape* (oil on canvas, 10 1/4 x 13 ins / 26 x 33 cm) DEM 3,500. LONDON, 5 July 1978, *The Goosegirl* (oil on canvas, 11 x 18 ins / 28 x 46 cm) GBP 1,300. COLOGNE, 24 May 1982, *Stagecoach in a Summer Landscape* (1950, tempera, 7 1/2 x 12 1/2 ins / 19 x 31.5 cm) DEM 3,000. MUNICH, 29 June 1983,

Uhlans Parading through a Small Town (gouache/chalk outline, 7 3/4 x 11 1/4 ins / 20 x 28.5 cm) DEM 1,800. MUNICH, 21 Sept 1983, *The Cab Drive* (oil on canvas, 15 3/4 x 25 1/2 ins / 40 x 65 cm) DEM 12,000. COLOGNE, 15 Oct 1988, *Summer in the Country* (watercolour, 6 x 12 1/4 ins / 15.5 x 31 cm) DEM 3,000. NEW YORK, 15 Oct 1991, *Feeding the Pigeons with Corn* (1908, watercolour and gouache/paper, 12 3/4 x 27 ins / 32.4 x 68.5 cm) USD 2,420. NEW YORK, 16 July 1992, *Rustic Landscapes* (watercolour and gouache/paper, a pair, 9 1/2 x 8 1/2 ins / 24.1 x 21.6 cm and 8 1/4 x 11 1/2 ins/21 x 28.9 cm) USD 4,950. MUNICH, 21 June 1994, *Harvest in the Dachau Region* (oil on canvas, 15 x 24 3/4 ins / 38 x 63 cm) DEM 13,800. NEW YORK, 10 Feb 1998, *An Unexpected Greeting; Walking along a Path* (watercolour and pencil, a pair, 8 3/4 x 7 1/2 ins / 22.2 x 19 cm) USD 3,450. VIENNA, 20 April 1999, *Landscape with Carriage* (oil on canvas, 10 x 17 ins / 25 x 42 cm) ATS 35,000. MUNICH, 22 March 2000, *Mother with Children by a Stream* (gouache over pencil, 7 x 11 ins / 19 x 29 cm) DEM 3,400. LUCERNE, 8 Nov 2000, *Children Playing on a Village Street* (watercolour and gouache, 8 x 14 ins / 21 x 35 cm) CHF 4,200. MUNICH, 5 Dec 2001, *Traveller at Dusk in a Snowy Village Street* (1890, oil on canvas, 20 x 37 ins / 50 x 95 cm) DEM 3,800. MUNICH, 20 March 2002, *Shepherd with Children* (gouache over pencil, 7 x 13 ins / 18 x 33 cm) EUR 4,500. COLOGNE, 11 April 2002, *Story of Poor Heinrich* (oil on canvas, five parts, 24 x 59 ins / 61 x 151 cm) EUR 10,000. COLOGNE, 17 May 2003, *Hay Harvest* (gouache on board, 30 x 37 ins / 75 x 94 cm) EUR 3,800. BERLIN, 27 Sept 2003, *Mother with Child Greeting Soldiers* (gouache, 9 x 14 ins / 22 x 35 cm) EUR 1,950. STAUFEN, 25 March 2004, *Peasant Woman and Children in Horse-drawn Cart* (watercolour, 9 x 8 ins / 23 x 21 cm) EUR 1,500. MUNICH, 25 June 2004, *Chat over the Garden Fence* (oil on canvas, 11 x 14 ins / 28 x 36 cm) EUR 3,900.

HEYART, Sylvie

French, 20th - 21st century.
Born 1961.
Engraver.

Heyart was nominated for the Prix Grav'x in 1991 by the Galerie Michèle Broutta in Paris.

BIBLIOGRAPHY:

'Sylvie Heyart ou la recherche de l'accord parfait' in *Art et Métiers du Livre* n° 189 p. 30-36, periodical, Paris, 1995.

HEYBEL, Jakob

German, 17th century.
Active in Regensburg.
Painter.

Heybel decorated the ceilings in Wörth Castle in 1676. He also executed religious paintings.

HEYBERG, Johannes Gerardus

Dutch, 19th century.
Born 1869, in Rotterdam.
Painter. Genre scenes.

He was a pupil at the academy in Rotterdam and won a gold medal at the Exposition Universelle in Paris in 1900.

HEYBOER, Anton

Indonesian, 20th century.
Born 1924, in Sabang, Indonesia.
Active in the Netherlands from 1938.
Engraver, painter, collage artist, sculptor, draughtsman.

A self-taught artist, Anton Heyboer lived in Curaçao in the Dutch Antilles from 1933 to 1938.

He was in a concentration camp in 1943 where he nearly died and his work is informed by this experience. He started off as a print maker in 1952 and took up painting around 1974 after a voluntary stay in a mental hospital. Since 1961 he has lived in a commune in the village of Den Ilp north of Amsterdam, with several women. His work is characterised at times by the use of Christian symbolism and by references to his mental and emotional state.

Heyboer produced a series of prints on the subject *The Flower of Fear*. His prints are characterized by 'scribbling', with pieces of writing in spaces filled with numbers. They combine furtively made graffiti from walls and childlike drawing with a narrative aspect found at times in 1960s pop art. Woman is a recurrent theme in his painting.

Heyboer has held a number of collective exhibitions including: Espace Gallery, Amsterdam (1957); Gemeente Museum, the Hague (1959, 1967-1968); Van Abbe Museum, Eindhoven; *Big Prints* exhibition, Arts Council of Great Britain, London (1982); Museum of Moden Art, New York (1966, 1971-1972); Documenta II and Documenta III Kassel, Germany (1959 and 1964); Venice Biennale (1960); Tokyo Biennale (1960, 1962, 1964); Pittsburgh International Exhibition (1970); County Museum of Art, Los Angeles (1975). Solo exhibitions include: Stedelijk Museum, Amsterdam (1958, 1968, 1975-1976) and Dutch Institute, Paris (1980). He was awarded the Paris Biennale prize (1959).

MUSEUMS AND GALLERIES:

AMSTERDAM (Stedelijk Mus.) - NEW YORK (MoMA) - ROTTERDAM (Mus. Boijmans Van Beuningen).

AUCTION RECORDS:

AMSTERDAM, 28 Nov 1978, *Nudes* (1973, etching, 49 1/2 x 39 1/4 ins / 126 x 100 cm) NLG 2,000. AMSTERDAM, 24 April 1979, *Composition* (1975, oil on canvas, 22 x 25 1/2 ins / 55 x 65 cm) NLG 4,400. MUNICH, 26 Nov 1979, *Composition* (1962, aquatint in colour, 20 1/4 x 18 1/2 ins / 51.3 x 46.8 cm) DEM 1,800. AMSTERDAM, 24 Oct 1983, *The Embrace* (bronze, h. 16 3/4 ins / 42.5 cm) NLG 5,200. AMSTERDAM, 8 Dec 1988, *Three Women* (1975, oil on canvas, 78 3/4 x 59 ins / 200 x 150 cm) NLG 27,600. AMSTERDAM, 10 April 1990, *New Life* (1988, acrylic/canvas, 56 x 78 ins / 142.5 x 198 cm) NLG 5,520. AMSTERDAM, 22 May 1990, *Composition* (1975, oil on canvas, 78 3/4 x 59 ins / 200 x 150 cm) NLG 25,300. NEW YORK, 6 Nov 1990, *Untitled* (1989, gouache/paper, 30 3/4 x 42 ins / 78.1 x 106.8 cm) USD 660. AMSTERDAM, 12 Dec 1990, *Innocence* (bronze, h. 9 1/2 ins / 24 cm) NLG 4,025. AMSTERDAM, 13 Dec 1990, *Untitled* (1975, oil on canvas, 39 1/4 x 51 1/4 ins / 100 x 130 cm) NLG 18,400. AMSTERDAM, 5-6 Feb 1991, *Do Not Defend God in Words* (1989, oil on canvas, 20 x 23 1/2 ins / 51 x 60 cm) NLG 1,955. AMSTERDAM, 11 Dec 1991, *Domitilla Cavaletti* (1976, oil on canvas, 78 3/4 x 59 ins / 200 x 150 cm) NLG 14,950. LOKEREN, 21 March 1992, *Madonna* (acrylic/canvas, 33 1/2 x 23 1/2 ins / 85 x 60 cm) BEF 48,000. LOKEREN, 23 May 1992, *Dog* (oil on paper, 54 x 63 3/4 ins / 137 x 162 cm) BEF 24,000. AMSTERDAM, 10 Dec 1992, *The Adornment of Shame* (1963, collage and mixed media/paper, 42 1/2 x 29 1/2 ins / 108 x 75 cm) NLG 2,530. AMSTERDAM, 14 Sept 1993, *Figures* (1976, acrylic/canvas, 51 1/4 x 39 1/4 ins / 130 x 100 cm) NLG 6,325. AMSTERDAM, 31 May 1995, *A Living is Giving* (eight engravings coloured by hand, each 39 1/4 x 25 1/2 ins / 100 x 65 cm) NLG 14,750. AMSTERDAM, 18 June 1996, *Composition* (1983, acrylic/canvas, 37 1/2 x 49 1/4 ins / 95 x 125 cm) NLG 1,150. LOKEREN, 8 March 1997, *Composition* (watercolour, 30 x 41 1/2 ins / 76.5 x 105.5 cm) BEF 19,000. AMSTERDAM, 4 June 1997, *Innosens as consciens Anton Heyboer as not normals* (1974, oil on canvas, diptych in a frame, 39 1/4 x 102 1/4 ins / 100 x 260 cm) NLG 23,064.

HEYBOM

German, 18th century.
Active in Berlin at the end of the 18th century.
Watercolourist.

HEYD, Johann Wolfgang

German, 18th century.
Died c. 1799.
Active in Kassel.

Sculptor.
Johann Heyd worked with his brother, Ludwig Daniel Heyd.

HEYD, Ludwig Daniel
German, 18th century.
Died 1801.
Active in Kassel.
Sculptor.
Ludwig Heyd worked with his brother, Johann Wolfgang Heyd, executing classically inspired sculptures.

HEYDE, Bartold von der
German, 16th century.
Active in Brunswick at the beginning of the 16th century.
Painter.

HEYDECK, Adolf von, called Poussin-Heydeck
German, 19th century.
Born 25 April 1787, in Dessau; died 23 January 1856.
Painter, engraver.
Von Heydeck worked mainly in Italy, where he copied and imitated Poussin and Dughet.

Stamp of sale

HEYDECK, Johannes
German, 19th - 20th century.
Born 2 July 1835, near Königsberg (now Kaliningrad, Russia); died 6 August 1910, near Königsberg.
Painter. History painting, portraits.
Johannes Heydeck studied with Rosenfelder at the academy in Königsberg. He became a teacher at the Berlin academy. He exhibited in Berlin from 1872, and also on several occasions in Munich.
Museums and Galleries:
Kaliningrad: *Immanuel Kant* (portrait); *Karl von Horn* (portrait).

HEYDEL, Paul
German, 19th century.
Born 7 February 1854, in Dresden.
Painter. Portraits, genre scenes.
Heydel studied at the Dresden academy of art. He first exhibited in Berlin in 1887 and then also in Dresden.

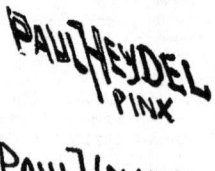

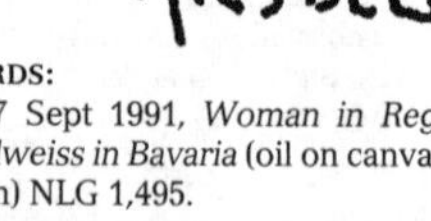

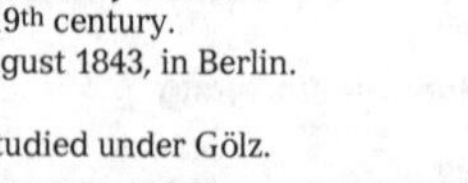

Auction records:
Amsterdam, 17 Sept 1991, *Woman in Regional Costume Holding an Edelweiss in Bavaria* (oil on canvas, 41 1/4 x 31 ins / 104.5 x 78.5 cm) NLG 1,495.

HEYDEMANN, Clara
German, 19th century.
Born 9 August 1843, in Berlin.
Painter.
Heydemann studied under Gölz.

HEYDEMANN, Willie. See **HEYDERMANN**

HEYDEN, August Jakob Theodor von
German, 19th century.
Born 13 June 1827, in Breslau (now Wroclaw, Poland); died 1 June 1897, in Berlin.
Painter. Historical scenes, genre scenes, portraits.
August von Heyden was a son of the poet, Friedrich von Heyden, and a pupil of Holbein and Steffeck in Berlin in 1860. In 1861 he went to Paris, where he studied under Gleyre and Couture. He returned to work in Berlin, then went on to travel for quite some time in Italy, where he devoted himself to painting Renaissance monuments.

In 1885, he was appointed professor in Berlin, where he had first exhibited around 1864. He regularly took part in the German Salons as well as exhibiting at the Paris Salons during his stay in France, being awarded a third-class medal in 1863. In 1873, he was awarded a medal in Vienna. He executed the decorative work in the Council Chamber in Berlin Town Hall, as well as that in Ludweiler Church depicting *St Barbara, Patron Saint of the Miners*. He was made a senior member of the Council of State in 1890.
Museums and Galleries:
Nuremberg: *Luther's Entrance into Worms*.

HEYDEN, Christian
German, 19th century.
Born 1854, in Cologne.
Painter. Portraits, genre scenes.
Christian Heyden, a pupil of Karl Heyden in Düsseldorf, also worked at the Antwerp academy of art, before returning to Düsseldorf under Baur's instruction.
Museums and Galleries:
Cologne: *Landsknecht*.
Auction records:
New York, 7 Oct 1977, *My Mother-in-law* (1886, oil on canvas, 34 x 22 ins / 86.5 x 56 cm) USD 1,500. Paris, 22 Nov 1982, *The First Bottle of Champagne* (1886, oil on canvas, 17 1/4 x 24 1/2 ins / 44 x 62 cm) FRF 12,500. Zurich, 19 March 1999, *Bad School Report* (oil on canvas, 24 x 31 ins / 61 x 78 cm) CHF 2,600. Warsaw, 3 June 2001, *Musician in a Coastal Scene* (oil on canvas, 25 x 26 ins / 64 x 67 cm) PLN 8,000.

HEYDEN, Hendrick van der
Flemish, 16th century.
Born c. 1502, in Louvain; died c. 1556, in Louvain.
Painter.
Louvain School, Flemish School.
Hendrick van der Heyden's father-in-law was the painter Jan Gossaert, known as Mabuse.

HEYDEN, Hubert von, or Heiden
German, 19th - 20th century.
Born 13 September 1860, in Berlin; died 20 January 1911, in Munich.
Painter. Genre scenes, animals.
Hubert von Heyden first exhibited in Hamburg in 1887. He then settled in Munich and exhibited there regularly after 1890.
Museums and Galleries:
Munich: *Henhouse*.

HEYDEN, Isaak van der
French, 16th - 17th century.
Active in Strasbourg.
Painter, engraver. Portraits.
Isaak van der Heyden was the son of Jan van der Heyden of Cologne and the brother of the French artist Jacob van der Heyden. He worked principally in Germany, as did his brother.

HEYDEN, J.C.J. van der, or Heijden
Dutch, 20th century.
Born 1928, in 's Hertogenbosch.
Painter, video artist. Multimedia.

Van der Heyden began painting in 1956. At first he produced monumental pictures using a minimal technique, then he reduced painting simply to a surface. At that stage, he showed canvases with two dark stripes on a light background. In 1967, he stopped painting and took up audio-visual techniques using video, computers and electro-acoustical materials and techniques. This led him to create cabins that resembled workshops, containing lamps, clocks, photographs and reproductions of paintings.

J.C.J. van der Heyden took part in the Paris Biennale in 1965. He featured in the exhibition *Art - Pays-Bas - XXe siècle - Du concept à l'image* (*Twentieth Century Dutch Art: From Concept to Image*) at the ARC, Musée d'Art Moderne, Paris in 1994. He is said to have had an exhibition in The Hague in 1966. His first solo show was at the Galerie Swart in Amsterdam, followed by others in 1967 and 1983 at the Stedelijk Van Abbemuseum in Eindhoven, 1977 at the Gemeentemuseum in The Hague, 1990-1991 at the Boymans van Beuningen Museum and 2002 at the Fondation ICAR in Paris.

AUCTION RECORDS:

AMSTERDAM, 22 May 1990, *Untitled* (oil and mixed media/canvas, 29½ x 29½ ins / 75 x 75 cm) NLG 4,600. AMSTERDAM, 11 Dec 1991, *Triptych* (oil on canvas and wood, 59½ x 24¼ ins / 151 x 61.5 cm) NLG 18,400. AMSTERDAM, 12 Dec 1991, *Untitled* (1960, watercolour and black chalk/paper, 9¼ x 19 ins / 23.5 x 48 cm) NLG 1,265. AMSTERDAM, 21 May 1992, *Untitled* (1956, oil on panel, 19¼ x 22½ ins / 49 x 57 cm) NLG 1,955. AMSTERDAM, 26 May 1993, *Four Times Four* (1985, oil on panel, 8 x 8½ ins / 20.5 x 21.7 cm) NLG 4,830. AMSTERDAM, 5 June 1996, *Red, Yellow, Blue* (1990, triptych in acrylic/canvas, 28¼ x 40½ ins / 72 x 103 cm) NLG 11,500. AMSTERDAM, 10 Dec 1996, *Tree* (1957, oil and sand/paper, 13½ x 16¼ ins / 34 x 41 cm) NLG 3,690. AMSTERDAM, 2-3 June 1997, *Juxtaposed Yellow Construction* (1966, oil/three separate canvases, 19¾ x 35¼ ins / 50 x 89.5 cm) NLG 18,880. AMSTERDAM, 1 Dec 1997, *Curved Horizon* (oil/cotton, 21¾ x 57¾ ins / 55.5 x 147 cm) NLG 15,930. AMSTERDAM, 28 Nov 2000, *Yellow Line* (1964, oil on canvas, 12 x 9 ins / 30 x 24 cm) NLG 5,200. AMSTERDAM, 3 Dec 2001, *Grote wolk* (1999, inkjet on canvas, 55 x 39 ins / 140 x 100 cm) NLG 9,000. AMSTERDAM, 3 Dec 2002, *Untitled* (1966, oil on canvas, diptych, 18 x 24 ins / 45 x 61 cm) EUR 17,000.

HEYDEN, Jacob van der

French, 16th - 17th century.
Born 1573, in Strasbourg; died 1645, in Brussels.
Painter, sculptor, engraver (burin). Mythological subjects, portraits, landscapes.

Jacob van der Heyden engraved portraits and subjects from mythology. He was the son of Jan van der Heyden, the Cologne painter, and a student of Rafael Coxie. He worked mostly in Germany for the courts of Hesse, Bade-Durlach and elsewhere.

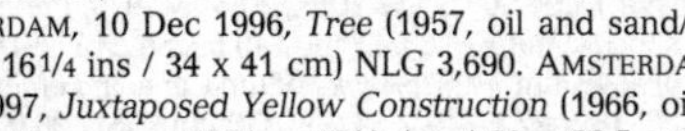

HEYDEN, Jacob van der

Dutch, 17th century.
Born in Arnhem.
Painter. History painting.

He established himself in Brussels, where he worked on the decoration of several churches.

HEYDEN, Jan van der

German, 16th century.
Active in Cologne.
Painter.

Jan van der Heyden was exiled from his birthplace because of his religious beliefs and settled in Strasbourg. He specialised in portrait painting.

HEYDEN, Jan van der

Flemish School, 17th century.
Born c. 1635, in Brussels; died c. 1686, in England.
Painter.

Active mostly in England, Wegerman has cited portraits of his at the homes of Lord Gainsborough, Milord Scherrard and at Bolovir Castle.

HEYDEN, Jan van der, or Hyde

Dutch, 17th - 18th century.
Born 1637, in Gorkum or Gorinchem; died 28 March 1712, in Amsterdam or Gorinchem.
Painter, draughtsman, engraver. Genre scenes, landscapes with figures, urban landscapes, architectural views.

His master was a painter of glass. At a very early age, he astounded those around him with his ability to draw houses, churches, palaces, castles, as though he were destined for architecture. Later, he learned to paint these buildings after nature, meticulously rendering the smallest details, including even cracks in the bricks, mossy gaps in stones, the slates of roofs, as well as the minute nuances and gradations of light. These abilities only sharpened with age, and Jan van der Heyden grew to become a painter of such sites so well loved by his fellow Dutchmen. They admired and appreciated his talent for detailing the minutiae of their daily lives, whether of domestic interiors, or of cityscapes where they worked and strolled, or of the fields where they cultivated flowers and worked the land. Van der Heyden responded by perfecting his technique in this genre. He succeeded in bringing to the fore the intriguing physicality of the most insignificant and ordinary details that would otherwise escape notice in everyday life. His fame spread, and he established himself in Amsterdam, turning for subjects to the beautiful buildings of that city: the Stock Exchange, the Offices of Weights, City Hall. The painting of this last edifice, now in the Louvre, is one of his masterpieces. The talent with which he was able to soften the hardness of the building, with skilful use of aerial perspective, plays of light and atmospheric fluidity, affirms the hand of a true master. The potential severity of the subject is also tempered by his adroit introduction of figures into the painting. These figures were in fact painted by Adriaen van de Velde, because Van der Heyden, scrupulously modest about his own abilities, felt he would not have been able to render them to his own satisfaction. Willem van de Velde, the painter of seascapes and Adriaen's brother, was another of his collaborators. Willem assisted Van der Heyden in his paintings of cities and villages, by introducing elements such as the mirroring of dormant canals or a sea filled with longboats and ships. Van der Heyden's highly esteemed *View of a Village on the Edge of a Canal*, was painted with the assistance of both Van de Velde brothers.

While passionately devoted to his art, he also made a study of the laws of physics and he worked on perfecting fire pumps. His work in this field paid him an allowance, and from that time on, he painted with less diligence.

He continued, however, to depict all kinds of compositions. He painted Dutch landscapes, punctuated by the outlines of trees, and half-French or half-Spanish castles or houses. These works, offering contrasts between masses of foliage and lighter elements in the distance, still retain their freshness and vigour.

It was nevertheless as a painter of architecture, and not of landscapes, that Van der Heyden remained famous. This was due to his special ability to render even the most ordinary buildings interesting. He did so by seeking out the details in the lines and in the gradations of tone, without compromising the unity of the composition.

Van der Heyden did not try merely to render the picturesque, such as it is often conceived, with wavy or broken lines creating accidents of light or contrasts that would be easy to reproduce. Instead, he succeeded in giving a great intensity of expression to smooth, monotonous surfaces, receding streets and good, solid walls. He had the means skilfully to break the uniformity of the lines and symmetry of buildings and effect a knowing infiltration of light. The figures in his landscapes are always introduced with great adroitness. His works, while less sought after following his death, have nevertheless retained their place in major public museums and galleries as well as in private collections.

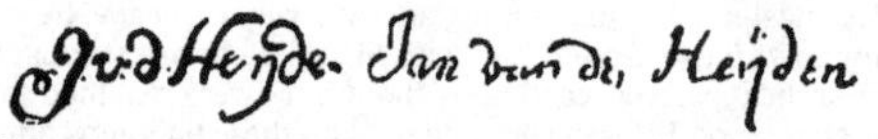

BIBLIOGRAPHY:

Schatborn, P., *Dutch Figure Drawing from the Seventeenth Century*, exhibition catalogue, Rijksmuseum, Amsterdam; Washington DC, N.G.A., 1981-1982 (pp. 124-6). Schwartz, G., *'Jan van der Heyden and the Huydecopers of Maarsseveen*, Getty Museum, J, xi, 1983 (pp. 197-220).

MUSEUMS AND GALLERIES:

AMSTERDAM: *Dutch City; View of Martelaarsgracht in Amsterdam; The Stone Bridge; The Drawbridge; Dam Square, Amsterdam* (c. 1668) - BERLIN: *The Gate of Haarlem in Amsterdam* - BUDAPEST: *Still-life* - COPENHAGEN: *Exterior of a Villa* - DOUAI: *The Quay at Haarlem* - DRESDEN: *View of Brussels; View of a Cloister; Old House; Street with Cloister and Castle* - EDINBURGH: *Forest Scene* - FLORENCE: *City Hall Square in Amsterdam* - FRANKFURT AM MAIN: *Castle in Holland; The Great Avenue* - GENEVA (Mus. Ariana): *Landscape* - GLASGOW: *Fortified Entrance to a Dutch City; Temple of Vesta; Arch of Titus* - HAMBURG: *Still-life; Houses in the Garden of Huis ten Bosch* - KASSEL: *Palace of the Duc de Bourgogne in Brussels; Before the Gate of a Fortified City* - LILLE: *Rest Before an Inn* - LONDON (Dulwich Picture Gal.): *Two Churches and a Town Wall* (c. 1660, oil/panel) - LONDON (NG): *An Architectural Fantasy* (1665-1670, oil/wood); *A View in Cologne* (1660-1665, oil/wood); *A Farm among Trees* (c. 1670, oil/wood); *A Square before a Church* (1678, oil/wood); *View of the Westerkerk, Amsterdam* (1660?, oil/wood); *The Huis ten Bosch at The Hague* (1665-1675, oil/wood); *An Imaginary View of Nijenrode Castle and the Sacristy of Utrecht Cathedral* (1665-1670, oil/wood) - LONDON (Wallace Collection): *A Street Scene in Cologne* (c. 1684, oil/panel); *View of the Westerkerk, Amsterdam* (1618, oil/panel); *Extrerior of a Church* (c. 1667-1772, oil/panel) - MONTPELLIER: *View of the Almshouse Convent in Ghent* - MONTREAL (Learmont Collection): *River Scene in Holland* - MOSCOW (Rumiantsev Mus.): *House Near The Hague; House with Garden and Strolling Figures; Landscape with Chateau and Church* - MUNICH: *Great Square of a City; Old Palace of Brussels and Zoological Garden* - OSLO: *Market and Church in Haarlem* - PARIS (Louvre): *View of City Hall, Amsterdam; Church and City Square in Holland; Village by the Edge of a Canal; Landscape* - ROTTERDAM: *Great Castle in Ruins* - ST PETERSBURG (Hermitage): *Street in Cologne; Interior View in Cologne; Gate of Haarlem in Amsterdam; Two Views of Castles; View of Amsterdam; View of Xanten; Two Views of Fortified Castles* - THE HAGUE: *View of the Church of Veere; Still-life; View of the Church of the Jesuits in Düsseldorf* - VIENNA: *Old Fortified Castle* - VIENNA (Czernin'sche Gemäldegal.): *Landscape*.

AUCTION RECORDS:

PARIS, 1832, *City Interior*, FRF 6,951; *View of a Gate of Amsterdam*, FRF 3,550. PARIS, 4-7 Dec 1901, *View of a Dutch Canal*, FRF 30,000. PARIS, 30 Nov 1908, *The Small Square*, FRF 22,500. LONDON, 20 Feb 1909, *Royal Palace in Amsterdam*, GBP 42. LONDON, 9 May 1910, *Street Scene*, GBP 11. LONDON, 12 Dec 1910, *Landscape with Ancient Buildings*, GBP 42. NEW YORK, April 1911, *Old House*, FRF 16,000; *Rotterdam Market*, FRF 6,500; *Village*, FRF 4,250. LONDON, 3 April 1911, *River Scene*, GBP 54. LONDON, 19 May 1911, *View of Vlakenhof in Nijmegen*, GBP 504. LONDON, 16 June 1911, *View of Amsterdam*, GBP 1,365. NEW YORK, 12 June 1919, *A Square in Holland*, FRF 20,300. LONDON, July 1922, *City Suburbs*, GBP 27. PARIS, 15 March 1923, *The Harteveld Residence near the Vecht, Utrecht*, FRF 5,200. PARIS, 21-22 May 1928, *Inn on a Canal Bank*, FRF 66,000. PARIS, 17 Dec 1935, *Leaving for the Hunt*, FRF 31,000. LONDON, 1 Dec 1944, *Interior of a Library*, GBP 231. LONDON, 19 Jan 1945, *House Under the Trees*, GBP 892. PARIS, 18 June 1945, *View of a Dutch City*, FRF 5,000. LONDON, 30 April 1947, *Landscape with Hills*, GBP 90. LONDON, 24 June 1959, *The Tolling Office, Maarsden*, GBP 7,800. LONDON, 24 March 1965, *Farm in a Dutch Landscape*, GBP 6,800. LONDON, 10 July 1968, *View of a Small Town in Holland*, GBP 23,000. LONDON, 6 Dec 1972, *View of Cologne*, GBP 46,000. LONDON, 29 June 1973, *View of a Square in Front of a Palace, with Figures*, Gns 34,000. LONDON, 11 July 1973, *View of Cologne*, GBP 42,000. LONDON, 26 Nov 1976, *View of the Porte du Rivage, Brussels* (oil on panel, 12 x 11 ins / 30.5 x 28 cm) GBP 18,000. LONDON, 14 Dec 1977, *View of Amsterdam* (oil on panel, 15 x 15 3/4 ins / 38.3 x 40 cm) GBP 28,000. LONDON, 7 July 1978, *Village Square with Cobbler's Workshop and Figures* (1676, oil on panel, 18 x 23 1/2 ins / 45.7 x 59.7 cm) GBP 190,000. NEW YORK, 30 May 1979, *Return of the Hunters* (oil on panel, 16 x 22 ins / 40.5 x 56 cm) USD 18,000. NEW YORK, 18 June 1982, *Banks of the Canal in Leiden* (oil on canvas, 21 1/2 x 27 3/4 ins / 54.9 x 70.8 cm) USD 26,000. NEW YORK, 7 June 1984, *View of a Fortified City in a Landscape* (oil on panel, 16 1/2 x 21 3/4 ins / 42 x 55.5 cm) USD 18,000. LONDON, 20 April 1988, *Landscape with Canal Lined with Trees and Houses* (oil on panel, 18 x 23 1/4 ins / 46 x 59 cm) GBP 77,000. NEW YORK, 31 May 1989, *The Park in the Old Palace in Brussels* (oil on canvas/panel, 14 x 16 3/4 ins / 35.6 x 42.5 cm) USD 16,500. NEW YORK, 2 June 1989, *Wooded Mountain Landscape* (oil/glass, 7 x 11 ins / 17.5 x 28 cm) USD 77,000. LONDON, 15 Dec 1989, *Village Scene with Peasants Talking on the Road* (oil on canvas, 12 x 17 ins / 30.5 x 43 cm) GBP 14,300. NEW YORK, 14 Jan 1993, *Village Entry with Peasants on a Road* (oil on panel, 12 x 17 ins / 30.5 x 42.9 cm) USD 28,600. LONDON, 9 July 1993, *City Square with Cobbler's Workshop and Church, with Two Turks Conversing with a Cleric* (1676, oil on panel, 18 x 23 3/4 ins / 45.7 x 60.2 cm) GBP 551,500. NEW YORK, 5 Oct 1995, *Falcon Hunt on Road Lining a River with Peasant on a Bridge in the Foreground* (oil/copper, 8 1/4 x 9 1/4 ins / 20.7 x 23.2 cm) USD 101,500. LONDON, 3 July 1997, *Düsseldorf, View of the Jesuit Church of St Andreas* (1666, oil on panel, 20 x 22 1/2 ins / 51 x 57 cm) GBP 661,500. LONDON, 3 Dec 1997, *Farm with Figures of Lesser Gentry By a Tree, Children Playing by a Pond, and Landscape with Bell-tower in the Distance* (1668, oil on panel, 9 x 13 ins / 22.9 x 33 cm) GBP 111,500. NEW YORK, 29 Jan 1998, *View of Goudestein With Woman and Child Walking Along a Dyke* (oil on panel, 9 x 11 1/4 ins / 23 x 28.5 cm) USD 79,500. PARIS, 8 Dec 1999, *Gentlemen and Turks before the Facade of a Baroque Palace* (oil on silvered copper, 4 x 6 ins / 11 x 16 cm) FRF 1,250,000. LONDON, 16 Dec 1999, *Brussels, Capriccio of the Porte du Rivage* (oil on panel, 12 x 11 ins / 30 x 27 cm) GBP 26,000. NEW YORK, 18 Oct 2000, *View of Goudesteyn Castle on the Vecht* (oil on panel, 7 x 11 ins / 18 x 28 cm) USD 26,000. ZURICH, 5 Sept 2001, *Landscape with Classical Ruins and Figures* (oil on canvas, 13 x 17 ins / 32 x 43 cm) CHF

15,000. NEW YORK, 25 Jan 2002, *View of the Interior of the Amsterdam Stock Exchange. Study of an Underground Water Supply* (graphite and black chalk with wash, a pair, 10 x 8 ins / 25 x 20 cm) USD 75,000. BUDAPEST, 6 Dec 2002, *Riverside Landscape with Castle* (oil on canvas, 19 x 23 ins / 48 x 58 cm) HUF 11,000,000. AMSTERDAM, 18 Feb 2003, *Hawking Party Returning to a Castle beside a River* (oil on panel, 19 x 24 ins / 49 x 62 cm) EUR 48,000. LONDON, 9 July 2003, *View of a Canal with a Village beyond, possibly the Vecht near Maarssen* (oil on panel, 18 x 24 ins / 46 x 60 cm) GBP 35,000.

HEYDEN, Karl
German, 19th - 20th century.
Born 4 November 1845, in Cologne; died 1939.
Painter. Portraits, genre scenes.

Karl Heyden studied at the Düsseldorf academy and exhibited for the first time in 1876 in Berlin. He also exhibited in Bremen, Magdeburg, Dresden and Düsseldorf.

AUCTION RECORDS:
VIENNA, 14 June 1977, *The Visit* (oil on canvas, 26 3/4 x 20 1/2 ins / 68 x 52 cm) ATS 22,000. COLOGNE, 22 Nov 1979, *Young Woman and Girl in a Boat* (oil on canvas, 41 3/4 x 33 ins / 106 x 84 cm) DEM 11,000. LUCERNE, 11 Nov 1987, *The Goat Girl* (oil on canvas, 41 3/4 x 23 1/2 ins / 106 x 60 cm) CHF 5,000.

HEYDEN, Otto Johann Heinrich
German, 19th century.
Born 8 July 1820, in Ducherow, near Auklam; died 21 September 1897, in Göttingen (Lower Saxony).
Painter, watercolourist. Historical scenes, genre scenes, portraits, landscapes.

Otto Heyden, having abandoned his theological studies, became a pupil of Wach and Von Klöber at the Berlin academy of art in 1843, before going on to study with L Cogniet in Paris in 1847. He lived in Italy from 1850 to 1854. Having exhibited first in Berlin around 1854, he subsequently also showed his work in Dresden, Cologne, Munich and Vienna.

Having settled in Berlin, he was appointed professor at the academy of art and painter to the court.

Heyden took part in the 1866 campaign following the German crown princes. His painting of *The Battle of Königgrätz* dates from this period and is on show in Berlin Museum. In 1869, he went to Egypt before returning to Germany to take part in the 1870 Franco-Prussian War. He was also a talented watercolourist.

MUSEUMS AND GALLERIES:
BERLIN: *The Battle of Königgrätz.*

AUCTION RECORDS:
ZURICH, 29 Nov 1985, *Banks of the Nile* (1869-1870, oil on canvas, 28 3/4 x 4 3/4 ins / 73 x 12 cm) CHF 40,000. LONDON, 13 Oct 1994, *Portrait of Otto von Bismarck Returning from the Hunt with his Dog and a Pheasant Hanging from to his Gamebag* (1897, oil on canvas, 43 1/2 x 31 ins / 110.5 x 78.7 cm) GBP 5,750. AMSTERDAM, 27 April 1999, *River Nile with Gizeh Pyramids* (c. 1869, oil on canvas, 16 x 27 ins / 40 x 68 cm) NLG 6,000. HAMBURG, 8 May 1999, *Emperor Wilhem I, War Council at Versailles, 6th December 1870* (oil on panel, 15 x 21 ins / 39 x 54 cm) DEM 8,000. PARIS, 17 Dec 2001, *On the Nile* (oil on canvas, 10 x 16 ins / 25 x 41 cm) FRF 20,000. AMSTERDAM, 29 April 2003, *In the Shade on the Banks of the River Nile* (oil on canvas, 10 x 17 ins / 25 x 42 cm) EUR 4,000.

HEYDEN, Pieter van der. See **MERICA Petrus A.**

HEYDENDAHL, Friedrich Joseph Nicolai
German, 19th century.
Born 4 September 1844, in Düsseldorf; died 6 February 1906, in Düsseldorf.
Painter. Genre scenes, landscapes.

Heydendahl studied at the Düsseldorf academy of art, then went on to exhibit in Düsseldorf and Dresden.

MUSEUMS AND GALLERIES:
ALTENBURG: *Leaving the Castle.*

AUCTION RECORDS:
NEW YORK, 21 Jan 1978, *Winter Landscape at Dusk* (oil on canvas, 32 x 42 1/4 ins / 81 x 107 cm) USD 4,000. LINDAU (B.), 9 May 1979, *Winter Landscape* (oil on canvas, 17 1/4 x 26 1/2 ins / 43.5 x 67.5 cm) DEM 8,500. LONDON, 21 May 1982, *Winter Landscape with Peasants on the Outskirts of a Village* (oil on canvas, 26 3/4 x 38 1/2 ins / 68 x 97.8 cm) GBP 4,000. MUNICH, 15 Sept 1983, *Dawn* (oil on canvas, 26 3/4 x 38 1/2 ins / 68 x 98 cm) DEM 15,000. BREMEN, 18 Oct 1986, *Winter Landscape at the Close of Day* (oil on canvas, 37 1/2 x 52 1/4 ins / 95 x 132.5 cm) DEM 8,000. STOCKHOLM, 19 April 1989, *Animated Winter Landscape with Buildings* (oil on canvas, 24 3/4 x 38 1/2 ins / 63 x 98 cm) SEK 10,000. NEW YORK, 16 July 1992, *Winter Landscape* (oil on card, a pair, each 10 1/4 x 16 ins / 26 x 40.6 cm) USD 3,575. AMSTERDAM, 21 April 1994, *Peasant Woman by a Building in a Wooded Valley with a Windmill in the Background* (oil on panel, 11 x 8 ins / 27 x 20.5 cm) NLG 2,875. AHLDEN, 20 May 2000, *Ice-skating Scene* (1900, oil on panel, 9 x 13 ins / 22 x 33 cm) DEM 7,500. COLOGNE, 30 Nov 2000, *Hunter in Winter Wood* (oil on canvas, 37 x 30 ins / 95 x 75 cm) DEM 4,500. STOCKHOLM, 27 Aug 2001, *Winter Landscape with Mother and Child Walking* (1882, oil on canvas, 44 x 34 ins / 113 x 87 cm) SEK 19,000. COLOGNE, 15 Dec 2001, *Winter Evening in a Dutch Village* (oil on canvas, 24 x 31 ins / 60 x 80 cm) DEM 4,400. COLOGNE, 11 April 2002, *Winter Landscape in Evening* (oil on canvas, 30 x 37 ins / 76 x 94 cm) EUR 1,900. SAN FRANCISCO, 15 May 2002, *Hunting Party Resting by the Edge of a Forest in a Winter Landscape* (oil on canvas, 37 x 50 ins / 94 x 127 cm) USD 4,500. LONDON, 7 Jan 2003, *Fishing Boat in a Norwegian Fjord by Moonlight* (oil on canvas, 37 x 52 ins / 94 x 132 cm) GBP 2,000. BRUSSELS, 13 May 2003, *Boars in a Forest* (oil on canvas, 37 x 51 ins / 94 x 130 cm) EUR 8,500.

HEYDER, Otto
German, 19th century.
Born 7 May 1863, in Barmen.
Painter.

Heyder worked in Karlsruhe.

HEYDER, Pierre Jean de
French, 19th century.
Active c. 1843.
Painter. Flowers, fruit, still-lifes.

HEYDER, Thomas
Swiss, 16th century.
Died 1597, in Solothurn.
Active in Überlingen.
Painter.

None of Thomas Heyder's works are known.

HEYDERMANN, Willie, or Heydemann
British, 19th - 20th century.
Active in London.
Engraver.

Willie Heydermann exhibited at the Royal Academy in London in 1886, and won an honourable mention at the 1900 Exposition Universelle in Paris.

HEYDON, Mary
British, 19th - 20th century.
Painter, watercolourist.

HEYDORN, Richard
Danish, 19th century.
Born 27 April 1858, in Pinneberg; died 9 August 1888.
Sculptor.
Richard Heydorn studied in Copenhagen.

HEYDRICH, Franz
Bohemian, 19th century.
Active in Gablontz c. 1800.
Miniaturist.
This is presumably the Franz Heydrich who died in Prague on 8 December 1811.

HEYDRICK, Georges
French, 20th century.
Born 2 December 1895, in Lyons; died 3 October 1951, in Lyons.
Painter (gouache), watercolourist, draughtsman.
Landscapes.
In 1914, Georges Heydrick left for the War and participated, in 1915, in the landing at the Dardanelles. He was called up again in 1939 and continued painting during the Occupation.

After the war, he became a member of the Comité Directeur de la Société Lyonnaise des Beaux-Arts receiving several awards and being eventually placed hors concours. He painted landscapes of villages and the banks of the river Azergues and the Loire region.

Georges Heydrick participated in collective exhibitions in Lyons including: Salon de l'Ouest Lyonnais and Salon des Artistes Viennois, Galerie R. Roger; Galerie de la Barre; Galerie Longhi. Retrospectives include: Maison de Lyon (1973) and Palais des Expositions (1977). He received the Palmes d'Officier from the Académie.

MUSEUMS AND GALLERIES:
LYONS.

HEYDT, Johann Wolfgang
German, 18th century.
Draughtsman, engraver.
Heydt worked in Wilhermsdorf, executing landscape drawings and engravings.

HEYDTMANN, Alexander Wilhelm
Russian, 18th century.
Born 1750; died 1795.
Painter.
Alexander Wilhelm Heydtmann worked in Riga.

HEYDUCK, Franz Moritz
German, 18th century.
Born 1728; died 1788.
Active in Dresden.
Sculptor.

HEYDUCK, Johann Gottfried
German, 18th century.
Died 1788, in Dresden.
Painter. Animals.

HEYE, André
Belgian, 20th century.
Born 1913, in Sinai.
Painter, engraver.
André Heye studied at the Académie St-Luc in Brussels and in Ghent. He was a teacher of fine arts.

HEYENBROCK, Herman, or Heijenbrock
Dutch, 19th - 20th century.
Born 24 July 1871, in Amsterdam; died 1948.
Painter, pastellist, lithographer. Local scenes.
Herman Heyenbrock studied in Rotterdam. He devoted himself to depicting the world of factory work, and his paintings provide important documentation of that aspect of his time.

AUCTION RECORDS:
AMSTERDAM, 8 Dec 1988, *Leaving the Factory* (pastel/paper, 17 1/4 x 24 ins / 44 x 61 cm) NLG 2,530. AMSTERDAM, 24 May 1989, *Workers in a Steelworks at Night* (pastel/paper, 25 1/2 x 36 1/2 ins / 65 x 93 cm) NLG 3,450. AMSTERDAM, 25 April 1990, *Steelworkers* (oil on canvas, 49 1/2 x 50 1/4 ins / 126 x 127.5 cm) NLG 5,750. AMSTERDAM, 5-6 Feb 1991, *Foundry Interior* (pastel and black chalk/paper, 25 1/2 x 38 ins / 65 x 96.5 cm) NLG 4,600. AMSTERDAM, 24 April 1991, *Steelworkers* (oil on canvas, 32 3/4 x 40 1/4 ins / 83.5 x 102 cm) NLG 6,900. AMSTERDAM, 17 Sept 1991, *Leaving the Factory at Midday* (pencil and pastel/grey paper, 21 x 13 3/4 ins / 52.5 x 35 cm) NLG 1,150. AMSTERDAM, 21 April 1993, *The Foundry* (pastel/paper, 25 1/2 x 37 1/2 ins / 65 x 95 cm) NLG 3,220. AMSTERDAM, 27-28 May 1993, *Ironfounders* (pastel/paper, 23 3/4 x 35 3/4 ins / 60.5 x 91 cm) NLG 2,760. AMSTERDAM, 9 Nov 1994, *Blast Furnace* (oil on canvas, 51 1/4 x 37 1/2 ins / 130 x 95 cm) NLG 7,130. AMSTERDAM, 19 Jan 1999, *Night of St Martin in Giethoorn with Lanterns on Trees* (oil on board, 28 x 20 ins / 70 x 50 cm) NLG 6,500. AMSTERDAM, 22 April 2002, *Quay Scene with Figures* (pastel, 24 x 36 ins / 62 x 92 cm) EUR 2,000. AMSTERDAM, 3 Sept 2002, *Factory in Burgerhout, Rotterdam* (oil on canvas, 40 x 80 ins / 101 x 202 cm) EUR 11,000. AMSTERDAM, 21 Jan 2003, *Gieterij Nering Bogel, Deventer* (colour chalk and pastel, 29 x 39 ins / 73 x 100 cm) EUR 3,500. AMSTERDAM, 27 Sept 2004, *Steel Workers near a Town* (oil on canvas, 138 x 49 ins / 350 x 125 cm) EUR 6,000. AMSTERDAM, 21 Dec 2004, *View of the Lutheran Church in Winter, Amsterdam* (pastel, 31 x 20 ins / 80 x 50 cm) EUR 1,900.

HEYER, Arthur
German, 20th century.
Born 28 February 1872, in Haarhausen; died 1931, in Rákospalota, near Budapest.
Active in Hungary.
Painter, illustrator. Landscapes, animals.
Arthur Heyer studied at the college of applied arts in Berlin. In 1896, he went into exile in Rákospalota, near Budapest, and eventually settled there permanently.

He began by painting landscapes and then developed into an animal painter, with a particular attraction for cats. He provided illustrations for books produced by the Franklinische Verlag, which specialised in books about animals. He also worked for *Shver's Familieblatt* (*Shver's Family Magazine*) and *Über Land und Meer* (*Over Land and Sea*).

AUCTION RECORDS:
LONDON, 3 Oct 1980, *Dog and Cats in an Interior* (oil on canvas, 38 1/2 x 30 1/4 ins / 97.7 x 76.8 cm) GBP 800. VIENNA, 17 March 1982, *Cat and Kittens in an Interior* (oil on canvas, 19 3/4 x 27 1/2 ins / 50 x 70 cm) ATS 35,000. LONDON, 26 Feb 1988, *A Dangerous Intruder* (oil on canvas, 23 1/4 x 31 ins / 59 x 79 cm) GBP 5,720; *Fox Terrier* (oil on canvas, 19 3/4 x 27 1/2 ins / 50 x 70 cm) GBP 990. LONDON, 7 June 1989, *Coloured Ball* (oil on canvas, 23 x 30 1/2 ins / 57.5 x 77.5 cm) GBP 3,300. LONDON, 14 Feb 1990, *White Persian Cat Chasing a Ladybird* (oil on card, 18 x 26 ins / 45.7 x 66 cm) GBP 2,420. LONDON, 11 May 1990, *The Intruder* (oil on canvas, 19 1/4 x 27 1/4 ins / 49 x 69 cm) GBP 4,400. AMSTERDAM, 11 Sept 1990, *Reindeer Leaving a Snow-covered Pine Forest to Drink at a Waterhole Where the Ice Had Thawed* (1917, oil on canvas, 31 x 36 1/2 ins / 79 x 93 cm) NLG 2,530. LONDON, 15 Jan 1991, *Young White Persian Cats Watching a Bee* (oil on canvas, 20 x 28 ins / 50.8 x 71.2 cm) GBP 2,420. LONDON, 16 July 1991, *Young White Angora Cats Watching a Beetle* (1929, oil on canvas, 21 3/4 x 26 3/4 ins / 55.3 x 67.9 cm) GBP 3,520. AMSTERDAM, 24 Sept 1992, *Salome with the Head of John the Baptist* (1909, oil on

canvas, 39¼ x 29¼ ins / 100 x 74 cm) NLG 2,300. LONDON, 28 Oct 1992, *Two White Cats in the Grass* (oil on canvas, 18¾ x 26¾ ins / 47.5 x 68 cm) GBP 770. NEW YORK, 16 Feb 1993, *Two White Angora Cats Watching a Bee* (oil on canvas, 19¾ x 27¾ ins / 50.2 x 70.5 cm) USD 2,200. LONDON, 27 Oct 1993, *Two White Cats and a Ladybird* (oil on canvas, 19¾ x 27½ ins / 50 x 70 cm) GBP 1,495. LONDON, 22 Feb 1995, *Chasing Butterflies* (oil on canvas, 19 x 27¼ ins / 48 x 69 cm) GBP 2,300. LONDON, 17 Oct 1996, *White Persian Cat and Jack Russell Terrier* (oil on canvas, 21 x 26 ins / 53.4 x 66 cm) GBP 2,300. LONDON, 10 July 1997, *Two White Persian Cats and Ladybird* (oil on panel, 19 x 26½ ins / 48.3 x 67.2 cm) GBP 1,725. LONDON, 18 Dec 1997, *Playtime* (oil on canvas, 31½ x 23½ ins / 80 x 59.6 cm) GBP 1,265. LONDON, 27 May 1999, *Deer in a Wooded Glade* (1908, oil on canvas, 39 x 39 ins / 100 x 100 cm) GBP 1,500. BILLINGSHURST, 20 July 1999, *Cat and Kittens at Play* (oil on canvas, 27 x 33 ins / 68 x 83 cm) GBP 2,000. RIDGEWOOD, 29 Jan 2000, *Dog and Cat at Play* (oil on canvas, 22 x 27 ins / 56 x 69 cm) USD 2,400. AHLDEN, 24 Nov 2000, *Angora Cat* (oil on masonite, 19 x 27 ins / 49 x 68 cm) DEM 3,300. LONDON, 8 Feb 2001, *Beast of Friends* (oil on canvas, 20 x 28 ins / 50 x 70 cm) GBP 2,000. LONDON, 8 Feb 2001, *Family of Cats at Play* (oil on canvas, 24 x 31 ins / 61 x 80 cm) GBP 4,000. LONDON, 17 Sept 2002, *Cat on Table* (oil on canvas, 22 x 27 ins / 55 x 68 cm) GBP 1,000. NEW YORK, 11 Feb 2003, *Old and the Young* (oil on canvas, 20 x 28 ins / 50 x 70 cm) USD 3,200. LONDON, 20 May 2003, *Curiosity* (oil on canvas, 22 x 27 ins / 56 x 69 cm) GBP 4,800. LONDON, 14 July 2004, *Best of Friends* (oil on canvas, 20 x 28 ins / 50 x 71 cm) GBP 2,500. LONDON, 1 Dec 2004, *Playtime* (oil on canvas, 20 x 28 ins / 50 x 70 cm) GBP 2,700.

HEYER, P. J.
German, 17th century.
Painter.
Heyer is known to have painted a signed *Landscape*.

HEYERDAHL, Hans Olaf
Norwegian, 19th - 20th century.
Born 8 July 1857, in Dalarna, Sweden; died 10 October 1913, in Christiania (now Oslo).
Painter. Religious subjects, genre scenes, portraits, landscapes.
Born in Sweden to Norwegian parents, Hans Olaf Heyerdahl studied first in Munich then, from the autumn of 1878, with Bonnat in Paris. In the same year, he won a third-class medal at the exhibition with his painting *Adam and Eve*. He also won a gold medal in Paris in 1889. At the beginning of 1880 he visited Florence, then returned to Norway, where he spent the rest of his life. He painted copies after Rembrandt, Raphael and Ribera.

MUSEUMS AND GALLERIES:
OSLO: *On the Beach*; *Two Sisters*; *The Dying Child*; *Portrait of the Artist* - STOCKHOLM: *In the Heart of Summer*.

AUCTION RECORDS:
PARIS, 21-23 May 1929, *Maternity*, FRF 1,120; *Young Boy*, FRF 420; *By the Stream*, FRF 220. STOCKHOLM, 19 April 1972, *The Artist's Studio*, SEK 6,000. NEW YORK, 27 Oct 1982, *The Beggar* (1881, oil on canvas, 30 x 19 ins / 76.2 x 48.3 cm) USD 6,800. NEW YORK, 27 May 1983, *The Beggar* (1881, oil on canvas, 30 x 19 ins / 76.2 x 48.3 cm) USD 3,500. LONDON, 27-28 March 1990, *View of Telemark* (oil on canvas, 19 x 29½ ins / 48 x 75 cm) GBP 10,450. STOCKHOLM, 30 Nov 1993, *Young Woman and Child near a Village at Dusk* (oil on canvas, 13¾ x 19¾ ins / 35 x 50 cm) SEK 22,000.

HEYERMANS, Jean Arnould
Belgian, 19th century.
Born 1837, in Rotterdam.
Painter. Genre scenes.
He exhibited in Antwerp and Dresden.

MUSEUMS AND GALLERIES:
MONTREAL: *Preparations for the Decoration of the Church*.

AUCTION RECORDS:
PARIS, 24 Nov 1922, *Little Girl Frightened By the Storm*, FRF 205. LONDON, 19 March 1980, *The Cobbler's Shop* (1874, oil on canvas, 33 x 27 ins / 84 x 68.5 cm) GBP 1,900. NEW YORK, 8 March 2000, *Children at Play* (1871, oil on canvas, 32 x 40 ins / 81 x 102 cm) USD 18,000. LONDON, 23 Nov 2000, *An Irresistible Offer* (oil on canvas, 32 x 46 ins / 82 x 118 cm) GBP 4,200. COLOGNE, 5 April 2001, *Village Scene with Three Boys* (oil on canvas, 21 x 26 ins / 54 x 65 cm) DEM 10,000. NEW YORK, 30 Oct 2001, *Festival of Flowers* (1863, oil on canvas, 37 x 49 ins / 93 x 124 cm) USD 26,000. BRUSSELS, 28 May 2002, *Children Playing Hide and Seek* (oil on canvas, 24 x 29 ins / 60 x 73 cm) EUR 8,000. LONDON, 21 June 2002, *Fond Memories* (oil on canvas, 34 x 28 ins / 86 x 71 cm) GBP 4,000. STOCKHOLM, 4 June 2003, *He Loves Me, He Loves Me Not* (oil on canvas, 23 x 17 ins / 58 x 44 cm) SEK 22,000. LONDON, 11 Nov 2003, *He Loves Me, He Loves Me Not* (oil on canvas, 24 x 18 ins / 60 x 45 cm) GBP 1,500.

HEYERMANS, Marie
Belgian, 19th century.
Born 19th century, in Rotterdam.
Painter. Genre scenes.
She obtained an honourable mention in 1891 in Paris.

HEYINGER, Franz Anton
Austrian, 18th century.
Active in Vienna.
Painter.
Heyinger executed religious paintings.

HEYL, Heinrich
German, 19th century.
Born c. 1850, in Berlin.
Painter.
Heinrich Heyl worked on the decoration of Kolberg Cathedral (now Kolobrzeg, Poland) and churches in Stralsund and Wittenberg.

HEYL, Marius or Marinus
Dutch, 19th century.
Born 22 March 1836, in Utrecht; died 1931.
Painter. Landscapes with figures, landscapes, animals.
He exhibited in Brussels, Amsterdam and Berlin.

AUCTION RECORDS:
NEW YORK, 15-16 March 1906, *Landscape*, USD 170. AMSTERDAM, 3 May 1988, *Ducks in the Reeds, Dud-Loosschecht* (oil on canvas, 15¾ x 24½ ins / 40 x 62 cm) NLG 3,910. AMSTERDAM, 2 May 1990, *Feeding the Ducks* (oil on canvas, 11½ x 17 ins / 29 x 43 cm) NLG 1,725. AMSTERDAM, 5 June 1990, *A Cabin in the Woods with a Peasant Woman Leading her Animals to a Stream* (oil on canvas, 45¼ x 31½ ins / 115 x 80 cm) NLG 4,025. LOKEREN, 23 May 1992, *Landscape with a Pool* (oil on canvas, 19¼ x 28¼ ins / 49 x 72 cm) BEF 90,000. AMSTERDAM, 11 April 1995, *Navigating in a Bay* (oil on card, 13¼ x 9¼ ins / 33.5 x 23.5 cm) NLG 1,180. AMSTERDAM, 25 Oct 1999, *Forest View with Children near Stream* (oil on canvas, 33 x 28 ins / 85 x 70 cm) NLG 7,800. AMSTERDAM, 19 April 2000, *Polders Landscape with Ducks at the Water's Edge* (oil on panel, 9 x 15 ins / 23 x 37 cm) NLG 4,000. PHILADELPHIA, 27 June 2004, *River Amstel, Amsterdam* (oil on panel, 18 x 30 ins / 45 x 75 cm) USD 3,250.

HEYL, Philipp Heinrich Georg
German, 19th century.
Born 26 June 1864, in Frankfurt am Main.
Painter, engraver. Portraits, genre scenes.
Philipp Heyl studied in Karlsruhe under Hasselhorst, Keller and Ritter.

HEYLAN, Ana
Flemish School, 17th century.

Active in Seville and Grenada.
Engraver.
She was the sister of Francisco Heylan.

HEYLAN, Bernardo
Flemish School, 17th century.
Active in Seville and Grenada.
Engraver.
He was the brother of Francisco and Ana.

HEYLAN, Francisco
Flemish School, 17th century.
Died c. 1650.
Active in Seville and Grenada.
Engraver.
Of Flemish origin, he settled in Spain with his brother and sister, and illustrated several works.

HEYLAND, Jean Christophe
Swiss, 19th century.
Born 1792, in Frankfurt am Main; died 29 August 1866, near Genoa.
Painter, watercolourist.
Heyland lived mainly in Switzerland.
MUSEUMS AND GALLERIES:
GENEVA (Mus. Ariana): two watercolours.

HEYLANDT, Ferdinand Ludwig
German, 19th century.
Born c. 1800, in Berlin.
Painter.
Heylandt executed portraits, genre and history paintings.

HEYLBROECK, Nicolas
Flemish School.
Engraver.
Nicolas Heylbroeck is mentioned by Siret.

HEYLBROECK, Norbert, the Elder
Flemish School, 18th century.
Born in Bruges; died March 1762, in Brussels.
Engraver.
This artist was the son of Michael Heylbrouck or Heylbroeck. He engraved plates for Despars' *Chronicle of Flanders*. His son was a professor in Bruges.

HEYLBROECK, Norbert, the Younger
Flemish School, 18th century.
Died 8 December 1785.
Active in Bruges.
Engraver.
In 1757, he went to Paris, and in 1775, became a professor in Bruges. He was the son of Norbert the Elder, with whom he collaborated.

HEYLBROECK, Robert
Belgian, 20th century.
Born 1901, in Ghent; died 1962.
Sculptor (including bronze), painter. Interiors.
Robert Heylbroeck studied with Georges Verbranck and Égide Rombaux.
AUCTION RECORDS:
ANTWERP, 18 April 1978, *Mother and Child* (bronze, h. 28 3/4 ins / 73 cm) BEF 30,000.

HEYLBROECK, Séraphin
Flemish School, 18th century.
Active in Bruges c. 1730.
Engraver.
He is known to have executed *The Mystical Marriage of St Catherine*, after Van Dyck.

HEYLBROUCK, Michael, or Helybruck or Heylbroeck
Flemish School, 17th - 18th century.
Born 1635, in Ghent; died 1733, near Brescia.
Painter, engraver.
He engraved after Sebastian Bourdon, Van Dyck, Antoine Coypel and Charles Le Brun. He was a pupil of Gerard Scotin the Younger.

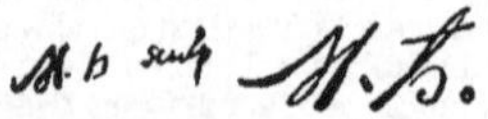

HEYLEN, Franciscus
Flemish School, 17th century.
Born in Antwerp.
Active in Seville c. 1608.
Engraver.

HEYLEN, Gonzalcs Frans van
Flemish School, 17th - 18th century.
Born 9 April 1661, in Antwerp; died 1720, in Antwerp.
Engraver, printer.
He executed mostly illustrations for publishers.

HEYLEN, Jan
Belgian, 20th century.
Born 1931, in Diest near Louvain; died 1967, in Genk (Flanders).
Sculptor, potter.
Jan Heylen was a pupil of La Cambre before studying with Ossip Zadkine in Paris. As well as ceramics, he worked with such materials as iron, copper and aluminium.

HEYLEN, Luce
Belgian, 20th century.
Born 1930, in Meerhout, near Turnhout.
Painter. Scenes with figures, genre scenes, landscapes.
Luce Heylen's paintings focus on animals, particularly cats, and flowers.

HEYLIGERS, Gustaaf Antoon François, or Heijligers
Dutch, 19th century.
Born 1828; died 1897.
Painter. Genre scenes.
He lived and worked mostly in Antwerp.
MUSEUMS AND GALLERIES:
MONTREAL: *A Tete-à-tete* (1860).
AUCTION RECORDS:
LONDON, 10 July 1908, *Dutch Interior* (1867) GBP 57. LONDON, 19 Dec 1924, *The Favoured Lamb*, GBP 21. LONDON, 5 Dec 1927, *The Town Crier of Bruges*, GBP 23. LONDON, 15 April 1929, *The Amateur*, GBP 42. VIENNA, 14 March 1978, *The Woman with the Parrot* (1872, oil on panel, 12 1/2 x 10 ins / 32 x 24.5 cm) ATS 50,000. LONDON, 20 June 1980, *An Elegant Figure at the Foot of a Stair* (1873, oil on panel, 18 1/2 x 14 1/4 ins / 47 x 36.1 cm) GBP 2,000. NEW YORK, 22 May 1991, *The Sleeping Cook* (1863, oil on panel, 11 1/2 x 14 1/2 ins / 29.2 x 36.8 cm) USD 24,200. LONDON, 7 April 1993, *The New Earrings* (1872, oil on panel, 12 1/2 x 9 1/2 ins / 32 x 24 cm) GBP 2,645. LOKEREN, 6 March 1999, *Winding up the Clock* (1866, oil on canvas, 20 x 25 ins / 51 x 64 cm) BEF 1,200,000. COLOGNE, 4 Dec 1999, *Young Woman at Spinning Wheel* (1863, oil on panel, 14 x 11 ins / 36 x 29 cm) DEM 24,000. LONDON, 28 Nov 2000, *Figures in a Laundryroom* (1864, oil on canvas, 25 x 19 ins / 63 x 48 cm) GBP 9,500. BRUSSELS, 11 Dec 2000, *Rest of a Musician and his Pupil* (oil on canvas, 26 x 20 ins / 65 x 52 cm) BEF 150,000. COLOGNE, 17 Nov 2001, *Homecomers from Market* (oil on panel, 9 x 7 ins / 22 x 19 cm) DEM 10,000. COLOGNE, 17 Nov 2001, *Young Couple Going through a Gate, Talking* (1852, oil on panel, 9 x 7 ins / 22 x 19 cm) DEM 10,500. LONDON, 17 June 2003, *Town Crier at Bruges* (1860, oil on panel, 11 x 13 ins / 27 x 33 cm) GBP 3,000. YORKSHIRE, 7 May 2004, *Girl Seated at Spinning Wheel in an Interior Scene with Doves* (oil on panel, 14 x 11 ins / 36 x 28 cm) GBP 6,500. NEU-

ILLY, 15 June 2004, *Scene with Figures in a Narrow Street* (1858, oil on panel, 14 x 18 ins / 35 x 46 cm) EUR 4,500.

HEYMA, Stanislaw
Polish, 19th century.
Born c. 1850, in Warsaw.
Painter.
Stanislaw Heyma worked in Warsaw, Berlin and Munich, painting genre scenes and portraits.

HEYMAN
Dutch, 15th century.
Active in Haarlem c. 1454.
Painter.

HEYMAN, Charles
French, 20th century.
Born 9 August 1881, in Paris; died 15 May 1915, on the battlefield.
Watercolourist, engraver, draughtsman. Landscapes, urban landscapes.
Charles Heyman was the grandson of Jean-François Millet. He engraved mainly landscapes of Paris, including the series, *Sites of Paris*, as well as landscapes of Normandy, and engraved plates about the railways. His body of work includes about 170 engravings both of artistic and documentary value.

An associate member of the Société Nationale des Beaux-Arts in Paris, he exhibited at the Salon at the beginning of the 20th century.

BIBLIOGRAPHY:
Sanchez, Pierre/Seydoux, Xavier, *Charles Heyman 1881-1915. Catalogue raisonné illustré de l'œuvre gravé*, L'Échelle de Jacob, Paris, 1999.

MUSEUMS AND GALLERIES:
PARIS (Bibliothèque d'Art et d'Archéologie, Fondation Jacques-Doucet) - PARIS (MNAM-CCI).

AUCTION RECORDS:
PARIS, 2 and 4 June 1920, *St-Nicolas du Chardonnet* (pen) FRF 385. PARIS, 11 and 12 June 1928, *The Bottom of Rue Mouffetard, Paris* (pen and watercolour) FRF 1,200. PARIS, 21 Dec 1942, *The Sea, Jobourg* (1912, pen) FRF 1,750. PARIS, 17 Dec 1943, *The Point, Jobourg* (1912, pencil and Indian ink wash heightened with white) FRF 3,000. PARIS, 11 June 1997, *The Railways* (c. 1910, watercolour, $7^3/_4$ x $11^1/_2$ ins / 19.5 x 29.5 cm) FRF 12,000.

HEYMAN, F. A.
Dutch, 19th century.
Active at the beginning of the 19th century.
Lithographer.
He executed mostly portraits.

HEYMAN, Maurice
Polish, 19th century.
Born in Kalisz; died May 1898, in Algiers.
Miniaturist.
Maurice Heyman studied with Cormon and exhibited at the Salon des Artistes Français.

HEYMANN, Balz
Swiss, 19th century.
Born 1775.
Active in Sarnen.
Painter.

HEYMANN, Charles. See **HEYMAN Charles**

HEYMANN, Joseph Anton
Swiss, 18th - 19th century.
Born 1758, in Wallis; died 8 March 1837, in Obwalden.
Painter.

MUSEUMS AND GALLERIES:
SARNEN (Historisches Mus. Obwalden): several works.

HEYMANN, Jules
French, 19th - 20th century.
Active in Viarmes.
Sculptor.
Jules Heymann was a member of the Société des Artistes Français from 1889.

HEYMANN, Moritz
German, 20th century.
Born 2 July 1870, in Breslau (now Wroclaw, Poland).
Painter, engraver.
Moritz Heymann was active in Munich and also spent much time travelling in Northern Italy.

HEYMANN, Octavie, or Heyman
Maiden name: Le Foye
French, 19th century.
Born in the 19th century, in Paris.
Painter, miniaturist, sculptor.
Octavie Heymann was a pupil of Levasseur and Madame Rélin. She first exhibited at the Paris Salon in 1878, and became a member of the Société des Artistes Français in 1883.

HEYMANS
Flemish School, 19th century.
Active c. 1842.
Painter. History painting.
This artist has been mentioned by Siret.

HEYMANS, Adriaan Josef
Belgian, 19th - 20th century.
Born 11 June 1839, in Antwerp; died December 1921, in Schaerbeek.
Painter, watercolourist. Genre scenes, landscapes, seascapes.
Groups: Société Libre des Beaux-Arts, Vie et Lumière. School of Kalmthout or 'École Grise'.
Adriaan Heymans was a student at the Koninklijke Academie voor Schone Kunsten in Antwerp. He became the prime mover of the Kalmthout school in Belgium, also known as the 'École du Gris', and then of the Termonde school. He was one of the founder members of the Société Libre des Beaux-Arts in Brussels, the Groupe des Vingt (Group of Twenty), L'Art Contemporain (Contemporary Art) and the art society Vie et Lumière (Life and Light). During a stay in France from 1855 to 1858, he was influenced by the painters Rousseau, Corot, Daubigny and Millet, and more generally by the Barbizon school, whose theories he promulgated in Belgium.

During the 1860s, he developed rapidly in the direction of an independent kind of Pre-Impressionism, which led him towards a very personal Luminism. He painted landscapes using the technique of 'touche divisée', working with hatching and small brushstrokes juxtaposed with colours so light as to be almost white, and broken shades, with a particular liking for capturing fleeting impressions of the union of sea and sky. He also painted sheep in the landscape of the Campine region.

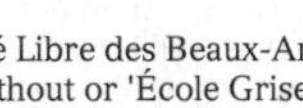

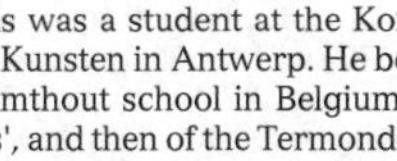

MUSEUMS AND GALLERIES:
ANTWERP: *Deepest Brittany* - BRUSSELS: *Heathland; Spring; Moonlit Evening* - GHENT: *Moorland Sunset* - LIÈGE: *Heathland in the Campine Area.*

AUCTION RECORDS:
PARIS, 6 April 1892, *Pond in Campine,* FRF 1,800. BRUSSELS, 26 March 1904, *Willows at Genck,* FRF 1,450. LONDON, 12 Nov 1970, *Windmill in Flanders,* GBP 500. BRUSSELS, 5 Oct

1971, *Landscape in the South of France,* BEF 100,000. ANTWERP, 3 April 1973, *Spring,* BEF 100,000. BRUGES, 10 April 1976, *Landscape with Windmill* (oil on canvas, 38 1/2 x 65 ins / 98 x 165 cm) BEF 82,000. BRUSSELS, 18 May 1977, *Landscape with River* (oil on canvas, 39 1/4 x 57 3/4 ins / 100 x 147 cm) BEF 90,000. BRUSSELS, 28 March 1979, *The Return of the Livestock* (oil on canvas, 18 1/2 x 23 1/2 ins / 47 x 60 cm) BEF 170,000. BRUSSELS, 27 Oct 1982, *Landscape with a Lily Pond* (oil on canvas, 38 1/4 x 57 1/2 ins / 97 x 146 cm) BEF 75,000. LOKEREN, 23 April 1983, *Peasant Woman picking Cabbages* (oil on canvas, 37 x 63 3/4 ins / 94 x 162 cm) BEF 180,000. LONDON, 26 March 1986, *Bridge in the Valley* (oil on canvas, 35 3/4 x 20 ins / 91 x 51 cm) GBP 24,000. ANTWERP, 27 Oct 1987, *Farm in a Landscape* (oil on canvas, 39 3/4 x 19 1/4 ins / 101 x 49 cm) BEF 200,000. PARIS, 7 Dec 1987, *Village in the Snow* (oil on canvas, 19 1/4 x 15 ins / 49 x 38 cm) FRF 5,000. PARIS, 5 Feb 1988, *Landscape with Farm* (oil on panel, 17 x 24 ins / 43 x 61 cm) FRF 7,500. LOKEREN, 5 March 1988, *The Drive in Autumn* (oil on canvas, 59 x 39 1/4 ins / 149 x 100 cm) BEF 500,000. LONDON, 19 Oct 1989, *Mine near Charleroi* (oil on canvas, 32 x 28 1/4 ins / 81 x 72 cm) GBP 33,000. BRUSSELS, 12 June 1990, *Sleeping Nude* (oil on canvas, 15 x 18 ins / 38 x 46 cm) BEF 75,000. LONDON, 3 Dec 1991, *Bridge in the Valley* (oil on canvas, 20 1/2 x 36 1/4 ins / 52 x 92 cm) GBP 18,700. AMSTERDAM, 2 Nov 1992, *Farm* (oil on panel, 10 1/2 x 14 ins / 26.5 x 35.5 cm) NLG 6,325. AMSTERDAM, 20 April 1993, *Cart on a Village Road* (oil on canvas, 19 3/4 x 35 1/4 ins / 50 x 89.5 cm) NLG 16,100. LOKEREN, 15 May 1993, *Cowgirl* (oil on canvas, 15 x 18 ins / 38 x 46 cm) BEF 90,000. LOKEREN, 28 May 1994, *Summer Landscape* (oil on canvas, 15 x 18 1/2 ins / 38 x 47 cm) BEF 600,000. LOKEREN, 10 Dec 1994, *Lily Pond* (oil on canvas, 45 1/4 x 75 1/4 ins / 115 x 191 cm) BEF 950,000. LOKEREN, 20 May 1995, *The Moors in the Afternoon* (oil on canvas, 30 x 45 1/4 ins / 76 x 115 cm) BEF 260,000. LOKEREN, 18 May 1996, *Sunset* (oil on canvas, 32 3/4 x 49 1/4 ins / 83.5 x 125 cm) BEF 290,000; *Avenue in Autumn* (c. 1880, oil on panel, 15 1/2 x 19 3/4 ins / 39.5 x 50 cm) BEF 80,000. LOKEREN, 7 Dec 1996, *Autumn* (oil on canvas, 30 1/4 x 46 ins / 77 x 116 cm) BEF 250,000. LOKEREN, 11 Oct 1997, *River Landscape in Summer* (oil on canvas, 18 3/4 x 24 ins / 47.5 x 61 cm) BEF 200,000. LOKEREN, 6 Dec 1997, *Autumn* (oil on canvas, 30 1/4 x 46 ins / 77 x 116 cm) BEF 240,000.

HEYMANS, J.
Dutch, 17th century.
Born 17th century, in Friesland.
Painter.
The details of his life are unknown. However, he is known to have executed several portraits of theologians.

HEYMANS, Jan Hendrik, or Heijmans
Dutch, 19th century.
Born 19 February 1806, in Leeuwarden; died 1888.
Painter. Portraits, genre scenes, interiors, landscapes, still-lifes.
He was a pupil of W.B. van der Kool. He was active in Munich and Dresden in 1840, and then in Zwoll.
AUCTION RECORDS:
AMSTERDAM, 20 April 1993, *Fishermen in the Moonlight* (1872, oil on panel, 7 1/2 x 9 3/4 ins / 19 x 25 cm) NLG 1,035. AMSTERDAM, 21 Jan 1998, *Still-life with Peaches and Grapes* (1872, oil on panel, 11 x 14 1/4 ins / 28 x 36.5 cm) NLG 1,960. TOESTORF, 5 May 2001, *Young Woman, Dead Bird and Dead Rabbit* (1878, oil on canvas, 34 x 26 ins / 87 x 65 cm) DEM 9,900.

HEYMANS, Johannes
Flemish School, 18th century.
Born 1757, in The Hague; died c. 1809, in The Hague.
Painter. History painting, landscapes, still-lifes.
He was a pupil of Davrance. In 1805, he entered into "Pictura", the painters' fraternity, in The Hague as a foreman.

HEYMANS, Pierre
Belgian, 20th century.
Born 1935, in Brussels.
Painter, draughtsman, sculptor, watercolourist.
Figures, nudes, portraits, landscapes, seascapes.

HEYMANS, Willem George Frederick
Dutch, 19th century.
Born 22 August 1797, in The Hague; died 13 May 1868, in The Hague.
Portrait painter.
He was a pupil of J.W. Pieneman.

HEYMHOWECK, Rombout
Dutch, 17th century.
Active in the Netherlands.
Engraver (burin).
He engraved mythological and religious subjects.

HEYMÜLLER
German, 18th century.
Died 1760, in Potsdam.
Sculptor.
Heymüller was heavily involved in the decoration of the Neues Palais (New Palace) in Potsdam.

HEYMÜLLER, Gottlieb
German, 18th century.
Born 1751, in Potsdam; died 5 December 1788, in Potsdam.
Sculptor.
Gottlieb Heymüller, a son of Heymüller who died in 1760, worked in Dresden, but mainly in Potsdam.

HEYN, August
German, 19th century.
Born 10 August 1837, in Sophienau.
Painter. Portraits, genre scenes.
August Heyn, a pupil of Raupp and Defregger at the Munich academy of art, first exhibited around 1864, before going on to exhibit mainly in Dresden and Munich. Heyn travelled in Germany, the Tyrol and Italy and then settled in Munich.
AUCTION RECORDS:
NEW YORK, 13 Oct 1978, *Young Smokers* (1876, oil on canvas, 18 x 14 3/4 ins / 45.5 x 37.5 cm) USD 10,000. LONDON, 9 May 1979, *At the Matchmaker's* (oil on canvas, 34 3/4 x 29 ins / 88.5 x 73.5 cm) GBP 3,000. LONDON, 8 Oct 1982, *Portrait of a Young Bavarian Woman* (oil on panel, 8 1/2 x 6 ins / 21.5 x 15.3 cm) GBP 1,000. NEW YORK, 24 May 1984, *The Punished Child* (oil on canvas, 36 3/4 x 32 1/2 ins / 93.5 x 82.5 cm) USD 3,100. MUNICH, 31 May 1990, *Undeserved Punishment* (1870, oil on canvas, 34 x 27 1/4 ins / 85.5 x 69.5 cm) DEM 77,000. SAN FRANCISCO, 15 Nov 2000, *The Broken Sled* (oil on canvas/board, 20 x 16 ins / 51 x 41 cm) USD 4,250. VIENNA, 29 Nov 2001, *First Shave* (oil on canvas, 29 x 24 ins / 73 x 62 cm) ATS 70,000. NEW YORK, 23 April 2002, *Blowing Bubbles* (1873, oil on canvas, 35 x 30 ins / 90 x 77 cm) USD 16,000.

HEYN, Ernst Friedrich
German, 19th century.
Born 7 September 1841, in Leipzig; died 14 January 1894, in Leipzig.
Painter, watercolourist. Landscapes.
Heyn studied at the Leipzig academy of art and first exhibited in 1868, before going on to show his work mainly in Dresden.
MUSEUMS AND GALLERIES:
LEIPZIG (Mus. der Bildenden Künste): watercolour.

HEYN, Erwin
French, 20th century.
Born 1 July 1941, in Vendenheim (Bas-Rhin).
Painter, engraver.

Heyn lives and works in Eckartswiller (Alsace). He has taken part in collective exhibitions, including the Biennale de la Gravure in Mulhouse in 1978, where he was awarded the special prize. His solo exhibitions include those in Strasbourg at the Galerie l'Empreinte in 1981 and the Galerie Rencontre d'Espaces in 1985.

MUSEUMS AND GALLERIES:
MONTPELLIER (Artothèque) - MULHOUSE (MBA, Prints Collection) - STRASBOURG (Musée D'Art Moderne et Contemporain, Graphic Arts Collection).

HEYN, Johann Christoph, or Heyne
German, 18th century.
Born 1754, in Pomerania; died 8 July 1800, in Dresden.
Miniaturist.

HEYN, Karl
German, 19th century.
Born 24 May 1834, in Leipzig; died 21 July 1906, near Dresden.
Painter. Genre scenes, landscapes.

Karl Heyn was the brother of Ernst Friedrich Heyn and a student at the Leipzig academy of art. He worked in Munich from 1860 to 1865, then in Weimer and Dresden. In 1891, he settled in Blasewitz, near Dresden. He exhibited in Dresden, Berlin and Vienna from about 1860.

HEYNACHER, Franz
German, 19th century.
Active in Berlin.
Painter. Historical scenes, portraits.

Heynacher first exhibited in Berlin around 1887.

HEYNDRICKX, Félix Jan Ferdinand
Flemish School, 19th century.
Born 9 January 1799, in Ghent; died c. 1833.
Painter. History painting, portraits.

He was a pupil of David and Gros.

AUCTION RECORDS:
AMSTERDAM, 1 Oct 1981, *The Milkmaid* (1825, oil on panel, 18 3/4 x 14 1/2 ins / 47.5 x 37 cm) NLG 15,000.

HEYNE, Heinrich
German, 20th century.
Born 16 June 1869, in Ohlau (now Olawa, Poland).
Painter, sculptor, lithographer.

Heinrich Heyne was active mainly in Berlin, Karlsruhe and Stuttgart. He also spent some time in Rome.

HEYNE, Ludwig Heinrich
German, 20th century.
Born 25 August 1878, in Düsseldorf; died 22 October 1914, in Douvrin, France.
Painter. Genre scenes, landscapes.

Ludwig Heyne studied with Claus Meyer in Düsseldorf. He died in battle.

HEYNERT, Johann Friedrich
German, 19th century.
Born 1857; died 6 June 1888, in Schandau.
Sculptor.

Heynert studied in Dresden and is best known for his portrait of the architect, Sendig.

HEYNES, E.
British, 19th century.
Painter. Seascapes.

MUSEUMS AND GALLERIES:
BRISTOL: *Shipwreck.*

HEYNRICKZ, Roeloff
German, 16th century.
Active in Utrecht in 1523.
Painter. History painting.

HEYNS, Jan
Flemish, 16th century.
Born 1542, in Antwerp; died 1582, in Antwerp.
Engraver, print publisher.
Antwerp School, Flemish School.

Jan Heyns was a pupil of Bernard van den Putte.

HEYNS, Jan
Flemish, 16th century.
Died 1536, in Utrecht.
Active in Mechelen in 1511.
Sculptor.
Flemish School.

HEYNS, Mattheus, pseudonym: Smets
Flemish, 16th century.
Died 1576, in Mechelen.
Active in Mechelen.
Sculptor, architect.
Mechelen School, Flemish School.

Mattheus Heyns was admitted into the Mechelen guild in 1519.

HEYNS, Rombout, the Elder
Flemish, 16th century.
Active in Mechelen.
Sculptor.
Flemish School.

HEYNS, Rombout, the Younger
Flemish School, 17th century.
Died 16 November 1615, in Mechelen.
Sculptor.

HEYNSIUS, Kees
Dutch, 20th century.
Born 29 April 1890, in Schoonhoven.
Painter. Landscapes.

Kees Heynsius painted landscapes in Belgium, Luxembourg, Holland and France. His works combine a robust use of colour with a meticulous technique, based on a rigorous, somewhat Spartan construction.

AUCTION RECORDS:
AMSTERDAM, 19 Sept 1989, *Landscape with a Farm* (oil on canvas, 15 1/2 x 21 1/2 ins / 39.5 x 54.5 cm) NLG 1,150. AMSTERDAM, 5 June 1990, *Bunch of Summer Flowers in a Brown Earthenware Pot* (oil on canvas, 19 x 15 1/4 ins / 48 x 39 cm) NLG 1,265. AMSTERDAM, 18 Feb 1992, *Cab on Rembrandtplein* (1919, oil on canvas, 14 1/4 x 20 3/4 ins / 36 x 53 cm) NLG 1,150.

HEYRAULT, Louis Robert
French, 19th - 20th century.
Born in Paris.
Painter. Genre scenes, hunting scenes, animals.

Louis Robert Heyrault was a pupil of P. Delaroche and Pico. He made his début at the Salon de Paris in 1877.

He specialised in the painting of animals and hunting scenes.

AUCTION RECORDS:
COMPIÈGNE, 4 Dec 1983, *Imperial Hunting Meet in the Compiègne Forest* (oil on canvas, 43 1/4 x 74 3/4 ins / 110 x 190 cm) FRF 36,000. MONTE CARLO, 21 June 1986, *Promenade in a Carriage* (1850, oil on canvas, 28 3/4 x 36 1/4 ins / 73 x 92 cm) FRF 90,000. PARIS, 7 April 1987, *Cavalier* (oil on canvas, 23 1/2 x 28 3/4 ins / 59.5 x 73 cm) FRF 18,000. PARIS, 12 Oct 1990, *The Obstacle Course* (1852, two oils on canvas, pendants, 17 x 21 1/4 ins / 43 x 54 cm and 15 1/4 x 21 ins/39 x 53.5 cm) FRF 42,000. PARIS, 5 Nov 1991, *English Harness* (oil on canvas, 28 3/4 x 36 1/4 ins / 73 x 92 cm) FRF 35,000. PARIS, 9 July 1992, *Promenade in the Wood* (oil on canvas, 23 1/4 x 35 1/2 ins / 59 x 90 cm) FRF 44,000. NEW YORK, 3 June 1994, *Promenade in a Cab* (1856, oil on canvas, 28 3/4 x 36 1/4 ins / 73 x 92.1 cm) USD 11,500.

HEYRMAN, Hugo
Belgian, 20th century.
Born 1942, in Antwerp.
Painter, performance artist.

Heyrman was a prize-winner at the Koninklijke Academie voor Schone Kunsten and the Nationaal Hoger Instituut voor Schone Kunsten in Antwerp. He won the Prix de la Jeune Peinture Belge in 1975. Heyrman has notably produced a piece of work on water: *Cycle of Water*.

Auction records:
Lokeren, 7 Oct 1995, *Still Morning* (1982, oil on canvas, 43 1/4 x 63 ins / 110 x 160 cm) BEF 85,000. Lokeren, 11 Dec 1999, *Snow Melting* (oil on canvas, 79 x 51 ins / 200 x 130 cm) BEF 220,000. Lokeren, 11 Dec 1999, *Track* (oil on canvas, 51 x 79 ins / 130 x 200 cm) BEF 220,000. Lokeren, 4 March 2000, *Puddles* (oil on canvas, 47 x 47 ins / 120 x 120 cm) BEF 130,000.

HEYSEN, Hans (Sir)
Australian, 20th century.
Born 1876 or 1877, in Germany; died 1968 or 1971.
Painter, watercolourist, draughtsman, engraver.
Landscapes, landscapes with figures.

Hans Heysen's father emigrated from Hamburg to Southern Australia, where he was joined by his wife and five children. Hans left school at the age of 14 and went to work in an ironmongery while studying part-time in James Ashton's Norwood Art School in Adelaide. He was supported financially by a number of businessmen who enabled him to visit Europe, including England, during the years 1899 to 1903. He studied in Paris at the Académie Julian and the École des Beaux-Arts before returning to Australia, where he settled in Hahndorf, a village near Adelaide founded by German immigrants.

Heysen observed the countryside with an attentive and careful eye, recording landscapes and scenes of rural life, often including eucalyptus trees in his paintings. At first he worked in a classical manner inspired by Poussin, then became a follower of Millet, Constable and the Barbizon school, before developing his own naturalistic style. His paintings reveal a preoccupation with the quality of Australian light, as well as a nostalgia for the bush, prompted by the increasing industrialisation of his adopted land. He exhibited in Melbourne.

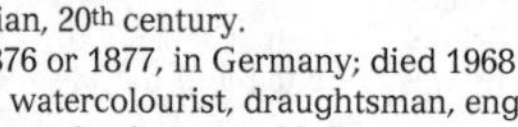

Bibliography:
North, Ian, '*Gum-Tree*' in *Creating Australia: 200 Years of Art 1788-1988*, exhibition catalogue, Art Gall. Board of South Australia, Adelaide, 1988.

Museums and Galleries:
Adelaide (AG of South Australia): *Red Gold* (1913) - Melbourne: *A Lord of a Bush*; *Sun and Shadow*; a watercolour - Sydney: *Coming Home*.

Auction records:
Melbourne, 11 and 12 March 1971, *Landscape in Summer* (watercolour) AUD 1,800. London, 30 April 1976, *Trees* (watercolour, 13 x 15 3/4 ins / 33 x 40 cm) GBP 800. Melbourne, 11 March 1977, *Ploughing Scene, Australia* (watercolour, 14 1/2 x 18 1/2 ins / 37 x 47 cm) AUD 2,200. Melbourne, 20 March 1978, *Wooded Landscape and River* (1938, watercolour, 12 3/4 x 16 ins / 32.3 x 39.7 cm) AUD 32,000. Melbourne, 19 June 1978, *Zinnias in a Bowl* (1926, oil on canvas, 19 3/4 x 15 1/2 ins / 50 x 39.5 cm) AUD 2,500. Sydney, 10 March 1980, *Steep Country* (watercolour, 9 3/4 x 16 1/2 ins / 25 x 42 cm) AUD 2,800. Sydney, 10 March 1980, *Landscape* (oil on card, 9 3/4 x 13 ins / 25 x 33 cm) AUD 3,800. Armadale, 12 April 1984, *The Two Red Gums* (1938, watercolour, 13 x 15 3/4 ins / 33 x 40 cm) AUD 6,500. Melbourne, 21 April 1986, *The Race Course* (1924, watercolour/paper, 19 x 25 ins / 48 x 63.5 cm) AUD 50,000. Sydney, 30 June 1986, *Morning Smoko* (charcoal and chalk, 15 3/4 x 12 1/2 ins / 40 x 32 cm) AUD 2,600. Melbourne, 26 July 1987, *Surrey Landscape* (c. 1901, oil on card, 9 1/2 x 12 1/2 ins / 24 x 32 cm) AUD 4,500. Sydney, 17 April 1988, *Cool Morning in Ambleside* (1917, oil on canvas, 12 1/4 x 15 ins / 31 x 38 cm) AUD 19,000. Sydney, 4 July 1988, *Landscape with Sheep* (pencil, 5 1/2 x 9 1/4 ins / 14 x 23.5 cm) AUD 1,400. Sydney, 21 Nov 1988, *Children under Tall Gum Trees* (1945, watercolour, 12 1/2 x 15 3/4 ins / 32 x 40 cm) AUD 17,000. London, 1 Dec 1988, *Rocks and Brushwood* (oil on canvas, 24 x 20 ins / 61 x 51 cm) GBP 3,960; *Gum Trees in Sunshine, Hahndorf* (1954, pencil and watercolour, 12 3/4 x 15 3/4 ins / 32.3 x 40.1 cm) GBP 24,200. London, 30 Nov 1989, *The Picnic* (oil on canvas, 48 x 36 1/4 ins / 122.2 x 92 cm) GBP 143,000. Sydney, 26 March 1990, *Livestock in the Meadow* (charcoal, 8 1/2 x 11 ins / 21.5 x 28 cm) AUD 1,600. Sydney, 2 July 1990, *Still-life, Flowers* (oil on canvas, 19 1/4 x 25 1/4 ins / 49 x 64 cm) AUD 20,000. London, 28 Nov 1991, *Sheep Grazing under Eucalyptus Trees* (pencil and watercolour, 12 3/4 x 10 ins / 32.4 x 25.4 cm) GBP 3,300. Melbourne, 20-21 Aug 1996, *The Stroll* (1920, watercolour, 20 1/4 x 26 1/4 ins / 51.5 x 66.5 cm) AUD 46,000. Hobart, 26 Aug 1996, *Willow Creek, Early Morning* (1924, watercolour, 19 x 24 1/2 ins / 48.5 x 62 cm) AUD 18,400. Melbourne, 29 April 1997, *Livestock Coming Home* (1920, watercolour, 20 x 23 1/2 ins / 50.5 x 59.5 cm) AUD 20,700; *Still-life* (1925, oil on canvas, 23 1/2 x 25 1/2 ins / 60 x 65 cm) AUD 23,000. Melbourne, 27 April 1999, *Still-life* (1925, oil on canvas, 24 x 26 ins / 60 x 65 cm) AUD 28,000. Victoria, 9 Nov 1999, *Morning Light, Ambleside, South Australia* (1957, oil on canvas, 19 x 24 ins / 48 x 60 cm) AUD 34,000. Melbourne, 2 May 2000, *Still-life of Mixed Flowers* (1927, oil on canvas, 25 x 22 ins / 63 x 55 cm) AUD 34,000. Melbourne, 2 May 2000, *Zinnias and Plums* (1925, oil on canvas, 25 x 31 ins / 64 x 79 cm) AUD 44,000. Melbourne, 27 Nov 2001, *Hahndorf* (watercolour and pencil, 12 x 16 ins / 31 x 40 cm) AUD 16,000. Melbourne, 27 Nov 2001, *Pastoral Landscape* (1926, oil on canvas, 26 x 32 ins / 66 x 81 cm) AUD 60,000. Melbourne, 30 April 2002, *Settler's Cottage* (1894, oil on canvas, 25 x 33 ins / 64 x 84 cm) AUD 70,000. Paddington, 25 Aug 2002, *Cows in the Pasture* (1936, watercolour, 19 x 24 ins / 48 x 61 cm) AUD 20,000. Melbourne, 6 May 2003, *Flower Piece* (1925, oil on canvas, 24 x 20 ins / 61 x 51 cm) AUD 32,000. Sydney, 27 Aug 2003, *Near Hahndorf* (1954, watercolour, 20 x 28 ins / 52 x 70 cm) AUD 32,000. Sydney, 20 July 2004, *Druids Range far North, Central Australia* (1932, oil on canvas, 16 x 28 ins / 40 x 70 cm) AUD 30,000. Melbourne, 8 Sept 2004, *Summer Late Afternoon* (1916, watercolour, 15 x 13 ins / 38 x 33 cm) AUD 30,000.

HEYSEN, Nora
Australian, 20th century.
Born 1911, in Adelaide.
Painter. Flowers.

Nora Heysen studied at the School of Fine Arts in Adelaide.

Auction records:
Sydney, 6 Oct 1976, *The Breakfast Table* (1934, oil on canvas, 20 x 18 ins / 50.5 x 46 cm) AUD 480. Sydney, 4 July 1988, *Portrait of Camille Gheysens* (1951, oil on canvas, 41 1/4 x 33 3/4 ins / 105 x 86 cm) AUD 700. Melbourne, 21 Aug 2000, *Still-life with Flowers in a Vase* (oil on canvas on board, 18 x 14 ins / 45 x 35 cm) AUD 11,500. Victoria, 21 Aug 2001, *Still-life with Fucschias* (1939, oil on board, 20 x 17 ins / 51 x 44 cm) AUD 27,000. Sydney, 28 Aug 2001, *Still-life with Spring Flowers in a Glass Bowl* (1982, oil on canvas, 23 x 19 ins / 59 x 49 cm) AUD 18,000. Paddington, 25 Aug 2002, *Still-life with Dahlias in a Jug* (oil on canvas, 16 x 13 ins / 40 x 33 cm) AUD 23,000. Melbourne, 6 May 2003, *Native Flower Posy* (oil on cardboard, 9 x 5 ins / 22 x 12 cm) AUD 3,500. Melbourne, 2 Sept 2003, *Flowers in a Window* (1938, oil on canvas, 20 x 16 ins / 51 x 40 cm) AUD 30,000. Melbourne, 16 June 2004, *Spring Flowers* (oil on canvas on board, 19 x 17 ins / 48 x 44 cm) AUD 26,000. Paddington, 24 Aug 2004, *Still-life* (oil on board, 21 x 17 ins / 53 x 43 cm) AUD 24,000.

HEYSER, Friedrich
German, 19th - 20th century.
Born 12 September 1857, in Gnoien (Mecklenburg-Vorpommern); died 7 October 1921, in Dresden.
Painter. History painting, portraits.
Friedrich Heyser studied with Leon Pohle in Dresden and Ferdinand Keller in Karlsruhe. He was active in Karlsruhe, then in Berlin. In 1891, he settled in Harzburg. He exhibited in Berlin from 1854.

HEYSINGER, Ernest W.
American, 20th century.
Born 1872, in Philadelphia.
Painter.
Ernest Heysinger studied under George R. Bonfield.

HEYSINGER, Julius
German, 19th century.
Active in Leipzig in the middle of the 19th century.
Painter.
MUSEUMS AND GALLERIES:
LEIPZIG: *Portrait.*

HEYVAERT, Pierre
Belgian, 20th century.
Born 1934.
Active from 1957 in Canada.
Sculptor.
Neo-Constructivism.
Pierre Heyvaert studied at the school of industrial and decorative arts in Elsene. His very geometrical sculptures play on the vertical and horizontal tension between half-formed three-dimensional spaces and surfaces that are cut into, for example, roughly triangular shapes.

HEYWARD, Katherine Bayard
American, 20th century.
Born 25 November 1886; died 1974.
Painter.
Also a teacher, Katherine Heyward was a member of the Pen and Brush Club and the American Federation of Arts.

HEYWOOD, Carl
Canadian, 20th century.
Born 6 June 1941, in Toronto (Ontario).
Active in France since 1967.
Engraver.
Carl Heywood trained at the Toronto School of Fine Art from 1959-1963. He settled in France in 1967. He has exhibited in Canada since 1969, and in France since 1972.

HEYWORTH
British, 19th - 20th century.
Painter. Landscapes.
From 1909, Heyworth exhibited at the Royal Academy in London and at the Salon des Artistes Français in Paris.

HI KANG. See **XI GANG**

HI KUMASHIRO. See **YU HI**

HIA K'AO-TCH'ANG. See **XIA KAOCHANG**

HIA K'OUEI. See **XIA KUI**

HIA KIN. See **XIA JIN**

HIA KOUEI. See **XIA GUI**

HIA PING. See **XIA BING**

HIA TCH'ANG. See **XIA CHANG**

HIA TCHE. See **XIA ZHI**

HIA TI. See **XIA DI**

HIA YONG. See **XIA YONG**

HIALTELIN, Thorstein Illia. See **HJALTELIN**

HIANG CHENG-MO. See **XIANG SHENGMO**

HIANG K'OUEI. See **XIANG KUI**

HIANG TÖ-SIN. See **XIANG DEXIN**

HIANG YUAN-PIEN. See **XIANG YUANBIAN**

HIAO LING-TCHO. See **XIAO LINGZHUO**

HIAO-NGAN. See **XIAO-AN**

HIBACK
French, 19th century.
Active in Paris c. 1840.
Engraver (wood).
Hiback is known for the vignettes he made for a publication entitled *Physiologies*.

HIBARNE, Juan Francisco de
Spanish, 17th century.
Born in Saragossa; died 18 November 1635, in Valladolid.
Sculptor.
Juan Francisco de Hibarne was a pupil of Gregorio Fernandez.

HIBBARD, Aldro Thompson
American, 20th century.
Born 25 August 1886, in Falmouth; died 1972.
Painter.
Aldro Hibbard worked in Belmont and Philadelphia.

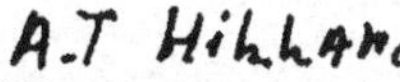

AUCTION RECORDS:
NEW YORK, 18 Sept 1980, *Vermont River Valley* (oil on canvas, 25 x 30 1/4 ins / 63.5 x 76.8 cm) USD 3,750. NEW YORK, 21 Oct 1982, *Winter Landscape* (oil on canvas, 17 1/2 x 23 1/2 ins / 44.5 x 60 cm) USD 2,000. NEW YORK, 8 Dec 1983, *Snowy Landscape* (oil on canvas, 30 x 36 ins / 76.2 x 91.4 cm) USD 9,500. NEW YORK, 29 May 1986, *Snowy Landscape* (oil on canvas, 30 1/4 x 34 ins / 76.8 x 86.4 cm) USD 11,000. NEW YORK, 23 June 1987, *Snowy Landscape* (oil on canvas, 24 1/4 x 32 1/4 ins / 61.5 x 82 cm) USD 5,000. NEW YORK, 30 Sept 1988, *Maple Sap Harvesters' Cabin* (oil on canvas, 17 3/4 x 25 ins / 45.4 x 63.5 cm) USD 4,950. NEW YORK, 24 Jan 1989, *Melting Snow in the Valley* (oil on canvas, 19 3/4 x 39 1/4 ins / 50 x 100 cm) USD 9,900. NEW YORK, 28 Sept 1989, *Jeffersonville, Vermont* (oil on canvas, 24 1/4 x 32 ins / 61.6 x 81.5 cm) USD 9,350. NEW YORK, 1 Dec 1989, *Winter in Vermont* (oil on canvas, 28 1/2 x 36 1/4 ins / 72.4 x 92.1 cm) USD 16,500. NEW YORK, 16 March 1990, *Pines Covered in Snow* (oil on canvas, 20 1/4 x 34 ins / 51.2 x 86.5 cm) USD 7,700. NEW YORK, 12 April 1991, *Snowy Landscape in Vermont with the River Winhall* (oil on canvas, 23 3/4 x 42 ins / 60.3 x 106.7 cm) USD 10,450. NEW YORK, 15 May 1991, *Mountains in Vermont* (oil on reinforced canvas, 17 x 21 ins / 43.2 x 53.3 cm) USD 2,475. NEW YORK, 18 Dec 1991, *First Snow* (oil on canvas, 22 x 30 ins / 55.9 x 76.2 cm) USD 2,970. NEW YORK, 10 March 1993, *Southern Vermont* (1924, oil on canvas, 30 x 34 ins / 76.2 x 86.4 cm) USD 10,925. NEW YORK, 17 March 1994, *Spring Returns to Shelburne in Vermont* (oil on canvas, 30 1/2 x 40 ins / 77.5 x 101.6 cm) USD 37,375. PARIS, 10 April 1995, *Snowy Landscape* (oil on canvas/card, 10 1/4 x 13 1/2 ins / 26 x 34 cm) FRF 9,500. NEW YORK, 21 May 1996, *Flags Flying on St Mark's Square, Venice* (oil on canvas, 25 x 21 ins / 63.5 x 53.5 cm) USD 29,900. NEW YORK, 3 Dec 1996, *Canal in Venice* (1914, oil on card, a pair, 11 x 9 ins / 28 x 22.8 cm) USD 5,520. MICHIGAN, 10 Nov 1999, *Covered Bridge, Vermont* (oil on canvas, 25 x 30 ins / 64 x 76 cm) USD 14,000. NEW YORK, 1 Dec 1999, *Christmas Eve, Swiftwater, New Hampshire* (oil on canvas, 24 x 30 ins / 62 x 76 cm) USD 22,000. NEW YORK, 4 Oct 2000, *Country Store, Rawsonville* (oil on canvas, 28 x 5 ins / 71 x 13 cm) USD 32,000. BOSTON, 10 Nov 2000, *Bald Mountain Brook at Jamaica, Vermont* (oil on canvasboard, 18 x 25 ins / 46 x 63 cm) USD 7,000. BOSTON, 16 Nov 2001, *Inlet, Provincetown* (oil

on canvasboard, 9 x 11 ins / 22 x 27 cm) USD 9,000. PHILADELPHIA, 9 Dec 2001, *Covered Bridge, Late Autumn* (oil on canvas, 24 x 30 ins / 61 x 76 cm) USD 8,500. NORTH BETHESDA, 9 Nov 2002, *Vermont Hills* (oil on canvasboard, 16 x 20 ins / 41 x 51 cm) USD 7,000. LOS ANGELES, 20 Nov 2002, *Snowy Valley* (oil on canvas, 38 x 50 ins / 96 x 127 cm) USD 10,000. BOSTON, 21 Nov 2003, *Wooden Bridge* (oil on canvas, 28 x 36 ins / 72 x 91 cm) USD 26,000. SAN FRANCISCO, 10 Dec 2003, *Winter Stream* (oil on canvas, 30 x 36 ins / 76 x 91 cm) USD 10,000. OREGON, 14 Sept 2004, *Dry Dock, Gloucester, Mass* (canvas on board, 18 x 20 ins / 46 x 51 cm) USD 13,000. BOSTON, 26 Sept 2004, *Snowy Mountain View* (oil on board, 18 x 15 ins / 46 x 38 cm) USD 7,500.

HIBBARD, Frederick Cleveland
American, 20th century.
Born 15 June 1881, in Canton (Missouri); died 1950, in Chicago.
Sculptor. Military subjects, portraits.
Frederick Hibbard studied at the Art Institute of Chicago. He was a member of the Chicago Society of Artists and the American Federation of Arts. He painted portraits and military subjects.

HIBBART, William
British, 18th - 19th century.
Active in Bath between 1760 and 1800.
Painter, engraver (etching).
William Hibbart engraved in the manner of Worlidge. His works include portraits of *Antoine Watteau, Laurence Delvaux* and *Samuel Derrick.*

HIBBERT (Miss)
British, 19th century.
Active in London.
Miniaturist.
Miss Hibbert exhibited in London at the Royal Academy and the Suffolk Street Gallery between 1836 and 1840.

HIBBERT, J.
British, 19th century.
Active at the beginning of the 19th century.
Engraver, lithographer.
J. Hibbert produced a number of portraits.

HIBINO, Katsuhito
Japanese, 20th century.
Painter, decorative artist, installation artist, performance artist. Multimedia.
Hibino Katsuhito graduated from the design division of the fine arts department of Tokyo University of Fine Arts and Music in 1982. He takes part in group exhibitions. He took part in the Sixth Sydney Biennial, and exhibited his work in a one-man show at Hajuku, Japan, in 1983. In 1985, he created *Hibino Theatre,* a video performance. His paintings seem to be a latter-day, more aggressive version of Fauvist painting.
AUCTION RECORDS:
PARIS, 13 April 1988, *Graceful People* (acrylic/card, 65 x 71 ins / 165 x 180 cm) FRF 8,000.

HIBLER, Sylvester
Bohemian, 18th century.
Active in Zasmuk at the beginning of the 18th century.
Miniaturist.

HIBON, Auguste
French, 19th century.
Born 1780, in Paris; died 1857, in Paris.
Engraver.
Hibon was a pupil of Percier and Fontaine, whose engravings were mostly on architectural subjects. He made his Salon début in 1817.

HIBON, Marianne
French, 18th century.
Painter.
Marianne Hibon was admitted into the Académie de St-Luc in 1749.

HICANUS
Sculptor.
Ancient Greek.
Hicanus is mentioned in Pliny the Elder.

HICHESK
19th century.
Painter. Landscapes.
Hichesk is mentioned by Florence Levy.
AUCTION RECORDS:
NEW YORK, 26-28 Feb 1902, *The Dunes,* FRF 2,300.

HICK, Jean
Belgian, 20th century.
Born 1933, in Seraing (Liège).
Painter, draughtsman, watercolourist.
Jean Hick studied at the Académie Ranson and in the studio of S.W. Hayter in Paris.

HICK, Mattheus Jansz.
Dutch, 17th century.
Born 1580, in Leiden; died c. 1650, in Leiden.
Painter.

HICKEL, Anton Karl
Austrian, 18th century.
Born 1745, in Ceský Krumlov, Bohemia (now Ceská Lípa, Czech Republic); died 30 October 1798, in Hamburg.
Painter. Portraits, genre scenes.
Anton Hickel worked with his brother, Joseph Hickel, and at the academy of art in Vienna. He visited the Tyrol and Switzerland, and stayed in France where he painted the portraits of *Marie-Antoinette* and the *Princess of Lamballe.* He exhibited at the Society of Artists in 1791 and at the Royal Academy in London from 1792 to 1796.

He lived in England during the French Revolution and it was during this period that he executed his famous painting depicting the *House of Commons* including about a hundred figures, in addition to the portrait of William Pitt.
MUSEUMS AND GALLERIES:
BASEL: *Portrait of Bürgermeister J de Bary* - LONDON (National Portrait Gal.): *Welbore Ellis, 1st Baron Mendip* (1793, oil on canvas); *William Pitt addressing the House of Commons on the French Declaration of War, 1793* (1793-1795, oil on canvas); *Charles James Fox* (1793-1794, oil on canvas) - VIENNA (Kunsthistorisches Mus.).
AUCTION RECORDS:
PARIS, 4 May 1921, *Portrait of a Woman in Disgrace,* FRF 1,900. LONDON, 19 March 1928, *William Wilberforce, Esq,* GBP 115. LONDON, 9 July 1993, *Portrait of a Nun Growing Vegetables in a Wood* (1790, oil on canvas, 26 3/4 x 20 3/4 ins / 68 x 53 cm) GBP 9,775.

HICKEL, Joseph
Austrian, 18th century.
Born 19 March 1736, in Böhmisch-Leipa (now Ceská Lípa, Czech Republic); died 28 March 1807, in Vienna.
Painter. Religious subjects, genre scenes, portraits.
Hickel was extremely precocious, being only 14 when he painted the altarpiece in the church in Hirschberg (Bohemia). When he came to Vienna, he was greatly appreciated by Empress Maria-Theresa who became his patron and sent him to Italy to make copies of the portraits of the Italian nobility. He left over 3,000 portraits, including many of *Emper-*

or *Joseph*, some of *Winck, Elector Charles-Theodore* and of many members of the Italian and Austrian aristocracy.

AUCTION RECORDS:

LONDON, 29 June 1928, *Joseph II, Emperor of Austria*, GBP 35. LONDON, 30 Nov 1977, *The Engaged Couple* (oil on canvas, 39 3/4 x 32 1/2 ins / 101 x 82.5 cm) GBP 1,800. NEW YORK, 7 Oct 1994, *Portrait of Prince Joseph Wenzel von Lichtenstein Wearing the Medal of the Order of the Golden Fleece* (oil on canvas, 29 x 23 ins / 73.7 x 58.4 cm) USD 13,800. LONDON, 9 Nov 1994, *Portrait of a Young Boy Playing in a Landscape with his Drum and Dog* (oil on canvas, 51 1/2 x 42 ins / 131 x 106.5 cm) GBP 3,450. LONDON, 8 July 1999, *Emperor Josef II Wearing Military Uniform, Orders* (oil on canvas, 36 x 29 ins / 92 x 74 cm) GBP 25,000. VENICE, 15 Dec 2000, *Portrait of Ferdinand, Archduke of Austria and Governor of Milan* (oil on canvas, 59 x 44 ins / 151 x 111 cm) ITL 45,000,000. VENICE, 15 Dec 2000, *Portrait of Maria Beatrice d'Este, Archduchess of Austria* (oil on canvas, 59 x 44 ins / 150 x 111 cm) ITL 45,000,000. LONDON, 11 Dec 2003, *Portrait of Maria-Theresia, Altgrafin Zu Salmreifferscheidt-Raitz, Half Length* (oil on canvas, 30 x 23 ins / 75 x 58 cm) GBP 7,500.

HICKEL, Joseph, or Hickl
German, 19th century.
Born 1781, in Schrobenhausen.
Painter. Historical scenes, portraits.

Joseph Hickel studied in Munich under Hauber.

HICKEY, Isabel
American, 20th century.
Born 25 October 1872, in Philadelphia; died 1931.
Painter.

Isabel Hickey studied at the Pennsylvania Academy of the Fine Arts, Philadelphia. She also worked in France, Italy and Spain. She was a member of the Pennsylvania Academy of the Fine Arts and the American Federation of Arts.

HICKEY, John
Irish, 18th century.
Born 1756, in Dublin; died 12 January 1795, in London.
Sculptor.

The younger brother of Thomas Hickey, John Hickey exhibited in London at the Royal Academy from 1777 to 1794.

HICKEY, Thomas
Irish, 18th - 19th century.
Born 1741, in Dublin; died 20 May 1824, in Madras.
Painter. Portraits.

Thomas Hickey studied at the Dublin Academy. His portraits include those of *Mrs Abington, John Duke of Bedford* and *George Marquess Townshend*. He went to Italy and also travelled to China with Lord Macartney. His works are of interest to collectors. He exhibited at the Royal Academy between 1772 and 1792.

MUSEUMS AND GALLERIES:

DUBLIN: *Portrait of Dr Samuel Madden.*

AUCTION RECORDS:

LONDON, 11 Dec 1909, *Portraits of the Earl of Sheffield and Colonel Ridley*, GBP 162. LONDON, 8 July 1927, *Sir George Staunton*, GBP 199. PARIS, 15 May 1931, *Full-length Portrait of Sir George Staunton as a Child*, FRF 5,200. NEW YORK, 18 April 1934, *Richard Westenra*, USD 250. LONDON, 5 July 1935, *Man in a Wine-Coloured Waistcoat*, GBP 78. LONDON, 16 July 1937, *Miss Charlotte Dee in Pink*, GBP 147. LONDON, 17 June 1966, *Portrait of Thomas Graham of Kinross*, Gns 1,800. LONDON, 6 April 1973, *Green Parasol*, Gns 750. LONDON, 21 March 1979, *Portrait of Mrs Frances Johnson* (oil on canvas, 29 1/2 x 24 1/2 ins / 75 x 62.5 cm) GBP 600. LONDON, 26 June 1981, *Baptism* (after 1798, oil on canvas, 77 3/4 x 99 1/2 ins / 197.5 x 252.7 cm) GBP 8,500. LONDON, 13 Dec 1982, *Portrait of Lieutenant Alexander Perkins Lindsay* (1787, oil on canvas, 18 x 15 ins / 46 x 38 cm) GBP 1,600. NEW YORK, 24 March 1983, *Portrait of a Man* (1782 and 1784, oil on canvas, a pair, oval, 10 1/4 x 8 ins / 26 x 20.5 cm) USD 2,200. NEW YORK, 17 Jan 1985, *Portrait of Miss Charlotte Dee, later Lady Nugent* (1781, oil on canvas, 35 1/4 x 29 1/4 ins / 89.5 x 74.5 cm) USD 12,000. LONDON, 15 July 1987, *Portrait of an Indian Princess* (oil on canvas, 29 1/2 x 24 1/2 ins / 75 x 62.5 cm) GBP 7,500. LONDON, 17 Nov 1987, *Portrait of a Young Lady* (1784, pencil, black and white chalks/grey paper, 15 x 11 1/4 ins / 38 x 28.8 cm) GBP 4,200. LONDON, 12 July 1989, *Boy with his Nurse* (oil on canvas, 53 1/2 x 66 1/4 ins / 136 x 168 cm) GBP 11,000. LONDON, 10 April 1991, *Portrait of a Lady of the Abergavenny Family and her Three Children* (four oils on canvas, oval, collection, 12 3/4 x 11 ins / 32.5 x 27 cm) GBP 2,640. LONDON, 15 Nov 1991, *Head and Shoulders Portrait of Mary Wathen in White by a Column in a Wooded Landscape* (1794, oil on canvas, 29 1/4 x 25 ins / 74.2 x 63.5 cm) GBP 7,150. LONDON, 6 April 1993, *Portrait of a Gentleman with his Wife at the Harpsichord* (1781, oil on canvas, 20 1/4 x 16 1/2 ins / 51.5 x 42 cm) GBP 4,600. LONDON, 12 July 1999, *Portrait of an Indian Princess* (oil on canvas, 30 x 24 ins / 75 x 62 cm) GBP 15,000. LONDON, 8 June 2000, *Portrait of a Young Girl with a Butterfly. Portrait of a Young Boy* (oil on canvas, oval, a pair, 12 x 10 ins / 30 x 25 cm) GBP 5,800. LONDON, 28 Nov 2002, *Portrait of a Young Officer* (oil on canvas, 10 x 8 ins / 26 x 20 cm) GBP 4,400.

HICKFORD
British, 18th century.
Active in Florence in the middle of the 18th century.
Painter.

Hickford was the first teacher of Cipriani.

HICKIN, George
British, 19th century.
Active in Greenwich.
Painter. Landscapes, still-lifes, animals.

George Hickin exhibited frequently in London at the Royal Academy, the British Institution and the Suffolk Street Gallery from 1858 to 1877.

AUCTION RECORDS:

LONDON, 16 July 1976, *Pont Aber Glaslyn* (oil on canvas, 20 x 30 1/2 ins / 51 x 77.5 cm) GBP 260. LONDON, 14 June 1979, *Woodgathering* (oil on canvas, 12 x 16 ins / 30.5 x 40.5 cm) GBP 580. EDINBURGH, 30 Aug 1988, *Wounded Grouse* (oil on canvas, 9 x 11 1/2 ins / 22 x 29 cm) GBP 550. LONDON, 27 Sept 1989, *Farmyard Poultry* (oil on canvas, 24 x 20 ins / 61 x 51 cm) GBP 2,420. LONDON, 3 Feb 1993, *Still-life with Game on an Entablature* (1853, oil on canvas, 17 1/4 x 23 1/2 ins / 44 x 60 cm) GBP 1,035. CREWKERNE, 18 Nov 1999, *Cock Fighting Set To. The Fight* (watercolour heightened with gouache, a pair, 6 x 8 ins / 16 x 21 cm) GBP 1,250. BATH, 6 Dec 1999, *Still-life with Fruit, Flowers and Bowl of Goldfish* (1847, oil on canvas, 30 x 24 ins / 75 x 62 cm) GBP 2,200. LONDON, 23 May 2001, *Guinea Fowl* (oil on canvas, 24 x 20 ins / 61 x 51 cm) GBP 2,000.

HICKMANN, Fritz
German, 19th century.
Born 6 January 1820, in Schiltz; died 24 May 1900, in Schiltz.
Painter, miniaturist, lithographer.

Hickmann worked in Frankfurt am Main, Cologne, Brussels and Ghent.

AUCTION RECORDS:

PARIS, 10 Dec 1992, *Family Portrait* (oil on canvas, 59 x 45 ins / 150 x 114 cm) FRF 38,000.

HICKMANN, Werner
German, 20th century.
Born in Meissen; died 11 January 1914, in Hermsdorf.
Painter.

Werner Hickmann lived in Freiberg and Langebrück.

HICKOK, Conde Wilson
American, 20th century.
Born in Batavia (Illinois).
Painter. Landscapes.

Primarily a landscape painter, Conde Hickok worked in Chicago and was a member of several artists' associations in that city.

HICKS, Edward
American, 18th - 19th century.
Born 4 April 1780, in Attleboro, now Langhorne (Pennsylvania); died 23 August 1849, in Newton (Pennsylvania).
Painter. Scenes with figures.
Folk Art.

Public attention will always focus on the abundance of Naive painting in the USA during the 19th century, and Edward Hicks is possibly the most accomplished and characteristic exponent of this style. It would be interesting to undertake a study of the style to attempt to define the differences between the climate of American Naive painting and that of French or European Naive painting from the same period; the findings would certainly indicate geographical, historical and social reasons underlying the differences. Hicks was a Quaker, a fervent preacher and a painter of carriages and signs. He gave himself to painting wholeheartedly but it weighed down on him as a reprehensible weakness, and he justified his art by depicting edifying subjects. In particular, he depicted the theme of the *Peaceable Kingdom* over 100 times, a theme in which humans and especially children and domestic animals live in peace with the most ferocious of beasts such as lions, tigers, leopards and wolves.

While the Naivety of his style, and its concomitant charm, are evident in his flat, stylised treatment of animals, his background landscapes, more skilfully evoked, are inspired by the American landscape artists of the time. The warmth of the colours, the abundance of decorative features in the composition and the heavy regard with which the animals and people bear down on the viewer all contribute to the strangeness of the poetic climate of these paradisiacal works.

Hicks' work featured in *L'Héroique et le Quotidien: Les Artistes Américains, 1820-1920* (*The Heroic and the Everyday: American Artists, 1820-1920*) at the Musée d'Art Américain in Giverny in 2001.

BIBLIOGRAPHY:

Price Mather, Eleanore/Canning Miller, Dorothy, *Edward Hicks: his Peaceable kingdoms and other paintings*, University of Delaware Press, Newark (DE), 1983. Ford, Alice, *Edward Hicks: his life and art*, Abbeville Press, New York, 1985. Weekley, Carolyn J., *The kingdoms of Edward Hicks*, Colonial Williamsburg Foundation, Williamsburg (VA), 1999.

MUSEUMS AND GALLERIES:

BUFFALO (Albright-Knox AG): *Peaceable Kingdom* (c. 1848, oil on canvas) - CHICAGO (Terra Foundation for American Art Collection): *Peaceable Kingdom and Quakers Bearing Banners* (c. 1827, oil on canvas) - MONTGOMERY (MFA, Blount Collection): *Peaceable Kingdom* (c. 1830-1832, oil on canvas) - PHILADELPHIA (MA): *Noah's Ark* (1846-1848, oil on canvas) - SYRACUSE (Everson MA): *Peaceable Kingdom* (c. 1840-1844, oil on canvas) - WORCESTER, MA (AM): *Peaceable Kingdom* (c. 1833, oil on canvas).

AUCTION RECORDS:

NEW YORK, 14 Nov 1973, *Golden Age*, USD 65,000. NEW YORK, 27 Oct 1977, *Peaceable Kingdom* (1847, oil on canvas, 24 x 32 ins / 61 x 81.2 cm) USD 125,000. NEW YORK, 21 Nov 1980, *Residence of David Twining* (oil on canvas, 26 x 29 3/4 ins / 66 x 75.5 cm) USD 270,000. NEW YORK, 29 Nov 1990, *Penn's Treaty with the Indians* (1847, oil on canvas, 25 x 30 ins / 63.5 x 76.2 cm) USD 990,000. NEW YORK, 3 Dec 1997, *Washington on the Banks of the Delaware* (oil on canvas, 32 1/2 x 31 1/2 ins / 82.5 x 80 cm) USD 233,500. NEW YORK, 21 Jan 2000, *William Penn's Treaty, 1681* (oil on canvas, 24 x 29 ins / 61 x 74 cm) USD 575,000. NEW YORK, 28 Nov 2001, *Grave of William Penn* (1847, oil on canvas, 24 x 31 ins / 60 x 79 cm) USD 115,000. NEW YORK, 16 Jan 2003, *Washington at the Delaware* (oil on canvas, 13 x 13 ins / 32 x 32 cm) USD 320,000.

HICKS, George Edgar or Elgar
British, 19th - 20th century.
Born 1824, in Lymington; died 1914, in London.
Painter. History painting, religious subjects, portraits, genre scenes.

George Edgar Hicks was member of the Royal Society of British Artists. He initially concentrated on scenes of contemporary life, but also produced a small number of paintings with biblical, historical and literary themes. From about the mid-1870s he began to paint portraits. Like many other well known Victorian painters he devoted himself to this lucrative activity for some 15 years. Around 1857 he painted several family portraits on the theme of the mother and child. This genre of portrait painting became his speciality: at least nine family portraits of aristocratic women and their children by him are known. From 1847 he exhibited in London, at the Royal Academy, the British Institution and the Suffolk Street Gallery.

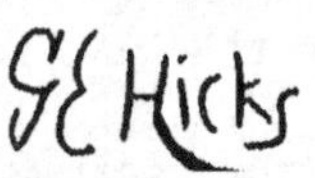

BIBLIOGRAPHY:

Allwood, Rosamond, *George Elgar Hicks, Painter of Victorian Life*, exhibition catalogue, Geffrye Museum, London, 1983.

MUSEUMS AND GALLERIES:

CAPE TOWN: *Cupid's Dream* - LONDON (Mus. of London): *The General Post Office - One Minute to Six* (1860).

AUCTION RECORDS:

PARIS, 25 Jan 1896, *The Count and Countess of Dashley*, FRF 536. LONDON, 28 Nov 1908, *Haymaking* (1864) GBP 6. LONDON, 18 March 1911, *Zilla* (1877) GBP 47. LONDON, 24 July 1911, *Leitah*, GBP 1. NEW YORK, 14 Nov 1941, *The Fisherman's Wife*, USD 360. LONDON, 5 Oct 1945, *Dividend Day*, GBP 84. LONDON, 8 July 1966, *Dividend Day*, Gns 1,500. LONDON, 19 Oct 1971, *The General Post Office - One Minute to Six*, GBP 7,200. LONDON, 15 Oct 1976, *Bayeux Tapestry* (1899, oil on canvas, 35 x 71 ins / 89 x 180.5 cm) GBP 1,000. LONDON, 2 Feb 1979, *Snowdrops* (1858, oil on canvas, 20 1/4 x 16 1/2 ins / 51.4 x 42 cm) GBP 1,900. THETFORD, 21 May 1984, *Portrait of Adelaide Maria, Countess of Iveagh* (1855, oil on canvas) GBP 120,000. LONDON, 12 April 1985, *Wars of the Roses* (1865, oil on canvas, 19 3/4 x 15 3/4 ins / 50 x 40 cm) GBP 8,000. LONDON, 26 June 1987, *Found* (1874, oil on canvas, 24 x 20 ins / 61 x 50.8 cm) GBP 11,000. LONDON, 23 Sept 1988, *Young Rose Seller* (1910, oil on canvas, 24 x 20 ins / 61 x 51 cm) GBP 4,950. NEW YORK, 23 Feb 1989, *Mrs Baxendale and her Children* (1887, oil on canvas, 83 3/4 x 65 1/2 ins / 212.8 x 166.2 cm) USD 33,000. STOCKHOLM, 14 Nov 1989, *Convalescence: Interior with Young Woman and Old Man in Bed* (1862, oil on canvas, 29 1/2 x 24 1/2 ins / 75 x 62 cm) SEK 57,000. LONDON, 13 Dec 1989, *The Blind Reader* (1872, oil on canvas, 16 1/2 x 23 1/2 ins / 42 x 60 cm) GBP 19,800. NEW YORK, 28 Feb 1990, *The Cherry* (1857, oil on canvas, 24 x 20 ins / 61 x 50.8 cm) USD 10,450. LONDON, 13 June 1990, *Croquet* (1864, oil on panel, 6 x 9 3/4 ins / 15.5 x 25 cm) GBP 4,400. LONDON, 19 June 1990, *The General Post Office - One Minute to Six* (1860, oil on canvas, 35 x 53 1/4 ins / 89 x 135 cm) GBP 231,000. LONDON, 30 Nov 1990, *Portrait of the Duchess of St Albans Seated with her Son on her Knees* (1875, oil on canvas, 36 x 28 ins / 91.5 x 71 cm) GBP 16,500. LONDON, 12 Nov 1992, *Young Companions* (1878, oil on card, 18 x 14 ins / 46 x 35.5 cm) GBP 14,300. LONDON, 9 June 1994, *Portrait of Adelaide Maria, Countess of*

Iveagh (oil on canvas, 64 1/4 x 90 1/2 ins / 163 x 230 cm) GBP 78,500. NEW YORK, 24 May 1995, *The Three Graces* (1866, oil on canvas, 48 x 30 ins / 121.9 x 76.2 cm) USD 34,500. PARIS, 13 Oct 1995, *Soirée dans un intérieur* (1862, oil on panel, 8 1/4 x 11 ins / 21 x 27 cm) FRF 25,000. LONDON, 6 Nov 1995, *Motherhood* (oil on canvas, 35 3/4 x 28 ins / 91 x 71 cm) GBP 10,580. LONDON, 6 Nov 1996, *The Butterfly* (1866, oil on canvas, 21 1/2 x 17 ins / 54.5 x 43 cm) GBP 36,700. LONDON, 12 March 1997, *Zilla* (1877, oil on card, a pair, 17 x 14 ins / 43 x 35.5 cm) GBP 47,700.

HICKS, Herbert
American, 20th century.
Born 26 June 1894, in Ohio; died after 1963, in Arlington (Virginia).
Painter, illustrator.

Herbert Hicks was a member of the Washington Watercolor Club.

HICKS, Lilburne
British, 19th century.
Died 1861.
Active in London.
Painter, watercolourist. Genre scenes.

A member of the New Water-Colour Society, Lilburne Hicks frequently exhibited there and also at the Royal Academy and the Suffolk Street Gallery between 1830 and 1860.

HICKS, Nicola
British, 20th - 21st century.
Born 1960.
Sculptor, draughtswoman. Figures, animals.

Nicola Hicks uses plaster and straw to produce fantastical half-men, half-animal figures. She also produces powerful drawings on brown paper. In 1995, she took part in the FIAC (Foire Internationale d'Art Contemporain) in Paris, presented by the Angela Flowers Gallery, London.

AUCTION RECORDS:
LONDON, 20 Sept 1990, *Walking Dog* (1984, pastel, charcoal and white chalk/brown paper, 39 1/4 x 59 ins / 100 x 150 cm) GBP 880. LONDON, 26 March 1993, *Oi* (1988, painted plaster and straw, h. 50 ins / 127 cm) HBP 2,300. LONDON, 26 Oct 1994, *Nice Little Earner* (1988, bronze, h. 41 ins / 104 cm) GBP 9,200. LONDON, 22 May 1996, *Nice Little Earner* (1988, bronze) GBP 6,325. LONDON, 23 Oct 1996, *Elephant* (1988, chalk/brown paper, in two parts, 66 1/2 x 73 1/2 ins / 169 x 187 cm) GBP 4,025. LONDON, 17 July 2001, *Standing Hare* (1986, charcoal, 44 x 32 ins / 111 x 81 cm) GBP 1,800. LONDON, 14 Nov 2001, *Pacific Dreaming 2* (1990, charcoal and chalk, 68 x 53 ins / 173 x 134 cm) GBP 1,800. LONDON, 12 March 2002, *Dog 3, Lying on Its Back* (1996, charcoal and pastel, 177 x 71 ins / 450 x 180 cm) GBP 4,000. LONDON, 12 March 2002, *Ready to Jump* (black patinated bronze, 45 x 50x26 ins / 115 x 128x65 cm) GBP 10,000. LONDON, 4 Feb 2004, *Nice Little Earner* (1988, grey patinated bronze, 41 x 34 ins / 104 x 86 cm) GBP 11,500. LONDON, 17 Nov 2004, *Nice Little Earner* (1988, brown patinated bronze, h. 42 ins / 107 cm) GBP 10,000.

HICKS, Robert
British, 19th century.
Reproductions engraver.

Robert Hicks provided illustrations for a number of publications.

HICKS, Sheila
American, 20th century.
Born 1934, in Hastings (Nebraska).
Painter, hand-weaver. Designs for tapestries.

Sheila Hicks started out as a painter, studying with Joseph Albers at Yale University from 1953 to 1959. Albers gave her a good understanding of materials and at the end of her studies she wrote a thesis on pre-Inca textiles. She then travelled to South America, visiting Venezuela, Bolivia, Ecuador, Argentina and Chile, before settling in Mexico the following year. This time spent in Latin America taught Hicks a great deal and the influence of the ancient Inca and Aztec finery can be seen in her work. However her research extended in all directions, from tradition to industry, that could help her to perfect her understanding of materials and techniques. During a stay in France in 1961 she became particularly interested in 17th and 18th-century passementerie. She then went back to Mexico, where she had her first exhibition of tapestries in 1962. After this her work was shown throughout the world, in both solo and group exhibitions, including all the tapestry biennales.

In 1964 Hicks moved to France, where she founded and led a workshop. In 1970 she went to Morocco at the invitation of the Moroccan government and, in 1972, opened another weaving workshop in Mexico with the benefit of the experience she had gained from the Taller Artesanal Huaquen (Huaquen Craft Workshop) she founded in Valparaíso in 1968. The 1960s were a period of great upheaval in tapestry, freeing it from the confines of the simple weaving of images. In this regard Hicks' work was very important.

Formally her tapestries are more like textile sculptures than traditional tapestries. Marie-France Aubert describes them as 'strange scalps coming down the wall, hairy fleeces, woolly cascades in which spidery architectures intertwine, where bundles of threads play at parallax, lianas bursting from the ceiling, wound round a column, silky masses crouching like drowsy animals', while the ethnologist Claude Lévi-Strauss wrote of Hicks' work, 'Reaching beyond centuries in which the incomparable works of Ancient Peru have been forgotten or ignored, Sheila Hicks has managed to recover and assimilate their tradition, combining it with others, such as those of Persia and India. Without ever copying them, she has given them new life through original ideas which adapt them to present-day raw materials, techniques and aspirations.'

She has held solo shows all over the world since 1958, notably at the Stedelijk Museum, Amsterdam, in 1974; at the Konstall, Lund, in 1978 and 1986; at the Israel Museum, Jerusalem, in 1980; at the Musée des Arts Décoratifs, Paris, in 1985; at Matsuya Ginza, Tokyo, in 1990; National Museum of Decorative Arts, Prague, in 1992; at the Museum of Nebraska Art, Kearney, in 1996; and the Kiryu Municipal Arts Center, Japan, in 1997.

HICKS, Thomas
American, 19th century.
Born 18 October 1823, in Newton (Pennsylvania); died 1890.
Painter. Religious subjects, genre scenes, portraits.

Thomas Hicks was a pupil of Couture in Paris. His works include a *Death of Abel*. He may have been the son of Edward Hicks.

AUCTION RECORDS:
NEW YORK, 21 and 22 Jan 1909, *By the Hearth*, USD 100. NEW YORK, 25 March 1931, *George Washington*, USD 650. LONDON, 12 March 1985, *Portrait of Elizabeth Sherman* (1862, oil on mounted canvas on board, oval, 29 1/4 x 24 1/2 ins / 74 x 62 cm) GBP 2,600. NEW YORK, 3 Dec 1987, *Portrait of Edward Hicks Painting the Peaceable Kingdom* (1839, oil on canvas, 36 x 28 3/4 ins / 91.4 x 73.2 cm) USD 270,000. NEW YORK, 24 May 1989, *Interior of a Country House* (1862, oil on canvas, 12 3/4 x 16 3/4 ins / 32.4 x 42.5 cm) USD 8,800. NEW YORK, 31 March 1993, *After Twenty Years of Marriage* (oil on canvas, 23 1/4 x 28 3/4 ins / 59.1 x 73 cm) USD 2,990. NEW YORK, 25 May 1995, *Frugal Meal* (1860, oil on canvas, 11 1/2 x 12 1/4 ins / 29.2 x 31.1 cm) USD 6,900. NEW YORK, 22 May 2002, *Red Jacket* (oil on canvas, 32 x 22 ins / 81 x 56 cm) USD 50,000. THOMASTON, 1 Feb 2003, *Home Stretch, Trout All Sold* (1864, oil on canvas) USD 2,750. NEW YORK, 31 March 2004, *No Place Like*

Home (1877, oil on canvas, 22 x 28 ins / 55 x 72 cm) USD 12,000.

HICKSON, Margaret (Miss)
British, 19th century.
Active in London.
Painter. Still-lifes.

Margaret Hickson frequently exhibited in London at the Royal Academy, the Suffolk Street Gallery and the New Water-Colour Society from 1879.

HIDAI, Nankoku
Japanese, 20th century.
Born 1912, in Kamakura.
Painter, calligrapher.

Hidai Nankoku studied calligraphy under his father, Hidai Tenru, who was a member of the Imperial Academy. He graduated from Tokyo Technical College in 1934 and became president of the Institute of Calligraphy Studies in 1939. In 1945, taking Chinese classic forms as his base, he moved towards abstraction, causing a major controversy. By 1948, the break with tradition was final. In 1954, he started working in the Hikaku style, the so-called 'flying ribbon style', which has influenced modern abstract calligraphy. In 1955, he did works using oil on canvas, and has since employed techniques mixing the old and the new, such as ink on card coated with lacquered fibres.

He has given talks at many American universities, including Rutgers and Columbia. During the 1960s, he was twice invited to Brooklyn College by Ad Reinhardt, and taught at the Rudolph Schaeffer School of Design in San Francisco. In 1948 he organised and took part in the exhibition *All Japanese Calligraphy*. In 1956 he organised the first annual Avant Garde Calligraphy Exhibition in memory of his father. In 1959, he showed his work in Holland, at the exhibition *Tradition and Renewal in Japanese Art*, and took part in the 5th São Paulo Biennale. In 1960, he had a one-man show at the San Francisco Fine Arts Museum. In 1961, 1963 and 1965, he had solo shows at the David Cole Gallery in Sausalito, the University of California, Berkeley, and the New York Nippon Club.

AUCTION RECORDS:
NEW YORK, 27 April 1994, *Work No. 59-11* (1959, ink/paper, 27 x 32 ins / 68.6 x 81.3 cm) USD 4,600.

HIDALGO, Antonio
Spanish, 17th century.
Active in Seville at the end of the 17th century.
Painter. Flowers.

HIDALGO DE AGÜERA, Fernando
Spanish, 19th - 20th century.
Born in Madrid.
Painter.

Fernando Hidalgo de Agüera studied at the Real Academia de Bellas Artes de San Fernando in Madrid. He took part in the Exposición Nacional de Bellas Artes until 1910, receiving an honourable mention in 1904 and distinctions in 1908 and 1912.

BIBLIOGRAPHY:
Arnáiz, José Manuel/López Jiménez, Javier/Merchán Díaz, Manuel (ed.), *Cien años de pintura en Espana y Portugal (1830-1930)*, Antiqvaria, Madrid, 1989.

HIDALGO DE CAVIEDES, Hipólito
Spanish, 20th century.
Born 13 July 1902, in Madrid; died 1994, in Madrid.
Painter. Figure compositions, figures, nudes.

Hipólito Hidalgo de Caviedes was the son of Rafael Hidalgo de Caviedes, who was also his teacher. He began exhibiting in Madrid while still a child, and later studied at the Real Academia de Bellas Artes de San Fernando. In 1933 he was awarded a bursary which enabled him to travel to Italy and Germany, studying at the Accademia di Belle Arti in Florence and taking lessons in Berlin. After 1935 he travelled in Europe, then made a long journey to Cuba, the USA and Puerto Rico. He finally returned to Spain in 1961.

Hidalgo de Caviedes took part in the Exposición Nacional de Bellas Artes from 1922. In 1929, he showed an important collection of paintings at the Spanish Society of the Friends of Art, and he continued to show his works in galleries in Spain and abroad. In 1935, he won the first prize awarded by the Carnegie Foundation of Pittsburgh, which established him as one of Spain's most important painters.

Hidalgo de Caviedes' technique was direct and unfussy. His work was figurative, but he synthesised forms, and his colours were naturalistic, but heightened. He aligned himself with the ideas of the École de Paris between the wars.

BIBLIOGRAPHY:
Arnáiz, José Manuel/López Jiménez, Javier/Merchán Díaz, Manuel (ed.), *Cien años de pintura en Espana y Portugal (1830-1930)*, Antiqvaria, Madrid, 1989.

MUSEUMS AND GALLERIES:
CÁCERES (Mus.) - HAVANA (Mus. Nacional, Palacio de Bellas Artes) - JAÉN (Mus. de Jaén) - LUGO (Mus. Provincial) - MADRID (Mus. Nacional Centro de Arte Reina Sofía) - MALABO (Mus. of the Republic of Equatorial Guinea) - PUERTO RICO (MA) - SARAGOSSA (Mus. Ibercaja Camón Aznar) - TOLEDO (MAC) - VALENCIA (MBA).

AUCTION RECORDS:
MADRID, 17 Oct 1979, *The Fates* (oil on canvas, 46 x 32 ins / 116 x 81 cm) ESP 160,000. NEW YORK, 19 Nov 1987, *Elvira and Tiberius* (1935, oil on canvas, 45½ x 61 ins / 115.5 x 155 cm) USD 9,500. NEW YORK, 2 May 1990, *Standing Male Nude* (1937, oil on canvas, 49½ x 30½ ins / 126 x 77.5 cm) USD 7,150. NEW YORK, 5 Nov 1991, *Seated Woman* (oil on canvas, 24 x 20 ins / 61 x 50.8 cm) USD 1,650. MADRID, 27 April 1999, *Nude with Head Lowered* (1975, oil on canvas, 51 x 32 ins / 130 x 81 cm) ESP 550,000. MADRID, 15 Dec 1999, *Chairs* (1964, oil on canvas, 35 x 45 ins / 89 x 115 cm) ESP 550,000. MADRID, 19 Dec 2000, *Boy with Donkey* (1985, oil on canvas, 13 x 16 ins / 32 x 40 cm) ESP 325,000. MADRID, 21 Jan 2003, *Girl with Doves* (oil on canvas, 39 x 30 ins / 100 x 75 cm) EUR 5,000. MADRID, 20 May 2003, *Plañideras II* (*Wailing Women II*) (oil on panel, 26 x 20 ins / 65 x 50 cm) EUR 2,000.

HIDALGO DE CAVIEDES, Rafael
Spanish, 19th - 20th century.
Born 1864, in Quesada near Jaén (Andalusia); died 1950, in Madrid.
Painter. Mythological subjects, figures, portraits, genre scenes, interiors, landscapes.

Rafael Hidalgo de Caviedes studied at the Real Academia de Bellas Artes de San Fernando in Madrid. He was awarded a travel bursary, which enabled him to continue his studies in Italy and other countries in Europe from 1885 to 1890. He took part in group exhibitions, especially the Exposición Nacional de Bellas Artes, winning bronze medals in 1890 and 1897, silver in 1904 and 1908 and distinctions in 1901 and 1912. He taught in Barcelona, became curator of the national archaeological museum, then professor at the school of applied arts in Madrid and deputy director of the national museum of modern art. He was made a Commander of the Order of Alfonso XII.

Hidalgo de Caviedes painted a variety of subjects, particularly figures, ranging from Venus to the Virgin Mary, using traditional 19th-century techniques and making clever use of chiaroscuro and back-lighting.

BIBLIOGRAPHY:
Arnáiz, José Manuel/López Jiménez, Javier/Merchán Díaz, Manuel (ed.), *Cien años de pintura en Espana y Portugal (1830-1930)*, Antiqvaria, Madrid, 1989.

MUSEUMS AND GALLERIES:
MADRID (Ateneo) - MADRID (Prado).

HIDALGO LINARES FERNANDEZ, Juan.
See **LINARES FERNÁNDEZ Juan Hidalgo**

HIDALGO Y PADILLA, Félix Resurrección
Spanish, 19th - 20th century.
Born 1857, in Manila, Philippines; died April 1915, in Paris.
Painter. History painting.

Felix Hidalgo y Padilla won a silver medal in Paris in 1889 and, in the same year, was created a chevalier of the Légion d'Honneur. He studied in Manila and Madrid, and won many awards, notably in Madrid, Paris and Chicago, as well as the major prize in St Louis in 1904.

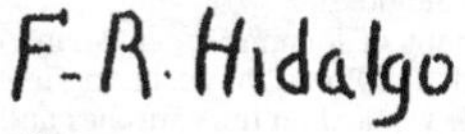

MUSEUMS AND GALLERIES:
TOURCOING: *Fabiola.*

HIDARI, Jingoro
Japanese, 16th century.
Born in Fushimi.
Active at the end of the 16th century.
Sculptor.

Hidari Jingoro is considered one Japan's greatest artists. His wood carving *Sleeping Cat*, one of the most famous works in Japan, is kept behind a silver grille in the Leyasu Temple. He was also an architect.

HIDDEMANN, Benno
German, 19th century.
Born 23 August 1861, in Düsseldorf; died 25 December 1907, in Düsseldorf.
Painter. Genre scenes, landscapes.

Benno Hiddemann first exhibited in Düsseldorf in 1902, only five years before his death.

HIDDEMANN, Friedrich Peter
German, 19th century.
Born 4 October 1829, in Düsseldorf; died 19 January 1892, in Düsseldorf.
Painter, lithographer. Genre scenes.

Friedrich Hiddemann was the father of Benno Hiddemann, and a pupil of Theodor Hildebrand and Schadow at the Düsseldorf academy of art. He first worked as a lithographer. After travelling in Germany, France, Belgium and Holland, he returned to settle in Düsseldorf. He was awarded a medal in Vienna in 1873 and another in Philadelphia in 1876.

MUSEUMS AND GALLERIES:
DÜSSELDORF: *A Bottle of Champagne* - KALININGRAD: *Quartet of Dilettanti.*

AUCTION RECORDS:
LONDON, 31 Oct 1928, *Fire-raiser*, GBP 46. PARIS, 15 June 1934, *School Scene*, FRF 1,000. CANNES, 30 Oct 1979, *The Children and the Clergyman* (1873, oil on canvas, 27 1/4 x 21 1/4 ins / 69 x 54 cm) FRF 30,000. NEW YORK, 28 Oct 1987, *Smoke Rings* (1870, oil on canvas, 27 1/4 x 22 ins / 69.2 x 55.8 cm) USD 11,000. LONDON, 19 June 1992, *The Quartet* (1865, oil on canvas, 26 x 31 ins / 66 x 78.7 cm) GBP 17,050. NEW YORK, 18 March 1998, *The Mysterious Traveller* (1892, oil on canvas, 24 x 29 ins / 61 x 73.7 cm) USD 12,650. COLOGNE, 20 May 2000, *After the Hunt, Children Looking at Dead Stag* (1862, oil on canvas, 16 x 13 ins / 41 x 34 cm) DEM 4,500. COLOGNE, 17 Nov 2001, *On the Terrace of a Village Inn* (1864, oil on panel, 9 x 13 ins / 22 x 32 cm) DEM 4,500. NEW YORK, 29 Sept 2004, *Catch of the Day* (1869, oil on canvas, 24 x 21 ins / 62 x 53 cm) USD 8,000.

HIDDING, Hermann
German, 19th century.
Born 9 May 1863, in Nottnen.
Sculptor.

Hidding studied in Düsseldorf and Berlin, and exhibited at the Berlin academy of art from 1891.

HIDDINGA
German, 18th century.
Born in Hamburg; died 1793.
Watercolourist.

Hiddinga, a pupil of Amama, was definitely related to Gerloff Hiddinga.

HIDDINGA, Gerloff
German, 18th century.
Died 1 April 1766, in Hamburg.
Painter, draughtsman.

Hiddinga was a pupil of Amama who went on to teach drawing in Hamburg. His paintings were primarily of flowers.

HIDE, Peter
British, 20th - 21st century.
Born 1944, in Carshalton (Surrey), England.
Active in Edmonton, Canada.
Sculptor (steel).

Peter Hide studied at the Croydon College of Art (1961-1964) and St Martin's School of Art in London (1964-1967), where he studied under Anthony Caro and was his part-time assistant. From 1968 to 1974 he taught at the Norwich School of Art, and from 1971 to 1978 taught at St Martin's School of Art. In 1978 he moved to Canada to teach at the University of Alberta. By his own admission, although he counts Caro among the sculptors who have most influenced him (along with David Smith and Michael Steiner), his move to Canada was prompted partly by a desire to get away from the influence of Caro, and to seek a space where he could develop and explore his individual style.

Hide works largely in steel, creating massive abstact pieces constructed from plates of steel which are grouped together in 'long pleats and folds', resulting in a 'stiffened, geometric drapery' (T. Fenton).

Hide has exhibited widely, particularly in Canada, but also in the USA and London. Solo exhibitions include: *Monumental Sculptures of Peter Hide* at the Millar Building in Edmonton in Canada (1990); *Peter Hide: In Context*, a retrospective exhibition held at the Edmonton Art Gallery (1998); *Sculpture in the Round* curated by Terry Fenton at Harcout House in Edmonton (2002); and *New Small Sculpture* at the Scott Gallery in Edmonton (2003). Group exhibitions include *Sculpture by Invitation* at the Edmonton Contemporary Art Society Show at the Prince of Wales Armouries (1998), and *Monumental Sculpture at Jesus College* in Cambridge, England (2003).

BIBLIOGRAPHY:
Morris, Derek, *Current British Sculpture*, Norwich School of Art, Norwich, 1979. Hide, Peter, '*Abstraction and the Figure: My Art in Context*' in *Edmonton Review*, vol 5, Issue 1, Summer 1999. '*Steel Hide Away*' in *Border Crossings*, vol 18, no. 1, Review of Exhibition at Edmonton Art Gallery, January 1999.

MUSEUMS AND GALLERIES:
ALGOMA, ONTARIO (Art Gallery of Algoma) - BARCELONA (Museu d'Art Modern) - EDMONTON (Edmonton Art Gallery, Alberta Art Foundation) - FREDERICTON, NEW BRUNSWICK (Beaverbrook Art Gallery) - LONDON (Tate Collection) - TORONTO (Art Gallery of North York) - WATERLOO, ONTARIO (Kitchener Art Gallery).

HIDEKEL, Lezar M.
Russian, 20th century.
Born 1904.
Painter.
Suprematism.

Lezar Hidekel was a pupil of Kazimir Malevich in Vitebsk and attended the Unovis school. In 1922 he left for Petrograd (now St Petersburg) with Malevich to work at GINKhUK (the state institute of culture). At the same time, he studied at the institute of civil engineering until 1928. He contributed to the movement for Suprematist Architecture.

AUCTION RECORDS:

LONDON, 16 Oct 1991, *Suprematist Composition* (oil on canvas, 26 x 32 1/4 ins / 66 x 82 cm) GBP 3,080.

HIDEKUNI, childhood name: Toyokawa
Japanese, 19th century.
Active c. 1825.
Print artist.

HIDEMARO, real name: Kitagawa Hidemaro, artist name: Shorinsai
Japanese, 19th century.
Active in Kyoto c.1823.
Print artist.

HIDENOBU, or Eishin, artist names: Hidenobu, Ungeisai
Japanese, 18th century.
Born 1764; died 1781.
Active in Osaka c. 1760-1770.
Painter, illustrator.

HIDENOBU, childhood name: Kose
Japanese, 19th century.
Active in Osaka c. 1800.
Painter.

HIDEUX, Abraham
French, 16th - 17th century.
Born in Valenciennes; died July 1616, in Tournai.
Sculptor.

In 1596 Abraham Hideux created the chimney-piece of the great hall in the municipal buildings in Lille, and its four carved statues, *France, Justice, Prudence* and *Temperance*.

HIDEUX, Estienne
French, 17th century.
Active in Tournai.
Sculptor.

Estienne Hideux was a member of the Académie de St-Luc in Paris in 1685.

HIDEUX, Isaac
French, 16th - 17th century.
Active in Tournai.
Architect, sculptor.

Isaac Hideux was the son of Abraham Hideux.

HIDEYORI, real name: Kano Joshin or Shoshin, artist name: Hideyori
Japanese, 16th century.
Died 1557.
Painter.
Kano School.

The son and disciple of Motonobu (1476-1559), Hideyori lived at Kyoto.

HIDEYUKI
Japanese, 20th century.
Sculptor (ivory).

HIDLEY, Joseph H.
American, 19th century.
Born 1830, in Poestenkill (New York); died 1872, in Poestenkill.
Painter.

Joseph H. Hidley is known mainly for his panoramic landscapes of his town and some of the surrounding villages. He also painted several religious subjects. The innocent primitivism of his style places him among the American Naive painters of the 19th century.

AUCTION RECORDS:

NEW YORK, 21 Nov 1980, *Poestenkill, New York: Winter* (c. 1865-1870, oil on panel, 18 3/4 x 29 ins / 47.7 x 73.6 cm) USD 65,000. PITTSFIELD, 8 Sept 2001, *Going to Town* (oil on canvas, 23 x 29 ins / 58 x 74 cm) USD 1,700. PITTSFIELD, 8 Sept 2001, *Banks of the Hudson* (oil on canvas, 14 x 24 ins / 36 x 61 cm) USD 2,250.

HIEBEL, Johann
German, 18th century.
Born 1681, in Ottobeuren (Bavaria); died 15 June 1775, in Prague.
Painter. Mythological subjects, religious subjects.
Bohemian School.

Hiebel was a pupil of Johann Siegelbein in Wangen, Kaspar Sing in Munich and Pozzo the Jesuit in Vienna, whose style he imitated. He worked on the churches and monuments in Prague, where he settled in 1709, and collaborated with Byss on the decoration of the house of the Count of Thun. He was represented in the exhibition, *Lumière et ténèbres, art et civilisation du Baroque en Bohême* (*Light and Darkness. Baroque Art and Civilisation in Bohemia*) at the Palais des Beaux-Arts in Lille in 2002.

BIBLIOGRAPHY:

Nevímová, Petra, '*Johann Hiebels Deckenfresko in der Prager Spiegelkapelle*' in *Kunst. Politik. Religion. Studien zur Kunst in Süddeutschland, Österreich, Tschechien und der Slowakei (Art. Politics. Religion. Studies of Art in Southern Germany, Austria, the Czech Republic and Slovakia)*, Imhof, Petersberg, 2000. Vlnas, Vit (ed.), *Lumière et ténèbres, art et civilisation du Baroque en Bohême*, exhibition catalogue, Palais des Beaux-Arts, Lille, Réunion des musées nationaux, Paris, 2002.

HIEBELER, Jakob
German, 17th century.
Active in Füssen.
Painter.

Jakob Hiebeler is best known for a *Dance of Death*.

HIEBELER, Johann Georg
German, 17th century.
Active in Füssen.
Painter.

We know Johann Hiebeler painted a copy after Rubens.

HIEBNER, Israel
Hungarian, 17th century.
Active in Eperjes (now Prešov, Slovakia).
Engraver.

HIEL, Napoléon
Belgian, 19th century.
Born 1823; died 21 January 1862, in Brussels.
Painter.

HIELM, Fanny
Swedish, 19th century.
Born 1858, in Lindesberg.
Miniaturist.

Fanny Hielm was a pupil at the academy in Stockholm around 1880.

HIELM, Karl Jakob
Swedish, 18th - 19th century.
Born 1771, in Falun; died 1827, in Stockholm.
Painter.

Karl Hielm was a pupil of Louis Jean Desprez, and for a long time painted decorative sets for the theatre in Stockholm.

HIEMER
German, 18th century.
Active in Ottobeuren (Bavaria) c. 1720.
Painter.

HIEMER, Franz Karl, or Hlemer
German, 18th century.
Born 1768, in Rottenacker.
Painter.
Franz Karl Hiemer worked in Stuttgart executing mostly portraits.
MUSEUMS AND GALLERIES:
MARBACH (Schiller Nationalmus.): *Portrait of Schiller.*

HIEN, Daniel
French, 18th century.
Born 1725, in Strasbourg; died 1773, in Zweibrücker.
Painter. Still-lifes, flowers.
Several paintings by Daniel Hien are to be found in the galleries in Augsburg and Schleissheim.

HIEN, J. van
Dutch, 18th century.
Active in 1771.
Painter.
He is known to have produced a portrait, dated, of *Salomon van Deventer.*

HIEN MAI VAN. See **MAI VAN HIEN**

HIEN-TSONG MING. See **XIANZONG MING**

HIENCK, J.
Painter. Birds.
J. Hienck is listed in *Art Prices Current.*
AUCTION RECORDS:
LONDON, 21 Dec 1907, *Muscovy Ducks and other Birds* (watercolour) GBP 10.

HIEPES, Tomás, or Yepes or Jepes
Spanish, 17th century.
Born c. 1610, in Valencia; died 16 June 1674, in Valencia.
Painter. Still-lifes (including flowers/fruit).
Tomás Hiepes worked mainly in Valencia, between 1642 and 1668.

His compositions are often balanced in a symmetrical fashion and include detailed depictions of fruit, flowers, fish and game, in the spirit of 17th-century Flemish still-lifes. There are examples of his works in a number of private collections in Madrid and Seville.
BIBLIOGRAPHY:
Jordan, William B./Cherry, Peter, *Spanish Still-life from Velázquez to Goya*, National Gallery, London, 1995 (pp.118-28).
MUSEUMS AND GALLERIES:
MADRID (Prado): *Still-life with Grapes; Table with Dishes; Still-life with Basket of Bread* (1668).
AUCTION RECORDS:
NEW YORK, 2 June 1989, *Young Girl Arranging Bouquets Surrounded by Pots of Flowers in Coloured Faience* (oil on canvas, 39 1/2 x 61 1/4 ins / 100.5 x 155.5 cm) USD 1,017,500. NEW YORK, 11 Jan 1990, *Still-life with Flowering Plants in Majolica Pots* (oil on canvas, a pair, 29 1/4 x 22 1/4 ins / 74.5 x 56.5 cm) USD 319,000. MADRID, 21 May 1991, *Still-life with a Bouquet of Flowers, Fruit and Doves* (oil on canvas, 34 1/4 x 49 1/2 ins / 87 x 126 cm) ESP 29,680,000. MADRID, 29 Oct 1991, *Still-life with a Vase of Flowers, an Artichoke, Fruit and a Salmon* (oil on canvas, 34 1/4 x 50 ins / 87 x 127 cm) ESP 21,280,000. MADRID, 20 Feb 1992, *Still-life with Fruit, Bread in a Basket, Cakes and an Ice Cream Maker on a Table* (oil on canvas, 29 3/4 x 44 ins / 75.5 x 111.5 cm) ESP 10,640,000. LONDON, 29 May 1992, *Teruel Pottery Jug, Decanter, Jar of Cherries, Boxes of Plums and Biscuits on a Bowl on a Table* (oil on canvas, 29 x 37 1/2 ins / 73.7 x 95.5 cm) GBP 60,500. MADRID, 27 Oct 1992, *Still-life with Kitchen Utensils, Fish, Vegetables and Flowers* (oil on canvas, 26 3/4 x 43 3/4 ins / 68 x 111 cm) ESP 8,000,000. PARIS, 23 June 1993, *Bouquet of Flowers in an Antique Style Vase* (oil on canvas, 44 1/2 x 35 3/4 ins / 113 x 91 cm) FRF 1,750,000. PARIS, 10 Dec 1993, *Still-life* (oil on canvas, 27 1/2 x 43 ins / 70 x 109 cm) FRF 780,000. NEW YORK, 12 Jan 1994, *Vine Stock in a Ceramic Pot with Pomegranates, Quinces, Pears and Apples on a Table and French Marigolds Growing in a Ceramic Vase* (1654, oil on canvas, 43 1/2 x 53 ins / 110.5 x 134.6 cm) USD 783,500. NEW YORK, 11 Jan 1995, *Lilies, Narcissi, Tulips, Roses, Passion Flowers, Jasmine and Other Assorted Flowers in a White China Vase Decorated with Bronze on a Table Covered in a Richly Embroidered Cloth* (oil on canvas, 44 1/4 x 35 3/4 ins / 112.5 x 91 cm) USD 442,500.

HIER VAN. See **HIERSCHL-MINERBI Joachim**

HIERBER, Friedrich
German, 18th century.
Active in Mannheim.
Painter. Stage sets (?).
Friedrich Hierber was a son of Georg Hierber the Elder.

HIERBER, Georg, the Elder
German, 18th century.
Died 1768.
Active in Mannheim.
Painter. Landscapes. Stage sets.

HIERBER, Georg, the Younger
German, 18th century.
Active at the end of the 18th century.
Painter. Stage sets.
Georg Hierber the Younger was probably the son of Georg Hierber the Elder.

HIERHOLTZ, Gustave, or Gustav
French, 20th century.
Born 5 August 1877, in Lausanne, to French parents.
Sculptor.
Gustave Hierholtz exhibited in Paris at the Salon des Artistes Français. He received an honourable mention in 1907, a 3rd class medal in 1908, and was a member from 1909.
AUCTION RECORDS:
LONDON, 8 Nov 1984, *Horse* (c. 1910, bronze, h. 16 3/4 ins / 42.5 cm) GBP 1,400.

HIERL-DERONCO, Otto
German, 19th century.
Born 28 July 1859, in Memmingen.
Painter. Historical scenes, portraits, genre scenes.
Hierl-Deronco, a pupil of Lofftz and W Diez at the Munich academy of art, won medals in London in 1884, in Barcelona in 1888 and in Paris at the Exposition Universelle in 1900. He exhibited in Munich and Berlin from 1888.
MUSEUMS AND GALLERIES:
MUNICH (Pinakothek): *At the Theatre.*
AUCTION RECORDS:
LONDON, 26 Nov 1980, *The Arrest of Louis XVI* (1883, oil on canvas, 70 x 99 1/4 ins / 178 x 252 cm) GBP 700. BERN, 30 April 1988, *Bavarian Peasant Woman in Traditional Costume* (oil on canvas, 18 1/2 x 15 3/4 ins / 47 x 40 cm) CHF 2,800. MUNICH, 22 March 2001, *Portrait of Young Woman* (1922, oil on canvas, 33 x 24 ins / 85 x 61 cm) DEM 4,800.

HIERLE, Louis
French, 19th century.
Born in L'Estréchure (Gard).
Painter. Mythological subjects, genre scenes, portraits.
Hierle first exhibited at the Salon in 1881.
MUSEUMS AND GALLERIES:
BAGNOLS: *Young Woman; Madame Garidel.*
AUCTION RECORDS:
NEW YORK, 20 Feb 1992, *Diana at Rest* (1887, oil on canvas, 47 1/2 x 78 1/2 ins / 120.7 x 199.4 cm) USD 13,200.

HIERLITZ, Franz
Austrian, 18th century.

Active in Steiermark.
Painter.
MUSEUMS AND GALLERIES:
GRAZ (Landesmus. Joanneum): *St Mark.*

HIERLOW, Rangvald Amandus.
See **HJERLOW**

HIERNAUX, Andrée Jeanne
Belgian, 20th century.
Painter.
Andrée Hiernaux exhibited at the Salon d'Automne and the Salon des Tuileries.

HIERNLE, Anton
German, 18th century.
Born 1676; died 1753.
Active in Landshut.
Sculptor.
Anton Hiernle executed many wood carvings of saints.

HIERNLE, Carl Joseph or Karel Josef
Bohemian, 18th century.
Born in Prague; died c. 1748, in Prague.
Sculptor. Religious subjects.
Bohemian School.
Carl Joseph Hiernle may have been related to the sculptors of Landshut and to Franz Matthias. He was represented in the exhibition *Lumière et ténèbres, art et civilisation du Baroque en Bohême* (*Light and Darkness. Baroque Art and Civilisation in Bohemia*) at the Palais des Beaux-Arts in Lille in 2002 by a polychrome wood sculpture of *St Anne with the Virgin and the Infant Jesus.*
BIBLIOGRAPHY:
Vlnas, Vit (ed.), *Lumière et ténèbres, art et civilisation du Baroque en Bohême*, exhibition catalogue, Palais des Beaux-Arts, Lille, Réunion des musées nationaux, Paris, 2002.

HIERNLE, Ferdinand Anton
German, 18th century.
Born 1703; died 1743.
Active in Landshut.
Sculptor.
Ferdinand Hiernle was a son of Anton Hiernle.

HIERNLE, Franz
Bohemian, 18th century.
Born 1736, in Prague.
Sculptor.
Franz Hiernle was the son or nephew of Carl Joseph Hiernle. He studied at the Akademie der Bildenden Künste in Vienna.

HIERNLE, Franz Matthias
German, 18th century.
Born 19 September 1677, in Landshut; died 1732, in Mainz.
Sculptor.
Franz Hiernle decorated the *Favourite* Park near Mainz for the Palatinate Prince Lothar Franz von Schönborn.

HIERNLE, Johann Michael
German, 18th century.
Born c. 1710; died 1770.
Active in Landshut.
Sculptor.
Johann Michael Hiernle was a son of Anton Hiernle. He was the most gifted and most famous member of his family.
MUSEUMS AND GALLERIES:
BERLIN (Bodemus.): several works.

HIERNLE, Johann Nepomuk Anton Ferdinand
German, 18th century.
Born 1731.
Active in Landshut.
Sculptor.
Johann Nepomuk Anton Ferdinand Hiernle was a son of Ferdinand Anton Hiernle.

HIERNLE, Kaspar
German, 18th century.
Born 25 February 1710, in Mainz; died 1755.
Sculptor.
Kaspar Hiernle was a son of Franz Matthias Hiernle and the brother of Sebastian Hiernle.

HIERNLE, Sebastian
German, 18th century.
Born 1705, in Mainz; died 4 May 1755, in Mainz.
Sculptor.
Sebastian Hiernle was a son of Franz Matthias Hiernle and worked with his brother, Kaspar, providing the decoration of many churches in Mainz.

HIERNOE, Jens Jensen
Danish, 18th century.
Born in Samsoe.
Sculptor.
Jens Jensen Hiernoe was the father of Jens Rasmussen Hiernoe.

HIERNOE, Jens Rasmussen
Danish, 18th century.
Born 2 June 1748, in Horsens; died 13 November 1801, in Horsens.
Sculptor.
Jens Hiernoe worked in Copenhagen before returning to his native Horsens.

HIÉRONIMUS, Alain
French, 20th century.
Born 22 February 1925, in Paris.
Painter, engraver, designer. Stage sets, designs for tapestries, designs for mosaics.
Both Alain Hieronimus' parents were actors and he grew up in the world of the theatre. From 1944, he was a pupil at the Académie de la Grande Chaumière in Paris. At the same time, he created sets for young theatre companies and was an assistant-decorator for film. He also received training in tapestry work, which was enjoying a resurgence due to Jean Lurçat and Marcel Gromaire. From 1947 to 1949, he stayed in Zurich, where he was influenced by Johannes Itten. In 1948, he met Gino Séverini, who initiated him to mosaic art. From 1949, he executed numerous tapestry cartoons, which were woven at Aubusson and Mechelen.

From 1949, Alain Hieronimus participated in collective exhibitions in his various art forms including: Salon des Indépendants, Salon d'Automne, Salon Comparaisons, and Salon des Artistes Décorateurs in Paris as well as abroad. He was a member of many associations and president of the Société des Artistes Décorateurs (SAD) in 1972 and 1973. The Musée de Gap organised a solo exhibition of his work in 1979. He was a professor at the École des Arts Appliqués in Paris from 1965 to 1973 and director of the École Nationale des Arts Décoratifs in Nice from 1973 to 1985.
BIBLIOGRAPHY:
A. Hiéronimus, exhibition catalogue, Musée de Gap, Gap, 1979 (full documentation).

HIERONYMI, Ernst
German, 19th century.
Born 31 January 1823, in Holle; died 23 October 1897, in Darmstadt.
Painter.
Ernst Hieronymi worked in Frankfurt am Main and in Munich.

HIERONYMI, Robert Philipp
German, 19th century.

Born 27 May 1868, in Frankfurt am Main.
Painter. Genre scenes.
Robert Hieronymi lived mainly in Bonn. In addition to genre scenes, he also painted religious subjects.

HIERONYMUS DE BRESCIA.
See **ROMANINO Girolamo**

HIERONYMUS DE FRANCFORT. See **GREFF Hieronymus**

HIERONYMUS OF SAMOTHRACE
4th (?) century BC.
Sculptor.
Ancient Greek.
Hieronymus worked in the Hellenistic period; no works can be attributed to him with any certainty.

HIERSCHEL, Gioachino
Italian, 19th century.
Born 19th century, in Trieste.
Landscape artist.
MUSEUMS AND GALLERIES:
TRIESTE (Civico Mus. Revoltella): *Dutch Landscape*.

HIERSCHL-MINERBI, Joachim, pseudonym: Van Hier
Austrian, 19th century.
Born 18 March 1834, in Trieste.
Painter, engraver. Genre scenes, landscapes, urban landscapes, waterscapes, seascapes.
Hierschl-Minerbi studied in Trieste before taking painting courses at the Akademie der bildenden Künste in Vienna. He made many trips to Holland, France and England and took part in collective exhibitions such as the Vienna Salon in 1856 and the Paris Salon from 1873.

Hierschl-Minerbi painted mainly waterscapes, most notably the port of Rotterdam, the canal in Venice and Dordrecht by night.
MUSEUMS AND GALLERIES:
NEVERS: *The Environs of Dieppe* - ROANNE: *Dordrecht by Night* - TRIESTE: *View of Trieste*.
AUCTION RECORDS:
PARIS, 14-16 Feb 1921, *The Scheldt*, FRF 200. PARIS, 4 July 1945, *Marine Landscape*, FRF 800. PARIS, 26 Feb 1947, *Marine Landscape*, FRF 4,100. NEW YORK, 2 May 1979, *Harbour Scene* (oil on canvas, 24 x 36 ins / 61 x 91.4 cm) USD 1,800. COLOGNE, 30 Nov 2000, *Coastal Fishermen Returning Before Storm* (oil on canvas, 24 x 36 ins / 61 x 91 cm) DEM 4,000.

HIERSING, Arne
Norwegian, 19th century.
Born 13 July 1860, in Saltdalen.
Painter. Genre scenes.
Arne Hiersing received an honourable mention at the Exposition Universelle in Paris in 1889.

HIERTA, Catherine de
Russian, 20th century.
Born in Russia.
Active in Finland.
Painter.
Catherine de Hierta exhibited regularly at the Salon des Indépendants in Paris from 1926.

HIERTHÈS, Frédéric
French, 19th century.
Born in the 19th century, in Paris.
Painter.
Hierthès, a pupil of Léon Cogniet, exhibited at the Salon in 1848 and 1864.

HIERY, Oswald
German, 20th century.
Sculptor.
Oswald Hiery's sculptures are markedly realist, although he puts the emphasis on expression.

HIERZIG, Hans
German, 17th century.
Born c. 1600, in Überlingen.
Sculptor.
Hierzig worked on Magdeburg Cathedral.

HIERZL, Hans Georg
Austrian, 18th century.
Active in Linz in 1703.
Sculptor.

HIESSE, Nicolas
French, 16th century.
Illuminator.
Nicolas Hiesse worked for Cardinal Georges d'Amboise on the great breviary of Pierre de La Poterne.

HIESZ, Geza
Hungarian, 20th century.
Born in Budapest.
Sculptor.
A student at the school of fine art in Budapest, Geza Hiesz exhibited at the Salon des Artistes Français in Paris from 1924.

HIETANEN, Reino
Finnish, 20th century.
Painter.
Figuration Libre.
Reino Hietanen exhibited in Paris at one of the Biennales des Jeunes Artistes. He works in a graphic style with calculated naiveties, perhaps inspired by the graffiti on walls and the poetry of children's drawings.

HIGASHIYAMA, Kaii
Japanese, 20th century.
Born 1908, in Yokohama; died 1999.
Painter. Landscapes.
Rokusokai group.
In 1929, while still a student of Gyokudo (Kawai), Eikyu (Matsuoka), and Kobori at the department of Japanese painting of Tokyo Fine Arts University, Higashiyama Kaii exhibited *Autumn in the Land of the Mountains* at the 10th *Teiten* (imperial exhibition). He became the disciple of Motoaki (Mutsushiro). He graduated from Tokyo Fine Arts University in 1931, assuming the artist name of Kaii. Higashiyama has since had an eminent official career with all the concomitant honours.

In 1934, he was the first Japanese to be awarded a study grant by the Hitler regime in Germany, studying for a year in the art history section of Berlin University. He interrupted his stay on the death of his father. In 1940, he married the daughter of the painter Kawasaki (Kotora) and settled in Tokyo. He then travelled to Manchuria and Korea. In 1944, he retired to Takayama (Gifu Prefecture), but was called up by the army. In 1947, he received the special prize at the Nitten (Japanese Art) exhibition for his painting *Zansho* (*Last Reflections of the Setting Sun*), which was purchased by the government. In 1949, he became a member of Nitten, and in 1950 a member of the jury. He then founded the Rokusokai group (Six Windows Society) with a number of colleagues from the university, including Hashimoto Akiharu, Kato Ezo, Yamada Shingo, Sato Kei, Suda Kotobuki, Ise Masayoshi, Onuki Shozo, the sculptors Kuroda Yoshiharu, Osuga Chikara, Nagasawa Kozo, Nonomura Kazuo, Naito Shiro, and the architect Yoshimura Junzo. In 1951, he was involved in the foundation of the Mikon society, along with Sakurai Kensodo, Yamamoto Okahito, Sugiyama Tei, Morita Sai, Hashimoto Akiharu and Kato Ezo. He continued to exhibit regularly with Nitten and, in 1956, won the fine arts academy's prize for *Evening Twilight*. The following year, he published his autobiography. In 1960, he finished a huge mural, *The Four Seasons*, for the imperial palace in Tokyo. It measures more than 75 feet long x 6 1/2 feet high (23 x 2 metres). In 1961, accompanied by his wife, he went on a grand tour of northern Europe, Germany and Austria. The same year, he painted *Green Hill* for the Casa Italo-Giapponese in Rome and published three books of reproductions of his works and travel souvenirs: *Voyage of White Night, Land of Forests and Lakes*, and *Dawn Tide*. In 1965 he became a member of the academy of fine arts and a member of the board of Nitten, the Japanese fine arts society, of which he would become a life member in 1969. In 1967, he published *Dialogue with Landscape*.

He then devoted himself to painting the murals in the new palace in the imperial palace complex in Tokyo, which he completed in 1968. In the same year, he was appointed to the Committee for the Protection of Cultural Property. In 1969, he was awarded the Medal for Culture and the Art Grand Prize by the journal *Mainichi* for his mural *Dawn Tide*, now in the Yamatane Museum of Art in Tokyo. In 1970, he was appointed member of the board of the National Museum of Art in Tokyo. In 1971, he published various books, including a travelogue, *Go Slowly Barrow, Painting the Old City*, an illustrated book, *Higashiyama: His Art and Characters*, and *Listening to the Fountain*, an essay. He then made sliding doors for the Toshodai-ji Temple at Nara, the first work in a cycle of decorative murals, which he would complete only in 1980. In 1973, he became a member of the Commission for the Preservation of Nature. In 1974, he was appointed General Administrator of Nitten, but resigned the following year.

Higashiyama painted water and objects reflected in it, autumn colours, snow-covered branches, and starry nights with an astonishing economy of means. He specialised in traditional, coloured landscapes, which he composed with masterly skill, imbuing them with peaceful and meditative serenity.

He exhibited in one-man shows. These included: 1938 *Drawings from a Trip to Europe*, Tokyo; 1963, *Exhibition of Nordic Landscapes*, Tokyo; 1963, *Masterpieces by Kaii Higashiyama*, an exhibition organised by *Kobe* magazine, Tokyo; 1972, Oyakama, Hiroshima. From 1976 he exhibited regularly at the Yoshii Gallery, Paris, notably in 1976, when he showed *Studies for the Murals in the Toshodaiji Temple*. In 1976 he showed *Chairs in the Place de la Concorde* at the Yoshii Gallery in Tokyo. In 1979 he exhibited in Leipzig; in 1981 at the National Museum of Modern Art, Tokyo. In 1993, UNESCO helped to organise the exhibition *Kaii Higashiyama, le dialogue avec les arbres* (*Kaii Higashiyama, Dialogue with Trees*) at the Yoshii Gallery, Paris.

BIBLIOGRAPHY:

Higashiyama, Kaii, *Nihon no Meiga 28*, Tokyo, 1972. *Kaii Higashiyama. Dialogue avec les arbres*, exhibition catalogue, Gal. Yoshii, Paris, 1982. *Kaii Higashiyama. Dialogue avec les arbres*, exhibition catalogue, Gal. Yoshii, Paris, 1993. Cortazzi, Sir Hugh, '*Traditional Japanese Painter Kaii Higashiyama*' in *Arts of Asia*, vol 26, no. 4, July-August 1996.

MUSEUMS AND GALLERIES:

ADACHI (Mus. of Art) - CHIBA (Prefectural Mus. of Art) - KITAKYUSHU (Municipal MA) - NAGANO (Shinano Art Mus., Higashiyama Kaii Gallery): more than 700 works - NAGAOKA (Niigata MMA) - NAGOYA (Aichi Prefectural Mus. of Art) - TOKYO (Metropolitan Art Mus.) - TOKYO (Nat. School of Fine Arts, House of Documentation) - TOKYO (National MMA) - TOKYO (Yamatane Mus. of Art) - YOKOHAMA (Mus. of Art).

HIGGINS, Edward

American, 20th century.
Born 1930, in South Carolina.
Sculptor.

Edward Higgins studied at the University of North Carolina and moved to New York in 1956. He uses metal and contemporary materials in works drawing on the world of machines.

Higgins participated in group exhibitions including *Recent Sculpture, USA* at the Museum of Modern Art, New York, in 1959; the *Sculpture Annual* exhibitions in New York in 1960 and 1962; the *Carnegie International*, Pittsburgh, in 1961; *Seattle World's Fair* in 1962 and at the Art Institute of Chicago in 1963. In 1961 he won the Tiffany Award.

BIBLIOGRAPHY:

Ier Salon international des Galeries Pilotes, exhibition catalogue, Musée cantonal, Lausanne, 1963.

HIGGINS, Eugene

American, 20th century.
Born February 1874, in Kansas City (Missouri); died 1958, in New York.
Painter (gouache), engraver.

In the first decade of the twentieth century Eugene Higgins spent time in Paris, where he studied with Jean-Léon Gérôme and Jean-Paul Laurens at the École des Beaux-Arts and also attended the Académie Julian. Higgins painted people from the lower social classes, to which he felt he also belonged, having experienced great poverty. He painted from memory and his figures had a primarily symbolic role in touching, realist compositions.

Higgins exhibited at the Salon des Artistes Français and the Société Nationale des Beaux-Arts in Paris and, on his return to New York in 1904, took part in the historic Armory Show exhibition in 1913. He was a member of many artists' associations in New York, the Salmagundi Club and the American Federation of Arts.

MUSEUMS AND GALLERIES:

WASHINGTON DC (Georgetown University): *Portrait of George M. Cohan* (c. 1915, pastel/paper).

AUCTION RECORDS:

NEW YORK, 4 May 1945, *Philosopher*, USD 200; *Interior*, USD 130. NEW YORK, 29 Jan 1970, *Woman in Green*, USD 1,400. NEW YORK, 27 March 1981, *Night's Loneliness* (charcoal and pastel, 18 1/2 x 12 1/2 ins / 47 x 31.8 cm) USD 800. LOS ANGELES, 3 May 1982, *Strange Land* (oil on canvas, 35 x 26 1/4 ins / 89 x 66.5 cm) USD 1,500. NEW YORK, 28 Sept 1983, *Emigrants* (oil on card, 11 3/4 x 15 ins / 30 x 38.2 cm) USD 3,000. NEW YORK, 30 Sept 1985, *Labourer* (oil on canvas, 26 x 33 1/4 ins / 66 x 84.5 cm) USD 2,200. NEW YORK, 17 March 1988, *Tree of Life* (oil on canvas, 11 x 11 ins / 28 x 28 cm) USD 1,320. NEW YORK, 30 Sept 1988, *Weary* (1905, oil on canvas, 30 3/4 x 22 ins / 78.1 x 56 cm) USD 6,600. NEW YORK, 14 Nov 1991, *Beggars* (charcoal/paper, 12 x 16 ins / 30.5 x 40.5 cm) USD 660. NEW YORK, 10 June 1992, *Hard Times* (gouache/paper, 20 1/4 x 14 1/4 ins / 51.5 x 36.3 cm) USD 4,400. NEW YORK, 9 Sept 1993, *Home from the Fields* (oil on canvas, 30 x 40 ins / 76.2 x 101.6 cm) USD 2,875. NEW YORK, 31 March 1994, *When the Mississippi Rises* (oil on canvas, 26 x 21 ins / 66 x 53.3 cm) USD 1,035. NEW YORK, 28 Sept 1995, *Dangerous Passage* (oil on canvas/card, 22 x 30 ins / 55.9 x 76.2 cm) USD 1,265. NEW YORK, 12 March 2002, *Woodsman Cutting Trees. Escape. Drinking by the Spring* (oil on canvasboard, set of three, 8 x 10 ins / 20 x 25 cm) USD 1,600. NEW YORK, 25 March 2004, *Brawl. Flight* (1935, oil on canvas, 16 x 20 ins / 41 x 51 cm) USD 1,900. NEW YORK, 25 March 2004, *Watering Place. Poor Fisherman* (oil on canvas, two, 16 x 20 ins / 41 x 51 cm) USD 2,000.

HIGGINS, Victor, or William Victor

American, 20th century.
Born 28 June 1884, in Shelbyville (Indiana); died 1949, in Taos (New Mexico).
Painter. Landscapes with figures, winter landscapes.

Victor Higgins studied at the Art Institute of Chicago and the Chicago Academy of Fine Arts from 1899, and then with Lucien Simon at the Académie de la Grande-Chaumière in Paris, after which he worked with Hans von Hyeck in Munich. On his return to Chicago he joined the Chicago Society of Artists and took a teaching post at the Academy of Fine Arts. He received prizes and awards, notably in 1917 and 1918, and painted a mural for the Englewood Theater in Chicago. Later he settled in Taos (New Mexico) with Walter Ufer, where they became members of the Taos Society of Artists.

Early in his career Higgins' style was rather academic with influences from the Impressionists. Then, in the 1920s, he developed in a more structured, post-Cézanne direction, which evolved throughout his life, showing the influence of Cubism. He was primarily a painter of typical New Mexican figures, as in *Pueblo of Taos* and *Fiesta Day*.

AUCTION RECORDS:

LOS ANGELES, 9 June 1976, *Ranch House* (oil on canvas, 24 x 27 1/4 ins / 61 x 69 cm) USD 2,300. NEW YORK, 25 Oct 1979, *Rural Landscape with Dwellings* (oil on canvas, 16 x 20 ins / 40.6 x 50.8 cm) USD 5,750. NEW YORK, 5 Dec 1980, *Blue Mountains* (watercolour, 20 x 14 ins / 50.8 x 35.6 cm) USD 8,500. NEW YORK, 3 June 1982, *Orange Landscape* (watercolour, 15 1/2 x 23 ins / 39.4 x 58.3 cm) USD 5,000. NEW YORK, 22 Oct 1982, *Canyon Drive, Santa Fe* (oil on canvas, 24 x 27 1/2 ins / 61 x 69.8 cm) USD 32,000. NEW YORK, 6 Dec 1984, *Cactus* (oil on canvas, 18 x 20 ins / 45.7 x 50.8 cm) USD 14,000. NEW YORK, 5 Dec 1986, *November: Country Landscape* (oil on canvas, 25 1/4 x 30 ins / 64 x 76.3 cm) USD 14,000. NEW YORK, 3 Dec 1992, *Adobe and Windmill* (watercolour/paper, 15 x 21 ins / 38.1 x 53.3 cm) USD 15,400. NEW YORK, 11 March 1993, *Cottonwood Trees in Winter* (watercolour/paper, 15 3/4 x 22 3/4 ins / 40 x 58 cm) USD 18,400. NEW YORK, 28 Sept 1995, *Watching the Boats* (watercolour/paper, 12 1/2 x 16 ins / 31.8 x 40.6 cm) USD 1,035. NEW YORK, 27 May 1999, *Taos in Winter* (1920-1921, oil on canvas, 30 x 36 ins / 76 x 91 cm) USD 280,000. CONNECTICUT, 9 Oct 1999, *Landscape* (oil on canvas, 16 x 22 ins / 41 x 56 cm) USD 2,900. MICHIGAN, 16 Feb 2000, *Pool in the Rio Grande* (oil on canvas, 14 x 15 ins / 36 x 38 cm) USD 23,000. NEW YORK, 28 Nov 2001, *River in Winter* (oil on panel, 14 x 18 ins / 36 x 46 cm) USD 32,500. NEW YORK, 28 Nov 2001, *Aspen Trees* (oil on canvas, 27 x 30 ins / 69 x 76 cm) USD 70,000. SANTA FE, 1 Nov 2003, *Sarah with her Horse* (1923, oil on panel, 14 x 20 ins / 36 x 51 cm) USD 25,000. SANTA FE, 1 Nov 2003, *New Mexico landscape* (1930-1940, watercolour, 14 x 20 ins / 36 x 51 cm) USD 27,500. HAYDEN, 24 July 2004, *Fish Ponds* (watercolour, 17 x 22 ins / 43 x 56 cm) USD 55,000. HAYDEN, 24 July 2004, *Meadow with Cattle* (oil on board, 12 x 17 ins / 30 x 43 cm) USD 85,000.

HIGGINTON, Fay

British, 20th century.
Born 1899, in London; died 1952.
Painter.

HIGGS

British, 18th century.
Active in London in 1774.
Painter.

HIGH PRIEST, Master of the. See **MASTERS**

HIGHAM, B.

British.
Active in England.
Painter.

B. Higham is mentioned in *Art Prices Current.*

AUCTION RECORDS:

LONDON, 20 March 1909, *Drifting and Paddling,* GBP 4. ST PETERSBURG (FLORIDA), 24 Jan 2004, *To a Higher Plane* (1917, watercolour on paper mounted on board, 29x29 ins / 74x74 cm) USD 5,000. BIRMINGHAM, 3 Dec 2004, *Lady in an Ornamental Garden* (watercolour, 12x17 ins / 30x43 cm) GBP 250.

HIGHAM, J. W.

British, 19th century.
Active in Norwich.
Enameller.

J.W. Higham exhibited in London at the Royal Academy and the Suffolk Street Gallery from 1821 to 1835.

AUCTION RECORDS:

LONDON, May 1922, *Sir Joshua Reynolds,* GBP 89.

HIGHAM, Thomas

British, 19th century.
Born 1796; died 1844.
Active in London.
Engraver.

Thomas Higham exhibited in London at the Royal Academy from 1824 to 1830.

HIGHMORE, Anthony

British, 18th century.
Born 1719; died 3 October 1799.
Painter. Portraits, landscapes, architectural views.

The son and pupil of Joseph Highmore, Anthony Highmore painted several views of Hampton Court and Kensington that were engraved by Tinney.

MUSEUMS AND GALLERIES:

MELBOURNE (Nat. Gal. of Victoria): *Joseph Highmore* (c. 1745-1747, oil on canvas).

HIGHMORE, Joseph

British, 18th century.
Born 23 June 1692, in London; died 1780, in Canterbury.
Painter. History painting, portraits.

One of the best English portrait artists, Joseph Highmore was a self-taught painter who came to the attention of Sir Godfrey Kneller because of his assiduous attendance at Kneller's Academy of Art in Great Queen Street. Encouraged by this encounter, Highmore devoted himself entirely to drawing and painting. He was employed by Pine in 1725 to illustrate a book on the *Order of the Bath,* providing it with some excellent portraits of the knights of the Order. Subsequently he painted a portrait of the *Duke of Cumberland.* His history paintings include those of *The Good Samaritan, Hagar and Ishmael* and *The Finding of Moses.* In 1744, he illustrated Richardson's novel *Pamela.* His style shows the influence of the French Rococo on 18th-century English art. He in turn was to influence the American portraitists of the period. He exhibited in London at the Society of British Artists and the Free Society in 1760 and 1761.

BIBLIOGRAPHY:

Paintings by Joseph Highmore, 1692-1780, London County Council, London, 1963. Mild, Warren, *Joseph Highmore of Holborn Row,* Phyllis Mild, Pennsylvania, 1990.

MUSEUMS AND GALLERIES:

BATH (Holburne Mus. of Art): *Portrait of Garton Orme* (c. 1725, oil on canvas) - LONDON (Foundling Mus.): *Hagar and Ishmael* (1746, oil on canvas); *Portrait of Thomas Emerson, a Governor of the Foundling Hospital* (1731, oil on canvas) - LONDON (National Portrait Gal.): *Samuel Richardson* (c. 1747, oil on canvas); *Henry Stebbing* (1757, oil on canvas).

AUCTION RECORDS:

NEW YORK, 22-23 Feb 1907, *Portrait of Mrs Adair Playing the Lute,* USD 400. LONDON, 27 Jan 1908, *Portrait of a Woman,* GBP 5. NEW YORK, 14-15 Jan 1909, *Portrait of a Woman,* USD 1,375. LONDON, 7 May 1909, *Portrait of a Lady,* GBP 367. LONDON, 19 May 1911, *Portrait of a Lady,* GBP 241. LONDON, 25-26 May 1911, *Portrait of Mrs Prichard,* GBP 787. LONDON, 14 July 1911, *The Grant Family,* GBP 37. LONDON, Feb 1922, *Mrs Bracegirdle in a White Dress,* GBP 17. LONDON, 31 Jan 1923,

Lady Claimed to be Flora MacDonald, GBP 50. London, April 1923, *Lady in a Brown Dress,* GBP 50. London, April 1923, *Thomas Western of Rivenhall Place, Essex, and Anne Western,* GBP 48. London, 28 July 1924, *Samuel Freake of Darrington House,* GBP 18. London, 16 Dec 1925, *George II,* GBP 125. London, 24 March 1926, *James Stuart,* GBP 52. London, 9 July 1926, *Maria Gunning, Countess of Coventry,* GBP 31. London, 4 March 1927, *Simon Welman,* GBP 367; *Isaac Welman,* GBP 336. London, 25 May 1927, *Colonel The Honorable Edward Byng,* GBP 185. London, 19 March 1928, *Lord Hill,* GBP 115. London, 20 April 1928, *Portrait of a Woman,* GBP 231. London, 30 July 1928, *Countess of Westmorland,* GBP 113. London, 22 Feb 1929, *John Reynes; Wife of John Reynes* (both) GBP 147. London, 26 April 1929, *Lord Hill,* GBP 283. London, 14 June 1929, *Miss Caroline Harsey,* GBP 178. London, 18 July 1930, *Lady in a Blue Dress,* GBP 220. London, 15 Dec 1933, *Edward Byng and his Wife Mary,* GBP 92. London, 12 Dec 1934, *Conversation,* GBP 120. London, 27 March 1936, *James Short,* GBP 52. London, 26 Feb 1937, *Barnstaple Bay,* GBP 46. London, 14 Feb 1938, *Ann Spencer.* London, 19 Jan 1945, *Miss Fryer,* GBP 294. New York, 17 March 1945, *Lady,* USD 175. London, 1 March 1946, *Lord Lempster and Lady Sophia Fermor,* GBP 52. London, 19 April 1961, *Portrait of a Gentleman,* GBP 1,180. London, 20 March 1963, *Portraits of William Wilberforce and his Wife Sarah,* GBP 1,100. London, 13 March 1970, *Portraits of Thomas Parker of Longton and his Wife* (two pendants) Gns 400. London, 17 Nov 1976, *Portrait of Isabella Lee* (oil on canvas, 28 1/2 x 17 1/4 ins / 72.5 x 44 cm) GBP 900. New York, 16 March 1979, *Portrait of Mrs Joshua Iremonger* (1742, oil on canvas, 49 x 39 ins / 124.5 x 99 cm) USD 7,000. London, 17 June 1983, *Portrait of a Lady* (1737, oil on canvas, 35 x 27 ins / 88.9 x 68.5 cm) GBP 2,400. London, 19 Nov 1986, *Portrait of a Lady* (1737, oil on canvas, 35 x 27 ins / 89 x 68.5 cm) GBP 2,400. New York, 15 Jan 1988, *Portrait of a Lady in a White Dress Holding a Letter* (oil on canvas, 50 x 40 ins / 127 x 101.5 cm) USD 6,600. New York, 21 Oct 1988, *Portrait of a Boy with a Pet Squirrel* (oil on canvas, 29 1/4 x 24 1/4 ins / 74.5 x 61.5 cm) USD 10,450. London, 20 July 1990, *Portrait of a Gentleman in a Blue Suit with a Red Waistcoat and a White Cravat* (1734, oil on canvas, 30 x 25 ins / 76.5 x 63.5 cm) GBP 2,750. New York, 10 Oct 1990, *Portrait of a Young Woman in a Blue and White Dress with Flowers on her Bodice* (oil on canvas, 30 1/4 x 25 1/4 ins / 76.8 x 64.2 cm) USD 2,750. London, 18 Nov 1992, *Three-Quarter Length Seated Portrait of Mrs Iremonger of Wherwell in a Blue Dress with a Lace Cap* (1745, oil on canvas, 49 1/4 x 39 1/4 ins / 125 x 100 cm) GBP 12,320. Vienna, 29-30 Oct 1996, *Three-Quarter Length Portrait of a Young Woman in a White Satin Dress with a Pink Bow* (1738, oil on canvas, 36 1/4 x 28 ins / 92 x 71 cm) ATS 51,750. London, 16 June 2000, *Portrait of the Duchess of Argyll* (1743, oil on canvas, 50 x 40 ins / 127 x 102 cm) GBP 3,000. London, 1 Dec 2000, *Three Girls, in Blue, Pink and Oyster Satin Dresses, in a Landscape* (oil on canvas, 50 x 41 ins / 127 x 103 cm) GBP 38,000. New York, 5 Oct 2001, *Portrait of a Lady. Portrait of a Gentleman* (oil on canvas, a pair, 50 x 40 ins / 127 x 102 cm) USD 20,000. London, 29 Nov 2001, *Portrait of a Gentleman in a Blue Coat and Scarlet Waistcoat, Naval Engagement beyond* (oil on canvas, 45 x 34 ins / 114 x 87 cm) GBP 6,000. London, 17 April 2002, *Portrait of a Lady in a White Dress in a Landscape* (oil on canvas, 50 x 40 ins / 127 x 102 cm) GBP 3,000. London, 27 Nov 2003, *Portrait of a Young Girl in a Cream Dress* (oil on canvas, 15 x 11 ins / 39 x 29 cm) GBP 9,200. London, 21 Jan 2004, *Portrait of George Leycester* (oil on canvas, oval, 28 x 24 ins / 72 x 60 cm) GBP 3,200. Dublin, 21 Sept 2004, *Portrait of a Lady in a White Dress with a Lace Cap* (oil on canvas, feigned oval, 30 x 25 ins / 76 x 64 cm) EUR 10,000.

HIGHMORE, Thomas

British, 18th century.

Born 1692; died 1720.

Painter.

The uncle of Joseph Highmore, Thomas Highmore was painter to William III. Sir James Thornhill was his pupil and successor.

HIGHMORE, Thomas

British, 19th century.

Born 1796, in Suffolk; died 3 January 1844, in Islington (London).

Engraver.

Thomas Highmore is known for his engravings of architectural subjects. He collaborated on the engraving of *The Coronation of Queen Victoria* after the painting by Hayter.

HIGHSTEIN, Jene

American, 20th - 21st century.

Born 1942, in Baltimore (Maryland).

Sculptor, environmental artist.

Jene Highstein studied at the University of Maryland, receiving a BA in 1963, at the University of Chicago (1963(1965), the New York Studio School (1965-1966), and the Royal Academy School, London (1967-1970). He was a member of the Anarchitecture Group, initiated in 1973, which examined alternative perceptions of architectual environments.

Highstein creates sculpture in stone, cast iron, steel, glass, concrete, fabric and plaster. His monolithic approach to sculpture is seen in the wood piece, *Palm I* (1983), the plaster work, *Palm III* (1993), or his site-specific steel work *Double Pipe Piece 1974/2003* at P.S.1 Contemporary Art Center, New York. Highstein's untitled work (1987-1988) at the Walker Art Center consists of three stone shapes, which he has scored with grooves using a diamond-tipped circular saw, and then chiselled between the cuts. An example of his glass work is *Bubble* (1992). In 2004, Highstein collaborated with Steven Holl in *The Snow Show* held in Kevi and Rovaniemi in Finland, where they created *Oblong Voidspace* in ice.

Highstein has exhibited since 1970 in the USA and Europe, including: 2000, *Bilbao Guggenheim,* Bilbao, Spain; 1984, *An International Survey of Recent Painting and Sculpture,* Museum of Modern Art, New York; 1979, solo show at the University Art Museum, Berkeley; and the 1975 Paris Biennale. Highstein has received awards from the National Endowment for the Arts (1994, 1984); St Gauden's Memorial Prize (1992); a Guggenheim Fellowship (1985); and a Sculpture Award, Creative Artists Public Service Program (1979). His works are held in the collections of more than 30 museums, including, Victoria and Albert Museum, London; Museum of Contemporary Art, Chicago; Los Angeles County Museum of Art; Rose Art Museum, Brandeis University, MA; Guggenheim Museum, New York; and Museum of Modern Art, New York.

Bibliography:

IXe Biennale de Paris, exhibition catalogue, Idea Books, Musée d'Art moderne de la Ville de Paris, Paris, 1975. Davies, Hugh Marlais, *Jene Highstein,* Exhibition catalogue, La Jolla Museum of Contemporary Art, La Jolla (CA), 1986. *Sculpture in the Landscape: Jene Highstein at Wave Hill,* Illustrated book, Wave Hill, New York, 1989. *Jene Highstein: Gallery/Landscape,* Exhibition catalogue, Santa Barbara Contemporary Arts Forum, Santa Barbara, 1991. *Jene Highstein,* Exhibition catalogue, Southeastern Center for Contemporary Art, Winston-Salem (NC), 1996. *Jene Highstein: Rooms and Interconnected Rooms,* Exhibition catalogue, University of Memphis, Memphis, 2001.

Museums and Galleries:

Chicago (MCA) - London (Victoria and Albert Mus.) - Los Angeles (County MA) - Minneapolis (Walker Art Center): *Untitled* (1987(1988, granite sculpture); *Untitled* (1987(1988, granite sculpture) - New York (Guggenheim Mus.) - New York (MoMA) - San Diego (MCA): *Untitled* (1981, pastel on paper) - WALTHAM (Rose AM, Brandeis University) - WASHINGTON DC (NGA): *Untitled* (1995, letterpress print).

AUCTION RECORDS:

NEW YORK, 12 Feb 2004, *Untitled* (1988, carved elm wood, 72 x 35x27 ins / 183 x 89x68 cm) USD 3,250. LAMBERTVILLE, 24 April 2004, *Untitled* (1971, graphite, 9 x 12 ins / 22 x 30 cm) USD 4,000.

HIGNETT, Reginald Arthur
British, 20th century.
Born in Liverpool.
Sculptor.

Reginald Arthur Hignett was a pupil of E. Winthey-Smith.

HIGNY, Michelle
French, 18th century.
Active in Paris in 1766.
Painter.

HIGO HOKKYÔ JÔKEI. See **JOKEI**

HIGS, Richard
British, 18th century.
Active in London.
Enameller.

Richard Higs exhibited in London at the Royal Academy from 1786 to 1796.

HIGTON, T.
British, 19th century.
Active in London.
Painter. Sporting subjects.

T. Higton exhibited regularly at the Royal Academy in London from 1801 to 1815.

HIGUERAS Y FUENTES, Jacinto
Spanish, 20th century.
Born in Santisteban del Puerto (Jaén).
Sculptor.

Jacinto Higueras y Fuentes trained in Madrid, and exhibited there from 1906.

HIJNER, Arend, or Hyner
Dutch, 19th - 20th century.
Born 18 September 1866, in Arnhem; died July 1916.
Painter. Portraits, genre scenes, landscapes, still-lifes.

Arend Hijner was a pupil of Schulman. He exhibited at the 1900 Exposition Universelle in Paris, where he received an honourable mention.

AUCTION RECORDS:

AMSTERDAM, 15 March 1983, *Woman and Two Children in an Interior* (oil on canvas, 26 x 38 1/2 ins / 66 x 98 cm) NLG 5,800. AMSTERDAM, 3 Nov 1992, *Flirt* (oil on canvas, 28 1/4 x 24 1/4 ins / 72 x 61.5 cm) NLG 2,300. AMSTERDAM, 21 April 1993, *The Object of Attention* (oil on canvas, 15 1/4 x 18 ins / 39 x 46 cm) NLG 5,520. AMSTERDAM, 8 Feb 1994, *Woman Watching a Pot on the Kitchen Fire* (oil on canvas, 18 1/4 x 15 ins / 46.5 x 38 cm) NLG 3,220.

HIKEI
Japanese, 19th century.
Active in Osaka c. 1831.
Painter.

HIKMET ONAT
Turkish, 20th century.
Born 1882, in Istanbul; died 1977.
Painter. Landscapes, seascapes.

Hikmet Onat was one of the elders of the young Turkish School, and introduced many innovations from Western art into Turkey. He completed his studies and began his career before the modernising reforms of Kemal Atatürk, from 1923 onwards, swept away many of the strictures of the Ottoman sultanate. In 1946 he presented a *View of the Golden Horn* at the exhibition of modern art held at the museum of modern art in Paris under the auspices of the United Nations.

AUCTION RECORDS:

LONDON, 17 Oct 1997, *Garden of a Mosque* (1953, oil on canvas, 21 1/4 x 28 1/4 ins / 54 x 72 cm) GBP 11,500.

HIKOBEI. See **HANKO**

HIKOKUNI, from his real name, Ashikawa, artist names: Ashikawa, Toyokawa (a signature from 1827), Arakawa
Japanese, 19th century.
Active c. 1821-1827.
Painter.

HIKOSAKA, Naoyuki
Japanese, 20th - 21st century.
Born 1946, in Tokyo.
Painter (mixed media).

Hikosaka Naoyuki studied at Taka University. Using visible wooden panels, he paints geometric abstract motifs in acrylics in the style of papiers découpés. He then assembles these components in space in patterns and correspondences related to the artistic traditions of the Far East, to form what he describes as 'composed paintings'. He has exhibited since 1970. In 1975, he took part in the Paris Biennale.

HILAIRE, Camille
French, 20th century.
Born 2 August 1916, in Metz; died 1988.
Painter (gouache), watercolourist. Figure compositions, figures, nudes, sporting subjects, horse racing scenes, flowers, landscapes with figures, animals. Murals, designs for tapestries, for stained glass and for mosaics.

Camille Hilaire was a pupil at the École des Beaux-Arts in Paris. He also worked in the free academies, including that of André Lhote, whose teaching had a major influence on his work.

He executed numerous mural decorations, tapestries, stained glass windows and mosaics for embassies, cruise liners and public buildings, especially in Nancy. His work was abundant and clearly decorative in a style of Post-Cubist construction with a broad range of colour in acid tones. He is particularly known for his *Orchestras, Horse Races* and 1950 *Greenhouses.* He taught at the École des Beaux-Arts first in Nancy, then in Paris.

Camille Hilaire participated in numerous collective exhibitions in Paris including: Salon d'Automne, Salon des Indépendants, Salon des Tuileries, Salon de Mai, Salon des Peintres Témoins de leur Temps. He also exhibited abroad. Solo exhibitions include: Paris (1951, 1957, 1961, 1965); New York (1954 and 1956; Geneva (1958). He received numerous awards: a travel grant from the French State (1947); Venice prize (1949); Antral and Casa Velázquez prizes (1950); Prix de la Société des Amateurs d'Art (1958).

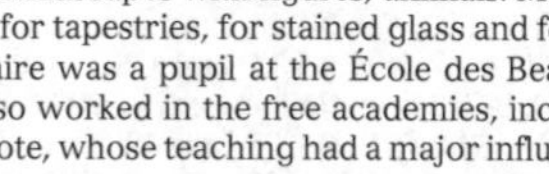

MUSEUMS AND GALLERIES:

ÉPINAL (Mus. départemental d'Art ancien et contemporain): *Landscape* - PARIS (MAMVP) - PARIS (MNAM-CCI).

AUCTION RECORDS:

VERSAILLES, 16 Dec 1973, *Jazz* FRF 6,500. PARIS, 3 March 1976, *Agile Dancer* (watercolour, 20 1/2 x 14 1/2 ins / 52 x 37 cm) FRF 2,300. VERSAILLES, 5 Dec 1976, *Landscape in the Mediterranean* (oil on canvas, 28 3/4 x 36 1/4 ins / 73 x 92 cm) FRF 6,000. VERSAILLES, 16 April 1978, *The Acrobats* (gouache and watercolour, 23 x 30 ins / 57.5 x 76.5 cm) FRF 4,500. LA TRINITÉ-SUR-MER, 3 June 1979, *Before Spring* (oil on canvas, 13 3/4 x 22 ins / 35 x 55 cm) FRF 9,000. AMSTER-

DAM, 11 May 1982, *Bathers* (oil on canvas, 28¼ x 35½ ins / 72 x 90 cm) NLG 6,000. VERSAILLES, 12 March 1983, *Before the Race* (oil on canvas, 13 x 22 ins / 33 x 55 cm) FRF 12,500. PARIS, 7 Nov 1986, *Cap d'Antibes* (1958, oil on canvas, 35½ x 46 ins / 90 x 116 cm) FRF 28,000. NANTERRE, 11 Oct 1987, *Riverbank* (watercolour, 22½ x 29½ ins / 57 x 75 cm) FRF 11,500. PARIS, 14 Dec 1987, *The Model in the Studio* (oil on canvas, 9 x 11 ins / 22 x 27 cm) FRF 8,500. ST-DIÉ, 14 Feb 1988, *The Weighing* (oil on canvas, 21¼ x 25½ ins / 54 x 65 cm) FRF 27,000. VERSAILLES, 20 March 1988, *Landscape* (oil on canvas, 19¾ x 23¾ ins / 50 x 60.5 cm) FRF 26,000; *The River* (1964, oil on canvas, 11¾ x 23½ ins / 30 x 60 cm) FRF 20,500. PARIS, 25 May 1988, *The Floods* (1955, oil on canvas, 28¾ x 36¼ ins / 73 x 92 cm) FRF 15,000. PARIS, 1 June 1988, *The Edges of a Pond* (c. 1965, oil on canvas, 15 x 18 ins / 38 x 46 cm) FRF 20,500. PARIS, 3 June 1988, *The Pool* (oil on canvas, 11¾ x 31½ ins / 30 x 80 cm) FRF 10,000. PARIS, 20 June 1988, *The Port in Antibes* (oil on canvas, 14¾ x 17¾ ins / 37.5 x 45 cm) FRF 13,500. PARIS, 23 June 1988, *Undergrowth* (watercolour, 21 x 27½ ins / 53.5 x 70 cm) FRF 23,000. PARIS, 20 Oct 1988, *The Two Friends* (watercolour, 20 x 26½ ins / 51 x 67 cm) FRF 4,000. PARIS, 16 Nov 1988, *Camargue* (tapestry, 60¼ x 76½ ins / 153 x 194 cm) FRF 36,000. PARIS, 22 March 1989, *Landscape with Trees* (oil on canvas, 28¾ x 36¼ ins / 73 x 92 cm) FRF 75,000. PARIS, 29 Sept 1989, *Portrait of Camille Renaud* (gouache/pencil, 14½ x 10¼ ins / 37 x 26 cm) FRF 4,000. VERSAILLES, 29 Oct 1989, *Nude* (wash and Indian ink, 17¾ x 22 ins / 45 x 56 cm) FRF 7,500. STRASBOURG, 29 Nov 1989, *The Orchard* (watercolour, 19¼ x 25¼ ins / 49 x 64 cm) FRF 25,000. NEUILLY, 5 Dec 1989, *Intimate Scene* (watercolour/paper, 22 x 14¼ ins / 55 x 36 cm) FRF 14,500. NEW YORK, 21 Feb 1990, *San-Tomá Lane, Venice* (oil on canvas, 36¼ x 28¾ ins / 92.2 x 73.1 cm) USD 20,900. CALAIS, 4 March 1990, *Bois Jérôme* (oil on canvas, 28¾ x 36¼ ins / 73 x 92 cm) FRF 139,000. PARIS, 25 June 1990, *The Orchestra* (oil on canvas, 23½ x 28¾ ins / 60 x 73 cm) FRF 136,000. PARIS, 6 Oct 1990, *Figures* (watercolour, 29¼ x 21¼ ins / 74 x 54 cm) FRF 27,000. LE TOUQUET, 11 Nov 1990, *Spring in Normandy* (1969, oil on canvas, 31½ x 51¼ ins / 80 x 130 cm) FRF 200,000. CALAIS, 9 Dec 1990, *July Flowers* (oil on canvas, 18½ x 22 ins / 47 x 55 cm) FRF 75,000. NEW YORK, 13 Feb 1991, *Weighing in Deauville* (oil on canvas, 35 x 45½ ins / 89 x 115.6 cm) USD 19,800. PARIS, 15 March 1991, *Jazz* (oil on canvas, 23½ x 28¾ ins / 60 x 73 cm) FRF 70,000. NEW YORK, 12 June 1991, *Weighing at Longchamp* (oil on canvas, 28½ x 36 ins / 72.4 x 91.4 cm) USD 12,100. CALAIS, 7 July 1991, *The Horse Competition* (oil on canvas, 23½ x 32 ins / 60 x 81 cm) FRF 115,000. CALAIS, 5 April 1992, *The Pool* (watercolour, 15¼ x 12¼ ins / 39 x 31 cm) FRF 12,500. CALAIS, 5 July 1992, *The House in the Trees* (oil on canvas, 23½ x 28¾ ins / 60 x 73 cm) FRF 77,500. LE TOUQUET, 30 May 1993, *Quartet* (oil on canvas, 32 x 25½ ins / 81 x 65 cm) FRF 125,000. NEW YORK, 29 Sept 1993, *The Great Orchestra* (1962, oil on canvas, 39½ x 39½ ins / 100.3 x 100.3 cm) USD 14,950. PARIS, 25 March 1994, *The Arrival* (1967, oil on canvas, 15¾ x 31¼ ins / 40 x 79.5 cm) FRF 41,000. MAYENNE, 11 Dec 1994, *Autumn Bouquet* (oil on canvas, 28¾ x 23½ ins / 73 x 60 cm) FRF 80,000. PARIS, 7 June 1995, *Nude with Bouquet* (oil on canvas, 35½ x 45¼ ins / 90 x 115 cm) FRF 47,000. CALAIS, 25 June 1995, *Sunbathing* (oil on canvas, 23½ x 28¾ ins / 60 x 73 cm) FRF 61,000. PARIS, 28 June 1996, *The Two Pines* (oil on canvas, 23½ x 23½ ins / 60 x 60 cm) FRF 24,500. CALAIS, 15 Dec 1996, *Reclining Nude* (watercolour and wash, 17¾ x 22 ins / 45 x 56 cm) FRF 10,200. PARIS, 20 Jan 1997, *Nude in the Studio* (oil on canvas, 15 x 18 ins / 38 x 46 cm) FRF 14,000. CALAIS, 23 March 1997, *The Trio* (oil on canvas, 13 x 18 ins / 33 x 46 cm) FRF 38,000. PARIS, 27 June 1997, *Weighing at Clairefontaine* (oil on canvas, 23½ x 28¾ ins / 60 x 73 cm) FRF 34,500. PARIS, 5 March 1998, *The Weighing at Deauville* (oil on canvas, 28¾ x 36½ ins / 73 x 93 cm) FRF 43,000. PARIS, 20 March 1998, *The Painter's Studio* (oil on canvas, 11¾ x 31½ ins / 30 x 80 cm) FRF 17,000. CAEN, 1 Jan 1999, *Spring* (oil on canvas, 8 x 24 ins / 20 x 60 cm) FRF 181,000. NEUILLY, 25 June 1999, *Sunbathing* (oil on canvas, 29 x 36 ins / 73 x 92 cm) FRF 88,000. STOCKHOLM, 15 May 2000, *Horses in the Paddock* (oil on canvas, 29 x 36 ins / 73 x 92 cm) SEK 110,000. PARIS, 15 Dec 2000, *Big Summer Bouquet* (oil on canvas, 38 x 64 ins / 97 x 162 cm) FRF 125,000. CALAIS, 6 May 2001, *Vase of Poppies* (oil on canvas, 37 x 29 ins / 93 x 73 cm) FRF 72,000. CALAIS, 6 May 2001, *Summer Light* (oil on canvas, 51 x 64 ins / 130 x 163 cm) FRF 127,000. CALAIS, 10 Nov 2002, *Horse Race* (1957, oil on canvas, 32 x 51 ins / 81 x 130 cm) EUR 10,000. CALAIS, 10 Nov 2002, *Canal in Venice* (oil on canvas, 29 x 36 ins / 73 x 92 cm) EUR 10,700. PARIS, 18 Nov 2003, *On Mont Boron* (c. 1968, oil on canvas, 35 x 46 ins / 89 x 116 cm) EUR 7,000. NEW YORK, 5 Dec 2003, *Paddock at Deauville* (oil on canvas, 29 x 36 ins / 74 x 91 cm) USD 12,000. PARIS, 3 March 2004, *Weigh-in at Deauville* (oil on canvas, 29 x 36 ins / 73 x 92 cm) EUR 5,800. CALAIS, 30 May 2004, *Venice* (oil on canvas, 21 x 26 ins / 54 x 65 cm) EUR 5,800.

HILAIRE, Jean Baptiste

French, 18th - 19th century.

Born 1753, in Audun-le-Tiche, near Metz; died after 1822, in Paris.

Painter, watercolourist, draughtsman, illustrator.

Portraits, genre scenes, local scenes, landscapes with figures.

Orientalism.

Jean Baptiste Hilaire studied under Leprince who had a strong influence on his illustration work. He exhibited at the Salon de la Jeunesse in the Place Dauphine in 1780 and at the Salon de la Correspondance in 1780.

The Louvre Museum owns *Music* and *Reading* by him. These two paintings, their gorgeous colour offsetting their somewhat vapid style, have stood Hilaire in good stead among artists of the end of the 18th century. Langlois and Malherbe engraved from his originals a beautiful series of Oriental costumes for the account of a tour of Eastern Europe and Turkey, making him a forerunner to Orientalists like Marilhat and Decamps. He is also known for his drawing of the *Cannibal* engraved by Mathieu, treating a murderer named Blaise Ferrage known as Seyé (1783).

MUSEUMS AND GALLERIES:

PARIS (Louvre): *Reading*; *The Music Lesson*.

AUCTION RECORDS:

PARIS, 29 June 1900, *The Travelling Showmen at the Palace*, FRF 3,505. PARIS, 26 March 1902, *The Declaration*, FRF 380. PARIS, 11-15 May 1903, *Park Peopled with Figures*, FRF 1,200. PARIS, 6 June 1907, *Adriatic Fishermen* (watercolour) FRF 230. PARIS, 13 Dec 1920, *The Country Concert*, FRF 7,700. PARIS, 21-22 June 1923, *View of an Eastern Town Square* (watercolour) FRF 880. PARIS, 22-23 May 1924, *The Boat Ride* (watercolour) FRF 9,500. PARIS, 22-23 April 1925, *Louveciennes Terrace* (watercolour and gouache) FRF 12,200. PARIS, 19 April 1928, *Gathering in the Park*, FRF 5,100; *The Embarkation for the Island of Love* (gouache) FRF 6,000. PARIS, 13-15 May 1929, *Ruins of Miletus and Course of the Meander River (Asia Minor)* (drawing) FRF 29,000; *Portrait of a Woman* (drawing) FRF 6,000. PARIS, 28 May 1931, *The Arbour* (watercolour) FRF 21,000. PARIS, 15 June 1938, *Macaw* (watercolour and gouache) FRF 30,000. PARIS, 15 Dec 1941, *Turkish Dance* (watercolour) FRF 800. PARIS, 3 March 1944, *The Singing Lesson in a Park*, FRF 230,000. NEW YORK, 4 Jan 1947, *Lady in a Pink and White Dress*, USD 1,300. PARIS, 4 June 1947, *Embarkation on the Lake* (gouache) FRF 12,000. PARIS, 25 Nov 1963, *Girls and Peasant Boy in a Landscape Trying to Catch Doves*, FRF 18,000. PARIS, 9 June 1971, *The Pantheon* (watercolour) FRF 7,800. VERSAILLES, 3 Dec 1972, *The Big Tree* (watercolour) FRF 8,600. VERSAILLES, 15 June 1977, *The Big Tree* (watercolour, 14 x 8½ ins / 35.5 x

21.5 cm) FRF 9,500. LONDON, 10 July 1979, *View of the City of Negroponte* (watercolour and pen heightened with white, 17 1/4 x 35 ins / 43.8 x 88.8 cm) GBP 1,900. LILLE, 14 March 1981, *Turqueries (Turkish Scenes); The Harem Bathing* (gouache, pen and wash, a pair, 12 1/2 x 16 1/4 ins / 32 x 41 cm) FRF 60,000. VERSAILLES, 18 Dec 1983, *Walk in a Park* (oil on canvas, 29 1/4 x 36 1/2 ins / 74 x 93 cm) FRF 14, 000. LONDON, 13 Dec 1984, *'The Romeca': Greek Women's Dance with a View of Istanbul in the Background* (pen and wash, 9 3/4 x 15 ins / 24.6 x 38.3 cm) GBP 9,500. NEW YORK, 16 Jan 1986, *Three Camels and Eastern Travellers* (red chalk and wash, 9 1/2 x 14 3/4 ins / 24.2 x 37.3 cm) USD 3,600. MONTE CARLO, 29 Nov 1986, *Young Women with a Parrot in a Park, Presumed to be at the Château de Louveciennes* (1793, watercolour and gouache, 19 3/4 x 25 ins / 50.4 x 62.6 cm) FRF 180,000. PARIS, 11 March 1988, *View of the Square in Kos* (drawing squared in black pen, 7 1/2 x 9 ins / 19 x 23 cm) FRF 8,000. PARIS, 12 Dec 1990, *Ruins of Miletus and Course of the Meander River (Turkey)* (black chalk and watercolour, 9 x 14 ins / 22 x 35.4 cm) FRF 70,000. NEW YORK, 8 Jan 1991, *Equestrian Portraits of a Turkish Officer and Soldier* (1783, watercolour and gouache/black chalk, a pair, each 10 x 7 1/2 ins / 25.5 x 18.9 cm) USD 17,600. LONDON, 11 Dec 1992, *Peasants Dancing the Tarantella on Marechiaro Beach* (oil on panel, 18 x 25 1/4 ins / 45.8 x 63.9 cm) GBP 8,800. NEW YORK, 13 Jan 1993, *Three Camels Resting* (red chalk, red-brown wash and black chalk lines, 9 1/2 x 15 ins / 24.2 x 37.2 cm) USD 7,700. PARIS, 6 July 1993, *Everyday Scene in Turkey* (1785, black chalk and brown wash, 9 x 14 ins / 22 x 35.6 cm) FRF 47,000. MONACO, 20 June 1994, *Veiled Women at the Foot of an Obelisk by the Nile River* (black chalk, ink and watercolour, 13 3/4 x 9 3/4 ins / 35.1 x 24.7 cm) FRF 33,300. PARIS, 25 Oct 1994, *Young Nude Captive Girl Set before the Pasha* (oil on canvas, 19 3/4 x 13 1/2 ins / 50 x 34 cm) FRF 160,000. PARIS, 29 March 1996, *Ruins of Miletus and Course of the Meander River* (black chalk and watercolour, 9 x 14 ins / 22 x 35.4 cm) FRF 41,000. PARIS, 16 Nov 1999, *Two Large Caravans at Palmyra, Valley of the Tombs* (oil on canvas, 31 x 60 ins / 80 x 152 cm) FRF 550,000. PARIS, 8 Dec 1999, *Pier* (oil on canvas, 32 x 48 ins / 81 x 122 cm) FRF 300,000. NEW YORK, 26 May 2000, *Lady Seated by a Stone Plinth Holding a Handkerchief. Lady Wearing a Hat Walking in Landscape* (oil on panel, a panel, 6 x 5 ins / 16 x 13 cm) USD 28,000. PARIS, 27 March 2001, *Oriental Shepherd with his Flock and a Camel* (watercolour over black crayon/colour wash, 13 x 8 ins / 34 x 21 cm) FRF 26,000. PARIS, 15 June 2001, *Dromedary* (oil on panel, 9 x 7 ins / 24 x 19 cm) FRF 60,000. PARIS, 28 June 2002, *Figures in Costume of Ottoman Empire* (gouache on paper/panel, set of four, 7 x 5 ins / 19 x 12 cm) EUR 23,000. PARIS, 28 June 2002, *Figures in Costume of ottoman Empire* (gouache on paper/panel, set of four, 7 x 5 ins / 19 x 12 cm) EUR 23,000. NEW YORK, 21 Jan 2003, *Country Fair with Girl on a Swing* (gouache/vellum, 13 x 10 ins / 32 x 26 cm) USD 2,100. ROME, 17 May 2004, *Flora* (1787, oil on canvas, 33 x 44 ins / 85 x 113 cm) EUR 11,000. LONDON, 30 Sept 2004, *View of Park, Sevigne* (ink/watercolour, 16 x 21 ins / 41 x 53 cm) GBP 1,000.

HILARIUS

4th century.
Born in Bithynia; died near Athens, murdered.
Active in Athens AD 364 to 379.
Painter.
Ancient Greek.

HILBERT, Georges

French, 20th century.
Born 22 March 1900, in Algeria; died 6 September 1982, in the Loiret region.
Sculptor. Animals.

A pupil at the École des Arts Décoratifs and the École des Beaux-Arts in Paris, Georges Hilbert was much inspired by the animal world which he had experienced in his childhood in Algeria. He sculpted using the direct cutting method. He executed five low reliefs for the section housing the large felines at the Jardin des Plantes in Paris, a baptismal font for the cathedral in the Grand Duchy of Luxembourg, sculptures for the cruise liner Normandie and for the baptistery in Strasbourg cathedral.

A member of the Salon d'Automne from 1925, Hilbert won same year the gold medal at the Exposition des Arts Décoratifs and participated in Salons in Paris. He also showed his work in Europe, as well as in the USA, where he was much appreciated. Awards include: Prix Blumenthal (1927) and Grand Prix of the Salon des Artistes Français (1973). He was elected to the Académie des Beaux-Arts in 1973.

MUSEUMS AND GALLERIES:
DENVER - LOS ANGELES - NEW YORK (Metropolitan Mus. of Art) - PARIS (MAMVP).

AUCTION RECORDS:
PARIS, 6 June 1990, *The Otter* (bronze, h. 18 ins / 46 cm) FRF 26,000. PONTOISE, 12 Nov 2000, *Fennec* (pink marble, h. 15 ins / 37 cm) FRF 32,000.

HILBERT, Jaro

20th century.
Born 24 June 1897, in Krsko, Slovenia, to Czech parents; died 1 March 1995, in Ville-d'Avray.
Since 1962 active and naturalised in France.
Painter, watercolourist, draughtsman. Figure compositions, figures, nudes, portraits, landscapes, seascapes, flowers.
Orientalism.

Jaro Hilbert studied at the art school in Prague from 1919 to 1925. In 1926 he settled in Cairo, where he founded a free art school. He travelled widely until 1961 from his home in Cairo. In 1962 he moved permanently to Ville d'Avray. Using a direct and sober technique, he painted a wide variety of pictures, and many landscapes around Cairo, in the Ile de France, Brittany, Normandy, Provence, Switzerland, Italy and Scotland. He is noted for his 1936 *Last Supper*.

He showed work in various collective exhibitions: in Cairo in 1927 and from 1963 to 1976 at the Salon des Artistes Français in Paris. His first solo retrospective was at Ljubljana in 1925, and he had other exhibitions during his travels in the Near East and in Europe. His solo exhibitions in France included a show in 1966 at the Egyptian Cultural Centre in Paris, and exhibitions in Ville d'Avray, Montreux, Lyons, St-Lô; in 1977 *60 années de peinture* (*60 Years of Painting*) at the Ville d'Avray château; in 1982 *Egypt 1926-1962* in Ville d'Avray; in 1984 *Les Pays de Loire* (*Lands of the Loire*), in Ville d'Avray; in 1989 a gift to the town of St-Lô after his death; and in 1998 at the Ville d'Avray cultural centre.

BIBLIOGRAPHY:
Bongnie, Émile de/Barret, Robert, *Jaro Hilbert: 60 années de peinture*, Blanchard, Le Plessis-Robinson, 1977. *Maisons d'ici et d'ailleurs. Jaro Hilbert*, exhibition catalogue, L'Orangerie, Ville-d'Avray, 1981.

MUSEUMS AND GALLERIES:
CAIRO (Mus.) - KOSTANJEVICA (Galerija Bozidar Jakac) - PRAGUE (Mus.) - TORONTO (Mus.).

HILBERTH, Iren

Hungarian, 19th - 20th century.
Born 1872, in Budapest.
Painter. Portraits, still-lifes.

Iren Hilberth exhibited from 1892.

HILBING, August

German, 19th century.
Born 1836, in Münster; died 1888, in Münster.
Painter.

MUSEUMS AND GALLERIES:
MÜNSTER: one work.

HILD, Eric
French, 20th - 21st century.
Born 15 February 1951, in Marseilles.
Sculptor, potter.

Hild's works are intentionnally baroque. He carefully works with space where light penetrates. Until 1973, he worked equally on sculpture and ceramics. Since then, he has created sculptures with several closely fitting elements. He held his first exhibition at the Musée d'Hyères in 1971. He then exhibited in Paris in 1973 and then again at the Musée d'Hyères in 1975.

HILD, Johann Franz
German, 18th century.
Active in Trier at the beginning of the 18th century.
Painter.

HILD, Johann Kaspar
German, 18th century.
Born 1676; died 15 August 1716, in Koblenz.
Painter.

Johann Kaspar Hild worked mainly in Trier.

HILDA, E. Baily
Austrian, 19th century.
Active in Paris.
Painter. Genre scenes.

Hilda, mentioned by Florence Levy, exhibited at the Salon des Artistes Français from 1895.

AUCTION RECORDS:

NEW YORK, 22 to 24 Nov 1896, *Guardian of the Tomb,* USD 270. NEW YORK, 2 Feb 1906, *Ruin Raiders in the Indies,* USD 300. NEW YORK, 12 Nov 1908, *An Intruder,* USD 340.

HILDBRAND, Leonhard
Swiss, 18th - 19th century.
Born 8 December 1766, in St Gall; died 28 October 1845, in St Gall.
Draughtsman.

Leonhard Hildbrand was a pupil of Melling in Strasbourg.

HILDEBRAND, Adam Wilhelm
German, 18th century.
Born 1678, in Erfurt; died 9 March 1735, in Leipzig.
Painter.

Bernigeroth engraved many portraits after Adam Hildebrand.

HILDEBRAND, Adolf Ernest Robert
German, 19th - 20th century.
Born 6 October 1847, in Marburg (Hesse); died 18 January 1921, in Munich.
Sculptor.

Adolf Hildebrand's father was the famous economist Bruno Hildebrand. As a young boy, Adolf showed a lively interest in art, particularly sculpture. After studying with Kreling in Nuremberg and Zumbusch in Munich, he went to Italy in 1867 and again in 1872 to study the classical Italian masters. They had a considerable influence on him, occasionally overcoming his inclinations towards realism. This duality can be seen in many of his works, which are sometimes very traditionalist and sometimes frankly modernist. He set out his opinions on the aesthetics of sculpture in a remarkable book, *The Problem of Form.* He achieved considerable success in Berlin and Vienna. Among his best-known works, apart from the statues on show in museums, is his *Monumental Fountain* in Munich dating from 1891-1894. He had earlier won the first prize for the national monument to Wilhelm I, but the Emperor refused to accept it. After 1897, he spent half his time in Munich and the other half in Florence, producing mainly isolated works that were the product of his own reflections, but also a few monuments, notably the equestrian statues of the Prince Regent Luitpold and Bismarck in Bremen. His friendship with Hans von Marées and his thoughts on Italian art had made him into one of the group known as the 'German Romans'. He is often thought of as one of the precursors of the Modern Style. He was much preoccupied with the representation of movement in his works. He considered it to be the 'spiritual material' of the sculptor, as opposed to simple 'optical representation'. It led him to create supple forms that flowed from a kind of organic growth. To his credit, he carved directly in stone or modelled directly in clay before casting his works in bronze. His ideas had some influence on the aestheticians Wölfflin and Strygowski.

MUSEUMS AND GALLERIES:

BASEL: *Portrait of Arnold Böcklin* - BERLIN: *Young Man; General Baeyer; The Painter Arnold Böcklin; Max von Pettenkofer; Werner van Siemens; The Philologist Philipp Heyse* - HAMBURG: *Bismarck* (plaquette); *Privy Councillor W. Bodé* (plaquette); *P.D. Fischer* (medal) - LEIPZIG: *Adam* (marble) - STRASBOURG: *Bust of Grand Councillor W. Bodé; Bust of Dr Otto Back* - WEIMAR: *Bust of Grand Duke Charles Alexander of Saxony.*

AUCTION RECORDS:

BERLIN, 8 Nov 1977, *Bust of Heinrich von Stephan* (black-patinated bronze, h. 17 3/4 ins / 45 cm) DEM 2,200.

HILDEBRAND, Bernard
French, 19th century.
Born in Montoillet; died 1903, in Paris.
Sculptor.

Bernard Hildebrand was a member of the Société des Artistes Français.

HILDEBRAND, C.
17th century.
Active c. 1680.
Engraver (burin).

C. Hildebrand is known to have engraved a portrait of Descartes.

HILDEBRAND, Claire, or Hildebrandt
French, 19th century.
Born in the 19th century, in Colmar.
Painter.

Claire Hildebrand was a pupil of Madame de Cool and Chaplin. She made her Salon début in 1873, and gained an honourable mention in 1885; she became a member of the Société des Artistes Français in 1887. Hildebrand often exhibited paintings on porcelain and enamel.

HILDEBRAND, Ernst
German, 19th century.
Born 8 March 1833, in Falkenberg.
Painter. Historical scenes, portraits, genre scenes, landscapes.

Ernst Hildebrand, a pupil of Steffeck in Berlin, went on to become a professor at the school of art in Karlsruhe in 1875 and also in Berlin in 1880, having become a member of the Berlin academy of art in 1878. He was awarded medals in Berlin in 1887 and in Melbourne and Munich in the following year.

MUSEUMS AND GALLERIES:

BERLIN: *Portrait of Professor Auwers; Queen Louise in January 1807* - COLOGNE: *By the Stream.*

AUCTION RECORDS:

LONDON, 25 May 1932, *Bust of a Red-haired Woman,* FRF 410. LONDON, 3 Nov 1976, *Fishing Boats* (1843, watercolour, 6 1/4 x 9 1/2 ins / 16 x 24 cm) GBP 250. NEW YORK, 16 July 1992, *Favourite Games* (oil on canvas, 23 3/4 x 31 ins / 60.3 x 78.7 cm) USD 1,650. NEW YORK, 22-23 July 1993, *The Request before the King* (oil on canvas, 24 1/2 x 41 ins / 62.2 x 104.1 cm) USD 920.

HILDEBRAND, Henri Théophile.
See **HILDIBRAND**

HILDEBRAND, Johannes, or Hildebrandt
Flemish, 16th century.
Died 19 December 1522, in Bruges.
Illuminator.
Flemish School.
The work of Johannes Hildebrand was for a long time thought to be that of Margarette van Eyck.

HILDEBRAND, Josef
French, 18th century.
Active in Metz in 1752.
Painter.
Josef Hildebrand is known to have executed a *St Peter* and a *St Angela*.

HILDEBRAND, Melchior
German, 17th century.
Born in Uelzen; died 1618.
Painter.
Hildebrand, dean of the bishopric of Bardowick (Lower Saxony), painted mainly religious subjects.

HILDEBRAND, Otto
French, 20th century.
Born 16 November 1874, in Metz.
Sculptor (bronze). Low reliefs.
Otto Hildebrand was a pupil of Auguste Dujardin in Paris.
MUSEUMS AND GALLERIES:
METZ: *Low relief* (bronze).

HILDEBRANDT, Christian
German, 17th century.
Active in Leipzig during the first half of the 17th century.
Painter.

HILDEBRANDT, Eduard
German, 19th century.
Born 9 September 1818, in Danzig (now Gdansk, Poland); died 25 October 1869, in Berlin.
Painter, watercolourist, illustrator. Landscapes, mountainscapes.
Orientalism.
Eduard Hildebrandt started out in building decoration before going on to study art in Berlin in the studio of Wilhelm Krause. He then went to Paris, where he knew Eugène Isabey and set up his own studio. However, *Wanderlust* soon took hold and he left for Brazil, America, the Far East, Asia Minor, Switzerland and Italy. He took part in various collective exhibitions, including, the Paris Salon from 1843, where he was awarded a gold medal, a private exhibition in London in 1866 and Crystal Palace, London, in 1868. He also exhibited in Brussels. He was represented in the exhibition *Expedition Kunst. Die Entdeckung der Natur von C. D. Friedrich bis Humboldt (Expedition Art. The Discovery of Nature from CD Friedrich to Humboldt)* at Hamburg Kunsthalle in 2002, an exhibition which demonstrated the links between the natural sciences and the painted landscape.

He brought back many watercolours from his travels. His illustrated journal was published in Berlin in 1867 under the title *Reise um die Erde (Journey Round the Earth)*.
BIBLIOGRAPHY:
Janda, Karl Heinz, *Eduard Hildebrandt. Aquarelle, Zeichnungen, aus Beständen der National-Galerie, von der Sowjetunion 1958 übergeben*, exhibition catalogue, Staatlichen Museen zu Berlin, Berlin, 1959. *Expedition Kunst. Die Entdeckung der Natur von C. D. Friedrich bis Humboldt*, exhibition catalogue, Hamburger Kunsthalle, Hamburg, 2002.
MUSEUMS AND GALLERIES:
BERLIN: *Kronborg Castle, near Helsingor; Forest in Winter; High Mountain Valley at Sunset* - COLOGNE: *Landscape from Northern Germany* - ROUEN (MBA): *After the Thunderstorm; Setting Sun.*
AUCTION RECORDS:
PARIS, 18 May 1897, *Horses at the Watering Place,* FRF 1,443. LONDON, 22 April 1911, *View of the Rhine* (1855) GBP 52. PARIS, 20 Feb 1929, *St Mark's Square in Venice* (gouache) FRF 1,450. VIENNA, 16 March 1971, *Peasants in a Winter Landscape,* ATS 45,000. ZURICH, 26 May 1978, *Old Clock Tower, Rouen* (1846, oil on canvas, 14 1/4 x 10 1/4 ins / 36 x 26 cm) CHF 7,800. NEW YORK, 3 May 1979, *Moonlight in Madeira* (oil on canvas, 35 1/2 x 46 3/4 ins / 90 x 119 cm) USD 3,500. PARIS, 16 May 1979, *Watercourse Flowing through a Town* (watercolour, 6 x 4 3/4 ins / 15 x 12 cm) FRF 1,600. HAMBURG, 4 June 1980, *Seaside Scene* (pen/paper, 12 x 18 1/4 ins / 30.3 x 46.6 cm) DEM 2,300. STOCKHOLM, 28 Oct 1981, *Winter Landscape* (1848, oil on canvas, 35 x 52 1/4 ins / 88 x 133 cm) SEK 53,000. HAMBURG, 10 June 1982, *Lake Hezekiah, Jerusalem* (1852, watercolour, 10 x 14 1/2 ins / 25.5 x 37 cm) DEM 3,400. GENEVA, 25 Nov 1983, *The Promenade* (1850, oil on canvas, 13 3/4 x 17 1/4 ins / 35 x 44 cm) CHF 9,000. MUNICH, 21 June 1994, *Sailing Ships off the Coast* (oil on canvas, 11 x 14 1/2 ins / 27 x 37 cm) DEM 8,625. LONDON, 21 Nov 1996, *Rear View of a House; View of a Street with a Gothic Church in the Background* (black chalk, watercolour and gouache, a pair, 8 1/4 x 5 ins / 20.8 x 12.9 cm) GBP 1,495. COLOGNE, 25 March 1999, *View of S Maria della Salute in Venice* (1852, oil on canvas, 31 x 45 ins / 78 x 115 cm) DEM 44,000. LONDON, 29 April 1999, *Rua do Ouvidor, Rio de Janeiro* (watercolour, 14 x 10 ins / 35 x 26 cm) GBP 6,000. HAMBURG, 2 Sept 2000, *People on Beach Looking at Russian Ships* (1840, oil on canvas, 41 x 61 ins / 105 x 155 cm) DEM 28,000. BREMEN, 8 Dec 2000, *Winter on the Lofoten Isles* (oil on canvas, 25 x 37 ins / 63 x 93 cm) DEM 16,000. LONDON, 26 Sept 2001, *Gloria, Rio de Janeiro* (1847, oil on canvas, 26 x 34 ins / 66 x 86 cm) GBP 180,000. NEW YORK, 20 Nov 2001, *Untitled* (1845, watercolour, 20 x 28 ins / 51 x 72 cm) USD 40,000. LONDON, 26 Sept 2002, *Loo Rock and Pontinha, Madeira, Sunset* (oil on canvas, 33 x 46 ins / 84 x 117 cm) GBP 4,500. LONDON, 25 Sept 2003, *Ein heiliger See in Birma* (oil on canvas, 33 x 46 ins / 84 x 117 cm) GBP 48,000. BREMEN, 26 Sept 2003, *Grand Canal, Venice in the Evening* (1852, oil on canvas, 31 x 45 ins / 78 x 115 cm) EUR 16,000. STUTTGART, 26 April 2004, *Brazilian Landscape* (oil on canvas, 27 x 40 ins / 68 x 102 cm) EUR 4,600. LONDON, 23 Sept 2004, *South American Landscape with Storks by a Lake at unset* (oil on canvas, 13 x 17 ins / 33 x 43 cm) GBP 1,500.

HILDEBRANDT, Ernst
German, 20th century.
Born 18 March 1876, in Tuchel (now Tuchola, Poland).
Painter. Portraits, genre scenes, landscapes.
Ernst Hildebrandt exhibited at the Berlin academy, showing mainly genre scenes.

HILDEBRANDT, Ferdinand Theodor
German, 19th century.
Born 2 July 1804, in Stettin (now Szczecin, Poland); died 29 September 1874, in Düsseldorf.
Painter, engraver. Historical scenes, portraits, genre scenes, landscapes.
Dusseldorf School.
Hildebrandt first studied at the Berlin academy of art in 1820, then went on in 1823 to the studio of Schadow, following him to Düsseldorf in 1826. He exhibited from 1824, most notably in Berlin and Vienna, and became a member of the Academies in both cities. In 1832, having spent two years travelling in Belgium and Italy, he returned to Germany and was appointed professor at the Düsseldorf academy of art.

Hildebrandt came to public attention through his qualities as a colourist and was one of the most prominent painters of the German Realist School. He is also well known for some engravings executed from his own paintings.

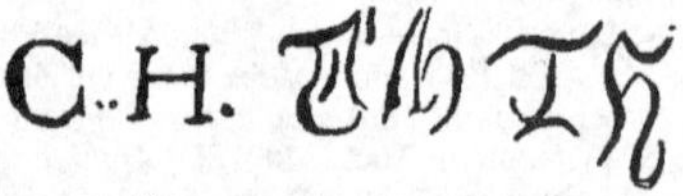

Museums and Galleries:
AMSTERDAM: *View of the River Neva at St Petersburg* - BERLIN: *Warrior with his Child; The Thief* - COLOGNE: *The Artist's Father; Portrait of the Engraver, Thelott* - DÜSSELDORF: *Portrait of Gustave Wappers.*
Auction records:
NEW YORK, 28 and 30 March 1904, *King Lear*, USD 580. COLOGNE, 18 Nov 1982, *Portrait of Prince George of Prussia* (oil on canvas, 5 x 37½ ins / 13 x 95 cm) DEM 8,000. MUNICH, 18 May 1988, *Portrait of Felix Mendelssohn-Bartholdy* (oil on canvas, 23½ x 21 ins / 59.5 x 52.5 cm) DEM 85,800. STOCKHOLM, 29 May 1991, *Farmyard with a Milkmaid Milking the Cows* (1867, oil on canvas, 30 x 48 ins / 76 x 121 cm) SEK 21,000. BRUSSELS, 24 April 2001, *The Letter* (oil on canvas, 12 x 14 ins / 30 x 36 cm) BEF 160,000. COLOGNE, 15 May 2002, *Artist's Studio* (1825, watercolour, 7 x 4 ins / 19 x 11 cm) EUR 3,600. NEW YORK, 22 Jan 2003, *Artist's Studio in Rome* (pencil and watercolour, 7 x 4 ins / 19 x 11 cm) USD 17,000.

HILDEBRANDT, Friedrich Fritz
German, 19th century.
Born 12 February 1819, in Danzig (now Gdansk, Poland); died 18 December 1885, in Rome.
Painter. Portraits, landscapes, seascapes. Murals.

Friedrich Hildebrandt was a brother of Eduard Hildebrandt and a pupil of Wilhelm Krause in Berlin and Eugène d'Isabey in Paris. He went to Italy in 1885.

Hildebrandt worked on the decoration of the Winter Palace in St Petersburg.

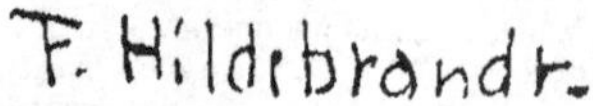

Museums and Galleries:
BERLIN: *Valley in the Pyrenees* - DIEPPE: *The Shore; Ship at the Coast.*
Auction records:
PARIS, 11 April 1945, *Fisherman's Daughter* (1844) FRF 9,500. STOCKHOLM, 15 Nov 1989, *Seascape with Sailing Ships, in Holland* (oil on panel, 13 x 20 ins / 33 x 51 cm) SEK 10,500. LONDON, 16 March 1994, *Winter Landscape with Figures by a Frozen River* (oil on canvas, 23¾ x 37½ ins / 60.5 x 95 cm) GBP 4,370.

HILDEBRANDT, Fritz
German, 20th century.
Born 1 January 1878, in Quedlinburg.
Painter. Portraits, landscapes.

Fritz Hildebrandt was active in Berlin.

HILDEBRANDT, Fritz
Swiss, 20th century.
Born 5 July 1890, in Winterthur; died 14 December 1918.
Painter, engraver.

Fritz Hildebrandt studied with Félix Valloton and Ker-Xavier Roussel.
Museums and Galleries:
WINTERTHUR: *Self-portrait.*

HILDEBRANDT, Howard Logan
Austrian, 19th - 20th century.
Born 21 November 1872, in Allegheny; died 1958.
Active in the USA.
Painter. Figures, still-lifes, flowers.

Howard Hildebrandt studied in Paris with Benjamin-Constant and Jean-Paul Laurens, and also at the École des Beaux-Arts. He settled in New York, where he became a member of the Salmagundi Club and the New York Watercolor Club.
Auction records:
NEW YORK, 18 Nov 1943, *Portrait of a Girl*, USD 650. BOLTON, 17 Nov 1983, *Esmeralda* (oil on canvas, 27¼ x 27¼ ins / 69 x 69 cm) USD 3,500. NEW YORK, 20 June 1985, *Young Woman Sitting in a Garden* (oil on canvas, 22 x 27 ins / 56 x 68.6 cm) USD 4,250. NEW YORK, 24 Jan 1989, *Still-life with Flowers in a Pewter Jug* (oil on canvas, 26½ x 22 ins / 67.5 x 55 cm) USD 1,320. PARIS, 9 Nov 1990, *Fisherman Pushing a Boat* (1843, watercolour, 7 x 11 ins / 17.5 x 28 cm) FRF 4,800.

HILDEBRANDT, J. W. C.
German, 19th century.
Active in Berlin c. 1800.
Sculptor.

J. W. C. Hildebrandt studied under Schadow at the Berlin academy of art.

HILDEBRANDT, Johann Heinrich, or Hillebrandt
German, 19th century.
Born 13 December 1840, in Hamburg.
Painter, lithographer.

Johann Hildebrandt was a pupil of Bach in Breslau (now Wroclaw, Poland).

HILDEBRANDT, Thomas
German, 17th century.
Active in Erfurt during the second half of the 17th century.
Painter. Portraits.

Thomas Hildebrandt painted portraits.

HILDEBRANDT, Tobias, the Elder
German, 17th century.
Active in Leipzig during the first half of the 17th century.
Painter.

HILDEBRANDT, Tobias, the Younger
German, 17th century.
Active in Leipzig during the second half of the 17th century.
Painter.

HILDEBRANT
German, 19th century.
Born in Bayreuth.
Sculptor.

Hildebrant exhibited his *Bust of the Poet, Jean Paul* at the Berlin academy of art in 1818.

HILDEGARDUS
German, 16th century.
Born to a family originally from Cologne.
Active c. 1523.
Painter.

Hildegardus painted the pictures in the monastery of Dortmund in Westphalia entitled *The Tables of the Rosary, Birth of Christ, The Seven Joys and Seven Sorrows of the Virgin,* and others.

HILDER, C.
17th century.
Active c. 1675.
Engraver (burin).

HILDER, G. Howard
British, 19th - 20th century.
Born 1868, in London.
Painter, illustrator.

Howard Hilder studied under William Bouguereau, Émile Jacque and Arthur (?) Perrier in Paris, and under Théophile de Bock in Amsterdam, where he became a member of the Kunst Vereeniging (art association). He was active in New York.

HILDER, Jesse Jewhurst
Australian, 20th century.
Born 1881; died 1916.
Painter, watercolourist. Landscapes.

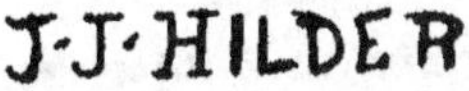

AUCTION RECORDS:
SYDNEY, 6 Oct 1976, *Cow Crossing Creek* (1915, watercolour, 7¾ x 9¾ ins / 20 x 25 cm) AUD 780. SYDNEY, 20 Oct 1980, *Winter Ploughing* (watercolour, 7 x 12¼ ins / 18 x 31 cm) AUD 6,000. SYDNEY, 28 June 1982, *Sheep in a Landscape* (watercolour, 9¾ x 6¾ ins / 25 x 17 cm) AUD 2,300. MELBOURNE, 8 Nov 1984, *Boatsheds, Hawkesbury River* (watercolour, 6¾ x 7¾ ins / 17 x 20 cm) AUD 5,000. SYDNEY, 23 Sept 1985, *Sheep Grazing* (watercolour, 9 x 8¼ ins / 23 x 21 cm) AUD 6,000. MELBOURNE, 6 April 1987, *Hawkesbury River* (1915, oil on panel, 5¾ x 9 ins / 14.5 x 23 cm) AUD 10,000. VICTORIA, 20 April 1999, *Morning Mist* (watercolour, 9 x 10 ins / 23 x 26 cm) AUD 4,000. VICTORIA, 9 Nov 1999, *Sydney Harbour* (5 x 10 ins / 12 x 26 cm) AUD 6,500. VICTORIA, 8 Aug 2000, *Country Bridge* (watercolour, 6 x 9 ins / 16 x 24 cm) AUD 3,200. PADDINGTON, 3 June 2001, *St Mary's Cathedral* (1911, watercolour and gouache, 8 x 7 ins / 20 x 18 cm) AUD 5,000. PADDINGTON, 25 Aug 2002, *Interior of Albers Home at Gordon* (watercolour, 11 x 7 ins / 27 x 19 cm) AUD 3,200. MELBOURNE, 2 April 2003, *Boy with Calf in a Meadow* (watercolour, 5 x 11 ins / 13 x 29 cm) AUD 11,000. SYDNEY, 27 Aug 2003, *Jetty* (watercolour, 6 x 10 ins / 16 x 26 cm) AUD 12,000. SYDNEY, 23 Aug 2004, *Old Street in Paddington* (oil on canvas on board, 6 x 9 ins / 15 x 24 cm) AUD 8,000. PADDINGTON, 24 Aug 2004, *Julian Ashton and Students at Narrabeen* (1906, 5 x 11 ins / 13 x 27 cm) AUD 10,000.

HILDER, P. John
British, 19th century.
Active in London.
Painter. Landscapes.
John Hilder exhibited in London very frequently between 1829 and 1839 at the Royal Academy, the British Institution and the Suffolk Street Gallery.
AUCTION RECORDS:
LONDON, 13 Feb 1909, *Canterbury*, GBP 10. LONDON, 30 Nov 1923, *Ferry*, GBP 35. LONDON, 21 Dec 1925, *Eton from the Thames*, GBP 44. LONDON, 15 Oct 1928, *Heron's Nest*, GBP 46. LONDON, 1 May 1931, *Ferry*, GBP 52. LONDON, 11 July 1947, *Last Load*, GBP 42. LONDON, 21 July 1978, *Wooded Landscape with River and Figures* (oil on panel, 11½ x 15 ins / 29.2 x 38 cm) GBP 900. LONDON, 11 April 1980, *Landscape with River and Cows and Sheep in a Ferryboat* (1837, oil on canvas, 24 ins / 61 cm 29 ins/73.6 cm) GBP 5,000. CREWKERNE, 31 Jan 2002, *Royal Oak Hotel and Gates to Lambard's Park, Sevenoaks, Kent* (1833, oil on canvas, 36 x 29 ins / 91 x 74 cm) GBP 5,000. LONDON, 1 Oct 2003, *Horse and Cart on a Wooded Track* (oil on canvas, 31 x 25 ins / 78 x 64 cm) GBP 1,200.

HILDER, Richard
British, 19th century.
Born 1813; died 1848.
Painter. Landscapes with figures, landscapes, animals.
Richard Hilder exhibited frequently in London between 1830 and 1851 at the Royal Academy, the British Institution and the Suffolk Street Gallery.
AUCTION RECORDS:
LONDON, 27 Jan 1908, *Stream*, GBP 1. LONDON, July 1922, *Farm Stream*, GBP 157. LONDON, Dec 1922, *Stream with Buildings, Figures etc.*, GBP 40. LONDON, 30 Nov 1923, *Landscape with Cottage and Figures*, GBP 42. LONDON, 20 June 1924, *Wooded River with Two Figures in a Boat*, GBP 37. LONDON, 3 July 1925, *Landscape*, GBP 75. LONDON, 23 July 1928, *View of Kent*, GBP 78. LONDON, 15 Oct 1928, *Hilly Landscape with Figures*, GBP 68. LONDON, 29 July 1929, *River with Bridge and Cattle*, GBP 50. LONDON, 22 June 1934, *Farm in Kent*, GBP 42. LONDON, 2 April 1937, *Country People*, GBP 110. LONDON, 23 April 1937, *Trout Stream*, GBP 60. LONDON, 17 Nov 1944, *Mousehold Heath, Norwich*, GBP 57. LONDON, 11 Dec 1946, *Landscape with Children Fishing in a Stream*, GBP 70. LONDON, 11 July 1947, *View near Sevenoaks*, GBP 126; *Landscape*, GBP 78. LONDON, 2 Nov 1966, *Wooded Landscapes*, GBP 750. LONDON, 17 June 1970, *Flocks in a Landscape*, GBP 850. LONDON, 27 June 1973, *Wooded Landscape with Figures*, GBP 2,300. LONDON, 14 July 1976, *Flocks at a Drinking Trough in a Wooded Landscape* (1843, oil on panel, 17¾ x 23¾ ins / 45 x 60.5 cm) GBP 1,500. LONDON, 29 July 1977, *Angler near a Bridge* (oil on panel, 13½ x 17½ ins / 34.3 x 44.4 cm) GBP 900. LONDON, 9 July 1980, *Country Road* (oil on panel, 23½ x 18 ins / 60 x 46 cm) GBP 2,000. LONDON, 7 July 1982, *Country People in a Wooded Landscape* (oil on panel, 18 x 24 ins / 46 x 61 cm) GBP 2,800. LONDON, 21 Dec 1983, *Near Cranbrook, Kent* (oil on canvas, 13¾ x 17¾ ins / 35 x 45 cm) GBP 1,300. LONDON, 11 March 1987, *Wooded Landscape with Cottages and Figures* (oil on canvas, 14¼ x 18 ins / 36 x 46 cm) GBP 4,500. LONDON, 29 Jan 1988, *Shepherds and Flocks on a Path in a Wooded Landscape* (oil on panel, 14¼ x 18¼ ins / 36.5 x 46.4 cm) GBP 2,860. LONDON, 26 May 1989, *Wooded Landscape with a Girl and her Herd of Cows* (oil on panel, 12 x 16 ins / 30.2 x 40.5 cm) GBP 4,840. LONDON, 26 Oct 1990, *Landscape with a Cottage, Country People and Cattle in the Foreground* (oil on canvas, 13½ x 17 ins / 34.3 x 42.9 cm) GBP 1,100. LONDON, 10 April 1991, *Kentish Homestead* (oil on panel, 13¾ x 20 ins / 35 x 50.5 cm) GBP 3,080. LONDON, 5 March 1993, *Milking Time* (oil on panel, 11¾ x 16 ins / 29.7 x 40.6 cm) GBP 2,990. ST ASAPH, 2 June 1994, *Wooded Landscape with Cattle Drinking* (oil on panel, 17 x 24 ins / 43 x 61 cm) GBP 3,450. LONDON, 9 Oct 1996, *Figures on a Path* (oil on panel, 13½ x 17¼ ins / 34.5 x 43.5 cm) GBP 1,725. LONDON, 13 March 1997, *Figures on a Path by a Village Pond* (oil on panel, 11¾ x 16 ins / 30 x 40.6 cm) GBP 2,200. LONDON, 9 Sept 1999, *Figures on a Path by a Bridge* (oil on canvas, 12 x 16 ins / 30 x 41 cm) GBP 3,800. LONDON, 30 Nov 1999, *Country Folk Resting by a Pond* (oil on panel, 14 x 18 ins / 35 x 46 cm) GBP 4,500. LONDON, 8 June 2000, *Figures on a Track in a Wooded Landscape, Cottage beyond* (oil on canvas, 14 x 24 ins / 35 x 60 cm) GBP 2,800. LEYBURN, 14 July 2000, *Surrey Farmstead* (oil on panel, 7 x 11 ins / 18 x 27 cm) GBP 1,200. DORCHESTER, 1 March 2001, *Rural Landscape with Cattle Grazing, Figure Approaching on a Track* (oil on canvas, 19 x 24 ins / 48 x 61 cm) GBP 1,400. LONDON, 8 Nov 2001, *Figures before a Cottage in a Wooded Landscape* (oil on canvas, 15 x 13 ins / 37 x 32 cm) GBP 2,000. CREWKERNE, 31 Jan 2002, *Rustics Watching a Chairmender near a Country Cottage* (oil on panel, 13 x 17 ins / 34 x 44 cm) GBP 3,000. BATH, 2 Dec 2002, *Winter Landscape with a Figure on a Path before a Cottage* (oil on panel, 10 x 13 ins / 25 x 34 cm) GBP 1,200. CREWKERNE, 15 May 2003, *Figure on Horseback on a Country Track. Gathering Brushwood* (oil on panel, a pair, 9 x 7 ins / 24 x 19 cm) GBP 3,000. EDINBURGH, 23 May 2003, *Woded River Landscape with Figures on a Country Path* (oil on panel, 12 x 16 ins / 30 x 40 cm) GBP 1,500. LONDON, 13 Jan 2004, *Extensive Country Landscape at Dusk with Figure and Horses* (oil on panel, 11 x 15 ins / 27 x 37 cm) GBP 1,100.

HILDER, Rowland
British, 20th century.
Born 28 June 1905, in Greatneck (Long Island), to British parents; died 1993.
Active in England.

Painter, illustrator, decorative artist. Landscapes, marine scenes.

Rowland Hilder came to England in 1915 and served in the army working on camouflage, illustrating the *Army Manual on Camouflage*. He studied etching and drawing under E.J. Sullivan from 1922 to 1925 at Goldsmith's College in London, where he also lectured. In 1924 he was awarded a travel scholarship to visit the Low Countries. He taught at the Central School of Arts and Crafts, the Royal College of Art and Farnham School of Art. He was influenced by the work of Muirhead Bone and Frank Brangwyn. He served as president of the Royal Institute of Painters in Watercolour from 1964 to 1974.

Hilder was involved in a number of fine art publication companies, doing pioneering work in silkscreening in Britain, and setting up Heron Press. From 1925 he was a noted illustrator of books, including work for R.L. Stevenson's *Treasure Island* (Oxford University Press, 1929); Herman Melville's *Moby Dick* (Jonathan Cape, 1926); John Masefield's *The Midnight Folk* (Heinemann, 1931); and G. Grigson's *Shell Guide to Flowers of the Countryside* (Phoenix House, 1955; assisted by his wife Edith Blenkiron). He also wrote instructional books on painting with watercolour.

Hilder was quite successful with his watercolour and oil paintings of the English countryside, especially of Kent, which featured a pre-industrial landscape, webs of trees and oast houses. As a sailor and owner of a coastguard cottage at Shell Ness, he enjoyed painting marine scenes and illustrating books of boys' sea adventure stories. He concentrated on painting rather than illustration after 1963, producing works such as *Fill Dyke No 1* (1975, oil); *Hop Fields and Oast Houses Near Shoreham, Kent* (1977, watercolour); *Shrimper off Gravesend* (1980, watercolour); and *The Swale* (1976, watercolour).

His work was exhibited at the Royal Academy (1926-1947); Fine Art Society (1936); Royal Institute of Painters in Watercolour; Royal Hibernian Academy; New English Art Club; a retrospective at Woodlands Art Gallery (1985); and the Duncan Campbell Gallery in London (from 1986). He was awarded the Order of the British Empire (OBE).

Bibliography:

Hilder, Rowland, *Starting with Watercolour*, Illustrated book, Studio Vista, 1966. Lewis, John, *Rowland Hilder: Painter and Illustrator*, Illustrated book, Barrie and Jenkins, London, 1978. Hilder, Rowland, *Painting Landscape in Watercolour*, Illustrated book, Collins, 1983. Hilder, Rowland, *Rowland Hilder's England: A Personal Record by the Artist*, Illustrated book, Herbert Press, London, 1986. Lewis, John Noel Claude, *Rowland Hilder: Painter of the English Landscape*, Illustrated book, Antique Collectors' Club, Woodbridge, 1987. Thomas, Denis (ed.), *Rowland Hilder Country: An Artist's Memoir*, Illustrated book, Herbert Press, London, 1987. Thomas, Denis (ed.), *Rowland Hilder Sketching Country*, Illustrated book, Herbert Press, London, 1991.

Museums and Galleries:

Canberra (Nat. Gal. of Australia): *Cable Ship, Greenwich* - London (UK Government Art Collection): *Canterbury Cathedral* (watercolour); *Late Autumn, North Downs* (watercolour); *Mountains in Snow, Skiddaw* (watercolour); *Toad Lane, Rochdale* (watercolour).

Auction records:

Billingshurst, 26 Oct 1999, *Shoreham Valley* (oil on canvasboard, 19 x 29 ins / 49 x 74 cm) GBP 3,500. London, 3 Nov 1999, *Lane and Cottage, East Anglia* (watercolour, pen and ink heightened with white, 14 x 21 ins / 35 x 53 cm) GBP 3,200. London, 17 July 2001, *Smallholding with Two Oasts* (1942, oil on board, 20 x 24 ins / 50 x 60 cm) GBP 6,000. Billingshurst, 18 July 2001, *Oast Houses and Elms, Kent* (watercolour, 15 x 22 ins / 37 x 57 cm) GBP 4,200. London, 4 July 2002, *Kent* (1960, ink, gouache and watercolour, 20 x 26 ins / 50 x 67 cm) GBP 5,500. London, 15 Oct 2002, *Suffolk Farm* (oil on board, 20 x 24 ins / 51 x 61 cm) GBP 3,080. London, 10 Sept 2003, *Winter Landscape in Kent* (oil on board, 24 x 32 ins / 60 x 81 cm) GBP 3,600. London, 2 Dec 2003, *Winter Landscape* (pen, ink and watercolour, 20 x 28 ins / 51 x 70 cm) GBP 2,800. London, 11 Feb 2004, *Morning Shadows over a Country Track* (watercolour, 21 x 29 ins / 53 x 73 cm) GBP 6,500. Lewes, 7 Sept 2004, *Shoreham Valley* (oil on board, 20 x 30 ins / 51 x 76 cm) GBP 3,800.

HILDIBRAND, Henri Théophile

French, 19th century.

Born 1824, in Paris; died 1897, in Paris.

Engraver (wood).

Hildibrand, who was a master of wood engraving and a pupil of Best and Leloir, received an honourable mention at the Salon of 1872. He made his Salon début in 1866 with two engravings after Gustave Doré, produced as illustrations for Dante's *Purgatorio*, and continued to participate regularly in the exhibitions held in Paris. Hildibrand made engravings for the top publishers of the day, from drawings by the finest graphic artists, including: Grenier, Riou, Therond, Foulquier, Lancelot, Doré, Karl Girardet, H. Clerget, Émile Bayard, Gransire, A. de Neuville, A. Marie, Allongé, Maillard, Valerio, Deyrole, Philippoteaux, Delort, Regamey, and Zier. He also illustrated the works of Théophile Gautier, and many books in the Bibliothèque Rose collection.

HILDITCH, George

British, 19th century.

Born 1803, in London; died 1857, in London.

Painter. Landscapes.

Many of George Hilditch's paintings, which show mainly views of the area around Richmond and landscapes of Wales, Germany and France, are owned by the dukes of Devonshire and Sutherland and the earls of Dysart and Wharncliffe. He exhibited regularly in London between 1823 and 1856 at the Royal Academy, the British Institution and the Suffolk Street Gallery, receiving a number of awards for his work.

Auction records:

London, 12 July 1967, *House by the Thames*, GBP 850. London, 15 Dec 1972, *The Avenue*, Gns 700. London, 23 Nov 1973, *Banks of the Thames*, Gns 600. London, 11 April 1980, *Wooded Landscape with Figures* (oil on card, 12½ x 19½ ins / 31.7 x 49.5 cm) GBP 1,600. London, 16 July 1982, *Landscape with Figures* (oil on card, 12½ x 19½ ins / 31.8 x 49.5 cm) GBP 1,300. London, 22 April 1983, *Backwater, Old Deer Park, Isleworth* (oil on card, 9½ x 13½ ins / 24.1 x 34.3 cm) GBP 850. London, 15 Dec 1993, *View of Petersham Eyot by the Thames near Richmond* (oil on canvas, 12 x 16 ins / 30.5 x 40.6 cm) GBP 1,840. London, 9 April 1997, *View of the Thames at Richmond* (oil on canvas, 29½ x 42½ ins / 75 x 108 cm) GBP 10,925. Crewkerne, 21 May 1999, *View of Richmond Hill* (oil on canvas, 13 x 19 ins / 32 x 47 cm) GBP 3,100. London, 14 July 1999, *View of Richmond with Star and Garter* (oil on panel, 13 x 20 ins / 32 x 50 cm) GBP 3,800. Amsterdam, 5 Sept 2000, *Pond Twickenham Park* (oil on panel, 9 x 13 ins / 24 x 34 cm) NLG 5,000.

HILDITCH, Richard H.

British, 19th century.

Active in London.

Painter. Waterscapes, urban landscapes, landscapes.

Richard Hilditch frequently exhibited in London at the Royal Academy, the British Institution and the Suffolk Street Gallery between 1823 and 1865.

HILEKEN, Jean Jacques

French, 18th century.

Born c. 1720, in Trèves (Trier); died 1799, in Salins (Jura).

Active in Salins between 1740 and 1799.
Painter.

HILER, Hilaire
American, 20th century.
Born 16 July 1898, in St Paul (Minnesota); died 1966.
Active in France.
Painter, decorative designer.

Hilaire Hiler mainly worked in Paris, where he exhibited at the Salon d'Automne and the Salon des Indépendants. He also exhibited in London and New York. He painted decorative works and created the tapestry *Fish-Sellers*.

AUCTION RECORDS:
NEW YORK, 24 June 1988, *Café-Brasserie du Dôme* (1928, oil on canvas, 17¾ x 25 ins / 45 x 63.3 cm) USD 3,080. NEW YORK, 30 Sept 1988, *Castles in Spain* (1931, oil on canvas, 28¾ x 21¼ ins / 73 x 54 cm) USD 4,180. NEW YORK, 4 March 1999, *Grey Shadow Series Run. Red and Green Complementary Harmony* (1956, oil on panel, 12 x 16 ins / 30 x 40 cm) USD 3,000. CHICAGO, 16 May 2004, *Bronson Gold* (1931, gouache, 12 x 18 ins / 30 x 46 cm) USD 14,000.

HILES, Frederick John, called Bartram
British, 19th - 20th century.
Born 1872, in Bristol; died 1927, in Clifton.
Painter, watercolourist. Landscapes, figures.

Frederick John Hiles grew up in Hotwells, a Bristol suburb located between Clifton and the River Avon. As a result of a tram accident, Hiles lost both his arms at the age of eight, but his disability did not deter him from becoming a successful artist. Hiles learnt to draw holding a paintbrush with his mouth, and went on to study art in London and Paris. He was a member of the Royal West of England Academy and signed his work as 'Bartram Hiles'. His work consists mainly of watercolours.

BIBLIOGRAPHY:
Reid, H. and Stops, S., *On the Waterfront: the Hotwells Story*, Redcliffe Press, Bristol, 2002.

HILFELING, Anna Maria
Maiden name: Lange
Swedish, 18th century.
Born 21 or 24 April 1714, in Stockholm; died 26 May 1789, in Romelanda.
Miniaturist.

Anna Hilfeling studied with Precht and Lafrensen. There is a *Portrait of a Woman* by her in the museum of Copenhagen.

HILFELING, Carl Gustaf Gottfried
Swedish, 18th - 19th century.
Born 1740, in Östergötland; died 1823, in Skövde.
Active in Copenhagen from 1785.
Painter. Architectural views.

HILGEMANN, Ewerdt
German, 20th century.
Born 1938, in Witten (Ruhr).
Active in the Netherlands.
Painter, sculptor.

Ewerdt Hilgemann featured in the exhibition *Aspects Historiques du Constructivisme et de l'Art Concret* (*Historical Aspects of Constructivism and Concrete Art*) at the Muséé d'Art Moderne in Paris in 1977. His works start from primary structures. At first he assembled low reliefs from wooden rods, then he developed systems of objects in space, and since 1970 he has been producing square reliefs and cubes.

HILGERS, Carl
German, 19th century.
Born 14 April 1818, in Düsseldorf; died 3 December 1890, in Düsseldorf.
Painter. Genre scenes, landscapes.

Hilgers studied at the Düsseldorf academy of art, then travelled in Germany, France, Belgium and Holland. Having first exhibited in 1838, he went on to exhibit mainly in Berlin and Dresden.

MUSEUMS AND GALLERIES:
DÜSSELDORF: three landscapes.

AUCTION RECORDS:
NEW YORK, 31 Jan 1946, *Winter Scene in Holland*, USD 450. COLOGNE, 15 Nov 1972, *Winter Hunting Scene*, DEM 25,000. COLOGNE, 15 June 1973, *Winter Landscape*, DEM 8,500. COLOGNE, 14 Nov 1974, *Winter Landscape*, DEM 7,000. COLOGNE, 14 June 1976, *Landscape with Mill* (1876, oil on canvas, 20¼ x 15½ ins / 51.5 x 39.5 cm) DEM 2,600. LONDON, 23 Feb 1977, *Winter Landscape* (1853, oil on canvas, 16¼ x 23¼ ins / 41 x 59 cm) GBP 5,800. COLOGNE, 30 March 1979, *Romantic Landscape* (1846, oil on canvas, 33 x 49½ ins / 84 x 126 cm) DEM 26,000. COLOGNE, 25 June 1982, *Winter Landscape with Figures* (1855, oil on panel, 19¼ x 24½ ins / 49 x 62.5 cm) DEM 14,000. NEW YORK, 17 May 1984, *Fox on a Frozen River* (1867, oil on canvas, 45 x 40 ins / 114 x 101.5 cm) USD 10,000. LONDON, 20 March 1985, *Winter Landscape* (1849, oil on canvas, 22½ x 32¾ ins / 57 x 83 cm) GBP 10,000. PARIS, 3 June 1992, *The Market in Winter* (1855, oil on canvas, 24¾ x 33 ins / 63 x 84 cm) FRF 80,000. NEW YORK, 20 Jan 1993, *Dutch Landscape in Winter* (oil on canvas, 20½ x 28¾ ins / 52.1 x 73 cm) USD 8,338. MUNICH, 7 Dec 1993, *Winter Pastimes* (1870, oil on panel, 6 x 9½ ins / 15 x 24 cm) DEM 10,350. LONDON, 18 March 1994, *Boats Moored on the Banks of a Frozen Lake* (1849, oil on canvas, 12¼ x 17½ ins / 31.1 x 44.2 cm) GBP 4,600. AMSTERDAM, 21 April 1994, *Winter: Horse-drawn Sleigh with Peasants on a Frozen Canal near a Town; Summer: Fishermen Chatting with Passers-by on the Shore* (1871, oil on panel, a pair, each 4¼ x 15 ins / 11 x 38 cm) NLG 20,700. AMSTERDAM, 27 Oct 1997, *Crowds of Skaters on a Frozen Canal near Amsterdam* (1859, oil on canvas, 30¼ x 50½ ins / 77 x 128 cm) NLG 147,500. AMSTERDAM, 27 April 1999, *Winter Landscape with Horse-drawn Sledge on Frozen River by Windmill* (1871, oil on panel, 15 x 18 ins / 37 x 46 cm) NLG 18,000. COLOGNE, 15 May 1999, *Fishermen around Fire in Coastal Landscape at Night* (1860, oil on canvas, 16 x 22 ins / 40 x 55 cm) DEM 6,000. KÖNIGSTEIN, 25 Nov 2000, *Winter Landscape* (1875, oil on canvas, 8 x 12 ins / 21 x 31 cm) DEM 13,000. LINDAU, 1 Dec 2000, *Enjoying the Ice* (oil on canvas, 20 x 29 ins / 52 x 73 cm) DEM 20,000. COLOGNE, 5 April 2001, *Winter Day with Frozen Canal* (oil on panel, 12 x 19 ins / 31 x 48 cm) DEM 26,000. COLOGNE, 17 Nov 2001, *Fishermen Hauling in Nets* (1877, oil on panel, 9 x 13 ins / 22 x 32 cm) DEM 10,000. AMSTERDAM, 24 April 2002, *Skaters on a Frozen Lake, with a Manor Beyond* (1849, oil on canvas, 38 x 57 ins / 96 x 145 cm) EUR 36,000. COLOGNE, 21 Nov 2002, *Soldiers by Tent in Winter Landscape* (oil on panel, 7 x 9 ins / 19 x 23 cm) EUR 2,800. COLOGNE, 10 April 2003, *Dutch Winter Landscape* (oil on panel, 16 x 23 ins / 40 x 58 cm) EUR 12,000. COLOGNE, 20 Nov 2003, *On the Coast in Winter with Riders Round Campfire* (1877, oil on panel, 9 x 13 ins / 24 x 32 cm) EUR 4,600. NEW YORK, 22 April 2004, *Hunters with their Dogs on a Frozen Stream by a Castle* (1858, oil on canvas, 12 x 18 ins / 30 x 46 cm) USD 10,000.

HILGERS, Georg
German, 20th century.
Born 23 January 1879, in Munich.
Painter.

Georg Hilgers studied at the Düsseldorf academy from 1904.

HILGERS, Karl
German, 19th century.
Born 17 January 1844, in Düsseldorf.
Sculptor.

Hilgers studied painting and sculpture at the Düsseldorf academy of art, then went on to work in Italy, staying there for three years before returning to settle in Düsseldorf. He became one of the most popular sculptors of the German

School of the 19th and 20th centuries. His best known works include his *Colossal Statue of William I*, unveiled in Szczecin in 1894, a *Monument to the Dead* in Düsseldorf and his *Statue of Frederick William I*. William II appointed Karl Hilgers as court sculptor. His overwhelming quality was a certain correctness that, despite being slightly cold, is always elegant.

MUSEUMS AND GALLERIES:
BERLIN: *Muse, Seated* - DÜSSELDORF: *The Spirit of Art*.

HILHOUSE, James Martin
British, 18th - 19th century.
Born 1748; died 1822.
Painter. Battles, seascapes.

James Hilhouse came from well-known family of ship-builders. By 1782, he was the most important ship-builder in Bristol. As a painter, he worked in collaboration with Nicholas Pocock.

AUCTION RECORDS:
LONDON, 30 May 1996, *The Battle of the Saints* (oil on canvas, 40 1/4 x 64 1/4 ins / 102.5 x 163.5 cm) GBP 25,300.

HILIGENSNYDER. See BELDENSNYDER

HILKER, Georg Christian
Danish, 19th century.
Born 5 June 1807, in Copenhagen; died 13 January 1875, in Copenhagen.
Painter.

Georg Hilker was a pupil of Baruël and Kongsler. He painted some landscapes but mostly executed decorative works.

HILL, Adrian
British, 20th century.
Born 1897, in Charlton (Kent); died 1977.
Painter, watercolourist. Landscapes.

AUCTION RECORDS:
LONDON, 12 May 1989, *On the Fal in Cornwall* (oil on card, 19 3/4 x 23 1/2 ins / 50 x 60 cm) GBP 605. TORONTO, 12 June 2000, *Art Show. Landscape* (oil on canvas, double-sided, 20 x 24 ins / 51 x 61 cm) CAD 2,400. SAN FRANCISCO, 19 Nov 2003, *By the Barbican, Plymouth* (oil on canvas, 20 x 24 ins / 51 x 61 cm) USD 2,000.

HILL, Amelia Robertson
Maiden name: Paton
British, 19th century.
Born in Dunfermline.
Sculptor. Figures. Busts.

The wife of David Octavius Hill, Amelia Hill exhibited at the Royal Academy in London in about 1870.

AUCTION RECORDS:
LONDON, 28 Oct 1976, *Bust of Shelley* (bronze, h. 37 ins / 94 cm) GBP 480.

HILL, Anthony
British, 20th century.
Born 1930, in London.
Painter, sculptor.

Anthony Hill lives and works in London. The son of an academic painter, he was initially interested in science but later turned to painting, and from 1947 to 1951 he attended St Martin's School of Art and the Central School of Arts and Crafts, London. It was at this time that he met the British painters Victor Pasmore, Robert Adams and Adrian Heath, who introduced him to abstract painting. In Paris in 1950 Hill met the Belgian painter Georges Vantongerloo, the Russian painter Sonia Delaunay, the French painter and writer Francis Picabia, the Czech painter František Kupka, and the Belgian painter and writer Michel Seuphor: through them he encountered Neo-Constructivism. In 1951 Hill's work appeared in *English Abstract Art*, the first exhibition of abstract art ever held in London. In 1959, he made his first visit to Holland; here he met artists and writers on art, and began contributing to the art journal *Structure*. The following year, he took part in *Art Concret* (*Concrete Art*), an exhibition organized by the Swiss artist and writer Max Bill, and in 1962 his work was shown in *Experiment in Constructie* (*Experiment in Constructivism*) at the Stedelijk Museum, Amsterdam.

In 1964 Hill travelled to the USA, where he met the Minimalist sculptor Donald Judd and the painter and writer Ad Reinhardt. In 1968 he edited *DATA: Directions in Art, Theory and Aesthetics*, an anthology of essays on the relationship between art and mathematics. After 1975, although he still working in an abstract Constructivist style, Hill created collages that he signed with the Dadaist pseudonym Redo (for Rembrandt's Doghsfoodt). In 1977, he took part in *Aspects historiques du Constructivisme et de l'Art Concret* (*Historical Aspects of Constructivism and Concrete Art*), an exhibition at the Musée d'Art Moderne, Paris, and in 1980 he featured in *Pier and Ocean*, which was shown at the Hayward Gallery, London, then at the Museum Kröller-Müller, Otterloo. A retrospective of his work was held at the Hayward Gallery in 1983.

Although Hill's early paintings, dating from 1948, seem to follow in the post-Dadaist tradition, he later joined the British Constructivist movement. He was influenced by historical Constructivism, by Max Bill and by De Stijl. His paintings and collages of 1950 to 1952 are similar to the early work of Victor Pasmore and Ben Nicholson. From 1956 Hill gave up painting and began to make reliefs. These are made up of basic geometric shapes arranged according to mathematical formulae and consisting of radically different materials, such as aluminium, vinyl, laminate, copper and wood, which he applied to a flat surface with no trace of manual work. Hill made an important contribution to British Constructivism, a movement completely at odds with figurative art and its major exponents. However, at the end of the 1970s, Hill abandoned Constructivism to devote himself to creating post-Dadaist collages.

BIBLIOGRAPHY:
Alloway, Lawrence, *Nine Abstract Artists, their Work and Theory: Robert Adams, Terry Frost, Adrian Heath, Anthony Hill, Roger Hilton, Kenneth Martin, Mary Martin, Victor Pasmore and William Scott*, Alec Tiranti, London, 1954.

MUSEUMS AND GALLERIES:
GRENOBLE (Mus. de Grenoble): *Relief-Construction* (1956-1960) - LONDON (Tate Collection): *Orthogonal/Diagonal Composition* (1954, painting/canvas); *Painting 55-56* (1955-1956, oil and painting/canvas); reliefs (plastic and metal); screenprints.

AUCTION RECORDS:
LONDON, 25 Nov 1993, *Maquette for a Relief in 5 Zones* (1963, acrylic and metal/card, 13 1/4 x 11 1/2 ins / 33.7 x 29.2 cm) GBP 1,035. LONDON, 22 Oct 1997, *Progression of Rectangles (Relief Construction)* (1954-1955, perspex, metal and wood construction, 36 x 36 x 2 3/4 ins / 91.5 x 91.5 x 7 cm) GBP 2,415. LONDON, 8 June 1999, *Relief Construction* (1956-1966, plastic and brass, 26 x 26 ins / 66 x 66 cm) GBP 2,500. LONDON, 2 June 2004, *Relief Construction* (1969, plastic and aluminium, 36 x 36 ins / 91 x 91 cm) GBP 4,000.

HILL, Arthur
British, 19th - 20th century.
Active from 1858 to 1893, in Nottingham.
Painter. Figures, nudes, genre scenes.

Arthur Hill was a member of the Society of British Artists. He exhibited at the Royal Academy and the Suffolk Street Gallery from 1958.

AUCTION RECORDS:
LONDON, 24 Feb 1908, *Water Carrier* (1881) GBP 1. LONDON, 2 Feb 1979, *Portrait of a Lady* (1905, oil on panel, 35 1/4 x 13 3/4 ins / 89.5 x 35 cm) GBP 2,000. LONDON, 23 March 1981, *The Slave* (oil on canvas, 59 1/2 x 22 1/2 ins / 151 x 57 cm) GBP 3,500. LONDON, 29 March 1983, *Before the Bath* (1881, oil on canvas, 36 x 18 ins / 91.5 x 46 cm) GBP 950. LONDON, 2 Nov 1989, *He Loves Me, He Loves me Not* (1875, oil on canvas, 30 x 17 ins / 76.2 x 43.2 cm) GBP 8,800. NEW YORK, 17 Jan 1990, *Young Woman Holding Prayer Book and Beads* (1876, oil on canvas, 46 x 29 ins / 116.8 x 73.7 cm) USD 2,530. LONDON, 25 March 1994, *The Naked Piper* (oil on canvas, 60 3/4 x 25 ins / 154.6 x 63.2 cm) GBP 13,800. LONDON, 7 March 2002, *Classical Piper* (1881, oil on canvas, 36 x 24 ins / 91 x 61 cm) GBP 3,500. LONDON, 27 May 2004, *Reflection* (1886, oil on canvas, 25 x 15 ins / 63 x 37 cm) GBP 5,000. NEW ORLEANS, 5 June 2004, *Dancer* (oil on canvas, 69 x 30 ins / 175 x 76 cm) USD 12,000.

HILL, Arthur Thurnbull
American, 19th century.
Born 26 April 1868, in New York; died 1929.
Painter. Landscapes.

MUSEUMS AND GALLERIES:
NEW YORK (Brooklyn Mus.): several works.

HILL, Carl Frederick
Swedish, 19th - 20th century.
Born 1849, in Lund; died 1911, in Lund.
Painter, draughtsman. Religious subjects, mythological subjects, landscapes with figures, landscapes.

After his early studies at the Stockholm academy, Carl Frederick Hill went to Paris in 1873 and followed Corot and Daubigny to Barbizon, working in the forest of Fontainebleau. Having been rejected by the Salon de Paris, he exhibited with the Impressionists at their third exhibition in 1877. He was intending to show 18 large paintings at the 1978 Exposition Universelle. His family destroyed these paintings, which they considered disturbed, and had him confined in Dr Blanche's clinic, where he spent two years. He was transferred to a Danish asylum, then taken home to Lund, where he spent 30 years shut away in the family home. In 1998, his paintings featured in the exhibition *Visions du Nord* (*Visions of the North*) at the Musée d'Art Moderne in Paris.

His work falls into two distinct periods. The first is the pantheistic contemplation of nature corresponding to his time in France. Then, during the last 30 years of his life after his return to Sweden, he sank into a state of pathological melancholia, producing around 4,000 drawings, in which he retraced the fantastic visions of his dreams and hallucinations - demons, wild animals, erotic scenes, descents into hell, projected into the world of classical mythology and the Bible. His favourite subjects were curses, monstrous creatures, scenes of destruction and ruin, desolate mental landscapes, deserted and frozen at the moment of cataclysm. In the black and white drawings, and the occasional paintings in which strident blues and yellows constantly reappear, he was obsessed with depicting the primitive elements, water and ice, fire, the mineral kingdom. His mental journey led him to the contemplation of nature at its most imposing, to a state of near-hallucination at the sight of all it had to offer, and opened the way to primitive mystery and fear.

BIBLIOGRAPHY:
Lassaigne, Jacques, *Carl Frederik Hill*, Paris, 1952. Lindwall, Bo, *Hill, Josephson, Strindberg*, exhibition catalogue, Malmö Museum, Malmö, 1970. Baselitz, Georg, *Carl Frederik Hill, Ball Season in Sweden*, Blondal, Hellerup, 1994. *Visions du Nord*, exhibition catalogue, Musée d'Art moderne de la Ville de Paris, Paris, 1998.

AUCTION RECORDS:
NEW YORK, 24-26 Oct 1946, *Landscape with River and Figures*, GBP 1,700. GÖTEBORG, 29 March 1973, *Landscape* (1872) SEK 10,000. STOCKHOLM, 20 April 1977, *Landscape with River* (1875, oil on canvas, 21 x 35 1/2 ins / 52.5 x 90 cm) SEK 98,000. STOCKHOLM, 30 Oct 1979, *Summer Landscape* (1875, pencil, 21 1/4 x 21 1/4 ins / 54 x 54 cm) SEK 14,200. STOCKHOLM, 30 Oct 1979, *The Forest of Fontainebleau in Summer* (1875, oil on canvas, 19 3/4 x 23 1/2 ins / 50 x 60 cm) SEK 111,000. STOCKHOLM, 26 April 1982, *Parnassus* (pen, 22 1/4 x 26 1/2 ins / 56.5 x 67.5 cm) SEK 16,000. STOCKHOLM, 26 April 1983, *The Cliffs, Luc-sur-Mer* (1876, oil on card, 15 x 19 ins / 38 x 48 cm) SEK 365,000. STOCKHOLM, 16 May 1984, *The Entrance to the Temple* (pen and Indian ink, 22 1/2 x 13 3/4 ins / 57 x 35 cm) SEK 26,000. STOCKHOLM, 29 Oct 1985, *Landscape with Huts* (charcoal and coloured chalk, 9 x 14 1/4 ins / 23 x 36 cm) SEK 15,000. STOCKHOLM, 4 Nov 1986, *The Forest of Barbizon* (1874, oil on canvas, 13 x 10 1/4 ins / 33 x 26 cm) SEK 64,000. LONDON, 27-28 March 1990, *The Bois de Boulogne* (1875, black chalk, 26 3/4 x 20 3/4 ins / 68 x 53 cm) GBP 33,000. STOCKHOLM, 19 May 1992, *Seaside Landscape with Cliffs* (oil on panel, 15 x 19 ins / 38 x 48 cm) SEK 470,000. STOCKHOLM, 5 Sept 1992, *Boats on a Pond II* (oil on canvas, 41 1/4 x 49 1/4 ins / 105 x 125 cm) SEK 800,000. STOCKHOLM, 10-12 May 1993, *Large Composition with Figures* (ink, 13 1/2 x 16 1/2 ins / 34 x 42 cm) SEK 31,000. STOCKHOLM, 30 Nov 1993, *Conifer Forest with Birds* (black ink, 6 3/4 x 8 1/2 ins / 17 x 21.5 cm) SEK 10,000.

HILL, Caroline
American, 20th century.
Born in Boston.
Sculptor, painter.

Caroline Hill studied under Antoine Bourdelle in Paris, where she exhibited at the Salon des Tuileries from 1929. She may be the same artist as Clara and Carrie Hill.

HILL, Carrie L.
American, 20th century.
Painter. Landscapes.

Carrie Hill won various prizes and awards. She was a member of the National Association of Women Painters and Sculptors in New York. She may be the same artist as Clara and Caroline Hill.

HILL, Charles Christopher
American, 20th - 21st century.
Born 1948, in Greensburg (Pennsylvania).
Painter (mixed media).

Charles Hill trained at the University of California, Irvine. The surfaces of his canvases are covered with free-hand strips which evolve from black to colour, before criss-crossing with other elements to define the space of the support.

Since 1972, Hill's work has featured in numerous group exhibitions, chiefly in cities in the USA. His paintings have also been shown in solo exhibitions, starting in Newport Beach in 1972, and subsequently throughout the USA, notably in Los Angeles. He has also exhibited internationally: 1973, Bern; 1975, Venice, Paris, Bern; 1976, Zurich, Paris; 1977, Bern, Edinburgh; 1978, Zurich, Edinburgh; 1981, Zurich; 1982, Bern and Galerie Baudoin Lebon, Paris; 1985, Galeria Dell Cavallino, Venice and Galerie Baudoin Lebon, Paris; 1991, Galerie Baudoin Lebon, Paris; 1997 Galerie Baudoin Lebon.

AUCTION RECORDS:
PARIS, 30 Jan 1989, *Composition* (1987, mixed media/paper, 11 x 9 ins / 28 x 23 cm) FRF 5,000.

HILL, Clara
American, 20th century.
Sculptor.

Clara Hill may be the same artist as Carrie and Caroline Hill. She studied in Paris and was a member of the American Federation of Arts.

HILL, David
American, 20th century.
Born in the USA.
Painter.

HILL, David Octavius
British, 19th century.
Born 1802, in Perth, Scotland; died 17 May 1870, in Edinburgh.
Painter, photographer. Genre scenes, landscapes, seascapes.

David Octavius Hill studied under Andrew Wilson in Edinburgh and held his first exhibition there in 1823. He painted scenes of rural Scottish life and later landscapes, publishing a series entitled *The Land of Burns* in 1841. However, he is better known as one of the pioneers of the art of photography.

In 1843 he and the photographer Robert Adamson were commissioned to photograph the founders of the Scottish Free Church. From then onwards the pair produced a great many landscapes, city views and especially portraits, gaining great acclaim for their sensitive use of what was then an extremely new technique.

BIBLIOGRAPHY:
The Works of David Octavius Hill, exhibition catalogue, Hunterian Museum, Glasgow, 1954. *Hill and Adamson: photographs from the J. Paul Getty Museum*, exhibition catalogue, J. Paul Getty museum, Los Angeles, 1999. Stevenson, Sara, *The Personal Art of David Octavius Hill*, Yale University Press, New Haven, 2002.

MUSEUMS AND GALLERIES:
GLASGOW: *Scene in a Cemetery* - MELBOURNE (Nat. Gal. of Victoria): *Seascape*.

AUCTION RECORDS:
SCOTLAND, 24 Aug 1976, *Bonfire at Taymouth* (c. 1835-1840, oil on canvas, 13 x 17 1/2 ins / 33 x 44.5 cm) GBP 700. LONDON, 28 Jan 1977, *View of Edinburgh* (oil on canvas, 27 1/2 x 53 1/2 ins / 70 x 136 cm) GBP 1,000. LOCH LOMOND, 30 June 1981, *Gareloch at Sunset* (1851, oil on canvas, 40 1/4 x 67 3/4 ins / 102 x 172 cm) GBP 1,000. GLASGOW, 5 Feb 1986, *The Royal Mile, Edinburgh* (oil on canvas, 53 1/2 x 76 ins / 136 x 193 cm) GBP 9,000. EDINBURGH, 26 April 1988, *View of Stirling* (oil on canvas, 19 1/4 x 36 ins / 49 x 91.5 cm) GBP 2,420. EDINBURGH, 19 Nov 1992, *Bruce's Castle at Turnberry, Carrick Shore* (1856, oil on canvas, 19 x 30 1/4 ins / 48.2 x 76.8 cm) GBP 990.

HILL, Derek
Irish, 20th century.
Born 1916.
Painter. Genre scenes, landscapes.

AUCTION RECORDS:
LONDON, 7 June 1990, *Hunting in Limerick* (oil on canvas, 30 x 45 1/4 ins / 76 x 115 cm) GBP 4,180. LONDON, 9 May 1996, *Tory Island, the East Coast* (1995, oil on card, 7 3/4 x 13 ins / 20 x 33 cm) GBP 3,450. LONDON, 20 May 1999, *Sienese Landscape* (oil on board, 11 x 16 ins / 27 x 41 cm) GBP 4,800. LONDON, 17 May 2001, *String Quartet, Teatro Municipale, Florence* (c. 1952, oil on canvas, 21 x 15 ins / 54 x 39 cm) GBP 9,000. LONDON, 17 May 2001, *Professor R.B. McDowell Leaving the Rubrics, Trinity College, Dublin* (oil on canvas, 16 x 18 ins / 41 x 46 cm) GBP 20,000. LONDON, 16 May 2002, *Tau Cross at West Town, 1963* (oil on canvas, 31 x 46 ins / 79 x 117 cm) GBP 11,000. LONDON, 16 May 2002, *From My Hut, Tory Island, Co. Donegal* (oil on canvas, 20 x 31 ins / 50 x 78 cm) GBP 16,000. LONDON, 15 May 2003, *Miss Pye's Washing Day* (oil on canvas, 17 x 13 ins / 43 x 33 cm) GBP 3,500. DUBLIN, 18 Nov 2003, *Tor Mor* (oil on canvas, 28 x 48 ins / 71 x 122 cm) EUR 6,200. LONDON, 11 May 2004, *Portrait of Yehudi Playing the Violin* (oil on canvas, 20 x 30 ins / 51 x 76 cm) GBP 3,500. LONDON, 14 May 2004, *Tory Gully* (oil on canvas, 36 x 20 ins / 91 x 51 cm) GBP 5,000.

HILL, Diana
British, 18th century.
Active in London.
Miniaturist.

Diana Hill exhibited three works at the Royal Academy in London in 1785.

HILL, Edith
British, 19th century.
Active in Edinburgh.
Sculptor.

Edith Hill exhibited at the Suffolk Street Gallery in London in 1883.

HILL, Ellen G. (Miss)
British, 19th century.
Active in London.
Painter. Figures.

Ellen Hill exhibited in London at the Royal Academy and the New Water-Colour Society from 1864.

HILL, Friedrich Jakob
German, 19th century.
Born 1785, in Darmstadt; died 1846, in Darmstadt.
Painter.

Friedrich Hill was a court painter and painted mostly miniatures.

HILL, Gary
American, 20th - 21st century.
Born 1951, in Santa Monica (California).
Also active in France.
Sculptor, installation artist, video artist.

Gary Hill trained at the Art Students League in New York in 1969, and travelled in Japan before settling in Seattle and France. He is the winner of numerous international prizes, including the Venice Biennale in 1995 and the Kurt Schwitters prize in 2000 (Sprengel Museum, Hanover). Hill's work explores the relationship between language, physicality and thought. Sound has remained an important element since his earliest sculptures in steel; tape recorders, soundtracks and video are used in real time, allowing him to 'think out loud'. His vast installations combine images with literary, philosophical and religious texts (Blanchot, Heidegger), sound and space. *Between Cinema and a Hard Place* comprises 23 screens of various sizes displaying an evolving image, decomposed at intervals into two or three scenes, which are subsequently shown at half, a third and a quarter of their normal speed. The images are accompanied by a text from Heidegger, evoking the close parallels between poetry and thought.

Hill's work has featured in a number of group exhibitions, since 1972: 1975, 1979, 1981, 1986, 1989, Museum of Modern Art, New York; 1979, Buffalo (New York), touring exhibition: American Center, Paris, ELAC (Espace Lyonnais d'Art Contemporain), Lyons and Musée Cantini, Marseille; 1982, Sydney Biennial; 1983, 1985, 1987, 1989, 1991, Biennale, Whitney Museum of American Art, New York; 1984, Venice Biennale; 1986, 1990, 1992, Musée National d'Art Moderne, Paris; 1987, 1990, Stedelijk Museum, Amsterdam; 1987, 1991, 1992, Institute of Contemporary Art, Boston; 1991, Martin Gropius, Berlin; 1995, Lyons Biennale (video art); 1997, Lyons Biennale; 2004, *Sons et Lumières. Une histoire du son dans l'art du 20ème siècle* (*Sons & Lumières. A History of Sound in 20th Century Art*), Centre Pompidou, Paris. Gary Hill's work has also been shown in numerous solo exhibitions: 1971, 1973, Woodstock (New York); 1980, Museum of Modern Art, New York; 1983, American Center, Paris; 1986, Whitney Museum of American Art, New York; 1990, Museum of Modern Art, New York;

1991, Museum of Contemporary Art, Helsinki; 1992, Watari Museum of Contemporary Art, Tokyo and Musée National d'Art Moderne, Paris; 1994-1995, Museum of Contemporary Art, Basel; 1996, Sydney Biennial; 2002, Barbara Gladstone Gallery, New York.

BIBLIOGRAPHY:

Gary Hill, exhibition catalogue, Musée national d'Art moderne, Paris, 1992. Liesbrock, Heinz, *Gary Hill, Midnight crossing*, exhibition catalogue, Westfälischer Kunstverein Münster, Münster, 1997 (text in German and English). Morgan, Robert C./Sarrazin, Stephen, *Gary Hill*, The John Hopkins University Press, Baltimore, London, 2000.

MUSEUMS AND GALLERIES:

AMSTERDAM (Stedelijk Mus.): *Beacon (two versions of the imaginary)* (1990) - CHÂTEAUGIRON (FRAC Bretagne): *And sat beside her (table and chair)* (1990) - LYONS (MAC): *Untitled* (1995) - PARIS (MNAM-CCI): *Disturbance (among the jars).*

HILL, H. (Mrs)
British, 18th century.
Active in London.
Miniaturist.

Mrs Hill exhibited in London at the Society of Artists and the Royal Academy between 1775 and 1791.

HILL, J.
British, 18th - 19th century.
Active in London.
Painter. Landscapes.

J. Hill exhibited in London at the Free Society and the Royal Academy between 1780 and 1825.

HILL, James
British, 18th century.
Active in London.
Sculptor.

James Hill often exhibited in London at the Society of Artists between 1761 and 1770.

HILL, James
American, 19th century.
Active in Charlestown in 1803.
Engraver.

James Hill produced the illustrations for a Bible.

HILL, James John
British, 19th century.
Born 1811, in Birmingham; died 1882, in Highgate.
Painter. Portraits, genre scenes.

A pupil of J. W. Barber at the Royal Academy, James Hill became a member of the Society of British Artists in 1842. From this year, he regularly exhibited at the Suffolk Street Gallery and the Royal Academy.

AUCTION RECORDS:

LONDON, 9 Dec 1907, *On the Sea*, GBP 2. LONDON, 7 March 1908, *Contemplation*, GBP 7. LONDON, 27 April 1908, *Women Gleaning* (1860) GBP 5. LONDON, 4 Dec 1909, *A Sister's Attentions*, GBP 40. LONDON, Nov 1921, *Affection*, GBP 17. LONDON, July 1922, *Ballad*, GBP 11. LONDON, 13 July 1925, *Shepherd Playing a Pipe*, GBP 10. LONDON, 18 June 1928, *Gleaning*, GBP 21. LONDON, 20 July 1976, *Peasant Girl Giving a Child a Drink* (oil on panel, 9 1/4 x 7 3/4 ins / 23.5 x 20 cm) GBP 300. LONDON, 12 Dec 1978, *The Fisherman's Daughters* (oil on canvas, 29 1/4 x 24 ins / 74 x 61 cm) GBP 2,600. LONDON, 20 March 1979, *Return of the Fisherman* (1875, oil on canvas, 11 x 15 ins / 28 x 38 cm) GBP 1,800. LONDON, 26 Oct 1979, *Little Shepherdess and Two Sheep* (1860, oil on canvas, 29 1/2 x 24 1/2 ins / 75 x 62.3 cm) GBP 1,700. LONDON, 16 Sept 1982, *Waiting* (1868, oil on canvas, 33 1/2 x 28 ins / 85 x 71 cm) GBP 1,150. LONDON, 14 July 1983, *Maternal Joy* (1868, oil on canvas, 36 1/4 x 27 1/4 ins / 92 x 69 cm) GBP 6,000. LONDON, 16 May 1986, *Sleeping Shepherd Boy* (1851, oil on canvas, 21 3/4 x 31 3/4 ins / 55.3 x 80.6 cm) GBP 8,000. LONDON, 23 Sept 1988, *Mother and Child* (oil on canvas, 30 1/4 x 25 1/4 ins / 77 x 64 cm) GBP 4,950. LONDON, 3 Nov 1989, *Young Beauty* (oil on canvas, 14 1/4 x 12 1/4 ins / 36 x 31 cm) GBP 1,100. NEW YORK, 19 July 1990, *Girl with a Terrier* (oil on canvas, 26 x 21 ins / 66.1 x 53.3 cm) USD 6,050. LONDON, 5 June 1991, *In the Fields* (oil on canvas, 26 x 22 ins / 66 x 56 cm) GBP 3,080. NEW YORK, 29 Oct 1992, *Boy on Horseback on a Forest Path* (1871, oil on canvas, 24 1/2 x 36 ins / 62.3 x 91.5 cm) USD 5,500. LONDON, 13 Nov 1992, *Fishing by the Burn* (oil on canvas, 24 1/4 x 19 ins / 61.5 x 48.3 cm) GBP 1,210. NEW YORK, 20 Jan 1993, *Idle Shepherd* (1878, oil on canvas, 20 x 24 ins / 50.8 x 61 cm) USD 3,220. LONDON, 4 Nov 1994, *Woodcutters' Hut* (1874, oil on canvas, 18 x 27 1/4 ins / 45.7 x 68.9 cm) GBP 2,300. LONDON, 10 March 1995, *She Looks and Looks, and Still with New Delight* (1870, oil on canvas, 44 x 34 ins / 111.8 x 86.3 cm) GBP 6,670. KNOWLE, 17 Feb 1999, *Young Harvest Girl Holding a White Terrier* (oil on canvas, oval, 25 x ? ins / 63 x ? cm) GBP 8,300. LONDON, 9 June 1999, *Hayfield* (1858, oil on canvas, 34 x 63 ins / 86 x 161 cm) GBP 40,000. NEW YORK, 15 Feb 2000, *Friends* (oil on canvas, 26 x 21 ins / 66 x 53 cm) USD 15,000. LEICESTER, 13 Dec 2000, *Portrait of a Mother, Sleeping Baby in Her Arms* (1863, oil on canvas, 36 x 28 ins / 91 x 71 cm) GBP 7,000. LONDON, 8 March 2001, *Stepping Stones* (oil on canvas, 30 x 22 ins / 76 x 56 cm) GBP 4,000. LONDON, 6 Sept 2001, *Ballad* (oil on canvas, 24 x 18 ins / 62 x 46 cm) GBP 6,000. TORONTO, 18 Nov 2002, *Harvest Girl* (oil on canvas, 36 x 28 ins / 91 x 71 cm) CAD 9,000. LONDON, 3 Dec 2002, *Portrait of a Lady in the Countryside* (1871, oil on canvas, 30 x 25 ins / 77 x 63 cm) GBP 3,000. SAN FRANCISCO, 14 May 2003, *On the Way to Market* (oil on canvas, 36 x 28 ins / 91 x 71 cm) USD 3,000. BATH, 29 March 2004, *Family Group at a Spring* (oil on canvas, 37 x 51 ins / 94 x 130 cm) GBP 2,000. NEW YORK, 27 Oct 2004, *Fern Gatherers* (1848, oil on canvas, 40 x 33 ins / 102 x 83 cm) USD 20,000.

HILL, James Stevens
British, 19th - 20th century.
Born 1854, in Exeter; died August 1921.
Painter. Landscapes, flowers.

James Hill began studying at the Royal Academy in 1873, and first exhibited there in 1875. In 1804 he became a member of the Royal Society of British Artists, and he joined the Society of Oil Painters in 1892 and the Royal Institution in 1898. As well as exhibiting at the Royal Academy, he also showed his work in the Suffolk Street Gallery, and in Paris, where he received an honourable mention in 1903.

AUCTION RECORDS:

PARIS, 4 and 5 March 1920, *Farm in a Meadow at Boscham*, FRF 450. NOTTINGHAM, 13 Feb 2002, *Still-life with Flowers in a Glass Vase* (oil painting, 14 x 12 ins / 35 x 30 cm.

HILL, John
British, 18th - 19th century.
Born 1770, in London; died 1850, in West Nyack.
Engraver.

John Hill made aquatints of a number of landscapes by Charles Dibdin. He left for America in 1822.

AUCTION RECORDS:

NEW YORK, 26 March 1981, *United States Military Academy* (1828, colour aquatint remounted on board, 13 3/4 x 19 1/2 ins / 35.2 x 49.8 cm) USD 5,500. NEW YORK, 21 Sept 1983, *View of the Landscape around the Hudson* (1822, etching and coloured aquatint, after William Guy Wall, 14 1/2 x 21 1/2 ins / 36.6 x 54.7 cm) USD 1,600.

HILL, John Henry
British, 19th - 20th century.
Born 1839; died 1922.
Active in London.
Painter, watercolourist, engraver. Landscapes, natural history (birds).

John Henry Hill, the son of John William Hill, exhibited in London at the Suffolk Street gallery from 1865 to 1879.
AUCTION RECORDS:
NEW YORK, 5 Dec 1980, *Seaside* (1907, watercolour, 17 x 29 1/2 ins / 43.3 x 75 cm) USD 2,600. LOS ANGELES, 9 Feb 1982, *Landscape* (1857, watercolour/mounted paper/card, round, diam. 12 ins / 30.5 cm) USD 2,400. NEW YORK, 21 Sept 1984, *Mountain Lake with Indian* (1873, watercolour, 9 1/2 x 15 ins / 24.2 x 38.2 cm) USD 900. NEW YORK, 1 Oct 1986, *Fishermen Beside a Mountain Stream* (1878, watercolour, 10 x 14 ins / 25.3 x 35.5 cm) USD 1,500. NEW YORK, 18 March 1987, *Niagara Falls* (oil on canvas remounted on board, 7 3/4 x 6 1/4 ins / 20 x 16 cm) USD 5,800. NEW YORK, 9 March 1996, *A Pond in Summer* (1865, watercolour/paper, 10 1/2 x 15 3/4 ins / 26.6 x 40 cm) USD 3,795. NEW YORK, 23 April 1997, *Waterlilies; Wild Flowers* (1905, watercolour and pencil/paper, a pair, 5 x 7 1/2 ins / 12.7 x 19 cm and 10 1/2 x 14 ins/26.7 x 35.6 cm) USD 20,700.

HILL, John William
American, 19th century.
Born 1812, in London; died 1879, in Nyack Turnpike (New York).
Painter (including gouache), watercolourist, engraver. Animals, landscapes with figures, landscapes, still-lifes (including flowers/fruit), natural history (botanical subjects/birds), flowers.

John William Hill's family emigrated to the USA when he was seven years old. His father, an engraver in New York, taught him the basics of art. In 1830 he worked for the New York Geological Survey. His career was determined by his reading of John Ruskin's treatise on art, *Modern Painters*, when he was 43 years old. He devoted himself to the painting of outdoor scenes in a simple style, depicting birds, flowers and fruit faithfully.
AUCTION RECORDS:
LOS ANGELES, 24 June 1980, *Ramapo Mountains* (1842, oil on mounted card, 10 1/2 x 14 1/2 ins / 26.5 x 37 cm) USD 1,300. NEW YORK, 21 Nov 1980, *View of New York* (c. 1837, watercolour and pen, 19 x 31 3/4 ins / 48.2 x 80.7 cm) USD 50,000. NEW YORK, 30 Sept 1982, *Sunset on the Hudson* (watercolour, gouache and pen, 14 x 21 ins / 35.6 x 53.4 cm) USD 1,000. NEW YORK, 23 March 1984, *Still-life with Fruit* (1874, watercolour, 10 x 15 ins / 24.5 x 38.2 cm) USD 3,600. NEW YORK, 15 March 1985, *Hudson River Valley* (1869, watercolour/mounted paper/card, 10 x 15 ins / 25.3 x 38.1 cm) USD 6,000. NEW YORK, 26 June 1986, *Hackensack near Clarksville, New York* (1877, oil on canvas, 24 x 36 ins / 61 x 91.5 cm) USD 2,500. NEW YORK, 20 March 1987, *Foliage* (1871, watercolour, 15 x 18 ins / 38 x 46 cm) USD 2,200. NEW YORK, 24 June 1988, *People on a Strand* (1859, watercolour/paper, 9 1/4 x 13 ins / 23.3 x 33.3 cm) USD 3,190. NEW YORK, 24 Jan 1989, *The Hudson near Albany* (watercolour and gouache, 11 3/4 x 18 1/2 ins / 30 x 46.8 cm) USD 2,090. NEW YORK, 24 Jan 1990, *Forest Interior* (1869, watercolour/paper/canvas, 16 1/4 x 14 ins / 41 x 35.7 cm) USD 2,200. NEW YORK, 17 Dec 1990, *Landscape with a Mountain Torrent* (1863, watercolour/paper/card, 13 1/4 x 17 ins / 33.7 x 43.3 cm) USD 3,630. NEW YORK, 25 Sept 1992, *Wooded Landscape with Figures* (1869, watercolour/paper, 16 x 14 ins / 40.6 x 35.6 cm) USD 990. NEW YORK, 3 Dec 1992, *Vast River Landscape with a Young Boy Angling* (1861, watercolour/paper, 9 x 13 1/2 ins / 22.9 x 34.3 cm) USD 16,500. NEW YORK, 30 Nov 1995, *Fawn's Leap at Catskill, New York* (oil on canvas, 19 1/2 x 25 1/2 ins / 49.5 x 64.7 cm) USD 13,800. NEW YORK, 4 Dec 1996, *Still-life with Grapes, Apples and Pears* (1877, watercolour/paper, 7 1/2 x 11 1/2 ins / 19.1 x 29.5 cm) USD 10,350. NEW YORK, 23 April 1997, *Blue Hydrangeas* (watercolour and pencil/paper, oval, 13 1/4 x 11 3/4 ins / 33.6 x 29.8 cm) USD 3,220. LONDON, 2 Dec 1999, *Still-life with Apples and Grapes* (watercolour heightened with gouache and gum arabic, 14 x 17 ins / 35 x 44 cm) GBP 7,500. NEW YORK, 4 Oct 2000, *Hudson River at Caldwell* (1866, watercolour over pencil on paper laid on paper, 8 x 13 ins / 20 x 34 cm) USD 13,000. NEW YORK, 28 Nov 2000, *Fishing in the White Mountains* (1868, watercolour, 11 x 17 ins / 28 x 44 cm) USD 3,600. EAST DENNIS, 16 Nov 2001, *River Valley Landscape* (watercolour, 11 x 18 ins / 28 x 46 cm) USD 1,700. NEW YORK, 17 July 2002, *Still-life with Peaches and Plums* (1877, watercolour, 5 x 9 ins / 13 x 23 cm) USD 3,500. NEW YORK, 4 Dec 2002, *Broadway Looking South from Liberty Street* (1831, watercolour, 17 x 25 ins / 44 x 63 cm) USD 110,000. NEW YORK, 21 May 2003, *Gone Fishing* (watercolour, 7 x 10 ins / 18 x 25 cm) USD 12,000. NEW YORK, 18 May 2004, *Fishing* (c. 1865, watercolour, 6 x 5 ins / 15 x 13 cm) USD 16,000. NEW YORK, 19 May 2004, *Hudson River at Caldwell* (1866, watercolour, 8 x 13 ins / 20 x 33 cm) USD 12,000.

HILL, Justus
British, 19th century.
Active in London.
Painter. Genre scenes.

Justus Hill exhibited at the Royal Academy in London from 1879 to 1891.

HILL, Léonard Raven. See **RAVEN-HILL**

HILL, Roswell Stone
American, 19th - 20th century.
Born 17 April 1861, in Lawrence (New York); died 1907.
Painter. Genre scenes, landscapes.

Roswell Stone Hill was a pupil of Gérôme and Bouguereau in Paris and later settled in New York.
MUSEUMS AND GALLERIES:
SYRACUSE (Everson MA): *Provincetown, Massachusetts* (oil on canvas); *Sunny Day* (1903, oil on canvas).

HILL, Rowland Henry
British, 19th - 20th century.
Born 1873, in Halifax; died after 1935.
Painter. Figures, genre scenes, seascapes.

Rowland Hill first worked in Halifax, then at Bradford School of Art. He later studied under the German-born painter Sir Hubert von Herkomer. He painted a variety of subjects.
MUSEUMS AND GALLERIES:
LEEDS (City AG): *The Road Makers, Ugthorpe* (1935, watercolour).
AUCTION RECORDS:
LONDON, 24 May 1910, *The Primrose Bank* (1906) GBP 7. PARIS, 22 Nov 1946, *The Ship in Peril*, FRF 2,500. LONDON, 21 May 1986, *The Marauders* (1897, oil on canvas, 26 x 20 ins / 66 x 51 cm) GBP 6,500. LONDON, 4 March 1987, *Children Picking Flowers* (1923, oil on canvas, 14 x 16 1/2 ins / 35.5 x 42 cm) GBP 2,800. BELFAST, 30 May 1990, *Chatting on the Path at Glenties in County Donegal* (oil on canvas, 18 1/4 x 24 3/4 ins / 46.3 x 62.9 cm) GBP 825. LEEDS, 30 June 1999, *Figures beside a Bridge at Sandsend* (1912, pencil and watercolour heightened with white, 14 x 20 ins / 35 x 50 cm) GBP 1,950. LEEDS, 16 Nov 1999, *Extensive Moorland Landscape with Figure* (1924, pencil, watercolour and gouache heightened with white, 15 x 20 ins / 38 x 52 cm) GBP 2,000. BURY ST EDMUNDS, 29 June 2000, *Rock Pool, Portrush, Co. Antrim* (oil on canvas-board, 14 x 20 ins / 35 x 51 cm) GBP 2,200. DUBLIN, 13 Dec 2000, *Carron Point, Co. Antrim* (oil on canvas, 20 x 30 ins / 51 x 76 cm) IEP 2,000. WHITBY, 26 April 2001, *Runswick Cobles and Fisherfolk with Village beyond* (1922, watercolour, 11 x 16 ins / 28 x 41 cm) GBP 3,200. WHITBY, 27 Sept 2001, *Towards the Cockpit, Runswick Bay* (1921, watercolour, 9 x 12 ins / 23 x 30 cm) GBP 2,500. LEEDS, 12 March 2002, *Study of a Little Girl* (1905, oil on board, 10 x 7 ins / 25 x 18 cm) GBP 3,100. SCARBOROUGH, 10 Sept 2002, *National Gallery and St Martin's in the Fields* (1921, watercolour, 11 x 15 ins / 27 x 37 cm) GBP 2,950. BIRMINGHAM, 11 Feb 2003, *Runswick Bay, Yorkshire* (1931, watercolour, 15 x 10in) GBP 2,200. SHEF-

FIELD, 12 Sept 2003, *Pickering Moor, North Yorkshire* (1923, oil on canvas, 34 x 41 ins / 86 x 104 cm) GBP 5,200. BILLINGSHURST, 13 Oct 2004, *Village Scene. Hunt Scene outside Village Pub* (1950, watercolour, a pair, 9 x 12 ins / 23 x 30 cm) GBP 3,100. BILLINGSHURST, 13 Oct 2004, *Village Scene. Moorland Scene. Snow Scene* (watercolour, three, 9 x 13 ins / 23 x 34 cm) GBP 4,300.

HILL, Samuel
American, 19th century.
Active in Boston c. 1800.
Engraver.

Samuel Hill produced a large number of portraits.

HILL, Thomas
British, 17th - 18th century.
Born 1661; died 1734, in Mitcham, near London.
Painter. Portraits.

Thomas Hill lived in London where he was a pupil of Faithorne.

MUSEUMS AND GALLERIES:

LONDON (National Portrait Gal.): *Humphrey Wanley* (1717, oil on canvas); *William Wake* (c. 1720-1725, oil on canvas).

HILL, Thomas
British, 19th century.
Active in London.
Painter. Landscapes.

Thomas Hill exhibited in London at the Royal Academy and the British Institution between 1800 and 1822.

HILL, Thomas
British, 19th century.
Active in London.
Painter. Portraits.

Thomas Hill frequently exhibited in London at the Royal Academy and the Suffolk Street Gallery from 1871.

HILL, Thomas
American, 19th - 20th century.
Born 11 September 1829, in Birmingham, England; died 1 July 1908, in Raymond.
Painter. Figures, landscapes.

Thomas Hill went to America at the age of 12 and studied at the Pennsylvania Academy of the Fine Arts, Philadelphia, but worked more or less alone. In 1961 he went west to seek his fortune and settled in San Francisco. He won first prize at the city's Art Union Club in 1865. Until then Hill had primarily painted portraits and figures, but late in his career he concentrated on landscapes and is particularly known for *Yosemite Valley*.

Hill took part in many American exhibitions and won 32 prizes, notably in Philadelphia in 1864. He was a member of the Boston Art Club and the San Francisco Art Union.

AUCTION RECORDS:

NEW YORK, 9 Feb 1906, *Yosemite Valley*, USD 275. LONDON, 25 Jan 1908, *In Yosemite Valley* (1880) GBP 3. LONDON, 14 May 1970, *The Yosemite. Party of Indians alongside a Road*, GBP 980. NEW YORK, 27 Oct 1971, *Yosemite Valley and Companion Piece* (pair) USD 2,800. LOS ANGELES, 23 May 1972, *Mountain Landscape*, USD 3,300. LONDON, 20 March 1973, *Yosemite Valley* (1863) GBP 1,800. LONDON, 12 Nov 1974, *Yosemite Valley* (1892) GBP 2,000. LOS ANGELES, 9 June 1976, *Boat-Trip* (oil on canvas, 14 x 22 ins / 35.5 x 56 cm) USD 2,500. LOS ANGELES, 8 Nov 1977, *Redwood Trees* (1898, oil on canvas, 36 x 18 ins / 91.5 x 45.8 cm) USD 3,400. LONDON, 2 Nov 1979, *Yosemite Landscape with Red Indians* (1889, oil on canvas, 29 1/2 x 36 3/4 ins / 74.9 x 93.4 cm) GBP 5,200. LOS ANGELES, 3 May 1982, *Yosemite Falls* (oil on canvas, 54 x 36 ins / 137 x 91.5 cm) USD 28,000. NEW YORK, 23 June 1983, *View of Lake Tahoe* (oil on card, 13 3/4 x 20 1/2 ins / 35 x 52 cm) USD 3,000. PORTLAND, 11 May 1985, *A Wary Moment* (1878, oil on canvas, 70 x 42 1/4 ins / 178 x 107 cm) USD 48,000. NEW YORK, 1 Oct 1987, *Mont Vista* (1871, oil on canvas, 23 1/4 x 30 ins / 58.8 x 76.5 cm) USD 16,000. LOS ANGELES, 9 June 1988, *Riders in the Redwood Forest* (1906, oil on canvas, 30 x 40 1/4 ins / 76 x 102 cm) USD 55,000. NEW YORK, 24 Jan 1989, *Yosemite Valley* (1888, oil on canvas, 29 1/2 x 19 3/4 ins / 75 x 50 cm) USD 7,150. LOS ANGELES-SAN FRANCISCO, 12 July 1990, *Indian Encampment at the Foot of Mount Hood* (1893, oil on canvas, 18 x 26 1/2 ins / 46 x 67 cm) USD 6,050. NEW YORK, 26 Sept 1990, *Lone Fisherman, Yosemite* (1891, oil on canvas, 36 1/4 x 53 1/4 ins / 92.1 x 135.2 cm) USD 52,800. LOS ANGELES-SAN FRANCISCO, 10 Oct 1990, *Vernal Falls, Yosemite* (1903, oil on canvas, 30 x 20 ins / 76 x 51 cm) USD 8,800; *Figures in Yosemite Valley* (1894, oil on canvas, 24 x 20 ins / 61 x 51 cm) USD 38,500. NEW YORK, 29 Nov 1990, *Resting by the Stream* (1866, oil on canvas, 24 x 32 ins / 61 x 81.3 cm) USD 63,250. NEW YORK, 22 May 1991, *Bridal Veil Falls, Yosemite* (oil on canvas, 29 1/2 x 19 1/2 ins / 75 x 49.6 cm) USD 24,200. NEW YORK, 26 Sept 1991, *Hunter and Pointers* (1861, oil on canvas, 20 x 30 ins / 51 x 76.2 cm) USD 18,700. NEW YORK, 15 April 1992, *Hunter with Two Setters in a Wooded Landscape* (oil on canvas, 14 x 13 ins / 35.6 x 33 cm) USD 9,350. NEW YORK, 9 Sept 1993, *Yosemite* (oil on panel, triptych, centre: 28 x 15 1/2 ins / 71.1 x 39.4 cm; side: 24 3/4 x 5 3/4 ins/62.9 x 14.6 cm) USD 5,175. NEW YORK, 25 May 1995, *Fishing by the Merced, Yosemite* (oil on canvas, 36 x 54 ins / 91.4 x 137.2 cm) USD 98,750. NEW YORK, 4 Dec 1996, *Niagara Falls* (oil on canvas, 40 1/4 x 49 ins / 102.3 x 124.4 cm) USD 90,500.

HILL, William Robert
British, 19th century.
Active in London during the second half of the 19th century.
Painter. Landscapes.

William Hill exhibited work between 1859 and 1884.

HILLA
German, 14th century.
Miniaturist.

Hilla is recorded together with her husband in a list of painters in Cologne in 1301.

HILLAIREAU, Georges
French, 20th century.
Born 1884, in St-Ouen; died 1954.
Painter. Figures, interiors with figures, landscapes, still-lifes.

For many years, Georges Hillaireau was obliged to attend to the family business and only painted intermittently. Only in 1940 painting became his principal occupation.

According to Pierre Courthion, he was 'a man driven by obscure, secret forces, which made him an ancestor of a new school'. At any rate, Hillaireau arrived at a quasi-nonfigurative expression. His rare works are abstractions of coloured outpourings fashioned in a generous, tormented texture with sombre tones lit only by a few glimmers of light, and areas feverishly joined according to a purely pictorial space. Such works foreshadowed those of Nicolas De Staël, who considered Hillaireau in a way 'like his master'. His first exhibition dates from 1941.

BIBLIOGRAPHY:

Courthion, Pierre, *L'Art indépendant*, Albin Michel, Paris, 1958.

AUCTION RECORDS:

PARIS, 9 April 1987, *Composition* (oil on canvas, 25 1/2 x 31 1/2 ins / 65 x 80 cm) FRF 28,000. PARIS, 19 March 1988, *Still-life with Flowers and a Bottle* (oil on cardboard, 18 x 24 3/4 ins / 46 x 63 cm) FRF 10,000. PARIS, 20-21 June 1988, *Composition* (oil on paper, 19 x 28 ins / 48 x 71 cm) FRF 15,000; *Figure* (oil on panel, 11 x 13 3/4 ins / 28 x 35 cm) FRF 5,600. PARIS, 21 Nov 1988, *Composition* (1950, oil on paper, 11 x 13 3/4 ins / 28 x 35 cm) FRF 3,550. PARIS, 14 Dec 1988, *Landscape* (oil on paper, 11 x 13 3/4 ins / 27 x 35 cm) FRF 5,800. PARIS, 8 Oct 1989, *Interior* (oil on paper, 9 x 11 ins / 22 x 27 cm) FRF 5,500.

HILLAIRET, Anatole Eugène
French, 20th century.
Born 1880, in Le Chay; died 1928.
Painter. Cityscapes.

Anatole Hillairet painted mainly cityscapes of Paris and exhibited in Paris at the Salon des Indépendants from 1907.

AUCTION RECORDS:
PARIS, 30 April 1919, *Notre Dame de Paris, the Seine and the Pont de l'Archevêché. Evening Effect*, FRF 75. PARIS, 15 June 1945, *Dusk on the Seine*, FRF 2,100. PARIS, 27 Nov 1946, *Place Blanche* FRF 3,100. BOURG-EN-BRESSE, 24 Feb 1980, *The Beach at Cabourg* (1921, oil on canvas, 18 x 22 ins / 46 x 55 cm) FRF 8,100. VERSAILLES, 19 Oct 1986, *Dawn at Auvers-sur-Oise* (1910, oil on canvas, 19 3/4 x 25 1/2 ins / 50 x 64.5 cm) FRF 17,500. LYONS, 21 May 1987, *Notre Dame and the Seine, Sunset* (oil on canvas) FRF 4,500. VERSAILLES, 21 Feb 1988, *The Jardin des Tuileries and the Louvre* (oil on canvas, 19 3/4 x 25 1/2 ins / 50 x 65 cm) FRF 5,800. VERSAILLES, 21 Feb 1988, *The Jardin des Tuileries and the Louvre* (oil on canvas, 19 3/4 x 25 1/2 ins / 50 x 65 cm) FRF 5,800. PARIS, 16 Oct 1988, *14 July at the Pont de la Concorde* (oil on canvas, 19 3/4 x 25 1/2 ins / 50 x 65 cm) FRF 20,000. PARIS, 16 Dec 1988, *Paris, the Quays* (oil on canvas, 19 3/4 x 25 1/2 ins / 50 x 65 cm) FRF 19,000. VERSAILLES, 5 March 1989, *The Jardin des Tuileries and the Louvre* (oil on canvas, 19 3/4 x 25 1/2 ins / 50 x 65 cm) FRF 7,000. PARIS, 21 March 1990, *Still-life with Oysters* (oil on canvas, 23 1/2 x 36 1/2 ins / 60 x 92.5 cm) FRF 35,000. PARIS, 13 June 1994, *Street in Auvers-sur-Oise* (1924, oil on canvas, 18 x 25 1/2 ins / 46 x 65 cm) FRF 5,500. PARIS, 18 March 1998, *Tall Tree in a Village Street* (1907, oil on canvas, 19 3/4 x 25 1/2 ins / 50 x 65 cm) FRF 3,400. AMSTERDAM, 10 June 1999, *Boats on River Seine, Paris* (oil on canvas, 15 x 22 ins / 38 x 55 cm) NLG 3,600.

HILLARD, William H.
American, 19th century.
Died April 1905, in Washington DC.
Painter. Genre scenes, portraits.

William H. Hillard had a considerable reputation in America. His most famous works include *Portrait of President Garfield* and *Tomb of Howard Payne*, author of the famous novel *Home, Sweet Home*.

HILLBOM, Henrick
Swedish, 19th - 20th century.
Born 1863; died 1928.
Painter. Scenes with figures.

AUCTION RECORDS:
LONDON, 24 March 1988, *A Ferry on the Hudson River* (oil on canvas, 14 x 18 ins / 35.5 x 45.9 cm) GBP 3,520.

HILLE, Andreas
German, 16th century.
Died 12 April 1598, in Hamburg.
Painter.

Andreas Hille painted portraits of Luther and Calvin.

HILLE, Anton
German, 19th - 20th century.
Born 1 August 1866, in Dresden; died 1921, in Dresden.
Painter.

Anton Hille studied with Guy and Preller.

HILLE, Jacques
Austrian, 19th century.
Born 21 April 1870, in Vienna.
Miniaturist.

HILLE, Jakob
Austrian, 19th century.
Active in Vienna.
Miniaturist.

Jakob Hille was the father of Jacques Hille.

HILLE, Pierre
German, 16th century.
Active in Frankfurt an der Oder.
Engraver (wood).

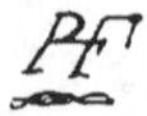

HILLEBRAND, Hans
German, 16th century.
Died 23 March 1567.
Active in Breslau (now Wroclaw, Poland).
Painter.

Hans Hillebrand was a pupil of Reinhart the Elder.

HILLEBRAND, Ignaz
German, 18th century.
Active in Türkheim (Swabia) at the beginning of the 18th century.
Sculptor.

Ignaz Hillebrand is best known for his works at Oberostendorf and at Bertoldshofen.

HILLEBRANDT, Johann Heinrich.
See **HILDEBRANDT**

HILLEGAERT, François, or Hilligaard
Dutch, 17th century.
Born c. 1627, in Amsterdam.
Painter.

He was the elder son of Pauwels van Hillegaert the Elder. His works are often confused with those of his father.

MUSEUMS AND GALLERIES:
AMSTERDAM (Rijksmus.): a painting.

HILLEGAERT, Pauwels van, the Elder, or Hilligaard
Dutch, 17th century.
Born c. 1595, in Amsterdam; died 1640, in Amsterdam.
Painter. Military subjects, portraits.

It is often wrongly claimed that his father, François van Hilligaert, was a painter. He was married in Amsterdam on 27 June 1620.

His paintings are quite rare. He often painted figures in the landscapes of Alexander Keirincx.

MUSEUMS AND GALLERIES:
AMSTERDAM: *Battle of Nieuport* (1600); *Dismissal of the Mercenaries in Utrecht* (1618); *Prince Frederick-Henry and Count Ernest-Casimir*; *Frederick Henry*; *Prince Maurice at the Hunt*; *Siege of Bois-le-Duc* (1629); *Evacuation of Bois-le-Duc* (1629) - ROTTERDAM: *Undergrowth with Hunters* - THE HAGUE: *Princes of Orange and Their Entourages in Front of the Binnenhof* - UTRECHT: *Dismissal of the Mercenaries in Utrecht*.

AUCTION RECORDS:
PARIS, 1 June 1901, *Camp Near a Fortified City*, FRF 310. LONDON, 28 March 1979, *The Ambush* (oil on panel, 11 1/2 x 16 1/4 ins / 29 x 41.5 cm) GBP 1,800. L'ISLE-ADAM, 24 March 1985, *Market Near a Fortified City* (oil on canvas, 17 1/4 x 22 ins / 44 x 56 cm) FRF 51,500. MONTE CARLO, 6 Dec 1987, *Vast Landscape with Skirmish* (1633, oil on panel, 16 1/2 x 24 1/4 ins / 42 x 61.5 cm) FRF 100,000. STOCKHOLM, 15 Nov 1988, *Advance of the Cavalry* (oil, 23 1/2 x 29 1/2 ins / 60 x 75 cm) SEK 51,000. ROME, 8 May 1990, *Battle* (oil on panel, 21 1/4 x 28 1/4

ins / 54 x 72 cm) ITL 12,500,000. AMSTERDAM, 8 Nov 2000, *Italianate River Landscape with Fortifications, Three Men by a Boat and Cattle* (pen, brown ink, brown and blue wash and black ink with framing lines, 7 x 11 ins / 19 x 27 cm) NLG 5,500. LONDON, 14 Dec 2000, *Siege of Grol, Groenlo, 1627* (oil on canvas, 50 x 85 ins / 127 x 215 cm) GBP 28,000. AMSTERDAM, 4 Nov 2003, *Wooded Landscape* (pen, brown ink and colour wash over black chalk, 9 x 13 ins / 23 x 32 cm) EUR 5,000. MADRID, 25 May 2004, *Landscape* (oil on canvas, 45 x 64 ins / 114 x 163 cm) EUR 6,000.

HILLEGAERT, Pauwels van, the Younger, or Hilligaard
Dutch, 17th century.
Born 1631, in Amsterdam; died 21 January 1658, in Amsterdam.
Painter, engraver.

He was the son and pupil of Pauwels van Hillegaert the Elder. In 1651, he married Cornelia de Vlieger, the daughter of Simon de Vlieger, painter of seascapes. His engraved works are not well known. He engraved mostly plates of animals.

HILLEKAMP, Maurice
French, 20th century.
Active in Paris.
Painter, engraver.

Maurice Hillekamp was a pupil of Merson and Morot.

HILLEMACHER, Eugène Ernest
French, 19th century.
Born 13 October 1818, in Paris; died 2 March 1887, in Paris.
Painter, engraver, illustrator. Religious subjects, portraits, genre scenes.

In 1838 Eugène Hillemacher went to study at the École des Beaux-Arts in Paris, in the studio of Léon Cogniet. He first exhibited at the Paris Salon in 1840, winning a second-class medal in 1848, and two first-class medals in 1861 and 1863. He was made a Chevalier of the Légion d'Honneur in 1865.

Hillemacher's best-known canvases are probably *Cordelia, Mother of the Gracchi* and *Cuirassier Resting*. He also made engravings of several of his works, most notably: *Molière Consulting His Maidservant, Philip IV and Velázquez, Mortimer and Richard Plantagenet, The Hand of Whist, Boileau and His Gardener* and *Brother Philip's Geese*. He also illustrated an edition of Racine's *Theatre*, which was engraved by his brother, Frédéric Hillemacher.

MUSEUMS AND GALLERIES:
AUCH: *Latona* - BESANÇON: *Ceres with the Peasants* - BREST: *Test of Resemblance; Turenne as a Young Man* - CHÂTEAU-THIERRY: *Allegorical Composition on the Crimean War* - COMPIÈGNE: *Brother Philip's Geese* - DIJON (MBA): *Aristides and the Peasant* - LUXEMBOURG: *A Confessional at St Peter's in Rome* - MELBOURNE: *Psyche in Hell* - MONTPELLIER: *Margaret of Anjou* - ROUEN (MBA): *A Chess Game under Louis XIII; The Besieged of Rouen.*
AUCTION RECORDS:
PARIS, 28 June 1897, *The Holy Family at Rest*, FRF 75. LONDON, 1 July 1927, *Crossing the Ditch*, GBP 35. PARIS, 1 Feb 1945, *Sitting for the Painter* (1863) FRF 22,100. PARIS, 10 June 1976, *Tarpeia* (1880, oil on canvas, 41¼ x 55 ins / 105 x 140 cm) FRF 2,650. ZURICH, 2 Nov 1979, *Don Juan* (1864, oil on canvas, 39¼ x 32 ins / 100 x 81.5 cm) CHF 20,000. PARIS, 10 Dec 1996, *Scene in a Studio at the École des Beaux-Arts* (c. 1835, oil on canvas, 18 x 15 ins / 46 x 38 cm) FRF 23,000. PARIS, 1 April 1998, *Gentleman Ranting in a Park* (1858, oil on canvas, 32 x 25½ ins / 81 x 65 cm) FRF 9,500. PARIS, 29 March 2002, *Interior Scene with Three Peasants* (1875, oil on canvas, 26 x 22 ins / 66 x 55 cm) EUR 5,800. STUTTGART, 25 March 2004, *French Nobleman with Two Italian Peasant Girls* (1864, oil on canvas, 31 x 39 ins / 80 x 100 cm) EUR 6,000.

HILLEMACHER, Frédéric Désiré
French, 19th century.
Born 23 June 1811, in Brussels; died 28 October 1886, in Paris.
Painter, engraver.

Frédéric was the brother of Eugène Ernest Hillemacher.

HILLEMACHER, Jean
French, 20th century.
Born 15 June 1889, in Verneuil; died 6 September 1914, in Blesme, on the battlefield.
Painter.

Jean Hillemacher exhibited in Paris in 1913 at the Salon des Artistes Français.

HILLEN, Edouard
Flemish School, 19th century.
Active c. 1842.
Landscape painter.

He has been mentioned by Siret.

HILLER, Heinrich or Heinz
German, 19th century.
Active in Berlin from 1866 to 1894.
Painter. Landscapes, seascapes.

Heinrich Hiller worked in Berlin, where he first exhibited around 1866, before subsequently showing his work in Dresden and Hanover.

MUSEUMS AND GALLERIES:
MAINZ: *Landscape with Beach.*
AUCTION RECORDS:
LONDON, 20 June 1979, *Alpine Landscape* (1879, oil on canvas, 31½ x 47 ins / 80 x 118.5 cm) GBP 700. COLOGNE, 26 March 1982, *View of the Rhine* (oil on canvas, 24½ x 34¾ ins / 62.5 x 88.5 cm) DEM 4,400. CALAIS, 8 Nov 1987, *Fishing Boat Run Aground near the Norwegian Coast* (1878, oil on canvas, 30 x 44 ins / 76 x 112 cm) FRF 28,000. COLOGNE, 15 June 1989, *Venice* (oil on canvas, 12½ x 10 ins / 32 x 25.5 cm) DEM 4,500. COLOGNE, 20 Oct 1989, *Rhenish Landscape* (oil on panel, 5 x 10½ ins / 13 x 26.5 cm) DEM 1,700. LONDON, 7 April 1993, *Coastal Scene* (oil on canvas, 11¾ x 20 ins / 30 x 51 cm) GBP 1,610. NEW YORK, 17 Jan 1996, *Alpine Landscape with Boatmen* (1879, oil on canvas, 32 x 47¼ ins / 81.3 x 120 cm) USD 4,600. WARSAW, 24 Oct 1999, *Alpine Lake Landscape* (oil on canvas, 25 x 39 ins / 63 x 99 cm) PLN 23,000. WARSAW, 4 June 2000, *Alpine Lake Landscape* (1879, oil on canvas, 32 x 47 ins / 81 x 120 cm) PLN 22,000. WARSAW, 22 Oct 2000, *Alpine Landscape with Chalet* (oil on canvas, 19 x 15 ins / 48 x 39 cm) PLN 17,000. WARSAW, 10 March 2002, *Königssee* (oil on canvas, 25 x 27 ins / 63 x 69 cm) PLN 12,000. MUNICH, 20 March 2002, *Berchtesgaden* (oil on canvas, 31 x 51 ins / 80 x 130 cm) EUR 3,000. COLOGNE, 20 Nov 2003, *Windmill. Peasant with Horse and Cart* (1871, oil on canvas, two, 19 x 17 ins / 48 x 42 cm) EUR 2,000. LINZ, 27 Nov 2003, *Lower Alpine Landscape with Old Farmhouse* (1872, oil on canvas, 24 x 35 ins / 62 x 88 cm) EUR 1,800. MUNICH, 26 March 2004, *Mountain Landscape with River and Cow Herder* (oil on canvas, 27 x 38 ins / 68 x 96 cm) EUR 3,200. COPENHAGEN, 8 Sept 2004, *From Helsingør Harbour towards Kronborg* (oil on canvas, 32 x 48 ins / 81 x 121 cm) DKK 25,000.

HILLER, J.
Bohemian, 18th century.

Active in Prague from 1716 to 1746.
Engraver (burin).
Bohemian School.

Hiller mainly engraved religious subjects after paintings by G. Severoni.

HILLER, Joseph, Jr

American, 18th - 19th century.
Born 1777, in Salem (Massachusetts); died 1795.
Engraver.

HILLER, Karol

Polish, 20th century.
Born 1891, in Lódz; died 1939, in Lódz, murdered.
Painter, graphic designer, illustrator.

Karol Hiller studied chemistry in Darmstadt in Germany, and then architecture in Moscow, before studying painting at the academy of fine art in Kiev in 1916. There he particularly focused on the techniques used in traditional Russian icon painting. During the Revolution of 1917, Hiller was commissar of art in Kiev. Returning to Lódz in 1921, he became closely involved in the cultural and particularly theatrical life there, collaborating with Witold Wandurski on the formation of a workers' theatre and writing many critical essays for the avant-garde review *Forma*, a publication he had helped establish in 1933. Well-known for his militant left-wing activities, he was executed by the Nazis shortly after the occupation of Poland.

Although his time was greatly taken up with his activities as an organiser and promoter of cultural activities, he continued his own painting and also produced posters and illustrations for a number of literary works. He explored various techniques derived from photography, including what he called 'heliography', to reproduce multiple copies of certain works so as to make them accessible to the greatest number of people. At the time of his return to Lódz, his painting consisted of compositions representing geometrically distorted scenes from working-class life set in cityscapes amidst factories and machines. From 1926, his painting developed rapidly from a post-Cubist style towards a progressive abandonment of figurative representation and a greater abstraction. Forms became simplified, mirroring the changes in form brought about by industrialism, an evolution that had its origins in Italian Futurism, the Purism of Ozenfant and Jeanneret and the Functionalism of the Bauhaus movement. From 1928, Hiller's paintings were properly abstract, without espousing the Neoplasticism of Mondrian. They are clearly interested in conveying a sense of three-dimensional space, partly through the use of a perspective as rigorous as that of industrial design, a feature of Hiller's work at this period that can be compared to the work of the Purists. In 1932, he began to include references to biological forms in his works, perhaps through a feeling of dissatisfaction with the strictly geometric forms of his earlier painting. The forms began to resemble the images produced by the Surrealists and can be seen as anticipating the post-war Art Informel movement. Outside Poland, publications discussing avant-garde painting in the inter-war period very rarely mention this important artist, whose work did not appear for sale in the international art market and consequently did not become widely known.

Karol Hiller's work has appeared in collective and thematic exhibitions, including *Vision Machine*, an exhibition of 'seeing machines' used by artists and architects, Musée des Beaux-Arts, Nantes (2000).

BIBLIOGRAPHY:

Porebski, Mieczyslaw, *Peinture moderne polonaise, sources et recherches*, exhibition catalogue, Musée Galliera, Paris, 1969. *Vision machine*, exhibition catalogue, Musée des Beaux-Arts, Nantes, Somogy, Paris, 2000.

MUSEUMS AND GALLERIES:

LÓDZ (Muz. Sztuki): numerous works.

HILLER, Margareta

Maiden name: Ehrenzeller
Swiss, 18th century.
Born 28 February 1695, in St Gall; died 19 June 1778, in St Gall.
Draughtswoman, engraver.

Margareta Hiller is known to have executed many portraits.

HILLER, Susan

American, 20th - 21st century.
Born 1940 or 1942, in Florida.
Active in England since 1973.
Painter, photographer, installation artist, video artist.

Susan Hiller studied at Smith College of Art, Northampton, MA, receiving a BA in 1961, and at Tulane University, New Orleans, receiving an MA in anthropology (Mesoamerican tribal art, linguistics and archaeology) in 1965. She has carried out anthropological field research in Mexico, Guatemala and Belize, and has travelled in Europe, North Africa, India and the Far East. She moved to London in 1973, where she taught at the Slade School of Art, London (1982-1990), was Professor of Fine Art at the School of Art and Design, University of Ulster, Belfast (1991-1997), and has held the Baltic Chair of Contemporary Art at University of Newcastle. Hiller has received a DAAD Fellowship in Berlin (2002-2003), and a Guggenheim Fellowship (1998).

Hiller has refused to confine herself to a single medium, working in painting, photography, performance, video, sculpture, installation art and language. She describes her work as originating in Minimalism and as a kind of archaeological investigation. Typically, it begins with modern cultural artefacts and often seeks to highlight the overlooked or anonymous aspects of social culture, as in *Dedicated to the Unknown Artists* (1972-1976), which contains hundreds of British 'rough sea' postcards, along with charts and notes, or *Monument* (1980-1981), comprising 41 colour photographs on a wall accompanied by a sound tape and park bench to accommodate viewers. Another ten-year project entitled *Photomat Portraits* used discarded photographs from photobooths. In the 1970s, she experimented with automatic writing as a basis for her art, as in *Sisters of Menon* (1972), and collaborated in a large-scale community performance, *Street Ceremonies* (1973), and an experiment in telepathy, *Dream Mapping* (1974). Video has been a regular feature of her installations, such as *Belshazzar's Feast, the Writing on your Wall* (1990), and *Psi Girls*.

Hiller has had numerous exhibitions throughout Europe and the US, including: 1990, *Signs of the Times*, Museum of Modern Art, Oxford; 1995, FIAC (Foire Internationale d'Art Contemporain), presented by Galerie Gimpel Fils, Paris; 1995, *Rites of Passage*, Tate Gallery, London; 1996, retrospective, Tate Gallery, Liverpool; 1998, *Out of Actions*, Museum of Contemporary Art, Los Angeles; 1998, Institute of Contemporary Art, Philadelphia; 1998, Experimental Art Foundation, Adelaide, Australia; 2000, *Bienale de Habana*, Havana, Cuba; 2001, *Intelligence*, Tate Britain; 2001, *Empathy*, Taidemuseon, Pori, Finland; 2002, Museet for Samidskunst, Roskilde, Denmark; 2003, *Apparition: The Action of Appearing*, Kettle's Yard, Cambridge.

BIBLIOGRAPHY:

Susan Hiller, Recent Works, exhibition catalogue, Kettle's Yard, Cambridge, 1978. Hiller, Susan, *Enquires=Inquiries*, exhibition catalogue, Gardner Center Gallery, University of Sussex, Brighton, 1979. *Susan Hiller 1973-83: The Muse My Sister*, exhibition catalogue, Orchard Gallery, Londonderry, 1984. Van den Bosch, Annette, '*Susan Hiller: Resisting Representation*' in *Artscribe*, vol 46, Journal article, May-July 1984. Kent, Sarah/Morreau, Jackie, '*A Conversation with Susan Hiller*' in *Women's Images of Men*, Book, Writers and Readers, London, New York, 1985. *Susan Hiller*, exhibition catalogue, Institute of Contemporary Arts, London, c. 1986.

Brett, Guy, '*Susan Hiller's Shadowland*' in *Art in America*, vol 79, Journal article, April 1991. Hiller, Susan, *Thinking about Art: Conversations with Susan Hiller*, Book, Manchester University Press, Manchester, 1996. *After the Freud Museum*, Illustrated book, Book Works, London, 1996. *Susan Hiller*, exhibition catalogue, Tate Gallery, Liverpool, 1996. *Witness*, CD-ROM, Art Angel Afterlives, London, 2000. Turner, Chris/ Higgs, Matthew, *Psi Girls*, exhibition catalogue, Site Gallery, Sheffield, 2000. Malbert, Roger, *Apparition: the action of appearing*, group exhibition catalogue, Arnolfini, Bristol, 2003. Lingwood, James (ed.), *Susan Hiller: Recall, Selected Works 1969(2004*, exhibition catalogue, Baltic, Gateshead, 2004.

MUSEUMS AND GALLERIES:

ADELAIDE (AG of South Australia) - COLOGNE (Mus. Ludwig) - LEEDS (City AG, Contemporary Art Collection): *Monument* (1980-1981, installation) - LONDON (Imperial War Mus.) - LONDON (Tate Collection): *Monument* (1980-1981, installation); *Belshazzar's Feast, the Writing on your Wall* (1983-1984, installation); *An Entertainment* (1990, installation); *From the Freud Museum* (1991-1996, installation, mixed media) - LONDON (Victoria and Albert Mus.) - OSLO (Henie-Onstad Kunstsenter).

HILLERMANN, Anna
German, 19th century.
Born in Hamburg.
Painter.

Hillerman studied under Herterich and Franz Simm.

HILLERN-FLINSCH, Wilhelm von
German, 20th century.
Born 26 March 1884, in Freiburg im Breisgau; died 11 April 1986, in Munich.
Painter, lithographer. Figures, portraits.

Wilhelm von Hillern-Flinsch was a career military officer who took to drawing and painting. He studied in 1920 at the J.A. Sailer College of Design in Munich and, in 1922, under Peter Halm's direction at the Munich fine arts academy. He was forced to cut short his career when he refused to swear allegiance to Adolf Hitler. He settled in Sweden from 1947 to 1953 before returning to Munich. At the age of 70 he started producing lithographs. He died in 1986 at the age of 102.

Examples of work by Hillern-Flinsch featured at *Verfemt. Vergessen. Wiederentdeckt. Schicksale expressiver Bildkunst im 20. Jahrhundert* (*Condemned. Forgotten. Rediscovered. The Fate of Expressive Art in the 20th Century*), an exhibition held in 2001 at the Cultural and Historical Museum in Osnabrück and designed to highlight the importance and influence of a generation of German and Austrian artists of the 1920s and 1930s whose work was consigned to oblivion by virtue of cultural and political pressure exerted by the Nazi regime.

BIBLIOGRAPHY:

Dokumente zu Leben und Werk des Malers Wilhelm von Hillern-Flinsch, exhibition catalogue, Germanisches Nationalmuseum, Nürnberg, 1978. *Wilhelm von Hillern-Flinsch*, Munich, 1983. *Verfemt. Vergessen. Wiederentdeckt. Schicksale expressiver Bildkunst im 20. Jahrhundert. Sammlung Gerhard Schneider*, exhibition catalogue, Kulturgeschichtiches Museum, Osnabrück, 2001.

AUCTION RECORDS:

MUNICH, 26 May 1992, *Storm at Sea* (oil on canvas, 15 1/4 x 28 ins / 39 x 71 cm) DEM 2,990.

HILLERO, Georges
French, 20th century.
Born in St-Ouen.
Painter.

Georges Hillero exhibited at the Salon des Indépendants from 1927.

HILLERS, Hans Andreas Joachim
German, 18th - 19th century.
Born 1750, in Hamburg; died 8 September 1817, in Hamburg.
Engraver.

Hillers made engravings of views and portraits.

HILLERSBERG, Lars
Swedish, 20th century.
Born 1937, in Frustuna.
Painter, draughtsman.

Lars Hillersberg attracted attention following an exhibition in 1960 but he subsequently suffered a few setbacks as the result of his outspokenness, and his paintings were rejected by the São Paulo Biennale in 1969. He is the driving force behind the magazine *Puss*, which he launched in 1968, covering the avant-garde 'underground' activities in the USA, which has a large readership among young artists in Sweden. He makes graphic contributions himself with his brutal satirical and political images, which are somewhat reminiscent of the aims and writings of George Grosz in his day.

Hillersberg professes his admiration for the Abstract Expressionism of painters such as Jackson Pollock. However, he does not appear to have gone in that direction himself, as the opinions he tries to express in his graphic and three-dimensional work are incompatible with the kind of abstract formulation he describes as 'inoffensive calligraphy'. His ink drawings and tempera paintings pursue the same polemical aim as his contributions to *Puss*. In his compositions, small cartoon figures are heaped together in catastrophic visions that result as much from a fanciful imagination as a violent satire on society, as is made clear by the captions inserted in numerous 'speech bubbles'. His most pictorial works, while remaining attached to his original critical roots, show a carnival world, whose grotesque character is reminiscent of the masks of James Ensor.

HILLERSTRÖM, Gustaf
Swedish, 18th century.
Active in Stockholm.
Painter. Genre scenes, architectural views.

For a long time Gustaf Hillerström was a weaver at the Gobelins factory. He favoured comic subjects.

HILLESTRÖM, Carl Peter
Swedish, 18th - 19th century.
Born 1760, in Stockholm; died 1812.
Painter. Seascapes.

Carl Hilleström was the son of Per Hilleström. Two of his gouaches are in the museum of Stockholm.

AUCTION RECORDS:

STOCKHOLM, 30 Oct 1979, *View of Riddarholmen* (1782, oil on canvas, 22 x 31 ins / 56 x 79 cm) SEK 40,000. STOCKHOLM, 26 April 1983, *Summer Landscape* (oil on canvas, 14 1/2 x 20 3/4 ins / 37 x 53 cm) SEK 10,500. STOCKHOLM, 9 April 1985, *Landscape* (1791, watercolour, 8 1/4 x 12 1/2 ins / 21 x 32 cm) SEK 9,000. HELSINKI, 28 Nov 1999, *Landscapes* (mixed media, semicircular, a pair, 20 x 39 ins / 50 x 100 cm) FIM 40,000. STOCKHOLM, 28 Nov 2001, *Summer Landscape with Water and Figures by House* (1789, oil on panel, 8 x 11 ins / 20 x 29 cm) SEK 51,000. STOCKHOLM, 28 May 2002, *Landscape with Buildings and Figures* (1799, watercolour, a pair, 15 x 20 ins / 37 x 50 cm) SEK 46,000. STOCKHOLM, 3 Dec 2003, *View of Haga Park from Old Haga* (watercolour, Works on paper, 16 x 22 ins / 40 x 56 cm) SEK 18,000.

HILLESTRÖM, Per or Pehr
Swedish, 18th - 19th century.
Born 18 November 1732, in Väddö; died 13 August 1816, in Stockholm.
Painter. Historical subjects, portraits, genre scenes, interiors with figures, still-lifes.

Per Hilleström studied fine arts in Paris and returned to Sweden in 1750. He became a teacher at the academy in Stockholm and then director in 1805. He had initially been a weaver.

Bibliography:

Winquist, M./Kruse, H., *Pehr Hillstrom*, exhibition catalogue, National Museum, Stockholm, 1979. Kent, N., *The Triumph of Light and Nature: Nordic Art, 1740-1940*, Thames and Hudson, London, 1987. Varnedoe, K., *Northern Light: Nordic Art at the Turn of the Century*, Yale University Press, New Haven and London, 1988.

Museums and Galleries:

Stockholm: *Peasant Selling Goods; The Old Match Seller; Interior of Swedish Thatched Cottage; Two Kitchen Scenes; Karl Mikael Bellman Writing; Morning Toilette; The Artist at 62; The Artist at 38; Travelling Salesmen; Stockholm in 1790; Young Girl Buying a Love Song; Kitchen Interior.*

Auction records:

Stockholm, 11 and 15 April 1967, *Young Girl in Interior Lit by a Candle*, SEK 12,100. Stockholm, 31 March 1971, *Interior with Two Young Women*, SEK 14,000. Paris, 10 June 1976, *Still-life* (oil on canvas, 19 x 23¼ ins / 48 x 59 cm) SEK 17,000. Stockholm, 20 April 1977, *Interior of the Royal Museum of Stockholm* (oil on canvas, 18¼ x 18½ ins / 46.5 x 47 cm) SEK 39,100. Stockholm, 30 Oct 1979, *Still-life* (oil on canvas, 20½ x 24 ins / 52 x 61 cm) SEK 24,000. Stockholm, 21 April 1982, *Couple in an Interior* (1779, oil on canvas, 19¼ x 15¼ ins / 49 x 39 cm) SEK 90,000. Stockholm, 26 April 1983, *The Storyteller* (oil on canvas, 22 x 26¾ ins / 56 x 68 cm) SEK 103,000. Stockholm, 4 Nov 1986, *Interior with Two Young Women Cleaning Copper Pots and Glasses* (1776-1779, oil on canvas, 23¼ x 28¾ ins / 59 x 73 cm) SEK 290,000. Stockholm, 20 April 1987, *Cathedral View* (c. 1790, oil on panel, 11¾ x 9¾ ins / 30 x 25 cm) SEK 45,000. Stockholm, 19 May 1992, *Interior with Seated Lady Reading and Servant Bringing a Cup of Tea* (oil on panel, 15¾ x 13½ ins / 40 x 34 cm) SEK 170,000. Stockholm, 5 Sept 1992, *Still-life with Ham on a Pewter Plate, with Bread and a Plate by a Bowl of Currants on a Table* (oil on canvas, 20½ x 26¾ ins / 52 x 68 cm) SEK 115,000; *Two Servants in a Kitchen* (c. 1775, oil on canvas, 12¼ x 17¼ ins / 31 x 44 cm) SEK 125,000. Stockholm, 30 Nov 1993, *Swedish Peasant with Two Women* (oil on canvas, 15 x 11¾ ins / 38 x 30 cm) SEK 24,000. London, 5 Dec 1997, *The Forge* (oil on panel, attributed, 22 x 17¼ ins / 55.8 x 43.8 cm) GBP 11,270. Uppsala, 5 Dec 1999, *Kitchen Interior with Two Girls, One Cleaning Bottles, One Polishing Knife* (oil on canvas, 20 x 17 ins / 50 x 42 cm) SEK 280,000. Stockholm, 28 Nov 2000, *Two Elegant Ladies Warming Themselves by the Open Fire* (oil on canvas, 20 x 16 ins / 50 x 40 cm) SEK 255,000. Stockholm, 5 Dec 2000, *Girl Peeling Carrots, Talking to a Lady While Another Cooks* (oil on canvas, 19 x 16 ins / 49 x 40 cm) SEK 320,000. Stockholm, 29 May 2001, *Interior Scene with Woman Ironing* (1795, oil on canvas, 20 x 16 ins / 51 x 41 cm) SEK 295,000. Stockholm, 4 Dec 2001, *Woman Polishing Copper* (oil on canvas, 22 x 17 ins / 55 x 42 cm) SEK 235,000. Stockholm, 28 May 2002, *Gustav III in Armour on Horseback at Skolsund 1776* (pencil, 24 x 17 ins / 60 x 44 cm) SEK 210,000. Stockholm, 29 May 2002, *Orpheus and Eurydice - Scene from the Opera* (oil on panel, 15 x 13 ins / 39 x 33 cm) SEK 115,000. Stockholm, 26 May 2003, *Young Girl Looking for Something by Candlelight in her Pantry* (oil on panel, 16 x 13 ins / 40 x 32 cm) SEK 290,000. Stockholm, 2 Dec 2003, *The Broken Plate* (c. 1776, oil on canvas, 21 x 17 ins / 54 x 43 cm) SEK 360,000. Stockholm, 26 May 2004, *Still-life with Fish, Onions and Wine on Table* (oil on canvas, 13 x 18 ins / 34 x 45 cm) SEK 92,000. Stockholm, 26 May 2004, *Young Woman Sweeping and Girl Untidying* (1774, oil on canvas, 15 x 12 ins / 39 x 30 cm) SEK 220,000.

HILLEVELD, Adrianus David

Dutch, 19th century.

Born 16 April 1838, in Amsterdam; died 1869.

Painter. Landscapes, seascapes.

He was a pupil of Valentin Bing and Abraham Hulk.

Auction records:

London, 26 Nov 1980, *Boats on a River* (oil on canvas, 28¼ x 35¾ ins / 72 x 91 cm) GBP 4,600. London, 9 Oct 1987, *Winter Landscape with Painters* (oil on panel, 10 x 14 ins / 25.3 x 35.5 cm) GBP 2,600. Amsterdam, 25 April 1990, *View of Katwijk* (1885, oil on panel, 6 x 9 ins / 15 x 23 cm) NLG 3,680. Amsterdam, 14 Sept 1993, *River Landscape with Peasants in a Boat near a Windmill* (oil on panel, 10½ x 12½ ins / 26.5 x 32 cm) NLG 4,600. Amsterdam, 14 June 1994, *Hillside Landscape with Figures on the Bank* (oil on panel, 12¾ x 21¼ ins / 32.5 x 54 cm) NLG 4,370. Edinburgh, 1 July 2000, *Ship of the Line Stranded off the Coast* (1862, oil on canvas, 19 x 24 ins / 47 x 62 cm) GBP 2,150. Amsterdam, 24 Oct 2000, *Daily Catch - Beach Scene in Summer with Fisherfolk* (1859, oil on canvas, 24 x 35 ins / 62 x 90 cm) NLG 30,000. Rotterdam, 6 Nov 2001, *Ships by the Shore* (1862, oil on canvas, 19 x 24 ins / 47 x 61 cm) NLG 7,800. Gravenhage, 7 Nov 2001, *Landscape with Figures on Turnpike Road* (oil on panel, 10 x 13 ins / 26 x 34 cm) NLG 17,000. Amsterdam, 21 Oct 2003, *Summer Landscape with Ships in a Waterway* (1858, oil on canvas, 17 x 23 ins / 42 x 59 cm) EUR 3,500. Munich, 26 March 2004, *Dutch Canal with Windmill and Houses* (oil on panel, 14 x 18 ins / 35 x 46 cm) EUR 4,000.

HILLFON, Hertha

Swedish, 20th century.

Born 1921.

Sculptor.

Hertha Hillfon works mainly in bronze, but also in terracotta.

Auction records:

Stockholm, 6 June 1988, *Face* (1975, bronze, h. 7¾ ins / 20 cm) SEK 16,000. Stockholm, 6 Dec 1989, *Relief of a Half-face, Nose and Mouth* (brown-patinated bronze, h. 8¾ ins / 22.5 cm) SEK 27,000. Stockholm, 30 Nov 1993, *Reclining Figure* (terracotta in two parts, h. 19¾ ins / 50 cm and 31½ x 27½ ins/80 x 70 cm) SEK 35,000. Stockholm, 6 Nov 2002, *Head* (terracotta, 35 x 31x20 ins / 90 x 78x52 cm) SEK 56,000.

HILLGAARD, Stefanny

Norwegian, 20th century.

Born in Sofia.

Sculptor.

Stefanny Hillgaard lives in Oslo. She trained in Rome and Paris, where she exhibited at the Salon de Mai. She also took part in the international sculpture exhibition at the Musée Rodin in Paris in 1966. Her work is figurative and expressionist, symbolising the horror of the human condition and full of weeping, sorrow and heartbreak.

HILLIARD, John

British, 20th century.

Born 1945, in Lancaster.

Sculptor, photographer.

Outsider Art.

John Hilliard studied Outsider Art at Lancaster College of Art from 1962 to 1964 and at St Martin's College from 1964 to 1967. He lives and works in London. While training, Hilliard constructed ephemeral assemblages which he recorded photographically. Since 1970, he has worked with photography transposed onto canvas but continues to create the environments or settings that he takes as a starting point for a variety of technical strategies. Hilliard exhibited in London at the Lisson Gallery from 1979 and in Paris at the Galerie Durand-Dessert from 1976. In 2001, he took part in the exhibition *UK in the Seventies* at the Galerie Liliane & Michel Durand-Dessert, Paris; in 2003 in *Phantom der Lust: Visionen des Machochismus in der Kunst* (*Phantom of Desire. Visions of Masochism in Art*), an exhibition devoted to Sacher-Masoch, who gave his name to masochism, held at the Neue Galerie am Ladesmuseum, Graz. In 1983, his work was shown at the Kunstverein, Cologne, and the Kunsthalle, Bremen. In 1984, it was shown at the Institute of Contemporary Art in London and the Frankfurt Kunstverein, at the Sprengel Museum in Hanover in 1987, at the University of Chicago in 1989, the Kunstverein, Stuttgart in 1990, at the Musée de La Chaux-de-Fonds in 1993, at Le Channel Gallery, formerly the post office, in Calais in 1994 and at the Krems Kunsthalle in 1997.

Bibliography:

Scene - John Hilliard, exhibition catalogue, Musée des Beaux-arts, La Chaux-de-Fonds, Le Channel, Gal. de l'Ancienne Poste, Calais, 1993-1994. *John Hilliard,* Verlag das Wunderhorn, Heidelberg, 2000. Weibel, Peter (ed.), *'Phantom der Lust. Visionen des Masochismus in der Kunst'* in *2 vol.*, exhibition catalogue, Neue Galerie am Landesmuseum, Graz, Belleville Verlag, Munich, 2003.

Museums and Galleries:

Dijon (FRAC Bourgogne): *She Seemed to Stare* (1977) - Stuttgart (Staatsgal.): *Arrested Curve/Curve Arrested* (1979).

HILLIARD, Laurence

British, 17th century.
Born c. 1581, in London; died c. 1640.
Miniaturist, goldsmith.

The son of Nicholas Hilliard, Laurence Hilliard inherited his father's privileges at court.

HILLIARD, Laurence Jermyn, or Lawrence

British, 19th century.
Born 1855; died 1887; at sea.
Active in Uxbridge.
Painter. Still-lifes.

The secretary of John Ruskin, Laurence Hilliard exhibited frequently between 1876 and 1887. He died on the Aegean Sea.

In 2003, his work appeared in the exhibition held at the Musée de Picardie, Amiens, *Ruskin - Turner. Dessins et Voyages en Picardie Romantique* (*Ruskin - Turner: Drawings and Travels in Romantic Picardy*).

Bibliography:

Gamble, Cynthia/Wildman, Stephen/Pinete, Matthieu, *Ruskin - Turner. Dessins et voyages en Picardie romantique*, group exhibition catalogue, Musée de Picardie, Amiens, 2003.

HILLIARD, Nicolas

British, 16th - 17th century.
Born 1547, in Exeter; died c. 1619, in London.
Miniaturist, jeweller.

Nicolas Hilliard, the son of a goldsmith, was apprenticed to his father's trade but preferred the art of the miniature. In 1570 his name appears on the register of the Goldsmiths' Company, and he became miniaturist and goldsmith to Queen Elizabeth I, of whom he painted a number of portraits, including one which shows her covered with jewels depicted in detail - he was, after all, a jeweller. He may have visited France and perhaps met Ronsard. In 1577 the Duke of Alençon made a payment to a Nicholas Belliart, who was probably the same person as Hilliard. In 1583-1584 he was appointed sole portrait painter to the queen, as he was later to James I, who in 1617 granted Hilliard an exclusive right to portrait painting at court. In 1598 he was asked to write a treatise on the art of the miniature, in which he defined his role as an English gentleman painter, friend of men of letters and court notables. He said that he greatly admired Holbein, a truth made evident by his sharp, clear, brilliant style. His principal subjects, especially during Elizabeth's reign, were men depicted in a romantic Shakespearean manner. One such portrait is the *Young Man by a Rosebush,* and another is the *Portrait of an Unknown Man against a Background of Flames*. His style later became tighter, and he moved on to painting portraits of women with flowing hair.

Museums and Galleries:

Amsterdam: *Two Portraits of Elizabeth; Lady in Fine Attire; Elderly Lady* - London (National Maritime Mus.): *George Clifford, Earl of Cumberland* - London (Victoria and Albert Mus.): *Portrait of a Man of Twenty-Four; Young Man by a Rosebush; Portrait of an Unknown Man against a Background of Flames.*

Auction records:

New York, 1-8 April 1908, *Queen Elizabeth,* USD 925. London, 28 Feb 1911, *Lady in Black and White,* GBP 58. London, 22 April 1911, *Post Horses in a Storm; River Scene,* GBP 4. London, June 1922, *Queen Elizabeth Wearing Black,* GBP 120. London, July 1922, *Lady Frances Reynell,* GBP 315. Paris, 6 Dec 1924, *Portrait of Sir Francis Drake* (attributed) FRF 12,000. London, 29 April 1932, *Queen Elizabeth,* GBP 840. London, 17 April 2000, *Portrait of a Noblewoman Wearing a Crown* (miniature, h. 2 ins / 5 cm) GBP 48,000. London, 6 June 2002, *Portrait of a Lady Wearing a Black Dress and Hat* (miniature, h. 2 ins / 6 cm) GBP 200,000. London, 10 Dec 2002, *Anne of Denmark* (miniature, h. 2 ins / 4 cm) GBP 6,000. London, 3 June 2003, *Gentleman in a Black Doublet and Cloak with High Collar* (1577, miniature, oval, h. 2 ins / 5 cm) GBP 105,000. London, 22 April 2004, *Henry Wriothesely, Third Earl of Southampton* (miniature, oval, h. 2 ins / 5 cm) GBP 110,000.

HILLIARD, Richard

British, 16th century.
Died 1560.
Miniaturist.

HILLIARD, William Henry

American, 19th century.
Born 1836, in Auburn (New York State); died April 1905, in Washington DC.
Painter, watercolourist, draughtsman. Portraits, genre scenes, landscapes.

William Henry Hilliard started his art studies under Émile Lambinet and Charles Cicéri in Paris. He worked in Boston and New York and then travelled to Europe. He settled in Paris in 1880, returning to live in the USA in 1884. He exhibited at the Royal Academy in London in 1880, and at the Paris Salon. His works include *Fight against the Clouds, Portrait of President Garfield* and *Tomb of Howard Payne*.

Auction records:

New York, 17-18 March 1809, *Dutch Village,* USD 145. Boston, 12 March 1999, *Peasant Girl on a Forest Path* (oil on canvas, 20 x 12 ins / 51 x 30 cm) USD 2,200. Philadelphia, 15 April 1999, *Bear Paw Creek, Adirondacks* (1868, oil on canvas, 29 x 36 ins / 74 x 91 cm) USD 4,100.

HILLIER, Tristram Paul, or Tristan

British, 20th century.
Born 11 April 1905, in Beijing; died 1983.
Painter. Landscapes, still-lifes, urban scenes, religious subjects.
Unit One Group.

Tristan Hillier trained at the Slade School in London under Henry Tonks in 1926, then in Paris at the Atelier Colarossi under André Lhote. In the 1930s he set up with other artists the group Unit One. Up to the outbreak of World War II he travelled extensively to Spain and Portugal (1935-1936) and France (1937-1940), painting scenes of sparsely populated villages under the bleaching sun. He also met Braque and studied Velázquez and his use of the colour black, which is a strong influence on some of his still-lifes, such as *Harness*. Later he lived at East Pennard, Shepton Mallet in Somerset.

His work is characterised by a disquieting, almost surreal stillness and a meticulous technique, and is reminiscent of that of Edwards Wadsworth, with whom he painted abroad.

He exhibited regularly at the Royal Academy and at Arthur Tooth's in London; a touring retrospective was organised by the Royal Academy in 1983. He also published an autobiographical book, *Leda and the Goose* (1954).

MUSEUMS AND GALLERIES:
ABERDEEN (AG and Mus.): *Slipway at Peniche* (1948) - LONDON (Tate Collection): *Harness.*
AUCTION RECORDS:
LONDON, 19 March 1971, *Viseu (Portugal),* Gns 450. LONDON, 19 May 1972, *Still-life with Apples and Bottle,* Gns 600. LONDON, 18 July 1973, *Yport* (1940) GBP 3,400. LONDON, 5 March 1976, *Train in Andalusia* (1953, oil on canvas, 15 x 22 ins / 38 x 56 cm) GBP 480. LONDON, 8 March 1978, *Pedrozo de Acim* (1971, oil on canvas, 19 3/4 x 23 1/2 ins / 50 x 60 cm) GBP 1,000. LONDON, 27 June 1979, *The Bridges at Espalion* (1964, oil on canvas, 21 1/2 x 35 1/4 ins / 54.5 x 89.5 cm) GBP 580. LONDON, 14 March 1983, *Shipbuilding at Peniche* (1947, oil on canvas, 24 x 32 ins / 61 x 81 cm) GBP 8,500. LONDON, 7 June 1985, *The Anchor* (oil on panel, 28 1/2 x 24 ins / 72.7 x 61 cm) GBP 17,000. LONDON, 12 June 1987, *Lake at Guijo de Coria* (1975, oil on canvas, 13 3/4 x 20 ins / 35 x 50.8 cm) GBP 4,200. LONDON, 3-4 March 1988, *Anchor on a Lee Shore* (oil on card, 17 3/4 x 14 3/4 ins / 45 x 37.5 cm) GBP 1,400. LONDON, 21 Sept 1989, *The Indian Ocean at Plattenberg* (1976, oil on canvas, 13 1/2 x 19 1/2 ins / 34.4 x 49.4 cm) GBP 3,300. LONDON, 10 Nov 1989, *Threshing Floor* (1947, oil on card, 6 3/4 x 9 3/4 ins / 17.1 x 24.8 cm) GBP 6,050. LONDON, 3 May 1990, *Lerana* (1970, oil on canvas, 13 1/2 x 15 1/4 ins / 34 x 39 cm) GBP 4,180. LONDON, 8 June 1990, *Hulks on a Portuguese Beach* (1967, oil on canvas, 20 x 24 ins / 51 x 61 cm) GBP 8,800. LONDON, 8 Nov 1991, *The Road to Binegar* (1944, oil on panel, 6 x 8 1/2 ins / 15 x 21.5 cm) GBP 4,620. LONDON, 12 March 1992, *The Cart* (1974, oil on card, 7 3/4 x 10 ins / 20 x 25.5 cm) GBP 4,025. LONDON, 14 May 1992, *Spanish Bread* (1972, oil on canvas, 16 1/4 x 20 ins / 41 x 51 cm) GBP 3,300. LONDON, 5 June 1992, *The Chateau-Lafitte Taster* (1963, oil on canvas, 18 x 14 1/4 ins / 46 x 36 cm) GBP 2,420. LONDON, 5 Nov 1999, *Surrealist Landscape, Men and Boat* (oil on panel, 33 x 30 ins / 84 x 77 cm) GBP 43,000. LONDON, 11 Nov 1999, *Still-life with Wine Bottle* (1969, oil on canvas, 20 x 24 ins / 51 x 61 cm) GBP 13,000. LONDON, 6 Sept 2000, *Godney Moor* (1975, tempera on canvas, 16 x 20 ins / 41 x 51 cm) GBP 4,000. LONDON, 6 Sept 2000, *La Guardia de La Mancha* (1973, tempera on board, 10 x 14 ins / 25 x 35 cm) GBP 4,800. LONDON, 4 July 2001, *Mountain Village, Aragon* (1958, oil on canvas, 24 x 32 ins / 61 x 81 cm) GBP 11,000. LONDON, 21 Nov 2001, *Beach at Ypres* (oil on canvas, 24 x 32 ins / 61 x 81 cm) GBP 10,000. CREWKERNE, 16 May 2002, *Portrait of Violet Wyndham* (1933, pencil, 9 x 9 ins / 24 x 23 cm) GBP 2,000. LONDON, 4 July 2002, *Fossils, February* (1957, oil on canvas, 14 x 18 ins / 35 x 45 cm) GBP 12,000. LONDON, 10 Sept 2003, *August Bees and Wasps* (oil on canvas, 14 x 18 ins / 36 x 46 cm) GBP 6,500. LONDON, 2 Dec 2003, *Clewer* (1943, oil on canvas, 16 x 20 ins / 40 x 50 cm) GBP 10,000. LONDON, 16 March 2004, *Mijas* (oil on panel, 6 x 9 ins / 15 x 23 cm) GBP 8,200. LONDON, 16 March 2004, *Provence* (1936, oil on canvas, 25 x 30 ins / 63 x 76 cm) GBP 9,000.

HILLIGAARD. See **HILLEGAERT**

HILLINGER, Peter, the Elder
Czech, 18th century.
Born 9 October 1698, in Glatz (now Klodzko, Poland).
Miniaturist.
Peter Hillinger worked mainly in Prague, painting portraits of notable citizens.

HILLINGER, Peter, the Younger
Bohemian, 18th century.
Born c. 1737, in Prague.
Miniaturist.
Peter Hillinger the Younger was taught by his father.

HILLINGFORD, Robert Alexander or Richard
British, 19th century.
Born 28 January 1828 or 1825, in London; died 1893 or 1904.
Painter. Military subjects, genre scenes.
Robert (or Richard) Hillingford made his debut in London in 1864. He exhibited at the Royal Academy, the British Institution and the Suffolk Street Gallery. His painting entitled *Yet Still a King,* now in Glasgow, was shown at the Royal Academy in 1888. His works are much sought after by collectors.
MUSEUMS AND GALLERIES:
GLASGOW: *Yet Still a King.*
AUCTION RECORDS:
PARIS, 20 April-1 and 2 May 1902, *Boat Trip,* FRF 200. NEW YORK, 28-30 March 1904, *Ravages of War,* USD 140. NEW YORK, 26 Jan 1906, *Between Love and Duty,* USD 325. LONDON, 7 Dec 1907, *Imperial Guard at Waterloo,* GBP 15. LONDON, 25 Jan 1908, *Oath to the Flag,* GBP 17. LONDON, 22 Feb 1908, *Battle of Malplaquet,* GBP 19; *Capture,* GBP 16. LONDON, 7 March 1908, *Pro Patria,* GBP 89. LONDON, 10 July 1908, *Sermon to the Soldiers,* GBP 6. LONDON, 21 Nov 1908, *Provisions for the Besieged,* GBP 21. LONDON, 30 Nov 1908, *Marlborough's Victory at Malplaquet,* GBP 26. LONDON, 4 June 1909, *Napoleon Entering Moscow,* GBP 44. LONDON, 17 June 1910, *Othello,* GBP 31. LONDON, Feb 1922, *Napoleon and his Troups; Royalists* (both) GBP 23. LONDON, March 1923, *Disembarkation of Men from the Vendée and Brittany near Lorient,* GBP 26. LONDON, 14 April 1924, *After the Battle,* GBP 13. LONDON, 17 April 1925, *Critical Moment at Quatre-Bras,* GBP 50. LONDON, 18 May 1925, *Council of War,* GBP 75. LONDON, 21 Jan 1927, *Men of the Vendée Disembarking,* GBP 42. LONDON, 17 June 1927, *Princess Elizabeth in the Tower,* GBP 29; *History of Adventure,* GBP 63. LONDON, 22 May 1930, *Duke of Wellington,* GBP 28. LONDON, 30 April 1931, *Don Quixote,* GBP 46. LONDON, 17 June 1932, *James II and Louis XIV at La Hougue,* GBP 37. LONDON, 26 April 1937, *Baron Münchhausen,* GBP 30. LONDON, 3 Aug 1944, *Countess of Derby,* GBP 50. LONDON, 19 Oct 1945, *Coming Home from the Feast of the Madonna at Pagliano,* GBP 52. LONDON, 25 Jan 1946, *Royalist Fugitive,* GBP 33. LONDON, 22 Feb 1972, *New Owners,* GBP 380. LONDON, 27 March 1973, *Departure of the Troops to Waterloo* (1898) GBP 3,200. LONDON, 14 May 1976, *Return from the Indies* (oil on panel, 14 x 17 1/2 ins / 35.5 x 44.5 cm) GBP 1,300. MILAN, 20 Dec 1977, *After the Carnival* (1863, oil on canvas, 44 x 61 ins / 112 x 155 cm) ITL 3,600,000. LONDON, 3 July 1979, *Othello Recounting his Adventures* (1869, oil on canvas, 19 1/2 x 28 1/2 ins / 49.5 x 72.5 cm) GBP 3,300. GÖTEBORG, 4 Nov 1982, *Wellington before the Battle of Waterloo* (oil on canvas, 20 x 30 ins / 51 x 76 cm) SEK 36,000. LONDON, 14 July 1983, *Peasants in the Roman Campagna* (1860, oil on canvas, 40 x 65 ins / 101.5 x 165 cm) GBP 6,000. LONDON, 16 April 1986, *Wellington at Waterloo* (1892, oil on canvas, 18 x 24 ins / 46 x 61 cm) GBP 4,200. LONDON, 18 March 1987, *Eve of the Battle of Waterloo, Wellington outside the Village Inn* (oil on canvas, 28 x 42 1/4 ins / 71 x 107 cm) GBP 12,000. LONDON, 24 June 1988, *Depature of the Regiment of the Coldstream Guards for Egypt* (oil on canvas, 36 1/4 x 24 ins / 92 x 61 cm) GBP 4,180. TORONTO, 30 Nov 1988, *Musicians of the Duke of Devonshire* (oil on canvas, 40 1/4 x 59 ins / 102 x 150 cm) CAD 11,000. LONDON, 2 June 1989, *Baron von Münchhausen Relating his Adventures* (oil on canvas, 17 1/4 x 26 1/4 ins / 43.5 x 66.5 cm) GBP 8,800. LONDON, 21 March 1990, *Wellington at Waterloo* (oil on canvas, 20 x 30 ins / 51 x 76 cm) GBP 13,750. COPENHAGEN, 25-26 April 1990, *Duel* (1869, oil on canvas, 11 3/4 x 15 3/4 ins / 30 x 40 cm) DKK 32,000. LONDON, 1 Nov 1990, *News from the Front* (oil on panel, 8 x 11 3/4 ins / 20.2 x 30 cm) GBP 3,080. NEW YORK, 28

Feb 1991, *Musical Gathering* (oil on canvas, 37 1/2 x 52 1/2 ins / 95.2 x 133.3 cm) USD 9,900. STOCKHOLM, 29 May 1991, *Cavalry Attacking* (oil on panel, 12 1/4 x 8 1/4 ins / 31 x 21 cm) SEK 12,000. LONDON, 11 Oct 1991, *The Battlefield at Waterloo* (oil on canvas, 20 x 30 ins / 50.8 x 76.2 cm) GBP 4,400. NEW YORK, 20 Feb 1992, *Tavern in the Roman Campagna* (1861, oil on canvas, 18 3/4 x 26 ins / 47.6 x 66 cm) USD 5,225. NEW YORK, 16 Feb 1994, *King James II Observing the Battle of La Hougue* (oil on canvas, 20 x 30 ins / 50.8 x 76.2 cm) USD 6,900. LONDON, 10 March 1995, *Under Fire* (oil on canvas, 18 x 24 1/4 ins / 46 x 61.6 cm) GBP 6,325. LONDON, 9 Oct 1996, *Mandolin Player* (1863, oil on canvas, 16 1/4 ins / 41 cm, 2 x 22 3/4 ins/5 x 58 cm) GBP 2,415. LONDON, 5 Nov 1997, *Cordelia and King Lear* (oil on canvas, 16 1/2 x 24 ins / 42 x 61 cm) GBP 2,070. LONDON, 4 Nov 1999, *Wellington and Blucher Meeting before the Battle of Waterloo* (c. 1815, oil on canvas, 23 x 17 ins / 59 x 44 cm) GBP 2,800. NEW ORLEANS, 17 March 2000, *Marlborough and His Ally Prince Eugene before Blenheim* (oil on canvas, 17 x 26 ins / 43 x 66 cm) USD 12,000. LONDON, 4 April 2000, *Peasant of the Campagna* (1860, oil on canvas, 40 x 65 ins / 102 x 165 cm) GBP 32,000. EXETER, 27 Feb 2001, *Interesting Story* (oil on canvas, 11 x 15 ins / 29 x 39 cm) GBP 3,800. LONDON, 8 March 2001, *Princess Elizabeth Arriving at the Tower of London* (1867, oil on panel, 24 x 20 ins / 61 x 51 cm) GBP 9,000. LONDON, 11 June 2002, *Morning of Waterloo* (oil on canvas, 18 x 24 ins / 46 x 61 cm) GBP 5,000. LONDON, 19 June 2002, *Fairy Dance* (oil on canvas, 16 x 21 ins / 41 x 53 cm) GBP 7,000. LEWES, 29 April 2003, *Battle of Waterloo* (oil on canvas, 19 x 29 ins / 48 x 74 cm) GBP 6,200. HASLEMERE, 5 Nov 2003, *Italian Serenade, Man Playing a Guitar with Figures and Dog round a Table* (oil on canvas, 26 x 36 ins / 66 x 91 cm) GBP 8,000. LONDON, 4 March 2004, *Adventures of Baron Münchausen* (oil on canvas, 23 x 35 ins / 58 x 90 cm) GBP 8,500. LONDON, 23 Nov 2004, *Three Caskets* (oil on canvas, 23 x 30 ins / 58 x 77 cm) GBP 7,500.

HILLMACKER
German, 19th century.
Active in San Sebastian c. 1840.
Painter. Historical scenes.

HILLNER, Franz
German, 18th - 19th century.
Born 1745, in Breslau (now Wroclaw, Poland); died 1812, in Potsdam.
Painter, draughtsman.

Hillner studied with B. Rode, and continued his artistic education himself by studying the paintings in Potsdam's Sanssouci Gallery, before completing his training later in Rome under Pompeo Battoni and executing many copies. On his return from Italy, he went to Potsdam where he taught drawing.

HILLS (Miss)
British, 18th century.
Active in London.
Painter. Flowers.

Miss Hills exhibited at the Royal Academy in London in 1799.

HILLS (Mrs)
British, 18th century.
Active in London.
Glass painter.

Mrs Hills exhibited at the Society of Artists in London in 1778.

HILLS, Charles John
British, 18th - 19th century.
Painter. Seascapes.

MUSEUMS AND GALLERIES:
MELBOURNE (Nat. Gal. of Victoria): *Dundee seen from Tayport.*

HILLS, Laura, later Mrs Coombs
American, 19th - 20th century.
Born 7 September 1859, in Newburyport (New York); died 1952.
Painter, pastellist, miniaturist. Still-lifes, flowers.

Laura Hills studied under Helen M. Knowlton and had many successes in both the USA and France. She won a bronze medal at the Exposition Universelle in Paris in 1900, second prize at the Corcoran Prize, Washington, in 1901, a silver medal in Buffalo in 1901 and Charleston in 1902, and a gold medal in St Louis in 1904. She became an associate member of the National Academy in 1903 and was vice-president of the Society of Miniaturists.

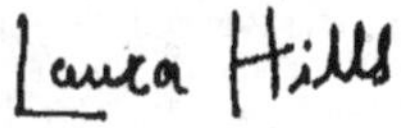

AUCTION RECORDS:
NEW YORK, 20 Sept 1984, *Flowers* (pastel, a pair, 11 1/4 x 14 ins / 28.5 x 35.5 cm and 12 x 10 1/4 ins/30.5 x 26 cm) USD 2,400. BOLTON, 15 May 1985, *Still-life with Flowers* (pastel, 21 x 18 ins / 53.5 x 45.7 cm) USD 3,100. NEW YORK, 26 May 1988, *Yellow Pansies* (pastel/card, 11 x 13 1/4 ins / 27.7 x 33.9 cm) USD 3,300. NEW YORK, 14 Feb 1990, *Pink and White Petunias* (1946, pastel/card) USD 4,950. NEW YORK, 9 March 1996, *Pink Dahlias* (pastel/card, 21 1/2 x 18 ins / 54.5 x 46 cm) USD 6,325. WASHINGTON, 18 Sept 1999, *Salpiglossis* (pastel, 22 x 17 ins / 55 x 44 cm) USD 8,000. HAMPTON, 2 April 2000, *Mixed Flowers No 2* (pastel, 27 x 23 ins / 69 x 58 cm) USD 12,000. BOSTON, 2 Dec 2001, *Trumpet Vine* (pastel on board, 21 x 18 ins / 53 x 46 cm) USD 18,000. BOSTON, 2 Dec 2001, *Little Bowl of Zinnias* (pastel, 13 x 12 ins / 33 x 30 cm) USD 19,000. NEW YORK, 22 May 2002, *Hollyhocks and Dahlias* (pastel on board, 28 x 24 ins / 72 x 60 cm) USD 22,500. EAST DENNIS, 1 Oct 2002, *Sweet Peas and Roses* (oil on canvas, 16 x 14 ins / 41 x 36 cm) USD 6,500. BOSTON, 2 June 2003, *Floral Still-life* (pastel on board, 16 x 16 ins / 41 x 41 cm) USD 12,000. BOSTON, 21 Nov 2003, *Portrait of a Young Girl, Possibly Lizzie Hills, the Artist Sister* (oil on canvas, 20 x 24 ins / 51 x 61 cm) USD 4,250. BOSTON, 14 May 2004, *Pansies and Red* (pastel on board, 15 x 13 ins / 38 x 32 cm) USD 14,000. BOSTON, 14 May 2004, *Peonies and Velvet* (pastel on board, 28 x 23 ins / 72 x 58 cm) USD 45,000.

HILLS, Robert
British, 18th - 19th century.
Born 22 June 1769, in Islington (London); died 1844, in London.
Painter, watercolourist, draughtsman. Portraits, landscapes, animals.

A pupil of Gresse, Robert Hills was one of the founders of the Society of Painters in Watercolours where, between 1791 and 1844, he exhibited 600 works. His collection of *Sketches of Flanders and Holland* appeared in 1816.

MUSEUMS AND GALLERIES:
LONDON (British Mus.): etchings of animals - LONDON (Victoria and Albert Mus.).

AUCTION RECORDS:
LONDON, 12 May 1910, *Girl in a White Dress*, GBP 12. LONDON, 4 March 1911, *Farm* (1806, drawing) GBP 3. LONDON, 9 Nov 1976, *Farmyard* (1928, watercolour, 14 3/4 x 19 3/4 ins / 37.7 x 50 cm) GBP 850. LONDON, 24 March 1977, *Stags in Knole Park* (1816, watercolour, 32 x 22 ins / 81.5 x 55 cm) GBP 700. LONDON, 28 Nov 1978, *Flocks in a Landscape* (1839, watercolour, 11 1/4 x 16 ins / 28.5 x 40.5 cm) GBP 650. LONDON, 29 Nov 1978, *Farmyard Scene* (1813, oil on panel, 7 x 9 ins / 18 x 23 cm) GBP 2,000. LONDON, 20 March 1979, *Scene in the Countryside* (1820, watercolour, 17 x 12 1/2 ins / 43 x 31.5 cm) GBP 700. PARIS, 7 Dec 1984, *Stags and Hinds in a Landscape* (1815, watercolour, 15 3/4 x 20 1/2 ins / 40 x 52 cm) FRF 16,500. LONDON, 19 Nov 1985, *Farmer and his Family* (watercolour,

10 x 7 3/4 ins / 25.5 x 19.7 cm) GBP 2,200. LONDON, 19 Nov 1987, *Harvesters Sitting by a Haycart* (watercolour/pencil outlines, 15 x 19 1/2 ins / 38 x 49.5 cm) GBP 2,800. NEW YORK, 25 Feb 1988, *Herd of Deer Resting in a Clearing* (watercolour, 19 x 31 1/2 ins / 48.2 x 80.2 cm) USD 7,700. MONACO, 8 Dec 1990, *Labourers* (1819, watercolour, 11 1/2 x 16 1/2 ins / 29 x 42 cm) FRF 9,990. LONDON, 13 July 1993, *Sleeping Herdsman* (1807, pencil and watercolour, 11 1/2 x 16 ins / 29.2 x 40.7 cm) GBP 1,495. LONDON, 11 Oct 1995, *Stag in the Highlands* (1830, watercolour, 16 x 11 ins / 40.5 x 28 cm) GBP 575. LONDON, 8 June 1999, *Figures, Horses and Oxen on a Road* (1839, pencil and watercolour heightened with white, 12 x 17 ins / 30 x 42 cm) GBP 2,500. CASTLECOMER, 14 Oct 1999, *Wooded Landscape with Deer* (oil on canvas, 33 x 54 ins / 84 x 138 cm) IEP 4,400. DRIFFIELD, 11 Feb 2000, *Farmyard Scene* (oil on canvas) GBP 1,900. LONDON, 29 Nov 2000, *Farmyard near Sevenoaks, Kent* (watercolour over pencil, 10 x 7 ins / 25 x 19 cm) GBP 2,400. LONDON, 27 June 2001, *Mill Stream at Gomershall, Surrey* (watercolour, 12 x 17 ins / 30 x 44 cm) GBP 2,400. MANCHESTER, 25 Sept 2001, *Wooded Lane with Cattle Driven by a Drover on a Donkey* (1811, watercolour, 17 x 12 ins / 43 x 30 cm) GBP 1,900. IPSWICH, 30 Sept 2002, *Deer by a Woodland Stream* (watercolour, 15 x 19 ins / 39 x 49 cm) GBP 1,850. LONDON, 5 Nov 2002, *Village in Snow* (1817, watercolour with scratching out, 20 x 28 ins / 51 x 71 cm) GBP 8,000. EXETER, 4 March 2003, *Peaceful Farmyard* (1806, watercolour, 19 x 29 ins / 48 x 73 cm) GBP 2,900. LONDON, 4 Nov 2003, *Cottage Children* (watercolour, 11 x 8 ins / 27 x 20 cm) GBP 1,900. LONDON, 13 Oct 2004, *Deer in a Woodland Pool* (watercolour, 12 x 17 ins / 31 x 42 cm) GBP 1,200.

HILLSMITH, Fannie or Fanny
American, 20th century.
Born 13 March 1911, in Boston.
Painter, draughtswoman, watercolourist, print artist, collage artist, assemblage artist, ceramicist, sculptor.
Figures, interiors with figures, landscapes, architectural views, still-lifes.
American Abstract Artists (AAA).

Fannie Hillsmith was the granddaughter of painter and interior decorator Frank Hill Smith, who later joined his second given name to his family name to form the name Frank Hillsmith. The fact that both of them had the name F. Hillsmith gives rise to some confusion.

From 1930 to 1934, Fannie Hillsmith studied at the Boston Museum School, which had been co-founded by her grandfather, and then at the Art Students League, New York, from 1934 to 1935. She returned to New York with her mother in 1939, this time settling in the city. After 1944 she was a member of the American Abstract Artists group. In the summer of 1945 she was invited to teach at Black Mountain College, North Carolina. From 1946 to 1950 she worked closely with European painters who had emigrated to New York in Atelier 17, a printmaking workshop that had been founded by Stanley William Hayter. In 1958 she travelled to Europe on an alumnus grant from the Boston Museum School, staying a year. She married the Cambridge mathematician Gordon Welchman but the marriage ended in divorce in 1970.

Hillsmith was influenced by Paul Klee, at first painting stripped-down abstracts based on fractures of cubist space, which attracted the attention of the critics, including Clement Greenberg. After making dolls and jewellery during the war, during the 1960s she created circular, compartmented constructions and sculptures, and in the 1970s boxes containing surrealistic assemblages such as miniature porcelain furniture or multiple mirrors designed to fragment the image seen by the viewer. She also made numerous miniature ceramic and bronze chairs, as well as embroideries.

Fannie Hillsmith took part in various group exhibitions, including *Art of the Century*, New York and 1944, *Spring Salon for Young Artists*, Guggenheim Museum, New York; in 1944, *Abstract and Surrealist Art in America*, a travelling exhibition organised by the Sidney Janis Gallery, New York; 1944, 1947, *American Abstract Artists* and in 1990, *America Gone Modern: From the Twenties to the Sixties*, Spanierman Gallery, New York. Her first solo exhibition was at the Norlyst Gallery, New York and others followed in 1945 at the Riverside Museum, New York; 1949, Charles Egan Gallery, New York; 1996, Black Mountain College Art Institute, Black Mountain College and in 2000, *Overview: The Art of Fannie Hillsmith and Walter Kamys*, Thorne-Sagendorph Art Gallery, Keene, New Hampshire.

BIBLIOGRAPHY:

Janis, Sidney, *Abstract and Surrealist Art in America*, group exhibition catalogue, Reynal & Hitchcock, New York, 1944. De Kooning, Elaine, '*Fannie Hillsmith*' in *Art News* vol. 48, periodical, New York, April 1949. Campbell, Laurence, '*Fannie Hillsmith*' in *Art News* vol. 53 n° 1, periodical, New York, March 1954. Campbell, Laurence, '*Fannie Hillsmith*' in *Art News* vol. 56 n° 2, periodical, New York, April 1957. Hillsmith, Fannie, *The Ups and Downs of Needlepoint*, A.S. Barnes and Co., Cranbury, 1976. Birmingham, Doris A., *Fannie Hillsmith*, Currier Gall. of Art, Manchester, 1987. Mecklenburg, Virginia M., *The Patricia and Phillip Frost Collection: American Abstraction, 1930-1945*, National Museuml of American Art, Smithsonian Institution Press, Washington DC, 1989. '*Fanny Hillsmith*' in *Black Mountain College Dossiers* n° 2, periodical, Black Mountain College Museum and Arts Center, Black Mountain, 1996.

MUSEUMS AND GALLERIES:

NEW YORK (Metropolitan Mus. of Art) - NEW YORK (MoMA).

AUCTION RECORDS:

NEW YORK, 14 Feb 1990, *Blue Lagoon* (1949, oil on canvas, 30 x 16 1/4 ins / 76 x 41 cm) USD 4,400. NEW YORK, 30 Sept 1997, *Desk* (1946, oil on canvas, 35 x 24 ins / 88.9 x 61 cm) USD 3,450.

HILLSMITH, Frank. See **SMITH Frank Hill**

HILLYARD, J. W.
British, 19th century.
Active in London, from 1833 to 1861.
Painter. Figures, genre scenes, animals.

AUCTION RECORDS:

AMSTERDAM, 19 Oct 1993, *Sleeping Coachman* (oil on canvas, 20 1/4 x 24 1/4 ins / 51.5 x 61.5 cm) NLG 19,550.

HILMAN
French, 18th century.
Engraver.

Hilman engraved most notably after J.-B. Leprince.

HILMAR, Jiri
Czechoslovak, 20th century.
Born 28 May 1937, in Hradec Králové.
Sculptor.
Neo-Constructivism, Op Art.

Jiri Hilmar studied in Prague from 1952 to 1956. He creates not so much sculptures as reliefs, sometimes in paper, whose optical effects and plastic structure can be placed in the tradition of Neo-Constructivism.

He held his first exhibition in Prague in 1967 when he was associated with the Art Concret movement. He exhibited in Munich (1969) and Frankfurt am Main (1969 and 1972).

HILPERICUS
9th century.
Active in Prüm c. 850.
Painter.

Hilpericus painted a picture of the martyrs *St Peter and St Marcellinus*.

HILPERT, Maximilien
Swiss, 20th century.
Born 28 May 1928, in Zurich.

Painter.

Maximilien Hilpert studied at the Naples academy. He arrived in France in 1950, and since then has exhibited in Lucerne, Zurich, Berlin and Paris, where he took part in the Salon des Surindépendants.

HILSCHER

German, 19th century.

Active during the first half of the 19th century.

Draughtsman, engraver.

HILSING, Werner

German (?), 20th century.

Painter. Figure compositions.

Werner Hilsing's works have rarely been seen. His compositions are crammed with figures, strange or monstrous creatures illustrating all kinds of anecdotes, and occupy an ambiguous position somewhere between the naive and the fantastic.

HILSOE, Hans

Danish, 19th - 20th century.

Painter. Interiors with figures.

AUCTION RECORDS:

COPENHAGEN, 20 Oct 1985, *Girl in an Interior* (1924, oil on canvas, 31 1/2 x 24 ins / 80 x 61 cm) DKK 25,000. LONDON, 7 June 1989, *Interior* (oil on canvas, 24 3/4 x 20 3/4 ins / 63 x 53 cm) GBP 3,740. LONDON, 29 March 1990, *Interior* (oil on canvas, 23 x 19 ins / 58.4 x 48.3 cm) GBP 8,250. LONDON, 17 May 1991, *Interior* (oil on canvas, 20 3/4 x 16 1/2 ins / 53 x 42 cm) GBP 3,850. LONDON, 22 May 1992, *Interior* (oil on canvas, 19 3/4 x 23 1/2 ins / 50 x 60 cm) GBP 2,750. LONDON, 17 Nov 1994, *Sunlit Interior* (oil on canvas, 18 1/2 x 22 1/4 ins / 47.3 x 56.5 cm) GBP 4,830. LONDON, 17 Nov 1995, *The Green Dining Room* (oil on canvas, 22 1/2 x 26 1/2 ins / 57 x 67.2 cm) GBP 2,300. COPENHAGEN, 1 Dec 1999, *Interior* (oil on canvas, 22 x 26 ins / 57 x 67 cm) DKK 16,000. COPENHAGEN, 29 Feb 2000, *Interior with Paintings on Walls in a Luxurious Home* (oil on canvas, 22 x 26 ins / 55 x 65 cm) DKK 19,000. LONDON, 5 April 2001, *Interior* (oil on canvas, 22 x 22 ins / 57 x 57 cm) GBP 3,200. VEJLE, 25 Sept 2001, *Interior Scene with Woman Sewing in Sunlit Sitting Room* (oil on canvas, 22 x 26 ins / 57 x 67 cm) DKK 15,500. LONDON, 21 March 2002, *Interior with a Lady Sewing* (oil on canvas, 22 x 26 ins / 55 x 65 cm) GBP 1,800. COPENHAGEN, 5 March 2003, *Interior Scene with Peep into Dining Room* (oil on canvas, 20 x 24 ins / 50 x 60 cm) DKK 15,000. COPENHAGEN, 2 March 2004, *Interior with View of the Green Sitting Room from the Pink One* (oil on canvas, 21 x 23 ins / 53 x 58 cm) DKK 12,000. LONDON, 25 March 2004, *Music Room* (oil on canvas, 22 x 17 ins / 57 x 44 cm) GBP 1,900.

HILST, J. C.

Dutch, 18th century.

Painter. Flowers, fruit.

He was an imitator of De Heem.

HILSUM, François

French, 20th century.

Born January 1929, in Paris.

Painter.

François Hilsum's mother, Marcelle Granjux, was a painter and a pupil of André Lhote. His father, René Hilsum, an important member of the Dada movement published *Sans Pareil* (*Unrivalled*) where appeared the first works by Breton, Aragon, Éluard, Soupault and Yourcenar. After studying at the École Nationale des Arts Décoratifs in Paris, François Hilsum divided his time between art, publishing, journalism and public life. He devoted himself to painting, his primary vocation, only from the 1980s.

Hilsum's painting has evolved from Figurative to Abstraction, transforming the initial motif into a series of rhythmic, coloured variations, that are rendered by the artist's ample, regular and decorative gesture. In the long-lived tradition of 'Ut pictura poesis' ('As is painting, so is poetry') and following Baudelaire or Breton, François Hilsum feels the need to establish a correspondence between his compositions and poetry involving in his quest Paul Élouard, Pierre Jean Jouve or René Char, whose metaphors translate the painted work better than any analytical discourse. Beyond the artificial opposition between Abstraction and Figuration, according to Hilsum painting, like poetry, is only meaningful when it is a metaphor for reality. He lives and works in Aubervilliers and in Guernes.

François Hilsum waited for quite a significant period before exhibiting his works. Collective exhibitions include: Salon de Mai (1996, 1997); Salon des Réalités Nouvelles (1996); *French Contemporary Art Fair*, Hong Kong (2001). Solo exhibitions include: a major event, Galerie Henri Bénézit, Paris (1995); double exhibition with René Hilsum, Galerie 1900-2000, Paris (1999); Centre Pablo Neruda, Bagnolet (1998); Orangerie du Sénat, Paris (2001).

BIBLIOGRAPHY:

Moulin, Raoul-Jean, *François Hilsum*, exhibition catalogue, Gal. Henri Bénézit, Paris, 1995. *François Hilsum*, exhibition catalogue, Centre Pablo-Neruda, Bagnolet, 1998. *René et François Hilsum*, exhibition catalogue, Gal. 1900-2000, Paris, 1999.

HILTEN, Hendrik van

Dutch, 18th century.

Active in Haarlem c. 1773.

Engraver.

He mostly engraved portraits.

HILTENSPERGER, Johann Georg

German, 19th century.

Born 21 February 1806, in Haldenwang; died 13 June 1890, in Munich.

Painter. Historical subjects.

Hiltensperger was a student at the Munich academy of art under Langer in 1822, and in Düsseldorf under Cornelius whom he followed to Munich in 1825. He executed the frescoes in the arcades in Munich's Hofgarten.

King Ludwig of Bavaria having taken him into his service, Hiltensperger left for Italy with the prince and was present at the excavations in Naples and Pompeii. He used his stay in Italy to study the Old Masters. On his return to Germany, he executed the decoration of the court theatre and various other monuments in Munich from the drawings of Schnorr and Schwanthaler. He was appointed professor at the academy of art in Munich.

HILTHROP, Jan van

Dutch, 18th century.

Active in Utrecht c. mid-18th century.

Engraver.

He worked mostly for booksellers.

AUCTION RECORDS:

PARIS, Oct 1945-July 1946, *The Church of the Hamlet* (1763, pen and wash) FRF 2,500.

HILTMANN, Jochen

German, 20th century.

Born 1935, in Hamburg.

Sculptor.

Jochen Hiltmann studied agronomy, but attended painting classes at the academies in Hamburg and Düsseldorf. In 1956, he won one of the prizes for the Villa Romana, which enabled him to spend time in Rome. He opted for sculpture in 1958, and has been entirely self-taught. He works with iron, casting his works in steel and bronze and leaving the marks of the casting and solidifying processes visible. His works retain the look and coarse substance of the products of intense heat, like volcanic lava or the clinker from a blast furnace. He works particularly with geometrical shapes, leaving them sometimes with a smooth surface and sometimes deeply scored.

He has featured in group and themed exhibitions, including *Zero aus Deutschland: 1957-1966. Und Heute* (*Zero out of Germany: 1957-1966. And Today*) at the Esslingen city gallery in 2000. His first exhibition took place in Düsseldorf in 1961, but since 1963 he has shown his work mainly in Frankfurt am Main and at the Cologne art fair.

BIBLIOGRAPHY:

Wiehager, Renate, *Zero aus Deutschland: 1957-1966. Und heute*, group exhibition catalogue, Gal. der Stadt, Esslingen, 2000.

AUCTION RECORDS:

COLOGNE, 17 May 1980, *Abstraction* (1958-1959, oil on canvas, 31 1/2 x 45 ins / 80 x 114.5 cm) DEM 2,000.

HILTON, Arthur Cyril

British, 20th century.

Painter.

Arthur Cyril Hilton was a member of the Manchester Group.

HILTON, Roger

British, 20th century.

Born 1911, in Northwood (Middlesex); died 1975, in St Just (Cornwall).

Painter (including gouache).

Roger Hilton studied at the Slade School of Art, London, from 1929 to 1931, and from 1932 to 1939 at the Académie Ranson, in Paris, where his teacher was the painter and sculptor Roger Bissière. After World War II, Hilton taught at various schools in London, including the Central School of Arts and Crafts from 1954 to 1956. He then settled in St Just in Cornwall, and associated with painters of the St Ives School. After meeting the Dutch artist Constant A. Nieuwenhuys, Hilton travelled to Paris and many times to Amsterdam, where he saw Mondrian's paintings.

Hilton's work developed through several, sometimes overlapping phases. He was initially influenced by Bissière's manner of combining different shapes, and the effects that Bissière achieved. His work comprises mainly abstract but smoothly executed paintings, metaphorical allusions to people, landscapes and still lifes. Through all phases of his output, his draughtsmanship has a certain conscious primitivism, which brings his style close to Art Brut. After seeing Mondrian's work, Hilton simplified his compositions and restricted his palette to three colours: black, red and ochre. The paintings dating from this period consist of cleanly defined shapes on impulsively drawn backgrounds, which may reflect his newly kindled interest in Abstract Expressionism. Hilton's simple, clean shapes, and the female silhouettes that he used in some paintings after 1961, bring to mind the paper cut-outs that Matisse made towards the end of his life. In his very last gouaches, Hilton used a broader palette to create subtle effects.

He had his first solo exhibition in London in 1952, and in the same year his work featured in the exhibition of British contemporary painting in Paris. He also exhibited in Zurich, at Documenta II at Kassel in 1957, and at the 1964 Venice Biennale, where he won the UNESCO Prize. Towards the end of his life he was bedridden because of acute neuritis, but he continued to paint, producing gouaches that he called *Night Letters*.

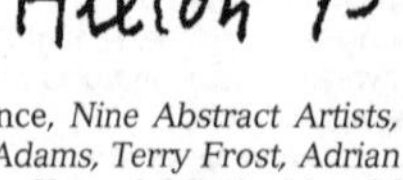

BIBLIOGRAPHY:

Alloway, Lawrence, *Nine Abstract Artists, their Work and Theory: Robert Adams, Terry Frost, Adrian Heath, Anthony Hill, Roger Hilton, Kenneth Martin, Mary Martin, Victor Pasmore, William Scott*, Tiranti, London, 1954. Roger Hilton (ed.)/Calger-Smith, Martin, *Roger Hilton*, catalogue, South Bank Centre, London, 1993. Lewis, Adrian, *Roger Hilton*, Aldershot, c. 2003.

MUSEUMS AND GALLERIES:

AMSTERDAM (Stedelijk Mus.) - LISBON (Centro de Arte Moderna José de Azeredo Perdigão, Fundação Calouste Gulbenkian): *Deserted Beach* (1960) - LONDON (Tate Collection): *Untitled* (1953, oil on canvas); *February 1954* (1954, oil on canvas); *January 1957* (1957, oil on canvas); *Grey Day by the Sea, February 1960* (1960, oil on canvas); *September 1961* (1961, oil on canvas); *Oi Yoi Yoi* (1963, oil and charcoal/canvas); *Foliage with Orange Caterpillar* (1974, gouache and charcoal); lithographs, other works.

AUCTION RECORDS:

LONDON, 18 July 1973, *April 1956*, GBP 550. LONDON, 21 Sept 1983, *Nude* (gouache, black chalk and pencil, 17 x 12 ins / 43 x 30.5 cm) GBP 520. LONDON, 27 Jan 1986, *Two Animals in a Landscape with Blue Lily* (1974, gouache and black chalk, 19 x 15 1/4 ins / 48 x 39 cm) GBP 950. LONDON, 25 Feb 1988, *Once Upon a Time* (1959, 30 x 40 ins / 76 x 101.5 cm) GBP 4,400. LONDON, 9 June 1989, *February 1957* (oil on canvas, 11 x 30 ins / 28 x 76.3 cm) GBP 4,950. LONDON, 10 Nov 1989, *December 1963* (oil on canvas, 60 x 50 ins / 152.6 x 127 cm) GBP 15,950. LONDON, 9 March 1990, *January 1965* (oil on canvas, 16 x 20 ins / 40.7 x 50.8 cm) GBP 10,120. LONDON, 24 May 1990, *Composition* (1967, oil on canvas, 36 x 36 ins / 91.5 x 91.5 cm) GBP 26,400. LONDON, 20 Sept 1990, *Abstract Composition* (1973, watercolour and gouache, 9 1/2 x 14 ins / 24 x 35.5 cm) GBP 2,200. LONDON, 18 Oct 1990, *Untitled* (1957, oil on paper/card, 27 x 19 3/4 ins / 68.5 x 50 cm) GBP 4,180. LONDON, 9 Nov 1990, *Untitled* (1970, oil on canvas, 55 x 60 1/4 ins / 140 x 153 cm) GBP 27,500. LONDON, 8 March 1991, *January 1969* (oil on canvas, 29 3/4 x 29 3/4 ins / 75.5 x 75.5 cm) GBP 12,100. LONDON, 18 Dec 1991, *Untitled* (colouring pencil, 7 1/2 x 7 3/4 ins / 19 x 20 cm) GBP 495. LONDON, 25 Nov 1993, *Black, White, Green and Ochre* (1961, oil on canvas, 20 x 15 3/4 ins / 50.8 x 40 cm) GBP 3,680. LONDON, 26 Oct 1994, *March 1961* (oil on canvas, 50 x 40 ins / 127 x 101.6 cm) GBP 14,950. LONDON, 25 Oct 1995, *Family Outing* (1974, lead pencil and gouache, 13 1/4 x 17 3/4 ins / 33.7 x 45 cm) GBP 2,645. LONDON, 30 May 1997, *Untitled* (1967, oil on canvas, 24 x 20 ins / 61 x 50.8 cm) GBP 5,980. LONDON, 2 Nov 1999, *févr-55* (1955, oil on canvas, 36 x 30 ins / 91 x 76 cm) GBP 7,000. LONDON, 2 Nov 1999, *sept-60* (1960, oil on canvas, 30 x 36 ins / 76 x 91 cm) GBP 8,000. LONDON, 5 April 2000, *Untitled* (1968, oil on canvas, 36 x 30 ins / 91 x 75 cm) GBP 13,000. LONDON, 6 June 2000, *Composition in Red, Blue, Orange and Black* (1953, oil on canvas, 24 x 20 ins / 60 x 51 cm) GBP 7,200. LONDON, 4 July 2001, *Composition 1963* (oil on canvas, 50 x 46 ins / 128 x 116 cm) GBP 24,000. LONDON, 5 Dec 2001, *Sickle Moon* (1960, oil on canvas, 25 x 30 ins / 63 x 76 cm) GBP 28,000. LONDON, 12 March 2002, *June - Sept '53* (oil on canvas, 13 x 18 ins / 33 x 46 cm) GBP 21,000. LONDON, 7 June 2002, *Untitled* (c. 1958, oil on canvas, 20 x 24 ins / 51 x 61 cm) GBP 9,000. LONDON, 6 June 2003, *Reclining Female Figure* (1973, crayon and gouache, 15 x 21 ins / 38 x 54 cm) GBP 6,000. LONDON, 3 Dec 2003, *Crouching Form* (charcoal and gouache, 19 x 22 ins / 47 x 57 cm) GBP 5,500. LONDON, 14 Oct 2004, *Untitled* (c. 1950, oil on canvas, 20 x 30 ins / 51 x 76 cm) GBP 10,000. LONDON, 17 Nov 2004, *Untitled* (1970, oil on canvas, 26 x 36 ins / 66 x 91 cm) GBP 10,000.

HILTON, Rose Julia

British, 20th century.

Born 15 August 1931, in Kent.

Painter. Figures, interiors, still-lifes, landscapes.

St Ives Group, Newlyn Society of Artists.

Rose Hilton studied at Beckenham Art School from 1948 to 1953, at the Royal College of Art from 1953 to 1957 and at the British School in Rome from 1958 to 1959 on an Abbey Minor Scholarship. She married the painter Roger Hilton in

1959 and put aside her painting to raise their children and take care of her ill husband at their home in Botallack, Cornwall. After Roger's death in 1975 she resumed painting, taking drawing lessons from Cecil Collins in the mid-1980s. Her paintings of informal figurative subjects are noted for the bright and vibrant colours which are the dominant force in her work, such as the oils *Blue Still-life, Stella in the Studio* and *Interior, St Ives*.

She has participated in group exhibitions including: Michael Parkin Gallery (1988); Oxford Gallery (1989); *Works on Paper*, Rainyday Gallery, Penzance (1995); *Godrevy*, St Elwyns Church, Hayle (2000); and *From the Heart: Newlyn Society of Artists Winter Exhibition*, Newlyn Art Gallery (2002). Solo exhibitions include: Newlyn Art Gallery (1977, 1987); David Messum Gallery in London (1991); frequently at Huddersfield North Light Gallery; with the Penwith Society; and in the Royal Academy Summer Show in London.

Bibliography:

Brown, David, *Rose Hilton 1991: an Exhibition of Recent Paintings*, Exhibition catalogue, David Messum Gallery, London, 1991.

Museums and Galleries:

Plymouth (County Museum) - Truro (County Museum).

Auction records:

London, 27 Jan 1999, *Still-life in Greys, Pots on the Table* (1980, oil on canvas, 48 x 48 ins / 122 x 122 cm) GBP 1,400. London, 14 July 1999, *Golden Still-life* (oil on canvas, 36 x 48 ins / 91 x 122 cm) GBP 1,200. London, 21 Nov 2000, *Wedding Guest* (oil on canvas, 24 x 20 ins / 60 x 50 cm) GBP 3,600. London, 22 Nov 2000, *St Elvyns, Hayle* (oil on canvas, 24 x 30 ins / 61 x 76 cm) GBP 1,000. Penzance, 16 Oct 2002, *Cat* (watercolour, 5 x 7 ins / 13 x 18 cm) GBP 1,200. Penzance, 16 Oct 2002, *Yellow Pot* (1983, oil on board, Oil Painting) GBP 1,600. Penzance, 27 March 2003, *Vase of Anemones* (oil on canvas, 20 x 20 ins / 51 x 51 cm) GBP 2,500. London, 10 Sept 2003, *Nude in Red Chair* (oil on canvas, 20 x 16 ins / 50 x 40 cm) GBP 1,000. London, 19 May 2004, *St Elvyns, Hayle* (oil on canvas, 24 x 30 ins / 61 x 76 cm) GBP 1,350. Penzance, 3 June 2004, *Wistful Woman, Nude Seated on a Bed* (oil on canvas, 19 x 11 ins / 49 x 29 cm) GBP 2,000.

HILTON, William, the Elder

British, 18th - 19th century.
Born 1752, in Newark; died 7 September 1822, in Lincoln.
Painter. Genre scenes, portraits.

The father of William Hilton the Younger, William Hilton the Elder painted portraits and genre scenes in Lincoln, Norwich and London. He exhibited at the Society of Artists and the Royal Academy between 1777 and 1783.

Auction records:

London, 19 Nov 1985, *Gentleman Standing beside a Seated Young Woman* (watercolour and pencil heightened with white, 10¼ x 9 ins / 26 x 22.8 cm) GBP 1,200.

HILTON, William, the Younger

British, 19th century.
Born 3 June 1786, in Lincoln; died 30 December 1839, in London.
Painter. Mythological subjects, genre scenes.

The son and pupil of William Hilton the Elder, William Hilton the Younger studied under John Raphael Smith and at the Royal Academy, of which he was made an associate in 1813 and a member in 1819. Several of his works were inspired by Milton and Spencer. There are a large number of his paintings in English museums and galleries.

Museums and Galleries:

Leeds: *Ganymede* - Leicester: *Rebecca at the Well* - Liverpool: *Crucifixion* - London: *Christ Crowned with Thorns* - London (National Portrait Gal.): *John Clare* (1820, oil on canvas) - London (Royal Academy of Arts): *The Rape of Ganymede* (c. 1806, oil on canvas) - London (Tate Collection): *Nature Blowing Bubbles for her Children* (exhibited in 1821, oil on canvas); *Rebecca and Abraham's Servant at the Well* (exhibited in 1833, oil on canvas) - London (Wallace Collection): *Venus in search of Cupid surprises Diana* (before 1820, oil on canvas) - Manchester: *Phaeton* - Newark: *Lazarus* - Oldham: *Cupid Disarmed by Venus*.

Auction records:

New York, 14 and 15 Jan 1909, *Flora*, USD 120. New York, 22-24 March 1911, *Lord Althorp*, USD 240. London, Jan 1923, *Cupid Disarmed*, GBP 8. New York, 12 April 1935, *Portrait of a Lady*, USD 600. London, 12 Sept 1941, *Harriet, Daughter of W. Hilton and her Daughter*, GBP 126. New York, 14 Jan 1943, *Bacchante Disarming Cupid*, USD 200. London, 21 July 1978, *Cupid and the Three Graces* (oil on canvas, 69 x 90¼ ins / 175 x 229.2 cm) GBP 1,200. London, 20 Nov 1992, *King Lear and his Three Daughters* (oil on canvas, 61 x 78 ins / 154.9 x 198.2 cm) GBP 7,700. London, 6 April 1993, *Comus and Lady Alice on the Enchanted Throne* (oil on canvas, 62 x 92½ ins / 157.5 x 235 cm) GBP 23,000. London, 12 April 1995, *King Lear and his Three Daughters* (oil on canvas, 61 x 78 ins / 155 x 198 cm) GBP 18,400.

HILTUNEN, Eila

Finnish, 20th century.
Born 1922, in Sortavala.
Sculptor (including stone/bronze/steel), medallist.
Figures, animals. Monuments, busts.

Eila Hiltunen studied at the Helsinki school of art. She travelled in Scandinavia, then a grant from the Ford-Leader Foundation enabled her to spend some time in the USA. After that, she received a grant from the French government, and also visited Austria. She has shown collections of her works in solo exhibitions, many of them in Helsinki, notably one in 1960 featuring her new style, and also in Copenhagen in 1953 and Paris in 1959.

In her early realist period she used marble, granite and cast bronze for war memorials, busts of officials and medals, including those for the Finnish president Juho Paasikivi, and the writer Frans Emil Sillanpää, who won the Nobel Prize for Literature. In 1960, she went over to welded steel for the works of her second period, in which she gave her imagination free rein, producing fabulous beasts bristling with aggressive spines.

Bibliography:

Elgar, Frank, *Dictionnaire de la sculpture moderne*, Hazan, Paris, 1960.

Museums and Galleries:

Helsinki (Suomen Kansallismus.) - Lahti (Lahden Kaupunginmuseo).

HILVERDING, Friedrich Fedor

Russian, 18th century.
Active in St Petersburg.
Painter, engraver, decorative designer.

Friedrich Fedor Hilverding worked primarily for Empress Catherine the Great.

HILVERDINK, Edouard Alexander

Dutch, 19th century.
Born 12 May 1846, in Amsterdam; died 12 October 1891, in Amsterdam.
Painter. Landscapes, urban landscapes.

He was the son and pupil of Johannes Hilverdink.

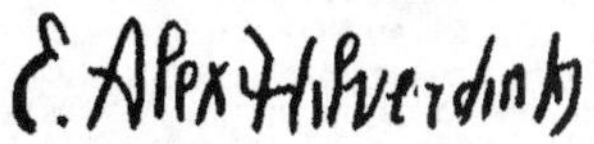

Museums and Galleries:

Amsterdam: *Singel Canal in Amsterdam; Rembrandt's House*.

Auction records:
London, 6 March 1974, *View of a City* (1869) GBP 900. Amsterdam, 25 Jan 1977, *View of Amsterdam* (1885, oil on canvas, 18 x 26 1/2 ins / 45.5 x 67 cm) NLG 8,000. Amsterdam, 30 Oct 1979, *Street Scene* (oil on panel, 14 x 11 ins / 35.5 x 27.7 cm) NLG 5,600. New York, 22 Jan 1982, *View of a City in Holland* (1887, oil on canvas, 18 x 30 1/4 ins / 46 x 77 cm) USD 2,600. Washington DC, 22 Sept 1985, *View of a City by a Canal in Holland* (1868, oil on panel, 9 1/2 x 14 ins / 24 x 35.8 cm) USD 3,600. Calais, 3 July 1988, *The Church Square* (oil on panel, 9 3/4 x 7 3/4 ins / 25 x 20 cm) FRF 18,000. Amsterdam, 24 April 1991, *The House of Suffering in Enkhuisen* (oil on panel, 10 1/2 x 9 ins / 26.5 x 22 cm) NLG 4,830. Amsterdam, 22 April 1992, *Winter: Amsterdam with Moored Boats and Figures Near a Frozen Canal and a Fallen Bridge; Summer: Amsterdam with Men Guiding the Transport of Wood on a Canal by Pole* (1869, oil on panel, a pair, 9 x 12 1/2 ins / 23 x 31.5 cm) NLG 17,250. New York, 29 Oct 1992, *Village Street in Winter* (1866, oil on canvas, 20 x 17 ins / 50.8 x 43.2 cm) USD 1,320. Amsterdam, 3 Nov 1992, *Dutch City in Winter* (oil on panel, 7 3/4 x 11 3/4 ins / 20 x 30 cm) NLG 8,280. Amsterdam, 20 April 1993, *View of the Groenburgwal in Amsterdam* (1891, oil on panel, 15 3/4 x 19 3/4 ins / 40 x 50 cm) NLG 11,500. Amsterdam, 7 Nov 1995, *View of the Grimburgwal in Amsterdam* (1877, watercolour, 28 1/4 x 24 ins / 72 x 61 cm) NLG 4,720. Amsterdam, 5 Nov 1996, *City Scene* (1881, oil on canvas, 15 3/4 x 11 ins / 40 x 28 cm) NLG 5,900. Amsterdam, 1 Sept 1999, *Watergraafsmeer, Amsterdam* (1874, oil on canvas, 24 x 37 ins / 61 x 95 cm) NLG 9,000. Amsterdam, 26 Oct 1999, *View of the Shipyard at Lijnbaansgracht, Amsterdam* (oil on canvas, 14 x 20 ins / 35 x 50 cm) NLG 18,000. London, 14 June 2000, *View of the Amstel River, Amsterdam* (1873, oil on canvas, 21 x 33 ins / 54 x 83 cm) GBP 6,800. New York, 7 Nov 2000, *Dutch Canal Scene with Figures beside a Drawbridge* (oil on canvas) USD 7,500. Amsterdam, 20 March 2001, *View of Amsterdam, with Schreierstoren on the Prins Hendrikkade* (1883, pencil, pen, black ink and watercolour heightened with white, 13 x 20 ins / 32 x 50 cm) NLG 5,000. Gravenhage, 25 April 2001, *View of Amsterdam* (oil on canvas, 18 x 30 ins / 45 x 76 cm) NLG 14,000. Toestorf, 17 Aug 2002, *Winter Scene with City Gate and Figures* (oil on panel, 10 x 8 ins / 25 x 21 cm) EUR 2,000. Amsterdam, 15 April 2003, *Snowy View of the Smedestraat* (1889, oil on canvas, 26 x 22 ins / 67 x 56 cm) EUR 14,000. Gravenhage, 7 May 2003, *Figures by the Gate of an Old Guesthouse in Achterburgwal in Amsterdam* (oil on panel, 13 x 10 ins / 34 x 25 cm) EUR 2,600. Amsterdam, 20 April 2004, *Canal in a Dutch Town* (oil on canvas, 26 x 22 ins / 65 x 56 cm) EUR 8,500. Bethesda, 7 May 2004, *Canal Scene in a Dutch City* (1868, oil on panel, 13 x 17 ins / 33 x 43 cm) USD 8,500.

HILVERDINK, Johann Jakob Anton

Dutch, 19th century.
Born 22 May 1837, in Amsterdam; died 21 October 1884, in Amsterdam.
Painter. Urban landscapes, seascapes.

He was a pupil of his father, Johannes Hilverdink. He exhibited in Holland and Germany.

Auction records:
New York, 28 April 1977, *Village by the Edge of a River* (oil on panel, 15 3/4 x 22 ins / 40 x 55 cm) USD 1,400. New York, 27 Oct 1982, *Fishing Boats in a Port* (oil on canvas, 16 x 24 3/4 ins / 40.6 x 62.9 cm) USD 1,800. Amsterdam, 30 Oct 1991, *View of the Amsterdam Nieumarkt with the Office of Weights and Numerous Figures at a Fish Market* (oil on canvas, 13 3/4 x 19 3/4 ins / 35 x 50 cm) NLG 12,650. Amsterdam, 19 Jan 1999, *Sailing Boats on the Amstel in Amsterdam with Stadhouderskade beyond* (oil on canvas, 16 x 22 ins / 40 x 57 cm) NLG 6,500. New Orleans, 22 May 1999, *Mountainous Landscape with Castle Ruins and Figures* (1870, oil on canvas, 16 x 28 ins / 41 x 71 cm) USD 5,750. Amsterdam, 4 Sept 2001, *View of the Binnen Amstel, Amsterdam* (oil on canvas, 16 x 22 ins / 40 x 56 cm) EUR 3,200.

HILVERDINK, Johannes

Dutch, 19th century.
Born 28 January 1813, in Groningen; died 1 October 1902, in Amsterdam.
Painter, watercolourist. Landscapes with figures, seascapes.

He was a pupil of Alexander Joseph Dawaille and Jan-Willem Pieneman. He was a member of the academy of Amsterdam.

Museums and Galleries:
Amsterdam (Rijksmus.): *Seascape* - Amsterdam (Stedelijk Mus.): *Outer Port of IJmniden.*

Auction records:
London, 19 May 1971, *Mediterranean Shore,* GBP 320. London, 23 July 1976, *Ferryboat* (1849, oil on canvas, 22 x 29 1/4 ins / 56 x 74 cm) GBP 1,800. Vienna, 12 Dec 1978, *Coast of Brittany, End of Summer* (1872, oil on canvas, 31 1/2 x 51 1/4 ins / 80 x 130 cm) ATS 90,000. Amsterdam, 22 April 1980, *View of Lake Annecy* (1876, oil on canvas remounted, 17 1/2 x 27 1/2 ins / 44.5 x 70 cm) NLG 4,600. Amsterdam, 15 March 1983, *Seascape* (oil on panel, 11 1/2 x 19 1/4 ins / 29 x 49.2 cm) NLG 6,200. Lokeren, 20 April 1985, *Scene by the Sea* (1844, oil on panel, 18 x 22 1/2 ins / 46 x 57 cm) BEF 160,000. Amsterdam, 5 June 1990, *Fishermen at Work on the Coast of Scheveningen* (1850, oil on panel, 10 3/4 x 15 1/4 ins / 27.5 x 38.5 cm) NLG 18,400. Amsterdam, 30 Oct 1990, *Mediterranean Hillside Landscape with Gypsies Camping on the Cliff* (1878, oil on canvas, 39 3/4 x 59 1/2 ins / 101 x 151 cm) NLG 16,100. Amsterdam, 6 Nov 1990, *Figures on a Road Lining a Valley River* (1865, oil on panel, 14 1/2 x 19 3/4 ins / 37 x 50 cm) NLG 4,600. Amsterdam, 17 Sept 1991, *Ruin in Brederode* (1890, watercolour/paper, 5 1/4 x 8 3/4 ins / 13.5 x 22.5 cm) NLG 1,035. Amsterdam, 3 Nov 1992, *Fisherman at a Cove in a River* (1889, oil on panel, 9 x 12 1/2 ins / 23 x 32 cm) NLG 2,300. Amsterdam, 19 Oct 1993, *Fishermen in a Longboat on a Lake with a Flight of Ducks by the Bank* (1881, 20 1/2 x 32 3/4 ins / 52 x 83.5 cm) NLG 12,650. Tel Aviv, 11 April 1996, *View of Jerusalem* (1855, oil on canvas, 31 1/2 x 52 ins / 80 x 132 cm) USD 52,900. Amsterdam, 5 Nov 1996, *Figures in a Longboat Near a Mill in Holland* (oil on panel, 9 1/2 x 12 1/4 ins / 24 x 31 cm) NLG 8,850. Amsterdam, 21 Jan 1998, *Mountain Landscape with a Traveller on a Sandy Road* (1831, oil on canvas, 14 3/4 x 18 ins / 37.5 x 46 cm) NLG 2,883. Amsterdam, 7 July 1999, *Winter Landscape with Skaters on a Frozen River by a Town Gate* (1843, oil on canvas, 24 x 31 ins / 62 x 78 cm) NLG 42,000. Amsterdam, 26 Oct 1999, *Seventeenth Century Naval Battle* (1864, oil on canvas, oval, 43 x 71 ins / 110 x 180 cm) NLG 28,000. Rotterdam, 2 Nov 1999, *Shipwreck by Rocky Coast* (1894, oil on canvas, 18 x 30 ins / 45 x 75 cm) NLG 7,400. Amsterdam, 18 April 2000, *Travellers on a Mountain Pass* (1863, oil on canvas, 17 x 24 ins / 44 x 62 cm) NLG 10,000. Amsterdam, 5 Sept 2000, *Norwegian Coast. Sea Landscape* (1872, oil on panel, a pair, 7 x 6 ins / 19 x 15 cm) NLG 7,000. Bremen, 29 June 2001, *River Landscape with Fishing Huts* (oil on canvas/panel, 19 x 30 ins / 47 x 77 cm) DEM 6,000. Lucerne, 24 May 2003, *Dutch Winter Landscape* (oil on canvas, 24 x 34 ins / 60 x 86 cm) CHF 11,000. Amsterdam, 3 Feb 2004, *Fisher Family Standing by a River on a Sunny Day* (1858, oil on canvas, 15 x 21 ins / 37 x 54 cm) EUR 10,000. Ahlden, 8 May 2004, *Winter Landscape with Figures* (oil on canvas, 20 x 24 ins / 50 x 60 cm) EUR 3,000.

HIMBLOT, Adrien

French, 17th century.
Active in Paris in 1608.
Sculptor.

HIMBLOT, Didier

French, 17th century.

Active in Paris at the beginning of the 17th century.
Sculptor.
Didier Himblot may have been Adrien Himblot's brother.

HIME, Harry
British, 19th century.
Active in Liverpool at the end of the 19th century.
Painter. Landscapes.
Harry Hime exhibited in London at the Royal Academy from 1885 to 1887.

HIMELY, Henri
Swiss, 19th century.
Active c. 1830.
Painter. Flowers, fruit.
Henri Himely was a brother of Sigismond Himely.

HIMELY, Sigismond
Swiss, 19th century.
Born 7 June 1801, in Neuveville; died 1872, in Paris.
Active in France where he was later naturalised.
Painter, watercolourist, engraver. Historical scenes, landscapes, urban landscapes.
Sigismond Himely was initially a pupil of Fielding in Switzerland, then went to Paris, where he studied in the studio of Victor Bertin. He exhibited at the Paris Salon from 1824 to 1869 and became a naturalised Frenchman.

Himely executed mainly watercolour landscapes and aquatint prints after various artists including Fielding, Callow, Perot, Garneray, Turner, Charlet, Decamps, Roqueplan and H. Bellangé.

MUSEUMS AND GALLERIES:
VERSAILLES: *Siege of Toulon, 19 November 1794 at 6 O'clock in the Morning; Siege of Toulon, 30 November in the Morning.*

AUCTION RECORDS:
PARIS, 14 Feb 1978, *Returning to the Village* (watercolour, 8 1/4 x 6 ins / 21 x 15 cm) FRF 400. PARIS, 15 Dec 1997, *View of Venice, The Dogana* (heightened colour aquatint) FRF 3,500.

HIMMELFARB, John
American, 20th - 21st century.
Born 1946.
Painter, draughtsman, engraver.
John Himmelfarb is an architecture graduate from Harvard University. He is an exponent of Abstract Expressionism whose development of line has been described as 'dramatic'. His often calligraphic drawings and paintings spring from jazz rhythms or an allusive imagery. Himmelfarb is best known for the gigantism of his 'works in progress' executed in full view of the public, much in the way of a performance. He has benefited from grants from the National Education Association and the Pollock-Krasner Foundation. He has shown his works in solo exhibitions mostly in the Midwest but also at the University of Connecticut, Fairfield, and at the Centre for Contemporary Art, Christchurch, New Zealand.

BIBLIOGRAPHY:
Meetings in the garden: the art of John Himmelfarb, exhibition catalogue, The Institute, Kalamazoo (MI), 1989.

MUSEUMS AND GALLERIES:
BALTIMORE (MA) - BOSTON (Public Library, Fine Arts Department) - CHICAGO (AI) - CLEVELAND (MA) - LONDON (British Mus.) - PARIS (MNAM-CCI) - WASHINGTON DC (Smithsonian American AM).

HIMMELHEBER, Julius Philipp Wilhelm Max
German, 19th century.
Born 12 November 1812, in Karlsruhe.
Engraver, lithographer.
Himmelheber was a pupil of Scheill and Haldenwang.

HIMMELSBACH, Paula Balano
German, 20th century.
Born 10 May 1878, in Leipzig.
Active in the USA.
Painter.
Paula Himmelsbach moved to Philadelphia early in her life, and began her training there. After winning a travel scholarship, she studied with Mucha in Paris in 1900-1901.

HIMMELSTOSS, Christian
German, 16th century.
Painter.
Christian Himmelstoss worked in the castle of Oldenburg at the end of the 16th century, and painted battle scenes.

HIMMELSTOSS, Karl
German, 20th century.
Born 12 July 1878, in Breslau (now Wroclaw, Poland).
Sculptor, decorative artist.
Karl Himmelstoss studied in Berlin, then in Munich, and worked for porcelain factories.

HIMMES, Henriette
French, 19th century.
Born in the 19th century, in Paris.
Painter, pastellist.
Himmes was a pupil of Maria Loustau. She exhibited at the Salon in 1865 and 1866.

HINARD, Émile
French, 19th century.
Born in Paris.
Painter (porcelain), draughtsman.
Hinard was a pupil of Collot, and made his Salon début in 1878.

HINCHCLIFF, John James
British, 19th century.
Born 1805; died 1875, in Walton-by-Clevedon.
Engraver.
The son of the sculptor John Elley Hinchliff, John James Hinchliff specialised in engravings of landscapes. The best known are those that appeared in the collections entitled *Gentlemen's Residences; Castles and Abbeys of England* and *Picturesque Views of Wales*.

HINCHIS. See **HINKIS**

HINCHLEY, Edith M.
Maiden name: Mason
British, 20th century.
Born 1870.
Miniaturist.
Edith Hinchley was a member of the Royal Society of Miniature Painters and an associate member of the Royal Cambrian Academy.

HINCHLIFF, John
British, 18th century.
Active in London.
Sculptor.
John Hinchliff exhibited in London at the Society of Artists in 1768 and 1772.

HINCHLIFF, John Elley
British, 19th century.
Born 1777; died 1867.
Active in London.
Sculptor.
John Elley Hinchliff frequently exhibited in London between 1814 and 1849 at the Royal Academy and the British Institution.

HINCHLIFF, Woodbine K.
British, 19th - 20th century.
Painter. Genre scenes, landscapes.
Woodbine Hinchliff lived in South Kensington, London. He was a member of the Ridley Art Club and in 1909 he exhibited at the Royal Society of New South Wales, Australia.

HINCHMAN, John Herbert
American, 20th century.
Born 4 April 1884, in Michigan; died 1948, in Laguna Beach (California).
Painter.
John Herbert Hinchman studied under André Lhote at his private academy in Paris, where he was a member of the Société des Artistes Américains de Paris.

HINCKELDEY, Ernst Paul
German, 20th century.
Born 12 April 1893, in Arnstadt.
Sculptor. Genre scenes. Busts.
Ernst Hinckeldey studied in Berlin and exhibited regularly there.

HINCKLEY, Robert
American, 19th century.
Born 3 April 1853, in Boston; died 1941, in Rehoboth Beach (Delaware).
Painter. Portraits.
Robert Hinckley was a pupil of Carolus Duran in Paris.

HINCKLEY, Thomas Hewer
American, 19th century.
Born 1813, in Milton (Pennsylvania); died 1896.
Painter. Animals, landscapes.
Thomas Hewer Hinckley produced a lot of work in Philadelphia, and then settled in Boston.
AUCTION RECORDS:
NEW YORK, 1 June 1944, *Mount Monadnock*, USD 285. NEW YORK, 2 Jan 1945, *Pasture Scene*, USD 150. NEW YORK, 13 Sept 1972, *Hunting Dog*, USD 1,600. NEW YORK, 28 Oct 1976, *Horses in a Landscape* (1844, oil on canvas, 20½ x 24 ins / 52 x 61 cm) USD 2,500. NEW YORK, 21 June 1979, *Livestock at Pasture* (1856, oil on canvas, 36 x 52½ ins / 91.4 x 133.3 cm) USD 4,000. NEW YORK, 3 Dec 1982, *Stags, Beaver River, Maine* (1884, oil on canvas, 36 x 29 ins / 91.2 x 72.8 cm) USD 4,800. NEW YORK, 5 June 1986, *Greyhound in a Landscape* (1854, oil on canvas, 33½ x 44 ins / 85 x 111.9 cm) USD 5,000. NEW YORK, 4 June 1993, *Portrait of a Terrier* (1870, oil on canvas, 25 x 30 ins / 63.5 x 76.2 cm) USD 2,760. NEW YORK, 3 June 1994, *Spaniel Scenting a Track* (1843, oil on canvas/synthetic resin, 39 x 49 ins / 99.1 x 124.5 cm) USD 8,050. NEW YORK, 11 April 1997, *Red and White Setter with her Pups* (1849, oil on canvas, 41 x 46 ins / 104.1 x 116.8 cm) USD 19,550. BOSTON, 12 March 1999, *Cattle and Sheep in Pasture* (1860, oil on canvas, 25 x 36 ins / 63 x 91 cm) USD 7,500. NEW YORK, 1 Dec 1999, *American Grouse* (1858, oil on canvas, 29 x 36 ins / 74 x 91 cm) USD 14,000. PORTSMOUTH, 3 Nov 2001, *Cows in a Landscape with Farmhouse in the Distance* (1855, oil on canvas, 26 x 36 ins / 66 x 91 cm) USD 8,000. CHICAGO, 17 Feb 2002, *Red Fox* (1870, oil on canvas, 30 x 40 ins / 76 x 102 cm) USD 19,000. BOSTON, 22 Nov 2002, *In the Pasture* (1837, oil on canvas, 40 x 54 ins / 102 x 137 cm) USD 9,000. EAST DENNIS, 31 July 2003, *Portrait of a Young Boy from Milton, Massachusetts* (oil on canvas, 12 x 10 ins / 30 x 25 cm) USD 13,000. BOSTON, 10 Sept 2004, *Cows at Pasture* (oil on canvas, 36 x 48 ins / 91 x 122 cm) USD 21,000.

HINCKS, William
Irish, 18th century.
Born in Waterford.
Active at the end of the 18th century.
Painter, engraver.
William Hincks exhibited in London between 1781 and 1797, showing miniatures, portraits and history paintings.

HINCZ, Gyula
Hungarian, 20th century.
Born 1904, in Budapest.
Painter, sculptor, illustrator. Murals, designs for tapestries.
A student at the school of fine art in Budapest, Gyula Hincz went to Paris in 1926 and to Berlin in 1928. In 1930-1931, he stayed in Rome as a member of the Hungarian college. A professor at the school of decorative arts in Budapest (1946) and at the school of fine art (1949), he was also the director of the school of decorative arts (1958 to 1963). His work, initially inclining towards the non-figurative, became increasingly expressionist in character.
He took part in collective exhibitions, notably with the Der Sturm group in Berlin in 1928. He also held solo exhibitions in Berlin (1928) and Hungary (1946). He was awarded the Kossuth and Munkácsy prizes and was given the title of 'artist emeritus'.

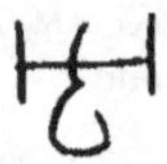

BIBLIOGRAPHY:
Hongrie 1968, Pannonia, Budapest, 1968. Csorba, Géza, *L'Art hongrois contemporain*, Musée Galliera, Paris, 1970.

HIND, Frank
British, 19th century.
Active in Leamington.
Painter.
Frank Hind frequently exhibited in London from 1885 at the Royal Academy and the Suffolk Street Gallery. He specialised in Spanish subjects.
AUCTION RECORDS:
LONDON, 5 Sept 1996, *Mosque in Tetouan, Morocco* (oil on canvas, 23 x 17¾ ins / 58.4 x 45 cm) GBP 1,380.

HIND, Her
British, 17th century.
Active in England c. 1675.
Engraver (burin).

HIND, J.
British, 17th century.
Active in England.
Engraver (burin).
J. Hind engraved mainly portraits.

HIND, Robert Neal
British, 19th century.
Born 1817; died 1879.
Draughtsman, watercolourist.
Robert Hind worked in London.
MUSEUMS AND GALLERIES:
LONDON (British Mus.): a work.

HINDE, Thomas
British, 17th century.
Active in England c. 1645 or 1675.
Engraver.
Thomas Hinde engraved portraits of *Charles II*, *Robert Rich, Earl of Warwick* and *Prince Rupert*.

HINDEMANN, Franz Joseph
Swiss, 19th century.
Born 1827, in Lucerne.
Lithographer.
Hindemann, a pupil of Eglin, worked mainly in Lucerne. He executed a map of Switzerland.

HINDEN VAN, Peter. See **VANHINDEN**

HINDENLANG, Charles
Swiss, 20th century.
Born 1 October 1894, in Basel; died 1960, in Basel.
Painter. Figure compositions, figures, portraits.
Gruppe 33.
Charles Hindenlang studied at the school of applied arts in Basel. He also trained in Paris and Italy. He painted a num-

ber of murals in Basel. His paintings show signs of Cubist influence.

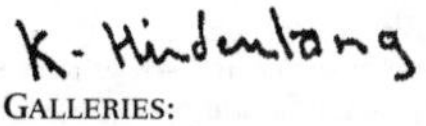

MUSEUMS AND GALLERIES:
BASEL: *Small Boys in the Forest*; numerous other works.
AUCTION RECORDS:
ZURICH, 12 Nov 1976, *The City of Basel* (1919, oil on canvas, 34 1/4 x 23 1/2 ins / 87 x 60 cm) CHF 2,400. ZURICH, 26 Jan 1983, *Village Scene* (1926, oil on canvas, 25 1/2 x 29 1/2 ins / 65 x 75 cm) CHF 7,000. LUCERNE, 15 May 2002, *Sketch for a Glass Window* (gouache and watercolour, 28 x 33 ins / 72 x 85 cm) CHF 3,000.

HINDER, Frank
Australian, 20th century.
Born 1906, in Sydney.
Painter, lithographer. Scenes with figures.

Frank Hinder began his art studies in Australia but then decided to go the USA, and continued his artistic training in Chicago, New York and New Mexico. He remained in the USA from 1927 - when he also travelled to Europe - until 1934. In New York he met the sculptor Margel Harris, who later became his wife. When he returned to Australia, Hinder introduced some modernity into the conservative art world of the mid-1930s. He also began teaching at the National Art School in Sydney, where he exerted a strong influence.

Unlike his peers who found their inspiration in the work of the French painter and teacher André Lhote, Hinder was never interested in Cubist-style still-life painting. His subject matter - people at work or crowds in the city streets - clearly has a more contemporary relevance. His paintings also reflect the futuristic ideals of the early 20th century and the Section d'Or without, however, endorsing any of their ideological excesses. Hinder owed his creative philosophy to the teaching of Emil Bisttram and his 'dynamic symmetry', according to which formal relationships and movement are essential within a composition. The restrained classicism of Cubism can be seen in Hinder's futuristic compositions, in which he put into practice the divisionist concept of matter, light and colour. His technique is sophisticated and precise, and his methods painstakingly polished. His compositions are highly fragmented - the elements within them being broken up into prismatic facets - and his broad palette produces deliberately sharp contrasts. In his time, Hinder was one of the very few Australian painters to take up the challenge of abstract painting.

BIBLIOGRAPHY:
Free, Renée, '*The crew escaped amid flames*' in *Creating Australia: 200 Years of Art 1788-1988*, exhibition catalogue, Art Gall. Board of South Australia, Adelaide, 1988.
MUSEUMS AND GALLERIES:
ADELAIDE (AG of South Australia): *Subway Escalator* (1953) - CANBERRA (Australian War Memorial): *Bomb Explosion* (1943-1949).
AUCTION RECORDS:
SYDNEY, 16 Oct 1989, *Jerry* (ink, 6 x 9 3/4 ins / 15 x 25 cm) AUD 700. SYDNEY, 17 Aug 1999, *Red Construction* (1967, tempera on canvas, 24 x 19 ins / 62 x 48 cm) AUD 4,500. MELBOURNE, 23 Nov 1999, *Untitled* (1954, oil on glass on board, 17 x 11 ins / 44 x 28 cm) AUD 4,000. MELBOURNE, 15 Aug 2000, *Figure Study* (1936, pencil and watercolour, 13 x 8 ins / 32 x 20 cm) AUD 3,000. SYDNEY, 21 Nov 2000, *Brown Construction* (1954, oil on masonite, 36 x 28 ins / 92 x 71 cm) AUD 9,800. VICTORIA, 1 May 2001, *Seated Female Nudes* (conte crayon, 27 x 20 ins / 68 x 51 cm) AUD 8,000. PADDINGTON, 25 Aug 2002, *Over the Bridge* (1957, oil on board, 37 x 29 ins / 95 x 74 cm) AUD 48,000. SYDNEY, 3 Dec 2002, *Dark Image* (electric motors, coloured lights and perspex, 18 x 15x7 ins / 46 x 37x18 cm) AUD 8,400. MELBOURNE, 4 May 2004, *City Building* (1957, oil on board, 6 x 7 ins / 14 x 19 cm) AUD 2,600. PADDINGTON, 24 Aug 2004, *Counterpoint* (1968, pastel, 22 x 31 ins / 55 x 78 cm) AUD 4,000.

HINDER, Margel Ina
Maiden name: Harris
American, 20th century.
Born 1906, in Brooklyn; died 1995.
Active in Australia.
Sculptor.

Margel Hinder studied sculpture in Buffalo and Boston and then, after settling in Australia, in Sydney. In their form and artisanal technique her sculptures show the influence of Australian Aboriginal art. In 1961 she took part in the *International Sculpture Exhibition* at the Musée Rodin, Paris.
AUCTION RECORDS:
SYDNEY, 16 Oct 1989, *Totem* (copper on plaster, 14 1/4 x 11 3/4 x 4 ins / 36 x 30 x 10 cm) AUD 1,900. SYDNEY, 26 March 1990, *Totem* (copper sheet/plaster, 13 3/4 x 13 1/2 x 4 ins / 35 x 34 x 10 cm) AUD 1,100. SYDNEY, 2 July 1990, *Abstraction* (beaten copper on plaster, 19 1/4 x 9 1/2 x 5 ins / 49 x 24 x 13 cm) AUD 4,800.

HINDERICKX, Jean Martin
Flemish School, 18th century.
Born 26 May 1744, in Ypres; died 10 August 1777, in Ypres.
Sculptor.

He was a pupil of Hendrik Pulincx. He worked mostly in Ypres and Bruges.

HINDERLING, Herman
Swiss, 19th century.
Born 1853, in Maur (Zurich).
Painter. Genre scenes.

Hinderling, a pupil of Gérôme, was awarded a bronze medal at the Paris Exposition Universelle of 1900.

HINDLE, W.
British, 19th century.
Watercolourist. Landscapes.
MUSEUMS AND GALLERIES:
BLACKBURN: two watercolours.

HINDLEY, Godfrey C.
British, 19th century.
Active in London.
Painter. Genre scenes, flowers.

Godfrey Hindley was a member of the Royal Institute of Oil Painters. He exhibited in London at the Royal Academy and the Suffolk Street Gallery from 1876.
MUSEUMS AND GALLERIES:
SUNDERLAND: *A Series of Accidents*.

HINDORF, Alfred
German, 19th century.
Born 12 May 1824, in Laiden (St Gall); died 10 September 1892.
Painter. Architectural views.

Hindorf was put in charge of the works in Hohenzollern Castle in 1863. On leaving the army in 1877, he settled in Charlottenburg.
MUSEUMS AND GALLERIES:
COLOGNE: *The Faulhorn* - WROCLAW: *Entrance of William I into Breslau* (1866).

HINDSBO, Sys
Danish, 20th century.
Born 12 March 1944, in Frederiksberg.
Painter, draughtswoman, engraver. Figure compositions.

From 1962 to 1965, Hindsbo attended the sculpture school of the Kongelige Danske Kunstakademi in Copenhagen, and later the Graphics School from 1965 to 1969. Since 1984 she has been a member of the academic council. Hindsbo produced a design for the conference centre in Herning in 1986 and for a secondary school in 1994. She exhibited her works for the first time in 1966, at the Charlottenborg Spring Exhibition. In 1994, she exhibited at the Maison du Danemark in Paris. She has won many prizes, and in 2003 appeared on a Danish postage stamp. Hindsbo tackles socio-political themes in her figurative works, such as the concept of power and its control, or scenes portraying certain actions in the process of being completed: *Man Trying to Grab* (1988); *Man Running* (1991); *Object under his Nose* (1991 - 1993); *Man Holding a Bird* (1993).

BIBLIOGRAPHY:

Tojner, Paul Erik (preface), *Sys Hindsbo*, exhibition catalogue, Maison du Danemark, Paris, 1994.

MUSEUMS AND GALLERIES:

COPENHAGEN (Prints Collection) - MALMÖ (Konstmus.) - OSLO (Nasjonalgal.).

HINE, Aleksandr Vasilevich. See **GUINET**

HINE, Harry T.

British, 19th century.

Born 27 February 1845, in London; died 1941.

Painter, watercolourist.

Harry Hine was a member of the Royal Institute of Painters in Watercolours, exhibiting there and at the Old Dudley Art Society, the Royal Academy and the Suffolk Street Gallery from 1873.

MUSEUMS AND GALLERIES:

LIVERPOOL: *Early Arrival of Autumn* - NORWICH (Castle Mus. and AG): *A Surrey Mill* (watercolour) - SYDNEY: *St Albans Cathedral*.

AUCTION RECORDS:

LONDON, 7 Dec 1907, *Green Village* (watercolour) GBP 4. LONDON, 26 June 1908, *Over Brayford Head* (watercolour) GBP 84.

HINE, Henry or Harry George

British, 19th century.

Born 15 August 1811, near Brighton; died 16 March 1895, in Hampstead.

Painter, watercolourist, engraver, draughtsman.

Landscapes.

Henry Hine was taught engraving by H. Meyer but taught himself painting. Returning to Brighton after a period in Rouen, he devoted himself entirely to painting seascapes. Most of his works depict the Sussex coast. He was a member of the Royal Institute. He often exhibited in London at the Royal Academy and the Suffolk Street Gallery between 1830 and 1851. He exhibited at the Society of British Artists from 1856. Three years later he sent his *Smugglers Waiting for a Lugger* for exhibition at the Royal Academy.

BIBLIOGRAPHY:

Hine, Henry George, *Henry George Hine 1811-1895: The South Downs in Watercolour*, exhibition catalogue, Towner Art Gallery, Eastbourne, 2003.

MUSEUMS AND GALLERIES:

BRIGHTON: *Sunset* - BRIGHTON (Mus. & AG): *Arundel* (watercolour) - CARDIFF: *Walking in the Meadow* - LONDON (Victoria and Albert Mus.): six watercolours - SYDNEY: watercolour; *East Cliff Hastings Sussex*.

AUCTION RECORDS:

LONDON, 1 Feb 1908, *Landscape* (1870, watercolour) GBP 13. LONDON, 15 Feb 1908, *Folking, Sussex* (1870, watercolour) GBP 42. LONDON, 7 March 1908, *Folkington Hills, Sussex* (1874, watercolour) GBP 283. LONDON, 26 June 1908, *Chanctonbury Hills* (watercolour) GBP 47. LONDON, 11 June 1909, *Corfe Castle* (watercolour) GBP 183. LONDON, 28 Nov 1910, *Amberley Castle* (watercolour) GBP 43. LONDON, 13 March 1925, *On the Hills near Lewes* (watercolour) GBP 173. LONDON, 2 March 1926, *Autumn Evening* (watercolour) GBP 49; *Old Chalk Pit* (watercolour) GBP 168; *Landscape near Midhurst* (watercolour) GBP 48; *Near Harting, Sussex* (watercolour) GBP 29. LONDON, 8 Feb 1928, *Hills near Lewes* (watercolour) GBP 35. LONDON, 19 April 1929, *Chalk Pit near Eastbourne* (watercolour) GBP 48. LONDON, 19 June 1929, *South Dune between Willington and Eastbourne* (watercolour) GBP 34. NEW YORK, 7 Jan 1981, *Sussex Landscape at Dusk* (1883, watercolour, 11 x 21 3/4 ins / 28.2 x 55.2 cm) USD 800. LONDON, 28 April 1983, *Holywell, Sussex* (1878, watercolour/pencil outlines, 14 3/4 x 25 1/2 ins / 37.5 x 65 cm) GBP 340. LONDON, 22 May 1986, *Amberley, Sussex* (1867, watercolour/pencil outlines heightened with gouache, 10 1/2 x 22 1/2 ins / 26.5 x 57 cm) GBP 1,600. LONDON, 28 April 1987, *Swanage Bay, Dorset* (1864, watercolour and pencil heightened with white, 8 x 21 1/2 ins / 20.3 x 54.5 cm) GBP 1,500. LONDON, 31 Jan 1990, *Corbridge Market Square, Northumberland* (1854, watercolour and gouache, 9 1/4 x 13 1/4 ins / 23.5 x 33.5 cm) GBP 1,760. LONDON, 26 Sept 1990, *Old Eastbourne* (1885, watercolour, 11 1/2 x 17 1/4 ins / 29 x 44 cm) GBP 935. LONDON, 5 March 1993, *Hexham Market Square* (pencil and watercolour, 13 3/4 x 10 ins / 34.9 x 25.4 cm) GBP 920. LONDON, 20 July 1994, *The Thames at Gravesend* (1867, watercolour, 13 1/2 x 23 1/2 ins / 34.5 x 60 cm) GBP 1,035. SCARBOROUGH, 22 April 1999, *Playing in the Pool* (1859, watercolour, 10 x 17 ins / 25 x 43 cm) GBP 2,350. HASLEMERE, 23 Feb 2000, *Haymaking near a Village at Sunset* (1860, 11 x 20 ins / 28 x 51 cm) GBP 1,100. LONDON, 5 Nov 2001, *Rabbits on the Sussex Downs* (1878, watercolour over pencil heightened with stopping out, 15 x 30 ins / 37 x 75 cm) GBP 1,050. LONDON, 3 June 2004, *Downs near Eastbourne* (1869, pencil and watercolour with scratching out, 14 x 24 ins / 35 x 61 cm) GBP 4,000. LONDON, 3 June 2004, *Chain Pier, Brighton during the Hurricane, 24 November 1824* (watercolour with scratching out, 9 x 27 ins / 23 x 69 cm) GBP 5,500.

HINE, William Egerton

British, 19th century.

Died 1926.

Active in London.

Painter. Landscapes, seascapes.

William Hine frequently exhibited from 1873, particularly at the Royal Academy.

HINES, Felrath

American, 20th century.

Born 9 November 1913, in Indianapolis; died 3 October 1993, in Silver Spring (Maryland).

Painter, draughtsman.

Spiral Group.

Felrath Hines graduated from the Art Institute, Chicago in 1946, the Pratt Institute, Brooklyn in 1948, and New York University in 1955. In 1963, he joined the Spiral Group, which sought to define an African-American aesthetic. In 1969 he joined the Black Emergency Cultural Coalition (BECC) protest against the photographic exhibition held in the Metropolitan Museum of Art, New York in 1968-1969, *Harlem on my Mind*, which did not include black artists and leaders. From 1972 to 1980 he was Chief Conservator at the National Portrait Gallery, Washington DC and from 1980 to 1984 Chief Conservator at the Hirshhorn Museum and Sculpture Garden, Washington DC.

Hines painted abstracts made up of simple forms and diffuse colours whose vibration set off a sort of suspended motion. He developed this illusionistic practice by adopting the principles of De Stijl, as in *Rite of Spring* (1987), where the surface of the picture is divided by lines crossing the planes of colour, which lose their intensity to the benefit of rhythm and tension.

Hines took part in various group exhibitions, including in 1976, *Two Centuries of Black American Art*, Los Angeles County Museum of Art, Los Angeles and in 1999, *To Con-*

serve a Legacy. American Art from Historically Black Colleges and Universities,* Studio Museum in Harlem, New York. He also had a number of solo exhibitions, including in 1951, Creative Gallery, New York and regularly from 1977 at the Franz Bader Gallery, Washington DC. Posthumous retrospectives of his work were held in 1995, at the Indianapolis Museum of Art and in 2002, at the June Kelly Gallery, New York.

BIBLIOGRAPHY:
Coleman, Floyd/Day, Holliday T., *Felrath Hines*, exhibition catalogue, Indianapolis Museum of Art, Indianapolis, 1995.
Passantino, Erika, *Felrath Hines. Encore: paintings: 1958-1991*, exhibition catalogue, June Kelly Gall., New York, 2002.

MUSEUMS AND GALLERIES:
CHAPEL HILL, NC (Ackland Art Mus., University of North Carolina): *Rite of Spring* (1987, oil on canvas) - WASHINGTON DC (GA, Howard University): *Façade II* (1988, oil on canvas).

HINES, Frederick
British, 19th - 20th century.
Painter, watercolourist. Figures, animals, landscapes.

Frederick Hines frequently exhibited at the Suffolk Street Gallery and at the Royal Academy, London, from 1875.

AUCTION RECORDS:
LONDON, 20 March 1911, *White Ladies* (1879) GBP 1. LONDON, 10 April 1973, *Hunting Scene* (1882) GBP 300. LONDON, 24 Sept 1987, *Dusk* (1899, watercolour and gouache, 20 1/2 x 29 1/2 ins / 52 x 75 cm) GBP 1,250. LONDON, 25-26 April 1990, *The Lost Lamb* (watercolour and gouache, 15 x 11 ins / 38 x 27 cm) GBP 550.

HINES, Theodore
British, 19th century.
Active in London.
Painter. Landscapes.

Theodore Hines frequently exhibited in London between 1876 and 1889 at the Royal Academy and the Suffolk Street Gallery.

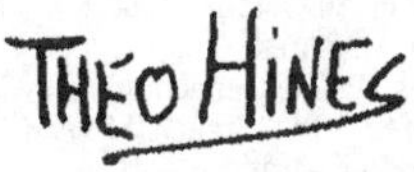

AUCTION RECORDS:
LONDON, 8 June 1976, *View of Eton* (oil on canvas, 19 3/4 x 29 1/2 ins / 50 x 75 cm) GBP 320. LONDON, 1 April 1980, *On the Slaney, Carlour, Ireland* (oil on canvas, 29 1/2 x 48 ins / 75 x 122 cm) GBP 1,300. LONDON, 2 Oct 1985, *Landscape near the Banks of the Thames* (oil on canvas, a pair, 20 x 30 ins / 51 x 76 cm) GBP 3,200. LONDON, 13 Dec 1989, *Whitchurch-on-Thames; The Thames near Streatley* (oil on canvas, a pair, each 10 x 14 ins / 25.5 x 35.5 cm) GBP 3,520. LONDON, 13 June 1990, *The Thames near Shiplake* (oil on canvas, 20 x 30 ins / 51 x 76 cm) GBP 2,200. ROME, 19 Nov 1992, *River Landscape with Fishermen* (1882, oil on canvas, 30 1/4 x 20 ins / 77 x 51 cm) ITL 4,025,000. LONDON, 12 May 1993, *Near Maple Durham on Thames; Clivedon on Thames* (oil on canvas, a pair, 18 x 32 ins / 46 x 81 cm) GBP 2,875. PERTH, 29 Aug 1995, *Through the Trossachs* (1896, oil on canvas, 18 x 14 ins / 46 x 35.5 cm) GBP 805. LONDON, 12 March 1997, *Henley Regatta* (1897, oil on canvas, 25 1/4 x 50 1/4 ins / 64 x 127.5 cm) GBP 6,900. BURY ST EDMUNDS, 24 March 1999, *Thames near Marlow* (1881, oil on canvas, 30 x 50 ins / 76 x 127 cm) GBP 2,900. LONDON, 29 Nov 1999, *In Glen, Arran* (oil on canvas, 30 x 20 ins / 76 x 51 cm) GBP 1,000. LONDON, 8 June 2000, *Eton College from the Thames* (oil on canvas, 20 x 30 ins / 51 x 76 cm) GBP 6,500. BOSTON, 10 Nov 2000, *View of a Park with Distant Buildings* (1888, oil on canvas, 20 x 30 ins / 51 x 76 cm) USD 2,800. LONDON, 8 March 2001, *Distant Loch, Loch Katrine* (1901, oil on canvas, 30 x 20 ins / 76 x 51 cm) GBP 1,500. NEW YORK, 23 April 2001, *Peasant Woman by Birch Trees* (oil on canvas, 30 x 50 ins / 76 x 127 cm) USD 2,400. LONDON, 1 May 2002, *Burnham Beeches* (oil on canvas, 30 x 50 ins / 76 x 128 cm) GBP 2,700. LONDON, 17 July 2002, *Geese in the Farmyard* (oil on canvas, 24 x 36 ins / 61 x 91 cm) GBP 2,000. LONDON, 6 March 2003, *Ellen's Isle, Loch Katrine* (oil on canvas, 16 x 12 ins / 41 x 30 cm) GBP 1,200. LEWES, 9 March 2004, *On the Lockay, Killin, Scotland* (oil on canvas, 20 x 30 ins / 51 x 76 cm) GBP 3,800.

HINESTROSA, Juan de
Spanish, 17th - 18th century.
Born 1670; died 1765, in Seville.
Sculptor.

Juan de Hinestrosa was self taught and most of his carvings were of animals. He also executed a number of religious works.

HING T'ONG. See **XING TONG**

HING TS'EN-TSING. See **XING CIJING**

HINGELBERG, M. C.
18th century.
Active in 1794.
Miniaturist.

One work, signed and dated, by M.C. Hingelberg is recorded.

HINGRE, Théophile, or Theo
French, 19th - 20th century.
Born 19th century, in Écouen; died 1911.
Painter, sculptor (including bronze), medallist. Figures, genre scenes, animals.

Louis Hingre was a pupil of Gervais and Passot. He made his début at the Salon of 1881 receiving an honourable mention in 1891 and a 3rd class medal in 1902. He received a bronze medal in 1889 and a gold medal in 1900 at the Paris Expositions Universelles. He was a member of the Société des Artistes Français from 1909.

AUCTION RECORDS:
PARIS, 22 March 1976, *The Valet Monkey and the Rat* (oil on canvas, 24 x 19 3/4 ins / 61 x 50 cm) FRF 4,800. NEW YORK, 16 Feb 1994, *Rabbits and Snails* (oil on canvas, 17 1/2 x 23 1/2 ins / 44.5 x 60 cm) USD 7,475. LONDON, 14 June 1995, *The Hunters' Break* (1897, oil on canvas, 11 1/2 x 9 1/4 ins / 29.5 x 23.5 cm) GBP 2,760. PARIS, 20 March 1998, *Heron Holding a Frog in its Beak* (patinated bronze, h. 8 3/4 ins / 22.5 cm) FRF 3,800.

HINIEU, Jean-Paul
French, 20th century.
Born 1942, in Langouria (Côtes-d'Armor).
Painter. Landscapes.

Hinieu studied at the École des Beaux-Arts in Paris for five years. He was influenced by his admiration for Bonnard and in particular Matisse. He takes part in the Salon des Indépendants in Paris and his work is shown in galleries in Paris and Pont-Aven.

HINKEL, Johann Daniel
German, 18th century.
Active in Danzig (now Gdansk, Poland).
Miniaturist.

Hinkel is best known for his miniature portrait of Christ. Loth.

HINKIS, Alexandre, pseudonym of Hinchis
Moldovan, 20th century.
Born 30 May 1913, in Chisinau; died 14 April 1997.
Active in France from 1932.
Painter, decorative artist. Figures, portraits, landscapes, still-lifes. Stage sets.

Alexandre Hinkis first studied at the academy of fine art in Chisinau from 1926 to 1931. From 1933-1934 he was a pupil of Fernand Léger at his private academy in Paris. He then attended the École des Arts Décoratifs, receiving his diploma in 1939. That same year, and then again from 1945 to 1956, he studied architecture at the École des Beaux-Arts. From 1950 to 1962, he worked as an architect and interior designer for the cinema and then, from 1963 to 1978, for television.

His works are characterised by the predominance of green and yellow enlivened by red. They depict, for example, views of roofs in confused perspective. He draws with colour using a kind of shorthand that stands out transparently against a white background that has often been prepared as if for watercolours.

He took part in collective exhibitions from 1934, mainly in Paris at the Salon d'Automne, of which he was a member from 1940, and the Salon des Tuileries. Solo exhibitions include: in his own studio (1995); Galerie Atelier dans la Cour, Paris (1996); Canada; Morocco; Russia; and Hungary. A retrospective, *Alexandre Hinkis. 60 ans d'expositions 1934-1994*, was held at the town hall in Cambrai in 1994.

BIBLIOGRAPHY:

Alexandre Hinkis - 60 ans d'expositions 1934-1994, exhibition catalogue, Hôtel de ville, Cambrai, 1994.

MUSEUMS AND GALLERIES:

CHISINAU - JERUSALEM (Yad Vachem Mus.) - MADAGASCAR (NM) - PARIS (Mus. d'Histoire Contemporaine): *War*.

HINMAN, Charles

American, 20th century.

Born 1932, in Syracuse (New York).

Painter.

Starting from the interplay of geometric forms superimposed on a succession of monochrome planes, Charles Hinman tries to find a solution to problems of suface and space. The orientation of the planes, which are more or less detached from the underlying support, is set in advance by a governing line.

AUCTION RECORDS:

NEW YORK, 27 Feb 1976, *68-4* (acrylic, 65 3/4 x 91 1/4 x 21 1/4 ins / 167 x 231.5 x 54 cm) USD 500. NEW YORK, 14 Dec 1976, *Sunspot in Blue* (1965, acrylic/canvas, 53 x 21 x 5 ins / 134.5 x 53.5 x 12.5 cm) USD 850. NEW YORK, 16 May 1980, *U.F.O.* (1966, acrylic/canvas, 72 x 102 x 10 ins / 183 x 259 x 25.5 cm) USD 9,000. NEW YORK, 13 May 1981, *Clipper* (1964, acrylic/canvas, irregular, 46 x 77 1/2 x 16 ins / 117 x 197 x 40.5 cm) USD 1,800. NEW YORK, 19 Nov 1981, *Untitled* (1966, acrylic/canvas, 24 1/2 x 40 1/4 x 7 ins / 62 x 102.5 x 18 cm) USD 2,000. NEW YORK, 10 Nov 1983, *Tan Butterfly* (1977, acrylic/canvas, irregular, 34 1/2 x 52 ins / 87.6 x 132.1 cm) USD 2,000. NEW YORK, 5 May 1986, *Vertical Waves* (1964, acrylic/canvas, irregular, 93 x 73 x 33 ins / 236.3 x 185.5 x 83.8 cm) USD 9,500. NEW YORK, 6 Oct 1987, *Tumbling* (1968, acrylic/canvas, 30 x 51 ins / 76.2 x 129.5 cm) USD 2,700. NEW YORK, 9 May 1989, *Vertical Waves* (1964, acrylic/shaped canvas, 88 x 33 1/2 x 30 ins / 223.3 x 85.4 x 76.2 cm) USD 5,500. NEW YORK, 5 Oct 1989, *Capillary Action* (1973, acrylic/canvas, 79 x 59 ins / 200.6 x 150 cm) USD 9,900.

HINNA, John Bernhard Jonassen

Norwegian, 19th - 20th century.

Born 11 June 1871, in Hetland, near Stavanger.

Painter. Landscapes.

John Hinna was a pupil of Johan Jacob Bennetter and also trained in Copenhagen. He exhibited at the Exposition Universelle in Paris in 1900, winning a silver medal.

HINNE, Charles Frederik

Danish, 19th century.

Born 14 November 1854, in Copenhagen.

Painter. Landscapes.

Charles Hinne was a pupil at the Kunstakademi in Copenhagen. He settled in Germany, living mostly in Solln near Munich.

HINRAKUSAI. See **SHOKEI**

HINRICHSEN

German, 17th century.

Active in Hamburg.

Painter.

HINRICHSEN, Kurt

Swiss, 20th century.

Born 26 October 1901, in Basel or St Gall, to a German father; died 2 July 1963, in Paris.

Active in France.

Painter, draughtsman, engraver. Figure compositions, figures, nudes, portraits, landscapes.

Kurt Hinrichsen's family settled in Basel in 1906. He settled permanently in Paris in 1924-1925, at the time when he decided to devote himself entirely to painting, while studying with Jules Adler. During a trip to Belgium in 1934, his painting was influenced by studying the works of Rubens in greater depth. In 1937, a bursary from the Basel museum enabled him to travel to Italy and Antwerp. From 1945, he often spent the summer in Sables-d'Olonne, which encouraged him to introduce new subjects into his work. Similarly, in 1946, he visited Savoy and painted landscapes there. He exhibited regularly at the Salon des Indépendants from 1929, and sometimes at the Salon d'Automne. He also exhibited from 1950 onwards at the Salon du Dessin et de la Peinture à l'Eau, and at the Salon Comparaisons in 1955 and 1957. He had about 15 solo exhibitions, mainly in Basel and Paris, including one at the Kunsthalle in Basel in 1946, and also in Le Havre and The Hague. His painting is very personal, characterised by drawing that is nervous, baroque, full of curls, curves and counter-curves, and he uses the pure colours of the Fauves, often slightly acid, placed on the canvas in scattered dots. He has painted many subjects, landscapes of various regions, mainly in France and Italy, portraits, a large number of female nudes and, above all, compositions containing figures in motion.

BIBLIOGRAPHY:

Fierens, Paul/Chappuis, Adrien, *Le Peintre Kurt Hinrichsen*, J. Frion, Paris, 1954. *Atelier Kurt Hinrichsen*, auction catalogue, L'Isle-Adam, 30 October 1988.

MUSEUMS AND GALLERIES:

BASEL (Kunstmus., Prints Collection): drawings and engravings - PARIS (MAMVP) - PARIS (MNAM-CCI): *Nude with Flowers* (1944); other paintings.

AUCTION RECORDS:

PARIS, 18 March 1985, *Woman Bathing* (1928, oil on canvas, 39 1/4 x 43 1/4 ins / 100 x 110 cm) FRF 15,000. PARIS, 11 Dec 1987, *Music-Hall Dancer* (oil on canvas, 9 1/2 x 13 ins / 24 x 33 cm) FRF 2,500. L'ISLE-ADAM, 31 Jan 1988, *Two Seated Women* (oil/hardboard, 31 1/2 x 25 1/2 ins / 80 x 65 cm) FRF 20,100. PARIS, 1 June 1988, *Young Woman Seated* (c. 1944-1945, oil on panel, 24 x 19 3/4 ins / 61 x 50 cm) FRF 7,500; *The Couple* (oil on canvas, 15 1/4 x 18 ins / 39 x 46 cm) FRF 7,500. PARIS, 27 Oct 1988, *The Lion of St Mark* (oil on canvas, 28 3/4 x 23 1/2 ins / 73 x 60 cm) FRF 9,000. L'ISLE-ADAM, 30 Oct 1988, *The Black-Eyed Woman* (oil on canvas, 28 3/4 x 23 1/2 ins / 73 x 60 cm) FRF 40,000; *Seated Women* (oil on panel, 28 3/4 x 36 1/4 ins / 73 x 92 cm) FRF 54,000; *It Is Raining* (oil on canvas, 32 x 39 1/4 ins / 81 x 100 cm) FRF 100,000. PARIS, 14 Dec 1988, *City Smoke* (oil on canvas remounted/panel, 14 1/2 x 18 1/4 ins / 37 x 46.5 cm) FRF 14,500. PARIS, 26 Jan 1990, *The Red Carpet* (oil on canvas, 15 x 18 ins / 38 x 46 cm) FRF 5,200. PARIS, 27 April 1990, *Gossip* (oil/hardboard, 32 x 39 1/4 ins / 81 x 100 cm) FRF 48,000. PARIS, 6 July 1990, *Scuola di San Rocco* (oil/hardboard, 28 3/4 x 23 1/2 ins / 73 x 60 cm) FRF 6,000. PARIS, 19 June 1991, *Venice: San Moise* (oil/hardboard, 25 1/2 x 21 1/4 ins / 65 x 54 cm) FRF 5,000.

HINRICHSEN, Lorenz Vilhelm

Danish, 19th - 20th century.

Born 4 January 1865, in Copenhagen; died 1929.

Painter. Landscapes.

Lorenz Hinrichsen received an honourable mention at the Paris Exposition Universelle in 1900.

MUSEUMS AND GALLERIES:

GÖTEBORG: *Landscape*.

AUCTION RECORDS:

LONDON, 16 Feb 1990, *Roskilde* (1904, oil on canvas, 48 x 72 ins / 122 x 183 cm) GBP 3,850. VEJLE, 19 Jan 2000, *Windswept Trees* (1919, oil on canvas, 40 x 60 ins / 102 x 153 cm) DKK 18,700. STOCKHOLM, 28 May 2002, *West Coast Idyll* (1911, oil on canvas, 15 x 23 ins / 39 x 59 cm) SEK 22,000.

HINSBERGER, Alexis

French, 20th century.

Born 18 September 1907, in Cartagena, Spain, to an Andalusian mother and a French father; died January 1996.

Painter, sculptor. Figure compositions, genre scenes.

Alexis Hinsberger studied at the school of fine arts, and then at the school of arts and crafts in Barcelona. He painted mostly actors and circus figures in a populist vein, in lighting effects that accentuated the Expressionist opposition between light and shade. His sculptures represented genre subjects: *Don Quixote and Sancho, Carmen, Guitarist, Pierrot Violinist*. He lived and worked in Paris. He participated in collective exhibitions in Paris including: Salon d'Automne, Salon Comparaisons, Salon des Artistes Français, Salon des Indépendants and the Salon Populiste. He had solo exhibitions in Paris (1951, 1959, 1961, 1969, 1982); Barcelona (1952); Murcia (1968); Madrid (1971).

AUCTION RECORDS:

HONFLEUR, 11 July 1976, *Dusk in Honfleur* (oil on canvas, 22 x 18 ins / 55 x 46 cm) FRF 2,600. VERSAILLES, 16 Oct 1988, *Blue Harlequin* (1987, oil on canvas, 28 3/4 x 21 1/4 ins / 73 x 54 cm) FRF 7,000. PARIS, 8 April 1990, *Place du Trocadero* (oil on cardboard, 23 1/2 x 28 3/4 ins / 60 x 73 cm) FRF 10,000. NANTES, 18 Nov 1990, *The Theatre* (oil on canvas, 51 1/4 x 38 1/4 ins / 130 x 97 cm) FRF 50,000. LE TOUQUET, 8 Nov 1992, *Dancer with Mask* (1982, oil on canvas, 24 1/2 x 15 ins / 62 x 38 cm) FRF 6,000. PARIS, 1 Feb 1996, *Foire du Trône* (oil on canvas, 28 3/4 x 46 ins / 73 x 116 cm) FRF 5,000.

HINSCH, Heinrich Wilhem

German, 19th century.

Born 28 March 1822, in Hamburg; died 21 June 1846, in Hamburg.

Painter.

Hinsch was primarily a landscape painter.

HINSCHELWOOD, Robert

British, 19th century.

Born 1812, in Edinburgh.

Engraver.

Robert Hinschelwood was the pupil of James Johnstone and W. Allen.

HINSDALE, Richard L.

American (?), 19th century.

Painter. Genre scenes.

AUCTION RECORDS:

NEW YORK, 26 March 1986, *Children's Games* (1855, oil on canvas, 12 1/2 x 12 ins / 32 x 30.5 cm) USD 14,000.

HINTERHOFER, Silvester

Austrian, 16th century.

Active in Innsbruck at the beginning of the 16th century.

Painter.

Silvester Hinterhofer was employed by Maximilian I and Ferdinand I.

HINTERHOLZER, Andreas

Austrian, 20th century.

Born 18 July 1875, in Lazsfons.

Sculptor.

Andreas Hinterholzer studied with Georg Werbas in Munich. In the early part of his life, he was also active in Hamburg, Münster, Nuremberg and Berlin. He later settled in Pradl, near Innsbruck.

HINTERHOLZER, Christian

German, 17th - 18th century.

Painter.

Christian Hinterholzer is known from an engraving of a landscape he painted.

HINTERHOLZER, Franz

German, 19th century.

Born 15 December 1851, in Salzburg.

Painter. Landscapes.

Franz Hinterholzer studied at the academy of art in Munich, where he went on to exhibit. In 2002, Salzburg's Carolino Augusteum Museum devoted an exhibition to him, *Der Landschaftsmaler Franz Hinterholzer (The Landscape Painter, Franz Hinterholzer)*.

HINTERMEISTER, Henry

American, 20th century.

Born 10 June 1897, in New York; died 1972.

Painter, watercolourist, illustrator. Genre scenes.

Henry Hintermeister was a member of the National Arts Club, New York and several watercolourists' associations.

AUCTION RECORDS:

LOS ANGELES, 17 Nov 1980, *Watch it, Grandpa* (oil on canvas, 30 x 22 ins / 76.2 x 56 cm) USD 3,750. LOS ANGELES, 16 March 1981, *Walking on Stilts* (oil on canvas, 26 x 24 ins / 66 x 61 cm) USD 2,200. NEW YORK, 14 Feb 1990, *Six Little Puppies* (oil on canvas, 19 x 28 1/4 ins / 48.5 x 72 cm) USD 8,800. NEW YORK, 17 Dec 1990, *Scout Feeding Girl, with Dog Nearby* (oil on canvas, 30 x 23 ins / 76.3 x 58.4 cm) USD 4,675. NEW YORK, 2 Dec 1992, *Flying a Kite* (oil on canvas, 22 1/4 x 24 1/4 ins / 56.5 x 61.5 cm) USD 2,420. NEW YORK, 11 March 1993, *Dog's Best Friend* (oil on canvas, 26 x 24 1/4 ins / 66.3 x 61.3 cm) USD 3,680. NEW YORK, 12 Sept 1994, *Spaniel Puppies* (oil on canvas, 19 x 28 1/4 ins / 48.3 x 71.8 cm) USD 13,800. NEW YORK, 6 Nov 1999, *Roller-skating Boy Sprawled as Dog Chases Cat* (1940, oil on canvas, 30 x 24 ins / 76 x 61 cm) USD 6,000. NEW YORK, 6 May 2000, *Man Fishing by the Brook* (oil on canvas) USD 5,000. MILFORD, 25 Oct 2001, *On the Hunt* (oil on canvas, 24 x 30 ins / 61 x 76 cm) USD 3,200. NEW YORK, 10 Nov 2001, *Policeman Crossing Guard in Rain* (oil on canvas, 12 x 9 ins / 30 x 22 cm) USD 17,000. NEW YORK, 11 May 2002, *Determined Uncle Sam at Rolltop Desk* (1950, oil on canvas, 30 x 22 ins / 76 x 56 cm) USD 4,750. HAYDEN, 27 July 2002, *Gramps* (oil on canvas, 30 x 22 ins / 76 x 56 cm) USD 6,000. HAYDEN, 26 July 2003, *Pat* (oil on canvas, 24 x 30 ins / 61 x 76 cm) USD 7,500. NEW YORK, 15 Nov 2003, *Mother Bear and Cubs Fishing, One Distracted by Beehive* (oil on canvas, 30 x 24 ins / 76 x 61 cm) USD 4,500. NEW YORK, 15 May 2004, *Boy to the Rescue as a Young Girl Chases Ball into Street* (oil on canvas, 30 x 22 ins / 76 x 56 cm) USD 2,800. NEW YORK, 15 May 2004, *Fisherman reeling in catch* (oil on canvas, 17 x 12 ins / 43 x 30 cm) USD 2,900.

HINTERREITER, Hans

Swiss, 20th century.

Born 1902, in Winterthur; died 1989, in Ibiza (Balearic Islands).

Painter, watercolourist.

Die Allianz Group.

Hans Hinterreiter studied mathematics from 1920 to 1921, then architecture, at the Zurich polytechnic, gaining his degree in architecture in 1925. From 1929 to 1934, he studied landscape painting with Wilhelm Ludwig Lehmann in Seelisberg, while studying the laws of colour according to Wilhelm Ostwald. From 1934 to 1936, he lived in Spain, where he learned about Moorish ornamentation. He returned to Switzerland during the Spanish Civil War, but settled in Ibiza in 1939. During the 1930s, he had written a work entitled *L'Art de la Forme Pure* (*The Art of Pure Form*), which was not published until 1978. In 1942, he joined the association Allianz and often exhibited with them. In the same year, Max Bill organised an exhibition of his works at the Zurich Kunsthaus. Hinterreiter's next exhibition was in Turin in 1947. He took part in the Salon des Réalités Nouvelles in Paris in 1948. In 1954, he took part in a group exhibition in Sweden and in 1960, he had another exhibition at the Zurich Kunsthaus. He later exhibited in Madrid, Ibiza, San Francisco, Berlin, London, Lausanne and other places.

His abstract, geometrical compositions exploit the phenomena of colour, mainly in watercolour until 1973, and are often structured serially, by intervals or rotation.

BIBLIOGRAPHY:

Geometrische Abstraktion 1910-1990, exhibition catalogue, Gal. Eremitage, Berlin, 1991.

AUCTION RECORDS:

NEW YORK, 7 June 1984, *Opus 130* (1961, watercolour, 19 3/4 x 15 ins / 50.3 x 38.2 cm) USD 1,000. NEW YORK, 27 Feb 1985, *Opus 117* (1960, tempera/paper, 12 x 9 1/4 ins / 30.5 x 23.5 cm) USD 1,500. NEW YORK, 14 Feb 1989, *Opus 105 A* (acrylic/canvas, 28 3/4 x 37 3/4 ins / 73.3 x 96.2 cm) USD 6,050. NEW YORK, 9 May 1992, *Study 138* (1933, gouache/paper, 6 1/4 x 8 1/2 ins / 15.9 x 21.6 cm) USD 3,080. LUCERNE, 15 May 1993, *SWF 62* (1973, acrylic/canvas, 35 1/2 x 26 1/2 ins / 90 x 67 cm) CHF 12,000. LUCERNE, 20 Nov 1993, *E.105* (acrylic/canvas, 26 3/4 x 35 3/4 ins / 68 x 91 cm) CHF 11,000. ZURICH, 24 Nov 1993, *Opus 54* (1951, acrylic/synthetic resin, 28 1/4 x 25 1/4 ins / 72 x 64 cm) CHF 6,900. NEW YORK, 7 June 1999, *Opus 59* (1943, tempera on masonite, 33 x 33 ins / 84 x 84 cm) USD 5,250. LUCERNE, 24 Nov 2001, *Opus 45* (1958, tempera on paper, 13 x 16 ins / 32 x 40 cm) CHF 3,200. LUCERNE, 24 Nov 2001, *Op 79* (1972, watercolour, 16 x 13 ins / 41 x 34 cm) CHF 4,400. LUCERNE, 1 June 2002, *Study 14* (tempera on canvas, 4 x 6 ins / 11 x 16 cm) CHF 4,000. ZURICH, 25 Nov 2003, *Untitled* (1949, tempera on canvas, 6 x 7 ins / 14 x 19 cm) CHF 5,000. ZURICH, 25 Nov 2003, *Opus 10* (1951, tempera on pavatex, 33 x 28 ins / 83 x 72 cm) CHF 16,000. ZURICH, 8 June 2004, *Opus 57F* (1943-1981, caparol, 14 x 12 ins / 36 x 30 cm) CHF 5,000. ZURICH, 8 June 2004, *Opus 79* (1958, tempera on pavatex, 32 x 32 ins / 82 x 82 cm) CHF 13,000.

HINTERSCHER, Josef

German, 20th century.
Born 16 March 1878, in Munich.
Sculptor.

Josef Hinterscher spent some time in Italy and then worked in Paris and Berlin.

HINTNER, Johann

Swiss, 19th century.
Born 1834, in Gsies (now San Martino in Casies, Italy); died 15 February 1892, in Bozen, South Tyrol (now Bolzano, Italy).
Painter.

Johann Hintner, a brother of Michael Hintner, was a pupil of Johann von Schrandolph in Munich, before going on to settle in Bozen. He painted mainly portraits and genre scenes.

HINTNER, Michael

German, 19th century.
Born 28 September 1842, in Pichl bei Wels; died 14 December 1900, in Munich.
Sculptor.

Michael Hintner, a brother of Johann Hintner, executed many sculptures of the *Madonna* and of the *Crucifixion*.

HINTON, Charles Louis

American, 19th - 20th century.
Born 18 October 1869, in Ithaca (New York); died 1950.
Painter, illustrator, sculptor. Figures, genre scenes.

Charles Hinton studied under William H. Low at the National Academy of Design, New York and Gérôme and Bouguereau in Paris. He mainly painted subjects linked to childhood.

AUCTION RECORDS:

NEW YORK, 24 April 1981, *Standing Nude* (dark-green-patinated bronze, fountain, h. 27 1/2 ins / 69.8 cm) USD 3,800. NEW YORK, 27 Sept 1990, *Bacchante* (bronze, fountain, h. 35 ins / 89.2 cm) USD 4,950.

HINTON, Erwald Stuart

American, 19th century.
Born 3 January 1866, in New York.
Active in Chicago.
Sculptor.

HINTZ, Julius

German, 19th century.
Born c. 1805, in Hamburg; died 1862, in Paris.
Active in France.
Painter. Seascapes, landscapes.

Hintz, having settled in France, exhibited reasonably regularly at the Paris Salons around the middle of the 19th century, receiving honourable mentions in 1857 and 1859. His paintings were mostly of harbours painted in pastel colours.

MUSEUMS AND GALLERIES:

MONTPELLIER: *View of the Town and Harbour of Sète* - ROANNE: *View of a Seaside Village in Brittany* - ROUEN: *Landscape* - TOURS: *Entrance to Dieppe Harbour*.

AUCTION RECORDS:

LONDON, 27 Sept 1985, *A Naval Review at Le Havre* (oil on panel, 19 1/2 x 33 ins / 49.5 x 84 cm) GBP 9,500. LE HAVRE, 17 Feb 2002, *Sailors on the Landing Stage on the Departure of the Ships* (1851, oil on canvas, 30 x 43 ins / 75 x 109 cm) EUR 6,200. LONDON, 10 Feb 2004, *Port of Dieppe* (oil on board, 15 x 24 ins / 39 x 61 cm) GBP 3,800.

HINTZE, Jedrzej

Polish, 19th century.
Active during the first half of the 19th century in Cracow.
Miniaturist.

Jedrzej Hintze probably worked in all the major cities in Poland and Germany, where his works are still to be found.

HINTZE, Johann Ferdinand Julius

German, 19th century.
Born 3 June 1849, in Wittingen; died 25 June 1877, in Munich.
Painter. Genre scenes.

Johann Ferdinand Hintze exhibited in Berlin around 1872.

AUCTION RECORDS:

LONDON, 14 Nov 1973, *Children Playing in the Snow* (1877) GBP 1,700.

HINTZE, Johann Heinrich

German, 19th century.
Born 1800, in Berlin; died c. 1860.
Painter. Architectural views, urban landscapes, landscapes.

Johann Heinrich Hintze, a pupil of Völcker, travelled in Germany and Austria and exhibited in Berlin from 1826.

MUSEUMS AND GALLERIES:

BERLIN: *Square in Hildesheim* - KALININGRAD: *Foundation of the Canons Regular of the Holy Cross in Prague*.

AUCTION RECORDS:

COPENHAGEN, 12 May 1969, *View of Vienna*, DKK 46,000. LONDON, 12 May 1974, *View of Vienna*, GBP 2,800. MUNICH, 5 June 1986, *View of the Old Berlin Museum* (after 1831, oil on canvas, 12 1/4 x 18 1/2 ins / 31 x 47 cm) DEM 37,000. ZURICH, 18

Oct 1990, *Berlin Panorama* (c. 1832, oil on canvas, 28 1/4 x 44 ins / 72 x 112 cm) CHF 40,000.

HINZE, Adolf
German, 19th century.
Active in Blankenburg.
Painter.
Hinze exhibited landscapes and paintings of historical subjects in Berlin and Dresden.

HINZENBERG, Karl Yakovlevich
Russian, 19th century.
Born 17 October 1814.
Painter.
Karl Yakovlevich Hinsenberg worked at the academy of art in St Petersburg.

HIOLIN, E. N.
Painter. Genre scenes.
E.N. Hiolin is listed in *Art Prices Current.*
AUCTION RECORDS:
LONDON, 21 Jan 1911, *Bathers,* GBP 2.

HIOLIN, Louis Auguste
French, 19th - 20th century.
Born 18 March 1846, in Septmonts; died May 1910, in Silly-la-Poterie.
Sculptor. Statues, groups.
Louis Hiolin was a pupil of Perray and Jouffroy and is known for the sculptural decoration in the chapel in Rue Jean-Goujon in Paris, which he carried out almost in its entirety. A member of the Société des Artistes Français in 1885, he had first exhibited at the Salon in 1874. He was awarded a number of medals at the Paris Expositions Universelles: 3rd class (1879), a 2nd class (1885), bronze (1889) and a silver (1900).
AUCTION RECORDS:
NEW YORK, 14 Dec 1982, *Wolf!* (patinated bronze, h. 33 ins / 84 cm) USD 2,800. LONDON, 20 March 1984, *Wolf!* (bronze, h. 31 ins / 79 cm) GBP 1,400. LONDON, 12 June 1986, *Wolf!* (c. 1888, brown-patinated bronze, h. 31 ins / 79 cm) GBP 5,000. NEW YORK, 25 May 1988, *Wolf! (group: a hunter a wolf)* (bronze, h. 30 3/4 ins / 78 cm) USD 6,600. NEW YORK, 14 Oct 1993, *Aguador (Water Carrier)* (polychrome bronze, h. 13 3/4 ins / 35 cm) USD 1,265. NEW YORK, 3 June 1994, *Wolf!* (bronze, h. 30 ins / 76.2 cm, l. 35 ins/88.9 cm) USD 5,175.

HIOLLE, Auguste
French, 19th century.
Born in the 19th century, in Paris.
Painter. Genre scenes.
Auguste Hiolle became a member of the Société des Artistes Français in 1895.

HIOLLE, Ernest Eugène
French, 19th century.
Born 5 May 1834, in Paris; died 5 October 1886, in Bois-le-Roi (Seine-et-Marne).
Sculptor.
Ernest Hiolle was a pupil of Jouffroy and Granfils, and entered the École des Beaux-Arts on 31 March 1853. He came second in the Prix de Rome competition of 1856 and won it in 1862. He was made a Chevalier of the Légion d'Honneur in 1873. Hiolle began exhibiting at the Salon from 1866, winning medals in 1867, 1869 and 1870. He also won a medal of honour in 1878 at the Exposition Universelle. His best-known works include: *Allegorical Figure,* in bronze-plated plaster, which he sculpted for the monument at Cambrai, erected in memory of the 'Children of Cambrai who died for their country'; *St John of Matha* (a statue for the church of Sainte-Geneviève); *General Foy* (a bronze statue for the town of Ham, northern France); *Lafayette,* a statue erected in Lafayette Square in Le Puy-en-Velay (Haute-Loire), France, in 1883; and *The Present Pediment of the Town Hall in Cambrai.*
MUSEUMS AND GALLERIES:
ABBEVILLE: *Brutus* - AIX: *Mirabeau* - LYONS: *Bust of Paul Chenavard* - PARIS (Louvre): *Narcissus; Arion Astride a Dolphin* - TROYES: *Eve* - VALENCIENNES: *Bust of Carpeaux; Narcissus; Allegorical Figure; A Sabine Woman; Rape of Europa; Rape of Deianeira; Arion Playing the Lyre, and Being Carried off by a Dolphin; Jesus Tempted by the Demon.*
AUCTION RECORDS:
LONDON, 20 March 1986, *Nude Man Pulling on His Stocking* (1885, brown-patinated bronze, h. 35 1/2 ins / 90 cm) GBP 2,600.

HIOLLE, Maximilien Henri
French, 19th century.
Born 4 April 1843, in Valenciennes.
Sculptor.
Maximilien Hiolle was a pupil of Jouffroy, and first exhibited at the Salon of 1869. He received honourable mentions in 1882 and in 1900 (at the Exposition Universelle).

HIPKISS, Chris
British, 20th - 21st century.
Born 1964, in London.
Draughtsman. Scenes with figures, landscapes.
After working as a cabinet maker with his father, Chris Hipkiss became a draughtsman and produced his early landscapes in ballpoint pen on paper. He lives and works in the village of Doddington, working on rolls of paper, sometimes 20 feet (6 metres) long, producing monochrome compositions with a vision of a dreamlike world. He has taken part in group exhibitions since 1993 in the USA, England and Ireland. In 2001, his work was shown as part of the exhibition *Noir sur Blanc: Mondes Intérieurs* (*Black on White: Inner Worlds*) at the Halle St-Pierre, Paris. He has also shown his work in solo exhibitions, including in 2000 at the John Michael Kohler Arts Center, Wisconsin.
BIBLIOGRAPHY:
Mason, Alpha, '*The Visionary World of Chris Hipkiss*' in *Raw Vision* No. 9. Gallien, Antoine/Lusardy, Martine/Pons, Louis, *Noir sur Blanc. Mondes intérieurs,* exhibition catalogue, La Halle Saint-Pierre, Paris, Travioles, Paris, 2001 (text in French and English).

HIPOLITE, Auguste
French, 18th - 19th century.
Born 18th century.
Painter, miniaturist, actor.
Auguste Hipolite exhibited at the Salon between 1799 and 1814. He had studied under J.-B. Regnault.

HIPPEL, Walter Gustav
German, 20th century.
Born 29 April 1888, in Berlin.
Painter, engraver.
Walter Hippel studied in Charlottenburg and Munich, and then moved to Paris.

HIPPELI, Kaspar
German, 18th century.
Active in Neustadt-am-See.
Sculptor.
Hippeli worked for churches, particularly those in Oberelsbach.

HIPPENMEYER, Jenny
Swiss, 19th century.
Born 31 May 1851, in Zurich.
Painter.
Hippenmeyer was a pupil of Anna Fries in Florence. She went on to exhibit in Paris, Cologne and Düsseldorf.

HIPPEUS
3rd century BC.
Born probably during the 3rd century BC, in Athens.
Painter.

Ancient Greek.
Pliny the Elder gives his name as Hippys.

HIPPIAS
4th century BC.
Sculptor.
Ancient Greek.
Hippias is named by Dio Chrysostom as one of Phidias' teachers.

HIPPIUS, Gustav Adolf
Estonian, 19th century.
Born 1 March 1792, in Pastorat-Nissy; died 24 September 1856, in Tallinn.
Painter, lithographer. Portraits.
Gustav Adolf Hippius studied under Höppner in Tallin. He travelled to Germany and Italy before settling in St Petersburg.

HIPPOLITE, Hector, or Hyppolyte
Haitian, 20th century.
Born 1894, in St-Marc; died 1948, in Port-au-Prince.
Painter. Scenes with figures.
Art Brut.
After travelling in America and Africa during his youth, Hector Hippolite became, like his father and grandfather before him, a 'houngan' or priest of the Voodoo cult, which originated in Africa and was the most widely practised religion of the black population of Haiti. Voodoo combines elements of African cults with practices of the Catholic religion and this is reflected in Hippolite's work in paintings such as *The Siren and St John Watch over Me*. As well as painting he ran the *À la Renaissance* inn. With Philomé Obin, he was one of Haiti's first naive painters and was discovered in 1943 by English teacher Dewitt Peters who brought together all the island's naive painters and founded the Port-au-Prince Art Centre. As result a school of naive painters was set up, as in Hlebine in Yugoslavia with Ivan Generalic, but in Haiti these artists were united around the Voodoo cult. Since Hippolite's work had preceded the foundation of the art centre, it cannot have influenced him.

When André Breton discovered him, Hippolite was living in poverty, which would explain why he painted using random implements and colours, even using his fingers to paint on pieces of stuck together cardboard. In fact, these materials suited his deliberately primitive form of expression very well. He composed without composing, without depth, scattering figures and objects around the rudimentary setting of the action, flattening and separating them for clarity on the surface to be painted in a style similar to children's drawings, or following their example, like Matisse in *The Red Studio*. Hippolite's paintings exorcise and glorify women's power to tempt, they evoke mythical heroes drawn from the island's warrior pantheon and invoke mythological voodoo spirits through the schematic and violent representation of obscure rites and conjurations. André Breton and Wilfredo Lam arranged for Hippolite's work to be shown at the 1947 Surrealist exhibition in Paris, which only added the confusion surrounding the artist who shows no real evidence of Surrealism. However, to classify him as naive, a term normally associated with the simple and felicitous, is equally misleading as it does not take into account the witchcraft element which relates his work to primitive art.

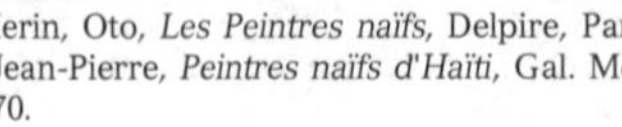

BIBLIOGRAPHY:
Bihalji-Merin, Oto, *Les Peintres naïfs*, Delpire, Paris, 1960.
Bouvet, Jean-Pierre, *Peintres naïfs d'Haïti*, Gal. Mona Lisa, Paris, 1970.

AUCTION RECORDS:
LOS ANGELES, 20 March 1976, *Three Women Bathing* (gouache, 19 3/4 x 32 3/4 ins / 50.3 x 83.2 cm) USD 2,600. NEW YORK, 20-21 April 1976, *Still-life with Fruit* (oil on card, 22 x 34 ins / 56 x 86.5 cm) USD 2,200. LOS ANGELES, 6 June 1978, *Ecce Agnus Dei* (oil on card, 36 x 27 ins / 91.5 x 68.5 cm) USD 2,600. NEW YORK, 4 Dec 1979, *Two Loas* (oil on card, 27 1/2 x 20 1/2 ins / 70 x 52 cm) USD 16,000. NEW YORK, 9 July 1981, *Two Nudes* (oil/hardboard, 24 x 30 ins / 61 x 76.2 cm) USD 23,000. NEW YORK, 30 Nov 1983, *The River* (c. 1946-1948, oil/hardboard, 23 x 28 1/2 ins / 57.5 x 72.5 cm) USD 33,000. NEW YORK, 30 May 1985, *Herzulie Freda Dahonmin* (oil on card, 31 x 27 1/2 ins / 78.7 x 69.6 cm) USD 22,000. NEW YORK, 19 Nov 1987, *Two Peasant Women* (c. 1947, oil on card, 28 3/4 x 23 3/4 ins / 73.3 x 60.6 cm) USD 21,000. NEW YORK, 21 Nov 1988, *Mistress Elizabeth* (oil/synthetic resin, 31 x 24 ins / 78.7 x 61 cm) USD 31,900. NEW YORK, 2 May 1990, *3 Marasa - 3 Plat Mister* (1948, oil/synthetic resin, 23 3/4 x 23 3/4 ins / 60.5 x 60.5 cm) USD 38,500. NEW YORK, 19-20 Nov 1990, *Fish with a Woman's Head* (oil on card, 47 3/4 x 29 1/4 ins / 121.5 x 74.5 cm) USD 44,000. NEW YORK, 15 May 1991, *Nude* (oil on card/card, 24 x 30 ins / 61 x 76.5 cm) USD 55,000; *Macanda* (oil on card, 18 x 20 1/4 ins / 45.5 x 51.5 cm) USD 24,200. NEW YORK, 20 Nov 1991, *Houngan Chango* (oil/synthetic resin, 24 1/4 x 23 3/4 ins / 61.5 x 60.3 cm) USD 16,500. NEW YORK, 19 May 1992, *President Florvil Hyppolite* (pencil and oil on card, 30 x 24 ins / 76 x 61 cm) USD 74,800. NEW YORK, 15 Nov 1994, *Female Nude with Birds* (oil on canvas, 17 1/4 x 19 1/2 ins / 43.8 x 49.5 cm) USD 13,800. NEW YORK, 21 Nov 1995, *Peasant Women* (oil on card, 13 x 19 ins / 33 x 48.2 cm) USD 12,650. NEW YORK, 29-30 May 1997, *Still-life* (c. 1946, tempera on panel, 30 x 24 1/4 ins / 76.2 x 61.6 cm) USD 35,650. LONDON, 27 June 2002, *Man Man-Man Dia* (oil on board, 30 x 23 ins / 75 x 59 cm) GBP 3,000. PARIS, 15 April 2003, *Mari Travo* (oil on card, 20 x 27 ins / 52 x 69 cm) EUR 31,000. PARIS, 15 April 2003, *Dee* (oil on card, 24 x 30 ins / 61 x 76 cm) EUR 34,000.

HIPPOLYTE-LUCAS, Marie Felix
French, 19th - 20th century.
Born 9 November 1854, in Rochefort-sur-Mer; died 17 April 1925, in Bougival.
Painter. Figures, portraits. Murals.
Marie Felix Hippolyte-Lucas was a pupil of Isidore Pils, Karl Lehmann and Évariste Luminais.

He executed decorative paintings for the casino in Monte Carlo, the conference centre at the Musée Océanographique in Monaco, and three ceilings in the Préfecture du Rhône.

A regular exhibitor from 1877 to 1924 at the Salon des Artistes Français, Hippolyte-Lucas received a number of awards including: honourable mention (1879); travel grant (1881); 3rd class medal (1884); 2nd class medal (1887); silver medal (1889) as well as a silver medal at the 1900 Exposition Universelle. He was Chevalier de la Légion d'Honneur.

AUCTION RECORDS:
LONDON, 5 Dec 1980, *La Loïe* (c. 1898, oil on canvas, 25 x 17 1/4 ins / 63.5 x 44 cm) GBP 1,400. NEW YORK, 17 Dec 1983, *Loïe Fuller* (c. 1900, oil on canvas, 34 x 45 ins / 86.5 x 114.5 cm) USD 8,000. NEW YORK, 31 Oct 1985, *Young Woman in a Park in Autumn* (oil on canvas, 65 1/4 x 36 ins / 165.8 x 91.5 cm) USD 7,000. NEW YORK, 31 Oct 1985, *The Engaged Couple* (oil on canvas, 64 1/2 x 39 3/4 ins / 164 x 101 cm) USD 7,500. PARIS, 22 March 1988, *Allegory at the Temple of Mercury* (oil on canvas, 21 1/4 x 26 1/2 ins / 54 x 67 cm) FRF 6,000. NEUILLY, 5 Dec 1989, *The Orchard* (oil on canvas, 30 3/4 x 22 ins / 78 x 55 cm) FRF 64,000. LONDON, 18 March 1992, *The Refreshment of Strawberries* (oil on canvas, 23 x 16 1/4 ins / 58.5 x 41.5 cm) GBP 2,420. AMSTERDAM, 20 April 1993, *Young Girl Holding Flowers* (oil on canvas, 17 1/2 x 23 1/4 ins / 44.5 x 59 cm) NLG 9,200. NEW YORK, 22-23 July 1993, *Young Woman on a Park Bench* (oil on canvas, 22 1/2 x 18 ins / 57.2 x 45.7 cm) USD

2,185. NEW YORK, 12 Oct 1994, *Portrait of Loïe Fuller* (oil on canvas, 35 x 46 ins / 88.9 x 116.8 cm) USD 8,337.

HIPPONICUS
1st century BC.
Active c. 1st century BC.
Sculptor.
Ancient Greek.
His name was found on a statue pedestal.

HIPPOTOMADES
4th century BC.
Sculptor.
Ancient Greek.
Hippotomades' name was found on a statue pedestal on the Acropolis at Athens.

HIPPYS. See **HIPPEUS**

HIPSCHMANN, Georg
German, 17th century.
Painter, engraver.
Georg Hipschmann is best known for his portraits.

HIPSCHMANN, Sigmund Gabriel
German, 17th century.
Born 1639, in Nuremberg.
Painter, engraver.
Sigmund Hipschmann painted mainly landscapes and portraits.

HIQUILY, Philippe
French, 20th century.
Born 27 March 1925, in Paris.
Sculptor. Figures, portraits.
From 1947 to 1951, Philippe Hiquily studied with Marcel Gimond and Alfred Janniot at the École des Beaux-Arts in Paris. He was influenced by Julio Gonzalés, Germaine Richier, Alberto Giacometti and African sculpture. He devoted himself exclusively to metallic sculpture from 1951.

Hiquily evolved in different directions. He retained an attachment to figuration after his time at the École des Beaux-Arts: from Gonzalés he took his technique of metalworking, from Germaine Richier, a certain familiarity with insects, and from the Surrealist Giacometti, a sense of the void (*The Invisible Object*) and an obsession with entrapment (*Palace at 4 o'clock in the Morning*).

Hiquily works with iron, oxidized bronze, brass, aluminium and stainless steel, with the precision of a clockmaker fashioning robots. He alternates full forms with plump bodies, thin elements, threadlike limbs, a fragile mix of generators of sensations. He creates strange beings from Surrealist mythology, combinations of giant insects and primitive humanoid figures, most often female normally with pinheads. His figures are often occupied in erotic activities, whether in couplings or through the intervention of sado-masochistic instruments, even a German machine-gun. Creatures of a pretty ugliness with delicately fashioned monstrosities, they are often placed on individual scaffoldings, at times in front of a mirror so that they can verify their physical appearance. Alternatively, they might be placed, like a squirrel in a cage, in a more spacious construction up to two metres high. Since 1956, Hiquily has constructed mobile figures executing slow gyrations, rotations, manoeuvres, gravitations, ingeniously generated by bizarre mechanisms which manipulate them by means of successive pulses. Depending upon the obstacles put in the way, the moving figures create hand-bell sounds or gong-like sonorities. Hiquily's work c. 1980 moved beyond grotesque figures, with animations and couplings towards a kinder production, lacking perhaps in the violence of the old sensation of anxiety. He celebrated the female body with elegant elongations and curves to the thighs, arms, neck and breasts, instead of the previous atrophied limbs. In this way, he restored to the female form the grace accorded to it by traditional Mannerism. Hiquily also executed numerous pieces of furniture inspired by his sculptures and 1967-1968 created a monumental sculpture for Mont-de-Marsan.

A sculptor of masterful technique, Hiquily's imagination is authentic: its humour, which compensates for cruelty, is at the origin of Kinetic art.

Philippe Hiquily has participated in numerous collective exhibitions including: Salon de Mai (from 1956); Salon de la Jeune Sculpture (from 1957); Carnegie International, Pittsburgh (1958); Paris Biennale (1959 winning the critics' prize); *Sculpture contemporaine*, Musée de St-Étienne (1960); *Sculpture Contemporaine Internationale*, Musée Rodin, Paris (1961); 8th Tokyo Biennale, Antwerp-Middelheim Biennale and *Groupe 1/65*, Musée National d'Art Moderne, Paris (1965). Solo exhibitions include: Paris (1954, 1958 and 1964); New York (1959 and 1961); Institute of Contemporary Art, London (1963); *Accouplements* (*Couplings*), Galerie H. Odermatt, Paris (1973); important retrospective, Maison de la Culture, Amiens (1975); retrospective, Galerie Fabien Boulakia, Paris, (1984); Galerie Ratton-Hourdé, Paris (2001).

BIBLIOGRAPHY:
George, Waldemar, '*Les Machines humaines de Hiquily*' in *Prisme des Arts* n° 19, periodical, Société Art et Industrie, Paris, 1959. Jaguer, Édouard, '*Sculpture 1950-1960 - Poétique de la sculpture*' in *coll. Le Musée de poche*, Georges Fall, Paris, 1960. Jonquet, François, *Philippe Hiquily, le métal direct*, Éd. Cercle d'Art, Paris, 1992.

MUSEUMS AND GALLERIES:
NEW YORK (MoMA) - NEW YORK (Solomon R. Guggenheim Mus.) - PARIS (MNAM-CCI) - ST-ÉTIENNE (Mus. d'Art et d'Industrie).

AUCTION RECORDS:
NEW YORK, 11 May 1966, *Pin-ball Machine* (steel) USD 2,100. PARIS, 17 Nov 1972, *Sculpture* FRF 7,500. NEW YORK, 5 May 1973, *Mobiloïde* (1961) USD 2,200. NEW YORK, 26 May 1976, *The Unstable* (1960, steel, h. 32 ins / 81.3 cm) USD 2,100. PARIS, 28 Feb 1978, *Clothilde* (1961, wrought iron, h. 35 3/4 ins / 91 cm) FRF 10,000. PARIS, 23 Nov 1984, *The Viscountess* (1960, patinated iron, h. 54 1/4 ins / 138 cm) FRF 75,000. PARIS, 6 Dec 1986, *Mobile Fountain* (1979, polished and soldered brass, h. 80 ins / 203 cm) FRF 120,000. PARIS, 27 Nov 1987, *Tightrope Walker* (patinated brass, h. 42 1/2 ins / 108 cm) FRF 54,000. PARIS, 20 March 1988, *Bust of a Woman* (1961, iron, h. 31 1/2 ins / 80 cm) FRF 40,000. PARIS, 28 Oct 1988, *Speed* (bronze and steel, h. 53 1/4 ins / 135 cm) FRF 52,000. PARIS, 20 Nov 1988, *The Prey II* (1976, brass, steel and Altuglass, 51 1/4 x 37 1/2 x 15 3/4 ins / 130 x 95 x 40 cm) FRF 27,000. NEW YORK, 21 Feb 1990, *Untitled* (1966, welded steel, h. 24 3/4 ins / 62.9 cm) USD 35,200. NEUILLY, 10 May 1990, *La Dame Pipi* (double-patinated bronze, 37 3/4 x 33 3/4 x 11 ins / 96 x 86 x 28 cm) FRF 140,000. PARIS, 19 June 1990, *Figure in Iron* (h. 26 1/2 ins / 67 cm) FRF 140,000. PARIS, 21 June 1990, *Sculpture Study* (ink/paper, 11 1/2 x 12 1/4 ins / 29 x 31 cm) FRF 3,800. PARIS, 23 Oct 1990, *Stabile with Water Projection* (1956, sculpture, h. 82 3/4 ins / 210 cm, diam. 78 3/4 ins/200 cm) FRF 105,000. PARIS, 3 Feb 1992, *Seated Nude* (1990, Indian ink, 41 1/4 x 47 1/4 ins / 105 x 120 cm) FRF 10,000. PARIS, 26 Nov 1992, *Happening Mask (exorcism)* (1962, iron, 67 x 47 1/4 ins / 170 x 120 cm) FRF 49,000. NEW YORK, 10 May 1993, *Hasch du H. 1961* (wrought iron, 48 1/2 ins / 123.3 cm) USD 4,370. PARIS, 29 Sept 1993, *Mimi Feet in the Air* (bronze, 43 1/4 x 26 x 7 1/4 ins / 110 x 66 x 18.5 cm) FRF 70,000. PARIS, 22 April 1994, *The Migraine* (bronze, 35 x 11 3/4 x 9 ins / 89 x 30 x 23 cm) FRF 44,500. PARIS, 29-30 June 1995, *Miroir aux alouettes* (*The Lure*) (iron, incrusted with glass and mirrors, h. 26 1/2 ins / 67.5 cm, w. 20 3/4 ins/52.8 cm) FRF 9,000. PARIS, 29 Sept 1995, *Untitled* (painted iron, h. 73 1/4 ins / 186 cm) FRF 70,000. PARIS, 27 March 1996, *Ermadrissa* (1974, gilded brass and iron trap, 22 1/2 x 18 ins / 57 x 46 cm) FRF 24,000. PARIS, 1 July 1996, *The Diamond Eater* (antique-green and dark-green pa-

tinated polished bronze, sculpture in two parts, 23 1/2 x 11 x 9 3/4 ins / 60 x 28 x 25 cm) FRF 17,500. Paris, 5 Oct 1996, *Seated Woman* (brown and black patinated bronze, h. 37 3/4 ins / 96 cm, w. 33 1/2 ins/85 cm, depth 9 3/4 ins/25 cm) FRF 50,000. Paris, 16 Dec 1996, *Trapped Woman* (gilded bronze, tortoiseshell and iron, h. 20 ins / 51 cm) FRF 54,000. Paris, 19 March 1997, *Sculpture* (metal, 14 1/4 x 17 3/4 x 5 ins / 36.5 x 45 x 13 cm) FRF 27,500. London, 29 May 1997, *Untitled* (fossilised wood and copper, 23 x 20 1/4 x 19 1/4 ins / 58.4 x 51.4 x 48.8 cm) GBP 5,175. Paris, 16 June 1997, *The Swimmer* (1989, embossed brass with brown and green patina, 15 x 12 1/4 ins / 38 x 31 cm) FRF 19,500. Paris, 3 Oct 1997, *Untitled* (c. 1960, beaten iron, 27 1/2 x 19 3/4 x 14 1/4 ins / 70 x 50 x 36 cm) FRF 32,000. Paris, Jan 1998, *Yen* (sculpture green-patinated brass, 33 1/2 x 20 3/4 ins / 85 x 53 cm) FRF 34,500. Paris, 5 Aug 1999, *The Banker* (1989, brown patinated bronze with metal safe, 74 x 41x26 ins / 187 x 104x67 cm) FRF 180,000. Paris, 18 Sept 1999, *Untitled* (c. 1966, iron, mobile with seven elements, h. 50 ins / 127 cm) FRF 80,000. Paris, 2 Aug 2000, *Hio-up la Boum* (brown patinated bronze, 44 x 31x6 ins / 113 x 78x14 cm) FRF 60,000. Versailles, 17 Dec 2000, *Untitled* (brown patinated bronze, 38 x 33x9 ins / 97 x 85x24 cm) FRF 65,000. Paris, 20 June 2001, *Woman* (brown patinated bronze, h. 56 ins / 142 cm) FRF 150,000. Paris, 2 Aug 2001, *Grapefruit Lady* (brown patinated bronze, 56 x 20x16 ins / 143 x 51x40 cm) FRF 78,000. Paris, 8 Feb 2002, *Suspended from your Breath* (gilt tin, h. 81 ins / 205 cm) EUR 29,000. Paris, 8 Feb 2002, *Claudie* (tin and wood, 94 x 47x53 ins / 240 x 120x135 cm) EUR 34,000. Paris, 9 Dec 2003, *La Celestine* (brown-green patinated bronze, 43 x 22 ins / 108 x 57 cm) EUR 10,100. Versailles, 14 Dec 2003, *Olympia* (brass, wood, screenprint on panel, 41 x 71 ins / 104 x 180 cm) EUR 6,000. Paris, 10 June 2004, *Woman Cigar Box* (gold brass, 15 x 20 ins / 38 x 50 cm) EUR 11,000. Paris, 29 June 2004, *Chrysalis* (1988, tin, 20 x 9 ins / 52 x 24 cm) EUR 5,800.

HIRAFUKU, Hyakusui, real name: Hirafuku Teizo, artist name: Hyakusui
Japanese, 20th century.
Born 1877, in Akita Prefecture; died 1933.
Painter, draughtsman, illustrator. Landscapes, flowers, birds.

Hyakusui was the son of the painter Hirafuku Suian. As Teizo he had a reputation as a poet. He started his artistic training at the school of Kawabata Gyokusho (1842-1913) in Tokyo, going on to continue at the Tokyo school of fine arts, from which he graduated in 1899. The following year, he founded a group of naturalist and realist painters. After experiencing difficulty in gaining acceptance in the art circles of the Bunten (the official Ministry of Education exhibition), he became a member of the Imperial Art Academy and professor at the Tokyo school of fine arts.

In 1900, he devoted himself to drawing from nature while striving to achieve a synthesis between Western and Eastern techniques. At the same time, he severely criticised contemporary society in his drawings that appeared in newspapers. With time, he seemed to draw closer to traditional Japanese art and studied the work of Sotatsu (active in about 1630) and Korin (1658-1716) as well as trends in decorative painting. In his last years, he approached the Nanga (scholar-painter) style, developing a delightful talent based on almost religious observation of nature.

Museums and Galleries:
Tokyo (Eisei-Bunko Mus.) - Tokyo (Maeda Ikutokukai Foundation) - Tokyo (National MMA).

HIRAGA, Kamesuke
Japanese, 20th century.
Born 25 September 1889, in Mie; died 5 November 1971, in Paris.
Active in France.
Painter, engraver (including etching). Figures, landscapes, flowers. Murals.

Hiraga Kamesuke studied under Jules Pagès at the San Francisco Art Institute, where he won the First Grand Prize, and under Paul-Albert Laurens and Lucien Simon at the Académie Julian in Paris. He painted decorations for the Japanese embassies in Berlin, Washington and Panama, and the Consulates General in Hong Kong and Honolulu. Primarily a landscape artist, he worked much in Brittany. He exhibited at the Salon de la Société Nationale des Beaux-Arts in Paris from 1926 to 1932, at the Salon d'Automne from 1927 to 1933, and at the Salon des Artistes Français, where he was awarded an honourable mention in 1934, a second medal in 1938 and a gold medal in 1954. He took part in the Paris Exposition Universelle of 1937. He was a member of the Society of French Etchers. In 1961, Emperor Hirohito conferred on him the Order of Konsanto, a very rare honour for a living person.

Museums and Galleries:
Gaillac: *Tréboul Landscape* - Kurume - Locronan: *Locronan Church* - Paris (Mus. d'Orsay): *Douarnenez Bay* - Rouen (MBA): *Bouquet of Flowers* - Yamada: *Woman with Fan.*

Auction records:
Paris, 23 Dec 1942, *Breton House,* FRF 4,100. Paris, 28 Feb 1996, *Houses in the Forest* (oil on panel) FRF 5,000. Bolton, 1 Feb 2001, *Fountaine ceret-pyr-or* (oil on canvas, 21 x 29 ins / 53 x 74 cm) USD 2,100. Lyons, 6 June 2004, *Washerwomen near the Port* (1930, oil on panel, 18 x 24 ins / 46 x 61 cm) EUR 1,700.

HIRAGA, Kei
Japanese, 20th century.
Born 1936, in Tokyo.
Painter. Scenes with figures.
Nouvelle Figuration.

After studying economics at Keio University, Tokyo, Hiraga Kei taught himself painting and starting in 1956 took part in group exhibitions. Essentially graphic, although raw colour does appear, Hiraga's work cannot be seen outside the Pop Art movement which was soon to sweep across Europe and engulf the world. The form it took, to use the term coined by Gérald Gassiot-Talabot, was narrative figuration. As he said about Hiraga: 'Looking at these sinister forms with their feet in the air and bowler hats on their heads in the midst of a forest of symbols, where sex and genitalia abound, trying to decipher these complicated tattoos, these tongue-like ties with their irreverent patterns, these questionable roses, these jolly sleepwalkers who seem to have forgotten all about the laws of gravity, the least one can say is that Hiraga is a painter who doesn't have his feet on the ground'.

From 1960, he took part in the exhibition of *Young Painters from Asia* and the *New Japanese Painting and Sculpture* exhibition at the Museum of Modern Art, New York. In 1963, he won the Shell prize in Tokyo and in 1964 the Kokuga-kai (National Painting Society) Salon Prize. The same year, he also won the prize at the third International Exhibition of Young Artists in Tokyo as well as a study grant to go to Europe. In 1965, he went for a year to Paris. In 1966, he took part in the *Narrative Figuration* exhibition organised by Gérald Gassiot-Talabot. In 1969, he took part in the São Paulo Biennale, in 1971 in the Brussels Exhibition of Japanese Painters Living in France, and in the Salon des Réalités Nouvelles in Paris. He exhibited collections of works in various one-man shows, including shows in Scotland and Paris in 1966, in Haarlem and Paris in 1967, in Rotterdam in 1970 and in Milan in 1972.

Bibliography:
Gassiot-Talabot, Gérald, *Key Hiraga*, exhibition catalogue, Gal. Lambert, Paris, 1967.

AUCTION RECORDS:
AMSTERDAM, 9 Dec 1992, *Windows* (1966, acrylic/canvas) NLG 3,680. AMSTERDAM, 8 Dec 1994, *Untitled* (1971, acrylic/canvas) NLG 1,380. PARIS, 31 Oct 1997, *Pop Character* (1968, oil and collage/canvas) FRF 5,500. AMSTERDAM, 4 March 2002, *Windows* (1966, oil on canvas, 51 x 63 ins / 130 x 160 cm) EUR 5,000.

HIRAKAWA, Seizo
Japanese, 20th century.
Born 1897; died 1964.
Engraver. Landscapes.
A wood engraver, preferably in black and white, Hirakawa exhibits with the Japanese Engraving Society. His technique is one of repetition of elements.

HIRAKAWA, Shigeko
Japanese, 20th - 21st century.
Born 14 March 1953, in Kurume (Fukuoka).
Sculptor, installation artist.
After studying at the Tokyo National University of Fine Arts and Music, Hirakawa Shigeko was awarded a scholarship by the French government. She settled in Paris in 1983, where she studied at the École Nationale des Beaux-Arts in Olivier Debré's studio from 1983 to 1986. Shigeko Hirakawa's work seeks to explore our relationship with the elements that surround us and to illustrate a balance between man and nature.

For an exhibition at the Maison des arts at Malakoff in 2001, the artist created four installations and sculptures exploring the notion of life tied to the theme of water. Her project *Domesticated Water*, which is on show in the garden, is made up of ten huge lenses containing water, in which the water is fluorescent and appears green and yellow, thus guiding the spectator into a playful environment. In *Water Underground*, the visitor is induced to look up at hanging glass bowls in which the water, coloured as ever, gives off a luminous halo made effervescent with bubbles. The installation *Water/Sky* is a metaphor for rain and the reappearance of water in the air, which is evoked by columns of blue cloth stretched between earth and sky.

Hirakawa received a special mention at the 17th International Painting Festival, Cagnes-sur-Mer, in 1985, and the Muranaka prize at the 3rd NAC (Nihonjinkaï Artistes Club exhibition) at Orly, 1986.She has taken part in a number of group shows, including: 1983, *16th Exhibition of Contemporary Art of Japan*, municipal museums of Tokyo and Kyoto; 1984, Salon d'Automne, Paris; 1985, Salon de la Jeune Peinture, Salon de Montrouge, Paris; 1995, Centre d'Art, Neuchâtel; 1997, *Touch Me*, Departmental Museum, Miyazaki (Japan); the 1998, NAC exhibition at the Japanese Cultural Centre, Paris. She has shown her installations at a number of solo shows, including: 1982, Gallery Te, Tokyo; 1986, Cité Internationale des Arts, Paris; 1991, Galerie Espace Archidé, Paris; 1994, Gallery Lunami, Tokyo; 1995, *More Than Ten Years in Paris*, Gallery Tom, Tokyo; 2001 *Water Followed*, Maison des Arts, Malakoff, France.

BIBLIOGRAPHY:
Delavallade, Olivier/Hirakawa, Shigeko, *Shigeko Hirakawa. Eau suivie...*, exhibition catalogue, Maison des Arts, Malakoff, 2001 (text in French and English).

HIRAKUSHI, Denchu, or Hiragushi
Japanese, 19th - 20th century.
Born 1872, in Okayama Prefecture; died 1979.
Sculptor. Religious subjects, mythological figures, local figures, portraits.
Hirakushi studied sculpture under Takamura Koun and was soon selected to take part in the Bunten (ministry of education) exhibition and exhibitions at the art institute. In 1914 he became a member of the art academy and the Saiko academy, and was appointed professor at the Tokyo University of Fine Arts. He was subsequently decorated with the Medal of Culture. From the 1920s until the mid-1930s, Hirakushi mainly produced portrait sculptures. Then, in 1935, he concentrated on carving wooden images, sometimes polychromed, of the legendary demons of Buddhism, mendicant monks, warriors from dynastic wars, high dignitaries, and old men from folklore. During this period of his maturity, he worked for 20 years on his life's work, the *Lion Dance*, which stands in the hall of the National Kabuki Theatre in Tokyo. Deeply imbued with Buddhist thought, his art refers back to tradition both in the subjects he treats and in the deliberately direct, spontaneous technique he uses. His vigorous style sometimes recalls that of Okakura Tenshin, one of the main figures of the Maiji and Taisho periods, who specialised in depicting Kabuki actors.

Several of his works are on show at the National Theatre, Tokyo. In 1973, the Museum of Modern Art in Tokyo granted him a large retrospective of his work, and in 1996, the Espace Mitsukoshi-Étoile in Paris organised an exhibition of his entire opus.

HIRALDEZ DE ACOSTA, Marcos
Spanish, 19th century.
Born c. 1830, in Seville.
Painter.
Marcos Hiraldez de Acosta was a pupil of Esquivel and Picot. After spending some time in Rome, he painted many mythological subjects.

HIRAMOTO, Masaji
Japanese, 20th century.
Born 8 December 1888, in Fukui.
Sculptor.
Hiramoto Masaji worked in Paris and the USA.

HIRATSUKA, Un'ichi
Japanese, 20th century.
Born 1895, in Matsue (Shimane Prefecture); died 1997.
Painter, engraver (wood). Religious subjects, nudes.
Sosaku Hanga.
The grandson of an architect and son of a carpenter, Hiratsuka graduated from Matsue Commercial School before studying Western painting with Ishii Hakutei and Umehara Ryuzaburo and woodblock printing with Igami Bonkotsu. He exhibited woodblock prints in the 1916 Niha (two disciplines - painting and sculpture) Salon. He was one of the cofounders of the Japanese Print Society. In 1939, one of his works on show at the Bunten (the ministry of education exhibition) was bought by the government, and he was appointed professor at the Fine Arts University in Tokyo and the National College of Art in Beijing. In 1948, he founded his own school. Among its students have been Munakata Shiko, Kitaoka Fumio and Hashimoto Okiie. In 1950, he founded the Hiratsuka Printing Institute, for the purpose of training young printmakers. In 1962, he settled in Washington DC, only returning to Japan in 1994. He was a member of the Kokuga-kai (National Painting Society) and the Japanese Print Society. The emperor named him a Sacred National Treasure.

Hiratsuka was one of the main figures in the Sosaku Hanga (creative print) movement. His figurative style and monochrome ink compositions are imbued with restrained sensitivity. He achieves interesting textures through his unusual woodblock technique, which relies almost entirely on the working of the chisel. He is fond of traditional religious subjects, where a taste for detail does not detract from a complex rhythm of verticals and horizontals. In 1991, the Hiratsuka Un'ichi Print Museum was founded at Suzaka, in Nagano Prefecture.

In 1957 and 1960, he took part in the International Print Biennale, Tokyo. In 2000, three years after his death, the Tokyo Station Gallery organised an exhibition of his entire work, which in 2001 travelled to the Art Institute of Chicago. His work was shown at the *Japanese Prints during the Allied Occupation, 1945-1952* exhibition held at the British Museum in 2000.

BIBLIOGRAPHY:

Un'ichi Hiratsuka: a retrospective exhibition of woodblock prints in celebration of the artist's 90th birthday, exhibition catalogue, Japanese American Cultural & Community Center, Los Angeles, 1985. Merrit, Helen/Yamada, Nanako, *Guide to Modern Japanese Woodblock Prints: 1900-1975*, University of Hawaii Press, Honolulu, 1992. Merrit, H. et al., *Hiratsuka: Modern Master*, Art Institute of Chicago, Chicago, 2001. Smith, Lawrence, *Japanese Prints during the Allied Occupation, 1945-1952: Onchi Koshiro, Ernst Hacker and the First Thursday Society*, The British Museum Press, London, 2002.

MUSEUMS AND GALLERIES:

BOSTON (MFA) - NEW YORK (Metropolitan Mus. of Art) - NEW YORK (Rockefeller Foundation) - SUZAKA (Hiratsuka Un'ichi Print Mus.) - TOKYO (MMA) - WASHINGTON DC (Library of Congress).

HIRAYAMA, Ikuo

Japanese, 20th century.
Born 1930, in Hiroshima Prefecture.
Painter.

Hirayama Ikuo entered the Department of Japanese Painting at the Tokyo National University of Fine Arts and Music, where he studied under Maeda Seison, graduating in 1953, and subsequently joining the faculty as an assistant. In 1953, he took part for the first time in the Exhibition of Japanese Art, Tokyo. In 1961, he won the prize of the art academy, of which he is a member. In 1966, he exhibited in New York. He shows his work in solo shows, the first of which was held in 1965.

His painting is decorative, with surrealist tendencies.

AUCTION RECORDS:

NEW YORK, 21 April 1989, *Oirase* (ink and colour/paper) USD 300,000. NEW YORK, 10 May 2000, *Kumamoto Castle, Shiroyama* (colour ink and gold, 21 x 13 ins / 53 x 33 cm) USD 130,000. NEW YORK, 10 May 2000, *Indus River Upstream, Eternally Flowing* (colour ink and gold, 26 x 36 ins / 65 x 92 cm) USD 150,000.

HIRAYAMA, Kantei

Japanese, 19th - 20th century.
Active in Tokyo.
Sculptor.

Hirayama Kantei won a bronze medal at the Paris Exposition Universelle of 1900.

HIREMY-HIRSCHL, Adolf

Hungarian, 19th - 20th century.
Born 31 January 1860, in Temesvár (now Timisoara, Romania); died 1933.
Painter, pastellist. History painting, genre scenes.

Hiremy-Hirschl was a pupil of L.K. Muller and Eisenmemger at the academy in Vienna. He worked and exhibited in Budapest, Vienna, Rome and Munich. He was awarded a place at the Vienna academy in Rome. He received medals in Munich (1888), Paris (1889 Exposition Universelle), an honourable mention in Berlin (1890) and the emperor's prize in Vienna (1891).

AUCTION RECORDS:

ROME, 15 March 1983, *End of the World* (oil on canvas, 55 x 89 3/4 ins / 140 x 228 cm) ITL 7,000,000. LONDON, 26 Feb 1988, *Faraway Thoughts* (oil on panel, 10 3/4 x 16 1/2 ins / 27.3 x 42 cm) GBP 1,320. ROME, 13 May 1991, *Untitled* (pastel and wax/paper, 16 1/2 x 17 1/4 ins / 42 x 44 cm) ITL 1,725,000. LONDON, 28 June 1999, *Venus Reclining in the Waves* (oil on canvas, 43 x 89 ins / 109 x 227 cm) GBP 22,000. LONDON, 7 June 2001, *Study of the Head of St Cecillia, Possibly for Ahasverus* (black and white chalk, 9 x 13 ins / 24 x 32 cm) GBP 1,100. ROME, 5 June 2002, *Stream Amongst Rocks* (watercolour, 21 x 7 ins / 53 x 17 cm) EUR 2,200. NEW YORK, 29 Oct 2002, *Studies for St Cecilia. Woman from the Back* (pencil, black and white chalk, two, 9 x 13 ins / 24 x 33 cm) USD 3,000. NEW YORK, 28 Oct 2003, *Portrait of the Artist's Daughter Maud* (graphite, black chalk and stumping, 17 x 10 ins / 42 x 25 cm) USD 2,500. LONDON, 3 Dec 2003, *Venus Reclining in the Waves* (oil on canvas, 43 x 108 ins / 109 x 274 cm) GBP 20,000. SYDNEY, 15 May 2004, *Ahasverus* (1888, oil on canvas, 55 x 90 ins / 139 x 229 cm) AUD 100,000.

HIRI, Guy-Max

French, 20th century.
Born 29 May 1928, in Paris.
Painter, draughtsman. Nudes, animals.

Guy-Max Hiri received advice from Metzinger, Brayer and Henri Goetz. His two favourite themes are the female body and horses which drew or painted with a knife, in thick touches, and in a palette of violent contrasts. He also painted bouquets of flowers and landscapes. Hiri lives and works in Paris in the Marais. He has participated in collective exhibitions in Paris, including the Salon d'Automne, and abroad and has also organised solo exhibitions.

HIRN, Jean Georges

French, 19th century.
Born 15 December 1777, in Mulhouse; died 9 April 1839, in Logelbach, near Colmar.
Painter. Still-lifes.

Hirn studied in Paris, then pursued a career in France. He won two medals at the Salon of 1812, which was his first appearance, and his work was featured there until 1838.

MUSEUMS AND GALLERIES:

MULHOUSE: *Flowers and Fruit* - PARIS (Louvre): *Flowers and Fruit*.

AUCTION RECORDS:

LONDON, 6 Oct 1982, *Still-life with Fish and Onions* (1817, oil/metal, 13 x 16 1/4 ins / 33 x 41.5 cm) GBP 1,500. MONTE CARLO, 6 Dec 1987, *Apples, Onions and Herrings near a Window* (1828, oil/copper, 26 3/4 x 22 1/2 ins / 68 x 57 cm) FRF 85,000. MONACO, 17 June 1989, *Basket of Grapes on a Marble Entablature Laden with Cut Peaches and Melons* (1815, oil/copper, 39 1/4 x 35 ins / 100 x 88 cm) FRF 366,300. NEW YORK, 28 Jan 1999, *Bouquet of Flowers in Urn on Black Stone Ledge* (1813, oil on panel) USD 65,000. PARIS, 27 June 2002, *Still-life with Onions and Herrings* (1817, oil on canvas/copper, 13 x 16 ins / 32 x 40 cm) EUR 11,000.

HIRN, Johann Michael

German, 18th century.
Active in Berlin in 1716.
Sculptor.

HIRN, Marian

Austrian, 18th century.
Born c. 1780, in Obermiemingen; died 1801, in Vienna.
Engraver.

Marian Hirn was a pupil of Peter Denifle in Innsbruck, then worked at the Akademie der bildenden Künste in Vienna.

HIRNE, François

French, 18th century.
Active in Paris in 1757.
Sculptor, painter.

HIRNSCHROT, Johann Andreas

German, 19th century.
Born 1799, in Nuremberg.
Miniaturist, enameller, glassmaker.

Hirnschrot studied at the Nuremberg academy of art. He went on to work at the Sèvres Porcelain Factory and then in Switzerland.

HIROCHIKA, real name: Tosa Hirochika (or Hirokane, Hirokata)
Japanese, 15th century.
Active 1459-1492.
Painter.

A painter in the court painting studio *(e-dokoro)*, Hirochika is supposed to have been the uncle of Mitsunobu (d. 1525).

HIROI, Risaburo
Japanese, 20th century.
Born 1937, in Gumma Prefecture.
Painter.

Hiroi Risaburo graduated from the department of painting of Tokyo National University of Fine Arts and Music in 1965. He had his first solo show in Tokyo in 1968.

HIROKANE. See **SADAHIRO II**

HIROKAWA, Toshio
Japanese, 20th century.
Born 1924, in Kosakai (Aichi Prefecture).
Painter.

Hirokawa Toshio's artistic training in the strict sense of the term lasted six months, at the Nishijin Obi Design School, Kyoto. His style, which is precise, fantastical and magical all at the same time, tends towards the decorative and may be described as bordering on the surrealist. Since 1950, he has exhibited at the New Creation Society, winning several prizes. In 1961, he travelled to Europe. In 1963, he became a member of the New Creation Society. In 1967, he took part in an exhibition in Houston, Texas.

HIROKUNI. See **HIROSADA** and **HIRONOBU II**

HIROMICHI. See **SUMIYOSHI**

HIROMOTO, Susumu
Japanese, 20th century.
Painter.

Hiromoto Susumu took part in the exhibition of Japanese art held in Paris in 1929.

HIRON, Adolf
Polish, 20th century.
Born c. 1887.
Painter. Landscapes.

Adolf Hiron was a student at the academy of Cracow.

HIRON, Antoine
French, 19th century.
Born 14 March 1823, in Ris-Orangis (Essonne).
Active in Paris.
Sculptor.

Hiron made his Salon début in 1848.

HIRONOBU I, childhood name: Kinoshita Hironobu, artist names: Hakusui, Hakusuisai, Goyotei, Gohotei, Torin, Ashinoya
Japanese, 19th century.
Born 1851; died 1870.
Print artist.

HIRONOBU II, real name: Kinoshita Hironobu, original first name: Hirokuni, artist names: Hakuho, Ryuto, Rosui, Ashimi
Japanese, 19th century.
Born 1844.
Active c. 1870-1880.
Engraver, print artist.

HIROSADA, real name: Utagawa Hirosada, original names: Tomikuni (1821), Tamikuni (1823-1826), Gocho (1826), Sadahiro (1830-1846) probably used simultaneously with Hirosada until 1851, Hirokuni I (1847). Childhood names: Suzuki, Konishi, Ishii, Utagawa. Artist names: Gosotei, Gorakutei
Japanese, 19th century.
Born c. 1810; died c. 1865.
Print artist.

From a print published in Edo (now Tokyo) in August 1852, it can be surmised that Hirosada was a pupil of Kunimasu. Between 1849 and 1852, his work was published by a variety of publishers: Konishi Gocho (Kinkado), Rankei (Kawaoto), Sada-han (Isekichi), Sada (Kinkodo), Kinsekido (Ikekichi), Ko (Meikodo), Han Sada (Daijin), Gocho (Tenki), Cho, Sadahiro and Gosotei.

HIROSE, Toho, real name: Hirose Hitoshi, artist name Toho
Japanese, 20th century.
Born 1875; died 1930.
Painter.

Toho took part in the exhibition of Japanese art held in Paris in 1929.

HIROSHIGE I, or Utagawa Hiroshige, real name: Ando Hiroshige, childhood names: Tokutaro, later Juemon, Tokube, Jubei; artist names: Ichiyusai, Ichiryusai, Ryusai, Tokaido Utashige
Japanese, 19th century.
Born 1797, in Edo (now Tokyo); died September 1858.
Print artist.

The uncontested master of the landscape print, Hiroshige is as well known in Japan as he is in the West. It is likely that no one has ever interpreted the beauties of the Japanese landscape with such understanding. Unanimously regarded as Japan's foremost landscape artist, Hiroshige, together with Hokusai (1760-1849) represents a peak of both *ukiyo-e* and the coloured woodblock print.

His father was a samurai firefighting official who, though of low rank, was quite comfortably off. Hiroshige showed a talent for drawing and painting at a very young age and started by working with a minor artist of the Kano school, before frequenting painters of the Shojo school. After being turned away by the studio of Toyokuni (1769-1825) because it was full, he entered the school of Toyokuni's brother Toyohiro (1774-1829) in 1811, and thereupon abandoned his father's trade. A very capable student, after only a year of study he received permission from Toyohiro to use the name Utagawa and a new first name, Hiroshige. He was only 15.

Toyohiro's gentle, restrained, highly subtle style was probably a determining influence on Hiroshige, as well as his study of landscape and *kacho* (bird-and-flower pictures). He was also interested in the different kinds of prints then in fashion - historical scenes, actor prints, and beautiful women.

Until the death of his master in 1829, Hiroshige's output was limited and is virtually indistinguishable from the usual prints of the time: some *surimono* (limited-edition prints for greeting cards, announcements, and so on), actor prints, heroic scenes influenced by Shuntei (d. 1820), and mother-and-child prints in the style of Eizan (1787-1867). Refusing to succeed Toyohiro as the head of the studio, Hiroshige turned to the study of nature and very quickly developed the style to which he would remain faithful all his life. From this period date the many *tanzaku* (small prints including a poem, to accompany a gift), delicate compositions of birds and flowering branches that already prefigure his magnificent *kacho* prints. From the same period come his first true landscapes, which caught the public eye: the series of 10 prints entitled *Toto meisho (Famous Spots in the Eastern Capital)*, published in 1831 or 1832 and followed, a year later, by the *Honcho-meisho (Famous Views of Japan)*, his first masterpiece. Despite considerable influence from Hokusai, one can already discern in these works the sure signs of Hiroshige's own hand, his characteristic composition and drawing.

In August 1832, quite by chance, he found himself accompanying an official messenger of the Tokugawa Shogunate to the imperial court at Kyoto. This took him in both directions along the great Tokaido highway. Overwhelmed by the beauty of the land he was crossing, he made countless sketches of the countryside and the life at the relay stations *(shukuba)*. His future was decided there and then. His own particular style followed, as did the full expression of his genius, the *Tokaido gojusan tsugi* (*53 Stations on the Tokaido*), which was published the following year, 1833-34, by the publisher Hoei-do. This work was an immediate success and has remained so ever since; which is why Hiroshige would make 40 different versions of it. But none would approach the artistic quality of the first, the so-called Great Tokaido.

Unlike the fiery Hokusai, Hiroshige bathes his landscapes with restrained lyricism and sensitivity, expressing them in delicate lines and harmonious colouring. His view of nature is coloured by softness and poetry yet is always deeply connected to the artist himself, the man who when the moment seizes him reveals his supreme draughtsmanship.

Even though his source of inspiration would gradually dry up as Tokaido series followed on Tokaido series, his lyrical sensitivity and artistic gift can be seen to deepen with *Omi Hakkei* (*Eight Views of Omi*) (1834), the *Meisho* (*Famous Spots of Kyoto and Edo*), even more so in his famous *Kiso kaido rokujukyu tsugi* (*69 Stations on the Kiso Highway*), the highway linking east and west by the central mountains, which appeared in about 1839 with the help of Eisen (1790-1848), and the very famous *Wakan Roeishu* (*Japanese and Chinese Poems*) (1840). From 1841, Hiroshige criss-crossed the country, sketchbook in hand, partly out of a love of travel, and partly in search of new subject-matter. But, faced with the need to produce more and more because of his success, the quality of his work can be seen to fall off. His compositions become sloppy and his colours lose their subtlety, luminosity and gradation. By 1852, his landscape prints took on a longer format, yet he could still produce fine work, such as the *Setsugekka* (1857), a series of three triptychs devoted to the theme of snow, moon and blossom, so dear to the Japanese. His final major work, *Meisho Edo hyakkei* (*One Hundred Famous Views of Edo*) was published between 1856-59. His disciples, Hiroshige II (1826-1869) and Hiroshige III (d. 1894), who had worked with him since 1852, continued to work in his style, signing works closely resembling his own.

Bibliography:

Takahashi, Seiichiro, *Traditional Woodblock Prints of Japan*, Weatherhill, New York, 1964. Narazaki, Muneshige, '*Hiroshige famous views*' in *coll. Masterworks of Ukiyo-e*, Kodansha International, Tokyo, Palo Alto (USA), 1968 (Palo Alto, CA (USA)). Kozyreff, C., in *Encyclopaedia Universalis* vol. VIII, Paris, 1970 (Encyclopaedia). Lee, Sherman E./Boorstin Buch, Daniel J., *The sketchbooks of Hiroshige*, G. Braziller, New York, 1984. Guth, Christine, *Japanese Art of the Edo Period*, Calmann and King, London, 1996. Jûzô, Suzuki, *Hiroshige. Paysages célèbres des soixante provinces du Japon*, Hazan, Paris, 1998. Fahr-Becker, Gabriele (ed.), *Japanese Prints*, Taschen, Cologne, 1999. White, Julia M., *Hokusai and Hiroshige: Great Japanese Prints from the James A. Michener Collection*, University of Washington Press, 1999. Smith, Henry D. and others, *Hiroshige: One Hundred Famous Views of Edo*, George Braziller, 2000. Boorstin, Daniel J./Lee, Sherman E., *Hiroshige: carnets d'esquisses*, Phébus, Paris, 2001. Faulkner, Rupert, *Hiroshige Fan Prints at the V & A*, V & A Publications, London, 2001. Impey, Oliver, *Hiroshige's Views of Fuji*, Ashmolean Museum Publications, Oxford, 2001.

Museums and Galleries:

Paris (Mus. National des Arts asiatiques-Guimet) - Tokyo (National Mus.).

Auction records:

New York, 22 Sept 1983, *The Monkey Bridge in Koshu Province* (hanging scroll in colour) USD 55,000. Paris, 14 Dec 1987, *Three Peasants in the Evening Snow* (print, $13^{3}/_{4}$ x $9^{1}/_{4}$ ins / 35.2 x 23.2 cm) FRF 14,500; *Shower on the Bridge, in the Rain, Passers-by Shelter under Umbrellas* (Oishi No. 52, $13^{1}/_{4}$ x $8^{3}/_{4}$ ins / 33.5 x 22.2 cm) FRF 30,000. New York, 16 April 1988, *Swallow Perched on Wisteria Branch* (print, $14^{3}/_{4}$ x 5 ins / 37.4 x 12.9 cm) USD 11,000; *Yahagi Bridge at Okazaki* (print, 10 x 15 ins / 25.3 x 37.8 cm) USD 3,850. London, 16 May 1988, *53 Stations on the Tokaido* (oban yoko-e, complete series of 55 prints published by Hoeido) GBP 77,000; *Oiso* (print, taken from 53 Stations on the Tokaido published by Hoeido) GBP 1,155. London, 16 June 1988, *Mishima* (oil on panel, taken from the Houx series, $11^{1}/_{4}$ x $7^{1}/_{4}$ ins / 28.8 x 18.5 cm) ITL 950,000. London, 9 Nov 1988, *Spring Rain* (Oban Yoko-e print, from the Hoeido Tokaido series, 10 x 15 ins / 25.5 x 38.2 cm) GBP 2,750; *100 Famous Views of Edo* (Oban Tate-e print, from the Meisho Edo hyakkei series, $14^{1}/_{2}$ x $9^{3}/_{4}$ ins / 37 x 24.8 cm) GBP 3,300. London, 15 Dec 1988, *Wooded Landscape* (Oban Yoko-e print, from the Hoeido Tokaido series, 10 x $15^{1}/_{4}$ ins / 25.5 x 38.8 cm) GBP 4,620. New York, 21 March 1989, *Hakone* (Oban Yoko-e print, from the series 55 Views of the Tokaido, $9^{1}/_{4}$ x $14^{1}/_{4}$ ins / 23.7 x 36.5 cm) USD 9,900; *White Rain at Shono* (Oban Yoko-e print, from the series 55 Views of the Tokaido, $9^{1}/_{4}$ x $14^{1}/_{4}$ ins / 23.7 x 35.9 cm) USD 60,500; *Fireworks at Ryogoku* (Oban Tate-e print, from the series 100 Famous Views of Edo, $14^{1}/_{4}$ x $9^{1}/_{2}$ ins / 36 x 24.3 cm) USD 110,000. London, 22 March 1990, *Night in the Snow at Kanbara* (Oban Yoko-e print, $9^{1}/_{4}$ x 15 ins / 23.7 x 37.8 cm) GBP 8,250. London, 6 June 1990, *The Great Bridge at Atake in a Shower* (Oban Tate-e print, from the series One Hundred Famous Views of Edo, $14^{1}/_{4}$ x $9^{3}/_{4}$ ins / 36.2 x 24.6 cm) GBP 13,200. New York, 15 June 1990, *Swallow Perched on a Wisteria Branch* (chu-tanzaku print, $14^{1}/_{2}$ x 5 ins / 37.1 x 13 cm) USD 20,900; *Figures on the Banks of the Sumida after a Snowfall* (Oban Tate-e print, triptych, each panel $14^{1}/_{2}$ x $9^{1}/_{2}$ ins / 36.9 x 24 cm) USD 49,500. New York, 27 March 1991, *Return of Fine Weather after Snow at Kameyama* (Oban Yoko-e print, $9^{3}/_{4}$ x $14^{3}/_{4}$ ins / 24.8 x 37.4 cm) USD 12,100; *Crescent Moon and Owl on a Pine-branch* (chu-tanzaku print, $14^{3}/_{4}$ x 5 ins / 37.4 x 12.4 cm) USD 52,800. Munich, 26 May 1992, *The Bridge at Fukagawa* (1857, oban tate-e woodblock) DEM 1,265. Paris, 22 March 1995, *The 15th Station (Kambura)* (Oban Yoko-e print, of Tokaido) FRF 27,000. Munich, 6 June 2000, *View of the Sumida River in Winter* (colour woodcut, triptych) DEM 10,000. Cleveland, 6 July 2000, *Fifty-three Stations of the Tokaido* (woodblock, album of 53) USD 65,000. London, 20 June 2002, *One Hundred Famous Views of Edo* (1856-1858, print, 120, 14 x 9 ins / 36 x 24 cm) GBP 480,000. New York, 25 March 2003, *Seba, Station 32* (colour print, 9 x 15 ins / 23 x 37 cm) USD 65,000. New York, 25 March 2003, *Fireworks, Ryogoku* (colour print, 14 x 9 ins / 36 x 24 cm) USD 110,000.

HIROSHIGE II, real name: Suzuki Chimpei, original name: Morita, artist names: Hiroshige II, original forename: Rissho, Ichiryusai, Ichyusai, Ichiyusai, Kisai, Ryusai, Ryusho, Shigenobu
Japanese, 19th century.
Born 1826; died 1869.
Active during the second half of the 19th century.
Painter, print artist.

Hiroshige II was Hiroshige's first son-in-law. In 1865, he renounced his master's name and went to Yokohama, where he settled. Lacking Hiroshige's talent, he copied his landscape style, peopling his prints with foreigners such as Russians, Americans and Englishmen.

Auction records:
London, 16 May 1988, *Fresh Snow in the Kiso Gorges, Shinano Province* (Oban print, series: 100 Famous Spots in the Provinces) GBP 1,210. New York, 21 March 1989, *Evening Shower at a Pawlonia Plantation at Akasaka* (Oban Tate-e print, 14 1/4 x 9 3/4 ins / 36.1 x 24.8 cm) USD 19,800. New York, 16 Oct 1989, *Iwakuni Bridge in Suo Province* (Oban Tate-e print, 14 1/4 x 9 1/2 ins / 36.2 x 24.3 cm) USD 2,860. New York, 15 June 1990, *Iwakuni Bridge in Suo Province* (Oban Tate-e print, 14 3/4 x 10 ins / 37.5 x 25.2 cm) USD 5,500. New York, 13 Sept 1999, *Mariko* (print) USD 4,500. Paris, 10 Nov 1999, *Irises in Flower by Horikiri Lake* (engraving) FRF 25,000. Paris, 6 June 2000, *Meisho Edo Hyakkei Series* (ohashi) FRF 62,000. Boston, 24 June 2000, *Shono from the Hoeido Tokaido, 1832* (print) USD 6,500. Paris, 2 Feb 2001, *Net Hung Out to Dry above the Waves and Boats under Sail* (ink on silk, 12 x 20 ins / 31 x 52 cm) FRF 15,500. Paris, 16 Dec 2002, *Halt* (print) EUR 3,200. Paris, 16 Dec 2002, *Halt* (print) EUR 4,800.

HIROSHIGE III, real name: Ando Tokukei, childhood name, Goto Torakichi, artist names: Hiroshige, Isshosai, Shiganasa, Shigeton
Japanese, 19th century.
Born 1843; died 1894.
Print artist.

Hiroshige III was Hiroshige's disciple and successor, taking over his master's studio in 1865. Together with Hoen, Kuniteru, Sadahide and Kunisada II, he was one of the last generation of *ukiyo-e* artists, whose works were chosen by the Tokugawa government to be shown at the 1867 Paris Exposition Universelle. These prints went on sale in Paris after the exhibition itself came to an end, and contributed to the first wave of fascination with all things Japanese that was soon to sweep Europe. Yet the true aesthetics of *ukiyo-e* had already become diluted in the mannerism of these relatively minor works, which are a far cry from the great masters of the 18th century. Like his contemporaries, Hiroshige III seems to revel in the novelties of his time, which he brings to life using the new aniline colours, with their harsh, strident tones. He seems fascinated with railways (the first line built in Japan ran between Tokyo and Yokohama) and the foreigners living in Yokohama after 1868. He liked to depict them enjoying themselves, especially in restaurants.

HIROTAKA, real name: Kose no Hirotaka, artist name Hirochika or Hirosane
Japanese, 11th century.
Active c. 1000.
Painter. Figures, landscapes.

Kose no Hirotaka, a descendant of Kose no Kanaoka (active late 9th century), was appointed head of the e-dokoro, the bureau of painting of the imperial court. He painted many works, both secular and religious, but nothing has come down to us. From written sources we may surmise that the depiction of the Japanese landscape and important people attained a maturity of style in his time that corresponded to the tastes of the aristocracy. One of the most eloquent testimonials to this flowering is the interior of the Phoenix Hall (Hoodo) of the Byodoin in Nara, which was built in 1053, and which gives an idea of what might have been Hirotaka's style, and that of his contemporaries.

HIROU, Ernest Marie, or Hiron
French, 19th century.
Born 5 January 1850, in Paris; died December 1900, in Paris.
Sculptor.

Ernest Hirou was a pupil of Aimé Millet and Bastet, and was a member of the Société des Artistes Français. He was awarded an honourable mention at the Salon of 1889 and won a bronze medal at the Exposition Universelle.

Museums and Galleries:
Abbeville: *Admiral Courbet; François de Poilly* - Le Mans: *Olivier Heuzé; The Republic; Maxime Echivard.*

HIROU, Jeanne
French, 19th century.
Born in the 19th century, in Paris.
Sculptor.

Jeanne Hirou exhibited at the Salon des Artistes Français and received received an honourable mention in 1886.

HIROYUKI, real name: Sumiyoshi Hiroyuki; court name: Naiki; artist name: Keikin en
Japanese, 18th - 19th century.
Born 1755; died 1811.
Painter.

The son of Keishu (1729-1797), Hiroyuki was adopted by Sumiyoshi Hiromori, the founder of the Sumiyoshi School, and became his disciple. A great specialist in ancient Japanese painting, he devoted himself to genre painting in the service of the Tokugawa government.

HIRSCH
French, 18th century.
Miniaturist. Portraits.

Museums and Galleries:
Valenciennes: *Portrait of Monsieur Charles de Berlaimont.*

HIRSCH, Albert
French, 20th century.
Born 25 February 1940, in Garches.
Sculptor.

Albert Hirsch was a pupil at the École des Arts Appliqués in Paris from 1958 to 1963. He produces elegant forms in bronze. He lives and works in the Somme region.

Hirsch participated in collective exhibitions including: Salon de la Jeune Sculpture, Paris (from 1969 to 1972); Salon des Grands et Jeunes d'Aujourd'hui and FIAC (Foire Internationale d'Art Contemporain), both in Paris (1981); Maison des Arts et Loisirs, Laon (1982). He has held solo exhibits in Paris since 1978.

HIRSCH, Alphonse
French, 19th century.
Born 1843, in Paris; died 18 July 1884, in Paris.
Painter. Portraits, genre scenes.

Alphonse Hirsch was a pupil of Bonnat. His work appeared at the Salon from 1869 to 1882.

Stamp of sale

Museums and Galleries:
Troyes: *Study of a Head.*

Auction records:
New York, 24 May 1989, *The Camando Children in the Winter Garden of their Private Mansion* (1875, oil on canvas, 45 x 57 1/2 ins / 114 x 146 cm) USD 55,000. London, 15 June 1994, *A Young Beauty* (oil on panel, 10 1/4 x 6 1/4 ins / 26 x 16 cm) GBP 4,370.

HIRSCH, Auguste Alexandre
French, 19th - 20th century.
Born 8 July 1833, in Lyons; died December 1912, in Paris.
Painter, lithographer.

Auguste Hirsch was a pupil of V. Vibert at the École des Beaux-Arts in Lyons (1851-1854), and of H. Flandrin and Gleyre at the École des Beaux-Arts in Paris which he entered in 1856. He made his début in Paris in 1857 with a drawing, *Moses,* and lithographs. From then, he exhibited, both in Paris and Lyons, history and genre paintings, portraits, figures and scenes from Morocco (paintings and watercolours), and drawings and watercolours after the Old Masters. Among the works he showed in Paris are: *Child Playing with a Lizard* (1861); *The Sacrifice of Abraham* (1869); *Jewesses of Oran* (1874); *Return of the Hadjis (Pilgrims)* (1880); *Country Dance* (1866); *Religious Instruction in Morocco* and *Idyll; Dauphiné* (1889, 3rd class medal); *The Feast of Carlina* (1891); *In Provence, from the Time of Caesar* (1985); *Pastoral* (1899); *Gathering the Lemons* (1906); *The Rebuffed Nest* (1909). He received an honourable mention, a bronze medal at the 1889 and 1900 Expositions Universelles and a gold in 1889. In Lyons, in 1877, he painted the ceiling of the Célestins theatre. He made lithographs mostly after H. Flandrin (*Mater Dolorosa, Saint Clair Healing the Blind,* and portraits).

MUSEUMS AND GALLERIES:

LYONS: *Rebecca* (1882) - MULHOUSE: *Portrait of Jean Zuber* - PÉRIGUEUX: *Calliope Teaching Music to Orpheus.*

AUCTION RECORDS:

LONDON, 20 June 1984, *The Return of the Hadji (Pilgrim)* (oil on canvas, 38 1/4 x 28 1/4 ins / 97 x 72 cm) GBP 13,000.

HIRSCH, C.

German, 18th century.
Miniaturist.

HIRSCH, Émile

French, 19th century.
Born in the 19th century, in Metz.
Painter.

Émile Hirsch entered the École des Beaux-Arts on 8 April 1852, where he received his artistic training from Eugène Delacroix and Hippolyte Flandrin. He exhibited portraits and designs for stained-glass windows for churches at the Paris Salon, from 1852 to 1900.

HIRSCH, G. V.

Dutch, 16th - 17th century.
Painter. History painting.

G. V. Hirsch was a painter of the Rembrandt School.

MUSEUMS AND GALLERIES:

BAYEUX: *The Flight into Egypt.*

HIRSCH, Gustav

German, 19th century.
Born 27 September 1867, in Hanover.
Painter, illustrator. Landscapes.

Gustav Hirsch studied at the Munich academy of art.

HIRSCH, Herman

German, 19th century.
Born 1806; died 1834, in Munich.
Active in Sulzbach.
Landscape artist.

HIRSCH, Hermann

German, 19th - 20th century.
Born 4 June 1861, in Rheydt, near Düsseldorf; died 1934.
Painter. Landscapes.

Hermann Hirsch studied at the Berlin academy.

AUCTION RECORDS:

LONDON, 6 Oct 1989, *In the Open Air* (1898, oil on card, 12 1/4 x 16 1/4 ins / 31 x 41 cm) GBP 6,600. AMSTERDAM, 21 Sept 1999, *Jacob Blessing the Sons of Joseph* (1923, oil on canvas, 67 x 79 ins / 170 x 200 cm) NLG 3,800.

HIRSCH, Joseph

American, 20th century.
Born 1910; died 1981.
Painter (gouache), watercolourist. Figures, nudes, genre scenes.

Joseph Hirsch often painted scenes showing theatrical performances, the circus, concerts or figures at the beach.

AUCTION RECORDS:

WASHINGTON DC, 6 June 1976, *Clown's Lunch* (gouache, 19 x 26 ins / 48.5 x 66 cm) USD 2,000. NEW YORK, 20 April 1979, *Lunch Counter* (1941, oil on canvas, 15 3/4 x 38 ins / 40 x 96.5 cm) USD 9,500. NEW YORK, 29 May 1981, *Four Artists* (oil on canvas, 35 x 51 ins / 89 x 129.5 cm) USD 18,000. NEW YORK, 6 Dec 1984, *Juggler* (oil on canvas, 38 x 22 ins / 96.5 x 55.9 cm) USD 16,000. NEW YORK, 4 Dec 1986, *Supper* (1963-1965, oil on canvas, 66 x 85 ins / 167.7 x 215.9 cm) USD 18,000. NEW YORK, 4 Dec 1987, *Reflecting Policeman* (oil on canvas, 18 x 14 1/4 ins / 46 x 36 cm) USD 4,000. NEW YORK, 26 May 1988, *Bathers* (oil on canvas, 35 x 40 1/4 ins / 89 x 102 cm) USD 8,800. NEW YORK, 1 Dec 1988, *Girl Juggler* (oil on canvas, 38 x 22 ins / 96.5 x 55.9 cm) USD 18,700. NEW YORK, 24 May 1989, *Allegory* (oil on canvas, 56 x 60 ins / 142.2 x 152.3 cm) USD 24,200. NEW YORK, 30 May 1990, *Pomona* (oil on canvas, 30 x 24 ins / 76.3 x 61 cm) USD 7,700. NEW YORK, 26 Sept 1990, *Sextet* (1965, oil on canvas, 14 x 20 ins / 35.5 x 50.8 cm) USD 10,450. NEW YORK, 27 Sept 1990, *Persuasion* (1937, oil/synthetic resin, 25 1/2 x 36 1/4 ins / 65 x 92 cm) USD 15,400. NEW YORK, 14 March 1991, *Chef* (oil on canvas, 25 1/2 x 18 ins / 65 x 46 cm) USD 2,860. NEW YORK, 14 Nov 1991, *Beach with Figures* (watercolour/paper, 11 x 15 1/2 ins / 27.9 x 39.3 cm) USD 660. NEW YORK, 23 Sept 1992, *The Nickel* (oil on canvas, 25 1/4 x 12 ins / 64.4 x 30.5 cm) USD 3,520. NEW YORK, 11 March 1993, *Nude and Picture Book* (oil on canvas, 23 1/2 x 28 3/4 ins / 60 x 73 cm) USD 17,250. NEW YORK, 9 Sept 1993, *Francis and the Bird* (1979, oil on canvas, 27 x 19 ins / 68.6 x 48.3 cm) USD 3,450. NEW YORK, 29 Nov 1995, *Man Drinking Milk* (1963, oil on canvas, 11 x 14 ins / 27.9 x 35.6 cm) USD 6,325. NEW YORK, 25 March 1997, *Woman with Grapes, Vendor* (1952, oil/linen, 36 1/2 x 23 3/4 ins / 92.4 x 60.3 cm) USD 4,887. NEW YORK, 15 June 2000, *Portrait of William Benton* (1959, oil on canvas, 20 x 16 ins / 51 x 41 cm) USD 2,000. DALLAS, 28 Oct 2000, *Grading the Harvest* (oil on canvasboard, 26 x 42 ins / 66 x 107 cm) USD 9,000. PHILADELPHIA, 24 June 2001, *Couple in Blue* (oil on canvas) USD 4,500. FLORIDA, 18 March 2003, *Kites on the Levee* (acrylic, 17 x 25 ins / 43 x 64 cm) USD 1,700. NEW YORK, 10 May 2003, *Men Pausing From Excavation work* (1940, oil on canvas, 25 x 11 ins / 64 x 28 cm) USD 3,750. PHILADELPHIA, 27 June 2004, *Wrestlers* (1932, oil on canvas, 16 x 20 ins / 41 x 51 cm) USD 17,000. MILFORD, 21 Oct 2004, *Bubble at Breakfast* (1979, oil on canvas, 17 x 20 ins / 43 x 51 cm) USD 3,000.

HIRSCH, Karl Jakob

German, 20th century.
Born 13 November 1892, in Hanover.
Painter, engraver.

Karl Hirsch studied in Munich, Berlin and Paris. After World War I, he was part of the Expressionist movement in Germany.

HIRSCH, Martin

German, 17th century.
Active in Waldsassen.
Sculptor.

Martin Hirsch decorated the church at Waldsassen.

HIRSCH, Peter

German, 20th century.
Born 24 August 1889, in Munich.
Painter. Religious subjects, portraits.

Peter Hirsch originally studied drawing and engraving at the Munich academy.

HIRSCH, Stefan
American, 20th century.
Born 1899; died 1964.
Painter.
Stefan Hirsch studied under Hamilton Easter Field.
AUCTION RECORDS:
NEW YORK, 30 Nov 1989, *Plants and Towers* (1920, oil on canvas, 19¾ x 16 ins / 50.2 x 40.6 cm) USD 39,600. NEW YORK, 22 Sept 1993, *Portrait of Aline Meyer Liebman* (1927, oil on card, 19¼ x 17 ins / 49 x 43 cm) USD 1,093.

HIRSCH, Suzanne
French, 20th century.
Born in Paris.
Painter.
Suzanne Hirsch exhibited in Paris at the Salon des Indépendants from 1924.

HIRSCH-RADO, Nelly
Hungarian, 19th - 20th century.
Born 22 May 1872, in Budapest; died 30 July 1915, in Vienna.
Painter, illustrator. Portraits.

HIRSCHAUTER, Joseph
Austrian, 19th century.
Born 6 May 1801, in Vienna; died 26 April 1859, in Vienna.
Sculptor.
Joseph Hirschauter, in addition to his decorative sculptures, also executed busts and statuettes.

HIRSCHBERG, Alice
Maiden name: Kerr Nelson
American, 19th century.
Born 12 February 1852, in England; died 1930.
Active in Buffalo (New York).
Painter.
Alice Hirschberg was the wife of the painter Carl Hirschberg. She studied in London and Paris, and settled in America in 1884.

HIRSCHBERG, Carl
American, 19th - 20th century.
Born 8 March 1854, in Berlin; died May 1923, in Danbury (Connecticut).
Painter.
Carl Hirschberg moved to New York at the age of six and began his studies there. He also studied under Cabanel at the École des Beaux-Arts in Paris.
AUCTION RECORDS:
NEW YORK, 25 Sept 1992, *Veteran* (1893, oil on canvas, 44 x 35 ins / 111.8 x 88.9 cm) USD 6,600.

HIRSCHBÜHL, Ludwig
Swiss, 20th century.
Born c. 1880, in Coire.
Painter.
Ludwig Hirschbühl was an officer in the Pope's Swiss Guards. He painted portraits in Rome.

HIRSCHEL, Abraham
Polish, 18th - 19th century.
Born 1764, in Kalisz; died 1836, in Kalisz.
Miniaturist.
Abraham Hirschel studied in Germany. He settled in Danzig (now Gdansk) where he painted many portrait miniatures. In 1804, he returned to Kalisz, where he continued working as a painter.

HIRSCHEL, Caspar, or Hirscheli
German, 18th century.
Born c. 1698, in Prague; died 15 January 1743, in Prague.
Painter. Flowers, fruit.
Hirschel studied under Angermayer.
MUSEUMS AND GALLERIES:
OBERSCHLEISSHEIM (Neues Schloss Schleissheim, Staatsgal.): several works.
AUCTION RECORDS:
VERSAILLES, 16 June 1971, *Bouquet in a Glass Vase*, FRF 7,000. PARIS, 5 Dec 1978, *Flowers in a Crystal Vase; Bouquet of Flowers in a Crystal Vase* (painting/wood, a pair, 13½ x 9¼ ins / 34 x 23.5 cm each) FRF 150,000. ZURICH, 16 May 1980, *Still-life with Fowl* (painting/metal, a pair, 8¾ x 6 ins / 22.2 x 15.5 cm) CHF 5,200.

HIRSCHFELD, Al
American, 20th century.
Born 21 June 1903, in St Louis (Missouri); died 20 January 2003, in New York.
Caricaturist, newspaper cartoonist, lithographer.
Al Hirschfeld studied drawing at the Art Students League, New York. Fascinated by the theatre from an early age, he started working for Goldwyn Pictures at the age of seventeen, making posters and portraits of comedians such as Laurel and Hardy, and Buster Keaton. He then started his own business, which went bankrupt, and was taken on by Warner Brothers. He happened to do a sketch of French actor Sacha Guitry in performance and it was published on the theatre page of the New York Herald Tribune, launching his career. Shortly afterwards he was contacted by the *New York Times* and offered a job for the theatre pages on an exclusive basis. During the 1930s he travelled to the Far East, where he discovered classical Japanese woodcuts (Hokusai, Utamaro, Harunobu). Although he experimented with solid black planes during the 1930s and 1940s, his style tended towards a purity of line, as can be seen in his numerous pictures of show business subjects, for example, the theatre, the cinema, rehearsals and portraits of all the great actors and characters of stage and screen. Dubbed the 'Fred Astaire of pen and ink', Hirschfeld lived through 1930s Broadway but also painted and drew political cartoons. Another Hirschfeld gesture, one that will probably go down in history, became known as the Nina Game. In 1945 his daughter Nina was born, and in celebration he hid the letters NINA in one of his drawings. For years after that, he would hide the same letters in his drawings and the practice became a game of hide-and-seek between himself and hundreds of thousands of his readers.
BIBLIOGRAPHY:
Hirschfeld, Al, *Hirschfeld: Art and Recollections from Eight Decades*, Prentice Hall and IBD, 1991. Hirschfeld, Al, *Hirschfeld on Line*, autobiography, Applause Theatre Book Pub, New York, 1998. Bell, Clare/Rich, Frank, *Hirschfeld's New York*, N. Abrams Inc, 2001 (illustrated by Al Hirschfeld). Leopold, David, *Hirschfeld's Hollywood: The Film Art of Al Hirschfeld*, N. Abrams Inc, 2001 (illustrated by Al Hirschfeld). Hirschfeld, Al, *Hirschfeld's Harlem*, Applause Theatre Book Publications, 2003. Hirschfeld, Al/Kahn, Gordon, *The Speakeasies of 1932*, Applause Theatre Book Publications, 2003.
AUCTION RECORDS:
NEW YORK, 24 Jan 1990, *The World of Suzie Wong* (ink on card, 21¾ x 28 ins / 55.4 x 71.1 cm) USD 2,200. NEW YORK, 17 Nov 1999, *Keystone Kops* (pen and ink, 11 x 22 ins / 29 x 57 cm) USD 8,500. NEW YORK, 17 Nov 1999, *Fiddler on the Roof* (pen and ink, 17 x 26 ins / 44 x 67 cm) USD 9,000. NEW YORK, 5 May 2001, *Charles De Gaulle Defending Himself Against the Brits* (gouache, 19 x 15 ins / 48 x 38 cm) USD 4,250. NEW YORK, 10 Nov 2001, *Couple Watch Christian Samurai Cut Off his Hair, Battle in Background* (pen and ink, 20 x 21 ins / 51 x 53 cm) USD 4,250. NEW YORK, 9 Nov 2002, *Writer Pauses Outside of Broadway Theatres* (pen, ink, wash and grisaille, 13 x 13 ins / 33 x 33 cm) USD 4,000. NEW YORK, 9 Nov 2002, *Katherine Hepburn and Sir Laurence*

Olivier with Emmy Award (pen and ink, 23 x 20 ins / 58 x 51 cm) USD 5,500. NEW YORK, 25 Sept 2003, *TV Totem Pole, Lucille Ball, Desi Arnaz, J. Gleason, J. Webb and Groucho Marx* (gouache and board, 21 x 16 ins / 53 x 41 cm) USD 28,000. NEW YORK, 25 Sept 2003, *Broadway at Night, Broadway on a Saturday Night* (pen, ink and blue watercolour heightened with gouache on board, 10 x 20 ins / 25 x 51 cm) USD 30,000. NEW YORK, 10 June 2004, *Spencer and Kate* (etching, 15 x 15 ins / 38 x 38 cm) USD 21,000. NEW YORK, 10 June 2004, *Katharine Hepburn and Spencer Tracy* (etching, 22 x 18 ins / 56 x 46 cm) USD 27,000.

HIRSCHFELD, Emil Benediktov
Ukrainian, 19th - 20th century.
Born 1867, in Odessa; died October 1922, in Concarneau, France.
Active in France.
Painter. Seascapes.

Emil Hirschfeld studied in Paris with William Bouguereau, Jules Lefebvre and Tony Robert-Fleury. He specialised in painting seascapes, mainly in Brittany and almost always of the port of Concarneau. He was particularly interested in the unusual effects of light at night, in moonlight and in the setting sun.

He exhibited regularly at the Salon des Artistes Français in Paris. He received an honourable mention (1892), a third class medal (1894) and a silver medal at the 1900 Exposition Universelle. He was awarded the Légion d'Honneur (1910).

AUCTION RECORDS:
PARIS, 7 May 1903, *Concarneau by Night*, FRF 85. PARIS, 21 Jan 1928, *Fishing Boats at Low Tide*, FRF 300. PARIS, 13 May 1942, *Port of Concarneau*, FRF 450. BREST, 18 May 1980, *View of the Sea near Concarneau* (oil on canvas, 12 1/2 x 17 3/4 ins / 32 x 45 cm) FRF 5,000. LORIENT, 27 June 1987, *Tuna Boats at the Passage-Lanriec, Concarneau* (oil on canvas, 22 3/4 x 31 1/4 ins / 58 x 79.5 cm) FRF 34,000. PARIS, 17 Feb 1988, *Sailing Boats by moonlight* (oil on canvas, 21 1/4 x 28 3/4 ins / 54 x 73 cm) FRF 11,000; *Sailing Boats at Sunset* (oil on canvas, 13 x 25 1/2 ins / 33 x 65 cm) FRF 8,000. PARIS, 27 Nov 1989, *Sketch for a View of the Port by Moonlight* (oil on canvas, 18 x 22 ins / 46 x 55 cm) FRF 15,500. AMSTERDAM, 30 Oct 1991, *Blessing the Catch* (oil on canvas, 64 1/2 x 90 1/2 ins / 164 x 230 cm) NLG 8,625. PARIS, 1 July 1992, *Tied-Up Sailing Boats* (oil on canvas, 13 x 16 1/4 ins / 33 x 41 cm) FRF 10,000. BREST, 19 Dec 1999, *Operations before Going to Sea* (oil on canvas, 21 x 28 ins / 53 x 72 cm) FRF 10,800.

HIRSCHFELD, Jules
French, 19th century.
Born 26 January 1866, in Sète.
Sculptor.

Hirschfeld studied under Bouguereau and A. Clerget.

MUSEUMS AND GALLERIES:
SÈTE: *Fantasy*.

HIRSCHFELD-MACK, Ludwig
German, 20th century.
Born 1893, in Frankfurt am Main; died 1965, in Sydney, Australia.
Active from 1940 in Australia.
Painter, engraver, sculptor.
Lumino-Kinetic Art.

In 1919, Ludwig Hirschfeld-Mack was a pupil of Adolf Hölzel at the Stuttgart academy. From 1920 to 1925, he was a student at the Bauhaus in Weimar, while working in the engraving studio. In 1926 and 1927, he was director of the *Vorkurs*, a preliminary course for the Bauhaus. From 1927 to 1935, he taught in various cities in Germany, then from 1935 to 1940 in England, and finally, from 1940 onwards in Australia, on a course concentrating mainly on materials.

It was at the Bauhaus in 1922-1923 that he created, with Kurt Schwendtfeger, the 'Reflektorische Lichtspiele' (Play of Reflections and Light), and in 1924 the 'Farbenlichtspiele' (Play of Coloured Light). These were shows based on projecting moving coloured lights in simple geometric shapes, accompanied by music, which at the time were well ahead of activities that would not become widespread until around 1970.

BIBLIOGRAPHY:
Popper, Frank, *Naissance de l'Art cinétique*, Gauthier-Villars, Paris, 1967. Leymarie, Jean/Herzogenrath, Wulf/Grote, Ludwig/Gropius, Walter, *Le Bauhaus*, exhibition catalogue, Württembergischer Kunsteverein, Stuttgart, Musée national d'Art moderne, Paris, 1969. Hapkemeyer, Andreas/Kent, Rachel/Sabin, Stefana/Stasny, Peter, *Ludwig Hirschfeld-Mack. Bauhäusler und Visionär*, Hatje Cantz, Ostfildern, 2000.

HIRSCHFELDER, Salomon
German, 19th century.
Born 16 May 1832, in Dettensee; died 10 May 1903, in Munich.
Painter. Genre scenes.

Hirschfelder was a student at the academy of art in Munich where he lived from 1853. He exhibited in Vienna and Munich from 1873.

MUSEUMS AND GALLERIES:
STUTTGART: *Office Table*.

AUCTION RECORDS:
ZURICH, 28 May 1976, *Checking the Bread* (1876, oil on canvas, 30 1/2 x 38 1/2 ins / 77.5 x 97.5 cm) CHF 15,000. NEW YORK, 30 May 1980, *Children's Games* (1872, oil on canvas, 25 1/2 x 20 1/2 ins / 64.5 x 52.1 cm) USD 10,000.

HIRSCHFIELD, Morris
Polish, 20th century.
Born 1872, in Poland; died 1946, in New York.
From 1890 active and naturalised in the USA.
Painter. Figures, animals.

As a small boy in Poland, Morris Hirschfield began to carve and paint from an early age. He carved, painted and gilded wooden statues of Esther, Xerxes and Aman and made a lectern formed by two lions supporting the Tablets of the Law for the synagogue of his village. He then worked as a dressmaker and tailor. When he arrived in New York, he opened a clothes shop and later ran a business making ladies' shoes. A long period of ill-health forced him to give up his commercial activities in 1937, but he began painting again in his room in Brooklyn. In 1939, he was discovered by Sidney Janis, the American specialist in naive art, who began to show Hirschfield's work. That same year, his first paintings were exhibited at *Unknown American Painters* and in 1946, the Museum of Modern Art in New York held a retrospective devoted to his work. The Surrealists who had taken refuge in the USA during the World War II discovered Hirschfield and saw him as one of the most important artists since Le Douanier Rousseau.

Morris Hirschfield was one of the major figures in naive American painting, although the description 'naive' does not take account of developments in his work in the last nine years of his life. His first two paintings, *Girl on a Beach* and *Angora Cat*, were produced in 1937. They were taken from pictures he had bought and to which he added a landscape background. By 1939, his technique had improved and he went on to paint 72 ever larger and more complex canvases, using the bright colours of folk art. Most of his works depict figures or animals against highly simplified backgrounds, their hieratic appearance endowing the works with a symbolic quality. His figures were mainly female at first, alone, or with a female friend or sometimes reflected in a mirror, in the nude or glamorously dressed in short skirts and evoking, though ill-proportioned, the disjointed mannequins in a shop window and the primitive erotic fascination of the stereotypical magazine pin-up with veiled references to Egyptian archaeology. When he began to paint animals he portrayed leopards, tigers and panthers, on their own or in groups, against stylised backgrounds of vegetation emphasising the hieratic and heraldic appearance of the animals. Recalling his childhood, he painted a number of snowy landscapes criss-crossed by sledges. Unusually, he depicted himself with one of his muses in *The Painter and his Model* (1945).

The rich texture of the multiple patches of colour in Hirschfield's work, his manner of painting hair, fur, tufts of grass, clouds or a woman's skin with minuscule brush-strokes juxtaposed in parallel or crossing over one another constantly call to mind the appearance of the woven fabrics with which he worked for so much of his life.

Bibliography:

Bihalji-Merin, Oto, *Peinture naïve*, Delpire, Paris.

Museums and Galleries:

New York (MoMA): *Tiger* (1940); *Girl before a Mirror* (1940) - Venice (Collezione Peggy Guggenheim): *Two Women before a Mirror* (1943).

Auction records:

New York, 12 Dec 1968, *Girl and Dog*, USD 18,000. New York, 30 May 1985, *Baby Elephant with Boy* (1943, oil on canvas, 32 x 44 ins / 81.3 x 111.7 cm) USD 30,000.

HIRSCHHORN, Thomas

Swiss, 20th - 21st century.
Born 1957, in Bern.
Active since 1984 in France.
Painter, assemblage artist, installation artist.
Neo-Conceptual Art.

Hirschhorn trained as a graphic designer. He lives and works in Paris. In 2001, he won the Prix Marcel Duchamp in Paris. Hirschhorn assembles elements salvaged at random, which he displays for their meaning and with no regard for any aesthetic consideration. In particular, he occupies space with protuberances of aluminium foil, which hang from the ceiling and emerge from the ground, portraying a place reminiscent of a grotto. His works highlight and reappraise the everyday object. In 1995, the Centre Genevois de Gravure Contemporaine published an illustrated book, which included several of his works, including press photographs accompanied with a caption, courtesy of Hirschhorn, and glued onto a piece of cardboard. In 2000, Hirschhorn had built a *Monument to Gilles Deleuze* at the bottom of an HLM block (habitation à loyer modéré: low rent housing), in a district of Avignon regarded as deprived.

Hirschhorn has participated in group exhibitions in Paris, Berlin and Cologne, notably 1997, *Skulptur. Projekte in Münster 1997* (*Sculpture. Projects in Münster 1997*); 2003, *Common Wealth*, Tate Modern, London; 2003, *L'État des Choses* (*The State of Things*), an exhibition which examined the status of the everyday object in contemporary art, held on the occasion of *Trésors Publics, 20 Ans de Création dans les Fonds Régionaux d'Art Contemporain (FRAC)* (*Public Treasury, 20 Years of Creation in the Regional Collection of Contemporary Art (FRAC)*), held at the Musée des Beaux-Arts, Nantes. He has held solo shows: 1994, the Galerie Nationale du Jeu de Paume, Paris; 1997, the Galerie Chantal Crousel, Paris; 1997, a mobile installation in a Burger King in Bordeaux; an appartment and later a shopping centre, at the Kunsthof in Zurich; 2000, the Art Institute, Chicago; 2001, an installation at the Centre Georges-Pompidou, Paris.

Bibliography:

David, Catherine, *Thomas Hirschhorn*, exhibition catalogue, Gal. nationale du Jeu de Paume, Paris, 1994. Rondeau, James/Ghez, Susanne/Walker, Hamza/Enwezor, Okwui, *Thomas Hirschhorn, Jumbo Spoons and Big Cake*, exhibition catalogue, The Art Institute, Chicago, 2000. Zahm, Olivier (preface), et al., *Trésors publics, 20 ans de création dans les Fonds régionaux d'art contemporain*, Flammarion, Paris, 2003 (text in French and English).

Museums and Galleries:

Marseilles (FRAC Provence-Alpes-Côte d'Azur): *Éponges* (1989-1990); *For Reto Fleury* - Paris (FNAC): *Untitled* (1988-1989) - Paris (MNAM-CCI): *Skulptur Sortier Station* (1997) - Villeneuve d'Ascq (MAM Lille Métropole): *Direct Sculpture* (1997).

HIRSCHING, August

German, 20th century.
Born 29 September 1889, in Unterheimbach (Württemberg).
Painter.

August Hirsching studied in Stuttgart and was advised by Karl Schmoll von Eisenwerth. He was active in Alsace for many years.

HIRSCHLER, Eduard

Austrian, 19th century.
Born 13 June 1828, in Vienna; died 9 June 1891, in Vienna.
Painter.

Eduard Hirschler studied under Hartinger and Wegmayr, and at the Akademie der bildenden Künste in Vienna. He is best known for his flower and fruit paintings.

HIRSCHLER-KUNWALD, Ernestine

German, 19th century.
Born c. 1843, in Munich; died 8 January 1904, in Weimar.
Painter. Genre scenes.

Hirschler-Kunwald exhibited in Berlin and Dresden from about 1888. In 1891, she settled in Weimar.

HIRSCHMANN, Andreas, the Elder

German, 18th century.
Born 1700, in Nuremberg; died 28 August 1759, in Nuremberg.
Draughtsman.

Andreas Hirschmann the Elder was a draughtsman and an engraver.

HIRSCHMANN, Andreas, the Younger

German, 18th century.
Born 1729, in Burgkundstadt.
Active in Bamberg (Bavaria), Germany.
Painter. Portraits.

Andreas Hirschmann the Younger was the father of Johann Baptist Hirschmann.

HIRSCHMANN, Johann, or Hirsman

German, 18th century.
Active in Bamberg (Bavaria), Germany.
Portrait painter.

Johann Hirschmann was a member of the Guild in The Hague in 1790.

HIRSCHMANN, Johann Baptist

German, 18th century.
Born 1770, in Bamberg.
Painter, pastellist, miniaturist.

A son of Andreas Hirschmann the Younger, it is highly probably that Johann Baptist Hirschmann is the artist mentioned by Dr Von Wurzbach under the name of Johann Hirschmann, born in Bamberg, and who entered the Guild of Painters in The Hague in 1790.

Auction records:

Amsterdam, 15 Nov 1994, *Portraits of a Lady and a Gentlemen* (1790, pastel, oval, a pair, 12 1/2 x 10 1/4 ins / 32 x 26 cm and 11 1/2 x 9 1/4 ins/29.5 x 23.5 cm) NLG 1,610.

HIRSCHMANN, Johann Hyeronimus
German, 18th century.
Born 1708, in Nuremberg; died 1765, in Berlin.
Landscape artist.

Johann Hyeronimus Hirschmann, a pupil of Ermels and Bemmel, worked initially in Regensburg, before moving on to settle in Berlin in 1731. He was the son of Johann Leonhard Hirschmann.

HIRSCHMANN, Johann Leonhard
German, 17th - 18th century.
Born 1 November 1672, in Nuremberg; died 13 November 1750, in Nuremberg.
Painter. Historical portraits.

MUSEUMS AND GALLERIES:
LONDON (National Portrait Gal.): *Sophia Dorothea, Queen of Prussia* (c. 1706, oil/copper, medallion, after J. L. Hirschmann).

AUCTION RECORDS:
COLOGNE, 23 Nov 1978, *Children's Party* (oil on canvas, 35 x 45 ins / 89 x 114 cm) DEM 9,500.

HIRSCHMANN, Sigmund Leonhard
German, 17th century.
Active in Frankfurt c. 1670.
Engraver (mezzotint).

HIRSCHMANN, Thomas
German, 17th century.
Active in Nuremberg in 1690.
Engraver (burin).

Thomas Hirschmann, the father of Johann Leonhard Hirschmann, engraved mostly portraits.

HIRSCHVOGEL, Augustin, or Hirssfogel
German, 16th century.
Born c. 1503, in Nuremberg; died 1553, in Vienna.
Painter (enamel), engraver (copper/etching). Figures, scenes with figures, landscapes, architectural views.

Augustin Hirschvogel received his earliest teaching from his father Veit Hirschvogel the Elder, a glass painter. As well as glass painting, Augustin studied painting on enamel, wood engraving, pottery, letters and the sciences. He spent some time in Vienna. His landscape etchings are remarkable.

In 2003 his work was included in the exhibition *Les Dieux comme les Hommes. Gravures rhénanes du XVIè siècle* (*Gods as Men: Rhenish Engravings of the 16th Century*), which showed the collections held by the Print and Drawing Collection of the Musée des Beaux-Arts in Strasbourg.

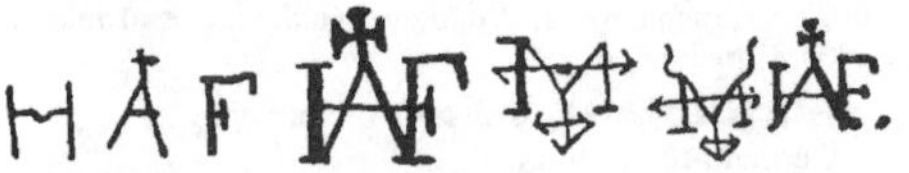

BIBLIOGRAPHY:
La Gravure allemande à la Renaissance, group exhibition catalogue, Musée des Beaux-Arts, Caen, 1999. Schefer, Jean Louis/Haus, Anny-Claire/Hergott, Fabrice (preface), et al., *Les Dieux comme les Hommes. Gravures rhénanes du XVIe siècle*, group exhibition catalogue, Musée des Beaux-Arts, Strasbourg, 2003. Jover, Manuel, *'Les Petits Maîtres de Nuremberg'* in *L'Œil* n° 544, periodical, Paris, February 2003.

MUSEUMS AND GALLERIES:
BUDAPEST: *Portrait of a Man and a Woman* - CONSTANCE: *Landscape* - STRASBOURG (MBA, Prints Collection): *Master of the Horses' Heads; Landscape with Fortified Castle; Nine Children Dancing and Making Music.*

AUCTION RECORDS:
LONDON, 7 Dec 1977, *Cleopatra in a Landscape* (etching, 4 x 6 ins / 10.1 x 15.4 cm) GBP 1,350. LONDON, 1 July 1980, *River Landscape with the Ruins of a Town and the Temptation of Christ* (etching, 3 3/4 x 7 ins / 9.8 x 17.5 cm) GBP 1,800. LONDON, 1 Dec 1981, *Landscape with the Conversion of St Paul* (etching, 4 x 10 ins / 10 x 25.4 cm) GBP 10,500. LONDON, 27 June 1984, *Coat of Arms of Lassla von Edlasperg* (engraving/copper, 11 x 7 1/4 ins / 28.1 x 18.6 cm) GBP 1,600. NEW YORK, 8 May 1985, *View of a Town by a River with Three Bridges* (1549, brown-black etching, 3 1/2 x 4 1/2 ins / 8.6 x 11.4 cm) USD 6,500. BERLIN, 26 Nov 1999, *Cleopatra Killing Herself with the Snake* (etching, 4 x 6 ins / 11 x 15 cm) DEM 7,000. BERN, 24 June 2000, *River Landscape with Town and Ruins and Temptation of Christ by the Devil* (etching) CHF 7,000. BERN, 24 June 2000, *River Landscape with Two Buildings by Water* (etching) CHF 19,000. LONDON, 6 Dec 2001, *View of Passau* (counterproof etching, 6 x 8 ins / 14 x 21 cm) GBP 7,500.

HIRSCHVOGEL, Jorg
German, 16th century.
Active in Nuremberg in 1509.
Painter.

HIRSCHVOGEL, Josias Sebald
German, 16th century.
Died in 1589.
Engraver.

Josias Sebald Hirschvogel was the nephew of Augustin Hirschvogel.

HIRSCHVOGEL, Veit, the Elder
German, 15th - 16th century.
Born 1461, in Nuremberg; died 24 December 1525, in Nuremberg.
Glass painter.
Nuremberg School.

HIRSCHVOGEL, Veit, the Younger
German, 16th century.
Born 1485, in Nuremberg; died 1553, in Nuremberg.
Glass painter.
Nuremberg School.

Veit Hirschvogel the Younger was the brother of Augustin Hirschvogel.

HIRSCHY, William
Swiss, 19th century.
Born 1838, in La Chaux-de-Fonds; died 5 May 1889.
Painter. Genre scenes.

MUSEUMS AND GALLERIES:
NEUCHÂTEL (MAH): *Head Study.*

HIRST, Claude Raguet
American, 19th - 20th century.
Born 1855; died 1942.
Painter. Still-lifes.

Claude Hirst specialised in still-lifes, often including identifiable books; he can be called a painter of portraits of books.

MUSEUMS AND GALLERIES:
COLUMBIA, MO (MAA, University of Missouri): *Still-life with Bowl (Lionel and Clarissa: A Comic Opera)* (c. 1890, oil on canvas).

AUCTION RECORDS:
NEW YORK, 2 Feb 1979, *German Poem* (oil on canvas, 7 x 9 ins / 17.8 x 22.9 cm) USD 8,000. NEW YORK, 29 Jan 1981, *Old Book* (oil on canvas, 7 x 9 ins / 17.8 x 22.8 cm) USD 8,750. NEW YORK, 28 Jan 1982, *My Favourite Satsuma* (watercolour, 8 1/2 x 10 1/2 ins / 21.5 x 26.6 cm) USD 3,500. NEW YORK, 23 March 1984, *Still-life with Books* (1939, oil on canvas, 20 x 24 ins / 50.8 x 61 cm) USD 2,600. NEW YORK, 21 Sept 1984, *Picture Book* (watercolour/mounted paper/card, 10 x 13 1/4 ins / 25.5 x 33.4 cm) USD 8,000. NEW YORK, 25 June 1986, *Book of Letters* (watercolour, 9 x 12 ins / 22.8 x 30.6 cm) USD 12,000. NEW YORK, 17 March 1988, *Still-life with Book and Candlestick* (watercolour/paper, 5 1/2 x 11 1/2 ins / 13.7 x 29.3 cm) USD 2,090. NEW YORK, 26 May 1988, *Poems of Oliver Goldsmith* (oil on canvas, 8 1/4 x 10 ins / 20.7 x 25.7 cm)

USD 26,400. NEW YORK, 28 Sept 1989, *Gentleman's Table* (oil on canvas, 18 x 32 ins / 45.7 x 81.2 cm) USD 44,000. NEW YORK, 27 Sept 1990, *Poems of William Cowper* (oil on canvas, 8 x 10 ins / 20.5 x 25.5 cm) USD 30,800. NEW YORK, 22 May 1991, *Some Interesting Books* (oil on canvas, 10 x 14 1/4 ins / 25.5 x 36 cm) USD 28,600. NEW YORK, 17 March 1994, *Still-life with Books and a Vase* (watercolour/paper, 10 x 8 ins / 25.4 x 20.3 cm) USD 10,350. NEW YORK, 21 Sept 1994, *Still-life with a Cup, a Jug and the Book 'Letters of Lord Chesterfield' on a Table* (oil on canvas, 8 x 10 ins / 20.3 x 25.4 cm) USD 23,000. NEW YORK, 14 Sept 1995, *German Poem* (oil on canvas, 7 x 9 ins / 17.8 x 22.9 cm) USD 23,000. NEW YORK, 9 March 1996, *Winter's Tale* (oil on canvas, 8 x 10 ins / 20.3 x 25.4 cm) USD 14,950. NEW YORK, 29 Sept 1999, *Book of British Classics* (oil on canvas, 9 x 12 ins / 23 x 30 cm) USD 15,000. NEW YORK, 1 Dec 1999, *Poem - The Pleasure of Memory* (oil on canvas, 8 x 10 ins / 20 x 25 cm) USD 42,500. MILFORD, 11 May 2000, *Chrysanthemums in Canton Jar* (oil on canvas, 16 x 12 ins / 41 x 30 cm) USD 7,750. NEW YORK, 30 Oct 2003, *Peaches on a Tabletop* (oil on canvas, 9 x 14 ins / 23 x 35 cm) USD 28,000.

HIRST, Damien
British, 20th - 21st century.
Born 7 June 1965, in Bristol.
Assemblage artist, installation artist, painter.
Conceptual Art, Young British Artists.

Damien Hirst studied at Goldsmiths College, London (1986-1989), and has been a leading figure in the Young British Artists Group of the 1990s. In 1988, Hirst curated the influential exhibition *Freeze*, which launched his career, along with that of a number of other young artists such as Mat Collishaw and Michael Landy. He was shortlisted for the Turner Prize in 1992, and won the Prize in 1995. In 1994, Hirst curated *Some Went Mad, Some Ran Away* at the Serpentine Gallery. Hirst has produced primarily three types of work, namely glass tank pieces, paintings and cabinet sculptures, often using media that challenges conventional ideas of high art and contemporary culture. He showed his greatest burst of creative work in the period of 1987 to 1997, when his work reflected changes in contemporary life. Following this period, he suffered from self-admitted substance-addiction problems, resulting in work which has been seen by some critics as repetitive and reductive, while others point to his successful exhibition at Gagosian Gallery in 2000 as evidence of continuing vitality. Much of his work has been made with the aid of assistants, causing some critics to question the validity of his authorship.

Hirst's work often deals with the processes of human existence, and society's unwillingness to cope with the idea of death. His *Natural History* series of dead animals preserved in formaldehyde included his best known work *The Physical Impossibility of Death in the Mind of Someone Living* (1991), a preserved tiger shark in a tank. This piece has become iconic, being much imitated and parodied in film and advertising, and was sold by the collector Saatchi to an American collector in 2005 for a reported sum of more than £6 million. Although Saatchi had purchased many pieces by Hirst, they had a falling-out in 2003, and Hirst bought back a number of his works. Some of his pieces remaining with Saatchi were destroyed in the warehouse fire of 24 May 2004. Another glass tank piece, *Away from the Flock*, was vandalised in 1993 by someone pouring black ink into the work. Many of these glass tank pieces have provoked shock and other strong emotions in viewers, such as his works involving pieces of animals, as in the flayed cow's head with maggots and flies, *A Thousand Years* (1989), or *Mother and Child Divided* (1993), which displayed a longitudinally bisected cow and calf.

In painting, Hirst has concentrated on his 'spot' and 'spin' works. The spot paintings are randomly spotted canvases with titles referring to pharmaceutical chemicals and narcotics, such as *Arachidic Acid* (1994). The spin paintings are created by using a spinning table to distribute the household gloss paint by centrifugal force, as in *Beautiful, Shattering, Slashing, Violent, Pinky, Hacking, Sphincter Painting* (1995). Hirst has also used the spinning technique to scratch copper plates for etchings, such as *Burning Wheel* (2002). He was commissioned to paint a simple colour pattern for calibrating cameras for the Beagle 2 space probe to Mars. In 2004, Hirst designed the cover for the *Band Aid 20* charity single recording.

Hirst's cabinet series consists of collections of items such as pill bottles or surgical tools displayed in an orderly manner on shelves. His theme of death continues in these works, such as *Forms without Life* (1986-1989), a cabinet of shells from Thailand, about which he has said, 'You kill things to look at them'.

Hirst has had solo exhibitions at *Internal Affairs*, Institute of Contemporary Arts, London (1991); *Pharmacy*, Cohen Gallery, New York (1992); *No Sense of Absolute Corruption*, Gagosian Gallery, New York (1996); and *Damien Hirst: Theories, Models, Methods, Approaches, Assumptions, Results and Findings*, Gagosian Gallery, London (2000). Other exhibitions include the Venice Biennale (1993); *New British Painting in the 1990s*, Museum of Modern Art, Oxford (1996); *Life/Live. La scène artistique au Royaume-Uni en 1996* (*Life/Live: The UK Art Scene in 1996*), Musée d'Art Moderne de la Ville de Paris (1996) *Un Siècle de Sculpture Anglaise* (*A Century of English Sculpture*), Galerie Nationale du Jeu de Paume, Paris (1996); *Collections Exhibitions: London/Screen*, Whitworth Art Gallery (1999-2000); *Hypermental*, Kunsthalle, Hamburg (2001); *Painting on the Move*, simultaneously at Kunstmuseum, Kunsthalle and Museum für Gegenwartskunst, Basel (2002); *The Dazzled Eye*, Whitworth Art Gallery, Manchester (2004); *Artists and Prints: Masterworks from the Museum of Modern Art*, Museum of Modern Art (2004-2005); and *Contemporary Voices: Works from the UBS Art Collection*, Museum of Modern Art, New York (2005).

BIBLIOGRAPHY:

Damien Hirst, exhibition catalogue, ICA/Jay Jopling, London, 1991. Bum, G. (ed.), *Damien Hirst: I Want to Spend the Rest of my Life Everywhere, with Everyone, One to One, Always, Forever, Now*, Monacelli Press, New York, 1997. *Damien Hirst: Theories, Models, Methods, Approaches, Assumptions, Results and Findings*, exhibition catalogue, Gagosian Gallery, London, 2000. *Damien Hirst: Pictures from the Saatchi Gallery, 28 Tablets*, exhibition catalogue, Booth-Clibborn Editions, London, 2001. Hirst, Damien/Burn, Gordon, *On the Way to Work*, illustrated book, Faber, London, 2001. Mendes Bürgi, Bernhard, et al., *Painting on the Move*, exhibition catalogue, Kunstmuseum, Kunsthalle, Museum für Gegenwartskunst, Basel, 2002.

MUSEUMS AND GALLERIES:

DUBLIN (Irish Museum of Modern Art): *Beautiful Soft Exploding Rainbow Painting* (2001, gloss household paint on canvas); *Untitled, London Portfolio* (1992, screenprint); *Acquired Inability to Escape* (1991, mixed media); *Breakthrough No. IV* (1973-1979/1980, mixed media) - LONDON (Tate Collection): *Forms without Life* (1991, installation); *London* (1992, set of 11 screenprints); *Pharmacy* (1992, installation); *The Last Supper* (1999, set of 13 screenprints) - LONDON (UK Government Art Collection): *Untitled (from London portfolio)* (1992, screenprint) - MANCHESTER (Whitworth Art Gallery): *Untitled* (1992, screenprint) - NEW YORK (MoMA): *Burning Wheel* (2002, etching).

AUCTION RECORDS:

LONDON, 22 May 1996, *Adrenochrome Semicarbazone Sulfonate* (1992, painting, household varnish/canvas, 65 x 75 ins / 165 x 190.5 cm) GBP 32,200. LONDON, 27 June 1996, *Abras Toxin* (1991, painting, household varnish/canvas, 45 1/2 x 31 3/4 ins / 115.5 x 80.5 cm) GBP 13,225. LONDON, 23 Oct 1996,

Ammonium Biborate (1993, varnish/canvas, 67 x 78¾ ins / 170 x 200 cm) GBP 36,700. NEW YORK, 7 May 1997, *Edge* (1988, wall painting, 85½ x 128¼ ins / 217.2 x 325.8 cm) USD 20,700. LONDON, 23 June 1997, *6-Bromo-4-Cyclohexene-1,2,3-Triol* (1996, household gloss paint/canvas, 1 x ½ ins / 2.5 x 1.3 cm) GBP 6,000. LONDON, 11 Dec 1997, *Anazolene Sodium* (gloss paint/canvas, 48 x 55 ins / 121 x 140 cm) GBP 43,300. NEW YORK, 16 Nov 1999, *My Way* (1990-1991, glass, steel, board, old drug bottles, 54 x 40x9 ins / 137 x 102x23 cm) USD 320,000. LONDON, 9 Dec 1999, *Untitled* (gloss house paint and butterflies on canvas, 99 x 98 ins / 251 x 248 cm) GBP 160,000. NEW YORK, 18 May 2000, *Out of Sight, Out of Mind* (glass, steel and two cows' heads in formaldehyde solution, in two parts, 18 x 33x18 ins / 46 x 84x46 cm) USD 500,000. NEW YORK, 13 Nov 2000, *In Love - Out of Love* (gloss household paint and butterflies on canvas, diptych, 48 x 96 ins / 121 x 244 cm) USD 680,000. LONDON, 7 Feb 2001, *Aminoantipyrine* (gloss household paint on canvas, 80 x 88 ins / 203 x 223 cm) GBP 200,000. NEW YORK, 14 May 2001, *Calcium Gluconate Injection* (1992, gloss household paint, 92 x 108 ins / 234 x 274 cm) USD 300,000. NEW YORK, 12 Nov 2002, *Beauty is in the Eye of the Beholder* (1998, butterflies and gloss household paint on canvas, ? x ? ins /? x ? cm) USD 480,000. NEW YORK, 13 Nov 2002, *Aicar Diphosphate* (1992, gloss household paint on canvas, 67 x 79 ins / 170 x 201 cm) USD 260,000. NEW YORK, 11 Nov 2003, *4-Chlororesorcinol - PFS* (1999, household gloss on canvas, four panels, 30 x 70 ins / 76 x 179 cm) USD 500,000. NEW YORK, 13 Nov 2003, *Something Solid Beneath the Surface of All Creatures Great and Small* (2001, animal skeletons in glass display unit, 81 x 148x48 ins / 205 x 376x122 cm) USD 1,050,000. NEW YORK, 13 May 2004, *We are Afraid of Nothing* (MDF, glass, steel, pharmaceutical drug containers, ladder, 72 x 108x12 ins / 183 x 274x30 cm) USD 950,000. NEW YORK, 9 Nov 2004, *Amodiaquin* (1993, gloss household paint on canvas, 82 x 78 ins / 208 x 198 cm) USD 750,000.

HIRST, Norman
British, 19th century.
Born 1 February 1862, in Liverpool.
Engraver (mezzotint).

HIRST, William
British, 18th century.
Active during the second half of the 18th century.
Draughtsman, engraver.
One of William Hirst's works is a *View of the Cape of Good Hope*.

HIRSZEL, Abraham. See **HIRSCHEL**

HIRSZENBERG, Samuel
Polish, 19th century.
Born 22 February 1865, in Lódz; died 1908, in Jerusalem.
Painter. Genre scenes.
Samuel Hirszenberg studied in Munich and Paris. In France, he won a silver medal in 1889 and a bronze medal in 1900. He later settled in Lódz, and then in Warsaw. One of his paintings, *The Talmudists' School*, used to hang in the museum in Cracow.
AUCTION RECORDS:
VIENNA, 14 June 1977, *Children Playing in a Park* (oil on canvas, 27½ x 14½ ins / 70 x 37 cm) ATS 40,000. TEL AVIV, 4 July 1999, *Houses by River* (1884, oil on canvas, 9x13 ins / 22x34 cm) USD 4,600.

HIRT, Caspar
Swiss, 17th century.
Born 1632, in Zurich; died 1700, in Zurich.
Glass painter.
Caspar Hirt was a pupil of Hans Jakob Nüscheler the Younger.
MUSEUMS AND GALLERIES:
ZURICH (Kunsthaus): several works.

HIRT, Friedrich Christoph
German, 18th century.
Born 26 November 1685, in Durlach; died 1763, in Frankfurt am Main.
Painter. Portraits, landscapes.
Friedrich Christoph Hirt, a son and pupil of Michael Conrad Hirt, went on to travel in France and Germany.

HIRT, Friedrich Wilhelm
German, 18th century.
Born 11 February 1721, in Frankfurt; died 19 January 1772, in Frankfurt.
Painter.
Friedrich Wilhelm Hirt, a son and pupil of Friedrich Christoph Hirt, was a painter in the service of the Duke of Saxe-Meiningen for a time, before going on to travel. He excelled at painting figures and animals, often executing them in the paintings of C.G. Schütz.
MUSEUMS AND GALLERIES:
BERN: two landscapes - FRANKFURT AM MAIN: *Hunters' Meet; Return of the Hunt; Cattle Grazing; Shepherd and Flock* - KASSEL: two landscapes - MAINZ: two landscapes - STOCKHOLM: *River Motif with Watermill; Landscape with High Mountains*.
AUCTION RECORDS:
LONDON, 17 Dec 1985, *Leopards Attacking a Stag* (1755, oil on panel, 13 x 13 ins / 33 x 33 cm) GBP 4,000. ZURICH, 20 June 2000, *Landscape with Trees, Figures and Animals* (1766, oil on canvas, 16 x 20 ins / 40 x 52 cm) CHF 13,500. LONDON, 11 July 2001, *Rhenish Landscape at Evening with Figures and Livestock* (oil on canvas, a pair, 13 x 16 ins / 34 x 41 cm) GBP 6,000. VIENNA, 5 June 2002, *Expansive River Landscape with Shepherd and Travellers* (oil on wood, 10 x 11 ins / 25 x 29 cm) EUR 5,500. ZURICH, 22 March 2004, *River Landscape with Herders and Grazing Animals* (1766, oil on canvas, 15 x 20 ins / 39 x 51 cm) CHF 7,000.

HIRT, Heinrich
German, 18th century.
Born 12 September 1727, in Frankfurt; died 3 September 1796, in Frankfurt.
Painter. Portraits, landscapes.
Heinrich Hirt was the second son of Friedrich Hirt.
AUCTION RECORDS:
MUNICH, 1 Dec 1982, *Die Ankunft der Schwalben* (*The Arrival of the Swallows*) (oil on canvas) DEM 58,000.

HIRT, Heinrich
German, 19th century.
Painter. Genre scenes.
Heinrich Hirt exhibited in Berlin and Munich from 1872 and specialised in painting childhood scenes.
AUCTION RECORDS:
LONDON, 26 April 1968, *Grandmother's Stories*, Gns 1,000. NEW YORK, 14 May 1976, *Dog Sitting Up and Begging* (oil on canvas, 19¼ x 15¼ ins / 49 x 39 cm) USD 5,500. LONDON, 20 Oct 1978, *One O'clock, Two O'clock...* (1879, oil on canvas, 17¼ x 11½ ins / 43.5 x 29.2 cm) GBP 1,800. SAN FRANCISCO, 12 June 1986, *Baby's Meal* (oil on canvas, 28 x 20¾ ins / 71 x 53 cm) USD 22,500. NEW YORK, 22 May 1990, *The Young Fashion Designer* (oil on canvas, 19¼ x 16 ins / 49 x 39.7 cm) USD 38,500. LONDON, 21 Nov 1996, *Baby's Meal* (oil on canvas, 30¼ x 24 ins / 77 x 61 cm) GBP 35,600. LONDON, 22 June 1999, *Helping Hand* (oil on canvas, 28 x 33 ins / 72 x 83 cm) GBP 14,000. COLOGNE, 28 Oct 1999, *School Girl on Path in Meadow Landscape Holding Dandelion* (1879, oil on panel,

17 x 12 ins / 44 x 30 cm) DEM 19,000. MUNICH, 27 Sept 2000, *Ladybird, Fly Away* (oil on canvas, 28 x 21 ins / 70 x 54 cm) DEM 35,000. MUNICH, 27 Sept 2000, *Peasant Man with Children Watching Arrival of the Swallows* (oil on canvas, 28 x 21 ins / 70 x 54 cm) DEM 60,000. BRUSSELS, 10 Oct 2001, *Little Girl in a Wheat Field* (1878, oil on canvas, 18 x 12 ins / 45 x 30 cm) BEF 400,000. MILFORD, 25 Oct 2001, *Young Peasant Girl* (oil on canvas, 18 x 12 ins / 46 x 30 cm) USD 7,500. MUNICH, 26 June 2002, *Making Dolls' Clothes* (oil on canvas, 20 x 15 ins / 50 x 39 cm) EUR 19,000. COLOGNE, 20 Nov 2003, *Hunter with Two Girls* (oil on canvas, 28 x 33 ins / 72 x 83 cm) EUR 4,400. MUNICH, 17 March 2004, *Small Girl with Rabbits* (oil on panel, 16 x 11 ins / 40 x 29 cm) EUR 6,500.

HIRT, Johann Christian
German, 19th century.
Born 4 March 1836, in Fürth; died 19 August 1897, in Munich.
Sculptor.

MUSEUMS AND GALLERIES:
BUCHAREST (Muz. National de Arta al României): *Andromeda*.

HIRT, Johannes
German, 19th - 20th century.
Born 27 April 1859, in Worms; died October 1917, in Karlsruhe.
Sculptor.

Johannes Hirt studied with Schaper in Berlin. He was active in Worms and Karlsruhe. He is best known for his monument to Hüchler, the minister of Hesse.

HIRT, Marthe
Belgian, 20th century.
Born 4 February 1890, in Liège; died 7 October 1984.
Active in Switzerland and in France.
Painter, draughtsman. Figures, portraits, landscapes, still-lifes.

Marthe Hirt's family came originally from Switzerland. She began painting in 1915, then enrolled in David Estoppey's life class at the Geneva art school. After the war, she settled in the Montparnasse district of Paris and enrolled in the Académie Ranson, where she was taught by Maurice Denis, Sérusier and Bonnard. Her work shows a great sense of unity between her three main subjects. Her figures - kitchen boys, clowns, young monks, girls - are almost always presented in isolation against a neutral background, after the manner of Soutine or Kisling. In her still-lifes, baskets containing a few indeterminate fruits and vegetables are presented on a napkin or a sketchy table, in dim light, or rather in semi-darkness. Her landscapes, wherever they were painted, are completely unindividualised, the elements and reliefs are synthesised into blocks, as with Cézanne, but in a quite different rhythmic and chromatic register. In all three types of subject, her painting is reclusive and secretive.

She exhibited once at the Salon des Indépendants during the 1920s, and at the Salon des Tuileries in 1930. She went off to paint landscapes in Brittany, Ancy-le-Franc in Burgundy and Mayenne. She exhibited in solo shows in Paris in 1942, 1943, 1944, 1948, and again in 1977, although she had abandoned all artistic activity at the beginning of the 1950s. However, in 1980, the Manoir de Martigny in Switzerland organised a retrospective exhibition of 120 of her paintings.

BIBLIOGRAPHY:
Marthe Hirt, exhibition catalogue, Manoir de Martigny, Martigny, 1980. *Atelier Marthe Hirt*, auction catalogue, Drouot Richelieu, Paris, 9 March 1989.

AUCTION RECORDS:
PARIS, 6 July 1983, *Seated Boy* (1936, oil on canvas, 24 x 18 ins / 61 x 46 cm) FRF 11,000. PARIS, 20 March 1988, *Portrait of a Girl* (oil on canvas, 26 x 19¾ ins / 66 x 50 cm) FRF 10,000. PARIS, 20 March 1988, *Portrait of a Girl* (oil on canvas, 26 x 19¾ ins / 66 x 50 cm) FRF 10,000. PARIS, 15 June 1988, *Still-life with Melon* (oil on canvas, 22 x 18 ins / 55 x 46 cm) FRF 11,000. VERSAILLES, 25 Sept 1988, *Still-life* (oil on canvas, 16¼ x 13 ins / 41 x 33 cm) FRF 6,500. VERSAILLES, 16 Oct 1988, *Still-life with Jug* (oil on canvas, 18 x 15 ins / 46 x 38 cm) FRF 7,000. VERSAILLES, 11 Jan 1989, *Still-life with Pears and a Decanter* (oil on canvas, 11 x 13¾ ins / 27 x 35 cm) FRF 5,000. PARIS, 9 March 1989, *The Girl in the Green Shawl* (oil on canvas, 21¼ x 25½ ins / 54 x 65 cm) FRF 10,500; *Contemplation* (oil on canvas, 39¼ x 25½ ins / 100 x 65 cm) FRF 8,200; *Child Clown and Maidservant* (oil on canvas, 39¼ x 25½ ins / 100 x 65 cm) FRF 10,800; *Portrait in a White Dress* (oil on canvas, 27¼ x 27¼ ins / 69 x 69 cm) FRF 13,600. PARIS, 13 Dec 1989, *Still-life with Potatoes, Pears and Jam* (oil on canvas, 15 x 18 ins / 38 x 46 cm) FRF 6,100. PARIS, 27 April 1990, *Family* (oil on canvas, 36¼ x 28¾ ins / 92 x 73 cm) FRF 28,000. PARIS, 9 Nov 1990, *Drowsy Model with Red Drapes* (oil on canvas, 19¾ x 24 ins / 50 x 61 cm) FRF 5,200. PARIS, 13 April 1992, *Still-life* (oil on canvas, 21¼ x 25½ ins / 54 x 65 cm) FRF 6,500. PARIS, 21 June 1993, *Young Man Seated* (oil on canvas, 28¾ x 19¾ ins / 73 x 50 cm) FRF 5,200. PARIS, 17 May 1995, *Portrait of Gisèle* (oil on canvas, 25½ x 21¼ ins / 65 x 54 cm) FRF 6,000. PARIS, 28 June 1995, *Young Woman with a Shawl and a Hat* (oil on canvas, 28¾ x 19¾ ins / 73 x 50 cm) FRF 6,000.

HIRT, Michael Conrad, or Hirth
German, 17th century.
Born c. 1615; died c. 1695.
Painter.

Michael Conrad Hirt, a court painter in Berlin, executed portraits and paintings of historical subjects. He is also well known for his work for Stendhal Cathedral.

HIRTH, Édouard
French, 20th century.
Born 14 September 1885, in Richwiller; died 1980.
Painter. Portraits, landscapes, still-lifes.

Édouard Hirth studied in Strasbourg, then part of Germany, and, until the World War I, exhibited regularly in Berlin and Bremen.

HIRTH DU FRÊNES, Rudolf
German, 19th - 20th century.
Born 24 July 1846, in Grafentonna, near Gotha; died 1 May 1916, in Miltenberg am Main.
Painter. Portraits, genre scenes.

From 1861 to 1864, Rudolf Hirth du Frênes was a pupil of Kreling at the Nuremberg art school. He then studied at the Munich academy under the direction of Artur von Ramberg, and spent five years travelling in Belgium, Holland and France. His career began in 1870. He exhibited in Vienna, Berlin and Munich, where he eventually settled. He was greatly influenced by the works of Courbet and Millet that were exhibited in Munich.

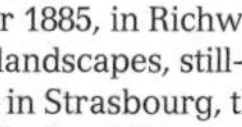

MUSEUMS AND GALLERIES:
FRANKFURT AM MAIN: *Self-portrait* - MUNICH: *Portrait of the Painter Schrich* - WROCLAW: *Hop-picking*.

AUCTION RECORDS:
COPENHAGEN, 6 Nov 1979, *Washerwomen on a River Bank* (oil on canvas, 26½ x 35½ ins / 67 x 90 cm) DKK 26,000. MUNICH, 15 March 1984, *Children Playing Outside a House* (oil on panel, 10 x 7¾ ins / 25.5 x 20 cm) DEM 5,000. LONDON, 8 Oct 1986, *Naughty Boy Stealing a Sausage* (oil on canvas, 29 x 23¼ ins / 73.5 x 59 cm) GBP 7,500. MUNICH, 27 June 1995, *Girl in Traditional Costume* (oil on canvas, 21¼ x 13¾ ins / 54 x 35 cm) DEM 6,900.

HIRTZ, Camille
French, 20th century.
Born 13 April 1917, in Kronembourg-Strasbourg; died 1987, in Strasbourg.
Painter, watercolourist, engraver.

In 1935, Camille Hirtz was a student at the École des Arts Décoratifs in Strasbourg, in 1938, at the École des Beaux-Arts in Paris, in the studio of F. Sabatté and, in 1941, he was back École des Arts Décoratifs in Strasbourg. He was drafted into the German army and sent to the Russian front, where he was taken prisoner. In 1946 he became professor of painting at the École des Arts Décoratifs in Strasbourg. He occupied that position, with increased responsibilities, until 1981.

He executed a number murals including one for the chapel in the St. Amand church in Strasbourg.

Camille Hirtz started as a figurative artist and soon evolved towards Abstraction, an abstraction both formally and technically comparable to Serge Poliakoff 's. His compositions have well-defined though not geometric figures with an alternation of curves and right angles. His works are characterised by a particularly elaborate pictorial technique involving the refined application of pigmented layers. These are created by delicate brushstrokes that allow the layer below to come through with deliberate optical effects. His colour harmonies are accentuated by this technique, some vivid, bright and gay, with other harmonies more measured, in muted, graver tones. Camille Hirtz was a well-known personality in Strasbourg's artistic milieu but he hardly sought to make himself know outside Alsace, which would explain why his work isn't more widely known. He participated in numerous collective exhibitions in Strasbourg, and in several cities in Alsace, as well as in Stuttgart, Munich, Karlsruhe, Ludwigshafen, Paris, Nice and Menton. He had regular solo exhibitions, especially in Strasbourg, at the Maison Alsacienne from 1949, and at the Maison d'Art Alsacienne in the Ancienne Douane from 1972.

BIBLIOGRAPHY:
Schneider, Joseph Paul, *Camille Hirtz peintre rhénan*, Éd. de La Dryade, Strasbourg, 1980. Schneider, Joseph Paul, et al., *Camille Hirtz*, Éd. Michel frères, Virton, 1988.

MUSEUMS AND GALLERIES:
STRASBOURG (MBA): several works - STRASBOURG (Prints and Drawings Collection).

HIRTZ, Hans
French, 15th century.
Active in Strasbourg between 1421 and 1460.
Painter. Religious subjects. Designs for stained glass.
School of Alsace.

Hans Hirtz is known to have worked for the cathedral and probably for the Dominican church in Strasbourg, and may also have produced plans for windows in the churches of St-Pierre-le-Vieux and St-Guillaume in the same city. According to Lilli Fischel, he painted the *Passion* retable, most of the scattered panels of which are now in the Karlsruhe museum.

His style of drawing is close to that of the Flemish primitives, but his composition can seem violent.

MUSEUMS AND GALLERIES:
COLOGNE (Wallraf-Richartz Mus.): *Arrest of Christ* - KARLSRUHE: *Carrying the Cross; Prayer on the Mount of Olives; Crowned with Thorns; Entombment.*

HIRTZ, Jacques
French, 20th century.
Born 20 February 1905, in Paris; died 16 January 1988, in Issy-les-Moulineaux.
Painter, draughtsman. Figures, scenes with figures, landscapes, urban landscapes.

Jacques Hirtz was the son of Lucien, enameller and studio supervisor of the Boucherin Jewellers. A pupil at the École des Arts Décoratifs, and then in Lucien Simon's studio at the Beaux-Arts in Paris, he was a resident at the Casa Velázquez in 1940 and was awarded its first prize.

Hirtz participated in collective exhibitions at the Salon de la Société Nationale des Beaux-Arts, of which he was a member. He received the Taylor Prize at the 1984 Salon du Dessin et de la Peinture à l'eau (Watercolour Painting and Drawing Exhibition), the Prix Roger Deverin, at the 1986 Salon des Artistes Français where he showed hors concours and received a medal. The Salon des Artistes Français paid homage to him in 1988, the year of his death, and the Fondation Taylor in Paris set up an exhibition of his works in 1992. Jacques Hirtz was Chevalier de la Légion d'Honneur.

HIRTZ, Johann
German, 17th century.
Born 1649, in Augsburg.
Painter.

HIRTZ, Lucien
French, 19th - 20th century.
Born 16 March 1864; died 1928, in Paris.
Painter, designer, enameller.

Lucien Hirtz studied at the École des Arts Décoratifs in Paris and in 1924 he became professor of enamelling in the enamellers' studio in the Sèvres factory. Until 1928, he was enameller and studio supervisor for the Boucheron-Radius jewellers.

A member of the Salon de la Société Nationale des Beaux-Arts in Paris and of the Association des Artistes Décorateurs, Hirtz exhibited at the Salon des Tuileries in Paris (1923), at the French exhibition in Madrid (1927) and at the Musée Galliera (1929). An exhibition of silverware and jewellery from the Boucheron studios, set up in Paris by the Institut de France and the Musée Jacquemart-André in 1988, paid homage to him. Lucien Hirtz was awarded medals and prizes at events in Paris (1899 and 1900), Milan (1906), Brussels (1897 and 1910) and London (1908).

MUSEUMS AND GALLERIES:
LIMOGES: three enamel plates - PARIS (former Mus. du Luxembourg): *The Round* (enamel panel); *La Gaieté* (enamel panel) - PARIS (Mus. des Arts décoratifs): *The Naiad* (enamel panel) - PARIS (Mus. Galliera).

HIRZEL, Heinrich
Swiss, 18th century.
Born 1729, in Zurich; died 1790, in Weiningen.
Painter. Landscapes.

Heinrich Hirzel was a pupil of Füssli.

AUCTION RECORDS:
ZURICH, 25 Nov 1977, *Horse Rider in a Mountain Landscape* (1757, oil on canvas, 8 3/4 x 12 1/4 ins / 22.5 x 31 cm) CHF 3,500. ZURICH, 22 May 1980, *Landscape* (1767, oil on canvas, 29 1/2 x 36 1/2 ins / 75 x 93 cm) CHF 7,000.

HIRZEL, Hermann
German, 19th - 20th century.
Born 1864, in Buenos Aires; died 1939, in Berlin.
Painter, draughtsman. Ex-libris, advertising art, designs (jewels/precious metalware).
Jugendstil.

Hermann Hirzel studied chemistry and pharmacy in Geneva and Berlin, then abandoned those studies in 1887 and entered the academy in Berlin. He lived in Italy from 1890 to 1893 and then returned to live in Berlin.

BIBLIOGRAPHY:
Hase, Ulrike von, *Schmuck in Deutschland und Österreich. Symbolismus, Jugendstil, Neohistorismus*, Prestel, Munich, 1977.

MUSEUMS AND GALLERIES:
DARMSTADT (Hessisches Landesmus.): *Brooch* (c. 1898) - PFORZHEIM (Schmuckmuseum): *Brooch* (c. 1898).

HIRZEL, Suzette
Swiss, 18th - 19th century.
Born 1769, in Zurich; died 1858, in Zurich.
Painter. Portraits.
Suzette Hirzel is best known for her portrait of *Frau Obmann Füssli*.

HIS, Jacques de
French, 17th century.
Active in Paris.
Engraver, painter.
Jacques de His studied under Oehlenhainz and Lancaster. He painted in oil and pastel. He is remembered for his portrait of the *Duke of Angoulême, Louis Emmanuel de Valois*.

HIS, René Charles Edmond, pseudonym: René-His
French, 19th - 20th century.
Born 15 February 1877, in Colombes; died 1960.
Painter. Landscapes, waterscapes.
René His was a pupil of Jules Lefebvre, Tony-Robert-Fleury and Henri Biva. He painted mostly landscapes of bodies of water, ponds and rivers and views of Provence and Algeria. He regularly exhibited in Paris at the Salon des Artistes Français, receiving honourable mention in 1898, and honourable mention again with a 3rd class medal in 1900, when he became a member on the occasion of the Exposition Universelle.
AUCTION RECORDS:
PARIS, 28 Dec 1923, *Pool in the Wood*, FRF 400. PARIS, 26 June 1942, *River Under the Trees*, FRF 2,650. PARIS, 19 March 1945, *Pool in the Forest*, FRF 12,000; *Riverbanks Shadowed by Trees*, FRF 20,000. PARIS, 30 April 1947, *River in the Wood*, FRF 5,100. LONDON, 20 Feb 1976, *Landscape in Normandy* (oil on canvas, 44 1/2 x 64 ins / 113 x 162.5 cm) GBP 500. PARIS, 28 Nov 1977, *Riverbanks* (oil on canvas, 23 1/2 x 32 ins / 60 x 81 cm) FRF 5,900. LONDON, 6 Feb 1987, *Sunny Landscape* (oil on canvas, 18 1/2 x 24 1/2 ins / 47 x 62 cm) GBP 2,600. LA VARENNE-ST-HILAIRE, 12 March 1989, *Landscape of the Eure* (oil on canvas, 19 3/4 x 25 1/2 ins / 50 x 65 cm) FRF 15,000. PARIS, 12 Oct 1990, *Landscape with Sheep* (oil on canvas) FRF 9,000. NEW YORK, 26 May 1992, *Wooded River Landscape* (oil on canvas, 24 x 32 ins / 61 x 81.3 cm) USD 2,640. NEW YORK, 29 Oct 1992, *A Winding River* (oil on canvas, 20 x 30 ins / 50.8 x 76.2 cm) USD 1,650. CALAIS, 14 March 1993, *River Edged with Trees* (oil on canvas, 20 x 30 ins / 51 x 76 cm) FRF 7,000. LONDON, 16 June 1993, *St-Jean-Cap-Ferrat* (oil on canvas, 25 1/4 x 31 3/4 ins / 64 x 80.5 cm) GBP 4,370. NEW YORK, 19 Jan 1995, *In the Forest* (oil on canvas, 23 3/4 x 22 ins / 60.3 x 55.9 cm) USD 2,185. LONDON, 22 Feb 1995, *River Landscape Bathed in Sunlight* (oil on canvas, 22 3/4 x 31 ins / 58 x 79 cm) GBP 5,175. LONDON, 31 Oct 1996, *Field of Peonies by a River* (oil on canvas, 23 1/2 x 32 ins / 59.5 x 81 cm) GBP 4,600. BURY ST EDMUNDS, 24 March 1999, *Arcade of Leaves* (oil on canvas, 20 x 26 ins / 51 x 65 cm) GBP 2,400. JERSEY, 29 Sept 1999, *Le Casier, Village in Normandy* (oil on canvas, 32 x 46 ins / 81 x 116 cm) GBP 3,600. BILLINGSHURST, 1 Feb 2000, *River Landscape with Sheep and Shepherd, Autumn* (oil on canvas, 19 x 25 ins / 48 x 63 cm) GBP 2,700. NEW YORK, 8 March 2000, *Washerwoman* (oil on canvas, 31 x 45 ins / 80 x 115 cm) USD 16,000. NEW YORK, 30 April 2001, *Waterlilies on a Tranquil Pond* (oil on canvas, 91 x 130 ins / 230 x 330 cm) USD 26,000. LONDON, 26 Sept 2001, *River Landscapes* (oil on canvas, a pair, 13 x 18 ins / 33 x 46 cm) GBP 3,500. LONDON, 1 May 2002, *Waterlillies* (oil on canvas, 20 x 26 ins / 51 x 65 cm) GBP 1,800. MELUN, 1 Dec 2002, *River Bank* (oil on canvas, 24 x 32 ins / 60 x 81 cm) EUR 4,000. LONDON, 5 June 2003, *Summer's Day at the Banks of the River* (oil on canvas, 21 x 29 ins / 53 x 74 cm) GBP 3,250. LONDON, 1 Oct 2003, *River Landscape* (oil on canvas, 26 x 36 ins / 65 x 91 cm) GBP 4,200. LONDON, 11 May 2004, *Woodland Pool* (oil on canvas, 45 x 63 ins / 114 x 161 cm) GBP 7,400. NEUILLY, 11 June 2004, *Encampment by the Wadi* (oil on canvas, 52 x 89 ins / 132 x 225 cm) EUR 75,000.

HISAMOTO, Haruno
Japanese, 20th century.
Painter.
Hisamoto Haruno took part in the exhibition of Japanese art in Paris in 1929.

HISBENS
German, 17th century.
Active in Nuremberg.
Portrait painter, engraver, draughtsman.
The critics are generally agreed that the prints originally attributed to Hisbens are in fact the work of Beham.

MUSEUMS AND GALLERIES:
RENNES: drawings.

HISCHBEIN
French, 18th century.
Portrait artist.
MUSEUMS AND GALLERIES:
VERSAILLES (Mus.): *Portrait of Count Waldner of Freundstein*.

HISCOX, George Dunkerton
British, 19th century.
Born 1840, in North Wootton; died 21 January 1901.
Painter.
Intended for a career in the church, George Hiscox changed direction, studying painting in Bristol at the art school and the academy. A number of his works were bought by Queen Victoria including *The Queen's Residence*. He taught art in Bristol and Windsor. He exhibited his painting *The Hour when the Splendour Dies* in London at the Royal Academy in 1884. His *Sun Setting over a Forest* of 1891 shows the same subject.

HISHIDA, Shunso, real name: Hishida Mioji, artist names: Seiten, Shuko, Shunso
Japanese, 19th - 20th century.
Born 1874, in Nagano Prefecture; died 1911.
Painter. Figures, scenes with figures, flowers, birds.
Hishida Shunso trained at the Tokyo school of fine arts and was involved, together with Okakura Tenshin and Hashimoto Kunio, in the foundation of the Art Institute. He was a member of the Bunten jury. He was appointed assistant at the school of fine arts. In 1903, he went to India and he visited Europe in 1904-1905. Inspired by the American Ernest Fenollosa, who from the 1880s was calling for the preservation of traditional styles, Hishida contributed as writer and theoretician to the founding of the so-called orientalist movement, together with Yokoyama Taikan (1868-1958) and Shimomura Kanzan (1873-1930).

Like that of his fellow members in the orientalist movement, Hishida's work drew inspiration from Japanese history and is characterised by the summary, subjective composition typical of traditional painting. It is also a way of transcribing space, particularly depth, that comes from Western art. He observes with lucidity and shows a keen sensitivity, replacing bold outlines with a softer, more nuanced touch, achieving almost impressionistic effects. Yet his work remains highly decorative. He had a marked influence on the Japanese artists who succeeded him during the first part of the 20th century, when his style was the dominant trend in nihon-ga (traditional Japanese painting).

MUSEUMS AND GALLERIES:
TOKYO (Eisei-Bunko Mus.): *Dead Leaves* (1909, two-panel screen).

HISIG, A.
Swedish, 18th century.
Active c. 1700.
Sculptor.
A. Hisig was a pupil of Burchard Precht.

HISPALENSE, Juan
Spanish, 15th century.
Active in Seville during the first half of the 15th century.
Painter.
The signature of Juan Hispalense is to be found on a triptych inspired by the Italian School that is in the Lazaro Galdeno collection, Madrid.

HISPANO, Antonio
Spanish, 16th century.
Active in Valladolid.
Sculptor.
In 1598, Antonio Hispano carved picture frames for two portraits: one of the emperor, the other of the king.

HISPANO, Marcos (Brother)
Spanish, 17th century.
Died 1679, in Madrid.
Painter. Religious subjects.

HISSARD, Jean-René
French, 20th century.
Born 1943.
Painter, engraver. Scenes with figures.
Hissard lives and works in Paris. His paintings deride the most striking points of 'modernity' in the form of diptychs, triptychs and polyptychs, in which he virulently caricatures various well-known avant-garde, historic or contemporary works.

He has taken part in collective exhibitions, including: Salon de la Jeune Peinture and Biennale des Jeunes Artistes, Musée d'Art Moderne de la Ville de Paris, 1967; Galerie Paul Fachetti, Paris, 1969; Biennale Internationale de l'Estampe, Paris, 1970; *Salammbô*, Carthage museum, 1987; Centre d'Art Contemporain, Ivry, 1988; Maison des Jeunes et de la Culture, Belleville-Paris, 1989; and *Dissonances*, Le 19 Centre Régional d'Art Contemporain, Montbéliard, 2000.

He showed a collection of paintings in solo exhibitions in 1991 at the Musée des Beaux-Arts in Mulhouse, the Maison d'Art Contemporain in Fresnes, and the École d'Art in Juvisy-sur-Orge; and in 1996 at the Galerie J. Barbier in Paris.
BIBLIOGRAPHY:
Jean-René Hissard, exhibition catalogue, Musée des Beaux-Arts, Mulhouse, 1991.

HISSINCK, Lambert
Dutch, 17th century.
Born c. 1619, in Amsterdam.
Painter.

HISTA, H.
French, 20th century.
Active in Paris.
Painter.
Hista was a member of the Société des Artistes Français.

HISTA, Louis
French, 19th century.
Born in the 19th century, in Aire-sur-la-Lys (Pas-de-Calais).
Painter, watercolourist. Landscapes.
Hista was a pupil of P.-V. Galland, and became a member of the Société des Artistes Français in 1886.

MUSEUMS AND GALLERIES:
ARRAS: five watercolours.
AUCTION RECORDS:
PARIS, 30 March 1925, *The Basin of Bacchus (Versailles) - The Green Carpet* (both) FRF 390. PARIS, 8 May 1925, *Terrace of the Sicaud Villa at Beaulieu - Les Rochers de St-Jean at Beaulieu*, FRF 200. PARIS, 5 April 1979, *Woodcutters' Huts in the Forest of St-Germain* (1874, oil on panel, 7¾ x 11¾ ins / 20 x 30 cm) FRF 4,500.

HISTAEUS
3rd century BC.
Active in Athens at the end of the 3rd century BC.
Sculptor.
Ancient Greek.
Histaeus' name was found on a pedestal from Thebes.

HISZPANSKA-NEUMANN, Maria
Polish, 20th century.
Born 28 October 1917, in Warsaw.
Painter.
Maria Hiszpanska-Neumann was a pupil of Stanislaw Ostoja Chrostowski at the academy of fine art in Warsaw from 1935 to 1939. She joined the Polish resistance during World War II and was arrested by the Gestapo in 1941 and deported to Ravensbrück until the end of the war. Her work is highly Expressionistic, often dealing with tragic subjects.

Since 1945 she has lived in Warsaw. A member of the society of Polish artists, she has taken part in collective exhibitions including: Düsseldorf, Bern, Geneva and Milan. Solo exhibitions include: Warsaw; Sofia (1954); Berlin (1959 and 1962); and Cairo and Alexandria (1960).
BIBLIOGRAPHY:
Bialostocki, J., *Maria Hiszpanska-Neumann*, Arkady, Warsaw, 1963 (in Polish and English).

HITA DEL CASTILLO, Benito
Spanish, 18th century.
Born 1706; died 1786.
Active in Seville.
Sculptor.
Benito Hita del Castillo worked for the church of S Juan de la Palma in Seville. He was almost certainly related to Agustino Hitta Del Castillo.

HITCH, F.- B.
British, 20th century.
Born 1877; died 1957.
Sculptor, painter.
F.B. Hitch lived and worked in Chelsea, and was a member of the Society of British Sculptors. He exhibited at the Royal Institute of Oil Painters in 1909, at the Royal Academy and at the Royal Cambrian Academy.

HITCHCOCK, Cecil. See **JAY**

HITCHCOCK, David Howard
American, 19th - 20th century.
Born 15 May 1861, in Hawaii; died 1943.
Painter, illustrator, sculptor. Landscapes.
David Hitchcock studied under William Bouguereau and Gabriel Ferrier in Paris and worked in Honolulu. He joined the Salmagundi Club in 1904. He mainly painted landscapes in the Hawaiian islands, which were annexed by the USA in 1898 and became one of the USA in 1959.
AUCTION RECORDS:
LOS ANGELES-SAN FRANCISCO, 7 Feb 1990, *View of the Outskirts of Honolulu* (1942, oil on canvas, 26 x 30 ins / 66 x 76 cm) USD 5,225. STOCKHOLM, 18 May 1999, *Landscape with Palms, Hawaii* (1915, oil on canvas laid on panel, 16 x 11 ins / 40 x 29 cm) SEK 36,000. SAN FRANCISCO, 17 June 1999, *Palace of Fine Arts Exposition at San Francisco* (1915, canvas board, 10 x 14 ins / 25 x 36 cm) USD 3,750. SOUTH DEERFIELD, 31 March 2000, *Beach Scene* (oil on board) USD 12,000.

HITCHCOCK, George
American, 19th - 20th century.
Born 29 September 1850, in Providence; died 2 August 1913, in Marken, the Netherlands.
Active in the Netherlands.
Painter, watercolourist, illustrator. Religious subjects, genre scenes, landscapes, flowers, figures.

George Hitchcock, son of portrait painter Charles Hitchcock, received a law degree from Harvard University in 1874, and was a practising lawyer in New York before turning to art in 1879. He studied in London, in Paris at the Académie Julian under Gustave Boulanger and Jules Lefebvre, in Düsseldorf, and in the Hague under H.W. Mesdag. In 1883 Hitchcock settled in Egmond-aan-Zee in the Netherlands, becoming the centre (along with Gari Melchers) of the Egmond School art colony. His exhibition of his *La Culture des Tulipes* at the 1885 Paris Salon received wide recognition. Hitchcock received an honourable mention in Paris (1887), and medals in New York (1887), at the Exposition Universelle in Paris (1889), in Chicago (1893), Berlin (1896), Dresden (1897), Vienna (1898), and Munich (1900). His work was noted for its technical sophistication, often showing brightly coloured Dutch landscapes and tulip fields. Hitchcock was known for paintings of visionary religious subjects containing subtle symbols while retaining an element of secularism, reflecting the 19th-century effort to reconcile faith and new scientific ideas. Examples of such works include *The Blessed Mother* (1892) and *The Flight into Egypt* (1892). He was the first American to receive the Officer's Cross of the Order of Franz Joseph of Austria, and the first American member of the Akademie der Bildenden Künste, Vienna. Hitchcock was also a Chevalier of the Légion d'Honneur.

BIBLIOGRAPHY:
George Hitchcock, exhibition catalogue, M. Knoedler Gallery, New York, 1906. Brinton, C. (ed), *George Hitchcock*, exhibition catalogue, Memorial Art Gallery, University of Rochester, Rochester (NY), 1915. Boswell, P., '*The George Hitchcock Memorial Exhibition to be Held at a New York Gallery*' in *Art & Decoration*, vol 14, journal article, 1921.

MUSEUMS AND GALLERIES:
ABERDEEN (AG and Mus.): *Maternity* (1889, oil) - CHICAGO (AI): *Flower Girl in Holland* (1887, oil); *The Annunciation* (1887, oil) - CLEVELAND (MA): *The Blessed Mother* (1892) - GRAND RAPIDS (Grand Rapids AM): *Purple Hyacinths* (c. 1890, oil) - NEW YORK (Metropolitan Mus. of Art): *Vespers* (c. 1895-1900, oil) - PARIS (Louvre): *Vaincu* - TELFAIR, GA (Telfair Museum of Art): *Early Spring in Holland* (c. 1887-1905, oil) - WASHINGTON DC (Smithsonian American AM): *The Flight into Egypt* (1892, oil).

AUCTION RECORDS:
PARIS, 17 Feb 1896, *Willow*, FRF 625; *Dunes at Egmond-aan-Zee*, FRF 1,500; *Dawn on the Dunes* (pastel) FRF 1,625. NEW YORK, 26 au 28 Feb 1902, *Dunes*, USD 460; *Windmill and Geese in Holland*, USD 290. NEW YORK, 4 Jan 1907, *Tulip Growing*, USD 1,200. NEW YORK, 7 April 1971, *Landscape with Church*, USD 1,500. LONDON, 12 March 1974, *The Bride*, GBP 700. LONDON, 29 June 1976, *Zealand Girl* (oil on canvas, 31 x 22 ins / 79 x 56 cm) GBP 1,800. NEW YORK, 21 June 1978, *Peasant Girl* (oil on canvas, 32 x 24 ins / 81.3 x 61 cm) USD 2,200. NEW YORK, 21 June 1979, *Flower Seller* (oil on canvas, 32 x 26 ins / 81.3 x 66 cm) USD 2,800. NEW YORK, 17 April 1982, *Canal in Holland* (1885, watercolour, 12 x 19 1/2 ins / 30.5 x 49.5 cm) USD 1,200. NEW YORK, 2 June 1983, *Noordwyke* (oil on canvas, 19 x 14 ins / 48.3 x 35.5 cm) USD 7,250. NEW YORK, 20 June 1985, *Boats at Anchor* (1884, oil on canvas, 28 x 50 1/4 ins / 71.1 x 127.6 cm) USD 6,750. NEW YORK, 29 May 1987, *The Stork's Nest* (oil on canvas, 22 1/4 x 17 1/4 ins / 56.5 x 43.8 cm) USD 22,000. NEW YORK, 24 June 1988, *Street with Figures in Holland* (oil on canvas, 24 1/4 x 20 1/2 ins / 61.4 x 52 cm) USD 4,675. NEW YORK, 30 Sept 1988, *The Siren* (1902, oil on panel, 10 x 6 ins / 25.4 x 15 cm) USD 6,600. NEW YORK, 16 March 1990, *Flight into Egypt* (1892, oil on canvas, 44 1/2 x 65 1/4 ins / 112.8 x 166 cm) USD 14,300. NEW YORK, 30 Nov 1990, *Farm in Normandy* (oil on canvas, 15 3/4 x 22 ins / 40.3 x 56 cm) USD 18,700. NEW YORK, 2 Dec 1992, *Girl in a Field of Flowers* (1889, oil on canvas, tondo, 24 1/4 x 24 1/2 ins / 61.4 x 62.5 cm) USD 4,620. NEW YORK, 31 March 1993, *Sailing in Choppy Waters* (1880, watercolour and pencil/paper/card, 20 3/4 x 14 1/4 ins / 52.7 x 36.2 cm) USD 1,035. NEW YORK, 27 May 1993, *Dunes in Holland* (1892, oil on canvas, 27 1/4 x 45 1/2 ins / 69.2 x 115.6 cm) USD 28,750. NEW YORK, 3 Dec 1993, *Baptism* (oil on canvas, 43 x 35 ins / 109.2 x 89 cm) USD 34,500. NEW YORK, 14 March 1996, *Spring Blossoms* (oil on canvas, 22 x 17 1/2 ins / 55.9 x 44.5 cm) USD 8,050. NEW YORK, 5 Dec 1996, *Stork's Nest* (oil on canvas, 22 1/4 x 17 1/4 ins / 56.5 x 43.8 cm) USD 21, 850. NEW YORK, 6 June 1997, *Spring Crocus Fields* (c. 1889, pastel/paper, 17 x 23 ins / 43.2 x 58.4 cm) USD 68,500.

HITCHCOCK, Harold
British, 20th century.
Born 1914, in London.
Painter, watercolourist. Landscapes.

Harold Hitchcock took part in group shows, including exhibitions at the Royal Academy and the Royal Society of British Artists in London, and also in the USA, Canada and Australia. In 1967 a retrospective of his work was held in London. Most of Hitchcock's output consists of watercolours painted in a style strongly influenced by Claude Lorraine, J.M.W. Turner and the Pre-Raphaelites. His subject matter, rendered in great detail, consists of imaginary landscapes and seascapes bathed in sunlight.

MUSEUMS AND GALLERIES:
LIDICA - LOUISIANA - WINSTON-SALEM.

HITCHCOCK, Lucius Wolcott
American, 19th - 20th century.
Born 2 December 1868, in West Williamsfield (Ohio); died 1942.
Painter (gouache), illustrator. Genre scenes.

Lucius Hitchcock studied at the Art Students League, New York, before going to Paris, where he received teaching from Jules Lefebvre, Benjamin-Constant and Jean-Paul Laurens, and also attended the Académie Colarossi. He lived mainly in New-Rochelle (New York). He joined the Salmagundi Club in 1905 and was also a member of the Royal Drawing Society in London. He painted scenes of everyday life and also more exceptional events.

Hitchcock participated in various group exhibitions, receiving prizes including a bronze medal at the Exposition Universelle in Paris in 1900, an honourable mention in Buffalo in 1901 and bronze and silver medals at St Louis in 1904. In 1909 he exhibited at the Walker Art Gallery, Liverpool.

AUCTION RECORDS:
LOS ANGELES, 29 June 1982, *Heated Discussion* (oil on canvas, 27 x 34 ins / 68.5 x 86.5 cm) USD 1,300. NEW YORK, 17 March 1988, *Taking Her Leave* (1915, oil on canvas, 25 1/2 x 33 1/2 ins / 65 x 85 cm) USD 1,870. NEW YORK, 24 June 1988, *Charmed by Music* (1911, oil on card, 23 1/2 x 18 1/4 ins / 60 x 46.3 cm) USD 770. NEW YORK, 24 Jan 1990, *Verdict* (1901, grisaille, gouache/paper/card, 15 1/2 x 23 ins / 39.5 x 58.2 cm) USD 880. NEW YORK, 10 May 2003, *Artist Carrying Canvas, Children Watching* (charcoal board, 25 x 17 ins / 64 x 43 cm) USD 1,800.

HITCHENS, Ivon
British, 20th century.
Born 3 April 1893, in London; died 1979.
Painter. Figure compositions, nudes, interiors with figures, landscapes, still-lifes, flowers. Murals.

Ivon Hitchens was the son of the painter Alfred Hitchens. From 1911 to 1918 he studied at St John's Wood School of

Art and at the Royal Academy, London. He was a member of the Seven and Five Society from 1922 to 1925, and joined the London Group in 1931. In 1940 he settled near Petworth in West Sussex.

Hitchens is considered to be one of the most important British painters of his generation. There are two aspects to his work: one consisting of traditional figurative painting; and the other in an abstract style. His early paintings, dating from a period when he was influenced by Henri Matisse, are mostly of interiors in which the handling of space is the dominant concern. Just before 1935, and influenced by Ben Nicholson, he turned to still-life painting; his increasingly structural approach to this genre brought him to the edge of abstraction. Soon afterwards, Wassily Kandinsky's theories on abstraction and on the relationship between painting and music led Hitchens even further towards abstraction. From that time, around 1937, he adopted the long, horizontal format that typifies his later work.

After moving to Sussex, Hitchens produced many series of landscapes in this format, repeatedly returning to each subject just as Claude Monet had done in his *Haystacks* series. In these landscapes, Hitchens reconciled his objective approach to painting with the principles of pure abstraction and with the expression of sensations that inspired him to paint these scenes, in which light melds together vegetation, water and sky. The paintings from this period have a lyrical abstraction whose emotional content, rather than the subject matter itself, is the defining factor. He executed these paintings with wide, mostly lateral brushstrokes, using bright, fluid colours on a white background, which is translucent with a few patches of impasto.

At the same time as his abstract paintings, Hitchens also painted classic subjects and created compositions with figures, particularly in the murals he made for the British Society of Popular Dance and Song in London, in 1954, and for Sussex University, near Brighton, in 1960. Having absorbed several influences, he broke away from conventional landscape painting, but perpetuated the tradition of British landscape painting, just as Constable and Turner had done before him.

He took part in many group exhibitions, including the *Exposition d'Art Moderne* (*Exhibition of Modern Art*) organised by UNESCO, and the *Exposition des Tableaux Britanniques Modernes de la Tate Gallery* (*Exhibition of Modern British Paintings from the Tate Gallery*) at the Musée du Jeu de Paume, in Paris in 1946, and the 1956 Venice Biennale. Between 1925 and 1962, Hitchens also had 19 solo exhibitions in London, as well as retrospectives in Leeds in 1945, and at the Tate Gallery, London, in 1963, at the Royal Academy in London in 1979, and at the Serpentine Gallery in London in 1989.

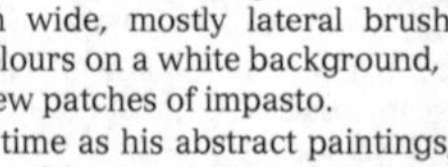

Bibliography:

Khoroche, Peter, *Ivon Hitchens*, A. Deutsch, London, 1990.

Museums and Galleries:

London (Tate Collection): *Balcony at Cambridge* (1929, oil on canvas); *Winter Stage* (1936, oil on canvas); *Forest Edge No. 2* (1944, oil on canvas); *A View from my Roof* (1978, oil on canvas); other paintings - Paris (MNAM-CCI).

Auction records:

London, 4 Nov 1959, *Green Pastures*, GBP 260. London, 6 July 1960, *Terwick Mill, on a Wet Evening No. 19*, GBP 800. London, 15 Dec 1965, *Bright April No. 2*, GBP 850. London, 1 May 1968, *The Front Doors*, GBP 1,700. London, 22 April 1970, *Reclining Nude (Algerian Girl) No. 3*, GBP 2,200. London, 12 May 1974, *Flowers* (1943) Gns 4,400. London, 10 Nov 1976, *Landscape* (oil on canvas, 16 x 42¼ ins / 40.5 x 107 cm) GBP 800. London, 16 Nov 1977, *Mill Pool, Coming Storm* (1951, oil on canvas, 16½ x 42¼ ins / 42 x 107.5 cm) GBP 1,700. London, 27 June 1979, *Corner of a Plantation* (oil on canvas, 19 x 36½ ins / 48 x 93 cm) GBP 2,200. London, 12 March 1982, *Yellow Glade No. 2* (oil on canvas, 18 x 43 ins / 45.7 x 109.5 cm) GBP 4,000. London, 10 June 1983, *Open Blue* (1966, oil on canvas, 20¼ x 41¼ ins / 51.5 x 105 cm) GBP 5,000. London, 13 June 1986, *Autumn Flowers in a Conservatory* (1957, oil on canvas, 20¼ x 41½ ins / 51.5 x 105.3 cm) GBP 6,500. London, 11 Nov 1987, *Still-life in the Studio* (oil on canvas, 25 x 33 ins / 63.5 x 84 cm) GBP 14,000. London, 3-4 March 1988, *Windy Countryside* (oil on canvas, 15¾ x 28½ ins / 40 x 72.5 cm) GBP 9,020; *The Lodge Gates* (oil on canvas, 20¼ x 38½ ins / 51.2 x 97.5 cm) GBP 9,900. London, 9 June 1988, *Wooded Landscape* (1956, oil on canvas, 15¾ x 35½ ins / 40 x 90 cm) GBP 14,300. London, 9 June 1989, *Clearing III* (1967, oil on canvas, 18 x 41½ ins / 45.5 x 105.4 cm) GBP 20,900; *Terwick Mill No. 9, Blue Morning* (1945, oil on canvas, 17 x 43 ins / 43.3 x 109.2 cm) GBP 37,400. London, 10 Nov 1989, *Flowers* (oil on canvas, 23¾ x 32½ ins / 60.3 x 82.7 cm) GBP 28,600. London, 9 March 1990, *Still-life with Torso and Plant* (oil on canvas, 20 x 18 ins / 50.8 x 45.5 cm) GBP 20,900. London, 8 June 1990, *Woodland Walk and Farm Fields* (1972, oil on canvas, 16½ x 41½ ins / 42 x 105.5 cm) GBP 29,700. London, 9 Nov 1990, *Interior with Red Projector* (1960, oil on canvas, 22 x 33 ins / 56 x 84 cm) GBP 23,100. London, 8 March 1991, *Trees and Barges* (1956, oil on canvas, 20 x 36 ins / 51 x 91.5 cm) GBP 17,600. London, 7 June 1991, *Landscape* (oil on canvas, 16 x 36 ins / 40.5 x 91.5 cm) GBP 17,050. London, 8 Nov 1991, *Spring in the Air* (1933, oil on canvas, 28 x 40¼ ins / 71 x 102 cm) GBP 26,400. London, 11 June 1992, *Interior at Moatlands* (1929, oil on canvas, 20¼ x 26¼ ins / 51.5 x 66.5 cm) GBP 23,100. London, 25 May 1994, *Flowers, Yellow and Green* (1948, oil on canvas, 32 x 39¼ ins / 81 x 100 cm) GBP 17,250. Mill House, Sonning (Berkshire), 22 June 1994, *Fir and Birch* (1934, oil on canvas, 21 x 24 ins / 53.3 x 60.9 cm) GBP 9,775. London, 26 Oct 1994, *Figure near a Doorway* (oil on canvas, 19 x 24 ins / 48.2 x 61 cm) GBP 12,650. London, 22 May 1996, *Still-life of Spring Flowers* (oil on canvas, 22 x 24 ins / 56 x 61 cm) GBP 24,150. London, 23 Oct 1996, *Willow Covered Pool* (c. 1960, oil on canvas, 16 x 36 ins / 40.6 x 91.5 cm) GBP 6,900. London, 2 Dec 1996, *Water, Rushes, and Reflections* (1964, oil on canvas, 16 x 36 ins / 40.8 x 91.4 cm) GBP 7,500. London, 11 Dec 1997, *Dinghy at Sea in Summer* (1957, oil on canvas, 16 x 29¼ ins / 40.6 x 74 cm) GBP 6,325. London, 5 March 1999, *Floral Still-life* (1932, oil on canvas, 22 x 33 ins / 56 x 84 cm) GBP 40,000. London, 2 Nov 1999, *Millpool in Haze* (c. 1957, oil on canvas, 17 x 35 ins / 42 x 90 cm) GBP 38,000. London, 9 June 2000, *Still-life with Daisies and Daffodils* (oil on canvas, 30 x 16 ins / 76 x 41 cm) GBP 32,000. Toronto, 12 June 2000, *Pattern of Poppies* (oil on canvas, 20 x 44 ins / 51 x 113 cm) CAD 57,000. London, 8 June 2001, *Land and Sky Spaces No.3 1963* (oil on canvas, 18 x 56 ins / 46 x 143 cm) GBP 29,000. London, 14 June 2001, *Cottage Interior* (1925, oil on canvas, 20 x 18 ins / 51 x 45 cm) GBP 35,000. London, 22 Nov 2002, *Spring Flowers and Blue Teapot* (c. 1934, oil on canvas, 29 x 24 ins / 74 x 61 cm) GBP 55,000. London, 3 Dec 2002, *River Rother, near Stedham* (1964, oil on canvas, 18 x 43 ins / 45 x 110 cm) GBP 34,000. London, 21 Nov 2003, *Orange Boy, John by Jordan no.3* (1942, oil on canvas, 16 x 30 ins / 41 x 75 cm) GBP 92,000. London, 21 Nov 2003, *Boy at Breakfast* (1943, oil on canvas, 25 x 36 ins / 64 x 91 cm) GBP 150,000. London, 2 June 2004, *Orange Bush 1* (oil on canvas, 18 x 30 ins / 46 x 76 cm) GBP 62,000. London, 19 Nov 2004, *Flowers and a Mirror* (1969, pencil and oil on canvas, 20 x 33 ins / 50 x 83 cm) GBP 22,000.

HITCHINGS, J.
British, 19th century.
Active in London.
Painter. Rustic scenes.
J. Hitchings exhibited in London at the Suffolk Street Gallery between 1860 and 1870.

HITMAYER, Johann Baptist
German, 18th - 19th century.
Born 1751, in Salzburg; died 1810, in Munich.
Painter. Historical scenes, portraits.
Hitmayer was a pupil of Streicher in Salzburg.

HITSU. See **TSUBAKI Chinzan**

HITTA DEL CASTILLO, Agustino
Spanish.
Active in Seville.
Sculptor.
Agustino Hitta del Castillo was a relative of Benito Hita del Castillo.

HITTELL, Charles J.
American, 19th century.
Born 4 August 1861, in San Francisco; died 1938, in Pacific Grove (California).
Painter. Genre scenes.
Charles J. Hittell studied in Munich and then in Paris.

HITTLE, Margaret A.
American, 20th century.
Born 19 April 1886, in Victor (Iowa).
Painter, engraver, illustrator. Genre scenes.
Margaret Hittle studied in Chicago.

HITZ, Conrad
Swiss, 19th century.
Born 23 December 1798, in Langnau; died 10 July 1866, in Munich.
Miniaturist, painter (porcelain).
Conrad Hitz worked in Munich and executed many paintings on porcelain.

HITZ, Dora
German, 19th - 20th century.
Born 31 March 1856, in Altdorf; died 1924.
Painter. Genre scenes, portraits.
Dora Hitz studied with Lindenschmit in Munich from 1870 to 1878. In 1878, she went to stay at the court of Queen Elisabeth of Romania in Bucharest until 1882, when she went to Paris and worked under the direction of Luc-Olivier Merson, Courtois, Benjamin Constant and Carrière. She remained there until 1891, winning a bronze medal at the 1889 Exposition Universelle. In 1891, she became an associate of the Société Nationale des Beaux-Arts, then she returned to Germany, settling first in Dresden and then in Berlin. She exhibited in Paris, Germany (in particular Munich, Dresden and Berlin), and also at the Royal Academy in London. However, her best works are the beautiful frescoes she painted at the royal castle of Peles in Sinaia, Romania.
MUSEUMS AND GALLERIES:
BERLIN: *Portrait of a Little Girl.*
AUCTION RECORDS:
BERN, 1 May 1980, *Maternal Tenderness* (oil on canvas, 26 x 41 ins / 66 x 104 cm) CHF 3,200. LONDON, 28 Nov 1985, *Two Girls* (pastel, 20 1/2 x 28 3/4 ins / 52 x 73 cm) GBP 1,200. ZURICH, 13 June 1986, *Mother and Child* (oil on canvas, 26 x 40 1/4 ins / 66 x 102.5 cm) CHF 6,500.

HITZ-BAY, Hanni
Swiss, 20th century.
Born 28 September 1885, in Belp (Bern).
Painter.
Hanni Hitz-Bay studied with Ernst Linck in Bern and then set up in Coire.

HITZBERGER, Otto
German, 20th century.
Born 2 October 1878, in Munich.
Sculptor.
Otto Hitzberger studied in Garmisch-Partenkirchen, before going to work in Munich and Stuttgart.

HITZENTHALER, Anton, the Elder
Austrian, 19th century.
Active in Linz c. 1800.
Painter.
Anton Hitzenthaler the Elder worked for several churches, including those of Feldkirchen, Helmansöd, Linz and Leonfelden.

HITZENTHALER, Anton, the Younger
Austrian, 19th century.
Active in Linz at the beginning of the 19th century.
Painter.
Anton Hitzenthaler the Younger, a son or brother of Anton Hitzenthaler the Elder, painted frescoes and restored religious paintings in Linz.

HITZL, Franz
Austrian, 19th century.
Born 22 May 1794, in Salzburg; died 29 January 1856, in Salzburg.
Sculptor.
Franz Hitzl, a son of Franz de Paula Hitzl, worked for the Peterskirche in Salzburg.

HITZL, Franz de Paula
Austrian, 18th - 19th century.
Born 1738, in Salzburg; died 22 January 1819, in Salzburg.
Sculptor.
Franz de Paula Hitzl, a son of Johann Georg Hitzl, assisted his father in his work and lived in Berlin, Vienna, Potsdam and Dresden.

HITZL, Jakob
Austrian, 18th century.
Active near Salzburg, c. 1750.
Sculptor.

HITZL, Johann Georg
Austrian, 18th century.
Born c. 1706; died 16 July 1781.
Active in Salzburg.
Sculptor.
Johann Georg Hitzl is best known for his work for the Peterskirche in Salzburg.

HITZL, Johann Paul
Austrian, 18th century.
Died 1799.
Active in Salzburg.
Sculptor.
Johann Paul Hitzl was a son of Johann Georg Hitzl.

HIU. See **XU YI**

HIU CHE-K'I. See **XU SHIQI**

HIU KING. See **XU JING**

HIU MENG-TS'AI. See **XU MENGCAI**

HIU PIN. See **XU BIN**

HIU TAO-NING. See **XU DAONING**

HIU TCHEN. See **XU ZHEN**

HIU YEOU. See **XU YOU**

HIU-KOU. See **XUGU**

HIVONNAIT, Guillaume
French, 19th century.
Born in Poitiers; died 1830, in Poitiers.
Painter, draughtsman. Animals.
MUSEUMS AND GALLERIES:
ROCHEFORT: red chalk.

HIWASAKI, Takao
Japanese, 20th century.
Born 1941, in Kochi Prefecture.
Engraver.
Hiwasaki Takao took part in the 7th International Print Biennale, held in Tokyo in 1970.

HIXON, James Thompson
British, 19th century.
Born 1836; died 30 July 1868, on Capri.
Watercolourist.
James Hixon worked for a long time in Algiers. He exhibited in London at the British Institution, the Suffolk Street Gallery and the New Water-Colour Society (of which he was a member) between 1856 and 1867.

HIXON, R.
British, 19th century.
Active in London in 1813.
Engraver.

HIXON, William J.
British, 19th century.
Active in London.
Painter. Animals.
William Hixon exhibited in London at the Royal Academy, the British Institution and the Suffolk Street Gallery from 1825 to 1857.

HIZALDI. See **ELEZADI Miguel**

HJALTELIN, Thorstein Illia
Danish, 18th - 19th century.
Born 1771, in Iceland; died 1815 or 1817, in Halle.
Active from c. 1800 in Germany.
Painter. Landscapes.
Thorstein Hjaltelin was a pupil of Johann Freidrich Weitsch. He lived in Iceland and then Copenhagen. He then settled in Germany, living in Brunswick before later moving to Königsberg and Halle.

HJERLOW, Rangvald Amandus
Norwegian, 19th century.
Born 20 February 1863, in Christiania (now Oslo).
Painter. Genre scenes, landscapes.
Rangvald Hjerlow was a pupil of Knut Bergslien. He received an honourable mention at the Exposition Universelle in Paris in 1889.

HJERTEN, Sigrid, married Isaac Grünewald
Swedish, 20th century.
Born 1885, in Sundsvall; died 1948.
Painter. Portraits, landscapes, interiors, still-lifes.
De Unga Group.
Sigrid Hjerten went to Paris in 1909 to learn the technique of painting on fabrics. In 1910, she became a pupil of Henri Matisse. Matisse considered her to have been the most gifted of his Scandinavian students. She married the painter Isaac Grünewald and travelled through Europe with him during the 1920s. Together with her husband and Leander Engström, she was a member of the De Unga group. During her first stay in Paris, she exhibited at the Salon des Indépendants and the Salon d'Automne in 1911 and 1913. She exhibited in Malmö in 1914, Berlin in 1915, Göteborg in 1916 and Venice in 1920. After 1935 she began to suffer mental problems, and stopped painting.

When she returned to Sweden after her first stay in Paris, the influence of Matisse lingered on in her painting. At that time, she was painting typical views of Stockholm and the city park, interior scenes, still-lifes, and portraits of her son Ivan. Then, while travelling with her husband, she was influenced by him to become more expressionist and create more elaborate compositions, painting the same subjects, especially the landscape of Provence, with a heightened range of colours.

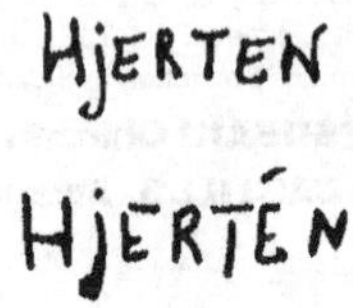

AUCTION RECORDS:
STOCKHOLM, 23 April 1980, *Two Figures in a Landscape, Cassis* (oil on canvas, 28 3/4 x 39 1/4 ins / 73 x 100 cm) SEK 57,000. STOCKHOLM, 25 Nov 1982, *Still-life with Flowers* (oil on canvas, 31 1/2 x 25 1/4 ins / 80 x 64 cm) SEK 138,000. STOCKHOLM, 23 April 1983, *Still-life with Orchids* (oil on canvas, 35 3/4 x 28 1/4 ins / 91 x 72 cm) SEK 35,000. STOCKHOLM, 16 May 1984, *Three Girls in an Interior* (mixed media, 14 1/2 x 10 1/4 ins / 37 x 26 cm) SEK 19,500. STOCKHOLM, 16 Nov 1985, *Still-life with Flowers* (oil on canvas, 28 1/4 x 23 1/4 ins / 72 x 59 cm) SEK 49,000. LONDON, 29 March 1990, *Vast Landscape* (oil on canvas, 24 1/2 x 20 1/2 ins / 62 x 52 cm) GBP 82,500. STOCKHOLM, 5 Sept 1992, *Portrait of a Man* (oil on panel, 12 1/2 x 9 ins / 32 x 23 cm) SEK 14,500. STOCKHOLM, 10-12 May 1993, *Fortified Village on a Mountain Spur in Provence* (1935, oil on canvas, 28 3/4 x 36 1/2 ins / 73 x 93 cm) SEK 155,000. STOCKHOLM, 30 Nov 1993, *Still-life on a Blue Background* (gouache, 19 x 24 3/4 ins / 48 x 63 cm) SEK 42,000. LONDON, 15 March 1996, *The Cousins* (oil on card, 28 1/2 x 26 ins / 72.5 x 66 cm) GBP 17,825. STOCKHOLM, 27 April 1999, *Berthe Embroidering* (tempera on canvas, 31 x 26 ins / 80 x 66 cm) SEK 500,000. STOCKHOLM, 22 Nov 1999, *Ester in a Blue Suit* (1916, oil on canvas, 39 x 29 ins / 100 x 73 cm) SEK 540,000. STOCKHOLM, 2 May 2000, *Self-portrait* (oil on canvas, 45 x 35 ins / 115 x 89 cm) SEK 1,450,000. STOCKHOLM, 7 Nov 2000, *Ivan and the Flowers* (c. 1918, oil on canvas, 22 x 20 ins / 55 x 50 cm) SEK 850,000. STOCKHOLM, 2 May 2001, *Woman in a Red Interior* (oil on canvas, 63 x 59 ins / 159 x 151 cm) SEK 2,450,000. STOCKHOLM, 6 Nov 2001, *Dora and Ivan in Granna* (oil on canvas, 39 x 32 ins / 100 x 81 cm) SEK 3,600,000. STOCKHOLM, 6 Nov 2002, *Woman in a Yellow Blouse* (1919, oil on canvas, 25 x 19 ins / 64 x 49 cm) SEK 430,000. STOCKHOLM, 6 Nov 2002, *Children* (1914, oil on canvas, 60 x 63 ins / 153 x 161 cm) SEK 3,000,000. STOCKHOLM, 28 April 2003, *Beach at Alassio* (gouache, 20 x 25 ins / 50 x 64 cm) SEK 250,000. STOCKHOLM, 4 Nov 2003, *Ivan Playing in a Heap of Sand* (1913, oil on canvas, 18 x 15 ins / 45 x 38 cm) SEK 630,000. STOCKHOLM, 26 April 2004, *Kornhamstorg - Market Scene with Figures* (1913, watercolour, 39 x 46 ins / 98 x 116 cm) SEK 495,000. STOCKHOLM, 26 April 2004, *Red Hoisting Cranes at Stadsgaarden* (oil on panel, 36 x 29 ins / 92 x 73 cm) SEK 1,450,000.

HJORTH, Brör Leonard
Swedish, 20th century.
Born 1894, in Marma (Uppsala); died 1968, in Uppsala.
Painter, sculptor (wood/bronze/clay). Figures, nudes, popular scenes, interiors with figures.
Färg och Form (Colour and Form) Group.
Brör Hjorth spent his youth among peasant folk and foresters. He studied first at the Stockholm academy until 1915, then with Einar Utzon-Frank at the Kunstakademi in Copenhagen. He then went to Paris for nine years, working for three years from 1921 to 1924 in the studio of Antoine Bour-

delle. He became particularly fascinated by the work of Gauguin, and was also interested in the Douanier Rousseau, and Chagall. On returning to Sweden in 1930, he became director of a school of sculpture in Stockholm. He was one of the co-founders of the group Färg och Form (Colour and Form). In 1929, he featured in the exhibition of Swedish art in Paris, and in 1945 in the exhibition of Swedish art at the Swedish Institute in London. From 1949 to 1959, he was professor of drawing at the Stockholm art college.

He was very drawn to folk art and also to Gauguin's attempts to achieve authentic Polynesian forms. During the 1920s, he was close to the Neo-Primitives, who liked to think of themselves as reacting against the European avant-garde, whom they considered too intellectual and divorced from reality. The paintings of his Paris years are mainly landscapes, some of them memories of his homeland. They are very like the naive art he was so fond of and the colours are rather crude. After his return to Sweden, he developed a more realistic style with more traditional, though bold, draughtsmanship. Like Gauguin, he was both a painter and a sculptor, and carved and painted the frames for his pictures. He painted figures, rustic nudes, scenes of working-class life and national folklore, with forms reduced to the essential and bold colours. His wood sculptures were also polychrome in order to add to their expressiveness.

MUSEUMS AND GALLERIES:
GÖTEBORG: *At the Kitchen Table* (1923) - STOCKHOLM (Nationalmus.): *Margit in the Garden* (1941) - STOCKHOLM (Waldemarsudde): *The Violin Lesson* (1946).

AUCTION RECORDS:
STOCKHOLM, 24 April 1947, *Nude Woman Reading,* SEK 3,300. STOCKHOLM, 22 March 1956, *Interior with Two Female Nudes,* SEK 3,150. STOCKHOLM, 7 Dec 1960, *Female Nude in a Rocking-Chair in front of a Curtain,* SEK 6,800. GÖTEBORG, 9 Nov 1977, *Margit* (oil on canvas, 36 1/4 x 28 3/4 ins / 92 x 73 cm) SEK 47,000. STOCKHOLM, 24 April 1980, *The Bride* (wood, painted relief, 13 3/4 x 7 ins / 35 x 18 cm) SEK 46,000. STOCKHOLM, 26 Nov 1981, *Summer Landscape* (c. 1950, oil on canvas, 19 1/4 x 31 1/2 ins / 49 x 80 cm) SEK 65,000. STOCKHOLM, 26 Nov 1982, *Rolande* (terracotta, l. 27 1/2 ins / 70 cm) SEK 17,200. STOCKHOLM, 27 April 1983, *Model with Violin* (1923, charcoal and watercolour, 22 x 13 3/4 ins / 55 x 35 cm) SEK 15,500. STOCKHOLM, 30 Nov 1983, *Skaldinnan* (1952-1954, polychrome wood relief, 43 3/4 x 26 1/2 ins / 111 x 67 cm) SEK 120,000. STOCKHOLM, 16 Nov 1985, *Snowy Landscape* (oil on canvas, 16 1/4 x 20 3/4 ins / 41 x 53 cm) SEK 155,000. STOCKHOLM, 7 Dec 1987, *Aphrodite* (1947, wood, painted relief, h. 39 1/4 ins / 100 cm) SEK 215,000. STOCKHOLM, 30 May 1991, *Little Girl with Her Dog* (stone, h. 10 1/4 ins / 26 cm) SEK 10,000. STOCKHOLM, 19 May 1992, *Girl with Violin* (brown-patinated bronze, h. 15 3/4 ins / 40 cm) SEK 41,000. STOCKHOLM, 22 Nov 1999, *Nude Girl in Rocking Chair* (c. 1945, oil on canvas, 25 x 21 ins / 64 x 53 cm) SEK 730,000. UPPSALA, 5 Dec 1999, *Girl in Garden* (1924, oil on canvas, 32 x 21 ins / 81 x 54 cm) SEK 120,000. STOCKHOLM, 2 May 2000, *Girl with Basket of Apples* (gold-patinated bronze, h. 16 ins / 40 cm) SEK 24,000. STOCKHOLM, 2 May 2000, *Girl Playing the Violin* (oil on panel, 7 x 4 ins / 18 x 10 cm) SEK 360,000. STOCKHOLM, 6 Nov 2001, *Cubist Girl* (1921, dark patinated bronze, h. 61 ins / 156 cm) SEK 800,000. STOCKHOLM, 27 Nov 2001, *Girl and Lion* (1966, oil on canvas, 39 x 41 ins / 100 x 105 cm) SEK 1,000,000. STOCKHOLM, 24 April 2002, *Irene and Yellow Flowers - Interior with Nude Model* (1947, oil on canvas, 18 x 15 ins / 46 x 38 cm) SEK 580,000. STOCKHOLM, 5 Nov 2002, *Love Scene I* (polychrome painted wood, 70 x 27 ins / 177 x 68 cm) SEK 750,000. STOCKHOLM, 4 Nov 2003, *Reclining Girl* (painted terracotta, w. 9 ins / 24 cm) SEK 29,000. STOCKHOLM, 5 Nov 2003, *Lady of the Woods and Fiddler* (1947, sculpted painted black oak, h. 33 ins / 84 cm, w. 20 ins/50 cm) SEK 800,000. STOCKHOLM, 26 April 2004, *Violinist on Horseback* (mixed media, 7 x 8 ins / 18 x 21 cm) SEK 70,000. STOCKHOLM, 27 April 2004, *Old Rattviks Road in Sjugare* (oil on canvas, 24 x 20 ins / 61 x 50 cm) SEK 330,000.

HJORTH NIELSEN, Søren

Danish, 20th century.
Born 1901, in Svostrup, near Silkeborg; died 1983.
Painter, engraver. Portraits, landscapes, urban landscapes.

From 1925, Søren Hjorth Nielsen studied painting and sculpture at the Kunstakademi in Copenhagen. He travelled in Scandinavia, Italy, France and Germany. He took part in many group exhibitions in Denmark and several other European countries. He was one of the co-founders of the Decembrists group and exhibited regularly at *den Frie Udstilling* (*the Free Exhibition*) in Copenhagen. He was a professor at the Kunstakademi in Copenhagen and was awarded the Eckersberg medal in 1940.

In his portraits and landscapes, often views of Copenhagen or typical village scenes, his palette became lighter over the years.

MUSEUMS AND GALLERIES:
AARHUS (Kunstmus.): *Winter* (1934) - COPENHAGEN (Statens Mus. for Kunst): *Vigerslev* (1937); *Aarhus Harbour* (1939); *Fredensbro* (1940).

AUCTION RECORDS:
COPENHAGEN, 11 Oct 1979, *Fishermen's Houses* (1957, oil on canvas, 32 x 39 3/4 ins / 81 x 101 cm) DKK 19,000. COPENHAGEN, 6 May 1987, *House by the Sea* (c. 1942, oil on canvas, 22 3/4 x 33 1/2 ins / 58 x 85 cm) DKK 24,000. COPENHAGEN, 2 March 1988, *View of a Country Village* (oil on canvas, 33 1/2 x 45 1/4 ins / 85 x 115 cm) DKK 80,000. COPENHAGEN, 4 May 1988, *Warehouses* (1976, 35 x 46 ins / 89 x 116 cm) DKK 27,000; *Summer Landscape at Askøy in Norway* (1951, 25 1/2 x 32 1/4 ins / 65 x 82 cm) DKK 6,000. COPENHAGEN, 30 Nov 1988, *View of Part of Holte Station* (1934, oil on canvas, 32 1/4 x 41 ins / 82 x 104 cm) DKK 4,000. COPENHAGEN, 10 May 1989, *Fredensbro* (oil on canvas, 27 1/2 x 40 1/4 ins / 70 x 102 cm) DKK 30,000. COPENHAGEN, 22 Nov 1989, *The Park in Silkeborg* (1927, oil on canvas, 21 1/4 x 28 3/4 ins / 54 x 73 cm) DKK 6,500. COPENHAGEN, 21-22 March 1990, *View of the Road through Christiansborg with the Canal* (oil on canvas, 34 1/4 x 42 1/2 ins / 87 x 108 cm) DKK 30,000. COPENHAGEN, 9 May 1990, *The Village of Fredensbro* (1942, oil on canvas, 42 1/4 x 51 1/4 ins / 107 x 130 cm) DKK 48,000. COPENHAGEN, 31 Oct 1990, *Summer Landscape* (oil on canvas, 41 1/4 x 47 1/4 ins / 105 x 120 cm) DKK 18,000. COPENHAGEN, 1 April 1992, *View of a Western District of Copenhagen* (oil on canvas, 26 1/2 x 34 1/4 ins / 67 x 87 cm) DKK 14,000. COPENHAGEN, 21 Oct 1992, *Still-life* (oil on canvas, 28 3/4 x 23 1/2 ins / 73 x 60 cm) DKK 7,000. COPENHAGEN, 13 April 1994, *View of the Harbour of Vesterø* (1960, oil on canvas, 35 x 51 1/4 ins / 89 x 130 cm) DKK 26,000. COPENHAGEN, 26 April 1995, *Road between the Trees* (oil on canvas, 25 1/2 x 22 3/4 ins / 65 x 58 cm) DKK 5,500. COPENHAGEN, 17 April 1996, *A Distant Hunting Ground* (1934, oil on canvas, 28 x 35 3/4 ins / 71 x 91 cm) DKK 9,400. COPENHAGEN, 6 Oct 1999, *Landscape with Houses* (oil on canvas, 30 x 37 ins / 75 x 95 cm) DKK 21,000. VEJLE, 19 Nov 1999, *Seated Woman* (1931, oil on canvas, 43 x 47 ins / 110 x 120 cm) DKK 18,000. AARHUS, 11 March 2000, *Model and Woman with Child* (1927, oil on canvas, 48 x 24 ins / 123 x 61 cm) DKK 14,000. COPENHAGEN, 2 Oct 2001, *Winter Scene, Sydhavnen* (oil on canvas, 31 x 37 ins / 80 x 95 cm) DKK 16,500. COPENHAGEN, 25 Oct 2001, *Coastal Landscape from Læsø* (1955, oil on canvas, 29 x 37 ins / 74 x 93 cm) DKK 15,000. COPENHAGEN, 10 April 2002, *Landscape from Svanninge Hills*

(oil on canvas, 36 x 46 ins / 92 x 116 cm) DKK 16,000. Copenhagen, 4 Dec 2002, *Summer Landscape, Asserbo* (oil on canvas, 26 x 36 ins / 65 x 92 cm) DKK 15,000. Copenhagen, 12 June 2003, *Summer Landscape, Falsted* (1956-1958, oil on canvas, 29 x 37 ins / 73 x 93 cm) DKK 17,000. Copenhagen, 7 Oct 2003, *View of Houses* (oil on canvas, 35 x 46 ins / 89 x 117 cm) DKK 28,000. Copenhagen, 29 March 2004, *Harbour View* (oil on canvas, 31 x 39 ins / 80 x 100 cm) DKK 22,000. Vejle, 9 Aug 2004, *Town in Winter* (1980, oil on canvas, 31 x 40 ins / 80 x 102 cm) DKK 22,000.

HJORTZBERG, Gustav Olof, or Hiortzberg, called Olle
Swedish, 19th - 20th century.
Born 14 November 1872, in Stockholm; died 1959.
Painter, watercolourist, engraver, draughtsman, illustrator, poster artist. Figures, portraits, landscapes with figures, still-lifes (including flowers/fruit). Wall decorations, designs for stained glass.

Gustav Olof Hjortzberg studied at the Stockholm academy from 1892 to 1896. He spent seven years travelling in France, Italy, Spain, Greece and Asia. After returning to Stockholm, he was professor of drawing at the academy from 1911 to 1917, and later its director from 1920 to 1941. Between 1921 and 1938, he instituted a school of decorative arts at the academy. He took part in group exhibitions, including the *Exposition d'Art Suédois* (*Exhibition of Swedish Art*) in Paris in 1929. He became a member of the Swedish academy of fine art.

In addition to his paintings on various themes, his main occupation was the painting of murals for many churches and public buildings, including Stockholm city hall and the church of the Annunciation in Saltsjöbaden. He designed posters for the Olympic Games in Stockholm in 1912 and also illustrated the *Gustav Vasa Bible*. His diverse works show Byzantine and Italian influences.

Museums and Galleries:
Göteborg: *View of Italy*.

Auction records:
Göteborg, 1 Nov 1972, *Still-life*, SEK 8,500. Göteborg, 24 March 1976, *Still-life with Flowers* (1944, oil on panel, 25 1/2 x 21 1/4 ins / 65 x 54 cm) SEK 18,200. Malmö, 2 May 1977, *San Gimignano* (1946, watercolour, 22 1/2 x 32 1/4 ins / 57 x 82 cm) SEK 7,000. Göteborg, 9 Nov 1977, *Still-life* (oil on canvas, 25 1/2 x 21 1/4 ins / 65 x 54 cm) SEK 28,000. Stockholm, 30 Oct 1979, *Summer Landscape* (1951, oil on canvas, 24 3/4 x 21 ins / 63 x 52.5 cm) SEK 14,000. Stockholm, 26 Oct 1982, *Still-life with Flowers* (1945, oil on panel, 28 1/4 x 23 1/4 ins / 72 x 59 cm) SEK 85,000. Stockholm, 26 April 1983, *Still-life with Flowers* (1945, oil on panel, 28 1/4 x 23 1/4 ins / 72 x 59 cm) SEK 82,000. Stockholm, 24 April 1984, *Still-life with Flowers* (1954, watercolour, 15 3/4 x 12 1/2 ins / 40 x 32 cm) SEK 25,000. Stockholm, 9 April 1985, *Bunch of Summer Flowers* (1943, oil on panel, 45 x 35 ins / 114 x 88 cm) SEK 380,000. Stockholm, 29 Oct 1985, *Still-life with Flowers* (watercolour, 18 x 15 ins / 46 x 38 cm) SEK 13,700. Stockholm, 20 Oct 1987, *Still-life with Summer Flowers* (1943, oil on panel, 46 x 33 3/4 ins / 116 x 86 cm) SEK 340,000. London, 16 March 1989, *The Spirit of the Waters* (oil on canvas, 115 1/2 x 68 3/4 ins / 293.5 x 174.5 cm) GBP 13,200. Stockholm, 22 May 1989, *Landscape with Trees and Buildings and a Man Guarding Cattle* (oil on panel, 17 3/4 x 14 1/2 ins / 45 x 37 cm) SEK 18,000. Copenhagen, 25 Oct 1989, *Portrait of an Old Woman* (oil on canvas, 28 x 21 1/4 ins / 71 x 54 cm) DKK 7,500. Stockholm, 6 Dec 1989, *Still-life with Apples and Grapes* (oil on panel, 15 x 18 ins / 38 x 46 cm) SEK 71,000. London, 27-28 March 1990, *A Red Rose* (1946, oil on canvas, 23 1/2 x 28 3/4 ins / 60 x 73 cm) GBP 23,100. Stockholm, 5-6 Dec 1990, *Peonies in a Silver Vase* (1945, oil on panel, 23 1/2 x 19 1/4 ins / 60 x 49 cm) SEK 78,000. Stockholm, 29 May 1991, *Still-life with a Yellow Rose in a Pottery Vase* (1952, oil on canvas, 25 1/4 x 19 1/4 ins / 64 x 49 cm) SEK 45,000. Stockholm, 19 May 1992, *Branch of a Rose-bush* (watercolour, 13 1/2 x 9 3/4 ins / 34 x 25 cm) SEK 16,500. Stockholm, 30 Nov 1993, *Still-life with an Earthenware Soup Tureen* (1945, oil on panel, 21 1/4 x 25 1/2 ins / 54 x 65 cm) SEK 32,000. Stockholm, 24 Nov 1999, *Meadowflowers* (1941, oil on panel, 29 x 24 ins / 73 x 60 cm) SEK 130,000. Stockholm, 24 Nov 1999, *Still-life with Pink Roses and Cornflower* (1948, oil on panel, 20 x 24 ins / 50 x 62 cm) SEK 135,000. Stockholm, 29 May 2000, *Hare-bells and Other Meadow Flowers* (1947, oil on panel, 37 x 29 ins / 93 x 73 cm) SEK 240,000. Stockholm, 29 May 2000, *Summer Flowers in Vase* (1944, oil on panel, 46 x 35 ins / 116 x 89 cm) SEK 385,000. Stockholm, 29 May 2001, *Wildflowers* (1946, oil on canvas, 24 x 20 ins / 61 x 50 cm) SEK 195,000. Göteborg, 24 Nov 2001, *Meadowflowers* (1943, oil on panel, 36 x 29 ins / 92 x 73 cm) SEK 200,000. Stockholm, 28 May 2002, *Still-life with Roses in Silver Vase and Apples* (1944, oil on panel, 36 x 29 ins / 92 x 73 cm) SEK 150,000. Stockholm, 3 Dec 2002, *Still-life of with Wildflowers* (1941, oil on canvas, 24 x 20 ins / 61 x 50 cm) SEK 105,000. Stockholm, 26 May 2003, *Midsummer Wildflowers* (1942, oil on panel, 39 x 32 ins / 100 x 81 cm) SEK 450,000. Stockholm, 4 June 2003, *Still-life with Yellow Roses in Silver Vase* (1946, oil on panel, 26 x 20 ins / 65 x 50 cm) SEK 120,000. Stockholm, 25 May 2004, *Still-life with Chrysanthemums* (1955, oil on panel, 39 x 32 ins / 100 x 81 cm) SEK 350,000. Stockholm, 25 May 2004, *Wildflowers in a Dish* (1951, oil on canvas, 20 x 24 ins / 50 x 61 cm) SEK 410,000.

HLADIK, Karel
Czech, 20th century.
Born 27 June 1912, in Prague; died 27 April 1967, in Prague.
Sculptor. Figures.

Karel Hladik was trained as a stone cutter. From 1929 to 1940 he worked in the studio of the sculptor V. Skoda in Hradec Králové. From 1940 to 1944 he was a pupil of Jan Lauda at the school of decorative arts in Prague. From 1945 to 1947 he studied with Karel Pokorny at the school of fine art, where he taught from 1947 until his death.

His sculpture is figurative, graceful and tender. It is Impressionist in feel, and his models in particular recall Degas, not least because he often portrayed dancers.

HLAVACEK, Avlov or Anton
Austrian, 19th - 20th century.
Born 7 May 1842, in Vienna; died 1926.
Painter, watercolourist. Landscapes.

Avlov Hlavacek studied with Steinfels at the Akademie in Vienna in 1859, and later with Zimmermann. After some study tours, he settled in Vienna, where he exhibited from 1871.

Museums and Galleries:
Vienna: *View of the Palatinate*; watercolour.

Auction records:
London, 16 Sept 1969, *View of Vienna*, ATS 55,000. Vienna, 11 March 1980, *View of Melk* (watercolour, 8 1/4 x 11 3/4 ins / 21 x 30 cm) ATS 25,000. London, 7 May 1980, *Tyrolean Landscape* (1893, oil on canvas, 26 x 39 3/4 ins / 66 x 101 cm) GBP 2,600. Vienna, 17 March 1982, *Alpine Landscape* (oil on canvas, 18 1/2 x 25 ins / 46.8 x 63.6 cm) AST 60,000. Vienna, 23 March 1983, *The Königssee* (mixed media/canvas, 9 3/4 x 13 3/4 ins / 25 x 35 cm) ATS 11,000. London, 26 Feb 1988, *Mountain Lake* (oil on canvas, 27 x 41 3/4 ins / 68.5 x 106 cm) GBP 3,300.

HLAVICA, Frantisek
Czech, 20th century.
Born 23 January 1885, in Vsetín.
Painter.
Hlavica worked in Brno.

HLAVIN, Bartolomej
Bohemian, 19th century.
Born 1846, in Bestin; died 19 December 1904, in Prague.
Painter.
Bartolomej Hlavin studied at the academy in Prague.

HLEMER, Franz Karl. See **HIEMER**

HLITO, Alfredo
Argentinian, 20th century.
Born 1923, in Buenos Aires; died 1993.
Painter, draughtsman.
Neo-Constructivism.
Groups: Arte Concreto Invención, Artistas Modernos de la Argentina.
Alfredo Hlito studied at the school of fine arts in Buenos Aires but soon came under the influence of Torres García. In 1946 he became one of the co-founders of the Arte Concreto-Invención group with Maldonado and Girola, with whom he signed the *Manifesto Invencionista* the same year. In 1953 he travelled in Europe and the same year won a prize at the 2nd São Paulo Biennale.

Around 1943, when he was about 20, Hlito painted in the Expressionist style. His first abstract works appeared in 1944. They have been described as: 'planes and finely shaded lines, reduced to the barest essentials'. Later, without renouncing the principles of Art Concret in any way, he went on to develop his own style, moving towards greater suppleness, particularly in his touch, and according to Impressionist techniques which he had discovered during his 1953 visit to Europe. His later works are more ambitious, their simple forms achieve a monumental effect and his colour register becomes more refined, ranging from bright tones to harmonious and subtle greys.

Hlito took part in collective exhibitions and published studies on *Art Concret* and the *New Vision*. His national and international exhibitions include: *Painting and Sculpture of the Present Century* at the national fine arts museum in Buenos Aires (1952); *Modern Artists of Argentina* at the Stedelijk Museum in Amsterdam, Rio de Janeiro museum, São Paulo Biennale (1953); Venice Biennale and *Exhibition of Argentinian Painting* in Washington (1956); *Art Concret* at the Kunsthaus, Zurich and the Buenos Aires International Exhibition (1960); *150 Years of Argentinian Painting and Sculpture* (1961). He also exhibited in solo exhibitions, the first of which took place in Buenos Aires in 1952. Others include: 1979, Galería Jacques Martinez, Buenos Aires; and 1987, Museo Nacional de Bellas Artes, Buenos Aires. A posthumous exhibition of his work, *Alfredo Hlito. Metaphors of the Visible* was held at the Fundación Telefónica in Madrid in 2002.

BIBLIOGRAPHY:
Chierico, Osiris, *Alfredo Hlito, efigies y simulacros, 1976-1979*, exhibition catalogue, Galería Jacques Martínez, Buenos Aires, 1979. Nanni, Martha, *Alfredo Hlito, Obra pictórica 1945-1985*, exhibition catalogue, Museo nacional de Bellas Artes, Buenos Aires, 1987. Alierta, César, et al., *Alfredo Hilto. Metaphors of the Visible*, exhibition catalogue, Fondacíon Telefónica, Madrid, 2002 (texts in English and Spanish).

AUCTION RECORDS:
NEW YORK, 17 May 1994, *Structure* (1945, oil on canvas, 27 1/2 x 19 3/4 ins / 70 x 50 cm) USD 21,850. NEW YORK, 18 May 1995, *Effigy in Orange* (1982, acrylic/canvas, 39 x 31 ins / 99.1 x 78.7 cm) USD 4,025. NEW YORK, 25 Nov 1997, *Development of a Theme* (1952, oil on canvas, 23 3/4 x 28 ins / 60.3 x 70.2 cm) USD 43,125. NEW YORK, 19 Nov 2001, *Untitled* (1952, oil on canvas, 28 x 28 ins / 70 x 70 cm) USD 20,000. BUENOS AIRES, 15 Nov 2002, *Monument* (1989, acrylic, 71 x 18 ins / 180 x 45 cm) USD 8,390. NEW YORK, 19 Nov 2002, *Composition* (1959, oil on canvas, 39 x 19 ins / 99 x 49 cm) USD 5,500. NEW YORK, 19 Nov 2003, *Construction* (1945, oil on canvas, 28 x 20 ins / 70 x 50 cm) USD 18,000. BUENOS AIRES, 30 March 2004, *Untitled* (oil on card, 20 x 14 ins / 50 x 35 cm) USD 11,000. BUENOS AIRES, 1 June 2004, *Ghost* (acrylic, 28 x 47 ins / 70 x 120 cm) USD 32,000.

HLOSICK, Valeria
Polish, 20th century.
Born 1908.
Painter. Flowers.

HLOZNIK, Ferdinand
Czechoslovak, 20th century.
Born 18 November 1921, in Svedernik.
Painter.
Ferdinand Hloznik lived in Bratislava, where he studied at the technical school between 1942 and 1946. Collective exhibitions include: Berlin (1964); São Paulo Biennale (1965); and *Fifty years of Czechoslovak Painting from the Collections of the Galleries, 1918-1958*, a touring exhibition in several museums in the country in 1968 on the 50th anniversary of the founding of Czechoslovakia.

HLOZNIK, Vincent
Czechoslovak, 20th century.
Born 22 October 1919, in Svedernik.
Painter, illustrator. Figures, animals.
Vincent Hloznik studied in Prague from 1937 to 1942 before settling in Bratislava. His work remains within that Expressionist tradition still very much alive in Central Europe, and is characterised by the inclusion of references to primitive art. Figures of humans and animals are used to convey the anguish of existence in an art that angrily expresses the painter's reaction to the oppressive regime set up after the defeat of Dubcek in 1968.

Collective exhibitions include: Venice Biennale (1958); São Paulo Biennale (1963 and 1967); *Fifty years of Czechoslovak Painting from the Collections of the Galleries, 1918-1958* a touring exhibition in several museums in the country in 1968 on the 50th anniversary of the founding of Czechoslovakia (with four works). Solo exhibitions of paintings and engravings include Bratislava; Budapest; Berlin; Mexico; Havana; Warsaw; Leningrad (now St Petersburg); Antwerp; Cairo; London; and Artothèque Sud, Nimes with a collection of his woodcuts produced from 1967 to 1972 (1992).

BIBLIOGRAPHY:
Fifty years of Czechoslovak Painting from the Collections of the Galleries, 1918-1958, exhibition catalogue, Slovenska Narodna Gal., Bratislava, 1968 (in commemoration of the 50th anniversary of the Republic of Czechoslovakia).

HMELKO, Mikhail Ivanovich
Russian, 20th century.
Born 1919.
Painter. Historical subjects, figure compositions, genre scenes, landscapes with figures, harbour scenes.
Mikhail Ivanovich Hmelko studied at the institute of fine art in Kiev and then in Odessa at the art institute with Muchnik. After serving in the army during World War II he received his diploma in Kiev in 1946. He was also a pupil of Trohimenko. Admitted into the union of artists, he was appointed professor at the institute of fine art in Kiev, later becoming dean. As an official painter, he executed many commissions for the Communist party. His work is academic in technique and almost photographic, the compositions bathed in an even golden light symbolic of the happiness made possible by the

new order. As well as illustrating events from the history of the Russian Revolution and the achievements of the Soviet regime, his paintings also show scenes from the everyday life of the fulfilled and praiseworthy citizens. He received many official honours, including the Order of Lenin, and was made an 'artist emeritus'.

AUCTION RECORDS:

PARIS, 18 March 1991, *Lenin Declaring Soviet Power* (1975, oil on card, 18 x 31 1/2 ins / 46 x 80 cm) FRF 5,000. PARIS, 19 June 1991, *The Port of Rotterdam* (1957, oil on card, 10 1/4 x 13 ins / 26 x 33 cm) FRF 4,800.

HNIEPPER, Hans, or Hnieper
Danish, 16th century.
Active in Denmark.
Painter.

Frederick II, King of Denmark and Norway, appointed Hans Hniepper to the post of king's painter in 1578. As well as other work, he produced a series of cartoons for tapestries to be made by another important artist, Antonius de Corte. After this commission was fulfilled, the king ordered him to make cartoons showing himself, his son Christian IV, and three of the kings who had ruled Denmark before him. Hniepper did further work of the same kind. Unfortunately the greater part of these fine tapestries, intended for Kronborg castle, were destroyed in a fire in 1629. The royal portraits were saved, however, and some of them were taken to Fredriksborg castle where they, too, later suffered fire damage. Some were rescued and are now in the Copenhagen museum of antiquities.

HO. See also **HOE**

HÖ. See also **HOE**

HO, Philip. See **HE BAILI**

HO CH'I-YUAN. See **HE QIYUAN**

HO CH'ING-T'AI. See **HE QINGTAI**

HO CH'UNG. See **HE CHONG**

HO CHAO-YE. See **HE SHAOYE**

HO CHING. See **HE JING**

HO HWAI-SHOUH. See **HE HUAISHUO**

HO I. See **HE YI**

HO KING. See **HE JING**

HO LEANG-KIUN. See **HE LIANGJUN**

HO LIANG-CHÜN. See **HE LIANGJUN**

HO LONG. See **HE LONG**

HO LUNG. See **HE LONG**

HO SHAO-YEH. See **HE SHAOYE**

HO T'ENG-CHIAO. See **HE TENGJIAO**

HO T'ENG-KIAO. See **HE TENGJIAO**

HO T'IEN-CHIEN. See **HE TIANJIAN**

HO T'IENKIEN. See **HE TIANJIAN**

HO TCH'ENG. See **HE CHENG**

HO TCH'ONG. See **HE CHONG**

HO TS'I-YUAN. See **HE QIYUAN**

HO TS'ING-T'AI. See **HE QINGTAI**

HO TSOUEN-CHE. See **HE ZUNSHI**

HO TSUN-SHIH. See **HE ZUNSHI**

HO YUAN. See **HE YUAN**

HOADLY, Peter
British.
Miniaturist.

MUSEUMS AND GALLERIES:

AMSTERDAM: *Mary Stuart and her Husband William III* (two portraits).

HOAI NAM
School of Indochina, 20th century.
Born 20th century, in Vietnam.
Painter, decorative artist.

Hoai Nam's paintings and lacquerware have been exhibited in Paris.

HOANG SUNG
Vietnamese, 20th century.
Born 1926, near Hanoi.
Painter (gouache). Scenes with figures, figures, portraits.

Hoang Sung graduated from the school of fine arts in Hanoi in 1960, and undertook postgraduate study in Cuba and the former USSR. In 1973 he spent some time in India. He is known for his lacquerware and his painting on silk, which is done in bright hues.

His work has been exhibited regularly as part of collective exhibitions in Germany (1972), Switzerland (1982), Italy, Belgium, and France (1991 and 1996). He has also received awards for work on cartoon films in Vietnam.

HOANG TICH CHU
Vietnamese, 20th century.
Born 1912, to a family originally from Ha Bac province.
Painter, lacquerer. Scenes with figures, figures, landscapes.

Hoang Tuch Chu graduated from the school of fine arts in Hanoi in 1941 and specialized in lacquer work. He favours themes from rural life, and his compositions are robust and well put together.

BIBLIOGRAPHY:

André-Pallois, Nadine/Ménonville, Corinne de, *Paris-Hanoï-Saigon, l'aventure de l'art moderne au Viêt Nam*, exhibition catalogue, Pavillon des Arts, Paris, 1998.

HOARD, Margaret
American, 19th - 20th century.
Born in Iowa.
Sculptor.

Margaret Hoard worked in New York and San Francisco.

HOARE
British, 17th century.
Engraver.

Hoare engraved Evelyn's sketches of Italy.

HOARE (Mrs)
British, 18th century.
Active in Bath.
Painter.

Mrs Hoare exhibited at the Royal Society of Artists in London in 1766.

HOARE, Prince, the Elder
British, 18th century.
Died 1769.
Active in Bath.
Sculptor.

Hoare the Elder was the brother of William Hoare and a pupil of Scheemakers. He carved the *Tomb of Mrs Margaret Rae* in Worcester Cathedral.

HOARE, Prince, the Younger
British, 18th - 19th century.
Born 1755, in Bath; died 22 December 1834, in Brighton.
Painter. History painting, portraits.

Hoare the Younger studied with his father William Hoare, and then at the Royal Academy in London and in Rome with Mengs. He exhibited at the Royal Academy between 1781 and 1815 but, finding little success with his painting, abandoned it in favour of art criticism.

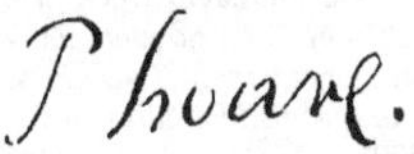

Museums and Galleries:
Florence (Uffizi): *Self-portrait* - London (Victoria and Albert Mus.): *Head of a Woman.*
Auction records:
London, June 1922, *Reverend Henry Pelham,* GBP 26. London, 3 July 1935, *Thomas Edward Freeman,* GBP 98. London, 12 Jan 1942, *Portrait of a Man,* GBP 39.

HOARE, Richard Colt (Bart.)
British, 18th - 19th century.
Born 9 December 1758, in Barn Elms (Surrey); died 19 May 1838, in Stourhead (Wiltshire).
Painter, writer. Landscapes.

Richard Hoare, a distinguished art lover, executed paintings of various places in Wiltshire. He also wrote about the history of Wiltshire.

HOARE, William, called Hoare of Bath
British, 18th century.
Born 1697 or 1706, in Eye (Suffolk); died 1792 or December 1799, in Bath.
Painter, pastellist. Religious subjects, portraits, mythological portraits.

William Hoare studied in London with the Italian painter Grisoni and then attended the school of Francesco Imperiale in Rome. After a period of nine years away, in which he took much inspiration from the works of the old masters, he returned to England, working in London and Bath. One of the founding members of the Royal Academy in London, he exhibited there and at the Society of Artists between 1761 and 1783. He produced a number of history paintings but his greatest successes were his portraits. His attractive works are much sought after.

Museums and Galleries:
Bath (Church): *Christ Carrying the Cross* (oil on canvas) - Bath (Holburne Mus. of Art): *Portrait of Lady Emily Kerr as a Bacchante* (oil on canvas) - Dublin: *Portrait of Philip, Earl of Chesterfield* - London (National Portrait Gal.): *Charles Fitzroy, 2nd Duke of Grafton* (c. 1735-1745, oil on canvas, attributed); *Henry Pelham* (1751, oil on canvas); *William Pitt, 1st Earl of Chatham* (c. 1754, oil on canvas, work of studio); *Richard Grenville-Temple, 2nd Earl Temple* (1760, oil on canvas); *Alexander Pope* (c. 1739-1784, pastel) - London (Tate Collection): *A Gentleman in Brown* (1750, oil on canvas) - London (Victoria and Albert Mus.): *Head of a Girl.*
Auction records:
London, 5 Dec 1908, *Portraits of a Naval Officer and a Lady,* GBP 50. London, 8 July 1910, *Portrait of the Countess of Northampton,* GBP 44. London, Feb 1922, *Earl of Chesterfield in a Red Suit,* GBP 54. London, 27 June 1924, *Lord Anson in Naval Uniform,* GBP 136. London, 21 Sept 1924, *Francesco Geminiani,* GBP 25. London, 12 Dec 1930, *Queen Charlotte,* GBP 47. New York, 4 Feb 1931, *Sir Jeffrey Amherst,* USD 275. London, 4 June 1937, *Sir Henry Clinton,* GBP 262. New York, 5 May 1939, *Henry Pelham,* GBP 115. New York, 5 April 1946, *The Honourable Henry Grenville,* GBP 47. London, 20 June 1978, *Portrait of Elizabeth Adlercron* (pastel, 23 1/2 x 19 1/2 ins / 59.5 x 49.5 cm) GBP 620. London, 24 Nov 1978, *Portrait of Lord Mount Stuart* (oil on canvas, 29 x 24 ins / 73.7 x 61 cm) GBP 1,800. London, 20 Nov 1979, *Portrait of a Gentleman* (pastel, 23 1/2 x 17 1/4 ins / 59.5 x 44 cm) GBP 650. London, 16 July 1981, *Portrait of Miss Harriet Isted* (1752, pastel, 18 x 12 ins / 45.5 x 30.5 cm) GBP 750. London, 20 March 1984, *Portrait of a Lady* (coloured chalk, 7 1/2 x 6 3/4 ins / 19 x 17.2 cm) GBP 1,500. London, 14 March 1985, *Figure Studies* (red chalk, pencil or pen, volume of 76 drawings) GBP 1,700. London, 19 Nov 1985, *The Seasons* (pastel, series of four, 23 x 17 1/4 ins / 58.5 x 44 cm) GBP 7,000. London, 18 Nov 1988, *Family Group, the Drakes of Fernhill in Berkshire* (oil on canvas, 84 x 107 ins / 213.2 x 271.6 cm) GBP 44,000. London, 18 Oct 1989, *Seated Portrait of John Meredith of Templerainey, County Wicklow, in a Brown Suit* (oil on canvas, 19 x 15 ins / 48 x 38 cm) GBP 2,640. London, 14 Nov 1990, *Three-quarter Length Seated Portrait of the Reverend William Freind in Clerical Garb with his Son Robert Standing beside him* (oil on canvas, 39 1/2 x 49 1/2 ins / 100.5 x 126 cm) GBP 7,150. New York, 20 May 1993, *Portrait of Richard, Earl of Cavan, in a Brown Suit* (oil on canvas, 29 x 23 1/4 ins / 73.7 x 59.1 cm) USD 4,313. London, 11 Oct 1995, *Portrait of a Lady* (pastel, 23 1/4 x 17 1/4 ins / 59 x 44 cm) GBP 747. London, 3 April 1996, *Portrait of the Reverend William Freind with his Son Robert in a Library* (oil on canvas, 39 1/2 x 49 1/2 ins / 100.5 x 126 cm) GBP 4,600. London, 31 March 1999, *Portrait of a Girl Holding a Rabbit* (pastel, 24 x 19 ins / 61 x 49 cm) GBP 5,000. London, 24 Nov 1999, *Portrait of the Pitt Family* (oil on canvas, 55 x 46 ins / 140 x 118 cm) GBP 10,000. London, 6 June 2002, *Portrait of Henrietta, Countess of Abergavenny* (pastel, 24 x 17 ins / 60 x 44 cm) GBP 4,800. London, 9 July 2002, *Portrait of a Lady, said to be Elizabeth, Dowager Countess of Aykesford* (oil on canvas, 50 x 40 ins / 128 x 102 cm) GBP 3,600. London, 25 Nov 2003, *Double Portrait of Elizabeth and Thomas Trower in a Landscape, with Their Dog* (1773, oil on canvas, 54 x 43 ins / 137 x 109 cm) GBP 17,500. Norfolk, 22 March 2004, *Portrait of a Lady with a Pearl Choker* (pastel, 24 x 17 ins / 60 x 44 cm) GBP 4,200. London, 26 May 2004, *Portrait of George Burges* (oil on canvas, 31 x 25 ins / 78 x 64 cm) GBP 2,000.

HOART, Jean Baptiste Auguste
French, 19th century.
Born 16 June 1800, in Paris; died 27 June 1847, in Paris.
Portrait painter.

Hoart entered the École des Beaux-Arts in Paris on 2 March 1820, where he was taught by Guérin. His only appearance at the Salon was in 1831, when he exhibited a portrait.

HOBART, Clark
American, 19th - 20th century.
Born 1868, in Rockville (Illinois); died 1948, in Los Gatos (California).
Painter, etcher. Landscapes, portraits.

Clark Hobart's family moved to California while he was still young. He studied at the San Francisco School of Design, the Art Students League in New York, and in Paris. From 1903 to 1911 he worked in New York as the art editor for the Burr-McIntosh magazine; he then moved to Monterey, California to devote himself to painting, and later to San Francisco and then Los Gatos. He produced paintings and colour monotype prints in an Impressionist style. He painted landscapes as well as portraits, including those of the artists Carl Oscar Borg and Gottardo Piazzoni and the wife of Leo Lentelli.

His first award was a silver medal in 1915 at the Panama Pacific International Exhibition. Subsequently he won the Crocker Prize in 1918, a first prize in 1921, a gold medal in 1922 and first prize at the Liberty Fair in 1918. In 1916 an entire room was devoted to his monotypes at the newly-opened Oakland Civic Art Gallery.

Bibliography:
Helgesen, N.R., *The Color-monotypes of Clark Hobart,* Hegelsen Galleries, San Francisco, 1915.

MUSEUMS AND GALLERIES:
MONTEREY (Peninsula Mus) - OAKLAND - RENO (Sierra Nevada Mus) - SAN FRANCISCO (MA).
AUCTION RECORDS:
LOS ANGELES, 28 Oct 1999, *Beside Still Waters* (oil on canvas on board, 24 x 30 ins / 61 x 76 cm) USD 7,000. PASADENA, 18 Feb 2003, *Along the Riverbank* (1897, oil on canvasboard, 11 x 16 ins / 28 x 41 cm) USD 5,000. PASADENA, 17 Feb 2004, *Monterey Coastal* (oil on canvas, 16 x 24 ins / 41 x 61 cm) USD 25,000.

HOBART, Elijah

American, 19th century.
Born in England.
Active in New York and Albany from 1845.
Engraver.

HOBBEMA, Meindert

Flemish School, 17th century.
Born 1638, in Amsterdam; died 7 December 1709, in Amsterdam.
Painter. Landscapes, landscapes with figures, ruins.

Little is known about this landscape artist. Even his place of birth is disputed. Some have claimed it could have been Antwerp, Cœwarden, Drent or Hamburg but Amsterdam is the more generally accepted location. It is known that he was a friend of Jan van Kessel and pupil and friend of Jacob van Ruysdael. He is cited for the first time on 4 June 1661, as a witness to a painting appraisal. This would suggest that if he was not yet a painter at that time, at least his artistic aptitudes were valued. Nevertheless, he signed his first painting at the age of 20. It is interesting to note that while the most highly esteemed artists of the time, such as Lingelbach, Van de Velde, Berchem and Wouwerman, would not deign to paint figures and animals in their landscapes, such elements in Meindert Hobbema's works went largely unnoticed by even the most enlightened among Dutch collectors. After his death, his paintings still only amounted to several florins' worth in public auctions. On 2 November 1668, Hobbema married Leltje Pieters Finck, four years his senior and servant to the Amsterdam official, Lambert Reynst. Through this alliance he obtained employment as a wine-gauger in the Amsterdam Excise. He retained this position for the rest of his life even though it proved to be hardly more lucrative than his painting prior to his employment. Indeed, both he and his wife, who died in 1704, were buried in poverty. Their son was born on 9 September 1669, and a daughter on 11 December 1671. She died in 1706.This artist, whose work is now highly valued, seemed then to have led such a difficult existence that he practically gave up painting from the moment of his Excise employment (1668). Certainly his painting output diminished significantly. The rare works that are known to be by him are dated no later than 1669. It was not until the end of the 18th century that British collectors began to value and seek out Hobbema's works. He painted mostly landscapes of the area surrounding Haarlem. They were limited to a few select subjects, such as ruins or watermills in bushy tree surroundings, motifs which he repeated continually throughout his work. He enjoyed depicting effects of evident contrast, using a fresh, pleasing palette of colours. The scope of his compositions was controlled, most often with a closed horizon, and his works thus yielded few surprises. The minutiae of these compositions were a contrast to the more ample views of van Ruysdael or Van Goyen. Only *Avenue of Middelharnis* was the exception, revealing an unexpected boldness in composition, theme and colouring. In it, one single road extends up the middle of the painting, effectively splitting the composition in two. This vertical division is accentuated by the two rows of somewhat spindly trees, which burst into foliage at their crowns. Another road cuts the first horizontally, while the figures animating the landscape do nothing to detract from the principal subject of the painting. The browns and red ochres contrast against the muted blue and blend smoothly with the grey of the clouded sky. Here, 'Hobbema defined even before the Impressionists what would become their space, and conferred a serene grandeur upon these mutilated trees'. Hobbema was featured in the exhibition *Twee gouden eeuwen: schilderkunst uit Nederland en Denemarken* (*Two Golden Ages: Masterpieces of Dutch and Danish Painting*) at the Rijksmuseum in Amsterdam in 2001.

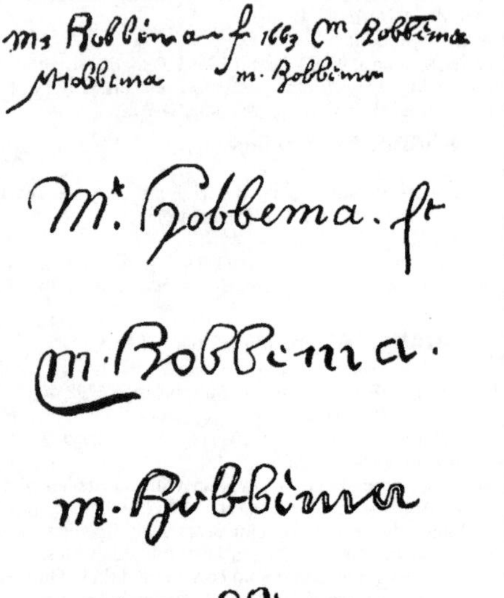

BIBLIOGRAPHY:
Broulhiet, Georges, *Meindert Hobbema*, Firmin-Didot, Paris, 1938. Dupont, Jacques/Mathey, François, *Le XVIIe sicèle, les tendances nouvelles en Europe de Caravage à Vermeer*, Skira, Paris, Geneva, 1951. Stechow, Wolfgang, *'The Early Years of Hobbema'* in *A.Q.*, Detroit, 1959 (pp. 3-18). *Masters of 17th-century Dutch Landscape Painting*, exhibition catalogue, ed. P.C. Sutton, Amsterdam, Rijksmuseum; Boston, Museum of Fine Arts; Philadelphia, Museum of Art, 1987-1988.

MUSEUMS AND GALLERIES:

AMSTERDAM: *Watermill* (same subject); *Peasant Dwelling* - ANTWERP: *Watermill* - AVIGNON: *Landscape* - BERLIN: *Forest Landscape* - BRUSSELS: *Watermill* - BUDAPEST: *Landscape with Small House* - COPENHAGEN (Statens Mus. for Kunst): *A Pool on the Fringe of a Wood* - DIJON: *Landscape* - DRESDEN: *Watermill; Landscape* - EDINBURGH (Nat. Gal. of Scotland): *A Waterfall in a Wood* (oil/panel); *Wooded Landscape* (oil on canvas) - FRANKFURT AM MAIN: *Entrance to a Wood; Thatched Cottage; Fishermen's Cabin* - GENEVA (Mus. Ariana): *Dutch Landscape* - GLASGOW: *two wooded landscapes;* two wooded landscapes; *Ruins of a Cottage; Group of Trees on the Edge of a River* - GRENOBLE: *Landscape* - HELSINKI: two landscapes with mills - LA FÈRE: four landscapes - LE PUY-EN-VELAY: *Landscape* - LONDON (Dulwich Picture Gal.): *Wooded landscape with a Water-mill* (c. 1660, oil/panel) - LONDON (NG): *A Woody Landscape with a Cottage* (c. 1665, oil on canvas); *A Woody Landscape* (c. 1665, oil/wood); *The Watermills at Singraven near Denekamp* (1665-1670, oil/wood); *A Road winding past Cottages* (c. 1667-1668, oil/wood); *The Ruins of Brederode Castle* (1671, oil on canvas); *The Avenue at Middelharnis* (1689, oil on canvas) - LONDON (Wallace Collection): *A Ruin on the Bank of a River* (1667, oil/panel); *A Stormy Landscape* (c. 1665, oil on canvas/relined); *A Wooded Landscape* (c. 1663, oil on canvas); *A Watermill* (c. 1662-1664, oil/panel); *The Outskirts of a Wood* (early 1660s, oil/panel) - MUNICH: *Landscape* - PARIS (Louvre): *Landscape; Watermill* - ROHRAU (Schlossmus., Graf Harrach'sche Familiensammlung): *Farm* - ROTTERDAM: two landscapes - STUTTGART: *Landscape* - VIENNA: *Wooded Landscape.*

AUCTION RECORDS:

PARIS, 1-3 June 1865, *The Mills,* FRF 81,000. PARIS, 6-9 March 1872, *The Watermill,* FRF 30,000; *Entry to the Forest,* FRF 81,000; *Dutch Country House,* FRF 50,000. PARIS, 6-7 April 1876, *The Mill,* FRF 100,000. PARIS, 25 June 1891, *Dutch Landscape on a Bright Summer Day,* FRF 249,600; *Small Wooded Landscape with River,* FRF 49,400; *Wooded Landscape with Travellers,* FRF 39,800. PARIS, 14-17 May 1898, *The Avenue,* FRF 51,000. LONDON, 6 May 1899, *Landscape with Figures,* FRF 238,875. LONDON, 30 March 1908, *Wooded Landscape,* GBP 44. LONDON, 8 May 1908, *Wooded Landscape,* GBP 84. LONDON, 25 June 1908, *Market Day* (engraved by Vinkels) GBP 273. NEW YORK, April 1910, *Landscape,* FRF 240,000. LONDON, 22 July 1910, *Landscape with Mill,* GBP 13,610. PARIS, 12 June 1919, *The Pond,* FRF 11,500. PARIS, 12 June 1919, *The Broken Bridge,* FRF 16,100. LONDON, March 1922, *Wooded Landscape,* GBP 73. LONDON, May 1922, *Castle on a Canal,* GBP 6,510; *Watermill,* GBP 6,510. LONDON, July 1923, *Wooded Landscape with Mill and Horsemen,* GBP 73. LONDON, 28 March 1924, *Forest Scene with Small Houses and Figures,* GBP 56. PARIS, 2 June 1924, *Farm in the Sunlight,* FRF 1,320,000; *Farm by the Water,* FRF 102,000; *Road Near the River,* FRF 110,000. PARIS, 17-18 June 1924, *The Pond,* FRF 30,000. LONDON, 1 May 1925, *Farm by the Water,* GBP 609. PARIS, 12-13 June 1925, *The Mill in the Forest,* FRF 370,000. PARIS, 27-28 May 1926, *The Barn,* FRF 155,000. LONDON, 19 Nov 1926, *River,* GBP 367. LONDON, 2 Feb 1927, *Landscape in a Wood,* GBP 215. LONDON, 27 July 1928, *River in the Woods,* GBP 525. LONDON, 1 Aug 1929, *Wooded Landscape,* GBP 204. LONDON, 18 July 1930, *Wooded Landscape,* GBP 357. NEW YORK, 22 Jan 1931, *Landscape with Figures,* USD 11,000. LONDON, 7 Dec 1933, *Winding Road,* GBP 483. LONDON, 7 Dec 1933, *Winding River,* GBP 737. LONDON, 1 June 1934, *Wooded River Scene,* GBP 3,570. GENEVA, 7 Dec 1935, *Landscape,* FRF 40,000. LONDON, 30 April 1937, *The Fishermen,* GBP 7,350. LONDON, 28 May 1937, *Wooded Landscape,* GBP 4,620. LONDON, 2 July 1937, *Watermill,* GBP 2,415. LONDON, 18 Nov 1938, *Wooded Landscape,* GBP 3,675. NEW YORK, Dec 1941, *View of Westphalia,* USD 30,000. LONDON, 7 Aug 1942, *Wooded Landscape,* GBP 52; *Wooded Landscape,* GBP 57. NEW YORK, 3 Dec 1942, *Small Houses in a Wood,* USD 3,900. PARIS, 12 March 1943, *Watermill* (school of M. H.) FRF 50,000. LONDON, 27 Oct 1943, *Wooded Landscape,* GBP 150. NEW YORK, 2 March 1944, *Stream in a Forest,* USD 2,100. LONDON, 9 June 1944, *View of Undulating Lansdscape,* GBP 441. LONDON, 21 March 1945, *Wooded Landscape,* GBP 150. PARIS, 25 May 1945, *The Old Oak* (attributed) FRF 885,000. NEW YORK, 25 Oct 1945, *Watermill,* USD 23,000. LONDON, 8 Feb 1946, *On the River,* GBP 162. NEW YORK, 5 June 1946, *Road in the Woods,* USD 1,400. NEW YORK, 9 Jan 1947, *Mill,* USD 5,750. AMSTERDAM, 21-28 Jan 1947, *Landscape,* NLG 8,000. LONDON, 9 May 1947, *Canal with Boat and Figures,* GBP 399. PARIS, 11-12 June 1947, *The Wild Duck Hunt* (attributed) FRF 205,000. PARIS, 30 May 1956, *View of Westphalia,* FRF 13,700,000. LONDON, 2 July 1958, *Wooded Landscape,* GBP 5,200. LONDON, 24 June 1959, *The Mill,* GBP 4,500. LONDON, 1 April 1960, *A Wooded River,* GBP 14,700. PARIS, 23 June 1961, *Thatched Cottage in the Woods,* FRF 14,500. LONDON, 6 July 1966, *Wooded Landscape with Thatched Cottages and Figures,* GBP 125,000. LONDON, 3 Dec 1969, *Wooded Landscape,* GBP 34,500. LONDON, 24 June 1970, *Wooded Landscape with Thatched Cottages and Figures,* GBP 120,000. NEW YORK, 20 May 1971, *Wooded Landscape with Two Hunters,* USD 22,000. LONDON, 29 June 1973, *Wooded Landscape,* Gns 90,000. LUCERNE, 22 June 1974, *Landscape with Mill* (1660) CHF 55,000. NEW YORK, 2 Dec 1976, *Wooded Landscape with Thatched Cottage* (oil on panel, 24 x 33 1/2 ins / 61 x 85 cm) USD 26,000. LONDON, 25 March 1977, *Wooded River Landscape* (oil on panel, 11 1/2 x 14 1/2 ins / 29.2 x 36.6 cm) GBP 14,000. LONDON, 18 April 1980, *Wooded Landscape with Thatched Cottages and Figures* (oil on panel, 21 x 28 1/4 ins / 53.3 x 71.7 cm) GBP 95,000. LONDON, 21 April 1982, *Wooded Landscape with Watermill* (oil on canvas, 38 1/2 x 50 1/2 ins / 98 x 128 cm) GBP 34,000. NEW YORK, 18 Jan 1983, *Wooded Landscape* (oil on panel, 23 x 32 3/4 ins / 58.5 x 83.2 cm) USD 55,000. NEW YORK, 17 Jan 1986, *The Watermill* (1662, oil on panel, 23 1/2 x 33 ins / 59.5 x 84 cm) USD 120,000. NEW YORK, 14 Jan 1988, *Entry to a Wood with a Farm and Horsemen on Two Roads* (oil on panel, 24 x 34 ins / 61 x 86.5 cm) USD 550,000. BERN, 30 April 1988, *Wooded Landscape with Watermill* (oil on oak panel, 23 1/2 x 35 1/2 ins / 59.5 x 90 cm) CHF 35,000. NEW YORK, 12 Jan 1989, *Farmers Bringing Home Cattle under a Menacing Sky* (oil on panel, 29 1/2 x 42 ins / 75 x 106.5 cm) USD 44,000. LONDON, 8 Dec 1989, *River Landscape with a House in the Under-brush and a Peasant on a Path* (oil on panel, 18 x 25 ins / 45.7 x 63.5 cm) GBP 38,500. LONDON, 6 July 1990, *Lake in a Clearing with Thatched Cottages and Fishermen* (oil on panel, 14 3/4 x 19 1/4 ins / 37.3 x 48.7 cm) GBP 550,000. LONDON, 13 Dec 1991, *Wooded Landscape with a Fiddler Arriving in a Hamlet and Welcomed by the Inhabitants* (oil, 35 1/4 x 42 ins / 89.5 x 105.8 cm) GBP 1,600,000. LONDON, 7 Dec 1994, *Wooded Landscape with Houses* (oil on canvas, 35 1/4 x 48 ins / 89.5 x 122 cm) GBP 3,741,500. LONDON, 5 July 1996, *Cabin at the Entry to a Wood* (oil on panel, 10 3/4 x 13 ins / 27.2 x 33 cm) GBP 80,000. LONDON, 11 Dec 1996, *Landscape with Figures By a Church* (c. 1659, oil on panel, 15 1/2 x 22 1/2 ins / 39.5 x 57 cm) GBP 65,300. LONDON, 3 July 1997, *Wooded Landscape with Figures on a Road and Cottages in the Distances* (c. 1660, oil on panel, 9 1/2 x 14 ins / 24.2 x 35.7 cm) GBP 38,900. LONDON, 3 Dec 1997, *Ruins of Brederode Castle* (oil on panel, 20 3/4 x 26 3/4 ins / 52.7 x 68 cm) GBP 56,500. LONDON, 3-4 Dec 1997, *Wooded Landscape* (1660, oil on panel, 20 3/4 x 27 ins / 52.9 x 68.5 cm) GBP 67,500. NEW YORK, 28 Jan 2000, *View of a Fish Pond with Boys Fishing on a Bridge and Other Figures* (oil on panel, 16 x 24 ins / 41 x 61 cm) USD 300,000. STUTTGART, 30 June 2000, *Watermill in Westphalia* (1670, oil on canvas, 32 x 26 ins / 81 x 65 cm) DEM 50,000. LONDON, 11 July 2001, *Wooded Landscape with Travellers on a Path through a*

Hamlet (oil on canvas, 38 x 52 ins / 96 x 131 cm) GBP 5,900,000. VIENNA, 2 Oct 2002, *River Landscape* (oil on canvas, 20 x 27 ins / 51 x 68 cm) EUR 30,000. ASHVILLE, 31 May 2003, *Landscape with Figures on a Road, Hunters and Dogs* (oil on canvas, 40 x 53 ins / 102 x 135 cm) USD 8,000. LONDON, 7 July 2004, *Wooded Landscape with Hunter and Other Figures on a Path* (oil on panel, 12 x 16 ins / 31 x 40 cm) GBP 130,000.

HOBBENNE
French, 18th century.
Painter.

AUCTION RECORDS:
PARIS, 13 Oct 1943, *Travellers Attacked by Bandits* (attributed) FRF 15,000.

HOBBS, G. W.
American, 18th century.
Painter, pastellist. Portraits.

G.W. Hobbs was also a pastor, being one of the founders of the black Methodist church, the African Methodist Episcopal Church (AME). He was active at the end of the 18th century in Baltimore as the official painter for this church. A picture attributed to him was the pastel portrait of Richard Allen (1784), a former slave who became a founder and later a bishop of the AME, then co-founded the Free African Society; however, we know of no work signed by Hobbs.

BIBLIOGRAPHY:
Dickason Cederholm, Theresa (ed.), *Afro-American Artists. A Bio-Bibliographical Directory*, Trustees of the Boston Public Library, Boston, 1973. Lewis, Samella, *Art: African American*, Harcourt Brace Jovanovich, New York, 1978.

MUSEUMS AND GALLERIES:
WASHINGTON DC (GA, Howard University): *Richard Allen* (1784, pastel).

HOBBS, George Thomson
American, 19th century.
Born 18 February 1846, in Philadelphia; died 1929.
Active in Philadelphia.
Painter, art restorer. Still-lifes.

George Thomson Hobbs was a pupil of Bouguereau and Tony Robert-Fleury in Paris.

AUCTION RECORDS:
NEW YORK, 19 March 1969, *Still-life*, USD 2,500. NEW YORK, 18 Nov 1976, *Still-life with Pipe* (1895, oil on canvas, 15 x 22 ins / 38 x 56 cm) USD 1,200. NEW YORK, 26 May 1988, *Still-life with Tankard and Pretzels* (oil on panel, 13 3/4 x 10 1/4 ins / 34.9 x 25.9 cm) USD 5,280.

HOBBS, Peter
British, 20th century.
Born 1930, in London.
Painter, sculptor.

Peter Hobbs studied at Ealing School of Art and at the Central School of Arts and Crafts, London. The elements in his paintings have a forceful dynamism.

HOBDAY, William Armfield
British, 18th - 19th century.
Born 1771, in Birmingham; died 17 February 1831, in London.
Painter, miniaturist.

William Hobday worked in London, Bath and Bristol. His portraits are much admired. He exhibited in London at the Royal Academy and the British Institution between 1794 and 1830.

MUSEUMS AND GALLERIES:
BRISTOL (City Mus. & AG): several portraits.

AUCTION RECORDS:
LONDON, 15 July 1983, *Portrait of the Boxer Henry Pearce, 'The Game Chicken'* (1805, oil on canvas, 24 1/2 x 19 1/4 ins / 62 x 49 cm) GBP 4,000. LONDON, 11 March 1999, *Portrait of General George Sackville Browne* (oil on canvas, 30 x 25 ins / 76 x 63 cm) GBP 2,200. LONDON, 17 April 2000, *Portrait of a Gentleman in a Blue Coat* (oval miniature, h. 2 ins / 6 cm) GBP 3,000. BILLINGSHURST, 24 July 2000, *Hannah Anderson with a String of Pearls* (oval miniature, h. 3 ins / 7 cm) GBP 3,000. LONDON, 28 May 2002, *Young Lady in a White Dress with a Frilled Collar* (oval miniature, h. 3 ins / 7 cm) GBP 1,100. LONDON, 5 Nov 2002, *Young Gentleman in a Dark Grey Coat, Cream Waistcoat and Frilled White Cravat* (oval miniature, h. 3 ins / 7 cm) GBP 2,900.

HOBDEN, Frank
British, 19th - 20th century.
Painter. Genre scenes.

Frank Hobden lived in South Benfleet in Essex, and was active from 1879 to 1930. He exhibited at the Royal Society of British Artists, of which he was a member, and in 1909 he also exhibited at the Royal Institute of Oil Painters.

AUCTION RECORDS:
LONDON, 2 Oct 1979, *Reading in the Garden* (oil on canvas, 20 x 16 1/4 ins / 51 x 41 cm) GBP 550. LONDON, 2 Nov 1989, *A Difficult Choice* (oil on canvas, 12 x 16 ins / 30.5 x 40.7 cm) GBP 3,080. CHELSEA, 13 April 1999, *Footsteps* (1900, oil on canvas, 24 x 35 ins / 60 x 90 cm) GBP 1,600. LONDON, 11 Jan 2000, *Reclining Lady in a Classical Bath* (oil on canvas, 8 x 12 ins / 20 x 30 cm) GBP 4,600.

HOBEN, Benedikt
German, 15th century.
Active in Magdeburg c. 1490.
Illuminator.

HOBERG, Reinhold
German, 19th century.
Born 4 October 1859, in Berlin.
Painter. Genre scenes.

Hoberg first exhibited in Berlin in 1888.

HOBI, pseudonym of Billstein, Horst
German, 20th century.
Born 12 June 1939, in Cologne.
From 1959 active in France.
Painter, illustrator. Landscapes.

Hobi studied at the national school of graphic and decorative arts in Cologne. He took part in many group exhibitions, being awarded various distinctions, in France, Switzerland, Italy, Spain, the Netherlands and the USA. In Paris he exhibited at the Salon des Artistes Français, of which he was a member, as well as the Salon des Indépendants and the Salon des Terres Latines. From 1959, he also showed his work in solo exhibitions at the Galerie Bernheim in Paris, and also in 1972 in Perpignan, 1973 in Aubonne, 1974 in Megève and 1979 in Cassis. His painting is figurative and he is essentially a landscape artist. He painted in Provence, Sologne and Venice. He was always inspired by the Impressionist vision, but adopted their soft colours rather than their separate brush strokes.

MUSEUMS AND GALLERIES:
CASSIS (Mus. Nat.) - PONT-AVEN (Mus. municipal) - VIENNA (NM).

HOBLEY, Edward G.
British, 19th century.
Born 1866; died 1916.
Painter. Genre scenes, animals.

Edward Hobley exhibited in London at the Royal Academy from 1893.

MUSEUMS AND GALLERIES:
BRADFORD (Cartwright Hall AG): *Cutting Stack Rods* - LIVERPOOL: *Shaft of Light*.

AUCTION RECORDS:
LONDON, 6 Dec 1909, *Cutting the Seed Potatoes; Setting Sun,* GBP 5. LONDON, 15 May 1911, *In the Stable,* GBP 11. LONDON, 16 Nov 1999, *Boy and Goat* (oil on canvas, 24 x 18 ins / 61 x 46 cm) GBP 1,800. KNOWLE, 22 Nov 2000, *Ready for Work* (1890, oil on canvas, 20 x 30 ins / 50 x 76 cm) GBP 1,600. LONDON, 8 March 2001, *End of the Day* (1890, oil on canvas, 20 x 30 ins / 51 x 76 cm) GBP 2,500.

HOBS, Michel
French, 18th century.
Active in Nantes in 1781.
Sculptor.

HOBSON, Alice Mary
British, 19th century.
Born 1860; died 1954.
Active in Leicester.
Watercolourist.
Alice Hobson showed many landscapes at the Society of Painters in Watercolours and the Royal Institute in London from 1879. She was a member of both societies.

HOBSON, C.J.
British, 19th century.
Painter. History painting.
MUSEUMS AND GALLERIES:
MELBOURNE: *St Elizabeth.*

HOBSON, H.
British, 19th century.
Active in London 1814-1822.
Engraver.

HOBSON, Henry E.
British, 19th century.
Active in Bath.
Painter. Genre scenes.
Henry Hobson exhibited in London at the Royal Academy and the British Institution between 1857 and 1866.
MUSEUMS AND GALLERIES:
LONDON (Victoria and Albert Mus.): *Country Girl.*
AUCTION RECORDS:
LONDON, 12 April 1985, *Setting Off for Market; People around a Well* (1861, oil on panel, a pair, 11 1/4 x 8 1/4 ins / 28.5 x 21 cm) GBP 2,100. TAUNTON, 24 Feb 2000, *Man, Woman and Children outside a Country Cottage* (1866, watercolour and gouache, 24 x 30 ins / 61 x 76 cm) GBP 1,050. LONDON, 23 May 2001, *At the Well* (oil on panel, 6 x 8 ins / 15 x 20 cm) GBP 1,800. NOTTINGHAM, 1 July 2004, *Well* (pencil and watercolour heightened with white, 15 x 11 ins / 37 x 27 cm) GBP 1,000. NOTTINGHAM, 1 July 2004, *Stile* (pencil and watercolour heightened with white, 18 x 14 ins / 45 x 35 cm) GBP 1,000.

HOBSON, Mabel E.
British, 19th century.
Active in London.
Miniaturist.
Mabel Hobson frequently exhibited at the Royal Academy in London from 1889.

HOBUN, real name: Kikuchi Tsunejiro; childhood name: Koki, artist name: Hobun
Japanese, 19th - 20th century.
Born 1862, in Kyoto; died 1918.
Painter.
Hobun was a pupil of Bairei (1844-1895) and a member of the Shijo School, who also taught at Kyoto Technical School. He specialised in landscapes, and pictures of birds and flowers.

HOCH, Franz Xaver
German, 19th - 20th century.
Born 25 May 1869, in Freiburg; died 17 June 1916, in Freiburg or in the Vosges.
Painter. Landscapes.
Franz Xaver Hoch studied with Gustav Schönleber at the Karlsruhe academy. He exhibited in Paris at the Salon des Artistes Français, where he won a bronze medal at the Exposition Universelle in 1900. He also won a medal in Munich in 1901.
MUSEUMS AND GALLERIES:
BERLIN: *Landscape with Village* - MUNICH: *Harvest Time.*
AUCTION RECORDS:
COLOGNE, 28 June 1991, *Italian Village in Summer* (oil on paper, 17 x 20 3/4 ins / 43 x 53 cm) DEM 3,300.

HOCH, Georg Friedrich
German, 18th - 19th century.
Born 1751, in Mainz; died 29 April 1812, in Mainz.
Painter, engraver (etching).
Georg Friedrich Hoch made engravings of historical subjects and worked mainly in Rome and Paris.
AUCTION RECORDS:
PARIS, Oct 1945-July 1946, *Parade of Troops; Convoy Passing a Ford* (two watercolours) FRF 5,200.

HÖCH, Hannah, or Hanna
German, 20th century.
Born 1 November 1889, in Gotha (Thuringia); died 1978 or 1979, in Berlin.
Painter, collage artist, sculptor, watercolourist, mixed media.
Dadaism.
Berlin Dadaist group.
Hannah Höch studied with Emil Orlik at the school of the museum of applied arts in Berlin from 1912 to 1914. In 1914, she received a bursary at the Werkbundausstellung in Cologne, then studied at the Charlottenburg art school. Her friendship with Raoul Hausmann dates from this period. In 1918, after the war, she participated in the activities of the Berlin Dada group. It was Kurt Schwitters who made her add an 'h' to the end of her forename so that it could be read backwards and forwards. She exhibited for the first time in 1919, together with Hausmann, George Grosz and John Heartfield, at the Neumann gallery in Berlin, showing watercolours and photomontages. Hausmann asked her to contribute politically inspired collages to the magazines *Der Dada* and *Schall und Rauch* (*Noise and Smoke*). In 1920, she showed reliefs and dolls, notably *The Dadaist Dictatorship*, at the International Dada Fair in Berlin. At the end of 1921, she took part in the Dada event in Prague with Schwitters and Hausmann. In 1922, she contributed to the review *Merz*, and joined the Novembergruppe (November Group), remaining a member until it came to an end in 1931. She also knew Van Doesburg, Moholy-Nagy and Arp, among others. From 1926 to 1929, she lived with her companion the poet Til Brugman in Holland, where she was in contact with the De Stijl group, before returning to Berlin. Her work featured in many group exhibitions in Germany, Holland, New York, and in 1996 at the Whitechapel Art Gallery in London. In the Hitler period and during the war, she lived discreetly on the outskirts of Berlin, and managed to preserve important archives of the Dada movement. In 1976, Paris and Berlin organised a joint exhibition of her work, which was seen in 1996 at the Walker Art Center in Minneapolis.

Her creative activities were always very varied, developing freely from the abstract to the figurative. At the very start of her career, she produced black and white abstract compositions in her photomontages of 1919. From 1922, she worked with Schwitters, and collaborated on his first *Merzbau*. From photomontage she moved on to collage, a technique she introduced into her paintings in 1925, when she progressed from the surrealist still-lifes of 1922 to ironic compositions with figures. She developed the theory of collage by bringing in all kinds of different elements - photos, of course, but also astronomical charts, a variety of textures, plants, dress patterns - in order to create dream landscapes, primitive sculptures in her 1928 *Ethnographisches Museum* (*Ethnographical Museum*), and grotesque dolls. In her mixed collages, she was a forerunner of the spirit and certain aspects of American Pop Art of the 1970s.

Her work is characterised by its polymorphism. She worked from impulse rather than deep consideration, and was very easily influenced by chance encounters and circumstances. It is not easy to define precise periods in her production, as she moved freely back and forth between techniques and movements. At different times, or sometimes simultaneously, she was attracted by the spirit of confrontation and the destructive nihilism of the Berlin Dada and the abstract plasticism of the Zurich Dada.

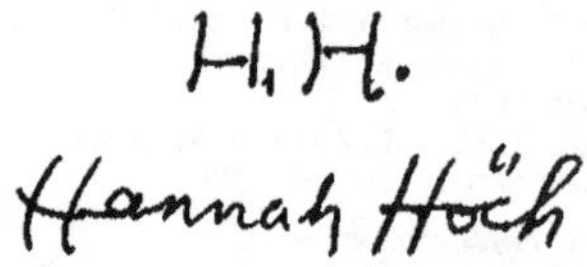

BIBLIOGRAPHY:

Dorival, Bernard/Hoog, Michel, *Dada*, group exhibition catalogue, Musée national d'Art moderne, Paris, 1966. Burmeister, Ralf/Fürlus, Eckhard/Ohff, Heinz/Roters, Eberhard, *Hannah Höch. Eine Lebenscollage 1921-1945*, Hatje Cantz, Ostfildern, 1996.

MUSEUMS AND GALLERIES:

BERLIN (Berlinische Gal.): *Roma* (1925); *Guardian Angel* (1927-1928) - BERLIN (National Mus.): *Cutting with a Kitchen Knife* (1919); *Collage with Arrow* (1919); *The Fly is Dead* (1922) - STUTTGART (ifa-Gal.): *Flight* (1931).

AUCTION RECORDS:

NEW YORK, 6 Dec 1972, *Landscape* (watercolour) USD 1,500. NEW YORK, 18 Oct 1973, *Twin Landscapes* (1946) USD 2,400. NEW YORK, 3 Nov 1978, *Composition* (1923, pen, 11½ x 7¾ ins / 29 x 19.5 cm) USD 3,300. COLOGNE, 2 Dec 1978, *Grotesque* (watercolour/black background, 10¼ x 10½ ins / 26 x 26.5 cm) DEM 1,900. BERN, 20 June 1979, *The Dada Mill* (c. 1920, collage/card and construction in metal, wood and string, h. 9½ ins / 24 cm) CHF 16,500. MUNICH, 26 Nov 1979, *Majesties* (c. 1940, collage, 4½ x 6 ins / 11.4 x 15.1 cm) DEM 2,250. MUNICH, 1 Dec 1980, *Vase of Flowers* (1925, gouache, 24 x 18 ins / 61 x 46 cm) DEM 7,000. MUNICH, 25 Nov 1981, *On a Green Background* (1919, watercolour, 12¼ x 7¾ ins / 31.2 x 19.5 cm) DEM 16,000. BERN, 23 June 1982, *Double Portrait* (1953, oil on canvas, 26½ x 23½ ins / 67 x 60 cm) CHF 13,000. BERN, 22 June 1983, *Skizze zu Geburt* (*Sketch of Birth*) (1921, watercolour, 16¼ x 16½ ins / 41 x 42 cm) CHF 13,000. BERN, 22 June 1983, *The Master* (1925, collage, 6¼ x 4½ ins / 16 x 11.2 cm) CHF 20,000. MUNICH, 29 Nov 1985, *Zwei Geschnäbelte* (*Two People with Strange Noses*) (1966, collage and Indian ink, 11½ x 15½ ins / 29.5 x 39.5 cm) DEM 5,500. LONDON, 4 Dec 1985, *Construction in Red* (1919, watercolour/pencil outline, 10¾ x 8¾ ins / 27.4 x 22.5 cm) GBP 4,500. MUNICH, 1 June 1987, *Still-life with Flowers* (watercolour and gouache/pencil outlines heightened with white, 28½ x 19½ ins / 72.3 x 49.4 cm) DEM 3,850. LONDON, 28 Nov 1989, *Hanging Forms* (oil on canvas, 35½ x 23½ ins / 90 x 60 cm) GBP 23,100. HEIDELBERG, 12 Oct 1991, *The Forest and Us, Tachiste Composition* (frottage, 8¾ x 5½ ins / 22.2 x 13.7 cm) DEM 1,100. HEIDELBERG, 11 April 1992, *Tracks in the Snow* (ink, 8¼ x 11½ ins / 21 x 29.3 cm) DEM 1,100. MILAN, 21 May 1992, *Fly, Fly* (1955, collage, 9¾ x 6¾ ins / 25 x 17 cm) ITL 1,600,000. LONDON, 29 June 1992, *The Priestess* (collage with wash, heightened with gold, 13 x 9½ ins / 33 x 24 cm) GBP 22,000. BERLIN, 27 Nov 1992, *Apollinaire's House* (ink and watercolour/Japanese paper, 6¾ x 7½ ins / 17 x 19 cm) DEM 11,300. PARIS, 10 March 1993, *The Master* (1925, photomontage, 6¼ x 4¼ ins / 15.6 x 11 cm) FRF 102,000. NEW YORK, 10 Nov 1994, *Untitled Composition* (1918, watercolour and ink/paper, 12¼ x 7½ ins / 31.1 x 19.3 cm) USD 9,775. LONDON, 11 Oct 1995, *Composition of a Landscape* (monotype and watercolour, 8¼ x 5¾ ins / 20.8 x 14.8 cm) GBP 690. NEW YORK, 10 Oct 1996, *The Little Stepfather* (1937, watercolour and black ink/paper, 9¼ x 5½ ins / 23.5 x 14 cm) USD 2,185. LONDON, 9 Oct 1997, *Face and Hand* (1947, collage/paper, 10 x 9¾ ins / 25.5 x 24.7 cm) GBP 4,600. COLOGNE, 28 April 1999, *Still-life with Flowers* (1914, watercolour and gouache, 20 x 18 ins / 52 x 45 cm) DEM 13,000. BERLIN, 27 Nov 1999, *From Gentle Things* (collage and pen on board, 7 x 5 ins / 17 x 12 cm) DEM 12,000. MUNICH, 6 May 2000, *Three Faces* (1940, oil on canvas, 26 x 21 ins / 65 x 53 cm) DEM 27,000. LONDON, 18 Oct 2000, *Portrait of Gerhard Hauptmann* (1919, ink and photographic collage on paper on card, 11 x 8 ins / 27 x 21 cm) GBP 58,000. HAMBURG, 9 June 2001, *Self-portrait* (1922, watercolour, tempera and Indian ink, 9 x 6 ins / 22 x 16 cm) DEM 25,000. BERLIN, 1 Dec 2001, *Forest Landscape* (oil on canvas, 31 x 28 ins / 80 x 70 cm) DEM 15,000. AHLDEN, 3 May 2002, *Abstract Composition* (1921, watercolour, 17 x 12 ins / 42 x 30 cm) EUR 7,000. HAMBURG, 15 June 2002, *Dominant Red* (1919, colour chalk, 11 x 6 ins / 28 x 16 cm) EUR 5,500. BERLIN, 26 April 2003, *Above the Clouds* (1971, collage on board, 12 x 9 ins / 31 x 23 cm) EUR 5,500. BERLIN, 26 April 2003, *Colourful Wall* (1961, 26 x 20 ins / 66 x 52 cm) EUR 5,600. NEW YORK, 17 Feb 2004, *Untitled* (photo collage, 10 x 6 ins / 25 x 16 cm) USD 21,000. PARIS, 8 June 2004, *Children* (oil on canvas, 19 x 15 ins / 49 x 37 cm) EUR 16,000.

HOCH, J. G.

Dutch, 18th century.

Draughtsman.

J.G. Hoch is almost certainly the same person as Johann Gustav Hoch.

HOCH, Johann Gustav

German, 18th century.

Born 23 April 1716, in Reutlingen; died 1779, in Mainz.

Painter. Historical subjects, portraits, landscapes.

Johann Gustav Hoch, a pupil of Leibold, travelled for many years through Europe before returning Germany to settle in Mainz.

AUCTION RECORDS:

LONDON, 7 Dec 1967, *Set of 85 Sheets of Studies Comprising 500 Species of Shellfish* (watercolour) GBP 3,400.

HOCH, Johann Jakob

German, 18th - 19th century.

Born 1750; died 2 April 1829.

Active in Mainz.

Painter. Military subjects, portraits, landscapes.

Johann Jakob Hoch was a brother of Georg Friedrich Hoch.

MUSEUMS AND GALLERIES:

MAINZ: *Rhine Landscape*; two battle scenes.

AUCTION RECORDS:

PARIS, 7 Dec 1918, *Church Interior*, FRF 360. LONDON, 9 Feb 1927, *View of Mainz*, GBP 22. NEW YORK, 23 March 1957, *Still-life*, USD 1,075. LONDON, 28 Nov 1985, *Visiting the Hermit* (1780, pen and wash, 17½ x 23 ins / 44.5 x 58.5 cm) GBP 800. NEW YORK, 13 Jan 1993, *Stags, Rabbits and Egrets by a Pond in a Forest* (1774, gouache, 9¾ x 10¼ ins / 24.6 x 25.9 cm) USD 9,200. COLOGNE, 19 May 2001, *Trompe l'Oeil Paintings* (oil on canvas, a pair, 17 x 14 ins / 42 x 35 cm) DEM 16,000. PARIS, 12 Oct 2001, *Portrait of a Young Woman in an Interior* (oil on panel, 17 x 15 ins / 43 x 37 cm) FRF 19,000.

Madrid, 18 June 2002, *Alchemist* (1790, tempera, 14 x 11 ins / 35 x 27 cm) EUR 5,000. Munich, 21 June 2002, *Interior of Gothic Church* (1787, copperplate, 17 x 20 ins / 43 x 52 cm) EUR 15,000.

HOCH, Johann Peter
German, 18th century.
Born 1741, in Mainz.
Painter.

Johann Peter Hoch was the son of Johann Gustav Hoch.

Museums and Galleries:
Mannheim: two grisailles.

HOCHAPFEL, Helwig Reinhard
German, 19th century.
Born 28 April 1823, in Kassel; died 7 June 1903, in Kassel.
Painter.

Hochapfel returned to Kassel after living in London and Munich, where he specialised in decorative painting.

HOCHARD, Gaston
French, 19th - 20th century.
Born c. 1863, in Orléans; died May 1913, in Paris.
Painter (gouache), pastellist. History painting, genre scenes, architectural views.

Gaston Hochard was a pupil of Eugène Carrière and Alfred Roll. He painted numerous urban landscapes, especially views of Rouen, as well as scenes from elegant Parisian life. He exhibited at the Salon de la Société Nationale des Beaux-Arts, of which he became a member in 1905.

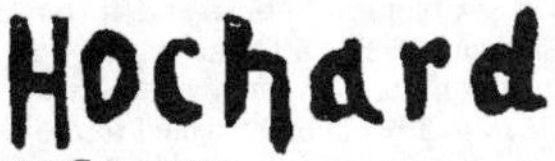

Museums and Galleries:
Rouen (MBA): *Rue du Bac in Rouen; Rue du Gros-Horloge in Rouen; Rue Martainville in Rouen; Tour St. Laurent and St. Godart in Rouen; Rue Eau-de-Robec; St-Maclou in Rouen; View of Rouen; Flaubert's House in Croisset; Rue Damiette in Rouen; Rouen Cathedral; Rue de l'Épicerie in Rouen; Rue St-Romain in Rouen; Rue St-Maclou in Rouen.*

Auction records:
Paris, 28 Jan 1924, *The Hurdy Gurdy Player* (gouache) FRF 62. Paris, 26 Feb 1934, *A Cantor in Rouen Cathedral,* FRF 140. Paris, 2 June 1993, *Elegant Ladies in the Rue du Gros-Horloge* (pastel, 57 x 45 1/4 ins / 145 x 115 cm) FRF 3,500.

HOCHAUSER, David
French, 18th century.
Active in Paris in 1750.
Painter, sculptor.

HOCHECKER, Franz
German, 18th century.
Born 1730, in Frankfurt; died 1782, in Frankfurt.
Painter, watercolourist. Landscapes.

Hochecker was pupil of Schütz the Elder.

Auction records:
London, 24 July 1929, *River Valley* (two paintings) GBP 32. Bern, 24 Oct 1979, *Riverscape* (oil on canvas, 14 3/4 x 22 1/2 ins / 37.5 x 57 cm) CHF 12,000. Cologne, 15 Oct 1988, *Romantic Landscape with a Boat at the Edge of a Lake with Mountains in the Background* (watercolour and gouache, 7 3/4 x 10 1/4 ins / 20 x 26.2 cm) DEM 3,750. Stuttgart, 24 Sept 1999, *Riders Resting* (1785, oil on canvas, 10 x 13 ins / 26 x 34 cm) DEM 9,000. Zurich, 6 Dec 1999, *River Landscapes* (oil on canvas, a pair, 15 x 20 ins / 39 x 52 cm) CHF 11,000. Vienna, 5 June 2002, *Mountainous River Landscape with Village and Figures* (oil on canvas, 11 x 14 ins / 29 x 36 cm) EUR 2,500. Munich, 26 June 2002, *Elegant Hunting Party amongst Trees with Waterfall* (oil on canvas, 10 x 12 ins / 25 x 30 cm) EUR 5,000. Munich, 19 Sept 2003, *River Landscape with Houses and Fishing Boats* (oil on canvas, 14 x 19 ins / 36 x 49 cm) EUR 7,500. Munich, 25 June 2004, *Landscape with Mill on River* (oil on canvas, 9 x 12 ins / 23 x 31 cm) EUR 2,500. London, 29 Oct 2004, *River Landscape with Peasants* (oil on canvas, 17 x 22 ins / 44 x 55 cm) GBP 1,500.

HOCHEISEN, Johann
German, 16th century.
Born in Memmingen.
Sculptor.

Johann Hocheisen worked in Butzbach on the building of a castle for Philip III, Landgrave of Hesse Butzbach.

HÖCHENWALDT, Michael Joseph
Austrian, 18th century.
Born in Linz; died before 1722, in Vienna.
Sculptor.

Höchenwaldt worked in Melk (Lower Austria).

HOCHFELD, Christoph
German, 18th century.
Active in Kassel.
Painter, engraver.

Hochfeld studied under Trevisani in Rome, then went on to take up the post as painter to the court in Kassel.

HOCHHAUS, Carl
German, 19th century.
Born 19 September 1852, in Berlin.
Painter. Portraits, genre scenes, landscapes.

Hochhaus studied under A von Werner and at the Berlin academy of art. He first exhibited in Berlin in 1876 and was awarded a gold medal in 1886.

HOCHHAUSER, Ephraïm
Austrian, 18th century.
Born in Banská Bystrica (Slovakia); died 13 December 1771.
Painter.

Hochhauser studied at the Akademie der bildenden Künste in Vienna.

HOCHHEIMER, Peter
German, 17th century.
Active c. 1600.
Painter.

Hochheimer worked in Frankfurt am Main.

HÖCHLE, Anton, or Hochl
German, 19th century.
Born 20 February 1820, in Munich; died 21 February 1897.
Painter, architect. Architectural views.

Anton Höchle lived in Munich.

Museums and Galleries:
Munich: *Landshut Gate.*

HOCHMANN, Daniel
German, 17th century.
Died 28 October 1633, in Freiburg im Breisgau.
Painter.

Daniel Hochmann executed religious paintings in the Freiburg area from 1596.

HOCHMANN, Franz Gustav
German, 19th century.
Born 17 January 1861, in Dresden.
Painter. Landscapes, animals.

Franz Hochmann studied at the school of fine art in Weimar, at the Dresden academy of art and under Professor Preller the Younger. He visited Rome in 1885, before setting up home in Karlsruhe from 1887 to 1890. He returned to Dresden and established himself from 1880, particularly in Dresden and in Munich, where he was awarded a medal in 1894, and also in Berlin and England, where he was awarded a silver medal in 1882.

Museums and Galleries:
Munich: *Winter Sun*.

Auction records:
Munich, 23 Nov 1978, *Riverscape* (oil on canvas, 23 1/2 x 31 1/2 ins / 60 x 80 cm) DEM 2,800.

HOCHMANN, Henryk
Polish, 20th century.
Born 1881, in Lublin.
Painter, sculptor.
Hochmann was a pupil of the sculptor Konstant Laszczka in Warsaw.

HOCHREIN, Jozsef
Hungarian, 19th century.
Born 1820, in Pécs; died 27 June 1905, in Pécs.
Painter.
Jozsef Hochrein was a pupil of Geiger and Eybl in Vienna, and was the father of Lajos Karoly Hochrein.

HOCHREIN, Lajos Karoly
Hungarian, 19th century.
Born 9 June 1853, in Pécs.
Painter.
Lajos Karoly Hochrein, son of Jozsef Hochrein, studied in Budapest with Szekely and Greguss. He is known for landscapes and still-lifes.

HÖCHSTÄDT, Anna
German, 19th century.
Born 26 February 1854, in Ratzeburg.
Painter.
Höchstädt was a pupil of Gussow in Berlin and of Fr Smith in Munich.

HOCHSTUHL, Karl, or Hochtuhl
German, 19th century.
Born 1849, in Strasbourg.
Painter. Landscapes.
Hochstuhl was a pupil of Grison.

Museums and Galleries:
Strasbourg: *Landscape*.

Auction records:
Nancy, 10 Feb 1980, *The Hunter* (oil on canvas, 14 1/2 x 11 ins / 37 x 28 cm) FRF 6,000.

HOCHU, real name: Nakamura Tatsuji, artist name: Hochu, Kakö
Japanese, 18th - 19th century.
Born in Kyoto.
Active at the end of the 18th and beginning of the 19th century.
Painter.
Hochu trained in the school of Korin (1658-1716) and worked all his life in Osaka.

Auction records:
New York, 17 Oct 1989, *Morning Glory* (hanging scroll, ink and colour/silk, 43 1/4 x 16 ins / 109.6 x 40.8 cm) USD 6,600. New York, 29 March 1990, *Iris* (hanging scroll, ink and colour/paper, 9 1/4 x 19 ins / 23.5 x 48.4 cm) USD 7,700.

HOCK, Cornelia Hock Shouter
Dutch, 19th century.
Born 1849, in Dordrecht.
Painter. Flowers.
Cornelia Hock was active in Nijmegen.

HOCK, Daniel
Austrian, 19th - 20th century.
Born 5 April 1858, in Vienna; died 1934.
Painter. History painting, genre scenes, still-lifes.
Daniel Hock exhibited in London and Vienna.

Auction records:
London, 18 June 1986, *Soap Bubbles* (oil on canvas, 12 x 17 3/4 ins / 30.5 x 45 cm) GBP 1,500. London, 19 June 1991, *Still-life with Peppers, a Basket of Fruit, a Crayfish and a Cat* (oil on canvas, 19 3/4 x 47 1/4 ins / 50 x 120 cm) GBP 7,150. London, 26 March 1997, *Still-life with Cat* (oil on canvas, 19 x 46 1/2 ins / 48.5 x 118 cm) GBP 10,350.

HÖCKERT, Johan Fredrik. See **HOECKERT**

HOCKNEY, David
British, 20th century.
Born 9 July 1937, in Bradford (West Yorkshire).
Active in the USA since 1975.
Painter (including gouache), watercolourist, collage artist, draughtsman, engraver (etching/aquatint), lithographer, illustrator, draughtsman, photographer. Portraits, scenes with figures, interiors with figures, landscapes, still-lifes. Stage sets, stage costumes, painted ceramics.
David Hockney studied at Bradford College of Art from 1953 to 1957, and at the Royal College of Art in London from 1959 to 1962. The exhibition *Picasso*, shown at the Tate Gallery, London, in 1960, made a deep impression on him. The following year he went to New York for the first time, then travelled to Egypt and Los Angeles in 1963, and to France and Italy in 1967. During his time in the USA, Hockney held several teachings posts: at the University of Iowa in 1964; at the University of Colorado in 1965; and in Los Angeles from 1966 to 1967. From 1968 to 1971 he travelled in Europe, the USA, Japan, Indonesia, Myanmar and Hawaii. He lived in Paris from 1973 to 1974, then returned to the USA in 1976. Hockney won a number of prizes and was awarded several honours: he graduated from the Royal College of Art with a gold medal in 1962; in 1963 he won the prize for the drawing at the Paris Biennale in 1963, and the prize for printmaking prize at the Ljubljana Biennale; and he won first prize at the 6th John Moores Exhibition in Liverpool in 1966.

He was regarded as one of the leaders of British Pop Art after the Young Contemporaries Exhibition in 1961. From 1965, Hockney worked in an abstact Expressionist style. At the time, and in step with contemporary trends, he was influenced by the American painter Jackson Pollock, and the British painter Roger Hilton, but also by the British painter Francis Bacon and the French painter and sculptor Jean Dubuffet. Hockney's friend R. B. Kitaj, the American painter who was prominent in the British Pop Art movement, persuaded him to abandon the abstraction of his early work and turn to figurative painting with a greater autobiographical theme. Although it is figurative, Hockney's paintings from this period still have an abstract quality, and are evocative rather than objective. His canvases of this period often feature poems written out in their entirety, or quotations relating to their subject matter. Here, Hockney created a surreal world in which wizards, hypnotists, nudes, elephants and snakes inhabit hazy landscapes. A multitude of incongruous details fills the canvas, and each element is rendered in flat colour, without concern for realism.

Soon afterwards, as Hockney became interested in the appearance of things, his style became highly figurative. Although his work was clearly influenced by the realism of Pop Art, the nearest he came to being a Pop artist was in his choice of subject matter, which is often taken from ordinary, albeit quite sophisticated, daily life. In 1963, in the drawings of Egyptian scenes commissioned by the *Sunday Times* (but never used), his style became more concise and objective. At this time he also produced a series of paintings of people taking a shower, then went on to other subjects, such as still-lifes, portraits and interiors, which often recurred in his work. He was then drawn towards Hyperrealism, producing icily cool canvases with a photographic objectivity (he also began taking photographs at this time). On flat, shadowless backgrounds, he painted figures in the hedonistic world portrayed by the media. These paintings have a certain irony. Hockney took obvious delight in depicting people, his parents, himself, Mr and Mrs Clark, in stiff poses, not looking at each other, like fictional characters in a sterilised world.

At the end of the 1970s, Hockney's work took another change of direction. Abandoning this rigorous style, he began to paint in a more intuitive, sensual way, with graceful touches reminiscent of Matisse and expressing the sensuous pleasure of painting. This was also a time when Hockney was frequently travelling, spending long stretches of time abroad, and his work reflects these stimulating episodes. In the final analysis, Hockney's work is autobiographical: not only does it document his travels and his perception of the countries he lived in and the cultures he experienced; it is also a record of his life, his friendships and close relationships. Each of his foreign travels resulted in a series of canvases painted in situ or back in his London studio. During his visit to Japan in 1970-1971 he also produced paintings strongly influenced by traditional Japanese painting and very typical of his output: two of these are *Japanese Rain* and *Mount Fuji*, both painted in 1972. It was also during this period that Hockney painted numerous portraits of his friend Peter Schlesinger, whom he left just before he went to California and who appears for the last time (a final souvenir) in *Portrait of an Artist* (a swimming-pool scene with two figures) of 1971.

Hockney's stay in California in 1971-1972 was an important time, primarily in his personal life but also as a painter. The pleasant climate, the relaxed way of life and the ease and luxury of Californian life are all expressed in Hockney's well-known swimming-pool paintings, the best-known being *A Bigger Splash* of 1968, now at the Tate in London. In 1978, still on the swimming-pool theme, Hockney experimented with a new technique. He made paper pulp, coloured it and pressed it into moulds. He produced 29 paintings in this way, the largest consisting of several canvases. Very early on in his career he began to work with Polaroids, which offered boundless possibilities for brilliantly representing three dimensions on a flat surface. He said it was what he had been looking for, and what he wanted to put into his paintings. Hockney, in fact, used his photographs, with enlargements and views from unusual angles, as references for his paintings. Later, in 1986, he began to work with photocopies and also produced many collages.

From an early age, Hockney was attracted by the theatre, and in 1966 he designed the sets and costumes for *Ubu Roi*. In 1979 he was asked to design the sets for the French musical cycle at the Metropolitan Opera House, New York, comprising *The Breasts of Tiresias* by Francis Poulenc and Guillaume Apollinaire, and *Parade* by Eric Satie and Jean Cocteau, and *L'Enfant et les Sortilèges* (*The Child and the Spells*) by Ravel and Colette. He also worked on three operas by Stravinsky: *The Rite of Spring, The Nightingale* and *Oedipus Rex* and in 1987 he produced paintings for the sets of Wagner's *Tristan and Isolde* at the Los Angeles Music Center. He also illustrated many works of fiction, most notably *Six Fairy Tales* by the Brothers Grimm and Cafavy's *Poems*. During the 1990s he completed a series of *Very New Paintings*, rendering the Californian landscape in an uncharacteristically abstract style.

Hockney is an unusual painter. Although he shot to fame in London, just as Andy Warhol had in New York, his painting remained traditional, even though it exploited the relaxed spirit of Pop Art, which took hold simultaneously in London and New York. Indeed, far from rejecting traditional painting, Hockney has always expressed a desire to respect it and preserve its place in a troubled age. Although he has undeniable skill as a draughtsman (drawing is a particularly important aspect in his paintings' composition), his style can be little clumsy. However, far from detracting from his work, this adds to its appeal. It has an innocent, exquisite beauty, with a deliberate lack of skill that, whether it confronts or identifies with Picasso, is far from being naive.

From 1963 Hockney exhibited two or three times a year. His work has been shown in about 100 group exhibitions, including *Nouvelle Subjectivité* (*New Subjectivity*), organised by Jean Clair at the Palais des Beaux-Arts, Paris, in 1979, to showcase the return of figurative and genre painting, and *The Big Americans* at the National Gallery of Australia, Canberra, in 2002. He had his first solo exhibition in 1960. This was followed by many others: at the Museum of Modern Art, New York, in 1964, 1968 and 1979; the Stedelijk Museum, Amsterdam, and the Palais des Beaux-Arts, Brussels, in 1966; a retrospective at the Whitechapel Art Gallery, London, in 1970; the Musée des Arts Décoratifs, Paris, in 1974; the National Gallery of Victoria, Melbourne, and the Museum of Modern Art, Tehran, in 1976; the Gulbenkian Foundation, Lisbon, in 1977 and 1985; the Albertina Museum, Vienna, in 1978; the Tate Gallery, London, in 1980 and 1986; the Musée National d'Art Moderne, Paris, in 1982; the Palazzo Grassi, Venice, and Walker Art Center, Minneapolis, in 1983; the Hayward Gallery, London, in 1983 and 1985; the Museum of Contemporary Art, Chicago, in 1984; the Museum of Modern Art, San Francisco, in 1985; the Museum of Modern Art, Toyoma, in 1986; the National Museum of Photography, Film and Television, Bradford, in 1986; a show of his graphic work at the Royal Academy of Arts, London, in 1995; in *Dialogue avec Picasso* (*Dialogue with Picasso*) at the Musée Picasso, Paris, in 1999; in *Peintures 1960-2000* (*Paintings 1960-2000*) at the Louisiana Museum for Moderne Kunst, Humlebaek, Denmark, in 2001; and in *Five Double Portraits: New Works by David Hockney* at the National Portrait Gallery, London, in 2003.

Bibliography:

Glazebrook, M., *David Hockey: Paintings, Prints and Drawings 1960-70*, exhibition catalogue, Whitechapel Art Gallery, London, 1970. Spender, Stephen/Restany, Pierre, *David Hockney - tableaux et dessins*, Musée des Arts décoratifs, Paris, 1974. Friedman, Martin, *Hockney Paints the Stage*, Thames & Hudson, London, 1983. Hockney, David/Geldzahler, Henry/Stangos, Nikos, *David Hockney, My early years*, Thames & Hudson, London, 1988. Barron, Stephanie/Tuchman, Maurice, *David Hockney, a Retrospective*, exhibition catalogue, County Museum of Art, Los Angeles, 1988. Kitaj, Ronald Brooks/Geldzahler, Henry/Knight, Christopher, et al., *David Hockney, a Retrospective*, exhibition catalogue, Los Angeles County Museum of Art, Los Angeles, Metropolitan Museum of Art, New York, Tate Gall., Thames & Hudson, London, 1988. Luckhardt, Ulrich/Melia, Paul, *David Hockney, a Drawing Retrospective*, exhibition catalogue, Royal Academy of Arts, London, Chronicle Books, San Francisco, 1995. Melia, Paul, *'David Hockney'* in *coll. critical introductions to art*, Manchester University Press, Manchester, 1995. Hockney, David/Stangos, Nikos, *That's the Way I See It*, Thames & Hudson, London, 1995 (2nd edition). Livingstone, Marco, *'David Hockney'* in *coll. World of art*, Thames & Hudson, London, 1996 (2nd edition). Greenhalf, Jim, *Salt and Silver, a story of hope*, Bradford Libraries, Bradford, 1998 (2nd edition). Ottinger, Didier/Livingstone, Marco, et al., *David Hockney, espace-paysage*, exhibition catalogue, Éd. du Centre Georges-Pompidou, Paris, 1999. Hockney, David/Livingstone, Marco/Richard, Gray, *David Hockney, space and line. Grand Canyon pastels on paper and works on paper 1966-1994*, exhibition catalogue, Richard

Gray Gall., New York, Annely Juda Fine Art, London, 1999. Régnier, Gérard/Ottinger, Didier, *David Hockney, dialogue avec Picasso*, exhibition catalogue, Musée Picasso, Paris, Réunion des musées nationaux, Paris, 1999. Melia, Paul and Luckhardt, Ulrich, *David Hockney: Paintings*, Prestel, Munich, New York, c. 2000. Hockney, David, *Secret Knowledge: Rediscovering the Lost Techniques of the Old Masters*, Thames & Hudson, London, 2001. Hockney, David, *Hockney on Art*, Little Brown, New York, 2002. Hockney, David/Livingstone, Marco, *David Hockney: Egyptian journeys*, American University in Cairo Press, Cairo, c. 2002. *David Hockney: Painting on paper, 17 January-1March, 2003*, Annely Juda Fine Art, London, c. 2003.

MUSEUMS AND GALLERIES:

CANBERRA (Nat. Gal. of Australia): *A Bigger Grand Canyon* - CHICAGO (AI) - COLOGNE (Mus. Ludwig) - LONDON (Arts Council Collection, Hayward Gal.): *We Two Boys Together Clinging* (1961, oil/panel) - LONDON (Royal Academy of Arts): *Double Study for Grand Canyon* (painting) - LONDON (Tate Collection): *The First Marriage (A Marriage of Styles I)* (1962, oil on canvas); *A Bigger Splash* (1967, acrylic/canvas); *Mr and Mrs Clark and Percy* (1970-1971, acrylic/canvas); *My Parents* (1977, oil on canvas); around 70 lithographs and prints - MELBOURNE (Nat. Gal. of Victoria): *The Second Marriage* (1963) - MINNEAPOLIS (Walker Art Center) - NEW YORK (MoMA) - PITTSBURGH (Carnegie MA): *He Inquired after the Quality* (1966, etching and aquatint) - PROVIDENCE (Rhode Island School of Design) - VIENNA (Mus. Moderner Kunst Stiftung Ludwig): *Self-portrait with Blue Guitar* (c. 1977) - WASHINGTON DC (Hirshhorn Mus. and Sculpture Garden): *Iowa* (1964, acrylic/canvas).

AUCTION RECORDS:

LONDON, 14 Dec 1966, *Two Men in a Swimming Pool*, GBP 950. LONDON, 7 April 1971, *My Carol for Comrades and Lovers*, GBP 650. NEW YORK, 26 Oct 1972, *I Saw in Louisiana a Live Oak Growing*, USD 17,000. LONDON, 5 July 1973, *The Splash*, GBP 25,000. MILAN, 6 Nov 1973, *Two Trees*, ITL 11,000,000. LONDON, 3 April 1974, *Building, Pershing Square (Los Angeles)*, GBP 24,000. LONDON, 29 Jan 1976, *Celia* (1969, etching and aquatint, 27 x 21 1/2 ins / 68.5 x 54.5 cm) GBP 520. LONDON, 1 July 1976, *Japanese Rain on Canvas* (acrylic/canvas, 48 x 48 ins / 122 x 122 cm) GBP 10,000. LONDON, 27 Jan 1977, *The Hypnotist* (1963, etching and aquatint in black and red, 20 x 20 ins / 50.8 x 50.5 cm) GBP 720. LONDON, 7 Dec 1977, *K's for King* (1962, oil on canvas, 31 1/2 x 22 1/2 ins / 80 x 57 cm) GBP 4,200. LONDON, 28 June 1978, *Still-life* (1965, watercolour and pen, 10 1/4 x 7 3/4 ins / 26 x 20 cm) GBP 500. LONDON, 13 July 1978, *Jungle Boy* (1964, etching and watercolour in black and red, 15 3/4 x 19 1/2 ins / 40 x 49.3 cm) GBP 900. NEW YORK, 19 Oct 1979, *Russ + Mo* (1966, ink, 19 1/2 x 15 3/4 ins / 49.5 x 40 cm) USD 3,200. LONDON, 4 Dec 1979, *Blue Interior with Two Still Lives* (1965, acrylic/canvas, 57 x 57 ins / 145 x 144.5 cm) GBP 37,000. BERN, 19 June 1980, *Contre-jour in the French Style* (1974, colour etching, 29 1/4 x 29 1/4 ins / 74 x 74.5 cm) CHF 4,700. ROME, 19 June 1980, *Small California Forest* (1965, tempera, 13 3/4 x 16 1/2 ins / 35 x 42 cm) ITL 3,000,000. LONDON, 3 Dec 1981, *Bianca* (1972, pencil, 30 1/4 x 13 3/4 ins / 77 x 35 cm) GBP 13,400. LONDON, 1 July 1982, *Cat* (1955, painted ceramic, l. 16 ins / 40.5 cm) GBP 1,250. LONDON, 24 March 1983, *Cat* (1955, painted ceramic, l. 16 ins / 40.5 cm) GBP 1,400. LONDON, 28 June 1983, *Boy About to Take a Shower* (1964, acrylic/canvas, 35 3/4 x 35 3/4 ins / 91 x 91 cm) GBP 62,000. NEW YORK, 9 Nov 1983, *The Duke's Nest* (1971, colouring pencil and graphite, 14 x 17 ins / 35.3 x 42.9 cm) USD 31,000. NEW YORK, 8 Nov 1984, *Still-life with Books* (1973, coloured lithograph, 27 1/4 x 22 ins / 69 x 56 cm) USD 7,250. NEW YORK, 2 May 1985, *Oversized Pool (Paper Pool 23)* (1978, paint and coloured papier mâché/paper, 81 1/2 x 92 1/2 ins / 207 x 235 cm) USD 145,000. NEW YORK, 119 Nov 1985, *Sun State I* (1973, lithograph and coloured silk-screen print, 36 x 30 ins / 91.5 x 76.2 cm) USD 9,300. NEW YORK, 13 Nov 1986, *Peking View, China* (1981, watercolour/paper, 14 x 17 ins / 35.5 x 43.2 cm) USD 14,000. NEW YORK, 5 Nov 1987, *House Behind Château Marmont* (1976, colouring pencil, 14 x 17 ins / 35.5 x 43.3 cm) USD 52,500. LONDON, 3 Dec 1987, *The Bedroom, Tarzana* (1967, acrylic and pencil/canvas, 95 x 95 ins / 241.2 x 241.2 cm) GBP 260,000. NEW YORK, 20 Feb 1988, *Peter at Carrennac* (1967, ink/paper, 14 x 17 ins / 35.3 x 43 cm) USD 3,850; *Plastic Sheet Floating in a Swimming Pool* (oil on canvas, 25 1/4 x 34 ins / 64 x 86.3 cm) USD 165,000. PARIS, 19 March 1988, *The Ghost* (etching in black, 9 x 11 ins / 23 x 27 cm) FRF 10,200. LONDON, 30 June 1988, *Demonstration of Versatility: Swiss Landscape* (1961, oil on canvas, 20 x 24 ins / 51 x 61 cm) GBP 49,500. NEW YORK, 8 Oct 1988, *Geography Book Illustration for a Simple Heart* (1973, pencil/paper, 14 x 17 ins / 35.5 x 43.2 cm) USD 17,600. NEW YORK, 9 Nov 1988, *Early Morning at Ste-Maxime* (1969, acrylic/canvas, 48 x 60 ins / 122 x 152.5 cm) USD 352,000. LONDON, 1 Dec 1988, *A Neat Lawn* (1967, acrylic/canvas, 96 x 96 ins / 244 x 244 cm) GBP 352,000. LONDON, 6 April 1989, *Dale and Mo* (1966, pencil/paper, 18 1/2 x 14 1/2 ins / 47 x 37 cm) GBP 6,050. NEW YORK, 2 May 1989, *A Grand Procession of Dignitaries in Semi-Egyptian Style* (1961, oil on canvas, 84 x 144 ins / 213.4 x 366 cm) USD 2,200,000. NEW YORK, 4 May 1989, *Portrait of Shinro* (pencil and coloured chalk/paper, 12 1/4 x 12 ins / 31.4 x 30.5 cm) USD 22,000. LONDON, 25 May 1989, *Sadyas* (1960, oil on card, 35 3/4 x 24 ins / 91 x 61 cm) GBP 11,000. NEW YORK, 5 Oct 1989, *Portrait of John St Clair* (1972, colouring pencil/paper, 14 x 17 ins / 35.5 x 43 cm) USD 33,000. NEW YORK, 31 Oct 1989, *Portrait of Robert Mapplethorpe* (1971, ink/paper, 17 x 14 ins / 43.2 x 35.5 cm) USD 77, 000. NEW YORK, 8 Nov 1989, *Deep and Wet Water* (1971, acrylic/canvas, 60 x 60 ins / 152.4 x 152.4 cm) USD 1,430,000. NEW YORK, 27 Feb 1990, *Lucca* (1973, colouring pencil/paper, 14 x 17 ins / 35.5 x 43.3 cm) USD 143,000. NEW YORK, 9 May 1990, *Terrace of a House in the Hollywood Hills with Banana Tree* (1983, gouache/paper, 51 x 65 3/4 ins / 129.8 x 167.3 cm) USD 319,000. LONDON, 24 May 1990, *The Pursuit* (1963, colouring pencil and graphite/paper, 12 1/4 x 10 ins / 31 x 25.5 cm) GBP 19,800. LONDON, 18 Oct 1990, *Peter* (1964, ink/paper, 12 1/4 x 19 3/4 ins / 31 x 50 cm) GBP 8,250. LONDON, 27 June 1991, *The Actor* (acrylic/canvas, 65 3/4 x 65 3/4 ins / 167 x 167 cm) GBP 264,000. NEW YORK, 12 Nov 1991, *Full Swimming Pool with Two Blue Shadows* (1978, pressed and coloured paper pulp, 74 1/4 x 86 3/4 ins / 188.5 x 220.5 cm) USD 418,000. LONDON, 26 March 1992, *Portrait of Gerad* (1974, colouring pencil/paper, 25 1/2 x 19 3/4 ins / 65 x 50 cm) USD 18,700. NEW YORK, 6 May 1992, *Curtain with Square Steps and Floorboards* (1979, colouring pencil/paper, 18 3/4 x 24 ins / 47.9 x 61 cm) USD 30,800. NEW YORK, 11 May 1992, *Portrait of Douglas Cooper* (1974, colouring pencil and graphite/paper, 17 x 14 ins / 43.2 x 35.6 cm) USD 17,600. STOCKHOLM, 21 May 1992, *Steps with an A-Shaped Shadow* (1978, collage of coloured papier mâché on strips of paper, 48 x 32 1/4 ins / 122 x 82 cm) SEK 180,000. LONDON, 11 June 1992, *Fredda Bringing Me and Ann a Cup of Tea* (1983, collage of photographs on green paper with a letter taped on, 59 x 67 1/2 ins / 149 x 171.5 cm) GBP 7,700. PARIS, 13 June 1992, *Beside the Swimming Pool* (colouring pencil, 11 x 13 1/2 ins / 27 x 34 cm) FRF 25,000. LONDON, 2 July 1992, *View from the Grand Hotel in Capri* (1970, colouring pencil, 16 3/4 x 13 1/2 ins / 42.5 x 34.5 cm) GBP 25,300. NEW YORK, 17 Nov 1992, *Henry Geldzahler and Christopher Scott in an Interior* (acrylic/canvas, 84 x 120 ins / 213.4 x 304.8 cm) USD 1,100,000. NEW YORK, 19 Nov 1992, *Gregory in the Swimming Pool* (1978, pressed and coloured paper pulp, 32 1/4 x 50 ins / 81.6 x 127 cm) USD 33,000. MUNICH, 1-2 Dec 1992, *Vase and Flowers* (1969, aquatint, 23 x 21 1/2 ins / 58.5 x 54.5 cm) DEM 7,705. LONDON, 3 Dec 1992, *Gregory and Mark* (1975, colouring pencil/paper, 14 x 16 3/4 ins / 35.6 x 42.5 cm) GBP 12,100. LON-

DON, 26 March 1993, *David Graves Looking Out of the Window* (1982, photo collage/green paper, 48 x 30 1/2 ins / 122 x 77.5 cm) GBP 12,650. NEW YORK, 3 May 1993, *Piscine on Sprayed Blue Paper with Green Top (Paper Pool 24)* (1978, colour on papier mâché, 72 x 85 1/2 ins / 182.9 x 217.2 cm) USD 321,500. NEW YORK, 10 Nov 1993, *Californian Collector* (1964, acrylic/canvas, 60 x 72 ins / 152.4 x 182.9 cm) USD 1,020,000. HEIDELBERG, 5-13 April 1994, *Ashtray with a Match and a Cigarette Butt* (1970, ink, 9 1/2 x 6 1/2 ins / 24.1 x 16.3 cm) DEM 1,800. NEW YORK, 5 May 1994, *Green Swimming Pool with Diving Board and its Shadow on the Water* (1978, coloured papier mâché pressed on paper, 49 1/2 x 31 3/4 ins / 125.7 x 80.6 cm) USD 90,500. LONDON, 29 June 1994, *The Cruel Elephant* (1962, oil on canvas, 48 x 60 ins / 121.9 x 152.4 cm) GBP 220,000. LOKEREN, 8 Oct 1994, *Remembering* (1966, aquatint, 13 3/4 x 9 ins / 35 x 22 cm) BEF 44,000. NEW YORK, 3 May 1995, *Portrait of Ben Sonnenberg* (1974, ink/paper, 17 x 14 ins / 43.2 x 35.6 cm) USD 9,775. AMSTERDAM, 30 May 1995, *Maurice Payne (s.a.c. 123)* (1971, etching, 26 3/4 x 21 1/4 ins / 68 x 54 cm) NLG 2,375. LONDON, 30 Nov 1995, *Ravel's Garden* (1980, oil on canvas, 20 x 30 ins / 51 x 76.5 cm) GBP 38,900. NEW YORK, 5 May 1996, *Celia in a Green Hat* (1985, coloured lithograph, 30 x 22 ins / 76 x 56 cm) USD 10,350. NEW YORK, 7 May 1996, *Marinka, Naked* (1977, chalk and pencil/paper, 17 x 14 ins / 43.2 x 35.6 cm) USD 46,000. NEW YORK, 9 Nov 1996, *A Picture of Celia* (1984-1986, coloured lithograph, 65 1/4 x 48 ins / 165.6 x 122 cm) USD 74,000. NEW YORK, 20 Nov 1996, *Armchair with Stanley, August* (1988, oil on canvas, 24 x 24 ins / 61 x 61 cm) USD 239,000. NEW YORK, 21 Nov 1996, *Yves-Marie of Paris* (1974, graphite and pencil/paper, 17 x 13 3/4 ins / 43.2 x 35 cm) USD 37,950. AMSTERDAM, 2-3 June 1997, *Ian Fountains Abbey, Yorkshire* (1983, photographic collage/paper, 49 1/2 x 38 3/4 ins / 125.5 x 98.5 cm) NLG 11,328. COPENHAGEN, 7 June 1997, *Artcurial* (lithograph) DKK 4,000. NEW YORK, 19 Nov 1997, *Berlin: A Souvenir* (1962-1963, oil on canvas, 84 x 84 ins / 213.4 x 213.4 cm) USD 635,000. NEW YORK, 6 and 7 March 1998, *Dark Mist* (1973, lithograph, 29 x 25 ins / 73.5 x 63.5 cm) USD 4,887. LONDON, 1 July 1999, *Red Bridge* (1989, acrylic on canvas, 36 x 24 ins / 91 x 61 cm) GBP 110,000. LONDON, 1 July 1999, *Green Pool with Diving Board and Shadow* (1978, liquid dyes and pulp on pressed colour paper, 50 x 31 ins / 126 x 80 cm) GBP 300,000. NEW YORK, 10 Nov 1999, *Near Bruges* (1995, oil on canvas, diptych, 21 x 60 ins / 53 x 153 cm) USD 420,000. NEW YORK, 17 May 2000, *Day Pool with Three Blues* (1978, coloured pressed paper pulp, 72 x 85 ins / 183 x 217 cm) USD 600,000. LOS ANGELES, 5 Dec 2000, *Study of Water, Phoenix, Arizona* (1976, colour pencil, 16 x 18 ins / 41 x 45 cm) USD 350,000. NEW YORK, 8 May 2001, *Picture of a Hollywood Swimming Pool* (1964, acrylic on canvas, 36 x 48 ins / 91 x 122 cm) USD 550,000. NEW YORK, 16 May 2001, *Pool on a Cloudy Day with Rain, Paper Pool 22* (1978, coloured pressed paper pulp, 72 x 85 ins / 183 x 216 cm) USD 550,000. NEW YORK, 12 Nov 2002, *Diving Board with Still Water on Blue Paper* (1978, coloured pressed paper pulp, 72 x 85 ins / 183 x 217 cm) USD 550,000. NEW YORK, 13 Nov 2002, *Portrait of Nick Wilder* (1966, acrylic on canvas, 72 x 72 ins / 183 x 183 cm) USD 2,600,000. NEW YORK, 14 May 2003, *Snake* (1962, oil, chalk and graphite on canvas, 72 x 72 ins / 183 x 183 cm) USD 280,000. NEW YORK, 12 Nov 2003, *Portrait of Nick Wilder* (1966, acrylic on canvas, 72 x 72 ins / 183 x 183 cm) USD 2,100,000. NEW YORK, 12 May 2004, *Antheriums* (1995, oil on canvas, 41 x 53 ins / 105 x 135 cm) USD 750,000. LONDON, 25 June 2004, *Gregory in the Pool* (1978, hand pressed colour pulp, 32 x 50 ins / 81 x 127 cm) GBP 80,000.

HOCKS, Teun
Dutch, 20th - 21st century.
Born 1947, in Leiden.
Installation artist.

Teun Hocks had a solo exhibition at the Galerie 15 as part of the 1995 *International Fair of Contemporary Art*.

He works from photographs, placing himself in scenes from daily life.

HOCQ, Marcel
Belgian, 20th century.
Born 16 March 1933, in Boignée.
Painter, sculptor, potter, photographer. Figures, nudes.

Marcel Hocq studied briefly at the École Supérieure des Arts St-Luc in Brussels. He became a professional photographer, living and working in Velaine-sur-Sambre. In 1977, an exhibition entitled *Hocq Sculpteur* was mounted in Fleurus town hall. Collections of his paintings were shown in 1990, 1993 and 1997 at the Galerie Le Roc d'Art in Balâtre. He was influenced first by Post-Impressionist techniques, then by Surrealist imagery, before developing a kind of Expressionism, with woman as the principal subject and justified by references to Modigliani, Magritte, Delvaux, Chagall and Kokoschka.

BIBLIOGRAPHY:

Mespouille, José, *Marcel Hocq*, Éd. du Roc d'Art, Balâtre, 1990. *M. Hocq*, E. D. Évolution Éd., Granville, 1991.

HOCQUART, Édouard
French, 19th century.
Engraver.

This artist worked in Paris, and appears to have mostly created industrial art. In 1824 he exhibited a machine that he had invented for engraving skies, portrait backgrounds and straight or undulating lines of shading for architectural drawings. This machine could also be used for tracing shapes - ovals, concentric circles, and so forth - on to steel and copper.

HOCQUART, Ildephonse
Belgian, 19th century.
Born 19 July 1819, in Geersberge.
Active in Antwerp.
Landscape artist.

Ildephonse Hocquart was a pupil of Ducorron and E.-F. de Block.

HOCQUET, Christian
Belgian, 20th century.
Born 1935, in Gosselies (Charleroi).
Painter, engraver, illustrator.

Christian Hocquet was awarded the Grand Prix de Peinture et des Arts Plastiques de Wallonie in 1981. He paints opulent, spontaneous scenes of everyday life and his local region.

HOCTYN, François
Dutch, 18th century.
Active in Leiden c. 1745.
Painter.

HOCXBERGEN, Frans van
Dutch, 17th century.
Born c. 1625, in Amsterdam; died 1679.
Painter.

Frans van Hocxbergen painted landscapes.

HODACK, Arnoldine
Moravian, 19th century.
Born 16 July 1822, in Brno; died 2 May 1893, in Brno.
Painter. Still-lifes (fruit).

A painting entitled *Fruits* by Arnoldine Holdack is in the museum in Brno.

HODART, Philippe, or Édouard, Odoarte, Oudart, Udart, Udarte, Uduarte
French, 16th century.
Born 16th century, in France.
Sculptor.

Philippe Hodart worked first in Spain, on stalls in Sto Domingo de la Calzada in 1522-1523, and then in Toledo. In 1534 he was in Coimbra in Portugal, where he made a monumental *Last Supper*, emphasising the tragic aspect.

Museums and Galleries:
Coimbra (Mus. Nacional de Machado de Castro): *Last Supper* (from the Holy Cross refectory in Coimbra).

HODDER, Albert
British, 19th century.
Active in Worcester.
Painter. Seascapes.

Albert Hodder exhibited in London at the Royal Academy between 1872 and 1890.

HODÉ, Pierre
French, 20th century.
Born 8 January 1889, in Rouen; died 1942.
Painter, illustrator. Scenes with figures, landscapes, urban landscapes, harbour scenes, architectural views, still-lifes. Stage sets, murals.
School of Normandy.

Pierre Hodé began painting in 1909. He left Rouen to live in Paris at the *Bateau Lavoir*, where he struck up a friendship with the painter Pierre Dumond. He was self-taught, but was influenced by Impressionism, Cézanne and Cubism before finally forging his own style close to nature, as can be seen in his landscapes of the Normandy coastline and in his still-lifes. Apart from murals in Rouen, he created theatre sets. He mainly worked in his native Normandy and became secretary-general of the Société des Peintres Normands.

He exhibited locally, as well as in Paris, at the Salon des Indépendants and the Salon d'Automne. He featured posthumously in *Autour de l'Impressionnisme: dix-neuf peintres de l'École Normande* (*Around Impressionism: Nineteen Painters from the School of Normandy*), Maison des Arts in Antony (2003).

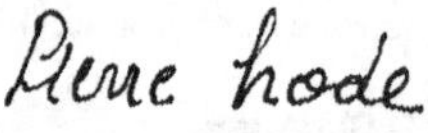

Bibliography:
Dubosc, Georges, *L'École de Rouen, ses peintres et ses ferronniers*, Lecerf fils, Rouen, 1914. *Ensemble... Capon, F.Z. Ebérl, Ed. Goerg, Pierre Hodé, Henry Ramey*, group exhibition catalogue, Gal. Balzac, Paris, 1923. *L'École de Rouen*, BDS, Rouen, 1972. *École normande, École de Rouen 1870-1930*, exhibition catalogue, Centre culturel du Palais Bénédictine, Fécamp, 1989. Lespinasse, François, *L'École de Rouen*, Lecerf, Rouen, 1995. *L'École de Rouen, de l'impressionnisme à Marcel Duchamp 1878-1914*, exhibition catalogue, Musée des Beaux-Arts, Rouen, 1996. *Autour de l'Impressionnisme: dix-neuf peintres de l'école normande*, exhibition catalogue, La Maison des Arts, Antony, 2003.

Auction records:
Paris, 7 June 1923, *Boats in the Port of Marseilles*, FRF 380. Paris, 3 April 1925, *Moulin de la Galette*, FRF 805. Paris, 4 Feb 1928, *Notre Dame de Paris* FRF 1,100. Paris, 3 May 1929, *Boats in Rouen*, FRF 1,550. Paris, 19 May 1930, *Roses and Apples*, FRF 310. Paris, 30 April 1931, *Still-life with Violin*, FRF 850. Paris, 31 Jan 1938, *The Port at Rouen*, FRF 430. Paris, 9 July 1942, *The Port at Rouen*, FRF 1,500. Paris, 2 April 1943, *The Apse of Notre Dame and the Quays*, FRF 10,500. Paris, July 1946, *Factories in Cormeilles-en-Parisis*, FRF 800. Paris, 2 Dec 1946, *The Table*, FRF 5,500. Paris, 30 April 1947, *Honfleur, the Lieutenance and Cheval Blanc Hotel*, FRF 16,000. Versailles, 1 March 1970, *The Port at Rouen*, FRF 16,000. Paris, 10 Dec 1971, *Bouquet of Flowers*, FRF 5,000. Paris, 9 June 1972, *The Port at Dieppe*, FRF 6,000. Rouen, 27 March 1973, *The Ball of the 14 of July in Paris*, FRF 9,900. Paris, 9 Dec 1974, *Cathedral and Roofs*, FRF 20,500. Honfleur, 11 July 1976, *The Lieutenance, Honfleur* (oil on canvas, 13 x 16 1/2 ins / 33 x 42 cm) FRF 6,200. Paris, 9 June 1977, *The Port at Rouen* (oil on canvas, 25 1/2 x 32 ins / 65 x 81 cm) FRF 13,000. Enghien-les-Bains, 18 Nov 1979, *The Port at Honfleur* (oil on canvas, 23 1/2 x 29 ins / 60 x 73.5 cm) FRF 24,600. Paris, 27 April 1982, *Old Houses in Argentan* (oil on cardboard, 17 x 21 1/4 ins / 43 x 54 cm) FRF 13,500. Paris, 17 March 1983, *The Port at Rouen* (oil on canvas, 17 3/4 x 32 ins / 45 x 81 cm) FRF 36,000. Paris, 27 Oct 1986, *Rouen: the Cathedral* (oil on canvas, 39 1/4 x 32 ins / 100 x 81 cm) FRF 108,000. Paris, 20 Nov 1987, *Still-life with Red Mullets and Vegetables* (oil on canvas, 15 x 22 ins / 38 x 55 cm) FRF 23,000. Paris, 17 Dec 1987, *The Port* (oil on canvas, 28 3/4 x 39 1/4 ins / 73 x 100 cm) FRF 190,000. Paris, 17 Dec 1987, *The Port* (oil on canvas, 28 3/4 x 39 1/4 ins / 73 x 100 cm) FRF 190,000. La Varenne-St-Hilaire, 29 May 1988, *Still-life with Pitcher and Roses* (oil on canvas, 21 1/4 x 28 3/4 ins / 54 x 73 cm) FRF 27,000. Versailles, 23 Oct 1988, *Mechanical Rhythm* (1937, gouache and paint/paper, 19 1/4 x 26 3/4 ins / 49 x 68 cm) FRF 40,500. Neuilly, 22 Nov 1988, *Still-life with Bouquet of Roses* (oil on canvas, 19 3/4 x 24 ins / 50 x 61 cm) FRF 80,000; *Boats in the Mist in the Port of Rouen* (oil on canvas, 15 x 18 ins / 38 x 46 cm) FRF 106,000. Versailles, 18 Dec 1988, *Still-life with Bust of the Artist* (oil on canvas, 31 3/4 x 39 1/4 ins / 80.5 x 100 cm) FRF 160,000. Paris, 13 March 1989, *Children in the Park* (oil on cardboard, 11 3/4 x 15 1/4 ins / 30 x 39 cm) FRF 17,000. Paris, 20 Nov 1989, *Composition on the Port of Dieppe* (oil on canvas, 23 1/2 x 28 3/4 ins / 60 x 73 cm) FRF 130,000. Amsterdam, 10 April 1990, *Boat* (1939, oil on cardboard, 15 1/4 x 19 ins / 38.5 x 48.5 cm) NLG 11,500. Paris, 21 June 1990, *The Port of Dieppe* (oil on panel, 19 3/4 x 24 ins / 50 x 61 cm) FRF 320,000. New York, 10 Oct 1990, *View of a Port* (oil on canvas, 21 1/4 x 25 1/2 ins / 53.9 x 64.8 cm) USD 49,500. Paris, 16 March 1991, *Honfleur, the Lieutenance* (oil on canvas, 25 1/2 x 32 ins / 65 x 81 cm) FRF 180,000. Calais, 2 Feb 1992, *The Suspended Bridge in Conflans, at the End of the Oise River* (oil on canvas, 21 1/4 x 25 1/2 ins / 54 x 65 cm) FRF 144,000. Paris, 18 Nov 1992, *The Ball of the 14th of July* (oil on card, 10 3/4 x 13 1/2 ins / 27.3 x 34.6 cm) FRF 78,000. Paris, 30 April 1993, *The Port of Rouen* (oil on canvas, 13 x 18 ins / 33 x 46 cm) FRF 60,000. Calais, 4 July 1993, *The Port of Rouen c. 1925* (oil on canvas, 13 x 18 ins / 33 x 46 cm) FRF 90,000. Paris, 22 March 1994, *Composition on the Port of Rouen* (1928, oil on canvas, 21 1/4 x 25 1/2 ins / 54 x 65 cm) FRF 90,000. Honfleur, 16 April 1995, *Construction on the Port of Rouen* (1927, oil on canvas, 31 x 25 1/4 ins / 79 x 64 cm) FRF 170,000. Paris, 13 Oct 1995, *Notre Dame de Paris* (oil on canvas, 23 1/2 x 28 3/4 ins / 60 x 73 cm) FRF 62,000. Paris, 28 June 1996, *Still-life with Bouquet of Flowers* (oil on canvas, 15 x 18 ins / 38 x 46 cm) FRF 5,000. Calais, 7 July 1996, *Paris, the Quays of the Seine* (oil on canvas, 21 1/4 x 25 1/2 ins / 54 x 65 cm) FRF 34,000. Paris, 10 March 1997, *The Lieutenance* (oil on canvas, 14 1/4 x 17 3/4 ins / 36 x 45 cm) FRF 26,000. Paris, 5 June 1997, *Still-life with Violin* (oil on canvas, 21 1/4 x 28 3/4 ins / 54 x 73 cm) FRF 18,000. Paris, 23 June 1997, *Tugboat at the Quay in Conflans-Ste-Honorine* (c. 1921, oil on canvas, 19 3/4 x 25 1/2 ins / 50 x 65 cm) FRF 37,000. Paris, 9 March 1998, *The Port of Dieppe* (oil on canvas, 28 1/4 x 23 1/2 ins / 72 x 60 cm) FRF 133,000. Paris, 1 April 1998, *Still-life with Jug and Bottle* (oil on canvas, 18 x 22 3/4 ins / 46 x 58 cm) FRF 20,000. Paris, 28 Jan 1999, *Steamer on the Quay* (oil on canvas, 20 x 26 ins / 50 x 65 cm) FRF 44,000. Paris, 8 Dec 1999, *City Walls* (oil on canvas, 21 x 26 ins / 54 x 65 cm) FRF 47,000. Calais, 5 Nov 2000, *Boats in Harbour* (oil on canvas, 26 x 32 ins / 65 x 81 cm) FRF 122,000. Paris, 10 Dec 2000, *Cubist Composition with*

Globe (1920-1922, oil on canvas, 24 x 28 ins / 60 x 72 cm) FRF 60,000. PARIS, 29 Jan 2001, *The Lieutenance in Honfleur* (oil on canvas, 25 x 20 ins / 63 x 50 cm) FRF 103,000. ZURICH, 4 Dec 2001, *Four Female Nudes* (oil on card, 15 x 11 ins / 37 x 28 cm) CHF 10,000. VERSAILLES, 7 April 2002, *Still-life* (oil on panel, 13 x 16 ins / 33 x 41 cm) EUR 3,800. VERSAILLES, 7 April 2002, *Fisherman* (oil on canvas, 15 x 18 ins / 38 x 46 cm) EUR 4,000. PARIS, 21 Oct 2003, *Paris, Notre-Dame Seen from the Quays* (oil on canvas, 21 x 26 ins / 54 x 65 cm) EUR 3,000. NEUILLY, 16 Dec 2003, *Boats on the Quay* (oil on canvas, 21 x 26 ins / 54 x 65 cm) EUR 22,000. PARIS, 2 March 2004, *Still-life with Violin* (oil on canvas, 21 x 26 ins / 54 x 65 cm) EUR 2,500. PARIS, 11 June 2004, *Still-life with Tall Hat* (1921, oil on canvas, 24 x 20 ins / 61 x 50 cm) EUR 6,000.

HODEBERT, Léon Auguste César

French, 19th - 20th century.

Born c. 1852, in St-Michel-sur-Loire; died 16 May 1914, in Neuilly-sur-Seine.

Active in Beauvais.

Painter, engraver. Figures, nudes, landscapes.

A painter, Léon Hodebert made his début at the Salon in 1877; he also executed engravings and lithographs. A member of the Société des Artistes Français from 1883, he received an honourable mention (1897), a 3rd class medal (1900) and a 1st class medal (1908). He received a bronze medal at the 1900 Exposition Universelle.

AUCTION RECORDS:

PARIS, 17-21 May 1904, *Female Nude seen from the Back*, FRF 125. LONDON, 29 May 1908, *Bathers* (1886) GBP 84. PARIS, 3 and 4 May 1923, *Getting Ready*, FRF 115. LONDON, 31 Nov 1928, *Bathers*, GBP 32. PARIS, 22 July 1942, *Le Déshabillé*, FRF 800; *The Flowered Steps*, FRF 320. NEW YORK, 30 Oct 1992, *The Bathers* (1880, oil on canvas, 37 1/2 x 46 1/4 ins / 95.2 x 117.5 cm) USD 13,200.

HODEL, Ernst, the Elder

Swiss, 19th century.

Born 8 February 1852, in Thun; died 13 May 1902, in Lucerne.

Painter. Landscapes.

Ernst Hodel the Elder, father of Ernst Hodel the Younger, worked in Lucerne, Geneva and Vevey.

HODEL, Ernst, the Younger

Swiss, 20th century.

Born 29 July 1881, in Lucerne; died 1955.

Painter. Genre scenes.

Ernst Hodel the Younger was the son of the landscape painter Hodel the Elder. He took part in the Exposition Internationale in Brussels in 1910.

MUSEUMS AND GALLERIES:

BERN: *The Cousin*.

AUCTION RECORDS:

ZURICH, 19 May 1979, *Peasant Woman with Two Cows* (oil on canvas remounted on board, 12 3/4 x 18 1/2 ins / 32.5 x 46.8 cm) CHF 2,000. PARIS, 25 Nov 1981, *Landsturm* (1914, oil on canvas, 30 1/2 x 42 1/4 ins / 77.5 x 107 cm) CHF 9,000. LUCERNE, 7 June 1984, *The House* (oil on canvas remounted/Pavatex, 17 1/4 x 24 ins / 44 x 61 cm) CHF 4,000. BERN, 30 April 1988, *Peasant Woman from the Valais with her Goats* (oil on canvas, 23 1/2 x 32 ins / 60 x 81 cm) CHF 3,900. ZURICH, 8 Dec 1999, *Engadin Houses in Sils Baselgia* (oil on board, 17 x 21 ins / 42 x 54 cm) CHF 6,000. ZURICH, 8 Dec 1999, *Engadin Winter Landscape* (oil on canvas, 24 x 30 ins / 60 x 76 cm) CHF 10,000. ZURICH, 13 Sept 2000, *Mountain Landscape with Stream* (oil on canvas, 66 x 78 ins / 168 x 198 cm) CHF 3,300. STOCKHOLM, 30 Oct 2000, *Alpine Landscape with Lake* (oil on canvas, 35 x 55 ins / 90 x 140 cm) SEK 24,000. LUCERNE, 14 Nov 2001, *Soldiers Wrestling* (oil on board, 27 x 17 ins / 69 x 44 cm) CHF 2,600. LUCERNE, 14 Nov 2001, *Shipyard with Pilatus beyond* (oil on canvas, 22 x 29 ins / 55 x 73 cm) CHF 4,000. ZURICH, 25 March 2002, *Mountain Landscape with Glacier* (oil on canvas, 31 x 39 ins / 80 x 99 cm) CHF 3,800. ZURICH, 26 May 2004, *Cows Drinking* (oil on canvas, 24 x 31 ins / 60 x 80 cm) CHF 3,000.

HODEL, Rudolf

Swiss, 18th century.

Painter.

Rudolf Hodel executed a reredos for the church in Kriens.

HODENIUS, C.

German, 19th century.

Active in 1833.

Draughtsman.

The signature of C Hodenius, an unknown artist, was discovered in a book in the collection of Duke Aribert von Anhalt Dessau.

HODGE

British, 18th century.

Active in London c. 1775.

Miniaturist.

HODGE, Albert

British, 20th century.

Born 1875, in Glasgow; died 1918.

Sculptor.

Albert Hodge lived and worked in Campden Hill. He was a member of the Society of British Sculptors and exhibited at the Royal Academy in London in 1909.

HODGE, R. P.

British, 18th century.

Active in London.

Painter. Fruit.

R.P. Hodge exhibited at the Free Society from 1769 to 1780.

HODGES, Charles

British, 19th century.

Born in London; died 1846, in Hamburg.

Engraver.

Charles Hodges was an amateur engraver who worked first in Munich, making copies of the Dutch masters.

HODGES, Charles Howard

British, 18th century.

Active in London.

Miniaturist.

Charles Hodges is likely to be the same person as the miniaturist Hodge whose works appeared without any first-name initial at the exhibitions of the Society of Artists and the Free Society in 1765 and 1775. Charles Hodges exhibited in London with these societies in 1768 and 1783.

HODGES, Charles Howard

British, 18th - 19th century.

Born 1764, in Portsmouth; died 24 July 1837, in Amsterdam.

Also active in the Netherlands.

Painter, pastellist, engraver.

Charles Howard Hodges was a student at the Royal Academy in 1782; it is likely that he received lessons from John Raphael Smith. He went to The Netherlands in 1788, spending most of his life there working in Amsterdam and The Hague. He painted portraits of many notables and made engravings after Rembrandt, Reynolds, Van Dyck and others. He was one of the most distinguished artists of the English School at the end of the 18th century to work in mezzotint and his prints are much sought after.

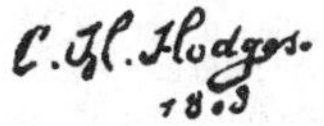

Bibliography:
Van der Felz, A.C.A.W., *Charles Howard Hodges (1764-1837)*, Van Gorcum, Assen, 1982.
Museums and Galleries:
Ajaccio: *Louis Bonaparte* - Amsterdam (Rijksmus.): *Self-portrait; King William I; Louis Napoleon King of Holland; Emma Jane Hodges; The Poet Willem Bilderdijk; Cornelis Apostool; Reinier Vinkeles; Joanna Cornelia Zieseni; Jacoba Vetter; Hendrik Bicker; Wilhelmina Jacoba van Hoorn; Jehan Fraser; Maria Antoinette Sanderson; Edward Fraser; Portrait of a Man; Portrait of a Woman* - Haarlem: *Louis Bonaparte King of Holland; Paulus Roeloff; Maria Fabricius.*
Auction records:
Amsterdam, 30 Oct 1990, *Three-Quarters Seated Portrait of a Lady thought to be Maria van de Graaf in a Brown Dress and a Lace Cap on a Terrace in Front of a Curtain* (pastel/vellum, 13 1/2 x 11 1/4 ins / 34 x 28.5 cm) NLG 3,220. Amsterdam, 24 April 1991, *Head and Shoulder Portrait of the Grand Duchess Catherine Paulovna of Russia in a Black Velvet Dress holding the Insignia of St Anne of Oldenburg* (1810, oil on canvas, 28 1/2 x 23 ins / 72.5 x 58.5 cm) NLG 14,950. Amsterdam, 13 Nov 1995, *Portrait of Jacobus Catharinus de Joncheere in a Black Suit with a Yellow Waistcoat and White Shirt; Three-Quarter Length Seated Portrait of Helena Cornelia Luberta de Joncheere in a Brown Silk Dress Ornamented with Lace* (oil on canvas, a pair, 29 x 24 1/2 ins / 73.4 x 62 cm and 29 x 24 1/4 ins/72.8 x 61.8 cm) NLG 14,950.
Amsterdam, 25 Oct 1999, *Portrait of Sebald Justinus Brugmans* (c. 1816, oil on canvas, 30 x 24 ins / 76 x 61 cm) NLG 8,500. Amsterdam, 29 March 2004, *Portrait of Herman Arnoldus Crommelin* (pastel, oval, 10 x 9 ins / 25 x 22 cm) EUR 2,500. Amsterdam, 3 Nov 2004, *Portrait of Anne Madeleine Henriette de Bosset* (pastel, oval, 10 x 9 ins / 26 x 22 cm) EUR 2,400.

HODGES, David
American, 20th - 21st century.
Born 1960, in Rockford (Illinois).
Painter, miniaturist. Genre scenes.

David Hodges studied philosophy before devoting himself to painting. He lives and works in Chicago. His works, often in oval wooden frames, feature old-fashioned scenes of 1930s life, sharply observed and often humorous. Their conventional appearance is subverted by their often voyeuristic quality, and by the commentary implicit in their titles.

Hodges' work has featured in a number of group exhibitions, notably: 1988, Hyde Park Art Center, Chicago; 1990, Frankfurt International Exhibition of Contemporary Art; 1990, *Real Allusions*, Whitney Museum of American Art, New York. He has also held solo exhibitions at Galerie Farideh Cadot in Paris, and New York.
Bibliography:
Un Regard autre, exhibition catalogue, Gal. Farideh Cadot, Paris, 1987. Chevrefils-Desbiolles, Annie, '*David Hodges*' in *Art Press* n° 150, periodical, Paris, September 1990.

HODGES, Edward. See BAILY Edward Hodges

HODGES, George Schuyler
American, 19th - 20th century.
Born 3 March 1864, in Pontiac (Michigan); died 1953, in (Pine Lake, Michigan).
Painter.

George Hodges studied under Gérôme at the École des Beaux-Arts, Paris, and lived and worked in Pontiac. He was a member of the Paris American Art Association.

HODGES, J. Sidney Willis
British, 19th century.
Born 4 April 1829, in Worthing; died July 1900.
Painter.

Sidney Hodges exhibited a large number of portraits at the Royal Academy and the British Institution in London between 1864 and 1893. They included those of the *Bishop of Exeter* and the *Duke of Northumberland* (1863). He also wrote several literary works including some on art.
Auction records:
London, May 1922, *Sir James Brooke*, GBP 10; *Henry Phillpotts*, GBP 4. Stockholm, 15 Nov 1989, *Lady Godiva* (oil on canvas, 40 1/2 x 28 3/4 ins / 103 x 73 cm) SEK 10,000. London, 11 Jan 2001, *Lord Hood of Avalon as a Midshipman, Bombay Harbour in the Distance* (watercolour heightened with white, 14 x 10 ins / 36 x 26 cm) GBP 1,000.

HODGES, James Newman
British, 19th century.
Born c. 1786; died 29 December 1821.
Active in London.
Engraver (mezzotint).

James Hodges was the son of Charles Howard Hodges and lived principally in Amsterdam.

HODGES, Jim
American, 20th - 21st century.
Born 1957.
Installation artist, draughtsman.

Jim Hodges, who works in New York, received a BFA from Fort Wright College in Spokane, Washington in 1980, and an MFA from the Pratt Institute, Brooklyn in 1986. He has been transforming ordinary objects such as paper napkins, light bulbs, scarves, chains, mirrors, tissue paper and silk flowers into art since the early 1990s. His labour-intensive work, which uses techniques normally associated with crafts, blurs the distinction between high and low art and seeks to communicate with the viewer on a basic human level. One series of work, *This Way In* (1999), comprised curtains sewn from fabric petals, and configurations of flower parts pinned to walls. Hodges' work *View*, a mosaic of mirror fragments, highlights the fragility of life. Other works include the collage *Picturing That Day* (2002), the light-bulb sculptures *Ahhha* (2000) and *Ultimate Joy* (2001), a woven sculpture of silver jewellery, *On We Go* (1996), and the installation *Colorsound* (2003). His *Subway Music Box* (2000) was a multi-projection video installation which documented subway musicians.

Hodges' solo shows include: 1994, *A Diary of Flowers*, at CRG Art, New York; 1998, *Jim Hodges: Welcome*, at the Kemper Museum of Contemporary Art, Kansas City, MO; 2002, *Jim Hodges: Constellation of an Ordinary Day*, at the Jundt Art Museum, Gonzaga University, Spokane, WA; 2003, at the Stephen Friedman Gallery, London; 2003, *Jim Hodges: Colorsound* at the Addison Gallery of American Art, Andover, MA; 2004, *Jim Hodges: Don't Be Afraid*, at the Worcester Art Museum, MA; and 2005, at the Museum of Contemporary Art, Cleveland.

Other exhibitions include: 1996-1997, *Just Past: The Contemporary in MOCA's Permanent Collection* and 1997, *Home: Selections from the Permanent Collection*, both at the Museum of Contemporary Art, Los Angeles; 1998-1999, *Every way*, at the Museum of Contemporary Art, Chicago; and 2005, *Heaven and Earth*, at the Centro Galego de Arte Contemporanea, Santiago de Compostella, Spain. He has also participated in an exhibition of banners, *Projects 70: Jim Hodges, Beatriz Milhazes, Faith Ringgold*, at the Museum of Modern Art, New York (2000).

He has received a Penny McCall Foundation Grant (1994), the Louis Comfort Tiffany Foundation Award (1995) and the Albert Ucross Prize (2001).

BIBLIOGRAPHY:

Edelman, Robert G., '*Jim Hodges*' in *Art Press* n° 189, periodical, Paris, March 1994. Cruz, Amanda, *Jim Hodges*, exhibition catalogue, Museum of Contemporary Art, Chicago, 1998. *Jim Hodges*, exhibition catalogue, CRG Gallery, New York, 2002. '*Jim Hodges*' in *Art on Paper*, vol 6, no. 6, journal article, July-August 2002. Harris, Susan, '*Jim Hodges at CRG*' in *Art in America*, journal article, January 2003.

MUSEUMS AND GALLERIES:

CHICAGO (AI) - CHICAGO (MCA): *The End from Where You Are* (1998, textile) - DALLAS (MA) - KANSAS CITY (Kemper MCA): *Dot* (1999, wood and metal panel, light bulbs) - LONDON (Tate Collection): *Everything We Know* (2003, cut photograph) - LOS ANGELES (MCA): *A Diary of Flowers - Above the Clouds* (1995, installation) - MIAMI (AM) - MILWAUKEE (AM) - NANTES (FRAC) - NEW YORK (Guggenheim Mus.) - NEW YORK (Whitney Mus. of American Art) - PARIS (MNAM-CCI) - WASHINGTON DC (Hirshhorn Mus. and Sculpture Garden): *This Way In* (1999, silk, plastic and wire); *View* (1998, mirror on canvas).

AUCTION RECORDS:

NEW YORK, 18 May 2000, *Diary of Flowers* (1993, ink on paper napkins, 26, 47 x 37 ins / 119 x 94 cm) USD 7,000. NEW YORK, 18 May 2000, *Line to You* (silk, plastic wire and thread, h. 211 ins / 536 cm) USD 35,000. NEW YORK, 16 May 2002, *Diary of Flowers/Just Blue* (1993, pen and blue ink on paper napkins, 84 x 53 ins / 213 x 135 cm) USD 13,000. NEW YORK, 12 Nov 2002, *Diary of Flowers* (1993, pen and ink on paper napkins) USD 13,000. NEW YORK, 23 Sept 2003, *Blue Love* (1992, ink on paper napkins, 21, 36 x 32 ins / 91 x 81 cm) USD 8,500. NEW YORK, 12 Nov 2003, *Trembling and Joy* (1994, metal chains) USD 165,000.

HODGES, John

British, 18th century.
Died 1802, in London.
Engraver (mezzotint).

John Hodges should perhaps be identified with Charles Howard Hodges or James Newman Hodges.

HODGES, William

British, 18th century.
Born 1744, in London; died 6 March 1797, in Brixham.
Painter. Landscapes.

William Hodges was the pupil of Wilson. He accompanied Captain Cook on his journey around the world bringing back some extremely interesting views of the places explored including some of the islands of the Pacific. He began exhibiting in London at the Royal Academy in 1777, becoming an associate member in 1786. He also exhibited at the Society of Artists and the Free Society.

MUSEUMS AND GALLERIES:

LONDON (Victoria and Albert Mus.): *Ruined Palace*; *Ludlow Castle*.

AUCTION RECORDS:

LONDON, 31 Jan 1924, *Landscape with River*, GBP 68. LONDON, 10 March 1965, *Hindu Temple*, GBP 900. LONDON, 17 March 1967, *Tomb of Sher Shah, Sasarem*, Gns 1,300. LONDON, 17 Nov 1971, *The Armenian Bridge*, GBP 1,300. LONDON, 22 June 1979, *Landscape near the Agra Reservoir* (oil on canvas, 38 1/2 x 48 1/2 ins / 97.8 x 123.2 cm) GBP 9,000. LONDON, 16 July 1982, *Old Bridge in Shrewsbury* (oil on panel, 22 x 32 1/4 ins / 56 x 82 cm) GBP 4,000. LONDON, 15 May 1988, *View of the Fort of Peteter* (oil on canvas, 24 x 28 1/2 ins / 61 x 72.4 cm) GBP 7,700. LONDON, 9 Nov 1994, *View of the Rhine in Germany*; *Mountains in Switzerland* (oil on canvas, a pair, each 14 1/4 x 18 1/2 ins / 36 x 47 cm) GBP 7,820. LONDON, 12 April 1995, *Tivoli: Temple of the Sibyl with the Roman Campagna in the Distance* (oil on canvas, 24 1/2 x 29 1/4 ins / 62 x 74.5 cm) GBP 5,750. LONDON, 31 March 1999, *View on Rhine* (oil on canvas, 17 x 21 ins / 44 x 54 cm) GBP 7,000. LONDON, 14 Dec 2000, *Matavie Bay in the Island of Otaheite, now Tahiti* (oil on canvas, 20 x 24 ins / 50 x 61 cm) GBP 340,000. LONDON, 21 March 2001, *View of an Italianate Coastline* (oil on panel, 19 x 25 ins / 47 x 64 cm) GBP 6,000. LONDON, 24 Sept 2003, *View of the Fort of Pateeta, near Chunar* (oil on canvas, 24 x 40 ins / 61 x 102 cm) GBP 24,000. LONDON, 24 Sept 2003, *View of the North End of the Fort of Chunar Gur* (oil on canvas, 25 x 30 ins / 64 x 76 cm) GBP 28,000.

HODGETTS, R. M.

British, 19th century.
Active in London.
Painter, engraver. Portraits, genre scenes.

R.M. Hodgetts was probably the son of Thomas Hodgetts. He exhibited from 1826.

HODGETTS, Thomas

British, 19th century.
Active in London.
Painter, engraver (mezzotint). Religious subjects, portraits, landscapes.

Thomas Hodgetts exhibited in London at the Royal Academy from 1801 to 1824, at the British Institution, and as an engraver at the Suffolk Street Gallery until 1846.

HODGINS, Henry

British, 18th century.
Active in London.
Landscape artist.

Henry Hodgins was a member of the Society of Artists and exhibited at the gallery in Suffolk Street in London from 1778 to 1783.

HODGINS, Henry

Irish, 18th century.
Born in Dublin; died 11 September 1796, in Maidstone.
Painter. Genre scenes.

Henry Hodgins was a pupil of Robert Carver. He was a scenery painter at Covent Garden Theatre, and may be the same person as the landscape artist of the same name.

HODGKIN, C. Eliot

British, 20th century.
Born 19 June 1905, in Purley (Berkshire); died 1987.
Painter. Plants, natural objects, landscapes, townscapes, still-lifes.

Eliot Hodgkin studied art in London at the Byam Shaw School of Art, and at the Royal Academy Schools under F. Ernest Jackson. He taught mural painting at Westminster School of Art and lived in London. From 1939 to 1945 he served as an air raid warden in World War II, during which time he painted scenes of the war in England.

Although he also painted murals, Hodgkin is best known for his small and highly detailed still-life paintings, which often resemble Victorian botanical illustrations. Flowers, fruit and vegetables were favoured subjects, as in his *Pink and White Turnips* (1971). He painted directly from his motif, and often depicted the objects at their actual size because he wished to show things exactly as they were, while giving them the aspect of being seen for the first time. He was also the author of *She Closed the Door* (1931), *55 Views of London* (1948) and *A Pictorial Gospel* (1949), and was a noted collector of art.

Hodgkin's first solo show was at the Picture Hire Gallery in 1936. He later exhibited at Leicester Galleries (1956); the Royal Academy; the New English Art Club; the Royal Society of British Artists; and Wildenstein & Company. In 1990 a memorial exhibition was held at Hazlitt, Gooden and Fox in London.

Bibliography:

Eliot Hodgkin, Terry Frost and Cecil Collins, exhibition catalogue, Leicester Galleries, London, 1956. *Eliot Hodgkin 1905-1987: Painter and Collector*, exhibition catalogue, Hazlitt, Gooden & Fox, London, 1990.

Museums and Galleries:

London (Tate Collection): *October* (1935, oil); *Undergrowth* (1941, tempera); *Pink and White Turnips* (1971, oil) - London (UK Government Art Collection): *Bamboo Grove on an Island near Ascona on Lake Maggiore* (1952-1956, tempera) - Manchester (Whitworth Art Gallery): *Two Hyacinth Bulbs* (ink).

Auction records:

London, 4 June 1999, *Shells* (tempera on gesso prepared panel, 4 x 6 ins / 9 x 16 cm) GBP 8,500. London, 5 Nov 1999, *July: Summer Fruits* (1955, tempera on canvas, 2 x 9 ins / 6 x 24 cm) GBP 17,500. London, 6 Sept 2000, *Violets II* (1959, tempera on board, 3 x 6 ins / 7 x 16 cm) GBP 44,000. London, 21 Nov 2000, *Autumn Leaves* (1959, tempera on board, 6 x 17 ins / 16 x 44 cm) GBP 28,000. Knowle, 14 Feb 2001, *Five Truffle Jars and a Rose* (1964, oil on board, 11 x 13 ins / 29 x 32 cm) GBP 14,600. Lewes, 4 Sept 2001, *London Wall* (1945, tempera on canvas, 13 x 11 ins / 33 x 28 cm) GBP 14,500. London, 3 July 2002, *Pheasant Eggs in a Punnet* (1958, tempera on board, 6 x 11 ins / 16 x 27 cm) GBP 25,000. London, 4 July 2002, *Christmas Still-life* (gouache, 6 x 9 ins / 16 x 23 cm) GBP 6,000. London, 5 June 2003, *Dead Leaves and Bird's Eggs* (1966, tempera on canvas, 5 x 11 ins / 13 x 29 cm) GBP 12,000. London, 3 July 2003, *Apricot in Paper* (1965, tempera on board, 5 x 7 ins / 12 x 19 cm) GBP 9,000. Haslemere, 5 May 2004, *Two Lemons, One Partly Peeled on a Pewter Dish* (1972, tempera on canvas, 7 x 12 ins / 18 x 30 cm) GBP 7,500. London, 4 June 2004, *La famille brioche* (1959, tempera on board, 10 x 11 ins / 25 x 29 cm) GBP 14,000.

HODGKIN, Howard (Sir)

British, 20th century.
Born 6 August 1932, in London.
Painter, printmaker.
School of London.

Howard Hodgkin studied at the Camberwell School of Art, London from 1949 to 1950, and from 1950 to 1954 at the Bath Academy of Art at Corsham Court, where he taught from 1956 to 1966. In 1966 he began teaching at Chelsea School of Art, and became a senior lecturer in 1970. He made several visits to India. He served as a trustee of the Tate Gallery, London, and won the Turner Prize in 1985. He was made a CBE in 1977 and knighted in 1992.

From an early stage in his career Hodgkin did not follow the then-fashionable trends of Pop Art but chose instead to concentrate on texture and pictorialism. Showing the influence of Matisse in his very late period, Hodgkin created paintings that at first seem to be totally abstract but in which human figures can be made out. The colours that he used, and the way his canvases tease the eye, are reminiscent of the Orphic Cubism of Robert Delaunay. Hodgkin also played with the concept of dissimulation: certain areas of his canvases are blurred or blank while the borders of his compositions are painted in the same colour as their centre. By contrast, his precise style is similar to that of Indian miniatures (which he collected). Considered to be one of the greatest British contemporary colourists, Hodgkin created vibrant, almost abstract paintings that seem to capture fleeting memories.

He first exhibited in about 1960 and represented Britain in a major retrospective at the Venice Biennale in 1984. He has also shown his work in many group exhibitions, including *Peinture Anglaise Aujourd'hui* (*English Painting Today*) at the Musée d'Art Moderne, Paris, in 1973, and *The Inward Eye: Transcendence in Contemporary Art* at the Contemporary Arts Museum, Houston, in 2001. He has also had several solo exhibitions, including *Howard Hodgkin: Prints, 1977-1983* at the Tate Gallery, London, in 1985; shows at the Musée de Nantes in 1990, and at the Scottish National Gallery of Modern Art, Edinburgh, in 1991, consisting of a selection of small-format paintings dating from 1975 to 1989; an exhibition at the Hayward Gallery, London, in 1996; *Howard Hodgkin: Retrospektive 1975 bis 1996* (*Howard Hodgkin: A Retrospective 1975-1996*) at Kustverein für die Rheinlande und Westfalen, Düsseldorf, also in 1996; and an exhibition at the National Gallery of Scotland, Edinburgh, in 2002, with 20 large paintings dating from 1984 onwards.

Bibliography:

Knowles, Elizabeth, *Howard Hodgkin: Prints, 1977 to 1983*, exhibition catalogue, Tate Gall., London, 1985. Graham-Dixon, Andrew, *Howard Hodgkin*, Thames & Hudson, London, 1994 (2nd extended edition, Thames & Hudson, New York, 2001). Auping, Michael/Elderfield, John/Sontag, Susan/Price, Marla, *Howard Hodgkin, Paintings*, catalogue raisonné, Modern Art Museum of Fort Worth, Thames & Hudson, London, 1995. Stecker, Raimund/Krajewski, Michael, *Howard Hodgkin Retrospektive 1975-1996*, exhibition catalogue, Kunstverein fur die Rheinlande und Westfalen, Edition Tertium, Ostfildern, 1996. Kendall, Richard/Rosenblum, Robert, *Howard Hodgkin: Large Paintings 1984-2002*, exhibition catalogue, National Galleries of Scotland, Edinburgh, 2002.

Museums and Galleries:

London (Tate Collection): *Interior of a Museum* (1956-1959, oil/wood).

Auction records:

London, 16 March 1977, *R.B.K.* (1969-1970, card, painted frame, 43 x 55 ins / 109 x 140 cm) GBP 2,800. London, 5 Dec 1978, *Electric Light* (1960-1963, oil on panel/hardboard, 36 x 36 ins / 91.5 x 91.5 cm) GBP 1,700. New York, 2 Nov 1983, *Moonlight* (1980, coloured lithograph, diptych, 44 1/2 x 30 ins / 113 x 76.5 cm) USD 800. New York, 9 Nov 1983, *David Hockney at Clandeboye* (c. 1968-1970, oil on panel, 41 3/4 x 50 ins / 106 x 127 cm) USD 27,000. New York, 119 Nov 1985, *For B. J.* (1979, hand-coloured lithograph, 41 x 30 ins / 104.2 x 76.2 cm) USD 4,200. London, 5 Dec 1985, *Portrait of Mr and Mrs Kasmin* (1964-1966, oil on canvas, 41 3/4 x 50 ins / 106 x 127 cm) GBP 60,000. London, 11 Nov 1987, *Teatime in America* (1948, varnished gouache/card, 10 1/4 x 14 1/4 ins / 26 x 36.5 cm) USD 11,000. London, 30 June 1988, *Guest* (oil on panel, 23 x 29 ins / 57.5 x 73.5 cm) GBP 81,400. New York, 8 Oct 1988, *Architecture* (1978, fabric dye/hand-made paper, 21 x 24 1/2 ins / 53.3 x 62.2 cm) USD 15,400. London, 23 Feb 1989, *Getting Up, from the Indian Leaves Series* (1978, textile dyes on handmade rag paper, 19 x 22 ins / 48.5 x 56 cm) GBP 22,000. New York, 2 May 1989, *Garden of the Bombay Museum* (oil on panel, 48 x 56 1/4 ins / 122 x 143 cm) USD 506,000. London, 29 June 1989, *Bedroom at Carennac* (oil on panel, 42 1/2 x 47 ins / 108 x 118.5 cm) GBP 154,000. New York, 8 Nov 1989, *Counting the Days* (oil on wood, 21 3/4 x 25 1/4 ins / 55.3 x 64.2 cm) USD 440,000. New York, 9 May 1990, *A Small Henry Moore at the Bottom of the Garden* (1976, oil on panel, 20 3/4 x 21 x 1 1/2 ins / 53 x 53.5 x 4 cm) USD 220,000. London, 24 May 1990, *On the Beach* (1962, oil on panel, 17 3/4 x 20 3/4 ins / 45 x 53 cm) GBP 39,600. New York, 30 April 1991, *Family Group* (1973, oil on canvas, 36 x 42 ins / 91.4 x 106.8 cm) USD 137,500. New York, 3 Oct 1991, *Electric Light* (oil on card, 36 x 36 ins / 91.5 x 91.5 cm) USD 66,000. New York, 13 Nov 1991, *Interior and Figures* (oil on wood, 49 1/4 x 56 1/4 ins / 125 x 143 cm) USD 165,000. London, 2 Dec 1993, *Small View of Venice* (oil on wood, 17 1/4 x 18 ins / 43.5 x 45.7 cm) GBP 54,300. New York, 2 Nov 1994, *In the Honeymoon Suite*. London, 30 Nov 1994, *Mr and Mrs*

P. Stringer (oil on canvas, 48 x 50 ins / 122 x 127 cm) GBP 56,500. LONDON, 30 Nov 1995, *Bathroom Mirror* (oil on wood in a frame by the artist, 26 1/4 x 30 1/4 ins / 66.5 x 77 cm) GBP 47,700; *Menswear* (oil on wood in a frame by the artist, 32 3/4 x 42 1/2 ins / 83 x 108 cm) GBP 117,000. NEW YORK, 5 May 1996, *A Storm* (1977, coloured lithograph heightened with gouache, 20 1/2 x 24 ins / 52 x 61 cm) USD 2,587. NEW YORK, 7 May 1996, *The Bay of Naples* (oil on panel, 54 x 60 ins / 137.2 x 152.4 cm) USD 486,500. NEW YORK, 20 Nov 1996, *Asphalt* (1985-1988, oil on wood, 27 1/4 x 33 ins / 69 x 84 cm) USD 178,500. NEW YORK, 7 May 1997, *First Portrait of Terence McInerney* (1981, oil on wood, 50 x 55 ins / 127 x 140 cm) USD 354,000. LONDON, 27 June 1997, *Night and Day* (1976-1977, oil on wood, 14 1/2 x 18 1/2 ins / 37 x 47 cm) GBP 41,100. NEW YORK, 6 and 7 March 1998, *Untitled* (1989, coloured lithograph, 26 3/4 x 33 ins / 68 x 84 cm) USD 1,035. NEW YORK, 18 Nov 1998, *In Central Park* (1983-1986, oil on canvas, 19 x 25 ins / 48 x 63 cm) USD 60,000. LONDON, 30 June 1999, *Interiors with figures* (c. 1977-1984, oil on panel, 49 x 56 ins / 125 x 143 cm) GBP 370,000. LONDON, 8 Dec 1999, *Cafeteria at the Grand Palais* (1975, oil on panel, 49 x 57 ins / 124 x 144 cm) GBP 220,000. LONDON, 29 June 2000, *In Guest Room* (1978-1980, oil on panel, 16 x 21 ins / 40 x 53 cm) GBP 65,000. LONDON, 26 Oct 2000, *Early Evening* (1996-1997, oil on wood, 19 x 20 ins / 47 x 52 cm) GBP 35,000. NEW YORK, 8 May 2001, *In a French Restaurant* (1977, oil on panel, 36 x 48 ins / 91 x 122 cm) USD 460,000. NEW YORK, 13 Nov 2001, *Interior with a Painting by Stephen Buckley* (1975-1976, oil on panel, 49 x 57 ins / 124 x 145 cm) USD 240,000. NEW YORK, 16 May 2002, *Fire in Venice* (1986-1989, oil on panel, 19 x 22 ins / 48 x 57 cm) USD 105,000. LONDON, 24 Oct 2002, *Venice Evening* (etching, aquatint, colour and embossing on 16 sheets, 63 x 77 ins / 160 x 196 cm) GBP 6,500. LONDON, 24 June 2003, *On the Beach* (oil on panel, 18 x 21 ins / 45 x 53 cm) GBP 28,000. LONDON, 27 June 2003, *Rain in Venice* (1985, oil on panel) GBP 30,000. LONDON, 5 Feb 2004, *After Dinner at Smith Square* (1980-1981, oil on panel, 31 x 41 ins / 79 x 104 cm) GBP 80,000. LONDON, 1 April 2004, *Portrait of Mr and Mrs Kasmin* (1964-1966, oil on canvas, 42 x 50 ins / 106 x 127 cm) GBP 68,000.

HODGKINS, Frances

New Zealander, 19th - 20th century.

Born 1869 or 1870; died 1947, in London.

Active mainly in England.

Painter, watercolourist. Landscapes, still-lifes, portraits. Frances Hodgkins had no formal training as a painter. She came to Europe in 1900 and settled in Paris in 1902. Soon afterwards she left for Morocco, and it was there that she began to paint seriously. She then returned to Paris, where she stayed for 10 years, also travelling to Holland and Italy and to Concarneau in Brittany. Here she attended classes at a watercolour school run by Charles Morice, a friend of Paul Gauguin. Back in Paris, she set up a watercolour school at the Académie Colarossi. She also became familiar with Post-Impressionist painting, the art of Marinetti and some Futurist painters, though none of them influenced her. In 1914 she settled permanently in Britain, where she became a member of the Seven and Five Society.

Hodgkins was fascinated by light and closely studied the work of other artists, from Claude Monet to Alfred Sisley and Auguste Renoir, and also that of Gauguin and Matisse. From 1914 to 1919 she painted Cornish scenes, and although she was primarily a landscape painter she also painted still-lifes and portraits. In Dorset, where she finally settled, she admired the rich light and luxuriant greenery of the surroundings. This is reflected in her use of luminous colours, which are the dominant feature of her sweeping, somewhat loosely organised paintings. Her watercolours have the strong tonal qualities of oil paintings.

She took part in the Exposition Internationale d'Art Moderne organised by UNESCO in Paris in 1946, and that same year in the *Exposition des Tableaux Britanniques Modernes de la Tate Gallery* (*Exhibition of Modern British Paintings from the Tate Gallery*) at the Musée du Jeu de Paume, Paris, where she showed two gouache paintings, *Two Women with Flower Basket, the Lake* and *The Broken-down Tractor*.

MUSEUMS AND GALLERIES:

LONDON (Tate Collection): *Loveday and Ann: Two Women with a Basket of Flowers* (1915, oil on canvas); *Flatford Mill* (1930, oil on canvas); *Wings over Water* (1930, oil on canvas).

AUCTION RECORDS:

LONDON, 2 May 1947, *Pleasure Garden,* GBP 50. LONDON, 23 July 1947, *Locomotive in a Landscape,* GBP 48. LONDON, 16 June 1976, *Still-life* (oil on canvas, 19 1/2 x 23 1/4 ins / 49.5 x 59 cm) GBP 1,700. LONDON, 10 Nov 1976, *Lemons* (watercolour, 14 x 18 1/2 ins / 35.5 x 47 cm) GBP 720. LONDON, 16 March 1977, *The Colonel's House* (watercolour heightened with gouache, 15 3/4 x 21 1/4 ins / 40 x 54 cm) GBP 1,450. LONDON, 7 June 1978, *Fruit and Flowers* (oil on canvas, 22 x 22 ins / 55 x 55 cm) GBP 1,500. LONDON, 2 March 1979, *Portrait of a Baby* (c. 1919, oil on canvas, 17 1/2 x 17 1/2 ins / 44.5 x 44.5 cm) GBP 1,300. LONDON, 19 Oct 1979, *Still-life with Flowers, Eggs and Lemon* (watercolour and pencil, 27 x 20 ins / 68.5 x 51 cm) GBP 1,400. LONDON, 11 March 1981, *Sabrina's Garden* (pencil, 17 x 21 1/2 ins / 43 x 54.5 cm) GBP 850. LONDON, 11 March 1981, *The Crimson Pond* (gouache and pencil, 18 x 13 3/4 ins / 45.5 x 35 cm) GBP 900. LONDON, 2 Nov 1983, *The Family* (oil on canvas, 29 x 24 ins / 73.5 x 61 cm) GBP 3,800. LONDON, 14 Nov 1984, *Beach Scene* (watercolour, 17 x 22 ins / 43 x 56 cm) GBP 12,000. LONDON, 15 May 1985, *The Japanese Lantern* (watercolour, 27 x 27 ins / 68.5 x 68.5 cm) GBP 24,000. LONDON, 119 Nov 1985, *The Kinema* (charcoal, 14 x 20 3/4 ins / 35.6 x 52.7 cm) GBP 4,200. LONDON, 12 June 1987, *Motor Transport* (1941, watercolour and gouache, 15 3/4 x 21 1/4 ins / 40 x 53.8 cm) GBP 16,000. LONDON, 9 June 1989, *Bridge over the River* (watercolour and gouache, 13 x 12 1/2 ins / 33.1 x 31.8 cm) GBP 2,200. LONDON, 28 Nov 1991, *Red Earth* (watercolour, 18 x 22 1/2 ins / 45.7 x 57.2 cm) GBP 4,510. LONDON, 12 March 1993, *Portrait of Lett Haines* (oil on canvas, 25 x 20 1/4 ins / 63.5 x 51.5 cm) GBP 17,250. LONDON, 26 Oct 1994, *Houses at Cassis* (watercolour and pencil, 21 x 17 1/2 ins / 52.5 x 44.5 cm) GBP 3,680. SYDNEY, 10 Aug 1999, *Still-life with Pineapple* (watercolour, 15 x 13 ins / 37 x 34 cm) AUD 35,000. LONDON, 5 Nov 1999, *Ibiza* (c. 1934, oil on canvas, 24 x 28 ins / 61 x 72 cm) GBP 23,000. LONDON, 6 June 2000, *Weir, Bradford on Tone* (oil on canvas, 24 x 34 ins / 60 x 86 cm) GBP 26,000. AUCKLAND, 28 July 2000, *The Cow* (gouache, 20 x 28 ins / 52 x 71 cm) NZD 80,000. AUCKLAND, 15 Aug 2001, *Figures Fishing in French Canal* (1905, watercolour, 12 x 9 ins / 30 x 22 cm) NZD 45,000. AUCKLAND, 8 Nov 2001, *Sur la plage* (watercolour, 12 x 12 ins / 30 x 31 cm) NZD 46,000. LONDON, 3 July 2002, *Dorset Landscape* (1943, watercolour and gouache, 19 x 28 ins / 48 x 70 cm) GBP 12,000. AUCKLAND, 4 Dec 2002, *Still-life* (pencil, watercolour and gouache, 19 x 25 ins / 47 x 63 cm) NZD 60,000. AUCKLAND, 8 April 2003, *Private Bathing* (c. 1936, gouache, 22 x 30 ins / 55 x 76 cm) NZD 150,000. AUCKLAND, 8 April 2003, *Still-life with Landscape* (c. 1930, oil on canvas, 30 x 24 ins / 75 x 62 cm) NZD 410,000. AUCKLAND, 25 March 2004, *Washerwomen, Morrocco* (1902, watercolour, 9 x 8 ins / 23 x 20 cm) NZD 51,000. AUCKLAND, 18 Aug 2004, *Reine* (c. 1930, pencil, 19 x 15 ins / 49 x 37 cm) NZD 28,000.

HODGKINS, Mary. See **GRACE, Mrs**

HODGKINS, Thomas F.

British, 19th century.

Died 1903.

Active in London.
Painter, lithographer. Landscapes.
Thomas Hodgkins exhibited in London at the Royal Academy between 1835 and 1875.

HODGKINSON, Frank
Australian, 20th century.
Born 1919, in Sydney.
Painter, illustrator.
After training as an artist from 1937 to 1939, Frank Hodgkinson worked as an illustrator for newspapers in Sydney and Melbourne. After World War II he came to Europe and studied in England, France, Spain and Italy from 1947 to 1953. He then returned to Australia, where he became a leading figure in Australian abstract painting. In 1958 Hodgkinson won the first Helena Rubinstein grant to be awarded and embarked on a second period of travels, staying in Spain from 1959 to 1960 and in the USA from 1961 to 1962. He exhibited frequently in Australia, and also in London (in 1960) and the USA.
MUSEUMS AND GALLERIES:
LONDON (Courtauld Institute of Art).
AUCTION RECORDS:
MELBOURNE, 11-12 March 1971, *Summer*, AUD 1,100. SYDNEY, 4 July 1988, *Marshland Vegetation* (gouache, 22 1/2 x 29 1/2 ins / 57 x 75 cm) AUD 1,100. VICTORIA, 3 Aug 1999, *Totalscape* (1973, oil and collage on board, 74 x 24 ins / 188 x 62 cm) AUD 7,500. SYDNEY, 8 Nov 1999, *Shikara Lane* (1988, oil on canvas, 32 x 77 ins / 82 x 196 cm) AUD 6,750. SYDNEY, 10 April 2000, *Crunch Crack* (1970, oil on masonite, 54 x 54 ins / 136 x 136 cm) AUD 2,750. MELBOURNE, 28 June 2000, *Drifting Form* (1964, gouache and charcoal on board, 41 x 28 ins / 105 x 71 cm) AUD 7,000. MELBOURNE, 28 June 2000, *Magic Christian* (1965, oil on panel, a pair, 76 x 91 ins / 193 x 230 cm) AUD 20,000. SYDNEY, 19 Nov 2001, *Grand Ultra Marine* (1988, oil on canvas, 72 x 84 ins / 183 x 213 cm) AUD 14,000. MELBOURNE, 11 Nov 2002, *Walsh Bay* (oil on canvas, 50 x 42 ins / 127 x 107 cm) AUD 7,000. MELBOURNE, 11 Nov 2002, *Night Fishing, Port Jackson IV* (1987, oil on canvas, 73 x 42 ins / 185 x 107 cm) AUD 8,000. SYDNEY, 27 Aug 2003, *Kakadu, Last of the Wet* (1989, watercolour and gouache, 21 x 29 ins / 54 x 74 cm) AUD 6,000. SYDNEY, 27 Oct 2003, *Symbol Man and Olga Wuhl Wuhl* (1983, mixed media, 22 x 30 ins / 57 x 75 cm) AUD 4,000. SYDNEY, 20 July 2004, *Lake Eyre Reflections* (oil on canvas, 71 x 60 ins / 181 x 152 cm) AUD 6,000. MELBOURNE, 8 Sept 2004, *Midnight, Darling Harbour* (1987, oil on canvas, 48 x 60 ins / 122 x 152 cm) AUD 8,000.

HODGSON (Miss)
British, 18th century.
Active in Scarborough.
Painter. Flowers.
Miss Hodgson exhibited in London at the Free Society between 1770 and 1775.

HODGSON, Charles
British, 18th - 19th century.
Painter. Genre scenes, architectural views.
Charles Hodgson was one of the Norwich Group of painters. He exhibited with the group and also in London at the Royal Academy and the British Institution between 1802 and 1824.

HODGSON, David
British, 19th century.
Born 1798, in Norwich; died 22 April 1864, in Norwich.
Painter. Genre scenes, landscapes, architectural views.
School of Norwich.
David Hodgson, the son of Charles Hodgson, was a member of the Society of Norwich Artists founded by Crome. This group of painters, known as the Norwich School, sought to revive the study of nature, but in a new Realist and Romantic manner. He exhibited in London at the Royal Academy, the British Institution and the Suffolk Street Gallery between 1818 and 1864.
BIBLIOGRAPHY:
Cundall, Herbert Minton, *The Norwich School*, The Studio, London, 1920.
MUSEUMS AND GALLERIES:
NORWICH (Castle Mus. and AG): *Old Fishmarket, Norwich*; *Norwich Cathedral from Cowgate*; *King Street Gates, Norwich*.
AUCTION RECORDS:
LONDON, 14 June 1968, *Market Scenes* (two matching panels) Gns 950. LONDON, 7 Oct 1983, *Children Fishing by a Pond* (oil on canvas, 29 1/2 x 24 3/4 ins / 75 x 62.8 cm) GBP 950. LONDON, 31 Oct 1990, *Farm in a Clearing* (oil on canvas, 22 1/4 x 29 1/4 ins / 56.5 x 74.5 cm) GBP 1,210. LONDON, 20 Nov 1992, *St Mary's Abbey, York* (oil on card, 14 x 10 ins / 35.6 x 25.4 cm) GBP 825. LONDON, 19 March 2003, *Drawings of Norwich* (pen, ink and wash over pencil, four, 8 x 5 ins / 20 x 13 cm) GBP 5,400. BURY ST EDMUNDS, 3 Sept 2003, *Debris of the Old Fish Market, Norwich* (oil on canvas, 8 x 10 ins / 21 x 26 cm) GBP 1,050. BURY ST EDMUNDS, 6 Oct 2004, *New Mills, Norwich* (oil on canvas, 30 x 25 ins / 76 x 63 cm) GBP 2,200.

HODGSON, Edward, or Hodgeson
Irish, 18th century.
Born c. 1719, in Dublin; died 1794, in London.
Painter. Flowers, fruit.
Edward Hodgson exhibited in London at the Royal Academy and the Free Society of Artists between 1762 and 1791.

HODGSON, John Evan
British, 19th century.
Born 1 March 1836 or 1831, in London; died 19 June 1895, in London.
Painter. History painting, genre scenes, local scenes, landscapes.
Orientalism.
John Hodgson spent the first years of his life in Russia, only returning to England at the age of 22. He then studied at the Royal Academy in London exhibiting his first work, *Arresting a Poacher*, there in 1857. He first painted historical subjects but after a visit to North Africa he devoted himself exclusively to scenes of oriental life. He became an associate member of the Royal Academy in 1873 and a full member in 1880. He was the Academy's librarian.
MUSEUMS AND GALLERIES:
CARDIFF: *A Challenge Refused* - HAMBURG: *Shepherds' Music*; *Woman of Algiers*; *Snake Charmer*; *Harbour*; *Arab Storyteller* - MELBOURNE: *J.E. Hodgson* - SYDNEY: *Oriental Question* - VICTORIA: *Pillage*; *Poet Laureate*.
AUCTION RECORDS:
LONDON, 23 March 1908, *Birdseller in Tunis* (1873) GBP 9. LONDON, 24 June 1909, *Moorish Woman* (1873) GBP 3. LONDON, 26 Nov 1910, *Robert Burns Ploughing* (1894) GBP 21. LONDON, 9 April 1920, *Visit to Holbein's Studio*, GBP 31. LONDON, Nov 1921, *Farmer's Dream*, GBP 2. LONDON, 23 Jan 1925, *Tricky Negotiation*, GBP 21. LONDON, 13 May 1977, *River Landscape with Fisherman* (oil on canvas, 18 x 14 ins / 45.7 x 35.5 cm) GBP 1,200. LONDON, 15 May 1979, *Candidate and Voter* (oil on canvas, 17 x 15 1/4 ins / 43 x 39 cm) GBP 3,400. LONDON, 5 June 1981, *Voter and Candidate* (oil on paper remounted/canvas, 20 x 16 ins / 50.8 x 40.6 cm) GBP 3,000. LONDON, 27 April 1983, *Tunisian Poultry Merchant* (1873, oil on panel, 16 x 12 ins / 40.5 x 30.5 cm) GBP 1,900. NEW YORK, 30 Oct 1985, *Poor Knife Grinder* (1873, oil on panel, 16 x 11 3/4 ins / 40.6 x 30.1 cm) USD 7,500. LONDON, 17 June 1987, *Art Lover* (1881, oil on canvas, 12 x 16 ins / 30.5 x 40.5 cm) GBP 2,200. LONDON, 3 Nov 1989, *Woman Snake Charmer in Tunis* (1884, oil on canvas, 42 1/4 x 23 1/4 ins / 107 x 59 cm) GBP 3,520. NEW YORK, 14 Oct 1993, *Reorganisation of the Army in*

Morocco (1872, oil on canvas, 60 1/4 x 34 1/4 ins / 153 x 87 cm) USD 11,500. NEW YORK, 2 May 2000, *Arab Prisoners* (1870, oil on canvas, 37 x 73 ins / 94 x 185 cm) USD 18,000. DRIFFIELD, 26 May 2000, *Plan of the White Horse of Kilburn, Yorkshire* (1857, pen and ink, 14 x 18 ins / 36 x 46 cm) GBP 2,400.

HODGSON, Thomas
British, 18th century.
Active at the end of the 18th century.
Engraver.

Thomas Hodgson worked for Bewick in 1776. He engraved chiefly on wood.

HÖDICKE, Karl Heinz, or Horst
German, 20th century.
Born 1938, in Nuremberg.
Painter, draughtsman, sculptor.
New Fauves.

Karl Heinz Hödicke studied with Fred Thieler at the Berlin academy in 1959, and has been teaching there since 1974. His students have included Helmut Middendorf and Rainer Fetting. He spent a year in New York in 1966, and the following year he received a bursary from the Villa Massimo in Rome. He has taken part in various group exhibitions. A retrospective of his work was held at the Kunstsammlung Nordrhein-Westfalen in Düsseldorf in 1986.

Up until the 1960s, in addition to his drawings, paintings and films, he produced objects that were a kind of witty trap, placed in an unexpected context that created new associations between things, giving rise to a narrative that could not have existed without the artist's creative initiative. Some of these objects play a part in his films. After drawing inspiration from themes of everyday life, he created paintings in which he placed mythological subjects in the heart of the sprawling modern city, mixing dragons with fire engines, before embarking on new subjects at the end of the 1980s. Each of his paintings tells a real story, whose characters - human faces with animal bodies, robots, puppets - seem to have come straight out of a dream. Having started as a Tachiste, Hödicke developed a world of his own, marked by violence and irony, on large surfaces painted with sweeping gestures making very bold use of contrast.

BIBLIOGRAPHY:
Merkert, Jörn, '*La Foire de la réalité sur l'art de K. H. Hödicke*' in *Artstudio*, periodical, Gal. Templon, Paris, autumn 1986.

MUSEUMS AND GALLERIES:
BERLIN (Berlinische Gal.): *Big Butcher* (1963).

AUCTION RECORDS:
COLOGNE, 4 Dec 1985, *Hands* (mixed media/paper, 39 1/4 x 27 1/2 ins / 100 x 70 cm) DEM 3,500. COLOGNE, 31 May 1986, *Gorgon's Head* (1983, acrylic/canvas, 67 x 90 1/2 ins / 170 x 230 cm) DEM 20,000. NEW YORK, 4 Nov 1987, *Medea* (acrylic/canvas, 78 3/4 x 118 ins / 199.9 x 299.8 cm) USD 4,000. NEW YORK, 7 May 1990, *Les Goudronneurs* (*The Tarrers*) (1977, acrylic/canvas, 74 3/4 x 98 1/2 ins / 190 x 250 cm) USD 33,000. LONDON, 3 Dec 1992, *Prometheus* (1984, acrylic/material, 116 1/4 x 79 ins / 295 x 200.7 cm) GBP 12,100. BERLIN, 27 Nov 1999, *Three Children's Heads* (1983, acrylic on canvas, 24 x 35 ins / 60 x 90 cm) DEM 6,000. BERLIN, 27 Nov 1999, *Black Kasper* (1984, acrylic on canvas, 102 x 75 ins / 260 x 190 cm) DEM 26,000. BERLIN, 23 Nov 2000, *Untitled* (mixed media and acrylic on paper, 39 x 27 ins / 99 x 69 cm) DEM 6,000. BERLIN, 23 Nov 2000, *Irish Folk Music* (1984-1986, oil on dispersion cloth, 67 x 91 ins / 170 x 231 cm) DEM 44,000. MUNICH, 19 May 2001, *Flames at the Brandenburger Gate* (tempera on canvas, 31 x 41 ins / 78 x 105 cm) DEM 6,500. MUNICH, 15 May 2003, *Melon* (1996, acrylic on canvas, 31 x 39 ins / 80 x 100 cm) EUR 4,200. COLOGNE, 13 Dec 2003, *Composition with Figure and Snakes* (1983, acrylic on cotton, 67 x 45 ins / 170 x 115 cm) EUR 11,500. NEW YORK, 29 June 2004, *Jaguar* (1983, oil on canvas, 67 x 91 ins / 170 x 230 cm) USD 6,500. BERLIN, 27 Nov 2004, *Untitled* (1985, gouache, 28 x 39 ins / 70 x 99 cm) EUR 3,600.

HODICO
German, 14th century.
Illuminator, copyist.

Hodico was a famous illuminator who in 1376 made a superb pontifical for Albert von Sternberg, Archbishop of Magdeburg and Bishop of Sentomischl. The work used to be in the library of the convent at Bruck, near Quaym in Moravia, then in that of Strakow. It contains 42 miniatures in capital letters.

HODIEUX, Marie, Mme Beloux-Hodieux since 1896
French, 19th century.
Born c. 1860, in Lyons; died 11 May 1897.
Painter. Flowers.

Hodieux studied under André Perrachon. She began exhibiting at the Lyons Salon in 1885, and won a second-class medal in 1892. Her work was first shown at the Salon des Artistes Français in 1895.

Hodieux painted many flower paintings, attaching more importance to their decorative aspect than to documentary accuracy.

MUSEUMS AND GALLERIES:
LYONS (MBA): *Roses and Cherry Blossom in a Blue Vase.*

HODIN, Daniel
French, 20th century.
Born 1918.
Sculptor. Figures, nudes, animals. Statuettes, groups.

AUCTION RECORDS:
PARIS, 1 Feb 1988, *Bull* (1987, welded iron and paint, 9 1/2 x 9 1/4 x 19 ins / 24 x 23.5 x 48 cm) FRF 3,200. PARIS, 7 Oct 1991, *Tenderness* (1985, bronze, 8 3/4 x 5 1/2 x 4 3/4 ins / 22.5 x 14 x 12 cm) FRF 17,000. PARIS, 3 Feb 1992, *Duo* (1960, bronze, 14 1/2 x 3 1/4 x 3 1/4 ins / 37 x 8.5 x 8.5 cm) FRF 13,000. PARIS, 18 May 1992, *Eros* (1958, bronze, 12 1/2 x 2 1/4 x 2 1/4 ins / 32 x 6 x 6 cm) FRF 6,000. PARIS, 31 Jan 1993, *Passion* (1950, bronze, 4 1/4 x 2 1/2 x 2 1/4 ins / 10.5 x 6.5 x 5.5 cm) FRF 4,500.

HODLER, Ferdinand
Swiss, 19th - 20th century.
Born 14 March 1853, in Bern; died 19 May 1918, in Geneva.
Painter, sculptor, draughtsman. History painting, portraits, genre scenes, landscapes, seascapes, animals.
Symbolism.

Ferdinand Hodler was born into a poor family. His father, a carpenter, died of tuberculosis when Hodler was eight, leaving five children in poverty. His mother soon remarried, this time to the painter Gottfried Schüpbach, a widower with many children. He taught the young Hodler the rudiments of painting, and the boy became keen on art. The large number of children born of the second marriage made life increasingly hard for the family. They moved to Steffisburg, where Schüpbach had originally come from, and where Hodler's mother died when he was only 13. Soon afterwards Hodler trained as a painter with Ferdinand Sommer in Thun, then with a relative in Langenthal, where he began to make a living from his art. In 1872, he moved to Geneva, where the influential painters of the time were Alexandre Calarne and François Diday. After a few years, he met Barthelemy Menn, who took an interest in his work. Although Hodler was still living in poverty he managed to produce a number of paintings during this period. Menn, a friend of Corot, was also an admirer of Ingres. He seems to have encouraged Hodler to apply geometry to his work. The theory of parallelism, which

Hodler formulated around 1880, also coincided with a religious crisis he was going through at the time, and he turned to symbolism. He said that symbolist art should suggest not the being but what it might become, not immobility but movement and transition, not the pose but motion. Hodler often used a variety of procedures derived from parallelism, indicating movement by regularly repeating the same figure throughout the composition or by breaking down a movement into its components and distributing the stages among the various figures in the composition. This is what caused Frank Popper to include Hodler in his book *The Origins and Development of Kinetic Art* (1968). Hodler first put the principles of parallelism into practice in his large composition from the 1880s entitled *Prayer in the Canton of Bern*, in which he painted the same figure in different poses. The first solo exhibition of his works was in Bern in 1887. In 1890, his composition *Night* attracted the public's attention to him. In 1892, his mystical preoccupations led him to take part in Sar Péladan's *Salon de la Rose-Croix* in Paris. In 1895, he won a painting competition in Zurich with *The Retreat from Marignan*. Among his large canvases are: the trilogy *Tired of Living, Dead Souls* and *Eurythmia* of 1891-1895, *The Day* (1900), *William Tell* and *The Emotions*.

Some critics tend to compare Hodler's symbolist compositions with the symbolist movement in the Latin countries, while others link them to German Expressionism. Dating as they do from the turning point between two periods, it might perhaps be fairer to consider them a separate effort. Although he had exhibited successfully at the Société Nationale in Paris in 1891, where he came to the attention of Puvis de Chavannes, Hodler's talent was not recognised until his exhibition at the Vienna Secession in the winter of 1903-1904. Despite continued criticism, his reputation continued to grow during the following years. He painted symbolist compositions, portraits, and numerous landscapes of the Bernese Oberland and Lake Geneva, with a very direct technique using large, simple, strong plane surfaces. This more spontaneous, less organised part of his work, in which expression is freed from stylistic constraints, became increasingly important during the latter part of his life. It is this side of his work that shows certain characteristics of German Expressionism: drawing simplified into large flat shapes, flat patches of colour, symbolic rather than imitative and pantheistic. At the time of the Vienna Secession in 1904 he was recognised as one of the masters of the 'Jugendstil'. As early as 1890, while on a visit to Switzerland, Nolde had appreciated how forward-looking Hodler's work was. Another of the Expressionist founders of the group Die Brücke (The Bridge) engraved a portrait of Hodler in 1910. During this period of portraits and landscapes, Hodler painted one or two more programmatic compositions: *Truth* in 1903, the *Volunteers Leaving for Jena* in 1908 and *Unanimity* in 1913. From then on, he was seen at his best in his landscapes, in which he gave direct expression to his mystical feeling for man and nature, despite the apparent modesty of the subject matter. He was awarded an honorary doctorate by the University of Basel, appointed an officer of the Légion d'Honneur and made an honorary citizen of Geneva. In 1983, a travelling exhibition was shown at the Petit Palais in Paris, the Nationalgalerie in Berlin and the Zurich Kunsthaus.

Hodler's chief characteristic is the powerful unity that governs his composition, drawing and colour. It has been suggested that, because of their rigorous balance, his works were based on geometrical figures. However, the passionate vitality and the emotion emanating from his pictures inform us that, without dismissing mathematical concepts, Hodler put his heart and soul into his painting.

In 2003, his work featured in the exhibitions *Swiss Drawings from the 1900s* at the Kunstmuseum in Bern and in the same year his landscapes were shown at the Musée Rath in Geneva.

Bibliography:
Frey, Adolf, *Ferdinand Hodler*, H. Haessel, Leipzig, 1922. Selz, P., *Ferdinand Hodler*, exhibition catalogue, Berkeley, U. CA Mus.; New York, Guggenheim; Cambridge, MA, Bush-Reisinger Mus., 1973. Brüschweiler, Jura, *Ferdinand Hodler: Selbstbildnisse als Selbstbiographie*, Brenteli, Bern, 1979. Mühlestein, Hans/Schmidt, Georg, *Ferdinand Hodler: sein leben und sein Werk*, Unionsverlag, Zurich, 1983. *Ferdinand Hodler, 1853-1918*, exhibition catalogue, Musée du Petit Palais, Paris, 1983. *Ferdinand Hodler: Landscapes*, exhibition catalogue, Schweiz. Inst. Kstwiss, Zurich; Los Angeles, UCLA, Wight A.G.; Chicago IL, A. Inst.; New York, N. Acad. Des., 1987. Eisenman, Stephen F., *Ferdinand Hodler: landscapes*, exhibition catalogue, Wight Art Gall., University of California, Los Angeles, Swiss Institute for Art Research, Zurich, 1987. Waldkirch, Bernhard von/Schindler, Rudolf/Steinhoff, Christina, *Ferdinand Hodler, vom Frühwerk bis zu Jahrhundertwende: Zeichungen aus der Graphischen Sammlung des Kunsthauses Zürich*, exhibition catalogue, Kunsthaus, Graphisches Kabinett, Zurich, 1990. Frodl, Gerbert, *Ferdinand Hodler un Wien*, exhibition catalogue, Österreichische Gal., Vienna, 1993. Lüthy, Hans A./Fischer, Peter/Brüschweiler, Jura/Bätschman, Oskar/Hirsh, Sharon, *Ferdinand Hodler: views and visions*, travelling exhibition catalogue, Swiss Institute for Art Research, Zurich, The Trust for Museum Exhibitions, Washington DC, 1994. Koella, Rudolf, *Ferdinand Hodler*, exhibition catalogue, Kunsthalle, Hirmer, Munich, 1999. Bätschmann, Oskar, *Ferdinand Hodler. Die Zeichnungen im Kunstmuseum Bern*, exhibition catalogue, Kunstmuseum, Bern, 1999. Bezzola, Tobia (ed.)/Lang, Paul/Müller, Paul, *Ferdinand Hodler, paysages*, exhibition catalogue, Musée d'Art et d'Histoire, Geneva, Somogy, Paris, 2003.

Museums and Galleries:
Aarau (Aargauer Kunsthaus): *Rhythmical Forms on the Shore of Lake Geneva; Mount Niesen* - Basel (Kunstmus.): *Episode from the Battle of Nafels; Landscape of Lake Geneva; Portrait of Pastor Jacques Probst; Portrait of Marie Rose Krebs-Schüpbach; Portrait of Marc Odier; The Schoolboy; A Soul in Torment; The Brave Woman; Looking into Infinity* - Bern (Kunstmus.): *Wounded Man; Day I; Louis Duchosal on his Deathbed; Girl with a Poppy; Prayer in the Canton of Bern; The Fall; Looking into Eternity; Augustine Dupin Pregnant; Intimate Dialogue; Emotion; The Chosen One; The Ascension; Lake Thun seen from Leissigen; Valentine Godé Darel and Paulette at the Cradle; Valentine Godé Darel Full-face* -

BERN (Town Hall): *Le Cortège des Lutteurs* (1882); *The Angry Man; Portrait of the Artist; Night* (1889-1890, allegory); *Disappointed Souls; Eurythmia* (allegory); *Day* (allegory); *After the Gymnastics Festival* - CHICAGO (AI): *Figure Study for the Students of Jena* - DALLAS (MA): *Der Holzfäller (The Woodcutter)* (1910, lithograph); *Armed Soldier, The Halberdier* (1895, oil and graphite on canvas) - ESSEN (Folkwang Mus.): *Spring I* (1901) - GENEVA (MAH): *Portrait of André Bourdillon* (1878); *The Carpenter in his Workshop* (1879); *Self-portrait* (1879-1880); *Peasant Meditating* (1882); *The Angry Soldier* (1883-1884); *Study for The Historian* (1886-1887); *Bertha Stucki with a Garter* (1887); *The New Grütli* (1887-1888); *Lilac* (1890); *Sadness* (1890-1892); *Parisian Self-portrait* (1891); *Moonlight in the Lauterbrunnen Valley* (1894); *The Retreat from Marignan* (1899); *Portrait of Georges Navazza* (1916); *Portrait of the Artist* (1917); *The Battle of Morat* (1917); *The Mont Blanc Range* (1918, drawing); *Last Self-portrait* (1918); *The Pensive Carpenter; Lansquenet; Woman in Ecstasy; The Small Tree; Lake Geneva with Swans and Dawn over the Mont Blanc Range* (several works); *The Stockhorn Range; The Banks of the Manzanares; Unanimity; Portrait of Matthias Mohardt; Portrait of James Vibert; Valentine on her Sickbed* (several works); *The Miller, His Son and the Donkey; The Angry Soldier* - LAUSANNE (Cantonal MFA): *Portrait of Doctor Bourget* (1889); *Lake Geneva seen from Chexbres* - LUCERNE (Kunstmus.): *The Breithorn; Watchmaker's Workshop in Madrid* (1879); *Day III* (1909-1910); *Portrait of Carl Spitteler* (1915) - MANNHEIM (Städtische Kunsthalle): *Distant Song* (1906); *Lake Thun with the Stockhorn Range* (1910) - MUNICH (Neue Pinakothek): *Die Lebensmüder (Tired of Living)* - NEUCHÂTEL: *Autumn* - NEUCHÂTEL (MAH): *Autumn Evening* - OLTEN (Kunstmus.): *Study for Day* - SARAJEVO (Muz. Grada Sarajevo): *The Reaper* (1909, design for a bank note) - SOLOTHURN (Kunstmus.): *Avalanche* (1887); *Mist Forming on the Wetterhorn* (1908); *Portrait of Miss Gertrude Müller; Group of Trees; Valentine in Bed, February 1914; William Tell* (1897) - STE-CROIX (Mus. des Arts et des Sciences): *Out of Work* (1881) - STUTTGART (Staatsgal.): *Jena Student Adjusting His Kitbag; The Retreat from Marignan* (1898); *Studies for Day; Self-portrait* (1900) - THE HAGUE (Gemeentemus.): *Study for New Year's Day* (1899) - VEVEY (Mus. Jenisch): *The Eiger, the Mönch and the Jungfrau with a Sea of Fog* - WINTERTHUR: *Tired of Living; Self-portrait with a Smile* (1908); *Adoration* (1893, drawing) - ZURICH: *The Swiss Retreat from the Battle of Marignan* (fresco) - ZURICH (Kunsthaus): *Valentine on her Deathbed; Portrait of Augustine Dupin; Distant Song II; Portrait of Helene Weigel in Profile; Fog Rising near Caux; The Cobbler Frédéric Neukomm at Work; The Student; The Carpenter; Mother and Child; Dark Genius; The Gymnasts' Feast; The Mouth of the Maggia, Ticino; Nude by a Stream; Stream in the Forest of Leissigen, Bernese Oberland; Portrait of Louise Delphine Duchosal; Lake Silvaplana in Autumn; Portrait of F.R. Martin; Sketch for Truth; Truth II; Study for the Portrait of Berthe Jacques* (drawing); *Study for the Battle of Morat; Study for the Wandering Jew* (drawing); *Holy Hour I* (1907); *Unanimity* (1911, sketch).

AUCTION RECORDS:

LUCERNE, 2 Sept 1935, *Watchmaker's Workshop in Madrid*, FRF 10,000; *Seascape*, FRF 8,000. GENEVA, 23 March 1937, *Bull in the Cowshed*, FRF 7,100; *Bernese Peasant Women*, FRF 4,350; *Willows at the Crossroads*, FRF 12,000; *The Standard-bearer*, FRF 8,060; *Young Woman in a Meadow*, FRF 9,750; *The Spring*, FRF 7,750; *Dancer*, FRF 8,100; *River at Néris*, FRF 6,950; *Looking into Infinity*, FRF 8,100; *Two Portraits of Lina*, FRF 8,910; *Female Nude Walking*, FRF 16,500. NEW YORK, 4 May 1944, *The Stockhorn Mountains*, USD 1,650. BERN, 27 Nov 1959, *Head of a Woman*, CHF 8,200. STUTTGART, 20 May 1960, *View of the Weiszhorn from Montana*, DEM 66,000. GENEVA, 13 June 1960, *Mountain Landscape* (pencil) CHF 980. STUTTGART, 3-4 May 1962, *Lake Thun with the Stockhorn Range*, DEM 64,000. GENEVA, 2 Nov 1963, *The Dying Woman, Portrait of Mme Darel-Godé*, CHF 59,000. BERN, 10 June 1966, *Bust of Madame Darel* (lost-wax bronze) CHF 9,000. BERN, 23 Nov 1968, *Young Woman Standing, Three-quarter Portrait* (study for the Reception) CHF 47,000. GENEVA, 24 April 1970, *Walk along the Edge of the Wood*, CHF 85,000; *Bust of Mme Darel* (bronze) CHF 6,500. GENEVA, 10 Dec 1970, *The Reader* (watercolour) CHF 4,000. LUCERNE, 20 Nov 1971, *The Reformer*, CHF 18,000. BERN, 18 Nov 1972, *Lake Thun*, CHF 218,000. ZURICH, 9 Nov 1973, *The Good Samaritan* (1886) CHF 135,000. ZURICH, 16 May 1974, *Standing Nude* (1917) CHF 195,000. ZURICH, 5 May 1976, *The Boules Players* (1881, oil on canvas, 11 x 9 1/2 ins / 27 x 24 cm) CHF 54,000. LONDON, 1 July 1976, *Portrait of a Woman* (c. 1912-1914, gouache, charcoal and oil on paper, 14 1/4 x 17 ins / 36 x 43 cm) GBP 6,800. BERN, 22 Oct 1976, *The Standard-bearer* (drawing, 12 1/2 x 6 1/4 ins / 31.5 x 16 cm) CHF 2,800. BERN, 8 June 1977, *Sheep at Villalba, Spain* (1879, watercolour, 5 1/2 x 9 ins / 13.7 x 22.6 cm) CHF 6,800. ZURICH, 25 Nov 1977, *Portrait of a Workman in a Blue Smock* (1884, oil on canvas, oval, 27 1/4 x 23 ins / 69 x 57.5 cm) CHF 42,000. ZURICH, 26 Nov 1977, *Self-portrait* (1916, lithograph) CHF 2,200. ZURICH, 26 May 1979, *Study for Arnold von Melchtal* (c. 1897, pencil, 6 x 12 3/4 ins / 15.2 x 32.6 cm) CHF 10,500. LONDON, 2 July 1979, *View of Lake Thun* (c. 1905, oil on canvas, 35 1/2 x 39 1/4 ins / 90 x 100 cm) GBP 295,000. HAMBURG, 5 June 1980, *Spring* (lithograph) DEM 4,000. LONDON, 30 June 1981, *Self-portrait* (c. 1916, wash and wax crayon, 15 3/4 x 13 3/4 ins / 40 x 35 cm) GBP 6,000. ZURICH, 13 May 1982, *Bust of Valentine Godé Darel* (green and gold patinated bronze, h. 13 ins / 33 cm) CHF 8,000. LUCERNE, 25 May 1982, *Lake Thun* (1904, oil on canvas, 28 x 41 1/4 ins / 71 x 105 cm) CHF 380,000. NEW YORK, 4 May 1983, *Holy Hour* (c. 1910, lithograph, 22 3/4 x 39 1/4 ins / 58 x 99.7 cm) USD 1,300. LUCERNE, 19 May 1983, *Portrait of Valentine Godé Darel* (bronze, h. 13 1/4 ins / 33.5 cm) CHF 16,000. LONDON, 5 Dec 1983, *Landscape of Majola* (1907, oil on canvas, 20 x 31 ins / 51 x 79 cm) GBP 240,000. LONDON, 6 Dec 1983, *Geneva, View of the Studio* (1890, watercolour and pen/paper, 14 1/2 x 20 ins / 37 x 51 cm) GBP 15,000. BERN, 19 June 1985, *The Woodcutter* (c. 1915, lithograph, 23 1/2 x 15 3/4 ins / 59.5 x 40 cm) CHF 2,300. BERN, 19-20 June 1985, *Joyful Woman I, Woman in Motion with Arms Outstretched* (oil on canvas, 50 1/4 x 29 1/4 ins / 127.5 x 74 cm) CHF 310,000. LONDON, 24 June 1985, *Autumn Snow in the Engadine* (1907, oil on canvas, 25 1/4 x 33 3/4 ins / 64 x 86 cm) GBP 220,000. BERN, 17 June 1987, *Head of Giulia Leonardi* (1910, bistre wash/colouring pencil and graphite, 10 3/4 x 8 1/2 ins / 27.2 x 21.5 cm) CHF 24,000. COLOGNE, 28 Nov 1987, *Portrait of Berthe Hodler* (tempera and oil on paper remounted/canvas, 13 1/4 x 11 1/4 ins / 33.4 x 28.6 cm) DEM 38,000. ZURICH, 3 Dec 1987, *Walnut Tree* (c. 1905-1909, oil on canvas, 28 1/2 x 25 ins / 72.5 x 63.5 cm) CHF 250,000. LUCERNE, 30 Sept 1988, *Kneeling Soldier Wearing a Beret* (lithograph, 20 x 17 1/4 ins / 51 x 44 cm) CHF 600. ZURICH, 18 Oct 1990, *Cow in the Alps* (watercolour, 5 1/4 x 8 3/4 ins / 13.5 x 22.5 cm) CHF 6,000. HEIDELBERG, 12 Oct 1991, *Spring* (lithograph, 26 3/4 x 17 1/4 ins / 67.8 x 43.6 cm) DEM 2,800. ZURICH, 4 June 1992, *Avalanche* (watercolour and pencil/paper, 14 1/4 x 11 ins / 36 x 27 cm) CHF 39,550; *Mountain Lake* (oil on canvas, 25 1/2 x 31 1/2 ins / 65 x 80 cm) CHF 802,300. ZURICH, 9 June 1993, *Mount Niesen* (oil on canvas, 15 1/4 x 19 1/2 ins / 38.5 x 49.5 cm) CHF 182,200. LONDON, 21 June 1993, *Lake Geneva with Mont Blanc at Sunrise* (1918, oil on canvas, 23 1/2 x 31 1/2 ins / 60 x 80 cm) GBP 265,500. LUCERNE, 20 Nov 1993, *Study for Looking into Infinity* (pencil/paper, 5 1/4 x 8 1/2 ins / 13.3 x 21.5 cm) CHF 1,800. ZURICH, 2 June 1994, *Walnut Tree* (1888, oil on canvas, 24 1/2 x 17 1/2 ins / 62 x 44.5 cm) CHF 148,300. ZURICH, 8 Dec 1994, *The Rhône Valley* (oil on canvas, 23 1/2 x 31 1/2 ins / 60 x 80 cm) CHF 453,400. ZURICH, 12 June 1995, *Woodcutter* (oil on paper/canvas, 19 x 15 1/4 ins / 48 x 39 cm)

CHF 182,200. LONDON, 29 Nov 1995, *Sketch for The Day* (1891, pencil/paper, 9 3/4 x 19 ins / 24.7 x 48.2 cm) GBP 5,000. ZURICH, 30 Nov 1995, *The Aar Canal near Scherzligen* (1880, oil on canvas, 30 x 35 1/4 ins / 76.5 x 89.5 cm) CHF 216,100. ZURICH, 5 June 1996, *Woodcutter* (1910, oil on canvas, 50 1/2 x 41 1/4 ins / 128 x 105 cm) CHF 1,357,400. ZURICH, 10 Dec 1996, *Woman by a Stream* (c. 1903, oil on panel, 47 1/4 x 46 1/2 ins / 120 x 118 cm) CHF 283,900. ZURICH, 14 April 1997, *Lake Thun with Reflections* (1904, oil on canvas, 32 x 39 1/4 ins / 81 x 100 cm) CHF 3,334,900; *The Gorges de l'Aar* (1907, oil on canvas, 35 3/4 x 26 3/4 ins / 91 x 68 cm) CHF 622,900. ZURICH, 4 June 1997, *Below Salève* (oil on canvas, 28 x 42 ins / 71 x 106.5 cm) CHF 566,400.

HODLER, Hermann

German, 20th century.

Born 1888, in Nidau; died 1965, in Oberdiessbach.

Painter.

Hermann Hodler studied at the Dresden and Munich academies. His work was influenced by Böcklin, F. Hodler and Puvis de Chavannes.

MUSEUMS AND GALLERIES:

BERN.

AUCTION RECORDS:

BERN, 26 Oct 1988, *Tree against the Light* (distemper, 13 x 15 3/4 ins / 33 x 40 cm) CHF 900.

HODRU, Jean

Belgian, 19th - 20th century.

Born 1870, in Louvain; died 1932.

Painter. Portraits, genre scenes, landscapes.

Jean Hodru was a student and later professor at the Académie des Beaux-Arts in Louvain.

HODSON, George Frederick (Sir)

Irish, 19th century.

Born 25 October 1806; died 2 April 1888.

Painter.

George Hodson exhibited paintings of figures and landscapes at the Royal Hibernian Academy in Dublin.

HODSON, John Francis

British, 20th century.

Born 19 August 1945, in Oxford.

Painter. Genre scenes, landscapes.

John Hodson is a self-taught artist who became a professional painter in 1970. He exhibits in England, France and Italy. His turbulent landscapes are enlivened by touches of contrasting colour.

MUSEUMS AND GALLERIES:

LONDON (Courtauld Institute of Art).

HODSON, Samuel John

British, 19th century.

Born c. 1836, in London; died 5 July 1908.

Painter, watercolourist. Genre scenes.

Samuel Hodson was a member of the Society of Painters in Watercolours, the Royal Society of British Artists and the Royal Cambrian Academy. He exhibited frequently after 1858.

MUSEUMS AND GALLERIES:

LONDON (Courtauld Institute of Art).

AUCTION RECORDS:

NEW YORK, 16 Feb 1993, *Children Picking Wild Flowers by the River* (1873, watercolour and gouache/paper, 13 1/4 x 18 1/4 ins / 33.7 x 46.3 cm) USD 1,320. NEW YORK, 10 Feb 1998, *Piazza Verona* (1895, watercolour and pencil/paper/panel, 22 x 31 ins / 55.9 x 78.8 cm) USD 8,625. LONDON, 15 June 2000, *Grande Place, Antwerp* (1875, watercolour heightened with gouache, 32 x 24 ins / 81 x 61 cm) GBP 3,000.

HOE, Nicolas de

Flemish School, 17th - 18th century.

Born 1626, possibly in Antwerp; died 1710, in Vienna.

Painter, engraver.

Nicolas de Hoe was a pupil of Matheus in Antwerp. He worked for Emperor Leopold.

HOEBEKE, Amaat

Belgian, 20th century.

Born 1922, in Woubrechtegem.

Painter.

Amaat Hoebeke studied at the academies of art in Alost and Ghent.

HOEBEKE, Maguy

Belgian, 20th century.

Born 17 February 1917.

Painter. Figures, nudes, portraits, interiors, landscapes, seascapes, still-lifes, flowers.

Maguy Hoebeke studied at the Brussels academy. She went on study tours to Normandy, Tunisia and Spain. Since 1945, she has shown her work in many group exhibitions in Belgium and in solo exhibitions, mainly in Brussels, but also in Ostend and Ghent in 1962, Anderlecht in 1963, 1977 and 1980, Courtrai in 1964 and Namur in 1995.

She is chiefly a landscape painter. In Belgium she paints in the Ardennes, Les Fagnes and on the coast, and in France in Normandy, Brittany and the Cevennes. Her favourite subjects are the sea and orchards in blossom.

HOEBER, Arthur

American, 19th - 20th century.

Born 23 July 1854, in New York; died 29 April 1915, in Nutley (New Jersey).

Painter, illustrator, art critic. Landscapes, landscapes with figures.

Arthur Hoeber went to Paris to study at the École des Beaux-Arts in Gérôme's studio. He received an honourable mention in Buffalo in 1901. He became a member of the Salmagundi Club in 1900 and an associate member of the National Academy of Design in 1909. He was also the art critic of the New York *Globe*.

AUCTION RECORDS:

NEW YORK, 31 Jan au 2 Feb 1900, *Road to the Sea,* USD 130. NEW YORK, 23 and 24 Jan 1901, *Landscape,* USD 165. NEW YORK, 6 Jan 1911, *Meadow with Animals,* USD 380. NEW YORK, 21 Oct 1983, *Salt Marshes, New Jersey* (oil on canvas remounted on board, 31 1/4 x 52 1/2 ins / 79.4 x 133.3 cm) USD 2,000. NEW YORK, 4 Dec 1986, *Story of the Voyage* (oil on canvas, 29 x 32 1/2 ins / 73.7 x 82.5 cm) USD 6,750. NEW YORK, 2 Dec 1992, *Landscape at Twilight* (oil on canvas, 25 1/4 x 40 1/4 ins / 64 x 102.2 cm) USD 4,400. NEW YORK, 11 March 1993, *Concarneau Beach* (oil on canvas, 22 x 32 ins / 56.1 x 81.2 cm) USD 3,680.

HOEBER, Max Marcus

German, 19th - 20th century.

Born 4 January 1870, in Würding.

Painter. Portraits, genre scenes.

Max Hoeber was active in Vienna and later in Munich.

HOEBOER, Wout

Dutch, 20th century.

Born 1910, in Rotterdam; died 1983, in Brussels.

Active in Belgium.

Painter.

Wout Hoeboer studied at the Rotterdam academy, then travelled in Italy, France and Germany. He took part in the exhibitions of the CoBrA group. His works, which are full of malicious fantasy, bear witness to a lively imagination.

AUCTION RECORDS:
LOKEREN, 28 May 1994, *Composition* (1967, collage, 21 x 28 ins / 53.5 x 71 cm) BEF 36,000.

HOEBRECHT, Pierre
Belgian, 20th century.
Born 1888, in Gellik; died 1966, in Brussels.
Painter.

HOECGEEST, Joachim Ottensz van. See **HOUCKGEEST**

HOECH, Hannah. See **HÖCH**

HOECHLE, Johann Baptist
Swiss, 18th - 19th century.
Born 19 October 1754, in Klingnau; died 1 January 1832, in Vienna.
Painter. Historical scenes, portraits.

Johann Baptist Hoechle studied with the painter Morat, and then at the academy of art in Augsburg. He went on to become a painter at the court of Prince Elector Karl Theodor of Bavaria and from 1802, was painter to Emperor Francis I. After working in Munich from 1780 to 1800, he settled in Vienna. He is best known for two portraits in the Vienna Museum.

HOECHLE, Johann Nepomuk
German, 19th century.
Born 1790, in Munich; died 12 December 1835, in Vienna.
Painter, draughtsman, lithographer. Historical subjects, military subjects, battles.

Johann Nepomuk Hoechle, a pupil of Kobell and Duvivier, went to work at the Akademie der bildenden Künste in Vienna and then became court painter, following Emperor Francis to Paris in 1815. He subsequently travelled to Italy, before returning to Austria, where he executed military sketches and paintings. He also left a large number of delicately tinted pen-and-ink drawings and some lithographs.

MUSEUMS AND GALLERIES:
VIENNA: *The Allies Crossing the Vosges Mountains* - VIENNA (Liechtenstein Mus.): *Battle Scene* (several).

AUCTION RECORDS:
VIENNA, 21 March 1972, *Emperor Francis I of Austria Inspecting the Troops*, ATS 65,000. VIENNA, 16 March 1976, *Emperor Francis I Inspecting a Regiment of Hussars* (oil on canvas, 22 x 28 ins / 55 x 71 cm) ATS 160,000.

HOECK, Frieda. See **RUSTI-HOECK**

HOECK, Jan van den, or Hoecke
Flemish School, 17th century.
Born 1611, in Antwerp; died 1651, in Brussels.
Painter. Religious subjects, allegorical subjects, portraits, still-lifes.

Jan van den Hoeck was baptised on 4 August 1611 in Antwerp. Almost nothing is known of the artist's work until he was about fifty years old. He studied under Rubens and left Antwerp at a young age. After a period of several years in Rome during which, according to the *Annales Antverpienses (Antwerp Annals)*, he copied numerous paintings 'both old and new', he went to Germany. He was summoned there by the Emperor Ferdinand II; the exact year is not known, but it must have been prior to 1637 as Ferdinand died that year. In Germany it appears he continued painting portraits and compositions for churches and palaces up to 1647; nothing is known of these works but they evidently established a widespread reputation for the artist, as Archduke Leopold summoned him to Brussels to work as a painter to the royal household. He spent the last three years of his life in the city and executed a considerable number of works; however, very little of this work remained in Belgium, no doubt because he mainly executed commissions sent to him from Italy and Germany. We know, for example, that the year he died he painted a bust portrait of the *Emperor of Germany, Ferdinand III, Crowned by Mars and Peace, Accompanied by Abundance*. An engraving of this piece by the line engraver Lucas Vorsterman the Younger carries the following inscription: *Joannes van Hoeck pictor dedicabat MDCL (1650)*. In the church of Notre-Dame in Mechelen there is a *Deposition* with Joseph of Arimathea, St John, the Virgin and Mary Magdalene and in the distance a man and woman crying; a *Bearing of the Cross* with half figures of two executioners, St John, the Virgin and Mary Magdalene; a *Holy Family* engraved by Paul Pontius with the Infant Jesus asleep in the crib and St Joseph; another *Holy Family*, an engraving of which by François van den Steen is dedicated to the Countess of Schwartzenberg, Van Hoeck's protector (*patronae suae*). The church of St Saviour in Bruges has a *Christ on the Cross* with the Virgin, St John and a monk of the Recollect order; there is a copper engraving by Corneille Galle (the Elder, died in 1656) of a *Dying Jesus* by Van Hoeck but the painting is unknown. The Antwerp museum has a *Virgin Presenting her Son to St Anthony of Padua*. Given that Van Hoeck is thought to have been a prolific artist, this is a somewhat meagre list, and Alfred Michiels has suggested that many of his paintings, particularly those that remained in Italy and Austria, may have been falsely attributed to Van Dyck.

MUSEUMS AND GALLERIES:
ANTWERP: *St Francis of Assisi in Adoration before the Infant Jesus* - BERGUES: *The Artist; The Artist's Wife* - BÉZIERS: *Portrait of a Woman; Portrait of a Man* - DIJON: *Martyrdom of St Mary of Cordoba* - DUNKIRK: *Christ on the Cross* - ST PETERSBURG (Hermitage): *The Holy Apostles Paul and Barnabas in Lystria* - VIENNA: *Allegory of Inconstancy; Archduke Leopold William; Flora; Pomona; September and October; February and January; May and June; July and August; Day and Night; Archduke Leopold William at Prayer; Cupid Triumphing over the Arts; March and April; November and December; Allegory of Day; Allegory of Night* - YPRES: *The Saviour of the World*.

AUCTION RECORDS:
PARIS, 10 March 1902, *Pilgrimage*, FRF 590. LONDON, 19 Nov 1910, *Portrait of a General in Armour*, GBP 9. COLOGNE, 11 Nov 1964, *Allegory of Abundance*, DEM 12,000. VERSAILLES, 17 Dec 1981, *Motherhood* (oil/copper, $11\frac{3}{4}$ x 9 ins / 30 x 23 cm) FRF 10,000. VERSAILLES, 20 Feb 1983, *Holy Family* (oil/metal, $11\frac{3}{4}$ x 9 ins / 30 x 23 cm) FRF 10,500. NEW YORK, 17 Jan 1985, *Allegory* (oil on canvas, $53\frac{3}{4}$ x $65\frac{3}{4}$ ins / 136.5 x 167 cm) USD 15,000. LONDON, 23 April 1993, *Bust Portrait of the Artist as a Shepherd* (oil on panel, $34\frac{3}{4}$ x $27\frac{1}{4}$ ins / 88.4 x 68.9 cm) GBP 16,100. NEW YORK, 20 May 1993, *Large Still-life with a Basket of Fruit, Silverware, Oysters, Bread and Lemons on a Table with a Mandolin on a Bench* (oil on canvas, $46\frac{3}{4}$ x 38 ins / 118.7 x 96.5 cm) USD 90,500. MILAN, 15 Oct 1996, *Still-life with Flowers and Fruit* (oil on canvas, $14\frac{3}{4}$ x $18\frac{1}{4}$ ins / 37.5 x 46.5 cm) ITL 34,950,000. PARIS, 17 Dec 1997, *Still-life with a Basket of Fruit, Vase of Flowers and Precious Plate on a Table* (panel oak, $27\frac{1}{2}$ x $42\frac{1}{2}$ ins / 70 x 108 cm) FRF 70,000.

HOECK, Pieter van
Flemish School, 17th century.
Active in Antwerp at the beginning of the 17th century.
Painter.

Pieter van Hoeck is almost certainly the same artist who studied under Tobias Verhaegt and was made a master in Brussels on 24 April 1626.

Auction records:
Amsterdam, 15 Nov 1995, *Undulating Landscape with Houses, a Bridge and a Church in the Distance* (ink, 7 x 10 ins / 18 x 24.5 cm) NLG 14,160.

HOECKE, Jules van

Belgian, 20th century.
Born 1899, in Ghent.
Painter. Landscapes.

Jules van Hoecke studied at the Ghent academy.

HOECKE, Kaspar or Caspar or Jasper van den

Flemish School, 17th century.
Born 1595; died c. 1648.
Active in Antwerp.
Painter. Flowers.

Kaspar Hoecke was the father of Jan van Hoecke, and studied under Juliaen Teniers in 1595. In 1603 he became a master in Antwerp. His pupils included Joost van Egmont.

Auction records:
London, 24 March 1976, *Esther and Ahasuerus* (oil on panel, 21¼ x 30¼ ins / 54 x 77 cm) GBP 2,000. London, 11 Dec 1984, *The Parable of the Prodigal Son* (1618, oil on panel, 18½ x 32½ ins / 47 x 82.5 cm) GBP 38,000. Monaco, 16 June 1989, *Bunch of Flowers* (oil/copper, 14¼ x 11 ins / 36 x 28 cm) FRF 1,165,500. Paris, 31 March 1994, *Croesus Displaying his Wealth* (oil on oak panel, 18 x 16½ ins / 46 x 42 cm) FRF 50,000. New York, 11 Jan 1995, *Large Floral Composition of Spring Flowers in a Terracotta Vase with Wild Currants and Strawberries on an Entablature* (oil on panel, 26½ x 17½ ins / 67.5 x 44.5 cm) USD 156,500. New York, 2 April 1996, *The Samian Sibyl* (oil on canvas, 42 x 30¼ ins / 106.7 x 76.8 cm) USD 6,900. New York, 28 May 1999, *The Feast of Belshazzar* (oil on panel, 25 x 42 ins / 64 x 107 cm) USD 24,000. Paris, 27 March 2000, *The Parable of the Prodigal Son* (oil on panel, 11 x 16 ins / 27 x 40 cm) FRF 160,000. Madrid, 26 Sept 2000, *Still-life with Two Figures, Basket of Fruit and Vegetables* (oil on canvas, 64 x 82 ins / 163 x 209 cm) ESP 8,000,000. Paris, 21 June 2004, *The Abduction of Proserpina* (oil on canvas, 45 x 54 ins / 114 x 136 cm) EUR 5,500.

HOECKE, Robert van den

Flemish School, 17th century.
Baptised 30 November 1622 in Antwerp; died 1668, in Bergues.
Painter. Religious subjects, historical subjects, military subjects, battles, genre scenes, landscapes with figures, winter landscapes.

Robert van den Hoecke studied under his father, Kaspar van den Hoecke. In 1625 he was made a master in Antwerp. He spent some time in Brussels before finally settling in Bergues around 1650.

He worked as a painter but was also controller of the fortifications of Flanders and painted a series of scenes of military life and encampments as well as battles. The church of St Victor in Bergues has some landscapes with religious scenes by this artist.

Bibliography:
Ollinger-Zinque, Gisèle, *Étude sur les peintres Van Hoecke*, 1961.

Museums and Galleries:
Dunkirk: *Encampment* - St Petersburg (Hermitage): *Attack on a Fortress* - Strasbourg: *Winter Landscape* - Vienna: *Route March; Ostend; Fire at Night; Encampment; Store Room in Holland; Encampment near Ruins; Night Encampment outside an Inn.*

Auction records:
New York, 12 Jan 1979, *Military Encampment* (metal, 9¼ x 12 ins / 23.5 x 30.5 cm) USD 7,250. London, 5 April 1995, *Cavalry Regiment Encampment* (oil on panel, 7 x 9 ins / 18 x 22.6 cm) GBP 17,250. Amsterdam, 7 May 1996, *Winter Landscape with Skaters on a Frozen River and a Carriage in the Background* (oil on panel, 9½ x 13¼ ins / 23.9 x 33.4 cm) NLG 40,250.

HOECKER, Adalbert, the Younger

German, 19th century.
Born c. 1800, in Breslau (now Wroclaw, Poland); died c. 1860, in Breslau.
Painter. Portraits, landscapes.

The son and pupil of painter Adalbert Höcker the Elder. In 1825, he joined the staff of the school of fine arts in Breslau.

Museums and Galleries:
Wroclaw: *Portrait of Sculptor Mächtig.*

HOECKER, Adalbert Longin, the Elder

German, 18th - 19th century.
Born 21 August 1761, in Albendorf (Silesia); died 22 February 1841, in Breslau (now Wroclaw, Poland).
Painter, decorative designer. Landscapes.

He studied at the academy in Dresden. The theatres in Karlsruhe and Oels (Olesnica, Silesia) have decorative work by him.

HOECKER, Paul

German, 19th century.
Born 11 August 1854, in Oberlangenau, near Glatz (Klodzko, Silesia); died 13 January 1910, in Munich.
Painter. Religious subjects, genre scenes, portraits.

He studied at the academy of fine arts in Munich, where he worked from 1874 to 1879. Then he paid visits to Paris and Holland before returning to Munich in 1884. He also spent some time in Berlin. In 1891, he succeeded F. A. von Kaulbach at the academy in Munich. He exhibited in Berlin, Nuremberg, Munich, Vienna and Paris, and gained a number of awards such as a gold medal in Berlin in 1886 and a bronze medal at the Universal Exhibition in Paris in 1889.

Museums and Galleries:
Munich: *Dutch Girl* - Stuttgart: *On the Chimney.*

Auction records:
New York, 9-10 Feb 1905, *The Fisherman's Fiancée*, USD 155. London, 19 June 1981, *Young Girl at the Spinning Wheel* (oil on panel, 12½ x 10½ ins / 31.8 x 26.6 cm) GBP 900. Vejle, 25 Sept 2001, *Interior Scene with Mother and Daughter Wearing Rural Costumes* (oil on canvas, 31 x 41 ins / 79 x 104 cm) DKK 17,000.

HOECKERT, Johan Fredrick, or Höckert

Swedish, 19th century.
Born 26 August 1826, in Jönköping; died 16 September 1866, in Göteborg.
Painter. History painting, genre scenes, landscapes.

Johan Hoeckert was a pupil at the fine arts academy in Stockholm. He also studied at the fine arts academy in Munich with Johan Kristofer Bökland under F. L. Storch until 1849. He went to Paris in 1851 and worked there until 1857. He returned definitively to Stockholm in 1857. He was named a member of the academy in Stockholm and was decorated with the Order of Gustav Vasa and the Order of the Northern Star in 1866. He travelled and worked a great deal in Holland, Belgium, England, Spain, Italy and Algeria.

He exhibited at the Salon de Paris in 1853 and 1855, and won a gold medal at the Exposition Universelle. Among his works are *Queen Christina Condemning Monaldeschi to Death* and *Service in a Chapel in Lapland*.

Bibliography:
Borelius, A., *Johan Fredrik Höckert*, P. A. Norstedt, Stockholm, 1927.
Museums and Galleries:
Lille (MBA): *Preaching in a Chapel in Swedish Lapland* - Stockholm (Nationalmus.): *Interior of a Lapp Hut; Wedding in Hornavan (Lapland); Fire at the Royal Palace of Stockholm in 1697*.
Auction records:
Stockholm, 26 April 1982, *A Small Accident* (oil on panel, 8 1/4 x 6 1/4 ins / 21 x 16 cm) SEK 24,000. Stockholm, 26 April 1983, *Rustic Scene in Summer Landscape* (oil on canvas, 31 1/2 x 53 1/2 ins / 80 x 136 cm) SEK 155,000. Stockholm, 22 May 2001, *Behind the Scenes* (oil on panel, 11 x 8 ins / 27 x 21 cm) SEK 51,000. Stockholm, 4 Dec 2001, *Visiting the Basket Maker* (oil on canvas, 20 x 26 ins / 52 x 65 cm) SEK 15,000.

HOECKHINGER, Daniel
German, 18th century.
Active in Augsburg.
Engraver.

HOECKLER
19th - 20th century.
Painter.
Hoeckler became a member of the Société Nationale des Beaux-Arts in 1890.

HOECKNER, Johann Caspar
German, 17th century.
Born 28 November 1629, in Weimar.
Active in Dresden.
Engraver, medallist.
He engraved mainly portraits.

HOECKNER, Rudolf
German, 19th century.
Born 28 July 1864, on the Hilmersdorf estate, near Wolkenstein (Saxony); died 1942.
Active in Munich.
Painter. Landscapes.
He worked initially in Weimar, then from 1889 in Munich.

HOEDER, Friedrich Wilhelm
German, 18th century.
Born in Cottbus; died c. 1761, in Berlin.
Active in Berlin.
Painter, engraver.
A painter in the Lancret genre, he decorated great houses in the French style and also worked at Charlottenburg Palace in Berlin.

HOEDRICH
Austrian, 18th century.
Active in Graz c. 1790.
Miniaturist.

HOEDT, J. C.
Dutch, 19th century.
Active in Rotterdam c. 1800.
Draughtsman, engraver.
J.C. Hoedt is known for his portrait of the actor *Ward Bingley*.

HOEDYCK, Nicolas
Flemish School, 17th century.
Painter. Genre scenes.
The Brussels museum has a *Dutch Interior* by Nicolas Hoedyck.

HOEF, Abraham van der, or Hoeff
Dutch, 17th century.
Painter. Military subjects, battles.
Little is known about Abraham van der Hoef, who was active between 1613 and 1649 in Delft.

Museums and Galleries:
St Petersburg (Hermitage): *Cavalry Skirmish*.
Auction records:
Amsterdam, 10 Nov 1970, *War Scene*, NLG 5,500. New York, 11 June 1981, *Cavalry Charge* (oil on panel, 18 1/2 x 25 ins / 47 x 63.5 cm) USD 3,400. Paris, 15 April 1988, *Cavalry Attack - Cavalry Encampment* (oil on panel, 19 x 25 ins / 47.4 x 63.5 cm and 18 3/4 x 25 ins/47.5 x 63.5 cm) FRF 50,000. New York, 13 Oct 1989, *Cavalry Engagement with a Bridge in the Distance* (oil on panel, 20 1/2 x 33 ins / 52 x 84 cm) USD 8,525. Monaco, 20 June 1992, *Battle Scene* (oil on panel, 12 x 15 ins / 30.5 x 38 cm) FRF 22,200. Paris, 14 Dec 1992, *Cavalry Charge* (oil on panel, 12 1/4 x 15 ins / 31 x 38 cm) FRF 28,000. Amsterdam, 10 May 1994, *Cavalry Engagement* (oil on panel, 12 1/2 x 16 1/4 ins / 31.5 x 41.5 cm) NLG 11,500. London, 6 July 1999, *Cavalry Skirmish in Italianate Landscape beside Rocky Outcrop* (oil on canvas, 19 x 25 ins / 48 x 64 cm) GBP 3,400. London, 6 July 1999, *Encampment Scene with Cavalry Officer Taking Refreshment and Other Soldiers* (1653, oil on panel, 19 x 25 ins / 47 x 63 cm) GBP 5,500. Bremen, 8 Dec 2000, *Huntsmen Resting* (1651, oil on canvas, 39 x 51 ins / 100 x 129 cm) DEM 65,000. London, 10 July 2001, *Elegant Huntsman Taking Refreshment from a Boy* (1651, oil on canvas, 51 x 39 ins / 129 x 98 cm) GBP 25,000. London, 13 Dec 2001, *Cavalry Engagement* (1639, oil on panel, 22 x 41 ins / 56 x 104 cm) GBP 9,000. London, 7 July 2004, *Cavalry Skirmish on a Plain* (oil on panel, 19 x 25 ins / 48 x 63 cm) GBP 5,000.

HOEF, C. J. van der
Dutch, 20th century.
Born c. 1875, in Amsterdam.
Sculptor, medallist.
C. J. van der Hoef is best known for his statuettes in bronze and wood.

HOEF, G. van der
Dutch, 20th century.
Born 2 March 1879, in Amsterdam.
Painter, engraver.
Van der Hoef studied at the Académie des Beaux Arts in Brussels and then settled in The Hague.

HOEFEL, Blasius
Austrian, 19th century.
Born 27 May 1792, in Vienna; died 17 September 1863, in Salzburg.
Engraver, lithographer.
After a difficult start, he worked at the academy in Vienna under the direction of Quirin Mark, whose daughter he later married. In 1820, he was appointed drawing master at the military academy in Neustadt, and subsequently became a member of the academy in Vienna. He made a number of important technical discoveries. Among his works are several portraits of the imperial family and religious paintings.

HOEFEL, Johann Nepomuk, or Höfel
Austrian, 19th century.

Born 1788, in Pest (Hungary); died 22 January 1864, in Vienna.

Painter. History painting, religious subjects, portraits.

The elder brother of Blasius Höfel, he was a pupil of Kraft and subsequently worked at the academy in Vienna. His painting of *Aegeus Recognising His Son Theseus* won him a prize in 1811. He subsequently visited Italy and settled in Munich.

His compositions were generally inspired by ancient history, but he also did altar paintings and portraits.

AUCTION RECORDS:

NEW YORK, 23 Feb 1989, *Napoleon and Josephine* (1825, oil on canvas, 33 x 36 1/2 ins / 83.8 x 92.7 cm) USD 8,800. BUDAPEST, 6 Dec 2002, *After Breakfast* (oil on canvas, 20 x 17 ins / 52 x 44 cm) HUF 450,000.

HOEFER, Adolf, or Hofer

German, 19th - 20th century.

Born 10 October 1869, in Munich.

Painter, illustrator. Portraits, landscapes.

Adolf Hoefer studied with Heterich and Hoecker.

HOEFERLIN, Johannes

Swiss, 19th century.

Died 1816, in Diegten.

Painter, engraver.

He was a drawing master in Basel. He produced a number of genre pictures.

HOEFFIUS

17th century.

Active c. 1650.

Painter.

A *Portrait of a Woman* signed by Hoeffius is recorded.

HOEFFLER, Adolf

German, 19th century.

Born 1826, in Frankfurt am Main; died 1898.

Painter, watercolourist, engraver. Landscapes.

He trained at the municipal institute in Frankfurt and the academies in Munich and Düsseldorf. In 1848, he set off for Canada, returning thence in 1853. He worked in Paris, Antwerp and Munich before settling for good in Frankfurt.

MUSEUMS AND GALLERIES:

FRANKFURT AM MAIN: *The Giant Oak.*

HOEFFLER, Heinrich Friedrich

German, 19th century.

Born 29 March 1793, in Frankfurt am Main; died 15 May 1844, in Frankfurt am Main.

Painter.

A pupil of Regges in Frankfurt and later Gros in Paris, he painted mainly religious paintings. He was the father of Adolf Hoeffler.

HOEFFLER, J. D.

German, 18th century.

Active in Dresden.

Painter.

He worked in Frankfurt am Main in the last years of the 18th century.

HOEFLE, R.

German, 19th century.

Active c. 1850.

Draughtsman.

He is known for his landscapes of Hesse, the Rhineland and Alsace.

HOEFLEIN, Otto

German, 19th century.

Born 1840; died 1 January 1899, in Pforzheim.

Sculptor.

He trained in Munich and Stuttgart.

HOEFLING, Bernhard

German, 19th century.

Active in Bonn c. 1850.

Draughtsman, lithographer.

He is known for an album of portraits of Düsseldorf artists.

HOEFLINGER, Albert

German, 19th century.

Born 28 August 1855, in Neustadt (Baden).

Painter.

He spent his childhood in Basel. In Paris, he was a pupil of Bonnat and Robert-Fleury. He is known for genre paintings and portraits.

HOEFLINGER, Louis

German, 19th century.

Born in Hesse.

Lithographer.

He is known for his *Views of Dorpat (Tartu, Estonia)* and *Views of Reval (Tallinn).*

HOEFNAGEL, Jakob

Flemish School, 17th century.

Born 1573 or 1575, in Antwerp; died c. 1630, in the Netherlands.

Painter, miniaturist, draughtsman, engraver (also of reproductions). Natural history (botanical subjects/insects), topographical views.

Prague School.

Jakob Hoefnagel was the son of Joris Hoefnagel. He produced original engravings and reproductions from various masters. He also executed a series of engravings from drawings of animals, flowers and insects made by his father and brought together under the title *Archetypa Studiaque Patris Georgii Hoefnagelii* (published in 1592). He continued his father's work for the *Civitates Orbis Terrarum* by Georg Braun and Franz Hogenberg (six volumes published between 1512 and 1617) which consisted of plans and views of mainly European towns and cities. In 1607 he was court painter to Emperor Rudolph.

BIBLIOGRAPHY:

DaCosta Kaufmann, Thomas, *L'École de Prague*, Flammarion, Paris, 1985.

MUSEUMS AND GALLERIES:

NEW YORK (Pierpont Morgan Library): *Orpheus Charming the Animals* (drawing).

AUCTION RECORDS:

LONDON, 11 Dec 1929, *Winter and Summer* (drawing) GBP 96. LONDON, 30 April 1947, *Butterflies*, GBP 22. AMSTERDAM, 26 Nov 1984, *Winter* (1618, watercolour with a gold border/parchment remounted/panel, 6 x 5 3/4 ins / 14.3 x 14.9 cm) NLG 30,000. LONDON, 6 July 2001, *River Landscape with the Rape of Psyche by Mercury* (engraving, 11 x 13 ins / 27 x 34 cm) GBP 3,000. LONDON, 10 July 2002, *Lethaeus Amor* (1611, brush and gouache on vellum, 7 x 9 ins / 17 x 24 cm) GBP 190,000.

HOEFNAGEL, Johann

Flemish School, 17th century.

Miniaturist, engraver.

Johann Hoefnagel was the son of Joris Hoefnagel and brother of Jakob Hoefnagel.

HOEFNAGEL, Joris or Georg or Georgius, or Hoefnagels or Hufnagel or Houfnaglius

Flemish, 16th century.

Born 1542, in Antwerp; died 9 September 1600, in Vienna.

Painter, watercolourist, draughtsman, miniaturist, engraver, illuminator. Mythological subjects, allegorical subjects, portraits, natural history (animals/botanical subjects), still-lifes, topographical views.

Prague School, Flemish School.

Joris Hoefnagel was a jeweller's son and was interested in art from an early age. He studied with Hans Bol, then visited Spain, Italy and Germany. After the sack of Antwerp in 1576 he returned to Germany in the company of the geographer Abraham Ortelins or Ortelius. For a number of years he was employed by Albert V, Elector of Bavaria, except for a short time spent in Rome working for Cardinal Farnese. Archduke Ferdinand noticed him in Munich and took him to Innsbruck, where he accomplished his masterpiece, the *Roman Missal*, as remarkable as anything by Giulio Clovio. His fame reached Emperor Rudolph, who gave him work in Prague. Hoefnagel then settled permanently in Vienna. A Renaissance man, he wrote Latin poems, spoke several languages and played a number of musical instruments.

In Prague Maximilian II and Rudolph II created the principal centre of botanical resources in the 16th century. They included it in a vast collection, the 'Kunstkammer', an assemblage of works of art and such curiosities as fossils, minerals, rough or worked, and scientific instruments. Hoefnagel was already known for his botanical and zoological work. Between 1591 and 1596, at the request of Rudolph II, he made drawings of flora and fauna to illustrate Georg Bocskay's *Mira Calligraphiae Monumenta* (1561-1562), a register of patterns of calligraphy. To the author's surprise, it was these illustrations that led to the book's success. They may not be scientifically exact - Hoefnagel made some of them livelier than nature required - but his work served as a basis for more rigorous studies. He also produced topographical drawings and maps. Several of his plates were included in the *Civitates Orbis Terrarum* by Georg Braun and Franz Hogenberg (six volumes published 1512-1617) consisting of views and plans of towns, European and others. In his qualities of Realism he was one of the finest miniaturists and last great artists among Flemish illuminators. He, along with Roelandt Savery and others at the court of Rudolph II, shared in an outburst of Naturalism which stripped the veil from the world around them.

Hoefnagel's work has been included in themed exhibitions: in 1998 *Durch die Blume: Natursymbolik um 1600* in the Staatliche Graphische Sammlung in Munich; in 2002 *Praga Magica. L'Art à Prague au temps de Rodolphe II* (*Praga Magica. Art in Prague under Rudolph II*) in the Magnin museum in Dijon; in 2002 *Deceptions and Illusions: Five Centuries of Trompe-l'oeil Painting* in the National Gallery of Art in Washington, USA; and again in 2002 *Das Flaemische Stilleben* (*Flemish Still-life Painting*) in the Kunsthistorisches Museum in Vienna.

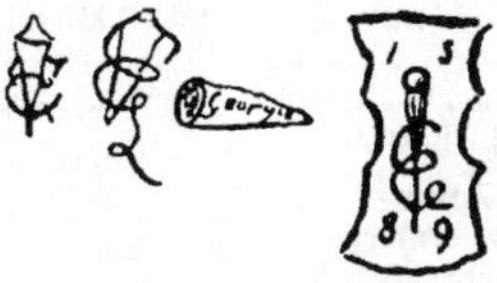

BIBLIOGRAPHY:

Popham, Arthur Ewart, *Georg Hoefnagel and the Civitates Orbis Terrarum*, A. E. Popham, 1936. DaCosta Kaufmann, Thomas, *L'École de Prague*, Flammarion, Paris, 1985. Hendrix, Marjorie L., *Joris Hoefnagel and the four elements: a study in 16th-century nature painting*, dissertation, Ann Arbor, 1989. Hendrix, Lee/Vignau-Wilberg, Thea, *Mira calligraphiae monumenta: a sixteenth-century calligraphic manuscript inscribed by Georg Bocskay and illuminated by Joris Hoefnagel*, J. Paul Getty Museum, Malibu (CA), 1992. *Praga Magica. L'Art à Prague au temps de Rodolphe II*, exhibition catalogue, Musée Magnin, Dijon, Réunion des musées nationaux, Paris, 2002.

MUSEUMS AND GALLERIES:

LILLE (MBA) - LOS ANGELES (Getty Mus.): *Mira Calligraphiae Monumenta* (1591-1596) - SAN FRANCISCO (California Palace of the Legion of Honor): *Archetypa studiaque patrisä* (1592, several engraved plates of this work) - SIBIU (Brukenthal Mus.) - WASHINGTON DC (NGA): *Animalia Qvadrvpedia et Reptilia (Terra)* (1575-1580, watercolour and gouache/vellum, several plates of this folio); *Animalia Volatilia et Amphibia (Aier)* (1575-1580, watercolour and gouache/vellum, several plates of this folio); *Animalia Rationalia et Insecta (Ignis)* (1575-1580, watercolour and gouache/vellum, several plates of this folio); *Animalia Aqvatilia et Cochiliata (Aqva)* (1575/1580, watercolour and gouache/vellum, several plates of this folio).

AUCTION RECORDS:

PARIS, 18-25 March 1901, *Diana Bathing*, FRF 330. LONDON, 13 May 1931, *Allegory of the Arts and Sciences*, GBP 26. LONDON, 6 July 1976, *Still-life with Flowers* (watercolour, 11 1/2 x 9 1/2 ins / 29 x 24 cm) GBP 7,500. LONDON, 30 June 1986, *View of Windsor Castle with Elegant Figures in the Foreground* (pen and brown ink with brown and blue wash, 10 1/2 x 16 1/4 ins / 26.4 x 41.5 cm) GBP 58,000.

HOEG, Josef van
Belgian, 19th century.
Active in Mechelen during the first half of the 19th century.
Painter. Genre scenes.

HOEG, Niels
Danish, 19th century.
Born 6 December 1858, in Sorring.
Sculptor.

Niels Hoeg studied at the Kunstakademi in Copenhagen. He executed mostly bust portraits.

HOEGEL, Mina
Austrian, 19th century.
Born 16 June 1849, in Vienna.
Painter.

A self-taught artist, she painted portraits and genre pictures.

HOEGEN, Peter
German, 19th century.
Born 2 July 1858, in Krefeld.
Painter.

He was a pupil of Steinles in Frankfurt.

HOEGENWALD, Matthias
German, 17th century.
Active in Passau at the end of the 17th century.
Sculptor.

He had a hand in the decoration of Passau Cathedral and sculpted the tomb of Archbishop Sebastian von Pötting.

HOEGER, Joseph
Austrian, 19th century.
Born 3 November 1801, in Vienna; died 13 May 1877, in Vienna.
Painter, watercolourist. Landscapes.

A pupil of Mössmer at the academy in Vienna, he was influenced by Rebell and his brother-in-law Gauermann, but it was mainly in the study of nature that he sought artistic expression. He travelled widely in Styria, South Tyrol and Upper Austria. In 1843, he became a member of the academy in Vienna, and in 1850 was appointed a professor there. He had great success with oil paintings and watercolours alike. His publications include several collections of model drawings and watercolours.

MUSEUMS AND GALLERIES:

VIENNA: *Part of Berchtesgaden Valley*; *Summer Landscape in the High Mountains*; 11 watercolours.

HOEGG, Alex Herman
Swedish, 19th century.
Born 19th century, in Sweden.
Engraver.

Alex Hoegg won a bronze medal at the Exposition Unverselle in Paris in 1889.

HOEGG, Joseph
German, 19th century.
Born 1826, in Koblenz.
Painter. Genre scenes.
He studied at the academy in Düsseldorf from 1840 to 1850 and with Rudolph Jordan. He exhibited from 1846.

HOEGGEEST, Cornelis
Dutch, 17th century.
Active in Holland c. 1625.
Engraver (etching/burin). Church interiors.
Cornelis Hoeggeest is known for his *Church Interior*.

HOEGGER, Andreas Renatus
Swiss, 19th century.
Born 19 April 1808, in St Gall; died 3 April 1854, in St Gall.
Painter, lithographer.
He was a pupil of J. J. Meyer in Meilen near Zurich, then studied at the academy in Munich. As a landscape artist, he was equally interested in painting and drawing. His favourite subject matter was the Swiss and Bavarian Alps.

HOEGGER, Augustus
American, 19th century.
Born c. 1846, in Switzerland; died 2 January 1908, in Philadelphia.
Painter.
Augustus Hoegger went to the USA while still a child. He died tragically as a result of burns suffered while attempting to save his work from a fire in his studio.

HØEGH, Niels
Danish, 19th - 20th century.
Born 6 December 1858, in Sorring; died 7 November 1912, in Aarhus.
Sculptor.
Høegh received an honourable mention at the Exposition Universelle in Paris in 1889.

HOEGLER, Anton Josef
German, 18th century.
Born c. 1705, in Würzburg; died 1786.
Painter.
A pupil of Kallenbach and then Byss, he initially painted landscapes, including views of Würzburg. Later he painted frescoes and subject pictures as well.

HOEGLER, Franz, or Högler
Austrian, 19th century.
Born 25 January 1802, in Vienna; died 12 May 1855, in Vienna.
Sculptor.
A student at the academy in Vienna, he sculpted mainly busts and statuettes. A noted work is a *Portrait of the Emperor Franz Joseph*.

HOEGLER, Jacob, or Högler
Austrian, 18th - 19th century.
Born 29 November 1763, in Vienna; died 13 March 1838, in Vienna.
Sculptor.

HOEGLER, Wolfgang, or Hôgler
Austrian, 17th - 18th century.
Born 29 October 1674, in Siezenheim, near Salzburg; died 1754, in Würzburg.
Miniaturist.
The father of Anton Hoegler, he worked for the cathedral and Archiepiscopal court in Salzburg.

HOEGNER, Simon
Austrian, 17th century.
Active in Tittmoning (Bavaria).
Sculptor.
A noted work by him is a *Crucifix* in the church at Anthering near Salzburg.

HOEHN, Georg
German, 19th century.
Born 1 July 1812, in Neustrelitz; died 21 January 1879, in Dessau.
Painter. Landscapes, architectural views.
A pupil of Blechen, he lived in Berlin and Dessau.
MUSEUMS AND GALLERIES:
HANOVER: *Landscape; Monument to Queen Louisa at Hohenzieritz.*

HOEK, Hans van
Dutch, 20th - 21st century.
Born 1947, in Deurne, near Antwerp.
Active in Canada and South Africa.
Painter. Figures, nudes, still-lifes.
From 1962 to 1969, Van Hoek attended the Koninklijke Academie voor Kunst en Vormgeving, in 's Hertogenbosch. He has participated in various group exhibitions, notably the 9th Biennale de Paris in 1975.
MUSEUMS AND GALLERIES:
AMSTERDAM (Stedelijk Mus.): *Still-life with Ivory Elephant* (1973-1974).
AUCTION RECORDS:
LONDON, 25 March 1993, *Buddha by a Vase Surrounded by Flowers* (1981, oil on canvas, 51¼ x 67¼ ins / 129.9 x 170.6 cm) GBP 9,200. AMSTERDAM, 31 May 1994, *Seated Nude* (pencil and watercolour/paper, 23 x 30 ins / 58.5 x 76.5 cm) NLG 3,220. AMSTERDAM, 10 Dec 1996, *Cellist* (brush and black ink/Japanese paper, 19¼ x 26½ ins / 49 x 67 cm) NLG 3,690. AMSTERDAM, 8 June 2000, *Dark Landscape: Banks of Winding Brook* (1986, oil on canvas, 78 x 180 ins / 198 x 458 cm) NLG 20,000. AMSTERDAM, 8 June 2000, *Black Water* (1982, oil on canvas, 78 x 98 ins / 197 x 249 cm) NLG 34,000. AMSTERDAM, 4 Dec 2001, *After Rubens* (pencil and charcoal, 59 x 43 ins / 150 x 110 cm) EUR 2,500. AMSTERDAM, 4 Dec 2001, *Untitled* (watercolour, 29 x 41 ins / 74 x 104 cm) EUR 2,800. AMSTERDAM, 3 Dec 2002, *Freesias* (1986, watercolour, 29 x 41 ins / 74 x 105 cm) EUR 3,000. AMSTERDAM, 3 Dec 2002, *Peelandschap* (1989, charcoal and watercolour, 29 x 40 ins / 73 x 102 cm) EUR 3,200. AMSTERDAM, 3 June 2003, *Cross between Trees* (1988, oil and chalk on canvas, 67 x 63 ins / 169 x 160 cm) EUR 4,000. AMSTERDAM, 2 Dec 2003, *Buddha with Vase Surrounded with Flowers* (1980-1981, oil on canvas, 51 x 67 ins / 130 x 170 cm) EUR 15,000. AMSTERDAM, 8 June 2004, *Crucifixion I* (watercolour and black chalk, 41 x 29 ins / 105 x 74 cm) EUR 3,000.

HOEK, Johan
Dutch, 18th century.
Died 20 February 1732.
Painter. Seascapes.
In 1725, Johan Hoek became a member of the Alkmaar painters' guild.

HOELBE, Rudolph
German, 19th century.
Born 6 October 1848, in Lemgo.
Sculptor.
He trained in Dresden and Leipzig, and under Schilling, subsequently working in Dresden. His work includes genre statuettes, busts and religious sculptures.

HOELLOFF, Curt
German, 20th century.
Born 29 May 1887, in Leipzig.
Engraver.

Hoelloff studied in Leipzig and Dresden. He was a sculptor for a while and went on to engrave many decorative bookplates.

HOELPERL, Anton
German, 19th century.
Born 1820, in Schlaggenwald (Horni Slavkov), Bohemia; died 1888, in Prague.
Painter. Portraits, genre scenes.
After working for porcelain makers, he specialised in portraits.

HOELTZ, Johann Georg
German, 18th century.
Active in Altheim (Württemberg).
Painter.
He worked for the church at Wurmlingen.

HOELZEL, Adolf. See **HÖLZEL**

HOELZEL, Bonaventura
Flemish School, 17th century.
Engraver (burin).

HOELZEL, Moritz
Bohemian, 19th century.
Born 18 January 1841, in Prague; died 24 July 1902, in Bardejov.
Sculptor.
Moritz Hoelzel studied at the academies in Prague and Vienna. He is known for both religious and non-religious sculptures. One of his most important works is the *Statue of the Poet Netzer* in Marburg.

HOELZL, Andreas
German, 18th century.
Painter. Portraits.
A work mentioned is the *Portrait of Caspar de Jacquemod and His Wife*. He worked mainly in Freising, near Munich.

HOELZL, Felix
German, 18th century.
Active in Ingolstadt in the middle of the 18th century.
Painter.
He decorated several churches in Ingolstadt and Straubing.

HOELZL, Josef
Austrian, 19th century.
Born 24 December 1809, in Obermais, Merann (now Merano, Italy); died 10 December 1891, in Wilten (Innsbruck).
Painter.
A student at the academy in Vienna, he subsequently painted portraits and religious paintings.
MUSEUMS AND GALLERIES:
INNSBRUCK: *Study of heads* - MERANO: five paintings.

HOELZL, Joseph
German, 18th century.
Born 1749, in Ingolstadt; died 1783.
Painter.
The son of Felix Hoelzl, he was his pupil and partner.

HOEN, real name: Nishiyama Seisho; childhood name: Shitatsu, artist names: Hoen, Chiichi, Kan'ei
Japanese, 19th century.
Born 1804; died 1867.
Print artist.
A pupil of Keibun (1779-1843), Hoen worked in Osaka as a bird-and-flower and figure painter. Together with Hiroshige III, Kuniteru, Sadahide and Kunisada II, he was one of the final generation of *ukiyo-e* masters, whose work was chosen by the Tokugawa government to be shown at the Paris Exposition Universelle in 1867.

HOEN, Alfred Georges
French, 19th - 20th century.
Born 3 January 1869, in Bar-le-Duc; died 26 November 1954, in Paris.
Active in the USA from 1918 to 1940.
Painter. Portraits.
After having learned the art of staining glass with Champigneulle, Alfred Hoen went to Paris in 1890. He studied at the École des Arts Décoratifs and the École des Beaux-Arts, where he was a pupil of Gérome. He was a society portrait artist in France, as well as in the USA but also painted landscapes, seascapes and scenes from both world wars. He settled in France in 1940.

Alfred Hoen exhibited at the Salon des Artistes Français, of which he became a member in 1910.
AUCTION RECORDS:
CORBEIL-ESSONNES, 9 March 1991, *A Corner of My Studio in New York Between 1932 and 1939* (oil on cardboard, 6 x 10 1/4 ins / 15.5 x 26 cm) FRF 12,500. PARIS, 10-11 April 1997, *Young Tunisian Woman with Green Apples* (oil on panel, 6 3/4 x 6 3/4 ins / 17 x 17 cm) FRF 8,000.

HOEN, Cornelis Petrus T', or Cornelis Peter
Dutch, 19th century.
Born 3 March 1814, in Amsterdam; died 1880.
Painter. Genre scenes, landscapes with figures.
Cornelis Hoen was a pupil of Antonie Waldorp.
AUCTION RECORDS:
LONDON, 19 May 1971, *Winter Landscape*, GBP 400. AMSTERDAM, 10 Feb 1988, *View of Nassaulaan in The Hague with the Old Riding School of King William II* (oil on canvas, 14 1/2 x 18 3/4 ins / 37 x 47.5 cm) NLG 1,495. AMSTERDAM, 5 June 1990, *Skaters on a Frozen River Lined by Mills* (oil on canvas, 17 3/4 x 25 3/4 ins / 45 x 65.5 cm) NLG 5,750. AMSTERDAM, 6 Nov 1990, *Mill by a Frozen River with Figures* (oil on panel, 9 1/4 x 11 1/2 ins / 23.5 x 29.5 cm) NLG 3,680. AMSTERDAM, 30 Oct 1991, *Winter Landscape with Skaters near Moored Vessels* (1849, oil on panel, 8 1/2 x 11 1/2 ins / 21.5 x 29 cm) NLG 14,950. AMSTERDAM, 14-15 April 1992, *Winter Landscape with Skaters on a Frozen River near a Ruined Tower* (oil on panel, 9 3/4 x 14 1/4 ins / 25 x 36 cm) NLG 17,250. AMSTERDAM, 8 Nov 1994, *Winter Landscape with Figures and Boats Trapped in Ice on the River* (1843, oil on panel, 14 1/4 x 18 3/4 ins / 36.5 x 47.5 cm) NLG 13,800. LONDON, 10 Feb 1995, *Frozen River Landscape with Skaters near a Windmill* (1846, oil on panel, 12 3/4 x 17 1/4 ins / 32.4 x 43.8 cm) GBP 3,680. AMSTERDAM, 5 Nov 1996, *Skaters on a Frozen River* (oil on panel, 9 1/2 x 12 1/2 ins / 24 x 31.5 cm) NLG 6,136. GRAVENHAGE, 7 Nov 2001, *Icy View* (oil on panel, 15 x 10 ins / 37 x 26 cm) NLG 5,000. AMSTERDAM, 23 April 2002, *Winter Landscape with Figures on the Ice* (oil on panel, 8 x 11 ins / 21 x 29 cm) EUR 8,000. AMSTERDAM, 23 April 2002, *River Landscape at Sunset* (1845, oil on panel, 9 x 11 ins / 22 x 29 cm) EUR 12,000. MUNICH, 17 March 2004, *Dutch Landscape in Winter* (oil on panel, 9 x 12 ins / 22 x 30 cm) EUR 1,800. AMSTERDAM, 21 April 2004, *Figures on the Ice at Dusk* (1846, oil on panel, 16 x 21 ins / 41 x 54 cm) EUR 12,000.

HOENDERMAN, G.
17th century.
Painter.
A landscape in the style of Berchem signed *G. Hoenderman* is recorded.

HOENDERMANS, Johannes
Dutch, 17th century.
Active in Delft c. 1680.
Painter. Figures.
AUCTION RECORDS:
PARIS, 10 June 1980, *The Gallant Smoker* (oil on wood, 9 1/2 x 7 ins / 24 x 18 cm) FRF 7,200.

HOENE, Max
German, 20th century.

Born 22 December 1884, in Rudolstadt.
Sculptor.
Hoene studied in Munich. He created several life-size and larger than life-size statues.

HOENEM, F. de
French, 19th century.
Active in Paris.
Painter. Genre scenes.
MUSEUMS AND GALLERIES:
PONTOISE: *Place Pigalle*.

HOENEMANN, Martin
German, 19th century.
Born 5 March 1858, in Berlin.
Painter, engraver.
He gained an honourable mention in Paris in 1909. He did many engravings from painters of the 19th century.

HOENERBACH, Margarete
German, 19th century.
Born 9 September 1848, in Deutz, Cologne.
Painter, sculptor, engraver.
A pupil of Rethel, she travelled widely in France and Italy. A notable work is her *Tomb of Rector Guido Hauck*.

HOENICH, Paul Konrad
Israeli, 20th century.
Born 1907, in Vienna.
Painter, installation artist.
Kinetic Art.
Paul Konrad Hoenich felt that his fauvist paintings did not succeed in representing light as he wished, and so embarked on the creation of works in which there would be movement deriving from the known course of the sun and the chance variations of the wind. He based his procedures on observations made at the Mount Carmel observatory near Haifa. He built a special installation for collecting rays of light which he called *Robot-Picture*.
BIBLIOGRAPHY:
Popper, Frank, *Naissance de l'Art cinétique*, Gauthier-Villars, Paris, 1967.

HOENIG, Georg Joseph
German, 18th - 19th century.
Born 21 October 1763, in Büchenbach (Bavaria); died 3 September 1816, in Allersburg (Bavaria).
Engraver.
He worked at the court of Count Drexel in Regensburg.

HOENIGER, Paul
German, 19th - 20th century.
Born 9 March 1865, in Berlin; died 1924.
Painter. Portraits, genre scenes, landscapes.
Hoeniger went to live in Paris after studying in Munich and Berlin. He painted portraits, landscapes and genre scenes. He exhibited his work at the Salon des Artistes Français in 1896, 1897 and 1904, and in Berlin from 1889.

AUCTION RECORDS:
LONDON, 27 Nov 1985, *Inside the Moulin de la Galette, Paris* (1894, oil on canvas, 39 1/4 x 28 ins / 100 x 71 cm) GBP 13,000. NEW YORK, 24 Nov 1987, *Parisian Woman* (1896, oil on canvas, 25 x 18 1/2 ins / 63.5 x 47 cm) USD 6,250. NEW YORK, 3 May 1989, *Village Street in Holland* (1918, oil on canvas, 23 3/4 x 28 3/4 ins / 60.3 x 73 cm) USD 72,150. NEW YORK, 19 July 1990, *Woman Wearing a Hat* (1896, oil on canvas, 25 x 18 1/2 ins / 63.5 x 46.8 cm) USD 6,600.

HOENIGSMANN, Rela
Austrian, 19th century.
Born 1865, in Lemberg (now Lviv, Ukraine).
Active in Munich and Austria.
Painter.
Rela Hoenigsmann exhibited in Munich and Berlin.

HOENING, Johann Lorenz
German, 18th century.
Active in Nuremberg c. 1700.
Engraver.
He is noted for his portraits of kings of Poland, also portraits of Charles XII of Sweden and Ferdinand III.

HOENINGHAUS, Adolf
German, 19th century.
Born 1811, in Krefeld; died 30 September 1882, in Krefeld.
Painter. Landscapes.
From 1829 to 1835, he was a pupil of J W Schirmer in Düsseldorf, after which he went to Italy to study. He did compositions in landscapes.
MUSEUMS AND GALLERIES:
COLOGNE: *View of St Peter's in Rome* - DÜSSELDORF (Kunstmus.): *Landscape*.

HOENOW, Max
German, 19th - 20th century.
Born 16 June 1851, in Berlin; died 3 February 1909, in Berlin.
Painter. Landscapes.
Hoenow painted portraits initially, then concentrated mainly on landscape painting. He studied at the academy in Berlin and with Steffeck. He exhibited his work in Berlin from 1883.
AUCTION RECORDS:
LINDAU, 7 Oct 1987, *Landscape with Mill* (oil on canvas, 20 1/2 x 24 3/4 ins / 52 x 63 cm) DEM 4,800.

HOENRAET, Luc
Belgian, 20th century.
Born 28 June 1941, in Alost.
Painter, draughtsman, engraver.
Hoenraet attended the Institut de St Luc, Schaerbeek. He lives and works in Brussels. He has exhibited since 1964 in Brussels, Antwerp, Rome and Paris. His painting is abstract, verging both on the informal and action painting.

HOENSTROP, Meynard
German, 14th century.
Active in Lübeck at the end of the 14th century.
Painter.

HOEPFINGER, Felix
German, 16th century.
Active in Nuremberg at the end of the 16th century.
Engraver.

HOEPPE, Ferdinand Bernhard. See **HOPPE**

HOEPPENER, Hugo
German, 19th century.
Born 8 October 1868, in Lübeck.
Painter, illustrator.
He trained in Lübeck and Munich, but subsequently settled in Woltersdorf near Berlin. A great traveller, he sent a number of drawings to newspapers. He also did paintings and symbolical drawings.

HOEPPNER, Julius
German, 19th century.
Born 27 October 1839, in Lichtenberg; died 26 February 1893, in Dresden.
Painter, watercolourist.
He studied at the academy of fine arts in Dresden.

HOER, Andreas
Swiss, 16th century.

Active in St Gall at the end of the 16th century.
Glass painter.

HOER, Joseph
German, 18th century.
Born 29 November 1732, in Blasiwald (Schluchsee, Black Forest); died 9 March 1785, in Freiburg.
Sculptor.
He studied in Riedlingen. He did decorative work for churches and castles in the small towns of the Black Forest region.

HOERBERG, Pehr
Swedish, 18th - 19th century.
Born 31 January 1746, in Småland; died 24 January 1816, in Falla.
Painter, engraver.
Pehr Hoerberg was the son of a peasant. Drawn to painting, he left his farming work to paint buildings and cultivate his art, hitherto expressed only in drawings. However, it was not until 1783, at the age of 37, that he became a pupil at the academy in Stockholm. There he developed his own style to which he would consistently adhere. He became a member of the academy in 1797 and Jean-Baptiste Jules Bernadotte, Charles XIV, gave him a stipend. He painted religious, history and genre subjects. Among his first works are numerous altarpieces that were sent throughout Småland and Golergötland. His painting had many qualities, for he had a rich imagination and a certain grandeur of conception. However, he was unable to surmount certain technical difficulties. His style was also evident in his work as a copper engraver, deriving from the work of the 15th- and 16th-century Italian masters.
MUSEUMS AND GALLERIES:
OSLO: *Christ Curing a Blind Man* - STOCKHOLM: *The Annointing of Saul as King; The Interiors of a Thatched Cottage and a Charcoal Burner's House in Småland.*

HOERBST, Baptist
Swiss, 19th century.
Born 1 December 1850, in Zurich.
Sculptor.
He was a pupil of J C Dielmann in Frankfurt. The son of Georg Hoerbst, he travelled widely in Austria and Italy.

HOERBST, Franz R.
German, 18th century.
Active in Laufen (Bavaria).
Painter.
He is noted for his religious works in Arnsdorf, Salzburg.

HOERBST, Georg
Swiss, 19th century.
Born 1823, in Tannheim (Tyrol); died 1876, in Zurich.
Sculptor.
He was the father of Baptist and Hans Hoerbst.

HOERBST, Hans
Swiss, 19th century.
Born 29 April 1859, in Zurich.
Sculptor.
This artist worked in Chicago, where he sculpted monuments and busts before returning to his native town for good.

HOERGER, Ferenc Antal
Hungarian, 18th century.
Active in Buda (Budapest) at the beginning of the 18th century.
Sculptor.

HOERL, Johann Franz
Austrian, 17th - 18th century.
Born 1653, in Vienna; died 3 May 1742, in Vienna.
Painter, decorative designer. Wall decorations.
He is credited with work at the castle of Laxenburg, near Vienna.

HOERLE, Heinrich. See **HÖRLE**

HOERLEN, Leonhart
German, 16th century.
Died c. 1513.
Active in Breslau (now Wroclaw, Poland).
Painter, sculptor (wood).

HOERLING, Johann Fredrik
Swedish, 18th century.
Born 1718, in Stockholm; died 12 November 1786, in Stockholm.
Painter. History painting, portraits.
Johann Hoerling worked a great deal in Italy towards the end of his life. Around 1740, he was a pupil of Carel van Loo in Paris.
MUSEUMS AND GALLERIES:
STOCKHOLM: *Portrait* (pastel).

HOERMANN, Franz Xaver
German, 19th century.
Born 29 November 1822, in Burg; died 1 April 1896, in Traunstein.
Sculptor.
He was a pupil of Schwanthaler in Munich.

HOERMANN, Joseph Ignaz
German, 19th century.
Born c. 1775, in Obergünzburg (near Kaufbeuren); died 30 May 1820, in Augsburg.
Engraver, caricaturist. Portraits, landscapes.
He was also a caricaturist of talent.

HOERMANN, Theodor von. See **HÖRMANN Theodor von**

HOERMANN VON GUTTENBERG, Christian Friedrich
German, 18th century.
Active in Augsburg.
Painter, engraver.
He did a noted portrait of Chancellor C. U. Ketelhodt.

HOERNER
Bohemian, 18th century.
Died in Budejovice.
Painter. Still-lifes.

HOERNER, Johan
Danish, 18th century.
Born 28 January 1711, in Edebo; died 10 March 1763, in Copenhagen.
Painter.
Johan Hoerner was a pupil of Johan Henrik Scheffel in Stockholm. He executed mostly portraits.
AUCTION RECORDS:
COPENHAGEN, 10-12 Sept 1997, *Portrait of Nils Lange* (1736, oil on canvas, 21 1/4 x 16 1/4 ins / 54 x 41.5 cm) DKK 10,000. COPENHAGEN, 1 June 1999, *Portrait of a Young Lady in a Pale Blue Dress* (oil on canvas, 30 x 24 ins / 75 x 61 cm) DKK 17,000. COPENHAGEN, 2 Dec 2002, *Portrait of Thalia Storm* (1756, oil on canvas, 29 x 25 ins / 74 x 64 cm) DKK 70,000. COPENHAGEN, 26 May 2003, *Portrait of a Nobleman in Armour and Red Jacket* (oil on canvas, 31 x 25 ins / 78 x 64 cm) DKK 15,000.

HOERSCHELMANN, Rolf E. von
German, 20th century.
Born 1885, in Tartu.
Painter, engraver.
Von Hoerschelmann was active in Munich. He mainly illustrated high-quality books.

HOERSTEN, B. van
German, 19th century.
Active in Oldenburg c. 1820.
Sculptor.
He worked mainly in Vienna.
MUSEUMS AND GALLERIES:
OLDENBURG: several works.

HOERTER, August
German, 19th century.
Born 5 August 1834, in Elberfeld; died 23 October 1906, in Karlsruhe.
Painter. Portraits, landscapes.
He studied at the academy in Düsseldorf and with Lessing in Karslruhe. He exhibited in Paris (1867), Dresden, Vienna, Munich and Berlin.

HOERUP
German, 17th century.
Painter. Portraits.
Noted for his portraits of *Count A G von Oldenburg* and *Duke John of Schleswig Holstein.*

HOERWARTER, Joseph Eugen
Austrian, 19th century.
Born 11 August 1854, in Vienna.
Painter. History painting.
He was a pupil of Eisenmenger.

HOESCH, Hans
German, 19th century.
Born 2 March 1855, in Nuremberg; died 14 January 1902, in Munich.
Painter. Portraits, genre scenes, interiors.
He completed his training in Munich, where he exhibited regularly from 1890.
AUCTION RECORDS:
NEW YORK, 2 April 1976, *Interior Scene* (oil on canvas, 28 x 21 ins / 71 x 53.5 cm) USD 3,400. NEW YORK, 21 Jan 1978, *The Young Widow* (1884, oil on canvas, 37 1/2 x 30 3/4 ins / 95 x 78 cm) USD 4,000.

HOËSE, Jean de La. See **LA HOËSE Jean de**

HOESEL, Oskar Erich
German, 19th century.
Born 5 April 1869, in Annaberg.
Sculptor.
A pupil of Schilling and W Diez at the academy in Dresden, he joined the staff of the academy in 1908. He gained gold medals in Berlin (1896) and Paris (Universal Exhibition, 1900).
MUSEUMS AND GALLERIES:
BERLIN: *On Horseback.*

HOESL, Fridolin Fritz
Swiss, 19th century.
Born 31 March 1848, in Glarus; died 1902, in Trübbach (near Buchs).
Painter, decorative designer.
He worked mostly in Zurich, Bern and St Gall.

HOESLINGER, Joseph
Austrian, 19th century.
Active in Vienna at the beginning of the 19th century.
Engraver.
Two landscapes by him are known.

HOESS, Eugen Ludwig
German, 19th century.
Born 1 October 1866, in Immenstadt.
Painter, engraver.
He worked mainly in Munich and Frankfurt.

HOESS, Nikolaus, the Elder
Austrian, 18th century.
Born 1736, in Salzburg; died January 1806.
Sculptor.
He worked for the Archbishop of Salzburg.

HOESS, Nikolaus, the Younger
Austrian, 19th century.
Born 1780, in Salzburg.
Draughtsman.
The son of the elder Nikolaus Hoess, he did views of Salzburg.

HOESSEIN, Dato' Mohd Enas
Indonesian, 20th century.
Born 1924, in Bogor, Indonesia; died 1995.
Active in Malaya from 1947.
Painter.
Hossein arrived in Malaya in 1947. The national art gallery in Kuala Lumpur organized a retrospective in his honour in 1966, and in 1990 he was awarded the title 'royal painter' by the Sultan of Selangoe.
AUCTION RECORDS:
SINGAPORE, 5 Oct 1996, *Head of a Bajau Man* (1993, pastel/paper, 18 1/4 x 12 1/4 ins / 46.5 x 31 cm) SGD 9,200. SINGAPORE, 27 Sept 1997, *Portrait* (1963, pastel/paper) SGD 9,200. SINGAPORE, 28 March 1999, *Portrait of a Nude* (oil on canvas, 26 x 22 ins / 67 x 57 cm) SGD 8,000.

HOESSEL, Herkules
German, 19th century.
Active at the beginning of the 19th century.
Draughtsman, engraver.
He worked at the court of Bavaria, principally producing views of towns.

HOESSEL, Johann Baptist
German, 18th - 19th century.
Active in Dessau.
Engraver (aquatint).
He appears to have travelled to Russia and England. He is credited with engravings after Reiffenstein and R Hackert.

HOESSLIN, George von
Hungarian, 19th - 20th century.
Born 20 March 1851, in Pest; died 1923, in Munich.
Painter. Mythological subjects, genre scenes, portraits.
George von Hoesslin went to America when young, returning in 1871 and settling in Munich. He spent some time in Italy and then returned again to Munich.
AUCTION RECORDS:
LONDON, 7 Dec 1907, *Reverie*, GBP 6. LONDON, 25 April 1912, *Art*, GBP 3. LONDON, 16 June 1978, *Young Archer* (oil on canvas, 17 1/4 x 19 1/2 ins / 43.5 x 49.5 cm) GBP 600. NEW YORK, 25 Jan 1980, *Student* (oil on canvas, 20 1/4 x 25 1/2 ins / 51.5 x 65 cm) USD 1,700. LONDON, 18 March 1992, *Ulysses Lured onto the Rocks by the Sirens* (oil on canvas, 42 1/4 x 72 1/2 ins / 107 x 184 cm) GBP 4,950. ZURICH, 21 March 2000, *Peaceful Evening* (oil on canvas, 33 x 49 ins / 83 x 125 cm) CHF 4,000.

HOET, Gérard, the Elder
Dutch, 17th - 18th century.
Born 22 August 1648, in Bommel; died 2 December 1733, in The Hague.
Painter, engraver. Religious subjects, mythological subjects, portraits, genre scenes, interiors with figures.
Utrecht School, The Hague School.
Gérard Hoet the Elder studied under his father, the glass painter Mozes Hoet, and later under Warnard van Ryzen and Cornelis van Poelenborch. When the French took Bommel in 1672 he decided to leave for The Hague and worked in the city for General Salis. He later went to Amsterdam and France before settling in Utrecht, where he founded a school around 1696. In 1715 he became a member of the Guild of St Luke in The Hague.

Even during his lifetime, Hoet's paintings were very fashionable and achieved high prices. He wrote a book on painting and as an engraver left some interesting examples of mezzotint work.

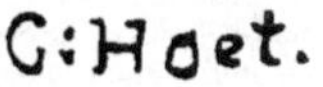

Museums and Galleries:
Amsterdam: *Two Idylls; Marriage of Alexander the Great; Homage Given to Alexander the Great; Family Group* - Avignon: *Armida Preparing to Follow Rinaldo* - Bergamo: *Catacombs* - Glasgow: *Callisto and Diana* - Leipzig: *Samson Overwhelmed; Idolatry of Solomon* - London (Dulwich Picture Gal.): *Apollo and Daphne* (oil on canvas); *Pan and Syrinx* (oil on canvas) - Orléans: *Young Man Playing the Flute* - Rouen: *Marriage of Alexander* - St Petersburg (Hermitage): *Adoration of the Magi* - Stockholm: *Achilles Disguised as a Woman, Recognised by Ulysses* - The Hague: *Card Players* - Utrecht: *The Generosity of Scipio* - Vienna: *Moses Striking the Rock; Venus and Adonis; Death of Endymion.*

Auction records:
Paris, 22 March 1897, *The Feast of Pomona,* FRF 600. Paris, 3-4 Dec 1903, *Guardroom Interior,* FRF 180. London, 27 Jan 1908, *Pomona and Omphale,* GBP 6. London, 16 March 1908, *Young Woman Playing the Guitar,* GBP 19. Paris, 29 May 1908, *Thomyri,* FRF 230. London, 16 July 1909, *Herodias Dancing before Herod,* GBP 16. Paris, 8 April 1910, *Scene from Roman History,* FRF 400. Paris, 27 Jan 1921, *Portrait of a Young Woman,* FRF 900. Paris, 17 June 1924, *Rinaldo in the Gardens of Armida,* FRF 960. Paris, 8 June 1925, *Rinaldo and Armida,* FRF 1,280. Paris, 29 Jan 1932, *Mercury's Message,* FRF 1,050. Paris, 25 June 1943, *The Fortunate Thief,* FRF 17,500. Paris, 16 Oct 1946, *Diana and Actaeon,* FRF 33,000; *Triumph of Silenus,* FRF 31,500. Vienna, 11 March 1980, *Tea Time* (oil on panel, 6 1/2 x 5 ins / 16.5 x 12.5 cm) ATS 180,000. Amsterdam, 18 Nov 1980, *Entellus Victorious over Dares* (pen and wash heightened with white/black chalk, 8 x 12 3/4 ins / 20.5 x 32.2 cm) NLG 2,100. London, 21 April 1982, *Judgement of Solomon* (oil on canvas, 50 x 81 ins / 127 x 206 cm) GBP 12,500. London, 15 April 1983, *Sacrifice to Ceres* (oil on canvas, 21 x 27 1/4 ins / 53.2 x 69.2 cm) GBP 4,800. London, 2 July 1985, *Aaron before the Pharaoh* (grey wash heightened with white, 12 3/4 x 8 1/2 ins / 32.5 x 21.5 cm) GBP 1,050. London, 11 Dec 1985, *Bacchanalia in an Italian Landscape* (oil on panel, 10 x 11 1/2 ins / 25.5 x 29.5 cm) GBP 8,200. Paris, 4 March 1988, *Joseph Sold by his Brothers* (brush and wash, 7 1/2 x 18 ins / 19 x 45.5 cm) FRF 3,000. Paris, 11 Oct 1988, *The Feast of Pomona* (oil on canvas, 17 3/4 x 20 3/4 ins / 45 x 53 cm) FRF 98,000. Paris, 31 Jan 1991, *Christ and the Children* (oil on canvas, 26 x 33 ins / 66 x 84 cm) FRF 45,000. Paris, 25 June 1991, *The Feast of Pomona* (oil on canvas, 17 3/4 x 20 1/2 ins / 45 x 52 cm) FRF 140,000. New York, 17 Jan 1992, *Diana and Callisto* (oil/copper, 13 3/4 x 17 1/4 ins / 34.9 x 43.8 cm) USD 41,800. New York, 21 May 1992, *Judgement of Solomon* (oil on canvas, 19 1/4 x 22 1/2 ins / 48.9 x 57.1 cm) USD 2,860. London, 23 Oct 1992, *Banter in a Park* (oil on canvas, 13 x 11 ins / 33 x 27 cm) GBP 7,700. New York, 14 Jan 1994, *Judgement of Paris* (oil on canvas, 14 3/4 x 18 1/4 ins / 37.5 x 46.4 cm) USD 5,750. Paris, 31 March 1994, *Antiochus and Stratonice* (oil on canvas, 16 1/4 x 20 1/2 ins / 41 x 52 cm) FRF 28,000. Monaco, 14 June 1996, *Diana and Cupid* (oil on panel, 10 x 13 3/4 ins / 25.6 x 35 cm) FRF 29,250. London, 30 Oct 1996, *Portrait of a Gentleman in a Blue Coat and Lightbrown Cloak with his Hands on a Marble Balustrade* (oil on canvas, 20 1/4 x 16 1/4 ins / 51.5 x 41 cm) GBP 2,300. Amsterdam, 10 Nov 1997, *Haman before Ahasuerus and Esther* (oil on panel, 11 1/2 x 13 3/4 ins / 29.2 x 34.8 cm) NLG 59,966. Vienna, 30 March 2000, *Portrait of a Gentleman* (oil on canvas, 26 x 21 ins / 65 x 54 cm) ATS 100,000. London, 5 July 2000, *Celebrants at the Shrine of Diana* (oil on canvas, 20 x 25 ins / 52 x 63 cm) GBP 8,000. London, 1 Nov 2001, *Portrait of the Botanist Jan Commelin* (oil on canvas, 20 x 18 ins / 52 x 45 cm) GBP 22,000. London, 11 Dec 2001, *Esther Presented by Mordecai to King Ahasuerus* (oil on canvas, 22 x 26 ins / 56 x 65 cm) GBP 9,000. London, 10 Dec 2002, *Rachel and Jacob. Rachel and Laban* (1674, oil on panel, a pair, 7 x 9 ins / 19 x 24 cm) GBP 9,500. London, 21 April 2004, *Market Scene with a Commedia dell'Arte Performance* (oil on canvas, 25 x 35 ins / 63 x 88 cm) GBP 30,000. London, 6 July 2004, *Cephalus and Procris* (oil on canvas, 14 x 11 ins / 36 x 27 cm) GBP 3,400.

HOET, Gérard, the Younger

Dutch, 18th century.
Born 1698; died 1760, in The Hague.
Painter. Portraits.

Gérard Hoet the Younger was the eldest son of Gérard Hoet. He was also his pupil and collaborator.

Auction records:
Amsterdam, 11 Nov 1997, *Bust Portrait of a Young Girl and Boy Playing with a Dog and Cockatoo in a Draped Window Opening* (oil on canvas/panel, 12 3/4 x 10 ins / 32.5 x 25.4 cm) NLG 9,225. New York, 28 Jan 1999, *Diana Discovering the Pregnancy of Callisto* (oil on copper, 14 x 17 ins / 35 x 44 cm) USD 50,000. London, 8 July 1999, *Mercury and Herse* (oil on copper, 22 x 27 ins / 56 x 68 cm) GBP 17,000. Vienna, 4 Oct 2000, *Rest on the Flight to Egypt* (oil on canvas, 15 x 20 ins / 38 x 50 cm) ATS 50,000. Malmö, 18 Nov 2000, *Moses Defending the Seven Daughters of Jethro* (oil on canvas, 14 x 19 ins / 36 x 49 cm) SEK 14,500. Vienna, 22 March 2001, *Abstinence of Scipio* (oil on panel, 15 x 19 ins / 37 x 47 cm) ATS 130,000. Venice, 7 July 2001, *Offer to Venus* (oil on canvas, 17 x 21 ins / 43 x 54 cm) ITL 8,000,000. Munich, 6 Dec 2002, *Odysseus and Calypso* (oil on panel, 13 x 17 ins / 33 x 43 cm) EUR 16,500.

HOET, H. D.

Dutch, 18th century.
Painter. Portraits, still-lifes.

Museums and Galleries:
Aachen (Suermondt-Ludwig Mus.): *Portrait of a Man.*

HOET, Hendrick Mozes

Dutch, 17th century.
Died c. 1665.
Active in Bomnuel.
Painter (glass).

Hendrik Mozes Hoet was the father of Gérard Hoet.

HOET, Hendrik Jacob

Dutch, 18th century.
Born c. 1693; died 1733, in The Hague.
Painter. Genre scenes, village scenes, flowers, fruit.

Hendrik Jacob Hoet was the second son of Gérard Hoet and painted in the style of Van Huysum. He died shortly after his father.

Auction records:
London, 22 April 1929, *Village Scenes* (two paintings) GBP 42. Cologne, 26 March 1982, *Tavern Scene* (oil on canvas, 25 1/4 x 30 1/4 ins / 64 x 77 cm) DEM 18,000. Amsterdam, 15 May 1984, *Elegant Figures at a Window* (oil on panel, 17 1/2 x 12 1/2 ins / 44.5 x 32 cm) NLG 26,000.

HOET, Jan

Flemish, 15th century.
Active in Antwerp, c. 1465-1474.
Painter (glass).
Flemish School.

HOETERICKX, Émile

Belgian, 19th - 20th century.
Born 1858, in Brussels; died May 1923, in Brussels.
Painter, watercolourist. Landscapes.

Hoeterickx spent some time in London. He was awarded a bronze medal at the Exposition Universelle in Paris in 1900.

Museums and Galleries:
Abbeville: *London* - Antwerp: *La Cambre Wood* - Lille: *London Docks*.
Auction records:
Lokeren, 18 Oct 1980, *Conjurer* (1880, oil on canvas, 17 3/4 x 29 1/2 ins / 45 x 75 cm) BEF 60,000. Lokeren, 11 Oct 1997, *On the Beach* (watercolour, 25 1/4 x 21 1/4 ins / 64 x 54 cm) BEF 54,000.

HOETGER, Bernhard

German, 19th - 20th century.
Born 4 May 1874, in Hörde (Westphalia); died 18 July 1949; in Interlaken or Beatenberg (Canton of Bern).
From 1933 active in Switzerland.
Sculptor (including bronze/majolica/ceramics), painter (including gouache), engraver, draughtsman, architect, graphic designer. Statuettes, figurines.
Jugendstil.

Darmstadt Artists' Colony, Worpswede Artists' Colony.
Bernhard Hoetger entered the Kunstakademie in Düsseldorf in 1898 after an apprenticeship as a stone-cutter where he was taught by Carl Janssen. From 1900 to 1907, he lived in Paris, where he met Rodin and even worked in his studio. In 1905, he was one of the first to exhibit at the Salon d'Automne. On his return to Germany, he was appointed to a professorship in Darmstadt in1911 where he remained until 1919. While there, he was closely involved with the artists' colony in Mathildenhöhe. In 1933-1934, when the Nazis came to power, he left Germany for Italy, then travelled to France, Spain, Portugal, and finally Switzerland.

At first, he was influenced by Rodin and Constantin Meunier; then he turned to archaic Greek sculpture. In the decade after 1910, it was his ambition to integrate sculpture groups within an architectural setting, as in *Fountain of Justice* in Eberfeld in 1910, or his much admired *Platanenhain* in Darmstadt, a decorative sculpture (four figures and a fountain) of a grove of plane trees, the theme of which was the cycle of life. From 1914 to 1929, he lived in the community of artists of Worpswede, near Bremen, on the North Sea. In Worpswede he designed furniture and buildings (Café Worpswede, Grosse Kunstschau, Kreatives Haus) and domestic houses, including his own, giving prominence to their fabric and construction.

He was self-taught as far as architecture was concerned, and was noted for his Neo-Baroque Expressionism and his brick constructions, typical of North Germany. He had no hesitation in mixing the formal traditions of different cultures, Gothic, Jugendstil and Cubism, while at the same time developing a certain modernity. After 1920, he worked in Bremen for the coffee merchant Ludwig Roselius. Roselius, who had made a fortune from decaffeinated coffee, asked him to renovate and re-design the Böttcherstrasse, a medieval street in Bremen. In doing this, he displayed a certain amount of theatrical romanticism. In this street, he also built the Paula Modersohn-Becker-Haus, an example of Expressionist architecture, to house the works of Paula Modersohn-Becker from Roselius' collection. Still in the same street, he created the Haus Atlantis. He also designed a project for the ideal housing estate for a commission by Hermann Bahlsen. Apart from his architectural works, he became known in the sphere of graphic arts for his social themes, inspired by Steinlen and Willette, the depiction of people in distress, girls from poor districts, sickly children, or neglected old women.

Bibliography:
Drost, Suse, *Bernhard Hoetger 1874-1949. Sein Leben und Schaffen*, Bremen, 1974. *Umelecka Kolonie Darmstadt, 1899-1914*, exhibition catalogue, Narodni Galerie, Prague, 1989. *Bernhard Hoetger: Skuptur, Malerei, Design, Architektur*, exhibition catalogue, Georg Kolbe Museum, Berlin, 1998.

Museums and Galleries:
Darmstadt (Mus. Künstlerkolonie): *Loïe Fuller* (1900, bronze); *Flight of Fancy* (1906) - Hamburg (Mus. für Kunst und Gewerbe): *Storm, Woman Dancing* (c. 1901) - Karlsruhe (Badisches Landesmus.): *Lion Cub* (c. 1911) - Mont-de-Marsan (Mus. Despiau-Wlérick): *The Sower* (1905, bronze) - Paris (Mus. d'Orsay): *Storm*; *The Human Machine* (1902).
Auction records:
Paris, 2 June 1933, *Woman's Torso* (green-patinated bronze) FRF 400. Paris, 23 April 1937, *Woman's Torso and Legs* (bronze) FRF 200. Munich, 24 May 1976, *Dancer* (1902, patinated bronze, h. 14 1/2 ins / 37 cm) DEM 2,600. Monte Carlo, 16 Dec 1978, *Female Nude Holding a Casket* (1901, bronze, l. 7 3/4 ins / 20 cm) FRF 9,100. Paris, 17 Dec 1982, *Young Woman Dozing* (green lustrous patinated bronze, h. 11 1/4 ins / 28.5 cm) FRF 16,500. Semur-en-Auxois, 4 April 1983, *Haulier* (bronze, h. 13 3/4 ins / 35 cm) FRF 29,100. Enghien-les-Bains, 25 March 1984, *Beggar* (1902, bronze, h. 10 1/4 ins / 26 cm) FRF 15,000. Cologne, 9 Dec 1986, *Head of Sent M'Ahesa* (1917, bronze, h. 14 3/4 ins / 37.5 cm) DEM 34,000. Munich, 8 June 1988, *Little Girl with Jug* (bronze, h. 9 1/4 ins / 23.5 cm) DEM 10,780. Heidelberg, 12 Oct 1991, *Beggar* (terracotta, h. 10 ins / 25.2 cm) DEM 3,800. Paris, 25 Nov 1994, *Bust of Female Nude* (bronze, h. 16 3/4 ins / 42.5 cm) FRF 53,000. Berlin, 5 June 1999, *Seated Lady* (c. 1904-1905, brown patinated bronze, 11 x 9x9 ins / 28 x 24x24 cm) DEM 22,000. Hamburg, 9 June 2000, *Seated Female Nude* (1905, watercolour over pencil, 15 x 15 ins / 39 x 37 cm) DEM 19,000. Bremen, 20 Oct 2000, *Dancer Sent M'Ahesa* (patinated bronze, h. 57 ins / 146 cm) DEM 26,000. Paris, 16 March 2001, *Coalman* (brown patinated bronze, h. 15 ins / 37 cm) FRF 49,000. New York, 5 Nov 2001, *Tug-of-war Participant* (brown patinated bronze, h. 11 ins / 27 cm) USD 9,000. Berlin, 30 May 2003, *Head of the Dancer Sent M'Ahesa* (artificial stone, h. 15 ins / 38 cm) EUR 16,000. Cologne, 26 Nov 2003, *Fountain - Child* (bronze, h. 43 ins / 109 cm, w. 20 ins/50 cm) EUR 17,000. Cologne, 5 June 2004, *Seated Man* (1903, bronze, 27 x 12x13 ins / 68 x 31x34 cm) EUR 13,000. London, 9 July 2004, *Fecondite* (patinated bronze, h. 19ins / 47 cm) GBP 7,000. Paris, 23 Nov 2004, *Coalman* (1902, black patinated bronze, h. 14 ins / 35 cm) EUR 7,000.

HOETZENDORF, Johann Samuel, or Hözendorf

Austrian, 18th century.
Born 1694, in Sulzbach; died 1742, in Vienna.
Painter. History painting, architectural views.

Mention is made of his paintings in the abbey of Gattweich.
Auction records:
New York, 9 Oct 1991, *Christ on the Road to Emmaus* (oil on canvas, 30 1/4 x 39 3/4 ins / 76.9 x 101 cm) USD 14,300.

HOEVEMEYER, August

German, 19th century.
Born 29 September 1824, in Bückeburg; died 13 January 1878, in Munich.
Painter. History painting, genre scenes.

A pupil of Kaulbach and Schwind, he worked at a residence of the king of Bavaria in Berchtesgaden. He first exhibited publicly around 1854. In 1864, he is documented as copying paintings by Raphael and Titian. A large proportion of the decorative paintings in Munich station are by him.

HOEVEN, Abraham van

Dutch, 17th century.
Born 1576; died 15 February 1621.
Painter. History painting.

Abraham van Hoeven was the son of Apert Fransz. van der Hoeven. He worked for a time in Rome.

HOEVEN, Aper Fransz. van

Dutch, 16th century.

Active in Delft in 1566.
Painter.
Fontainebleau School.
Aper Fransz. van Hoeven worked in Fontainebleau with Jan de Meyer, Denys van Utrecht and Jerome Franck. He studied under Frans Floris.

HOEVEN, Gilliam van den
Flemish School, 17th century.
Died 1696.
Painter.
Gilliam van den Hoeven is mentioned in 1670 as a member of the Antwerp painters' guild.

HOEVEN, Valerius van der
Flemish School, 17th century.
Active in Antwerp at the beginning of the 17th century.
Painter.
Valerius van der Hoeven is known to have painted portraits.

HOEVEN, Willem van der
Flemish School, 17th century.
Sculptor.
Willem van der Hoeven is mentioned by Houbraken as the teacher of Hendrik van der Streck in 1659.

HOEVENAAR, Cornelis Willem, the Elder
Dutch, 19th century.
Born 22 December 1802, in Utrecht; died 14 July 1873, in Utrecht.
Painter. Fruit.
Cornelis Hoevenaar the Elder was a pupil of C. van Geelen. The Utrecht museum has a paintings of *Fruit* by this artist.

HOEVENAAR, Cornelis Willem, the Younger
Dutch, 19th century.
Born 11 October 1847, in Utrecht; died 29 June 1884, in Utrecht.
Painter. Landscapes, landscapes with figures, animals.
Cornelis Hoevenaar the Younger was the son and pupil of Cornelis Willem Hoevenaar the Elder. The Utrecht museum has a painting by him of *Calves in a Meadow*.

HOEVENAAR, Jozef
Dutch, 19th century.
Born 30 September 1840, in Utrecht; died 1926.
Painter. Genre scenes.
Jozef Hoevenaar was the son and pupil of Willem Pieter Hoevenaar. His painting *Decorating the Christmas Tree* is in the Utrecht museum.
AUCTION RECORDS:
NEW YORK, 30 Oct 1985, *Young Woman Feeding Pigeons* (oil on canvas, 18 1/2 x 14 1/4 ins / 47 x 36.5 cm) USD 5,000.

HOEVENAAR, Pieter
Dutch, 17th century.
Active in Rotterdam at the beginning of the 17th century.
Painter. Portraits.
Pieter Hoevenaar also worked in Delft.

HOEVENAAR, Willem Pieter
Dutch, 19th century.
Born 16 March 1808, in Utrecht; died 31 October 1863, in Utrecht.
Painter, engraver. Genre scenes.
Willem Pieter Hoevenaar was a pupil of B. van Straaten, Van Geeben and P.-C. Wonder.

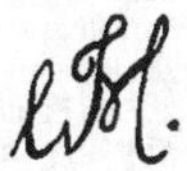

MUSEUMS AND GALLERIES:
AMSTERDAM: *The Slipsteenens* - UTRECHT: *Making Music*.

AUCTION RECORDS:
PARIS, 30 April 1919, *The First Loss*, FRF 170. AMSTERDAM, 30 Oct 1996, *A Recital* (oil on canvas, 29 1/2 x 26 ins / 75 x 66 cm) NLG 32,289. AMSTERDAM, 24 April 2001, *Soldiers Playing Backgammon in a Tavern* (oil on panel, 13 x 18 ins / 34 x 46 cm) NLG 16,000. AMSTERDAM, 24 April 2002, *Young Lady Doing Needlework in an Interior* (1842, oil on panel, 15 x 12 ins / 39 x 31 cm) EUR 8,000. BERN, 6 Nov 2002, *Figures Round a Table* (1835, oil on canvas, 29 x 35 ins / 73 x 90 cm) CHF 25,000.

HOEVENAGEL
Flemish School, 19th century.
Born 1811, in Bruges; died 1843, in Naples.
Sculptor.
In 1842, Hoevenagel worked for the church of St Walburge in Bruges.

HOEVISCH, Adolf
Danish, 18th century.
Born 1709, in Copenhagen.
Painter.
Adolf Hoevisch was a pupil of Hendrik Krock.

HOEWAER, Lidy
Belgian, 20th century.
Born 1943, in Hasselt (Limburg).
Sculptor.
Hoewaer attended the art academy in Hasselt and the Académie de La Cambre, in Brussels. She is a professor of ceramics at the art academy in Ghent.

HOEWEL VON
German, 19th century.
Active in Danzig (Gdansk) c. 1812.
Painter.
He exhibited military scenes in Berlin.

HOEY, Claude de, also called Doué
French, 17th century.
Born 1585, in Troyes; died 10 January 1660, in Fontainebleau.
Painter.
Claude de Hoey was the son of Jan de Hoey and took over his father's position as warden of the paintings at Fontainebleau. He held this position until 1635 when he passed it on to his nephew Jean Dubois. He worked with his father on the decoration of the palace.

HOEY, Dammerts, or Dammesz. Claesz. van
Dutch, 16th century.
Born in Utrecht; died c. 1560, in Leiden.
Painter.
Dammerts van Hoey was the son-in-law of Lucas van Leyden and the father of Lucas D. van Hoey and Jan. D van Hoey.

HOEY, Françoise de
French, 17th century.
Died 30 June 1648, in Fontainebleau.
Painter.
Françoise de Hoey was married to the painter A. Dubois who died in 1614. She was the daughter of Jan D. van Hoey.

HOEY, Guillaume de
French, 16th century.
Painter.
Fontainebleau School.
Guillaume de Hoey's name occurs in the royal building accounts. He worked at the Château de Fontainebleau around 1540.

HOEY, Jacques de
French, 17th century.
Born in Troyes.

Painter (?).
Jacques de Hoey was the son of Jan D. van Hoey. He was the warden of the paintings cabinets in the Louvre from 1618 to 1643.

HOEY, Jan Dammerts van, or Jean van Haey or Hooy or Doc or Dhoc
Dutch, 16th - 17th century.
Born 1545, in Leiden; died 8 September 1615, in Avon, near Fontainebleau.
Painter, engraver (etching).
Second School of Fontainebleau.
Jan Dammerts van Hoey was the son of Dammerts C. van Hoey and the grandson of Lucas van Leyden. He studied under his brother Lucas Dammerts van Hoey. He visited Italy, then France, and became a naturalised Frenchman in 1570. He was chamberlain to King Henri IV, who put him in joint charge of the decoration of the Château de Fontainbleau with Ambroise Dubois, and appointed him director of his picture gallery. Van Hoey also worked at the abbey of Barbeaux. The painter Cornelisz. Vroom seems to have been his pupil in Paris.

HOEY, Joseph Ignace van
Belgian, 19th century.
Born in Mechelen.
Painter, engraver. Genre scenes, landscapes.
Joseph van Hoey was a pupil of Wappers. He may be the same person as the artist J.-J. Dehoy, who was born in 1843, and is mentioned by Siret.
AUCTION RECORDS:
NEW YORK, 25 Feb 1988, *A School in Belgium* (1872, oil on canvas, 37 3/4 x 47 1/4 ins / 96.2 x 120 cm) USD 3,850.

HOEY, Lucas Dammerts van
Dutch, 16th century.
Born c. 1533, in Leiden; died 1604, in Utrecht.
Painter.
Utrecht School.
Lucas Dammerts van Hoey was the son of Dammerts C. van Hoey and the grandson of Lucas van Leyden. He was a master in Utrecht in 1569 and taught his brother Jan van Hoey.

HOEY, Nickolaus van, or Nikolaus, or Nicolas, the Elder, or Hoy, Hoje
Flemish School, 17th century.
Born 1631, in Antwerp; died 25 June 1679, in Vienna.
Painter, draughtsman, engraver.
Nickolaus van Hoey the Elder was a pupil of Matheusz. in Antwerp. He worked for Emperor Leopold and for Duke Leopold Wilhelm around 1667. He settled in Vienna, where he was appointed painter to the court, a position he held until his death and in which his son Nickolaus Hoey the Younger appears to have succeeded him. He decorated the chapel of the Order of St Augustine and engraved religious scenes and mythological subjects after Veronese, Barocci and Raphael.

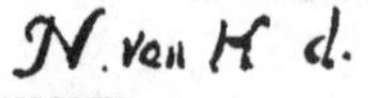

MUSEUMS AND GALLERIES:
VIENNA: *Battle Scene* (two paintings).

HOEY, Nickolaus van, or Nikolaus, or Nicolas, the Younger, or Hey, Hoje
Flemish School, 17th - 18th century.
Born c. 1660; died c. 1710, in Vienna.
Active in Antwerp.
Painter. Battles.
Nickolaus van Hoey the Younger was the son of Nickolaus van Hoey the Elder. He succeeded his father as court painter in Vienna.

HOEY, Nicolas de, or Hoeyen, Hoy
Flemish, 16th century.
Died 3 August 1521, in Antwerp.
Painter.
Flemish School.
Nicolas de Hoey was probably a pupil of Mattheus Matheussens.

HOEY, Nicolas de, also known as Doué
French, 16th - 17th century.
Painter.
Nicolas de Hoey was employed by Henri IV. Dutch by birth, he was related to the Lucas van Leyden family. His name appears from 1590 to 1611 in the royal account books. His main works were the two paintings in the collegiate church of Fribourg in Switzerland, signed and dated 1585, and the 1592 triptych in the Trinity chapel of the church in Vitteaux in the Côte d'Or.
BIBLIOGRAPHY:
Réau, Louis, *La Peinture française du XIVe au XVIe siècle*, Éd. Hypérion, Paris, 1939.

HOEY, Nicolas de
French, 17th century.
Baptised 15 May 1597 in Paris, in the church of St-Germain-l'Auxerrois; died probably before 1621.
Painter.
Nicolas de Hoey was the son of Jan van Hoey and is sometimes known as Jan the Younger.

HOEYDONCK, Patrick van
Belgian, 20th century.
Born 1959, in Merksem; died 1984.
Sculptor.
Van Hoeydonck attended the art academy in Mechelen. He produced classical work which is not without a certain romanticism.

HOEYDONCK, Paul van
Belgian, 20th century.
Born 1925, in Antwerp.
Painter, sculptor.
Van Hoeydonck studied at the institute for the history of art and archaeology in Antwerp, but was self-taught as an artist and sculptor. He lives and works in Wynegem. He started out as a still-life artist, then developed towards abstraction and finally practised assemblage art. He used existing objects from everyday life, such as mannequins' faces or even their disembodied arms and legs: he assembled these - sometimes piled up together - in the style of Arman, in order to bring out their symbolic potential.

He shows a certain humour in his treatment of the key symbols of modern society, particularly the conquest of space, which forms a very significant part of his work. It is difficult to classify Van Hoeydonck's 'futurology', which is a development of Dada and has links to a current of Surrealism that has always been strong in Flanders. It often bears similarities to Pierre Restany's New Realists' use of everyday objects to create artwork, but really belongs to Flemish Fantastic Art, in which he is considered to be one of the most important contemporary Flemish artists.

Van Hoeydonck took part in many group exhibitions, such as the Biennales in Venice, São Paulo and Tokyo, *Antagonismes* (*Antagonisms*) in Paris and Documenta in Kassel. He held the first of many private exhibitions in Antwerp in 1952. He was awarded the Belgian art critics' prize in 1963.

Bibliography:
Chevalier, Denys, *Nouveau dictionnaire de la sculpture moderne*, Hazan, Paris, 1972.
Museums and Galleries:
Brussels (MAM) - New York (MoMA) - Ostend (Mus. voor Schone Kunsten): *Astronaut.*
Auction records:
Antwerp, 10 Oct 1972, *Flight in Space*, BEF 45,000. Brussels, 29 Oct 1974, *Spacetrees* (1963) BEF 160,000. Antwerp, 7 April 1976, *Aeronautics* (1965, oil on panel, 48 1/2 x 17 3/4 ins / 123 x 45 cm) BEF 10,000. Breda, 26 April 1977, *Spacetree* (1963, oil on panel, 84 1/4 x 48 ins / 214 x 122 cm) NLG 2,600. Lokeren, 31 March 1979, *Sphinx* (bronze, h. 5 1/2 ins / 14 cm, w. 4 3/4 ins/12 cm) BEF 95,000. Lokeren, 14 April 1984, *Young Girl with Rose* (bronze, h. 13 ins / 33 cm) BEF 75,000. Antwerp, 22 April 1986, *Head* (bronze, h. 13 ins / 33 cm) BEF 55,000. Lokeren, 28 May 1988, *Hybo-man* (1979, bronze, h. 61 ins / 155 cm) BEF 140,000. Brussels, 13 Dec 1990, *Figure* (assemblage of metal and various materials/card, 24 x 20 ins / 61 x 51 cm) BEF 91,200. Brussels, 13 Dec 1990, *Moonlight* (1961, mixed media/card, 31 1/2 x 22 ins / 80 x 55 cm) BEF 171,000. Paris, 15 April 1991, *Space Mirror with Flying Madonna* (1964, mixed media/panel, 28 x 28 ins / 71 x 71 cm) FRF 12,000. Lokeren, 10 Oct 1992, *Two Figures* (bronze, h. 11 ins / 28 cm, w. 7 1/2 ins/19 cm) BEF 70,000. Lokeren, 15 May 1993, *Two Figures* (bronze, h. 11 ins / 28 cm, w. 7 1/2 ins/19 cm) BEF 60,000. New York, 29 Sept 1993, *Inhabited Planet I* (1962, coating/synthetic resin and white paint, 48 x 48 ins / 121.9 x 121.9 cm) USD 2,300. Lokeren, 8 Oct 1994, *Caskets from Kyoto* (1989, bronze relief and other materials, 27 1/2 x 42 1/4 ins / 70 x 107 cm) BEF 180,000. Amsterdam, 6 Dec 1995, *Untitled* (1960, collage and oil/synthetic resin); *Collage* (1960) NLG 2,530. Lokeren, 8 March 1997, *Hand with Rose* (bronze, 5 x 6 3/4 ins / 12.5 x 17 cm) BEF 28,000. Brussels, 8 May 2001, *Composition* (1989, oil on plexi panel, 29 x 44 ins / 74 x 111 cm) BEF 85,000. Lokeren, 6 Oct 2001, *Alexandra* (1986, painted bronze, 22 x 7 ins / 55 x 18 cm) BEF 70,000. Antwerp, 23 April 2002, *Astronaut* (1969, assemblage, h. 17 ins / 42 cm) EUR 1,900. Antwerp, 22 Oct 2002, *Kyoto Box* (1989, mixed media, 29 x 44 ins / 74 x 111 cm) EUR 28,000. Antwerp, 27 April 2004, *Head of a Woman and Ball* (bronze, h. 21 ins / 53 cm) EUR 1,700. Antwerp, 27 April 2004, *Electronic Virgin* (1966, sculpture, 83 x 48 ins / 210 x 122 cm) EUR 3,000.

HOEYE, Franciscus van
Dutch, 17th century.
Born c. 1591, in Amsterdam; died 1636, in Amsterdam.
Engraver.

Franciscus was the father of Rombout van Hoeye.

HOEYE, Rombout van den
Dutch, 17th century.
Born 1622, in Amsterdam.
Engraver, printer.

Rombout van den Hoeye is known for his equestrian portrait of *King Christian IV of Denmark.*

HOEYER, Christian Faedder
Danish, 19th century.
Born 24 January 1775, in Reerslev; died 23 June 1855, in Copenhagen.
Active in Rome and Copenhagen.
Painter, miniaturist.

Christian Hoeyer was the son and pupil of Cornelis Hoeyer. His *Hero Awaiting Leander* is in the Copenhagen museum.

HOEYER, Cornelius F., or Høyer
Danish, 18th century.
Born 1741, in Copenhagen; died 2 June 1804, in Copenhagen.
Miniaturist, painter. Genre scenes.

Cornelius Hoeyer was a pupil at the Kunstakademi in Copenhagen from 1755 to 1764. He gained a travel grant from King Frederick V enabling him to go to Paris. From 1765 he attended the École des Beaux-Arts and became the favourite pupil of Jean-Baptiste Massé. He also worked in Italy from 1766 to 1767. He then stayed in Dresden to paint the (now lost) familial portrait of Elector Fredrick Augustus III and became a member of the academy. He returned to Copenhagen in 1770 when he was named miniaturist to the Danish court. He was received into the academy and became its secretary in 1777. He was then summoned to St. Petersburg by Catherine II, and remained in Russia from 1780 to 1797.

Bibliography:
Colding, T.H., *Cornelius Høyer, 1741-1804: Selskabet til Udgivelse af Skrifter om Danske Mindesmaerker*, Gad, Copenhagen, 1961. Colding, T.H., *Miniature og Emaillemaleri i Danmark, 1606-1850*, Gyldendal, Copenhagen, 1991.

HOF, Gijs Jacobs van den
Dutch, 20th century.
Born 1889; died 1965.
Sculptor.

Bibliography:
Scheerder, Henk, *Gijs Jacobs Van den Hof, 1889-1965: beeldhouwer*, Museum Jacobs van den Hof, Amersfoort, 1995.
Auction records:
Amsterdam, 5 June 1996, *Gijsberta* (fire-clay, h. 13 3/4 ins / 35 cm) NLG 5,750. Amsterdam, 12 Dec 2001, *Seated Faun* (c. 1920, rosewood, h. 4 ins / 11 cm) NLG 9,000.

HOFACKER, Georg
German, 16th century.
Active in Schwäbisch Hall.
Sculptor.

Georg Hofacker worked in the castle of Grosskomburg, Württemberg.

HOFBAUER, Arnost
Czech, 19th - 20th century.
Born 26 April 1869, in Prague.
Painter, engraver.

Arnost Hofbauer was a student at the academy of fine art in Prague. He stayed for a long time in Paris, Venice and Berlin. He was also a writer.

HOFBAUER, Ferdinand
Austrian, 19th century.
Born 18 October 1801, in Vienna; died 8 August 1864, in Vienna.
Painter, engraver, lithographer. Military subjects, portraits. Miniatures.

His oeuvre comprises miniatures, portraits and military scenes painting in oils.

Auction records:
New York, 25 Oct 1989, *The Wreck* (oil on canvas, 28 3/4 x 39 1/2 ins / 73 x 100.4 cm) USD 6,600.

HOFBAUER, Janos
Hungarian, 19th century.
Born in Gyor.
Active in Vienna c. 1846.
Painter.

Janos Hofbauer painted portraits of the Hungarian nobility.

HOFBAUER, Karl
Austrian, 19th century.
Painter.

In 1855, he painted a *Christ on the Cross* at Persenbeug on the Danube.

HOFBAUER, Louis
Russian, 20th century.
Born 26 October 1889, in Yalta.

Painter. Religious subjects, portraits.

Louis Hofbauer spent his youth in Vienna. He stayed in Rome, the city that inspired him to paint religious works such as his *Mary Magdalene at the Foot of the Cross.*

HOFBAUER, Ludwig

Austrian, 19th century.

Born 5 August 1843, in Vienna.

Painter, watercolourist, draughtsman. Genre scenes, landscapes.

He is noted mainly for his watercolours.

AUCTION RECORDS:

MUNICH, 21 June 1994, *The New Market in Vienna* (1894, pencil and watercolour/paper, 7 x $9\frac{1}{2}$ ins / 18 x 24 cm) DEM 4,370.

HOFELICH, Friedrich Ludwig

German, 19th century.

Born 30 October 1842, in Leipzig; died 13 January 1903, in Munich.

Painter.

He began his artistic training in Berlin, then worked in Leipzig under the direction of Flegel. From 1860 to 1864 he lived in St Petersburg. From 1864, he lived in Germany and exhibited in Berlin, Munich, Dresden and Leipzig.

AUCTION RECORDS:

LUCERNE, 12 Nov 1982, *Woman Gathering Firewood* (oil on canvas, $31\frac{1}{2}$ x $43\frac{1}{4}$ ins / 80 x 110 cm) CHF 4,800. MUNICH, 22 March 2000, *Herder with Cattle Watering* (oil on canvas, 26 x 39 ins / 67 x 98 cm) DEM 6,000.

HOFEMANN, Martin

Bohemian, 17th century.

Active in Krombach at the beginning of the 17th century.

Creator of stained glass.

HÖFER, Alexander, or Hoefer

German, 20th century.

Born 16 January 1877, in Keuern.

Sculptor. Animals. Busts.

Höfer studied under Epler and Diez at the academy of fine arts in Dresden, where he lived and was active. He exhibited his work in Berlin in 1909.

HOFER, André

French, 20th century.

Born in Autun.

Painter, illustrator.

André Hofer has a well-established reputation as an illustrator. In addition to working on numerous periodicals, he also illustrated Kipling's *Des Voyages et des Parfums* and Pearl S. Buck's *The Patriot.* He exhibited regularly in Paris at the Salon des Indépendants from 1912.

AUCTION RECORDS:

NEUILLY, 5 Dec 1989, *The Luncheon on the Grass* (oil on canvas, 32 x $39\frac{1}{4}$ ins / 81 x 100 cm) FRF 11,000. VERSAILLES, 21 Oct 1990, *Landscape with River* (1956, oil on canvas, $19\frac{3}{4}$ x 24 ins / 50 x 61 cm) FRF 4,000. PARIS, 15 Dec 1990, *Large Cubist Nude* (1921, oil on canvas, $38\frac{1}{4}$ x $57\frac{1}{2}$ ins / 97 x 146 cm) FRF 23,000. ST-DIÉ, 23 June 1991, *The Two Friends* (1950, oil on canvas, $39\frac{1}{4}$ x 32 ins / 100 x 81 cm) FRF 18,000.

HOFER, Andreas

German, 18th century.

Active in Nuremberg.

Engraver.

He was a pupil of Nunzer.

HOFER, Andreas W.

Swiss, 20th century.

Born in Lützelflüh.

Painter.

HOFER, Daniel

French, 17th century.

Born 2 July 1637, in Mulhouse; died 8 May 1702, in Mulhouse.

Painter.

Daniel Hofer studied under H. D. Bodan and decorated the Mulhouse town hall.

HOFER, Franz

Austrian, 20th century.

Born 24 December 1885, in Graz; died 1915.

Painter, engraver. Religious subjects, landscapes.

Hofer studied in Dresden and Vienna.

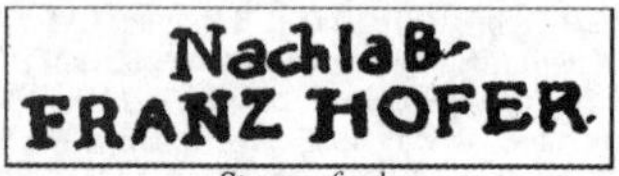

Stamp of sale

HOFER, Gottfried

Austrian, 19th century.

Born 27 March 1858, in Bozen, South Tyrol (now Bolzano, Italy).

Painter. Genre scenes, portraits.

From 1876 to 1883 he was a pupil of Löfftz at the academy in Munich. He subsequently spent 1883 to 1887 in Italy. After a short spell in Paris, where he gained a bronze medal at the Universal Exhibition in 1889, he returned to Germany, working successively in Munich, Bremen, Leipzig and Hamburg. He also exhibited in Berlin.

MUSEUMS AND GALLERIES:

BREMEN (Kunsthalle): *Portrait of Mayor Otto Gildemeister.*

AUCTION RECORDS:

LINDAU, 7 May 1980, *Portrait of a Woman* (oil on canvas, 46 x $34\frac{1}{4}$ ins / 117 x 87 cm) DEM 4,800.

HÖFER, Heinrich

German, 19th century.

Born 1825, in Eisfeld (near Coburg); died 1878, in Munich.

Painter. Genre scenes, landscapes with figures, landscapes.

He started out painting porcelain, then studied landscape with Carl Millner in Munich. His travels in Switzerland, Tyrol and Italy provided subject matter for his paintings. He exhibited in Munich, Dresden and Vienna.

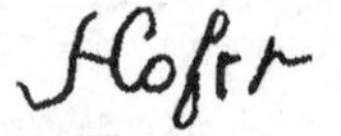

MUSEUMS AND GALLERIES:

WROCLAW: *Bavarian Village in Winter.*

AUCTION RECORDS:

COLOGNE, 25 Nov 1976, *Landscape with Mill* (1861, oil on canvas, 20 x $26\frac{1}{2}$ ins / 50.5 x 67 cm) DEM 7,500. NEW YORK, 13 Oct 1978, *The Forge in Winter* (1865, oil on canvas, $16\frac{1}{2}$ x 21 ins / 42 x 52.5 cm) USD 8,500. NEW YORK, 26 Jan 1979, *Traveller outside a Mill* (1868, oil on canvas, 22 x 17 ins / 55 x 43 cm) USD 7,500. VERSAILLES, 27 March 1983, *The Torrent* (1862, oil on canvas, $28\frac{1}{4}$ x $35\frac{3}{4}$ ins / 72 x 91 cm) FRF 30,000. LIMOGES, 17 June 1984, *View of Königsee Lake* (oil on canvas, $31\frac{1}{2}$ x $23\frac{1}{2}$ ins / 80 x 60 cm) FRF 20,000. NEW YORK, 31 Oct 1985, *Woodcutters on a Frozen River* (1873, oil on canvas, $30\frac{3}{4}$ x $41\frac{3}{4}$ ins / 78 x 106 cm) USD 9,500. LONDON, 24 June 1988, *Woodcutters Carrying Timber on a Frozen River* (1873, oil on canvas, $30\frac{3}{4}$ x $41\frac{3}{4}$ ins / 78.1 x 106 cm) GBP 14,300. LONDON, 17 Nov 1995, *Figures on a Frozen Lake in a Forest* (1854, oil on canvas, $16\frac{1}{4}$ x $27\frac{1}{2}$ ins / 41.3 x 69.8 cm) GBP 7,130. MUNICH, 22 June 1999, *Farmer Resting in Woodland Clearing* (1869, oil on canvas, 16 x 20 ins / 41 x 52 cm) DEM 12,000. COLOGNE, 29 June 2000, *Goat Herder before Mill*

(1860, oil on canvas, 17 x 20 ins / 42 x 52 cm) DEM 10,000. MUNICH, 27 Sept 2000, *Horse-drawn Sledge and Figures Standing on Frozen River* (1867, oil on panel, 13 x 16 ins / 32 x 41 cm) DEM 30,000. MUNICH, 27 June 2001, *Old Smithy near Berchtesgaden* (1861, oil on canvas, 15 x 21 ins / 39 x 53 cm) DEM 15,000. MUNICH, 6 Dec 2002, *Winter Landscape with Houses on Shore* (1871, oil on canvas, 19 x 26 ins / 48 x 66 cm) EUR 7,500.

HOFER, Henri, or Hoffer
French, 19th century.
Born 3 March 1827, in Paris; died 1 July 1862.
Painter. Portraits.

Hofer was a pupil of Thomas Couture, and exhibited at the Salon from 1848 to 1861. He committed suicide by hanging himself in his studio.

MUSEUMS AND GALLERIES:
NIORT: *Portrait of Jules Hardouin Mansart.*

HOFER, Ignaz
Austrian, 19th century.
Born 15 June 1790, in Schwanberg (near Graz); died 2 August 1862, in Graz.
Painter. Still-lifes.

He trained in Graz, then spent time in Trieste and Bologna before returning to Graz, where he was appointed director of the art academy.

MUSEUMS AND GALLERIES:
GRAZ (Landesmus. Joanneum): *Circlet of Flowers; Fruit; Still-life* (three).

HOFER, Josef
Austrian, 20th century.
Born 1945, in Wegscheid (Bavaria).
Draughtsman. Figures.
Art Brut.

Josef Hofer is a deaf mute who grew up with no formal schooling on the family farm in Bavaria. On the death of his father in 1982, he, his mother and his similarly handicapped brother were put in care of a female cousin. Hofer started to draw at around the age of 40, but it was not until 1997 that art historian Elisabeth Telsnig discovered examples of his drawings. In 2003, the Art Brut Collection in Lausanne exhibited Hofer's work for the first time, showing that his hatched drawings possess a remarkably expressive quality.

BIBLIOGRAPHY:
Telsnig, Elisabeth/Thévoz, Michel/Peiry, Lucienne, *Josef Hofer*, exhibition catalogue, Collection de l'Art Brut, Lausanne, 2003.

MUSEUMS AND GALLERIES:
LAUSANNE (Collection de l'Art Brut): bequest of some 70 drawings.

HOFER, Karl
German, 18th century.
Active in Passau c. 1750.
Sculptor.

HOFER, Karl or Carl
German, 20th century.
Born 11 October 1878, in Karlsruhe; died 1955, in Berlin.
Painter, engraver, draughtsman. Figures, scenes with figures, still-lifes.
Symbolism, Magical Realism.

Hofer studied at the academy of fine arts in Karlsruhe from 1896 until 1900. The Nazis classed his work as 'degenerate art' - the term they applied to the works of Expressionist and Abstract painters - and as a result 150 of his canvases were destroyed along with his studio. After the defeat of Germany in 1945 Hofer was appointed director of the school of fine arts in Berlin. He published a theoretical study entitled *Wege der Kunst* (*Methods in Art*) in 1947, and an autobiography *Aus Leben und Kunst* (*Of Life and Art*) in 1952.

During his studies, Hofer was strongly influenced by the classicism of his teacher, Hans Thoma, and the Fantastic Realism of Böcklin's works. He went to live in Italy between 1903 and 1908 and accompanied Hans von Marees, painting large classically inspired compositions. He then went to Paris, where he stayed until 1913; there, he was inspired and influenced by the works of Cézanne, which encouraged him to develop a modern interpretation of form along with a classical construction in his work. He joined the new association of Munich artists around 1909, an eclectic group with lively tendencies that was in the process of breaking away from the declining Nouveau Style and would soon develop into the two diverging currents of Expressionism and the Blaue Reiter group. However, Hofer's works cannot easily be classified as Expressionist and they certainly do not fall into the abstract category of the Blaue Reiter. They are characterised by a classical construction similar to that of Derain. As well as his paintings he also produced many lithographs.

Hofer was awarded first prize by the Carnegie Institute in Pittsburgh in 1938. His first major exhibition took place in 1924, but it was the retrospective exhibition of his work held in 1928 to mark his fiftieth birthday that brought him fame and established his reputation as an artist. Another retrospective exhibition was dedicated to him at the Kunsthalle in Berlin in 1978.

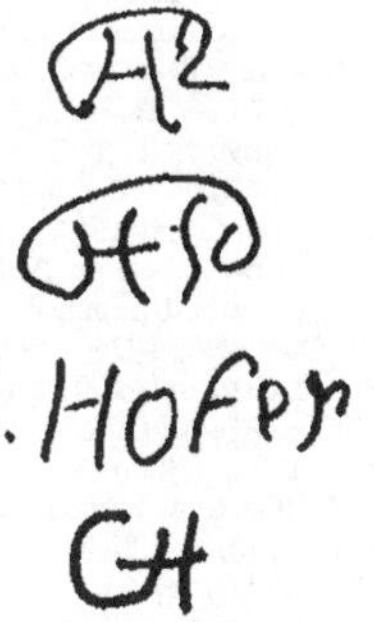

BIBLIOGRAPHY:
Cichy, Bodo, *Moderne Malerei, Beginn und Entwicklung*, E. E. Thoma, Munich, 1965.

MUSEUMS AND GALLERIES:
BERLIN (Berlinische Gal.): *Prisoners* (1933); *Night of the Black Moon* (1944) - BERLIN (Neue Nationalgal.): *Head of Young Girl* (1920) - COLOGNE (Wallraf-Richartz Mus.): *Mascarade* (1922); *Three Masks* (1922); *Landscape in Ticino* (1925); *Female Nude with Basket of Fruit* (1928) - ESSEN (Folkwang Mus.): *Two Women* (1907) - HAMBURG (Kunsthalle): *Friends* (1923-1924) - HANOVER (Niedersächsisches Landesmus.): *Houses in Montagnola* (1925) - KASSEL (Staatliche Kunstsammlungen): *Man in the Ruins* (1937) - MUNICH (Pinakothek): *Girls Playing Cards* (1937); *Carnival* - PORTLAND (MA): *Early in the Morning* (1935) - ULM (Ulmer Mus.): *Card Players* (1924) - WUPPERTAL (Von der Heydt Mus.): *Ascent to San Salvatore* (1925).

AUCTION RECORDS:
PARIS, 8 March 1934, *Young Girl with Flower Pot*, FRF 680. COLOGNE, 28 Oct 1958, *Interior with Three Female Nudes*, DEM 19,000. STUTTGART, 29 May 1959, *View of Carona in Ticino*, DEM 23,000. STUTTGART, 20 May 1960, *Woman in Red Wearing a Hat*, DEM 18,500. STUTTGART, 3 May 1961, *Ticino Landscape: Lavena*, DEM 30,500. STUTTGART, 3 and 4 May 1962, *St Gothard Pass* (c. 1936) DEM 12,500. HAMBURG, 18 May 1963, *Peri*, DEM 17,000. COLOGNE, 26 May 1964, *Young Girl with Fruit*, DEM 19,000. COLOGNE, 8 and 9 Dec 1966,

Imaginary Farewell, DEM 22,000. MUNICH, 8 June 1967, *Self-portrait with Wife,* DEM 28,000. HAMBURG, 25 June 1968, *Boy with a Cloth around his Head,* DEM 42,000. NEW YORK, 19 Nov 1969, *Three Bathers,* USD 5,500. BERLIN, 2 July 1970, *Landscape in Ticino,* DEM 15,500. HAMBURG, 4 June 1971, *Landscape in Lugano,* DEM 26,000. MUNICH, 23 Nov 1973, *Autumn Flowers* (1917) DEM 36,000. COLOGNE, 4 Dec 1974, *Dream,* DEM 44,000. COLOGNE, 21 May 1976, *Three Women in a Mountainous Landscape* (oil on canvas, 32 x 20 1/2 ins / 81 x 52 cm) DEM 16,000. MUNICH, 28 Nov 1977, *Young Woman at the Mirror* (1943, oil on canvas, 39 1/4 x 25 1/2 ins / 100 x 65 cm) DEM 19,500. COLOGNE, 3 Dec 1977, *Head of Young Girl* (watercolour and Indian ink, 17 x 12 1/4 ins / 43 x 31 cm) DEM 3,000. COLOGNE, 6 May 1978, *Two Girls Embracing* (c. 1923, lithograph, 7 1/2 x 7 ins / 19 x 17.5 cm; 18 x 14 3/4 ins/45.5 x 37.5 cm) DEM 1,700. COLOGNE, 6 May 1978, *König von Thules* (1911, black chalk, 15 1/4 x 12 1/2 ins / 39 x 31.5 cm) DEM 2,900. HAMBURG, 2 June 1978, *Couple (Two Heads)* (watercolour and gouache, 19 3/4 x 12 1/4 ins / 50 x 31 cm) DEM 3,800. MUNICH, 28 May 1979, *Woman in Red* (1928-1930, oil on canvas, 43 1/4 x 32 ins / 110 x 81 cm) DEM 74,000. MUNICH, 30 Nov 1979, *Muzzano in Ticino* (c. 1926, etching) DEM 2,500. MUNICH, 30 June 1981, *Two Lovers II* (pen and wash, 15 3/4 x 14 1/2 ins / 40 x 37 cm) DEM 9,400. MUNICH, 30 June 1981, *Harlequin Standing* (1921-1922, watercolour/pen outline, 11 1/2 x 7 3/4 ins / 29 x 20 cm) DEM 36,000. BREMEN, 22 May 1982, *Still-life* (oil on canvas, 17 1/4 x 27 1/4 ins / 43.5 x 69 cm) DEM 32,000. MUNICH, 29 June 1983, *Three Nudes Dancing* (c. 1913-1915, oil on card, 27 1/4 x 21 3/4 ins / 69 x 55.5 cm) DEM 40,000. COLOGNE, 7 Dec 1983, *Reading* (1924, etching and dry-point, 8 1/2 x 7 ins / 21.7 x 17.7 cm) DEM 1,700. MUNICH, 26 Nov 1984, *Novices* (c. 1922, pen and wash, 17 1/4 x 9 3/4 ins / 43.5 x 25 cm) DEM 8,500. MUNICH, 30 Nov 1984, *Head of Young Girl* (watercolour, 16 1/4 x 11 3/4 ins / 41 x 30 cm) DEM 6,800. COLOGNE, 4 Dec 1985, *Muzzano in Ticino* (1926, etching and dry-point/paper, 9 1/2 x 13 ins / 24.3 x 33.3 cm) DEM 2,000. COLOGNE, 4 Dec 1985, *Couple* (1954, tempera/canvas, 39 1/4 x 29 1/2 ins / 100 x 75 cm) DEM 25,000. ZURICH, 13 June 1986, *Group of Women* (1908, oil on canvas, 43 1/4 x 39 1/4 ins / 110 x 100 cm) CHF 57,000. COLOGNE, 30 May 1987, *Triplet* (1953, tempera/canvas, 32 x 24 ins / 81 x 61 cm) DEM 27,000. LONDON, 29 March 1988, *Three Nudes* (pencil/paper, 18 x 13 3/4 ins / 45.7 x 35 cm) GBP 3,300. LONDON, 21 Oct 1988, *Dreamer* (1952, oil on canvas, 31 x 20 3/4 ins / 79 x 53 cm) GBP 18,150. LONDON, 29 Nov 1988, *Portrait* (1935, oil on canvas, 35 1/2 x 25 ins / 90.2 x 63.5 cm) GBP 18,700. MUNICH, 7 June 1989, *Female Nude Standing in Front of Window* (1923, gouache, 13 1/2 x 10 ins / 34 x 24.5 cm) DEM 26,400. MUNICH, 13 Dec 1989, *Portrait of Little Girl* (1945, oil on canvas, 18 x 14 1/4 ins / 46 x 36.4 cm) DEM 60,500. NEW YORK, 26 Feb 1990, *Dialogue* (1935, oil on canvas, 35 x 45 ins / 89 x 114.3 cm) USD 82,500. MUNICH, 31 May 1990, *Bowl of Pears* (oil on canvas, 14 x 22 ins / 35.5 x 56 cm) DEM 74,800. NEW YORK, 9 May 1991, *Malcescine* (1937, oil on canvas, 19 1/2 x 31 1/2 ins / 49.7 x 80 cm) USD 39,600. BERLIN, 30 May 1991, *Landscape in Ticino* (1935, oil on canvas, 26 x 32 ins / 66 x 81 cm) DEM 122,100. AMSTERDAM, 11 Dec 1991, *View of a Village in Ticino* (oil on canvas, 23 1/2 x 31 1/2 ins / 60 x 80 cm) NLG 218,500. HEIDELBERG, 11 April 1992, *Three Women* (lithograph, 13 1/2 x 6 3/4 ins / 34.3 x 17.2 cm) DEM 3,000. MUNICH, 26 May 1992, *Still-life with Pears in a Fruit Bowl* (1952, oil on canvas, 14 x 17 3/4 ins / 35.5 x 45 cm) DEM 41,400. NEW YORK, 12 Nov 1992, *Couple with Yellow Flag* (gouache and watercolour/paper, 24 x 19 ins / 61 x 48.2 cm) USD 7,700. MUNICH, 1-2 Dec 1992, *Heads of Two Girls* (pencil, 12 1/4 x 9 ins / 31 x 23 cm) DEM 4,830. HEIDELBERG, 3 April 1993, *Two Lovers* (dry-point, 4 1/4 x 4 1/4 ins / 10.9 x 10.6 cm) DEM 1,180. LONDON, 20 May 1993, *Landscape in Ticino I* (1935, oil on canvas, 24 1/4 x 31 3/4 ins / 61.7 x 80.7 cm) GBP 49,900. LONDON, 13 Oct 1994, *Card Players* (1933, oil on canvas, 13 3/4 x 19 ins / 35 x 47.4 cm) GBP 21,850. ZURICH, 7 April 1995, *Two Women* (ink wash, 16 1/2 x 11 ins / 42 x 28 cm) CHF 3,600. LONDON, 11 Oct 1995, *Young Women Throwing Flowers* (1934, oil on canvas, 48 1/2 x 38 3/4 ins / 123.3 x 98.6 cm) GBP 232,500. NEW YORK, 2 May 1996, *Portrait of Freda Braun* (1929, oil on canvas, 45 x 31 1/2 ins / 114.3 x 80 cm) USD 43,125. ZURICH, 17-18 June 1996, *Still-life of Fruit* (oil on canvas, 13 3/4 x 21 1/4 ins / 35 x 53.8 cm) CHF 34,000. LONDON, 24 June 1996, *Feast Day* (oil on canvas, 51 1/4 x 41 ins / 130 x 104 cm) GBP 551,500. LUCERNE, 23 Nov 1996, *Woman Bathing* (1912, oil on canvas, 35 x 25 1/2 ins / 89 x 65 cm) CHF 40,000. LONDON, 3 Dec 1996, *Lover at the Window* (1925, oil on canvas, 39 1/2 x 35 1/2 ins / 100.5 x 90 cm) GBP 155,500. AMSTERDAM, 18 June 1997, *Young Girl* (1943, oil on canvas, 19 3/4 x 18 ins / 50 x 45.5 cm) NLG 38,055. LONDON, 9 Oct 1997, *Woman with Hat* (1912, oil on canvas, 35 1/2 x 25 1/4 ins / 90 x 64 cm) GBP 133,500. BERLIN, 4 June 1999, *Daphnis and Chloe* (1913, oil on canvas, 43 x 31 ins / 110 x 80 cm) DEM 360,000. LONDON, 6 Oct 1999, *After Bathing* (1934, oil on canvas, 39 x 27 ins / 99 x 69 cm) GBP 220,000. BERLIN, 26 May 2000, *Three Girls* (1943, oil on canvas, 26 x 22 ins / 67 x 57 cm) DEM 250,000. LONDON, 17 Oct 2000, *Bathers* (1945, oil on canvas, 45 x 36 ins / 114 x 91 cm) GBP 110,000. BERLIN, 29 June 2001, *Three Girls at a Window* (1939, oil on canvas, 40 x 31 ins / 102 x 80 cm) DEM 810,000. BERLIN, 30 Nov 2001, *Portrait of Cornelia* (oil on canvas, 18 x 15 ins / 46 x 38 cm) DEM 580,000. LONDON, 9 Oct 2002, *Seated Female Nude* (1927, oil on canvas, 37 x 33 ins / 95 x 85 cm) GBP 90,000. BERLIN, 29 Nov 2002, *Girl Throwing Flowers* (1945, oil on canvas, 41 x 32 ins / 104 x 81 cm) EUR 210,000. LONDON, 3 Feb 2003, *Peasant Couple in the Moonlight* (1938, oil on canvas, 40 x 42 ins / 102 x 106 cm) GBP 85,000. BERLIN, 28 Nov 2003, *Woman Reading* (oil on canvas, 38 x 27 ins / 96 x 69 cm) EUR 90,000. LONDON, 23 June 2004, *Two Young Nudes in front of a Curtain* (c. 1927, oil on canvas, 46 x 35 ins / 117 x 90 cm) GBP 80,000. ZURICH, 23 June 2004, *Masquerade* (oil on canvas, 43 x 34 ins / 109 x 87 cm) CHF 560,000.

HOFER, Konrad

Swiss, 20th century.
Born 1928, in Langnau.
Painter.

Hofer painted abstract landscapes and was greatly influenced by the work of Nicolas de Staël. The museum in Basel owns three of his works entitled *Sierra*, *Cordillera* and *La Theurre*.

HOFER, Ludwig von

German, 19th century.
Born 20 June 1801, in Ludwigsburg; died 8 March 1887, in Stuttgart.
Sculptor. Animals. Statues, monuments.

He trained in Munich and later in Rome (in Thorvaldsen's studio). His work includes marble busts, monuments and monumental sculptures of mythological inspiration.

MUSEUMS AND GALLERIES:

LAUSANNE (Cantonal MFA): *Dressage* (bronze, a set of two).

HOFER-GROSJEAN, Edouard

German, 19th century.
Born in Mulhouse; died 1890.
Painter. Genre scenes.

A pupil of Hayon.

MUSEUMS AND GALLERIES:

MULHOUSE: *Interioron the Meggerhorn.*

HOFF, Adriaan van 't

Dutch, 20th century.
Born 1893; died 1939.
Painter. Landscapes, flowers.

Van 't Hoff was featured in *De blijvende verlokking: Nederlandse kunstenaars in Italië, 1806-1940* (*Lasting Attraction:*

Dutch Artists in Italy, 1806-1940), an exhibition showing how travel to Italy had influenced Dutch artists, which was held at the Kunsthal in Rotterdam in 2003.

Bibliography:

De blijvende verlokking: Nederlandse kunstenaars in Italië, 1806-1940, exhibition catalogue, Kunsthal, Rotterdam, 2003.

Auction records:

Vienna, 23 June 1987, *Archery* (1928, oil on canvas, 66 1/4 x 45 ins / 168 x 114.5 cm) ATS 70,000. Amsterdam, 19 Sept 1989, *Roses and Peonies in a Vase* (oil on canvas, 19 3/4 x 15 3/4 ins / 50 x 40 cm) NLG 5,750. Amsterdam, 19 May 1992, *San Domenico near Florence* (oil on canvas, 11 3/4 x 15 3/4 ins / 30 x 40 cm) NLG 1,725. Amsterdam, 5 June 1996, *Still-life of Flowers* (oil on canvas, 19 3/4 x 15 3/4 ins / 50 x 40 cm) NLG 4,370. Gravenhage, 7 Nov 2001, *Heron in Water* (chalk and watercolour heightened with white) NLG 5,500. Gravenhage, 12 May 2004, *Florence, Italy, Garden of Villa S Girolamo* (1928, oil on canvas, 30 x 23 ins / 77 x 59 cm) EUR 2,200.

HOFF, Carl

German, 19th century.
Died 7 March 1862, in Dresden.
Draughtsman, engraver, miniaturist.

He was the brother of Johann Nikolaus Hoff and pupil of Wendelstadt in Frankfurt. Subsequently he was based in St Petersburg and did a large number of portraits there.

HOFF, Carl Heinrich, the Elder

German, 19th century.
Born 8 September 1838, in Mannheim; died 13 May 1890, in Karlsruhe.
Painter. Genre scenes, figures, landscapes.

From 1855 to 1858 he was a pupil of J W Schirmer and Des Coudres at the school of fine arts in Karlsruhe. Subsequently he studied at the academy in Düsseldorf under the direction of Vautier. He travelled in France, Italy and Greece, returning to Germany in 1863. From then until 1878 he was based in Düsseldorf, moving thence to teach in the academy in Karlsruhe, where he remained for the rest of his life. He exhibited and won medals in Berlin (1872), Vienna, London, Munich and Melbourne.

Museums and Galleries:

Hamburg: *The Eavesdropper.*

Auction records:

Paris, 18 June 1930, *A Scene from Tartuffe*, FRF 2,300. Paris, 17 March 1932, *The Notary*, FRF 2,605. New York, 30 Oct 1985, *Soldier Saying Goodbye to His Mother* (1888, oil on canvas, 83 1/2 x 52 1/2 ins / 212.1 x 133.3 cm) USD 12,000. Munich, 11 Nov 1987, *The Young Widow* (1886, oil on canvas, 46 x 25 3/4 ins / 117 x 65.5 cm) DEM 25,000. New York, 27 May 1993, *The Card Party* (oil on canvas, 30 x 35 3/4 ins / 76.2 x 90.8 cm) USD 14,950. Vienna, 29-30 Oct 1996, *Sta Maria della Salute, Venice* (oil on canvas, 21 3/4 x 41 ins / 55.5 x 104 cm) ATS 575,000. San Francisco, 26 May 1999, *Hope for Recovery* (1867, oil on canvas, 47 x 60 ins / 119 x 152 cm) USD 8,500. New York, 8 Sept 2004, *Lover's Tryst* (oil on canvas, 35 x 25 ins / 90 x 63 cm) USD 3,200.

HOFF, Carl Heinrich, the Younger

German, 19th - 20th century.
Born 17 September 1866, in Düsseldorf; died 1904.
Painter, engraver. Portraits, genre scenes.

Hoff was the son and student of Carl Heinrich Hoff the Elder. He was active both in Paris and Brittany, then in the Black Forest and the Tyrol. He settled in Paris in 1892. He produced engravings as well as paintings.

18 |€| 29

HOFF, Conrad

German, 19th century.
Born 19 November 1816, in Schwerin; died 18 February 1883, in Munich.
Painter. History painting, architectural views.

He trained at the academies in Dresden and Munich. Before he went over to architectural subjects, he had been a decorative painter. He is noted for a number of pictures showing interiors of churches in Venice and palaces in Germany. He was based in Dresden and Munich.

Museums and Galleries:

Hanover: *The Morning after the Banquet* - Munich: *Interior of Würzburg Residenz.*

Auction records:

New York, 4 May 1979, *Fishing Boats, Venice* (oil on canvas, 12 1/2 x 23 1/2 ins / 32 x 60 cm) USD 1,400. Munich, 5 July 2000, *Mother and Child in Interior Looking at Evening Sky* (1849, oil on canvas, 25 x 30 ins / 64 x 76 cm) DEM 6,500. Munich, 19 March 2003, *Venice by Moonlight* (oil on canvas, 14 x 11 ins / 36 x 29 cm) EUR 3,500.

HOFF, Dirck Claesz.

Dutch, 17th century.
Died c. 1627.
Active in Rotterdam.
Painter.

HOFF, Friedrich

German, 19th - 20th century.
Born 19 July 1832, in Frankfurt am Main; died 1913, in Frankfurt am Main.
Painter, art critic.

Hoff was the son of Johann Nikolaus Hoff. He painted landscapes and views of monuments.

HOFF, Heinrich

German, 18th century.
Born in Duderstadt, near Göttingen.
Painter.

He worked for the Dominican convent in Brno, where he painted a *St Dominic* in 1734.

HOFF, Izaak van T'

Dutch, 18th century.
Painter, draughtsman. Portraits.

Izaak van T'Hoff is known through his engravings after portraits that he painted.

HOFF, Jakob

German, 19th century.
Born 14 June 1838, in Frankfurt am Main; died 28 December 1892, in Frankfurt am Main.
Painter. Genre scenes, portraits.

A pupil of sculptor Zwerger and painter Jacob Becker, he began his career in 1861, travelling subsequently to France and Belgium. He also exhibited in Amsterdam and London, notably at the Royal Academy in 1877.

HOFF, Johann Nikolaus

German, 19th century.
Born 4 May 1798, in Frankfurt; died 6 March 1873, in Frankfurt.
Engraver, lithographer.

A pupil of G van Muller, he is notable for three particularly remarkable engravings: a *Madonna* after Vincenzo of San Gimignano, a *Deposition* after Perugino, and a *Madonna, Child and St Catherine* after Leonardo da Vinci.

HOFF, Jost von

German, 16th century.
Died 24 February 1592, in Kassel.
Painter.

Jost von Hoff painted a series of portraits in the castle at Kassel.

HOFF, Margo

American, 20th century.

Born 1912, in Tulsa (Oklahoma).
Painter. Landscapes.

Margo Hoff studied at the art school of the Art Institute of Chicago. She settled in New York but has travelled widely.

MUSEUMS AND GALLERIES:
LONDON (Courtauld Institute of Art).

AUCTION RECORDS:
NEW YORK, 21 May 1991, *In the Cathedral* (oil on reinforced canvas, 30 x 19 3/4 ins / 76.2 x 50.1 cm) USD 1,870.

HOFF, Philipp
German, 19th century.
Born 25 October 1833, in Frankfurt am Main.
Sculptor.

He was the son of Johann Nikolaus Hoff. A noted work is his *St Mark* in the church at Nied.

HOFFART, Johannes
German, 19th century.
Born 22 January 1851, in Mannheim.
Sculptor.

He trained at the academy in Munich. A noted work is his *Tomb of Prince Karl Friedrich of Baden*

HOFFBAUER, Charles Constantin Joseph
French, 19th - 20th century.
Born 28 June 1875, in Paris; died 1957.
Painter (gouache), watercolourist. History painting, portraits, genre scenes.

The son of Theodor Joseph Hubert Hoffbauer, the architect known for his reconstitution of ancient buildings, Charles Hoffbauer was taught by Flameng, Corman and Moreau. He was a remarkable artist with a delicate talent with an exceptional composition and a highly personal palette.

Charles Hoffbauer first showed in 1898, receiving an honourable mention; he was awarded a second medal in 1899 and a bronze at the 1900 Exposition Universelle in Paris. He was quickly successful. In 1902, he received the Prix Rosa Bonheur, as well as a travel grant and won the Prix National at the Salon des Artistes Français in Paris in 1906.

MUSEUMS AND GALLERIES:
BUCHAREST: *In Cairo* - MULHOUSE: *At the Ball* - PARIS (MAM): *Battlescene* - PHILADELPHIA: *Revolt of the People of Flanders* - ROUEN: *The Beggars* - SYDNEY: *On the Rooftops*.

AUCTION RECORDS:
PARIS, 18 June 1927, *Triumph of a Condottiere,* FRF 360. PARIS, 15 May 1944, *A Dinner on the Rooftops,* FRF 4,800. PARIS, July 1946, *Procession on the Square of Notre Dame in Paris in the Middle Ages* (gouache) FRF 3,500. PORTLAND, 7 July 1979, *Street Scene in the Snow* (oil on canvas, 18 x 22 ins / 46 x 56 cm) USD 3,100. NEW YORK, 30 Sept 1982, *On the Rooftops* (oil on canvas, 16 x 12 ins / 40.4 x 30.5 cm) USD 1,500. CHARLEVILLE-MÉZIÈRES, 9 Oct 1983, *Arabian Market* (oil on canvas, 23 1/2 x 31 1/2 ins / 60 x 80 cm) FRF 25,000. NEW YORK, 30 May 1986, *The Ball* (watercolour, gouache and pencil/brown paper, 9 x 11 1/2 ins / 22.9 x 29.5 cm) USD 8,500. MONTE CARLO, 6 Dec 1987, *Broadway in the Rain* (oil on canvas, 20 x 24 ins / 50.5 x 61 cm) FRF 75,000. MONACO, 20 Feb 1988, *Reconstruction of The Storming of the Bastille* (1918, watercolour, 18 x 33 ins / 46 x 84 cm) FRF 22,200. MONACO, 2 Dec 1988, *Reconstitution of a Roman City* (1914, gouache, 10 x 8 ins / 25.5 x 20.5 cm) FRF 8,880. LONDON, 7 June 1989, *On the Deck* (oil on canvas, 12 1/2 x 20 1/2 ins / 32 x 52 cm) GBP 3,300. VERSAILLES, 29 Oct 1989, *The Deck of the Boat* (oil on canvas, 11 1/2 x 21 1/4 ins / 29.5 x 54 cm) FRF 10,000. NEW YORK, 31 May 1990, *The Ball* (oil on canvas/panel, 7 3/4 x 9 3/4 ins / 20 x 25 cm) USD 3,080. PARIS, 19 June 1990, *Beach Scene* (oil on canvas, 11 3/4 x 17 3/4 ins / 30 x 45 cm) FRF 55,000. NEW YORK, 14 Nov 1991, *German Prisoners after the Battle of the Somme* (watercolour/paper, 10 1/2 x 14 ins / 26.7 x 35.5 cm) USD 825. LONDON, 17 June 1992, *The Gardens of Versailles* (oil on canvas, 31 1/2 x 39 1/4 ins / 80 x 100 cm) GBP 4,840. NEW YORK, 24 May 1995, *Broadway in the Snow in Front of the Astor Hotel in New York* (1925, oil on panel, 28 3/4 x 38 ins / 73 x 96.5 cm) USD 11,500. NEW YORK, 6 June 1997, *A Street in New York in the Rain* (c. 1912, oil on canvas, 31 1/4 x 25 1/4 ins / 79.4 x 64.1 cm) USD 68,500. PARIS, 6 April 1998, *Profile of a Woman; Scene in the Trench* (charcoal drawing and a watercolour, 11 1/4 x 8 1/2 ins / 28.5 x 21.5 cm and 11 1/2 x 8 3/4 ins/29.5 x 22.5 cm) FRF 1,100. NEW YORK, 5 May 1999, *Masked Ball at Versailles* (1901, oil on canvas, 22 x 30 ins / 56 x 77 cm) USD 18,000. ENGLEWOOD, 15 Nov 1999, *Cityscape* (oil on canvas, 24 x 30 ins / 61 x 76 cm) USD 11,000. NEW YORK, 15 June 2000, *Dance Hall* (oil on canvas laid on board, 8 x 10 ins / 20 x 25 cm) USD 2,600. NEW YORK, 28 Nov 2000, *Venetian Scene* (oil on canvas, 9 x 13 ins / 23 x 32 cm) USD 4,000. CHICAGO, 11 June 2001, *Wintry Evening in Times Square* (oil on canvas, 13 x 16 ins / 33 x 41 cm) USD 3,750. NEW YORK, 3 Dec 2003, *New York at Night* (oil on canvas, 20 x 16 ins / 50 x 40 cm) USD 15,000. NEW YORK, 3 Dec 2003, *Wintry Evening in Times Square* (c. 1927, oil on canvas, 18 x 24 ins / 45 x 60 cm) USD 27,500. PORTLAND, 6 Aug 2004, *Bacino di San Marco* (oil on board, 9 x 12 ins / 23 x 30 cm) USD 3,500.

HOFFBAUER, Theodor Josef Hubert
German, 19th - 20th century.
Born 1839, in Neuss near Düsseldorf; died 1922.
Active then naturalised in France.
Painter, watercolourist, draughtsman. Historical subjects, architectural views.

Hoffbauer was an important architect and one of the first organisers of Dioramas in Paris. He wrote many works on architecture, including *Le Vieux Paris* (*Old Paris*) and *Paris à travers les âges* (*Paris Through the Ages*), which are a very important source of information. He also produced various drawings of ancient Rome. Towards the end of his life he concentrated exclusively on making three-dimensional models of Paris in past times. He exhibited at the Salon des Artistes Français in Paris, of which he became a member in 1886.

MUSEUMS AND GALLERIES:
PARIS (Mus. Carnavalet): *Île de la Cité* (model).

AUCTION RECORDS:
PARIS, 30 Nov 1927, *Two Views of the Plaster Monument Erected for the Return of the Army from Italy: Two Drawings* (graphite) FRF 260.

HÖFFELE, B.
18th century.
Active at the end of the 18th century.
Miniaturist.

Miniatures by B. Höffele were exhibited in Vienna and Berlin in the early 20th century.

HOFFENBACH, Marie Jeanne
French, 20th century.
Born 15 March 1929, in Paris.
Collage artist.

Marie Jeanne Hoffenbach studied at the École des Beaux-Arts in Marseilles, and then in Paris, where she had her first solo exhibition in 1971.

She produced collages, using objects or images, which she brings together in a very personal way. Her paintings express a kind of fantastical poetry, not devoid of a slightly kitsch atmosphere.

HOFFERT, Joseph Kasimirovich
Russian, 19th century.
Born 20 April 1826; died 1906, in St Petersburg.

Painter.
Joseph Kasimirovich Hoffert is mainly known for watercolour and miniature portraits.

HOFFET, Wilhelm Johann
Russian, 19th century.
Born 25 August 1823; died 4 May 1906, in St Petersburg.
Painter.
Wilhelm Johann Hoffet is known for his miniatures.

HOFFLACK, Jacob
Dutch, 16th century.
Born in Amersfoort.
Painter.
A *Christ on the Cross* by Jacob Hofflack is mentioned in a will of 1599.

HÖFFLER, Josef, or Hoeffler
German, 20th century.
Born 18 March 1879, in Kaiserslautern (Rhineland-Palatinate); died 28 March 1915, in Bergzabem.
Sculptor.
Höffler studied under Schwert in Kaiserslautern and then travelled in France, Austria and Germany. He lived in Hamburg for a long time.

HOFFMAN, Belle
American, 20th century.
Born 28 April 1889, in Ohio; died 1961, in Cleveland (Ohio).
Painter.
Belle Hoffman studied at the Art Students League, New York and became a member of the Association of Women Painters and Sculptors and the American Federation of Arts.

HOFFMAN, Charles Herman
Belgian, 20th century.
Born 1900, in Vorst (Antwerp); died 1973, in Brussels.
Painter, sculptor, draughtsman. Portraits, genre scenes, still-lifes.
Hoffman studied at the Académie Royale des Beaux Arts in Brussels.

HOFFMAN, Francis, or Hoffmann
German, 18th century.
Of German origin.
Active in England c. 1711.
Engraver.
He is known for his portraits.

HOFFMAN, Frank B.
American, 20th century.
Born 28 August 1888, in Chicago; died 11 March 1958, in Taos (New Mexico).
Painter, illustrator, sculptor. Western scenes, figures, horses, animals.
Frank B. Hoffman studied with the portrait painter J. Wellington Reynolds from about 1910 to 1915. He grew up in New Orleans, where his father owned racing stables, which gave him the opportunity to draw the anatomy and movement of horses. He worked as an illustrator for the *Chicago American* daily newspaper, where he drew many subjects including boxing matches and operas, and was promoted to head of his department. He travelled to the American West, visiting ranches and living with Native Americans. He worked at Glacier National Park as a public relations director, where he met the artist John Singer Sargent. In 1920, he came to the Taos Art Colony in New Mexico, meeting Leon Gaspard.

Hoffman became one of New Mexico's most successful illustrators, contributing works on Western subjects to many national magazines, including *McCalls*, the *Saturday Evening Post* and *Cosmopolitan*. He also handled advertising illustration for General Motors and General Electric, and did works for books by Jack London, Zane Grey, Courtney Ripley Cooper and Gene Stratton Porter. His success allowed him to buy the Hobby Horse Rancho farm at Taos, where he raised quarter horses, longhorn cattle, dogs, eagles, burros and even a bear, all of which he used as models for his work.

Hoffman's paintings were known for their vibrant colours and bold brush-strokes, as seen in his cowboy paintings *A Sure Catch* and *Quick Action*, or other scenes such as *Wagon Train* and *Fisherman's Luck*. From 1940 to 1954, Hoffman worked under exclusive contract for Brown and Bigelow, producing 150 paintings on Western subjects for calendars. Although primarily a painter, he also sculpted models of animals in the 1930s.

BIBLIOGRAPHY:
Zimmer, Stephen, '*Frank B. Hoffman: The Calendar Years*' in *Southwest Art*, September 1995.

MUSEUMS AND GALLERIES:
BARTLESVILLE, OK (Woolaroc Museum) - CANYON, TX (Panhandle-Plains Historical Museum) - INDIANAPOLIS (Eiteljorg Mus. of American Indians and Western Art) - OKLAHOMA CITY (National Cowboy and Western Heritage Mus.) - OMAHA, NE (Joslyn Art Museum) - PUEBLO, CO (Sangre de Cristo Arts Center) - TRINIDAD, CO (A.R. Mitchell Museum).

AUCTION RECORDS:
HAYDEN, 31 July 1999, *Cowboy* (watercolour, 16 x 11 ins / 41 x 28 cm) USD 6,500. HAYDEN, 31 July 1999, *Wagon Train* (oil on board, 18 x 24 ins / 46 x 61 cm) USD 18,000. HAYDEN, 29 July 2000, *Cowboy Contentment* (oil on board, 12 x 16 ins / 30 x 41 cm) USD 8,500. HAYDEN, 29 July 2000, *Bringing in the Remuda* (oil on board, 10 x 14 ins / 25 x 36 cm) USD 10,000. NEW YORK, 7 June 2001, *Riders up: Saddling for the Point to Point* (oil on canvas, 24 x 31 ins / 61 x 79 cm) USD 32,000. HAYDEN, 28 July 2001, *Buffalo on the Plains* (oil on board, 14 x 16 ins / 36 x 41 cm) USD 25,000. NEW YORK, 18 April 2002, *Jockeys up!* (oil on canvas) USD 26,000. HAYDEN, 27 July 2002, *Disputed Prize* (oil on board, 18 x 24 ins / 46 x 61 cm) USD 22,500. SAN FRANCISCO, 10 Dec 2003, *Racehorse* (oil on canvas, 40 x 50 ins / 102 x 127 cm) USD 16,000. SAN FRANCISCO, 10 Dec 2003, *No Dinner Tonight* (oil on masonite, 28 x 36 ins / 71 x 91 cm) USD 22,000. HAYDEN, 24 July 2004, *Cowboy Camp* (oil on canvasboard, 18 x 24 ins / 46 x 61 cm) USD 16,000. HAYDEN, 24 July 2004, *Trapper* (oil over grisaille on canvas, 30 x 20 ins / 76 x 51 cm) USD 16,000.

HOFFMAN, Georg
German, 20th century.
Born 1924.
Painter, sculptor.
Hoffman's works are non-figurative.

HOFFMAN, Hans
Austrian, 20th century.
Born 1928, in Ybbs (Danube).
Painter. Insects.
Hoffman produced a series of appliquéd and printed pictures of insects on unframed canvases.

AUCTION RECORDS:
NEW YORK, 3 May 1988, *Nocturne* (1952, oil on canvas, 60 x 48 ins / 152.4 x 122 cm) USD 319,000.

HOFFMAN, Harry Leslie
American, 19th - 20th century.
Born 1871, in Cressona (Pennsylvania); died 1964.
Painter. Genre scenes, landscapes, seascapes, still-lifes.
After studying under Jean-Paul Laurens in Paris, Harry Hoffman settled in New York. He was a member of many New York artists' associations, the Salmagundi Club and the American Federation of Arts.

AUCTION RECORDS:
NEW YORK, 28 Nov 1995, *Nassau Docks* (oil on card, 6 x 7 3/4 ins / 15 x 20 cm) USD 1,380. CONNECTICUT, 24 May 1999, *West Wind* (oil on board, 14 x 16 ins / 36 x 41 cm) USD 2,100. MILFORD, 21 Oct 1999, *Artist's Wife Bea at Loom* (oil on board, 16 x 12 ins / 41 x 30 cm) USD 3,000. PASADENA, 14 Nov 2000, *Figures and Boat* (oil on board, 2 x 3 ins / 6 x 8 cm) USD 1,600. CONNECTICUT, 21 June 2001, *Fishing in Lyme* (oil on canvas, 24 x 26 ins / 61 x 66 cm) USD 5,750. MILFORD, 25 Oct 2001, *Yesterday's snow* (1913, canvasboard, 7 x 10 ins / 18 x 25 cm) USD 5,500. BOSTON, 10 May 2002, *Reef* (1916, oil on canvas, 24 x 26 ins / 61 x 66 cm) USD 2,000. CEDAR FALLS, 14 June 2003, *Indefatigable Shore, Galapogos* (1923, oil on panel, 18 x 20 ins / 46 x 51 cm) USD 3,000. MILFORD, 6 May 2004, *In the Garden* (oil on board, 10 x 8 ins / 25 x 20 cm) USD 12,000. MILFORD, 21 Oct 2004, *Gathering Flowers* (oil on board, 8 x 10 ins / 20 x 25 cm) USD 4,000.

HOFFMAN, Juan

French (?), 20th century.

Painter. Landscapes, still-lifes.

AUCTION RECORDS:
PARIS, 12 April 1943, *In the Park*, FRF 600; *Notre Dame* (1910) FRF 1,100.

HOFFMAN, L.

German (?), 19th century.

Painter. Genre scenes, animals.

First mentioned in *Art Prices Current*.

AUCTION RECORDS:
LONDON, 17 Feb 1908, *Geese on the watch*, GBP 4. COPENHAGEN, 28 April 1981, *The (Female) Poultry Vendor* (1841, oil/metal, 15 1/4 x 12 1/2 ins / 39 x 32 cm) DKK 14,000.

HOFFMAN, Malvina Cornell

American, 20th century.

Born 15 June 1887, in New York; died 1966, in New York.

Sculptor, painter, printmaker. Figures, dancers.

Malvina Hoffman studied painting under John White Alexander at the Art Students League, and studied sculpture with Gutzon Borglum and in Paris with Auguste Rodin in 1910, where she learned carving, modelling and foundry techniques. She came from an artistic family, and had modelled her first sculpture by the age of 21. From 1910 to 1914, Hoffman also studied anatomy at the College of Physicians and Surgeons in New York to learn more about human physiognomy. Hoffman created mostly portraits or allegorical figures and she was regularly commissioned to make public monuments and commemorative medallions. She was particularly known for her sculptures of dancer Anna Pavlova, who posed for her on many occasions. Her *Bacchanale Frieze* (1915-1924) is a 26-panel plaster tribute to Pavlova. In 1929, Hoffman was commissioned by the Field Museum of Natural History in Chicago to make the series of 104 life-size sculptures, *The Living Races of Man*. She travelled to places such as Japan, China, the South Pacific, the Dutch Indies, India and the Malay Peninsula to make models, producing such pieces as *Jaipur Woman* (1932).

BIBLIOGRAPHY:
Alexandre, Arsène, *Malvina Hoffman*, E.J. Pouterman, Paris, 1930. Hoffman, Malvina, *Heads and Tales in Many Lands*, Scribner, New York, 1937. *Malvina Hoffman*, W.W. Norton, New York, 1948. *Malvina Hoffman, 1885-1966*, exhibition catalogue, FAR Gallery, New York, 1980. Conner, Janis, *A Dancer in Relief: Works by Malvina Hoffman*, exhibition catalogue, The Hudson River Museum, New York, 1984. Hill, May Brawley, *The Woman Sculptor Malvina Hoffman and her Contemporaries*, exhibition catalogue, Berry-Hill Galleries, New York, 1984. Conner, Janis/Rosenkranz, Joel, *Rediscoveries in American Sculpture: Studio Works, 1893-1939*, exhibition catalogue, University of Texas Press, Austin (TX), 1989.

MUSEUMS AND GALLERIES:
CEDAR RAPIDS (Cedar Rapids Museum of Art): *Bacchanale Triangle (Pavlova and Mordkin)* (1914, woodcut); *Boy and Panther Cub* (1915, bronze); *Bacchanale Frieze* (1915-1924, plaster); *Roger Kahn* (1916, marble); *Jaipur Woman* (1932, bronze); *Girl on the Beach* (marble) - CINCINNATI (University of Cincinnati): *Portrait of Pierre Teilhard de Chardin* (1948, bronze) - DETROIT (IA): *Russian Dancers* (1911, bronze) - GLENS FALLS, NY (Hyde Collection): *Dancers* (1912, bronze) - LONDON (Courtauld Institute of Art) - LOS ANGELES (County MA): *Column of Life* (1917, bronze) - NEW YORK (National Academy of Design Mus.): *Bali Boy and Fighting Cock* (1928, bronze) - SAN FRANCISCO (FAM): *Cambodian Dancer* (1937, bronze); *Pavlova and Mordkin in 'Bacchanale Russe'* (1912, bronze); *Daboa, African Dancer* (1931, bronze); *The Mandolin* (1915, lithograph); *Pavlova* (lithograph); *Egyptian Dancer* (1933, bronze) - WASHINGTON DC (National Mus. of Women in the Arts): *Anna Pavlova* (1926, bronze) - WASHINGTON DC (Smithsonian American AM): *Self-portrait* (1929, limestone); *Giovanni Boldini* (1928, bronze); *Katharine Cornell* (1961, bronze); *Marcel Griaule* (1935, bronze); *Modern Crusader* (c. 1917-1919, bronze); *Paderewski 'The Man'* (1923, bronze).

AUCTION RECORDS:
NEW YORK, 20 April 1972, *Indian Standing* (patinated bronze) USD 2,400; *Saint's Head* (1926, white marble, h. 13 1/2 ins / 34.5 cm) USD 3,800. NEW YORK, 13 May 1977, *Kili Sleeping* (1929, patinated bronze, diam. 11 ins / 27 cm) USD 1,000. NEW YORK, 24 Nov 1978, *Pavlowa the Incomparable* (1914, coloured lithograph poster mounted on canvas, 60 1/4 x 33 3/4 ins / 153 x 86 cm) USD 1,600. NEW YORK, 18 Sept 1980, *Bust of an African Woman* (black-patinated bronze, h. 14 3/4 ins / 37.4 cm) USD 5,000. NEW YORK, 2 Dec 1982, *La Gavotte - Anna Pavlova* (1915, golden-brown-patinated bronze, h. 14 ins / 35.6 cm) USD 8,250. NEW YORK, 1 June 1983, *Borneo Native Climbing a Palm Tree* (bronze, h. 17 3/4 ins / 45.1 cm) USD 9,500. NEW YORK, 28 Sept 1989, *Mask of Anna Pavlova* (gilded bronze, h. 7 3/4 ins / 20 cm) USD 6,600. NEW YORK, 1 Dec 1989, *Bill Working* (bronze/marble plinth, h. 9 1/4 ins / 23.5 cm) USD 22,000. NEW YORK, 14 Feb 1990, *Nymph* (1920, bronze, h. 12 1/4 ins / 31 cm) USD 3,080. NEW YORK, 16 March 1990, *Egyptian Dancer Nyota Inyoka* (1932, partially gilded bronze, h. 10 1/2 ins / 26.7 cm, l. 12 1/2 ins/32 cm) USD 11,000. NEW YORK, 21 May 1991, *Mask of Anna Pavlova* (bronze, h. 8 ins / 19.4 cm) USD 3,080. NEW YORK, 25 Sept 1991, *Breton Wrestlers* (1929, bronze, h. 19 3/4 ins / 50.2 cm) USD 5,500. NEW YORK, 15 April 1992, *Struggle - Elemental Man* (brown-patinated bronze, h. 25 1/4 ins / 64.1 cm) USD 5,225. NEW YORK, 4 Dec 1992, *Hindu Incense Burner* (bronze, h. 10 3/4 ins / 27.3 cm) USD 5,280. NEW YORK, 9 Sept 1993, *La Frileuse (Shivering Girl)* (1912, bronze, h. 11 ins / 27.9 cm) USD 1,150. NEW YORK, 21 Sept 1994, *Russian Dancers* (1911, bronze, h. 10 3/4 ins / 27.3 cm, w. 13 ins/33 cm) USD 20,700. PARIS, 30 Jan 1995, *Pavlova and Mordkin in Bacchanale* (1920, original plaster in bronze patina, 23 1/4 x 17 ins / 59 x 43 cm) FRF 10,000. NEW YORK, 13 March 1996, *La Gavotte* (bronze, h. 14 ins / 35.6 cm) USD 6,900. NEW YORK, 26 Sept 1996, *Napping Cat* (black marble, l. 9 1/2 ins / 24.1 cm) USD 6,900. NEW YORK, 4 Dec 1996, *Bill Working* (bronze, h. 9 1/4 ins / 23.5 cm) USD 28,750. NEW YORK, 23 April 1997, *Pavlova and Novikoff Dancing* (1914, red-brown-patinated bronze, group, h. 11 1/2 ins / 29.2 cm) USD 9,200. PARIS, 12 Dec 1997, *Bust of Eugène Rudier* (1929, h. 20 ins / 51 cm) FRF 11,000. NORWALK, 18 April 1999, *Memento de Verdad, Matador with Sword and Cape in Hand* (gilt green patinated bronze, 8 x 3 ins / 20 x 8 cm) USD 1,750. CHICAGO, 6 May 2000, *La Frileuse (Shivering Girl)* (green patinated bronze, h. 39 ins / 99 cm) USD 7,500. ZOFINGEN, 1 Dec 2000, *Russian Bacchanale* (1911, bronze, 13 x 10 ins / 32 x 26 cm) CHF 6,000. NEW YORK, 21 May 2002,

Russian Dancers (1911, reddish brown patinated bronze, 11 x 13 ins / 27 x 33 cm) USD 22,000. NEW YORK, 5 Dec 2002, *La Frileuse* (*Shivering Girl*) (1912, green patinated bronze, h. 39 ins / 100 cm) USD 45,000. NEW YORK, 4 March 2003, *Tibetan Jewel Merchant* (brown patinated bronze, h. 12 ins / 31 cm) USD 9,000. NEW YORK, 3 Dec 2003, *La Frileuse* (*Shivering Girl*) (brown green patinated bronze, h. 38 ins / 96 cm) USD 30,000. NEW YORK, 3 March 2004, *Daboa* (1933, brown red patinated bronze, h. 15 ins / 37 cm) USD 6,000. NEW YORK, 18 May 2004, *Modesty* (brown patinated bronze, h. 8 ins / 20 cm) USD 6,500.

HOFFMAN, Nancy M.
American, 20th - 21st century.
Born 24 June 1949, in Boston (Massachusetts).
Painter.

Nancy Holt's work features regularly in solo and group exhibitions in New York.

AUCTION RECORDS:
PARIS, 16 Dec 1990, *Tipped tourmaline n° 1* (1990, oil on canvas, 53 1/4 x 53 1/4 ins / 135 x 135 cm) FRF 12,000.

HOFFMAN, Vlastimil, or Hofmann
Czech, 20th century.
Born 1881, in Prague.
Active in Poland.
Painter. Religious subjects, genre scenes.

After studying with Gérôme in Paris, Vlastimil Hoffman lived and worked in Cracow and Vienna. He was an associate member of the Salon de la Société Nationale des Beaux-Arts in Paris. In 1921, two of his works, *Confession* and *Legend*, were shown at the exhibition of work by Polish artists held at the Salon de la Société Nationale des Beaux-Arts in Paris.

MUSEUMS AND GALLERIES:
CRACOW: *Christmas Eve* - VIENNA: *The Virgin*.

HOFFMAN, Wilmer
American, 20th century.
Born 1 August 1889, in Calonsville (Maryland); died 1954.
Active in France.
Sculptor.

Wilmer Hoffman studied at the Pennsylvania Academy of the Fine Arts, Philadelphia and received a travel bursary. He exhibited in America before moving to Paris, where he exhibited at the Salon d'Automne and at the Tuileries. He specialised in sculpting busts of Indians and black people, exaggerating the forms to facilitate the effects of light.

HOFFMANN, Alexander
German, 20th century.
Born 28 August 1878, in Grimma.
Painter, engraver.

Hoffmann studied at the academy of fine arts in Dresden and was active in Lauenstein and Lübeck.

HOFFMANN, Anker
Danish, 20th century.
Born 13 April 1904, in Holte; died 9 June 1985, in Kongens Lyngby.
Sculptor. Figures, portraits. Statuettes, groups, busts.

AUCTION RECORDS:
COPENHAGEN, 28 April 1976, *Couple Seated, Back to Back* (1965, bronze, 11 x 17 ins / 27 x 43 cm) DKK 5,500. COPENHAGEN, 11 May 1977, *Couple Back to Back* (1968, bronze, h. 11 ins / 27 cm, w. 17 ins/43 cm) DKK 5,600. COPENHAGEN, 27 Oct 1982, *Seated Nude* (1939, stone, h. 31 1/2 ins / 80 cm) DKK 10,000. COPENHAGEN, 9 May 1990, *Young Girl* (1964, bronze, h. 15 3/4 ins / 40 cm) DKK 16,500. COPENHAGEN, 1 April 1992, *Head of Young girl* (1963, bronze, h. 12 1/4 ins / 31 cm) DKK 3,600. COPENHAGEN, 21 Oct 1992, *Little Girl* (1957, bronze, h. 13 3/4 ins / 35 cm) DKK 4,000. COPENHAGEN, 21 April 1993, *Little Girl* (lost-wax bronze, h. 21 1/4 ins / 54 cm) DKK 6,000. COPENHAGEN, 13 April 1994, *Young Girl Standing* (1956, bronze, h. 17 ins / 43 cm) DKK 5,000. COPENHAGEN, 17 April 1996, *Young Girl Reclining No. 3* (1961, bronze, h. 8 1/4 ins / 21 cm) DKK 5,500. COPENHAGEN, 12 April 2000, *Girl Kneeling* (1960, bronze, 11 x 17 ins / 27 x 42 cm) DKK 15,000. COPENHAGEN, 10 April 2002, *Young Devotion* (1979, green patinated bronze, 11 x 12 ins / 27 x 31 cm) DKK 16,000. COPENHAGEN, 26 Nov 2003, *Girl Seated with Bent Knees* (1961, bronze, h. 13 ins / 33 cm, w. 19 ins/47 cm) DKK 19,000. COPENHAGEN, 29 March 2004, *Reclining Female Nude* (1945, dark patinated bronze, h. 10 ins / 25 cm, w. 17 ins/42 cm) DKK 15,000. COPENHAGEN, 29 March 2004, *Reclining Female Nude* (dark green patinated bronze, h. 10 ins / 25 cm, w. 16 ins/41 cm) DKK 18,000.

HOFFMANN, Anselm Franz
German, 18th century.
Born 20 April 1708, in Mainz; died 6 April 1782, in Frankfurt.
Painter, decorative designer. Architectural views.

His works are frescoes.

HOFFMANN, Anton
German, 19th - 20th century.
Born 10 April 1863, in Bayreuth; died 1938.
Painter, illustrator. Genre scenes.

Hoffmann exhibited his work in Berlin in 1909. He spent most of his time in Munich and illustrated high quality books.

AUCTION RECORDS:
MUNICH, 21 Sept 1978, *Soldiers of the Emperor Maximilian I* (oil on panel, 6 1/4 x 9 1/2 ins / 16 x 24 cm) DEM 4,000. LONDON, 3 Oct 1979, *Soldiers on a Road* (oil on canvas, 26 x 39 ins / 66 x 99 cm) GBP 900. MUNICH, 8 May 1985, *Cavalry Engagement During the American War of Independence of 1775-1783* (oil on canvas, 23 1/2 x 31 ins / 60 x 79 cm) DEM 5,000. MUNICH, 27 Feb 1999, *Farmhands on Moving Horse-drawn Cart* (oil on panel, 4 x 6 ins / 10 x 14 cm) DEM 4,300. STUTTGART, 2 Dec 1999, *Peasants on the Move during the Thirty Years War* (oil on canvas, 20 x 30 ins / 50 x 76 cm) DEM 4,300. NEW YORK, 28 March 2000, *Skirmish* (1918, oil on canvas, 37 x 60 ins / 94 x 152 cm) USD 2,200. LYONS, 4 March 2001, *Odalisques* (oil on canvas) FRF 37,000. MUNICH, 24 Oct 2001, *Cavalry Battle* (1917, oil on canvas, 38 x 53 ins / 96 x 135 cm) DEM 3,600. NEW ORLEANS, 22 March 2002, *Skirmish* (1918, oil on canvas, 37 x 60 ins / 94 x 152 cm) USD 2,600. WARSAW, 19 Oct 2003, *Wandering Troops during Summer War* (c. 1900, oil on canvas, 24 x 32 ins / 61 x 81 cm) PLN 14,000. LINDAU, 5 Dec 2003, *Medieval Military Camp* (oil on canvas, 22 x 35 ins / 56 x 88 cm) EUR 1,500.

HOFFMANN, Arthur
German, 19th - 20th century.
Born 20 July 1874, in Potsdam.
Sculptor.

Hoffmann's works include *Hamlet; German Warrior*. He exhibited in Berlin in 1909.

HOFFMANN, August
German, 19th century.
Born 1 August 1810, in Elberfeld; died 20 October 1872, in Berlin.
Engraver.

He learnt engraving from Thelott at the academy in Düsseldorf, though completing his training with Keller. He engraved from Raphael, Kaulbach, Cornelius etc. Among works by him is *The Hussites' Sermons*, after Lessing, in Raczynski's *History of Modern Art in Germany*. He worked in Munich, Berlin and Paris, and in 1857 gained a third-class medal.

HOFFMANN, Bartholomeus
German, 15th - 16th century.
Died before 1522.
Active in Breslau (now Wroclaw, Poland).
Painter.
Bartholomeus Hoffmann was a pupil of Paul Glaser from 1479 to 1482.

HOFFMANN, C. A.
French (?), 19th century.
Painter, watercolourist. Landscapes.
This artist exhibited his work at the Paris Salon between 1842 and 1847.

HOFFMANN, C. Heinrich
German, 19th century.
Painter. Genre scenes, landscapes.
He worked in Dresden and Munich, launching his career in 1866.

HOFFMANN, Didier
Belgian, 20th - 21st century.
Born 1 November 1959.
Active in France.
Painter.
In 1981, Hoffmann studied painting at the École Van der Kelen et Logelain in Brussels. He has participated in group exhibitions and has held solo shows since 1987, notably in Paris. Between 1983 and 1985, he was producing décors in Paris. Thickly applied paint and drips saturate the surface of the canvas in his works.

HOFFMANN, E. Conrad
German.
Engraver (burin).
E. Conrad Hoffmann made engravings after Govaert Flinck.

HOFFMANN, Eduardo
Argentinian, 20th century.
Painter.
Eduardo Hoffmann lives and works in Buenos Aires. In 1993 he took part in the Salon Découvertes in Paris. He exhibits in Argentina. Hoffmann paints on wood.

HOFFMANN, Émilie Marguerite
French, 19th century.
Active in Rueil-Malmaison (Hauts-de-Seine).
Painter, draughtsman. Portraits.
Émilie Hoffmann's work (consisting chiefly of drawings) was exhibited at the Salon of 1848.

HOFFMANN, Engelhard
German, 16th century.
Died 18 February 1550.
Active in Überlingen.
Painter.
Engelhard Hoffmann painted a retable for the church in Überlingen.

HOFFMANN, Ernst Christoph
German, 17th century.
Born 7 April 1642, in Waldheim (Saxony); died 2 September 1678, in Dresden.
Painter.
He was the court painter of Johann Georg II, Prince Palatine of Saxony.

HOFFMANN, Ernst Theodor Amedeus
German, 19th century.
Born 24 January 1776, in Königsberg (now Kaliningrad, Russia); died 25 June 1822, in Berlin.
Painter, draughtsman.
A famous storyteller and musician in his time, this universally gifted genius also ventured in caricatures and decorative art.

HOFFMANN, Felicita. See **SARTORI**

HOFFMANN, Franz Xaver
Austrian, 19th century.
Active in Vienna c. 1835.
Painter.
His oeuvre includes portraits and still lifes.

HOFFMANN, Friedrich
German, 18th century.
Born 21 November 1755, in Frankenheim.
Painter.
The brother of Georg Andreas Hoffmann, he worked mostly in Berlin, where he painted portraits of children.

HOFFMANN, Gaston
French, 20th century.
Born 12 January 1883, in Paris.
Painter. Genre scenes.
Gaston Hoffmann was a pupil of Bonnat, Lefebvre, L.O. Merson and J. Marcher. He became a member of the Société des Artistes Français in 1909.
AUCTION RECORDS:
PARIS, 28 Dec 1942, *Female Nude*, FRF 750.

HOFFMANN, Georg
German, 17th century.
Active in Brieg (now Brzeg, Poland) at the beginning of the 17th century.
Painter.
A noted work is a *Death of Abel.*

HOFFMANN, Georg
German, 18th - 19th century.
Born 24 December 1749, in Kromach; died 23 April 1817, in Bamberg.
Sculptor.
A pupil of J B Kamm, he worked mainly in Mainz and Würzburg.

HOFFMANN, Georg Andreas
German, 18th century.
Born 28 October 1752, in Frankenau (Saxony); died 1808, in Berlin.
Painter, copyist. Portraits.
Hoffmann was a deaf-mute. During his time at the Heineck Institute, he had to learn drawing at the academy in Leipzig, and worked subsequently in Dresden under the guidance of Professor Casanova. He was an excellent copyist and reproduced inter alia Correggio's *Night* and several of Raphael's canvases. He also did some very good portraits.
AUCTION RECORDS:
LONDON, 28 April 1924, *Summer - Bavaria*, GBP 9. PARIS, 6 March 1942, *The Violin Lesson*, FRF 2,900.

HOFFMANN, George Jan or George Johannes
Dutch, 19th century.
Born 24 January 1833, in The Hague; died 28 November 1873, in The Hague.
Painter. Seascapes.
George Hoffmann studied under Louis Meyer and exhibited at The Hague exhibition of 1857.
MUSEUMS AND GALLERIES:
THE HAGUE (Gemeentemus.): *Restless Water.*
AUCTION RECORDS:
AMSTERDAM, 5 Nov 1996, *Sailing Boats in a Sound* (oil on panel, 13 1/2 x 17 3/4 ins / 34 x 45 cm) NLG 4,012. AMSTERDAM, 27 Oct 1997, *Sailing Boats at Sea* (oil on panel, 12 x 16 3/4 ins / 30.5 x 42.5 cm) NLG 20,650. AMSTERDAM, 20 April 1999, *Full-rigged Koff in the Breeze, Paddle Steamer beyond* (oil on

canvas, 14 x 20 ins / 36 x 50 cm) NLG 8,500. AMSTERDAM, 30 Jan 2001, *Hay Barge Unloading, Dutch Frigate in the Distance* (oil on panel, 16 x 21 ins / 40 x 54 cm) NLG 9,000. BERN, 10 May 2001, *Seascape* (oil on panel, 11 x 16 ins / 27 x 41 cm) CHF 3,000.

HOFFMANN, Gottfried Augustin
German, 18th century.
Active in Schweidnitz (now Swidnica, Poland), c. 1724.
Sculptor.
He worked on the decoration of Fürstenstein (Ksiaz) castle, near Sorgau (Troska), Silesia.

HOFFMANN, Gustav Adolf
German, 19th century.
Born 28 January 1869, in Cottbus.
Engraver.
He was a pupil of K Marr in Munich.

HOFFMANN, Hans, called Lani
German, 16th century.
Died 1568, in Freiburg im Brisgau.
Painter.
Hans Hoffmann did decorative painting in the Freiburg im Brisgau town hall.

HOFFMANN, Hans or Johann
German, 16th century.
Born c. 1530, in Nuremberg (?); died perhaps c. 1591, in Prague.
Painter, watercolourist. Religious subjects, portraits, animals, flowers.
Prague School.
As well as flowers and insects, Hans Hoffmann painted some portraits, including one of Hans Sachs. He principally used watercolours. He was in the service of Emperor Rudolph in Prague in 1584. He drew inspiration from the work of Dürer.

BIBLIOGRAPHY:
DaCosta Kaufmann, Thomas, *L'École de Prague*, Flammarion, Paris, 1985.
MUSEUMS AND GALLERIES:
BUDAPEST: *St Peter in Prison* - LOS ANGELES (Getty Mus.): *Hare in the Forest* (c. 1585, oil/panel) - VIENNA: *Portrait of a Man*.
AUCTION RECORDS:
LONDON, 14 Dec 1923, *Head of St John the Baptist,* GBP 18. LONDON, 24 April 1929, *Squirrel* (watercolour) GBP 115. LONDON, 10 July 1936, *Study of a Dead Jay* (watercolour) GBP 178. VIENNA, 22 Sept 1970, *Ecce Homo,* ATS 50,000. LONDON, 30 March 1976, *Squirrel Eating a Hazelnut* (1578, watercolour heightened with white, 10 x 7 ins / 25.1 x 17.7 cm) GBP 27,000. LONDON, 7 April 1981, *Squirrel Eating a Hazelnut* (1578, watercolour heightened with white/parchment, 10 x 7 ins / 25.1 x 17.7 cm) GBP 70,000. LONDON, 30 Nov 1983, *Hare among Plants, with a Lizard and Insects* (oil on panel, 24 3/4 x 31 ins / 63 x 78.5 cm) GBP 370,000. NEW YORK, 25 Jan 2001, *Hare in a Forest* (oil on panel, 62 x 78 ins / 157 x 198 cm) USD 2,400,000.

HOFFMANN, Hans Ruprecht, the Elder
German, 16th - 17th century.
Born c. 1540, in Trier; died 1616, in Trier.
Sculptor.
Hans Ruprecht Hoffmann the Elder studied under Dietrich Shro in Mainz. He worked almost entirely for the archbishops of Trier and specialised in altars and tombs.

HOFFMANN, Hans Ruprecht, the Younger
German, 17th century.
Born 1596, in Trier.
Sculptor.
He was the son of sculptor Heinrich Hoffmann. He worked for the church in Klüsserath (Moselle Valley).

HOFFMANN, Heinrich
German, 16th - 17th century.
Died 1623.
Active in Mainz c. 1570.
Sculptor.
Heinrich Hoffmann was the son and collaborator of Hans Ruprecht Hoffmann the Elder and worked in the church of Bernkastel.

HOFFMANN, Heinrich
German, 19th century.
Born 27 August 1816, in Darmstadt; died 14 March 1891, in Darmstadt.
Painter. Landscapes, urban landscapes.
An army officer professionally, he took up painting much later. He painted landscapes and views of towns in a Dutch 17th-century style.

HOFFMANN, Heinrich
German, 19th century.
Born 30 August 1859, in Kassel.
Painter, sculptor.
He was a pupil of Louis Kolitz and Hermann Knackfuss at the academy in Kassel. He was active in Heidelberg.

HOFFMANN, Heinrich Adolf Valentin
German, 19th century.
Born 18 October 1814, in Frankfurt am Main; died 11 June 1896, in Frankfurt am Main.
Painter. Landscapes.
A pupil of Jacob Recker at the Städelsches Institut in Frankfurt from 1843 to 1850, he travelled around Germany, Switzerland and Austrian Tyrol before returning to Frankfurt to settle. He often exhibited in France.
MUSEUMS AND GALLERIES:
FRANKFURT AM MAIN (Städel): *Impression of November.*
AUCTION RECORDS:
COLOGNE, 12 June 1970, *Landscape in the Frankfurt Area,* DEM 5,300. ZURICH, 20 June 2000, *Extensive Lake Landscape with Chapel and Figures* (oil on canvas, 26 x 43 ins / 66 x 108 cm) CHF 4,300.

HOFFMANN, Heinrich Bernhard Martin Johannes
Danish, 19th - 20th century.
Born 17 July 1844, in Schleswig; died 20 June 1920, in Copenhagen.
Sculptor.
Hoffmann studied under Herman Vilhelm Bissen at the Kongelige Danske Kunstakademi in Copenhagen in 1862. He left for Italy in 1874 and settled in Rome.
MUSEUMS AND GALLERIES:
BASEL: *Youth* - COPENHAGEN (Statens Mus. for Kunst): *Psyche* (1876).

HOFFMANN, Hermann
German, 19th century.
Born 6 January 1862, in Berlin.
Painter. Genre scenes.
He was a student at the academy in Berlin. His debut was in 1890.

HOFFMANN, Israel
Argentinian, 20th century.
Born in Argentina.
Sculptor.

HOFFMANN, Jacob
German, 19th century.
Born 4 June 1852, in Frankfurt am Main; died 5 June 1903, in Oberursel (Bad Homburg).
Landscape artist.
The son and pupil of Heinrich Adolf Valentin Hoffmann, he began to work professionally around 1880. He exhibited in Frankfurt, Munich and Hamburg.

HOFFMANN, Jakob
Swiss, 16th century.
Active c. 1576.
Painter.
Jakob Hoffmann is mentioned in the chronicle of Abbot Christoph Silberisen of Wettingen.

HOFFMANN, Janos
Hungarian, 18th century.
Active in Buda (Budapest).
Sculptor.

HOFFMANN, Jeanne Juliette Joséphine
French, 19th - 20th century.
Born in Paris.
Engraver, draughtswoman.
A pupil of George-Sauvage, Jeanne Hoffmann exhibited in Paris at the Salon des Artistes Français, of which she became a member in 1905. She executed numerous lithographs.

HOFFMANN, Johann
Austrian, 18th century.
Active in Prerau (Prerov/Moravia) in the middle of the 18th century.
Painter.
He worked in Kremsier (Kromeríz) and for the church of St Michael in Prerov, Moravia.

HOFFMANN, Johann. See also **HOFFMANN Heinrich Bernhard Martin Johannes**

HOFFMANN, Johann Daniel
German, 18th century.
Born c. 1730, in Wiesbaden; died 1777.
Painter. History painting, portraits.
He is known for a *Mutius Scævola* dated 1760.

HOFFMANN, Johann Franz
German, 18th century.
Born in Grüssau (now Krzeszow, Poland); died c. 1766, in Prague.
Painter, engraver.
Johann Franz Hoffmann was a pupil of Willmann in Breslau (now Wroclaw). He worked for the church in Hirschberg (now Jelena Góra, Poland).

HOFFMANN, Johann Joseph
German, 18th century.
Born 17 March 1762, in Guhlau (Gola), Silesia.
Sculptor.
He was a pupil of Stein and then Prokop. A known work is his *Bust of the Philosopher Garve*.

HOFFMANN, Johann Leonhard
German, 18th - 19th century.
Born 25 August 1740, in Neustadt; died c. 1812.
Draughtsman, miniaturist. Landscapes.
A student at Erlangen University, he was later a drawing master. He travelled in Italy, Russia and Poland.

HOFFMANN, Johann Valentin
Austrian, 17th century.
Painter.
Active in Vienna, he is known for a still life dated 1658.

HOFFMANN, Jonas
Swedish, 18th century.
Born 1731, in Örebro; died 1780, in Stockholm.
Painter.
Jonas Hoffmann worked in France and Italy and then returned to Sweden to settle in 1770. There is a *Still-life* by him in the National Museum, Stockholm.

HOFFMANN, Josef
Austrian, 19th century.
Born 22 July 1831, in Vienna; died 31 January 1904, in Vienna.
Painter, watercolourist. Genre scenes, landscapes.
He displayed a marked interest in drawing at an early age, and went on a study tour to Serbia and Slavonia. On his return to Vienna, he studied with Anton (?) Rath and Leitung (?) until 1854. From 1856 to 1858 he travelled in Italy and Greece, immersing himself in the study of Italian landscape painting. He subsequently went on an extensive journey through Norway before returning to Vienna again. In 1867, he became a member of the academy of fine arts in Vienna. In 1878, he did the stage sets for Wagner's *Ring* at the Festspielhaus in Bayreuth.

HOFFMANN, Josef
Czech, 19th - 20th century.
Born 1870; died 1956.
Active in Austria from 1894.
Designer.
Art Nouveau.
Wiener Werkstätte group.
Born in Moravia, Josef Hoffmann first studied there before going to train in Germany. In 1894, he entered the academy of fine art in Vienna, working under Otto Wagner. While there, he met Olbrich and Moser and with them set up the Siebener Klub (Club of Seven). In 1897, he was one of the founders of a Viennese group of architects and designers who styled themselves as the Secession group in order to establish their anti-establishment credentials.. From this time until World War I saw the full flowering of his work as a designer and architect. His achievement was to create a style of interior and furniture design that was more minimal and geometrically elegant than anything seen before. Through his connection with the Kunstgewerbeschule from 1898 he became interested in the idea of artistic collaboration, which led, in 1903, to the setting up of the Wiener Werkstätte (Vienna workshop) with Fritz Wärndorfer and Koloman Moser.

AUCTION RECORDS:
LONDON, 23 Sept 1993, *Geometric Design* (pencil and ink, 11 1/2 x 8 1/4 ins / 29.5 x 21 cm) GBP 1,955.

HOFFMANN, Joseph
German, 18th - 19th century.
Born 28 October 1764, in Cologne; died 6 March 1812, in Cologne.
Painter. Murals.
He was a pupil of his father Valentin Hoffmann, then studied with Lambert Krähe and Johann Peter von Langer at the academy in Düsseldorf. In 1793, he did the ceiling paintings for Groß Sankt Martins Kirche in Cologne. Following a brief visit to Paris in 1797, he did some large decorative paintings in Kassel in partnership with Johann August Nahl for a competition established by Goethe. Other works include ceiling paintings for the schloss in Weimar.

HOFFMANN, Karl
German, 19th century.
Born 1816, in Wiesbaden; died c. 1872.
Sculptor. Statues.
In 1837 he was in Paris, presumably remaining there for some time since his son was born in Paris in 1841, but later he went to Rome. His sculpture was much influenced by

Thorvaldsen. He did a marble *Pietà* for the church of St Moritz in Cologne.

HOFFMANN, Karl
German, 19th century.
Born 11 October 1841, in Paris, of a German father; died after 1909.
Painter. Portraits, genre scenes.

The son of sculptor Karl Hoffmann, he was born during the latter's years in Paris. He lived in Rome for quite a while, possibly as a result of his father's visit to the city, but finally settled in Germany. He exhibited initially in Berlin, then (from 1876) Dresden.

MUSEUMS AND GALLERIES:
ANTWERP: *Portrait of the Painter Johann Friedrich Overbeck.*

AUCTION RECORDS:
MUNICH, 21 Sept 1978, *The Animal Lover* (oil on panel, 9 x 13 ins / 23 x 33 cm) DEM 7,000.

HOFFMANN, Leni
German, 20th - 21st century.
Born 1962, in Bad Pyrmont.
Environmental artist.

Hoffmann set up the publishing house, Kobro. She lives and works in Nuremberg. Using plasticine, a material generally intended for children, which she sometimes combines with foam, Hoffmann produces colour-rich spaces, modifying them at will by simple pressure of the finger.

She has participated in group exhibitions: 1998, the Kunsthalle, Nuremberg; 1990, Cologne; 1991, Vevey; 1992-1993, *Qui, quoi, où?* (*Who, what, where?*), at the Musée d'Art moderne de la Ville de Paris; 1995, the Société Jet Lag K, in Malakoff; 2003, *Un Tableau dans le Décor. Peintures 1970-2000* (*A Painting in the Décor: Paintings 1970-2000*), an exhibition on the occasion of 20 years of the FRAC (Fonds Régionaux d'Art Contemporain - regional contemporary art collections), the Château des Ducs de Bretagne, Nantes. Hoffmann has held solo shows in Nuremberg, Bayreuth, Cologne, Mainz, and Frankfurt; in 1995, at the Musée d'Art moderne de la Ville de Paris within the context of a series of interventions *Migrateurs* (*Migrants*); 1999, at the Städtische Galerie im Lenbachhaus.

MUSEUMS AND GALLERIES:
DUNKIRK (FRAC Nord-Pas de Calais): *Iluka* (2001).

HOFFMANN, Magdalena, wife of Stuewarts
Swiss, 17th century.
Born in Zurich; died 1671, in Amsterdam.
Active in Holland.
Painter. Flowers.

She was the daughter of Swiss painter Samuel Hoffmann, who had married a Dutch woman during his long stay in Antwerp. She moved to her mother's homeland, establishing herself in Amsterdam.

HOFFMANN, Max
German, 19th - 20th century.
Born 9 July 1873, in Dresden-Loschwitz.
Painter.

Hoffmann studied at the Kunstakademie in Dresden, where his teachers were Gey and Pohle.

HOFFMANN, Max
German, 20th century.
Painter, engraver. Landscapes, portraits.

Hoffmann was active in Marburg in 1915.

HOFFMANN, Maximilian
Bohemian School, 16th - 17th century.
Painter.
Prague School.

Maximilian Hoffmann worked for Emperor Rudolph II in Prague around 1600.

BIBLIOGRAPHY:
DaCosta Kaufmann, Thomas, *L'École de Prague*, Flammarion, Paris, 1985.

HOFFMANN, Michael
German, 17th - 18th century.
Born c. 1700, in Weissenfels (Saxony).
Painter. Religious subjects, portraits. Murals.

Among other things, he carried out paintings for the church in Hohenmölsen, near Weissenfels. A person of the same name, probably the same artist, painted portraits in Leipzig around the same period.

HOFFMANN, Nicolaus
German, 18th - 19th century.
Born 1740, in Darmstadt; died c. 1823, in Darmstadt.
Painter. Genre scenes.

He was a pupil of Sekatz.

MUSEUMS AND GALLERIES:
DARMSTADT (Kunstgal.): *School Mistress; Elementary School Teacher.*

HOFFMANN, Oskar Adolfovich, or Gofman
Estonian, 19th - 20th century.
Born 24 January 1851, in Tartu; died c. 1913, in St Petersburg.
Painter. Genre scenes, landscapes with figures, landscapes.

Oskar Hoffmann was a pupil of Eugen Gustav Dücker at the academy of fine art in Düsseldorf. He settled in St Petersburg, becoming a member of the academy. He received a bronze medal at the 1889 Exposition Universelle in Paris.

AUCTION RECORDS:
LONDON, 19 March 1910, *Going to Market,* GBP 9. NEW YORK, 29 May 1981, *Peasants Going to Market* (oil on canvas, 25 1/2 x 47 ins / 64.8 x 119.4 cm) USD 11,000. LONDON, 6 Oct 1988, *Breakfast by the Baltic* (1892, oil on card, 8 3/4 x 6 1/4 ins / 22.3 x 16 cm) GBP 880. LONDON, 27 Nov 1992, *Village Crossroads* (oil on canvas, 21 3/4 x 47 3/4 ins / 55.5 x 121.3 cm) GBP 11,550.

HOFFMANN, Paul
German, 19th century.
Born 19th century, in Breslau (now Wroclaw, Poland).
Painter. Landscapes.

He settled in Düsseldorf, his debut being around 1878.

AUCTION RECORDS:
LONDON, 9 May 1979, *A Letter for the Master; Amorous Conversation* (two oils on canvas, 15 1/4 x 10 1/4 ins / 39 x 26 cm) GBP 2,000.

HOFFMANN, Philipp Heinrich
German, 19th - 20th century.
Born 26 February 1863, in Saarlouis (Saarland).
Painter.

Hoffmann made his debut in Berlin in 1891. He was related to H. Hoffmann-Saarlouis.

HOFFMANN, Richard
German, 20th century.
Born 1930, in Lebach (Saarland).
Painter, sculptor.

Hoffmann studied at the school of art and crafts in Saarbrücken from 1949 until 1954. He held a scholarship at the Académie de la Grande Chaumière in Paris in 1954-1955, followed by a scholarship at the École des Beaux-Arts in 1955-1956 and then the college of fine arts in Berlin from 1957 until 1962.

From 1963 until 1983 Hoffmann created sculptures in bronze and synthetic stone for public places in various towns in the Saar region; among these was the 1976 peace memorial and altar for Tholey. After 1983, he once again devoted a large part of his time to painting. He was fascinated by the natural world and animals. His paintings, like his sculptures, are evocative of visceral masses, as though he is attempting to reconstruct indeterminate bodies or parts of the human body.

Hoffmann took part in collective exhibitions in Germany and other countries from 1951. He participated in an international symposium of sculpture in Homburg in the Saar area in 1973, but did not take part in any public exhibitions after 1974.

HOFFMANN, Robert
German, 19th century.
Born 10 February 1868, in Stuttgart.
Painter.
Kronberg painters' colony.

He was a student at the academy in Karlsruhe, continuing his training with Lefebvre and Robert-Fleury in Paris.

BIBLIOGRAPHY:
Wiederspahn, August, *Die Kronberger Malerkolonie*, Verlag Waldemar Kramer, Frankfurt am Main, c. 1971.

AUCTION RECORDS:
LONDON, 5 Dec 1980, *Portrait of the Father of Ibn Saud* (1923, oils mounted on card, 7 3/4 x 7 3/4 ins / 20 x 20 cm) GBP 550.

HOFFMANN, Rudolf
Austrian, 19th century.
Active in Vienna c. 1840.
Lithographer, miniaturist.

He is credited with a lithograph after J B Metzler.

HOFFMANN, Samuel, or Hoffman
Swiss, 17th century.
Born c. 1592, in Zurich; died 1648, in Frankfurt.
Painter. History painting.

He was initially a pupil of Gotthard Ringgli, but later went to Antwerp to study with Rubens. He soon established himself as a distinctive talent among the disciples of the Flemish master, and he achieved great success on his return to Switzerland. He painted mainly portraits and still lifes of fruit and game, but a number of history paintings by him are also known.

MUSEUMS AND GALLERIES:
DESSAU: *The Child Jesus and St John* - FRANKFURT AM MAIN: *Portrait of a Woman* - FRIBOURG: *Equestrian Portrait of Peter König* - STUTTGART: *Kitchen Interior* - WINTERTHUR: two portraits - ZURICH: *Miniature Portrait of Hans Heinrich Holzhalt.*

AUCTION RECORDS:
ZURICH, 3 Dec 1987, *Portrait of Johannes Caspar Bauhin* (1644, oil on canvas, 23 3/4 x 23 ins / 60.5 x 57.5 cm) CHF 16,000. LONDON, 24 Nov 1999, *Brown-haired Gentleman with Moustache Wearing Black Cloak* (miniature, oval, h. 3 ins / 8 cm) GBP 3,700. LONDON, 16 Dec 1999, *Portrait of Wilhelm Baudart* (c. 1616, oil on panel, 37 x 28 ins / 94 x 71 cm) GBP 3,800.

HOFFMANN, Theodor
German, 19th century.
Active in Berlin c. 1835.
Painter. History painting.

A pupil of Wach.

HOFFMANN, Thomas
Bohemian, 19th century.
Died 1865.
Active in 1810.
Painter.

Works by Thomas Hoffman are in the museum in Prague.

HOFFMANN VON VESTENHOF, August
German, 19th century.
Born 18 June 1849, in Olmütz (Olomouc), Moravia.
Painter, illustrator, sculptor.

He worked in Munich, exhibiting there and in Berlin.

MUSEUMS AND GALLERIES:
VIENNA (Österreichische Gal. Belvedere): *Amor Janitor.*

HOFFMANN-CANSTEIN, Olga
Austrian, 19th - 20th century.
Born 4 November 1872, in Lemberg (now Lviv, Ukraine).
Painter. Landscapes, flowers.

Olga Hoffmann-Canstein was a pupil of Karl Karger and Alfred Zoff. She exhibited regularly in Vienna.

HOFFMANN-FALLERSLEBEN, Franz, or Hoffman-Fallersleben
German, 19th century.
Born 19 May 1855, in Weimar.
Painter. Landscapes.

He was the son of poet Heinrich Hoffmann von Fallersleben (author of *Deutschland Deutschland über Alles*). He trained at the academies of Düsseldorf and Weimar, where his teacher was T Hagen. He went on long study tours in Italy and around Germany before settling in Düsseldorf, which he later abandoned for Weimar and finally Berlin (1888). He exhibited from 1878, particularly in Berlin (where he won a gold medal in 1906), Munich and Düsseldorf.

MUSEUMS AND GALLERIES:
BERLIN: *First Snow* - WEIMAR: *The Castle in the Forest* - WROCLAW: *Kyffhauser.*

AUCTION RECORDS:
AMSTERDAM, 28 Oct 1992, *Trees in a Summer Landscape* (oil on paper/card, 7 x 12 1/4 ins / 17.5 x 31 cm) NLG 1,495. COLOGNE, 30 Nov 2000, *Avenue in Augustenburg Park, Alsen* (1889, oil on canvas, 11 x 14 ins / 27 x 35 cm) DEM 3,300. AHLDEN, 28 Sept 2001, *Winters Day, Thuringen, Weimar* (1883, oil on canvas, 38 x 52 ins / 96 x 132 cm) DEM 11,000. MUNICH, 5 Dec 2001, *Autumn Wood* (1907, oil on canvas, 43 x 24 ins / 110 x 61 cm) DEM 5,500. AHLDEN, 28 Nov 2003, *Country House* (1908, oil on canvas/board, 14 x 11 ins / 36 x 27 cm) EUR 1,450.

HOFFMANN-FALLERSLEBEN, Joachim
German, 20th century.
Painter, engraver. Landscapes.

Hoffmann-Fallersleben was the son of the landscape painter Franz Hoffmann-Fallersleben. He lived and was active in Berlin. He exhibited his work from 1909.

AUCTION RECORDS:
MUNICH, 6 Dec 1994, *Portcullis at Corvey Castle and the Weser* (oil/plywood, 25 1/2 x 19 ins / 65 x 48 cm) DEM 6,900.

HOFFMANN-SAARLOUIS, H.
German, 20th century.
Painter. Genre scenes.

Hoffmann-Saarlouis lived and was active in Frankfurt. He exhibited his work in Berlin in 1909. He was related to Philipp Heinrich Hoffmann.

HOFFMANN-TEDESCO, Julia or Giulia.
See **TEDESCO-HOFFMANN**

HOFFMANS, Martinus
Painter. Portraits.

Martinus Hoffmans is listed in an auction catalogue.

AUCTION RECORDS:
AMSTERDAM, 26-29 Nov 1901, *Portrait of Linnaeus in Lapp Dress*, FRF 420.

HOFFMEISTER, Adolf
Czech, 20th century.
Born 1902, in Prague; died 24 July 1973, in Ricky.
Painter, draughtsman, illustrator.

Aldolf Hoffmeister produced fiercely political caricatures until 1939, when he left for the USA. After World War II, he returned to Prague and held various official cultural positions in Czechoslovakia, including that of cultural representative in Paris between 1948 and 1951. He taught animation at the school of applied arts in Prague.

His frequent trips abroad enabled him to meet many famous figures, whom he recorded in an irreplaceable collection of caricature portraits full of poetry and psychological insight. These often combine drawing and a type of collage derived from 19th century woodcuts, and are reminiscent of some of Max Ernst's work. He illustrated works by Maiakovsky, Jules Vernes, Cendrars and Elsa Triolet.

His work has appeared in many exhibitions since 1927 in cities including Prague, Paris and Brussels.

HOFFMEISTER, C. L.
Austrian, 19th century.
Active in Vienna.
Glass painter.

Probably the same artist as the landscape painter L. C. Hoffmeister.

HOFFMEISTER, Christian
German, 19th century.
Born 28 March 1818, in Karlsruhe; died 29 December 1871, in Frankfurt am Main.
Engraver.

He was a pupil of E. Schüler in Karlsruhe. He illustrated Lamotte-Fouqué's fairy romance *Undine* and an edition of Shakespeare's plays.

HOFFMEISTER, Heinz
German, 19th century.
Born 24 June 1851, in Saarlouis; died 5 March 1894, in Berlin.
Sculptor, painter, scholar. Statues.

He was a pupil of Cauer in Kreuznach. He travelled widely, visiting North Africa, Spain and the east. A noted work is his statue of *L. Ravené* at the French church in Berlin.

HOFFMEISTER, J. H.
Dutch, 19th century.
Active in Rotterdam in 1857.
Lithographer.

J.H. Hoffmeister is known for his portraits.

HOFFMEISTER, Johann Peter
German, 18th century.
Born 1740, in Heidelberg; died 6 December 1772, in Mannheim.
Painter.

He was the son of Johann Philipp Hoffmeister. A noted work is his *Portrait of Countess Heydeck* dated 1770.

HOFFMEISTER, Johann Philipp
German, 18th century.
Died April 1771.
Active in Mannheim.
Painter.

He was a pupil of J. L. Lippe, and likewise worked in Heidelberg.

HOFFMEISTER, L. C.
Swiss (?), 19th century.
Painter. Scenes with figures, landscapes with figures.

AUCTION RECORDS:
BERN, 26 Oct 1988, *Composition with Figures in a Park and a Structure with Turrets in the Background* (1829, oil on panel, 18 x 21 1/4 ins / 46 x 54 cm) CHF 4,500. KLAGENFURT, 19 Nov 2003, *Italian Garden* (1892, oil on canvas, 20 x 24 ins / 50 x 62 cm) EUR 1,600.

HOFFMEISTER, Louis
German, 19th century.
Active in Munich.
Engraver.

He was a pupil of C. L. Frommel in Karlsruhe.

HOFFMEISTER, Samuel
Swedish, 18th - 19th century.
Born 1765; died 1818, in Stockholm.
Sculptor. Medallions, busts.

Samuel Hoffmeister was a pupil of Johan Tobias Sergel. He executed mostly portraits, in bust or medallion form.

MUSEUMS AND GALLERIES:
STOCKHOLM: *Benjamin Franklin; J.-G. Sack; Strandberg; Mrs Strandberg; An Unknown.*

HOFFNAS, Johann Wilhelm, or Hofnass
German, 18th century.
Born 19 June 1727, in Ohaus; died 16 August 1795, in Mannheim.
Painter. Portraits.

At the age of 16, he was apprenticed to a glass painter. In 1753, he went to Rome to study with Mengs. On returning to Germany in 1760, he was appointed painter at the court of the Elector Palatine and a member of staff at the academy in Mannheim. A large number of his portraits are found in the towns of the Palatinate.

MUSEUMS AND GALLERIES:
MAINZ: *Portrait of a Woman* (two paintings).

HOFFNAS, Lorenz, or Hofnass
German, 18th - 19th century.
Born 1772, in Mannheim; died 1837, in Regensburg.
Miniaturist, draughtsman.

The son and pupil of Johann Wilhelm Hoffnass. His miniatures were much sought after, but he also did religious drawings.

HOFFSTADT, Friedrich
German, 19th century.
Born 1802, in Amorbach; died 7 September 1846, in Aschaffenburg.
Painter, sculptor, engraver, collector. Church decoration.

He studied a wide range of subjects in Munich. Among other things, he decorated the Catholic church in Nördlingen (Bavaria).

HOFFSTÄDTER, Bedrich
Slovak, 20th century.
Born 15 November 1910, in Trencín, 10 August 1954.
Painter. Military subjects, local scenes, cityscapes.

Bedrich Hoffstädter studied at the academy of fine art in Prague from 1929 to 1930, and with V. Nowak in Prague from 1930 to 1936. He then studied in Paris for a time.

His paintings of daily life, street scenes or military subjects are in an Expressionist style similar to that of Daumier, with a solid construction created by the simplifying effects of strong light and shade.

His work was included in exhibitions of contemporary Czechoslovak art, including *Fifty years of Czechoslovak Painting from the Collections of the Galleries, 1918-1958* organised on the occasion of the 50th anniversary of the founding of the republic.

BIBLIOGRAPHY:
Fifty years of Czechoslovak Painting from the Collections of the Galleries, 1918-1958, exhibition catalogue, Slovenska Narodna Gal., Bratislava, 1968 (in commemoration of the 50th anniversary of the Republic of Czechoslovakia).

HOFHERR, Johannes
German, 17th century.
Active in Ulm c. 1674.
Painter. History painting, landscapes.

HOFHUIZEN, Josée
Dutch, 20th - 21st century.
Born 1946, in Maastricht.
Painter. Figures, nudes.

Hofhuizen attended the art academy in Maastricht. She has exhibited in many Dutch towns, in addition to abroad: Italy, and particularly Belgium.

HOFIG, Gustav

German, 20th century.
Active in Charlottenburg.
Painter. Genre scenes.

Hofig exhibited his work in Berlin in 1909.

HOFKER, Willem Gerard

Dutch, 20th century.
Born 1902, in The Hague; died 1980 or 1981.
Painter, pastellist. Figures, portraits, scenes with figures, local scenes, architectural views.
Orientalism.

Hofker studied at the academy of art in The Hague and the Rijksakademie in Amsterdam. In 1938 he moved to Bali with his family and stayed there until 1944. He painted the Balinese people going about their daily activities, giving his pictures a touch of mysticism. He frequently depicted traditional costumes in an Impressionist style.

AUCTION RECORDS:

AMSTERDAM, 25 April 1990, *Woman near a Temple in Bali* (pastel and black chalk, 18½ x 11½ ins / 47 x 29 cm) NLG 34,500. AMSTERDAM, 5-6 Nov 1991, *Ni-Dantih the Young Weaver* (1938, pastel, 17¼ x 11 ins / 44 x 27 cm) NLG 33,350. AMSTERDAM, 18 Feb 1992, *Montelbaanstoren in Amsterdam* (1956, oil on canvas, 27½ x 22 ins / 70 x 55 cm) NLG 11,500. AMSTERDAM, 14-15 April 1992, *Native of Bali* (1938, oil on canvas, 15 x 10¼ ins / 38 x 26 cm) NLG 27,600. AMSTERDAM, 2-3 Nov 1992, *Two Young Balinese Women on the Steps of a Temple* (1948, pastel, 25¼ x 21¾ ins / 64 x 55.5 cm) NLG 25,300. AMSTERDAM, 20 April 1993, *Young Balinese Girl* (1936, oil on canvas/panel, 15¾ x 11 ins / 40 x 27 cm) NLG 28,750. AMSTERDAM, 19 Oct 1993, *Temptation: Young Balinese Woman Reclining* (1942, oil on canvas, 12 x 15¾ ins / 30.5 x 40 cm) NLG 51,750. AMSTERDAM, 9 Nov 1993, *Young Balinese Woman on the Steps of a Temple* (pastel, 18 x 11 ins / 46 x 28 cm) NLG 43,700. AMSTERDAM, 19 April 1994, *Young Balinese Woman in Galoet Dress* (pastel, 18 x 12¼ ins / 45.5 x 31 cm) NLG 46,000. AMSTERDAM, 23 April 1996, *Still-life with Dolls on a Shelf* (1954, oil on canvas, 13¼ x 15¼ ins / 33.5 x 39 cm) NLG 11,800. SINGAPORE, 5 Oct 1996, *Portrait of Ni Danti Lebah* (1939, pencil/paper, 19¼ x 11¾ ins / 49 x 30 cm) SGD 201,750. SINGAPORE, 27 Sept 1997, *Portrait* (1939, charcoal/paper, 21 x 13¾ ins / 52.5 x 35 cm) SGD 41,400. SINGAPORE, 28 March 1999, *In the Sawahs, Bali* (1941, oil on canvas, 22 x 13 ins / 57 x 32 cm) SGD 60,000. SINGAPORE, 3 Oct 1999, *Woman with Offering* (1941, crayon and pastel, 18 x 13 ins / 46 x 32 cm) SGD 24,000. AMSTERDAM, 21 May 2000, *Houses on the Gelder Pier, Amsterdam* (1931, oil on panel, 10 x 11 ins / 25 x 28 cm) NLG 23,000. SINGAPORE, 1 Oct 2000, *Self-portrait* (1935, oil on canvas, 24 x 16 ins / 60 x 40 cm) SGD 15,000. SINGAPORE, 30 Sept 2001, *Portrait of Gusti Compian* (1940, pastel, 12 x 16 ins / 30 x 40 cm) SGD 26,000. SINGAPORE, 30 Sept 2001, *Ni Noneh, Ni Asoeg and Gusti Kompiang* (pastel, 19 x 15 ins / 48 x 37 cm) SGD 35,000. HONG KONG, 28 April 2002, *Portrait of Anak Agoeng Ngoerah* (1941, pastel and white chalk, 19 x 12 ins / 48 x 30 cm) HKD 320,000. HONG KONG, 27 Oct 2002, *Under the Banyan Tree at the Temple of the Dead near the House in Abangan, Bali* (1941, conte crayon and colour pigment, 19 x 12 ins / 47 x 30 cm) HKD 400,000. HONG KONG, 6 July 2003, *Ni Gemblong, Klandis Bali* (1939, black chalk and pastel, 15 x 10 ins / 38 x 25 cm) HKD 380,000. HONG KONG, 6 July 2003, *Balinese Beauties* (1943, oil on canvas, 30 x 19 ins / 75 x 49 cm) HKD 2,500,000. SINGAPORE, 4 April 2004, *Ni Tjawan* (watercolour on cardboard, 18 x 12 ins / 46 x 30 cm) SGD 140,000. SINGAPORE, 10 Oct 2004, *Tjawan and Sadri* (1939, oil on canvas, 34 x 21 ins / 86 x 54 cm) SGD 520,000.

HOFKUNST, Alfred

Austrian, 20th century.
Born 30 December 1942, in Vienna.
Active in Switzerland.
Painter, draughtsman.

Before devoting himself to drawing and engraving in 1965, initially Hofkunst served as an apprentice in a typography studio and later contributed to the creation of theatre sets. He has worked in Marseilles and Montet-sur-Cudrefin; he lives in Missy (Vaud). In the 1970s, his works were deemed to be an expression of the Hyperrealist movement; later, they could be conceived as an expression of the Fantastic Realism trend, or even Surrealist. However, Hofkunst's drawings are distinguishable from Hypperealism, as his work mainly appears in the USA. His drawings are more a frontal substitution of the object by its image, which is always perceived as two-dimensional, than a sketchy description of an object isolated from its context (light bulb, mattress, ping-pong table). In this sense, Hofkunst's drawings could also be similar to certain principles in Conceptual Art, in particular those expounded by American experimental artist Joseph Kosuth in the mid 1960s. In addition to everyday objects, Hofkunst sets out to capture the atmosphere of places, firmly conveying his own perception of his environment. In 1980, for a series dedicated to Marseilles, Hofkunst tackled a new technique, based on enlarged photographic clichés and transposing the image onto huge canvases, using acrylic, pastel and pencil.

The group exhibitions in which he has participated indicate the sense and direction of his work: 1996, *Art Fantastique et Surréalisme* (*Fantastic Art and Surrealism*), at the Musée de Bern; 1967, 1969, the international engraving exhibition, Ljubljana; 1969, *Fantastic Figuration*, Zurich; 1969, *22 Young Swiss Artists*, at the museums in Amsterdam and Bern; 1969, *Jeune Gravure Suisse* (*Young Swiss Engraving*), a travelling exhibition in Chile and Argentina; 1969, the 3rd international drawing exhibition in Darmstadt; 1971, *Avant-Garde Suisse* (*Swiss Avant-Garde*), the cultural centre, New York; 1971, the 10th São Paulo Biennale; 1972, *Dessin Suisse au XXe Siècle* (*20th Century Swiss Design*), the Munich Museum, Winterthur, Geneva and Bonn; 1972, *31 Suisses* (*31 Swiss Artists*) at the Galeries Nationales du Grand Palais, Paris; 1972, *Bianco e Nero* (*Black and White*), the Exposition Nationale de Gravure, Lugano; 1972, *Magic Realism*, the Ulm Museum; 1974, *Hyperréalistes Américains et Réalistes Européens* (*American Hyperrealists and European Realists*), at the CNAC (Centre National d'Art Contemporain), Paris; 1979, *Nouvelle Subjectivité* (*New Subjectivity*), an exhibition devised by Jean Clair about the return of figurative expression and the genre scene in painting at the turn of the century, held at the Palais des Beaux-Arts, Brussels. Hofkunst has held many solo shows in Switzerland and abroad: 1967 and 1970, Biel; 1968 and 1969, Bern; 1970, Basel and Zurich; 1972, Stedelijk Van Abbemuseum, Eindhoven; 1976 and 1983, the Musée Cantini, Marseilles; 1980, Aarau; 1982, the Musée Cantonal des Beaux-Arts, Lausanne and 2002 Cent pour Jean, an exhibition of work inspired by, and later acquired by, Jean Tinguely, at the Musée d'Art et d'Histoire in Fribourg. Hofkunst has won many prizes and distinctions: 1968, the international drawing prize, Buenos Aires; 1971, the São Paulo Biennale prize; 1972, the Lugano prize.

BIBLIOGRAPHY:

Alfred Hofkunst, exhibition catalogue, Stedelijk Van Abbemuseum, Eindhoven, 1972. *L'Art moderne à Marseille. La Collection du musée Cantini*, catalogue, Musée Cantini, Marseilles, 1988.

MUSEUMS AND GALLERIES:

EINDHOVEN (Van Abbe Mus.).

AUCTION RECORDS:
BERN, 19 June 1980, *Winter* (1969, pencil, 37 1/4 x 27 1/2 ins / 94.4 x 69.7 cm) CHF 12,500. BERN, 20 June 1984, *Bed of Nails* (double-sided pencil drawing/panel, 39 1/4 x 27 1/2 ins / 100 x 70 cm) CHF 6,000. BERN, 20 June 1986, *Window and Rain* (1970, pencil, 39 1/4 x 27 1/4 ins / 99.4 x 69.5 cm) CHF 9,000. AMSTERDAM, 10 April 1990, *Safety Pin* (1970, pencil/paper, 39 x 27 1/4 ins / 99 x 69 cm) NLG 2,760. ZURICH, 13 Oct 1994, *Composition with Cuttlefish* (1983, mixed media/paper/canvas, 12 3/4 x 9 ins / 32.5 x 23 cm) CHF 800. ZURICH, 3 April 1996, *Packet* (1970, mixed media/wood, 39 1/4 x 27 1/4 ins / 100 x 69.5 cm) CHF 2,000. ZURICH, 21 March 2000, *Bather* (1987, mixed media on paper, 14 x 11 ins / 36 x 28 cm) CHF 3,500. ZURICH, 21 March 2000, *Tile Reaching the Sky* (1993, painted tile, 20 x 8 ins / 50 x 20 cm) CHF 4,000. ZURICH, 13 Nov 2001, *Blind* (1970, graphite on paper laid on board, 77 x 57 ins / 196 x 146 cm) CHF 11,000. PARIS, 6 Feb 2002, *Rouleau* (pencil and red felt, 35 x 50 ins / 90 x 128 cm) EUR 6,000. ZURICH, 25 Nov 2002, *Sunset I* (1980, pastel and acrylic on paper, 59 x 67 ins / 150 x 170 cm) CHF 6,000.

HOFLAND, Thomas Christopher
British, 19th century.
Born 1777, in Worksop; died 3 January 1843, in Leamington.
Painter. Landscapes.

Thomas Hofland was a pupil of John Rathbone. He taught art in Derby, then in 1811 settled in London where he produced copies of works by artists including Claude Lorraine, Poussin, Wilson and Gainsborough. He became well known for his paintings of lakes. He went to Italy in 1839 and made a large number of interesting sketches and drawings of Naples, the area around Castellammare, Pompeii, Rome, Tivoli and Florence. He fell ill with a fever and was forced to return to England, where he died shortly afterwards. Hofland exhibited at the Royal Academy in London from 1798.

MUSEUMS AND GALLERIES:
LONDON (Victoria and Albert Mus.): *Hampstead Heath*.

AUCTION RECORDS:
LONDON, 8 Feb 1908, *Ship in Distress near Scarborough*, GBP 6. LONDON, 26 Feb 1910, *Hills near Richmond*, GBP 52. LONDON, 13 June 1927, *Greenwich Hospital*, GBP 21. LONDON, 5 April 1935, *View of Hampstead*, GBP 27. LONDON, 4 March 1938, *The Thames at Twickenham*, GBP 42. LONDON, 25 June 1965, *View of White Knights; View of White Knights with a Young Woman Reading* (matching pair) Gns 1,700. LONDON, 10 Dec 1971, *View of the Thames*, Gns 4,800. LONDON, 19 Nov 1976, *Wooded Landscape* (oil on canvas, 29 3/4 x 40 1/2 ins / 75.5 x 103 cm) GBP 380. LONDON, 6 July 1977, *View of Castellamare* (oil on canvas, 52 3/4 x 72 1/2 ins / 134 x 184 cm) GBP 9,000. LONDON, 24 Nov 1978, *Wooded Landscape with Figures* (oil on canvas, 8 1/4 x 11 3/4 ins / 21 x 30 cm) GBP 1,600. LONDON, 19 Nov 1982, *Wooded Landscape with Shepherd and Cottage* (oil on canvas, 29 x 40 1/4 ins / 73.6 x 102.2 cm) GBP 2,600. LONDON, 14 March 1984, *View from Hampstead Looking towards St Paul's Cathedral* (oil on canvas, 18 1/2 x 30 ins / 47 x 76 cm) GBP 8,000. LONDON, 13 March 1985, *Harrow from Hampstead* (oil on card, 9 3/4 x 13 1/2 ins / 25 x 34.5 cm) GBP 5,500. LONDON, 18 Nov 1992, *Castellamare Seen from the New Sorrento Road* (oil on canvas, 52 1/2 x 73 ins / 133.5 x 185.5 cm) GBP 41,800. LONDON, 30 Aug 2000, *Fisherman, Loch Awe* (oil on panel, 11 x 16 ins / 27 x 41 cm) GBP 16,000. LONDON, 10 June 2003, *Cromack Waters* (oil on canvas, 20 x 30 ins / 51 x 77 cm) GBP 2,600.

HOFLAND, Thomas Richard
British, 19th century.
Born c. 1816; died 2 January 1876, in West Hartlepool.
Painter, watercolourist. Landscapes.

Thomas Richard Hofland, the son and pupil of Thomas Christopher, devoted much of his career to teaching. He exhibited two landscapes in London at the Royal Academy, in 1844 and 1845.

AUCTION RECORDS:
LONDON, 30 Nov 1907, *Castle and Town*, GBP 3.

HOFLEHNER, Rudolf
Austrian, 20th century.
Born 1916, in Linz.
Sculptor.

Hoflehner learned the skills of turning, forging and welding at the technical school of mechanical construction in Linz. He then studied at the Akademie der Bildenden Künste in Vienna. He became a teacher at the school of arts and crafts in Linz in 1945. He moved to Vienna in 1951 and concentrated exclusively on his creative work.

After initially working in wood, Hoflehner began to use iron and steel after 1951. In 1954 UNESCO awarded him a bursary to travel to the Ionian Islands; until then his work had been abstract, but his travels in Greece led him to return to the human form. From 1958 he produced constructions simplified by the constraints of working with metal, and which were sometimes reminiscent of Gonzalez, although cruder in spite of a certain softening in form. Hoflehner took part in many group exhibitions, including the Venice Biennale in 1954, 1956 and 1960, and the Documenta in Kassel in 1959 and 1964. He held private exhibitions of his work in Vienna, Linz, Basel (1963), Amsterdam (1964) and New York (1965).

BIBLIOGRAPHY:
Schmied, Wieland, *Hoflehner: Skulptur, Malerei, Zeichnung*, catalogue raisonné, Klett-Cotta, Stuttgart, 1988.

AUCTION RECORDS:
LONDON, 7 Dec 1977, *Small Idol* (1960, iron, h. 23 1/2 ins / 60 cm) GBP 250. NEW YORK, 9 May 1990, *Dea Mediterranea* (iron, h. 79 ins / 200.6 cm) USD 33,000. MUNICH, 1-2 Dec 1992, *Four Figures* (1960, coloured inks, 7 1/2 x 10 1/2 ins / 19 x 26.5 cm) DEM 1,725. HAMBURG, 3 Dec 1999, *72 K* (black-brown polished steel, 13 x 8x4 ins / 34 x 21x10 cm) DEM 5,000. VIENNA, 27 Nov 2002, *Untitled* (1948, mixed media, 37 x 43 ins / 95 x 110 cm) EUR 7,000. VIENNA, 20 May 2003, *Poros - Figure 12 K* (iron, h. 29 ins / 73 cm) EUR 15,000.

HOFLER, Christoph
Austrian, 17th century.
Active in Salzburg.
Painter.

He is noted for a miniature depicting *Jesus, Mary, St Joseph and St John the Baptist*.

HOFLER, Johann Wolfgang
Austrian, 17th century.
Died 1702.
Active in Salzburg.
Painter.

He was the son of Christoph Hofler, and worked for several monasteries in the city.

HOFLING, Salomon
Swedish, 19th century.
Born 1788; died 18 January 1827, in Stockholm.
Miniaturist.

There is a *Portrait of U. A. Sahlstedt* by Salomon Hofling in the museum of Stockholm.

HOFLINGER, Albert
German, 19th - 20th century.
Born 1855, in the Black Forest; died 1936.
Painter.

Hoflinger began his studies with L.A. Kellerborn in Basel. He then went to Paris in 1877 and studied under Bonnat. After he returned to Basel he continued to go back to Paris every year to work at the Académie Julian. He painted the *Portrait of J.-J. Falkeyser*, the curator of the art collections at the museum in Basel.

MUSEUMS AND GALLERIES:
BASEL: *Portrait of J.-J. Falkeyser.*
AUCTION RECORDS:
NEW YORK, 19 Oct 1984, *Ready for the Masked Ball* (oil on canvas, 20 1/4 x 12 3/4 ins / 51.5 x 32.5 cm) USD 1,750.

HOFMAN, Alfred
Austrian, 20th century.
Born 28 November 1879, in Vienna.
Sculptor. Busts.
Hofman studied under Anton Brenek and spent time in Naples, Florence and Rome.

HOFMAN, Pieter
Dutch, 18th - 19th century.
Born 31 August 1755, in Dordrecht; died 9 April 1837, in Dordrecht.
Painter. Landscapes, fruit.
Pieter Hofman was a pupil of Joris Ponse and Dirk Kuipers and was a co-founder of the *Pictura* art society in Dordrecht.

HOFMAN VON ALPERNBURG, Edmund
Hungarian, 19th century.
Born 2 November 1847, in Buda.
Sculptor.
Edmund Hofman von Alpernburg studied in Vienna with F. Bauer. His sculpture of *Orestes Pursued by a Fury* is worthy of note.

HOFMAN-GRÖTZINGEN, Gustav
German, 20th century.
Born 14 September 1889, in Grötzingen.
Painter. Landscapes.
Hofman-Grötzingen studied under Trübner at the academy of fine arts in Karlsruhe.
MUSEUMS AND GALLERIES:
POZNAN: *Bridges.*

HOFMANN, Charles C.
American, 19th century.
Born 1821; died 1882.
Painter. Landscapes.
The lack of information on Charles C. Hofmann is surprising, given the high price obtained for his work in the auction records.
AUCTION RECORDS:
NEW YORK, 1 Feb 1986, *View of the Schuylkill County Almshouse Property, Pennsylvania* (1875, oil on canvas, 31 x 43 ins / 78.7 x 109.1 cm) USD 115,000.

HOFMANN, Christoph
German, 17th century.
Sculptor.
He was active in Schweinfurt in 1628.

HOFMANN, Egon
Austrian, 20th century.
Born 1884, in Linz; died 1972.
Painter.
Hofmann studied in Munich, Vienna and Innsbruck. He attended the academy of fine arts in Stuttgart from 1909 until 1913, then the Dresden academy until 1915. He also studied at the Académie de la Grande Chaumière during a stay in Paris in 1921.

HOFMANN, Elias
German, 16th century.
Died c. 1591.
Active in Frankfurt am Main.
Painter.

HOFMANN, G. W.
German, 18th century.
Active in Berlin.
Painter.
Documented for drawings and miniature portraits.

HOFMANN, Georg
German, 17th - 18th century.
Born in Coburg.
Sculptor.
He is documented for his tomb of Superintendant Laurentius Hartmann in Königsberg in Franconia (1703).

HOFMANN, Hans
German, 20th century.
Born 21 March 1880, in Weissenberg (Bavaria); died 1965 or 1966, in New York.
Active in the USA from 1930 and naturalised from 1941.
Painter.
School of New York.
Hofmann began his study of painting with Willi Schwartz in Munich in 1896. During this period he was influenced by the Secessionist movement, bringing together the Jugendstil trends in Germany. He was encouraged to go to Paris by Freudenberg, and stayed there for ten years from 1904 until 1914. While he was there he received the most important part of his education in circles frequented by the Fauvists and Cubists, becoming a close friend of Delaunay in particular. When he returned to Munich in 1915 he opened an art school, which marked the beginning of a long and successful career as a teacher. He taught for some years in the Bavarian mountains, Dalmatia, Italy and France.

In 1930 and 1931, Hofmann gave summer courses at the University of California, and taught at the Art Students League in New York in 1932-1933. He opened private schools in New York in 1933 and Provincetown in 1934. Most of the young artists who would go on to establish the new American school passed through his studio. Hofmann is considered to have had an influence on all the young American painters - even those whom he did not teach personally - especially Clifford Still and Jackson Pollock. He won several prizes, including those awarded by the University of Illinois in 1950 and the Contemporary Art Society in 1952. Through his teaching, Hofmann provided the inspiration for American Abstract Expressionism.

Hofmann's importance as a teacher has often unjustly been regarded as taking precedence over his work as an artist. In his own works he often created a synthesis of the different European movements in which he had been involved. He did not develop the freedom of form that gave his work its own individual character until after 1940. Between 1940 and 1948 his works were characterised by a fluid, vigorous style reminiscent of Kandinsky and Klee and the precursor of Pollock, visible in *Spring* from 1940, *Fairy Tale* from 1944 and *Cataclysms*, a series of paintings in which he began to develop a much more informal, or Tachist, technique that predominated during the period that followed, from 1948 to around 1955. The paintings he produced during this time contain very free elements balanced by flat, almost geometric surfaces, violently coloured but still maintaining a uniformity of light, such as *Bowl of Fruit* from 1950 and *Exuberance* painted in 1955. After 1955, the fields of colour in his compositions became more rectilinear, more geometric, as can be seen in *Cathedral*, painted in 1959.

Unrestrained at some times and more disciplined at others, Hofmann's work is always joyful and celebratory. He made a name for himself by introducing the notion of 'Spannung' (tension). The Expressionists considered a work to be the unity achieved through the equilibrium of many tensions counterbalanced by relaxation of the superficial form; tensions resulting from the necessity to put real objects mentally to one side so that the mind might be free to achieve the ultimate in expressiveness. Allowing radical freedom from all the norms to instant, spontaneous, irrational, inorganic expressiveness was a determining factor in the development of the early style of the New York school, Action Painting - the bridge between the spontaneity of the Surrealists and the neo-formalism of the German Expressionists. Although concerned with the theoretical aspects of tension, Hofmann is often regarded as a gestural theorist. He himself distinguished two parallel currents in his work: the 'painterly' and the 'naturalistic'; the former resulting in more defined shapes and materials in response to his concerns for form, the latter in spontaneous unelaborated expressions.

Hofmann staged a private exhibition of his paintings in Berlin in 1910, but did not put on any other exhibitions until 1931 in San Francisco and then 1940 at the Delgado Museum in New Orleans. From 1944 he exhibited more frequently, particularly in New York, including a retrospective at the Arts Club of Chicago in 1944; an exhibition of his work in Paris in 1949, which passed completely unnoticed; the Baltimore Museum of Art in 1954; and a retrospective in New York in 1959. His significant participation in the Venice Biennale in 1960 was perhaps the determining factor that finally drew attention to his own work. In the same year an exhibition of about a hundred of his works was toured around the principal towns in Germany, beginning in Nuremberg, then throughout Europe. Retrospective exhibitions held since his death have included: 1977, Museum of Fine Arts, Houston; and 1988, *Hans Hofmann: Late Paintings*, Tate Gallery, London.

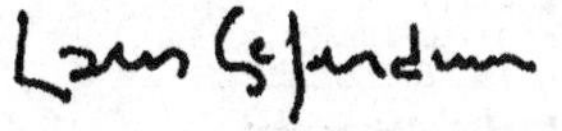

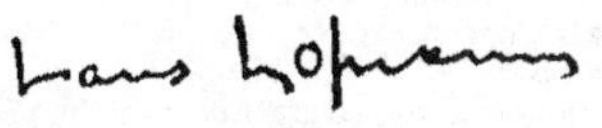

BIBLIOGRAPHY:

Greenberg, Clement, '*Most important teacher of our time*' in *The Nation*, periodical, New York, April 21, 1945. '*Hans Hofmann*' in *Derrière le miroir special edition*, periodical, Maeght, Paris, January 1949. Ashton, D., '*Hofmann*' in *Cimaise*, periodical, Paris, January 1959. Greenberg, Clement, '*Hans Hofmann*' in *coll. Musée de poche*, Georges Fall, Paris, 1961. *Hans Hofmann*, exhibition catalogue, Museum of Modern Art, New York, 1963. Tapié, Michel, *Hans Hofmann*, Gal. Anderson-Meyer, Paris, 1963. Bannard, Walter Darby, *Hans Hofmann: a retrospective exhibition*, exhibition catalogue, The Museum of Fine Arts, Houston, 1976. Varley, Christopher, *Hans Hofmann. 1880-1966. an introduction to his paintings*, exhibition catalogue, Edmonton Art Gall., 1982. *Hans Hofmann: the Renate series*, exhibition catalogue, Fort Worth Art Museum, Fort Worth, 1985. Goodman, Cynthia, *Hans Hofmann*, Abbeville Press, New York, 1986. *Hans Hofmann: late paintings*, exhibition catalogue, Tate Gall., London, 1988. Friedel, Helmut, *Hans Hofmann*, Hudson Hills Press, New York, 1998. Stella, Frank, '*Hans Hofmann en l'an 2000 Ça va barder!*' in *Art Press* n° 278, periodical, Paris, April 2002.

MUSEUMS AND GALLERIES:

AUSTIN (Jack S. Blanton MA, University of Texas): *X Orange* (1959); *Elysium* (1960); *Cascade* (1960) - BERKELEY (AM, University of California): *The Vanquished* (1959) - BUFFALO (Albright-Knox AG): *Exuberance* (1955) - CLEVELAND (MA): *Smaragd, Red, and Germinating Yellow* (1959, oil on canvas) - GRENOBLE (Mus. de Grenoble) - NEW YORK (Metropolitan Mus. of Art) - NEW YORK (MoMA): *Memoria in Aeternum* (1962) - NEW YORK (Solomon R. Guggenheim Mus.) - NEW YORK (Whitney Mus. of American Art).

AUCTION RECORDS:

NEW YORK, 27 Jan 1966, *Succulence*, USD 2,600. NEW YORK, 6 April 1967, *Opinion*, USD 8,500. NEW YORK, 14 May 1970, *Pleiades*, USD 4,500. NEW YORK, 17 Nov 1971, *Floral Composition*, USD 15,000. NEW YORK, 26 Oct 1972, *Branch in Blossom*, USD 9,000. NEW YORK, 4 May 1973, *Joy Spark of the Gods* (1965) USD 50,000. LOS ANGELES, 27 Feb 1974, *The Hague* (1950) USD 7,000. MILAN, 6 April 1976, *Capriccio I* (tempera and oil on card, $20\frac{3}{4}$ x $25\frac{1}{4}$ ins / 53 x 64 cm) ITL 2,600,000. NEW YORK, 21 Oct 1976, *Capriccio I* (1959, oil on card, $20\frac{3}{4}$ x $25\frac{1}{4}$ ins / 53 x 64 cm) USD 8,500. NEW YORK, 17 Nov 1977, *Blue in Blue* (1954, oil on canvas, 50 x 40 ins / 127 x 101.5 cm) USD 42,000. NEW YORK, 2 Nov 1978, *House and Studio* (1943, watercolour, $17\frac{1}{4}$ x 24 ins / 44 x 61 cm) USD 5,000. NEW YORK, 18 May 1979, *Pleiades* (1946, oil on card remounted/canvas, 31 x $41\frac{1}{2}$ ins / 79 x 105.5 cm) USD 28,000. NEW YORK, 19 Oct 1979, *Study of Landscape* (1942, ink and colouring pencil, $13\frac{3}{4}$ x $16\frac{3}{4}$ ins / 35 x 42.5 cm) USD 4,600. NEW YORK, 13 Nov 1980, *Times Square* (1945, gouache/mounted paper/card, $21\frac{1}{2}$ x $25\frac{1}{2}$ ins / 54.5 x 65 cm) USD 7,500. NEW YORK, 13 May 1981, *Untitled* (1944, watercolour and pencil, 24 x $17\frac{3}{4}$ ins / 61 x 45 cm) USD 9,000. NEW YORK, 9 Nov 1982, *X* (1955, oil on canvas, 60 x 48 ins / 152.4 x 122 cm) USD 110,000. NEW YORK, 20 May 1983, *Lunar Passage* (1957, oil on canvas, 60 x 72 ins / 152.4 x 182.9 cm) USD 135,000. NEW YORK, 10 Nov 1983, *Landscape* (1938, Indian ink, 14 x 17 ins / 35.5 x 43.1 cm) USD 2,900. NEW YORK, 2 Nov 1984, *Oil on Paper No. 6* (1962, watercolour and oil on paper, $24\frac{3}{4}$ x 19 ins / 62.7 x 48.3 cm) USD 6,500. NEW YORK, 3 May 1985, *Untitled* (1943, colouring pencil, 18 x 24 ins / 45.7 x 61 cm) USD 19,000. NEW YORK, 1 Oct 1985, *Fish* (1945, gouache, $21\frac{1}{2}$ x 26 ins / 54.7 x 66 cm) USD 15,000. NEW YORK, 5 May 1986, *Swamp-elegy* (1962, oil on canvas, 50 x 40 ins / 127 x 101.6 cm) USD 220,000. NEW YORK, 6 May 1987, *Untitled* (1944, gouache and pencil/paper, 17 x 14 ins / 43.2 x 35.6 cm) USD 11,000. NEW YORK, 20 Feb 1988, *Untitled* (1944, gouache/paper, $21\frac{3}{4}$ x 30 ins / 55.5 x 75.9 cm) USD 16,500; *Red-Brown-Blue: Chromatic Series I* (1962, gouache/paper, 18 x $23\frac{1}{2}$ ins / 45.8 x 60 cm) USD 8,800. NEW YORK, 3 May 1988, *Port of Provincetown* (1938, oil on card, 30 x 36 ins / 76.3 x 91.5 cm) USD 110,000. NEW YORK, 8 Oct 1988, *Untitled Self-portrait* (1932, watercolour/paper, 11 x $8\frac{1}{2}$ ins / 27.9 x 21.6 cm) USD 13,200; *Untitled* (1943, gouache and ink, $17\frac{3}{4}$ x 24 ins / 45 x 61 cm) USD 66,000. NEW YORK, 9 Nov 1988, *Untitled* (1945, oil on panel, 43 x 31 ins / 109.2 x 79 cm) USD 165,000. LONDON, 1 Dec 1988, *Landscape* (oil on card, 30 x 35 ins / 76.2 x 88.8 cm) GBP 41,800. NEW YORK, 14 Feb 1989, *Untitled* (oil on panel, $19\frac{1}{2}$ x $23\frac{1}{2}$ ins / 49.8 x 59.7 cm) USD 60,500. NEW YORK, 2 May 1989, *Opinion* (1959, oil on canvas, 72 x 60 ins / 183 x 152.5 cm) USD 550,000. NEW YORK, 5 Oct 1989, *Ravine* (1954, oil on card, 24 x 36 ins / 61 x 91.5 cm) USD 242,000. NEW YORK, 8 Nov 1989, *Mirage II* (1963, oil on canvas, 50 x 40 ins / 127 x 101.5 cm) USD 506,000. NEW YORK, 27 Feb 1990, *Still-life of Large Table* (1944, gouache/paper, $27\frac{1}{4}$ x $39\frac{1}{4}$ ins / 69 x 100 cm) USD 44,000. NEW YORK, 8 May 1990, *Swamp Series II, Autumn Glory* (1957, oil on canvas, 48 x 60 ins / 122 x 152.5 cm) USD 682,000. NEW YORK, 9 May 1990, *Magical Vision of Nature* (1963, oil on canvas, 30 x 24 ins / 76.2 x 61 cm) USD 385,000. NEW YORK, 15 Feb 1991, *Untitled* (gouache/paper, $23\frac{3}{4}$ x 19 ins / 60.4 x 48 cm) USD 16,500. NEW YORK, 13 Nov 1991, *Objects of Worship* (1951, oil on canvas, 30 x 24 ins / 76.2 x 61 cm) USD 44,000. NEW YORK, 25-26 Feb 1992, *Dragon* (1947, oil on card, 23 x $21\frac{1}{2}$ ins / 57.5 x 54.3 cm) USD 49,500. NEW YORK, 5 May 1992, *Ocean* (1957, oil on canvas, $59\frac{3}{4}$ x $71\frac{3}{4}$ ins / 152 x 182.5 cm) USD 550,000. NEW YORK, 6 May 1992, *Spring* (1962, oil on canvas, 50 x 40 ins / 127 x 101.6 cm) USD 440,000. NEW YORK, 18 Nov 1992, *Ancient Wealth* (1964, oil on canvas, 84 x 52 ins / 213.4 x 132.1 cm) USD 363,000. NEW YORK, 11 Nov 1993, *Almost Harvest Time* (1958, oil on panel, 36 x $47\frac{1}{2}$ ins / 91.4 x 120.7 cm) USD 228,000. ZURICH, 23 June 1995, *Composition* (1945, oil on paper/plywood, 22 x 26 ins / 55.9 x 66 cm) CHF 28,000. NEW YORK, 14 Nov 1995, *Terpsichore* (1958, oil on canvas, $59\frac{3}{4}$ ins / 152 cm, $1\frac{1}{2}$ x $48\frac{1}{2}$ ins/4 x 123.2 cm) USD 420,500. NEW YORK, 8 May 1996, *Succulence* (1946, oil/synthetic resin,

22$^{1/2}$ x 15 ins / 57.2 x 38.4 cm) USD 34,500. NEW YORK, 19 Nov 1996, *Untitled* (1944, pen, brush, black ink, pencil and graphite/paper, 17 x 14 ins / 43.2 x 35.5 cm) USD 10,350. NEW YORK, 20 Nov 1996, *Gloria in Excelsis* (1963, oil on canvas, 50 x 40 ins / 127 x 101.6 cm) USD 750,500. NEW YORK, 20 Nov 1996, *Red Domination* (1949, oil on canvas, 60 x 42 ins / 152.4 x 106.7 cm) USD 112,500. NEW YORK, 6 May 1997, *Red Spot* (1956, oil on canvas, 30 x 25 ins / 76.2 x 63.5 cm) USD 277,500. NEW YORK, 8 May 1997, *Untitled* (1936, oil on panel, 24$^{3/4}$ x 30 ins / 62.8 x 76.2 cm) USD 40,250. NEW YORK, 18-19 Nov 1997, *Paling Moon* (1965, oil on canvas, 72 x 60 ins / 182.8 x 152.4 cm) USD 717,500. NEW YORK, 19 Nov 1997, *Wind und Weide* (1959, oil on panel) USD 101,500. NEW YORK, 20 Nov 1997, *Ave Maria* (1965, oil on canvas, 72 x 48 ins / 182.9 x 121.9 cm) USD 211,500. NEW YORK, 13 May 1999, *Autumn Chill and Sun* (1962, oil on canvas, 60 x 52 ins / 152 x 132 cm) USD 520,000. NEW YORK, 10 Nov 1999, *Scotch and Burgundy* (oil on canvas laid on panel, 61 x 41 ins / 155 x 103 cm) USD 170,000. NEW YORK, 17 May 2000, *Salut au matin (Hail to the Morning)* (1965, oil on canvas, 48 x 36 ins / 122 x 91 cm) USD 360,000. NEW YORK, 15 Nov 2000, *Proprie Mto* (1965, oil on canvas, 60 x 52 ins / 152 x 132 cm) USD 450,000. NEW YORK, 8 May 2001, *Towering Clouds* (1958, oil on canvas, 50 x 84 ins / 128 x 213 cm) USD 720,000. NEW YORK, 17 May 2001, *Quartet* (1949, oil on canvas, 50 x 50 ins / 127 x 127 cm) USD 48,000. NEW YORK, 13 Nov 2002, *Calliope - Muse of Epic Poetry* (1963, oil on canvas, 76 x 60 ins / 193 x 152 cm) USD 510,000. NEW YORK, 14 Nov 2002, *Opulence* (1954, oil on canvas, 40 x 50 ins / 102 x 127 cm) USD 450,000. NEW YORK, 12 Nov 2003, *Violin Concerto* (1962, oil on canvas, 50 x 40 ins / 127 x 102 cm) USD 350,000. NEW YORK, 12 Nov 2003, *In Upper Regions* (1963, oil on canvas, 60 x 48 ins / 152 x 122 cm) USD 980,000. NEW YORK, 11 May 2004, *Tourbillon (Whirlwind)* (1960, oil on board, 48 x 46 ins / 122 x 118 cm) USD 700,000. NEW YORK, 12 May 2004, *Conjuntis Viribus* (1963, oil on canvas, 72 x 60 ins / 183 x 152 cm) USD 600,000.

HOFMANN, Jakob
German, 17th century.
Active in Stuttgart c. 1600.
Painter.

Known for a signed portrait dated 1614.

HOFMANN, Jakob
German, 20th century.
Born 17 February 1876.
Sculptor. Religious subjects. Busts.

Hofmann studied in Munich. He was active in Aschaffenburg, Neuburg and Brunswick.

HOFMANN, Johann
German, 17th century.
Active in Bozen, South Tyrol (now Bolzano, Italy) c. 1650.
Painter.

He worked for the church of Assling.

HOFMANN, Johann
Austrian, 18th century.
Active in Graz.
Painter.

HOFMANN, Johann Benedikt, the Elder
Polish, 17th - 18th century.
Born 1668, in Sorau (now Zary, Poland); died 1745, in Danzig (now Gdansk).
Painter, decorative designer.

Johann Benedikt Hofmann the Elder is known for his portraits and a few ceilings, painted in the French style of the beginning of the 18th century. He studied with Mock in Warsaw and became a court painter.

HOFMANN, Johann Benedikt, the Younger
Polish, 18th century.
Died c. 1775, in Danzig (now Gdansk).
Painter.

Johann Benedikt Hofmann the Younger was the son and pupil of Johann Benedikt Hofmann the Elder. He may be the painter of the *Portrait of King Carl XII of Sweden* and the *Portrait of Landgrave Charles of Hesse*, which are sometimes attributed to his father.

HOFMANN, Johann Jakob
Austrian, 17th - 18th century.
Active in Vienna.
Engraver.

HOFMANN, Johann Michael Ferdinand Heinrich
German, 19th - 20th century.
Born 19 March 1824, in Darmstadt; died 23 June 1911, in Dresden.
Painter. History painting, portraits.

Hofmann studied under E. Rauch and with T. Hildebrand and Schadow at the academy in Düsseldorf in 1842. He studied at the academy in Antwerp in 1846 and then went to Paris and Italy. He settled in Dresden in 1862, where he was appointed teacher at the academy of art on 1 June 1870. His works include: *Portrait of Young Woman in Grey* and *Departure Scene from Romeo and Juliet*. He was the uncle of Ludwig von Hofmann.

MUSEUMS AND GALLERIES:
DARMSTADT: *Jesus Held Captive*.

HOFMANN, Johannes
Danish, 18th century.
Active in Copenhagen.
Miniaturist.

Johannes Hofmann worked at the court of King Frederik IV.

HOFMANN, Karl
Austrian, 19th century.
Born 10 September 1852, in Lienz (Tyrol); died 1926.
Painter. Landscapes.

He exhibited regularly in Vienna and later in Berlin from 1899.

AUCTION RECORDS:
VIENNA, 22 June 1979, *Wooded Landscape* (oil on canvas, 42$^{1/2}$ x 59 ins / 108 x 150 cm) ATS 18,000. VIENNA, 16 May 1984, *A Prayer in the Fields* (1877, oil on panel, 15 x 11$^{3/4}$ ins / 38 x 30 cm) ATS 120,000.

HOFMANN, Ludwig, or Hofmann-Zeitz
German, 19th century.
Born 11 November 1832, in Zeitz; died 28 September 1895, in Heidelberg.
Painter. History painting, genre scenes.

He was a pupil of Jaeger at the academy in Leipzig and of Schwind in Munich in 1862. In 1886, he was appointed inspector of the Grand Duke of Hessen-Darmstadt's picture gallery. He exhibited in Berlin (winning a gold medal there in 1896), Munich and Vienna. Noted pictures include *Surprise* and *The Days of Sedan*.

HOFMANN, Ludwig von
German, 19th - 20th century.
Born 17 August 1861, in Darmstadt (Hesse); died 23 August 1945, in Pillnitz, near Dresden.
Painter, lithographer, engraver, illustrator, pastellist, decorative designer. Mythological subjects, genre scenes, landscapes.
Symbolism, Jugendstil.
Group of Eleven (Gruppe der Elf).

Ludwig von Hofmann was born into the wealthy middle class in Germany. His father was a senior adviser to Bismarck, and his uncle was the painter Johann Michael Heinrich Hofmann. Later, he would be taught by his uncle at the Kunstakademie, Dresden (1883-1886), but first he studied law. He completed his art education in the academies of Karlsruhe, under the supervision of Ferdinand Keller, from 1886 to 1888, and Munich. In 1889, he went to study at the Académie Julian in Paris, where he discovered Puvis de Chavannes and Albert Besnard. From 1891 to 1894, he lived in Berlin and Munich, and became interested in the work of Hugo von Marées, before moving to Rome. In 1892, he became a founder member of the Group of Eleven with Corinth, Liebermann, Skarbina and Leistikow, precursors of the Berlin Secession of 1899. In 1903, he became a professor at the Kunstakademie in Weimar, and in 1916 professor of mural art at the Kunstakademie Dresden, where he remained until 1931. He was a founder member of the Deutscher Künstlerbund (German Federation of Artists). 1918 saw the publication of a monograph by Edwin Redlob: *Ludwig von Hofmann. Handzeichnungen* (*Ludwig von Hofmann. Drawings*).

He demonstrated brilliant qualities as a colourist and a special skill in representing the female nude. He had a predilection for figures of ancient, even archaic, art, in compositions that were sometimes close to academism. But it was this desire to achieve an ideal harmony between man and nature, allied to the German Jugendstil, that gave his works their originality. Influenced by Impressionism, then by Art Nouveau, he evolved, introducing symbolic motifs, towards solid and decorative compositions, and then went on to become interested in the discoveries of the Cubists, structuring his canvases and freeing himself from concern with volumes and focusing on planes.

As an artist, he was very closely linked with certain artistic and literary milieus, associating, in particular, with Max Klinger, Stefan George, Böcklin and Rilke, who would dedicate two poems to him: *Spiel* (*Play*) and *Die Bilder entlang* (*Along the Pictures*). He collaborated on *Pan*, the periodical published in Berlin, in the year of its founding, 1895, and produced pastels and illustrations for the works of Hugo von Hofmannsthal, Stefan George, Théodor Däublen, and for *The Iliad and The Odyssey* (1919-1927). He created a mural (1907) for the Weimar theatre (now the Nationaltheater), and another mural, *The Muses*, for the University of Jena (1909), as well as two mural compositions for the library in Leipzig.

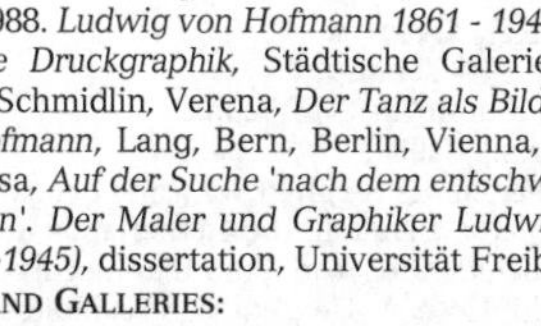

BIBLIOGRAPHY:
Hammer, Klaus, *Ludwig von Hofmann. Maler und Werk*, Dresden, 1988. *Ludwig von Hofmann 1861 - 1945 Zeichnungen Pastelle Druckgraphik*, Städtische Galerie, Albstadt, 1995. Senti-Schmidlin, Verena, *Der Tanz als Bildmotiv: Ludwig von Hofmann*, Lang, Bern, Berlin, Vienna, 1999. Roberts, Contessa, *Auf der Suche 'nach dem entschwebten Land der Griechen'. Der Maler und Graphiker Ludwig von Hofmann (1861-1945)*, dissertation, Universität Freiburg, 2001.

MUSEUMS AND GALLERIES:
ALTENBURG (Lindenau-Mus.): *Pastoral Landscape* (c. 1900) - AUGSBURG (Staatsgalerie) - BERLIN (Berlinische Gal.) - BERLIN (Deutsches Historisches Mus.) - BERLIN (Nationalgal.): *Cliff* (1898) - BERLIN (Stadtmuseum) - COLOGNE (Wallraf-Richartz Mus.) - DARMSTADT (Hessisches Landesmus.) - DRESDEN (Gemäldegal. Neue Meister): *Frauen am Wasser* (*Women by the Water*) (1899, oil on canvas) - FLORENCE (Uffizi) - GINGINS (Fondation Neumann) - HAMBURG (Kunsthalle) - HAMBURG (Mus. für Kunst und Gewerbe) - KARLSRUHE (Badisches Landesmus.) - KARLSRUHE (Staatliche Kunsthalle) - LEICESTER (New Walk Mus. and AG): *Gathering* - LEIPZIG (Mus. der bildenden Künste) - LONDON (Courtauld Institute of Art) - LOS ANGELES (County MA) - MUNICH (Neue Pinakothek): *Nocturne* (c. 1897, oil on canvas) - OSLO (Nasjonalgal.) - POZNAN (Muz. Narodowe) - RIGA: *Near the Spring* - STUTTGART: *Women beside the Sea* - VIENNA (Graphische Sammlung Albertina) - VIENNA (Österreichische Gal. Belvedere) - WEIMAR: *Dances* - WROCLAW (Muz. Narodowe) - WUPPERTAL (Von der Heydt Mus.) - ZURICH (Ludwig-von-Hofmann-Archiv).

AUCTION RECORDS:
BERLIN, 2 July 1970, *Women Bathing* (pastel) DEM 13,300. HAMBURG, 9 June 1972, *Sunny Street*, DEM 6,000. HAMBURG, 15 June 1973, *Spring*, DEM 3,600. ZURICH, 12 Nov 1976, *Nude in a Landscape* (oil on canvas, 13 x 26 1/4 ins / 33 x 66.5 cm) CHF 3,000. MUNICH, 23 May 1977, *Young girl by a Stream* (pastel, 14 1/4 x 25 1/4 ins / 36.5 x 64 cm) DEM 2,000. COLOGNE, 21 May 1977, *Wooded River Landscape with Washing Drying* (1889, oil on canvas, 19 3/4 x 27 1/2 ins / 50 x 70 cm) DEM 5,000. COLOGNE, 26 March 1982, *Women Bathing* (oil on canvas, 20 x 15 3/4 ins / 51 x 40 cm) DEM 5,300. HEIDELBERG, 15 Oct 1983, *Spring* (oil on card, 15 3/4 x 26 3/4 ins / 40 x 68 cm) DEM 16,500. MUNICH, 14 June 1985, *Totenklage* (pastel, 19 1/4 x 26 ins / 49 x 66 cm) DEM 6,200. PARIS, 8 Dec 1987, *Bay* (oil on canvas, 18 x 22 ins / 46 x 55 cm) FRF 25,000. LONDON, 19 Oct 1988, *Landscape with Naked Boys and Girls* (pastel, 24 1/4 x 39 1/2 ins / 61.5 x 100.6 cm) GBP 7,150. COLOGNE, 20 Oct 1989, *Study for a Seascape* (oil on card, 10 x 13 1/4 ins / 24.5 x 33.5 cm) DEM 2,200. NEW YORK, 9 Jan 1991, *Study of Woman Wrapped in a Veil in a Landscape with a Rocky Stream* (pastel and brown wash/tinted paper, 6 1/4 x 9 3/4 ins / 15.6 x 24.7 cm) USD 1,100. TEL AVIV, 6 Jan 1992, *Standing Female Nude* (sepia, 18 1/2 x 9 3/4 ins / 47 x 25 cm) USD 600. HEIDELBERG, 11 April 1992, *Women Bathing on a Beach* (coloured chalks, 7 x 9 1/4 ins / 17.8 x 23.7 cm) DEM 1,400. MUNICH, 1-2 Dec 1992, *Two Riders* (pastel, 12 1/4 x 17 1/4 ins / 31 x 44 cm) DEM 3,795. NEW YORK, 12 Oct 1994, *Paradise* (oil on canvas, 26 1/2 x 20 3/4 ins / 67.3 x 52.7 cm) USD 12,650. LONDON, 20 March 1996, *Landscape with Women and Children* (pastel, 24 1/4 x 39 1/2 ins / 61.5 x 100.6 cm) GBP 4,600. LONDON, 23 Oct 1996, *Quelltrunk* (c. 1920, pastel/paper, 30 3/4 x 22 ins / 78 x 56 cm) GBP 4,370. AHLDEN, 23 April 1999, *Summer - Flautist and Other Figures* (oil on canvas, 31 x 26 ins / 78 x 65 cm) DEM 6,000. BERLIN, 25 Nov 2000, *Male Nude* (1894, charcoal, 17 x 10 ins / 42 x 26 cm) DEM 3,600. BERLIN, 25 Nov 2000, *Bathers* (pastel, 20 x 32 ins / 52 x 81 cm) DEM 26,000. STOCKHOLM, 2 May 2001, *Women Sunbathing* (oil on canvas, 29 x 38 ins / 74 x 96 cm) SEK 56,000. COLOGNE, 4 Dec 2001, *Dancers* (oil on canvas, 30 x 24 ins / 76 x 62 cm) DEM 14,000. MUNICH, 7 June 2002, *In the Outdoors* (oil on canvas, 19 x 35 ins / 48 x 89 cm) EUR 4,600. NEW YORK, 29 Oct 2002, *Bathers* (pastel, 9 x 15 ins / 24 x 37 cm) USD 4,750. BERLIN, 31 May 2003, *Spring Dance* (1905, oil on canvas, 43 x 27 ins / 108 x 69 cm) EUR 26,000. BERLIN, 29 Nov 2003, *Three Women Bathing* (oil on canvas, 29 x 38 ins / 74 x 97 cm) EUR 48,000. MUNICH, 26 March 2004, *Spring* (oil on canvas, 19 x 35 ins / 48 x 90 cm) EUR 4,800. MUNICH, 13 May 2004, *March Sun* (pastel and chalk on paper on board, 13 x 17 ins / 32 x 43 cm) EUR 3,000.

HOFMANN, Michael

Austrian, 19th century.
Born 8 October 1797, in Vienna; died 12 October 1867, in Vienna.
Engraver.

He is noted for some plates for the Belvedere gallery.

HOFMANN, Otto

German, 20th century.
Born 1907.
Active in Italy.
Painter, watercolourist.

Hofmann exhibited at the Goethe Institute in Brussels in 1933. Influenced by Klee and Kandinsky, he painted shapes freely and simply on the canvas.

HOFMANN, Rudolf
German, 19th century.
Born 29 January 1820, in Darmstadt; died 28 October 1882, in Darmstadt.
Painter. History painting, genre scenes.
He trained in Düsseldorf, Munich and Rome. He was inspector of the Grand-Duke of Hessen-Darmstadt's painting collection.

HOFMANN, Thomas
German, 17th century.
Born in Landshut; died 5 December 1646, in Munich.
Painter.
In 1635, he painted a *Crucifixion* for the church in Beuerberg, south of Munich.

HOFMANS, Pieter, also known as Janitzer or Geannizzero
Flemish School, 17th century.
Born c. 1642, in Antwerp; died 30 February 1692, in Rome.
Painter. Battles.
In 1657, Pieter Hofmans was a pupil of Nicolas van Eyck and later, in 1660, of Il Borgignone. He made a trip to Turkey in the company of the landscape artist Zantruiter.

HOFMEIER, Eugen
German, 19th century.
Born 23 March 1843, in Rottenburg.
Painter. Genre scenes.
He was a pupil of Alexander Wagner, Ramberg and Piloty at the academy of Nuremberg and in Munich. He taught drawing at the University of Tübingen, and from 1873 exhibited in Vienna, Munich and Stuttgart.

HOFMEIER, Heinrich
German, 19th - 20th century.
Born 9 January 1869, in Nuremberg.
Painter. Landscapes.
Hofmeier exhibited his work in Berlin in 1909. He lived in Munich.

HOFMEISTER. See also **HOFFMEISTER**

HOFMEISTER, Johannes or Johs
Danish, 20th century.
Born 1 December 1914, in Hjørring; died 26 August 1990, in Hjørring.
Painter. Landscapes with figures, seascapes.
Hofmeister's landscapes frequently depict specific locations rather than anonymous places.

AUCTION RECORDS:
COPENHAGEN, 11 May 1977, *Figure in a Landscape* (oil on canvas, 25 1/4 x 27 1/2 ins / 64 x 70 cm) DKK 10,000. COPENHAGEN, 23 Jan 1979, *Figure on the Beach* (oil on canvas, 26 x 38 1/2 ins / 66 x 98 cm) DKK 15,000. COPENHAGEN, 4 May 1988, *Figure in a Landscape* (19 3/4 x 24 ins / 50 x 61 cm) DKK 14,000. COPENHAGEN, 10 May 1989, *Figure in a Landscape* (11 1/2 x 14 1/2 ins / 29 x 37 cm) DKK 10,000. COPENHAGEN, 22 Nov 1989, *Landscape with Figures near Klanhøj* (oil on canvas, 30 3/4 x 37 3/4 ins / 78 x 96 cm) DKK 22,000. COPENHAGEN, 21-22 March 1990, *Landscape with Figures* (painting/wood, 30 1/4 x 37 3/4 ins / 77 x 96 cm) DKK 26,000. COPENHAGEN, 14-15 Nov 1990, *Landscape with Figures* (oil on canvas, 19 3/4 x 23 1/2 ins / 50 x 60 cm) DKK 13,000. COPENHAGEN, 4 March 1992, *Figure in a Landscape* (oil/synthetic resin, 37 1/2 x 25 1/2 ins / 95 x 65 cm) DKK 8,500. COPENHAGEN, 21 Oct 1992, *Figures in a Landscape* (oil/synthetic resin, 17 x 20 3/4 ins / 43 x 53 cm) DKK 9,000. COPENHAGEN, 21 April 1993, *Landscape at Vennebjerg* (painting/synthetic resin, 23 1/2 x 27 1/2 ins / 60 x 70 cm) DKK 12,000. COPENHAGEN, 19 Oct 1994, *Seascape with Figures at Læsø* (1957, oil on canvas, 26 x 34 1/4 ins / 66 x 87 cm) DKK 15,000. COPENHAGEN, 17 April 1996, *Landscape with Figures* (oil on paper, 15 1/4 x 17 1/4 ins / 39 x 44 cm) DKK 4,800. COPENHAGEN, 23 March 1999, *Two Figures by a House* (oil on panel, 19 x 25 ins / 47 x 64 cm) DKK 19,000. COPENHAGEN, 23 March 1999, *Landscape with Figures* (oil on panel, 30 x 38 ins / 77 x 96 cm) DKK 20,000. COPENHAGEN, 28 March 2000, *Figure by a Cliff near the Sea* (oil on masonite, 20 x 24 ins / 50 x 60 cm) DKK 18,000. COPENHAGEN, 20 June 2000, *Two Figures by the Sea* (oil on canvas, 20 x 26 ins / 50 x 65 cm) DKK 21,000. COPENHAGEN, 7 Feb 2001, *Landscape with Figures* (oil on masonite, 41 x 48 ins / 103 x 122 cm) DKK 54,000. BERN, 10 May 2001, *Lake at Zurich and surroundings after La Nature* (etching, 10 x 48 ins / 26 x 122 cm) CHF 18,000. COPENHAGEN, 29 May 2002, *Figure in Landscape* (oil on panel, 14 x 18 ins / 35 x 45 cm) DKK 23,000. BERN, 14 Nov 2002, *Town of Rapperschweil by Lake Zurich* (colour etching, 6 x 10 ins / 16 x 26 cm) CHF 5,200. VEJLE, 22 Sept 2003, *Coastal Landscape with Figures and Houses* (oil on canvas, 49 x 157 ins / 125 x 400 cm) DKK 31,000. VEJLE, 22 Sept 2003, *Coastal Landscape with Figures* (oil on canvas, 49 x 99 ins / 125 x 251 cm) DKK 32,000. VEJLE, 12 Jan 2004, *Houses and Figures by the Sea* (oil on canvas, 20 x 27 ins / 51 x 69 cm) DKK 26,000. COPENHAGEN, 5 Oct 2004, *Figures with Houses, Sea beyond* (1969, oil on canvas, 20 x 24 ins / 50 x 60 cm) DKK 24,000.

HOFMULLER, Hans
German, 20th century.
Born 4 October 1888, in Darmstadt; died 21 June 1916, in Verdun.
Painter, illustrator. Stage sets.

HOFNER, Johann Baptist
German, 19th - 20th century.
Born 30 April 1832, in Aresing; died 29 June 1913, in Munich.
Painter. Genre scenes, still-lifes, animals.
Hofner studied under Piloty and lived in Munich. He exhibited his work in Munich and Vienna from 1863.

MUSEUMS AND GALLERIES:
MUNICH: *Still-life*.

AUCTION RECORDS:
LONDON, 17 Feb 1908, *Sheep Shearing* (1872) GBP 17. LONDON, 26 Nov 1982, *Shepherdess* (1866, oil on canvas, 47 1/2 x 35 3/4 ins / 120.5 x 90.8 cm) GBP 8,500. NEW YORK, 27 Oct 1983, *Sheep and Rabbits in the Cowshed* (oil on canvas, 38 1/2 x 59 1/4 ins / 97.7 x 150.3 cm) USD 20,000. NEW YORK, 24 Feb 1987, *Farm Animals* (1884, oil on canvas, 25 x 42 ins / 63.5 x 106.8 cm) USD 4,400. MUNICH, 31 May 1990, *Poultry by a Dead Fox* (1870, oil on canvas, 36 1/2 x 52 ins / 93 x 132 cm) DEM 38,500.

HOFNER, Otto
Austrian, 20th century.
Born 29 March 1879, in Vienna.
Sculptor, medallist.
Hofner studied under Stephan Schwartz before travelling to France, England, Belgium, the Netherlands and Germany. His works include the large tomb that he carved for his father Leopold Hofner. He regularly exhibited in Vienna, Hamburg, Berlin and Rome.

HOFREITER, Karl
German, 18th century.
Active in Eger (Cheb), Bohemia c. 1724.
Painter.
He painted frescoes in the library of the monastery of Waldsassen in Germany, not far from his birthplace.

HOFREUTER, Kaspar
German, 16th century.

Active in Eger c. 1550.
Painter.
Kaspar Hofreuter's work includes a *View of Eger*.

HOFRICHTER, Martha
Czech, 19th - 20th century.
Born 1872, in Brno.
Painter. Figures.
Martha Hofrichter lived for a while in Munich and then mainly in Vienna.
AUCTION RECORDS:
LONDON, 11 Feb 1987, *Girl with Lyre* (oil on canvas, 25 1/4 x 27 1/4 ins / 64 x 69 cm) GBP 1,600.

HOFSCHEN, Edgar
German, 20th century.
Born 1941, in Tapiau, East Prussia (now Gvardeysk, Russia).
Painter.
Hofschen has lived in Radevormwald since 1956. He exhibited in West Germany (before German unification), in Cologne, Frankfurt and Hamburg since 1971. He was invited to the Biennale de Paris in 1973. Hofschen covers large areas of the canvas in his Abstract painting, which are almost monochrome; they are simply defined by darker strips at the sides.
AUCTION RECORDS:
HAMBURG, 8 June 1979, *Composition* (1973, mixed media/mounted paper/canvas, 36 x 27 3/4 ins / 90.5 x 70.3 cm) DEM 2,600.

HOFSESS, Georg
German, 19th century.
Born 3 October 1826, in Frankfurt am Main.
Sculptor.
He did sculptures of animals.

HOFSTADT, Gabriel van. See **HOOCHSTADT**

HOFSTADT, Pieter van der, or Hoffstadt, called de Vocht
Flemish, 16th century.
Active in Louvain from 1523 to 1551.
Painter.
Flemish School.
In 1523 Pieter van der Hofstadt painted a canopy for the church of St James.

HOFSTED VAN ESSEN, G.
German, 17th - 18th century.
Born probably, in Essen.
Painter.
He worked in Amsterdam, where he painted a *Monumental View of the Ruins of Palmyra*.

HOFSTEIN, Hugo O. von
Swedish, 19th century.
Born 20 June 1865, in Sweden.
Painter, illustrator.
Hugo von Hofstein established himself in America after completing his studies in Stockholm.

HOFSTETTEN, Franz Xaver von
German, 19th century.
Born 1811, in Munich; died 1883, in Waidhaus, Bavaria.
Painter. Landscapes.
His debut was in 1851.
AUCTION RECORDS:
MUNICH, 26 Oct 1977, *Landscape* (oil on canvas, 16 1/4 x 19 1/4 ins / 41 x 49 cm) DEM 5,000. MUNICH, 15 Sept 1983, *Hunters in a Wooded Landscape with a Mediaeval Castle* (1848, oil on canvas, 22 x 30 ins / 55 x 76 cm) DEM 9,000.

HOFSTETTER, William Alfred
American, 20th century.
Born 15 July 1884; died 22 September 1970, in Pennsylvania.
Painter.
William Hofstetter worked in Philadelphia, where he was a member of several artists' associations. He exhibited annually with the Pennsylvania Academy of the Fine Arts' for about forty years.

HOFSTÖTTER, Franz
German, 19th - 20th century.
Born 1871, in Munich.
Painter, sculptor.
Hofstötter studied under Hackl at the academy of fine arts in Munich.

HOFTEN, Dirck von
Dutch, 17th century.
Active in Amsterdam c. 1646.
Painter.

HOGAI, real name: Kano Enshin, childhood name Kotaro, artist names: Enshin, Hogai, Shokai, Shorin
Japanese, 19th century.
Born 1828, in Shimonoseki; died 1888.
Painter.
A pupil of Shosen (1823-1880), Kano Hogai lived in Tokyo. His father, Kano Seiko, seems to have been a good painter. He developed an interest in Chinese poetry and the *Noh* theatre at a very early age; at 15 he painted his first work, *Bakan Shinkei Zukan*, an illustrated scroll of the Shimonoseki countryside painted in minute detail but already betraying a greater sense of freedom than that normally found in work of the Kano School of the same period. His bird-and-flower album *Kacho Gasatsu*, which he painted at the age of 16, is regarded as one of his masterpieces. Under the influence of Watarai Tomei, a painter of the Tosa school and friend of his father, he tried his hand at *yamato-e* (Japanese painting) before resuming his studies in Edo (now Tokyo), in the Katsukawa studio founded by Shonsho (1726-1792), from which he would soon be expelled because of his Kano affiliations. Yet he would remain one of the best-known Katsukawa painters, working with Hashimoto Sentaro, Kano Shogyoku and Kimura Ryugaku. In 1860, he restored the murals in Edo Castle. He was already 34 when he assumed his artist name, Hogai. To survive, he painted ceramics and lacquer.

In 1885, he took part in the second Japanese Salon in Paris, where he exhibited his *Kannon Zu*, today in the Freer Gallery of Art, Washington. His meeting with Ernest Fenollosa, who had arrived in Japan in 1878 to teach at Tokyo University, was a turning point in his life: together with Hashimoto Kunio, he would revive the ideal of Asian painting for the American. Together they created the *Kanga Kai* (art appreciation society), which would go on to organise many events. Hogai was also involved in the founding of the Tokyo school of fine arts but died before the school could open. His work shows the influence of Sesshu (1420-1506) while remaining true to the style of the Kano School, albeit (following the advice of Fenollosa) with a certain realism in form and colour.
MUSEUMS AND GALLERIES:
WASHINGTON DC (Freer Gal. of Art): *The Bodhisattva Kannon* (1883, ink, colour and gold on silk, hanging scroll).

HOGAN, Joâo
Portuguese, 20th century.
Painter. Landscapes.
Joâo Hogan's stony desert landscapes, in which human beings have no place, evoke a distant, as yet unexplored, planet.

HOGAN, John
Irish, 19th century.

Born 14 October 1800, in Tallow (Waterford); died 27 March 1858, in Dublin.

Sculptor. Busts.

John Hogan exhibited in London at the Royal Academy from 1833 to 1850.

Museums and Galleries:

Dublin: *Bust of Archbishop Murray.*

HOGAN, John Valentine

British, 19th - 20th century.

Sculptor.

John Valentine Hogan was the son of John Hogarth, under whom he studied and several of whose paintings he completed after his death. He spent much of his life in Rome.

HOGARTH, Burne

American, 20th century.

Born 25 December 1911, in Chicago; died 1996.

Painter, draughtsman, engraver. Comic strips.

Burne Hogarth studied drawing and anthropology at Columbia University. In 1937 he succeeded Harold Foster in drawing the Tarzan comic strip, now regarded as an art form in itself. Serious analysis has attempted to deconstruct Hogarth's world, seeing in it his admiration for the baroque artists, German Expressionism, the arts of the Far East and Michelangelo. He was also a painter and engraver and closely followed developments in Op Art. He was co-founder of the Visual Arts School in New York.

HOGARTH, T. C.

British, 19th century.

Active in Edinburgh and London.

Painter, engraver.

T.C. Hogarth exhibited in London at the Royal Academy from 1859.

HOGARTH, William

British, 18th century.

Born 10 November 1697, in London; died 25 October 1764, in London.

Painter, draughtsman, engraver. History painting, portraits, genre scenes.

William Hogarth played a crucial part in establishing an English School of painting. In 1713 he was apprenticed to Ellis Gamble, a silver-plate engraver. By 1720 he was in business on his own and in 1721, he engraved the first of his satires, *South Sea Scheme*. Hogarth studied life drawing at the St Martin's Lane Academy from 1720 with Vanderbank and Chéron, but by 1724 this had closed and he joined James Thornhill's academy in the Great Piazza, Covent Garden; he later married Thornhill's daughter.

Hogarth is best known for his satires and moral pieces and these themes are evident in his work from the start of his career. In the mid-1720s, *The Bad Taste of the Town* provided an early example of the artist's xenophobia in which he attacked Italian opera and the Palladian taste in architecture current at that time. Similar sentiments resurfaced in *O the Roast Beef of Old England (The Gate of Calais)* (1748) in which he satirised the French after his arrest in Calais on a charge of spying. In 1726, he provided 12 illustrations for Samuel Butler's satirical poem, *Hudibras*, which were a precursor to his later moral progresses. His first major oil painting was *The Beggar's Opera* (1728) of which several versions exist.

The first of what Hogarth termed his 'modern moral subjects' was *A Harlot's Progress* (1731). This work initially began life as a genre painting of low life, in this case, a prostitute in her room about to be apprehended by a magistrate. Hogarth then expanded it to included scenes from her previous and subsequent history, ending with her death. Other moral subjects include *A Rake's Progress* (1733-1774) and *Marriage à la Mode* (1743) in which he satirised the upper classes by depicting the events and sad end of an arranged marriage. In his later work, Hogarth adopted a reforming stance directed at the vices of the poorest members of society, in which his subjects, for example, *Industry and Idleness* (1747) and *Beer Street* and *Gin Street* (both 1751) were conceived as engravings from the start and published as cheaply as possible.

Hogarth also painted portraits and during the early 1730s was greatly in demand at a painter of conversation pieces, for example *Family Party* (c. 1730-1735). In the 1740s, he produced portraits of contemporary worthies like *George Arnold, Mary Edwards* and *Captain Thomas Coram,* the founder of the Foundling Hospital of which Hogarth was a keen supporter. Although he worked at the highest level of society in the execution of portraits, he also painted likenesses of famous criminals, for example the murderer *Sarah Malcolm in Prison* (1733).

Many exhibitions of Hogarth's work have been held, including, in 2002, *William Hogarth: Dirne, Wüstling und eine Moderne Ehe* (*William Hogarth: Harlots, Rakes and a Modern Honour*) at the Kunsthalle in Hamburg and, in 2003, *William Hogarth: Conversation Piece* at the Pallant House Gallery, Chichester. Examples of Hogarth's work also formed an exhibition, *Master of Satire: the World of William Hogarth,* at the Meadows Museum of Art, Centenary College Louisiana, in 2004.

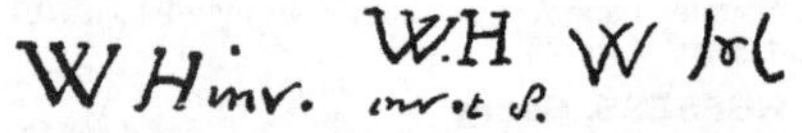

Bibliography:

Oppé, A.P., *The Drawings of William Hogarth,* Phaidon Press, London, 1948. Gowing, L., *Hogarth,* exhibition catalogue, Tate, London, 1971-1972. Einberg, E., *Manners and Morals: Hogarth and British Painting 1700-1760,* exhibition catalogue, Tate, London, 1987-1988. Einberg, E./Egerton, J., *The Age of Hogarth: British Painters Born 1675-1709,* Tate, London, 1988 (Tate Gallery Collections, vol. 2). *Hogarth's Graphic Works,* Print Room, London, 1989 (commentary by R. Paulson). Paulson, R., *Hogarth,* Lutterworth Press, Cambridge, 1992-1994 (3 vols). Bindman, David, *Hogarth and His Time: Serious Comedy,* University of California Press, Berkeley, 1997. Hogarth, William/Paulson, R. (ed.), *The Analysis of Beauty,* Yale University Press, New Haven, 1997. Uglow, J.S., *Hogarth: a Life and a World,* Faber, London, 1997. Hallet, Mark, *The Spectacle of Difference: Graphic Satire in the Age of Hogarth,* Yale University Press, New Haven, 1999. Mitchell, E.L., *Death by Hogarth,* exhibition catalogue, Harvard University Press, Cambridge (MA), 1999. Fort, Bernadette/Rosenthal, Angela (ed.), *The Other Hogarth: Aesthetics of Difference,* essays, Princeton University Press, Princeton, 2001. Paulson, R., *Hogarth's Harlot: Sacred Parody in Enlightenment England,* Johns Hopkins University Press, Baltimore, 2003.

Museums and Galleries:

Cambridge (Fitzwilliam Museum): *Dr Benjamin Hoadley* (late 1730s, oil on canvas); *A Musical Party, the Mathias Family* (1730s, oil on canvas) - Cardiff (National Museum and Gallery): *The Jones Conversation Piece* (1731, oil on canvas) - Dublin (NG of Ireland): *Family of George II* (c. 1732, drawing) - Edinburgh (Nat. Gal. of Scotland): *Interiors with figures and Portrait of an Old Man* (drawings); *Sarah Malcolm* (*Sarah Malcolm in Prison*) (1733, oil on canvas) - London (Courtauld Institute of Art): *Head of a Man Turned Slighty to the Right* (chalk on paper) - London (Foundling Mus.) - London (National Maritime Mus.) - London (National Portrait Gal.): *The Gaols Committee of the House of Commons* (c. 1729, oil on canvas); *William Hogarth* (c. 1757, oil on canvas) - London (NG): *Marriage à la Mode: 1 The Marriage Settlement; 2 The Tête a Tête; 3 The Inspection; 4 The Toilette; 5 The*

Bagnio; 6 The Lady's Death (c. 1743, oil on canvas); *The Shrimp Girl* (c. 1740-1745, oil on canvas) - London (Tate Collection): *Lavinia Fenton, Duchess of Bolton* (c. 1740-1750, oil on canvas); *O the Roast Beef of Old England (the Gate of Calais)* (1748, oil on canvas); *Heads of Six of Hogarth's Servants* (c. 1750-1755, oil on canvas); *Sigismunda Mournin Over the Heart of Guiscardo* (1759, oil on canvas); *The Strode Family* (c. 1738, oil on canvas); *James Quin, Actor* (c. 1739) - New Haven (Yale Center For British Art): *The Beggar's Opera* (1729, oil on canvas); portrait*John and Elizabeth Jeffreys and their children* (1730, oil on canvas); portrait*William Cavendish, Marquess of Hartington (later 4th Duke of Devonshire)* (1741, oil on canvas); *Family Party* (c. 1730-1735); *William Augustus, Duke of Cumberland* (c. 1732) - New Haven (Yale Center for British Art): *A Night Encounter* (c. 1738).

Auction records:

Paris, 2 May 1881, *The Gate of Calais,* FRF 68,500. Paris, 30 and 31 Jan 1894, *Preacher in a Church,* FRF 1,200; *Gambling Scene,* FRF 800. Paris, 17 April 1899, *Evening During the Reign of George II* (sepia) FRF 1,800. London, 2 Dec 1907, *Last Throw,* GBP 9. London, 21 Dec 1907, *Portrait of Mrs Garrick,* GBP 131. London, 29 Feb 1908, *Portrait of Lord Holland,* GBP 50. New York, 12-14 April 1909, *Viscountess Townshend,* USD 1,550. London, 3 June 1909, *Portrait of Peg Woffington,* GBP 21. London, 23 July 1909, *Portrait of Handel,* GBP 94. London, 18 Dec 1909, *Voltaire with a Group of Gentlemen,* GBP 81. London, 4 July 1910, *Portrait of a Young Woman,* GBP 241. New York, 16 and 17 Feb 1911, *Portrait of Peg Woffington,* USD 2,200. London, 25 Feb 1911, *Portrait of Peg Woffington in White,* GBP 525; *Portrait of a Gentleman and his Family,* GBP 52. London, 14 July 1911, *Lady in Blue,* GBP 105. London, 17 July 1911, *Lady in Red,* GBP 73. Paris, 31 Jan 1921, *Portrait of Mary Walcot,* FRF 520. London, Jan 1922, *Lady in Yellow,* GBP 39. London, Feb 1922, *Bishop Hoadley,* GBP 10. London, May 1922, *Auction Sale at Christie's,* GBP 241; *Group of Frenchmen and Women,* GBP 36. London, July 1922, *Young Chief of the MacKinnon Clan,* GBP 68. London, Dec 1922, *Lady Thought to be Mrs Hoadley,* GBP 29. London, July 1923, *Lady in a White Satin Dress,* GBP 1,050. London, 3 March 1924, *The Court,* GBP 19. London, 20 April 1925, *Miss Ral,* GBP 99. London, 12 Feb 1926, *James, 1st Earl of Charlemont,* GBP 399. London, 28 July 1926, *House of Cards* (both) GBP 315. London, 13 April 1927, *Bard,* GBP 210. London, 13 May 1927, *Mrs Garrick,* GBP 273. London, 8 July 1927, *Midnight Conversation,* GBP 268. London, 15 June 1928, *Lord and Lady Grey as Children,* GBP 1,155. London, 2 July 1928, *Wagg Family,* GBP 315. London, 8 July 1929, *Frederick Frankland,* GBP 168. London, 27 June 1930, *Lady in a Slate-coloured Dress,* GBP 120. London, 12 Dec 1930, *Anne Wolstenholme,* GBP 2,257. Philadelphia, 30 March 1932, *Portrait of a Man,* USD 250. New York, 12 April 1935, *Mary Hogarth,* USD 550. London, 28 Feb 1936, *Little Girl in Blue and White,* GBP 157. London, 4 June 1937, *Benjamin Hoadley,* GBP 1,470; *Southwark Fair,* GBP 3,045. London, 27 May 1938, *Morning and Night* (both) GBP 2,520. London, 18 Nov 1938, *Man in Brown,* GBP 89. London, 12 Jan 1942, *Theodore Jacobsen,* GBP 735. Paris, 21 Dec 1942, *Portrait of a Young Woman in a Cap* (attributed) FRF 3,950. London, 16 July 1943, *Captain Joseph,* GBP 1,365. New York, 5 April 1944, *Little Girl in a Sunhat,* USD 3,000. London, 14 July 1944, *Bowl of Punch,* GBP 115. New York, 20 Feb 1946, *Viscount Monck,* USD 300. London, 2 Oct 1946, *Miss Elisabeth Brightwell,* GBP 200. London, 31 July 1947, *Lady in a Yellow Dress,* GBP 105. London, 25 June 1958, *Portrait of a Lady,* GBP 1,900. London, 15 July 1959, *Men's Club,* GBP 3,000. London, 23 March 1960, *Portrait of Mrs Margaret Woffington,* GBP 3,000. Lucerne, 25 Nov 1960, *Portrait of the Actor David Garrick,* CHF 5,000. London, 14 June 1961, *The Threepenny Opera, Act III Scene 2; Makky with Lucy and Polly,* GBP 30,000. London, 29 May 1963, *The Clarke Brothers of Swakeleys Drinking Wine,* GBP 3,200. London, 25 June 1965, *Portrait of Daniel Lock,* Gns 50,000. London, 7 July 1967, *Portrait of Thomas Herring Archbishop of York,* Gns 19,000. London, 20 Nov 1970, *Merry Company,* Gns 1,500. London, 18 June 1971, *Scene from The Tempest,* GBP 12,000. London, 22 June 1973, *Southwark Fair* (1733) Gns 55,000. London, 6 July 1977, *Portrait of HRH William Augustus, Duke of Cumberland* (1732, oil on canvas, 17 3/4 x 13 1/2 ins / 45 x 34 cm) GBP 65,000. London, 16 July 1981, *The Industrious Prentice Married and Furnishing his House (recto)* (pen and wash/pencil outlines); *The Idle Prentice Returned from Sea and in a Garret with a Common Prostitute (verso)* (pencil) GBP 29,000. London, 22 April 1983, *Portrait of the Right Honorable Richard Mouteney, 1st Baron of the Exchequer in Ireland* (oil on canvas, 29 x 24 1/2 ins / 73.6 x 62.2 cm) GBP 60,000. London, 16 March 1984, *Portrait of William Jones* (1740, oil on canvas, 50 x 40 1/4 ins / 127 x 102 cm) GBP 260,000. London, 27 June 1985, *The Works of Hogarth* (1764-1789, etching and burin) GBP 4,600. London, 12 July 1989, *Seated Portrait of a Gentleman in a Grey Suit lined with Pink* (oil on canvas, 33 1/4 x 27 ins / 84.5 x 68.5 cm) GBP 126,500. London, 14 Nov 1990, *Chiswick House, Middlesex* (oil on canvas, painted in collaboration with G. Lambert, 30 1/2 x 40 1/2 ins / 77.5 x 103 cm) GBP 220,000. London, 10 July 1991, *The Edwards Hamilton Family on the Terrace of their House in Kensington* (oil on canvas, 27 x 33 3/4 ins / 68.5 x 86 cm) GBP 401,500. Stockholm, 19 May 1992, *Choir* (oil on canvas, 56 1/4 x 44 1/2 ins / 143 x 113 cm) SEK 15,000. London, 15 June 2000, *Portrait of Gentleman, Standing in a Landscape with Dog, Wearing a Blue Coat* (oil on canvas, 16 x 13 ins / 40 x 33 cm) GBP 35,000. London, 6 Dec 2000, *Midnight Modern Conversation* (engraving) GBP 3,000. London, 15 June 2001, *Portrait of Mary Hogarth and Anne Hogarth, the Artist's Sisters* (oil on canvas laid on panel, a pair, oval, 19 x 17 ins / 47 x 42 cm) GBP 82,000. London, 6 July 2001, *Harlot's Progress* (album of 85 etchings and engravings, 24 x 19 ins / 61 x 48 cm) GBP 12,000. London, 12 June 2002, *Antiquaries, Group of Men Seated at a Circular Table in an Interior* (oil on canvas, 25 x 30 ins / 63 x 76 cm) GBP 60,000.

HOGE, Oscar

Belgian, 20th century.

Born 1884, in Ghent.

Painter. Figures, landscapes, still-lifes.

Hoge studied at the academy of fine arts in Ghent. He decorated the thermal baths in Ostend and the church in Middelkerke.

HOGEN, Leendert van

Dutch, 18th century.

Portrait artist.

HOGENBERG, Hans or Johann-Nicolas, the Elder, or Hoogenberg or Hogenbergh

Flemish, 16th century.

Born c. 1500, in Mechelen; died 1544, probably in Mechelen.

Painter, engraver. Religious subjects.

Flemish School.

Hans Hogenberg the Elder was a brother or other relative of Nicolas Hooghenberg from Munich who settled in Liège at the beginning of the 16th century. Hogenberg visited Italy as a young man. Van Mander includes him in the German School and attributes to him several paintings in churches in Mechelen, especially those of St-Rombout and St-Romuald.

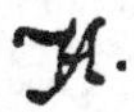

HOGENBERG, Johann

Flemish School, 17th century.

Born c. 1550.
Engraver. Historical subjects, portraits, animals.

The son of Franz Hogenberg and brother of Abraham, he was in Cologne around 1600. Mostly he engraved portraits and history subjects.

HOGENBERG, Nikolas or Nikolaus, or Hoochbergh, Hooberghe
Flemish, 16th century.
Born c. 1500; died before 23 September 1539.
Active in Mechelen in 1527.
Painter, engraver. History painting.
Flemish School.

Nikolas Hogenberg was the father of Remigius and Franz Hogenbergh. Some place him in the German School, as he came from Munich. His works include an engraving of the *Entrance of Charles V and Pope Clement VII into Bologna.*

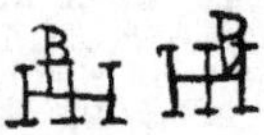

Bibliography:
Hollstein, Friedrich Wilhelm Heinrich, *'Hollstein's German engravings, etchings and woodcuts 1400-1700'* in vol. 13, Van Gendt, Amsterdam, 1984.

Auction records:
London, 9 April 1981, *The Entombment* (pen, diam. 13 ins / 33 cm) GBP 750. London, 5 Dec 1985, *Oedipus Consulting the Sphinx* (1524, engraving/copper, 4 3/4 x 3 1/4 ins / 12 x 8.2 cm) GBP 10,000.

HOGENBERGH, Abraham, or Hoogenbergh
Flemish School, 17th century.
Engraver. Urban landscapes, topographical views. Frontispieces.

Abraham Hogenbergh was the son of Franz Hogenbergh and brother of Johann Hogenbergh. He is known to have been in Cologne as early as 1590 and 1593. He assisted his father with the plates he engraved for the work *Theatrum Orbis Terrarum* by the geographer and cartographer Abraham Ortelius.

HOGENBERGH, Franz
Flemish, 16th century.
Born c. 1535, in Mechelen; died 1590, in Cologne.
Draughtsman, engraver. Urban landscapes.
Flemish School.

Franz Hogenbergh was one of the two sons of Nikolas Hogenberg. Some biographers place his birth in England in 1555; this is an improbable date as his engraving, *Portrait of Mary Tudor,* is dated that same year. He was born in Mechelen and is thought to have accompanied his brother Remigius to England. In 1560 he was working in Poitou in France. By 1570 he had settled in Cologne. There are references to him in Hamburg in 1585 and in Copenhagen in 1588. He had two sons, Johann and Abraham, both engravers.

Hogenbergh was one of the principal engravers contributing to the *Civitates Orbis Terrarum* by Georg Braun (six volumes published 1512-1617), which consists of plans and views of European and other towns, and he may even have originated the idea for the books. He also collaborated on the *Theatrum Orbis Terrarum* by the geographer and mapmaker Abraham Ortelius.

Bibliography:
Old European cities: thirty-two 16th-century city maps and texts from the Civitates orbis terrarum of Georg Braun & Franz Hogenberg, Thames & Hudson, London, 1965 (with a contribution by Ruthardt Oehme). Skelton, R.A. (preface), *Civitates orbis terrarum, 1572-1618,* Theatrvm Orbis Terrarum, Amsterdam, 1965. *Cartes anciennes des grandes villes d'Europe: une sélection des plus beaux plans de Braun et Hogenberg,* Solar, Paris, 1992. *Le Dictionnaire des Peintres belges du XIVe siècle à nos jours depuis les premiers maîtres des anciens Pays-bas méridionaux et de la Principauté de Liège jusqu'aux artistes contemporains,* La Renaissance du Livre, Brussels, 1995.

Auction records:
London, 4-5 and 6 July 1911, *Collection of around Two Hundred Military Subjects* (1614, album in its original binding) GBP 24.

HOGENBERGH, Remigius
Flemish, 16th century.
Born c. 1536, in Mechelen; died after 1573; c. 1588 according to the Grove Dictionary of Art.
Engraver (burin). Portraits, topographical views.
Flemish School.

Remigius Hogenbergh was the son of Nikolas Hogenberg and the brother of Franz Hogenbergh. Around 1570 he was working for the archbishop of Canterbury in England, and probably also in France. He specialised in engraving portraits, including those of *Henry IV, Charles, Duke of Lorraine, François de Valois,* and *Parker, Archbishop of Canterbury* (1573), as well as a *Genealogy of the Kings of England* (1574). Hogenbergh used only a burin when engraving, and his works are rare.

HOGENDORPS-JACOB, Adrienne Jacqueline van (Baroness)
Dutch, 19th - 20th century.
Born 1857, in Batavia, now Jakarta; died 1920.
Painter. Still-lifes, flowers.

Van Hogendorps-Jacob studied under M. Roosenborn. She took part in the Exposition Universelle in Paris in 1900.

Auction records:
Amsterdam, 30 Oct 1991, *Still-life of Peonies on a Chinese Dish* (oil on canvas, 17 1/4 x 26 3/4 ins / 44 x 68 cm) NLG 7,475.

HOGENHEYM, Emmanuel Jacob van
Dutch, 17th century.
Active in Leiden in 1642.
Painter.

Emmanuel van Hogenheym was almost certainly the father of Jacob van Hogenheym.

HOGENHEYM, Jacob van
Dutch, 17th century.
Active in Amsterdam c. 1680.
Painter.

HOGENHUYZEN, Elisabeth Georgine van
Dutch, 18th century.
Born 1776, in The Hague; died 28 May 1794, in The Hague.
Painter. Fruit, flowers.

Auction records:
Paris, 16 Nov 1977, *Rose, Tulip, Peony and Other Flowers in a Glass Vase* (1790?, wood, 18 3/4 x 14 1/2 ins / 47.5 x 37 cm) FRF 29,000. Blois, 26 Nov 1984, *Vase of Flowers and Fruit on an Entablature* (1792, oil on panel, 21 1/4 x 17 3/4 ins / 54 x 45 cm) FRF 186,000.

HÖGER, Otto
German, 20th century.
Born 27 May 1881, in Hamburg; died 4 December 1918, in Rastatt (Baden-Württemberg).
Painter, engraver, sculptor. Landscapes.

Höger studied under Olde and Hofmann at the academy of fine arts in Weimar. He travelled in Denmark and Germany for a long time.

HOGERS, Jacob
Dutch, 17th century.

Baptised 16 January 1614 in Deventer; died after 1660.
Painter.

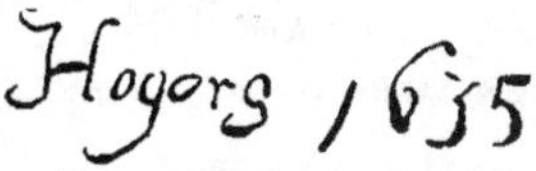

Museums and Galleries:
Amsterdam: *Esau and Jacob Meet.*
Auction records:
Milan, 6 May 1971, *Solomon Adoring the Idols,* ITL 3,700,000.

HOGERVORST, Hendrik
Dutch, 18th century.
Active at the beginning of the 18th century.
Portrait artist.

HOGERWAARD, Frans
Dutch, 20th century.
Born 10 November 1882, in Batavia, now Jakarta; died 15 June 1921, in The Hague.
Painter, engraver. Portraits, landscapes.
Hogerwaard studied in Haarlem.
Auction records:
Amsterdam, 30 Oct 1990, *Early Morning in Montmartre, Paris* (oil on canvas, 15 1/4 x 23 3/4 ins / 38.5 x 60.5 cm) NLG 2,185. Amsterdam, 4 March 2002, *Sunny Afternoon* (oil on canvas, 48 x 36 ins / 121 x 91 cm) EUR 10,000.

HOGERWAARD, George or Georges
Dutch, 20th century.
Born 9 September 1878, in Surabaya, Indonesia; died 1939.
Painter. Nudes, still-lifes (flowers).
Hogerwaard studied under Thyssen in The Hague. He was the brother of Frans Hogerwaard.
Auction records:
Amsterdam, 5-6 Feb 1991, *Pink Roses in a Crystal Vase in front of a Green Curtain* (oil on canvas/card, 13 1/4 x 16 1/4 ins / 33.5 x 41.5 cm) USD 1,380. Amsterdam, 20 April 1993, *Still-life of Flowers* (1927, oil on canvas, 26 x 23 1/2 ins / 66 x 60 cm) NLG 1,438. Amsterdam, 18 June 1996, *Semi-reclining Nude* (1935, oil on canvas, 31 1/2 x 27 1/2 ins / 80 x 70 cm) NLG 2,415. Amsterdam, 7 July 1999, *Dahlias in a Jug* (oil on canvas, 26 x 24 ins / 65 x 60 cm) NLG 4,200.

HOGEVEEN, G. van
Dutch, 18th century.
Active in Amsterdam.
Painter.
G. van Hogeveen is known for his decorative work.

HÖGFELDT, Robert
Swedish, 20th century.
Born 1894; died 1986.
Painter. Genre scenes, landscapes, waterscapes.

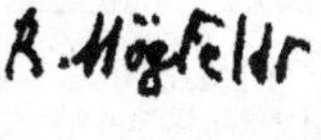

Auction records:
Stockholm, 23 April 1980, *Conversation* (pencil/paper, 15 1/4 x 12 1/2 ins / 39 x 31.5 cm) SEK 4,500. Stockholm, 27 Oct 1981, *Rascals' Parade* (watercolour, 20 3/4 x 20 1/4 ins / 53 x 51.5 cm) SEK 18,000. Stockholm, 26 April 1983, *Musical Hour* (oil on panel, 13 x 16 1/4 ins / 33 x 41 cm) SEK 15,200. Stockholm, 30 Oct 1984, *Plums* (watercolour, 11 x 15 3/4 ins / 27 x 40 cm) SEK 21,000. Stockholm, 9 Dec 1986, *Little Girl and the Sorcerer* (watercolour, 11 3/4 x 19 ins / 30 x 48 cm) SEK 36,000. Stockholm, 26 May 1987, *Nudes on the Beach* (pencil, 17 3/4 x 21 1/4 ins / 45 x 54 cm) SEK 13,500. Stockholm, 6 June 1988, *Landscape with a Tree near a Lake in Summer* (mixed media, 17 3/4 x 21 1/4 ins / 45 x 54 cm) SEK 10,000. Stockholm, 21 Nov 1988, *Family of Gnomes* (coloured chalks, 9 1/2 x 11 1/2 ins / 24 x 29 cm) SEK 4,500. Stockholm, 20 Feb 1989, *Daily Bread* (ink, 4 1/4 x 9 1/2 ins / 11 x 24 cm) SEK 5,200. Stockholm, 6 Dec 1989, *Women Bathers on a Beach* (oil on canvas, 19 1/4 x 24 3/4 ins / 49 x 63 cm) SEK 15,500. Stockholm, 14 June 1990, *Wooded Landscape with a Lake in the Distance* (oil on panel, 17 3/4 x 21 1/4 ins / 45 x 54 cm) SEK 10,500. Stockholm, 5-6 Dec 1990, *At the Antique Dealer's* (oil on canvas, 28 3/4 x 23 1/2 ins / 73 x 60 cm) SEK 15,500. Stockholm, 28 Oct 1991, *Summer Landscape* (oil on panel, 12 1/2 x 15 1/4 ins / 32 x 39 cm) SEK 11,000. Stockholm, 13 April 1992, *Lake Landscape in Spring* (oil on panel, 12 1/2 x 15 3/4 ins / 32 x 40 cm) SEK 9,500. Stockholm, 26 May 1999, *Together on the Swings* (watercolour, 10 x 12 ins / 25 x 30 cm) SEK 30,000. Stockholm, 24 Nov 1999, *Susanna in the Bath* (oil on panel, 18 x 22 ins / 46 x 55 cm) SEK 48,000. Stockholm, 16 May 2000, *Spring Hats* (oil on panel, 13 x 16 ins / 32 x 40 cm) SEK 23,000. Stockholm, 28 Nov 2000, *Pair of Trolls* (oil on panel, 18 x 15 ins / 46 x 38 cm) SEK 21,000. Stockholm, 28 Nov 2001, *Hunter's Hunt* (watercolour, 9 x 7 ins / 24 x 19 cm) SEK 20,000. Stockholm, 4 Dec 2001, *In the Studio* (oil on canvas, 33 x 37 ins / 83 x 94 cm) SEK 19,000. Stockholm, 29 May 2002, *Hunting the Hunter* (watercolour, 9 x 7 ins / 24 x 19 cm) SEK 15,000. Stockholm, 8 March 2004, *Susanna in the Bath* (oil on panel, 24 x 29 ins / 61 x 74 cm) SEK 14,200.

HOGG, Franz
German, 19th century.
Portrait artist.
He was active in Koblenz.

HOGG, Herbert W.
British, 19th century.
Active in Derby.
Sculptor.
Herbert Hogg exhibited at the Royal Academy in London from 1883 to 1885.

HOGG, Jacob or James
British, 18th century.
Active during the second half of the 18th century.
Engraver.
Jacob Hogg engraved a number of plates after Angelica Kauffmann and Kirke for the Shakespeare (or Boydell) Gallery. He is probably the same person as the engraver James Hogg mentioned as an engraver of portraits by Le Blanc.

HOGG, Paul
Swiss, 20th century.
Born 11 September 1892, in Fribourg.
Painter.
Hogg exhibited his work in Paris at the Salon d'Automne, the Salon des Indépendents and the Salon des Tuileries.
Auction records:
Paris, 29 Oct 1926, *Still-life,* FRF 1,400.

HOGGER, Janos
Hungarian, 18th century.
Active in Szegedin c. 1754.
Painter.
Janos Hogger worked for a church in the town of Szegedin.

HOGHENS, Daniel François
French, 17th century.
Active in Roubaix in 1668.
Painter.
Daniel François Hoghens painted a *Virgin Mary with St Dominic* for the church of St-Martin.

HOGLE, Richard
British, 20th century.
Installation artist.
Lumino-Kinetic Art.

In 1968 Richard Hogle exhibited at the Institute of Contemporary Art, London. He showed a set of coloured ramps that lit up when people walked over them, with a double row of lights for men and a single row for women.

HOGLER
French, 19th century.
Sculptor.
The works that Hogler exhibited at the Salon, between 1836 and 1838, were mostly bas-reliefs in wood. He was in all probability a member of the Hoegler family.

HOGLEY, Stephen E.
British, 19th century.
Active in Holmfirth.
Painter, watercolourist. Landscapes with figures, landscapes, animals.
Stephen Hogley exhibited in London at the Suffolk Street Gallery in 1874 and 1881.
AUCTION RECORDS:
LONDON, 29 Jan 1910, *On the Esk,* GBP 11. LONDON, 9 March 2000, *Church Pool, Betws-y-Coed, Wales* (oil on canvas, 20 x 36 ins / 51 x 91 cm) GBP 3,800.

HOGNON, François
French, 18th century.
Active in Paris in 1783.
Painter (?), sculptor (?).

HOGOLL, Peter
German, 19th century.
Active in Breslau (now Wroclaw).
Portrait artist.

HOGOMMAT, André
French, 20th century.
Born 15 October 1925, in Nantes.
Sculptor. Figures, animals.
From 1948 to 1953, André Hogommat was a pupil of Marcel Gimond at the École Nationale Supérieure des Beaux-Arts in Paris. He is a figurative sculptor of the classical tradition and specialised in race horses. He does not however, define himself as an animal artist. For him, humans or horses are above all 'sculpted beings'. He treats them with a great sense of movement and balance, using the effects of the material in such a way that light plays upon the surface of the bronze. He taught for more than 20 years at the École des Beaux-Arts in Nîmes.

André Hogommat participated in collective exhibitions including: Salon d'Automne, of which he was a member; Salon de la Jeune Sculpture; Salon des Terres Latines; Salon Comparaisons; and Salon des Artistes Français (gold medal - 1992, 1st prize for Sculpture - 1994). Solo exhibitions include: Galerie J.C. Bellier, Paris (1967); Musée de Mont-de-Marsan (1975); Galerie Sculptures, Paris (1984), Association des Arts Plastiques, Champigny (1986); Galerie Univers du Bronze, Paris (1993). After a success in the Concours de Rome in 1952, he was awarded the Prix Suisse (1955), a grant from the French State (1960) and the Prix Despiau (1974).
MUSEUMS AND GALLERIES:
MONT-DE-MARSAN (Mus. Despiau-Wlérick) - PARIS (MAM-VP) - PARIS (MNAM-CCI).
AUCTION RECORDS:
PARIS, 16 Oct 1988, *The Hurdle Jump* (golden-brown-patinated bronze, h. 7 ins / 18 cm) FRF 4,500. PARIS, 22 May 1989, *Jumping the Obstacle* (greenish-brown-patinated bronze, 11 1/2 x 11 x 4 1/4 ins / 29 x 28 x 11 cm) FRF 8,000. PARIS, 5 Feb 1990, *The Leap* (green-patinated bronze, 11 1/2 x 9 3/4 x 3 1/2 ins / 29 x 25 x 9 cm) FRF 9,000. PARIS, 21 May 1990, *Polo Players* (1989, black-patinated bronze, 9 x 11 3/4 x 2 3/4 ins / 23 x 30 x 7 cm) FRF 30,000. NEUILLY, 3 Feb 1991, *Sulky* (1989, bronze, 7 3/4 x 4 3/4 x 14 1/4 ins / 20 x 12 x 36 cm) FRF 12,000. PARIS, 7 Oct 1991, *The Thinker* (bronze, 12 3/4 x 9 x 7 3/4 ins / 32.5 x 22 x 20 cm) FRF 12,000. PARIS, 3 Feb 1992, *The Rearing Horse* (1989, bronze, 11 x 11 x 4 3/4 ins / 27 x 28 x 12 cm) FRF 8,500. PARIS, 18 May 1992, *Two Polo Players* (1991, bronzes, h. 18 ins / 46 cm and 16 1/2 ins/42 cm) FRF 18,000.

HOGUER, Lucie, later Mme Thurot
French, 19th century.
Born 30 April 1786, in Versailles.
Painter (including porcelain). Portraits.
Lucie Hoguer was a pupil of Regnault.

HOGUET, Charles
French, 19th century.
Born 21 November 1821, in Berlin, to French parents; died 4 August 1870, in Berlin.
Painter. Genre scenes, landscapes, waterscapes, seascapes, still-lifes.
Hoguet was a pupil of the seascape painter Wilhelm Krause in Berlin. He continued his artistic training in Paris, under Bertin, Paul Delaroche, Hildebrand and Isabey. He visited England, then in 1848 moved to the German capital for good. In 1869 he was admitted as a member of the Berlin Academy. Hoguet won medals in Paris in 1848, and in Berlin in 1859. He was nicknamed the 'Raphael of Windmills'.
MUSEUMS AND GALLERIES:
BERLIN: *Dead Bustard and Other Birds; Plucked Turkey near a Cauldron* - CHARTRES: *Landscape in the Rain* - HAMBURG: *The Marketplace at Wernigerode* - KALININGRAD: *Sheep near a Shore* - LEIPZIG: *Seascape* - LONDON (Victoria and Albert Mus.): *Fountain near the Beach; Windmill* - WROCLAW: *Forest Landscape.*
AUCTION RECORDS:
PARIS, 18 May 1897, *Seascape,* FRF 412. PARIS, 29 May 1897, *Undulating Terrain,* FRF 285. PARIS, 9 May 1898, *Arab Scene,* FRF 650. NEW YORK, 10 April 1900, *Landscape,* USD 180. COLOGNE, 19-29 Oct 1904, *Kitchen Interior,* FRF 100; *Return from the Countryside,* FRF 1,112. NEW YORK, 15 Nov 1906, *Village on the Banks of the Rhine,* FRF 1,400. PARIS, 13 Nov 1918, *Windmill,* FRF 405. PARIS, 5 Feb 1923, *Path to the Farm,* FRF 300. LONDON, June 1923, *Beach Scene, with Washed-up Boats,* GBP 15. PARIS, 30 April 1926, *Landscape with a River Running through it,* FRF 1,040. PARIS, 1 March 1934, *Windmill,* FRF 410. PARIS, 29 Nov 1937, *Beach at Low Tide* (watercolour) FRF 200. PARIS, 20-21 July 1942, *Old Windmill,* FRF 10,000. VIENNA, 17 March 1970, *The Pont-Neuf and the Île de la Cité,* ATS 50,000. BERLIN, 7 July 1971, *The Pont-Neuf and the Île de la Cité,* DEM 9,000. COLOGNE, 15 Nov 1972, *Wooded Landscape,* DEM 3,800. PARIS, 10 Dec 1976, *Beach in Normandy* (1854, oil on canvas, 29 1/2 x 40 1/2 ins / 75 x 103 cm) FRF 8,500. ZURICH, 20 May 1977, *Windmill* (1861, oil on canvas, 17 x 25 1/2 ins / 43 x 65 cm) CHF 10,500. MUNICH, 29 Nov 1979, *Normandy Landscape with Windmill* (1850, oil on canvas, 22 3/4 x 17 ins / 58 x 43 cm) DEM 17,000. HAMBURG, 10 June 1982, *Fishermen on the Beach* (1844, oil on canvas, 14 1/2 x 23 ins / 37 x 58.2 cm) DEM 7,500. STOCKHOLM, 27 April 1983, *Woman Selling Poultry* (oil on canvas, 38 1/4 x 54 ins / 97 x 137 cm) SEK 35,000. COLOGNE, 20 May 1985, *Peasant Woman in a Rustic Interior* (1852, oil on canvas, 12 3/4 x 18 1/4 ins / 32.5 x 46.2 cm) DEM 9,000. LONDON, 27 Nov 1987, *Landscape with Stormy Sky* (1854, oil on canvas, 39 1/2 x 55 ins / 100.5 x 140 cm) GBP 11,000. LONDON, 22 Sept 1988, *Fishing Boats in a Storm* (1885, oil on canvas, 27 1/4 x 39 ins / 69.2 x 99 cm) GBP 1,540. PARIS, 11 Oct 1988, *Pumpkin* (oil on panel, 13 3/4 x 11 1/2 ins / 35 x 29 cm) FRF 18, 000. NEW YORK, 23 Feb 1989, *Well-stocked Marketplace* (oil on canvas, 18 1/4 x 15 1/4 ins / 46.3 x 39 cm) USD 6,050. NEW YORK, 17 Oct 1991, *People on top of the Cliffs at Étretat* (oil on canvas, 21 1/4 x 39 3/4 ins / 54 x 101 cm) USD 11,000. RHEIMS, 15 March 1992, *Still-life with Vegetables and Basin* (oil on panel, 7 3/4 x 13 3/4 ins / 20 x 35 cm) FRF 8,000. NEW YORK, 29 Oct 1992, *Preparing a Meal in a Barn* (1864, oil on canvas, 10 1/2 x 12 3/4 ins / 26.6 x 32.2 cm)

USD 2,640. LONDON, 18 June 1993, *The Marksburg near the Rhine* (1869, oil on canvas, 46½ x 56 ins / 118 x 142 cm) GBP 8,050. MUNICH, 6 Dec 1994, *Cavalier near a Stream in a Forest* (oil on canvas/panel, 38½ x 26½ ins / 98 x 67.5 cm) DEM 5,750. VIENNA, 29-30 Oct 1996, *The Good Samaritan* (1855, oil on canvas, sketch, 21¾ x 31 ins / 55.5 x 78.5 cm) ATS 27,600. MUNICH, 27 Feb 1999, *Old Windmill on Sea Shore* (oil on panel, 11 x 12 ins / 28 x 31 cm) DEM 6,500. MUNICH, 27 Feb 1999, *Rocky Coastal Landscape, possibly Britanny* (oil on canvas, 17 x 33 ins / 44 x 83 cm) DEM 6,500. COLOGNE, 25 Nov 2000, *Peasant Kitchen* (oil on canvas, 30 x 23 ins / 75 x 59 cm) DEM 10,000. COLOGNE, 25 Nov 2000, *In the Dining Room* (oil on canvas, 30 x 23 ins / 75 x 59 cm) DEM 10,000. STOCKHOLM, 22 May 2001, *Kitchen Interior with Cooks* (1863, oil on canvas, 29 x 26 ins / 74 x 65 cm) SEK 50,000. MUNICH, 27 June 2001, *Old Harbour Tower* (oil on canvas, oval, 17 x 33 ins / 44 x 84 cm) DEM 5,000. COLOGNE, 11 April 2002, *Shepherd with Flock in Extensive Landscape with Windmill* (1864, oil on canvas, 8 x 15 ins / 21 x 39 cm) EUR 3,000. LONDON, 8 Oct 2002, *Extensive Landscape with Windmill, Pond and Figure Fishing from Rock in the Foreground* (1846, oil on canvas, 19 x 29 ins / 49 x 73 cm) GBP 2,600. NEW YORK, 24 April 2003, *Straying from the Herd* (oil on canvas, 36 x 29 ins / 91 x 73 cm) USD 8,000. LONDON, 12 Nov 2003, *Château Kitchen* (1863, oil on canvas, 29 x 26 ins / 74 x 65 cm) GBP 5,000. COLOGNE, 1 April 2004, *Kitchen Still-life with Saucepan on Little Stove* (oil on panel, 6 x 5 ins / 15 x 13 cm) EUR 3,200.

HOGUET, Louis
German, 19th century.
Painter. Landscapes, seascapes.
Established in Potsdam, he made his Berlin debut in 1866.

HOHBACH, Friedrich
German, 19th century.
Born 23 January 1809, in Polsingen (Bavaria); died 6 July 1877, in Munich.
Painter, lithographer. Genre scenes.
He was a student at the academy in Munich, and later a member of staff there.
AUCTION RECORDS:
VIENNA, 14 Sept 1976, *The Love Letter* (1841, oil on canvas, 18½ x 16¾ ins / 47 x 42.5 cm) ATS 55,000.

HOHE, Friedrich
German, 19th century.
Born 1802, in Bayreuth; died 7 June 1870, in Munich.
Painter, reproductions lithographer. Landscapes, animals.
He was taught by his father before being admitted to the academy in Munich in 1820. In 1823, he took up lithography full-time. In 1826, he and Karl Rottmann went to Italy together. Hohe returned thence to Munich, and in 1828 made his debut at the Leuchtenberger gallery. He and A Brugger jointly produced lithographs of paintings by the principal contemporary artists, notably Bayer, Fearnley, Foltz, Haider, Heideck, Heinlein, Ruben, Stieler Wagenbauer and Weller.

HOHE, Nicolaus Christian
German, 19th century.
Born 1798, in Bayreuth; died 22 June 1868, in Bonn.
Painter, draughtsman. Portraits, landscapes.
The elder brother of Friedrich Hohe, he was a drawing instructor at the University of Bonn. He had a hand in the decorations of Cologne Cathedral and various monuments in the area.
AUCTION RECORDS:
COLOGNE, 27 May 1971, *Mountainous Landscape*, DEM 4,600.

HOHEI, real name: Satake Seii; artist names: Hohei and Kibunshujin
Japanese, 18th century.
Born 1750, in Nagano Prefecture; died 1807.
Painter. Landscapes.
Nanga School.
Hohei was one of the pupils of Ike.

HOHENBERG, Enrico
Italian, 19th century.
Active in Trieste.
Painter. Still-lifes.
MUSEUMS AND GALLERIES:
TRIESTE (Civico Mus. Revoltella): *Still-life*.

HOHENBERG, Martin. See **ALTOMONTE Martino**

HOHENBERG, Rosa
German, 19th century.
Active in Munich.
Painter. Genre scenes.
She exhibited in Hanover and Munich from 1880.

HOHENBERGER, Franz
Austrian, 19th century.
Born 14 August 1867, in Vienna; died 1941.
Painter.
He was a pupil of Gervex and Robert-Fleury in Paris. After spending some time in France and Germany, he settled in Vienna, painting landscapes, portraits and still lifes in a realistic style.
AUCTION RECORDS:
VIENNA, 14 June 1977, *Young Girl by a Stream* (pastel, 14¼ x 25¼ ins / 36.5 x 64 cm) DEM 2,000. VIENNA, 21 Sept 1979, *Market Scene* (1913, oil on canvas, 26¼ x 24 ins / 66.5 x 61 cm) ATS 60,000. VIENNA, 19 March 1986, *Flowers* (oil on panel, a pair, 11¾ x 15¾ ins / 30 x 40 cm) ATS 140,000.

HOHENFELDEN, Georgii Vasilevich
Russian, 19th century.
Born 29 March 1828, in St Petersburg; died 26 January 1908, in St Petersburg.
Engraver, lithographer.
Georgii Vasilevich Hohenfelden is known mainly for his book illustrations.

HOHENHAUSEN, Leopold von (Baron)
German, 18th century.
Active in Mannheim in 1758.
Engraver.

HOHENLEITER Y CASTRO, Francisco
Spanish, 20th century.
Born 24 February 1889, in Cádiz; died 1968, in Seville.
Painter, illustrator. Nudes, scenes with figures.
Francisco Hohenleiter y Castro studied at the school of fine arts in Cádiz, where he was taught by the genre painter Felipe Abarzuza y Rodriguez de Arias. In 1918, he settled permanently in Seville, participating in many exhibitions there, notably those of 1920, 1921 and 1922.Much of his work consisted of illustrations for literary works and magazines. He also produced posters, including the one for Holy Week in Seville in 1924. He decorated a number of public buildings, several in San Fernando, including the church of the Capuchin Fathers, and also the church of San Antonio in Cádiz.His paintings are often composed of a multitude of figures, either carrying on some activity in a vast landscape, as in *The Procession of the Virgin*, or in a state of great excitement, with a view of a city in the background, as in *Festival in Cordova*. There is often an obvious reference to Goya, particularly in his festival scenes and his nudes.

BIBLIOGRAPHY:
Arnáiz, José Manuel/López Jiménez, Javier/Merchán Díaz, Manuel (ed.), *Cien años de pintura en Espana y Portugal (1830-1930)*, Antiqvaria, Madrid, 1989.

HOHENLOHE-INGELFINGEN, Emilie
(Princess)
German, 19th century.
Active at the beginning of the 19th century.
Painter. Portraits.
She and her sister Sophia amused themselves painting miniature portraits of members of their family.

HOHENLOHE-INGELFINGEN, Sophie
German, 18th - 19th century.
Born 10 September 1762, in Magdeburg; died 29 April 1831, in Ingelfingen.
Painter, miniaturist.
Sophie Hohenlohe-Ingelfingen painted portraits of members of the Hohenlohe family.

HOHENLOHE-KIRCHBERG, Friedrich Carl Ludwig von (Prince)
German, 18th century.
Born 19 November 1751, in Kirchberg; died 12 September 1791, in Weikersheim.
Painter.
He had to give up his position in the Austrian army because of an accident, and so began to develop the artistic talents he had already displayed with Valentin Tischbein. He worked on the Oeser in Leipzig. He is noted for paintings and drawings, but also did ivory carvings.

HOHENLOHE-LANGENBURG, Viktor (Prince, Count Gleichen)
German, 19th century.
Born 11 November 1833, in Langenburg; died 31 December 1891, in London.
Active in England.
Sculptor, watercolourist.
Von Hohenlohe-Langenburg was an honorary member of the Royal Institute of Painters in Watercolours. He frequently exhibited in London at the Royal Academy and the Grosvenor Gallery between 1868 and 1890.

HOHENSTEIN, Adolf
German, 19th - 20th century.
Born 18 March 1854, in St Petersburg; died 1917.
Painter. Portraits, genre scenes, landscapes.
Hohenstein lived in Italy then Germany and painted genre scenes, landscapes and portraits.
AUCTION RECORDS:
AMSTERDAM, 21 April 1994, *Peasant Woman near a Hay Cart Pulled by Oxen* (oil on canvas, 11 3/4 x 17 3/4 ins / 30 x 45 cm) NLG 1,265.

HOHENZOLLERN-SIGMARINGEN, Antonia de (Infanta of Portugal). See **ANTONIA de HOHENZOLLERN-SIGMARINGEN**

HOHFELDER, Carl
German, 19th century.
Active in Munich.
Lithographer.
He is known mainly for occasional engravings.

HOHFELDER, Friedrich
German, 19th century.
Born 1821, in Munich; died 20 September 1905, in Munich.
Painter. Religious subjects.
He is noted for doing the *Stations* in the church of St Anna in Munich (1878).

HOHLENBERG, Johannes Edouard
Danish, 20th century.
Born 21 May 1881, in Copenhagen; died 10 May 1960, in Copenhagen.
Painter. Portraits.

HÖHLER, Georg Johan
German, 20th century.
Born 1 December 1890, in Langenberg.
Painter, engraver.
Höhler was mainly active in Darmstadt.

HOHLFELD, Bruno
Austrian, 19th - 20th century.
Born 21 March 1862, in Freiwaldau; died 18 January 1917, in Salzburg.
Painter.
Hohlfeld's works include flower paintings and portraits.

HOHLWEG, Georg
German, 19th century.
Active in Munich in 1826.
Landscape artist.

HOHLWEIN, Ludwig
German, 19th - 20th century.
Born 27 July 1874, in Wiesbaden; died 15 September 1949, in Berchtesgaden.
Painter, watercolourist, draughtsman, poster artist, interior designer. Figures, landscapes, animals.
Designs (ceramics).
Jugendstil.
Ludwig Hohlwein began drawing illustrations and making models of jewellery and bookbindings, parallel to his architectural studies, which he began in 1895 at the Technische Hochschule, Munich, He completed his training at the academy in Dresden and then travelled to London and Paris. He returned to Germany and settled in Munich.

From 1904, he regularly showed his watercolours and other paintings at the Glaspalast in Munich. Around 1900, he was responsible for the interior design of several houses and other buildings, including the Hotel Continental in Munich, and for steamships, but his most important work was poster design, in which he was self-taught. From 1906, he created many highly stylised posters on mainly animal themes (*Hellabrunn Zoo*) and sport. He designed the posters for the Brussels Exposition Universelle of 1910, the Grosse Berliner Kunstausstellung (Great Berlin Art Exhibition) of 1913, worked for well-known brands and created propaganda posters at the time of World War I. In the 1920s, he soon broke away from Jugendstil stylisation in favour of a more pictorial technique featuring contrasts, shapes and colours. Among his many posters and designs (especially book jackets), of which more than 3,000 have been counted, the best are: *Sun on Demand*, *Winter in Bavaria*, and *Munich Zoo*.
BIBLIOGRAPHY:
Ludwig Hohlwein: Plakate der Jahre 1906-1940 aus der Graphischen Sammlung Staatsgalerie Stuttgart, exhibition catalogue, Staatsgalerie, Stuttgart, 1985. Duvigneau, Volker/Götz, Norbert, *Ludwig Hohlwein, 1874-1949: Kunstgewerbe und Reklamekunst*, Klinkhardt & Biermann, Munich, 1996.
MUSEUMS AND GALLERIES:
BERLIN (Deutsches Historisches Mus.): *Pelikan Künstler-Farben* (*Pelikan Artists' Colours*) (1913) - NEW YORK (MoMA): *Zooligischer Garten München* (*Munich Zoo*) (1912, lithograph) - SARREGUEMINES (Musée des faïences): several items after models by the artist - STUTTGART (Staatsgal.): *Riquet-Tee* (*Riquet Tea*) (c. 1921, important collection).
AUCTION RECORDS:
NEW YORK, 13 March 1982, *Zoological Gardens, Munich* (1912, coloured lithograph, 47 1/4 x 33 1/4 ins / 120 x 84.7 cm)

USD 2,200. HAMBURG, 9 June 1986, *Vase of Flowers* (1909, gouache/grey-brown card, 17 1/2 x 19 1/4 ins / 44.5 x 49 cm) DEM 3,400. MUNICH, 1-2 Dec 1992, *Avenue of Birches in the Marshes* (watercolour, 10 3/4 x 15 ins / 27.5 x 38 cm) DEM 2,300. MUNICH, 11 Nov 1999, *Munich Zoo* (gouache and bodycolour on board, 6 x 4 ins / 14 x 11 cm) DEM 26,000. MUNICH, 18 Nov 2000, *Flamingo* (c. 1912, colour lithograph, 49 x 36 ins / 124 x 91 cm) DEM 8,000. KEMPTEN, 12 Jan 2001, *Wooded Landscape with Stag* (charcoal and watercolour, 8 x 11 ins / 20 x 29 cm) DEM 3,500. KEMPTEN, 4 April 2002, *Deer in a Clearing* (tempera on canvas, 17 x 21 ins / 43 x 54 cm) EUR 1,900. MUNICH, 26 March 2003, *Wild Ducks* (1908, gouache, 17 x 17 ins / 43 x 42 cm) EUR 1,500. NEW YORK, 15 May 2004, *Woman and Two Men Having Drinks* (1917, gouache and watercolour, 12 x 12 ins / 30 x 30 cm) USD 2,100. KEMPTEN, 4 Nov 2004, *Deer in Winter Mountains* (1921, pencil and watercolour, 14 x 16 ins / 35 x 40 cm) EUR 1,700.

HOHMANN, B. B.

German, 19th century.
Active in Leipzig c. 1854.
Painter.

He is known for a portrait.

HOHMANN, Heinz

German, 20th century.
Born 28 January 1879, in Rüsselheim.
Painter, illustrator.

Hohmann studied at the Académie Julian in Paris.

HÖHME, Gerhard

German, 20th century.
Born 5 February 1920, in Greppin (Saxony-Anhalt); died 1989.
Painter (mixed media), watercolourist.
Gruppe 53.

Höhme did not begin painting until after 1945 and studied art from 1947 until 1952. He taught at the school of fine arts in Düsseldorf from 1960. Until 1955 he achieved success with a style developed from *Art Informel* (Tachism) and abstract landscape painting, and which already showed significant influences of different materials. His research into materials then became his main focus as he developed a form of collage incorporating a wide range of materials, particularly plastics and plastic textiles. In this second phase of his work he experimented with non-standard formats.

In 1954 Höhme was awarded the Düsseldorf art prize and in 1957 he won a prize at the Annual Exhibition of Graphic Arts in New York. He also won the Prix de Rome in 1960 and one of the Marzotto prizes in 1962. He took part in very many group exhibitions, including the Premio Lissone on several occasions and Documenta II in Kassel in 1959. He showed his work in private exhibitions in Berlin, Bern, Boston, Düsseldorf, Hanover and Munich. The Kunstmuseum in Bonn staged a retrospective of his work in 1998.

BIBLIOGRAPHY:

La Motte, Manfred de, *Gerhard Hoehme, Bilder - Objekte - Aquarelle*, exhibition catalogue, Galerie Neher, Essen, 1994.
Gerhard Hoehme. Die Energie der Farbe. Werke 1956 bis 1989, exhibition catalogue, Kunstmuseum, Bonn, 1998.

AUCTION RECORDS:

HAMBURG, 9 June 1972, *View from the Window*, DEM 3,900. DÜSSELDORF, 12 June 1973, *The Fourth Sex* (1952) DEM 9,000. COLOGNE, 3 Dec 1977, *Composition* (1961, watercolour, Indian ink and collage, 23 1/2 x 16 3/4 ins / 60 x 42.5 cm) DEM 2,600. MUNICH, 28 May 1979, *Herzog der Stille* (1956, oil on canvas, 27 1/2 x 22 ins / 70 x 55 cm) DEM 6,800. COLOGNE, 24 June 1983, *Vogelzart* (1956, oil on canvas, 39 1/4 x 31 1/2 ins / 100 x 80 cm) DEM 7,000. MUNICH, 2 June 1986, *Bei Nazca und Palpa* (1958, watercolour/chalk outlines, 23 1/2 x 18 3/4 ins / 60 x 47.5 cm) DEM 4,400. HAMBURG, 12 June 1987, *Schritt, Zeichen, Raum* (1961, watercolour and Indian ink, 23 3/4 x 17 ins / 60.2 x 43.1 cm) DEM 7,200. ROME, 7 April 1988, *Composition* (1963, mixed media, 27 1/2 x 19 3/4 ins / 70 x 50 cm) ITL 6,000,000. ROME, 15 Nov 1988, *Minenbild* (1965, mixed media, 47 1/4 x 25 1/4 ins / 120 x 64 cm) ITL 10,500,000. LONDON, 17 Oct 1991, *Red Signs* (1952, oil on canvas, 29 x 39 3/4 ins / 73.5 x 101 cm) GBP 19,800. LONDON, 5 Dec 1991, *Letter from Berlin* (1966, pencil and fabric collage/canvas, diptych, 78 3/4 x 141 3/4 ins / 200 x 360 cm) GBP 154,000. LONDON, 2 July 1992, *Tribute to Feininger* (1961, oil and ink/canvas, 78 3/4 x 39 1/4 ins / 200 x 100 cm) GBP 52,800. AMSTERDAM, 9 Dec 1992, *Untitled* (1962, ink and paper collage, 27 1/4 x 19 3/4 ins / 69.5 x 50 cm) NLG 11,500. AMSTERDAM, 9 Dec 1993, *Composition No. 5* (1954, oil on canvas, 31 1/4 x 14 3/4 ins / 79.5 x 37.5 cm) NLG 39,100. LONDON, 9 Oct 1997, *Wild Blue Image* (1956-1957, oil on canvas, 67 x 47 1/2 ins / 170.2 x 120.5 cm) GBP 45,500. LONDON, 25 March 1999, *De Profundis* (1961, oil and ink wash on paper with collage, 39 x 25 ins / 99 x 64 cm) GBP 6,500. ZURICH, 1 June 1999, *Versponnenes Blatt* (1962, mixed media, 39 x 25 ins / 98 x 63 cm) CHF 12,000. COLOGNE, 10 Nov 2000, *Untitled* (1957, collage and watercolour on board, 20 x 13 ins / 52 x 34 cm) DEM 6,500. MUNICH, 2 Dec 2000, *Impressions in Silvery Grey* (1954, oil on canvas, 39 x 35 ins / 100 x 90 cm) DEM 76,000. MUNICH, 19 May 2001, *Gouache Obscure* (1960, mixed media and gouache heightened with white Indian ink on board, 39 x 26 ins / 100 x 65 cm) DEM 27,000. LONDON, 10 Oct 2001, *Berlin Letter* (1966, acrylic and graphite on canvas, two parts, 79 x 142 ins / 200 x 360 cm) GBP 90,000. COLOGNE, 5 June 2002, *Untitled* (1959, Indian ink, pen and brush on canvas on masonite, 40 x 20 ins / 101 x 51 cm) EUR 3,000. COLOGNE, 3 Dec 2002, *Mondrian's Garden - Homage* (1959, oil on canvas with collage, 43 x 39 ins / 109 x 100 cm) EUR 32,000. MUNICH, 5 Dec 2003, *Paravent B* (acrylic on canvas, 79 x 197 ins / 200 x 500 cm) EUR 65,000. MUNICH, 5 Dec 2003, *Paravent A* (acrylic on canvas, 79 x 197 ins / 200 x 500 cm) EUR 65,000. MUNICH, 14 May 2004, *Untitled* (watercolour, pencil, white bodycolour and chalk, double-sided, 16 x 20 ins / 40 x 50 cm) EUR 2,500. COLOGNE, 4 June 2004, *Portinguez* (1958, oil, gouache and resin on paper collage, 38 x 27 ins / 96 x 68 cm) EUR 16,500.

HÖHN, Wolfang

German, 20th century.
Born 1930.
Painter.

Höhn painted in an abstract style that appears to have derived from the Cobra Group.

HOHNBAUM, Franz

German, 19th century.
Born 1825, in Hildburghausen; died 19 January 1867, in Hildburghausen.
Painter. Genre scenes.

A pupil of F. Preller in Weimar, he exhibited in Munich and Cologne from 1854.

HOHNE, K. F.

German, 19th century.
Painter. Genre scenes.

He lived in Weimar. He made his debut in Berlin in 1870.

HOHNECK, Adolf

German, 19th century.
Born 3 February 1812, in Dresden; died 2 February 1879, in Oberlössnitz (Harz).
Painter, lithographer. Portraits, genre scenes, landscapes.

He studied at the academy in Dresden, then under T. Hildebrand in Düsseldorf. He exhibited mainly in Dresden.

AUCTION RECORDS:

COLOGNE, 30 March 1979, *Lake Landscape* (oil on canvas, 10 3/4 x 15 1/2 ins / 27.5 x 39.5 cm) DEM 2,600. LONDON, 17 April 1996, *Portrait of Charles Dickens Wearing a Grey Coat,*

Seated (1840, oil on canvas, 11 x 8 1/4 ins / 28 x 21 cm) GBP 4,830. STUTTGART, 30 June 2000, *Hilly Landscape with Ruined Castle* (1866, oil on board, 11 x 15 ins / 28 x 39 cm) DEM 3,500. STUTTGART, 25 Sept 2003, *Extensive Winter Landscape with Frozen Lake* (oil on canvas, 21 x 28 ins / 53 x 72 cm) EUR 3,200.

HOHR, Franz Xaver Ludwig
French, 18th - 19th century.
Born 1766, in Colmar; died 1848, in Colmar.
Miniaturist. Portraits.

MUSEUMS AND GALLERIES:
COLMAR: portraits.

HOIGAIRDEN, Joost van
Flemish, 16th century.
Born probably, in 's Hertogenbosch.
Active in Antwerp.
Painter.
Flemish School.

HOIJTEMA, Antoinette Agathe van
Dutch, 20th century.
Born 1875, in Delft; died 1967 in The Hague.
Painter. Landscapes with figures.

Hoijtema painted in a quasi-Pointillist style in which the accent is less on colour and more on formal subdivision.

HOIN, Claude Jean Baptiste
French, 18th - 19th century.
Born 25 June 1750, in Dijon; died 16 June 1817, in Dijon.
Miniaturist, watercolourist, pastellist, painter (gouache), draughtsman, engraver. Portraits, genre scenes.

Claude Jean Baptiste Hoin studied under Greuze and Desvosges. He took part in the Salon de la Correspondance in 1782 with a gouache (now in the Dijon museum) and in 1783 with two pastels. He exhibited at the Louvre in 1801 and 1802. He was a member of the Toulouse and Dijon Académies and the curator of the Dijon museum.

This museum holds the interesting gouache showing a landscape including both his father's and his mother's graves, and a *Portrait of François Jacques Hoin, Professor of Surgery* thought to be Hoin's father. Claude Hoin was first and foremost a miniaturist and a pastel and gouache painter and showed unquestionable skill in these techniques. He engraved after H. Fragonard, Boichot, Madame Labille-Guillard (whose portrait he painted in 1785), Anton van Dyck and Jean-Baptiste Greuze. He bequeathed several of his paintings to his native city. His works are rated by connoisseurs.

MUSEUMS AND GALLERIES:
BORDEAUX (Mus. des Arts décoratifs): *Madame Elisabeth and Louis XVII* (after 1794, miniature) - DIJON: *Three Heads* (studies); *Phlox*; *Madame Hoin*; *Self-portrait* (pastel); *Madame Berlier*; three landscapes; *Portrait of Jacques Hoin* - TOULOUSE: *Head of a Girl*; *Head of an Old Man*.

AUCTION RECORDS:
PARIS, 15-17 Feb 1897, *Madame Dugazon Playing the Part of Nina* (gouache) FRF 19,000. PARIS, 1899, *Madame Dugazon Playing the Part of Nina or The Love-sick Woman* (gouache) FRF 18,000; *Girl Gazing at her Reflection in the Water* (watercolour) FRF 2,250; *Mid-length Portrait of a Young Woman* (miniature/box) FRF 1,100. PARIS, 17 Dec 1900, *Portrait of a Musician and his Wife* (drawing) FRF 600. PARIS, 22 Feb 1901, *Allegory on the Marriage of the Dauphin and Marie-Antoinette* (gouache) FRF 725. PARIS, 13-15 March 1905, *The Girl with the Roses* (gouache) FRF 1,400; *The Gathering in the Park* (gouache) FRF 6,100. PARIS, 6 and 7 May 1920, *A Bacchante*, FRF 8,000. PARIS, 21 and 22 June 1920, *Sharing a Secret* (sepia) FRF 19,000. PARIS, 6-8 Dec 1920, *The Tryst* (watercolour) FRF 13,200. PARIS, 22 June 1921, *Portrait of a Young Woman*; *Young Woman Holding a Basket of Flowers and Grapes* (two pastels) FRF 4,850. PARIS, 22 Nov 1923, *Self-portrait*, FRF 8,900; *The Girl with the Roses*, FRF 10,650. PARIS, 6 and 7 March 1925, *The Garter* (gouache) FRF 17,600. PARIS, 21 and 22 March 1927, *Landscapes Peopled with Small Figures* (two drawings) FRF 19,000. PARIS, 22-24 June 1927, *Madame Dugazon Playing the Part of Nina, or The Love-Sick Woman* (gouache) FRF 101,000. PARIS, 7 and 8 June 1928, *Portrait of a Girl with a Blue Ribbon in her Hair* (drawing in coloured chalks) FRF 24,500; *Family Scene* (drawing à trois crayons) FRF 7,200. PARIS, 10 and 11 Dec 1928, *Portrait of Rembrandt as a Young Man* (pastel) FRF 13,000. PARIS, 22 April 1929, *Portrait of Jean-Jacques-Louis Hoin* (pastel) FRF 18,000. PARIS, 25 June 1931, *Self-portrait* (pencil) FRF 1,000. PARIS, 12 and 13 June 1933, *The Shepherds' Rest*, FRF 21,300. PARIS, 7 Dec 1934, *Sharing Secrets* (pencil, sepia wash and watercolour with dabs of gouache) FRF 12,000. PARIS, 17 Dec 1935, *Madame Dugazon Playing the Part of Nina* (gouache) FRF 65,000. PARIS, 12 May 1937, *Park in Autumn* (drawing) FRF 9,600. PARIS, 15 June 1938, *The Love Letter*, FRF 14,500. PARIS, 13 and 14 Feb 1941, *Portrait of a Young Woman* (drawing à trois crayons and stump, attributed) FRF 28,500. PARIS, 20 Nov 1941, *Young Woman in a Park* (watercolour and gouache) FRF 25,100. PARIS, 30 Nov 1942, *La Dugazon Chased by Cupids* (watercolour) FRF 34,000. PARIS, 12 Feb 1943, *Fisherman at the Foot of a Torrent* (1804, gouache) FRF 13,000. PARIS, 22 March 1945, *Woman Sitting* (miniature) FRF 15,000. LONDON, 26 June 1963, *Waiting in the Park*, GBP 1,200. VERSAILLES, 13 May 1970, *Madame Dugazon Playing the Part of Nina* (watercolour) FRF 8,500. LYONS, 28 March 1972, *Young Woman Sitting and Composing Music* (gouache) Gns 550. PARIS, 19 March 1976, *Mademoiselle Dugazon* (watercolour and gouache, 6 3/4 x 5 ins / 17 x 13 cm) FRF 3,200. PARIS, 23 Feb 1978, *The Worship of Virtue* (1841, watercolour, 7 1/4 x 9 ins / 18.5 x 23 cm) DEM 2,000. NEW YORK, 30 April 1982, *Young Woman Arranging Flowers* (graphite, gouache and wash, 7 x 5 ins / 17.7 x 13 cm) USD 3,000. VERSAILLES, 27 Nov 1983, *Portrait of a Young Woman Holding a Basket of Flowers* (oil on canvas, 35 1/2 x 28 ins / 90 x 71 cm) FRF 66,000. ENGHIEN-LES-BAINS, 23 Dec 1984, *Portrait of M. Nizard* (pastel, 21 1/2 x 17 1/2 ins / 54.5 x 44.5 cm) FRF 31,500. PARIS, 20 Nov 1985, *Portrait of M. Brizard, Actor at the Comédie-Française* (1783, pastel, 21 1/2 x 17 1/2 ins / 54.5 x 44.5 cm) FRF 90,000. LONDON, 30 June 1986, *Study of a Man Sitting* (recto; *Study of a Woman* (black chalk heightened with white and stump, verso, 20 3/4 x 13 ins / 52.6 x 33 cm) GBP 12,500. PARIS, 8 June 1988, *Portrait of a Young Woman* (pastel, 15 1/4 x 12 1/4 ins / 39 x 31 cm) FRF 12,000. NEW YORK, 12 Jan 1989, *Lady Sitting on a Bench in a Park with her Pet Spaniel in her Lap* (oil on panel, 14 1/4 x 12 1/2 ins / 36 x 32 cm) USD 14,300. PARIS, 9 June 1993, *Bust Portrait of a Woman* (black chalk heightened with white/paper, 20 3/4 x 17 1/4 ins / 53 x 44 cm) FRF 20,000. PARIS, 17 June 1994, *Portrait of a Man* (pastel, 13 3/4 x 9 ins / 35 x 22 cm) FRF 33,000. NEW YORK, 10 Jan 1995, *An Artist Worshipping the Statue of Virtue* (1783, watercolour and black chalk heightened with white, 16 x 10 3/4 ins / 40.7 x 27.5 cm) USD 9,200. PARIS, 27 March 1995, *Louis XVI, Protector of the Arts* (lead pencil and colour, diam. 8 1/4 ins / 21 cm) FRF 8,500. PARIS, 11 April 1995, *Bust of a Young Man in Three-quarter Profile to the Right* (1779, oil on canvas, 25 1/2 x 21 1/4 ins / 65 x 54 cm) FRF 45,000. PARIS, 29 March 1996, *The Young Archeologist's Eagerness* (Indian ink, black chalk and watercolour, 8 1/4 x 6 1/2 ins / 20.9 x 16.4 cm) FRF 21,000. PARIS, 20 Dec 1996, *Head of a Child* (lead pencil heightened with white chalk/gouache/paper, 9 1/2 x 7 3/4 ins / 24 x 20 cm) FRF 6,500. NEW YORK, 28 Jan 1998, *Study of a Girl with her Head Resting on her Hand* (coloured chalks, 12 1/2 x 15 1/4 ins / 32 x 39 cm) USD 4,255. PARIS, 20 Oct 1999, *Portrait of Pastel Artist* (oil on canvas, oval, 9 x 8 ins / 24 x 20 cm) FRF 23,000. LONDON, 22 May 2001, *Young Gentle-*

man in a Brown Coat and Frilled Cravat (miniature) GBP 3,200. PARIS, 27 June 2001, *Portrait of Young Woman with White Ribbon* (pastel, 23 x 19 ins / 59 x 48 cm) FRF 75,000. PARIS, 21 March 2002, *Group of Women near Waterfall* (pen/ink/watercolour heightened with white, 11 x 15 ins / 28 x 37 cm) EUR 9,000. PARIS, 27 Nov 2002, *Portrait of Young Man* (colour chalk, 22 x 17 ins / 55 x 44 cm) EUR 6,000.

HOITSU, real name: Sakai Tadamoto, childhood name: Kishin, artist names: Keikyo Dojin, Kuzento, Nison'an, Niwabyoshi, Osan, Toryu, Ukaan
Japanese, 18th - 19th century.
Born 1 August 1761, in Edo (now Tokyo); died 9 January 1828, in Edo (now Tokyo).
Painter. Screens.

The second son of Sakai, the lord of Himeji Castle, Hoitsu was born to a life far removed from worldly care. From the earliest age, he devoted himself to the pleasures of art, studying *haiku* (the Japanese 17-syllable verse form), calligraphy and painting. He tried his hand at all styles, from the Kano School to *ukiyo-e* and Toyoharu (1735-1814), until he discovered Korin (1658-1716), whom he then devoted himself to restoring to the public eye. In the process, he became one of the great painters of the Korin School. In 1793, he left for Kyoto, to enter the priesthood. In 1815, he celebrated Korin's centenary himself, commemorating him in his *Korin hyakuzu* (*100 Masterpieces by Korin*), *Ogata-ryu ryaku impu* (*Collection of Seals of the Ogata School*), and *Kenzan gafu* (*Works of Kenzan*). At the same time, in order to restore Korin to honour, he painted a number of works, especially bird-and-flower paintings. Thus on the reverse of the screens *Wind and Thunder Gods*, which Korin had painted after Sotatsu, Hoitsu added two compositions in the same spiritual vein as the main subject, *Summer Rain* and *Autumn Grasses*. Against a background of silver (as opposed to the gold background on the front), he expresses all the lyricism of nature with great delicacy. A highly sensual colourist, he is known for his brilliant, light watercolours.

BIBLIOGRAPHY:
Akiyama, Terukazu, *La Peinture japonaise*, Skira, Geneva, 1961. Guth, Christine, *Japanese Art of the Edo Period*, Calmann and King, London, 1996.

MUSEUMS AND GALLERIES:
ST LOUIS (AM): *Fans and Stream* (1820-1828, ink, colour, gold and silver/silk, pair of screens) - TOKYO (Commission For the Protection of Cultural Property): *Wind and Thunder Gods* (screens painted by Korin after Sotatsu) - WASHINGTON DC (Freer Gal. of Art): *36 Master Poets* (colours/silk).

AUCTION RECORDS:
NEW YORK, 16 April 1988, *Imperial Messenger Approaching Figures in a Bower* (ink and colour/silk, 12$1/2$ x 17$1/4$ ins / 31.5 x 44 cm) USD 2,420. NEW YORK, 17 Oct 1989, *Jurojin Riding the Deer* (ink and colour/silk, hanging scroll, 38$1/2$ x 15 ins / 97.7 x 37.2 cm) USD 4,180. NEW YORK, 29 March 1990, *Sping, Mount Fuji, Bamboo and Hummingbird* (ink and diluted colour/silk, handscroll, 12 x 205$3/4$ ins / 30.3 x 522.5 cm) USD 44,000. NEW YORK, 29 March 1990, *Autumn Vegetation* (ink and colour/silk, hanging scroll, 43 x 16$1/4$ ins / 109.3 x 41 cm) USD 12,100. NEW YORK, 16 Oct 1990, *Autumn Plants in Blossom* (ink and colour/silk, hanging scroll, 42$1/4$ x 16 ins / 107.2 x 40.7 cm) USD 4,950. NEW YORK, 23 Oct 1991, *Maple Branch* (ink and colour/gold-leaf/paper, fan, 7$1/2$ x 19 ins / 19.1 x 48.2 cm) USD 16,500.

HOJEDA, Cristóbal de
Spanish, 16th century.
Active in Seville in 1553.
Sculptor.

Cristóbal de Hojeda worked for the churches of Seville and then requested permission to move with some assistants to work in Peru. He obtained the necessary licences to emigrate on 14 March 1554.

HOJEDA, Sebastián de
Spanish, 16th century.
Active in Seville in 1549.
Painter.

Between 1549 and 1553, Sebastián de HojedaHH painted very large works in a number of palaces.

HOKANE
Japanese, 20th century.
Painter. Figures, landscapes, still-lifes.

Hokane exhibited with honour at the Salon d'Automne in Paris until 1943. He paints in the tradition of Japanese contemporary masters.

HOKE, Giselbert
German, 20th century.
Born 1927, in Warnsdorf.
Painter.

Giselbert Hoke studied in Vienna. His work is inspired by the imagination, evoking past civilisations such as those of the Aztecs and Indians.

HOKKAI, artist name: Shunshisai; first name: Tohonan Hokusei
Japanese, 19th century.
Active c. 1832.
Print artist.

Hokkai's name is given on a print from August 1832 as Shunshisai Hokkai.

HOKKAKU. See **HOKUGAN**

HOKKEI, artist name: Ran'yosai
Japanese, 19th century.
Active c. 1820.
Painter.

HOKKEI, original names: Kintaro Shun'yo and Shun'yosai; artist name: Shun'yosai; seal: Santokaku
Japanese, 19th century.
Painter.

Hokkei was active in about 1818-1820. His work is very similar to that of Shunshi, who was active in Osaka in about 1826-1828.

HOKKEI, Toyota, or Uoya ('fishmonger') Hokkei, real name: Iwakubo Tatsuyuki; childhood name: Hatsugoro or Shogoro, later Kin'emon; artist names: Kosai, Kiko (Aoigaoka), Kien, Kyosai, Tyota, Hokkei
Japanese, 19th century.
Born 1780; died 1850.
Active c. 1800-1850.
Painter.

A pupil of Kano Yosen and then Hokusai (1760-1849), Hokkei was a fishmonger before becoming an artist. He drew many *surimono* (limited-edition greeting cards, announcements) and illustrated collections of *kyoka* (comic poems), notably the *Hokuri Juni Toki (Twelve Hours in Yoshiwara, a Northern Village)*.

BIBLIOGRAPHY:
Fahr-Becker, Gabriele (ed.), *Japanese Prints*, Taschen, Cologne, 1999.

MUSEUMS AND GALLERIES:
MELBOURNE: seven prints - PARIS (Musée Guimet): prints; eight prints in an album, various types of shell on mica and lightly embossed background.

AUCTION RECORDS:
LONDON, 16 May 1988, *Chinese General Kori Striking the Rock with his Sword to bring forth Water* (print) GBP 1,045. NEW YORK, 21 March 1989, *Figure hanging on a Rock in a Wild Torrent (Water, from the series The Five Elements)* (Kakubuan print, 8$1/2$ x 7$1/4$ ins / 21.3 x 18.1 cm) USD 3,300.

HOKKO. See **HOKUCHO**

HOKKO
Japanese, 19th century.
Active c. 1810-1830.
Painter.
Hokko was a pupil of Hokusai (1760-1849).

HOKKO, childhood name: Katsushika; artist name: Gakyojin
Japanese, 19th century.
Active c. 1820.
Painter.

HOKUBA, real name: Avisaka, original name: Hoshino, childhood names: Gorohachi, Mitsutaka; artist names: Teisai, Shunshunsai, Shunshuntei, Shuen, Hokuba
Japanese, 18th - 19th century.
Born 1771; died 27 September 1844.
Active in Edo (now Tokyo).
Painter.
A pupil of Hokusai (1760-1849), Hokuba designed some beautifil *surimono* (limited-edition prints used as greeting cards, announcements, etc) and illustrated collections of *kyoka* (comic poems). He also painted *bijin-ga* (pictures of beautiful women). Apparently, he was also an assistant to the painter Buncho (1763-1840).

HOKUBOKU
Japanese.
Painter.

HOKUCHO, artist names: Shungyosai, Shunchosai
Japanese, 19th century.
Active c. 1850.
Painter.
Hokucho may be the same artist as the Hokucho who was active in about 1822-1830.

HOKUCHO, real name: Inove, artist names: Shunshosai, Hokucho, Shunsho
Japanese, 19th century.
Active c. 1822-1830.
Painter.
Hokucho is supposed to have studied under Shunko and Shunkosai. He may be the same artist as the Hokucho who was active around 1850.

HOKUEI, first name: Shunko, artist names: Shunkosai (1829-1833), Shunbaisai (1833-1837), Sekkaro (1836), Sekka and Shun'yosai; (seals): Fumoto no yuki, Fumoto no ume, Koshiji no ume
Japanese, 19th century.
Died 1837.
Active c. 1824?-1837.
Painter.
Hokuei is said to have been a pupil of Shunkosai.

HOKUGA, artist names: Nan'yosai, Nan'yo
Japanese, 19th century.
Active 1812-1826.
Painter.

HOKUGAN, known erroneously as Hokkaku; original names: Toshikuni (1816?-1832) and Toyokawa; artist names: Rodo, Juyodo, Shun'yodo (1826), Shunkisai (1832); seal: Magari
Japanese, 19th century.
Active c. 1816?-1832.
Painter.
Hokugan is thought to have been a pupil of Ashikuni and Yoshikuni. His change of name Toshikuni to Hokugan appears on a print dated September 1832.

HOKUJU, first name: Shunju, artist names: Shunshosai, Shun'eisai (1836), Goryuken
Japanese, 19th century.
Active c. 1828?-1836.
Painter.
Hokuju was a pupil of Hokuei.
AUCTION RECORDS:
NEW YORK, 20 April 1989, *Enoshima* (Oban Yoko-e print, 9 3/4 x 15 ins / 25 x 37.2 cm) USD 2,200. NEW YORK, 15 June 1990, *Promenade at Edo* (Oban Yoko-e print, 10 x 15 1/4 ins / 25.2 x 38.8 cm) USD 1,100.

HOKUJU, Shotei, real name: Kazumasa; artist names: Shosai, Shotei, Hokuju
Japanese, 18th - 19th century.
Born 1763; died after 1824.
Active in Edo (now Tokyo).
Painter.
A disciple of Hokusai (1760-1849), Hokuju learned the elements of western painting from his master and developed a unique landscape style, based on interlocking triangles, a sort of cubism before the fact. His work is remarkable for its freshness, its carefully sought atmosphere and its treatment of light. Though he was not so fine a draughtsman as his master, Hokuju often made his colours even more transparent.
BIBLIOGRAPHY:
Fahr-Becker, Gabriele (ed.), *Japanese Prints*, Taschen, Cologne, 1999.

HOKUJUN. See **HOKUCHO**

HOKUMEI, real name: Katsushika Hokumei, artist names: Gakyojin, Kyukyushin
Japanese, 19th century.
Active c. 1830.
Painter.
Hokumei Gakyushin was a pupil of Shunkosai.

HOKUMEI, childhood names: Ikuta and Tezuka; artist name: Kisseido Togetsu
Japanese, 19th century.
Active c. 1830.
Painter.
Hokumei Gakyushin was a pupil of Shunkosai.

HOKUMYO, artist names: Shunpusai (1830-1833), Sekkotei (1837)
Japanese, 19th century.
Active c. 1830-1837.
Painter.
Hokumyo may be a late name of Shunyosai Shunshi, and it is even possible this artist was a woman. Hokumyo is mentioned as a portraitist.

HOKURAI
Japanese, 19th century.
Active c. 1810-1820.
Painter.

HOKUROKU, artist name: Shun'yosai
Japanese.
Painter.

HOKUSAI, real name: Katsushika Tamekazu, original name: Nakajima, childhood names: Tokitaro, Tetsuzo; artist names: Katsukawa Shunro, Soshunro, Gumbatei, Gyobutsu, Tawara-ya Sori, Kako, Tatsumasa, Hokusai, Shinsai, Kintaisha, Tamekazu, Raito, Raishin, Gakyojin, Manji-o, Manjirojin
Japanese, 18th - 19th century.
Born September 1760, in Honjo Wari-Gesui, now Tokyo; died 1849.

Painter, print artist, illustrator, draughtsman. Figures, portraits, landscapes, seascapes.

While Hiroshige (1797-1858) is unanimously admired both in Japan and in the West, no Japanese artist has ever been so admired in the West and been regarded as so controversial in Japan as Hokusai. 'The old man mad with painting', to whom Edmond de Goncourt would pay so touching a tribute, left behind a corpus so monumental and so varied that wittingly or unwittingly no artist of his time would remain untouched by it, and his originality was so marked as to be intimidating, even offputting. Until he arrived, the Japanese print had concentrated on the female figure and portraits of actors, and had reached its peak at the end of the 18th century. With Hokusai, it found new life in a new field: landscape. 'I was born at the age of 50,' he would say, hinting at the long years when, rather like a pilgrim, he nurtured and refined his art until, as the 18th century drew to a close, it was ready to burst forth.

Hokusai's life is a moving story, for it is nothing less than a quest for perfection. A total individualist, he painted and drew admirably, but was never satisfied, and his curiosity was boundless. In a word, he was the archetypal artist who lives for his art alone and who will not let anything get in the way of reaching his goal. Born on the eastern, still almost rustic, outskirts of Edo, he never lost the old Katsushika County peasant spirit. At the age of three, he was adopted by Nakajima Ise, a mirror polisher in the service of the Tokugawa Shogunate. In about 1769, he assumed the name Tetsuzo and apparently left the Nakajima household at the same time. Yet he would retain the name until his death. After trying his hand at various trades, in 1778 he entered the studio of Katsukawa Shunsho (1726-1792), one of the leading masters of the time, and worked there for some 15 years, making actor portraits and book illustrations under the name Shunro. It is not impossible that he also worked for Kano Yusen at the same time. On Shunsho's death in 1792, the Katsukawa School went into a slow decline, and Hokusai left after a falling out with his colleague Shunko. Thereafter, he worked on his own, studying with startling intensity the traditional styles and techniques of the Kano and Tosa Schools (or at least its derivative, the Sumiyoshi School), and the Rimpa (Sotatsu-Korin) School, as well as Chinese aesthetics and Dutch engravings. His encounter with the West would be crucial to the development of his style.

Hokusai is known to have used some 30 different names, an impressive number, as each change signified a new approach, style and vision. The name Hokusai itself dates from 1798. His first success came with his book illustrations for novelettes by Santo Kyoden and Kyokutei Bakin, *surimono* (limited-edition prints intended for use as greeting cards, announcements, etc.), a series of *bijin-ga* (portraits of beautiful women) in the manner of Kiyonaga (1752-1815) and Utamaro (1753-1806) and a series of pure, 'Western-style' landscapes inspired by Dutch engravings. In them views of Edo and nautical scenes are rendered with exaggerated perspective, a use of chiaroscuro that contrasts strangely with the way the figures are sketched in. In some of them the artist's name appears in an imitation of Western calligraphy, with Japanese hiragana characters masquerading as Roman letters.

For the first time, Hokusai here adopts a single, low viewpoint, something totally alien to Japanese tradition. And, as if symbolically of the encounter between East and West, these two principles lie at the source of all his masterpieces.

Henceforth he would move slowly away from the classical world of the *ukiyo-e*, the images of the floating world, the world of pleasure, and devote himself to landscape and the common working people. In 1804, he published views of the Tokaido and the Eastern Capital (Edo). In these works his line hardens, as if a reflection of his increasing determination to represent life in all its movement and reality. The period of his maturity starts after 1820: the *Fugaku-Sanju-Rokkei* (*36 Views*), the first series of prints of Mount Fuji, which, despite its title, actually contains 46 prints.

These stunningly powerful images (*The Red Fuji*, *Mt Fuji in a Thunderstorm*, and *Beneath the Wave off Kanagawa* spring immmediately to mind) are astonishing studies of space and rhythm in which the brilliant graphic representation is heightened by a highly original, not to say personal, use of colour. Other series go hand-in-hand with the *36 Views*: the *Shokoku meikyo kiran* (*Bridges*), and the *Shokoku taki-meguri* (*Tour of Japanese Waterfalls*). Now over seventy years old, Hokusai was planning a grandiose sequel, the *Fugaku hyakkei* (*100 Views of Fuji*), for publication in 1834; but at that point his place in the limelight was suddenly taken by his younger rival, Hiroshige, whose *53 Stations on the Tokaido* appeared to unexpected success in 1833.

While Hokusai was also a great painter, he became famous for his woodcuts. Together with Ishikawa Maronobu (d. 1695), he is perhaps the most prolific illustrator in the entire history of the Japanese book, producing nearly 13,500 plates. Starting with drawings for *kibyoshi* (the cheap, popular novelettes of the time), he went on to illustrate an enormous number of novels and *kyoka* (comic poems). Yet his masterpiece in this genre remains the *Hokusai manga* (*Random Sketches*), a vast encyclopedia of images which he started to publish in 1814 and which would eventually contain his entire draughtsman's repertoire. Thirteen volumes were published while he was still alive, and a further two after his death. His *100 Views of Mt Fuji* appeared in 1834, each plate a masterpiece of drawing, composition, finesse and printing he would never equal. By now a proud and solitary old man, he continued to work in more mannered a style than ever. And defiant as ever, he writes towards the end of the first volume of the *100 Views*: 'of all I drew prior to my 70th year there is truly nothing of any great note... in my 90th I shall have penetrated even further the deeper meaning of things.' He went on to say that in his 100th year he would become a real painter and at 110 would attain perfection! In the event, he was to reach the end of his sad life on 18 April 1849, aged 90.

Among the retrospectives devoted to Hokusai were: 1900, Japan Fine Art Association, Uyeno Park, Tokyo; 1980, *Le Fou de peinture. Hokusai et son temps* (*Man Mad with Painting: Hokusai and his Time*), Centre Culturel du Marais, Paris; and 1990, *Hokusai: Prints and Drawings*, Royal Academy of Arts, London.

BIBLIOGRAPHY:

Bowie, Theodore Robert, *The Drawings of Hokusai*, Greenwood Press, Westport, 1964 (2nd edition, Indiana University Press, Bloomington, 1979). Narazaki, Muneshige, '*Hokusai: the thirty-six views of Mt. Fuji*' in *coll. Masterworks of Ukiyo-e*, Kodansha International, Tokyo, Palo Alto (CA), 1968 (Palo Alto, Ca (USA)). Guillaud, Jacqueline/Guillaud, Maurice, *Le Fou de peinture. Hokusai et son temps: dessins, estampes, livres, peintures, bronzes, kimono, laques, netsuke*, exhibition catalogue, Centre culturel du Marais, Paris, 1980. Smith, Henry D., *One Hundred Views of Mont Fuji*, Braziller, New York, 1988. Goncourt, Edmond de/Forrer, Matthi, *Hokusaï*, Flammarion, Paris, 1988. Morse, Peter, *Hokusaï, cent poètes*, Anthèse, Arcueil, 1989. White, Kenneth, *Hokusaï ou l'horizon sensible*, Terrain vague, Paris, 1990. Forrer, Matthi, *Hokusai: Prints and Drawings*, exhibition catalogue, Royal Academy of Arts, London, Prestel, Munich, 1991. Guth, Christine, *Japanese Art of the Edo Period*, Calmann and King, London, 1996. Fahr-Becker, Gabriele (ed.), *Japanese Prints*, Taschen, Cologne, 1999. Forrer, Matthi, *Hokusai: Prints and Drawings*, Prestel Publishing, 2001. Pollard, Clare, *The Art of Hokusai: Masterpieces of Japanese Printing in the*

Chester Beatty Library, Town House, 2003. Claza, Gian Carlo, ed., *Hokusai*, Phaidon, 2004.

MUSEUMS AND GALLERIES:

LA ROCHELLE (MBA): *100 Views of Mount Fuji* (vol. 1 and 3); *Hokusai manga* (vol. 6 and 7); *Hokusai gafu* (vol. 1); *Models of Designs for Artisans* (vol. 2 and 4) - PARIS (Mus. National des Arts asiatiques-Guimet) - TOKYO (National Mus.).

AUCTION RECORDS:

PARIS, 9 March 1944, *Sennin Gamma Making His Toad Dance to the Sound of His Drum* (Indian ink) FRF 2,600; *Hotel with Grimacing Child* (Indian ink) FRF 1,400; *Lord Sheathing his Sabre* (Indian ink) FRF 1,300. NEW YORK, 17 Nov 1986, *Soko Protecting Lady Fujiyo from Danger* (brush and grey and black wash, 11 3/4 x 12 1/2 ins / 29.8 x 31.5 cm) USD 50,000. PARIS, 14 Dec 1987, *Inume Pass in Kai Province* (print, 14 1/2 x 9 1/4 ins / 36.7 x 23.6 cm) FRF 9,000. LONDON, 16 May 1988, *Yahagi Bridge at Okazaki on the Tokaido* (print) GBP 2,090. LONDON, 16 June 1988, *Hodogaya on the Tokaido* (Oban Yoko-e print, from the series 36 Views of Mount Fuji, 10 x 14 1/2 ins / 25.5 x 36.9 cm) GBP 4,955. NEW YORK, 21 March 1989, *Ono Falls on the Kiso Highway* (Oban Tate-e print, from the series a Tour of Japanese Waterfalls, 15 1/4 x 10 1/4 ins / 38.6 x 26.3 cm) USD 121,000; *Lilies* (Oban Yoko-e print, 10 x 14 1/4 ins / 25.3 x 36.4 cm) USD 104,500. NEW YORK, 20 April 1989, *Mt Fuji on a Snowy Morning* (ukiyo-e print, from the series 36 Views of Mount Fuji, 10 x 15 ins / 24.5 x 37.2 cm) USD 16,500. PARIS, 19 Dec 1989, *Young Woman in Walking Clothes* (hanging scroll, painting) FRF 750,000. LONDON, 22 March 1990, *Pilgrims Washing in the Oyama Falls in Sagami Province* (Oban Tate-e print, 14 x 10 ins / 35.7 x 24.5 cm) GBP 11,000. MONTREAL, 30 April 1990, *Landscape with Figures* (woodcut/rice paper, 9 3/4 x 14 1/4 ins / 25 x 36 cm) CAD 3,300. LONDON, 6 June 1990, *Stalls near Ryogoku Bridge* (Oban Yoko-e print, 10 1/4 x 15 1/4 ins / 26.1 x 38.5 cm) GBP 1,100. NEW YORK, 15 June 1990, *Porters Coming down the Hill* (Oban Yoko-e print, from the series 100 Poems My Nanny Used to Tell Me, 10 1/2 x 15 ins / 26.5 x 38 cm) USD 33,000. NEW YORK, 27 March 1991, *Beneath the Wave off Kanagawa* (Oban Yoko-e print, from the series 36 Views of Mount Fuji, 10 1/4 x 15 ins / 25.9 x 38.1 cm) USD 220,000. PARIS, 3 June 1992, *Mount Fuji Reflected in Lake Misaka, Kai Province* (Oban print, from the series 36 Views of Mount Fuji, 10 1/4 x 15 ins / 25.8 x 37.8 cm.-,) FRF 21,000. PARIS, 26 May 1993, *Kajikawasa, Kai Province* (Oban Yoko-e print, 10 x 14 3/4 ins / 25.3 x 37.4 cm) FRF 100,000. LONDON, 23 June 2000, *Waterwheel at Onden* (print from series 'Fugaku Sanju Rokkei') GBP 5,500. PARIS, 16 Dec 2002, *Poem* (print) EUR 6,200. PARIS, 7 March 2003, *Oban Yoko-e* (print, 14 x 9 ins / 36 x 24 cm) EUR 23,000. LONDON, 11 Dec 2003, *Going around Waterfalls in Various Provinces* (oil on canvas, 15 x 10 ins / 38 x 25 cm) GBP 6,500.

HOKUSEI. See **HOKKAI**

HOKUSETSU, artist name: Shun'yusai
Japanese, 19th century.
Active c. 1830.
Painter.

'Hokusetsu' is probably a misreading of 'Hokuun'.

HOKUSHIN, artist names: Shunkantei, Shunkosai
Japanese, 19th century.
Active c. 1830.
Painter.

Hokushin was a pupil of Hokuei.

HOKUSHO, real name: Takehara Nobushige, original name: Matsumoto, first name: Shuncho (1815-1821); childhood names: Matsumoto, Takehara; artist names: Shunchosai, Hokusho; personal names: Nobushige, Monji
Japanese, 19th century.
Born 1772; died 1801.
Active c. 1815?-1830.
Painter.

HOKUSHO, first name: Shuncho (1822-1823); artist name: Shunchosai
Japanese, 19th century.
Active c. 1822-1832.
Painter.

It is possible that Hokusho and Hokushu were the same artist.

HOKUSHU, personal name: Shima Jinsen; artist names: Shunko (1810-1818, as poet from 1806), Shunkosai, Shokosai (1811), Shunkosai (1818-1832), Sekkatei (1819); seal: Yoshinoyama
Japanese, 19th century.
Active c. 1810-1832.
Painter.

The change of name from Shunko to Shokosai is recorded on a print dated September 1811.

HOKUSOO. See **ITCHO**

HOKUSUI. See **YOSHITOYO**

HOKUSUI
Japanese, 19th century.
Active c. 1860.
Painter.

Hokusui worked with Tokyo on the *Miyako hyakkei*.

HOKUTO, artist name: Shokosai or Shunkosai
Japanese, 19th century.
Active c. 1835.
Painter.

HOKUUN, real name: Katsushira Goro, original name: Okubo, familiar names: Bungoro, Kyugoro, artist name: Tonansei
Japanese, 19th century.
Active c. 1828.
Painter.

From a print dated 1828, Hokuun would have been a pupil of Shunkosai (Hokuei). There is, however, little doubt that he bears no relation to Hokusai's pupil Katsushika Tonansai.

HOKUYO, childhood name: Katsushika; artist names: Tanseido, Senkakutei (1819), Senkakudo
Japanese, 19th century.
Active c. 1819-1830.
Painter.

HOKUZAN, childhood name: Kano
Japanese, 19th century.
Active c. 1810.
Painter.

Hokuzan also made portrait and actor prints, which were published in Kyoto.

HOLAN, Karel
Czech, 20th century.
Born 1893, in Prague; died 1953, in Prague.
Painter. Scenes with figures, landscapes.

Karel Holan studied architecture in Prague in 1914, before studying painting with Maximilian Pirner and Karl Krattner from 1915 to 1921. He went several times to France and Italy.

In the early part of his career he painted compositions with figures depicting the dramas of everyday life, such as *Ambulance* and *Drowned Woman*. Later he began to paint landscapes.

He exhibited mainly in Prague from 1933 onwards.

BIBLIOGRAPHY:

Fifty years of Czechoslovak Painting from the Collections of the Galleries, 1918-1958, exhibition catalogue, Slovenska

Narodna Gal., Bratislava, 1968 (in commemoration of the 50th anniversary of the Republic of Czechoslovakia).

HOLANDA, DE. See first name

HOLAREK, Emil
Czech, 19th - 20th century.
Born 1867, in Laun; died 26 February 1919, in Laun.
Painter, engraver. History painting.
A pupil of Pirner at the Prague academy, Emil Holarek specialised in historical scenes.
AUCTION RECORDS:
NEW YORK, 23 May 1997, *Beauty Exhibited* (oil on canvas, 41 x 53 ins / 104.1 x 134.6 cm) USD 23,000.

HOLBAN, Fausto
Italian, 20th century.
Born 25 April 1940, in Modena.
Painter, engraver. Interiors.
Holban is of Romanian origin, although he has always lived in Modena, Italy. While studying literature and philosophy at Modena University he simultaneously followed a course in archaeology, painting and engraving. He has exhibited in many group exhibitions in Italy and abroad. Since 1970 he has shown his work in solo exhibitions and in 1972 he was awarded the Ambroglio d'Oro medal in Milan. He uses a limited palette of red, white, brown and black to depict a world which sunlight never enters.

HOLBE, Rudolph
German, 19th - 20th century.
Born 1848; died 1926.
Sculptor. Mythological subjects, allegorical subjects.
Rudolph Holbe created the allegorical group, *Art*, on the door of the Albertinum in Dresden.
MUSEUMS AND GALLERIES:
DRESDEN (Albertinum, Skulpturensammlung): *Waldnymphe (Wood Nymph)* (1895).

HOLBECH, Carl Frederik
Danish, 19th century.
Born 27 February 1811; died 23 July 1880, in Rome.
Sculptor.
There is a *Child Bacchus* by Carl Holbech in the museum of Copenhagen. He collaborated with Thorvaldsen.
AUCTION RECORDS:
LONDON, 30 Nov 1983, *Cupid; Child Bacchus* (1843 and 1844, marble, two, h. 34¼ ins / 87 cm and 28¾ ins/73 cm) GBP 2,800.

HOLBECH, Niels Peter
Danish, 19th century.
Born 14 September 1804; died 11 January 1889, in Karlshamn.
Painter.
Niels Holbech studied with Christian August Lorentzen before travelling throughout Germany and England. He executed portraits, genre paintings and religious paintings, such as the altarpiece for a church in Flodstrup.

HOLBEIN
German (?), 19th century.
Active in Russia.
Painter. Portraits.
He was active in Kiev in 1850. Overbeck engraved a portrait of him.

HOLBEIN, Ambrosius
German, 16th century.
Born c. 1493 or 1495, in Augsburg; died probably between 1519 and 1526.
Painter, engraver (wood).
Augsburg School.
Little is known about Ambrosius Holbein. He was the son of Hans Holbein the Elder and probably an older brother of Hans Holbein the Younger. Some biographers say that he was born in Basel, but this was not so; he and his younger brother only arrived in Basel in 1514. He joined the 'Guild Zum Himmel' in 1517. He may have died and certainly was no longer working when Hans the Younger left Basel for the first time in 1526.

It is highly likely that the two brothers worked together, and when Hans the Younger later became famous, any joint productions, wood engravings or portraits, perhaps with an altered forename, would easily be attributed to him. The list below records works by Ambrosius now in museums, and includes the 1516 *Portrait of the Painter Johannes Herbster* who was his teacher. He made drawings for wood engravings and is thought to be the creator of the *Calumny of Apelles* dated 1517, which was used at various times in works printed in Basel by Froben. He is also believed to be the author of some 40 other drawings, among them the *Garden of Hylthodus* in Thomas More's *Utopia*, and *Lucretia and Collatinus*.
MUSEUMS AND GALLERIES:
BASEL: *Christ and God the Father Surrounded by Angels; Portrait of the Painter Johannes Herbster; Portrait of a Fair-haired Child; Portrait of a Dark-haired Child; Portrait of a Gentleman of Rudyswyler; Two Death's Heads in a Window* - ST PETERSBURG (Hermitage): *Portrait*.

HOLBEIN, Eduard Carl Friedrich
German, 19th century.
Born 1807, in Berlin; died 19 February 1875, in Berlin.
Painter, engraver. History painting, genre scenes.
He was a student at the academy in Berlin, then a pupil of Carl Begas from 1832 to 1839. His professional debut in Berlin was c. 1830. In 1853, he became a professor at the academy in Berlin.
AUCTION RECORDS:
VIENNA, 11 Nov 1987, *The Death of the Pilgrim* (1835, oil on canvas, 41¼ x 48 ins / 105 x 122 cm) ATS 40,000. MUNICH, 12 Dec 1990, *The Death of the Old Pilgrim* (1835, oil on canvas, rounded at the top, 53¼ x 60¼ ins / 135 x 153 cm) DEM 33,000.

HOLBEIN, Friedrich Wilhelm
German, 19th century.
Sculptor.
He was the brother of Eduard Holbein, and active in Berlin in the early 19th century. He exhibited at the academy in Berlin from 1832.

HOLBEIN, Hans, the Elder
German, 15th - 16th century.
Born between 1460 and 1465, in Augsburg; died 1524, in Issenheim.
Painter. History painting, portraits.
Swabian School.
Hans Holbein the Elder does not seem to have had an easy life. He was the son of Michael Holbein, a tanner who settled in Augsburg in 1448. Through his mother Anna Mair he was related to important artists in the area. He is thought to have worked in the studio of Martin Schongauer in Colmar and to have been indirectly influenced there by Rogier van der Weyden. Works attributed to him from this period echo van der Weyden's style. In any case, Hans Holbein the Elder was established in Augsburg by 1494, as his name appears with that date on the city registers instead of his father's. He must have produced a considerable output, considering how much is still extant, yet he was always poor, more than once being taken to court for quite small debts, particularly by his brother Sigmund. Tradition asserts that he married a sister of Hans Burgkmair, but the identity of his wife is not known for certain. Although he worked hard, he could not support himself and in 1514, when his sons moved to Basel, Hans left

Augsburg for Issenheim where he lived for the rest of his life.

Among his first known works are those he painted for the Benedictine monastery at Weingarten - four altar paintings taken from *Scenes from the Life of the Virgin* (now in Augsburg Cathedral) and two small Madonnas (now in the gallery in Nuremberg). In 1499 Hans was granted citizenship in Ulm. In the same year he painted *Thirteen Scenes from the Passion* in a single frame, the triptych *The Basilica of S Maria Maggiore* (in Augsburg museum), and a *Madonna with the Infant Jesus* (in Nuremberg museum). In 1501 Hans was working in Frankfurt am Main where he painted *The Death of the Virgin* (in Basel museum), and made an altar painting for the Dominicans which included *The Last Supper, Christ's Entry into Jerusalem, The Expulsion of the Merchants from the Temple* and a *Tree of Jesse*. In 1502 at the Dominican Klosterkirche in Kaisheim near Donauwerth he painted a decoration consisting of some 20 subjects, including a *Descent from the Cross*, an *Entombment* and 16 scenes from *The Life of the Virgin* (now in the gallery in Munich). From the same period come his *Twelve Scenes from the Passion* (in the Furstenberg collection in Donaueschingen) and the *Transfiguration* and *Christ Crowned with Thorns* (now in the Augsburg gallery). In 1503 and 1504 he produced the *Scenes from the Life of St Paul* in which he painted his own portrait and that of his two sons Ambrose and Hans. Hans the Younger was then six years old, so we can give an approximate date to his birth. In 1506, 1507 and 1508 Hans the Elder worked in the church of St Maurice and other religious establishments in Augsburg.

Much of the elder Holbein's work has been attributed to his son Hans, including his masterpiece *The Martyrdom of St Sebastian*, an altar painting he made for St Catherine's abbey in Augsburg, now in the Munich museum and correctly attributed. The elder Holbein was not only a fine painter himself but a fine teacher, who taught his son Hans the Younger. Father and son are known to have collaberated on some projects, including the Oberried altarpiece in Freiburg-im-Breisgau Cathedral from 1520-1521.

For a long time the younger son's fame eclipsed the father's. Hans Holbein the Elder was one of those who, like Lucas Cranach, held firmly to his own national tradition and preferred to reject fashionable Renaissance ideas throughout much of his career, even though this meant that potential patrons rejected him.

In 2002 the Staatsgalerie in Stuttgart exhibited 26 of the most important works in the Fürstenberg Collection in Donaueschingen deriving from the late medieval Swabian School, including some by Hans Holbein the Elder.

Bibliography:

Hans Holbein der Ältere und die Kunst der Spätgotik, exhibition catalogue, Augsburg-Rathaus, Augsburg, 1965. Bushart, Bruno, *Hans Holbein, der Ältere*, Hofmann, Augsburg, 1987.

Museums and Galleries:

Augsburg (Schaezler-Palais, Staatsgal.): *The Basilica of S Maria Maggiore* (triptych); *The Transfiguration; Christ Crowned with Thorns* - Basel: *Death of Mary among the Apostles* (two canvases) - Darmstadt: *Mourning the Christ; Resurrection; Portrait of Hans Holbein the Younger* - Donaueschingen (Fürstlich Fürstenbergisches Sammlungen): *Scenes of the Passion* (c. 1495, 12 panels) - Graz: *Portrait of a Practitioner* - Hanover: *Christ and the Virgin at Golgotha* - Munich: *Christ on the Mount of Olives; Arrest of Christ; Christ before Pilate; The Scourging; Crown of Thorns; Ecce Homo; Carrying the Cross; Resurrection; Welcome of Mary at the Temple; The Angel's Greeting; The Visitation; The Nativity; Adoration of the Kings; The Circumcision; Presentation in the Temple; Death of the Virgin; Martyrdom of St Sebastian; St Barbara; St Elisabeth of Thuringia* - Nuremberg (Gal.): *Madonna and the Infant Jesus* - Strasbourg: *Suffering Christ* - Stuttgart (Staatsgal.): *Virgin and Child with an Augustinian Canon as Donor* (c. 1493-1494); *Grey Passion* (c. 1495) - Zurich: *The Seven Wounds of Christ*.

Auction records:

Cologne, 1862, *Portrait of a Man; Portrait of a Woman* (two) FRF 273. Paris, 1871, *Portrait of a Scholar*, FRF 700. London, 12 Feb 1926, *St Peter and St Paul* (drawing) GBP 75. London, 10 July 1936, *Study of a Woman* (drawing) GBP 367; *Virgin and Child* (drawing) GBP 54. London, 2 July 1965, *Public Scribe*, Gns 2,000. London, 24 June 1970, *Portrait of a Bearded Man with a Carnation*, GBP 9,000. London, 6 Dec 1995, *Virgin and Child (The Madonna of Montenuovo)* (oil on pine panel, 18 x 13 1/2 ins / 45.5 x 34.5 cm) GBP 106,000.

HOLBEIN, Hans, the Younger

German, 16th century.

Born probably in 1497 or 1498, in Augsburg; died November 1543, in London.

Active in Switzerland from 1514, then in England from 1531.

Painter, draughtsman, engraver. Religious subjects, portraits. Murals.

Like his brother Ambrosius, Hans Holbein the Younger studied under his father Hans Holbein the Elder. He probably worked with him until 1514, when the family separated and the sons went to Basel and the father to Issenheim, where he died ten years later. The young men may have gone to Basel in the hope of finding work as draughtsmen and wood engravers in a town where there were so many printers: Adam Petri, Cratander, Wolff and Jean Froben. This hope was realised and the young Holbeins produced numerous drawings for title pages and illustrations, especially for Froben. In 1519, he became member of the Basel Guild and in 1524 he went to France to become painter for the court of Henry the VIII. The decision by Hans in 1519 to leave Basel, torn apart as it was by religious quarrels, may have been suggested by Erasmus, with whom he had made friends. When he set off on his travels to France and England, he certainly had with him letters of introduction to Sir Thomas More. He travelled down the Rhine, stopping in Antwerp to visit Quentin Matsys to whom Erasmus had also given him an introduction. According to Karel van Mander, More gave Holbein a warm welcome and had him stay with him in Chelsea. Some biographers dispute this. Holbein had married young and when he returned home to Basel he painted a portrait of his wife and their two children. His travels had brought him enough money to buy a house on the banks of the Rhine. His adoptive fellow citizens made him welcome and the city magistrates commissioned him to paint the two murals still lacking in the council chamber. But the political and economic situation in Basel had not improved and Hans set off once again for England. He then settled in London in 1531 not far from the headquarters of the German merchants. There is a tradition that he lived in one of the houses on London Bridge. He died in the plague which devastated London in 1543. A later date is sometimes given, but is incorrect. Hans the Younger's superiority over his elder brother seems to have been clear from the beginning of their time in Basel. His first known dated work, *The Virgin and the Child Jesus* (1514, now in the Basel museum), shows that Hans was already a very talented painter when he was scarcely 17. Two years later his *Portraits of Jakob Meier and his Wife* (also in the Basel museum) showed him firmly established as a portrait painter. Among his work from the first period in Basel (up to 1526), mention should also be made of the *Portrait of Bonifacius Amerbach* (1519), *Christ in the Tomb* (1521), *The Virgin of Solothurn* (1522) in Solothurn, two altar panels in Fribourg Cathedral (1522), the *Portraits of Erasmus* (1523), the famous *Christ in the Tomb* (1525) in the Basel museum, and *The Madonna of the Meier*

Family (1526) owned by the museum in Darmstadt. During the same period a number of important decorative works were commissioned from him. In 1517 the Hertenstein family had him go to Lucerne to adorn their home there. This building was demolished in 1824. When he returned to Basel in 1519 he is thought to have painted murals in a number of houses there. He certainly painted *The Lady's House* which survived until the 18th century, a decorative work whose existence is proved by a drawing in the artist's hand kept in the Berlin museum and copies of the drawing in the museum in Basel. The city officials also commissioned him to paint murals in the council chamber in the town hall in 1521. These have also been lost. Among the many friends of young Hans there was a famous one, Erasmus. By 1515 they knew each other well enough for Erasmus to write the name 'Holbein' over a picture of a drunken peasant in one of the pen and ink drawings with which Hans illustrated his *In Praise of Folly, Encomium Moriae*. In 1519 Hans engraved a frontispiece for Erasmus' *Epistles of St Paul*. Also in 1519 he painted the *Portrait of Bonifacius Amerbach, Jurist of Basel*. His famous *Portrait of Erasmus of Rotterdam, Writing* in the museum in Basel dates from 1523.

During his first period in England, Sir Thomas More and his friends employed Holbein to paint their portraits. The Basel museum has a pen and ink drawing of a large *Portrait of the Family of Chancellor Thomas More in London*. The portrait was painted in 1527 but has disappeared; Holbein took the drawing home with him to Basel in 1528. Extant works from this time are *Portrait of William Warham, Archbishop of Canterbury* (1527), *Sir Henry Guilford* (1527), and in Windsor Castle *Nicolas Kratzer* (1528), *Thomas Godsalve and his Son* (1528) and *Sir Bryan Tuke*. Before leaving England, Holbein engraved a block for the very scarce *The Pastime of the People, or the Chronicles of Divers Realms, and most especially of the Realm of England*. This was a large quarto printed by J. Pastell in 1529 and reprinted in 1811 by T.F. Dibdin.

The *Madonna with Burgomaster Meyer 'of Darmstadt'* may have been painted during Holbein's brief return to Basel in 1528. The carpet on which the donors kneel does not seem to lie flat, and a number of theories have been based upon this detail. Settled once again in London and prospering as a portrait painter, Holbein was now commissioned to paint two large pieces for the City of London's headquarters. Highly successful but now lost, these were *Triumph of Wealth* and *Triumph of Poverty*. A sketch of the former survives together with an engraving of the second, kept in the Louvre. In 1532 he painted the *Portrait of the Merchant Georg Gisze* (now in the museum in Berlin), which is remarkable for the number of objects grouped around the subject, both in the still-life on the table and in the trompe-l'œil on the wall. The *Double Portrait of Jean de Dinteville and Georges de Selve, 'The Ambassadors'*, dated 1533, is one of Holbein's most accomplished works, if only for the profusion of objects scattered about as in a still-life, the sumptuous rendering of the fabrics and, particularly, the startling presence of a distorted and floating skull. Holbein's *Portrait of Thomas Cromwell*, master of the jewel-house of Henry VIII, which he painted in 1534, had a considerable influence on his career as it is thought to have been Cromwell who made him known to the king. Some think that Holbein entered court circles with the help of Thomas More, but if so, it would surely have happened during his first visit to London. Whatever the case, Holbein is not listed among the painters of Henry VIII until 1536. His *Portrait of Sir Richard Southwell* (now in the Uffizi in Florence) dates from this year. The following year saw the production of the famous *Portrait of Henry VIII and his Father*, which was destroyed in a fire at Whitehall in 1698 (the study is in the collection of the Duke of Devonshire); that of *Jane Seymour*; that of *Lady Vaux* (in Prague); and that of *Charles Solier de la Morette*. It was probably in 1539-1540 that he painted the impressive and disturbing *Portrait of Henry VIII of England*, of which there is an old copy in Rome. An inscription on the canvas gives the king's age as 49.

In 1538 Holbein went to Belgium to paint the *Portrait of Christina of Denmark, Duchess of Milan*, a masterpiece on loan to the National Gallery in London. In the same year he was sent to Burgundy (it is not known why) and visited Lyons and Basel. His journey may have coincided with the publication in Lyons by Gaspar and Melchior Trechsel of the *Simulacres et Histories Faces de la Mort*, a large octavo with 41 plates, and the *Historiarum Vete in Testamentum Icones Advivum Expressae*, a small quarto with 92 plates with Latin captions, the engravings of which had been made by Hans Lützlburger. Proofs from these two publications exist, probably taken in Basel before Holbein first went to England in 1526, and are kept in the print rooms of Paris, London, Karlsruhe, Munich, and Basel. Le Blanc gives 1530 for the date of printing of the *Dance of Death* and says that the edition with German captions consisted of only 40 plates. Between 1538 and 1562 no fewer than 12 editions of this work were published in Lyons and Basel, with different captions and additional plates. The most recent had 58.

During his last period in Basel, Holbein does not seem to have had time to work. He agreed to a contract with the city council by whose terms he would become painter to the town once he had returned for good, but had permission to travel abroad to practise his art. In 1539 he left England again to paint the *Portrait of Anne of Cleves*. Other paintings from this time are the *Portrait of Thomas Howard, Duke of Norfolk* (1540) and that of *John Chambers* (1542), Henry VIII's physician. His *Self-portrait at the Age of Forty-five*, a drawing in colour in the Uffizi museum, also dates from 1542-1543. His last known work is a drawing now in the British Museum, dated 1543, of the model of a clock intended for the king.

Hans Holbein the Younger painted many religious pictures, perfect in composition and execution if not in spirituality, but it is for his portraits he is famous, both for the beauty of their settings and for the brilliance with which he caught and showed the individuality of the sitters.

In 1997 the National Gallery in London mounted an exhibition entitled *Making and Meaning: Holbein's Ambassadors*.

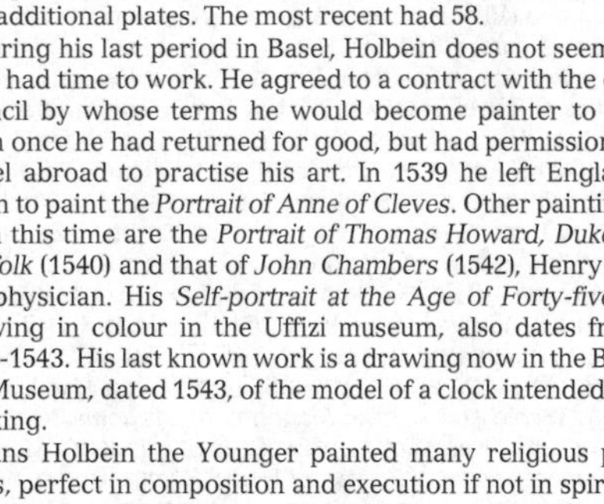

BIBLIOGRAPHY:

Ganz, Paul, *Paintings of Hans Holbein (Translation of Hans Holbein: Die Gemälde)*, Phaidon Press, London, 1950 (Introduction translated by R.H. Boothroyd, catalogue by Marguerite Kay). Rowlands, J./Bartum, G., *Drawings by German Artists in the Department of Prints and Drawings in the British Museum: The Fifteenth Century and the Sixteenth Century by Artists born before 1530, 2 vols*, London, 1993. Bätschmann, Oskar/Griener, Pascal, *Hans Hol-*

bein, Reaktion, London, 1997. Wilson, Derek A., *Hans Holbein: Portrait of an Unknown Man*, Phoenix Giants, London, 1997. Roskill, Mark/Hand, John Oliver (eds.), *Hans Holbein: Paintings, Prints, and Reception*, National Gallery of Art, Washington, c. 2001.

MUSEUMS AND GALLERIES:

AVIGNON: *Portrait of a Man* - BASEL (Öffentliche Kunstsammlung): *The Virgin and the Child Jesus; The Last Supper; Christ on the Mount of Olives; Christ in Prison; Pilate Washing his Hands; The Scourging of Christ; Head of St John on a Blue Background; Head of the Virgin on a Blue Background; A Master and Two Scholars; School for Boys and Girls with the Master and his Wife; Portraits of Mayor Jacob Meier (or Meyer) and his Wife; Adam and Eve with the Apple; Portrait of Bonifacius Amerbach, Jurist of Basel* (1519); *The Passion in Eight Pictures; The Last Supper; The Man of Sorrows and Mater Dolorosa; Christ in the Tomb* (1525); *Portrait of Erasmus of Rotterdam, Writing* (1523); *The Organ of Basel Cathedral, Emperor Heinrich II and his Wife; Magdalena Offenburg as Laïs of Corinth; Magdalena Offenburg as Venus; Portrait of Erasmus of Rotterdam, Writing; The Family of Thomas More in London* (1527, pen and ink drawing); *Young Woman; Man Wearing Furs; Head and Hands of the King; Heads of the Samnite Envoys; Heads of Zaleukus and a Spectator in The Justice of Zaleukus* (album of drawings and plans for ornaments and jewels known as the 'English Sketchbook') - BERLIN (Gemäldegal.): *Portrait of the Merchant Georg Gisze* (1532); *Portraits of Two Young Men; Portrait of an Old Man* - BERLIN (Kupferstichkabinet): book*Historiarum Vete in Testamenti Icones Advivum Expressae; Simulacra* (book) - BERN: *Two Heads* - BÉZIERS: *Portrait of a Man* - BOOTLE (AG and Mus.): *The Virgin and the Meyer Family; Henry VIII; Thomas More* - BORDEAUX: *Portrait of a Man* - BRUSSELS: *Thomas More* - CHÂLONS-EN-CHAMPAGNE: *Portrait of a Man* - DARMSTADT (Schlossmus.): *The Madonna of Burgomaster Meyer (or Meier) 'of Darmstadt'* (1526) - DIJON: *Portrait of a Man; Entombment* - DUBLIN: *Portrait of Henry Wyatt* - DUNKIRK: *Portrait of Luther or Melanchthon* - ÉPINAL: *Head of a Man; Calvin; Luther Writing* - FLORENCE (Palazzo Pitti): *Portrait of a Man* - FLORENCE (Uffizi): *Portrait of Richard Southwell; Portrait of the Artist Aged Forty-five* (1542-1543, drawing in coloured pencil); *Portrait of a Man; The Reformer Zwingli; Thomas More; Portrait of a Woman* - FORT WORTH (Kimbell AM): *Portrait of Sir Thomas Le Strange of Hunstanton* (1536, oil and tempera/panel) - FRANKFURT AM MAIN: *George of Cornwall* - GENEVA (Mus. Ariana): *Lord Goven; Sigismond von Föh* - GENOA: *St Jerome* - HANOVER: *Edward VI; Portrait of a Man; Philip Melanchthon* - KARLSRUHE (Prints Collection): *Historiarum Vete in Testamenti Icones Advivum Expressae* (book); *Simulacra* (book) - LILLE: *Charity* - LONDON (British Mus.): album of 185 drawings and plans for ornaments and jewels - LONDON (NG): *Portrait of Erasmus* (1523, tempera/wood, on loan from a private collection); *A Lady with a Squirrel and a Starling* (1526-1528, oil/wood); *Jean de Dinteville and Georges de Selve ('The Ambassadors')* (1533, oil/wood); *Christina of Denmark, Duchess of Milan* (1538, oil/wood) - LONDON (Wallace Collection): *Edward VI as Prince of Wales* (after 1792, oil/paper/panel, after the artist) - MADRID: *Portrait of an Old Man* - MONTAUBAN: *Portrait of a Monk* - MOSCOW (Rumiantsev Mus.): *Portrait of Erasmus; Portrait of a Man* - MUNICH: *Portraits of Dreick Born, Bryan Tuke, and Derick Berck* - MUNICH (Staatliche Graphische Sammlung): *Historiarum Vete in Testamenti Icones Advivum Expressae* (book); *Simulacra* (book) - NANTES: *Portrait of a Man* - NEW YORK (Frick Collection): *Sir Thomas More* (1527, oil on oak panel) - PARIS: *Portrait of the Artist* (miniature) - PARIS (BNF, Prints Collection): *Historiarum Vete in Testamenti Icones Advivum Expressae* (book); *Simulacra* (book) - PARIS (Louvre): *Portrait of Nicolas Kratzer; Portrait of William Warham; Portrait of Erasmus; Portrait of Thomas More; Portrait of Anne of Cleves; Portrait of Richard Southwell; Portrait of Sir Henry Wyatt; Portrait of a Man* - ROME (Gal. Colonna): *Laurent Colonna, Brother of Martin V* - ROME (Gal. Nazionale d'Arte Antica di Palazzo Barberini): *Henry VIII of England* (old copy) - SÃO PAULO: *Henry Howard, Earl of Surrey* - ST LOUIS (AM): *Mary, Lady Guildford (Portrait of Mary Wotten, Wife of Sir Henry Guildford)* (1527, oil/panel) - ST PETERSBURG (Hermitage): *Erasmus of Rotterdam* - THE HAGUE: *Robert Cheseman* - TOLEDO (MA): *Portrait of a Woman of the Cromwell Family* - VIENNA: *John Chambers; Two Portraits of a Man; Two Portraits of a Woman; Dirck Tybis* - VIENNA (Kunsthistorisches Mus.): *Jane Seymour, Queen of England (Jane Seymour)* - VIENNA (Schönborn-Buckheim): *Portrait of a Man* - WINDSOR (Windsor Castle, Royal Collection): series of paintings representing Henry VIII and the members of his court.

AUCTION RECORDS:

PARIS, 1831, *Portrait of Stephen Gardiner*, FRF 66,700. PARIS, 20-22 June 1898, *Portrait of Cardinal Fisher*, FRF 10,300. AMSTERDAM, 26-29 Nov 1901, *Self-portrait* (miniature) FRF 420. NEW YORK, 30 Jan 1902, *Portrait of a Churchman*, USD 4,000. PARIS, 26-29 April 1904, *Calvin's Mother*, FRF 30,000. PARIS, 28 and 29 March 1906, *Lord Antoine Humbert*, FRF 39,000. LONDON, 8 May 1908, *Portrait of Éléonore, Wife of Francis I*, GBP 89; *Portrait of Isabelle, Wife of Christian II of Denmark*, GBP 71. LONDON, 7 May 1909, *Portrait of a Woman*, GBP 73. LONDON, 18 June 1909, *Portrait of a Gentleman and Lady* (drawing, in one frame) GBP 367. LONDON, 23 July 1909, *Portrait of Mary Tudor*, GBP 63. LONDON, 8 July 1910, *Portrait of the Artist*, GBP 189. LONDON, 5 May 1911, *Portrait of a Gentleman*, GBP 220. LONDON, 14 July 1911, *Portrait of a Donor and his Wife, Kneeling*, GBP 194. PARIS, 26 and 27 May 1919, *Portrait of a Man* (drawing in coloured chalks) FRF 66,000. PARIS, 30 May -1 June 1921, *Portrait of a Man*, FRF 250,100. LONDON, May 1922, *Francis, Prince of Thurn and Taxis*, GBP 336. LONDON, July 1922, *Man in Black*, GBP 204. LONDON, July 1923, *Erasmus*, GBP 441. LONDON, 27 June 1924, *Henry VIII in a Yellow Embroidered Doublet*, GBP 136. LONDON, 18 July 1924, *Gentleman, said to be the Protector Somerset*, GBP 399. LONDON, 10 June 1925, *Sir John Seymour*, GBP 493. LONDON, 12 June 1925, *Portrait of a Gentleman*, GBP 336. LONDON, 26 June 1925, *Sir Henry Guildford*, GBP 787. LONDON, 12 April 1926, *Henry VIII, Queen Mary, Philip II, Elizabeth and Edward VI*, GBP 315. PARIS, 10 and 11 May 1926, *St Nicholas* (pen and Indian ink) FRF 7,000. LONDON, 20 June 1927, *Portrait of the Artist at Sixteen*, GBP 315. LONDON, 8 July 1927, *Thomas Cromwell*, GBP 787; *Sir Bryan Tuke*, GBP 168. LONDON, 14 Dec 1928, *Gentleman in Black with Plum-coloured Sleeves*, GBP 735. LONDON, 21 Dec 1928, *Edward VI*, GBP 220. LONDON, 15 March 1929, *Gentleman in Black*, GBP 1,522. LONDON, 28 March 1929, *Thomas Cromwell, Earl of Essex*, GBP 210. LONDON, 12 July 1929, *Edward VI*, GBP 9,975; *Henry VIII*, GBP 1,155. LONDON, 27 April 1934, *Lady, said to be Anne Boleyn*, GBP 903. LONDON, 29 March 1935, *Man in Black*, GBP 241. LONDON, 24 May 1935, *Henry Howard, Earl of Surrey*, GBP 483. LONDON, 26 June 1936, *Mary Tudor*, GBP 924. LONDON, 8 April 1938, *Duchess of Suffolk*, GBP 220. LONDON, 1 July 1938, *Anne Boleyn*, GBP 235. LONDON, 18 Nov 1938, *Sir Henry Sydney*, GBP 367. LONDON, 16 July 1943, *Sir Robert Sheffield*, GBP 1,890; *Lady Sheffield*, GBP 1,050; *The Earl of Surrey*, GBP 1,785. LONDON, 9 June 1944, *Lady (Anne Boleyn)*, GBP 1,995. LONDON, 19 Jan 1945, *Edward VI*, GBP 997; *Henry VIII*, GBP 3,360. LONDON, 18 Jan 1946, *Gentleman*, GBP 3,885. LONDON, 26 June 1946, *Armorial Bearings* (drawing) GBP 1,850. LONDON, 6 Dec 1946, *Young Woman*, GBP 7,350. LONDON, 31 Jan 1947, *The Marchioness of Dorset*, GBP 378. LONDON, 27 June 1958, *Portrait of Sir Thomas Cromwell, Earl of Essex* (miniature) GBP 1,680. LONDON, 29 May 1959, *Portrait of a Man*, GBP 787. BERN, 16 June 1960, *Christ's Body in the Tomb* (heightened drawing) CHF 7,100. NEW YORK, 15 Nov 1961, *Portrait of Sir George Nevill, Fifth*

Lord Bergavenny (c. 1533-1535) USD 35,000. LONDON, 30 June 1965, *Portrait of Catherine Parr, Last Wife of Henry VIII*, GBP 4,000. LONDON, 17 Nov 1977, *Death and the Abbot* (engraving/wood, 2 1/2 x 2 ins / 6.6 x 4.9 cm) GBP 500. LONDON, 30 Nov 1979, *Portrait of the Engraver Johann Froben of Basel* (oil and tempera/panel, round, diam. 3 3/4 ins / 9.5 cm) GBP 17,000. MUNICH, 29 May 1980, *Erasmus of Rotterdam* (engraving/wood) DEM 3,400. BERN, 24 June 1983, *Die Mutter Gottes zwischen den Schuzpatronen der Stadt Friburg* (*The Mother of God between the Patrons of the City of Friburg*) (1519, engraving/wood) CHF 5,400. LONDON, 3 July 1984, *Portrait of a Scholar or a Churchman* (black and red chalk, brush, ink and wash/pale pink base, 8 1/2 x 7 1/4 ins / 21.8 x 18.4 cm) GBP 1,450,000. HEIDELBERG, 15-16 Oct 1993, *Way of the Cross* (ink wash, 17 1/4 x 12 1/4 ins / 43.5 x 31.2 cm) DEM 3,600. NEW YORK, 28 Jan 1998, *Tantalus* (pen, black ink and watercolour heightened with gold, round, diam. 2 ins / 5.1 cm) USD 745,000. LUCERNE, 13 Oct 1999, *Whore of Babylon* (grey pen and brush wash, 11 x 9 ins / 27 x 23 cm) CHF 4,400. NEW YORK, 23 Jan 2001, *St Thomas* (1527, pen, black ink and grey wash heightened with white, 8 x 4 ins / 20 x 10 cm) USD 140,000. LONDON, 11 July 2001, *St Paul* (1527, pen, black ink and grey wash heightened with white, 7 x 4 ins / 18 x 10 cm) GBP 70,000.

HOLBEIN, Sigmund
German, 15th - 16th century.
Born between 1465 and 1470, in Augsburg; died 1540, in Bern.
Painter, engraver.

Sigmund Holbein was the younger brother of Hans Holbein the Elder. His name appears on the Augsburg tax register from 1505 to 1509. He is then thought to have left Augsburg to settle in Bern where he bought a house and other property and was granted citizenship. In 1540 he made his will, bequeathing his goods to his nephew Hans Holbein the Younger, and died soon afterwards.

His authentic work is rare and includes a *Virgin and the Child Jesus* painted on a golden background and now in the Nuremberg museum. The museum in Vienna possesses two small portraits of a man, and the National Gallery in London has a portrait of a Swiss woman, attributed to Sigmund Holbein. He engraved copies of work by Martin Schongauer and Albrecht Dürer.

MUSEUMS AND GALLERIES:
NUREMBERG (Germanisches Nationalmus.): *Virgin and the Child Jesus* - VIENNA: *Two Small Portraits of a Man* (attributed).

AUCTION RECORDS:
PARIS, 20-22 June 1898, *Portrait of a Young Man*, FRF 4,000. LONDON, 26 Nov 1965, *Christ Blindfolded, Scourged and Mocked*, Gns 2,400.

HOLBEIN, Thérèse
Austrian, 19th century.
Born 1785, in Graz; died 1859, in Vienna.
Painter, watercolourist, draughtsman, engraver. Landscapes.

She worked in Vienna from 1814. Le Blanc mentions a series of thirty landscapes by her.

AUCTION RECORDS:
VIENNA, 12 Sept 1985, *View and Landscape of Austria* (watercolour, series of 30 works, 11 3/4 x 19 3/4 ins / 30 x 50 cm) ATS 32,000.

HOLBEK, Johannes
Danish, 19th century.
Born 13 November 1872, in Aarby; died 14 May 1903, in Copenhagen.
Draughtsman, caricaturist, painter.

Johannes Holbek studied in Paris with Gustave Moreau and Jean-Léon Gérôme. He worked mostly as a caricaturist.

HOLBEN, H.
German, 16th century.
Painter. Portraits.

Gotha museum possesses a triple portrait by H. Holben.

HOLBERG, Richard A.
American, 20th century.
Born 11 March 1889, in Wisconsin; died 1942.
Painter, illustrator.

Richard Holberg was a member of the Salmagundi Club and the Boston Arts Club.

HOLBERTON, Wakeman
American, 19th century.
Born 1 September 1839, in New York; died 4 January 1898.
Painter. Genre scenes.

Wakeman Holberton was a great lover of hunting and sport, both of which provided numerous subjects for his work.

HOLBLOCK, Jan Cornelis
Dutch, 17th century.
Born c. 1612; died 1679; buried 3 September in Amsterdam.
Painter.

Jan Cornelis Holblock painted Italianate landscapes in the style of Lingelbach and Both.

HOLBÖ, Kritsen
Norwegian, 19th century.
Born 13 September 1869, in Vaage.
Landscape artist.

Kritsen Holbö participated in the Exposition Universelle of 1900 in Paris.

HOLBROOKE, John
Irish, 19th century.
Born c. 1778.
Engraver, lithographer.

John Holbrooke worked in Dublin.

HOLBROOKE, William Henry
Irish, 19th century.
Born 1805, in Dublin.
Engraver.

William Holbrooke was the son and collaborator of John Holbrooke. He continued his father's work after the latter's death.

HOLCK, Cathalyutje Willems van der
Dutch, 17th century.
Died 1651.
Painter.

In 1648, Cathalyutje Willems van der Holck was a member of the painters' guild in The Hague.

HOLCK, Olaus Kröger
Norwegian, 19th century.
Born c. 1820; died 31 May 1876.
Active in Christiania (now Oslo).
Miniaturist, lithographer.

There is a known *Self-portrait* in miniature by Olaus Holck.

HOLD, Abel
British, 19th century.
Born 1815; died 1891.
Painter. Genre scenes, still-lifes, animals.

Abel Hold was active in London from 1849 and 1890.

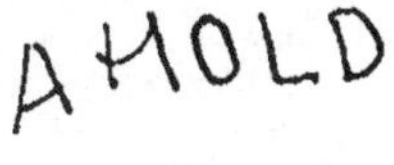

AUCTION RECORDS:
AUCHTERARDER, 28 Aug 1979, *Pheasants and Capercaillies* (1899, oil on canvas, a pair, 11 x 15 ins / 28 x 38 cm) GBP 750. EDINBURGH, 30 Aug 1988, *Opening of the Grouse Shooting Season* (1884, oil on canvas, 27 1/4 x 35 3/4 ins / 69 x 91 cm) GBP 4,950. PERTH, 28 Aug 1989, *Red-legged Partridge* (1876, oil on canvas, 12 x 18 1/2 ins / 30.5 x 47 cm) GBP 880. EDINBURGH, 22 Nov 1989, *Pair of Red-legged Partridge in the Heather* (1886, oil on canvas, 25 x 30 ins / 63.5 x 76.2 cm) GBP 935. GLASGOW, 6 Feb 1990, *Grouse-shooting* (oil on canvas, 18 x 24 ins / 46 x 61 cm) GBP 2,310. GLASGOW, 5 Feb 1991, *Grouse* (oil on canvas, 22 1/2 x 31 ins / 57 x 79 cm) GBP 1,540. LONDON, 7 Oct 1992, *Grouse* (oil on canvas, 16 x 20 ins / 40.5 x 51 cm) GBP 880. GLASGOW, 1 Feb 1994, *Pair of Grouse* (oil on canvas, 12 x 10 ins / 30.5 x 25.5 cm) GBP 690. LONDON, 15 March 1994, *Dead Grouse in the Heather* (1887, oil on canvas, 16 1/4 x 20 1/2 ins / 41.4 x 52 cm) GBP 4,025. LONDON, 7 Nov 1996, *Bird's Nest* (1853, oil on canvas, 10 x 12 ins / 25.4 x 30.4 cm) GBP 2,070. LONDON, 8 Nov 1996, *Squirrels* (oil on canvas, 16 1/4 x 20 ins / 41 x 51.1 cm) GBP 8,500. LONDON, 18 Dec 1997, *Dead Woodcock* (1882, oil on panel, 14 x 18 ins / 35.5 x 45.7 cm) GBP 747. BILLINGSHURST, 14 Sept 1999, *Still-life with Partridge in a Landscape. Still-life with Grouse in a Landscape* (1854, 1859, oil on canvas, a pair, 18 x 24 ins / 46 x 61 cm) GBP 12,000. BILLINGSHURST, 24 July 2000, *Grouse on the Moor* (oil on canvas, 19 x 25 ins / 49 x 64 cm) GBP 2,800. LEYBURN, 23 Nov 2000, *Dead Game on a Moor* (1857, oil on canvas, 27 x 36 ins / 69 x 92 cm) GBP 3,000. AYLSHAM, 3 Aug 2001, *Still-life with Dead Grouse and Snipe on a Bank* (1878, oil on canvas, 20 x 29 ins / 51 x 74 cm) GBP 2,100. LONDON, 5 Sept 2001, *Dead Grouse* (oil on canvas, 17 x 21 ins / 43 x 54 cm) GBP 1,400. LONDON, 15 April 2002, *Cock, Red Grouse and Snipe on the Moor* (1878, oil on canvas, 22 x 30 ins / 56 x 76 cm) GBP 4,500. LONDON, 23 Jan 2003, *Day's Bag* (1849, oil on canvas) GBP 1,500.

HOLD, Ferdinand
British, 18th century.
Active at the end of the 18th century.
Miniaturist.

HOLDA, Stany
Polish, 20th century.
Born 1919, in Nyniov Wicktorowka.
Active in Belgium.
Painter, draughtsman.
Stany Holda studied at the Académie des Beaux-Arts in Charleroi.
MUSEUMS AND GALLERIES:
BAYONNE - CHARLEROI - MAUBEUGE.

HOLDBY
British, 18th century.
Active in Reigate.
Landscape artist.
Holdby exhibited six works at the Society of Artists in London in 1777.

HOLDEN, Albert William
British, 19th century.
Born 1848; died 1932.
Active in London.
Painter. History painting, genre scenes.
Albert Holden exhibited in London at the Royal Academy and the Suffolk Street Gallery from 1881.

MUSEUMS AND GALLERIES:
SYDNEY: *Theft of the Crown Jewels from the Tower of London by Captain Blood in 1671.*

AUCTION RECORDS:
LONDON, 6 Nov 1996, *Billiard Room* (1902, oil on canvas, 34 1/4 x 44 ins / 87 x 112 cm) GBP 5,520. LONDON, 26 Nov 1999, *Storey's Gate and Great George Street looking towards Big Ben* (1883, oil on canvas, 12 x 18 ins / 30 x 46 cm) GBP 1,700. MELBOURNE, 24 Nov 2003, *Tempora Mutantur - Dressed for the Occasion* (oil on canvas, 38 x 20 ins / 96 x 50 cm) AUD 4,200.

HOLDEN, Evelyn B.
British, 19th - 20th century.
Died 1920.
Illustrator.
Evelyn Holden exhibited in London at the Royal Academy and at the Society of Women Artists. In collaboration with her sister Violet, she illustrated many children's books.
BIBLIOGRAPHY:
Osterwalder, Marcus (ed.), *Dictionnaire des illustrateurs 1800-1914*, Ides et Calendes, Neuchâtel, 1989.

HOLDEN, Luisa Jane (Miss)
British, 19th century.
Active in London.
Miniaturist.
Luisa Holden exhibited in London at the Royal Academy between 1840 and 1843.

HOLDEN, Samuel
British, 19th century.
Active in Greenwich.
Painter. Flowers.
Samuel Holden exhibited in London at the Royal Academy between 1845 and 1847.
MUSEUMS AND GALLERIES:
WARRINGTON: six watercolours.

HOLDEN, Sara B.
Canadian, 20th century.
Active in the USA.
Painter. Genre scenes.
After working in Canada, Sara Holden settled in Colorado.
MUSEUMS AND GALLERIES:
MONTREAL: *Widowed but not Abandoned* (1894).

HOLDENRIEDER, Ignaz
German, 18th century.
Active in Mainz in 1727.
Engraver.
He illustrated a Bible.

HOLDER, Edward Henry
British, 19th - 20th century.
Born in Scarborough; died after 1922; c. 1922 according to some sources.
Painter. Figures, landscapes with figures, landscapes.
Edward Holder exhibited frequently in London at the Royal Academy and, from 1864, particularly at the Suffolk Street Gallery.
MUSEUMS AND GALLERIES:
LONDON (Victoria and Albert Mus.): *October in the County of Surrey.*
AUCTION RECORDS:
LONDON, 5 March 1910, *View of Wales*, GBP 6. LONDON, 10 April 1910, *Welsh House* (1882) GBP 5. LONDON, 30 March 1976, *View of a Village* (1890, oil on canvas, 19 1/2 x 29 1/4 ins / 49.5 x 74 cm) GBP 420. PERTH, 19 April 1977, *Flock of Sheep in a Mountain Landscape* (oil on canvas, 23 1/4 x 35 ins / 59 x 89 cm) GBP 600. LONDON, 27 March 1979, *Gomshall, near Dorking, Surrey* (oil on canvas, 19 1/4 x 29 1/4 ins / 49 x 74.5 cm) GBP 1,300. LONDON, 23 Nov 1982, *Sheep in a Landscape* (oil on canvas, 13 x 33 ins / 33 x 84 cm) GBP 1,050. LONDON, 13 June 1984, *Hilly Landscape* (oil on canvas, 24 x 40 ins / 61 x 101.5 cm) GBP 2,200. LONDON, 3 June 1988, *The Bathers* (1886, oil on canvas, 36 1/4 x 28 1/4 ins / 92 x 71.7 cm) GBP

3,740. LONDON, 21 March 1990, *Child Playing near Village Houses* (1891, oil on canvas, 20 x 30 ins / 51 x 76 cm) GBP 7,920. LONDON, 5 June 1991, *Harvest Time* (1896, oil on canvas, 13 x 34 ins / 33 x 86.5 cm) GBP 3,080. LONDON, 3 Feb 1993, *Night Clouds Coming up Reigate Heath, Surrey* (1894, oil on canvas, 13 x 34 ins / 33 x 86.5 cm) GBP 782. LONDON, 6 Nov 1995, *Lynmouth in Devon* (oil on canvas, 20 x 30 1/4 ins / 50.7 x 77 cm) GBP 3,220. BOSTON, 12 March 1999, *Ifley Mill on the Thames* (oil on canvas, 13 x 34 ins / 33 x 86 cm) USD 2,900. BILLINGSHURST, 18 May 1999, *Children Playing beneath an Apple Tree near a Farmhouse* (oil on canvas, 12 x 33 ins / 31 x 85 cm) GBP 4,500. LONDON, 3 June 1999, *Streatly on Thames* (oil on canvas, 20 x 30 ins / 51 x 76 cm) GBP 6,000. LONDON, 8 June 2000, *On Reigate Heath* (1893, oil on canvas, 13 x 34 ins / 33 x 86 cm) GBP 1,900. MARKET HARBOROUGH, 5 Sept 2000, *Landscape with Figures in the foreground* (1893, oil on canvas, 13 x 35 ins / 33 x 88 cm) GBP 2,000. CAMBRIDGE, 22 March 2001, *Farmyard with Figures Resting beside a Hay Cart* (1896, oil on canvas, 20 x 31 ins / 51 x 80 cm) GBP 3,000. LEYBURN, 25 April 2002, *Hackness, near Scarborough, Yorkshire* (1885, oil on board, 13 x 18 ins / 34 x 46 cm) GBP 1,000. LONDON, 7 Nov 2002, *Thunderstorm Passing over Lands End* (oil on canvas, arched top, 40 x 30 ins / 102 x 76 cm) GBP 4,200. LONDON, 23 Jan 2003, *Lynton and Lynmouth from Haliday Hill* (oil on canvas, 20 x 30 ins / 51 x 76 cm) GBP 1,500. COPENHAGEN, 2 Sept 2003, *Waterway through Gorge* (1880, oil on canvas, 24 x 18 ins / 61 x 45 cm) DKK 25,000. HARROGATE, 11 March 2004, *Cliveden on Thames. Figure Fishing from a Punt* (1893, oil on canvas, a pair, 11 x 17 ins / 28 x 44 cm) GBP 1,800. LONDON, 27 May 2004, *First Gleam, Early Morning on Reigate Heath* (1894, oil on canvas, 13 x 34 ins / 33 x 86 cm) GBP 1,800.

HOLDER, Edwin
British, 19th century.
Active in Isleworth.
Painter. Landscapes with figures, landscapes, seascapes.

Edwin Holder exhibited in London at the British Institution from 1856 to 1864.

HOLDER, Franz von
Belgian, 20th century.
Born 26 October 1882, in Ixelles (Brussels); died 15 March 1919, in Geneva, Switzerland.
Painter. Portraits, genre scenes, landscapes.

Von Holder studied under his father and Alfred Cluysenaar at the Académie des Beaux Arts in Brussels. His portraits and genre subjects are usually situated against landscape backgrounds.

MUSEUMS AND GALLERIES:
BRUGES (Groeningemus.): *Interior* - BRUSSELS - GHENT - IXELLES.

AUCTION RECORDS:
LOKEREN, 21 Feb 1987, *Sunny Garden* (1912, oil on panel, 20 x 27 3/4 ins / 50.5 x 70.5 cm) BEF 360,000. LOKEREN, 28 May 1988, *The Artist's Father* (1911, oil on panel, 22 x 15 1/4 ins / 55 x 39 cm) BEF 240,000. LOKEREN, 9 March 1996, *Sunny Landscape* (1910, oil on canvas, 31 1/2 x 39 1/4 ins / 80 x 100 cm) BEF 95,000.

HOLDER, Johann Michael
German, 19th century.
Born 18 January 1796, in Hildrizhausen (Württemberg); died 27 March 1861, in Stuttgart.
Painter, miniaturist.

He trained in Stuttgart, Munich, Dresden, Prague and Paris. In 1834, he was an honorary member of the Dresden academy.

HOLDERIUS, pseudonym of Van Holder, Jan
Belgian, 20th century.
Born 1908, in Ruislede; died 1980, in Laethem-St-Martin.
Painter, draughtsman.

Holderius was a self-taught artist. His paintings are in a traditional style.

HOLDERMANN, Carl Wilhelm
German, 19th century.
Active in Weimar in 1824.
Painter, engraver (etching).

HOLDERNESS
British, 17th century.
Active in England at the time of Charles I.
Painter.

No works by Holderness have been identified.

HOLDING, Frederick
British, 19th century.
Born 1817; died 1874.
Watercolourist.

Frederick Holding was the brother of Henry James Holding.

HOLDING, G.
British, 19th century.
Sculptor. Allegorical subjects.

HOLDING, Henry James
British, 19th century.
Born 1833, in Manchester; died 9 August 1872, in Paris.
Painter. Landscapes, seascapes.

Henry James Holding, one of a family of painters, made a reputation for himself in Manchester. He went to Paris, where he was to die of consumption. He exhibited in London from 1867 to 1870, but showed his work mainly in Manchester.

AUCTION RECORDS:
NEW YORK, 29 Oct 1992, *Fishermen on a Rocky Coast in Rough Weather* (1863, oil on canvas, 33 1/2 x 50 1/4 ins / 85.4 x 127.6 cm) USD 2,860. LONDON, 11 June 2004, *Logging Wagon* (1858, oil on canvas, 35 x 50 ins / 88 x 128 cm) GBP 7,500.

HOLDSTOCK, Alfred Worsley
Canadian, 19th century.
Born 1820; died 1901.
Pastellist, draughtsman. Landscapes, waterscapes.

AUCTION RECORDS:
TORONTO, 5 Nov 1979, *On the Gatineau, Montreal* (oil on canvas, 12 1/2 x 19 1/2 ins / 32 x 49.5 cm) CAD 1,500. TORONTO, 26 May 1981, *Rapids* (watercolour, 7 1/2 x 10 1/2 ins / 18.8 x 26.6 cm) CAD 3,200. TORONTO, 27 May 1981, *Scocomie River* (coloured chalk, 13 1/4 x 21 1/4 ins / 33.8 x 53.8 cm) CAD 1,600. MONTREAL, 17 Oct 1988, *On the Becancour River in Quebec Province* (pastel, 13 x 22 ins / 33 x 55 cm) CAD 2,200. TORONTO, 12 June 1989, *Niagara Falls* (pastel, 16 1/2 x 26 1/4 ins / 41.8 x 66.7 cm) CAD 2,600. MONTREAL, 30 April 1990, *Encampment at Ottawa River* (pastel, 12 1/2 x 19 1/4 ins / 32 x 49 cm) CAD 2,750. MONTREAL, 5 Nov 1990, *Thousand Islands from Wolfe Island* (pastel, 12 1/4 x 19 1/4 ins / 31 x 49 cm) CAD 1,430. MONTREAL, 4 June 1991, *Around Gore Island* (pastel, 13 x 19 3/4 ins / 33 x 50.2 cm) CAD 1,200. TORONTO, 24 May 2000, *River with Hares. Wahasee Rapids, CW* (pastel, a pair, 14 x 21 ins / 36 x 53 cm) CAD 2,500. CALGARY, 28 May 2001, *On the Ottawa* (oil and pastel on canvas, 13 x 20 ins / 34 x 52 cm) CAD 2,400. MONTREAL, 10 Dec 2002, *Fishing near the Waterfalls in Autumn* (oil on board, 10 x 14 ins / 25 x 35 cm) CAD 2,500. MONTREAL, 10 Dec 2002, *Lower Falls* (pastel, 13 x 22 ins / 34 x 55 cm) CAD 3,200.

HOLE, Henry
British, 19th century.
Active at the beginning of the 19th century.

Engraver (wood).
Henry Hole worked with Bewick, collaborating with him on a book about the birds of England. A large inheritance led to his abandoning his artistic career.

HOLE, William
British, 17th century.
Active in London c. 1613.
Engraver (burin).
William Hole is known mainly for portraits and for the frontispieces he engraved for bookshops.

HOLE, William Brassey
British, 19th - 20th century.
Born 7 November 1846, in Salisbury; died 22 October 1917, in Edinburgh.
Painter, watercolourist, engraver. Religious subjects, genre scenes.
William Brassey Hole was a member of the Royal Scottish Academy, the Royal Society of Painters in Watercolours and the Royal Society of Painter-Etchers and Engravers. He showed two etchings at the Royal Academy from 1873, and exhibited *If Thou Had'st Known* in Edinburgh in 1885 and in Brussels in 1897.

MUSEUMS AND GALLERIES:
EDINBURGH (Royal Scottish Academy): *If Thou Had'st Known* (1885, oil on canvas).
AUCTION RECORDS:
AUCHTERARDER, 1 Sept 1981, *The End of the '45* (1878, oil on canvas, 33 x 49 ins / 84 x 124.5 cm) GBP 6,000. AUCHTERARDER, 28 Aug 1984, *Matters of State* (1878, oil on canvas, 36 x 28 ins / 91.4 x 71.1 cm) GBP 3,600. GLASGOW, 30 Jan 1985, *The End of the '45* (1878, oil on canvas, 33 3/4 x 49 1/4 ins / 86 x 125 cm) GBP 6,000. LONDON, 3 Nov 1989, *The Heretic's Hiding Place* (1878, oil on canvas, 32 3/4 x 42 1/4 ins / 83 x 107 cm) GBP 935. GLASGOW, 6 Feb 1990, *The Book-lover* (1878, oil on canvas, 18 1/4 x 15 ins / 46.5 x 38 cm) GBP 935. CHELSEA, 7 March 2000, *Lesson in Astronomy* (1879, oil on canvas, 14 x 17 ins / 35 x 44 cm) GBP 1,600.

HOLEMAN, Marguerite
Belgian, 19th century.
Died 8 June 1905, in Uccle, near Brussels.
Painter.
Marguerite Holeman is known primarily for her humorous genre pieces.

HOLENSTEIN, Werner
Swiss, 20th century.
Born 1932; died 1985.
Painter. Landscapes, seascapes, interiors with figures, flowers.
AUCTION RECORDS:
ZURICH, 2 Dec 1994, *Interior with a Bouquet* (1975, oil on canvas, 25 1/2 x 32 ins / 65 x 81 cm) CHF 2,900. ZURICH, 3 April 1996, *On the Coast near Positano* (1977, oil on canvas, 23 3/4 x 28 3/4 ins / 60.5 x 73.2 cm) CHF 1,600.

HOLESZ, Ludwig
Polish, 20th century.
Born 1920, near Katowice.
Painter. Scenes with figures.
A self-taught painter, Ludwig Holesz paints symbolic scenes representing the past or the future.

HOLEWELL, Thomas
French, 15th century.
Active in Nantes in 1408.
Sculptor.
Thomas Holewell worked for Nantes Cathedral.

HOLEWINSKY, Josef
Polish, 19th - 20th century.
Born 1848, in Warsaw; died 20 January 1917, in Warsaw.
Painter, engraver.
Josef Holewinsky was a pupil of Gerson and Styli. He is known particularly for his portraits.

HOLFELD, Hippolyte Dominique
French, 19th century.
Born 22 November 1804, in Paris; died 13 January 1872, in Paris.
Painter. History painting, portraits, local scenes.
Holfeld's masters were Abel de Pujol and Hersent. He entered the École des Beaux-Arts on 9 November 1822. He came second in the Rome Prize in 1832. His work was regularly featured at the Salon from 1831 to 1870 - particularly his portraits. There was a retrospective exhibition of his works in 1872. His paintings have also been frequently reproduced as lithographs. He was an archivist for the Association of Painters, Sculptors, etc., which was founded by Baron Taylor.
MUSEUMS AND GALLERIES:
BORDEAUX: *Marie Antoinette in Prison* (studies for the painting of the same name) - CAMBRAI: *African Hunters and a Young Arab Woman* - SENS: *Baptism of Constantine.*
AUCTION RECORDS:
PARIS, 12 June 1929, *Portrait of the Empress Eugénie,* FRF 1,350. ENGHIEN-LES-BAINS, 17 June 1979, *Young Girl in a Red Dress* (1871, oil on canvas, 28 3/4 x 23 1/2 ins / 73 x 60 cm) FRF 4,800. LONDON, 8 Oct 1986, *Religious Education* (1845, oil on canvas, oval, 23 x 28 ins / 58.5 x 71 cm) GBP 1,800. NEW YORK, 17 Oct 1991, *Little Girl; Little Boy* (1863, oil on canvas, a pair, each 26 x 21 1/4 ins / 65.1 x 54 cm) USD 22,550. PARIS, 30 March 2004, *Homage to the Emperor, Paris* (1863, oil on cardboard, oval, 10 x 15 ins / 26 x 39 cm) EUR 7,100.

HOLGATE, Edwin Headley
Canadian, 20th century.
Born 19 August 1892, in Allandale (Ontario); died 1977, in Montreal.
Painter, engraver (wood). Nudes, portraits, landscapes. Murals.
Group of Seven.
In 1904 Edwin Holgate enrolled at the school of the Art Association of Montreal, where he studied under William Brymner. In Paris in 1912 he worked at the Académie de la Grande-Chaumière with Claudio Castelucho, then with Lucien Simon and René Ménard. After World War I, which he spent in France in the Canadian army, Holgate returned to Canada, then returned to spend two years in France, from 1920 to 1922, and enrolled at the Académie Colarossi. In 1922 he opened a wood engraving studio at the School of Fine Arts in Montreal. In 1930 he belatedly joined the Group of Seven, but was primarily associated with the Montreal painters of Beaver Hall and was a founder member, in 1933, of the Canadian Group of Painters. He exhibited mainly in Montreal, in 1922, 1931, 1933, 1937, 1946, 1947, 1953 and 1970, but also in Quebec City in 1944 and Ottawa in 1975.

Holgate was primarily a painter of nudes and portraits, which he set in landscapes, giving each aspect equal value. This is true of *Nude*, at the Art Gallery of Ontario, Toronto, painted in 1930, and of *Portrait of Herman 'Jackrabbit' Johannsen* at the Montreal Museum of Fine Arts, painted around 1935. The woman's body and rocks on which she is lying on one side, the portrait of the skier on the other and the mountain landscape in the background, are all lit in the same way, giving them all the same sculptural quality, so that figures and natural elements are united by colour, the rendition of the forms and the space.

The same characteristics can be seen in Holgate's wood engravings. He also painted murals for hotels in Ottawa and Vancouver and was very interested in the totem poles he had discovered in British Colombia, painting *Totem Poles, Gitsegiuklas* in 1927.

Bibliography:

Reid, Dennis, *A Concise History of Canadian Painting*, Oxford University Press, Toronto, 1988. *Regards sur les collections du Musée des Beaux-Arts de Montréal*, Musée des Beaux-Arts, Montreal, 1992.

Museums and Galleries:

Hamilton, NJ (AG): *Old Breton Woman* (1921); *Blue Net Festival, Concarneau* (1921); *Ski Tracks* (1935); *Uncle George* (1947) - Montreal (MBA): *Skier: Portrait of Hermann Johannsen, known as Jackrabbit* (c. 1935); *Bathers* (1937) - Ottawa (NG. of Canada): *Suzy* (1921); *Tsimshian Chief* (1926); *Totem Poles, Gitsegiuklas* (1927); *Blacksmith* (1928, wood); *Ludovine* (1930); *Nude in a Landscape* (1930); *Bathers* (1931, wood); *Women Reading* (1933, wood); *Early Autumn* (1938); *Portrait of Stephen Leacock* (1943); *Rainy Day, Heavy Bombers Station* (1943) - Quebec (Mus. du Quebec): *Coolie Girl, Jamaica; Daisy Field, Gaspe Coast* (1936); *Portrait of a Naturalist* (1941) - Toronto (AG of Ontario): *Nude* (1930); *Interior* (1933); *French Submarine* (1941); *Laurentian Cemetery* (1948); *April Thaw* (1950).

Auction records:

Toronto, 27 Oct 1977, *Bidon's Barn, October* (1964, oil on panel, 8½ x 11 ins / 21.5 x 27 cm) CAD 2,900. Toronto, 5 Nov 1979, *Study of a Woman* (1957, oil on panel, 10½ x 8½ ins / 26.5 x 21.5 cm) CAD 3,900. Toronto, 1 June 1982, *St Paul's Bay* (1924, oil on canvas, 17¾ x 21¼ ins / 45 x 53.8 cm) CAD 26,000. Vancouver, 18 Nov 1999, *Great Bug Pond, Cache River* (1939, oil on canvas, 26 x 30 ins / 66 x 76 cm) CAD 110,000. Toronto, 7 Dec 1999, *Lake Reflections, Mt Tremblant* (oil on canvas, 24 x 24 ins / 60 x 60 cm) CAD 62,000. Vancouver, 9 Nov 2000, *Winter Scene* (1932, pencil, 13 x 9 ins / 32 x 23 cm) CAD 3,250. Toronto, 21 Nov 2000, *Trout Stream, Laurentian Mountains* (oil on panel, 13 x 16 ins / 32 x 40 cm) CAD 46,000. Calgary, 19 Nov 2001, *Nude by a Lake* (wood engraving, 8 x 6 ins / 20 x 16 cm) CAD 3,900. Toronto, 4 Dec 2001, *Laurentian Landscape - Blackberry Island, Lac Tremblant, Quebec* (oil on panel, 12 x 13 ins / 31 x 34 cm) CAD 36,000. Toronto, 18 Nov 2002, *Bathers* (wood engraving, 5 x 4 ins / 12 x 11 cm) CAD 8,500. Toronto, 3 Dec 2002, *Reclining Nude* (charcoal, 21 x 29 ins / 53 x 74 cm) CAD 8,000. Toronto, 18 Nov 2003, *Laurentian Farm* (1952, oil on board, 20 x 22 ins / 51 x 56 cm) CAD 60,000. Toronto, 18 Nov 2003, *The River at Simon Morin Heights* (oil on panel, 9 x 11 ins / 22 x 27 cm) CAD 12,000. Toronto, 31 May 2004, *Mutton Bay, Quebec* (1930, oil on canvas, 9 x 11 ins / 22 x 27 cm) CAD 30,000. Toronto, 1 June 2004, *Beach Logs* (1960, oil on panel, 8 x 10 ins / 21 x 26 cm) CAD 12,000.

HOLIDAY, Gilbert Joseph

British, 20th century.
Born 1879; died 1937.
Painter (gouache), watercolourist, pastellist, draughtsman. Scenes with figures, animals.

Gilbert Joseph Holiday specialised in racing and hunting scenes, although he also painted all kinds of horses, including carthorses.

Auction records:

London, 17 Oct 1984, *The Winning Post* (1929, coloured chalk, 12 x 19 ins / 30.5 x 48 cm) GBP 4,200. London, 30 May 1985, *Through the Gate* (charcoal and coloured chalk, 14 x 21½ ins / 35.5 x 54.5 cm) GBP 3,000. London, 12 June 1986, *29th Division of the Royal Horse Artillery Crossing Hohenzollern Bridge, Cologne, 18 December 1918* (watercolour and gouache, 14¾ x 11½ ins / 37.5 x 29.2 cm) GBP 1,000. London, 4 March 1987, *Waiting for a Mount* (oil on canvas remounted on board, 14 x 18 ins / 35.5 x 46 cm) GBP 3,000. New York, 9 June 1988, *Day at the Races* (gouache and watercolour/paper, 15 x 9¼ ins / 38.1 x 23.5 cm) USD 9,900. London, 8 June 1989, *The Derby at Tattenham Corner* (watercolour and gouache and pastel, 14½ x 24½ ins / 37 x 62.2 cm) GBP 23,100. London, 7 March 1991, *Gone Away, Irish Hunt* (pastel and colouring pencil, 15 x 23½ ins / 38 x 59.5 cm) GBP 7,150. London, 2 May 1991, *Carthorses* (pencil and watercolour, 9 x 11¾ ins / 22 x 30 cm) GBP 1,320. London, 6 June 1991, *Well Turned Out* (watercolour and gouache heightened with white, 15 x 12¾ ins / 38.1 x 32.4 cm) GBP 7,150. London, 18 Dec 1991, *Kelp Cart in Guernsey* (watercolour and gouache, 12¼ x 9 ins / 31 x 23 cm) GBP 1,815. London, 25 Sept 1992, *Finish at Goodwood* (1929, pastel, 11¾ x 18¾ ins / 30 x 47.5 cm) GBP 7,700. London, 24 March 1999, *Grand National* (gouache laid down on card, 6 x 15 ins / 15 x 37 cm) GBP 3,600. Lymington, 29 Sept 1999, *Fall at the Fence, Aintree* (gouache, 11 x 18 ins / 28 x 45 cm) GBP 5,200. London, 26 May 2000, *Well Turned Out* (black crayon, watercolour and gouache heightened with white, 15 x 13 ins / 38 x 33 cm) GBP 14,000. London, 15 June 2000, *Glorious Goodwood* (charcoal and pastel, 14 x 22 ins / 35 x 57 cm) GBP 11,000. Billingshurst, 18 July 2001, *Carry On Sir* (pastel, 17 x 15 ins / 43 x 37 cm) GBP 5,500. Bristol, 2 Oct 2001, *Ascot* (pastel, 13 x 23 ins / 34 x 58 cm) GBP 8,200. Haslemere, 6 Feb 2002, *Six Horses and Three Soldiers Pulling a Cannon in World War I* (watercolour, 9 x 15 ins / 23 x 38 cm) GBP 3,600. Bishops Stortford, 30 April 2002, *Grand National* (oil on canvas, 18 x 24 ins / 46 x 61 cm) GBP 16,000. London, 12 June 2003, *Grand National* (oil on canvas, 18 x 24 ins / 46 x 61 cm) GBP 9,500. Lewes, 21 Oct 2003, *Leppin Fantasia, Grand National* (oil on canvas) GBP 5,500. London, 15 June 2004, *Ireland* (pastel, 15 x 21 ins / 37 x 53 cm) GBP 1,700.

HOLIDAY, Henry James

British, 19th - 20th century.
Born 17 June 1839, in London; died 15 April 1927, in London.
Painter, watercolourist, draughtsman, illustrator, stained glass painter. History painting, portraits, genre scenes.

Henry James Holiday worked in London, where he exhibited at the Royal Academy and at the Grosvenor Gallery from 1858. In 1876 he illustrated the first edition of Lewis Carroll's poem *The Hunting of the Snark*. These illustrations have a fantastical quality that anticipates Surrealism.

Museums and Galleries:

Liverpool (Walker AG): *Dante and Beatrice* (1883, oil on canvas).

Auction records:

London, 29 Oct 1991, *Study for an Allegory of Virtue* (black chalk heightened with white/brown paper, 20¼ x 11¼ ins / 51.5 x 28.3 cm) GBP 1,045. London, 12 June 1992, *Portrait Bust of Mrs Wheeler* (pencil and red chalk, 10½ x 7¾ ins / 26.7 x 19.7 cm) GBP 990. London, 4 Nov 1994, *Workmen Building an Observatory for the Solar Eclipse at Poodoocottah in 1871* (watercolour heightened with white, 10 x 7 ins / 25.1 x 17.5 cm) GBP 3,680. London, 25 Nov 2004, *Duet* (pencil and chalk, 15 x 21 ins / 38 x 53 cm) GBP 3,400. London, 25 Nov 2004, *Duet* (watercolour, 30 x 43 ins / 77 x 108 cm) GBP 8,500.

HOLINBERG, Gustaf Wermer
Swedish, 19th century.
Born 1830, in Helsinki; died 24 September 1860, in Düsseldorf.
Painter.
Gustaf Holinberg was a pupil of Hans Frederik Gude.

HOLL, Benjamin
American, 19th century.
Born 11 March 1808; died June 1884, in Marisania.
Engraver.
Benjamin Holl was the brother of William Holl the Younger. He engraved portraits in London before settling in the USA.

HOLL, Charles
British, 19th century.
Died 1882.
Engraver.
Charles Holl was the son of William Holl the Elder. He executed several portraits.

HOLL, Elias or H. F.
German, 17th century.
Active in Nuremberg c. 1638.
Engraver.
He engraved from Cesare Reverdino. He used to signed *H. F.*, which suggests that the name Elias was wrong. Le Blanc mentions a series of 12 plates by him depicting *The Months of the Year*. He was also a goldsmith.

HOLL, Erwin
20th - 21st century.
Born 1957.
Painter.
Erwin Holl exhibited his work in 1992-1993 at the museum in Valence. His work developed, and he now creates image-objects rather than actual pictures.

HOLL, Francis
British, 19th century.
Born 23 March 1815, in London; died 14 January 1884, in Milford.
Engraver.
Francis Holl was the son and pupil of William Holl the Younger. He is known particularly for his portrait engravings after drawings by George Richmond. He was also the author of a number of very rare prints depicting members of the family of Queen Victoria, of which only those of Prince Albert and Princess Alice have been published. He also made some engravings of genre subjects. He was made an associate member of the Royal Academy in 1883.

HOLL, Francis Montague, called Frank (Sir)
British, 19th century.
Born 4 July 1845, in London; died 31 July 1888.
Painter. History painting, portraits, genre scenes.
Frank Holl was the son of the engraver Francis Holl. He studied at the Royal Academy Schools in London and was awarded a travel bursary in 1868 for his painting *The Lord Giveth and the Lord Taketh Away*. He only spent a year away, returning to take his place among the young English painters of his day. The works he showed at the Royal Academy brought him considerable fame, particularly his painting *Newgate* of 1879. Thereafter, he was to receive many commissions for portraits. His early death was due to a serious heart problem.

Holl is considered one of the best portraitists of his period. He was made an associate member of the Royal Academy in 1878 and a full member in 1883.

BIBLIOGRAPHY:
Reynolds, A.M., *The Life and Work of Frank Holl*, Methuen, London, 1912.

MUSEUMS AND GALLERIES:
BIRMINGHAM (Mus. and AG): *John Bright*; *Edmond Tonks* - BRISTOL (City Mus. & AG): *Portrait of James Harvey* (oil on canvas); *Miss Rachel Harvey of Shirehampton* (oil on canvas) - LEEDS (City AG): *'I am the Resurrection and the Life' (The Village Funeral)* (1872, oil on canvas) - LONDON (Corporation of Trinity House): *King Edward VII* (1887) - LONDON (National Portrait Gal.): *Francis Montague ('Frank') Holl* (1863, oil on canvas) - LONDON (Royal Academy of Arts): *Portrait of Sir John Everett Millais* (1886, oil on canvas, competition piece) - LONDON (Tate Collection): *Hush!* (1877, oil on canvas); *Hushed* (1877, oil on canvas); two portraits - MELBOURNE (Nat. Gal. of Victoria): *Returning from the Frontier*; *Burial of the First-born* - READING: *Portrait of W.I. Palmer*.

AUCTION RECORDS:
LONDON, 12 June 1908, *Alone* (1873) GBP 39. LONDON, 24 June 1909, *Departure of the Emigrants*, GBP 147. LONDON, 9 July 1909, *Newgate*, GBP 94. LONDON, 4 Dec 1909, *In Spring* (1880) GBP 44. LONDON, 4 July 1910, *Anxiety*, GBP 36. LONDON, 18 March 1911, *Hidden* (1879) GBP 63. LONDON, 9 June 1911, *Portrait of General Wolseley*, GBP 304. LONDON, Dec 1921, *Gone*, GBP 21. LONDON, June 1922, *Burial of the First-born*, GBP 33. LONDON, 20 March 1925, *Fairies' Gifts*, GBP 94; *Girl Resting in a Wheatfield*, GBP 33. COLOGNE, 22 June 1979, *Children Fishing by the Thames* (oil on canvas, 24 1/2 x 20 ins / 62 x 51 cm) DEM 7,500. LONDON, 6 March 1981, *Desperate Hope* (1875, oil on canvas, 37 1/2 x 53 1/2 ins / 95.2 x 136 cm) GBP 4,000. LONDON, 15 March 1983, *First-born* (1877, oil on card, 13 3/4 x 20 ins / 35 x 50.5 cm) GBP 2,800. MONTEVIDEO, 8 May 1986, *Deserter* (1874, oil on canvas, 36 1/2 x 54 ins / 93 x 137 cm) USD 10,200. LONDON, 26 June 1987, *Deserter* (1874, oil on canvas, 36 1/4 x 53 1/2 ins / 92 x 136 cm) GBP 8,000. LONDON, 23 Sept 1988, *Rest on the Roadside* (1879, oil on card, 15 1/4 x 19 1/4 ins / 39 x 49 cm) GBP 1,870. NEW YORK, 28 Feb 1990, *Convalescent Girl* (1867, oil on canvas, 18 1/2 x 22 1/4 ins / 47 x 56.5 cm) USD 104,500. LONDON, 5 Nov 1993, *By the Fireside* (1878, oil on canvas, 14 x 18 ins / 35.5 x 45.7 cm) GBP 7,130. LONDON, 9 June 1994, *Deserter* (1874, oil on canvas, 36 1/4 x 53 1/2 ins / 92 x 136 cm) GBP 11,500. LONDON, 10 March 1995, *Soldier in a Railway Carriage* (oil on canvas, 22 1/4 x 18 ins / 56.2 x 46 cm) GBP 2,760. LONDON, 5 June 1996, *Waiting* (1879, oil on canvas, 35 x 46 1/2 ins / 89 x 118 cm) GBP 36,700. LONDON, 7 Nov 1997, *Hidden* (1879, oil on canvas, 30 x 43 1/4 ins / 76 x 110 cm) GBP 40,000. CASTLECOMER, 27 July 1999, *Portrait of General Lord Wolseley* (c. 1883, oil on canvas, 58 x 38 ins / 147 x 96 cm) IEP 4,250. BILLINGSHURST, 14 Sept 1999, *Contemplation* (oil on canvas, 22 x 16 ins / 56 x 40 cm) GBP 2,000. LONDON, 26 March 2002, *Children of the Sea* (oil on canvas, 30 x 22 ins / 76 x 56 cm) GBP 3,800. LONDON, 28 Nov 2002, *Wide Wide World* (1873, oil on canvas, 30 x 25 ins / 76 x 64 cm) GBP 45,000. LONDON, 23 March 2004, *Boulogne Fisher Girl* (1866, oil on canvas, 22 x 16 ins / 56 x 41 cm) GBP 4,500. LONDON, 9 June 2004, *Absconded* (1879, oil on canvas, 30 x 43 ins / 76 x 110 cm) GBP 76,000.

HOLL, John
British, 18th century.
Engraver (burin).

HOLL, Mina
Maiden name: Geyer
German, 19th century.
Born 14 April 1836, in Augsburg; died 15 September 1871.
Painter.
She is credited with a *Portrait of Luther*.

HOLL, William, the Elder
British, 18th - 19th century.
Born 1771; died 1 December 1838, in London.
Engraver.

William Holl the Elder was a pupil of Benjamin Smith. He is known particularly for his engravings of the antique marbles in the British Museum. He was the father of William Holl the Younger and Francis Holl.

HOLL, William, the Younger
British, 19th century.
Born February 1807, in Plaistow (Essex); died 30 January 1871, in London.
Engraver.

William Holl the Younger was the son and pupil of William Holl the Elder. He mainly engraved portraits, often using a stippling technique. He also provided an illustration to Moore's poems and engraved some genre subjects after Frith, Goodall and George Richmond. He exhibited 22 works at the Royal Academy in London between 1860 and 1871.

HOLLAENDER, Alphons or Alfonso
German, 19th - 20th century.
Born c. 1845, in Berlin or in Regensburg; died 1923, in Florence.
Painter. Genre scenes, landscapes, architectural views.

Hollaender made his debut in Berlin around 1868 and continued to take part in exhibitions there, but he settled in Florence in 1870.

AUCTION RECORDS:
MILAN, 15 March 1977, *Washerwoman* (oil on panel, 23 x 83/4 ins / 57.5 x 22.5 cm) ITL 1,100,000. MILAN, 20 March 1980, *Woodcutter* (oil on canvas, 193/4 x 251/2 ins / 50 x 65 cm) ITL 2,000,000. MILAN, 23 March 1983, *Sacristy* (oil on canvas, 121/2 x 193/4 ins / 32 x 50 cm) ITL 3,500,000. MILAN, 25 Oct 1995, *Trawlers Grounded on a Beach* (oil on panel, 6 x 10 ins / 15 x 24.5 cm) ITL 8,050,000.

HOLLAGAN, M. J.
British, 18th - 19th century.
Painter. Landscapes. Stage sets.

M.J. Hollagan exhibited frequently at the Royal Academy in London between 1795 and 1809.

HOLLAIN, Louis
French, 19th century.
Born 14 July 1813, in Iwuy (Nord).
Sculptor. Figures. Statues.

The town of Cambrai in northern France granted Hollain a pension to go and study at the École des Beaux-Arts in Paris.

MUSEUMS AND GALLERIES:
CAMBRAI: *Young Slave* (statue).

HOLLAIN, N. F. J.
French, 18th century.
Born c. 1761, in Valenciennes.
Painter, sculptor. Portraits, landscapes.

N. F. J. Hollain exhibited at the Salon between 1791 and 1799.

AUCTION RECORDS:
LONDON, 9 Dec 1976, *Bust of an Old Man Smiling; Bust of an Old Woman* (terracotta, h. 71/2 ins / 19 cm) GBP 500. PARIS, 21 March 1980, *Bust of a Man* (terracotta, h. 171/4 ins / 44 cm) FRF 9,600.

HOLLAMS, Mabel Frances
British, 19th - 20th century.
Active from 1897 to 1934 in Tonbridge.
Painter. Genre scenes.

AUCTION RECORDS:
NEW YORK, 9 June 1988, *Portait of the Fox-terriers Raffle and Rally of the North Cotswold Pack* (oil on panel, 17 x 21 ins / 43.2 x 53.3 cm) USD 3,300; *Nero* (oil on panel, 13 x 18 ins / 33 x 45.7 cm) USD 2,420. LONDON, 14 Feb 1990, *Sally and Susan, a Couple of Red Setters* (oil on panel, 5 x 171/2 ins / 13 x 44.6 cm) GBP 715. LONDON, 19 Dec 1991, *Peasant Turning a Haycart* (oil on canvas, 491/2 x 73 ins / 125.7 x 185.4 cm) GBP 7,700. LONDON, 3 June 1992, *Anne on Twinkle; Young Boy on a Chestnut Pony* (1934, oil on card, a pair, each 16 x 20 ins / 40.5 x 51 cm) GBP 2,860. NEW YORK, 3 June 1994, *The Hunter St Andrew* (oil on panel, 131/2 x 18 ins / 34.3 x 45.7 cm) USD 8,625. LONDON, 17 Oct 1996, *Silverlane, a Thoroughbred; Sandboy, a Thoroughbred* (oil on panel, a pair, 131/2 x 173/4 ins / 34.3 x 45 cm) GBP 2,875. LONDON, 10 July 1997, *A Red Setter* (oil on canvas, 15 x 12 ins / 38.2 x 30.5 cm) GBP 1,380. LONDON, 18 Dec 1997, *Midget, A Dapple-grey Pony in the Stable Yard* (1924, oil on panel, 121/2 x 16 ins / 31.8 x 40.6 cm) GBP 747. LONDON, 26 Nov 1999, *Judith, Chestnut Hunter* (1928, oil on canvas, 12 x 17 ins / 30 x 43 cm) GBP 3,000. LONDON, 26 Nov 1999, *Wusie, a Long-haired Dachshund* (1950, oil on panel, 15 x 19 ins / 37 x 49 cm) GBP 3,800. BILLINGSHURST, 24 July 2000, *Turning the Wagon* (1901, oil on canvas, 48 x 72 ins / 122 x 184 cm) GBP 3,200. BILLINGSHURST, 23 Oct 2000, *Jubie and Kirstie* (oil on panel, 14 x 20 ins / 36 x 51 cm) GBP 2,600. CHESTER, 28 Feb 2001, *Meg, a Grey Mare* (oil on panel, 13 x 18 ins / 34 x 45 cm) GBP 3,600. LONDON, 14 June 2001, *Favourite Hunter* (1937, oil on board, 17 x 21 ins / 43 x 53 cm) GBP 6,500. NEW YORK, 12 Feb 2002, *Scrap, a Sealyham* (1948, oil on board, 15 x 20 ins / 39 x 52 cm) USD 6,500. LONDON, 7 March 2002, *Saddled Liver Chestnut Hunter in a Paddock* (1927, oil on canvas, 16 x 21 ins / 41 x 54 cm) GBP 2,500. LONDON, 26 March 2003, *Chestnut Hunter in a Field* (1948, oil on canvas, 13 x 20 ins / 34 x 50 cm) GBP 2,000. LONDON, 27 Nov 2003, *Monmouthshire Hunt* (1937, oil on canvas, 31 x 39 ins / 80 x 100 cm) GBP 6,000. LONDON, 10 June 2004, *Susie, a Terrier* (1928, oil on panel, 13 x 9 ins / 33 x 24 cm) GBP 2,200. LONDON, 3 Nov 2004, *Violet Seeley on Henry of Navarre* (oil on canvas, 30 x 35 ins / 76 x 89 cm) GBP 5,000.

HOLLAN, Alexandre
Hungarian, 20th century.
Born 1933, in Budapest.
Active in France from 1956.
Painter, watercolourist, draughtsman. Landscapes, still-lifes.

Alexandre Hollan studied at the École des Arts Decoratifs and École des Beaux-Arts in Paris. He settled in France, dividing his time between Paris and the Gard region in the south of France.

His works feature water, trees (he once spent a whole summer in the Gard region painting nothing but one tree again and again) and still-lifes of jars, jugs and fruit, painted in an abstract-nuagiste style where things and objects dissolve in the floods of black washed with green or red and pierced through with light. Sometimes he only uses charcoal, with which he conveys both the brightness of dawn and the deepest shadows of dusk. The poet Yves Bonnefoy, who has written several times about Hollan's work, most notably in his book *La Journée d'Alexandre Hollan* (*A Day in the Life of Alexandre Hollan*), has said: 'a little of the absolute can still be glimpsed showing through the branches and shining on the water of the spring'.

Collective exhibition from 1979 include: Munich Salon (1982); Stockholm and the FIAC (Foire Internationale d'Art Contemporain), Paris (1983); Salon d'Art Graphique Actuel (SAGA), Paris (1988); *L'Oeuvre - Le Sacré*, Annemasse, Joigny and Clamecy (1991); *L'Oeuvre et le Regard*, Brussels, Villeneuve-d'Ascq and Hattingen (1993); and *Yves Bonnefoy*, Tours château.

Solo exhibitions include: Munich (1978); Hanover (1980, 1982, 1985, 1987 and 1992); Galerie Nane Stern, Paris (1983, 1986 and 1991); Geneva and Munich (1989; Maubeuge museum (1991); Montpellier and Lille (1992); Villeneuve-d'Ascq, Joigny and Clamecy museum and at Vasarely Museum, in Budapest (1993); Galerie Vieille-du-Temple, Paris (1994); Galerie Cantoisel, Joigny, Sens museum and Geneva (1995); Paris (1996 and 1997); *À l'écoute du visible: Giorgio Morandi et Alexandre Hollan* (*Listening to the Visible: Giorgio Moran-*

di and Alexandre Hollan), Musée Jenisch, Vevey (2001); and Galerie Vieille-du-Temple in Paris (2002).

Bibliography:

Hardy-Marais, Laurence, *Alexandre Hollan*, exhibition catalogue, Musée de Maubeuge, Maubeuge, 1991. Bonnefoy, Yves, *La Journée d'Alexandre Hollan*, Le Temps qu'il fait, Cognac, 1995. Bonnefoy, Yves, *Alexandre Hollan, dessins*, William Blake, Bordeaux, 2003.

Museums and Galleries:

Budapest (Országos Széchényi Könyvtár) - Chamalières (MAC) - Düren (Leopold-Hoesch Mus.) - Hanover (Sprengel Mus.) - Maubeuge (Musée Henri-Boez) - Munich (Bayerische Staatsbibliothek) - Paris (BNF) - Paris (MNAM-CCI).

HOLLAND
British, 18th century.
Painter.

Holland painted a *Portrait of King George I.*

HOLLAND, Ada R. (Miss)
married name: Sachs
British, 19th century.
Painter.

Ada Holland exhibited in London at the Royal Academy and the Suffolk Street Gallery from 1888.

HOLLAND, Henry
British, 18th century.
Engraver (aquatint).

HOLLAND, J.
British, 18th century.
Active in London c. 1755.
Engraver.

Holland produced a *Turk's Head.*

HOLLAND, James, or Hollande
British, 19th century.
Born 1799, in Burslem; died 12 February 1870, in London.
Painter, watercolourist. Landscapes, urban landscapes, architectural views, flowers.

James Holland first worked as a flower painter at a china factory. He went to London when he was 19, where he supported himself by giving lessons and selling small flower paintings. After a visit to Paris in 1831, he painted some successful landscapes. He visited Italy, Switzerland, Portugal, Holland and France, all countries that provided him with subjects for his paintings. He exhibited in London at the Royal Academy from 1824, and also showed work at the Society of Painters in Watercolours, the Society of British Artists and the British Institution.

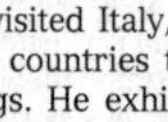

Bibliography:

Bauer, Gérald, *L'Éloquence de la couleur ou le génie des émules de Bonnington*, Clem arts, Lavallois-Perret, 2003.

Museums and Galleries:

Boston: *Ruins* (watercolour) - Brighton (Mus. & AG): *Grand Canal, Venice* (1851, oil on canvas) - Cardiff: *Palace of Philip the Fair* - Dublin: *Ampitheatre in Verona* (watercolour) - Edinburgh (Nat. Gal. of Scotland): *Rialto, Venice* (oil on canvas) - Glasgow: *Grand Canal, Venice; Grand Canal, Venice* - Leicester: *English Landscape* - Liverpool: *Port of Genoa; Moonlight* - London (Tate Collection): *The Grand Canal, Venice* (c. 1835-1855, oil/board); *Greenwich Hospital as it was in 1837* (1862, oil/board); *A Recollection of Venice* (oil/board); *The Thames below Woolwich* (1843, oil on canvas) - London (Victoria and Albert Mus.): three Landscapes; *Flowers* - Manchester: two watercolours - Montreal: *Lake Garda; Night Scene* - Sheffield: *Rialto Bridge, Venice.*

Auction records:

London, 9 Dec 1907, *Aucey (Savoie)*, GBP 7. London, 18 Jan 1908, *On the Balcony (Venice)*, GBP 14. London, 4 April 1908, *Piazzetta San Marco, Venice* (1859) GBP 262. London, 11 April 1908, *Doge's Palace, Venice*, GBP 63. London, 21 May 1908, *Canal in Venice* (1845) GBP 78. London, 25 June 1908, *Venice*, GBP 1,207; *Colleoni Monument*, GBP 651; *Venice*, GBP 693; *Greenwich Hospital*, GBP 367. London, 26 June 1908, *View of the Grand Canal, Venice* (watercolour) GBP 614; *On the Giudecca, Venice* (watercolour) GBP 420. London, 27 March 1909, *The Rialto*, GBP 88; *Piazza San Marco* (1859) GBP 178. London, 7 May 1909, *Tower of Philip the Fair in Paris* (1845) GBP 31. London, 11 June 1909, *The Rialto* (1862, watercolour) GBP 210; *Rotterdam* (watercolour) GBP 52. London, 2 July 1909, *Square in Venice* (1844) GBP 105; *Jesuit Church, Venice* (watercolour) GBP 257. London, May 1922, *Peacocks and Poultry in a Landscape*, GBP 315. London, May 1923, *Herne Bay, Kent*, GBP 120. London, June 1923, *Venice, Sunset*, GBP 47. London, Sept 1923, *View of Venice*, GBP 68. London, May 1924, *View of the Grand Canal, Venice*, GBP 48. London, July 1924, *Rialto, Venice*, GBP 50; *Street in Venice: Bridge, Gondolas and Figures*, GBP 78. London, 13 March 1925, *Entrance to the Grand Canal, Venice*, GBP 168; *Venice after Rain*, GBP 210. London, 18 Dec 1925, *Venice with Gondolas and Figures*, GBP 86. London, 30 April 1926, *The Dogana and Doge's Palace*, GBP 273. London, 2 March 1927, *San Giorgio Maggiore*, GBP 71; *View of Venice*, GBP 71. London, 30 Nov 1928, *Rialto, Venice*, GBP 89. London, 3 March 1930, *Giudecca, Venice*, GBP 99. London, 4 April 1935, *Greenwich Hospital*, GBP 200. London, 26 June 1936, *View of Venice with Procession*, GBP 46. London, 29 Jan 1943, *Rialto*, GBP 31. London, 17 Nov 1944, *Venice*, GBP 42. London, 6 Dec 1946, *Doge's Palace, Venice*, GBP 189. London, 6 June 1958, *Colleoni Monument, Venice*, GBP 339. London, 22 April 1959, *Greenwich Hospital*, GBP 1,800. London, 19 April 1961, *Leaning Tower of San Giorgio dei Greci*, GBP 140. London, 28 June 1963, *View of the Rialto*, Gns 700. London, 16 July 1965, *The Lagoon, Venice*, Gns 950. London, 9 Nov 1971, *S Maria dei Miracoli, Venice* (watercolour) Gns 550. London, 21 March 1972, *Scaglieri Monument, Verona*, GBP 1,400. London, 9 March 1976, *View of Villa Nova, Portugal* (oil on canvas, $11\frac{1}{2}$ x $17\frac{1}{2}$ ins / 29 x 44.5 cm) GBP 950. London, 15 June 1976, *View of Venice* (1860, watercolour heightened with gouache, $18\frac{1}{2}$ x $28\frac{1}{4}$ ins / 47 x 72 cm) GBP 600. London, 1 March 1977, *Estrella Church* (1837, watercolour and pencil heightened with white, 10 x $17\frac{1}{4}$ ins / 25.5 x 43.5 cm) GBP 1,600. London, 7 July 1977, *La Salute, Venice* (1853, watercolour and pencil, $9\frac{3}{4}$ x $6\frac{3}{4}$ ins / 25 x 17 cm) GBP 950. London, 25 Oct 1977, *View of Venice* (oil on card, 9 x $6\frac{3}{4}$ ins / 22 x 17 cm) GBP 1,200. New York, 11 Oct 1979, *S Maria dei Miracoli, Venice* (oil on canvas, 35 x $27\frac{1}{4}$ ins / 89 x 69 cm) USD 6,000. London, 18 Nov 1980, *Rialto Bridge* (watercolour and pencil heightened with white, $5\frac{1}{2}$ x 10 ins / 14 x 25.5 cm) GBP 1,300. London, 29 March 1983, *Walmer Castle* (1850, oil on canvas, $18\frac{1}{2}$ x 31 ins / 47 x 79 cm) GBP 2,500. London, 21 Nov 1984, *Lions of St Mark, Venice* (1866, watercolour and gouache/pencil outlines, $13\frac{1}{2}$ x $18\frac{1}{4}$ ins / 34.5 x 46.5 cm) GBP 5,500. London, 9 July 1985, *Corte dei Miracoli, Venice* (1846, watercolour and black chalk heightened with white, 16 x $12\frac{1}{2}$ ins / 40.5 x 31.5 cm) GBP 2,400. London, 9 July 1986, *Hillfield House* (oil on canvas, $16\frac{3}{4}$ x 28 ins / 42.5 x 71 cm) GBP 6,000. London, 17 Nov 1987, *Paris, Church of St-Sulpice* (1831, watercolour and pencil, $7\frac{1}{2}$ x $3\frac{3}{4}$ ins / 19 x 9.8 cm) GBP 5,000. Paris, 19 April 1989, *The Four Seasons* (oil on canvas, four, each $11\frac{3}{4}$ x $9\frac{3}{4}$ ins / 30 x 25 cm) FRF 72,000. London, 2 June 1989, *The Piazzetta in Venice* (1855, oil on panel, $12\frac{1}{2}$ x $18\frac{1}{4}$ ins / 32 x 46.5 cm) GBP 4,400. London, 12 July 1989, *Langford Family in the*

Drawing Room (oil on canvas, 23 1/2 x 32 1/4 ins / 59.5 x 82 cm) GBP 34,100. LONDON, 28 Feb 1990, *Dogana and Church of La Salute in Venice* (1848, oil on panel, 12 x 16 1/2 ins / 30.5 x 42 cm) GBP 1,980. LONDON, 30 May 1990, *Busy Port* (oil on panel, 7 x 10 ins / 18 x 25.5 cm) GBP 1,100. LONDON, 15 June 1990, *Painted Hall Staircase at Greenwich Hospital* (1862, oil on paper/canvas, 18 x 12 ins / 45.7 x 30.5 cm) GBP 1,980. LONDON, 11 July 1990, *Court of Honour in a Venetian Palazzo* (oil on canvas, 33 1/4 x 23 1/4 ins / 84.5 x 59 cm) GBP 4,620. LONDON, 30 Jan 1991, *Washerwomen beneath the Walls of a Castle in Genoa* (1868, watercolour heightened with gouache, 18 x 11 1/2 ins / 45.5 x 29 cm) GBP 2,200. NEW YORK, 21 May 1991, *Venice, the Rialto Bridge* (oil on canvas/synthetic resin, 24 x 36 ins / 61 x 91.5 cm) USD 4,400. LONDON, 10 July 1991, *Largo da Sé Velha in Coimbra, Portugal* (1838, oil on canvas, 20 3/4 x 15 ins / 53 x 38 cm) GBP 16,500. LONDON, 7 Oct 1992, *Capriccio of Greenwich Palace from the Thames by Moonlight* (1852, oil on card, 11 x 11 ins / 28 x 28 cm) GBP 1,540. LONDON, 13 Nov 1992, *Country Fair* (oil on canvas, 16 1/4 x 25 1/2 ins / 41 x 65 cm) GBP 11,000. LONDON, 14 July 1993, *Interior of the Museum in Greenwich* (oil on panel, oval, 11 1/4 x 15 ins / 28.5 x 38 cm) GBP 1,265. NEW YORK, 19 Jan 1994, *Figures in a Public Garden* (watercolour and pencil/paper, 12 1/2 x 9 1/2 ins / 31.8 x 24.1 cm) USD 9,775. LONDON, 4 Nov 1994, *Church of S Maria del Rosario in Venice* (1863, oil on canvas, 16 1/2 x 30 ins / 41.6 x 76.5 cm) GBP 14,950. LONDON, 10 March 1995, *Billingsgate Market* (oil on canvas, 31 1/4 x 44 1/4 ins / 79.4 x 112.4 cm) GBP 13,800. LONDON, 5 Sept 1996, *Yarmouth* (oil on canvas, 10 x 14 1/4 ins / 25.4 x 36.2 cm) GBP 1,150. BURY ST EDMUNDS, 24 March 1999, *Gypsy Encampment with Donkeys and Horses before a Windmill* (oil on canvas, 24 x 36 ins / 61 x 91 cm) GBP 1,800. SHREWSBURY, 14 April 1999, *Figure on a Venetian Quayside. Ferry about to Land, Venice* (oil on board, a pair, 7 x 9 ins / 18 x 23 cm) GBP 3,000. LONDON, 7 April 2000, *Venice, Evening* (pencil, watercolour and gum arabic heightened with white and scratching out, 11 x 20 ins / 28 x 50 cm) GBP 15,000. LONDON, 7 April 2000, *Orange Market with Rialto Bridge beyond, Venice* (1867, pencil, watercolour, gouache and gum arabic, 11 x 22 ins / 29 x 57 cm) GBP 16,000. LONDON, 7 June 2001, *Grand Canal, Venice* (1843, pencil, watercolour and gum arabic with scratching out, 9 x 7 ins / 23 x 18 cm) GBP 4,800. LONDON, 5 Sept 2001, *October Morning, Rotterdam* (1849, oil on canvas, 30 x 4 ins / 76 x 11 cm) GBP 10,000. SALISBURY, 9 Oct 2002, *Grand Canal, Venice* (oil on canvas, 26 x 35 ins / 67 x 90 cm) GBP 6,800. LONDON, 16 Dec 2002, *Serra Convent, Oporto* (1838, oil on canvas, 15 x 21 ins / 37 x 53 cm) GBP 22,000. LONDON, 10 June 2003, *Colleoni Monument, Venice* (1845, oil on canvas, 40 x 50 ins / 101 x 127 cm) GBP 30,000. NEW YORK, 29 Oct 2003, *Church of the Gesuati, Venice* (1863, oil on canvas, 16 x 30 ins / 41 x 76 cm) USD 26,000. AMSTERDAM, 20 April 2004, *View of Venice* (oil on canvas, 30 x 50 ins / 76 x 126 cm) EUR 5,000. LONDON, 25 Nov 2004, *Mrs Hixon's House* (1847, oil on canvas, 12 x 15 ins / 30 x 39 cm) GBP 4,200.

HOLLAND, John

British, 18th century.

Painter.

John Holland exhibited in London at the Society of Artists between 1764 and 1770.

HOLLAND, John, called Henry Bromley

British, 18th century.

Active at the end of the 18th century.

Engraver.

John Holland engraved several portraits after Faithorne and also produced a *Catalogue of English Portraits*, published in 1793 under the pseudonym of Henry Bromley.

HOLLAND, John

British, 19th century.

Painter. Landscapes.

John Holland was active in Nottingham and exhibited in London at the British Institution and the Suffolk Street Gallery between 1831 and 1879.

MUSEUMS AND GALLERIES:

NOTTINGHAM: *View of Sherwood Forest.*

AUCTION RECORDS:

LONDON, 22 Feb 1972, *Fête Champêtre*, GBP 650. LONDON, 14 May 1976, *Return of the Fishermen* (oil on canvas, 29 1/4 x 59 ins / 74 x 150 cm) GBP 800. LONDON, 2 Feb 1979, *Lechlade-on-Thames* (oil on canvas, 13 1/2 x 21 ins / 34.3 x 52.5 cm) GBP 2,200. NEW YORK, 27 Oct 1982, *Fishermen by the Sea* (oil on canvas, 16 x 24 ins / 40.6 x 61 cm) USD 3,000. LONDON, 2 March 1984, *Boats off Dover* (oil on canvas, 25 x 41 ins / 63.5 x 104.2 cm) GBP 1,200. LONDON, 22 Feb 1985, *Spa Bridge, Crag Valley* (1869, oil on canvas, 25 x 30 ins / 63.5 x 76.2 cm) GBP 1,400. LONDON, 15 June 1988, *Whitby from Larpool* (oil on canvas, 28 1/4 x 42 ins / 72 x 106.5 cm) GBP 2,200. MONTRÉAL, 17 Oct 1988, *Fishermen on a Rocky Coast with a Castle in the Background* (oil on canvas, 16 1/4 x 24 ins / 41 x 61 cm) CAD 5,000. LONDON, 31 May 1989, *Territory of the Gulls* (oil on canvas, 30 x 51 1/4 ins / 76.5 x 130 cm) GBP 495. LONDON, 3 Nov 1989, *Llamphey Palace in Pembrokeshire* (oil on canvas, 20 x 29 1/2 ins / 51 x 75 cm) GBP 2,750. COPENHAGEN, 28 Aug 1991, *Rocky Coast with Fishermen at Port-du-Moulin (Island of Sark)* (oil on canvas, 24 x 36 1/4 ins / 61 x 92 cm) DKK 10,000. NEW YORK, 20 July 1995, *Remains of the Castle of King Arthur at Tintagel in Cornwall* (oil on canvas, 20 x 30 ins / 51.1 x 76.5 cm) USD 2,587. LONDON, 6 Nov 1997, *Wooded Landscape with Horseman and Inhabitants on a Path, a Village in the Background* (oil on canvas, 25 x 30 ins / 63.5 x 76.3 cm) GBP 3,220. CRANBROOK, 2 Oct 2000, *Horses and Cart* (oil on panel, 13 x 11 ins / 33 x 28 cm) GBP 1,450. NEWBURY, 30 Jan 2002, *Yorkshire Coast near Scarborough* (oil on canvas, 18 x 30 ins / 46 x 76 cm) GBP 1,650. GUERNSEY, 20 March 2003, *Les Autelets, Sark* (oil on canvas, 11 x 17 ins / 28 x 43 cm) GBP 1,300. NORFOLK, 22 March 2004, *Portrait of a Young Girl by a Fence* (1864, oil on canvas, 21 x 17 ins / 53 x 43 cm) GBP 1,300. LONDON, 26 May 2004, *Outside the Canterbury Arms Hotel* (oil on canvas, 36 x 52 ins / 91 x 132 cm) GBP 10,500. LEWES, 22 July 2004, *Sark, Channel Islands, with Lobstermen on the Shore* (oil on canvas, 12 x 18 ins / 30 x 46 cm) GBP 1,300.

HOLLAND, John Joseph

British, 19th century.

Born 1776, in London; died in the USA.

Painter, architect. Landscapes.

John Joseph Holland was a pupil of Marinelli. He worked mainly in New York.

AUCTION RECORDS:

LONDON, 14 Feb 1978, *Rustic Scene* (oil on canvas, 19 1/2 x 29 1/4 ins / 49.5 x 74.5 cm) GBP 1,350.

HOLLAND, Peter

British, 18th century.

Miniaturist. Landscapes.

Peter Holland exhibited in London at the Royal Academy from 1781 to 1793.

HOLLAND, Philip

British, 19th century.

Painter. Still-lifes.

Philip Holland exhibited frequently in London at the Royal Academy and the Suffolk Street Gallery between 1850 and 1883.

HOLLAND, Philip Sidney

British, 19th century.

Born October 1855; died January 1891.

Painter. Genre scenes.

Philip Sidney Holland settled in London where he exhibited fairly regularly at the Royal Academy and the Suffolk Street Gallery from 1877.
MUSEUMS AND GALLERIES:
NORWICH (Castle Mus. and AG): *The Monk's Repentance.*

HOLLAND, R.
British, 19th century.
Draughtsman (?).
R. Holland is known to have produced a *Portrait of Philip Henry.*

HOLLAND, Tom
American, 20th century.
Born June 1936, in Seattle.
Painter (mixed media).
Tom Holland studied at Berkeley University. His early painting was very similar to what is called funk art - expressive art somewhere between painting and sculpture, which is in deliberate bad taste; its content is frequently pornographic or scatological.

Holland's art has evolved in the direction of 'anti-form'. He produces nearly monochrome banners, using synthetic fibres and epoxy resin. He has exhibited since 1962 in San Francisco, then in New York and Los Angeles.
AUCTION RECORDS:
NEW YORK, 27 Feb 1976, *Untitled* (1971, polyester resin, 16 1/4 x 86 1/2 ins / 41 x 220 cm) USD 900. NEW YORK, 28 May 1976, *North Side* (1973, polyester resin, 66 x 102 ins / 167.5 x 259 cm) USD 2,250. NEW YORK, 13 May 1981, *Ellis* (1972, acrylic/fibreglass/copper, collage, 48 x 96 ins / 122 x 244 cm) USD 4,000. NEW YORK, 13 Nov 1986, *Avilla* (1980, epoxy and oil/aluminium, 67 1/4 x 64 1/2 x 36 1/2 ins / 170.6 x 163.8 x 92.4 cm) USD 8,000. NEW YORK, 8 Oct 1988, *Untitled* (1982, mixed media, 24 1/2 x 29 ins / 62.3 x 73.7 cm) USD 4,400. NEW YORK, 3 May 1989, *Tori* (1983, woven fibreglass, 78 x 53 1/2 x 4 ins / 198 x 136 x 10 cm) USD 13,200. NEW YORK, 21 Feb 1990, *Untitled* (1971, acrylic/fibreglass, 19 x 86 ins / 47.4 x 218.7 cm) USD 1,925. NEW YORK, 23 Feb 1990, *Hurley* (1983, acrylic and rubber lacquer/fibreglass with rivets, 33 x 73 ins / 83.8 x 185.4 cm) USD 3,300. NEW YORK, 6 Nov 1990, *Helli* (1980, varnish and resin on fibreglass, 116 x 78 3/4 x 30 ins / 294.6 x 200 x 76.2 cm) USD 10,450. NEW YORK, 7 May 1993, *Mola, Mural Relief* (1987, oil, resin and black felt on fibreglass and aluminium, 18 x 32 1/4 x 2 ins / 45.5 x 82 x 5 cm) USD 2,300. NEW YORK, 20 Nov 1996, *Amaro* (1979, epoxy/fibreglass, 72 x 45 ins / 182.9 x 114.3 cm) USD 4,312. SAN FRANCISCO, 22 April 1999, *TA* (1982, mixed media on fibreglass, 84 x 76 ins / 213 x 194 cm) USD 6,000. SAN FRANCISCO, 24 Oct 2000, *Lacy* (1979, mixed media on fibreglass, 73 x 56 ins / 185 x 141 cm) USD 2,000. SAN FRANCISCO, 8 May 2001, *Untitled* (1971, oil on fibreglass, 35 x 116 ins / 90 x 295 cm) USD 2,000. SAN FRANCISCO, 23 April 2002, *FA Baja Series No. 10* (1952, mixed media, h. 48 ins / 122 cm) USD 2,500. SAN FRANCISCO, 14 Oct 2002, *Black Fish Series No. 8* (1991, aluminium and fibreglass, 48 x 61 ins / 122 x 155 cm) USD 4,250.

HOLLAND, William Langford
Irish, 18th century.
Miniaturist.
William Holland studied at the Dublin Society.

HOLLANDA DE. See first name

HOLLANDE, Jean de. See **JEAN de Hollande**

HOLLANDER, Hendrik
Dutch, 19th century.
Born 7 August 1823, in Leeuwarden; died 1 June 1884, in Amsterdam.
Painter. Portraits, genre scenes.
Hendrik Hollander was a pupil of J.-W. and N. Pienemann.
MUSEUMS AND GALLERIES:
AMSTERDAM: *Self-portrait.*
AUCTION RECORDS:
LONDON, March 1924, *In Memory of Van Dyck,* GBP 8. AMSTERDAM, 16 March 1976, *Couple in an Interior* (1841, oil on panel, 18 3/4 x 14 1/2 ins / 47.5 x 37 cm) NLG 6,000. AMSTERDAM, 28 Nov 1978, *Young Woman Feeding a Parrot* (oil on panel, 13 3/4 x 11 ins / 35 x 27 cm) NLG 7,000. LONDON, 26 Nov 1980, *The Letter* (1849, oil on panel, 22 1/4 x 18 ins / 56.5 x 45.5 cm) GBP 3,000. NEW YORK, 29 May 1981, *Bed Time* (1862, oil on panel, 20 1/4 x 16 3/4 ins / 51.5 x 42.5 cm) USD 3,500. AMSTERDAM, 25 April 1990, *The Jeweller* (oil on panel, 7 1/2 x 6 ins / 19 x 15 cm) NLG 2,990. AMSTERDAM, 5-6 Feb 1991, *The Letter* (oil on panel, 10 3/4 x 9 ins / 27.5 x 22 cm) NLG 4,025. AMSTERDAM, 17 Sept 1991, *The Contract* (oil on panel, 8 x 7 ins / 20.5 x 18 cm) NLG 2,760. AMSTERDAM, 11 April 1995, *Johan de Wit Reading the Act of Renunciation* (oil on canvas, 28 1/4 x 22 ins / 72 x 56 cm) NLG 3,776. MUNICH, 5 July 2000, *Rembrandt Painting 'The Nightwatchman'* (1857, oil on canvas, 40 x 31 ins / 102 x 80 cm) DEM 6,000. WARSAW, 10 Dec 2000, *Untitled* (oil on canvas) PLN 38,000. AMSTERDAM, 4 March 2002, *Return of the Hunter* (oil on panel, 9 x 11 ins / 23 x 27 cm) EUR 3,200. LEYBURN, 21 Nov 2002, *Interior with Woman Sewing by a Window, with a Spaniel at her Feet* (oil on panel, 7 x 6 ins / 19 x 15 cm) GBP 1,100. EAST DENNIS, 14 May 2004, *Interior Scene with Man and Woman at a Table with an Infant, Child and Servant* (oil on canvas, 29 x 22 ins / 74 x 56 cm) USD 3,200.

HOLLANDERS, Johannes
Italian, 19th century.
Born 17 March 1821, in Oosterhout, the Netherlands.
Painter. History painting, portraits.
Hollanders was a pupil of N. de Keyser in Antwerp.

HOLLANDINE, Louise de (Palatine Princess).
See **LUISE de Hollandine**

HOLLAR, Wenceslaus, or Wenzel von Prachna
Bohemian, 17th century.
Born 23 July 1607, in Prague; died 25 March 1677, in London.
Engraver, reproductions engraver, draughtsman, watercolourist, illustrator. Historical subjects, portraits, urban landscapes, landscapes, animals, costume studies. Maps.
Bohemian School.
Wenceslaus Hollar was the son of a clerk at the court of justice in Prague, and his family intended him to take up a legal career. However, he left Prague in 1627 and settled in Frankfurt, where he became a pupil of Matthaus Merian the Elder, from whom he learned the art of cartography. He travelled across Germany, making numerous drawings and engravings of the towns he visited. After stays in Strasbourg, Frankfurt and Mainz, he met the Earl of Arundel, English ambassador to Ferdinand III, in Cologne and returned with him to Prague. From there he accompanied him to Vienna and finally to England, where he arrived in 1637.

The Earl employed him to make engravings of the works of art in his collection. He also engraved views of London. In 1641, Hollar married one of the ladies-in-waiting to Lady Aletheia Talbot, Countess of Arundel. He was presented to Charles I and gained favour with the king. He was commissioned to make engravings of the festivities on the occasion of Maria de' Medici's visit to England. The Civil War of 1645 put an end to his success. He was arrested, but managed to escape and he fled to Antwerp, where he was reunited with the Earl of Arundel.

In Antwerp Hollar resumed work, but the death of his protector left him in abject poverty. At the time of the Restoration of Charles II, he returned to England, but never regained his previous popularity. He was deeply affected by the death of his wife and son in the plague of 1665 and the print sellers took advantage of his misfortune. The following year, he engraved a number of views of London during the Great Fire.

In 1668, Hollar left for Africa in the company of Lord Howard, grandson of the Earl of Arundel, with a commission to produce drawings and engravings, but received little payment for this work. He returned to England in 1672 and worked there until his death, drawing and engraving views of Lincoln, Southwell and York. He died in poverty.

Hollar's works comprise between 2,500 and 2,730 items. Some are extremely rare and have achieved high prices. He was a very talented engraver, but was the victim of events. Rembrandt owned some of his plates and used one of his subjects.

BIBLIOGRAPHY:
Hind, Arthur Mayger, *Wenceslaus Hollar and his Views of London and Windsor in the XVIIth. Century*, John Lane, London, 1922. Urzidil, J., *Hollar, a Czech emigré in England*, The 'Czechoslovak', London, 1942. *Van Dyck, Wenceslaus Hollar & the miniature-painters at the court of the early Stuarts*, exhibition catalogue, The Queens's Gall., Buckingham Palace, London, 1968. Denkstein, Vladimir, *Hollar drawings*, Arabis Books, New York, 1979. Pennington, Richard, *A descriptive catalogue of the etched work of Wenceslaus Hollar, 1607-1677*, catalogue raisonné, Cambridge University Press, New York, 1982. Godfrey, Richard T., *Wenceslaus Hollar: A Bohemian Artist in England*, exhibition catalogue, Yale Centre for British Art, New Haven, 1994. Doggett, Rachel (ed.), *Impressions of Wenceslaus Hollar*, exhibition catalogue, Folger Shakespeare Library, Washington DC, 1996. Vlnas, Vit (ed.), *Lumière et ténèbres, art et civilisation du Baroque en Bohême*, exhibition catalogue, Palais des Beaux-Arts, Lille, Réunion des musées nationaux, Paris, 2002. Tindall, Gillian, *The Man who Drew London: Wenceslaus Hollar in Reality and Imagination*, Chatto & Windus, London, 2002.

AUCTION RECORDS:
PARIS, 22 March 1928, *Cathedral* (pen) FRF 750. LONDON, 4 July 1979, *Muffs and Lace* (etching with touches of burin and dry-point, 4 1/4 x 8 ins / 10.8 x 20.3 cm) GBP 1,900. LONDON, 23 March 1982, *Klingenberg am Main* (black chalk, pen and wash, 3 1/4 x 10 ins / 8.1 x 25.2 cm) GBP 4,500. LONDON, 18 June 1982, *Fur Muff and Stole* (etching, 315 3/4 x 4 1/2 ins / 802 x 11.2 cm) GBP 950. LONDON, 12 April 1983, *Wooden Gate at Duren* (black chalk, pen, wash and watercolour, 3 3/4 x 7 1/4 ins / 9.8 x 18.5 cm) GBP 1,900. NEW YORK, 3 May 1983, *Peace between Spain and the Netherlands* (1648, etching, 9 x 13 1/2 ins / 22 x 34 cm) USD 900. LONDON, 30 June 1986, *Grande Place and the Town Hall in Brussels* (black chalk, 11 x 15 ins / 27.9 x 38.3 cm) GBP 23,000. LONDON, 30 June 1986, *View of Eltville on the Rhine* (watercolour and pen/traces of black chalk, 6 1/2 x 12 ins / 16.7 x 30.7 cm) GBP 19,500. LONDON, 16 July 1987, *Lambeth Palace from the River Thames* (pen and wash/pencil outlines, 4 3/4 x 10 3/4 ins / 12 x 27.5 cm) GBP 7,500. NEW YORK, 27 Jan 1999, *View of Ober Alteich on Danube* (pen, brown ink, brown/grey wash, 4x9 ins / 11x23 cm) USD 30,000. LONDON, 26 Nov 1999, *The Long View of London from Bankside* (1647, etching, h. 19 ins / 48 cm) GBP 41,000. BERLIN, 24 Nov 2000, *Bird's Eye View of Jerusalem* (etching, 17x43 ins / 42x109 cm) DEM 8,000. LONDON, 28 Nov 2000, *View of the Town and Fort, Tangier. View from the Bowling Green, Tangier* (pencil, pen and brown ink, double-sided, 7x24 ins / 19x62 cm) GBP 11,000. LONDON, 6 Dec 2001, *Five Muffs* (etching, 4x8 ins / 11x20 cm) GBP 9,400. LONDON, 6 Dec 2001, *Dark Fur Muff with Brocade Band* (etching, 3x4 ins / 8x11 cm) GBP 5,000. LONDON, 24 May 2002, *Long View of London from Bankside* (etching on five sheets, 20x78 ins / 50x199 cm) GBP 9,000. LONDON, 24 May 2002, *London and Westminster* (etching on four sheets, 12x61 ins / 30x155 cm) GBP 2,500. LONDON, 6 July 2004, *View of Regensburg* (black chalk, pen and ink wash, 2x5 ins / 4x13 cm) GBP 26,000.

HOLLART, Charles
French, 20th century.
Born 14 October 1891, in Arras.
Painter. Figures.

Charles Hollart was a pupil of Cormon and Winter. He exhibited in Paris at the Salon des Artistes Français.

HOLLEBECQUE, Jean
French, 20th century.
Born 27 October 1914, in Wervicq; died 27 April 1983, in St-Martin-de-Lamps.
Painter, watercolourist. Portraits, landscapes, urban landscapes, landscapes with figures, still-lifes.

From 1930 to 1935, Jean Hollebecque was a pupil at the École des Arts et Industries Textiles in Roubaix. From 1942 to 1945, he studied at the École des Beaux-Arts in Paris. He settled definitively in the Berry region in 1945. He painted mostly landscapes of the Berry and Creuse regions.

Jean Hollebecque took part in collective exhibitions in Paris, including: Salon des Indépendants (between 1939 and 195); Salon des Artistes Français (1944 and 1952), Solo exhibitions include: Musée de Châteauroux (1947, 1955, 1963); Musée de La Châtre (1948); Galerie Art du Berry de Châteauroux (1944 to 1960); Galerie Bourgeois, Châteauroux (1965 to 1979). Retrospectives include: Château de Bouges (1991); Musée de Châteauroux and Centre Culturel Buzançais (1993).

Hollebecque participated in the Prix de la Jeune Peinture (1947), the Prix Othon Friesz (1963) and won the Prix Legay-Lebrun (1952).

BIBLIOGRAPHY:
Maurice Croze, et al., *Hollebecque 1914-1983*, Association des Amis de Jean Hollebecque, St-Martin-de-Lamps, 1991.

MUSEUMS AND GALLERIES:
CHÂTEAUROUX - LA CHÂTRE.

HOLLEBEKE, Bruno Jean Charles van
Belgian, 19th century.
Born 1817, in Bruges; died 1892, in Brussels.
Painter. History painting.

The Bruges museum has a painting by Bruno Hollebeke entitled *The Condemned Man's Final Day*. He also painted many portraits.

HOLLECK-WEITHMANN, Karl
German, 19th - 20th century.
Born 23 August 1872, in Grottkau.
Draughtsman, engraver.

Holleck-Weithmann exhibited his work in Berlin in 1909.

HOLLEGHA, Wolfgang
Austrian, 20th century.
Born 1929, in Klagenfurt (Carinthia).
Painter.

Hollegha studied from 1947 until 1954 at the Akademie der Bildenden Künste in Vienna, where he became a member of the art club as one of Josef Mikl's entourage. He travelled to Germany, England and the USA. He took part in Documenta III in Kassel in 1963 and from 1952 regularly participated in exhibitions in Vienna, also exhibiting his paintings in New York in 1960, and in Los Angeles. The London Institute of Contemporary Art organised an exhibition of his work in 1961, and he exhibited in Cologne in 1964. He was awarded the Guggenheim Prize for Austria in 1958, and received a prize from the Carnegie Institute in Pittsburgh in 1961.

MUSEUMS AND GALLERIES:
PITTSBURGH (Carnegie MA): *Composition* (1957, oil on canvas) - VIENNA (Albertina Mus.) - VIENNA (Mus. Moderner Kunst Stiftung Ludwig).

HOLLENBERG, Felix

German, 19th - 20th century.

Born 15 December 1868, in Sterkrade.

Painter, engraver. Landscapes.

Hollenberg studied at the academies in Düsseldorf and Stuttgart, where his teacher was Albert Kappis. He was awarded a bronze medal at the Exposition Universelle in Paris in 1900.

MUSEUMS AND GALLERIES:

STUTTGART: *Morning in May.*

HOLLENSTEIN, Stephanie

Austrian, 20th century.

Born 18 July 1886, in Lustenau; died 1944.

Painter, watercolourist, draughtswoman. Religious subjects, village views, landscapes.

Hollenstein was active in Vienna.

AUCTION RECORDS:

VIENNA, 13 June 1980, *View of a Village* (oil on card, 12¼ x 16½ ins / 31 x 42 cm) ATS 38,000. VIENNA, 22 March 1983, *Sunrise* (oil on canvas, 27½ x 33½ ins / 70 x 85 cm) ATS 50,000. VIENNA, 29 Nov 2000, *Village by a Lake* (watercolour, 13 x 17 ins / 32 x 44 cm) ATS 45,000. VIENNA, 27 Nov 2002, *Lake Zoi, Dolomites* (watercolour, 5 x 8 ins / 13 x 21 cm) EUR 2,600. VIENNA, 27 Nov 2002, *Lake Zoi, Dolomites* (oil on canvas, 32 x 50 ins / 82 x 126 cm) EUR 12,000.

HÖLLER, Carsten

German, 20th - 21st century.

Born 1961, in Brussels.

Installation artist, video artist.

From 1979 to 1985 Höller studied agronomy in Kiel, before embarking on his artistic career. His work is based on the future and the Darwinian theory of the evolution of the species as developed most famously by biologist Richard Dawkins. This theory repudiates, as far as evolution is concerned, any notion of romanticism about universal love and the well-being of species. Effectively, genes programme the living organism in a selfish way; their primary function is replication. So Carsten Höller's works, which are mainly interactive installations, take pleasure in demythologizing our so-called altruistic, but unconsciously selfish, behaviour and propose new approaches to the subject, particularly in the fields of sex and passion. Nevertheless, the human species has the ability to operate in the cultural domain, as demonstrated in his video, *Chaffinches of Love*, in which the artist teaches love songs to chaffinches.

He has participated in various group exhibitions in Germany, Finland, Poland, and France, notably: 1995, the Biennale de Lyons; 1997, *Connexions Implicites* (*Implicit Connections*), the École des Beaux-Arts, Paris; 2000, *Vision Machine*, an exhibition about 'future machines' by artists and architects, the Musée des Beaux-Arts, Nantes; 2000, *Présumés Innocents: l'Art Contemporain et l'Enfance* (*Presumed Innocent: Contemporary Art and Childhood*), the Capc Musée d'Art Contemporain, Bordeaux; 2002, the Museum für Moderne Kunst, Kittelman, Frankfurt; 2002, *Relation Aesthetics from the 1990s*, the San Francisco Art Institute; 2003, *Common Wealth*, the Tate Modern, London; 2003, *L'État des Choses* (*The State of Things*), an exhibition which examined the status of the everyday object in contemporary art, held on the occasion of *Trésors Publics, 20 Ans de Création dans les Fonds Régionaux d'Art Contemporain (FRAC)* (*Public Treasury, 20 Years of Creation in the Regional Collection of Contemporary Art (FRAC)*), the Musée des Beaux-Arts, Nantes; 2003, *C'est Arrivé Demain* (*It Happened Tomorrow*), the Biennale in Lyons; 2003, *Berlin-Moscow/Moscow-Berlin 1950-2000*, an exhibition overview, which, following the exhibition covering the period 1900-1950, opened up to debate 50 years of German-Russian artistic and cultural relations, influenced by political change, and was held at the Martin Gropius-Bau Gallery, Berlin and the Tretyakov Gallery, Moscow. Höller has held solo shows; 1997, 2002, the Galerie Air de Paris; 1999, alongside Rosemarie Trockel, at the Musée d'Art moderne de la Ville de Paris; 2003, *Half Fiction*, the ICA, Boston.

BIBLIOGRAPHY:

Carsten Höller. Glück, Skop, travelling exhibition catalogue, Centraal Museum, Utrecht; Secession, Vienna; Kunstverein, Hamburg; Oktagon, Cologne, 1996. *Carsten Höller. Neue Welt*, exhibition catalogue, Museum für Gegenwartskunst, Basel, 1998. Barmann, Stefan, *Maisons (Häuser): Carsten Höller, Rosemarie Trockel*, exhibition catalogue, Musée d'Art moderne de la Ville de Paris, Oktagon, Cologne, 1999 (text in French and German). Bernadac, Marie-Laure/Moisdon-Tremblay, et al., *Présumés innocents: l'art contemporain et l'enfance*, exhibition catalogue, Capc-Musée d'Art contemporain, Bordeaux, 2000. Zahm, Olivier (preface), et al., *Trésors publics, 20 ans de création dans les Fonds régionaux d'art contemporain*, Flammarion, Paris, 2003 (text in French and English). *'Berlin-Moskau/Moskau-Berlin 1950-2000'* in *2 vol*, exhibition catalogue, Martin-Gropius-Bau, Berlin, 2003 (text in German).

MUSEUMS AND GALLERIES:

ANGOULÊME (FRAC Poitou-Charentes): *Komm Kleines, Kriegst was Feines* (*Come Little one, Have Something Nice*) (1991, installation); *Mind of Animals* (1994, assemblage) - LYONS (MAC).

HOLLERITH, Lucia Beverly

American, 20th century.

Born 1 July 1891, in Washington; died 1982.

Painter.

Lucia Beverly Hollerith was a member of the main art associations of Washington.

MUSEUMS AND GALLERIES:

WASHINGTON DC (Georgetown University): *Orange and Gray* (1934, oil on canvas).

HOLLESTELLE, Jacob Huijbrecht

Dutch, 19th - 20th century.

Born 19 November 1858, in Middelburg; died 1920.

Painter. Landscapes.

Hollestelle was first active in The Hague.

AUCTION RECORDS:

AMSTERDAM, 25 April 1990, *Winter Landscape with a Cart near a Bridge* (1893, oil on canvas, 29¼ x 19 ins / 74 x 48 cm) NLG 2,185.

HOLLEY-TRASENSTER, Francine

Belgian, 20th century.

Born 23 November 1919, in Liège.

Active in France.

Painter, collage artist.

Holley-Trasenster studied first at the Académie des Beaux-Arts in Liège and then in Paris, where she was taught by André Lhote in 1947, Fernand Léger in 1948, and Dewasne and Pillet at the Atelier d'Art Abstrait in 1950. In the 1950s she was influenced by Dewasne in particular. Her work can be classified as Abstract Geometric. After producing works in black and white she reintroduced colour into her paintings, using flat tints of sober colours and freely arranging planes and shapes in carefully balanced complex compositions. She was also interested in painting signs or geometric circuits on the canvas, breaking down the motifs into their individual components and isolating them. She produced several murals and illustrations.

Holley-Trasenster took part in many collective exhibitions including: 1952, 1954, 1955, 1968, 1972 to 1977 at the Salon des Réalités Nouvelles in Paris; 1953 and 1954 at the Quadriennale in Belgium; 1955 at the Palais des Beaux-Arts in Brussels; 1959 at the Salon du Musée des Beaux-Arts in Liège; 1964 at the Musée d'Art Wallon in Liège; 1965 to 1967 at the Salon d'Automne in Paris; 1974 to 1984 at the Salon Grands et Jeunes d'Aujourd'hui in Paris; 1978 to 1980 and 1982 to 1984 at the Salon Comparaisons in Paris; 1987 at the Museum in Ostend; and 1988 at the Palais des Congrès in Liège. She put on solo exhibitions in Paris and Belgium from 1943; at the museum of art and history in Meudon in 1995; and at the art gallery in the Hotel Astra in Paris in 1996. In 1990 the Musée des Beaux-Arts in Verviers organised a retrospective exhibition of her work.

HOLLIDAY, Edward
British, 19th century.
Painter. Fruit.

Edward Holliday exhibited frequently at the Royal Academy and the Suffolk Street Gallery in London from 1874 to 1884.

AUCTION RECORDS:

COPENHAGEN, 10-12 Sept 1997, *Still-life with Fruit and a Jug* (1875, oil on canvas, 20 x 24 ins / 51 x 61 cm) DKK 11,000.

HOLLIDAY, Lily
British, 19th century.
Painter. Flowers.

Lily Holliday exhibited in London at the Suffolk Street Gallery between 1879 and 1884.

HOLLIER, Jean François
French, 18th - 19th century.
Born 1772, in Chantilly; died January 1845, in Paris.
Miniaturist.

Jean François Hollier studied under David and Isabey. He exhibited at the Salon from 1804 to 1838 and was awarded medals in 1817 and 1824.

AUCTION RECORDS:

PARIS, 8 April 1919, *Portrait of Countess de Mniszech, Princess Radziwill, later Marquess de Ville* (miniature) FRF 3,750. PARIS, 10 June 1925, *Portrait of Marshal Ney* (miniature) FRF 1,300. PARIS, 12 Dec 1932, *Talma*, FRF 205. PARIS, 12 March 1945, *Brown-haired Young Woman in a Low-cut Dress* (miniature) FRF 10,500. PARIS, 24 March 1947, *The Empress Josephine* (miniature) FRF 10,000.

HOLLINGDALE, Horatio R.
British, 19th century.
Painter. Waterscapes, landscapes.

Horatio Hollingdale was a member of the Royal Society of British Artists. He exhibited in London at the Royal Academy and the Suffolk Street Gallery from 1881.

AUCTION RECORDS:

LONDON, 18 March 1987, *Lily Pond* (oil on canvas, 30 x 50 ins / 76 x 127 cm) GBP 2,100.

HOLLINGDALE, Richard
British, 19th century.
Painter. Genre scenes, portraits.

Richard Hollingdale exhibited frequently in London at the Royal Academy, the British Institution and the Suffolk Street Gallery from 1850.

HOLLINGSWORTH, Alvin
American, 20th century.
Born 1931, in New York.
Painter (mixed media), watercolourist, draughtsman, print artist, sculptor, illustrator. Figure compositions, figures, nudes, landscapes. Murals.
Spiral Group.

Alvin Hollingsworth was born into a family of West Indian origin. He studied at the Art Students League and New York City College, graduating in 1959. He taught at City University of New York. In 1963 he joined the Spiral Group, a group of African-American artists seeking to define their cultural identity at the height of the civil rights movement. He settled in New York.

In 1958, he worked with fluorescent paint and ultraviolet light. He went on to create protest collages of city trash (fragments of glass, cloth, paper, fishbones, and so on) for his series *Cry City* (1964-65). One of the paintings in this series, *Why: Black Guernica* (1965) shows children in silhouette on the walls of a street where a sign 'No Coloreds' recalls the poverty and segregation that was rife in America's cities. Hollingsworth's interest in matter is a constant in his career: his forms seem to dissolve in coloured backgrounds painted in with thick strokes and warm tones. In this way he plays with the effect of figures appearing and disappearing, and evokes a dramatic or poetic atmosphere. He has also painted murals, such as that at 55 W. 125th Street Harlem, where President Clinton had his offices, has written a children's book *I'd like the Goo-Gen-Heim* (Reilly & Lee, Chicago, 1972), and has illustrated *Black Out Loud: An Anthology of Modern Poems by Black Americans* (Macmillan, New York, 1970).

Hollingsworth has taken part in various group exhibitions including *Harlem '69*, Studio Museum in Harlem, New York in 1969, and has had a number of solo exhibitions, including in 1961, Ward Eggleston Gallery, New York; 1965, Terry Dintenfass Gallery, New York and 1972, Lee Nordness Galleries, New York.

BIBLIOGRAPHY:

Honig Fine, Elsa, *The Afro-American Artist. A Search for Identity*, Holt, Rinehart and Winston, New York, 1973.

MUSEUMS AND GALLERIES:

ASHEVILLE (MA) - NEW YORK (Brooklyn Mus.) - NEWARK, NJ (Rutgers University).

HOLLINGSWORTH, Dennis
American, 20th century.
Painter.

Dennis Hollingsworth combines wax and painting, working the material using a scraper, stencilling figures on it, and subtly alternates colours and smooth surfaces. He showed his works at the Bennet Roberts Fine Arts Gallery in Los Angeles in 1995, and featured in the exhibition *Smoggy Abstraction; Recent Los Angeles Painting* at the Haggerty Museum of Art, Marquette University, in 1996.

BIBLIOGRAPHY:

Dennis Hollingsworth: Enough is Enough, the Bridge, Smear Tactics, exhibition catalogue, Bennett Roberts Fine Art, Los Angeles, 1995. Scarborough, James, '*Dennis Hollingsworth*' in *Art Press* n° 204, periodical, Paris, July-August 1995. Colpitt, Frances, *Dennis Hollingsworth*, Smart Arts Press, Santa Monica, 1996.

HOLLINS, John
British, 19th century.
Born 1 January 1798, in Birmingham; died 7 March 1855, in London.
Painter, miniaturist, watercolourist. Portraits, genre scenes, landscapes.

John Hollins seems to have been the pupil of his father, a painter on glass. He made his début at the Royal Academy in 1818, settling in London and working as a portrait painter and miniaturist in 1822. In 1825, he set off for Italy where he remained for two years.

His works, confident in draughtsmanship and attractively coloured, earned Hollins numerous successes at the Royal Academy exhibitions. In the early years of his career he mainly painted subjects taken from the poets and novelists of the day; later, he came to concentrate more on landscapes. He became an associate member of the Royal Academy in 1842.

MUSEUMS AND GALLERIES:

LONDON (Victoria and Albert Mus.): two watercolours.

AUCTION RECORDS:

LONDON, Jan 1924, *Scene on Loch Etive*, GBP 4. PERTH, 1 Sept 1992, *Young Fisherman* (1854, oil on canvas, 33 3/4 x 44 ins / 86 x 112 cm) GBP 4,400. LONDON, 10 Feb 2000, *Portrait of a Gentlemen* (1840, oil on canvas, 56 x 45 ins / 143 x 114 cm)

GBP 1,300. LONDON, 11 May 2004, *Portrait of Emily, Wife of Carteret John William Ellis* (oil on canvas, 51 x 41 ins / 129 x 104 cm) GBP 1,600.

HOLLINS, Peter
British, 19th century.
Born 1800, in Birmingham; died 16 August 1886, in Birmingham.
Sculptor.

Peter Hollins was the elder son of the sculptor William Hollins. He studied with his father and also studied drawing with J.V. Barber. He helped his father in many of his projects and, for a while, worked in the studio of Chambrey, probably as an assistant. He settled in London in about 1828 where he was very successful.

The death of his father brought Hollins back to Birmingham in 1843. The works he produced after this date include statues of Sir Robert Peel and Sir Rowland Hill and sculptural work at the Priory Church in Malvern, at Lichfield Cathedral and at the church in Weston. He was vice-president of the Society of Birmingham Artists. Despite the importance of his work, he does not seem to have made much money. He often exhibited at the Royal Academy in London between 1822 and 1871.

MUSEUMS AND GALLERIES:
BIRMINGHAM: *William Scholefield; Felix Mendelssohn; Matthew Davenport Hill; David Cox.*

AUCTION RECORDS:
LONDON, 13 April 1983, *Seated Girl* (1833, marble, h. 24 1/4 ins / 61.5 cm and w. 29 1/4 ins/74 cm) GBP 800.

HOLLINS, William
British, 18th - 19th century.
Born 1754, possibly in Birmingham; died 1843, in Birmingham.
Sculptor, architect.

William Hollins was the father of Peter Hollins. He enjoyed a considerable reputation in Birmingham and exhibited in London at the Royal Academy from 1821 to 1825.

HOLLIS, George
British, 19th century.
Born 1792, in Oxford; died 2 January 1842, in Walworth.
Engraver (burin).

George Hollis was a pupil of George Cooke. He engraved portraits, views of the Oxford colleges and, in collaboration with his son Thomas, a series of *Views of the Monuments of Great Britain.*

HOLLIS, Thomas
British, 19th century.
Born 1818; died 4 October 1843, in Walworth.
Draughtsman, engraver.

Thomas Hollis was the son and pupil of George Hollis. He also studied with H.W. Pickersgill and attended classes at the Royal Academy. It is not always easy to distinguish his works from those of his father, with whom he frequently collaborated.

HOLLISTER, Antoinette B.
American, 19th - 20th century.
Born 19 August 1873, in Chicago.
Sculptor.

Antoinette B. Hollister trained at the Art Institute of Chicago, and worked under Rodin in Paris.

AUCTION RECORDS:
NEW YORK, 14 Nov 1980, *Pan* (green-patinated bronze, h. 48 1/2 ins / 123.2 cm) USD 4,600.

HOLLMANN, Karl
German, 19th century.
Born 18 July 1863, in Berlin.
Painter.

He worked at the academy of Karlsruhe. He is credited with a number of genre sculptures.

HOLLO, Barnabas
Hungarian, 19th - 20th century.
Born 16 May 1866, in Also-Hangony; died 2 November 1917, in Budapest.
Sculptor.

A pupil of Aloyse Strohl, Barnabas Hollo received a silver medal at the 1900 Exposition Universelle.

HOLLO, Zsigmund
Hungarian, 19th century.
Born 1858, in Miskolc; died 11 February 1896, in Pécs.
Painter.

Zsigmund Hollo worked at the academy in Budapest.

HOLLOGAN, J.
British, 18th century.
Painter, pastellist.

J. Hollogan exhibited in London at the Society of Artists in 1790.

HOLLOSY, Simon
Hungarian, 19th - 20th century.
Born 2 February 1857, in Mamarossziget; died 8 May 1918, in Técso.
Painter.

A pupil of Szekely, Simon Hollósy was influenced by French Impressionism. He is known particularly for his landscapes and illustrations such as those for the poetry of Jozsef Kiss.

MUSEUMS AND GALLERIES:
BUDAPEST (Magyar Nemzeti Gal.): *Peasant Courtyard; Standard-Bearer.*

HOLLOWAY, Charles Edward
British, 19th century.
Born 10 May 1838, in Christchurch; died 5 March 1897, in London.
Painter, watercolourist, draughtsman. Seascapes, landscapes.

Charles Holloway studied first with Leigh alongside Fred Walker, D. Linton and Charles Green. From 1866, he concentrated entirely on painting. He travelled to Venice in 1875 and 1895 and to The Netherlands in 1883. Notable for their skilful drawing and striking use of colour, his works are full of feeling and harmony. He is considered one of the best English landscape and seascape painters. He exhibited fairly regularly in London from 1866, particularly at the Royal Academy, the Suffolk Street Gallery and the New Water-Colour Society.

MUSEUMS AND GALLERIES:
LONDON (Victoria and Albert Mus.): *Windy Day.*

AUCTION RECORDS:
LONDON, 24 Feb 1908, *Game* (1885, watercolour) GBP 1. LONDON, 6 March 1909, *Entering Harbour* (1881, watercolour) GBP 14. LONDON, April 1922, *St Paul's Cathedral from the River* (watercolour) GBP 6. LONDON, 19 and 20 March 1946, *The Thames at Chelsea* (watercolour) GBP 38. MONTRÉAL, 19 Nov 1991, *The Thames at Limehouse in Winter* (watercolour, 10 x 13 1/2 ins / 25.5 x 34.2 cm) CAD 800. LONDON, 17 Nov 1995, *The Painter's Studio* (1885, pencil and watercolour heightened with gouache, 22 1/4 x 29 1/2 ins / 56.5 x 74.7 cm) GBP 5,750. LONDON, 3 March 1999, *Artist's Studio* (1885, pencil and watercolour heightened with gouache, 22 x 30 ins / 56 x 75 cm) GBP 2,400.

HOLLOWAY, Edgar
British, 20th century.
Born 6 May 1914.
Engraver (line-engraving).

HOLLOWAY, Evan
American, 20th - 21st century.

Born 1967, in La Mirada (California).
Sculptor.
Evan Holloway graduated in 1989 with a BA from the University of California, Santa Cruz and later studied for a Master's degree in Fine Art at University of California, Los Angeles, graduating in 1997. His work is concerned with the interaction between nature and culture.

Holloway's work has featured in several solo exhibitions, including *Black Cabinet* at Marc Foxx in Los Angeles in 1997, another show at Marc Foxx in 1999 and at The Approach in London in 2001. His work *Grey Scale*, a delicate sculpture made from tree branches shaped into right angles to create a structure painted in tones ranging from white to grey to black, was selected for the Whitney Biennial in 2002. In 2004 Holloway showed *Map*, a similar structure with one side painted in grey tones and the other in colour.

BIBLIOGRAPHY:
Erickson, Karl, '*Evan Holloway, Marc Foxx*' in *Flash Art*, no. 220, p. 104, Milan, 2001. *Whitney Biennial 2002*, Exhibition catalogue, Harry N. Abrams, New York, 2002.

MUSEUMS AND GALLERIES:
LOS ANGELES (MOCA).

HOLLOWAY, George
British, 19th century.
Born c. 1820, in Christchurch; died 12 July 1843, in Christchurch.
Painter.
George Holloway, a pupil of Patten, exhibited in London in 1842.

HOLLOWAY, L.
British, 19th century.
Painter.
L. Holloway exhibited several times at the Royal Academy in London between 1857 and 1865.

HOLLOWAY, Thomas
British, 18th - 19th century.
Born 1748, in London; died February 1827, in Coltishall, near Norwich.
Painter, engraver (burin).
Thomas Holloway engraved mainly portraits and illustrations for magazines. Between 1773 and 1792, he exhibited in London at the Society of Artists and the Royal Academy.

HOLLPEIN, Heinrich
Austrian, 19th century.
Active in Vienna c. 1836.
Painter.
He is noted for portraits of *The Singer Wild* and *The Poet Grillparzer*.

HÖLLRIGL, Karl A.
Austrian, 20th century.
Born 1907; died 1987.
Painter.
Art Brut.
Höllrigl was active in Coire.

MUSEUMS AND GALLERIES:
COIRE (Bündner Kunstmus.) - LAUSANNE (Coll. de l'Art Brut).

AUCTION RECORDS:
LUCERNE, 20 May 1995, *Fragmented Plant* (1982, mixed media/paper, 11 1/2 x 8 1/4 ins / 29.5 x 21 cm) CHF 750.

HOLLSTAINER, Christoph
Austrian, 17th century.
Sculptor.
He worked in Upper Styria.

HOLLSTEIN, Eduard
German, 19th century.
Active in Berlin c. 1840.
Painter. Landscapes.
He is documented for landscapes of Switzerland.

MUSEUMS AND GALLERIES:
KALININGRAD: *Sun Setting over the Alps*; *View of Ischl*.

HOLLWAY, Janet (Miss)
British, 19th century.
Miniaturist.
Janet Hollway exhibited in London at the Royal Academy from 1887.

HOLLY ROMERO, Diego
American, 20th - 21st century.
Born 1965.
Ceramicist. Scenes with figures.
Folk Art.
Diego Holly Romero featured in 2001 in *Un art populaire* (*An Art of the People*) presented at Fondation Cartier pour l'Art Contemporain in Paris. The exhibition brought together artists creating objects representative of the peoples of the world's everyday life. He showed ceramics in the traditional *pueblo* style, distinguished by the fact that the scenes decorating the bottom of his pots represented, in a style both earthy and elaborate, erotic episodes of Native American life.

BIBLIOGRAPHY:
Un art populaire, exhibition catalogue, Fondation Cartier, Paris, 2001.

HOLLYERS, Samuel
British, 19th - 20th century.
Born 1826, in London; died 29 December 1919.
Engraver, lithographer.
Samuel Hollyers spent much of his life in New York. Among his best-known works is *Charles Dickens in his Study*

HOLM, Adolf
German, 19th century.
Born 21 April 1858, in Mücheln, near Merseburg.
Painter, writer.
He painted landscapes, still lifes, portraits and genre pictures. He was also a lithographer.

HOLM, Anders
Swedish, 18th - 19th century.
Born c. 1751 or 1770; died c. 1822 or 1824.
Painter. Scenes with figures, landscapes with figures.
Anders Holm studied at the academy in Stockholm. He executed compositions after antiquity, as well as landscapes.

MUSEUMS AND GALLERIES:
HELSINKI: *Landscape with Stream*.

AUCTION RECORDS:
STOCKHOLM, 29 May 1991, *Classical Landscape with Christian and Moor Horsemen* (oil on panel, a pair, each 8 1/4 x 11 1/2 ins / 21 x 29 cm) SEK 15,000. STOCKHOLM, 19 May 1992, *Landscape with Boat and Bridge in Background* (oil on canvas, 27 1/4 x 36 1/2 ins / 69 x 93 cm) SEK 30,000. HELSINKI, 24 April 1999, *Landscapes* (oil on panel, a pair, 8 x 12 ins / 20 x 30 cm) FIM 21,000. STOCKHOLM, 18 May 1999, *Lake Landscapes with Buildings and Figures* (1809, oil on panel, a pair, 15 x 21 ins / 39 x 53 cm) SEK 47,000. STOCKHOLM, 2 Dec 2003, *River Landscape with Figures and Boats* (1800, oil on canvas, 25 x 32 ins / 64 x 82 cm) SEK 52,000.

HOLM, Axel Peter Jorgen
Danish, 19th century.
Born 14 March 1861, in Rodby.
Painter, engraver.
Axel Holm was a pupil of Godfred Christensen. He painted mostly landscapes.

HOLM, Christian Frederik Carl
Danish, 19th century.
Born 18 February 1804, in Copenhagen; died 24 July 1846, in Tivoli.

Painter, engraver (etching). History painting, landscapes with figures, landscapes, animals.

The son of a silversmith, Christian Holm rejected his father's artform early on and devoted himself to painting and engraving. He travelled to Dresden in 1829. Between 1830 and 1834 he was in Munich, and in 1844 he travelled to Rome. He also worked in Sweden and Norway.

He had a particular gift for painting animals and Le Blanc mentions two of his animal plates. He also executed several historical paintings.

MUSEUMS AND GALLERIES:

COPENHAGEN: *View of the Alps; Tyrolean Hunters.*

AUCTION RECORDS:

COPENHAGEN, 5 May 1976, *Landscape with Horses* (oil on canvas, 37 1/2 x 50 1/2 ins / 95 x 128 cm) DKK 10,500. AHLDEN, 9 May 2003, *Taking the Cows up to the Mountain Pasture* (1838, oil on canvas, 28 x 39 ins / 72 x 98 cm) EUR 5,500.

HOLM, Ebba

Danish, 20th century.

Born 29 May 1889, in Frederiksberg; died 30 November 1967, in Copenhagen.

Painter, engraver (wood), illustrator, decorative artist. Designs (wallpapers).

Holm studied at the Kongelige Danske Kunstakademi in Copenhagen. She travelled and was active throughout Europe, especially in Italy. Her artwork was very varied; in addition to painting she also produced illustrations, wood engravings and wallpaper.

AUCTION RECORDS:

NEW YORK, 20 July 1995, *Lady in Oriental Dress Writing at a Desk* (1922, oil on canvas, 24 1/2 x 18 1/2 ins / 62.2 x 47.3 cm) USD 1,495.

HOLM, Emil Niels Severin

Danish, 19th century.

Born 1823, in Aarhus; died 29 December 1863, in Copenhagen.

Painter. Military subjects, landscapes.

Emil Holm is known for his landscapes and military scenes.

AUCTION RECORDS:

LONDON, 25 Feb 1970, *The Ruins of Messina*, GBP 380. LONDON, 30 Nov 1977, *Landscape with the Strait of Messina* (1859, oil on canvas, 33 x 52 ins / 84 x 132 cm) GBP 8,000. COPENHAGEN, 5 Feb 1992, *Fishing Village in Summer* (1844, oil on canvas, 23 1/2 x 34 1/4 ins / 60 x 87 cm) DKK 9,500. COPENHAGEN, 4 Sept 2002, *Herrevadskloster in Skåne, Summer of 1852* (oil on canvas, 9 x 13 ins / 22 x 32 cm) DKK 12,000. COPENHAGEN, 25 Feb 2004, *View towards Catania with Etna in Background, Sicily* (1867, oil on canvas, 15 x 22 ins / 37 x 56 cm) DKK 58,000.

HOLM, Frederick

Danish, 18th century.

Painter.

Frederick Holm worked for King Frederik IV.

HOLM, Harald Martin Hansen

Danish, 19th - 20th century.

Born 26 August 1866, in Horne; died 22 February 1920, in Genoa.

Painter. Flowers.

Holm received an honourable mention at the Exposition Universelle in 1900.

MUSEUMS AND GALLERIES:

COPENHAGEN (Statens Mus. for Kunst): *Orkidéer* (*Orchids*) (1900).

AUCTION RECORDS:

LONDON, 16 Feb 1990, *Asters* (1899, oil on canvas, 21 x 16 1/4 ins / 53.4 x 41.3 cm) GBP 1,980. LUND, 30 Oct 1999, *Still-life with Flowers* (1917, oil on canvas, oval, a pair, 20 x 16 ins / 52 x 40 cm) SEK 16,000.

HOLM, Heinrich Gustav Ferdinand

Danish, 19th century.

Born 23 April 1803; died May 1861, in Copenhagen.

Painter.

Heinrich Holm was the son of Jens Holm. He painted landscapes.

AUCTION RECORDS:

COPENHAGEN, 3 May 1977, *View of Nytorv Palace* (gouache and pen, 8 x 12 1/4 ins / 20.5 x 31 cm) DKK 31,000. COPENHAGEN, 29 Nov 1978, *Street Scene* (watercolour, 5 x 6 3/4 ins / 13 x 17 cm) DKK 16,500. COPENHAGEN, 27 March 1979, *Winter Landscape* (drawing in sepia ink, 7 3/4 x 9 3/4 ins / 20 x 25 cm) DKK 15,000. COPENHAGEN, 27 March 1979, *The University Courtyard* (watercolour, 7 1/2 x 9 ins / 19 x 22 cm) DKK 14,500. COPENHAGEN, 2 Dec 1998, *Figures at Kongen's Nytorv* (watercolour, 7 x 9 ins / 17 x 22 cm) DKK 19,000. COPENHAGEN, 23 Feb 1999, *Part of Amelie Street 15-17* (c. 1850, pen and watercolour, Works on paper, 4 x 6 ins / 11 x 15 cm) DKK 12,000. COPENHAGEN, 23 Feb 1999, *The General Hospital seen from Amalie Street* (c. 1848, pen and watercolour, Works on paper, 7 x 9 ins / 18 x 23 cm) DKK 20,000. COPENHAGEN, 29 Feb 2000, *Hoigaard Home Farm near Aldershvile* (pen and watercolour, Works on paper, 9 x 14 ins / 22 x 35 cm) DKK 18,000. COPENHAGEN, 4 Sept 2000, *View of the East Coast of Sjaelland with Large Trees* (pencil and watercolour, 8 x 12 ins / 21 x 31 cm) DKK 17,000. COPENHAGEN, 29 Nov 2000, *Street scene, Kronprinsessegade, Copenhagen* (watercolour, 4 x 4 ins / 9 x 11 cm) DKK 16,000. COPENHAGEN, 29 Aug 2001, *Schonberg's Place at Gamle Kongevei* (1834, watercolour, 4 x 7 ins / 11 x 18 cm) DKK 12,000. VEJLE, 25 Sept 2001, *View of Copenhagen with Dehn's Palace* (watercolour, 6 x 8 ins / 15 x 21 cm) DKK 12,500. COPENHAGEN, 6 Feb 2002, *View across Gammel Avlsgaard towards the Round Tower* (c. 1840, watercolour, 6 x 8 ins / 16 x 20 cm) DKK 13,000. VEJLE, 5 May 2003, *Schonberg's Country Home, Gammel Kongevej* (1834, watercolour, 5 x 7 ins / 12 x 18 cm) DKK 24,000.

HOLM, Hildegard

German, 20th century.

Born 14 October 1924, in Duisburg (Rhineland).

Active in the USA from 1950.

Painter.

Holm studied for a BA degree at the University of California in Los Angeles. She exhibited mainly in California.

HOLM, Jens

Danish, 19th century.

Born 1776, in Copenhagen; died 24 December 1859, in Copenhagen.

Painter, engraver.

Jens Holm spent part of his youth in Rome and specialised in landscapes.

HOLM, Jesper Johansen

Danish, 18th - 19th century.

Born 1748, in Copenhagen; died 7 January 1828, in Copenhagen.

Sculptor, medallist.

Jesper Holm was a pupil of Johannes Wedewelt. He produced silver medals and works in porcelain.

HOLM, Just Jean Christian

Danish, 19th century.

Born 8 May 1815, in Randers; died 20 March 1907.

Painter.

Just Holm studied at the Kunstakademi in Copenhagen. He spent long periods in Munich and Paris.

AUCTION RECORDS:

NEW YORK, 26 Feb 1986, *Fanny and Alexander on a Swing* (1847, oil on canvas, 61 1/2 x 53 1/4 ins / 156.2 x 135.5 cm) USD 6,000. AHLDEN, 23 April 1999, *Portrait of a Man against the Silhouette of Munich* (1843, oil on canvas, 38 x 29 ins / 96 x 73 cm) DEM 12,000. VEJLE, 20 May 1999, *Woman seen from behind Standing by Open Window* (oil on canvas, 13 x 11 ins / 33 x 28 cm) DKK 20,000.

HOLM, Lauritz
Danish, 18th century.
Active in London.
Sculptor.
Lauritz Holm exhibited from 1761 to 1773.

HOLM, Niels
Danish, 19th century.
Born 14 February 1860, in Slagelse.
Sculptor.
Niels Holm is known to have produced busts and statuettes.

HOLM, Per Daniel
Swedish, 19th - 20th century.
Born 11 September 1835, in Malingsbo; died 1903, in Stockholm.
Painter, watercolourist. Landscapes, flowers.
Holm studied under Nils Anderson. He was active in Stockholm, Düsseldorf, Munich, Karlsruhe and Paris. He belonged to the generation following Carl Johan Fahlcrantz, 'the father of Swedish landscape painting'. He was one of the first artists to paint the Nordic landscapes of his country. The small studies in oil that he produced while he was on his travels are the first examples of painting in the open air. His most well-known painting *Saggat-träsk, Kvikkjokk* (*Saggat Swamp, Kvikkjokk*), kept at the national museum in Stockholm, was produced in Lapland, an area almost unknown at that time, and has been reproduced in historical and ethnographical works on the region.
MUSEUMS AND GALLERIES:
STOCKHOLM: *Forested Landscape*; *Saggat-träsk, Kvikkjokk* (*Saggat Swamp, Kvikkjokk*); four small watercolours.
AUCTION RECORDS:
GÖTEBORG, 24 March 1976, *Landscape* (1870, oil on canvas, 12 1/4 x 18 ins / 31 x 46 cm) SEK 4,700. LONDON, 19 April 1978, *Landscape in Lapland* (1866, oil on canvas, 44 1/4 x 67 ins / 112.5 x 170 cm) GBP 4,200. STOCKHOLM, 26 Oct 1982, *Summer Landscape* (1876, oil on canvas, 17 1/4 x 27 1/2 ins / 44 x 70 cm) SEK 20,000. STOCKHOLM, 26 April 1983, *Summer Landscape* (1862, oil on canvas, 14 1/2 x 23 1/4 ins / 37 x 59 cm) SEK 10,200. STOCKHOLM, 13 Nov 1987, *Summer Landscape* (1866, oil on canvas, 26 1/2 x 39 3/4 ins / 67 x 101 cm) SEK 51,000. STOCKHOLM, 27 April 1988, *Undergrowth with Young Girl and a Sheep near a Stream* (1869, oil on canvas, 24 1/2 x 18 ins / 62 x 46 cm) SEK 5,800. STOCKHOLM, 15 Nov 1988, *Forest Lake at Sunset* (oil, 12 1/4 x 17 3/4 ins / 31 x 45 cm) SEK 34,000. STOCKHOLM, 19 April 1989, *Undergrowth* (1859, oil on canvas, 10 1/4 x 13 3/4 ins / 26 x 35 cm) SEK 8,500. STOCKHOLM, 15 Nov 1989, *Reflections of the Sun on a Lake in a Forest* (oil, 12 1/4 x 17 3/4 ins / 31 x 45 cm) SEK 22,000. LONDON, 29 March 1990, *Forest near a Meadow Shrouded in Early Morning Mist* (1880, oil on paper, 7 1/4 x 11 ins / 18.5 x 27 cm) GBP 3,080. COPENHAGEN, 28 Aug 1991, *Roses in a Stone Urn* (1863, paint/mahogany panel, 13 3/4 x 15 3/4 ins / 35 x 40 cm) DKK 8,000.

HOLM, Rasmus Andersen
Danish, 19th century.
Born 1781; died 4 February 1874.
Painter.
Rasmus Holm was a pupil of J. P. Møller. He devoted himself to landscape painting.

HOLM, Rosalie
Maiden name: Petit
British, 19th century.
Born 1807; died 1873.
Engraver.
Rosalie Petit, an engraver, married Christian-Frederik Holm.

HOLM, Victor S.
American, 19th - 20th century.
Born 6 December 1876, in Copenhagen, Denmark; died 1935.
Sculptor, medallist.
Victor S. Holm studied at the Art Institute of Chicago, and was a member of the National Society of Sculpture of New York. Many monuments in universities and hospitals, as well as commemorative medals, are attributed to him.

HOLMA, Claude
Finnish, 20th century.
Active in France.
Painter.
Holma lived in Paris, where he married a French woman. He became a soldier in 1940. He wrote a book on David.

HOLMAN, Francis
British, 18th century.
Died 1790.
Painter. Military subjects, seascapes.
Francis Holman exhibited in London at the Royal Academy between 1774 and 1784.
MUSEUMS AND GALLERIES:
LONDON (Corporation of Trinity House): *Yacht Approaching the River Humber to Inspect Spurn Point Lighthouse, 7 April 1778* (painting).
AUCTION RECORDS:
LONDON, 27 Jan 1908, *Ships at the Mouth of a River*, GBP 2. LONDON, 12 Jan 1911, *Lord Hood Repelling the Attack by the Comte de Grasse, January 1782*, GBP 20. LONDON, 20 Feb 1925, *Blackwall Yard*, GBP 220. LONDON, 6 July 1934, *Near Cape St Vincent*, GBP 68. LONDON, 26 Oct 1945, *Warships off the Coast*, GBP 42. LONDON, 17 April 1964, *Seascape*, Gns 750. LONDON, 16 July 1965, *Seascape*, Gns 800. LONDON, 22 Nov 1967, *Sailing-ships Passing a Lighthouse*, GBP 3,200. LONDON, 3 April 1968, *Seaside with Many Figures*, GBP 8,500. LONDON, 23 June 1978, *The 'Columbus' off the Coast* (oil on canvas, 27 x 48 ins / 68.5 x 122 cm) GBP 4,500. LONDON, 23 March 1979, *Frigate 'Jamaica' off Dover* (1780, oil on canvas, 24 1/4 x 50 3/4 ins / 61.5 x 129 cm) GBP 6,500. LONDON, 26 Aug 1982, *The 'Elizabeth' and Other Ships off the Dutch Coast* (1774, oil on canvas, 32 3/4 x 58 ins / 83.5 x 147.5 cm) GBP 4,200. LONDON, 18 Nov 1983, *Shipping off Cornet Castle, Guernsey* (1785, oil on canvas, 34 1/2 x 59 1/2 ins / 87.6 x 151.1 cm) GBP 8,500. LONDON, 19 July 1985, *The 'Betsy' in Two Positions* (1774, oil on canvas, 25 x 39 3/4 ins / 63.5 x 101 cm) GBP 16,000. LONDON, 24 April 1987, *English Frigate with a Captured Dutch Merchant Ship* (1789, oil on canvas, 30 x 44 ins / 76.2 x 111.8 cm) GBP 16,000. LONDON, 9 Feb 1990, *Procession of Warships off Deal* (oil on canvas, 20 1/4 x 38 1/2 ins / 51.2 x 98 cm) GBP 6,600. LONDON, 20 April 1990, *Frigate and Other Ships in the Mediterranean* (oil on canvas, 25 1/2 x 56 1/4 ins / 64.8 x 142.7 cm) GBP 8,800. LONDON, 22 Nov 1991, *Merchant Ships off Yarmouth* (oil on canvas, 25 3/4 x 58 1/2 ins / 65.3 x 148.6 cm) GBP 14,300. LONDON, 20 Jan 1993, *The 'London', the 'Integrity', the 'Elizabeth' and the 'Nancy' off Yarmouth* (oil on canvas, 34 x 59 ins / 86.5 x 150 cm) GBP 27,600. LONDON, 9 Nov 1994, *English Warship and Other Ships at Sea* (oil on canvas, 27 1/2 x 52 1/2 ins / 70 x 133.5 cm) GBP 5,750. LONDON, 12 April 1995, *English Warship and Other Ships off Dover*; *Frigate and Other Ships off Portsmouth* (oil on canvas, a pair, each 20 1/2 x 26 1/2 ins / 52 x 67.5 cm) GBP 9,200. LONDON, 30 May 1996, *HMS 'Hyaena' Capturing Three Dutch Ships off Saint Eustatius* (1782, oil on canvas, 29 x 41 1/4 ins / 73.5 x 104.5 cm) GBP 4,025. LONDON, 9 July 1997, *Three-Master and Frigate in Rough Sea* (1781, oil on canvas, 34 x 68 ins / 86.5 x 173 cm) GBP 32,200. NEW YORK, 17 Feb 1999, *Four Views of the Antonetta* (1775, oil on canvas on

panel, 30 x 47 ins / 75 x 120 cm) USD 20,000. LONDON, 11 May 2000, *Ships of the Fleet off Naval Dockyard* (oil on canvas, 22 x 32 ins / 55 x 81 cm) GBP 7,000. LONDON, 19 June 2002, *Fifth Rate in Tow Positions, One under Sail and One at Anchor, in the Channel off Dover* (oil on canvas, 33 x 51 ins / 85 x 130 cm) GBP 15,000. LONDON, 21 May 2003, *Cutter Mermaid Running into the Fleet Anchorage at the Downs* (1778, oil on canvas, 18 x 14 ins / 46 x 36 cm) GBP 1,400. LONDON, 1 July 2004, *Action between Lord Hood and the Count de Grasse* (oil on canvas, 39 x 72 ins / 98 x 183 cm) GBP 55,000.

HOLMAN, Frank
American, 19th century.
Born 15 January 1865, in Attleboro (Massachusetts); died 1930, in Paris.
Painter.

Frank Holman was a pupil at the École des Beaux-Arts in Paris, and of Cabanel and Carolus-Duran. He received an honourable mention at the Exposition Universelle in Paris in 1900.

HOLMBERG, Adam Peter
Danish, 18th - 19th century.
Born 1762; died 1819.
Painter.

Adam Holmberg studied with Louis Jean Desprez in Stockholm.

HOLMBERG, August Johann
German, 19th - 20th century.
Born 1 August 1851, in Munich; died 7 October 1911, in Munich.
Painter. Genre scenes, portraits.

Holmberg studied sculpture at the school of arts and crafts in Munich, and painting at the academy in 1868 under Wilhelm Diez. He went to Italy in 1875 and Paris in 1878. He was awarded medals in Vienna in 1873, London in 1875, Munich in 1897, Düsseldorf and Berlin in 1880, Antwerp in 1885, Vienna in 1888, and Paris in 1900 (a silver medal at the Exposition Universelle).

MUSEUMS AND GALLERIES:
BERLIN: *Füssen Castle in Upper Bavaria* - GRAZ: *Landscape with Mill* - LEIPZIG: *Goldsmith in his Studio* - MUNICH: *Young Scholar*.

AUCTION RECORDS:
LONDON, 27-31 May 1898, *Far from the World*, FRF 1,800. LONDON, 16 March 1936, *Critical Moment*, GBP 42. NEW YORK, 18 Oct 1944, *Prisoners*, USD 200. VIENNA, 18 Sept 1979, *Convent Library* (oil on canvas, 37 x 50 1/4 ins / 94 x 127.5 cm) ATS 70,000. LONDON, 19 June 1981, *Child Reciting the Catechism* (oil on canvas, 29 3/4 x 34 3/4 ins / 75.6 x 88.2 cm) GBP 1,700.

HOLMBERG, Gustaf Werner
Finnish, 19th century.
Born 1 November 1830, in Helsinki; died 24 September 1860, in Düsseldorf.
Painter. Architectural views, landscapes.

Gustaf Holmberg was a pupil of Magnus von Wright and Pehr Adolf Kruskopf (1805-1852) in Finland. He exhibited in Cologne and Bremen and was a follower of the Düsseldorf School. In Düsseldorf his development as a landscape artist would be influenced by Johann Wilhelm Schirmer, who had founded an academy for landscape painting in 1827. He disappeared at the height of his fame. His work is particularly interesting for its representation of Finnish landscape. He was also influenced by Dutch and Norwegian art. Among his most noted and typical works is *The Kyrö Waterfall* (1854).

MUSEUMS AND GALLERIES:
HELSINKI: *The Kyrö Waterfall; The Park at a German Castle; View of the Kuru Chapel; View of the Kuru Chapel in Daylight; A Farm in Kuru; The Land of a Fiefdom; Finnish Landscape; Forrest Land Near Nasijarvi; Twastland Landscape* - OSLO: *Forest; Study*.

AUCTION RECORDS:
LONDON, 5 July 1978, *Wooded Landscape with Lake* (oil on canvas, 22 3/4 x 35 ins / 58 x 89 cm) GBP 1,700. COLOGNE, 15 June 1989, *Autumn in the Norwegian Highlands* (1866, oil on canvas, 10 x 17 ins / 25.5 x 43 cm) DEM 2,200. HELSINKI, 13 May 2000, *Old Man Filling his Pipe* (c. 1848, oil on canvas, 15 x 12 ins / 37 x 30 cm) FIM 70,000. HELSINKI, 2 Dec 2001, *Approaching Storm - Men with Horses and Wagon* (1856, oil on canvas, 24 x 33 ins / 62 x 84 cm) FIM 1,600,000.

HOLMBERGSSON, Johan
Swedish, 19th century.
Born 1804; died 1835, in Lund.
Draughtsman, engraver.

Johan Holmbergsson was a pupil at the academy in Stockholm. He painted Swedish historical subjects.

HOLMBOE, Thorolf
Norwegian, 19th - 20th century.
Born 10 May 1866, in Vefsen; died 1935, in Oslo.
Painter, draughtsman. Landscapes, seascapes, portraits. Designs (ceramics/decorative objects).
Art Nouveau.

Holmboe was taught at first by a Norwegian landscape artist before going on to study with Gude in Berlin and at the royal school of art in Christiania (now Oslo). He also studied under Cormon in Paris. He is best known for his decorative landscapes of northern Norway but painted seascapes as well. He worked on decorative arts between 1890 and 1915, producing Art Nouveau-style objects, and produced designs for ceramics.

Holmboe took part in exhibitions in Munich in 1891 and Paris in 1900. In 2001 some of his landscapes were entered in the exhibition *Da Dahl a Munch, Romanticismo, realismo e simbolismo nella pittura di paesaggio norvegese* (*From Dahl to Munch: Romanticism, Realism and Symbolism in Norwegian Landscape Painting*) at the Palazzo dei Diamanti in Ferrara.

BIBLIOGRAPHY:
Lange, Marit (ed.), *Da Dahl a Munch. Romanticismo, realismo e simbolismo nella pittura di paesaggio norvegese*, exhibition catalogue, Palazzo dei Diamanti, Ferrara Arte editore, Ferrara, 2001.

MUSEUMS AND GALLERIES:
OSLO (Nasjonalgal.): *Frozen Landscape below a Dyke* (1902, oil on canvas); *Pine Tree on the Coast in the Moonlight* (1902, oil on canvas).

AUCTION RECORDS:
LONDON, April 1922, *Norway: Sunset*, GBP 4. STOCKHOLM, 15 Nov 1988, *Sailing Ship off a Group of Islands in Summer* (oil, 27 1/4 x 38 1/2 ins / 69 x 98 cm) SEK 70,000. AMSTERDAM, 16 Nov 1988, *Coastal Landscape with Norwegian Vessels Moored in Calm Weather* (oil on canvas, 44 x 38 3/4 ins / 112 x 98.5 cm) NLG 3,680. LOKEREN, 4 Dec 1993, *View of a Park* (1904, oil on canvas, 24 x 19 3/4 ins / 61 x 50 cm) BEF 44,000. NEW YORK, 23 Oct 1997, *Little Girl in White Hat* (1905, oil on canvas, 48 x 47 1/2 ins / 121.9 x 120.7 cm) USD 14,950. OSLO, 22 Nov 1999, *Children Hoisting the Norwegian Flag* (1910, oil on canvas, 52 x 41 ins / 133 x 105 cm) NOK 200,000. OSLO, 7 Dec 1999, *In the Avenue - Woman and Child by a House* (1904, oil on canvas, 28 x 31 ins / 70 x 80 cm) NOK 82,000. OSLO, 8 May 2000, *Summer's Day in the Country near Arendal - Women Hanging Washing Out* (1906, oil on canvas, 48 x 39 ins / 123 x 100 cm) NOK 65,000. OSLO, 4 Dec 2000, *Evening in the Wood - Girl by Trees* (mixed media, 17 x 12 ins / 43 x 30

cm) NOK 48,000. OSLO, 11 June 2001, *Vessel by the Coast, possibly Heligoland* (oil on canvas, 35 x 43 ins / 90 x 110 cm) NOK 53,000. OSLO, 6 Nov 2001, *Dronningen, Bygdøy - View with Many Sailing Boats in Frognerkilen* (oil on canvas, 26 x 35 ins / 66 x 90 cm) NOK 115,000. LONDON, 21 March 2002, *Young Girl Laying the Tea Table in the Garden* (1905, oil on canvas, 48 x 47 ins / 122 x 120 cm) GBP 9,000. OSLO, 30 May 2002, *Girl Standing by Laid Table in Garden* (1905, oil on canvas, 48 x 48 ins / 122 x 121 cm) NOK 180,000. COPENHAGEN, 5 March 2003, *Evening with Horse Chestnut in Flower* (1912, watercolour, crayon and Indian ink, 24 x 22 ins / 61 x 57 cm) DKK 42,000. LYSAKER, 13 Dec 2003, *Christmas Shopping on Karl Johan, Oslo* (oil on canvas, 22 x 17 ins / 55 x 43 cm) NOK 110,000. OSLO, 25 May 2004, *Bare Rock-face and Boats* (oil on canvas, 28 x 35 ins / 70 x 90 cm) NOK 80,000. LONDON, 14 July 2004, *Midnight Sun at the North Cape* (oil on canvas, 45 x 65 ins / 114 x 164 cm) GBP 6,800.

HOLME, A.
British.
Portrait artist.
A. Holme is listed in *Art Prices Current*.
AUCTION RECORDS:
LONDON, 1 Feb 1908, *Portrait of Handel*, GBP 2.

HOLME, Dora
British, 19th century.
Miniaturist.
Dora Holme contributed many illustrations to the journal *The Studio*.

HOLME, Geoffrey
British, 19th - 20th century.
Active in London.
Illustrator, caricaturist.
Geoffrey Holme was a regular contributor to the art periodical *The Studio*.

HOLME, John Francis, called Frank
American, 19th century.
Born 29 June 1868, in Corinth (Illinois); died 27 July 1904, in Denver.
Newspaper cartoonist, illustrator, engraver.
John Francis Holme produced a number of drawings for American newspapers, and then founded a school of illustration in Chicago. His health forced him to move to Phoenix, where he founded the Bandar Log Press. He was also a teacher.

HOLME, Lauritz. See **HOLM**

HOLME, R.
British, 18th century.
Active in the second half of the 18th century.
Engraver.

HOLME, Siv
Swedish, 20th century.
Painter, draughtsman. Portraits, landscapes, interiors, still-lifes.
Holme exhibited his work at the Institut Tessin in Paris in 1946.

HOLME, William
British, 19th century.
Painter. Genre scenes.
William Holme exhibited work between 1833 and 1849.

HOLMEAD, Clifford H. Phillips
American, 20th century.
Born 1889; died 1975.
Painter. Figures, landscapes.
Clifford Holmead was acquainted with Soutine and Modigliani. He often painted tragic faces in which fierce humour was discernible, and his landscapes are just as tormented.

HOLMENS, Gérard
Belgian, 20th century.
Born 29 September 1934, in Ostend.
Sculptor.
Holmens studied at the academies of fine art in Ostend, Ghent and Antwerp, and at the Académie de la Grande Chaumière in Paris. After first producing figurative works he turned to the creation of more abstract forms, usually in white marble. The museum of fine arts in Ostend staged a solo exhibition of his work in 2001.
MUSEUMS AND GALLERIES:
COURTRAI - DETROIT - KNOKKE - MONS (MBA) - OSTEND - YPRES.
AUCTION RECORDS:
LOKEREN, 13 March 1976, *Bat* (1970, marble, h. 17 1/4 ins / 44 cm) BEF 60,000. BREDA, 26 April 1977, *Figure* (1964, marble, h. 17 3/4 ins / 45 cm) NLG 2,200. LOKEREN, 21 March 1992, *Figure* (pink-veined white marble, h. 78 3/4 ins / 200 cm and w. 27 3/4 ins/70.5 cm) BEF 360,000. LOKEREN, 12 March 1994, *Form* (marble, h. 58 1/4 ins / 148 cm and w. 9 1/2 ins/24 cm) BEF 220,000. LOKEREN, 9 Dec 1995, *Abstraction* (1960, lead on a marble plinth, h. 10 1/2 ins / 26.5 cm) BEF 60,000. LOKEREN, 11 Dec 1999, *Insect* (1965, marble, 12 x 9 ins / 31 x 22 cm) BEF 70,000. ANTWERP, 4 April 2000, *Composition* (marble, h. 56 ins / 143 cm) BEF 240,000. LOKEREN, 11 May 2002, *Form* (1964, white marble, 10 x 10 ins / 25 x 25 cm) EUR 1,700. ANTWERP, 21 Oct 2003, *Composition* (marble, h. 49 ins / 124 cm) EUR 2,400. LOKEREN, 15 May 2004, *Fish* (marble, 28 x 61 ins / 72 x 155 cm) EUR 9,000. LOKEREN, 15 May 2004, *Communication* (white marble, 75 x 26 ins / 190 x 65 cm) EUR 11,000.

HOLMES, Basil
British, 19th century.
Painter. Landscapes.
Basil Holmes exhibited in London at the Royal Academy from 1844 to 1850.

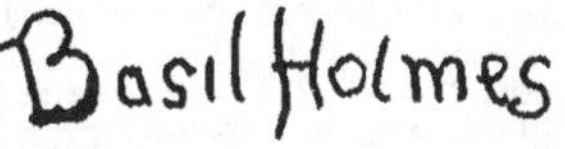

AUCTION RECORDS:
NEW YORK, 25 May 1988, *Afternoon near Sevenoaks, Kent* (oil on canvas, 20 x 27 ins / 50.8 x 68.8 cm) USD 10,450.

HOLMES, Charles John (Sir)
British, 19th - 20th century.
Born 11 November 1868, in Preston; died 1936, in London.
Painter, engraver, watercolourist. Landscapes.
Charles Holmes exhibited at the New English Art Club, of which he was a member, and in 1909 in Manchester. He was an associate of the Royal Society of Painters in Watercolours and Director of the National Portrait Gallery and then the National Gallery, London. He was knighted in 1921.
MUSEUMS AND GALLERIES:
LONDON (Tate Collection): *The Red Ruin* (1907, oil on canvas); *The Burning Kiln* (1914, oil on canvas) - OXFORD (Ashmolean Mus.): *Coniston Old Man from Levens Water* (painting); *Saddleback from the South-west* (painting).
AUCTION RECORDS:
LONDON, May 1924, *High Cup Nick Seen from Middle Tongue*, GBP 78. LONDON, 30 Nov 1928, *View of Murton Fell from Middle Tongue*, GBP 60. LONDON, 22 June 1934, *Church at Simmerton*, GBP 42. LONDON, 5 Sept 2002, *Harter Fell* (1909, oil on canvas, 20 x 24 ins / 51 x 61 cm) GBP 1,800.

HOLMES, Edward
British, 19th century.
Painter. Genre scenes, landscapes.

Edward Holmes was a member of the Royal Society of British Artists. He exhibited very frequently in London at the Royal Academy, the British Institution and the Suffolk Street Gallery between 1841 and 1891.

Auction records:

London, 23 May 1924, *Waiting,* GBP 10. London, 13 Dec 1989, *A New Trick* (1884, oil on canvas, 17 x 20 3/4 ins / 43 x 53 cm) GBP 2,750. New York, 21 Nov 1999, *Nibble* (oil on canvas, 19 x 27 ins / 48 x 69 cm) USD 1,800. Billingshurst, 24 July 2000, *Leading the Way* (oil on canvas, 19 x 30 ins / 49 x 75 cm) GBP 4,200. New Orleans, 29 July 2000, *Young Angler* (oil on canvas, 21 x 17 ins / 53 x 43 cm) USD 3,000. Nottingham, 24 May 2001, *Prawn Fishers* (oil on canvas, 17 x 22 ins / 43 x 56 cm) GBP 5,900. London, 25 June 2002, *Nearest Way Home* (oil on canvas, 20 x 30 ins / 52 x 75 cm) GBP 2,400. Lund, 16 Nov 2002, *Landscape with Girl and Dog* (oil on canvas, 17 x 20 ins / 44 x 52 cm) SEK 19,000. London, 29 May 2003, *Chasing the Ducks* (18541, oil on canvas, 20 x 30 ins / 51 x 76 cm) GBP 3,250.

HOLMES, George

Irish, 18th - 19th century.
Painter, engraver. Landscapes.

George Holmes is probably the artist of that name still exhibiting in Dublin in 1843.

HOLMES, George Augustus

British, 19th - 20th century.
Died 1911.
Active in London between 1852 and 1911.
Painter. Genre scenes, animals.

George Holmes exhibited frequently at the Royal Society of British Artists, of which he was a member, from 1852, and also at the Royal Society of British Artists of Birmingham and at the British Institution.

Auction records:

New York, 23 and 24 Jan 1901, *Friendly Greetings,* USD 240. London, 4 May 1908, *Returning Home,* GBP 6. London, 4 June 1908, *Newfoundland Puppy,* GBP 5. London, 4 Dec 1909, *Kiss Me* (1876) GBP 26. London, 18 March 1980, *Circle of Friends* (oil on canvas, 22 1/2 x 28 1/2 ins / 57 x 72.5 cm) GBP 1,600. London, 23 Sept 1988, *Young Friends* (1876, oil on canvas, 26 3/4 x 20 1/2 ins / 68 x 52 cm) GBP 8,250. Göteborg, 1 Oct 1988, *Farewell* (oil on canvas, 10 3/4 ins / 27.38 cm) SEK 20,000. London, 2 June 1989, *First Meeting* (1881, oil on canvas, 20 1/2 x 29 ins / 52 x 73.5 cm) GBP 9,680. Bern, 12 May 1990, *Lack of Experience* (oil on canvas, 19 3/4 x 26 ins / 50 x 66 cm) CHF 3,500. London, 1 Nov 1990, *A Prickly Problem* (oil on canvas, 20 x 26 1/4 ins / 51.1 x 66.7 cm) GBP 2,640. London, 12 May 1993, *Noisy Family* (oil on canvas, 15 x 20 ins / 38 x 51 cm) GBP 3,910. New York, 28 May 1993, *Live and Let Live* (oil on canvas, 25 1/2 x 21 1/2 ins / 64.7 x 54.6 cm) USD 10,350. London, 27 March 1996, *Friends* (1894, oil on canvas, 23 1/2 x 35 1/2 ins / 60 x 90 cm) GBP 4,945. Bath, 6 Dec 1999, *Welcome Home* (oil on canvas, 13 x 10 ins / 34 x 26 cm) GBP 4,800. Billingshurst, 29 Jan 2001, *Pushing Family* (oil on canvas, 21 x 26 ins / 54 x 67 cm) GBP 7,200. London, 14 June 2001, *An Inquisitive Terrier* (oil on canvas, 11 x 9 ins / 27 x 23 cm) GBP 1,800. Clevedon, 21 Nov 2002, *Doctor* (oil on board, 14 x 17 ins / 36 x 42 cm) GBP 6,000. London, 8 April 2003, *Rivals* (oil on canvas, 9 x 7 ins / 22 x 17 cm) GBP 1,500. London, 4 Sept 2003, *But They Who Come Mid Frost and Flood, Peeping from Bank* (1968, oil on canvas, painted oval, 18 x 22 ins / 46 x 56 cm) GBP 6,000. London, 4 March 2004, *Rivals* (oil on canvas, 9 x 7 ins / 23 x 18 cm) GBP 2,200. London, 17 Nov 2004, *The Favourite* (1964, oil on canvas, 13 x 12 ins / 33 x 30 cm) GBP 3,800.

HOLMES, Henry (Mrs)

British, 19th century.
Sculptor.

Mrs Holmes was exhibiting work in around 1881.

HOLMES, J. (Jr.)

British, 19th century.
Painter.

J. Holmes exhibited in London at the Royal Academy and, particularly, at the Suffolk Street Gallery from 1836 to 1859.

HOLMES, James

British, 19th century.
Born 1777, in Burslem; died 24 February 1860.
Miniaturist, watercolourist.

James Holmes was one of George IV's favourite painters. A member of the Society of Painters in Watercolours, he exhibited there between 1813 and 1822. In 1819, he began exhibiting in London at the Royal Academy. As one of the founder-members of the Society of British Artists, he took part in its exhibitions from 1850.

Auction records:

London, 10 July 1984, *Armado and Jaquenetta* (1828, watercolour heightened with white, 9 3/4 x 8 1/4 ins / 25 x 21 cm) GBP 1,100. London, 8 Sept 1999, *Officer of East Indian Regiment, probably Madras Light Cavalry* (oval miniature, h. 2 ins / 6 cm) GBP 1,200. London, 6 March 2001, *Portrait of a Lady in a White Dress* (1831, miniature, h. 5 ins / 12 cm) GBP 1,700. London, 30 Oct 2001, *Lady Reclining in a White Dress and Pink Shawl* (miniature, h. 4 ins / 10 cm) GBP 1,000. Exeter, 4 March 2003, *Rt Hon George Gordon Byron, later Lord Byron* (1816, oil on canvas, 4 x 3 ins / 11 x 8 cm) GBP 3,500.

HOLMES, John

British, 20th century.
Born 1935, in London.
Painter.

John Holmes exhibited in London in 1962, and also showed his work in the USA, Canada, Denmark, Belgium and Holland.

HOLMES, Marcus

British, 20th century.
Born 1875; died 1951.
Active in Monmouth.
Painter.

Marcus Holmes was a member of the Royal Drawing Society.

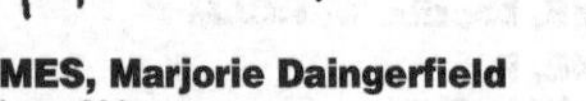

HOLMES, Marjorie Daingerfield

American, 20th century.
Born in New York.
Sculptor.

Marjorie Daingerfield Holmes was a member of the National Arts Club of New York.

HOLMES, P.

British, 17th century.
Active in London at the end of the 17th century.
Engraver.

P. Holmes was one of the engravers to play a major role in the publication of *Emblems,* which appeared in 1696. His first name may have been Philip.

HOLMES, P.

Dutch, 19th century.
Active in Amsterdam c. 1820.
Landscape artist.

HOLMES, Ralph William

American, 20th century.
Born 1876, in Illinois; died 1963.

Painter, illustrator. Landscapes.

Ralph William Holmes trained in Chicago and Illinois. He was a member of the Arts Club of California.

AUCTION RECORDS:

LOS ANGELES-SAN FRANCISCO, 12 July 1990, *Rim Canyon* (oil on canvas, 24 x 28 ins / 61 x 71 cm) USD 1,650. NEW YORK, 27 Sept 1996, *Californian Coastline (San Pedro)* (oil/Masonite, 17½ x 20 ins / 44.4 x 50.8 cm) USD 805. PASADENA, 19 Oct 1999, *Paramont Ranch* (oil on canvas, 24 x 30 ins / 61 x 76 cm) USD 3,750. LOS ANGELES, 3 May 2000, *Lost City, Bryce Canyon* (oil on canvas, 24 x 28 ins / 61 x 71 cm) USD 1,800. PASADENA, 14 Nov 2000, *Summer Landscape* (oil on canvas, 24 x 28 ins / 61 x 71 cm) USD 1,500. PASADENA, 13 Feb 2001, *Landscape* (oil on canvas, 28 x 32 ins / 71 x 81 cm) USD 3,000. SAN FRANCISCO, 13 June 2001, *Red Barn in a Landscape* (oil on canvas on masonite, 16 x 20 ins / 41 x 51 cm) USD 2,500. PASADENA, 11 June 2002, *House in Foothill Landscape* (oil on masonite, 16 x 20 ins / 41 x 51 cm) USD 1,700. PASADENA, 29 Oct 2002, *Landing* (oil on canvas, 34 x 36 ins / 86 x 91 cm) USD 6,000. PASADENA, 17 June 2003, *River Landscape* (oil on canvas, 24 x 30 ins / 61 x 76 cm) USD 2,000. PASADENA, 17 June 2003, *Landscape with Road to the Snow* (oil on canvas, 24 x 28 ins / 61 x 71 cm) USD 3,000.

HOLMES, Richard Rivington (Sir)
British, 19th - 20th century.
Born 16 November 1835, in London; died 22 March 1911, in London.
Painter. Landscapes.

Richard Holmes exhibited in London at the Royal Academy from 1874 to 1878, and at the Grosvenor Gallery between 1872 and 1891. He is best known as an archaeologist and art historian.

AUCTION RECORDS:

LONDON, 3 April 1911, *San Gimignano dalle Belli Torri*, GBP 1.

HOLMES, William Henry
American, 19th - 20th century.
Born 1 December 1846, in Cadiz (Ohio); died 1933, in Royal Oak (Michigan).
Active in Washington DC.
Painter, watercolourist.

William H. Holmes occupied the difficult post of curator of the National Gallery at the Smithsonian Institute in Washington DC. During his artistic career he was awarded the Corcoran Prize for Watercolours in 1900, and the Parsons Prize in 1902.

HOLMGREN, Fritz
Swedish, 19th century.
Died 1857, in Stockholm.
Miniaturist.

HOLMLUND, Josephina or Josefina
Swedish, 19th - 20th century.
Born 1827, in Stockholm; died 1905.
Painter. Landscapes with figures, landscapes.

Holmlund studied under Billing.

AUCTION RECORDS:

GÖTEBORG, 9 Nov 1977, *Seashore* (1899, oil on canvas, 18½ x 28¾ ins / 47 x 73 cm) SEK 10,000. STOCKHOLM, 30 Oct 1979, *Landscape* (oil on canvas, 11 x 15¾ ins / 27 x 40 cm) SEK 5,800. COPENHAGEN, 22 April 1982, *View of a Fjord* (1894, oil on canvas, 17 x 28¾ ins / 43 x 73 cm) DKK 16,000. STOCKHOLM, 1 Nov 1983, *Mountain Landscape* (1861, oil on canvas, 15¾ x 22½ ins / 40 x 57 cm) SEK 14,800. STOCKHOLM, 29 Oct 1985, *Mountain Landscape with Stream* (1897, oil on canvas, 45¼ x 32 ins / 115 x 81 cm) SEK 30,000. STOCKHOLM, 20 April 1987, *View of a Fjord* (oil on canvas, 15¼ x 23½ ins / 39 x 60 cm) SEK 35,000. STOCKHOLM, 27 April 1988, *Fjord Landscape with a Steamboat against a Background of Mountains* (oil on canvas, 15 x 22 ins / 38 x 56 cm) SEK 9,000. STOCKHOLM, 15 Nov 1988, *Swedish Landscape with Farm Buildings near a Lake in the Woods* (1889, oil, 24¾ x 36¼ ins / 63 x 92 cm) SEK 41,000. STOCKHOLM, 19 April 1989, *Coastal Cliffs with Houses and Figures* (1875, oil on canvas, 22 x 32 ins / 55 x 81 cm) SEK 29,000. STOCKHOLM, 16 May 1990, *Coastal Landscape with Fishermen near the Cabins in their Boats* (oil on canvas, 23½ x 37½ ins / 60 x 95 cm) SEK 31,000. STOCKHOLM, 19 May 1992, *Mountain Stream with a Woman and Child near a Footbridge* (oil on canvas, 45¼ x 35¾ ins / 115 x 91 cm) SEK 18,500. STOCKHOLM, 30 Nov 1993, *Boats Moored on Pontoons in Furusund at Twilight* (oil on canvas, 14½ x 22¾ ins / 37 x 58 cm) SEK 26,000.

HOLMLUND, Margaretha
Maiden name: Abom
Swedish, 19th century.
Born 1781, in Stockholm; died 1821.
Painter.

HOLMSKOV, Helge
Danish, 20th century.
Born 11 December 1912, in Sakskøbing; died 10 February 1982, in Dragstrup (Nordsjælland).
Sculptor.

Holmskov was initially a blacksmith, but turned to sculpture after undertaking study trips to Norway, Sweden, Africa and France. His sculptures are figurative and show a certain naivety in their rigidity and stylised poses. He made his debut at the Salon d'Automne in Paris in 1942 and took part in an exhibition at the Musée Rodin in 1961.

AUCTION RECORDS:

COPENHAGEN, 14-15 Nov 1990, *Young Woman Standing* (bronze, h. 12¼ ins / 31 cm) DKK 10,000. COPENHAGEN, 30 May 1991, *Abstract Sculpture* (1975, bronze, h. 7 ins / 18 cm) DKK 7,000. COPENHAGEN, 2-3 Dec 1992, *Little Girl Skipping* (1979, stainless steel sculpture, h. 37½ ins / 95 cm) DKK 56,000. COPENHAGEN, 21 April 1993, *Little Girl Walking* (1974, iron sculpture, h. 15¾ ins / 40 cm) DKK 7,000. COPENHAGEN, 7 June 1995, *Wings* (1972, stainless steel on a granite plinth, h. 102¼ ins / 260 cm) DKK 30,000. COPENHAGEN, 5 Oct 1999, *Composition* (1972, pink marble, h. 25 ins / 64 cm) DKK 28,000.

HOLMSTRAND, Cajsa
Swedish, 20th - 21st century.
Born 1951.
Painter, draughtswoman.
Neo-Constructivism.

Holmstrand lives and works in Stockholm. She participated in the exhibition *Art construit- Tendances actuelles en France et en Suède* (*Art Construit. Current Trends in France and Sweden*), at the Centre Culturel Suédois, Paris, in 1986.

HOLMSTRÖM, Otto Alexis
Swedish, 19th - 20th century.
Born 1866, in Göteborg; died 1915.
Painter. Landscapes.

Holmström studied under Larsson in Göteborg.

HOLMSTRÖM, Tora
Swedish, 20th century.
Born 2 March 1880, in Tottarp.
Painter.

Holmström was active in Paris and Stuttgart.

HOLMSTRÖM, Torsten
Swedish, 20th century.
Born May 1884, in Tottarp.
Painter, engraver, draughtsman.

Holmström was the brother of Tora Holmstroem. He produced many illustrations for newspapers and magazines.

HOLNPACH, Franz Willibald
Austrian, 17th century.
Active in Emmersdorf (near Melk) c. 1674.
Painter.

HOLOKA, Andrzei
Polish, 18th century.
Engraver.
Andrzei Holoka mainly engraved religious subjects.

HOLROYD, Charles (Sir)
British, 19th - 20th century.
Born 9 April 1861, in Leeds; died 17 November 1917.
Painter, engraver.
Charles Holroyd was primarily a painter in his early years as an artist, and the first works that he exhibited at the Royal Academy, London, were genre paintings. Later, he turned to the medium of aquatint, and his prints are much sought after. Holroyd was a member of the Royal Drawing Society, the New Gallery, the International Society of Sculptors, Painters and Engravers, and the Royal Society of Painter-Etchers and Engravers. He was Director of the National Gallery, and knighted in 1903. His work also includes some interesting views of Venice.
AUCTION RECORDS:
LONDON, March 1923, *Preparing to go Herring Fishing, Cornwall*, GBP 5.

HOLROYD, Newmann
British, 20th century.
Painter.
Newmann Holroyd worked in Ryde on the Isle of Wight. He exhibited at the Royal Society of British Artists, of which he was member, in 1909.

HOLROYD, T.
British, 19th century.
Painter. Landscapes.
T. Holroyd exhibited in London at the Royal Academy, the British Institution and the Suffolk Street Gallery between 1860 and 1878.
AUCTION RECORDS:
LONDON, 18 Oct 1990, *Rocky Islets off Capri* (1867, oil on canvas, 21 x 32 1/2 ins / 53.5 x 82.5 cm) GBP 9,350.

HOLSBEECK, Herwig van
Belgian, 20th century.
Born 1945, in Alost.
Painter, sculptor.
Van Holsbeeck specialised in furnishings at the St-Lucas Academie in Ghent. He is self-taught in painting and sculpture.

HOLSBEEK, Albert van
Belgian, 20th century.
Born 1877, in Brussels; died 1948, in Etterbeek.
Painter, draughtsman, engraver. Portraits, landscapes, still-lifes.
Van Holsbeek studied at the academies of fine arts in Antwerp and Brussels.
AUCTION RECORDS:
BRUSSELS, 27 March 1990, *Still-life* (oil on canvas, 19 3/4 x 23 1/2 ins / 50 x 60 cm) BEF 360,000.

HOLSBY, Paul
Swedish, 20th century.
Painter, engraver.
Holsby practised Abstract *Art Informel* (Tachist Abstraction), combining both clear and indistinct forms with pure colours.

HÖLSCHER, Constantin
German, 19th - 20th century.
Born 15 May 1861, in Bad Godesberg (North Rhine-Westphalia); died 3 February 1921, in Berlin.
Painter. Landscapes, portraits.
Hölscher studied in Düsseldorf and Berlin.
AUCTION RECORDS:
COLOGNE, 24 March 1972, *Watermill*, DEM 2,600. LONDON, 16 July 2003, *Boarding* (1893, oil on canvas, 30 x 38 ins / 77 x 97 cm) GBP 3,800.

HÖLSCHER, Richard, or Hoelscher
German, 19th - 20th century.
Born 5 February 1865, in Alsfeld (Hesse).
Painter, engraver. Local scenes.
Hölscher lived in Darmstadt from 1890 as a member of a Künstlerkolonie (artists' colony), where he painted scenes of everyday life in the region.

HOLSELMANN, Heinr.
German (?), 16th century.
Miniaturist.
Heinr. Holselmann wrote and painted miniatures in an antiphonary in 1543. The work was completed after his death by Euch Gleich.

HOLSLAG, Edward J.
American, 19th - 20th century.
Born 1870, in Buffalo; died 1925, in DeKalb (Illinois).
Painter.
Edward J. Holslag studied in New York, then worked in Chicago and Washington.

HOLSMAN, Elisabeth Tuttle
American, 19th - 20th century.
Born 25 September 1873; died 1956, in Evanston (Illinois).
Painter, sculptor. Portraits. Busts.
Elisabeth Tuttle Holsman trained at the Art Institute of Chicago, and was a member of several art associations in Chicago. She executed many portraits of key figures of her time.

HOLSØE, Carl Vilhelm
Danish, 19th - 20th century.
Born 12 March 1863, in Aarhus; died 7 November 1935, in Asserbo.
Painter. Genre scenes, interiors, landscapes.
Holsøe was active in Lyngby. He received an honourable mention at the Exposition Universelle in Paris in 1889 and a medal in Munich in 1891.

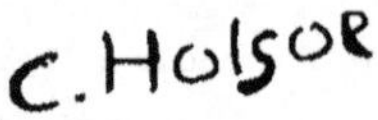

MUSEUMS AND GALLERIES:
COPENHAGEN: *Landscape; Three Interiors* - MUNICH: *Interior with Little Girl.*
AUCTION RECORDS:
COPENHAGEN, 8 Feb 1972, *Young Woman in an Interior*, DKK 7,800. COPENHAGEN, 3 June 1976, *Rear View of Young Woman at her Window* (oil on canvas, 19 3/4 x 21 1/4 ins / 50 x 54 cm) DKK 19,000. COPENHAGEN, 27 Sept 1977, *Interior* (oil on canvas, 24 3/4 x 25 1/4 ins / 63 x 64 cm) DKK 15,000. COPENHAGEN, 30 May 1979, *Young Woman Sewing in an Interior* (oil on canvas, 26 x 24 ins / 66 x 61 cm) DKK 28,500. COPENHAGEN, 3 Nov 1982, *Rear View of Young Woman in an Interior* (oil on canvas, 25 1/4 x 22 ins / 64 x 56 cm) DKK 27,000. COPENHAGEN, 1 March 1983, *Rear View of Young Woman Preparing the Table for Lunch* (oil on canvas, 36 1/2 x 35 1/2 ins / 93 x 90 cm) DKK 38,000. COPENHAGEN, 16 April 1986, *Young Woman Embroidering with her Child in an Interior* (oil on panel, 20 1/2 x 17 1/4 ins / 52 x 44 cm) DKK 290,000. STOCKHOLM, 19 Oct 1987, *Rear View of Young Woman in an Interior Looking towards the Window* (oil on canvas, 29 1/2 x 27 1/4 ins / 75 x 69 cm) SEK 420,000. LONDON, 24 March 1988, *Interior, Woman Looking through Windows* (oil on canvas, 18 x 13 3/4 ins / 46 x 35 cm) GBP 11,000. LONDON, 22 Sept 1988, *Port of*

Nakskov in Denmark (oil on canvas, 20 x 25 3/4 ins / 50.8 x 65.5 cm) GBP 4,400. STOCKHOLM, 15 Nov 1988, *Old Woman Sewing near a Window in an Interior* (oil, 18 x 22 ins / 46 x 56 cm) SEK 50,000. LONDON, 16 March 1989, *Young Girl Sewing in an Interior* (oil on canvas, 19 1/2 x 15 ins / 49.5 x 38 cm) GBP 25,300. STOCKHOLM, 19 April 1989, *Landscape with Canals in Holland* (oil on canvas, 19 3/4 x 25 1/2 ins / 50 x 65 cm) SEK 32,000. NEW YORK, 24 Oct 1989, *Silver Goblet* (oil on canvas, 31 x 26 3/4 ins / 78.7 x 68 cm) USD 17,600. LONDON, 27-28 March 1990, *Breakfast in the Sun* (oil on canvas, 28 1/4 x 26 1/2 ins / 72 x 67 cm) GBP 66,000. LONDON, 6 June 1990, *Woman with a Tray* (oil on canvas, 14 1/2 x 11 ins / 37 x 28 cm) GBP 4,180. NEW YORK, 23 Oct 1990, *At the Window* (oil on canvas, 32 1/4 x 35 1/2 ins / 82 x 90.1 cm) USD 55,000. STOCKHOLM, 14 Nov 1990, *Interior with Woman Peeling Vegetables near a Table* (oil on panel, 18 x 22 ins / 46 x 56 cm) SEK 27,000. LONDON, 30 Nov 1990, *Woman Reading in an Interior* (oil on canvas, 22 1/2 x 20 ins / 57.2 x 50.7 cm) GBP 13,200. COPENHAGEN, 6 Dec 1990, *Little Girl Drawing in an Interior* (oil on mahogany panel, 18 1/2 x 20 3/4 ins / 47 x 53 cm) DKK 70,000. COPENHAGEN, 1 May 1991, *Study of Sunbeams in an Interior* (oil on canvas, 19 x 16 1/2 ins / 48 x 42 cm) DKK 88,000. LONDON, 17 May 1991, *Woman in an Interior* (oil on canvas/panel, 20 x 15 3/4 ins / 50.5 x 40.3 cm) GBP 11,000. COPENHAGEN, 28 Aug 1991, *Interior* (oil on canvas, 12 1/2 x 11 3/4 ins / 32 x 30 cm) DKK 48,000. STOCKHOLM, 5 Sept 1992, *Interior with Young Girl Sitting near a Window* (oil on canvas, 18 1/2 x 20 1/2 ins / 47 x 52 cm) SEK 52,000. COPENHAGEN, 18 Nov 1992, *Interior with Woman Feeding her Baby* (oil on canvas, 30 x 23 1/4 ins / 76 x 59 cm) DKK 80,000. LONDON, 27 Nov 1992, *Woman Reading in an Interior* (oil on canvas, 31 3/4 x 27 1/2 ins / 80.6 x 69.8 cm) GBP 9,020. LONDON, 18 Nov 1994, *Motherhood* (oil on canvas, 38 3/4 x 32 1/2 ins / 98.5 x 82.5 cm) GBP 20,700. COPENHAGEN, 17 May 1995, *Woman in a Rural Landscape* (oil on canvas, 17 1/4 x 22 ins / 44 x 55 cm) DKK 6,600. LONDON, 15 March 1996, *Woman Reading in an Interior* (oil on panel, 21 1/4 x 18 ins / 53.8 x 45.9 cm) GBP 16,100. NEW YORK, 24 Oct 1996, *Looking at the Sea through the Window* (oil on canvas, 22 x 15 ins / 55.9 x 38.1 cm) USD 54,625. LONDON, 20 Nov 1996, *Woman Reading in an Interior* (oil on canvas, 25 1/4 x 23 1/2 ins / 64 x 60 cm) GBP 33,350. LONDON, 21 March 1997, *Saucer of Milk* (oil on canvas, 30 3/4 x 27 3/4 ins / 78 x 70.5 cm) GBP 20,700. LONDON, 13 June 1997, *Women in a Candlelit Interior* (oil on canvas, 29 1/4 x 27 1/4 ins / 74 x 69 cm) GBP 11,500. LONDON, 19 Nov 1997, *Interior with a Young Woman* (oil on canvas, 18 1/2 x 16 1/4 ins / 47 x 41 cm) GBP 25,875. NEW YORK, 5 May 1999, *Morning Room* (oil on canvas, 33 x 28 ins / 85 x 71 cm) USD 72,500. NEW YORK, 1 Nov 1999, *Saucer of Milk* (oil on canvas, 31 x 28 ins / 78 x 70 cm) USD 90,000. COPENHAGEN, 6 Sept 2000, *The Artist's Wife Setting the Table* (oil on canvas, 29 x 26 ins / 73 x 65 cm) DKK 580,000. COPENHAGEN, 4 Dec 2000, *Interior with the Artist's Wife Seated by a Sunlit Window* (oil on canvas, 19 x 21 ins / 48 x 54 cm) DKK 540,000. COPENHAGEN, 5 March 2001, *Interior with Young Girl Reading* (oil on canvas, 31 x 28 ins / 80 x 70 cm) DKK 450,000. LONDON, 6 June 2001, *In the Spring Sun* (oil on canvas, 23 x 17 ins / 59 x 43 cm) GBP 45,000. COPENHAGEN, 3 June 2002, *Lady at the Spinet by Candlelight* (oil on canvas, 20 x 17 ins / 50 x 43 cm) DKK 300,000. NEW YORK, 30 Oct 2002, *Interior with Stove and View into Dining Room* (oil on canvas, 28 x 24 ins / 70 x 60 cm) USD 42,000. STOCKHOLM, 4 June 2003, *Interior with Lady Seated at a Window* (oil on canvas, 26 x 20 ins / 66 x 52 cm) SEK 490,000. COPENHAGEN, 2 Sept 2003, *Interior with Woman Reading by a Window* (oil on wood, 24 x 19 ins / 60 x 48 cm) DKK 450,000. LONDON, 15 June 2004, *Lady Reading* (oil on panel, 28 x 24 ins / 70 x 62 cm) GBP 65,000. LONDON, 16 June 2004, *Mother and Child in a Dining Room* (oil on canvas, 30 x 27 ins / 75 x 68 cm) GBP 48,000.

HOLSØE, Niels

Danish, 19th - 20th century.
Born 21 December 1865, in Copenhagen; died 5 December 1928, in Charlottenlund.
Painter. Genre scenes, interiors with figures.

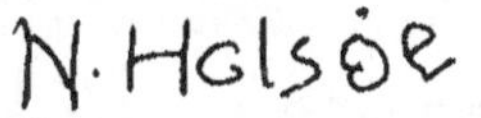

MUSEUMS AND GALLERIES:
STOCKHOLM: *Window*.
AUCTION RECORDS:
COPENHAGEN, 21 Feb 1990, *Interior* (oil on canvas, 19 3/4 x 15 1/4 ins / 50 x 39 cm) DKK 9,500. LONDON, 29 March 1990, *Interior with a Chair near a Window* (1907, oil on canvas, 21 x 18 ins / 53.3 x 45.7 cm) GBP 4,180. COPENHAGEN, 25-26 April 1990, *Interior Seen from the Garden* (oil on canvas, 17 3/4 x 14 1/2 ins / 45 x 37 cm) DKK 6,300. LONDON, 17 May 1991, *White Room* (oil on canvas, 20 x 24 ins / 51 x 61 cm) GBP 2,420. LONDON, 22 May 1992, *Interior Lit by Candles* (oil on canvas, 19 1/2 x 17 1/2 ins / 49.5 x 44.5 cm) GBP 2,090. COPENHAGEN, 2 Feb 1994, *Interior* (oil on canvas, 19 3/4 x 22 1/2 ins / 50 x 57 cm) DKK 4,700. LONDON, 17 June 1994, *Woman in an Interior* (1915, oil on canvas, 20 3/4 x 20 ins / 52.8 x 50.8 cm) GBP 1,610. COPENHAGEN, 23 May 1996, *Child Reading in an Interior* (1915, oil on panel, 14 1/2 x 17 3/4 ins / 37 x 45 cm) DKK 14,000. NEW YORK, 25 Oct 2000, *Cosy Corner* (oil on panel, 18 x 15 ins / 46 x 37 cm) USD 6,500. COPENHAGEN, 4 Dec 2000, *Interior with Chest of Drawers and Wall with Pictures* (oil on canvas, 23 x 25 ins / 58 x 63 cm) DKK 13,000. LONDON, 22 May 2001, *Interior with Dresser and Pictures on the Walls* (oil on board, 20 x 18 ins / 51 x 46 cm) GBP 1,000.

HOLST, Frans

Belgian, 20th century.
Born 1876, in Molenbeek-St-Jean; died 1935, in Etterbeek.
Painter, draughtsman, watercolourist, pastellist. Landscapes, urban landscapes.

Holst's works, which are almost romantic, create an association between dreams and reality.

HOLST, Johann

Dutch, 17th - 18th century.
Born in Hamburg, Germany.
Painter.

In 1700, Johann Holst was a member of the painters' guild in The Hague. He is known for his landscapes and animal paintings.

HOLST, Johann Gustaf von

Swedish, 19th - 20th century.
Born 15 March 1841, in Stockholm; died 1917, in Stockholm.
Painter. Genre scenes, animals.

Von Holst studied under Verlat in Antwerp and went to the academy of fine arts in Stockholm. He exhibited his works in Vienna in 1882 and Munich in 1888.

AUCTION RECORDS:
STOCKHOLM, 26 April 1983, *Hunting Dog with its Prey* (1878, oil on canvas, 31 x 44 ins / 79 x 112 cm) SEK 25,000. STOCKHOLM, 19 May 1992, *Landscape with a Fox Flushing out a Brood of Partridges* (oil on canvas, 35 x 47 1/4 ins / 89 x 120 cm) SEK 20,000.

HOLST, Johann Karl

Swedish, 18th century.
Born 1746; died 1797, in Rome.
Painter.

Johann Holst painted *Views of the Castle in Nyköping*.

HOLST, Laurits Bernhard
Danish, 19th - 20th century.
Born 20 August 1848, in Bogense; died 19 July 1934, in Bournemouth.
Painter, watercolourist. Seascapes.

Holst made his debut at the Royal Academy in London in 1878 and continued to send works there at fairly irregular intervals.

MUSEUMS AND GALLERIES:
LONDON (Corporation of Trinity House): *View of the Europa Lighthouse* (1895).

AUCTION RECORDS:
LONDON, 22 April 1911, *Squally Weather on the Norwegian Coast* (1883, watercolour) GBP 9. LONDON, 15 Feb 1924, *Rising Tide*, GBP 3. COPENHAGEN, 8 Feb 1977, *Sailing Ships off the Cape of Good Hope* (oil on canvas, 32¼ x 53¼ ins / 82 x 135 cm) DKK 11,500. COPENHAGEN, 25 April 1979, *Seascape* (1885, oil on canvas, 16¼ x 24 ins / 41 x 61 cm) DKK 7,200. LONDON, 20 Oct 1981, *Sir Francis Drake on Board the Revenge* (oil on canvas, 20 x 36 ins / 51 x 91.5 cm) GBP 3,900. NEW YORK, 24 Jan 1989, *Coast at Monterey* (1870, oil on canvas, 14¾ x 28½ ins / 37.5 x 72.5 cm) USD 1,540. STOCKHOLM, 19 April 1989, *Coast at Bournemouth* (1912, oil on canvas, 14½ x 20¾ ins / 37 x 53 cm) SEK 4,500. LONDON, 18 Oct 1990, *Mediterranean Port* (oil on canvas, 15½ x 24 ins / 39.5 x 61 cm) GBP 495. LONDON, 22 May 1991, *Off Gibraltar* (1892, oil on canvas, 16¼ x 27 ins / 41 x 68.5 cm) GBP 2,200. COPENHAGEN, 18 Nov 1992, *Fort on the Atlantic Coast of France* (1898, oil on canvas, 15¼ x 27½ ins / 39 x 70 cm) DKK 5,000. COPENHAGEN, 15 Nov 1993, *Seascape with Danish Sailing Ships* (oil on canvas, 29½ x 50¾ ins / 75 x 129 cm) DKK 13,000. LONDON, 22 Nov 1996, *Raging Fjord* (1882, oil on canvas, 22 x 19 ins / 56 x 48.2 cm) GBP 1,092. LONDON, 26 March 1997, *French Fleet and the Marengo before Kronborg* (1891, oil on canvas, 32 x 50½ ins / 81 x 128 cm) GBP 2,760.

HOLST, Richard Nicolas Roland
Dutch, 19th - 20th century.
Born 1868 or 1869, in Amsterdam; died 1938, in Amsterdam.
Painter, engraver, draughtsman, illustrator, fresco artist. Designs for stained glass, murals.
Symbolism, Constructivism.

Holst studied at the Hogeschool voor de Kunsten in Amsterdam from 1885 until 1890 and taught there from 1918. He was also its director from 1926 until 1934. He spent a year in England, where he discovered Beardsley and the Pre-Raphaelites. He turned to Symbolism between 1891 and 1895 under the influence of Rossetti, then moved towards Constructivism, publishing articles on Constructivist art and artists and painting pictures and decorations to support his theses. He had many lithographs published in magazines such as *De Nieuwe Gids* (*The New Guide*) and *Van Nu en Straks* (*Today and Tomorrow*), both published in Brussels. He executed murals for the diamond exchange in Amsterdam, and cartoons for stained glass windows for the high school and town hall in Amsterdam and the cathedral in Utrecht.

BIBLIOGRAPHY:
Osterwalder, Marcus (ed.), *Dictionnaire des illustrateurs 1800-1914*, Ides et Calendes, Neuchâtel, 1989.

MUSEUMS AND GALLERIES:
AMSTERDAM (Stedelijk Mus.): *Anangkè* (1892) - THE HAGUE (Gemeentemus.): *Entrance of Helga* (1894).

HOLST, Theodor Matthias von
British, 19th century.
Born 3 September 1810, in London; died 14 February 1844, in London.
Painter, draughtsman. Figure compositions, figures, genre scenes.

Von Holst, of a German family from Livonia (modern Livoniya), showed a remarkable talent for drawing from a young age. He spent a considerable amount of time copying the antique marbles in the British Museum and then attended classes at the Royal Academy. He was an admirer of the work of Sir Thomas Lawrence, perhaps to the detriment of cultivating his own style; his work has a certain heaviness.

MUSEUMS AND GALLERIES:
LONDON (Victoria and Albert Mus.): *Figure Studies*.

AUCTION RECORDS:
LONDON, 20 April 1990, *Fantasy Inspired by Goethe's 'Faust'* (1834, oil on canvas, 44 x 28¾ ins / 112 x 73 cm) GBP 14,300. LONDON, 12 April 1991, *Hero and Leander on a Beach by Moonlight* (oil on canvas, 50½ x 40 ins / 128.5 x 101.5 cm) GBP 3,850.

HOLSTEIN, Bent
Danish, 20th century.
Born 1942.
Painter (including mixed media), watercolourist, engraver, draughtsman. Landscapes, still-lifes.

Holstein participated in SAGA in Paris in 1992. He is represented by the Galerie Galise Petersen in Thonon-les-Bains. In the 1970s, his drawings were similar to the Hyperrealist Gäfgen. Since then, Holstein has produced compositions, reconciling recollections of Pop Art and Abstraction, which evoke certain collages.

AUCTION RECORDS:
COPENHAGEN, 10 May 1989, *Still-life* (1975, oil on canvas, 43¼ x 39¼ ins / 110 x 100 cm) DKK 7,000. COPENHAGEN, 1 Oct 2002, *African Baroue I* (1983, oil on canvas, 58 x 45 ins / 147 x 114 cm) DKK 12,000. COPENHAGEN, 5 Oct 2004, *Golden Tide* (1998, oil on canvas, 71 x 51 ins / 180 x 130 cm) DKK 19,000. COPENHAGEN, 5 Oct 2004, *Tenkyo - Composition* (1995, oil on canvas, 75 x 55 ins / 190 x 140 cm) DKK 22,000.

HOLSTEIN, Gustav
Lithuanian, 20th century.
Born 20 December 1876, in Vilnius.
Active in Germany.
Painter, engraver. Landscapes.

Gustav Holstein worked at the academy of fine art in Berlin.

HOLSTEIN, Pieter
Dutch, 20th century.
Born 1934, in Enschede.
Painter, engraver, illustrator.

Holstein draws objects scattered in apparent disorder on the canvas, thus creating an intricate co-occurrence of ideas, often full of humour, fantasy and poetry. He staged his first exhibition in Amsterdam in 1964 and exhibited there again in 1965 and 1966. He took part in the Paris Biennale in 1969 and 1975 and the Tokyo Biennale in 1970.

AUCTION RECORDS:
AMSTERDAM, 10 Dec 1996, *Bock-Book* (c. 1961, brush, ink and gouache/paper, cover in wood, leather, pins and collage, 53 drawings together in a single volume, each page 17¼ x 15¼ ins / 44 x 39 cm, cover 20 x 16½ ins/51 x 42 cm) NLG 8,649.

HOLSTEYN, Cornelis
Dutch, 17th century.
Born 1618, in Haarlem; died 1658; buried 2 December in Amsterdam.
Painter (including glass), draughtsman, engraver.
Mythological subjects, portraits, genre scenes.

Cornelis Holsteyn studied under his father Pieter Holsteyn the Elder. He has often been confused with Cornelis Cornelissen. Bryan states that he was senior member of the Delft painters' guild in 1661, but this date conflicts with the date of his death as given by von Wurzbach.

Holsteyn engraved numerous plates from his own drawings and produced engravings for the famous collection known as *The Reysist Cabinet*.

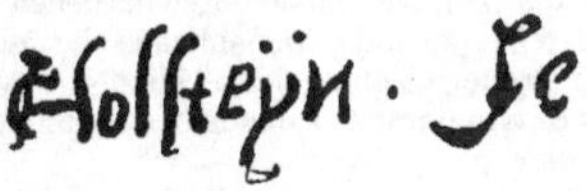

Museums and Galleries:
Amsterdam: *Distribution of Peat to the Poor* - Haarlem: *Vineyard Country; Venus Mourning the Death of Adonis* - Hanover: *Children's Round; Children's Games* - Vienna: *Ariadne and Bacchus*.

Auction records:
London, Dec 1922, *Venus with Cherubs*, GBP 7. London, 28 July 1926, *Children's Revelries*, GBP 21. London, 6 Nov 1964, *Portrait of Reynier Pauw and his Family in their Garden*, Gns 2,800. Paris, 2 Dec 1987, *The Heliades Witnessing the Fall of their Brother Phaeton into the River Eridanus* (drawing in black chalk/paper, 16 1/4 x 11 1/2 ins / 41 x 29 cm) FRF 10,000. Munich, 26 Sept 2001, *Satyr Family and Goats in Grotto* (oil on panel, 16 x 21 ins / 41 x 53 cm) DEM 5,500.

HOLSTEYN, Lorenz
German, 17th century.
Active in Germany c. 1630.
Engraver (burin).

HOLSTEYN, Pieter, the Elder
Dutch, 17th century.
Born c. 1580, in Haarlem; died 23 July 1662, in Haarlem.
Watercolourist, painter (glass/gouache), engraver, draughtsman. Portraits, animals, birds, insects.

By 1620, Pieter Holsteyn the Elder was already active in Haarlem. In 1637 he counted Balten Joppen, Erasmus Gerritsz. den Otter of Haarlem and Frederik van Steencoyck as his pupils. He is known primarily as a portrait engraver, but also for his drawings.

Auction records:
London, 4 July 1972, *Insect Studies* (watercolour) Gns 950. Amsterdam, 21 March 1977, *Two Ducks* (watercolour, 6 1/4 x 8 1/4 ins / 15.6 x 20.8 cm) NLG 2,000. London, 24 June 1980, *Turkey Cock* (watercolour and pen heightened with white, 5 1/4 x 6 3/4 ins / 13.6 x 17.4 cm) GBP 500. Amsterdam, 14 Nov 1988, *Studies of a Moth and Other Insects* (1654, watercolour and gouache, 6 x 8 ins / 15.5 x 20.1 cm) NLG 8,740; *Red Parrot in a Desert Landscape* (watercolour, 6 1/4 x 8 ins / 15.7 x 20.3 cm) NLG 8,510. Amsterdam, 25 Nov 1991, *White-Eared Puffins* (watercolour and gouache, 7 x 8 1/2 ins / 17.8 x 21.9 cm) NLG 4,830. Paris, 16 Nov 1993, *Curlews* (pen, watercolour and gouache, 6 x 7 3/4 ins / 15 x 19.5 cm) FRF 6,500. Amsterdam, 15 Nov 1995, *Crane* (ink, watercolour and gouache, 6 1/4 x 7 3/4 ins / 15.6 x 20 cm) NLG 2,950. London, 6 July 1999, *Mottled Longhorn Beetle, Musk Beetle, Rhinoceros Beetle and Other Beetles* (1636, chalk, wash and bodycolour on vellum, 6 x 8 ins / 16 x 21 cm) GBP 30,000. London, 28 Nov 2001, *Waders and Ducks by a River, Town in the Distance* (gouache on vellum, 8 x 13 ins / 21 x 33 cm) GBP 1,800. Munich, 4 Dec 2001, *Horse* (watercolour and Indian ink over pencil, 6 x 7 ins / 15 x 18 cm) DEM 3,200. Heidelberg, 11 April 2003, *Gibbon* (watercolour over pencil, 6 x 8 ins / 15 x 20 cm) EUR 2,900. Heidelberg, 11 April 2003, *Dromedary* (watercolour and Indian ink over pencil, 6 x 7 ins / 15 x 17 cm) EUR 3,200. Heidelberg, 2 April 2004, *Lucky Cat* (watercolour and Indian ink over pencil, 6 x 7 ins / 14 x 18 cm) EUR 2,600.

HOLSTEYN, Pieter, the Younger
Dutch, 17th century.
Born c. 1614, in Haarlem; died 1673 or 2 March 1687, in Haarlem.
Watercolourist, painter (glass/gouache), engraver.
Portraits, still-lifes, flowers, animals.

Pieter Holsteyn the Younger was the son and pupil of Pieter Holsteyn the Elder. He worked for many years in Zwolle and Münster and is known mainly as a portrait engraver.

Auction records:
Amsterdam, 26 Nov 1984, *Shrike* (watercolour, black chalk and gouache, 6 1/4 x 8 ins / 15.6 x 20.3 cm) NLG 3,500. London, 11 April 2002, *Two Red Admiral Butterflies, Moth and a Weevil* (1660, black chalk, watercolour and bodycolour, 8 x 12 ins / 21 x 31 cm) GBP 17,000. London, 11 April 2002, *Tulips* (watercolour and bodycolour, book with 42 drawings, 12 x 8 ins / 31 x 20 cm) GBP 110,000. Hamburg, 24 Oct 2003, *Tulip* (watercolour and Indian ink, 12 x 7 ins / 30 x 17 cm) EUR 2,500. Amsterdam, 4 Nov 2003, *Black-tailed Godwit* (pen, black ink and watercolour, 6 x 8 ins / 16 x 20 cm) EUR 3,600. London, 6 July 2004, *Wall Lizard* (black chalk, pen, ink wash, watercolour and bodycolour with framing lines, 5 x 8 ins / 12 x 20 cm) GBP 6,000. London, 8 July 2004, *Tulip - Semper Augustus* (watercolour and bodycolour over traces of black chalk, 12 x 8 ins / 31 x 21 cm) GBP 5,500.

HOLSTMARK, Karen
Norwegian, 20th century.
Born 1907.
Painter.

HOLSWILDER, Jan Pieter
Dutch, 19th century.
Born 1850, in Leiden; died 1890, in The Hague.
Caricaturist, lithographer.

Jan Pieter Holswilder is known for his political caricatures.

HOLT, Alf Krogh
Norwegian, 20th century.
Born 19 September 1919, in Tvedestrand.
Active in France since 1962.
Painter, pastellist. Nudes, interiors, landscapes, still-lifes.

Holt studied at the school of fine arts in Oslo, then went to Paris, where he entered the studio of André Lhote in 1951. He settled there in 1962. His paintings are moderate in style with links to Neo-Impressionism and Cubism. In his landscape paintings, he places the accent on light using a mosaic of diverse tones. His still-lifes, on the other hand, are built up of geometric planes derived from Cubism.

Holt took part in collective exhibitions including: at the autumn salon in Oslo; regular appearances at the Salon d'Automne in Paris, where he was a member; at the Salon de Mai from 1954 until 1962; and at the Salon Comparaisons in 1984. He also put on solo exhibitions in such places as the gallery of Modern Art in Oslo from 1954 to 1985, the art association of Stavanger in 1984, the Galerie Camille Renaud in Paris from 1971 to 1973 and the Galerie Art-Melt in Paris in 1989.

Bibliography:
Alf K. Holt, exhibition catalogue, Gal. Art-Mel, Paris, 1989.

HOLT, Edwin Frederick
British, 19th century.
Active in London 1850-1897.
Painter. History painting.

Edwin Holt exhibited in London at the Royal Academy, the British Institution and the Suffolk Street Gallery between 1850 and 1865.

Auction records:
London, 8 May 1908, *Hunters Resting* (1864) GBP 5. London, 13 March 1979, *Old Houses in Exeter* (oil on canvas, 22 3/4 x

18¾ ins / 58 x 47.5 cm) GBP 600. LONDON, 23 June 1981, *Departure from the Farm in the Morning* (1893, oil on canvas, 20 x 29¼ ins / 51 x 74 cm) GBP 850. NEW YORK, 4 June 1982, *Gamekeeper* (1870, oil on canvas, 20 x 30 ins / 50.8 x 76.2 cm) USD 13,000. NEW YORK, 10 June 1983, *Puggy and Jack in a Loose Box* (1888, oil on canvas, 18¼ x 24 ins / 46.3 x 61 cm) USD 1,500. LONDON, 12 June 1985, *Dogs and Puppies* (oil on canvas, 23½ x 17¼ ins / 60 x 44 cm) GBP 2,600. LONDON, 13 Feb 1987, *Albert Memorial, London* (1877, oil on canvas, 32 x 30 ins / 81.3 x 76.2 cm) GBP 11,000. LONDON, 15 July 1988, *Sergeant-Major and a Detachment of the Scots Greys near the Royal Pavilion at Aldershot* (1874, oil on canvas, 20 x 27¼ ins / 51.1 x 68.9 cm) GBP 4,620. LONDON, 13 Dec 1989, *Stolen Scraps in the Dog Food* (1884, oil on canvas, 24 x 20 ins / 61 x 51 cm) GBP 1,320. LONDON, 14 Feb 1990, *Cat Stealing Food from a Plate on a Table while Four Young Mastiffs Fight on the Carpet* (1887, oil on canvas, 20 x 30 ins / 50.8 x 76.2 cm) GBP 1,870. LONDON, 13 June 1990, *Horses in a Farmyard* (1891, oil on canvas, 16¼ x 24 ins / 41 x 61 cm) GBP 880. LONDON, 26 Sept 1990, *Going, Going, Gone!* (1863, oil on canvas, 28 x 35¾ ins / 71 x 91 cm) GBP 3,300. LONDON, 27 Sept 1994, *Proud Cottagers* (1901, oil on canvas, 15¾ x 24 ins / 40.5 x 61 cm) GBP 862. NEW ORLEANS, 9 April 1999, *Stable Interior* (1888, oil on canvas, 16 x 24 ins / 41 x 61 cm) USD 2,750. LONDON, 9 Sept 1999, *Elizabeth I, Henry VIII, Queen Mary, Queen Adelaide, Sir Walter Raleigh and Lucy Harrington* (1903, oil on canvas, 16 x 20 ins / 41 x 51 cm) GBP 1,200. NEW YORK, 15 Feb 2000, *Proud Mother* (1872, oil on canvas, 20 x 30 ins / 51 x 76 cm) USD 8,000. LEOMINSTER, 20 Sept 2000, *Farm Animals with Two Youths and a Horse in Parkland with Avenue* (1893, oil on canvas, 34 x 45 ins / 86 x 114 cm) GBP 3,700. LEWES, 15 March 2001, *Study of a Saddled Chestnut Cavalry Mount in a Stable* (1866, oil on canvas, 18 x 23 ins / 46 x 58 cm) GBP 1,100. KNOWLE, 6 Feb 2002, *Cattle Grazing before a House. Cattle, Sheep and Donkeys in Pasture* (1900, oil on canvas, a pair, 16 x 24 ins / 41 x 61 cm) GBP 9,200. MADRID, 19 Nov 2002, *Hunting Scene* (oil on canvas, 28 x 35 ins / 70 x 90 cm) EUR 12,000. NEW YORK, 4 June 2003, *Trip to the Farriers* (1892, oil on canvas, 20 x 30 ins / 51 x 76 cm) USD 1,800. LONDON, 12 June 2003, *Huntsman with Pointers on a Moor* (1883, oil on canvas, 20 x 30 ins / 51 x 76 cm) GBP 1,500. LONDON, 10 Feb 2004, *Sportsman's Rendezvous* (1878, oil on canvas, 27 x 20 ins / 69 x 51 cm) GBP 1,400. SAN FRANCISCO, 30 March 2004, *Dan, a Special Poodle* (1879, oil on canvas, 25 x 31 ins / 64 x 80 cm) USD 11,000.

HOLT, Heinrich van
German, 15th - 16th century.
Born in Calcar.
Active from 1514.
Sculptor.

HOLT, J.
British, 19th century.
Active in London.
Sculptor.

J. Holt exhibited at the Royal Academy in 1855.

HOLT, Sara
American, 20th - 21st century.
Born 14 March 1946, in Los Angeles.
Active in France since 1969.
Sculptor, installation artist.

Sara Holt trained at the University of Colorado and Pasadena City College. She travelled to Europe in 1968, and settled in France in 1969. Since 1966, her work has explored the use of transparent polyester resins in sculpture. Her themes and materials recall works by Jean-Claude Fahri, although Holt's sculpture is more craftsmanlike in approach. Fahri works in an industrial, 'factory' context using technological means of production, while Holt casts, chases and assembles her own pieces. Her experiments with colour mixtures have allowed her to develop a number of innovative techniques. Her sculptures emerge within simple forms (cylinders, lens shapes, sinusoids, cones), thanks to a technique involving successive layers of different-coloured hardened resins. The resulting play of light and colour animates the interior of her forms with strange colours and (seemingly) moving forms. Her series of photographs extends her experiments in her chosen medium.

Holt exhibits mainly in Paris, where her work has featured at the Salon de Mai since 1970. She held a solo exhibition at the Musée d'Art Moderne de la Ville de Paris in 1971-1972.

BIBLIOGRAPHY:
Sara Holt, exhibition catalogue, Musée d'Art moderne de la Ville de Paris, Paris, 1971.

HOLT, Winifred
American, 20th century.
Born 1870, in New York; died 1945.
Sculptor.

Winifred Holt was a pupil of Trentanove and Augustus Saint-Gaudens in New York. She also studied in Italy.

HOLTE, A. Brandish
British, 19th century.
Painter. Landscapes.

Holte exhibited in London at the Suffolk Street Gallery in 1875.

MUSEUMS AND GALLERIES:
CARDIFF: *Among the Birch Trees.*

HOLTE, Johann
German, 17th century.
Active in Heide in 1699.
Painter.

HOLTEN, Ragnar von
Swedish, 20th century.
Born 1934, in Gleiwitz, Germany (now Gliwice, Poland).
Painter, collage artist, draughtsman.
Phases.

Von Holten is a writer as well as a visual artist. He became a specialist on Gustave Moreau, whom he linked with his interest in (and practice of) Surrealism. He organised a Surrealist exhibition at the Moderna Museet in Stockholm in 1970. He was represented in the exhibition *Le Mouvement Phases de 1952 à l'horizon 2001* (*The Phases Movement from 1952 to the New Millennium*) at the Kiosque Centre Culturel in Mayenne and the Centre Noroit in Arras in 2000. As a visual artist he exhibited mainly drawings and collages.

HOLTEN, Sofie
Danish, 19th century.
Born 12 August 1858.
Painter.

Sofie Holten studied in Paris with Alfred Stevens.

HOLTEN, Susette Cathrine
Maiden name: Skovgaard
Danish, 19th century.
Born 29 January 1863, in Copenhagen.
Painter.

Susette Holten is known to have painted genre scenes, portraits and landscapes.

HOLTER, Carl Johan
Norwegian, 19th - 20th century.
Born 6 June 1870, in Soon.
Painter.

Holter was a student and follower of Munch.

AUCTION RECORDS:
LONDON, 19 March 1980, *Coast of Norway* (oil on canvas, 15½ x 26 ins / 39.5 x 66 cm) GBP 800.

HOLTER, Georg Frederik
Norwegian, 19th century.

Born 10 January 1816, in Drammen; died 4 September 1857, in Drammen.
Painter.
Georg Holter worked a great deal in Copenhagen.

HOLTER, Wenzel
German, 19th century.
Born 22 August 1827, in Haslau (Haslov), Bohemia; died 1872, in Haslau (Haslov).
Painter.
Noted for his portraits and genre paintings.

HOLTER, Wilhelm Franz
Norwegian, 19th - 20th century.
Born 1 June 1842, in Drammen; died 27 July 1916, in Christiania (now Oslo).
Painter. Portraits, landscapes.
Holter went to Berlin when he was very young and made his debut there around 1879. He was appointed as a teacher at the academy of Leipzig in 1884. He was awarded a medal in Berlin in 1891.

HOLTERHOFF DE HARVEN, Alice
Belgian, 20th century.
Active in Antwerp.
Sculptor.
Holterhoff de Harven took part in the Brussels Exhibition in 1910.

HOLTHAUSEN, Ludwig
German, 19th century.
Born 1807, in Uerdingen; died 13 April 1890.
Painter. Genre scenes, flowers.
He trained at the academy in Düsseldorf, and made his debut there c. 1833. He likewise exhibited in Berlin.

HOLTHE, Jan van
Dutch, 20th century.
Born 1923, in Surabaya, Indonesia.
Sculptor.
Van Holthe recycled rubbish and articles of useless scrap in an imaginative way. After assembling these discarded objects in the most inventive way possible he painted them in dreamlike colours.
AUCTION RECORDS:
AMSTERDAM, 17-18 Dec 1996, *Untitled* (assemblage of painted bicycle parts, chains and alarm clocks, h. 14 1/2 ins / 37 cm) NLG 2,360.

HOLTHUYS, Andreas
German, 15th century.
Born in Cleves.
Sculptor.
Andreas Holthuys worked for the church of St Victor in Xanten.

HOLTICH, Petrus van
Dutch, 17th century.
Painter. Landscapes.

HOLTMANN, Theodor
German, 17th century.
Active in Cologne.
Engraver.

HOLTS, Ruprecht von dem
Flemish, 16th - 17th century.
Born in Mechelen.
Painter.
Flemish School.

HOLTY, Carl Robert
German, 20th century.
Born 21 June 1900, in Freiburg im Breisgau; died 1973.
Active and naturalised in the USA.
Painter, draughtsman, watercolourist.
Abstraction-Creation group.
Holty studied in New York and Munich, where he was taught by Hans Hofmann. He taught in colleges and art schools in America for 28 years. Before the World War II he was a member of the Abstraction-Creation group. He was profoundly influenced by Cubism and Abstract art, although he always took great care to retain his own individual style. A great admirer of the work of Juan Gris, he aimed to produce rigorous and definitive compositions in which each element has its own value. The human element is still present at the heart of his combinations of lines and surfaces. The austerity of his work fits easily with the harshness of the dark aspects of art, for which he clearly had a preference.

Holty exhibited both in the USA and Europe. He participated in many group exhibitions, for example at the Whitney Museum in New York; in exhibitions at the Carnegie International Institute in Pittsburgh; and at the Corcoran Biennales, with the group of Abstract American artists of which he was a founding member. In Europe he appeared at the Salon des Tuileries in Paris in 1930, and in a group exhibition in Paris again in 1947. His work was shown in many solo exhibitions, in 1936, 1938, 1944, 1946, 1948, 1951, 1952, 1955, 1958, 1959 and 1960.
MUSEUMS AND GALLERIES:
MILWAUKEE (IA).
AUCTION RECORDS:
NEW YORK, 23 May 1979, *Swift's Premium* (1947, oil on card, 38 x 30 ins / 96.5 x 76 cm) USD 1,500. NEW YORK, 3 June 1982, *Footballers No. 1* (1945, oil/hardboard, 20 1/4 x 18 ins / 51.5 x 45.7 cm) USD 3,200. NEW YORK, 3 June 1983, *The Bridegroom's Party* (oil on canvas, 55 3/4 x 46 ins / 141.9 x 116.9 cm) USD 2,200. NEW YORK, 4 Dec 1987, *Odalisque* (1937, oil/hardboard, 35 3/4 x 24 ins / 90.7 x 61 cm) USD 7,000. NEW YORK, 24 Jan 1989, *Victor* (1945, oil/synthetic resin, 29 1/2 x 23 1/2 ins / 75 x 60 cm) USD 7,700. PARIS, 9 Nov 1989, *Composition* (watercolour, 8 1/4 x 11 ins / 21 x 28 cm) FRF 18,000. NEW YORK, 24 Jan 1990, *Untitled* (pastel/paper/card, 12 x 8 ins / 30.5 x 20.3 cm) USD 2,200. NEW YORK, 14 Feb 1990, *Odalisque* (1937, oil/synthetic resin, 35 3/4 x 24 ins / 90.7 x 61 cm) USD 6,600. NEW YORK, 30 May 1990, *Moonlight* (1947, oil/synthetic resin, 18 x 14 ins / 45.5 x 35.6 cm) USD 1,870. NEW YORK, 30 May 1990, *Untitled* (1944, watercolour/paper, 11 x 8 1/4 ins / 28 x 20.9 cm) USD 4,125. NEW YORK, 17 Dec 1990, *Europa II* (1947, oil/synthetic resin, 18 x 14 ins / 45.5 x 35.6 cm) USD 1,870. NEW YORK, 21 May 1991, *Untitled* (oil on canvas/synthetic resin, 12 x 9 ins / 30.5 x 22.9 cm) USD 825. NEW YORK, 18 Dec 1991, *Untitled* (oil/synthetic resin, 36 x 42 ins / 91.4 x 106.7 cm) USD 1,320. NEW YORK, 25 Sept 1992, *Dune Landscape* (1947, oil on canvas, 24 x 30 ins / 61 x 76.2 cm) USD 1,650. NEW YORK, 2 Dec 1992, *Abstraction in Blue, Green and Red* (1948, oil on canvas/synthetic resin, 36 x 24 ins / 91.5 x 61 cm) USD 2,200. NEW YORK, 31 March 1993, *Flamenco* (1948, oil on canvas, 47 x 36 ins / 119.4 x 91.4 cm) USD 2,185. NEW YORK, 25 March 1997, *Soldier's Bouquet* (1944, oil/Masonite, 35 3/4 x 29 1/4 ins / 90.8 x 74.6 cm) USD 5,175.

HOLTZ, Franz Viktor
German, 19th century.
Born 13 November 1859, in Berlin.
Painter.
He painted mainly portraits.

HOLTZ, Johann
German, 20th century.
Born 2 March 1875, in Tondern.
Painter, engraver.
Holtz studied at the Académie Julian in Paris.

HOLTZ, Karl
German, 20th century.
Born 1899, in Berlin.
Painter, lithographer.

HOLTZAPPFEL, Jules
French, 19th century.
Born 1826, in Strasbourg; died 12 April 1866, in Paris, committed suicide.
Painter. Genre scenes, portraits.
Holtzappfel was a pupil of Léon Cogniet, and his works were shown at the Paris Salon from 1852 to 1865. In 1866 he sent two paintings to the Salon: *The Father's Advice* and *Foolishness*. When he learned that the admissions jury had rejected his paintings, he killed himself with a pistol shot.
MUSEUMS AND GALLERIES:
STRASBOURG: *Orphan*.
AUCTION RECORDS:
PARIS, 16 Feb 1927, *'Pay to Enter'*, FRF 135.

HOLTZBECHER, Eberhard Dietrich
German, 17th century.
Active in Hamburg.
Painter.

HOLTZBECHER, Hans
German, 19th century.
Born 22 February 1861, in Berlin.
Painter. Portraits, genre scenes.
A student at the Berlin academy, he made his debut in Berlin c. 1887.

HOLTZBECHER, Johann Christoph
Danish, 18th century.
Born 1700; died 6 November 1762, in Copenhagen.
Painter, decorative artist.
Johann Holtzbecher worked mostly at Frederiksborg castle.

HOLTZBECHER, Johannes Simon
German, 17th century.
Active in Hamburg in 1690.
Painter. Still-lifes.

HOLTZMAN, Harry
American, 20th century.
Born 1912, in New York; died 1987, in Lyme (Connecticut).
Painter.
Harry Holtzman was a pupil at the Art Students League (ASL) of New York from 1928 to 1933, taught by Hans Hofmann. He made a visit to Paris in 1934 to meet Mondrian, which was the beginning of a long friendship. Upon returning to New York in 1935, he helped to found the American Abstract Artists Group.

It was Holtzman who made it possible for Mondrian to emigrate to America in 1940, and Mondrian made him his sole legatee. He stopped painting to teach and from 1950 edited the review *Transformation*. Apart from Neoplastic paintings, he produced several 'framed' sculptures.
MUSEUMS AND GALLERIES:
SAN FRANCISCO (MoMA): *Horizontal Volume* (1938-1946, oil on linen).

HOLTZMANN, Carl Friedrich
German, 18th - 19th century.
Born 4 April 1740, in Dresden; died 18 May 1811, in Dresden.
Painter, engraver.
A pupil of Dietrich, he devoted himself mainly to watercolour portraits, of which he is supposed to have done more than 2,000. He also did engravings, and published a collection called *Aquatint Reproductions of Drawings by Various Masters*.

HOLTZMANN, Eugen
French, 20th century.
Born 1887, in Börsch.
Painter, engraver. Genre scenes.
Eugen Holtzmann worked mainly in Strasbourg.

HOLUB, Georg
Czech, 19th - 20th century.
Born 29 November 1861, in Brno; died April 1919, in Vienna.
Painter. Landscapes.
Georg Holub worked in Vienna, exhibiting there in 1891.
MUSEUMS AND GALLERIES:
LINZ: painting.
AUCTION RECORDS:
VIENNA, 23 March 1983, *Mountain Pasture* (1891, oil on canvas, 19¾ x 32½ ins / 50 x 82.5 cm) ATS 25,000. VIENNA, 10 April 2001, *View of Salzburg* (1888, oil on canvas) ATS 50,000. VIENNA, 24 Nov 2003, *Nymph Callisto* (oil on canvas, 39 x 68 ins / 100 x 172 cm) EUR 5,000.

HOLWECK, Louis
French, 19th - 20th century.
Born in Paris.
Sculptor.
Louis Holweck was a pupil of Charles Gauthier and Thomas. A member of the Société des Artistes Français in 1887, he received a 3rd class medal in 1888, bronze medals at the Expositions Universelles in 1889 and 1900, a 2nd class medal in 1893 and a travel grant in 1891.
AUCTION RECORDS:
NEW YORK, 21 Sept 1981, *Wine* (green-patinated bronze, h. 35¼ ins / 89.5 cm) USD 2,000.

HOLWECK, Oskar
German, 20th century.
Born 1924, in St Ingbert (Saarland).
Painter.
Holweck studied at the school of arts and crafts in Saarbrücken from 1946 until 1949, then at the equivalent school in Paris from 1949 to 1951. He taught at his former school in Saarbrücken from 1956. His works, consisting of random groupings or, conversely, repetitive structures (often designed in relief), are particularly intended to bring architecture to life. His free paintings are often limited to the use of black and white.

Holweck exhibited in Germany as well as taking part in group exhibitions in Paris, Lausanne, Milan, Antwerp, Amsterdam and Bern. His work has appeared in collective and themed exhibitions, including *Zero aus Deutschland: 1957-1966. Und heute* (*Zero out of Germany: 1957-1966. And Today*), held at the Galerie der Stadt, Esslingen in 2000.
BIBLIOGRAPHY:
Wiehager, Renate, *Zero aus Deutschland: 1957-1966. Und heute*, group exhibition catalogue, Gal. der Stadt, Esslingen, 2000.

HOLWEG, Gustav, or Glantschnigg
Austrian, 19th century.
Born 1855, in Graz; died 1890, in Vienna.
Painter. Genre scenes.
He lived in Venice, Vienna and Munich, and exhibited in Vienna and Munich from 1881.
AUCTION RECORDS:
LONDON, 1 April 1911, *Examining the Bronze* (1883) GBP 8. MUNICH, 9 March 1978, *The Oboist* (1880, oil on panel, 9½ x 6½ ins / 24 x 16.5 cm) DEM 8,500. LONDON, 30 Jan 1980, *The Letter* (1880, oil on panel, 10¼ x 6½ ins / 26 x 16.5 cm) GBP 900. LONDON, 17 Aug 2000, *Game of Cards* (1878, oil on panel, 6 x 6 ins / 15 x 16 cm) GBP 1,000.

HOLWELL, W.. See **CARR William Holwell**

HOLWORTHY, James
British, 19th century.
Born 10 April 1781, in Bosworth (Leicestershire); died 10 June 1841, in London.
Painter, watercolourist. Landscapes with figures, landscapes.

James Holworthy was one of the founding-members of the Society of Painters in Watercolours in 1804. He also exhibited some landscapes of Wales at the Royal Academy in London in 1803 and 1804. From 1824, the year in which he married, he stopped exhibiting.

Museums and Galleries:

London (Victoria and Albert Mus.): *Raglan Castle* (watercolour); *Landscape with Animals* (watercolour).

HOLY, Adrien

Swiss, 20th century.

Born 1898, in St-Imier (Bern); died 1979, in Geneva.

Painter, draughtsman, decorative artist. Portraits, genre scenes, landscapes.

Holy studied first in La Chaux-de-Fonds in 1915-1916 and then in Geneva in 1917-1918, before going to Paris in 1920. He effectively settled there until 1939, although he continued to travel in Italy and Norway. He taught at the École Supérieure des Beaux-Arts in Geneva from 1961 until 1966.

While he was in Paris, Holy was commissioned to paint decorative panels for the theatres in Pigalle and on the Champs-Élysées and to produce decorations for Gaston Baty and Louis Jouvet. Poncelet, Planson and Chapelain-Midy took him under their wings and the critics regarded him as a member of their group. Together with these artists he began to experiment with a form of art that was directly Realist, but severe in its principles, in a reaction to the complex experimentation of the Cubists. What made his style instantly recognisable was his particular feeling for his materials, shown in the way he superimposed and scraped off the paint. He created murals at the Asile Suisse in Paris, the École Tremblay in Geneva, and at Grand-Fontaine.

Holy exhibited his work mainly in Switzerland, particularly in Geneva at the Musée de l'Athénée in 1940 and 1965, and the Musée Rath in 1968. He also took part in the Salon des Indépendents and the Salon d'Automne in Paris and exhibited in Norway, which he visited every year from 1930 onwards.

Auction records:

Paris, 29 Oct 1926, *Landscape in La Corrèze,* FRF 500. Paris, 14 Oct 1942, *Self-portrait,* FRF 2,000. Paris, 28 Feb 1944, *Tennis Player* (gouache) FRF 3,100. Paris, 28 March 1947, *Urban Landscape,* FRF 9,000. Zurich, 28 Nov 1974, *St Peter's Square, Rome* (1954) CHF 2,600. Bern, 22 Oct 1976, *Rooftops in Paris* (1936, oil on canvas, 19 3/4 x 25 1/2 ins / 50 x 65 cm) CHF 2,000. Lucerne, 18 Nov 1978, *Standing Nude* (1935, oil on canvas, 25 1/2 x 19 3/4 ins / 65 x 50 cm) CHF 4,000. Zurich, 6 June 1980, *1st August 1932* (gouache, 24 1/2 x 25 1/4 ins / 62 x 64 cm) CHF 2,400. Geneva, 20 June 1980, *Pipe Shooting Gallery* (1942, oil on canvas, 38 1/4 x 51 1/4 ins / 97 x 130 cm) CHF 4,100. Lucerne, 13 Nov 1982, *Shooting Range* (1948, oil on canvas, 38 1/4 x 51 1/4 ins / 97 x 130 cm) CHF 14,000. Bern, 6 May 1983, *Three Young Italians* (1929, tempera, 9 1/2 x 6 3/4 ins / 24 x 17 cm) CHF 1,900. Zurich, 7 Oct 1987, *Portrait of Woman* (oil on canvas, 25 1/2 x 21 1/4 ins / 65 x 54 cm) CHF 3,800. Bern, 26 Oct 1988, *Working in the Fields in Early Spring* (1950, oil on canvas, 19 3/4 x 25 1/2 ins / 50 x 65 cm) CHF 3,200. Zurich, 4 June 1992, *Palace in Venice* (oil on paper, 14 1/4 x 22 1/2 ins / 36.5 x 57 cm) CHF 2,260. Zurich, 2 June 1994, *Palace in Venice* (1953, oil on paper, 14 1/4 x 22 1/2 ins / 36.5 x 57 cm) CHF 1,725. Zurich, 8 Dec 1994, *Nude Woman with a Sash* (1954, oil on canvas, 36 1/2 x 26 ins / 93 x 66 cm) CHF 2,875. Bern, 11 May 2000, *Busy Street Scene* (1972, oil on canvas, 13 x 18 ins / 33 x 45 cm) CHF 4,000. Bern, 3 Nov 2000, *Portrait of Rosetta Leins* (1950, oil on canvas, 23 x 31 ins / 59 x 80 cm) CHF 2,600. Zofingen, 8 June 2001, *Young Lady* (1922, oil on canvas, 28 x 23 ins / 72 x 58 cm) CHF 2,600. Bern, 8 Nov 2001, *Figures in a Locarno Street* (1944, oil on canvas, 13 x 18 ins / 33 x 46 cm) CHF 3,200. Zurich, 3 June 2002, *Fairground* (1938, oil on canvas, 26 x 20 ins / 65 x 50 cm) CHF 3,000. St Gall, 6 Nov 2002, *Studio Interior* (1947, oil on canvas, 29 x 36 ins / 73 x 92 cm) CHF 2,600.

HOLY, Miloslav

Czech, 20th century.

Born 1897, in Prague.

Painter. Scenes with figures, figure compositions, landscapes.

Miloslav Holy studied at the academy of fine art in Prague from 1918 to 1924. In the early years of his career he painted mainly figure compositions, emphasising the social and psychological elements of the scene. Later he turned to landscape painting, depicting the many countries to which he travelled.

He took part in many exhibitions of contemporary Czechoslovak painting in various European countries and the USA. He has shown his work in many solo exhibitions, mainly in Prague.

Bibliography:

Fifty years of Czechoslovak Painting from the Collections of the Galleries, 1918-1958, exhibition catalogue, Slovenska Narodna Gal., Bratislava, 1968 (in commemoration of the 50th anniversary of the Republic of Czechoslovakia).

Museums and Galleries:

Brno (Moravská Gal.) - Prague (Národní Gal.).

HOLYMAN, Michel

Belgian, 20th century.

Born 1925; died 1966.

Painter, enameller.

HOLYOAKE, Rowland

British, 19th - 20th century.

Active in London, from 1880 to 1907.

Painter. Genre scenes.

Rowland Holyoake frequently showed his work in London from 1880 at the Royal Academy and at the Suffolk Street Gallery.

Auction records:

London, 2 Feb 1979, *The Gentleman's Arrival* (oil on canvas, 16 x 12 1/4 ins / 40.6 x 31 cm) GBP 450. London, 31 July 1987, *The Art Lover* (1893, oil on canvas, 30 x 21 1/2 ins / 76 x 54.5 cm) GBP 5,800. London, 6 Nov 1995, *The Fisherman and the Mermaid* (oil on canvas, 29 1/4 x 35 1/2 ins / 74 x 90 cm) GBP 2,300. Toronto, 12 June 2000, *Maid Pouring a Drink for a Gentleman* (oil on canvas, 24 x 20 ins / 61 x 51 cm) CAD 3,100. Toronto, 7 Dec 2000, *Hunter Outside an Inn* (oil on panel, 13 x 9 ins / 32 x 24 cm) CAD 3,400. Chelsea, 5 June 2001, *Reading by the Fireside* (oil on canvas, 12 x 10 ins / 31 x 25 cm) GBP 1,200. Bury St Edmunds, 6 May 2002, *Out for the Day* (oil on canvas, 24 x 20 ins / 61 x 51 cm) GBP 2,600. Woodbridge, 24 June 2003, *Portrait of a Young Girl* (oil on canvas, 13 x 11 ins / 33 x 28 cm) GBP 2,200.

HOLYOAKE, William

British, 19th century.

Born 1834, in Birmingham; died 17 January 1894, in London.

Painter. Genre scenes.

William Holyoake was a member of the Royal Society of British Artists. He frequently exhibited in London at the Royal Academy and the Suffolk Street Gallery between 1858 and 1888.

Museums and Galleries:

Glasgow: *In the Front Row at the Opera.*

Auction records:

London, 14 March 1908, *Overture,* GBP 9. London, 13 Oct 1978, *Fortune Teller* (oil on canvas, 37 1/2 x 47 1/4 ins / 95.2 x

120 cm) GBP 5,000. LONDON, 2 Oct 1979, *Waiting* (oil on canvas, 23½ x 19¾ ins / 60 x 50 cm) GBP 700. ROME, 13 May 1986, *Peasant Women at the Well* (oil on canvas, 28 x 39¾ ins / 71 x 101 cm) ITL 4,400,000. LONDON, 21 March 1990, *Lady Spectators Watching a Regatta* (oil on canvas, a pair, each 20 x 24 ins / 51 x 61 cm) GBP 29,700. LONDON, 1 Nov 1990, *Vows of Love* (oil on canvas, 40 x 48 ins / 101.5 x 122 cm) GBP 13,200. LONDON, 12 May 1993, *Rebecca, Jewish Girl* (oil on panel, 12 x 10 ins / 30.5 x 25.5 cm) GBP 713. LONDON, 30 March 1994, *Lovers' Vows* (oil on canvas, 40 x 48 ins / 101.5 x 122 cm) GBP 12,075. NEW YORK, 10 Feb 1998, *Day at the Races* (oil on canvas, 24 x 20 ins / 61 x 51 cm) USD 3,450. LONDON, 17 Feb 1999, *In a Summer Garden* (oil on canvas, 22 x 30 ins / 57 x 76 cm) GBP 1,100. EDINBURGH, 28 Feb 2000, *Children Playing by a Pier* (oil on canvas, 30 x 19 ins / 75 x 49 cm) GBP 1,500. LONDON, 13 June 2000, *Patience* (oil on canvas, 38 x 48 ins / 96 x 122 cm) GBP 25,000. LONDON, 9 Nov 2000, *Gathering Mussels* (oil on canvas, 30 x 20 ins / 76 x 51 cm) GBP 2,200. LONDON, 10 June 2003, *Receiving the Love Note* (oil on canvas, 20 x 16 ins / 52 x 41 cm) GBP 3,200. NEW YORK, 22 April 2004, *Patience* (oil on canvas, 38 x 48 ins / 96 x 122 cm) USD 45,000.

HOLZ, Hermann
German, 19th century.
Born 20 May 1821, in Bremen; died 16 October 1883, in Munich.
Painter.
He mostly painted portraits.

HOLZ, Johann Daniel
German, 19th - 20th century.
Born 26 January 1867, in Bremen; died 1945, in Fürstenfeldbruck.
Painter. Landscapes, animals.
Holz was active in Munich.

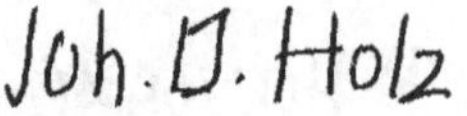

MUSEUMS AND GALLERIES:
BUCHAREST (Muz. National de Arta al României): *Cattle Returning* - MUNICH: *Evening in the Forest.*
AUCTION RECORDS:
MUNICH, 26 Nov 1976, *Flock in the Pasture* (oil on canvas remounted/panel, 15 x 14¼ ins / 38 x 36 cm) DEM 2,800. COLOGNE, 11 May 1977, *Summer Morning* (oil on canvas, 27½ x 40¼ ins / 70 x 102 cm) DEM 4,200. COLOGNE, 19 Oct 1979, *Peasant Woman and Two Cows in front of the Cowshed* (oil on canvas, 27¾ x 39½ ins / 70.5 x 100.5 cm) DEM 4,500. COLOGNE, 20 March 1981, *Flocks in the Pasture* (oil on canvas, 27½ x 39¼ ins / 70 x 100 cm) DEM 4,800. COLOGNE, 23 March 1990, *Flock of Sheep on the Banks of a Stream* (oil on canvas, 32 x 44½ ins / 81 x 113 cm) DEM 3,500. AMSTERDAM, 21 April 1993, *Smallholding* (oil on canvas, 23½ x 31½ ins / 60 x 80 cm) NLG 6,900. DRESDEN, 19 June 1999, *Peasant Girl with Calves in a Meadow* (oil on canvas, 19 x 27 ins / 48 x 68 cm) DEM 3,000. HELSINKI, 9 Dec 2000, *Cows Standing in Water* (oil on canvas, 28 x 37 ins / 70 x 95 cm) FIM 20,000. WARSAW, 10 Dec 2000, *Cattle Watering* (oil on canvas, 31 x 46 ins / 80 x 117 cm) PLN 14,000. NURNBERG, 26 April 2001, *Peasant with Cattle* (oil on canvas, 24 x 31 ins / 60 x 80 cm) DEM 4,500. AUGSBURG, 15 March 2002, *Cows by a River* (oil on canvas, 28 x 37 ins / 70 x 94 cm) EUR 4,000. MUNICH, 6 Dec 2002, *Cowherd with Cattle by a Wood* (oil on canvas, 34 x 46 ins / 87 x 118 cm) EUR 1,700. WARSAW, 30 March 2003, *Pasture Scene* (c. 1900, oil on canvas, 35 x 47 ins / 88 x 120 cm) PLN 12,000. MUNICH, 2 July 2003, *Peasant Woman with Cow and Goat* (oil on canvas, 35 x 41 ins / 88 x 104 cm) EUR 2,200. MUNICH, 30 Nov 2004, *Horses in Water* (oil on canvas, 28 x 37 ins / 70 x 95 cm) EUR 1,800.

HOLZAMER, C.
German, 19th century.
Active in Worms in 1860.
Draughtsman, lithographer.

HOLZAPFEL, Carl
German, 19th - 20th century.
Born 30 November 1865, in Berlin.
Painter. Landscapes.
MUSEUMS AND GALLERIES:
WEIMAR: *In the Mountains of Thuringia; Autumn Day in the Country.*

HOLZAPFL, Joseph Michael
German, 19th - 20th century.
Born 28 October 1860, in Munich; died 1914, in Munich.
Draughtsman, engraver, painter.
Holzapfl studied at the Munich academy in 1878, then at the art school run by J.-L. Raabs. He was awarded a silver medal at the Exposition Universelle in 1900.

HÖLZEL, Adolf, or Hoelzel
German, 19th - 20th century.
Born 13 May 1853, in Olmütz (now Olomouc, Czech Republic); died 1934, in Stuttgart.
Painter, pastellist. Religious subjects, figures, landscapes. Murals, designs for stained glass.
Dachau Artists' Colony.
Hölzel studied under Wurzinger, Griepenkerl and Eisenmeyer at the Akademie der bildenden Künste in Vienna from 1874 to 1876, then with Barth and W. Diez at the academy of fine arts in Munich. He went to Paris in around 1880, where he spent time in the studios of Manet and Monet. He returned and settled near Munich in 1888 and founded an art school, where Nolde was a student. He was appointed to the academy of fine arts in Stuttgart in 1905.

Hölzel invented the theory of visual counterpoint and harmony, which was inspired by musical theory and influenced by the ideas of Seurat. During the second decade of the 20th century he attempted to demonstrate this theory in his works. He is best known for designing the stained glass windows in Stuttgart's town hall and the Balsen factory in Hanover.

MUSEUMS AND GALLERIES:
BERLIN: *Before Sunset* - HANOVER (Pelikan Kunstsammlungen): *Composition in Red I* (1905) - MUNICH: *Meditation* - STUTTGART (Staatsgal.): *Savage; Abstraktion II.*
AUCTION RECORDS:
STUTTGART, 20 Nov 1959, *Abstraction*, DEM 7,000. STUTTGART, 20 May 1960, *Adoration* (pastel) DEM 4,700. COLOGNE, 3 Dec 1970, *Christ on the Mount of Olives* (pastel) DEM 3,500. HAMBURG, 4 July 1971, *Composition* (pastel) DEM 9,200. HAMBURG, 9 June 1972, *Biblical Scene*, DEM 4,200. MUNICH, 28 May 1976, *Young Boy in a Frozen Landscape* (1902, oil on canvas, 33 x 26½ ins / 84 x 67 cm) DEM 3,500. COLOGNE, 21 May 1977, *Birth of Christ* (pastel, 9¾ x 13¼ ins / 25 x 33.5 cm) DEM 6,500. NEW YORK, 7 Oct 1977, *Letter* (oil on canvas, 33 x 27 ins / 84 x 68.5 cm) USD 16,000. LONDON, 6 Dec 1977, *Composition* (coloured chalks, 9 x 11½ ins / 23 x 29 cm) GBP 1,800. HAMBURG, 2 June 1978, *Clown* (c. 1914, oil on card, 7¼ x 9½ ins / 18.5 x 24 cm) DEM 10,500. COLOGNE, 19 May 1979, *Composition* (pastel, 10 x 13¼ ins / 24.5 x 33.5 cm) DEM 12,000. VIENNA, 22 June 1979, *Resting in the Fields* (oil on canvas, 12½ x 15¾ ins / 32 x 40 cm) ATS 90,000. COLOGNE, 4 Dec 1980, *Composition* (pastel and graphite, 22 x 8¾ ins / 55 x 22.1 cm) DEM 19,000. MUNICH, 1 June 1981, *Suffer the Children to Come Unto Me* (c. 1912-1913, charcoal/canvas, 49½ x 43 ins / 126 x 109.5 cm) DEM

6,800. HAMBURG, 12 June 1981, *Composition in Yellow, Orange, Red* (c. 1930, pastel, 12 1/2 x 17 ins / 31.6 x 43.2 cm) DEM 16,000. HAMBURG, 11 June 1982, *Village Scene* (soft chalk, 7 1/2 x 6 1/2 ins / 19.2 x 16.6 cm) DEM 5,400. MUNICH, 26 Nov 1982, *Composition* (c. 1917-1918, oil on card, 9 3/4 x 7 3/4 ins / 25 x 20 cm) DEM 16,000. COLOGNE, 7 Dec 1984, *Houses in a Landscape* (pastel and pencil, 6 1/2 x 9 1/4 ins / 16.8 x 23.7 cm) DEM 6,400. MUNICH, 25 Nov 1985, *Petition* (coloured chalks, 11 1/2 x 9 ins / 29 x 23 cm) DEM 12,500. MUNICH, 29 Nov 1985, *Abstract Composition* (pastel, 9 x 11 3/4 ins / 23 x 30 cm) DEM 3,500. MUNICH, 1 June 1987, *Petition* (c. 1925, pastel and pencil, 5 3/4 x 4 1/2 ins / 14.5 x 11.6 cm) DEM 9,100. MUNICH, 26-27 Nov 1991, *Group of Figures* (charcoal, 9 x 14 ins / 23 x 35.5 cm) DEM 3,450. MUNICH, 26 May 1992, *Composition* (pastel and pencil, 12 1/2 x 9 1/2 ins / 32 x 24 cm) DEM 16,100. BERLIN, 27 Nov 1992, *Figures and Houses in a Landscape with a Yellow Sky* (pastel and graphite, 12 1/2 x 10 ins / 31.9 x 25.1 cm) DEM 29,380. ZURICH, 26 March 1996, *Figures in a Landscape* (pastel, 12 3/4 x 9 3/4 ins / 32.3 x 24.9 cm) CHF 7,500. BERN, 20-21 June 1996, *Train of Pilgrims* (c. 1924-1930, pastel/pencil, 9 3/4 x 13 1/2 ins / 24.8 x 34.3 cm) CHF 15,000.

HOLZER, Adalbert

German, 20th century.
Born 31 December 1881, in Munich.
Painter. Landscapes.

Holzer studied under C. von Marr.

HOLZER, Fred André

Swiss, 20th century.
Born 1935, in Moulier.
Painter, watercolourist. Landscapes.

Holzer studied painting and mosaics with Coghuf. He went to Paris and in 1958 he studied at the Académie de la Grande Chaumière. He created a poetic atmosphere in his paintings by bathing his landscapes in diffused light, with the shapes only alluded to by touches of colour. He took part in various group exhibitions in France and Switzerland and put on his first solo exhibition in Paris in 1973.

HOLZER, J. A.

Swiss, 19th - 20th century.
Born 30 October 1858, in Bern.
Active in the USA.
Painter, sculptor, fresco artist.

Holzer studied first under Fournier in Paris, then went to New York and worked there with Auguste St-Gaudens and La Fage. He mainly concentrated on painting murals.

AUCTION RECORDS:

PARIS, 11 Dec 1995, *Interior of Mosque in Damascus* (1898, oil on canvas, 26 x 19 1/4 ins / 66 x 49 cm) FRF 33,000.

HOLZER, Jenny

American, 20th - 21st century.
Born 29 July 1950, in Gallipolis (Ohio).
Installation artist, intervention artist.
Neo-Conceptual Art.

Jenny Holzer studied at Duke University, Durham, North Carolina (1968-1970), where she took general arts courses, and at the University of Chicago, where she studied painting, printmaking and drawing. Later she attended: Ohio University, Athens, obtaining a BFA in 1972; the Rhode Island School for Design, where she received an MFA in 1977; and the Independent Study Program at the Whitney Museum of American Art (1977).

Holzer has worked exclusively with language as a medium since she began to record her *Truisms* series in 1977, creating phrases like 'Abuse of power comes as no surprise', or 'Money creates taste' on broadsheets. She then pasted these sheets on walls and fences throughout Manhattan. She has since moved on to other series, such as *Laments* and *Messages* (1988-1989), placing these texts in unexpected places of normal signage, as when she displayed her work on the signboard in Times Square in 1982. Her messages have appeared on other signboards in Piccadilly Circus, Belfast and Plymouth, as art breaks on the MTV television channel, on video monitors in subway stations, and on cash till receipts in Virgin record shops. Her *Truisms* have also been seen on baseball caps and T-shirts. Holzer's purpose is to use technology to access a large public audience which would not normally take the time to consider 'art', and to challenge accepted ideas about where art should be shown. Her favoured medium is the LED (light emitting diode) sign, which she used in her 1989 retrospective show at the Guggenheim Museum, New York, in 1989.

Holzer's solo exhibitions include: 1991, at the Albright-Knox Art Gallery, Buffalo, the Walker Art Gallery, Minneapolis, and the Guggenheim Museum, New York. Her work has also been shown in other exhibitions, including: 1985, Musée d'Art Contemporain, Montreal;1990, *Language in Art*, Aldrich Museum of Contemporary Art; 1993, *Don't Ask, Don't Tell, Don't Pursue*, Fairfield University, CT; 1993, *American Art in the 20th Century Travelling Show*, Royal Academy of Arts, London; 1993, *Virtual Reality: An Emerging Medium*, Guggenheim Museum, New York; 1994, *Translucent Writings*, Neuberger Museum of Art, New York; 2002, Musée d'art moderne, Lille Métropole, Villeneuve d'Ascq; and 2002, *Heaven's Gift*, Contemporary Art Tower, MAK, Vienna. She received the Blair Award at the 79th Americans Show, Art Institute of Chicago (1982).

BIBLIOGRAPHY:

Holzer, Jenny, *Eating Friends*, illustrated book, Hallwells, Buffalo, 1981. Holzer, Jenny, *Truism and Essays*, Cologne, 1983. Holzer, Jenny, *Truisms and Essays*, book, Press of the Nova Scotia College of Art and Design, Halifax (NS), 1983. Holzer, Jenny, *Sign on a Truck*, video, School of the Art Institute of Chicago, Chicago, 1984. Domino, Christophe, '*Le Discours à l'œuvre*' in *Artstudio* n° 15, periodical, Gal. Templon, Paris, winter 1989. Holzer, Jenny, *Laments*, video, Dia Art Foundation, New York, 1989. Schjeldahl, Peter, '*Jenny Holzer*' in *Art Press* n° 147, periodical, Paris, May 1990. *Jenny Holzer: The Venice Installation*, exhibition catalogue, Albright-Knox Art Gallery, Buffalo, 1991. Auping, Michael, *Jenny Holzer*, illustrated book, Universe, New York, 1992. *Jenny Holzer: The Living Series*, exhibition catalogue, Tallgrass Press, New York, 1992. *L'Art au corps - Le Corps exposé de Man Ray à nos jours*, group exhibition catalogue, Musée d'Art contemporain, Marseille, Réunion des musées nationaux, Paris, 1996. Joselit, David, *Jenny Holzer*, illustrated book, Phaidon Press, London, 1998. *Jenny Holzer oh*, exhibition catalogue, Capc musée d'Art contemporain, Bordeaux, Réunion des musées nationaux, Paris, 2001 (text in French and English). *Archival Segments*, video, Inner-Tube Video, New York, 2001. Noever, Peter (ed.), *heaven's gift. A new programmatic strategy for the presentation of contemporary art*, exhibition catalogue, MAK, Vienna, 2002 (editions in German and English). Durand, Régis, et al., *Sans commune mesure. Image et texte dans l'art actuel*, exhibition catalogue, Éd. Léo Scheer, Paris, 2002.

MUSEUMS AND GALLERIES:

BOSTON (MFA): *Selection from the Survival Series* (1983-1985, cast aluminium) - CHICAGO (MCA) - EINDHOVEN (Van Abbe Mus.) - HAMBURG (Kunsthalle): *Ceiling Snake* (1996, installation) - LETHBRIDGE (University of Lethbridge): *Selections from Truisms* (1992, LED sign) - LONDON (Tate Collection): *from Inflammatory Essays* (1979-1982, print on paper) - NEW YORK (Guggenheim Mus.): *Untitled (Selections from Truisms, Inflammatory Essays, The Living Series, The Survival Series...)* (1989, electronic-display signboard) - NEW YORK (MoMA): *Truisms* (1977-1987, photocopied paper) - PARIS (FNAC): *Untitled, with selection from Truisms* (1985) - REGINA (MacKenzie AG): *Survival Series* (1991, graphite pencils, text, in cardboard box) - SAN FRANCISCO (MoMA): *I Am A Man* (1987, electronic LED and diodes).

AUCTION RECORDS:

VERSAILLES, 15 June 1986, *Selection from Truisms* (metal, glass, electronics, French version, 5 1/2 x 30 x 5 1/2 ins / 14 x 76 x 14 cm) FRF 20,500. NEW YORK, 27 Feb 1990, *Little Queenie* (painting/metal, 21 x 23 ins / 53.3 x 58.4 cm) USD 19,800. NEW YORK, 8 May 1990, *Selection from the Survival Series* (1983, red LED message machine, 6 1/2 x 124 x 4 ins / 16.5 x 315 x 9.9 cm) USD 82,500. PARIS, 20 Jan 1991, *Selection from the Truisms* (1984-1985, 2 3/4 x 29 1/2 x 5 1/2 ins / 7 x 75 x 14 cm) FRF 135,000. NEW YORK, 13 Feb 1991, *Selection from the Survival Series* (moulded aluminium wall plaque, 6 x 10 ins / 15.2 x 25.4 cm) USD 2,860. NEW YORK, 2 May 1991, *Untitled, From the Living Series* (1981, enamel/metal, 21 x 23 ins / 53.3 x 58.4 cm) USD 6,600. NEW YORK, 12 Nov 1991, *Selection from the Survival Series* (moulded aluminium wall plaque, 3 x 10 ins / 7.7 x 25.4 cm) USD 1,650. NEW YORK, 27 Feb 1992, *Untitled, Selection from the Living Series* (varnish/aluminium, 21 x 23 ins / 53.4 x 58.4 cm) USD 3,850. NEW YORK, 5 May 1992, *Untitled* (1990, three coloured LED message machine, 9 1/2 x 176 1/4 x 4 1/2 ins / 24 x 447.6 x 11.4 cm) USD 66,000. NEW YORK, 17 Nov 1992, *Selection from the Survival Series* (moulded aluminium wall relief, 3 x 10 ins / 7.6 x 25.4 cm) USD 1,870. NEW YORK, 19 Nov 1992, *Untitled* (1983, coloured LED machine, 6 1/2 x 61 x 4 1/4 ins / 16.2 x 154 x 10.5 cm) USD 28,600. NEW YORK, 5 May 1993, *Living Series* (engraved white granite bench, 16 3/4 x 35 1/2 x 17 3/4 ins / 42.5 x 90.2 x 45 cm) USD 40,250. NEW YORK, 3 Nov 1994, *Untitled (Selection From the Survival Series)* (red LED message machine, 6 1/4 x 120 1/2 x 3 3/4 ins / 15.8 x 306 x 9.6 cm) USD 36,800. NEW YORK, 3 May 1995, *Truisms* (1988, brown granite from the Baltic, 16 1/2 x 23 x 15 3/4 ins / 41.6 x 58.4 x 40 cm) USD 18,400. NEW YORK, 15 Nov 1995, *Truisms* (1988, brown granite from the Baltic, 16 1/4 x 23 x 15 3/4 ins / 41.2 x 58.4 x 40.2 cm) USD 32,200. PARIS, 27 March 1996, *Selection from Truisms* (red LED message machine) FRF 19,000. NEW YORK, 6-7 May 1997, *Lamentations* (1989, black granite and LED message machine, sarcophagus 82 x 30 x 24 1/4 ins / 208.3 x 76.2 x 61.9 cm and LED 128 x 10 x 4 1/2 ins/325.1 x 25.4 x 11.4 cm) USD 68,500. NEW YORK, 8 May 1997, *Untitled (Selection from the Survival Series)* (1983-1984, red LED message machine, 6 1/2 x 60 1/4 x 4 1/2 ins / 16.5 x 153 x 11.4 cm) USD 17,250. LONDON, 23 June 1997, *Truisms 3* (1994, three-coloured LED message machine, 4 3/4 x 4 ins / 12.2 x 10.1 cm) GBP 3,200. NEW YORK, 19 Nov 1997, *Untitled with a Selection of Truisms* (royal Danby marble, 17 x 54 x 25 ins / 43.2 x 137.3 x 63.5 cm) USD 34,500. LONDON, 8 Dec 1999, *Untitled* (enamel on metal, 21 x 23 ins / 53 x 59 cm) GBP 2,800. LONDON, 8 Dec 1999, *Laments, I Have a Hot Hole* (black granite sarcophagus with LED sign, 128 x 10x4 ins / 325 x 25x11 cm) GBP 40,000. NEW YORK, 17 May 2000, *Laments* (green and yellow signboard and granite sarcophagus, 93 x 9x5 ins / 235 x 24x13 cm) USD 70,000. NEW YORK, 19 May 2000, *Selection from Survival Series* (enamel and metal, 15 x 18 ins / 38 x 46 cm) USD 4,000. LONDON, 8 Feb 2001, *Selection from the Survival Series* (1983, silk screen on brushed aluminium, 15 x 18 ins / 38 x 46 cm) GBP 3,500. NEW YORK, 13 Nov 2001, *Survival Series: In a Dream You Saw a Way* (1998, marble, 17 x 24x17 ins / 43 x 61x43 cm) USD 55,000. NEW YORK, 15 May 2002, *Untitled C-11* (1990, green and red LED signboard, 9 x 176x5 ins / 24 x 448x13 cm) USD 30,000. SYDNEY, 26 June 2002, *Xenon* (photos, eighteen, 16 x 20 ins / 40 x 50 cm) AUD 38,000. NEW YORK, 29 April 2003, *Little Queenie* (enamel on metal, 21 x 23 ins / 53 x 59 cm) USD 2,200. NEW YORK, 13 Nov 2003, *I Am a Man* (LED sign and colour diodes, 112 x 9x4 ins / 284 x 24x11 cm) USD 35,000. NEW YORK, 13 May 2004, *Untitled* (1986, electronic LED sign with red diodes, 5 x 29x4 ins / 13 x 74x11 cm) USD 18,000. CHICAGO, 16 May 2004, *Selection for the Living Series* (enamel on aluminium, 21 x 23 ins / 53 x 58 cm) USD 6,500.

HOLZER, Johann Evangelist

Austrian, 18th century.

Born 24 December 1709, in Burgeis (S Tyrol); died 21 July 1740, in Clemenswerth (Sögel).

Painter, fresco artist, engraver. Religious subjects, allegorical subjects, mythological subjects, portraits.

A pupil of Nicolas Auer in Meran (now Merano, Italy), then J.G. Bergmuller in Augsburg from 1732 to 1736, he subsequently worked with publisher J.A. Pfeffel. He furnished a large number of public monuments in Augsburg with frescoes, also the dome of St Anton in Partenkirchen (1736) and the episcopal summer palace in Eichstätt (1737). In 1740, he did a portrait of Elector Clement in Bonn. The following year he died, just after being commissioned to do the decoration of the hunting lodge at Clemenswerth. He did engravings of mythological subjects from his own drawings and from Bergmuller.

Holzer's style was notable for its realism, and he portrayed saintly figures in the guise of labourers flanked by farm girls and chubby-faced children taken from life, in settings of imaginary architecture with dramatic lighting such as the age loved. Along with J.W. Baumgartner and G.B. Gös, he was one of the best representatives of the Augsburg School of the 18th century.

MUSEUMS AND GALLERIES:

AUGSBURG (Kunsthalle, Staatsgal.): *Christian Georg and Maria Magdalena von Köpf.*

AUCTION RECORDS:

NEW YORK, 12 May 1960, *Apotheosis,* USD 450. COLOGNE, 7 June 1972, *The Mystic Marriage of St Catherine,* DEM 3,200. LONDON, 21 June 1978, *Allegory of the House of Habsburg* (oil on canvas, 22 1/2 x 12 1/2 ins / 57 x 32 cm) GBP 9,000. LONDON, 12 April 1983, *The Emperor Charles VI on His Throne Surrounded by Arts* (1732, pen and wash heightened with white, 22 1/4 x 17 3/4 ins / 56.4 x 45.4 cm) GBP 3,800. MUNICH, 8 June 1999, *Adoration of the Three Kings* (1733, pen/wash/heightened white over graphite, 9 x 7 ins / 23 x 18 cm) DEM 9,000. MUNICH, 30 Nov 1999, *Adoration of the Kings* (pen over pencil/wash/heightened white, 6 x 4 ins / 14 x 10 cm) DEM 10,000. BERLIN, 30 Nov 2001, *Saint Kneeling on Pouch* (pen/brush/heightened white, ? x 2 ins /? x 6 cm) DEM 3,200.

HOLZER, Joseph

Austrian, 19th century.

Born 20 March 1824, in Vienna; died 17 January 1876, in Vienna.

Painter, lithographer. Landscapes.

He started out as a student of engraving under the direction of Kleber, then went over to paintings, becoming a pupil of Ender and Steinfeld. In 1840, he was elected a member of the academy in Vienna. After travelling in Germany, Belgium and Switzerland, he finished up in Munich, remaining there from 1856 to 1859. He was a talented landscape painter, and his works were quite sought after at one time.

MUSEUMS AND GALLERIES:

GRAZ: *Landscape* - VIENNA: *Carpathian Landscape; Tranquil Part of the Forest.*

AUCTION RECORDS:

VIENNA, 19 June 1979, *Wooded Landscape* (watercolour, 15 3/4 x 11 1/2 ins / 40 x 29.5 cm) ATS 18,000. VIENNA, 19 May 1981, *Walk at the Edge of the Wood* (oil on canvas, 26 3/4 x 22 ins / 68 x 55 cm) ATS 80,000. MUNICH, 30 June 1983, *Autumn Landscape* (oil on canvas, 31 1/2 x 46 ins / 80 x 116 cm) DEM 4,600. LUCERNE, 7 Nov 1985, *Mountainous Landscape* (oil on canvas, 26 3/4 x 20 1/2 ins / 68 x 52 cm) CHF 5,500. NEW YORK, 23 Feb 1989, *Dachstein Mountain* (oil on canvas, 27 1/4 x 37 1/4 ins / 69.3 x 94.6 cm) USD 8,800. VIENNA, 20 May 1999, *View of Schneeberg, Wooded Mountain Landscape* (oil on canvas, 15 x 20 ins / 39 x 52 cm) ATS 50,000. VIENNA, 14 June 2000, *Wood Landscape with Figures* (1854, oil on canvas, 28 x 38 ins / 70 x 96 cm) ATS 75,000. VIENNA, 29 Nov 2001, *Theben Cliffs with Theben Fortress Ruins on the Donau* (oil on canvas, 28 x 37 ins / 70 x 95 cm) ATS 90,000. VIENNA, 16 May 2002, *Idyllic River Landscape with Figures* (1848, oil on canvas, 26 x 31 ins / 66 x 78 cm) EUR 5,500. VIENNA, 28 Nov 2002, *Zellersee with View of Zell am See and the Kitzsteinhorn* (oil on canvas, 27 x 37 ins / 68 x 95 cm) EUR 10,000. VIENNA, 24 Nov 2003, *Zellersee with Kitzsteinhorn* (1854, oil on canvas, 28 x 37 ins / 70 x 94 cm) EUR 17,000.

HOLZHALB, Adolf Rudolf
Swiss, 19th century.
Born 13 July 1835, in Zurich; died 5 August 1885.
Painter. Architectural views.
He was a pupil of Gude and a student at the academy in Düsseldorf. After travelling widely in Germany, Austria, France and Italy, he was appointed to the staff of the Polytechnicum in Zurich.

HOLZHALB, Heinrich
Swiss, 16th century.
Died 3 September 1570, in Zurich.
Active in Andelfingen and Grüningen.
Glass painter.

HOLZHALB, Jacob
Swiss, 17th - 18th century.
Born in Zurich.
Painter.
In 1705, he was living in Rotterdam.

HOLZHALB, Johann Jacob
German, 17th century.
Active in Zurich in 1690.
Engraver (burin).

HOLZHALB, Johann Rudolph
Swiss, 18th century.
Born 1723, in Zurich; died 21 September 1806.
Engraver.
He engraved mostly portraits and illustrations for Fuseli's book of *Swiss Painters*.
AUCTION RECORDS:
BERN, 24 June 1983, *Prospect of the City of Zurich* (1778, engraving/copper, three items, 14 1/2 x 21 ins / 37 x 52.5 cm) CHF 13,000. LUCERNE, 8 Nov 2000, *Varenna on Lake Como* (1862, oil on canvas, 15 x 22 ins / 38 x 55 cm) CHF 7,000. COLOGNE, 5 April 2001, *Wooded Landscape with Ruin* (1880, oil on canvas, 34 x 49 ins / 87 x 125 cm) DEM 5,500.

HOLZHAUER, Emil
American, 19th - 20th century.
Born 1887; died 1986.
Painter.
Emil Holzhauer is featured at the Art Institute of Chicago.

HOLZHAUSEN, Fritz von
Austrian, 19th - 20th century.
Born 12 April 1857, in Troppau (now Opava, Czech Republic); died 7 December 1923, in Hinterberg.
Painter, scholar.
Von Holzhausen studied under Laufberger.

HOLZHAUSEN, Olga von
Austrian, 19th - 20th century.
Born 21 January 1871, in Vienna.
Painter.
Von Holzhausen was the sister-in-law of Fritz von Holzhausen.

HOLZHAUSEN PORTRAITS, Master of the.
See **MASTERS**

HOLZHEY, Sebastian
German, 18th century.
Born 1728, in Heilbronn.
Painter.
He worked in Ludwigsburg.

HOLZINGER
German, 18th century.
Miniaturist.

HOLZINGER, Franz Joseph Ignatius
Austrian, 18th century.
Born c. 1690, in Schörfling (Salzkammergut); died 14 August 1775, in St Florian.
Sculptor.
His main output was plasterwork and decorative sculpture.

HOLZINGER, Johann Georg
Austrian, 18th century.
Sculptor.
He was the brother and partner of Franz Joseph Holzinger.

HOLZMAIER, Josef
German, 19th century.
Born 21 November 1809, in Frauenchiemsee (near Rosenheim); died 29 December 1859, in Munich.
Painter. History painting.
He trained at the academy in Munich and with Joseph Schlorthauer.

HOLZMAIR, Hans
German, 17th century.
Active in Munich c. 1600.
Painter.

HOLZMAIR, Johann Wilhelm
German, 17th century.
Active in Munich c. 1660.
Painter.
He also worked in Ingolstadt.

HOLZMAIR, Melchior
German, 17th century.
Active in Munich.
Painter.

HOLZMAIR, Thomas
German, 17th century.
Active in Munich c. 1630.
Painter.

HOLZMANN, Adolf
Swiss, 20th century.
Born 1890, in Zurich.
Painter. Portraits, landscapes, still-lifes.

HOLZMANN, Johann. See **HULSMAN**

HOLZMANN, Johann Michael
German, 18th century.
Active in Lower Franconia c. 1780.
Sculptor.

HOLZMEYER, Peter
German, 16th century.
Active in Berlin c. 1578.
Engraver (wood).

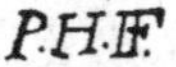

HOLZMÜLLER, Andreas
Swiss, 18th century.
Died 1728, in Basel.
Painter.
He did landscapes in the style of Claude Lorraine.

HOLZNER, Sebastian
German, 19th century.
Active in Augsburg.
Painter.
He also worked in Munich and Salzburg.

HOLZSCHUH, Rudolf
German, 19th century.
Born 27 March 1865, in Merseburg.
Painter. Landscapes.
MUSEUMS AND GALLERIES:
WEIMAR (Goethe-Nationalmus.): *In the Forest* (oil on canvas).

HOM, Georg
German, 19th - 20th century.
Born 27 June 1838, in Frankfurt am Main; died 23 October 1911, in Berlin.
Portrait artist.
Hom studied under Jacob Becker. He exhibited his work in Berlin from 1878 onwards.
MUSEUMS AND GALLERIES:
FRANKFURT AM MAIN: *Portrait of the Explorer Eduard Rüppel.*

HØM, Poul or Paul
Danish, 20th century.
Born 2 May 1905, in Ballerup; died 25 September 1994, in Gudhjem.
Painter. Figures, genre scenes, interiors, flowers.
Høm mainly painted young mothers and little girls either daydreaming or busy with their tasks.
AUCTION RECORDS:
COPENHAGEN, 28 April 1976, *Reverie* (1943, oil on canvas, 31 1/2 x 39 1/4 ins / 80 x 100 cm) DKK 12,200. COPENHAGEN, 11 May 1977, *Little Girls at the Window* (oil on canvas, 29 1/2 x 39 1/4 ins / 75 x 100 cm) DKK 13,500. COPENHAGEN, 5 March 1980, *Two Girls with Flowerpots* (1942, oil on canvas, 55 x 39 1/4 ins / 140 x 100 cm) DKK 20,000. COPENHAGEN, 31 March 1982, *Garden* (1942, oil on canvas, 17 3/4 x 25 1/2 ins / 45 x 65 cm) DKK 23,000. COPENHAGEN, 26 Feb 1986, *Seated Model* (1939, oil on canvas, 51 1/4 x 33 ins / 130 x 84 cm) DKK 27,000. COPENHAGEN, 2 March 1988, *Little Girl Reclining* (oil on canvas, 26 3/4 x 55 ins / 68 x 140 cm) DKK 33,000. COPENHAGEN, 20 Sept 1989, *Arum Lilies* (1942, oil on canvas, 27 1/2 x 35 1/2 ins / 70 x 90 cm) DKK 10,000. COPENHAGEN, 22 Nov 1989, *Little Girl Playing* (oil on canvas, 25 1/2 x 32 ins / 65 x 81 cm) DKK 30,000. COPENHAGEN, 9 May 1990, *Young Girl Reading* (oil on canvas, 28 3/4 x 21 1/4 ins / 73 x 54 cm) DKK 27,000; *Little Girl* (oil on canvas, 28 1/4 x 19 3/4 ins / 72 x 50 cm) DKK 5,500. COPENHAGEN, 10 March 1993, *Mother and Child* (oil on canvas, 31 1/2 x 23 1/2 ins / 80 x 60 cm) DKK 8,500. COPENHAGEN, 21 April 1993, *Little Girl* (oil on canvas, 25 1/2 x 13 ins / 65 x 33 cm) DKK 8,000. COPENHAGEN, 20 Oct 1993, *Interior with Mother and Children* (1947, oil on canvas, 32 x 41 1/4 ins / 81 x 105 cm) DKK 14,500. COPENHAGEN, 26 April 1995, *Young Girl* (1954, oil on canvas, 27 1/2 x 19 3/4 ins / 70 x 50 cm) DKK 8,800. COPENHAGEN, 12-14 Nov 1997, *Boy and Girl* (1941, oil on canvas, 65 x 49 1/4 ins / 165 x 125 cm) DKK 23,000. VEJLE, 22 Jan 1999, *Interior with Boy Sleeping* (oil on canvas, 39 x 49 ins / 100 x 125 cm) DKK 20,000. COPENHAGEN, 20 Oct 1999, *Boy and Girl* (oil on canvas, 65 x 49 ins / 165 x 125 cm) DKK 17,000. COPENHAGEN, 10 Oct 2001, *Interior with Young Girl Reading* (1970, oil on canvas, 26 x 36 ins / 65 x 92 cm) DKK 15,500. COPENHAGEN, 23 April 2002, *Portrait of Julie* (1967, oil on canvas, 20 x 24 ins / 50 x 61 cm) DKK 16,000. COPENHAGEN, 18 June 2002, *Mother and Child* (oil on canvas, 46 x 28 ins / 116 x 72 cm) DKK 20,000. COPENHAGEN, 26 Feb 2003, *Julie* (c. 1958, oil on canvas, 38 x 28 ins / 97 x 70 cm) DKK 15,000. COPENHAGEN, 29 March 2004, *Kirsten - the Artist's Wife* (oil on canvas, 59 x 39 ins / 150 x 98 cm) DKK 30,000. HAVNEN, 24 April 2004, *Passage of Life - Composition with Figures* (1940, oil on canvas, 81 x 59 ins / 205 x 150 cm) DKK 22,000.

HOMAN, Gertrude (Miss)
British, 19th century.
Active in London.
Painter. Portraits, genre scenes.
Gertrude Homan exhibited in London at the Royal Academy and the Suffolk Street Gallery from 1886.
AUCTION RECORDS:
LONDON, 16 June 1993, *Arab Sitting outside his Shop* (1887, oil on canvas, 29 1/2 x 24 3/4 ins / 75 x 63 cm) GBP 3,220. NEW YORK, 17 Feb 1994, *Cavaliers in a Room in a Palace* (1897, oil on canvas, 32 x 36 ins / 81.3 x 91.5 cm) USD 6,900.

HOMAN, Margot
Dutch, 20th - 21st century.
Born 1950, in Oss.
Sculptor. Statues, groups.
Homan studied at the art academy in Tilburg, where she lives. She works in bronze and marble, with close attention to detail. She has exhibited regularly in the Netherlands.
BIBLIOGRAPHY:
Nieuwendijk, Koen, *Met engelengeduld (The Patience of a Saint)*, exhibition catalogue, Gal. Lieve Hemel, Amsterdam, 1995.

HOMANN, Andreas Christoph
German, 19th century.
Born 23 August 1790, in Bremen; died 3 June 1841, in Bremen.
Draughtsman.
He was a pupil of J H Menken.

HOMANN, Johann Baptista
German, 17th - 18th century.
Born 20 March 1664, in Kambach; died 1 July 1724, in Nuremberg.
Engraver (burin), print publisher.
He engraved plates for illustrations.

HOMBERG, Franz Friedrich
German, 19th century.
Born 12 April 1851, in Magdeburg.
Engraver, medallist.
He worked in Berlin and then Bern.

HOMBERG, Louis Marie
French, 20th century.
Born in Paris.
Painter.
A pupil of Etcheverry, Louis Homberg featured regularly at the Salon des Artistes Français in Paris from 1914.

HOMBRON, Henri
French, 19th century.
Born in the 19th century, in Lambézellec.
Painter. Genre scenes, landscapes, still-lifes.
Hombron was a pupil of L. Caradec, and exhibited at the Paris Salon from 1876 onwards.
MUSEUMS AND GALLERIES:
BREST: *Inside a Kitchen; Culinary Preparations; Woodcocks; Lunch Has Begun.*
AUCTION RECORDS:
PARIS, 24 June 1991, *Headrace at Kerno Lesneven* (oil on canvas, 11 3/4 x 18 3/4 ins / 30 x 47.5 cm) FRF 3,500. NEW YORK, 23 Oct 1997, *Dahlias in Japanese Vases* (1897, oil on canvas, oval, 45 3/4 x 35 ins / 116.2 x 88.9 cm) USD 10,350.

HOMBURG, Jacob
French, 18th century.
Born in Alsace.
Draughtsman, engraver.
Jacob Homburg worked mostly in Frankfurt am Main where he specialised in the engraving of portraits.

HOMBURG, Karl
German, 19th - 20th century.
Born 25 June 1874, in Berlin.
Engraver, painter. Landscapes.
Homburg exhibited his work in Berlin in 1909.

HOMCH, Louis
French, 17th century.
Active in Haguenau c. 1625.
Sculptor.
Louis Homch worked at the church of Bitche.

HOME, David (Sir)
British.
Painter. Portraits.
Sir David Home is mentioned in *Art Prices Current*.
AUCTION RECORDS:
LONDON, 14 July 1911, *Portrait of Lord Crossrig*, GBP 12.

HOME, Gordon
British, 20th century.
Painter. Landscapes.
Gordon Home worked in Epsom in 1900. He exhibited at the Royal Academy in London.

HOME, Juan de
French, 15th century.
Active in Pamplona in 1410.
Sculptor.
Juan de Home was employed by Carlos III, King of Navarre.

HOME, Robert
British, 18th - 19th century.
Born 6 August 1752, in Hull; died 12 September 1834, in India.
Painter. History painting, portraits, genre scenes.
Robert Home studied first with Angelica Kauffmann and then in Rome. He worked for a while in Dublin and London and then left for India in 1790. He made a fortune there as official painter to Ghazi-ud-Din Haidar, the king of Oudh. He exhibited his portraits in London at the Royal Academy between 1770 and 1813.
MUSEUMS AND GALLERIES:
DUBLIN: *Portrait of Miss Frances Barnett Woollery* - LONDON (Royal Collection): *White Leopard; Arthur Wellesley, Later First Duke of Wellington; Ghazi-ud-Din Haidar, King of Oudh, Receiving Tribute*.
AUCTION RECORDS:
LONDON, Nov 1922, *Captain Harris*, GBP 50. LONDON, 26 June 1981, *Portrait of King Ghazi-ud-Din Haidar* (c. 1820, oil on canvas, 82 x 52 ins / 208.3 x 132 cm) GBP 9,500. LONDON, 17 June 1983, *Portrait of a Lady* (oil on canvas, 30 1/2 x 25 1/2 ins / 77.5 x 64.8 cm) GBP 1,100. GLASGOW, 6 Feb 1990, *Bridgend, Ceres* (oil on canvas, 28 1/4 x 36 1/4 ins / 72 x 92 cm) GBP 2,970. LONDON, 18 Nov 1992, *Three-quarter Length Portrait of Major Carlo Jospeh Doyle in Uniform* (oil on canvas, 38 1/2 x 30 1/4 ins / 97.5 x 77 cm) GBP 3,000. LONDON, 10 Nov 1993, *Portrait of Mrs Braddyl Seated at a Writing Desk* (oil on canvas, 29 1/2 x 24 1/2 ins / 75 x 62 cm) GBP 2,760. NEW YORK, 29 Jan 1999, *Portrait of a Lady as the Cumcaen Sibyl* (oil on canvas, 30 x 25 ins / 76 x 63 cm) USD 40,000. LONDON, 17 Oct 2002, *Portrait of Mordant Ricketts* (gouache on ivory, 40 x 37 ins / 101 x 93 cm) GBP 2,400.

HOMELL, Antonio
Spanish, 16th century.
Born in Girona.
Active in Girona c. 1500.
Painter.
Antonio Homell worked for the cathedral of Vic.

HOMENKO, Boris
Russian, 20th century.
Born 1930, in Leningrad (now St Petersburg).
Painter. Scenes with figures.
Boris Homenko studied at the Ilya Repin academy in Leningrad (now St Petersburg). Alongside a number of hallucinatory works, he takes Socialist-Realist themes, freely interpreting them in his own way. He was a member of the union of artists of the USSR.
MUSEUMS AND GALLERIES:
JITOMIR (MFA) - MOSCOW (Ministry of Culture) - ST PETERSBURG (Academy).
AUCTION RECORDS:
PARIS, 18 Feb 1991, *Roundabout* (oil on canvas, 32 1/4 x 33 1/2 ins / 82 x 85 cm) FRF 6,000. PARIS, 24 Sept 1991, *Theatre at Taormina* (oil on canvas, 33 3/4 x 39 3/4 ins / 86 x 101 cm) FRF 4,000.

HOMER, Winslow
American, 19th - 20th century.
Born 24 February 1836, in Boston (Massachusetts); died 29 September 1910, in Prout's Neck (Maine).
Painter (gouache), watercolourist, engraver, draughtsman. Genre scenes, landscapes, seascapes. Symbolism.
Winslow Homer was employed by a lithographer in Boston at the age of 19, and sent some of his engravings to *Harper's Weekly*. In 1859, he was in New York, working as a freelance illustrator for *Ballou's Pictorial* and *Harper's Weekly*. He became the latter's correspondent during the Civil War as a 'reporter through images'. Instead of producing war scenes, he preferred to show life in the camps, demonstrating sensitivity and humour. After this experience, he executed a large painting entitled *Prisoners from the Front*, which he exhibited in 1866. The preceding year he had been elected to the National Academy of Design, New York.

Once the war was over, Homer toured New England during the summer months, drawing and making notes of its landscapes. Back in New York in winter, he executed paintings using his detailed sketches, like the majority of painters of American landscapes at this time. His themes were pleasant rustic scenes, and scenes of family life, where mother and child featured prominently. However, he employed dark colours for the backgrounds, broken up with a few bright touches for the foregrounds. His trip to France between 1866 and 1867 had little influence on his painting, unlike his illustrations. The style of the latter became more cheerful and showed evidence of the fashion for Japanese engraving.

In 1873, Homer started learning the watercolour technique, which he afterwards preferred to pencil for doing his rough sketches. Children's worlds fascinated him; this can be seen in paintings such as *Farandole* and *Breezing up (A Fair Wind)*. The latter painting shows evidence of his liking for the sea. Its composition was quite daring. The boat, kept upright by young boys and a man accompanying them, steers a marked diagonal course, which is offset on a pictorial level by a dark yacht on the horizon steering in an almost vertical direction.

Homer communed more and more with nature and, in 1881, left America and spent two years in Tynemouth, a small fishing village in England on the shores of the North Sea. The life of the fishermen and their women inspired him to produce austere paintings. These were the first signs of what would mainly occupy him in future and for which he is best known - representation of the power and solitude of the sea and the contest of man with the forces of nature. The sea and the frequent danger it poses for man is the predominant theme, and his watercolours have an uneasy feeling about them. Upon returning to America, he moved to Prout's Neck, a fishing village in a desolate spot on the Maine coast, and lived in a house by the sea which had a balcony facing the sea which seemed like the gangway of a boat. This contact with the elements was accompanied by an ever-increasing solitude.

Homer painted scenes of shipwrecks in dark colours with dramatic effects. He put out to sea with the fishermen, which allowed him to execute monumental paintings like *The Herring Net*, and *The Fog Warning*. If we compare the latter to *Breezing up (A Fair Wind)*, the link in terms of the composition is obvious. The diagonal line of the boat in the foreground is offset by a dark vertical yacht on the horizon. But the atmosphere is very different. In (*Breezing up (A Fair Wind)*) the sea is bathed in sunlight with hardly any threatening waves, and in the other, the sea is dark and surging. This contest of man against the forces of nature found its apotheosis in *Gulf Stream* (1899).

During the last few years of his life Homer varied his compositions more. Some were influenced by Japanese engravings, like *Kiss by Moonlight*, some had strange layouts, like the *Right and Left*, and some were brighter, like his last watercolours. Homer was one of the greatest realist painters in America at the turn of the century.

After his death, his work appeared in many exhibitions of American painting, notably: 1947, Milch Galleries, New York; 1972, Whitney Museum of American Art, New York; 1989, *200 Ans de Peinture Américaine. Collection du Wadsworth Atheneum* (*200 Years of American Painting. The Wadsworth Atheneum Collection*) at Galeries Lafayette, Paris; 1995, a dozen of his works were exhibited at the Musée d'Art Américain, Giverny; and 2001, *L'Héroïque et le quotidien: les artistes américains, 1820-1920* (*The Heroic and the Everyday: American Artists, 1820-1920*), Musée d'Art Américain, Giverny.

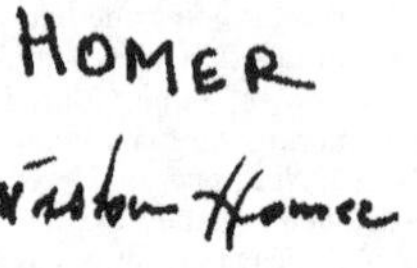

BIBLIOGRAPHY:

Gelman, Barbara, *The Wood Engravings of Winslow Homer*, Bounty Books, New York, 1969. Hendricks, Gordon, *The Life and Works of Winslow Homer*, Abrams, New York, 1979. Copper, Helen A., *Winslow Homer Watercolors*, exhibition catalogue, National Gall. of Art, Washington DC, 1986. Jennings, Kate F., *Winslow Homer*, Magna Books, Wigston, 1990. Ahrweiler, Hélène/Mandle, Roger/Atkinson, D. Scott/Gerdts, William H./Shelby, Carole L./Wierich, Jochen, *Lasting Impressions: American Painters in France 1865-1915*, exhibition catalogue, Musée d'Art américain, Giverny, Terra Foundation for the Arts, Evanston (IL), 1992. Cikovsky Jr., Nicolai/Kelly, Franklin/Walsh, Judith/Brock, Charles, *Winslow Homer*, National Gall. of Art, Washington DC, Yale University Press, New Haven, 1995. Jennings, Kate F., *Winslow Homer*, Knickerbocker Press, New York, 1998. Kushner, Marilyn S., *Winslow Homer: Illustrating America*, exhibition catalogue, Brooklyn Museum of Art, New York, 2000. Unger, Miles, *The Watercolors of Winslow Homer*, W.W. Norton, New York, 2001. Johns, Elizabeth, *Winslow Homer: the Nature of Observation*, University of California Press, Berkeley, 2002. Wood, Peter H., *Weathering the Storm: Inside Winslow Homer's Gulf Stream*, University of Georgia Press, Athens (GA), 2004.

MUSEUMS AND GALLERIES:

BALTIMORE (Peabody Art Collection): *Waiting an Answer* (1872, oil on canvas) - BOSTON (MFA): *The Fog Warning* (1885, oil on canvas); *Long Branch* - CHICAGO (AI): *The Herring Net* (1885, oil on canvas) - CHICAGO (Terra Foundation for American Art Collection): *The Watch* (1864, oil on canvas); *Haymakers* (1867); *Game of Croquet* (1868-1869, oil on card); *Garden in Nassau* (1885, watercolour, gouache, pencil/paper) - HARTFORD (Wadsworth Atheneum): *Boy in a Dory* (c. 1881, watercolour/paper); *Red Feather* (1864, oil on canvas) - NEW YORK (Metropolitan Mus. of Art): *Prisoners Captured at the Front* (1866); *Gulf Stream*; *Prisoners from the Front* - NORTHAMPTON, MA (MA, Smith College): *Shipyard in Gloucester* (1871) - PARIS (Mus. d'Orsay): *Summer Night* (1890, oil on canvas (76,7x102)) - PHILADELPHIA (MA): three other paintings*A Huntsman and Dogs* (1891, oil on canvas) - PORTLAND, ME (MA): *Sharpshooter* (1863, oil on canvas); *Artists Sketching in the White Mountains* (1868, oil/panel); *Taking an Observation* (c. 1886); *Weatherbeaten* (1894); *Wild Geese in Flight* (1897) - SPRINGFIELD, MA (MFA): *Promenade on the Beach* (1880, oil on canvas) - WASHINGTON DC (NGA): *Breezing Up (A Fair Wind)* (c. 1873-1876, oil on canvas); *Right and Left* (1909, oil on canvas) - WILMINGTON, DE (Delaware AM): *Milking Time* (oil on canvas) - WORCESTER, MA (AM): *Boys and Kitten* (1873, watercolour and gouache); *The Gale* (1883-1893, oil on canvas).

AUCTION RECORDS:

NEW YORK, 31 Jan-2 Feb 1900, *Sunday Morning in Virginia*, USD 400; *Battered by the Storm*, USD 4,000. NEW YORK, 9 Jan 1902, *Autumn*, USD 120. NEW YORK, 9-10 Feb 1905, *Watching the Breakers*, USD 2,700. NEW YORK, 15-16 April 1909, *Charmed*, USD 350. NEW YORK, 6 Jan 1911, *Music Amateurs*, USD 450. LONDON, 1 April 1911, *Gathering the Cotton* (1876) GBP 141. NEW YORK, 6 May 1937, *Miss Williams* USD 300. NEW YORK, 4 June 1942, *Haymaking*, USD 925. NEW YORK, 16 March 1944, *Shall I Tell Your Fortune?*, USD 1,600. NEW YORK, 18-19 Oct 1946, *Party in the Bay*, USD 5,400. NEW YORK, 13 May 1959, *Shepherdess* (pencil) USD 4,000. NEW YORK, 18 Feb 1960, *Shepherdess* (pencil) USD 1,100. LONDON, 15 Feb 1961, *Fisherman's Family Awaiting the Return of the Boats* (drawing) GBP 5,600. NEW YORK, 21 March 1962, *The Saguenay, Grand Discharge* (watercolour) USD 24,000. NEW YORK, 23 April 1964, *Country Store*, USD 26,000. NEW YORK, 11 May 1966, *Farm on a Hill* (watercolour) USD 21,000. NEW YORK, 19 March 1969, *Farm Girl* (watercolour and pencil/bluish-grey paper) USD 12,000. NEW YORK, 21 May 1970, *Florida Landscape* (watercolour) USD 14,000. NEW YORK, 10 Dec 1970, *View from Cape Diamond, Levis, Quebec* USD 8,000. NEW YORK, 28 Oct 1971, *Girl on a Hillside*, USD 8,000. NEW YORK, 18-19 Oct 1972, *Adirondack Catch*, USD 37,500; *Gallows Island, Bermuda* (watercolour) USD 65,000. NEW YORK, 29 April 1976, *Young Girl Sitting in a Garden* (c. 1878, oil on canvas, 22¼ x 15½ ins / 56.8 x 39.4 cm) USD 28,000. LONDON, 30 Nov 1976, *Shepherdess* (1878, drawing, 9 x 13 ins / 23 x 33 cm) GBP 8,000. NEW YORK, 21 April 1977, *The Watch, Eastern Shore* (1894, watercolour, 15½ x 22 ins / 39.4 x 55 cm, 2¼ ins/6 cm) USD 120,000. NEW YORK, 21 April 1977, *Croquet Match* (c. 1868-1869, oil on card, 9¾ x 15½ ins / 25 x 39.4 cm) USD 210,000. NEW YORK, 18 May 1977, *Perils of the Sea* (1888, etching, 16½ x 22 ins / 42.2 x 56 cm) USD 3,000. NEW YORK, 22 March 1978, *Day is Done* (1878, watercolour, 13¾ x 20 ins / 35 x 50.5 cm) USD 57,500. NEW YORK, 25 Oct 1979, *Woman and Dog Seen from Behind* (1900, charcoal and pencil, 8 x 6¼ ins / 20.3 x 16 cm) USD 11,000. NEW YORK, 25 April 1980, *Orange Trees with a Gate* (1885, watercolour, 14¼ x 20¾ ins / 36.4 x 52.7 cm) USD 165,000. NEW YORK, 24 Sept 1980, *Eight Bells* (1887, etching, 19½ x 25 ins / 49.5 x 63.6 cm) USD 27,000. NEW YORK, 17 Oct 1980, *The Signal of Distress* (1892, oil on canvas, 24½ x 38¼ ins / 62.2 x 97.2 cm) USD 1,700,000. PORTLAND, 4 April 1981, *Tynemouth Beach* (1883, watercolour, 5¼ x 18¾ ins / 13.3 x 47.8 cm) USD 90,000. NEW YORK, 24 April 1981, *High Sea* (1884, charcoal and white chalk/mounted paper/card, 15½ x 24 ins / 39.3 x 60.9 cm) USD 88,000. NEW YORK, 23 Sept 1981, *Eight Bells* (1887, etching, 19¼ x 25 ins / 48.9 x 63.2 cm) USD 15,000. NEW YORK, 22 Oct 1982, *Sharpshooter on Picket Duty* (1863, oil on canvas, 12¼ x 16½ ins / 31.2 x 42 cm) USD 320,000. NEW YORK, 2 June 1983, *Easthampton Beach, Long*

Island (1874, oil on canvas, 10 x 21 1/2 ins / 25.4 x 54.6 cm) USD 430,000. NEW YORK, 21 Sept 1983, *Fly Fishing, Lake Saranac* (1889, etching and aquatint, 14 x 20 1/2 ins / 35.7 x 51.8 cm) USD 22,000. NEW YORK, 26 Oct 1984, *Portrait of John Murray Brown* (lead pencil, 12 x 8 1/2 ins / 30.5 x 21.6 cm) USD 9,000. NEW YORK, 6 Dec 1984, *Inland Water, Bermuda* (1901, watercolour, 13 3/4 x 21 ins / 34.9 x 53.3 cm) USD 290,000. NEW YORK, 6 March 1985, *Yachting Girl* (1880, lithograph heightened with white/greyish paper, 7 3/4 x 12 1/2 ins / 20 x 32 cm) USD 39,000. NEW YORK, 5 Dec 1985, *Solitude* (1889, watercolour/paper, 13 1/2 x 19 1/2 ins / 34.3 x 49.5 cm) USD 320,000. NEW YORK, 5 Dec 1985, *Enchanted* (1874, oil on canvas, 12 x 20 ins / 30.5 x 50.8 cm) USD 650,000. NEW YORK, 29 May 1986, *Group of Seamen on a Pier* (charcoal, 8 x 11 3/4 ins / 20.3 x 29.8 cm) USD 31,000. NEW YORK, 28 May 1987, *In Charge of Baby* (1873, watercolour/paper, 9 1/2 ins / 24 cm, 1/2 x 13 1/2 ins/1 x 34.4 cm) USD 700,000. NEW YORK, 26 May 1988, *Return to Camp* (1892, watercolour, gouache and pencil/paper, 15 1/4 x 21 1/2 ins / 38.5 x 54.5 cm) USD 440,000. NEW YORK, 1 Dec 1988, *Pond Lilies* (1884, charcoal and gouache/paper, 17 x 23 ins / 43.2 x 58.4 cm) USD 88,000; *Fresh Flowers* (1885, watercolour and pencil/paper, 14 1/4 x 20 1/4 ins / 36.5 x 51.5 cm) USD 429,000. NEW YORK, 25 May 1989, *Honeymoon* (1875, pencil heightened with white, 8 3/4 x 11 1/4 ins / 22.5 x 28.5 cm) USD 121,000. NEW YORK, 30 Nov 1989, *Initials* (1864, oil on canvas, 16 x 12 1/4 ins / 40.6 x 31.1 cm) USD 880,000. NEW YORK, 1 Dec 1989, *Picking Flowers* (watercolour, gouache and pencil/paper, 10 x 16 1/2 ins / 25.4 x 42.2 cm) USD 352,000. NEW YORK, 23 May 1990, *Quiet Pool on a Sunny Day* (1889, watercolour and pencil/card, 12 3/4 x 19 3/4 ins / 32.4 x 50.1 cm) USD 308,000. NEW YORK, 14 March 1991, *Boy Frightening Birds* (1879, pencil heightened with white/tinted paper, 9 x 12 ins / 23 x 30.5 cm) USD 59,400. NEW YORK, 25 Sept 1991, *Girls on Pebbly Beach* (pencil and white watercolour/greyish paper, 6 3/4 x 12 1/2 ins / 17.1 x 31.8 cm) USD 22,000. NEW YORK, 27 May 1992, *Young Woman with a Parasol* (1880, watercolour/paper, 9 1/2 x 13 1/4 ins / 24.1 x 33.7 cm) USD 550,000; *Backrush* (oil on canvas, 22 x 29 ins / 55.9 x 73.7 cm) USD 1,100,000. NEW YORK, 3 Dec 1992, *The Unruly Calf* (1875, oil on canvas, 24 1/4 x 38 1/2 ins / 61.6 x 97.8 cm) USD 1,210,000. NEW YORK, 27 May 1993, *Looking out to Sea* (1872, oil on canvas, 15 1/2 x 22 1/2 ins / 39.4 x 57.2 cm) USD 706,500. NEW YORK, 21 Sept 1994, *Girl in a Farmyard* (pencil/paper, 5 1/2 x 8 ins / 14 x 20.3 cm) USD 54,625. NEW YORK, 1 Dec 1994, *Entering the First Rapid, Grand Discharge - Shooting the Rapid* (1897, watercolour/paper, 13 1/2 x 20 1/2 ins / 34.3 x 52.1 cm) USD 332,500. NEW YORK, 25 May 1995, *Diamond Shoal, Seascape* (1905, watercolour/paper, 13 3/4 x 21 3/4 ins / 35.2 x 55.2 cm) USD 1,817,500. NEW YORK, 22 May 1996, *Fishing in the Adirondacks* (1889, watercolour/paper, 14 x 20 ins / 35.6 x 50.8 cm) USD 442,500. NEW YORK, 27 Sept 1996, *Returning from the Spring* (1874, oil on panel, 8 x 6 ins / 20.3 x 15.2 cm) USD 629,500. NEW YORK, 30 Oct 1996, *The Clara; Man Lying on Ground; Uncle's Cow* (pencil/paper, three sketches, 2 1/4 x 2 3/4 ins / 5.7 x 7 cm; 2 1/2 x 3 3/4 ins/6.4 x 9.5 cm and 3 1/4 x 4 3/4 ins/8.3 x 12 cm) USD 8, 050. NEW YORK, 4 Dec 1996, *How Many Eggs?* (1873, watercolour and gouache/paper, 13 x 9 ins / 33 x 22.8 cm) USD 717,500. NEW YORK, 5 June 1997, *Home, Sweet Home* (oil on canvas, 21 1/2 x 16 1/2 ins / 54.6 x 41.9 cm) USD 2,642,500; *Fog Warning* (1883, watercolour/paper, 13 3/4 x 20 3/4 ins / 34.9 x 52.7 cm) USD 325,000. NEW YORK, 5 June 1997, *Horse and Plowman, Houghton Farm* (watercolour/paper, 6 1/4 x 11 ins / 15.9 x 27.9 cm) USD 140,000. NEW YORK, 4 Dec 1997, *Two Girls on the Beach, Tynemouth* (1881, watercolour/paper, 14 x 20 ins / 35.6 x 50.8 cm) USD 1,652,500. NEW YORK, 27 May 1999, *Woodshopper in the Adirondacks* (c. 1870, oil on canvas, 11 x 16 ins / 27 x 40 cm) USD 900,000. NEW YORK, 1 Dec 1999, *Red Canoe* (1889, watercolour, 14 x 20 ins / 35 x 51 cm) USD 4,400,000. NEW YORK, 24 May 2000, *Uncle Ned at Home* (1875, oil on canvas, 14 x 22 ins / 36 x 56 cm) USD 2,600,000. NEW YORK, 25 May 2000, *Girl Reading under Oak Tree* (1879, oil on canvas, 15 x 22 ins / 39 x 57 cm) USD 1,700,000. NEW YORK, 23 May 2001, *Boys Fishing, Gloucester Harbor* (1880, watercolour, 9 x 14 ins / 23 x 35 cm) USD 340,000. NEW YORK, 29 Nov 2001, *Sponge Fishermen, Bahamas* (watercolour, gouache and pencil, 11 x 20 ins / 28 x 51 cm) USD 900,000. NEW YORK, 25 April 2002, *Hilly Landscape* (1894, watercolour, 15 x 22 ins / 38 x 55 cm) USD 600,000. NEW YORK, 5 Dec 2002, *Girl in the Hammock* (1873, oil on canvas, 13 x 20 ins / 34 x 51 cm) USD 1,500,000. NEW YORK, 3 Dec 2003, *In the Garden* (1874, watercolour and gouache, 9 x 7 ins / 23 x 17 cm) USD 1,500,000. NEW YORK, 4 Dec 2003, *Last Days of Harvest* (1874, oil on canvas, 12 x 20 ins / 31 x 51 cm) USD 1,000,000. NEW YORK, 18 May 2004, *Young Man Reading* (1873, oil on canvas, 14 x 16 ins / 36 x 41 cm) USD 450,000. NEW YORK, 18 May 2004, *Farmer with a Pitchfork* (c. 1874, oil on board, 9 x 13 ins / 24 x 34 cm) USD 2,100,000.

HOMERE, Stavros
British, 19th - 20th century.
Born in London.
Engraver.

Stavros Homere studied in Paris under Jules Lefebvre and Tony Robert-Fleury.

HOMERO, pseudonym of Homero Panagiotopulos
Argentinian, 20th century.
Born 1919, in Argentina, to a Greek father.
Active in France from 1985.
Painter, decorative artist. Figures, nudes, portraits, landscapes, still-lifes. Stage sets.

Homero studied at the school of fine arts in Buenos Aires before continuing his training in Europe. He taught drawing and painting in Buenos Aires and from 1985 in Carpentras in France where he settled in 1995.

AUCTION RECORDS:
NEUILLY, 27 Nov 1997, *The Tightrope Walker* (oil on canvas, 24 x 19 3/4 ins / 61 x 50 cm) FRF 3,000.

HOMET, Louis Jacques
French, 18th century.
Active in Paris in 1778.
Painter (?), sculptor (?).

HOMEVILLE, François
French, 18th century.
Active in Paris in 1743.
Painter, sculptor.

HOMICSKO, Athanasius
Hungarian, 19th - 20th century.
Born 1864, in Nagyberezna; died 2 November 1916, in Budapest.
Caricaturist.

Homicsko worked for most of the newspapers of Budapest.

HOMINE, Jacques
French, 16th century.
Painter.

HOMIUS, Joan
Dutch, 17th century.
Active in Utrecht c. 1686.
Engraver.

HOMMEL, Konrad
German, 20th century.
Born 16 February 1883, in Mainz.
Painter.

Hommel studied under J. P. Laurens in Paris. He was mainly active in Munich and Darmstadt.

HOMMENBUT, Henri
French, 17th century.

Active in Tours c. 1682.
Sculptor.

HOMO, Alexandre
French, 19th century.
Born c. 1840, in Paris; died 22 July 1889, in Paris.
Painter, watercolourist. Landscapes.
Alexandre Homo was a pupil of Péquenot, and began showing his work at the Salon in 1877.
MUSEUMS AND GALLERIES:
BERNAY: *Environs of Honfleur; View of Bernay; Boucheville Bridge; Charenton Woman* - LOUVIERS (Galerie Roussel): *Rue de la Grosse-Horloge, in Rouen* (watercolour).
AUCTION RECORDS:
PARIS, 8 March 1919, *Rocks near Villerville,* FRF 75. PARIS, 6 Feb 1929, *Morning in a Street in Old Paris* (watercolour) FRF 110. NICE, 24 May 1945, *The Rue de Bièvre in Paris* (watercolour) FRF 1,110.

HOMO, Arsène Pierre
French, 19th century.
Born c. 1830; died 1896.
Painter, draughtsman. Waterscapes, landscapes.
Arsène Homo showed his work at the Salon of the Société des Artistes Français, of which he was a member. He chiefly painted small-scale landscapes depicting places in Normandy and Brittany.

HOMOLATSCH, Otto
Austrian, 20th century.
Born 17 November 1883, in Vienna.
Painter, draughtsman. Portraits, genre scenes.
Homolatsch was mainly active in Saalbach.
MUSEUMS AND GALLERIES:
VIENNA (Albertina Mus.): *Portrait.*

HOMOLOICHUS
2nd century BC.
Sculptor.
Ancient Greek.

HOMPESCH, Daniel
Belgian, 20th - 21st century.
Born 1948.
Engraver.
Hompesch attended the Institut des Beaux-Arts de St Luc, Liège.

HOMPS, Henri
French, 20th century.
Born 1924, in Narbonne.
Painter.
A pupil of Augustin Hanicotte, Henri Homps featured at the Salon d'Automne in Paris in 1976 and 1978, and at the Salon international in Béziers. He held his first solo exhibition at the age of 19.
BIBLIOGRAPHY:
Vingt cinq ans d'acquisitions (1959-1984), exhibition catalogue, Musée d'Art et d'Histoire, Narbonne, 1984.
MUSEUMS AND GALLERIES:
NARBONNE (MAH): *In La Clape; Les inférets* (1983).

HOMS, Gaspar I
Spanish, 17th century.
Active in Majorca (Balearic Islands).
Sculptor.

HOMS, Gaspar II
Spanish, 17th - 18th century.
Born in Palma.
Sculptor.
Gaspar Homs II was the son of Gaspar Homs I. He studied under his brother Juan Antonio.

HOMS, Gaspar III
Spanish, 18th century.
Active in Majorca (Balearic Islands).
Sculptor.
Gaspar Homs III was the son of Juan Antonio and the father of Jaime and Pablo Homs.

HOMS, Jaime
Spanish, 19th century.
Died c. 1820.
Active in Majorca (Balearic Islands).
Sculptor.
Jaime Homs studied under his father Gaspar Homs III.

HOMS, Juan Antonio
Spanish, 18th century.
Died 29 February 1748, in Palma (Majorca), Balearics.
Sculptor.
Juan Antonio Homs worked for the monastery of Sto Domingo in Palma.

HOMS, Marcel
French, 20th century.
Born 10 March 1910, in Céret.
Sculptor, fresco artist.
Marcel Homs lived in Abidjan, Ivory Coast, where he had been sent to found a fine-arts school. His style slowly evolved from a classical, though dynamic, sculpture towards an often lyrical Abstraction. He exhibited in Paris at the Salon des Indépendants, the Salon d'Automne and, since its creation, the Salon de la Jeune Sculpture. He came second in the Prix de Rome in 1939.

HOMS, Pablo
Spanish, 19th century.
Died before 1820.
Sculptor.
Pablo Homs was the son of Gaspar Homs III. He worked in Majorca.

HOMULIN, Andreas. See **GOMULIN**

HON, Henri, or Le Hon
Belgian, 19th century.
Born 20 January 1809, in Ley-Pommereul; died 1872, in San Remo (Italy).
Painter. Landscapes, seascapes.
Henri Hon taught at the military academy in Brussels. He exhibited *The End of the Squall* at the Salon of 1842 and *Ostend Beach* in 1845.
Hon was one of the first painters to paint the sea as a subject in its own right.
MUSEUMS AND GALLERIES:
BRUSSELS: *Seascape.*
AUCTION RECORDS:
CARCASSONNE, 27 Oct 1984, *Small Fishing Port* (1859, oil on canvas, 13 1/2 x 23 3/4 ins / 34 x 60.5 cm) CHF 3,400. LOKEREN, 10 Dec 1994, *Blankenberghe Beach* (1857, oil on canvas, 17 3/4 x 29 1/2 ins / 45 x 75 cm) BEF 140,000. LOKEREN, 9 Dec 1995, *Blankenberghe Beach* (1857, oil on canvas, 17 3/4 x 29 1/2 ins / 45 x 75 cm) BEF 130,000.

HÖNA-SENFT, Hedwig
Bohemian, 19th century.
Born 17 October 1855, in Prague.
Painter, miniaturist. .
Hedwig Höna-Senft was a pupil of Lauffer, and spent some time in Munich, Dresden, Berlin and Vienna.

HONAMI KOETSU. See **KOETSU**

HOND. See **HONDIUS**

HOND, David de
Flemish School, 17th century.
Active in Flanders.
Painter. Military subjects.

The Rennes museum has a painting entitled *Naval Battle between the Turks and the Spanish* catalogued under the name of David de Hond and stating that the artist was a pupil of Teniers the Younger. There may have been an error in the forename, as this might conceivably be the work of Lambert de Hondt.

MUSEUMS AND GALLERIES:
RENNES: *Naval Battle between the Turks and the Spanish.*

HONDA, Kinkichiro, artist names: Keizan, Kogai
Japanese, 19th - 20th century.
Born 1850; died 1921.
Active in Tokyo.
Painter.

A disciple of Kunisawa Shinkuro, Honda specialised in Western-style painting, landscapes in particular. He taught at the Tokyo Military Academy before succeeding his master as the head of the Shogido School, which he had founded. Honda trained many artists.

HONDA, Shingo
Japanese, 20th century.
Born 1944, in Niigata Prefecture.
Painter.
Mono-ha (school of things); Conceptual Art.

Honda Shingo specialises in conceptual art and photographic collage. After interrupting his studies at Tokyo University of Fine Arts and Music in mid-programme, he had his first solo shows in Tokyo in 1969 and 1970. That year, he also took part in the 5th Japan Art Festival Association (JAFA) exhibition. In 1973, he was part of an international art exhibition at Tokyo and Kyoto and in the exhibition *Japanese Art Today* held at the museum of contemporary art in Montreal.

HONDECOETER, Adriaen de
Dutch, 16th century.
Born in Mechelen.
Painter.

Adriaen de Hondecoeter settled in Delft where he married in 1590.

HONDECOETER, Gillis Claesz. de
Dutch, 17th century.
Born 1575, in Antwerp; died September 1638, in Amsterdam.
Painter, draughtsman. Religious subjects, figures, landscapes, landscapes with figures.

Gillis de Hondecoeter is believed to have been the father of Gysbert and grandfather of Melchior d'Hondecoeter. He lived first in Delft and then in Utrecht where, in 1602, he was married. After being widowed he married again in 1628 in Amsterdam. In 1636 he was a member of the Amsterdam painters' guild. It is uncertain whether he was the father or brother of Gysbert d'Hondecoeter, but he was definitely the father-in-law of the painter J.-B. Weenix. He is believed to have been a pupil of Gillis van Coninxloo.

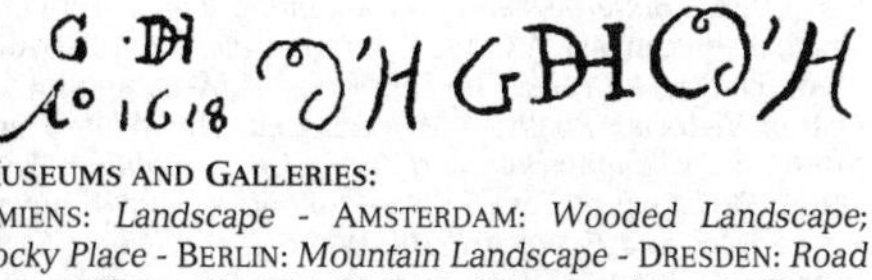

MUSEUMS AND GALLERIES:
AMIENS: *Landscape* - AMSTERDAM: *Wooded Landscape; Rocky Place* - BERLIN: *Mountain Landscape* - DRESDEN: *Road near a Village Church* - KASSEL: *River Landscape* - STOCKHOLM: *Orpheus Charming the Animals with the Sound of his Flute* - STRASBOURG: *Mountains.*

AUCTION RECORDS:
PARIS, 20 May 1925, *Woman Bather at the River Bank,* FRF 750. BERLIN, 20 Sept 1930, *Landscape,* DEM 900. PARIS, 17 Dec 1942, *Village in the Trees,* FRF 125,000. LONDON, 26 June 1957, *Rocky Landscape with a Woodcutter and Miners,* GBP 550. LONDON, 24 June 1959, *Landscape,* GBP 800. STOCKHOLM, 26 Oct 1960, *Wooded Landscape,* SEK 13,000. PARIS, 23 March 1968, *View of a Village,* FRF 23,000. VIENNA, 1 Dec 1970, *Hunt in the Palace Forest,* ATS 450,000. COLOGNE, 24 Nov 1971, *Landscape with Poultry,* DEM 19,000. VIENNA, 28 Nov 1972, *Village in Flanders,* ATS 350,000. LONDON, 9 May 1973, *Jesus on the Road to Emmaus* (1630) GBP 3,900. PARIS, 3 April 1979, *Mountain Landscape with Lake* (1612, oil/metal, 10 x 13¾ ins / 25.5 x 35 cm) FRF 142,000. LONDON, 11 Dec 1986, *Wooded Landscape with Village View, Shepherd, Flock and Pilgrim* (oil on panel, 16¾ x 31 ins / 42.8 x 78.8 cm) GBP 26,000. NEW YORK, 21 Oct 1988, *Vast Rocky Landscape with a Town in the Distance* (1619, oil on panel, 10 x 14¾ ins / 24.5 x 37.5 cm) USD 22,000. PARIS, 14 April 1989, *Landscape with Animals near a Pond* (oil on panel, 18 x 26¾ ins / 46 x 68 cm) FRF 105,000. AMSTERDAM, 28 Nov 1989, *Hunters near a Village, in a Wood with a Hermit, a Lion and a Donkey* (1606, oil on panel, 23¼ x 34½ ins / 58.9 x 87.8 cm) NLG 402,500. NEW YORK, 10 Jan 1990, *Vast Wooded Landscape with Christ on the Road to Emmaus* (oil on canvas, 25 x 42¼ ins / 63.5 x 107.3 cm) USD 93,500. AMSTERDAM, 12 June 1990, *Garden of Eden* (oil on panel, 22 x 36½ ins / 55.7 x 92.7 cm) NLG 391,000. LONDON, 6 July 1990, *Wooded Landscape with a Couple of Farmers Walking with their Dog* (oil on panel, 13 x 24½ ins / 32.8 x 62 cm) GBP 60,500. LONDON, 2 July 1991, *Village Walls with a Ruined Arch* (black chalk, brown ink and wash, 6 x 6¼ ins / 14.4 x 15.6 cm) GBP 1,760. LONDON, 3 July 1991, *Christ Curing a Blind Man in a Vast Wooded Landscape* (1608, oil on panel, 38½ x 55 ins / 97.5 x 139.5 cm) GBP 44,000. LONDON, 1 April 1992, *Landscape with Christ on the Road to Emmaus* (oil on panel, 13¼ x 24 ins / 33.5 x 61 cm) GBP 22,000. PARIS, 22 June 1992, *Landscape with Cows* (oil on canvas, 6¼ x 9 ins / 16 x 23 cm) FRF 25,000. LONDON, 9 Dec 1992, *Rocky River Landscape with Travellers on a Road* (oil on panel, 15¼ x 24¼ ins / 39 x 61.5 cm) GBP 16,500. LONDON, 6 Dec 1995, *River Landscape with Cattle and Swans* (oil on panel, 13¼ x 10½ ins / 33.6 x 26.7 cm) GBP 14,950. PARIS, 12 Dec 1995, *River Landscape in the Mountains with Two Stags* (oil on oak panel, 25¼ x 19½ ins / 64 x 49.5 cm) FRF 40,000. AMSTERDAM, 19-20 Feb 1997, *Cattle and Sheep on a Hill* (oil on panel, 5¼ x 9½ ins / 13.2 x 24 cm) NLG 11,532. LONDON, 30 Oct 1997, *Rocky River Landscape with Herdsmen and their Animals at Rest* (oil on panel, 16¼ x 28¼ ins / 41.5 x 71.7 cm) GBP 8,050. AMSTERDAM, 11 Nov 1997, *Christ on the Road to Emmaus* (1609, oil on panel, 28½ x 43½ ins / 72.4 x 110.6 cm) NLG 74,958. LONDON, 17 Dec 1999, *Town in Wooded River Landscape with Huntsmen and Other Figures* (1606, oil on panel, 12 x 34 ins / 30 x 86 cm) GBP 78,000. ZURICH, 22 Sept 2000, *Landscape with Cows* (oil on panel, 7 x 15 ins / 19 x 38 cm) CHF 24,000. PARIS, 18 Dec 2000, *River Landscape with Fishermen* (oil on panel, 19 x 29 ins / 48 x 74 cm) FRF 150,000. LONDON, 24 April 2001, *Wooded Landscape with Drover and Cattle on a Track* (oil on panel, 15 x 23 ins / 39 x 59 cm) GBP 12,000. AMSTERDAM, 9 May 2001, *Deer, Goat, Cat, Fox and Birds in a Wooded Landscape* (oil on panel, 18 x 26 ins / 45 x 66 cm) NLG 60,000. LONDON, 10 July 2002, *Wooded Landscape with Sportsman* (1612, oil on copper, 10 x 13 ins / 25 x 33 cm) GBP 80,000. LONDON, 11 Dec 2002, *Wooded River Landscape with Travellers and Dog. Wooded River Landscape with Figures* (oil on panel, a pair, 8 x 10 ins / 20 x 26 cm) GBP 32,000. LONDON, 9 April 2003, *Wooded River Landscape with Huntsman on a Track, Village beyond* (1613, oil on panel, 11 x 14 ins / 27 x 35 cm) GBP 15,000. AMSTERDAM, 27 Sept 2004, *Cows and Horses in a*

Summer Landscape (oil on panel, 10 x 15 ins / 25 x 37 cm) EUR 1,800.

HONDECOETER, Gysbert Gillisz. or Gysbrecht

Dutch, 17th century.

Born 1604, in Amsterdam or in Utrecht; died 29 August 1653, in Utrecht.

Active in Amsterdam.

Painter. Mythological subjects, landscapes, landscapes with figures, animals.

Gysbert d'Hondecoeter studied under either his father or his brother Gillis d'Hondecoeter. He had a son, Michiel d'Hondecoeter, and was chiefly active in Amsterdam.

MUSEUMS AND GALLERIES:

AMSTERDAM: *Water Birds* - COPENHAGEN (Statens Mus. for Kunst): *Birds* - HANOVER: *Diana and Nymphs Bathing* - ROTTERDAM: *Mountain Landscape; Cockerel and Hens* - THE HAGUE: *Cockerel and Hens.*

AUCTION RECORDS:

PARIS, 2 March 1921, *Peacocks,* FRF 180. PARIS, 6 May 1925, *Dead Birds,* FRF 1,250. NEW YORK, 4-5 Feb 1931, *Animals,* USD 80. COLOGNE, 26 May 1971, *Poultry,* DEM 28,000. LONDON, 29 Nov 1977, *Landscape with Poultry* (gouache, 7 3/4 x 11 1/2 ins / 19.6 x 29.5 cm) GBP 500. VERSAILLES, 16 April 1978, *Cock Fight* (oil on panel, 32 1/4 x 48 ins / 82 x 122 cm) FRF 24,000. LONDON, 14 Oct 1983, *Landscape with Poultry* (1650, oil on canvas, 31 x 40 3/4 ins / 78.8 x 103.5 cm) GBP 5,000. LONDON, 21 July 1989, *Rocky Landscape with Dromedary, Stallion, Cow, Goat and Egret* (oil on panel, 20 1/2 x 32 1/4 ins / 52 x 82 cm) GBP 6,600. AMSTERDAM, 6 May 1993, *Farmyard with Peacock, a Bucket of Cabbages and Onions, Poultry and a Rabbit* (oil on canvas, 52 3/4 x 27 1/4 ins / 134.3 x 69 cm) NLG 10,350. LONDON, 11 Dec 1996, *Farmyard* (1643, oil on canvas, 31 x 26 1/4 ins / 78.7 x 66.4 cm) GBP 27,600. LONDON, 16 Dec 1999, *Cockerel and Hens* (1649, oil on canvas, 28 x 36 ins / 71 x 91 cm) GBP 90,000. AMSTERDAM, 9 May 2000, *Hen and Chicks in a Landscape* (oil on panel, 16 x 28 ins / 40 x 72 cm) NLG 140,000. STUTTGART, 19 Sept 2002, *Poultry Yard* (oil on panel, 22 x 28 ins / 55 x 72 cm) EUR 21,500. NEW YORK, 22 Jan 2004, *Garden of Eden* (1644, oil on panel, 17 x 26 ins / 42 x 65 cm) USD 27,000. VIENNA, 16 June 2004, *Orpheus Enchanting the Animals and Trees* (1642, oil on panel, 26 x 41 ins / 66 x 105 cm) EUR 24,000.

HONDECOETER, Hans Claesz. de

Dutch, 17th century.

Active in Mechelen.

Painter.

Hans de Hondecoeter was made a citizen of Delft on 9 July 1612.

HONDECOETER, Melchior de, or Eondekoeter

Dutch, 17th century.

Born 1636, in Utrecht; died 3 April 1695, in Amsterdam.

Painter, engraver (mezzotint). Animals, birds, farmyard scenes, still-lifes.

Melchior de Hondecoeter studied under his father Gysbert Hondecoeter and his uncle J.-B. Weenix. From 1659 to 1663, he worked in The Hague before settling in Amsterdam where he received citizen's rights in 1668. Hondecoeter specialised in painting animals, and birds in particular. He excelled in this genre and was known as the "Raphael of the Birds". He is also known for his mezzotint engravings.

Hondecoeter's work is often anecdotal, taking fables as its subject. He displayed meticulous realism and remarkable talent as a draughtsman and colourist and was a great influence on late 17th-century and 18th-century still-life painters and painters of animals. Houbraken mentions Willem van Royen as one of his most notable pupils.

MUSEUMS AND GALLERIES:

AMIENS: *Cock Fight* - AMSTERDAM: *Dead Birds; Plants and Fungi; The Philosophical Magpie; House in the Country; The Duck Pond; The Startled Throng; The Menagerie; The Floating Feather; Game; Birds; The Farmyard; Poultry* - ANGOULÊME: *Turkey Cocks; Cockerel and Hare* - ANTWERP: *Birds; The Farmyard; Poultry* - BERLIN: *Water Fowl* - BREMEN: *Farmyard* - BRUSSELS: *Entrance to the Park; Cock Crow; Still-life* - BUDAPEST: *Cockerel and Peacock Fighting; Various Animals* - CAEN: *Hen with her Chicks* - CHANTILLY: *Farmyard Fowl* - CHERBOURG: *Monkey and Parrot* - COLOGNE: *Farmyard; Same Subject* - COPENHAGEN: *Farmyard at a Manor House* - DIJON: *Birds* - DOUAI: *Peacock Attacked by a Cockerel* - DRESDEN: *Bird of Prey in a Farmyard; Hens at Rest; Spoils of the Hunt; Still-life and Kingfisher; Choir of Birds* - DUBLIN: *Stork and Vulture; Poultry* - FLORENCE (Palazzo Pitti): *Farmyard Fowl* - FRANKFURT AM MAIN: *Cockerel and Bird of Prey* - GENEVA: *Group of Large Fowl* - GLASGOW: *Domestic Fowl* - HAMBURG: *Hen House; Disturbance in the Hen House* - KASSEL: *Choir of Birds; White Hen with Chick; Cockerel and Turkey Cock Fighting; White Peacock; Cock Fight* - LA FÈRE: *Birds and Monkeys* - LE HAVRE: *Dog Protecting Game* - LE MANS: *Still-life* - LEIPZIG: *A Farmyard* - LILLE: *Birds* - LONDON (NG): *Birds, Butterflies and a Frog among Plants and Fungi* (1668, oil on canvas); *A Cock, Hens and Chicks* (c. 1668-1670, oil on canvas) - LYONS: *The Hen House* - MELBOURNE (Nat. Gal. of Victoria): *Poultry* - MONTPELLIER: *The White Hen* - MUNICH: *Cock Fight; Hens and Turkey Cocks Fighting* - NOTTINGHAM: *Group of Fowl* - OSLO: *Still-life* - PARIS (Louvre): *Two Eagles in a Farmyard; The White Turkey Cock; Farmyard Fowl* - RHEIMS (MBA): *Young Girl with Peacock* (c. 1680) - ROTTERDAM: *Dead Fowl and Hunting Gear* - ROUEN: *Various Unusual Animals* - ST PETERSBURG (Hermitage): *Three Pic-*

tures of Birds; Hunting Trophy - ST-BRIEUC: *Birds in a Park* - STOCKHOLM: *Dead Fowl and Hunting Gear* - STUTTGART: *Farmyard with Magpie and Jay; Poultry* - THE HAGUE: *The Crow Stripped of the Feathers with which it had adorned itself; Prince William III's Menagerie at Loo Palace; Geese and Ducks; Hens and Ducks* - VENICE (Gal. Reale): *Hen with her Chicks; Cock Fight* - VIENNA: *Poultry; Same Subject* - VIENNA (Czernin'sche Gemäldegal.): *Landscape with Cockerel and Hens.*

AUCTION RECORDS:

PARIS, 7-8 April 1876, *Morning; Evening* (forming a pair) FRF 35,500. PARIS, 26-29 April 1904, *The White Hen,* FRF 13,100. LONDON, 14 Dec 1907, *Poultry and Birds,* GBP 13. LONDON, 21 Dec 1907, *Farmyard Animals,* GBP 46. LONDON, 19 Dec 1908, *Hens and Geese,* GBP 52. LONDON, 28 Feb 1910, *Poultry, Pigeons and Ducks,* GBP 68. LONDON, 22 July 1910, *Choir of Birds,* GBP 115. LONDON, 11 Feb 1911, *Turkey Cocks and Poultry,* GBP 84. LONDON, 25 Feb 1911, *Poultry and Pigeons,* GBP 336. LONDON, 5 May 1911, *Cock Fight,* GBP 147. LONDON, 25-26 May 1911, *Poultry,* GBP 115. PARIS, 16-19 June 1919, *Hunting Trophy,* FRF 13,500. PARIS, 18 June 1920, *Choir of Birds,* FRF 19,000. LONDON, 2 March 1923, *Cock Fight,* GBP 945. PARIS, 14 June 1923, *Cockerel and Hens,* FRF 7,100. LONDON, 6 July 1923, *Palace Gardens* (1677) GBP 4,095. PARIS, 28-29 Nov 1923, *Motherly Concern,* FRF 17,000. PARIS, 27-28 May 1926, *Spoils of the Hunt,* FRF 15,000. LONDON, 17-18 May 1928, *Assembly of Birds,* GBP 1,312. PARIS, 6 July 1928, *Cock Fight,* FRF 6,000. LONDON, 7 March 1930, *Eagle Attacking a Hen House,* GBP 609. NEW YORK, 22 Jan 1931, *Farmyard,* USD 500. LONDON, 19 June 1935, *Farmyard,* GBP 105. LONDON, 18 Dec 1936, *Dead Game,* GBP 46. LONDON, 12 March 1937, *Poultry,* GBP 194. LONDON, 22 July 1937, *Birds,* GBP 230. LONDON, 3 May 1940, *Peacock and Other Birds,* GBP 168. PARIS, 11 Jan 1943, *The Farmyard,* FRF 73,000. LONDON, 17 March 1944, *Eagle Attacking Poultry,* GBP 162. LONDON, 28 April 1944, *Peacocks and Poultry,* GBP 210. LONDON, 17 Oct 1945, *Garden Scene with Birds,* GBP 120. NEW YORK, 17-19 Jan 1946, *Peacocks and Poultry,* USD 130. PARIS, July 1946, *The Farmyard,* FRF 600,000. LONDON, 5 Oct 1946, *Peacock, Hens and Ducks in the Gardens of a Palace,* GBP 84. LONDON, 31 Jan 1947, *Hens, Turkey Cocks and Ducks in a Garden,* GBP 168. ROTTERDAM, 12 March 1947, *Landscape with Birds,* NLG 800. PARIS, 11 June 1947, *The Farmyard - The White Hen,* FRF 420,000. LONDON, 14 June 1961, *Palace Interior,* GBP 450. LONDON, 25 Nov 1962, *Geese and Ducks by a Pond,* Gns 2,200. NEW YORK, 25 March 1964, *Fowl in a Landscape,* USD 3,100. VIENNA, 18 May 1965, *Peacock Surrounded by Fowl,* ATS 120,000. LONDON, 26 March 1971, *Cock Fight,* Gns 1,800. NEW YORK, 4 April 1973, *Fowl in a Landscape,* USD 37,000. LONDON, 29 June 1973, *Peacocks and Other Fowl on a Balcony,* Gns 3,400. LONDON, 28 June 1974, *Fowl in a Landscape,* Gns 4,500. LONDON, 24 March 1976, *Swan and Other Fowl in a Park* (1675, oil on canvas, 82¼ x 99½ ins / 209 x 253 cm) GBP 26,000. LONDON, 4 Feb 1977, *Goats and Fowl in a Landscape* (oil on canvas, 58¼ x 79¼ ins / 148 x 201 cm) GBP 11,000. LONDON, 28 March 1979, *Fowl in a Park* (oil on canvas, 67¾ x 102¼ ins / 172 x 260 cm) GBP 45,000. NEW YORK, 12 June 1981, *The Menagerie* (oil on canvas, 60 x 73½ ins / 152.5 x 187 cm) USD 290,000. NEW YORK, 20 Jan 1983, *Bird of Prey Attacking a Farmyard* (oil on canvas, 55½ x 69¾ ins / 141 x 177 cm) USD 20,000. LONDON, 10 July 1987, *Fowl in a Landscape* (1681, oil on canvas, 46¾ x 56¼ ins / 119 x 143 cm) GBP 160,000. LONDON, 8 July 1988, *Ducks on a Rocky River Bank* (oil on canvas, 35 x 31 ins / 89 x 78.5 cm) GBP 46,200. NEW YORK, 12 Jan 1989, *Hunting Picture with Two Rabbits and Small Birds Placed on Hunting Gear* (oil on canvas, 22 x 18¾ ins / 56 x 47.5 cm) USD 49,500. NEW YORK, 1 June 1989, *Peacock and Other Fowl by a Lake* (oil on canvas, 66½ x 85 ins / 169 x 216 cm) USD 242,000. PARIS, 12 Dec 1989, *Still-life with Woodcocks* (canvas, 32¼ x 27¼ ins / 82 x 69.5 cm) FRF 190,000. PARIS, 16 May 1990, *Hen in the middle of her Brood with a Dove Flying away* (oil on canvas, 31½ x 25½ ins / 80 x 64.5 cm) FRF 78,000. NEW YORK, 1 June 1990, *Choir of Birds* (oil on canvas, 39¼ x 49 ins / 99.5 x 124.5 cm) USD 165,000. AMSTERDAM, 12 June 1990, *Peacocks, Pelican, Pheasant, Ducks and Other Birds in a Park* (oil on canvas, 44½ x 55½ ins / 113 x 141.2 cm) NLG 46,000. AMSTERDAM, 14 Nov 1990, *Landscape with Fox by a Slaughtered Lamb and Goose with Poultry in the Background* (oil on canvas, 54¼ x 66½ ins / 138 x 169 cm) NLG 109,250. LONDON, 24 May 1991, *Poultry, Ducks and Pigeon in a Park* (oil on canvas, 40¼ x 47 ins / 102.2 x 118.5 cm) GBP 77,000. STOCKHOLM, 10-12 May 1993, *Fowl in a Landscape* (oil on canvas/two panels, each 73¼ x 52 ins / 186 x 132 cm) SEK 77,000. LONDON, 9 July 1993, *A Pelican, Crowned Crane and other Exotic Birds by a Pond in a Park* (oil on canvas, 60½ x 73¼ ins / 153.5 x 186.2 cm) GBP 331,500. AMSTERDAM, 18 Nov 1993, *Dead Pheasant Hanging by One Foot with a Sporting Gun, a Flask, a Powder Bag and a Game Pouch* (oil on canvas, 32 x 25 ins / 81.3 x 63.8 cm) NLG 161,000. NEW YORK, 14 Jan 1994, *Pair of Peacocks and Other Exotic Birds in a Park* (oil on canvas, 73 x 57½ ins / 185.4 x 146.1 cm) USD 354,500. LONDON, 3 July 1996, *Cock Fight in a Park* (oil on canvas, 46¾ x 49½ ins / 119 x 126 cm) GBP 45,500. LONDON, 13 Dec 1996, *Cocks Fighting in a Garden with a Palace in the Background* (oil on canvas, 34½ x 43 ins / 87.7 x 109.3 cm) GBP 54,300. NEW YORK, 29 Jan 1999, *Chinese and Egyptian Geese, Muscovy Ducks, Hoopoe* (oil on canvas, 52 x 61 ins / 131 x 154 cm) USD 410,000. LONDON, 17 Dec 1999, *Chinese Goose, Egyptian Goose, Muscovy Duck, Wigeon and Teal by a Pond* (oil on canvas, 49 x 42 ins / 124 x 106 cm) GBP 210,000. LONDON, 19 April 2000, *Peacock, Peahen, Pheasant and Turkey by Wall, Landscape beyond* (oil on canvas, 50 x 61 ins / 126 x 154 cm) GBP 170,000. NEW YORK, 25 May 2000, *Poultry at the Edge of a Wood* (oil on canvas, 35 x 31 ins / 88 x 78 cm) USD 260,000. NEW YORK, 25 Jan 2001, *Pelican, Crested Crane, Hen and Rooster with Various Ducks in a Landscape* (oil on canvas, 70 x 66 ins / 179 x 168 cm) USD 150,000. AMSTERDAM, 9 May 2001, *Hen Protecting her Chickens against a Cockerel, with Pigeons on a Fence* (oil on canvas, 36 x 44 ins / 92 x 113 cm) NLG 200,000. LONDON, 17 April 2002, *Concert of Birds* (oil on canvas, 44 x 49 ins / 113 x 124 cm) GBP 265,000. LONDON, 11 Dec 2002, *Forest Floor Still-life with Birds* (oil on canvas, 27 x 23 ins / 68 x 59 cm) GBP 95,000. LONDON, 10 July 2003, *Still-life with Game and a Knife upon a Marble Tabletop and Green Cloth* (oil on canvas, 29 x 25 ins / 73 x 64 cm) GBP 12,000. PARIS, 2 Dec 2003, *Poultry in a Garden* (1670, oil on canvas, 50 x 65 ins / 126 x 164 cm) EUR 80,000. MADRID, 26 Jan 2004, *Landscape with Birds* (oil on canvas, 51 x 65 ins / 130 x 164 cm) EUR 33,000. MUNICH, 26 March 2004, *Birds on Branch* (oil on panel, 26 x 20 ins / 66 x 51 cm) EUR 7,800.

HONDECOETER, Niclaes Gillisz. de
Dutch, 17th century.
Born c. 1607; died July 1642, in Amsterdam.
Painter. Landscapes.

Niclaes Hondecoeter married in Delft in 1638.

HONDECOETER, Niclaes Jansz. de
Flemish, 16th century.
Died 1609, in Delft.
Painter.
Antwerp School, Flemish School.

Niclaes Jansz. de Hondecoeter is mentioned in 1585 as a member of the Antwerp guild.

HONDERMARCQ, Jacqueline
Belgian, 20th century.
Born 1936, in Hyon-lez-Mons (Hainaut).
Painter.

Hondermarcq became known in the context of the Fantasmagie group. The group brought together the old Belgian Surrealists, such as Mesens, and exponents of the traditional Fantastic movement still alive in Flanders, such as Aubin Pasque (the promoter of the group) with younger artists attracted to this new idea. Her works are a mix of the fantastic and lyrical abstraction.

HONDIUS, Abraham Danielsz., or Hond or Hont
Dutch, 17th century.
Born c. 1625, in Rotterdam, in 1636 according to Bryan's Dictionary; died 1693 or 1695, in London.
Painter, engraver, draughtsman. Religious subjects, battles, hunting scenes, animals, dogs.

In 1653, Abraham Hondius married Gertruyd-Willems van der Eyck. In 1659 he was still working in Rotterdam but later went to Amsterdam and is believed to have travelled to England in around 1666.

Abraham Hondius painted and engraved hunting scenes, animals (particularly dogs), and occasionally battle scenes. He displayed a remarkable realism and use of colour in his work.

MUSEUMS AND GALLERIES:

AMSTERDAM: *Annunciation to the Shepherds; Adoration of the Shepherds* - AVIGNON: *Wounded Heron Pursued by Dogs* - DRESDEN: *Boar Hunt* - FLORENCE (Uffizi): *Hunt* - GLASGOW: *Swan Attacked by Dogs* - MONTPELLIER: *Boar Hunt* - MOSCOW (Rumiantsev Mus.): *Fight between Dogs and Lions* - NEW YORK: *Hunting Scene* - PARIS (Louvre): *The Pigeon Seller* - ROTTERDAM: *Wolf Grappling with Dogs; Bear Attacked by Dogs* - ST PETERSBURG (Hermitage): *Stag Attacked by a Pack of Hounds; Boar Hunt; Family Celebration; Guardroom Interior.*

AUCTION RECORDS:

PARIS, 30 April 1891, *Two Tom Cats,* FRF 800. PARIS, 24 Jan 1899, *Hunting Scene,* FRF 150. LONDON, 17 July 1908, *Dogs, Ducks and Livestock,* GBP 3. LONDON, 27 May 1909, *Bear Hunt,* GBP 6. LONDON, 3 June 1920, *Bear Hunt,* FRF 500. LONDON, April 1922, *Landscape with Two Falcons,* GBP 1. LONDON, March 1923, *Dogs Pursued by a Crane,* GBP 13. LONDON, 28 March 1924, *Dogs Attacking a Bittern,* GBP 16. PARIS, 22 May 1925, *Bear Hunt,* FRF 7,100. PARIS, 10 March 1928, *Stag at Bay Attacked by Dogs,* FRF 15,500. PARIS, 12 June 1933, *Christ at Emmaus,* FRF 2,000. PARIS, Oct 1945-July 1946, *Ducks and Goose* (school of Abraham Hondius) FRF 50,000. VIENNA, 19 March 1968, *Vegetable Merchant,* ATS 65,000. BRUSSELS, 25 Feb 1969, *Adoration of the Shepherds,* BEF 110,000. MILAN, 16 Dec 1971, *Hunting Scene,* ITL 1,400,000. LONDON, 28 March 1979, *Market Scene* (1666, oil on panel, 18 x 24 1/2 ins / 46 x 62.5 cm) GBP 5,000. LONDON, 9 July 1982, *Allegory of the Four Winds* (oil on canvas, 41 1/4 x 59 ins / 104.8 x 149.8 cm) GBP 6,500. LONDON, 4 April 1984, *Hunters' Repose* (oil on panel, 36 1/2 x 49 1/4 ins / 92.5 x 125 cm) GBP 13,500. LONDON, 11 April 1986, *Huntsman and his Dogs Resting at an Inn* (1651, oil on panel, 34 1/4 x 42 3/4 ins / 87 x 108.5 cm) GBP 110,000. LONDON, 20 April 1988, *Spaniels Preparing to Take a Heron Brought Down by a Bird of Prey* (oil on canvas, 27 1/2 x 31 ins / 70 x 79 cm) GBP 4,950. LONDON, 13 May 1988, *Dog Attacking a Boar in a Wood* (oil on canvas, 21 1/2 x 27 1/4 ins / 54.9 x 69.2 cm) GBP 5,720. LONDON, 31 March 1989, *Spaniel Taking a Pheasant* (oil on canvas, 39 3/4 x 50 ins / 101 x 126.7 cm) GBP 2,200. NEW YORK, 1 June 1989, *Boar Hunt* (oil on canvas, 60 1/2 x 75 1/2 ins / 153.5 x 191.7 cm) USD 33,000. NEW YORK, 10 Jan 1990, *Dogs Attacking a Heron* (oil on panel, 11 x 13 1/2 ins / 28 x 34.3 cm) USD 16,500. AMSTERDAM, 12 June 1990, *Hunting Dogs Pursuing a Bird* (oil on panel, 6 1/2 x 7 3/4 ins / 16.2 x 19.9 cm) NLG 4,370. LONDON, 2 July 1990, *Greyhound* (ink and red wash/red chalk, 9 1/4 x 13 3/4 ins / 23.8 x 35 cm) GBP 14,850. LONDON, 12 Dec 1990, *Heron Attacked by Dogs in an Italian Landscape One Afternoon* (oil on panel, 15 1/4 x 13 3/4 ins / 39 x 35 cm) GBP 5,280. PARIS, 18 Dec 1991, *Assembly of the Gods* (oil on canvas, 18 1/2 x 14 1/2 ins / 47 x 37 cm) FRF 28,000. LONDON, 28 Oct 1992, *Entrance into Jerusalem; Mary Magdalene Washing Christ's Feet* (oil on panel, a pair, each 14 1/2 x 19 1/2 ins / 37 x 49.5 cm) GBP 5,500. AMSTERDAM, 10 May 1994, *Dogs Attacking a Crane* (1670, oil on panel, 11 x 14 ins / 28 x 35.5 cm) NLG 12,650. NEW YORK, 11 Jan 1995, *Dogs Attacking a Heron* (oil on panel, 11 x 12 1/2 ins / 28 x 31.8 cm) USD 2,990. LONDON, 8 Dec 1995, *Crowd Gathered around a Bear Leader in a Public Square* (oil on canvas, 30 1/2 x 34 1/4 ins / 77.5 x 87.3 cm) GBP 52,100. PARIS, 13 Dec 1995, *Dogs Pursuing a Heron and Dogs Pursuing a Swan* (1663, oil on panel, a pair, around 10 x 13 3/4 ins / 25.5 x 35 cm) FRF 40,000. PARIS, 29 March 1996, *Pack of Hounds Attacking a Boar* (oil on canvas, 51 1/4 x 74 3/4 ins / 130 x 190 cm) FRF 170,000. NEW YORK, 16 May 1996, *Serving Girl Bringing a Huntsman a Drink outside an Italian Inn with Dogs Resting after the Hunt* (1651, oil on panel, 34 1/4 x 42 1/4 ins / 87 x 107.3 cm) USD 162,000. LONDON, 16 April 1997, *Stag Hunt* (oil on canvas, 25 x 30 ins / 63.7 x 76.2 cm) GBP 4,025. LONDON, 5 Dec 1997, *The Angel Appearing to the Shepherds* (oil on canvas, 29 1/2 x 49 1/4 ins / 74.9 x 124.8 cm) GBP 3,450. AMSTERDAM, 9 March 1999, *Hounds Bringing Down a Bear* (oil on canvas, 22 x 25 ins / 56 x 64 cm) NLG 6,000. NEW YORK, 26 May 2000, *Hounds Chasing a Wounded Bittern* (oil on canvas, 26 x 57 ins / 65 x 145 cm) USD 15,000. VIENNA, 4 Oct 2000, *Hunting Party at Rest* (oil on panel, 36 x 49 ins / 91 x 124 cm) ATS 300,000. LONDON, 26 April 2001, *Two Dogs Playing on a Red Cushion* (oil on canvas, 15 x 20 ins / 37 x 52 cm) GBP 2,500. LONDON, 1 Nov 2001, *Feeding the Dogs* (oil on canvas, 25 x 30 ins / 63 x 77 cm) GBP 4,500. LONDON, 17 April 2002, *Evening Landscape with Dogs Flushing a Heron* (oil on panel, 15 x 14 ins / 39 x 35 cm) GBP 7,000. BAYSWATER, 23 Sept 2002, *Landscape with Huntsman and Hounds* (1685, oil on canvas, 33 x 55 ins / 85 x 140 cm) GBP 10,000. AMSTERDAM, 13 May 2003, *Swan being Chased from Nest by Hounds. Stork Frightened by Hounds* (oil on panel, a pair, 11 x 14 ins / 28 x 35 cm) EUR 6,800. LONDON, 10 July 2003, *Hounds Attacking a Stag* (oil on canvas, 47 x 70 ins / 119 x 177 cm) GBP 12,000.

HONDIUS, Hendrik, the Elder, or Hond
Dutch, 16th - 17th century.
Born 9 June 1573, in Duffel; died c. 1649.
Engraver, draughtsman.
The Hague School.

Hendrik Hondius the Elder studied with J. Wierix and later with Jan Fredeman de Vries. He worked in Mechelen, then in Antwerp, Brussels, Cologne, Paris and London. He then moved to The Hague, where he married. In 1597 he belonged to the guild of The Hague.

He specialised in engraving portraits of leaders of the Reformation and of contemporary artists, and also engraved plates after Dürer, Holbein, Brueghel, van Mander and Moestart.

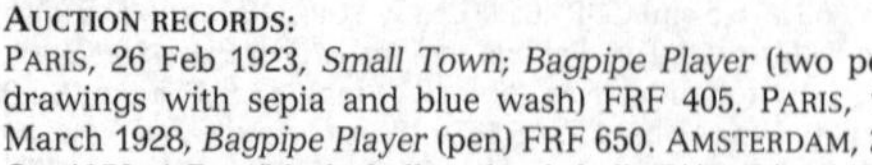

AUCTION RECORDS:

PARIS, 26 Feb 1923, *Small Town; Bagpipe Player* (two pen drawings with sepia and blue wash) FRF 405. PARIS, 19 March 1928, *Bagpipe Player* (pen) FRF 650. AMSTERDAM, 29 Oct 1979, *A Dog* (black chalk and red chalk, 5 1/4 x 5 ins / 13.3 x 12.7 cm) NLG 3,200. LONDON, 9 Dec 1982, *Memento Mori*

(1625, engraving/copper, 8 1/2 x 10 3/4 ins / 21.6 x 27.4 cm) GBP 1,600. Amsterdam, 18 Nov 1985, *Kasteel Spangen, near Rotterdam* (black chalk, pen and wash, 8 3/4 x 13 1/4 ins / 22.4 x 33.4 cm) NLG 7,500. Amsterdam, 25 Nov 1992, *Bagpipe Player* (1649, ink, 6 1/4 x 4 1/2 ins / 15.7 x 11.4 cm) NLG 13,800. Amsterdam, 10 May 1994, *Windmill and Farm Buildings by a River* (1625, ink and wash, 4 3/4 x 6 3/4 ins / 12.1 x 17 cm) NLG 20,700. New York, 22 Jan 2004, *Farmstead with Windmill by a Pond* (1625, pen, brown ink, grey wash, 5 x 7 ins / 12 x 17 cm) USD 10,000.

HONDIUS, Hendrik, the Younger, or Hond
Dutch, 17th century.
Born c. 1597, in Amsterdam or in London; died c. 1644.
Painter, engraver, draughtsman.

Hendrik Hondius the Younger was the son and pupil of Jodocus Hondius and in 1635 was a member of the painters' guild in The Hague. He engraved genre pieces, landscapes but mainly portraits. An engraving of *The Funeral of Charles V* has been attributed to him, but is possibly the work of Hendrik the Elder.

HONDIUS, Isac
Dutch, 18th century.
Died 20 April 1716, in Rotterdam.
Painter.

Isac Hondius was almost certainly the son of Abraham Hondius.

HONDIUS, J., or Hond
Dutch, 16th - 17th century.
Painter.

Kramm mentions a *Magdalene at Prayer* signed *J. Hondius* and dated 1600. J. Hondius may be the same person as Jodocus Hondius, and perhaps also the same as the son of Hendrik Hondius the Younger.

HONDIUS, Jodocus or Josse, the Elder or I, or Hond
Dutch, 16th - 17th century.
Born 14 October 1563, in Wacquin according to Moreri, in Ghent according to other sources; died 16 February 1611, in Amsterdam.
Engraver, cartographer. Maps.

During the troubles in the Netherlands Jodocus Hondius the Elder went to London in 1583 and became known there as an engraver and map-maker. He married in London in 1586 and then returned to Amsterdam, where he made a number of plates for a work by Sir Francis Drake.

HONDIUS, Jodocus or Justus, the Younger or II
Dutch, 17th century.
Born 9 November 1593; died 1629.
Engraver. Maps.

Jodocus Hondius the Younger was the son of Jodocus Hondius the Elder and brother of Hendrik Hondius the Younger. He worked in Amsterdam around 1628 and produced mainly portrait engravings of the princes and princesses of Orange.

HONDIUS, Willem, or Hond
Dutch, 17th century.
Born c. 1597, in The Hague; died 1652, in Danzig (now Gdansk, Poland).
Draughtsman, engraver.

Willem Hondius studied under his father Hendrik Hondius, and worked for a time in Holland before moving to Danzig, where he became court painter to Wladyslaw IV Vasa of Poland (r. 1632-48). His engravings are signed in Latin: *Guilliel-mus Hondius Hago Batavus Sculpsit cum Gratia et Privilegio S R M Poloniae et Sueciae* (*Sculpted by Willem Hondius of The Hague in the Netherlands, by the Grace and Favour of His Majesty the King of Poland and Sweden*). He engraved mainly portraits after the paintings and drawings of Van Dyck. In 1629 he was a member of the painters' guild in The Hague.

HONDORFF, Joachim
German, 19th century.
Died 2 August 1846, in Breslau (now Wroclaw, Poland).
Painter.

He worked for the church of St Elisabeth in his native city.

HONDRIESAR, Frédéric
French, 19th century.
Died 1906.
Sculptor.

Hondriesar was a member of the Société des Artistes Français.

HONDROGEN, Nicolas
American, 20th - 21st century.
Born 5 January 1952, in Concord (New Hampshire).
Active in France.
Painter, draughtsman.

Nicolas Hondrogen graduated from Boston Museum of Fine Art in 1971, by which time his work had already featured in a number of group exhibitions in the city. He settled in France in 1972, and exhibited with the Salons des Grands et Jeunes d'Aujourd'hui in 1973. In 1974 his work featured at the Salon des Réalités Nouvelles, and the Salon de Mai. He held his first solo exhibition in the same year. Hondrogen's paintings and drawings provide an interesting commentary on the problem of pictorial space, defining its extent and scale, and finally apprehending the material qualities of the resulting space through the use of 'scratchmarks'.

Bibliography:
Dexeus, Victoria Combalía, *Nicolas Hondrogen: Polígrafia*, Barcelona, 1977.

Auction records:
Stockholm, 6 June 1988, *Extension No. 2* (mixed media, 51 1/4 x 76 1/2 ins / 130 x 194 cm) SEK 7,000. Stockholm, 22 May 1989, *Siamise Progression No. 8* (mixed media, 22 x 18 1/2 ins / 56 x 47 cm) SEK 5,000.

HONDT, Bernard d'
Belgian, 19th century.
Died 1863, in Eecloo.
Painter.

Bernard d'Hondt taught at the Ghent academy.

HONDT, C.
Dutch (?).
Painter. Portraits.

C. Hondt's name occurs in a sale catalogue.

Auction records:
Paris, 29 June 1900, *Portrait of a Child*, FRF 237.

HONDT, Franciscus Johannes de
Flemish School, 19th century.
Born 2 October 1786, in Bruges; died 18 May 1862, in Bruges.
Engraver.

Franciscus Hondt studied under his brother Jan, who died in Paris.

HONDT, Hendrick Pieters de
Dutch, 17th century.
Painter.
Hendrick Hondt studied under Salomon Ruysdael in Haarlem, and in 1645 was a member of the Haarlem guild. He painted genre pieces.

HONDT, Jan de, the Elder
Flemish School, 17th century.
Active in Mechelen.
Painter.
Jan d'Hondt the Elder was the brother of Lambert d'Hondt and father of Jan the Younger.

HONDT, Jan de, the Younger
Flemish School, 17th - 18th century.
Baptised 13 October 1649 in Mechelen; died 19 June 1726, in Mechelen.
Painter.
In 1672, Jan d'Hondt the Younger was senior member of the Guild of St Luke in Mechelen.

HONDT, Karl de
Flemish School, 18th - 19th century.
Painter. Genre scenes.

HONDT, L. de
French, 18th century.
Active in Paris c. 1700.
Painter.
L. de Hondt painted cartoons for the Gobelins tapestry works.

HONDT, Lambert de
Flemish School, 17th century.
Born before 1620; died c. 1665, in Mechelen.
Painter. Mythological subjects, battles, genre scenes, landscapes with figures.
Lambert d'Hondt was the brother of Jan de Hondt and a pupil of David Teniers the Younger. He worked in Mechelen and, according to Nagler, also lived in Munich. He is known primarily for his battle scenes.

Museums and Galleries:
Dresden: *Horseman in Battle* - Frankfurt am Main: *The Unforeseen Attack* - Périgueux: *Battle on a Bridge*.
Auction records:
Paris, 6 Dec 1924, *Convoy of Troops Passing through a Village*, FRF 3,800. Paris, 12 Feb 1925, *Horsemen in Battle at the Edge of a Wood; Defending the Ford* (both) FRF 2,000. Paris, 12 June 1926, *The Escort*, FRF 7,000. London, 22 April 1977, *At the Blacksmith's* (oil on canvas, 15 1/2 x 23 1/2 ins / 39.4 x 59.7 cm) GBP 4,000. Paris, 7 June 1985, *Wladyslaw, King of Poland, Making War against the Turks* (oil on canvas, 32 3/4 x 43 3/4 ins / 83 x 111 cm) FRF 80,000. Paris, 2 July 1987, *Spanish Dignitary on a Road in Flanders* (oil on canvas, 17 x 23 1/2 ins / 43 x 60 cm) FRF 100,000. London, 13 May 1988, *Skirmish between Horsemen on a Bridge* (oil on canvas, 16 1/4 x 23 1/2 ins / 41 x 60 cm) GBP 5,500. Paris, 1 July 1988, *Gathering at an Inn* (oil on panel, 17 1/4 x 25 1/2 ins / 44 x 64.5 cm) FRF 3,400. Paris, 7 July 1988, *Horsemen Attacking a Convoy at the Edge of a Wood* (oil on panel, 7 x 10 ins / 17.5 x 25.7 cm) FRF 17,000. London, 1 March 1991, *Orpheus Enchanting the Animals; The Wave* (oil on canvas, a pair, each 23 1/2 x 16 1/2 ins / 59.7 x 41.9 cm) GBP 26,400. London, 30 Oct 1996, *Landscape with Horsemen and Other Travellers* (oil on canvas, 12 1/4 x 15 3/4 ins / 31 x 40 cm) GBP 4,600. Paris, 9 Dec 1996, *Orpheus Enchanting the Animals; Noah's Ark* (copper, a pair, 9 3/4 x 13 3/4 ins / 25 x 35 cm) FRF 300,000. London, 16 April 1997, *Huntsmen and Dogs Running in a Landscape* (oil on card, 35 x 46 1/2 ins / 88 x 117.8 cm) GBP 28,750. Madrid, 2 Dec 1999, *Cavalry Battle* (oil on canvas, 11 x 15 ins / 27 x 39 cm) ESP 600,000. Amsterdam, 9 May 2001, *Expulsion from the Garden of Eden* (oil on canvas, 24 x 33 ins / 60 x 85 cm) NLG 30,000.

HONDT, Philipp de
Flemish School, 18th century.
Active in Brussels.
Painter. Religious subjects.
Philipp d'Hondt painted a *Life of St Cyprian* for the church of Ninove.
Auction records:
London, 14 Oct 1983, *Moses and the Daughters of Jethro* (oil on canvas, 73 1/2 x 53 1/4 ins / 186.6 x 135.2 cm) GBP 2,600. New York, 31 Jan 1997, *Rachel at the Well; Joseph Sold into Slavery* (oil on canvas, a pair, 91 x 68 3/4 ins / 231 x 174.6 cm) USD 29,900.

HONE, A. (Jr.)
British, 19th century.
Sculptor.
A. Hone may be connected with the sculptor Alfred Hone. He exhibited a work at the Royal Academy in London in 1856.

HONE, Alfred
British, 19th century.
Sculptor.
Alfred Hone exhibited in London at the Royal Academy.

HONE, Evie
Irish, 20th century.
Born 1894, in Dublin; died 13 March 1955, in Rathfarnham.
Painter.
Evie Hone studied in Paris under the French painters André Lhote and Albert Gleizes, and was strongly influenced by the spirit of Gleizes's work. In Paris, she worked to breathe new life into religious painting. She then returned to Ireland, where she exerted a strong influence on younger generations of painters. This may have been because, with Mainie Jellet and other painters, she had been instrumental in the formation of the Irish Exhibition of Living Art. Founded in 1943, this organisation still plays an important part in the diffusion of contemporary Irish art. Although the influence of Hone's own work was not as important as is sometimes claimed, she was highly successful in promoting modern Irish art. She began to work with stained glass around 1933 and produced windows for Ardcame church, near Boyle, Co. Roscommon, in 1934 and for Eton College Chapel, Windsor (1948-1952).

She was a member of the group Abstraction-Création, and exhibited from 1930 to 1931 at the Salon des Surindépendants, Paris. In 1978 her work featured in the exhibition *Abstraction-Création 1931-1936* at the Westfälisches Landesmuseum, Münster, and the Musée d'Art Moderne, Paris. In Ireland she took part in the activities of the Irish Exhibition of Living Art.
Bibliography:
Fabre, Gladys C., *Abstraction-Création 1931-1936*, exhibition catalogue, Westfälisches Landesmuseum für Kunst und Kulturgeschichte, Münster, Musée d'Art moderne de la ville de Paris, Paris, 1978.
Auction records:
Slane Castle, 13 May 1980, *Two Children Playing with their Dogs in a Park* (oil on card, 10 x 13 ins / 25.5 x 33 cm) GBP 750. Dublin, 29 Sept 1999, *Bride Bar, near Athlone* (1940, gouache, 22 x 30 ins / 56 x 76 cm) IEP 12,000. Dublin, 8 Dec

1999, *Pond at Marley* (1947, gouache, 13 x 19 ins / 33 x 48 cm) IEP 6,700. DUBLIN, 29 March 2000, *Composition* (gouache, 13 x 19 ins / 33 x 48 cm) IEP 5,600. DUBLIN, 13 Dec 2000, *Graveyard at Ardmore* (oil on board, 17 x 28 ins / 43 x 71 cm) IEP 5,700. DUBLIN, 13 March 2001, *Crucifixion, 1947* (gouache on board, 30 x 23 ins / 76 x 58 cm) IEP 6,200. LONDON, 17 May 2001, *Cloister at Arles, Southern France* (oil on board, 17 x 24 ins / 43 x 61 cm) GBP 4,800. DUBLIN, 19 Feb 2002, *Marley Wood* (1943, oil on board, 23 x 33 ins / 58 x 83 cm) EUR 9,600. DUBLIN, 29 May 2002, *View from the Balcony, France* (1948, gouache, 14 x 9 ins / 36 x 24 cm) EUR 8,000. DUBLIN, 16 Sept 2003, *Man with Accordion* (stencil, silkscreen and gouache, 17 x 10 ins / 42 x 25 cm) EUR 5,200. DUBLIN, 16 Sept 2003, *Windowsill Still-life with Oil Lamp and Chrysanthemums* (oil on canvas, 24 x 36 ins / 61 x 91 cm) EUR 26,000. LONDON, 14 May 2004, *Cubist Composition* (gouache, 20 x 28 ins / 51 x 71 cm) GBP 7,000. DUBLIN, 29 Sept 2004, *Chateau de Fontguitaro, Tarn, France* (mixed media, 14 x 9 ins / 36 x 24 cm) EUR 5,200.

HONE, Horace

British, 18th - 19th century.

Born 1756, in London; died 24 May 1825, in London.

Painter, miniaturist, enameller, engraver.

Horace Hone was the son of Nathaniel Hone the Elder. He painted in oils and watercolours but was chiefly known for his miniatures. He lived for most of his life in London. In 1795, he was appointed miniaturist to the Prince of Wales. He exhibited in London at the Royal Academy from 1772, becoming an associate member in 1799.

MUSEUMS AND GALLERIES:

DUBLIN: *Self-portrait; Lord Edward Fitzgerald; James Gandon; Bishop Marlay.*

AUCTION RECORDS:

LONDON, 12 March 1937, *Lady Holding a Child,* GBP 44.

HONE, John

British, 18th century.

Painter.

John Hone exhibited in London at the Free Society between 1778 and 1782.

HONE, John Camillus

Irish, 18th - 19th century.

Born 1745; died 23 May 1836, in Dublin.

Painter, watercolourist.

John Hone was the son of Nathaniel Hone the Elder. He exhibited in London at the Royal Academy from 1777 to 1780 before going to India, where he was to spend many years. On his return, he was granted a pension by the government in Dublin.

AUCTION RECORDS:

NEW YORK, 21 March 1906, *Portrait of a Boy,* USD 425. LONDON, 6 April 1993, *Portrait of a Girl in a Pink Dress and a White Lace Bonnet* (1776, oil on canvas, 20 1/2 x 15 3/4 ins / 52 x 40 cm) GBP 4,140. LONDON, 16 May 1996, *Portrait of Colonel John Bateman Fitzgerald, 24th Knight of Glin, in Uniform Leaning on a Cannon* (1784, watercolour, 14 x 11 ins / 35.5 x 28 cm) GBP 1,265.

HONE, Nathaniel, the Elder

Irish, 18th century.

Born 24 April 1718, in Dublin; died 14 August 1784, in London.

Painter, miniaturist, enameller, engraver. Portraits, genre scenes.

Nathaniel Hone, the son of a Dublin merchant, was a self-taught artist. He went to London when very young, living for a time in York where he married a rich bride before returning to London. In 1753, he spent a month in Paris.

Hone was a skilled engraver and his aquatint showing *Two Monks Celebrating* became very popular. He quickly made a name for himself in London as a portrait painter in oils, in miniature and in enamel, particularly the last of these. He was a charming man, combining good looks and a lively wit. Much has been written about his quarrels with Sir Joshua Reynolds and Angelica Kauffmann. At one point, two paintings that he had sent for exhibition at the Royal Academy in 1775 were interpreted by the academicians as an attack on his two illustrious colleagues and so were rejected. His response to this was to hold his own exhibition of 66 of his works, including the rejected paintings, an event that has been seen as the first ever solo exhibition of an artist's work.

Hone bore no grudge against his colleagues and sent work for exhibition the following year as usual and continued to do so every year until his death. He had a large family: four sons, two of whom - Horace and John Camillus - were painters like their father, and four daughters. His portraits of two of his daughters were engraved by Charles Philips and Greenwood. He was a member of the Society of Artists and one of the founder-members of the Royal Academy.

MUSEUMS AND GALLERIES:

DUBLIN: *Self-portrait; Portrait of a Man; Boy Smoking a Pipe; Gentleman* - LONDON (National Portrait Gal.): *Nathaniel Hone* (1760s, enamel/copper); *Sir John Fielding* (1762, oil on canvas); *John Wesley* (c. 1766, oil on canvas); several miniatures including a self-portrait - LONDON (Tate Collection): *Mary Hone, the Artist's Wife* (1760?, oil on canvas); *Edward Orpin, Parish Clerk of Bradford-upon-Avon* (c. 1760-1774, oil on canvas); *Sketch for 'The Conjuror'* (1775, oil/wood, sketch for a painting rejected by the Royal Academy); *Portrait of a Lady in a Blue Dress, possibly Mrs Mary Barnardiston* (1779, oil on canvas).

AUCTION RECORDS:

NEW YORK, 7 and 8 April 1904, *Sir James Mac Douglas,* USD 170. NEW YORK, 9 and 10 April 1908, *Portrait of Shelley,* USD 200. LONDON, 8 April 1911, *Signora Zamperini,* GBP 28. LONDON, Feb 1922, *Gentleman in a Landscape,* GBP 21. LONDON, March 1922, *The Actress Miss Smyth,* GBP 63. LONDON, April 1923, *Head of Lord Charlemont,* GBP 21. LONDON, July 1923, *Lady in a Black Dress and Hat,* GBP 18; *Lady in a Low-necked Green Dress,* GBP 11. LONDON, 13 Feb 1925, *Portrait of a Girl,* GBP 136. LONDON, 30 Nov 1927, *Portrait of a Man,* GBP 199. LONDON, 9 Dec 1927, *The Honorable George Douglas,* GBP 115. LONDON, 17 May 1928, *Portrait of a Young Woman,* GBP 236. LONDON, 22 June 1928, *Naval Officer,* GBP 131. LONDON, 15 March 1929, *Lady in a White Muslin Dress,* GBP 105. LONDON, 26 July 1929, *Mrs Anastasia Blake Forster,* GBP 2,940. LONDON, 8 Feb 1930, *Head and Shoulders of a Gentleman in Uniform,* GBP 162. LONDON, 20 June 1930, *Signora Zamperini in 'Cecchina',* GBP 756. NEW YORK, 2 April 1931, *Girl with a Dog,* USD 275. LONDON, 18 March 1932, *Mrs Ann Gardiner and her Son,* GBP 173. LONDON, 9 July 1937, *Man in Olive Green,* GBP 105. LONDON, 1 July 1938, *Lord Fielding,* GBP 252. LONDON, 1 Dec 1944, *Conjurer,* GBP 262. LONDON, 2 Dec 1959, *Portrait of a Young Man,* GBP 680. LONDON, 18 Nov 1970, *Portrait of Christopher O'Brien,* GBP 550. LONDON, 14 July 1976, *Portrait of Henry Angelo Tremamondo* (1769, oil on canvas, 29 1/4 x 24 1/4 ins / 74.5 x 61.5 cm) GBP 900. LONDON, 23 March 1979, *Portrait of a Lady* (oil on canvas, 29 x 24 ins / 73.6 x 61 cm) GBP 1,800. NEW YORK, 18 June 1982, *The Bird Nesters: Portrait of Lord Morton and his Brother* (1769, oil on canvas, 27 1/4 x 35 ins / 69 x 89 cm) USD 10,000. NEW YORK, 20 April 1983, *Portrait of Lord Morton and his Brother Holding a Bird's Nest* (1769, oil on canvas, 27 1/4 x 35 ins / 69 x 89 cm) USD 38,000. LONDON, 12 March 1986, *Bird's Nest* (oil on canvas, 23 x 19 ins / 58.5 x 48.5 cm) GBP 4,600. LONDON, 20 Nov 1987, *Green Boy* (1782, oil on canvas, 24 1/4 x

20$\frac{1}{4}$ ins / 61.9 x 51.4 cm) GBP 30,000. LONDON, 12 July 1989, *Portrait of a Little Girl with her Pomeranian Dog* (oil on canvas, 19$\frac{1}{4}$ x 15$\frac{3}{4}$ ins / 49 x 40 cm) GBP 8,800; *Portrait of David Garrick in a Red Waistcoat* (oil on canvas, 25 x 21$\frac{1}{2}$ ins / 63.5 x 54.5 cm) GBP 23,100. LONDON, 10 July 1991, *Portrait of a Little Girl with her Dog* (oil on canvas, 21$\frac{1}{4}$ x 17 ins / 54 x 43 cm) GBP 9,350. LONDON, 15 Nov 1991, *Half Portrait of a Little Girl in a White Dress with a Blue Sash Holding a Melon in a Landscape* (oil on canvas, 22$\frac{1}{4}$ x 17$\frac{3}{4}$ ins / 56.5 x 45.1 cm) GBP 9,350. LONDON, 8 April 1992, *Three-Quarters Portrait of Miss Gardner in a Landscape Wearing a White Dress with a Blue Sash and Bonnet* (oil on canvas, 36 x 27$\frac{3}{4}$ ins / 90.5 x 70.5 cm) GBP 7,700. LONDON, 7 April 1993, *The Whitefoord Children in a Wood* (oil on canvas, 41 x 50$\frac{1}{2}$ ins / 103.2 x 128.3 cm) GBP 41,100. LONDON, 2 June 1995, *Portrait of a Lady with her Three Daughters* (oil on canvas, 36 x 46 ins / 91.5 x 117 cm) GBP 26,450. LONDON, 11 Sept 1997, *Portrait of a Gentleman traditionallly believed to be Captain Lambert Brabazon* (1783, oil on canvas, 30 x 25 ins / 76.2 x 63.5 cm) GBP 2,300. LONDON, 21 June 1999, *Young Gentleman in a Gold-bordered Lilac Coat* (1750, enamel on copper, oval miniature, h. 2 ins / 5 cm) GBP 4,200. LONDON, 12 July 1999, *Portrait of Gentleman Playing a Mandolin* (oil on canvas, 29 x 24 ins / 73 x 61 cm) GBP 9,500. LONDON, 19 May 2000, *Portrait of Captain Robert Boyle Walsingham MP, with View of Louisbourg, Canada* (1760, oil on canvas, 94 x 58 ins / 239 x 147 cm) GBP 220,000. LONDON, 21 Nov 2000, *Young Lady in a Lace-bordered White Silk Dress* (1751, enamel on copper, h. 2 ins / 5 cm) GBP 2,800. LONDON, 30 Oct 2001, *Portrait of a Gentleman in a Gold Figured Royal Blue Coat* (1749, enamel, oval miniature, h. 2 ins / 4 cm) GBP 1,600. LONDON, 11 Dec 2001, *Portrait of a Gentleman in Eastern European Costume with Fur-trimmed Robe* (oil on canvas, 30 x 25 ins / 76 x 64 cm) GBP 24,000. LONDON, 26 Nov 2002, *Double Portrait of General Richard Wilford and Sir Levett Hanson* (1777, oil on canvas, 54 x 54 ins / 137 x 137 cm) GBP 60,000. LONDON, 10 Dec 2002, *Young Lady in a Black Dress* (1749, enamel on copper, miniature, h. 2 ins / 4 cm) GBP 3,200. LONDON, 3 June 2003, *Young Gentleman in a White Coat with a Red Velvet Collar* (1762, enamel, oval miniature, h. 1 in/ 3cm) GBP 2,200. LONDON, 27 Nov 2003, *Portrait of Master Meynell in Van Dyck Dress* (oil on canvas, oval, 29 x 24 ins / 74 x 62 cm) GBP 10,500. NORFOLK, 22 March 2004, *Portrait of a Lady, believed to be Lady Juliana Colyer* (1757, oil on canvas, 30 x 25 ins / 76 x 63 cm) GBP 20,000. LONDON, 14 May 2004, *Gentleman, believed to be John, 7th Earl of Galloway, Facing Right* (1759, oval miniature, h. 1 in/3 cm) GBP 1,500. LONDON, 14 May 2004, *Portrait of the Artist, Half-length, in a Brown Coat, Holding a Canvas and Pen* (oil on canvas, 30 x 25 ins / 76 x 63 cm) GBP 105,000.

HONE, Nathaniel, the Younger

Irish, 19th - 20th century.

Born 26 October 1831, in Dublin; died 14 October 1917, in St Dolough's Park.

Painter. Portraits, landscapes, seascapes.

Nathaniel Hone the Younger was the grandson of the Irish painter of the same name. He studied in Paris under the French painters Yvon and Couture.

AUCTION RECORDS:

LONDON, 9 June 1978, *Sailing Ships at Sea* (oil on canvas, 20 x 27$\frac{1}{4}$ ins / 51 x 69 cm) GBP 2,200. LONDON, 8 June 1979, *Seagulls on the Shore* (oil on canvas, 24 x 40 ins / 61 x 101.5 cm) GBP 1,600. LONDON, 13 Nov 1985, *Flock of Sheep in a Wooded Landscape* (oil on canvas, 18 x 24 ins / 46 x 61 cm) GBP 2,200. LONDON, 9 June 1988, *Landscape* (oil on canvas, 27$\frac{1}{2}$ x 35$\frac{1}{2}$ ins / 70 x 90 cm) GBP 6,050. DUBLIN, 24 Oct 1988, *Breakers on the Reefs* (oil on canvas, 10 x 14$\frac{1}{4}$ ins / 25.7 x 35.9 cm) IEP 3,080. BELFAST, 28 Oct 1988, *Heavy Seas off St Marhocks* (oil on canvas, 17 x 27$\frac{1}{4}$ ins / 43.2 x 69.3 cm) GBP 3,520. NEW YORK, 11 Jan 1989, *Portrait of Mary Edwards in a Blue Dress with a Jewelled Bow* (oil on canvas, oval, 30 x 25 ins / 76.2 x 63.5 cm) USD 3,850. BELFAST, 30 May 1990, *Cattle in a Meadow at Malahide* (oil on canvas, 16$\frac{3}{4}$ x 25$\frac{1}{4}$ ins / 42.5 x 64.2 cm) GBP 2,750. DUBLIN, 12 Dec 1990, *Windswept Road at Dusk* (oil on canvas, 25 x 36 ins / 63.5 x 91.4 cm) IEP 4,000. DUBLIN, 26 May 1993, *On the Banks of the Seine* (oil on canvas, 24 x 36 ins / 61 x 91.5 cm) IEP 31,900. LONDON, 2 June 1995, *Coastal Landscape* (oil on canvas, 24$\frac{1}{2}$ x 39$\frac{3}{4}$ ins / 62 x 101 cm) GBP 17,250. LONDON, 16 May 1996, *Menton in the Evening* (oil on canvas, 24 x 40$\frac{1}{2}$ ins / 61 x 103 cm) GBP 18,400. LONDON, 20 May 1999, *Houses by Bay* (watercolour, 7 x 9 ins / 18 x 23 cm) GBP 1,200. DUBLIN, 26 May 1999, *On the Malahide Sands* (oil on canvas, 26 x 39 ins / 66 x 99 cm) IEP 25,000. DUBLIN, 31 May 2000, *Landscape* (watercolour, 4 x 7 ins / 10 x 18 cm) IEP 2,100. DUBLIN, 15 Nov 2000, *Cows in a Field* (oil on canvas on board, 13 x 20 ins / 34 x 52 cm) IEP 9,000. DUBLIN, 28 March 2001, *Coastal Scene at Etretat* (watercolour, 7 x 11 ins / 19 x 27 cm) IEP 2,900. LONDON, 17 May 2001, *Boating on the River* (oil on canvas, 25 x 36 ins / 63 x 91 cm) GBP 70,000. DUBLIN, 29 May 2002, *Seaweed Gatherers, Portmarnock* (oil on canvas, 2 x 36 ins / 6 x 91 cm) EUR 88,000. DUBLIN, 19 Nov 2002, *Sand Bunker* (6 x 9 ins / 16 x 24 cm) EUR 2,400. DUBLIN, 25 Nov 2003, *Coastal Landscape, Malahide* (oil on canvas on board, 11 x 18 ins / 29 x 46 cm) EUR 8,000. DUBLIN, 25 Nov 2003, *Cattle in Pasture, Malahide* (oil on canvas on board, 10 x 14 ins / 26 x 36 cm) EUR 8,000. DUBLIN, 26 May 2004, *Cows at Malahide* (oil on canvas, 14 x 20 ins / 36 x 52 cm) EUR 23,000. DUBLIN, 29 Sept 2004, *Orange Trees and Path in the Sunshine* (watercolour, 10 x 12 ins / 25 x 30 cm) EUR 1,900.

HONE, Robert

Irish (?), 19th century.

Painter. Landscapes.

A landscape by Robert Hone is recorded as having been sold in 1986. There are no other references to an artist of this name. If the landscape is indeed of Madras, then it seems likely that the artist was John Camillus Hone.

AUCTION RECORDS:

LONDON, 18 April 1986, *Landscape outside Madras (?)* (oil on canvas, 26$\frac{3}{4}$ x 50$\frac{1}{4}$ ins / 68 x 127.6 cm) GBP 35,000.

HONE, Samuel

Irish, 18th century.

Born 8 September 1726, in Dublin; died in Jamaica.

Painter.

Samuel Hone was the brother of Nathaniel Hone the Elder. He worked mainly in Dublin.

HONEGGER, Gottfried

Swiss, 20th century.

Born 12 June 1917, in Zurich.

Active in France.

Painter, sculptor, illustrator.

Honegger studied at the school of arts and crafts in Zurich in 1931-1932, then from 1932 until 1935 took an apprenticeship in decorating techniques. He opened his own publicity and graphics agency with his first wife, Warja Honegger-Lavater, in 1937. He decided to concentrate exclusively on art in 1958 and from then until 1960 he lived in New York, where he met Sam Francis, Mark Rothko, Barnett Newman and Alexander Calder, and where he worked as a director in the field of design. After 1960 he divided his time between Paris and Zurich. He always supported the art world, building up a collection of concrete art with his companion Sybil Albers-Barrier, which can be seen at the Château de Mouans-Sartoux in the Alpes-Maritimes.

After producing Figurative works, Honegger went through an *Informel* period from 1945 until 1950. Then, between 1950 and 1955, he was influenced by analytical Cubism, before he finally turned to a style approaching Neo-Plasticism, through which he expressed his ideas using a wide diversity of techniques. In his paintings and sculptures alike, a mathematical-geometric approach to surface and space is immediately apparent. The shape is created purely using a ruler and compass; he gives an added perspective to this geometric severity with his use of monochrome. The combination of straight lines and curves is only visible through the subtle play of light on slight differences of relief achieved through various processes, which he called 'bevelling', using simple card as a medium.

He managed nevertheless to break the principle of tableau-relief-monochrome in some respects, particularly in his works after 1967, large parts of which are covered in aluminium plate. It is quite probable that the only emotions he wanted to provoke with his simple works were modest Pythagorean feelings of accuracy, balance and harmony, similar sometimes to the American Minimalists. And yet, although the choice of precisely applied monochrome laquers in red, blue or black that predominate in his works is based on a simulated chance, being programmed on the computer or selected on the throw of the dice, they have an air of poetic communication. After 1949, He illustrated various texts, including the poems by Michel Seuphor published in 1964 under the title *Hommage à Cercle et Carré* (*Homage to the Circle and Square*), using lithography and other techniques.

Honegger soon took up sculpture alongside painting - only a small step from his 'relief-paintings' which already emerged from the face of the wall to allow the better play of light on their surfaces and to more easily become part of the environment. His sculptures, composed of basic three-dimensional shapes such as spheres and cubes and in which he combines raw materials and pure forms, are, in effect, based on the same principles as his paintings. They play with the division of geometric shapes, creating the feeling of movement towards the exterior, towards an open space, obeying 'random programming' in the same way as nature. But it was in the area of monumental sculpture that he found most satisfaction in later years, creating art that is an integral part of architecture and that can be a 'contribution to the ecology of beauty'. In 1987 he also designed some abstract stained glass windows for the cathedral in Nevers, their structure inspired by the architecture of the building.

Honegger received many public commissions in Europe and the USA after 1971, especially in France and Switzerland: the university in Dijon; Renault Corporation in Cacia; Geneva; Lille; CES in Nevers; Renault Corporation and the Arche de la Défense in Paris; the university and the underground in Zurich. In 1985 he was made Chevalier of the Ordre des Arts et des Lettres and in 1987 he was awarded the Grand Prix by the city of Zurich. He took part in many international collective exhibitions, among which were: the museum of fine arts in Neuenburg (1957); the Kunsthalle in Basel (1958, 1971); the Museum of Modern Art in New York (1960); the Carnegie International in Pittsburgh, where he won the major J. M. Bovard Purchase Prize (1962, 1964, 1967, 1970); the Guggenheim International Award in New York (1964); the Salon de Mai in Paris (1964, 1966, 1968); the Stedelijk Museum in Amsterdam (1964); the Salon des Réalités Nouvelles in Paris (1965, 1966, 1968, 1975); the Musée Cantini in Marseilles (1969, 1985); the Kunsthaus in Zurich (1970, 1978, 1988); the Galeries Nationales du Grand Palais in Paris (1972); the University Art Museum in Austin and the Kunstmuseum in Aarau (1973); the Salon Grands et Jeunes d'Aujourd'hui in Paris (1974, 1975, 1984); the international Biennale of engraving in Ljubljana (1977, 1979); the Musée d'Art Moderne de la Ville in Paris, the Van Abbemuseum in Eindhoven and the Kunsthaus in Zurich (1978); the Musée du Luxembourg in Paris (1983); the Kunsthaus in Zug (1984, 1987); the Fondation Cartier in Jouy-en-Josas (1985); the Venice Biennale (1987); FNAC (Fonds National d'Art Contemporain) in Paris (1989); and the French Institute in Naples and FRAC Bretagne (Fonds Régional d'Art Contemporain) in Nantes (1992).

He showed his works in a great number of solo exhibitions: in Zurich (1950, 1952, 1954, 1958, 1966, 1967 (Kunsthaus), 1971, 1974, 1976, 1979, 1983, 1985, 1986, 1991); New York (1951, 1960, 1964, 1970); Paris (1961, 1963, 1974, 1975, 1978 (Musée d'Art Moderne de la Ville), 1983, 1986 (at the Galerie Gilbert Brownstone after this date), 1988, 1989, 1991, 1993, 1996); London (1964, 1968, 1979, 1983, 1988); Essen (1965, 1970); Stuttgart (1966 (Kunstverein), 1974, 1980, 1982, 1987, 1989); Dortmund, at the Museum am Ostwall (1968); Dallas (1969, 1972); the Sao Paulo Biennale (1975); Ulm, at the Ulmer Museum (1981); Stockholm, at the Konstruktiv Tendens Gallery (1984, 1988, 1989, 1991); Marseilles, at the Musée de la Vieille-Charité (1985); Lyons, at the Musée St-Pierre (1986); Reutlingen (1989); Mouans-Sartoux, at the Espace de l'Art Concret (1990); Crestet, at the Art Centre (2001); and in Saumur, at the Centre d'Art Contemporain (2002).

BIBLIOGRAPHY:

Read, Herbert, *A Letter to a Young Painter*, Horizon Press, New York, 1962. Wehrli, René/Seuphor, Michel/Kultermann, Udo, *Gottfried Honegger*, exhibition catalogue, Kunsthaus, Zurich, 1967. Lemoine, Serge, *Sculptures 1953-1983*, Gal. Liliane et Michel Durand-Dessert, Paris, 1984. Lemoine, Serge, *Tableaux-reliefs, sculptures 1970-1983*, Waser, Zurich, 1984. Besset, M., *Gottfried Honegger*, exhibition catalogue, Musée d'Art moderne de la Ville de Paris, Paris, 1987. Gassiot-Talbot, Gérald/Argence, Guy, '*Gottfried Honegger*' in *Opus international* n° 103, periodical, Paris, winter 1987. *Gottfried Honegger*, exhibition catalogue, Gal. Dorothea Van der Koelen, Mainz, 1990. Honegger, Gottfried, '*Pour un art concret*' in *Nouvelles de l'Estampe*, periodical, Bibliothèque nationale de France, Paris, 2000. Honegger, Gottfried/Anselm, Guy (preface), *Lettres à...: des écrits inventés et vécus*, J. Chambond, Paris, 2003.

MUSEUMS AND GALLERIES:

BOSTON (University MFA) - BUFFALO (Albright-Knox AG) - DALLAS (MA): *Z-BI-73* (1964, oil on Masonite); *Lbisy* (1971, acrylic and tempera on canvas) - GRENOBLE (Mus. de Grenoble): *P 907* - HUMLEBÆK (Louisiana Mus. for Moderne Kunst) - JERUSALEM (Israel Mus.) - MARSEILLES (Mus. Cantini): *Relief-painting P 1* (1962-1963); *P 880* (1983) - NEW YORK (MoMA) - OTTERLO (Kröller-Müller Mus.) - PARIS (FNAC): *Z 889* (1973); *Z 779* (1978); *P 961* (1987) - PARIS (MNAM-CCI): *P 537* (1967) - PHOENIX (AM): *Synonyme* (1960, oil on canvas) - PITTSBURGH (Carnegie MA): *Tableau-Relief W Z 425* (1966, oil and collage on canvas, relief-painting) - PRINCETON (AM, Princeton University) - TOULOUSE (FRAC Midi-Pyrénées): *P-1044* (1994) - VALENCIA (MBA) - WASHINGTON DC (Hirshhorn Mus. and Sculpture Garden): *Configuration* (1960, oil and collage); *Metamorphose* (1962, bronze); *Tableau Relief - Blue-Gold* (1963, oil and synthetic polymer) - WASHINGTON DC (NGA): *Germinating* (1955, colour lithograph) - ZURICH (Kunsthaus).

AUCTION RECORDS:

ZURICH, 10 May 1978, *Axiom* (1958, mixed media/canvas, 23 1/2 x 23 1/2 ins / 60 x 60 cm) CHF 60,000. ZURICH, 23 Nov 1978, *Axiom* (1958, mixed media/canvas, 23 1/2 x 23 1/2 ins / 60 x 60 cm) CHF 3,800. ZURICH, 27 May 1982, *Z 619* (1970, acrylic and tempera, 71 x 55 ins / 179.5 x 140 cm) CHF 5,000. ZURICH, 6 June 1984, *Z 619* (1970, acrylic/canvas, 71 x 55 ins / 179.5 x 140 cm) CHF 7,500. LONDON, 22 Oct 1986, *Relief-painting PZ 32* (1963, oil on card, 30 3/4 x 39 1/4 ins / 78 x 100 cm) GBP 1,800. PARIS, 20 July 1989, *Assimilas* (1960, oil on canvas, 31 1/2 x 31 1/2 ins / 80 x 80 cm) FRF 80,000. ZURICH, 25 Oct 1989, *P + 52* (1964, wood relief darkened with chalk/white background, 50 1/2 x 50 3/4 ins / 128.5 x 129 cm) CHF 19,000. PARIS, 21 June 1990, *Project 698 First Version* (acrylic/paper and cut-outs, 30 x 21 1/2 ins / 76 x 54.5 cm) FRF

9,000. PARIS, 15 Oct 1990, *Monoform 26* (bronze, 10¼ x 10¼ x 2½ ins / 26 x 26 x 6.5 cm) FRF 4,000. LUCERNE, 24 Nov 1990, *Relief-painting PZ32* (1963, oil/synthetic resin, 30¾ x 39¼ ins / 78 x 100 cm) CHF 15,000. ZURICH, 29 April 1992, *Relief-painting P 485* (1968, mixed media/canvas, 39¼ x 39¼ ins / 100 x 100 cm) CHF 8,500. LUCERNE, 20 Nov 1993, *Inclusion* (1955, oil on canvas, 23½ x 11¾ ins / 60 x 30 cm) CHF 10,000. LUCERNE, 4 June 1994, *Relief-paintings P 896* (1984, acrylic and collage/canvas, 59 x 63 ins / 150 x 160 cm) CHF 29,000. PARIS, 24 June 1994, *White Composition* (mixed media, 27½ x 15¾ ins / 70 x 40 cm) FRF 13,000. LUCERNE, 20 May 1995, *Relief-painting Z 587* (1969, white acrylic/polyester, 40½ x 40½ ins / 103 x 103 cm) CHF 15,000. PARIS, 19 June 1996, *IV P 994* (1989, acrylic/canvas, 94½ x 48¼ ins / 240 x 122.5 cm) FRF 85,000. LUCERNE, 23 Nov 1996, *Relief Painting* (1972, mixed media and oil on card/canvas, 46 x 30 x 1½ ins / 117 x 76 x 3.5 cm) CHF 6,200. ZURICH, 8 April 1997, *Z 619* (1970, acrylic and tempera, 71 x 55 ins / 179.5 x 140 cm) CHF 19,000. ZURICH, 23 March 1999, *Bevelling Z-121* (oil on pavatex on canvas, 30 x 30 ins / 75 x 75 cm) CHF 10,000. LONDON, 28 June 2001, *Tableau Relief, Red with Blue Border* (1966, oil and collage on canvas, 59 x 59 ins / 150 x 150 cm) GBP 9,500. STOCKHOLM, 6 Nov 2001, *Z 580* (1969, mixed media relief, 41 x 41 ins / 103 x 103 cm) SEK 30,000. LUCERNE, 23 Nov 2002, *Pole* (nickeled aluminium, h. 35 ins / 89 cm) CHF 6,600. LUCERNE, 23 Nov 2002, *Bevelling* (1969, acrylic over board relief, 40 x 30 ins / 102 x 76 cm) CHF 11,000. AMSTERDAM, 3 June 2003, *Sculpture Division 2* (1986, marble, h. 22 ins / 55 cm) EUR 2,400. ZURICH, 24 June 2003, *Z91* (1977, acrylic on canvas, two parts, 55 x 24 ins / 140 x 60 cm) CHF 12,000. STOCKHOLM, 27 April 2004, *Fragment 18* (steel, h. 16 ins / 41 cm) SEK 20,000. ZURICH, 29 Nov 2004, *Z 843* (1980, acrylic and oil on canvas, 14 x 9 ins / 36 x 22 cm) CHF 25,000.

HONEGGER, Paul
Austrian, 17th century.
Born in Bad Mergentheim; died 23 May 1649, in Innsbruck.
Painter.

A noted work is *The Virgin Appearing to St Bernard*. Possibly related to Kaspar Lindenfelder.

MUSEUMS AND GALLERIES:
INNSBRUCK: painting.

HONEGGER-LAVATER, Warja. See **LAVATER**

HONEIN, Alphonse Célestin Hermann
French, 19th century.
Born 27 October 1814, in Paris.
Painter. Genre scenes, portraits.

Honein entered the École des Beaux-Arts on 2 October 1838, and became a pupil of Drolling. His portraits and genre paintings were featured at the Salon from 1841 to 1859. He is best known for: *Death of Lara*; *First Joys*; *The Final Moments of Mary Stuart*; *Fortune Teller*; *Italian Family*; and *Jocelyn*.

HÖNEL, Friedrich Jakob Lorenz
German, 20th century.
Born 6 July 1888, in Hinterbrühl.
Painter. Scenes with figures, landscapes.

Hönel is known for his scenes of children.

HONER, Marie Edmond
French, 19th century.
Born in Nancy.
Engraver.

Honer was a pupil of Paul Maurou, and became a member of the Société des Artistes Français in 1889. He received an honourable mention in 1893, and won a third-class medal in 1895, a second-class medal in 1898, and a silver medal in 1900 (at the Exposition Universelle).

AUCTION RECORDS:
PARIS, 12 March 1919, *Stream beneath the Woods*, FRF 90.

HONERBACH, Margarete
German, 19th century.
Active in Berlin.
Engraver.

She engraved genre subjects.

HONERT, Martin
German, 20th - 21st century.
Born 1953, in Bottrop (Westphalia).
Sculptor.

Honert's sculptures reveal his attachment to the world of childhood, often his own. He has participated in many group exhibitions in Germany and abroad: 1988, Munich; 1990, the Fondation Cartier in Jouy-en-Josas; 1991, the Galleria Communale d'Arte Moderna in Bologna; 1992, the Sydney Biennial; the Musée d'Art moderne de la Ville de Paris. He also has held solo shows notably in 1991, 1994, 1996 and 2003 at the Matthew Marks Gallery in New York.

MUSEUMS AND GALLERIES:
MONTREAL (MBA): *Lime-Tree* (1990).

AUCTION RECORDS:
FRANKFURT AM MAIN, 14 June 1994, *Choir Children* (two sculptures in painted polyester, h. appro x . 23½ ins / 60 cm) DEM 11,500.

HONERVOGT, Jacques. See **HONNERVOGT**

HONET, Jean or Jehennin de. See **JEAN de Honet**

HONG, Anna Helga
American, 20th century.
Born 21 February 1894; died 1984, in Santa Barbara.
Painter.

Anna Helga Hong was a member of the Art Club of California and Art Institute of Chicago. She was awarded various prizes.

HONG RUILIN, or Hung Jui-lin
Chinese, 20th century.
Born 1911, in Taipei.
Painter. Figure compositions.

Hong Ruilin was raised in a cultured milieu, receiving his first art lessons from his father. In 1927, he entered the Taiwan Painting Institute and took part in the city's first exhibition in the same year. In 1930, he went to Japan to study at the Imperial Art Academy. After graduating, he returned to Taiwan, where he developed towards oil painting. His paintings often featured in exhibitions in Taiwan and Japan. He lived in a mining area and was deeply aware of his fellow citizens and their harsh working conditions. Their lives were one of his main themes. His style is painterly: he draws his forms in rapidly, leaving his brushstrokes still visible. Many of his paintings are based on neutral beige or gray.

AUCTION RECORDS:
HONG KONG, 30 March 1992, *Miners* (1952, oil on card, 11½ x 11½ ins / 29 x 29 cm) HKD 374,000. TAIPEI, 18 Oct 1992, *Miner* (1948, charcoal and watercolour/paper, 7¾ x 5¾ ins / 20 x 14.5 cm) TWD 198,000. TAIPEI, 18 April 1993, *Coalminers* (1956, black ink and wash/paper, 13¾ x 17¾ ins / 35 x 45 cm) TWD 345,000. TAIPEI, 10 April 1994, *Coalminers at Work* (1950, ball-point and wash/paper, 10½ x 15 ins / 26.5 x 38 cm) TWD 230,000. TAIPEI, 16 Oct 1994, *Childhood* (1935, oil on canvas, 19¾ x 23½ ins / 50 x 60 cm) TWD 4,450,000. TAIPEI, 14 April 1996, *Sunset over Fishing Village* (1980, oil on canvas/card, 15½ x 21 ins / 39.2 x 52.5 cm) TWD 736,000.

HONG TONG, or Hung Tung
Chinese, 20th century.
Born 1920, in Tainan; died 1987.
Painter (mixed media), watercolourist. Scenes with figures.

Orphaned at an early age, Hong Tong was raised by his uncle. He only took up painting at the age of 50, exhibiting soon thereafter. Two years later, he was already known to collectors' circles, where his work rapidly achieved acceptance. Self-taught, he painted scenes from fantasy, full of childlike images, creating a fairy-tale atmosphere peopled with fantastic animals and weightless figures hanging from magical kites.

Hong composed his pictures as if they were hanging scrolls, with highly ornamental borders surrounding the whole of the main composition. He would then develop his themes, painting them in a profusion of tiny detail like an immensely complicated piece of embroidery. His art lies midway between naive and raw, a combination of Western imagery complete with cowboys for his main themes, and the exotic for his minor themes, in which decorative narrative elements, small clown-like figures, improbable aircraft and imaginary plants all swarm together. His first solo show was held in 1976. After his death in 1987, the American Cultural Center and *Artist Magazine* organised a retrospective.

AUCTION RECORDS:

HONG KONG, 2 May 1991, *Queen* (hanging scroll, ink and colour/paper, 52 3/4 x 26 3/4 ins / 134 x 68 cm) HKD 143,000. TAIPEI, 22 March 1992, *Imaginary Figures and Birds* (hanging scroll, ink and colour/paper, 47 1/2 x 23 1/2 ins / 120.5 x 59.5 cm) TWD 440,000. HONG KONG, 30 April 1992, *Imaginary Figures in Red* (1974, ink and colour/paper, 42 1/4 x 14 3/4 ins / 107 x 37.5 cm) HKD 187,000. TAIPEI, 18 Oct 1992, *The World of Hong Tong* (ink and colour/paper, 64 1/4 x 16 1/2 ins / 163 x 42 cm) TWD 440,000. TAIPEI, 16 Oct 1994, *White Moon* (oil/synthetic resin, 23 1/4 x 23 1/4 ins / 59 x 59 cm) TWD 1,260,000. TAIPEI, 15 Oct 1995, *Chinese* (1977, mixed media/paper, 72 x 29 1/2 ins / 183 x 75 cm) TWD 460,000. TAIPEI, 13 April 1997, *Flower God* (acrylic/paper, 28 1/4 x 11 3/4 ins / 72 x 30 cm) TWD 287,500. TAIPEI, 19 Oct 1997, *Guanyin and Mazu* (oil on paper, 38 1/4 x 30 1/4 ins / 97 x 77 cm) TWD 3,570,000. TAIPEI, 11 April 1999, *Heavenly Treasures* (mixed media on paper, 60 x 17 ins / 153 x 42 cm) TWD 900,000. TAIPEI, 18 April 1999, *Auspicious Dolls* (1971, ink and colour, 37 x 14 ins / 93 x 36 cm) TWD 120,000. HONG KONG, 26 Oct 2003, *Festival* (mixed media on paper/board, 54 x 17 ins / 138 x 43 cm) HKD 200,000. HONG KONG, 26 Oct 2003, *Phoenix and Lion* (c. 1972-1976, mixed media on board, 24 x 48 ins / 62 x 122 cm) HKD 450,000.

HONG WU, or Hong Wou, Hung Wu, Gushan beizi, nicknames: Shuzhai, Zuiyu, artist names: Yaohua daoren, Yiru jushi
Chinese, 18th century.
Active during the reign of the Qing emperor Qianlong (1736-1796).
Painter. Landscapes, flowers.

Hong Wu was the grandson of the Qing emperor Kangxi (1662-1722).

MUSEUMS AND GALLERIES:

KYOTO (Yurinkan): *Winter Landscape, signed.*

HONG-JEN. See **HONGREN**

HONGO, Shin
Japanese, 20th century.
Born 1905, in Sapporo (Hokkaido); died 1980.
Sculptor.

Hongo Shin graduated from the Tokyo School of Decorative Arts in 1928. He took part in the International Sculpture Exhibition held at the Musée Rodin, Paris, in 1966. His work is figurative and fairly traditional, with Expressionist tendencies.

HONGRE LE. See **LE HONGRE**

HONGREN, or Hong-jen or Hung-jen, childhood name: Jianjiang, artist name: Meihua guna; monk's name Jiang Tao or Jiang Fang
Chinese, 17th century.
Born c. 1610, in Xiexian (Anhui Province); died 1663 or 1664.
Painter, draughtsman. Landscapes.

Hongren lost his father when he was still young and took up painting to support his mother and himself. When the Ming dynasty collapsed in 1644, he became a monk. He is regarded as one of the Eight Masters of Anhui (a province near the mouth of the Blue River), a regional group who because of their subject matter and to some extent their style seem to be rooted in the very ground of their native region. What has come down to us of his work dates from late in his life. Critics often associate his landscapes with the style of Ni Zan (1301-1374) and in several of his inscriptions Hongren himself mentions the connection. But his mature style borrows so little from Ni Zan and displays such originality that the most one can talk about is a shared taste, especially when it comes to clarity and purity, the desire to reduce a landsape to its essence and build a firm, cohesive structure. Hongren draws his mountain masses as if they were in fact built. His overlapping, sharply-angled slopes are carefully defined by long blue lines drawn in with a dry brush and a minimum of light wash, with here and there a few touches of pale colour. Then he adds isolated groups of trees and houses, leaving us with a blueprint of a mountain landscape on a very clear day. Yet the real world is no less present. Hongren had a number of disciples, including Yao Song (active in about 1700).

BIBLIOGRAPHY:

Cahill, James, *Chinese Painting*, Skira, Geneva, 1960. Reardon, Jackie, *'Structural Tension in the Paintings of Hongren'* in *Oriental Art*, vol 34, no. 1, Spring 1988. Kuo, Jason C., *'The Art of Hongren'* in *Orientations*, vol 25, no. 1, January 1994. Yang Xin and others, *Three Thousand Years of Chinese Painting*, Yale University Press, 1997.

MUSEUMS AND GALLERIES:

BEIJING (Palace Mus.): *Landscape* (after Ni Zan, poem by the artist, dated 1660) - BOSTON (MFA): *Lake Zhiyang and the Eastern Lake* (signed and dated 1663, ink and light colours/paper, handscroll) - HONOLULU (Academy of Arts): *Coming of Autumn* (ink/paper, vertical scroll, signed, with artist's seal and two collectors' seals) - PARIS (Mus. National des Arts asiatiques-Guimet): *Trees Covered in Frost* (signed and dated 1658, ink/paper, inscription) - STOCKHOLM (Nationalmus.): *Hills and Rivers Without End* (light colours, handscroll, inscription signed and dated 1661); *Farm at the Foot of Rocky Mountains* (from the inscription, painted for the artist's friend Shi An).

AUCTION RECORDS:

NEW YORK, 31 May 1994, *Landscape* (1658, ink/gilded paper, fan painting, 6 1/4 x 19 1/4 ins / 15.9 x 48.9 cm) USD 8,625.

HONGRIE, Henry de
French, 17th century.
Active in Paris.
Sculptor, painter.

Henry de Hongrie was the son of Philippe de Hongrie and the brother of Nicolas de Hongrie.

HONGRIE, Jehan de
French, 16th century.
Active in Paris at the end of the 16th century.
Painter.

HONGRIE, Julien de
French, 17th century.
Active in Paris in 1643.
Painter.

HONGRIE, Nicolas de
French, 17th century.
Active in Paris in 1672.
Painter, sculptor.

HONGRIE, Philippe de
French, 17th century.
Died 23 January 1661, in Paris.
Painter, sculptor.

HONGRIE, Thomas de
French, 17th century.
Active in Paris at the beginning of the 17th century.
Painter.

HONGRIS, Jean
French, 17th century.
Died 1651, in Paris.
Painter.

HONICH, Adriaen, or Honing
Dutch, 17th century.
Born 1644, in Dordrecht; died after 1683.
Painter. Landscapes.

According to Houbraken, Adriaen Honich was born in Dordrecht. In 1663 his father, 'Huybert Honingh', received 14 florins on behalf of his son, who was 'ill in Paris', in payment 'for a painting of the town hall executed by this painter'. In 1673 Adriaen was in Rome, where he took the name of Lossenbruig in the painters' guild. He is also known as a landscape artist.

HÖNICH, Heinrich
German, 19th - 20th century.
Born 5 October 1873, in Niederhanichen.
Painter, engraver. Landscapes.

Hönich studied in Dresden and Prague.

HONIG (Frau). See **GREIL Augusta**

HONIG, Ethelyn
American, 20th century.
Painter.
Minimal Art.

Ethelyn Honig trained at the Art Students League (ASL), New York in 1953. Her works explore the qualities of props, starting with glued paper and paper which has been distorted by glue.

HONIG, Paulina van den
Dutch, 16th - 17th century.
Born in London, of Dutch parents.
Miniaturist.

Paulina van den Honig was a lady in waiting to Queen Elizabeth of England.

HONNERVOGT, Jacques, the Elder
German, 16th century.
Born in Cologne.
Engraver, print publisher.

Jacques Honnervogt the Elder settled in Paris in 1608. He was the father of Jacques Honnervogt the Younger.

HONNERVOGT, Jacques, the Younger, or Honervogt
French, 17th century.
Active in Paris.
Engraver (burin), print publisher.

Jacques Honnervogt, who is essentially remembered for religious engravings, some paintings and some coats of arms, was Isaac Brissot's publisher. He published his famous series of costumes after St Igny, Élie du Bois and Léonard Gaultier. He lived in Rue St-Jacques under the sign of *The City of Cologne*. It seems likely that the Jollains took over his business.

HONNET, Alexandre Romain
French, 18th - 19th century.
Born 18th century, in Paris.
Painter. History painting.

HONNET, Gabriel
French, 16th century.
Born in Paris; died 1592, in Paris.
Painter. History painting, landscapes.
Second School of Fontainebleau.

Gabriel Honnet was a pupil of Toussaint Dubreuil. He worked in the Louvre and in the palaces of Fontainebleau and St-Germain.

HONNET, Pierre
French, 17th century.
Born in Troyes.
Painter.

Pierre Honnet was Gabriel's nephew.

HONNÊTE, Jean François
French, 18th century.
Born 1735, in Blamont; died c. 1793, in Frankfurt am Main.
Active in Frankfurt am Main.
Pastellist, miniaturist. Portraits.

HONNINCKX. See **CONINCK Jacob de**

HONNORÉ-ALATERRE, Yamina
French, 20th century.
Born in St-Jean-de-Braye.
Painter.

Yamina Honnoré-Alaterre exhibited at the Salon des Indépendants from 1921.

HONORÉ (Maître)
French, 13th century.
Active from 1288 to 1296.
Miniaturist, illuminator.

This artist worked in Paris with his son-in-law Richard de Verdun, and Thomassin. In 1288 he sold a *Decrees of Gratian* for 50 Parisian pounds; in 1296 he received 20 pounds from Philippe le Bel in payment for work.

The *Breviary of Philippe le Bel* is attributed to him. His art tends towards the careful observation of nature, his colours are bright, and the figures stand out against a light, evocative background. He and his workshop opened up the way for Parisian art of the beginning of the 14th century, and for Jean Pucelle, who may have been a pupil of his.

MUSEUMS AND GALLERIES:
PARIS (BNF): *Breviary of Philippe le Bel* (lat. 1023, attributed) - TOURS (Library): *Decrees of Gratian* (1288, ms. 588).

HONORÉ, family of artists
French, 16th century.
Painters.

Louis Honoré was living in Lyons in 1515, and Laurent Honoré was there in 1515 and 1524.

HONORÉ
French, 17th century.
Active in Sillé-le-Guillaume (Sarthe) in 1689.
Painter.

HONORÉ
French, 18th century.
Miniaturist.

Honoré ran an art school in Angers in the second half of the 18th century.

HONORÉ, Andrée
French, 20th century.
Born 5 March 1945, in Tourcoing.
Sculptor.

Honoré has taken part in collective exhibitions in Paris, including: Salon de Mai (1975-1977); Salon Grands et Jeunes d'Aujourd'hui and the Salon de la Jeune Sculpture (since

1975); and Salon des Réalités Nouvelles (1980). She has held solo exhibitions, for example at the Galerie de l'Université in Paris in 1980 and in Mexico in 1981.

Auction records:

Paris, 26 Sept 1989, *Sculpture* (1989, lacquered wood, 33 1/2 x 19 3/4 x 11 1/2 ins / 85 x 50 x 29 cm) FRF 5,800.

HONORÉ, Caroline
French, 20th century.
Born 6 January 1878, in Bohain; died 2 November 1953, in Bohain.
Painter, watercolourist.

A pupil of Faux-Froidure, Caroline Honoré regularly exhibited in Paris at the Salon des Artistes Français.

HONORÉ, Georges
French, 18th century.
Sculptor.

Georges Honoré was working at the church of Mezières-sous-Lavardin in 1702.

HONORÉ, Louis
French, 20th century.
Born 28 February 1891, in Elbeuf.
Painter.

Louis Honoré exhibited in Paris at the Salon des Artistes Français.

HONORÉ, Paul
American, 20th century.
Born 30 May 1885, in Crawford County (Pennsylvania); died 1956, in Philadelphia.
Painter, illustrator, decorative designer.

Paul Honoré trained at the Pennsylvania Academy of the Fine Arts, Philadelphia. He was a member of the National Art Club in New York, and was awarded various prizes. He executed murals in Michigan.

HONORÉ, Pierre
French, 20th century.
Born 20 June 1908, in Paris.
Sculptor.

Pierre Honoré was a pupil of Coutan, and later taught at the École des Beaux-Arts in Dijon. He received many commissions from both the State and the municipalities between 1930 and 1960. He exhibited in Paris at the Salon des Artistes Français from 1924 and won the Grand Prix de Rome in 1928

Museums and Galleries:

Dijon.

HONORÉ-THOUVENIN. See **THOUVENIN**

HONOWE, Peter
French, 15th century.
Active in Strasbourg c. 1400.
Sculptor.

HONRATH, Theodore
Painter. Rustic scenes.

T. Honrath is mentioned by Florence Levy.

Auction records:

New York, 15 Feb 1907, *Ploughing*, USD 325.

HONSBERG, P. A.
German, 19th century.
Active in Emden c. 1806.
Painter. History painting.

He exhibited a drawing called *Abraham's Sacrifice* in Berlin.

HONT, P.
Dutch, 17th century.
Painter. Genre scenes, seascapes.

Auction records:

Paris, 5 May 1945, *Fishermen's Stalls on a Beach*, FRF 8,000.

HONT, Pieter d'
Dutch, 20th century.
Born 1917.
Sculptor.

D'Hont studied at the Hogeschool voor de Kunsten in Amsterdam and produces figurative sculptures. He exhibited his work in Amsterdam, Rotterdam, The Hague, Malmö and Paris.

HONTA, Renee, later Mrs Roderic O'Connor (?)
Irish, 20th century.
Painter.

Auction records:

Dublin, 26 May 1993, *Apples* (oil on panel, 5 1/4 x 7 3/4 ins / 13.3 x 19.7 cm) IEP 1,320. Dublin, 29 April 2003, *Still-life with Fruit* (oil on canvas, 21x25 ins / 53x64 cm) EUR 8,000.

HONTHORST, Domenicus Aerstsz. van
Dutch, 16th century.
Active in Utrecht.
Painter.

HONTHORST, Gerrit van or Gerard van, called Gherardo della Notte
Dutch, 17th century.
Born 4 November 1592, in Utrecht; died 27 April 1656, in Utrecht.
Also active in Italy and England.
Painter, engraver, draughtsman, decorative artist.
Historical subjects, religious subjects, allegorical subjects, figures, portraits, historical portraits, genre scenes, scenes with figures. Church decoration.

Gerrit van Honthorst was the son of a painter and tapestry maker, and studied under Abraham Bloemart in Utrecht. He went to Italy as a young man and was greatly impressed by the energetic style of Caravaggio and his striking lighting effects. Between 1610 and 1621 he established a reputation as an artist in Rome and became known as 'Gherardo della notte'. He was known in particular for his mural paintings in the church of S Maria della Scala. When he returned to Utrecht in 1622, he joined the painters' guild and opened a school that was attended by the upper classes. According to Walpole, the queen of Bohemia and her children were among his pupils. Honthorst was senior guild member in 1625, 1628 and 1629. Also, during this period he was summoned to London by Charles I and in 1628 was employed to work on the decoration of the palace of Whitehall. He painted various allegorical subjects and also portraits of the king, the queen, their children and many English noblemen. He later returned to Holland and settled in The Hague in 1637. On 22 May 1637 he became a member of the guild of painters of The Hague. He succeeded Mierevelt as official court painter, a post he held until 1652, and was summoned to decorate the royal residences of Rijswijk and Honselaersdijk. As his career progressed, Honthorst began to concentrate more on portraiture; he executed some fifteen portaits of princes of the House of Orange and of the most distinguished members of the court. The king of Denmark commissioned several paintings from Honthorst, depicting events from Danish history; the Berlin court commissioned him to paint a large number of portraits. Honthorst amassed a considerable fortune, and in 1652 retired to his native city of Utrecht.

Gerrit van Honthorst's work can be divided into two periods: the paintings of the first period of his life are, historically, the best known; his later work, executed during the period when he enjoyed greatest public acclaim, particularly in The Hague, is devoted mainly to formal portraiture, or is in a lighter style, taking its inspiration from Van Dyck, whom Honthorst had met in England. In the works of his first period - before and after his return to Utrecht, when he clearly imitated the themes and manner of Caravaggio - his figures are generally lit by the artificial light of torches, lamps and candles, often from a concealed source, with a powerful contrast of light and shade in a chiaroscuro setting. Examples of such works are *Adoration of the Shepherds* of 1621 (Uffizi Gallery, Florence), *The Denial of St Peter* (Musée des Beaux-Arts, Rennes) and a *Descent from the Cross* at Ghent Cathedral. Honthorst in fact proved a worthy imitator of Caravaggio, not aspiring to the same grandiose quality as Caravaggio's major religious compositions, but rather limiting himself to genre pieces such as drinking scenes, fortune tellers and other popular subjects. Examples include *The Merry Musician* of 1623 (Rijksmuseum, Amsterdam) and *The Tooth Puller* (in the Louvre, Paris). During the second period he occasionally reverted to his nocturnal style, notably in familiar scenes such as *Suzanna and the Elders* of 1655 (Borghese Gallery, Rome). His work had an undeniable influence on Rembrandt and possibly also on Georges de la Tour. Honthorst's mastery of chiaroscuro made him the clear intermediary between Caravaggio, whose works remained difficult to access, and later painters such as Rembrandt. The nocturnal pieces from Honthorst's early period are, like many other works, currently enjoying renewed popularity, as the result of a revival of interest in everything associated with Caravaggio and Caravaggism.

In 1997-1998, a number of Honthorst's works were featured in the exhibition *Masters of Light: Dutch Painting from Utrecht in the Golden Age*, which toured the Fine Arts Museum of San Francisco, the Walters Art Gallery in Baltimore and the National Gallery in London.

BIBLIOGRAPHY:
Judson, Jay Richard, *Gerrit van Honthorst; a discussion of his position in Dutch Art*, Nijhoff, The Hague, 1959. Braun, Hermann, *Gerard und Willem van Honthorst*, Göttingen, 1966. Nicolson, Benedict, *The International Caravaggesque Movement*, Oxford, 1979 (review by L.J. Slatkes in Similous, xii (1981-82), pp,167-183). Spicer, Joaneath A./Orr, Lynn Federle/Bok, Marten, et al., *Masters of Light: Dutch Painting from Utrecht in the Golden Age*, travelling exhibition catalogue, Fine Arts Museums of San Francisco, San Francisco, Walters Art Gall., Baltimore, National Gall., London, Yale University Press, New Haven, 1997. Judson, J. Richard/Ekkart, Rudolf E., '*Gerrit van Honthorst, 1592-1656*' in *coll. Aetas aurea*, Davaco, Doornspijk, 1999. Papi, Gianni, '*Gherardo delle Notti: Gerrit van Honthorst in Italia*' in *coll. I Cardini*, Edizioni dei Soncino, Soncino, 1999.

MUSEUMS AND GALLERIES:
AJACCIO: *Christ Insulted by the Jews; Beheading of St John the Baptist* - AMSTERDAM: *Self-portrait; Sophia Coopmans; Merry Musician; Prince William II; Prince Frederick Henry and his Family; Frederick William, The Great Elector of Brandenburg, and his Wife; Prince William II and his Wife; Prince Frederick Henry; Amalia von Solms; Louisa Cristina von Solms* - ANGERS: *Violin Player* - AVIGNON: *Woman Playing with her Cat* - BASEL: *Hunting for Fleas* - BERGAMO: *Man with a Banner; Man Lighting a Candle* - BERLIN: *Portrait of Amalia von Solms; Portrait of Princess Mary Stuart; Puff's Fire* - BORDEAUX: *St Mary Magdalene* - BUDAPEST: *Cimon and Peron* - CALAIS: *Young Shepherd* - CHAMBÉRY: *Avarice; St Luke* - CHANTILLY: *The Supper at Emmaus* - COLOGNE: *Adoration of the Shepherds* - CONSTANCE: *Petition for Love* - COPENHAGEN: *Old Man with his Son* - DIJON: *Adoration of the Shepherds* - DRESDEN: *The Dentist; Old Men at Table; Old Men Holding Candles* - DUBLIN: *Christ Betrayed* - FLORENCE (Uffizi): *The Fortune Teller; Evening Meal; Holy Family, Two Angels Adoring the Infant Jesus; Adoration of the Shepherds; Self-portrait* - FONTAINEBLEAU: *Woman Playing the Lute* - GLASGOW: *Portrait of Frederick Henry of Nassau, Prince of Orange* - GRENOBLE: *The Disciples at Emmaus* - HAARLEM: *Woman Singing* - HANOVER: *Frederick V; Frederick V; Elisabeth, Wife of Frederick V* - KASSEL: *The Merry Couple* - LA FÈRE: *Infant Jesus Sleeping* - LONDON (National Portrait Gal.): *King Charles I* (1628, oil on canvas); *Frederick V, King of Bohemia* (1635, oil on canvas) - LONDON (NG): *Christ before the High Priest* (c. 1617, oil on canvas); *St Sebastian* (c. 1623, oil on canvas); *Elizabeth Stuart, Queen of Bohemia* (1642, oil on canvas) - MADRID (Prado): *The Incredulity of St Thomas* - MAINZ: *The Concert* - MILAN (Pinacoteca di Brera): *Male Figure* - MOSCOW (Rumiantsev Mus.): *The Swindlers* - MUNICH: *The Prodigal Son; The Prodigal Son in the Arms of a Courtesan; Angel Releasing St Peter from Prison; Ceres Searching for her Daughter Proserpina Carried off by Pluto; Cimon and Peron* - NANTES: *Adoration of the Shepherds* - PARIS (Louvre): *Pilate Washing his Hands before the People; Concert; Portrait of Charles Louis, Count Palatine of the Rhine; Portrait of the Brother of Charles Louis; Man Tuning his Lute; The Tooth Puller* - RENNES: *St Peter Denying Christ* - RHEIMS: *Jesus Examined by Pilate* - ROME (Mus. e Gal. Borghese): *Chaste Susannah and the Elders; Musicians; Lot Made Drunk by his Daughters; Man with a Lamp; The Evening Reading; The Last Supper* - ROME (Palazzo Doria Pamphili): *Young Man with a Bat; Adolescent's Head in Candlelight; Young Man with a Lantern; Young Man; Young Girl Illuminated by a Small Flame* - ROTTERDAM: *Soldier Smoking; Head of an Old Man* - ROUEN: *St Sebastian Dead in the Arms of the Holy Women; Jesus Christ before Pilate* - SALFORD (Museum and AG): *The Woman taken in Adultery; Lady Frances Honywood; Sir Robert Honywood* - SEATTLE (AM): *Pastoral* (1627, oil on canvas) - ST PETERSBURG (Hermitage): *Christ before Caiaphas; The Concert; Charles Louis, Count Palatine of the Rhine; Rupert, Count Palatine of the Rhine; The Bon Vivant; The Merry Musician; The Spinner; Young Woman at her Toilette; The Evening Prayer* - STOCKHOLM: *Old Man Holding a Lighted Candle in his Hand* - THE HAGUE: *Wife of the Stadholder William II of Nassau, Prince of Orange; Portrait of William III of Nassau as a Child and Maria of Nassau; Nude Portrait of a Young Girl; Portrait of the Elector Frederick William I and his Family; Portrait of the Stadholder Frederick*

Henry of Nassau, Prince of Orange and his Wife; Portrait of Frederick Henry in Old Age - THE HAGUE (Gemeentemus.): *Portrait of Princess Amalia von Solms; Portrait of Louisa Henrietta, Daughter of Prince Frederick Henry* - UTRECHT: *Death of Seneca; St Peter Praying* - VIENNA: *Boy with a Dog; St Jerome Praying* - VIENNA (Czernin'sche Gemäldegal.): *Young Man Drinking* - YPRES: *The First Crime; The Surprise.*

AUCTION RECORDS:

NEW YORK, 9-10 March 1900, *Lute Player,* USD 300. PARIS, 10-11 May 1900, *Tambourine Player,* FRF 210. PARIS, 9-10 and 11 April 1902, *Portrait of a Dutch Woman,* FRF 9,500. PARIS, 25 April 1907, *The Interrupted Game,* FRF 1,920. LONDON, 29 Feb 1908, *The Female Captive,* GBP 5. LONDON, 5 Dec 1908, *Christ at the House of Simon,* GBP 30. LONDON, 12 Dec 1908, *Portrait of Charles I* (1630) GBP 120. LONDON, 7 July 1911, *Portrait of George of Buckingham,* GBP 162. PARIS, 13 March 1920, *The Guitar Player,* FRF 660. LONDON, March 1922, *The Card Players,* GBP 25. LONDON, April 1922, *The Duet,* GBP 17. LONDON, May 1922, *Lady Playing the Mandolin,* GBP 42. LONDON, March 1923, *Brouwer in Prison,* GBP 11. LONDON, March 1923, *Musical Conversation,* GBP 294. LONDON, April 1923, *Five Children and Pet Dog,* GBP 73. LONDON, April 1923, *Young Man in Armour with a Brown Sash,* GBP 34. LONDON, March 1924, *Lord Falconberg in a Grey Doublet,* GBP 21. LONDON, 21 Nov 1924, *Sir Robert Honywood; Lady Honywood* (both) GBP 115. PARIS, 15 March 1925, *Motherhood,* FRF 3,100. LONDON, 12 Feb 1926, *Charles II as a Child,* GBP 131. LONDON, 25 March 1927, *Cavalier,* GBP 42. LONDON, 6 July 1927, *Lute Player,* GBP 29. PARIS, 25 Jan 1928, *Monarch Being Received in a Palace,* FRF 3,400. LONDON, 10 Feb 1928, *Portrait of a Woman,* GBP 28. LONDON, 1 June 1928, *The Laughing Musician,* GBP 78. PARIS, 28 Nov 1928, *The Merchant and his Wife Writing up their Accounts* (drawing) FRF 1,800. LONDON, 5 Dec 1928, *Young Man Playing the Mandolin,* GBP 90. LONDON, 22 Feb 1929, *Countess Emilia of Salms,* GBP 136. LONDON, 3 May 1929, *Young Man with a Glass of Wine,* GBP 294. LONDON, 13 Dec 1929, *Man in Armour with a Blue Sash,* GBP 52. LONDON, 27 Feb 1931, *Man in a Leather Tunic,* GBP 125. NEW YORK, 29 March 1934, *The Hurried Meal,* USD 250. LONDON, 22 Nov 1935, *Sir Hatton Fermor,* GBP 105. LONDON, 23 June 1937, *Two Musicians,* GBP 240. NEW YORK, 20 April 1939, *Thomas, Count Falconberg,* USD 1,100. LONDON, 4 Oct 1942, *Fruit Seller,* GBP 52. LONDON, 18 Feb 1944, *Musical Gathering,* GBP 336. NEW YORK, 20 Jan 1945, *The Stock Exchange,* USD 900. LONDON, 22 June 1945, *The Gentleman,* GBP 105. NEW YORK, 8 May 1957, *Woman with Miniature,* USD 1,200. LONDON, 4 Dec 1964, *Young Hermit Reading by Candlelight,* Gns 1,500. LONDON, 24 March 1965, *Portrait of King Charles I,* GBP 4,000. LONDON, 27 Nov 1968, *Frederick, King of Bohemia,* GBP 4,600. LONDON, 10 April 1970, *Musicians on a Balcony,* Gns 12,000. BRUSSELS, 23 March 1977, *The Tricksters* (oil on canvas, 64 1/4 x 86 1/2 ins / 163 x 220 cm) BEF 160,000. NEW YORK, 12 Jan 1979, *Portrait of a Young Man* (oil on panel, oval, 29 1/4 x 21 1/2 ins / 74 x 54.5 cm) USD 4,000. LONDON, 12 Dec 1980, *Portrait of Princess Hohenzollern-Hechingen* (1649, oil on panel, 51 1/4 x 37 ins / 130.2 x 94 cm) GBP 16,000. PARIS, 2 Dec 1982, *Diana Leaving for the Hunt* (oil on canvas, 38 1/4 x 63 ins / 97 x 160 cm) FRF 520,000. LONDON, 15 April 1983, *Portrait of Prince William of Orange* (1640, oil on canvas, 84 3/4 x 60 ins / 215.3 x 152.5 cm) GBP 13,000. LONDON, 19 April 1985, *Adoration of the Shepherds* (1632, oil on canvas, 48 x 39 3/4 ins / 122 x 101 cm) GBP 155,000. LONDON, 9 Dec 1987, *Man with a Glass of Wine* (oil on canvas, 29 3/4 x 25 1/2 ins / 75.5 x 65 cm) GBP 160,000. MILAN, 25 Oct 1988, *Ulysses and his Companions Blinding the Cyclops* (oil on canvas, 40 1/4 x 52 1/4 ins / 102 x 133 cm) ITL 105,000,000. STOCKHOLM, 15 Nov 1988, *The Infant Jesus Watched over by Angels* (oil, 72 3/4 x 54 ins / 185 x 137 cm) SEK 31,000. LONDON, 27 Oct 1989, *Bust Portrait of William, First Count Craven Wearing Armour* (oil on panel, 29 1/4 x 23 1/4 ins / 74 x 59 cm) GBP 4,620. LONDON, 11 July 1990, *Bust Portrait of a Lady Wearing a Yellow Dress and a Red Coat* (1647, oil on canvas, 28 1/4 x 22 1/2 ins / 71.5 x 57 cm) GBP 6,600. LONDON, 12 Dec 1990, *Phryne and Xenocrates* (1623, oil on canvas, 60 x 81 3/4 ins / 151.5 x 207.5 cm) GBP 209,000. NEW YORK, 14 Jan 1993, *Portrait of a Man Dressed in Black with a White Collar in a Painted Alcove* (oil on panel, 29 1/4 x 23 1/4 ins / 74.4 x 59.1 cm) USD 8,800. LONDON, 9 Dec 1994, *Bust Portrait of a Gentleman Wearing a Hat and a Black Costume with a White Collar* (1631, oil on canvas, 28 x 22 3/4 ins / 70.2 x 57.9 cm) GBP 46,600. LONDON, 4 July 1997, *Young Woman and her Maidservant* (oil on canvas, 43 1/4 x 35 1/4 ins / 110 x 89.5 cm) GBP 155,500. NEW YORK, 28 Jan 1999, *Courtesan in a Straw Hat with Viola da Gamba* (oil on canvas, 32 x 25 ins / 81 x 64 cm) USD 200,000. LONDON, 8 July 1999, *Portrait of Laughing Violinist in a Blue and Yellow Striped Doublet and Cap* (1624, oil on canvas, 32 x 26 ins / 82 x 65 cm) GBP 280,000. LONDON, 19 April 2000, *Portrait of Prince Edward of the Palatinate in Armour and Red Mantle* (1640s, oil on canvas, 43 x 35 ins / 110 x 88 cm) GBP 38,000. LONDON, 3 Nov 2000, *Portrait of King Frederick V of Bohemia a la Romaine* (1633, oil on panel, feigned oval, 20 x 15 ins / 50 x 39 cm) GBP 55,000. NEW YORK, 26 Jan 2001, *Young Woman Playing a Viola da Gamba* (oil on canvas, 33 x 26 ins / 84 x 66 cm) USD 450,000. LONDON, 9 July 2003, *The Tooth Extracter* (oil on canvas, 57 x 84 ins / 145 x 214 cm) GBP 5,000. NEW YORK, 29 Jan 2004, *The Crucifixion of St Peter. Man Holding a Post* (pen and ink, double-sided, 10 x 8 ins / 25 x 20 cm) USD 1,900. PARIS, 11 June 2004, *Portrait of a Woman with Pearls* (1644, oil on panel, 29 x 23 ins / 74 x 59 cm) EUR 3,800.

HONTHORST, Hendrik Aerstsz. van

Dutch, 17th century.

Painter.

Hendrik van Honthorst was active in Utrecht in 1622.

HONTHORST, Herman van

Dutch, 17th century.

Sculptor.

Herman van Honthorst was the brother of Gerrit and Willem van Honthorst. Originally from Utrecht, he moved to Antwerp and worked in that city.

HONTHORST, Tolnis

Dutch, 16th century.

Active in Utrecht in 1569.

Painter.

Tolnis Honthorst was the son of Domenicus Aerstsz. van Honthorst.

HONTHORST, Willem van

Dutch, 17th century.

Born 1594 or 1604, in Utrecht; died 1666; buried 19 February in Utrecht.

Painter. Portraits, genre scenes.

Having studied initially under Abraham Bloemart, Willem van Honthorst later received instruction from his elder brother Gerrit. On 21 June 1643 he married Sophia van Honthorst in The Hague and in 1646 left for Berlin to become court painter to Louisa Henrietta, daughter of Prince Frederick-Henry and wife of the Great Elector of Brandenburg. He remained in Germany until 1664 but eventually returned to his home city of Utrecht, where he died and was buried in the church of St Catherine.

Willem van Honthorst painted portraits of various royal personages, including Prince Frederick-Henry and Prince William II. In Germany he painted portraits of princes and princesses. As he signed his work with the same monogram as his brother, Gerrit van Honthorst, several of his pieces have been wrongly attributed to the latter. However,

Willem's style of painting was markedly different from that of his brother towards the end of his life.

Bibliography:

Braun, Hermann, *Gerard und Willem van Honthorst*, Göttingen, 1966.

Museums and Galleries:

Amsterdam: *Prince William II; Princes William II, Frederick-Henry-William II And William III* - Berlin: *Three Portraits: Prince and Princesses of Orange* - Copenhagen: *Portrait of a Woman* - Hanover: *Frederick, Prince Elector of the Palatinate; Frederick V; Wife of Frederick V; Miss de Valkenberg and d'Osimal; Amelia van Solms; Portrait of Charles-Louis of the Palatinate; Princess of Hohenzollern; Portrait of a Lady* - Utrecht: *Portrait of a Young Woman as Diana*.

Auction records:

London, June 1924, *Lady of Sixty-five in a Black Fur-Trimmed Gown*, GBP 26; *Adolescent in Black Costume with Slashes*, GBP 7. Paris, 14 Dec 1935, *Young Musician*, FRF 5,300. London, 15 July 1987, *Portrait of Prince Rupert* (oil on panel, oval, 29 1/4 x 23 ins / 74.5 x 58.5 cm) GBP 7,500. New York, 31 May 1990, *Portrait of a Gentleman in Armour with a Blue Sash; Portrait of a Lady in a Black Gown with a Lace Collar, Wearing a Pearl Necklace* (oil on panel, a pair, each 27 3/4 x 22 1/2 ins / 70.3 x 57.2 cm) USD 16,500. Paris, 13 June 1997, *The Young Singer* (1645, panel, three panels, 29 1/4 x 22 3/4 ins / 74 x 58 cm) FRF 145,000. North Bethesda, 10 Dec 1999, *Queen Henrietta Maria* (1633, oil on canvas, 44 x 34 ins / 112 x 86 cm) USD 5,500.

HONTI, Nandor
Hungarian, 20th century.
Born 25 April 1878, in Budapest.
Painter.

Nandor Honti studied at the Académie Julian in Paris.

HONTOIRE, Arnold
Flemish School, 17th century.
Born c. 1630, in Liège; died 5 May 1709, in Liège.
Sculptor, architect.

Arnold Hontoire worked primarily for the cathedral of St Lambert.

HONY, Thérèse Michèle
French, 18th century.
Active in Paris from 1752.
Painter.

HOO MOJONG, pseudonym of Ho Mojong
Chinese, 20th century.
Born 1929, in Shanghai, of Brazilian origin.
Active and naturalised in France.
Painter, engraver.

Hoo Mojong lives and works in Paris. In 1992 her work featured in *De Bonnard à Baselitz: Dix Ans d'Enrichissements du Cabinet des Estampes 1978-1988* (*From Bonnard to Baselitz: A Decade of Acquisitions by the Prints Collection 1978-1988*) in the Bibliothèque Nationale in Paris.

Museums and Galleries:

Paris (BNF): *Drunkards* (1982, etching).

HOOCH, Charles Cornelisz. de, or Carl, or Carel, or Hoogh
Dutch, 17th century.
Died 2 July 1638, in Utrecht.
Painter, engraver. Landscapes with figures, landscapes, interiors, ruins.

Little is known about the painter Charles de Hooch. He joined the Utrecht painters' guild in 1633, but had already made a gift of a landscape to the St Job hospice in 1628. He is believed to have died young, leaving a wife and young children. Hooch also worked as an engraver. In Berlin there is a series of four engravings executed by an unknown engraver after drawings by this artist. His paintings are characteristic of the period, which boasted gifted painters such as P. Molyn, Adam Willaerts and other landscape artists; Hooch ranks alongside them.

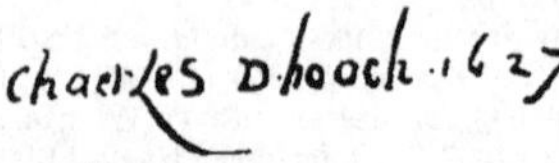

Museums and Galleries:

Amsterdam: *Landscape* - Château-Thierry: *Landscape* - Épinal: *Interior Ruins of a Town at the Thermal Baths of Titus in Rome* - Utrecht: *The Pigeon House*.

Auction records:

Paris, 14 Oct 1898, *Dutch Interior*, FRF 4,700. Paris, 26 Feb 1936, *Cavern Interior*, FRF 255. Vienna, 30 Nov 1976, *Bacchus, Venus and Ceres in a Landscape* (oil on panel, 21 x 38 3/4 ins / 53.5 x 98.5 cm) ATS 12,000. Vienna, 15 Sept 1982, *Bacchus, Venus and Ceres in a Landscape* (oil on panel, 21 x 38 3/4 ins / 53.5 x 98.5 cm) ATS 70,000. Paris, 15 June 1983, *River Landscape with Mill, in the Morning* (1624, oil on panel, 28 x 39 1/4 ins / 71 x 100 cm) FRF 25,000. London, 24 Oct 1986, *Peasants at a Well* (oil on panel, 25 x 30 1/2 ins / 62.6 x 77.2 cm) GBP 3,000. Amsterdam, 2 May 1991, *Travellers Admiring Classical Ruins in a Grotto* (oil on panel, 16 1/4 x 21 1/4 ins / 41.5 x 54 cm) NLG 9,200. London, 5 July 1991, *Gentleman by a Well at the Entrance to a Grotto containing a Sarcophagus* (oil on panel, 24 3/4 x 19 1/2 ins / 62.9 x 49.5 cm) GBP 23,100. Amsterdam, 17 Nov 1993, *Figures near Ruins* (oil on panel, 16 1/2 x 20 3/4 ins / 42 x 53 cm) NLG 9,430. Amsterdam, 11 Nov 1997, *Capriccio of Roman Tombs and Classical Ruins in a Grotto with Vagabonds Playing Cards at the Foot of a Column* (24 1/4 x 25 1/2 ins / 61.5 x 64.6 cm) NLG 10,378. London, 7 July 1999, *Open Landscape with Travellers Resting before a Dovecote* (oil on canvas, 15 x 19 ins / 37 x 48 cm) GBP 5,000. Paris, 24 March 2000, *Ruinous Landscape with Shepherds* (oil on panel, 11 x 17 ins / 28 x 43 cm) FRF 62,000. London, 18 April 2000, *Figures among Italianate Ruins* (oil on panel, 25 x 31 ins / 63 x 78 cm) GBP 3,600.

HOOCH, Gerrit de
Dutch, 17th century.
Active in The Hague c. 1670.
Painter.

Gerrit de Hooch is known to have painted landscapes.

HOOCH, Horatius de, or Hoogh
Dutch, 17th century.
Painter. Landscapes, waterscapes.

In 1669, Horatius de Hooch was a member of the Malerkollegium in Utrecht.

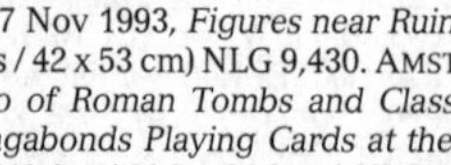

Museums and Galleries:

Copenhagen (Statens Mus. for Kunst): *Landscape with Ruins* - Stockholm: *Italian Landscape*.

Auction records:

London, June 1923, *Bay with Boats and Figures*, GBP 9. Paris, 11 Dec 1946, *River in a Mountain Landscape*, FRF 13,500. Amsterdam, 23 Nov 1971, *Italian Landscape*, NLG 9,000. New York, 16 June 1976, *River Landscape with Figures* (oil on canvas, 19 1/2 x 25 1/4 ins / 49.5 x 64 cm) USD 4,750. London, 19 April 1985, *Italian Landscape with Horseman by a Bridge* (oil on panel, 14 1/4 x 20 1/4 ins / 36.4 x 51.7 cm) GBP 5,500. Paris, 22 Oct 1999, *Peasants Stopping on the Edge of a Village* (oil on canvas, 31 x 27 ins / 79 x 69 cm) FRF 200,000.

BERLIN, 18 May 2001, *Temptation of St Anthony after Jacques Callot* (pen, 13 x 19 ins / 34 x 48 cm) DEM 4,400. PARIS, 19 Dec 2001, *River Landscape with Satyrs* (oil on panel, 15 x 21 ins / 38 x 54 cm) FRF 30,000. MADRID, 30 June 2003, *Italianate Landscape* (oil on canvas, 32 x 42 ins / 81 x 106 cm) EUR 16,000. LONDON, 29 Oct 2003, *Group Portrait of a Family in an Italianate Landscape* (oil on canvas, 36 x 48 ins / 91 x 121 cm) GBP 2,600. COLOGNE, 1 July 2004, *Southern River Landscape with a Bridge and Figures* (oil on canvas, 33 x 40 ins / 85 x 102 cm) EUR 7,500.

HOOCH, Pieter de, or Hoogh or Hooghe
Dutch, 17th century.
Born 1629, in Rotterdam; died 1684, in Haarlem.
Painter. Genre scenes, interiors with figures.
Delft School.

Born in Rotterdam in 1629, Pieter de Hooch was three years older than Vermeer and younger than Van Ostade, Jan Steen and Terborch. Almost nothing is known about his life, although we do know that he was a pupil of Berchem and perhaps also of Rembrandt.

At the end of the 16th century in the Low Countries a major historical event took place that was to have enormous political, social and artistic consequences - in 1566 the Protestant provinces of the north embarked on a struggle for liberation from Catholic Spain. This struggle, which continued until 1609, saw the formation of an independent federal republic - the first in Europe - while the provinces of the south (Flanders) remained a Spanish dependency. Thus, while the populace of Flanders upheld their Catholic traditions and remained under the influence of Spain, from the early 17th century onwards Protestant Holland developed its own identity, and its artists found their most important sources of inspiration in studying the region's landscape and the daily lives of its inhabitants, avoiding religious subjects.

Unlike his contemporaries Jan Steen and Van Ostade, Pieter de Hooch remained on the margins of the celebration of Flemish life. The rupture that took place between the provinces of the north and those of the south can be clearly seen in his work: the young republic turned in upon itself and the Protestant religion encouraged the pleasant austerity that can be seen in his interiors and which to some extent became the keynote of his art. His profound feeling for the intimate and his love of these homely houses protected from the strong light of his native country are his trademark and although he may perhaps not attain the impossible perfection of Vermeer, he nevertheless merits comparison. One of the differences between the two artists is that Vermeer adopts a highly polished approach to the use of colour, filtering the light in an intimate, soft, hazy fashion by reducing each scene to a self-contained space and by concentrating the interest of the composition on the interiorised expression of the central characters. In the work of Pieter de Hooch, however, the colour is smooth, reflecting a light that is harsh and bright like metal; closed and open spaces alternate in skilful geometry with each element opening on to the exterior; the characters of his paintings exist only physically, not mentally - they are figures placed there to bring life to the setting. In Vermeer everything moves from the exterior towards the interior, whereas for De Hooch the movement is from the interior to the exterior.

Pieter de Hooch also painted many exteriors - a somewhat simplistic and traditional term but one that is highly appropriate here, since his exteriors closely interact with the interiors of which he was so fond. The subject is almost invariably the courtyard of a Dutch house, in which quiet figures go calmly about their business. However, the painter's concern with light and his determination to use it methodically is ever-present. Similarly, when he paints interiors, it is unusual not to find doors giving on to staircases or revealing glimpses of trees in a garden, giving the simultaneous impression that the main painting is the antechamber or complement to another picture; De Hooch was the master of extending the intimacy of the Dutch house out into the street.

Pieter De Hooch was harshly judged by critics in succeeding centuries. In the 18th century, Descamp in his *Vie des Peintres* (*Painters' Lives*) remained impervious to the merits and originality of Pieter de Hooch, appearing to make little distinction between him and Metsu or Mieris: 'His touch is broader than that of Mieris or Metsu but his paintings fail to capture the same polished finish! He cannot therefore be considered to occupy the same rank'. For many years this harsh judgement remained the received opinion. Even Vermeer, several of whose works were attributed to De Hooch (*Woman Reading* in the Dresden museum), had to wait until the end of the 19th century to gain the recognition he deserved. On the other hand, Fromentin in his *Maîtres d'Autrefois* (*Masters of the Past*) (1875) barely mentions Vermeer but devotes several very comprehensive pages to De Hooch. Pieter De Hooch's work has featured in various thematic exhibitions, including: in 2001, *Twee gouden eeuwen: schilderkunst uit Nederland en Denemarken* (*Two Golden Ages: Masterpieces of Dutch and Danish Painting*) at the Rijksmuseum, Amsterdam; 2003, *Vermeer y el interior holandés* (*Vermeer and the Dutch Interior*) at the Prado Museum in Madrid.

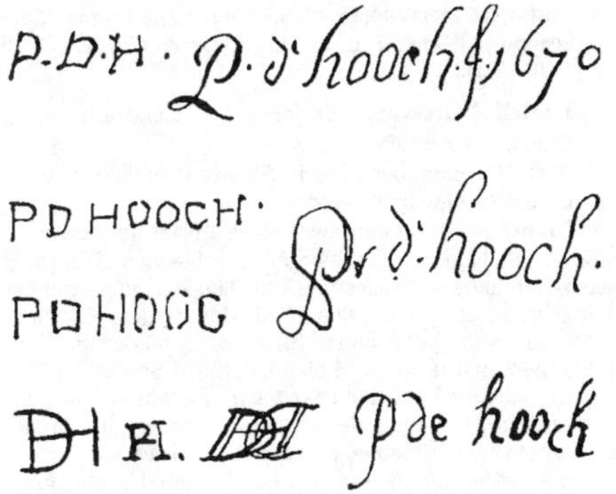

BIBLIOGRAPHY:

Sutton, Peter C., *Pieter de Hooch*, Phaidon, Oxford, 1980. Sutton, Peter C., *Peter de Hooch, 1629-1684*, exhibition catalogue, Wadsworth Museum in Association with Yale University Press, Hartford, 1998. Vergara, Alejandro/Westermann, Mariët, *Vermeer and the Dutch Interior*, group exhibition catalogue, Museo Nacional del Prado, Madrid, 2003 (texts in Spanish and English).

MUSEUMS AND GALLERIES:

AIX: *Interior of a House* - AMSTERDAM (Rijksmus.): *The Storeroom; Interior; Interior with a Mother delousing her Child's Hair (A Mother's Duty)* (1658-60); *House in the Country; Maternal Joy; Interior with Women by a Linen Chest* - BERLIN: *The Dead Pig; Interior of Dutch Dwelling House* - BERLIN (Gemäldegal.): *The Mother* - COPENHAGEN (Statens Mus. for Kunst): *Couple Dancing a Minuet; Musical Society; Mother of a Family Giving Orders* - DARMSTADT: *Interior Scenes* - DUBLIN: *Backgammon Players* - HAMBURG: *Messenger of Love* - LILLE: *Interior of a Dutch House* - LONDON (NG): *A Man with Dead Birds, and Other Figures, in a Stable* (c. 1655, oil/wood); *The Courtyard of a House in Delft* (1658, oil on canvas); *An Interior, with a Woman drinking with Two Men, and a Maidservant* (1658?, oil on canvas); *Woman and her Maid in a Courtyard* (1660-1661, oil on canvas); *A Musical Party in a Courtyard*

(1677, oil on canvas) - LONDON (Wallace Collection): *A Woman Peeling Apples* (c. 1663, oil on canvas); *A Boy Bringing Bread* (c. 1650-1665, oil on canvas) - MONTREAL: *Interior* - MONTREAL (Learmont Collection): *Dutch Interior* - MUNICH: *Dutch Interior* - NUREMBERG: *Genre Painting* - PARIS (Louvre): *Two Dutch Interiors* - ROME (Mus. e Gal. Borghese): *Around a Flute Player* - ROTTERDAM (Mus. Boijmans Van Beuningen): *The Empty Glass; The Fish* - ST PETERSBURG (Hermitage): *A Lady and her Cook; A Concert; Interior* - STOCKHOLM: *Interior* - STRASBOURG: *The Outing* - VIENNA: *The Mother.*

AUCTION RECORDS:

PARIS, 1831, *The Wet Nurse,* FRF 12,000. LONDON, 30 June 1971, *Interior with a Young Woman Feeding a Parrot,* GBP 32,000. LONDON, 9 July 1999, *Mother and Child with Serving Woman in Interior, Hallway beyond* (oil on panel, 17 x 15 ins / 43 x 38 cm) GBP 140,000. LONDON, 9 July 1999, *Interior with Two Gentlemen and a Woman beside a Fire* (oil on canvas, 17 x 21 ins / 44 x 53 cm) GBP 160,000. NEW YORK, 28 Jan 2000, *Interior with Lady Feeding Parrot with a Gentleman Handing her a Letter* (oil on canvas, 22 x 20 ins / 57 x 51 cm) USD 80,000. NEW YORK, 25 May 2000, *Lady and Gentleman Making Music with Dancing Dogs* (oil on canvas, 24 x 21 ins / 62 x 53 cm) USD 120,000. LONDON, 12 July 2001, *Man and Serving Woman behind a Screen, with Card Players beyond* (oil on canvas, 35 x 32 ins / 88 x 81 cm) GBP 170,000. LONDON, 12 Dec 2002, *Interior with Mother Nursing her Children before a Fireplace* (oil on canvas, 33 x 32 ins / 84 x 82 cm) GBP 80,000. LONDON, 7 July 2004, *Card Players at Table* (oil on canvas, 42 x 37 ins / 107 x 93 cm) GBP 1,100,000. VIENNA, 29 Sept 2004, *The Visitor - Cavalier Visiting an Elegant Lady* (oil on canvas, 29 x 25 ins / 73 x 64 cm) EUR 28,000.

HOOCH, Romeyn de, or Hooge, Hooghe
Dutch, 17th century.
Born 10 September 1646, in Amsterdam; died 1708; buried 15 June in Haarlem.
Painter, sculptor, engraver, illustrator, draughtsman.

Romeyn de Hooch was the nephew of Pieter de Hooch. He worked initially in Amsterdam and Haarlem before going to Paris in 1662 at the invitation of Van der Meulen. He worked in Paris for some years and in 1675 was granted letters of nobility there by the king of Poland, John III Sobieski (r.1674-96). In 1683 he is known to have been a member of the painters' guild in The Hague. He returned to Haarlem in 1687, and appears to have remained there until his death.

Romeyn de Hooch was a highly original artist, full of verve, and also an outstanding engraver, although his work can sometimes be criticised for a lack of precision in the draughtsmanship. He engraved mythological subjects, portraits, historical subjects and landscapes. He also illustrated La Fontaine's *Contes et Nouvelles en Vers* (published in Amsterdam by Henry Desbordes in 1685), producing 58 drawings of figures and engravings.

MUSEUMS AND GALLERIES:

AMSTERDAM: *Allegorical Composition.*

AUCTION RECORDS:

AMSTERDAM, 19 April 1982, *View of Dunkirk* (pen and wash/outline in black chalk/three joined sheets of paper, 9 3/4 x 62 ins / 24.8 x 157.2 cm) NLG 3,600. PARIS, 17 April 1985, *The Three Graces* (pen, 7 x 4 3/4 ins / 18 x 12 cm) FRF 13,000. PARIS, 4 March 1988, *Esther and Ahasuerus* (pen and wash, 6 x 3 3/4 ins / 15 x 9.5 cm) FRF 2,500. PARIS, 22 Nov 1988, *Allegory of William of Orange* (pen and grey wash, 12 1/2 x 8 1/2 ins / 32 x 21.5 cm) FRF 6,000. MONACO, 5-6 Dec 1991, *Two Warriors on Horseback* (red chalk, a pair, 8 x 6 1/4 ins / 20.5 x 16 cm) FRF 14,430. AMSTERDAM, 9 Nov 1999, *The Brothers de Witt Set Upon by a Crowd* (brush and brown ink wash heightened with white over black chalk, 8 x 13 ins / 21 x 32 cm) NLG 10,000. AMSTERDAM, 9 Nov 1999, *Arrival of Johan de Witt at The Hague* (brush and brown ink wash heightened with white over black chalk, 8 x 13 ins / 21 x 32 cm) NLG 10,000. LONDON, 12 July 2001, *Italianate Landscape with Herders and Animals among Roman Ruins* (oil on copper, 6 x 7 ins / 16 x 18 cm) GBP 23,000.

HOOCHSTADT, Gabriel van, or Ofstadt, Hofstadt
Flemish School, 17th century.
Born 1625, according to Descamps; died 1690.
Active in Antwerp.
Painter.

According to Clément de Ris, Gabriel van Hoochstadt painted altarpieces in Brussels. In 1685 he joined the Antwerp painters' guild. Hoochstadt is possibly the same person as the artist known by the forename Geeraert, who worked in Brussels.

HOOD, George Percy Jacomb. See **JACOMB-HOOD**

HOOD, George Washington
American, 19th - 20th century.
Born 2 September 1869, in New York; died 1949.
Illustrator.

George Washington Hood trained at the National Academy of Design, New York. He illustrated works on China, Brazil, Sweden and Spain.

HOOD, Gilles
Flemish, 15th century.
Active in Mechelen c. 1430.
Sculptor (wood).
Flemish School.

HOOD, John
British, 18th century.
Active in Limehouse.
Painter, watercolourist. Seascapes.

John Hood exhibited in London at the Society of Artists and the Free Society from 1762 to 1771.

HOOD, Thomas, the Elder
British, 19th century.
Born 23 May 1799, in London; died 3 May 1845, in London.
Engraver, illustrator, poet, humorist.

Thomas Hood the Elder, a pupil of Le Keux, was best known as an illustrator.

HOOD, Thomas, the Younger, called Tom Hood
British, 19th century.
Born 13 January 1835, in Wapstead; died 20 November 1874, in Peckham Rye (London).
Engraver, draughtsman.

Tom Hood contributed to a number of satirical magazines.

HOOF
German, 19th century.
Active in Berlin in the early 19th century.
Architect, painter. Architectural views.

HOOF, Jef van
Belgian, 20th century.
Born 1928, in Brussels.
Painter, draughtsman. Landscapes.

Van Hoof studied at the school of fine arts in La Cambre in Brussels at the same time as studying at the university for a degree in literature, history of art, archaeology, and ethnography (in which he specialised). He was essentially a landscape painter and violently depicted the psychological climate in an Impressionist style reminiscent of Permeke. He exhibited in solo exhibitions in Brussels in 1959, 1960 and 1962, Antwerp in 1964, Paris in 1967, and elsewhere.

MUSEUMS AND GALLERIES:

BRUSSELS (Bibliothèque royale Albert Ier, Prints Collection).

AUCTION RECORDS:
CALAIS, 5 April 1992, *Walking on a Deserted Moor* (oil on canvas, 22 x 25 1/2 ins / 55 x 65 cm) FRF 6,500. PRATO, 8 May 2003, *Pagliaio* (oil on canvas, 39 x 47 ins / 100 x 120 cm) EUR 5,500.

HOOFT, J.
Dutch, 17th century.
Painter. Landscapes.
J. Hooft has sometimes been confused with Nicolas Hooft.

HOOFT, Nicolas
Dutch, 17th - 18th century.
Born 1664, in The Hague; died 21 January 1748, in The Hague.
Painter. History painting, genre scenes, landscapes with figures, landscapes.
Nicolas Hooft was a pupil of Daniel Mytens, Doudyns and, in 1687, of Aug. Terwesten.

MUSEUMS AND GALLERIES:
LEIPZIG: *Landscapes* (several versions) - STOCKHOLM: *Landscapes* (several versions).
AUCTION RECORDS:
AMSTERDAM, 15 May 1979, *Wooded Landscape with Figures* (oil on panel, 19 x 25 1/4 ins / 48 x 64 cm) NLG 17,000.

HOOFT, Pieter Adriaensz.
Dutch, 17th century.
Active in The Hague in 1639.
Sculptor.
Pieter Hooft also worked in Utrecht.

HOOFT, R.
Dutch, 17th century.
Active in 1656.
Painter. Landscapes.
There is a landscape signed and dated by *R. Hooft*.

HOOFT, W. J.
Dutch, 19th century.
Active in Amsterdam c. 1818.
Painter. Landscapes, still-lifes.

HOOFT, Willem Dirks
Dutch, 17th century.
Active in Amsterdam in 1617.
Glass painter.
Willem Hooft worked for various clients, including the church of Schermehoorn.

HOOG. See also **HAAG**

HOOG, Johan Friedrick Christian. See **HAAG**

HOOG, Johann Bernhard de
Dutch, 19th - 20th century.
Born 1866 or 1867, in Amsterdam; died 1943, in The Hague.
Painter. Portraits, genre scenes.
De Hoog painted very straightforward genre scenes, concentrating on everyday domestic scenes, especially interiors, motherhood and children's games. He signed his works *B. de Hoog*.

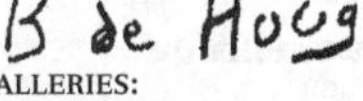

MUSEUMS AND GALLERIES:
BLACKBURN (Mus. & AG): *Dutch Interior* (oil on canvas).
AUCTION RECORDS:
NEW YORK, 19 April 1907, *Dutch Baby*, USD 230. LONDON, 18 Jan 1908, *Frugal Meal*, GBP 56. LONDON, 4 July 1910, *Midday Meal*, GBP 86. NEW YORK, 15-17 March 1911, *Humble Interior*, USD 1,000. LONDON, Nov 1921, *Happy Family*, GBP 152. LONDON, Feb 1922, *Rustic Home*, GBP 136. LONDON, 20 July 1923, *Motherhood*, GBP 68. LONDON, 23 Jan 1925, *Happy Family*, GBP 147. LONDON, 1 and 2 June 1927, *At the Seaside*, GBP 99. GLASGOW, 18 June 1931, *Mother and Children on the Beach*, GBP 86. LONDON, 24 Nov 1933, *Motherhood*, GBP 78. LONDON, 15 Dec 1939, *Interior Scene*, GBP 21. LONDON, 3 July 1942, *Midday Meal*, GBP 57. LONDON, 8 Oct 1943, *Mother at Work*, GBP 94. GLASGOW, 8 March 1945, *Happy Moments in Childhood*, GBP 180. NEW YORK, 29 March 1945, *Peasant Woman and Child*, USD 600. LONDON, 22 Nov 1946, *Mother's Caresses*, GBP 120. LONDON, 2 Nov 1973, *Mending*, Gns 1,100. LONDON, 12 June 1974, *Little Brother*, GBP 1,200. LOS ANGELES, 9 June 1976, *Motherhood* (oil on canvas, 30 x 24 ins / 76 x 61 cm) USD 2,300. NEW YORK, 7 Oct 1977, *Preparing Dinner* (oil on canvas, 19 1/4 x 17 ins / 49 x 43 cm) USD 7,000. LONDON, 20 April 1979, *Maternal Love* (oil on canvas, 38 3/4 x 49 ins / 98.5 x 124.5 cm) GBP 4,500. NEW YORK, 28 May 1982, *Woman Sitting near a Cradle* (oil on canvas, 24 x 30 ins / 61 x 76.2 cm) USD 5,000. NEW YORK, 27 May 1983, *Newborn* (oil on canvas, 31 3/4 x 39 3/4 ins / 80.6 x 101 cm) USD 5,000. LONDON, 25 March 1987, *Young Peasant Woman Washing Clothes* (oil on canvas, 39 1/4 x 25 1/2 ins / 100 x 65 cm) GBP 8,500. LONDON, 26 Feb 1988, *Paternal Love* (oil on canvas, 20 x 17 1/4 ins / 51 x 44 cm) GBP 4,400. NEW YORK, 25 May 1988, *Helping Mummy* (oil on canvas, 19 3/4 x 25 3/4 ins / 50.1 x 65.4 cm) USD 8,250. COLOGNE, 15 Oct 1988, *Young Woman Sitting near a Window with her Child* (oil on panel, 7 1/4 x 5 ins / 18.5 x 13 cm) DEM 2,000. TORONTO, 30 Nov 1988, *Dutch Interior with a Young Mother Breast-feeding her Baby* (oil on canvas, 19 1/2 x 15 1/4 ins / 49.5 x 39 cm) CAD 6,000. NEW YORK, 23 May 1989, *Still-life with Vase of Roses and Marguerites* (oil on card, 13 3/4 x 10 1/2 ins / 35 x 26.7 cm) USD 23,100. LONDON, 7 June 1989, *Sewing Lesson* (oil on canvas, 11 1/2 x 15 1/4 ins / 29 x 38.5 cm) GBP 7,700. MONTREAL, 30 Oct 1989, *Interior Scene with Mother and Children* (oil on canvas, 16 1/4 x 20 ins / 41 x 51 cm) CAD 8,800. EDINBURGH, 22 Nov 1989, *Breakfast Time* (oil on canvas, 31 3/4 x 39 3/4 ins / 80.6 x 100.9 cm) GBP 4,620. NEW YORK, 17 Jan 1990, *Maternal Tenderness* (oil on canvas, 27 x 22 1/2 ins / 68.6 x 57.4 cm) USD 6,050. LONDON, 14 Feb 1990, *Mother and Little Girl Playing with Dolls* (oil on canvas, 15 3/4 x 11 3/4 ins / 40 x 30 cm) GBP 3,960. AMSTERDAM, 2 May 1990, *Taking Care of the Baby* (oil on canvas, 36 x 28 1/2 ins / 91.5 x 72.5 cm) NLG 10,925. STOCKHOLM, 16 May 1990, *Mother with her Baby in her Arms Sitting in front of the Fire* (oil on canvas, 26 3/4 x 22 ins / 68 x 56 cm) SEK 23,000. NEW YORK, 23 May 1990, *In the Dunes* (oil on canvas, 32 x 43 1/2 ins / 81.2 x 110.5 cm) USD 11,000. LONDON, 5 Oct 1990, *Young Family* (oil on canvas, 40 x 47 1/2 ins / 101.6 x 120.7 cm) GBP 13,200. NEW YORK, 24 Oct 1990, *Mother and Child in an Interior* (oil on canvas, 20 x 15 1/2 ins / 50.8 x 39.4 cm) USD 10,450. GLASGOW, 22 Nov 1990, *Newborn* (oil on canvas, 16 x 20 ins / 40.7 x 50.8 cm) GBP 4,400. AMSTERDAM, 24 April 1991, *Waiting for Father to Return* (oil on canvas, 15 3/4 x 19 3/4 ins / 40 x 50 cm) NLG 8,625. MONTREAL, 4 June 1991, *Youngest Sister* (oil on canvas, 20 x 25 1/2 ins / 50.8 x 65 cm) CAD 5,000. LONDON, 4 Oct 1991, *Little Crybaby* (oil on canvas, 27 x 22 1/2 ins / 68.6 x 57.1 cm) GBP 6,820. NEW YORK, 15 Oct 1991, *Family in an Interior* (oil on canvas, 35 3/4 x 47 1/4 ins / 90.8 x 120.3 cm) USD 7,150. MONTREAL, 19 Nov 1991, *Feeding the Baby* (oil on canvas, 18 x 21 3/4 ins / 46 x 55.5 cm) CAD 7,000. NEW YORK, 20 Feb 1992, *Helping Mummy* (oil on canvas, 24 x 30 ins / 61 x 76.2 cm) USD 10,450. AMSTERDAM, 14-15 April 1992, *Happy Family* (oil on canvas, 24 3/4 x 20 1/4 ins / 63 x 51.5 cm) NLG 22,425. NEW YORK, 18 Feb 1993, *Mother and Children Sitting near a Sunny Window* (oil on canvas, 49 1/2 x 37 1/2 ins / 126 x 95.2 cm) USD 15,400. AMSTERDAM, 19 Oct 1993, *Happy Family* (oil on canvas, 59 1/2 x 47 1/4 ins / 151 x 120 cm) NLG 32,200. LOKEREN, 12 March 1994, *Interior Scene* (oil on canvas, 23 1/2 x 22 ins / 60 x 56 cm) BEF 180,000. LONDON, 18 March 1994, *Sewing Room* (oil on canvas, 31 x 38 1/2 ins / 78.7 x 97.8 cm) GBP 18,400. NEW YORK, 16 Feb 1995, *Morning Conversation*

(oil on canvas, 31 3/4 x 39 3/4 ins / 80.6 x 101 cm) USD 12,650. AMSTERDAM, 7 Nov 1995, *Blue Blouse* (oil on canvas, 19 1/4 x 15 3/4 ins / 49 x 40 cm) NLG 11,210. AMSTERDAM, 5 Nov 1996, *Happy Family* (oil on canvas, 20 x 24 ins / 50.5 x 61 cm) NLG 9,440. LONDON, 22 Nov 1996, *Mother and Children in an Interior* (oil on canvas, 12 x 16 ins / 30.5 x 40.6 cm) GBP 1,610. MONTREAL, 3 Dec 1996, *Little Girls' Wooden Horse and Cart* (oil on canvas, 24 x 29 1/2 ins / 61 x 75 cm) CAD 9,000; *Peeling Apples* (oil on canvas, 20 x 16 ins / 50.8 x 40.5 cm) CAD 5,250. LONDON, 26 March 1997, *Having a Break* (oil on canvas, 32 1/2 x 39 3/4 ins / 82.5 x 101 cm) GBP 13,800. AMSTERDAM, 22 April 1997, *Breakfast* (oil on canvas, 25 3/4 x 38 1/2 ins / 65.5 x 97.5 cm) NLG 43,660. NEW YORK, 23 Oct 1997, *Mealtime* (oil on canvas, 21 x 25 ins / 53.3 x 63.5 cm) USD 8,050. LONDON, 21 Nov 1997, *Feeding the Baby* (oil on canvas, 40 x 47 1/2 ins / 100.7 x 120.6 cm) GBP 9,430. NEW YORK, 12 Feb 1998, *Domestic Interior* (1903, oil on canvas, 47 1/2 x 58 1/2 ins / 120.7 x 148.6 cm) USD 18,400. AMSTERDAM, 27 April 1999, *Domestic Family Scene* (oil on canvas, 20 x 25 ins / 50 x 64 cm) NLG 32,000. AMSTERDAM, 25 Oct 1999, *Ideal Domestic Circle* (oil on canvas, 60 x 80 ins / 152 x 202 cm) NLG 34,000. AMSTERDAM, 24 Oct 2000, *Young Family* (oil on canvas, 36 x 30 ins / 91 x 76 cm) NLG 37,000. AMSTERDAM, 25 Oct 2000, *Birthday* (1925, oil on canvas, 31 x 39 ins / 80 x 99 cm) NLG 52,000. COLOGNE, 5 April 2001, *Interior with Family* (oil on canvas, 52 x 25 ins / 131 x 64 cm) DEM 22,000. DUBLIN, 16 May 2001, *Mother, Child and Sleeping Infant* (oil on canvas, 20 x 26 ins / 50 x 65 cm) IEP 12,000. AMSTERDAM, 23 Oct 2002, *Washing Day* (oil on canvas, 39 x 31 ins / 100 x 80 cm) EUR 25,000. UPPSALA, 25 May 2003, *Interior with Family* (oil on canvas, 24 x 30 ins / 60 x 75 cm) SEK 65,000. AMSTERDAM, 1 July 2003, *Doctor's Visit* (oil on canvas, 37 x 50 ins / 95 x 126 cm) EUR 8,500. AMSTERDAM, 21 April 2004, *Playing in the Dunes* (oil on canvas, 26 x 33 ins / 65 x 85 cm) EUR 18,000. LONDON, 17 Nov 2004, *Happy Family* (oil on canvas, 0 x 48 ins / 0 x 121 cm) GBP 8,500.

HOOGCARSPEL, Olfert
Dutch, 18th century.
Died 5 December 1778, in Alkmaar.
Painter.

HOOGE, Jan van der
Dutch, 17th century.
Active c. 1680.
Painter.
Jan van der Hooge is mentioned by Houbraken, with the soubriquet 'Charon'.

HOOGENBERG. See **HOGENBERGH**

HOOGENHOUCK
Dutch, 17th century.
Active in Haarlem.
Painter.
In 1636, a painting by Hoogenhouck is mentioned in a lottery in Haarlem.

HOOGENRAAD, Andries
Dutch, 20th - 21st century.
Born 1955, in Utrecht.
Sculptor.
From 1977 to 1983 Hoogenraad attended the Van Eyck art academy in Maastricht. He shows his works in many exhibitions in the Netherlands and abroad. His sculptures, which are arrangements of metal pieces, look like impressive machines.

HOOGERHEYDEN, Engel
Dutch, 18th century.
Born 1740, in Middelburg; died 1809, in Middelburg.
Painter. Seascapes.
MUSEUMS AND GALLERIES:
AMSTERDAM: two seascapes.
AUCTION RECORDS:
LONDON, 30 Jan 1970, *Fishing Boat Returning to Port; Three-Master in Heavy Seas* (two panels) Gns 800. AMSTERDAM, 30 Oct 1979, *Sailing Ships off the Coast* (1807, two oils on panel, 6 1/2 x 9 1/4 ins / 16.5 x 23.5 cm) NLG 17,500. AMSTERDAM, 17 Nov 1994, *The Vessel of the "Slot ter Hooge" Indies Company Preparing to Go to Sea* (oil on canvas, 34 x 53 3/4 ins / 86.1 x 136.7 cm) NLG 32,000.

HOOGERS, Hendrik
Dutch, 18th - 19th century.
Born 24 March 1747, in Nijmegen; died 24 October 1814, in Nijmegen.
Painter, draughtsman. History painting, portraits, genre scenes, landscapes.
AUCTION RECORDS:
HANOVER, 16 June 1979, *Flight into Egypt* (1792, oil on panel, 14 x 17 1/4 ins / 35.5 x 43.5 cm) DEM 20,000. PARIS, 4 March 1988, *Study of a Woman* (lead pencil heightened with white, 13 x 11 ins / 33 x 27 cm) FRF 2,000. AMSTERDAM, 11 Nov 1997, *Noah Warning Men of the Flood* (1773, pen, brown and grey ink, wax/black chalk, 9 1/4 x 10 ins / 23.2 x 25.5 cm) NLG 6,136. PARIS, 3 April 1998, *Scene from Parisian Life* (1771, grey wash, 7 x 7 ins / 16.9 x 18 cm) FRF 4,000.

HOOGERS, Willem Carel
Dutch, 18th - 19th century.
Born 3 September 1774, in Nijmegen.
Watercolourist.
Willem Hoogers was the son of Hendrick Hoogers and a pupil of Jacob van Eynden.

HOOGEVEEN, G. van
Dutch, 18th century.
Active in Amsterdam.
Draughtsman.
G. van Hoogeveen painted sets for the theatre in Amsterdam.

HOOGH, Charles, Horatius and Pieter de.
See **HOOCH**

HOOGH, Dirck de
Dutch, 17th century.
Born 1613, in The Hague.
Painter. Portraits.
Dirck de Hoogh was a pupil of Pieter Gruast. He worked in Amsterdam and later in Königsberg, East Prussia (now Kaliningrad, Russia).

HOOGH, Eliseus de
Dutch, 17th century.
Active in Rotterdam in 1698.
Painter.

HOOGHE, Anthonie de
Flemish School, 17th century.
Born 1630, in Bruges; died 4 August 1662.
Miniaturist. Landscapes.

HOOGHE, Balthasar Richard de
Flemish School, 17th century.
Baptised 6 October 1636 in Bruges; died 2 December 1697.
Landscape artist.
In 1656, Balthasar de Hooghe entered Dunes abbey. He was the brother of Anthonie de Hooghe.

HOOGHE, Cornelis de
Dutch, 16th century.
Born in The Hague; died 29 March 1583, in The Hague.
Engraver.
Cornelis de Hooghe studied with P. Galle, worked for some time in England and then settled in Delft. He produced maps and views of cities and monuments, including a map of Holland dated 1567. He seems also to have been an adventurer,

working for the Spanish interest and claiming to be a natural son of Charles V. He was apparently protected by the Duke of Gelderland. He was beheaded in The Hague after an attempt on the life of William of Orange.

HOOGHE, Pieter and Romeyn de.
See **HOOCH**

HOOGHENBERG, Hans or Johann
Dutch, 16th - 17th century.
Active in Cologne c. 1594-1605.
Engraver.

Hans Hooghenberg was probably a brother of Abraham Hogenbergh. He mostly engraved portraits and historical subjects.

HOOGHSCHILT, David
Dutch, 17th century.
Died c. 1691, in Leiden.
Painter.

HOOGHSTAEL, Gérard van, or Hoogstad, Hoostadt
Flemish School, 17th century.
Born 1625, in Brussels.
Painter.

Gerard van Hooghstael painted a number of works for various churches in Brussels, including a *Passion of Christ* at the church of St Gudula.

HOOGHSTOEL, Jean Marie
French, 18th century.
Born 1765, in Paris.
Painter, art restorer.

Jean Marie Hooghstoel studied under David, Vincent, Doyen and his own father. He exhibited at the Salon in 1793 and 1799. A restorer, he worked for the galleries of such Empire grandees as the duke of Dalmatia (Marshal Soult) and the duke of Padua, Napoleon's first cousin. He worked at the Louvre for Pajou and then for Denon.

HOOGKAMER, Willem H.
Dutch, 19th century.
Died 1864, in Arnhem.
Active in Utrecht.
Draughtsman, engraver.

Willem Hoogkamer is known for his *Battle of Waterloo*.

HOOGLAND, William
American, 19th century.
Active in New York.
Engraver.

William Hoogland produced portraits of *Lafayette* and *Queen Maria Christina of Spain*.

HOOGSAAT, Jan, or Hoogzaat
Dutch, 17th - 18th century.
Born 12 March 1664, in Amsterdam; died c. 1730, in Amsterdam.
Painter. History painting, genre scenes.

Jan Hoogsaat was a pupil of Lairesse. He worked at Loo Palace for William III.

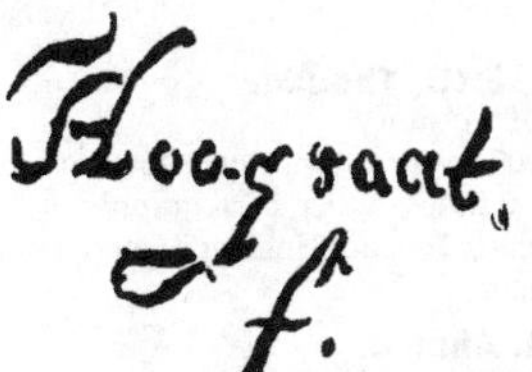

MUSEUMS AND GALLERIES:
GRENOBLE: *Young Woman Holding Flowers* - STOCKHOLM: *St Paul Welcoming a Disciple; Christ Healing a Leper.*

HOOGSTEYNS, Jan
Belgian, 20th century.
Born 9 October 1935, in Beverlo.
Painter, draughtsman. Figures, nudes, landscapes, still-lifes.

Hoogsteyns was influenced by various different movements in his early years as an artist. His biographer, Guy van Hoof, pinpointed the emergence of his individual style with his winning of the Renaix prize in 1970. Hoogsteyn himself agrees with this assessment: 'Around that time my works were shrouded in mist'. The colours he used, barely tinted shades of white or lightly coloured shades of pale grey, were made softer by this misty effect.

As with the Impressionists, the role of drawing - and consequently that of the subject - became minimal in Hoogsteyn's paintings as he developed the subtleties in his new harmonies of colour. The subject became simply a pretext and prop for his poetic creations of colour. Nevertheless, both his shaded and line drawings continued to demonstrate his perfect mastery of the skill. His landscapes, usually covered in snow, can hardly be seen through the iridescent effect of the mist that envelops them; the hazy nudes become purely an evocative but nevertheless discreetly sensual suggestion of the form; his still-lifes, showing little in the way of detail with the sudden colour of the objects piercing the delicate blue or golden expanse of the table, have a luminist quality similar to paintings by Morandi. In the arbitrary categorisation of artists' work it is rare that a painter can be classified so justifiably as an Intimist, in the style developed by Pierre Bonnard.

Hoogsteyns took part in collective exhibitions in Belgium, in several other European countries and the USA. He showed collections in solo exhibitions in Brussels and many other towns in Belgium; in The Hague and several other places in the Netherlands; in London and other places in Great Britain; in some towns, including Düsseldorf, in Germany; in Paris; and in the USA. He won the *Limburgse Dag* first prize in 1956, the Renaix town prize in 1974, the Aarschot town prize in 1972 and the Oudenaarde town prize in 1974.

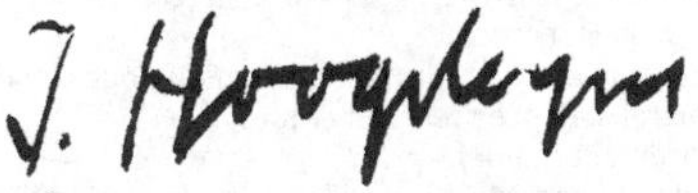

BIBLIOGRAPHY:
Van Hoof, Guy, *Jan Hoogsteyns*, Antiqua Tessenderlo, Antwerp, 1980 (extensive documentation). Van Wilderode, Anton, *Jan Hoogsteyns*, Ars Libris, Brussels, 1998.

MUSEUMS AND GALLERIES:
LA LOUVIÈRE (Mus. Ianchelevici) - MONS (MBA) - TOURNAI (MBA).

HOOGSTRAATEN, Abraham van
Dutch, 18th century.
Born in The Hague; died 1736, in The Hague.
Painter, engraver.

In 1687, Abraham van Hoogstraaten was a pupil of Daniel Haaring. In 1694 he was a member of the painters' guild in The Hague.

HOOGSTRATEN, C. A. van
Dutch, 18th century.
Engraver.

Engravings by C.A. van Hoogstraten are mentioned in a Leiden catalogue of 1816.

HOOGSTRATEN, Dirk van
Flemish School, 17th century.

Born c. 1596, in Antwerp; died 20 December 1640, in Dordrecht.
Painter, engraver.

Dirk van Hoogstraten was the son of Jan Hoogstraten. He worked first as an engraver and goldsmith but on his return from a trip to Germany devoted himself to painting. In 1624 he joined the Dordrecht guild and in 1635 had a pupil named Konvenberch. He painted historical subjects.

Museums and Galleries:
Amsterdam: *Mary, St Anne and the Infant Jesus.*
Auction records:
Paris, 21 April 1896, *Moses Rescued from the Water,* FRF 580.

HOOGSTRATEN, Jan or Hans
Flemish, 16th century.
Born c. 1568; died 14 May 1605.
Painter.
Antwerp School, Flemish School.

Jan Hoogstraten was a member of the Antwerp guild in 1593. He was the father of Dirk van Hoogstraten.

HOOGSTRATEN, Jan van
Dutch, 17th century.
Born between 1629 and 1631, in The Hague; died 19 May 1654, in Vienna.
Painter. History painting, portraits, genre scenes.

Jan van Hoogstraten was the younger brother of Samuel van Hoogstraten and son of Dirk van Hoogstraten. According to Houbraken, in 1649 he became a member of the Dordrecht guild. For many years he was painter to the emperor of Austria.

Museums and Galleries:
Vienna (Österreichische Gal. Belvedere): *Interiors with figures.*
Auction records:
Paris, 26 June 1900, *Walk in the Park,* FRF 1,050. London, 27 May 1927, *Virgin and Child,* GBP 330.

HOOGSTRATEN, Samuel van, or Hoogstraeten
Flemish School, 17th century.
Born 2 August 1627, in Dordrecht; died 19 October 1678, in Dordrecht.
Painter, engraver, draughtsman. Religious subjects, portraits, genre scenes, still-lifes.
Dordrecht School.

Samuel van Hoogstraten studied under his father Dirk van Hoogstraten, and in 1642 became a pupil of Rembrandt in Amsterdam. In 1651, he worked in Vienna for the emperor. In 1653 he was in London and in 1668 was a member of the painters' guild in The Hague. He later returned to Dordrecht, where he ran an academy.

Hoogstraten's pupils included Golfried Schalcken, Arend de Gelder, Cornelis Vermeulen and Arnold Houbraken. He was a cultivated man and also produced some literary work, including an account of his travels in Italy and a treatise on painting entitled *The Illuminated World and the Sightless World.* This artist's work was featured in the exhibition *Twee gouden eeuwen: schilderkunst uit Nederland en Denemarken* (*Two Golden Ages: Masterpieces of Dutch and Danish Painting*) at the Rijksmuseum in Amsterdam in 2001.

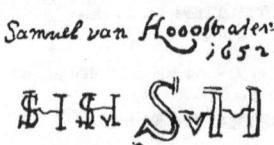

Museums and Galleries:
Amsterdam (Rijksmus.): *Mattheus van den Broucke; The Invalid; Feeble Young Girl* - The Hague: *Young Lady Walking* - Vienna: *The Palace Square in Vienna; Man at the Window* - Wroclaw: *Portrait of an Elderly Man.*
Auction records:
Paris, 21-22 Feb 1919, *Boats* (pencil and Indian ink) FRF 50. London, Dec 1923, *Glances,* GBP 283. London, 10 April 1930, *Man in Black,* GBP 99. London, 28 May 1930, *Martyrdom of St John the Baptist,* GBP 105. New York, 11 Dec 1930, *Christ Appearing to his Disciples,* USD 425. Paris, 15 May 1931, *Portrait of a Lady of Quality,* FRF 3,600. London, 30 April 1937, *First-born,* GBP 220. Paris, 29 April 1942, *Portrait of a Woman,* FRF 18,500. London, 20 June 1947, *Sir John Finch,* GBP 420. London, 25 July 1958, *Interior,* GBP 787. London, 27 April 1960, *Interior with a Young Lady,* GBP 250. London, 21 June 1968, *Still-life,* Gns 2,000. Amsterdam, 26 May 1970, *Portrait of an Eastern Prince,* NLG 8,200. London, 20 July 1973, *Child Seated* (1645) Gns 5,000. Amsterdam, 7 May 1974, *Portrait of a Young Man,* NLG 31,000. Amsterdam, 6 June 1977, *Two Apostles Visiting John the Baptist in Prison* (pen and wash heightened with white gouache, 7 1/2 x 9 1/2 ins / 19 x 24.4 cm) NLG 22,000. London, 30 March 1979, *Portrait of a Young Man* (oil on canvas, 28 x 23 1/2 ins / 71 x 59.7 cm) GBP 9,000. London, 9 April 1981, *Studies of Figures* (pen and wash, 5 1/2 x 6 3/4 ins / 14 x 17.4 cm) GBP 2,000. New York, 7 June 1984, *Interior of Westminster Abbey* (oil on canvas, 61 x 43 ins / 155 x 109 cm) USD 21,000. Munich, 28 Nov 1985, *Study of Three Figures Standing* (pen and wash, 4 1/2 x 3 ins / 11.5 x 7.5 cm) DEM 5,200. New York, 31 May 1989, *A White Cockerel* (1669, oil on canvas, 30 x 25 1/2 ins / 76.5 x 65 cm) USD 33,000. London, 17 Nov 1989, *Portrait of Thomas Godfrey of Burton Aleph Dressed in Black over a White Shirt with a Lace Ruff and with a Spaniel nearby* (1663, oil on canvas, 41 3/4 x 31 1/4 ins / 106 x 79.5 cm) GBP 17,600. New York, 31 May 1990, *Portrait of Count Ferdinand von Werdenberg at the Foot of a Staircase with a Breton Spaniel* (oil on canvas, 75 3/4 x 64 3/4 ins / 192.4 x 164.6 cm) USD 220,000. New York, 16 Jan 1992, *Immaculate Conception* (oil on canvas, 26 1/2 x 21 ins / 67.6 x 53.3 cm) USD 22,000. London, 9 Dec 1994, *Doctor Visiting a Young Woman Invalid in her Bedroom* (oil on canvas, 27 1/4 x 22 ins / 69.2 x 55.9 cm) GBP 16,100. Amsterdam, 8 Nov 1999, *Gipsy Telling the Fortune of Young Couple under Arcade* (oil on canvas, 27 x 22 ins / 68 x 55 cm) NLG 110,000. London, 6 July 2000, *Portrait of Axel Gustafsson, Count Oxenstierna* (1665, oil on canvas, 30 x 27 ins / 76 x 68 cm) GBP 14,000. New York, 23 Jan 2001, *St Peter in Prison Visited by the Angel* (colour ink, 7 x 9 ins / 19 x 22 cm) USD 6,500. New York, 23 Jan 2001, *Studies of Three Standing Figures and of Head* (colour ink wash, 4 x 3 ins / 11 x 8 cm) USD 14,000. London, 11 April 2002, *Angel Appearing to the Two Marys at the Tomb* (red and black chalk, pen and ink heightened with white, 13 x 11 ins / 32 x 29 cm) GBP 12,000. London, 10 July 2002, *Bathsheba Imploring David to Appoint Solomon as his Successor* (pen and ink wash, arched top, 4 x 4 ins / 11 x 10 cm) GBP 12,000. London, 10 July 2003, *Young Boy Preparing to Bathe in a Stream, Watched by a Girl* (oil on canvas, arched top, 37 x 30 ins / 95 x 75 cm) GBP 65,000. London, 7 July 2004, *Portrait of a Young Man in a Brocade-lined Cloak and Black Velvet Cap* (oil on canvas, 20 x 17 ins / 52 x 44 cm) GBP 22,000.

HOOIBERG, Theodor
Dutch, 19th century.
Born 1809, in Harderwijk; died 1899, in Eje.
Engraver, lithographer, cartographer.

For many years, Theodor Hooiberg worked in The Hague as a cartographer.

HOOK, Allan J.
British, 19th century.

Born 1853, in London.
Active in Farnham.
Painter. Landscapes, waterscapes, seascapes.
Allan Hook exhibited in London at the Royal Academy from 1876.
Auction records:
Paris, March 1924, *On the Devon Coast*, GBP 15. London, 23 Sept 1988, *Herring Boats off the West Coast* (1886, oil on canvas, 27½ x 41¾ ins / 70 x 106 cm) GBP 2,200.

HOOK, Bryan
British, 19th century.
Active in Silberbeck.
Painter. Portraits, landscapes, seascapes.
Bryan Hook exhibited regularly in London at the Royal Academy from 1879.
Auction records:
London, 23 March 1908, *Summer on the Corniche* (1880) GBP 2.

HOOK, Eliza (Mrs)
British, 18th century.
Active in London.
Miniaturist.
Eliza Hook exhibited in London at the Free Society and the Royal Academy between 1773 and 1786.

HOOK, James Clarke
British, 19th - 20th century.
Born 21 November 1819, in London; died 14 April 1907, in Churt (Surrey).
Painter. Religious subjects, historical subjects, figures, genre scenes, fishing scenes, waterscapes, seascapes, animals.
James Hook studied at the Royal Academy Schools, London. He became an associate member of the Royal Academy in 1851 and a full member in 1860, and exhibited there from 1839. He was awarded a gold medal at the Exposition Universelle in Paris in 1889. His output includes paintings illustrating episodes in Italian history (particularly Venetian history) and the life of William Shakespeare.
Museums and Galleries:
Birmingham (Museum and Art Gallery): *Fish from the Dogger Bank: Scheningen, Holland* (oil on canvas); *Breakfasts for the Porth* (oil on canvas) - Brighton (Museum and Art Gallery): *The Gull Catcher* (1877, oil on canvas) - Bristol: *The Dredgers* - Hamburg: *Kelp Gatherer on the Normandy Coast* - Leicester: *Farmer Pengelly* - London (Royal Academy of Arts): *Gathering Limpets* (1886, oil on canvas, competition piece) - London (Tate Collection): *Home with the Tide* (1880, oil on canvas); *The Stream* (1885, oil on canvas); *Young Dreams* (1887, oil on canvas); *The Seaweed Raker* (1889, oil on canvas); *Wreckage from the Fruiter* (1889, oil on canvas) - Manchester: *Downpour in Devonshire*; *Castle with Lake* - Preston: *Deliverance of the Venetian Financiers* - Sydney: *Jetsam and Flotsam*.
Auction records:
London, 3 April 1908, *Yo Heave Ho!* (1885) GBP 294. London, 27 March 1909, *Stand Clear* (1860) GBP 141. London, 24 June 1909, *Chimney Sweeps* (1868) GBP 420. London, 5 March 1910, *Ravages of a Herd of Cows* (1867) GBP 84. London, 6 May 1910, *Eel Catchers*, GBP 152. London, 27 May 1910, *View of the Shore at Hall*, GBP 210. London, 17 June 1910, *Dream of Venice*, GBP 105. London, 24 June 1910, *Lobster Catchers* (1868) GBP 294. London, 9 June 1911, *Sailors Setting off to Fish in the North Sea*, GBP 178. London, May 1922, *Prawn Catchers*, GBP 54. London, Feb 1923, *View of Hard Lines*, GBP 99. London, Feb 1923, *Morning, After the Storm*, GBP 178. London, Jan 1924, *Viola Disguised as a Pageboy, and Olivia*, GBP 15. London, May 1924, *Ragworms*, GBP 57. London, 24 April 1925, *Skye Salmon*, GBP 105. London, 29 Jan 1926, *The Cider Makers*, GBP 99. London, 13 April 1928, *Washerwomen in Brittany*, GBP 75. London, 30 Nov 1928, *Kelp Burners in the Shetlands*, GBP 57. London, 6 Dec 1929, *Tending a Cow*, GBP 60. London, 20 Oct 1936, *Return from Torello*, GBP 46. London, 26 April 1946, *Fisherman's Return*, GBP 52. London, 11 Oct 1968, *Making Cider*, Gns 1,300. London, 28 Nov 1972, *Rugged Coastline*, GBP 700. London, 15 June 1973, *Catching Butterflies* (1857) Gns 1,800. London, 16 July 1976, *Picking Mushrooms* (1879, oil on canvas, 42½ x 57¾ ins / 108 x 147 cm) GBP 950. London, 8 March 1977, *Coral Pickers, Amalfi* (1878, oil on canvas, 31 x 54 ins / 79 x 137 cm) GBP 1,000. London, 20 March 1979, *Gathering Shells* (1879?, oil on canvas, 42¼ x 58¼ ins / 107 x 148 cm) GBP 2,600. London, 6 March 1981, *Fruits of the Sea* (1870, oil on canvas, 30 x 55 ins / 76.2 x 139.6 cm) GBP 1,300. London, 14 Feb 1986, *Colin, Thou Ken'st the Southerne Shepheard's Boye* (1855, oil on panel, 19¼ x 29½ ins / 49 x 75 cm) GBP 10,000. London, 13 Feb 1987, *Seagull Catcher* (1877, oil on canvas, 47 x 37 ins / 119.3 x 94 cm) GBP 2,400. London, 26 Sept 1990, *Gratitude of the Mother of Moses Saved by the Pharaoh's Daughter* (1855, oil on canvas, 50 x 32¼ ins / 127 x 82 cm) GBP 6,820. London, 8 Feb 1991, *Fishermen's Return* (oil on canvas, 25½ x 39½ ins / 64.8 x 100.3 cm) GBP 2,860. London, 16 July 1993, *Disasters of a Stormy Night* (oil on canvas, 38 x 61 ins / 96.5 x 154 cm) GBP 11,270. London, 7 June 1996, *Romeo and Juliet* (oil on canvas, 32½ x 27 ins / 82.5 x 68.6 cm) GBP 7,820. London, 29 May 1997, *Off the Fishing Ground* (oil on canvas, 20½ x 31½ ins / 52 x 80 cm) GBP 4,600. Billingshurst, 26 Jan 1999, *The Old Steps* (1870, oil on panel, 15 x 12 ins / 37 x 30 cm) GBP 1,700. Sweden, 1 Dec 1999, *Coastal Landscape with Fishing Boats and Figures* (oil on canvas, 35 x 55 ins / 88 x 139 cm) SEK 21,000. London, 13 June 2000, *Dutch Pedlar* (1890, oil on canvas, 37 x 61 ins / 95 x 156 cm) GBP 9,000. London, 30 Nov 2000, *Rest while Gathering* (oil on canvas, 33 x 48 ins / 84 x 123 cm) GBP 14,000. London, 20 Feb 2003, *Gull Catcher* (1877, oil on canvas, 48 x 37 ins / 122 x 94 cm) GBP 32,000. London, 11 June 2004, *Cow Tending* (1874, oil on canvas, 34 x 54 ins / 87 x 136 cm) GBP 15,000. London, 11 June 2004, *Olivia and Viola* (oil on panel, 24 x 29 ins / 60 x 74 cm) GBP 26,000.

HOOK, Sandy, pseudonym of Georges Taboureau
French, 19th - 20th century.
Born 1879, in Paris; died 1960, in Paris.
Painter (including gouache), draughtsman, poster artist. Seascapes, boats.
Sandy Hook was official painter to the Navy. He worked for numerous maritime companies, creating their posters. He camouflaged boats for the national navy. He exhibited his works at the Musée de la Marine in Paris. The Salon du Livre Maritime of Concarneau showed his works at the chapel of the Trinité, Ville-Close (1998).
Auction records:
Paris, 10 July 1983, *Flanders* (watercolour, 30¾ x 26½ ins / 78 x 67 cm) FRF 24,000. London, 11 Nov 1999, *Whaler James Clark Ross* (1931, pencil and watercolour heightened with white, sold with two others, 19 x 28 ins / 47 x 71 cm) GBP 1,300. Paris, 28 Nov 1999, *Steamship on a Choppy Sea with Gulls* (1928, watercolour and gouache, 16 x 22 ins / 40 x 57 cm) FRF 17,000. Paris, 24 Sept 2000, *The Tugboat 'Skjun' from the Port of Göteborg* (1954, watercolour and gouache, 17 x 21 ins / 42 x 53 cm) FRF 27,000. Paris, 24 Sept 2000, *S Sysalou, ME Tawa. SS New Lambton, MS Swedru, SS Saale, and others* (watercolour, set of 14) FRF 80,000. Rennes, 4 March 2003, *Le Saverne Manoeuvring in a Harbour* (1919, gouache and watercolour, 21 x 34 ins / 54 x 86 cm) EUR 3,500. Le Havre, 26 Oct 2003, *Freighters and Junks* (gouache, a pair, 8 x 15 ins / 21 x 37 cm) EUR 2,800. Boulogne, 17 April 2004, *Freighter in the English Channel* (1959, watercolour, 11 x 14 ins / 28 x 36 cm) EUR 1,700.

HOOKE, Richard
British, 19th century.
Born c. 1823; died 1887, in Manchester.
Painter.
Richard Hooke is known for his *Portrait of the Marchioness of Downshire.*

HOOKER, William
American, 19th century.
Active in New York, and in Philadelphia in 1805.
Engraver.
William Hooker's works include a copy of David's *Napoleon Crossing the Saint Bernard.*

HOOKER, William
British, 19th century.
Active in London c. 1810.
Painter. Flowers.
William Hooker was a pupil of Ferdinand Bauer.

HOOL, Gilbert van
Belgian, 20th century.
Born 1929, in Antwerp.
Painter, draughtsman, engraver, pastellist.
Gilbert van Hool was a student at the Koninklijke Academie voor Schone Kunsten and Hoger Instituut voor Schone Kunsten in Antwerp.

HOOL, H.
18th century.
Miniaturist.
H. Hool painted a *Portrait of John Pocock.*

HOOL, Johannes Baptista van, the Elder
Flemish School, 18th - 19th century.
Born 1 March 1769, in Antwerp; died 14 June 1837, in Antwerp.
Sculptor.
From 1780 to 1802, Johannes Hool the Elder was a pupil of Frans van Ursel. In 1812 he was a teacher at the Koninklijke Academie voor Schone Kunsten in Antwerp. He worked for churches in Rotterdam, Amsterdam, Arnhem, Bosch, Breda and Oosterhout.

HOOL, Johannes Baptista van, the Younger
Belgian, 19th century.
Born 1812, in Antwerp; died 16 December 1883, in Antwerp.
Sculptor.
Johannes Hool the Younger was the son and pupil of Johannes Hool the Elder. He later became a teacher at the Koninklijke Academie voor Schone Kunsten in Antwerp.

HOOLARN, G. H.
Dutch, 18th century.
Born c. 1716, in Dordrecht; died 1772.
Painter, glass painter, engraver. Portraits.
G.H. Hoolarn created stained glass windows after drawings by A. van Ostade and other Dutch masters.
MUSEUMS AND GALLERIES:
RENNES: *Landscape.*

HOOMIS, Elias
Dutch, 17th century.
Died 1636, in Amsterdam.
Painter.
Elias Hoomis painted landscapes and seascapes.

HOOMIS, Jasper
Dutch, 17th century.
Born 1630, in Amsterdam; died c. 1681.
Painter.
Jasper Hoomis was the son of Elias Hoomis.

HOONE, Galyon
British, 16th century.
Active in London at the beginning of the 16th century.
Glass painter.
Galyon Hoone worked in King's College Chapel in Cambridge.

HOOP, Douwe de
Dutch, 19th century.
Born 24 March 1800, in Workum; died 27 October 1830, in Amsterdam.
Painter.
Douwe de Hoop was a pupil of C. Kruseman. He painted historical subjects and still-lifes.

HOOPER (Miss)
British, 18th century.
Painter.
Miss Hooper exhibited two flower paintings at the Free Society in London in 1762.

HOOPER, Annie Blakeslee (Mrs)
American, 20th century.
Born in California.
Active in New York.
Painter, illustrator.
Annie Blakeslee Hooper began her studies in San Francisco, and also worked at the Art Students League, New York. She was a member of the New York Watercolor Club.

HOOPER, Grace
American, 19th century.
Born November 1850, in Boston (Massachusetts).
Active in Boston.
Sculptor, painter.
Scarab Club.
Grace Hooper started her studies in Boston with Cyrus Dallin, and then went to work in Paris with Injalbert.

HOOPER, Harold
British, 20th century.
Painter.
Harold Hooper lives in Paris and rarely exhibits his work, tending to keep out of the public eye. Characterised by a sparing use of colour and line, his paintings seem to express anxiety and melancholy. Some of his work is reminiscent of that of the Italian painter Giorgio Morandi.

HOOPER, John Horace
British, 19th century.
Painter. Landscapes, seascapes.
John Hooper made his début in London at the Suffolk Street Gallery, exhibiting there between 1877 and 1878. An interesting painter, he was active in London until 1899.
AUCTION RECORDS:
NEW YORK, 11-13 Feb 1903, *Seascape,* USD 100. LONDON, 30 Nov 1907, *Harvest; Near Rickmansworth* (matching pair) GBP 5. LONDON, 25 April 1908, *High Tide,* GBP 10. LONDON, 6 March 1909, *Dusk over the Upper Thames,* GBP 7. LONDON, 18 June 1909, *Fairlight Glen, Hastings,* GBP 17. LONDON, 5 March 1910, *Evening after Rain,* GBP 7. LONDON, Feb 1922, *Pangbourne,* GBP 11; *View of Redhill, Surrey,* GBP 22. LONDON, April 1923, *On the Kennet,* GBP 10. PARIS, 16 Nov 1923, *English Landscape,* FRF 510. LONDON, Dec 1923, *Harvest near Fairlight, Hastings,* GBP 10. LONDON, 8 Dec 1931, *Landscape,* GBP 42. LONDON, 25 July 1972, *River Landscape,* GBP 480. LONDON, 23 April 1974, *River Landscape,* GBP 1,000. LONDON, 29 June 1976, *Autumn Landscape at Nightfall* (oil on canvas, 26 1/4 x 34 1/4 ins / 66.5 x 87 cm) GBP 900. LONDON, 14 June 1977, *Haycart* (oil on canvas, 23 1/4 x 41 1/4 ins / 59 x 105 cm) GBP 1,800. LONDON, 20 March 1979, *Ferry* (oil on canvas, 23 x 41 ins / 58.5 x 104 cm) GBP 1,200. LONDON, 17 Feb 1984, *Summer in Shiplake-on-Thames* (oil on canvas, 30 x 50 1/4 ins / 76.2 x 127.6 cm) GBP 2,400. LONDON, 18 Dec 1985, *Cornfield near Littlehampton* (oil on canvas, 48 x 68 ins / 122 x 173 cm)

GBP 5,000. LONDON, 13 Feb 1987, *On the Wye near Guildford* (oil on canvas, 20 x 30 ins / 50.7 x 76.2 cm) GBP 2,600. LONDON, 23 Sept 1988, *Summer in Ockley, Surrey* (oil on canvas, 24 x 42½ ins / 61 x 108 cm) GBP 5,280. LONDON, 27 Sept 1989, *Fishing in a Mountain Stream* (oil on canvas, 50 x 40¼ ins / 127 x 102 cm) GBP 6,600. LONDON, 9 Feb 1990, *Banks of the Kennet* (oil on canvas, 24 x 42 ins / 61 x 106.7 cm) GBP 4,180. LONDON, 13 Feb 1991, *Diss, Norfolk* (oil on canvas, 24 x 40 ins / 61 x 101.5 cm) GBP 1,870. LONDON, 11 Oct 1991, *Children Paddling in a River* (oil on canvas, 16 x 24 ins / 40.6 x 61 cm) GBP 1,650. NEW YORK, 20 Jan 1993, *Winter Landscape with Figures Walking Past the Churchyard* (oil on canvas, 20 x 30 ins / 50.8 x 76.2 cm) USD 1,380. LONDON, 3 Nov 1993, *Fishing in the Evening* (oil on canvas, 24 x 36 ins / 61 x 91.5 cm) GBP 1,035. LONDON, 9 June 1994, *Cornfield by a River* (oil on canvas, 30 x 49½ ins / 76 x 126 cm) GBP 11,500. LONDON, 6 Nov 1995, *Haymaking on the Riverbank* (oil on canvas, 24 x 42 ins / 61 x 106.8 cm) GBP 2,530. LONDON, 6 June 1996, *At Eventide* (oil on canvas, 24 x 42 ins / 61 x 106.7 cm) GBP 4,140. LONDON, 16 Sept 1999, *Harvesting Pulborough, Sussex* (oil on canvas, 26 x 42 ins / 66 x 107 cm) GBP 3,200. LONDON, 14 Dec 1999, *End of the Day* (oil on canvas, 24 x 42 ins / 61 x 107 cm) GBP 2,800. LONDON, 16 March 2000, *In Southampton* (oil on canvas, 16 x 24 ins / 40 x 61 cm) GBP 2,500. LONDON, 14 June 2000, *Golden Harvest* (oil on canvas, 24 x 42 ins / 61 x 107 cm) GBP 3,500. WASHINGTON, 15 Sept 2001, *Marsh Landscape with Cows Watering, Sunset* (oil on canvas, 24 x 42 ins / 61 x 106 cm) USD 4,400. BELFAST, 25 Oct 2001, *Streatley on Thames* (oil on canvas, 24 x 42 ins / 61 x 107 cm) GBP 3,800. FRANKFURT, 23 Nov 2002, *Figure with Geese in an English Evening Landscape* (oil on canvas, 24 x 42 ins / 62 x 107 cm) EUR 2,000. NEW YORK, 15 Jan 2003, *Summer Afternoon* (oil on canvas, 23 x 39 ins / 59 x 100 cm) USD 4,000. LONDON, 20 May 2003, *Berkshire Cornfield* (oil on canvas, 36 x 60 ins / 91 x 152 cm) GBP 2,300. MELBOURNE, 3 May 2004, *On the River* (oil on canvas, 24 x 41 ins / 61 x 105 cm) AUD 5,500. COPENHAGEN, 8 Sept 2004, *Evening Sunshine Reflecting in the Water* (oil on canvas, 24 x 36 ins / 61 x 91 cm) DKK 30,000.

HOOPER, Luther
British, 19th century.
Active in London.
Painter. Genre scenes.

Luther Hooper exhibited work between 1870 and 1891.

HOOPER, Rosa
American, 20th century.
Born 1876, in San Francisco; died 1963, in Milbrae (California).
Painter. Genre scenes.

Rosa Hooper worked in Paris and Dresden before returning to California.

HOOPER, S.
British, 18th century.
Draughtsman.

S. Hooper executed some drawings for Richard Gough's *Monumental Antiquities*.

HOOPER, Will Philip
American, 20th century.
Painter, illustrator.

Will Philip Hooper trained at the Art Students League (ASL), New York. He worked in Boston, and worked on various magazines. He is a member of the New York Watercolor Club and Salmagundi Club.

HOOPER, William G.
British, 19th century.
Active in London.
Painter. Genre scenes.

William Hooper exhibited between 1870 and 1891.

HOOPER, William Harcourt
British, 19th - 20th century.
Born 22 February 1834; died 24 February 1912, in London.
Engraver.

William Hooper was a pupil of Bolton. He worked mostly for newspapers.

HOORDE, Ernest van
Belgian, 20th century.
Born 1922, in Ghent.
Painter.

Van Hoorde was a student at the fine arts academies in Ghent and Antwerp. He has taught in various art schools in Ghent. His work has been shown at a number of annual exhibitions, and he has been awarded various prizes. His art is figurative, and he aligned himself with the German Expressionists.

HOOREN, Egbert van
Dutch, 17th century.
Active in Amsterdam.
Painter.

Egbert van Hooren collaborated with Isaack Jacobsz., who was almost certainly his brother.

HOOREN, Isaack Jacobsz. van
Dutch, 17th century.
Died 30 April 1649, in Amsterdam.
Painter. Portraits, genre scenes.

Isaack Hooren is known to have painted a number of family portraits.

AUCTION RECORDS:
LONDON, March 1923, *Two Boys with a Dead Bird*, GBP 31. LONDON, June 1923, *Lady in a Black Dress*, GBP 78. LONDON, July 1924, *Family Group*, GBP 33. AMSTERDAM, 29 Nov 1988, *Portrait of a Gentleman Dressed in Red with a Lace Collar* (1646, oil on panel, 6½ x 5 ins / 16.6 x 12.7 cm) NLG 16,100.

HOOREN, Melchisedech van
Flemish, 16th century.
Active in Antwerp, in 1550.
Painter, engraver.
Flemish School.

Melchisedech van Hooren engraved *Views of Brussels*.

HOORICK, Adrien van
Flemish, 16th century.
Active in Audenarde c. 1530.
Sculptor.
Flemish School.

Adrien van Hoorick did work for the town hall in Audenarde.

HOORICKX, Ernest
Belgian, 19th century.
Active in Brussels.
Painter. Landscapes.

Ernest Hoorickx exhibited in Munich in 1892.

HOORN, Gérard van, or Hoorne, called Gerardo Orniero and Ornerio Frisio
Dutch, 16th century.
Born 16th century.
Painter (glass).

Gérard van Hoorn worked in Florence and in Bologna, where he made five windows for the church of St Peter in 1575.

HOORN, Jordanus
Dutch, 18th - 19th century.
Born 26 February 1753, in Amersfoort; died 3 July 1833, in Amersfoot.
Painter, draughtsman. Portraits, landscapes.

Jordanus Hoorn was a pupil of Gerrit Torenbourg. He went to Haarlem in 1772.

AUCTION RECORDS:

AMSTERDAM, 14 Nov 1988, *Soldier Standing Holding a Musket* (chalk/paper, 12 3/4 x 11 ins / 32.7 x 27.7 cm) NLG 632. AMSTERDAM, 12 May 1992, *Horseman by a Forge* (1781, oil on panel, 11 1/2 x 14 1/4 ins / 29 x 36 cm) NLG 7,820. AMSTERDAM, 14 May 2002, *River Landscape with Elegant Townsfolk. View of Arnhem with the St Walburgskerk* (1776, oil on canvas, a pair, 11 x 15 ins / 28 x 39 cm) EUR 11,000. AMSTERDAM, 17 May 2004, *Portrait of Two Children and their Dog* (1792, pastel, 28 x 21 ins / 70 x 53 cm) EUR 2,000.

HOORN, Klaes Jansz.

Dutch, 17th century.
Probably active in Leiden.
Painter.

Klaes Hoorn is known to have painted a *St John the Baptist*.

HOORNE (Mrs)

British, 18th century.
Active in London.
Miniaturist.

Mrs Hoorne exhibited in London at the Society of Artists in 1776.

HOORNE, Emiel

Belgian, 20th - 21st century.
Born 1951, in Roulers (West Flanders).
Draughtsman, engraver.

Hoorne attended the art academies in Izegem and Ghent. He borrows from Pop Art and Nouvelle Figuration (a resurgence of figurative painting in the early 1960s), in order to portray everyday objects such as toasters and blenders, but also eccentric machines, including a machine to pump out sadness and to make dreams visible. Hoorne uses a very wide variety of graphic techniques: etching, engraving, linocut, silk-screen printing and offset. He exhibited at the Musée Provincial d'Art Moderne, Ostend in 1991.

HOOSTE, Jef van

Belgian, 20th century.
Born 1884, in St Niklaas-Waas; died 1940.
Painter, pastellist. Interiors, landscapes, waterscapes, seascapes.

AUCTION RECORDS:

LOKEREN, 28 May 1994, *Village Church* (oil on canvas, 39 3/4 x 28 3/4 ins / 101 x 73 cm) BEF 55,000. LOKEREN, 5 Oct 1996, *Barges* (oil on canvas, 33 x 39 1/4 ins / 84 x 100 cm) BEF 48,000.

HOOVEN, Herbert Nelson

American, 20th century.
Born 31 January 1898.
Painter.

Herbert Nelson Hooven trained at the Pennsylvania Academy of the Fine Arts, Philadelphia, and became a member. He also became a member of the American Artists Professional League and Society of Independent Artists.

HOOYKAAS

Dutch, 20th century.
Painter, engraver.

Hooykaas is known for his violently Colourist work, which evolved towards Abstract art.

HOPE, E.

British, 19th century.
Active in London in 1868.
Miniaturist.

HOPE, Edith A.

British, 19th - 20th century.
Born in Australia.
Painter, lithographer.

Edith Hope initially worked in London, and later exhibited in Paris, Brussels, Düsseldorf and Rome.

HOPE, James

American, 19th century.
Born 29 November 1818, in Drygrange (Scotland); died 1892, in Watkins Glen (New York).
Painter. Portraits, landscapes, battle scenes.

James Hope, born in Scotland, came to Canada as a child, but was orphaned at the age of 12. He was apprenticed to a wagon maker in Vermont in the USA, attended Castleton Vermont Seminary for a year, and began to paint portraits. He pursued his career as a painter in West Rutland, Vermont in 1843, but moved to Montreal from 1844 to 1846 to take advantage of a better market for art. When he returned to Castleton in 1846, he began to paint landscapes while also teaching at the seminary. His style may have been influenced by the work of Frederic Church. He opened a painting studio in New York in 1853.

During active duty in the American Civil War, Hope sketched many studies, which he later used to paint a series of large battle scenes, such as the oil *Army of the Potomac* (1865). These war paintings achieved popular success throughout the USA. In 1872 he established a studio and art gallery in Watkins Glen, New York, where he painted the geological formations of the local landscape.

Hope exhibited at the American Art Union in 1849, and with the National Academy of Design from 1854. He continued to show with the Academy for twenty-five years, being elected an Associate Member in 1871. He also exhibited with the Brooklyn Art Association, and in Boston, Philadelphia, Buffalo, Cincinnati, Detroit, Utica, Chicago and St Louis. Noted examples of his landscape work are *Gem of the Forest* and *Forest Glen*.

MUSEUMS AND GALLERIES:

BARRE (Vermont Historical Society): *Anna Gray Child* (1856, oil); *Mary Wallis Goodrich* (1856, oil) - BOSTON (MFA): *Marble Quarry* (1851, oil); *Bird Mountain, Castleton, Vermont* (1855, oil); *Army of the Potomac* (1865, oil) - CHATTANOOGA (Hunter Museum of American Art) - MANCHESTER, NH (Currier Gallery of Art) - NASHVILLE (Tennessee State Museum) - NEW YORK (Metropolitan Mus. of Art) - PROVO, UT (Museum of Art, Brigham Young University) - SANTA BARBARA (Santa Barbara Museum of Art) - SHELBURNE (Shelburne Museum) - SYRACUSE (Everson MA) - WASHINGTON DC (Corcoran Gal. of Art) - YOUNGSTOWN (Butler Institute of American Art).

AUCTION RECORDS:

NEW YORK, 27 June 1999, *Elm Cottage, Winter, Mount Hope, Castleton, VT* (1860, oil on canvas, 12 x 16 ins / 30 x 41 cm) USD 7,250. NEW YORK, 26 Sept 1999, *Landscape at the Foot of Mt Marcy* (oil on canvas, 40 x 51 ins / 102 x 130 cm) USD 10,000. NEW YORK, 18 Feb 2000, *Landscape Uptown, W. Rutland, Vermont* (oil on canvas, 31 x 48 ins / 79 x 122 cm) USD 18,700. NEW YORK, 30 Nov 2000, *Rainbow Falls, Watkins Glen, New York* (1871, oil on canvas, 78 x 60 ins / 198 x 152 cm) USD 130,000. NEW YORK, 25 May 2001, *Cavern Gorge, Watkins Glen* (1870, oil on canvas, 35 x 29 ins / 89 x 74 cm) USD 7,500. NEW YORK, 5 Dec 2001, *View of Yosemite* (oil on canvas, 49 x 38 ins / 124 x 97 cm) USD 9,500. NEW YORK, 21 Jan 2002, *Spearing Fish, Watkins Glen* (oil on canvas, 25 x 20 ins / 64 x 51 cm) USD 6,500. BOSTON, 22 March 2002, *Forest Glen* (oil on canvas, 40 x 51 ins / 102 x 129 cm) USD 15,000. NEW YORK, 4 March 2003, *Study of Rainbow Falls, Watkins Glen* (1872, oil on canvas, 36 x 30 ins / 91 x 76 cm) USD 7,000. THOMASTON, 26 July 2003, *Army of the Potomac at Cumberland Landing on the Pamunky River Virginia* (oil on canvas) USD 75,000. MILFORD, 21 Oct 2004, *Civil War Captain at Rest* (oil on board, 8 x 10 ins / 20 x 25 cm) USD 7,500.

HOPE, Jimi, or Koffi Mokpokpo Senaya

Togolese, 20th - 21st century.

Born 12 October 1956, in Lomé.
Painter, sculptor.

Jimi Hope is a self-taught artist. He studied architecture at the Da Silva Institute in Lomé, but then turned to painting, sculpture and song. He fills his paintings with African faces.

BIBLIOGRAPHY:

Persin, Patrick-Gilles, *L'École de Lomé. Artistes togolais d'aujourd'hui*, exhibition catalogue, Association Grands et Jeunes d'Aujourd'hui, Paris, 2001.

HOPE, Laura Elizabeth Rachel
Maiden name: Troubridge
British, 19th century.
Born 1858.
Pastellist.

Laura Hope made several portraits of members of the English royal family towards the end of Queen Victoria's reign.

HOPE, Robert
British, 19th century.
Born 1869, in Edinburgh; died 1936.
Painter. History painting, genre scenes, portraits, landscapes.

Robert Hope exhibited mainly in London and Munich.

AUCTION RECORDS:

LONDON, 13 July 1929, *Guitar Player,* GBP 35. LONDON, 28 March 1930, *Proud Maisie,* GBP 46. EDINBURGH, 30 April 1986, *Market Scene, Bruges* (oil on canvas, 16 x 20 ins / 40.6 x 50.8 cm) GBP 2,400. LONDON, 29 July 1988, *Girl Choosing Silks* (oil on canvas, 16 3/4 x 15 ins / 42.5 x 38.2 cm) GBP 1,760. PERTH, 29 Aug 1989, *Landscape with Sheep* (oil on canvas, 18 x 30 ins / 46 x 76.5 cm) GBP 1,870. GLASGOW, 6 Feb 1990, *Knowe Mill in East Lothian* (oil on canvas, 18 x 24 ins / 46 x 61 cm) GBP 2,200. SOUTH QUEENSFERRY, 1 May 1990, *Portrait of a Lady* (oil on canvas, 50 1/2 x 40 1/2 ins / 128 x 103 cm) GBP 2,420. EDINBURGH, 28 April 1992, *Sketching near Berwick* (oil on card, 10 x 14 ins / 25.5 x 35.5 cm) GBP 880. GLASGOW, 1 Feb 1994, *Fishing Port* (oil on canvas, 18 x 24 ins / 45.5 x 61 cm) GBP 2,530.

HOPE, Thelma Paddock
American, 20th century.
Born 6 November 1898, in Indiana; died 1991.
Painter.

Thelma Paddock Hope trained at the Art Institute of Chicago, and became a member of this institute.

HOPE, Thomas
Dutch, 18th - 19th century.
Born c. 1770; died 3 February 1831.
Painter, architect. Landscapes, still-lifes.
Orientalism.

Thomas Hope lived on the outskirts of Haarlem before spending eight years travelling around the Mediterranean. He painted many landscapes while on his travels, mainly in the Orientalist style.

AUCTION RECORDS:

PORTLAND, 5 July 1980, *Still-life with Melons* (oil on canvas, 19 x 27 1/4 ins / 48.3 x 69 cm) USD 3,500.

HOPE-PINKER, Henry Richard. See **PINKER Henry Richard Hope**

HOPF, Anny or Annie Stebler. See **STEBLER-HOPF**

HOPF, Fredy
Swiss, 20th century.
Born 28 June 1875, in Thoune (Bern).
Painter. Landscapes.

MUSEUMS AND GALLERIES:

BERN: *Boat on the Seine* (study); *Autumn Symphony by the Water.*

HOPF, Sonia
German, 20th century.
Born 1 May 1940, on Sylt.
Active in France.
Engraver.

Sonia Hopf studied at the fine arts school in Munich from 1960 to 1963 and then settled in Paris, where she got to know the painter Fossier. She is a professor at the École des Beaux-Arts in Marseilles. Her work was shown at the Salon de Mai in Paris in 1966, and then at the first Paris Print Biennale (1968). She also exhibited at the second Print Biennale, entitled *Le Désespoir du Peintre* (*The Painter's Despair*), at the Maison de la Culture in Grenoble, an exhibition devised by Jean Clair. This event acted as a precursor to an exhibition held a few months later that year, entitled *Nouvelle Subjectivité* (*New Subjectivity*), under the auspices of the Festival d'Automne in Paris.

From 1962 to 1968, Hopf produced black and white etchings that developed the theme of man as machine, intimating the existence of an ambiguous universe in which it is impossible to tell whether man is becoming a machine or vice versa. She subsequently produced aquatints with organic forms that are half-animal, half-vegetable.

HOPFER, Bartholomaeus, the Elder
German, 15th century.
Born c. 1431.
Active in Kaufbeuren.
Painter.

Bartholomaeus Hopfer the Elder was the son of Peter Hopfer and the father of Daniel Hopfer.

HOPFER, Bartholomaeus, the Younger
German, 17th century.
Active in Augsburg, then Strasbourg c. 1650.
Painter.

MUSEUMS AND GALLERIES:

STRASBOURG: *Portrait of Counsellor Johan-Adam Schraa.*

HOPFER, C. B.
Dutch, 16th century.
Engraver (burin).

C.B. Hopfer engraved genre scenes and subjects from mythology.

HOPFER, C. W.
German, 19th century.
Active in Berlin c. 1800.
Painter, engraver.

He was the son of Johann Bernhard Gottfried Hopfer.

HOPFER, Daniel
Dutch, 15th - 16th century.
Born c. 1470, in Kaufbeuren; died 1536, in Augsburg.
Engraver.

Daniel Hopfer was the son of Bartholomaeus Hopfer the Elder. His own sons are thought to have been Hieronymus and Lambert Hopfer. He engraved religious and historical subjects as well as portraits and genre scenes. Abbot Marolles was probably incorrect when he identified him as the *Master of the Candlestick,* a title in fact belonging to his son Hieronymus.

AUCTION RECORDS:
LONDON, 19 April 1909, *St John on Patmos* (four other drawings by Schaefein and Elsheimer) GBP 22. LONDON, 1 Nov 1978, *Christ on the Cross Pierced by the Lance* (etching, 13½ x 8½ ins / 34.2 x 21.9 cm) GBP 600. NEW YORK, 3 May 1983, *Presentation of the Virgin* (etching, 12 x 8½ ins / 30.5 x 21.3 cm) USD 2,000. LONDON, 5 Dec 1985, *St George* (etching, 8¾ ins / 22.4 cm x 6 ins/15.3 cm) GBP 4,200. BERLIN, 4 June 1999, *Interior of St Catherine's Cathedral in Augsburg* (iron etching, 11 x 8 ins / 28 x 20 cm) DEM 5,000. MUNICH, 17 May 2001, *Adam and Eve* (etching, 11 x 4 ins / 29 x 11 cm) DEM 36,000. NEW YORK, 6 Nov 2003, *Crucifixion* (c. 1525, etching, 13 x 9 ins / 34 x 22 cm) USD 7,000.

HOPFER, G. Thomas
German, 17th century.
Painter. Portraits.
Court painter to the Duchy of Württemberg, Hopfer did a *Portrait of Luther* for the church of St Martin in Ebingen (Albstadt) in 1674.

HOPFER, Hieronymus
Dutch, 16th century.
Active in Augsburg from 1520 to 1535.
Painter, engraver (etching/burin). Religious subjects, allegorical subjects, genre scenes, portraits.
Hieronymus Hopfer was probably the son of Daniel Hopfer. He engraved religious and genre subjects, also portraits and allegories, and made many engravings after Dürer. He sometimes made copies of work by his father Daniel. Some of his prints are very valuable.

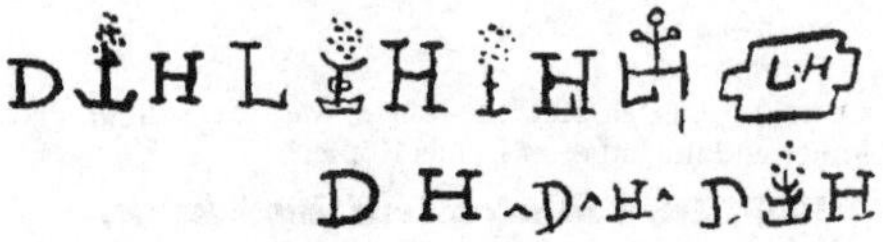

AUCTION RECORDS:
LONDON, 12 July 1963, *Portrait of a Prelate,* Gns 7,000. HAMBURG, 6 June 1985, *St Jerome* (etching) DEM 1,400.

HOPFER, Johann Bernhard Gottfried
German, 18th century.
Born c. 1716, in Rödelsee (near Würzburg); died 1789, in Berlin.
Painter, draughtsman.
A pupil of his father and Johann C. Sperling, he went to Berlin in 1754 and was appointed draughtsman to the academy of sciences. In this role, he did anatomical and physics drawings of remarkable precision.

HOPFER, Johann Sebastian Ludwig
German, 17th century.
Active second half of the 17th century.
Painter, draughtsman.
He worked in the principality of Ansbach-Bayreuth. Possibly the same artist as the engraver called simply Johann Hopfer working in the same period.

HOPFER, Lambert
Dutch, 16th century.
Active in Augsburg.
Engraver (etching/burin).
Lambert Hopfer engraved religious and historical subjects and allegories. He was the son of Daniel Hopfer and the brother of Hieronymus Hopfer.

HOPFER, Leonhard
German, 15th century.
Active in Kaufbeuren in 1497.
Painter.
Leonhard Hopfer was the brother of Bartholomaeus Hopfer the Elder.

HOPFER, Nikolaus
Dutch, 16th century.
Active probably in Augsburg.
Engraver (copper/wood).
Nikolaus Hopfer engraved religious, historical and genre subjects.

HOPFER, Peter
German, 15th century.
Died before 1484.
Active in Kaufbeuren.
Painter.
Peter Hopfer was the father of Bartholomaeus Hopfer the Elder and the grandfather of Daniel Hopfer.

HOPFER, Wolfgang Ludwig
German, 17th century.
Born 4 January 1648, in Nuremberg; died 29 October 1698, in Nuremberg.
Painter.
A pupil of G. Strauch and later Johann Spielberger in Vienna. After working in Italy for nine years, he was appointed painter to the Elector Palatine.

HOPFGARTEN, August Ferdinand
German, 19th century.
Born 17 March 1807, in Berlin; died 26 July 1896, in Berlin.
Painter. History painting, religious subjects, mythological subjects, genre scenes.
Admitted to the academy in Berlin in 1820, he studied with Neudlich, Dähling and Wach there. Around 1827, he set off for Italy, remaining there until 1832. On his return to Berlin, he became a member of the academy in 1841 and was appointed professor there in 1854. He is credited with the decoration of the ducal chapel in Wiesbaden and part of the work at the chapel of the Stadtschloss in Berlin.

MUSEUMS AND GALLERIES:
KALININGRAD: *Bacchus's Youth.*
AUCTION RECORDS:
PARIS, 26 March 1996, *Crowning of Tasso, the Poet* (1838, oil on canvas, 31 x 25¾ ins / 79 x 65.5 cm) FRF 28,000. MUNICH, 5 May 2003, *Portrait of the Artist Senff, Two Italian Women Strolling along* (pencil, double-sided, 8 x 5 ins / 21 x 12 cm) EUR 3,000. MADRID, 27 April 2004, *Young Neapolitan Women* (1849, oil on canvas, 23 x 23 ins / 59 x 58 cm) EUR 1,900.

HOPFGARTEN, Bodo von
German, 19th century.
Born 1810, in Breslau (now Wroclaw, Poland).
Painter.
He spent several years in Rome and Naples, later exhibiting genre pictures in Berlin.

HOPFGARTEN, Emil Alexander
German, 19th century.
Born 3 April 1821, in Berlin; died 12 September 1856, in Biebrich.
Sculptor.
A pupil of L Wichmann, he exhibited busts and mythologically inspired sculptures in Berlin from 1844.

HOPKIN, Robert
American, 19th century.
Born 3 January 1832, in Glasgow, Scotland; died 21 March 1909, in Detroit.
Painter, watercolourist. Waterscapes, seascapes.
Robert Hopkin went to the USA with his parents in 1843, and went on to occupy a place among American painters. Notable works include six paintings decorating the Cotton

Exchange in New Orleans. He was president of the Detroit Association of Arts, and a member of the Society of Western Artists.

AUCTION RECORDS:

DETROIT, 1 June 1980, *Sailing Ships at Sea* (oil on canvas, 14 x 20 ins / 35.5 x 51 cm) USD 1,600. DETROIT, 20 March 1983, *Two Sailing Ships at Sea* (oil on canvas, 14 x 20 ins / 35.5 x 50.8 cm) USD 1,600. NEW YORK, 21 Nov 1986, *Sailing Ships at Sea* (oil on canvas, 30 x 25 ins / 76.2 x 63.5 cm) USD 3,750. NEW YORK, 31 March 1993, *Isle of Arran* (1871, oil on canvas, 27 1/2 x 40 ins / 69.9 x 101.6 cm) USD 3,450. DETROIT, 16 Nov 2001, *Close Hauled* (oil on canvas, 12 x 18 ins / 30 x 46 cm) USD 1,900. DETROIT, 14 June 2002, *Fisherman* (oil on canvas, 23 x 19 ins / 58 x 48 cm) USD 2,000. DETROIT, 13 Dec 2002, *Sailing Ships at Night* (oil on canvas, 20 x 24 ins / 51 x 61 cm) USD 2,500. DETROIT, 18 July 2003, *Seascape with Sailing Ship* (oil on canvas, 18 x 24 ins / 46 x 61 cm) USD 3,000. DETROIT, 19 Sept 2003, *In the Channel* (oil on canvas, 24 x 18 ins / 61 x 46 cm) USD 3,000. NEW YORK, 3 March 2004, *Shipping Offshore in Rough Winters* (1872, oil on canvas on board, 26 x 40 ins / 66 x 102 cm) USD 3,200. DETROIT, 17 Sept 2004, *Sea at Night* (oil on canvas, 61 x 47 ins / 155 x 119 cm) USD 2,100.

HOPKIN, T.

British, 19th century.
Active in London.
Sculptor.

T. Hopkin exhibited in London at the Royal Academy in 1854.

HOPKINS, Arthur

British, 19th century.
Born 1848; died 1930.
Active in London.
Painter, watercolourist, engraver, draughtsman.
Mythological subjects, genre scenes.

Arthur Hopkins was a very productive artist and served as treasurer of the Royal Society of Painters in Watercolours in London. He exhibited in London for the first time in 1872 and continued regularly to show work at exhibitions at the Royal Academy and the Royal Society of Painters in Watercolours.

AUCTION RECORDS:

LONDON, 24 July 1911, *Rough Sea* (watercolour) GBP 5. LONDON, 24 March 1981, *The Only Way* (1913, watercolour heightened with gouache, 19 x 27 1/2 ins / 48 x 70 cm) GBP 600. NEW YORK, 26 Oct 1983, *Boys' Paradise* (1878, watercolour, 24 1/2 x 35 ins / 62 x 89 cm) USD 11,000. LONDON, 30 May 1985, *Haycart* (1913, watercolour, 20 x 27 1/2 ins / 51 x 70 cm) GBP 3,200. LONDON, 25 Jan 1988, *Danae and her Son Perseus Drifting towards the Island of Seriphos* (1911, watercolour, 22 3/4 x 37 3/4 ins / 58 x 96 cm) GBP 1,780. LONDON, 30 Jan 1991, *Under-gardener* (watercolour, 8 1/4 x 6 1/4 ins / 21 x 16 cm) GBP 4,180. LONDON, 19 Dec 1991, *The Torn Gown* (1909, pencil and watercolour, 21 1/4 x 13 3/4 ins / 54 x 34.9 cm) GBP 7,150. NEW YORK, 19 Feb 1992, *Leader of the Gang* (watercolour/paper, 23 x 32 ins / 58.5 x 81.3 cm) USD 7,150. LONDON, 5 Nov 1993, *Orchard by the Sea* (1914, pencil and watercolour, 11 1/4 x 15 1/4 ins / 28.5 x 38.8 cm) GBP 2,760. LONDON, 25 March 1994, *Tired of Waiting* (1881, pencil and watercolour, 22 1/4 x 29 3/4 ins / 56.5 x 75.5 cm) GBP 3,680. LONDON, 10 March 1995, *Little Glutton* (pencil and watercolour heightened with white, 19 1/4 x 14 3/4 ins / 49.2 x 37.3 cm) GBP 2,070. NEW YORK, 18-19 July 1996, *Boys' Paradise* (1878, watercolour and gouache/paper, 24 1/2 x 35 ins / 62.2 x 88.9 cm) USD 5,750. LONDON, 5 Nov 1997, *Picking Flowers* (1886, watercolour heightened with scratches, 14 1/4 x 11 ins / 36 x 28 cm) GBP 5,520. JOHANNESBURG, 11 Oct 1999, *On the Lookout* (1879, oil on canvas, 41 x 63 ins / 104 x 159 cm) ZAR 38,000. LONDON, 17 April 2000, *Hartland Point, North Devon* (watercolour and gouache, 14 x 19 ins / 35 x 49 cm) GBP 1,900. SANDBACH, 14 March 2001, *Hartland Point, North Devon* (watercolour, 14 x 19 ins / 36 x 48 cm) GBP 3,300. CREWKERNE, 26 April 2001, *Haymaking Games* (1899, watercolour with scratching out, 22 x 28 ins / 55 x 71 cm) GBP 4,000. DORCHESTER, 4 July 2002, *Daphne, All Is Fair and Sweet* (watercolour, 11 x 15 ins / 28 x 38 cm) GBP 1,100. LONDON, 11 March 2003, *RSVP* (1910, watercolour, 15 x 19 ins / 37 x 49 cm) GBP 2,400. NEWCASTLE, 18 March 2003, *Daphne, All Is Fair and Sweet* (oil on canvas, 11 x 15 ins / 29 x 39 cm) GBP 1,050. LONDON, 9 March 2004, *Young Girl Carrying Violets* (watercolour, 18 x 15 ins / 46 x 37 cm) GBP 4,600. LONDON, 14 Sept 2004, *Coming In to Shore* (1897, watercolour heightened with white, 22 x 33 ins / 55 x 83 cm) GBP 2,000. LONDON, 9 Nov 2004, *By the Mill Stream, Spring* (watercolour heightened with gouache, 18 x 14 ins / 45 x 36 cm) GBP 4,600.

HOPKINS, Edna Boies

Maiden name: Boies
American, 19th - 20th century.
Born 1872, in Hudson (Michigan); died 1937.
Active in France.
Painter, engraver (wood), watercolourist. Flowers, plants.
Japonisme.
Provincetown Artists' Colony.

Edna Boies Hopkins studied at the Pratt Institute of Design, New York, under Arthur Wesley Dow, then at Ohio State University and in Paris. She married James R. Hopkins, an artist from Ohio, in 1904, and lived in Paris from 1905 to 1914, and from 1920 to 1923. She became a member of the Société Nationale des Beaux-Arts, and was an active member of the Provincetown (Massachusetts) Artists' Colony, a group of American students, formed in Paris, which produced woodcuts inspired by Japonisme.

Hopkins made colour woodcuts, essentially representations of plants, often at the moment when they were wilting, like *Datura* (1910) or *Lily of the Valley* (Muguet), creating a melancholy and even unsettling atmosphere, as in *Pea Pods* (Cosses de Petits Pois), where the plant is represented on the stalk, in the manner of a naturalistic illustration, but with empty pea pods.

Hopkins' work has featured posthumously in themed exhibitions: 2002, *From Paris to Provincetown; Blanche Lazzell and Color Woodcut*, Cleveland Museum of Art, Cleveland; 2002, *Le Japonisme en Amérique: œuvres sur papier, 1880-1930* (*Japonisme in America: Works on Paper, 1880-1930*), Musée d'Art Américain/Terra Foundation for the Arts, Giverny.

BIBLIOGRAPHY:

Arnold, Edwin (Sir), *Japonica*, C. Scribner's Sons, New York, 1891. *Le Japonisme en Amérique: œuvres sur papier, 1880-1930*, exhibition catalogue, Musée d'Art américain, Giverny, Terra Foundation for the Arts, Evanston (IL), 2002. Shapiro, Barbara Stern, *From Paris to Provincetown: Blanche Lazzell and the Color Woodcut*, exhibition catalogue, MFA Publications, Cleveland, 2002.

MUSEUMS AND GALLERIES:

BERLIN (Kunstgewerbemus.) - CINCINNATI (AM) - DETROIT (IA) - PARIS (Bibliothèque d'Art et d'Archéologie, Fondation Jacques-Doucet): *Datura* (woodcut); *Achillea* (woodcut) - SAN FRANCISCO (San Francisco Museums of Art): *Petunia* (c. 1910, woodcut); *Pea Pods* (c. 1910, watercolour) - SPRINGFIELD, USA, OH (MA) - STOCKHOLM (Nationalmus.) - WASHINGTON DC (Library of Congress).

HOPKINS, Everard

British, 19th - 20th century.

Born 1860, in London; died 17 October 1928.
Painter, watercolourist, draughtsman, illustrator.
Everard Hopkins studied at the Slade School of Fine Art. He exhibited at the Royal Academy, the New Water-Colour Society from 1884, and the Royal Institute of Painters in Watercolours. He contributed to the satirical magazine *Punch*.
BIBLIOGRAPHY:
Osterwalder, Marcus (ed.), *Dictionnaire des illustrateurs 1800-1914*, Ides et Calendes, Neuchâtel, 1989.

HOPKINS, Frances Anne, Mrs Edward Hopkins
Maiden name: Beechey
British, 19th century.
Active in London.
Painter. Genre scenes.
Frances Hopkins exhibited some Canadian scenes at the Royal Academy and the Society of Painters in Watercolours in London from 1872.
AUCTION RECORDS:
LONDON, 10 June 1986, *Mounting a Rapid: Autumn, Canada* (oil on canvas, 36 1/2 x 53 1/2 ins / 92.7 x 135.9 cm) GBP 75,000. TORONTO, 14 May 2002, *Le Tréport, Normandy* (1895, watercolour and gouache, 12 x 18 ins / 31 x 46 cm) CAD 4,600. TORONTO, 1 June 2004, *Pastoral Scene with Cattle and Farm Workers* (watercolour, 13 x 19 ins / 34 x 47 cm) CAD 3,600. TORONTO, 22 Nov 2004, *Setting Sail* (watercolour and gouache on cardboard, 12 x 2 ins / 30 x 4 cm) CAD 11,000.

HOPKINS, George Edward
American, 19th century.
Born 30 July 1855, in Covington (Maryland).
Active in Baltimore.
Painter.
George Edward Hopkins was a pupil of Franck Duveneck and Gabl at the academy in Munich.

HOPKINS, Hannah H. (Mrs)
British, 19th century.
Active in Odiham (Hampshire).
Painter. Genre scenes.
Hannah Hopkins was married to William Hopkins. She exhibited in London, sometimes at the Royal Academy and the Suffolk Street Gallery, between 1871 and 1879.

HOPKINS, J.
British, 18th - 19th century.
Active in London.
Miniaturist. Landscapes.
J. Hopkins exhibited frequently at the Royal Academy in London between 1791 and 1809. He painted a *Portrait of Nelson*.

HOPKINS, James Roy
American, 20th century.
Born 1877, in Irwin (Ohio); died 1969, in Mechanicsburg (Ohio).
Active in Philadelphia, and in Paris from 1902 to 1914.
Painter, engraver, illustrator. Nudes, portraits.
James Roy Hopkins trained at Columbus Art School and Cincinnati Art Academy under the painter Frank Duvenek. He went to Paris in 1902 where he met the Impressionist painters. He married the engraver Edna Boies in 1904. He painted the inhabitants of Cumberland Mountain (Tennessee) and female nudes.

Hopkins was a member of the International Society of Colour Engravers, the International Society of Wood Engravers, the Société Nationale des Beaux-Arts, and the American Art Association of Paris. He ran the Department of Art at Ohio State University from 1923 to 1947, and was awarded the Lippincott Prize in 1908.
MUSEUMS AND GALLERIES:
SPRINGFIELD, USA, OH (MA): *The Bamboo Screen* (c. 1912, oil on canvas).

HOPKINS, John
British, 19th century.
Sculptor (bronze). Busts.
John Hopkins is known only by two pieces in the museum in Boulogne.
MUSEUMS AND GALLERIES:
BOULOGNE: two busts in bronze.

HOPKINS, John
Australian, 20th century.
Born 1943, in Melbourne.
Painter.
John Hopkins first worked as a designer but around 1972 decided to become a professional painter. He has taken part in several group exhibitions since 1969 and exhibited in Melbourne in 1970 and 1971.

HOPKINS, Mark
American, 20th century.
Born 9 February 1881, in Williamstown; died 1935, in Pau, France.
Also active in France.
Sculptor.
Mark Hopkins trained under Mac Monnies, and was a member of the Société des Artistes Français in Paris, and of the International Union of Fine Arts. He lived in Giverny (Eure) and Williamstown.

HOPKINS, Thomas
British, 18th century.
Died 4 August 1794, in London.
Miniaturist, enameller.
Thomas Hopkins was a pupil of H. Bone.

HOPKINS, W.
British, 19th century.
Active in London.
Painter.
W. Hopkins exhibited in London at the Suffolk Street Gallery in 1846 and 1870.

HOPKINS, W.
British, 19th century.
Active in Windsor Castle.
Painter, engraver.
W. Hopkins exhibited in London at the Royal Academy from 1803 to 1811.

HOPKINS, W. A.
British, 19th century.
Active in London.
Sculptor.
W.A. Hopkins exhibited in London at the Royal Academy in 1844.

HOPKINS, William
British, 19th century.
Pastellist.
Only one work by William Hopkins has been identified.

HOPKINS, William H.
British, 19th century.
Died 18 October 1892.
Active in Keynsham (Bath).
Painter. Landscapes, animals.
William H. Hopkins exhibited many paintings of sporting scenes in London at the Royal Academy, the British Institution and the Suffolk Street Gallery between 1853 and 1890.
AUCTION RECORDS:
LONDON, Feb 1923, *Hunt Followers*, GBP 18. LONDON, 27 Feb 1925, *Hunting Scenes*, GBP 33. LONDON, 7 Dec 1928, *Burgundy, Kate and Amy with a Stable Boy in a Landscape*, GBP 42. LONDON, 14 Feb 1978, *Lunch on the Moors* (1869, oil on canvas, 18 3/4 x 29 1/4 ins / 47.5 x 74 cm) GBP 800. NEW YORK, 25 May 1984, *King of the West Held by a Rider* (oil on canvas, 25

x 29 3/4 ins / 63.5 x 75.5 cm) USD 2,500. LONDON, 19 July 1985, *Rowley Mile, Newmarket* (1892, oil on canvas, 13 1/4 x 19 1/2 ins / 33.7 x 49.5 cm) GBP 4,000. NEW YORK, 4 June 1987, *Over the Hedge* (1878, oil on canvas, 20 x 30 ins / 50.8 x 76.2 cm) USD 21,000. EDINBURGH, 9 June 1994, *End of the Day in the Grouse-shooting Season* (1868, oil on canvas, 16 1/2 x 27 1/2 ins / 42 x 69.8 cm) GBP 3,450. LONDON, 6 Nov 1996, *Earl of Hardwick with Two Hunters and a Stable Lad* (oil on canvas, 33 x 52 ins / 84 x 132 cm) GBP 11,500. LEYBURN, 13 April 2000, *Brenda, Bay Hunter in an Open Landscape* (1879, oil on canvas, 23 x 28 ins / 58 x 71 cm) GBP 2,800. TORONTO, 12 June 2000, *Shooting Party, Loch Ericht* (1871, oil on canvas, 30 x 46 ins / 75 x 118 cm) CAD 52,000. LONDON, 5 Sept 2001, *Shooting Party, Loch Ericht* (1871, oil on canvas, 30 x 46 ins / 75 x 118 cm) GBP 40,000. MELBOURNE, 26 Nov 2001, *Threshing the Harvest* (1860, oil on canvas, 24 x 43 ins / 61 x 108 cm) AUD 21,000. LEYBURN, 25 April 2002, *Grey Hunter, Griselda, in a Stable* (1882, oil on canvas, 24 x 29 ins / 60 x 73 cm) GBP 1,500. ANTWERP, 10 Dec 2002, *Hunting Scene* (oil on panel, a pair, 13 x 23 ins / 34 x 58 cm) EUR 7,000. NEW YORK, 10 Feb 2004, *Pug* (oil on canvas, 29 x 33 ins / 74 x 84 cm) USD 10,000.

HOPKINSON, Charles Sydney
American, 19th - 20th century.
Born 27 July 1869, in Cambridge, MA; died 1962.
Active in the USA.
Painter, watercolourist. Portraits, genre scenes, landscapes, seascapes.

Charles Hopkinson studied at Harvard University, then at the Art Students League in New York, where his teacher was the American painter John Twachtman, a co-founder of the innovative artists' group known as The Ten. Hopkinson then went to Paris, where he studied at the Académie Julian. Later, he returned to the USA and settled in Boston. He is known for his portraits and picturesque scenes of childhood, and often painted members of his own family.

He took part in several group exhibitions, including the Salon des Artistes Français in Paris in 1895; at the Academy of the Fine Arts of Philadelphia and at the Dallas Fair in 1924; at the Los Angeles County Museum of Art in 1925; and at several events organised by the group known as the Boston Five. He had a solo exhibition at the Danforth Museum of Art in Framingham in 1988-1989. He was awarded gold medals in Buffalo in 1901 and in St Louis in 1904. He won second prize ($200) at Worcester in 1902 and 1905.

AUCTION RECORDS:
NEW YORK, 6 Dec 1984, *Windy Anchorage* (1899, oil on canvas, 31 3/4 x 25 1/2 ins / 80.6 x 64.7 cm) USD 15,000. NEW YORK, 24 May 1989, *Portrait of a Young Child* (oil on canvas, 32 x 27 1/2 ins / 81.3 x 69.8 cm) USD 11,000. NEW YORK, 12 April 1996, *Portrait of Henry G. Vaughan* (1903, oil on canvas, 65 x 46 ins / 165.1 x 116.8 cm) USD 13,800. NEW YORK, 21-22 May 1996, *Three Dancing Girls* (1923, oil on canvas, 66 x 78 1/4 ins / 167.6 x 198.8 cm) USD 112,500; *Shipwreck at Dana Passage* (oil on canvas, 30 1/4 x 32 1/4 ins / 77 x 82 cm) USD 2,530.

HOPKINSON, Robert
British, 18th century.
Active in London.
Painter. Landscapes.

Robert Hopkinson exhibited in London, at the Society of Artists and the Free Society from 1762 to 1788 and at the Royal Academy in 1774, 1781 and 1788.

HOPLEY, Edward William John
British, 19th century.
Born 1816; died 30 April 1869, in London.
Painter. Portraits, genre scenes.

Edward Hopley embarked on the study of medicine but abandoned this in favour of painting. He worked in Lewes and later in London, where he exhibited at the Royal Academy and the British Institution from 1851.

HOPP, H. W.
German, 18th - 19th century.
Born in Groningen, Holland.
Painter, miniaturist. Portraits.

He exhibited in Berlin from 1804 to 1838. A noted work is his *Portrait of Tsar Alexander I of Russia*.

HOPPE, Aemilius Samuel
Dutch, 17th century.
Born 1643.
Active in Dordrecht.
Sculptor.

According to Houbraken, Aemilius Hoppe was the master of Abraham van Kalroai.

HOPPE, Bror Christian
Danish, 19th century.
Born 28 November 1859, in Ystad.
Active in Malmö and Copenhagen.
Painter.

HOPPE, C. A. W.
German, 19th century.
Active in Berlin.
Painter.

He painted genre scenes and still lifes.

HOPPE, C. F.
German, 19th century.
Active c. 1810.
Lithographer.

He produced a series of *Views of Silesia*.

HOPPE, Erik
Danish, 20th century.
Born 1897, in Ødis; died 1968.
Painter. Portraits, landscapes with figures, landscapes.

Erik Hoppe was a student at the Kongelige Danske Kunstakademi in Copenhagen from 1918 to 1920, and his work has been shown at many exhibitions of contemporary Danish painting. He is one of the most representative figurative painters in twentieth-century Danish art. Although landscape is often the initial inspiration for his paintings, their subject is really the play of light.

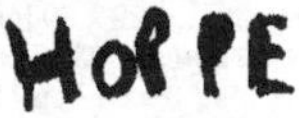

MUSEUMS AND GALLERIES:
COPENHAGEN (Statens Mus. for Kunst): *Figures on a Lawn* (1944).

AUCTION RECORDS:
COPENHAGEN, 25 April 1972, *Figure*, DKK 12,000. COPENHAGEN, 10 Oct 1973, *Summer Day*, DKK 15,500. COPENHAGEN, 25 Nov 1976, *Summer Day* (1946, oil on canvas, 26 3/4 x 32 ins / 68 x 81 cm) DKK 10,500. COPENHAGEN, 5 Oct 1977, *The Frederiksholms Canal* (1935, oil on canvas, 27 1/4 x 32 3/4 ins / 69 x 83 cm) DKK 16,000. COPENHAGEN, 14 March 1978, *Two Women in a Summer Landscape* (1932, oil on canvas, 43 1/4 x 50 1/2 ins / 110 x 128 cm) DKK 18,600. COPENHAGEN, 10 Oct 1979, *Figure in a Landscape* (oil on canvas, 33 1/2 x 40 1/2 ins / 85 x 103 cm) DKK 17,500. COPENHAGEN, 8 April 1981, *Street Scene* (oil on canvas, 25 1/2 x 27 1/2 ins / 65 x 70 cm) DKK 25,000. COPENHAGEN, 13 Feb 1985, *Landscape with Church* (1945, oil on canvas, 19 3/4 x 24 ins / 50 x 61 cm) DKK 27,000. COPENHAGEN, 26 Nov 1986, *Landscape* (1954, oil on canvas, 26 1/2 x 33 1/2 ins / 67 x 85 cm) DKK 24,000. NEW YORK, 4 June 1987, *Tables and Chairs in a Garden* (1930, oil on canvas, 39 1/4 x 39 1/4 ins / 100 x 100 cm) DKK 52,000. COPENHAGEN, 2 March 1988, *Figure in Søndermarken* (35 x 38 1/2 ins / 89 x 98 cm) DKK 38,000. COPENHAGEN, 4 May 1988, *Two People Lying on a Lawn* (1948, 25 1/2 x 32 ins / 65 x 81 cm) DKK 26,000; *Sunlight on the Fields* (11 3/4 x 17 ins / 30 x 43

cm) DKK 15,000. COPENHAGEN, 30 Nov 1988, *Figure in Søndermarken* (oil on canvas, 17¼ x 20 ins / 44 x 51 cm) DKK 10,000. COPENHAGEN, 10 May 1989, *The Barns in Summer* (oil on canvas, 32 x 35½ ins / 81 x 90 cm) DKK 29,000. COPENHAGEN, 20 Sept 1989, *Red Sun* (oil on canvas, 19¾ x 24 ins / 50 x 61 cm) DKK 19,000. COPENHAGEN, 9 May 1990, *Figure in Søndermarken* (1938, oil on canvas, 33½ x 35½ ins / 85 x 90 cm) DKK 27,000. COPENHAGEN, 31 Oct 1990, *Figures in Søndermarken* (oil on canvas, 26 x 32¼ ins / 66 x 82 cm) DKK 27,000. COPENHAGEN, 4 Dec 1991, *Figure in a Sunlit Field* (oil on canvas, 20 x 24¾ ins / 51 x 63 cm) DKK 18,000. COPENHAGEN, 1 April 1992, *Self-portrait* (1932, oil on canvas, 16½ x 16¼ ins / 42 x 41 cm) DKK 4,500. COPENHAGEN, 21 Oct 1992, *Figure in Søndermarken* (1951, oil on canvas, 35 x 38½ ins / 89 x 98 cm) DKK 25,000. COPENHAGEN, 21 April 1993, *View of Nekselo* (1919, oil on canvas, 22 x 25¼ ins / 56 x 64 cm) DKK 33,000. COPENHAGEN, 19 Oct 1994, *Round Church at Østerlars* (oil on canvas, 29¼ x 36¼ ins / 74 x 92 cm) DKK 70,000. COPENHAGEN, 26 April 1995, *Wilder's Square* (oil on canvas, 31½ x 35½ ins / 80 x 90 cm) DKK 36,000. COPENHAGEN, 17 April 1996, *Garden at the Lindekroen Inn* (1930, oil on canvas, 39¼ x 39¼ ins / 100 x 100 cm) DKK 35,000. COPENHAGEN, 29 Jan 1997, *Sunlit Glade in Søndermarken* (oil on canvas, 15¾ x 20 ins / 40 x 51 cm) DKK 24,000. COPENHAGEN, 16 April 1997, *View of the Painter's Studio* (1950, oil on canvas, 17¼ x 21¼ ins / 44 x 54 cm) DKK 11,000. COPENHAGEN, 12-14 Nov 1997, *Girl in Søndermarken* (oil on canvas, 19¾ x 23¼ ins / 50 x 59 cm) DKK 14,500. COPENHAGEN, 23 March 1999, *Summer Landscape* (oil on canvas, 24 x 28 ins / 61 x 71 cm) DKK 27,000. COPENHAGEN, 20 Oct 1999, *From Sondermarken* (oil on canvas, 35 x 39 ins / 90 x 100 cm) DKK 28,000. COPENHAGEN, 15 March 2000, *Landscape from Sondermarken with Figures Walking in Avenue* (oil on canvas, 39 x 43 ins / 100 x 110 cm) DKK 41,000. COPENHAGEN, 7 Dec 2000, *Mother and Daughter in Sondermarken* (oil on canvas, 19 x 26 ins / 48 x 65 cm) DKK 38,000. COPENHAGEN, 7 Feb 2001, *Figure in Sondermarken* (oil on canvas, 27 x 32 ins / 68 x 81 cm) DKK 40,000. COPENHAGEN, 30 May 2001, *Figures in Sondermarken* (oil on canvas, 28 x 31 ins / 70 x 80 cm) DKK 40,000. COPENHAGEN, 23 April 2002, *Middle of Summer in Sondermarken* (1956, oil on canvas, 26 x 32 ins / 67 x 81 cm) DKK 36,000. COPENHAGEN, 23 Oct 2002, *Figure among Trees, Sondermarken* (oil on canvas, 29 x 39 ins / 73 x 100 cm) DKK 36,000. COPENHAGEN, 29 April 2003, *Figure in Sondermarken* (oil on canvas, 15 x 19 ins / 39 x 47 cm) DKK 25,000. COPENHAGEN, 7 Oct 2003, *Walking in Sondermarken* (oil on canvas, 26 x 31 ins / 67 x 80 cm) DKK 24,000. COPENHAGEN, 25 Feb 2004, *Figure in Sondermarken, sunshine* (oil on canvas, 32 x 39 ins / 81 x 100 cm) DKK 48,000. COPENHAGEN, 29 March 2004, *Summer's Day in Sondermarken* (oil on canvas, 20 x 26 ins / 51 x 66 cm) DKK 50,000.

HOPPE, Erna
German, 19th - 20th century.
Born in Hamburg.
Painter. Landscapes.

Hoppe lived in Paris, and her work was exhibited there between 1906 and 1914.

AUCTION RECORDS:

PARIS, 15 June 1945, *Banks of the Seine*, FRF 1,700.

HOPPE, Ferdinand
German, 19th century.
Born 23 February 1848, in Tartu, Estonia; died 2 December 1890, in Cologne.
Painter. Landscapes, seascapes.

He was a pupil of Dücker, and worked mainly in Düsseldorf and Berlin.

AUCTION RECORDS:

COLOGNE, 18 March 1989, *Sun Setting on Ost Lake* (1884, oil on canvas, 29½ x 46½ ins / 75 x 118 cm) DEM 3,500. MUNICH, 5 Dec 2003, *Still-life* (1863, oil on canvas, 13 x 11 ins / 33 x 27 cm) EUR 2,400. MUNICH, 26 March 2004, *Still-life with Wine Glass and Grapes* (1863, oil on canvas, 13 x 11 ins / 33 x 27 cm) EUR 2,400.

HOPPE, Ferdinand Bernhard, or Hoeppe
Dutch, 19th century.
Born 20 February 1831, in Cleves.
Watercolourist. Landscapes.

From 1851 to 1854, Ferdinand Hoppe studied under G. van Merkensteyn in Nijmegen and in 1870 in Düsseldorf. He later settled in The Hague and frequently exhibited in Munich and Berlin.

MUSEUMS AND GALLERIES:

MONTREAL: *Arrival at Port* - THE HAGUE (Gemeentemus.): *In the Woods*.

AUCTION RECORDS:

LONDON, 29 April 1911, *Dutch Canal with Barges and Boats* (watercolour) GBP 27 60. AMSTERDAM, 5 Sept 2000, *Peasant Woman on Birch-lined Road* (oil on canvas, 20 x 29 ins / 52 x 73 cm) NLG 3,800. AMSTERDAM, 1 Sept 2004, *Watermill in Winter* (1896, oil on canvas, 44 x 59 ins / 111 x 151 cm) EUR 2,200.

HOPPE, Georg
German, 19th century.
Born in Hanover.
Painter.

He lived mainly in Berlin.

HOPPE, Hedwig
German, 19th century.
Born 19th century, in Berlin.
Painter. Portraits, still-lifes.

She first exhibited in Berlin around 1886. Probably identical with Hedwig Hausman-Hoppe.

HOPPE, Jochim
German, 16th - 17th century.
Born in Hamburg.
Painter.

HOPPE-CAMPHAUSEN, Curt
German, 20th century.
Born 11 April 1877, in Düsseldorf.
Painter. History painting, portraits, landscapes.

HOPPEN, Karol
Polish, 19th century.
Born 1798, in Radom; died 21 December 1849, in Radom.
Painter.

Karol Hoppen studied in Dresden and Rome. His painting *Baptism of Christ* is in the Protestant church in Radom.

HOPPENBROUWERS, Johannes Franciscus
Dutch, 19th century.
Born 16 April 1791, in The Hague; died 18 July 1866, in The Hague.
Painter, watercolourist, draughtsman. Hunting scenes, landscapes, waterscapes.

Johannes Hoppenbrouwers was a pupil of Andreas Schelfhout.

MUSEUMS AND GALLERIES:

AMSTERDAM (Stedelijk Mus.): *Stag Hunt* - THE HAGUE (Gemeentemus.): six landscapes.

AUCTION RECORDS:

PARIS, 23 April 1925, *View of a Canal in Holland*, FRF 350. PARIS, 28-29 June 1926, *Winter Landscape* (sepia) FRF 120. PARIS, 23 May 1935, *Troops on the March*, FRF 105. LONDON, 15 March 1974, *Winter Landscape* (1864) Gns 1,000. MUNICH, 25 Nov 1976, *Hunter's Repose* (1851, oil on canvas, 23¼ x 31¼ ins / 59 x 79.5 cm) DEM 2,800. LONDON, 10 May 1979, *Peasants on a Frozen Canal* (watercolour, 13½ x 19¾ ins /

34.5 x 50 cm) GBP 900. AMSTERDAM, 30 Oct 1979, *Landscape with Stormy Sky* (1844, oil on panel, 20 x 26¼ ins / 50.5 x 66.7 cm) NLG 16,500. AMSTERDAM, 11 May 1982, *Mountain Landscape at Twilight* (oil on panel, 22½ x 31½ ins / 57 x 80 cm) NLG 6,800. BRUSSELS, 22 Nov 1984, *Winter Landscape* (oil on canvas, 23½ x 35 ins / 60 x 89 cm) BEF 120,000. AMSTERDAM, 15 April 1985, *Skaters in a Winter Landscape* (oil on panel, 6 x 8¾ ins / 15 x 22.5 cm) NLG 7,600. LONDON, 23 March 1988, *Farm in a Storm* (1863, watercolour, 15 x 21¼ ins / 38 x 54 cm) GBP 1,100. AMSTERDAM, 19 Sept 1989, *Hilly Landscape with a Peasant and his Mule accompanied by a Dog on a Sandy Road* (oil on canvas, 19 x 24¾ ins / 48.5 x 63 cm) NLG 7,475. AMSTERDAM, 2 May 1990, *Summer Landscape with a Peasant Woman and her Dog on a Road Leading to a Windmill* (oil on panel, 8 x 11¼ ins / 20.5 x 28.8 cm) NLG 4,830. AMSTERDAM, 17 Sept 1991, *Winter Landscape with a Skater Pushing a Sledge on a Frozen River* (oil on panel, 9¼ x 11¾ ins / 23.5 x 30 cm) NLG 4,830. AMSTERDAM, 28 Oct 1992, *Winter Landscape with Skaters on a Frozen Canal* (oil on panel, 8 x 12¼ ins / 20.5 x 31 cm) NLG 5,750. AMSTERDAM, 3 Nov 1992, *Winter Landscape with Figures on a Frozen River* (oil on canvas/panel, 13½ x 17¼ ins / 34.5 x 44 cm) NLG 3,680. AMSTERDAM, 21 April 1993, *Hunting Party in an Undulating Landscape at Sunset* (oil on panel, 9¼ x 11½ ins / 23.5 x 29.5 cm) NLG 2,760. AMSTERDAM, 21 April 1994, *Winter Landscape with a Huntsman and a Dog on a Snowy Road* (1950, oil on panel, 7¾ x 10½ ins / 19.5 x 26.5 cm) NLG 12,650. AMSTERDAM, 8 Nov 1994, *Figures on a Frozen River* (1852, oil on panel, 21½ x 28¾ ins / 54.5 x 73 cm) NLG 14,950. LONDON, 15 Nov 1995, *Winter Landscape* (1846, oil on panel, 13¾ x 18½ ins / 35 x 47 cm) GBP 5,175. AMSTERDAM, 28 April 1999, *House on Bank of Frozen River* (oil on panel, 12 x 16 ins / 30 x 40 cm) NLG 28,000. LEYBURN, 25 Nov 1999, *Summer. Winter* (oil on panel, a pair, 9 x 13 ins / 23 x 32 cm) GBP 5,800. BRUSSELS, 20 March 2000, *Woodgatherers in Winter* (oil on panel, 9 x 11 ins / 22 x 29 cm) BEF 340,000. AMSTERDAM, 20 March 2001, *After the Harvest* (1849, oil on panel, 15 x 21 ins / 38 x 54 cm) NLG 22,000. AMSTERDAM, 4 Sept 2001, *Winter Landscape with Peasant near Windmill* (oil on canvas, 18 x 23 ins / 45 x 59 cm) EUR 3,600. AMSTERDAM, 22 Oct 2002, *Winter Landscape with Skaters near a Koek en Zopie* (oil on canvas, 21 x 28 ins / 54 x 70 cm) EUR 7,500. AMSTERDAM, 23 Oct 2002, *Woodgatherers on the Ice on a Windy Day* (1853, oil on panel, 22 x 29 ins / 55 x 73 cm) EUR 10,000. AMSTERDAM, 29 April 2003, *Snow-covered Pine Trees in a Winter Landscape* (oil on panel, 5 x 7 ins / 12 x 18 cm) EUR 2,500. BREMEN, 26 Sept 2003, *Winter Landscape with Ice Skaters* (oil on panel, 15 x 18 ins / 38 x 46 cm) EUR 2,500. AMSTERDAM, 3 Feb 2004, *Smoking Eels on a River in Moonlight* (1854, oil on panel, 15 x 22 ins / 39 x 56 cm) EUR 4,000. AMSTERDAM, 19 May 2004, *Winter Landscape* (1854, watercolour, 9 x 13 ins / 23 x 32 cm) EUR 4,200.

HÖPPENER, Hugo. See **FIDUS**

HOPPENER, Jacobus
German, 15th century.
Active in Lübeck at the beginning of the 15th century.
Painter.

MUSEUMS AND GALLERIES:
HANOVER: works attributed - SCHWERIN: works attributed.

HOPPENHAUPT
German, 18th century.
Born 18th century.
Engraver.

She was the daughter of Johann Michael Hoppenhaupt junior.

HOPPENHAUPT, Johann Christian
German, 18th century.
Died c. 1780, in Berlin.
Sculptor.

He was probably the son of Johann Michael Hoppenhaupt senior. He worked for Frederick the Great all his life, having a hand in the completion of the decoration of Sanssouci and also working on the Neues Schloss in Potsdam and Charlottenburg Palace.

HOPPENHAUPT, Johann Michael, the Elder
German, 17th - 18th century.
Born in Zittau.
Sculptor.

He worked mainly for the churches in Zittau and Hainewalde in Saxony.

HOPPENHAUPT, Johann Michael, the Younger
German, 18th century.
Born 1709, in Merseburg.
Sculptor.

The son of Johann Michael Hoppenhaupt senior, he worked at various royal palaces in Vienna, Dresden and Berlin.

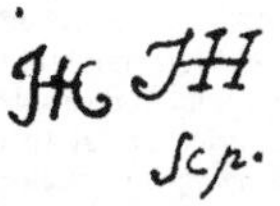

HOPPENSACH, Alfred Valdemar
Danish, 19th century.
Born 16 September 1854, in Copenhagen; died 27 October 1886, in Copenhagen.
Sculptor, painter.

Alfred Hoppensach is known for his *Landscapes*.

HOPPER, Edward
American, 20th century.
Born 22 July 1882, in Nyack (New York); died 15 May 1967, in New York.
Painter (gouache), watercolourist, engraver, draughtsman, illustrator. Scenes with figures, nudes, urban landscapes, animals.

Edward Hopper was an apprentice at the New York School of Art from 1900 to 1906; his teachers were William Merrit Chase, Kenneth Hayes Miller and notably Robert Henri. The latter had a great formative influence on his art. He travelled to Europe and settled in Paris until 1907, developing his knowledge of Impressionism. He would have encountered the avant-garde artists of the time, such as Matisse and Picasso. His stay in Paris was interspersed with short trips to London and Amsterdam - where he discovered Hals, Vermeer and Rembrandt - Berlin and Brussels. In 1910 he returned to Paris, and seized the opportunity to visit Madrid and Toledo.

Upon returning to New York, Hopper earned his living as an illustrator in advertising and for magazines. But from 1912 onwards he devoted himself to painting the architecture of New England during summers spent in Gloucester, though it was not until 1924 that he abandoned his work as a commercial illustrator to dedicate himself to painting.

Like the majority of his American contemporaries, Hopper was a great admirer of Impressionism. Steeped in the art of Degas and Valloton, he executed several Pointillist works in Paris, but abandoned this style because he found it too French. From 1916 to 1918 he executed a series of very gestural oil paintings. He attracted critical attention during an exhibition in 1924. He then abandoned etching - a technique he had used from 1915, as it was particularly suitable for the play of light and shade he enjoyed producing - for watercolours (in works of minor importance) and oil painting. For a long time he had wanted to extricate himself from French painting, to 'withdraw American art from its French mother', but was unable to do this. When he understood, about

1925, that he could borrow its style while removing its themes and selecting a new world - the America of Faulker, Capra, Chandler, Goodis or Hammett, 1920s America, somewhere between prohibition and unemployment - he found his own style.

From then on, Hopper travelled from east to west across the USA, as far as Mexico, in search of new and typically American subjects. Offices, façades, bars, petrol pumps, railroads, hotel bedrooms and self-service places became engraved in his memory. This earned him the reputation of a 'regionalist', the movement which notably dominated the 1930s 'as a reaction against the art being imported from Europe and seeking to bestow on America an art form all its own' (François Marc Gagnon and Hazan). His style, however, seemed unrelated to this.

Isolated from the avant-garde artists of the time, Hopper devoted himself to landscapes, and more notably to cities, their single-storey suburban houses and the provincial realities of American life, in paintings like *Railroad Crossing* 1922-1923, *Lighthouse Hill* 1927, *Coast Guard Station* 1927, and *Railroad Sunset* 1929. He attached great importance to architecture, notably to Victorian buildings and prefabricated bungalows lost in a wild and desolate environment, representative of an America about to disappear. But apart from this striking realism, he developed a pure style and profoundly original manner, in treating banal subjects.

In 1930 Hopper had said: 'My aim in painting has always been the most exact transcription possible of my most intimate impressions of nature', producing a universe which was so everyday that it became enigmatic. The special light which surrounds the dynamic forms which have been solidly constructed with huge monochrome panels of colours, conveys a brooding sense of emptiness and solitude. Mankind occupies an essential place in his works from the end of the 1930s, though it seems to merge into the architecture, specifically because it shares some of the characteristics of this dehumanised environment. The astonishing contrasts of light, the play of diagonal and oblique lines, the unusual angles of view and zoom effects, which owed much to the cinema, highlight this ambient solitude. There is a lack of detail, embellishment and action, only a chilly ascetic universe of fixed anonymous figures, who never look each other in the eye: office employees, a couple caught unawares in private through a window in a hotel bedroom, as if 'stuck' in a distorted space (*Hotel by a Railroad*), or a woman half-dressed on the doorstep at midday, looking into the distance (*High Noon*).

Women occupy a primordial place in Hopper's works (he used his wife Jo as his model, but was not interested in rendering a true likeness). They appear mysterious and sensual, and often provocative, seemingly waiting and looking straight ahead with a strained expression on their faces. But the real subject-matter can be found in the strange light which surrounds every scene, as Hopper himself said: 'What I am really trying to paint is the light of the sun on the façade of a house, and not the grimaces or gestures of people'. We learn nothing about the private life of this couple (*Hotel by a Railroad*). The woman in her slip is reading while her husband is smoking at the window. We learn nothing about the woman with white shoulders (*Night Windows*) surprised from behind one evening while alone and in the process of getting undressed. Metaphysical anguish is born from a seemingly randomly built set, or non-event. Like the figures in *People in the Sun*, spectators feel drawn to look beyond the painting itself.

Edward Hopper has confused the critics more than any other artist. He was a scrupulous realist and some regarded him as the founder of Pop Art for the manner in which he handled everyday subjects. Yet he often incorporated an adherence to the followers of abstract art, such as De Kooning, Diebenkorn and Rothko. He was committed to a realistic depiction of the urban landscapes of twentieth-century American life, yet was a figurative painter of abstract reality.

Hopper took part in a great many collective exhibitions, notably: 1908 *Paintings and Drawings by Contemporary American Artists* held in New York; 1909 Independent Artists' Exhibition in New York (equivalent to the Salon des Refusés in Paris); 1912 MacDowell Club of New York; 1913 Armory Show in New York; 1923 Brooklyn Museum; 1929 Museum of Modern Art, New York; 1952 Venice Biennale, and others. He exhibited in numerous solo exhibitions: 1920, 1922, 1950, 1964, 1979, 1980-1981 and 1995 at the Whitney Museum of American Art, New York; 1933 Museum of Modern Art, New York; 1934 Arts Club, Chicago; 1937 Carnegie Institute, Pittsburgh; 1950 Museum of Fine Arts, Boston, and Detroit Institute of Arts; 1952 Venice Biennale, where he represented America; 1959 Currier Gallery of Art, Manchester (New Haven), and Rhode Island School of Design, Providence; 1962 Philadelphia Museum of Art, and Worcester Art Museum; 1965 Art Institute of Chicago, Detroit Institute of Arts and City Museum, St-Louis; 1967 São Paulo Biennale; 1980 Museum of Modern Art, San José (California); 1981 Hayward Gallery, London, Stedelijk Museum, Amsterdam, Städtische Kunsthalle, Düsseldorf, Art Institute of Chicago and Museum of Modern Art, San Francisco; 1982 Art Gallery of South Australia, Adelaide, and Art Gallery of New South Wales, Sydney; 1989 Musée Cantini, Marseilles; 1993 Palais des Beaux Arts, Brussels; and 2003 High Museum, Atlanta.

After his death, his wife bequeathed all Hopper's works to the Whitney Museum of American Art, New York. He was awarded a great many prizes and distinctions: in 1943, the medal and a tribute from the Logan Institute at the Art Institute of Chicago, and membership of the National Institute of Arts and Letters. The latter presented him with a gold medal for painting in 1955. The Huntingdon Hartford Foundation offered him a travelling scholarship to Pacific Palisades (California), where he spent six months.

BIBLIOGRAPHY:

Zigrosser, C, *The Etchings of Edward Hopper*, Prints C. Zigrosser, New York, 1962. Seitz, W.C./Goodrich, L., *Edward Hopper/Environment USA, 1957-1967*, exhibition catalogue, Smithsonian Inst, Washington, 1967. Goodrich, L., *Edward Hopper*, New York, 1971. Levin, G., *Edward Hopper as Illustrator*, exhibition catalogue, Whitney Museum, New York, 1979. Levin, G., *Edward Hopper: The Complete Prints*, W.W. Norton & Company, New York, 1979. *Edward Hopper - Das Frühwerk*, exhibition catalogue, Wetphalisches Landesmuseum, Munich, 1981. Levin, G., *Edward Hopper*, New York, 1984. Levin, Gail, *Hopper's Places*, New York, 1985.

MUSEUMS AND GALLERIES:

BOSTON (MFA): *Room in Brooklyn* (1932) - CHICAGO (AI): *Nighthawks* (1942, oil on canvas) - CHICAGO (Terra Foundation for American Art Collection): *Two Pigeons* (c. 1920, etching); *Nocturnal Shadows* (1921, etching); *Yacht* (1922, etching) - COLUMBUS, OH (MA): *Morning Sun* (1952) - DALLAS (MA): *Lighthouse Hill* (1927, oil on canvas) - INDIANAPOLIS (MA): *Hotel Lobby* (1943) - LUGANO (Thyssen-Bornemisza Collection) - MINNEAPOLIS (Walker Art Center): *Office at Night* (1940) - MONTGOMERY (MFA): *Light at Two Lights* (1927, watercolour/paper); *New York Office* (1962, oil on canvas) - NEW HAVEN (AG, Yale University): *Rooms for Tourists* (1945) - NEW YORK (Metropolitan Mus. of Art): *The Lighthouse at Two Lights* (1929, oil on canvas); *View of Williamsburg Bridge* - NEW YORK (MoMA): *House by Railroad* (1925); *New York Movie* (1939); *Gas* (1940) - NEW YORK (Whitney Mus. of American Art): large collection of works; *Quai des Grands-Augustins* (1909); *Railroad Sunset* (1929); *Early Sunday Morning* (1930); *Seven A. M.* (1948) - NORTHAMPTON, MA (MA, Smith College): *Pretty Penny* (1939) - PHILADELPHIA

(MA): *American Landscape* (1920) - PHILADELPHIA (Pennsylvania Academy of the Fine Arts Gal.) - PITTSBURGH (Carnegie MA): *Cape Cod Afternoon* (1936, oil on canvas) - RICHMOND (Virginia MFA): *House at Dusk* (1935, oil on canvas) - SYRACUSE (Everson MA): *Charleston Doorway* (1929, watercolour/paper) - WASHINGTON DC (Smithsonian American AM): *People in the Sun* (1960, oil on canvas) - WEST PALM BEACH (Norton MA): *August in the City* (1945, oil on canvas) - WILLIAMSTOWN (MA, Williams College): *Morning of a City* (1944) - WILMINGTON, DE (Delaware AM): *Summertime* (oil on canvas).

AUCTION RECORDS:

NEW YORK, Feb 1913, *Sailing* USD 250. NEW YORK, 7 Dec 1923, *Mansard Roof* USD 100. NEW YORK, 24 Oct 1968, *Steep Landscape* (watercolour) USD 17,000. NEW YORK, 4 March 1970, *North Truro, Massachusetts* (watercolour) USD 36,000. NEW YORK, 18 Oct 1972, *Lighthouse* (watercolour) USD 50,000. NEW YORK, 29 April 1976, *Boat on the Beach* (c. 1929, watercolour, 13 1/2 x 19 1/2 ins / 34.3 x 49.5 cm) USD 24,000. NEW YORK, 28 Oct 1976, *Hotel Room* (oil on canvas, 60 x 65 1/4 ins / 152.4 x 165.7 cm) USD 200,000. NEW YORK, 10 Nov 1976, *Locomotive* (1923, etching, 8 x 10 ins / 20.2 x 25.3 cm) USD 3,000. NEW YORK, 21 April 1977, *River Banks, Vermont* (charcoal, 15 x 22 ins / 38 x 56 cm) USD 5,250. NEW YORK, 21 April 1977, *Near the Connecticut River, Bellows Falls, Vermont* (1927, watercolour, 14 x 20 ins / 35.5 x 50.5 cm) USD 26,000. NEW YORK, 11 Nov 1977, *Locomotive* (1923, etching, 7 3/4 x 9 3/4 ins / 20 x 25 cm) USD 3,800. NEW YORK, 9 Nov 1978, *Evening Wind* (1921, etching, 7 x 8 1/4 ins / 17.7 x 21.2 cm) USD 6,500. NEW YORK, 20 April 1979, *Locomotive* (pencil, 13 1/4 x 19 1/4 ins / 33.7 x 49 cm) USD 14,500. NEW YORK, 25 Oct 1979, *Lee Shore* (1941, oil on canvas, 31 x 43 ins / 77.8 x 109.2 cm) USD 230,000. NEW YORK, 25 Sept 1980, *Near Eastham* (1947, charcoal/paper, 10 1/4 x 16 ins / 26 x 40.5 cm) USD 18,000. NEW YORK, 13 Nov 1980, *Evening Wind* (1921, etching, 7 x 8 1/4 ins / 17.6 x 21.1 cm) USD 13,500. NEW YORK, 4 Dec 1980, *Gloucester* (1923, watercolour and pencil, 14 x 20 ins / 35.5 x 50.8 cm) USD 23,000. NEW YORK, 4 May 1983, *Locomotive* (1913, etching, 7 3/4 x 9 3/4 ins / 20 x 25 cm) USD 17,000. NEW YORK, 2 June 1983, *Dead Trees, Gloucester* (1923, watercolour/paper, 13 1/4 x 19 1/4 ins / 33.7 x 48.9 cm) USD 40,000. NEW YORK, 9 Dec 1983, *Night on the El Train* (charcoal, 10 1/4 x 11 ins / 26.1 x 27.9 cm) USD 65,000. PORTLAND, 11 May 1985, *Family House at Long Island, Casco Bay, Maine* (watercolour, 9 x 13 ins / 22 x 33 cm) USD 75,000. NEW YORK, 15 Nov 1985, *Evening Wind* (1921, etching, 7 x 8 1/4 ins / 17.6 x 21.1 cm) USD 16,000. NEW YORK, 29 May 1986, *Study for Portrait of Orleans* (1950, charcoal and red Conté pencil, 10 1/2 x 16 ins / 26.7 x 40.6 cm) USD 17,000. NEW YORK, 3 Dec 1987, *Maine in the Fog* (1929, charcoal, 15 x 22 ins / 38.1 x 55.9 cm) USD 47,500. NEW YORK, 3 Dec 1987, *Captain Upton's House* (1927, oil on canvas, 28 1/2 x 36 1/4 ins / 72.5 x 92 cm) USD 2,100,000. NEW YORK, 1 Dec 1988, *Trees in East Gloucester* (1926, watercolour/paper, 13 1/2 x 19 1/2 ins / 34.2 x 49.4 cm) USD 25,300. NEW YORK, 24 May 1989, *A Stifling Day* (watercolour/paper, 13 1/2 x 19 1/4 ins / 34.3 x 48.9 cm) USD 137,500. NEW YORK, 1 Dec 1989, *Mount Moran* (watercolour and pencil/paper, 20 3/4 x 28 1/2 ins / 52.7 x 72.4 cm) USD 132,000. NEW YORK, 16 March 1990, *Male Nude Seated* (charcoal/paper, 24 1/4 x 18 3/4 ins / 61.5 x 47.5 cm) USD 18,700. NEW YORK, 26 Sept 1990, *Study of Cats* (charcoal/paper, 15 x 21 3/4 ins / 38.1 x 55.3 cm) USD 11,000. NEW YORK, 29 Nov 1990, *Church of South Truro* (1930, oil on canvas, 29 x 43 ins / 73.6 x 109.2 cm) USD 2,420,000. NEW YORK, 25 Sept 1991, *Church of South Truro* (watercolour/paper, 3 3/4 x 9 ins / 9.5 x 22.9 cm) USD 30,800. NEW YORK, 26 Sept 1991, *Yellow House* (watercolour/paper, 11 3/4 x 18 ins / 30 x 45.7 cm) USD 220,000. NEW YORK, 3 Dec 1992, *Gloucester Houses* (watercolour/paper, 16 x 21 3/4 ins / 40.6 x 55.2 cm) USD 330,000. NEW YORK, 2 Dec 1993, *Coastline in Oregon* (1941, watercolour/paper, 19 1/2 x 27 1/2 ins / 49.5 x 69.9 cm) USD 85,000. NEW YORK, 25 May 1994, *Sierra Madre in Monterey* (1943, watercolour/paper, 21 1/4 x 29 3/4 ins / 53.7 x 75.6 cm) USD 123,500. NEW YORK, 29 Nov 1995, *Runner of the Six-Day Event in France* (oil on canvas, 17 1/4 x 19 1/4 ins / 43.8 x 48.9 cm) USD 772,500. NEW YORK, 23 May 1996, *Last Study for The Night Birds* (pencil, charcoal and white chalk/paper, 11 x 15 ins / 27.9 x 38.2 cm) USD 827,500. NEW YORK, 27 Sept 1996, *Five Cats* (pencil/paper, study, 13 x 12 ins / 33 x 30.5 cm) USD 18,400. NEW YORK, 3 Dec 1996, *Shoe* (charcoal/paper, study, 7 x 9 1/2 ins / 17.8 x 24.2 cm) USD 5,520. NEW YORK, 5 Dec 1996, *Model Draped in a Towel Sitting on a Trunk* (oil on canvas, 12 x 10 ins / 30.5 x 25.4 cm) USD 37,375. NEW YORK, 23 April 1997, *Young Girl in White* (oil on canvas, 22 x 18 ins / 56 x 45.7 cm) USD 29,900. NEW YORK, 3 Dec 1997, *Squam Light* (oil on canvas, 24 x 29 ins / 61 x 73.7 cm) USD 1,267,500. NEW YORK, 3 May 1999, *American Landscape* (1920, etching, 7 x 12 ins / 18 x 31 cm) USD 43,000. NEW YORK, 27 May 1999, *Monhegan Houses, Maine* (c. 1916-1919, oil on board, 9 x 13 ins / 24 x 33 cm) USD 220,000. NEW YORK, 2 May 2000, *Locomotive* (etching, 8 x 10 ins / 20 x 25 cm) USD 24,000. NEW YORK, 30 Nov 2000, *Freight Car at Truro* (1931, watercolour, 14 x 20 ins / 35 x 50 cm) USD 370,000. NEW YORK, 23 May 2001, *Charleston* (watercolour, 16 x 25 ins / 41 x 63 cm) USD 1,700,000. NEW YORK, 29 Nov 2001, *Mount Moran* (watercolour, 22 x 31 ins / 57 x 79 cm) USD 450,000. NEW YORK, 5 Dec 2002, *Oregon Coast* (watercolour, 20 x 28 ins / 50 x 70 cm) USD 450,000. NEW YORK, 5 Dec 2002, *Clamdigger* (oil on canvas, 24 x 30 ins / 62 x 76 cm) USD 1,300,000. NEW YORK, 21 May 2003, *House on Hill Top - House on Dune, South Truro* (watercolour, 14 x 20 ins / 36 x 51 cm) USD 525,000. NEW YORK, 22 May 2003, *House and Trees, Gloucester* (1922, charcoal, 12 x 18 ins / 30 x 46 cm) USD 220,000. NEW YORK, 30 April 2004, *Cat Boat* (etching, 8 x 10 ins / 20 x 25 cm) USD 60,000. NEW YORK, 19 May 2004, *Shacks at Pamet Head* (1937, watercolour, 20 x 22 ins / 51 x 56 cm) USD 620,000.

HOPPER, Humphrey

British, 18th - 19th century.
Active in London.
Sculptor.

Humphrey Hopper exhibited in London at the Royal Academy from 1799 to 1834.

HOPPIN, Augustus

American, 19th century.
Born 1828, in Providence (Rhode Island); died 1896, in Flushing (New York).
Engraver, illustrator.

Augustus Hoppin was a member of Brown University. He worked mainly in illustration.

HOPPIN, Thomas Frederick

American, 19th century.
Born 15 August 1816, in Providence (Rhode Island); died 1872, in Providence.
Painter, sculptor, engraver.

Thomas Frederick Hoppin was the brother of Augustus Hoppin. He studied in Philadelphia and then went to Paris, where he was a pupil of Delaroche. He returned to America in 1837 and settled in New York, where he designed the figures of *St Peter* and *St Paul* for Trinity Church. He also worked in illustration.

HOPPNER, John

British, 18th - 19th century.
Born 25 April 1758, in London; died 23 January 1810, in London.
Painter, watercolourist, engraver. Portraits, landscapes.

John Hoppner's mother was a servant of German origin in the service of the royal family, as was her husband. It was said that Hoppner was the illegitimate son of George III, and he was not inclined to discourage such speculation. He was a chorister in the king's chapel. Showing a remarkable talent for drawing from a young age, and this being brought to the attention of the king, he was admitted to the Royal Academy Schools in 1775 with a small royal pension. He studied under Sir Joshua Reynolds and proved to be a remarkable pupil. In 1782, he married the daughter of Mrs Wright, an artist famous for her wax models.

At the beginning of his career, Hoppner was drawn towards landscape painting, although the need to make a living meant that he had to concentrate on the more lucrative genre of portrait painting. His abilities as a painter of the picturesque can be clearly seen in a series of landscape studies in charcoal in the British Museum, made during his rare leisure hours. His connections at court meant that he was kept busy with portraits. In 1785, he exhibited those of the princesses Sophia, Amelia and Maria. In 1789, he was appointed official painter to the Prince of Wales. He also produced portraits of the Duke and Duchess of York and the Duke of Clarence. In 1786, the king commissioned him to paint a picture of *Mrs Jordan as the Comic Muse*, now at Hampton Court.

Hoppner's works, particularly his portraits of women, have a certain voluptuous poetry that is more pronounced than in the work of Reynolds. He excelled in the depiction of women and children, perhaps drawing on his experience of his own family, which he painted with obvious affection. His male portraits, dry and lacking intimacy, are (with a few exceptions, including that of *Lord Nelson*) less successful. Nonetheless, his portraits are considered worthy to be placed alongside those of Reynolds, Gainsborough, Romney and Lawrence. Hoppner's works were engraved by S.W. Reynolds, J.R. Smith, W. Ward and C. Turner; he was a skilled engraver of mezzotints himself.

Hoppner exhibited for the first time at the Royal Academy in 1780. In 1782, he was awarded the gold medal for his painting of *King Lear*. In 1793, he was made an associate member and, in 1795, a full member of the Royal Academy. He exhibited there until the end of his life, his last work being shown in 1809.

MUSEUMS AND GALLERIES:

BATH (Holburne Mus. of Art): *Mrs Catherine Cussans* (oil on canvas) - BAYONNE: *Head of a Woman* - BUDAPEST: *Portrait of a Lady; Portrait of Mrs Swete* - CARDIFF: *David Williams* - DUBLIN: *Self-portrait; Mrs Musters or Mary Chaworth* - LONDON (Corporation of Trinity House): *Captain Joseph Huddart FRS* - LONDON (National Maritime Mus.): *Rear-Admiral Sir Horatio Nelson* (c. 1800, oil on canvas, sketch); other s - LONDON (National Portrait Gal.): *Dorothy Jordan* (exhibited in 1791, oil on canvas, on loan from the Tate Collection); *John Hoppner* (c. 1800, oil on canvas); *William Wyndham Grenville, 1st Baron Grenville* (c. 1800, oil on canvas); *Charles Abbott, 1st Baron Colchester* (c. 1802, oil on canvas); *William Pitt* (1804-1805, oil on canvas, work of studio) - LONDON (Royal Academy of Arts): *Self-portrait of John Hoppner* (c. 1800, oil on canvas, competition piece) - LONDON (Tate Collection): *A Gale of Wind* (c. 1794, oil on canvas); *Jane Elizabeth, Countess of Oxford* (1797, oil on wood); *Portrait of a Lady* (oil on canvas) - LONDON (Victoria and Albert Mus.): *Miss Mary Linwood* - LONDON (Wallace Collection): *George IV as Prince of Wales* (oil on canvas) - MONTREAL (Learmont Coll.): *E. Forbes Mackenzie; Lady Byng* - NOTTINGHAM: *Henry Pirke White* - PARIS (Louvre): *Portrait of a Woman; Countess of Oxford* - PARIS (Mus. Jacquemart-André): *Mrs Inchbald; Young Woman* - SALFORD (Museum and AG): *William Beckford.*

AUCTION RECORDS:

NEW YORK, 10-11 April 1902, *Mrs Sutherland,* USD 1,500. NEW YORK, 23 Jan 1903, *Portrait of Mrs Gwyn,* USD 22,200. NEW YORK, 7 and 8 April 1904, *Miss Kelvin,* USD 9,300. PARIS, 26 April 1907, *Portrait of Lady Pilkington,* FRF 5,500. PARIS, 16-18 May 1907, *Portrait of Mrs Horne,* FRF 78,000; *Portrait of Miss Raine,* FRF 102,000; *Portrait of Mrs Jordan,* FRF 11,600. LONDON, 28 March 1908, *Portrait of Lady Ponsonby,* GBP 220. NEW YORK, 1-3 April 1908, *Miss Elizabeth Sulfnell,* USD 6,200. LONDON, 8 May 1908, *Portrait of a Young Gentleman,* GBP 283. LONDON, 22 May 1908, *Gypsy,* GBP 577. LONDON, 10 Dec 1908, *Portrait of Miss Gray,* GBP 304. PARIS, 1 April 1909, *Portrait of a Young Man,* FRF 3,100. LONDON, 10 June 1909, *Portrait of Lady Langham,* GBP 5,460. LONDON, 2 July 1909, *Portrait of a Woman,* GBP 1,522. LONDON, 11 Dec 1909, *Portrait of the Countess of Sheffield,* GBP 2,940; *Portrait of the Earl of Chichester* (1807) GBP 789. LONDON, 6 May 1910, *Portrait of Mrs Augustus Phipps,* GBP 5,355. LONDON, 8 July 1910, *Portrait of Miss Matilda Fielding as a Peasant Girl,* GBP 7,927. LONDON, 8 April 1911, *Portrait of Mrs Bridge,* GBP 6,510. LONDON, 9 May 1911, *Portrait of Mrs Dousion,* GBP 3,045. LONDON, 16 June 1911, *Portrait of Vice-Admiral Samuel Hood,* GBP 2,310. PARIS, 22 May 1919, *Portrait of Jane Molesworth, married to the Honourable Stephenson on 3 September 1792,* FRF 10,000; *Man in a Blue Suit,* FRF 11,300. PARIS, 6-8 Dec 1920, *Young Woman Sitting in a Park* (pencil) FRF 6,550. PARIS, 14 June 1921, *Portrait of a Young Officer,* FRF 8,000. PARIS, May 1922, *The Artist in a Red Coat,* GBP 1,417; *Lady as Hebe*; *William Pitt,* GBP 7,350. PARIS, May 1922, *Lady in White,* GBP 273; *Lady Vernon,* GBP 441. PARIS, May 1923, *Mrs Belloc,* GBP 1,207. PARIS, May 1923, *Georgina Grenfell and her Child,* GBP 1,732. PARIS, May 1923, *John Cotes MP,* GBP 210. PARIS, May 1923, *Lady Southampton,* GBP 840. PARIS, July 1923, *Lady in a White Muslin Dress,* GBP 1,680. PARIS, July 1923, *Lady in a Short White Dress,* GBP 1,470. PARIS, July 1923, *Brigadier General James Law,* GBP 220. PARIS, July 1923, *Sir Francis Basset,* GBP 241. PARIS, June 1924, *1st Lady de Dunstanville,* GBP 300. PARIS, July 1924, *Mrs Augustus Phipps,* GBP 2,940. PARIS, July 1924, *Brigadier General Alexander Beatson,* GBP 420. PARIS, July 1924, *Thomas Grylls,* GBP 357. PARIS, 1 May 1925, *John, 4th Earl of Darnley,* GBP 3,255. PARIS, 3 July 1925, *Three Young Princesses,* GBP 110. PARIS, 7 May 1926, *Portrait of the Honourable Leicester Stanhope,* GBP 6,300. PARIS, 14 May 1926, *Portrait of Miss Holcroft,* GBP 1,312. PARIS, 24 June 1926, *The Bowden Children,* GBP 11,550; *Lady Louisa Manners,* GBP 18,900; *Mrs Jermingham,* GBP 7,350. PARIS, 22-24 June 1927, *Portrait thought to be of Lady Fitzherbert,* FRF 192,000. LONDON, 22 July 1927, *Portrait of a Girl,* GBP 1,260. LONDON, 18 Nov 1927, *Lady Elisabeth Le Despencer,* GBP 1,732. LONDON, 22 Dec 1927, *Lady Vernon,* GBP 1,787. LONDON, 10 Feb 1928, *Reverend Thomas Gishorne,* GBP 210. LONDON, 16 May 1928, *Elizabeth Harriet Warren,* GBP 840. LONDON, 13 July 1928, *Sir John Chardin Musgrave,* GBP 1,102. LONDON, 27 July 1928, *Portrait of a Man,* GBP 378. LONDON, 14 Dec 1928, *Lady Charlotte Campbell,* GBP 3,570. LONDON, 3 May 1929, *Sleeping Child,* GBP 273. LONDON, 3 May 1929, *John and Henry Cust,* GBP 10,500. LONDON, 20 Feb 1930, *Lady in White,* GBP 651. LONDON, 27 June 1930, *Miss Charlotte Augusta Sapendick,* GBP 14,700. LONDON, 18 July 1930, *Lady Waldegrave,* GBP 2,310. PARIS, 10 Dec 1930, *Meditation* (lead pencil, heightened with watercolour) FRF 9,100. LONDON, 12 Dec 1930, *Jane Wilson,* GBP 945. NEW YORK, 4 Feb 1931, *Mrs Fuller,* USD 2,100. NEW YORK, 2 April 1931, *Mrs Sarah Barnes,* USD 4,600. PARIS, 3 June 1931, *Young Woman Sketching,* FRF 40,000. LONDON, 10 July 1931, *Miss Larpent,* GBP 442. NEW YORK, 12 Nov 1931, *Maria Ellenwood,* USD 1,050. NEW YORK, 20 Nov 1931, *John Corbet,* USD 1,250. NEW YORK, 22 April 1932, *Miss Larpent,* USD 3,000. NEW YORK, 29 April 1932, *Master Mordant Ricketts,* USD 4,300; *Miss Elizabeth Jemina Blake,* USD 4,800. NEW YORK, 16 Nov 1933, *Mrs Sophia Dawson,* USD 6,000; *Mrs Sarah Dawson,* USD 3,200. NEW YORK, 18 April 1934, *Mrs Sarah*

Barnes, USD 800; *Girl Gleaning*, USD 12,500. LONDON, 1 June 1934, *Miss Gale*, GBP 1,470. LONDON, 13 June 1934, *Master William Russell*, GBP 3,400. LONDON, 29 March 1935, *Admiral Rainier*, GBP 525. LONDON, 31 May 1935, *Hurdy-Gurdy Player*, GBP 5,040; *Mrs Hoppner*, GBP 12,075. NEW YORK, 15 Nov 1935, *Keith Jopp*, USD 3,800; *Mrs Gibson*, USD 4,000; *Mrs Jopp of Aberdeen*, USD 4,600. LONDON, 3 April 1936, *Richard Drummond*, GBP 168. LONDON, 5 June 1936, *Lady Braithwaite*, GBP 651. PARIS, 18 March 1937, *Portrait of a Woman*, FRF 22,000. LONDON, 2 July 1937, *Lady Langham*, GBP 1,732. LONDON, 29 April 1938, *Sir John Morris*, GBP 1,102. LONDON, 8 July 1938, *Lady Leighton*, GBP 2,310. LONDON, 24 Feb 1939, *Reverend Inigo Jones*, GBP 241. LONDON, 19 May 1939, *Henry and Keppel Berkeley*, GBP 262. LONDON, 20 Dec 1940, *Miss Kemble*, GBP 159. LONDON, 28 May 1941, *Seated Youth*, GBP 390. NEW YORK, 4 Dec 1941, *Miss Frances Beresford*, USD 39,000. LONDON, 25 Sept 1942, *Sir Thomas Munro*, GBP 78; *Countess of Dysart*, GBP 819. LONDON, 16 July 1943, *Mrs W. Dundas*, GBP 1,627. NEW YORK, 15 Jan 1944, *Leicester Stanhope*, USD 57,000. NEW YORK, 18 Nov 1944, *Mrs Jordan*, USD 4,000; *Samuel Braddram*, USD 2,500; *Sir Humphrey Davy*, USD 3,750. PARIS, 27 May 1946, *Portrait of Mrs Home*, FRF 65,000. LONDON, 5 Feb 1947, *Portrait of Lord Grenville*, GBP 105. NEW YORK, 9-10 May 1947, *Elizabeth, Duchess of Devonshire*, USD 1,900. LONDON, 4 Dec 1957, *Portrait of William Locke*, GBP 800. PARIS, 6 Dec 1957, *Portrait of a Man*, FRF 300,000. NEW YORK, 10 Dec 1958, *Elizabeth, Duchess of Devonshire*, USD 1,600. LONDON, 29 May 1959, *Portrait of the Countess of Oxford and her Daughter; Child; Lady Jane Elizabeth Harley*, GBP 1,470. LONDON, 24 Feb 1960, *Portrait of Mrs Mowbray*, GBP 620. PARIS, 9 March 1961, *Portrait of Lady Basset* (1781-1855) FRF 28,000. LONDON, 27 June 1962, *Portrait of Elizabeth Bligh as a Girl*, GBP 2,800. LONDON, 3 July 1963, *Portrait of Georgiana Elizabeth, Duchess of Bedford*, GBP 9,000. LONDON, 17 Nov 1967, *Portrait of Miss Maria Bover*, Gns 2,200. LONDON, 27 Nov 1968, *Keppel Richard Craven and Henry Augustus Berkeley Craven*, GBP 3,400. LONDON, 28 Nov 1969, *Portrait of Lady Coote of Donnybrook*, Gns 1,800. LONDON, 13 March 1970, *Portrait of a Boy; Portrait of a Girl* (two canvases) Gns 10,500. NEW YORK, 6 March 1971, *Lady Sykes*, USD 4, 000. LONDON, 27 June 1973, *Portrait of Elizabeth Countess of Mexborough*, GBP 7,000. LONDON, 17 July 1974, *Portrait of Mrs Jordan*, Gns 1,000. PARIS, 7 April 1976, *Portrait thought to be of Miss Crouch* (oil on canvas, 30 x 23 1/2 ins / 76 x 60 cm) FRF 14,000. LONDON, 25 Nov 1977, *Portrait of Lady Arundel of Wardour* (oil on canvas, 50 x 39 ins / 127 x 99 cm) GBP 3,500. NEW YORK, 5 June 1979, *Portrait of HRH Princess Amelia* (oil on canvas, oval, 30 x 24 3/4 ins / 76.5 x 63 cm) USD 15,000. LONDON, 19 Nov 1981, *Head of a Girl* (pencil and coloured chalk, 9 1/4 x 7 ins / 23.5 x 18 cm) GBP 420. LONDON, 16 July 1982, *Portrait of HRH Frederica Charlotte Ulrica, Princess Royal of Prussia and Duchess of York* (oil on canvas, 107 x 83 ins / 271.7 x 210.7 cm) GBP 150,000. NEW YORK, 18 Jan 1983, *Portrait of Miss Emma Laura Whitbread* (oil on canvas, 50 x 40 ins / 127 x 101.5 cm) USD 48,000. NEW YORK, 17 Jan 1985, *Portrait of Her Royal Highness Princess Amelia* (oil on canvas, oval, 30 x 24 3/4 ins / 76.5 x 63 cm) USD 29,000. LONDON, 29 Jan 1988, *Portrait of Mrs Billington Seated in a White Dress with a Yellow Sash* (oil on canvas, 35 x 24 ins / 88.9 x 61 cm) GBP 8,800. PARIS, 14 April 1988, *Three-quarter Length Portrait of a Young Woman Looking to the Left* (oil on canvas, 28 1/4 x 22 1/2 ins / 72 x 57 cm) FRF 25,000. PARIS, 1 July 1988, *Portrait of a Woman* (oil on canvas, 29 x 24 1/4 ins / 73.5 x 61.3 cm) FRF 26,000. LONDON, 15 July 1988, *Portrait of William Pitt in a Black Suit on a Terrace* (oil on canvas, 55 3/4 x 43 1/2 ins / 141.7 x 110.2 cm) GBP 24,200. NEW YORK, 7 April 1989, *Portrait of Sarah Erle Drax Grosvenor Seated in a White Dress with a Yellow Ribbon in her Hair* (oil on canvas, 35 x 27 1/2 ins / 89 x 70 cm) USD 6,050. LONDON, 12 July 1989, *Portrait of Jane Countess of Westmorland as Hebe* (oil on canvas, 28 3/4 x 25 1/2 ins / 73 x 65 cm) GBP 33,000. LONDON, 15 Nov 1989, *Portrait of Sir John Osborn of Chicksands Priory in Bedfordshire* (oil on canvas, 29 1/2 x 24 1/2 ins / 75 x 62 cm) GBP 39,600. NEW YORK, 19 July 1990, *Portrait of J.H. Smyth* (sketch, oil on canvas, 29 1/4 x 24 1/2 ins / 74.3 x 62.3 cm) USD 4, 950. NEW YORK, 31 May 1991, *Portrait of Mrs Shaw of Green's Norton Standing by a Balustrade in a Black Dress and a White Shawl* (oil on canvas, 50 3/4 x 57 1/2 ins / 128.8 x 146 cm) USD 10,450. LONDON, 12 July 1991, *Portrait of the Honourable Mrs Grenfell and her Son Pascoe St Leger Standing in a White Dress and holding a Hoop and a Black Hat with a Feather in an Interior Opening onto a Terrace with Hollyhocks* (oil on canvas, 90 x 60 ins / 228.6 x 152.4 cm) GBP 44,000. NEW YORK, 17 Jan 1992, *Portrait of Mrs Sophia Fielding* (1787, oil on canvas, 31 x 24 3/4 ins / 78.7 x 62.9 cm) USD 79,750. LONDON, 20 Nov 1992, *Portrait of Sophia Lady Burrell in a White Dress with a Book on her Lap* (oil on canvas, 36 1/2 x 28 1/4 ins / 93 x 71.8 cm) GBP 49,500. LONDON, 10 Nov 1993, *Portrait of Miss Elizabeth Beresford in a White Dress and a Black Hat with White Ostrich Feathers* (oil on canvas, 30 x 25 ins / 76 x 63.5 cm) GBP 44,400. NEW YORK, 11 Jan 1995, *Three-quarter Length Portrait of William Pitt Standing in a Green Suit and White Cravat* (oil on canvas, 55 1/4 x 45 3/4 ins / 140.3 x 116.2 cm) USD 34,500. LONDON, 12 July 1995, *Head and Shoulders Portrait of Edward Viscount Lascelles in a Red Coat with a Fur Collar, Buff-Coloured Waistcoat and White Cravat* (oil on canvas, 45 1/2 x 38 ins / 115.5 x 96.5 cm) GBP 23,000. LONDON, 10 July 1996, *Head and Shoulders Portrait of the Honourable Mary Rycroft in a White Dress and Turban* (oil on canvas, 29 1/4 x 24 ins / 74 x 61 cm) GBP 8,050. NEW YORK, 4 Oct 1996, *Portrait of the Honourable Miss Emma Crewe Seated in a Landscape with her Dog* (oil on canvas, 50 x 40 1/2 ins / 127 x 103 cm) USD 5,750. NEW YORK, 30 Jan 1997, *Portrait of Captain George Porter 6th Baron Hochepied* (1789, oil on canvas, 91 x 56 1/2 ins / 231.1 x 143.5 cm) USD 101,500. NEW YORK, 31 Jan 1997, *Portrait of a Lady with her Daughter in a Landscape* (oil on canvas, 30 1/4 x 25 ins / 76.9 x 63.5 cm) USD 32,200. NEW YORK, 13 Nov 1997, *Head and Shoulders Portrait of the Honourable Mrs Augustus Philipps* (oil on canvas, 30 x 25 ins / 76.2 x 63.5 cm) USD 7,475. LONDON, 31 March 1999, *Portrait of Henry Howard* (oil on canvas, 29 x 24 ins / 74 x 61 cm) GBP 7,000. LONDON, 12 July 1999, *Sir Foster Cunliffe, 3rd Baronet of Acton Park, Denbigh* (oil on canvas, 94 x 56 ins / 239 x 143 cm) GBP 45,000. NEW YORK, 27 Jan 2000, *Portrait of Lady Boothby in a Grey Dress with Plume in Her Hair, Landscape beyond* (oil on canvas, 50 x 40 ins / 127 x 101 cm) USD 18,000. NEW YORK, 25 May 2000, *Portrait of Rear Admiral John Sprat Rainer in Naval Uniform* (oil on canvas, 29 x 24 ins / 74 x 62 cm) USD 12,000. LONDON, 7 June 2001, *Study of an Elegant Young Lady, identified as Emma Hamilton* (pencil crayon, chalk and watercolour, 7 x 9 ins / 18 x 22 cm) GBP 3,400. LONDON, 4 July 2001, *Portrait of a Gentleman in a Red Coat and White Stock* (oil on canvas, 28 x 24 ins / 72 x 61 cm) GBP 8,200. EDINBURGH, 24 May 2002, *Portrait of Robert Dundas of Arniston* (oil on canvas, 30 x 25 ins / 75 x 63 cm) GBP 4,200. LONDON, 4 July 2002, *Portrait of Samuel Brandram* (oil on canvas, 30 x 24 ins / 75 x 62 cm) GBP 5,200. LONDON, 25 Nov 2003, *Portrait of Eleanor Agnes, Wife of Robert, 4th Earl of Buckingham, in a Wooded Landscape* (oil on canvas, 50 x 40 ins / 127 x 102 cm) GBP 21,500. LONDON, 27 Nov 2003, *Portrait of a Lady as Evelina* (oil on canvas, 27 x 21 ins / 68 x 53 cm) GBP 150,000. NEW YORK, 27 May 2004, *Portrait of Henry Wellesley, Baron Cowley* (oil on canvas, 30 x 25 ins / 76 x 63 cm) USD 25,000. LONDON, 25 Nov 2004, *Portrait of Anne, Lady Romilly* (oil on canvas, 30 x 24 ins / 75 x 62 cm) GBP 15,000.

HOPPNER, Lascelles H.
British, 19th century.
Born 1 June 1788.

Painter. Portraits, genre scenes.
Lascelles Hoppner, the son of John Hoppner, studied at the Royal Academy in London, receiving a gold medal in 1807. He exhibited there from 1811 until 1875.

HÖPPNER, Oskar
German, 19th - 20th century.
Born 5 June 1871, in Luckenwalde.
Painter, illustrator. Portraits.
Höppner exhibited his work in Berlin in 1909.

HOPPNER, Richard Belgrave
British, 19th century.
Born 9 January 1786; died 6 August 1872.
Active in London.
Painter. Seascapes.
Richard Hoppner was the son of John Hoppner and the brother of Lascelles. He exhibited in London at the Royal Academy and the British Institution from 1807 to 1827.

HOPS, Franz Magnus
German, 18th century.
Born 6 September 1717, in Mietingen (near Ulm); died 3 January 1756, in Sigmaringen.
Sculptor.
The son of Johann Baptist Hops senior, his oeuvre was mainly ornaments sculpted in the French style.

HOPS, Johann Adam
German, 18th century.
Born 31 July 1708, in Mietingen (near Ulm).
Sculptor.
The son of Johann Baptist Hops senior, he is known to have worked in Hüttisheim and Dellmensingen.

HOPS, Johann Baptist, the Elder
German, 18th century.
Born 6 May 1681, in Eggenthal.
Painter, sculptor.
He worked in the south German villages of Mietingen, Aulendorf, Heiligkreuztal, Grundsheim and Oberdischingen.

HOPS, Johann Baptist, the Younger
German, 18th century.
Born in Mietingen; died 3 August 1788, in Sigmaringen.
Sculptor.
Possibly the son of Johann Adam, his work is found in Messkirch, Storzingen, Lautlingen and Effendorf among other places.

HOPS, Josef Anton
German, 18th century.
Born 2 June 1720, in Mietingen; died 23 May 1761, in Villingen.
Sculptor, painter.
The son of Johann Baptist senior, he worked for churches and monasteries in Rottenburg, Villingen, Hedingen and Donauschingen.

HOPSON, Henry
Irish, 18th century.
Active in Dublin at the end of the 18th century.
Painter.
Henry Hopson is known from an engraved a portrait by J.P. Durran.

HOPSON, William Fowler
American, 19th - 20th century.
Born 30 August 1849, in Watertown (Connecticut); died 1935, in New Haven.
Active in New Haven (Connecticut).
Engraver.
William Fowler Hopson was a pupil of L. Sanford in New Haven, and of Pelter and August Will in New York. He received an honourable mention in Buffalo in 1901.

HOPWOOD, Henry Silkstone
British, 19th - 20th century.
Born 12 January 1860, in Markfield; died 1914, in Edinburgh.
Painter, watercolourist. Genre scenes.
Henry Hopwood, who was active in Manchester, was a member of the Royal Society of Painters in Watercolours.
MUSEUMS AND GALLERIES:
LEEDS (City AG): *Butter Market, Montreuil* (1912, drawing); *Spring* (oil on canvas); *The Breakfast Table* (1907, watercolour and gouache) - LONDON (Tate Collection): *Industry* (1894, watercolour/paper).
AUCTION RECORDS:
LONDON, Jan 1924, *The Mealtime*, GBP 9. LONDON, 11 Nov 1981, *Woman Reading* (oil on panel, 8 1/2 x 10 1/2 ins / 21.5 x 26.5 cm) GBP 1,100. NEW YORK, 14 Oct 1993, *Marketplace in Tangier* (1910, watercolour and gouache/paper, 17 x 19 1/4 ins / 43.2 x 49 cm) USD 2,760. MELBOURNE, 27 April 1999, *Morning Aboard Ship* (c. 1888, oil on canvas, 10 x 13 ins / 26 x 34 cm) AUD 18,000. LONDON, 13 Oct 1999, *Market Square, Tangier* (1910, oil on board, 17 x 19 ins / 42 x 47 cm) GBP 1,800. LEEDS, 14 Nov 2000, *Cottage Service in Hebrides* (watercolour, 37 x 39 ins / 93 x 100 cm) GBP 3,800. LEEDS, 20 Nov 2001, *Glimpsing Daybreak* (1906, watercolour over pencil, 23 x 17 ins / 58 x 42 cm) GBP 4,500. PHILADELPHIA, 9 Dec 2001, *Public Gardens, Venice* (1909, watercolour, 15 x 18 ins / 38 x 46 cm) USD 5,500. CHELSEA, 29 Jan 2002, *Workshop* (watercolour, 12 x 9 ins / 30 x 24 cm) GBP 1,600. LEEDS, 19 Nov 2002, *On the Sands* (oil on panel, 5 x 6 ins / 12 x 16 cm) GBP 1,200. LONDON, 16 Sept 2003, *Draught Players, Tunis* (oil on canvasboard, 9 x 11 ins / 22 x 28 cm) GBP 1,300. LONDON, 16 Sept 2003, *Tunis Doorway* (oil on canvasboard, 11 x 9 ins / 28 x 22 cm) GBP 1,600. WORTHING, 17 June 2004, *Cottage Prayer Meeting* (1898, watercolour, 9 x 10 ins / 23 x 25 cm) GBP 4,600. SCARBOROUGH, 14 Sept 2004, *Fisherwoman Stoking the Grate* (watercolour, 11 x 14 ins / 27 x 36 cm) GBP 3,100.

HOPWOOD, James, the Elder
British, 18th - 19th century.
Born c. 1752, in Beverley; died 28 September 1819, in London.
Engraver.
James Hopwood the Elder was a self-taught artist and was little known before 1797, when he was working in London in collaboration with James Heath.

HOPWOOD, James, the Younger
British, 19th century.
Born 1795.
Active in London.
Engraver, painter.
James Hopwood the Younger was the son and pupil of James Hopwood the Elder. His works include portraits of *King Louis-Philippe and Queen Marie-Amélie* and *Queen Victoria and Albert the Prince Consort*. He exhibited in London at the Royal Academy between 1802 and 1825.

HOPWOOD, William
British, 19th century.
Active at the beginning of the 19th century.
Painter, engraver, illustrator.
William Hopwood, the son of James Hopwood the Elder, exhibited in London at the Royal Academy from 1801 to 1804.

HOQUART, Édouard
French, 19th century.
Engraver.

HOQUET, Marie
French, 18th century.
Active in Paris in 1765.
Painter.

HORA, Janos Alajos
Hungarian, 19th century.
Born 11 October 1812, in Zsombolya.
Painter.
Janos Alajos Hora studied in Vienna, and painted portraits and genre scenes.

HORA, Louis Jules
French, 19th century.
Portrait painter.
Hora exhibited at the Paris Salon from 1839 to 1845.

HORADAM, Franz
German, 19th century.
Born 7 December 1846, in Bamberg; died 1925, in Munich.
Active in Munich.
Painter, draughtsman. Landscapes.
He exhibited in Munich and Berlin.
MUSEUMS AND GALLERIES:
WEIMAR: *Autumn Day*.
AUCTION RECORDS:
HEIDELBERG, 15-16 Oct 1993, *Copse in the Region of Dachau* (charcoal, 20 x 27 1/2 ins / 50.5 x 70 cm) DEM 1,250.

HORATIO, or Horacio
Mexican, 20th century.
Born 1912; died 1972.
Painter. Genre scenes, figures.
AUCTION RECORDS:
NEW YORK, 20 Dec 1980, *No Me Olvides* (*Forget Me Not*) (oil on canvas, 23 3/4 x 18 ins / 60.2 x 45.7 cm) USD 5,250. NEW YORK, 9 July 1981, *Young Girl with Cat* (oil on canvas, 24 x 18 1/4 ins / 61.2 x 46.2 cm) USD 5,750. NEW YORK, 27 Nov 1985, *Young Girl by a Fountain* (1878, oil on canvas, 23 3/4 x 18 1/4 ins / 60.4 x 46.3 cm) USD 8,000. NEW YORK, 18 Nov 1987, *Summer Day* (oil on canvas, 32 x 25 1/2 ins / 80.4 x 65 cm) USD 5,000. NEW YORK, 21 Nov 1988, *Portrait of a Young Girl with Doves* (oil on canvas, 23 3/4 x 18 ins / 60.3 x 46 cm) USD 7,700; *Portrait of a Young Girl in a Kitchen* (oil on canvas, 23 1/2 x 18 ins / 60 x 46 cm) USD 8,250. NEW YORK, 17 May 1989, *Young Girl with Fish and Fruit* (oil on canvas, 23 1/2 x 18 1/4 ins / 59.5 x 46.45 cm) USD 8,800. NEW YORK, 20 Nov 1989, *Young Girl with a Broody Hen in a Basket* (oil on canvas, 25 x 18 3/4 ins / 63.5 x 47.5 cm) USD 7,700. NEW YORK, 2 May 1990, *Portrait of a Young Girl* (oil on canvas, 23 1/4 x 18 ins / 59 x 46 cm) USD 8,800. NEW YORK, 19-20 Nov 1990, *Portrait of a Young Girl* (oil on canvas, 23 1/2 x 18 ins / 60 x 46 cm) USD 7,975. NEW YORK, 15 May 1991, *Young Girl with Birds* (oil on canvas, 23 1/2 x 18 1/4 ins / 60 x 46.5 cm) USD 9,350. NEW YORK, 19 May 1992, *Young Boy in Military Uniform* (oil on canvas, 23 3/4 x 18 1/4 ins / 60.5 x 46.5 cm) USD 9,350. NEW YORK, 25 Nov 1992, *Young Girl Carrying a Tea Tray* (oil on canvas, 23 1/2 x 18 ins / 60 x 46 cm) USD 7,480. NEW YORK, 23-24 Nov 1993, *Young Girl with a Basket of Fruit* (oil on canvas, 22 3/4 x 19 ins / 57.7 x 48 cm) USD 6,900. NEW YORK, 18 May 1994, *Young Girl on a Terrace* (oil on canvas, 23 3/4 x 18 ins / 60.3 x 46 cm) USD 8,050. NEW YORK, 16 May 1996, *Young Girl Opposite the Plaza Mayor* (oil on canvas, 24 x 18 1/4 ins / 61 x 46.3 cm) USD 4,025. NEW YORK, 10 Oct 1996, *Bouquet of Youth* (oil on canvas, 23 1/2 x 18 ins / 60 x 45.7 cm) USD 5,175. NEW YORK, 17 Nov 1999, *Portrait of Young Girl Seated in an Interior with a Display of Fruit* (oil on canvas, 24 x 18 ins / 60 x 46 cm) USD 4,500. LONDON, 2 Dec 1999, *Portrait of Maria Puente at the Age of Seven* (oil on canvas, 24 x 18 ins / 60 x 45 cm) GBP 2,800. SAN FRANCISCO, 24 Oct 2000, *Boy with Cat and Dogs. Girl with Birds* (oil on board, a pair, 24 x 18 ins / 60 x 46 cm) USD 6,000. BOSTON, 10 Nov 2000, *Portrait of Girl* (oil on canvas, 20 x 15 ins / 51 x 39 cm) USD 2,300. NEW YORK, 31 May 2001, *Portraits of Girls* (c. 1950, oil on canvas, a pair, 24 x 18 ins / 60 x 46 cm) USD 16,000. MIAMI, 10 June 2001, *Children's Games* (oil on canvas, 24 x 18 ins / 61 x 46 cm) USD 4,000. NEW YORK, 29 May 2002, *Portraits of Girls* (c. 1945, oil on canvas, a pair, 24 x 19 ins / 60 x 47 cm) USD 9,500. NEW YORK, 20 Nov 2002, *Portraits of Girls* (c. 1945, oil on canvas, a pair, 24 x 18 ins / 61 x 46 cm) USD 22,000. LOS ANGELES, 2 May 2004, *Portrait of a Young Girl with a Village and Figures in the Distance* (oil on canvas, 24 x 18 ins / 60 x 45 cm) USD 3,250. NEW YORK, 3 June 2004, *Portrait of a Little Girl in a Red Dress Holding a Cardinal* (1879, oil on canvas, 24 x 18 ins / 60 x 46 cm) USD 8,500.

HORAVSKY. See **GOROVSKY**

HORBECK, Egidius
German, 16th century.
Active probably in Munich c. 1585.
Painter, engraver.
There is a portrait of *Ambroise Paré* painted by Egidius Horbeck.

HORCHERT, Joseph
German, 20th century.
Born 4 May 1874, in Hechingen.
Sculptor.
Horchert was a student at the arts institute in Frankfurt am Main and at the academy in Munich. He sculpted a fountain in St Louis (in memory of Guggenheim) and figures for the Friedrichsbrücke in Berlin.

HORCHOLLE, Arthur
French, 19th century.
Born in the 19th century, in Paris.
Engraver (wood).
Horcholle was a pupil of Quartley, and made his début at the Paris Salon in 1867.

HORCICKA, Franz
Bohemian, 19th century.
Born 29 June 1776, in Prague; died 5 April 1856, in Prague.
Painter. Religious subjects, portraits.
Franz Horcicka is best known for the large religious paintings with which he decorated many churches in Bohemia.

HORD, Donal
American, 20th century.
Born 26 February 1902, in Prentice (Winsconsin); died 29 June 1966, in San Diego (California).
Sculptor.
Donal Hord worked in New York.
MUSEUMS AND GALLERIES:
SAN DIEGO (MA): *Young Maize* (1931, wood); *Thunder* (c. 1946-1947, nephrite).

HORDAING, Colart de. See **COLART de Hordaing**

HORDYK, Gérard
Dutch, 20th century.
Born 12 September 1899, in The Hague; died 1958.
Painter. Urban landscapes, still-lifes.
Work by Hordyk was exhibited in Paris.
AUCTION RECORDS:
AMSTERDAM, 23 April 1980, *View of New York* (oil on canvas, 25 x 31 1/2 ins / 63.5 x 80 cm) NLG 2,800. AMSTERDAM, 21 May 1992, *Still-life* (oil on canvas, 22 x 15 1/4 ins / 55 x 39 cm) NLG 1,035. AMSTERDAM, 7 Dec 1995, *The Place de Paris* (oil on canvas, 20 1/2 x 23 1/2 ins / 52 x 60 cm) NLG 1,416. AMSTERDAM, 4 June 1996, *View of Grand Army Plaza in New York* (oil on canvas, 26 x 32 1/4 ins / 66 x 82 cm) NLG 7,552. AMSTERDAM, 28 Nov 2000, *Still-life with Oranges* (oil on canvas, 11 x 14 ins / 27 x 35 cm) NLG 5,200. AMSTERDAM, 28 Nov 2000, *Ile St Louis, Paris* (oil on canvas, 21 x 26 ins / 54 x 65 cm) NLG 9,500. GRAVENHAGE, 25 April 2001, *Vermont Landscape* (oil on canvas, 20 x 26 ins / 52 x 65 cm) NLG 11,000. GRAVENHAGE, 12 May 2004, *Window with Flowers and Bottle* (oil on

canvas, 26 x 20 ins / 65 x 50 cm) EUR 2,600. AMSTERDAM, 21 Dec 2004, *Manhattan New York* (oil on canvas, 14 x 11 ins / 35 x 27 cm) EUR 2,800.

HORE, Jean Baptiste de
German, 18th century.
Active at Ehrenbreitstein Castle (Koblenz) in 1701.
Sculptor.
He also worked in the town of Koblenz itself.

HORE, Sommath
Indian, 20th century.
Born 1921, in Chittagong, Bangladesh.
Engraver.
Sommath Hore lives in Bangladesh. In 1974-1975, his work was shown at the Tokyo print biennale.

HOREBOUT, Cornelis, or Horembout
Flemish School, 17th century.
Active in Ghent c. 1618.
Painter.
Cornelis Horebout may be the same person as the artist Cornelis Horenbolt.

HOREBOUT, Gérard, or Horenbout, or Horenbolt, or Harembourg
Flemish, 15th - 16th century.
Born c. 1465, in Ghent; died c. 1540, in Ghent.
Active also in England.
Painter, illuminator. Religious subjects, portraits, genre scenes, landscapes.
Ghent School, Flemish School.
Gérard Horebout is often referred to as Gerard Harembourg and his name occurs in a variety of spellings. It seems probable that he was the Gerard Horebout or Huerebout mentioned by Albrecht Dürer in his *Tour in the Low Countries* and whose daughter or granddaughter Suzanne gained a brilliant reputation at the court of Henry VIII of England. But it must be remembered that there were 19 artists of this name working in Ghent between 1414 and 1540.

He probably qualified as a master in Ghent in 1487 and lived in Mechelen from 1517 to 1521. After working at the English court, he returned to Ghent and settled there permanently. He has been identified with the miniaturist who painted the *Hortolus Animae* (*The Little Garden of the Soul*), a breviary which he illuminated with shining landscapes and genre scenes in broken colours which must certainly have inspired Bruegel the Elder. As Gerard Harembourg he completed several important pieces for Margaret of Austria in 1521, including a *Portrait of Christian II of Denmark*, her nephew. He also did the illuminations in a handsome book of hours. This book, known as the Sforza Hours, had been commissioned by Bona of Savoy, widow of Galeazzo Sforza, Duke of Milan, and illuminated in 1490 by Giovan Pietro Birago. Some of these illuminations were stolen, and in 1519-1520 Margaret of Austria, Bona Sforza's niece, ordered replacements from Gerard Horenbout. Whatever the many spellings of his name, he should not be confused with Gerard David, known as Gerard of Bruges.

BIBLIOGRAPHY:
Evans, Mark, *The Sforza Hours*, British Library, London, 1992. Calkins, Robert G., '*Gerard Horenbout and his associates: illuminating activities in Ghent, 1480 - 1521*' in *detail: new studies of Northern Renaissance art in honor of Walter S. Gibson*, Brepols, Turnhout, 1998.

MUSEUMS AND GALLERIES:
LONDON (British Library): *The Sforza Hours*.

AUCTION RECORDS:
PARIS, 30-31 May 1892, *Holy Family*, FRF 2,550. LONDON, 11 March 1911, *Henry VIII with Gloves and Staff*, GBP 115. LONDON, July 1923, *Head of Henry VIII*, GBP 29. LONDON, 29 April 1932, *Henry VIII*, GBP 231.

HOREBOUT, Lukas, the Elder, or Horenbolt
Flemish, 16th century.
Died c. 1544, in London.
Painter, miniaturist. History painting, portraits.
Flemish School.
Lukas Horebout the Elder was the son of Gérard Horebout, with whom he went to London.

HOREBOUT, Lukas, the Younger
Flemish School, 17th century.
Died 26 April 1626, in Ghent.
Painter.
Lukas Horebout the Younger was active from around 1600 onwards.

HOREBOUT, Susanna, later Mrs Parker
Flemish, 16th century.
Born 1503; died 1545, in Worcester.
Miniaturist.
Flemish School.
According to Vasari and others Susanna Horebout was a sister of Gérard Horebout, but a note on Vasari by Lemonnier says that 'Susanna, born about 1500, was not the sister but the daughter of Lukas. She was in Antwerp when Albrecht Dürer was passing through and he bought from her for a florin a miniature of Christ, saying, 'It is a miracle to see a child paint so well'. Soon afterwards she married John Parker, Henry VIII's treasurer.

HOREGSSY
Austrian, 19th century.
Active in Vienna.
Painter, lithographer.

HOREJC, Jaroslav
Czech, 20th century.
Born 15 June 1886, in Prague.
Sculptor, medallist.
Jaroslav Horejc is best known as a medallist.

AUCTION RECORDS:
LONDON, 22 Feb 1995, *Market in the Middle East* (oil on canvas, 22 3/4 x 30 3/4 ins / 58 x 78 cm) GBP 1,610. PRAGUE, 20 Nov 1999, *Black Female Dancer* (painted wood, h. 21 ins / 54 cm) CZK 160,000. PRAGUE, 13 Oct 2001, *Salome* (polychrome plaster, h. 21 ins / 54 cm) CZK 150,000.

HOREL, E. Albert
French, 20th century.
Born 25 June 1876, in Aubevoye; died 1964.
Painter. Waterscapes, urban landscapes, village views, panoramas, architectural views.
Orientalism.
Albert Horel exhibited in Paris at the Salon des Artistes Français.

AUCTION RECORDS:
PARIS, 22 June 1990, *Lane in Fez (Morocco)* (oil on canvas, 25 3/4 x 21 3/4 ins / 65.5 x 55.5 cm) FRF 5,500. NANCY, 24 June 1990, *Barge on the Bank of the Canal* (1904, oil on canvas, 25 1/2 x 21 1/4 ins / 65 x 54 cm) FRF 21,000. METZ, 14 Oct 1990, *The Village of Amance* (oil on canvas, 23 1/2 x 31 3/4 ins / 60 x 80.8 cm) FRF 25,000. PARIS, 19 May 1995, *The Tea Room* (oil on canvas, 23 1/2 x 32 ins / 60 x 81 cm) FRF 6,000. PARIS, 12 June 1995, *Panoramic View of Fez (Morocco)* (1933, oil on canvas, 26 x 36 1/2 ins / 66 x 93 cm) FRF 10,000. CALAIS, 24 March 1996, *Nancy - The Tea Room at the Magasins Réunis* (oil on canvas, 24 x 31 1/2 ins / 61 x 80 cm) FRF 11,000. PARIS, 14 Nov 2000, *View of Fez* (1935, oil on canvas laid on panel, 25 x 36 ins / 64 x 91 cm) FRF 22,000. PARIS, 23 Oct 2002, *Medina* (oil on canvas, 25 x 36 ins / 64 x 92 cm) EUR 1,800.

HOREMANS, Francis
Belgian, 20th century.
Died 6 June 1965.
Painter.

HOREMANS, Jan Josef, the Elder, called le Brun
Flemish School, 17th - 18th century.
Baptised 16 November 1682 in Antwerp; died 7 August 1759, in Antwerp.
Painter, draughtsman. History painting, allegorical subjects, genre scenes, interiors with figures.

Jan Horemans the Elder was a pupil of the sculptor Michiel van der Voort and later of Jan van Pel. In 1706 he became a master of the Guild of St Luke in Antwerp.

He continued in the tradition of Teniers, producing some familiar anecdotal pieces, including: *The Denounced Poacher; The Card Players; In the Tavern;* and *Visit to a Woman in Childbed.*

Museums and Galleries:
Aix: *The Card Players* - Antwerp: *Reception of the Abbot of St Michel* - Besançon: *Spectacles Seller* - Budapest: *Card Players; Skittles Players* - Dijon: *Lunching on Oysters; Musical Performance* - Dresden: *Shoemaker in his Workshop; Mother Sewing with her Child* - Florence (NG): *Woman Praying before Eating; Tailor's Family; The Tea Seller; The Card Players; Kitchen of a Poor Family* - Geneva (Mus. Ariana): *The Dying Woman* - Graz: *Poultry Market; Fish Market; Wine Sampling; Card Players* - Hanover: *Peasant Family; Same Subject* - Kassel: *Peasants Playing; Room in the Inn* - Leipzig: *Skittles Players* - Melbourne (Nat. Gal. of Victoria): *Scene in Holland; Killing a Pig* - Nottingham: *Interior, Card Game; Interior with Smokers* - Toul: *Studio Interior* - Vienna: *Shoemaker's Workshop; Village School.*

Auction records:
Paris, 30 April 1900, *Return from the Hunt,* FRF 680. Amsterdam, 8 Nov 1999, *Fishmarket* (oil on canvas, 28 x 32 ins / 72 x 81 cm) NLG 19,000. London, 3 Nov 2000, *Interior of Cobbler's Shop* (oil on canvas, 13 x 16 ins / 32 x 40 cm) GBP 23,000. Amsterdam, 8 Nov 2000, *Small Girl Seen from behind* (red chalk, 7 x 5 ins / 18 x 12 cm) NLG 16,000. Brussels, 8 May 2001, *Blacksmith in his Smithy* (oil on canvas, 19 x 22 ins / 47 x 57 cm) BEF 380,000. Amsterdam, 4 Sept 2001, *Gentleman Eating Oysters in a Kitchen* (oil on canvas, 12 x 15 ins / 31 x 38 cm) EUR 1,800. Amsterdam, 6 Nov 2002, *Elegant Company Dancing and Feasting on a Terrace* (1719, oil on canvas, 19 x 24 ins / 47 x 60 cm) EUR 4,500. London, 13 Dec 2002, *Lawyer's Office* (oil on canvas, 14 x 13 ins / 35 x 32 cm) GBP 7,500. London, 11 July 2003, *Courtyard in a Town with a Mussel Seller and Other Figures* (oil on canvas, 19 x 24 ins / 47 x 60 cm) GBP 16,000. Amsterdam, 2 Sept 2003, *Elegant Company Dancing and Feasting on a Terrace* (1719, oil on canvas, 19 x 24 ins / 47 x 60 cm) EUR 5,500. Amsterdam, 18 May 2004, *Farm Scene with Woman Putting Apples in a Basket. Market Scene with Trader Selling Fruit* (1756, oil on canvas, a pair, 21 x 24 ins / 54 x 62 cm) EUR 58,000. New York, 27 May 2004, *Interior Scene with Figures by Hearth. Interior Scene with Figures at Table* (oil on canvas, a pair, 18 x 23 ins / 46 x 59 cm) USD 45,000.

HOREMANS, Jan Josef, the Younger, called le Clair
Flemish School, 18th century.
Born 15 January 1714, in Antwerp; died c. 1790.
Painter. History painting, portraits, genre scenes.

Jan Horemans the Younger was a great imitator of his father Jan Josef Horemans the Elder. He was a master in Antwerp in 1767 and became senior guild member in 1768.

Like his uncle Peter Jacob Horemans, he was a talented decorative artist, painting scenes of country life and blending the Flemish style with touches of the French. He was also a highly regarded portraitist of the Antwerp bourgeoisie.

Museums and Galleries:
Amsterdam: *A New Air; Merry Company* - Antwerp: *The Joyful Entry of Charles of Lorraine in Antwerp in 1749.*

Auction records:
Paris, 4 Dec 1924, *The Schoolmistress,* FRF 360. Paris, 22 Dec 1927, *Dance outside the Inn,* FRF 1,250. Paris, 27 Dec 1927, *The Feast,* FRF 2,200. London, 13 March 1946, *At the Money Changer's,* GBP 54; *Visit to the Doctor,* GBP 54. Brussels, 27 Jan 1947, *Meeting at a Scholar's House,* BEF 22,000. Brussels, 7 June 1974, *Huntsmen on a Terrace,* Gns 1,900. Vienna, 13 March 1979, *Interior with People Merrymaking* (1750, oil on canvas, 24 x 29¼ ins / 61 x 74.5 cm) ATS 200,000. Paris, 13 Dec 1982, *Smokers and Drinkers Sitting at Table by a Fireplace* (oil on canvas, 19¼ x 22 ins / 49 x 56 cm) FRF 39,000. Zurich, 14 May 1983, *Still-life with Flowers* (oil on canvas, 25¼ x 30 ins / 64 x 76 cm) CHF 5,000. London, 19 April 1985, *Hunters Resting in a Park* (1762, oil on canvas, 112 x 98½ ins / 284.5 x 250 cm) GBP 12,000. New York, 15 Oct 1987, *Fish Market on the Quay* (1762, oil on canvas, 114 x 115 ins / 289.5 x 292 cm) USD 15,000. London, 27 Oct 1988, *Satyr Taking the Sleeping Diana by Surprise* (oil on canvas, 18¾ x 23 ins / 47.8 x 58.4 cm) GBP 1,320. Amsterdam, 29 Nov 1988, *The Sculptor's Workshop with a Servant Serving Drinks* (1714, oil on canvas, 21¼ x 26½ ins / 53.9 x 67.6 cm) NLG 17,250. Amsterdam, 20 June 1989, *A Man on a Kitchen Doorstep Talking with a Woman Peeling Vegetables* (oil on canvas, 16 x 12½ ins / 39.8 x 31.7 cm) NLG 9,200. New York, 9 Oct 1991, *Country Fair* (1756, oil on canvas, 35½ x 25 ins / 90 x 63.5 cm) USD 7,150. London, 9 Dec 1992, *Two Hermits by a House* (oil on canvas, 16 x 19 ins / 40.6 x 48 cm) GBP 1,870. Paris, 28 June 1993, *Family Meal; Woman in the Kitchen Surrounded by her Children* (oil on canvas, a pair, 15¾ x 13 ins / 40 x 33 cm) FRF 82,000. London, 29 Oct 1993, *Bourgeois Family Taking Tea in a Garden; Farmer Serving Wine and a Young Girl Bringing Apples; Seller and Purchaser Concluding the Sale of a Bull in a Courtyard* (oil on canvas, group of three, each 19 x 16 ins / 48.5 x 40.4 cm) GBP 12,650. Mayenne, 11 June 1995, *At the Alchemist's; At the Money Changer's* (oil on canvas, a pair, each 25½ x 32¾ ins / 65 x 83 cm) FRF 90,500. Paris, 16 June 1995, *Military Celebrations* (oil on canvas, 24½ x 23¼ ins / 62 x 59 cm) FRF 25,000. Amsterdam, 14 Nov 1995, *Schoolmaster Being Given Eggs* (oil on panel, 14½ x 12 ins / 37 x 30.5 cm) NLG 29,500. Amsterdam, 11 Nov 1997, *Two Common Women Playing Cards while another Woman Holds a Mirror* (oil on canvas, 24 x 20 ins / 61 x 50.5 cm) NLG 7,080. London, 13 April 1999, *Elegant Family Dining in Interior* (oil on canvas, 19 x 22 ins / 48 x 56 cm) GBP 7,800. New York, 3 Nov 1999, *Musical Gathering* (oil on canvas, 23 x 19 ins / 58 x 49 cm) USD 10,000. London, 12 Dec 2000, *The Four Seasons* (oil on canvas, four, 15 x 20 ins / 38 x 50 cm) GBP 45,000. London, 14 Dec 2000, *Kitten Still-life with Apples and Pears in Baskets and Other Objects on a Wooden Table* (oil on panel, 17 x 24 ins / 44 x 61 cm) GBP 42,000. London, 11 July 2001, *Doctor Bleeding a Patient* (oil on canvas, 19 x 23 ins / 49 x 58 cm) GBP 2,600. London, 12 July 2001, *Domestic Interior with Family Quarrelling over a Meal* (oil on canvas, 19 x 23 ins / 48 x 58 cm) GBP 2,000. London, 16 April 2002, *Interior with Merry Company* (oil on canvas, 13 x 16 ins / 34 x 40 cm) GBP 3,500. Madrid, 7 Oct 2002, *Inn Interior* (oil on canvas, 25 x 30 ins / 63 x 76 cm) EUR 5,400. London, 9 April 2003, *Cauliflower, Onions and Peaches with Jug on a Table* (1773, oil on panel, 17 x 24 ins / 44 x 61 cm) GBP 25,000. Paris, 17 Oct 2003, *Country Interior Scenes* (oil on canvas, a pair, 15 x 13 ins / 39 x 32 cm) EUR 19,000. London, 21 April 2004, *Sliced Melon, Apples, Pears and Plums and Two Pewter Plates with a Wicker Basket Hanging from the Wall* (oil on canvas, 17 x 24 ins / 44 x 60 cm) GBP 19,000. Milan, 1 June

2004, *Kitchen Interiors with figures* (oil on canvas, 18 x 22 ins / 45 x 56 cm) EUR 4,500.

HOREMANS, Peter
Flemish School, 18th century.
Born 1714, in Antwerp.
Painter.

HOREMANS, Peter Jacob
Flemish School, 18th century.
Baptised 26 October 1700 in Antwerp; died 1776, in Munich.
Painter, decorative artist. Religious subjects, allegorical subjects, figures, portraits, scenes with figures, genre scenes, interiors with figures, fruit.

In 1714, Peter Jacob Horemans was a pupil of his brother Jan Josef Horemans the Elder. In 1725 he went to Munich and in 1727 was appointed court painter to Karl Albrecht, the Prince Elector of Bavaria. He decorated the castles of Schleissheim and Nymphenburg.

MUSEUMS AND GALLERIES:
FLORENCE (Uffizi): *Children's School; Tavern Interior; Dance in a Tavern; Dice Players; Skittles Players* - NUREMBERG: *Fruit; Kant, Valet to the Elector of Cologne, and his Wife; Johanna of Lasande; The Wife of Friedrich Michaels von Zweibrücken* - OSLO: *Fatherly Admonition.*

AUCTION RECORDS:
PARIS, 25 May 1921, *Costume Ball,* FRF 2,700. PARIS, 21 Feb 1925, *Dance,* FRF 600. PARIS, 28-29 June 1926, *Baptismal Meal; Visit to a Woman in Childbed* (both) FRF 13,000. BERN, 1-2 Nov 1946, *The Singers,* CHF 1,750. LONDON, 20 Oct 1972, *The Painter's Studio; The Sculptor's Studio,* Gns 5,000. VIENNA, 22 June 1976, *Carnival Scene* (1760, oil on canvas, 20 x 24 1/2 ins / 51 x 62 cm) ATS 120,000. LONDON, 23 April 1982, *Elegant Society on a Terrace* (two oils on canvas, 42 x 34 ins / 106.8 x 86.3 cm) GBP 10,000. NEW YORK, 18 Jan 1984, *Elegant Figures Making Music by a Portico* (1739, oil on canvas, 35 x 43 ins / 88 x 109.2 cm) USD 32,000. LONDON, 8 July 1987, *Allegories of Spring and Summer* (one canvas dated 1738, oil on canvas, a pair, 25 1/4 x 32 ins / 64 x 81 cm) GBP 38,000. AMSTERDAM, 14 Nov 1990, *Elegant Society Taking Tea in an Interior* (oil/copper, 11 x 14 1/4 ins / 28 x 36 cm) NLG 7,590. LONDON, 5 July 1991, *Peasants Paying their Dues in Produce from their Farms to the Lord of the Manor in his Library* (oil on canvas, 25 3/4 x 32 1/4 ins / 65.4 x 81.9 cm) GBP 8,800. LONDON, 5 July 1995, *Bedroom Interior with a Woman about to give Birth Surrounded by her Family and Doctors; Group of Doctors Admiring a Baby with other Figures* (1734, oil on canvas, a pair, 28 1/4 x 35 1/2 ins / 71.5 x 90 cm) GBP 41,100. PARIS, 12 Dec 1995, *Return from the Hunt* (oil on canvas, 40 1/2 x 49 1/2 ins / 103 x 126 cm) FRF 120,000. LONDON, 17 April 1996, *Elegant Figures Dining in Palace Rooms; Elegant Society Dancing in Palace Rooms* (1745, oil on canvas, a pair, each 31 1/2 x 40 1/2 ins / 80 x 103 cm) GBP 31,050. LONDON, 30 Oct 1996, *Two Gentlemen in a Library, One Seated Writing at his Desk* (1745, oil on canvas, 21 x 16 3/4 ins / 53.2 x 42.5 cm) GBP 6,900. NEW YORK, 16 Oct 1997, *Interior with Ladies and Gentlemen Drinking and Playing Cards* (oil on canvas, a pair, 19 1/2 x 24 ins / 49.5 x 61 cm) USD 18,400. LONDON, 30 Oct 1997, *Interior with the Holy Family, St Anne and St John the Baptist* (1744, oil on canvas, a pair, each 19 x 24 1/2 ins / 48.2 x 62.4 cm) GBP 14,950. LONDON, 6 July 2000, *Self-portrait* (1736, oil on panel, 10 x 8 ins / 26 x 21 cm) GBP 14,000. LONDON, 1 Nov 2001, *Interior with the Holy Family and St Anne. St John the Baptist* (1744, oil on canvas, a pair, 19 x 24 ins / 48 x 62 cm) GBP 5,500. PARIS, 19 Dec 2001, *Interior Scene with Food* (oil on canvas, 30 x 23 ins / 77 x 58 cm) FRF 40,000. VIENNA, 21 March 2002, *Holy Family with St Elizabeth and St John in Workshop* (1744, oil on canvas, 19 x 24 ins / 48 x 62 cm) EUR 8,500. VIENNA, 21 March 2002, *Holy Family with St Anne and St John in workshop* (1744, oil on canvas, 19 x 24 ins / 48 x 62 cm) EUR 8,500.

HORENBANT, Joseph
Belgian, 19th - 20th century.
Born 7 March 1863, in Ghent; died 1956.
Painter. Genre scenes, landscapes with figures.

Horenbant was awarded a bronze medal at the Exposition Universelle in Paris in 1900.

AUCTION RECORDS:
NEW YORK, 1 and 2 March 1906, *Dutch Interior,* USD 300. LOKEREN, 11 March 1995, *Vegetable Market* (oil on canvas, 15 1/4 x 19 3/4 ins / 38.5 x 50 cm) BEF 40,000. LOKEREN, 7 Oct 1995, *Old Working-class Quarter* (oil on canvas, 16 x 23 ins / 40.5 x 58.5 cm) BEF 36,000. LEWES, 5 Sept 2000, *Peasants' Meal* (oil on canvas, 66 x 52 ins / 168 x 132 cm) GBP 2,000. LOTS ROAD, 14 May 2002, *Family Having Supper* (oil on canvas, 66 x 52 ins / 168 x 132 cm) GBP 1,700.

HORENBOLT, Cornelis
16th - 17th century.
Active in Ghent c. 1555-1624.
Painter (glass).

HORENBOUT. See **HOREBOUT Gérard**

HORENBURG, Nikolai Carlovich
Russian, 20th century.
Born 1874.
Painter.

Horenburg worked in St Petersburg.

HORER, Balthasar
Austrian, 18th century.
Born 1705, in Kauns; died 1760, in Passau.
Sculptor.

He was a sculptor at the episcopal court in Passau.

HORFELIN, Antonio de
Spanish, 17th century.
Born 1597, in Saragossa; died 1660, in Saragossa.
Painter. History painting.

Antonio de Horfelin was the son of the little-known painter Pedro Horfelin. He was taught the basics of his art by his father before being sent to Rome to study Raphael and Michelangelo. He also worked with Poultier. One of his principal works is a painting of *St Joseph* in the church of the discalced Augustinian order in Saragossa.

HORFELIN, Pedro de, called Pierre l'Orphelin
French, 16th - 17th century.
Born c. 1560, perhaps in Poitiers; died c. 1620, in Saragossa.
Painter.

Pedro de Horfelin was the father of Antonio.

HORGNIES (Merrouw), or Horgines
later Mme Paelinck
Belgian, 19th century.
Active in 1846 in Brussels.
Painter. Historical subjects, genre scenes.

MUSEUMS AND GALLERIES:
NICE: *The Schoolmaster.*

AUCTION RECORDS:
BRUSSELS, 19 Dec 1989, *Interior Scene* (oil on panel, 19 3/4 x 15 3/4in/50 x 40cm) BEF 105,000.

HORGNIES, Norbert Joseph
Belgian, 19th century.
Active in Brussels in the middle of the 19th century.
Painter. Genre scenes.

AUCTION RECORDS:
LONDON, 11 July 1983, *The Breakfast* (1848, oil on panel, 26 x 21 3/4in/66 x 55.5cm) GBP 1,500. LEWES, 11 March 2003, *Boys Selling Fish at a Doorway* (oil on canvas, 19 x 15 ins / 48 x 38 cm) GBP 1,400. TORONTO, 10 June 2003, *Boy Blowing on his Soup. Boy Kneeling in Snow with Bird and Birdcage* (oil on panel, a pair, 7 x 6 ins / 19 x 15 cm) CAD 4,250. LONDON, 21 Jan 2004, *Fish Sellers* (oil on canvas, 19 x 15 ins / 49 x 37 cm) GBP 3,200.

HORGUES, Miguel
Spanish, 20th century.
Painter. Landscapes.
Miguel Horgues trained in Granada. He took part in the 1910 Exposition de Bruxelles.

HORI, Keikin, real name: Hori Chiyoko
Japanese, 20th century.
Born 15 November 1907, in Tokuyama (Yamaguchi Prefecture).
Painter, calligrapher.
Hori Keikin studied under Shokin Hidai and Kaikaku Niwa, and was appointed director of the Kana-shodo (Japanese calligraphy) artists society in 1965. She teaches at the Japanese Calligraphy School and is in the mainstream of Japanese calligraphy. In 1955, she took part in a travelling exhibition of Japanese calligraphy using Indian ink that went to Europe. She has also exhibited in Pittsburgh, New York and Los Angeles. The Mitsukoshi Gallery in Tokyo organised a retrospective of her work. In 1983, the Galerie Marcel Bernheim in Paris exhibited her work as well as that of 19 of her pupils.

HORI, Kosai
Japanese, 20th - 21st century.
Born 1947, in Toyama.
Painter.
Hori Kosai studied at Tama art school. Using various media, his work explores pictoriality, tending towards abstraction, which he attempts to reconcile with the Japanese tradition. He took part in the 1977 Paris Biennale.

HORION, Alexander de
Flemish School, 17th century.
Born c. 1591, in Liège; died 30 May 1659, in Liège.
Painter. Portraits.
Alexander de Horion is known for his paintings in the churches of Liège and the convent of St Claire.

HORIONS, Johan
Dutch, 17th century.
Active in Utrecht c. 1655.
Painter.
There was a painter by the name of Johan Horions who was also an engraver and draughtsman.

HORIOT, Marceline
French, 19th century.
Born in Auxerre.
Painter.
Horiot exhibited at the Paris Salon in 1878.

HORIUCHI, Masakazu
Japanese, 20th century.
Born 1911, in Kyoto; died 2001.
Sculptor.
After studying sculpture in Tokyo, Horiuchi Masakazu later taught at the Kyoto Municipal College of Art. He tended to detach himself from his works so that they, in his words, lost whatever human flavour they had and became lucid and transparent like air and water, leaving the ego far behind. His technique is uncompromising, using just a few simple materials, such as paper, glue, adhesive tape, wire and scissors. This economy of means is paralleled by an extreme economy of form, his forms constituting the fruit of his meditation. When proceeding to create the finished work - most often in metal - from the model, he imposed the strictest discipline on himself, refusing to accept any idea that might strike him along the way and thus cause him to modify his original conception. From the 1980s, he designed geometric forms, always in this sober fashion.

In 1929 Horiuchi took part in his first Nika exhibition (Salon of the two disciplines of sculpture and painting), and was a member of Nika from 1947 to 1965. In 1957 he took part in the São Paulo Biennale and thereafter in many international modern sculpture exhibitions, especially shows of contemporary Japanese sculpture, such as *One Hundred Masterpieces of Contemporary Japanese Art* held at the National Modern Art Museum in Tokyo on the occasion of the 1964 Olympic Games, and the 2nd JAFA Exhibition held in 1967 in Houston in Texas.

HORKY, Franz Wilhelm
Moravian, 19th century.
Active in Mahrisch-Trübau (Moravská Trebova) c. 1800.
Painter, art restorer.
Franz Horky's wife Rosa was also a painter.

HÖRL, Ottmar
German, 20th century.
Installation artist.
Hörl's work has been shown at solo exhibitions, including ones in 1993 in Zurich and Munich. The objects he produces fall somewhere between 'ready-made' and Minimalism. He also works as a photographer.

HORLACHER, Emma
German, 19th century.
Active in Stuttgart.
Painter. Genre scenes.
She exhibited, from 1882, in Hanover, Munich and Bremen.

HÖRLE, Angelika
German, 20th century.
Born 1899, in Cologne; died 1923.
Painter.
Dadaism.
Cologne Dadaist.
Angelika Hörle was the wife of Heinrich Hörle. Her Dadaist drawings and collages were reproduced in the Dada movement's journals, *Bulletin D, Die Schammade* (*The Maggot of Shame*) and *Stupid*, founded by her husband. These works bear witness to Hörle's extraordinary proto-Surrealist talent, whose development was cut short by her early death.

HÖRLE, Heinrich
German, 20th century.
Born 1 September 1895, in Cologne; died 3 July 1936, in Cologne.
Painter, draughtsman, engraver.
Dadaism.
Cologne Dadaist, Stupid Group, Gruppe Progressiver Künstler (Progressive Art Group).
Before dedicating himself to painting, Heinrich Hörle travelled to Belgium and the Netherlands. He then had a somewhat episodic training at the applied arts school in Cologne. He founded Die Progressiven (Progressive Art Group) in Cologne together with Seiwert. In Cologne in 1919, he founded the Stupid group and a journal with the same name. He was a friend of Max Ernst and collaborated on *Bulletin D*, as well as on the journal *Die Schammade* (*The Maggot of Shame*), in 1920. In 1919, he published a collection of lithographs entitled *Krüppelmappe* (*The Cripple File*). He also collaborated with Baargeld, Otto Freundlich and Max Ernst on the journal *The Ventilator* and the *Der Strom* (*The Current*) publications.

Although Hörle was initially influenced by Expressionism, Dada and the metaphysical paintings of De Chirico, his works gradually developed more political connotations. He depicts modern man, annihilated by technology and reduced to the level of a machine. These figures are reminiscent of those by Léger and De Chirico, but also those of George Grosz and Otto Dix.

HOERLE14

BIBLIOGRAPHY:

Dorival, Bernard/Hoog, Michel, *Dada*, exhibition catalogue, Musée national d'Art moderne, Paris, 1966.

AUCTION RECORDS:

COLOGNE, 3 Dec 1976, *Still-life* (oil on card, 9 1/2 x 11 1/2 ins / 24 x 29 cm) DEM 2,000. COLOGNE, 6 May 1978, *Vase of Flowers* (gouache, 24 3/4 x 19 ins / 63 x 48 cm) DEM 2,400. BERN, 19 June 1980, *Figure, Faces, Houses* (c. 1920, charcoal, 15 3/4 x 11 3/4 ins / 40 x 30 cm) CHF 3,200. LONDON, 2 Dec 1982, *Still-life with a Jug and Fruit* (oil on paper remounted/panel, 23 1/2 x 15 3/4 ins / 59.7 x 40 cm) GBP 4,000. HAMBURG, 9 June 1983, *Composition with Figures and Houses* (c. 1916, chalk, 15 1/2 x 11 3/4 ins / 39.4 x 29.7 cm) DEM 4,800. NEW YORK, 16 Feb 1984, *Woman's Head* (1925, gouache/mounted paper/card, 27 x 20 ins / 67.7 x 50.8 cm) USD 2,400. COLOGNE, 25 Oct 1985, *Still-life with Flowers* (c. 1920-1925, gouache, 16 1/4 x 20 1/2 ins / 41 x 52 cm) DEM 4,000. LONDON, 5 Dec 1985, *Prosthesis* (pen and Indian ink, 19 1/4 x 12 3/4 ins / 48.6 x 32.5 cm) GBP 3,000. COLOGNE, 9 Dec 1986, *People Passing* (1931, oil on card, 18 x 11 1/4 ins / 46 x 28.5 cm) DEM 17,000. PARIS, 3 June 1992, *Composition* (sepia ink and graphite/paper, 10 1/4 x 7 ins / 26 x 18 cm) FRF 22,000. PARIS, 12 May 1993, *Figure* (ink/paper, 11 3/4 x 7 1/2 ins / 30 x 19 cm) FRF 9,500. LONDON, 13 Oct 1994, *Two People (Seiwert and Hörle)* (1931, oil on card, 4 3/4 x 3 1/2 ins / 12 x 9 cm) GBP 4,370.

HORLIAT, Pierre

French, 18th century.
Active in Paris in 1769.
Painter, sculptor.

HORLOR, F.

British, 19th - 20th century.
Active in England.
Painter. Seascapes.

F. Horlof is mentioned in *Art Prices Current.*

AUCTION RECORDS:

LONDON, 12 Jan 1911, *Cornish Coast,* GBP 4.

HORLOR, George William

British, 19th century.
Painter. Landscapes with figures, animals.

George Horlor worked in Cheltenham. He often exhibited in London at the Royal Academy, the British Institution and the Suffolk Street Gallery between 1849 and 1890.

AUCTION RECORDS:

LONDON, 2 Dec 1907, *On the Heath* (1894) GBP 7. LONDON, 9 Dec 1907, *Evening in the Forest,* GBP 12. LONDON, 5 Dec 1908, *Dogs and Dead Birds* (1849) GBP 6. LONDON, 4 Dec 1909, *Ewe and Lamb,* GBP 8. LONDON, 7 March 1910, *Highland Sheep,* GBP 16. LONDON, Feb 1923, *Mealtime,* GBP 26. LONDON, Jan 1924, *Scene in the Highlands with Cattle and Ponies,* GBP 25. LONDON, 25 Jan 1974, *Landscape with Figures,* Gns 280. GLASGOW, 30 Nov 1976, *The Mothers* (1859, oil on canvas, 27 1/4 x 35 ins / 69 x 89 cm) GBP 550. LONDON, 21 Oct 1977, *Setters* (1867, oil on canvas, 14 x 16 1/2 ins / 35.5 x 42 cm) GBP 750. LONDON, 3 July 1979, *Hunter's Friends* (1851, oil on canvas, 30 x 25 ins / 76 x 63.5 cm) GBP 1,800. LONDON, 26 June 1981, *Hunters and their Dogs in a Landscape* (oil on canvas, 14 x 18 ins / 35.5 x 45.6 cm) GBP 3,500. CHESTER, 5 May 1983, *End of the Day* (oil on canvas, 15 1/4 x 23 1/2 ins / 39 x 59.5 cm) GBP 1,000. NEW YORK, 5 June 1986, *Young Squire* (c. 1844, oil on canvas, 25 1/2 x 30 1/4 ins / 65 x 77 cm) USD 20,000. NEW YORK, 4 June 1987, *A Ticklish Customer* (1883, oil on canvas, 16 x 20 ins / 40.6 x 50.8 cm) USD 6,500. LONDON, 2 Nov 1989, *Young Cowherd* (oil on canvas, 18 x 28 ins / 45.8 x 71.2 cm) GBP 2,090. LONDON, 13 Dec 1989, *Returning from Hunting on the Moors* (1864, oil on canvas, 40 1/4 x 60 ins / 102 x 152.5 cm) GBP 13,200. LONDON, 14 Feb 1990, *Watching the Flocks* (1873, oil on canvas, 24 x 36 ins / 60.9 x 91.5 cm) GBP 3,520. NEW YORK, 24 Oct 1990, *Calves Eating* (1856, oil on panel, 15 3/4 x 20 ins / 40 x 50.9 cm) USD 7,150. STOCKHOLM, 14 Nov 1990, *Pony and Two Calfs Guarded by a Dog in a Meadow* (oil on canvas, 26 x 40 1/4 ins / 66 x 102 cm) SEK 10,500. NEW YORK, 16 Oct 1991, *Companions* (1882, oil on canvas, 16 1/4 x 22 ins / 41.2 x 55.8 cm) USD 14,300. LONDON, 13 March 1992, *Children in the Mist* (1858, oil on canvas, 20 1/4 x 55 ins / 51.4 x 139.6 cm) GBP 4,620. AMSTERDAM, 28 Oct 1992, *Pack of Hounds Resting* (1852, oil on canvas, 25 1/4 x 30 ins / 64 x 76 cm) NLG 9,200. PERTH, 31 Aug 1993, *Ponies and Dogs in the Highlands* (1885, oil on canvas, 23 3/4 x 32 ins / 60.5 x 81.5 cm) GBP 20,700. LONDON, 29 March 1995, *Maltese Terrier* (1879, oil on canvas, 16 x 20 ins / 40.5 x 51 cm) GBP 3,450. LONDON, 7 June 1995, *Protection* (oil on canvas, 17 x 23 ins / 43 x 58.5 cm) GBP 6,325. LONDON, 6 Nov 1996, *In the Fields* (1879, oil on canvas, 16 1/4 x 24 ins / 41 x 61 cm) GBP 4,600. LONDON, 5 Nov 1997, *Sheep in the Highlands* (1877, oil on canvas, 24 1/4 x 36 1/2 ins / 61.5 x 92.5 cm) GBP 3,910. LONDON, 3 June 1999, *Standing Guard* (1890, oil on canvas, 18 x 24 ins / 46 x 61 cm) GBP 5,500. LONDON, 14 Dec 1999, *Day's Sport in Perthshire, Preparing for the Return* (1855, oil on canvas, 49 x 60 ins / 125 x 152 cm) GBP 62,000. CANTERBURY, 11 April 2000, *Portrait of a King Charles Spaniel with a Blue Ribbon* (oil on board, 9 x 9 ins / 23 x 23 cm) GBP 2,800. CRANBROOK, 26 June 2000, *Peasant Family with a Child on a Pony* (oil on canvas, 22 x 30 ins / 56 x 76 cm) GBP 2,000. LONDON, 8 March 2001, *Calves and Black Faced Ewes with a Sheepdog* (1872, oil on canvas, 24 x 36 ins / 61 x 91 cm) GBP 4,200. NEW YORK, 6 June 2001, *Terriers* (oil on canvas, 20 x 30 ins / 51 x 76 cm) USD 9,500. LONDON, 17 Sept 2002, *Dead Game* (1845, oil on canvas, 17 x 25 ins / 43 x 64 cm) GBP 1,800. LONDON, 28 Nov 2002, *Bran, property of the Author* (1877, oil on board, 9 x 12 ins / 23 x 30 cm) GBP 1,800. LONDON, 27 Aug 2003, *Setters in a Highland Landscape* (1866, oil on canvas, 34 x 44 ins / 86 x 112 cm) GBP 23,000. LONDON, 30 Oct 2003, *Day's Bag* (1855, oil on canvas, 44 x 59 ins / 113 x 151 cm) GBP 38,000. LONDON, 8 June 2004, *Sheep in a Mountain Landscape* (oil on canvas) GBP 1,800. LONDON, 10 June 2004, *Spaniels with the Day's Bag* (oil on canvas, 10 x 14 ins / 25 x 35 cm) GBP 1,600.

HORLOR, Joseph

British, 19th century.
Born 1809; died 1887.
Active in Bath.
Painter. Landscapes, waterscapes, seascapes.

Joseph Horlor exhibited in London at the British Institution and the Suffolk Street Gallery from 1834 to 1866.

AUCTION RECORDS:

PARIS, 5 April 1943, *On the Shore,* FRF 3,200. LONDON, 15 Oct 1976, *River Landscape* (1871, oil on canvas, 14 x 19 1/2 ins / 35.5 x 49.5 cm) GBP 480. LONDON, 13 Oct 1978, *Fishermen on the Banks of a River* (1859, oil on canvas, 17 x 24 3/4 ins / 43 x 63 cm) GBP 1,100. LONDON, 29 Feb 1980, *Woodcutters in a Landscape* (oil on canvas, 23 3/4 x 35 1/2 ins / 60.3 x 90.2 cm) GBP 750. LONDON, 15 June 1988, *Woodcutters on the Devonshire Coast* (oil on canvas, 25 x 37 1/2 ins / 63.5 x 95.5 cm) GBP 2,420. LONDON, 22 Sept 1988, *Fishermen on a Beach at Low Tide* (oil on canvas, 12 x 20 ins / 30.5 x 51 cm) GBP 935. LONDON, 2 June 1989, *Landscape in Wales with Cattle Crossing a Bridge near a House* (oil on canvas, 29 1/4 x 46 1/2 ins / 74 x 118 cm) GBP 1,650. LONDON, 9 Feb 1990, *Cwm Gwilly in Car-*

marthen (1861, oil on card, 12 x 18 ins / 30.5 x 46 cm) GBP 1,430. LONDON, 5 June 1991, *Salmon Stream* (oil on canvas, 18 x 24 ins / 46 x 61 cm) GBP 990. PARIS, 3 July 1991, *Landscape with Cowherds* (oil on canvas, 11 3/4 x 17 3/4 ins / 30 x 45 cm) FRF 25,000. LONDON, 27 Sept 1994, *Windermere from near Low Wood; Derwent Water in Cumberland* (oil, a pair, each 16 x 28 1/4 ins / 40.5 x 71.5 cm) GBP 1,495. NEW YORK, 17 Jan 1996, *Welsh Landscape* (oil on canvas, 36 x 60 ins / 91.4 x 152.4 cm) USD 3,220. RUMBEKE, 20-23 May 1997, *On the Beach* (1865, oil on canvas, 26 1/4 x 40 1/4 ins / 66.4 x 102 cm) BEF 75,744. LONDON, 5 June 1997, *Lake in a Broad Landscape with Wood Gatherers* (oil on canvas, 18 x 25 ins / 45.7 x 63.5 cm) GBP 2,300. UPPSALA, 9 May 1999, *Scottish Mountain Landscape with Cattle by Water* (oil on canvas, 35 x 59 ins / 90 x 150 cm) SEK 28,000. CRANBROOK, 26 July 1999, *Rustic Figure with Shire Horse before Rural English Thatched Cottage* (1860, oil on canvas, 7 x 13 ins / 18 x 33 cm) GBP 1,300. PORTLAND, 2 Aug 2000, *Working the River Barges* (oil on canvas, 24 x 35 ins / 61 x 89 cm) USD 4,000. LONDON, 7 Sept 2000, *Figure before a Cottage in a Lake Landscape. Figures Resting in a Mountainous Landscape* (oil on canvas, a pair, 12 x 20 ins / 30 x 51 cm) GBP 1,300. LONDON, 30 Aug 2001, *Fisherfolk on the Shore. Cattle Watering in an Extensive River Landscape* (1866, oil on canvas, a pair, 9 x 14 ins / 22 x 36 cm) GBP 1,600. LONDON, 6 Sept 2001, *Drover with Cattle on a Bridge in a Highland Landscape* (oil on canvas, 24 x 40 ins / 60 x 101 cm) GBP 1,300. AYLSHAM, 15 Feb 2002, *Extensive Scottish Loch and Mountain Landscape with Figures, Cattle and Dog on a Riverbank* (oil on canvas, 22 x 37 ins / 56 x 94 cm) GBP 1,550. CASTLECOMER, 5 March 2002, *Pastoral Landscape with Cattle* (oil on board, 9 x 13 ins / 24 x 34 cm) EUR 4,200. HOUSTON, 2 Feb 2003, *Coast of North Shields* (1867, oil on canvas, 11 x 19 ins / 28 x 48 cm) USD 3,500. EXETER, 1 July 2003, *At Carmarthen, Vale of Towy. On the Irvon. At Abergwesyn on the Irvon.Trawler on Shore* (1853, oil on board, four, 4 x 6 ins / 11 x 15 cm) GBP 1,700. LONDON, 23 March 2004, *Wooded River Landscape with Figure in the Foreground* (1860, oil on canvas, 18 x 26 ins / 46 x 66 cm) GBP 1,500. BURY ST EDMUNDS, 23 June 2004, *Landscape near Bath* (oil on board, four, 5 x 7 ins / 13 x 18 cm) GBP 2,300.

HORMANN, Sophie Fessy
German, 19th century.
Born in Blischolz-Schambeck.
Painter, sculptor.

She worked mainly in Munich, but also exhibited in Paris from 1893 to 1896.

HÖRMANN, Theodor von, or Hoermann
Austrian, 19th century.
Born 13 December 1840, in Imst; died 1 July 1895, in Graz.
Painter. Landscapes with figures, landscapes.

A pupil of Eduard Lichtenfels and Anselm Feuerbach at the academy in Vienna, he set out to run military and artistic careers side by side, being a drawing master and fencing master at the military school in St Pölten. He finally opted for an artistic career in 1884 and between 1886 and 1890 was in Paris to train in Raphaël Collin's studio. He exhibited mainly in Vienna, but gained an honourable mention at the Universal Exhibition in Paris in 1889. He was rediscovered posthumously at the Secession Exhibition in Vienna in 1899. His bright-coloured paintings give an impression of movement which is also achieved by the use of inversed perspective and by layering the elements of his compositions.

MUSEUMS AND GALLERIES:
VIENNA (Österreichische Gal. Belvedere): *View of the Tuileries, Paris; Evening Skating Party (Nocturnal Celebration); Znaim (Znojmo) in Winter; View of Prague* (1890).

AUCTION RECORDS:
LONDON, 7 May 1971, *Place St-Sulpice in Paris*, Gns 1,200. VIENNA, 16 March 1976, *View of Znaim (Znojmo)* (oil on canvas, 19 3/4 x 23 1/2 ins / 50 x 60 cm) ATS 160,000. VIENNA, 15 March 1977, *Calvary* (oil on canvas, 14 1/2 x 11 ins / 37 x 27 cm) ATS 40,000. COLOGNE, 11 June 1979, *The Water Mill* (1876, oil on panel, 7 1/2 x 15 1/4 ins / 19 x 38.5 cm) DEM 4,600. VIENNA, 15 Sept 1982, *The Village Church* (1888, oil on canvas, 19 3/4 x 15 1/4 ins / 50 x 39 cm) ATS 75,000. NEW YORK, 25 Oct 1984, *Winter Landscape with Figures* (1892, oil on canvas, 28 x 40 1/4 ins / 70.2 x 102.2 cm) USD 31,000. LONDON, 8 Oct 1986, *Children around a Fire in an Autumn Landscape* (1875, oil on panel, 19 x 31 1/2 ins / 48 x 80 cm) GBP 15,000. LONDON, 26 June 1987, *View of a Salzkammergut Village* (oil on panel, 14 3/4 x 21 1/2 ins / 37.5 x 54.5 cm) GBP 19,000. NEW YORK, 24 Oct 1989, *Flower Market outside the Madeleine* (oil on canvas, 18 x 24 ins / 46 x 61 cm) USD 63,250. MUNICH, 22 June 1993, *Summer in the Garden in Znaim (Znojmo)* (oil on canvas, 30 3/4 x 38 3/4 ins / 78 x 98.5 cm) DEM 419,700. MUNICH, 7 Dec 1993, *Forester Family Making Charcoal in Samois* (oil on canvas, 14 1/2 x 21 1/2 ins / 37 x 54.5 cm) DEM 43,700. MUNICH, 21 June 1994, *The Tower of Gmunden Church* (oil on canvas, 19 1/2 x 13 1/4 ins / 49.5 x 33.5 cm) DEM 46,000. LONDON, 11 Oct 1995, *Children in School Lane* (oil on panel, 11 x 11 1/2 ins / 28 x 29.2 cm) GBP 51,000. MUNICH, 25 June 1996, *Landscape with Houses* (oil on card, 12 1/4 x 20 1/4 ins / 31 x 51.5 cm) DEM 31,200. VIENNA, 20 May 1999, *Vienna Forest in Spring* (oil on canvas, 15 x 22 ins / 38 x 55 cm) ATS 130,000. VIENNA, 20 May 1999, *Charcoal Burners in Forest of Fontainbleau* (oil on panel, 11 x 14 ins / 27 x 35 cm) ATS 180,000. DÜSSELDORF, 31 Jan 2000, *Villagers outside Miskolez* (oil on canvas, 13 x 23 ins / 34 x 58 cm) DEM 60,000. VIENNA, 23 May 2000, *Farm House Garden* (oil on panel, 11 x 8 ins / 27 x 21 cm) ATS 80,000. VIENNA, 29 Nov 2001, *Fruit Trees in Blossom* (oil on canvas, 11 x 16 ins / 27 x 41 cm) ATS 220,000. VIENNA, 29 Nov 2001, *Walk in the Woods* (oil on panel, 8 x 11 ins / 21 x 27 cm) ATS 400,000. VIENNA, 22 May 2003, *Residence with Garden in the Neighbourhood of St Polten* (1882, oil on canvas, 22 x 27 ins / 56 x 68 cm) EUR 12,000. VIENNA, 27 May 2003, *Estate in Spring* (oil on canvas, 14 x 20 ins / 36 x 50 cm) EUR 27,000. VIENNA, 22 June 2004, *Study of Dorfbrand* (oil on canvas/board, 8 x 12 ins / 20 x 31 cm) EUR 4,500. MUNICH, 30 June 2004, *Mill by Stream* (1885, oil on board, 14 x 6 ins / 36 x 16 cm) EUR 1,600.

HORMANN, W.
Painter. Landscapes.

MUSEUMS AND GALLERIES:
CAPE TOWN (museum): *In the Forest* (oil on canvas).

HORMUTH-KALLMORGEN, Margarete
German, 19th - 20th century.
Born 22 August 1858, in Heidelberg; died 7 July 1916, in Heidelberg.
Painter. Still-lifes, flowers.

Hormuth-Kallmorgen was a student of Ferdinand Keller in Karlsruhe from 1878 to 1885. Her work was exhibited in Bremen, Berlin and Düsseldorf.

HORN, Bartholomeus
Dutch, 17th century.
Active in Groningen.
Painter. Still-lifes.

HORN, C.
British, 19th century.
Active in London.
Painter. Genre scenes.

C. Horn exhibited eight times at the Royal Academy in London between 1819 and 1830.

AUCTION RECORDS:
NEW YORK, 29 Jan 1902, *Still-life*, USD 115. PARIS, 14 March 1931, *Cleopatra* (pen drawing) FRF 25.

HORN, Carl
German, 20th century.
Born 27 April 1874, in Kassel.
Painter.
Horn is known for his landscapes and portraits.

HORN, David
German, 20th century.
Born 1937.
Active in Britain.
Sculptor.
David Horn studied in London at the Chelsea School of Art and (from 1960 to 1964) at the Royal College of Art in London. Work by him was shown at the Young Sculptors' Exhibitions from 1959 onwards. He taught at St Martin's School of Art in London.

HORN, Lex
Dutch, 20th century.
Born 1916, in Nijmegen; died 1968.
Painter.
Lex Horn arrived in Amsterdam at the age of eighteen and began studying at the fine arts school, where he worked with Campendock. After 1939, he travelled to the south of France and to Italy, but his worked remained distinctively Dutch. He was the foremost figure in a renaissance of mural art in the Netherlands and produced typically Flemish Expressionist mosaics and ceramics that sometimes bordered on the abstract.
AUCTION RECORDS:
AMSTERDAM, 30 May 1995, *Urban Landscape* (oil on paper/card, 16 1/2 x 22 1/2 ins / 42 x 57 cm) NLG 1,400.

HORN, Melchior
German, 17th century.
Born in Michelau; died 1615, in Brieg (now Brzeg, Poland).
Painter.

HORN, Paul
German, 20th century.
Born 22 July 1876, in Merseburg.
Sculptor, decorative designer.
Paul Horn was a student of Topfmeyer in Hanover and worked mainly in Halle-Gröllwitz.

HORN, Rebecca
German, 20th century.
Born 1944, in Michelstadt.
Also active in the USA.
Sculptor, performance artist, installation artist, film producer, video artist.
From 1964 to 1969, Horn studied painting and sculpture at the art academy in Hamburg, which was renowned for its complete educational freedom, and its new exploration of aesthetics. She discovered the writings of Jean Genest, Franz Kafka, the films of Luis Bunuel and Pier Paolo Pasolini at the academy. Having Swiss nationality, she settled first in Geneva and later came to divide her time between Paris and Zell-Bad König, near Berlin. She travels extensively. In 1971-1972 she obtained a grant to work at St Martin's School of Art, London. In 1974, she was invited to teach at the California Art Institute (University of San Diego), then in 1991 at the art academy in Berlin to teach multimedia courses. In 1975, she won the Deutscher Kritiker Preis (Critics' Prize) at the Berlin Film Festival; the Kunstpreis Glockengasse (prize) in Cologne in 1977; the Documenta prize in Kassel in 1986; the Carnegie International prize of Pittsburgh in 1988; in 1992, the prestigious Trägerin des Kaiserrings, Goslar.

Following a year's interruption of her work due to poisoning, from the polyurethane she used for her sculptures at the art academy in Hamburg, Horn started writing scenarios for performances. These portrayed her friends, for whom she also made objects, 'body sculptures', which they wore. Simultaneously, she made films of them, such as *Head Extension*. More than a documentary of her performances, *Berlin Exercises: Dreaming under Water* (1974-1975) was her first film made purely for the cinema. All her productions, objects, films and performances have become part of her history in one way or another, and more specifically part of the relationship she maintains between the body and the environment - one of the recurrent elements throughout her work. Horn belongs to the tradition of the European and American artists, heirs of the avant-garde, who became known at the beginning of the 1970s, and openly questioned the autonomy of the aesthetic object and the institutional frameworks that preserve it. Initially, Horn used the body in its own right as her starting point. With *Overflowing Blood Machine* (1970), she aimed, for example, to establish correlations and connections between the inside of the human body - comparable to a hidden, mysterious machine - and the exterior, revealed through a system of transparent pipes, which envelop the body and through which blood flows. Elsewhere, in *The Feathered Prison Fan* (1978), she dressed up the body with a prosthesis made of feathers. Half-animal, half-human, the installation mixes organic matter with different forms. Rebecca Horn is primarily known for her strange 'machines', which she also sets up in the form of installations, for example: *Night and Day on the Back of the Two-headed Snake*, the Musée d'Art moderne de la Ville de Paris, 1986. They are composed of ill-assorted elements, including water, metal, mercury, mirror, peacock feather, goose egg, and funnels; their lightness is suggested, their transparency is visible and their fragility is assessed. They are sometimes guided by an operator, or more frequently, are autonomous and thus the mechanics of rotation or hammering are an integral part. These 'machines' do not produce any work: their function is purely artistic. They express a set of links, emotions and contradictory forces (including tenderness and aggression. The feathers of crows in *Little Widow* (1988), move in a semi-circle, then return to their original position, thanks to a small motor; or the mercury that covers an oblong box *Hydra Piano* (or *Snake Piano*), is deployed in fine drops. 'Perhaps this sensation of a permanent flow maintaining the movement of things is why I use water so often, as well as flashes of light'. Her choice of organic materials also comes from her interest in alchemy and her fascination in the transformation of matter, stemming from a chain of processes. The book *Die Chymische Hochzeit des Christian Rosenkreutz* (*The Chemical Wedding of Christian Rosenkreutz*), written at the beginning of the 17th century and usually attributed to Johann Valentin Andreae, has triggered many things in her, according to her statements. While she does not confirm the existence of a direct relationship with the 'bachelor machines', of Marcel Duchamp, Rebecca Horn reveals her interest in the work of Raymond Roussel, which includes *Locus Solus*, with its really 'fluid', formal, combinatory elements. Alone, but in no way abandoned, Rebecca Horn's 'machines' have a genuine interpretation. Attributed with a sexual or mythological symbolism, they dismiss the aesthetics of fundamental instinct, of Surrealist origin, such as the machine irrigating her 'feminine' sculpture, installed for her retrospective at the Guggenheim Museum in 1993: from one of the two funnels resembling enormous breasts a milky liquid, drips into a pool, situated about 49feet (15 metres) down below, into the middle of which gushes a fountain, like a penis. Other pieces, which are always viewed as symbols to decipher, combine several levels of interpretation, from which ideas of death, sex, freedom and life join forces in an implacable, sometimes aggressive, not to say pathological, 'machine'; an example of this is the two Winchester rifles in *High Moon* (1991), suspended from the ceiling which, revolving around the room, take aim at the visitors. When these two weapons, which are connected up to two funnels, two 'breasts', filled with a blood-red liquid, eventually stabilize opposite each other, they fire.

Horn has participated in group exhibitions, including 1972, Documenta V, Kassel; 1975, the Biennale de Paris; 1977, the Documenta VI, Kassel; 1978, the *Videosymposium*, Tokyo; 1980, the Festival of Spoletto; 1981, *La Ferdinanda* (*La Ferdinanda*), the Staatliche Kunsthalle, Baden-Baden; 1981, the Stedelijk Museum, Amsterdam; 1982, the Documenta VII, Kassel; 1984, *Von Hier aus* (*From Here On*), Düsseldorf; 1986, the Documenta, Kassel; 1986, the Venice Biennale; 1987, *Skulptur Projekte* (*Sculpture Projects*), Münster; 1988, the Sydney Biennial; 1989, *Les Magiciens de la Terre* (*Magicians of the Earth*), the Centre Georges-Pompidou, Paris; 1992, the Documenta IX, Kassel; 2002, *Les Années 70: l'Art en Cause* (*The 1970s: Art in Question*), the Capc-Musée d'Art Contemporain, Bordeaux; 2003, the Tate Collection, Liverpool; 2003, *Phantom der Lust. Visionen des Masochismus in der Kunst* (*Phantom of Desire. Visions of Masochism in Art*), an exhibition dedicated to Sacher-Masoch, the Austrian novelist who described masochism, which was held at the Neue Galerie am Landesmuseum, Graz; 2003, *Berlin-Moscow/Moscow-Berlin 1950-2000*, an exhibition overview, which, following the exhibition covering the period 1900 - 1950, opened up to debate 50 years of German-Russian artistic and cultural relations, influenced by political change, held at the Martin-Gropius-Bau, Berlin and the Tretyakov Gallery, Moscow.

Horn has held solo shows, including 1975, the Galerie René Block, Berlin; 1975, the Galerie Nächst Sankt-Stephan, Vienna; 1976, the René Block Gallery, New York; 1977, the Kölnischer Kunstverein, Berlin; 1978, the Kestner-Gesellschaft, Hanover; 1979, the Stedelijk Van Abbemuseum, Eindhoven; 1981, the Staatliche Kunsthalle, Baden-Baden; 1983, the Centre d'Art Contemporain, Geneva; 1983, the Kunsthaus, Zurich; 1985, the Museum of Contemporary Art, Chicago; 1986, *Nuit et Jour sur le Dos d'un Serpent à Deux Têtes* (*Night and Day on the Back of a Two-headed Snake*), the Musée d'Art moderne de la Ville de Paris; 1986, the PS1, New York; 1987, 1988, 1990, 1991, the Marian Goodman Gallery, New York; 1988, 1991, 1992, the Galerie de France, Paris; 1989, the Galerie Konrad Fischer, Düsseldorf; 1990, the Museum of Modern Art, Los Angeles; 1990, the Galerie Eric Franck within the context of the Foire Internationale d'Art Contemporain (international contemporary art fair), Paris; 1991, the Galerie Élisabeth Kaufmann, Basel; 1991, 1992, the Galerie Franck & Schulte, Berlin; 1993-1995, a travelling exhibition at the Guggenheim Museum of New York; the Stedelijk Van Abbemuseum, Eindhoven; the National Gallery, Berlin; the Kunsthalle, Vienna; the Tate Gallery, London; the Musée de Grenoble; 2004, the K20 Kunstsammlung North Rhine-Westphalia, Düsseldorf; 2005, Hayward Gallery, London.

BIBLIOGRAPHY:

Horn, Rebecca, *Carnets de notes*, Gal. de France, Paris. *Rebecca Horn*, Kunsthaus, Zurich, Museum of Contemporary Art, Chicago, 1983. *Rebecca Horn: nuit et jour sur le dos du serpent à deux têtes*, Musée d'Art moderne de la Ville de Paris, Paris, 1986. Martin, Jean-Hubert/Mark, Francis/Magnin, André/Marcadé, Bernard, *Les Magiciens de la terre*, group exhibition catalogue, Éd. du Centre Georges-Pompidou, Paris, 1989. Bourriaud, Nicolas, *'Les Machines malades de Rebecca Horn'* in *Artstudio* no. 22, periodical, Gal. Templon, Paris, 1991. Durand, Régis, *'Interview: Rebecca Horn, danger imminent'* in *Art Press* no. 181, periodical, Paris, 1993. Weibel, Peter (ed.), *'Phantom der Lust. Visionen des Masochismus in der Kunst'* in *2 vol*, exhibition catalogue, Neue Galerie am Landesmuseum, Graz, Belleville Verlag, Munich, 2003. *'Berlin-Moskau/Moskau-Berlin 1950-2000'* in *2 vol*, exhibition catalogue, Martin-Gropius-Bau, Berlin, 2003 (text in German).

MUSEUMS AND GALLERIES:

NANTES (MBA) - PARIS (FNAC): *Hydra Piano* (1988); *Wings of Chinese Feathers* (1993) - ROCHECHOUART (Mus. Départemental d'Art Contemporain): *Metamorphosis* (1986) - VILLEURBANNE (FRAC Rhône-Alpes): *Ocean Dewdrop*.

AUCTION RECORDS:

NEW YORK, 2 May 1991, *Henry and Frederico Quivering* (1988, two butterflies on steel wire with an electric motor, 54 x 50 x 5 1/2 ins / 137.1 x 127 x 14 cm) USD 33,000. NEW YORK, 13 Nov 1991, *Drawing Machine* (1986, electric motor, goose egg, hook and charcoal sticks, 98 x 15 x 15 ins / 248.9 x 38.1 x 38.1 cm) USD 26,400. NEW YORK, 19 Nov 1992, *Untitled* (1987, steel, feathers and electric motor, 49 x 14 1/2 x 7 1/4 ins / 124.5 x 37.1 x 18.4 cm) USD 18,700. NEW YORK, 24 Feb 1993, *Spoon Sleep* (1989, electric motor and two silver spoons, 11 1/2 x 12 1/4 x 3 1/2 ins / 29.2 x 31.4 x 8.9 cm) USD 33,000. NEW YORK, 5 May 1993, *Untitled (Shoes)* (1989, steel wire, leather shoes and an electric motor, h. 78 1/4 ins / 198.8 cm) USD 43,700. LONDON, 24 June 1993, *Upside down Marriage* (1985, painted wood, 27 1/2 x 11 x 8 ins / 69.8 x 28 x 20.2 cm) GBP 4,830. NEW YORK, 10 Nov 1993, *Ostrich* (black and white photograph, collage of graphite paper and coloured pencil, 27 1/2 x 39 1/4 x 2 ins / 69.8 x 100 x 5 cm) USD 4,025. NEW YORK, 5 May 1994, *The Unconsciousness of Feelings* (1985, aluminium construction with an electric motor, 19 1/2 x 11 1/4 x 8 1/4 ins / 49.5 x 28.6 x 21 cm) USD 27,600. NEW YORK, 3 May 1995, *Small Painting School* (1988, steel, electric motor, brush, metal wire and canvas, 116 x 17 x 43 ins / 294.6 x 43.2 x 109.2 cm) USD 33,350. NEW YORK, 8 May 1996, *Painting Machine* (steel, electric motor, brush, metal wire and wooden stretcher, h. variable, w. 43 ins / 109.2 cm, d. 17 ins/43.2 cm) USD 34,500. LONDON, 27 June 1996, *Seraphine's Soul* (1987, writing in felt in a glass case with feathers, 11 3/4 x 7 3/4 x 3 1/4 ins / 30 x 20 x 8.5 cm) GBP 3,450. NEW YORK, 19 Nov 1997, *Gold Rush* (1985, steel, motor, resin with gold paint and coal, 94 x 9 1/2 x 10 ins / 238.7 x 24.1 x 25.4 cm) USD 43,700. NEW YORK, 19 May 1999, *Death in Venice* (1990, shoes, metal, motor, hammer, pigment, sieve) USD 40,000. PARIS, 13 Oct 1999, *Kangaroo* (1976, black ink and coloured crayon on paper, 11 x 8 ins / 27 x 21 cm) FRF 11,000. NEW YORK, 15 Nov 2000, *Oyster Piano* (steel, oyster shells, pearls and mechanical parts, 3 x 15x15 ins / 8 x 38x38 cm) USD 16,000. BERLIN, 23 Nov 2000, *La Ferdinanda* (c. 1981, iron, glass and feather, 28 x 8 ins / 70 x 20 cm) DEM 26,000. NEW YORK, 16 May 2001, *Arthur* (1987, pair of shoes, charcoal, hammer with motor) USD 20,000. NEW YORK, 18 May 2001, *Spoons* (1990, electric motor and spoons, 10 x 10 ins / 25 x 25 cm) USD 20,000. LONDON, 28 June 2002, *Three-armed Painting School* (1989, sculpture, 145 x 74x69 ins / 368 x 188x174 cm) GBP 10,000. LONDON, 22 Oct 2002, *Love Thermometer* (crystal, liquid metal, butterflies and text mounted on on wall, 37 x 14x4 ins / 95 x 36x9 cm) GBP 5,800. NEW YORK, 12 Nov 2003, *Seamless* (1990, wood, spools, thermometer and other objects, 41 x 28x7 ins / 105 x 71x19 cm) USD 9,500. ZURICH, 25 Nov 2003, *Untitled* (1978, mixed media, pencil, coloured pen, fingerprints, collage and polaroids, 27 x 39 ins / 68 x 98 cm) CHF 4,500. LONDON, 25 June 2004, *Libelle* (1986, electric motor, wire, metal and feathers, h. 50 ins / 127 cm) GBP 27,000. PARIS, 30 Nov 2004, *Robert Walser's Library* (1994, steel, glass, feather, book and engine, 39 x 28x8 ins / 100 x 70x20 cm) EUR 26,000.

HORN, Roni

American, 20th - 21st century.
Born 1955, in New York.

Sculptor, painter, collage artist, installation artist, photographer, draughtswoman. Artists' books. Conceptual Art.

Roni Horn studied at the Rhode Island School of Design in 1975 and at Yale in 1978. She lives and works in New York, where she teaches at the School of Arts, Columbia University.

Roni Horn's work is heterogeneous in its approach. Her early experiments in sculptural form were Minimalist in style, using industrial, machine-tooled objects and incorporating elements of language. She has also produced artist's books (the *Top Place* series) reflecting her passion for the geology, topography and landscapes of Iceland. Her later work includes photographic images incorporated into mixed-media installations (sculptures, drawings, photos) or presented as installations in their own right. *Ellipsis II* (1988) comprises 64 such images, showing the interior architecture (corridors, doors, walls) of a municipal swimming baths. Through the formal repetition of certain motifs (notably the peepholes surreptitiously gouged into the doors of the changing cubicles), and the piece's overall composition (the photographs are all identical in size), the building's space is compartmentalised and resembles an endless labyrinth. Repetition remains a central feature of her work, although the repeated images are never wholly identical. Her landscapes and portraiture are the vehicles for in-depth exploration of the subject's subtle variations, enabling the artist to question the concepts of identity, difference and similarity.

Horn's work has featured in a number of group exhibitions: 1996, *From Beuys to Trockel. Contemporary Drawings from the Kunstmuseum Basel*, Centre Georges Pompidou, Paris; 1998, Sydney Biennial; 2001, *The Inward Eye: Transcendence in Contemporary Art*, Contemporary Arts Museum, Houston; 2002, *Moving Pictures* (exhibition exploring the use of photography, film and video in art since the late 1960s), Solomon R. Guggenheim Museum, New York; 2002, *Sans commune mesure. Image et texte dans l'art actuel* (*Without Common Measure: Image and Text in Contemporary Art*), Musée d'Art Moderne Lille Métropole, Villeneuve d'Ascq. Her work has also been shown in a number of solo exhibitions, including: 1988, Galerie Daniel Lelong, Paris; 1995, Kunsthalle, Basel; 1995, 1997, 1999, Matthew Marks Gallery, New York; 1995, 1998, Museum für Gegenwartskunst, Basel; 1999, *Events of Relation*, Musée d'Art Moderne de la Ville de Paris; 1999, *Water*, CAPC-Musée d'Art Contemporain, Bordeaux; 1999, Staatsgalerie Moderner Kunst, Munich; Whitney Museum of American Art, New York; 2003, Centre Georges Pompidou, Paris.

BIBLIOGRAPHY:

Goldstein, Ann/Kertess, Klaus, *Roni Horn*, exhibition catalogue, Museum of Contemporary Art, Los Angeles, 1990. Koepplin, Dieter, *Roni Horn: Zeichnungen [Drawings]*, exhibition catalogue, Museum für Gegenwartskunst, Basel, Cantz, Ostfildern, 1995 (text in German and English). Bossé, Laurence/Spector, Nancy, et al.., *Events of Relation*, solo exhibition catalogue, Musée d'Art Moderne de la Ville de Paris, Paris, 1999 (text in French and English). Schulz-Hoffmann, Carla/Strobl, Andreas, *Roni Horn. Photoinstallation*, exhibition catalogue, Staatsgalerie Moderner Kunst, München, Hatje Cantz, Ostfildern-Ruit, 1999 (English edition, Hatje Cantz, Ostfildern-Ruit, 2000). Neri, Louise/Cooke, Lynne/DeDuve, Thierry, *Roni Horn*, Phaidon, London, 2000. *Moving Pictures*, exhibition catalogue, Solomon R. Guggenheim Museum, New York, 2002.

MUSEUMS AND GALLERIES:

LOS ANGELES (County MA) - NEW YORK (Solomon R. Guggenheim Mus.): *Untitled (Flannery)* (1996-1997); *Dead Owl* (1997) - SAN FRANCISCO (MoMA).

AUCTION RECORDS:

NEW YORK, 23-25 Feb 1993, *Thicket #1* (1990, resin and brushed aluminium, 21/4 x 64 x 481/4 ins / 5.4 x 162.6 x 122.6 cm) USD 20,700. NEW YORK, 5 May 1993, *Sphere V* (1989, wrought copper, diam. 12 ins / 30.5 cm) USD 18,400. NEW YORK, 11 Nov 1993, *The XIII* (powdered pigments and varnish/paper, 251/2 x 37 ins / 64.8 x 94 cm) USD 6,038. NEW YORK, 23 Feb 1994, *The XXXVI* (1988, pigment and varnish on a collage of paper/paper, 181/4 x 253/4 ins / 46.4 x 65.4 cm) USD 4,600. NEW YORK, 3 Sept 1999, *When Dickenson Shuts her Eyes* (plastic and aluminium, 5 x 5 ins / 13x13 cm) USD 26,000. NEW YORK, 18 Nov 1999, *Steven's Bouquet* (aluminum and Plexiglas, 42 x 50x15 ins / 107 x 127x38 cm) USD 55,000. ZURICH, 19 June 2001, *Untitled* (pigment and varnish on paper, 13 x 15 ins / 34 x 37 cm) CHF 13,000. VIENNA, 27 Nov 2001, *Untitled* (1979, pencil, 8 x 10 ins / 20 x 26 cm) ATS 25,000. NEW YORK, 13 Nov 2002, *When Dickinson Shut her Eyes* (1993, plastic and aluminium, 55 x 35x25 ins / 140 x 89x63 cm) USD 40,000. CHICAGO, 19 Nov 2002, *Untitled* (pastel and pigment on cut-out shapes, a pair, 4 x 6 ins / 11 x 16 cm) USD 5,500. NEW YORK, 13 Nov 2003, *Untitled, Pigment Drawings* (1986, pigment, varnish and pencil, a pair, 16 x 19 ins / 40 x 49 cm) USD 13,000. NEW YORK, 14 Nov 2003, *Dead Owl* (1997, iris print, 22 x 22 ins / 57 x 57 cm) USD 18,000. NEW YORK, 14 May 2004, *The XXIX* (acrylic and collage on paper, 25 x 31 ins / 63 x 80 cm) USD 16,000. LONDON, 25 June 2004, *Still Water - River Thames, for Example - Images C, G, J* (three offset lithographs, 30 x 41 ins / 77 x 105 cm) GBP 15,000.

HORN-ZIPPELIUS, Dora

German, 20th century.
Born 22 August 1876.
Painter, engraver.

Horn-Zippelius was a student at the Karlsruhe academy.

HORNBERGER, Wilhelm

German, 19th century.
Born 21 February 1819, in Ilbesheim (Rhineland); died c. 1880.
Sculptor.

He worked in Mannheim and Ludwigshafen.

HORNBROOK, Thomas Lyde

British, 19th century.
Born c. 1808; died 1855.
Painter. Seascapes, naval battles.

AUCTION RECORDS:

LONDON, Dec 1923, *Capture of the American Flotilla*, GBP 216. LONDON, July 1924, *Naval Battles*, GBP 27. LONDON, 28 May 1930, *Montréal*, GBP 168. LONDON, 11 Dec 1931, *Engagement on a River in America*, GBP 100. LONDON, 23 March 1979, *View of the Port of Corunna* (oil on canvas, 161/2 x 231/2 ins / 42 x 59.7 cm) GBP 1,700. LONDON, 13 Dec 1982, *Anglo-American Action on Lake Borge, New Orleans, in 1814* (oil on canvas, 231/2 x 351/2 ins / 60 x 90 cm) GBP 24,000. LONDON, 6 July 1983, *English Frigates at Anchor in the Port of Corunna* (oil on canvas, 17 x 24 ins / 43 x 61 cm) GBP 2,000. LONDON, 21 Nov 1986, *English Warship at Anchor off Port Mahon, Minorca* (oil on canvas, 171/4 x 36 ins / 43.8 x 90.5 cm) GBP 3,500. LONDON, 17 July 1992, *Tamar Estuary in Plymouth with a Frigate at Anchor and other Ships* (oil on canvas, 12 x 353/4 ins / 30.3 x 90.8 cm) GBP 4,400. LONDON, 29 May 1997, *Ships on a Calm Sea* (oil on canvas, 15 x 22 ins / 38 x 56 cm) GBP 7,475. LONDON, 28 April 1999, *Man-o'-war in Devonport, Plymouth* (oil on canvas, 18 x 24 ins / 45 x 61 cm) GBP 19,000. LONDON, 17 Aug 1999, *View of Belem Castle, Lisbon* (pencil and watercolour, 12 x 15 ins / 30 x 39 cm) GBP 3,200. WELLINGTON, 30 Aug 2000, *Battle of Trafalgar* (oil on canvas, 14 x 18 ins / 35 x 45 cm) NZD 12,000. NEWBURY, 11 Oct 2000, *Estuary Scene with Naval Shipping, Mount Edgecumbe House beyond* (oil on canvas, 24 x 36 ins / 60 x 91 cm) GBP

4,600. LONDON, 17 Jan 2001, *Battle of San Domingo* (1831, oil on canvas, 23 x 38 ins / 58 x 97 cm) GBP 6,400. LONDON, 15 June 2001, *Frigate Hove-to and Signalling for a Pilot off Approaches to Guernsey* (oil on canvas, 20 x 30 ins / 52 x 75 cm) GBP 5,500. LONDON, 16 Jan 2002, *HMS Grasshopper Being Attacked. Action off Cadiz. Two Spanish Merchants* (oil on canvas, three, 24 x 36 ins / 61 x 91 cm) GBP 9,000. LONDON, 31 Oct 2002, *Royal Naval Frigate Announcing Its Arrival in the Hamoaze, Plymouth Sounds* (oil on canvas, 15 x 21 ins / 38 x 53 cm) GBP 2,600. LONDON, 25 Nov 2003, *Aftermath of the Great Gale: Frigate in Distress in Plymouth Sounds* (oil on panel on board, 11 x 15 ins / 29 x 39 cm) GBP 4,000. LONDON, 25 Nov 2003, *Frist Making Her Way down Plymouth Sounds in a Still Breeze with Drake's Island* (oil on panel on board, 12 x 16 ins / 31 x 41 cm) GBP 5,000. LONDON, 14 Sept 2004, *Royal Navy Frigate in Plymouth Sound* (watercolour, 13 x 19 ins / 34 x 47 cm) GBP 1,400.

HORNBY, Lester George
American, 20th century.
Born 27 March 1882, in Lowell (Massachusetts); died 1956.
Painter, engraver, draughtsman, illustrator.

Lester George Hornby studied at Rhode Island School of Design before moving to Boston. He travelled for a long time in England and then France, where he trained under J.P. Laurens. He is known in England for his drawings, and as an illustrator of the World War I.

HORNDASH, Ulrich
German, 20th - 21st century.
Born 1951, in Munich.
Painter, mixed media. Murals.

Horndash lives and works in Munich. He uses multiple forms of expression and combines cultural references from the Suprematism of Russian painter Kasimir Malevich to the Constructivism of Russian painter, sculptor and graphic artist Eliezer Markowich Lissitzky. Notably, he produces monumental murals on glass, painted from the block, and inscribes signs, scripts and geometric forms onto the vast surface.

Horndash has participated in group exhibitions: 1981, the Kunstverein, Munich; 1984, the Kunstverein, Cologne; 1985, the Fine Arts Museum, Taipei; 1986, 1990, the Palais des Beaux-Arts, Charleroi; 1987, the Kunstverein, Bonn; 1988: the Kunstverein, Frankfurt, FRAC (Fonds Régional d'Art Contemporain), Rhône-Alpes, in St-Étienne; the Vienna Secession; the Institute of Contemporary Art, Boston; the Internationaal Culturel Centrum, Antwerp; 1989, the Institute of Art, Minneapolis; 1990, the Civico Museo, Trieste; 1991: the Stadtmuseum, Munich; the Centraalmuseum, Utrecht; the Salon de Montrouge; 1995, the City Art Centre, Edinburgh. Horndash has held solo shows: 1982, the Kunstforum, Munich; 1984, Rotterdam; 1986, Graz and New York; 1987, Brussels and Cologne; 1989, Le Magasin, the Centre National d'Art Contemporain, Grenoble; 1991, the Contemporary Art Gallery, Vancouver; 1992: the Lenbachhaus, Munich; the Gemeentemuseum, The Hague; the Kunstverein, Salzburg; 1996 - 1997, the Galerie Renos Xippas, Paris.

BIBLIOGRAPHY:
Ulrich Horndash, exhibition catalogue, Centre national d'Art contemporain Le Magasin, Grenoble, 1989. Boulbès, Carole, '*Ulrich Horndash*' in *Art Press* no. 221, periodical, Paris, February 1997.

HORNEBOLTE, Lucas
Flemish, 16th century.
Born c. 1490; died 1544.
Active in Great Britain.
Painter, miniaturist.
Flemish School.

Lucas Hornebolte was one of a family of illustrators belonging to the guild of Ghent and Bruges. He, his sister and their father Gerard left Flanders for England around 1520. He is credited with having introduced the art of the miniature into England. Recent research attributes 23 miniatures to him, mostly royal portraits, including one of Henry VIII aged 35 (in the collection of the duke of Buccleuch). This is confirmed by the record of the first payments made to both father and son in the royal accounts for 1528. From 1531 he was considered to be the king's painter, a post guaranteed to him for life in 1534.

To render his sitters' features, Hornebolte used red and grey hatching on a pink background over the cheeks and forehead. Hair and beards are treated in the same way on an opaque background.

MUSEUMS AND GALLERIES:
CAMBRIDGE (Fitzwilliam Mus.): *Henry VIII 1491-1547* (1525-1527, watercolour/vellum/card).

AUCTION RECORDS:
PARIS, 18 Nov 1994, *New Portrait of Henry VIII, King of England* (gouache heightened with gold, diam. 2 1/4 ins / 6 cm) FRF 400,000.

HORNECKER, Léon
French, 19th - 20th century.
Born 13 April 1864, in Strasbourg; died 8 January 1924, in Paris.
Painter. Portraits.

A pupil of Gysis and L. von Loefftz, Léon Hornecker received honourable mention in Paris at the Salon de Paris (1894) and a 3rd class medal (1903).

MUSEUMS AND GALLERIES:
MULHOUSE: *Portrait* - STRASBOURG: *Portraits of an Old Woman, Old Man and a Little Girl; Portrait of the Actress Jane Hato.*

HORNEL, Edward Atkinson
British, 19th - 20th century.
Born 1864, in Victoria, Australia; died 1933.
Painter. Landscapes with figures.
Glasgow School.

Edward Hornel's father, a Scot, brought him to Scotland from Australia in 1866. He began to study in Edinburgh in 1881, but two years later he left to work in Antwerp for two years with Verlat. He returned to Scotland in 1885. He travelled to Japan in 1893 and 1894, then settled in Kirkcudbright, Scotland. He first exhibited at the Edinburgh Exhibition in 1883, and also showed his work at the Grosvenor Gallery in London in 1890. He was a member of the International Society of Painters and Engravers and an associate member of the New Gallery.

MUSEUMS AND GALLERIES:
BRADFORD (Cartwright Hall AG): *The Pool* (1904, oil on canvas) - GLASGOW: *The Coming of Spring* - LEEDS (City AG): *Tamil Water Carriers* (1909, oil on canvas); *Springtime* (1904, oil on canvas) - LIVERPOOL: *The Captive Pavilion* - LIVERPOOL (Art Gallery, University): *Two Girls on a Beach* - LIVERPOOL (Walker AG): *Summer* (1891).

AUCTION RECORDS:
Picking Yellow Flags at Brighouse Bay. LONDON, 26 April 1809, *Easter Eggs*, GBP 94; *The Old Orchard* (1898) GBP 73. LONDON, July 1924, *Autumn*, GBP 17. LONDON, 18 June 1926, *April*, GBP 78. LONDON, 26 March 1929, *Picking Snowdrops*, GBP 131. LONDON, 12 June 1930, *In a Japanese Shop*, GBP 50. LONDON, 27 March 1931, *At a Burmese Well*, GBP 31. GLASGOW, 2 Nov 1933, *Caught!*, GBP 290. GLASGOW, 14 June 1938, *Offerings to Buddha*, GBP 90. GLASGOW, 12 June 1945, *Amusement*, GBP 560. GLASGOW, 8 Nov 1946, *Picking Water Lilies*, GBP 190. LONDON, 12 June 1970, *Girls Picking Snowdrops*, Gns 1,700. LONDON, 14 Dec 1973, *The Geisha* (1894) Gns 3,000. NEW YORK, 9 Oct 1974, *Water Lilies* (1900) USD

7,000. SCOTLAND, 24 Aug 1976, *By the Lake* (1917, oil on card, 19 1/2 x 15 1/4 ins / 49.5 x 39 cm) GBP 1,600. LONDON, 4 March 1977, *Water Lilies* (1910, oil on canvas, 40 1/4 x 30 ins / 102 x 76.5 cm) GBP 3,400. AUCHTERARDER, 28 Aug 1979, *Girls at the Seaside* (1917, oil on canvas, 23 1/2 x 19 3/4 ins / 60 x 50 cm) GBP 6,000. GLASGOW, 8 July 1982, *Lily Pond* (1904, oil on canvas, 37 3/4 x 30 ins / 96 x 76 cm) GBP 15,500. GLASGOW, 7 July 1983, *Lily Pond* (1899, oil on canvas, 24 x 20 ins / 61 x 50.8 cm) GBP 7,500. PERTH, 26 Aug 1986, *Spring-time Roundelay* (1910, oil on canvas, 25 1/2 x 35 1/2 ins / 65 x 90 cm) GBP 20,000. SOUTH QUEENSFERRY, 29 April 1987, *Primrose Time* (oil on canvas, 36 x 30 ins / 91.5 x 76 cm) GBP 29,000. EDINBURGH, 26 April 1988, *Burmese Girls Catching Butterflies* (1919, oil on canvas, 24 x 20 1/2 ins / 61 x 52 cm) GBP 28,600. EDINBURGH, 30 Aug 1988, *The Magic Wood* (1917, oil on canvas, 30 1/4 x 40 1/4 ins / 77 x 102 cm) GBP 46,200; *Young Burmese Girls* (1922, oil on canvas, 40 1/4 x 30 ins / 102 x 76 cm) GBP 26,400. EDINBURGH, 22 Nov 1988, *Swans and Water Lilies* (oil on canvas, 20 x 16 ins / 50.8 x 40.6 cm) GBP 24,000. PERTH, 29 Aug 1989, *Feeding the Ducks* (1918, oil on canvas, 24 1/2 x 20 ins / 62 x 51 cm) GBP 19,800. EDINBURGH, 22 Nov 1989, *Easter Eggs* (1905, oil on canvas, 60 1/4 x 48 1/2 ins / 153 x 123 cm) GBP 60,500. GLASGOW, 6 Feb 1990, *Blind Man's Buff* (1909, oil on canvas, 35 3/4 x 30 ins / 91 x 76 cm) GBP 33,000. SOUTH QUEENSFERRY, 1 May 1990, *Picking Apple Blossom* (1917, oil on canvas, 29 1/2 x 24 ins / 75 x 61 cm) GBP 26,400. PERTH, 27 Aug 1990, *Little Goose Girl* (1916, oil on canvas, 30 x 36 ins / 76 x 91.5 cm) GBP 46,200. GLASGOW, 5 Feb 1991, *Wood Sprite* (1910, oil on canvas, 20 x 24 1/2 ins / 51 x 62 cm) GBP 22,000. EDINBURGH, 2 May 1991, *Vanity* (1900, oil on canvas/panel, 21 3/4 x 9 ins / 55.4 x 22.9 cm) GBP 10,450. EDINBURGH, 28 April 1992, *Crown of Spring Flowers* (1917, oil on canvas, 28 x 30 ins / 71 x 76 cm) GBP 37,400. EDINBURGH, 19 Nov 1992, *Song of the Woods* (1906, oil on canvas, 30 x 36 ins / 76.2 x 91.4 cm) GBP 24,200. EDINBURGH, 13 May 1993, *Geisha* (oil on canvas, 24 x 20 ins / 61 x 50.8 cm) GBP 9,350. PERTH, 30 Aug 1994, *Spring* (1910, oil on canvas, 30 x 36 1/4 ins / 76 x 92 cm) GBP 29,900. PERTH, 29 Aug 1995, *Young Japanese Girls* (oil on canvas/panel, 30 x 13 1/2 ins / 76 x 34 cm) GBP 19,550. NEW YORK, 1 Nov 1995, *Lily Pond* (1902, oil on canvas, 46 x 40 1/2 ins / 116.8 x 102.9 cm) USD 79,500. EDINBURGH, 23 May 1996, *Water Lilies* (1901, oil on canvas, 36 x 19 1/4 ins / 91.4 x 49.2 cm) GBP 20,700. PERTH, 26 Aug 1996, *Picking Primroses* (1905, oil on canvas, 36 1/4 x 19 1/4 ins / 92 x 49 cm) GBP 28,750. EDINBURGH, 27 Nov 1996, *In the Middle of White Rhododendrons* (1900, oil on canvas, 24 x 24 ins / 60.9 x 60.9 cm) GBP 17,250. LONDON, 15 April 1997, *Among the Flowers* (1916, oil on canvas, 30 x 24 1/2 ins / 76 x 62 cm) GBP 18,400. EDINBURGH, 15 May 1997, *Flowering, Brighouse Bay* (1917, oil on canvas, 30 x 25 ins / 76.1 x 63.5 cm) GBP 11,500. AUCHTERARDER, 26 Aug 1997, *Wild Flowers* (1917, oil on canvas, 16 x 20 ins / 40.5 x 51 cm) GBP 9,200. EDINBURGH, 7 May 1999, *Amusements* (1908, oil on canvas, 46 x 40 ins / 116 x 102 cm) GBP 21,000. LONDON, 28 Oct 1999, *Goatherd* (1896, oil on canvas, 24 x 20 ins / 61 x 51 cm) GBP 30,000. LONDON, 10 April 2000, *Gathering Waterlillies* (1905, oil on canvas, 30 x 36 ins / 76 x 91 cm) GBP 46,000. LONDON, 26 Oct 2000, *Dancing Geisha Girl* (1894, oil on canvas, 48 x 24 ins / 122 x 61 cm) GBP 58,000. LONDON, 5 Sept 2001, *Japanese Dancing Girls* (1894, oil on canvas on panel, 27 x 36 ins / 68 x 91 cm) GBP 60,000. LONDON, 1 Nov 2001, *Pool in the Woods* (1890, oil on canvas, 16 x 20 ins / 41 x 51 cm) GBP 27,000. LONDON, 28 Aug 2002, *Swan Lake* (1905, oil on canvas, 24 x 24 ins / 61 x 61 cm) GBP 48,000. LONDON, 31 Oct 2002, *Easter Eggs* (1901, oil on canvas, 30 x 25 ins / 77 x 63 cm) GBP 50,000. DONCASTER, 27 April 2003, *Sea Breeze* (1913, oil on canvas, round, 24 x 24 ins / 61 x 61 cm) GBP 14,500. LONDON, 30 Oct 2003, *In the Woods* (1904, oil on canvas, 20 x 16 ins / 51 x 41 cm) GBP 23,000. LONDON, 19 April 2004, *Little Goatherd* (1912, oil on canvas, 25 x 31 ins / 63 x 80 cm) GBP 20,000. LONDON, 1 Sept 2004, *Flowers of Japan* (1896, oil on canvas, 16 x 12 ins / 41 x 31 cm) GBP 28,000.

HORNEMAN, Sara
Norwegian, 19th century.
Born 1863.
Active in Christiania (now Oslo).
Painter. Genre scenes.

Sara Horneman participated in the Exposition Universelle in Paris in 1900.

HORNEMANN
German, 19th century.
Active in Lübeck in 1801.
Painter.

HORNEMANN, Christian
Danish, 18th - 19th century.
Born 1765, in Copenhagen; died 1844, in Copenhagen.
Miniaturist.

Christian Hornemann was a pupil at the Kunstakademi in Copenhagen from 1782 and became a member in 1805. In the interim, he travelled in Germany and Italy. In 1804 he was named miniaturist to the Danish court. He also executed pastels.

HORNEMANN, Friedrich Adolf
German, 19th century.
Born 19 May 1813, in Hanover; died 22 December 1890, in Düsseldorf.
Painter, lithographer. Portraits, genre scenes.

A pupil of the Corneliuses in Munich, he also worked in Paris and St Petersburg, where he was a member of the academy. In 1867 he returned to Germany, settling in Düsseldorf.

MUSEUMS AND GALLERIES:
HAMBURG: *Russian Officer Prisoners*.

AUCTION RECORDS:
COPENHAGEN, 9 Nov 1977, *The Birthday Cake* (1871, oil on canvas, 31 x 27 1/2 ins / 79 x 70 cm) DKK 54,000. COLOGNE, 22 June 1979, *Peasant Woman and Children in anInterior* (oil on canvas, 30 x 23 1/2 ins / 76 x 60 cm) DEM 26,000. NEW YORK, 24 May 1984, *The Village Doctor* (1868, oil on canvas, 34 3/4 x 48 ins / 88.3 x 122 cm) USD 26,000. COLOGNE, 4 July 2002, *Walker with Heavy Backpack in a Fight with Two Eagles on the High Mountain* (1868, oil on canvas, 57 x 43 ins / 144 x 109 cm) EUR 3,600. STUTTGART, 5 Dec 2002, *Gypsies Playing for Peasant Family round a Table* (oil on canvas, 35 x 48 ins / 90 x 122 cm) EUR 7,000. FRANKFURT AM MAIN, 22 Nov 2003, *Peasant at Weekly Market with Fruit, Poultry and Flowers* (oil on canvas, 50 x 45 ins / 126 x 115 cm) EUR 6,000.

HORNEMANN, Hans Adolf
German, 19th - 20th century.
Born 2 December 1866, in Hamburg; died 20 April 1916, in Düsseldorf.
Painter. Portraits, genre scenes, still-lifes.

Work by Hornemann was exhibited in Munich and Düsseldorf.

AUCTION RECORDS:
LONDON, 11 May 1990, *Distributing Grain for the Chickens* (oil on canvas, 31 1/2 x 39 1/4 ins / 80 x 100 cm) GBP 4,950.

HORNEMANN, Jens Jakob Brochner
Danish, 19th century.
Born 1796, in Copenhagen; died 2 November 1853.
Miniaturist.

Jens Hornemann is known for his *Death of Cleopatra*.

HORNER, Friedrich
Swiss, 19th century.
Born 1800, in Basel; died 1864, in Basel.
Painter.

He spent a long time in Italy, returning with a large number of landscapes and views of ruins.

AUCTION RECORDS:
ZURICH, 19 July 1984, *View of Basel* (oil on canvas, 13 3/4 x 18 3/4 ins / 35 x 47.5 cm) CHF 11,000. LONDON, 19 June 1986, *Rome* (watercolour and pencil, 11 1/4 x 16 1/4 ins / 28.5 x 41.2 cm) GBP 2,400. ZURICH, 22 March 1999, *View of Bay of Naples* (watercolour, 16 x 23 ins / 41 x 59 cm) CHF 7,500. BERN, 5 Nov 1999, *View of Sultan Ahmed Mosque* (watercolour/pencil, 19 x 28 ins / 48 x 71 cm) CHF 8,500. MUNICH, 7 Nov 2001, *View of Rome from Villa Borghese* (watercolour, 26 x 39 ins / 65 x 99 cm) DEM 15,500. LUCERNE, 14 Nov 2001, *Country Fair outside the Walls of Rome* (watercolour, 11 x 16 ins / 29 x 40 cm) CHF 3,000. LONDON, 10 July 2002, *View of Rome, with Peasants Resting by Trees in the Foreground* (watercolour/bodycolour over black chalk, 26 x 38 ins / 65 x 97 cm) GBP 11,000. BERN, 14 Nov 2002, *Hilly Landscape with Ruins in Upper Italy* (watercolour, 15 x 20 ins / 37 x 50 cm) CHF 2,600. SWITZERLAND, 4 June 2004, *View towards Genua* (oil on canvas, 16 x 22 ins / 41 x 55 cm) CHF 4,800.

HORNER, G. Christopher
American (?), 19th century.
Active during the middle of the 19th century.
Painter. Animals.

AUCTION RECORDS:
NEW YORK, 6 June 1986, *Cheshire Hunt* (1852, oil on canvas, 28 x 36 ins / 71.1 x 91.5 cm) USD 12,000.

HORNER, Maree
New Zealander, 20th - 21st century.
Born 6 June 1951, in Okinawa.
Sculptor.

Maree Horner studied at the Auckland School of Fine Arts. Her work is related to the kinetic art movement.

HORNES, Jacques de, or Horen, Hoorn
Flemish School, 17th century.
Born c. 1618, in Mechelen; died 11 December 1674, in Mechelen.
Painter. Historical subjects.

Jacques de Hornes was a pupil of Grégoire Berincx. In 1648, he was a master in Mechelen, and was elected senior guild member there in 1669. The church of St John in Mechelen has a fresco by him entitled *The Holy Sacrament Carried by Angels.*

HORNES, Jehan de
French, 16th century.
Active in Lille in 1535.
Painter.

HORNES, Léonard
Flemish, 16th century.
Active in Liège c. 1520.
Painter.
Flemish School.

HORNICK, Erasmus
Dutch, 16th century.
Active in Nuremberg c. 1550.
Engraver (burin).

Le Blanc mentions Erasmus Hornick's set of 18 plates representing vases.

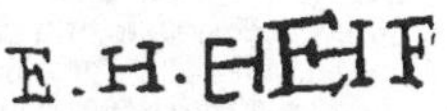

HORNIG, Charles Guillaume
French, 19th century.
Born 1824, in Strasbourg.
Painter. Genre scenes.

Hornig trained with Cambon and Thierry. He showed his work at the Paris Salon from 1865 to 1873, and is mostly remembered for his views of Constantinople.

AUCTION RECORDS:
LONDON, 21 March 1997, *Hagia Sofia, Constantinople* (1870, oil on canvas, 35 1/2 x 55 ins / 90 x 140 cm) GBP 33,350.

HÖRNIGK, Hans
German, 20th century.
Born 25 March 1878, in Berlin.
Painter. Seascapes.

Hörnigk studied in Leipzig. Emperor Wilhelm II owned some of his paintings in his private collection.

HORNIK, Jiri
Czech, 20th century.
Born 1916, in Libici nad Doubravkou, in Libici nad Doubravkou; died 30 April 1961.
Painter. Landscapes.

Jiri Hornik was a student at the Prague academy from 1935 to 1939. He resumed his studies at the École des Beaux-Arts in Paris from 1947 to 1948. He has taken part in a number of exhibitions of contemporary Czechoslovak painting in Eastern Europe and also in Paris.

BIBLIOGRAPHY:
Fifty years of Czechoslovak Painting from the Collections of the Galleries, 1918-1958, exhibition catalogue, Slovenska Narodna Gal., Bratislava, 1968 (in commemoration of the 50th anniversary of the Republic of Czechoslovakia).

MUSEUMS AND GALLERIES:
PRAGUE.

HÖRNLEIN, Friedrich Wilhelm
German, 20th century.
Born 1873; died 1945.
Medallist. Portraits.

Friedrich Wilhelm Hörnlein produced very many portraits for medals, as well as portraits of well-known personalities and members of his family.

BIBLIOGRAPHY:
Arnold, Paul/Fischer, Max, *Friedrich Wilhelm Hörnlein: 1873 - 1945*, catalogue raisonné, Staatliche Kunstsammlungen, Münzkabinett, Dresden, 1992.

MUSEUMS AND GALLERIES:
DRESDEN (Albertinum, Münzkabinett): *Internationale Hygiene-Austellung, Dresden, 1911* (*International Hygiene Exhibition, Dresden, 1911*) (medal).

HORNN, François
French, 20th century.
Born 23 March 1942, in Saigon (now Ho Chi Minh City, Vietnam).
Sculptor. Murals.

Hornn moved to France in 1956. His painted murals are magical, dreamlike compositions. He creates large-scale sculptures. He has shown his works in collective exhibitions, including: Mitam Salon, Milan (1966-1969); Biennale Internazionale Dantesca, Ravenna (1975, 1977); and the 4th Biennale Internationale d'Art Contemporain, Abbaye St-Vincent, Senlis (2001).

HORNO-POLAWSKY, Stanislaw
Polish, 20th century.
Born 1902, in the Caucasus.
Sculptor.

Stanislaw Horno-Polawski completed his studies at the school of fine art in Warsaw in 1931. A member of the Forma group, he has exhibited in Poland since 1923 and took part in exhibitions of Polish sculpture between 1945 and 1960. He also took part in a sculpture exhibition held at the Musée Rodin in Paris in 1961. He won the commission to make the monument to Adam Mickiewicz, completed in 1955 in Warsaw. He received many prizes from the Polish state. From 1956 he taught at the Gdansk school of fine art.

HORNOECK, Franz Xaver
German, 18th century.

Born 1751, in Schönau.
Painter, collector. Historical portraits.
Noted works are his portraits of *Francis, Emperor of Germany* and *The King of Bavaria*.

HORNONG
French, 18th century.
Active in 1783.
Miniaturist.

HORNOR, Thomas
British, 19th century.
Draughtsman, engraver, watercolourist. Panoramas.

AUCTION RECORDS:
LONDON, 10 July 1986, *Panorama of the Vale of Neath* (1816, watercolour/pencil outlines, 16 1/4 x 102 1/4 ins / 41 x 259.5 cm) GBP 9,500. BILLINGSHURST, 19 Oct 1999, *River Neath, near Aberdulais* (watercolour over pencil, 7 x 13 ins / 17 x 32 cm) GBP 1,400. BILLINGSHURST, 19 Oct 1999, *Spirit of the Vale of Neath: Day and Night* (watercolour over pencil, a pair, 17 x 23 ins / 44 x 58 cm) GBP 2,100.

HORNSBY, W.
British, 19th century.
Active in London.
Miniaturist.
W. Hornsby exhibited his *Portrait of a Woman* at the Royal Academy in London in 1821.

HORNSEY, J.
British, 18th century.
Active c. 1795.
Draughtsman. Perspectives.

HORNUNG, David
German, 17th century.
Active in 1671.
Painter.

HORNUNG, Émile Charles Moïse
Swiss, 20th century.
Born 16 December 1883, in Geneva.
Painter.
Preben Hornung was a student of T. Steinlein in Paris.

HORNUNG, Franz
German, 18th century.
Died 1755, in Stuttgart.
Sculptor.

HORNUNG, Gottfried
German, 18th century.
Active in Stuttgart.
Sculptor.
He worked for Hohenheim Castle.

HORNUNG, Johann David
German, 18th century.
Active in Stuttgart in 1772.
Sculptor.

HORNUNG, Johann Michael
German, 17th century.
Born 20 September 1646, in Schwäbisch Hall; died 4 May 1706, in Schwäbisch Hall.
Sculptor.
Noted for his work in Langenburg church and Waldenburg castle near Schwäbisch Hall.

HORNUNG, Joseph
Swiss, 19th century.
Born 25 January 1792, in Geneva; died 4 February 1870, in Geneva.
Painter, engraver. History painting, portraits, genre scenes.
Initially he specialised in woodcuts, but then went over to painting. He was influenced by the French Romantic school. Among his works, there are many that relate to the history of the Reformation.

MUSEUMS AND GALLERIES:
GENEVA (MAH): *Calvin's Farewells; Catherine de' Medici Gazing at the Head of Coligny; Study for the head of Coligny; A Prisoner; Portraits of the Artist and the Poet Albert Richard; Return from the Grape Harvest in Bonn; Portrait of a Child; Reformationist Froment Haranguing the Crowd* - GENEVA (Mus. Ariana): *The Education of Henri IV; Admiral Coligny Awaiting His Assassins; Torture of Servet (Miguel de Villanueva); The Fight of the Tertasse Scaling the Walls of Geneva*.

AUCTION RECORDS:
LUCERNE, 8 Nov 1984, *The Return of the Soldier* (1859, oil on panel, 18 3/4 x 15 ins / 47.5 x 38 cm) CHF 4,500. ZURICH, 8 Nov 1985, *After the St Bartholomew's Massacre* (oil on canvas, 51 3/4 x 39 3/4 ins / 131.5 x 101 cm) CHF 16,000. PARIS, 13 Nov 1996, *Nude in the Bath* (oil on canvas, 51 1/4 x 33 3/4 ins / 130 x 86 cm) FRF 80,000. ZOLLIKON, 3 Sept 2001, *Over-excited Children in Classroom* (oil on canvas, 35 x 44 ins / 88 x 113 cm) CHF 11,000. FLORENCE, 17 March 2003, *King of Sweden Meeting his Daughter* (oil on canvas, 50 x 39 ins / 128 x 99 cm) EUR 9,500.

HORNUNG, Lorenz
German, 17th century.
Died 1624, in Pirna (Saxony).
Sculptor.
He sculpted the altar for Türmitz (Trmice) church near Aussig (Ústí nad Labem), Bohemia.

HORNUNG, Preben
Danish, 20th century.
Born 22 July 1919; died 3 August 1989.
Painter. Interiors, landscapes.
Hornung developed his subjects in series of variations, sometimes taking them to the edge of abstraction.

AUCTION RECORDS:
COPENHAGEN, 28 April 1976, *Composition* (1958, oil on canvas, 56 3/4 x 37 3/4 ins / 144 x 96 cm) DKK 7,000. COPENHAGEN, 23 Jan 1979, *Composition* (1950, oil on canvas, 26 3/4 x 31 1/2 ins / 68 x 80 cm) DKK 6,200. COPENHAGEN, 26 Nov 1986, *Composition* (1953, oil on canvas, 31 x 44 ins / 79 x 112 cm) DKK 43,000. COPENHAGEN, 25 Nov 1987, *Composition* (1951, oil on canvas, 44 x 31 ins / 112 x 79 cm) DKK 40,000. COPENHAGEN, 10 May 1989, *View of Langebro* (oil on canvas, 82 3/4 x 27 1/2 ins / 210 x 70 cm) DKK 26,000. COPENHAGEN, 20 Sept 1989, *Composition* (1951, oil on canvas, 33 1/2 x 23 1/2 ins / 85 x 60 cm) DKK 37,000. COPENHAGEN, 22 Nov 1989, *Slagtekrop* (1968, oil on canvas, 44 x 31 1/2 ins / 112 x 80 cm) DKK 18,000. COPENHAGEN, 21-22 March 1990, *Studio* (1978, oil on canvas, 43 1/4 x 51 1/4 ins / 110 x 130 cm) DKK 50,000. COPENHAGEN, 14-15 Nov 1990, *Love* (oil on canvas/synthetic resin, 21 1/4 x 17 3/4 ins / 54 x 45 cm) DKK 9,000. COPENHAGEN, 13-14 Feb 1991, *View of Langebro* (1952, oil on canvas, 19 3/4 x 28 3/4 ins / 50 x 73 cm) DKK 24,000. COPENHAGEN, 30 May 1991, *Composition* (1950, oil on canvas, 38 1/2 x 25 1/4 ins / 98 x 64 cm) DKK 27,000. COPENHAGEN, 4 Dec 1991, *Railway Theme* (1959, oil on canvas, 17 1/4 x 16 1/4 ins / 44 x 41 cm) DKK 29,000. COPENHAGEN, 4 March 1992, *Animal Carcass* (1969, oil on canvas, 44 x 31 ins / 112 x 79 cm) DKK 28,000. COPENHAGEN, 10 March 1993, *Studio* (1970, oil on canvas, 51 1/4 x 36 1/4 ins / 130 x 92 cm) DKK 24,000. COPENHAGEN, 1 Dec 1993, *Reflections of Langebro* (oil on canvas, 32 x 39 1/4 ins / 81 x 100 cm) DKK 41,000. COPENHAGEN, 2 March 1994, *Variation on a Railway Theme* (1958, oil on canvas, 80 3/4 x 143 3/4 ins / 205 x 365 cm) DKK 80,000. COPENHAGEN, 7 June 1995, *View of Langebro* (1954, oil on canvas, 26 x 21 1/4 ins / 66 x 54 cm) DKK 36,500. COPENHAGEN, 15 March 1997, *Composition* (coloured lithograph) DKK 1,600. COPENHAGEN, 22-24 Oct 1997, *Composition* (1962, oil on canvas, 32 x 51 1/4 ins / 81 x 130 cm) DKK 30,000. COPENHAGEN, 5 Oct 1999, *Composition* (1950,

oil on canvas, 49 x 31 ins / 125 x 78 cm) DKK 70,000. COPENHAGEN, 6 Oct 1999, *Constructive Composition* (1949, oil on canvas, 31 x 44 ins / 79 x 112 cm) DKK 62,000. COPENHAGEN, 28 March 2000, *Composition* (oil on canvas, 61 x 81 ins / 155 x 205 cm) DKK 48,000. COPENHAGEN, 28 March 2000, *Composition* (oil on canvas, 63 x 83 ins / 160 x 212 cm) DKK 50,000. COPENHAGEN, 19 Sept 2001, *Composition* (1953, tempera, 17 x 15 ins / 44 x 37 cm) DKK 18,000. COPENHAGEN, 10 April 2002, *Impression from the Street* (1966, oil on canvas, 59 x 122 ins / 150 x 310 cm) DKK 50,000. COPENHAGEN, 4 Dec 2002, *Railway Theme* (1959, oil on canvas, 77 x 45 ins / 196 x 115 cm) DKK 123,000. COPENHAGEN, 7 Oct 2003, *White Composition* (oil on canvas, 87 x 57 ins / 220 x 145 cm) DKK 52,000. COPENHAGEN, 26 Nov 2003, *Sergel's Birds - Shape is Made Up* (oil on canvas, 62 x 49 ins / 157 x 125 cm) DKK 48,000. COPENHAGEN, 5 Oct 2004, *Red on White* (oil on canvas, 64 x 51 ins / 162 x 130 cm) DKK 47,000. COPENHAGEN, 5 Oct 2004, *Concrete Composition* (1950, oil on canvas, 35 x 49 ins / 89 x 125 cm) DKK 100,000.

HORNY, Conrad
German, 18th century.
Born November 1764, in Mainz; died 7 November 1807, in Weimar.
Painter, engraver.

The father of Franz Horny.

MUSEUMS AND GALLERIES:
WEIMAR: *Landscape* (watercolour).

HORNY, Franz Theobald
German, 19th century.
Born 23 November 1798, in Weimar; died June 1824, in Olevano, Italy.
Painter, draughtsman. Genre scenes, landscapes, still-lifes.

He was a pupil of J A Koch in Rome, and worked in Munich, Rome and Olevano. He was first and foremost a painter of Italy. He had it in him to become the best of the 'Romanising Romantics' of the time, but his untimely death put paid to that.

He was represented at the *Expedition Kunst. Die Entdeckung der Natur von C.D. Friedrich bis Humboldt* (*Expedition Art. The Discovery of Nature from C.D. Friedrich to Humboldt*) exhibition at the Kunsthalle in Hamburg in 2002, which focused on the links between natural sciences and painted landscapes. A retrospective of his works was put on in Weimar in 1998.

BIBLIOGRAPHY:
Scheidig, Walther, *Franz Horny*, Berlin, 1954. Hohl, Hanna, et al., *Franz Theobald Horny: ein Romantiker im Lichte Italiens*, exhibition catalogue, Kunstsammlungen zu Weimar, Weimar, 1998. *Expedition Kunst. Die Entdeckung der Natur von C.D. Friedrich bis Humboldt*, exhibition catalogue, Hamburger Kunsthalle, Hamburg, 2002.

AUCTION RECORDS:
HEIDELBERG, 13 Oct 1979, *A Mountain Village* (pen/outline in black chalk, 9 3/4 x 16 1/2 ins / 24.6 x 41.7 cm) DEM 3,400. MUNICH, 28 Nov 1979, *Flowers* (1817, watercolour/pencil outlines, 10 x 7 3/4 ins / 24.5 x 19.5 cm) DEM 28,000. MUNICH, 29 June 1982, *Setting Off on the Hunt* (oil on canvas, 22 x 26 1/2 ins / 55 x 67 cm) DEM 85,000. HEIDELBERG, 12 April 1986, *A Village in the Sabine Hills* (c. 1820, pen and brown ink/lines in black chalk, 9 3/4 x 16 1/2 ins / 24.6 x 41.7 cm) DEM 3,400. NEW YORK, 26 May 1993, *Asters, Clusters of Black Grapes, Medlars and a Piece of Walnut* (watercolour, gouache and pencil/paper, 13 1/4 x 9 1/4 ins / 33.7 x 23.2 cm) USD 27,600. LONDON, 13 Oct 1994, *Urchin under a Tree (recto); Woman Sorting Out a Skein (verso)* (pencil and ink/paper, 7 1/4 x 4 1/2 ins / 18.4 x 11.4 cm) GBP 2,760. MUNICH, 30 Nov 1999, *Poplar Study* (1814, Indian ink, 17 x 8 ins / 42 x 21 cm) DEM 3,600. BERLIN, 26 May 2000, *Study of Chestnut Tree* (pen/wash, 13 x 17 ins / 34 x 43 cm) DEM 270,000. NEW YORK, 23 May 2001, *Italianate Landscape with Ruins* (1824, oil on canvas, 33 x 43 ins / 83 x 109 cm) USD 27,000.

HOROVSKI. See **GOROVSKY**

HOROWITZ, Frank
American, 20th century.
Born 1889, in Odessa, Ukraine.
Painter.

Frank Horowitz was a pupil at the Pennsylvania Academy of Fine Arts, Philadelphia. He was a member of the American Artists Professional League. He is known for his still-lifes.

HOROWITZ, Jonathan
American, 20th - 21st century.
Born 1966, in New York.
Video installation artist.

Jonathan Horowitz studied philosophy at Wesleyan University and graduated with a BA in 1986. From the beginning of his career, he was interested in video art and early works include *Document and Dream* (1989), *Unlearning* (1991), *Pre-Existing Condition* (1994), *Sex Drugs and Explosives* (1995) and *Facing the Millennium* (1995).

Horowitz's work has formed part of numerous art fairs and group exhibitions, including *Over the Edges* (2000) at the Stedelijke Museum voor Actuele Kunst in Ghent, *The Americans: New Art* (2001) at the Barbican Gallery in London, *Non-places* (2002) at the Frankfurter Kunstverein, and *Love* (2003) at the Vorarlberger Kunstverein. In *The Jonathan Horowitz Show* (2000), he placed seven television monitors in a circle showing the 'highlights' of his own life. In *Pillow Talk* (2002), Horowitz considered the role of the celebrity couple or partnership in society through a series of photographs showing pairs of pillow cases printed with the names of well-known couples such as Ben and Jerry, Liza and David, Laverne and Shirley, and Dumb and Dumber. Horowitz also works with interactive media, such as in *Name My Cat* (2003) for the Galerie Yvon Lambert in Paris, where the audience was asked to email Horowitz with suggestions of a name for the cat whose picture could be seen at the gallery and on the printed PR material.

BIBLIOGRAPHY:
'*Jonathan Horowitz in der Kunsthalle*' in *Kunst-Bulletin*, no. 12, p 57, Zurich, 2001. Uta, Grosenick, *Art Now*, Taschen, Cologne, 2002. Ilaria, Bonacossa, '*The Americans: New Art*' in *Flash Art*, no. 222, p 48, Milan, 2002.

MUSEUMS AND GALLERIES:
GHENT (Stedelijke Museum voor Actuele Kunst) - NEW YORK (New Mus. of Contemporary Art) - PARIS (MNAM-CCI).

HOROWITZ, Leopold
Hungarian, 19th - 20th century.
Born 11 January 1838, in Rozgony; died 16 November 1917, in Vienna.
Painter. Portraits, genre scenes.

After studying at the academy of fine art in Vienna, Leopold Horowitz worked in Berlin, Dresden, Munich and then Paris. He returned to Berlin, settling there in 1891 and winning a gold medal. He was the contemporary of the first Jewish artists emerging from the ghettos, including Isidor Kaufmann, Mauricy Gottlieb and Jozef Israels.

His work includes one of the best portraits of Emperor Franz-Josef I and *Portrait of Janos Aeany*.

He took part in various collective exhibitions in Berlin, Vienna, Munich where he received a medal in 1888 and Paris where he received a 3rd class medal in 1889, a gold medal in the same year at the Exposition Universelle and then a silver medal at the 1900 Exposition Universelle.

AUCTION RECORDS:
PARIS, 2 and 3 June 1926, *Portrait of a Woman*, FRF 175. LONDON, 23 March 1988, *Little Girl Leaning on an Armchair* (oil

on canvas, 46 3/4 x 13 ins / 119 x 33 cm) GBP 1,980. TEL AVIV, 20 June 1990, *Portrait of a Girl* (1886, watercolour, 21 x 16 1/4 ins / 52.5 x 41 cm) USD 3,300. NEW YORK, 16 July 1992, *Studying the Talmud* (1887, oil on panel, 8 1/2 x 11 1/2 ins / 21.6 x 29.2 cm) USD 2,860. PARIS, 24 Nov 1993, *Young Woman* (1896, oil on canvas, 61 x 43 ins / 154 x 109 cm) FRF 19,000. TEL AVIV, 14 Jan 1996, *Tish'a B'av* (1887, oil on panel, 7 3/4 x 11 ins / 20 x 28 cm) USD 11,040. VIENNA, 8 April 1999, *Kaiserin Elisabeth von Osterreich* (1899, oil on canvas, 63 x 43 ins / 160 x 110 cm) ATS 800,000.

HOROWITZ-EDWARDS, Fernande
French, 20th century.
Born 27 January 1887, in Asnières.
Painter. Landscapes.

Fernande Horowitz-Edwards exhibited in Paris at the Salon des Artistes Français from 1926 and at the Salon des Artistes Indépendants. Her works include landscapes of the Creuse region.

HOROZCO, Gomez de. See **GOMEZ de Horozco**

HOROZCO, Juan de. See **JUAN de Horozco**

HORRAK, Johann
Austrian, 19th century.
Born March 1815, in Milotitz (Milotice); died 1870.
Painter, watercolourist, engraver, draughtsman. Portraits.

He lived in Vienna and London.

MUSEUMS AND GALLERIES:

EDINBURGH (Scottish National Portrait Gallery): *John Scott* (1816, portrait).

AUCTION RECORDS:

LONDON, 11 Feb 1994, *Group Portrait of the Klein Brothers in an Interior* (1851, pencil and watercolour, 18 1/4 x 22 1/2 ins / 46.1 x 57.1 cm) GBP 1,552. NEW ORLEANS, 2 Oct 1999, *Afternoon in the Tavern* (oil on canvas, 32 x 39 ins / 81 x 99 cm) USD 3,000.

HORRAK, T.
British, 19th century.
Active in London.
Painter.

T. Horrak exhibited in London at the Royal Academy from 1858 to 1862.

HORRI, Koha
Japanese, 20th century.
Painter.

Horri Koha took part in the exhibition of Japanese art held in Paris in 1929.

HORRIE, Félix Charles
French, 19th century.
Born in Ruffec (Charente).
Engraver (wood).

Félix Horrie was awarded an honourable mention in 1893.

HORRIE, Gustave Théophile Charlemagne
French, 19th century.
Born in the 19th century, in Nantes.
Engraver (wood).

Gustave Horrie was a pupil of Dumont, and exhibited at the Paris Salon in 1880.

HORRIE, Hendrik
Belgian.
Active in Rosselaere.
Painter.

Hendrik Horrie founded the Rosselaere Academy.

HORRIENS, Sebastian de
Spanish, 16th century.
Born 1547.
Active in Valladolid.
Sculptor.

He worked for the church of San Eutropio, Espinar, in 1569.

HORRIX, Henricus or Hendrikus Mattheus
Dutch, 19th century.
Born 30 May 1845, in The Hague; died 1923.
Painter, draughtsman. Genre scenes.

Henricus Horrix studied in Louvain under Philippe Sadée.

AUCTION RECORDS:

AMSTERDAM, 16 Nov 1988, *Childish Affections in the Meadow* (oil on canvas, 14 1/4 x 21in/36 x 53.5cm) NLG 13,800. LONDON, 30 March 1990, *A Captivating Story* (pencil and watercolour heightened with white, 12 1/2 x 8 1/2in/31.7 x 21.3cm) GBP 770. AMSTERDAM, 24 April 1991, *Kitchen Interior with a Peasant Family in Zeeland Costume around a Stove* (oil on canvas, 20 1/4 x 26in/51.5 x 66cm) NLG 3,220. AMSTERDAM, 22 April 1992, *The Wheelbarrow* (oil on canvas, 23 x 29 3/4in/58.5 x 75.5cm) NLG 10,925. AMSTERDAM, 21 April 1993, *Peasant Woman Carrying a Basket* (oil on canvas, 22 x 14in/55 x 35.5cm) NLG 1,725. AMSTERDAM, 21 April 1994, *Children Playing with a Wheelbarrow* (oil on canvas, 22 1/2 x 29 3/4in/57 x 75.5cm) NLG 13,800. AMSTERDAM, 19-20 Feb 1997, *The Reading Lesson* (oil on canvas, 14 1/4 x 11 3/4in/36 x 30cm) NLG 2,075; *Old Woman Feeding Poultry in a Farmyard* (oil on canvas, 22 x 15 1/2in/55 x 39.5cm) NLG 3,459. AMSTERDAM, 19 April 2000, *In the Flower Garden* (oil on canvas, 16 x 9 ins / 40 x 22 cm) NLG 4,000. AMSTERDAM, 22 Oct 2001, *Among the Roses* (oil on canvas, 16 x 9 ins / 41 x 23 cm) NLG 4,800. AMSTERDAM, 19 April 2004, *Early Love, Zeeland* (oil on canvas on panel, 13 x 19 ins / 32 x 48 cm) EUR 1,900. AMSTERDAM, 19 April 2004, *Two Girls from Zeeuw in National Costume with Flowers* (oil on canvas, 30 x 22 ins / 75 x 57 cm) EUR 6,000.

HORRO, Koha
Japanese, 20th century.
Painter.

Horro Koha took part in the exhibition of Japanese art held in Paris in 1929.

HORSBURGH, John
British, 19th century.
Born 16 November 1791, in Prestonpans (East Lothian); died 24 September 1869, in Edinburgh.
Engraver.

John Horsburgh studied in Edinburgh and with the engraver Robert Scott. He engraved mainly portraits after Sir William Allan, Sir Thomas Lawrence, Taylor and Turner.

HORSBURGH, T.
British, 19th century.
Engraver.

T. Horsburgh provided an engraving after S. Prout for *The Landscape Annual*.

HORSCHELT, Friedrich
German, 19th century.
Born 22 November 1824, in Munich; died 27 July 1881, in Munich.
Painter. Portraits.

He was court painter. He exhibited in Munich from 1851.

HORSCHELT, Theodor
German, 19th century.
Born 16 March 1829, in Munich; died 3 April 1871, in Munich.
Painter. Battles, local scenes, animals.

He was a pupil of Anschutz and Romberg at the academy in Munich, then of Albert Adam and Klaubach. In 1858, he was commissioned to paint the horses at the royal stables in Stuttgart. Subsequently he travelled to Italy and Algeria, returning with numerous studies. Invited to Russia by the Emperor Alexander II, he followed the campaign in the Caucasus in

1858. He won medals in Paris (1867) and Munich (1869), and was a member of the academies in St Petersburg, Munich and Vienna.

Museums and Galleries:

Munich: *Arab on Horseback.*

Auction records:

New York, 3 and 4 Feb 1898, *Arab Horseman,* FRF 1,000. New York, 1 Nov 1995, *Midday Break near Algiers* (1855, oil on canvas, 44 1/4 x 61 ins / 112.4 x 154.9 cm) USD 57,500. Copenhagen, 9 Dec 2003, *Cossacks - Vier Kaukas, Reiter* (1866, watercolour/pencil, 17 x 13 ins / 44 x 34 cm) DKK 180,000. Stuttgart, 24 June 2004, *Battle Scene with Cossacks in Mountain Landscape* (1853, oil on canvas, 42 x 34 ins / 107 x 87 cm) EUR 36,000.

HORSDUBOIS, Nicolas

French, 17th - 18th century.

Painter. History painting.

Nicolas Horsdubois came first in the Prix de Rome competition with *Moses Dicovered on the Nile.*

HORSETZKY, Mélanie Von

Austrian, 20th century.

Born 7 April 1882, in Vienna.

Sculptor.

Horsetzky was for a while a student of Rodin in Paris.

HORSFALL, Carolyn Sarah

American, 20th century.

Born 3 July 1901, in Hartford (Connecticut).

Painter.

Carolyn Sarah Horsfall was a member of several New York art associations.

HORSFALL, Charles Mendelssohn

German, 20th century.

Born 1865; died 1942.

Painter.

Work by Horsfall was exhibited in Berlin from 1909 onwards.

Auction records:

London, 20 March 1992, *Portrait of a Woman in Blue Sitting under a Tree* (oil on canvas, 77 1/4 x 57 1/2 ins / 196 x 146 cm) GBP 6,050. London, 17 June 1999, *Portrait of Lady in a White Silk and Chiffon Dress, in a Chair* (1906, oil on canvas, 55 x 41 ins / 140 x 105 cm) GBP 4,500.

HORSFALL, Robert Bruce

American, 20th century.

Born 21 October 1869, in Clinton; died 1948.

Illustrator.

Robert Bruce Horsfall worked in Cincinnati, Munich and Paris before settling in New York.

HORSFIELD, Craigie

British, 20th - 21st century.

Born 1949, in Cambridge.

Active in London and New York.

Photographer.

Craigie Horsfield lived in Cracow from 1972 to 1979, during which time he studied graphics at the academy of arts and taught at the academy of sciences.

Horsfield usually prints negatives many years after the time the photographs were originally taken. The photos thus become significant as representations of and links between both past and present, taken in the past but effectively created in the here and now. This is fundamental to Horsfield's thinking: his manner of working ensures the photographs exist as entities in themselves (with a connection to the present) and are not merely images of the past. His photographs are strikingly like paintings, many resembling Old Masters in composition, the poses of the subjects and the effects of light, mood and atmosphere. They are also large in format, resembling life-size portraits. These similarities are consciously created: the position of the nude figure in his work *E. Horsfield. Well Street, East London, March 1986,* for example, is a 'quotation' from Masaccio's *Expulsion of Adam and Eve.* Horsfield is interested in finding 'an epic dimension within the intimacy of his portraits' (Tate Galleries, display caption, September 2004), but also wishes to challenge the notion of history as the 'mythical past'. The similarity of his photographs to paintings creates resonances of the epic, but also of mythic function. He was shortlisted for the Turner Prize in 1996 for his work shown in solo exhibitions at the Fundació Antoni Tàpies in Barcelona and the Barbara Gladstone Gallery in New York.

Since 1996 Horsfield has worked on a series of collaborative projects in Barcelona, the Canary Islands and Holland. For the *El Hierro Project* in the Canary Islands he continues to work with the 5,000 inhabitants of El Hierro in order to give an account of the island's present through the relations of the island's citizens. Society, connection and human relations are central to Horsfield's work, as is his desire to create, document and encourage the importance of these themes to human existence and humanity. Although he is best known for his photographs, his later collaborations have taken his work into new arenas, including sound installations and film.

Solo exhibitions include: the Palais des Beaux-Arts in Brussels (2000); *What Film May Be. A New Proposal for Film* (collaboration) at the Royal Film Museum of Belgium in Brussels (2000-2001); *Middelburg Soundwork. Soundwork 4.0* (collaboration) at the Vleeshal in Middelburg, The Netherlands (2002); Documenta 11 in Kassel (2002); and *Irresponsible Drawings* at the Frith Street Gallery in London (2003).

Bibliography:

Matter of Facts: Photographie Art Contemporain en Grande-Bretagne, exhibition catalogue, Musée des Beaux Arts, Nantes, 1988. Nusser, Uta (ed.), *Craigie Horsfield im Gespräch/Conversation,* Württemburgischer Kunstverein, Stuttgart, 2000 (to accompany the Rotunda Installation in Stuttgart in 1999).

Museums and Galleries:

Amsterdam (Stedelijk Mus.) - Dublin (Irish Museum of Modern Art) - Ghent (Museum van Hedendaagse Kunst) - Jerusalem (Israel Mus.) - Lisbon (Gulbenkian Foundation) - London (Tate Collection): *E. Horsfield. Well Street, East London, March 1986; Andrzej Klimowski. Crouch End Road, North London, October 1969; E. Horsfield. Well Street, East London, August 1987; Bankside Power Station, London, December 1994* - Minneapolis (Walker Art Center) - Nantes (Museé des Beaux-Arts) - Paris (Fondation Nationale d'Art Moderne) - Prato (Museo d'Arte Contemporanea) - Rotterdam (Boymans van Beuningen Museum) - San Francisco (MoMA) - St-Étienne (Musée d'Art Moderne) - Stuttgart (Staatsgal.).

Auction records:

London, 28 June 2000, *Plaça de Braus de la Monumental, Barcelona, October 1995* (black and white photograph, 39 x 38 ins / 99 x 96 cm) GBP 5,500. London, 28 June 2000, *Wall Street, East London, August 1986* (black and white photograph, 56 x 57 ins / 142 x 144 cm) GBP 11,000. London, 23 Oct 2001, *Sarah Horsfield, Hayesfield Park, Bath, September 1979* (black and white photograph, 58 x 54 ins / 148 x 137 cm) GBP 3,500.

HORSFORD, A. J.

American, 19th century.

Born towards the middle of the 19th century; died 1877, in New York.

Painter. Genre scenes.

A.J. Horsford exhibited at the Royal Academy, the British Institution and the Royal Society of British Artists in London between 1859 and 1872.

AUCTION RECORDS:
LONDON, 6 Nov 1995, *Ballet Dancers* (oil on canvas, 28 1/4 x 35 3/4 ins / 72 x 91 cm) GBP 3,910. NEW YORK, 23 May 1996, *Precocious Spirit* (oil on canvas, 28 x 36 ins / 71 x 91.4 cm) USD 29,900.

HORSIN-DÉON, Léon
French, 19th century.
Born in Paris.
Painter. History painting.
Léon was the son of Simon Horsin-Déon. He received his artistic training from Cornu, Cabanel and Léon Cogniet. He made his Salon début in 1873 with *Jesus Christ in the Sepulchre*, and continued to exhibit religious paintings and portraits up until 1880.

HORSIN-DÉON, Simon
French, 19th century.
Born 23 July 1812, in Sens; died October 1882, in Paris.
Painter.
Simon Horsin-Déon was taught to paint by Rioult, and entered the École des Beaux-Arts on 6 October 1831. He showed portraits and other types of painting at the Paris Salon from 1833 to 1861. He was appointed restorer for the national museums of France. He also wrote a book, entitled *Conservation et Restauration des tableaux* (*Conservation and Restoration of Paintings*).

HORSLEY (Master)
British, 18th century.
Active in London.
Painter.
Horsley exhibited in London at the Free Society in 1774.

HORSLEY, Charles
British, 19th - 20th century.
Painter.
Charles Horsley was active in Beckenham, Kent. He was a member of the Royal Society of British Artists and exhibited at the Suffolk Street gallery, most notably in 1909. He may also have worked under the name Walter Charles Horsley.

HORSLEY, Gerald Calcott
British, 19th century.
Active in London.
Painter. Architectural views.
Gerald Horsley frequently exhibited at the Royal Academy in London from 1882.

HORSLEY, Hopkins Horsley Hobday
British, 19th century.
Born 1807; died 1890.
Active in Birmingham.
Painter. Landscapes with figures, waterscapes, landscapes, architectural views.
Hopkins Horsley exhibited in London at the British Institution and the Suffolk Street Gallery from 1832 to 1866 and at the Royal Academy until 1857.
AUCTION RECORDS:
LONDON, 8 March 1977, *Winter* (oil on canvas, 26 x 35 1/2 ins / 66 x 90 cm) GBP 1,800. LONDON, 3 July 1979, *Signpost* (oil on canvas, 16 1/2 x 30 1/4 ins / 42 x 77 cm) GBP 700. SEVENOAKS, 26 April 1999, *Study of Snowdrifts, Carlton near Rugeley Jan 7th 1881* (1881, oil on canvas, 23 x 35 ins / 59 x 90 cm) GBP 1,250. BATH, 30 Jan 2001, *Beach Scenes with Numerous Figures* (1877, oil on canvas, a pair, 8 x 12 ins / 20 x 30 cm) GBP 3,000. BILLINGSHURST, 23 May 2001, *Busy Beach Scene with Archers. Figures in a Rocky Cove* (1877, oil on canvas, a pair, 7 x 11 ins / 19 x 29 cm) GBP 4,000.

HORSLEY, John Calcott
British, 19th - 20th century.
Born 29 January 1817, in London; died 18 October 1903.
Painter, miniaturist, draughtsman. Portraits, genre scenes.
Cranbrook School.
John Calcott Horsley joined the Royal Academy Schools in 1831, and later taught at the Somerset House School of Drawing. He became an associate member of the Royal Academy in 1855, exhibiting there from 1860 and becoming a full member in 1864. He travelled to Egypt in about 1878.
MUSEUMS AND GALLERIES:
LONDON (National Portrait Gal.): *Isembard Kingdom Brunel* (1857, oil on canvas) - LONDON (Royal Academy of Arts): *Pleasant Spot* (1865, oil on canvas, competition piece) - LONDON (Tate Collection): *Pride of the Village* (1839, oil/wood, exhibited in 1839) - LONDON (Victoria and Albert Mus.): *Old Man and Child Going into a Church; Waiting for the Answer; The Rivals* - SHEFFIELD: *Grandmother's Gift* - SYDNEY: *Portrait of the Artist* (miniature).
AUCTION RECORDS:
LONDON, 25 Jan 1908, *Reunion* (1862) GBP 22. LONDON, 22 Feb 1908, *The Duenna* (1867) GBP 46. LONDON, 25 June 1908, *My Lady's Keeping Warm; Sir is Keeping Warm* (1871, two pendants) GBP 14. LONDON, 18 June 1909, *The Jailer's Daughter* (1869) GBP 22; *Jane Gray; Roger Ascham,* GBP 33. LONDON, 6 May 1910, *Frequenting Society,* GBP 71. LONDON, 26 Nov 1910, *The New Dress* (1864) GBP 39; *Malvolio* (1849) GBP 25. LONDON, April 1923, *Secret Message,* GBP 31. LONDON, June 1924, *Orange Blossom,* GBP 50. LONDON, 4 April 1927, *Under the Mistletoe,* GBP 37. LONDON, 15 July 1938, *Valentine's Day,* GBP 31. LONDON, 21 Jan 1943, *Drowsiness,* GBP 44. LONDON, 17 Feb 1971, *My Lady's Keeping Warm,* GBP 620. LONDON, 5 Oct 1973, *The Poet* (1874) Gns 1,300. LONDON, 14 June 1977, *Queen Victoria with her Children* (oil on canvas, 47 1/4 x 33 ins / 120 x 84 cm) GBP 2,500. LONDON, 20 March 1979, *Fête Galante* (1866, oil on canvas, 23 1/2 x 18 ins / 60 x 46 cm) GBP 1,450. LONDON, 15 June 1982, *Cupboard Love* (oil on canvas, 36 x 28 ins / 91.5 x 71 cm) GBP 5,500. LONDON, 2 March 1984, *Oblivious to the World: Sunday Afternoon in Kensington Gardens* (1780, oil on canvas, 34 1/4 x 48 1/4 ins / 87 x 122.5 cm) GBP 7,000. LONDON, 28 Nov 1986, *The New Dress* (1864, oil on canvas, 33 3/4 x 44 ins / 86 x 112 cm) GBP 8,000. CHESTER, 8 Oct 1987, *Rent Day at Haddon Hall* (1868, oil on canvas, 59 1/2 x 59 1/2 ins / 151 x 151 cm) GBP 3,900. LONDON, 3 June 1988, *Rent Day at Haddon Hall* (oil on canvas, 60 x 60 ins / 152.4 x 152.4 cm) GBP 6,050. LONDON, 21 Nov 1989, *The Valentine's Letter* (oil on canvas, 24 x 29 1/2 ins / 61 x 75 cm) GBP 14,300. NEW YORK, 28 Feb 1990, *Oblivious to the World: Sunday Afternoon in Kensington Gardens* (1780, oil on canvas, 34 x 48 ins / 86.4 x 121.9 cm) USD 22,000. LONDON, 13 June 1990, *The Poet's Muse* (oil on canvas, 53 1/2 x 42 1/4 ins / 136 x 107 cm) GBP 14,850. LONDON, 10 March 1995, *The Visitor* (1884, oil on canvas, 6 3/4 x 8 1/4 ins / 17.2 x 20.9 cm. LONDON, 29 March 1996, *On Valentine's Morning* (1865, oil on canvas, 17 x 20 ins / 43.2 x 50.8 cm) GBP 3,220. LONDON, 14 March 1997, *A Pleasant Place* (1866, oil on canvas, 32 x 23 1/2 ins / 81 x 59.7 cm) GBP 9,200. LONDON, 12 May 1999, *Attracting Attention* (1867, oil on canvas, 29 x 25 ins / 73 x 63 cm) GBP 3,400. LONDON, 9 June 1999, *Country Flower Girl* (1858, oil on canvas, 36 x 28 ins / 92 x 71 cm) GBP 78,000. NEW YORK, 3 Oct 2001, *Troubadour* (1868, oil on canvas, 29 x 19 ins / 74 x 48 cm) USD 1,800. LONDON, 1 July 2004, *Hunting Morning* (1861, oil on canvas, 21 x 26 ins / 54 x 65 cm) GBP 6,500. LONDON, 25 Nov 2004, *Morning of St Valentine* (oil on canvas, 24 x 28 ins / 60 x 71 cm) GBP 40,000.

HORSLEY, T. J.
British, 19th century.
Active in London c. 1825.
Miniaturist.

HORSLEY, Walter Charles
British, 19th - 20th century.

Born 1848 or 1855; died 1921.
Painter. Genre scenes, landscapes.
Orientalism.

Walter Horsley, the son of John Calcott Horsley, was active in London. In 1874 he entered the Royal Academy Schools; that year he began to exhibit in London.

Bibliography:
Ackerman, Gérald M., *Les Orientalistes de l'école britannique*, ACR Édition, Courbevoie, 1991.

Museums and Galleries:
Sheffield: *The French in Cairo* (1884).

Auction records:
London, 24 Nov 1976, *Old Man and Child Praying in a Mosque* (1878, oil on canvas, 31 1/4 x 29 1/4 ins / 79.5 x 74 cm) GBP 1,050. London, 18 Oct 1978, *Old Arab Recounting his Battles* (1883, oil on canvas, 48 3/4 x 38 1/4 ins / 124 x 97 cm) GBP 3,400. London, 22 March 1985, *The Prisoners* (1894, watercolour, 21 1/2 x 15 1/2 ins / 54.6 x 39.3 cm) GBP 700. London, 17 June 1987, *Arabs Talking* (oil on canvas, 36 x 28 ins / 91.5 x 71 cm) GBP 10,000. Paris, 18-19 March 1996, *Striking a Deal* (oil on canvas, 35 3/4 x 28 ins / 91 x 71 cm) FRF 100,000. London, 6 Nov 1996, *A Prisoner* (oil on canvas, 41 3/4 x 37 ins / 106 x 94 cm) GBP 109,300.

HORSSEN, Winand Bastian van
Dutch, 19th century.
Born 8 May 1863, in Rijwik.
Painter.

Winand van Horssen studied at the academy of The Hague.

HORST, Emil Carl Wilhelm
German, 19th century.
Born 3 September 1854, in Hamburg; died 1910, in Hamburg.
Painter.

His work is mainly humorous.

HORST, Gerard van der
Dutch, 17th century.
Active in Rheimbach from 1610 to 1628.
Landscape artist.

HORST, Gerrit Willemsz.
Dutch, 17th century.
Born c. 1612; died 1652; buried on 15 October in Amsterdam.
Painter. Religious subjects, allegorical subjects, still-lifes.

Gerrit Horst studied under Anthony Hendrikz. in Amsterdam. He and the artist known as Anthony Gerrit van den Horst, who married in Amsterdam in 1637, appear to be the same person.

Bibliography:
Sumowski, Werner, *Gemälde des Rembrandt-Schüler*, PVA, Landau, 1983.

Museums and Galleries:
Berlin: *The Blessing of Jacob; The Generosity of Scipio; Fruit* - Dublin: *Admonishment of Solomon by the Dying David* - Stockholm: *Esau Meets Jacob*.

Auction records:
Amsterdam, 10 Dec 1968, *Still-life*, NLG 18,000. Cologne, 26 March 1971, *Still-life*, DEM 15,000. New York, 18 June 1982, *Still-life with Fruit* (oil on canvas, 37 x 29 1/4in/94 x 74.5cm) USD 6,500. New York, 3 June 1988, *Allegory of Music* (oil on canvas, 48 x 38 1/4in/122 x 97cm) USD 88,000. New York, 10 Oct 1990, *Still-life with Fruit with a Pot of Ginger and a Glass on a Draped Ledge* (oil on panel, 37 x 29 1/4in/94 x 74.2cm) USD 15,400.

HORST, Heinrich
Polish, 16th century.
Active in Brzezany c. 1582.
Sculptor.

HORST, Jan van or van der
Dutch, 16th century.
Active c. 1572.
Painter. Religious subjects.

Jan van Horst imitated the work of Pieter Aarsten.

Auction records:
Stockholm, 29 May 1991, *Christ at Emmaus: Kitchen Scene with Table Covered with Foodstuffs* (oil on panel, 31 1/2 x 46 3/4 ins / 80 x 119 cm) SEK 117,000.

HORST, Ludwig
German, 19th century.
Born 28 December 1829, in Büdingen (Hesse); died 19 August 1891, in Degerloch (Stuttgart).
Portrait artist.

He studied at the academy in Düsseldorf, but worked subsequently in Munich and Rome.

HORST, Martin Erich
German, 20th century.
Painter. Genre scenes.

Horst worked in Berlin and exhibited there in 1909.

HORST, Nicolaus van der
Flemish School, 17th century.
Born c. 1598, in Antwerp; died 1646, in Brussels.
Painter, draughtsman.
Brussels School.

According to De Bie, Nicolaus van der Horst was a pupil of Rubens and himself taught Johannes Mytens. He travelled in Germany, Italy and France. On his return to Flanders he settled in Brussels.

Auction records:
London, 14 Dec 1907, *Portrait of a Burgomaster and his Wife*, GNS 7. Versailles, 14 June 1981, *Young Pageboy and his Dogs Following the Hunt* (oil on canvas, 35 1/2 x 43 3/4in/90 x 111cm) FRF 26,000.

HORST, Philipp
German, 17th century.
Active in Jena in 1626.
Painter.

HORST, Wilhelm
German, 19th century.
Born 13 September 1852, in Pfungstadt (near Darmstadt).
Painter.

He was a pupil of Hofmann and Hiltensperger.

HORST-SCHULZE, Paul
German, 20th century.
Born 5 October 1876, in Naunhof.
Painter, engraver, illustrator.

Horst-Schulze studied in Leipzig, Munich and Düsseldorf. He was a prolific illustrator of children's books.

HORSTIG, Eugen
German, 19th century.
Born 1843; died 7 August 1901.
Active in Munich.
Painter. Genre scenes, landscapes.

He was a pupil of W von Diez.

AUCTION RECORDS:
MUNICH, 27 June 1984, *A Pair of Farmers and a Flock at the Gate* (1878, oil on canvas, 15 x 20 1/2 ins / 38 x 52 cm) DEM 5,500.

HORSTINK, Warnaar
Dutch, 18th - 19th century.
Born 1 November 1756, in Haarlem; died 2 November 1815, in Haarlem.
Painter, engraver, draughtsman. Portraits, landscapes with figures.

Warnaar Horstink studied under C. van Noorde and Wybrand Hendriks. In 1778, he was a master in the Haarlem guild. He engraved portraits and landscapes.

AUCTION RECORDS:
VERSAILLES, 14 June 1981, *Gentry Meeting in the Park* (oil on canvas, 20 1/2 x 25in/52 x 63.5cm) FRF 18,000. AMSTERDAM, 30 Nov 1987, *Family in a Garden* (1796, black chalk, pencil, pen, grey ink and watercolour, 17 1/2 x 22in/44.2 x 56cm) NLG 8,000. AMSTERDAM, 25 Nov 1992, *Travellers Resting by a Road on the Outskirts of a Village; Farm in a Wooded, Undulating Landscape with Fishermen* (1793, pencil, ink and watercolour, a pair, 9 1/2 x 14 1/2in/24.3 x 37cm) NLG 4,370.

HORSTMANN, Johann Carl
German, 19th century.
Born 1797, in Lübeck; died 15 April 1852, in Lübeck.
Painter, miniaturist. Portraits.

He spent some time in Berlin and Dresden.

HORSTMEYER, Wilhelm
German, 19th century.
Born 1880, in Arnsberg; died 30 October 1901, in Berlin.
Painter.

He worked mainly as an illustrator.

HORSTOK, Johannes Petrus van
Dutch, 18th - 19th century.
Born 1 April 1745, in Overveen near Haarlem; died 20 March 1825, in Haarlem.
Painter. Genre scenes, landscapes with figures.

Johannes van Horstok studied under Tako Hoyo Jelgersma and P. Barbiers. His pupils include A. de Visser and Jan Reekers. He worked in Alkmaar and Haarlem.

MUSEUMS AND GALLERIES:
AMSTERDAM: *Village Inn; Peasant Wedding in Brabant* - HAARLEM: *Deception.*

AUCTION RECORDS:
BRUSSELS, 15 June 1983, *Family Scene in an Interior* (1813, painting/wood, two pendants, 13 x 18in/33 x 46cm) BEF 85,000. AMSTERDAM, 19 April 1994, *Merry Company outside a House* (1800, oil on panel, 25 x 18in/63.5 x 46cm) NLG 8,510. BRUSSELS, 22 Feb 1999, *Child with Toy* (1780, oil on panel, 6 x 5 ins / 16 x 12 cm) BEF 155,000. LONDON, 14 Dec 2000, *Figures in a Courtyard* (1800, oil on panel, 25 x 18 ins / 63 x 46 cm) GBP 6,000.

HORTALA, Philippe
French, 20th century.
Born 21 July 1960, in Toulouse; died 3 October 1998.
Painter, pastellist.
Nouvelle Figuration.

Hortala studied at the École des Beaux-Arts in Toulouse from 1978 until 1982. In 1983, he was awarded a scholarship to go and work in Barcelona for a few months. His paintings are in a 'kitsch' style with disorientated perspectives and garish colours, the subjects ranging from his early cream cakes to scenes of hunters and African safaris, deep-sea fauna, interiors composed of objects, to views in kitchen gardens such as *Slug and Geometrid* of 1996, touching briefly on figures and nudes taken from advertising design or comic strips.

Hortala took part in collective exhibitions at the Musée de Toulouse, the Basel Fair in 1984, the Arte Feria in Bologna and the Réfectoire des Jacobins in Toulouse. Solo exhibitions include: Galerie Axe Sud, Toulouse, Belgrade, and the French Institute, Barcelona, 1984; Centre Régional d'Art Contemporain, Labège, 1987; a collection of paintings presented at the FIAC (Foire Internationale d'Art Contemporain) by the Galerie Loft at the Grand Palais, Paris, 1988; Musée des Beaux-Arts Denys-Puech, Rodez, and Galerie Piltzer, Paris (with a collection of works by Jean Hélion), 1996; Musée de l'Abbaye Ste-Croix, Les Sables-d'Olonne, 2000; and Galerie Girard, Toulouse, 2002.

BIBLIOGRAPHY:
Leydier, Richard, '*Philippe Hortala*' in *Art Press* n° 261 p. 84, periodical, Paris, October 2000.

AUCTION RECORDS:
PARIS, 30 March 1989, *Cakes* (1987, oil on canvas, 51 1/4 x 76 3/4 ins / 130 x 195 cm) FRF 6,500. PARIS, 8 Oct 1989, *Cakes* (1987, oil on canvas, 19 3/4 x 25 1/2 ins / 50 x 65 cm) FRF 3,800.

HORTART, Jean or Janin, called of Scotland
French, 15th century.
Active in Lyons in 1412 and 1465.
Illuminator, glass painter, embroiderer.

On 30 December 1412 Jean Hortart of Scotland was appointed master painter for the church of St-Jean in Lyons, where he painted the choir in 1420. In 1463 he worked on the preparations for the ceremonial entry of Louis XI.

HORTE, Max
German, 19th century.
Born 5 June 1865, in Berlin.
Painter, engraver (etching).

He gained an honourable mention in Paris in 1899, He engraved a large number of old masters.

HORTEMELS (Mme). See **COCHIN Louise Madeleine**

HORTEMELS, Frédéric
French, 18th century.
Born c. 1688, in Paris; died 5 November 1738.
Engraver (burin).

Frédéric Hortemels engraved mythological and religious subjects after Giorgione, Veronese, Tintoretto and other Italian masters.

HORTEMELS, Marie Anne Hyacinthe
French, 18th century.
Born 1682; died 24 March 1727.
Active in Paris.
Engraver.

Marie Anne Hyacinthe Hortemels married the engraver N. H. Tardieu. She engraved works by Le Brun and Mignard.

HORTER, Earl
American, 20th century.
Born 1881; died 1940.
Painter (gouache), watercolourist, draughtsman. Still-lifes, landscapes.

AUCTION RECORDS:
NEW YORK, 28 Sept 1989, *Table Top Abstraction* (oil on panel, 20 x 24 ins / 50.8 x 61 cm) USD 66,000. NEW YORK, 24 Jan 1990, *City Beyond Walls* (watercolour/paper/card, 20 1/2 x 17 3/4 ins / 52.1 x 45.1 cm) USD 4,620. NEW YORK, 16 March 1990, *Still-life No 2* (1939, watercolour and ink and pencil/paper, 17 1/2 x 22 ins / 44.7 x 56 cm) USD 11,000. NEW YORK, 5 Dec 1991, *Still-life with Cherries, Apple and Pear* (1939, watercolour/paper, 16 1/2 x 21 3/4 ins / 41.9 x 55.2 cm) USD 7,700. NEW YORK, 31 March 1993, *Coke Factory* (ink and gouache/paper, 8 x 10 1/4 ins / 20.6 x 26 cm) USD 575. NEW YORK, 26 Sept 1996, *Still-life* (oil on canvas, 18 x 30 ins / 45.7 x 76.2 cm) USD 23,000. NEW YORK, 9 March 2000, *Still-life with Vases* (watercolour, 13 x 17 ins / 34 x 44 cm) USD 3,000.

NEW YORK, 23 May 2000, *Newcastle, Delaware* (watercolour, 12 x 19 ins / 31 x 48 cm) USD 7,000. PHILADELPHIA, 9 Dec 2001, *Reclining Female Nude* (watercolour and pencil, 13 x 19 ins / 33 x 48 cm) USD 3,750. BOSTON, 26 Sept 2004, *Gloucester* (1932, crayon, 12 x 14 ins / 30 x 36 cm) USD 2,000. PHILADELPHIA, 1 Oct 2004, *Boats on the Shore* (oil on board, 8 x 11 ins / 20 x 28 cm) USD 3,750.

HORTER, Karl
American, 20th century.
Painter, engraver.

Karl Horter studied in the museums of America and Europe. He was awarded many prizes for his engravings and watercolours. His work *Gloucester Harbor* was shown at the exhibition at Worcester Art Museum in 1933.

HORTHY, Bela von
Hungarian, 19th - 20th century.
Born 4 February 1871, in Mezokaszony.
Painter.

Bela von Horthy studied with Simon Hollósy in Munich and then with Bouguereau in Paris.

HORTI, Pol
Hungarian, 19th century.
Born 18 June 1865, in Budapest; died 25 May 1907, in Bombay.
Painter.

Pol Horti spent some time in Mexico and New York.

HORTIGOSA
Spanish, 16th century.
Active in Seville in 1571.
Sculptor.

HORTIGOSA, Pedro
Spanish, 19th century.
Born 1811, in Segovia; died 1870, in Madrid.
Painter, engraver.

Pedro Hortigosa is known for a portrait engraving of *Queen Isabella II*.

HORTON, Carrie. See **BLACKMAN**

HORTON, Harriet Hutchinson
American, 20th century.
Died July 1922, in Bald Eagle Lake.
Painter, miniaturist. Portraits.

Harriet Hutchinson Horton always worked in the state of Minnesota.

HORTON, Percy
British, 20th century.
Born 8 March 1897, in Brighton; died 1970, in Lewes.
Painter, draughtsman. Figures, portraits, landscapes.
Artists' International Association.

The brother of the artist Ronald Horton, Percy Horton trained at the Brighton School of Art (1914-1916) under Louis Ginnett, at the Central School of Arts and Crafts (1918-1920) under F. Jackson and A.S. Hartrick, and at the Royal College of Art (1922-1925) under Rothenstein, Randolph Schwabe and Allan Gwynne-Jones. He taught at the Royal College (1930-1939) and then was appointed Ruskin Master of Drawing at Oxford University (1949). A conscientious objector in World War I, Horton believed that artists should be socially committed. An early member of the Artists' Association and a contributor to the *New Left Review*, he painted portraits in a restrained, conservative style and in a realist vein influenced by Cézanne (*The Invalid, Portrait of an Unemployed Man*). He lived in Lewes.

Horton exhibited at the Royal Academy, at the Goupil Gallery, at the Institute of Education, University of Oxford (drawings and paintings, 1962) and at Sheffield City Gallery (*Percy Horton: Artist and Absolutionist*, Sheffield City Art Galleries, 1984). He also featured in *Les Années Trente en Europe. Le Temps Menaçant* (*Europe in the 1930s: The Gathering Storm*), Musée d'Art Moderne de la Ville de Paris (1997).

BIBLIOGRAPHY:
Horton, Percy, *An exhibition of drawings and paintings by Percy Horton, M.A., Ruskin Master of Drawing*, solo exhibition catalogue, Institute of Education, University of Oxford, 1962. Barnes, James, *Percy Horton: Artist and Absolutionist*, solo exhibition catalogue, Sheffield City Art Galleries, Sheffield, 1982. Pagé, Suzanne/Winock, Michel/Michaud, Éric/Vidal, Aline, *Les Années trente en Europe. Le Temps menaçant*, exhibition catalogue, Musée d'Art moderne de la Ville de Paris, Paris musées, Flammarion, Paris, 1997.

MUSEUMS AND GALLERIES:
BRIGHTON (Brighton and Hove Museums): *Portrait of the Artist's Mother* (c. 1939) - LONDON (National Portrait Gal.): *George Edward Moore* (1947, pencil and chalk); *George Edward Moore* (1952, chalk, pen and wash) - LONDON (Tate Collection): *The Invalid (Portrait of the Artist's Mother)* - SHEFFIELD (City Mus. and Art Gallery): *Portrait of an Unemployed Man* (1936).

HORTON, William Samuel
American, 19th - 20th century.
Born 16 November 1865, in Grand Rapids; died 1936.
Also active in France.
Painter, pastellist, draughtsman, illustrator. History painting, genre scenes, landscapes, mountainscapes, waterscapes, still-lifes.

William Samuel Horton trained at the Art Students League (ASL) and National Academy, New York; under J.P. Laurens in Paris and under Benjamin-Constant at the Académie Julian. He occupied Winterhalter's former studio in Paris. He travelled to Europe and took refuge in England in 1914, returning to the USA in 1919. He was awarded medals at several exhibitions in the French provinces. He was a member of the Société du Salon d'Automne.

At the age of 14 Horton drew Indian reservations for the *North West Magazines*

MUSEUMS AND GALLERIES:
PARIS (MAMVP) - PARIS (Mus. Carnavalet) - STOCKHOLM (Nationalmus.) - WASHINGTON DC: *Pershing's March across Paris*.

AUCTION RECORDS:
PARIS, 1 July 1943, *Small Church of St-Léger*, FRF 1,000. NEW YORK, 4 Nov 1960, *Skaters and Snow in Gstaad*, USD 475. NEW YORK, 22 Oct 1969, *Ritz Tower, New York* (1936, pastel/maroon paper) USD 3,000. NEW YORK, 15 April 1970, *Flock of Sheep in a Landscape*, USD 3,200. LOS ANGELES, 22 May 1972, *View of Gstaad*, USD 1,100. LONDON, 7 July 1973, *Beach Scene*, Gns 3,200. VERSAILLES, 25 June 1976, *Mountainscape* (pastel, 17 3/4 x 23 1/2 ins / 45 x 60 cm) FRF 2,000. NEW YORK, 21 April 1977, *Riviera* (oil on canvas, 25 x 29 1/4 ins / 63.5 x 74 cm) USD 3,600. NEW YORK, 28 April 1978, *Children Playing in a Village* (1918, watercolour); *Beach Scene* (watercolour and pencil, 8 x 10 ins / 20.3 x 25.4 cm) USD 3,000. NEW YORK, 20 April 1979, *Snow in the Mountains* (oil on card, 25 x 30 ins / 63.5 x 76.2 cm) USD 6,250. LOS ANGELES, 23 June 1981, *Peonies* (1924, oil on card, 21 x 22 3/4 ins / 53.5 x 58 cm) USD 11,750. NEW YORK, 2 June 1983, *Concert on the Sands, Hythe, England* (oil on canvas, 25 1/4 x 30 1/4 ins / 64.3 x 76.8 cm) USD 37,000. NEW YORK, 5 Dec 1985, *Summer at the Seashore* (oil on canvas, 25 x 30 ins / 63.5 x 76.2 cm) USD 24,000. NEW YORK, 29 May 1986, *Under the Trees* (watercolour, charcoal and gouache/mounted paper/canvas, 23 3/4 x 28 3/4 ins / 60.4 x 73 cm) USD 3,000. NEW YORK, 1 Oct 1987, *Old City* (pastel/card, 21 1/4 x 17 1/4 ins / 54 x 43.7 cm) USD 2,600. PARIS, 11 April 1988, *Landscape of Blue and Orange Snow* (pastel, 15 3/4 x 22 ins / 40 x 55 cm) FRF 9,500. LA VARENNE-ST-HILAIRE, 29 May 1988, *River Bank in Autumn* (pastel, 18 x 24 ins / 46 x 61 cm) FRF 11,000. VERSAILLES, 15 June 1988, *Gstaad Valley* (oil on

canvas, 25 1/4 x 30 1/4 ins / 64 x 77 cm) FRF 40,000. PARIS, 23 June 1988, *Village under Snow* (oil on canvas, 25 1/4 x 30 1/4 ins / 64 x 77 cm) FRF 27,000. NEW YORK, 30 Sept 1988, *Broadstairs Beach* (1906, oil on panel, 14 1/2 x 18 ins / 37 x 46 cm) USD 24,200. NEW YORK, 1 Dec 1988, *In the Garden* (1910, oil and gouache/card, 25 x 30 ins / 63.5 x 76.2 cm) USD 12,100. NEW YORK, 24 Jan 1989, *Trees in Winter* (1922, oil on card, 14 x 17 ins / 35.7 x 43.2 cm) USD 2,530. NEW YORK, 24 Jan 1990, *Mountainside Village, Winter Evening* (pastel/blue paper/card, 18 3/4 x 24 1/4 ins / 47.9 x 61.8 cm) USD 3,300. NEW YORK, 31 May 1990, *Still-life of Flowers* (1934, oil on card, 24 x 28 ins / 61 x 71 cm) USD 1,980. NEW YORK, 27 Sept 1990, *The Seine* (oil on card, 14 3/4 x 18 ins / 37.5 x 45.5 cm) USD 6,050. PARIS, 4 March 1991, *Beach* (oil on panel, 15 x 18 ins / 38 x 46 cm) FRF 52,000. NEW YORK, 6 Dec 1991, *On the Beach at Broadstairs* (oil on card, 25 x 30 ins / 63.5 x 76.3 cm) USD 104,500. NEW YORK, 27 May 1992, *Whitby Beach* (1913, oil on canvas, 25 x 30 1/2 ins / 63.5 x 77.5 cm) USD 30,800. NEW YORK, 28 May 1992, *Beach in the Sun* (1914, oil on canvas, 25 1/4 x 30 1/4 ins / 64 x 76.9 cm) USD 38,500. NEW YORK, 28 Sept 1995, *Shepherd and His Flock* (oil on card, 9 1/4 x 13 ins / 23.5 x 33 cm) USD 4,312. NEW YORK, 23 May 1996, *Children on a Beach* (oil on panel, 15 x 18 ins / 38.1 x 45.7 cm) USD 32,200. NEW YORK, 11 March 1999, *Ritz Tower, New York* (1928, oil on canvas, 36 x 42 ins / 92 x 106 cm) USD 11,000. CLEVELAND, 30 Sept 1999, *Still-life, Tulips in Vase on a Red Lacquer Stand* (oil on canvas, 29 x 24 ins / 74 x 61 cm) USD 6,500. LYONS, 7 June 2000, *Beach Games* (gouache, 21 x 22 ins / 53 x 57 cm) FRF 28,000. LONDON, 21 June 2000, *Gstaad* (1912, oil on panel, 17 x 21 ins / 44 x 53 cm) GBP 2,000. OAK PARK, 11 Feb 2001, *Gstaad, Switzerland* (1912, oil on panel, 17 x 21 ins / 43 x 53 cm) USD 7,500. MILFORD, 26 April 2001, *Skaters at Pontarlier* (oil on board on panel, 25 x 30 ins / 64 x 76 cm) USD 12,000. MAINE, 4 Aug 2002, *Venetian Canal* (oil on board, 18 x 24 ins / 46 x 61 cm) USD 2,600. NEW YORK, 4 Dec 2002, *Garden and Bridge at Sonning* (oil on board, 17 x 21 ins / 42 x 53 cm) USD 25,000. NEW YORK, 5 March 2003, *Waves, Rocks and Little People on the Beach* (oil and panel, 2 x 18 ins / 6 x 45 cm) USD 7,000. NEW YORK, 5 March 2003, *Evening Lights, Broadstairs Harbour. Stream in Front of Château* (oil on board on panel, two, 25 x 30 ins / 63 x 76 cm) USD 12,000. BOSTON, 14 May 2004, *Blackbirds and Falling Snow* (oil on board, 25 x 30 ins / 63 x 76 cm) USD 31,000. BOSTON, 10 Sept 2004, *View of Gstaad, Switzerland* (1905, oil on canvas, 26 x 31 ins / 65 x 79 cm) USD 20,000.

HORVAI, Janos
Hungarian, 20th century.
Born 1873, in Pécs.
Sculptor. Busts, monuments.

Janos Horvai studied and worked in Budapest. He is known for a number of busts and a monument to Kossuth in Budapest.

HORVATH, Adorian
Hungarian, 20th century.
Born 15 February 1874, in Gyor.
Sculptor.

Adorian Horvath completed his studies in Munich, Rome and Paris before settling in Budapest.

AUCTION RECORDS:
VIENNA, 17 March 1982, *Violin Maker* (1893, oil on canvas, 22 x 27 1/4 ins / 56 x 69 cm) ATS 30,000.

HORVATH, Bela
Hungarian, 20th century.
Born 25 March 1888, in Pinkafo, Hungary (now Pinkofeld, Austria); died 6 January 1973, in Pompano (Florida), USA.
Active from 1948 in the USA.
Sculptor, medallist. Figures, portraits, landscapes, still-lifes, flowers. Monuments, murals.

Bela Horvath studied at art school in Budapest from 1904 to 1909, then attended classes in architecture and painting at the Akademie der Bildenden Künste in Munich, from 1909 to 1911. He continued his studies at the Académie de la Grande Chaumière in Paris from 1911 to 1914. From 1914 to 1924, he travelled to Austria, Germany, Belgium, Holland and Italy with the assistance of a grant from the Hungarian government. From 1924 to 1941, he was a professor at the school of art and sculpture in Budapest. He was selected by the Hungarian government to assess the paintings that Hitler's Third Reich had banned from German museums, so that the Hungarian government could acquire them and save them from destruction. He was then made director of the Society of Fine Arts. He left Budapest in 1944, wishing to settle in France, but was only able to get as far as Austria. From 1946 to 1958, he taught at the Free Academy of Fine Arts in the province of Salzburg in Austria. He then went to the USA, where he taught in Dayton, Ohio, from 1950 to 1952, then to Sedona in Arizona. He was a member of the World Federation of Hungarian Artists.

Bela Horvath painted portraits and figures, created a number of sculptures, and produced monuments for cemeteries, as well as medals both in Hungary and the USA. He also did murals, notably for the Holy Name Church in Dayton (Ohio) in 1962. His underlying motivation was the quest for true artistic reproduction and the inspiration of beauty.

Horvath showed his works at solo exhibitions in 1950, Jane Reece Gallery, Dayton (Ohio); 1951, South Gallery Miami Beach Art Center, Miami (Florida); 1953, Loretto Guild, Dayton and in 1953, Tucson (Arizona).He received various awards including in 1929, highly commended for his work; 1930, Gyorgy Rath Award, in Hungary; 1934, Silver Medal from the Hungarian Society of Fine Arts; 1940, a professional medal from the Union of Hungarian Artists; 1942, Gold Medal from the Union of Hungarian Artists and in 1947, Austrian Alps Award.

MUSEUMS AND GALLERIES:
BUDAPEST (Budavári Palata) - BUDAPEST (Fővárosi Képtár).

HORVATH, Endre
Polish.
Painter.

Endre Horvath painted a *Portrait of Josef Ben.*

HORVATH, Geza
Hungarian, 20th century.
Born 1879, in Tîrgu Mures.
Sculptor, medallist.

Geza Horvath was a pupil of Strobl at the Budapest academy.

HORVATIC, Hrvoje
Croat, 20th century.
Active in England from 1991.
Video artist. Multimedia.

Born in Zagreb, Hrvoje Horvatic settled in London in 1991. He works with Breda Beban producing videos.

BIBLIOGRAPHY:
Taking on a Name: Breda Beban and Hrvoje Horvatic, Whitechapel Art Gall., London, 1994.

HORWELL, Charles
British, 18th - 19th century.
Active in London.
Sculptor.

Charles Horwell frequently exhibited at the Royal Academy in London from 1785 to 1805.

HORWITT, Will
American, 20th century.
Born 1934, in New York.
Sculptor.

Will Horwitt studied at the Art Institute of Chicago from 1952 to 1954, and lives in New York. He took part in the Antwerp Biennale in 1971. His sculpture is abstract, based on the distribution and balancing of blocks with very little carving. They are stacked in 'ruiniform' piles.

HORWITZ, E.
British, 20th century.
Active in the 1920s.
Painter.
E. Horwitz worked in South Kensington, London. He was a member of the Ridley Art Club and in 1909 he exhibited at the Royal Academy and the Royal Hibernian Academy.

HORWITZ, Helena (Miss)
British, 19th century.
Active in London.
Miniaturist.
Helena Horwitz exhibited at the Royal Academy in London in 1889 and 1890.

HORWITZ, Louise B. (Miss)
British, 19th century.
Active in London.
Miniaturist.
Louise Horwitz exhibited at the Royal Academy in London in 1892.

HORWOOD (Mrs)
British, 20th century.
Active in London.
Painter.
Mrs Horwood was a member of the Ridley Art Club.

HORY, Elmyr von, pseudonym of Hoffmann Elementer
Hungarian, 20th century.
Born 1905 or 1911, in Budapest; died December 1976 or 1978, in Palma (Majorca).
Painter. Nudes, portraits, seascapes, urban landscapes.
Elmyr Hory arrived in Paris shortly after the end of World War II and began painting. Unable to interest anyone in his own work, he achieved fame by becoming one of the greatest forgers of the 20th century. He was at the heart of the 'Meadows affair' involving faked paintings and taking its name from the Texan collector who paid a million dollars for a group of pictures consisting of faked works by Picasso, Derain, Modigliani and Matisse. Hory's story is told in Clifford Irving's book *Fake* (London, 1970).

Those paintings to which he put his own name present an amalgam of styles derived from the artists that he most frequently imitated.

AUCTION RECORDS:
BARCELONA, 8 Oct 1980, *Portrait of a Woman* (oil on canvas, 32¼ x 20½ ins / 82 x 52 cm) ESP 200,000. LONDON, 2 June 1982, *Portrait* (oil on canvas, after Modigliani, 39¼ x 28½ ins / 99.7 x 72.4 cm) GBP 1,200. LONDON, 26 Oct 1983, *Walk by the Sea* (oil on canvas, after Dufy, 19½ x 26 ins / 49.8 x 65.1 cm) GBP 3,800. MADRID, 14 March 1985, *Venice* (oil on canvas, 25½ x 32 ins / 65 x 81 cm) ESP 480,000. RAMBOUILLET, 13 Dec 1987, *Seascape* (watercolour, after Raoul Dufy, 19¾ x 25½ ins / 50 x 65 cm) FRF 17,000. TEL AVIV, 20 Oct 1992, *Nude* (oil on canvas, 25¾ x 19¾ ins / 65.3 x 50.4 cm) USD 1,980.

HOSAEUS, Kurt Hermann
German, 20th century.
Born 6 May 1875, in Eisenach (Thuringia).
Sculptor.
Hosaeus was a student of Herter and Begas. He worked successively in Dresden, Nuremberg and Munich, and was awarded a gold medal in Berlin in 1908.

MUSEUMS AND GALLERIES:
BERLIN: *After Battle.*

HOSANG, Ernst
German, 19th century.
Born 10 February 1857, in Berlin.
Painter. Genre scenes.
He was a student at the academy in Berlin, and exhibited in Berlin from 1879.

HOSCH, Eduard
Swiss, 19th century.
Born 13 June 1843, in Basel; died 1908, in Lausanne.
Glass painter, architect.
He did stained glass windows in Bern and Geneva Cathedral, among other places.

HOSCH, Friedrich Karl
German, 19th century.
Active in Munich.
Painter. Genre scenes.
AUCTION RECORDS:
LONDON, 7 June 1989, *The Lesson* (oil on canvas, 25¼ x 22 ins / 64 x 55 cm) GBP 2,310. FURTH, 14 May 2004, *Watchmaker in an Interior Studying a Wrist Watch* (1858, oil on canvas, 21 x 23 ins / 53 x 59 cm) EUR 3,700.

HÖSCH, Hans. See **HOESCH Hans**

HOSCH, Karl
Swiss, 20th century.
Born 1900, in Yvedon-les-Bains (Vaud); died 1972, in Zurich.
Painter, engraver. Figures, landscapes, waterscapes.
Hosch worked mainly in Richterswil on Lake Zurich. In 2002, the Zurich gallery Zäune 8/Irène Ringier presented a retrospective of his works.
AUCTION RECORDS:
ZURICH, 5 May 1976, *Reclining Woman* (1948, oil/hardboard, 15¾ x 19½ ins / 40 x 49.5 cm) CHF 1,300. ZURICH, 2 Nov 1979, *Cherry Trees in Glarus Canton* (1968, oil on canvas, 21¼ x 25½ ins / 54 x 65 cm) CHF 1,700. ZURICH, 28 Oct 1981, *Village on Lake Zurich* (1946, oil on canvas, 21½ x 30¾ ins / 54.5 x 78 cm) CHF 3,800. ZURICH, 9 Nov 1983, *Lake Zurich* (1939, oil on card, 15¼ x 21¼ ins / 39 x 54 cm) CHF 3,200. ZURICH, 14 Nov 1986, *Three Women Sitting in the Corner by the Fire* (1942, gouache, 19¾ x 26½ ins / 50 x 67.5 cm) CHF 2,000. COLOGNE, 15 June 1989, *Alpine Lake* (oil on canvas, 19 x 25¼ ins / 48 x 64 cm) DEM 1,400. ZURICH, 25 Oct 1989, *View of Oberrieden* (1934, oil on canvas, 36¾ x 48¾ ins / 93.5 x 124 cm) CHF 14,000. ZURICH, 29 April 1992, *Conversation* (oil/synthetic resin, 8 x 14¼ ins / 20.5 x 36 cm) CHF 1,300. ZURICH, 24 Nov 1993, *Shores of a Lake* (1926, oil on canvas, 20 x 26 ins / 51 x 66 cm) CHF 1,725. ZURICH, 5 June 1996, *Thiele-sur-Yverdon* (1947, oil on canvas, 35¾ x 28¾ ins / 91 x 73 cm) CHF 6,900. ST GALL, 8 May 2001, *Lake Landscape* (1949, oil on canvas, 30 x 42 ins / 76 x 106 cm) CHF 3,200. ZURICH, 10 Dec 2001, *Winter Landscape near Schonenberg* (1925, oil on canvas, 22 x 29 ins / 55 x 73 cm) CHF 3,000.

HOSCHEDÉ-MONET, Blanche
French, 19th - 20th century.
Born 1865, in Paris; died November 1947.
Painter. Landscapes.
Blanche Hoschedé-Monet was the daughter-in-law of Claude Monet who taught her. Her charming works, always well-received, were regularly shown in the annual exhibitions.

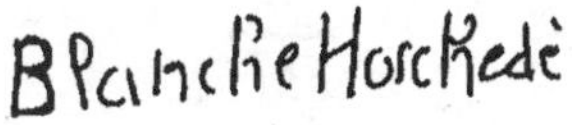

AUCTION RECORDS:
PARIS, 7 June 1923, *Pond among the Poplars,* FRF 155. PARIS, 28 Nov 1928, *The Stacks,* FRF 1,000. NEW YORK, 11 Feb 1971, *The Epte,* USD 900. PARIS, 9 April 1973, *View of the Garden at Giverny* (1930) FRF 2,400. PARIS, 13 Dec 1976, *Monet's Garden in Giverny* (oil on canvas, 19¾ x 24 ins / 50 x 61 cm) FRF 4,000. PARIS, 27 March 1980, *Houses in the Trees* (oil on canvas, 32 x 25½ ins / 81 x 65 cm) FRF 10,500. PARIS, 26 Nov 1982, *View of Rouen* (1902, oil on canvas, 23½ x 28¾ ins / 60 x 73 cm) FRF 10,500. VERSAILLES, 27 Nov 1983, *Snow Effect* (oil on canvas, 17¾ x 22 ins / 45 x 56 cm) FRF 19,500. PARIS, 11 Dec 1987, *Village* (oil on canvas, 19¼ x 23¼ ins / 49 x 59 cm) FRF 6,600. VERSAILLES, 15 May 1988, *The Primroses* (1928, oil on canvas, 23½ x 20 ins / 60 x 50.5 cm) FRF 38,000. PARIS, 23 June 1988, *The Apple Trees in the Snow* (oil on canvas, 25½ x 32 ins / 65 x 81 cm) FRF 46,000. PARIS, 26 March 1990, *Swiss Landscape* (oil on canvas, 17 x 24½ ins / 43 x 62 cm) FRF 29,000. NEUILLY, 11 June 1991, *The Haystack* (oil on canvas, 18 x 22 ins / 46 x 55 cm) FRF 123,000. LE TOUQUET, 8 Nov 1992, *The Haystacks* (oil on canvas, 19¾ x 24 ins / 50 x 61 cm) FRF 40,000. CALAIS, 14 March 1993, *Park in Bloom in the Shade* (oil on canvas, 25¼ x 32 ins / 64 x 81 cm) FRF 36,500. LONDON, 23 June 1993, *Azalea* (1928, oil on canvas, 23¾ x 39½ ins / 60.5 x 100.5 cm) GBP 13,800. NEW YORK, 17 Feb 1999, *Corner of Claude Monet's Garden at Giverny* (1930, oil on canvas, 18 x 26 ins / 46 x 65 cm) USD 14,000. NEW YORK, 30 Sept 1999, *Homage to Monet, Banks of the Seine* (1904, oil on canvas, 21 x 29 ins / 54 x 73 cm) USD 12,000. NEW YORK, 23 Feb 2000, *Banks of the Seine* (oil on canvas, 24 x 29 ins / 60 x 74 cm) USD 16,000. NEW YORK, 23 Feb 2000, *Corner of a Garden in Spring, Giverny* (oil on canvas, 21 x 29 ins / 54 x 73 cm) USD 26,000. NEW YORK, 23 Feb 2001, *Nympheas* (1946, oil on canvas, 18 x 15 ins / 46 x 38 cm) USD 16,000. NEW YORK, 21 Feb 2002, *Rose Garden at Monet's House in Giverny* (oil on canvas, 24 x 29 ins / 60 x 73 cm) USD 20,000. NEW YORK, 21 Feb 2002, *Monet's Garden in Giverny* (1928, oil on canvas, 29 x 36 ins / 73 x 92 cm) USD 42,500. NEW YORK, 12 Feb 2003, *By the River* (oil on canvas, 21 x 26 ins / 54 x 65 cm) USD 18,000. PARIS, 23 June 2003, *Countryside near Giverny* (oil on canvas, 26 x 32 ins / 65 x 81 cm) EUR 11,500. NEW YORK, 11 Feb 2004, *Claude Monet's Garden, Giverny* (1928, oil on canvas, 29 x 37 ins / 74 x 93 cm) USD 15,000. NEW YORK, 11 Feb 2004, *Monet's Rose Garden, Giverny* (1927, oil on canvas, 26 x 32 ins / 65 x 81 cm) USD 37,500.

HOSE, Heinrich
German, 18th - 19th century.
Born 1765, in Tannroda (near Weimar); died 1841, in Eisenach.
Painter, sculptor.

He did a lot of work for the palace in Weimar. Noted pieces include his busts of *Duke Frederick Augustus of Brunswick* and *Duchess Anna Amelia of Saxony-Weimar.*

HOSE, Henriette
German, 19th century.
Born 1795, in Eisenach; died 1823, in Munich.
Painter.

She was the daughter of Heinrich Hose.
MUSEUMS AND GALLERIES:
WEIMAR: *Self-portrait.*

HOSEMANN, Theodor Friedrich Wilhelm Heinrich
German, 19th century.
Born 24 September 1807, in Brandenburg; died 15 October 1875, in Berlin.
Painter, engraver. Genre scenes.

Hosemann was mainly an illustrator and lithographer. In 1857, he became a professor at the academy in Berlin.

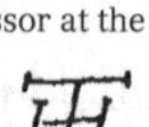

MUSEUMS AND GALLERIES:
BERLIN (Nationalgal.): *Carters at the Market; The Cabaret.*
AUCTION RECORDS:
MUNICH, 6 June 1968, *Rider Resting in a Mountainous Landscape,* DEM 15,800. MUNICH, 2 Dec 1971, *The Masons At Rest,* DEM 10,000. VIENNA, 10 Feb 1976, *The Farmyard* (1854, oil on card, 7¾ x 10 ins / 20 x 25.5 cm) ATS 40,000. MUNICH, 24 May 1977, *Children in a Landscape* (1854, oil on card, 6½ x 9 ins / 16.5 x 22 cm) DEM 4,000. MUNICH, 27 May 1978, *The Policeman and Two Vagrants* (1864, oil on panel, 6 x 8¼ ins / 15.5 x 21 cm) DEM 10,000. LUCERNE, 30 May 1979, *The Toy Vendor* (1860, oil on canvas, 14 x 11½ ins / 35.7 x 29 cm) CHF 10,000. MUNICH, 29 May 1980, *Children in a Coach* (1837, watercolour, 6¼ x 8¾ ins / 16 x 22.5 cm) DEM 10,000. MUNICH, 30 June 1983, *The Open-Air Café* (1868, oil on canvas remounted on board, 13½ x 17½ ins / 34.5 x 44.5 cm) DEM 5,000. HAMBURG, 7 June 1984, *The Itinerant Artistes* (1836, watercolour heightened with white, 8½ x 11 ins / 21.9 x 27.8 cm) DEM 15,000. COLOGNE, 21 Nov 1985, *The Sunday Fishermen* (1846, oil on canvas, 9 x 13½ ins / 22 x 34.5 cm) DEM 12,000. LONDON, 21 March 1986, *Introspection* (1853, watercolour and pencil, 5 x 4 ins / 12.9 x 9.3 cm) GBP 1,400. BERLIN, 22 May 1987, *The Talented Painters* (watercolour/pencil outlines heightened with white, 5½ x 4¼ ins / 13.7 x 10.8 cm) DEM 3,600. HEIDELBERG, 12 Oct 1991, *Children Playing with a Goat* (brown ink drawing and wash, 7¼ x 9¼ ins / 18.5 x 23.5 cm) DEM 1,100. HEIDELBERG, 15 Oct 1994, *Two Schoolchildren Finding a Child Lying in the Snow on the Way Home* (1860, watercolour and pencil, 5 x 4 ins / 12.5 x 10.3 cm) DEM 2,700. MUNICH, 6 Dec 1994, *Two Vagrants with a Policeman* (1864, oil on canvas, 20 x 25 ins / 50.5 x 63.5 cm) DEM 17,250. MUNICH, 27 June 1995, *Waiting to Leave* (1860, oil on canvas, 18¾ x 26¾ ins / 47.5 x 68 cm) DEM 24,150. MUNICH, 22 June 1999, *Two Children in Cornfield* (1846, watercolour, 4 x 6 ins / 9 x 14 cm) DEM 4,500. BERLIN, 26 Nov 1999, *Three Young Children Looking in a Box* (1835, watercolour/gouache over pencil, 5 x 3 ins / 12 x 8 cm) DEM 7,000. LONDON, 25 May 2000, *Worse for Wear* (1836, oil on canvas, 7 x 10 ins / 18 x 25 cm) GBP 1,300. BERLIN, 26 May 2000, *Der Uckermarker und die Importierten - Three Hunting Figures with Dogs* (oil on panel, 6 x 9 ins / 16 x 23 cm) DEM 7,000. LONDON, 28 Nov 2001, *Sunday Promenade* (oil on canvas, 11 x 13 ins / 27 x 34 cm) GBP 3,000. BERLIN, 31 May 2003, *Rendezvous in the Country* (1853, oil on board, 7 x 9 ins / 18 x 24 cm) EUR 5,000. COLOGNE, 15 Nov 2003, *Shepherd Having Fun* (1846, oil on canvas, 17 x 15 ins / 44 x 37 cm) EUR 5,800.

HOSENFELDER, Christian Friedrich
German, 18th century.
Born 1706, in Krossen (Prussia); died 19 May 1780, in St Petersburg.
Painter. Animals.

He worked in Frankfurt (Oder), Berlin and St Petersburg, becoming a member of staff at the academy in the last-named in 1777. He was mainly a painter of horses.
AUCTION RECORDS:
NEW YORK, 5 June 1986, *Riding School Horses* (oil on canvas, a pair, 18½ x 21¼ ins / 47 x 54 cm) USD 14,000. LONDON, 30 Oct 1991, *Grey in a Stormy Landscape* (oil on canvas, 19¾ x 24¾ ins / 50 x 63 cm) GBP 4,400.

HOSENFELLER, Henrich Christian Friedrich,
or Osenfeldt
German, 18th century.
Born c. 1723, in Berlin; died c. 1801, in Norway.
Painter.

Initially a painter on porcelain, he subsequently did landscapes and portraits. Some of his works are now in the Oslo Museum.

HOSHI, Joichi
Japanese, 20th century.

Born 1913, in Niigata Prefecture; died 1979.
Engraver.

Hoshi Joichi made much use of the natural woodgrain in his blocks, which he combined with his Abstract compositions. After graduating from Tainan Normal School in Formosa (now Taiwan), he taught in that country for 13 years before being repatriated to Japan after World War II. He then started to study stencilling techniques and to exhibit with the Japan Print Association, which awarded him a prize in 1949. In 1956 he graduated from the Western painting department of Musashino University, near Tokyo, turned to woodblock printing and went on to exhibit with the Kokugakai (National Painting Society), which awarded him a prize in 1959. From 1960 he exhibited regularly at the Tokyo International Print Biennale and in 1967 took part in the São Paulo Biennale.

HOSHOJI TAMENOBU. See **TAMENOBU**

HOSHU. See **HYAKUSEN**

HOSIASSON, Philippe

Ukrainian, 20th century.
Born 15 February 1898, in Odessa; died 13 July 1978.
Active from 1924 and from 1928 naturalised in France.
Painter (including gouache/mixed media), watercolourist, decorative painter, illustrator.

Philippe Hosiasson was introduced to painting early on by his uncle Leonid Pasternak. He was in Rome in 1920 studying the history of art and in 1921 he was working in Berlin for Boris Romanov's Ballets Romantiques Russes. He travelled with the company to Paris in 1924 and while there carried out a number of decorative projects for, among other things, the Printemps stores. He also designed the decorations of the Martinique pavilion at the Exposition Universelle in Paris. He was wounded at Dunkirk in 1939. After the war he illustrated Aragon's *Crève-cœur* and executed a number of decorative works including *The Liberation of Marseilles*. He was the vice-president of the Salon des Surindépendants in Paris.

Waldemar George, in the review *Formes*, describes Hosiasson as one of the promoters, along with Christian Bérard, of a return to a Latin Classicism and the values of western culture through his use of a traditional and neo-Realist style. An admirer of Poussin and Cézanne, at his first exhibition in Rome Hosiasson showed works depicting Roman crowds against an antique architectural background. Another exhibition in Paris in 1931 again featured figures in architectural surroundings, painted in thickly applied colours. After the war, around 1947, he began to experiment with Informal Abstraction, taking advantage of his gift for composition and delight in the materials of painting. He used a mixture of oil paint, gouache, powders and sand reminiscent of Fautier but unlike the work of this artist in the readability of the canvas. As an artist with a long career and much experience, Hosiasson became something of an example to younger painters. Hosiasson's tumultuously mixed layers of dark, fused impasto well up in monochrome extrusions like the first suggestions of life, where the animal, vegetable and mineral worlds are still undifferentiated; we see the beginning of the creation of the world still undecided between the flank of a hill or the arm of a tree or the undulating valleys of a woman's body. After 1959, Hosiasson abandoned his dark palette in favour of lighter colours and, from 1967, moved towards what the *Le Robert Dictionnaire Universel de la Peinture* (1975) calls 'a world of organic ghosts'. His paintings were often produced in series including *Materials* (1956-1958), *Chaos* (1959-1960), *Walls* (1960-1962) and *Blazons* (1973-1975). Although long ignored by the critics, Hosiasson eventually gained recognition.

Collective exhibitions include: Salon des Réalités Nouvelles; Salon d'Automne; and the Salon des Tuileries as well as Italy; Germany; and Russia (from 1920). Solo exhibition include: Galleria Bragaglia, Rome (1920 or 1921?); Galerie du Haut Pavé, Paris (1955); Galerie Stadler, Paris (1956); Galerie Flinker, Paris (1961 and 1966); Musée National d'Art Moderne, Paris (1973); Kootz Gallery, New York (1956, 1957, 1958 and 1959); Martha Jackson Gallery, New York (1962); Primus Stuart Gallery, Los Angeles (1963); Verviers museum (1965); Galerie Regards, Paris (1975, 1976, 1978, 1979, 1980 and 1981). A retrospective was held at the Centre de la Vieille Charité in Marseilles (1989).

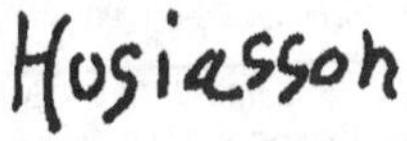

BIBLIOGRAPHY:

Courthion, Pierre, '*Philippe Hosiasson*' in *XXe Siècle* n° 32, Paris, 1969. *Philippe Hosiasson*, exhibition catalogue, Musée national d'Art moderne, Paris, 1973. Boissier, Pierre, *Hosiasson, genèse d'un expresionnisme abstrait*, Gal. Regards, Paris, 1982.

MUSEUMS AND GALLERIES:

BUFFALO (Albright-Knox AG) - CAMBRIDGE, MA (Fogg AM, Harvard University) - CHARLOTTESVILLE (University of Virginia) - EXETER, NH, USA (Lamont Gallery, Philipps Exeter Academy) - LOS ANGELES (UCLA) - LUXEMBOURG (Mus. national d'histoire et d'art) - NEW YORK (Columbia University) - NEW YORK (Metropolitan Mus. of Art) - NEW YORK (MoMA): *Red and Black* (1956) - NEW YORK (New York University) - NEW YORK (Solomon R. Guggenheim Mus.) - NEWARK (Mus.) - PARIS (MAMVP) - PARIS (MNAM-CCI): *Painting* (1961) - ROME (Gal. Nazionale d'Arte Moderna) - SAARBRÜCKEN (Saarlandmus., Moderne Galerie) - SKOPJE (Muzej na Sovremena Umetnost) - ST-ÉTIENNE (Mus. d'Art et d'Industrie) - STOCKHOLM (Moderna Mus.) - TEL AVIV (MMA) - VERVIERS (Mus. communal des Beaux-Arts et de la Céramique) - VIENNA (Mus. Moderner Kunst Stiftung Ludwig).

AUCTION RECORDS:

VERSAILLES, 12 May 1976, *Alba* (1963, watercolour and gouache, 22 x 18 ins / 55 x 46 cm) FRF 2,100. PARIS, 21 June 1979, *Composition* (1970, oil on canvas, 46 x 35 ins / 116 x 89 cm) FRF 8,500. PARIS, 6 Dec 1986, *Untitled - Tyrian Pink and Yellow* (1966, oil on canvas, 51 1/4 x 38 1/2 ins / 130 x 98 cm) FRF 34,000. PARIS, 1 June 1988, *Composition* (1963, gouache, 17 3/4 x 21 1/4 ins / 45 x 54 cm) FRF 7,000. NEUILLY-SUR-SEINE, 16 March 1989, *Composition* (1960, 25 1/2 x 36 1/4 ins / 65 x 92 cm) FRF 30,000. PARIS, 16 April 1989, *1971* (oil on canvas, 25 1/2 x 32 ins / 65 x 81 cm) FRF 22,000. STOCKHOLM, 22 May 1989, *Composition* (oil on canvas, 25 1/2 x 35 3/4 ins / 65 x 91 cm) SEK 13,500. NEUILLY, 6 June 1989, *New York* (1962, watercolour and gouache, 29 x 22 ins / 73.5 x 55 cm) FRF 28,000. PARIS, 21 May 1990, *Untitled* (1947, oil on canvas, 18 x 15 ins / 46 x 38 cm) FRF 16,000. NEW YORK, 10 Oct 1990, *Composition* (1961, oil on canvas, 39 x 31 1/2 ins / 99.1 x 80.1 cm) USD 11,000. PARIS, 26 Oct 1990, *Untitled* (1971, oil/gouache/canvas, 28 3/4 x 23 1/2 ins / 73 x 60 cm) FRF 25,000. STOCKHOLM, 5-6 Dec 1990, *Composition* (1959, oil on canvas, 31 1/2 x 25 1/4 ins / 80 x 64 cm) SEK 21,000. PARIS, 14 Feb 1991, *Untitled* (1960, oil and pigment/canvas, 31 3/4 x 25 1/2 ins / 80.5 x 64.5 cm) FRF 42,000. NEW YORK, 7 May 1991, *Four Squares* (1962, oil and dry pigments/canvas, 35 x 50 3/4 ins / 89 x 129 cm) USD 7,700. LONDON, 17 Oct 1991, *Dark Border* (1959, oil on canvas, 63 3/4 x 51 1/4 ins / 162 x 130 cm) GBP 3,520. PARIS, 20 Nov 1991, *Histories of the Earth* (1959, oil on canvas, 38 1/4 x 63 1/2 ins / 97 x 161 cm) FRF 40,000. NEW YORK, 17 Nov 1992, *Counter-Space* (1955, oil on canvas, 57 1/2 x 45 ins / 146 x 114 cm) USD 4,400. PARIS, 6 Dec 1993, *Composition* (1958, oil on canvas, 36 1/4 x 28 3/4 ins / 92 x 73 cm) FRF 28,000. PARIS, 24 June 1994, *Composition* (1961, watercolour and gouache, 29 1/2 x 43 1/4 ins / 75 x 110 cm) FRF 9,000. PARIS, 7 Oct 1995, *Composition No. 10* (1974, oil on canvas, 46 x 35 ins / 116 x 89 cm) FRF 13,500. PARIS, 29 Nov 1996, *Composition* (1968, oil and gouache/canvas, 76¾ x 51¼ ins / 195 x 130 cm) FRF 16,000. PARIS, 16 March 1997, *Untitled* (1964, oil on canvas, 25½ x 32 ins / 65 x 81 cm) FRF 8,500. PARIS, 24 March 1997, *Composition* (1963, watercolour and gouache/paper, 21¼ x 18 ins / 54 x 45.5 cm) FRF 3,000. PARIS, 28 April 1997, *Untitled* (1961, gouache/paper, 19¼ x 25¼ ins / 49 x 64 cm) FRF 3,500.

HOSKIN, John
British, 20th century.
Born 1921, in Cornwall; died 1990.
Sculptor.

John Hoskin was a self-taught sculptor. He began exhibiting in 1957 in London. He also showed his work in Antwerp in 1959 and took part in the 1963 Tokyo Biennale. He executed a sculpture, *Christ*, for Southmead church in Bristol in 1959, and another for a chapel in Oxford in 1961.

MUSEUMS AND GALLERIES:
LISBON (Centro de Arte Moderna José de Azeredo Perdigão, Fundação Calouste Gulbenkian) - LONDON (Tate Collection): *Black Beetle* (1957, iron); *Standing Figure* (1960, metal); *Square Flat* (1963, painted steel) - LONDON (Victoria and Albert Mus.).

HOSKINS, John, the Elder
British, 17th century.
Born c. 1595; died February 1664, in London.
Painter, miniaturist. Portraits.

John Hoskins the Elder originally painted portraits in oil and subsequently concentrated on miniatures, with which he achieved considerable success, particularly at the court of Charles I, whose portrait he painted along with that of Queen Henrietta and those of a number of high-ranking members of the English nobility. Such was the extent of his success that the public is said to have appreciated his works even more than those of Van Dyck, whose portraits he was sometimes asked to reproduce in miniature. Among his pupils were Samuel and Alexander Cooper and his son John Hoskins the Younger.

MUSEUMS AND GALLERIES:
LONDON (National Portrait Gal.): *Dudley North, 4th Baron North* (c. 1628, watercolour/vellum, miniature); *Henry Capel, 2nd Baron Capel* (c. 1655, watercolour/vellum, medallion) - LONDON (Wallace Collection).

HOSKINS, John, the Younger
British, 17th century.
Miniaturist.

John Hoskins the Younger was the son and pupil of John Hoskins the Elder. He was a remarkably talented miniaturist and his works are very sought after. He painted the portrait of James II in 1686 and was paid ten pounds five shillings for it. His monogram is similar to that of his father with the one difference that the I and the H are separated.

MUSEUMS AND GALLERIES:
AMSTERDAM: *Henrietta-Maria of France; same subject; Charles I; Elizabeth of England; Mary of England* - BERLIN: *Cromwell* - LONDON (National Portrait Gal.): *Prince Rupert* - LONDON (Wallace Collection): *A Gentleman; Edward, Second Viscount of Conway*.

AUCTION RECORDS:
LONDON, 15 June 1928, *The Honourable Anchitell Grey*, GBP 36. LONDON, 28 April 1999, *Gentleman in Black Doublet and White Lawn Collar* (c. 1645, miniature) GBP 1,200. STUTTGART, 17 March 2000, *Portrait of Sir Algenon Percy, Earl of Northumberland* (miniature) DEM 7,000. LONDON, 21 Nov 2000, *Lady called Mrs. Cromwell in Black Dress, Fur Cloak, Black Hood* (miniature) GBP 3,800. LONDON, 6 March 2001, *Portrait of Officer in Full Armour* (miniature) GBP 4,200. LONDON, 30 Oct 2001, *Gentleman with Small Beard, in a Black Doublet* (miniature) GBP 10,000. LONDON, 5 Nov 2002, *George Villiers, Duke of Buckingham with Blue Sash of the Garter* (watercolour on vellum, miniature) GBP 6,000. LONDON, 5 Nov 2002, *Robert Carr, Earl of Somerset Wearing Armour with Brass Studs* (miniature) GBP 16,000. NOTTINGHAM, 10 June 2003, *Lady, possibly Mary Cromwell, Wearing a Pearl Necklace* (1651, miniature) GBP 17,500. LONDON, 25 May 2004, *Sir Arthur Hesilrige, in Gilt Studded Armour* (1652, miniature) GBP 9,000.

HOSKOPFF, Sébastien. See **STOSKOPFF Sébastien**

HOSLET, Jean Joseph
Belgian, 20th century.
Born 1899, in Ixelles (Brussels); died 1981, in Brussels.
Painter, draughtsman.

Hoslet was a student at the fine arts academies in Ixelles (Brussels) and St-Josse-ten-Noode.

MUSEUMS AND GALLERIES:
BRUSSELS (Bibliothèque royale Albert Ier, Prints Collection) - MONS (MBA).

HOSMER, Harriet
American, 19th century.
Born 6 October 1830, in Watertown (Massachusetts); died 21 February 1908, in Watertown.
Sculptor. Statues, busts.

Harriet Hosmer was a pupil of Lenoe, and studied drawing and sculpture in Boston. After working on anatomy at the medical college of St Louis she went to Rome, where she was a pupil of the English sculptor Gibson. She produced the statue of *Beatrice Cenci* in the public library of St Louis, as well as a statue of *Puck*. She was also famous as a poet and prose writer.

BIBLIOGRAPHY:
Sherwood, Dolly, *Harriet Hosmer, American Sculptor, 1830-1908*, University of Missouri Press, Columbia (MO).

MUSEUMS AND GALLERIES:
ST LOUIS (GA, Washington University): *Daphne* (1854, marble); *Oenone* (1854-1855, marble); *Portrait of Wayman Crow Senior* (1866, marble) - SYDNEY: *Puck; Faun; Beatrice Cenci*.

AUCTION RECORDS:
LONDON, 16 March 1977, *Sleeping Faun* (c. 1864, marble, h. 50 ins / 127 cm, w. 60 ins/152.5 cm) GBP 12,000. LOS ANGELES, 18 June 1979, *Puck* (white marble, h. 31 ins / 78.5 cm) USD 9,000. BOLTON, 15 May 1986, *Will o' the Wisp* (white marble, h. 32¾ ins / 83 cm) USD 17,000. NEW YORK, 22 May 1996, *Medusa* (white marble, h. 27½ ins / 69.9 cm) USD 71,250. NEW YORK, 9 Nov 2001, *Figure of Puck* (marble, h. 31 ins / 79 cm) USD 15,000. ST LOUIS, 21 June 2003, *Winged Boy Seated on a Toadstool* (white marble, h. 40 ins / 102 cm) USD 27,000. LONDON, 8 July 2003, *Sleeping Faun* (white marble, h. 32 ins / 81 cm, w/ 41 ins/118 cm) GBP 22,000.

HOSODA, Eishi, also called: Kabane Tokitomi, then Yasaboro, Go, Chobonsai, Fujiwara
Japanese, 18th - 19th century.
Born 1756; died 1 August 1829.
Painter.
Ukiyo-e school.

Hosoda Eishi studied painting under Kano Eisen-in, turning later to wooden sculpture, and worked with Hokusai. His paintings are much appreciated in Japan. His *Thirty-six Immortal Women Poets* is well known.

HOSODA JIBUKYO TOKITOMI. See **EISHI**

HOSOTTE, Georges
French, 20th century.
Born 6 June 1936, in Paris.
Painter, watercolourist. Portraits, genre scenes, landscapes, landscapes with figures, still-lifes. Murals.

Georges Hosotte describes himself as self-taught. His portraits, especially those of old people, are colourful, and possess an undeniable depth while his landscapes in an ochre-brown palette, convey his love of happy, rustic nature set in a steadfast silence. He also works in watercolour in order to better evoke the fluid poetry of landscapes by the water's edge. Georges Hosotte has participated in numerous collective exhibitions. Solo exhibitions include: Galerie du Temple Auxerre (1958, 1964, 1967, 1968); Galerie St-Placide, Paris (1965, 1966); Galerie Vendôme, Paris (1971); Galerie d'Art de la Place Beauvau, Paris (1975, 1978, 1982, 1984); Galerie Main de Fer, Perpergnan (1976); retrospective, Abbaye-St-Germain d'Auxerre, Auxerre (1986).

BIBLIOGRAPHY:
Sautet, Camille, *Hosotte*, F. Labruyère, Paris, 1983. Ravignant, Patrick, *Hosotte. La Mémoire du présent*, 1986. *Hosotte. Rétrospective*, exhibition catalogue, Société des Amis des Musées d'Auxerre, abbaye-Saint-Germain, Auxerre, 1986.

MUSEUMS AND GALLERIES:
AUXERRE (Mus. du Coche D'eau) - FONTAINEBLEAU (Mus. d'Art Figuratif Contemporain) - PARIS (FMAC).

AUCTION RECORDS:
ST-JEAN-CAP-FERRAT, 16 March 1993, *Village in Provence* (oil on canvas, 44 1/2 x 57 1/2 ins / 113 x 146 cm) FRF 17,000.

HOSP, Franz
Austrian, 18th century.
Born in Imst.
Sculptor.

HOSPENTHAL, Franz von
Swiss, 18th century.
Born 18th century, in Arth.
Painter.

HOSPENTHAL, Melchior Anton von
Swiss, 18th century.
Painter.
He worked in Wylen.

HOSPITAL OF THE HOLY SPIRIT, Master of the. See **MASTERS**

HOSPODAR, Stephen von
Hungarian, 20th century.
Born 3 January 1902, in Nagymihaly.
Active in the USA.
Painter, engraver.

HOSS, Lorenz
German, 17th century.
Active in Nuremberg in 1629.
Painter.

HOSSE
German, 18th century.
Sculptor.

HOSSE, Adolph
German, 20th century.
Born 26 July 1875, in Hanau (Hesse).
Painter.
Hosse worked in Rothenburg and exhibited in Berlin from 1919 onwards.

HOSSE, Henriette. See **HOSE**

HOSSFELD, Friedrich
German, 19th century.
Born 1809, in Schulpforta (near Naumburg); died 1881, in Berlin.
Painter, illustrator.
He trained at the academy in Leipzig. Mostly he painted landscapes.

HÖSSLI, Philipp
Swiss, 19th - 20th century.
Born 25 February 1873, in Andeer (Grisons); died February 1917, in Schaffhausen.
Painter. Portraits, genre scenes, landscapes.
Hössli exhibited at the Kunsthaus in Zurich.

HOSSON, F. C.
Flemish School, 18th century.
Born 1717, in Bentheim; died 1799, in Groningen.
Painter. Historical subjects, portraits.
F. C. Hosson was the son and pupil of the painter M. C. Hosson, who was court painter to the count of Bentheim. He worked for many years in Germany.

HOSSPANION, J., or Hofspanion
Flemish School, 17th century.
Engraver, draughtsman.
Kramm refers to J. Hosspanion's *Portrait of Petrus de Witle*, who died in 1669.

HØST, Oluf, or Holst
Danish, 20th century.
Born 1884, in Svaneke; died 1966.
Painter. Genre scenes, landscapes with figures, landscapes.
School of Bornholm.
Oluf Høst spent a brief period at the Kongelige Danske Kunstakademi in Copenhagen, having been a sailor as a young man. In 1910 he went to study at Johan Rohde's painting school, in Harald Giersing's studio. He visited Italy, Paris and Scandinavia. From 1926 he was a member of the Den Frie artists' society in Copenhagen. His work was shown at many exhibitions of contemporary Danish painting; at the Carnegie International Exhibition in Pittsburgh (1927); and at the Venice Biennale (1934). He was awarded the Eckersberg Medal in 1933, and the Thorvaldsen Medal in 1943.

Høst was an artist of the Bornholm School, which came together in 1911 and was the last great colony of artists in Denmark after the Skagen and Funen schools of the second half of the nineteenth century. He was the only artist actually native to Bornholm. The Bornholm School thrived on new approaches to painting that were governed by the effects of colour and form. Høst mainly painted landscapes of his native island, Bornholm. The Swedish Painter Karl Isakson gave him a detailed introduction to the work of Van Gogh and Cézanne.

BIBLIOGRAPHY:
Johansen, Annette, et al., *Danske Kunstnerkolonier: Skagen, Fyn, Bornholm*, group exhibition catalogue, Aarhus Kunstmuseum, Aarhus, 2000.

MUSEUMS AND GALLERIES:
COPENHAGEN (Statens Mus. for Kunst): *Winter* (1931); *Winter Sunset* (1931); *Slaughtering Pigs* (1941) - HUMLEBÆK (Louisiana Mus. for Moderne Kunst) - RANDERS (Kunstmus.): *Winter in Gudhjem* (1936); *Winter* (1940).

AUCTION RECORDS:
COPENHAGEN, 1 March 1957, *Farm with a Woman Farmer Standing under a Tree*, DKK 6,600. COPENHAGEN, 2 March 1960, *Landscape with a Tree without Leaves in the Left Foreground*, DKK 9,200. COPENHAGEN, 11 Oct 1966, *Autumn Evening*, DKK 23,000. COPENHAGEN, 18 March 1970, *Goats in a Landscape*, DKK 22,000. COPENHAGEN, 1 Nov 1972, *After the Rain*, DKK 38,000. COPENHAGEN, 20 Oct 1976, *Landscape with Cottage* (1933, oil on canvas, 20 1/2 x 25 1/2 ins / 52 x 65 cm) DKK 17,000. COPENHAGEN, 5 Oct 1977, *Landscape with Cottage* (oil on canvas, 34 1/4 x 57 ins / 87 x 145 cm) DKK 57,000. COPENHAGEN, 10 Oct 1979, *Landscape with Tree and House* (oil on canvas, 38 1/2 x 51 1/2 ins / 98 x 131 cm) DKK 57,000. COPENHAGEN, 27 Oct 1982, *Winter Landscape* (oil on canvas, 25 1/2 x 39 1/4 ins / 65 x 100 cm) DKK 45,000. COPENHAGEN, 1 June 1983, *Cottage, Bognemark* (gouache, 17 1/4 x

22½ ins / 44 x 57 cm) DKK 22,500. COPENHAGEN, 1 June 1983, *Winter Day, Bognemark* (oil on canvas, 29½ x 32 ins / 75 x 81 cm) DKK 24,000. COPENHAGEN, 25 Sept 1985, *Landscape* (1943, oil on canvas, 32 x 46 ins / 81 x 116 cm) DKK 75,000. COPENHAGEN, 16 Sept 1987, *Bognemark in the Snow* (oil on canvas, 29¼ x 46 ins / 74 x 117 cm) DKK 210,000. COPENHAGEN, 4 May 1988, *Icy Landscape with Blue Reflections on Bornholm* (1947, 35 x 57½ ins / 89 x 146 cm) DKK 240,000. COPENHAGEN, 8 Feb 1989, *Bognemark on Bornholm* (1935, oil on canvas, 28¾ x 46 ins / 73 x 116 cm) DKK 100,000. COPENHAGEN, 10 May 1989, *Mist Coming Down* (1943, oil on canvas, 35½ x 57 ins / 90 x 145 cm) DKK 245,000. COPENHAGEN, 9 May 1990, *Blueish Cold in Bognemark on Bornholm* (1947, oil on canvas, 35 x 57½ ins / 89 x 146 cm) DKK 222,000. COPENHAGEN, 31 Oct 1990, *Composition* (oil on canvas, 19¾ x 17¾ ins / 50 x 45 cm) DKK 42,000. COPENHAGEN, 4 Dec 1991, *Bognemark Farm on Bornholm* (watercolour and gouache/paper/canvas, 17¼ x 22 ins / 44 x 56 cm) DKK 26,000. COPENHAGEN, 1 April 1992, *Winter Day in Gughjem* (oil on canvas, 24 x 46 ins / 61 x 116 cm) DKK 130,000. COPENHAGEN, 21 Oct 1992, *North Wind* (1938, oil on canvas, 35 x 57½ ins / 89 x 146 cm) DKK 186,000. AMSTERDAM, 31 May 1994, *Round Church at Osterlars* (1955, oil on canvas). COPENHAGEN, 26 April 1995, *Bognemark in Winter* (oil on canvas, 28¾ x 46 ins / 73 x 116 cm) DKK 75,000. COPENHAGEN, 16 April 1997, *Winter, Bognemark* (1941, oil on canvas, 11 x 18 ins / 28 x 46 cm) DKK 28,000; *North Wind* (1950, oil on canvas, 28¾ x 46 ins / 73 x 116 cm) DKK 157,000. COPENHAGEN, 12-14 Nov 1997, *Summer Landscape* (oil on canvas, 22 x 24 ins / 55 x 61 cm) DKK 58,000; *Bognemark* (oil on canvas, 19¾ x 32 ins / 50 x 81 cm) DKK 75,000. COPENHAGEN, 23 March 1999, *Bognemark in Snow with Farmyard and Cat* (c. 1950, oil on canvas, 35 x 58 ins / 89 x 147 cm) DKK 260,000. COPENHAGEN, 5 Oct 1999, *Bognemark at Sunset* (1954, oil on canvas, 26 x 46 ins / 65 x 116 cm) DKK 200,000. COPENHAGEN, 28 March 2000, *Sunset over Osterlars* (oil on canvas, 35 x 56 ins / 89 x 143 cm) DKK 270,000. COPENHAGEN, 3 Oct 2000, *Osterlar's Round Church* (c. 1946, oil on canvas, 24 x 36 ins / 61 x 91 cm) DKK 210,000. COPENHAGEN, 2 April 2001, *Bognemark* (c. 1955, oil on canvas, 26 x 46 ins / 65 x 116 cm) DKK 275,000. COPENHAGEN, 2 Oct 2001, *Spring in the Garden, Norresand* (oil on canvas, 32 x 57 ins / 82 x 146 cm) DKK 240,000. COPENHAGEN, 4 April 2002, *Summer Landscape* (1941, oil on canvas, 35 x 58 ins / 90 x 148 cm) DKK 100,000. COPENHAGEN, 10 April 2002, *Landscape, Bognemark in Afternoon Sunshine* (c. 1955, oil on canvas, 32 x 57 ins / 81 x 146 cm) DKK 240,000. COPENHAGEN, 12 June 2003, *Sunset over Norresund* (1963, oil on canvas, 35 x 57 ins / 90 x 146 cm) DKK 76,000. COPENHAGEN, 7 Oct 2003, *Sunset, Winter* (1952, oil on canvas, 38 x 51 ins / 96 x 130 cm) DKK 85,000. COPENHAGEN, 29 March 2004, *Bognemark* (oil on canvas, 32 x 51 ins / 81 x 130 cm) DKK 380,000. COPENHAGEN, 5 Oct 2004, *Bognemark in Evening, Woman Feeding Chickens* (c. 1945, oil on canvas, 32 x 57 ins / 81 x 146 cm) DKK 420,000.

HOSTE, Constant Prosper

Belgian, 19th - 20th century.
Born 1873, in Ledeberg; died 1917, in Ghent.
Painter, draughtsman. Portraits, landscapes, seascapes, boats, flowers.

Hoste was a student of Louis Tytgat.

AUCTION RECORDS:

LOKEREN, 23 May 1992, *Sailing Boats among the Breakers in the Bay* (1906, oil on canvas, 18¼ x 36 ins / 46.5 x 91.5 cm) BEF 70,000.

HÖSTE, Einar

Swedish, 20th century.
Born 1930, in Stockholm.
Sculptor.
Neo-Constructivism.

Einar Höste was one of a group of eight Swedish artists in Paris in 1971, and his work was shown at the exhibition *Art Construit. Current Trends in France and Sweden* at the French Institute in Stockholm in 1986. He creates spaces for optical effects, and his thought processes are tied in with technological research. His vast, refined forms can only be conceived of within an architectural context; indeed, it would be desirable to have Höste collaborate on the conceptions of buildings themselves.

AUCTION RECORDS:

STOCKHOLM, 6 Dec 1989, *Composition in Black and Blue* (acrylic/canvas, 39¼ x 27½ ins / 100 x 70 cm) SEK 15,000. STOCKHOLM, 2 Nov 2004, *P34 - Composition* (acrylic, 39 x 28 ins / 100 x 70 cm) SEK 21,000.

HOSTE, Guillaume

Flemish, 16th century.
Active in Oudenaarde in 1515.
Painter.
Flemish School.

HOSTEIN, Édouard Jean-Marie

French, 19th century.
Born 30 September 1804, in Pléhédel (Côtes-d'Armor); died 25 August 1889, in Paris.
Painter, draughtsman, illustrator, lithographer.
Portraits, landscapes.

Hostein was an employee at a bank, who also worked as an illustrator in Paris between 1827 and 1833. His work was regularly featured at the Paris Salon, from 1833 to 1859, and he won several medals: a third-class in 1835, a second-class in 1837, and a first-class in 1841. Several of his drawings were shown at the Musée de Toulon in 1971. He was honoured with the title of Chevalier of the Légion d'Honneur in 1846.

Hostein was a prolific artist, who produced many paintings and lithographs of views of the various regions of France. He also worked on several publications, including: *France in Ancient Times* by Baron Taylor; *Stony Arabia* by M. Delaborde; and *Tour of the World* and *Journey to Simplon* by Dumont d'Urville.

MUSEUMS AND GALLERIES:

AMIENS (Mus. de Picardie): *Lake Geneva* - AURILLAC: *View of the Forest of Compiègne* - AVIGNON (Mus. Calvet): *The Saône Valley on the outskirts of Lyons* - AVRANCHES: *The Beach at Dieppe* - BLOIS: *Les Montils* - CHÂTEAU-THIERRY: *The Team* - CHÂTEAUROUX: *Market in Spain* - DIEPPE: *View of the Beach at Dieppe; View of Italy* - LYONS (MBA): *Entrance to the Forest of Saverne, near Strasbourg* - ST-BRIEUC: *Portrait of the Artist; View from L'Arbresle; Ruins of the Château de Chabrillan* - ST-OMER: *View of the Town of Bressuire* - TOULON: *View of the Pines at Tauroentum* - VERSAILLES: *Charles VII Entering Acquapendente*.

AUCTION RECORDS:

ROUEN, 21 March 1982, *View of Rouen* (oil on canvas, 20½ x 31½ ins / 52 x 80 cm) FRF 11,500. PARIS, 24 Oct 1986, *Brickyard near Toulon Harbour* (pen and gouache) FRF 10,000. PARIS, 9 May 1994, *Portrait of a Little Girl* (1851, oil on canvas, de oval, 22 x 17¾ ins / 55 x 45 cm) FRF 5,800. NEW ORLEANS, 30 Jan 1999, *Granville* (1845, oil on canvas, 20 x 29 ins / 51 x 74 cm) USD 2,400. RHEIMS, 24 Oct 1999, *Country Landscape* (oil on canvas, 14 x 17 ins / 36 x 44 cm) FRF 16,000. PARIS, 22 June 2000, *Landscape* (1845, oil on canvas, 70 x 101 ins / 179 x 256 cm) FRF 155,000. NEW YORK, 31 Oct 2000, *View of the City of Lyons* (1857, oil on canvas, 39 x 85 ins / 98 x 216 cm) USD 33,000.

HOSTELAIN, Robert

French, 16th century.
Sculptor.

Robert Hostelain worked on the decoration of the town hall chapel in Béthune.

HOSUI, real name: Kaneko Tokuho, popularly known as: Kenshiro, pseudonyms: Miyagawa, Mokei
Japanese, 19th century.
Born 1815; died 1864.
Active c. 1850.
Draughtsman. Portraits.

Hosui produced prints of actors which were published in Kyoto.

HOT, Georges
French, 20th century.
Born 2 July 1920, in Rodez.
Painter, sculptor.
Symbolism.

Georges Hot graduated from the Faculté de Droit and the Faculté de Lettres in Paris and trained at the École des Arts Décoratifs in Paris and at the private academies in Montparnasse. He lived in Paris until 1958, and then abroad, mainly in Africa where he was magistrate until 1976. From 1977 he lived and worked in Roquefort-les-Pins in the south of France. He is linked to the Lyrical Abstraction movement. With laboriously mixed materials and occasionally mixing his technique, Hot evokes landscape interiors. Around 1982, he seems to have returned to a type of figurative symbolism, notably with the *Shrines* series.

Georges Hot has taken part in collective exhibitions in the south of France. In Paris, he has showed at the Salon d'Automne, the Salon des Indépendants, and was a member of the group, Lyrical Abstraction at the Salon Comparaison until the death of the painter Istrati. He also held solo exhibitions in Africa, and from 1987, at the Galerie Arcadia in Paris, and in 1994, at the Galerie Ariane in Paris. Hot was secretary-general of *Défense des Arts Plastiques* (*Defence of the Fine Arts*), an association organising collective exhibitions in the Côte d'Azur region.

BIBLIOGRAPHY:
Cent-vingt ans de gravure toulousaine, École des beaux-arts de Toulouse, Toulouse, 1986. Gaudet, Michel/Collot, André, *Georges Hot*, Gal Ariane, Paris, 1993.

AUCTION RECORDS:
PARIS, 12 Feb 1989, *Dépouille V* (1987, oil on canvas, 25½ x 19¾ ins / 65 x 50 cm) FRF 7,000. PARIS, 28 Oct 1990, *Untitled* (acrylic/canvas, 28¾ x 23½ ins / 73 x 60 cm) FRF 11,500. PARIS, 1 Oct 1993, *Figure* (oil on canvas, 28¾ x 23½ ins / 73 x 60 cm) FRF 10,000.

HOTCHKISS, T. H.
American, 19th century.
Active in New York c. 1857.
Painter. Landscapes.

MUSEUMS AND GALLERIES:
BOSTON: four watercolours.

HOTELIN, Laurent
French, 19th century.
Born in the 19th century, in Vallant-St-Georges (Aube).
Engraver (wood).

A pupil of Caillois, Hotelin made his début at the Paris Salon of 1863.

HOTHAM, Amelia
British, 18th century.
Active in 1793.
Painter. Landscapes.

MUSEUMS AND GALLERIES:
LONDON (British Mus.): watercolour, signed.

HOTIN, Auguste Emmanuel, called le Graveur Dieppois
French, 19th - 20th century.
Born December 1850, in Dieppe; died 16 June 1910, in Paris.
Painter, draughtsman, engraver.

Auguste Hotin was a little-known artist. Infirm from a very young age, he could only walk with crutches. His physical disadvantage was compounded by an extreme modesty which him to live away from the world. He worked tirelessly; his reproductions include: *The Laughing Child*, after Frans Hals, *Democritus*, after Coypel, a pen drawing for which the Administration des Beaux-Arts paid 1000 francs, and other engravings after Gerrit Dou, Rubens, Roybet, Antoine Vechte, Luc Olivier Merson. He also made interesting original etchings, most notably: *The Treasure of Saint John* or *The Frieze of Savages* and *View of the Gate of the Tour St. Jacques in Dieppe*. He is also known for a considerable number of drawings (over 6000), portraits, oil landscapes, watercolours, and some very remarkable works in *pyrogravure* (an engraving technique sometimes known as poker-work). Hotin died suddenly of an embolism, in the very midst of executing prints of his *Democritus*.

HOTTENIER, Adrien Joseph
French, 19th century.
Died 1908.
Painter.

Hottenier was a member of the Société des Artistes Français.

HOTTENROTH, Edmond
German, 19th century.
Born 9 October 1804, in Blasewitz (Saxony); died 12 April 1889, in Rome.
Painter. Landscapes, architectural views.

He settled in Rome in 1830.

AUCTION RECORDS:
LONDON, 10 Feb 1995, *The Colosseum from the Palatine* (1856, oil on canvas, 23¼ x 31 ins / 59 x 79 cm) GBP 6,325.

HOTTENROTH, Ernst
German, 20th century.
Born 1872, in Frankfurt am Main; died 27 February 1908.
Painter, decorative designer. Stage sets, wall decorations.

Ernst Hottenroth worked a great deal in Berlin, and also at the castle in Primkenau (now Przemków, Poland) and at the central theatre in Dresden.

HOTTENROTH, Friedrich
German, 19th century.
Born 6 February 1840, in Johannesberg.
Lithographer.

He worked in Frankfurt (Main).

HOTTENROTH, Joseph
German, 19th century.
Active in Frankfurt.
Sculptor.

He was the father of Ernst Hottenroth.

HOTTENROTH, Woldemar
German, 19th century.
Born 20 August 1802, in Blasewitz, near Dresden; died 6 September 1894, in Wachwitz, near Dresden.
Painter. History painting, portraits, genre scenes.

He was a pupil of Hartmann at the academy in Dresden. He won a travel bursary to Rome, where he remained for 14 years.

HOTTIN, Charles, the Elder
French, 17th century.
Born c. 1658, in Laon (Aisne); died 1 July 1701, in Laon.
Sculptor.

In 1683 Charles Hottin the Elder took on the execution of a retable for the church at Remies (Aisne)

HOTTIN, Charles, the Younger
French, 18th century.

Born 1687.
Active in Laon.
Sculptor.

Charles Hottin the Younger was the son of Charles Hottin the Elder.

HOTTIN, Claude
French, 17th century.
Active in Laon.
Sculptor.

Claude Hottin was the father of Charles Hottin the Elder.

HOTTINGER, Johann Konrad
Austrian, of Swiss origin, 19th century.
Born 1788, in Vienna; died 1828, in Lenzburg, Switzerland.
Painter.

He was a pupil of Overbeck in Rome, and one of the first members of the Brotherhood of St Luke. He worked mostly in Vienna, then Munich.

HOTTOT, Louis
French, 19th century.
Born 1834; died 1905, in Neuilly-sur-Seine.
Sculptor.

Hottot was a member of the Société des Artistes Français.

AUCTION RECORDS:

NEW YORK, 21 Sept 1981, *Slave* (polychrome bronze, h. 57 ins / 145 cm) USD 2,600. ENGHIEN-LES-BAINS, 16 Oct 1983, *Young Oriental Playing the Harp* (bronze and white marble, h. 18 ins / 46 cm) FRF 45,000. LONDON, 20 June 1985, *Young Woman Lying down* (bronze, h. 17 ins / 43 cm) GBP 1,650. PARIS, 24 April 1988, *Oriental Harp Player* (babbitt metal in brown and gold patina, h. 29 1/2 ins / 75 cm) FRF 23,000. PARIS, 8 Dec 1989, *Odalisque Reclining* (polychrome babbitt metal and brown patina, h. 17 ins / 43 cm l. 31 ins/79 cm) FRF 35,000. PARIS, 22 March 1994, *Water Carrier* (bronze, h. 26 3/4 ins / 68 cm, diam. 10 1/4 ins/26 cm) FRF 38,000. PARIS, 23 April 1996, *Oriental Couple* (pair of polychrome plates in babbitt metal, 33 1/2 x 17 ins / 85 x 43 cm) FRF 29,000. PARIS, 10-11 April 1997, *Soufraghi Wearing Earrings* (babbitt metal, proof, h. 39 1/4 ins / 100 cm) FRF 15,500. PARIS, 26 March 1998, *Young Oriental Woman with a Harp* (polychrome bronze, h. 23 1/2 ins / 60 cm) FRF 33,000. MUNICH, 24 Nov 1999, *Young Woman in Morning Dress in Chair* (sculpture, white metal, bronzed, h. 26 ins / 66 cm) DEM 3,500. PARIS, 18 June 2001, *Two Neapolitans Carrying Baskets* (sculpture, polychrome paint, a pair, h. 41 ins / 105 cm) FRF 200,000. NEW YORK, 2 Nov 2001, *Orientalist Vases* (sculpture, metal polychrome, h. 46 ins / 118 cm) USD 20,000. BILLINGSHURST, 21 May 2002, *Girl on the Moon* (sculpture, zinc rectangular base, stone pedestal) GBP 27,000. LONDON, 28 Oct 2002, *Figural Clock Group with Arab Woman* (sculpture, spelter, h. 43 ins / 108 cm) GBP 3,000. PARIS, 16 June 2003, *Couple of Orientals Holding a Plate* (sculpture, polychrome, rectangular socle, a pair, h. 42 ins / 107 cm) EUR 20,000. LUCERNE, 15 Nov 2003, *Young Oriental Woman Holding Playing Cards* (sculpture, patinated bronze/ivory, h. 26 ins / 67 cm) CHF 2,500. CEDAR FALLS, 12 March 2004, *An Arab Card Receiver* (sculpture, zinc patinated/polychrome, h. 43 ins / 109 cm) USD 2,300. PARIS, 1 April 2004, *Oriental Woman Spinning* (sculpture, colour patinated alloy, h. 20 ins / 51 cm) EUR 1,800.

HOTVEDT, Clarence Arnold
American, 20th century.
Born 16 April 1900, in Wisconsin; died 1991, in Wichita (Kansas).
Painter.

Clarence Arnold Hotvedt studied at the University of Minnesota and the Art Institute of Chicago, becoming a member of the latter. Most of his career was spent in Wichita, where he was a charter member of the Prairie Print Makers. His drypoint works include *Three Score Years and Ten* and *Old & Tired*.

HOU, Axel
Danish, 19th century.
Born 13 July 1860, in Copenhagen; died 1948.
Painter, engraver. Religious subjects, mythological subjects, portraits, genre scenes.

Axel Hou is known for his paintings inspired by mythological and Biblical subjects, such as those of *Susanna Bathing* and *Moses Rescued from the Water*.

AUCTION RECORDS:

LONDON, 9 May 1979, *The Outskirts of a City* (1903, oil on canvas, 17 1/4 x 22 1/4 ins / 44 x 56.5 cm) GBP 480. LONDON, 23 March 1988, *Young Girl at a Piano* (oil on canvas, 26 3/4 x 34 ins / 68 x 86.5 cm) GBP 9,350. LONDON, 17 May 1991, *The Artist's Musical Salon* (1939, oil on canvas, 28 1/4 x 34 1/4 ins / 72 x 87 cm) GBP 9,900.

HOU, followed by a second name. See **HU** followed by the name

HOU CHE-K'OUEN. See **HU SHIKUN**

HOU CHIN-LANG, or Jinlang
Chinese, 20th century.
Born 1937, in Jiayi, Taiwan.
Painter. Figures.

Hou Chin-lang trained at the National Taiwan Normal University from which he graduated in 1963 and where he later joined the faculty. In 1967 he was awarded a scholarship to enable him to continue his studies in France, where he worked for the Musée Guimet. He returned to Taiwan in 1984 and held his first solo exhibition in 1989.

AUCTION RECORDS:

TAIPEI, 10 April 1994, *Family* (1992, oil on canvas, 39 3/4 x 30 ins / 101 x 76 cm) TWD 218,500.

HOU CHOUEN-TCH'EN. See **HU SHUNCHEN**

HOU K'AO. See **HU KAO**

HOU KAO. See **HU GAO**

HOU KOUEI. See **HU GUI**

HOU MEI, or Heou Mei, nickname: Laiying, pseudonym: Chuhua Buyi
Chinese, 18th century.
Born in Luxian (Jiangsu).
Active c. 1770.
Painter.

Hou Mei was a landscape and figure artist who is known for the single signed and dated work entitled *Listening to a Stream from a Pavilion*.

HOU MOUGONG, or Heou Meou-kong, Hou Moukung, nickname: Yanshang, pseudonym: Yimen
Chinese, 16th century.
Born in Suzhou (Jiangsu); died c. 1604.
Active late 16th century.
Painter.

Hou Mougong was a landscape painter and pupil of Wen Zhengming (1470-1559). A number of scrolls by him, signed and sometimes dated, are in private collections.

MUSEUMS AND GALLERIES:

TAIPEI (National Palace Mus.): *Mountain Landscape* (after a Yuan master, signed, colophon by Dong Qichang); *Mountain Path following a River Bed* (in Yuan style).

HOU SI-KOUEI. See **HU XIGUI**

HOU SIBING, or Heou Sseu-ping, Hou Ssu-ping, nickname: Sizong, pseudonym: Yucun Xiaoyin
Chinese, 17th century.
Born in Luoqing (Zhejiang).

Active c. 1664.
Painter.
Hou Sibing is known for a *Mountain Landscape under Snow*, signed and dated 1664.

HOU SSU-PING. See **HOU SIBING**

HOU T'ING-HOUEI. See **HU TINGHUI**

HOU T'ING-LOU. See **HU TINGLU**

HOU TCHANG. See **HU ZHANG**

HOU TCHE-FOU. See **HU ZHIFU**

HOU TCHEN-K'AI. See **HU ZHENKAI**

HOU TCHENG-YEN. See **HU ZHENGYAN**

HOU TS'AO. See **HU CAO**

HOU TSING. See **HU JING**

HOU TSONG-JEN. See **HU ZONGREN**

HOU TSONG-SIN. See **HU ZONGXIN**

HOUANG TSIUAN. See **HUANG JUAN**

HOUASSE, François, called Houasse le neveu
French, 17th century.
Active in Paris.
Painter.
François Houasse, son of Nicolas Houasse, won prizes from the Académie de Paris from 1691 to 1696.

HOUASSE, Michel-Ange
French, 18th century.
Born 1680, in Paris; died 30 September 1730, in Arpajon (Essonne).
Active also in Spain.
Painter. History painting, mythological subjects, portraits, genre scenes.
Michel-Ange Houasse studied under his father René Antoine Houasse. He was admitted into the Académie des Beaux-Arts in Paris on 24 September 1707 on presentation of *Hercules Throwing Lichas into the Sea*. He spent time in Spain when he took over from his father as first painter to King Philippe V in 1715. He was exceedingly well received in Spain, possibly with regrettable consequences; the decadence of the Spanish School has been associated with a dilution of Spanish character instigated by French painters. Visiting France in 1730 with the king's permission, he fell ill on the return journey and died in Arpajon - not in Spain as some biographers assert.

He painted portraits, historical paintings and rustic themes in an easy, graceful hand. In his most ambitious compositions, such as *Bacchanalia* (1719) and *Sacrifice to Bacchus* (1720), he somewhat painstakingly emulated Poussin. His elegance shines through in the portraits attributed to him and in *The Holy Family with St John* (1726). Houasse has also painted landscapes from the area around Madrid, such as his *View of the Royal Monastery of San Lorenzo del Escorial*. He took a keen interest in his adopted country's popular traditions, people and pursuits. In this regard he foreshadowed Goya whose *St Francis Borgia* may well have been inspired by the *Life of St John Francis Regis* which Houasse painted for the Jesuits' noviciate in Madrid. This would be a testament indeed to the 'pernicious influence' he may have had on the Spanish School.

MUSEUMS AND GALLERIES:
MADRID (Prado): *Holy Family with St John; Portrait of the Infante Philippe, Duke of Parma; Portrait of a Young Infanta; Bacchanalia; Sacrifice in Honour of Bacchus; View of the Royal Monastery of San Lorenzo del Escorial* - TOURS: *Hercules Throwing Lichas into the Sea.*

AUCTION RECORDS:
PARIS, 29 Oct 1980, *Portrait of the Marchioness of Villeneuve Bargemont* (oil on canvas, oval, 27 1/4 x 22 ins / 69 x 56 cm) FRF 13,000. LONDON, 29 May 1992, *Young Bacchus with a Child Satyr* (oil on canvas, 39 1/4 x 32 ins / 100 x 81 cm) GBP 19,800. LONDON, 5 July 1993, *Four Decorative Panels Showing Children's Games* (oil on canvas, each 36 1/2 x 14 1/2 ins / 93 x 37 cm) GBP 9,200. NEW YORK, 5 Oct 1995, *Street Scene Showing a Woman Leaning over a Bridge Parapet; Gardener Raking over the Gravel by a Fountain in the Park of a Palalce* (oil on canvas, a pair, each 14 1/2 x 36 3/4 ins / 36.8 x 93.3 cm) USD 8,050. LONDON, 6 July 1999, *St Joseph Seated, Looking to Right, his Hands Clasped* (chalk/wash, 11 x 7 ins / 29 x 19 cm) GBP 4,200.

HOUASSE, Nicolas
French, 17th century.
Painter.
Nicolas Houasse was the brother of René Antoine Houasse.

HOUASSE, René Antoine
French, 17th - 18th century.
Born c. 1645, in Paris; died 27 May 1710, in Paris.
Active also in Spain.
Painter. History painting, religious subjects, mythological subjects, portraits, landscapes, landscapes with figures. Murals, designs for tapestries.
René Antoine Houasse studied under Charles Le Brun and faithfully followed in his master's footsteps. He was admitted into the Académie in 1673 and showed at the Paris Salon of that year. According to Papillon de la Ferté, he was called to Spain by King Charles II and returned in 1692. However, Bermudez states that he was in the retinue accompanying Philip V (grandson of Louis XIV and hitherto the duke of Anjou) to Madrid where he handed over his position as painter to the king to his son Michel-Ange Houasse in 1701. It can be established that René Antoine Houasse was director of the Académie Royale in Paris in 1701, hence his presence in that city. In 1704 he was appointed director of the Académie de France in Rome.

He worked with Le Brun at the Tuileries Palace and more importantly in Versailles, where he was responsible for the ceilings in the Venus Room and the *Salon de l'Abondance* where he depicted *Regal Splendour* and an *Allegory of the Progress of the Fine Arts*. In the Mars Room he illustrated *Earthly Powers in the Clutch of Terror, Fear, Fury and Dread*. In the Grand Trianon he painted several mythological canvases including *Minerva's Story*. In 1675 he produced *St Stephen Taken to Be Executed*, which was that year's painting offered by the guild of goldsmiths to the chapter of Notre-Dame. He had also undertaken major works in Madrid where, according to Bailly's inventory and contrary to prevailing usage, he also painted landscapes. His son was to continue the practice with views of the Madrid countryside.

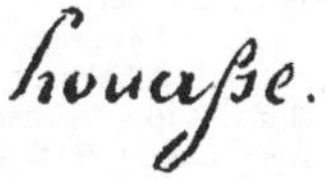

MUSEUMS AND GALLERIES:
ARRAS: *Equestrian Portrait of Louis XIV* - MADRID (Prado): *Portrait of a Young Woman* - NARBONNE: *Diana and Endymion* - ORLÉANS: *A Tomb Desecrated by a Soldier* - PARIS (Louvre): *St Stephen Taken to Be Executed; Portico with an Orange Tree; Vulcan and Minerva Attended by Flora and Pomona* (cartoon for a carpet) - RHEIMS: *Christ on the Cross* - VERSAILLES (Château): *Diana, Mars and Abundance* (ceiling paintings for the halls); four supra portas (overdoor decora-

tion) in the Council Chamber - VERSAILLES (Mus. Lambinet): *Minerva Back from War, Watering her Horses in the Ocean; Minerva and Perseus; Minerva and Tiresias; Minerva and Arachne; Narcissus.*

HOUAT, André
French, 18th century.
Active in Lyons in 1726 and 1727.
Engraver (burin).
André Houat engraved among others a *Devotional Image* signed *Houat fecit Lugduni 1726* (*Done by Houat in Lyons 1726*) and an *Ancient Urn Found in Lyons in 1727* signed *Sculpted by Houat.*

HOUAT, Claude
French, 18th century.
Active in Nancy in 1708.
Engraver. Portraits.

HOUAT, François
French, 17th century.
Active in Paris.
Engraver.

HOUAT, Jean Charles
French, 18th century.
Born 1683.
Active in Paris.
Engraver.

HOUBAR, Michael
Flemish School, 17th century.
Born in Liège.
Painter.

HOUBEN, Charles
Belgian, 20th century.
Born 19 February 1871, in Verviers; died 1931.
Painter. Landscapes.
Charles Houben was a student of Alfred Bastien and of the sculptor J. Lambeaux in Brussels. He travelled in France and Algeria.

AUCTION RECORDS:
PARIS, 12 May 1928, *In Front of the Farm,* FRF 350. LOKEREN, 8 Oct 1988, *By the Sea* (oil on canvas/panel, 18½ x 23 ins / 47 x 57.5 cm) BEF 33,000.

HOUBEN, Henri
Belgian, 19th - 20th century.
Born 1858; died 1931.
Painter. Figures, portraits, genre scenes, landscapes.
Houben was a student at the Koninklijke Academie voor Schone Kunsten in Antwerp and subsequently became a professor there. His work was shown at the Antwerp exhibition in 1910.

AUCTION RECORDS:
NEW YORK, 23-24 April 1903, *Dutch Serving Women,* USD 220. NEW YORK, 18-20 April 1906, *Shepherd and his Flock,* USD 250. LOKEREN, 5 Nov 1977, *Shepherd in a Landscape* (oil on canvas, 43¼ x 63 ins / 110 x 160 cm) BEF 70,000. NEW YORK, 30 May 1980, *Return of the Flock* (oil on panel, 17½ x 21¼ ins / 44.5 x 54 cm) USD 1,500. ANTWERP, 27 May 1986, *Shepherd in the Wood* (oil on canvas, 39¼ x 59 ins / 100 x 150 cm) BEF 115,000. PARIS, 30 March 1992, *Rosy-cheeked Flemings* (oil on canvas, 15 x 17¾ ins / 38 x 45 cm) FRF 5,000. LOKEREN, 10 Oct 1992, *Hunting Scene* (oil on canvas, 42 x 65¾ ins / 106.5 x 167 cm) BEF 70,000. LOKEREN, 28 May 1994, *Ferry Arriving at the Landing Stage* (oil on canvas, 36 x 55½ ins / 90.5 x 141 cm) BEF 500,000. LOKEREN, 10 Dec 1994, *Meadow Idyll* (oil on canvas, 31½ x 42¼ ins / 80 x 107 cm) BEF 280,000. LOKEREN, 20 May 1995, *View of a Flower Market in a Town* (oil on canvas, 27¾ x 21¾ ins / 70.5 x 55.5 cm) BEF 160,000. AMSTERDAM, 19-20 Feb 1997, *Flower Market along a Canal in Antwerp* (oil on canvas, 27¾ x 21¾ ins / 70.5 x 55.5 cm) NLG 5,189. LOKEREN, 8 March 1997, *By the Pump* (oil on canvas, 30¾ x 37¾ ins / 78 x 96 cm) BEF 275,000.

HOUBIGANT, Gustave Armand
French, 19th century.
Born 1789, in Paris; died 1862, in Paris.
Engraver.
Houbigant is known for a series of engravings on the subject of *Russian Dress.*

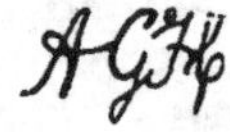

HOUBION, Sadi
Belgian, 20th century.
Died 1968.
Painter.

HOUBOLT, Eduard
Dutch, 20th century.
Born 9 August 1885, in Delft; died 1954.
Painter. Landscapes, harbour scenes.
Houbolt's works include a *View of Amsterdam.*

AUCTION RECORDS:
AMSTERDAM, 25 April 1990, *Sailing Vessels in a Port* (oil on panel, 22½ x 30¼ ins / 57 x 77 cm) NLG 3,450.

HOUBRAKEN, Anthonyna
Dutch, 17th - 18th century.
Baptised 30 May 1686 in Dordrecht; died 12 December 1736, in Amsterdam.
Draughtswoman.
Anthonyna Houbraken was the sister of Arnold Houbraken.

HOUBRAKEN, Arnold
Dutch, 17th - 18th century.
Born 28 March 1660, in Dordrecht; died 14 October 1719, in Amsterdam.
Painter, engraver, draughtsman. Historical subjects, religious subjects, portraits, genre scenes.
In 1672, Arnold Houbraken was a pupil of Willem Drillenburg and later of Jacob de Vecq and Samuel van Hoogstraesten. His drawings are more highly regarded than his paintings. As an engraver, he mainly produced etchings of genre pieces and religious subjects, but his most interesting contribution was as a writer on art. He wrote a book on Dutch, Flemish and German painting which, although somewhat incomplete today, was quite remarkable for the period.

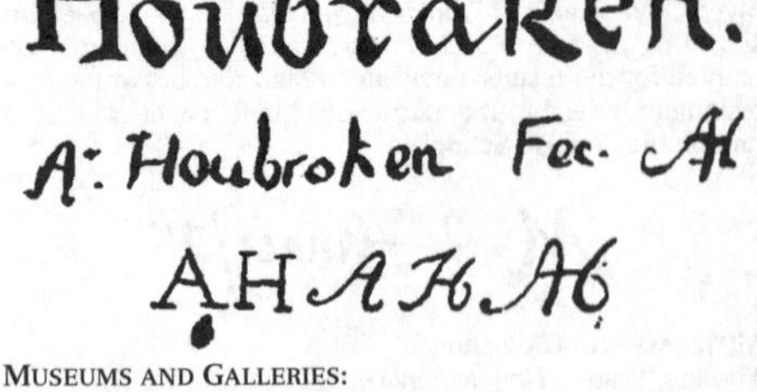

MUSEUMS AND GALLERIES:
ARRAS: *The Smoker* - FRANKFURT AM MAIN: *Portrait of Rudoph von Loen.*

AUCTION RECORDS:
PARIS, 27 March 1893, *Artemisia at the Tomb of Mausolus,* FRF 130. PARIS, 20 March 1901, *Studio Scene,* FRF 210. LONDON, May 1924, *Suzanna and the Elders,* GBP 4. LONDON, 12 May 1937, *Portrait of a Woman,* FRF 1,100. LONDON, 20 Oct 1972, *Young Girl Writing at a Window; Two Children with a Dog at a Window* (two pendants) Gns 2,200. NEW YORK, 9 Jan 1980, *Allegory of the Arts and Sciences* (oil on canvas, 23 1/2 x 19 1/2in/60 x 49.5cm) USD 2,800. MUNICH, 29 May 1980, *The Invalid* (red chalk, 11 x 8 3/4in/28 x 22.5cm) DEM 1,800. LONDON, 15 June 1984, *Young Girl at a Window* (oil on panel, 11 x 9in/28 x 22.8cm) GBP 2,200. LONDON, 31 March 1989, *The Sacrifice of Iphigenia* (oil/copper, 19 x 23 1/2in/48.2 x 60cm) GBP 5,500. AMSTERDAM, 28 Nov 1989, *Anthony and Cleopatra* (oil on canvas, 54 1/2 x 50 1/4in/138.5 x 127.5cm) NLG 27,600. NEW YORK, 11 April 1991, *Portrait of a Gentleman against a Extensive Landscape* (1686, oil on canvas, 45 1/2 x 36 1/4in/115.5 x 92cm) USD 4,950. AMSTERDAM, 12 May 1992, *Portrait of a Gentleman* (oil on canvas, 16 1/4 x 12 1/2in/41 x 32cm) NLG 2,070. LONDON, 3 July 1996, *Agamemnon Sacrificing Iphigeneia* (oil on canvas, 25 x 31 1/4in/63.4 x 79.5cm) GBP 16,100. AMSTERDAM, 9 March 1999, *Eternity and Wisdom by a Fire* (oil on canvas, 66 x 46 ins / 168 x 118 cm) NLG 9,500. PARIS, 15 March 1999, *Vertumnus and Pomona* (oil on panel, 35 x 25 ins / 88 x 63 cm) FRF 21,000. LONDON, 21 Feb 2002, *Portrait of a Young Man Leaning on a Stone Plinth* (oil on panel, 19 x 15 ins / 48 x 39 cm) GBP 1,800.

HOUBRAKEN, Ettore van
Flemish School, 17th century.
Active in Messina.
Painter.

Ettore van Houbraken was the son of Giovanni van Houbraken.

HOUBRAKEN, Giovanni van
Flemish School, 17th century.
Active in Messina.
Painter.

Giovanni van Houbraken was born in Flanders. He studied under Rubens and imitated his style.

HOUBRAKEN, Jacobus
Dutch, 18th century.
Born 25 December 1698, in Dordrecht; died 14 November 1780, in Amsterdam.
Draughtsman, engraver (burin).

Jacobus Houbraken was the son of Arnold Houbraken. He engraved religious subjects, portraits, historical subjects and genre pieces.

MUSEUMS AND GALLERIES:
EDINBURGH (Nat. Gal. of Scotland, Print Room): *Dr Andries Bicker, Burgomaster of Amsterdam* (engraving, after Bartolomeus van der Helst).

AUCTION RECORDS:
PARIS, 11 April 1924, *Portrait of a Young Man Seated Holding a Book* (wash) FRF 290; *Portrait of a Young Woman Seated* (wash) FRF 320.

HOUBRAKEN, Niccola, Niccolo or Niccolino van, or Vanhoubracken, Vanderbrach, Van Bubrachen, Wan-oubru-Ken, Valdubrochen, also called Niccola Messinese
Italian, 17th - 18th century.
Born c. 1660, in Messina; died 1723.
Painter. Portraits, still-lifes, flowers.

Noccola Houbraken was the son of Ettore. He was born in Sicily to a family of Flemish painters who settled in Livorno in 1674. He notably worked in Livorno and Florence. His paintings were known and bought in many different towns and cities in Italy. There is very little informaton on his life, but in the archives of the era it is possible to find evidence of his participation at exhibitions held in the cloister of the Holy Annunciation in Florence in 1706 and 1729.

BIBLIOGRAPHY:
Spike, John T., *Italian Still-life Paintings from Three Centuries,* Centro Di, Firenze, National Academy of Design, Old Masters Exhibitions Society, New York, 1983.

MUSEUMS AND GALLERIES:
FLORENCE (Uffizi): *Portrait of Francesco Riviere.*

AUCTION RECORDS:
ROME, 1 June 1982, *Still-life of Fruit and Monkey* (oil on canvas, 24 3/4 x 36 1/2 ins / 63 x 93 cm) ITL 5,000,000. PARIS, 17 March 1987, *Garlands and Flowers Surrounding Medallions* (oil on canvas, a pair, 40 1/4 x 29 1/4 ins / 102 x 74 cm) FRF 40,000. LONDON, 5 July 1989, *Still-life of Wild Plants and Mushrooms with Broken Earthenware Pots* (oil on canvas, 36 3/4 x 49 1/2 ins / 93.5 x 126 cm) GBP 14,300. NEW YORK, 31 May 1991, *Still-life with Fennel, Sausage, Onions and a Bottle of Wine; Fennel, Piece of Meat and White Wine* (oil on canvas, a pair, 18 1/2 x 25 ins / 47 x 63.2 cm) USD 49,500. ROME, 26 Nov 1992, *Undergrowth with Viper and Skull of Animal* (oil on canvas, 38 1/2 x 28 1/4 ins / 98 x 72 cm) ITL 36,000,000. AMSTERDAM, 17 Nov 1993, *Still-life with Mushrooms and Poppies at the Foot of a Bush* (oil on canvas, 26 3/4 x 34 1/4 ins / 68 x 87 cm) NLG 21,850. ROME, 10 May 1994, *Undergrowth* (oil on canvas, 38 1/2 x 28 1/4 ins / 98 x 72 cm) ITL 34,500,000. PARIS, 21 Dec 1994, *Study of Leaves and Flowers* (oil on canvas, 19 3/4 x 25 1/2 ins / 50 x 65 cm) FRF 48,000.

HOUBRON, Frédéric Anatole
French, 19th century.
Born c. 1851, in Paris; died October 1908, in Paris.
Painter (gouache), watercolourist, draughtsman.
History painting, genre scenes, landscapes, urban landscapes, architectural views.

Houbron began exhibiting in 1877, first at the Paris Salon, and then at the Salon des Artistes Français, where he won a bronze medal in 1900, at the Exposition Universelle.

Houbron produced a great many views of Paris, in oils, watercolours and chalk. He also created designs for fans in gouache.

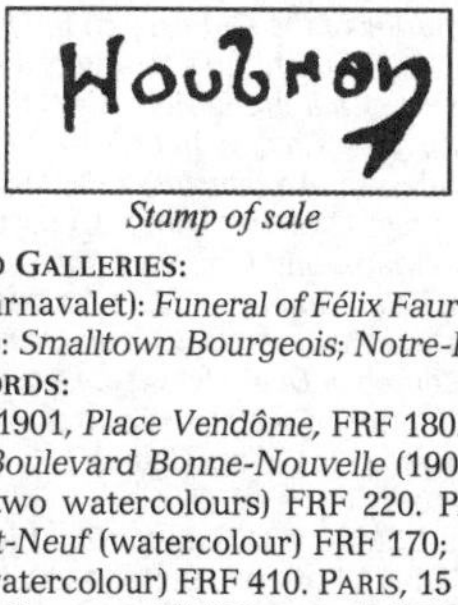

Stamp of sale

MUSEUMS AND GALLERIES:
PARIS (Mus. Carnavalet): *Funeral of Félix Faure* - PARIS (Mus. du Petit Palais): *Smalltown Bourgeois; Notre-Dame.*

AUCTION RECORDS:
PARIS, 8 April 1901, *Place Vendôme,* FRF 180. PARIS, 14 and 15 Dec 1925, *Boulevard Bonne-Nouvelle* (1902; *The Apse in Notre Dame* (two watercolours) FRF 220. PARIS, 9 March 1939, *The Pont-Neuf* (watercolour) FRF 170; *The Church of St-Eustache* (watercolour) FRF 410. PARIS, 15 Dec 1941, *Paris, the Pont du Carroussel* (1903, gouache) FRF 9,000. PARIS, 3 Feb 1944, *Place de la République,* FRF 3,500; *Place de la Bourse* (1907) FRF 5,200. NEW YORK, 21 Nov 1980, *Place de la Concorde* (1908, watercolour, gouache and pencil, 7 3/4 x 13 1/4 ins / 20 x 33.7 cm) USD 1,300. PARIS, 28 Sept 1984, *Boulevard Poissonnière* (watercolour, 12x18 ins / 31x44 cm) FRF 28,000. NEW YORK, 24 May 1985, *Paris, Place de la Concorde* (1908, watercolour and gouache/pencil outlines, 7 3/4 x 13 ins / 19.6 x 33.3 cm) USD 1,300. ST-DIÉ, 15 Oct 1989, *Entertainment in the Place de la Concorde* (1904, wax painting/panel, 14 1/4 x 24 3/4 ins / 36 x 63 cm) FRF 26,500. CALAIS, 14 March 1993, *London: Bridge over the Thames and St Paul's Cathedral* (1904, oil on panel, 14 1/4 x 27 1/2 ins / 36 x 70 cm) FRF 8,000. PARIS, 26 Feb 1998, *Firework Display on the Viaduct at*

Auteuil (1896, oil/paper, 15 1/4 x 22 3/4 ins / 39 x 58 cm) FRF 4,000. CALAIS, 14 March 1999, *Paris, Place de la Bourse with Figures* (1907, gouache/watercolour, 14 x 17 ins / 36 x 44 cm) FRF 39,000. LONDON, 16 Sept 1999, *Paris Street Scene* (1904, watercolour/bodycolour over pencil/canvas, 17 x 24 ins / 44 x 60 cm) GBP 3,200. BRUSSELS, 13 May 2003, *View of the Seine from Conflans-Sainte-Honorine* (1900, panel, mixed media, 7 x 13 ins / 19 x 33 cm) EUR 2,000.

HOUCH, Roger
French, 20th century.
Born in Alfortville.
Painter.

A pupil of E. Delbos, Roger Houch, he exhibited at the Salon des Artistes Français from 1925, and at the Salon des Artistes Indépendants.

HOUCK, Peter
Dutch, 17th century.
Active c. 1606.
Draughtsman.

AUCTION RECORDS:
AMSTERDAM, 15 Nov 1983, *Wooded Landscape with Pond* (pen and wash heightened with white/traces of black chalk, 5 3/4 x 7 1/2in/14.7 x 19.3cm) NLG 7,600.

HOUCKGEEST, Gerard or Gerrit, or Hoecgest or Hoeckgeest
Dutch, 17th century.
Born c. 1600, in The Hague; died 1661, in Bergen op Zoom.
Painter, engraver. Architectural views, church interiors. Delft School.

Gerard Houckgeest was the nephew of Joachim Houckgeest. In 1625, he was a member of the guild of The Hague and, in 1639, of the Delft guild. He mainly painted church interiors.

MUSEUMS AND GALLERIES:
AMSTERDAM: *Interior of the Old Church in Delft* - ANTWERP: *Interior of the New Church in Delft; Interior of a Protestant Church* - BRUSSELS: *Church Interior* - COPENHAGEN (Statens Mus. for Kunst): *Two Church Interiors* - EDINBURGH (Nat. Gal. of Scotland): *An Architectural Fantasy with Figures* (1638, oil on canvas) - LONDON (Royal Collection): *Charles I, Queen Henrietta Maria, and Charles, Prince of Wales, Dining in Public* (1635); *Palace Interior* - ST PETERSBURG: *Church Interior* (two works) - STOCKHOLM: *Mausoleum of William of Orange in the Church in Delft* - STRASBOURG: *Church Interior* - THE HAGUE: *Interior of the New Church in Delft; Tomb of William I of Orange in the Same Church.*

AUCTION RECORDS:
LONDON, 11 and 12 May 1911, *Interior of a Church with Gentlemen* (1656) GBP 31. LONDON, 12 Dec 1930, *Church Interior,* GBP 162. PARIS, 2 March 1942, *Church Interior,* FRF 53,000. LONDON, 13 Feb 1946, *New Church in Delft,* GBP 52. LONDON, 8 July 1977, *The Tomb of the Prince of Orange in the New Church in Delft* (1650, oil on panel, 20 x 16 1/2in/51 x 42cm) USD 5,000. LONDON, 28 March 1979, *Royal Tomb in the New Church in Delft* (oil on panel, rounded at the top, 23 1/2 x 16 1/4in/60 x 41cm) GBP 5,500. PARIS, 12 Dec 1995, *Interior of a Renaissance Church* (oil on panel, 16 1/4 x 12 1/2in/41 x 32cm) FRF 115,000. PARIS, 13 June 1997, *View of an Imaginary Town beside a River* (oak panel, two panels, 25 1/2 x 27 1/4in/65 x 69cm) FRF 580,000. AMSTERDAM, 11 Nov 1997, *Meeting of the Hunt in a Loggia of a Renaissance Palace, a Fountain with a Sculpture of Mercury in the Centre, a Pleasure Garden and a Palace in the Distance* (oil on panel, 21 1/2 x 30in/54.6 x 75.3cm) NLG 34,596. LONDON, 2 Nov 2001, *Interior of a Church Looking East, with Elegant Company in the Foreground* (oil on panel, 33 x 43 ins / 83 x 108 cm) GBP 15,000. CHICAGO, 19 Oct 2003, *Interior of the Old Church, Amsterdam* (oil on canvas, 21 x 25 ins / 53 x 64 cm) USD 2,200.

HOUCKGEEST, Joachim Ottensz van, or Hoecksgeest
Dutch, 17th century.
Born c. 1580; died c. 1644.
Active in The Hague.
Painter. Religious subjects, portraits.

In 1610, Joachim van Houckgeest was a member of the guild of The Hague; he was elected senior member in 1628 and 1632.

MUSEUMS AND GALLERIES:
ÉPINAL: *The Blessing* - ST PETERSBURG (Hermitage): *Christ and the Sick Woman* - THE HAGUE: *Flag Bearer.*

AUCTION RECORDS:
LONDON, 20 April 1928, *The Circumcision,* GBP 126.

HOUDAILLE, Marie Alix
French, 20th century.
Born 24 February 1888, in Versailles.
Painter.

A pupil of Henri Royer, Marie Alix Houdaille exhibited at the Salon des Artistes Français.

HOUDAILLE, Marin
French, 17th century.
Active in Paris from 1607.
Painter, sculptor.

HOUDAIN, André d'
French, 19th century.
Born 1860, in Cambrai; died 15 February 1904, in Paris.
Sculptor.

A pupil of Cavelier, André d'Houdain made his début at the Paris Salon in 1881. He was also a Chevalier of the Légion d'Honneur. The former Museum of Luxembourg once possessed several marble sculptures by this artist.

HOUDAN, Jean
French, 18th century.
Active in Paris c. 1775.
Engraver.

HOUDARD, Charles
French, 20th century.
Painter, engraver. Landscapes.

Charles Houdard's first exhibition was held in Paris in 1905 at the Galerie Georges Petit. He made coloured etching including: *The Seed - After the Downpour - The Trawlers at Grand-Camp - Summer.*

BIBLIOGRAPHY:
Dictionnaire de l'estampe en France, 1830-1950, Arts et Métiers Graphiques, Flammarion, Paris, 1985.

HOUDARD, Charles Louis M.
French, 19th century.
Born in Neuilly-sur-Seine.
Painter, engraver (etching).

Houdard studied under were J Lefebvre and Boulanger. He received an honourable mention in 1900 at the Exposition Universelle, and joined the Société des Artistes Français in 1893.

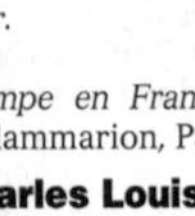

Stamp of sale

HOUDARD, Suzanne
French, 20th century.
Born in Puteaux.
Painter.
Suzanne Houdard exhibited in Paris at the Salon des Indépendants.

HOUDART, François
French, 20th century.
Born 19 August 1943, in Neuilly-sur-Seine.
Painter. Designs for mosaics.
Houdart attended the studios of sculpture and mosaics at the École des Beaux-Arts in Paris, then studied engraving in Friedlander's studio. He exhibited at the Salon des Surindépendants in Paris in 1964.

HOUDART, Marie, Mme Lacretelle
French, 19th - 20th century.
Active in Paris.
Painter.
Marie Houdart became a member of the Société des Artistes Français in 1896.

HOUDAU, J.
French, 18th century.
Active in Paris c. 1775.
Draughtsman, engraver (etching).
J. Houdau engraved a series of booklets showing vases.

HOUDÉ, Paul Alexandre
French, 19th century.
Born in the 19th century, in Paris.
Painter. Landscapes.
Houdé was a pupil of Didier and Pradelles, and made his Salon début in 1868.

HOUDEMON, Louis Pierre
French, 18th century.
Active in Sablé in 1720.
Sculptor.
Louis Pierre Houdemon, son of Louis, worked at the church of St-Cyr-de-Sargé (Loir-et-Cher)

HOUDERON, Andries von
Dutch, 17th century.
Active c. 1664.
Painter. Animals.

HOUDIAKOV, Leonid
Russian, 20th century.
Born 1915.
Painter. Portraits, landscapes, landscapes with figures, still-lifes, flowers.
Leonid Houdiakov studied at the Repin institute in Leningrad (now St Petersburg), where he later taught.

The subjects and composition of his works are very traditional, painted in a style sometimes reminiscent of Post-Impressionism.

A member of the association of painters of Leningrad, he took part in many exhibitions in Moscow and Leningrad from 1943 onwards. He featured in *50 Masterpieces from Soviet Museums*, Prague (1978) and in *Soviet Art*, Tokyo (1980). He was awarded the first prize by the ministry of Soviet culture at the exhibitions *Young Painters of Leningrad* and *The Nation's Youth* (1956 and 1958).

BIBLIOGRAPHY:
L'École de Léningrad, auction catalogue, Drouot, Paris, 19 November 1990.

MUSEUMS AND GALLERIES:
KIEV (Mus. of Russian Art) - KRASNOYARSK (MFA) - MOSCOW (Ministry of Culture) - NOVGOROD (MFA) - ST PETERSBURG (Academy) - ST PETERSBURG (Gosudarstvennyj Muz. Istorii) - STAVROPOL (Gal. of Contemporary Art) - VOLGOGRAD (Mus. of Contemporary Soviet Art).

AUCTION RECORDS:
PARIS, 11 June 1990, *Still-life with Fruit* (1957, oil on canvas, 25 1/2 x 22 ins / 65 x 55 cm) FRF 14,000. PARIS, 19 Nov 1990, *Voyage au long court* (1946, oil on canvas, 12 1/2 x 23 1/2 ins / 32 x 60 cm) FRF 7,000. PARIS, 4 March 1991, *Reverie on the Beach* (1950, oil on canvas, 22 3/4 x 31 ins / 58 x 79 cm) FRF 9,000.

HOUDIN, Robert. See **ROBERT-HOUDIN Georges**

HOUDOIN, Guy, pseudonym: Odon
French, 20th century.
Born 1 November 1940, in Le Mans.
Painter.
Guy Houdoin trained as an engraver. In 1978, he abandoned conventional pictorial technique for a more matter-oriented artform using a 'plaited' language. This involved cutting paper painted on both sides twisting the material onto itself (notably in the series, *Crossbreeding*). Until 1989, he produced polychromed low reliefs made of plaits, followed by rolled and twisted Kraft wrapping paper, spirals no longer defined or framed, but continuing indefinitely. Houdoin sees in the spiral 'the form fulfilled in each instant and unceasingly interminable'. He later devoted of his efforts to the interpretation of the human face. He lives and works in Nogent-sur-Marne.

Guy Houdoin has participated in collective exhibitions, including: *Fragments*, an exhibition of his Avant-garde work alongside Max Charvolen and Marcel Alocco, Maison des Arts, Antony (2001). His solo exhibitions were prefaced by Catherine Paysan and by Gilbert Lascaut. *Racines au ciel* (*Roots in the Sky*), a retrospective, was held at the Epau abbey in Sarthe in 2002.

BIBLIOGRAPHY:
Fragments, exhibition catalogue, Maison des Arts, Antony, 2001.

MUSEUMS AND GALLERIES:
NEW YORK (American Craft Mus.) - SÉLESTAT (FRAC Alsace).

HOUDON, Firmin Marc
French, 18th century.
Active in Paris in 1736.
Sculptor.

HOUDON, Jean Antoine
French, 18th - 19th century.
Born 20 March 1741, in Versailles; died 15 July 1828, in Paris.
Sculptor, founder. Religious subjects, figures, portraits, anatomical subjects. Busts.
Jean Antoine Houdon's father, Jacques Houdon, was successively servant to Monsieur de Lamotte, wine merchant and, more significantly, in 1743 caretaker of the Louvre École des Élèves Protégés. This last position would determine his son's future. From his earliest years, Jean Antoine Houdon hung around the studios in the company of masters and students in preference to anything else. In a memoir in his own hand, Houdon states that he was already sculpting at the age of nine, having benefited from the advice of various artists before he even set foot in the École de l'Académie. He entered Slodtz's studio at a very young age and won a third medal in 1756 for the Prix de Rome alongside Clodion. He won outright in 1761 but did not leave for Rome until 1764. Approved by the Académie in 1771, Houdon became a full member in 1777 and obtained a chair in 1778. In 1786 he married Marie-Ange Langlois with whom he had three daughters. In 1796 he was a member of the Institut, recently created to bring all the Académies under one single body, and taught at the École des Beaux-Arts from 1805. After producing several busts and statues of Napoleon, Houdon was awarded the Légion d'Honneur in 1809. He featured

regularly at the Salons from the moment he became a member of the Académie in 1777 and exhibited until 1814.

When he arrived in Rome, Houdon was thrilled with the recent discoveries in Herculaneum and Pompeii, but he was more drawn to the Renaissance masters and studied Michelangelo with particular care. Among the works undertaken by Houdon whilst in Italy, the following are best remembered: a *St Bruno* for the church of S Maria degli Angeli; a *St John the Baptist* at the church of the Carthusian Fathers in Rome; and *L'Écorché* (*The Flayed Man*) known as *Écorché de Houdon* (*Houdon's Écorché*). Houdon said that he had had two aims in his career; to master anatomy and to reclaim the craft of 16th and 17th-century bronze-casters and smelters. With *L'Écorché* he had achieved his first aim, thanks to his attendance at the dissection hall attached to San Luigi dei Francesi.

In 1768 Houdon was back in France facing numerous commissions. He was twice called to the court of Saxe-Gotha and spent two months there each time, in 1771 and 1773. In 1781 he executed his *Statue of Voltaire*. The following year he produced a bust of the famous philosopher and offered copies to his colleagues at the Académie. He worked indefatigably and, because of his popularity, earned a lot of money. Houdon would sometimes complain of losses incurred at the hands of forgers. His most famous busts, particularly that of Rousseau and his *L'Écorché*, were copied and re-cast and the copies fraudulently sold. For Monsieur de St-Waast's town house he executed *Winter* (which became known as *La Frileuse* (*The Cold Girl*)) and *Summer*.

In March 1772 he had obtained a studio on the Faubourg du Roule in buildings belonging to the city of Paris. He set up his furnaces and after many attempts cast two figures of his *Diana* and his *La Frileuse*. When this facility was withdrawn in 1787, he bought a house opposite the site he had just vacated and three weeks later he was able to continue with his sculpture and foundry work.

A close friend of Franklin and Jefferson, Houdon was chosen by the American Congress to produce a statue of Washington. He left for Philadelphia on 2 July 1785 and carried out several studies of the great American patriot. On 4 January 1786 he was back in France and set to work. His marble statue was put on display in his studio in 1792. He was paid 25,000 francs, transport costs excluded. In 1801 Houdon produced a bust of Washington. His rendering of Jefferson, whom he met when he was in Paris, survives in the Jefferson dollar and the nickel.

Apart from those already listed, Houdon lists as his principle works: a marble *Morpheus* presented for his admission at the Académie; a *Priest of the Lupercalia* and a large relief of *Our Lord Jesus Handing over the Keys to St Peter* cast in bronze, set at the pediment of the church of St-Geneviève and destroyed when it was closed down; two marble tombs for Russia; a marble bath into which a *Leaden Negro Woman Pours Water* for the Monceau Garden; a life-size *Naiad*; a marble life-size *Vestal Virgin*; *The Marshal of Tourville* in Ennery near Pontoise; *The Summer* in marble; *Ceres*; and *Philosophy* in marble, intended for the Convention's debating chamber. He is renowned for the numerous busts he sculpted of the great figures of his time, psychologically acute and technically flawless to such a degree that he has been called the 'preferred sculptor of the Enlightenment'.

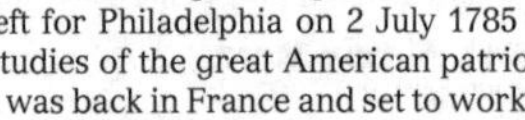

BIBLIOGRAPHY:
Giacometti, Georges, *Le Statuaire Jean-Antoine Houdon et son époque*, Jouve, Paris, 1918 (with catalogue of oeuvre). Réau, L., *Houdon, 2 vols*, Paris, 1964. Arnason, H. H., *The Sculptures of Houdon [with extensive bibliography]*, London, 1975.

MUSEUMS AND GALLERIES:
AIX: *Busts of Paesiello and the Bailli de Suffren* - ALENÇON: *Franklin; Voltaire; Rousseau* - ANGERS: *Marble Bust of Voltaire; Dumouriez; Franklin; Mirabeau* - AUCH: *Louis XVI* - BERLIN: *Head of a Woman; Bust of Prince Henry of Prussia, Brother of Frederick the Great; Bust of Voltaire; The Triumph of Mardocheus* - CAMBRAI: *Jean-Jacques Rousseau* - CHARTRES: *Colin d'Harleville* - DIEPPE: *Marie-Joseph Florent* - DIJON: *St Bruno; Buffon* - FORT WORTH (Kimbell AM): *Aymard-Jean de Nicolay, First President of the Chambre des Comptes* (1779, marble) - GENEVA (MAH): *Busts of Necker and Dr Tronchin* - GRENOBLE: *Barnave; The Marquess of Franquières* - LANGRES: *Denis Diderot* - LE MANS: *La Fayette* - LE PUY-EN-VELAY: *Diana the Huntress* - MONTPELLIER: *Winter (The Cold Girl); Voltaire; Summer; Molière; Turgot; Denis Cochin* - NANTES: *Voltaire* - NEUCHÂTEL (MAH): *Buffon; Isabelle de Charrière* (bust) - ORLÉANS: *President Haudry; Portrait of M. de Miroménil* - PARIS (Louvre): *Voltaire; Voltaire; Duquesnoy; Lavoisier; Louise Brongniart; Alexandre Brongniart; Madame Houdon; Sabine Houdon; Anne-Ange Houdon; Vestal Virgin; Model of the Tomb for a Prince Galitzine; Drawing for the Tomb; Winter; Diderot; Morpheus; Abbot Aubert; J.-J. Rousseau; Voltaire; Franklin; Buffon; Washington; Diana* - PARIS (Mus. Galliera): *War* - SEMUR-EN-AUXOIS: *Buffon; Daubenton; Voltaire* - STOCKHOLM: *The Duchess of Biron; The Countess of Egmont; The Count of Provence; The Composer Gluck* - STRASBOURG: *Marble Bust of Louis XVI* - THE HAGUE: *Admiral Pierre-André de Suffren* - TRIESTE (Civico Mus. Revoltella): *Napoleon I* - TROYES: *Diderot* - VERSAILLES: *Napoleon I; The Empress Josephine; Marshal Ney; Marie-Joseph Paul Lafayette; Intendant Trudaine; Joseph Valbelle; Louis XVI; The Sculptor Falconet; Benjamin Franklin; Molière; Tourville; Washington; General Joubert; Denis Diderot; Statue of Voltaire; Bust of Voltaire.*

AUCTION RECORDS:
PARIS, 11 June 1892, *Jean-Jacques Rousseau* (marble bust) FRF 1,000. PARIS, 13-15 May 1929, *Suffering Consoled by Justice Showing Fame to Her* (drawing) FRF 5,000. PARIS, 22-23 March 1933, *Bust of Bordas-Pardoux, Judge* (tinted plaster) FRF 10,000; *Bust of Gerbier, Lawyer* (plaster) FRF 18,500; *Bust of Napoleon I, Emperor of the French* (plaster, life-size) FRF 60,000. PARIS, 12-14 June 1933, *Bust of Dorothy Rodde* (original plaster) FRF 7,500; *Bust of Franklin* (dated 1778, terracotta, from the collection of the Grand-Duke of Saxe-Weimar) FRF 6,000; *A Bather Upstanding* (Lorraine earthenware) FRF 3,800. PARIS, 8 Feb 1934, *Portrait Presumed to be of Buffon (1707-1788)* (sculpted stone bust) FRF 12,100. PARIS, June 1936, *Bust Showing Voltaire's Portrait* (1770, terracotta) FRF 11,000. PARIS, 30 Nov-1 Dec 1936, *Voltaire Sitting* (1781, plaster, life-size statue) FRF 60,500. PARIS, 13 Feb 1941, *Bust of Louise Brongniart* (plaster) FRF 60,000. PARIS, 18 June 1963, *Bust of Jean de La Fontaine* (white marble) FRF 72,000. PARIS, 16 June 1967, *Molière* (white marble) FRF 205,000. LONDON, 28 Nov 1968, *Little Lise* (marble) GBP 8,500. PARIS, 26 Nov 1969, *Jeanne Adélaïde Olivier* (marble) FRF 98,000. PARIS, 10 June 1970, *Winter (The Cold Girl)* (terracotta) FRF 20,000. NEW YORK, 7 May 1971, *Voltaire Aged 84* (marble) USD 9,000. PARIS, 28 Nov 1972, *Bust* (white marble) FRF 140,000. PARIS, 10 June 1974, *Diana* (patinated plaster, terracotta) FRF 10,000. PARIS, 22 March 1977, *Bust of a Young Girl* (1781, white marble, h. 19 ins / 48 cm) FRF 500,000. LONDON, 23 March 1978, *Study of Benjamin Franklin's Head* (recto; *Study of a Man's Legs* (black chalk and white chalk/blue paper, verso, 12 x 9 ins / 30.2 x 23 cm) GBP 5,400. PARIS, 13 Dec 1980, *Bust of Voltaire* (white marble, h. 13 3/4 ins / 35 cm) FRF 300,000. PARIS, 1 March 1982, *Bust of the Abbot Barthélémy* (marble, h. 21 ins / 52.5 cm) FRF 128,000. PARIS, 20 March 1984, *Madame de Thelusson* (plaster, h. 27 1/2 ins / 70 cm) FRF 315,000. LONDON, 22 April 1986, *Bust of a Man Wearing a Myrtle Crown* (1775, white marble,

h. 19 ins / 48.5 cm) GBP 50,000. New York, 29 May 1987, *Bust of Thomas Jefferson* (plaster) USD 2,860,000. New York, 29 May 1987, *Thomas Jefferson* (plaster, h. 28 3/4 ins / 73 cm) USD 2,600,000. Paris, 11 March 1988, *Diana the Huntress* (tinted plaster, h. 23 1/4 ins / 59 cm) FRF 260,000. New York, 1 Dec 1989, *Bust of Robert Fulton* (original painted plaster, h. 27 ins / 68.5 cm) USD 880,000. Cologne, 28 June 1991, *Daina the Huntress* (bronze, h. 32 ins / 81 cm) DEM 1,600. Lokeren, 10 Oct 1992, *Diana* (bronze with dark green patina, h. 23 3/4 ins / 60.5 cm, w. 9 3/4 ins/25 cm) BEF 65,000. Paris, 11 June 1997, *Portrait Supposed to be of Madame Élisabeth* (1784, marble, h. 26 1/2 ins / 67 cm) FRF 445,000. Paris, 2 March 1998, *Claudine Houdon* (c. 1793, terracotta) FRF 95,000. Venice, 14 Nov 1999, *Mythological Figures* (brown patinated bronze, a pair, h. 30 ins / 75 cm) ITL 42,000,000. Paris, 12 March 2000, *Shivering Woman* (brown/green patinated bronze, 22 x 8x10 ins / 56 x 21x25 cm) FRF 14,500. Lokeren, 6 Oct 2001, *Diana* (dark/green patinated bronze marble base lit., 24 x 10 ins / 60 x 26 cm) BEF 85,000. Paris, 9 Dec 2002, *Portrait of Marie-Joseph Chenier* (terracotta, 22 x 11x9 ins / 56 x 28x23 cm) EUR 180,000. Paris, 13 Dec 2002, *Portrait of Marquis de Bire* (1785, white marble, h. 31 ins / 80 cm) EUR 630,000. Paris, 21 May 2003, *Portrait of Unknown Woman* (c.1775, plaster, 33 x 19x12 ins / 84 x 48x31 cm) EUR 6,800.

HOUE, Friedrich Heinrich von

Dutch, 17th century.
Born c. 1625, in Haarlem.
Engraver (burin).

Friedrich von Houe made engravings of historical portraits.

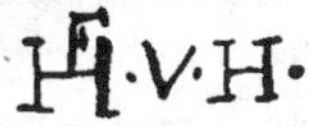

HOUEL, Charles François

French, 19th century.
Born 8 March 1819, in Paris; died July 1849, in Paris.
Painter. Portraits, architectural views.

Charles Houel entered the École des Beaux-Arts on 7 April 1838, where he was a pupil of Couder. He won a third-class medal in 1846. His portraits appeared at the Salon exhibitions from 1839 to 1849.

Museums and Galleries:
Besançon: *The Capitol in Rome.*

HOUEL, Jean Baptiste

French, 20th century.
Born in Condé-sur-Noireau.
Painter. Landscapes.

Jean Baptiste Houel exhibited in Paris at the Salon des Indépendants.

HOUEL, Jean Benjamin

French, 19th century.
Born c. 1778, in Rouen.
Painter.

Jean Houel was a relative and pupil of Jean Pierre Louis Laurent Houel. He entered the École des Beaux-Arts on 30 Vendémiaire, Year V of the Republican calendar (22 October 1805).

HOUËL, Jean Pierre Louis Laurent

French, 18th - 19th century.
Born 1735, in Rouen; died 14 November 1813, in Paris.
Painter (including gouache), watercolourist, engraver, draughtsman, illustrator. Genre scenes, portraits, landscapes with figures, scenes with figures, natural history, animals.

Jean Houël, though a minor master, deserves closer scrutiny. His subtle and witty drawing, a prerequisite to any 18th-century artistic endeavour, might explain why a number of his compositions have been ascribed to better known painters. Endowed with a sound Classical education and a fine intellect, Houël began to work in his native city with Descamp. He later went to Paris and studied under Francesco Casanova (in 1764) and Le Mire for painting, and Lebas for engraving. He was granted royal funding to continue his studies in Italy. He was approved by the Académie Royale on 29 October 1774 and featured at the 1775, 1781, 1789, 1791, 1804, 1806, and 1807 Salons. He also exhibited at the Salon de la Correspondance in 1781 and 1783, most memorably Italian landscapes.

Monographic exhibitions include *A Visit to Sicily* at the Louvre Museum, Paris (1990) and *Jean Houël: Paintings, Drawings, Etchings* for which the Rouen Musée des Beaux-Arts mustered gouaches, drawings, illustrated books and an assortment of etchings (2001).

Houël painted and drew many views of Paris and its surrounding countryside. During a second Italian tour he visited Sicily, the Aeolian Isles and Malta. On his return to Paris, the sketches he drew on this trip formed the basis for the 264 plates illustrating his *oyage pittoresque des îles de Sicile, de Malte et de Lipari* (*Picturesque Journey to the Islands of Sicily, Malta and Lipari*) which consisted of four folio volumes published from 1782 to 1787. Catherine II bought the original drawings from him. Besides some poems in longhand, Houël also produced several natural history works. He enjoyed the patronage of the duke of Choiseul and executed many works for his manor house in Chanteloup, in particular six paintings for its concert hall.

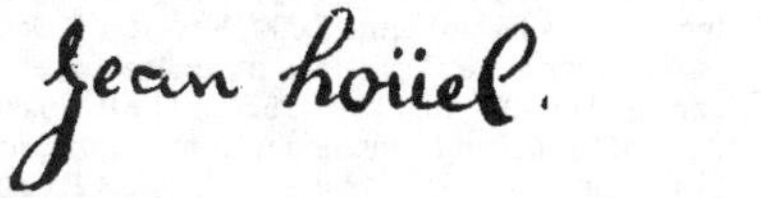

Bibliography:
Pinault, Madeleine, et al., *Houël: voyage en Sicile, 1776-1779*, Musée du Louvre, Paris, Herscher, Paris, 1990 (translation of publication: Houël: A trip to Sicily). Pinault Sørensen, Madeleine, *'Jean Hoüel (Rouen 1735-Paris 1813)'* in *Cahiers du Cabinet des dessins*, Musée des Beaux-Arts, Rouen, 2001 (a special edition accompanying the exhibition at the Musée des Beaux-Arts in Rouen).

Museums and Galleries:
Angers: *Landscape with Figures* - Paris (Louvre): *The Hermitage* (painting); *Halt of Travellers* (1774, painting); *Italian Landscape* (1774, painting) - Rouen (Bibliothèque Municipale): background sketch - Rouen (MBA): *Traditional Caux Doorway; View of the Ste-Catherine Coastline; View of the Tivoli Waterfalls; Cellar used for Storage in Dieppevalle; Gargantua's Seat; 18th-century Girl; Caumont Caves; Landscape; Two Women Wearing the Mantilla* - St Petersburg (Hermitage) - Tours: *View of the Loire River near Ambroise; View of St-Ouen, near Ambroise* (dated 1759); *View of the Seine in Paris near the Arsenal; Landscape with Shepherdess.*

Auction records:
New York, 7 Jan 1843, *Landscape with Figures,* USD 320. Paris, 1897, *Landscape with Old Building,* FRF 190; *A Wooded Hill,* FRF 130. Paris, 1899, *Country Subjects* (two pen drawings heightened with watercolour) FRF 390. Paris, 10-12 May 1900, *View of Maecenas's Villa,* FRF 260. Paris, 29 April 1920, *The Visit to Agrippa's Tomb* (red chalk) FRF 500. Paris, 21-22 Nov 1922, *View at Maecenas's Villa* (watercolour and gouache) FRF 4,000. Paris, 23 Nov 1927, *Mountain Road alongside a Torrent; Waterfall in a Gorge* (two washes) FRF 2,800. Paris, 15 Nov 1928, *Landscape Peopled with Figures* (gouache) FRF 3,700. Paris, 28 May 1931, *The Halt on the Wayside* (gouache) FRF 5,600. Paris, 8 May 1934, *Halt of Convoys* (watercolour/pen outline) FRF 980. Paris, 14 Dec 1936, *House on Stilts* (Indian ink wash heightened with white) FRF 700. Paris, 15 June 1938, *Out for a Walk in Aix-*

en-Provence (gouache) FRF 30,500. PARIS, 24 June 1942, *Landscape* (pen and wash heightened with white) FRF 1,650. PARIS, 9 March 1954, *Out for a Walk in Aix-en-Provence,* FRF 330,000. LONDON, 5 Dec 1961, *View of Maecenas's Villa* (watercolour and gouache) GBP 178. PARIS, 15 Dec 1969, *The Fountain amidst Ruins; Water Trough in the Roman Countryside* (two gouaches) FRF 14,000. LONDON, 13 July 1972, *View of a Garden in Italy* (watercolour) GBP 340. PARIS, 15 June 1978, *Hunting Halt* (1768, metal, 5 1/4 x 11 ins / 13.5 x 27 cm) FRF 10,000. MONTE CARLO, 11 Feb 1979, *View of Tours* (black chalk and brown wash, 8 3/4 x 14 1/2 ins / 22.1 x 37 cm) FRF 11,000. LONDON, 9 July 1981, *Figures on the Edge of a Pond* (drawing in wash/outline in black chalk heightened with white/blue paper, 15 1/2 x 20 3/4 ins / 39.2 x 52.6 cm) GBP 480. MONTE CARLO, 26 June 1983, *Out for a Walk in Aix-en-Provence* (1773, watercolour and gouache, 17 1/2 x 22 ins / 44.5 x 56 cm) FRF 80,000. PARIS, 23 May 1986, *Shepherd and Shepherdess in an Italian Landscape* (brown and pink wash, pen and Indian ink, 10 3/4 x 15 1/4 ins / 27.5 x 38.5 cm) FRF 15,000. PARIS, 17 June 1986, *The Discovery of the Ruins at Paestum* (oil on canvas, 18 x 40 1/2 ins / 46 x 103 cm) FRF 60,000. PARIS, 24 Feb 1987, *The Arethusa Spring* (oil on canvas, 9 3/4 x 13 ins / 25 x 33 cm) FRF 21,000. LONDON, 27 Oct 1989, *Wooded Landscape with a Shepherd Leading his Flock to the River* (oil on panel, 14 1/4 x 22 ins / 36.5 x 55 cm) GBP 2,200. PARIS, 14 Dec 1989, *People Conversing near the Ruins of a Building* (oil on canvas, 12 3/4 x 16 ins / 32.5 x 40.5 cm) FRF 14,000. PARIS, 23 April 1990, *Conversation near the Ruins of a Building in the Countryside* (oil on canvas, 12 3/4 x 16 ins / 32.5 x 40.5 cm) FRF 15,000. MONACO, 7 Dec 1990, *View of the Château de Chanteloup (near Ambroise)* (1769, oil on canvas, 31 x 49 1/2 ins / 79 x 125.5 cm) FRF 310,800. PARIS, 10 April 1991, *Italian Landscape with the Conveying of an Ancient Statue* (gouache, 13 x 20 1/2 ins / 33.2 x 52.3 cm) FRF 23,000. MONACO, 22 June 1991, *The Naples Solfatara* (gouache, 11 1/4 x 16 3/4 ins / 28.7 x 42.6 cm) FRF 31,080. PARIS, 28 April 1994, *Roman Architecture* (gouache, 10 x 13 ins / 25.5 x 33 cm) FRF 15,000. LONDON, 3 July 1996, *A Classical Roman Statue Pulled out of the Ruins* (watercolour and gouache, 13 x 20 3/4 ins / 33.1 x 52.6 cm) GBP 5,750. PARIS, 25 April 1997, *View of the Colosseum* (1769, watercolour and gouache, 25 1/4 x 18 3/4 ins / 64 x 47.5 cm) FRF 78,000.

HOUET, Laurens
French, 17th century.
Active in Paris at the beginning of the 17th century.
Painter (?), sculptor (?).

HOUET, Lois
French, 17th century.
Active in Paris from 1609.
Painter (?), sculptor (?).

HOUETTE, Louis
French, 20th century.
Born in Melun.
Painter.
Louis Houette exhibited at the Salon des Indépendants from 1912 and at the Salon d'Automne.

HOUETTE, Nicolas
French, 18th century.
Active in Paris in 1754.
Painter.

HOUETTE, Paul
French, 19th century.
Born c. 1815, in Paris; died c. 1905.
Painter, watercolourist. Mountainscapes, landscapes.
Houette was a friend of Corot and Daubigny. He often painted the woods of the Orléanais region and the Île-de-France, as well as mountain landscapes inspired by trips to Switzerland and the Vosges region of eastern France.

HOUFFLIN, André
Belgian, 20th century.
Born 1945, in Erquelinnes.
Painter, draughtsman, designer. Murals, designs for stained glass, designs for mosaics.
André Houfflin studied at the art academy in Mons and then became a teacher. He has painted frescoes and murals, notably in collaboration with Dubrunfaut.

HOUFNAGLIUS, Georges and Jacob
16th century.
Painters.
AUCTION RECORDS:
PARIS, 16 Dec 1942, *Diana and Actaeon* (1597, gouache) FRF 100,000.

HOUGARDY, Émile
Belgian, 20th century.
Born 18 March 1899, in Herstal-les-Liège.
Engraver.
Hougardy took artistic advice from Armand Rassenfosse. He mainly produced dry-point portrait engravings.
MUSEUMS AND GALLERIES:
BRUSSELS (Bibliothèque royale Albert Ier, Prints Collection) - LIÈGE (Drawings and Prints Collection) - LIÈGE (Galerie Wittert, Université) - PARIS (Prints Collection).

HOUGET, Fernand
Belgian, 20th century.
Active in Verviers.
Landscape artist.
Houget exhibited at the Brussels exhibition in 1910.

HOUGH, Walter
American, 19th century.
Born 23 April 1859; died 1935, in Washington DC.
Painter.
Walter Hough was a member of the New York Watercolor Society and the American Federation of Arts.

HOUGH, William B.
British, 19th century.
Born 1819; died 1897, in Wolverhampton.
Active 1857-1894.
Painter, watercolourist. Still-lifes.
William Hough was a painter of still-lifes and birds' nests. He exhibited at the Royal Academy between 1857 and 1894 as well as at the Royal Society of British Artists and the New Water-Colour Society. He was influenced by William Henry Hunt and closely followed his paintings of flowers and fruit.
BIBLIOGRAPHY:
Lambourne, Lionel/Hamilton, Jean, *British Watercolours in the Victoria and Albert Museum,* Sotheby Park Bernet, London, 1980.
MUSEUMS AND GALLERIES:
GLASGOW (AG and Mus.): *Fruits* - LONDON (Victoria and Albert Mus.): *Fruit: Pineapples, Plums and Grapes* (watercolour).
AUCTION RECORDS:
LONDON, 9 Dec 1907, *Fruits and Still-life,* GBP 5. LONDON, 27 April 1908, *Peaches and Grapes* (watercolour) GBP 4; *Raspberries* (watercolour) GBP 6. LONDON, July 1923, *Plums,* GBP 7. NEW YORK, 7 Jan 1981, *Still-life with Apples and Grapes* (watercolour, round, diam. 11 ins / 27 cm) USD 1,100. LONDON, 27 Oct 1983, *Plums* (watercolour heightened with gouache, 7 1/2 x 10 ins / 19 x 25.5 cm) GBP 580. LONDON, 16 Oct 1986, *Still-life with Apples and Plums* (watercolour/pencil outlines heightened with gouache, 11 x 15 ins / 28 x 38 cm) GBP 1,500. LONDON, 26 Jan 1987, *Still-life with Apples, Plums and Grapes on a Ledge* (watercolour heightened with gouache, 18 x 27 ins / 46 x 68.5 cm) GBP 3,600. LONDON, 25 Jan 1988, *Victoria Plums* (watercolour, 16 x 22 ins / 40.5 x 55 cm) GBP 2,860. LONDON, 25 Jan 1989, *Still-life of Roses in a*

Dish (watercolour, 10 x 14 ins / 25.5 x 35.5 cm) GBP 1,540. NEW YORK, 17 Jan 1990, *Still-life with Grapes and a Pear* (watercolour and gouache/card, 5 1/2 x 8 ins / 14 x 20.3 cm) USD 825. LONDON, 31 Jan 1990, *Still-life of Peaches, Plums and Strawberry* (watercolour heightened with white, 9 3/4 x 13 3/4 ins / 25 x 35 cm) GBP 2,970. LONDON, 30 Jan 1991, *Plums on a Stone Ledge; Primroses on a Stone Ledge* (watercolour heightened with gouache, a pair, each 7 x 5 ins / 18 x 13 cm) GBP 2,200. EDINBURGH, 2 May 1991, *Plums; Strawberries and Peach* (watercolour heightened with gouache, each 4 1/4 x 5 1/2 ins / 10.8 x 14 cm) GBP 1,210. LONDON, 29 Oct 1991, *Still-life with Bunch of Grapes, Nuts, Peach and Gooseberries* (watercolour and gouache, 8 1/2 x 11 1/2 ins / 21.7 x 29.2 cm) GBP 1,320. LONDON, 19 Dec 1991, *Still-life with a Nest and Primroses on a Mossy Bank* (watercolour and gouache, 9 x 12 ins / 22.9 x 30.7 cm) GBP 3,520. LONDON, 11 June 1993, *Still-life with a Nest, Primroses and Violets* (watercolour and gouache, 11 x 14 1/2 ins / 28 x 36.8 cm) GBP 3,450. LONDON, 5 June 1996, *Still-life with Plums, Apricots and Peach* (watercolour and gouache, 10 1/4 x 14 1/2 ins / 26 x 37 cm) GBP 1,495. LONDON, 14 June 2000, *Still-life of Plums and Grapes* (watercolour, 15 x 22 ins / 39 x 56 cm) GBP 1,800. CHESTER, 22 June 2000, *Plums, Strawberries and Pear on Mossy Bank* (watercolour, 9 x 13 ins / 23 x 34 cm) GBP 1,600. LONDON, 27 June 2001, *Still-life of Plums on a Mossy Bank* (watercolour and gouache, 9 x 12 ins / 24 x 31 cm) GBP 2,000. LONDON, 7 Nov 2001, *Still-life of Plums, Strawberries, Currants and Pear, on a Mossy Bank* (gouache and watercolour, 9 x 13 ins / 23 x 34 cm) GBP 1,800. BURY ST EDMUNDS, 6 May 2002, *Grapes, Peach and Strawberries on a Mossy Bank* (watercolour and gouache, 9 x 12 ins / 23 x 30 cm) GBP 1,300. SAN FRANCISCO, 14 May 2003, *Still-life with Blackberries and Ivy on a Mossy Bank* (oil on canvas, 15 x 19 ins / 38 x 48 cm) USD 11,000. LONDON, 4 Sept 2003, *Pears and Plums on a Mossy Bank* (1875, oil on canvas, 30 x 25 ins / 77 x 64 cm) GBP 2,500. LONDON, 21 Jan 2004, *Still-life of Cherry Blossoms and Bird's Nest* (watercolour and gouache, 10 x 15 ins / 26 x 38 cm) GBP 1,500.

HOUGHTON, Arthur Boyd
British, 19th century.
Born 1836, in Kotagiri, Madras; died 23 November 1875, in London.
Painter, watercolourist, draughtsman. Genre scenes.

After spending a long time as an illustrator Arthur Houghton exhibited at the Royal Academy in London from 1860 to 1870. In 1871 he became an associate of the Society of Painters in Watercolours. He mostly depicted subjects from the Middle Ages.

MUSEUMS AND GALLERIES:
LONDON (British Mus.): *Don Quixote and Rocinante* - LONDON (Victoria and Albert Mus.): *Transformation of King Beder; Oriental Presenting Monkeys.*

AUCTION RECORDS:
LONDON, 21 Nov 1908, *Scene from Roman Kenilworth; The Compromising Letter* (two pendants) GBP 2. LONDON, 3 April 1909, *On the Shore,* GBP 5. LONDON, 30 July 1936, *Holborn in 1861,* GBP 35. LONDON, 26 June 1987, *At the Water's Edge. Pegwell Bay near Ramsgate* (oil on canvas, 10 x 12 ins / 25.3 x 30.5 cm) GBP 6,000. LONDON, 25 March 1994, *Arabs Taking a Break Beside a River* (pencil, watercolour and gouache, 20 x 23 3/4 ins / 50.5 x 60.3 cm) GBP 1,725. LONDON, 20 Feb 2003, *Brother and Sister of the Artist Playing Chess* (oil on canvas, 10 x 12 ins / 26 x 30 cm) GBP 4,000.

HOUGHTON, John
Irish, 18th century.
Died c. 1775.
Active in Dublin.
Sculptor.

John Houghton's works include *St Paul Preaching in Athens.*

HOUGHTON, Margaret
Canadian, 19th - 20th century.
Born in Montreal.
Painter. Landscapes.

Margaret Houghton painted many landscapes of Brittany and exhibited in Paris in 1905 and 1907.

HOUGRAND, Jaspar
Belgian, 20th century.
Born 1884 or 1897, in Liège or in Hodimont-lez-Verviers.
Painter. Landscapes, genre scenes, interiors with figures.

Hougrand was a student of Theunissen and was a familiar face at the studios of Évariste Carpentier and A. Donnay.

HOUGUENADE, Julien P.
French, 19th century.
Died 1902.
Painter.

Houguenade was a member of the Société des Artistes Français.

HOUISTE
French, 18th century.
Active in Paris in 1727.
Sculptor.

HOUISTE, François
French, 19th century.
Born 11 December 1794, in Paris.
Engraver.

Houiste was a pupil of Pomel.

HOULIÈRE, Robert de La. See **LA HOULIÈRE Robert de**

HOUNSOM, G.
British, 18th - 19th century.
Active in London.
Miniaturist.

G. Hounsom exhibited his work frequently at the Royal Academy in London from 1796 to 1806.

HOUPLAIN, Jacques
French, 20th century.
Born 10 August 1920, in Luneray.
Painter, engraver, illustrator.

After working in painting studios, Jacques Houplain turned to engraving in 1945 receiving advice from Bersier, Goerg and Guastalla. He illustrated numerous works for bibliophiles including: *Les Chants de Maldoror* (*The Songs of Maldoror*) and *La Genèse* (*The Genesis*). His main technique is etching and his method of filling in objects with multiple tiny forms and small signs recalls Persian tapestry. A member of the Société des Peintres Graveurs Français, Jacques Houplain featured in the *Le Signe et la Marge* (*The Sign and the Margin*) exhibition with 16 other contemporary engravers, Musée d'Art Moderne Richard Anacréon, Granville (2002). He participated in the second Salon de Mai in 1946.

BIBLIOGRAPHY:
Les Peintres graveurs français - 80e anniversaire, Société des peintres-graveurs français, Paris, 1969. Houplain, Jacques, '*Matière et texture*' in *Nouvelles de l'Estampe* n° 164, periodical, Bibliothèque nationale de France, Paris, 1999.

HOURCASTREMÉ
French, 18th century.
Active in Paris in 1796.
Engraver.

HOURDAIN, C.
French, 18th century.
Engraver.

C. Hourdain is remembered for his *Portrait of Louis XVII* after Bertaux.

HOURDÉ, Daniel
French, 20th - 21st century.
Born 1947, in Boulogne-Billancourt.
Sculptor (bronze), draughtsman. Figures.
Hourdé studied at the École des Beaux-Arts in Grenoble in 1967 and 1968, and at the École des Beaux-Arts in Paris in 1969. He carves tall figures surging forward, showing clear attention to the body and the muscles. He has shown his works in solo exhibitions, including: Galerie Jean Claude Riedel, Paris, 1980; Galerie Charles Sablon, Paris, 1989; and Galerie Laarock-Granoff, 2002.

HOURDEAUX, Maurice
French, 20th century.
Born 30 October 1902, in La Flamengrie.
Painter.
The tenth child of a family of lumbermen, Maurice Hourdeaux attended the École Boulle and then the École Nationale des Arts Décoratifs, where he studied with G. Corlin, E. Fougerat and Legueult.. His *Still-life with White Parasol* was acquired by the French state in 1945. Hourdeaux first exhibited in Paris at the Salon des Indépendants in 1934 and also featured in the Salon de l' École Nationale des Arts Décoratifs and the Salon d'Automne.

HOURDEL, Gilles
French, 18th century.
Active in Le Mans in 1723.
Sculptor (wood).
Gilles Hourdel worked for the church of Chevaigné (Maine)

HOURLIER, Armand
French, 19th century.
Painter, decorative artist. Ornaments.
MUSEUMS AND GALLERIES:
LAVAL: ornaments (painting).

HOURLIER, Pierre
French, 18th century.
Active in Paris in 1741.
Painter (?), sculptor (?).

HOURLIER, Pierre Joseph
French, 18th century.
Active in Paris in 1773.
Sculptor, painter.

HOURLIER, Pierre Nicolas
French, 18th century.
Active in Paris in 1769.
Sculptor, painter.

HOURRIEZ, Georges
French, 19th - 20th century.
Born in Valenciennes.
Engraver.
Georges Hourriez was a pupil of Stéphane Pannemaker. He engraved the *Mercury* stamp for the Ministère des Postes, the French telecommunication ministry in 1938. He received an honourable mention at the Salon des Artistes Français (1896) and at the 1900 Exposition Universelle, as well as a 3rd class medal (1910).

HOURS, Laurent
French, 20th - 21st century.
Born 9 September 1946, in Neuilly-sur-Seine.
Painter.
Hours studied in Bertholle's studio at the École des Beaux-Arts in Paris. His work is based on printing. He models and carves his designs, which he then moulds in resin. He then uses this medium to create his dreamlike designs of buildings, columns, terraces, peristyles and figures bathed in an atmosphere of warm colours. He took part in the Salon des Réalités Nouvelles in Paris in 1972 and exhibited at the Centre d'Art Septentrion in the north in 1972 and 1973. He has shown his works at the Musée de St-Maur in La Varenne-St-Hilaire.

HOURS OF MARÉCHAL DE BOUCICAUT, Master of the. See **MASTER of the HOURS OF MARÉCHAL DE BOUCICAUT (Maître du Livre d'Heures du Maréchal de Boucicaut)**

HOURSOLLE, Pierre
French, 19th century.
Born 1853, in Bordeaux; died 1877.
Sculptor.
Hoursolle trained under Jouffroy and Delaplanche. He first exhibited at the Salon in 1896.
MUSEUMS AND GALLERIES:
BORDEAUX: *This Age is without Pity.*

HOURTAL, Henri
French, 20th century.
Born 1877, in Carcassonne; died 1944.
Painter. Urban landscapes, landscapes.
Henri Hourtal exhibited in Paris from 1904 at the Salon des Indépendants, the Société Nationale des Beaux-Arts and the Salon d'Automne.
AUCTION RECORDS:
AMSTERDAM, 24 March 1980, *In the Café, Paris* (oil/panel, oval, 14 1/2 x 18 1/2 ins / 37 x 47 cm) NLG 4,500. PARIS, 15 Feb 1988, *Moroccan Women* (oil on canvas, 32 x 39 1/4 ins / 81 x 100 cm) FRF 4,200. PARIS, 21 March 2003, *Rue Quinquempois in Paris* (oil on canvas, 21 x 18 ins / 53 x 45 cm) EUR 2,000. PARIS, 16 June 2003, *Two Moroccans* (watercolour, gouache and charcoal, 12 x 9 ins / 31 x 24 cm) EUR 1,600.

HOURVEL, François
French, 17th century.
Active in Paris in 1609.
Painter (?), sculptor (?).

HOURY, Charles Borromée Antoine
Belgian, 19th century.
Born 1823, in Soignies; died January 1898, in Paris.
Active in France.
Painter. Portraits, genre scenes, still-lifes.
Charles Houry studied under Cogniet at the school of fine arts and later joined the Sèvres porcelain works. He exhibited at the Salon in Paris from 1850, and is known for his portraits and genre subjects painted on faïence.
AUCTION RECORDS:
PARIS, 7 June 1943, *Still-life,* FRF 2,100. PARIS, 13 Feb 1973, *Young Woman Standing at a Piano,* FRF 3,000. NEW YORK, 17 Feb 1994, *The Composer Louis Gottshalk* (oil on panel, 15 1/2 x 12in/39.5 x 30.5cm) USD 1,150.

HOURY, Paul Louis
French, 20th century.
Born 26 August 1889, in Montfermeil.
Sculptor.
Paul Houry was a pupil of Mercié and exhibited in Paris at the Salon des Artistes Français.

HOUSE, Gordon
British, 20th century.
Born 1932, in Pontadarm (Glamorgan).
Painter.
Gordon House exhibited in London. The theme of his paintings centres on the visual perception of squares.
AUCTION RECORDS:
LONDON, 19 Oct 1983, *Geometric Drawings* (1976-1977, coloured woodcut, set of eight, 8 1/2 x 3 ins / 21.4 x 7.5 cm) GBP 700.

HOUSE, James
American, 18th century.
Active in Philadelphia in 1799.
Painter. Portraits.

HOUSEMAN, F.
British.
Engraver (mezzotint).
F. Houseman engraved a *Portrait of Nancy Parsano* after Lady Maynard.

HOUSER, Allan C., or Haozous, Ha-o-zous
American, 20th century.
Born 30 June 1914, near Apache (Oklahoma); died 22 August 1994, in Santa Fe (New Mexico).
Sculptor (bronze, wood, stone), painter. Figures, Native American subjects. Murals.
Native Art.

Allan C. Houser, a Chiracahua Apache, grew up in the farming and ranching area near Apache, Oklahoma. He was much influenced by his parents, who spoke Apache and sang traditional Native songs, particularly by his father, Sam Haozous, who had previously been imprisoned for 27 years for his part in the 1886 Chiracahua uprising, and who had been translator for the famous chief Geronimo. Houser studied painting at the Santa Fe Indian School under Dorothy Dunn from 1934, receiving the Arts and Crafts Award in 1936 for best work by a student, and later studied with Olle Nordmark, a Norwegian muralist, at Fort Sill Indian School in Oklahoma. It was Nordmark who encouraged him to start work in sculpture. Houser was artist in residence at the Inter-Mountain Indian School, Brigham City, Utah (1951-1962). He taught at the Institute of American Indian Arts in Santa Fe from 1962, becoming head of the sculpture department from 1971 until 1975, when he retired to concentrate on his sculpting work.

Houser painted in oil, casein and egg tempera, and did fresco and secco murals. His early works, which demonstrated his skilled drawing technique, were typical of the Santa Fe Indian school in their flat and conventional Southwest style. His first sculptures were executed in wood and stone; he cast his first bronze works in 1968. His style progressed from a naturalistic to a more experimental approach, as seen in the simplified, monumental forms of his sculpture.

Houser has been credited with bringing Native American sculpture into the contemporary art world, while preserving customary values and qualities. His graceful figures depict traditional subjects and activities, such as Apache mothers and children, Plains chieftains and hunters, and Navajo shepherds. He stated that his work honours the American Indian, and addresses the issue of living in harmony with nature. His work has influenced other Native American artists, including Doug Hyde and Bill Prokopiof, and his son Bob Haozous is also a sculptor.

Houser received many commissions for public work, including a mural (with Navajo painter Gerald Nailor) for the Department of the Interior building in Washington DC (1939); a mural for the Golden Gate Exposition in San Francisco (1939); a sculpture for the Haskell Institute, Lawrence, Kansas (1948); the memorial sculpture *Comrade in Mourning* to honour Native Americans who died in service in World War II; and the 59th medal for the American Society of Medalists. His sculpture *Offering to the Great Spirit* (1985), a medicine man holding a pipe in outstretched arms to the Great Spirit, was installed in the US Mission to the United Nations as an international symbol of peace.

Houser's work was shown in collective exhibitions including the World's Fair, New York (1936). Solo exhibitions include: Glenn Green Galleries, Santa Fe (1987); Museum of New Mexico, Santa Fe (1991, tour); and *A Life in Art*, Eiteljorg Museum, Indianapolis (1993). He received a Guggenheim Fellowship for Painting and Sculpture; a Palmes Académique award from the government of France; the Waite Phillips Trophy from Philbrook Art Center, Oklahoma; a Gold Medal from the Heard Museum, Phoenix (1973); Governor's Awards in the Visual Arts in New Mexico (1980, 1983, 1984); induction into the Oklahoma Hall of Fame (1985); an Honorary PhD in Fine Arts, University of Maine (1987); the American Indian Distinguished Achievement Award from the American Indian Resources Institute in Washington DC (1989); and in 1992 he was the first Native American to received the National Medal of Arts.

BIBLIOGRAPHY:

Perlman, Barbara H., *Allan Houser (Ha-o-zous)*, exhibition catalogue, Glenn Green Galleries, Santa Fe, 1987. *Allan Houser: A Life in Art*, exhibition catalogue, Museum of New Mexico, Santa Fe, 1991. Lowe, Truman T. (ed.), *Native Modernism: The Art of George Morrison and Allan Houser*, exhibition catalogue, Smithsonian Institution, Washington DC, 2004. Rushing, W. Jackson, *Allan Houser, an American Master*, Harry N. Abrams, New York, 2004.

MUSEUMS AND GALLERIES:

DENVER (AM) - GILREASE (Gilrease Museum) - INDIANAPOLIS (Eiteljorg Museum): *Morning Prayer* (1987-1988, bronze sculpture) - JACKSON HOLE (National Museum of Wildlife): *Lament* (1990, bronze sculpture) - MONTCLAIR, NJ (Montclair Art Museum): *Earth Mother* (1986, bronze sculpture) - NORMAN, OK (Fred Jones Jr Museum of Art, University of Oklahoma): *Respite (Seated Woman)* (sculpture); *Hunting Song* (painting); *Apache Family* (painting); *Corn Grinder* (sculpture); *Tending the Flock* (sculpture); *Homeward Bound* (sculpture); *May We Have Peace* (sculpture) - ORANGE, TX (Stark Museum of Art): *Chant of the Rio Grande* (bronze sculpture); *Acorn Harvest* (bronze sculpture) - PHILBROOK (Philbrook Art Center) - SANTA FE (Wheelwright Museum of the American Indian) - WASHINGTON DC (National Portrait Gal.) - WASHINGTON DC (Smithsonian American AM): *Buffalo Dance* (1983, stone relief sculpture).

AUCTION RECORDS:

SANTA FE, 20 Nov 1999, *Respect* (bronze, 58 x 14x13 ins / 147 x 36x33 cm) USD 14,000. NEW YORK, 29 Nov 2000, *Apache Buffalo Hunt* (oil on canvas, 6 x 4 ins / 16 x 11 cm) USD 25,000. SANTA FE, 9 Nov 2002, *Jicarilla Apaches* (bronze, 9 x 5x2 ins / 23 x 13x5 cm) USD 3,250. NEW YORK, 13 Jan 2003, *Pensive Maiden* (bronze, h. 14 ins / 36 cm) USD 12,000. SANTA FE, 1 Nov 2003, *Sacred Rain Arrow II* (bronze, 12 x 6x6 ins / 30 x 15x15 cm) USD 12,000.

HOUSEZ, Charles Gustave
French, 19th century.
Born 17 December 1822, in Condé; died c. 1880, in Valenciennes.
Painter. History painting, portraits, genre scenes.

Housez embarked on his artistic training at the École de Valenciennes, before entering the École des Beaux-Arts in Paris on 7 April 1838. He taught at the Académie de Valenciennes, and exhibited at the Paris Salon between 1845 and 1880.

MUSEUMS AND GALLERIES:

POITIERS: *Mary Stuart and Chatelard* - RHEIMS: *Psyche in a Faint*.

AUCTION RECORDS:

LONDON, 3 Oct 1979, *Ulysses Disguised as a Beggar, Recognised by Eurycleia* (oil on canvas, 44 x 57 ins / 112 x 145 cm) GBP 1,800. MONTE CARLO, 22 June 1985, *Death of Vitellius* (oil on canvas, 45 x 57¾ ins / 114 x 147 cm) FRF 90,000. NEW YORK, 1 Nov 1995, *Little Girl Lost in Paris* (1877, oil on canvas, 23 x 18½ ins / 58.4 x 47 cm) USD 11,500. NEW YORK, 23 Oct 1997, *Death of Vitellius* (oil on canvas, 45 x 57½ ins / 114.3 x 146.1 cm) USD 27,600.

HOUSHIARY, Shirazeh
Iranian, 20th - 21st century.
Born 1955, in Iran.
Active in England.
Sculptor.

Houshiary lives and works in London. She shows her work in solo exhibitions, such as *Breath* at the Lisson Gallery, London. She has also exhibited at the Rath Museum in Geneva (in 1988) and at the centre for contemporary art in Grenoble (in 1995), as well as in Munich and Maastricht.

Houshiary sculpts in clay, straw, metal, sheets of copper, aluminium and zinc, which she oxidises. In her work, she seeks to express 'the intervening space' between the formal dualities expressed by her sculptures.

BIBLIOGRAPHY:

Savadori, F., *Shirazeh Houshiary*, Musée Rath, Geneva, 1988.

HOUSMAN, Laurence

British, 19th - 20th century.

Born 18 July 1865 or 1867, in Bromsgrove; died 1959, in Street (Somerset).

Painter, draughtsman, illustrator.

Laurence Housman studied in Lambeth and at the South Kensington School of Art. Because of his failing eyesight he abandoned book illustration and became an art critic for the *Manchester Guardian*. He was also an author and playwright. Among Housman's best work as a writer and illustrator are *All-Fellows* (1896); *The Field of Clover* (1898); *The Little Land* (1899); and *New Child's Guide to Knowledge* (1911). He also illustrated *The End of Elfintown* by J. Barlow; *At the Back of the North Wind* by MacDonald; and *The Sensitive Plant* by P. B. Shelley. A major source of inspiration was the English poet and painter William Blake.

BIBLIOGRAPHY:

Osterwalder, Marcus (ed.), *Dictionnaire des illustrateurs 1800-1914*, Ides et Calendes, Neuchâtel, 1989.

HOUSONS, P. d'

British, 19th century.

Active c. 1800.

Painter (?), draughtsman (?).

A portrait engraved after Housons is extant.

HOUSSAR, Feuillan

Flemish School, 18th century.

Born 1757, in Namur.

Sculptor.

Feuillan Houssar worked in Everboden.

HOUSSARD, Charles Claude

Belgian, 20th century.

Born 18 February 1884, in Liège; died 30 September 1958, in Brussels.

Painter. Landscapes, seascapes.

Houssard took painting lessons in Liège, in the studios of A. Donnay and Évariste Carpentier, and then in Brussels, with Baron Frederick. He undertook study trips to the Netherlands, France, Italy and England (among other places), and his work was shown in collective exhibitions, including the Brussels Triennale (1914); at the Royal Academy of Art in London (1915); in Stockholm (1916); and at the Salon d'Automne in Paris, where he was awarded a prize for his canvas *Storm in Nieuport*. There were also solo exhibitions of his work, in Mons, Paris and Brussels.

He painted landscapes of the Ardennes and the Walloon countryside, and the North Sea.

HOUSSAY, Alain

French, 17th century.

Born c. 1649.

Active in Nantes.

Sculptor.

It seems likely that Alain Houssay's sons, Michel and Nicolas, were also sculptors.

HOUSSAYE, Frédéric

French, 19th century.

Born 2 February 1827, in Paris; died June 1899, in Paris.

Sculptor.

A pupil of Luc, Frédéric Houssaye made his Salon début in 1869.

HOUSSAYE, Joséphine, or Houssay

French, 19th century.

Born 25 December 1840, in Nantes.

Painter, watercolourist. History painting, portraits.

Joséphine was the sister of the sculptor Frédéric Houssaye, and a pupil of Robert Fleury and Henner. She began exhibiting at the Salon in 1868 and became a member of the Société des Artistes Français in 1883, winning a third-class medal in 1892, then a silver medal in 1900 (at the Exposition Universelle).

AUCTION RECORDS:

LONDON, 16 Feb 1979, *Waiting* (oil/parchment, 6½ x 5 ins / 16.5 x 12.6 cm) GBP 520.

HOUSSAYE DE LÉOMÉNIL, Adolphe Étienne

French, 19th century.

Born 15 March 1808, in Cherusco, to French parents; died 2 July 1871, in Léoménil.

Painter, watercolourist. Landscapes.

Adolphe Houssaye de Léoménil was a pupil of Watelet, and exhibited at the Salon between 1833 and 1845.

MUSEUMS AND GALLERIES:

BAGNÈRES: *View of Auvergne*.

HOUSSAYE DE LÉOMÉNIL, Laure (Mme)

Maiden name: Girard

French, 19th century.

Born 7 August 1806, in Condé; died 30 January 1866, in Léoménil.

Painter, pastellist. Portraits.

Laure Houssaye de Léoménil won a third-class medal in 1835, and her portraits were featured at the Paris Salon from 1834 to 1852. She was highly renowned in Parisian society during the reign of Louis-Philippe, and was particularly admired for her pastel drawings.

MUSEUMS AND GALLERIES:

VERSAILLES: portraits of famous figures.

AUCTION RECORDS:

PARIS, 24 May 1996, *Nude Young Woman* (oil on canvas, 57 x 29¼ ins / 145 x 74 cm) FRF 13,200.

HOUSSE, Jean de

Belgian, 17th century.

Born in Liège.

Sculptor.

HOUSSEAU HASSID, Mireille

French, 20th century.

Born 23 January 1933, in Tresson.

Painter (gouache), draughtsman. Landscapes.

Mireille Housseau Hassid studied at the École des Beaux-Arts in Versailles; she has shown at the Salon des Indépendants (from 1987), the Salon d'Automne (1989 and 1990) and the Salon des Artistes Français (1989 and 1990).

HOUSSEAUX, Alfred

French, 19th century.

Born in the 19th century, in Provins.

Painter.

Housseaux was a pupil of Allongé, and made his Salon début in 1874.

HOUSSELIN, Alexis Louis Pierre

French, 19th century.

Born in the 19th century, in St-Ingevert (Pas-de-Calais).

Painter, engraver.

Housselin studied under Drolling and Biennoury. His work first appeared at the Salon in 1867.

HOUSSET, E.

French, 19th - 20th century.

Miniaturist. Portraits.

AUCTION RECORDS:

PARIS, 21 April 1921, *Three-Quarter Portrait of a Woman* (miniature) FRF 2,210.

HOUSSIN, Édouard Charles Marie

French, 19th - 20th century.

Born 13 September 1847, in Douai; died 15 May 1917, in Paris.

Sculptor. Figures. Busts.

Édouard Houssin was a pupil of Jouffroy, A. Millet and studied in Douai on a scholarship. He executed numerous monuments in the north and his bronze bust of *Henry Berthoud* is in Douai. He exhibited from 1873 at the Salon de Paris receiving honourable mentions (1879, 1881, 1883, 1885), a 3rd class medal (1887), a 2nd class medal (1889) and a bronze (1900) for the Exposition Universelle.

MUSEUMS AND GALLERIES:

DOUAI: *Academic Figures; Man Armed with a Club; Man Throwing a Stone; Cupid Stung by a Bee* - LA ROCHELLE: *Leda.*

AUCTION RECORDS:

DOUAI, 13 May 1984, *Leaving to go Fishing* (1901, bronze, 31½ x 78¾ x 15¾ ins / 80 x 200 x 40 cm) FRF 55,000.

HOUSSOT, Louis

French, 19th century.

Born 24 May 1824, in Nancy; died 1890, in Paris.

Painter. History painting, genre scenes.

Houssot was taught by Drolling, and exhibited at the Paris Salon in 1857.

MUSEUMS AND GALLERIES:

AJACCIO: *Sunrise; Supper Time* (two pendants, attribution) - CHAMBÉRY (MBA): *The People of Chambéry Voting in 1860.*

HOUSTON, Caroline A.

American, 20th century.

Born 1871, in Brooklyn (New York City).

Painter, miniaturist.

Caroline A. Houston trained under Franck du Mond, Collin and Trasset. She took part in the World Fair in Paris in 1900.

HOUSTON, Frances C.

American, 19th - 20th century.

Born 14 January 1867, in Hudson (Michigan); died 1906, in Windsor.

Painter.

Frances C. Houston studied in Paris with Jules Lefebvre and Boulanger. She married M.W.C. Houston. She was a member of the major watercolour societies in Boston and New York, and received an honourable mention at the Exposition Universelle in Paris in 1900.

AUCTION RECORDS:

BOLTON, 13 Sept 1984, *Seated Nude* (1900, pastel, 19 x 14 ins / 48.3 x 35.5 cm) USD 1,500.

HOUSTON, George

British, 19th - 20th century.

Born 1869, in Dairy, Scotland; died 1947.

Painter, watercolourist. Landscapes, waterscapes, seascapes.

George Houston was a member of the Royal Scottish Society of Painters in Watercolours and the Royal Scottish Academy. He took part in exhibitions in Glasgow and Edinburgh.

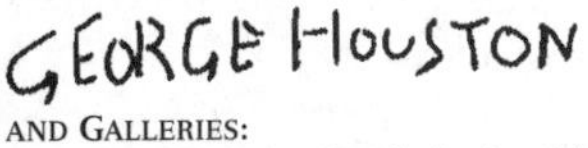

MUSEUMS AND GALLERIES:

EDINBURGH (Royal Scottish Academy): *An Ayrshire Glen* (oil on canvas).

AUCTION RECORDS:

GLASGOW, 3 March 1943, *Bonawe Ferry,* GBP 28. GLASGOW, 16 Nov 1945, *Autumn Landscape with River,* GBP 67. SCOTLAND, 24 Aug 1976, *Cairngow* (1917, oil on canvas, 27 x 35½ ins / 68.5 x 90 cm) GBP 700. GLASGOW, 19 April 1984, *Loch Fyne Head,* GBP 1,000. QUEENSFERRY, 29 April 1986, *Children near a Waterfall* (oil on canvas, 28 x 35¾ ins / 71 x 91 cm) GBP 2,600. SOUTH QUEENSFERRY, 29 April 1987, *View of Dalry, Ayrshire* (1901, oil on canvas, 36 x 72 ins / 91.5 x 183 cm) GBP 2,300. EDINBURGH, 30 Aug 1988, *The Road to Inverary* (watercolour, 9½ x 13½ ins / 24 x 34 cm) GBP 638; *Beside the River* (oil on canvas, 18 x 24 ins / 46 x 61 cm) GBP 2,970. EDINBURGH, 22 Nov 1988, *Lochgair on Loch Fyne* (oil on canvas, 28 x 36 ins / 71.2 x 91.5 cm) GBP 22,000. GLASGOW, 7 Feb 1989, *Highland Landscape* (oil on canvas, 40¼ x 60 ins / 102 x 152.5 cm) GBP 3,960. GLASGOW, 6 Feb 1990, *Ayrshire* (oil on canvas, 28 x 36 ins / 71 x 91.5 cm) GBP 1,320. EDINBURGH, 26 April 1990, *Crinan* (oil on canvas, 20 x 24 ins / 50.8 x 61 cm) GBP 2,420. SOUTH QUEENSFERRY, 1 May 1990, *Yellow Landscape* (oil on canvas, 35½ x 54 ins / 90 x 137 cm) GBP 1,045. PERTH, 27 Aug 1990, *View of the Artist's Garden* (oil on canvas, 39¾ x 59¾ ins / 101 x 152 cm) GBP 6,050. GLASGOW, 22 Nov 1990, *Spring at Loch Awe* (oil on canvas, 28 x 36 ins / 71.2 x 91.5 cm) GBP 1,540. EDINBURGH, 2 May 1991, *Lochgair on Loch Fyne* (oil on canvas, 28 x 36 ins / 71.2 x 91.4 cm) GBP 14,300. PERTH, 26 Aug 1991, *The River Stinchar in Ayrshire* (oil on canvas, 28 x 36 ins / 71 x 91.5 cm) GBP 1,870. NEW YORK, 20 Feb 1992, *Near the Waterfalls* (oil on canvas, 28 x 36 ins / 71.1 x 91.4 cm) USD 6,875. PERTH, 1 Sept 1992, *The Thaw* (oil on canvas, 40 x 50 ins / 101.5 x 127 cm) GBP 1,320. EDINBURGH, 23 March 1993, *Winter Landscape* (oil on canvas, 30¾ x 44¾ ins / 78 x 113.5 cm) GBP 6,900. GLASGOW, 1 Feb 1994, *Moorland near Kirkintilloch* (oil on canvas, 18 x 24 ins / 46 x 61 cm) GBP 4,600. PERTH, 26 Aug 1996, *Around a Farm* (oil on canvas, 40¼ x 49½ ins / 102 x 126 cm) GBP 6,325. GLASGOW, 31 Oct 1996, *Loch Road, Lochgilphead, Argyll* (oil on canvas, 28 x 36 ins / 71 x 91.3 cm) GBP 1,495. GLASGOW, 20 Feb 1997, *Loch Aweside, Argyll* (oil on canvas, 28 ins / 71 cm, ¾ x 36 ins/2 x 91.4 cm) GBP 3,105. GLASGOW, 25 Aug 1997, *Coastal Landscape with Figures on a Country Road* (oil on canvas, 13 x 15 ins / 33 x 38.2 cm) GBP 1,495. BURY ST EDMUNDS, 23 June 1999, *Croft on a Hillside* (oil on canvas, a pair, 18 x 24 ins / 46 x 61 cm) GBP 2,000. EDINBURGH, 25 Aug 2000, *Crisp Winter's Day on a Farm near Dalry, Ayrshire* (oil on canvas, 33 x 48 ins / 85 x 121 cm) GBP 8,200. LONDON, 30 Aug 2000, *Sledging* (oil on canvas, 28 x 36 ins / 71 x 91 cm) GBP 22,000. LONDON, 9 April 2001, *View of Arran. Loch Tay* (oil on canvas, a pair, 18 x 24 ins / 45 x 61 cm) GBP 4,800. LONDON, 1 Nov 2001, *Late Autumn, near Dalry, Ayshire* (1913, oil on canvas, 28 x 36 ins / 71 x 91 cm) GBP 5,800. LONDON, 7 March 2002, *Looking to Arran from Argyll* (oil on canvas, 18 x 24 ins / 46 x 61 cm) GBP 6,800. LONDON, 31 Oct 2002, *Returning from School* (oil on canvas, 40 x 50 ins / 102 x 127 cm) GBP 15,000. EDINBURGH, 21 Aug 2003, *Bridge at Inveraray* (oil on canvas, 28 x 36 ins / 71 x 91 cm) GBP 5,000. LONDON, 30 Oct 2003, *Loch Fyne Side* (oil on canvas, 28 x 36 ins / 71 x 91 cm) GBP 9,000. LONDON, 19 April 2004, *Spring Snows at Loch Fyne* (oil on canvas, 28 x 36 ins / 71 x 91 cm) GBP 6,800. LEYBURN, 21 April 2004, *Scottish River Landscape* (oil on canvas, 28 x 36 ins / 71 x 91 cm) GBP 6,000.

HOUSTON, H. H.

Irish, 18th century.

Engraver.

H. H. Houston was active in Dublin in 1790. He subsequently settled in the USA and worked mainly in Philadelphia.

HOUSTON, John

British, 20th century.

Born 1930, in Buckhaven, Scotland.

Painter.

John Houston attended Edinburgh College of Art from 1948 to 1954. His work is pleasing to the eye and has a decorative quality similar to the work of painters of the Paris School in

the interwar years. He showed his work in solo exhibitions in Edinburgh in 1958, 1960 and 1962.
AUCTION RECORDS:
PERTH, 27 Aug 1990, *The Yellow Café* (1981, oil on canvas, 10 x 12 ins / 25.5 x 30.5 cm) GBP 1,100. PERTH, 31 Aug 1993, *Roses* (oil on card, 24 x 30 ins / 61 x 76 cm) GBP 1,955. GLASGOW, 30 April 1999, *Still-life with Flowers and Jug* (1963, oil on canvas, 24 x 30 ins / 62 x 75 cm) GBP 2,200. EDINBURGH, 14 Dec 1999, *Low Tide, Luskentyre, Harris* (oil on canvas, 34 x 40 ins / 86 x 102 cm) GBP 2,100. LONDON, 26 Oct 2000, *Oriental Poppies* (1991, oil on canvas, 22 x 18 ins / 56 x 46 cm) GBP 4,200. LONDON, 26 Oct 2000, *Sunset over the Forth* (1973, oil on canvas, 47 x 76 ins / 119 x 193 cm) GBP 4,800. EDINBURGH, 24 Aug 2001, *Sunflowers* (1964, 24 x 20 ins / 60 x 50 cm) GBP 3,300. LONDON, 5 Sept 2001, *Oriental Poppies and Imari Plates* (1989, oil on canvas, 44 x 44 ins / 112 x 112 cm) GBP 4,000. LONDON, 7 March 2002, *Niesen, Lake Thun, Switzerland* (1972, oil on canvas, 36 x 36 ins / 91 x 91 cm) GBP 4,000. LONDON, 31 Oct 2002, *Blue Still-life* (oil on canvas, 25 x 30 ins / 63 x 76 cm) GBP 3,500. LONDON, 6 March 2003, *Flowers on Yellow* (1963, oil on canvas, 22 x 30 ins / 56 x 76 cm) GBP 3,800. LONDON, 27 Aug 2003, *Summer Sea, Gullane* (oil on canvas, 48 x 48 ins / 122 x 122 cm) GBP 3,000. LONDON, 1 Sept 2004, *After the Storm* (oil on canvas, 30 x 40 ins / 76 x 102 cm) GBP 3,000. LONDON, 1 Sept 2004, *Still-life with Daisies. Figure on a Pavement* (oil on canvas, double-sided, 28 x 36 ins / 71 x 91 cm) GBP 3,600.

HOUSTON, John Adam Plimmer

British, 19th century.
Born 25 December 1812, in Gwydyr Castle, Wales, to Scottish parents; died 2 December 1884, in London.
Painter, watercolourist. History painting, genre scenes.

John Houston was a pupil at the Academy of Fine Arts in Edinburgh and concluded his artistic studies in Germany and in Paris. He subsequently returned to settle in Edinburgh where he lived from 1840 to 1858 and became a member of the Royal Scottish Academy in 1845. Between 1840 and 1877 he took part in the majority of the big London exhibitions, mainly at the Royal Academy, the Society of British Artists and the British Institution. He also exhibited at the Society of Painters in Watercolours of which he became an associate in 1874 and a member in 1879.
MUSEUMS AND GALLERIES:
EDINBURGH (Royal Scottish Academy): *The Good Samaritan* (oil on canvas) - GLASGOW: *View of Glasgow*.
AUCTION RECORDS:
LONDON, 2 Dec 1907, *Death of the Count of Warwick* (1872) GBP 10. LONDON, 21 Nov 1908, *Knock Castle* (watercolour) GBP 5. LONDON, 5 March 1910, *Faithful Unto Death* (watercolour) GBP 15. NEW YORK, 12 Nov 1971, *The Fugitive Slave* (1853) USD 700. SCOTLAND, 25 Aug 1972, *Day in the Country*, GBP 850. LONDON, 2 Oct 1973, *Little Girl Returning from Mass* (1854) GBP 620. LONDON, 26 March 1974, *Seaside, Inverary, Argyllshire*, GBP 680. LONDON, 14 May 1976, *Wahabee Sheikh* (oil on canvas, 23 1/2 x 17 1/2 ins / 59.7 x 44.5 cm) GBP 420. LONDON, 13 Oct 1978, *Solicitude* (1862, oil on canvas, 15 x 19 3/4 ins / 38 x 50.3 cm) GBP 1,500. EDINBURGH, 2 July 1981, *Sunday* (1854, oil on card, 23 1/2 x 17 ins / 60 x 43 cm) GBP 1,200. LONDON, 18 Feb 1983, *Wahabee Sheikh* (oil on canvas, 24 1/4 x 18 1/4 ins / 61.5 x 46.5 cm) GBP 2,800. LONDON, 23 May 1985, *The Venetian Ambassador's Room, Knowle, Kent* (watercolour/pencil outlines heightened with gouache, 11 x 17 1/2 ins / 28 x 44.5 cm) GBP 1,500. EDINBURGH, 30 April 1986, *Sisters* (1874, oil on canvas, 20 x 27 ins / 51 x 68.5 cm) GBP 2,000. LONDON, 3 June 1992, *Skipping Rope* (1863, oil on canvas, 21 1/2 x 14 1/2 ins / 54.5 x 37 cm) GBP 1,540. LONDON, 20 Jan 1993, *Christopher Columbus Spotting Land* (1844, oil on canvas, 30 x 25 ins / 76 x 63.5 cm) GBP 3,680. PERTH, 29 Aug 1995, *Highland Produce* (1858, oil on panel, 14 x 9 3/4 ins / 35.5 x 25 cm) GBP 4,370. NEW YORK, 27 Sept 2000, *Captured Banner* (1869, oil on canvas, 31 x 40 ins / 79 x 102 cm) USD 2,700. EDINBURGH, 24 Aug 2001, *Night* (1862, oil on board, 11 x 9 ins / 29 x 24 cm) GBP 2,200. LONDON, 23 May 2002, *Warlike Gear of Old, the Matchlike* (1874, oil on canvas, 36 x 28 ins / 91 x 71 cm) GBP 3,000. EDINBURGH, 22 Aug 2002, *Skylark* (1861, oil on canvas, 24 x 35 ins / 60 x 90 cm) GBP 3,000. EDINBURGH, 21 Aug 2003, *Expectancy* (1850, oil on panel, 17 x 16 ins / 44 x 41 cm) GBP 4,800. LONDON, 25 March 2004, *Eastern Question* (1880, oil on canvas, 17 x 23 ins / 44 x 58 cm) GBP 2,800. LONDON, 19 April 2004, *His Favourite Toy* (1867, oil on canvas, 31 x 23 ins / 79 x 58 cm) GBP 3,200.

HOUSTON, Richard

Irish, 18th century.
Born c. 1721, in Dublin; died 14 August 1775, in London.
Painter, engraver (mezzotint).

Richard Houston was a pupil of J. Brooks in Dublin. He went to London while still fairly young, where he led a dissipated life, was imprisoned for debt and was only freed in 1760, on the accession of George III. He engraved mythological and historical subjects, portraits and genre subjects. His works are extremely sought after, in particular his portraits after Joshua Reynolds, of which the one of the Duchess of Marlborough and her child is one of the most perfect examples, and also his etchings after Rembrandt.
AUCTION RECORDS:
LONDON, May 1922, *Glyn, Mr. Sergeant, John Wilkes and the Reverend John Horne Tooke*, GBP 126.

HOUSTON, Robert

British, 20th century.
Born 1891; died 1942.
Painter. Landscapes, landscapes with figures, waterscapes.

Robert Houston worked mostly in Scotland.
AUCTION RECORDS:
WEST LOTHIAN, 30 April 1985, *November* (watercolour, 15 3/4 x 19 3/4 ins / 40 x 50 cm) GBP 950. GLASGOW, 6 Feb 1990, *Birch and Bracken at Loch Lomond* (oil on canvas, 28 x 36 ins / 71 x 91.5 cm) GBP 2,640. PERTH, 27 Aug 1990, *Panorama from Arisaig* (oil on canvas, 25 x 30 ins / 63.5 x 76 cm) GBP 2,200. EDINBURGH, 28 April 1992, *The Coast Road* (oil on canvas, 28 x 36 ins / 71 x 91.5 cm) GBP 1,320. PERTH, 1 Sept 1992, *The Flock's Return* (oil on canvas, 28 1/4 x 36 1/4 ins / 71.5 x 92 cm) GBP 1,980. GLASGOW, 14 Feb 1995, *Loch Lomond* (oil on canvas, 24 x 36 ins / 61 x 91.5 cm) GBP 575. PERTH, 29 Aug 1995, *View of Arran from Largs* (oil on canvas, 28 x 35 1/2 ins / 71 x 90 cm) GBP 1,265. PERTH, 26 Aug 1996, *The Clyde Estuary* (oil on canvas, 27 1/2 x 36 ins / 70 x 91.5 cm) GBP 2,415. EDINBURGH, 25 Aug 2000, *Arran from Fairlie* (oil on canvas, 31 x 36 ins / 78 x 92 cm) GBP 4,500. LONDON, 5 Sept 2001, *Western Highlands* (oil on canvas, 28 x 36 ins / 71 x 91 cm) GBP 1,500. LONDON, 5 Sept 2001, *Linlithgow Castle and Loch. Elderslie, Birthplace of Wallace* (oil on canvas, a pair, 24 x 36 ins / 61 x 91 cm) GBP 1,900. LONDON, 27 May 2004, *Arrochar, Loch Long, Argyll* (oil on canvas, 25 x 30 ins / 63 x 75 cm) GBP 1,600. LONDON, 28 Oct 2004, *Landscape with Ruined Castle by a Loch* (oil on canvas, 12 x 16 ins / 30 x 40 cm) GBP 1,400.

HOUSTRAET, Jacobus

Dutch, 17th century.
Active in Amsterdam.
Painter. Genre scenes, landscapes.

HOUT, H. J. van den

Dutch, 19th century.
Active in Rotterdam.
Lithographer.

H. J. van den Hout created plates after Charlet.

HOUT, Louis Edmond
French, 20th century.
Born in Épinac-les-Mines.
Painter.
Louis Hout exhibited in Paris at the Salon des Indépendants from 1926.

HOUT, Madeleine
French, 20th century.
Born 1915, in Paris.
Painter.
A pupil of Cheval, Madeleine Hout began by executing decorative works. She painted nudes and landscapes.

HOUTE, Adrian van den, the Elder
Flemish, 16th century.
Active in Mechelen in 1513.
Glass painter.
Flemish School.

HOUTE, Adrian van den, the Younger
Flemish, 16th century.
Active in Mechelen.
Painter.
Antwerp School, Flemish School.
Adrian van den Houte was admitted into the Antwerp guild in 1582 and was also mentioned in 1589.

HOUTE, Pierre van den
Flemish, 16th century.
Active in Mechelen.
Glass painter.
Flemish School.
In 1526 Pierre van den Houte painted a window for the church of St-Rombout.

HOUTE, Rambout van den
Dutch, 17th century.
Painter.
Rambout van den Houte worked in Lyons, France, in 1613. He mainly painted watercolours.

HOUTELET, François
French, 18th century.
Active in Paris in 1765.
Painter (?), sculptor (?).

HOUTEN, Barbara Elisabeth van, later Mme Behrend-Croiset van der Kop
Dutch, 19th century.
Born 8 April 1862, in Groningen.
Painter, engraver.
Barbara van Houten was the niece of Mrs Mesdag, and was partly brought up in the artistic residence of her uncle Mesdag who was a great influence on her career. She went to Paris to learn wood engraving under the direction of Perrichon. She worked mainly from life and started engraving with the aid of a treatise by Lalanne. In addition to her work as an engraver she also produced some very fine paintings. The Mesdag museum in The Hague has her works *Dead Birds* and *Suns*. She was awarded a silver medal at the Paris Universal Exhibition of 1900.

HOUTEN, C.
Dutch, 18th century.
Active at the beginning of the 18th century in Utrecht.
Portrait painter, draughtsman.

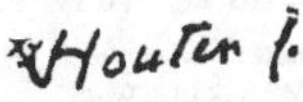

HOUTEN, Carel van
Dutch, 17th century.
Active during the first half of the 17th century.
Painter.

HOUTEN, Christian Gottfried Schutze van
Dutch, 19th century.
Born 12 July 1807, in Rotterdam; died 6 September 1869, in Rotterdam.
Engraver. Still-lifes (flowers).
Christian van Houten was a pupil of G. de Meyer.
AUCTION RECORDS:
LONDON, 4 May 1977, *Still-life with Flowers* (oil on panel, 16 x 11 3/4in/40.5 x 30cm) GBP 680.

HOUTEN, F. van
Flemish School, 17th century.
Painter.

HOUTEN, Georges
Belgian, 20th century.
Born 1888, in Antwerp.
Active in France.
Painter. Nudes, portraits, landscapes, seascapes, flowers.
Houten seems to have spent most of his life in Paris, and his work was shown at various salons there, including the Salon des Indépendants (1910) and the Salon d'Automne (1919). He had a solo exhibition at the Galerie Sauvage in Paris in 1919.

HOUTEN, Gerard van
Flemish, 17th century.
Born in Breda; died 1706, in Amsterdam.
Painter, draughtsman, engraver. Allegorical subjects.
Flemish School.
Gerard van Houten made engravings after Nicolas Poussin, and also painted glass.
AUCTION RECORDS:
PARIS, 8 March 1920, *Print Collector,* FRF 3,500. NEW YORK, 11 Jan 1989, *Sculptor in his Studio* (red chalk and ink, 6 1/4 x 4 ins / 16 x 10.3 cm) USD 880. AMSTERDAM, 25 Nov 1991, *Plan for a Frontispiece: Allegory of Peace* (1682, red chalk, wash and ink, 17 3/4 x 11 3/4 ins / 45 x 30.1 cm) NLG 1,840.

HOUTEN, H. L. van den
Dutch, 19th century.
Lithographer.
AUCTION RECORDS:
MELBOURNE, 11-12 March 1971, *Marysville,* AUD 1,600.

HOUTEN, Hans van
Flemish School, 17th century.
Born in Antwerp.
Painter.
Hans van Houten also worked in Amsterdam.

HOUTEN, Jan Jakobsz. van
Dutch, 17th century.
Born in Haarlem.
Active in 1642 in Amsterdam.
Engraver.

HOUTEN, Jan van
Dutch, 18th century.
Active in Amsterdam in 1707.
Painter.

HOUTEN, Katrine Van
American, 20th century.
Born 1940, in the USA.
Active in France.
Engraver.
Katrine Van Houten studied at the Western College in Ohio, and then at the Art Students League, New York. She went to Europe, attended the Academia di Brera in Milan and settled in Paris where she worked at *Atelier 17* with Hayter. Her art bears a direct resemblance to the geometric abstraction movement.

Van Houten took part in collective exhibitions, notably the Salon des Réalités Nouvelles in Paris in 1968, the Engraving Biennale in Paris in 1970, and the Engraving Biennale in Cracovic, also in 1970. In 1972, she appeared in the graphics section of the Venice Biennale. She staged her first solo exhibition in Paris in 1968.

HOUTEN, Sientje Mesdag Van. See **MESDAG VAN HOUTEN Sientje**

HOUTEN, T. van, or van Houtter
Flemish School, 17th century.
Active in Brussels.
Painter.

T van Houten worked in the same genre as Teniers.

HOUTHUESEN, Albert
Dutch, 20th century.
Born 1903, in Amsterdam; died 1979.
Active in England.
Painter.

Albert Houthuesen came to London while very young and settled there. He studied at St Martin's School of Art from 1917 to 1923 and, after winning a scholarship, at the Royal College of Art from 1923 to 1927. In 1961 he had his first solo show at the Reid Gallery in London. His work is kept by the Tate Gallery. His paintings show imaginary scenes lit by the light of a full moon, which is reflected in the nature he depicts.

AUCTION RECORDS:
LONDON, 13 June 1980, *Italian Peaches* (1961, oil on canvas, 28 x 36 ins / 71.2 x 91.5 cm) GBP 850. LONDON, 25 June 1980, *Head* (red and black chalks, 30 x 21 1/4 ins / 76 x 54 cm) GBP 400.

HOUTHUYSEN, Jan Jansz. van
Flemish School, 17th century.
Born c. 1609; died 1662.
Active in Amsterdam.
Painter. Figures, landscapes, waterscapes, hunting scenes.

This artist is almost certainly the Jan van Houthuysen who also worked in The Hague.

AUCTION RECORDS:
VIENNA, 16 March 1971, *River Landcape with Mill,* ATS 80,000. LONDON, 22 Feb 1984, *Hunters in a River Landscape* (oil on panel, 20 x 26 3/4in/50.5 x 68cm) GBP 2,700. AMSTERDAM, 10 Nov 1997, *Huntsman on a Road by a Wood in the Dunes* (oil on panel, 17 x 19in/43.2 x 48.1cm) NLG 9,802.

HOUTIN, François
French, 20th - 21st century.
Born 25 August 1950, in Craon.
Engraver (etching/dry-point), draughtsman (wash).
Landscapes, landscapes with figures.

François Houtin was a student in Jean Delpech's studio and has lived and worked in Paris since 1971. He won the Lacourière prize for engraving in 1981.

His etchings and dry point engravings explore imaginary gardens with astonishing precision worthy of encyclopaedic prints. These imaginary gardens may be in the French style or, as in the case of the *Fantaisies Romaines* (*Roman Fantasies*), of Italian inspiration, or more simply, *Jardins d'Évasion* (*Gardens of Escape*).

Houtin takes part in group exhibitions such as the 2003 St-Maur Print Biennale, St-Maur-des-Fossés. Solo exhibitions of his work include: Galerie Condillac, Bordeaux, 1978; Librairie Nicaise, Paris, 1980; Galerie de l'Ours, Bourges, 1981; French Cultural Centre, Rome, 1984; Galerie Roubaux, Munich, 1985 ND 1988; Galerie Flottbek, Hamburg, 1984 and 1987; French Cultural Centre, Palermo, 1985; Galerie l'Angle Aigu, Brussels, 1987; Galerie Eolia, Paris, 1989; Bagatelle, 1992; Galerie Michèle Broutta, Paris, 1982, 1993 and 2002.

BIBLIOGRAPHY:
François Houtin. Catalogue raisonné de l'œuvre gravé 1973-2002, catalogue raisonné, Gal. Michèle Broutta, Paris, 2002. *Biennale de l'Estampe de Saint-Maur,* exhibition catalogue, Musée de Saint-Maur, St-Maur-des-Fossés, 2003.

HOUTMAN, Cornelis
Dutch, 18th century.
Died 1806, in Maarssen, near Utrecht.
Painter. Flowers, fruit.

AUCTION RECORDS:
PARIS, 19 May 1927, *Vase of Flowers on a Stone Ledge* (watercolour) FRF 1,600.

HOUTMAN, J. P.
Dutch, 19th century.
Lithographer.

J. P. Houtman was a printer and almost certainly a lithographer in Utrecht around 1830. He either did the work himself or signed the plates he commissioned from other artists.

HOUTMAN, M.
Dutch, 18th century.
Born probably in Utrecht.
Active at the end of the 18th century.
Draughtsman, engraver.

HOUTMAN, Sipke Cornelis
Dutch, 20th century.
Born 1871, in Dokkum; died 1945, in Amsterdam.
Painter.

Houtman began to paint at the age of 16, while he was working in a bakery. In order to emphasise the fact that he was self-taught, he would write 'Our saviour Jesus Christ taught me ' on the back of his pictures. It was only when he was about 60 that he began to concentrate seriously on painting, depicting people and things from his immediate surroundings, as is often the case with naive artists. His works include *Birds in a Cage* and *Garden of the Old People's Home in Amsterdam*, whose endlessly crossing walkways have symbolic value.

BIBLIOGRAPHY:
Bihalji-Merin, Oto, *Les Peintres naïfs*, Delpire, Paris, 1960.

MUSEUMS AND GALLERIES:
AMSTERDAM (Stedelijk Mus.).

HOUTMANN, M., or Houtman
Dutch, 19th century.
Active in Amsterdam.
Painter. Landscapes, still-lifes, flowers.

M. Houtmann is mentioned by Kramm as working around 1820. He may be a relative of, or the same artist as, the draughtsman and engraver M. Houtman.

AUCTION RECORDS:
LONDON, 25 Jan 1908, *River in Switzerland,* GBP 2. NEW YORK, 5 April 1990, *Still-life with Peaches, Grapes, Apples and Pears in a Basket; Still-life with a Melon, Grapes, Apples and Pears in a Blue and White Faïence Dish* (1816, watercolour/paper, a pair, 24 3/4 x 20in/63 x 51cm) USD 17,600.

HOUVE, Hyacinthe
French, 17th century.
Painter.

Hyacinthe Houve was admitted into the Académie de St-Luc in 1690.

HOUVE, Paul de La. See **LA HOUVE**

HOUVEN, Henri
Dutch (?), 19th - 20th century.
Painter. Genre scenes, scenes with figures.

Despite the appearance of this name at a London sale, no information can be traced concerning any artist of this or a similar name.

Auction records:
London, 26 Nov 1986, *Flower Market, Amsterdam* (1916, oil on canvas, 33 x 48½ ins / 84 x 123 cm) GBP 16,000.

HOUVRER, Melchior
French, 18th century.
Active in 1765.
Painter, sculptor.

HOUWEN, Joris
Belgian, 20th century.
Born 1925, in Lichtervelde.
Painter, draughtsman, lithographer. Figures, scenes with figures, landscapes.

Auction records:
Amsterdam, 8 Dec 1993, *The Beach* (1981, oil on card, 31½ x 48 ins / 80 x 122 cm) NLG 2,300.

HOUWENS, Johannes
Dutch, 17th century.
Active in Rotterdam c. 1658.
Painter.

HOUX, Jacques
French, 17th century.
Active in Tours in 1663.
Painter.
Jacques Houx worked for the church of St-Julien.

HOUYOUX, Léon J.-J.
Belgian, 19th - 20th century.
Born 24 November 1856, in Brussels; died 1940, in Brussels.
Painter. Figures, nudes, interiors with figures, landscapes.
Houyoux was a student at the Académie des Beaux Arts in Brussels, in the studio of Jean François Portaels. He was a member of the Société Nationale des Beaux-Arts in Paris from 1896.

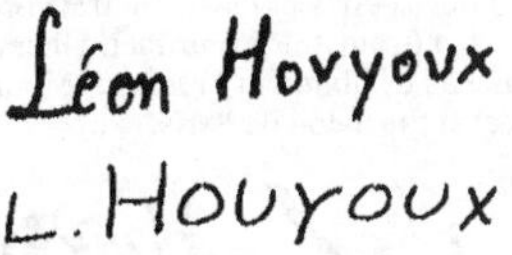

Auction records:
Amsterdam, 20 April 1993, *Female Nude on a Leopard Skin* (oil on canvas, 30¾ x 38½ ins / 78 x 98 cm) NLG 2,300.

HOUZÉ, A.
French, 19th - 20th century.
Born 1863; died 1931.
Active in Lille.
Landscape artist.

Auction records:
Paris, 16 March 1925, *Setting Sun*, FRF 105.

HOUZÉ, Florentin
French, 19th century.
Born 1812, in Tournai.
Painter. History painting.
Houzé was a pupil of Hennequin and Nicaise de Keyser. The Musée de Tournai owns his *Cardinal Visiting a Hospital*.

Auction records:
Brussels, 17 June 1982, *Discussion at the Gaming Table* (oil on canvas, 20¾ x 22 ins / 53 x 56 cm) BEF 85,000.

HOUZEAU
French, 18th century.
Painter.
Between 1793 and 1796 Houzeau exhibited mythological and allegorical subjects at the Salon and, significantly, at his last Salon, an allusion to the emancipation of Black slaves.

HOUZEAU, Jacques
French, 17th century.
Born 1624, in Bar-le-Duc; died 18 May 1691, in Paris.
Sculptor.
Jacques Houzeau was approved as a master sculptor in 1656 and was appointed sculptor to the king in 1663. He created several works, engraved by Thomassin and owned by Versailles Palace. He was made an Académicien on 29 November 1664.

Museums and Galleries:
Versailles (Château, Jardins): *Thalia*; *Momus*; *Terpsichore*; *Pan*; *Tiger Pinning a Bear to the Ground*; *Bloodhound Bringing Down a Stag*; *Bad-tempered Man*; *Faun*; four lead vases; four candelabra.

HOUZELOT, Alphonse Alexandre
French, 19th century.
Born 8 April 1802, in Troyes; died 2 February 1857, in Troyes.
Sculptor. Figures.
Houzelot initially learned sculpture from his father, J.B.T. Houzelot, then went to Paris, where he became a regular attendee at Bosio's studio.

Museums and Galleries:
Troyes: *Abbott Cortier*.

HOUZELOT, Jean Baptiste Thomas
French, 18th century.
Active in Troyes and Brienne.
Draughtsman.
Jean Baptiste Thomas Houzelot taught drawing at the military school in Brienne and then at the college of Troyes. He was the father of the sculptor Alphonse Houzelot.

HOVART, Giovanni, called Giovannino di Lamberto
Flemish School, 17th century.
Died 1668.
Painter. Historical subjects, portraits.
After studying in Antwerp, Giovanni Hovart settled in Genoa. His son was also a painter. He studied under Lucas and Cornelis de Wael.

HOVAS, Michel Ange. See **HOUASSE**

HOVE, Andreas van
Flemish School, 17th century.
Active in Antwerp at the end of the 17th century.
Painter.

HOVE, Bart van
Dutch, 19th - 20th century.
Born 18 March 1856, in The Hague; died 9 February 1914, in Amsterdam.
Sculptor. Busts.

Museums and Galleries:
Amsterdam (Stedelijk Mus.): *Bust of C. Rochussen*; *Bust of J. Bosboom*.

HOVE, Bartholomeus Johannes van
Dutch, 19th century.
Born 28 October 1790, in The Hague; died 8 November 1880, in The Hague.
Painter, watercolourist, draughtsman. Genre scenes, landscapes, urban landscapes, architectural views.
Bartholomeus van Hove was a pupil of Johannes Hendricus Adrianus Albertus Broekenheymer, and was a painter at the theatre of The Hague.

Museums and Galleries:
Amsterdam: *Corner of Town*; *View of Mauritshuis in The Hague* - Rotterdam: *Town View* - The Hague (Gemeentemus.): *The Former Hospice for Old Women and Children*; *View of Leiden*; *The Buitenhof*.

Auction records:
London, 2-9 June 1911, *View of a Dutch Town* (drawing) GBP 4. London, March 1923, *View of Leiden,* GBP 33. London, April 1923, *View of The Hague in Winter,* GBP 12. Paris, 9 Feb 1928, *View of a Dutch Town* (watercolour) FRF 375. London, 22 Dec 1937, *Leiden,* GBP 30. London, 17 Oct 1945, *Sea Scene, Holland,* GBP 60. London, 21 March 1947, *View of Amsterdam,* GBP 46. Amsterdam, 1-4 July 1947, *Town View,* NLG 2,200. London, 17 May 1961, *Canal Scene with Barges,* GBP 500. London, 17 May 1967, *Fortifications of a Dutch Town,* GBP 900. Amsterdam, 25 Nov 1969, *View of Amsterdam,* NLG 25,000. London, 17 Feb 1971, *Canal Scene,* GBP 2,300. Dordrecht, 12 Dec 1972, *View of a Town beside a River,* NLG 36,000. Amsterdam, 7 Sept 1976, *River Landscape* (oil on panel, 11 x 11¼in/28 x 28.5cm) NLG 9,800. Amsterdam, 25 April 1978, *Snowy Landscape* (oil on panel, 11 x 11¼in/28 x 28.5cm) NLG 23,000. Amsterdam, 7 Nov 1978, *View of a Town beside a River* (watercolour, 7 x 10¾in/17.5 x 27.3cm) NLG 7,200. London, 28 Nov 1979, *View of Haarlem* (1829, oil on panel, 22 x 29½in/56 x 75cm) GBP 10,000. Amsterdam, 28 Oct 1980, *View of Düsseldorf* (watercolour, 11¾ x 15¾in/30 x 40.3cm) NLG 3,200. Amsterdam, 19 May 1981, *View of a Town in Holland* (oil on panel, 13¾ x 19¼in/35 x 49cm) NLG 34,000. Amsterdam, 15 March 1983, *Riverside Scene, Haarlem* (1840, oil on canvas, 28¼ x 36¼in/71.5 x 92.2cm) NLG 34,000. London, 21 June 1984, *View of Haarlem with the Church of St Bavo* (1850, watercolour and pencil, 13¼ x 17¾in/33.6 x 45cm) GBP 2,400. Amsterdam, 28 May 1986, *Street in a Dutch Town with Figures* (watercolour and pencil, 16½ x 15in/42 x 38cm) NLG 5,500. Amsterdam, 10 Feb 1988, *Craft by a Lift Bridge on a Village Canal* (pencil and watercolour/paper, 9½ x 13½in/24 x 34.5cm) NLG 1,265. London, 24 June 1988, *The Court of Justice in The Hague* (oil on panel, 15½ x 19½in/39.4 x 49.5cm) GBP 7,150. Amsterdam, 16 Nov 1988, *Flemish Town with Craft Moored at the Edge of a Canal and a Cathedral in the Background* (1839, oil on panel, 29½ x 39¼in/75 x 100cm) NLG 109,250. Paris, 28 Sept 1989, *View of Bruges with Canals* (oil on canvas, 23¾ x 31in/60.5 x 78.5cm) FRF 190,000. New York, 25 Oct 1989, *A Canal in Holland* (watercolour, 7¼ x 10¾in/18.5 x 27.3cm) USD 1,760. London, 28 March 1990, *Street Scene in Amsterdam* (1828, oil on panel, 14¾ x 17in/37.5 x 43cm) GBP 22,000. Amsterdam, 2 May 1990, *Capriccio of a Dutch Town with Fishermen in the Foreground* (oil on panel, 18 x 23¼in/46 x 59cm) NLG 62,100. Amsterdam, 30 Oct 1991, *Deventer with the Brink in Winter* (oil on panel, 11½ x 15¼in/29 x 39cm) NLG 27,600. Amsterdam, 22 April 1992, *Capriccio of Haarlem with Townspeople on the Quay beside the Canal and the Bakenessekerk in the Background* (oil on panel, 16½ x 13in/42 x 33cm) NLG 36,800. Paris, 10 Dec 1992, *Views of a Town in Holland* (oil on panel, 11¾ x 15in/30 x 38cm) FRF 80,000. Amsterdam, 21 April 1993, *View of the Hospice and the Orphanage in The Hague with People Walking along the Bierkade in Winter* (1826, oil on canvas, 27¼ x 37½in/69 x 95cm) NLG 94,300. Copenhagen, 7 Sept 1994, *Canal in a Town in Holland* (oil on panel, 15 x 17in/38 x 43cm) DKK 285,000. Amsterdam, 11 April 1995, *Townspeople on a Frozen River* (watercolour, 14¼ x 12in/36.5 x 30.5cm) NLG 7,080. Rennes, 13 June 1995, *View of a Dutch Town* (1845, oil on mahogany panel) FRF 105,000. London, 11 Oct 1995, *Capriccio of a View of The Hague* (oil on panel, 15¼ x 12¼in/39 x 31cm) GBP 2,070. Amsterdam, 7 Nov 1995, *View of a Dutch Town* (oil on panel, 9½ x 12½in/24 x 32cm) NLG 22,420. Amsterdam, 16 April 1996, *People on a Frozen Canal in Haarlem* (oil on panel, 11½ x 16½in/29 x 42cm) NLG 23,600. Amsterdam, 5 Nov 1996, *View of a Dutch Town* (watercolour, 17¼ x 14¼in/44 x 36cm) NLG 10,030. New York, 23 May 1997, *Ferryboat Crossing a Canal in Haarlem* (oil on canvas, 21 x 28in/53.3 x 71.1cm) USD 61,900. London, 13 June 1997, *People by a Canal in Delft* (oil on panel, 16 x 22in/40.6 x 55.8cm) GBP 26,450. Amsterdam, 27 Oct 1997, *People by a City Gate with a Cathedral in the Background* (watercolour, 12½ x 9¾in/32 x 25cm) NLG 7,316. Amsterdam, 27 April 1999, *Capriccio View with Figures Leaving Church in Winter* (1846, oil on panel, 11 x 9 ins / 29 x 22 cm) NLG 25,000. Amsterdam, 27 April 1999, *Sunlit Town View with Figures Gathered in Square along Canal* (1873, oil on panel, 14 x 16 ins / 35 x 40 cm) NLG 35,000. Amsterdam, 24 Oct 2000, *Cappriccio View of the Hooglands Kerk, Leiden, in Winter* (1857, oil on canvas, 22 x 19 ins / 57 x 47 cm) NLG 65,000. Amsterdam, 8 Nov 2000, *Design for a Gothic Stage Set for Hoogduitsche Schouwburg, Amsterdam* (watercolour and black chalk, 12 x 17 ins / 30 x 42 cm) NLG 6,000. Rotterdam, 5 May 2001, *Boat and Figures seen through an Arch* (1863, oil on panel, 13 x 17 ins / 32 x 42 cm) NLG 40,000. London, 9 Nov 2001, *Riverside Town* (1834, oil on canvas, 24 x 28 ins / 60 x 71 cm) GBP 12,000. Leyburn, 25 April 2002, *View of a Sunlit Town with Figures amongst Logs* (oil on panel, 12 x 19 ins / 31 x 47 cm) GBP 6,600. Brussels, 28 May 2002, *View of Haarlem* (1832, oil on panel, 10 x 8 ins / 26 x 21 cm) EUR 15,000. Vienna, 30 Sept 2003, *Haarlem Canal* (watercolour, 7 x 10 ins / 18 x 26 cm) EUR 2,200. Lyons, 30 Nov 2003, *A Port at Brunswick in the Snow, and in Spring* (1824, oil on panel, a pair, 16 x 14 ins / 41 x 35 cm) EUR 32,000. Amsterdam, 29 March 2004, *View of a Town in Summer with Canal Activity* (watercolour, 18 x 24 ins / 45 x 62 cm) EUR 4,400.

HOVE, Denys van
Flemish School, 17th century.
Active in Antwerp in 1604.
Painter.

HOVE, Edmond Theodor van
Belgian, 19th - 20th century.
Born 7 June 1853, in Bruges; died 1913, in Ghent.
Painter. Religious subjects, genre scenes, portraits.

Edmond van Hove was a student of Alexandre Cabanel at the École des Beaux-Arts in Paris. He travelled in Italy and lived in Antwerp (from 1899) and then Ghent (from 1902). Work by him was exhibited in Stuttgart, Munich and (from 1879 onwards) at the Salon de Paris.

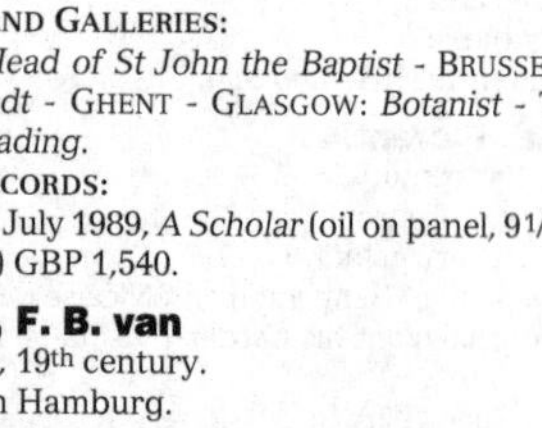

Museums and Galleries:
Antwerp: *Head of St John the Baptist* - Brussels: *Jacques Van Laerlandt* - Ghent - Glasgow: *Botanist* - Tourcoing: *Old Man Reading.*

Auction records:
Chester, 20 July 1989, *A Scholar* (oil on panel, 9½ x 11½ ins / 24 x 29 cm) GBP 1,540.

HOVE, F. B. van
German, 19th century.
Active in Hamburg.
Lithographer.

HOVE, Frederick Hendrik van den
Dutch, 17th century.
Born c. 1628, in The Hague; died 17 October 1698, in London.
Active in The Hague.
Draughtsman, engraver.

Frederick van den Hove studied under F. Bouttats in Antwerp. He was working in London around 1692.

HOVE, Hubertus or Huib van
Dutch, 19th century.
Born 13 May 1814, in The Hague; died 14 November 1865, in Antwerp.
Painter, watercolourist, draughtsman. Figures, genre scenes, interiors with figures, landscapes, architectural views.

Hubertus van Hove lived in Antwerp. He was the son of Bartholomeus Johannes van Hove and was taught by Van de Sande Bakhuyzen. At the start of his career he painted landscapes, but later produced interiors.

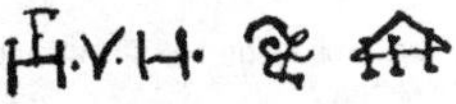

Museums and Galleries:
Graz: *The Housewife* - Leipzig: *Room at the Town Hall in The Hague* - Munich: *Staircase of an Old Palace* - Rotterdam: *View of the Marshes near Rotterdam* - Stuttgart: *Staircase of a Dutch House* - The Hague (Gemeentemus.): *Synagogue.*

Auction records:
Paris, 1869, *Interior,* FRF 1,080. Paris, 1883, *The Sale of Rembrandt's Furniture,* FRF 2,600. Paris, 1895, *Paying the Rent* (watercolour) FRF 270. London, 27 Feb 1925, *The Housewife,* GBP 157. London, 2 June 1939, *Interior,* GBP 39. Paris, 7 Feb 1951, *Young Woman Cooking Waffles,* FRF 32,000. London, 12 Feb 1969, *The Lamp Maker,* GBP 1,450. London, 28 Feb 1973, *Young Woman Washing her Hands in the Hallway of a Dutch House,* GBP 8,000. Vienna, 12 March 1974, *Preparing the Table,* ATS 140,000. Amsterdam, 16 March 1976, *The Breakfast Tray* (1849, oil on panel, 20 1/2 x 16 1/2in/52 x 42cm) NLG 7,600. London, 19 April 1978, *The Servant* (1851, oil on panel, 22 1/2 x 17 1/2in/57 x 44.5cm) GBP 8,000. London, 16 Feb 1979, *The Cook and her Lover* (oil on panel, 14 1/2 x 19in/37 x 48.2cm) GBP 1,000. London, 18 April 1983, *Saying Grace* (1861, oil on panel, 11 3/4 x 14 3/4in/30 x 37.5cm) GBP 1,500. London, 21 June 1985, *Couple in a Dutch Interior* (1842, oil on panel, 26 1/2 x 21 1/2in/67.5 x 54.5cm) GBP 9,000. Amsterdam, 10 April 1990, *Lady Standing by a Table* (1854, ink, wash and watercolour heightened with white/paper, 3 1/4 x 2 1/4in/8.5 x 5.5cm) NLG 1,092. Amsterdam, 22 April 1992, *The Secret Letter* (1847, oil on panel, 19 1/2 x 15 3/4in/49.5 x 40cm) NLG 9,775. Paris, 29 March 1993, *Lacemaker and Child* (oil on panel, 13 1/4 x 11in/33.5 x 28cm) FRF 3,600. London, 18 March 1994, *The Inventory* (1864, oil on panel, 20 3/4 x 17in/52.7 x 43.1cm) GBP 3,450. Amsterdam, 27 April 1999, *Guest's Arrival* (1863, oil on panel, 31 x 24 ins / 78 x 60 cm) NLG 20,000. London, 22 June 1999, *Pantry Maid in Hallway* (1838, oil on panel, 18 x 13 ins / 46 x 34 cm) GBP 4,500. Amsterdam, 18 April 2000, *Bringing over the Little Visitor* (1859, oil on panel, 14 x 12 ins / 36 x 30 cm) NLG 14,000. Amsterdam, 30 Jan 2001, *The Eavesdropper* (oil on panel, 6 x 5 ins / 14 x 13 cm) NLG 6,000. Brussels, 11 Nov 2002, *The Generous Servant* (1849, oil on panel, 24 x 19 ins / 60 x 47 cm) EUR 8,500. Vienna, 27 May 2004, *Mother with Child in Entrance Hall* (oil on panel, 7 x 9 ins / 19 x 24 cm) EUR 2,200.

HOVE, Johannes Hubertus van
Dutch, 19th century.
Born 7 March 1827, in The Hague; died 3 November 1881, in The Hague.
Painter, sculptor. Genre scenes.

Johannes van Hove was the brother of Hubertus.

Auction records:
London, 31 Oct 1996, *The Flood* (1850, oil on panel, 23 x 17 3/4in/57.5 x 45cm) GBP 2,645. Vienna, 2 Oct 2002, *The Letter* (oil on panel, 27 x 22 ins / 68 x 56 cm) EUR 12,000.

HOVE, Martinus van den
Dutch, 17th century.
Active in Delft in 1674.
Painter.

HOVE, Mattheus
Dutch, 17th century.
Born 1590, in Amsterdam.
Painter.

HOVE, Mattheus van den
Flemish, 15th century.
Active in Rome in 1463.
Painter.
Flemish School.

Mattheus van den Hove worked for the church of S Maria dell'Anima.

HOVE, Pierre van
Dutch, 18th century.
Active in Mechelen c. 1700.
Painter.

Together with Jean de Handt, Pierre van Hove executed decorative work in Mechelen.

HOVE, Victor van
Belgian, 19th century.
Born 6 September 1825, in Renaix; died 16 March 1891, in Hockelberg.
Painter, sculptor. Religious subjects, figures, portraits, church interiors, genre scenes, interiors with figures.

At this period, Rude was living and working in Belgium, yet this did little to breathe new life into Belgian sculpture, which was still in the grip of academicism under the Geefs and Simonis. After studying art, Victor van Hove realised that Belgian sculptors needed to return to a more in-depth approach to nature and life. This resulted in *Slave after Flogging,* a piece noted for its realism.

Museums and Galleries:
Brussels: *Young Dutch Girls; Self-portrait;* paintings - Liège: *Young Dutch Women on their Way to Church* - Ypres: *The Good Mother after the Judgement of Solomon; The Bad Mother after the Judgement of Solomon* (sculpture).

Auction records:
Amsterdam, 27 April 1976, *Church Interior* (oil on panel, 11 x 7 3/4in/27 x 20cm) NLG 4,400. Brussels, 23 Oct 1979, *Young Woman with Dog* (oil on wood, 9 x 6 3/4in/22 x 17cm) BEF 40,000. Vienna, 17 Nov 1981, *Dutch Girl Writing a Letter* (oil on panel, 13 3/4 x 19 1/4in/35 x 49cm) NLG 34,000. Enghien-les-Bains, 21 Oct 1984, *Slave Recumbent after Gaining his Freedom* (1859, bronze, 28 3/4 x 102 1/4 x 43 1/4in/73 x 260 x 110cm) FRF 240,000. New York, 25 Oct 1984, *Three Young Women in an Interior* (oil on canvas, 38 1/2 x 42 3/4in/98.1 x 108.6cm) USD 6,000. Paris, 3 Dec 1987, *Fisherman's Family* (oil on canvas, 52 1/4 x 43 1/4in/133 x 110cm) FRF 9,500. London, 17 June 1994, *Le nouveau tour* (oil on canvas, 46 x 34in/117 x 85.5cm) GBP 2,875. London, 29 Sept 1999, *Child Playing with Cat* (brown patinated bronze, h. 35ins / 88cm) GBP 4,000. Brussels, 17 March 2004, *Lecture in Shadow* (oil on panel, 14 x 10 ins / 35 x 26 cm) EUR 2,500.

HOVECKE, C. van
Flemish, 16th century.
Active in Ypres in 1598.
Sculptor (wood).
Flemish School.

C. van Hovecke worked for the church of St-Martin.

HOVEN, Gottfried von
German, 19th - 20th century.
Born 17 June 1868, in Frankfurt am Main; died 1921, in Munich.
Painter. Landscapes, landscapes with figures.

Views of Italy, the Netherlands and Germany by Von Hoven are extant.

HOVENDEN, Thomas
Irish, 19th century.
Born 23 December 1840, in Dunmanway (County Cork); died 14 August 1895, near Worristown (Pennsylvania).
Active in the USA.
Painter. Portraits, genre scenes.

Thomas Hovenden was a pupil at the School of Fine Arts in Cork. He went to America in 1863 and was a pupil at the National Academy in New York. Around 1874 he returned to Europe and worked in Paris in the studio of Alexandre Cabanel. He spent some time in Pont Aven in Brittany. He finally settled in the USA in 1880 and became a teacher at the Pennsylvania Academy of Fine Arts. He was influenced by Courbet and painted painted realist genre scenes which enjoyed great success in America.

He exhibited his work in the USA in 1878 and in 1893 at the Universal Exhibition in Chicago.

MUSEUMS AND GALLERIES:
DETROIT (IA): *In Hoc Signo Vinces* (1880) - PHILADELPHIA (MA): *Breaking Home Ties* (1890).

AUCTION RECORDS:
NEW YORK, 31 Jan-2 Feb 1900, *Seller of Breton Images,* USD 120. LONDON, April 1924, *Footpath to the Spring,* GBP 10. NEW YORK, 18 Oct 1972, *Village Blacksmith,* USD 11,000. NEW YORK, 28 Oct 1976, *Old Man with Pipe and Banjo* (1882, watercolour, 16 x 12 ins / 40.5 x 30.5 cm) USD 3,750. BOLTON, 12 May 1983, *A Stitch in Time* (1881, oil on canvas, 20 x 14 ins / 50.8 x 35.5 cm) USD 20,000. NEW YORK, 29 May 1986, *Young Breton Woman Lying in the Grass* (1878, oil on canvas, $37^{3}/_{4}$ x $53^{1}/_{2}$ ins / 95.8 x 135.8 cm) USD 8,000. NEW YORK, 30 Sept 1988, *Return of the Sailor* (1892, oil on canvas, 36 x 57 ins / 91.5 x 145 cm) USD 17,600. NEW YORK, 21 Sept 1994, *A Delicate Missive* (oil on canvas, 14 x 20 ins / 35.6 x 50.8 cm) USD 23,000. NEW YORK, 1 Dec 1994, *Self-portrait in the Attic* (oil on canvas, 24 x 19 ins / 61 x 48.3 cm) USD 18,400. NEW YORK, 30 Sept 1997, *The Crossing* (1873, oil on canvas, 18 x $24^{1}/_{2}$ ins / 45.7 x 62.2 cm) USD 10,062. NEW YORK, 15 March 2000, *Story of the Hunt* (1880, oil on canvas, 25 x 31 ins / 63 x 79 cm) USD 55,000. NEW YORK, 13 June 2001, *Couple in an Interior* (oil on canvas, 10 x 15 ins / 25 x 38 cm) USD 3,000. DUBLIN, 5 Dec 2001, *Old Couple in Interior* (oil on canvas, 10 x 15 ins / 25 x 38 cm) IEP 4,600. NEW YORK, 4 Dec 2002, *Special Correspondent* (oil on canvas, 14 x 20 ins / 36 x 51 cm) USD 37,500. SAN FRANCISCO, 14 May 2003, *Wayside Chat* (1875, oil on canvas, 33 x 24 ins / 83 x 62 cm) USD 35,000.

HOVER, H.
Painter. Genre scenes.

H. Hover is mentioned by Florence Levy.

AUCTION RECORDS:
NEW YORK, 8 April 1911, *The Love Letter,* USD 75.

HOVEY, Otis
American, 19th century.
Born 1788.
Active in New York, then in Oxford (New York).
Painter. Portraits.

HOVI, Mikko
Finnish, 20th century.
Born 1879.
Sculptor.

Mikko Hovi studied at the central school of industrial arts in Helsinki from 1907 to 1911, and also in 1916. He had his first exhibition in 1915, and his work was subsequently shown at exhibitions of Finnish art in various European countries, as well as at the Venice Biennale (1960). Hovi was initially a decorative sculptor and only began to work as an artist in about 1960.

He made a large number of wooden sculptures for churches in Finland and was also an advocate of sculpture in miniature. He was heavily influenced by popular imagery, and his sculptures take their inspiration and form from a particularly vivid form of Primitivism.

HOVIS, Caspar
Flemish, 16th century.
Active in Bari in 1596.
Painter.
Flemish School.

Caspar Hovis did work for the church of S Maria de Martiri near Molfetta.

HOVIV, René, pseudonym of Hovivian
French, 20th century.
Born 1929, in Vienne; died 28 May 2005.
Active in Russia from 1945 to 1964.
Draughtsman. Comic strips.

René Hoviv was born to Armenian parents. He attended the École des Beaux-Arts in Lyons and published his first comic strips in 1946 then he settled with his family in Armenia in 1947, where he worked as an electric welder in a factory. Deported with his family to Siberia and liberated in 1956, he settled in Moscow in 1957, where he worked in film studios. At that time he began his career as a humorist, publishing his drawings in several magazines and journals in Moscow, including: *Krokodil, Ogonek, The Moscow News.* Back in France in 1964, Hoviv regained his French citizenship and worked with *Marius* (*Le Hérisson*), *Paris Match, Lui, Ici Paris, VSD, Playboy, Femme, Télé 7 jours.* He made political drawings for the *Quotidien de Paris.* Hoviv's drawings are also published in numerous magazines abroad.

AUCTION RECORDS:
PARIS, 27 Nov 1993, *'To Bed Quickly, Honey, I'm Hungry'* (black and coloured ink/paper, $9^{1}/_{2}$ x $14^{1}/_{4}$ ins / 24 x 36 cm) FRF 3,000.

HOVREVELDE
Dutch.
Painter. Portraits.

The catalogue of Rochefort Museum attributes a *Portrait of a Dutch Woman* to a Hovrevelde, but perhaps mistakenly, as the name does not appear elsewhere.

MUSEUMS AND GALLERIES:
ROCHEFORT?.

HOW, Beatrice Julia
British, 19th - 20th century.
Born 1867, in England; died 1932, in Paris.
Painter, pastellist. Figures, portraits, genre scenes.

Beatrice How became a member of the Société Nationale des Beaux-Arts in Paris in 1910. She specialised in portraits of young children.

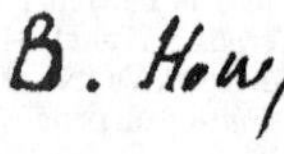

AUCTION RECORDS:
PARIS, 10 Nov 1933, *Young Mother Suckling her Child* (pastel) FRF 1,650. PARIS, 1 July 1943, *Near the Poet* (pastel) FRF 800. PARIS, 15 June 1945, *The Sideboard,* FRF 260. PARIS, 28 June 1950, *The Reader* (pastel) FRF 11,500. LONDON, 29 July 1988, *Study of a Baby* (oil on canvas, $13^{1}/_{2}$ x $10^{1}/_{2}$ ins / 34.5 x 26.8 cm) GBP 880. EDINBURGH, 26 April 1990, *Baby with a Toy* (pastel, $12^{1}/_{4}$ x $9^{1}/_{2}$ ins / 31 x 24.2 cm) GBP 3,850. PARIS, 4 March 1991, *The Model* (pastel, $17^{3}/_{4}$ x $21^{1}/_{4}$ ins / 45 x 54 cm) FRF 11,000. PARIS, 4 July 1995, *Motherhood and Tambourine* (oil on canvas, $18^{1}/_{2}$ x 15 ins / 47 x 38 cm) FRF 8,000. LONDON, 17 Feb 1999, *Maternity* (oil on canvas, 26 x 32 ins / 65 x 81 cm)

GBP 1,800. PARIS, 31 March 2000, *Maternity* (oil on canvas, 18 x 20 ins / 45 x 51 cm) FRF 18,000. EDINBURGH, 11 April 2002, *Mother, Child and Parakeet* (oil on canvas, 16 x 20 ins / 41 x 51 cm) GBP 1,500. LONDON, 7 Nov 2002, *Woman by the Fireplace* (oil on canvas, 17 x 14 ins / 43 x 36 cm) GBP 2,500. LONDON, 14 May 2004, *Man with a Cat* (oil on canvas, 20 x 15 ins / 51 x 38 cm) GBP 1,100.

HOW, L.
British, 19th century.
Engraver.
How is remembered for his *Portrait of Tsar Alexander I* dated 1815.

HOWARD, Annie (Miss)
British, 19th century.
Active in London.
Miniaturist.
Annie Howard exhibited in London at the Royal Academy from 1859.

HOWARD, Cecil de Blaquiere
American, 20th century.
Born 2 April 1888, in Clifton (Canada), to English parents; died 5 September 1956, in New York.
Sculptor. Figures. Monuments.
Cecil de Blaquiere Howard became a naturalised American in 1895. He studied at the Albright-Knox Art Gallery Art School, Buffalo, and at the Art Students League (ASL) under the sculptor James Earle Fraser. In 1905, he worked in France, simultaneously exhibiting in Paris and America, where he was a member of the National Society of Sculpture of New York. He appeared in the Salon des Tuileries in Paris. His entire works were displayed in the Galerie Vallois in Paris in 1994.

His works are in the classical genre and are harmonious, yet ample in form, using terracotta, plaster and wood. He executed a great number of portraits and sculptures of polychrome figures in the post-Cubist genre, taking musicians, dancers and athletes as his subject-matter. He also produced two war memorials in Seine-Maritime, at Hautôt-sur-Mer and Ouville-la-Rivière.

MUSEUMS AND GALLERIES:
BUFFALO (Albright-Knox AG): *Dancer* - NEW YORK (Brooklyn Mus.) - NEW YORK (New York University): *Bust of Walter Reed* - NEW YORK (Whitney Mus. of American Art) - PARIS (Mus. de la Ville): *Sunbathing*.

AUCTION RECORDS:
NEW YORK, 29 Sept 1977, *Wrestlers* (patinated bronze, h. 11 ins / 28 cm) USD 1,500. NEW YORK, 14 Nov 1980, *Knockout* (greenish-brown-patinated bronze, h. 23 1/2 ins / 59.6 cm) USD 3,000. NEW YORK, 21 Sept 1994, *Heavyweight Boxer* (lost-wax bronze, h. 30 1/2 ins / 77.5 cm) USD 17,250. NEW YORK, 26 Sept 1996, *Knockout* (1935, brown-patinated bronze, h. 24 ins / 61 cm) USD 9,200. PARIS, 16 June 1997, *Woman with a Cigarette* (c. 1913, brown-patinated bronze, 8 1/4 x 11 x 9 ins / 21 x 27 x 22 cm) FRF 14,500. PARIS, 14 March 2001, *Bather with Arm Raised* (brown patinated bronze, h. 18 ins / 45 cm) FRF 22,000. LONDON, 11 July 2001, *Standing Nude* (brown patinated bronze, h. 18 ins / 45 cm) GBP 4,000. NEW YORK, 22 May 2003, *Heavyweight Boxer* (brown patinated bronze, h. 30 ins / 76 cm) USD 26,000.

HOWARD, Charles
American, 20th century.
Born 1899, in California.
Painter.
Charles Howard's career began in 1924 and he worked in France, Italy, London and New York. He is nowadays linked with the non-figurative art movement. In Paris, he exhibited in the Salon des Réalités Nouvelles in 1946 with a painting which was very characteristic of his manner. In this painting the abstraction of forms is not irreconcilable with the eloquent expression of a distinctly eerie atmosphere. He was often mentioned in the USA, before World War II, as an artist influenced by Surrealism.

AUCTION RECORDS:
LONDON, 7 June 1985, *The Figure Meter or Variation on Circle No 27* (1951, oil on canvas, 15 3/4 x 20 ins / 40 x 50.5 cm) GBP 2,600. LONDON, 9 June 1988, *Variable Point of View* (oil on canvas, 17 3/4 x 23 1/2 ins / 45 x 60 cm) GBP 1,650.

HOWARD, Charlotte E. (Miss)
later Mrs Lugard
British, 19th century.
Active in Oakhurst.
Miniaturist.
Charlotte Howard exhibited her work in London at the Royal Academy from 1885.

HOWARD, Clara E.
American, 19th century.
Born 1866, in Poughkeepsie (New York); died 1933.
Miniaturist.
Clara E. Howard was a pupil of William Merritt Chase.

HOWARD, E. Stirling
British, 19th century.
Active in Sheffield.
Painter, watercolourist. Landscapes.
E. Stirling Howard exhibited his work for the first time in London in 1834 and continued to appear at irregular intervals at the Royal Academy and Suffolk Street until 1870.

MUSEUMS AND GALLERIES:
LONDON (Victoria and Albert Mus.): *Dolwyddelan Castle (Wales)* (1868, watercolour).

HOWARD, Edith Lucile
American, 20th century.
Born 1885, in Bellows Falls (Vermont); died 1960.
Painter, watercolourist. Genre scenes.
Edith Lucile Howard was a member of the Watercolorists Club of New York and the Plastic Club, and was awarded a great many prizes. She was also a teacher.

AUCTION RECORDS:
NEW YORK, 7 Oct 1987, *Young Woman at Her Piano* (oil on canvas, 40 1/4 x 35 1/2 ins / 102 x 90.3 cm) USD 3,200. PHILADELPHIA, 8 Oct 1999, *Figures in French Town* (oil on canvas-board, four, 11 x 14 ins / 27 x 35 cm) USD 1,800. PHILADELPHIA, 9 Dec 2001, *Lake in the Bog, County Donegal* (oil on canvas, 25 x 30 ins / 64 x 77 cm) USD 2,100. PHILADELPHIA, 9 Dec 2001, *At the Piano* (oil on canvas, 40 x 35 ins / 102 x 90 cm) USD 7,000. NEW YORK, 23 June 2004, *Drama in Grey, Mont St-Michel* (oil on canvas, 39 x 49 ins / 99 x 124 cm) USD 3,250.

HOWARD, Elisabeth
Flemish School, 18th century.
Died 17 December 1761.
Illuminator.
Elisabeth Howard was a Dominican nun and decorated devotional books.

HOWARD, Francis
British, 20th century.
Born 1874; died 1954.
Painter.
Francis Howard, a member of the International Society of Painters, Sculptors and Engravers, worked in London. He exhibited at the Walker Art Gallery in Liverpool.

HOWARD, Frank
British, 19th century.
Born c. 1805, in London; died 29 June 1866, in Liverpool.
Painter, draughtsman, engraver. Mythological subjects.

Frank Howard was the son and pupil of Henry Howard. He also worked in the studio of Sir Thomas Lawrence at the Royal Academy. He began his career around 1825. In 1842 he settled in Liverpool where he remained until his death. He published various works on painting and highly regarded engravings.

HOWARD, George James (Count of Carlisle)
British, 19th - 20th century.
Born 13 August 1843, in London; died 16 April 1911, in Hindhead.
Painter, watercolourist, draughtsman. Landscapes.

George Howard was one of the few Victorian aristocrats to be a serious artist. Placing his wife in charge of his extensive estates, he devoted himself to painting. On the recommendation of the British painter Frederick Lord Leighton he went to Rome to work with Giovanni Costa, who encouraged him to give up traditional English watercolour painting and take up oil painting.

A great traveller, Howard painted numerous watercolours, recording scenes that he saw on his travels in Italy, Egypt, the Indies and East Africa. He exhibited frequently in London from 1868 to 1889, and from 1889 to 1893, under the name Carlisle, at the Royal Academy, the Royal Society of Painters in Watercolours and the New Gallery.

AUCTION RECORDS:
LONDON, 28 May 1908, *The Residence, Lucknow* (drawing) GBP 2. LONDON, 16 June 1982, *Fort of Bocca d'Arno* (oil on canvas, 19 1/2 x 43 ins / 49.5 x 109 cm) GBP 2,600. LONDON, 1 March 1984, *Wooden Bridge* (watercolour heightened with white, 10 1/2 x 14 1/4 ins / 26.5 x 36.5 cm) GBP 650. LONDON, 26 Sept 1985, *Lady in a Garden Chair* (oil on panel, 21 1/4 x 14 1/4 ins / 54 x 36 cm) GBP 1,600. LONDON, 24 Sept 1987, *Portrait of Sir Edward Coley Burne-Jones* (oil on card, 13 x 9 1/2 ins / 33.2 x 24 cm) GBP 1,800. LONDON, 21 March 1990, *Jodhpur* (oil on panel, 7 3/4 x 14 ins / 20 x 35.5 cm) GBP 2,750. LONDON, 3 June 1992, *Temple at Luxor* (oil on canvas, 15 x 36 ins / 38 x 91.5 cm) GBP 3,520. LONDON, 12 Nov 1992, *Jodhpur in Rajhastan* (oil on canvas, 32 x 56 ins / 81.5 x 142 cm) GBP 5,060. NEW YORK, 14 Oct 1993, *Estuary at Tangier* (watercolour and gouache/paper, 20 1/2 x 14 1/2 ins / 52.1 x 36.8 cm) USD 3,450. LONDON, 5 Nov 1993, *Monte Pelligrino from Palermo* (1886, oil on panel, 11 x 14 1/4 ins / 27 x 36.5 cm) GBP 3,220. LONDON, 7 June 1995, *Coast of Northumberland at Bamburgh* (oil on canvas, 17 1/4 x 40 1/4 ins / 44 x 102 cm) GBP 3,680. LONDON, 6 Nov 1995, *Costa Belle near Hyères (Var)* (1897, pencil and watercolour heightened with white, 10 1/4 x 14 1/4 ins / 26 x 36.2 cm) GBP 828. LONDON, 29 March 1996, *Wood in Algeria* (pencil and watercolour, 8 1/2 x 12 3/4 ins / 21.6 x 32.3 cm) GBP 805. LONDON, 6 Nov 1996, *Port of Genoa Seen from the Sixth Floor of the Hotel* (1865, watercolour/pencil outlines, 9 3/4 x 13 3/4 ins / 25 x 35 cm) GBP 1,150. LONDON, 5 Nov 1997, *Ruins* (oil on panel, 5 3/4 x 9 1/2 ins / 14.5 x 24 cm) GBP 1,495. LONDON, 3 June 1999, *Portrait of Sir Edward Coley Burne-Jones. Study of a Figure* (pencil, double-sided, 7 x 6 ins / 18 x 15 cm) GBP 1,600. LONDON, 12 June 2001, *Bordighera* (oil on canvas, 30 x 45 ins / 75 x 114 cm) GBP 8,500. LONDON, 14 June 2001, *The Palatine, Rome* (oil on canvas, 24 x 38 ins / 61 x 96 cm) GBP 13,000.

HOWARD, Henry
British, 18th - 19th century.
Born 31 January 1769, in London; died 5 October 1847, in Oxford.
Painter. Genre scenes.

Henry Howard was a pupil of Philip Reinagle and was accepted on to the courses of the Royal Academy in 1788. He subsequently went to work in Italy and then returned to England where he was made an associate of the Royal Academy in 1800 and a member in 1808. In 1811 he became secretary of the Royal Academy and in 1833 a teacher of painting. Howard was one of the most appreciated artists of the English School.

MUSEUMS AND GALLERIES:
LONDON (National Portrait Gal.): *John Flaxman* (c. 1797, oil/panel); *Anne Flaxman (née Denman)* (c. 1797, oil/panel); *Sarah Trimmer* (exhibited in 1798, oil on canvas); *William Hayley* (c. 1800, oil/panel); *Cuthbert Collingwood, Baron Collingwood* (1828, oil on canvas, after Giuseppe Politi) - LONDON (Royal Academy of Arts): *The Sixth Trumpet Soundeth* (1804, oil on canvas, competition piece) - LONDON (Tate Collection): *The Florentine Girl ('The Artist's Daughter')* (exhibited in 1827, oil on canvas) - LONDON (Victoria and Albert Mus.): *Peasants of Subiaco, Sabrina; Pygmalion.*

AUCTION RECORDS:
LONDON, 1827, *The Pleiad,* FRF 5,515. LONDON, 1875, *The Pleiad,* FRF 3,675. NEW YORK, 29-30 March 1905, *Hebe Feeding the Bird of Jupiter,* USD 875. LONDON, 18 Jan 1908, *Child with Shells,* GBP 2. LONDON, 8 Feb 1908, *Rising Sun,* GBP 10. LONDON, 28 March 1908, *Lavinia, Countess Spencer,* GBP 68. LONDON, 27 Feb 1909, *Birth of Venus,* GBP 15. LONDON, March 1922, *Miss Charlotte Astle,* GBP 8. LONDON, 27 July 1928, *The Bishop of Winchester,* GBP 42. LONDON, 3 May 1940, *Message from the Sea,* GBP 57. LONDON, 2 Feb 1979, *Olympus* (oil on canvas, 42 3/4 x 54 3/4 ins / 108.6 x 139 cm) GBP 900. LONDON, 16 April 1982, *Venus and Cupid* (oil on canvas, 36 1/2 x 30 3/4 ins / 92.7 x 78 cm) GBP 2,400. LONDON, 11 July 1984, *Venus and Cherubs* (1809, oil on canvas, 36 1/2 x 30 3/4 ins / 93 x 78 cm) GBP 3,600. LONDON, 12 May 1999, *Hebe* (oil on canvas, 30 x 21 ins / 76 x 54 cm) GBP 1,100. LONDON, 12 Nov 1999, *Fairies on the Sea Shore* (oil on canvas, 20 x 24 ins / 51 x 61 cm) GBP 3,000. LONDON, 14 June 2000, *Diana and Nymphs* (oil on canvas, 50 x 41 ins / 127 x 103 cm) GBP 9,500. LONDON, 18 Jan 2001, *Sunset on Civetta* (1897, oil on canvas, 34 x 52 ins / 86 x 132 cm) GBP 1,500. LONDON, 4 July 2001, *Portrait of Maria Reinagle in a White Dress* (oil on panel, 7 x 6 ins / 18 x 14 cm) GBP 1,600. NEW YORK, 29 May 2003, *Birth of Venus* (oil on canvas, 13 x 16 ins / 33 x 40 cm) USD 4,500.

HOWARD, Hugh
Irish, 17th - 18th century.
Born 7 February 1675, in Dublin; died 17 March 1737, in London.
Painter. Portraits.

Hugh Howard worked in Holland and Italy, then returned to live first of all in Dublin and then in London.

AUCTION RECORDS:
LONDON, 24 April 1987, *Portrait of Arcangelo Corelli Seated and Holding a Musical Score with the Muse of Music in the Background* (oil on canvas, 50 x 40 ins / 126.9 x 101.6 cm) GBP 12,000.

HOWARD, Hugh Huntington
American, 19th century.
Born 1859, in Cherry Valley (New York); died 1927.
Active in Cleveland.
Painter.

Hugh Huntington Howard taught himself by studying nature. He was a member of the major art associations in Cleveland.

HOWARD, Isabella (Countess of Carlisle)
British, 18th century.
Born 1721, in England; died 1795.
Engraver.

Isabella Howard executed a few good plates, in particular those which she executed after Rembrandt's engravings.

HOWARD, Ken
British, 20th century.
Born 1932.
Painter. Figures, nudes, landscapes with figures.

Ken Howard studied at Hornsea College of Art (1949-1953) and the Royal College of Art (1955-1958) and received a British Council scholarship to study in Florence. He was appointed official artist in Northern Ireland (1973-1978) by the Imperial War Museum, and worked in the army in Germany, Oman, Cyprus, Hong Kong, Nepal, Norway, Canada, Belize and Brunei (1973-1980). He has carried out a number of commissions including for the Drapers' Company, The Haberdashers' Company and the United Nations.

Howard's work is characterised by a distinctive technique, though his subject matter is wide-ranging, from informal studio interiors to urban and rural landscapes. His paintings cast him as an invisible observer: often his model is portrayed in repose or turned away, and he frequently views streets from unusual angles. The manipulation of light (filtered, dappled or falling in clear-cut shafts over a composition) defines the mood of an image in his work.

Howard first exhibited at the Art Centre in Plymouth in 1955, and has frequently shown his work at the New Grafton Gallery in London (1971-1986).

BIBLIOGRAPHY:

Spender, Michael, *The Painting of Ken Howard*, Royal Academy Books, London, 1999. Howard, Ken, *Ken Howard a Personal View: Inspired by Light (Atelier Series)*, David & Charles Publishers, Newton Abbot, 2001.

MUSEUMS AND GALLERIES:

LONDON (Imperial War Mus.) - LONDON (National Army Mus.) - PLYMOUTH (City Art Gal.).

AUCTION RECORDS:

LONDON, 12 June 1987, *Deckchairs on the Beach in Brighton* (1978, oil on canvas, 19½ x 23½ ins / 49.5 x 59.5 cm) GBP 2,000. LONDON, 8 March 1990, *Marika* (oil on canvas, 23½ x 17½ ins / 59.7 x 44.6 cm) GBP 1,650. LONDON, 7 June 1990, *Nude Seated in a Studio* (1986, oil on canvas, 19 x 23 ins / 48 x 58.5 cm) GBP 2,200. LONDON, 9 Nov 1990, *Danny and Omani Coffee Pot* (oil on canvas, 48 x 40¼ ins / 122 x 102 cm) GBP 3,300. LONDON, 25 Jan 1991, *Female Nude Sleeping on a Deckchair* (oil on canvas, 16 x 20 ins / 40.5 x 51 cm) GBP 2,035. LONDON, 8 March 1991, *Flying the Kite, Sennen Cove, Cornwall* (oil on canvas, 38½ x 48 ins / 98 x 122 cm) GBP 4,400. LONDON, 2 May 1991, *Nude in Front of a Window* (oil on canvas, 23½ x 19¼ ins / 60 x 49 cm) GBP 2,200. LONDON, 6 June 1991, *Nude Reclining Below a Window* (oil on canvas, 24 x 20 ins / 61 x 51 cm) GBP 2,860. LONDON, 6 March 1992, *Nude Seated in a Studio* (oil on canvas, 24 x 20 ins / 61 x 51 cm) GBP 3,850. LONDON, 12 March 1992, *St Michael's Mount* (1990, oil on canvas, 20 x 24 ins / 50.8 x 61 cm) GBP 2,530. LONDON, 14 May 1992, *Red Umbrella* (oil on canvas, 24 x 20 ins / 61 x 51 cm) GBP 2,640. LONDON, 5 March 1999, *St Mark's Square, Venice* (oil on canvas, 46 x 57 ins / 117 x 145 cm) GBP 5,200. LONDON, 10 Nov 1999, *Yellow Culottes* (oil on canvas, 40 x 48 ins / 102 x 122 cm) GBP 7,200. LONDON, 28 April 2000, *Flying the Kite, Cornwall* (oil on canvas, 40 x 48 ins / 102 x 122 cm) GBP 5,700. LONDON, 13 July 2000, *The Silk Shirt* (oil on canvas, 48 x 40 ins / 122 x 102 cm) GBP 5,000. LONDON, 5 Sept 2001, *High Summer* (oil on canvas, 12 x 24 ins / 30 x 61 cm) GBP 3,000. LONDON, 23 Nov 2001, *Dora in a Blue Dress* (oil on canvas, 24 x 20 ins / 61 x 51 cm) GBP 3,800. LONDON, 12 Sept 2002, *St Martin-within-Ludgate, London* (oil on board, 42 x 22 ins / 106 x 56 cm) GBP 8,000. LONDON, 27 Nov 2002, *Model in an Artist's Studio* (oil on canvas, 48 x 36 ins / 122 x 92 cm) GBP 10,000. LONDON, 3 June 2003, *Standing Nude, the Artist's Studio* (oil on canvas, 48 x 40 ins / 122 x 102 cm) GBP 6,000. PENZANCE, 2 Oct 2003, *Summer Haze, Sennon Cove, Cornwall* (oil on canvas, 40 x 48 ins / 101 x 122 cm) GBP 8,000. SALISBURY, 18 May 2004, *Artist and Model, Bo Hilton at an Easel in the background* (oil on canvas, 48 x 40 ins / 122 x 101 cm) GBP 12,000. LONDON, 24 Nov 2004, *Merika at Oriel* (oil on canvas, 48 x 40 ins / 122 x 102 cm) GBP 10,500.

HOWARD, Mary R., later Mrs Brodbury
American, 19th century.
Born 22 December 1864, in Cambridge (Massachusetts); died 1963, in Palo Alto (California).
Active in Berkeley (California).
Painter.

Mary R. Howard was the wife of J.G. Howard. She was a pupil at the Art Students' League in New York and at the Académie Delecluse in Paris. She was a member of the New York Women's Club.

HOWARD, Mildred
American, 20th century.
Born 1945, in San Francisco.
Assemblage artist, installation artist, collage artist.

Mildred Howard is based in Oakland (California), having studied at the College of Alameda then at John F. Kennedy University, Orinda. Her work is a labour of memory: she creates assemblages and installations celebrating the African-American experience: photo-portraits transferred on to panes and set in window sashes, installations centred on witness accounts of slavery and the history of the black people of the USA. Her universe is nostalgic, its figures rising from the past, either through photography or scraps of clothing, of bodies, evidence of their presence. She acts on her assemblages by punctuating them with dashes of colour which stress their poignancy. While this Modernist transposition only serves to heighten a sense of loss and regret, Mildred Howard is equally capable of a poetic celebration of human resilience. In *Crossings* (1997), an installation addressing slave deportation across the ocean, she has set in rows hundreds of ceramic eggs alluding to a humanity yet to be born, equal and united. She took part in the exhibitions *In Transit*, New Museum of Contemporary Art, New York; *A Visual Arts Encounter: African Americans and Europe*, Galerie Resche, Paris; and *Let Freedom Ring: An Exhibition of Contemporary Art at Four Historic Sites on Boston's Freedom Trail*, Institute of Contemporary Art, Boston. She has shown her works in solo exhibitions in San Francisco, San Jose (California), Leicester (England) and Cairo.

BIBLIOGRAPHY:

Ten Little Children Standing in A Line (one got shot and then there were nine): Mildred Howard, exhibition catalogue, Art Institute, San Francisco, 1991. Driskell, David C., *African American Visual Aesthetics: A Post-modernist View*, Smithsonian Institute Press, Washington DC, 1995. Janson, H.W., *History of Art*, Harry N. Abrams, New York, 1995. *Mildred Howard: In the Line of Fire*, exhibition catalogue, The City Gall., Leicester, 1999.

MUSEUMS AND GALLERIES:

HARTFORD (Wadsworth Atheneum) - OAKLAND (Mus. of California).

HOWARD, Sarah T. (Miss)
British, 19th century.
Active in London.
Miniaturist.

Sarah Howard exhibited 44 works in London at the Royal Academy from 1840 to 1851.

HOWARD, Squire
British, 19th - 20th century.
Active in England.
Painter. Landscapes.

MUSEUMS AND GALLERIES:

MANCHESTER: *Hall I'lh'wood, Bolton* (1892).

HOWARD, Vernon
British, 19th - 20th century.
Active in London.

Painter, watercolourist. Landscapes.
Vernon Howard exhibited in London at the Suffolk Street gallery and at the New Water-Colour Society from 1864.
MUSEUMS AND GALLERIES:
LONDON (Victoria and Albert Mus.): watercolours - NOTTINGHAM (Castle Museum and Art Gallery): *Sand Dunes on the Lincolnshire Coast* (1902).

HOWARD, Wil, called Wil de Vray
German, 20th century.
Born 20 March 1879, in Leipzig.
Painter, engraver, sculptor. Portraits, landscapes.
Howard was a student at the Académie Julian and exhibited at the Salon d'Automne in Paris.

HOWARD, William
Dutch, 17th century.
Active in London c. 1665.
Painter, engraver (burin). Landscapes.
William Howard was a pupil of W. Hollar and made engravings of seascapes.

AUCTION RECORDS:
LONDON, 8 June 1976, *View of a Town in Holland* (oil on canvas, 29¼ x 49½in/74 x 126cm) GBP 250. LONDON, 5 June 1991, *A Crowded Port* (oil on canvas, 30 x 50in/76 x 127cm) GBP 2,420.

HOWARTH, Albany E.
British, 20th century.
Born 1872; died 1936.
Engraver.
Albany Howarth worked at Hutton in Essex, and exhibited in London at the Royal Academy from 1906.

HOWARTH, F. M.
American, 19th century.
Died 22 September 1908, in Philadelphia.
Illustrator.

HOWE, J.
British, 19th century.
Active in London.
Sculptor.
J. Howe exhibited in London at the Royal Academy between 1829 and 1842.

HOWE, James, or Howe of Stirling
British, 19th century.
Born 30 August 1780, in Stirling; died 11 July 1836, in Edinburgh.
Painter. Animals.
James Howe worked first of all in Edinburgh before moving to London, where he did studies of the royal stables. He returned to Scotland and then in 1815 visited the battlefield of Waterloo and painted a canvas of the battle.
AUCTION RECORDS:
LONDON, 22 June 1922, *Falconing*, GBP 31. LONDON, 12 Oct 1945, *Duck Hunting*, GBP 52. PERTH, 15 April 1980, *The Horse Fair at Grassmarket, Edinburgh* (oil on canvas, 36 x 45 ins / 91.5 x 114.5 cm) GBP 700. NEW YORK, 5 June 1986, *John Forgie with Two Favourite Ponies, a View of Champfleurie Beyond* (oil on canvas, 23 x 30 ins / 58.5 x 76.2 cm) USD 13,000. WOODBRIDGE, 21 June 2000, *Portrait of a Grey Mare in a Landscape with Two Dogs to Foreground* (oil on canvas, 24 x 29 ins / 61 x 74 cm) GBP 1,600.

HOWE, William Henry
American, 19th - 20th century.
Born 1846, in Ravenna (Ohio); died 1929.
Active in Bronxville.
Painter. Genre scenes, landscapes, animals.
William Henry Howe trained under Otto de Thoren and Vuillefroy, and worked in Paris, painting scenes from rustic life in Normandy. He also exhibited in America, Munich and Berlin. He received many awards, notably a third-class medal at the Salon de Paris in 1888, silver medal at Paris in 1889, gold medal at Boston in 1890 and at Atlanta in 1895, and a silver medal at Buffalo in 1901. He was a member of the Jury at St-Louis in 1904, a member of the National Academy in 1897, and made a chevalier de la Légion d'Honneur in 1899.
AUCTION RECORDS:
NEW YORK, 21 Jan- 2 Feb 1900, *In the Orchard*, USD 150. NEW YORK, 23-24 Jan 1901, *Drinkers*, USD 180. NEW YORK, 26-28 Feb 1902, *Cows by the Water*, USD 360. NEW YORK, 3 Feb 1905, *Return from the Pasture*, USD 675. NEW YORK, 15 June 1984, *Truants* (1888, oil on canvas, 42¼ x 32¾ ins / 107 x 83 cm) USD 1,300. NEW YORK, 14 Feb 1990, *Cows Grazing near a Pond* (1924, oil on canvas, 30¼ x 38 ins / 77 x 96.5 cm) USD 1,210. NEW YORK, 31 March 1993, *Cows in a Meadow* (1885, oil on canvas, 20 x 30 ins / 50.8 x 76.2 cm) USD 690.

HOWELL, A.P.
British, 19th century.
Active in London.
Sculptor.
A.P. Howell exhibited his work in London at the Royal Academy in 1854.

HOWELL, Ada M.
British, 19th century.
Active in Eastbourne (Sussex).
Miniaturist.

HOWELL, C.
British, 18th - 19th century.
Active in London.
Sculptor.
C. Howell exhibited in London at the Royal Academy in 1798 and 1807.

HOWELL, Felicie Waldo
American, 20th century.
Born 8 September 1897, in Honolulu; died 1968.
Painter, watercolourist. Landscapes, marine scenes, figures, interiors.
Felicie Waldo Howell studied at the Corcoran Art School in Washington DC with E.C. Messer; at the Philadelphia School of Design for Women; and with H.B. Snell. She taught at the New York School of Fine and Applied Art and Design in 1933, and at a summer school in Gloucester, Massachusetts. She lived in Washington DC from 1914 to 1916, in New York City from 1917 to 1962, and in Philadelphia from 1962. Her earliest work concentrated on interior scenes, later moving to landscape and scenes from sea and shore. Her husband, George W. Mixter, was a keen yachtsman, and many of Howell's watercolours of the New England coast were done while cruising on their schooner *Teragram*, including her series on the America's Cup race (1937).

Howell's exhibitions, in many of which she won awards, include the National Association of Women Artists (1916, prize); the Concord Art Association (1919); the Society of Washington Artists (1921, silver medal; 1922, bronze medal); the National Academy of Design (1921, prize); the Washington Watercolor Club (1921, medal); Doll and Richards, Boston (1921); the Art Institute of Chicago (1921, Augustus Peabody Prize); the State Fair at Aurora, IL (1922); Macbeth Galleries, New York City (1927); Vose Gallery, Boston (1927); the International Watercolor Club Exhibition, Art Institute of Chicago (1927, Tuthill Purchase Prize); and shows at the Museum of Modern Art, New York, and in Venice, Italy.

Museums and Galleries:
Boston (MFA): *Assembly House, Salem, Massachusetts* (1920, oil) - Chicago (AI) - Gloucester, MA (American Legion Building): *The Avenue of the Allies* - Indianapolis (Herron Gallery at Herron School of Art): *Gramercy Park, New York* - Mystic, CT (Maritime Gallery at Mystic Seaport) - New York (Metropolitan Mus. of Art): *Pierce-Nichol House, Salem* - New York (Mus. of the City) - New York (National Arts Club) - Savannah (Telfair Museum of Art): *Flower Women* - Washington DC (Corcoran Gal. of Art): *New England Street* - Washington DC (NGA) - Washington DC (Smithsonian American AM).
Auction records:
Maine, 27 March 1999, *Young Lady Window Shopping* (1919, gouache, 5 x 7 ins / 13 x 18 cm) USD 1,800. Amsterdam, 26 Oct 1999, *Wall Street, the Noon Hour* (1925, oil on canvas, 40 x 30 ins / 102 x 76 cm) NLG 210,000. Boston, 22 Sept 2000, *Residence at 1609 Sixteenth Street, NW, Washington DC* (1917, gouache, 15 x 12 ins / 39 x 30 cm) USD 4,000. Maine, 4 Aug 2001, *Georgetown* (oil on canvas, 24 x 30 ins / 61 x 76 cm) USD 7,200. San Francisco, 12 Dec 2001, *Assisi* (1927, oil on canvas, 20 x 24 ins / 51 x 61 cm) USD 5,500. Boston, 21 Nov 2003, *Pigeon Cove* (gouache, 11 x 15 ins / 29 x 39 cm) USD 3,750.

HOWELL, Samuel
British, 19th century.
Active in London.
Painter. Portraits.
Samuel Howell frequently exhibited in London at the Royal Academy and at Suffolk Street from 1829 to 1854.
Auction records:
London, 14 June 1946, *Lady*, GBP 37. Shrewsbury, 7 Nov 2001, *Portrait of a Lady Wearing a Black Dress, her Young Daughter on her Knee* (1843, oil on canvas, 37 x 29 ins / 94 x 74 cm) GBP 1,800.

HOWELL, Sophia H.M.
British, 18th century.
Active in London.
Miniaturist.
Sophia Howell exhibited her work in London at the Royal Academy from 1781 to 1788.

HOWEN, Ridder
Belgian, 19th century.
Active between 1808 and 1834.
Draughtsman.
Ridder Howen was a lieutentant colonel and worked on the illustration of *Scenic Journeys in the Low Countries*.

HOWENSCHOELD
Swedish, 19th century.
Active c. 1800.
Miniaturist.
Howenschoeld painted a *Portrait of Bernadotte, King of Sweden*.

HOWES, B.
British, 19th century.
Active in London.
Sculptor.
B. Howes exhibited in London at the Royal Academy in 1852 and 1853.

HOWES, John
British, 18th century.
Miniaturist, enameller. Portraits, genre scenes.
John Howes exhibited his work in London at the Royal Academy from 1772 to 1793.

HOWET, Marie
Belgian, 20th century.
Born 24 March 1897, in Libramont (Ardennes); died 1984.
Painter, draughtsman, watercolourist. Figures, nudes, portraits, landscapes.
Howet was a student at the academy of art in Brussels where she won first prize. She worked in Paris in 1916 and travelled in Italy, Greece and Ireland. She was a member of the Salon d'Automne in Paris from 1922 onwards, the year in which she won the Grand Prix de Rome.

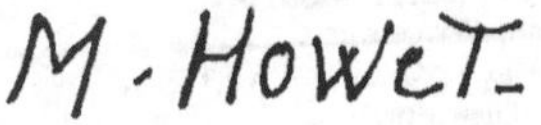

Museums and Galleries:
Antwerp - Brussels - Dublin - Ghent - Ixelles - Liège - Namur - Riga.
Auction records:
Brussels, 7 April 1973, *The Refugees*, BEF 47,000. Brussels, 28 Oct 1987, *Still-life* (oil on canvas, 27 1/4 x 41 ins / 69 x 104 cm) BEF 100,000. Brussels, 19 Dec 1989, *Still-life* (watercolour, 31 1/2 x 23 1/2 ins / 80 x 60 cm) BEF 32,000. Lokeren, 21 March 1992, *Café* (1929, gouache, 21 1/2 x 29 1/2 ins / 54.5 x 75 cm) BEF 30,000. Lokeren, 11 March 1995, *Slope* (oil on paper, 28 x 20 3/4 ins / 71 x 53 cm) BEF 60,000. Lokeren, 8 March 1997, *Ardenne Interior* (watercolour, 26 1/2 x 39 1/4 ins / 67 x 100 cm) BEF 55,000. Brussels, 11 Dec 2000, *View of Ardennes Village From Above* (oil on canvas, 28 x 39 ins / 70 x 100 cm) BEF 110,000. Brussels, 17 March 2003, *In my Kitchen at Rochehaut - Bouillon* (oil on canvas, 28 x 24 ins / 70 x 60 cm) EUR 1,800. Brussels, 13 Sept 2004, *Notre Dame des Sees in Sartre* (oil on panel, 25 x 20 ins / 64 x 50 cm) EUR 2,600. Brussels, 21 Dec 2004, *Elegant Woman on a Sofa* (oil on canvas, 31 x 39 ins / 80 x 100 cm) EUR 1,800.

HOWETT, S.
British, 18th - 19th century.
Active in England.
Engraver.

HOWGATE, William Arthur
British, 19th century.
Active in Leeds.
Painter. Landscapes, harbour scenes.
William Howgate exhibited his work at the Royal Academy and at Suffolk Street in London from 1884.
Auction records:
Stockholm, 16 May 1990, *Barges Moored in a Small Fishing Village* (oil on canvas, 11 3/4 x 20 ins / 30 x 51 cm) SEK 7,200.

HOWIS, William, the Elder
Irish, 19th century.
Born 1804; died 7 October 1882, in Dublin.
Painter. Landscapes.
William Howis the Elder imitated the works of James A. O'Connor.
Auction records:
London, 18 Nov 1987, *Lough Tay, County Wicklow* (1852, oil on canvas, 36 x 52 1/4 ins / 91.5 x 133 cm) GBP 3,400. London, 9 Nov 2000, *On the Dargle, Co Wicklow, from the Powerscourt Estate* (1862, oil on canvas, 18 x 24 ins / 46 x 61 cm) GBP 1,500. Castlecomer, 12 Nov 2002, *View on the Dargle* (1862, oil on canvas, 18 x 24 ins / 46 x 61 cm) EUR 1,900. Dublin, 24 Sept 2003, *The Salmon Leap, Leixlip* (oil on canvas, 20 x 28 ins / 52 x 71 cm) EUR 4,600.

HOWIS, William, the Younger
Irish, 19th century.
Born 19 September 1827, in Dublin; died 1857.
Painter.
William Howis the Younger was the son of William the Elder. His work includes many landscapes.

HOWISON, William
British, 19th century.
Born 1798, in Edinburgh; died 20 December 1850, in Edinburgh.
Engraver.

William Howison was a pupil of Wilson and D.O. Hill. He was elected to the position of Associate of the Royal Scottish Academy in 1838. He engraved genre scenes after Faed Harvey and Allan.

HOWITT, John Newton
American, 20th century.
Born 7 May 1885, in New York; died 1958.
Painter, illustrator.

John Newton Howitt trained at the Art Students League (ASL), New York. He was a member of the Society of Illustrators of New York and the Salmagundi Club.

HOWITT, William Samuel
British, 18th - 19th century.
Born 1756; died 1822, in London.
Painter, watercolourist, engraver, draughtsman.
Hunting scenes, sporting subjects, animals.

William Howitt was self-taught. After exhibiting some of his works in London, he left for the Indies around 1793 and lived for several years in Bengal. He mainly drew scenes of hunting. In 1801 he published 50 engravings from these drawings. He also executed 70 colour plates for *The British Sportsman* (1812), as well as *Aesops Fables* (1814), *Foreign Sports* (1814, 100 plates), *British Preserves* (1827), and 36 etchings. His drawing is particularly interesting.

He exhibited in London at the Society of Artists and at the Royal Academy from 1783 to 1815.

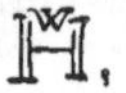

MUSEUMS AND GALLERIES:
LONDON (Victoria and Albert Mus.): drawings - MANCHESTER: drawings.

AUCTION RECORDS:
LONDON, 11 May 1908, *Hunting Subjects* (watercolour, four items) GBP 22. LONDON, 6 March 1909, *The White Horse Inn; Cranford Bridge* (two pendants in a frame) GBP 11. LONDON, 20-21 March 1911, *21 Watercolours for Aesop's Fables*, GBP 14. LONDON, 20 July 1925, *Fox Hunting* (drawing) GBP 199. LONDON, 16 April 1926, *The Chase* (drawing) GBP 57. LONDON, 29 June 1939, *Hunting Scenes*, GBP 90; *Hunting in the East* (several) GBP 48. PARIS, 2 June 1954, *Two Illustrations for Aesop's Fables* (two watercolours) FRF 6,500. LONDON, 16 Nov 1965, *Hunting Scenes* (six drawings) Gns 700. LONDON, 12 Nov 1968, *Two Jaguars* (watercolour) Gns 430. LONDON, 14 Oct 1969, *Mail Coach Going Through a Village* (watercolour) Gns 1,100. LONDON, 3 March 1970, *Hunting Scenes* (two watercolours) Gns 950. LONDON, 6 June 1972, *Relay* (watercolour and pen) Gns 350. LONDON, 22 Nov 1977, *Does Quenching their Thirst in a River* (1792, watercolour and pen, 8 x 10$\frac{3}{4}$ ins / 20.5 x 27.5 cm) GBP 480. LONDON, 13 March 1980, *Carriage and Travellers on a Road* (watercolour and pen/pencil outlines, 5$\frac{1}{2}$ x 9 ins / 14 x 23 cm) GBP 1,700. LONDON, 22 Oct 1981, *Elegant Group at the Seaside* (pen and watercolour, 5$\frac{1}{2}$ x 8$\frac{1}{4}$ ins / 14 x 21 cm) GBP 400. LONDON, 18 March 1986, *Arriving at the Race* (1792, watercolour and pen, 8$\frac{3}{4}$ x 12$\frac{3}{4}$ ins / 22.5 x 32.7 cm) GBP 2,400. LONDON, 25 Jan 1988, *Canada Goose; Bird of Prey* (watercolour, two pendants, each: 11$\frac{1}{2}$ x 9 ins / 29.5 x 22 cm) GBP 418; *Pair of Tigers* (watercolour, 9$\frac{1}{4}$ x 12$\frac{1}{2}$ ins / 23.5 x 32 cm) GBP 605. LONDON, 1 March 1991, *Leopard in a Tree above Two Antelopes in a Tropical Landscape* (oil on canvas, 24 x 20 ins / 61 x 50.8 cm) GBP 11,000. NEW YORK, 7 June 1991, *Hunting Near a Bay; Sugar Cane; Hunting Peacocks* (watercolour/paper, three watercolours, each 11$\frac{1}{2}$ x 17 ins / 29.5 x 43.2 cm) USD 12,100. LONDON, 25 Nov 1999, *Royal Oak Huntsman and Hounds* (pen, black ink, watercolour and pencil, 6 x 8 ins / 14 x 20 cm) GBP 1,800. LONDON, 25 Nov 1999, *Huntsman and Dogs in Open Landscape* (1791, watercolour and pencil heightened with gouache, 7 x 11 ins / 19 x 29 cm) GBP 1,800. LONDON, 21 Sept 2000, *Chase after the Hog. Hog at Bay* (pencil, pen, ink and watercolour, two, 12 x 17 ins / 30 x 43 cm) GBP 5,200. LONDON, 21 Sept 2000, *Pair of Tigers* (pencil and watercolour, 18 x 26 ins / 45 x 66 cm) GBP 9,500. PARIS, 7 June 2002, *Hunting Scene, The Pack* (1812, crayon and brown wash, 14 x 20 ins / 36 x 52 cm) EUR 1,800. PARIS, 18 March 2004, *Hounds Chasing Deer and Rabbts* (1812, black chalk, pen, brown ink, colour wash, 14 x 21 ins / 35 x 54 cm) EUR 3,900. LONDON, 26 March 2004, *Huntsmen and Dogs Hare Coursing in Rocky Landscape. Huntsmen and Dogs with Hare* (pen, ink and watercolour over pencil, a pair, 9 x 13 ins / 22 x 32 cm) GBP 4,600.

HOWLAND, Alfred Cornelius
American, 19th - 20th century.
Born 12 February 1838, in Walpole; died 17 March 1909, in Pasadena (California).
Painter. Landscapes.

Alfred Cornelius Howland studied successively in Boston and New York, then at the Royal Academy in Düsseldorf and under Albert Flamm, and finally trained under Émile Lambinet in Paris. He was an honorary member of the National Academy in 1874 and was elected to the Academy in 1882. He exhibited frequently in Paris, Munich and New York.

MUSEUMS AND GALLERIES:
MILWAUKEE - NEW HAVEN (Yale University).

AUCTION RECORDS:
NEW YORK, 31 Jan-2 Feb 1900, *Street beneath the Cap. Quebec*, USD 160. NEW YORK, 23 May 1979, *Autumn Chores* (oil on canvas, 20 x 26 ins / 50.5 x 66 cm) USD 2,500. SAN FRANCISCO, 21 June 1984, *Hoeing the Cabbage Patch* (oil on canvas, 11 x 9 ins / 28 x 23 cm) USD 3,250. NEW YORK, 24 April 1985, *Farm Scene* (oil on canvas, 14$\frac{1}{4}$ x 18$\frac{1}{4}$ ins / 36 x 46.2 cm) USD 3,750. NEW YORK, 9 Sept 1993, *Hay Stacks* (oil on canvas/card, 7$\frac{1}{2}$ x 11$\frac{3}{4}$ ins / 19.1 x 29.8 cm) USD 805. NEW YORK, 3 Dec 1993, *On the Bridge* (oil on canvas, 17$\frac{1}{4}$ x 23$\frac{1}{4}$ ins / 44 x 59 cm) USD 21,850. NEW YORK, 30 Oct 1996, *Country Lane in Vermont* (oil on canvas/card, 11$\frac{1}{2}$ x 12$\frac{1}{4}$ ins / 29.2 x 30.8 cm) USD 4,312. NEW YORK, 3 Dec 1996, *Farm House and Water Pump* (oil on canvas, 10$\frac{3}{4}$ x 11$\frac{3}{4}$ ins / 27.4 x 30 cm) USD 3,450.

HOWLAND, George (Sir). See **BEAUMONT George Howland, Sir**

HOWLAND, George
American, 19th century.
Born 12 February 1865, in New York; died 1928, in New York.
Active in Paris.
Painter.

George Howland was a pupil of Benjamin-Constant, Collin and Jean-Paul Laurens.

AUCTION RECORDS:
PARIS, 23 Feb 1949, *Eastern Seascape*, FRF 20,000.

HOWLETT, Bartholomew
British, 18th - 19th century.
Born 1767, in Louth; died 12 December 1827, in Newington.
Painter, draughtsman, engraver.

Howlett studied engraving with James Heath. He engraved architectural scenes and landscapes.

HOWS, John A.
American, 19th century.
Born 1831; died 1874, in New York.
Painter, draughtsman, engraver, writer.

John A. Hows produced many illustrations for various New York magazines. He also produced oil paintings and was a member of the National Academy of Design in New York.

HOWSE, George
British, 19th century.
Died c. 1860.
Active in London.
Painter, watercolourist, draughtsman. Landscapes, architectural views.

George Howse exhibited at the Institute of Painters in Water Colours and became a member of this Association in 1837. His work was also shown at the Royal Academy in London.

MUSEUMS AND GALLERIES:
DUBLIN: *A Street in Rouen; Around Gorcum (Holland); Dolbadarn Castle (Wales); River Bank at Hastings; Windsor Castle; Rochester Castle; Rider* - LONDON (Victoria and Albert Mus.).

AUCTION RECORDS:
LONDON, 29 March 1983, *The Clock Tower, St. Albans* (watercolour and pencil heightened with white, 16 1/4 x 20 3/4 ins / 41 x 53 cm) GBP 1,200. LONDON, 26 March 2004, *Figures Unloading Fishing Boats on the Shore* (watercolour and pencil heightened with gouache, 10 x 19 ins / 26 x 49 cm) GBP 1,700.

HOWSON, Peter
British, 20th - 21st century.
Born 27 March 1958, in London.
Painter, printmaker. Figures, military subjects.
Glasgow Boys.

Peter Howson moved to Scotland at the age of four. He studied at the Glasgow School of Art from 1975 to 1976, but left to join the Lothian branch of the Royal Highland Fusiliers for nine months. Howson worked as a nightclub bouncer and did bodybuilding, with over-developed bodies becoming a feature of much of his early painting. He returned to the Glasgow School of Art where he was taught by Alexander 'Sandy' Moffat, graduating in 1981. Howson was a central figure in the Glasgow Boys movement, which included painters such as Ken Currie. He became known for his bold, large-format pictures of the urban working class and the down-trodden of Glasgow, with his subject matter drawn from his experience of the economic depression in Scotland in the 1970s and 1980s. Howson was also noted in the 1980s for his series of satirical portrayals of institutional violence. In 1993, Howson went to Bosnia as official war artist with the British UN Peacekeeping Force, where he was much affected by the cruelty and suffering he saw there, as depicted in the oils *Plum Grove* (1994) and *Cleansed* (1994). Later works include a series based on Stravinsky's opera, *The Rake's Progress*, and a series of paintings documenting his own decline and recovery from substance addition. Howson moved his studio to London in 1995.

Howson's solo exhibitions include Crawford Centre for the Arts, University of St Andrews (1985); *The Twilight Zone*, Cleveland Gallery in Middlesborough, and Quay Art Centre on the Isle of Wight (1988); *New Works on Paper*, Scottish Gallery, Edinburgh (1988); his collection of Bosnian paintings at the Paris Art Fair (1997); and MacLaurin Gallery, *Ayr* (2002). Howson has received the Lord Provost's Prize, Glasgow (1998, 1995); an Honorary Doctorate from University of Strathclyde (1996); a Henry Moore Foundation Prize (1988); and the Edwin Morgan Artists' Prize, Glasgow League (1986). In 1998, he was commissioned to design a millennium stamp for the Royal Mail. Howson's work has been collected by many celebrities, including Madonna, David Bowie and Bob Geldof.

BIBLIOGRAPHY:
Saracen Heads: Peter Howson, exhibition catalogue, Angela Flowers Gallery, London, 1987. *Peter Howson*, exhibition catalogue, E. Flowers, London, 1989. Cohen, Carolyn/Lucie-Smith, Edward/Higgins, Judith, *The New British Painting*, Phaidon, Oxford, 1990. *Peter Howson: Blind Leading the Blind*, exhibition catalogue, E. Flowers, London, 1991. Heller, Robert, *Peter Howson*, illustrated book, Mainstream, Edinburgh, 1993. *Peter Howson: Bosnia*, exhibition catalogue, Imperial War Museum, London, 1994. Jackson, Alan, *A Different Man: Peter Howson's Art, from Bosnia and Beyond*, illustrated book, Mainstream, Edinburgh, 1997. *Peter Howson*, exhibition catalogue, E. Flowers, London, 1998. Heller, Robert, *Peter Howson*, illustrated book, Momentum, London, 2003.

MUSEUMS AND GALLERIES:
ABERDEEN (AG) - AYR (Rozelle House Gallery): *Judas* (2002, oil) - BRADFORD (Cartwright Hall AG) - CAMBRIDGE (Fitzwilliam Museum) - DUNDEE (AG) - EDINBURGH (City Arts Centre) - EDINBURGH (Scottish Arts Council) - EDINBURGH (Scottish Nat. Gal. of Modern Art) - GLASGOW (Glasgow Museums) - GLASGOW (Hunterian Museum) - GLASGOW (Royal Concert Hall) - HALIFAX (Bankfield Museum) - LISBON (Gulbenkian Collection) - LONDON (British Council) - LONDON (British Mus.) - LONDON (Imperial War Mus.): *Cleansed* (1994, oil); *M.F.U. 1994* (1994, pastel drawing); *Entering Gornji Vakuf 1993-1994* (1993-1994, oil); *Three Miles from Home 1993-1994* (1993-1994, oil); *Checkpoint Guard with Frightened Boy 1993* (1993, pastel drawing); *Travnik 1993-1994* (1993-1994, pastel drawing) - LONDON (Tate Collection): *Plum Grove* (1994, oil on canvas); *Saracen Heads* (1987, intaglio print/paper, incomplete series); *The Noble Dosser* (1987, relief print/paper); *The Noble Dosser* (1987, relief print/paper) - LONDON (Victoria and Albert Mus.) - NEW YORK (Metropolitan Mus. of Art) - NEW YORK (MoMA) - NOTTINGHAM (Castle Mus. and AG) - OSLO (National Gallery of Norway) - PAISLEY (AG) - SOUTHAMPTON (AG): *Peter* (1987, etching) - WASHINGTON DC (Library of Congress) - WOLVERHAMPTON (AG): *Wolverhampton Dream* (2000, oil).

AUCTION RECORDS:
SOUTH QUEENSFERRY, 23 April 1991, *Girl and Boy* (mixed media/card, 14 1/2 x 10 1/2 ins / 37 x 26.5 cm) GBP 1,100. GLASGOW, 1 Feb 1994, *Portrait on a Rainy Day* (oil on card, 24 x 48 ins / 61 x 122 cm) GBP 1,495. LONDON, 25 May 1994, *Men Staggering by Moonlight* (1988, pastel/black paper, 11 1/2 x 8 1/4 ins / 29 x 21 cm) GBP 920. PERTH, 30 Aug 1994, *Scream* (oil on canvas, 36 x 24 ins / 91.5 x 61 cm) GBP 2,185. LONDON, 26 Oct 1994, *Bridge to Nowhere* (oil on canvas, 48 x 36 ins / 122 x 91.5 cm) GBP 6,900. LONDON, 23 Oct 1996, *Silent Scream* (1991, oil on canvas, 72 x 48 ins / 183 x 122 cm) GBP 6,900. LONDON, 30 May 1997, *Embrace* (c. 1986, acrylic/paper/card, 50 x 40 ins / 127 x 101.8 cm) GBP 5,060. LONDON, 28 Oct 1999, *Lowland Hero 32* (coloured chalk, 11 x 8 ins / 29 x 20 cm) GBP 1,100. LONDON, 28 Oct 1999, *Lowland Hero 2* (coloured chalk, 11 x 12 ins / 29 x 30 cm) GBP 1,400. EDINBURGH, 29 Jan 2000, *Profile Portrait of a Boxer* (oil on canvas, 24 x 30 ins / 61 x 76 cm) GBP 2,600. EDINBURGH, 12 May 2000, *Exotic Dancer* (1986, oil on board, 55 x 39 ins / 140 x 100 cm) GBP 3,000. LONDON, 9 April 2001, *Game Boys* (oil on canvas, 24 x 36 ins / 61 x 91 cm) GBP 3,200. EDINBURGH, 24 Aug 2001, *Self-portrait* (oil on canvas, 30 x 24 ins / 76 x 61 cm) GBP 5,800. EDINBURGH, 22 Aug 2002, *Last Mohican* (oil on canvas, 72 x 48 ins / 183 x 122 cm) GBP 6,000. LONDON, 31 Oct 2002, *Pocket Full of Poesies* (oil on canvas, 72 x 84 ins / 183 x 213 cm) GBP 17,000. LONDON, 30 Oct 2003, *Face of Britain IV* (1991, oil on canvas, 84 x 60 ins / 213 x 152 cm) GBP 7,200. LONDON, 18 Nov 2003, *Riding the Gauntlet* (oil on canvas, 96 x 72 ins / 244 x 183 cm) GBP 7,500. LONDON, 1 Sept 2004, *Stool Pigeon* (oil on canvas, 110 x 74 ins / 280 x 189 cm) GBP 20,000. LONDON,

1 Sept 2004, *Age of Apathy* (oil on canvas, 36 x 95 ins / 91 x 242 cm) GBP 54,000.

HOY, Nikolaus Van. See **HOEY Nickolaus van**

HOYAU
French, 19th century.
Active in Paris c. 1850.
Draughtsman.
Hoyau worked on a book entitled *Illustration*.

HOYAU, Charles
French, 17th century.
Died c. 1644.
Active in Le Mans.
Sculptor (terracotta). Religious subjects. Statues, groups.
Charles Hoyau, together with Gervais de la Barre and Pierre Biardeau, is regarded as one of the most important representatives of terracotta sculptors in the region of Le Mans in the 17th century. He was most probably related to the architect Hoyau, who from 1604 to 1610, restored Le Mans Cathedral. He left a sufficient number of signed statues to enable us to determine his style. In 1631, he made statues for the high altar of the Church of the Minims, Plessis-lès-Tours: the Virgin, four Evangelists, two angels; and three figures in the Chapel of the Tomb. In 1632, he was commissioned to create a nativity group for the Abbey of Beaumont-lès-Tours; the following year, he sculpted an *Entombment* (1635) and a figure of St Francis of Assisi for the church of St-Rémy at Marolles-lès-Braults (Sarthe). The Magdalene in this *Entombment*, along with the *St Cécile* of St-Julien Cathedral, Le Mans, is characteristic of a physical type that recurred in his work, that is, a girl with round face, smooth forehead, small mouth and rounded cheeks. In the work of Charles Hoyau, the body is more expressive than the face. In 2003, he was represented at the thematic exhibition *Terre et Ciel, Sculptures du Maine en terre cuite XVIe - XVIIe siècles* (*Earth and Sky. 16th and 17th Century Terracotta Sculptures from the Maine region*), at the Abbey of l'Épau, Le Mans.
BIBLIOGRAPHY:
Bresc-Bautier, Geneviève/Le Boeuf, François/Ménard, Michèle, *Terre et Ciel, la sculpture en terre cuite du Maine, XVIe - XVIIe siècle*, exhibition catalogue, Abbaye de l'Épau, Le Mans, 2003.
MUSEUMS AND GALLERIES:
LE MANS (cathédrale St-Julien): *Vierge de douleur* (*Sorrowing Virgin*) (terracotta); *La Vierge et l'Enfant* (*Virgin and Child*) (terracotta, attributed); *Sainte Marguerite* (*St Margaret*) (1635, terracotta, attributed); *Sainte Cécile jouant de l'orgue* (*St Cecilia Playing the Organ*) (1633, terracotta) - MAROLLES-LES-BRAULTS (église St-Rémy): *Lamentation for Christ* (1635, terracotta, group) - PARIS (Louvre): *Éducation de la Vierge* (*Education of the Virgin*) (c. 1630-1635, terracotta); *Sainte* (*Saint*) (c. 1630-1640, terracotta) - PARIS (Mus. des Arts décoratifs): *La Vierge assise tenant l'Enfant assis sur ses genoux* (*Seated Virgin Holding Child Sitting on her Knee*) (terracotta).

HOYAU, Jean
French, 16th century.
Active in Orléans.
Sculptor.
In 1516 Jean Hoyau did the woodwork for the large and the small organ in the collegiate church in Cléry-sur-Loire.

HOYAUX, Émile Joseph
Belgian, 19th century.
Born 14 June 1823, in Mons.
Sculptor.
Émile Hoyaux is known mainly for his busts and low reliefs.

HOYDONCKX, Hendrik
Belgian, 20th century.
Born 1924, in Tessenderlo-on-Lommel.
Painter, engraver.
Hoydonckx was a student at the institute in Antwerp, at the Slade School of Fine Art and the Royal College of Art in London, and at Michael's School in Cape Town. He was awarded the Limburg province sculpture prize in 1983.

HOYECK, Youssef
Lebanese, 20th century.
Born 1883, in Halta; died 1965.
Painter, draughtsman, sculptor. Mythological subjects, figures, portraits.
Youssef Hoyeck studied in Paris, where he was taught by the sculptor Henri Bourdelle, and later in Rome. In 1939 he returned to Beirut, where he taught sculpture. He was awarded the Lebanese Order of the Cedar. He frequently exhibited work in Paris, and in 1939 in the Lebanese Pavilion of the *International Fair* in New York.
BIBLIOGRAPHY:
Liban. Le Regard des peintres. 200 ans de peinture libanaise, exhibition catalogue, Institut du Monde Arabe, Paris, 1989.

HOYEK
Lebanese, 20th century.
Born in Beirut.
Sculptor. Monuments.
Hoyek created the monument erected in a square in Beirut to commemorate the Lebanese men and women who died for France.

HOYEL, Jan van der
Flemish School, 17th century.
Born in Brussels.
Sculptor.
In 1669, Jan van der Hoyel worked in The Hague and later in Amsterdam.

HOYER, Anton
German, 18th century.
Active in Celle (Hanover).
Sculptor.
There are works by this artist in the churches of Steinwedel and Langenhagen, near Hanover.

HOYER, Bonaventura Gottlieb
German, 18th century.
Born 1710; died 5 May 1782.
Active in Meissen.
Painter. Figures, landscapes.
He did models for a porcelain manufactory.

HOYER, David
German, 17th - 18th century.
Born 1670, in Potsdam; died 27 May 1720, in Leipzig.
Painter. Portraits.
He was the official painter to several German royal and princely courts. A *Portrait of the King of Prussia* by him is known.
MUSEUMS AND GALLERIES:
BERLIN (Nationalgal.): *Portrait* (1693).

HOYER, Friedrich Hermann
German, 17th century.
Engraver.

HOYER, G. R.
German, 17th century.
Active c. 1600.
Draughtsman.

HOYER, Hermann Otto
German, 20th century.
Born 1893, in Bremen.
Painter. History painting.

Hermann Hoyer was a student at the fine arts academy in Munich. He painted Hitler making a speech to the party faithful, giving the picture the biblical title *In the Beginning was the Word*. The painting was shown for the first time in Munich in 1937, at the exhibition organised as a counterpart to the *Entartete Kunst* (*Degenerate Art*) exhibition, which brought together avant-garde artists of the time. The painting was also shown at the 1997 exhibition *Les Années trente en Europe. Le temps menaçant* (*Europe in the 1930s: The Gathering Storm*) at the Musée d'Art Moderne de la Ville de Paris.

Bibliography:

Pagé, Suzanne/Winock, Michel/Michaud, Éric/Vidal, Aline, *Les Années trente en Europe. Le Temps menaçant*, exhibition catalogue, Musée d'Art moderne de la Ville de Paris, Paris musées, Flammarion, Paris, 1997.

Museums and Galleries:

Washington DC (US Army Center Military History): *In the Beginning was the Word* (1937).

HOYER, Jean Louis Joseph

Swiss, 18th - 19th century.
Born 1 February 1762, in Lausanne; died 10 July 1829, in Soissons, France.
Painter, watercolourist. Landscapes, architectural views.

Museums and Galleries:

Soissons: numerous watercolours.

HOYER, Johann

German, 16th century.
Active in Berlin c. 1580.
Painter, illuminator.

HOYER, Johann Arent

German, 17th century.
Died 1674.
Active in Hanover.
Sculptor.

He was a pupil of Cordt Frömeling.

HOYER, Johann Georg

German, 18th century.
Active in Nordhausen.
Painter.

HOYER, L.

French, 17th century.
Painter. History painting.

L. Hoyer is remembered for three paintings in the church of Grasse: *St Roch, St Agnes* and *The Education of Orphans*.

HOYER, Philipp

German, 17th century.
Died 1610.
Active in Leipzig.
Painter, sculptor.

David may have been one of his descendants.

HOYER, Thorwalt Arenst

Danish, 20th century.
Born 1872, in Copenhagen.
Active in the USA.
Painter. Landscapes.

Hoyer lived in Chicago from 1915 and had his first solo exhibition there in 1936. He worked as an acrobat and travelled round the world. He had always loved painting and would visit museums during his travels.

When he began to paint himself, he imitated the painstaking techniques of his forebears in a sort of spontaneous pointillism, endeavouring accurately to translate the effects of light and shade and to impress the viewer with the contrast of light and dark. There are no people in Hoyer's landscapes, and their only geometry comes from the shadows that divide up the space.

Bibliography:

Bihalji-Merin, Oto, *Les Peintres naïfs*, Delpire, Paris, 1960.

Museums and Galleries:

New York (MoMA): *Interior of a Barn* (1937).

HOYER, Wolf von

German, 19th century.
Born c. 1806, in Dresden; died 1873, in Dresden.
Sculptor.

He worked at the Prussian royal palace at Sanssouci, but mostly for the King of Saxony's palaces in Eillnitz and Weesenstein.

HOYER, Wolfgang

Bohemian, 17th century.
Active in Prague c. 1600.
Painter.

Wolfgang Hoyer worked for Emperor Rudolph II.

HOYER VAN BRAKEL, Louiza Aletta

Dutch, 19th century.
Born 1805, in Rotterdam.
Painter. Flowers, fruit.

Louiza Hoyer van Brakel was a pupil of Groenendaal van der Berg and Robin.

HOYLAND, John

British, 20th century.
Born 12 October 1934, in Sheffield.
Painter (including gouache), watercolourist, engraver.

John Hoyland attended Sheffield College of Art from 1951 to 1960, then the Royal Academy Schools in London. In 1957 he travelled in the South of France and on Italy's Adriatic coast. He then began teaching: at Croydon School of Art from 1962; at Chelsea School of Art until 1970; at St Martin's School of Art and the Royal Academy Schools until 1977, and at the Slade School of Fine Art from 1974 until 1989. He was elected to the Royal Academy in 1991 and was appointed Professor of Painting at the Royal Academy Schools in 1999. A grant from the Peter Stuyvesant Foundation in 1964 allowed him to travel to New York for the first time; he returned there for a few months in 1972. Hoyland regularly produced prints, lithographs and monotype engravings in workshops in Britain and abroad, including the Atelier Lacourière-Frélaut in Paris. He won several awards, including the International Young Artists' Prize in Tokyo in 1964; prizes at the John Moores Liverpool Exhibition in 1965 and 1979; first prizes at the Edinburgh Open 100 in 1967, and at the Chichester National Art Exhibition in 1975; and a prize from the Arts Council of Great Britain in 1985.

Hoyland's early work is in a figurative style influenced by the watercolours of J.M.W. Turner. This is particularly true of the landscapes that he painted at St-Cyr in France. However, from 1958 his style acquired a flat geometric abstraction, with optical effects created by coloured lines. From 1964, under the influence of the American painters Robert Motherwell, Barnett Newman and Helen Frankenthaler and the Australian painter Sidney Noland, his work moved closer to the style of contemporary American painting. This can be seen in the paintings he produced from 1965: he began to give the coloured geometric elements in his work greater structure and arranged them more independently of one another on a more pronounced background. Around 1969 he re-engaged with certain aspects of American abstact painting - for example, applying paint very thickly - without, however, abandoning his methodical approach to composition. From 1970 to 1977 he explored the various effects of paint, including paint sprayed on to the canvas. He then turned to producing paintings with geometrically arranged areas of colour, applied in a way reminiscent of walls rendered in plaster. Around 1982 the geometric quality of his compositions began to be replaced by softer shapes painted in thickly applied, darker colours. From then on Hoyland's paintings acquired a dreamlike character; although they also have a violent quality, these paintings are somewhat to those of the Spanish painter Joan Miró.

Hoyland has taken part in group exhibitions since 1956, including the 4th Biennale des Jeunes in Paris in 1964; the 1967 Paris Biennale; the 1969 São Paulo Biennale; *British Painting and Sculpture 1960-1970* at the National Gallery of Art, Washington DC, in 1970-1971; *La Peinture Anglaise Aujourd'hui* (*English Painting Today*) at the Musée d'Art Moderne, Paris, in 1973; *British Painting 1952-1977* at the Royal Academy, London, in 1977; *English Expressionism* at the Warwick Arts Trust, London, in 1984; *British Art in the 20th Century: The Modern Movement* at the Royal Academy, London, in 1987; Tate Gallery, Liverpool and the Barbican Gallery, London, in 1993; at Galerie Josine Bokhoven, Amsterdam, and the Serpentine Gallery, London, in 1994. He has had solo exhibitions at the Marlborough New London Gallery in 1964; the Andre Emmerich Gallery, New York, in 1970 and 1972; the Galleria dell'Ariete, Milan, in 1970; the Harcus Krakow Gallery, Boston, in 1972; the Waddington Galleries, London, in 1974, 1975, 1976, 1981, 1983, 1985, 1987 and 1990; at the Galerie Krammer, Hamburg, in 1980. A retrospective of his work was held at the Serpentine Gallery, London, in 1979, and at the Royal Academy, London, in 1999..

BIBLIOGRAPHY:

Lassaigne, Jacques, *Peinture anglaise aujourd'hui*, exhibition catalogue, Musée d'Art moderne de la Ville de Paris, Paris, 1973. *John Hoyland, Paintings 1967-1979*, exhibition catalogue, Serpentine Gall., London, 1979. *John Hoyland Paintings Australia 1980*, Melbourne University Gallery, Melbourne, c. 1980. Gooding, Mel, *John Hoyland*, John Taylor in association with Lund Humphries, London, c. 1990. *John Hoyland*, Waddington Galleries Limited, London, 1990.

MUSEUMS AND GALLERIES:

ADELAIDE (AG of South Australia) - BELFAST (Ulster Mus.): *3-8-68* (1968, acrylic/canvas) - BIRMINGHAM (Museum and Art Gallery): *10.9.75* (oil on canvas) - BUFFALO (Albright-Knox AG) - HELSINKI (Ateneumin Taidemus.) - LEVERKUSEN (Schloss Morsbroich, Städtisches Museum) - LIVERPOOL (Walker AG) - LONDON (Arts Council Collection, Hayward Gal.): *Wotan* (1977, acrylic/canvas) - LONDON (British Council): *8-1-69* (1969, oil, acrylic/canvas); *22.5.75* (1975, acrylic/canvas); *31.8.76* (1976, acrylic/canvas) - LONDON (Courtauld Institute of Art): *Downland* (20th century, acrylic/canvas); *Verge* (20th century, acrylic/canvas) - LONDON (Gulbenkian Foundation) - LONDON (Royal Academy of Arts): *Taking a Dive* - LONDON (Tate Collection): *28. 5. 66* (1966, acrylic/canvas); *Saracen* (1977, acrylic/canvas); *North Sound* (1979, acrylic/canvas); screenprints, lithographs, prints - LONDON (Victoria and Albert Mus.) - LOS ANGELES (Frederick R. Weisman Art Foundation) - MANCHESTER (City AG) - MANCHESTER (Whitworth Art Gallery) - MELBOURNE (University Gallery) - NEW YORK (Neuberger Mus., University of New York) - PHOENIX (AM): *18.9.72* (1972, acrylic/canvas) - PITTSBURGH (Carnegie MA): several screenprints, two etchings - PROVIDENCE (Rhode Island School of Design) - RIO DE JANEIRO (MAM) - TEHRAN (Honarhaye Moaser) - TOLEDO (MA) - TORONTO (AG of Ontario).

AUCTION RECORDS:

LONDON, 10 Nov 1976, *Composition* (1973, acrylic, 36 x 36 ins / 91.5 x 91.5 cm) GBP 240. LONDON, 2 Dec 1980, *Untitled* (1969, acrylic/canvas, 84 x 36 1/4 ins / 213.5 x 92 cm) GBP 1,100. LONDON, 30 June 1983, *Untitled* (1966, oil on canvas, 50 x 40 ins / 127 x 101.6 cm) GBP 1,000. LONDON, 26 Feb 1986, *Composition* (1965, oil on canvas, 61 x 112 ins / 155 x 284.5 cm) GBP 2,300. LONDON, 13 Nov 1987, *19.12.65* (oil on canvas, 61 x 111 1/2 ins / 155 x 283 cm) GBP 3,200. NEW YORK, 4 May 1989, *Turn, Turn...* (1983, acrylic/canvas, 100 x 90 ins / 254 x 228.6 cm) USD 6,600. LONDON, 12 May 1989, *Abstract Rose* (1971, acrylic/paper, 22 x 31 ins / 55 x 78.7 cm) GBP 1,210. LONDON, 9 June 1989, *'Ormolu'* (1972, acrylic/canvas, 72 x 60 ins / 183 x 152.6 cm) GBP 4,180. LONDON, 10 Nov 1989, *'Hoo Ha Ha 7.1.84'* (1984, acrylic/canvas, 24 x 24 ins / 61 x 61 cm) GBP 4,620. LONDON, 9 March 1990, *Untitled* (1961, oil on canvas, 60 x 60 ins / 152.6 x 152.6 cm) GBP 2,145. NEW YORK, 6 Nov 1990, *Untitled* (1975, acrylic/canvas, 30 x 24 ins / 76.2 x 61 cm) USD 4,950. LONDON, 9 Nov 1990, *Untitled* (1978, oil and acrylic/paper, 29 1/4 x 22 ins / 74 x 55 cm) GBP 2,310. LONDON, 8 March 1991, *23.4.76* (acrylic/canvas, 30 x 24 ins / 76 x 61 cm) GBP 2,530. LONDON, 7 June 1991, *Abstract Composition - 24.8.76* (1976, oil on canvas, 24 x 30 ins / 61 x 76 cm) GBP 3,080. LONDON, 11 June 1992, *17/1/69* (oil on canvas, 120 x 72 ins / 305 x 183 cm) USD 3,080. LONDON, 25 May 1994, *Palindrome* (1975, oil on canvas, 90 1/4 x 80 ins / 229 x 203 cm) GBP 5,060. LONDON, 21 March 1996, *Cupid's Work* (1986, acrylic/canvas, 55 x 24 ins / 140 x 61.2 cm) GBP 1,610. LONDON, 30 Sept 1999, *Red on Green* (watercolour, 13 x 21 ins / 33 x 53 cm) GBP 1,100. LONDON, 5 Nov 1999, *Paramaribo 24.11.88* (1988, acrylic on cotton duck, 100 x 60 ins / 254 x 152 cm) GBP 4,500. LONDON, 1 June 2000, *Sat* (1988, acrylic on canvas, 100 x 93 ins / 254 x 236 cm) GBP 3,800. LONDON, 1 June 2000, *Carib* (1989, acrylic on canvas, 100 x 93 ins / 254 x 236 cm) GBP 4,500. LONDON, 1 March 2001, *Untitled* (oil on canvas, 145 x 78 ins / 368 x 199 cm) GBP 3,500. LONDON, 20 March 2001, *Untitled* (1967, gouache, 30 x 10 ins / 75 x 26 cm) GBP 1,400. LONDON, 4 July 2002, *Untitled* (acrylic on canvas, 84 x 120 ins / 213 x 304 cm) GBP 2,600. LONDON, 4 July 2002, *Oceano* (1980, acrylic on duck, 84 x 84 ins / 213 x 213 cm) GBP 3,500. LONDON, 27 March 2003, *Abstract* (1964, oil on canvas, 84 x 84 ins / 213 x 213 cm) GBP 2,800. LONDON, 2 Dec 2003, *Untitled* (acrylic on canvas, 66 x 72 ins / 167 x 184 cm) GBP 7,000. LONDON, 2 June 2004, *7.7.75* (1975, acrylic on canvas, 90 x 80 ins / 229 x 203 cm) GBP 9,500. LONDON, 17 Nov 2004, *1.7.74* (1974, oil on canvas, 72 x 66 ins / 183 x 167 cm) GBP 6,500.

HOYLANDT, Werner van

French, 20th century.

Painter. Still-lifes.

Werner van Hoylandt is of Flemish origin. He has participated in regional collective exhibitions, receiving various distinctions. He has also exhibited in Paris, as a member of the Salon d'Automne. The Campo gallery in Antwerp and the Galerie J. Auriel in Toulouse exhibit several of his works.

HOYLE, Annie Elizabeth

American, 19th century.

Born 29 April 1851; died 1931, in Washington DC.

Painter, illustrator.

Annie Elizabeth Hoyle studied at the Académie Julian in Paris. She was a member of the Arts Club of Washington and the American Federation of Arts. She illustrated many works.

HOYNCK, Otto

Dutch, 17th century.

Born c. 1630, in The Hague; died possibly in England.

Portrait artist.

In 1661, Otto Hoynck was a member of the guild of St Luke. He studied under Arnold van Ravestyn.

AUCTION RECORDS:

LONDON, 23 March 1943, *Greyhound*, GBP 31.

HOYNCK VAN PAPENDRECHT, Jan.

See **PAPENDRECHT Jan Hoynck van**

HOYOIT

British, 18th century.

Active in London.

Painter. Flowers.
Hoyoit exhibited regularly at the Free Society from 1771 to 1783.

HOYOLL, Philipp
German, 19th century.
Born 1816, in Breslau (now Wroclaw, Poland).
Painter, miniaturist, lithographer. Genre scenes.
He was a pupil of Schadow at the academy in Düsseldorf. From 1836, he exhibited in Berlin, Hanover and Stuttgart. He took part in the great exhibitions in London between 1864 and 1875.
AUCTION RECORDS:
LONDON, 23 Oct 1981, *Serenely Waiting for Coming Events* (oil on canvas, 13 x 11 ins / 33 x 28 cm) GBP 1,100. LONDON, 21 Sept 1983, *Very Wise Politicians* (oil on canvas, 12 x 9 1/2 ins / 30.5 x 24 cm) GBP 850. LONDON, 11 June 1986, *Children at a Window* (oil on canvas, 20 x 24 ins / 51 x 61 cm) GBP 3,500. LONDON, 25 March 1994, *An Exacting Rival* (1872, oil on canvas, 12 x 10 ins / 30.5 x 25.4 cm) GBP 920. EDINBURGH, 15 May 1997, *A Very Prudent Female Politician* (1857, oil on canvas, oval, 13 x 11 ins / 33 x 28 cm) GBP 2,185. LONDON, 9 Sept 1999, *Put Salt on their Tails, So Catch Them* (1871, oil on canvas, 21 x 17 ins / 53 x 43 cm) GBP 10,000. LONDON, 7 March 2002, *Spilt Milk* (1868, oil on canvas, 13 x 11 ins / 33 x 28 cm) GBP 1,200. NEW YORK, 5 Feb 2003, *Over her Shoulder* (1867, oil on canvas, 13 x 11 ins / 33 x 28 cm) USD 2,200.

HOYOS, Alonso de
Spanish, 16th century.
Born c. 1550, in Cuenca de Campos.
Painter.
He was a nephew of Francisco de Hoyos and worked in Tordesillas.

HOYOS, Ana Mercedes
Colombian, 20th century.
Born 1942.
Painter. Local scenes, scenes with figures, figures, still-lifes.
AUCTION RECORDS:
NEW YORK, 21 Nov 1988, *Palisade 4 - 44PM* (1987, oil on canvas, 59 x 59 ins / 150 x 150 cm) USD 16,500. NEW YORK, 17 May 1989, *Woman of Palenque* (1988, oil on canvas, 59 x 59 ins / 150 x 150 cm) USD 24,200. NEW YORK, 20 Nov 1989, *Woman of Palenque* (1988, oil on canvas, 39 1/4 x 39 1/4 ins / 100 x 100 cm) USD 18,700. NEW YORK, 21 Nov 1989, *Still-life* (1985, oil on canvas, 47 1/4 x 47 1/4 ins / 120 x 120 cm) USD 18,700. NEW YORK, 2 May 1990, *Bazurto* (1988, oil on canvas, 59 x 59 ins / 150 x 150 cm) USD 27,500. NEW YORK, 19-20 Nov 1990, *Fruit Sellers at Domingo III* (1988, oil on canvas, 43 x 43 ins / 109.5 x 109.5 cm) USD 16,500; *Display of Exotic Fruit* (1989, oil on canvas, 39 1/4 x 78 1/2 ins / 100 x 199.5 cm) USD 24,200. NEW YORK, 15-16 May 1991, *Still-life with Exotic Fruit from Palenque* (1989, oil on canvas, 59 x 59 ins / 150 x 150 cm) USD 49,500. NEW YORK, 20 Nov 1991, *Watermelon* (1990, acrylic/canvas, 19 3/4 x 94 1/2 ins / 50 x 240 cm) USD 26,400. NEW YORK, 25 Nov 1992, *Mis Americas* (*My Americas*) (1991, oil on canvas, 78 x 39 1/4 ins / 198 x 99.5 cm) USD 41,800. NEW YORK, 18 May 1993, *Inverapuestas el Perro* (1992, oil on canvas, 59 x 59 ins / 150 x 150 cm) USD 46,000. NEW YORK, 23-24 Nov 1993, *Display* (1991, oil on canvas, 78 3/4 x 39 1/4 ins / 200 x 100 cm) USD 55,200. NEW YORK, 17 May 1995, *Display of Exotic Fruit* (1991, oil on canvas, 70 3/4 x 70 3/4 ins / 180 x 180 cm) USD 48,875. NEW YORK, 14-15 May 1996, *Still-life of La Bahia* (1992, oil on canvas, 46 3/4 x 46 3/4 ins / 118.7 x 118.7 cm) USD 23,000. NEW YORK, 28 May 1997, *Palenquera Arena* (1996, oil on canvas, diptych, 19 3/4 x 114 1/4 ins / 50 x 290 cm) USD 34,500. NEW YORK, 24-25 Nov 1997, *Bazurto, Julia's Universe* (1995, oil on canvas, 49 1/4 x 116 1/4 ins / 125 x 295 cm) USD 52,900. NEW YORK, 2 June 1999, *Bazurto* (1998, oil on canvas, 46 x 46 ins / 118 x 118 cm) USD 35,000. NEW YORK, 22 Nov 1999, *Patillas de la cordialidad* (1997, oil on canvas, 47 x 94 ins / 119 x 239 cm) USD 40,000. NEW YORK, 21 Nov 2000, *Bananas* (c. 1990, oil on canvas, 12 x 12 ins / 30 x 30 cm) USD 5,000. NEW YORK, 28 May 2002, *Bazurto* (1988, oil on canvas, 47 x 94 ins / 120 x 240 cm) USD 35,000.

HOYOS, Francisco de
Spanish, 16th century.
Born c. 1540, in Cuenca de Campos.
Painter.
He worked in Valladolid.

HOYOS, Gaspar de
Spanish, 16th century.
Died c. 1586.
Painter. History painting.
Gaspar de Hoyos was a pupil of Becerra and worked in Astorga and Madrid.

HOYOS, Rafael de
Spanish, 16th century.
Born c. 1550, in Cuenca de Campos.
Painter.
He was a nephew of Francisco de Hoyos.

HOYOS LIMON, Andres de
Spanish, 19th century.
Active in Seville.
Painter.
Andrés de Hoyos Limon exhibited in Madrid and Paris.

HOYOUX, Bertin
Flemish School, 17th century.
Born 17th century, in Jupille.
Portrait artist.
Bertin Hoyoux worked around 1637.

HOYTEMA, Antoinette Agathe van
Dutch, 19th - 20th century.
Born 1875, in Delft; died 1967.
Painter. Portraits, still-lifes.
Hoytema studied at the art academy in Arnhem. She travelled a great deal, and although it has not been established whether she spent any time in Indonesia, her still-lifes and portraits of people from Indonesia suggest sensitivity to and genuine knowledge of the region.
BIBLIOGRAPHY:
Haks, Leo, *Haks & Maris Lexicon of Foreign Artists who Visualized Indonesia, 1600-1950: Surveying Painters, Watercolourists, Draughtsmen, Sculptors, Illustrators, Graphic and Industrial Artists*, Archipelago Press, Singapore, 1995.
AUCTION RECORDS:
SINGAPORE, 5 Oct 1996, *Wayang Puppets* (1929, oil on canvas, 17 1/2 x 17 1/2 ins / 44.5 x 44.5 cm) SGD 3,220.

HOYTEMA, Theodoor van
Dutch, 19th - 20th century.
Born 18 December 1863, in The Hague; died 29 August 1917, in The Hague.
Painter, watercolourist, pastellist, engraver, lithographer. Animals.
Hoytema was a student at the fine arts academy in The Hague. He was awarded a bronze medal at the Exposition Universelle in Paris in 1900. He engraved animals.
AUCTION RECORDS:
AMSTERDAM, 10 Feb 1988, *Storks, Swallows and Herons in Flight above Trees in Flower* (oil on canvas, 72 x 148 ins / 183 x 375 cm) NLG 3,910. AMSTERDAM, 12 Dec 1991, *Peacocks* (1912, watercolour and pastel/paper, 24 1/4 x 29 1/2 ins / 61.5 x 75 cm) NLG 5,520. AMSTERDAM, 11 April 1995, *Peacocks in a Tree* (oil on canvas, 85 3/4 x 41 3/4 ins / 218 x 106 cm) NLG 10,030.

HOZELL, Hans
German, 18th century.

Active in Bamberg early 18th century.
Painter.

HOZO, Dzevad
Serb, 20th century.
Born 10 May 1938, in Uzice.
Engraver, draughtsman.

Dzevad Hozo studied at the academy of fine art in Ljubljana. Using the style of Informal Abstraction, his work explores the effects on materials of, particularly, shadows and contrasts.

He exhibited work in Celje (1965), in Ljubljana (1966) and took part in the engraving Biennale in Ljubljana (1965).

HRACHOWINA, Karl
Austrian, 19th century.
Born 28 January 1845, in Budapest; died 21 February 1896, in Vienna.
Engraver.

He worked mainly in Vienna, teaching drawing there.

HRADICZKY, Lukacs
Hungarian, 18th century.
Active in Nyitra (now Nitra, Slovakia) c. 1750.
Painter.

HRADIL, Rudolf
Austrian, 20th - 21st century.
Born 1952, in Salzburg.
Painter, watercolourist, engraver, lithographer.
Landscapes, still-lifes.

Rudolf Hrabil studied in Vienna, Paris and London. He is best known for his views of Salzburg, which are quickly sketched with clear, open lines. The Rupertinum museum of modern and contemporary art in Salzburg mounted a solo exhibition of his watercolours in 2001.

HRDLICKA, Alfred
Austrian, 20th century.
Born 1928, in Vienna; died 1989.
Sculptor, draughtsman, engraver.

Alfred Hrdlicka initially studied painting from 1946 to 1953 at the Akademie der Bildenden Künste in Vienna, where his professors were Gütersloh and Dobrowsky. From 1953 to 1957, he was a student of Wtruba, and he also took Christian Martin's engraving course. His output has only one theme: man oppressed by the modern world and its alienating forces, and man's revolt. From 1972, he began to commemorate the French Revolution, depicting fallen heroes and dashed hopes with nervous, incisive strokes. Elsewhere in his output, he depicts the torments and tragedy of war, from the extermination of the Jews to the despair of broken love. His obsession with the demeaned, degraded and tortured body means that he can be grouped with Egon Schiele, Otto Dix and Georges Grosz.

Hrdlicka's work was shown at collective exhibitions, including the Venice Biennale (1964) and the São Paulo Biennale (1967). There have been regular exhibitions of his work in Austria, as well as in London (from 1968), Lübeck (1980), Vienna (1983) and Mexico (1984). The Galerie Hilger in Paris presented an exhibition of his work at the International Contemporary Art Fair at the Grand Palais, and he exhibited at the Centre Régional d'Art Contemporain Midi-Pyrénées in Labège-Innopole. The Musée-Galerie de la Seita in Paris presented a collection of his sculptures and works on paper in 1997, and in 2002 there was an exhibition of his sculptures entitled *Masterworks 1972-2001* at the Palais Harrach in Vienna.

BIBLIOGRAPHY:
Chobot, Manfred, *Graphik*, Propyläen, Berlin, 1973. Lewin, Michael, '*Alfred Hrdlicka. Das Gesamte Werk. Bildhauerei*' in *3 vols.*, Europaverlag, Zurich, Vienna, 1985.

AUCTION RECORDS:
VIENNA, 4 Dec 1974, *Portrait of Oskar Kokoschka* (bronze) ATS 45,000. VIENNA, 25 June 1976, *Torso* (1957, red marble from Romania, h. 72 ins / 182 cm) ATS 450,000. VIENNA, 18 March 1981, *The Step* (1974, white and red pencil/brown paper, 18 1/4 x 25 ins / 46.5 x 63.5 cm) ATS 16,000. VIENNA, 20 May 1981, *Seated Nude* (1980, bronze, h. 13 1/2 ins / 34 cm) ATS 12,000. MUNICH, 30 Nov 1984, *Young Girl Undressing* (bronze, h. 7 3/4 ins / 20 cm) DEM 3,500. MUNICH, 6 June 1986, *Mimmi Kaiserallee* (1981, bronze, h. 7 3/4 ins / 20 cm) DEM 2,200. COLOGNE, 28 Nov 1987, *Loving Couple* (patinated bronze, h. 26 1/2 ins / 67 cm) DEM 42,500. HEIDELBERG, 9 Oct 1992, *New Regime - Old Regime* (1985, dry-point, 23 1/2 x 39 1/4 ins / 59.5 x 99.6 cm) DEM 1,200. LONDON, 13 Oct 1994, *Small Female Torso* (1964, white marble, h. 16 ins / 40.5 cm) GBP 6,900. LONDON, 6 Oct 1999, *Stele with Female Figure* (1975, white Carrara marble, 53 x 8x8 ins / 135 x 20x20 cm) GBP 19,000. VIENNA, 13 Oct 1999, *Working Sketch* (1967, pencil on paper on canvas, 87 x 59 ins / 220 x 150 cm) ATS 380,000. VIENNA, 11 April 2000, *The King is Dead - Long Live the Emperor* (1986, brush and pencil, 20 x 30 ins / 50 x 75 cm) ATS 40,000. HAMBURG, 8 June 2001, *Wrestlers* (bronze, 15 x 11x8 ins / 39 x 28x21 cm) DEM 8,000. BERN, 21 June 2001, *Chess Player* (charcoal, colour chalk, watercolour, Works on paper, 22 x 30 ins / 56 x 77 cm) CHF 6,000. VIENNA, 23 April 2002, *Marsyas II* (1970, 29 x 12x12 ins / 73 x 30x30 cm) EUR 14,000. VIENNA, 27 Nov 2002, *Kaiserallee II - Tree Study* (dark brown patinated bronze, 35 x 8x8 ins / 88 x 21x20 cm) EUR 11,000. VIENNA, 28 Oct 2003, *Returning Aristocracy Assaulting the Corpse of the Revolution* (1985, oil and charcoal on canvas, 79 x 63 ins / 200 x 160 cm) EUR 45,000. COLOGNE, 27 Nov 2003, *Upright Male Figure* (1968, brown patinated bronze, h. 27 ins / 69 cm) EUR 11,500. AMSTERDAM, 8 June 2004, *Untitled* (1982, pastel, 26 x 19 ins / 67 x 49 cm) EUR 6,000. VIENNA, 23 Nov 2004, *Johann Joachim Winckelmanns Ende* (white marble, 17 x 24x10 ins / 42 x 62x25 cm) EUR 40,000.

HRNCIR, Thomas
Austrian, 19th - 20th century.
Born 31 October 1855, in Vienna; died October 1917, in Vienna.
Painter, engraver.

Thomas Hrncir was a student of Louis Jacoby in Vienna. He subsequently spent time in Paris. He specialised in portraits, both painted and engraved.

HRNCYRZ, Emma
Austrian, 19th - 20th century.
Born in Vienna.
Engraver.

Emma Hrncyrz was a student of L. Michalek.

HROCH, Vladimir
Czech, 20th century.
Born 1907.
Painter.

MUSEUMS AND GALLERIES:
PRAGUE (Národní Gal.).

HRODOGARIUS
9th century.
Miniaturist.

Hrodogarius transcribed and illustrated a copy of *Terence* which is now in the Vatican Library.

HRUBY, Rehar
Bohemian, 16th century.
Miniaturist.

Rehar Hruby wrote a book (now in the library in Prague) for Ladislas of Sleruberg in 1514, which he illustrated with miniatures.

HRUCIK, Maximilian
Austrian, 19th century.
Born c. 1810, in Lemberg (now Lviv, Ukraine).
Miniaturist. Landscapes.
Maximilian Hrucik studied in Vienna and travelled in Italy, before finally settling in his native city.

HRUTSKIJ, Ivan Timofeivich. See **CHRUTZKY**

HRYNKOWSKY, Jan Piotr or Yan
Polish, 20th century.
Born 15 June 1891, in Telechow; died 21 March 1971, in Cracow.
Painter, draughtsman, engraver (wood), lithographer, sculptor. Stage sets.
Jan Piotr Hrynkowski studied at the Cracow academy of fine art with Pankiewicz and then in Paris at the André Lhote studio in 1921. He started as a painter but also made woodcuts, lithographs and some sculptures.

He participated in the first exhibition of Polish Expressionism held in Cracow in 1917. This lead to the Formist movement with which Hrynkowski was associated until 1921. He lived in France in 1931-1932 and again in 1938. Collective exhibitions include: Brussels and London (1922); Prague (1924); Helsinki, Stockholm and Prague (1927); Budapest and Paris (1928); The Hague, Amsterdam and Brussels (1929); Copenhagen and Bucharest (1930); Philadelphia, New York, Chicago and Moscow (1933). He exhibited two paintings of flowers, a *Portrait of a Young Girl* and a *Landscape* (the latter a watercolour) in the Polish section of the Salon d'Automne in Paris, organised by the society for literary and artistic exchange between France and Poland and by the Cercle des Artistes Polonais de Paris. He held solo exhibitions in Cracow, Warsaw, Poznan and Bytom.
MUSEUMS AND GALLERIES:
CHICAGO (Polish Mus. of America) - CRACOW (Muz. Narodowe) - HARTFORD (Art School of University) - JAGELLON (Prints Coll.) - ŁÓDZ (Muz. Sztuki) - POZNAN (Muz. Narodowe) - PRAGUE - WARSAW (Muz. Narodowe) - WARSAW (Muz. Plakatu w Wilanowie) - WROCLAW (MA).

HSI KANG. See **XI GANG**

HSI-CHIN CHÜ-SHIH. See **XIJIN JUSHI**

HSIA CH'ANG. See **XIA CHANG**

HSIA CHIH. See **XIA ZHI**

HSIA CHIN. See **XIA JIN**

HSIA K'AO-CH'ANG. See **XIA KAOCHANG**

HSIA K'UEI. See **XIA KUI**

HSIA KUEI. See **XIA GUI**

HSIA PING. See **XIA BING**

HSIA TI. See **XIA DI**

HSIA YUNG. See **XIA YONG**

HSIANG K'UEI. See **XIANG KUI**

HSIANG SHENG-MO. See **XIANG SHENGMO**

HSIANG TE-HSIN. See **XIANG DEXIN**

HSIANG YÜAN-PIEN. See **XIANG YUANBIAN**

HSIAO. See **XIAO**

HSIAO CH'EN. See **XIAO CHEN**

HSIAO CH'IEN-CHUNG. See **XIAO QIANZHONG**

HSIAO CHAO. See **XIAO ZHAO**

HSIAO CHIN, or Xiao Jin
Chinese, 20th century.
Born 1935, in Shanghai.
Active in Italy since 1957.
Painter.
Hsiao Chin trained with Li Zhongsheng in Taipei before moving to Europe in 1956. In 1957, he co-founded the Ton Fan group and settled in Milan. Among his exhibitions are: 1966, 1970, Bochum; 1967, Berlin; 1980, Wuppertal Museum; 1982, Goethe Institut, Paris, Bourges Museum, Goethe Institut, London, Edinburgh Festival; 1983, Mülheim Museum.
AUCTION RECORDS:
COLOGNE, 31 May 1986, *TY 1* (1961, acrylic on canvas, 27 1/2 x 31 1/2 ins / 70 x 80 cm) DEM 2,000. MILAN, 19 Dec 1989, *Untitled* (1969, acrylic on canvas, 35 1/2 x 23 1/2 ins / 90 x 60 cm) ITL 1,800,000. MILAN, 27 March 1990, *Tuannn!!* (1964, tempera on canvas, 39 1/4 x 39 1/4 ins / 100 x 100 cm) ITL 1,800,000. MILAN, 27 Sept 1990, *Painting GH* (1959, oil on canvas, 23 1/2 x 27 1/2 ins / 60 x 70 cm) ITL 1,700,000. PARIS, 27 March 1995, *Pu-g* (1961, oil on canvas, 27 1/2 x 23 1/2 ins / 70 x 60 cm) FRF 11,500. MILAN, 12 Dec 1995, *Painting EU* (1959, oil on canvas, 35 1/2 x 23 1/2 ins / 90 x 60 cm) ITL 1,150,000. PARIS, 5 Oct 1996, *Untitled* (1960, watercolour and ink on paper, 22 1/2 x 16 1/4 ins / 57 x 41 cm) FRF 3,000. PARIS, 25 June 1999, *Geometry* (1963-1964, oil on canvas, 51 x 77 ins / 130 x 195 cm) FRF 50,000. AMSTERDAM, 8 June 2000, *To Him Who Teaches the Truth* (1963, acrylic on canvas, 31 x 31 ins / 80 x 80 cm) NLG 5,000. AMSTERDAM, 8 June 2000, *To Him Who Gives Power to the Spirit of Man* (1963, acrylic on canvas, 31 x 39 ins / 80 x 100 cm) NLG 5,000. MILAN, 30 May 2001, *Tension* (1967, oil on canvas, 45 x 45 ins / 115 x 115 cm) ITL 7,200,000. AMSTERDAM, 12 June 2001, *Light Composition no. 4* (1964, acrylic on canvas, 31 x 31 ins / 80 x 80 cm) NLG 4,500. COPENHAGEN, 18 June 2002, *Thunderstorm 30* (1981, oil on paper on canvas, 25 x 49 ins / 63 x 125 cm) DKK 15,000. PARIS, 4 Oct 2002, *The Tao* (oil on canvas, 39 x 28 ins / 100 x 70 cm) EUR 1,800. ROME, 13 Nov 2003, *Big Black Cloud* (oil on canvas, 44 x 74 ins / 112 x 187 cm) EUR 2,600. MILAN, 24 Nov 2003, *Best Wishes, Poland* (acrylic on canvas, 30 x 39 ins / 75 x 100 cm) EUR 1,700. LONDON, 6 May 2004, *Untitled* (oil on canvas, 35 x 27 ins / 89 x 69 cm) GBP 1,100. MILAN, 24 May 2004, *Composition* (1959, tempera on paper on canvas, 69 x 12 ins / 176 x 30 cm) EUR 1,800.

HSIAO HAI-SHAN. See **XIAO HAISHAN**

HSIAO JU SUNG, Ju-Sung, or Xiao Rusong
Chinese, 20th century.
Born 1922, in Kao-Hsiung, Taiwan; died 1992.
Painter, watercolourist. Landscapes.
Hsiao Ju Sung studied at the National Taiwan Normal University and won a great number of art prizes and honours in his country. In 1972 the China Art Society awarded him its gold cup for best watercolourist. He represented Chinese painting at the China-Japan cultural exchange exhibition. He was invited to many Chinese art events in the USA both as a painter and in his official role as inspector of fine arts in Hsin-chu Province and professor at Hsin-Chu Higher School. His watercolours, of robust landscapes and nudes, lack shading and lightness, and show hardly any sign of seeking transparency.
AUCTION RECORDS:
TAIPEI, 22 March 1992, *Field of Flowers* (watercolour on paper, 21 x 28 1/2 ins / 53.2 x 72.6 cm) TWD 396,000. TAIPEI, 18 Oct 1992, *Seaside* (watercolour on paper, 21 x 28 3/4 ins / 53.4 x 72.9 cm) TWD 462,000. TAIPEI, 16 Oct 1994, *Abstract Still-life* (watercolour on paper, 15 1/4 x 20 3/4 ins / 38.7 x 53 cm) TWD 287,500. TAIPEI, 13 April 1997, *Wall* (1982, watercolour on paper, 20 3/4 x 26 1/2 ins / 53 x 67.5 cm) TWD 667,000. TAIPEI, 19 Oct 1997, *Early Spring* (c. 1986, watercolour on pa-

per, 28 x 39 1/4 ins / 71 x 100 cm) TWD 1,865,000. TAIPEI, 11 April 1999, *Maid* (watercolour, 27 x 17 ins / 69 x 42 cm) TWD 400,000. HONG KONG, 26 Oct 2003, *Window Scene* (watercolour, 28 x 39 ins / 71 x 100 cm) HKD 480,000.

HSIAO LING-C'HO. See **XIAO LINGZHUO**

HSIAO YÜ. See **XIAO YU**

HSIAO YÜN-TS'UNG. See **XIAO YUNCONG**

HSIAO YUNG. See **XIAO YONG**

HSIAO-AN. See **XIAO-AN**

HSIEH CH'ENG. See **XIE CHENG**

HSIEH CH'Ü-SHENG. See **XIE QUSHENG**

HSIEH CHIH-LIU. See **XIE ZHILIU**

HSIEH CHIN. See **XIE JIN**

HSIEH HAI-YEN. See **XIE HAIYAN**

HSIEH HUAN. See **XIE HUAN**

HSIEH KUNG-CHAN. See **XIE GONGZHAN**

HSIEH LAN-SHENG. See **XIE LANSHENG**

HSIEH PIN. See **XIE BIN**

HSIEH PO-CH'ENG. See **XIE BOCHENG**

HSIEH SHIH-CH'EN. See **XIE SHICHEN**

HSIEH SUI. See **XIE SUI**

HSIEH SUN. See **XIE SUN**

HSIEH TZU-WEN. See **KIE ZIWEN**

HSIEH YÜ-CH'IEN. See **XIE YUQIAN**

HSIEH YUAN. See **XIE YUAN**

HSIEN-TSONG MING. See **XIANZONG MING**

HSIEN-YÜ SHU. See **XIANYU SHU**

HSIN TZ'U-CHING. See **XING CIJING**

HSING T'UNG. See **XING TONG**

H'SSICEN, Saâdi, real name Hacen
Algerian, 20th century.
Painter.

Saâdi H'ssicen began painting in 1959. He is also a singer and composer. He held a solo exhibition of his works at the Centre Culturel Algérien in Paris in 2003.

HSÜ. See **XU BIN**

HSÜ CH'UNG-CHÜ. See **XU CHONGJU**

HSÜ CH'UNG-SSÙ. See **XU CHONGSI**

HSU CHEN. See **XU ZHEN**

HSÜ CHIEH-MIN. See **XU JIEMIN**

HSÜ CHING. See **XU JING**

HSÜ FANG. See **XU FANG**

HSÜ HSI. See **XU XI or SIU HI**

HSÜ I. See **XU YI**

HSÜ JUNG. See **XU RONG**

HSÜ LIN. See **XU LIN**

HSÜ MEI. See **XU MEI**

HSÜ MENG-TS'AI. See **XU MENGCAI**

HSÜ MOU-WEI. See **XU MOUWEI**

HSÜ PEI-HUNG. See **XU BEIHONG**

HSÜ PEN. See **XU BEN**

HSÜ SHIH-CH'ANG. See **XU SHICHANG**

HSÜ SHIH-CH'I. See **XU SHIQI**

HSÜ T'AI. See **XU TAI**

HSÜ TAN. See **XU DAN**

HSÜ TAO-NING. See **XU DAONING**

HSÜ WANG-HSIUNG. See **XU WANGXIONG**

HSÜ WEI. See **XU WEI**

HSÜ WEI-JEN. See **XU WEIREN**

HSÜ YANG. See **XU YANG**

HSÜ YEN-SUN. See **XU YANSUN**

HSÜ YU. See **XU YOU**

HSU YU-JEN, or Hsü Yüan-wen, Xu Yuren, or Siu Yuanwen, nickname: Gongsu, pseudonym: Lizhai
Chinese, 17th century.
Born 1634, in Kunshan (Jiangsu); died 1691.
Painter.

He was a scholar painter. He held a post at the Hanlin academy and was president of the revenues office. He was also a landscape painter.

HSÜ YÜAN. See **XU YUAN**

HSÜ YÜAN-WEN. See **HSU YU-JEN**

HSÜ-KU. See **XUGU**

HSÜ-KU. See **XUGU**

HSÜAN-TSUNG MING. See **XUANZONG MING**

HSÜEH HSÜAN. See **XUE XUAN**

HSÜEH SU-SU. See **XUE SUSU**

HSÜEH WU. See **XUE SUSU**

HSÜEH-CHIEN. See **XUEJIAN**

HSUEH-YAI. See **XUEYA**

HU, Charles V. E.
French, 19th century.
Died 1899, in Paris.
Painter. Landscapes.

Charles Hu was a member of the Société des Artistes Français.

HU, Salomon de La. See **LA HU**

HU CAO, or Hu Ts'ao, nickname: Shigong
Chinese, 17th century.
Born in Jiangning (Jiangsu).
Active at the end of the 17th century.
Painter.

One of the Eight Scholars of Jinling, Hu Cao was a figure, chrysanthemum and landscape painter.

HU CHANG. See **HU ZHANG**

HU CHEN-K'AI. See **HU ZHENKAI**

HU CHENG-YEN. See **HU ZHENGYAN**

HU CHIH-FU. See **HU ZHIFU**

HU CHING. See **HU JING**

HU GAO, or Hu Kao, nickname: Gongmai
Chinese, 17th century.
Born in Nanjing.
Active in the first half of the 17th century.
Painter.

Hu Gao was sent on a mission to Korea with General Zhao Yu during the Tianqi period (1621-1627). Consequently, his landscapes are much appreciated in that country.

HU GUI, or Hu Kuei
Chinese, 10th century.

Of Khitan origin.
Active during the Later Tang dynasty (923-935).
Painter. Local scenes, animals.

Hu Gui was a Khitan Mongol. He is mainly known for his horse paintings and his scenes of tribal and nomadic life. His compositions are well organised, with some emphasis on the empty space around his lightly shaded hills and groups. He used a wolf-hair brush and in his horse painting achieved a highly refined treatment with very fine outlines, well-defined, subtly shaded angles and luxuriant manes and tails. His son continued in the same style.

Museums and Galleries:
Beijing (Palace Mus.): *Mongol with a Musical Instrument, with a Camel Lying on the Ground* (painting on fan, formerly attributed) - Boston (MFA): *Khitan Falconer with Horse* (painting on fan, formerly attributed) - Taipei (National Palace Mus.): *Hunters Returning with Greyhounds* (ink and colour/silk, with a seal of the Song Emperor Huizong, attributed); *Four Mongols on Horseback with Falcons Ready for Hunting* (light colours, large sheet of an album); *Three Mongols on Horseback on a Sandy Plain with a Large Dog* (colours on silk, large sheet of an album).

HU GUI, or Hu Kuei, nickname: Yuexiang
Chinese, 18th century.
Born in Suzhou (Jiangsu).
Active c. 1785.
Painter.

A court painter, Hu Gui painted landscapes and flowers in the style of Yun Shouping (1633-1690).

HU HSI-KUEI. See **HU XIGUI**

HU JIANCHENG
Chinese, 20th - 21st century.
Born 1959, in Harbin.
Painter. Figures, landscapes, landscapes with figures.

Hu Jiancheng studied oil painting at the Lu Xun Art Academy in Shengyuan until 1988. The following year he worked under the direction of Claude Yvel, a French painter who was teaching at Lu Xun in 1989, and was strongly influenced by him. A Realist by style, Hu has a real predilection for using unusual details to capture a melancholy scene. He has taken part in many exhibitions in China, in particular in Beijing and Shanghai.

HU JING, or Hu Ching, nickname: Xianqing, monastic name: Chengxue
Chinese, 16th - 17th century.
Born in Nanping (Fujian).
Active probably in the late 16th and early 17th century.
Painter.

Hu Jing became a monk. He travelled to the Liuqiu Islands, bringing back a considerable number of landscape sketches.

HU KAO, or Hu K'ao
Chinese, 20th century.
Painter, cartoonist.

A cartoonist in the Realist style, Hu Kao worked in Shanghai before leaving for Yenan during the second Sino-Japanese War.

Cartoon art has a very important place in 20th-century China as it is closely connected with the social upheaval the country underwent during this century. As a movement, cartoon art emerged in the 1930s, drawing inspiration at first from the novels of Lu Xun (1881-1936) and the urban jungle that Shanghai had become immediately after the Nationalist revolution.

Its graphic style was influenced by woodcuts, especially those of Grosz. and Kollwitz, as well as the work of the Soviet graphic artists who exhibited in Shanghai in 1935 at the large Exhibition of Soviet Graphic Art. It fell to the Chinese cartoonists to depict the horror and cruelty of this bloody time and to paint a portrait of Shanghai society as it became driven by the lust for money and political power. When the war started, many of the cartoonists, including Hu Kao, fled to Yenan. Henceforth, the target of their art would be the Japanese invaders.

Bibliography:
Sullivan, Michael, *Chinese Art in the Twentieth Century*, University of California Press, Berkeley, Los Angeles, London, 1959. Andrews, Julia F., *Painters and Politics in the People's Republic of China: 1949-1979*, University of California Press, Berkeley, 1994.

HU KAO. See also **HU GAO**

HU KUEI. See **HU GUI**

HU NIANZU
Chinese, 20th century.
Born 1927, in Hunan.
Painter.

Hu Nianzu studied painting at the fine art academy of Nanjing, where he later became one of Huang Junbi's favourite pupils. He taught Chinese painting at the University of New York and then took up a post at the National Taiwan Art Academy. He showed his work in solo and group exhibitions in his own country and the USA.

Auction records:
Hong Kong, 18 May 1989, *Landscape* (ink and pigments on paper, kakemono, 49 1/4 x 25 1/4 ins / 124.8 x 64.4 cm) HKD 165,000. Hong Kong, 30 March 1992, *Misty Mountains in the Evening* (ink and pigments on paper, mounted makemono, 15 3/4 x 46 3/4 ins / 40 x 119 cm) HKD 60,500. Taipei, 18 Oct 1992, *Huang Shan* (1991, ink and pigments on paper, 37 x 85 1/2 ins / 94 x 217 cm) TWD 550,000.

HU PEIHENG
Chinese, 20th century.
Born 1891; died 1962.
Painter. Landscapes.

Hu Peiheng painted in traditional *guohua* style with ink and coloured pigments on paper, sometimes in the form of *kakemono* (hanging scrolls).

Bibliography:
Andrews, Julia F., *Painters and Politics in the People's Republic of China: 1949-1979*, University of California Press, Berkeley, 1994. Yang Xin and others, *Three Thousand Years of Chinese Painting*, Yale University Press, 1997.

Auction records:
Hong Kong, 15 Nov 1990, *Landscape* (1951, ink and pigments on paper, kakemono, 33 1/2 x 12 ins / 84.8 x 30.5 cm) HKD 17,600. New York, 26 Nov 1990, *Landscape* (ink and pigments on paper, kakemono, 50 x 10 1/4 ins / 127 x 26 cm) USD 1,100. Hong Kong, 30 April 1992, *Landscape* (1962, ink and pigments on paper) HKD 41,800. Hong Kong, 29 Oct 1992, *Landscape* (1928, ink and pigments on paper, kakemono, 40 x 13 1/2 ins / 101.5 x 34 cm) HKD 13,200. New York, 31 May 1994, *Landscape with Fishermen* (ink and pigments on paper, kakemono, 51 1/4 x 29 3/4 ins / 130.2 x 75.6 cm) USD 1,840. Hong Kong, 26 April 2004, *Sailing in Autumn* (1951, ink and colour, 6 x 40 ins / 16 x 101 cm) HKD 52,000. Hong Kong, 26 April 2004, *Monastery in Zhejiang* (1953, ink and colour, hanging scroll, 58 x 17 ins / 148 x 43 cm) HKD 85,000.

HU PEIHUNG
Chinese, 20th century.
Born 1894, in I-Hsing (Jiangsu); died 1953, in Beijing.
Painter. Animals.

Hu Peihung received his initial art training in China, where he absorbed the traditional *guohua* style and techniques and studied Chinese art history. He then went to Paris and Berlin for a number of years, where he assimilated various aspects of Western painting. He was appointed director of the Central Art Institute upon the foundation of the Republic of China. His work had considerable success in China, where a museum was dedicated to him. This success then spread to the West.

Hu drew his inspiration from traditional subjects. He specialised in painting galloping horses, which he depicted using techniques and skills from Western art.

HU SHIKUN, or Hu Shih-k'un, nickname: Yuanqing, pseudonym: Yuanrun
Chinese, 17th century.
Active towards the middle of the 17th century.
Painter. Landscapes, flowers.
Hu Shikun specialised in painting orchids.

HU SHUNCHEN, or Hu Shun-ch'en
Chinese, 12th century.
Born in Zheijiang Province.
Painter.
Hu Shunchen was a disciple of Guo Xi (c. 1020-1100).

HU TINGHUI, or Hu T'ing-hui
Chinese, 14th century.
Born in Wuxing (Zhejiang).
Active c. 1300.
Painter. Landscapes.

HU TINGLU, or Hu T'ing-lu
Chinese, 20th century.
Born in Wuxi (Jiangsu).
Painter.
Hu Tinglu was affiliated with the traditional scholar-painter school.

HU TS'AO. See **HU CAO**

HU TSUNG-HSIN. See **HU ZONGXIN**

HU TSUNG-JEN. See **HU ZONGREN**

HU XIGUI, or Hu Hsi-kuei, nickname: Sanqiao, pseudonym: Hongyin Guanzhu
Chinese, 19th - 20th century.
Born 1839, in Changzhou (Jiangsu); died 1910.
Painter, draughtsman. Figures.
Hu Xigui specialised in figure painting in the *pai-miao* manner (ink drawing with very fine outlines). He worked in the style of Yan Liben (d. 673) and Li Gonglin (1040-1106).
AUCTION RECORDS:
NEW YORK, 25 Nov 1991, *Paintings of Women* (ink and pigments on paper, group of four works, each 56 x 15 1/2 ins / 142.2 x 39.1 cm) USD 3,300. HONG KONG, 3 Nov 1994, *Court Lady in a Garden* (1878, ink and pigments on paper, kakemono, 45 1/2 x 12 1/2 ins / 115.5 x 32 cm) HKD 59,800. NEW YORK, 28 Nov 1994, *Young Beauty in Moonlight* (1892, ink and pigments on paper, kakemono, 37 x 12 1/4 ins / 94 x 31.1 cm) USD 1,725. NEW YORK, 21 March 1995, *Zhongkui* (ink and pigments on paper, kakemono, 31 1/2 x 12 ins / 79.7 x 30.2 cm) GBP 1,380. HONG KONG, 4 May 1995, *Lady with a Fan* (ink and pigments on paper, kakemono, 52 1/4 x 20 1/2 ins / 132.4 x 51.8 cm) HKD 32,200.

HU YÜ-K'UN. See **HU YUKUN**

HU YUAN, or Hu Yuan, nickname: Gongshou, pseudonyms: Shouhao, Hengxue Shanmin
Chinese, 19th century.
Born 1823, in Huating (Jiangsu); died 1886.
Painter.
Hu Yuan was a calligrapher and painter who specialised in landscapes and plum blossom. He settled in Shanghai in 1861. Several of his works survive in private collections.
AUCTION RECORDS:
NEW YORK, 31 May 1989, *Landscape* (ink and pigments on paper, kakemono, 53 1/2 x 15 ins / 135.9 x 38.1 cm) USD 990. NEW YORK, 6 Dec 1989, *Flowers and Rock* (ink and pigments on paper, kakemono, 72 x 18 1/2 ins / 182 x 47 cm) USD 3,300. NEW YORK, 26 Nov 1990, *Four Landscapes* (1885, ink and pigments on paper, group of four kakemono, 67 3/4 x 17 1/4 ins / 172 x 43.5 cm) USD 2,750. NEW YORK, 25 Nov 1991, *Bamboo and Rocks* (ink and pigments on silk, kakemono, 51 1/2 x 13 ins / 131.1 x 33 cm) USD 1,320.

HU YUKUN, or Hu Yu-k'un, nickname: Yuanrun
Chinese, 17th century.
Active in the first half of the 17th century.
Painter. Landscapes.
The nephew of the painter Hu Zongren (active c. 1600), Hu Yukun was a landscape and flower painter in the family tradition.
AUCTION RECORDS:
NEW YORK, 29 Nov 1993, *Album of Landscapes* (1652, ink and pigments on paper, 12 sheets, each 8 x 11 1/4 ins / 19.4 x 28.3 cm) USD 200,500.

HU ZHANG, or Hu Chang, nickname: Tiemei
Chinese, 19th century.
Born in Tongcheng (Anhui).
Active in Shanghai c. 1870.
Painter.
Hu Zhang was the son of the painter Hu Yin. He is known to have travelled once to Japan. Some of his landscapes and flower paintings survive, all signed and dated.

HU ZHENGYAN, or Hu Cheng-yen, nickname: Yuecong
Chinese, 17th century.
Born 1584, in Xinan (Anhui); died after 1667.
Painter.
Hu Zhengyan published an anthology of paintings and calligraphy entitled *Shizhu Zhai Shuhua Pu*, which he illustrated with a number of drawings of flowers and birds, and some wood engravings.

HU ZHENKAI, or Hu Chen-k'ai, nickname: Xunfei, pseudonyms: Sean, Erkong Jushi
Chinese, 17th century.
Born in Wu Cheng (Zhejiang).
Active towards the middle of the 17th century.
Painter.
Hu Zhenkai passed the *juren* examination (the third level of the triennial provincial capital civil service examinations) in 1639. He specialised in painting on stone, but also painted some landscapes.

HU ZHIFU, or Hu Chih-fu
Chinese, 13th (?) century.
Painter. Figures, landscapes.

HU ZONGREN, or Hu Tsung-jen, nickname: Pengju, pseudonym: Changbo
Chinese, 17th century.
Born in Nanjing.
Active c. 1600.
Painter.
A poet and painter, Hu Zongren painted landscapes in the style of the Yuan masters.

HU ZONGXIN, or Hu Tsung-hsin, nickname: Kefu
Chinese, 17th century.
Born in Shangyuan (Jiangsu).
Active at the beginning of the 17th century.
Painter.
Hu Zongxin is known for one landscape, *Scholar's Study under the Trees at the Foot of Misty Mountains*, signed and dated 1604.

HU-YIN
Chinese, 16th century.
Active during the Ming period.
Painter. Birds.

HUA CHUN-WU. See **HUA JUNWU**

HUA GUAN, or Hua Kuan, real name: Hua Qingguan or Dian, nickname: Qingji, pseudonym: Jiyai
Chinese, 18th century.
Born in Wuxi (Jiangsu).
Active during the second half of the 18th century.
Painter.

A well-known portrait painter, Hua Guan also painted people using the *baimiao* technique (ink drawing with very fine outlines), as well as landscapes, trees and flowers. He is known for a landscape signed and dated 1766 (?), on the theme *If You Buy Wine, Your Friends Will Be Many*.

HUA GUANGREN, or Hua Kuang-jen, nickname: Zhongren
Chinese, 11th century.
Born in Zheijiang Province.
Active 1087-1093.
Painter. Flowers.

Hua Guangren was a Buddhist monk who painted plum trees in blossom.

HUA I-LUN. See **HUA YILUN**

HUA JUNWU, or Hua Chun-wu, Hwa Chun-wu
Chinese, 20th century.
Born 1930, in Xushou (Jiangsu).
Painter, cartoonist.

With a number of his contemporaries, Hua Junwu studied at the Lu Xun Academy at Yan'an, China's first revolutionary art school. In the late 1960s he was forced to attend struggle meetings and undergo public 'criticism', as were many of his colleagues.

BIBLIOGRAPHY:
Yang, Gladys (trans), *Satire and Humour: Selected Cartoons of Hua Junwu*, China Today Press, 1991. Andrews, Julia F., *Painters and Politics in the People's Republic of China: 1949-1979*, University of California Press, Berkeley, 1994.

HUA KUAN. See **HUA GUAN**

HUA KUANG-JEN. See **HUA GUANGREN**

HUA QINGGUAN. See **HUA GUAN**

HUA SHIQING
Chinese, 20th century.
Born 1942, in Jiangyin (Jiangsu).
Painter. Landscapes.

Huan Shiqing trained in his native province at the Wuxi Calligraphic Arts Institute. He took part in the 1980 exhibition *Peintres Traditionnels de la République Populaire de Chine* (*Traditional Painters of the People's Republic of China*) held at the Galerie Daniel Malingue in Paris.

HUA T'IEN-YU. See **HUA TIANYOU**

HUA TIANYOU, or Hua T'ien-yu
Chinese, 20th century.
Born 1902, in Huaiyin (Jiangsu); died 1986.
Active in France.
Painter, draughtsman, sculptor.

After studying at the National Central University in Nanjing from 1930 to 1933, Hua Tianyou left for France, entering the École des Beaux-Arts in Paris, where he studied under Bouchard. His first years in France were a time of great poverty and indifference on the part of his contemporaries. Finally, in 1936, he started to collect prizes and medals. In 1947 he returned to China and was appointed professor at the National Art Academy in Beijing. He was a member of the Association of Chinese Artists in France.

At first, Hua became a total convert to the European sculptural tradition and was a very good Academic sculptor. Then, just before leaving Paris, he started to change his style to something a little different, making slightly romanticised figures of Chinese peasants as he imagined them from his exile. It is interesting to note that when working on Chinese subjects he abandoned the solidity of his earlier busts, using the flatter line characteristic of traditional Chinese sculpture.

Hua first exhibited in Paris in 1935. He exhibited at the following: the Salon des Artistes Français, where he won a number of medals, including the 1941 silver medal and the 1943 gold medal; the Salon des Indépendants, where he showed his decorative, mannered *Nudes*; the Exposition d'Art Moderne held at the Musée d'Art Moderne in Paris under the auspices of the United Nations in 1946; and the Salon d'Automne, where he showed other stylised works.

BIBLIOGRAPHY:
Sullivan, Michael, *Chinese Art in the Twentieth Century*, University of California Press, Berkeley, Los Angeles, London, 1959.

HUA YAN, or Hua Yen, nickname: Qiuyue, pseudonym: Xinluo Shanren
Chinese, 18th century.
Born 1682, in Shanghang (Fujian); died 1756 or 1762.
Painter, draughtsman. Figures, landscapes, flowers, animals.

Poet, calligrapher and painter, Hua Yan was one of the Yangzhou Baguai (Eight Eccentrics of Yangzhou), named after the city in which, apart from a few visits to Hangzhou, he spent all his life. Together with Jin Nong (1687- after 1764) and Luo Ping (1733-1799), Hua was not only one of the three truly great artists in the group but also one of the most talented and versatile; he was certainly the most technically skilful of the eight. During his lifetime he was appreciated mainly for his paintings of flowers, birds, insects and animals, much less so for his landscapes. But today the best of his landscapes, especially his album sheets, are regarded as small masterpieces of concision. No other Yangzhou painter could organise better than he the elements of a landscape and their spatial relationship while preserving their dynamic balance. His clear, dry-brush graphic style was gentle without being weak, his compositions subtly off balance, yet not from any non-conformist urge, but rather, delicately, to heighten the sentimental qualities of a given scene while retaining the necessary firmness of touch. He is far from the dark eye of the Southern Song landscape artists and the powerful vision of the 18th-century individualists. Hua's spirit is more likeable, more human; one does not feel in him any profound need to convey his own intimate comprehension of the universe, nor yet to reconstruct a microcosm in the image of the macrocosm. Instead, he looks with serenity, even detachment, at changing nature and the passing of time.

BIBLIOGRAPHY:
Cahill, James, *Chinese Painting*, Skira, Geneva, 1960. Yang Xin and others, *Three Thousand Years of Chinese Painting*, Yale University Press, 1997.

MUSEUMS AND GALLERIES:
BEIJING (Palace Mus.): *Self-portrait Sitting on the Rocky Bank of a Stream* (dated 1727, ink and light colours); *Studies of Insects, Animals and Flowers* (eight album sheets, signed); *Bird on a Rose Branch* - BOSTON (MFA): *Hymn to Autumn* (painting on fan, illustration for a poem by Ouyang Xiu, after Tang Yin, with inscription by Hua Yan dated 1730); *Green Hills Appearing behind Mist* (signed, one of a series of 10 paintings on fans); *Cottage under Pine Trees, with Surrounding Wall* (signed, one of a series of 10 paintings on fans) - CLEVELAND (MA): *Autumn Conversation* (dated 1732, ink and colours on paper, hanging scroll, inscription, two seals of Hua Yan, three colophons) - HONG KONG (Ho Kuan-Wu): *Flower and Bird* (signed and dated 1747) - NEW YORK (Metropolitan Mus. of Art): *White Peonies near a Rock* (signed and dated

1752); *Peony and Rocks* (signed) - OSAKA (Municipal Mus. of Art): *Autumn Noises* (ink and colours on paper, hanging scroll, illustration for a poem by Ouyang Xiu (1007-1072)); *Bird Singing on Bamboo* (dated 1721); *Six Squirrels in an Old Tree* (dated 1721, with an inscription by Hua Yan) - PARIS (Mus. National des Arts asiatiques-Guimet): *Flowers, Trees in Blossom, Plants, Insects and Landscapes* (ink and light colours on paper, album of eight paintings) - SHANGHAI: *Peach Blossom and Mandarin Ducks* (colours on paper, hanging scroll); *Lin Xu Wandering in the Mountains* (colours on paper, hanging scroll); *Montain Village in Fog* (signed) - ST LOUIS (AM): *Visiting Chrysanthemum Flowers* (dated 1753, ink and colours on paper, hanging scroll, with an inscription by Hua Yan and two seals of Hua Yan) - STOCKHOLM (Nationalmus.): *Two Mynah Birds near a Plum Tree and Some Narcissi* (signed and dated 1758); *Two Birds on a Bare Branch* (poem, signed) - TAIPEI (National Palace Mus.): *Zhong Kui at the Feast of the Fifth Month* (ink and colours on paper, hanging scroll, inscription) - WASHINGTON DC (Freer Gal. of Art): *Album of Landscapes* (ink and light colours on paper, 15 sheets, with inscriptions by Hua Yan, the last dated 1729).

AUCTION RECORDS:

NEW YORK, 2 June 1988, *Autumn Landscape* (ink on paper, fan, 21 x 7 1/4 ins / 53.3 x 18.5 cm) USD 6,050; *Hunter* (ink on paper, kakemono, 49 1/4 x 20 1/2 ins / 125.2 x 52 cm) USD 82,500. NEW YORK, 1 June 1989, *Three Birds on a Bamboo Branch* (ink and pigments on paper, kakemono, 44 x 20 ins / 112 x 51 cm) USD 82,500. NEW YORK, 31 May 1990, *Figures in a Landscape* (ink and pigments on paper, kakemono, 66 1/2 x 37 ins / 169 x 94 cm) USD 7,150. NEW YORK, 26 Nov 1990, *Archer and Horse* (ink and diluted pigments, kakemono, 47 x 22 1/4 ins / 119.6 x 56.2 cm) USD 110,000. NEW YORK, 29 May 1991, *Figures in Landscapes* (1745, ink on paper, ink and pigments on paper, 12-sheet album, each sheet 11 x 11 3/4 ins / 27 x 29.9 cm) USD 154,000. NEW YORK, 25 Nov 1991, *Landscape* (ink and pigments on paper, kakemono, 44 x 11 3/4 ins / 111.7 x 29.9 cm) USD 30,800. NEW YORK, 1 June 1993, *Landscape with Figure* (ink and pigments on paper, kakemono, 51 x 23 3/4 ins / 128.6 x 60.3 cm) USD 48,875. NEW YORK, 31 May 1994, *Scholars beneath Pine Trees* (1748, ink and pigments on paper, fan, 6 1/2 x 19 1/4 ins / 16.5 x 48.9 cm) USD 10,350. NEW YORK, 28 Nov 1994, *Mongol with Camel* (ink and pigments on paper, kakemono, 50 x 19 3/4 ins / 127 x 50.2 cm) USD 74,000. HONG KONG, 4 May 1995, *Birds in Spring* (ink and pigments on paper, kakemono, 74 1/2 x 37 3/4 ins / 189.3 x 96.2 cm) HKD 570,000.

HUA YEN. See **HUA YAN**

HUA YILUN, or Hua I-lun
Chinese, 19th century.
Active in the second third of the 19th century.
Painter.

Critic, collector, painter and official, Hua Yilun drew his inspiration from Wang Yuanqi (1642-1715). At the same time, to free himself from formulaic academicism, he also travelled widely to rediscover the original source that had inspired the ancients; nature itself. In his theoretical work, the *Hua Shuo*, a collection of rambling reflections on aesthetics, criticism and technique seen from a penetrating, personal viewpoint, he attached great importance to the direct observation of nature.

BIBLIOGRAPHY:

Ryckmans, Pierre, *Les "Propos sur la peinture" de Shitao. Traduction et commentaires pour servir de contribution à l'étude terminologique et esthétique des théories chinoises de la peinture*, Institut belge des hautes études chinoises, Brussels, 1970.

HUA-LIN. See **HUALIN**

HUALIN, or Hua-lin, nickname: Ying
Chinese, 17th century.
Born 1597, in Sanshan (Fujian); died 1667.
Painter.

A Buddhist monk, Hualin left for Japan in 1660, where he became a priest. Many of his landscapes and flower and bamboo paintings are thus to be found in Japan.

HUALIN, or Hua-lin
Chinese, 19th century.
Active in the middle of the 19th century.
Painter.

Hualin placed such high demands on himself that he destroyed every work he painted as soon as he had finished it. He followed the orthodox academic style of Wang Yuanqi (1642-1715) of the Southern School and advocated unquestioning adherence to the classical models. He is the author of the *Nanzong Juemi* (1843), a treatise on painting which, despite its theoretical bias, is the work of a practising artist, in that each of the 30 sections that make it up is based on solid experience. The book discusses technical problems competently, and is for that reeason not without merit.

BIBLIOGRAPHY:

Ryckmans, Pierre, *Les "Propos sur la peinture" de Shitao. Traduction et commentaires pour servir de contribution à l'étude terminologique et esthétique des théories chinoises de la peinture*, Institut belge des hautes études chinoises, Brussels, 1970.

HUANG, Guinbi, or Kuin-Pi Huang
Chinese, 20th century.
Born 1899, in Guangding.
Painter. Landscapes.

Guinbi Huang was included in the Exposition Internationale d'Art Moderne held in 1946 in Paris under the auspices of the United Nations.

HUANG ANREN, Anren
Chinese, 20th century.
Born 1924, in Guangdong Province.
Painter. Landscapes.

Huang Anren trained at the Guangdong Art Institute. His primary inspiration in his landscape painting is the Lingnan School. He took part in the 1980 exhibition *Peintres Traditionnels de la République Populaire de Chine* (*Traditional Painters of the People's Republic of China*) at the Galerie Daniel Malingue in Paris.

HUANG BAI
Chinese, 20th century.
Born in Shanghai.
Painter.

Huang Bai exhibited at the 1928 Salon d'Automne, in Paris.

HUANG BANRUO, or Huang Pan-jo
Chinese, 20th century.
Born 1901 or 1903, in Guangdong; died 1968.
Painter, draughtsman. Scenes with figures.

Huang Banruo was co-founder of the Guangdong Hua Yanjiuhui (Guangdong Association for the Study of Chinese Painting).

BIBLIOGRAPHY:

Yang Xin and others, *'Huang Banruo'* in *Three Thousand Years of Chinese Painting*, Yale University Press, 1997.

AUCTION RECORDS:

HONG KONG, 15 Nov 1989, *Guanyin above Clouds of Flames* (1943, ink and pigments on silk, kakemono, 35 1/2 x 12 3/4 ins / 90 x 32.4 cm) HKD 35,200. HONG KONG, 28 Sept 1992, *Guanyin in a Grotto* (ink and pigments on paper, kakemono, 47 x 17 1/4 ins / 119.5 x 43.5 cm) HKD 35,200. HONG KONG, 29 April 1996, *Hong Kong Scene* (ink and pigments on paper, 11 3/4 x 36 1/2 ins / 29.8 x 92.5 cm) HKD 23,000.

HUANG BI, or Huang Pi, nickname: Xiaochi
Chinese, 18th century.
Born in Chaozhou (Guangdong).
Active c. 1720.
Painter.

A calligrapher and landscape painter, Huang Bi worked in the style of Wu Zhen (1280-1354). Some works of his still survive, such as *Misty Landscape*, signed and dated 1720.

HUANG BINHONG, or Huang Chih, also known as: Huang Zhi, Huang Pin-hong, Huang Pin-hung, nickname: Pucun, Yuxiang, pseudonym: Binhong
Chinese, 19th - 20th century.
Born 1865, in Tandu (Anhui); died 1955, in Hangzhou.
Painter, draughtsman, engraver. Landscapes, flowers. Seals.

Born into an artistic and scholarly milieu, Huang Binhong received excellent training from a very early age, concentrating on painting and seal carving. His long career would see him teach at various art schools (at Anhui, Shanghai, Nanjing, Beijing and Hangzhou), publish a number of essays on the aesthetic theory, history and technique of Chinese painting, identify and catalogue the works in the former imperial collections in Beijing, and edit the monumental *Meishu Congshu*, the anthology of classical writings on the arts, 120 fascicles of which were published in Shanghai in 1911.

From the age of 10 until the very last month of his life, Huang painted every day, incessantly, never once deviating from his chosen path, stubbornly going deeper and deeper into his painting, oblivious to the urgings of the public, to the calls of fame and fashion. And in reality, all he did until he was nearly 70 was to hone the tools that would make possible the extraordinary creative explosion of the last 20 years of his life. He also left behind a multitude of sketches of rivers and mountains.

In 20th-century Chinese painting there are two main streams; some artists decided to break with a tradition that for them had become stifling, while others, the majority, clung to it as to a ship in peril. Together with a few other isolated figures, Huang was one of the rare artists who managed to reconcile classical Chinese painting with the modern world, one who could include bold innovation in his work while remaining true to a value system that had become part of his nature and that he saw no reason to question. In his artistic career he remained true to his own dictum: 'At the beginning, art must have rules; at its end, it must do away with them. At the beginning, painting must strive to be true to life; at its end it must do away with being true to life in every way.' Another of his favourite quotations was: 'Outside, I am no more than the pupil of the Creator; within, I tap the source of my own heart.' Huang learned the rules by copying and studying the ancients (he developed a remarkable ability to capture their essence) and then translated them into his own language.

At the same time, he was a tireless traveller, displaying the same ability when looking at nature. In his drawings, the great rhythms of the earth take graphic, linear form and become as one with the inner force driving his brush. Mountains, trees and rocks become metamorphosed into marks, mists and rivers become sinuous white spaces that enliven the masses of dark ink. In the presence of the creative act, the artist is freed from the rules only because he has total mastery of them. Huang's style was not widely appreciated in his lifetime.

Huang Binhong was one of the artists featured in the exhibition *Cinq Grands Peintres Chinois: La Tradition au XXème Siècle* (*Five Great Chinese Painters: Tradition in the 20th Century*) held at the Musée d'Art Moderne in Paris in 1982.

Bibliography:

Sullivan, Michael, *Chinese Art in the Twentieth Century*, University of California Press, Berkeley, Los Angeles, London, 1959. Ryckmans, P., in *Encyclopaedia Universalis*, vol VIII, Paris, 1970. Oi, Lam, *An album by Huang Pin-hung*, Museum of Far Eastern Antiquities, Stockholm, 1972. Boissier, Jean-Louis, *Cinq grands peintres chinois - la tradition au XXème siècle*, group exhibition catalogue, Musée d'Art moderne de la Ville de Paris, Paris, 1982. Shen, Fu, *'Huang Binhong's Shanghai Period Landscape Paintings and His Late Floral Works'* in *Orientations*, vol 18, no. 9, September 1987. Kuo, Jason C., *'The Art of Huang Binhong'* in *Orientations*, vol 20, no. 12, December 1989. Andrews, Julia F., *Painters and Politics in the People's Republic of China: 1949-1979*, University of California Press, Berkeley, 1994. Clunas, Craig, *Art in China*, Oxford University Press, Oxford, New York, 1997. Yang Xin and others, *Three Thousand Years of Chinese Painting*, Yale University Press, 1997.

Museums and Galleries:

Cologne (Mus. für Ostasiatische Kunst): *Landscape in the Style of Li Tang* (1917) - Hangzhou (Huang Binhong-Qixialing Mus.).

Auction records:

Hong Kong, 12 Jan 1987, *The God of Wealth* (ink and colours on paper scroll, 23 x 11 1/2 ins / 58.5 x 29.2 cm) HKD 48,000. New York, 2 June 1988, *Boat near a Riverside Village* (ink on paper, kakemono, 48 x 17 ins / 122 x 43.2 cm) USD 7,150. Hong Kong, 17 Nov 1988, *Peonies* (1951, ink and pigments on paper, 16 1/2 x 12 1/2 ins / 41.8 x 31.6 cm) HKD 41,800; *Landscape* (ink and pigments on paper, 20 3/4 x 50 1/4 ins / 53 x 127.4 cm) HKD 198,000. Hong Kong, 16 Jan 1989, *Peonies* (ink and pigments on paper, 26 3/4 x 13 1/2 ins / 68 x 34 cm) HKD 20,900. Hong Kong, 18 May 1989, *Green Mountains* (1941, ink and pigments on paper, makemono, 16 1/4 x 45 1/4 ins / 41.5 x 115 cm) HKD 88,000. Hong Kong, 15 Nov 1989, *Landscape after Fan Kuan* (ink and pigments on paper, kakemono, 28 x 15 1/2 ins / 71.3 x 39.6 cm) HKD 286,000; *River Landscape* (1938, ink and diluted pigments on paper, makemono, 7 1/4 x 59 ins / 18.6 x 149 cm) HKD 484,000. New York, 6 Dec 1989, *Landscape* (ink and pigments on paper, makemono, 12 1/2 x 46 1/4 ins / 31.8 x 117.2 cm) USD 6,050. New York, 31 May 1990, *Scholar in a Landscape* (ink and pigments on paper, kakemono, 26 1/2 x 13 1/4 ins / 67 x 33.7 cm) USD 4,675. Hong Kong, 15 Nov 1990, *Landscape after Li Cheng* (1943, ink and pigments on paper, kakemono, 39 3/4 x 19 1/2 ins / 101 x 49.7 cm) HKD 93,500. New York, 26 Nov 1990, *Landscape* (ink and pigments on paper, 29 x 15 1/4 ins / 73.7 x 38.8 cm) USD 7,150. Hong Kong, 2 May 1991, *Landscape* (1952, ink and pigments on paper, kakemono, 34 1/4 x 14 3/4 ins / 87.3 x 37.5 cm) HKD 154,000. New York, 29 May 1991, *Guilin Landscape* (ink and pigments on paper, kakemono, 31 3/4 x 13 1/4 ins / 80.6 x 33.7 cm) USD 6,600. Hong Kong, 31 Oct 1991, *Landscape* (ink and pigments on paper, kakemono, 47 1/2 x 18 1/2 ins / 120.7 x 47 cm) HKD 242,000. Hong Kong, 30 March 1992, *View of Min River* (ink and pigments on paper, kakemono, 58 1/2 x 31 1/4 ins / 148.8 x 79.2 cm) HKD 385,000. Hong Kong, 28 Sept 1992, *Mountain Cottage in the Evening* (ink and pigments on paper, kakemono, 69 1/4 x 36 1/2 ins / 176 x 92.5 cm) HKD 415,000. Hong Kong, 22 March 1993, *Returning to Pine Mountain* (ink and pigments on paper, kakemono, 40 1/2 x 11 1/2 ins / 103 x 29 cm) HKD 138,000. New York, 16 June 1993, *Colour of the Mountains at Tonglu* (ink and pigments on paper, makemono, 13 1/2 x 53 1/2 ins / 34.3 x 136.2 cm) USD 20,700. Hong Kong, 3 Nov 1994, *Landscapes* (ink and pigments on paper, four kakemonos, each 60 x 16 ins / 152.4 x 40.6 cm) HKD 845,000. Hong Kong, 29 April 1996, *Landscape after Wang Jinqing* (1925, ink and pigments on paper, 33.6 x 536 cm) HKD 172,500. Hong Kong, 4 Nov 1996, *Landscape* (ink and pigments on paper, kakemono, 53 1/2 x 26 ins / 136 x 66 cm) HKD

195,500. HONG KONG, 28 April 1997, *Gathering of Scholars* (1924, ink and pigments on paper, kakemono, 33 1/2 x 15 ins / 85 x 38 cm) HKD 115,000. HONG KONG, 2 Nov 1997, *Landscape* (ink/paper, album of four sketches, 14 3/4 x 10 1/2 ins / 37.6 x 26.4 cm) HKD 86,250. HONG KONG, 26 April 1999, *Reading in Studio* (seals, ink and pigments, hanging scroll, 26 x 13 ins / 65 x 34 cm) HKD 90,000. HONG KONG, 26 April 1999, *Sailing at Night* (1953, seal, ink and pigments, hanging scroll, 27 x 17 ins / 69 x 43 cm) HKD 90,000. NEW YORK, 20 March 2000, *Forested Landscape with Cottages* (1950, ink and pigments, 28 x 14 ins / 72 x 35 cm) USD 4,750. HONG KONG, 28 Oct 2001, *Landscape* (1946, ink and pigments, scroll, 45 x 14 ins / 114 x 35 cm) HKD 60,000. HONG KONG, 28 Oct 2001, *Landscape* (1946, ink and pigments, scroll, 8 x 23 ins / 20 x 59 cm) HKD 70,000. HONG KONG, 6 May 2002, *Tranquil Landscape* (ink, scroll, 54 x 17 ins / 136 x 43 cm) HKD 75,000. HONG KONG, 28 April 2003, *Landscape of Yang Shuo* (ink and pigments, hanging scroll, 39 x 14 ins / 100 x 35 cm) HKD 240,000. HONG KONG, 27 Oct 2003, *Spring Landscape* (ink and pigments, hanging scroll, 41 x 23 ins / 104 x 59 cm) HKD 500,000. HONG KONG, 25 April 2004, *Landscape in the Shores* (ink and pigments, hanging scroll, 43 x 16 ins / 109 x 41 cm) HKD 340,000. HONG KONG, 26 April 2004, *Autumn Landscape* (1952, ink and pigments, hanging scroll, 34 x 15 ins / 87 x 37 cm) HKD 1,650,000.

HUANG CH'I-MIN. See **HUANG QIMIN**

HUANG CH'UAN. See **HUANG QUAN**

HUANG CHI. See **HUANG JI**

HUANG CHIH. See **HUANG BINHONG**

HUANG CHIN. See **HUANG JIN**

HUANG CHONGPI
Chinese, 20th century.
Born in China.
Painter.

In 1946 Huang Chongpi exhibited *Woodcutter on the Way Home* at the International Modern Art Exhibition held in Paris under the auspices of the United Nations.

HUANG CHU. See **HUANG JU**

HUANG CHU-TS'AI. See **HUANG JUCAI**

HUANG CHUAN. See **HUANG JUAN**

HUANG CHUN. See **HUANG JUN**

HUANG CHUN-PI. See **HUANG JUNBI**

HUANG DAOZHOU, or Huang Tao-chou, nicknames: Youxuan, Chiruo, pseudonym: Shizhai
Chinese, 17th century.
Born 1584 or 1585, in Zhangpu (Fujian); died 1646.
Painter, calligrapher. Landscapes.

Huang Daozhou was a scholar and landscape specialist and head of the Bureau of Rites. In 1644, when the Ming dynasty collapsed, he was taken prisoner by the Manchus and put to death in 1646. Some of his paintings survive in private collections, including the following: *Cabbages and Other Vegetables* (a handscroll, signed and dated 1625); *Ancient Pine on a Rocky Bank* (signed, and with a poem by the artist dated 1635); *River Landscape with a Pavilion on a Bank* in the manner of Ni Zan (signed and dated 1641); and *Bamboo, Epidendrums, Ferns and Stones* (signed and dated 1642).

MUSEUMS AND GALLERIES:

OSAKA (Municipal Mus. of Art): *Pines and Rocks* (ink on silk, roll opening horizontally, two colophons, three seals and signatures of the artist, eleven collector's seals).

AUCTION RECORDS:

NEW YORK, 29 May 1991, *Calligraphy in Running Script* (ink on satin, handscroll, 10 1/2 x 102 3/4 ins / 26.7 x 261 cm) USD 3,300.

HUANG DING, or Huang Ting, nickname: Zungu, pseudonyms: Guangting, Duwangke, and others
Chinese, 17th - 18th century.
Born 1660, in Jiangsu; died 1730.
Painter, draughtsman. Landscapes.

A great landscape specialist, Huang Ding worked with Wang Hui (1632-1717) and Wang Yuanqi (1642-1715), but had his own, original style, which recalls that of the Yuan master Wang Meng (1298-1385). He was a keen traveller who sketched much from nature.

MUSEUMS AND GALLERIES:

CAMBRIDGE, MA (Fogg AM, Harvard University): *Four Trees and Sheer Cliffs* (after Ni Zan, handscroll, signed and dated 1723, colophons are more recent) - HAMBURG: *Autumn Mountains* (after Dong Yuan, signed, colophon dated 1722) - HONOLULU (Academy of Arts): *Autumn Mountains* (ink and light colours on paper, after Wang Meng, hanging scroll, signed and dated 1697, inscription and two seals of the artist, four colophons) - TAIPEI (National Palace Mus.): *View of Stream and Grove* (dated 1713, ink and colours on paper, hanging scroll); *Autumn Retreat* (ink and light colours on paper, hanging scroll); *Travelling in a Landscape* (ink on paper, hanging scroll); *Sunshine on Mountains after Snow* (ink and light colours on silk, hanging scroll).

AUCTION RECORDS:

NEW YORK, 25 Nov 1991, *Landscape after Wang Meng* (ink and pigments on silk, 70 3/4 x 20 3/4 ins / 179.8 x 53 cm) USD 3,025.

HUANG ERH-NAN. See **HUANG ERNAN**

HUANG ERNAN, or Huang Erh-Nan
Chinese, 20th century.
Born 1883, in Hebei Province.
Active in Japan from 1903.
Painter. Landscapes, flowers.

Huang Ernan worked in Japan from the age of 20. On his return to China, he founded the Zhangdong Art School and thereafter devoted himself to teaching.

HUANG GONGWANG, or Huang Kong-wang, Huang Kung-wang, nickname: Zijiu, pseudonyms: Yifeng, Dazhi, Jingxi Daoren
Chinese, 13th - 14th century.
Born 1269, in Changzhou (Jiangsu); died 1354.
Painter.

Huang Gongwang was the eldest of the Four Masters of Yuan, the others being Wu Zhen (1280-1354), Ni Zan (1301-1374) and Wang Meng (1298-1385). These four artists determined the character of Yuan landscape painting and their influence dominated literati painting during the Ming and Qing dynasties. Huang's career as a scholar-painter is every bit as exemplary as his art itself. He divided his time between the intellectual and artistic circles in Suzhou and Hangzhou, which after the Southern Song had become the main cultural centres of China, and frequent retreats into the Lu and Fuchun Mountains south-west of Hangzhou. After first serving as an official, he retired from bureaucracy at the age of about 45 and took up the life of a wandering, uncommitted, free spirit. By stepping outside the reigning political order in this way, he was following the common practice of the intellectual elite of his time. From time to time he practised the profession of fortune-teller, as wandering monks and intellectuals often did. At the age of about 60, deeply interested in philosophy and religion, he accepted Neo-Taoist teachings. Then he withdrew for some years to Mount Lu, devoting himself to wine and the contemplation of nature. At the age of 80 he returned once more to the solitude of the Fuchun Mountains in the company of a monastic friend. The Fuchun Mountains would be the inspiration for the most famous of his paintings; communion with nature and a life in intimate proximity with the mountains were the basic elements of his artistic and spiritual development. It was his habit to sketch from nature. As he said: 'The painter should always have with him some brushes in a bag, then when he comes across some startling trees in a beautiful landscape, he should at once make sketches of them so as to preserve their natural idea. They will add life to paintings.' Huang really only started painting at about the age of 50. He had previously merely cultivated the art as a scholar's pastime. But his art would be recognised as a yardstick by those who came after, and literati painting would bear the indelible mark of his influence for at least five centuries.

Only one painting survives that can be attributed to him with certainty. It is a splendid piece entitled *Dwelling in the Fuchun Mountains*, now in the National Palace Museum in Taipei, which actually has two copies of the scroll, although only one of them is authentic. Huang painted this scroll when he was between 78 and 80 years old at a time when he was at the peak of his genius. It is one of the basic milestones in the history of Chinese landscape painting. He started it in the Fuchun Mountains and would work on it for the next three or four years, adding scenes as the inspiration took him, a typically scholarly approach. 'The work is flawless in its consistency: it has the rhythmic unity of a preliminary sketch and the solidity of a slow, sustained meditation' (P. Ryckmans). It is also quite new; at the most can be found echoes of Dong Yuan (d. 962), the first of the great southern landscape artists whose style Huang had studied.

Huang never seeks to impress but contents himself with very ordinary decorative touches that convey everyday life in its full flavour and emotional content. He represents things as they are, drawing them as they appear, alone, in unblemished light. His is an interior, spontaneous art far from the studied spectacular art of Southern Song painting. He replaces the rapid, infallible school methods with what at first seems like a lack of resolve but which conceals a deeper, more subtle certainty. Huang builds his works gradually, stroke by stroke, starting with pale ink before moving on to darker and darker inks, using an ever drier brush. He proceeds stroke by stroke, each making its own slight addition to the overall texture, which only gradually takes shape. He handles his outlines in the same way, placing ever stronger accents, rising in intensity until he completes everything with a scattering of dabs of creamy ink just like classic punctuation in which the rhythm of the entire painting reaches its culmination. The work seems to be of disconcerting simplicity. The viewer seems to stand right in the midst of the landscape, where everything is natural, clear, transparent and profoundly true, true as the creative movements of the artist's hand, true as nature itself.

BIBLIOGRAPHY:

Sirén, Osvald, '*Chinese painting, Leading Masters and Principles*' in vol IV, VI, Ronald Press, New York, 1956-1958. Cahill, James, *Chinese painting*, Skira, Geneva, 1960. Ryckmans, P., in *Encyclopaedia Universalis*, vol VIII, Paris, 1972. Clunas, Craig, *Art in China*, Oxford University Press, Oxford, New York, 1997. Yang Xin and others, *Three Thousand Years of Chinese Painting*, Yale University Press, 1997.

MUSEUMS AND GALLERIES:

BEIJING (Former Manchu Imperial Palace): *Orchid Pavilion* (painting, large-leaf album, inscription by Huang Gongwang dated 1342, generally thought to be authentic); *Sunshine on a River after Snow* (attributed); *Trees in Autumn Mist* (signed and dated 1342, short handscroll, attributed); *Landscapes* (signed and dated 1342, poem by Hua Yan dated 1417) - BEIJING (Palace Mus.): *Light Snow on the Nine Peaks* (signed and dated 1349, according to the inscription, generally thought to be authentic) - SHANGHAI: *Spirit Dwelling in Rocks* (colours on silk, hanging scroll, painted for the poet Zhang Yu); *Gentle Wooded Hills* (signed and dated 1338, seal of Huang Gongwang and colophon by Ni Zan) - TAIPEI (National Palace Mus.): *Dwelling in the Fuchun Mountains* (ink/paper, handscroll, genuine inscription by Huang Gongwang dated 1347-1350, colophons by Shen Zhou dated 1488, Wen Peng dated 1570, Wang Chichang dated 1571 and Dong Qichang (all artists)); *Dwelling in the Fuchun Mountains* (handscroll, inscription by Huang Gongwang dated 1338, several colophons and numerous inscriptions by Emperor Qianlong as well as the emperor's seals); *Stone Cliffs of Tianchi* (ink and light colours on silk, hanging scroll, colophon); *Temples on Cliffs on the Clouds* (ink on paper, album sheet); *Two Fishermen in Boats on a River* (album sheet) - WASHINGTON DC (Freer Gal. of Art): *View of Mount Lu* (ink and colour, inscription dated 1342, late copy); *Wooded Mountains* (ink on silk, free copy).

HUANG HEIMAN

Chinese, 20th - 21st century.
Born 1952, in Beijing.
Painter.

An infant prodigy, Huang Heiman started drawing when he was a small child and between 1956 and 1959 carried off five first prizes and gold medals in international young people's competitions in England, Germany and India. In 1978 he settled in Hong Kong, where he became a publisher of art magazines. In 1980 he worked in Italy at the Design Faculty of Milan Polytechnic and with the sculptor Virgilio Mortet. In 1983 he was part of the team organizing the travelling exhibition *Art and Civilisation during the Italian Renaissance* for Olivetti. In 1985 he set up his own design company in Hong Kong. He exhibited at the 1986 Venice Biennale, in 1987 at a solo show in Aspen in Colorado, and in 1990 at another solo exhibition at the Hong Kong Art Centre.

AUCTION RECORDS:

HONG KONG, 30 March 1992, *Singing Dragon* (1991, oil on sacking on canvas, 45 x 44 ins / 114 x 112 cm) HKD 71,500.

HUANG HSIANG-CHIEN. See **HUANG XIANGJIAN**

HUANG HSIEN-CHIH. See **HUANG XIANZHI**

HUANG HUANWU

Chinese, 20th century.
Born 1906; died 1985.
Painter. Genre scenes, landscapes with figures, landscapes.

AUCTION RECORDS:

HONG KONG, 17 Nov 1988, *Huang Shan* (ink and light colour highlights on paper, kakemono, 38 x 13 1/4 ins / 96.5 x 33.5 cm) HKD 27,500. HONG KONG, 15 Nov 1989, *Delivering Coal in the Snow* (1941, ink and pigments on paper, kakemono, 56 x 27 ins / 142.2 x 68.3 cm) HKD 93,500. HONG KONG, 15 Nov 1990, *Delivering Coal in the Snow* (1941, ink and pigments on paper, kakemono, 56 x 27 ins / 142.2 x 68.3 cm) HKD 44,000. HONG KONG, 2 May 1991, *Landscape* (1945, ink and pigments on paper, makemono, 12 1/4 x 45 3/4 ins / 31.2 x 116.5 cm) HKD 27,500. NEW YORK, 25 Nov 1991, *Pines* (ink and pigments on paper, kakemono, 55 3/4 x 16 ins / 141.6 x 39.7 cm) USD 2,200. NEW YORK, 16 June 1993, *Bamboos and Birds* (ink and pigments on paper, kakemono, 41 1/2 x 14 ins / 105.4 x 35.6 cm) USD 3,738. HONG KONG, 30 Oct 1995, *Huang Shan Emerging from a Sea of Clouds* (ink and pigments on paper, kakemono, 38 x 13 1/4 ins / 96.5 x 33.5 cm) HKD 17,250.

HUANG I. See **HUANG YI**

HUANG JI, or Huang Ki, Huang Chi, nickname: Lianqi

Chinese, 18th century.
Born in Wucheng (Zhejiang).
Painter. Landscapes, flowers.

Huang Ji specialised in painting peonies. It is not impossible that he and Huang Jishan (nickname: Duankui, pseudonym:

Lianqi) were one and the same, although the latter seems to have come from Tongxiang (Zhejiang).
MUSEUMS AND GALLERIES:
LONDON (British Mus.): *Numerous Boats at the Customs Gate* (signed and dated, probably 1752).

HUANG JI, or Huang Ki, Huang Chi
Chinese, 18th - 19th century.
Born in Nanjing.
Active during the reign of the Qing Emperor Jiaqing (1798-1820).
Painter.
Huang Ji was an official.

HUANG JIN, or Huang Kin, Huang Chin, nickname: Jinqing
Chinese, 13th - 14th century.
Born 1277, in Yiwu (Zhejiang); died 1357.
Painter.
Huang Jin was a scholar of the Hanlin Academy, an official, and reader of the classics to the emperor. He is recorded in the official biographies, but not as a painter. He worked in the style of Huang Gongwang (1269-1354) and Wang Meng (1298-1385).
MUSEUMS AND GALLERIES:
TAIPEI (National Palace Mus.): *Study in a Plum Tree Garden at the Foot of High Wooded Mountains* (signed and dated 1347, colophons by Huang Jin and Li Yong, the latter dated 1454).

HUANG JINSHENG, Jinsheng
Chinese, 20th century.
Born 1935, in Jilin.
Painter. Figure compositions.
Huang Jinsheng studied from 1956 to 1961 under Wu Zuoren at the Central Academy of Fine Arts in Beijing.
MUSEUMS AND GALLERIES:
BEIJING (NG).
AUCTION RECORDS:
HONG KONG, 28 Sept 1992, *Tibetan Woman* (1989, oil on canvas, 30 x 22 ins / 76 x 56 cm) HKD 38,500. HONG KONG, 4 May 1995, *Mother and Child* (1989, oil on canvas, 24 x 32 ins / 61 x 81.3 cm) HKD 40,250. HONG KONG, 30 Oct 1995, *Shepherd on a High Plateau* (1989, oil on canvas, 20 x 25 ins / 50.8 x 63.5 cm) HKD 36,800.

HUANG JINXIANG
Chinese, 20th - 21st century.
Born 1943, in Wenzhou (Zhejiang).
Active in the USA.
Painter. Landscapes.
Huang Jinxiang attended preparatory classes and then studied oil painting at the fine arts academy of Zhejiang, where he accepted a teaching post after graduating in 1968. The following year he left for the University of Montana in the USA. He now lives in the USA and is totally detached from the Asian tradition. He has an anonymous technique reminiscent of the Western Academic style of the 19th century. He took part in a number of exhibitions in the USA, winning second prize on one occasion.
AUCTION RECORDS:
HONG KONG, 22 March 1993, *Autumn Stream* (1992, oil on canvas, 24 x 35 3/4 ins / 61 x 91 cm) HKD 18,400.

HUANG JIZU. See **HUANG NIANZU**

HUANG JU, or Huang Kiu, Huang Chu, nickname: Qiushi
Chinese, 19th century.
Born c. 1800, in Songjiang (Jiangsu); died 1860.
Active in Suzhou.
Painter.
A flower and landscape painter in the style of Yun Shouping (1633-1690) and Wang Hui (1632-1717), Huang Ju also painted figure paintings.

HUANG JUAN, or Huang Chuan, nickname: Sengmo
Chinese, 16th century.
Active in Putian (Fujian).
Painter. Figures, landscapes.

HUANG JUCAI, or Huang Kiu-ts'ai, Huang Chu-ts'ai, nickname: Boluan
Chinese, 10th century.
Born 933; died after 993.
Painter. Landscapes, animals, flowers.
The younger son of Huang Quan (c. 900-965), the famous bird and flower painter, Huang Jucai also specialised in bird, flower and landscape painting. Like his father, he was at the court of the Later Shu at Chengdu (934-965) before working at the court of the Song Emperors Taizu (960-976) and Taizong (976-997) at Kaifeng. His work is characterised by the slightly concave, continuous outline he gives his rocks, which he shades with soft washes, and by his strongly emphasised leaves.
MUSEUMS AND GALLERIES:
BEIJING (Palace Mus.): *Sparrows Playing in Reeds* (painting on fan, attributed); *Two Small Birds on Reeds* (painting on fan, attributed); *Flock of Birds on Bare Trees and Snow-covered Rocks* (album sheet, attributed) - BOSTON (MFA): *Parrot on Peach Branch in Blossom* (album sheet, probably from the 13th century) - NEW YORK (Metropolitan Mus. of Art): *Two White Camelia Flowers with a Small Bird on a Branch* (painting on fan, Huang Jucai's name inscribed) - TAIPEI (National Palace Mus.): *Pheasants and Thorn Bushes*; *Pheasants and Sparrows among Rocks and Bushes* (ink and colours on silk, hanging scroll, several imperial seals, including that of the Song Emperor Huizong (1101-1126), inscription).

HUANG JUI. See **HUANG RUI**

HUANG JUN, or Huang Kiun, Huang Chun, nickname: Guyuan, pseudonym: Xiangchou
Chinese, 19th century.
Born 1775, in Suzhou (Jiangsu); died 1850.
Painter, draughtsman. Landscapes.
Huang Jun painted in the style first of Huang Ding (1660-1730) then of Wang Shimin (1592-1680). Several scrolls by him survive in private collections, signed and often dated.
AUCTION RECORDS:
NEW YORK, 31 May 1994, *Landscapes after Old Masters* (1836, ink and pigments on paper, album of eight sheets, 11 1/2 x 11 1/2 ins / 29.2 x 28.9 cm) USD 8,050.

HUANG JUNBI, or Huang Kiun-pi, Huang Chun-pi
Chinese, 20th century.
Born 1899, in Canton (now Guangdong); died 1991.
Painter.
Together with Fu Baoshi (1904-1965), Huang Junbi is one of the two traditional scholar-painters from the region of Nanjing who became famous both in China and abroad. He was a great lover of nature and a tireless traveller, going to Japan in 1930, a visit that would later influence his work. He taught at the municipal art school of Canton until 1935, when he was appointed to the National Art Academy in Nanjing.

The brushwork in his landscapes is very modern, and while he does look back to ancient Chinese techniques, it is not to the meticulous style of the academy, but rather to that of the Yuan masters, to which he adds a certain decorative touch.
BIBLIOGRAPHY:
Sullivan, Michael, *Chinese Art in the Twentieth Century*, University of California Press, Berkeley, Los Angeles, London, 1959.

AUCTION RECORDS:
NEW YORK, 6 Dec 1989, *Dragon Gate* (1941, ink and pigments on paper, kakemono, 38 1/4 x 17 ins / 97.2 x 42.3 cm) USD 6,050. NEW YORK, 11 April 1990, *Landscape* (ink on paper, makemono, 13 1/2 x 26 1/4 ins / 34.3 x 66.6 cm) USD 1,430. HONG KONG, 15 Nov 1990, *Sailing in Autumn* (1958, ink and pigments on paper, 21 3/4 x 36 ins / 55.3 x 90.5 cm) HKD 82,500. NEW YORK, 26 Nov 1990, *Waterfall Landscape* (1945, ink and pigments on paper, kakemono, 58 1/2 x 28 1/2 ins / 148.3 x 72.3 cm) USD 8,800. HONG KONG, 31 Oct 1991, *Scholar in a Landscape* (1940, ink and pigments on paper, kakemono, 46 x 9 ins / 117 x 22 cm) HKD 143,000. HONG KONG, 30 March 1992, *Sailing by a Cliff* (ink on paper, mounted makemono, 23 x 41 1/2 ins / 57.5 x 105.5 cm) HKD 110,000; *Scholar Contemplating a Waterfall beneath Pine Trees* (ink and pigments on paper, mounted makemono, 37 x 91 3/4 ins / 94 x 233 cm) HKD 286,000. NEW YORK, 2 Dec 1992, *Landscape* (ink and pigments on paper, kakemono, 38 x 22 3/4 ins / 96.5 x 58.1 cm) USD 5,500. HONG KONG, 29 April 1993, *Landscapes of the Four Seasons* (ink and pigments on paper, set of four paintings, each 46 3/4 x 23 1/2 ins / 119 x 59.5 cm) HKD 299,000. NEW YORK, 16 June 1993, *Scholar Contemplating a Waterfall* (1945, ink and pigments on paper, 19 1/4 x 32 1/2 ins / 48.6 x 82.6 cm) USD 9,200. HONG KONG, 5 May 1994, *Riding a Donkey in an Autumn Landscape* (1948, ink and pigments on paper, fan, 7 x 18 1/2 ins / 17.8 x 47 cm) HKD 29,900. HONG KONG, 30 Oct 1995, *Waterfall* (1973, ink and pigments on paper, kakemono, 23 1/2 x 23 1/2 ins / 59.5 x 60 cm) HKD 52,900. HONG KONG, 29 April 1996, *Excursion into the Mountains* (1942, ink and pigments on paper, kakemono, 63 x 23 1/2 ins / 160 x 59.4 cm) HKD 69,000. HONG KONG, 2 Nov 1997, *Waterfalls* (ink and pigments on paper, 35 x 74 1/2 ins / 89 x 189.2 cm) HKD 149,500. NEW YORK, 20 March 2000, *Autumn Landscape* (ink and colour, 15 x 24 ins / 38 x 60 cm) USD 2,200. HONG KONG, 6 May 2002, *Excursion* (ink, scroll, 24 x 12 ins / 60 x 31 cm) HKD 25,000. HONG KONG, 25 April 2004, *Landscape* (1933, ink and colour, scroll, 32 x 15 ins / 82 x 37 cm) HKD 42,000. HONG KONG, 25 April 2004, *Waterfall* (1984, ink and colour, scroll, 24 x 47 ins / 60 x 120 cm) HKD 140,000.

HUANG K'I-MIN. See **HUANG QIMIN**

HUANG KI. See **HUANG JI**

HUANG KIN. See **HUANG JIN**

HUANG KIU. See **HUANG JU**

HUANG KIU-TS'AI. See **HUANG JUCAI**

HUANG KIUN. See **HUANG JUN**

HUANG KIUN-PI. See **HUANG JUNBI**

HUANG KONG-WANG. See **HUANG GONGWANG**

HUANG KUNG-WANG. See **HUANG GONGWANG**

HUANG LIU. See **HUANG LU**

HUANG LU, or Huang Liu, nickname: Cihuang, pseudonym: Fengliu Shanren
Chinese, 18th century.
Born in Xiexian (Anhui).
Active c. 1700.
Painter. Landscapes, animals, flowers.

The son of the painter Huang Sheng, Huang Lu specialised in landscapes, birds and flowers.

AUCTION RECORDS:
NEW YORK, 4 Dec 1989, *Landscapes* (ink and pigments on paper, album of 10 sheets, each 5 3/4 x 7 1/2 ins / 14.5 x 19 cm) USD 3,300.

HUANG MING-CH'ANG, Ming-ch'ang
Chinese, 20th - 21st century.
Born 1952, in Hua-lien, Taiwan.
Painter.

Huang Ming-ch'ang graduated from the University of Chinese Culture in 1975 and continued at the National Higher Art Institute. On completing his studies in 1984, he returned to a teaching position in Taiwan. In 1985 several of his works were purchased by the city of Paris (Cultural Affairs Division) and are now in its permanent collection of Chinese painting. His series *Fields in the Wind* is painted with meticulous care, leaving nothing to chance, not even the slightest blade of grass, which leaves the viewer with a sense of world-weariness, no doubt deliberate. He first exhibited in 1978, had his first solo show in 1985 and another in 1991.

AUCTION RECORDS:
TAIPEI, 22 March 1992, *Field in the Wind* (1991, oil on canvas, 'Paddy Fields' series, no. 7, 28 1/2 x 39 1/4 ins / 72.4 x 99.7 cm) TWD 462,000. TAIPEI, 18 April 1993, *Wind* (1992, oil on canvas, 'Fields' series, no. 13, 38 x 57 1/4 ins / 96.7 x 145.5 cm) TWD 1,150,000. TAIPEI, 10 April 1994, *Twilight* (1993, oil on fabric, 'Paddy Fields' series, no. 18, 53 1/4 x 76 1/2 ins / 135 x 194 cm) TWD 1,920,000. TAIPEI, 15 Oct 1995, *Golden Rice Field XXII* (1995, oil on fabric, 55 1/4 x 79 1/2 ins / 140.5 x 202 cm) TWD 1,150,000. TAIPEI, 14 April 1996, *Tang Lady and Matisse* (1996, oil on fabric, 35 3/4 x 28 1/2 ins / 91 x 72.5 cm) TWD 437,000. TAIPEI, 20 Oct 1996, *Summer Ocean* (1996, oil on canvas, 44 x 67 1/2 ins / 112 x 171.5 cm) TWD 1,590,000. TAIPEI, 13 April 1997, *Call of the Island* (1996, oil on linen, 4th in the series 'On Look Sea', 38 1/4 x 57 ins / 97 x 145 cm) TWD 1,260,000. TAIPEI, 11 April 1999, *Rice Field with Red Dragonfly, Rice Field Series* (1998, oil on linen, 31 x 46 ins / 80 x 116 cm) TWD 720,000.

HUANG MINGZHE, also known as Michell Hwang
Chinese, 20th - 21st century.
Born 1948, in Ilan, Taiwan.
Painter. Figure compositions.

Huang Mingzhe trained in England. He has taken part in many exhibitions. In 1981-1982 he won the first-place Provincial Art Exhibition Prize.

AUCTION RECORDS:
TAIPEI, 10 April 1994, *Love* (1989, oil on canvas, 21 1/2 x 25 ins / 54.5 x 63.5 cm) TWD 184,000. TAIPEI, 16 Oct 1994, *Hope* (1990, oil on canvas, 70 3/4 x 35 1/2 ins / 180 x 90 cm) TWD 713,000. TAIPEI, 18 April 1999, *Child's Birthplace* (oil on canvas, 24 x 24 ins / 61 x 61 cm) TWD 100,000. TAIPEI, 18 April 1999, *Shepherd Boy* (oil on canvas, 24 x 24 ins / 61 x 61 cm) TWD 110,000. TAIPEI, 14 Oct 2001, *Hope* (1990, oil on canvas, 35 x 71 ins / 90 x 180 cm) TWD 850,000. TAIPEI, 14 Oct 2001, *Women in Downtown Taipei* (1991, oil on canvas, 54 x 71 ins / 136 x 180 cm) TWD 1,000,000.

HUANG NIANZU, or Huang Nien-tsu
Chinese, 18th century.
Born in Xinan (Anhui).
Active in Wuxing (Zhejiang) probably at the end of the 18th century.
Painter.

Huang Nianzu is not recorded in the painters' biographies and is probably identical with Huang Jizu (variants: Huang Ki-tsu, Huang Chi-tsu, nickname: Gongliang, pseudonym: Qiushan). He painted birds and flowers in the style of Xu Wei (1521-1593) and Chan Shun (1483-1544). He is noted for his *Two Magpies on an Old Tree*, signed and dated 1791.

HUANG NIEN-TSU. See **HUANG NIANZU**

HUANG OUBO, Oubo
Chinese, 20th century.
Born 1917, in Chiayi, Taiwan.
Painter. Landscapes.

Huang Oubo graduated from the Kawabata Art Institute and taught at the National Art Academy of Taipei. He held his first solo exhibition in Taiwan in 1952.
AUCTION RECORDS:
TAIPEI, 18 Oct 1992, *Forest Path* (1992, gouache on paper, 16 1/2 x 24 1/2 ins / 42 x 62 cm) TWD 330,000.

HUANG PAN-JO. See **HUANG BANRUO**

HUANG PI. See **HUANG BI**

HUANG PIN-HONG. See **HUANG BINHONG**

HUANG PIN-HUNG. See **HUANG BINHONG**

HUANG QIMIN, or Huang K'i-min, Huang Ch'i-min, later Huang Riguan, Huang Je-kuan, Huang Jih-kuan, Huang Sheng (or Huang Cheng), nickname: Fumeng, pseudonym: Xiangshan
Chinese, 17th century.
Born in Xixian (Anhui).
Active during the second half of the 17th century.
Painter, writer. Landscapes.

HUANG QIUSHI, pen name: Guan Dong Shan Qiao
Chinese, 20th century.
Born 1928, in Chifeng, Inner Mongolia.
Painter. Landscapes.
Huang Qiushi is fascinated by the snow-covered landscape of north-eastern China. He is a painter at the Jilin Artistic Creations Bureau, a member of the China Artists Association and the China Calligraphers Association, a director of the International Artists Federation, a member of the Art Committee of China Poem Calligraphy and Painting Academy, honorary president of the Jilin Province Painting and Calligraphy Academy, and a researcher for the Jilin Province Culture and History Research Institute.

HUANG QUAN, or Huang Ts'iuan, Huang Ch'uan, nickname: Yaoshu
Chinese, 10th century.
Born c. 900, in Chengdu (Sichuan); died 965.
Painter. Religious subjects, flowers, birds.
Huang Quan was a painter in the service of Meng Cheng of the Later Shu kingdom. He painted religious subjects, both Buddhist and Taoist, but mainly flowers and birds, and it was as a flower and bird painter that he was highly appreciated at the Shu court academy. These paintings are very realistic in their detail and imbued with an intense vitality, thanks to a new technique, the so-called *mogu* (boneless) style, or painting with submerged outlines, which consisted of applying the colours lightly in thin layers or washes, without first drawing in the ink outline. The story goes that one day the lord of Shu, having received six unusual cranes in 938 from the governor of Hainan, asked Huang to paint them. Huang did so, painting them in very life-like postures: 'Quivering under the dew, pecking at the moss, washing their feathers, adjusting their wings, crying at the heavens, and raising their feet; with their exquisite colours, their appearance surpassed reality itself.' The room in which this work was housed was called the Liuhe dian (Six Cranes). Commissions for similar paintings came from far and wide.
BIBLIOGRAPHY:
Yang Xin and others, *Three Thousand Years of Chinese Painting*, Yale University Press, 1997.
MUSEUMS AND GALLERIES:
BEIJING (Palace Mus.): *Studies after Nature: Birds and Insects* (colours on paper, small handscroll, according to the inscription made for Huang Quan's son Jubao); *Flowers, Grasses and Insects* (album sheet, attributed); *Ducks among Reeds*; *Sparrow by a Stream among Autumn Plants* (album sheet, attributed) - NEW HAVEN (Yale University): *Group of Birds by a Willow Pond* (thick colours on paper, long handscroll, title and name of Huang Quan inscribed in the style of Emperor Huizong, numerous seals and inscriptions, the oldest dating from 1032) - TAIPEI (National Palace Mus.): *Birds and Grains* (album sheet); *Four Crows in a Bare Willow and Two Ducks in the Water, under Snow* (album sheet, probably from the Southern Song).

HUANG RIGUAN. See **HUANG QIMIN**

HUANG RUI, or Huang Jui
Chinese, 17th century.
Active probably at the end of the Ming dynasty (1368-1644).
Painter.

HUANG RUNHUA
Chinese, 20th century.
Born 1932, in Shijiazhuang (Hebei).
Painter. Landscapes.
Huang Runhua graduated from the Central Art Institute in 1956, where he had studied traditional *guohua* painting. He became the deputy director of the institute. His style recalls that of the great Li Keran. He took part in the 1980 exhibition in Paris entitled *Peintres Traditionnels de la République Populaire de Chine* (*Traditional Painters of the People's Republic of China*) held at the Galerie Daniel Malingue.

HUANG SHEN, nicknames: Gongmou, Yingpiaozi, pseudonym: Yingpiao
Chinese, 18th century.
Born 1687, in Ninghua (Fujian); died after 1768.
Painter, calligrapher. Figures, portraits, genre scenes, landscapes, flowers, animals.
Huang Shen settled in Yangzhao (Jiangsu) around 1723, and would later become one of the group known as the Yangzhao Baguai (Eight Eccentrics of Yangzhao). In the middle of the 18th century, Yangzhao, which lies on the Blue River at the southern end of the Grand Canal, was a vibrant city. Merchants who had grown rich on the salt trade found a new social mobility and with it discovered that they could mix with scholars and members of the aristocracy. Groups of new patrons soon formed, attracting artists. Huang Shen started as a traditional, popular artist, specialising in figure painting, genre scenes, flowers, insects and landscapes, just as he had learned from his master, a minor painter from his native province. But in Yangzhao he would meet Zheng Xie (1693-1765), another of the Eight Eccentrics, and his painting gradually developed a playful, rather untidy style, yet without being wild. In Huang's landscapes, the surface interests him more than the structure, but his brushstrokes are alive and original. Many of his works survive in private collections.
BIBLIOGRAPHY:
Yang Xin and others, *Three Thousand Years of Chinese Painting*, Yale University Press, 1997.
MUSEUMS AND GALLERIES:
BEIJING (Palace Mus.): *Portrait of the Artist's Brother Holding an Inkstone*; *Studies of Fruit and Landscapes* (six sheets of an album) - SHANGHAI: *Flowers* (album sheet) - STOCKHOLM (Nationalmus.): *Plants, Flowers and Landscapes* (12-sheet album, signed).
AUCTION RECORDS:
NEW YORK, 2 June 1988, *Calligraphy* (ink on paper, kakemono, 53 1/2 x 22 3/4 ins / 136 x 58 cm) USD 4,400. NEW YORK, 6 Dec 1989, *Tao Yuanming with Chrysanthemums* (ink and pigments on paper, kakemono, 51 3/4 x 24 1/4 ins / 131.5 x 61.5 cm) USD 11,000. NEW YORK, 31 May 1990, *Figures in a Landscape* (ink and pigments on paper, makemono, 11 1/2 x 106 1/2 ins / 29.2 x 270.5 cm) USD 31,900. NEW YORK, 25 Nov 1991, *Snow-covered Landscape* (ink on silk, kakemono, 16 x 19 3/4 ins / 40.6 x 50.4 cm) USD 3,850. NEW YORK, 1 June 1992, *Narcissus Bulbs* (ink and pigments on paper, kakemono, 9 x 11 1/2 ins / 22.9 x 29.2 cm) USD 1,760. NEW YORK, 28 Nov

1994, *Immortals* (ink and pigments on silk, kakemono, 78 1/2 x 63 1/4 ins / 199.4 x 160.7 cm) USD 32,200. HONG KONG, 26 April 1999, *Gentleman Appreciating Chrysanthemums* (ink and colour on silk, hanging scroll, 15 x 33 ins / 39 x 83 cm) HKD 70,000. HONG KONG, 28 Oct 2001, *Old Scholar* (ink and colour, 11 x 15 ins / 27 x 38 cm) HKD 48,000. HONG KONG, 26 Oct 2003, *Plum Blossoms* (ink and colour, 32 x 18 ins / 81 x 45 cm) HKD 45,000. HONG KONG, 26 Oct 2003, *Scenes from Travels* (ink and colour, twelve, 10 x 16 ins / 25 x 41 cm) HKD 420,000. HONG KONG, 25 April 2004, *Flower Seller* (1727, ink and colour, hanging scroll, 44 x 16 ins / 111 x 41 cm) HKD 70,000.

HUANG SHENG. See **HUANG QIMIN**

HUANG SHIFU, or Huang Shih-fu, nickname: Qiren
Chinese, 17th century.
Active in Fujian Province at the end of the Ming dynasty (1368-1644).
Painter.

Huang Shifu specialised in women's portraits in the style of Zhou Fang (active c. 780-810).

HUANG SHIH-FU. See **HUANG SHIFU**

HUANG TAO-CHOU. See **HUANG DAOZHOU**

HUANG TING. See **HUANG DING**

HUANG TS'IUAN. See **HUANG QUAN**

HUANG WAN-CHUNG. See **HUANG WANZHONG**

HUANG WANZHONG, or Huang Wan-chung
Chinese, 18th century.
Active probably during the reign of the Qing Emperor Qianlong (1736-1796).
Painter.

Huang Wanzhong is not recorded in the painters' biographies. Yet two paintings by him, signed and forming a pair, survive in a private collection: *Four Mynah Birds in a Tree* and *Two Pheasants and a Rock*.

HUANG WEI, nickname: Kuiyuan
Chinese, 19th century.
Born in Wujin (Jiangsu).
Active c. 1800.
Painter. Flowers.

MUSEUMS AND GALLERIES:
TAIPEI (National Palace Mus.): *Plum Branch in Blossom* (signed and dated 1816).

HUANG WEN-LI. See **HUANG WENLI**

HUANG WENLI, or Huang Wen-li, nickname: Zhixian
Chinese, 17th century.
Active at the end of the Ming dynasty (1368-1644).
Painter.

Huang Wenli is not recorded in the painters' biographies. One of his paintings, *Scholar Teaching his Son in an Open Pavilion at the Foot of High Mountains*, signed and dated 1644, is in a collection in Japan.

HUANG XIANGJIAN, or Huang Hsiang-chien, nickname: Duanmu
Chinese, 17th century.
Born 1609, in Changshu (Jiangsu); died 1673.
Painter. Landscapes.

Huang Xiangjian is famous for his filial piety. He painted landscapes in the style of Wang Meng (1298-1385).

MUSEUMS AND GALLERIES:
BEIJING (Palace Mus.): *Juyong Pass* (poem by Huang Xiangjian) - HONG KONG (Ho Kuan-Wu): album of landscape studies illustrating Huang Xiangjian's trip to Yunnan.

AUCTION RECORDS:
NEW YORK, 31 May 1990, *Good Son Searching for his Parents* (ink/paper, ink and pigments on paper, 10-sheet album, each 10 x 8 1/4 ins / 25.5 x 21 cm) USD 159,500. NEW YORK, 31 May 1994, *Landscapes* (ink on paper, 12-sheet album, 9 1/4 x 6 1/4 ins / 23.8 x 15.6 cm) USD 10,350. NEW YORK, 22 Sept 1997, *Landscapes* (1656, ink on paper, 13-sheet album, each 9 1/4 x 12 1/2 ins / 23.2 x 31.7 cm) USD 9,200.

HUANG XIANZHI, or Huang Hsien-chih
Chinese, 20th century.
Born in Hangzhou (Zhejiang).
Painter.

A painter of the Modern School, Huang Xianzhi studied under Xu Beihong (1896-1953) at Nanjing National University. He then left for France.

HUANG XINRUI, or Wong Sun-yui
Chinese, 20th - 21st century.
Born 1946, in Hong Kong.
Painter. Landscapes, still-lifes.

Huang Xinrui graduated from Linghai Art School in 1968 and taught there until 1974. From 1974 until 1979 he studied at the École des Beaux-Arts in Paris. Returning to Hong Kong, he lectured at the Institute of Visual Arts from 1982 to 1984. He has exhibited in Hong Kong since 1974, has taken part in various group exhibitions abroad, such as the 1982 Salon d'Automne in Paris, and has held solo exhibitions in Macau (1984), San Francisco and Taipei.

AUCTION RECORDS:
HONG KONG, 30 March 1992, *Trompe-l'oeil: Photograph with Insurance Policy* (1982, oil on canvas, 24 x 30 ins / 61 x 76 cm) HKD 82,500. HONG KONG, 28 Sept 1992, *Landscape of Tansui in Taiwan* (1992, oil on canvas, 19 3/4 x 24 ins / 50 x 60.9 cm) HKD 30,800.

HUANG YAN, or Huang Yen
Chinese, 20th - 21st century.
Born 1966, in Guangdong Province.
Engraver.

A self-taught wood engraver, Huang Yan graduated from Changchun Normal University in 1987. He likes large-scale detailed compositions. His work betrays a certain Russian influence in both subject matter and treatment.

BIBLIOGRAPHY:
New Art from China: Post-1989, Marlborough, 1993.

HUANG YANG-HUI. See **HUANG YANGHUI**

HUANG YANGHUI, or Huang Yang-hui
Chinese, 20th century.
Born 1911, in Wuxi (Jiangsu).
Painter, calligrapher.

Huang Yanghui was a painter of the so-called Modern School and a renowned calligrapher. After graduating from the National Art Academy he took up a teaching post at the Central Academy in Beijing in 1946.

HUANG YE, or Huang Yeh
Chinese, 18th century.
Active c. 1775.
Painter. Figures.

MUSEUMS AND GALLERIES:
PRINCETON (AM, Princeton University): *Two Horses and a Groom* (signed and dated 1775).

HUANG YEH. See **HUANG YE**

HUANG YEN. See **HUANG YAN**

HUANG YI, or Huang I, nickname: Dayi, pseudonym: Xiaosong
Chinese, 18th century.

Born 1744; died 1801.
Active in Hangzhou (Zhejiang).
Painter. Landscapes, flowers.

Huang Yi was also an archaeologist and an eminent seal carver.

Museums and Galleries:

Boston (MFA): *Bay Surrounded on Three Sides by Mountains* (small handscroll, seal of Huang Yi); *Winter Landscape* (signed and dated 1794, ink on paper, handscroll, inscription by Huang Yi).

Auction records:

New York, 2 June 1988, *Bamboo, Trees and Rocks* (ink on paper, kakemono, 39 1/4 x 12 3/4 ins / 99.5 x 32.5 cm) USD 3,520. New York, 31 May 1990, *Landscape* (ink and touches of pigment on paper, painted fan, 7 x 20 1/2 ins / 17.8 x 52.1 cm) USD 3,025.

HUANG YING-SHEN. See **HUANG YINGSHEN**

HUANG YINGHAO
Chinese, 20th - 21st century.
Born 1949, in Shanghai.
Active in Shanghai.
Painter, sculptor. Figure compositions.

Huang Yinghao studied sculpture at the fine arts academy of Zhejiang in 1966. From 1969 to 1981 he did artwork for various magazines in Shanghai. In 1982 he returned to his studies, this time to the painting section of Jiaotong University in Shanghai. He exhibits both in China and abroad.

Auction records:

Hong Kong, 30 March 1992, *Profile* (1990, oil on canvas, 32 x 25 1/2 ins / 81 x 65 cm) HKD 55,000.

HUANG YINGSHEN, or Huang Ying-shen, nickname: Jingyi, pseudonym: Jianan
Chinese, 17th century.
Born in Shundian (Henan).
Active at the court in Beijing during the Shunzhi period (1644-1661).
Painter.

A painter who specialised in figures, children and ghosts, Huang Yingshen entered the painting academy in 1658. The landscape elements in his paintings are stable; his inks are light, his colours brilliant, and his figures still show the influence of the artists of the Ming court (1368-1644).

Museums and Galleries:

London (British Mus.): *Zhong Kui* (signed and dated 1676) - Taipei (National Palace Mus.): *Illustration of the Humble House Inscription* (ink and colours on silk, hanging scroll).

HUANG YONGPING, or Huang Yong Ping
Chinese, 20th - 21st century.
Born 1954, in Xiamen (Fujian).
Active in France from 1989.
Installation artist.
Conceptual Art.

Huang Yongping graduated from the fine arts academy of Zhejiang in 1982. He was active in the Xiamen Dada group. He left China for Paris in 1989 after the Tiananmen Square massacre and has lived there ever since.

In 1989 he expressed clear defiance and scepticism towards institutional culture when he exhibited *A Comprehensive History of Chinese Painting and A Concise History of Modern Western Painting Washed in a Washing Machine for Two Minutes*. Subsequently, with *Bridge with Wire Fencing in the Form of a Snake and Tortoise Table*, he asked questions about the relationship between men and animals to highlight the contradictions that govern the world. In an exhibition at the Centre Georges-Pompidou in Paris in 1994, he continued on the same lines, exploring the analogy between the human race and the animal kingdom. This time his installation *Yellow Peril*, in which thousands of living insects could be seen devouring each other, brought such vigorous protests from animal rights groups that the installation had to be withdrawn from the exhibition.

Huang has shown his work in group exhibitions, including the following: *Les Magiciens de la Terre* (*Magicians of the Earth*) at the Centre Georges-Pompidou and the Grande Halle de la Villette in Paris (his first foreign show, 1989); *Galerie des Cinq Continents* (*Gallery of the Five Continents*) at the Musée National des Arts d'Afrique et d'Océanie (National Museum of African and Oceanic Art) in Paris (1995-1996); *Skulptur. Projekte in Münster 1997* (*Sculpture. Projects in Münster 1997*) in Münster in Germany (1997); and *Paris pour Escale* (*Stop-over in Paris*) at the Musée d'Art Moderne in Paris (2000); *Alors, la Chine?* (*What About China?*), Centre Georges Pompidou (2003). He has also held a number of solo exhibitions, including at the following: the Galerie Froment-Putman in Paris (1992); the Musée National des Arts d'Afrique et d'Océanie, Paris; the Fondation Cartier in Paris (1997); and the Musée Denon in Chalon-sur-Saône with Yan Peiming (2003).

Bibliography:

Huang Yong Ping, exhibition catalogue, Réunion des Musées Nationaux, Paris, 1995 (exhibition held at the Musée National des Arts d'Afrique et d'Océanie in Paris). Gao Minglu (ed), *Inside Out: New Chinese Art*, University of California Press, Berkeley, 1998.

Museums and Galleries:

Lyons (MAC).

HUANG YONGYU, or Huang Yong-yu, Huang Yung-yu
Chinese, 20th century.
Born 1924, in Fenghuang (Hunan).
Engraver, cartoonist, painter.

After the end of World War II, disillusionment affected a number of the most independent Chinese artists, namely those who were opposed to any form of art in the service of propaganda. Particularly affected were a number of cartoonists, whose chosen field would seem particularly suited to that form of art. In the 1950s and 1960s, Huang Yongyu refused to join the Party and attracted criticism for his apparent lack of interest in politics. Along with other art tutors, he was beaten, tortured and imprisoned by the Red Guard on the Central Academy of Fine Arts (CAFA) campus during the Cultural Revolution and later sent to the countryside. In the early 1970s, Huang was reported to the authorities for producing a work depicting a winking owl, interpreted as a comment against the regime. In the early 1990s he went into voluntary exile in Hong Kong after publishing cartoons which attacked Li Peng, but returned to Beijing in 1998.

While the politically steadfast continued to serve the Realist cause, others searched for a more personal style. Huang is a case in point. With his light-hearted yet deeply humane approach, he would raise wood engraving to new heights. Tinged with romanticism, his sensibility comes as a breath of fresh air, bringing immense relief after the sombre Realism of Socialist art.

Huang exhibited in a black painting exhibition in Beijing in 1974, where the masses were encouraged to make criticisms against the artists with work on display.

Bibliography:

Sullivan, Michael, *Chinese Art in the Twentieth Century*, University of California Press, Berkeley, Los Angeles, London, 1959. Laing, Ellen Johnston, *The Winking Owl: Art in the People's Republic of China*, University of California Press, Berkeley, 1988. Andrews, Julia F., *Painters and Politics in the People's Republic of China: 1949-1979*, University of California Press, Berkeley, 1994.

Auction records:
New York, 24 Feb 1982, *Crab and Chrysanthemums* (ink and colours on paper, 37 3/4 x 35 ins / 96 x 89 cm) USD 5,000. Hong Kong, 15 Nov 1990, *Landscape in Snow* (1981, ink and pigments on paper, kakemono, 40 1/4 x 40 1/2 ins / 102 x 103 cm) HKD 104,500. New York, 26 Nov 1990, *Young Woman* (ink and pigments on paper, 54 1/4 x 27 ins / 137.7 x 68.3 cm) USD 4,125. Hong Kong, 28 Sept 1992, *Red Lotus* (ink and pigments on paper, 33 1/4 x 59 3/4 ins / 84.2 x 152 cm) HKD 66,000. Hong Kong, 3 Nov 1994, *Vase with Peach Blossoms* (1982, ink and pigmens on paper, 48 x 45 1/4 ins / 121 x 115 cm) HKD 103,500. Hong Kong, 28 April 2003, *Buddhist Monk* (1990, ink and colour, hanging scroll, 57 x 35 ins / 144 x 89 cm) HKD 130,000. Hong Kong, 27 Oct 2003, *Ethnic Girl* (1959, ink and colour, 21 x 16 ins / 54 x 40 cm) HKD 50,000.

HUANG YONGZAN, or Huang Yung-tsan
Chinese, 20th century.
Born in Sichuan.
Engraver.

Huang Yongzan was born in Chongging, one of four Sichuanese (the others being Wang Qi, Liu Pingchi and Zhang Yongxi) to occupy an important place in 20th-century Chinese wood engraving. During the war he worked with a theatre group in southern China, where he acquired a passion for trains and railways, which often appear in his work.

HUANG YUE, or Huang Yueh, nicknames: Zuotian, Zuojun
Chinese, 18th - 19th century.
Born 1750 or 1751, in Dangtu (Anhui); died 1841.
Painter, calligrapher. Landscapes, flowers.

A senior official and scholar, Huang Yue painted in the style of Wang Hui (1632-1717) and Yun Shouping (1633-1690). He also wrote two treatises on painting: *Huayou Lu* and *Huapin*.

Auction records:
New York, 21 March 1995, *Callligraphy in Running Script* (ink on paper, kakemono, 52 1/4 x 22 ins / 132.7 x 55.9 cm) USD 1,380.

HUANG YUEH. See **HUANG YUE**

HUANG YUNG-TSAN. See **HUANG YONGZAN**

HUANG YUNG-YU. See **HUANG YONGYU**

HUANG ZHI. See **HUANG BINHONG**

HUANG ZHONGFANG, called Harold Wong
Chinese, 20th century.
Born 1943.
Painter. Landscapes.

Bibliography:
Maudsley, Catherine, *Means of Self-Expression: Recent Paintings of Harold Wong (Huang Zhongfang)*, Hong Kong, 1993. Lee, Nancy Chang, '*Recent Paintings by Harold Wong*' in *Orientations*, vol 24, no. 10, October 1993. Munro, Susan, '*The Chinese Paintings of Harold Wong*' in *Arts of Asia*, vol 24, no. 5, September-October 1994. Doran, Valerie C., '*Ink, Brush, Light, Dark: A Conversation with Harold Wong*' in *Orientations*, vol 28, no. 10, November 1997. '*Unperturbed: The Art of Huang Zhongfang (Harold Wong)*' in *Kaikodo Journal XVIII*, November 2000.

Auction records:
Hong Kong, 15 Nov 1990, *Landscape* (1968, ink and pigments on paper, kakemono, 50 1/2 x 16 1/2 ins / 128 x 42 cm) HKD 18,700. Hong Kong, 2 May 1991, *Landscape* (1990, ink and pigments on paper, 26 3/4 x 26 3/4 ins / 68 x 68 cm) HKD 35,200. Hong Kong, 31 Oct 1991, *Landscape* (ink and pigments on paper, 26 3/4 x 53 1/2 ins / 68 x 136 cm) HKD 38,500. New York, 1 June 1992, *Landscape* (ink and pigments on paper, kakemono, 26 1/2 x 26 1/2 ins / 67.3 x 67 cm) USD 2,200.

HUANG ZHOU, or Chou
Chinese, 20th century.
Born 1925, in Hebei Province; died 1997.
Painter. Figure compositions, landscapes with figures, animals.

Huang Zhou taught drawing at a primary school in 1939 but resigned so he could study painting at Xian. He studied under the landscape painter Zhao Wangyun whom he accompanied on various trips, notably to Gansu and Xinjiang in 1947. In 1949 he joined the revolutionary army and was assigned to reorganising artistic life in Langzhou and the north-east of the country. In Beijing in 1955 he received official blessing as a painter and was awarded the gold medal at the World Youth Festival in 1957. During the Cultural Revolution of 1966-1969 he was forbidden to do anything connected with art. Afterwards, he worked with great intensity.

Huang's work is highly varied. He liked to paint the Muslim peoples of Xinjiang, where he stayed on a number of occasions. Later, towards 1980, he developed a particular interest in the people of southern China. He drew silhouettes with large, bold brushstrokes, such as in *Three Hunchbacks*, whose facial expressions are captured in just a few telling lines. He painted traditional genres such as flowers, animals, cats, fish, pigs, monkeys, donkeys, camels and squirrels, capturing and rendering their vitality. When wielding his brush, he would spread the ink, mark by mark, to create the general shape of the animal's body, and then add a few, precise marks with an energetic brush to capture its individual characteristics.

Huang was the subject of an exhibition at the Musée Cernuschi in Paris in 1995.

Bibliography:
Andrews, Julia F., *Painters and Politics in the People's Republic of China: 1949-1979*, University of California Press, Berkeley, 1994. Yang Xin and others, *Three Thousand Years of Chinese Painting*, Yale University Press, 1997.

Auction records:
Hong Kong, 12 Jan 1987, *Fan Dance* (ink and colour on paper scroll, 48 x 27 1/4 ins / 122 x 69.5 cm) HKD 21,000. Hong Kong, 16 Jan 1989, *One Hundred Donkeys* (1980, ink on paper, makemono, 11 3/4 x 58 1/4 ins / 30 x 147.7 cm) HKD 132,000. Hong Kong, 30 March 1992, *Dressage* (ink and pigments on paper, makemono, 54 x 27 1/4 ins / 137.4 x 69.2 cm) HKD 30,800. Hong Kong, 28 Sept 1992, *Young Girl Leading a Caravan of Mules* (ink and pigments on paper, kakemono, 33 x 19 ins / 84 x 48 cm) HKD 38,500. New York, 16 June 1993, *Woman Carrying a Basket of Fruit* (ink and pigments on paper, kakemono, 30 1/2 x 19 1/4 ins / 77.2 x 49.2 cm) USD 1,840. Hong Kong, 3 Nov 1994, *Nine Donkeys* (1982, ink on paper, 53 1/2 x 26 1/2 ins / 136 x 67 cm) HKD 43,700. New York, 20 March 2000, *Mother and Infant* (1973, ink and pigments, 15 x 20 ins / 37 x 50 cm) USD 2,000. Hong Kong, 6 July 2003, *Donkeys* (ink, scroll, 15 x 254 ins / 37 x 645 cm) HKD 45,000.

HUARD
French, 17th century.
Born 1637; died 8 November 1675, in Paris.
Sculptor.

Huard may be the same artist as Gérard Herard.

HUARD, Antoine
French, 17th century.
Active in Angers from 1669 to 1674.
Glass painter.

HUARD, Charles
French, 20th century.
Born 2 June 1874, in Poncey-sur-l'Ignon (Côte-d'Or); died 30 March 1965, in Poncey-sur-l'Ignon.
Painter, engraver, watercolourist, draughtsman, illustrator.

Charles Huard attended the Julian studio around 1900. An illustrator and draughtsman, he collaborated on publications such as *Le Rire* (*Laughter*); *Le Journal amusant* (*The Funny Paper*); *L'Assiette au beurre* (*The Buttered Plate*); and *Le Sourire* (*The Smile*). His favourite occupation was to sketch the failings of provincial figures in comic silhouettes. He is well-known for his illustration of the complete works of Balzac. In the same genre, he illustrated Flaubert's *Bouvard et Pécuchet* (*Bouvard and Pécuchet*). His engraved work comprises hundreds of plates and etchings, retracing his passion for travel and foreign cities. He produced numerous series of engravings on *Granville; The Thames; London As I Saw It; Mornings in Marseilles; Paris As I Saw It; New York As I Saw It*; and *Berlin As I Saw It*. He also illustrated G. Clémenceau's *Figures de Vendée* (*Figures of the Vendée*).

Though Huard rarely signed his works, he often applied a stamp with a pansy motif. In Paris, he was friends with Toulouse-Lautrec, Forain, Steinlein and Wilette. The least-known of his works are his paintings and drawings of landscapes, landscapes with figures, cityscapes and genre scenes demonstrating his great technical mastery. A retrospective exhibition of his work was held at the Musée de Montmartre in 1974.

Bibliography:

HUARD, E., or Huart
Dutch, 19th century.
Painter. Genre scenes.

E. Huard worked in Brussels in 1839, and later in Antwerp.

HUARD, François
French, 19th century.
Born 1793, in Salon; died 1857, possibly in Arles (Bouches-du-Rhône).
Painter, lithographer. Historical subjects, portraits.

This artist taught himself to paint, receiving only the most limited guidance from Granet. He is known for a *Portrait of Louis XVIII*, in the town hall in Arles (Provence), France. There is also a series of lithographs he made, depicting the antiquities of Arles.

Museums and Galleries:
Arles (Town Hall): *Portrait of Louis XVIII*.

HUARD, Louis
French, 19th century.
Born in Aix-en-Provence; died 1842, in London.
Painter, watercolourist. History painting, portraits, landscapes, still-lifes.

Louis Huard worked in Brussels for many years, and then in England. While in London, he exhibited at the British Institute.

Museums and Galleries:
Sydney: *Boar Hunter* (watercolour).

Auction records:
Paris, 18 May 1908, *Peasant Woman Seated* (watercolour) FRF 34. Paris, 4-5 Dec 1918, *Cavalrymen of Louis XV Crossing a Ford*, FRF 90. Paris, 24 Nov 1995, *Landscape with Two Cavalrymen Arresting a Vagabond* (oil on panel, 19 x 25 1/2 ins / 48 x 64.5 cm) FRF 11,500.

HUARD, Pierre
French, 19th century.
Born in Paris; died 1857, in Paris.
Painter. Architectural views.

A pupil of Legay, Pierre Huard exhibited at the Salon from 1831 to 1855. He worked at the Sèvres porcelain manufactory, and was also director of both the École de Dessin and the Musée d'Antiquité in Arles (Bouches-du-Rhône).

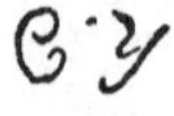

HUART
French, 14th century.
Active in Arras between 1370 and 1376.
Glass painter.

HUART, Benoît
French, 16th century.
Died c. 1552.
Active in Rouen.
Sculptor, founder, metal worker.
Gaillon School.

Benoît Huart worked at the Château de Gaillon.

HUART, Claude
French, 17th century.
Active in St-Mihiel.
Sculptor.

HUART, Claude
French, 20th century.
Born 1931.
Engraver. Landscapes.

Huart became director of the École des Beaux-Arts in Lorient in 1964. Since 1977, he has been a member of Xylon, an international society of wood engravers with which he exhibits. He was represented in 1979 and 1981 at the Biennale d'Art Contemporain in Brest.

HUART, Estienne
French, 16th century.
Active in Caen.
Painter.

Estienne Huart was employed in 1584 on the decorations for the entry of the Duke of Joyeuse into Caen.

HUART, Ferdinand d'
Luxembourg, 19th - 20th century.
Born 1859, in Sonlez; died 1919, in Luxembourg.
Painter. Portraits, flowers.

D'Huart was a student of Michel Engels in Luxembourg, then at the fine arts academy in Munich, and then, from 1880 to 1886, at the Académie des Beaux-Arts in Paris, where was taught by Alexandre Cabanel. His work was shown at the Brussels exhibition in 1910, and at the exhibitions of the Luxembourg Artists' Circle, of which he was president from 1910 to 1919.

Bibliography:
Cent cinquante ans d'Art luxembourgeois, exhibition catalogue, Musée national d'Histoire et d'Art du Luxembourg, Luxembourg, 1989.

Museums and Galleries:
Luxembourg (Mus. national d'histoire et d'art): *Portrait of Félix Blochhausen; Portrait of Grand Duke William IV; Portrait of Dr Michel Welter; Roses; Gladioli.*

HUART, Nicolas
French, 17th century.
Active in Paris in 1672.
Painter.

HUART, Philippe
French, 20th - 21st century.
Born 1953, in Clamart.
Painter. Scenes with figures, figures.
Nouvelle Figuration.

Philippe Huart was originally an illustrator and graphic designer for literary publishers and record companies. Since 1991 he has devoted himself to painting. His figurative representations are like superimposed catalogues of images in which words are integrated and have a readable and smooth appearance. They echo sources close to Pop Art or Narrative Figuration. He produces series of works: faces, animal portraits and various fragments of reality such as mouths, pills, etc. Houart has taken part in collective exhibitions such as:

the Salon de la Jeune Peinture, Paris, 1983, 1984; Salon Grands et Jeunes d'Aujourd'hui, Paris, 1984 and the Galerie Loft, Paris, 1995. Solo exhibitions of his work include: Centre d'Art Contemporain in Arches, Clermont-Ferrand, 1986; Boulogne-Billancourt Cultural Centre, 1995; Galerie Magda Danysz, Paris, 2001.

HUARTE DE MENDICOA, Francisco
Spanish, 16th century.
Active in Seville.
Painter.
His painting was mainly decorative.

HUAS, Pierre Adolphe
French, 19th century.
Born September 1838, in La Rochelle; died 8 April 1900, in Paris.
Painter, pastellist. Portraits, genre scenes.
Huas first exhibited at the Salon in 1863.
MUSEUMS AND GALLERIES:
LA ROCHELLE: *Portrait of R.P. Etourneau, of the Preaching Friars.*
AUCTION RECORDS:
PARIS, 20-24 Feb 1893, *Pretty Flower Girl,* FRF 225. PARIS, 30 March 1925, *Carmen: Three Silhouettes,* FRF 750. MUNICH, 26 Oct 1978, *Young Woman with a Lapdog* (1873, pastel, 27 1/2 x 22 ins / 70 x 55 cm) DEM 3,500.

HUAULT, Amy
Swiss, 17th - 18th century.
Born 9 August 1657; died 16 November 1724.
Active in Geneva.
Miniaturist, enameller.
Like his brother Jean Pierre, he was miniaturist to the court in Berlin.

HUAULT, Jean Pierre
Swiss, 17th - 18th century.
Born 28 July 1655, in Geneva; died 6 February 1723.
Miniaturist, enameller.
The brother of Amy Huault, with whom he mostly frequently collaborated.

HUAULT, Pierre, or Huaut or Huaud
Swiss, 17th century.
Born 2 February 1647, in Geneva; died c. 1698.
Miniaturist.
The brother of Amy and Jean Pierre, he went with them to Germany to work at the court of Prince Palatine Frederick III and in Berlin. Noted works include *The Abduction of Helen, Actæon* and a *Portrait of Frederick III.*

HUAULT-DUPUY, Valentin René
French, 19th - 20th century.
Born 1844, in Angers; died 1912.
Painter, engraver. Landscapes.
Huault-Dupuy was a student of C. Sauvageot and Toussaint. He is better known for his engraved work than for his painting. In Paris, he exhibited at the Salon, and the Salon des Artistes Français, receiving an honourable mention in 1903 and a third-class medal in 1908.

HUB, Emil
German, 20th century.
Born 2 February 1876, in Frankfurt am Main.
Sculptor.
Hub worked initially in Paris, where he had been a student at the Académie Julian. He was subsequently active in Germany, mainly in Frankfurt am Main, but he also exhibited in Wiesbaden, Munich, Darmstadt and Stuttgart.

HUBAC, Joseph
French, 18th century.
Born c. 1720, in Toulon; died 11 January 1761, in Toulon.
Sculptor.
Joseph Hubac was Louis Joseph's grandfather. He worked at the church of La Seyne-sur-Mer and for the Arsenal in Toulon.

HUBAC, Louis Joseph
French, 19th century.
Born 28 November 1776, in Toulon; died 13 March 1830, in Toulon.
Sculptor, draughtsman. Figures.
Hubac was director of sculpture work at the Arsenal de Toulon (Var), France.
MUSEUMS AND GALLERIES:
TOULON: *Janus and Hebe Pouring Nectar for Jupiter.*
AUCTION RECORDS:
PARIS, 16 June 1993, *Design for a Boat for Napoleon I* (pen and watercolour, 5 3/4 x 22 ins / 14.5 x 55 cm) FRF 9,000.

HUBACEK, Josef
Czech, 20th century.
Born 1899, in Prague; died 1931, in Prague.
Painter.
Josef Hubacek studied painting in Prague from 1922 to 1926. His travels in Yugoslavia (1924), France and Corsica (1926 and 1931), North Africa (1927) and Italy (1928) inspired many of his landscapes.
BIBLIOGRAPHY:
Fifty years of Czechoslovak Painting from the Collections of the Galleries, 1918-1958, exhibition catalogue, Slovenska Narodna Gal., Bratislava, 1968 (in commemoration of the 50th anniversary of the Republic of Czechoslovakia).

HUBACEK, William John
American, 19th - 20th century.
Born 15 October 1866 or 1871, in Chicago; died 14 June 1958, in San Bruno (California).
Painter. Landscapes, still-lifes.
William Hubacek came to San Francisco by covered wagon at the age of five with his family. He had begun to paint by the age of 12 and later studied at the Mark Hopkins Institute under Yelland, Mathews and Joullin. He travelled to France, Germany and Italy for more studies, and taught at the Mark Hopkins Institute when he returned to San Francisco. In 1938 he moved to San Bruno, where he established his studio and taught privately. His students referred to him as 'The Old Master'.

Hubacek was a highly skilled painter of realistic still-lifes and landscapes, such as his oils *Coconuts* (1891) and *Mount Tamalpais* (1894). His still-life paintings were of California flowers, fruits and vegetables, as well as fish and game. His refined and highly detailed work suggested physical and material comfort. Much of his early work was lost when his studio was destroyed in the San Francisco earthquake and fire of 1906.

Hubacek's exhibitions include the World's Columbian Expo in Chicago (1893); the California Midwinter International Expo (1894); the Mark Hopkins Institute (1898, 1906); the San Francisco Art Association (1903-1904); the Panama Pacific International Expo (1915); the Golden Gate International Expo and the New York World's Fair (1939); various San Mateo County Fairs and California State Fairs; and a retrospective at the San Bruno Public Library (1958).
MUSEUMS AND GALLERIES:
OAKLAND (Mus. of California) - SAN BRUNO (San Bruno Public Library).
AUCTION RECORDS:
SAN RAFAEL, 8 May 1999, *California Farm Scene* (oil on canvas, 14 x 20 ins / 36 x 51 cm) USD 2,250. SAN FRANCISCO, 12 Dec 2001, *Still-life with Pineapples, Plums and Copper Pot* (oil on canvas, 16 x 24 ins / 41 x 61 cm) USD 4,500. SAN FRAN-

CISCO, 11 June 2003, *Floral Still-life with Roses* (oil on canvas, 36 x 26 ins / 91 x 66 cm) USD 4,000. SAN FRANCISCO, 8 June 2004, *Still-life with Apples, Plums, Bananas and Watermelon* (1911, oil on canvas, 20 x 34 ins / 50 x 86 cm) USD 5,500.

HUBACHER, Hermann
Swiss, 20th century.
Born 14 August 1885, in Biel (Bern); died 1976.
Sculptor, engraver.

Hubacher studied in Geneva and Vienna. He worked in Bern and Munich before spending some time in Paris. He won a prize at the Venice Biennale in 1938. Initially, he was heavily influenced by Maillol, and produced generously proportioned nudes. He then began to produce portrait sculptures of men, women and children of distinct ethnic types. However, he continued to paint figures, some of which were nudes, both men and women, integrating the volumes of the faces into the volumes of the body as a whole.

BIBLIOGRAPHY:
Fierens, Paul, *Hermann Hubacher*, Quatre Chemins, Paris, 1932.

AUCTION RECORDS:
ZURICH, 5 May 1976, *Standing Nude* (bronze, h. 22 ins / 56 cm) CHF 2,600. ZURICH, 1 Nov 1979, *Nude Holding a Bird in the Left Hand* (patinated bronze, h. 59 3/4 ins / 152 cm) CHF 10,500. ZURICH, 6 June 1986, *Head of a Young Girl* (bronze, h. 14 1/4 ins / 36.5 cm) CHF 4,400. ZURICH, 29 May 2000, *Italian Woman* (bronze, h. 13 ins / 34 cm) CHF 4,000. ZURICH, 7 Dec 2000, *Torso* (1924, bronze, h. 48 ins / 122 cm) CHF 7,000. ZURICH, 26 May 2004, *Horse's Head* (bronze, h. 7 ins / 17 cm) CHF 2,400. ZURICH, 26 May 2004, *Girl with Mirror* (bronze, h. 9 ins / 24 cm) CHF 3,600.

HUBARD, William James
British, 19th century.
Born 1807, in England; died 25 February 1862, in Richmond, USA.
Painter. Portraits.

William Hubard settled in America from 1824 and lived in New York and then in Boston and Philadelphia. It was especially at this time that he painted a large number of portraits of American personalities of his time.

HUBATSCH, Hermann
German, 20th century.
Born 16 May 1878, in Berlin.
Sculptor.

Hubatsch was a student of Manzel and Haverkamp. He mainly produced busts.

HUBAULT, J.
Maiden name: Gauthier
French, 19th - 20th century.
Active in Paris.
Painter.

J. Hubault became a member of the Société des Artistes Français in 1891.

HUBAUT, Joël
French, 20th - 21st century.
Born 1947, in Amiens.
Painter, sculptor, collage artist, installation artist, film producer, performance artist. Multimedia.

Joël Hubaut lives in Réville and teaches at the École des Beaux-Arts in Caen. A multimedia designer whose work is a kind of semiotic restless wandering, Hubaut makes references to artists such as Giotto, Duchamp, Pissarro and Beuys as well as writers such as Raymond Roussel, Lewis Carroll or Jules Verne, by weaving slogans, inscriptions and quotations into his sculptures and assemblages. For Pierre Restany, by mixing an all-consuming enthusiasm with a scattered and varied number of signs, word play, images and sound components, Hubaut's works are a critique of a kind of 'information pollution'.

He has taken part in collective shows such as: ARC, Musée d'Art Moderne de la Ville de Paris, 1980; the eighth Foire d'Art Actuel, Palais des Beaux-Arts, Brussels, 1983; *L'Écriture dans la Peinture* (*Writing in Painting*), Centre National d'Art Contemporain, Nice, 1984; *Trans-figurations*, Centre d'Art Contemporain Pablo-Neruda, Corbeil-Essonnes, 1988.

His main solo exhibitions, performances and installations include: *Portrait d'Eric Satie*, Galerie de l'Estuaire in Honfleur, 1972; Galerie Noire, Paris, 1975; Galerie Lara Vincy, Paris, 1979, 1980, 1982, 1983; Galerie Arlogos, Nantes, 1983; Musée d'Art Moderne, Villeneuve d'Ascq, 1984; Ruth Siegel Gallery, New York, 1985; *La Peinture Loupée* (*Painting Defect*), Galerie Galea, Caen, 1988; *Peinture-Diode* (*Diode Painting*), Galerie Krief, Paris, 1988; *Chauf-âge-météors*, Galerie Janos, Paris, 1992; *Zig-zag Invisible* (*Invisible Zig-zag*), A.B. Galeries, Paris, 1992; *Muséè du Lapin Sémiotique*, Hôtel de Sponeck, Montbéliard, 1994; Centre d'Art Contemporain, La Ferme du Buisson, Noisiel, 1996; Le Parvis-Centre d'Art Contemporain, Ibos-Tarbes, 2001, Musée du Périgord, Périgueux, 2003.

BIBLIOGRAPHY:
Hubaut, Joël, *Robe grillée*, Gal. de l'Estuaire, Honfleur, 1972. Hubaut, Joël, *Hobby or not Hobby*, Westport books, New York, 1983. '*Écritures dans la peinture*' in vol. I, Villa Arson-Centre national des Arts plastiques, Nice, 1984. Hubaut, Joël, *Poèmes construct*, Éd. de la Nèpe, 1988.

MUSEUMS AND GALLERIES:
PARIS (FNAC): *Paella* (1988-1989).

AUCTION RECORDS:
HONFLEUR, 3 Oct 1976, *Composition* (1947, oil on canvas, 47 1/4 x 35 3/4 ins / 120 x 91 cm) FRF 1,900. PARIS, 12 Feb 1989, *Panda* (1988, acrylic/canvas, 45 x 46 ins / 114 x 116 cm) FRF 950,000. PARIS, 12 Feb 1990, *Rabbit Generation* (1989, relief and mixed media/panel, 11 x 18 ins / 28 x 46 cm) FRF 3,800. PARIS, 4 Oct 1991, *Seville-Barcelona* (1989, oil on canvas, 25 1/2 x 21 1/4 ins / 65 x 54 cm) FRF 12,000.

HUBAY, Paul
Hungarian, 20th century.
Born 23 November 1930, in Subotica.
Active in France from 1955.
Sculptor, painter, draughtsman. Figures, nudes, portraits, landscapes, still-lifes.

Paul Hubay studied art in Sarajevo, Zagreb, Munich, Madrid and then Paris. He met the singer and composer Georges Brassens in 1972, whose bust he carved. He was also executed the *Léon Rabot Monument* commissioned for the sports centre in Puteaux. He made the war memorial in Ponteilla (1981) and carved a group of 35 sculptures in marble and stone for a chapel in Céret (1984). He showed work at the Salon d'Automne (1956) and the Salon des Indépendants (1973 to 1978), and held a solo exhibition in Paris (1975).

AUCTION RECORDS:
PARIS, 16 May 1988, *Seated Model* (pastel, 9 x 11 3/4 ins / 23 x 30 cm) FRF 220. PARIS, 27 Jan 1989, *Helena* (marble, 7 3/4 x 4 1/4 x 6 3/4 ins / 20 x 11 x 17 cm) FRF 3,800. PARIS, 5 Feb 1990, *Crouching Woman* (brown-patinated bronze, 3 1/4 x 4 1/2 x 3 1/4 ins / 8 x 11.5 x 8 cm) FRF 5,200. PARIS, 19 Jan 1992, *Tactile* (black marble, 15 1/4 x 5 1/2 x 4 3/4 ins / 39 x 14 x 12 cm) FRF 3,500. PARIS, 5 Oct 1992, *Belle Époque* (1991, bronze, 11 1/2 x 5 x 6 3/4 ins / 29.5 x 13 x 17 cm) FRF 6,000. PARIS, 4 April 1993, *Tenderness* (bronze, 5 3/4 x 3 3/4 x 4 1/4 ins / 14.5 x 9.5 x 11 cm) FRF 3,500.

HUBBARD, Bennett
British, 19th century.
Born 1806; died 1870.
Active in London.
Painter. Portraits, animals.

Hubbard was a painter in Louth in Lincolnshire from 1839 to 1864.

AUCTION RECORDS:

COPENHAGEN, 23 May 1996, *Haidee, a Young Girl in Oriental Costume* (oil on canvas, 12½ x 12½ ins / 32 x 32 cm) DKK 4,000. LONDON, 6 Nov 1997, *A Shorthorn Heifer, Lady Horsley in a Landscape with a Farm in the Background* (oil on canvas, 25 x 30 ins / 63.5 x 76.3 cm) GBP 5,175. LONDON, 22 Nov 2001, *Young Boy with his Favourite Terrier* (1855, oil on canvas, 36 x 28 ins / 91 x 71 cm) GBP 4,800. NEW ORLEANS, 8 Feb 2003, *Young Boy with his Favourite Terrier* (1855, oil on canvas, 36 x 28 ins / 91 x 71 cm) USD 5,000.

HUBBARD, Charles Daniel

American, 20th century.

Born 14 July 1876, in New York; died 1951.

Painter, illustrator.

Charles Daniel Hubbard was a member of the Salmagundi Club and American Artists Professional League.

AUCTION RECORDS:

NEW YORK, 14 Feb 1990, *Murray House in Guillford, Connecticut* (oil on card, 7½ x 11 ins / 19 x 28 cm) USD 660.

HUBBARD, Eric Hesketh

British, 20th century.

Born 16 November 1892, in London.

Painter. Genre scenes, landscapes.

Eric Hubbard travelled extensively in Europe and exhibited in major British cities.

HUBBARD, John

American, 20th century.

Born 1931, in Ridgefield (Connecticut).

Active in Rome from 1958, in England from 1961.

Painter. Landscapes.

John Hubbard was educated at Harvard University. He did three years of military service based in Japan, where he became interested in Japanese painting, gardens and architecture. From 1956 to 1958 he studied at the Art Students League in New York City and with Hans Hoffman.

Hubbard went to Europe in 1958, travelling there and living in Rome until 1960. He married and moved to Dorset in England in 1961, where his work became identified with the English landscape, as in *Dorset Landscape* (1964) and *Winter Afternoon* (1965). He taught as visiting teacher of painting at the Camberwell School of Art in London (1963-1965), was resident artist at Poet's House, New Harmony, Indiana in 1988, and worked as a guest of the National Gallery of Malaysia in 1990. From 1993 to 1997 he was a member of the advisory panel at Tate St Ives.

Hubbard views himself as an unconventional landscape painter, combining elements of Chinese painting with contemporary Abstraction. During the 1960s he tended to used large brushstrokes to suggest form and directional emphasis, but a visit to Morocco in 1969 resulted in a shift to a more calligraphic approach to painting and a wider range of colours, as in *Moroccan Landscape* (1969). He has since used thinned oil paint and glazes to increase flexibility in his painting.

In the mid-1970s, Hubbard did a series of stone paintings, such as the oils *Encrusted Stone* and *Stone Group* (both 1976). A 1987 trip to Granada supplied ideas from Spanish courtyards for fusing architecture and plant material, as in his *Sevilla* (1991). From 1999 to 2000, he was commissioned by Lord Rothschild to design large areas of carpet bedding of plants at Waddesdon Manor in Berkshire. He has also designed sets and costumes for the Dutch national ballet and the Royal Ballet at Covent Garden.

Hubbard has participated in group exhibitions, including: *Scottish Paintings 1993-96*, Maclaurin Art Gallery, Ayr (1996); *Eight Variations on a Drawing by Rubens*, Fitzwilliam Museum, Cambridge (1998); *Paintings, Drawings and Millennium Garden*, Waddesdon Manor (2000); and the New Art Centre Sculpture Park and Gallery, Roche Court, East Winterslow (2002). He has had solo exhibitions at Dorset County Museum, Dorchester (1983); Center for British Art, Yale University, New Haven (1986); Museum of Modern Art, Oxford (1985); Poole Arts Centre, Dorset (1988); and Charleston Farmhouse, Sussex (1995). He was the winner of the Jerwood Prize in 1996.

BIBLIOGRAPHY:

John Hubbard: Paintings and Drawings 1975-1979, exhibition catalogue, Fischer Fine Art Ltd. Gallery, London, 1979. *John Hubbard*, exhibition catalogue, Center for British Art, Yale University, New Haven, 1986. *John Hubbard, Alhambra: Paintings, Drawings and Related Works*, exhibition catalogue, Fischer Fine Art Ltd. Gallery, London, 1988. Hall, Douglas, *John Hubbard: Scottish Paintings*, exhibition catalogue, Purdy Hicks Gallery, London, 1996.

MUSEUMS AND GALLERIES:

BELFAST (Arts Council of Northern Ireland) - BIRKENHEAD (City Art Gallery) - BRISTOL (City Art Gallery) - CAMBRIDGE (Fitzwilliam Museum) - EDINBURGH (Scottish Nat. Gal. of Modern Art) - KUALA LUMPUR (National Gallery of Malaysia) - LONDON (Arts Council of Great Britain) - LONDON (Tate Collection): *Autumn on the Chesil Bank* (1962, oil); *Light Structure* (1966, oil); *Stone Group Porthmeor Beach* (1977, charcoal); *Haytor Quarry* (1980-1981, oil); *Study for Winter Skies* (1963, oil) - LONDON (UK Government Art Collection): *Composition with Pink* (1962, oil); *New Grass* (1966, oil); *Quarry* (1976, oil); *Seascape, Lyme Bay* (1965, oil); *Study for Winter Skies* (1963, oil) - LONDON (Victoria and Albert Mus.) - MELBOURNE (Nat. Gal. of Victoria) - NEW HAVEN (Center for British Art, Yale University) - NEW SOUTH WALES (Ballarat Art Gallery) - PHILADELPHIA (MA) - PHILADELPHIA (Pennsylvania Academy of Fine Arts) - PORTSMOUTH (City Art Gallery) - TORONTO (AG of Ontario).

HUBBARD, Mary Wilson

American, 20th century.

Born 1871, in Massachusetts.

Painter.

Mary Wilson Hubbard worked in New York. She trained at the Art Students League (ASL), New York and also studied in Paris.

HUBBARD, Richard William

American, 19th century.

Born 1816 or 1817, in Middletown (New York); died 1888.

Painter. Landscapes.

Richard William Hubbard was a pupil of Morse and Huntingdon.

AUCTION RECORDS:

NEW YORK, 29 April 1976, *Shallows of the Hudson* (1877, oil on canvas, 32¼ x 55 ins / 82 x 140 cm) USD 2,500. NEW YORK, 27 June 1979, *View near Dover, New York* (oil on canvas, oval, 11¾ x 17½ ins / 30 x 44.5 cm) USD 2,750. NEW YORK, 27 Jan 1984, *Sailboat off Rocky Coast* (oil on canvas, 20 x 30 ins / 50.8 x 76.2 cm) USD 3,000. NEW YORK, 31 Jan 1985, *Cattle in Valley Landscape* (oil on canvas, 16¾ x 14¼ ins / 42.5 x 36.2 cm) USD 1,800. NEW YORK, 23 May 2000, *Afternoon by the River* (oil on board, 8 x 7 ins / 21 x 18 cm) USD 18,000. BETHESDA, 7 Feb 2004, *Landscape* (1885, oil on canvas, 14 x 24 ins / 36 x 61 cm) USD 3,750. NEW YORK, 27 Sept 2004, *Lake George* (1874, oil on canvas, 14 x 24 ins / 36 x 61 cm) USD 38,000.

HUBBELL, Henry Salem

American, 20th century.

Born 25 December 1870, in Paola, Canada; died 1949.

Painter. Landscapes.

Henry Salem Hubbell began his training in America. He went to work in Paris under Whistler, Colin, Laurens and

Benjamin Constant. He was an honorary member of the National Academy in 1906; a member of the Société des Peintres Américains de Paris and the Salmagundi Club. He exhibited at the Salon de Paris, and received an honourable mention in 1901, and a third silver medal in St Louis in 1904.
MUSEUMS AND GALLERIES:
PARIS (former Mus. du Luxembourg).
AUCTION RECORDS:
NEW YORK, 2 June 1983, *Tea Time* (oil on canvas, 32¾ x 22 ins / 83.2 x 55.9 cm) USD 32,000. LIMOGES, 12 May 1985, *Young Girl Sitting near the Window* (1906, oil on canvas, 23½ x 17 ins / 60 x 43 cm) FRF 60,000. NEW YORK, 14 March 1986, *At Grandmother's* (oil on canvas, 16¾ x 23½ ins / 42.7 x 59.8 cm) USD 2,000. NEW YORK, 15 May 1991, *Garden Seat* (oil on canvas, 23 x 16½ ins / 58.4 x 41.9 cm) USD 4,675. NEW YORK, 25 March 1997, *Augusta at the Parish Fête* (oil on canvas, 24 x 20 ins / 61 x 50.8 cm) USD 7,475. NEW YORK, 12 Jan 1999, *Young Boy with Globe* (oil on canvas, 36 x 30 ins / 91 x 76 cm) USD 2,400. AMSTERDAM, 7 March 2000, *Pont Neuf, Paris* (1897, oil on board, 7 x 5 ins / 19 x 13 cm) NLG 5,000. PARIS, 30 Jan 2002, *Young Girl with Hat and Flower* (c. 1900, oil on canvas, 33 x 22 ins / 83 x 56 cm) EUR 29,620. PARIS, 30 Oct 2002, *Huuse with a Red Roof in a Landscape* (oil on canvas, 11 x 16 ins / 27 x 41 cm) EUR 2,500. CHICAGO, 21 March 2004, *Portrait of Ricard W. Sears* (oil on canvas, 57 x 38 ins / 145 x 97 cm) USD 5,000. ST LOUIS, 26 June 2004, *Landscape River View from Alton Bluffs* (oil on canvas, 30 x 35 ins / 76 x 89 cm) USD 14,500.

HUBBERT

American, 16th century.
Active during the second half of the 16th century.
Painter. Portraits.

HUBBUCH, Karl

German, 20th century.
Born 21 November 1891, in Karlsruhe; died 26 December 1979, in Karlsruhe.
Painter, watercolourist, draughtsman, engraver, lithographer.
Neue Sachlichkeit (New Objectivity).

From 1908 to 1912, Karl Hubbuch took courses at the fine arts academy in Karlsruhe, where he associated with Rudolf Schlichter, George Scholz and Willi Müller-Hufschmid. From 1912 to 1914, he was a student at the applied arts museum school in Berlin, when it was run by Orlik and Walter Conz. Other sources suggest he may have taught at the fine arts academy in Berlin from 1912 to 1914, together with George Grosz. He fought in World War I, after which he took up engraving, particularly lithography. He became a professor at the fine arts school in Karlsruhe in 1925, but was dismissed from his post by the Nazis. He made several trips to France. It was only after World War II that he was able to start teaching again: he taught at the technical university in Karlsruhe in 1947, and at the Karlsruhe academy in 1948. From 1957 to 1979, he lived and worked as an independent artist in Karlsruhe.

Together with Dix, Grosz and Schlichter, Hubbuch was one of the verist tendency of the *Neue Sachlichkeit* movement, which grew up in Weimar Germany between 1918 and 1925 as a reaction to Expressionism. His reputation in France was established by two exhibitions at the Centre Georges Pompidou, *Paris-Berlin* (1978) and *Realisms* (1980). In the earliest stage of his career he produced works that both depict humans and are a vehicle for biting social criticism. The caricatures in his early works give way to a 'tidier topographic distribution of motifs', as seen in his studies for nudes and urban landscapes. His hard, precise strokes became more compact and darker in the 1920s, and he often used a soft-lead pencil for his lithographs. At the same time he began to integrate colour into his work. He was always ready to study the Old Masters. His universe is that of man in society, and he represented man with quasi-sociological precision: his behaviour, his social aspirations, his environment, and his modest idealism. He maintained a lively interest in France, which resulted in the publication, at the artist's expense, of his work *France* and the production of a series of fifty-five drawings entitled *The Capital* in 1970.

Work by Hubbuch was shown at a number of collective exhibitions, including the first *Neue Sachlichkeit* exhibition, at the Kunsthalle in Mannheim (1925); the Nierendorfgalerie in Berlin, with Otto Dix and Grosz (1927); the *Sezession* in Berlin (1928); the *Neue Sachlichkeit* exhibition in Amsterdam (1929); *Self-portraits by Artists from the Baden Region* at the Kunstverein in Karlsruhe (1930); *German Art Today* in Baden-Baden (1947); *Children and Art* at the Kunsthalle in Mannheim (1949); the *Third Exhibition of German Art* in Dresden (1953); the international art exhibition in Warsaw (1954); *Die Neue Sachlichkeit, Haus am Waldsee* in Berlin (1961); *Die Neue Sachlichkeit* at the Galerie Zwirner in Cologne (1966); *Realism in Painting in the 1920s* at the Kunstverein in Hamburg and Frankfurt am Main (1968); *Aspects of the New Realism* in Innsbruck (1972); *Realism in Germany 1919-1933* at the Musée d'Art et d'Industrie in St-Étienne and at the Musée d'Art et d'Histoire in Chambéry (both 1974); *Paris-Berlin* at the Centre Georges Pompidou in Paris (1978); *Realisms* at the Centre Georges Pompidou (1980); and *Phantom of Desire. Visions of Masochism in Art*, an exhibition dedicated to Sacher-Masoch (after whom masochism is named) at the Neue Galerie am Landesmuseum in Graz (2003).

There have been solo exhibitions of Hubbuch's work, and a number of posthumous retrospectives, including a retrospective at the Neue Münchner Galerie in Munich (1967); a retrospective of his graphic works in Freiburg (1969); *Hubbuch as a Young Man 1911-1925* at the Kunsthalle in Bremen (1974); a retrospective at the Badischer Kunstverein in Karlsruhe, the Kunsthalle in Berlin and the Kunstverein in Hamburg (1981); and an exhibition at the Galerie Karl Flinker in Paris (1984). In 1959 he was awarded the Silver Peace Medal in Leipzig, and in 1965 he was a guest of honour at the Villa Massimo in Rome.

BIBLIOGRAPHY:
Schmidt, Diether, *Karl Hubbuch*, exhibition catalogue, Gall. del Levante, Limes Verlag, Munich, 1976. Spies, Werner, '*Karl Hubbuch: chroniqueur de son siècle*' in *Karl Hubbuch, peintures, aquarelles, dessins, gravures des années 20 et 30*, exhibition catalogue, Gal. Karl Flinker, Paris, 1984. Weibel, Peter (ed.), '*Phantom der Lust. Visionen des Masochismus in der Kunst*' in *2 vol.*, exhibition catalogue, Neue Galerie am Landesmuseum, Graz, Belleville Verlag, Munich, 2003.
MUSEUMS AND GALLERIES:
MANNHEIM (Städtische Kunsthalle): *Woman Swimmer from Cologne* - MUNICH (Staatsgal. Moderne Kunst): *Hilde* (1923, two versions) - STUTTGART (Staatsgal.): *Duck Thieves*.
AUCTION RECORDS:
MUNICH, 12 Dec 1978, *Jannowitz Bridge* (1922, etching and dry-point, 9¾ x 12¼ ins / 25 x 31 cm) DEM 2,100. MUNICH, 26 Nov 1979, *Lissy in a Good Mood* (1927, pen, 22½ x 17¼ ins / 57 x 43.5 cm) DEM 4,000. ROME, 23 Nov 1981, *Orator* (1923-1924, pencil, 16¼ x 12¼ ins / 41 x 31 cm) ITL 1,500,000. MUNICH, 25 Nov 1981, *Standing Nude* (watercolour/pencil outlines, 24½ x 8¼ ins / 62 x 21 cm) DEM 3,000. LONDON, 26 June 1984, *Financial Difficulties* (c. 1926-1927, pen and black ink heightened with white, 19 x 21 ins / 48.5 x 53.5 cm) GBP 3,200. HAMBURG, 7 June 1985, *Congress* (watercolour and pencil, 42 x 39¾ ins / 106.4 x 101 cm) DEM

33,000. London, 26 Feb 1986, *Street Scene, Berlin* (pencil, 12½ x 9¾ ins / 31.5 x 25 cm) GBP 900. London, 30 June 1987, *Street Scene* (pen, 14¾ x 14¾ ins / 37.5 x 37.5 cm) GBP 1,200. London, 30 June 1987, *Still-life with Flowers* (watercolour, 22¾ x 16¾ ins / 58 x 42.5 cm) GBP 3,000. Munich, 8 June 1988, *Murder* (oil on canvas, 27¼ x 30¾ ins / 69 x 78 cm) DEM 15,400; *Chez Nous* (ink heightened with white, 17½ x 23¼ ins / 44.5 x 59 cm) DEM 5,390. Rome, 17 April 1989, *Central Section of a Transatlantic Liner* (pencil and pastel/paper, 19¾ x 15¾ ins / 50 x 40 cm) ITL 7,500,000. Rome, 6 Dec 1989, *Flowers* (1930, watercolour and pencil/paper, 23½ x 19¾ ins / 60 x 50 cm) ITL 6,900,000. Berlin, 30 May 1991, *Edith* (watercolour and pencil/paper, 39½ x 21¾ ins / 100.5 x 55.5 cm) DEM 31,080. Heidelberg, 12 Oct 1991, *Angler* (ink, 12 x 8¼ ins / 29.6 x 21.2 cm) DEM 1,300. Munich, 26-27 Nov 1991, *War Game* (1959, mixed media, 17¼ x 22¾ ins / 44 x 58 cm) DEM 1,840. Rome, 9 Dec 1991, *The Kiss that Kills* (1931, ink/card, 19¼ x 20½ ins / 49 x 52 cm) ITL 8,625,000. Berlin, 29 May 1992, *Three Sisters* (pencil, 16¼ x 22¼ ins / 41.5 x 56.3 cm) DEM 8,475. Heidelberg, 5-13 April 1994, *Young Woman from Essen (Martha)* (1925, dry-point, 9 x 9 ins / 22.7 x 22.6 cm) DEM 1,200. Heidelberg, 8 April 1995, *Study for a Nude* (pencil, watercolour and black chalk, 29¾ x 11½ ins / 75.7 x 29 cm) DEM 17,500. London, 17 April 1996, *Model in the Nude* (pencil, 12¾ x 9¾ ins / 32.3 x 25 cm) GBP 920. London, 9 Oct 1997, *Everyone Shows What He Has (Bruno and his Women)* (1930- 1932, oil on canvas, 59½ x 61½ ins / 151 x 156 cm) GBP 128,000. London, 6 Oct 1999, *Local Carnival* (1953, oil on masonite, 31 x 37 ins / 80 x 93 cm) GBP 15,000. London, 6 Oct 1999, *Myriam with Cat* (c. 1952-1954, oil on masonite, 53 x 31 ins / 135 x 79 cm) GBP 23,000. London, 18 Oct 2000, *Self-portrait* (lithographic crayon on paper on board, 20 x 14 ins / 52 x 36 cm) GBP 70,000. London, 18 Oct 2000, *Waitress* (c. 1926, watercolour, wash, pencil, 39 x 20 ins / 99 x 50 cm) GBP 75,000. London, 22 June 2001, *Frau im mantel. Figures Studies* (charcoal, double-sided, 26 x 19 ins / 65 x 47 cm) GBP 5,500. London, 11 Oct 2001, *In the Hamock* (1928, watercolour, pencil, tempera on paper on card, 26 x 26 ins / 65 x 67 cm) GBP 15,000. London, 9 Oct 2002, *Die drillinge - Triplets* (c. 1927, oil on canvas, 58 x 62 ins / 148 x 157 cm) GBP 150,000. Berlin, 29 Nov 2002, *Four Woman Talking* (c. 1930-1935, oil on canvas, 15 x 19 ins / 38 x 47 cm) EUR 22,000. London, 3 Feb 2003, *Akt im Badezimmer* (oil on canvas on board, 42 x 30 ins / 107 x 75 cm) GBP 68,000. Berlin, 30 May 2003, *Lona with Flowers* (oil on canvas, 39 x 37 ins / 100 x 95 cm) EUR 55,000. Berlin, 12 June 2004, *Roundabout* (c. 1960, oil on panel, 17 x 32 ins / 44 x 82 cm) EUR 5,000. London, 22 June 2004, *Afternoon Tea* (1933-1935, oil on panel, 8 x 12 ins / 21 x 31 cm) GBP 32,000.

HUBEL, Karl or Lucazs
Polish, 18th century.
Born 19 January 1722, in Chvaïnice; died 20 April 1793, in Lubieszow.
Active in Cracow and Vilna (now Vilnius, Lithuania).
Painter.

HUBER
German, 16th century.
Active in Leipzig at the end of the 16th century.
Miniaturist.

HUBER, Adam
German, 19th century.
Born 1825, in Traustein; died 25 February 1863, in Munich.
Painter. History painting.
He exhibited in Munich and Cologne.
Museums and Galleries:
Munich: *The Virgin with Jesus and St John.*

HUBER, Alexander
Swiss, 18th century.
Born in Basel.
Painter.
He lived in France and Italy for a long time.

HUBER, Alexius
Swedish, 20th century.
Born 1939.
Sculptor.
Neo-Constructivism.
Huber studied in Germany, taking courses at the decorative arts school in Pforzheim. His work has been exhibited in Sweden, Germany and Switzerland. In 1986, he was one of the artists featured in the exhibition *Five Swedish Constructivists* in Paris.

HUBER, Anton
Austrian, 18th - 19th century.
Born 1763, in Fügen (Zillertal); died 1840, in Fügen.
Sculptor, painter.
He illustrated religious subjects.
Museums and Galleries:
Innsbruck: several works.

HUBER, Arnold Pankraz
Swiss, 20th century.
Born 17 June 1873, in Wil (St Gall).
Painter. Landscapes, portraits.
Huber was a student of Léon Bonnat. He painted mainly landscapes and portraits.

HUBER, Christoffel
Swiss, 16th century.
Active in Lucerne at the end of the 16th century.
Sculptor (wood).

HUBER, Conrad
German, 18th - 19th century.
Born 24 November 1752, in Altendorf-Weingarten; died 17 May 1830, in Weissenhorn (near Ulm).
Painter.
A pupil of Brucker in Salmannsweiler (Salem in Baden) and then Kuen in Weissenhorn. After a successful spell at the academies of Karlsruhe and Stuttgart, he went to Italy, then returned to settle in Weissenhorn. He was above all a fresco painter, and decorated a large number of churches including those in Weissenstein, Schiessen and Aufgheim.
Auction records:
Milan, 19 Oct 1993, *David and Bathsheba* (1815, oil on canvas, 23¼ x 19 ins / 59 x 48 cm) ITL 5,060,000. Paris, 30 Oct 1996, *Jacob and Rachel at the Well* (1808, canvas, 20½ x 28 ins / 52 x 71 cm) FRF 27,000. Kempten, 8 April 1999, *Virgin Mary's Assumption* (oil on canvas, 15 x 11 ins / 37 x 28 cm) DEM 4,600. Stuttgart, 8 Dec 2000, *Portrait of St Paul. Portrait of St Peter* (oil on canvas, 13 x 9 ins / 32 x 24 cm) DEM 4,500. Kempten, 10 July 2003, *The Last Supper* (1825, oil on canvas, 27 x 35 ins / 69 x 89 cm) EUR 3,700. Stuttgart, 25 Sept 2003, *Jacob and Rachel* (1810, oil on canvas, 20 x 28 ins / 52 x 70 cm) EUR 5,500.

HUBER, Eduard
Austrian, 19th century.
Active in Vienna.
Painter.

HUBER, Emil
Swiss, 19th century.
Born 24 April 1858, in Lucerne; died 25 July 1896, in Sarnen (near Lucerne).
Sculptor.
He was a pupil of Amlehn.

HUBER, Ernst
Austrian, 20th century.
Born 15 July 1895, in Vienna; died 1960 or 1961, in Vienna.
Painter, engraver, illustrator. Mythological subjects, genre scenes.

Huber was initially a lithographer and ornament designer, but gradually began to produce paintings of mythological subjects and genre scenes.

AUCTION RECORDS:
VIENNA, 17 March 1976, *Harvest Scene* (1933, oil on canvas, 23 1/2 x 28 3/4 ins / 60 x 73 cm) ATS 18,000. MUNICH, 31 May 1979, *Cagnes* (1929, oil on canvas, 28 3/4 x 23 1/2 ins / 73 x 60 cm) DEM 2,000. VIENNA, 18 April 1980, *Salzburg* (watercolour, 18 x 23 1/2 ins / 45.5 x 59.5 cm) ATS 14,000. VIENNA, 4 Dec 1984, *Winter Landscape with Figures* (1923, oil on canvas, 29 1/2 x 35 3/4 ins / 75 x 91 cm) ATS 100,000. VIENNA, 19 March 1985, *Still-life with a Bouquet of Flowers* (mixed media/card, 25 1/2 x 21 1/4 ins / 65 x 54 cm) ATS 22,000. VIENNA, 3 Dec 1986, *Summer Landscape* (oil on canvas, 21 1/4 x 25 1/2 ins / 54 x 65 cm) ATS 40,000. MUNICH, 3 Dec 1996, *Wagram in Winter* (watercolour heightened with white/paper, 8 x 11 1/4 ins / 20.5 x 28.5 cm) DEM 5,040. MUNICH, 23 June 1997, *Draga in Istria* (1956, oil/synthetic fibres, 23 1/2 x 28 3/4 ins / 60 x 73 cm) DEM 12,000. VIENNA, 26 Jan 1999, *Donau Canal with Stephanskirche in Winter* (1959, oil on canvas, 32 x 41 ins / 82 x 105 cm) ATS 65,000. VIENNA, 3 Nov 1999, *Celebration in the Forest* (oil on panel, 23 x 17 ins / 58 x 43 cm) ATS 50,000. MUNICH, 18 May 2000, *Small Town in Winter* (1927, oil on canvas on board, 37 x 43 ins / 95 x 110 cm) DEM 32,000. VIENNA, 25 May 2000, *Rocky Landscape with Road* (1923, oil on canvas, 19 x 28 ins / 48 x 70 cm) ATS 180,000. BERN, 9 May 2001, *Village with Figures in Hilly Landscape* (oil on canvas on board, 12 x 16 ins / 30 x 40 cm) CHF 10,000. BERN, 9 May 2001, *Village on Rise* (oil on canvas, 24 x 31 ins / 60 x 80 cm) CHF 13,000. VIENNA, 14 May 2002, *Woodland Stream in Early Spring, Wagrain* (1947, oil on canvas, 29 x 39 ins / 73 x 100 cm) EUR 12,000. VIENNA, 11 June 2002, *Donau with Kahlenberg* (oil on canvas, 50 x 35 ins / 126 x 89 cm) EUR 12,000. VIENNA, 27 May 2003, *Village in Lower Austria* (oil on canvas, 24 x 31 ins / 60 x 80 cm) EUR 9,500. VIENNA, 27 May 2003, *Bunch of Flowers* (oil on canvas, 24 x 20 ins / 60 x 50 cm) EUR 12,000. VIENNA, 21 April 2004, *South Seas* (1925, oil on board, 22 x 29 ins / 56 x 73 cm) EUR 13,000. VIENNA, 12 Oct 2004, *Puchberg am Schneeberg in Winter* (oil on canvas, 31 x 39 ins / 78 x 100 cm) EUR 15,000.

HUBER, Franz Michael
Austrian, 18th century.
Died 22 May 1746, in Innsbruck.
Painter, fresco artist. History painting.

He was court painter to Karl Philipp in Innsbruck (Grandy Duchy of Tyrol), and worked on the decoration of the palace there.

HUBER, Franz Xaver
Dutch, 18th century.
Born 1755, in Eischtatt.
Engraver (burin).

HUBER, Hans
Swiss, 16th century.
Died 1598, in Bern.
Glass painter.

HUBER, Hans
German, 19th century.
Born 19th century, in Salzburg; died in Salzburg.
Landscape artist.

He settled in Munich.

HUBER, Hermann
Swiss, 20th century.
Born 13 September 1888, in Zurich; died 1968, in Sihlbrugg.
Painter, engraver. Figure compositions, figures, genre scenes.

Huber studied in Germany and then spent time in Rome, Paris and Algeria. He was quite strongly influenced by Hodler.

AUCTION RECORDS:
ZURICH, 8 March 1974, *Rider* (1936) CHF 3,000. ZURICH, 12 Nov 1976, *In the Garden* (oil on canvas, 29 1/2 x 25 1/4 ins / 75 x 64 cm) CHF 3,800. ZURICH, 20 May 1977, *Sihlbrugg* (oil on canvas, 32 x 39 1/4 ins / 81 x 100 cm) CHF 3,000. BERN, 20 June 1979, *Three Young Girls in a Landscape* (c. 1920, oil on canvas, 32 3/4 x 72 ins / 83 x 182 cm) CHF 2,000. ZURICH, 16 April 1986, *Im Schooren (Kilchberg)* (oil on panel, 27 1/2 x 35 1/2 ins / 70 x 90 cm) CHF 5,200. ZURICH, 6 June 1986, *View of Zurich* (1930, pen, 19 x 25 1/2 ins / 48 x 64.5 cm) CHF 4,000. ZURICH, 22 May 1987, *Sons of the Artist with Friends in a Wood* (oil on canvas, 39 1/4 x 55 ins / 100 x 140 cm) CHF 6,000. LUCERNE, 3 Dec 1988, *Girls and Boys in a Wooded Landscape with Rabbits* (oil on canvas, 23 1/2 x 29 1/2 ins / 60 x 75 cm) CHF 1,600. ZURICH, 22 June 1990, *Women Bathing* (oil on canvas, 19 3/4 x 20 3/4 ins / 50 x 53 cm) CHF 1,500. ZURICH, 24 Nov 1993, *Torrent in the Woods* (oil on canvas, 33 3/4 x 23 ins / 86 x 57.5 cm) CHF 8,050. ZURICH, 23 June 1995, *Four Children on a Low Wall* (oil on canvas, 37 1/2 x 50 3/4 ins / 95 x 129 cm) CHF 2,600. ZURICH, 3 April 1996, *Morning* (1910, oil on canvas, 39 3/4 x 34 3/4 ins / 101 x 88.5 cm) CHF 9,500. ZURICH, 5 June 1996, *Mountain Landscape* (1912, oil on canvas, 25 1/4 x 19 ins / 64 x 48 cm) CHF 6,900. ZURICH, 12 Nov 1996, *Three Graces* (oil on canvas, 50 x 59 1/4 ins / 127 x 150.5 cm) CHF 2,800. ZURICH, 10 Dec 1996, *Stream Bed near Grächen* (oil on canvas, 30 3/4 x 20 ins / 78 x 51 cm) CHF 10,350. ZURICH, 19 Nov 1997, *Composition* (oil on canvas, 37 1/2 x 28 ins / 95 x 71 cm) CHF 700. ZURICH, 15 June 1999, *Figurative Composition with Dog* (oil on canvas, 35 x 39 ins / 89 x 100 cm) CHF 2,600. ZURICH, 13 Nov 2001, *The Morning* (1910, oil on canvas, 40 x 35 ins / 101 x 88 cm) CHF 6,500. ZURICH, 3 Dec 2001, *Jagerhaus Sihlbrugg* (oil on canvas, 28 x 35 ins / 71 x 90 cm) CHF 5,000. ZURICH, 25 March 2002, *Portrait of Reinhold Kundig* (c. 1916-1917, oil on canvas, 11 x 9 ins / 28 x 23 cm) CHF 5,200. ZURICH, 3 June 2002, *Bunch of Flowers* (1966, oil on canvas, 39 x 32 ins / 100 x 81 cm) CHF 3,600. ST GALL, 24 Oct 2003, *Early Spring Landscape* (oil on canvas, 22 x 19 ins / 55 x 48 cm) CHF 3,600. ZURICH, 25 Nov 2003, *Landscape* (oil on canvas, 39 x 23 ins / 100 x 58 cm) CHF 4,200.

HUBER, Hugo
German, 19th - 20th century.
Born 7 November 1852, in Durbach; died 24 December 1913, in Munich.
Painter. History painting.

Huber was a student at the Munich academy.

HUBER, Jakob
Swiss, 16th - 17th century.
Born 1536, in Schaffhausen; died 1608, in Schaffhausen.
Painter.
Schaffhausen School.

HUBER, Jean, called Huber-Voltaire
Swiss, 18th century.
Born 13 January 1721, in Chambéry (France); died 1786, in Lausanne.
Painter, engraver.

He was intended for a military career, and was stationed for a while in Kassel. In 1751, he was in Turin, in the service of the Kingdom of Sardinia, and it was there he gave up his military career. In 1752, he is documented in Geneva, where he was a member of the city's Great Council and where two years later he met Voltaire, whose family deeds he would illustrate. He was also interested in aerostations and wrote works on this subject and the flight of birds.

MUSEUMS AND GALLERIES:

GENEVA (MAH): *Hunting Scene; Horses by the River* - GENEVA (Mus. Ariana): *Landscape and Animals.*

AUCTION RECORDS:

ZURICH, 25 Nov 1977, *Hunting Scene*; oils on canvas, 23 1/4 x 28 3/4 ins / 59 x 73 cm) CHF 9,000. ZURICH, 17 June 2002, *Voltaire and the Peasants* (oil on panel, 12 x 8 ins / 31 x 21 cm) CHF 2,400.

HUBER, Jean Daniel

Swiss, 18th - 19th century.

Born 9 October 1754, in Geneva; died 31 January 1845.

Painter (gouache), watercolourist, engraver, draughtsman, lithographer. Genre scenes, hunting scenes, landscapes, waterscapes, animals.

The son of Jean Huber, he was a forerunner of the naturalistic rural landscape which became popular in Switzerland in the mid-19th century. A retrospective exhibition was devoted to him at the Musée d'Art et d'Histoire in Geneva in 1983. His engravings mostly feature animals.

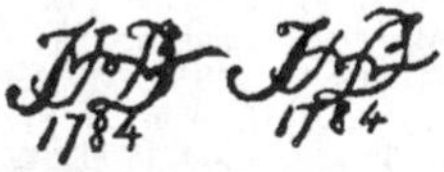

MUSEUMS AND GALLERIES:

GENEVA (MAH): *Banks of a River; Market Day.*

AUCTION RECORDS:

LUCERNE, 18 June 1971, *River Landscape,* CHF 7,500. LUCERNE, 29 June 1973, *Landscape,* CHF 10,000. BERN, 25 Nov 1976, *Pastorale* (oil on canvas, 23 1/2 x 19 3/4 ins / 60 x 50 cm) CHF 1,900. LUCERNE, 30 May 1979, *Alpine Landscape* (oil on canvas, 42 1/2 x 67 1/4 ins / 108 x 170.5 cm) CHF 9,000. ZURICH, 8 Dec 1999, *Cascade* (oil on canvas, 39 x 53 ins / 100 x 135 cm) CHF 7,000. LUCERNE, 2 May 2001, *Milking in Bernese Oberland* (oil on canvas, 30 x 41 ins / 76 x 105 cm) CHF 8,000. ZURICH, 28 Nov 2002, *Shore of Lake Geneva with Figures and Animals* (oil on canvas, 33 x 39 ins / 83 x 100 cm) CHF 8,500.

HUBER, Johann

Austrian, 18th century.

Active in Innsbruck.

Sculptor.

He was a pupil of Balthasar Moll.

HUBER, Johann Baptist

Austrian, 17th century.

Born in Neustift, near Brixen, South Tyrol (now Bressanone, Italy); died 1690.

Painter. History painting, architectural views.

He worked in Rome, then returned to Neustift, where he did numerous paintings at the theatre in Brixen (Bressanone), South Tyrol and the monastery of Neustift.

HUBER, Johann Heinrich

Swiss, 18th century.

Born 1677, in Zurich; died 1712.

Engraver.

He worked in Vienna.

HUBER, Johann Joseph, known as Joseph

German, 18th - 19th century.

Born 22 July 1737, in Augsburg; died 26 October 1815, in Augsburg.

Painter, fresco artist, engraver. Mythological subjects.

He was a pupil of Bergmuller and G. B. Götz. In 1784, he was elected director of the academy in Augsburg. He did a large number of frescoes, notably in various churches in Augsburg, Oberhausen and Kobel. As an engraver, his preference was for etchings.

AUCTION RECORDS:

LONDON, 11 March 1993, *Samson and Delilah; The Death of Samson* (a pair, 39 x 56 1/4 ins / 99 x 143.. cm 3 1/4 ins/8 cm) GBP 8,050.

HUBER, Johann Kaspar

Swiss, 18th - 19th century.

Born 1752, in Glattfelden, near Zurich; died 17 April 1827, near Zurich.

Painter, watercolourist, engraver. Landscapes, seascapes.

He was a pupil of F. Zimmermann. He worked in Basel, Strasbourg, Frankfurt and finally Amsterdam, where he remained four years. Subsequently he moved on to Düsseldorf, where he was admitted to membership of the academy. He returned to Switzerland only in 1789. He produced etchings.

MUSEUMS AND GALLERIES:

BASEL: *Seascape* - BERN: *Rural Idyll* - STUTTGART: *View of Koblenz.*

AUCTION RECORDS:

LONDON, April 1924, *Landscape with Little Houses and Figures beside a River,* GBP 4. LUCERNE, 15 Nov 1974, *Romantic Landscape* (1792) CHF 3,200. BERN, 25 Nov 1976, *Pastorale* (oil on canvas, 40 1/2 x 50 1/2 ins / 103 x 128 cm) CHF 7,000. ZURICH, 16 May 1980, *Landscape with Stone Bridge and Travellers* (1795, oil on canvas, 26 1/4 x 33 3/4 ins / 66.5 x 86 cm) CHF 10,000. ZURICH, 14 May 1982, *Landscape with Waterfall* (1784, oil on canvas, 23 1/2 x 32 ins / 60 x 81 cm) CHF 13,000. ZURICH, 25 May 1984, *Vessel in Difficulty off a Shore with Cliffs* (oil on panel, 10 x 16 1/4 ins / 25.5 x 41.5 cm) CHF 9,000. LUCERNE, 23 May 1985, *River Landscape with Figures* (oil on canvas, two pendants, 32 x 65 1/4 ins / 81.5 x 166 cm) CHF 22,000. HEIDELBERG, 3 April 1993, *Wooded Landscape in Switzerland* (watercolour, 11 3/4 x 17 1/4 ins / 30 x 44.1 cm) DEM 1,800.

HUBER, Johann Nepomuk

Austrian, 19th century.

Born 14 May 1802, near Innsbruck; died 24 May 1885, in Innsbruck.

Painter. Religious subjects, portraits.

He trained at the academy in Munich.

MUSEUMS AND GALLERIES:

INNSBRUCK: *Pietà.*

AUCTION RECORDS:

AMSTERDAM, 18 June 1997, *Portrait of Two Young Ladies Holding a Letter* (1840, oil on canvas, 35 x 28 1/4 ins / 89 x 71.5 cm) NLG 10,378.

HUBER, Johann Rudolph, the Elder

Swiss, 17th - 18th century.

Born 1668, in Basel; died 28 February 1748, in Basel.

Painter. Historical subjects, portraits.

The son of Alexis Huber, he studied with Kaspar Mayer and Joseph Werner, with whom he went to Italy, visiting Mantua, Venice and Rome and remaining in the latter for six years. Subsequently he moved to France, returning to Switzerland in 1693 and settling in Basel. He was successively painter to the Margrave of Baden-Durlach, then the Duke of Württemberg, who invited him to Stuttgart in 1696. He is credited with over 3,000 portraits. His prodigious facility earned him the nickname of the Swiss Tintoretto.

MUSEUMS AND GALLERIES:

BASEL: *Two Portraits of Dr Franz Platter; Mayor Emmanuel Socin; Portrait of a Painter; Portrait of the Artist* - BERN: *Portraits of J A Tillier and J H Steiger* - VERSAILLES: *Congress of Rastatt, 1714.*

AUCTION RECORDS:

ZURICH, 25 May 1979, *Portrait of Daniel Tschiffeli* (1705, oil on canvas, oval, 28 1/4 x 23 1/4 ins / 72 x 59 cm) CHF 5,000. BERN, 19 Nov 1984, *Portrait of F L Fischer* (oil on canvas, 35 x 28 1/4 ins / 88 x 72 cm) CHF 5,300. ZURICH, 22 Sept 2000, *Portrait of Michael Freudenreich* (1723, oil on canvas, 33 x 25 ins / 83 x 64 cm) CHF 3,000. ZURICH, 22 Sept 2000, *Portrait of Ursula von Freudenreich* (1723, oil on canvas, 33 x 25 ins / 83 x 64 cm) CHF 4,000. BERN, 13 May 2004, *Portrait of Man as Hunter* (1719, oil on canvas, 31 x 26 ins / 80 x 65 cm) CHF 2,400.

HUBER, Johann Rudolph, the Younger
Swiss, 18th century.
Died 1779.
Active in Basel.
Painter.

MUSEUMS AND GALLERIES:
BASEL (Kunstmus.): two portraits.

HUBER, Johann Rudolph
Swiss, 18th century.
Born 12 February 1766, in Basel; died 1806, in Basel.
Engraver.

HUBER, Jörg
German, 15th century.
Born in Passau (Bavaria).
Sculptor.

Jörg Huber was working in Cracow around 1500, including on the decoration of the cathedral.

HUBER, Josef
Austrian, 18th century.
Born 1730, in Imst (Tyrol); died 1772, in Imst.
Painter.

He trained initially with his father, then under a Salzburg painter, finally going to Rome. He returned to Prague to study under Bradel. He had a difficult relationship with his father who was likewise a painter.

HUBER, Joseph Ignaz
German, 18th century.
Born 16 April 1759, in Augsburg.
Draughtsman, engraver (burin).

The son of Johann Joseph Huber, he was a pupil of Nilson in Augsburg, then of Wille in Paris.

HUBER, Jozsef
Hungarian, 19th century.
Born 27 April 1777, in Porsony.
Sculptor.

Jozsef Huber studied with Franz Reindl in Vienna.

HUBER, Karl Georg
German, 20th century.
Born 13 February 1872, in Munich.
Sculptor.

HUBER, Léon Charles
French, 19th - 20th century.
Born 11 January 1858, in Paris; died 25 August 1928, in Paris.
Painter. Animals, cats, still-lifes.

Léon Charles Huber, who specialised in painting cats, was a student at the École des Beaux-Arts in Dawant and of Jules Grün. He received a mention in 1903.

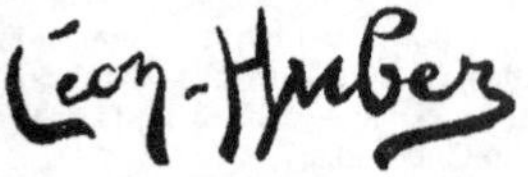

AUCTION RECORDS:
PARIS, 15-16 June 1923, *Cats Playing with a Ball*, FRF 400; *Basket of Peaches and Plums*, FRF 400; *Play*, FRF 400. PARIS, 20 Dec 1934, *Apples and Grapes*, FRF 650. PARIS, 23 Dec 1943, *Cat and Basket of Flowers*, FRF 1,250. PARIS, July 1946, *Two Young Cats Beside a Stand of Roses*, FRF 3,890; *Cats* (four canvases) FRF 1350-3200. LONDON, 27 Sept 1946, *Little Cats*, GBP 105. PARIS, 21 Oct 1946, *Reflections* (1914) FRF 5,000. PARIS, 10 Dec 1946, *Young Cats Playing*, FRF 5,000; *Young Cats and Aquarium*, FRF 6,250. PARIS, 21-22 Dec 1953, *Still-lifes with Game* (two pendants) FRF 14,000. VIENNA, 16 Oct 1973, *Cat* (1908) ATS 9,000. LUCERNE, 26 June 1976, *Cat and Kittens* (oil on panel, 16 1/2 x 23 1/2 ins / 42 x 60 cm) CHF 2,400. VERSAILLES, 11 Dec 1977, *Cats* (1926, oil on canvas, 25 1/4 x 17 3/4 ins / 64 x 45 cm) FRF 5,000. PARIS, 3 July 1979, *Young Cats* (oil on canvas, 16 1/2 x 13 ins / 42 x 33 cm) FRF 6,100. NEW YORK, 28 Oct 1982, *Kittens* (1907, oil on canvas, 15 1/2 x 18 1/2 ins / 39.5 x 47 cm) USD 6,500. LONDON, 8 Feb 1985, *Interior with Kittens Playing* (oil on canvas, 17 1/2 x 21 1/4 ins / 44.5 x 54 cm) GBP 7,000. NEW YORK, 29 Oct 1987, *Kittens Playing with Flowers* (oil on canvas, 21 1/2 x 25 3/4 ins / 54.6 x 65.3 cm) USD 14,000. LONDON, 26 Feb 1988, *Kitten* (oil on panel, 12 x 9 1/2 ins / 30.5 x 24.1 cm) GBP 990. VERSAILLES, 17 April 1988, *Kittens Near the Hearth* (oil on canvas, 15 x 18 ins / 38 x 46 cm) FRF 5,600. BERN, 26 Oct 1988, *Still-life with Grapes and Plums in a Wicker Basket* (oil on panel, 9 1/2 x 13 ins / 24 x 33 cm) CHF 4,200. PARIS, 21 Nov 1988, *Interior with Kittens and Parrot* (oil on canvas, 22 x 18 ins / 55 x 46 cm) FRF 22,000. NEW YORK, 23 Feb 1989, *Kittens Gambolling Around a Brass Bucket* (1914, oil on canvas, 32 x 25 3/4 ins / 81.5 x 65.4 cm) USD 17,600. LONDON, 6 Oct 1989, *Kittens' Game* (oil on canvas, 15 x 18 ins / 38 x 46 cm) GBP 8,580. AMSTERDAM, 2 May 1990, *Young Cats* (oil on canvas, 10 3/4 x 16 1/4 ins / 27.5 x 41.5 cm) NLG 18,975. MONTREAL, 4 June 1991, *Kittens with a Brass Pot* (1917, oil on canvas, 20 3/4 x 25 1/2 ins / 53 x 65 cm) CAD 5,500. LONDON, 16 July 1991, *Cat and Her Young Waiting for Their Mash* (oil on canvas, 15 x 21 1/2 ins / 38.1 x 54.5 cm) GBP 2,860. PARIS, 26 June 1992, *Kittens with Mimosas and Violets* (oil on canvas, 15 1/4 x 21 3/4 ins / 39 x 55.5 cm) FRF 20,000. NEW YORK, 29 Oct 1992, *Young Cat Playing with an Upset Basket of Flowers* (oil on canvas, 14 1/2 x 28 1/2 ins / 36.9 x 72.5 cm) USD 3,850. NEW YORK, 20 Jan 1993, *Still-life with Peaches in a Basket* (oil on canvas, 14 3/4 x 17 3/4 ins / 37.5 x 45.1 cm) USD 2,070. LONDON, 17 Nov 1993, *Waiting to Scratch* (oil on canvas, 19 x 25 1/4 ins / 48 x 64 cm) GBP 14,375. PARIS, 6 Dec 1993, *Still-life with Fruit* (oil on canvas, 14 1/2 x 17 1/2 ins / 37 x 44.5 cm) FRF 5,500. NEW YORK, 16 Feb 1995, *Spying Kittens* (oil on canvas, 27 1/2 x 45 1/4 ins / 69.9 x 114.9 cm) USD 9,200. LONDON, 12 June 1996, *New Basket of Cats* (1901, oil on canvas, 15 x 17 3/4 ins / 38 x 45 cm) GBP 2,530. PARIS, 8 Dec 1996, *Young Kittens* (oil on canvas, 15 x 18 ins / 38 x 46 cm) FRF 11,100. PARIS, 27 Oct 1997, *Kittens Playing* (1926, oil on canvas, 18 x 15 ins / 46 x 38 cm) FRF 10,000. PARIS, 5 Dec 1997, *Coco and Folette (Monkey Playing with a Brass Plate)* (1889, oil on canvas, 35 x 51 1/4 ins / 89 x 130 cm) FRF 21,000.

HUBER, Louis Édouard
French, 19th century.
Painter.

Huber exhibited at the Salon between 1842 and 1853.

HUBER, Max
German, 19th century.
Born 1824, in Munich; died 21 July 1877, in Munich.
Painter.

He was principally a fresco painter, and illustrated religious subjects.

HUBER, Max
Swiss, 20th century.
Born 1919, in Baar.
Painter, draughtsman, lithographer.
Neo-Constructivism.

Max Huber lives and works in Sagno. He was a student in Zurich and at the Accademia de Belle Arti in Milan. From 1944 to 1947 he was a member of the Modern Swiss Artists' Association Allianz (Alliance) and professor of graphics at the Scuola Rinascita in Milan. From 1949 to 1952, he was a member of MAC (the Movimento Arte Concreta). He was professor of graphics at the Scuola Umanitaria in Milan from 1959 to 1962; professor of graphics at the Scuola Politecnica di Design in Milan from 1971 to 1977; and professor of design and typography at the industrial art centre in Lugano from 1979 to 1984. He was principally a graphic artist and produced black and white designs of a rigorous, flat geometrical construction.

His work was shown from 1942 onwards at collective exhibitions of *art concret* (especially with the groups of which he was a member), in Zurich, Basel, Milan, Turin and Bologna; the second exhibition of the Salon des Réalités Nouvelles in Paris (1948); the Swiss *art concret* graphics exhibition at the University of Austin, Texas (1975); at the exhibition *Constructed Art 1915-1945* at the Winterthur Museum (1987); and at the *Art and Science* exhibition at the Venice Biennale (1987). There have also been solo exhibitions, in Tokyo (1965); regularly at the Suzanne Bollag Gallery in Zurich (since 1975); Milan (1980 and 1987); Como (1981, 1984 and 1987); Cadaquès (1986), and elsewhere.

MUSEUMS AND GALLERIES:

AUSTIN (Jack S. Blanton MA, University of Texas): two lithographs from 'Arte Concreta' (1949); *Due Gruppi (Two Groups)* (1973, silk screen print) - ZURICH (Kunsthaus).

HUBER, Max Emanuel

Swiss, 20th century.
Born 1903, in Bern; died 1987.
Painter.

AUCTION RECORDS:

BERN, 12 May 1990, *Reclining Female Nude* (1945, oil on canvas, 15¾ x 21¼ ins / 40 x 54 cm) CHF 1,000.

HUBER, Patriz

German, 20th century.
Born 19 March 1878, in Stuttgart; died 20 September 1902, in Berlin.
Architect, interior designer, designer. Designs for furniture, objets d'art, jewels, silverware and fabrics.
Jugendstil.
Darmstadt Artists' Colony.

Patriz Huber's father was a teacher at the Kunstgewerbeschule in Mainz, and Patriz was taught by him. With the intention of becoming a painter, he moved to Munich, where he studied interior architecture and decorative arts. He achieved a high reputation for his models and his alphabets, which were published by Alexander Koch, and this enabled him to work for the Artists' Colony of Mathildenhöhe in Darmstadt from 1899 to 1902, where he did decorative work and designed furniture. He then opened his own studio in Berlin in 1902. With his brother, Anton, an architect, he was commissioned to work on a private housing estate near Posen (now Poznan). He took his own life at the age of 24.

He designed the interiors of the homes of Ludwig Habich and the furniture maker Julius Glückert. He designed models of jewellery, which were later made in Theodore Fahrner's factory in Pforzheim, the centre of the jewellery industry between 1900 and 1930. His style is characterised by spiral ornamentation but is simple and precise in conception.

BIBLIOGRAPHY:

Umelecka Kolonie Darmstadt, 1899-1914, exhibition catalogue, Narodni Galerie, Prague, 1989. Ulmer, Renate, *Patriz Huber: ein Mitglied der Darmstädter Künstlerkolonie*, exhibition catalogue, Institut Mathildenhöhe, Darmstadt, 1992.

MUSEUMS AND GALLERIES:

DARMSTADT (Hessiches Landesmuseum): *Fabric* (1902) - KARLSRUHE (Badisches Landesmus.): *Gürtelschliesse (Belt Buckle)* (1900) - PFORZHEIM (Schmuckmuseum): *Brooch* (c. 1900) - STUTTGART (Landesmuseum): *Pendant* (c. 1900-1901).

HUBER, Paul

German, 20th century.
Born 25 February 1871, in Stuttgart.
Painter.

Genre scenes and landscapes by Huber were exhibited in Munich.

HUBER, Rudolf

Swiss, 18th - 19th century.
Born 1770, in Basel; died 1844, in Basel.
Painter, engraver.

He lived in Odessa and St Petersburg for a long time, then in Strasbourg.

HUBER, Rudolf Carl S.

Austrian, 19th century.
Born 15 August 1839, in Schleinz; died 22 August 1896, in Vienna.
Painter. Landscapes, animals.

He was a student at the academy in Vienna, where he later joined the staff. He exhibited mainly in Vienna, but was awarded a medal in Munich in 1883.

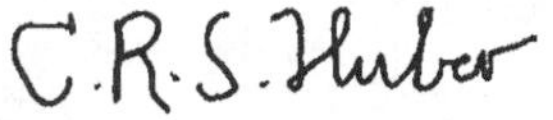

MUSEUMS AND GALLERIES:

VIENNA: *Archduke Rudolph Hunting Bears in Munkács (Mukacseve).*

AUCTION RECORDS:

COPENHAGEN, 19 Nov 1974, *Livestock at the Trough* (1887) DKK 18,000. VIENNA, 18 May 1976, *Landscape* (oil on canvas, 15¼ x 20 ins / 39 x 50.5 cm) ATS 10,000. VIENNA, 14 Nov 1978, *Stags Drinking* (1863, oil on canvas, 13½ x 18¾ ins / 34.5 x 47.5 cm) ATS 25,000. VIENNA, 10 Sept 1986, *Pair of Peasants Seated Beneath a Tree* (1892, oil on canvas, 24½ x 30¾ ins / 62 x 78 cm) ATS 60,000. VIENNA, 20 May 1999, *Shepherd with his Flock in Heath Landscape* (1863, oil on canvas, 10 x 20 ins / 25 x 50 cm) ATS 40,000. DÜSSELDORF, 31 Jan 2000, *Furstin Salm Riding Lipizzaner* (oil on panel, 22 x 17 ins / 56 x 44 cm) DEM 10,000. LONDON, 17 Oct 2001, *Kamele in der wuste - Camels in the Desert* (1876, oil on canvas, 37 x 26 ins / 94 x 67 cm) GBP 6,000. COLOGNE, 1 April 2004, *Hunting Dogs* (oil on canvas, 25 x 31 ins / 64 x 79 cm) EUR 8,500.

HUBER, Stephan

German, 20th - 21st century.
Born 1952, in Lindenberg/Allgäu.
Sculptor, installation artist, video artist.

Stephan Huber studied at the Akademie der Bildenden Künste in Munich from 1971 to 1978 and on a bursary at the PS1 in New York in 1980-1981. He lives and works in Munich. He was appointed professor at the Akademie der Bildenden Künste in Munich in 2004. He has won a number of prizes, including the Karl Hofer prize in Berlin in 1985. He is mainly known for his architectural reconstitutions of living spaces and places that have left a mark on his memory. His installations are autobiographical and invite the viewer to the thresholds of doors or windows, smaller than life size, behind which he portrays sometimes harrowing situations, deformed spaces such as *Ich liebe dich (I Love You)*, 1983, or sculptures like *Arbeiten im Reichtum (Working in Wealth)*, also from 1983.

He appeared on the international art scene in the 1980s, and has participated in many group exhibitions, such as Documenta in Kassel in 1987 and the Venice Biennale in 1999. He also shows in solo exhibitions. These have included *Das Spielzimmer (The Playroom)* at the Bonn Kunstverein in 1984, a joint exhibition with Raimund Kummer at the Hamburg Kunsthalle in 1991, and exhibitions in 2001 at the Hanover Kunstverein and 2002 at the Museum der Bildenden Künste in Leipzig and the Städtische Galerie im Lenbachhaus in Munich.

BIBLIOGRAPHY:

Bauplatz, exhibition catalogue, Kunsthalle, Mannheim, 1994 (interview with Jochen Kronjäger). Schmidt-Wulffen,

Stephan, *Stephan Huber, In-situ-Projekte: Kunst im Dialog mit ihrem Ort*, Prestel, Munich, 1998. *Stephan Huber*, exhibition catalogue, Kunstverein, Hanover, 2001.

HUBER, Thomas

German, 18th century.

Born 26 December 1700, in Rheinfels; died 1779, in Berlin.

Painter. History painting, portraits, animals, landscapes, decorative motifs (chinoiseries).

He trained at the academy in Berlin and under Georg Liszewski. He worked for the palace of Sanssouci from drawings by Le Sueur and was court painter in Berlin. He specialised in chinoiseries.

BIBLIOGRAPHY:

Huber, Thomas, *Die Urgeschichte der Bilder [The Prehistory of Paintings]*, exhibition catalogue, Museum für Gegenwartskunst, Basel, 1987.

AUCTION RECORDS:

AMSTERDAM, 2 May 1991, *Portrait of a Lady, Presumed to be Countess von Kavenhüller, Dressed in a Gown and Dark Red Velvet Hat and White Camisole* (oil on canvas, 25 3/4 x 21 1/2 ins / 65.5 x 54.3 cm) NLG 12,650. COLOGNE, 3 Dec 2002, *Stage* (watercolour over pencil, 28 x 45 ins / 71 x 114 cm) EUR 1,900. PARIS, 21 March 2003, *Old Man* (1741, oil on canvas, 15 x 12 ins / 37 x 31 cm) EUR 2,500.

HUBER, Thomas

Swiss, 20th - 21st century.

Born 1955, in Zurich.

Active in Germany.

Painter, draughtsman, watercolourist, installation artist.

Thomas Huber began studying at the Kunstgewerbeschule in Basel in 1977, continued at the Royal College of Art in London in 1979, and completed his studies at the Staatliche Kunstakademie in Düsseldorf from 1980 to 1983. He was a pupil of Joseph Beuys.

Thomas Huber's painting comes in a variety of simple, eclectic forms: landscapes in a style that borders on the naive, still-lifes or geometrical figures. He takes charge of the presentation of his works, commenting on them in writings or in lectures. His first three paintings gave rise to public presentations of this kind at the Kunstakademie in Düsseldorf, entitled *Rede über die Sintflut* (*Speech about the Flood*), *Rede zur Schöpfung* (*Speech about the Creation*) and *Rede in der Schule* (*Speech in School*). His 'speeches', which may be likened to performance art, describe the confrontation between the spectator, the work and the exhibition space, using well-orchestrated poetical rhetoric consisting of metaphors ornamented with symbolic objects. By doing this, in addition to the theatrical aspect, he attempts to situate the work in reality and define its limits. In his opinion, an artist must also think about the presentation of works of art, 'but I also think the viewer is an invention of the artist, there is no real viewer, only an image. And it is for this image that I paint.'

He has taken part in group exhibitions, including *Von Hier Aus* in Düsseldorf in 1984, *Skulptur Projekte* in Münster in 1987, *The Prehistory of Paintings* at the Museum für Gegenwartskunst in Basel in 1998, *Art et langage, années 80, œuvres choisies* (*Art and Language, the 1980s, Selected Works*) at the University of Rennes II in 1988, and in 2003, *L'état des choses* (*The State of Things*), a look at the status of the everyday object in contemporary art, presented on the occasion of *Trésors publics. 20 ans de création dans les Fonds régionaux d'art contemporain (FRAC)* (*Public Treasury, 20 Years of Creation in the Regional Collection of Contemporary Art (FRAC)*) at the Musée des Beaux-Arts in Nantes.

He has also exhibited in solo shows, including 1982, Galerie Rüdiger Schöttle, Munich; 1984, Galerie Philomène Maggers, Bonn; 1985, *Tout et bien plus encore: l'ABC poétique* (*Everything And a Lot More Besides: The Poetic ABC*) at the Kunsthalle in Bern; 1989, Musée d'Art Moderne, Strasbourg; 1989, Centre Georges Pompidou, contemporary galleries, Paris; 1997, Musée des Beaux-Arts, Lausanne; 1997, La Criée and the Galerie du TNB in Rennes; 2002 FRAC Franche-Comté, Musée des Beaux-Arts, Dole; and 2003, *Thomas Huber: Sonnez les Matines* at the Musée Départemental d'Art Contemporain, Rochechouart.

BIBLIOGRAPHY:

Poinsot, Jean-Marc, '*Le Colloque pictural de Thomas Huber*' in *Art Press*, periodical, Paris, 1988. Bordaz, Jean-Pierre, '*Thomas Huber*' in *Cnac magazine*, periodical, Éd. du Centre Georges-Pompidou, Paris, November 1988. '*Thomas Huber le rêve de Jacob*' in *Art Press* n° 224, periodical, Paris, May 1997. Zahm, Olivier (preface), et al., *Trésors publics, 20 ans de création dans les Fonds régionaux d'art contemporain*, Flammarion, Paris, 2003 (text in French and English).

MUSEUMS AND GALLERIES:

CHÂTEAUGIRON (FRAC Bretagne): *Wohnatelier* (*Living Studio*) (1994); *Das Bilderlager II* (*The Picture Store II*) (1989-1993); *The Reserve* (1989-1993, wooden shelf, 14 boxes and 5 ceramics) - METZ (FRAC Lorraine): *Das Wesen der Bilder* (*The Essence of Pictures*) (1993); *Preparatory Drawing for At Home with Us* (1994); *Preparatory Drawing for Sleep* (1994).

AUCTION RECORDS:

ZURICH, 30 Nov 1995, *1/2* (oil on canvas, 23 1/2 x 11 3/4 ins / 60 x 30 cm) CHF 5,980.

HUBER, Wilhelm

Swiss, 19th century.

Born 6 December 1787, in Düsseldorf; died 3 June 1871, in Zurich.

Painter, engraver (etching). Landscapes, waterscapes.

A pupil of his father, Johann Kaspar Huber.

AUCTION RECORDS:

NEW YORK, 25 Jan 1980, *The Naples Road* (1820, oil on canvas, 13 1/2 x 18 1/2 ins / 34 x 47 cm) USD 4,200. MONTE CARLO, 26 June 1983, *Road beside an Italian Lake* (1821, oil on canvas, 17 x 13 3/4 ins / 43 x 35 cm) FRF 30,000. ZURICH, 8 Dec 1999, *Italian Coastal Landscape with View of Rome* (1812, watercolour, two, 11 x 17 ins / 29 x 44 cm) CHF 16,000. ZURICH, 22 March 2002, *Eruption of Vesuvius* (1824, oil on canvas, 36 x 52 ins / 91 x 131 cm) CHF 32,000. ZURICH, 25 March 2002, *Italian Landscape with Town* (1808, oil on canvas, 23 x 28 ins / 58 x 72 cm) CHF 8,000. LONDON, 8 July 2003, *View of the Bay of Baia near Naples, Town of Pozzuoli Beyond* (1840, oil on canvas, 24 x 33 ins / 60 x 83 cm) GBP 6,800.

HUBER, Wolf

German, 16th century.

Born c. 1490, in Feldkirch; died June 1553, in Passau.

Painter, engraver (wood). Portraits, landscapes.

Danube School.

Wolf Huber was long thought to have been taught by Altdorfer. He engraved religious, mythological and genre subjects. He was one of the greatest of the German primitives, but little is known of him. In 1509 he was in Passau, where he became painter to the bishop's court and city architect. Between 1515 and 1521 in Feldkirch, probably his birthplace, he painted a retable for the confraternity of St Anne; fragments survive in Feldkirch and Vienna. Between 1529 and 1531 he travelled down the Danube, sketching landscapes as he went, so that he was just as much a 'master of the Danube School' as Altdorfer. This perception of nature is characteristic of German 16th-century painting and is also seen in Dürer's watercolours, in Grünewald, Baldung Grien and the Cranachs. Marcel Brion wrote that Huber 'could convey the panic terror of nature, sometimes so tranquil, sometimes seething with the excess of a cosmic sap incessantly welling up; this is why he is compared with Altdorfer, so long thought to have been his teacher'. These drawings were not filed and forgotten. In his *Portrait of the Humanist Jacob Ziegler*, for instance, the background landscape reveals a true sense of nature which is not present in much of the ornamental landscape painting of the time. But Huber did not limit himself to just landscapes. In one of his few surviving pieces, the Vienna *Crucifixion*, the strength of the bystanders' expressions and the Christ set almost in profile show why Huber has been so favourably compared with Altdorfer.

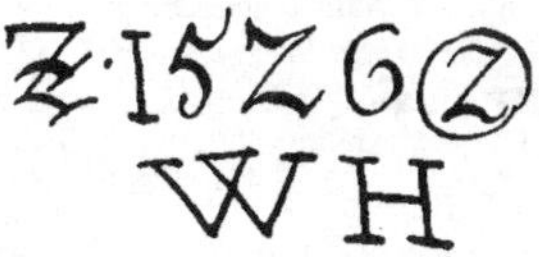

BIBLIOGRAPHY:
Voss, Hermann, *Albrecht Altdorfer und Wolf Huber*, Klinkhardt & Biermann, Leipzig, 1910. Buschbeck, Ernst H., *Primitifs autrichiens*, Éd. de la Connaissance, Brussels, 1937.

MUSEUMS AND GALLERIES:
CONSTANCE: *Camel Hunting* - DUBLIN: *Portrait of Antoine Hindertplund* - VIENNA (Kunsthistorisches Mus.): *Jakob Ziegler* (*Portrait of the Humanist Jacob Ziegler*); *Crucifixion*.

AUCTION RECORDS:
PARIS, 23 Jan 1928, *Rider Helping a Man on the Ground* (pen heightened with gouache) FRF 440. PARIS, 23 May 1928, *Watermill* (pen) FRF 2,700. LONDON, 10 May 1961, *A Camel* (pen and ink) GBP 300. LONDON, 27 March 1963, *Portrait of a Lady of Quality*, GBP 900. LONDON, 26 June 1969, *Full-length Study of a Peasant* (drawing) GBP 9,000. LONDON, 26 June 1970, *Portrait of a Man with a Short Beard*, Gns 5,500. MUNICH, 27 May 1977, *St George Fighting the Dragon* (1520, engraving/wood) DEM 1,700. LONDON, 20 June 1978, *Portrait of a Man in a Large Flat Hat* (1522, black, red and white chalk, 10¾ x 8½ ins / 27.6 x 21.5 cm) GBP 105,000. BERLIN, 24 Nov 2000, *Adoration of the Three Kings* (woodcut, 5 x 4 ins / 12 x 9 cm) DEM 9,000. LONDON, 6 July 2001, *Dream of Paris* (c. 1518, woodcut, 5 x 4 ins / 12 x 9 cm) GBP 6,500. NEW YORK, 5 Nov 2001, *Christ on the Cross* (c. 1517, woodcut, 5 x 4 ins / 13 x 9 cm) USD 3,400. BERLIN, 31 May 2002, *Crucifixion* (woodcut, 5 x 4 ins / 12 x 9 cm) EUR 6,500.

HUBER-FELDKIRCH, Josef
German, 19th century.
Born 16 March 1858, in Feldkirch (Baden).
Painter.

He trained in Munich, then Paris. He regularly exhibited in Munich, and taught the history of art at the academy in Düsseldorf.

HUBER-SULZEMOOS, Hans
German, 20th century.
Born 21 March 1873, in Sulzemoos.
Painter, illustrator. Religious subjects.

Huber-Sulzemoos was a student at the Munich academy. He specialised in religious painting.

HUBERLAND, Jeannette
French, 20th century.
Born 6 April 1904, in Aubergenville (Yvelines).
Painter. Landscapes.

Jeannette Huberland is known for her landscapes of Corsica.

HUBERT
French, 15th century.
Active in Roye (Somme).
Sculptor, designer of ornamental architectural features.

Hubert collaborated in 1448 on the decoration of the church of St-Pierre in Roye.

HUBERT
French, 18th century.
Active in Paris in 1725.
Painter.

Hubert decorated the chapel of the poorhouse in Bicêtre.

HUBERT
French, 18th century.
Active in Paris.
Sculptor.

Hubert sat on the board of the Académie de St-Luc. In 1752, 1753 and 1756 he exhibited mythological subjects in bronze or clay for this society.

HUBERT
French, 18th century.
Died in Paris.
Enameller, draughtsman. Portraits.

Hubert exhibited at the Salon de la Correspondance in 1779 a *Portrait of the Queen* and at the Exposition de la Jeunesse in 1788. It is conceivable that the *Portrait of Necker* kept in Poitiers museum and made around 1788 could be attributed to Hubert. He was reputed to capture a good likeness.

MUSEUMS AND GALLERIES:
POITIERS: *Portrait of Necker* (c. 1788).

HUBERT, Alain
French, 20th century.
Born 29 May 1942.
Painter. Figures, interiors with figures, urban landscapes.

Alain Hubert studied law and then specialised in town planning matters, taking a course at the Institut d'Urbanisme (School of Town Planning) in Paris in 1970. He was a self-taught painter. He was the main instigator of the plan to create a permanent contemporary art fair in Paris to bring together artists and collectors outside the usual circuit.

Hubert's painting takes a series of subjects from everyday life and through the composition and interpretation of his work makes them totally unusual. His work is distinguished by a restrained use of resources, both from the point of view of form that demands a meticulous structure, while any concern for detail is avoided, and the choice and use of clear tones that contribute to an almost unreal atmosphere. His solo exhibitions include: Galerie Helof, Paris, 1983; Galerie Nesle, Paris, 1985; *Le Coude Fou* restaurant, Paris, 1986; Espace Lucernaire, Paris, 1989; Association Espace des Fêtes, Paris, 1990 and *Le Reflet* restaurant, Paris, 1993.

HUBERT, Albert
Austrian, 20th century.
Born 1 December 1878, in Vienna.
Painter. Landscapes, still-lifes.

AUCTION RECORDS:
AMSTERDAM, 19 April 1994, *Still-life of Flowers* (1903, oil on canvas, 19¾ x 23¾ ins / 50 x 60.5 cm) NLG 1,265.

HUBERT, Alfred
Belgian, 19th century.
Born 1830, in Liège; died 1902, in Brussels.
Painter. Military subjects, genre scenes.

Alfred Hubert worked in Liège and Brussels. He also exhibited in Vienna and Dresden.

MUSEUMS AND GALLERIES:
BRUSSELS: *The Cuirassiers of Waterloo* - HELSINKI: *View of the Mountains of Italy* - LIÈGE: *Evening Battle*; *Stables of a Travelling Circus*; *Gypsy Horses*.

HUBERT, Edgar
British, 20th century.
Born 1907, in Billingshurst (Sussex); died 1985.
Painter.

Edgar Hubert, an abstract painter, took part in an exhibition of the work of British painters held at a major Parisian art gallery in 1947. Stylistically, his work is closer to some of Wasily Kandinsky's dramatically spontaneous paintings than to the rationally planned abstraction of Dutch and Italian painters of the time.

HUBERT, Édouard
French, 19th - 20th century.
Born 1834, in Romorantin; died 1923, in Paris.
Illustrator.
Édouard Hubert collaborated on the *Monde Illustré (Illustrated World)*.

HUBERT, Élisa
French, 19th century.
Painter, pastellist. Genre scenes.
Élisa Hubert's work was featured at the Salon in 1848 and 1849.

HUBERT, Ernest
Swiss, 20th century.
Born 1899, in Frauenfeld (Thurgau).
Painter.
Work by Hubert was exhibited in Paris, at the Salon des Indépendants, the Salon d'Automne, and the Salon des Tuileries, as well as at the 1937 Exposition Universelle.

HUBERT, F.
German, 19th century.
Active in Germany.
Painter. Landscapes.
MUSEUMS AND GALLERIES:
GLASGOW: *Clearing in a Forest*.

HUBERT, François
French, 18th century.
Born 2 February 1744, in Abbeville; died 14 February 1809, in Paris.
Engraver.
François Hubert studied under Beauvarlet. He engraved portraits, genre scenes and military uniforms.

HUBERT, G., called Thimothée
French, 17th century.
Painter.

HUBERT, H.L.
British, 19th century.
Active in London.
Sculptor.
Hubert exhibited in London at the Royal Academy between 1878 and 1889.

HUBERT, Hel.
French, 19th century.
Active in Paris in 1828.
Engraver (stippling).

HUBERT, Henri
French, 17th century.
Active in Lorraine.
Painter.

HUBERT, Honoré
French, 18th century.
Active in Paris in 1753.
Painter, sculptor.

HUBERT, Jean
French, 15th century.
Illuminator, copyist.
In 1464 Jean Hubert wrote *La Somme des Vices et des Vertus par Frère Laurent*, for Duchess Isabelle, daughter of the King of Scotland. The work is now in the Bibliothèque Nationale in Paris, and contains beautiful miniatures, probably the copyist's own work.

HUBERT, Jean
French, 16th century.
Active in Paris.
Miniaturist. Religious subjects.
Jean Hubert painted a large-scale *Life of the Virgin* which was given to Henry II in 1548. After appearing in the 1848 Paris exhibition, the painting was taken to the Bibliothèque Municipale in Rouen where it remains to this day
MUSEUMS AND GALLERIES:
ROUEN (Bibliothèque Municipale): *Life of the Virgin* (with 42 miniatures).

HUBERT, Jean
French, 17th - 18th century.
Active in Paris.
Painter.
Jean Hubert is known to have painted a *Portrait of John Law*.

HUBERT, Jean Jacques
French, 18th century.
Active in Paris from 1760 to 1793.
Engraver (burin).

HUBERT, Jean-Baptiste Louis
French, 19th century.
Born 15 October 1801, in Paris.
Painter, watercolourist, draughtsman. Landscapes.
Jean-Baptiste Hubert's work was regularly featured at the Paris Salon from 1819 to 1865, and he was awarded a second-class medal in 1831.

Hubert was exclusively a landscape painter, and found inspiration in Switzerland, the various regions of France and the province of Prussian Rhineland.
MUSEUMS AND GALLERIES:
BÉZIERS - LE HAVRE - LE PUY-EN-VELAY - PARIS (Louvre) - PERPIGNAN.
AUCTION RECORDS:
PARIS, 1868, *Pool* (drawing) FRF 100. PARIS, 10 Nov 1922, *Village Parade* (wash) FRF 300. PARIS, 4 Dec 1944, *Village Road* (watercolour) FRF 900. PARIS, 26 June 1991, *Landscape with a Hunter* (1833, watercolour, 10 3/4 x 14 1/4 ins / 27.6 x 36.2 cm) FRF 3,800.

HUBERT, Laurent
French, 18th century.
Died c. 1780.
Active in Paris.
Sculptor.

HUBERT, Léon
French, 20th century.
Born 3 July 1887, in Lille.
Painter. Portraits, landscapes.
AUCTION RECORDS:
LUCERNE, 13 Dec 1986, *Still-life with Fruit* (oil on canvas, 12 1/2 x 16 1/4 ins / 32 x 41 cm) CHF 4,000. NEW YORK, 26 Feb 1997, *A Dog's Life* (oil on canvas, 31 1/2 x 23 3/4 ins / 80 x 60.3 cm) USD 6,325. CALAIS, 14 March 1999, *Cat and Mouse* (oil on panel, 13 x 9 ins / 33 x 24 cm) FRF 11,000.

HUBERT, Marcel
Belgian, 20th century.
Born 1926, in Florennes near Namur; died 1976.
Painter, engraver.
Hubert was a student at the fine arts academy in Mons. He made burin and dry-point engravings.

HUBERT, Marie Gabriel
French, 19th century.
Born 23 March 1861, in Paris.
Painter. Landscapes.
Marie Gabriel was the father of Léon Hubert, and worked mostly in Lille (Nord).

HUBERT, Nicolas
French, 17th century.
Born in Dompaire; died 21 May 1689, in Orléans.
Sculptor.
Nicolas Hubert produced works for a number of private and religious buildings in his native city. Most noteworthy among those are: a cross at the Portereau Tudelle (one of the fortified gateways in Orléans); *Blessed Virgin Holding the Child Jesus* on the old bridge; a *Statue of St Francis of Paola* for the Minim brothers; a *Statue of St Bruno* for the Carthusian monks; and stone statues of the *Twelve Apostles* for the convent of the Visitation Sainte Marie.

HUBERT, Nicolas
French, 17th century.
Born 1660, in Paris.
Engraver.

HUBERT, Noël
French, 18th century.
Active in Paris in 1771.
Painter, sculptor.

HUBERT, Pierre
Belgian, 20th century.
Born 1940, in Tamines.
Painter.
Hubert was a student at the Académie Royale des Beaux Arts in Liège. In 1972, he was awarded the Young Painters' Prize in Belgium.

HUBERT, Pierre Alain
French, 20th century.
Born 5 June 1944, in Chatou.
Sculptor, performance artist, pyrotechnician.
Pierre Alain Hubert studied at the École des Arts Appliqués in Paris in 1962 and then the École Normale Supérieure d'Enseignement Technique in Paris in 1967. He lives in Marseilles and teaches technology at the Lycée Technique Marie Curie in Marseilles. He has made contributions to public shows, happenings and lectures. He made soft sculptures and environments that could be walked over, and then gave up concrete creations to concentrate on happenings. Since then he has travelled all over the world putting on shows with a firework display as the focal point and is an internationally renowned pyrotechnic expert.

He has taken part in collective exhibitions in France, such as the Paris Biennale in 1975, and also abroad, especially in Poland. Solo exhibitions include: *Les Œuvres Enterrées* (*Forgotten Works*), Galerie Ben, Nice, 1971; *Dialectique de la Durée*, Galerie Entre, Paris, 1974; *Substances et Phénomènes* (*Substances and Phenomena*), Galeria Dois, Oporto, Portugal, 1974; *Hommage à Maître Wù* (*Homage to Master Wu*), Krysztofory Gallery, Cracow, 1974; *L'Homme-Artifice* (*Man-Effects*), Galerie Entre, Paris, 1975.

BIBLIOGRAPHY:
IXe Biennale de Paris, exhibition catalogue, Idea Books, Musée d'Art Moderne de la Ville de Paris, Paris, 1975.

HUBERT, Raphael
French, 20th century.
Born 19 June 1884, in Paris.
Sculptor.
Raphael Hubert was a student of Barrias and Coutan. He exhibited in Paris at the Salon des Artistes Français.

HUBERT, Simon
French, 18th century.
Active in Paris.
Painter. History painting.
Simon Hubert was admitted into the Académie de St-Luc on 17 October 1750.

HUBERT, Sophie, or Odiot
French, 19th century.
Painter. Genre scenes.
Sophie Hubert exhibited portraits and other paintings at the Paris Salon from 1836 to 1845.

HUBERT, Stéphanie Louise (Mme)
French, 19th - 20th century.
Active in Paris.
Painter.
Stéphanie Louise Hubert became a member of the Société des Artistes Français in 1889.

HUBERT, Victor
French, 19th century.
Born 23 May 1786, in Bourth (Eure).
Painter. History painting, religious subjects.
Victor Hubert entered the École des Beaux-Arts in Paris on 9 March 1816, where he trained under the guidance of David and Guérin; his work was exhibited at the Salon from 1837 to 1850. Hubert painted mostly religious subjects, and worked for a number of churches in the French provinces. He was also the inventor of the *Polymetre*.

AUCTION RECORDS:
PARIS, 14 Dec 1989, *The Duke On Horseback during the Spanish Campaigns* (oil on canvas, 46 x 74 3/4 ins / 117 x 190 cm) FRF 50,000.

HUBERT, Vincent Honoré
French, 18th century.
Active in Paris.
Sculptor.
Vincent Honoré Hubert exhibited for the Académie de St-Luc.

HUBERT DE CASTELLA. See **CASTELLA Hubert de**

HUBERT DE CASTEX, Renée
French, 20th century.
Born 21 June 1904, in Rennes.
Painter.
Renée Hubert de Castex was a student of Henri Royer. She exhibited at the Salon des Artistes Français in Paris.

HUBERT DE SAINT-DIDIER, Balthazar
French, 19th century.
Born 1779, in Lyons; died 1863.
Painter, draughtsman. Landscapes, flowers.
Hubert de Saint-Didier was passionate about botany, and travelled around eastern France, visiting Dauphiné, Forez, Bresse, Velay and the Burey region. He made a great many sketches and, from 1837 onwards, published various albums of his work, including *Itinéraire pittoresque du Bugey* (*Picturesque Journey through Bugey*) and *Album des vues du Bugey* (*Album of Views of Bugey*).

HUBERT-DESCOURS. See **DESCOURS**

HUBERT-GAUTHIER, Jean
French, 20th century.
Born 30 June 1872, in Mondieu (Lot-et-Garonne).
Painter.
Jean Hubert-Gauthier was a student of Maignan. He exhibited at the Salon des Artistes Français in Paris. His works include *The Rest* and *The Cathedral*.

HUBERT-JACQUES, Claude
French, 20th century.
Born in Paris.
Painter.
Claude Hubert-Jacques exhibited in Paris at the Salon des Artistes Indépendants.

HUBERT-LAMALLE, Jane
French, 20th century.

Born 14 November 1868, in Claye-Souilly (Seine-et-Marne); died 19 July 1958.
Engraver.
Jane Hubert-Lamalle was a student of Dochy. She exhibited at the Salon des Artistes Français in Paris, of which she became a member in 1909.

HUBERT-ROBERT. See **ROBERT Hubert**

HUBERT-ROBERT, Marius
French, 19th - 20th century.
Born in Paris.
Painter. Local scenes, landscapes, seascapes.
Marius Hubert-Robert exhibited in Paris at the Salon des Indépendants from 1929.
AUCTION RECORDS:
PARIS, 7 Feb 1927, *Breton Village*, FRF 2,400. PARIS, 11 April 1927, *Gust of Wind*, FRF 2,400. PARIS, 2 June 1992, *The Great Caravan* (oil on card, 15 x 22 ins / 38 x 55 cm) FRF 6,000. PARIS, 5 April 1993, *Conversation Under the Arcades* (1914, oil on canvas, 21 1/4 x 28 1/4 ins / 54 x 72 cm) FRF 21,000. PARIS, 9 Dec 1996, *Square with Figures* (oil on canvas, 21 1/4 x 25 1/2 ins / 54 x 65 cm) FRF 18,500.

HUBERT-SAUZEAU, J. Gabriel
French, 19th century.
Born 3 September 1856, in Prahecq (Deux-Sèvres).
Active in Paris.
Painter.
Hubert-Sauzeau became a member of the Société des Artistes Français in 1901.

HUBERTI, Adrian, the Elder, or Huybrechts
Flemish, 16th - 17th century.
Died c. 1614.
Engraver.
Antwerp School, Flemish School.
Adrian Huberti was a member of the Antwerp guild in 1573 and was mentioned again in 1585.

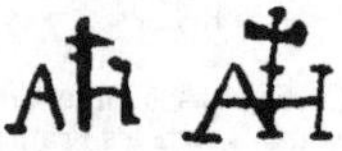

HUBERTI, Adrian, the Younger, or Huybrechts
Flemish School, 17th century.
Died 1648.
Active in Antwerp.
Illustrator.

HUBERTI, Antonio, pseudonym of an artist thought to be named Bernhard Globermann
Spanish, 20th century.
Born 1907.
Active in France.
Painter (including gouache), collage artist, draughtsman, sculptor.
Little is known about the life of Antonio Huberti. There is doubt about the date of his birth and also the date, around 1920-1923, when he left Spain and settled in Paris. He was self-taught and painted in the Cubist style of Braque, Picasso and Gris.
AUCTION RECORDS:
PARIS, 19 Dec 1988, *Constructivist Composition in Claret and Yellow* (gouache, 16 1/2 x 11 3/4 ins / 42 x 30 cm) FRF 8,200; *Harlequin with Banjo* (gouache, 23 1/4 x 17 ins / 59 x 43 cm) FRF 20,000; *Composition with Circle and Trapezium* (gouache, 17 3/4 x 12 1/2 ins / 45 x 32 cm) FRF 6,900. LA VARENNE-ST-HILAIRE, 3 Dec 1989, *Musical Composition* (gouache, 15 3/4 x 12 1/2 ins / 40 x 32 cm) FRF 12,500. PARIS, 26 Feb 1990, *Café Waiter* (collage, 25 1/4 x 20 1/2 ins / 64 x 52 cm) FRF 25,000. PARIS, 26 March 1990, *Person Playing the Recorder* (collage, 24 3/4 x 20 1/2 ins / 63 x 52 cm) FRF 30,000. PARIS, 14 April 1991, *Man in a Cap* (collage, 25 1/2 x 21 1/4 ins / 65 x 54 cm) FRF 15,000. PARIS, 6 July 1992, *Composition with Bottle* (oil and collage/paper, 21 1/4 x 15 3/4 ins / 54 x 40 cm) FRF 5,500. LUCERNE, 21 Nov 1992, *Violin* (collage and gouache/paper, 26 3/4 x 19 ins / 68 x 48 cm) CHF 1,900. PARIS, 19 March 1994, *Harlequin* (oil and collage/paper, 20 x 16 1/4 ins / 51 x 41 cm) FRF 5,000.

HUBERTI, Éduard Jules Joseph
Belgian, 19th century.
Born 6 January 1818, in Brussels; died 12 June 1880, in Brussels.
Painter. Landscapes.
Société Libre des Beaux-Arts. Barbizon School, Tervuren School.
Éduard Huberti was originally a musician. He studied architecture at the Antwerp school of fine arts and then painting with Théodore Fourmois. In 1868, he was a member of the Société Libre des Beaux-Arts. He painted landscapes from nature in Tervuren, the Belgian Barbizon, under the direction of Hippolyte Boulenger. In 1874, he joined the Barbizon School in the Île de France.
Huberti remained loyal to the Romantic approach of Boulenger and his work reveals a feeling of reverie.

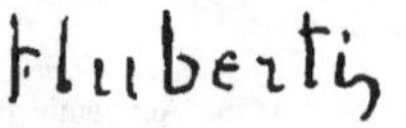

MUSEUMS AND GALLERIES:
ANTWERP: *Marshland in the Campine* - BRUSSELS (MBA): *Dull Weather*.
AUCTION RECORDS:
LOKEREN, 9 March 1996, *Landscape with a Pond* (black chalk, 18 x 11 3/4in/45.5 x 30cm) BEF 30,000. BRUSSELS, 15 Jan 2002, *Collection of Sketches with Drawings in Crayon, Charcoal, Watercolour and Ink* (mixed media) EUR 1,900. LOKEREN, 15 March 2003, *Edge of the Forest* (oil on canvas, 63 x 80 ins / 160 x 203 cm) EUR 6,000.

HUBERTI, F.
17th century.
Engraver.
Poitiers Museum has several engravings on copper signed *F. Huberti*, a name that is not found elsewhere. Perhaps identical with François Hubert.
MUSEUMS AND GALLERIES:
POITIERS: engravings.

HUBERTS, C.
Flemish School, 18th century.
Active in Amsterdam c. 1720.
Engraver.
C. Huberts worked for booksellers.

HUBIN, Louis, or Hubein
French, 17th century.
Active in Paris in 1683.
Enameller.

HUBIN, Nicolas
French, 15th century.
Active in Troyes from 1483 to 1488.
Painter.
Nicolas Hubin worked in the church of St Stephen.

HUBLIER, Charlotte (Mme)
later Mme Nicolas Henri Jacob
Maiden name: Mast
French, 19th century.
Born 1817, in Paris.
Painter, watercolourist. Still-lifes (flowers/fruit).
Charlotte Hublier was the pupil of N.-H. Jacob, whom she subsequently married. Her watercolours were exhibited at the Paris Salon between 1837 and 1844.

AUCTION RECORDS:
MONTE CARLO, 26 Oct 1981, *Still-life with Vase of Flowers and Fruit* (gouache, 33½ x 26 ins / 85 x 66 cm) FRF 52,000.

HUBLIN, Émile Auguste
French, 19th century.
Born 2 July 1830, in Angers.
Painter. Portraits, genre scenes.

On 6 April 1855 Hublin entered the École des Beaux-Arts in Paris, and became the pupil of Picot. He exhibited at the Paris Salon from 1861 to 1880.

His paintings are generally thought to be rather overblown and affected, with somewhat melodramatic subjects.

MUSEUMS AND GALLERIES:
LEICESTER: *Orphan Girl.*

AUCTION RECORDS:
LONDON, 26 Nov 1910, *Sick Child* (1873) GBP 5. LONDON, 1922, *Bargaining for a Kiss,* GBP 10. LONDON, Feb 1923, *Cherry Seller,* GBP 18. LONDON, 18 June 1934, *Begging for Alms,* GBP 31. LONDON, 7 Feb 1947, *Cherry Seller,* GBP 105. LONDON, 29 Nov 1991, *A Friend in Need* (1872, oil on canvas, 33¼ x 24 ins / 84.5 x 61 cm) GBP 14,300.

HÜBNER. See also **HUEBNER**

HUBNER, Louis Leonart
British, 18th century.
Born in Berlin; died 1769.
Painter. Landscapes with figures, still-lifes, animals.

Louis Hubner was one of the first artists to settle in Norwich around 1740 and remained there for almost 30 years. He himself organised sales of his paintings at the Union Coffee House in Norwich and thus became a precursor of sales by auction. He liked to scatter all sorts of birds and fruits in his compositions either as part of nature or as still-lifes. On his death in 1769 the *Norwich Mercury* singled out his ability as a still-life painter, praising the meticulousness, great perception and elegance of colour evident in most of his works.

AUCTION RECORDS:
LONDON, 12 July 1989, *Cockerels, Hens, Chickens, Pigeons and a Bullfinch in a Landscape* (oil on canvas, 38½ x 48½ ins / 98 x 123.5 cm) GBP 7,700. LONDON, 10 April 1991, *Still-life of Birds in a Landscape: Kingfisher, Quail, Partridge, Hoopoe, Wagtail etc...* (oil on canvas, 27¼ x 34½ ins / 69.5 x 87.5 cm) GBP 3,300. LONDON, 18 Nov 1992, *'Dismal', Grey Thoroughbred with Jockey up* (1746, oil on canvas, 40 x 50½ ins / 101.5 x 128 cm) GBP 8,800. NEW YORK, 12 Jan 1996, *A Squirrel Eating Chestnuts on a Tree Trunk with Apples, Plums and Pears on the Ground* (oil on canvas, 28 x 35 ins / 71.1 x 88.9 cm) USD 18,400. LONDON, 16 Dec 1999, *Still-life of Carnations, Roses, Tulips and Other Flowers in Gilt Urn, upon Marble Ledge* (oil on canvas, 24 x 26 ins / 60 x 65 cm) GBP 1,900. LONDON, 28 Nov 2002, *Duckwing Game Cock, Chickens, Pigeons and Bullfinch in a Landscape* (oil on canvas, 39 x 48 ins / 98 x 123 cm) GBP 7,000.

HUBNER, Peter Paul
German, 20th century.
Born 29 June 1870, in Feichenberg, Bohemia; died 31 August 1928, in Benfleet (Essex, England).
Active in England.
Painter.

Peter Paul Hubner studied at the art school in Jablonec nad Nisou (Gablonz) in 1988 and subsequently travelled around the country, developing his skills as a painter, draughtsman and lithographer, until 1891, when he was called up. From 1894 to 1897, he travelled around Austria, Germany and the Netherlands, while continuing to paint. He finally joined his brother in England, settling in Manchester. At this period, he worked as a decorator and designer for the Royal Worcester Porcelain factory. He married and settled in Dudley with his wife Laura. Once his situation was more settled, he concentrated more on painting and was able to travel in England. After World War I he set up a lithography studio, where his three sons worked with him. He had made a name for himself as a lithographer, but had no reputation as a painter, until he was eventually rediscovered. He is also remembered for having invented slogans and designed logos that are still in use today.

Hubner's painting was initially impersonal in style, as he tried to conform to the tastes of the country whose landscapes he was painting (heavy and Expressionist in Germany; almost monochrome in the Netherlands), but he later began to paint places he liked with great sensitivity, his colorations governed by light, the time of day, the season of the year, and the climate. He also painted portraits of his wife, his children, and his friend Paul Buck. His final years were very difficult, and he withdrew from society and spent his time retouching finished works.

HÜBNER, Ulrich
German, 19th - 20th century.
Born 17 June 1872, in Berlin; died 1932.
Painter. Landscapes, seascapes.

Hübner was awarded a medal at the 1901 Munich exhibition. He was influenced by the style of Claude Monet.

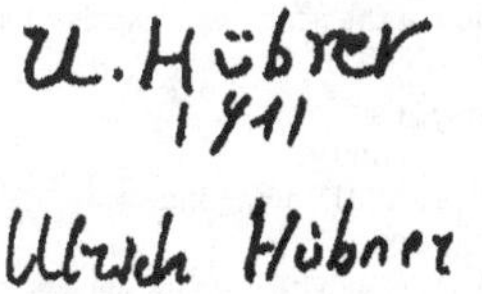

AUCTION RECORDS:
COLOGNE, 20 March 1981, *View from the Painter's Studio* (1913, oil on canvas, 31½ x 24 ins / 80 x 61 cm) DEM 5,000. HAMBURG, 5 Dec 1986, *Friedrichstrasse, Berlin* (oil on canvas, 27¾ x 23½ ins / 70.5 x 60 cm) DEM 15,000. NEW YORK, 19 Jan 1994, *Sailing Boats near the Quays* (oil on canvas, 24 x 30 ins / 61 x 76.2 cm) USD 4,888. AMSTERDAM, 18 June 1996, *Dutch and Swedish Ships in a Port* (oil on panel, 14½ x 18 ins / 37 x 46 cm) NLG 3,680. VIENNA, 26 Jan 1999, *Fishing Boats at Anchor* (oil on board, 12 x 16 ins / 30 x 40 cm) ATS 20,000. ZOFINGEN, 28 May 1999, *View of Harbour* (1918, oil on canvas, 21 x 26 ins / 54 x 65 cm) CHF 8,500. BERLIN, 25 Nov 2000, *Landscape* (oil on canvas, 32 x 40 ins / 82 x 102 cm) DEM 11,000. HAMBURG, 2 Dec 2000, *Landing-stage in Travemunde* (oil on canvas, 20 x 30 ins / 50 x 76 cm) DEM 11,200. BERLIN, 30 June 2001, *At the Sea* (1919, oil on canvas, 20 x 30 ins / 50 x 76 cm) DEM 12,000. LONDON, 11 Sept 2003, *Dutch Canal* (oil on canvas, 27 x 37 ins / 69 x 93 cm) GBP 2,500. BERLIN, 12 June 2004, *Courtyard with Trees* (1908, oil on canvas, 32 x 28 ins / 81 x 70 cm) EUR 8,000. BERLIN, 12 June 2004, *Canal Scene in Potsdam* (oil on canvas, 27 x 36 ins / 69 x 92 cm) EUR 8,500.

HUBRECHT, Amalda Bramine Louise
Dutch, 19th - 20th century.
Born 21 July 1855, in Rotterdam; died 5 November 1913, in England.
Painter, engraver, illustrator.

Work by Hubrecht was exhibited in Munich in 1888, when she was awarded a medal.

AUCTION RECORDS:
NEW YORK, 9 Dec 1982, *End of the School Day* (oil on canvas, 38½ x 35 ins / 98 x 88 cm) USD 1,600.

HUBRECHT, Martin
French, 20th century.
Born 29 March 1892, in Sélestat.

Painter, watercolourist. Interiors with figures, genre scenes.

Martin Hubrecht showed in Paris at the Salon d'Automne.

Auction records:

Paris, 28 Feb 1947, *Little Girl Sewing in Her Bed* (watercolour) FRF 300. Versailles, 8 July 1990, *Woman at the Washhouse* (1928, watercolour, 10¾ x 14½ ins / 27.5 x 37 cm) FRF 3,800.

HUBRICH, Paul

German, 19th - 20th century.
Born 9 November 1869, in Gebhardsdorf.
Sculptor.

Work by Hubrich was exhibited in Berlin in 1909.

HUBRICHS

British, 18th century.
Active in London.
Portrait artist.

Hubrichs exhibited his work in London at the Society of Artists in 1769.

HUBSCH, Francisca

German, 19th century.
Born 20 August 1857, in Philippsburg (near Karlsruhe).
Painter. Landscapes.

She was a pupil of the academy in Karlsruhe. She exhibited in Munich from 1888.

HUC, Eugène

French, 20th century.
Born 22 April 1891, in Bayonne.
Painter. Figures.

Eugène Huc was a student of Jean-Paul Laurens and Etcheverry. He exhibited in Paris at the Salon des Artistes Français.

HUCHE, Charles

French, 18th century.
Active in Paris in 1738.
Painter, sculptor.

HUCHET, Urbain

French, 20th century.
Born 1930, in Rennes.
Active in the USA.
Painter, illustrator. Landscapes.

Urbain Huchet trained himself in Pont-Aven, copying the works of Gauguin and Émile Bernard. He travelled across Europe, the Middle East, and particularly Latin America. He brought back views from his travels, which he then compiled into albums. He also illustrated Hervé Bazin's *Vipère au poing* (*Viper in the Fist*) and Alain Decaux's *La France* (*France*).

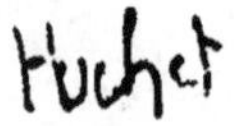

Auction records:

Rheims, 9 June 1991, *The Seine and the Trocadero* (oil on canvas, 22 x 18 ins / 55 x 46 cm) FRF 3,800.

HUCHON

French, 15th century.
Active in Arras.
Sculptor (wood).

Huchon was one of those who in 1497 carved the stalls of the abbey of St-Bertin near St-Omer.

HUCHTENBURG, Jacob van

Dutch, 17th century.
Born c. 1639-1640, in Haarlem; died 1675, in Amsterdam.
Painter. Battles, landscapes.

The brother of Jan van Huchtenberg, Jacob studied under Nicolaes Berchem. He developed a reputation as an artist in Italy.

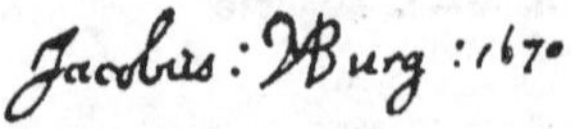

Museums and Galleries:

Copenhagen (Statens Mus. for Kunst): two landscapes.

Auction records:

Paris, 24 May 1923, *Cavalry Engagement,* FRF 300. Cologne, 18 Nov 1965, *View of a Park with Figures,* DEM 11,000. London, 25 Nov 1970, *Cavalry Engagement,* GBP 1,600. Vienna, 16 March 1971, *Scene from the Parthian War,* ATS 55,000. London, 4 April 1986, *The Campo Vacchino in Rome with Figures* (oil on canvas, 33 x 44in/82.9 x 112cm) GBP 15,000. Milan, 12 Dec 1988, *View of the Roman Forum with Figures and Animals* (oil on canvas, 15 x 18½in/38 x 47cm) ITL 48,000,000. London, 8 Dec 1989, *The Piazza del Popolo in Rome* (1673, oil on canvas, 14 x 20½in/35.8 x 52cm) GBP 30,800. London, 23 March 1990, *The Milvio Bridge on the Tiber with Rome in the Distance* (oil on panel, 11¼ x 8½in/28.5 x 21.3cm) GBP 4,180. London, 8 July 1992, *Figures and Livestock among Classical Ruins* (1674, oil on canvas, 25½ x 31½in/64.5 x 80cm) GBP 13,200. Paris, 5 June 2002, *Battle on Mount Kammel* (oil on canvas, 33 x 41 ins / 85 x 105 cm) EUR 12,000.

HUCHTENBURG, Jan van, or Hughtenburgh

Dutch, 17th - 18th century.
Born 20 November 1647, in Haarlem; died 1733, in Amsterdam.
Painter, engraver. Battles, portraits, hunting scenes, landscapes with figures.

Jan van Huchtenberg studied under Thomas Wyck but mainly followed the style of Philips Wouwerman. Around 1667, he went to Paris where he continued his studies under F. A. van der Meulen. From Paris he went to Italy, where in 1708 and 1709 he was commissioned by Prince Eugene of Savoy to paint scenes of the victories won by the prince. In 1711, he was at the court of the Elector Palatine. On 10 January 1670, a Jan van Hughtenburgh of Haarlem joined the reformed church and on 7 October of that year married Elisabeth Momneers; it has not been shown that this person was the same as the artist Van Huchtenberg. Shortly before his death, Van Huchtenberg went to Amsterdam to live in his daughter's house, where he eventually died. His paintings and engravings are generally of battles or military subjects.

Museums and Galleries:

Amsterdam: *Cavalry Charge; Battle of the Boyne* - Antwerp: *The Horrors of War* - Basel: *Travellers Attacked by Robbers* - Brussels: *Cavalry Charge; Battle Scene* - Copenhagen

(Statens Mus. for Kunst): *Street Scene in Rome; Market in Rome; Military Review* - Dijon: *Battle* - Dresden: *Battle* (six) - Fontainebleau: *Cavalry Charge; View of a Town Preparing for Siege* - Frankfurt am Main: *Encampment Scene* - Geneva (Mus. Ariana): *A Fight* - Haarlem: *Cavalry Encampment; Courtyard* - Hanover: *Near the Horse Market; Market of Italian Horses* - Kassel: *Piazza Colonna; The Siege of Fort Cuneo* - Liège: *Cavalry Charge; Cavalry Fight* - London (NG): *A Battle* (c. 1680, oil/canvas/panel) - Nuremberg: *Meal after the Hunt* - Rotterdam: *Fight between the Imperial Cavalry and the Turkish Cavalry* - Stockholm: *Battle between Austrians and Prussians; Cavalry Skirmish*; same subject - The Hague: *Stathouder Henry Casimir II Commanding a Battle; A Sortie; Convoy Attacked by Soldiers* - Utrecht: *Fight* - Valenciennes: *Attack on a Convoy* - Vienna: *Unexpected Attack* - Vienna (Czernin'sche Gemäldegal.): *Landscape with Figures and Ruins* - Vienna (Schönborn-Buckheim): *Battle; Cavalry Engagement* - Wroclaw: *Hunters in a Park.*

Auction records:

Paris, 23 March 1891, *Return from the Hunt,* FRF 3,000. Paris, 30 April 1891, *Cavalry Charge,* FRF 1,700. Paris, 30 May 1903, *Horsemen in Battle,* FRF 750. Paris, 16 May 1904, *Presumed Self-portrait,* FRF 330. London, 23 Nov 1907, *Battle Scene,* GBP 18. London, 24 Dec 1907, *Soldiers near a Fortress,* GBP 14. Paris, 23 March 1908, *Horsemen in Battle,* FRF 110. London, 2 July 1909, *General and his Staff in Battle,* GBP 19. London, Dec 1922, *Cavalry Engagement,* GBP 6. London, April 1923, *Landscape with Figures and Wagon for the Harvest,* GBP 25. London, June 1923, *Encampment outside a Town,* GBP 37. London, Dec 1923, *Cavalry Engagement,* GBP 23. London, 19 Nov 1925, *Gardens,* GBP 26. Paris, 25 Nov 1927, *Cavalry Battle,* FRF 1,980. London, 22 Feb 1929, *Louis XIV in a Carriage,* GBP 42. London, 11 April 1930, *Battle of Cassani; Battle of Belgrade* (both) GBP 68. Paris, 12 April 1943, *Cavalry Charge* (attributed) FRF 3,550. Paris, 13 Oct 1943, *Cavalry Charge* (red chalk, attributed) FRF 1,300. London, 1 March 1946, *Cavalry Engagement,* GBP 42. Paris, 26 May 1949, *Riding Out,* FRF 230,000. Paris, 11 June 1959, *Visit to an Encampment,* FRF 320,000. Vienna, 5 Dec 1960, *Cavalry Engagement in a Wooded Landscape,* ATS 20,000. Vienna, 18 June 1963, *Leaving for the Hunt,* FRF 5,500. London, 26 June 1964, *Battle of Chiari,* Gns 380. New York, 26 April 1967, *Italian Landscape,* USD 1,000. Versailles, 12 June 1969, *Cavalry Battle,* FRF 8,500. London, 25 Nov 1970, *Cavalry Engagement,* GBP 1,600. Vienna, 28 Nov 1972, *Market Scene in Rome,* ATS 160,000. London, 1 June 1973, *Horse Market,* Gns 9,000. New York, 18 June 1974, *Cavalry Engagement* (1675) USD 4,000. London, 21 May 1976, *Military Encampment* (oil on canvas, 20 x 26in/51 x 66cm) GBP 3,500. Vienna, 14 March 1978, *At the Blacksmith's* (oil on canvas, 12 1/2 x 15in/32 x 38cm) ATS 180,000. London, 16 April 1980, *Piazza Navona, Rome* (1674, oil on panel, 12 1/2 x 9 3/4in/31.5 x 25cm) GBP 7,500. London, 8 July 1983, *Soldiers Looting a Village* (oil on canvas, 28 x 33in/71.1 x 83.8cm) GBP 5,200. London, 3 July 1985, *Battle near Namur* (oil on canvas, 57 3/4 x 76 1/2in/147 x 194cm) GBP 17,000. Paris, 16 Dec 1987, *Battle Scene* (oil on canvas, 41 3/4 x 52 1/4in/106 x 133cm) FRF 85,000. Paris, 16 Dec 1987, *Battle Scene* (oil on canvas, 41 3/4 x 52 1/4in/106 x 133cm) FRF 85,000. Paris, 13 Dec 1988, *Attack on a Convoy* (oil on card, 10 x 14 1/4in/25.5 x 36cm) FRF 16,000. Paris, 15 March 1989, *Leaving for the Hunt* (oil on canvas, 25 1/4 x 30 3/4in/64 x 78cm) FRF 300,000. London, 19 May 1989, *Cavalry Engagement* (oil on panel, 24 1/2 x 35in/62 x 89.2cm) GBP 4,180. New York, 13 Oct 1989, *Cavalry Engagement with Artillery and Infantry in the Background* (oil on canvas, 26 x 34 1/2in/66 x 87.5cm) USD 9,900. Paris, 12 Dec 1989, *The Siege of Namur* (oil on canvas, 26 3/4 x 34 3/4in/68 x 88.5cm) FRF 140,000. London, 31 Oct 1990, *Landscape with Horsemen* (oil on canvas, 19 x 23 1/4in/48 x 59cm) GBP 4,950. Stockholm, 14 Nov 1990, *Cavalry Skirmish* (oil on panel, 11 x 14 1/4in/27 x 36cm) SEK 16,500. Paris, 31 Jan 1991, *Battle Scene* (oil on panel, 24 1/2 x 35in/62 x 89cm) FRF 40,000. London, 7 Feb 1991, *Cavalry Engagement* (oil on canvas, 23 x 29 1/4in/57.5 x 74.5cm) GBP 5,280. London, 19 April 1991, *Cavalry Skirmish* (oil on canvas, 14 3/4 x 16 1/4in/37.5 x 41.5cm) GBP 3,300. Amsterdam, 2 May 1991, *Italian Landscape with Hunting Party* (oil on canvas, 25 1/2 x 31in/64.8 x 78.5cm) NLG 32,200. Paris, 9 Dec 1991, *Dressage Scene* (oil on canvas, 18 x 22 1/2in/46 x 57cm) FRF 22,000. London, 11 Dec 1991, *Cavalry Engagement* (oil on canvas, 20 1/2 x 24 1/2in/52 x 62cm) GBP 9,020. London, 28 Oct 1992, *Horsemen and Passers-by on a Roman Road* (1717, oil on canvas, 16 1/2 x 22 1/4in/41.6 x 56.3cm) GBP 12,100. Paris, 11 Dec 1992, *Horsemen by a Fountain* (oil on canvas, 19 3/4 x 25 3/4in/50 x 65.5cm) FRF 50,000. Paris, 28 May 1993, *Two Horsemen Sounding the Trumpet* (brown ink and Indian ink wash, 10 1/2 x 8 1/2in/26.8 x 21.5cm) FRF 3,100. New York, 8 Oct 1993, *Horsemen outside an Inn* (oil on canvas, 23 1/2 x 32 1/2in/59.7 x 82.6cm) USD 5,750. London, 6 July 1994, *Prince Eugene of Savoy Beating the Turks at the Battle of Belgrade in 1717* (oil on canvas, 18 x 26 1/2in/45.8 x 67cm) GBP 17,825. London, 7 Dec 1994, *William III, Prince of Orange and King of England Entering an Occupied Town (Xanten?)* (oil on canvas, 33 1/4 x 43 1/4in/84.5 x 110cm) GBP 45,500. New York, 11 Jan 1995, *The Horse Fair* (oil on canvas, 21 x 25in/53.3 x 63.5cm) USD 19,550. Paris, 24 Nov 1995, *The Halt; After the Hunt* (oil on canvas, 25 1/2 x 31in/64.5 x 78.5 cm and 25 1/2 x 31in/64.5 x 79cm) FRF 125,000. London, 5 July 1996, *The Battle of Kahlenberg* (1683, oil on canvas, 25 1/4 x 38 3/4in/64 x 98.5cm) GBP 8,000. Paris, 9 Dec 1996, *William III Besieging a Town* (oil on canvas, 30 3/4 x 41 1/4in/78 x 105cm) FRF 160,000. London, 11 Dec 1996, *Italian Landscape with Travellers in a Square* (1717, oil on canvas, 16 1/4 x 22in/41.3 x 55.9cm) GBP 8,050. London, 31 Oct 1997, *Elegant Hunting Party near a Palace* (oil on canvas, 26 3/4 x 32 1/4in/68 x 82cm) GBP 24,150. Copenhagen, 3 March 1998, *Battle in the Mountains* (oil on canvas, 33 x 44 ins / 85 x 112 cm) DKK 55,000. Cologne, 4 Dec 1999, *Slaughter at Malplaquet on 11 September 1709* (oil on canvas, 58 x 67 ins / 148 x 169 cm) DEM 95,000. London, 17 Dec 1999, *Hunting Party by Fountain outside Mansion* (oil on canvas, 25 x 31 ins / 63 x 79 cm) GBP 40,000. Cologne, 6 April 2000, *The Fight by the Bridge* (oil on canvas, 33 x 41 ins / 83 x 105 cm) DEM 28,000. London, 2 Nov 2000, *Cavalry Engagment before a Burning Church* (oil on canvas, 25 x 31 ins / 64 x 78 cm) GBP 8,500. London, 26 April 2001, *Military Encampment in an Open Landscape with Cavaliers Conversing by a Pool* (oil on canvas, 21 x 27 ins / 53 x 69 cm) GBP 7,000. London, 13 July 2001, *Cavalry Engagement before a Fortified Town* (oil on canvas, 33 x 48 ins / 84 x 123 cm) GBP 14,000. Ahlden, 3 May 2002, *Cavalry Battle* (oil on canvas, 26 x 40 ins / 67 x 102 cm) EUR 11,000. Amsterdam, 5 Nov 2002, *Battle at Blenheim, near Hochstadt* (1704, oil on canvas, 17 x 26 ins / 44 x 66 cm) EUR 25,000. London, 10 April 2003, *Cavalry Skirmish* (oil on canvas, 17 x 21 ins / 44 x 53 cm) GBP 5,500. London, 22 April 2004, *Battle Scene with Cavalry Skirmishing before a Walled Town* (oil on canvas, 20 x 26 ins / 50 x 67 cm) GBP 8,000. Amsterdam, 7 Sept 2004, *Alexander Battle* (oil on canvas, 33 x 44 ins / 83 x 113 cm) EUR 16,000.

HUCHTHAUSEN, David

American, 20th - 21st century.

Born 1951.

Glassmaker.

Auction records:

New York, 25-26 Feb 1994, *Fantasy tableware* (1979, multicoloured blown glass, h. 13 ins / 32.1 cm) USD 1,840.

HUCK, Auguste Eugène

French, 19th century.

Born in the 19th century, in Nevers (Nièvre).

Active in Sedan, France.
Enameller.

Huck exhibited at the Salon between 1867 and 1879.

HUCK, Johann Gerhard

German, 18th - 19th century.
Born c. 1759, in Düsseldorf; died 16 August 1811, in Hanover.
Draughtsman, engraver (burin).

He engraved genre subjects, portraits and religious pictures. He worked in Düsseldorf, England and Hanover.

HUCK, Karl

Austrian, 20th century.
Born 16 March 1876; died 1926.
Painter. Animals.

AUCTION RECORDS:

LONDON, 15 Feb 1991, *Falcon Ready for the Hunt in a Mountainous Landscape (recto); Stag in a Wooded Landscape (verso)* (oil on canvas, 83¾ x 75 ins / 213 x 190.5 cm) GBP 5,500.

HUCKLEBRIDGE, M. (Miss)

British, 19th century.
Active in London.
Miniaturist. Portraits.

M. Hucklebridge frequently exhibited in London at the Royal Academy and in Suffolk Street from 1837 to 1852.

HUCLEUX, Jean-Olivier

French, 20th century.
Born 1923, in Chauny (Aisne).
Painter, draughtsman.

From 1940 to 1945, Jean-Olivier Hucleux worked as a photo retoucher. He did not begin to paint seriously until 1968. While practising what was essentially a photographic realism, he showed two gigantic canvases, one representing a cemetery, the other, a cemetery of cars. In 1973 he began painting portraits such as *Étienne-Martin* (1974) and *Jean Le Gac* (1977). He also painted portraits of *Bacon, Beckett,* and more recently, *Erik Dietman.* While still unknown in France, he was invited to Documenta V in Kassel in 1972, in the section dedicated to Hyperrealism. He was also invited to the Biennale in Venice in 1976. Hucleux has taken part in other collective exhibitions, including *Le Portrait s'envisage...* (*The Portrait Visualizes Itself...*) (2002) at the Château de Tanlay; and *Les Années 70: l'art en cause* (*The 1970s: Art in Question*) (2002) at the CAPC-Musée d'Art Contemporain, Bordeaux. He has held solo exhibitions at the Musée National d'Art Moderne, Paris (1979); the Maison d'Art Contemporain Chaillioux, Fresnes (1995); the Galerie Barbier-Beltz, Paris (1995); and the Galerie Slotine-Perkowsky, Le Havre (1995).

BIBLIOGRAPHY:

Lamarche-Vadel, Bernard, *Hucleux, 12 dessins suivis du catalogue de l'oeuvre*, exhibition catalogue, La Différence, Paris, 1987. Raspail Thierry, et al., *Jean Olivier Hucleux 1971-1999*, Musée d'Art contemporain, Lyons, 1999. Fréruchet, Maurice, et al., *Les Années soixante-dix: l'art en cause*, exhibition catalogue, Capc musée d'Art contemporain, Bordeaux, 2002.

MUSEUMS AND GALLERIES:

COLOGNE (Mus. Ludwig): *Portrait of Professor Ludwig and His Wife* - LYONS (MAC) - PARIS (FNAC): *Portrait of Antonin Artaud* (1986).

AUCTION RECORDS:

PARIS, 1 Oct 1992, *Portrait of Céline* (1988, graphite on paper, 59¾ x 63 ins / 152 x 160 cm) FRF 92,000. PARIS, 26 Nov 1994, *Portrait of Camille and Her Father* (1994, graphite, 87½ x 59¾ ins / 222 x 152 cm) FRF 190,000. PARIS, 27 Oct 2000, *Portrait of Celine* (crayon drawing heightened with gouache, 61 x 59 ins / 155 x 149 cm) FRF 112,000. PARIS, 23 June 2001, *Portrait of Bernard Lamarche-Vadel* (crayon, 88 x 59 ins / 223 x 149 cm) FRF 90,000.

HUDDE, Jean

French, 16th century.
Active in Bourges.
Sculptor.

Jean Hudde was working on the decoration of Bourges Cathedral in 1513.

HUDDESFORD, George

British, 18th - 19th century.
Born 1749; died 1909.
Painter. Portraits.

George Huddesford exhibited at the Royal Academy in London in 1775.

HUDE, Jürgen Matthias van der

German, 18th century.
Born 1690, in Lübeck; died 4 July 1751.
Miniaturist. Portraits.

HUDE, Paula van der

German, 20th century.
Born 15 March 1874, in Berlin.
Sculptor.

Van der Hude worked in Berlin, Munich and Paris.

HUDECEK, Antonin

Czech, 20th century.
Born 14 July 1872, in Bechyne or Lucka; died 1941, in Castolovice.
Painter.

Antonin Hudecek studied at the academies of Prague and Vienna. His work shows the successive influences of the major movements in art. In his *Procession* (1914), the influence of Symbolism is very clear, later he was receptive to Fauvism and then Expressionism and even, to some extent, Cubism. He can be placed alongside artists such as Kupka, Kubista, Spala and Filla as one of the creators of modern Czechoslovakian painting. He received an honourable mention at the 1900 Exposition Universelle in Paris.

MUSEUMS AND GALLERIES:

PRAGUE (Národní Gal.): *Procession.*

AUCTION RECORDS:

MUNICH, 1-2 Dec 1992, *Meadow with Flowers* (oil and tempera/card, 17¼ x 23½ ins / 44 x 59.5 cm) DEM 1,150. PRAGUE, 27 May 2000, *On a Stream* (1902, oil on canvas, 30 x 39 ins / 77 x 99 cm) CZK 300,000. PRAGUE, 17 Nov 2001, *Meadow in Bloom* (oil on canvas, 39 x 59 ins / 100 x 150 cm) CZK 100,000. BRATISLAVA, 1 Oct 2002, *Shade* (c. 1920-1923, oil on canvas, 37 x 51 ins / 94 x 130 cm) SL.K 148,000. PRAGUE, 22 May 2004, *Brook in Forest* (oil on canvas, 37 x 53 ins / 95 x 135 cm) CZK 120,000.

HUDECEK, Frantisek

Czech, 20th century.
Born 7 April 1919, in Nemcice.
Painter.

Frantisek Hudecek studied in Prague from 1928 to 1931, the city where he spent most of his career.

From the start, he aligned himself unequivocally with the Czechoslovakian avant-garde, working in various experimental techniques, particularly collage. He was attracted to Surrealism in his search for a new vision of the world, but was at the same time experimenting with purely plastic ideas which led him at times to produce work reminiscent of de Chirico's Metaphysical period.

Collective exhibitions include: Paris, Brussels, Lucerne, Warsaw, Tokyo and Los Angeles. He held solo exhibitions in Prague (1944, 1945, 1947 and 1965).

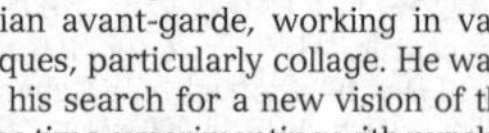

BIBLIOGRAPHY:
Fifty years of Czechoslovak Painting from the Collections of the Galleries, 1918-1958, exhibition catalogue, Slovenska Narodna Gal., Bratislava, 1968 (in commemoration of the 50th anniversary of the Republic of Czechoslovakia).

HUDEK, Émil
German, 20th century.
Born 1877.
Painter.
Hudek studied in Breslau (now Wroclaw, Poland).

HUDEL, Louis
French, 19th century.
Born in the 19th century, in Paris.
Painter. Genre scenes.
Hudel was a pupil of Monvoisin. He exhibited porcelain, earthenware, paintings and drawings at the Salon, between 1859 and 1866.

HUDELET, Henry Paul
French, 19th century.
Born 20 December 1849, in Langres (Haute-Marne); died 1878.
Sculptor.
Hudelet was taught by A. Dumont. He exhibited a statue at the Paris Salon of 1876, and a bronze medallion in 1877.
MUSEUMS AND GALLERIES:
LANGRES: *Discobolos; Fishermen Finding the Head of Orpheus on the Banks of the Hebrus* (low relief); *Dice Player* (bronze statue).

HUDELMAIER, Martin
German, 20th - 21st century.
Born 24 March 1949, in Plüderhausen.
Painter.
Martin Hudelmaier's paintings used to tend towards a complex realisation of fantasies in which archetypes were described by a free use of line and colour. Since 1973, he has painted directly onto his own body. He had a number of exhibitions in Germany in 1970.

HUDELOT, Anna
French, 20th century.
Born 19th century, in Neufchâteau.
Engraver.
Anna Hudelot exhibited regularly in Paris at the Salon des Artistes Français, of which she became a member in 1909. She received an honourable mention in 1910. Her engravings were on wood.

HUDETZ, Johann Michael
Austrian, 18th century.
Died 8 October 1745, in Innsbruck.
Painter.

HUDIER, Charles
French, 18th century.
Active in Paris in 1739.
Painter, sculptor.

HUDIER, Pierre François
French, 18th century.
Active in Paris in 1765.
Sculptor.

HUDLER, August
German, 19th century.
Born 12 December 1868, in Odelzhausen (near Munich); died 21 November 1905, in Dresden.
Sculptor.
He was a pupil of Ruemann and von Diez in Munich.

HUDSON (Mrs)
British, 18th century.
Active in London.
Painter.
Hudson exhibited his work at the Free Society in 1764.

HUDSON, Anna Hope
American, 19th - 20th century.
Born 1869, in New York; died 1957.
Painter.
Anna Hope Hudson trained in Paris under Carrière.
AUCTION RECORDS:
LONDON, 4 Nov 1983, *Violin Solo* (c. 1913, oil on canvas, 24 x 20 ins / 61 x 50.8 cm) GBP 3,000.

HUDSON, Benjamin
British, 19th century.
Active in London.
Painter. Portraits.
Benjamin Hudson exhibited his work in 1852 at the Royal Academy in London.
AUCTION RECORDS:
PARIS, 24 May 1943, *Portrait of a Man,* FRF 700. LONDON, 10 April 1992, *Portrait of Sir William Brooke O'Shaughnessy with his Hand on the Telegraph Machine* (oil on canvas, 50 x 40 ins / 127 x 101.5 cm) GBP 4,950. LONDON, 15 Dec 1993, *Portrait of Framji Nasserwanji Patel, Co-Founder of the Anglo-Indian Company Wallace and Co. Wearing a White Suit and Turban* (oil on canvas, 36 x 28¾ ins / 91.5 x 73 cm) GBP 16,100. MARKET HARBOROUGH, 14 Oct 1999, *Portrait of W.E. Gladstone* (oil on canvas, 30 x 25 ins / 76 x 64 cm) GBP 1,100.

HUDSON, Charles Bradford
American, 19th century.
Born 27 January 1865, in Ontario; died 1939, in Pacific Grove (California).
Painter.
Charles Bradford Hudson was a pupil of Bouguereau in Paris, and won a prize at the Exposition Universelle in 1900. He produced mural paintings and his works feature in important private collections.

HUDSON, Charles William
American, 20th century.
Born 21 August 1871, in Boston (Massachusetts); died 1943.
Painter. Landscapes.
Charles William Hudson trained under Grundmann and Tarbell.

HUDSON, Elmer Forrest
American, 19th century.
Born 14 August 1862, in Boston.
Active in Allston (USA).
Painter. Seascapes.
A member of the Arts Club in Boston and the Salmagundi Club.

HUDSON, Eric
American, 19th century.
Born in Boston (Massachusetts).
Active at the end of the 19th century.
Painter. Seascapes.
Eric Hudson was a member of the Salmagundi Club and the National Arts Club in New York.

HUDSON, F.H.
British, 19th century.
Active in London.
Painter. Portraits.
F.H. Hudson exhibited his work in London at the Royal Academy from 1843 to 1855.

HUDSON, Grace Carpenter (Mrs)
American, 19th - 20th century.

Born 21 February 1865, in Potter Valley; died 1937, in Ukiah (California).
Active in Ukiah.
Painter. Figures.

Grace Carpenter Hudson trained under Virgil Williams in San Francisco. She painted Native American children, and acquired a reputation in this genre. She received an honourable mention in Chicago in 1891.

BIBLIOGRAPHY:

Searles R. Boynton, *The painter lady Grace Carpenter Hudson*, Sun House Guild, Ukia (CA), c. 1978.

AUCTION RECORDS:

NEW YORK, 4 Jan 1907, *Indians*, USD 1,010. LOS ANGELES, 22 May 1973, *Young Indian Holding a Hare*, USD 6,000. LOS ANGELES, 4 March 1974, *Portrait of a Young Indian* (1904) USD 3,200. NEW YORK, 27 Oct 1977, *Topsy* (1934, oil on canvas, 34 1/4 x 18 1/4 ins / 87 x 46.3 cm) USD 11,000. LOS ANGELES, 18 June 1979, *Tihon Girl* (1902, oil on canvas, 3 1/2 x 7 ins / 8.9 x 17.8 cm) USD 12,000. NEW YORK, 23 April 1982, *Border Land* (1922, oil on canvas, 16 1/4 x 20 ins / 41.2 x 50.8 cm) USD 27,000. DETROIT, 30 Sept 1984, *Indian Child with an Apple* (oil on canvas, 16 x 12 ins / 40.5 x 30.5 cm) USD 12,000. NEW YORK, 4 Dec 1986, *Woodpecker (Ka-Totch)* (1915, oil on canvas, 24 1/4 x 18 ins / 61.6 x 45.7 cm) USD 40,000. NEW YORK, 28 May 1987, *Mendocino Products* (1895, oil on canvas, 13 1/4 x 25 1/4 ins / 33.8 x 64.1 cm) USD 51,000. CALIFORNIA, 3 Feb 1988, *Culin: Indian Child with an Apple* (oil on canvas, 20 x 14 3/4 ins / 51 x 37.5 cm) USD 17,600; *Nourishing Rain: the passing of Makila Madtha* (oil on canvas, 24 x 18 ins / 61 x 46 cm) USD 2,200. NEW YORK, 31 May 1990, *Little Beggar* (oil on card, 9 1/2 x 7 ins / 24 x 17.7 cm) USD 3,850. NEW YORK, 17 Dec 1990, *Mollie Wright's Little Dog* (1905, oil on card, 5 x 7 ins / 12.7 x 17.8 cm) USD 22,000. NEW YORK, 3 Dec 1992, *Chubome: the Orphan* (1917, oil on canvas, 19 1/2 x 13 1/2 ins / 49.5 x 34.3 cm) USD 26,400. NEW YORK, 21 Sept 1994, *Fiancée (Tale-a)* (1922, oil/synthetic resin, 20 3/4 x 16 3/4 ins / 52.7 x 42.5 cm) USD 16,100. LOS ANGELES, 29 April 1999, *Hunter - Tick-E-Dy* (1916, oil on canvas, 22 x 16 ins / 56 x 41 cm) USD 45,000. SAN FRANCISCO, 17 June 1999, *Harvesters, Mary Angel* (1923, oil on canvas, 17 x 14 ins / 43 x 36 cm) USD 25,000. LOS ANGELES, 30 Oct 2000, *Cornfield* (oil on board, 11 x 9 ins / 27 x 22 cm) USD 2,600. LOS ANGELES, 13 Dec 2000, *Profile Portrait of Pomo Indian Woman* (oil on paper on board, 16 x 12 ins / 41 x 30 cm) USD 3,500. NEW YORK, 14 March 2001, *Jack Rabbit* (1919, oil on canvas, 22 x 14 ins / 57 x 36 cm) USD 30,000. LOS ANGELES, 7 Nov 2001, *Matron Da-Sho-Ya* (1910, oil on canvas, 26 x 17 ins / 66 x 43 cm) USD 16,000. LOS ANGELES, 19 June 2002, *Spring Fever - Ya A Tole* (1904, oil on canvas, 24 x 18 ins / 61 x 46 cm) USD 24,000. HAYDEN, 27 July 2002, *Indian Girl* (gouache, oval, 10 x 8 ins / 25 x 20 cm) USD 4,500. BOSTON, 7 March 2003, *Baby* (1995, oil on canvas, 10 x 8 ins / 26 x 20 cm) USD 18,000. BOSTON, 7 March 2003, *Basket Weavers* (1906, oil on canvas, 14 x 18 ins / 36 x 46 cm) USD 42,500. BOSTON, 14 May 2004, *Guarding the Baby* (1905, oil on board, 7 x 5 ins / 18 x 13 cm) USD 14,000. SAN FRANCISCO, 8 June 2004, *Abalone* (1908, oil on canvas, 14 x 11 ins / 35 x 27 cm) USD 16,000.

HUDSON, Henry

British, 18th century.
Active in London between 1782 and 1793.
Engraver.

Henry Hudson's *Sir William Hamilton* after Joshua Reynolds is mentioned by Leblanc. He also engraved after Rembrandt, Castelli, Morland and Mather Brown.

AUCTION RECORDS:

LONDON, 13 Nov 1997, *Saved from the Alligator; Brook Watson and the Shark; another work* (1786, colour mezzotint, three items) GBP 3,220.

HUDSON, Henry John

British, 19th century.
Active in London.
Painter. Portraits, genre scenes.

Henry John Hudson exhibited his work at the Royal Academy in London from 1881.

MUSEUMS AND GALLERIES:

BRADFORD (Cartwright Hall AG): *Neaera Reading a Letter from Catullus* (c. 1894, oil on canvas).

AUCTION RECORDS:

CHESTER, 10 July 1986, *The Letter* (oil on canvas, 20 x 16 ins / 51 x 40.5 cm) GBP 1,800. NEW YORK, 19 July 1990, *Mother and Daughter* (oil on canvas, 35 1/2 x 28 1/2 ins / 90.3 x 72.5 cm) USD 4,950. LONDON, 12 June 1992, *Portrait of Mary Doris Reed Seated in an Armchair and Wearing a White Dress* (1910, oil on canvas, 50 x 40 ins / 127 x 101.6 cm) GBP 2,750.

HUDSON, Julien

American, 19th century.
Born 1811; died 1844.
Painter, miniaturist. Portraits, battles.

Julien Hudson was an Afro-American active in New Orleans during the years 1830-1840. His father was a British merchant and his mother was of mixed race living in New Orleans. He is believed to have studied under a painter in the city in 1826 and 1827, then under Alexandre Abel de Pujol in Paris. In 1831, he opened a studio as a miniaturist and portraitist in New Orleans, where he also gave drawing lessons.

Only four portraits bearing his signature are known. These include his *Self-portrait* (1839). In this, he appears as an elegant young man, with brown hair and a dark complexion, inset in a landscape. His dress indicates that he belongs to the middle class of the period. The details are painted with meticulous care, to the point that certain facial features seem exaggerated, such as the long, lean nasal bone structure or the bushy eyebrows. He also painted *Battle of New Orleans*

In the 20th century, he featured in group exhibitions including in 1967, *Ten Afro-American Artists of the 19th Century*, Howard University, Washington DC; 1974, *American Self-portraits 1670-1973*, travelling exhibition, National Portrait Gallery, Washington, DC; 1976, *Selections of Nineteenth-Century Afro-American Art*, Metropolitan Museum of Art, New York; 1976, *Two Centuries of Black American Art*, Los Angeles County Museum of Art, Los Angeles, and Brooklyn Museum of Art, Brooklyn.

BIBLIOGRAPHY:

Porter, James Amos, *Ten Afro-American Artists of the 19th Century*, group exhibition catalogue, Howard University, Washington DC, 1967. Frankenstein, Alfred/Van Devanter, Ann C., *American Self-portraits 1670-1973*, group exhibition catalogue, National Portrait Gall., International Exhibitions Foundation, Washington DC, 1974. Driskell, David C., *Two Centuries of Black American Art*, group exhibition catalogue, Los Angeles County Museum of Art, Los Angeles, Alfred A. Knopf, New York, 1976. Lewis, Samella, *African American art and artists*, group exhibition catalogue, University of California Press, Berkeley, 1994.

MUSEUMS AND GALLERIES:

NEW ORLÉANS (Louisiana State Mus.): *Jean Michel Fortier III; Self-portrait* (1839, oil on canvas).

HUDSON, Robert

British, 19th century.
Died 6 April 1884, in Sheffield.
Painter. Genre scenes, landscapes.

Robert Hudson exhibited his work at the Royal Academy in London from 1873.

HUDSON, Thomas

British, 18th century.
Born 1701, in Devon; died 26 January 1779, in Twickenham.

Painter. Portraits.

Thomas Hudson was a pupil of Jonathan Richardson and also became his son-in-law. He was a member of the group of artists, which included Hogarth, Allan Ramsay and Francis Hayman, who met at Old Slaughter's Coffee House in the mid-1740s, and with them, promoted the Foundling Hospital as the first public exhibition space for artists in London. Hudson became on of the leading portrait painters in London and executed at least 400 pictures. He followed the common practice of delegating the completion of his works to drapery painters, for example Jospeh van Aken. Examples of his portraits include *Theodore Jacobson* (1746) and *Charles Erskine* (c. 1747-1748). Hudson also executed group pictures like the *Family of Charles Spencer, Third Duke of Marlborough* (c. 1755) and exhibited at the Society of Artists in 1761 and 1766. He had a number of pupils, including Joshua Reynolds, who later became a rival.

BIBLIOGRAPHY:

Miles, E./Simon, J. (ed.), *Thomas Hudson 1701-1779, Portrait Painter and Collector: a Bicentenary Exhibition*, exhibition catalogue, Kenwood House, London, 1979. Simon, J. (ed.), *Handel, a Celebration of his Life and Times (1685-1759)*, exhibition catalogue, National Portrait Gallery, London, 1985. Einberg, E./Egerton, J., *The Age of Hogarth: British Painters Born 1675-1709*, Tate, London, 1988 (Tate Gallery Collections, vol. 2).

MUSEUMS AND GALLERIES:

LONDON (Dulwich Picture Gal.): *A Man, Possibly the 4th Duke of Leeds* (oil on canvas, portrait) - LONDON (Foundling Mus.) - LONDON (National Maritime Mus.) - LONDON (National Portrait Gal.): *Sir John Willes* (1744, oil on canvas); *George Frederick Handel* (1756, oil on canvas); *King George II* (1744, oil on canvas) - LONDON (Royal Collection) - LONDON (Tate Collection): *Samuel Scott the Marine Painter* (c. 1731-1733, oil on canvas); *Mrs Sarah Ingram* (c. 1750-1755, oil on canvas).

AUCTION RECORDS:

PARIS, 17 Feb 1896, *Portrait of a Woman,* FRF 1,750. PARIS, 10 May 1904, *Portrait of a Young Girl,* FRF 1,500. NEW YORK, 24 March 1905, *Mrs Colley Cibber,* USD 450. LONDON, 14 Dec 1907, *Portraits of Two Young Women,* GBP 30. LONDON, 28 March 1908, *Joseph Soyer,* GBP 52; *Mrs Lydia Soyer,* GBP 63. LONDON, 17 July 1908, *Portrait of the Young Son of M. Vanderveld,* GBP 63. LONDON, 11 Dec 1909, *Portrait of Mrs George Speke,* GBP 178. LONDON, 8 July 1910, *Miss Chetwynd Dressed as a Shepherdess,* GBP 65. LONDON, 19 Nov 1910, *Portrait of Mrs Pleydell,* GBP 39. LONDON, 25 Feb 1911, *Dame Francis Shirley,* GBP 18. LONDON, 12 April 1911, *Mrs Weston,* GBP 56. LONDON, 5 May 1911, *Gentleman in a Brown Suit,* GBP 162. LONDON, 1 June 1911, *Edward Hay,* GBP 35. PARIS, 9 Dec 1920, *George Frederick Handel, Composer* (pencil) FRF 2,400. LONDON, Feb 1922, *John Gray,* GBP 39. LONDON, June 1922, *Lady in a Blue Dress,* GBP 14. LONDON, July 1922, *Lady Ashbrook,* GBP 35; *Lord Ashbrook,* GBP 52. LONDON, July 1922, *Madame Pierce Taylor,* GBP 9. LONDON, Dec 1922, *Two Gentlemen Seated, Drinking Liqueurs,* GBP 84. LONDON, Jan 1923, *Lady in a White Satin Dress,* GBP 16. PARIS, 15 Feb 1923, *Portrait of Mrs Edward Gibbon in a Park,* FRF 1,420. LONDON, March 1923, *Portrait of a Lady,* GBP 37. LONDON, March 1923, *Lady Collingwood,* GBP 28; *Lady in a White dress and Blue Coat,* GBP 28. LONDON, July 1923, *John Campbell, Customs Officer,* GBP 28. LONDON, Feb 1924, *Jenny Cameron in a White Dress,* GBP 54. LONDON, July 1924, *Swift,* GBP 23. PARIS, 22 May 1925, *Portrait of a Young Lord,* FRF 8,000. LONDON, 11 June 1926, *Portrait of a Woman,* GBP 105. LONDON, 2 March 1928, *Mrs Benjamin,* GBP 173. LONDON, 15 June 1928, *Lady Mary Booth,* GBP 189; *The Honourable John Grey,* GBP 325; *Sir Richard Wrottesley,* GBP 367; *George Hunt,* GBP 819; *Portrait of a Man,* GBP 609. LONDON, 27 July 1928, *David Garrick,* GBP 273. LONDON, 9 Oct 1928, *Sir Edward Dering,* GBP 315. LONDON, 21 Dec 1928, *Sir Charles Trevelyan,* GBP 441. LONDON, 1 Aug 1929, *Lady of the Savile Family,* GBP 50. LONDON, 18 Nov 1929, *Carlos Cony,* GBP 136. LONDON, 7 March 1930, *Man in Grey,* GBP 115. LONDON, 18 July 1930, *Mrs Harvey,* GBP 819. LONDON, 12 Dec 1930, *Catherine, Countess of Egmont,* GBP 94; *John, 2nd Earl of Egmont,* GBP 199. NEW YORK, 2 April 1931, *Viscount Bolingbroke,* USD 475. LONDON, 24 June 1932, *Admiral William Rowlet,* GBP 147. NEW YORK, 18 April 1934, *Admiral Sir Charles Hardy,* USD 375. LONDON, 20 July 1934, *Lady Oxcuden,* GBP 220. LONDON, 14 Dec 1934, *William, Duke of Devonshire,* GBP 210. NEW YORK, 4 Jan 1935, *Lady Monnyfenny,* USD 700. NEW YORK, 15 Jan 1937, *Sir Thomas Aston and his Sisters,* USD 275. PARIS, 30 June and 1 July 1941, *Portrait of a Young Lord,* FRF 5,100. NEW YORK, 11 Nov 1942, *William Blair,* USD 210. NEW YORK, 9 March 1944, *A Lady,* USD 400. LONDON, 9 June 1944, *Mrs Watson,* GBP 189. NEW YORK, 29 March 1945, *Mrs John Durrant,* USD 900. NEW YORK, 20 Feb 1946, *Lady,* USD 575. LONDON, 3 May 1946, *the Earl of Galloway and his Wife,* GBP 262. NEW YORK, 9 May 1947, *David Garrick,* USD 225. PARIS, 7 Dec 1950, *Portrait of a Young Woman,* FRF 70,000. LONDON, 2 July 1958, *Mrs Emma Harvey,* GBP 400. LONDON, 18 Nov 1960, *Portrait of a Gentleman,* GBP 168. NEW YORK, 20 Jan 1961, *Portrait of a Girl with a Cat,* USD 425. LONDON, 25 March 1966, *Lady Elizabeth Cecil,* Gns 1,700. LONDON, 7 July 1967, *Handel,* Gns 9,000. LONDON, 17 June 1970, *Dr John Andrews,* GBP 500. NEW YORK, 21 April 1971, *Portrait of a Lady of Quality,* USD 2,000. LONDON, 13 Dec 1972, *Anne Dixie,* GBP 2,800. LONDON, 6 April 1973, *John and Robert, Sons of the 2nd Duke of Roxburgh,* Gns 16,000. LONDON, 22 March 1974, *Portrait of Young Woman,* Gns 22,000. LONDON, 31 March 1976, *Portrait of Woman* (1743, oil on canvas, 16 x 19 3/4 ins / 40.5 x 50 cm) GBP 32,000. LONDON, 25 Nov 1977, *Portrait of a Young Lady* (oil on oval canvas, 28 3/4 x 23 3/4 ins / 73.3 x 60.3 cm) GBP 3,000. LONDON, 27 June 1980, *George Hunt* (1750, oil on canvas, 48 3/4 x 38 3/4 ins / 123.8 x 98.5 cm) GBP 10,000. NEW YORK, 17 June 1982, *Henry Harvey Aston of Aston as a Youth* (oil on canvas, 46 3/4 x 37 ins / 119 x 94 cm) USD 6,500. LONDON, 13 May 1983, *Sir Watkin Williams Wynn* (oil on canvas, 49 3/4 x 40 ins / 126.4 x 101.5 cm) GBP 2,000. LONDON, 12 March 1986, *Alexander Thistlewayte, his Wife Sarah and their Daughters Anne and Catherine* (oil on canvas, 76 3/4 x 86 1/2 ins / 195 x 220 cm) GBP 40,000. LONDON, 30 Jan 1987, *Portrait of a Lady with a Lace Shawl* (oil on canvas, 50 1/4 x 40 1/2 ins / 127.6 x 102.9 cm) GBP 6,000. LONDON, 15 July 1988, *Nancy Fortescue Wearing a Dark Blue, Goldbraided Riding Habit* (oil on canvas, 50 x 40 ins / 127 x 101.6 cm) GBP 38,500. NEW YORK, 21 Oct 1988, *Phillip Chetwynd, Wearing a Brown Doublet with his Right Hand in the Pocket of a Blue Waistcoat* (oil on canvas, 48 x 39 1/4 ins / 122 x 100 cm) USD 9,900. NEW YORK, 28 Oct 1988, *John Ker, Future 3rd Duke of Roxburgh, with his Brother Robert* (1752, oil on canvas, 53 x 65 1/2 ins / 134.5 x 166.2 cm) USD 198,000. LONDON, 15 Nov 1989, *Thomas Popham of Bagborough; Sarah Popham, his Wife* (oil on canvas, a pair, each 49 1/2 x 40 ins / 126 x 101.5 cm) GBP 34,100. NEW YORK, 5 April 1990, *Portrait of an Elegant Gentleman* (oil on canvas, 49 1/2 x 39 ins / 126 x 99 cm) USD 11,000. LONDON, 10 July 1991, *Portrait of a Gentleman Dressed in a Brown Suit and a White Satin Waistcoat* (1749, oil on canvas, 49 1/4 x 39 1/4 ins / 125 x 100 cm) GBP 4,400. LONDON, 12 July 1991, *Portrait of Admiral Richard Tyrell in Uniform and Carrying his Tricorn under his Arm* (oil on canvas, 49 1/2 x 40 ins / 126 x 101.5 cm) GBP 7,150. LONDON, 15 Nov 1991, *Portrait of a Girl Wearing a White Dress and Garlanded with Flowers* (oil on canvas, oval 23 x 20 1/2 ins / 58.5 x 52 cm) GBP 4,950. STOCKHOLM, 19 May 1992, *Portrait Mrs Harris Wearing a White Dress and a Blue Stole* (oil on canvas, 50 x 39 3/4 ins / 127 x 101 cm) SEK 21,000. LONDON, 20 Nov 1992, *William Huddleston of Millom Castle in a Brown Velvet Suit, Seated at his Desk* (oil on canvas, 50 x 40 1/4 ins / 127 x 102.2 cm) GBP 4,950. LONDON, 6 April 1993, *Three-quarter Portrait of Lady Frances Coningsby Wearing a White Satin Dress* (oil on canvas, 35 1/4 x 27 1/4 ins / 89.5 x 69 cm) GBP 7,360. NEW YORK, 20 May 1993, *Three-quarter Standing Portrait of a Lady, Thought to be Isabelle Courtenay, in a Straw-coloured Dress with Blue Laces* (1751, oil on canvas, 49 x 38 3/4 ins / 124.5 x 98.4 cm) USD 9,200. LONDON, 13 July 1994, *Portrait of Lady Mary Osborn Wearing a White Dress and a Blue Stole, Standing near a Parapet, with Fruit and Flowers* (oil on canvas, 78 x 58 ins / 198 x 147.5 cm) GBP 20,700. NEW YORK, 19 May 1995, *Standing Portrait of a Lady in a Blue Dress Holding a Hat with an Ostrich Feather* (oil on canvas, 49 1/2 x 40 ins / 125.7 x 101.6 cm) USD 27,600. NEW YORK, 15 May 1996, *Three-quarter Standing Portrait of Sir John Berker, his Hand Resting on the Edge of a Table, Dressed in a Brown Velvet Suit and an Embroided Wasitcoat* (oil on canvas, 50 x 40 ins / 127 x 101.7 cm) USD 12,650. LONDON, 13 Nov 1996, *Walter Radcliffe and his Family* (oil on canvas, 126 x 174 ins / 320 x 442 cm) GBP 41,100. LONDON, 9 April 1997, *Miss Beaumont.* NEW YORK, 16 Oct 1997, *Three-quarter Portrait of a Lady, Thought to be Isabella Courtenay, Wearing a Yellow Satin Dress with a Blue Bow and a Shawl, Standing Beside an Orange Tree* (1751, oil on canvas, 50 x 40 ins / 127 x 101.6 cm) USD 11,500. LONDON, 12 Nov 1997, *Charles Jennens* (oil on canvas, 48 x 39 ins / 122 x 99 cm) GBP 13,800. LONDON, 31 March 1999, *Portrait of Lady Camilla Fleming* (1785, oil on canvas, 49 x 40 ins / 125 x 101 cm) GBP 13,000. LONDON, 11 June 1999, *Portrait of Lady Frances Courtenay, Daughter of Heneage Finch, 2nd Earl of Aylesford* (oil on canvas, 50 x 40 ins / 127 x 102 cm) GBP 30,000. LONDON, 16 June 2000, *Portrait of Joseph Gulston* (oil on canvas, 50 x 50 ins / 127 x 126 cm) GBP 25,000. LONDON, 16 June 2000, *Portrait of Alexander, Earl of Galloway* (1749, oil on canvas, a pair, 50 x 40 ins / 127 x 101 cm) GBP 30,000. LONDON, 15 June 2001, *Portrait of John Fytch Barker, Aged Three* (oil on canvas, 50 x 42 ins / 127 x 106 cm) GBP 65,000. LONDON, 28 Nov 2001, *Portrait of Study of the Clock Maker, George Graham* (red chalk, 11 x 7 ins / 27 x 17 cm) GBP 21,000. NEW YORK, 24 Jan 2002, *Portrait of a Lady in a Blue Gown* (oil on canvas, 50 x 40 ins / 126 x 102 cm) USD 48,000. LONDON, 21 March 2002, *Portrait of Miss Denison, Wife of Jonathan Midgley of Beverley, Yorkshire* (oil on canvas, 50 x 39 ins / 126 x 100 cm) GBP 26,000. VIENNA, 28 Oct 2003, *Duke of Kent* (oil on canvas, 49 x 39 ins / 124 x 100 cm) EUR 20,000. LONDON, 25 Nov 2003, *Portrait of Sir Watkin William Wynn, 3rd Bt., Wearing Dark Blue Coat and Red Trousers* (oil on canvas, 50 x 40 ins / 126 x 102 cm) GBP 19,000. LONDON, 1 July 2004, *Portrait of a Lady* (oil on canvas, 49 x 39 ins / 125 x 100 cm) GBP 9,000. LONDON, 25 Nov 2004, *Portrait of Lady Mary Osborn* (oil on canvas, 78 x 58 ins / 198 x 147 cm) GBP 42,000.

HUDSON, William

British, 19th century.
Born 1782; died 1847.
Active in Croydon.
Painter. Portraits.

William Hudson exhibited his work very regularly in London at the Royal Academy, Suffolk Street and the New Water-Colour Society (of which he was a member) from 1803 to 1846.

AUCTION RECORDS:

PARIS, 23 March 1923, *Young Mother Watching Over her Slumbering Child* (watercolour) FRF 150. LONDON, 2 July 2001, *Young Lady, in a Yellow Dress and Brimmed Bonnet* (1830, miniature) GBP 1,300. LONDON, 2 July 2001, *Lady, a Baby on her Lap, and Landscape Beyond* (1830, miniature) GBP 1,500. NEW YORK, 21 May 2003, *Political Debate between Two Irishmen* (oil on canvas, 30 x 20 ins / 76 x 51 cm) USD 9,000.

HUDSPETH, Robert Norman

American, 19th - 20th century.
Born 2 July 1862, in Caledonia (Ontario), Canada; died 1943.
Miniaturist.

Robert Norman Hudspeth was a pupil of Bouguereau in Paris.

HUDY, Joanny

French, 19th century.
Died 1890.
Painter.

Hudy was a member of the Société des Artistes Français.

HUE, Alexandre

French, 19th century.
Active in Versailles.
Painter. History painting, landscapes.

Alexandre Hue was the pupil and eldest son of Jean-François Hue. He exhibited at the Salon from 1810 to 1842.

HUE, Alexandre Laurent

French, 19th century.
Active in Paris.
Watercolourist, draughtsman. Landscapes.

Alexandre Laurent was the son of Jean-François Hue, and taught drawing at the Lycée in Versailles (Yvelines). He exhibited some watercolours at the Salon, between 1833 and 1835.

HUE, C.B.

British, 19th century.
Active in London.
Painter. Seascapes.

HUE, Charles Désiré

French, 19th century.
Born 1842, in Meaux; died 1899.
Painter, watercolourist, lithographer. Genre scenes, seascapes.

Charles Hue was a pupil of Robert Fleury and Caraud. He exhibited at the Paris Salon, and gained an honourable mention in 1883.

Hue enjoyed painting 18th-century scenes, and often used Jean-Jacques Rousseau and his works - as well as Prévost's novel *Manon Lescaut* - as his subjects.

MUSEUMS AND GALLERIES:

ST-BRIEUC: *Shipwreck.*

AUCTION RECORDS:

LONDON, 6 March 1911, *Genre Scene,* GBP 3. PARIS, 22-24 Feb 1923, *The Salon of Louis XVI,* FRF 135. PARIS, 4 Oct 1925, *Reading the Letter,* FRF 1,500. PARIS, 20 Dec 1944, *Woman at a Window,* FRF 2,600. PARIS, 7 Feb 1945, *Seascape,* FRF 10,500. LONDON, 4 May 1973, *The Forbidden Letter,* Gns 1,200. LONDON, 3 Oct 1980, *Widow* (oil on canvas, 31 x 21 ins / 79 x 53.4 cm) GBP 500. PARIS, 19 Feb 1982, *Teatime* (1860, oil on panel, 22 x 17 3/4 ins / 56 x 45 cm) FRF 14,500. ROUBAIX, 27 Feb 1983, *The Elegant Hairdresser* (1865, oil on canvas, 31 1/2 x 25 1/4 ins / 80 x 64 cm) FRF 23,000. NEW YORK, 15 Feb 1985, *Romantic Conversation* (oil on canvas, 39 x 28 ins / 99 x 71 cm) USD 4,000. LONDON, 26 Feb 1988, *Convalescence* (1865, oil on panel, 14 1/2 x 18 ins / 36.9 x 45.7 cm) GBP 2,640. NEW YORK, 9 Feb 1999, *Summer Picnic* (oil on canvas, 10 x 13 ins / 26 x 34 cm) USD 9,000. LONDON, 25 March 1999, *The Young Maid* (oil on canvas, 18 x 15 ins / 46 x 38 cm) GBP 12,500. PARIS, 6 June 2002, *Household Scene* (oil on canvas, a pair, 25 x 21 ins / 64 x 53 cm) EUR 8,500. NEW YORK, 21 Nov 2002, *Games of Love* (oil on canvas, a pair, 26 x 21 ins / 65 x 54 cm) USD 14,000. NEUILLY, 9 April 2004, *The Fabric Merchant* (1864, oil on panel, 18 x 25 ins / 46 x 64 cm) EUR 10,500.

HUE, Ernest
French, 19th century.
Active in Paris.
Sculptor.
Ernest Hue became a member of the Société des Artistes Français in 1883.

HUE, Jean Armand
French, 18th century.
Active in Paris in 1787.
Painter (?), sculptor (?).

HUE, Jean-François
French, 18th - 19th century.
Born 1 December 1751, in St-Arnould-en-Yvelines (Seine-et-Oise); died 26 December 1823, in Paris.
Painter (gouache). History painting, battles, genre scenes, landscapes, seascapes.
Jean-François Hue was apprenticed to Joseph Vernet in whose studio he worked assiduously. He was approved by the Académie on 25 November 1780 and was received as an Académicien on 30 November 1782. He featured at the Paris Salon from 1781 to 1822.

Hue was a prolific artist. He produced a few historical paintings but essentially concentrated on landscapes and seascapes. He was brought in to continue the series of French harbours started by Joseph Vernet, and the paintings he created in this genre are kept at the Musée de la Marine in Paris.

MUSEUMS AND GALLERIES:
ALENÇON: *Fishing by Torchlight* - ANGERS: *The Ship 'Le Formidable' in Combat* - CHÂTEAU-THIERRY: *Landscape* - CHERBOURG: *View of the Port and Harbour of Lorient; The Waterfall at Tivoli* - COMPIÈGNE: two landscapes - LE HAVRE: *Moonlit Sea; Sunset with Figures* - NANTES: *Waterfall under a Rocky Arch* - PARIS (Louvre): *Lorient; Moonlight; St-Malo; Brest Harbour; Brest Roads; Brest, the Cover Dock* - ST PETERSBURG (Hermitage): *Shipwreck* - VERSAILLES: *The Capture of Granada; Naval Battle for the Island of Granada; The French Army Crossing the Danube; The French Army Entering Genoa; Napoleon Visiting the Cape of Boulogne.*

AUCTION RECORDS:
PARIS, 8 June 1937, *View of a Harbour,* FRF 290. PARIS, 14 May 1945, *Fishing by Moonlight,* FRF 5,500. PARIS, 11 Dec 1946, *The Wreck Survivors,* FRF 5,100. PARIS, 4-5 May 1955, *Shepherds at the Foot of a Waterfall Overlooked by a Castle,* FRF 40,000. PARIS, 30 Nov 1978, *River Landscape* (oil on canvas, 18 x 22 ins / 46 x 55 cm) FRF 20,000. NEW YORK, 30 May 1979, *The Shipwreck* (oil on canvas, 49 x 66 ins / 124.5 x 167.5 cm) USD 4,100. PARIS, 13 Feb 1981, *View of a Harbour* (oil on canvas, 19 1/4 x 24 ins / 49 x 61 cm) FRF 11,500. MONTE CARLO, 26 June 1983, *Palombière at Daybreak* (oil on canvas, 32 x 46 ins / 81 x 117 cm) FRF 110,000. PARIS, 12 June 1986, *The Country Dance* (oil on canvas, 25 3/4 x 32 ins / 65.5 x 81.5 cm) FRF 53,000. MONACO, 17 June 1988, *Sunrise and Sunset* (oil on canvas, a pair, each 25 1/2 x 31 1/2 ins / 65 x 80 cm) FRF 111,000. AMSTERDAM, 13 Nov 1990, *Capriccio of a Mediterranean Port with Fishermen in the Foreground* (oil on canvas, 12 3/4 x 15 3/4 ins / 32.5 x 40.2 cm) NLG 12,650. PARIS, 18 April 1991, *Landscape with Waterfalls* (oil on panel, 8 1/4 x 12 1/2 ins / 21 x 32 cm) FRF 44,000. PARIS, 22 June 1992, *Seascape in Stormy Weather* (oil on canvas, 36 1/4 x 48 ins / 92 x 121 cm) FRF 85,000. PARIS, 4 Dec 1992, *Stairs Leading to a Quay* (gouache, 7 3/4 x 10 1/4 ins / 20 x 26 cm) FRF 3,000. LONDON, 11 Dec 1992, *Wrecked Frigate on a Howling Sea with Castaways on a Beach* (oil on canvas, 22 1/4 x 31 1/4 ins / 56.8 x 79.6 cm) GBP 8,800. NEW YORK, 15 Jan 1993, *Landscape in the Roman Countryside with Dancing Peasants* (1787, oil on canvas, 44 3/4 x 58 1/4 ins / 113.7 x 148 cm) USD 41,400. PARIS, 28 June 1993, *Landscape with a Waterfall* (oil on oak panel, 8 1/4 x 12 1/2 ins / 21 x 32 cm) FRF 40,000. MONACO, 4 Dec 1993, *Mediterranean Port at Sunset with Fishermen below a Fort* (1791, oil on canvas, 23 1/4 x 25 1/2 ins / 58.9 x 64.8 cm) FRF 55,500. NEW YORK, 28 Jan 1999, *Landscape with Woman Bathing near Waterfall* (oil on canvas, 22 x 28 ins / 57 x 72 cm) USD 13,000. PARIS, 20 Dec 1999, *Port Scene. Scene of Shipwreck* (oil on panel, a pair, 9 x 11 ins / 23 x 28 cm) FRF 40,000. NEW YORK, 23 May 2000, *View of the Hotel de Chassins Curtilly* (oil on canvas, 51 x 63 ins / 130 x 160 cm) USD 17,000. NEW YORK, 23 May 2000, *Views of the Chateau de Mousseaux and its Gardens* (oil on canvas, four, 30 x 34 ins / 75 x 86 cm) USD 220,000. PARIS, 5 Feb 2001, *Fishermen on the Shore* (oil on canvas, 21 x 28 ins / 53 x 72 cm) FRF 92,000. NEW YORK, 23 May 2001, *Fishermen and Other Figures Along a Shoreline* (oil on panel, 20 x 28 ins / 50 x 72 cm) USD 10,000. NEW YORK, 7 June 2002, *Moonlit River Landscape* (oil on canvas, 25 x 39 ins / 64 x 99 cm) USD 22,000.

HUE, Joseph
French, 19th century.
Painter. Landscapes.

AUCTION RECORDS:
PARIS, 29 June 1945, *Goats Resting, near a Wood* (1822) FRF 1,450.

HUE, Lambertus Janz de
Dutch, 17th century.
Born 1623; died 14 February 1681, in Amsterdam.
Painter.
Lambertus de Hue was active in Amsterdam in 1653 and in 1664 in The Hague. Between 1665 and 1676 he was again working in Amsterdam.

MUSEUMS AND GALLERIES:
AMSTERDAM: *Portrait of Margaretha Munter.*

HUE, Magdelaine or Madeleine
French, 20th century.
Born 1882; died 1943.
Painter. Urban landscapes, landscapes.
Hue was a painter of the Rouen School.

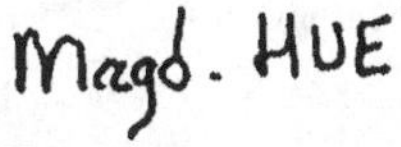

AUCTION RECORDS:
SCEAUX, 18 Nov 1990, *Wood near Tancarville* (oil on panel, 11 3/4 x 15 3/4 ins / 30 x 40 cm) FRF 4,200. PARIS, 2 June 1993, *The Quays of Rouen in the Snow* (oil on canvas, 23 1/2 x 28 3/4 ins / 60 x 73 cm) FRF 18,000. PARIS, 19 Nov 1995, *Bouquet of Blue Hortensias* (oil on card, 24 3/4 x 33 1/2 ins / 63 x 85 cm) FRF 4,000. PARIS, 15 June 2004, *Port of Rouen* (oil on canvas, 25 x 34 ins / 63 x 86 cm) EUR 2,200.

HUE D'ARRAS
French, 14th century.
Born at the beginning of the 14th century, in Arras.
Active in St-Omer in 1323.
Glass painter.

HUE DE BRÉVAL (Mlle). See **ROUSSEAU Virginie**

HUEBENER, Zacharias
German, 17th century.

Active in Hamburg.
Sculptor.

HUEBER, Hans
Austrian, 19th century.
Born 10 December 1813, in Waizenkirchen; died 15 November 1889, in Waizenkirchen.
Painter. Landscapes.

He was a student at the academy in Munich.

AUCTION RECORDS:

VIENNA, 14 Sept 1976, *River Landscape* (1845, oil on canvas, 16 x 19¾ ins / 40.5 x 50 cm) ATS 32,000.

HUEBER, Johann Franz
German, 18th century.
Active in Gars (Bavaria).
Painter.

HUEBER, Lorenz
German, 18th century.
Died 1737.
Active in Munich.
Painter.

Mention is made of his views of the Ratshaus (Town Hall) in Munich.

HUEBER, Luc, or Huber
French, 20th century.
Born 27 September 1888, in Ste-Croix-en-Plaine (Bas-Rhin); died 24 April 1974, in Strasbourg.
Painter.

Hueber was influenced by the work of Manet and was well-known in artistic cirlces in his native Alsace. He exhibited in Paris at the Salon des Artistes Français and the Salon d'Automne. He belonged to the Groupe de Mai (1919-1934), a group of ten artists who worked in a post-Cezanne style, led first by Simon Lévy and then by Hans Haug, painter and curator of the Musée de Beaux-Arts in Strasbourg. In 2003, the historical museum in Haguenau presented a solo exhibition of Luc Hueber's work.

BIBLIOGRAPHY:

Le Groupe de Mai, 1919-1934, exhibition catalogue, Musée Historique, Haguenau, 2002.

MUSEUMS AND GALLERIES:

STRASBOURG: *Walk*; *Portrait*.

HUEBER, Martin Joseph
German, 17th century.
Active in Kötzting (Bavaria) in 1689.
Painter.

HUEBER, Maximilian
German, 18th century.
Died 1789.
Active in Munich.
Engraver.

He produced devotional pictures.

HUEBER, Sebastian
German, 18th century.
Active in Pfarrkirchen (Bavaria) c. 1750.
Painter.

HUEBLER, Douglas Charles
American, 20th century.
Born 1924, in Ann Arbor (Michigan); died 1997.
Painter, sculptor, draughtsman, photographer, installation artist.
Conceptual Art, Appropriation Art.

Douglas Charles Huebler studied at the Cleveland Institute of Art at the University of Michigan, then at the Académie Julian, Paris. Like numerous young American artists who, despite the wave of Pop Art, remained loyal to Abstract art, his research led him, in terms of his early work, to 'minimal art'; his main preoccupation seemed to be gigantic dimensions. But in less than three years he switched to work which was more or less equivalent to Conceptual Art, and ultimately became one of its leading exponents, along with Joseph Kosuth, Sol Lewit, Robert Barry and Lawrence Weiner. His Conceptual Art enquiries focused on 'interpreting' the range of life of forms in multiple signs and places, rather than the internalising or integrity of objects typical of the 'minimalist' genre.

Huebler was respectful of the natural order of things, such as that advanced by Zen philosophy, and no longer desired a brutal confrontation with nature - unlike his early 'minimal' sculptures in plywood covered with Formica. Instead, he sought harmonic coordination between his action and this nature to achieve a conscious undiluted experience of things. It was at this time that he famously stated: 'The world is full of fairly interesting objects and I have no desire to add any more. I prefer to make do with stating the existence of things in terms of time and/or place.' This statement echoed the ideas developed by author Alain Robbe-Grillet in *For a New Novel* (1963), translated into English in 1965. Just like him, Huebler wanted to reach a portal somewhere beyond traditional communication, which would offer the possibility of removing all the historico-psychologico-symbolic connotations, which we are too often dependent on when we attempt to interpret a work of art. So he began to hammer simple nails into the ground and drew simple forms without building them.

But the major turning point occurred at the time of *Sculpture Sites*, c. 1967-1968. This was a series of personal appearances performed by the artist at various different geographic locations: 'Because work occurs somewhere beyond perceptual experience, a documentation system enables [people] to become aware of its existence. The documentation takes the form of photos, maps, plans, drawings and written descriptions.' Everything was pieced together in the imagination of spectators. According to Huebler, 'conceptual' initially meant 'Imagine this' without denying [yourselves] the phenomenal experience. His conceptual elements can be divided into three categories: *Duration Pieces, Location Pieces* and *Variable Pieces*. The first category was distinguished by the use of a time factor within the work itself, for example, the doubling of the duration of time which elapsed between each photo taken of the same place, e.g. 1, 2, 4, 8, 16 seconds etc. *Duration Piece No 5* (1970) is a series of 12 photographs arranged according to a time system. Each photo was taken following a lapse of time which reduced by half each time. This lapse of time was used by the artist to walk in a given direction and then take a new photo. The *Location Pieces*, the second direction in terms of his conceptual system, are locations randomly selected from a map, and identified photographically or via postal receipts. Thus *42° Parallel* (1968) tracked down 14 town locations situated exactly or approximately on the 42nd parallel latitude in the USA. The *Variable Pieces* were generated by contact between several often unknown people. *Variable piece No 4* (1970) began as follows: On 7 January 1970, a point representing a place photographically identified was marked on a map of Paris. This was the 'work step'. The owner of the work had to continue the system within the time and space allotted, 60 days after acquiring it. Its final form was unknown.

Generally speaking, Huebler's work was initially a confrontation between language and image, a way of articulating linguistically about phenomena: 'Reception (of a work) depends entirely on language. In my case, there is a time limit or text for every visual phenomenon.' From 1985, Huebler was interested in reinterpreting and commenting on art history painting (Bruegel, Monet, Matisse, Mondrian and Ad Reihardt), using texts, humorous narration, photographs and copies of works. The image of the original painting, the style of the painting, and the context in which the painting was perceived were the key elements at the end of the twentieth century and for the continuation of his research on the possibilities of thinking about art in terms of a medium, and searching in his own way for how to communicate by art and on art.

Huebler took part in many collective exhibitions, including: 1953, *Concepts for Examining Concepts* held at the Philipps Gallery, Detroit; 1957, *First Biennale*, held at Columbia Museum; 1966, *Primary Structures*, held at the Jewish Museum, New York; 1967, *Cool Art*, held at the Aldrich Museum, Ridgefield; 1969, Seth Siegelaub Gallery, New York; 1969, *Conception/Perception*, held at the Eugenia Butler Gallery, Los Angeles; 1969, *When Attitudes Become Forms*, held at the Kunsthalle, Bern; 1970, *Software*, held at the Jewish Museum, New York; *Conceptual Art Conceptual Aspects*, held at New York Cultural Center, New York; 1970, *Information*, held at the Museum of Modern Art, New York; 1971, *Books and Multiples*, held at Philadelphia Museum of Art; 1972, *Conceptual Art*, held at the Kunstmuseum, Basel; 1972, Documenta V, Kassel; 1989-1990, *L'Art conceptuel une perspective* (*Conceptual Art: A Perspective*), held at the Musée d'Art Moderne, Paris; 2002, *Les Années 70: l'art en cause* (*The 1970s: Art in Question*), held at Capc-Musée d'Art Contemporain, Bordeaux; 2002, *Sans commune mesure. Image et texte dans l'art actuel* (*Without Common Measure: Image and Text in Contemporary Art*), held at the Musée d'Art Moderne Lille Métropole, Villeneuve d'Ascq.

He had his first solo exhibition in 1953 at the Phillips Gallery, Detroit, then: 1967, Obelisk Gallery, Boston; 1968, Seth Siegelaub Gallery, New York; 1969, Eugenia Buttler Gallery, Los Angeles; 1970, 1971, Konrad Fischer, Düsseldorf; 1970, *Duration Pieces*, then *Variable Works in Progress*, held at Galleria Sperone, Turin; 1970, *Variable Works*, held at the Galerie Yvon Lambert, Paris; 1970, Galerie Art & Language, Amsterdam; 1971, *Variable Pieces: 11, 44, 45, 46, 47, 48, 49*, held at the Leo Castelli Gallery, New York; 1972, *Variable Pieces: 1, 2, 3, 4, 5*, held at the Galerie Yvon Lambert, Paris; 1972, *Variable Pieces: 20, 21, 22, 23, 24*, held at the Konrad Fischer Gallery, Düsseldorf; 1972, Museum of Fine Arts, Boston; 1973, Westfälischer Kunstverein, Münster; 1979, Stedelijk Museum, Amsterdam; 1988, Museum of Contemporary Art, La Jolla, California; 1989, Musée St-Pierre, Lyons; 1994, Palais des Beaux-Arts, Brussels; and 2002 Camden Arts Centre, London.

BIBLIOGRAPHY:

Douglas Huebler, exhibition catalogue, Stedelijk Van Abbemuseum, Eindhoven, 1979. Onorato, Ronald J., *Douglas Huebler*, exhibition catalogue, La Jolla Museum of Contemporary Art, La Jolla (CA), 1979. '*Sabotage or Trophy? Advance or Retreat?*' in *Artforum*, periodical, New York, May, 1982. Hugunin, James, *Douglas Huebler, the Map and the Territory*, Center for photographic Studies, Los Angeles, 1984. *Crocodile Tears*, Museum of Contemporary Art, Los Angeles, 1986. Denizot, René, et al., *Douglas Huebler: "variable", etc.*, exhibition catalogue, Fonds régional d'Art contemporain du Limousin, Limoges, 1993 (text in French and English). Ryoux, Jean Christophe, '*Douglas Huebler Alain Robbe-Grillet, le creux du sujet*' in *Galeries Magazine*, periodical, Paris, April-May 1993. Godfrey, Mark, *Douglas Huebler*, exhibition catalogue, Camden Arts Centre, London, 2002. Durand, Régis, et al., *Sans commune mesure. Image et texte dans l'art actuel*, exhibition catalogue, Éd. Léo Scheer, Paris, 2002.

MUSEUMS AND GALLERIES:

GRENOBLE: *Variable Piece n° 70 in Process* (1971) - LYONS (MBA): *Crocodile Tears II: The Great Corrector Mondrian III* (1989) - SANTA FE (MFA): *Duration piece #5, New York, April 1969* (photographs).

AUCTION RECORDS:

PARIS, 20 Jan 1991, *Variable Piece #70* (photos and typed text, 22 x 25 1/2 ins / 56 x 65 cm) FRF 43,000. NEW YORK, 3 May 1993, *Variable Piece #99* (1973, seven photographs/paper and pastel/card, 31 1/2 x 31 1/2 ins / 80 x 80 cm) USD 4,025. NEW YORK, 17 May 2000, *Crocodile Tears II. Buried Treasure - Monet* (oil, gelatin and silver with printed text, print, three, 37 x 16 ins / 95 x 41 cm) USD 6,500. PARIS, 19 June 2002, *Represented Above are the Vertical Edges of Two Planes of Colour* (1968, coloured crayon and ink, 22 x 30 ins / 55 x 76 cm) EUR 8,000. PARIS, 19 June 2002, *Variable Piece 13* (1971, collage over photograph, 19 x 35 ins / 49 x 88 cm) EUR 16,000. LONDON, 26 June 2003, *Working Drawings* (coloured felt tip, pencil and text on paper, three, 51 x 40 ins / 130 x 102 cm) GBP 10,800. LAMBERTVILLE, 24 April 2004, *Untitled* (1978, graphite, ink and coloured pencil, 5 x 5 ins / 12 x 13 cm) USD 3,750.

HUEBNER. See also HÜBNER

HUEBNER, Anastasius

Moravian, 19th century.
Born 1789; died 28 September 1856, in Brno.
Painter.

Anastasius Huebner is known for his portraits and paintings on porcelain.

HUEBNER, Anton

Moravian, 19th century.
Born 15 July 1818, in Brno; died 26 May 1892.
Painter.

Anton Huebner, the son of Anastasius Huebner, studied in Vienna.

HUEBNER, Bartholomaus

German, 18th century.
Born 1727, in Augsburg; died c. 1795, in Basel.
Engraver.

A pupil of J D Herz. He is documented in Basel from 1770, working in the studio of Christian von Mechel. He mostly engraved portraits.

HUEBNER, Carl

German, 19th century.
Born 13 January 1797, in Berlin; died 14 October 1831, in Paris.
Engraver, lithographer.

A pupil of Buchorn, he settled in Paris in 1828.

HUEBNER, Carl Wilhelm

German, 19th century.
Born 17 June 1814, in Königsberg (now Kaliningrad, Russia); died 5 December 1879, in Düsseldorf.
Painter. Genre scenes.

A pupil of J Wolf in Königsberg, then of Schadow and Karl Sohn at the academy in Düsseldorf. In 1874 and 1875, he travelled to North America. From 1864, he taught at the Rhenish academy.

MUSEUMS AND GALLERIES:

DÜSSELDORF: *The Consolation of Prayer* - HANOVER: *Abandoned; The Hunter and His Son; The Unexpected Return of the Son* - KALININGRAD: *The Seizure* - OSLO: *German Emigrants Visiting the Tombs of Their Relatives* - WROCLAW: *The Marriage Proposal*.

AUCTION RECORDS:

NEW YORK, 7 Feb 1901, *The Twins*, USD 160. NEW YORK, 7 March 1902, *The Young Wife*, USD 350. NEW YORK, 4 Jan 1931, *Widow's Tale*, USD 200. NEW YORK, 22 March 1958, *The First Grandchild*, USD 300. COLOGNE, 5 Feb 1960, *Young*

Woman in Regional Costume, DEM 1,700. NEW YORK, 4 March 1961, *The First Grandson,* USD 190. MUNICH, 30 Nov 1978, *Good News* (oil on canvas, 35½ x 43¼ ins / 90 x 110 cm) DEM 53,000. MUNICH, 30 May 1979, *The Tasting Cup* (1878, oil on canvas, 30¾ x 36¾ ins / 78 x 93.5 cm) DEM 11,000. NEW YORK, 26 Feb 1982, *Young Peasant Tickling a Sleeping Girl* (1868, oil on canvas, 43¼ x 32¾ ins / 110 x 83 cm) USD 4,800. MUNICH, 21 Sept 1983, *The Love Letter* (1861, oil on canvas, 33 x 35¾ ins / 84 x 91 cm) DEM 15,000. COLOGNE, 28 June 1985, *Peasant Women at the Well* (1859, oil on canvas, 24 x 20½ ins / 61 x 52 cm) DEM 26,000. COLOGNE, 15 Oct 1988, *The Birthday* (1849, oil on canvas, 24½ x 30¾ ins / 62 x 78 cm) DEM 6,000. STOCKHOLM, 19 April 1989, *Waiting - Fisherman's Wife and Child on the Coast* (oil on canvas, 23½ x 15¾ ins / 60 x 40 cm) SEK 14,000. NEW YORK, 29 Oct 1992, *The Marriage Proposal* (1853, oil on canvas, 25 x 30¾ ins / 63.5 x 78.1 cm) USD 7,150. NEW YORK, 17 Feb 1993, *The Letter* (1865, oil on canvas, 42¼ x 33½ ins / 107.3 x 85.1 cm) USD 10,638. NEW YORK, 16 Feb 1994, *Memories* (oil on canvas/synthetic resin, 28¾ x 37¾ ins / 73 x 95.9 cm) USD 5,750. MUNICH, 24 March 1999, *The Marriage Proposal* (1859, oil on canvas/board, 23 x 28 ins / 58 x 72 cm) DEM 4,800. ERLANGEN, 18 Sept 1999, *The Birthday* (1852, oil on panel, 20 x 25 ins / 52 x 63 cm) DEM 14,000. HEIDELBERG, 10 May 2003, *Young Seducer* (1835, oil on canvas, 24 x 30 ins / 60 x 77 cm) EUR 4,000. NEW YORK, 30 Sept 2003, *Farewell* (1856, oil on panel, 24 x 30 ins / 60 x 76 cm) USD 4,200.

HUEBNER, Eduard
German, 19th century.
Born 27 May 1842, in Dresden.
Painter, sculptor. Genre scenes, portraits.

The son and pupil of Julius Hübner. From 1860 to 1867 he was a pupil of his uncle Bendemann at the academy in Düsseldorf. He worked subsequently in Italy and Paris, returning to Berlin (c. 1881) and finally settling in Dresden. He exhibited in Germany, Dresden and Berlin.

HUEBNER, Ferdinand
German, 19th century.
Active in Berlin.
Painter. Portraits, genre scenes.

HUEBNER, Heinrich
German, 17th century.
Active in Bayreuth.
Sculptor.

HUEBNER, Heinrich
German, 19th century.
Born 21 August 1869, in Berlin.
Painter, draughtsman, engraver.

He was influenced by Liebermann and French Impressionism.

HUEBNER, Jacob
Dutch, 18th - 19th century.
Active in Augsburg from 1787 to 1816.
Engraver (burin). Natural history.

Jacob Huebner made natural history engravings.

HUEBNER, Joseph
German, 19th century.
Born 1817, in Gablenz (Saxony).
Painter.

His oeuvres consists of portraits, landscapes and religious paintings.

HUEBNER, Julius, or Hübner
German, 19th century.
Born 1842, in Düsseldorf; died 30 December 1874, in Düsseldorf.
Painter. History painting, portraits, genre scenes.

The second son and pupil of Karl Wilhelm Hübner.

AUCTION RECORDS:
LONDON, 9 May 1979, *The Evening Reading* (1871, oil on panel, 6½ x 7¾ ins / 16.5 x 20 cm) GBP 2,700. NEW YORK, 27 May 1983, *Man Consulting a Barometer* (oil on panel, 7½ x 6 ins / 19 x 15.2 cm) USD 1,800.

HUEBNER, Rudolf Julius Benno, or Hubner
German, 19th century.
Born 27 January 1806, in Öls (Olesnica, Silesia); died 7 November 1882, in Loschwitz (Dresden).
Painter. Scenes with figures, religious subjects, portraits.

A pupil of Schadow in Berlin, whom he accompanied to Düsseldorf, he later taught at the academy there. He was a member of the academies in Berlin, Dresden and Philadelphia. He won a gold medal in Brussels, and also worked in Italy. He exhibited in Paris in 1867 (Universal Exhibition), and published several works on the museum in Dresden.

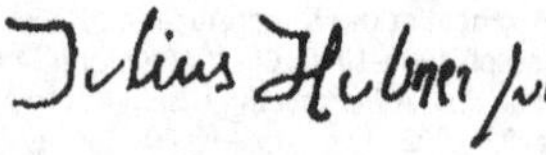

MUSEUMS AND GALLERIES:
BERLIN: *Portraits of Painters Lessing, Sohn and Hildebrandt; Gottfried Schadow* - BREMEN: *The Golden Age* - DÜSSELDORF: *Portrait of J Keller; Roland* - FRANKFURT AM MAIN: *Job and His Friends* - HANOVER: *Recompense of Work; Armed Horseman* - LEIPZIG: *Holy Family* - WROCLAW: *Bliss and Sleep.*

AUCTION RECORDS:
NEW YORK, 20 April 1905, *Young Shepherd,* USD 305. LONDON, 28 Nov 1980, *The Departure of the Warrior; The Death of the Warrior* (1853, canvas, a pair, 20 x 10 ins / 51 x 25.5 cm) GBP 6,500. MUNICH, 4 June 1981, *Three Women in a Landscape* (oil on canvas, 25 x 42 ins / 63.5 x 106.5 cm) DEM 21,000. MUNICH, 29 June 1982, *Ruth and Naomi* (1828, watercolour and gold, 9½ x 7½ ins / 24 x 19 cm) DEM 8,200.

HUEBSCHMANN, Donat
German, 16th century.
Born c. 1540, in Leipzig; died 1583, in Vienna.
Painter, draughtsman.

Donat Huebschmann worked principally in Vienna at the court of Emperors Rudolph II and Maximilian II.

HUECK, Georges von
Russian, 20th century.
Born 17 April 1904, in St Petersburg; died 25 June 1964, in Paris.
Active then naturalised in Finland.
Painter.

Georges von Hueck studied at the Athenaeum in Helsinki with the painter Akseli Gallen-Kallela. He took Finish nationality in 1923. He then went to study at the academies of Amsterdam, Antwerp and Brussels and finally worked with André Lhote in Paris.

His work, figurative until 1947 then more abstract in style, has been admired for its freshness, its rigorous construction and an internal richness.

He was a member of the Salon des Surindépendants and exhibited with Roland Oudot, Legueult and Terechkovich.

AUCTION RECORDS:
PARIS, 12 June 1991, *Abstract in Ultramarine Blue* (oil on canvas, 39¼ x 28¾ ins / 100 x 73 cm) FRF 14,500.

HUECKSTÄDT, Ludwig
German, 19th century.
Born c. 1800, in Güstrow.
Painter. Portraits.

He worked mainly in Güstrow in Mecklenburg-Schwerin.

HUEFFER, Catherine. See **BROWN Catherine Madox**

HUEGEL, Hieronymus von, called Kolle
German, 20th century.
Born 24 February 1899, in Charlottenburg.
Painter, lithographer.
Huegel worked initially in Bern, and then in Munich, Berlin and Paris. Wilhelm Uhde owned several of his works.

HUEGIN, Karl
Swiss, 20th century.
Born 18 July 1887, in Trimbach.
Painter, engraver.
Huegin worked in Basel and Stuttgart.

HUEGLI, Constance
Swiss, 19th century.
Born 1849, in La Chaux-de-Fonds.
Painter. Portraits, landscapes.
She was a pupil of W Hirschy.
MUSEUMS AND GALLERIES:
LA CHAUX-DE-FONDS (MBA): a painting.

HUEL, C.
German, 19th century.
Active in Mainz.
Miniaturist.

HUELIN, Michel
Swiss, 20th - 21st century.
Born 1962, in Saignelégier.
Painter.
Michel Huelin lived in France from 1989 to 1992 and now lives and works in Lausanne. His paintings come in three main variations. Firstly there are the 'skins of paint', which are crusts of superimposed layers of paint. Then there are landscapes created by means of a special technique of photographic projection onto a canvas already covered in acrylic paint. Finally, there are paintings of skin: the epidermis as the object of representation.

He has taken part in group exhibitions including those at the Bern Kunsthalle and the Schedhalle in Zurich in 1986, the Centre d'Art Contemporain in Geneva in 1987 and 1989, and the Birla Academy of Art in Calcutta and the Gallery of Modern Art in New Delhi in 1991. He has had solo exhibitions in 1983 at the Galerie Patrick Roy in Lausanne and the Galerie Alain Veinstein in Paris, in 1999 and 2002 at the Galerie Zürcher in Paris and in 2000 at the Centre d'Art Contemporain in Castres.
BIBLIOGRAPHY:
Comment, Bernard, '*Michel Huelin oscillation, dislocation*' in *Art Press*, periodical, Paris, February 1993. Huelin, Michel/Loock, Ulrich, *Michel Huelin*, exhibition catalogue, Gal. Patrick Roy, Lausanne, 1995.

HUELLMANN, Gottlieb Wilhelm
German, 18th - 19th century.
Born 22 May 1765, in Meissen (Saxony-Anhalt); died c. 1828, in Dresden.
Engraver.
Mention is made of his portraits of *Jérôme Bonaparte* and *Louis XVIII*.

HUELMA, Garcia de. See **BUELMA**

HUELMAN, François
French, 18th century.
Active in Lunéville.
Sculptor.
François Huelman was working in 1730 at the nunnery in Gerbevilliers.

HUELSENBECK, Richard. See **HULBECK Charles R.**

HUELSER, Joseph
German, 19th century.
Born 1819, in Kleinenbroich; died 1850, in Düsseldorf.
Painter. Landscapes.
MUSEUMS AND GALLERIES:
BERLIN (National Mus.).
AUCTION RECORDS:
LONDON, 12 Oct 1984, *Flock in a Wooded Landscape* (1844, oil on canvas, 28 1/2 x 43 1/4 ins / 72.5 x 110 cm) GBP 2,000.

HUELVA, José de
Spanish, 18th century.
Active in Seville.
Glass painter.
José de Huelva is believed to have worked for Seville Cathedral in 1794.

HUEN, Victor
French, 19th - 20th century.
Born 21 March 1874, in Colmar; died 15 December 1939, in Nancy.
Painter, lithographer. Military subjects, hunting scenes, horses.
Victor Huen studied in Paris with Gérome and G. Ferrier, and in Munich with Zügel and C. Marr. He exhibited at the Salon des Artistes Français until 1922. He made use of precise documentation on the old army for his compositions. As a lithographer, he collaborated with J. Waltz (Hansi) on the *Histoire d'Alsace racontée aux petits enfants d'Alsace et de la France* (*History of Alsace Recounted to the Grandchildren of Alsace and France*).
MUSEUMS AND GALLERIES:
COLMAR: *The Regiment of Alsace in the Battle of Heylissen, 18 July 1705*.

HUENE, Andreas Caspar
German, 18th - 19th century.
Born c. 1759, in Hamburg; died 2 October 1813, in St Petersburg.
Painter.
Invited to the Russian court by Catherine II, he devoted himself to painting portraits. In 1774, he had been in Italy after being a pupil of Schönemann in Hamburg. He applied himself to studying the works of Mengs and Torelli.

HUENE, Stephan von
American, 20th century.
Born September 1932, in Los Angeles.
Active in Germany.
Sculptor, painter, draughtsman, installation artist.
Stephan von Huene studied at Pasadena College (California) from 1950 to 1952, at the University of California, Los Angeles from 1952 to 1953, at the Chouinard Art Institute, Los Angeles from 1955 to 1959, and again at the University of California, Los Angeles from 1963 to 1965. He moved to Germany in the 1970s, and taught at the Hochschule für Gestaltung, Karlsruhe from 1993. He lives and works in Hamburg.

During the 1960s, von Huene visited John Cage, Ed Kienholz and Allan Kaprow. He created assemblages inspired by Pop Art, and developed an interest in integrating sound and movement into his works, as in *Kaleidophonic Dog* (1964-1967). In the 1970s, he integrated musical instruments into his sculptures, genuine robots and acoustic objects. Thus in *Dancing on Tables* (1987-1993), artificial legs really danced on stela, while historic speeches travelled round a loop circuit. His works are designed from genuine installations combining sound, movement and sometimes also drawing.

Von Huene has taken part in group exhibitions, including: 1967, *American Sculpture of the Sixties*, held at County Museum, Los Angeles; 1969, *Electromagica*, Tokyo; 1987, Documenta, Kassel; 1995, Venice Biennale. He has also shown his works in solo exhibitions, including: 1966, D. Stuart Gallery,

Log Angeles; 1984, Museum Ludwig, Cologne; 1999, *Sonic Boom - the Art of Sound*, held at Hayward Gallery, London; 2003, a retrospective, *Stephan von Huene. Tune the World. The Retrospective*, held at Hamburger Kunsthalle, Hamburg.

BIBLIOGRAPHY:

Stephan von Huene: Klangskulpturen, exhibition catalogue, Kunsthalle, Baden Baden, 1983. *Stephan von Huene, Lyd skulpturer (Sound sculptures)*, exhibition catalogue, Louisiana Museum, Humlebæk, 1990. Huene, Stephan von, *What's wrong with culture?*, exhibition catalogue, Neues Museum Weserburg, Bremen, 1998 (texts in German and English). Brockhaus, Christoph, *Stephan von Huene. Tune the world. Die Retrospektive*, exhibition catalogue, Hamburger Kunsthalle, Hamburg, 2003.

HUENERWADEL, Arnold
Swiss, 20th century.
Born 10 December 1877, in Lenzburg.
Sculptor.

Huenerwadel was a student of Barrias at the École des Beaux-Arts in Paris. His surviving works are mainly terracottas.

HUENERWADEL, Jérome
Swiss, 19th century.
Born 6 January 1829, in Schaffhausen; died 7 May 1859, in Fribourg.
Painter. Portraits.

After completing his studies in Antwerp, he returned to Schaffhausen, where he mainly painted portraits.

HUENTEN, Emil Johann, or Hünten
German, 19th century.
Born 19 January 1827, in Paris, of German origin; died 1 February 1902, in Düsseldorf.
Painter.

A pupil of Flandrin and Vernet in Paris, Wappers and Dyckmans in Antwerp and Lessing and Camphausen in Düsseldorf, he painted mainly history pictures and military scenes, following Crown Prince Frederick of Prussia on the Schlewsig-Holstein campaign and military operations generally from 1866 to 1870. In 1878, he became a member of the academy in Berlin. Medals were awarded to him in Berlin in 1872 and 1892 (Universal Exhibition) and in Vienna in 1873.

MUSEUMS AND GALLERIES:

BERLIN: *Cavalry Onslaught at Wörth* - DÜSSELDORF: *Battle of Gravelotte*.

AUCTION RECORDS:

NEW YORK, 13 and 14 Feb 1900, *French Prisoners in the Rearguard*, USD 575. MUNICH, 30 Oct 1907, *Military Courier*, FRF 875; *Rough Sea*, FRF 1,125.

HUENTEN, Franz Johann Wilhelm
German, 19th century.
Born 2 May 1822, in Hamburg; died 2 March 1887, in Eimsbüttel (Hamburg).
Painter. Seascapes.

From 1847 to 1850, he was a pupil of J W Schirmer at the academy in Düsseldorf. He undertook numerous voyages across the North Sea, the Atlantic and the Mediterranean, and specialised entirely in seascapes. He first went public in 1851, exhibiting in Düsseldorf, Hamburg, Hanover, Vienna, Dresden and Munich.

MUSEUMS AND GALLERIES:

DÜSSELDORF: *Storm at Sea*.

HUENTEN, Max
German, 19th - 20th century.
Born 25 September 1869, in Düsseldorf.
Painter. Military subjects.

Max Huenten was the brother of Émil Huenten. Like his brother, he studied in Paris, before returning to Germany to settle. His works comprise military and hunting scenes.

HUENTEN, Richard
German, 19th - 20th century.
Born 13 August 1867, in Hamburg.
Painter. Seascapes.

Work by Huenten was exhibited in Berlin in 1909.

HUEPSCHI, Albrecht
Swiss, 16th century.
Born c. 1521; died 1596, in Bern.
Active in Bern and Burgdorf.
Glass painter.

HUEPSCHI, Hans Jacob
Swiss, 16th century.
Active in Bern.
Glass painter.

Hans Jacob Huepschi was the son of Albrecht Huepschi.

HUERLIMANN, Johann
Swiss, 19th century.
Born 2 May 1793, in Uster; died 17 March 1850, in Paris.
Engraver (aquatint).

His work features mainly genre subjects. He did engravings from Boulanger, A Deveria, Banne, Ledieu and L Robert. A notable work was plates for the Prince of Wied's *Voyage to America*.

HUERNER, Joannes
German, 16th - 17th century.
Died 7 June 1613, in Ellwangen.
Active in Biberach.
Sculptor.

HUERNLIMANN, Christoffel
Swiss, 17th century.
Active in Lucerne c. 1640.
Glass painter.

HUERNLIMANN, J. B.
Swiss, 17th century.
Engraver.

He worked at Willisau, near Olten, among other places.

HUERT, or Heurck, Horick
Flemish School, 17th century.
Active in Mechelen.
Painter. Historical subjects.

Huert was a pupil of Michiel Coxie. He worked around 1622.

HUERTA, Jean de La. See **JEAN DE LA HUERTA**

HUERZELER, Hieronymus
Swiss, 19th century.
Born 7 October 1815, in Gretzenbach; died 19 September 1899, in Solothurn.
Draughtsman.

He is most noted for his landscapes, particularly his *Views of the Alps*.

HUESCA, Angel de (Fray)
Spanish, 18th century.
Active in Saragossa c. 1737.
Monk, engraver.

HUESSENER, Auguste
German, 19th century.
Born 1789, in Stettin (now Szczecin, Poland); died 13 February 1877, in Berlin.
Engraver.
A pupil of Buchhorn, she is noted for reproductions of German artists published in the pocket calendars of 1838 and 1843. She also did religious subjects and portraits.

HUESSENER, Elise
German, 19th century.
Born 1809, in Stettin (now Szczecin, Poland).
Sculptor.
She was the sister of Auguste and Julie.

HUESSENER, Julie, later Frau Ratti
German, 19th century.
Born in Stettin (now Szczecin, Poland).
Painter.
She was a pupil of W. Hensel in Berlin.

HUET
French, 16th century.
Active in Le Mans.
Sculptor.
Huet made a number of stone busts in 1550, and in 1554 he and Boiseleret worked on the rood screen of the Dominicans' church in Le Mans. The screen was destroyed in 1813.

HUET, the Younger
French, 18th century.
Active in Paris.
Painter. Flowers, fruit.
Huet exhibited for the Académie de St-Luc in 1753, 1756 and 1762. He was probably related to Nicolas Huet the Elder, perhaps his brother.

HUET, Alain
French, 20th century.
Born 27 April 1936.
Painter.
Alain Huet lives and works near Jurançon. He paints using a variety of media, in large sweeps, either horizontal or vertical. The titles of his paintings indicate the origin of his abstract propositions: *Labour, Fields, Lake, Creek* and *Autumn*. He took part in collective exhibitions from 1961 in Toulouse, Carcassonne, Pau and Bordeaux. In 1990, he showed at the Salon des Artistes Indépendants in Paris. He held solo exhibitions in Toulouse in 1961 and 1968, and in Pau in 1987.
AUCTION RECORDS:
PARIS, 7 Oct 1991, *Blue Vertical* (oil on canvas, 57 1/2 x 45 ins / 146 x 114 cm) FRF 7,000; *Flashes* (oil on canvas, 63 3/4 x 51 1/4 ins / 162 x 130 cm) FRF 8,000.

HUET, Alexandre
French, 16th century.
Active in Amiens.
Sculptor (wood).
In 1509 Alexandre Huet was commissioned to make the stalls on the left of the Amiens Cathedral choir; those on the right had already been made by the sculptor Arnould Boudin.

HUET, André
French, 18th century.
Active in Paris in 1774.
Painter.

HUET, Antoine
French, 20th century.
Born in Briançon.
Painter.
Antoine Huet was a student of Fougerat. From 1924, he exhibited in Paris at the Salon des Artistes Français and at the Salon des Indépendants.

HUET, Bernard
French, 15th century.
Born c. 1450, in Avignon.
Painter.

HUET, Charles Jean
French, 18th century.
Born c. 1760, in Paris.
Painter.
Charles Jean Huet was admitted into the École des Élèves Protégés of the Académie de Peinture on 25 March 1783. He studied under Gois.

HUET, Christophe
French, 18th century.
Born 1694; died 2 May 1759.
Painter, decorative designer, draughtsman. Figures, animals.
Little is known of Christophe Huet. Like Joue, Gillot, Claude Audran and Berrain, he belongs to that set of 18th-century painters whose craft was dedicated to the embellishment of aristocratic houses. He lived in Paris on the Rue Meslay and was in the financial position to own a country house in Bagnolet.

He is now generally credited for Chantilly's enchanting singeries, *Large Singerie* and *Small Singerie* long ascribed to Antoine Watteau. The ledgers of the Condé family incidentally have an entry regarding a 'settlement to M. Huet, painter, upon Mademoiselle de Clermont's inheritance', dated 1741. He also painted Chinese people and monkeys at the Hôtel de Rohan. It is highly likely that he also painted for the Opera House.
MUSEUMS AND GALLERIES:
NANTES: *Dog Pointing at Partridges* (1740, signed C. Huet) - VALENCIENNES: *Collection of Monkeys* (seven drawings in red chalk) - VIRE: *Music and Painting under the Guise of Two Monkeys in the Middle of a Decorative Panel.*
AUCTION RECORDS:
PARIS, 15 and 17 Feb 1897, *Duck Taking Flight,* FRF 75. PARIS, 12 June 1919, *The Attributes of Hunting; The Attributes of Fishing* (two sepia wash watercolours) FRF 1,050. PARIS, 26 March 1926, *Monkey and Parrot* (wash and gouache) FRF 380. PARIS, 22 March 1928, *Decorative Panel: The Monkey Falconer,* FRF 3,100. PARIS, 30 May 1930, *Dogs Pointing* (two canvases) FRF 5,300. PARIS, 18 Nov 1935, *Set of Six Monochrome Panels with Motives of Fountains, Folliage Scrolls, Flower Garlands and Monkey Musicians,* FRF 7,000. PARIS, 12 May 1939, *Fruit and Pheasant at the foot of a Stone Pedestal; Fruit and Pheasant by a Pedestal Supporting a Group of Cupids* (collection) FRF 4,500. PARIS, 30 June and 1 July 1941, *The Boar Kill* (1728) FRF 34,000. PARIS, 17 Nov 1948, *Spider Monkey with Pomegranate,* FRF 212,000. PARIS, 4 March 1981, *Study of Birds, Ducks, Hares and Dog Heads* (pen and watercolour, 11 3/4 x 7 3/4 ins / 30 x 20 cm) FRF 5,000. NEW YORK, 21 Jan 1982, *Spaniel Hound after a Duck* (1728, oil on canvas, 37 x 49 3/4 ins / 94 x 126.5 cm) USD 7,000. PARIS, 21 March 1984, *Poodle Seizing a Duck; Dog Pointing at a Pheasant* (1730, oil on canvas, a pair, 40 1/2 x 52 1/4 ins / 103 x 133 cm) FRF 155,000. MONTE CARLO, 22 Feb 1986, *Allegories of Hunting* (oil on canvas, set of three monochrome gold paintings/cream background, 33 1/2 x 48 3/4 ins / 85 x 124 cm) FRF 550,000. PARIS, 9 March 1988, *Hunting Scene* (1741, red chalk, 12 x 8 ins / 30.5 x 20.5 cm) FRF 1,988. NEW YORK, 2 June 1989, *Hound Hunting for Partridges in a Landscape* (oil on canvas, two pendants, each 38 1/2 x 58 1/4 ins / 98 x 148 cm) USD 77,000. NEW YORK, 31 May 1991, *Bitch with her Litter* (1734, oil on canvas, 50 x 57 1/2 ins / 127 x 146 cm) USD 71,500. NEW YORK, 17 Jan 1992, *The Hot Drink; The Cold Drink; Picnic Break during the Hunt; Meal in a Park* (oil on canvas, collection of four panels, the first two 119 1/2 x 53 1/4 ins / 303.5 x 135.3 cm, the other two 119 1/2 x 44 1/4 ins/303.5

x 112.4 cm) USD 165,000. LONDON, 11 Dec 1992, *A Mastiff and a Spaniel with Three Dressed-up Monkeys* (oil on canvas, 17 1/2 x 28 1/4 ins / 44.4 x 71.7 cm) GBP 2,860. LONDON, 28 March 1996, *A Mastiff with its Puppies in a Barn* (1734, oil on canvas, 50 1/4 x 57 3/4 ins / 127.5 x 146.5 cm) GBP 34,500. NEW YORK, 28 May 1999, *Wooded Landscape with Black Spider Monkey at Base of Tree* (oil on canvas, 17 x 21 ins / 44 x 54 cm) USD 72,500. NEUILLY, 12 Dec 1999, *Birds Perched in a Tree in Undulating Landscape* (1755, oil on canvas, 36 x 28 ins / 91 x 72 cm) FRF 460,000. PARIS, 27 April 2001, *Still-life, Fruit and Parrot* (1732, oil on canvas, 30 x 42 ins / 77 x 106 cm) FRF 165,000. NEW YORK, 23 Jan 2004, *Spaniel Retrieving a Duck from a Pond* (1728, oil on canvas, 37 x 50 ins / 95 x 127 cm) USD 15,000. PARIS, 18 March 2004, *Monkey Preaching in a Farm-Yard, Foxes Hiding Disguised as Priests* (gouache, 11 x 14 ins / 29 x 36 cm) EUR 4,300.

HUET, Ernestine
French, 19th century.
Born in the 19th century, in La Fère (Aisne).
Painter, pastellist. Portraits.

Ernestine Huet studied under Thomas Couture. She exhibited at the Paris Salon from 1848 to 1870.

AUCTION RECORDS:

NEW YORK, 14 Feb 1990, *Elderly Woman Knitting* (oil on panel, 13 1/2 x 11 ins / 34 x 27 cm) USD 880.

HUET, Felix Victor
French, 19th - 20th century.
Born 1 March 1861, in St-Pierre-les-Elbeuf (Seine-Maritime); died 27 August 1933, in St-Pierre-les-Elbeuf.
Sculptor.

Huet was a student of Decorchemont. On several occasions, he exhibited in Paris at the Salon des Artistes Français, of which he became a member in 1893. He received honourable mentions in 1885 and 1886 and a bronze medal in 1889 at the Exposition Universelle in Paris.

HUET, François, called Villiers-Huet or Huet-Villiers
French, 18th - 19th century.
Born 14 January 1772, in Paris; died 28 July 1813, in London.
Painter, watercolourist, miniaturist. Genre scenes, landscapes, animals.

According to Redgrave, François Huet was the son of a wildlife artist who settled in England at the beginning of the French Revolution. (This could make him the youngest son of Jean-Baptiste Huet who was quite likely still alive in 1799. In 1799 Huet exhibited at the Salon *The Portrait of Citizen Huet, Father of the Author*.) Whatever the case, Huet met with success in London. He had the title of painter to the king of France and miniaturist painter to the duchess of York. He exhibited in Paris in 1799, 1800, 1801, and 1812. In London he often featured in exhibitions between 1803 and 1813, particularly those of the Royal Academy. British biographers enter him under Villiers but the name seems to have been adopted by Huet after he settled in England.

AUCTION RECORDS:

PARIS, 26 Nov 1919, *Marie Thérèse Charlotte de France* (red chalk) FRF 400. PARIS, 27-29 May 1929, *Portrait of Chateaubriand* (miniature) FRF 1,900. PARIS, 7 and 8 Dec 1953, *Portrait of a Woman in a White See-through Dress*, FRF 50,000. LONDON, 12 July 1991, *A Donkey Tied up with a Sheep and some Chickens in a Barn* (oil on canvas, 14 3/4 x 18 1/2 ins / 37.5 x 46.7 cm) GBP 2,200.

HUET, Georges
French, 19th - 20th century.
Born 14 April 1860, in Elbeuf (Seine-Maritime); died 1935.
Painter.

Georges Huet exhibited in Paris at the Salon des Artistes Français. He was a curator at the Musée d'Orléans, in which he devoted a room to his own studies.

HUET, Hippolyte
French, 19th century.
Active in Paris.
Engraver (burin), lithographer.

Hippolyte Huet appears to have been an amateur, rather than a professional, burin engraver. He was an artist at the Opéra-Comique and a member of the King's Chapel. He made a lithograph of his *Portrait*, after Riesener, and another of *La Vessie*, after David Teniers. At the Salon of 1831 he exhibited some burin engravings, after Albrier, which were for the *Story of Frederick the Great*.

HUET, Jacques
Canadian, 20th century.
Born 1932, in Montreal.
Sculptor.

Jacques Huet appeared in the Salon de la Jeune Sculpture in Paris in 1935, and in the 2nd Symposium in Quebec. As a sculptor he is self-taught, and produces sculpture according to the assembly methods used for the frames of farmer homes in Canada.

HUET, Jacques
French, 20th century.
Born 4 December 1937, in Elbeuf (Seine-Maritime).
Painter. Landscapes, landscapes with figures.

A mechanic by profession, Jacques Huet took painting classes in Petit-Quevilly in Seine-Maritime. His painting celebrates nature. He is a member of the Salon des Artistes Français in Paris. He has taken part in collective exhibitions and has also held solo exhibitions, particularly in Seine-Maritime.

AUCTION RECORDS:

VERSAILLES, 21 Oct 1990, *Boats on the Seine* (oil on canvas, 18 x 22 ins / 46 x 55 cm) FRF 4,000. SCEAUX, 18 Nov 1990, *The Port of Rouen* (oil on canvas, 19 3/4 x 23 1/2 ins / 50 x 60 cm) FRF 9,000. NEUILLY, 3 Feb 1991, *The Water Lilies in Giverny* (oil on canvas, 23 1/2 x 28 3/4 ins / 60 x 73 cm) FRF 11,000. CALAIS, 14 March 1993, *Banks of the Seine at Rouen* (oil on canvas, 20 x 28 3/4 ins / 51 x 73 cm) FRF 4,300.

HUET, Jean
French, 16th century.
Active in Paris.
Sculptor (wood).

In 1562 Jean Huet was commissioned to work on carvings in the Château de Madrid in the Bois de Boulogne.

HUET, Jean
Belgian, 20th century.
Born 1903, in Wortel; died 1976, in Antwerp.
Painter.

Huet painted country scenes.

HUET, Jean-Baptiste, the Elder
French, 18th - 19th century.
Born 15 October 1745, in Paris; died 27 January 1811, in Paris.
Painter (including gouache), watercolourist, pastellist, engraver, draughtsman. History painting, mythological subjects, portraits, genre scenes, landscapes, landscapes with figures, animals. Designs for tapestries.

Jean-Baptiste Huet the Elder was the son of the wildlife painter Nicolas Huet the Elder. Having first practised drawing with C. Renou, he became J.-B. Leprince's pupil in 1764 and soon counted among this master's favourite students. Huet also worked with Boucher and Dagomer. Approved by the Académie on 30 July 1768 upon presentation of his painting *A Mastiff Chasing Geese*, he was made an Académicien on 29 July 1769.

From the outset Huet was a huge success with Paris society and the list of his Salon exhibits shows that many were commissions. He made his début at the Paris Salon in 1769 and featured at the exhibitions given in the Place Dauphine in 1770 and 1772 with *Landscapes Painted in Lantara's Style*. He continued to take part in the Salon until 1802. Of his many genre compositions he is best remembered for his 1775 *Return from the Market* and *Farmer's Wife Feeding her Chickens* of 1777. In 1790 he was assigned to the textile factories of Jouy, Beauvais and Gobelins. His supple, ready talent was wonderfully suited to the task and in this line his compositions are almost on a par with Boucher and Oudry. He was an outstanding engraver as well and etched an important body of landscapes with figures and animal studies. A large number of his drawings were etched or engraved in aquatint or 'à la manière de crayon' by Demarteau, Lebas and Bonnet.

Huet seems to have been particularly close to the latter and there is good reason to believe that he was the author of many a courtly subject represented without a painter's name in the famous engraver's output. It has to be admitted that he showed less elegance and more license than Baudoin, Fragonard and Lavreince in creations which came dangerously close to prurience. Huet was married twice, to Geneviève Marie Chevalier and then Marie-Madeleine Vacavant. He had many children with both of them. Two of his sons, Nicolas and Jean-Baptiste, followed their father's artistic calling.

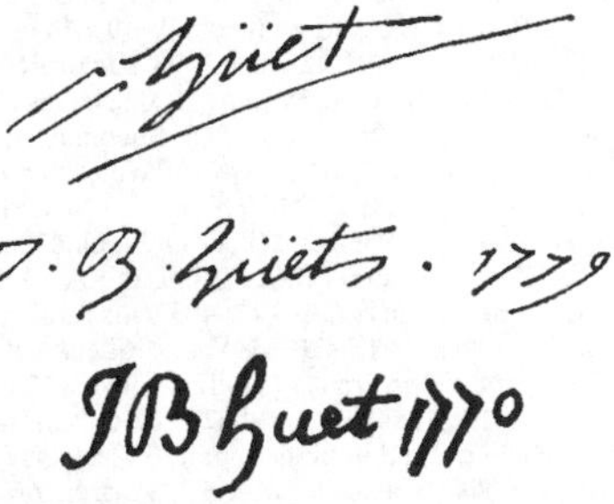

Museums and Galleries:

Amiens: *Doves* - Bourges: *Sheep and Goats; Sheep* - Chantilly: *Various Animals* (ten decorative panels) - Dijon: pastoral subject - Lyons: *Attributes of the Countryside* - Nantes: *Cattle Grazing; Horses and Sheep in a Pasture* - Orléans: *Shepherd with his Dog, Watching a Flock by the Ruins of a Temple* - Paris (Louvre): *Dog Chasing Two Geese* - Rennes: two drawings - Rouen: *Muleteers.*

Auction records:

Paris, 1892, *Little Shepherds,* FRF 3,280. Paris, 1897, *A Shepherdess* (pastel) FRF 3,050; *A Farm; Farmyard* (two drawings) FRF 4,500. Paris, 1898, *The Mound,* FRF 4,200; *Country Bridge,* FRF 4,200. Paris, 1899, *Pastoral* (drawing in red chalk) FRF 3,200. Paris, 22-24 April 1901, *Portrait of Marie-Joseph Chénier,* FRF 960. Paris, 11-15 May 1903, *Shepherd's Return,* FRF 13,200. London, 23 May 1903, *Pastoral,* FRF 10,750. Paris, 19 March 1905, *Pastoral,* FRF 5,400. Paris, 10 June 1909, *Rest* (watercolour) FRF 1,050. Paris, 21 April 1910, *Shepherd's Rest,* FRF 1,600. Paris, 7 Dec 1918, *Shepherdess, Cows and Sheep,* FRF 4,610. Paris, 21 Dec 1918, *Small Flock* (drawing heightened with pastels) FRF 4,800. Paris, 7-9 May 1919, *Gruel* (watercolour) FRF 10,000. Paris, 12 and 13 May 1919, *Jupiter and a Nymph* (watercolour) FRF 29,000. Paris, 4-6 Dec 1919, *Pastoral* (Indian ink wash) FRF 2,600. Paris, 8 March 1920, *Young Shepherdess* (coloured pencil) FRF 7,000; *La Jardinière* FRF 22,000. Paris, 13 March 1920, *Finder's Keeper's,* FRF 19,000. Paris, 10-11 May 1920, *Portrait of a Little Dog,* FRF 30,900. Paris, 18 Dec 1920, *Pastoral Scene,* FRF 31,000. Paris, 21 April 1921, *Pastorals* (two paintings) FRF 30,000. Paris, 27 April 1921, *Return to the Farm,* FRF 5,600. London, March 1922, *Jealousy: Boy with Two Girls in a Landscape,* GBP 54. London, July 1922, *Pastoral,* GBP 84. Paris, 17 March 1923, *Getting up,* FRF 15,600. Paris, 7 and 8 May 1923, *Hercules and Omphale* (pencil and wash) FRF 11,000. Paris, 18 May 1923, *Preparing for the Masked Ball* (drawing with watercolour and gouache) FRF 9,000. Paris, 4 June 1923, *Water Mill* (watercolour) FRF 19,000. Paris, Feb 1925, *Young Woman Holding a Basket Full of Flowers* (pencil) FRF 2,550. Paris, 17-18 June 1925, *Boat Bridge at Moulin-Joly* (pencil, pen and watercolour wash) FRF 6,600. London, 12 Feb 1926, *Blind Man's Buff,* GBP 1,522. Paris, 21-22 March 1927, *Sleeping Shepherdess* (pencil and wash) FRF 26,000. Paris, 11 May 1927, *Lovers* (pen and watercolour wash) FRF 5,050. London, 19 March 1928, *The Swing,* GBP 44. Paris, 1 June 1928, *Captive Dove* (watercolour/outlines in pen and ink) FRF 17,000. Paris, 7-8 June 1928, *Romantic Tête-à-tête* (drawing) FRF 13,200. Paris, 15 June 1928, *Faites le Beau* (black chalk heightened) FRF 13,500. Paris, 28 Nov 1928, *Milliner's Shop* (drawing) FRF 18,250. Paris, 13-15 May 1929, *Maternal Permission* (drawing) FRF 47,000; *Livestock Resting; Livestock Setting off* (two drawings) FRF 172,000; *Crossing the Ford* (gouache) FRF 25,000; *Frightened Livestock; Livestock Meeting* (two drawings) FRF 14,000. London, 16 May 1929, *Children Playing Bilind Man's Buff,* GBP 152. Paris, 12 June 1929, *Shepherdess Crowned by Love* (drawing) FRF 11,000. Paris, 28 May 1931, *Love* (watercolour/outlines in pen and ink) FRF 7,000. Paris, 3 June 1931, *Crossing the Ford,* FRF 76,000. Paris, 1 and 2 Dec 1932, *Little Bell* (pen and watercolour wash) FRF 24,000; *Servant Girl Vindicated,* FRF 24,000. London, 5 April 1934, *Shepherd and Shepherdess,* GBP 141. Paris, 8 May 1934, *Return from the Market* (watercolour) FRF 6,500. Paris, 14 May 1935, *Farm Interior* (watercolour/outlines in pen and ink) FRF 12,200. Paris, 22 Feb 1937, *Gypsies' Market* (red chalk) FRF 2,600. Paris, 22 June 1938, *The Graces Disarming Cupid; Cupid Crowned by the Graces* (two watercolours) FRF 9,000; *Cupid Punished* (pen and wash heightened with white) FRF 3,200. Paris, 11 July 1941, *Shepherd with his Dog* (drawing heightened with white) FRF 2,000. Paris, 28 Nov 1941, *Papillon the Dog,* FRF 30,000; *Poultry Yard,* FRF 38,000. Paris, 20 May 1942, *The Sculptor* (watercolour) FRF 5,600. New York, 7 Jan 1943, *Girl with a Basket of Flowers,* USD 525; *Pastoral Landscape,* USD 1,300. Paris, 29 Jan 1943, *Crossing the Ford; Métairie by the Water* (pen and bistre wash, matching pair) FRF 33,500; *Captive Dove* (1776, pen and watercolour wash) FRF 46,000. Paris, 15 March 1943, *Cat's Dinner; Children and Dog* (a pair of red chalk drawings) FRF 18,000. Paris, 19 March 1943, *Shepherdesses* (1782, gouache) FRF 55,000. Paris, 31 March 1943, *Caravan* (1768, pen, red chalk and wash) FRF 16,000; *Girl Plucking the Petals off a Flower* (1783, black chalk and chalk) FRF 10,000; *Cupid and the Graces* (1785) FRF 68,000. New York, 22 Nov 1944, *Farm Entrance,* USD 900. Paris, 7 Feb 1945, *Shepherd's Family* (1780, pen and wash) FRF 42,000. Paris, 16 May 1947, *Young Poultry Seller* (pen and watercolour wash heightened with gouache) FRF 215,000. Paris, 15 Dec 1948, *Dovecote* (heightened watercolour) FRF 220,000. Paris, 14 June 1955, *Sleeping Shepherdess; Young Fisherman* (two pastels) FRF 700,000. London, 7 July 1959, *Figures on a Terrace,* GBP 210. Bern, 16 June 1960, *Street Scene* (pen and watercolour) CHF 2,700. Paris, 4 Dec 1963, *Angler,* FRF 16,000. London, 11 March 1964, *Revellers Boarding a Boat* (gouache) GBP 900. Nice, 24 Sept 1969, *Nudes Reclining on a Couch* (matching pair) FRF 42, 000. Paris, 29 May 1970, *Sheep and Ram,* FRF 5,000. Paris, 23 March 1971, *Water Spaniel Flushing Two Nesting Ducks out of the Reeds,* FRF

16,000. LONDON, 7 July 1972, *Shepherd and his Flock*, Gns 7,000. LONDON, 20 March 1973, *Young Gentlewoman Angling* (watercolour and pencil) Gns 2,600. LONDON, 28 June 1974, *Fortune-teller*, Gns 2,400. PARIS, 23 March 1976, *Water Spaniel Flushing Two Nesting Ducks out of the Reeds* (1770, oil on canvas, 32 1/4 x 52 ins / 82 x 132 cm) FRF 16,000. LONDON, 30 March 1976, *Tree Trunk* (1780, black chalk and wash, 7 1/4 x 5 3/4 ins / 18.4 x 14.6 cm) GBP 420. PARIS, 6 April 1976, *View of a Farm* (1790, gouache, 11 1/4 x 13 1/4 ins / 28.5 x 33.5 cm) FRF 20,000. VERSAILLES, 26 Feb 1978, *Dog beside a Loaded Donkey* (oil on panel, 12 1/2 x 16 1/4 ins / 32 x 41 cm) FRF 6,500. MONTE CARLO, 11 Feb 1979, *Study Sheets Representing Madame Huet* (black chalk and watercolour, 9 3/4 x 12 1/2 ins / 25 x 32 cm) FRF 21,000. PARIS, 7 Nov 1979, *Pastoral* (1784, watercolour, pen and wash, 7 3/4 x 10 1/4 ins / 20 x 26 cm) FRF 9,500. PARIS, 8 Feb 1980, *The Joys of Motherhood* (1770, black chalk, bistre wash and watercolour, 7 3/4 x 11 1/2 ins / 19.5 x 29 cm) FRF 37,000. VERSAILLES, 17 June 1981, *Pastoral Scene* (gouache, 5 x 7 ins / 12.5 x 18 cm) FRF 7,000. PARIS, 9 Dec 1981, *The Market* (pen and wash, black chalk, red chalk, stump and white gouache, 17 1/2 x 22 ins / 44.5 x 56 cm) FRF 40,000. NEW YORK, 17 June 1982, *Venus and Cupid* (oil on canvas, 29 1/2 x 36 3/4 ins / 75 x 93.5 cm) USD 35,000. VERSAILLES, 17 April 1983, *Shepherds' Rest; Livestock Setting off* (1781, two watercolours/outlines in pen and ink, 14 1/2 x 17 1/2 ins / 37 x 44.5 cm) FRF 50,000. LONDON, 30 Nov 1983, *Shepherd and Shepherdess in a Wooded Landscape* (oil on canvas, 51 1/2 x 43 1/4 ins / 130.5 x 110 cm) GBP 18,500. LONDON, 25 Oct 1985, *Rural Idyll* (oil on canvas, oval, 18 1/2 x 22 ins / 47 x 55.9 cm) GBP 65,000. PARIS, 13 June 1986, *Pastoral* (1781, gouache/mounted paper/canvas, 29 x 48 3/4 ins / 73.5 x 124 cm) FRF 75,000. LONDON, 9 Dec 1986, *Shepherdess Sitting with a Goat and a Lamb* (1782, red, black, white and blue chalk, 10 3/4 x 12 ins / 27.3 x 30.4 cm) GBP 14,000. MONTE CARLO, 20 June 1987, *The Proposal* (1786, oil/copper, 10 3/4 x 9 ins / 27.3 x 22 cm) FRF 310,000. MONACO, 20 Feb 1988, *Washerwomen by a Cottage* (1773, black chalk and chalk, 16 x 13 ins / 39.8 x 33 cm) FRF 3,552. PARIS, 9 March 1988, *Offering of Doves to the God of Love* (1782, pen and brown wash, 9 x 7 ins / 23 x 17.5 cm) FRF 26,000. NEW YORK, 11 Jan 1989, *Landscape with a Shepherd and his Flock by a Farm; Riverscape with an Oxherd Fishing near his Cattle* (1788, gouache, a pair, 7 1/4 x 10 1/2 ins / 18.1 x 26.9 cm) USD 23,100. NEW YORK, 7 April 1989, *Rural Landscape with Country Folk and Cattle near a Brook* (oil on canvas, oval, 22 3/4 x 18 1/2 ins / 58 x 47 cm) USD 34,100. MONACO, 16 June 1989, *Shepherd and Shepherdess with their Flock in a Riverscape; Falcon Hunting by a Ruin* (1763, oil on panel, a pair, each 27 1/4 x 22 1/2 ins / 69.5 x 57 cm) FRF 199,800; *Romantic Scene in a Park* (oil on canvas, 12 1/2 x 9 1/2 ins / 32 x 24 cm) FRF 444,000. PARIS, 27 Nov 1989, *Landscape with Torrent and Fishermen* (charcoal heightened with white/grey paper, 17 1/4 x 13 1/4 ins / 44 x 33.5 cm) FRF 40,500. NEW YORK, 12 Jan 1990, *Study of a Sheep near a Basket of Flowers in a Landscape* (red chalk, 7 3/4 x 6 1/4 ins / 20 x 16 cm) USD 3,300. ROME, 8 March 1990, *Game of Backgammon in an Interior* (oil on canvas, 35 1/2 x 28 ins / 90 x 71 cm) ITL 7,000,000. PARIS, 7 Nov 1990, *Billy Goat Heads* (black chalk, 11 3/4 x 10 1/2 ins / 30 x 26.5 cm) FRF 20,000. PARIS, 5 Dec 1990, *War; Peace* (1790, oil on canvas, a pair, 44 x 51 1/2 ins / 112 x 131 cm) FRF 1,000,000. PARIS, 6 Dec 1990, *Landscape with a Peacock and a Hen on a Ledge* (oil on canvas, 15 3/4 x 12 1/2 ins / 40 x 32 cm) FRF 75,000. LONDON, 12 Dec 1990, *Transhumance* (oil on paper/card, 22 1/4 x 39 1/4 ins / 56.5 x 99.5 cm) GBP 44,000. NEW YORK, 8 Jan 1991, *A Sheep* (brown wash heightened with white, 5 x 7 1/4 ins / 13 x 18.2 cm) USD 2,750. NEW YORK, 9 Jan 1991, *Young Shepherdess Sitting on a Stone near a Goat and its Kid* (1782, red, black, white and blue chalk/parchment paper, 10 3/4 x 12 ins / 27.3 x 30.4 cm) USD 18,700. NEW YORK, 22-23 March 1991, *Studies of Animals: Donkeys with their Peck of Oats, Wolves and Foxes, Sheep, Goats, Cow and Suckling Calf, Does and Fawns* (ink and wash, six drawings, 3 x 3 3/4 ins / 7.6 x 9.7 cm) USD 6,600; *Couple Carving Entwined Hearts on a Tree Trunk* (1783, watercolour heightened with white, 7 1/4 x 5 3/4 ins / 18.5 x 14.8 cm) USD 3,520. LE TOUQUET, 10 Nov 1991, *Billy Goats and Nanny Goats in a Pasture* (red chalk, charcoal and Indian ink heightened with gouache, 19 x 23 1/2 ins / 48 x 60 cm) FRF 29,000. MONACO, 5-6 Dec 1991, *Young Artists* (1765, ink and watercolour heightened with white gouache, 5 x 6 ins / 11.8 x 15 cm) FRF 6,660; *Shepherd and Shepherdess in a Landscape* (oil on canvas, 23 1/2 x 31 1/2 ins / 60 x 80 cm) FRF 133,200. NEW YORK, 17 Jan 1992, *Pastoral Scene with a Shepherd* (oil on canvas, 24 1/2 x 60 ins / 62.5 x 152.4 cm) USD 14,300. NEW YORK, 15 Jan 1993, *Venus Reclining Seen from Behind with Two Doves* (oil on canvas, 40 1/2 x 58 1/4 ins / 102.9 x 148 cm) USD 211,500. PARIS, 1 April 1993, *Studies of Flowers* (1780, black chalk and red chalk, 10 1/2 x 16 3/4 ins / 26.5 x 42.5 cm) FRF 15,500. MONACO, 2 July 1993, *Pastoral Scenes* (oil on canvas, a pair, 22 x 25 1/2 ins / 55 x 65 cm) FRF 111,000. STOCKHOLM, 30 Nov 1993, *Pastoral with a Youth Waking up a Girl* (oil on panel, 15 1/4 x 21 1/4 ins / 39 x 54 cm) SEK 27,000. LONDON, 8 Dec 1993, *Dove Nest; Basket of Roses* (1785, oil on canvas, a pair, each 27 1/2 x 33 1/2 ins / 70 x 85 cm) GBP 128,000. PARIS, 10 Dec 1993, *Scene in a Sheep Barn* (1786, pencil heightened with pastels, 15 1/4 x 22 ins / 38.7 x 55 cm) FRF 42,000. NEW YORK, 11 Jan 1994, *Cottage in a Wood with Pine Trees* (black chalk/brown paper, 13 x 16 ins / 32.9 x 40.6 cm) USD 3,680. PARIS, 24 June 1994, *Study for a Cheetah* (oil on canvas, 24 x 20 ins / 61 x 50.5 cm) FRF 68,000. NEW YORK, 10 Jan 1996, *Study of Branches with Leaves and Berries* (red and white chalk, 19 x 14 3/4 ins / 48 x 37.5 cm) USD 3,450. PARIS, 12 April 1996, *Pastoral Scene with Cottage* (1789, ink and watercolour, 10 x 12 1/2 ins / 24.5 x 32 cm) FRF 20,000. LONDON, 3 July 1996, *Shepherdess and her Animals by a Brook* (1772, ink, wash and watercolour, 10 1/4 x 7 3/4 ins / 26.2 x 20 cm) GBP 2,070. PARIS, 26 Nov 1996, *Rural Scene* (pen, black ink wash and black chalk/blue paper, 11 3/4 x 18 1/4 ins / 29.8 x 46.5 cm) FRF 12,000. LONDON, 11 Dec 1996, *Flower Girl* (oil on canvas, 54 3/4 x 48 3/4 ins / 139 x 124 cm) GBP 43,300. PARIS, 16 Dec 1996, *Young Shepherdess Spinning Wool in the Farmyard* (1771, oil on canvas, 12 1/2 x 15 ins / 32 x 38 cm) FRF 24,000. PARIS, 20 Dec 1996, *Pastoral Scenes* (watercolour/engraved outlines, a pair, 6 1/4 x 9 ins / 15.8 x 22 cm) FRF 11,000. PARIS, 29 Jan 1997, *Portrait of a Young Woman in a Pink Dress in a Landscape* (oil on canvas, 27 1/2 x 23 1/2 ins / 70 x 60 cm) FRF 95,000. NEW YORK, 30 Jan 1997, *Pastoral Landscape with Women Preparing the Laundry* (1777, gouache/paper/canvas, 25 1/2 x 40 1/2 ins / 64.8 x 102.9 cm) USD 189,500. CANNES, 7 Aug 1997, *Ram in a Landscape* (1791, watercolour, 11 x 9 1/4 ins / 27 x 23.2 cm) FRF 29,000. NEW YORK, 21 Oct 1997, *A Family of Lions* (1803, oil on canvas, 38 1/4 x 51 1/2 ins / 97.3 x 130.5 cm) USD 442,500. NEW YORK, 30 Jan 1998, *Venus Asleep on a Bed with Two Doves at her Feet* (oil on canvas, oval, 40 1/2 x 58 1/4 ins / 102.9 x 148 cm) USD 233,500. PARIS, 30 March 1998, *Women and Children* (1776, pen, brown ink and grey wash, 6 x 4 1/2 ins / 15 x 11.2 cm) FRF 4,300. VIENNA, 6 Oct 1999, *Pastoral Scene near Fountain in Wooded River Landscape* (oil on canvas, 18 x 32 ins / 46 x 81 cm) ATS 150,000. NEW YORK, 14 Oct 1999, *Boy and Girl by Edge of Pond with Dog. Boys Playing Pipes with Dog* (oil on canvas, a pair, 18 x 14 ins / 45 x 36 cm) USD 37,500. LONDON, 19 April 2000, *Marie Joseph Chenier, Seated at Table, a Quill in his Left Hand* (1788, oil on panel, 12 x 9 ins / 30 x 23 cm) GBP 8,000. NEW YORK, 18 Oct 2000, *Flower Seller Setting Off for Market* (oil on canvas, 54 x 49 ins / 138 x 125 cm) USD 40,000. NEW YORK, 23 Jan 2001, *Two Studies of Boar's Head* (black ink/watercolour, 9 x 12 ins / 23 x 30 cm) USD 31,000. NEW YORK, 26 Oct 2001, *Flute Lesson. The Kite* (oil on canvas, a pair, 94 x 63 ins / 239 x 159 cm) USD 55,000. LONDON, 11 April 2002, *Nymph with a Female Satyr and Putti*

(1781, pen/ink/watercolour, oval, 6 x 9 ins / 16 x 22 cm) GBP 6,500. PARIS, 28 June 2002, *Shepherdesses Refreshing Themselves at a Spring* (1781, watercolour/ink/pen, 8 x 11 ins / 20 x 28 cm) EUR 5,500. PARIS, 2 Dec 2003, *Putti Dragging a Goat. A Young Woman Playing the Tambourine* (black chalk, a pair, 3 x 13 ins / 8 x 33 cm) EUR 3,200. PARIS, 12 Dec 2003, *Trophy, a Cockerel* (black crayon/pastel, 16 x 10 ins / 40 x 25 cm) EUR 3,000. PARIS, 19 March 2004, *Bunch of Flowers* (1770, colour crayon, 13 x 11 ins / 33 x 28 cm) EUR 11,000. PARIS, 19 March 2004, *Bunch of Flowers* (1770, colour crayon, 13 x 11 ins / 33 x 28 cm) EUR 28,000.

HUET, Jean-Baptiste, the Younger
French, 18th - 19th century.
Born 29 December 1772, in Paris.
Painter, engraver. Figures, landscapes.

Jean-Baptiste Huet the Younger was the son of J.-B. Huet the Elder. Having lost his right arm at the momentous battle of Jemmappes, he went on undaunted to master the skill of engraving left-handed.

AUCTION RECORDS:
PARIS, 1890, *Landscape*, FRF 780. PARIS, 21-22 Feb 1919, *Little Fishermen* (Indian ink) FRF 360.

HUET, Léon Armand
French, 19th - 20th century.
Born in Vitry-sur Seine.
Painter. Landscapes.

Léon Armand Huet exhibited regularly in Paris at the Salon des Artistes Français. He received an honourable mention in 1901.

AUCTION RECORDS:
LONDON, 30 Nov 1907, *Near Glaucoe* (1882) GBP 32. NEW YORK, 13 Feb 1985, *Robinson Crusoe and Friday* (oil on canvas, 76 x 40 ins / 193 x 101.5 cm) USD 4,000. PARIS, 1 July 1992, *The Model* (1899, oil on canvas, a pair, each 39¼ x 32 ins / 100 x 81 cm) FRF 120,000.

HUET, Louis
French, 18th century.
Active in Paris in 1740.
Painter, sculptor.

HUET, Marie
French, 19th - 20th century.
Active in Solesmes.
Painter.

Marie Huet became a member of the Société des Artistes Français in 1887.

HUET, Nicolas, the Elder
French, 18th century.
Born probably c. 1718; died after 1780.
Active still in Paris in April 1780.
Painter, watercolourist. Hunting scenes, still-lifes, animals.

Nicolas Huet the Elder was a painter for the Garde-Meuble (furniture depository) in the royal household. He was probably the first master of his more famous son, Jean-Baptiste Huet the Elder. He taught at the Académie de St-Luc and regularly featured in its exhibitions between 1751 and 1762. He lived on Rue Basse du Rempart and was married to Marie-Madeleine Colart. It is likely that Huet the Younger, Christophe Huet, and Nicolas Huet the Elder are related. Nicolas could be Christophe's brother and one and the same with Huet the Younger.

He painted sheep, dogs, birds and would have worked for the gentry.

AUCTION RECORDS:
PARIS, 10 Dec 1926, *Huntsmen* (watercolour) FRF 630. VERSAILLES, 27 May 1979, *Water Spaniel Chasing a Goose* (1744, oil on canvas, 48½ x 34¼ ins / 123 x 87 cm) FRF 15,000.

HUET, Nicolas, the Younger
French, 18th century.
Born c. 1770, in Paris; died 1828.
Painter, watercolourist, draughtsman, engraver.
Natural history (animals).

Nicolas Huet the Younger was the son of Jean-Baptiste Huet the Elder. He was the painter delegated to the Muséum d'Histoire Naturelle and to the scientific and artistic commission which Bonaparte took to Egypt and whose major research would be published by F. G. Levrault (Paris 1828). He was also painter to Empress Josephine's menagerie.

AUCTION RECORDS:
PARIS, 20 Dec 1993, *Adult Female Pyrale Moth* (watercolour, 15 x 10 ins / 38 x 24.5 cm) FRF 33,500. NEW YORK, 9 Jan 1996, *Royal Giraffe* (watercolour, gouache and ink/vellum, 17½ x 12¼ ins / 44.5 x 30.9 cm) USD 40,250. LONDON, 3 July 1996, *Tiger* (gouache/vellum, 9¼ x 15 ins / 23.5 x 38.3 cm) GBP 47,700.

HUET, Paul
French, 19th century.
Born 3 October 1803, in Paris; died 8 January 1869, in Paris.
Painter, watercolourist, engraver, draughtsman, lithographer. Genre scenes, animals, landscapes with figures, landscapes, waterscapes, seascapes, flowers. Panoramas.
Honfleur (or St-Siméon) School.

Paul Huet was a pupil of Pierre-Narcisse Guérin, but soon became disenchanted with his master's adherence to the academic style. He far preferred setting up his easel outdoors and painting from nature, in the Parc de St-Cloud near Paris, and the Île Seguin in the Seine Valley, which was still part of the countryside at that time. From 1819 to 1822 Huet studied at the studio of Antoine-Jean Gros, where he met the British landscapist Richard Parkes Bonington, who had moved from England to France in 1817. Together with Bonington, he painted seascapes on the Channel coast, at Honfleur and Trouville, which was then just a small port in Normandy; these canvases show him to be an excellent painter of raging seas. During this same period (around 1820) he also frequented the École des Beaux-Arts, and attended the Académie Suisse, in 1822. In this same year, he made the acquaintance of Delacroix.

In his early works, from 1821 and 1822, Huet painted the theme of the solitary cavalryman, with his back to the viewer, riding off into the heart of the forest or into a romantic landscape; and, in 1821, the theme of the *Return of the Napoleonic Soldier*, to which he would regularly return throughout his career. Thus, from the outset, Paul Huet may be regarded as a Romantic artist, in terms of the subjects he tackled, the feeling of anxiety that characterizes them, and the frenzied technique he used, which favours expressive eloquence over detail. His paintings are a visual record of his own state of mind, represented by mysterious forests or oppressive, stormy skies. However, on the occasions when he found inner peace, he produced far more serene pictures, such as his *Elms at St-Cloud* of 1823 (Paris, Petit Palais). It is highly probable, given his friendship with Bonington, that he saw the Constable exhibition that was held in Paris in 1824, and studied the paintings closely. In Constable's works he would have discovered the same sense of natural light observed outdoors, and the same dramatisation of the landscape, that were cornerstones of his own painting. He shared the same ideas as Théodore Rousseau, Diaz and Jules Dupré, about the need to paint directly from nature, but was also, like them, harshly judged by the official juries. Nevertheless, he first won them over with his work *View of the Environs of La Fère*, which was accepted for exhibition at the Salon of 1827. In 1829 he painted panoramic views for the 'Diorama', a painted illusion of nature created by a variety of separate backgrounds and lighting effects (which, incidentally, is how the photographic pioneer Louis Daguerre began his career). In painting these panoramic backgrounds, Paul Huet perfected his sense of space, through extreme contrasts of distance and lighting: all of which is clearly evident in his *View of Rouen from the Mont-aux-Malades* of 1831 (now in the Musée de Rouen). He made engravings on wood and stone, and also made lithographs: for Huet, engraving was above all a means of accentuating effects of dark and light, and playing with contrasts. In 1831 he provided the illustrations for a book by Taylor and Nodier, entitled *Picturesque Journeys*. In 1831 he sent nine oil paintings and four watercolours to the Salon, which brought him to the public attention. From then on he regularly participated in the Salon exhibitions, and was awarded a second-class medal in 1833, the Légion d'Honneur in 1841, and first-class medals in 1848 and 1855. In 1836 he started teaching drawing to the Duchess of Orléans. As an artist of the Romantic movement he shared in its success, but also its decline in popularity among the public. He greatly admired his friend Delacroix, and shared his admiration for the English landscape painters. He was also a personal friend of the Fielding brothers. His pantheistic sense of nature, along with his open mind and cultivated spirit, earned him the esteem of Michelet, Hugo, Saint-Beuve and Lamartine. Huet travelled around provincial France in search of motifs, looking for picturesque, wild or grandiose places that lent themselves to the expression of his tormented state of mind, and found them on the Île-de-France, in Normandy at Houlgate, and in central France at Le Mont-Dore. He also travelled to Italy, but found the skies there too serene.

As a fully-fledged member of the Romantic movement, Paul Huet may be counted among the precursors of Impressionism; furthermore, the accuracy of his observations from nature, and his feeling for space, fresh air and light, undoubtedly influenced the painters of the Barbizon School. His allusive, feverish strokes of colour herald the greater artistic freedoms to come, and can be found in the work of Diaz. He understood all that was presaged in the paintings of Turner, and there are echoes of Turner's influence in the pastel drawings he made towards the end of his life; his *Pont-Neuf* of 1847 can be regarded as a bridge between Turner's shimmering mists and Claude Monet's views of London.

Paul Huet's work has been featured in some collective thematic exhibitions, including: in 2003, *Lamartine et le paysage romantique autour de Paul Huet* (*Lamartine and the Romantic Landscape around Paul Huet*), at the Musée des Ursulines and the Musée Lamartine, in Mâcon, southern France. There have only been a few solo exhibitions celebrating his work, including: in 1938, at the Galerie Guy Stein in Paris; in 1965, at the Musée des Beaux-Arts in Rouen; in 1969, at the Pavillon des Arts in Paris; and *Paul Huet*, in 1995, at the Galerie Antoine Laurentin in Paris.

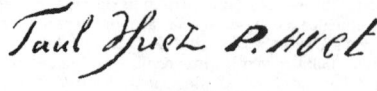

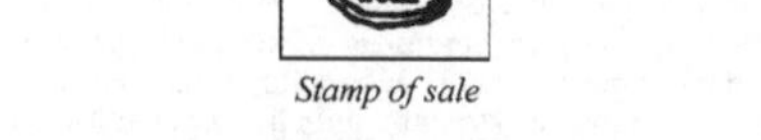

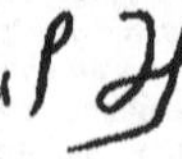

Stamp of sale

BIBLIOGRAPHY:

Huet, René-Paul, *Paul Huet, d'après ses notes, sa correspondance, ses contemporains*, Laurens, Paris, 1911. Delteil, Loys, '*Le Peintre-graveur illustré, Paul Huet*' in vol. VII, Chez l'auteur, Paris, 1911. Miquel, Pierre, *Paul Huet, de l'aube romantique à l'aube impressionniste*, Éd. de la Martinelle, Maurs-la-Jolie, 1962. *Paul Huet*, exhibition catalogue, Musée de Rouen, Rouen, 1965. *Paintings by Paul Huet (1803-1869) and some contemporary French sculpture*, exhibition catalogue, London, 1969 (winter exhibition 16th January-20th February 1969). Focillon, Henri, *La Peinture au XIXe siècle*, Flammarion, Paris, 1991 (reprinted). Comment, Bernard, *Le XIXe siècle des panoramas*, Adam Biro, Paris, 1993. *Paul Huet*, exhibition catalogue, Gal. Antoine Laurentin, Paris, 1995. Burty, Philippe, *Paul Huet*, Paris, 1995 (with a catalogue of those works exhibited in the Salons of the Union artistique). Cahen, Antoine, '*Paul Huet et l'eau-forte: les années romantiques*' in *Nouvelles de l'Estampe* n° 162, periodical, Bibliothèque nationale de France, Paris, 1999.

MUSEUMS AND GALLERIES:

AJACCIO: *Gate on the Road from Uriage to Vizille* - ALENÇON: *Interior of a Forest* - AMIENS: *Doves* - AVIGNON: *Gust of Wind, Memory of Auvergne; Torrent in Italy; View of Avignon, the Palais des Papes and the St-Bénézet Bridge* - BÉZIERS: *A Farm in Bourron* - BORDEAUX: *View of the Cliffs at Houlgate between Dives and Trouville* - BOURGES: *View of Spoleto* - CAEN: *Landscape* - LA ROCHELLE: *Landscape* - LE PUY-EN-VELAY: *Landscape* - LILLE: *Rocks at Nice; Environs of Abbeville; Evening* - MONTPELLIER: *Mountain Stream Bursting its Banks; Landscape; View from Bas-Meudon* - ORLÉANS: *View of the Arques Valley and Château, near Dieppe; Wood at La Haye*; two watercolours - PARIS (Louvre): *Flood at St-Cloud; Interior of a Forest; Hunters; Breakers on the Headland at Granville; The Park at St-Cloud; Farm; Cottage; Norman Horse; Interior of a Forest at Compiègne; Sunset at Seine-port; Morning Calm* - PARIS (Mus. du Petit Palais): *Elms at St-Cloud* (1823) - RHEIMS: *Death Valley at the Foot of the Sancy* - ROUEN: *View of Rouen from the Mont-aux-Malades* (1831) - VALENCIA: *Sunset* - VIRE: *The Abyss*.

AUCTION RECORDS:

PARIS, 1883, *Cascade in Italy*, FRF 1,250. PARIS, 1891, *Italian Landscape*, FRF 800. PARIS, 18-21 Dec 1918, *Landscape in Normandy*, FRF 140. PARIS, 2-4 June 1920, *Eu Valley* (heightened pencil) FRF 485. PARIS, 10-11 June 1921, *View from the Environs of Rouen*, FRF 530. PARIS, 11 March 1925, *In the Park at St-Cloud*, FRF 460. PARIS, 19 May 1926, *Flood at St-Cloud* (sketch) FRF 4,600. PARIS, 20 May 1927, *Landscape on the Banks of the Seine* (watercolour) FRF 1,400. PARIS, 11 May 1931, *Château-Gaillard* (watercolour) FRF 300; *Cliffs*, FRF 3,600. PARIS, 30 March 1942, *Rainbow*, FRF 4,000. PARIS, 23 June 1943, *Cliffs beneath the Clouds*, FRF 4,400; *Windmill at Luzarches*, FRF 6,800. PARIS, 25 March 1944, *The Bay at Antibes* (watercolour) FRF 7,400; *The Valley of St-Laurent du Pont* (watercolour) FRF 4,500. PARIS, 25 Nov 1946, *Landscape* (drawing) FRF 27,000. PARIS, 11 July 1947, *Cows*, FRF 7,000. PARIS, 1-2 April 1954, *Entrance to the Woods in the Environs of La Fère*, FRF 11,000. VERSAILLES, 20 Nov 1962, *View of Rouen* (watercolour) FRF 4,200; *Datura et Volubilis*, FRF 7,300. VERSAILLES, 19 April 1964, *Bouquet*, FRF 9,000. PARIS, 16 June 1966, *Seascape*, FRF 3,500. VERSAILLES, 7 June 1967, *Space*, FRF 3,000. VERSAILLES, 22 Nov 1972, *Landscape with Windmill*, FRF 7,500. ENGHIEN-LES-BAINS, 2 June 1977, *Riverbank with Poplars* (oil on card, 8 3/4 x 13 3/4 ins / 22.5 x 35 cm) FRF 5,000. PARIS, 16 May 1979, *Eu Valley in Stormy Weather* (heightened pencil, 10 x 15 1/4 ins / 25.5 x 39 cm) FRF 6,500. PARIS, 28 May 1979, *Environs of Antibes* (1855, oil on canvas, 38 1/2 x 63 3/4 ins / 98 x 162 cm) FRF 52,000. NEW YORK, 25 Feb 1982, *Woods at Bas-Bréau, Fontainebleau* (1852, oil on canvas, 23 1/2 x 32 1/4 ins / 59.5 x 82 cm) USD 7,750. LONDON, 17 March 1983, *Les Échelles, Savoy* (c. 1858, watercolour and pencil, 12 x 18 1/2 ins / 30.5 x 47 cm) GBP 1,700. PARIS, 14 June 1985, *Le Tréport at Low Tide* (watercolour, 5 x 9 3/4 ins / 13 x 25 cm) FRF 18,000. MONACO, 20 Feb 1988, *Pond at Ville d'Avray* (watercolour and charcoal, 6 1/2 x 10 ins / 16.2 x 25.7 cm) FRF 6,105. PARIS, 28 March 1988, *Paris, near the Meudon Hills* (1868, oil on panel, 14 1/4 x 23 ins / 36.5 x 57.5 cm) FRF 24,000. BERN, 30 April 1988, *Wooded Landscape with a Fisherman in a Boat on a Stream* (oil on canvas, 23 1/2 x 32 ins / 60 x 81 cm) CHF 3,000. PARIS, 14 June 1988, *Spring on the Banks of the Seine* (oil on canvas, 12 3/4 x 9 1/2 ins / 32.5 x 24 cm) FRF 8,000. PARIS, 10 April 1989, *The Artist Surrounded by Nature* (oil on paper, 10 x 13 3/4 ins / 25.5 x 35 cm) FRF 22,000. CALAIS, 10 Dec 1989, *Children in the Woods* (oil on panel, 9 1/2 x 13 3/4 ins / 24 x 35 cm) FRF 32,000. PARIS, 18 Dec 1989, *Oasis, Normandy* (oil on panel, 9 x 5 1/2 ins / 22 x 14 cm) FRF 41,000. PARIS, 10 April 1990, *Entrance to the Desert of La Grande Chartreuse* (oil on canvas, 13 x 16 1/4 ins / 33 x 41 cm) FRF 20,000. MONACO, 16 June 1990, *Landscape with the Château d'Arques la Bataille* (oil on canvas, 18 3/4 x 29 3/4 ins / 47.5 x 75.5 cm) FRF 55,500. PARIS, 5 July 1990, *Entrance to the Desert of La Grande Chartreuse* (oil on canvas, 13 x 16 1/4 ins / 33 x 41 cm) FRF 16,500. PARIS, 24 May 1991, *Cascade at Mortain-en-Manche* (oil on canvas, 19 x 27 1/4 ins / 48.5 x 69 cm) FRF 21,000. MONACO, 6 Dec 1991, *Spring Morning* (1834, oil on canvas, 38 1/2 x 63 1/2 ins / 98 x 161 cm) FRF 249,750. PARIS, 2 Nov 1992, *Torrent at La Grande Chartreuse* (charcoal and white gouache, 18 x 22 ins / 46 x 56 cm) FRF 10,000. NEW YORK, 28 May 1993, *Children Playing on a Beach* (watercolour/paper, 5 1/2 x 14 1/2 ins / 14.2 x 37 cm) USD 1,840. PARIS, 10 Dec 1993, *La Rance* (watercolour, 6 3/4 x 9 3/4 ins / 17.2 x 24.6 cm) FRF 9,000. PARIS, 15 Feb 1995, *Valley of St-Laurent-du-Port at the Foot of La Grande Chartreuse* (watercolour and pencil, 10 3/4 x 12 1/2 ins / 27.5 x 32 cm) FRF 7,000. PARIS, 24 March 1995, *Cascades at Tivoli* (oil on canvas, 21 1/4 x 33 ins / 54 x 84 cm) FRF 75,000. FONTAINEBLEAU, 31 March 1996, *Nymphs Bathing* (oil on panel, 25 1/2 x 40 1/2 ins / 65 x 103 cm) FRF 54,000. PARIS, 21 June 1996, *Rocks at Carabasco* (oil on canvas, study, 12 3/4 x 18 ins / 32.5 x 46 cm, 2 ins/5 cm) FRF 18,000. PARIS, 17 Oct 1997, *Sun Setting over the Plain* (oil on card, 5 1/2 x 10 1/4 ins / 14 x 26 cm) FRF 14,000. FONTAINEBLEAU, 6 June 1999, *Wood near the Town of Auray* (1863, oil on canvas/panel, 13 x 18 ins / 32 x 45 cm) FRF 50,500. LONDON, 4 July 2000, *View of Mont Ussy in the Forest of Fontainebleau* (black chalk/watercolour, 7 x 10 ins / 17 x 26 cm) GBP 4,200. LONDON, 15 Dec 2000, *Seascape at Twilight* (gouache, 11 x 13 ins / 27 x 34 cm) GBP 6,800. NEW YORK, 1 May 2001, *Salt Marshes near Saint Valley in Somme, Picardy* (oil on canvas, 38 x 64 ins / 97 x 162 cm) USD 25,000. PARIS, 16 Nov 2001, *The Pont de Toucques near Trouville* (oil on canvas, 18 x 31 ins / 46 x 78 cm) FRF 60,000. PARIS, 18 Nov 2002, *Study for Flood* (oil on canvas, 13 x 18 ins / 33 x 46 cm) EUR 5,400. PARIS, 30 March 2004, *The Elms of St-Cloud* (c. 1823, oil on panel, 14 x 11 ins / 36 x 27 cm) EUR 24,000. PARIS, 30 March 2004, *Study of the Sea, English Channel* (oil on panel, 14 x 26 ins / 35 x 66 cm) EUR 32,000.

HUET, Raf
Belgian, 20th century.
Born 1941, in Wortel.
Sculptor.
Raf Huet studied at the Académie de St-Luc in Schaerbeck. He now teaches at the Institut du Sacré-Cœur in Turnhout.

HUET, Raoullin
French, 16th century.
Active in Caen in 1588.
Painter.

HUET, René Ernest
French, 19th - 20th century.
Born 18 April 1876, in Villers-Bocage (Calvados); died 17 December 1914; on active service.
Painter. Genre scenes.
René Ernest Huet was a student of Merson and V. Gilbert. He exhibited in Paris at the Société des Artistes Français.

HUET, René Paul
French, 19th - 20th century.
Born 28 November 1844, in Nice; died 1928.
Painter, engraver. Genre scenes, landscapes.
René Paul Huet studied with his father Paul, and with Pils. He was a delicate artist, rendering various aspects of nature with great emotion. His etchings are very interesting, and he is also known for his wood engravings. He exhibited at the Salon de Paris from 1866, and then at the Salon des Artistes Français. He received an honourable mention in 1882, a third-class medal in 1887 and a bronze in 1900 at the Exposition Universelle.
MUSEUMS AND GALLERIES:
CAEN: *Ulysses Finding His Father.*
AUCTION RECORDS:
PARIS, 27 March 1947, *Seashores; The Shrimp Fishing Woman* (two paintings) FRF 1,000. PARIS, 13 June 1994, *Straw, the Artist's Family in Front of his Chalet in Chaville* (oil on panel, 17 3/4 x 30 3/4 ins / 45 x 78 cm) FRF 4,000. PARIS, 15 Dec 1994, *Horsewoman in Costume and her Greyhounds* (oil on panel, 19 3/4 x 13 1/4 ins / 50 x 33.5 cm) FRF 4,000.

HUET-VILLIERS. See **HUET François**

HUETHER, Julius
German, 20th century.
Born 4 November 1881, in Cannstatt, near Stuttgart.
Painter. Landscapes.
Huether was a student of Van Hackl and Van Loefftz. He settled in Munich and painted mainly landscapes.

HUETT, Hans. See **EWOUTSZ**

HUETTER, Elias
Austrian, 19th century.
Born 1775, in Vienna; died c. 1863.
Sculptor.
He was a pupil of Grassi and worked for porcelain manufactories before going over to sculpting primarily busts.

HUETTER, Lukacs
Hungarian, 18th century.
Died 13 November 1760, in Eger.
Painter.
Lukacs Huetter worked for the convents and churches in Eger.

HUETTIG, Paul Gottfried
German, 19th century.
Born 10 December 1865, in Leipzig.
Sculptor.
He studied at the academy in Dresden, then settled in Berlin.

HUEVA, Barbara Maria de
Spanish, 18th century.
Born 1733, in Madrid; died 23 April 1772, in Segovia.
Painter, engraver.
In 1752, Barbara Maria de Hueva became a member of the Real Academia de San Fernando.

HUEVOS VON BOGTA, Laszlo
Hungarian, 20th century.
Born 1883, in Budapest.
Sculptor.
Lazlo Huevos von Bogta worked in Paris where he sculpted works including busts of *Beethoven* and *Puccini*.

HUEY, A.
British, 19th century.
Active in London.
Miniaturist.
A. Huey exhibited his work in London at the Royal Academy from 1814 to 1818.

HUEZ, D'. See **D'HUEZ**

HUEZ, Jean Baptiste Cyprien d'
French, 18th century.
Born c. 1728, in Arras; died 27 October 1793, in Paris.
Sculptor.
Jean Baptiste Cyprien d'Huez studied under J.-B. Lemoine. In 1761 he was approved by the Académie and became an Académicien in 1763. In the 1770s he progressed through the teaching hierarchy, having exhibited at the Paris Salon from 1761 to 1773. The Louvre has a *St Andrew* by him and the Musée de la Comédie-Française has a *Bust of Crébillon*.

HUF, Fritz
Swiss, 20th century.
Born 14 August 1888, in Lucerne; died 1970, in Gentilino.
Sculptor, draughtsman. Busts.
Fritz Huf studied with a silversmith in Lucerne from 1906 to 1909. In 1911, he went to Paris with Jean Arp. After travelling in Italy for a while, he worked in Berlin from 1914 to 1923. During this period he was in contact with artists of *Der Sturm* (*The Storm*). From 1924 to 1940, he lived in France, first in Toulon (1924-25) and then in Paris (1925 onwards), where he associated with the Abstraction-Création group. Work by him was featured at the retrospective of the group at the Musée d'Art Moderne de la Ville de Paris in 1978 entitled *Abstraction-Création 1931-1936*. There were also solo exhibitions of his work, at the Kunstverein in Frankfurt (1913); at the Kunstmuseum in Lucerne (1962); and in Helmhaus, near Zurich (1969).
BIBLIOGRAPHY:
Fritz Huf, exhibition catalogue, Helmhaus, Zurich, 1969. Fabre, Gladys C., *Abstraction-Création 1931-1936*, exhibition catalogue, Westfälisches Landesmuseum für Kunst und Kulturgeschichte, Münster, Musée d'Art moderne de la ville de Paris, Paris, 1978.
AUCTION RECORDS:
BERN, 10 June 1971, *Head of Rainer Maria Rilke* (bronze) CHF 4,500. BERN, 22 June 1983, *Eleonore Duse* (1927-1928, bronze, h. 11¼ ins / 28.5 cm) CHF 1,600. LUCERNE, 21 Nov 1992, *Dusk 47* (1961, pastel/paper, 15¼ x 20½ ins / 38.5 x 52 cm) CHF 1,300. LUCERNE, 20 Nov 1993, *Drawing I* (1959, charcoal/paper, 17 x 19 ins / 43 x 48 cm) CHF 1,600; *Ursula* (1941, terracotta, h. 11¾ ins / 30 cm) CHF 1,700. LUCERNE, 4 June 1994, *Nude Lying Down* (1930, terracotta and plastic, h. 6¼ ins / 16 cm and l. 12½ ins/31.5 cm) CHF 2,200. ZURICH, 15 June 1999, *Water is the Best - Pike and Trout* (oil on canvas, 29 x 51 ins / 73 x 130 cm) CHF 4,100.

HUFFAM, A.W.
British, 19th century.
Active in Edmonton near London.
Engraver, lithographer.
A.W. Huffam's works include a *Portrait of King William IV* among others.

HUFFEL, Pieter van
Belgian, 18th - 19th century.
Born 17 April or 17 August 1769, in Geraardsbergen, Flanders; died 12 August 1844, in Ghent.
Painter. Historical subjects, portraits.
Pieter van Huffel studied under G. J. Herrxeyns in Mechelen and at the Ghent academy. He also worked in Paris. When he returned to Ghent, he was appointed director of the academy.
MUSEUMS AND GALLERIES:
ANTWERP: *Portrait of Napoleon Bonaparte, First Consul.*

HUFNAGEL. See **HOEFNAGEL Joris** or **Georg or Georgius**

HUFTIER, Jean Paul
French, 20th century.
Born 17 September 1944, in Lallaing.
Painter (mixed media), draughtsman, performance artist.
Jean Paul Huftier lives and works in Paris. He co-founded the magazine *Hors-Commerce* in 1981.
In Huftier's work traces of vigorously brushed colours permeate the surface of the canvas and the paint flows in vertical lines, creating a colour-matter assemblage theatre which is sometimes aggravated or blurred in an informal efflorescence. He also paints female nudes.
The many collective exhibitions in which he has taken part include: Salon des Réalités Nouvelles, Paris, 1972, 1973 and 1975; *Tendances de l'Art en France 1968-1978/9* (*Trends in French Art 1968-1978/9*), Musée d'Art Moderne de la Ville de Paris, 1979; Salon International, Musée des Beaux-Arts, Toulon, 1980; *Actualité du Dessin* (*Relevance of Art*), Grenoble Community Arts Centre, 1980; Salon de Montrouge, 1981 and 1982; *De Matisse à Nos Jours* (*From Matisse to the Present Day*), Musée des Beaux-Arts, Lille, 1982; *Vingt Ans de Peinture en France 1960-1980* (*Twenty Years of Painting in France 1960-1980*), Marcelin Pleynet's choice, travelling exhibition in Germany, Luxemburg and Italy, 1983; *Histoire de Peintures* (*History of Painting*), Musée du Berry, Bourges, 1985; Salon de Mai, Paris, 1985; *Aspects de la Jeune Peinture Abstraite* (*Aspects of Young Abstract Painting*), Maison des Jeunes et de la Culture les Hauts de Belleville, Paris, 1986; Musée des Beaux-Arts, Rennes, 1986; *Tradition et Réalités de la Peinture* (*Tradition and Reality of Painting*), Centre d'Action Culturelle de St-Brieuc and Château de la Roche-Jagu, 1987; *Présence d'Art Contemporain Français à Prague* (*Contemporary French Art in Prague*), National Gallery, Prague, 1988; Art Jonction International, Galerie Rivages, Nice, 1988; Salon de la Jeune Peinture, Paris, 1988.
Solo exhibitions of his work include: Librairie-Galerie Josie Peron, Paris, 1970; La Galerie de Paris, 1972; La Cour des Miracles, Paris, 1975, Galerie Galea, Caen, 1976; Atrium, Lyons, 1978; *La Peinture Déroulée* (*Painting Unfolded*), Maison de la Culture, Amiens, 1979; Nouveau Musée, Crédit Lyonnais Tower, Lyons, 1980; Galerie Stadler, Paris, 1981, 1982, 1983, 1984, 1986 and 1989; Haydn-Türk, Munich, 1984 and 1985.
BIBLIOGRAPHY:
Pleynet, Marcelin, '*Tendances de l'art en France 1968-1978*' in *Art Press*, periodical, Paris, October 1979. Dufau, Alain, *Jean Paul Huftier*, film, 1983. Zurcher, Bernard, *Jean-Paul Huftier*, Éd. B. et G. Zurcher, Paris, 1985. *Huftier*, exhibition catalogue, Gal. Stadler, Paris, January 1989.
MUSEUMS AND GALLERIES:
AMIENS (FRAC Picardie) - CARQUEFOU (FRAC Pays de la Loire) - CHÂTEAUGIRON (FRAC Bretagne) - GRENOBLE (Mus. de Grenoble) - PARIS (FNAC) - PARIS (MAMVP) - ST-ÉTIENNE (MAM).
AUCTION RECORDS:
PARIS, 21 Sept 1989, *Jorairatar IV* (1984, mixed media/canvas, 35¾ x 30¾ ins / 91 x 78 cm) FRF 6,500. PARIS, 8 July 1993, *La Cité Interdite* (*Forbidden City*) (1985, oil on canvas, 59 x 78¾ ins / 150 x 200 cm) FRF 9,000.

HUG, Charles
Swiss, 20th century.
Born 22 June 1899, in St Gall; died 1979.
Painter, fresco artist, lithographer. Designs for mosaics.
Work by Charles Hug has been exhibited at the principal museums in Switzerland, in Basel, Geneva and Zurich. There are also works by him in Paris, Berlin and New York. He produced lithographs of circus scenes, and his work was shown at the Paris exhibition *From Ingres to Picasso*.

AUCTION RECORDS:
ZURICH, 17 Nov 1976, *Horse Race* (oil on canvas, 18 x 25 3/4 ins / 45.5 x 65.5 cm) CHF 2,700. ZURICH, 26 May 1978, *Figures by the Nile* (1953, oil on canvas, 11 x 9 ins / 27 x 22 cm) CHF 2,200. ZURICH, 8 Nov 1980, *The Rhône in Spring* (1955, oil on canvas, 25 1/2 x 21 1/4 ins / 65 x 54 cm) CHF 5,500. ZURICH, 20 Nov 1987, *Lake Constance in Spring* (1943, oil on canvas remounted/panel, 23 1/2 x 28 1/4 ins / 60 x 72 cm) CHF 7,500. ZURICH, 30 Nov 1995, *Still-life of Flowers* (1929, oil on canvas, 22 x 18 ins / 55 x 46 cm) CHF 2,875. ST GALL, 10 Dec 1999, *Forest Path* (1934, oil on canvas on board, 26 x 37 ins / 66 x 94 cm) CHF 3,400. ST GALL, 10 May 2000, *Mountain Landscape* (oil on canvas, 24 x 29 ins / 60 x 73 cm) CHF 5,800. ZOFINGEN, 16 June 2000, *Artist's Garden in Greifenstein in the Summer* (oil on canvas) CHF 5,000. ST GALL, 21 Nov 2001, *Autumn Abundance* (1943, oil on canvas, 53 x 37 ins / 135 x 95 cm) CHF 14,500. ST GALL, 22 May 2002, *Still-life with Bunch of Flowers* (1970, oil on canvas on panel, 29 x 23 ins / 73 x 58 cm) CHF 9,000. ZURICH, 26 Nov 2002, *Peaches* (1948, oil on pavatex, 7 x 9 ins / 19 x 24 cm) CHF 3,200. ST GALL, 1 Oct 2004, *Garden Landscape with Trees near Greifenstein* (oil on canvas, 29 x 24 ins / 73 x 60 cm) CHF 5,800. ST GALL, 1 Oct 2004, *Musical Clown* (oil on canvas, 26 x 18 ins / 65 x 46 cm) CHF 8,500.

HUG, Fritz
Swiss, 20th century.
Born 1921; died 1989.
Painter. Landscapes, landscapes with figures, animals.

AUCTION RECORDS:
ZURICH, 17 Nov 1976, *Mountainous Landscape* (oil on canvas, 19 3/4 x 25 1/2 ins / 50 x 65 cm) CHF 2,700. ZURICH, 19 July 1984, *The Torrent* (oil on canvas, 21 1/4 x 28 3/4 ins / 54 x 73 cm) CHF 6,000. LUCERNE, 7 June 1986, *View of Zurich* (oil on canvas, 21 1/4 x 32 ins / 54 x 81 cm) CHF 4,600. ZURICH, 25 Oct 1989, *Kitten* (gouache, 9 1/2 x 6 1/2 ins / 24.3 x 16.8 cm) CHF 2,000. ZURICH, 22 June 1990, *Young Fawn* (oil on canvas, 11 x 13 3/4 ins / 27 x 35 cm) CHF 2,600. LUCERNE, 24 Nov 1990, *On the Meknès Road* (oil on card, 11 1/2 x 18 ins / 29 x 46 cm) CHF 1,100. ZURICH, 7-8 Dec 1990, *Owl in a Starry Sky* (oil on canvas, 13 3/4 x 11 ins / 35 x 27 cm) CHF 6,000. ZURICH, 21 June 1991, *Abyssinian Cat* (oil on canvas, 27 3/4 x 16 ins / 70.5 x 40.5 cm) CHF 4,800.

HUG, Hans Melchior
Swiss, 16th - 17th century.
Active in Wil.
Glass painter.

MUSEUMS AND GALLERIES:
ZURICH: *The Annunciation and the Holy Women at Christ's Tomb* (1608, stained-glass window); *The Sacrifice of Abraham and the Arms of Ulrich Hertzig* (stained-glass window).

HUG, Huguette Dupont
French, 20th century.
Born in Neuilly-sur-Seine.
Painter.
Hug exhibited in Paris at the Salon des Indépendants from 1929.

HUG, Nicolaus
Swiss, 18th - 19th century.
Born 14 June 1771, in Konstanz; died 2 December 1852, in Konstanz.
Painter, engraver.
He trained at the academy in Munich.

HUGAART, Willem, or Hugaerts
Dutch, 18th century.
Born 1683, in Haarlem; died 1727.
Painter.
Willem Hugaart was a pupil of Dirck Maes.

HUGARD
French, 20th century.
Sculptor. Figures, nudes. Statuettes.
Hugard studied at the École des Beaux-Arts in Rheims. From 1978, she participated in numerous collective regional exhibitions and showed in Parisian galleries. She works in stone and marble and sometimes casts her works in bronze, notably at the Landowski foundry. From her classical training, she has evolved towards much greater freedom of interpretation of the human body, to the point of joining arms and legs in *Ring*. Existential pain is a theme that seems to inhabit many of her sculptures: *Wounded Young Man, The Broken Woman, Behind the Mask of Solitude, The Torment, Birth of a Woman* and *Fall of a Young Girl*.

AUCTION RECORDS:
PARIS, 5 Feb 1990, *Behind the Mask, Solitude* (1988, brown-patinated bronze) FRF 28,000. PARIS, 21 May 1990, *The Opening* (1986, brown-patinated bronze, 11 3/4 x 14 1/4 x 6 3/4 ins / 30 x 36 x 17 cm) FRF 38,000. NEUILLY, 3 Feb 1991, *The Spider* (1988, bronze, 7 3/4 x 11 3/4 ins / 20 x 30 cm) FRF 32,000. PARIS, 3 June 1991, *The Gesture of Dressing* (1987, bronze, 9 x 7 3/4 x 6 ins / 22 x 20 x 15 cm) FRF 6,000. PARIS, 7 Oct 1991, *Quarry Interior* (1989, bronze, 19 3/4 x 16 1/4 x 13 1/2 ins / 50 x 41 x 34 cm) FRF 21,000. PARIS, 23 Jan 1995, *The Prayer* (original stone from St-Maximin, 19 3/4 x 15 3/4 ins / 50 x 40 cm) FRF 23,000; *The Ring* (brown-patinated bronze, h. 12 1/2 ins / 32 cm) FRF 15,000. PARIS, 13 May 1996, *Omnipresent* (patinated bronze, 24 1/2 x 11 3/4 x 9 3/4 ins / 62 x 30 x 25 cm) FRF 27,000. PARIS, 22 March 1998, *Shadow of a Reclining Woman* (brown-patinated bronze, 20 1/2 x 9 x 6 3/4 ins / 52 x 22 x 17 cm) FRF 11,000.

HUGARD, Claude S.
French, 19th - 20th century.
Born 5 June 1861, in Paris.
Painter, engraver (etching). Rustic scenes, genre scenes, landscapes, mountainscapes, waterscapes.
Hugard was a student of Cormon. He became a member of the Société des Artistes Français in 1901. He received an honourable mention in 1905.

AUCTION RECORDS:
PARIS, 30 April 1919, *The Flood,* FRF 200. PARIS, 12 June 1920, *The Dream,* FRF 1,200. PARIS, 21 Jan 1926, *The Flood in the Mountain,* FRF 320. PARIS, 6 Nov 1935, *Livestock at the Trough,* FRF 300. PARIS, 24 March 1941, *The Lake,* FRF 350. LONDON, 20 Nov 1996, *Women Sewing* (oil on panel, 9 x 11 1/4 ins / 23 x 28.5 cm) GBP 4,830.

HUGARD DE LA TOUR, Claude Sébastien
French, 19th century.
Born April 1818, in Cluses (Haute-Savoie); died 1886, in Paris.
Painter. Mountainscapes, landscapes.
Hugard de la Tour was taught to paint by Alexandre Calame in Geneva, and then by François Diday. He participated in the Paris Salon, from 1844 to 1880, and was awarded a third-class medal in 1844, and a second-class medal in 1846.

Hugard found inspiration for a great many of his canvases in the Alps, and also painted views of Normandy, Brie and the Pyrenées.

MUSEUMS AND GALLERIES:
AURILLAC: *Morning in the Cluses Valley* - BAGNÈRES-DE-BIGORRE: *View of the Gavarnie Circus; Lake Thann; View of Mont-Blanc from Mount Grammont; The Gavarnie Circus* - BÉZIERS: *Daybreak on the Gers Peak* - CHAMBÉRY (MBA):

Sunset on the Mont-Blanc Range; Flood at Chamonix; The Sea of Ice - MOULINS.

AUCTION RECORDS:

BERN, 1 May 1980, *Alpine Landscape* (oil on canvas, 13 x 23 1/2 ins / 33 x 60 cm) CHF 5,500. PARIS, 19 June 1991, *Mountain Landscape* (oil on canvas, 19 x 25 1/2 ins / 48.5 x 64.5 cm) FRF 28,000. PARIS, 22 June 1992, *Italian Countryside* (1858, oil on canvas, 15 1/4 x 22 ins / 39 x 56 cm) FRF 7,200. COPENHAGEN, 31 Aug 1999, *Cattle Watering in Woodland Tarn* (oil on canvas, 52 x 75 ins / 133 x 190 cm) DKK 20,000.

HUGART, Lina (Mme)
French, 19th century.
Died 1907.
Painter.

HUGEL
French, 19th century.
Engraver.

In 1870 Hugel exhibited the *Portrait of Madame Mère* at the Salon.

HUGEL, E.
British, 19th century.
Active in London at the beginning of the 19th century.
Miniaturist.

HUGEN, Jan
Dutch, 19th century.
Engraver.

In 1835, Jan Hugen received a state commission to engrave a picture of Guido Reni.

HUGENET, Thomas
French, 17th century.
Active in Paris in 1676.
Painter, sculptor.

HUGENHOLTZ, Ar
Dutch, 19th century.
Born 20 September 1851, in Haarlem.
Painter, engraver.

Ar Hugenholtz studied at the Amsterdam academy.

HUGENOT
German, 18th century.
Active in Hamburg.
Painter. Landscapes.

HUGENSZ., Dirck, or Huygenz or Huigens
Dutch, 16th century.
Active between 1527 and 1538.
Painter.

Dirck Hugensz. was the brother of Lucas van Leyden.

HUGENTOBLER, Iwan Edwin
German, 20th century.
Born 1886, in Degersheim; died 1972, in Zurich.
Painter, draughtsman. Military subjects, animals.

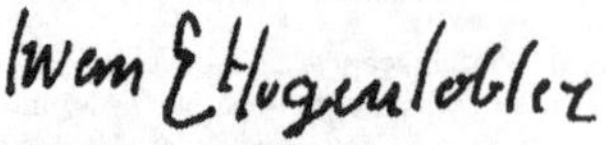

AUCTION RECORDS:

BERN, 23 Oct 1986, *Officer of the Swiss Cavalry* (1933, charcoal, 18 x 15 ins / 46 x 38 cm) CHF 2,300. LUCERNE, 30 Sept 1988, *Harvest Scene* (gouache, 11 x 11 ins / 27 x 27 cm) CHF 3,200. ST GALL, 21 April 1999, *Scene from Wallis* (1917, oil on canvas, 31 x 23 ins / 80 x 58 cm) CHF 5,000. ST GALL, 21 Nov 2001, *Village with Church in Bundnerland* (1916, oil on canvas, 22 x 17 ins / 55 x 42 cm) CHF 4,500. ST GALL, 22 May 2002, *Horse with Vet* (1924, oil on board, 10 x 10 ins / 26 x 25 cm) CHF 6,500. ST GALL, 26 Nov 2002, *Two Friends* (1915, oil on canvas, 23 x 30 ins / 59 x 75 cm) CHF 7,000. LUCERNE, 16 June 2004, *Two Horses Being Attached to the Plough* (1936, oil on canvas, 24 x 30 ins / 60 x 77 cm) CHF 3,000.

HUGFORD, Ignazio Enrico
Italian, 18th century.
Born 1703, in Pisa, to English parents; died 16 August 1778, in Florence.
Painter, engraver, scholar. Religious subjects, portraits.

Hugford studied art in Florence.

MUSEUMS AND GALLERIES:

FLORENCE (Church of S Felicità): *St Raphael* - FLORENCE (Mus.): several paintings.

HUGGENBERG, Sebastian
German, 17th century.
Born in Augsburg.
Sculptor, medallist.

He worked a lot in Wolfenbüttel and Salzdahlum.

HUGGINS, W.
British, 18th century.
Active in London.
Sculptor.

W. Huggins exhibited his work at the Royal Academy in London in 1790.

HUGGINS, William, called Huggins of Liverpool
British, 19th century.
Born May 1820, in Liverpool; died 25 February 1884, in Christleton, near Chester.
Painter, watercolourist, draughtsman. Portraits, genre scenes, animals, still-lifes.
School of Liverpool.

William Huggins, who held a distinguished position in the Liverpool School, exhibited his work in London at the Royal Academy, the British Institution and Suffolk Street from 1842 to 1875.

MUSEUMS AND GALLERIES:

BLACKBURN: *Head of a Lioness* - LIVERPOOL: *Three Friends; Ass and Poultry; Landscape; Portraits of the Artist and his Wife; William Taylor; Christians and Lions.*

AUCTION RECORDS:

LONDON, 4 April 1908, *Sleeping Lions* (1863) GBP 38; *Lion and Lioness* (1872, watercolour) GBP 23. LONDON, June 1922, *Duck*, GBP 9. LONDON, July 1922, *Poultry*, GBP 8. LONDON, 29 Jan 1926, *The Millennium*, GBP 33. LONDON, 30 April 1926, *Cheshire Cattle*, GBP 52; *Horse and Goats*, GBP 71. LONDON, 8 Feb 1968, *Head of a Leopard*, GBP 320. LONDON, 26 June 1968, *Fowl*, GBP 450. LONDON, 6 March 1970, *Lion Head*, Gns 530. LONDON, 16 June 1970, *Lioness and Cubs* (watercolour) Gns 400. LONDON, 28 Nov 1972, *Giraffes*, GBP 5,800. LONDON, 20 Nov 1973, *The Golden Age* (card) GBP 1,800. LONDON, 9 April 1974, *Two Sleeping Tigers* (1861) GBP 6,500. LONDON, 16 July 1976, *Still-life with Flowers* (1870, oil on card, 23 1/4 x 17 3/4 ins / 59 x 45 cm) GBP 700. LONDON, 9 Feb 1982, *Lion, Lioness and their Young* (1880, pencil, coloured chalk and watercolour/light-grey paper, 14 1/2 x 21 1/4 ins / 37 x 54.2 cm) GBP 4,500. LONDON, 15 May 1984, *Ducks* (1882, pencil and coloured chalk/greyish-brown paper, 10 x 14 1/4 ins / 25.5 x 36.5 cm) GBP 1,500. NEW YORK, 29 Oct 1986, *A Brown Study* (1853, oil on canvas, 36 1/4 x 28 1/4 ins / 92.1 x 72 cm) USD 22,000. LONDON, 25 Jan 1988, *Cats Asleep* (1860, coloured chalk, 6 1/4 x 5 1/4 ins / 16 x 13.5 cm) GBP 1,320. LONDON, 3 June 1988, *The Farmyard* (oil on card, 11 1/2 x 15 ins / 29.4 x 38.3 cm) GBP 2,200. EDINBURGH, 22 Nov 1988, *Study of a Terrier Seated in Front of a Chinese Vase* (1868, watercolour and coloured chalk/paper, 21 3/4 x 17 1/2 ins / 55.2 x 44.4 cm) GBP 5,500. LONDON, 26 May 1989, *A Cow and Poultry* (1855, oil on card, 25 x 17¾ ins / 63.2 x 45 cm) GBP 3,300. LONDON, 21 March 1990, *Cattle and Chickens* (1881, oil on canvas, 25 x 30 ins / 63.5 x 76 cm) GBP 3,850. LONDON, 15 June 1990, *Lion in a Jungle Landscape* (1867, oil on canvas, 28 x 36 ins / 71.1 x 91.5 cm) GBP 6,600. LONDON, 10 April 1991, *A Representative of the Working Class* (1864, oil on canvas, 28¾ x 24 ins / 73 x 61 cm) GBP 15,400. LONDON, 8 April 1992, *Schooner off the Coast of Dover* (1834, oil on canvas, 34 x 49½ ins / 85.5 x 126 cm) GBP 4,400. NEW YORK, 5 June 1992, *Tiger's Head* (1872, oil on canvas, diam. 9 ins / 22.9 cm) USD 5,500. LONDON, 3 March 1993, *Two Horses near a Pump* (1851, oil on card, 25 x 30 ins / 63.5 x 76 cm) GBP 18,975. LONDON, 8-9 June 1993, *Lion* (1876, coloured chalk, 10 x 13¾ ins / 24.5 x 35 cm) GBP 3,680. LONDON, 25 March 1994, *Head of a Tabby Cat* (oil on card, diam. 8¾ ins / 22.2 cm) GBP 8,625. NEW YORK, 3 June 1994, *King of the Jungle* (1867, oil on canvas, 28 x 36 ins / 71.1 x 91.4 cm) USD 13,800. LONDON, 9 Nov 1994, *Group of Wild Animals* (1840, oil on canvas, 22¾ x 33½ ins / 58 x 85 cm) GBP 36,700. NEW YORK, 9 June 1995, *Study in Brown* (1853, oil on canvas, 36¼ x 28¾ ins / 92.1 x 73 cm) USD 24,150. CLWYD, 26 Oct 1999, *Standing Donkey and Reclining Cow in a Landscape* (oil on canvas, 17 x 16 ins / 43 x 41 cm) GBP 4,800. LONDON, 4 Nov 1999, *Study of a Terrier, Sitting before a Cantonese Famille Rose Vase* (1868, coloured chalk and watercolour heightened with white, 22 x 17 ins / 55 x 43 cm) GBP 3,000. LONDON, 14 June 2000, *Bideston Farmhouse with Cattle and Ducks. Bideston Farmhouse* (oil on canvas, a pair, 22 x 16 ins / 56 x 41 cm) GBP 5,000. LONDON, 28 Nov 2000, *North American Indian in an Extensive Landscape* (oil on board, 24 x 16 ins / 60 x 40 cm) GBP 11,000. NEW YORK, 13 Feb 2001, *Faithful Friends, Border Collie and Two Terriers in a Landscape* (oil on canvas, 28 x 36 ins / 72 x 91 cm) USD 12,000. NEW YORK, 1 June 2001, *Study of Mallards* (1867, oil on board, 11 x 9 ins / 29 x 22 cm) USD 12,000. LONDON, 19 June 2002, *Lion* (watercolour, pencil, gouache and coloured chalk, 15 x 20 ins / 37 x 52 cm) GBP 2,500. LONDON, 19 June 2002, *Terrier Seated before a Canton Famille Rose Vase* (1868, coloured chalk and watercolour over pencil, 21 x 17 ins / 53 x 43 cm) GBP 6,000. LONDON, 20 May 2003, *Study of a Lion and his Pride* (1871, pencil and red chalk, 4 x 7 ins / 9 x 18 cm) GBP 1,700. CHESTER, 4 June 2003, *Tabby Cat* (oil on board) GBP 1,800. LONDON, 9 Nov 2004, *Sleeping Lion* (1875, pencil and pastel, 7 x 10 ins / 18 x 26 cm) GBP 1,500. LONDON, 9 Nov 2004, *The Pride of Lions* (pencil and pastel, 15 x 23 ins / 38 x 58 cm) GBP 1,600.

HUGGINS, William John

British, 19th century.

Born 1781; died 19 May 1845, in London.

Painter, draughtsman. Battles, seascapes.

After serving in the English East India Company, William John Huggins exhibited his work at the Royal Academy in London from time to time, and in 1834 became seascape painter to William IV.

MUSEUMS AND GALLERIES:

CAPE TOWN: *Seascape* - LONDON (Royal Collection): *The Beginning of the Action; The Close of the Action; The Storm after the Battle.*

AUCTION RECORDS:

LONDON, 17 Nov 1924, *Frigate*, GBP 46. LONDON, 9 Feb 1927, *The 'Viscount Melbourne' off Folkestone*, GBP 39. LONDON, 8 July 1927, *The 'Elizabeth' at Sea near the Eddystone Lighthouse*, GBP 21. LONDON, 15 March 1929, *The 'Windsor Castle' Arriving in Liverpool*, GBP 84. LONDON, 20 Oct 1930, *Old Friends*, GBP 112. LONDON, 13 March 1946, *Battle of Saint Vincent*, GBP 48. LONDON, 1 March 1963, *Boat with a View of Newcastle*, Gns 310. LONDON, 24 May 1968, *The 'Daedalus' on the Ceylon Route*, Gns 680. LONDON, 20 Nov 1970, *The 'William Fairlie' of the East India Company*, Gns 550. LONDON, 19 July 1972, *Seaside*, GBP 650. LONDON, 17 July 1974, *Boats off Penang*, GBP 2,000. LONDON, 24 June 1977, *Naval Battle* (1840, oil on canvas, 17¼ x 22¼ ins / 43.8 x 56.5 cm) GBP 2,000. LONDON, 27 June 1980, *Regatta off the Isle of Wight* (oil on canvas, 34 x 49½ ins / 86.3 x 125.7 cm) GBP 13,000. LONDON, 7 Oct 1980, *Lions* (1880, coloured chalk, 14¼ x 20¾ ins / 36 x 53 cm) USD 2,000. LONDON, 19 Nov 1982, *A Frigate at Sea off the Eddystone Lighthouse* (1820, oil on canvas, 31½ x 49¼ ins / 80 x 125 cm) GBP 3,800. LONDON, 22 April 1983, *The 'British Empire' off the Coast of Whitby* (1841, oil on canvas, 34 x 50¼ ins / 86.3 x 127.6 cm) GBP 2,600. LONDON, 12 March 1986, *'Red Rover' off the Coast of China* (oil on canvas, 26½ x 37½ ins / 67.5 x 95.5 cm) GBP 21,000. BOLTON, 19 Nov 1987, *Three-Master at Sea* (1835, oil on canvas, 24 x 36 ins / 61 x 91.5 cm) USD 9,000. NEW YORK, 13 Oct 1993, *King George IV Inspecting the 'Lightning'* (1823, oil on canvas, 32 x 48 ins / 81.3 x 121.9 cm) USD 18,400. LONDON, 12 April 1995, *The 'Lady Melville' with Captain R. Clifford Speeding Past South Foreland on 23rd April 1823* (oil on canvas, 31 x 49¼ ins / 79 x 125 cm) GBP 19,550. NEW YORK, 17 Feb 1999, *Barque, Florentina under Reduced Sail off Cliffs of Dover* (1839, oil on canvas, 24 x 36 ins / 61 x 91 cm) USD 5,000. LONDON, 11 Jan 2001, *East Indiaman under Full Sail in Two Position off Dover* (oil on canvas, 36 x 60 ins / 91 x 152 cm) GBP 24,000. LONDON, 25 Sept 2001, *Royal George on her Return from Ireland with his Late Majesty on Board* (oil on canvas, 33 x 50 ins / 85 x 127 cm) GBP 3,000. PORTSMOUTH, 17 Aug 2002, *Duke of York* (oil on board, set of five, 17 x 22 ins / 43 x 56 cm) USD 40,000. LONDON, 31 Oct 2002, *Gallant Encounter between HMS Boadicea and the French Warship Le Duguay-Trouin* (1822, oil on canvas, 32 x 50 ins / 81 x 127 cm) GBP 30,000. EASTBOURNE, 10 Sept 2003, *East Indiaman Earl Balcarres, Dropping a Pilot off Dover* (1832, oil on canvas, 26 x 37 ins / 65 x 93 cm) GBP 11,500. LONDON, 27 Nov 2003, *Blackwall Frigate Madagascar off Dover* (1841, oil on canvas, 36 x 51 ins / 91 x 130 cm) GBP 10,000.

HUGGLER, Arnold

Swiss, 20th century.

Born 12 February 1894, in Brienz (Bern); died 1988, in Zurich.

Sculptor.

Work by Arnold Huggler was exhibited from 1923 onwards, in Switzerland and Paris (at the Salon d'Automne, the Société Nationale des Beaux-Arts and the decorative arts exhibition in 1925). His work is Neo-Realist in inspiration.

AUCTION RECORDS:

ZURICH, 25 May 1978, *Picador and Bull* (gold-patinated bronze, 12¼ x 12¼ x 5¾ ins / 31 x 31 x 14.5 cm) CHF 1,500. ZURICH, 9 Nov 1983, *Dauphin* (1973, bronze, total height 30¾ ins / 78 cm) CHF 12,000. ZURICH, 21 March 1986, *Woman Dancing* (patinated bronze, h. 28¾ ins / 73 cm) CHF 3,400. ZURICH, 24 Nov 1993, *Horse* (lost-wax bronze, h. 14¾ ins / 37.5 cm) CHF 4,830. ZURICH, 10 Dec 1996, *Foal* (bronze, h. 10 ins / 25.5 cm) CHF 4,025. ZURICH, 8 April 1997, *Roe Deer Running* (bronze, 6¼ x 7¾ x 3¾ ins / 16 x 19.5 x 9.5 cm) CHF 1,200. ZURICH, 18 Nov 1997, *Toucan* (bronze, 15¼ x 4½ ins / 39 x 11.5 cm) CHF 3,600. ZURICH, 9 June 1999, *Standing Female Nude* (bronze, h. 18 ins / 45 cm) CHF 3,000. ZURICH, 6 July 2000, *Fish Otter* (1952, bronze, h. 28 ins / 72 cm) CHF 3,200. BERN, 9 Nov 2000, *Small Animal* (dark patinated bronze, h. 10 ins / 25 cm) CHF 3,200.

HUGH, Hugo

12th century.

Illuminator. Religious subjects.

Hugh ornamented the *St Jerome's Commentaries on Isaiah* now in Oxford, following the style of the Devonshire *Benedictional.*

MUSEUMS AND GALLERIES:

OXFORD (Bodleian Library): *St Jerome's Commentaries on Isaiah.*

HUGH OF ST ALBANS
British, 14th century.
Died 1361.
Painter. Religious subjects.
Hugh of St Albans worked on the decoration of the chapel of St Stephen in the Palace of Westminster in London.

HUGHE, Jean, or Hughesone
Flemish, 15th century.
Active in 1455.
Painter.
Flemish School.
Jean Hughe's pupils included Pierre van der Borch in 1460, Roland van der Heyden in 1467, Henri Hoos in 1475, and Reghin de Hooghe in 1477. Hughe's name also occurs in 1480.

HUGHE, Willem
Flemish, 15th century.
Active in Ghent.
Sculptor.
Flemish School.

HUGHES, Arthur
British, 19th century.
Born 5 July 1805, in Devon, England; died 5 November 1838, in Dresden.
Painter. Genre scenes, animals.
He exhibited at the Royal Academy in London in 1831.
AUCTION RECORDS:
LONDON, 24 May 1984, *Little Lamb, Who Made Thee?* (watercolour, 10 x 7 ins / 25.5 x 18 cm) GBP 1,900. LONDON, 17 June 1987, *You Cannot Barre Love Oute* (oil on panel, 14 x 7 ins / 35.5 x 18 cm) GBP 4,800.

HUGHES, Arthur
British, 19th - 20th century.
Born 27 January 1832, in London; died 22 December 1915.
Painter, fresco artist, draughtsman, illustrator.
Religious subjects, allegorical subjects, genre scenes.
Arthur Hughes was a prominent member of the Pre-Raphaelite school. He enrolled at the Royal Academy Schools in 1847 and was awarded a medal in 1849. He exhibited at the Royal Academy for the first time in 1849, and in the early 1950s several of his paintings - *Ophelia, The Eve of St Agnes* and *April Love* - won the admiration of Sir Edward Burne-Jones, Holman Hunt and Dante Gabriel Rossetti, all of whom encouraged him. Rossetti even invited him to collaborate on *The Death of Arthur*, a fresco for the Union Debating Room at Oxford University, on which Burne-Jones and William Morris also worked. Hughes's most noteworthy paintings include *The Nativity*, which was praised by John Ruskin while Hughes was at the Royal Academy, and *The Long Engagement* (1859), which shows the artist's meticulous treatment of detail. Hughes was also known as an illustrator.
BIBLIOGRAPHY:
Roberts, Leonard/Wildman, Stephen, *Arthur Hughes: his Life and Works: a Catalogue Raisonné*, Antique Collectors' Club, Woodbridge, 1997.
MUSEUMS AND GALLERIES:
BIRMINGHAM (Museum and Art Gallery): *The Annunciation* (oil on canvas); *The Nativity* (oil on canvas); *The Long Engagement* (1859, oil on canvas); *The Young Poet* (oil on canvas); *The Lost Child* (oil on canvas); *Musidora* - BRISTOL (City Mus. & AG): *The Guarded Bower* (1866, oil on canvas).
AUCTION RECORDS:
LONDON, 26 April 1909, *The Painted Heart*, GBP 210. LONDON, 21 Jan 1911, *Flemish Wedding*, GBP 18. LONDON, 11 Feb 1911, *Farm Favourite*, GBP 33. LONDON, 1921, *Burnhour Pond*, GBP 18; *Evening of Life*, GBP 18; *First Easter*, GBP 26; *Return from Work*, GBP 10; *Guardian's House*, GBP 9; *Moonrise*, GBP 18; *The Rescue*, GBP 26; *Rosaline*, GBP 9; *Sir Galahad*, GBP 11. LONDON, May 1924, *Palm Sunday Eve*, GBP 21; *The Artist's Daughter*, GBP 19; *Viola d'Amore*, GBP 52. LONDON, 5 March 1926, *The Rescue*, GBP 21. LONDON, 22 Nov 1946, *Ophelia: 'Will He Never Return?'*, GBP 47. LONDON, 18 June 1969, *Lady of Shalott*, GBP 1,100. LONDON, 15 Dec 1972, *Silver and Gold*, Gns 6,500. LONDON, 16 March 1973, *Adoration of the Shepherds*, Gns 1,900. LONDON, 24 Oct 1978, *Birthday Picnic* (oil on canvas, rounded at the top, 39 x 50 ins / 99 x 127 cm) GBP 22,000. LONDON, 19 March 1979, *Study for 'The Lady of Shalott'* (oil on canvas, 6 x 7¾ ins / 15 x 20 cm) GBP 3,800. LONDON, 23 June 1981, *The Nativity* (pencil, 10¼ x 9 ins / 26 x 23 cm) GBP 650. LONDON, 16 June 1982, *Sketch for the Threads of Fate* (1887, oil on canvas, 9 x 11 ins / 22 x 28 cm) GBP 1,300. LONDON, 22 June 1984, *Knight of the Sun* (oil on canvas, 39¾ x 52¼ ins / 101.1 x 132.5 cm) GBP 160,000. LONDON, 18 June 1985, *The Rescue* (c. 1890-1895, oil on canvas, 43 x 20¾ ins / 109 x 53 cm) GBP 27,000. LONDON, 2 June 1989, *Faith* (oil on panel, 19 x 14 ins / 48 x 35.5 cm) GBP 6,820. LONDON, 20 June 1989, *'Jack o'Lantern'* (1872, oil on canvas, 19 x 29 ins / 48 x 73.5 cm) GBP 12,100. LONDON, 2 Nov 1989, *Gathering Kelp* (oil on canvas, 10 x 16 ins / 25.5 x 40.7 cm) GBP 2,640. LONDON, 19 June 1990, *Goodnight!* (oil on canvas, 39 x 25½ ins / 99 x 64.8 cm) GBP 55,000. LONDON, 25 Oct 1991, *Silver and Gold* (oil on canvas, 39 x 26½ ins / 99 x 67.3 cm) GBP 220,000. LONDON, 12 June 1992, *Forget-me-not* (oil on canvas, 41¾ x 24¾ ins / 106 x 63 cm) GBP 11,000. LONDON, 13 Nov 1992, *Valiant Knight's Conquest* (oil on panel, 20¾ x 17 ins / 52.7 x 43.2 cm) GBP 11,000. LONDON, 8-9 June 1993, *The Convent* (oil on canvas, 18 x 28 ins / 46 x 71 cm) GBP 3,910. LONDON, 5 Nov 1993, *Enid and Geraint* (oil on canvas, 10¼ x 14¾ ins / 26 x 37.5 cm) GBP 58,700. LONDON, 4 Nov 1994, *Ophelia* (oil on panel, 20 x 36 ins / 50.8 x 91.4 cm) GBP 595,500. LONDON, 6 Nov 1995, *Youth and Old Age* (1911, oil on panel, 11½ x 18½ ins / 29.3 x 47 cm) GBP 5,750. LONDON, 27 March 1996, *Orlando* (oil and pencil/card, 7¾ x 3½ ins / 20 x 9 cm) GBP 10,350. LONDON, 4 June 1997, *The Starting Signal* (oil on canvas, 40¾ x 35¾ ins / 103.5 x 91 cm) GBP 67,500. LONDON, 5 Nov 1997, *Adoration* (oil on panel, 13¾ x 10½ ins / 35 x 26.5 cm) GBP 9,200. LONDON, 12 May 1999, *Convent Boat* (oil on canvas, 14 x 23 ins / 36 x 59 cm) GBP 5,000. LONDON, 30 Nov 1999, *The Property Room* (1879, oil on canvas, 45 x 33 ins / 115 x 83 cm) GBP 290,000. LONDON, 28 Nov 2000, *Coastal Scene* (oil on board, 10 x 18 ins / 26 x 46 cm) GBP 5,000. LONDON, 28 Nov 2000, *The Rescue* (oil on canvas, 43 x 21 ins / 110 x 53 cm) GBP 12,000. LONDON, 3 April 2001, *Forget-me-not* (oil on canvas, 43 x 25 ins / 108 x 64 cm) GBP 18,000. LONDON, 7 June 2001, *Motherhood* (colour chalk, 11 x 6 ins / 27 x 15 cm) GBP 6,500. NEW YORK, 30 Oct 2002, *Asleep in the Woods* (oil on canvas, 14 x 18 ins / 35 x 46 cm) USD 13,000. LONDON, 2 Dec 2002, *Returning Home* (oil on canvas, 19 x 30 ins / 49 x 75 cm) GBP 5,500. LONDON, 19 Feb 2003, *Birthday Picnic: Portrait of the Children of William and Anne Pattinson of Felling* (oil on canvas, painted arch, 40 x 50 ins / 102 x 128 cm) GBP 340,000. LONDON, 25 Nov 2003, *Sir Galahad* (oil on canvas, 35 x 44 ins / 89 x 113 cm) GBP 50,000. LONDON, 25 Nov 2004, *Lucy Hill* (1888, oil on canvas on panel, 17 x 10 ins / 42 x 26 cm) GBP 4,000. LONDON, 25 Nov 2004, *Perran Point, Cornwall* (oil on board, 11 x 16 ins / 29 x 40 cm) GBP 7,200.

HUGHES, Arthur Ford
British, 19th - 20th century.
Born 1856; died 1934.
Active in London.
Painter, watercolourist. Genre scenes, landscapes with figures.
AUCTION RECORDS:
LONDON, 9 March 1976, *Psyche* (watercolour, 23 x 39 ins / 58.5 x 99 cm) GBP 500. LONDON, 1 Nov 1990, *Sheep in a Meadow with Buildings Behind* (watercolour, 6¾ x 13½ ins

/ 17.1 x 34.4 cm) GBP 440. LONDON, 6 Nov 1995, *A Stranger Among Them* (watercolour/paper/panel, 27 x 36¼ ins / 68.5 x 92 cm) GBP 4,370. LONDON, 11 March 2003, *Lesson in Arcadia* (watercolour, 26 x 41 ins / 65 x 105 cm) GBP 1,800. BIRMINGHAM, 7 Oct 2003, *Farmyard Doves* (1873, oil on canvas, 24 x 19 ins / 62 x 47 cm) GBP 2,000. BISHOPS STORTFORD, 20 July 2004, *Below Stairs* (watercolour, 18 x 11 ins / 46 x 28 cm) GBP 1,200. LONDON, 9 Nov 2004, *Finding of Leander* (watercolour, 26 x 41 ins / 66 x 104 cm) GBP 6,200.

HUGHES, Edward
British, 19th century.
Born 14 September 1832, in Pontonville; died 14 May 1908, in London.
Painter. Portraits, genre scenes.

Edward Hughes was the son of George Hughes. He exhibited his work at the Royal Academy in London at a very young age. He is known for his portraits of the English royal family.

MUSEUMS AND GALLERIES:
LEEDS (Lotherton Hall): *Portrait of Mrs. Laura Gascoigne and her Son Alvary* (oil on canvas).

AUCTION RECORDS:
LONDON, 21 July 1978, *The Well* (1875, oil on canvas, 25¾ x 19½ ins / 65.3 x 49.5 cm) GBP 850. LONDON, 18 March 1983, *First Visit to the Dentist* (1866, oil on canvas, 24 x 20 ins / 61 x 50.9 cm) GBP 8,000. LONDON, 10 May 1985, *Young Woman and Child* (1899-1905, oil on canvas, 93 x 56¾ ins / 236.3 x 144 cm) GBP 3,800. LONDON, 2 Nov 1994, *Christmas Wishes* (1882, oil on canvas, 63½ x 49 ins / 161 x 124.5 cm) GBP 13,800. LONDON, 11 March 1999, *Return of Sir Henry Lee to his Hall at Woodstock* (1857, oil on canvas, 25 x 30 ins / 63 x 75 cm) GBP 5,800. NEW YORK, 6 May 1999, *English Artist Collecting Costumes in Brittany* (1862, oil on canvas, 34 x 48 ins / 87 x 123 cm) USD 28,000. LONDON, 9 Nov 2000, *Portrait of a Lady, in a White Dress and Black Shawl and Hat* (1906, oil on canvas, 58 x 40 ins / 147 x 102 cm) GBP 1,200. LONDON, 20 Nov 2001, *Secret Letter* (1867, oil on canvas, 21 x 25 ins / 53 x 63 cm) GBP 6,000. LONDON, 19 June 2002, *Debutante* (1886, oil on canvas, 68 x 50 ins / 173 x 127 cm) GBP 15,000. KNOWLE, 2 Oct 2002, *Incident in the Life of Paganini* (1869, oil on canvas, 29 x 40 ins / 73 x 102 cm) GBP 4,750. LONDON, 10 June 2003, *Rescue* (oil on canvas, 38 x 48 ins / 96 x 123 cm) GBP 14,000.

HUGHES, Edward John
Canadian, 20th century.
Born 1913, in North Vancouver.
Painter, draughtsman, watercolourist.

BIBLIOGRAPHY:
Thom, Ian M., *E.J. Hughes*, Douglas and McIntyre, Vancouver, 2002.

MUSEUMS AND GALLERIES:
TORONTO (AG of Ontario): *Unloading Merchandise; Kiska* (1945).

AUCTION RECORDS:
TORONTO, 19 Oct 1976, *South of Chilliwack, BC* (1962, watercolour, 15 x 18 ins / 38 x 46 cm) CAD 2,000. TORONTO, 3 May 1983, *Toronto from Olympic Island* (watercolour, 17½ x 23½ ins / 44.4 x 59.4 cm) CAD 4,200. TORONTO, 14 May 1984, *Artillery Drill* (1941, pencil and wash, 9½ x 13½ ins / 24.4 x 34.4 cm) CAD 3,000. TORONTO, 3 June 1986, *Wharves at Chemainus* (1952, oil on canvas, 20 x 24 ins / 50.8 x 61 cm) CAD 22,000. VANCOUVER, 27 May 1999, *Echo Bay* (1953, oil on canvas, 24 x 18 ins / 61 x 46 cm) CAD 68,000. MONTREAL, 13 Dec 1999, *Hopkin's Landing, Howe Sound* (1952, oil on canvas, 21 x 26 ins / 53 x 66 cm) CAD 64,000. VANCOUVER, 9 Nov 2000, *Harbour Scene, Nanaimo* (1970, oil on canvas, 32 x 40 ins / 81 x 102 cm) CAD 95,000. TORONTO, 15 Nov 2000, *Maple Bay* (1984, acrylic on canvas, 25 x 32 ins / 63 x 81 cm) CAD 32,500. VANCOUVER, 9 May 2001, *Beach Southeast of Crofton* (1973, oil on canvas, 25 x 32 ins / 63 x 81 cm) CAD 45,000. VANCOUVER, 8 Nov 2001, *Finlayson Arm - on Vancouver Island near Victoria, BC* (1965, oil on canvas, 32 x 48 ins / 81 x 122 cm) CAD 85,000. VANCOUVER, 2 May 2002, *Above Cowichan Bay* (1962, oil on canvas, 25 x 32 ins / 63 x 81 cm) CAD 45,000. VANCOUVER, 14 Nov 2002, *Roberts Bay, BC* (1953, oil on canvas, 24 x 25 ins / 61 x 63 cm) CAD 80,000. VANCOUVER, 15 May 2003, *Courtenay, BC* (1950, oil on canvas, 36 x 40 ins / 91 x 102 cm) CAD 190,000. TORONTO, 3 June 2003, *Store at Allison Harbour, BC* (1955, oil on canvas, 24 x 31 ins / 62 x 80 cm) CAD 110,000. VANCOUVER, 27 May 2004, *South Thompson Valley at Chase, BC* (1957, oil on canvas, 25 x 32 ins / 63 x 81 cm) CAD 190,000. TORONTO, 31 May 2004, *Departure from Nanaimo* (1964, oil on canvas, 32 x 48 ins / 81 x 122 cm) CAD 280,000.

HUGHES, Edward Robert
British, 19th - 20th century.
Born 1851, in London; died 1914, in St Albans.
Painter, watercolourist, draughtsman. Portraits, genre scenes, landscapes.

Edward Hughes was an associate member of the Royal Society of Painters in Watercolours. He exhibited at the Royal Academy in London from 1870.

MUSEUMS AND GALLERIES:
SYDNEY: watercolours.

AUCTION RECORDS:
LONDON, 17 Feb 1908, *The Poor Minstrel; The New Hat* (by W. Hemsley) GBP 3. LONDON, 23 March 1908, *Near Bruges* (1872, watercolour) GBP 12. LONDON, 23 June 1944, *Bertruccio's Fiancée*, GBP 44. LONDON, 23 June 1944, *He Who Writes Signs*, GBP 39. LONDON, 24 July 1973, *Pastorale* (gouache) GBP 290. LONDON, 25 Sept 1979, *Portrait of Anthony Freeman* (1903, watercolour, 11¾ x 10¼ ins / 30 x 26 cm) GBP 1,400. LONDON, 15 June 1982, *Midsummer Eve* (watercolour heightened with gouache, 44½ x 29½ ins / 113 x 75 cm) GBP 18,000. LONDON, 17 Oct 1984, *Heart of Snow* (watercolour heightened with gouache, 29½ x 44½ ins / 75 x 113 cm) GBP 14,000. LONDON, 27 Feb 1985, *Portia* (red chalk/card, 20½ x 28¼ ins / 52 x 72 cm) GBP 1,600. NEW YORK, 19 July 1990, *Biancabella and her Snake-Sister Samaritana* (1894, gouache/paper, 36 x 26½ ins / 91.6 x 67.4 cm) USD 7,150. LONDON, 1 Nov 1990, *Portrait Bust of Hilda Virtue Tebbs* (1897, red chalk, 24 x 20 ins / 61 x 50.8 cm) GBP 3,740. LONDON, 30 Jan 1991, *In the Corner Armchair* (1891, red chalk, 28 x 20½ ins / 71 x 52 cm) GBP 1,870. LONDON, 29 Oct 1991, *Bertuccio's Wedding (Nights at Straparola)* (pencil and watercolour, 39½ x 30 ins / 100.3 x 76.1 cm) GBP 88,000. YORK, 12 Nov 1991, *Mediterranean Landscape* (oil on canvas, 16¼ x 22 ins / 41 x 56 cm) GBP 2,420. LONDON, 8-9 June 1993, *Misty River* (oil on card, 10¼ x 14¼ ins / 26 x 36 cm) GBP 920. LONDON, 4 Nov 1994, *Return from the Fields* (oil on canvas, 16¾ x 22½ ins / 42.5 x 57 cm) GBP 1,610. LONDON, 17 April 1996, *Portrait of Hilda Virtue Tebbs* (1897, red chalk/card, 32¼ x 28¼ ins / 82 x 71.5 cm) GBP 5,980. LONDON, 30 Nov 1999, *Portrait of a Shepherdess* (oil on panel, 17 x 12 ins / 42 x 31 cm) GBP 2,800. LONDON, 15 June 2000, *Night and Day* (watercolour, gouache and charcoal heightened with gold and white, a pair, 10 x 7 ins / 25 x 18 cm) GBP 78,000. NOTTINGHAM, 28 Sept 2000, *Head of a Girl* (colour chalk, 13 x 9 ins / 32 x 23 cm) GBP 1,700. LONDON, 10 April 2001, *Returning Home* (watercolour heightened with scratching out, 20 x 28 ins / 50 x 70 cm) GBP 6,000. LONDON, 5 Nov 2001, *Making Music* (pastel, 28 x 20 ins / 71 x 52 cm) GBP 15,000. LONDON, 6 June 2002, *Portrait of Margaret Webster* (1897, red chalk, 24 x 20 ins / 61 x 51 cm) GBP 9,000. STOCKHOLM, 4 Dec 2002, *Nymph Running Away* (1898, watercolour, 37 x 29 ins / 93 x 73 cm) SEK 280,000. LONDON, 20 Feb 2003, *Byram's Tryst* (oil on canvas, 23 x 17 ins / 59 x 44 cm) GBP 7,000. LONDON, 27

Nov 2003, *Coward* (1898, colour chalk and watercolour, 18 x 13 ins / 45 x 33 cm) GBP 20,000. LONDON, 22 April 2004, *William Holman Hunt OM, Full Bearded* (oval miniature, h. 2 ins / 4 cm) GBP 13,000. LONDON, 9 June 2004, *Night. Day* (pencil and watercolour heightened with gold and gouache, a pair, 10 x 7 ins / 25 x 18 cm) GBP 62,000.

HUGHES, Edwin
British, 19th century.
Active in London.
Painter. Genre scenes.

Edwin Hughes exhibited his work at the Royal Academy in London from 1872 to 1890.

AUCTION RECORDS:
LONDON, 21 Dec 1925, *Prohibitive Prices*, GBP 23. LONDON, 14 Dec 1976, *Caught* (oil on canvas, 15 1/2 x 21 1/2 ins / 39.5 x 54.5 cm) GBP 620. LONDON, 2 Feb 1979, *No Fool Like the Old Fool* (1889, oil on canvas, 24 1/2 x 23 1/4 ins / 62.2 x 59.1 cm) GBP 1,400. LONDON, 2 Oct 1985, *A Convivial Host* (1888, oil on canvas, 24 x 35 3/4 ins / 61 x 91 cm) GBP 5,000. LONDON, 18 March 1987, *The Peacemaker* (1882, oil on canvas, 17 x 20 3/4 ins / 43 x 53 cm) GBP 2,800. STOCKHOLM, 16 May 1990, *Interior of a Forge with Figures* (1888, oil on canvas, 11 3/4 x 16 1/4 ins / 30 x 41 cm) SEK 15,000. LONDON, 3 Nov 1993, *Expected* (1881, oil on panel, 12 x 8 ins / 30.5 x 20.5 cm) GBP 2,185. LONDON, 7 March 2002, *Checkmate* (1889, oil on canvas, 16 x 22 ins / 41 x 56 cm) GBP 5,000. LONDON, 9 Sept 2004, *Love at the Window* (1892, oil on canvas, 22 x 16 ins / 56 x 41 cm) GBP 2,800.

HUGHES, George
British, 19th century.
Painter. Portraits, landscapes with figures, landscapes.

George Hughes's work includes satirical works among others.

HUGHES, George
British, 19th - 20th century.
Active in Liverpool.
Painter. Portraits, genre scenes.

HUGHES, Hugh
British, 19th century.
Born 1790, in Pwllygwichiaid; died 11 March 1863, in Great Malvern.
Painter, engraver (wood). Portraits.

Hugh Hughes's work includes satirical works.

HUGHES, John
Irish, 19th century.
Active in Dublin.
Sculptor.

John Hughes was a member of the Dublin Academy and the Society of British Sculptors.

MUSEUMS AND GALLERIES:
DUBLIN: two busts.

HUGHES, John
British, 19th century.
Born 2 January 1790; died 13 December 1857, in London.
Painter, engraver, sculptor.

John Hughes exhibited his work in London between 1819 and 1838.

HUGHES, John Joseph
British, 19th century.
Born 1820; died 1909, in West Bromwich.
Painter. Landscapes.

John Joseph Hughes took part in large London exhibitions between 1838 and 1867.

AUCTION RECORDS:
LONDON, 5 June 1996, *Extensive View over Windermere* (oil on canvas, 16 1/2 x 20 1/2 ins / 42 x 52 cm) GBP 2,070. MALMÖ, 8 April 2000, *English Landscape with Figures and Waterfall* (oil on canvas, 22 x 36 ins / 56 x 92 cm) SEK 15,500. LONDON, 17 Jan 2002, *Cows Watering near an Angler in a River, Church Beyond* (1874, oil on canvas, 24 x 36 ins / 62 x 91 cm) GBP 1,000.

HUGHES, Lily Jones
British, 19th - 20th century.
Active in Wales.
Miniaturist.

Lily Jones Hughes exhibited at the Royal Academy in London from 1896 to 1910.

HUGHES, Mary Kathleen
Irish, 20th century.
Born 9 September 1877, in Pole Hore; died 21 August 1918, in Hindhead.
Painter, engraver. Landscapes.

Mary Hughes regularly exhibited her work, particularly her landscapes, in London and Berlin.

HUGHES, Patrick
British, 20th century.
Born October 1939, in Birmingham.
Painter. Landscapes, seascapes, interiors. Wall reliefs.

Patrick Hughes initially trained as a teacher in English literature. His aesthetic ideas have been influenced by Paul Klee and Rene Magritte, and his complex use of spatial design is reminiscent of M.C. Escher.

Hughes describes his work as 'paradoxical perspectives'; it is sometimes considered as Surrealist because it plays with perception and the subconscious. He uses architectural elements to enhance the perspective illusionism that characterises most of his work, and constructs three-dimensional surfaces on which he paints landscapes and interiors. His first three-dimensional painting was made in 1964. His painted wall reliefs become 'moving images' that bewilder the viewers and prompt them to question the veracity of what is perceived. The shape of his canvases and his use of perspective create a *tromp l'oeil* effect which encourages interaction between the images and the viewer. For example, his *Paradoxymoron* (1996), on public display at the British Library, is a three dimensional composition in which the bookshelves of a library move around with the viewer.

In terms of content, Hughes uses rectilinear forms (doors, walls, buildings, bookshelves, and so on), which open into landscapes or lead the viewer towards open spaces. His work is also self-referential - some of his compositions portray gallery walls displaying the work of modern artists (*After Magritte*, 2002; *Cut-Outs Sticking Out*, 2004; *Andy Capp*, 2004). Another recurrent element of his work is libraries and bookshelves, which he uses to create more illusionist perspectives. He has also played with the materiality of rainbows, depicting stylised rainbows that appear solid or flaccid (*From the Domestic Life of the Rainbow*, 1979). He has co-authored three books on visual and verbal rhetoric.

Hughes's first solo exhibition was held in 1961 at the Portal Gallery, London, and from 1970 he has held regular exhibitions at the Angela Flowers Gallery, London. In 2002, he participated in the group exhibition *Head On: Art with the Brain in Mind*, organised by the Science Museum in London. Examples of his work can be found in the Tate Gallery, London; the Glasgow Museum and Art Gallery; Denver Art Museum; and the Duke University Museum of Art.

BIBLIOGRAPHY:
Hammond, Paul/Hughes, Patrick, *Upon the Pun: Dual Meaning in Words and Pictures*, Star Books, London, 1978. Hughes, Patrick, *Behind the Rainbow: Patrick Hughes Prints 1964-1983*, Paradox Publishing, London, 1983. Slyce, John, *Patrick Hughes: Perverspective*, Momentum Publishing, London, 1998. *Patrick Hughes: Whopperspective: Paintings and Mul-*

tiples, exhibition catalogue, Flowers East Gallery, London, c. 2003.

Museums and Galleries:

London (Tate Collection): *Over the Moon* (1978, screenprint on paper); *Infinity* (1976, Screenprint on paper); *Collected Works (part two)* (1971, Mixed media).

Auction records:

London, 6 June 2000, *Cloud Variations* (oil on board, 15 x 24 ins / 38 x 61 cm) GBP 1,000. London, 24 Nov 2000, *Uptown* (1994, oil on board construction, 40 x 42 ins / 101 x 107 cm) GBP 7,000. London, 2 July 2002, *Book Corner* (1994, oil on board, 30 x 72 ins / 76 x 182 cm) GBP 5,000. London, 12 Sept 2002, *Rainbow in a Cage* (gloss paint on board, 48 x 72 ins / 123 x 184 cm) GBP 2,400. London, 24 Nov 2004, *Deja Vu Revisited* (1988, oil on canvas, 36 x 48 ins / 91 x 122 cm) GBP 2,800.

HUGHES, R.
British, 18th century.
Active in London.
Painter.

R. Hughes exhibited landscapes at the Royal Academy between 1794 and 1799.

HUGHES, Robert Ball
British, 19th century.
Born 1806; died 5 March 1868, in Boston.
Also active in the USA.
Sculptor.

Robert Ball Hughes exhibited his work at the Royal Academy in London between 1822 and 1828.

HUGHES, S.G.
British, 19th century.
Engraver.

S.G. Hughes tended to favour aquatint. He is known for his views of Manchester and Liverpool.

HUGHES, Talbot
British, 19th - 20th century.
Born 1869, in London; died 1942.
Painter. Genre scenes, landscapes.

Talbot Hughes exhibited at the Royal Institute of Oil Painters, of which he was a member, from 1871, at the Royal Academy in London and the Walker Art Gallery, Liverpool.

Auction records:

London, June 1924, *The Rose Season,* GBP 5. London, 25 July 1930, *Confidences,* GBP 29. London, 12 May 1944, *Played Out,* GBP 63. London, 22 Feb 1946, *Meeting,* GBP 39. London, 29 June 1976, *Fate Carrying Away Two Women* (oil on canvas, 38 1/4 x 59 3/4 ins / 97 x 152 cm) GBP 1,100. London, 15 May 1979, *Nothing to Wear* (oil on panel, 20 x 12 1/2 ins / 51 x 32 cm) GBP 1,200. London, 15 June 1982, *Watching the Kittens* (1890, oil on panel, 13 1/2 x 11 1/2 ins / 34 x 29 cm) GBP 950. London, 6 May 1983, *In Disgrace* (1892, oil on panel, 7 x 9 ins / 17.8 x 22.8 cm) GBP 1,400. London, 17 Dec 1986, *Played Out* (1903, oil on canvas, 43 x 56 ins / 109 x 142 cm) GBP 5,500. Göteborg, 18 May 1989, *Beside a Stream* (1900, oil on panel, 11 3/4 x 9 ins / 30 x 23 cm) SEK 7,500. New York, 25 Oct 1989, *Game of Chance* (1891, oil on panel, 20 x 24 ins / 50.5 x 61 cm) USD 18,700. London, 2 Nov 1989, *The Games Room* (1895, oil on panel, 15 1/4 x 11 1/4 ins / 38.5 x 28.5 cm) GBP 3,850. London, 21 March 1990, *The Games Room* (1895, oil on card, 15 x 11 ins / 38 x 28 cm) GBP 4,180. New York, 22 May 1991, *Nature's Splendour* (1897, oil on panel, 24 x 20 ins / 61 x 50.8 cm) USD 11,000. London, 3 June 1992, *A Difficult Declaration* (1890, oil on panel, 7 3/4 x 10 ins / 20 x 25.5 cm) GBP 2,200. London, 3 Nov 1993, *Diana* (1904, oil on canvas, 53 1/4 x 91 1/4 ins / 135 x 232 cm) GBP 8,280. Newcastle, 23 March 1999, *Tavern Maid Lighting the Pipe of a Young Gentleman* (1890, oil on panel, 13 x 10 ins / 32 x 26 cm) GBP 3,600. Oxford, 30 March 2000, *Maid Serving Claret to a Gentleman in a Library* (1890, oil on panel, 9 x 12 ins / 22 x 30 cm) GBP 2,900. London, 30 Nov 2000, *Sweet Scent of Summer* (1897, oil on canvas, 24 x 20 ins / 61 x 50 cm) GBP 6,200. Vejle, 16 Jan 2001, *Island of the Sacred Swans* (oil on canvas, 54 x 65 ins / 136 x 166 cm) DKK 132,000. London, 10 May 2001, *Shadows* (1901, oil on panel, 19 x 26 ins / 49 x 65 cm) GBP 5,500. London, 13 Feb 2002, *Spring Dance* (1912, watercolour, 20 x 28 ins / 52 x 71 cm) GBP 2,200. London, 23 May 2002, *Sewing for Victory* (1900, oil on panel, 12 x 10 ins / 30 x 25 cm) GBP 17,000. London, 13 Nov 2003, *Story of The Hare That Got Away* (1898, oil on panel, 20 x 24 ins / 51 x 61 cm) GBP 8,000. London, 20 Nov 2003, *Starlight* (1905, colour chalks on buff paper, 11 x 9 ins / 28 x 22 cm) GBP 3,500. London, 10 March 2004, *Arrest* (oil on canvas, 42 x 31 ins / 107 x 80 cm) GBP 1,000. London, 14 Sept 2004, *Card Room* (1895, oil on panel, 15 x 11 ins / 37 x 27 cm) GBP 4,000.

HUGHES, Thomas
British, 19th century.
Active in London.
Sculptor.

Thomas Hughes exhibited his work at the Royal Academy in London between 1826 and 1836.

HUGHES, Thomas John
British, 19th century.
Painter. Genre scenes.

Thomas John Hughes exhibited mainly at the Royal Academy in London from 1851 to 1865. He is probably the same artist as Thomas John, who exhibited his work at Suffolk Street Gallery from 1879 to 1892.

Auction records:

London, 15 May 1979, *The First Attempt* (1860, oil on canvas, 29 1/2 x 23 1/4 ins / 75 x 59 cm) GBP 1,000. London, 13 Feb 1987, *The First Attempt* (1860, oil on canvas, 30 x 24 ins / 76.3 x 61 cm) GBP 1,900. London, 12 June 1992, *The First Attempt* (1860, oil on canvas, 30 x 23 1/2 ins / 76 x 60 cm) GBP 2,420.

HUGHES, Vernon
British, 19th century.
Active in London.
Painter. Genre scenes.

Auction records:

Chester, 12 July 1985, *The Rape of the Lock* (oil on canvas, 24 3/4 x 30 1/2 ins / 63 x 77.5 cm) GBP 5,000.

HUGHES, William
British, 19th century.
Born 1793, in Liverpool; died 11 February 1825, in London.
Engraver.

William Hughes was a pupil of Henry Hale and soon joined the ranks of the finest English wood engravers. He collaborated on the illustration of several important works, including Thomas Dibdin's *Bibliographical Decameron* (1817), John Johnson's *Typographia* and William Young Ottley's *Inquiry into the Origin and Early History of Engraving.* His works are rather dry but with genuine qualities. Also recorded are copies of two wood engravings after Holbein.

HUGHES, William
British, 19th century.
Active in London.
Painter. Landscapes.

William Hughes sometimes exhibited his work in London at the Royal Academy and Suffolk Street from 1830 to 1853.

HUGHES, William
British, 19th century.
Born 1842, in Lanarkshire, Scotland; died 18 December 1901, in Brighton.
Painter. Still-lifes (fruit/game).

William Hughes was a pupil of Lance and William Hunt. He painted many decorative paintings. He began his career in

London in 1862 at the British Institution. He subsequently exhibited very regularly at the Royal Academy and in the large London Salons.

Museums and Galleries:

Cape Town: *Fruit.*

Auction records:

London, 19 July 1909, *Fruits* (1873-1874, two pendants) GBP 4. London, June 1924, *Still-life,* GBP 6. Cologne, 23 March 1973, *Still-life with Fruits,* DEM 5,000. London, 3 Feb 1978, *Still-lifes* (1866, an oil on canvas and an oil on card, 14 x 17 3/4 ins / 35.5 x 45 cm) GBP 750. London, 5 Oct 1984, *Still-life with Fruit* (1867, oil on canvas, 20 x 24 ins / 50.8 x 61 cm) GBP 1,100. London, 2 Oct 1985, *Still-life with Fruit* (1872, oil on canvas, 28 x 35 3/4 ins / 71 x 91 cm) GBP 10,500. New York, 25 Feb 1988, *Still-life of Dead Game and Fruit* (1872, oil on canvas, 28 x 35 3/4 ins / 71.1 x 91 cm) USD 5,280. London, 3 June 1988, *Apples, Grapes and Bird's Nest on a Mossy Entablature* (1862, oil on canvas, 12 x 16 ins / 30.5 x 40.5 cm) GBP 2,640. Perth, 28 Aug 1989, *Still-life with a Teal* (1861, oil on canvas/card, 11 1/2 x 15 1/4 ins / 29 x 39 cm) GBP 1,980. Edinburgh, 22 Nov 1989, *The Bullfinches' Banquet* (1895, oil on canvas, 24 x 20 ins / 61 x 50.8 cm) GBP 4,950. New York, 24 Oct 1990, *Still-life with Grape, Pears, Peaches, Ewer and Butterfly* (1873, oil on canvas, 32 x 25 1/4 ins / 81 x 64.1 cm) USD 7,700. New York, 26 May 1992, *Plums Fallen onto Moss* (1866, oil on card, 14 x 18 ins / 35.6 x 45.7 cm) USD 2,420. London, 12 Nov 1992, *Still-life of Grape, Apple, Pear and a Wine Flask of Glazed Stoneware; Still-life of Grape, Peaches and Pears near a Chipped Jug* (oil on canvas, a pair, each 14 x 18 ins / 35.5 x 45.5 cm) GBP 4,400. London, 11 June 1993, *Sloes and Apples on Mossy Ground* (1867, oil on card, 14 x 18 ins / 35.5 x 45.7 cm) GBP 2,300. London, 6 Nov 1995, *Still-life with a Branch of Apples in a Japanese Vase; Still-life with a Branch of Plum Tree in a Japanese Vase* (1880, gold paint and oil on canvas, a pair, each 40 x 17 1/2 ins / 101.5 x 44.5 cm) GBP 16,100. London, 5 June 1996, *Still-life with Apples and Sloes* (1900, oil on canvas, 13 x 17 ins / 33 x 43 cm) GBP 1,725. London, 9 Oct 1996, *Still-life of Grape, Apple and Pineapple* (1878, oil on canvas, 20 x 16 ins / 50.5 x 40.5 cm) GBP 2,300. London, 6 June 1997, *Red Admiral with Bunches of Grapes in a Willow Basket and Plums, Apples, Plums and Strawberries on a Stone Entablature* (1874, oil on canvas, 36 x 28 ins / 91.5 x 71 cm) GBP 19,550. London, 18 March 1999, *Still-life with Mixed Fruit in Wicker Basket on Stone Ledge* (1883, oil on canvas, 36 x 28 ins / 91 x 71 cm) GBP 5,800. Stockholm, 23 Nov 1999, *Still-lifes with Grapes and Other Fruit* (oil on panel, a pair, 14 x 18 ins / 35 x 45 cm) SEK 66,000. London, 26 May 2000, *Still-life of Game Birds, a Tankard, Rifle and Powder Flask* (1876, oil on canvas, 36 x 28 ins / 91 x 71 cm) GBP 4,200. Amsterdam, 4 July 2000, *Branch with Plums against a Gold Background* (1885, oil and gold paint on canvas, 30 x 16 ins / 76 x 41 cm) NLG 11,000. Bern, 10 May 2001, *Exotic Birds* (1886, oil and gold leaf, 55 x 29 ins / 140 x 73 cm) CHF 14,000. London, 1 Nov 2001, *Still-life with Blossom, Bird's Nest and Butterfly* (1868, oil on canvas, 12 x 16 ins / 30 x 40 cm) GBP 2,500. Melbourne, 26 Nov 2002, *Still-life with Apples and Grapes* (1869, oil on panel, 12 x 16 ins / 30 x 40 cm) AUD 4,000. Bath, 2 Dec 2002, *Still-life of Strawberries, Grapes and Other Fruit in a Basket* (1882, oil on canvas, 14 x 18 ins / 36 x 46 cm) GBP 1,850. Johannesburg, 1 April 2003, *Black Grapes. White Grapes* (1881, oil on canvas, a pair, 4 x 22 ins / 11 x 57 cm) ZAR 62,000. London, 12 June 2003, *Grapes and Oranges on a Silver Salver, Decanter of Wine on a Ledge* (1867, oil on canvas, 20 x 24 ins / 51 x 61 cm) GBP 5,000. Salisbury, 7 April 2004, *Still-life with Grapes and Peaches* (1875, oil on canvas, 15 x 19 ins / 39 x 47 cm) GBP 1,500. Aylsham, 15 Oct 2004, *Study of Pineapple and Other Fruit on Mossy Bank* (1862, oil on canvas, 13 x 17 ins / 33 x 43 cm) GBP 1,150.

HUGHES-STANTON, Blair

British, 20th century.

Born 1902; died 1981.

Painter, engraver, illustrator.

Blair Hughes-Stanton, the son of the painter Herbert Hughes-Stanton, studied at the Byam Shaw School of Art from 1919 to 1921, and at the Royal Academy Schools. He then enrolled at the Brook Green Art School in Hammersmith, founded by the British artist and teacher Leon Underwood, which exposed him to new ideas.

Hughes-Stanton married the artist Gertrude Hermes in 1926. Both he and his wife were to leave their mark on the history of British woodcut engraving, particularly through their illustrations for *The Seven Pillars of Wisdom* by T. E. Lawrence and *Pilgrim's Progress* by John Bunyan, published by the Cresset Press in 1926. Blair later specialised in illustration and the production of illustrated books for such small-scale publishers as the Golden Cockerel Press, the Cresset Press, the Gregynog Press and his own Gemini Press. A retrospective exhibition of his work as an illustrator and producer of illustrated books was organised at The Minories in Colchester in 1984, and an exhibition of prints by Blair and Gertrude was shown at the Ashmolean Museum in Oxford in 1995.

Books illustrated by Hughes-Stanton include: *The Revelation of St John the Divine,* published by the Gregynog Press in 1932; *The Eustace Diamonds* by Anthony Trollope; *Epithalamion* by Ida Grave (1934); *Four Poems by John Milton* (1933); *Primeval Gods* by Christopher Sandford (1934); *Maya* by Simon Gantillon (1930); *Birds, Beasts and Flowers* by D. H. Lawrence (1930); *Erewhon* by Samuel Butler (1932); *The Wreck of the Golden Mary* by Charles Dickens and Wilkie Collins (1956); and *The Devil and All* by John Collier (1934).

Bibliography:

Hughes-Stanton, Penelope, *Wood Engravings of Blair Hughes-Stanton,* Oak Knoll Press, 1991. Eustance, Katherine, *Undewood's Children. The Wood Engravings of Gertrude Hermes & Blair Hughes-Stanton,* exhibition catalogue, Ashmolean Museum, University of Oxford, Oxford, 1995.

HUGHES-STANTON, Herbert Edwin Pelham (Sir)

British, 19th - 20th century.

Born 1870, in Chelsea (London); died 1937, in London.

Painter. Landscapes.

Herbert Hughes-Stanton was an associate member of the Royal Society of Painters in Watercolours and a member of the Royal Institute of Oil Painters and the Société des XXV. He exhibited most notably at the Royal Academy in London. His work also appeared in Parisian exhibitions; in Paris he won an honourable mention in 1904, a bronze medal in 1907 and a silver medal in 1908. He also took part in exhibitions at the Scottish Academy in 1912 and 1917. Hughes-Stanton spent some time in France, where he painted *Across the Dunes, Pas-de-Calais* and *Moonlight, Avignon.*

Museums and Galleries:

Bradford (Cartwright Hall AG): *Evening Twilight, Studland, Dorset* - Dundee (University, Fine Art Collection): *Noon, Avignon, France 1918* (1918) - Liverpool: *Sunny Day; Lelant, Cornwall; Château Gaillard, Les Andelys.*

Auction records:

London, 19 May 1911, *Hampstead Heath,* GBP 16. London, May 1923, *Bras de mer, Pas-de-Calais,* GBP 52. London, June 1924, *The Goose Girl,* GBP 57. London, 1 Dec 1925, *Landscape with River,* GBP 21. London, 19 July 1927, *Mail on the Road to Etaples,* GBP 25. London, 3 May 1935, *Morning on the Thames,* GBP 35. London, 13 March 1981, *View from Brithdor to Barmouth, North Wales* (oil on canvas, 39 3/4 x 48 1/2 ins / 101 x 123.5 cm) GBP 1,200. London, 30 March 1983, *Morning on the Thames* (1921, oil on canvas, 30 1/2 x 36 ins / 77.5 x 91.5 cm) GBP 1,300. London, 5 March 1987, *Les Baux-de-Provence* (1909, oil on canvas, 39 x 49 1/4 ins / 99 x

125 cm) GBP 1,800. LONDON, 12 May 1989, *Brithdir near Dolgelly* (1917, oil on canvas, 24 1/2 x 31 1/2 ins / 62.5 x 80 cm) GBP 935. LONDON, 21 Sept 1989, *Track Lined with Willows at Sunbury-on-Thames* (1912, oil on canvas, 12 x 18 ins / 30.5 x 45.5 cm) GBP 770. LONDON, 3 May 1990, *First World War* (1918, oil on canvas, 58 x 78 ins / 147.5 x 198 cm) GBP 1,210. HASLEMERE, 23 Feb 2000, *The Watermill, Young Woman on a Footbridge* (1898, oil on canvas, 32 x 40 ins / 81 x 102 cm) GBP 2,000. LONDON, 14 June 2000, *Avignon Looking on to Villeneuve* (1923, watercolour, 21 x 30 ins / 53 x 76 cm) GBP 1,600. LONDON, 1 March 2001, *Sunset at Paul du Var seen from Venice* (1928, oil on canvas, 35 x 44 ins / 88 x 112 cm) GBP 1,000. LONDON, 26 June 2001, *Haut de Cagnes* (oil on canvas, 20 x 27 ins / 51 x 68 cm) GBP 12,500. LONDON, 23 May 2002, *Harrow on the Hill* (oil on board, 9 x 10 ins / 24 x 26 cm) GBP 1,600. CHESTER, 26 June 2002, *Studland Bay, Dorset* (1904, oil on canvas, 21 x 31 ins / 54 x 80 cm) GBP 1,600. EXETER, 4 March 2003, *Evening, Cagnes* (1931, oil on canvas, 15 x 19 ins / 39 x 49 cm) GBP 1,250. LONDON, 18 Nov 2003, *Greek Views* (1935, watercolour, four, 19 x 26 ins / 48 x 65 cm) GBP 2,800.

HUGHTENBURGH. See **HUCHTENBURG Jan van**

HUGHTO, Darryl

American, 20th century.
Born 1943, in Watertown (New York).
Painter.

Daryl Hughto studied in Buffalo until 1969. He teaches at the University of Syracuse. His abstract paintings explore the concept of open space, taking spiral forms as their starting-point.

AUCTION RECORDS:

NEW YORK, 9 Nov 1983, *Summertime* (1976, acrylic/canvas, 76 3/4 x 56 ins / 195 x 142.5 cm) USD 1,800. NEW YORK, 27 Feb 1990, *Suzanne's House* (1976, acrylic/canvas, 72 x 63 ins / 182.9 x 160 cm) USD 5,500. NEW YORK, 7 May 1991, *'Monkey Shines'* (1978, acrylic/canvas, 74 3/4 x 56 ins / 189.9 x 142.2 cm) USD 1,650. NEW YORK, 26 Feb 1993, *Slipping and Sliding* (1976, acrylic/canvas, 66 x 99 ins / 167.6 x 251.5 cm) USD 3,450.

HÜGI, Jürg

Swiss, 20th century.
Born 1944, in Basel.
Painter.

Jürg Hügi has exhibited in Basel, Zurich and Morges, and in 1975 in Paris.

HÜGIN, Karl Otto

Swiss, 20th century.
Born 1887, in Trimbach; died 1963, in Bassersdorf.
Painter.

Karl Otto Hügin was a student at the arts and crafts school in Basel from 1901 to 1903. From 1904 to 1906 he worked as an industrial designer in Stuttgart, and in 1906 he settled in Zurich, concentrating fully on painting and drawing after 1918. He travelled to Berlin, Italy, Marseilles and Tunis, and from 1932 to 1939 was professor the fine arts school in Zurich. Work by him was shown at many collective exhibitions in the main Swiss cities, as well as in Berlin, Brussels, Florence, Grenoble, Leipzig, Manchester, Venice and Vienna. He painted landscapes and figural scenes.

MUSEUMS AND GALLERIES:

AARAU - BASEL - BERN - ZURICH.

AUCTION RECORDS:

ZURICH, 30 May 1979, *Three Women* (c. 1934-1935, oil on paper, 18 1/2 x 14 ins / 47 x 35.5 cm) CHF 3,000. ZURICH, 13 June 1986, *Café Scene* (oil on canvas, 25 1/2 x 39 1/4 ins / 65 x 100 cm) CHF 7,000. BERN, 26 Oct 1988, *Circus Rider* (watercolour, 18 1/2 x 12 1/4 ins / 47 x 31 cm) CHF 600. ZURICH, 24 Nov 1993, *The Port in Marseilles* (oil on canvas, 17 3/4 x 21 3/4 ins / 45 x 55.5 cm) CHF 2,990. ZURICH, 10 Dec 1996, *Sport* (tempera/Pavatex, study, 13 3/4 x 9 ins / 35 x 22 cm) CHF 4,370. ZURICH, 4 Nov 2000, *Worry Free Life* (oil on board, 19 x 20 ins / 47 x 52 cm) CHF 5,500.

HUGNES, E. Lucas

British, 19th century.
Painter. Landscapes.

Hugnes is cited by *Art Prices Current*.

AUCTION RECORDS:

LONDON, 7 March 1910, *A Corner of Bridston Wood* (1908) GBP 1.

HUGNET, Georges

French, 20th century.
Born 1904 or 1906, in Paris; died 1974, in St-Martin-de-Ré (Charente-Maritime).
Painter, collage artist, photomontage artist.

Georges Hugnet spent his childhood in Argentina, returning to France in 1913. He aligned himself with the Surrealists in 1932, but was excluded from the movement in 1939. In 1935, he created his *book-objects*, whose bindings are striking (an example is Bellmer's *The Doll*). He was also a writer, poet, critic (*Dictionnaire du dadaïsme* (*Dictionary of Dadaism*), 1971), screenwriter and the editor of Tzara and G. Stein.

In 2003, he was included in the collective exhibition *Phantom der Lust. Visionen des Masochismus in der Kunst* (*Phantom of Desire. Visions of Masochism in Art*), dedicated to Sacher-Masoch, the inventor of masochism, at the Neue Galerie am Ladesmuseum in Graz. The Galerie Zabriskie, in Paris, organised a retrospective of his collages from 1950 to 1960, and in 1984 the Galerie 14-16 Verneuil in Paris showed his collages and photomontages from the 1930s.

BIBLIOGRAPHY:

Hugnet, Georges, *Pleins et déliés: souvenirs et témoignages, 1926-1972*, G. Authier, La Chapelle-sur-Loire, 1972. *Pérégrination de Georges Hugnet*, exhibition catalogue, Musée national d'Art moderne, Paris, 1978. Weibel, Peter (ed.), *'Phantom der Lust. Visionen des Masochismus in der Kunst'* in *2 vol.*, exhibition catalogue, Neue Galerie am Landesmuseum, Graz, Belleville Verlag, Munich, 2003. Stourdzé, Sam (ed.), *Georges Hugnet, collages*, exhibition catalogue, L. Scheer, Paris, 2003.

AUCTION RECORDS:

LONDON, 3 Dec 1980, *Collage* (photograph and collage, 10 1/4 x 8 ins / 26 x 20.3 cm) GBP 800. NEW YORK, 27 Nov 1987, *The Source Itself* (1936, cut-outs, collage, 12 3/4 x 9 3/4 ins / 32.5 x 25 cm) USD 22,000. PARIS, 27 Nov 1987, *The Source Itself, Poem-cut-out for the 'La Septième Face du dé'* (1936, oil on canvas, 12 3/4 x 9 3/4 ins / 32.5 x 25 cm) FRF 22,000. NEW YORK, 6 Oct 1988, *Decal Art* (1936, gouache, 12 3/4 x 9 3/4 ins / 32.5 x 25 cm) USD 2,420. LONDON, 29 Nov 1989, *Poem-cut-out for 'La Septième Face du dé'* (collage of newspaper cutouts, photos and straw/paper, 12 3/4 x 9 3/4 ins / 32.5 x 25 cm) GBP 7,150. PARIS, 29 Nov 1989, *Untitled* (1961, collage, 13 1/2 x 9 3/4 ins / 34 x 25 cm) FRF 10,000. PARIS, 13 June 1992, *Untitled* (1961, collage, 12 x 9 3/4 ins / 30.5 x 25 cm) FRF 10,000. PARIS, 10 June 1993, *Untitled* (1961, collage, 8 1/4 x 5 1/4 ins / 21 x 13.5 cm) FRF 5,500. LONDON, 4 Dec 2000, *Exquisite Corpse* (1935, pencil, 10 x 7 ins / 25 x 18 cm) GBP 8,000. LONDON, 4 Dec 2000, *C'est Qu'elle Sait Etre Plus Jolie Encore la Machine Infernale* (*The Infernal Machine Can Be Even More Pretty*) (1936, collage, 12 x 9 ins / 31 x 22 cm) GBP 14,000. PARIS, 12 Dec 2001, *Cut-up Poem* (c. 1935, collage) FRF 41,000. LONDON, 6 Feb 2002, *Second Columne of the Millennium* (1935, collage on card, 12 x 12 ins / 31 x 30 cm) GBP 3,500. LONDON, 6 Feb 2002, *Destin sur qui gisent epars des vetements hatifs* (1935, collage on card, 11 x 8 ins / 29 x 21 cm) GBP 6,500. PARIS, 6 Dec 2003, *Pope with Hand Raised, in which He*

Seems to Hold a Woman with an Anxious Expression (collage, 10 x 10 ins / 25 x 25 cm) EUR 2,600. STOCKHOLM, 26 April 2004, *Untitled* (collage, 9 x 7 ins / 23 x 17 cm) SEK 29,000. LONDON, 24 June 2004, *Who Invents* (1936, paper collage on board, 22 x 16 ins / 56 x 40 cm) GBP 12,000.

HUGO
French, 10th century.
Sculptor, painter.

Active in Châlons-sur-Marne in 999, this artist decorated the city's cathedral. He may have been the abbot of the monastery of Montier-en-Der (Haute Marne).

HUGO (Friar), or Hugo D'Oignies
Walloon School, 13th century.
Born in Walcourt; died after 1240.
Worker in precious metals, miniaturist. Religious furnishings.

Friar Hugo went to live with four brother priests at Oignies, in Hainaut, where they founded a religious community. Before long, they had set up a goldsmith's workshop. Hugo made many pieces for the Treasury. His work included religious objects such as reliquaries, phylacteries, a gospel-book, a manuscript, an engraved chalice and a cross. In 2003, the Musée Provincial des Arts Anciens du Namurois presented the exhibition, *Autour de Hugo d'Oignes* (*Hugo d'Oignies and his World*)

BIBLIOGRAPHY:
Toussaint, Jacques, *Autour de Hugo dOignies*, exhibition catalogue, Musée provincial des Arts anciens du Namurois, Namur, 2003.

MUSEUMS AND GALLERIES:
NAMUR (Couvent des Sœurs de Notre-Dame): items from the Trésor d'Oignies.

HUGO, Antoine
French, 18th century.
Active in Paris in 1731.
Painter.

HUGO, Georges Charles Victor Leopold, called Georges-Victor
French, 19th - 20th century.
Born 16 November 1868, in Brussels; died 5 February 1925, in Paris.
Painter, draughtsman. Genre scenes.

AUCTION RECORDS:
PARIS, 24 Jan 1945, *Dispute over Prices* (pencil and wash) FRF 950. PARIS, Oct 1945-July 1946, *Café-Concert Dancer*, FRF 2,800. PARIS, 7 March 1978, *Ship in a Storm* (gouache, 11 x 14 1/4 ins / 27 x 36 cm) FRF 4,500. PARIS, 27 May 1993, *Woman Reading* (watercolour, 7 3/4 x 10 1/2 ins / 20 x 26.5 cm) FRF 5,000. PARIS, 27 April 1994, *Amazonian* (watercolour, 17 1/4 x 11 ins / 44 x 28 cm) FRF 8,000. PARIS, 19 April 1996, *Brittany, the Painter's House at Carentec* (oil on card, 13 x 18 ins / 33 x 46 cm) FRF 4,200. PARIS, 2 Dec 1999, *View of St-Malo, View of the Beach from the Lock at Dinard* (oil on canvas, 23 x 29 ins / 59 x 74 cm) FRF 42,000.

HUGO, Jean
French, 20th century.
Born 19 November 1894, in Paris; died 1984, in Lunel.
Painter (including gouache), draughtsman, illustrator.
Stage costumes and sets.

Jean Hugo was the great-grandson of Victor Hugo. He was self-taught, and studied literature before devoting himself to painting. He related his experiences in World War I in *Le Regard de la mémoire* (*The Perspective of Memory*). After the war he associated himself with Cocteau, Radiguet, the composers known as Groupe des Six (Group of Six), as well as Satie, Max Jacob, Picasso, Diaghilev and Stravinsky. He was married to Valentine Gross. From the 1920s he turned towards religion, and in 1929 he retreated to Mas de Fourques, near Lunel. He became particularly known for his stagings of Victor Hugo's dramas. He had a romantic temperament, and was most at home with gouache, quicker to dry than oil, and thus more apt for capturing fleeting inspiration, and a more substantial medium than watercolour. He was able to adapt medieval and romantic sources to a more contemporary treatment. It was by means of this somewhat Baroque side of his imagination that he often brushed with Surrealism, as is evidenced in his humorous, strange costume and set designs which he conceived in 1921 for *Mariés de la Tour Eiffel* (*Wedding on the Eiffel Tower*) by Jean Cocteau. The latter was a production of the Swedish Ballet, for which he developed a whole comical series of '1900' characters, such as cyclists and bathers. He also designed for the ballet-pantomime *Romeo and Juliet*, mounted in 1924, by the company, Soirées de Paris (Paris Evenings). Both productions were conceived by Jean Cocteau. Hugo then withdrew to the Midi region, where he painted still-lifes, and gouache landscapes in lively tones of the Languedoc, England, Paris and Russia. He was also an imaginative illustrator, some of his compositions including *Les Joues en feu* (*Cheeks on Fire*) by Raymond Radiguet; *Les Mariés de la Tour Eiffel* (*Wedding on the Eiffel Tower*) by Jean Cocteau and *Climats* (*Climates*) by André Maurois, one of his strangest illustrative works. He also illustrated many other works, such as those of Max Jacob, Péguy, René Char and Pierre-André Benoît.

In 1994, a collection of his works was shown at the Musée-bibliothèque Pierre-André Benoît in Alès. In 1995, the Musée National de la Coopération Franco-Américaine organised an exhibition at the Château de Blérancourt in Chauny of drawings executed at the front during World War I. A retrospective of his work was shown at the Maison de Victor Hugo in Paris in 1995, and another was presented at the Musée Fabre de Montpellier in the same year.

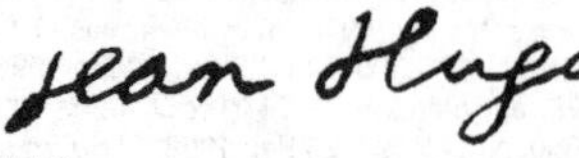

BIBLIOGRAPHY:
Hugo, Jean, *Le Regard de la mémoire*, Actes Sud, Arles, 1983. Hugo, Jean, *Carnets 1946-1984*, Actes Sud, Arles, 1995. *Jean Hugo*, exhibition catalogue, Maison de Victor Hugo, Paris, 1995. *Dessins des années de guerre (1915-1919)*, exhibition catalogue, Musée national de la coopération franco-américaine, Château de Blérancourt, 1995. Jourdan, Patrick, *Jean Hugo: la Bretagne et la mer*, Musée des Jacobins, Morlaix, 2001.

MUSEUMS AND GALLERIES:
MONTPELLIER (Mus. Fabre): *Eater of the Striped Sweater (Self-portrait)* (1940, oil on canvas); *The Beaulieu Quarries* (1953, oil on card); *Soulatgets* (1972, oil on canvas); *The Imposter* (1931, tempera/wood); *La Baie des Trépassés (Tréboul, Brittany)* (1931, oil on wood).

AUCTION RECORDS:
NEW YORK, 1 May 1946, *Bullfight* (drawing) USD 350. LONDON, 28 Oct 1981, *The Aperitif* (1921, pencil, 10 3/4 x 8 1/4 ins / 27.3 x 21 cm) GBP 1,000. LONDON, 28 Oct 1981, *The Forgotten Bathrobe* (1931, gouache, 19 x 12 1/2 ins / 48.3 x 31.7 cm) GBP 1,400. LONDON, 8 June 1983, *Two Houses in the Garrigue* (1953, oil on panel, 10 x 15 1/2 ins / 25.7 x 39.5 cm) GBP 900. LONDON, 28 March 1984, *The Blue Crosses* (1831, gouache, 11 1/4 x 8 1/4 ins / 28.5 x 21 cm) GBP 1,400. PARIS, 27 Nov 1985, *The Fishermen* (oil on canvas, 18 x 24 ins / 46 x 61 cm) FRF 19,000. LONDON, 2 April 1987, *The Bay of Beaulieu* (gouache, 10 x 12 1/4 ins / 25.5 x 31 cm) GBP 1,500. NEW YORK, 18 Feb 1988, *The News* (distemper/canvas, 24 x 19 3/4 ins / 61 x 50.2 cm) USD 13,200. LONDON, 18 April 1988, *Scene in Provence* (oil on canvas, 9 x 15 1/2 ins / 22.7 x 39.5 cm) GBP 2,420. LONDON, 19 Oct 1988, *Man Seated Between Two Women* (1928,

oil on panel, 9 x 12 1/2 ins / 22.7 x 31.7 cm) GBP 3,300. LONDON, 21 Oct 1988, *Landscape* (gouache/card, 6 3/4 x 9 3/4 ins / 17.2 x 24.8 cm) GBP 462. PARIS, 12 Dec 1988, *Door Opening Out onto a Landscape* (oil on canvas, 99 1/2 x 63 ins / 253 x 160 cm) FRF 43,000. NEW YORK, 10 Oct 1990, *Dream in Obscure Night* (gouache/panel, 11 3/4 x 7 1/2 ins / 30 x 19.1 cm) USD 5,225. MONACO, 11 Oct 1991, *Set Design for Orphée* (gouache, 5 3/4 x 9 1/4 ins / 14.5 x 23.5 cm) FRF 41,070. PARIS, 7 July 1992, *Costume Designs for Romeo and Juliet* (three gouaches/black paper, each approx. 11 x 9 ins / 28 x 22 cm) FRF 23,100. LONDON, 15 Oct 1992, *The Fair at Chipping Campden* (gouache/pencil, 6 1/2 x 14 1/4 ins / 16.2 x 36 cm) GBP 1,760. PARIS, 23 Oct 1992, *Rue de l'Arbre Sec* (1926, gouache, 6 1/4 x 9 ins / 16 x 22 cm) FRF 21,000. NEW YORK, 10 Nov 1992, *Nocturne* (tempera/panel, 19 1/4 x 24 ins / 49.2 x 61 cm) USD 14,300. MONACO, 6 Dec 1992, *St-Jean-Cap-Ferrat* (1922, gouache/paper, 2 1/2 x 4 ins / 6.4 x 9.3 cm) FRF 19,980; *The Breton Cottage at Guelvouarn* (1931, egg tempera/canvas, 8 1/4 x 13 1/4 ins / 21 x 33.8 cm) FRF 27,750. NEW YORK, 29 Sept 1993, *Village Square in Catalonia, Three-panelled Screen* (1969, oil on canvas, each panel 88 1/2 x 35 1/2 ins / 224.8 x 90.2 cm) USD 6,325. NEW YORK, 9 May 1994, *The Grove* (gouache/canvas, 11 1/2 x 14 ins / 29 x 35.5 cm) USD 4,830. PARIS, 26 Nov 1994, *Nocturnal Landscape* (gouache miniature, 1 1/2 x 2 1/2 ins / 4 x 6.5 cm) FRF 7,200. PARIS, 30 Jan 1995, *The 100 Kisses* (gouache, decor, 5 x 7 3/4 ins / 13 x 19.5 cm) FRF 10,000. LONDON, 25 Oct 1995, *Man Seated Between Two Draped Women* (1928, paper collage of glass and oil on panel, 8 3/4 x 13 ins / 22.5 x 33 cm) GBP 10,580. NEW YORK, 10 Oct 1996, *Working the Land* (gouache/paper/panel, 8 x 10 ins / 20.3 x 25.1 cm) USD 690. NEW YORK, 12 Nov 1996, *Houses on the River* (gouache/paper/card, 6 x 8 1/2 ins / 15.5 x 21.3 cm) USD 5,520. PARIS, 23 Feb 1997, *Saturargues* (1942, oil on card, 6 1/4 x 9 ins / 16 x 22 cm) FRF 17,000. PARIS, 18 June 1997, *The Kiosk on the Bank of the Loing* (1927, oil on card, 7 1/4 x 10 ins / 18.5 x 24.5 cm) FRF 26,000. PARIS, 19 Oct 1997, *Portrait of Paul Morand* (c. 1923, pencil/paper, 10 x 7 1/4 ins / 24.5 x 18.5 cm) FRF 8,000. PARIS, 4 June 1999, *Centaurs and Bull* (gouache, 5 x 8 ins / 12 x 20 cm) FRF 40,000. PARIS, 26 Nov 1999, *Pleasures of the Beach* (1928, oil on canvas, 90 x 53 ins / 228 x 135 cm) FRF 2,000,000. LONDON, 30 June 2000, *Still-life with Green Bottle* (oil on board, 18 x 14 ins / 46 x 35 cm) GBP 2,800. LONDON, 30 June 2000, *Fisherman on the Riverbank* (oil on board, 8 x 11 ins / 21 x 27 cm) GBP 3,200. CALAIS, 7 July 2002, *Vase of Dahlias and Zinnias* (oil on canvas, 29 x 24 ins / 73 x 60 cm) EUR 7,600. PARIS, 19 Dec 2002, *Landscapes* (oil on panel, set of six works, 3 x 5 ins / 8 x 13 cm) EUR 7,000. PARIS, 20 May 2003, *Still-lifes* (c. 1950, gouache and ink, four works) EUR 7,500. PARIS, 20 May 2003, *Illustration of Views of Boats or Houses* (c. 1950, gouache, six catalogue works) EUR 7,500. BANTAM, 14 July 2004, *Mazet in Ruin* (1971, oil on canvas, 10 x 13 ins / 25 x 33 cm) USD 2,300. NEW YORK, 5 Oct 2004, *Figures on Horseback and Cattle in a Misty Valley* (oil on panel, 9 x 13 ins / 24 x 33 cm) USD 3,200.

HUGO, Léopold Armand
French, 19th century.
Born in the 19th century, in Paris.
Sculptor.

A pupil of Horace Vernet, Hugo first exhibited at the Salon in 1874.

HUGO, Louise Rose Julie (Countess).
See **DUVIDAL DE MONTFERRIER**

HUGO, Marie
French, 20th century.
Also active in Britain.
Painter.

Marie Hugo is the daughter of the painter Jean Hugo. She studied at the École des Beaux-Arts in Montpellier. She executed a series on gardens, evoking an interiorised, imaginary universe. She favours the use of colour and simple, suggestive forms, in order to reveal the poetic character of the world. She has had solo exhibitions, most notably in London.

HUGO, Melchior von
German, 20th century.
Born 23 March 1872, in Unsingen.
Painter, sculptor, engraver.

Hugo was a student of Carrière in Paris. He worked in Stuttgart and Nuremberg, among other places.

HUGO, Valentine
Maiden name: Gross
French, 20th century.
Born 1890, in Boulogne-sur-Mer; died 1968, in Paris.
Painter, draughtswoman, illustrator. Stage sets.

Born Valentine Gross, this artist married Jean Hugo in 1919. She studied with Humbert, and made her début in Paris at the Salon des Artistes Français, where she received an honourable mention in 1909. A remarkable draughtswoman, she would represented subjects from the world of dreams, illustrating Surrealist-inspired literary works. Her drawings for Paul Éluard's *Hommes et Bêtes* (*Men and Beasts*), are perfect achievements in this sense, which evoke the mystery of Odilon Redon's charcoals. She painted numerous sets for the theatre, including *Les Mariés de la Tour Eiffel* (*Wedding on the Eiffel Tower*) by Jean Cocteau (Swedish Ballet, 1921), *Romeo and Juliet*, *Quadrille* (*Square Dance*), *Île de la Raison* (*Isle of Reason*), and in 1947, Débussy's opera *Pelléas et Mélisande*. She also painted numerous portraits, including those of *Salie*, *Stravinsky*, *Picasso*, *Max Ernst*, *Valéry* and *Éluard*. She executed illustrations for *Ondine* by la Motte-Fouqué, *Contes Bizarres* (*Bizarre Tales*) by Achim von Arnim, and *Promenoir des deux Amants* (*The Promenade of the Two Lovers*) by Guy Lévis-Mano.

BIBLIOGRAPHY:
Margerie, A. de, *Valentine Hugo*, Jacques Damase, Paris, 1983. Seguin, Béatrice (ed.), *Valentine Hugo: écrits et entretiens radiophonique*, Actes Sud, Arles, 2002 (followed by "Le Surréalisme de Valentine Hugo" by Jean-Pierre Cauvin).

AUCTION RECORDS:
LONDON, 6 June 1979, *Nijinsky in 'Le Spectre de la Rose'* (c. 1912, pastel, 11 x 7 ins / 28 x 18 cm) GBP 750. NEW YORK, 6 Dec 1979, *Nijinsky in 'Le Spectre de la Rose'* (oil on canvas, 25 3/4 x 19 3/4 ins / 65.5 x 50.2 cm) USD 2,000. LONDON, 13 March 1980, *Nijinsky in 'Le Spectre de la Rose'* (1913, pencil/paper, 10 3/4 x 7 ins / 27.5 x 18 cm) GBP 1,100. PARIS, 6 June 1983, *The Pink She-cat* (oil on panel, oval, 10 x 7 3/4 ins / 25.5 x 20 cm) FRF 20,000. LONDON, 26 Oct 1983, *Nijinsky in 'Le Spectre de la Rose'* (c. 1912, pastel, 11 x 7 ins / 28 x 18 cm) GBP 900. LONDON, 26 Feb 1986, *Portrait of Moira* (c. 1950, oil on canvas, 11 x 9 ins / 27 x 22 cm) GBP 1,200. PARIS, 1 July 1987, *Carnival: Karsavina and Nijinsky* (1912, oil on panel, 16 1/4 x 12 1/2 ins / 41 x 32 cm) FRF 15,200. PARIS, 12 Oct 1988, *Portrait of André Breton* (1931, pencil, 12 1/2 x 9 ins / 32 x 23 cm) FRF 17,000. PARIS, 27 June 1990, *"Le Spectre de la Rose", Nijinsky and Karsavina* (1912, oil on panel) FRF 160,000. PARIS, 25 Oct 1990, *Self-portrait* (pastel/paper, 22 1/2 x 16 1/2 ins / 57 x 42 cm) FRF 8,000. PARIS, 24 Nov 1992, *Portrait of Lise Deharme* (1938, oil on card, 11 x 9 ins / 27 x 22 cm) FRF 39,000. MONACO, 6 Dec 1992, *Portrait of Hubert de Saint Senoch* (1944, oil and mixed media/card, 8 3/4 x 8 ins / 22.3 x 20.6 cm) FRF 46,620. PARIS, 4 May 1993, *Costume Design for Heathcliff, 'Wuthering Heights' Act I* (colouring pencil, 13 x 8 1/4 ins / 33 x 21 cm) FRF 8,800. PARIS, 4 March 1994, *'Like a Fish Thrown from the Sea...'* (1954, blue wash, 28 1/4 x 20 3/4 ins / 72 x 53 cm) FRF 13,100. PARIS, 21 June 1994, *Profile of*

Suzanne Tezenas (pastel/paper, 17 1/4 x 11 3/4 ins / 44 x 30 cm) FRF 4,500. PARIS, 30 Jan 1995, *Le Spectre de la Rose: Nijinsky* (1912, woodcut on silk painted over in gouache heightened with gold and silver, 6 x 7 1/4 ins / 15 x 18.5 cm) FRF 58,000. PARIS, 28 March 1996, *Mademoiselle Susana* (oil on panel, 24 3/4 x 11 ins / 63 x 27 cm) FRF 26,000. LONDON, 19 Dec 1996, *Nijinsky in 'Le Spectre de la Rose'* (1913, pencil/tracing paper, 11 x 7 ins / 28 x 18 cm) GBP 2,760. PARIS, 19 Oct 1997, *Portrait of Jean Cocteau* (c. 1920, graphite/paper, 7 x 5 1/4 ins / 18 x 13.5 cm) FRF 25,000. PARIS, 21 Nov 1997, *Igor Stravinsky* (1938, mixed media/porcelain, diam. 10 ins / 24.5 cm) FRF 38,000. GENEVA, 19 May 1999, *Portrait of Raymond Radiguet* (crayon, 10 x 8 ins / 26 x 20 cm) CHF 10,000. PARIS, 27 Oct 2000, *Portraits of Rimbaud* (1934, ink on glass, 7 x 5 ins / 17 x 13 cm) FRF 160,000. PARIS, 27 Oct 2000, *Portrait of Surrealist Poets* (1932, oil on panel, 47 x 39 ins / 120 x 100 cm) FRF 1,800,000. PARIS, 11 Dec 2001, *Portrait of Jean Marais* (c. 1940, graphite, 10 x 8 ins / 26 x 20 cm) EUR 2,287. PARIS, 4 Dec 2002, *Portrait of Dominique Eluard* (c. 1945, Indian ink and graphite heightened with gouache, 15 x 11 ins / 37 x 28 cm) EUR 4,400.

HUGO, Victor Marie
French, 19th century.
Born 26 February 1802, in Besançon; died 23 May 1885, in Paris.
Painter, watercolourist, draughtsman, caricaturist.
Figures, genre scenes, landscapes, seascapes.

Victor Hugo was not only one of France's greatest writers, but also a prolific artist. Although little is known about his art, it is thought that he produced around 3,500 and 4,000 works. Hugo himself was extremely modest about his art. He told the poet Baudelaire that his drawings were "clumsily scrawled on paper by a fellow who has quite another task at hand". The fact that art was not his chief occupation was part of the reason why he could allow himself the freedom to be bold and experimental. It is thought that he drew throughout his life, particularly during his exile (1851-1870), and on his travels: through Normandy (1834); Picardy (1835); Brittany (1836); Belgium (1837); Alsace, the Rhineland and Burgundy (1839); the Rhine Valley (1840, 1865 and 1869); Spain (1843); and Waterloo (1861). Even though Hugo never went to art school, he learned the rudiments of drawing, geometry and optics as a boy.

In Edmond Bacot's 1864 account of his visit to Hauteville House (Victor Hugo's residence in Guernsey), published under the title *Un Passant chez Victor Hugo* (*A Passerby at Victor Hugo's House*), there is the following description of the drawings decorating the billiard room:

'There are ten fantastic pages enhanced by sepia tones and a few touches of gold, gently glinting through the sombre shades of the composition... They are views of Spain, Brittany, the Rhine, Jersey and Guernsey. Seeing them is like glimpsing a reflection of the magical pictures in prose and verse that the poet has painted onto our memories... The frames are made of fir, but against this white wood background are flowerets of the imagination, twisting and opening, along with perfectly realistic butterflies. When Victor Hugo produces a drawing he makes the frame at the same time, and occasionally he sculpts a piece of oak to separate the frame from the wall. He is a craftsman just like the artists of the Middle Ages.'

With time, it has become clear that Hugo's graphic art is highly diverse in several ways. His works vary enormously in size; they are sometimes executed over a long period of time, while at other times they seem to have been barely started. His subjects - which are now known to comprise caricatures, figures, landscapes, and views of old towns, houses or ruins - may be drawn as patterns, from memory, or simply from the imagination. Then there are other works that draw attention to their subject, with their expressive spots and drips of colour, while others again invite the viewer to examine the process by which they were created: through stamps, stencils, shadow prints and collage. Hugo used traditional materials, like lead pencil, pen and wash, chalk, charcoal, gouache and watercolour, but he was also very much an innovator, who would 'cook up' all sorts of other materials. Hugo was well aware of the artistic conventions for representing objects. Some of his drawings are tinged with a serenity that has almost a narrative quality, while others, created using different methods and procedures, convey insane passions, romantic freedom, and fantastical apparitions (for example his views of castles and ruins). He also presented images as reveries: rebellious expressions of the supernatural. For Hugo, drawing and writing were two aspects of a single creative force. In his introduction to Pierre Gorgel's book *Notes sur les Dessins de Victor Hugo* (*Notes on the Drawings of Victor Hugo*), Maurice Clouard wrote:

'It was about more than just relaxation for him; it was above all a *document* - a way of putting into concrete form the vision in his mind, more quickly and precisely than he could in writing. His imagination would be stirred by an old crumbling wall or a ruined turret, and his pencil would immediately create a castle balanced on top of a rock, or one of these mythical towns with a thousand pinnacles; or a half-dead tree trunk, or a bizarrely contorted branch, would on paper or canvas become a forest of sinister trees. Drawing, therefore, is the ideal medium for the inexpressible. Just like poetry, it is an art form that by its very nature is inclined to lyricism and visionary inspiration.'

The few previously undiscovered artworks that have been recently unearthed from the Victor Hugo archives are a good indication of the experimental nature of his work. The 2001 exhibition *Du chaos dans le pinceau... Victor Hugo dessins* (*Chaotic Brushstrokes: Victor Hugo's Drawings*) at Victor Hugo's House in Paris attempted to demonstrate how the stamps (or prints made with lace, vegetables, or even fingers), spots, drips, stencils, folded paper, collage and silhouettes used by Hugo were forms of expression that predate by almost a century the stamps, frottage and grattage used by the Surrealists and informal abstract painters.

There is also an extensive collection of caricatures poking fun at the bourgeoisie and authority figures. Many of these caricatures are held in Victor Hugo's house in Paris: some were put together in an album by Madame P. Meurice, while others used to belong to A Vacquerie and Philippe Burty. Many of his caricatures are accompanied by captions: *My friend, I am no romantic; Traitor, what state have you reduced me to; The man who looks at Constantinople*; and, on a cruelly allusive silhouette: *But it was I who brought trouble to that household*. M.J. Bertaut said that these caricatures "reveal Victor Hugo's satirical nature in an astonishing light". Indeed, as an artist, Victor Hugo never left the spectator indifferent.

Hugo's work was never exhibited during his lifetime. However in 1888, three years after his death, the first exhibition of his drawings and manuscripts was held at the Georges Petit Gallery in Paris. In 1881 he added a clause to his will in favour of the French national library, the Bibliothèque Nationale, which read: 'I bequeath all my manuscripts, and any other writings or drawings that are found, to the National Library in Paris, which one day will be the Library of the United Nations of Europe'. Works from the collections of the Bibliothèque Nationale and Victor Hugo's House in Paris are regularly displayed in temporary exhibitions all over the world. The most notable of these so far include: *Victor Hugo et les artistes romantiques* (*Victor Hugo and the Romantic Artists*), at Victor Hugo's House in Paris, in 1951; an exhibition celebrating the 150th anniversary of his birth at the Bibliothèque Nationale, Paris, in 1952; *Dessins de*

Victor Hugo (*Victor Hugo's Drawings*), at Victor Hugo's House in Paris, in 1972 (an important exhibition, being arguably the first to recognise Victor Hugo as an artist in his own right); *Soleil d'encre* (*The Ink Sun*), an exhibition on the centenary of his death in 1985, at the Petit Palais, Paris; *Victor Hugo peintre* (*Victor Hugo the Painter*) at the Galleria d'Arte Moderna Ca'Pesaro, Venice, in 1993; *Shadows of a Hand* at The Drawing Center, New York, in 1998; and *Du chaos dans le pinceau... Victor Hugo dessins* (*Chaotic Brushstrokes: Victor Hugo's Drawings*) at Victor Hugo's House in Paris and the Museo Thyssen-Bornemisza, Madrid, in 2001. For the bicentenary of his birth in 2002, the Bibliothèque Nationale held an exhibition entitled *Victor Hugo, l'homme océan* (*Victor Hugo, Man of The Ocean*). This was a display of 380 items from its collection, including original manuscripts of his poetry and prose, letters, drawings, caricatures, and pages from his notebooks and albums. Other exhibitions were also held to commemorate the bicentenary in 2002, including: *Victor Hugo et les siens: deux siècles d'art et d'artistes* (*Victor Hugo and His Countrymen: Two Centuries of Art and Artists*), at the art gallery of the Conseil Général (General Council) of Bouches-du-Rhône, in Aix-en-Provence; *L'Œil de Victor Hugo: graphisme* (*Victor Hugo's Eye: Graphic Art*), a conference at the Musée d'Orsay, Paris; *Aubes. Rêveries au bord de Victor Hugo* (*Dawn: Thoughts of Victor Hugo*), an exhibition comparing Victor Hugo's drawings with works by 20th-century artists, at Victor Hugo's House in Paris; and *Victor Hugo vu par Rodin* (*Victor Hugo as Seen by Rodin*), at the Musée des Beaux-Arts et d'Archéologie, Besançon, north-east France.

With the passage of time, appreciation of Hugo's artistic work continues to grow. His contemporary, the writer Théophile Gautier, said of him: 'If he had not been a poet, Victor Hugo would have been a first-class painter'; and in 2002, Pierre Rosenberg delivered a lecture to the Académie Française, entitled: 'A great painter named Victor Hugo'.

BIBLIOGRAPHY:

Picon, Gaëtan (preface), *Victor Hugo dessinateur*, Éd. du Minotaure, Paris, 1963 (notes and captions by Roger Cornaille and Georges Herscher). Delalande, Jean, *Victor Hugo dessinateur génial et halluciné*, Nouvelles Éditions Latines, Paris, 1964. Écalle, Martine/Lumbroso, Violaine, *Album Hugo*, Gallimard, Paris, 1964. Grynberg, Bernadette/Massin, Jean/Georgel, Pierre, '*Victor Hugo. Œuvre graphique*' in *3 vol., coll. Œuvres Complètes*, Club Français du Livre, Paris, 1967, 1969, 1970. Georgel, Pierre, *Dessins de Victor Hugo*, exhibition catalogue, Musée Victor-Hugo, Villequier, Maison de Victor Hugo, Paris, 1971-1972. *Dessins et ébauches de Victor Hugo*, exhibition catalogue, S.n., Paris, 1972 (from the Hugo legacy). Pierrot, Roger, et al., *Soleil d'encre. Manuscrits et dessins de Victor Hugo*, exhibition catalogue, Musée du Petit Palais, Paris, 1985. Lebel, Jean-Jacques, et al., *Victor Hugo peintre*, exhibition catalogue, Gall. d'Arte Moderna Ca'Pesaro, Venice, 1993. Molinari, Danielle/Butor, Michel/Hofmann, Werner, *Du chaos dans le pinceau... Victor Hugo dessins*, exhibition catalogue, Museo Thyssen-Bornemisza, Maison de Victor Hugo, Madrid, Paris, 2001. Georgel, Pierre, *Victor Hugo et les siens*, exhibition catalogue, Gal. d'art du Conseil général des Bouches-du-Rhône, Aix-en-Provence, 2002. Rosenberg, Pierre, '*Un grand peintre nommé Victor Hugo*' in *Le Monde*, periodical, Paris, 1 March 2002 (excerpt from a speech delivered at the Académie Française on 28 February 2002).

MUSEUMS AND GALLERIES:

PARIS (BNF): legacy of the artist, manuscripts and drawings - PARIS (Maison de Victor Hugo): *The House where I Live in Vianden* - VILLEQUIER (Musée Victor Hugo).

AUCTION RECORDS:

PARIS, 4 July 1919, *The Château du Moine (Île de St-Honorat)* (pen) FRF 110. PARIS, 31 March 1920, *Belfry* (sepia) FRF 515. PARIS, 11-13 June 1923, *Old Village in Ruins* (Indian ink wash, heightened with watercolour) FRF 4,100. PARIS, 20 March 1926, *Houses Halfway up a Hill* (pen and wash) FRF 185. PARIS, 14-16 Nov 1927, *Ruins of a Feudal Castle on a Mountain* (pen and wash) FRF 7,000; *Feudal Castle on the Tip of a Rock with People* (pen and wash) FRF 3,100; *View of an Old Castle by a Path* (pen and wash) FRF 6,600; *Landscape with Stream: Night* (pen and wash) FRF 4,000. PARIS, 3 and 4 June 1929, *Fortified Town* (sepia) FRF 7,100. PARIS, 22 Feb 1937, *Storm over the Town (Abbeville)* (pen and sepia wash) FRF 2,700; *Military Organisation* (pen and sepia wash) FRF 3,050. PARIS, 12 May 1937, *Village* (pen and Indian ink wash) FRF 510; *Roof and Tree Branch* (ink wash) FRF 260. PARIS, 8 Dec 1937, *Cottage* (Indian ink) FRF 1,500; *Feudal Castle* (watercolour) FRF 2,000. PARIS, 31 Jan 1938, *Seascape* (Indian ink wash) FRF 400. PARIS, 20 March 1940, *Wash Drawing*, FRF 500. PARIS, 30 Oct 1940, *Vision* (1865, wash) FRF 420. PARIS, 29 March 1943, *Old Village* (two wash drawings) FRF 3,200. PARIS, 2 July 1943, *After the Storm* (wash) FRF 8,000. PARIS, 17 Dec 1943, *Portrait of a Woman* (pen) FRF 5,000. PARIS, 9 July 1947, *St-Valéry-sur-Somme* (Indian ink wash) FRF 8,200. PARIS, 28 Nov 1949, *Phantom Vessel* (wash) FRF 14,000. PARIS, 30 June 1961, *Landscape* (watercolour) FRF 1,450. GENEVA, 29 June 1968, *Path to the Church* (soft pencil) CHF 4,500. GENEVA, 14 June 1970, *Seascape* (pastel) CHF 5,500. PARIS, 15 June 1973, *In the Ardennes* (wash) FRF 11,800. PARIS, 19 Nov 1976, *Village, Evening* (wash with gouache, 6¾ x 8½ ins / 17 x 21.5 cm) FRF 27,000. LONDON, 23 Nov 1978, *Montorgueil Castle in Jersey* (1855, charcoal, Indian ink and coloured chalks, 10 x 7¾ ins / 25.5 x 20 cm) GBP 5,200. PARIS, 14 Nov 1980, *The Mythical Castle at Freudenburg* (1863, Indian ink wash, 8¼ x 13 ins / 21 x 33 cm) FRF 215,000. PARIS, 19 June 1981, *Town in the Middle Ages* (pen and brown wash heightened with white, 10½ x 6¾ ins / 26.5 x 17 cm) FRF 190,000. PARIS, 16 Nov 1983, *Chevet of a Gothic Chapel in the Heart of a City in the Nord, with Nocturnal Lighting Effects* (Indian ink wash heightened with watercolour, gilding, varnish and roughened areas/white-laid paper, 7 x 8¾ ins / 17.8 x 22.2 cm) FRF 235,000. PARIS, 28 June 1985, *Village by Moonlight* (1866, brown pen and grey wash, gouache and pencil, 14¼ x 11½ ins / 36 x 29.5 cm) FRF 150,000. PARIS, 18 March 1987, *Cart Drivers in a Storm* (pen and brown wash, 1 x 5 ins / 2.7 x 13 cm) FRF 60,000. PARIS, 24 June 1988, *The Tower of St-Rombaud de Malines in the Centre of an Imaginary Town* (1850, ink, wash, charcoal and gouache, 19 x 24¾ ins / 48 x 63 cm) FRF 720,000; *Planet* (pen and brown ink, brown ink wash, 12¼ x 14½ ins / 31 x 37 cm) FRF 400,000. PARIS, 17 March 1989, *Village* (1875, pen and Indian ink, 5¾ x 8¾ ins / 14.5 x 22.2 cm) FRF 72,000. NEW YORK, 22 May 1990, *Mythical Castle in a Landscape* (black ink wash, gold paint and brown ink heightened with coloured gouache, 7 x 9 ins / 17.7 x 22 cm) USD 68,200. PARIS, 22 June 1990, *Landscape in Guernsey* (1875, brown wash, 6¾ x 10 ins / 17 x 25.4 cm) FRF 135,000.

PARIS, 12 June 1991, *Mythical Castle* (brown ink wash and pen, 7 3/4 x 5 ins / 20 x 12.9 cm) FRF 280,000. PARIS, 18 June 1993, *Landscape* (ink and brown wash, 3 1/2 x 6 ins / 9 x 15 cm) FRF 72,000. PARIS, 29 April 1994, *Village on a Stormy Night* (ink and wash, 3 1/2 x 7 ins / 9 x 17.5 cm) FRF 132,000. PARIS, 27 May 1994, *Mythical Castle at Dusk* (1857, Indian ink wash, 12 1/4 x 18 ins / 31 x 46 cm) FRF 700,000. MONACO, 20 June 1994, *Block of Medieval Houses* (1866, ink and brown wash, 10 1/4 x 6 3/4 ins / 26 x 17 cm) FRF 288,600. BORDEAUX, 16 Feb 1995, *Ruined Castle* (ink and wash heightened with white gouache, 74 x 9 3/4 ins / 188 x 25 cm) FRF 43,000. PARIS, 1 Feb 1996, *Tall Trees* (ink and white gouache, 5 3/4 x 3 1/4 ins / 14.5 x 8.5 cm) FRF 30,000. PARIS, 22 Nov 1996, *Mythical Castles* (ink, 2 x 4 1/4 ins / 5 x 10.5 cm) FRF 23,100. PARIS, 11 June 1997, *Castle by the Sea* (1848, Indian ink wash and watercolour, 2 3/4 x 8 1/2 ins / 7 x 21.5 cm) FRF 145,000. PARIS, 15 Dec 1997, *Landscape at Dusk with Ray of Light and Solitary Cavalier* (pen and brown ink wash, 8 3/4 x 11 ins / 22.3 x 28 cm) FRF 8,800. PARIS, 29 Oct 1999, *The Château of the Lake* (1857, brown ink/brush, 10 x 15 ins / 26 x 38 cm) FRF 172,000. PARIS, 20 Nov 2000, *Landscape. Landscape Sketch: Souvenir of the Rhine* (pen/brown ink/charcoal, two in frame, 2 x 10 ins / 6 x 25 cm) FRF 150,000. PARIS, 29 Nov 2000, *River Landscape* (1867, pen/brown ink/wash, double-sided, 6 x 9 ins / 14 x 22 cm) FRF 230,000. PARIS, 17 Dec 2001, *Untitled* (1861, pen/wash/watercolour, 7 x 13 ins / 18 x 32 cm) FRF 220,000. PARIS, 19 Dec 2001, *Landscape with the Name 'Victor Hugo'* (pen/ink/watercolour, 4 x 7 ins / 11 x 17 cm) FRF 242,000. PARIS, 16 Oct 2002, *Nameless Town in Neckarsteinach* (1857, sepia wash, drawing, 19 x 12 ins / 49 x 31 cm) EUR 240,000. PARIS, 29 Nov 2002, *Souvenir of the Heath* (pen/ink/Indian ink, 9 x 13 ins / 24 x 32 cm) EUR 56,000. NEW YORK, 22 Jan 2004, *Castle Seen across a Lake* (1863, pen/brown ink/colour wash, 4 x 6 ins / 10 x 15 cm) USD 22,000. NEW YORK, 22 Jan 2004, *Ruins in an Imaginary Landscape* (pen/brown ink/wash, 4 x 10 ins / 9 x 26 cm) USD 80,000.

HUGO D'OIGNIES (Friar). See **HUGO**

HUGO DE LA MODE

Flemish School.

Glass painter, draughtsman. Religious subjects.

No details are known about Hugo de la Mode, whose pen and ink drawing heightened with white, *The Virgin Nursing the Child Jesus*, is held in Lille Museum.

MUSEUMS AND GALLERIES:

LILLE (MBA, Wicar Collection): *The Virgin Nursing the Child Jesus* (drawing).

HUGO DE PLALIACO

French, 13th century.

Sculptor.

Among Hugo's works is the tomb of Queen Ingeburg of Denmark, wife of Philippe-Auguste, in the monastery church of St-Jean-en-l'Isle, Corbeil.

HUGON, Jean Baptiste

French, 19th century.

Born 26 January 1797, in Lyons; died 24 July 1860, in Lyons.

Draughtsman, engraver.

Hugon produced a series of at least 25 landscape drawings and etchings, and also engraved his own portrait, after Duclaux.

HUGONIET, Guillaume

French, 15th century.

Active in Langres.

Miniaturist.

HUGONNET, Aloys

Swiss, 20th century.

Born 21 October 1879, in Morges (Vaud); died 1938.

Painter. Nudes, landscapes, flowers.

Aloys Hugonnet was a student of Fernand Cormon and Joseph Bail in Paris, where he exhibited at the Salon des Indépendants. He painted generously proportioned nudes, landscapes and flowers in thick, sensuous colours. He achieved a certain degree of renown in Switzerland as a Post-Impressionist. He was the first artist since Hodler to work in this traditional vein, which was barely affected by changes in taste and technical developments.

AUCTION RECORDS:

PARIS, 19 May 1920, *Retreat*, FRF 360. PARIS, 15 June 1945, *Retreat* (1904) FRF 700. ST-GERMAIN-EN-LAYE, 6 May 1979, *Young Woman with a Parasol near the Pont-Marie* (oil on canvas) FRF 7,600. ZURICH, 15 May 1982, *Waiting* (1908, oil on canvas, 51 1/4 x 37 1/2 ins / 130 x 95 cm) CHF 3,800. PARIS, 24 March 1988, *Casket* (1912, oil on canvas, 25 1/4 x 20 3/4 ins / 64 x 53 cm) FRF 8,000. ZURICH, 21 April 1993, *Bouquet of Flowers* (oil on canvas, 24 1/4 x 19 1/2 ins / 61.5 x 49.5 cm) CHF 1,800. AHLDEN, 20 May 2000, *Spring No. X* (1917, oil on canvas, 29 x 37 ins / 73 x 93 cm) DEM 4,000.

HUGOT, Édouard Charles

French, 19th century.

Born 6 February 1815, in Coulanges-la-Vineuse (Yonne).

Painter, watercolourist, lithographer. Genre scenes.

Édouard Hugot was taught by Thomas Couture, and specialised in genre painting. He exhibited at the Paris Salon from 1835 to 1880.

AUCTION RECORDS:

ENGHIEN-LES-BAINS, 7 Dec 1980, *The Meal* (1848, oil on canvas, 18 x 15 ins / 46 x 38 cm) FRF 15,000.

HUGOT, Étienne

French, 19th century.

Born 11 February 1808.

Engraver.

HUGOT, François

French, 18th century.

Active in Le Mans in 1777.

Painter.

HUGOT, Jules Jean Marie Joseph

French, 19th century.

Born in the 19th century, in Toulouse.

Engraver.

Jules Hugot was taught engraving by his father, Étienne Hugot. He made his Salon début in 1868.

HUGOT, Louis Ernest

French, 19th century.

Active in Paris.

Painter. Genre scenes.

Louis Hugot made his début at the Salon in 1879.

HUGOULIN, Émile

French, 19th century.

Born 8 April 1848, in Aix (Bouches-du-Rhône).

Sculptor.

Hugoulin was a pupil of A. Dumont. From 1876, he began exhibiting busts and sculptures on fantasy subjects at the Paris Salon. He won a second-class medal in 1876. Hugoulin also sculpted the medallions in the friezes on the lateral pavilions of the Musée de Toulon (Var), France.

HUGREL, Claude Honoré

French, 20th century.

Born 12 June 1880, in Mâcon; died 13 February 1944, in Mâcon.

Painter, pastellist. Animals.

AUCTION RECORDS:

LYONS, 28 Nov 1984, *Stream in the Snow* (1924, gouache, 28 x 35 3/4 ins / 71 x 91 cm) FRF 7,000. PARIS, 15 Feb 1985, *Shepherd and His Flock* (1929, gouache, 40 1/2 x 46 ins / 103 x 117 cm) FRF 8,000. PARIS, 27 April 1990, *Moor at Dusk* (1908, oil on panel, 23 1/2 x 28 ins / 60 x 71 cm) FRF 12,000. PARIS, 2 June 1997, *Spray on the Crests of the Saône* (1931, tempera heightened with pastels/panel, 22 3/4 x 27 1/2 ins / 58 x 70 cm) FRF 7,000. PARIS, 20 Oct 2000, *Stonemason* (oil on card, 37 x 29 ins / 93 x 73 cm) FRF 14,000. NICE, 28 March 2001, *White Goats* (pastel on card, 36 x 43 ins / 92 x 110 cm) FRF 21,000.

HUGREL, Pierre Honoré
French, 19th century.
Born 17 November 1827, in Paris.
Painter. Mythological subjects, portraits, architectural views.

Hugrel was a pupil of Charles Gleyre. He exhibited at the Paris Salon from 1850 to 1880, and won a medal in 1868.

MUSEUMS AND GALLERIES:
NICE (MBA): *Sacrifice to the God Pan.*

HUGUE, Piercequin
French, 15th century.
Sculptor (wood).

In 1448 the duke of Orléans commissioned Piercequin Hugue to carve ornamental woodwork for a ship.

HUGUELIN DE CHAMPDIVERS
French, 14th century.
Illuminator.

Huguelin de Champdivers illuminated *Les Grandes Heures* (*The Great Hours*) for the Duke of Touraine in 1387.

HUGUENET, Jacques Joseph
French, 19th century.
Born 25 July 1815, in Versailles.
Engraver (etching).

A pupil of Olivier, Huguenet won a third-class medal in 1853, and a second-class medal in 1855 (at the Exposition Universelle).

HUGUENIN
French, 15th century.
Born in Navarre.
Active in Lyons from 1452 to 1499.
Sculptor.

Huguenin made three statues for the gable above the façade of the church of St-Jean in Lyons. He was one of those who signed the statutes of the carvers, painters and glass painters of Lyons confirmed in 1496 by Charles VIII. There is some resemblance between Huguenin and Huguenin Bailly.

HUGUENIN, Alphonse Adrien
French, 19th century.
Born in Arbois (Jura).
Painter.

Alphonse Huguenin was taught by his father, Victor Huguenin, and exhibited at the Salon between 1866 and 1868.

HUGUENIN, Auguste
French, 20th century.
Born 5 May 1886, in the Haute-Saône.
Sculptor.

Auguste Huguenin exhibited regularly in Paris at the Salon des Artistes Français.

HUGUENIN, J. B.
French, 19th century.
Painter. Genre scenes.

MUSEUMS AND GALLERIES:
TOULOUSE: *Arab Cafe.*

HUGUENIN, Jacques
French, 16th century.
Active in Paris in 1586.
Painter.

HUGUENIN, Jean Pierre Victor
French, 19th century.
Born 21 February 1802, in Dôle; died 8 January 1860, in Paris.
Sculptor. Historical figures. Busts, statues, groups, medallions.

Jean Huguenin was the son of a musician. From 1818 to 1820 he studied in the studio of a master from Salins. He entered the École des Beaux-Arts in Dijon on 11 April 1825, where he became a pupil of Ramey the Younger, and remained there until 1829. Huguenin taught at the École d'Arbois, in the Jura region on the Swiss border, then in 1833 went on to teach at the École des Beaux-Arts in Besançon, before finally moving to Paris for good in 1835. He had regular work there: he started teaching at the St-Jacques Institution for Deaf Mutes in 1838, and received a number of state commissions. In the early part of his career he worked within the Romantic aesthetic of the time, favouring scenes from the life of medieval French sovereigns and monumental works. He then gradually adopted a more rigid academic style.

Huguenin exhibited busts, statues and groups at the Salon, from 1835 to 1859. The statue of *Valentine of Milan* in the Luxembourg Gardens is his.

In 2002 there was a retrospective exhibition of Huguenin's work at the Musée des Beaux-Arts in Dôle, eastern France.

BIBLIOGRAPHY:
Dotal, Christiane/Frelin, Virginie, *Victor Huguenin. Un sculpteur romantique*, exhibition catalogue, Musée des Beaux-Arts, Dole, 2002.

MUSEUMS AND GALLERIES:
ANGERS: *Charles VI and Odette de Champdivers* - BOURG: same subject - CAMBRAI: *Charles VI and Odette de Champdivers* - DÔLE (Musée des Beaux-Arts): *Charles VI and Odette de Champdivers* (1839, marble group); *Prometheus Tied to a Rock* (1825, group in plaster); *General Delort* (bronze bust); *General Bonaparte* (c. 1840-1841, plaster, medallion) - LILLE: *Hebe* - LONS-LE-SAUNIER (Musée des Beaux-Arts): *Antide Janvier* (1836, marble bust) - VERSAILLES: *Marble Bust of Rameau the Musician*; *Bust of Brigadier Jean Rambures.*

HUGUENIN, Oscar
Swiss, 19th century.
Born 18 December 1842, in La Sagne; died 13 February 1903, in Boudry (Vaud).
Painter, draughtsman, writer.

After careers as a joiner and primary school teacher, Huegenin became a self-taught artist. The war of 1871 furnished him with subjects for numerous drawings. He caught the attention of the painter Léon Berthoud, who gave him advice. Huguenin wrote works that he illustrated with very conscientious pen drawings. He also did oil portraits and landscapes that are interesting for their sincerity.

MUSEUMS AND GALLERIES:
NEUCHÂTEL (MAH): 15 drawings illustrating the artist's texts.

HUGUENIN, Paul
Swiss, 19th - 20th century.
Born 18 September 1870, in Le Locle.
Painter, watercolourist, illustrator. Landscapes.

Hugenin settled in La Tour-de-Peilz. He travelled a great deal in Italy, the Netherlands, Germany, and as far as Polynesia.

HUGUENIN, Pierre
French, 20th century.
Born in Nice.
Painter.

Pierre Hugenin's painting is abstract, composed of simple, geometric planes and volumes. He uses colour to enlarge the visual field of the canvas. From 1947, he exhibited in the provinces and in Paris, where in 1948 he took part in the Salon de la Jeune Peinture, in 1969 the Salon Terres Latines and in 1970 the Salon Comparaisons.

HUGUENIN-LASSANGUETTE, Fritz Édouard
Swiss, 19th - 20th century.
Born in Neuchâtel.
Painter. Landscapes.

Hugeunin-Lassanguette was the father of Paul Hugeunin.

MUSEUMS AND GALLERIES:
GENEVA (MAH): *Landscape with Animals* - NEUCHÂTEL: *Autumn in Chatelot; The Banks of the Doubs beneath Saut.*

AUCTION RECORDS:
GENEVA, 1 Nov 1984, *Farmworkers' Return, Anniviers Valley* (oil on canvas, 34 1/4 x 50 1/2 ins / 87 x 128 cm) CHF 5,500. PARIS, 14 Feb 1990, *Léman Landscape* (oil on canvas, 19 x 28 3/4 ins / 48.5 x 73 cm) FRF 23,000.

HUGUENIN-PANCHAUD, Augustin
Swiss, 19th century.
Born c. 1806, in Vaud canton.
Miniaturist, lithographer.

He worked in Geneva.

HUGUENIN-VIRCHAUX, Henri Édouard
Swiss, 20th century.
Born 1878, in Le Locle (Neuchâtel); died 1958, in Brig.
Active in Portugal and in France.
Sculptor.

MUSEUMS AND GALLERIES:
LAUSANNE (Cantonal MFA): *Soul of a Child (Head of a Little Girl)* (1912).

HUGUENIOT, Guillaume. See **HUGONIET Guillaume**

HUGUENOT, family of artists
French, 17th - 18th century.
Active in Lyons.
Painters.

Émilien Huguenot, born around 1654, registered in Lyons to be taken into the Charité hospital. Jean Huguenot was a master painter in 1717.

HUGUENY, Jean
French, 18th - 19th century.
Born 6 March 1768, in Mulhouse; died 6 June 1817, in Mulhouse.
Draughtsman.

MUSEUMS AND GALLERIES:
MULHOUSE: drawings.

HUGUENY, Laurent Joseph
French, 18th - 19th century.
Born 9 May 1767, in Valenciennes; died 17 September 1814, in Valenciennes.
Painter. Self-portraits.

MUSEUMS AND GALLERIES:
VALENCIENNES: *Self-portrait.*

HUGUES
Swiss, 15th - 16th century.
Active in Geneva c. 1500.
Painter.

Hugues worked at the court of Savoy from 1499 to 1511.

HUGUES, Dominique Jean Baptiste
French, 19th - 20th century.
Born 15 April 1849, in Marseilles; died 28 October 1930.
Sculptor.

Hugues studied with Dumont and Bonassieux. He made his début at the Salon de Paris in 1878. He won the Prix de Rome in 1875, a third-class medal in 1878, a second-class medal in 1881, a first-class medal in 1882 and gold medals in 1889 and 1900 at the Expositions Universelles. He was named Chevalier, then Officier of the Légion d'Honneur.

BIBLIOGRAPHY:
Noet, Laurent, *Jean-Baptiste Hugues: un sculpteur sous la IIIe république*, catalogue raisonné, Thélès, Paris, 2002.

MUSEUMS AND GALLERIES:
PARIS (Louvre): *Œdipus at Colonna.*

HUGUES, E. P.
British, 20th century.
Painter.

E.P. Hughes was a member of the Royal Drawing Society.

HUGUES, Edouard
British, 19th century.
Active in England.
Painter. Genre scenes, landscapes.

Edouard Hugues is cited by *Art Prices Current.* He is probably the same artist as Edward Hughes.

AUCTION RECORDS:
LONDON, 7 March 1910, *Light-Hearted Chatter in Papa's Studio,* GBP 4. LONDON, 11 Feb 1911, *The Love Song* (1897) GBP 6.

HUGUES, Jean
Flemish, 15th century.
Active in Hesdin.
Painter.
Flemish School.

Jean Hugues was the son of Hugues de Boulogne.

HUGUES, Jeanne-Michèle
French, 20th century.
Born 25 September 1920, in Paris.
Painter. Urban landscapes, seascapes, landscapes.

After her secondary studies, Jeanne-Michèle Hugues attended the École des Arts Décoratifs from 1939. She paints in oil with a knife, using almost exclusively horizontal and vertical strokes. She received many distinctions, including the following: from 1967 until 1995, secretary-general of the Fédération des Associations d'Artistes Plasticiens Auprès des Pouvoirs Publics; from 1970, member of the presidency of the France-Czechoslovakia and France-Hungary committees; in 1977, vice-president of the Salon des Indépendants; 1980, member of the French committee of UNESCO's international association for fine art; 1980, silver-gilt medal from the city of Paris; 1983, the Taylor Foundation prize; 1991, after several years as vice-president, president of the Salon d'Automne (elected honorary president in 1995); 1991, after several years as Chevalier, promoted to Officier in the Ordre National du Mérite; Chevalier, then in 1996, Officier, of the Légion d'Honneur. Her work has been purchased by the French government, the city of Paris, and in municipalities and regions both in France and abroad. From 1956, she participated in numerous collective exhibitions in France, Europe, the USA, the Middle East and Japan. Most notably, she exhibited in Paris from 1957, at the Salon des Indépendants from 1960; at the Salon d'Automne from 1962 (where a homage was paid to her in 1983); at the Salon des Peintres Témoins de leur Temps; at the Salon du Dessin et de la Peinture à l'Eau; at the Salon Comparaisons; at the Salon de la Société Nationale des Beaux-Arts, and at the Salon de la Marine. Her first solo exhibition was in Paris in 1956, followed by numerous others in Paris, the provinces and abroad.

HUGUES, Lucile
French, 19th - 20th century.
Painter.

Lucile Hugues lived and worked in Dammarie-les-Lys. In Paris, she became a member of the Salon des Artistes Français in 1904.

HUGUES, Patrice
French, 20th century.
Born 10 April 1930, in Courbevoie.
Painter, sculptor, designer. Designs for mosaics, stained glass windows.

In 1946, Patrice Hugues frequented the studio of Fernand Léger in Montrouge, while attaining a teaching qualification in history. From 1955 to 1959 he taught in Nantes. As a painter, Hugues has attracted attention mostly for a series on *Cemeteries of Cars*. In 1965, he executed a monumental sculpture in cement and glass flagstones in Hennebont. In 1966, he executed a mosaic for the gymnasium in Épinay-sur-Seine, and in 1968, a monumental motif in polychromed polyester in Notre-Dame de Gravenchon in Normandy, decorative works for schools in Harfleur and Le Havre, and a stained glass window for the Hôtel-de-Ville in Le Havre. He exhibited as a painter in Paris at the Salon de la Jeune Peinture, the Salon d'Automne and the Salon des Indépendants. His first solo exhibition of paintings was in Nantes. He took up sculpture in 1965. As such, he participated regularly in the Salon de la Jeune Sculpture and Salon Comparaisons, and showed at the São Paulo Biennale. In 1968, he had a solo exhibition of his sculptures in Paris, another at the Musée du Havre, and in 1969 at the Maison des Jeunes in Colombes. From 1966 to 1969, he was curator at the Musée du Havre.

HUGUES, Paul Jean
French, 20th century.
Born 6 March 1891, in Paris.
Painter, pastellist. Interiors with figures.

Hugues was a student of Fernand Cormon and Henri Royer. He exhibited regularly in Paris at the Salon des Artistes Français, of which he became a member in 1923. He was named *hors concours* from 1925. He also exhibited at the Salon des Tuileries. He was a member of various associations.

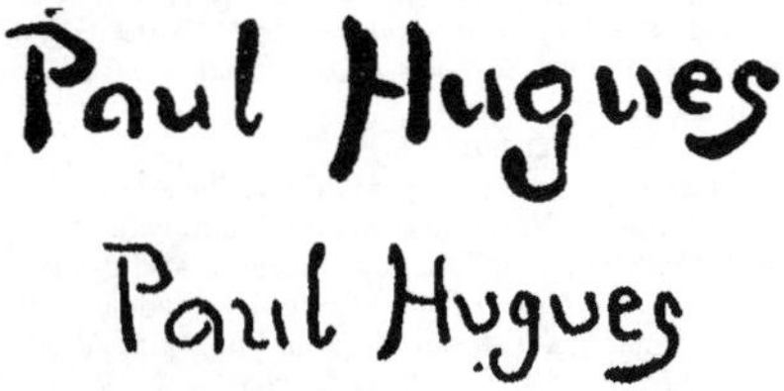

MUSEUMS AND GALLERIES:
AVIGNON - BELFORT - DIJON - LE MANS - PARIS (Mus. du Petit Palais) - TOURCOING.

AUCTION RECORDS:
PARIS, 21 Nov 1980, *Interior of Ruhlmann* (1922, oil on canvas, $17\frac{1}{4}$ x $13\frac{1}{2}$ ins / 44 x 34 cm) FRF 1,300. PARIS, 2 Dec 1991, *Interior* (pastel and gouache, $14\frac{1}{2}$ x $17\frac{1}{4}$ ins / 37 x 44 cm) FRF 3,700. LONDON, 17 Nov 1995, *Lounge Interior* (pastel, 18 x 21 ins / 44.8 x 53.3 cm) GBP 2,300. LOS ANGELES, 15 Sept 1999, *Convenient Interior* (c. 1920, oil on canvas, 18 x 15 ins / 46 x 38 cm) USD 4,800. LONDON, 10 April 2000, *Interior* (oil on canvas, 18 x 15 ins / 46 x 38 cm) GBP 1,700. PARIS, 22 April 2001, *Scene of Interior* (oil on canvas, 22 x 18 ins / 55 x 46 cm) FRF 24,000. PARIS, 5 July 2002, *Salon* (oil on canvas, 21 x 26 ins / 54 x 65 cm) EUR 2,500. CAMBRIDGE, 16 Nov 2003, *Interior* (oil on canvas, 16 x 13 ins / 41 x 33 cm) USD 3,500. CHELTENHAM, 26 Feb 2004, *Salon Interiors* (oil on canvas, a pair, 21 x 24 ins / 53 x 61 cm) GBP 3,800. LONDON, 14 July 2004, *Study of an Interior* (oil on canvas, 22 x 19 ins / 55 x 47 cm) GBP 1,800.

HUGUES, Stephen
British, 20th - 21st century.
Born 30 December 1957, in Harare, Zimbabwe.
Sculptor.

Stephen Hugues studied at Goldsmith's College, London, from 1984 to 1987. He assisted Richard Deacon from 1990 to 1992. His work is an invitation to go on a journey of discovery, to plunge into the depths of sealed containers or carefully wrought wooden boxes that are crying out to be opened. Inside, one discovers all sorts of brightly coloured dismantalable polyethylene toys, but these cannot be removed from their wrapping without destroying them. In 1993, he created new objects, piles of letters made of black and white polystyrene, glued together randomly. They invite the viewer to decipher them but convey a sense of unreadability. Hugues has taken part in group exhibitions since 1985 in London and Paris. He has also shown his work in solo exhibitions, notably in London, and in Paris at the Galerie Philippe Casini.

BIBLIOGRAPHY:
Dagbert, Anne, '*Stephen Hugues*' in *Art Press* n° 158, periodical, Paris, June 1991. Van Caeneghem, Marie Odile, '*Stephen Hugues - lettres plastiques*' in *Opus international* n° 132, periodical, Paris, autumn 1993.

HUGUES, Victor Louis
French, 19th century.
Born 30 June 1827, in Bordeaux.
Painter.

Hugues was a pupil of Gleyre. He exhibited landscapes and a few genre subjects at the Paris Salon, from 1859 to 1879, and is chiefly known for views of the environs of Paris and Normandy.

AUCTION RECORDS:
PARIS, 27 and 28 Dec 1926, *Bathers* (two) FRF 310. PARIS, 28 and 29 Nov 1940, *Pygmalion in Love with His own Statue*, FRF 2,000.

HUGUES DE BOULOGNE, or Hue de Boulogne
Flemish, 15th century.
Active in Hesdin.
Painter.
Flemish School.

Hugues de Boulogne worked for the dukes of Burgundy, especially Philip the Good, mainly in Hesdin. He was 'painter and controller of the clock, jails, glass windows and entertainment machinery at the said castle of Hesdin'. His name occurs in the duke's account books from 1417 to 1449.

HUGUES DE GAND. See **GOES Hugo van der**

HUGUES-ROYANNEZ, Jeanne Clovis (Mme)
French, 19th century.
Born 5 November 1855, in Paris.
Sculptor.

Jeanne Hugues-Royannez became a member of the Société des Artistes Français in 1888. She was a pupil of L. Coutan-Montorgueil.

HUGUET
French, 16th century.
Active in Châlons.
Sculptor, architect.

Together with Simon Avigny and Jean Lecomte, Huguet made a stone pulpit which was installed in the Augustinian monastery in 1535. In 1550 a Hugues Lallemant carved the wooden doors for the south entrance of the cathedral and two chimneypieces which are now in the Cluny museum, one bearing a *Diana Surprised by Actaeon* and the other a *Jesus at the Well*. Huguet and Hugues Lallemant are probably identical.

MUSEUMS AND GALLERIES:
CLUNY (MAA): two chimneypieces.

HUGUET, A.
French, 19th century.
Painter. Military subjects.

This artist painted military subjects; the Musée de Pontoise has a painting by him, which is signed and dated 1844.
MUSEUMS AND GALLERIES:
PONTOISE: *Episode from the Conquest of Algeria, with an Injured Soldier* (1844).

HUGUET, Antonio

Spanish, 15th century.
Active during the second half of the 15th century in Barcelona.
Painter.
The brother of Jaime Huguet the Elder, he collaborated with him in making large retables.

HUGUET, Claude

French, 18th century.
Active in Paris in 1775.
Painter, sculptor.

HUGUET, Fanny Françoise (Mme)

Maiden name: Lecomte
French, 19th century.
Born 10 March 1809, in Paris.
Landscape painter.
Fanny Huguet was taught by her father, Hippolyte Lecomte, and also by Watelet.
She exhibited at the Salon from 1833 to 1839.

HUGUET, Jaime, the Younger

Spanish, 16th century.
Active in Crexa in 1571.
Painter.
In 1572, Jaime Huguet the Younger was living in Bari, Italy.

HUGUET, Jaime or Jaume, the Elder

Spanish, 15th century.
Born c. 1415, in Valls (Tarragona); died 1492, in Barcelona.
Painter.
Catalan School.
Jaime Huguet the Elder was brought up by his uncle Pedro Huguet, a minor painter who worked in the cathedral in Barcelona, and there is no doubt that he was apprenticed to Martorell between 1435 and 1440. With him, Huguet may have learned the technique of tempera to which he remained attached, working in a style that takes no account of what was happening in Flemish art. Between 1440 and 1447, Huguet was in Aragon; he settled in Saragossa and worked for small neighbouring churches.

The altarpiece *Cervera de la Cañada* and the *Alloza* triptych, which are attributed to him, date from the Saragossa period, as does the *St George* retable, a delicate work with elongated, melancholic figures, in which the colours mixed with white take on an opaque quality. The modelling here is extremely delicate. However, his style was soon to change, and the *Epiphany* is a transitional painting that emphasises the rich garments of the figures. About 1448, Huguet went to Barcelona and opened a workshop that several painters joined, including his brother Antonio, Miguel Nadal and Pedro Ramirez. He began a collaboration with the Vergos family that gave his painting a more decorative aspect which would later weigh down his works. About 1450, he carried out the *St Vincent of Sarrià* retable, only the central panel of which is his. With this piece, new elements enter his art, which broadens and becomes more balanced, begins to make use of a great deal of gold, and depicts with some coarseness and in a rather dry style certain popular characters. In 1455, Huguet began a long series of retables that always involved the assistance of other artists. These include the retables of *St Anthony the Abbot* (1455-1458), no longer extant, and of *St Abdon and St Senen* (1459-1460), which is gently modelled and balanced in its colour composition, but which has a gold background that only allows a small landscape to peep through. In 1462, he carried out commissions for the chamber of commerce, the skinners and the guild of the Holy Spirit. Then came the retables of *St Bernard and the Angel, Constable Don Pedro of Portugal* (1465), and finally *St Augustine*, which had originally been commissioned from Luis Dalmau and was finished in 1487. All these retables are rich, grandiose, and loaded with gold, inlaid work and gilded reliefs. They announce the end of an artistic era. Jaime Huguet swings between a style that is delicate, gently modelled, but always underpinned by precise drawing that accentuates the forms, and an art brilliant with gilding, reliefs and colour, though the latter is toned down by his tempera technique. His painting is often harmed by the number of artists he involved in it, and makes no concessions to newfangled foreign techniques.

Jaime Huguet has been represented in two thematic exhibitions: in 2002, *The Age of Jan Van Eyck: the Mediterranean world of early Netherlandish painting, 1430-1530* at the Groeninge museum, Bruges, and in 2003 *La pintura gótica hispano flamenca: Bartolomé Bermejo y su época* (*Hispano-Flemish Gothic Painting. Bartolomé Bermejo and His Time*) at the Museu Nacional d'Art de Catalunya in Barcelona. There was a solo exhibition of his work at the Valls Museum in 1993.
BIBLIOGRAPHY:
Rowland, Benjamin, *Jaime Huguet, a Study of Late Gothic Painting in Catalonia*, Harvard University Press, Cambridge (MA), 1932. Ricart, Jose Gudiol/Ainaud de Lasarte, Juan, *Huguet*, Barcelona, 1948. Molina i Figueras, Joan, *Jaume Huguet*, Historia 16, Madrid, 1992. Jardi, Eulàlia (ed.), *Jaume Huguet: 500 anys*, exhibition catalogue, Museu de Valls, 1993 (includes proceedings from the 1992 symposium). Borchert, T., *The Age of Jan Van Eyck: the Mediterranean world of early Netherlandish painting, 1430 - 1530*, exhibition catalogue, Groeningemuseum, Bruges, Thames and Hudson, London, 2002. *Hispano-Flemish Gothic Painting. Bartolomé Bermejo and his time*, group exhibition catalogue, Museu Nacional d'Art de Catalunya, Barcelona, 2003 (Spanish, Catalan and English edition).
MUSEUMS AND GALLERIES:
BARCELONA (Cathedral): *St Bernard and the Angel Retable* - BARCELONA (Mus. Nacional d'Art de Catalunya): *St Augustine Retable; St Vincent Retable; St George and the Princess Retable* - BARCELONA (Palace of Santa Agueda): *Constable Retable* - TERRASSA (Church of Santa Maria): *St Abdon and St Senen Retable* - VIC: *Epiphany Retable.*

HUGUET, Jean

French, 20th century.
Born 1934, in Levroux (Indre).
Painter.
Jean Huguet studied in Bourges and in Paris. He sometimes uses chalk. He uses elementary forms to try to capture reality with a limited palette of colours. In 1962, he participated in a collective exhibition at the Musée des Arts et Traditions Populaires in Paris. He has also shown at exhibitions at the Musée Cantini in Marseilles, in Florence, in Tours and at the Maison de la Culture in Bourges.

HUGUET, Jean Charles, the Elder

French, 19th century.
Born 6 November 1815, in Paris.
Engraver.
A pupil of Olivier and Hibon, Jean Huguet exhibited at the Salon between 1857 and 1861. He gave up engraving, and went to Antwerp to work as a restorer.

HUGUET, Jean François (fils)

French, 18th century.
Born 29 December 1679, in Rennes; died 7 July 1749, in Rennes.
Draughtsman. Landscapes, architectural views. Maps.

Jean François Huguet fils worked all his life in Rennes and produced views of buildings as well as plans.

HUGUET, Michel
French, 20th century.
Born 12 December 1934, in Maurepas (Yvelines).
Painter, watercolourist, collage artist.
Nouvelle Figuration.

From 1953 to 1973, Michel Huguet was a bank employee. Self-taught, he has been painting since 1958, and has also taught, including at the municipal Atelier in Bagneux. The human figure is omnipresent in Huguet's work, represented by deformed faces and abused bodies, with an abstractly coloured décor. He divides the canvas into various scenes or moments that are unexpected and full of humour. His figuration is nonetheless freed from all convention, and retains the freshness of childhood. He has taken part in collective exhibitions such as the Biennale d'Arts Plastiques in Gennevilliers (1965, 1968 and 1970) and the Salon d'Arts Plastiques in Bagneux (1975, 1986 and 1988). He has held solo exhibitions at the Galerie Edouard Manet in Gennevilliers (1975 and 1976) and the Galerie Sud, Centre Culturel Communal, in Bagneux (1990).

BIBLIOGRAPHY:
Huguet, exhibition catalogue, Gal. sud, Centre culturel communal, Bagneux, 1990.

HUGUET, Pedro
Spanish, 15th century.
Painter.

It was once thought that he was the father of Jaime Huguet the Elder, but it seems that in fact he was his uncle. He worked in the cathedral in Barcelona between 1434 and 1448.

HUGUET, Victor Pierre
French, 19th century.
Born 1 May 1835, in Le Lude (Sarthe); died 16 August 1902, in Paris.
Painter, watercolourist. Local scenes, landscapes. Orientalism.

This artist studied in Marseilles under the direction of the painter Émile Loubon. At the age of 17 he visited Egypt, then in 1853 accompanied Durand Brager to Crimea, just before the siege of Sebastopol. He also travelled to Algeria, and what he saw on this trip became the subject for many of his paintings. In 1859 he exhibited *Lavoir in Provence* and *Cairo during the Flood* at the Paris Salon. In 2001 his work was featured in the exhibition *Les Peintres et la Sarthe* (*Painters and the Sarthe Region*) at the Musée de la Reine Bérengère (for the 19th-century works) and at Épau Abbey (20th-century works) in Le Mans.

Even early on in his career, Huguet's works were highly sought after by art lovers, and have lost nothing of their value today. He liked to introduce horses into his Orientalist paintings. Over the years, his technique gradually became more Impressionist, and his colours grew progressively brighter.

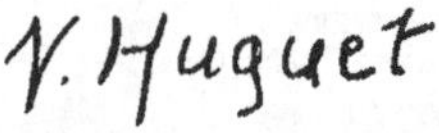

BIBLIOGRAPHY:
Thornton, Lynne, *La Femme dans la peinture orientaliste*, ACR Édition, Courbevoie, 1985 (text in French and English).
Arpentinier, Jean, *Sarthe, terre d'artistes*, Éd. de la Reinette, Le Mans, 2001.

MUSEUMS AND GALLERIES:
ALGIERS: *Landscape* - ROUEN: *Arab Cavalrymen*.

AUCTION RECORDS:
PARIS, 8 May 1900, *Arab Cavalrymen Taking a Break*, FRF 600. PARIS, 16 May 1900, *Biskra*, FRF 850. PARIS, 21 June 1900, *Caravan*, FRF 1,050. NEW YORK, Dec 1900, *Bedouin Camp*, USD 500. PARIS, 29 April 1901, *Bathing the Horses*, FRF 705. NEW YORK, 1902, *Caravan en Route to Algiers*, USD 750. PARIS, 1 March 1902, *Caravan Crossing a Wadi*, FRF 1,500. PARIS, 14-15 May 1902, *Arab Camp*, FRF 340. NEW YORK, 9-10 Feb 1905, *Arab Falconers*, USD 500. PARIS, 8 May 1905, *Fountain*, FRF 340. NEW YORK, 4 Jan 1907, *Arabs Bathing Their Horses*, USD 400. PARIS, 4 Feb 1919, *Taking a Break*, FRF 460. PARIS, 6-7 May 1920, *Bathing the Horses near Algiers*, FRF 1,980. PARIS, 10 Dec 1920, *Bathing the Horses on the Beach (Algeria)*, FRF 1,200. PARIS, 18 April 1921, *Arabs on the Move, Crossing a Ford*, FRF 1,250. PARIS, 20 Nov 1925, *Market at Sinop*, FRF 1,800. NEW YORK, 30 Jan 1930, *Arab Scene*, USD 1,100. PARIS, 20 Feb 1942, *Arabs Taking a Break*, FRF 3,800. NEW YORK, 31 Jan 1946, *Caravan of Emigrants*, USD 200. PARIS, July 1946, *At the Oasis, North Africa*, FRF 9,100; *Washerwomen by a Riverbank* (watercolour) FRF 2,050. PARIS, 8 Nov 1946, *Algerian Landscape*, FRF 15,000. PARIS, 17 March 1950, *Travelling on a Dromedary*, FRF 13,800. PARIS, 19 May 1954, *Hunting Falcon*, FRF 37,500. NEW YORK, 28 Feb 1968, *Arab Caravan*, USD 1,100. LONDON, 22 July 1971, *Arab Woman* (1871) Gns 300. VERSAILLES, 18 March 1973, *Camel Driver near an Arab Town*, FRF 3,400. PARIS, 6 Nov 1974, *Crossing the Ford*, FRF 6,500. PARIS, 17 June 1976, *View of Alcantara* (oil on canvas, 14 1/4 x 19 1/4 ins / 36 x 49 cm) FRF 2,500. LONDON, 3 Nov 1977, *Caravan* (oil on canvas, 39 x 31 ins / 99 x 78.7 cm) GBP 1, 700. LONDON, 9 May 1979, *Falcon Hunting* (1871, oil on canvas, 30 3/4 x 42 1/4 ins / 78 x 107 cm) GBP 5,000. LONDON, 20 March 1981, *Arabs in the Desert* (oil on canvas, 22 x 34 1/2 ins / 56 x 87.5 cm) GBP 4,500. ENGHIEN-LES-BAINS, 16 Oct 1983, *Cavalrymen outside a Mosque* (oil on panel, 18 x 15 ins / 46 x 38 cm) FRF 110,000. MONTEVIDEO, 14 Aug 1986, *Entrance to Medina* (oil on canvas, 25 1/2 x 41 1/4 ins / 65 x 105 cm) UYU 2,305,500. PARIS, 6 May 1988, *Arab Cavalrymen Resting beneath the Trees* (oil on canvas, 16 1/4 x 11 ins / 41 x 27 cm) FRF 34,000. PARIS, 17 June 1988, *Arab Cavalrymen Setting off* (oil on panel, 14 3/4 x 18 ins / 37.5 x 46 cm) FRF 29,000. VERSAILLES, 5 March 1989, *Arabs and Cavalrymen near the Coast* (oil on canvas, 26 1/4 x 33 3/4 ins / 66.5 x 86 cm) FRF 66,500. LONDON, 21 June 1989, *Resting at the Caravanserai* (oil on panel, 15 1/4 x 11 1/2 ins / 39 x 29 cm) GBP 4,180. NEW YORK, 24 Oct 1989, *Caravan Crossing a Bridge* (oil on canvas, 21 1/4 x 25 3/4 ins / 54 x 65.4 cm) USD 9,350. PARIS, 8 Dec 1989, *Camp* (oil on panel, 14 1/4 x 19 1/2 ins / 36.5 x 49.5 cm) FRF 75,000. PARIS, 14 March 1990, *Horses Resting* (oil on panel, 12 1/2 x 9 1/2 ins / 32 x 24 cm) FRF 17,000. PARIS, 6 April 1990, *Arab Cavalrymen Watering Their Horses in a River* (oil on canvas, 25 3/4 x 33 3/4 ins / 65.5 x 86 cm) FRF 122,000. NEW YORK, 23 May 1991, *Arab Women by a Watering Place* (oil on canvas, 25 1/2 x 33 1/2 ins / 64.7 x 85 cm) USD 10,450. PARIS, 19 Nov 1991, *Large Caravan in the Desert* (oil on canvas, 39 1/4 x 32 ins / 100 x 81 cm) FRF 300,000. LONDON, 18 March 1992, *Crossing the Wadi* (oil on panel, 14 3/4 x 18 ins / 37.5 x 46 cm) GBP 5,500. NEW YORK, 14 Oct 1993, *Arab Cavalryman at a Watering Place* (oil on canvas, 42 1/2 x 32 ins / 108 x 81.2 cm) USD 25,300. CALAIS, 12 Dec 1993, *Cavalrymen Taking a Break* (oil on panel, 6 1/4 x 10 1/4 ins / 16 x 26 cm) FRF 15,500. LONDON, 17 June 1994, *Mountain Trail* (1869, oil on panel, 23 1/4 x 31 1/2 ins / 59.1 x 80 cm) GBP 21,850. NEW YORK, 1 Nov 1995, *Arab Cavalrymen* (oil on panel, 14 3/4 x 18 ins / 37.5 x 45.7 cm) USD 6,900. PARIS, 11 Dec 1995, *Crossing the Wadi* (oil on panel, 14 3/4 x 18 ins / 37.5 x 46 cm) FRF 42,000. PARIS, 9 Dec 1996, *At the Water Trough* (oil on panel, 18 x 14 3/4 ins / 46 x 37.5 cm) FRF 38,000. LONDON, 21 March 1997, *Watering the Horses* (oil on panel, 14 3/4 x 18 ins / 37.5 x 45.5 cm) GBP 5,060. PARIS, 10-11 June 1997, *Camp* (oil on panel, 12 1/2 x 16 1/4 ins / 32 x 41 cm) FRF 29,500; *Taking a Break by the Side of a Wadi* (oil on panel, 14 3/4 x 18 ins / 37.4 x 46 cm) FRF 50,000. PARIS, 17 Nov 1997, *Tribe on the Move* (1864, oil on panel, 19 3/4 x 32 3/4 ins / 50 x

83 cm) FRF 52,000. Paris, 5 Feb 1998, *Horses* (oil on panel, with a sketch of a town on the back, 12 1/2 x 9 1/4 ins / 31.5 x 23.5 cm) FRF 6,000. Paris, 8 March 1999, *Meeting beside a Wadi* (oil on panel, 15 x 18 ins / 38 x 46 cm) FRF 65,000. Paris, 29 Nov 1999, *Halt at the Spring* (oil on canvas, 18 x 6 ins / 46 x 16 cm) FRF 130,000. London, 22 June 2000, *Arabs at the River's Edge* (oil on panel, 15 x 18 ins / 38 x 46 cm) GBP 3,800. London, 22 June 2000, *Arab Horsemen* (oil on canvas, 26 x 36 ins / 65 x 92 cm) GBP 4,200. Paris, 18 June 2001, *View of Cairo during a Flood* (1859, oil on canvas, 22 x 33 ins / 57 x 84 cm) FRF 72,000. Calais, 1 July 2001, *Halt of Bedouins at a Well* (1863, oil on canvas, 13 x 18 ins / 34 x 45 cm) FRF 65,000. Paris, 12 Feb 2002, *Caravan* (c. 1895, oil on canvas, 52 x 80 ins / 131 x 202 cm) EUR 82,000. Paris, 24 June 2002, *Market Scene before Ramparts* (oil on canvas, 26 x 42 ins / 66 x 106 cm) EUR 58,000. Paris, 16 June 2003, *Falcon Hunting* (oil on canvas, 23 x 28 ins / 59 x 72 cm) EUR 30,000. Paris, 12 Dec 2003, *Sandstorm* (oil on canvas/wood, 14 x 17 ins / 35 x 44 cm) EUR 5,800. Neuilly, 9 April 2004, *The Halt of the Horsemen* (oil on canvas, 9 x 13 ins / 24 x 32 cm) EUR 4,800. Paris, 3 June 2004, *Horseman before a Large Gate* (oil on canvas, 24 x 16 ins / 60 x 40 cm) EUR 9,000.

HUGUET-MOLINE, A.
French, 19th century.
Born 1815, in Alès.
Painter. Figures.
Museums and Galleries:
Sète: *Study of a Head.*

HUGUETI, John
British, 15th century.
Illuminator.

HUGWARTH, Élias
French, 17th century.
Active in Strasbourg.
Painter.
Élias Hugwarth was apprenticed to Brendel.

HUHN, Friedrich Wilhelm
German, 19th century.
Born 1821, in Thorn (West Prussia).
Painter.
He worked in Danzig (Gdansk) and exhibited in Berlin.

HUHN, Karl Theodor Fidorovitch
Livonian, 19th century.
Born 1 December 1830, in Sissegal (Livonia); died 28 January 1877, in Davos.
Painter. History painting.
He was a member of staff at the academy in St Petersburg. Stylistically, he was an imitator of Paul Delaroche. He exhibited in Vienna from 1872.

HUHSIEN. See **HUXIAN peasant painters of**

HUI-CH'UNG. See **HUI-CHONG**

HUI-CHONG, or Hui-ch'ung
Chinese, 11th century.
Born in Jianyang (Fujian).
Active at the beginning of the 9th century.
Painter. Animals, landscapes with figures.
Hui-chong was a monk and is known for his small landscapes and waterfowl paintings. The poet Su Dongpo (1036-1101) wrote a poem about one of his works.
Museums and Galleries:
Beijing (Palace Mus.): *Spring Dawn on Streams and Mountains* (handscroll, poems by the Qing Emperor Qianlong, colophons by Dong Qichang and other Ming Dynasty connoisseurs) - Taipei (National Palace Mus.): *Two Mandarin Ducks by an Autumn Stream* (ink and colours on paper, album sheet, seal of the artist Shen Zhou (1427-1509), attributed); *Two Geese on a Bank* (painting, fan).

HUI-TSUNG. See **HUIZONG**

HUIAN GIAN, Gian
Chinese, 19th - 20th century.
Born 1833; died 1910.
Painter.
Auction records:
Hong Kong, 19 May 1988, *Dragon* (1895, ink on paper, kakemono, 42 x 18 1/2 ins / 106.5 x 47 cm) HKD 22,000.

HUIDEKOPER, Christiaan
Dutch, 20th century.
Born 2 June 1878, in Groningen; died 1939.
Painter. Figures, interiors.
Huidekoper studied in Amsterdam and travelled in the Netherlands and Italy.
Auction records:
Amsterdam, 9 Dec 1992, *Spanish Countryfolk* (1907, oil on card, 14 x 11 ins / 35.6 x 27.7 cm) NLG 1,783.

HUIDOBRO LAPLANA, Luis
Spanish, 19th - 20th century.
Born 12 December 1870, in Madrid; died 1936.
Painter, sculptor. Nudes, genre scenes, landscapes, landscapes with figures.
Luis Huidobro Laplana was a self-taught artist. He painted various subjects, but the qualities of his composition are most obvious in his hilly landscapes with figures of peasants working the land or shepherds with their flocks.

Huidobro Laplana took part in many group exhibitions, including the Exposición Nacional de Bellas Artes from 1897 to 1932. He was awarded honourable mentions in 1904 and 1906, a bronze medal in 1910, silver in 1912, and bronze for decorative arts in 1913. In 1908, he won a medal at the Hispano-French Exhibition in Zaragoza. He was decorated in 1920.
Bibliography:
Arnáiz, José Manuel/López Jiménez, Javier/Merchán Díaz, Manuel (ed.), *Cien años de pintura en Espana y Portugal (1830-1930)*, Antiqvaria, Madrid, 1989.
Museums and Galleries:
Madrid (Mus. de Arte Moderno).

HUIGENS. See **LUCAS van LEYDEN**

HUIJSUM, van. See **HUYSUM**

HUILLARD, Esther
French, 19th - 20th century.
Born in Sedan.
Painter. Figures.
Esther Huillard lived and worked in Neuilly-sur-Seine. She studied with Jules Machard.

Museums and Galleries:
Draguignan: *Young Girl in White.*

HUILLIOT, Claude
French, 17th century.
Born c. 1632, in Rheims; died 6 August 1702, in Paris.
Painter, decorative designer. Landscapes, still-lifes (flowers/fruit).
Claude Huilliot was admitted into the Académie on 7 November 1664. He exhibited still-lifes in 1673 and 1699. He appears to have essentially been a decorator. Besides flowers and fruit, he painted the prevalent landscapes fashionable at the time. A *Flowers* canvas by him is on view at Fontainebleau Palace.

MUSEUMS AND GALLERIES:
RHEIMS: *Flowers in a Vase* (two paintings).
AUCTION RECORDS:
PARIS, 14 Dec 1979, *Parrot by a Fountain Bedecked with Flowers; Fountain Bedecked with Flowers* (two oils on canvas, making a pair, each 64 1/4 x 47 ins / 163 x 118.5 cm) FRF 120,000. VERSAILLES, 20 June 1982, *Vase with Roses and Tulips* (oil on canvas, 32 x 22 1/2 ins / 81 x 57 cm) FRF 40,000. PARIS, 13 Dec 1992, *Flower Arrangements in Ormolu Vases* (oil on canvas, a pair, 37 3/4 x 51 1/4 ins / 96 x 130 cm) FRF 90,000. PARIS, 26 March 1996, *Flower Arrangements in Ormolu Vases* (oil on canvas, a pair, each 37 3/4 x 51 1/4 ins / 96 x 130 cm) FRF 65,000. PARIS, 28 March 2001, *Vase of Flowers on a Ledge: poppy, anemonies, carnations, tulip and jasmins* (oil on canvas, 30 x 39 ins / 77 x 100 cm) FRF 56,000.

HUILLIOT, Pierre
French, 17th century.
Active in Rheims.
Painter.

HUILLIOT, Pierre Nicolas
French, 17th - 18th century.
Born 1674, in Paris; died 20 December 1751, in Paris.
Painter. Allegorical subjects, landscapes, animals, still-lifes (flowers/fruit/musical instruments). Decorative schemes.
Pierre Nicolas Huilliot was the son of Nicolas and was apprenticed to him, very likely assisting and continuing his work as a painter of symbols and decoration. He was admitted into the Académie on 31 December 1722. He exhibited at the Paris Salon between 1737 and 1750.

He was a prolific artist who painted the simplest of subjects with flair: animals, furniture, flowers, fruit, vegetables, and pretty landscapes.
AUCTION RECORDS:
PARIS, 24 and 25 April 1907, large decorative panel) FRF 1,200. PARIS, 24 March 1939, *Buffet in a Park,* FRF 7,200. LONDON, 1 Nov 1972, *Still-life with Musical Instruments,* GBP 2,400. VERSAILLES, 20 Nov 1977, *Flowers* (oil on canvas, matching pair, 59 x 49 1/4 ins / 150 x 125 cm) FRF 44,000. MONTE CARLO, 26 Oct 1981, *Bunches of Flowers* (oil on canvas, a pair, ovals, each 32 3/4 x 26 ins / 83 x 66 cm) FRF 60,000. PARIS, 9 June 1983, *Flower Garland Thrown around a Stone Sphinx* (oil on canvas, 37 1/2 x 39 1/4 ins / 95 x 100 cm) FRF 22,000. PARIS, 17 June 1986, *Flower Bowl on a Fruit-strewn Entablature* (oil on canvas, 43 3/4 x 59 1/2 ins / 111 x 151 cm) FRF 145,000. PARIS, 4 Dec 1987, *Flower Bowl and Fruit Bowl* (oil on canvas, 30 x 43 ins / 76 x 109 cm) FRF 54,000. PARIS, 4 Dec 1987, *Flower Bowl and Fruit Bowl on a Stone Entablature* (oil on canvas, 30 x 43 ins / 76 x 109 cm) FRF 54,000. NEW YORK, 10 Oct 1990, *Still-llife of Flower Arrangements in Silver Urns on Entablatures in front of Red Curtains* (oil on canvas, a pair, ovals, 48 1/2 x 44 1/2 ins / 123.2 x 113 cm and 47 3/4 x 43 3/4 ins/121.3 x 111 cm) USD 30,800. PARIS, 8 April 1991, *Vases of Flowers and Fruit on an Entablature* (oil on canvas, 35 x 39 ins / 88 x 99 cm) FRF 85,000. PARIS, 29 Nov 1991, *Vase of Flowers and Fruit on an Entablature* (oil on canvas, 35 x 39 ins / 88 x 99 cm) FRF 140,000. PARIS, 26 June 1992, *Still-life with Ewer, Lance, Flowers and Fruit* (oil on canvas, 33 3/4 x 39 ins / 86 x 99 cm) FRF 36,000. PARIS, 25 Jan 1993, *Concert of Birds* (oil on canvas, 28 x 46 ins / 71 x 117 cm) FRF 80,000. PARIS, 15 Dec 1993, *Still-life with Musical Instruments* (oil on canvas, 34 1/4 x 45 3/4 ins / 87 x 116.5 cm) FRF 135,000. VIENNA, 4 Oct 2000, *Decorative Bouquet of Flowers in a Gilt Vase* (oil on canvas, 34 x 39 ins / 86 x 98 cm) ATS 160,000. PARIS, 20 Dec 2000, *Still-life with Side-board of Fruit, Dog and Parrot* (oil on canvas, 9 x 62 ins / 24 x 158 cm) FRF 100,000. PARIS, 13 Dec 2001, *Vase of Flowers, Fruit and Shell-fish* (oil on canvas, 41 x 35 ins / 105 x 88 cm) FRF 120,000. PARIS, 11 March 2003, *Monkey by Bunch of Flowers* (oil on canvas, 103 x 39 ins / 262 x 100 cm) EUR 9,500. NEW YORK, 30 Sept 2003, *Flowers in a Vase with Foliage in an Urn, and Fruit on a Ledge* (oil on canvas, 60 x 57 ins / 153 x 145 cm) USD 20,000. PARIS, 7 April 2004, *Wild Duck and Frogs. Pigeons and Poultry* (oil on canvas, a pair, 31 x 28 ins / 80 x 72 cm) EUR 2,500.

HUIN
French, 18th century.
Active in Strasbourg.
Painter. Portraits.

HUIN (Mlle)
French, 18th - 19th century.
Miniaturist.
Huin studied under David and exhibited at the Salon between 1796 and 1801.

HUIN, Antoine
French, 18th century.
Active in Paris in 1786.
Painter.
Antoine Huin was a pupil at the École des Élèves Protégés.

HUIN, Charles Marc, known as Fitting
Swiss, 19th century.
Born 1819, in Geneva; died 1883.
Sculptor.

HUIN, Marguerite
French, 19th century.
Born in Rouen.
Painter. Genre scenes.
Huin studied at the École des Beaux-Arts in Paris, and was also a pupil of E Lefebvre. She showed a painting entitled *Preparations for a Meal* at the Angers Exhibition.

HUIS, Joseph
French, 18th century.
Active in Paris in 1750.
Painter, sculptor.

HUISKEN, Hermann
German, 19th century.
Born 13 June 1861, in Celle; died 22 September 1899, in Brunswick.
Painter. Genre scenes.
He exhibited in Berlin, Vienna and Munich.
AUCTION RECORDS:
LONDON, 15 June 1979, *An Amsterdam Beauty* (1897, oil on canvas, 32 x 25 1/4 ins / 81.2 x 64.2 cm) GBP 1,100. COLOGNE, 22 March 1985, *The Palace Guard in Karlsruhe* (1892, oil on canvas, 43 x 31 ins / 109 x 78.5 cm) DEM 7,000.

HUISMANS, Sipke
Dutch, 20th century.
Born 1938, in Amsterdam.
Engraver. Scenes with figures.
Spike Huismans had solo exhibitions at the Stedelijk Museum, Amsterdam, in 1966 and at the museum in The Hague in 1967. He mainly produced etchings. The atmosphere of his engravings is poetic, sometimes verging on the surreal. His work is figurative, and his style reminiscent of children's drawings, though his splintered composition gives his works a dreamlike quality.
MUSEUMS AND GALLERIES:
AMSTERDAM (Stedelijk Mus.) - THE HAGUE.

HUITE, Joseph
French, 19th century.
Painter.
Joseph Huite was admitted into the Académie de St-Luc on 17 October 1850.

HUITEL, Éloïse Caroline, called Vuitel
French, 19th century.
Born 1827, in Forges; died c. 1896, in Paris.
Painter. History painting, portraits, genre scenes.

Huitel was a pupil of both Léon Cogniet and Delorme, and made her début at the Paris Salon in 1863.

MUSEUMS AND GALLERIES:
AMIENS: *Young Girl Reading.*

HUIXU. See **HYE Ho**

HUIZONG, or Hui-Tsung
Chinese, 12th century.
Born 1082; died 1135.
Painter. Flowers, birds.

The last of the Northern Song emperors, Huizong was less a monarch who cultivated the arts than an artist who had somehow strayed onto a throne. A painter, calligrapher and great music-lover, he drew sustenance from literary, cultural and Taoist works, but neglected the affairs of state at a time when the empire needed a strong hand more than ever. In 1127 the Jurchen Mongols captured his capital, Kaifeng, and led him off into captivity. He survived the collapse of his power for eight years and died in exile.

In its brilliance and refinement, Huizong's reign marks one of the high points in the history of Chinese art and sensibility, and he himself would leave his mark on posterity as a collector, as inspiration and guiding light, and as a painter. His collections of ancient works are among the most splendid that ever existed in China. Yet the most important aspect of his legacy was the imperial painting academy, which he organised, developed and supervised, enabling him to lay down the direction for all the art of his time. For even though it is true that an academy existed before him, he was to change it forever, both in its structure and in its character. Under his direction, it ceased to be a body of elite craftsmen and was transformed into a training centre, with entrance examinations directly supervised by the emperor himself, and was dedicated to illustrating his aesthetic ideas. The academician-painters had superb conditions in which to work: dream-like gardens of flowers and birds which Huizong had specially laid out for them: access to the imperial collections, and frequent meetings with the emperor himself.

When it came to painting itself, Huizong was equally passionate. What he demanded was that his painters keep to the appearance of things. 'Painters must not imitate their predecessors', in the words of an academy edict at the beginning of his reign, '...they must paint things as they are and remain faithful to their forms and colours'. It is easy to imagine the sort of dead academicism to which rules like these might lead, had Huizong not been so brilliant a painter himself.

It is not easy nowadays to isolate the emperor's work from that of the academy, not only because his own paintings were copied hundreds of times but also because he would place his seal, and sometimes even his own signature, on those copies that pleased him most. On the other hand, there are a number of extant pieces of calligraphy by his hand, which are proof of his stunning command of the brush. In general, Huizong's work, like that of his academy, has certain unmistakable characteristics: a meticulous yet supple technique; a fidelity to nature that is both meticulous and yet curiously stylised in the perfection of its execution, the clarity of its presentation, and the skilful organisation of space; and a taste for telling a tale in a familiar way. Nature has never endowed her flowers, birds and insects with such elegant lines or such crystalline clarity as they have in these works, where they seem to exist in a dream-like perfection that could have been conceived only in the mind, a wholly different order of reality from that in which they had their being. As Huizong said: 'The painter does not merely convey the appearance of what is, but also the spiritual essence of these things, which takes hold of the mind of the viewer as if he were in the spot that is being depicted, as if he really had before his eyes the scene presented to him on the silk.

BIBLIOGRAPHY:
Cahill, James, *Chinese Painting*, Skira, Geneva, 1960. Ryckmans, P., in *Encyclopaedia Universalis*, vol VIII, Paris, 1970. Clunas, Craig, *Art in China*, Oxford University Press, Oxford, New York, 1997. Yang Xin and others, *Three Thousand Years of Chinese Painting*, Yale University Press, 1997.

MUSEUMS AND GALLERIES:
BEIJING (Palace Mus.): *Landscape with Figures and Pavilions* (handscroll, according to the inscription painted for Prince Yun, inscriptions by numerous Yuan artists); *Two Quails and Some Jujube Branches* (signed); *Two Quails* (album sheet, attributed); *Bird on the Branch of an Old Cedar, with Butterflies* (painting on fan, signed); *Bird on a Haitang Branch Catching an Insect* (album sheet, imperial seal); *Scholar Seated under a Large Tree Playing the Lute for Two Visitors* (colours on silk, signed, poem written by Cai Jing); *Pheasant Perched on a Branch of a Flowering Bush* (colours on silk, inscription by Emperor Huizong) - BERLIN (Staatliche Mus.): *Bird on a Flowering Branch* (colours on silk, album sheet, signature and imperial seal, attributed) - BOSTON (MFA): *Ladies of the Court Preparing Newly Woven Silk* (early 12th century, ink, colour and gold on silk, handscroll, after Zhang Xuan); *Five-coloured Parakeet* (early 12th century, ink and colours on silk, album sheet) - HAKONE: *Bird on a Branch of a Fruit Tree in Blossom* (attributed) - KYOTO (National Mus.): *Autumn and Winter Landscapes* (colours on silk, a pair of hanging scrolls) - SHANGHAI: *Four Magpies on a Bare Weeping Willow and Four Ducks on a Bank under Bamboo* (ink and colours on paper, handscroll, with Emperor Huizong's signature and several of his seals, and colophons) - TAIPEI (National Palace Mus.): *Birds in a Thicket of Bamboo and Plum Trees* (ink and colours on silk, hanging scroll); *Meeting of Scholars* (ink and colours on silk, hanging scroll, calligraphy by Emperor Huizong); *Autumn Colours on a Bank* (ink on paper, handscroll, decorated with floral motifs, with inscription) - TOKYO (Nezu Institute of Fine Arts): *Small Bird on a Large Pomegranate Tree* (colours on silk, album sheet); *Two Small Birds on the Branches of a Bush among Large White Flowers* (colours on silk, fan).

HUJER, Ludwig
German, 19th - 20th century.
Born 2 July 1872, in Wilhelmshöhe.
Sculptor, medallist.

Hujer travelled a great deal in Germany, France and England.

MUSEUMS AND GALLERIES:
GRAZ: sculpture.

HUKAN, Karol
Polish, 20th century.
Born 1888, near Kolomyia.
Sculptor.

Karol Hukan worked mainly in Cracow.

HULA, Zdenek
Czechoslovak, 20th - 21st century.
Born 25 February 1948, in Prague.
Painter.

Zdenek Hula attended the academy of fine arts in Prague from 1966 to 1972. His brightly coloured abstract compositions are embellished with dots, squares, lines and circles. His collective exhibitions have in particular included Prague (1972, 1976 and 1988) Bohemia (1979, 1985, 1987 and 1988), Poland (1983 and 1984) and Japan, 1986. He had solo exhibitions at the national museum of porcelain and ceramics in Bohemia in 1975 and 1978, in Prague 1980 and 1983, in Torougne, Poland, in 1980, in Bohemia in 1982 and 1986, in Moravia in 1987, and in Brno and Cracow in 1988.

HULBE, Georg
German, 19th - 20th century.
Born 1851, in Kiel; died 1917, in Hamburg.
Binder. Designs (furniture, book-binding, objets d'art).
Jugendstil.
Georg Hulbe was a bookbinder in Kiel from 1876. He moved to Hamburg in 1880. He then acquired his own leather workshop and, around 1900, after doing Neo-Renaissance decoration, he turned to Art Nouveau. He was awarded a gold medal at the Exposition Universelle in Paris. He worked from models designed by Peter Behrens.
BIBLIOGRAPHY:
Katthöfer, Anja, *Georg Hulbe (1851-1917). Ein Hamburger Kunsthandwerker im Zeitalter des Historismus* (university dissertation, Kiel, 1998). Franzke, Irmela, *Jugendstil. Glas, Graphik, Keramik, Metall, Möbel, Skulpturen und Textilien von 1880 bis 1915*, exhibition catalogue, Badisches Landesmuseum, Karlsruhe, 1987.
MUSEUMS AND GALLERIES:
HAMBURG (Mus. für Kunst und Gewerbe): *Mirror in Leather, Screen* - KARLSRUHE (Badisches Landesmuseum Leder) - OFFENBACH (Deutsches Ledermuseum/Schuhmuseum): *Writing Desk* (c. 1890).

HULBECK, Beate
German, 20th century.
Born 1903, in Berlin.
Active in the USA.
Painter, collage artist.
American Abstract Artists (AAA).
The wife of Charles R. Hulbeck, Beate Hulbeck was a member of the American Abstract Artists Association. Her work was shown at collective exhibitions, including two at the Salon des Réalités Nouvelles in Paris (1955 and 1957), and at solo exhibitions in Paris (1950) and Berlin (1956).

HULBECK, Charles R., pseudonym of Hülsenbeck, Richard, or Huelsenbeck
German, 20th century.
Born 23 April 1892, in Frankenau.
Active in the USA.
Painter.
Dadaism.
Zurich and Berlin Dadaist groups.
After being invalided out of the army during World War I, Charles R. Hulbeck took refuge in Zurich in 1916, where he was active in the Dada group (together with Hugo Ball, Tzara, Janco and Arp) as a poet. He returned to Berlin in 1917 and founded a Dada group together with Raoul Hausmann and Franz Jung. He continued to be active as a Dada poet until 1921. He subsequently led a colourful life: he began working as a doctor, then settled in New York and worked as a psychiatrist, adopting the name Hulbeck. It was only late in life that he began to paint, in the abstract manner, perhaps encouraged by his wife. It is worth recalling that in 1920 he had written in *En Avant Dada*: 'Dada should be a rallying point for all energies focused on abstract matters.'
BIBLIOGRAPHY:
Read, Herbert, *Histoire de la peinture moderne*, Somogy, Paris, 1960. Dorival, Bernard/Hoog, Michel, *Dada*, exhibition catalogue, Musée national d'Art moderne, Paris, 1966.

HULBERT, Charles Allen
American, 19th - 20th century.
Born in the Sacramento Valley (California); died 1939.
Painter.
Charles Allen Hulbert was a pupil at the San Francisco School of Design, the National Academy of Design, New York, and also trained under John Ward Simson. He moved to South Egremont (Massachusetts) in 1907-1908. He was a member of the Salmagundi Club.

HULBERT, Katherine Allmond
American, 19th - 20th century.
Born 1859; died 1937.
Painter.
Katherine Allmond Hulbert was the widfe of the painter Charles Allen Hulbert.

HULETT, James
British, 18th century.
Died 1771, in Clerkenwell.
Active in London.
Engraver (burin).
James Hulett engraved plates after G. Smith and Janet, notably the portraits of *Mary Stuart, Fairfax* and *Robert Devereux, Count of Essex*. He worked mainly for bookshops, in particular on Walker's work *The Life of Queen Anne*, for *The History of the Arts and Sciences* by Coetlogon and Fielding's *Joseph Andrews*.

HULGAL, Jacques
French, 17th century.
Born in Antwerp.
Painter.
Jacques Hulgal settled in Lyons in 1632. He became French by naturalisation in 1652 and became a master painter in 1666.

HULGAL, Luc
French, 17th century.
Born in Brabant.
Painter.
Luc Hulgal became a 'reçu habitant' (accepted citizen) of the city of Lyons in January 1664 and became a master craftsman in 1666 and 1670.

HULIN, Ernest
French, 20th century.
Born 29 September 1882, in Coutances; died during World War I (1914-1918), on the battlefield.
Sculptor.
Ernest Hulin exhibited in Paris at the Salon des Artistes Français, receiving an honourable mention in 1908.

HULIN, Jean
20th century.
Born 8 October 1920, in Mamers (Sarthe), France.
Painter, watercolourist, draughtsman. Figures, nudes, scenes with figures, landscapes, seascapes, Still-lifes.
Jean Hulin was taught by Roland Oudot and Maurice Brianchon at the École des Arts Décoratifs in Paris, and by René Jaudon at the École des Beaux-Arts. He showed work in Paris and won honours and medals at the Salon des Artistes Français, the Salon d'Automne and the Salons of Drawing, of Watercolour and of Seascapes, and was connected with various groups in French provinces and abroad. He also had solo exhibitions in several cities. Jean Aubert and André Grimaud have written about this artist.

He was a skilled draughtsman, and both his wash drawings and his watercolours are sharp and perceptive, especially the panoramic or foreshortened landscapes and the studies of trees on the edge of woodland. His oil paintings, nudes, figures and landscapes do not show the same light touch.

HULINGS, Clark
American, 20th century.
Born 1922.
Painter.
Clark Hulings' paintings are evocative of the American West. He took part in the exhibition: *À la Découverte de l'Ouest Américain* (*Discovering the American West*), organised by the Salon d'Automne, in Paris, in 1987, and the National Cowboy and Western Heritage Museum.

MUSEUMS AND GALLERIES:
OKLAHOMA CITY (National Cowboy and Western Heritage Mus.): *Grand Canyon, Kaibob Trail* (1973).

HULK
French, 19th century.
Active in Paris from 1800 to 1830.
Draughtsman, engraver (burin/stippling).
Hulk worked for the *Musée Français*. He engraved genre subjects and was also known for some vignettes after Moreau the Younger, for *Count Valmont* and *The History of France*, and for works by Ovid and Racine.

HULK, A. Pietersz.
Dutch, 18th century.
Draughtsman.

HULK, Abraham
British, 19th century.
Born 1 May 1813, in Amsterdam, in London according to some sources; died 1897, in London.
Painter, watercolourist, lithographer. Landscapes, seascapes.
Abraham Hulk was a pupil of J.A. Daiwaille in Rotterdam. He went to America in 1833. He exhibited his work in London at the Royal Academy and Suffolk Street from 1875.

MUSEUMS AND GALLERIES:
SUNDERLAND: *Dutch Fishing Boats.*
AUCTION RECORDS:
LONDON, 4 Dec 1909, *On the Coast,* GBP 4. LONDON, 4 Feb 1911, *On the Zuydersee,* GBP 2. LONDON, June 1924, *Mouth of a Dutch River with Fishing Boats,* GBP 11. LONDON, 9 Dec 1927, *Boats on the Waves,* GBP 27. LONDON, 16 Dec 1931, *Evening on the Scheldt; Morning on the Scheldt* (both) GBP 32. LONDON, 11 Jan 1946, *River Mouth,* GBP 63. LONDON, 5 Nov 1969, *Canal Scene,* GBP 850. AMSTERDAM, 10 Nov 1970, *Landscapes* (four pendants) NLG 10,600. LONDON, 8 Nov 1972, *Estuary Scene at Sunset,* GBP 2,500. LONDON, 27 July 1973, *Estuary Scene,* Gns 3,400. LONDON, 2 Nov 1973, *Seaside* (watercolour) Gns 1,200. LONDON, 6 March 1974, *Estuary Scene at Sunset,* GBP 2,300. LONDON, 11 Feb 1976, *Estuary Scene* (oil on canvas, 23 1/2 x 35 1/2 ins / 59.5 x 90 cm) GBP 1,800. LONDON, 11 Feb 1977, *Estuary Scene at Dusk* (oil on panel, 11 x 15 1/2 ins / 27 x 39.5 cm) GBP 3,000. COLOGNE, 11 June 1979, *Fishing Boats on the Beach* (oil on canvas, 15 3/4 x 26 ins / 40 x 66 cm) DEM 18,000. PARIS, 14 Dec 1981, *Sailing Boats Approaching the Jetty* (oil on canvas, 25 1/2 x 36 1/2 ins / 65 x 93 cm) FRF 52,000. ROUBAIX, 23 Oct 1983, *Landing Stage on a Canal in Amsterdam* (oil on canvas, 24 1/2 x 35 3/4 ins / 62 x 91 cm) FRF 59,000. LONDON, 28 Nov 1986, *Fishing Boats in an Estuary* (oil on canvas, 25 1/2 x 33 3/4 ins / 64.7 x 85.7 cm) GBP 5,000. LONDON, 24 June 1987, *Sailing Boats in an Estuary* (oil on canvas, 21 3/4 x 33 1/2 ins / 55.5 x 85 cm) GBP 13,000. LONDON, 25 March 1988, *Fishing Boats Anchored in an Estuary, Fishing Boats on a Rough Sea* (oil on canvas, two pendants, each 15 x 21 1/2 ins / 38 x 54.6 cm) GBP 25,300. MONTREAL, 17 Oct 1988, *Estuary with Boats* (oil on panel, 7 x 9 3/4 ins / 18 x 25 cm) CAD 4,200. AMSTERDAM, 16 Nov 1988, *Boat Striking its Sails in Sight of the Jetty* (1848, oil on panel, 10 1/4 x 14 1/4 ins / 26 x 36 cm) NLG 31,050. LONDON, 31 May 1989, *Fishing Boats at Dawn* (oil on panel, 11 x 16 1/4 ins / 28 x 41.5 cm) GBP 10, 450. LONDON, 4 Oct 1989, *Outside the Harbour* (1848, oil on canvas, 17 x 23 3/4 ins / 43 x 60.5 cm) GBP 8,250. LILLE, 25 March 1990, *Seascape* (oil on canvas, 24 3/4 x 35 1/2 ins / 63 x 90 cm) FRF 260,000. AMSTERDAM, 25 April 1990, *Sailing Boats off the Coast* (oil on panel, 7 x 10 ins / 17.5 x 25.5 cm) NLG 19,550. LONDON, 11 May 1990, *Fishing and Sailing Boats at Anchor in a Quiet Cove* (1888, oil on panel, 11 1/2 x 16 ins / 29.2 x 40.6 cm) GBP 6,050. LONDON, 30 May 1990, *Calm Weather on the Dutch Coast* (oil on canvas, 14 x 18 ins / 35.5 x 46 cm) GBP 8,800. NEW YORK, 24 Oct 1990, *Sailing Boats at Sunset* (oil on canvas, 22 1/4 x 34 1/4 ins / 56.8 x 86.7 cm) USD 15,400. AMSTERDAM, 30 Oct 1990, *Sailing Boat on a Stormy Sea at Dusk* (oil on panel, 11 1/2 x 17 ins / 29 x 43 cm) NLG 11,500. STOCKHOLM, 29 May 1991, *Shipping in a Storm near a Rocky Coast* (oil on canvas, 16 1/2 x 24 ins / 42 x 61 cm) SEK 15,000. NEW YORK, 17 Oct 1991, *Small Sailing Boats Sailing off the Coast* (oil on canvas, 22 1/4 x 34 ins / 56.8 x 86.4 cm) USD 13,200. AMSTERDAM, 30 Oct 1991, *Shipping in an Estuary with Fishermen in a Boat in the Shelter of a Jetty* (oil on canvas, 12 x 18 ins / 30.5 x 46 cm) NLG 23,000. LONDON, 29 Nov 1991, *Shipping in an Estuary; Shipping on the Waves in a Light Breeze* (oil on panel, 6 1/4 x 9 3/4 ins / 16 x 25 cm) GBP 7,150. NEW YORK, 20 Feb 1992, *Coming Alongside* (oil on panel, 9 x 12 ins / 22.9 x 30.5 cm) USD 11,000. LONDON, 2 Oct 1992, *Fishermen in an Estuary at Dusk* (oil on panel, 7 3/4 x 16 1/4 ins / 20 x 41 cm) GBP 4,950. AMSTERDAM, 2 Nov 1992, *Sailing Vessels in an Estuary* (oil on panel, 7 x 10 ins / 17.5 x 25.5 cm) NLG 8,625. NEW YORK, 26 May 1993, *Fishing Boats at Anchor at the End of the Day* (oil on canvas, 24 x 42 ins / 61 x 106.7 cm) USD 13,225. AMSTERDAM, 19 Oct 1993, *Fishing Boats in an Estuary with Sailors in a Dinghy Bringing in the Nets* (oil on canvas, 23 1/2 x 35 1/2 ins / 60 x 90 cm) NLG 13,800. LONDON, 11 May 1994, *Shipping on a Calm Sea* (1849, oil on canvas, 24 1/2 x 33 1/2 ins / 62 x 85 cm) GBP 21,850. AMSTERDAM, 11 April 1995, *Fishing Boats Near the Coast* (oil on panel, 7 x 9 3/4 ins / 17.5 x 25 cm) NLG 11,800. LOKEREN, 9 Dec 1995, *Sailing Boats on a Calm Sea* (oil on panel, 7 3/4 x 12 ins / 20 x 30.5 cm) BEF 100,000. NEW YORK, 17 Jan 1996, *Fishing Boats on a Stormy Sea* (oil on panel, 16 3/4 x 23 1/4 ins / 42.5 x 59.1 cm) USD 8,050. AMSTERDAM, 19-20 Feb 1996, *Sailing Ship in the Storm, a Three-Master in the Background* (oil on panel, 6 x 9 ins / 15 x 22 cm) NLG 2,998. LONDON, 30 May 1996, *Fishing Near the Coast on a Stormy Sea* (oil on canvas, 24 1/2 x 36 1/2 ins / 62.5 x 92.5 cm) GBP 31,050. LONDON, 31 Oct 1996, *Towards the River Mouth* (oil on canvas, 10 1/4 x 16 ins / 26 x 40.5 cm) GBP 5,175. AMSTERDAM, 5 Nov 1996, *Sailing Ship on a Wild Sea* (oil on canvas, 9 1/4 x 12 1/2 ins / 23.5 x 32 cm) NLG 10,620. LONDON, 21 March 1997, *Vessels on the Scheldt* (oil on panel, a pair, 7 x 10 ins / 17.8 x 25.5 cm) GBP 18,400. LONDON, 29 May 1997, *Fishing Boats off the Coast* (oil on canvas, 7 x 10 1/4 ins / 18 x 26 cm) GBP 4,830. LONDON, 11 June 1997, *At Sea* (oil on panel, 14 3/4 x 20 1/4 ins / 37.5 x 51.5 cm) GBP 10,925. LONDON, 13 June 1997, *Sailing Ships on an Estuary at Sunset; Sailing Ships on the Scheldt* (oil on panel, 11 3/4 x 16 ins / 29.7 x 40.6 cm) GBP 37,800. LONDON, 21 Nov 1997, *Dutch Sailing Ships on a Calm Sea at Sunset* (oil on panel, 8 x 11 1/4 ins / 20.3 x 28.3 cm) GBP 8,625.

HULK, Abraham (Jr.)
British, 19th - 20th century.
Born 1851; died 1922.
Active in Dorking.
Painter. Landscapes with figures, landscapes.

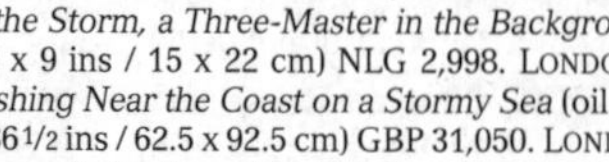

AUCTION RECORDS:
LONDON, 30 March 1908, *Near Owestrig,* GBP 1. LONDON, 12 May 1972, *Fishing Boats off the Coast,* Gns 550. LONDON, 23 April 1974, *River Landscape,* GBP 580. LONDON, 4 May 1977, *Fishing Boats off the Coast* (two canvases, 6 3/4 x 9 3/4 ins / 17 x 25 cm) GBP 850. LONDON, 9 May 1979, *Sailing Boats at Dusk* (oil on canvas, 23 1/4 x 41 1/2 ins / 59 x 105.5 cm) GBP 1,900. NEW YORK, 30 Oct 1985, *Fishing Boats in an Estuary* (oil on canvas, 16 x 24 ins / 40.6 x 61 cm) GBP 2,800. COPENHAGEN, 23 Nov 1987, *Sailing Boats off the Coast* (oil on canvas, 14 1/2

x 20½ ins / 37 x 52 cm) DKK 82,000. Amsterdam, 30 Aug 1988, *Cows near a Stream in a Wooded Landscape* (oil on canvas, 24 x 20 ins / 61 x 51 cm) NLG 1,035. London, 23 Sept 1988, *Walk beside the Sea* (1883, oil on canvas, 30¼ x 50½ ins / 77 x 128 cm) GBP 2,420. Stockholm, 19 April 1989, *Sailing Boats at the Mouth of a River with Figures on the Shore* (oil on panel, 7¼ x 11 ins / 18.5 x 28 cm) SEK 17,000. London, 9 Feb 1990, *Wooded Landscape near Dorking* (oil on canvas, 24 x 36 ins / 61 x 91.5 cm) GBP 2,420. London, 26 Sept 1990, *Albury Pond in Surrey* (oil on canvas, 40¼ x 29½ ins / 102 x 75 cm) GBP 2,200. Amsterdam, 23 April 1991, *Near Guildford* (oil on card, 7 x 6¼ ins / 18 x 16 cm) NLG 3,220. Amsterdam, 24 Sept 1992, *Peasant Leading a Horse-drawn Cart and Talking to Travellers in a Wooded Landscape; Firewood Gatherers in a Wooded River Landscape* (oil on canvas, a pair, each 24¾ x 36 ins / 63 x 91.5 cm) NLG 6,900. London, 3 March 1993, *Hay Barges at Dawn* (oil on canvas, 23¾ x 42 ins / 60.5 x 106.5 cm) GBP 2,415. New York, 22-23 July 1993, *Fishing Boats on a River* (oil on panel, 6¾ x 10 ins / 17.1 x 25.4 cm) USD 4,600. Penrith, 13 Sept 1994, *Near Albury in Surrey; Path in Surrey* (1877, oil on canvas, a pair, each 30 x 24 ins / 76 x 61 cm) GBP 5,175. New York, 19 Jan 1995, *Country Landscape* (oil on canvas, 30 x 50½ ins / 76.2 x 128.3 cm) USD 4,600. London, 6 June 1996, *Harvest* (oil on canvas, 22½ ins / 57 cm, 3¼ x 33 ins/8 x 83.8 cm) GBP 3,680. London, 4 June 1997, *Near West Clandon, Surrey* (1886, oil on canvas, 30 x 50 ins / 76 x 127 cm) GBP 2,760. London, 12 July 1999, *Shipping off the Dutch Coast* (oil on canvas, a pair, 7 x 10 ins / 18 x 25 cm) GBP 4,500. Salisbury, 12 Oct 1999, *Garnshall Avenue, Surrey* (1897, oil on canvas, a pair, 40 x 30 ins / 101 x 76 cm) GBP 1,600. Billingshurst, 24 July 2000, *Entering Harbour. Low Tide* (oil on canvas, a pair, 9 x 13 ins / 24 x 34 cm) GBP 3,000. London, 7 Sept 2000, *View of Albury Heath, Surrey* (1883, oil on canvas, 24 x 36 ins / 61 x 91 cm) GBP 2,600. Leeds, 22 June 2001, *Extensive Landscape with a Boy Seated beside a Path and Cottage beyond* (oil on canvas, 30 x 51 ins / 76 x 130 cm) GBP 1,400. New Orleans, 13 Oct 2001, *Country Landscape with Peasant Girl* (oil on canvas, 24 x 16 ins / 61 x 41 cm) USD 1,800. London, 21 June 2002, *Shipping at Low Tide* (oil on panel, 8 x 10 ins / 21 x 26 cm) GBP 1,500. Cologne, 4 July 2002, *Fishing Boat Landed on the English Coast* (oil on canvas, 11 x 17 ins / 28 x 44 cm) EUR 3,600. Helsinki, 9 Feb 2003, *Woodland Road* (oil on canvas, 14 x 10 ins / 35 x 25 cm) EUR 1,900. Stockholm, 26 May 2003, *Dutch Fishing Boats* (oil on canvas, 15 x 21 ins / 37 x 53 cm) SEK 100,000. The Hague, 12 May 2004, *English River Landscape* (oil on canvas, 19 x 29 ins / 49 x 74 cm) EUR 1,700.

HULK, Abraham Jacobsz.
Dutch, 18th - 19th century.
Engraver.

Abraham Hulk worked around 1776-1811.

HULK, Hendrik
Dutch, 19th - 20th century.
Born 1842, in Amsterdam; died 1937, in Haarlem.
Painter. Seascapes, waterscapes.

Auction records:

London, 10 Nov 1971, *Estuary Scene*, GBP 750. London, 23 Feb 1977, *Landscape with River, Boat and Sailing Boat* (oil on canvas, 6¾ x 11½ ins / 17 x 29 cm) GBP 650. New York, 25 Jan 1980, *Fishing Boats on a Canal* (oil on canvas, 17 x 26 ins / 43 x 66 cm) USD 3,200. Amsterdam, 19 May 1981, *Boats near the Coast* (oil on canvas, 16¾ x 25¾ ins / 42.5 x 65.5 cm) NLG 9,000. London, 22 June 1983, *Barge by the Banks of a River* (oil on canvas, 11½ x 17¼ ins / 29 x 44 cm) GBP 1,000. Amsterdam, 3 Sept 1988, *Small Boat Tacking in a Strong Wind on a Stormy Sea with Other Boats and Jetty* (oil on canvas, 11¾ x 18 ins / 30 x 46 cm) NLG 2,760. Amsterdam, 16 Nov 1988, *Fisherman Collecting Shellfish near the Coast* (oil on canvas, 17¼ x 26½ ins / 44 x 67.5 cm) NLG 10,925. Amsterdam, 28 Feb 1989, *Landscape with a River, Moored Sailing Boat, and Other Small Boats in the Background* (oil on panel, 13 x 17 ins / 33 x 43 cm) NLG 2,070. London, 5 May 1989, *Sailing Boats in a River Estuary* (oil on canvas, 12 x 18 ins / 30.5 x 45.7 cm) GBP 1,870. Cologne, 23 March 1990, *Sailing Boats at Anchor* (oil on canvas, 17½ x 26½ ins / 44.5 x 67 cm) DEM 2,800. Amsterdam, 25 April 1990, *Seascape* (oil on canvas, 11½ x 17¼ ins / 29 x 44 cm) NLG 8,050. Amsterdam, 24 April 1991, *Boats and Fishermen on the Coast at Zandvoort* (oil on canvas, 25½ x 36½ ins / 65 x 93 cm) NLG 17,250. Amsterdam, 19 Oct 1993, *Sailor in a Boat Approaching a Hay Barge* (1891, oil on panel, 6½ x 8 ins / 16.5 x 20.5 cm) NLG 4,025. Amsterdam, 21 April 1994, *Boats on a Beach with Zandvoort in the Background* (oil on canvas, 17¼ x 26½ ins / 44 x 67 cm) NLG 9,775. Amsterdam, 7 Nov 1995, *Boat Run Aground* (oil on canvas, 18 x 26½ ins / 46 x 67 cm) NLG 3,304.

HULK, Johannes Frederick
Dutch, 19th - 20th century.
Born 9 January 1829, in Amsterdam; died 12 July 1911, in Amsterdam.
Painter. Landscapes with figures, landscapes, waterscapes.

A student of his brother Abraham, Johannes Hulk was John Frederik Hulk's father.

Auction records:

London, 20 April 1979, *Fishermen and Boats on the Bank of a River* (1869, oil on canvas, 24¾ x 36¼ ins / 62.8 x 92 cm) GBP 2,600. Amsterdam, 19 May 1981, *Street Scene* (oil on panel, 12¼ x 16 ins / 31 x 39.7 cm) NLG 8,800. London, 16 March 1983, *Fishing Boats in Amsterdam* (oil on canvas, 24 x 35¼ ins / 61 x 89.5 cm) GBP 2,800. London, 12 Feb 1986, *Canal Scene, Amsterdam* (oil on canvas, 23¼ x 30 ins / 59 x 76.5 cm) GBP 4,000. London, 26 June 1987, *Street Scene in the Netherlands; Canal Scene in the Netherlands* (oil on canvas, a pair, 39 x 29 ins / 99 x 73.5 cm) GBP 14,000. London, 16 Feb 1990, *Street Scene in Amsterdam* (oil on canvas, 25¾ x 32 ins / 65.5 x 81 cm) GBP 7,150. Amsterdam, 6 Nov 1990, *The Spaarne in Haarlem* (oil on canvas, 23½ x 35¾ ins / 60 x 91 cm) NLG 25,300. Amsterdam, 24 April 1991, *View of a Dutch Village, with a Sailing Boat Tied Up on a Canal* (oil on panel, 18 x 15 ins / 45.5 x 38 cm) NLG 12,075. New York, 17 Oct 1991, *Fishermen Getting their Boats Ready* (oil on panel, 12½ x 15¾ ins / 31.8 x 40 cm) USD 9,900. New York, 29 Oct 1992, *Boats on a Canal in a Village* (oil on canvas, 24 x 36 ins / 61 x 91.5 cm) USD 6,050. Amsterdam, 2-3 Nov 1992, *Canal in a Dutch Village* (oil on canvas, 23½ x 35½ ins / 60 x 90 cm) NLG 13,800. Amsterdam, 20 April 1993, *View of a Dutch Port* (1863, oil on canvas, 24¾ x 34 ins / 63 x 85.5 cm) NLG 13,800. Amsterdam, 21 April 1993, *Idealised View of Haarlem with Boats Tied up on the Spaarne* (oil on canvas, 22¾ x 32 ins / 58 x 81 cm) NLG 23,000. New York, 20 July 1994, *The Singel in Amsterdam* (oil on canvas, 31½ x 25½ ins / 80 x 64.8 cm) USD 6,612. London, 22 Feb 1995, *Huntsman and Dog* (oil on canvas, 14½ x 17½ ins / 37 x 44.5 cm) GBP 1,150. New York, 9 June 1995, *Beaufort Pack in Action* (oil on canvas, 31 x 49½ ins / 78.7 x 125.7 cm) USD 11,500. Amsterdam, 19-20 Feb 1997, *Idealised View of Utrecht* (oil on panel, 16 x 13 ins / 40.5 x 33 cm) NLG 11,532.

HULK, John Frederik
Dutch, 19th - 20th century.
Born 17 November 1855, in Amsterdam; died June 1913.

Painter, watercolourist, engraver. Genre scenes, hunting scenes, landscapes.
Work by John Frederik Hulk was shown at the Brussels Exhibition in 1910.

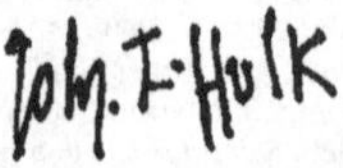

Auction records:
London, 25 Jan 1908, *End of the Race,* GBP 4. London, 5 Feb 1910, *View of Amsterdam,* GBP 3. London, 6 May 1910, *Woman Arriving at a Box in the Theatre,* GBP 19. London, 9 Oct 1970, *Street Scene, Amsterdam,* Gns 900. London, 12 May 1972, *View of Amsterdam,* Gns 1,800. London, 24 Nov 1976, *View of Amsterdam* (oil on panel, 12 x 15 ins / 30.5 x 38 cm) GBP 1,700. London, 25 Oct 1977, *Appointments for the Season* (1888, oil on canvas, 33 x 57¾ ins / 84 x 147 cm) GBP 950. London, 21 June 1989, *Elegant Young Woman with a Dog in a Park* (oil on panel, 26½ x 20¾ ins / 67 x 53 cm) GBP 3,520. London, 14 Feb 1990, *The Chase; The Kill* (1891, oil on canvas, a pair, 80 x 124 ins / 203.2 x 315 cm) GBP 3,190. Amsterdam, 5 June 1990, *Pigsty* (1909, oil on canvas, 23¼ x 37¾ ins / 59 x 96 cm) NLG 3,680; *Hunters in a Boat on a Lake* (1910, oil on canvas, 31½ x 43 ins / 80 x 109.5 cm) NLG 14,950. Amsterdam, 23 April 1991, *Ducks near a Pond* (1906, oil on canvas, 11 x 18 ins / 28 x 46 cm) NLG 2,300. Amsterdam, 14 Sept 1993, *Hare-hunting in the Dunes* (oil on canvas, 12¼ x 18 ins / 31 x 46 cm) NLG 2,070. Amsterdam, 14 June 1994, *Ducks in a Field* (oil on canvas/panel, 8 x 10½ ins / 20.5 x 26.5 cm) NLG 3,450. London, 17 Oct 1996, *The Kill* (oil on canvas, 34½ x 23¼ ins / 87.5 x 59 cm) GBP 2,760. Amsterdam, 5 Nov 1996, *Ducks on a Pond* (watercolour, 15¾ x 23 ins / 40 x 57.5 cm) NLG 10,030.

HULK, William Frederik

British, 19th - 20th century.
Born 1852; died 1906.
Active in London.
Painter, watercolourist. Landscapes with figures, animals.

William Hulk exhibited frequently in London at the Royal Academy, the Suffolk Street gallery and New Water-Colour Society from 1875.

Auction records:
New York, 1-2 Feb 1905, *Landscape with Cattle,* USD 115. London, 13 June 1973, *Canal Scene, Amsterdam,* GBP 3,700. London, 8 June 1976, *River Landscape* (oil on canvas, 8½ x 17¾ ins / 21.5 x 45 cm) GBP 380. London, 5 Oct 1979, *Flock of Sheep in a Landscape* (oil on canvas, 19½ x 29½ ins / 49.4 x 75 cm) GBP 600. Amsterdam, 30 Oct 1990, *Cattle near Dorking in England* (oil on canvas, 40¼ x 30 ins / 102 x 76 cm) NLG 6,325. London, 22 Nov 1990, *Cattle Beside a Pond* (oil on canvas, a pair, each 20 x 16 ins / 50.8 x 40.7 cm) GBP 1,210. London, 5 June 1991, *Cattle at Daybreak* (oil on canvas, 30 x 40 ins / 76 x 101.5 cm) GBP 1,650. Amsterdam, 17 Sept 1991, *Polder Landscape with Cows in a Meadow Crossed by a Stream* (oil on canvas, 20¼ x 30 ins / 51.5 x 76.5 cm) NLG 3,220. Amsterdam, 28 Oct 1992, *The Little Cow Girl* (oil on canvas, 30 x 40¼ ins / 76.5 x 102 cm) NLG 8,050. London, 12 May 1993, *Cattle Passing near the Farm* (oil on canvas, 16 x 24 ins / 40.5 x 61 cm) GBP 1,035. London, 6 June 1996, *Manor House in a Meadow* (oil on canvas, 35 x 24½ ins / 88.8 x 62.2 cm) GBP 1,840. Chester, 11 Dec 2000, *Cattle in a Watermeadow* (oil on canvas) GBP 1,350. Doncaster, 17 Dec 2000, *Cattle in a Country Lane* (oil on canvas, 24 x 20 ins / 60 x 50 cm) GBP 1,200. Haslemere, 21 Feb 2001, *Landscape with Cattle* (oil on canvas, four, 11 x 8 ins / 28 x 20 cm) GBP 1,800. Antwerp, 22 Oct 2001, *Cows in Pasture* (oil on canvas, 24 x 42 ins / 61 x 107 cm) BEF 115,000. Newmarket, 30 Jan 2002, *Cattle on a Lane by a Fence* (oil on board, 7 x 6 ins / 19 x 14 cm) GBP 1,250. The Hague, 6 Nov 2002, *Meadow with Cows Resting at the Water* (oil on canvas, 29 x 50 ins / 73 x 126 cm) EUR 1,900. Aylsham, 20 June 2003, *In the Meadow* (1978, oil on canvas, 29 x 48 ins / 74 x 122 cm) GBP 2,000. London, 21 Jan 2004, *Cattle Watering* (oil on canvasboard, a pair, 12 x 9 ins / 30 x 22 cm) GBP 1,250. Leominster, 27 Oct 2004, *Cattle Watering. Cattle on a Riverbank* (oil on board, a pair, 7 x 6 ins / 19 x 14 cm) GBP 1,100.

HULL, Clementina

British, 19th century.
Active in London.
Painter.

Clementina Hull exhibited her work from 1866 to 1904.

HULL, Edward

British, 19th century.
Active in London.
Draughtsman, lithographer.

Edward Hull worked from 1820 to 1834.

HULL, Edward

British, 19th century.
Active in London.
Painter, watercolourist. Genre scenes.

Edward Hull exhibited his work in London at the Royal Academy and Suffolk Street from 1827 to 1877.

Auction records:
London, 24 May 1909, *Eynsford Castle* (watercolour) GBP 1. New York, 8 June 1984, *Arrival of the Race* (oil on canvas, 9 x 12½ ins / 22.8 x 31.8 cm) USD 1,700. Monte Carlo, 22 Feb 1986, *Departure for the Hunt* (watercolour, 13 x 19¾ ins / 33 x 50 cm) FRF 10,000. London, 29 Oct 1991, *Farm Behind a Hedge* (1864, watercolour heightened with white, 8¾ x 12¼ ins / 22.2 x 31 cm) GBP 715. London, 14 Oct 2003, *The 2nd Life Guards on Manoeuvres* (watercolour over pencil heightened with gouache, 9 x 13 ins / 23 x 33 cm) GBP 2,400.

HULL, James

British, 20th century.
Born 1921.
Painter.

James Hull's work featured in a number of group exhibitions in London, in 1949, 1951 and 1953. He took part in an exhibition of contemporary British artists in Paris in 1952.

Auction records:
Paris, 14 March 1990, *Composition* (1952, gouache, 19¾ x 24½ ins / 50 x 62.5 cm) FRF 5,000.

HULL, Marie Atkinson

American, 20th century.
Born 28 September 1890, in Mississippi; died 1980.
Painter.

Marie Atkinson Hull trained at Pennsylvania Academy of the Fine Arts, Philadelphia. She became a member of this academy and of the American Art Union.

HULL, Thomas H.

British, 18th century.
Died 1800.
Active in London.
Miniaturist.

Thomas H. Hull exhibited in London at the Royal Academy from 1775 to 1800.

HULL, William

British, 19th century.
Born 6 March 1820, in Graffham; died 15 March 1880, in Rydal.
Painter, watercolourist. Landscapes.

William Hull exhibited in London at the Royal Academy from 1858 to 1877.

Auction records:
London, 25 June 1909, *Street in Conway; Street in Chelsea* (watercolour) GBP 8. Edinburgh, 25 Nov 1997, *St-Aubins, Jersey* (watercolour heightened with gouache, 9 x 13 ins / 22.9 x 33 cm) GBP 483. Edinburgh, 22 June 2000, *Figures Harvesting Potatoes* (1857, watercolour and gouache, 13 x 21 ins / 33 x 53 cm) GBP 1,350.

HULLAND, William T.
British, 19th century.
Active in London.
Engraver.

HULLE, Anselmus van. See **HEBBELYNCK Anselmus** or **Anselmus Van Hulle**

HULLEBROECK, Joseph
Belgian, 20th century.
Born 1876, in Gentbrugge.
Sculptor. Statues, busts.

Joseph Hullebroeck was a student of Jules Pierre van Biesbroeck. He became director of the fine arts academy in Deinze. His output consists of portrait busts, commemorative plaques and religious statues.

HULLEGAERDE, Jan van
Dutch, 17th century.
Active in Middelburg.
Painter.

HULLEGARDEN, Carel van
Dutch, 17th century.
Active in The Hague.
Painter. Still-lifes.

Auction records:
London, 9 July 1976, *Still-life* (1647, oil on panel, 21 1/2 x 33 1/2in/54.5 x 85cm) GBP 1,700.

HULLESHOVEN, L. von
German, 19th century.
Painter. Portraits.

Museums and Galleries:
Cologne: *Portrait of a Woman.*

HULLET, Martinus
Flemish School, 18th century.
Active in Brussels in 1729.
Painter.

HULLEY, H.
British, 18th century.
Active from 1783 to 1800.
Painter. Landscapes.

H. Hulley exhibited landscapes in London at the Royal Academy between 1783 and 1787.

Auction records:
London, 10 July 1996, *Lime Kiln in Hammersmith* (1784, oil on canvas, 18 3/4 x 24 1/2 ins / 47.5 x 62 cm) GBP 5,175.

HULLGREN, Oscar
Swedish, 19th - 20th century.
Born 10 August 1869, in Malilla; died 1948.
Painter. Seascapes.

Oscar Hullgren travelled along the Atlantic and North Sea coasts. His work was shown at the Salon d'Automne in Paris. He was a guest of the Carnegie Institute in Pittsburgh, won a medal in Munich in 1905, and became a member of the Stockholm academy of fine arts in 1917. He produced many views of the coasts he had visited, and he added ships to his seascapes, which generally portrayed rough seas.

Museums and Galleries:
Stockholm: *Storm at Sea; When the Lighthouse is Lit.*

Auction records:
Stockholm, 19 April 1972, *By the Sea*, SEK 6,200. Malmö, 2 May 1977, *By the Sea* (oil on canvas, 25 1/2 x 32 ins / 65 x 81 cm) SEK 8,000. Stockholm, 1 Nov 1983, *By the Sea* (oil on canvas, 27 1/4 x 36 1/4 ins / 69 x 92 cm) SEK 10,500. Stockholm, 10 Dec 1986, *Seascape* (1917, oil on canvas, 36 1/4 x 53 1/4 ins / 92 x 135 cm) SEK 15,000. Stockholm, 27 April 1988, *Sun on the Sea, with a Sailing Boat* (oil on canvas, 25 1/2 x 39 ins / 65 x 99 cm) SEK 20,000. Stockholm, 6 June 1988, *Rocky Coast* (oil, 16 1/2 x 20 3/4 ins / 42 x 53 cm) SEK 17,000. Stockholm, 15 Nov 1988, *Storm in Brittany* (oil, 26 3/4 x 35 3/4 ins / 68 x 91 cm) SEK 35,000. Stockholm, 19 April 1989, *Storm on a Rocky Coast* (1895, oil on canvas, 29 1/4 x 48 1/2 ins / 74 x 123 cm) SEK 49,000. Stockholm, 15 Nov 1989, *Open Seas off the Coast of Cornwall in Heavy Weather* (oil, 16 1/4 x 19 3/4 ins / 41 x 50 cm) SEK 34,000. Stockholm, 16 May 1990, *Sailing Boat on the Open Seas in Rough Weather* (1916, oil on canvas, 24 3/4 x 33 ins / 63 x 84 cm) SEK 36,000. Stockholm, 14 Nov 1990, *Eddies on the Reef* (oil on canvas, 15 3/4 x 19 3/4 ins / 40 x 50 cm) SEK 12,500. Stockholm, 28 Oct 1991, *Boats near a Pontoon* (1931, oil on canvas, 14 1/4 x 16 1/4 ins / 36 x 41 cm) SEK 9,000. Stockholm, 19 May 1992, *Breakers on the Rocks* (oil on canvas, 19 1/4 x 24 3/4 ins / 49 x 63 cm) SEK 9,000. Stockholm, 29 May 2000, *Cliffs and Breakers* (oil on canvas, 31 x 37 ins / 78 x 95 cm) SEK 31,000. Stockholm, 4 Dec 2002, *At the Outer Skerries* (1938, oil on canvas, 37 x 50 ins / 93 x 127 cm) SEK 15,000. Norrköping, 26 Nov 2003, *Archipelago* (1896, oil on canvas, 35 x 46 ins / 88 x 118 cm) SEK 13,000.

HULLIN, E.
19th century.
Painter. Genre scenes.

E. Hullin is mentioned by Florence Levy.

Auction records:
New York, 10-20 April 1906, *The Love Letter*, USD 290.

HULLIN-BOISCHEVALLIER, Anne Louis Félix de
French, 19th century.
Born 5 August 1818, in Paris.
Painter. Portraits.

Hullin-Boischevallier entered the École des Beaux-Arts on 2 October 1837, where he was a pupil of P. Delaroche. He appeared at the Salon from 1827 to 1853, and always exhibited under the name of Boischevallier.

Museums and Galleries:
Versailles (Mus.): *Portrait of Cardinal Arnaud d'Ossat.*

HULLIOT, Pierre Nicolas
French, 18th century.
Active in Paris in 1706.
Painter.

HULLMANDEL, Charles Joseph
British, 19th century.
Born 15 June 1789, in London, of German parents; died November 1850, in London.
Lithographer.

A pupil of Faraday, he produced lithographs from Cattermole, Stanfield, Hague Harding, Roberts and Nash. He published views of Italy, Paris and London.

HULME, Frederick William
British, 19th century.
Born 22 October 1816, in Swinton; died 14 November 1884, in London.
Painter. Genre scenes, landscapes with figures, landscapes.

Frederick William Hulme was a pupil of a Yorkshire artist. He went to London in 1844. He began by doing drawings for engravers and then devoted himself to painting.

Museums and Galleries:

Leicester: *Sussex Landscape* - Liverpool: *Rivington Valley* - Montreal: *Surrey Forest.*

Auction records:

London, 15 Feb 1908, *Woking Council* (1857) GBP 4. London, 13 April 1908, *Rainy Day,* GBP 3. London, 25 April 1908, *Pandy Mill* (1876) GBP 5. London, 13 March 1909, *Barden Tower,* GBP 19. London, 3 April 1909, *Cattle* (in collaboration with Willis) GBP 30. London, 17 Dec 1910, *Pont Cefyn, Wales* (1878) GBP 13. London, Nov 1921, *Panorama with Figures,* GBP 10. London, April 1923, *Surrey Footpath with Sheep,* GBP 15. London, 29 Jan 1926, *Scene near Ripley, Surrey,* GBP 31. London, 14 April 1967, *Midday Break,* Gns 190. London, 5 June 1968, *Harvest,* GBP 190. London, 5 June 1970, *Riverside,* Gns 400. London, 19 May 1971, *The Waning Year,* GBP 1,500. London, 5 Oct 1973, *Summer Landscape,* Gns 8,000. London, 29 June 1976, *Osterley Park* (oil on canvas, 23¼ x 19½ ins / 59 x 49.5 cm) GBP 2,200. London, 28 Jan 1977, *Conversation Along the Way* (1863, oil on canvas, 17½ x 23½ ins / 44.5 x 59.7 cm) GBP 3,500. London, 14 Feb 1978, *The Hunter's Greeting* (1863, oil on canvas, 17¼ x 23¼ ins / 44 x 59 cm) GBP 4,800. New York, 26 Jan 1979, *Sheep in a Wooded Landscape* (oil on canvas, 28 x 23 ins / 71 x 58.5 cm) USD 4,000. London, 20 Oct 1981, *Figures on a Country Road* (1850, oil on canvas, 28 x 22¾ ins / 71 x 58 cm) GBP 3,000. London, 19 Oct 1983, *Shady Lanes* (oil on card, a pair, 14 x 12 ins / 35.5 x 30.5 cm) GBP 5,800. London, 31 Oct 1986, *Fisherman at the River's Edge* (1875, oil on canvas, 27 x 35 ins / 68.5 x 89 cm) GBP 4,000. New York, 21 May 1987, *Resting Beside a Stile* (1879, oil on canvas, 30¼ x 50¼ ins / 76.8 x 127.6 cm) USD 17,000. New York, 25 May 1988, *The Way Home* (1881, oil on canvas, 24 x 20 ins / 61 x 51 cm) USD 3,300. London, 15 June 1988, *Surrey Meadows* (1866, oil on canvas, 30 x 50 ins / 76 x 127 cm) GBP 10,780. London, 23 Sept 1988, *Autumn* (1870, oil on canvas, 17 x 24 ins / 43 x 61 cm) GBP 1,650. Montreal, 1 May 1989, *Farm Scene* (1881, oil on canvas, 24 x 20 ins / 61 x 51 cm) CAD 5,600. London, 21 March 1990, *Shepherd and his Flock* (1870, oil on canvas, 18 x 24 ins / 46 x 61 cm) GBP 3,080. London, 15 June 1990, *English Country Scene* (1865, oil on canvas, 30 x 50 ins / 76.2 x 127 cm) GBP 34,100. London, 8 Feb 1991, *Betws-y-Coed in North Wales* (oil on canvas, 20 x 28 ins / 51 x 71 cm) GBP 5,280. London, 5 June 1991, *Sweet Summer Time* (1860, oil on canvas, 48 x 78 ins / 122 x 198 cm) GBP 16,500. New York, 29 Oct 1992, *Collecting Firewood in the Storm* (oil on canvas, 14 x 25 ins / 35.5 x 63.5 cm) USD 1,980. London, 13 Nov 1992, *Landscape with a Welsh River* (oil on canvas, 42 x 60 ins / 106.8 x 152.4 cm) GBP 5,720. London, 12 May 1993, *River Bordered with Trees* (1874, oil on canvas, 30 x 50 ins / 76 x 127 cm) GBP 2,185. London, 30 March 1994, *Harvest Scene with the Ruins of an Abbey in the Background* (oil on canvas, 12½ x 20 ins / 32 x 50.5 cm) GBP 7,820. London, 29 March 1995, *On the Footbridge* (1864, oil on canvas, 17¾ x 23½ ins / 45 x 60 cm) GBP 13,225. London, 6 June 1996, *River Landscape with Children Playing and a Manor House* (1872, oil on canvas, 20¼ x 29¼ ins / 51.4 x 74.2 cm) GBP 1,610. London, 5 Sept 1996, *Wayside Gossip; Rest along the Way* (1858, oil on canvas, a pair, 13½ x 9½ ins / 34.2 x 24.2 cm) GBP 1,725. London, 8 Nov 1996, *Surrey Meadows* (1866, oil on canvas, 30 x 50 ins / 76 x 127 cm) GBP 17,000. London, 7 Nov 1997, *Moel Siabod from near Bryntyrch, North Wales* (1856, oil on canvas, 28 x 36¼ ins / 71.2 x 91.9 cm) GBP 5,175. Newmarket, 16 Sept 1999, *Summer at Ockham, Surrey* (oil on canvas, 41 x 59 ins / 103 x 151 cm) GBP 20,000. London, 4 Nov 1999, *Wayside Conversation* (1863, oil on canvas, 18 x 24 ins / 45 x 61 cm) GBP 12,000. Newmarket, 3 May 2000, *At Ockham, Surrey, in Summer* (1867, oil on canvas, 30 x 50 ins / 76 x 127 cm) GBP 13,500. San Francisco, 17 May 2000, *Pastoral Landscape with Shepherd and Flock Resting in Sunny Glade* (1865, oil on canvas, 28 x 23 ins / 71 x 58 cm) USD 19,000. Boston, 9 March 2001, *Welsh River* (1871, oil on canvas, 35 x 52 ins / 88 x 133 cm) USD 7,000. London, 8 Nov 2001, *Resting by the Old Oak* (1881, oil on canvas, 30 x 50 ins / 76 x 128 cm) GBP 6,000. London, 11 June 2002, *Surrey Glade* (1871, oil on canvas, 30 x 50 ins / 76 x 127 cm) GBP 5,500. London, 26 Nov 2002, *Sheep Resting in Woodland Glade, Traveller Looking on* (1865, oil on canvas, 28 x 23 ins / 71 x 59 cm) GBP 28,000. London, 11 March 2003, *Surrey Landscape* (1870, oil on canvas, 30 x 50 ins / 76 x 127 cm) GBP 3,000. London, 11 June 2004, *Near the Common, Working, Surrey* (1859, oil on canvas, 20 x 26 ins / 51 x 67 cm) GBP 8,000. London, 14 July 2004, *Shepherd and his Flock* (1873, oil on canvas, 24 x 20 ins / 60 x 51 cm) GBP 9,800.

HULMET, Louis
French, 18th century.
Active in Paris in 1762.
Painter, sculptor.

HULOT, Caroline
French, 19th century.
Active in Paris c. 1800.
Engraver.

Hulot engraved the works of Boilly, among others.

HULOT, Étienne
French, 17th - 18th century.
Sculptor.

Étienne Hulot was the youngest son of Philippe Hulot. He is mentioned in 1719.

HULOT, Guillaume
French, 17th century.
Active also in Germany.
Sculptor.

According to Dussieux, Guillaume Hulot worked in Berlin with Jean de Bodt and produced for the Arsenal four large statues: *Arithmetic, Geometry, Mechanics* and *Pyrotechnics.* He also worked at the Berliner Tor (Berlin Gate) in Wesel. In their dictionary, Bellier de la Chavignerie and Auvray state that he returned to France and worked at Versailles; this seems unlikely. If the authoritative *France Protestante* (*Protestant France*) is to be believed, Guillaume Hulot, a Huguenot, sought refuge from religious persecution in Prussia. The artist who worked in Versailles could be Jacques-Philippe Hulot or one of his sons.

HULOT, Jacques, or Hullot
French, 17th century.
Active in Paris.
Sculptor.

Jacques Hulot was called as a witness on 16 September 1674.

HULOT, Nicolas
French, 17th - 18th century.
Active in Paris.
Sculptor.

Nicolas Hulot was Guillaume Hulot's brother.

HULOT, Philippe
French, 17th century.
Active in Paris in 1680.
Sculptor, painter.

HULOT, Philippe, or Hullot
French, 18th century.

Active in Paris.
Sculptor.
Philippe Hulot was member then rector of the Académie de St-Luc and sculptor to Philippe, Duke of Orléans, Regent of France. He married Madeleine Plisson with whom he had two sons, Pierre and Étienne, both sculptors. They were related to the painter François Bertault.

HULOT, Pierre
French, 17th - 18th century.
Born in Paris.
Sculptor.
Pierre Hulot was Philippe Hulot's eldest son and probably his pupil. He is cited in 1719.

HULSBERG, Hendrik
Dutch, 18th century.
Born in Amsterdam; died 1729, in London.
Engraver.
Hendrik Hulsberg worked in London for booksellers. He mainly produced architectural engravings, as well as some portraits.

HULSCHER, Johannes
Dutch, 17th century.
Active in The Hague in 1646.
Painter. Still-lifes.

HULSDONCK, Gillis van
Dutch, 17th century.
Born 1626, in Amsterdam; died after 1670.
Painter. Still-lifes (fruit).
Gillis van Hulsdonck was the son of Jacob van Hulsdonck and studied under his father.
AUCTION RECORDS:
LONDON, 16 July 1980, *Still-life* (oil on panel, 14¾ x 11in/37.5 x 28cm) GBP 5,400. LONDON, 19 May 1989, *Still-life with Various Fruits on a Pewter Dish on a Draped Ledge* (oil on panel, 18¼ x 23in/46.1 x 58.5cm) GBP 20,900. MILAN, 28 May 1992, *Still-life with Fruit* (oil on panel, 18 x 22¾in/46 x 58cm) ITL 48,000,000. LA FLÈCHE, 2 April 1995, *Still-life with a Bowl of Plums, Vase of Flowers, Lemons and Cherries on a Ledge* (oil on panel, 19¼ x 25½in/49 x 65cm) FRF 395,000. LONDON, 9 July 1999, *Partly Peeled Lemon and Orange in Blue and White Wanli Porcelain Dish and Rose* (oil on panel, 19 x 15 ins / 48 x 38 cm) GBP 19,000. LONDON, 17 Dec 1999, *Grapes, Pomegranates, Plums in a Bowl, Orange, Rummer and Tazza on a Table* (oil on canvas, 22 x 20 ins / 56 x 51 cm) GBP 6,000.

HULSDONCK, Jacob van
Flemish, 16th - 17th century.
Born 1582, in Antwerp; died 1647, in Antwerp.
Painter. Still-lifes (flowers/fruit).
Antwerp School, Flemish School.
Jacob van Hulsdonck worked first in Middelburg but joined the Antwerp guild in 1609.

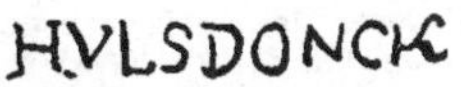

AUCTION RECORDS:
NEWCASTLE, 29 Oct 1941, *Still-life*, GBP 30. PARIS, 16 Dec 1942, *Lemons, Oranges and Pomegranates*, FRF 410,000. LONDON, 3 May 1946, *Fruit*, GBP 99; *Carnations in a Vase*, GBP 325. PARIS, 12 June 1953, *Vase of Flowers*, FRF 300,000. LONDON, 25 Nov 1966, *Still-life with Strawberries*, Gns 4,000. LONDON, 4 Oct 1967, *Still-life with Flowers*, Gns 9,200. LONDON, 27 June 1969, *Still-life with a Basket of Fruit*, Gns 11,000. PARIS, 17 March 1970, *Bowl of Plums*, FRF 100,000. LONDON, 26 Nov 1971, *Basket of Fruit*, Gns 11,000. LONDON, 8 Dec 1972, *Still-life with Flowers*, Gns 15,000. LONDON, 21 March 1973, *Still-life with Fruit*, GBP 8,000. LONDON, 29 Nov 1974, *Still-life with Grapes, Oranges and Lemons*, Gns 12,000. ZURICH, 12 Nov 1976, *Still-life* (oil on panel, 11 x 16¼ ins / 28 x 41 cm) CHF 34,000. LONDON, 8 July 1977, *Still-life with Fruit* (oil on panel, 10½ x 15 ins / 26.8 x 38.3 cm) GBP 32,000. PARIS, 28 March 1979, *Still-life with a Dish of Herrings* (oil on wood, 19½ x 25½ ins / 49.5 x 64.5 cm) FRF 150,000. NEW YORK, 9 Jan 1981, *Peaches and Plums in a Chinese Bowl* (oil on panel, 13¼ x 18¾ ins / 33.5 x 47.5 cm) USD 65,000. LONDON, 12 Dec 1984, *Still-life with Plums and a Rose* (oil/copper, 12½ x 16 ins / 32 x 40.5 cm) GBP 110,000. NEW YORK, 15 Jan 1985, *Still-life with Fruit* (oil on panel, 13 x 19 ins / 33 x 48.2 cm) USD 75,000. PARIS, 19 June 1986, *Peaches and Grapes on an Earthenware Dish* (oil on panel, 11 x 13½ ins / 28 x 34 cm) FRF 450,000. NEW YORK, 15 Jan 1987, *Still-life with a Basket of Grapes, Peaches, Plums and Cherries* (oil on panel, 24 x 35¾ ins / 61 x 91 cm) USD 130,000. PARIS, 14 Dec 1987, *Basket of Fruit on an Entablature* (oil on panel, 20¼ x 28 ins / 51.5 x 71 cm) FRF 660,000. LONDON, 21 April 1989, *Plums and Apricots in a Chinese Porcelain Bowl with a Carnation and a Rose on a Covered Entablature* (oil on panel, 12¼ x 15½ ins / 30.8 x 39.5 cm) GBP 60,500. PARIS, 9 April 1990, *Peaches and Bunches of Grapes in a Chinese Pottery Bowl on an Entablature with Plums, Cherries and Apricots* (oil on oak panel, 16 x 20¾ ins / 40.5 x 53 cm) FRF 1,400,000. LONDON, 11 April 1990, *Still-life with Plums and Peaches in a Basket* (oil on panel, 19 x 25¼ ins / 48 x 64 cm) GBP 236,500. LONDON, 8 July 1992, *Still-life with Apricots, Plums, Cherries, Radishes and Asparagus in a Basket on a Table* (oil on panel, 16 x 20½ ins / 40.5 x 51.9 cm) GBP 82,500. AMSTERDAM, 11 Nov 1992, *Still-life with Oranges, Lemons and Pomegranates in a Blue and White Pottery Bowl* (oil on panel, 12½ x 16¾ ins / 32 x 42.5 cm) NLG 759,000. PARIS, 4 Dec 1992, *Basket of Fruit and Flowers Placed on an Entablature* (oil on panel, 27 x 38 ins / 68.5 x 96.5 cm) FRF 7,550,000. FONTAINEBLEAU, 20 Dec 1992, *Still-life with Wang-Li Porcelain and a Bunch of Carnations; Still-life with a Basket of Grapes* (oil on panel, a pair, each 16¾ x 28½ ins / 42.5 x 72.5 cm) FRF 2,500,000. ST-GERMAIN-EN-LAYE, 31 March 1996, *Basket of Fruit Placed on an Entablature* (oil on panel, 20½ x 30 ins / 52 x 76 cm) FRF 4,400,000. NEW YORK, 30 Jan 1997, *Still-life of Peaches, Plums and Grapes in a Basket on an Entablature with a Lemon* (oil on panel, 16½ x 21¾ ins / 41.9 x 55.3 cm) USD 68,500. PARIS, 11 March 1997, *Basket of Fruit on an Entablature* (panel, 19½ x 25¼ ins / 49.5 x 64 cm) FFR 750,000. NEW YORK, 29 Jan 1998, *Peaches and Plums in a Wanli Kraak Porcelain Bowl with Cherries, a Plum and Pieces of Pomegranate on a Wooden Table* (oil on panel, 13½ x 18¾ ins / 34 x 47.6 cm) USD 310,500. LONDON, 16 Dec 1999, *Still-life of Whole Lemon and Pomegranate on Table Top* (oil on copper, 7 x 9 ins / 18 x 23 cm) GBP 30,000. LONDON, 13 Dec 2000, *Grapes on the Vine and Peaches in a Basket on a Table, with a Butterfly, Beetle and a Fly on a Ledge* (oil on panel, 20 x 25 ins / 50 x 64 cm) GBP 150,000. LONDON, 14 Dec 2000, *Still-life of Wild Strawberries and Carnation in a Ming Bowl, Cherries and Redcurrants on a Ledge* (oil on copper, 11 x 14 ins / 28 x 36 cm) GBP 470,000. LONDON, 11 Dec 2002, *Bunch of Grapes on the Vine* (oil on copper, 7 x 9 ins / 18 x 23 cm) GBP 80,000. NEW YORK, 27 May 2004, *Still-life of Fruit in Basket and Flowers in Basket* (oil on panel, 19 x 26 ins / 49 x 65 cm) USD 700,000. PARIS, 25 June 2004, *Still-life with Prunes and Apricots in a Basket* (oil on panel, 16 x 25 ins / 41 x 64 cm) EUR 370,000.

HULSEBOOM, Gerrit
Dutch, 19th century.
Born 1784, in Amsterdam; died 1863.
Painter, engraver, draughtsman. Landscapes.
Gerrit Hulseboom taught drawing at the H. van Niel Institute in Vaasen.
AUCTION RECORDS:
AMSTERDAM, 17 Nov 1993, *The Grimnessersluis in Amsterdam from the Rokin with the Old Church in the Distance* (ink and watercolour, 16½ x 13in/42 x 33cm) NLG 5,520. AMSTERDAM, 22 April 2002, *Country Road with Travellers* (oil on canvas, 20 x 26 ins / 50 x 65 cm) EUR 5,000.

HULSEN, Ezajas van, or Hulseen or Hulsius
Dutch, 16th - 17th century.
Born 1570, in Middelburg; died before 1626, in Stuttgart.
Engraver (burin), print publisher.

Ezajas van Hulsen engraved ornaments for jewellery, and plates of grotesques. He was the brother of Froedrich van Hulsen.

HULSEN, Friedrich van, or Hulseen or Hulsius
Dutch, 17th century.
Born 1580, in Middelburg; died c. 1665, in Frankfurt.
Draughtsman, engraver (burin).

Friedrich van Hulsen engraved historical portraits and mythological subjects. He lived in Frankfurt and later in London, where he worked for booksellers. He is believed to have been a pupil of Théodore de Bry.

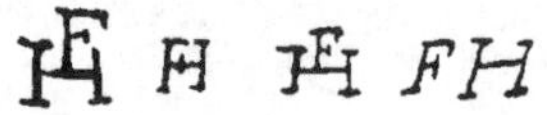

HÜLSENBECK, Richard. See **HULBECK Charles R.**

HULSER. See **HUELSER**

HULSHOFF POL, Albertus Gerhard
Dutch, 20th century.
Born 1883; died 1957.
Painter. Genre scenes, landscapes.

Albertus Hulshoff Pol worked by the River Gein from 1903 to 1906 with his friends Piet Mondrian and Simon Maris.

AUCTION RECORDS:
AMSTERDAM, 2 May 1990, *Two Girls with Umbrella on a Path* (oil on canvas on card, 9 1/4 x 11 3/4 ins / 23.5 x 30 cm) NLG 5,175. AMSTERDAM, 17 Sept 1991, *Impression: River* (oil on canvas, 24 1/2 x 34 3/4 ins / 62.5 x 88.5 cm) NLG 2,070. AMSTERDAM, 19 Jan 1999, *T'Gein, near Abcoude* (oil on canvas, 30x37 ins / 75x95 cm) NLG 3,200.

HULSMAN, Jan Jansz.
Dutch, 17th century.
Born in Oldenburg.
Painter.

Jan Hulsman appears to have worked in Amsterdam and Haarlem.

HULSMAN, Johann, or Holzmann
German, 17th century.
Painter, engraver. Mythological subjects, religious subjects, portraits, genre scenes.

Active in Cologne from 1634 to 1644. He was a pupil of Augustin Braun.

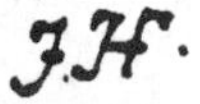

MUSEUMS AND GALLERIES:
COLOGNE: *St Veronica* - HANOVER: *Portrait of Princess Louise Hollandine.*

AUCTION RECORDS:
COLOGNE, 18 Nov 1982, *Tobias and the Angel* (1637, oil/copper, 11 1/4 x 17 3/4 ins / 28.5 x 45 cm) DEM 34,000. LONDON, 30 Oct 1997, *Tiresias Struck Blind by Minerva* (oil on canvas, 55 1/4 x 50 1/4 ins / 140.5 x 127.4 cm) GBP 6,325. LONDON, 7 July 1999, *Diana and Nymphs Resting on Edge of Forest* (oil on canvas, 55 x 54 ins / 139 x 138 cm) GBP 8,500. COLOGNE, 20 May 2000, *The Return of Commander Jephte* (oil on canvas, 37 x 53 ins / 95 x 135 cm) DEM 4,500. LONDON, 7 Aug 2000, *Portrait of King and Queen with Son as Donor* (oil on canvas, 43 x 27 ins / 109 x 69 cm) GBP 1,100.

HULST, Bartholomeus Jan van
Dutch, 18th century.
Born in Maasluis.
Painter. Portraits.

Bartholomeus van Hulst studied at the Koninklijke Academie voor Schone Kunsten in Antwerp.

HULST, Frans de
Flemish School, 17th century.
Born c. 1610, in Haarlem; died 29 December 1661, in Haarlem.
Painter. Landscapes with figures, landscapes, waterscapes.

In 1631, Frans de Hulst was a member of the Haarlem guild. He married in the city in 1640. In his landscapes, Hulst took inspiration from the technique of Ruysdael, R. de Vries and J. van Goyen.

MUSEUMS AND GALLERIES:
AMSTERDAM: *View of the Valkhof at Nijmegen* - ROTTERDAM: *View of the Old Gate and of Hoorn; View of Nijmegen* - STOCKHOLM: *Palace Wall by the Waterside* - TOURS: *Landscape with River.*

AUCTION RECORDS:
AMSTERDAM, 17 Oct 1905, *Town Walls*, FRF 1,500. LONDON, 5 April 1909, *River Scene*, GBP 9. PARIS, 12 June 1919, *View of Nijmegen*, FRF 1,250. LONDON, June 1922, *River Scene with Sailing Boats*, GBP 16. PARIS, 12 June 1931, *River Banks*, FRF 4,800. LONDON, 1 May 1946, *Dutch Fishing Boats*, GBP 30. PARIS, 5 April 1965, *Riverbank*, FRF 17,000. VIENNA, 14 March 1967, *Landscape with Figures*, ATS 60,000. AMSTERDAM, 26 May 1970, *Summer Landscape*, NLG 15,000. COLOGNE, 26 May 1971, *Outskirts of Scheveningen*, DEM 20,000. AMSTERDAM, 20 Nov 1973, *River Landscape*, NLG 21,000. NEW YORK, 15 June 1977, *River Landscape with a Fortified Town and a Ferryboat* (oil on panel, 15 3/4 x 27in/40 x 68.5cm) USD 9,000. LONDON, 30 Nov 1979, *Landscape with Cottage* (oil on panel, 11 x 16in/27.9 x 40.6cm) GBP 13,000. LONDON, 8 April 1981, *River Landscape with Fortress* (oil on panel, 15 1/2 x 24in/39.5 x 61cm) GBP 6,200. NEW YORK, 20 Jan 1983, *Fortified Town by a River* (oil on panel, 11 3/4 x 15 1/2in/30 x 39.5cm) USD 8,000. LONDON, 12 Dec 1986, *Landscape with Peasants and Travellers* (oil on panel, 11 1/2 x 16 1/4in/29 x 41.5cm) GBP 30,000. LONDON, 1 March 1991, *View of the Rhine with a Ferryboat Transporting a Cart* (oil on panel, 16 1/4 x 24 1/4in/41 x 61.3cm) GBP 6,600. PARIS, 25 March 1991, *Views of Villages in Holland* (oil on oval oak panel, a pair, each 15 3/4 x 20 3/4in/40 x 53cm) FRF 58,000. LONDON, 21 April 1993, *Extensive Landscape with Figures and a Ruined Church* (oil on panel, 14 1/2 x 27 1/2in/37 x 70cm) GBP 8,050. AMSTERDAM, 13 Nov 1995, *The Valkhof at Nijmegen with a Ferryman on the Wahal* (oil on panel, 12 1/4 x 19 1/2in/30.8 x 49.3cm) NLG 43,700. PARIS, 26 March 1996, *View of Dutch River Towns* (oil on panel, a pair, 14 x 22 3/4in/35.5 x 58cm) FRF 150,000. NEW YORK, 15 May 1996, *River Landscape with Fishermen Pulling in their Nets by a Castle* (oil on panel, 14 1/2 x 25 3/4in/37 x 65.7cm) USD 19,550. PARIS, 24 May 1996, *Still-life with Roemer Glass and Fruit* (oil on canvas, 15 x 22in/38 x 55cm) FRF 66,000. LONDON, 30 Oct 1996, *River Landscape with Fishermen; View of a Tower on a River* (oil on oval panel, a pair, each 12 1/2 x 16 1/4in/31.5 x 41.5cm) GBP 13,800. NEW YORK, 23 May 1997, *The River Waal at Nijmegen with the Valkhof and a Ferryboat in the Foreground* (oil on panel, 13 1/2 x 22 3/4in/34.6 x 57.8cm) USD 26,450. LONDON, 19 April 2000, *Roadside Inn in a Wooded Landscape* (oil on panel, 8 x 11 ins / 21 x 29 cm) GBP 12,000. ZURICH, 22 Sept 2000, *Canal Landscape* (oil on panel, oval, 15 x 20 ins / 39 x 52 cm) CHF 33,000. PARIS, 19 March 2001, *Medieval Fortress before a River Landscape* (oil on canvas, 30 x

45 ins / 75 x 114 cm) FRF 92,000. GRAVENHAGE, 7 Nov 2001, *City Wall on a River* (oil on panel, 26 x 17 ins / 66 x 42 cm) NLG 15,000. VIENNA, 2 Oct 2002, *Resting Peasants outside Village among Dunes* (oil on panel, 16 x 21 ins / 41 x 53 cm) EUR 20,000. COLOGNE, 21 Nov 2002, *Fortified Tower on Dutch River* (oil on panel, oval, 15 x 20 ins / 39 x 52 cm) EUR 7,500. COLOGNE, 15 Nov 2003, *River Landscape with Tower. Monastery by River* (oil on panel, 24 x 33 ins / 62 x 85 cm) EUR 24,000. MUNICH, 17 March 2004, *Riverside Castle with Towers and Landing Jetty with Sailing Boats* (oil on panel, 22 x 32 ins / 55 x 82 cm) EUR 6,500. VIENNA, 16 June 2004, *River Landscape with Anchoring Boats* (1637, oil on panel) EUR 8,000.

HULST, Hendrik van
Dutch, 18th century.
Born 24 December 1685, in Delft; died 5 April 1754.
Painter. Portraits.
Hendrik van Hulst studied under Mat Terwesten. He became a member of the Académie Royale de Peinture et de Sculpture in Paris, where he painted a *Portrait of Louis XIV*. He also worked in Italy.

HULST, Jan Baptist van der
Belgian, 19th century.
Born 22 March 1790, in Louvain; died 16 May 1862, in Brussels.
Painter. Religious subjects, portraits, landscapes.
Jan Baptist van der Hulst was a pupil of J. G. Geeds. He went to Paris in 1819, but finally settled in Holland, where he became painter to the court and a member of the fine arts academy of Amsterdam.

MUSEUMS AND GALLERIES:
AMSTERDAM: *William I, King of the Netherlands; Wilhemina, Princess of Prussia, Queen of the Netherlands; Count van der Duyn van Maasdam* - HAARLEM: *Portraits of Van Leyenburg and his Wife* - LEIDEN: *The Knight Jean van Hoogenhonck.*

AUCTION RECORDS:
AMSTERDAM, 30 Oct 1991, *Extensive River Landscape with a Fisherman on the Bank by a House* (1854, oil on panel, 13 1/2 x 16in/34 x 40.5cm) NLG 4,600. LOKEREN, 4 Dec 1993, *St Joseph and the Angels* (1861, oil on panel, 14 x 17 3/4in/35.5 x 45cm) BEF 40,000. MELBOURNE, 27 April 1999, *Portrait of a Young Woman* (1844, oil on panel, 17 x 15 ins / 43 x 37 cm) AUD 6,800. BRUSSELS, 23 Nov 1999, *Portrait of a Lady* (1850, oil on canvas, 49 x 37 ins / 124 x 95 cm) BEF 150,000.

HULST, Jan van der
Belgian, 19th century.
Active in Antwerp.
Painter.

HULST, Jehan
French, 14th century.
Active in Dijon.
Sculptor.
Flemish in origin, Jehan Hulst worked under Claus Sluter on the decoration of the door of the Carthusians of Champmol in Dijon in 1398 and 1399. In the same period he worked on the well placed in the centre of the cloister.

HULST, Maerten Fransz. van der
Dutch, 17th century.
Born 1605; died 1645.
Painter. Genre scenes, landscapes, seascapes.
Maerten van der Hulst worked in Leiden from 1630 to 1645. He followed the style of Ruysdael. Modern experts agree almost unanimously that he was the same artist as the painter Franz de Hulst.

MUSEUMS AND GALLERIES:
LEIDEN: *Fish Being Sold on the Beach.*

AUCTION RECORDS:
AMSTERDAM, 26 May 1970, *Summer Landscape*, NLG 15,000. LONDON, 30 May 1973, *Steep Landscape with Figures*, GBP 4,000. AMSTERDAM, 18 May 1976, *Harvest Scene* (oil on panel, 11 1/2 x 15 3/4in/29 x 40cm) NLG 24,000. NEW YORK, 19 March 1981, *Fishing Boats on a Canal* (oil on panel, 13 3/4 x 22 3/4in/35 x 58cm) USD 7,000. MONTE CARLO, 22 June 1985, *Dutch Seascape with Fishermen* (oil on panel, 15 3/4 x 21 3/4in/40 x 55.5cm) FRF 72,000. LONDON, 13 Dec 1991, *Landscape with Windmills beside a Canal* (oil on panel, 23 3/4 x 32 1/4in/60.5 x 82.2cm) GBP 33,000. PARIS, 31 March 1994, *Fishing Scene near the Dutch Coast* (oil on canvas, 19 x 25 1/4in/48.5 x 64cm) FRF 40,000. NEW YORK, 3 Nov 1999, *River Landscape with Fishermen in Rowing Boat* (oil on panel, 9 x 11 ins / 23 x 28 cm) USD 3,000. AMSTERDAM, 4 Nov 2003, *Two Figures Fishing from a Bridge over a Stream* (1643, black chalk, 6 x 9 ins / 15 x 22 cm) EUR 2,600. NEW YORK, 21 Jan 2004, *Travellers on a Coastal Road* (oil on panel, 10 x 16 ins / 26 x 40 cm) USD 11,000.

HULST, Pieter I van der
Dutch, 17th century.
Born c. 1583, in Dordrecht; died c. 1628.
Painter, engraver (etching).
Pieter van der Hulst I was a portrait engraver. He was probably a pupil of Ghielis Vinbons in Antwerp.

HULST, Pieter II van der
Flemish School, 17th century.
Active in Antwerp.
Painter.
Pieter van der Hulst II was the son of Pieter van der Hulst I, and was active from 1623.

HULST, Pieter III van der
Flemish School, 17th century.
Active in Antwerp.
Painter. Village scenes.
Pieter van der Hulst III was a master artist in 1647. He was almost certainly the son of Pieter van der Hulst II.

AUCTION RECORDS:
TOULOUSE, 1 March 1983, *Village Fair* (oil on panel, 29 1/4 x 36 1/4in/74 x 92cm) FRF 150,000. AMSTERDAM, 5 Nov 2001, *Amphitrite and Triton* (oil on canvas, 11 x 14 ins / 27 x 35 cm) NLG 4,000.

HULST, Pieter IV van der, or Hult or Verhulst
Dutch, 17th - 18th century.
Born 26 February 1651, in Dordrecht; died 1727, in Dordrecht.
Painter, engraver.
Pieter van der Hulst IV was a pupil of Willem Doudyns. In 1653, he was a member of the Camera in The Hague. In 1674, he went to Italy and worked in Rome. He also painted portraits.

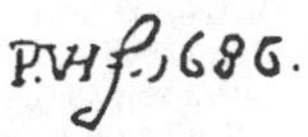

HULSTAERT, Albert
Belgian, 20th century.
Born 1918, in Melsele-Waas.
Painter. Landscapes with figures, seascapes.
Hulstaert painted mainly aquatic landscapes, polder landscapes and seascapes. His works are often enlivened by references to local customs and ancient myths.

HULSTEIJN, Johan Cornelis. See **HULSTYN Cornelis Johannes van**

HULSTER, Jan
Dutch, 17th century.

Active in The Hague.
Painter. Portraits.

In 1656, Jan Hulster was a member of the guild of The Hague. Around this period he painted a *Portrait of Prince Willem of Nassau*.

HULSTKAMP, J.

Dutch, 18th century.
Active c. 1786.
Engraver.

HULSTYN, Cornelis Johannes van

Dutch, 19th century.
Born 10 August 1813, in Jutfaas; died c. 1887.
Painter. Flowers, fruit.

Cornelis van Hulstyn was a pupil of Cornelis Johannes de Bruyn.

Auction records:

PARIS, 12 June 1942, *Flowers* (watercolour) FRF 14,500. LONDON, 15 Feb 1978, *Still-life with Flowers* (oil on canvas, 25 3/4 x 20 1/4in/65.5 x 51.5cm) GBP 1,000. AMSTERDAM, 2 Sept 1997, *17th-Century Interior with Elegant Woman Embroidering* (oil on canvas, 21 3/4 x 15 1/4in/55.5 x 38.5cm) NLG 1,037. AMSTERDAM, 19 June 2001, *Still-life with Grapes, Peaches and Plums in a Landscape* (1861, oil on canvas, 24 x 19 ins / 60 x 49 cm) NLG 7,000. PRAGUE, 22 May 2004, *Flowers* (1871, oil on canvas, 15 x 11 ins / 39 x 28 cm) CZK 50,000.

HULSWIT, Jan

Dutch, 18th - 19th century.
Born 11 April 1766, in Nieuwer Amstel; died 8 August 1822, in Amsterdam.
Painter, draughtsman. Landscapes, animals.

Jan Hulswit was a pupil of Pieter Barfiers Pietersz.

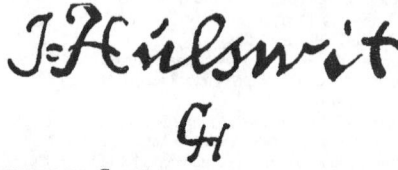

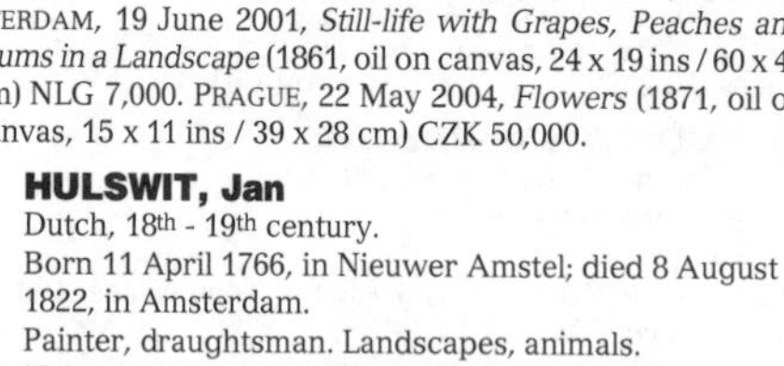

Museums and Galleries:

AMSTERDAM (Rijksmus.): *Landscape of Gooi; City Gate* - AMSTERDAM (Stedelijk Mus.): *Landscape* - FRANKFURT AM MAIN: *Landscape*.

Auction records:

PARIS, 18 Oct 1907, *Hilly Landscape,* FRF 225. LONDON, 27 May 1908, *Landscape* (drawing) GBP 4. LONDON, 13 Dec 1910, *Landscape* (drawing) GBP 3. PARIS, 7 July 1932, *Dutch Landscape,* FRF 22. PARIS, 8 Dec 1938, *Sunset on the River* (pen and wash) FRF 750. DORDRECHT, 1 Dec 1971, *Landscape with Small Bridge,* NLG 2,800. COLOGNE, 23 March 1973, *Wooded Landscape,* DEM 6,500. COLOGNE, 20 Oct 1989, *Romantic Landscape* (oil on canvas, 24 x 32 1/4in/61 x 82cm) DEM 11,000. AMSTERDAM, 2 May 1991, *The Singel in Amsterdam with Sailors Loading a Barge in the Foreground* (oil on canvas, 15 3/4 x 21 3/4in/40 x 55.3cm) NLG 9,775. PARIS, 22 Nov 1991, *Landscape with Bridge and Mill* (lead pencil, 3 3/4 x 6 1/4in/9.8 x 15.8cm) FRF 3,800. PARIS, 24 March 1995, *Landscape with Figures* (oil on canvas, 11 x 16 1/4in/27 x 41cm) FRF 19,000. AMSTERDAM, 8 Nov 2000, *Winter Scene in Drenthe with Soldiers and Travellers* (black chalk and watercolour, 9 x 12 ins / 22 x 31 cm) NLG 7,500. AMSTERDAM, 5 Nov 2002, *Wooded Landscape with Houses, Sheep and Cow near a Stream, and Two Shepherds Paddling beyond* (oil on canvas, 31 x 41 ins / 78 x 103 cm) EUR 10,000. HASLEMERE, 21 July 2004, *Shepherd and Sheep on Roadway* (oil on canvas, 18 x 22 ins / 46 x 56 cm) GBP 5,500.

HULTBERG, John Phillip

American, 20th century.
Born 1922, in Berkeley (California).
Painter (gouache), watercolourist. Scenes with figures.

John Phillip Hultberg began to paint at the age of 13. After studying in Fresno (California), he served as a lieutenant in the US marines from 1943 to 1946. When he was demobbed, he studied at the National Polytechnic Institute, Mexico, and then at the San-Miguel de Allende School of Fine Arts, Mexico. In 1947 he trained at California School of Fine Arts, San Francisco, and from 1949 to 1951 at the Art Students League, New York. In 1952-1953, he taught at Brooklyn Museum School, New York. From 1954 to 1959, he lived in Paris, and also travelled to Italy and Spain. In 1956 he received a bursary from the Guggenheim Foundation. In 1960, he taught at the Art Students League, New York, in 1964 was the 'artist in residence' at Portland Museum (Oregon), and in 1967 taught at the Art Academy, Honolulu.

Hultberg's work defies classification. His friendships with Clifford Still and Mark Rothko are not connected with any shared aesthetic motivation. He perhaps modelled his work on that of Hans Hofmann, like many Americans of the time. His Surrealist involvement is obvious, but not exclusive enough to classify him as one. He is figurative with no inhibitions and no possibility that his figurative art could be labelled 'Pop Art'. Figures with empty eyes, constantly escaping from their own image, avoid each other carefully in the congested semi-darkness of vast hangars. Hope meanwhile attempts to flee in the direction of the sky via the implacable light from behind of multiple gaping openings repeated in forgotten mirrors. Hultberg himself states that his paintings show 'a universe more dead than alive'.

Hultberg took part in a considerable number of group exhibitions, including: Corcoran Biennale, Washington, 1955 and 1958 Carnegie International, Pittsburgh, 1956 Venice Biennale, from 1962 the annual exhibition *Art in America* held at the Whitney Museum of American Art, New York, from 1962 the Salon de Mai, Paris, and 1965 São Paulo Biennale, etc. He very often showed series of his works in solo exhibitions: 1949 Sausalito (California), 1953 (and almost on an annual basis) New York, 1954 Fresno College Gallery (California), 1956 Institute of Contemporary Arts (ICA), London, 1957 (and frequently) Galerie du Drago, Paris, 1957 Florence, Milan, Washington, Chicago and several American universities, 1960, 1962, 1964 Santa Barbara (California), 1961 London, 1962 Museums in Malmö (Sweden) and Pasadena (California), 1963 Fresno College, 1965 London and Lausanne, 1967 Art Academy, Honolulu, and 1968 Liège (Belgium) and Southampton College, New York.

Hultberg was awarded several prizes: 1948 The San Francisco Prize for Watercolors, 1949 The San Francisco Prize for Painting, 1955 First Prize at the Corcoran Biennale, Washington, and an honourable mention at the Carnegie International, Pittsburgh, 1956 The Guggenheim Prize, 1957 The Hallmark Prize, 1963 The Tamarind Prize, and 1964 The Ford Foundation Prize.

Bibliography:

Hultberg, exhibition catalogue, Gal. du Dragon, Paris, 1970. *John Hultberg: Painter of the In-Between*, exhibition catalogue, F.L. Emerson Gallery, Hamilton College, Clinton (NY), 1985. *John Hultberg: Visionary Theatre*, exhibition catalogue, Denise Bibro Gallery, New York, 1994.

Museums and Galleries:

BUFFALO (Albright-Knox AG) - MARSEILLES (Mus. Cantini) - NEW YORK (Metropolitan Mus. of Art) - NEW YORK (Whitney Mus. of American Art).

Auction records:

MILAN, 15 March 1973, *Wings* (1959) ITL 1,700,000. STOCKHOLM, 27 May 1986, *Windows* (1960, oil on canvas, 38 1/2 x 50 ins / 98 x 127 cm) SEK 19,100. NEW YORK, 26 Feb 1993, *Great*

Empty Sky (1962, oil on canvas, 50 x 68 ins / 127 x 172.7 cm) USD 1,840. NEW YORK, 10 Oct 1996, *Reaper; Near Miss* (1959, oil on canvas, a pair, 35 x 51 ins / 88.9 x 129.5 cm and 25 x 35 ins/63.5 x 88.9 cm) USD 2,300.

HULTÉN, Carl Otto
Swedish, 20th century.
Born 1916, in Malmö.
Painter.
Groups: Minotaurgruppen, Imaginistgruppen, CoBrA.

A self-taught artist, Carl Otto Hultén was one of the co-founders in 1943 (together with Max Walter Svanberg and the Hungarian Endre Nemes, who had fled to Sweden) of the Minotaurgruppe (Minotaur group), and in 1945 of the Imaginistgruppe (Imaginist group). At the time, these groups were a focus and inspiration for Surrealism in Sweden. Hultén made several trips in Europe. He came into contact with Jorn in Denmark and, through him, Christian Dotremont and the CoBrA group. In 1950, he exhibited with the Imaginist group in Paris and Florence, as well as with the CoBrA group in Brussels. In Malmö he painted murals and laid a mosaic.

In 1947, within the context of his Surrealist work, Hultén produced a series of 'frottages' entitled *Dreams of a Leaf's Hands*. His style developed freely from fantastical representations through Expressionism to Abstraction, and from Surrealism to the spontaneous art of the CoBrA group. Like the Cobra artists, his drawing style is eloquent and violently primitive, and his coloration extreme. Together with Dotremont, Hultén also produced 'word-paintings'.

BIBLIOGRAPHY:
Stokvis, Willemijn, *Cobra*, Gallimard, Paris, 2001.

AUCTION RECORDS:
COPENHAGEN, 18 March 1970, *Composition*, DKK 7,500. STOCKHOLM, 6 June 1988, *Composition* (enamel, 5¼ x 10½ ins / 13.5 x 26.5 cm) SEK 5,000. LONDON, 26 Oct 1989, *Head* (oil on panel, 12½ x 10¾ ins / 32 x 27.2 cm) GBP 12,100. STOCKHOLM, 5-6 Dec 1990, *Dogonland* (oil on canvas, 28¾ x 36¼ ins / 73 x 92 cm) SEK 34,000. AMSTERDAM, 21 May 1992, *Beautiful Mask* (oil on canvas/card, 7¾ x 16½ ins / 20 x 42 cm) NLG 7,475. STOCKHOLM, 25 Nov 1999, *Cloud Symbol* (1963, oil on canvas, 29 x 24 ins / 73 x 60 cm) SEK 24,000. STOCKHOLM, 25 Nov 1999, *Mother and Child* (1950-1951, oil on canvas, 13 x 22 ins / 34 x 57 cm) SEK 33,000. STOCKHOLM, 15 May 2000, *Red Interior* (1958, oil on canvas, 25 x 31 ins / 64 x 80 cm) SEK 29,000. STOCKHOLM, 7 Nov 2000, *Untitled Composition* (1989, oil on canvas, 28 x 36 ins / 71 x 91 cm) SEK 35,000. STOCKHOLM, 21 May 2001, *Untitled Composition* (mixed media, 12 x 16 ins / 31 x 40 cm) SEK 19,000. STOCKHOLM, 6 Nov 2001, *Blue Coition* (oil on canvas, 18 x 22 ins / 45 x 56 cm) SEK 42,000. STOCKHOLM, 4 Nov 2003, *Dialogue with Landscape* (oil on canvas, 33 x 39 ins / 83 x 100 cm) SEK 36,000. STOCKHOLM, 4 Nov 2003, *The Wall* (oil on canvas, 57 x 66 ins / 144 x 168 cm) SEK 135,000. STOCKHOLM, 26 April 2004, *The Red Watchman* (oil on canvas, 39 x 32 ins / 100 x 81 cm) SEK 47,000. STOCKHOLM, 2 Nov 2004, *Community Transformation* (1954, oil on canvas, 26 x 44 ins / 67 x 112 cm) SEK 50,000.

HULTGREN, Anders
Swedish, 18th - 19th century.
Born 1763, in Arboga; died probably c. 1840, in Stockholm.
Painter.

Anders Hultgren decorated the royal castle in Stockholm.

HULTON, William
Italian, 20th century.
Died 1921.
Active in London.
Painter. Landscapes.

Hulton exhibited from 1882 and worked very often in Venice and Britain.

HULTZSCH, Hermann
German, 19th century.
Born 20 April 1837, in Dresden; died 17 December 1905, in Blasewitz.
Sculptor.

His forte was busts. He worked mainly in his native city.

HULURI, Martin de
Spanish, 16th century.
Active in Seville in 1542.
Sculptor.

HUMAIR, Daniel
Swiss, 20th century.
Born 23 May 1938, in Geneva.
Active in France.
Painter.

All three strands of Humair's career (as a well-known jazz drummer,as a musical *animateur* at the Musée d'Art Moderne de la Ville de Paris, and a painter) are tied together by music. The rhythm and spirit of freedom found in jazz can also be found in his paintings, rendered in spatial terms. During his various travels as a musician, he works on paper; this work is subsequently stuck to canvas. His painting is close in spirit to that of the artists of the CoBrA group, and he is inspired by the moment and the automatic nature of what results. As he has said: 'I never throw anything away.' Through his non-figurative compositions, which are generally lively and brightly coloured (though occasionally rendered in more muted and serious tones), Humair conjures up the fluidity of musical expression with sequences of multi-coloured ovoid forms that float on and punctuate neutral grounds. His painting has the spontaneity of graffiti, and the sensuality of his colours-as-subject-matter is indicative of his technical command. As in jazz, serial repetition of a riff forms the basis of an endless series of improvised variations.

Work by Humair has been shown at collective exhibitions since 1969, notably at the Salon de Mai in Paris. There have also been many solo exhibitions of groups of his works, for example in Paris and other French cities; Geneva (1978); Denmark (1978, 1980 and 1984); Zurich (1987); the Institut Français in Aachen (1988); the Centre Culturel in St-Yrieix-la-Perche (1997). Regular solo exhibitions have been held in Paris by the Galerie Erval (1980, 1983, 1986, 1987 (at the International Contemporary Art Fair), 1989, 1992 and others.).

BIBLIOGRAPHY:
Daniel Humair, Fragments, Paris, 2003.

AUCTION RECORDS:
PARIS, 29 Jan 1988, *Untitled* (1976, gouache, 19¾ x 25½ ins / 50 x 65 cm) FRF 6,800. PARIS, 26 Sept 1989, *Palöte* (1985, acrylic, 22 x 17¼ ins / 56 x 44 cm) FRF 6,000. COPENHAGEN, 14-15 Nov 1990, *Green Raga I* (1977, acrylic/paper/canvas, 39¼ x 39¼ ins / 100 x 100 cm) DKK 5,000.

HUMAIR, Michel
Swiss, 20th century.
Born 1926.
Active in France.
Painter.

Humair exhibited frequently at the Salon des Réalités Nouvelles in Paris. In 1993, 1996 and 1998, the Galerie Bellint in Paris presented solo exhibitions of his work. His painting is completely gestural, and he is generous with brightly coloured paint.

HUMANN, O. Victor
American, 20th century.
Painter.

O. Victor Humann was a pupil at the Art Institute of Chicago, and Art Students League, New York, under Arthur Dow. He became a teacher at the Worcester Art Museum School.

HUMAYER, Erzsebet
Hungarian, 20th century.
Born 17 July 1891, in the Czongrád region.
Painter. Flowers.
Erzsebet Humayer worked in Budapest.

HUMBACH, Jonas
Painter, draughtsman.
Jonas Humbach is mentioned by Ris-Paquot in the *Dictionnaire Encyclopédique des Marques et Monogrammes, Chiffres, Lettres, Initials, Signes Figuratifs*, 1893.

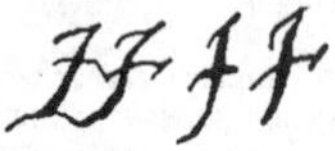

AUCTION RECORDS:
PARIS, 19 and 20 Jan 1942, *The Scourging* (drawing in red chalk) FRF 1,000.

HUMBEECK, Pierre van
Belgian, 20th century.
Born 27 April 1891, in Brussels; died 1964, in Herent.
Painter. Figures, portraits, genre scenes.
Pierre van Humbeeck was a student at the fine arts academy in St Joost-ten-Node and then of Jean Delville, Constant Montald, Émile Fabry and Victor Rousseau at the Brussels academy. He was awarded the Prix Godecharle. He married the painter Marie Piron. He visited Paris and Italy and with his wife was a founder member of the group Art et Louange (Art and Praise), whose aim was to spread the neo-Thomist approach to art. He settled in Louvain and founded the Van Humbeeck-Piron Museum.

He started out making decorative panels, and he and his wife divided their time between the Brabant and the Belgian Ardenne region. In addition to his genre scenes, Van Humbeeck painted mainly portraits, figurative works, and little girls. He was an artist of the Idealist-Expressionist trend that grew up in Belgium after World War I.

BIBLIOGRAPHY:
Bendère, R. de, *Pierre et Marie Van Humbeeck-Piron*, Brussels, 1927. Brucher, Roger/Fumet, Stanislas/Nothomb, Pierre, *Pierre et Marie Van Humbeeck-Piron, peintres du regard intérieur*, Éd. La Dryade, Vieux-Virton, 1960.
MUSEUMS AND GALLERIES:
LOUVAIN (Provinciaal Van Humbeeck-Pironmus.).

HUMBEECK-PIRON, Marie van
Belgian, 20th century.
Born 1888, in Philippeville; died 6 April 1969, in Louvain.
Painter, engraver, draughtsman. Portraits, landscapes.
Marie van Humbeeck-Piron was a student of Omer Dierickx at the academy in Louvain academy, and of Jean Delville and Herman Richir at the academy in Brussels. She was the wife of Pierre van Humbeeck, and they split their time between the Brabant and the Belgian Ardenne region. Together with her husband, she was co-founder of the Art et Louange (Art and Praise) group, whose aim was to spread the neo-Thomist approach to art. She was a member of the Académie des Beaux-Arts of Luxembourg and the Société Royale des Beaux-Arts in Belgium.

Most of Van Humbeeck-Piron's paintings, engravings and drawings were inspired by the Belgian Ardenne region.

BIBLIOGRAPHY:
Bendère, R. de, *Pierre et Marie Van Humbeeck-Piron*, Brussels, 1927. Brucher, Roger/Fumet, Stanislas/Nothomb, Pierre, *Pierre et Marie Van Humbeeck-Piron, peintres du regard intérieur*, Éd. La Dryade, Vieux-Virton, 1960.
MUSEUMS AND GALLERIES:
LOUVAIN (Provinciaal Van Humbeeck-Pironmus.).

HUMBELET, Jean
French, 16th century.
Active in Troyes.
Sculptor, architect.
Jean Humbelet was one of those who worked on the rood screen of the church of Mary Magdalene in Troyes in 1516.

HUMBELOT, Didier
French, 17th century.
Active at the beginning of the 17th century.
Painter, sculptor.
Didier Humbelot enjoyed the protection of Cardinal François de la Rochefoucauld. He worked for a number of Paris churches.

HUMBELOT, Jacques
French, 18th century.
Active in Paris c. 1760.
Engraver (burin).
Jacques Humbelot engraved portraits.

HUMBELOT, Jean Baptiste
French, 17th century.
Active in Paris.
Engraver.

HUMBERDOT, C. S. (Mme)
Maiden name: Lachaise
French, 19th - 20th century.
Active in Versailles.
Painter.
Humberdot became a member of the Société des Artistes Français in 1893.

HUMBERT, A.
French, 19th century.
Sculptor.
The Musée de Metz has a plaster low relief by this artist, dated 1852, entitled *Two Cavaliers Fighting*.

HUMBERT, Adèle
French, 19th century.
Born in Metz.
Painter. Genre scenes, portraits.
Adèle Humbert was a pupil of Hussenot. She exhibited at the Salon in 1846 and 1848. The Musée de Metz has a *Magdalene* by this artist, which was bought by the state after the 1846 exhibition.

HUMBERT, Albert
French, 19th century.
Born 24 February 1835, in Vesoul (Haute-Saône); died 1886, in Paris.
Caricaturist.
Albert Humbert's work of 1868, *Lantern of Boquillon*, brought him considerable success.

HUMBERT, André Louis Maxime
French, 20th century.
Born 27 November 1879, in Paris.
Painter. History painting, genre scenes.
Humbert was a student of Léon Bonnat. He regularly exhibited in Paris at the Salon des Artistes Français, winning a third-class medal in 1901, a second-class medal in 1904 and a travel grant in 1907.
MUSEUMS AND GALLERIES:
PÉRIGUEUX: *The Stoning of St Stephen*.
AUCTION RECORDS:
PARIS, 23 April 1945, *Nocturnal Dinner*, FRF 350. CALAIS, 3 July 1994, *The Wine Harvest* (oil on canvas, 103½ x 70 ins / 263 x 178 cm) FRF 20,000. NEW YORK, 1 Nov 1995, *At the The-*

atre: *Mlle Simone Frevalles* (1913, oil on canvas, 84½ x 41½ ins / 214.9 x 105.1 cm) USD 13,800.

HUMBERT, Cécile
French, 19th century.
Painter. Genre scenes, portraits.

Cécile Humbert exhibited at the Salons of 1846 and 1848.

HUMBERT, Charles-Jean Ferdinand.
See **HUMBERT Jean Charles Ferdinand**

HUMBERT, Dominique
French, 18th century.
Active in Lunéville in 1724.
Painter. Religious subjects, portraits.

HUMBERT, Frédéric
French, 19th - 20th century.
Painter, poet.

Frédéric Humbert was a student of Roybet. He exhibited at the Salon.

AUCTION RECORDS:
PARIS, 24 and 25 June 1902, *Louis XIII and Mlle de Hautefort*, FRF 5,400. PARIS, 9 Oct 1942, *A Bridge Over the Seine in Paris*, FRF 700. PARIS, 4 July 1945, *Village* FRF 700; *Springtime Landscapes* (two canvases) FRF 1,500.

HUMBERT, Jacqueline
French, 20th century.
Born 1937, in Paris.
Painter, designer.

Jacqueline Humbert has exhibited in Paris since 1969 at the Salon des Femmes Peintres et Sculpteurs. Her painting is closer to Pop Art than Naïve Art. She depicts greenery, flowers, birds and butterflies and often paints in stencil, in a manner recalling Mexican or Polish paper cut-outs. She decorated the façades of the Auxerre covered market.

HUMBERT, Jacques Fernand
French, 19th - 20th century.
Born 8 October 1842, in Paris; died 1934.
Painter. Religious subjects, mythological subjects, portraits, genre scenes.

Jacques Fernand Humbert entered the École des Beaux-Arts in Paris in 1861, and trained under the direction of François Édouard Picot, Alexandre Cabanel and Eugène Fromentin. Humbert executed two large decorative panels for the town hall of the fifteenth arrondissement in Paris. In their austerity of composition and their lifeless tonalities, these panels recall the work of Puvis de Chavannes. He showed regularly in Paris at the Salon, and then at the Salon des Artistes Français. He won medals in 1866, 1867, 1869 and 1878. He received a medal of honour in 1900. He was decorated with the Légion d'Honneur in 1878, promoted to Officier in 1885, and then Commandeur in 1906. He became a member of the Institut de France in 1902.

MUSEUMS AND GALLERIES:
AURILLAC: *Œdipus and Antigone* - AUTUN (Mus. Rolin): *The Abduction* - DIJON (MBA): *Lady in Grey* - GENEVA (Mus. Ariana): *Lady in Costume for a Ball* - LE HAVRE: *St John the Baptist* - LYONS (MBA): *Maternity* - MULHOUSE: *The Adulterous Woman* - PARIS (Louvre): *The Virgin, Christ Child and St John the Baptist; Young Girl on a Donkey* - PARIS (Mus. du Petit Palais): *Sketch for the Decoration of the City Hall* - THE HAGUE (Mus. Mesdag): *Fantasy*.

AUCTION RECORDS:
PARIS, 2 April 1897, *Leda Surprised by Jupiter*, FRF 700. NEW YORK, 15 Feb 1900, *Parisian Woman*, USD 475. NEW YORK, 1 Dec 1940, *The Virgin, Christ Child and St John*, USD 115. PARIS, 2 Dec 1946, *The Virgin and Child*, FRF 5,000. LONDON, 17 May 1991, *Diana at the Bath* (1886, oil on canvas, 32 x 43 ins / 81.2 x 109.2 cm) GBP 2,750. LONDON, 4 Oct 1991, *The Dance* (oil on canvas, 49 x 26 ins / 124.5 x 66 cm) GBP 2,090. NEW YORK, 17 Jan 1996, *Elegant Figure with Dog by the Seashore* (1881, oil on canvas, 80½ x 42¼ ins / 204.2 x 107 cm) USD 7,475. PARIS, 20 Oct 1997, *Elegant Figure with Muff* (1911, oil on canvas, 49¼ x 35½ ins / 125 x 90 cm) FRF 45,000.

HUMBERT, Jan
Dutch, 18th century.
Born 7 May 1734, in Amsterdam; died October 1794, in Amsterdam.
Painter. Historical subjects, portraits.

Jan Humbert was a pupil of J. Fournier. He studied art in Paris before returning to Holland and working in Amsterdam and The Hague. He became director of the school of drawing in The Hague.

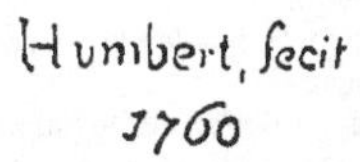

HUMBERT, Jean Charles Ferdinand
Swiss, 19th century.
Born 26 December 1813, in Geneva; died 30 March 1881, in Geneva.
Painter. Landscapes, animals.

He was a pupil of Ingres in Paris, but subsequently returned to Geneva and settled there, becoming a pupil of Diday. In 1842, he won a medal in Paris. He was a member of the St Petersburg academy.

MUSEUMS AND GALLERIES:
BASEL: *Cows Drinking* - BERN: *Livestock Crossing a River* - GENEVA (MAH): *Grazing; The Ford* - GENEVA (Mus. Ariana): *Meadow with Cows Grazing; Mountain Landscape with Animals; Landscape and Sheep Grazing; The Forge at Corraterie.*

AUCTION RECORDS:
LONDON, May 1924, *Spa*, GBP 33. GENEVA, 5 Oct 1972, *Landscape with Figures*, CHF 4,600. LUCERNE, 21 July 1974, *Grazing* (1876) CHF 4,200. BERN, 7 May 1976, *Animals beside the Water* (1875, oil on oval card, 9 x 16¼ ins / 23 x 41 cm) CHF 1,800. VIENNA, 10 May 1977, *Animals at the Trough* (1865, oil on canvas, 35 x 49¼ ins / 88 x 125 cm) ATS 65,000. BERN, 21 Nov 1978, *Animals in an Alpine Landscape* (1855, oil on canvas, 9 x 16¼ ins / 23 x 41.5 cm) CHF 3,000. BERN, 3 May 1979, *Cows beside an Alpine Lake* (1862, oil on canvas, 18½ x 29½ ins / 47 x 75 cm) CHF 3,500. BERN, 11 May 1984, *Autumn Landscape - The Woodcutter's Cart* (1876, oil on canvas, 35½ x 51¼ ins / 90 x 130 cm) CHF 8,500. LONDON, 23 May 1985, *Goats and Sheep in a Mountain Landscape* (oil on canvas, 38 x 54½ ins / 96.5 x 138.5 cm) CHF 10,000. BERN, 26 Oct 1988, *The Good Friends* (oil on card, 14¼ x 17 ins / 36.5 x 43 cm) CHF 2,200. BERN, 12 May 1990, *A Pool* (1878, oil on canvas, 12½ x 19¼ ins / 32 x 49 cm) CHF 4,400. PARIS, 5 June 1992, *Pastorale* (oil on canvas, 19 x 28¾ ins / 48 x 73 cm) FRF 15,000. AMSTERDAM, 2-3 Nov 1992, *Cows in a Mountain Landscape* (1873, oil on canvas, 35 x 50½ ins / 88 x 128 cm) NLG 6,900. ZURICH, 1 Dec 1999, *Cows in Alpine Pasture* (1869, oil on canvas, 26 x 39 ins / 65 x 99 cm) CHF 5,500. SWITZERLAND, 3 Dec 1999, *Girl Herding Cows and Goats Home* (1871, oil on canvas, 30 x 45 ins / 76 x 115 cm) CHF 6,000. ZURICH, 4 Nov 2000, *Oxcart by Lake Geneva* (1874, oil on canvas, 35 x 51 ins / 89 x 129 cm) CHF 5,500. BERN, 8 Nov 2001, *Officer on Horseback Taking a Break with other Soldiers* (1853, oil on canvas, 15 x 21 ins / 39 x 54 cm) CHF 4,000.

BERN, 8 Nov 2001, *Stormy Mountain Landscape with Cows* (1877, oil on canvas, 33 x 49 ins / 83 x 125 cm) CHF 9,000. ZURICH, 16 Sept 2002, *Landscape with Horses and Sheep* (oil on canvas, 17 x 24 ins / 44 x 61 cm) CHF 2,800. BERN, 9 May 2003, *Cattle Watering* (1879, oil on canvas, 31 x 50 ins / 79 x 128 cm) CHF 6,000. BERN, 9 May 2003, *Landscape with Riders* (1849, oil on canvas, 13 x 19 ins / 33 x 49 cm) CHF 6,000.

HUMBERT, Jules Eugène
French, 19th century.
Born 28 September 1821, in Strasbourg; died 8 July 1870, in Paris.
Painter.

Jules Humbert was a pupil of Picot and Gleyre. He exhibited his drawings at the Salon from 1851 to 1866, and was employed as a painter at the Sèvres porcelain manufactory. His best-known paintings include: *The Secret Surprise, Thisbe the Actress at the House of Catarina Brogadini* and *The Oracle*.

HUMBERT, Lambillion. See **LAMBILLON Humbert**

HUMBERT, Louis
French, 19th century.
Born 13 March 1835, in Alençon (Orne).
Painter. Landscapes.

Louis Humbert first exhibited at the Salon in 1865.

HUMBERT, Paulette
French, 20th century.
Born 5 July 1904, in Paris.
Painter, illustrator.

Paulette Humbert graduated from the École des Arts Décoratifs in Paris. She illustrated *Le Réveil des morts* (*The Awakening of the Dead*) by Roland Dorgelès, *La Brière* by Alphonse de Châteaubriant, *Dominique* by Eugène Fromentin, *Émaux et Camées* (*Enamels and Cameos*) by Théophile Gautier, *Raphaël* by Alphonse de Lamartine, *René* by Chateaubriand, and *La Porte étroite* by André Gide. She exhibited regularly at the Salon, of which she was a member.

BIBLIOGRAPHY:

Mornand, Pierre/Thomé, Jules-René, *Vingt artistes du livre*, A. Cymboliste, Paris, 1950.

HUMBERT, Pierre
French, 20th century.
Born 1929, in Paris.
Painter.

Pierre Humbert practices an informal, matter-oriented abstraction which recreates an allusive, tactile and sensual perception of landscape. In the early post-war years, he exhibited at the Galerie Maeght with the Mains Éblouies (Dazzled Hands) group, which presented to the public the new generation of Abstraction. In 1993, a Parisian gallery held an exhibition of his recent works, in the wider context of his work as a whole.

HUMBERT, Pierre
Swiss, 20th century.
Born 1920, in Le Locle; died 1992.
Active in France.
Painter. Still-lifes.

Pierre Humbert studied initially at the art college in La Chaux-de-Fonds, then moved to Paris to study under Othon Friesz, Ossip Zadkine and Goerg. He settled in Paris from 1968 and then in Saint-Laurent-la-Vernède in the Uzès region of France.

Critics and art lovers such as Jean-Jacques Levêque, Jean-Marie Drot and Jean-Marie Dunoyer have expressed interest in Humbert's work, which is distinguished by his accomplished treatment of light effects which invade and transform his essentially figurative compositions.

Humbert made his solo debut in 1958 at the Galerie Sholler in Paris. In 1994, the Georges Borias Museum in Uzès mounted a tribute exhibition and went on to exhibit a dozen or so of his canvases in 2000.

HUMBERT, Sébastien
French, 18th century.
Born c. 1749, in Metz.
Sculptor.

HUMBERT DE SUPERVILLE, David Pierre Giottino
Dutch, 18th - 19th century.
Born 18 July 1770, in The Hague; died 9 January 1849, in Leiden.
Draughtsman, engraver, lithographer.

David Humbert de Superville was the son of a protestant pastor. He studied art in Italy. In 1997-1998, the Musée Fabre in Montpellier and the Institut Néerlandais in Paris held exhibitions of his work entitled *Virtuose et Savant, DPG Humbert de Superville (1770-1849)* (*Virtuoso and Scholar, DPG Humbert de Superville (1770-1849)*) and *DPG Humbert de Superville: Dessins Néo-Classiques du Cabinet des Estampes de l'Université de Leyde* (*DPG Humbert de Superville: Neo-Classical Drawings from the Engravings Collection of the University of Leiden*).

Humbert de Superville was both a scholar and a highly talented artist. The University of Leiden has, in addition to his scientific writings, around 2,000 drawings and some 50 engravings by him in its engravings collection. His drawings cover a wide range of subjects: theoretical studies; classical studies; studies after the old masters including Benozzo Gozzoli, Raphael and Dürer; anatomical and historical subjects; model architectural plans; even fantastical monuments and portraits of his contemporaries and relations.

In 1827, he published a work on art entitled *Essai sur les Signes Inconditionnels dans l'Art* (*Essay on Absolute Signs in Art*) which addresses the expressive qualities of line and colour and, in modern terms, their synthetic potential. Charles Blanc, author of *Grammaire des Arts du Dessin* (*Grammar of the Art of Drawing*) introduced this work to Seurat and other Neo-Impressionists. These various works form the premise for a semiology of the graphic arts.

BIBLIOGRAPHY:

Superville, D.P.G. Humbert de, *Essai sur les signes inconditionnels dans l'art*, Leiden, Paris, 1998.

MUSEUMS AND GALLERIES:

LEIDEN (Universiteit Leiden, Prints Collection): approximately 2000 drawings and 50 engravings.

HUMBERT ESTEVE, Manuel
Spanish, 20th century.
Born 1890, in Barcelona; died 1975.
Painter, illustrator. Figure compositions, figures, portraits, landscapes.

Manuel Humbert Esteve studied at the school of fine arts in Barcelona and the academy of Francisco Gali. He spent some time in Paris in 1909, which inspired him to draw Parisian subjects. In his early years he became known as a magazine illustrator, but he also illustrated literary works, including Espronceda's *Student of Salamanca*, Rojas' *La Celestina* and the works of Juan Maragall and Miguel Llor.

Humbert Esteve's paintings, especially the compositions with figures such as *The Rural Council* or figures like his *Pensive Woman*, are solidly constructed according to an overall design. Three-dimensionality is strongly indicated by the use of light and shade and the contrast of warm and cool tones, as if distantly echoing the teachings of Cézanne.

Humbert Esteve took part in many group exhibitions, including the Barcelona Exposición de Bellas Artes from 1918 onwards and the Exposición Nacional de Bellas Artes in Madrid from 1919 to 1942. He also exhibited in Paris, Buenos

Aires and New York. He was president of the Montjuic Salon, an important spring show for Catalan artists.

BIBLIOGRAPHY:

Arnáiz, José Manuel/López Jiménez, Javier/Merchán Díaz, Manuel (ed.), *Cien años de pintura en Espana y Portugal (1830-1930)*, Antiqvaria, Madrid, 1989.

MUSEUMS AND GALLERIES:

BARCELONA (MAM del Mus. Nacional d'Art de Catalunya) - MADRID (Mus. de Arte Moderno).

AUCTION RECORDS:

BARCELONA, 8 Oct 1980, *Still-life with Sardines* (oil on canvas, 24 x 28¾ ins / 61 x 73 cm) ESP 240,000. BARCELONA, 14 May 1981, *Seated Girl* (oil on canvas, 27½ x 22½ ins / 70 x 57 cm) ESP 320,000. MADRID, 9 March 1999, *Portrait of Woman* (1959, oil on canvas, 26 x 21 ins / 65 x 54 cm) ESP 300,000. MADRID, 9 March 1999, *Portrait of Woman* (oil on canvas, 24 x 20 ins / 61 x 50 cm) ESP 325,000. MADRID, 10 July 2000, *Sitting Figure* (oil on canvas, 29 x 24 ins / 73 x 60 cm) ESP 630,000. MADRID, 6 Nov 2000, *The Painter's Model* (oil on canvas, 32 x 26 ins / 81 x 65 cm) ESP 625,000. MADRID, 25 Feb 2002, *Female Nude* (oil on canvas, 24 x 20 ins / 61 x 50 cm) EUR 3,400.

HUMBERT-VIGNOT, Léonie

French, 19th - 20th century.
Born in Lyons.
Painter. Portraits, genre scenes, still-lifes.

Léonie Humbert-Vignot studied with Alexandre Bonnardel and Édouard Toudouze at the École des Beaux-Arts in Lyons. She was a painter of genre scenes, such as *Good Fortune* (1901); *Last Touches* (1903); *At the Curiosity Shop* (1905); *The Poor People*, *Convalescing Woman* and *Interrupted Reading* (1908); and the triptych *Strike Evening* (1910). She exhibited at the Salon in Lyons from 1896. She received a second-class medal in 1901, a *rappel de médaille* (recognition for a previous award of a medal) in 1903, and a first medal in 1908. She also exhibited in Paris from 1905 at the Salon des Artistes Français, receiving an honourable mention in 1908 and a third-class medal in 1910.

MUSEUMS AND GALLERIES:

DIGNE-LES-BAINS: *Good Fortune*.

AUCTION RECORDS:

PARIS, 12 Oct 1990, *The Little Diva* (oil on canvas, 46½ x 36½ ins / 118 x 93 cm) FRF 13,500. PARIS, 10 Feb 1993, *Elegant Woman* (oil on canvas, 42 x 35¾ ins / 106.5 x 91 cm) FRF 8,500. PARIS, 3 April 2000, *Oriental Market* (oil on canvas, 18 x 15 ins / 46 x 38 cm) FRF 12,000. EVREUX, 30 Sept 2001, *Orientalist Nude* (oil on canvas, 24 x 15 ins / 61 x 38 cm) FRF 19,500.

HUMBLE, D. George

British, 16th century.
Active in London.
Painter. Portraits.

HUMBLET, Théo

Belgian, 20th century.
Born 1919, in Louvain.
Painter, engraver, illustrator.

Humblet was a student at the St Luke Academy in Schaerbeek and at the fine arts academy in Louvain. He won the Prix de Rome and became director of the academy in Louvain.

MUSEUMS AND GALLERIES:

BRUSSELS (Bibliothèque royale Albert Ier, Prints Collection).

AUCTION RECORDS:

LOKEREN, 11 March 1978, *Head* (1967, ceramic, h. 19¾ ins / 50 cm) BEF 30,000.

HUMBLOT, Antoine

French, 18th century.
Died 1758.
Active in Paris.
Draughtsman.

Antoine Humblot is responsible for many book illustrations.

HUMBLOT, Didier

French, 18th century.
Active in France.
Engraver (burin).

HUMBLOT, Émile Joseph

French, 19th - 20th century.
Born 6 June 1862, in Joinville; died 21 December 1931, in Paris.
Painter, engraver. Landscapes.

Émile Joseph Humblot was a student of Hector Guiot and of Edmond or Hippolyte Petitjean. He exhibited regularly at the Salon des Artistes Français in Paris. He was the director of the Musée de Dijon, and also supervised the Manufacture de Beauvais and the Musée Rodin in Paris. He was president of the art group at the Sénat.

MUSEUMS AND GALLERIES:

CHAUMONT: *Interior of the Church of St-Jean in Chaumont* - DIJON (MBA): *The Four Hours* - LANGRES (MAH): *Reverie in Champlitte*.

HUMBLOT, Emmeline

German, 19th century.
Born 18 March 1816, in Berlin; died 24 March 1895, in Eisenach.
Painter. Flowers.

She worked in Berlin, Dresden and Munich.

HUMBLOT, Léon

French, 20th century.
Painter.

HUMBLOT, Robert

French, 20th century.
Born 13 May 1907, in Fontenay-sous-Bois; died 14 March 1962, in Paris.
Painter. Scenes with figures, allegorical subjects, figures, portraits, still-lifes, landscapes. Murals.
Group Forces Nouvelles.

At the age of 24, Humblot abandoned his studies in natural science at the Museum National d'Histoire Naturelle in Paris and turned instead to drawing classes, notably at the Académie de la Grande-Chaumière. In 1931, he entered the studio of Lucien Simon at the École des Beaux-Arts in Paris, where he worked until 1934. He travelled in Italy, especially Venice, in Spain, Provence and Brittany. He often returned from such travels having painted numerous works. He then travelled to Holland, Africa, the Antilles and Mexico. In 1935, with Georges Rohner, whom he had met at the Beaux-Arts, and with Henri Jannot, he participated in the creation of the Forces Nouvelles (New Forces) group, with which he exhibited until World War II. He was taken prisoner in the war, but escaped in 1941. He returned from Germany and the Austrian Tyrol with drawings and landscapes. He rejoined the group in Oppède-le-Vieux, taking shelter in Villefranche-sur-Mer, then the Auvergne, before finally settling in the forest of Fontainebleau.

In Paris in 1934, two exhibitions had an impact on his formative years: *Les Peintres de la réalité en France au XVIIe siècle* (*Painters of Reality in 17th-Century France*) at the Musée de l'Orangerie, and *Les Le Nain* (*The Le Nains*) at the Musée du Petit Palais. Unlike contemporaries who followed Cubism and Fauvism or Impressionism, Humblot and his friends Rohner and Jeannot were inspired by the synthetic realism of Georges de la Tour, the Le Nain brothers and Baugin. The Forces Nouvelles group believed that a return to tradition was the most desirable option in the circumstances. Other painters influenced by them include Pierre Tal-Coat, André Marchand and perhaps Francis Grüber. The group extolled a 'return to drawing, to the conscious metier of tradition' in order to depict the world directly. *The Dead Child* (1936), *The Loves of the Minotaur* and *The Horrors of War* (both 1937) are examples of Humblot's interest in the contemporary. In 1954, he painted the allegorical composition *Hunger and Fear*. His style reduces lines, forms and colours to the bare essentials. Volumes, limbs, heads and eyelids tend towards the cylindrical or spherical. His landscapes and seascapes are typically serene and contemplative, and as he grew older he painted increasing numbers of still-lifes of fish, birds and mushrooms.

Humblot participated in numerous collective exhibitions from 1932. In Paris, he showed at the Salon des Independents and the Salon d'Automne. He also showed in Sofia, Brussels, Luxembourg, Madrid and New York. His first solo exhibition was held at the Galerie Billet-Worms in Paris in 1936, followed by numerous others in the French capital. In 1941, after his return from captivity, he showed landscapes from the Ile d'Ouessant, which drew fresh attention to him. From 1943 to 1950, he showed at the Vander Klip and Barreiro galleries; in 1950 and 1951, at the Galerie Framond; from 1955 to his death, at the Galerie Romanet. He had an exhibition in 1958 at the Musée de l'Athénée in Geneva. After his death, the Musée Galliera in Paris organised a retrospective of the ensemble of his work. Other posthumous homages were paid to him, most notably: 1966, Musée de Cagnes and Musée Calvet in Avignon; 1968, Musée Toulouse-Lautrec in Albi, Musée des Beaux-Arts in Quimper; 1976, 1987, Salon d'Automne in Paris; 1979, Musée du Bastion St-André in Antibes; 1980, Musée d'Art Figuratif Contemporain in Fontainebleau; 1985, Salon de Fontainebleau; 1988, 1998, Galerie Bernheim-Jeune in Paris; 1991, 20th Salon de Montmorency and Centre Culturel Nicolas Pomel in Issoire. In 1952, he received the Prix Conté-Carrière and in 1953 the Prix de la Biennale in Menton.

BIBLIOGRAPHY:

Vanuxem, Roland, '*Robert Humblot 1907-1962*' in *Châteaux de France*, periodical, Paris, December 1984. *Robert Humblot*, exhibition catalogue, Bernheim-Jeune, Paris, 1988. Rollin, Jean, '*Le Métier consciencieux*' in *L'Humanité*, periodical, Paris, 20 December 1988. *Robert Humblot*, exhibition catalogue, Centre culturel Nicolas-Pomel, Issoire, 1991.

MUSEUMS AND GALLERIES:

ALBI (Mus. Toulouse-Lautrec) - ANGERS (MBA) - GENEVA (Petit Palais) - GRENOBLE (Mus. de Grenoble): *Sleeping Nude* (c. 1935) - LOUVIERS (Mus. municipal) - MENTON (MBA) - MONTEVIDEO (Mus.): *Shipwrecked* (1946) - NICE (Mus.) - PARIS (MAMVP): *Hunger and Fear* (1949) - PARIS (MNAM-CCI): *The Sardine Merchant* (1938); *Port of Villefranche* (1941); *The Shepherd's Instruments* (1942, other works) - PARIS (Mus. Carnavalet): *Portrait of Juliette Gréco* (1956) - SAN FRANCISCO (FAM) - SCEAUX (Mus. de l'Île-de-France).

AUCTION RECORDS:

PARIS, 12 Dec 1946, *Seascape*, FRF 8,500. PARIS, 24 Nov 1950, *The Rooster*, FRF 15,100. PARIS, 12 April 1954, *Mushrooms*, FRF 64,100. VERSAILLES, 11 June 1965, *Outskirts of Fontainebleau*, FRF 11,000. GENEVA, 13 June 1970, *Landscape of Les Baux*, CHF 8,000. PARIS, 4 Dec 1972, *Cap d'Ail* FRF 13,000. VERSAILLES, 18 Nov 1973, *The Cottage*, FRF 19,000. GENEVA, 8 June 1974, *Landscape in Brittany* (1956) CHF 12,000. VERSAILLES, 15 June 1976, *The Moor at Kérity* (1960, oil on canvas, 15 x 24 ins / 38 x 61 cm) FRF 9,000. VERSAILLES, 8 June 1977, *Landscape in Provence* (1955, oil on canvas, 23 1/2 x 36 1/4 ins / 60 x 92 cm) FRF 20,000. VERSAILLES, 13 June 1979, *Church in Noisy-sur-École* (oil on canvas, 32 x 39 1/4 ins / 81 x 100 cm) FRF 24,000. GENEVA, 4 May 1981, *Hunting Scene* (1943, oil on canvas, 23 1/2 x 36 1/4 ins / 60 x 92 cm) CHF 13,000. PARIS, 10 July 1983, *Hunting Dogs in the Forest* (oil/hardboard, 19 3/4 x 98 ins / 50 x 249 cm) FRF 50,000. VERSAILLES, 11 June 1986, *Strelitzia and Lilies* (1946, oil on canvas, 28 3/4 x 39 1/4 ins / 73 x 100 cm) FRF 67,000. VERSAILLES, 11 June 1986, *Vase of Lilies and Pipes on the Table* (1946, oil on canvas, 28 3/4 x 39 1/4 ins / 73 x 100 cm) FRF 67,000. PARIS, 8 Dec 1987, *View of Village Houses* (1932, oil on canvas, 24 x 36 1/4 ins / 61 x 92 cm) FRF 32,000. VERSAILLES, 20 March 1988, *Village in the Ardèche* (1952, oil on canvas, 23 1/2 x 36 1/4 ins / 60 x 92 cm) FRF 49,000; *Boats at St-Pierre (Pen'March)* (1958, oil on canvas, 15 x 24 ins / 38 x 61 cm) FRF 52,000; *Les Baux-de-Provence* (1957, oil on canvas, 15 x 24 ins / 38 x 61 cm) FRF 38,000. VERSAILLES, 15 June 1988, *Les Alpilles* (oil on canvas, 23 1/2 x 36 1/4 ins / 60 x 92 cm) FRF 90,000. PARIS, 23 June 1988, *Le Baou de St-Jeannet* (1953, oil on canvas, 23 1/2 x 36 1/4 ins / 60 x 92 cm) FRF 39,000. CALAIS, 3 July 1988, *Les Baux-de-Provence* (1957, oil on canvas, 15 x 24 1/2 ins / 38 x 62 cm) FRF 38,000. VERSAILLES, 23 Oct 1988, *Landscape of the Midi* (oil on canvas, 11 x 13 3/4 ins / 27 x 35 cm) FRF 27,000. PARIS, 16 Jan 1989, *The St-Pierre Breakwater in Brittany* (1959, oil on canvas, 23 1/2 x 36 1/4 ins / 60 x 92 cm) FRF 60,000. PARIS, 12 Feb 1989, *The Port in the Midi* (oil on canvas, 23 1/2 x 36 1/4 ins / 60 x 92 cm) FRF 90,000. AVIGNON, 25 June 1989, *The Church of Gréolières* (1953, oil on canvas, 35 x 51 1/4 ins / 89 x 130 cm) FRF 101,000. BELFORT, 22 Oct 1989, *Les Bigoudens* (1956, oil on canvas, 7 1/2 x 9 1/2 ins / 19 x 24 cm) FRF 23,500. PARIS, 23 Oct 1989, *Port of St-Pierre* (1961, oil on canvas, 15 x 24 ins / 38 x 61 cm) FRF 42,000. LE TOUQUET, 12 Nov 1989, *Breton Port at Low Tide* (oil on canvas, 6 3/4 x 9 1/2 ins / 17 x 24 cm) FRF 54,000. BAYEUX, 17 Dec 1989, *Mas d'Aigret* (c. 1954, oil on canvas, 15 x 24 ins / 38 x 61 cm) FRF 70,000. AURILLAC, 13 April 1990, *The Solidor Tower in St-Servan* (1950, oil on canvas, 23 1/2 x 36 1/4 ins / 60 x 92 cm) FRF 116,000. PARIS, 26 April 1990, *The Port of Menton* (1952, oil on canvas, 23 1/2 x 36 1/4 ins / 60 x 92 cm) FRF 120,000. PARIS, 16 Dec 1991, *Village in Brittany* (oil on canvas) FRF 22,500. PARIS, 7 Feb 1992, *The Port of Villefranche-sur-Mer* (1954, oil on canvas, 32 x 46 ins / 81 x 116 cm) FRF 92,000. CANNES, 11 Aug 1992, *The Port of Villefranche-sur-Mer* (1954, oil on canvas, 32 x 46 ins / 81 x 116 cm) FRF 100,000. CALAIS, 4 July 1993, *The Farm* (1943, oil on canvas, 18 1/2 x 24 ins / 47 x 61 cm) FRF 11,000. PARIS, 1 Oct 1993, *Red Mullet and Lemons* (1960, oil on canvas, 23 1/4 x 35 3/4 ins / 59 x 91 cm) FRF 22,000. NEW YORK, 2 Nov 1993, *Houses Near the Canal* (1955, oil on canvas, 11 x 13 3/4 ins / 27 x 35 cm) USD 2,300. LONDON, 23-24 March 1994, *The Almond Trees* (1960, oil on canvas, 15 x 24 ins / 38 x 61 cm) GBP 1,610. NEW YORK, 9 May 1994, *Cyprus Hedge* (1960, oil on canvas, 23 3/4 x 14 1/2 ins / 60.3 x 36.8 cm) USD 3,680. LE TOUQUET, 22 May 1994, *The Almond Trees in Provence* (1960, oil on canvas, 15 x 24 ins / 38 x 61 cm) FRF 27,500. CALAIS, 24 March 1996, *House in Provence* (oil on canvas, 13 1/2 x 18 ins / 34 x 46 cm) FRF 18,000. PARIS, 3 April 1996, *The Village* (1943, oil on canvas, 28 3/4 x 46 ins / 73 x 116 cm) FRF 40,000. NEW YORK, 30 April 1996, *Venice* (1954, oil on canvas, 23 1/2 x 36 1/4 ins / 60 x 92 cm) USD 4,025. PARIS, 28 June 1996, *Alpilles with Olive Trees* (1959, oil on canvas, 23 1/2 x 36 1/4 ins / 60 x 92 cm) FRF 30,000. PARIS, 12 Dec 1996, *Provençal House* (oil on canvas, 14 1/2 x 23 1/2 ins / 37 x 60 cm) FRF 20,000. PARIS, 12 Dec 1997, *House in Provence* (oil on canvas, 15 x 24 ins / 38 x 61 cm) FRF 12,500. PARIS, 17 Nov 1999, *Gondolas in front of S Giorgio Maggiore in Venice* (1954, oil on canvas, 24 x 36 ins / 60 x 92 cm) FRF 70,000. PARIS, 17 Nov 1999, *Dancer* (1960, oil on canvas, 64 x 44 ins / 162 x 113 cm) FRF 95,000. CALAIS, 5 Nov 2000, *Port of Dieppe* (oil on canvas, 24 x 32 ins / 60 x 81 cm) FRF 28,000. PARIS, 27 Nov 2000, *Provence* (1954, oil on canvas, 24 x 36 ins / 60 x 92 cm) FRF 38,000. LONDON, 6 April 2001, *Les Baux* (1959, oil on canvas, 32 x 52 ins / 81 x 131 cm) GBP 3,800. PARIS, 22 June 2001, *Landscape* (1959, oil on canvas, 32 x 51 ins / 81 x 130 cm) FRF 64,000. PARIS, 11 April 2002, *Port of St-Guenole* (oil on canvas, 15 x 24 ins / 38 x 61 cm) EUR 5,200. PARIS, 16 April 2002, *Farmhouse in the Alpilles* (1961, oil on canvas, 24 x 36 ins / 60 x 92 cm) EUR 4,810. PARIS, 26 March 2003, *Boats at Low Tide* (1958, oil on canvas, 20 x 29 ins / 50 x 73 cm) EUR 4,400. PARIS, 2 Dec 2003, *Still-life with Bouquet of Roses* (1956, oil on canvas, 29 x 23 ins / 73 x 59 cm) EUR 3,500. PARIS, 17 May 2004, *Landscape of Provence* (oil on canvas, 15 x 24 ins / 38 x 61 cm) EUR 2,700. CALAIS, 30 May 2004, *Vase of Roses* (oil on canvas, 15 x 10 ins / 38 x 25 cm) EUR 2,500.

HUMBORG, Adolf

Austrian, 19th - 20th century.

Born 17 January 1847, in Oravitza; died 1913 or 1921.

Painter. Genre scenes.

Humborg was a student at the fine arts academies in Vienna and Munich, where he settled. His work was exhibited in Berlin and Hanover.

AUCTION RECORDS:

LONDON, 29 April 1911, *Unhappiness* (1887) GBP 26. LOS ANGELES, 8 April 1973, *Monastery Kitchen,* USD 5,000. VIENNA, 10 Feb 1976, *Good Catch* (oil on panel, 9 x 6 ins / 22 x 15 cm) ATS 15,000. MUNICH, 24 May 1977, *Joys of the Wine Cellar* (oil on panel, 13 1/2 x 10 1/4 ins / 34.5 x 26 cm) DEM 5,300. VIENNA, 19 June 1979, *Monk Doing the Washing Up* (oil on canvas, 24 1/2 x 19 3/4 ins / 62 x 50 cm) ATS 90,000. COLOGNE, 18 March 1983, *A Good Drink* (oil on canvas, 19 1/2 x 15 1/4 ins / 49.5 x 39 cm) DEM 5,500. MUNICH, 5 Nov 1986, *New Wine* (1886, oil on canvas, 30 x 48 1/2 ins / 76 x 123 cm) DEM 73,000. VIENNA, 18 March 1987, *Baby's Meal* (1877, oil on canvas, 24 3/4 x 19 3/4 ins / 63 x 50 cm) ATS 55,000. LONDON, 11 May 1990, *Preparing the Feast in the Monks' Kitchen* (oil on canvas, 31 1/2 x 43 1/4 ins / 80 x 110 cm) GBP 4,950. NEW YORK, 28 May 1992, *New Wine!* (oil on canvas, 32 1/2 x 48 ins / 82.6 x 121.9 cm) USD 38,500. NEW YORK, 26 May 1993, *Cleaning the Wine Cellar* (oil on panel, 17 x 23 3/4 ins / 43.2 x 60.3 cm) USD 8,625. NEW YORK, 27 May 1993, *Wine Connoisseurs* (1883, oil on panel, 19 1/4 x 15 3/4 ins / 49 x 40 cm) USD 11,500. LONDON, 19 Nov 1993, *Welcome* (oil on panel, 16 1/2 x 21 3/4 ins / 42.1 x 55.1 cm) GBP 6,900. NEW YORK, 16 Feb 1994, *Easter Cake* (oil on canvas, 32 x 43 1/2 ins / 81.3 x 110.5 cm) USD 34,500. LONDON, 10 Feb 1995, *The Blessed Cook* (1881, oil on canvas, 19 x 23 3/4 ins / 48.5 x 60.5 cm) GBP 6,900.

HUME, Alexander

British, 19th century.

Born 1800, in Kelso, Scotland; died 1830.

Painter.

Alexander Hume studied in Edinburgh.

HUME, Amelia. See **FARNBOROUGH**

HUME, Edith

Maiden name: Dunn

British, 19th - 20th century.

Active in London.

Painter.

Edith Hume was the wife of Thomas O. Hume. She exhibited genre scenes and landscapes at the Royal Academy and the Suffolk Street Gallery from 1870.

AUCTION RECORDS:

LONDON, 19 Nov 1970, *Children Playing on a Beach,* Gns 320. TORQUAY, 12 June 1979, *Seaside Scene* (oil on canvas, 15 x 23 1/4 ins / 38 x 59 cm) GBP 1,300. LONDON, 29 March 1984, *The Model Boat* (oil on canvas, 16 x 24 ins / 40.5 x 61 cm) GBP 5,200. LONDON, 12 April 1985, *Children Playing at the Waterside* (oil on canvas, 11 1/2 x 15 ins / 29 x 38 cm) GBP 3,900.

HUME, Gary

British, 20th - 21st century.

Born 1962, in Tenterden, Kent.

Painter, printmaker, graphic artist. Figures, architecture.

Young British Artists.

Gary Hume studied at the Liverpool Polytechnic from 1985 to 1986, and at Goldsmiths College in London from 1986 to 1988. He describes his subject matter as 'embarrassingly personal', including everyday objects and people like feet, animals, toys, women, flowers and media celebrities, such as the British radio DJ Tony Blackburn. Hume draws images from mass media and popular culture sources like fashion magazines, and he suggests that his superficial subject-matter is secondary to his focus on structure, surface and colour. His paintings are executed by careful layers of high-gloss paint to create flat, brightly coloured images, as in *Whistler* (1996, enamel paint on aluminium panel). Hume painted a successful series based on swing doors in schools and hospitals done in pale monochromes, shown in groups of four in which geometric shapes were used to give the impression of actual doors. In the mid-1990s, he changed from panel to aluminium support.

Hume's exhibitions include Esther Schipper, Cologne (1989); Lorence Monk Gallery, New York City (1989); *The British Art Show,* South Bank Centre (1990, tour); Hayward Gallery, London (1994); San Pasquale Monastery, Venice (1995); a solo at the Institute of Contemporary Art, London (1995); *New British Painting in the 1990s,* Museum of Modern Art, Oxford (1996); the São Paulo Biennale (1996); a show with Fiona Rae, Saatchi Gallery, London (1997); *Collaborations with Parkett: 1984 to Now,* Museum of Modern Art, New York (2001); *Painting on the Move,* simultaneously at Kunstmuseum, Kunsthalle and Museum für Gegenwartskunst, Basel (2002); a solo at White Cube Gallery, London (2002); a solo at the Irish Museum for Modern Art, Dublin (2003); and *Gary Hume: The Bird Has a Yellow Beak,* Kunsthaus, Bregenz (2004). Hume was shortlisted for the Turner Prize in 1996, and received the Jerwood Prize in 1997.

BIBLIOGRAPHY:

Gary Hume: Paintings, exhibition catalogue, ICA, London, 1995. *Gary Hume: British Pavilion, XLVIII Venice Biennale,* exhibition catalogue, British Council, London, 1999. *Gary Hume,* exhibition catalogue, Whitechapel Art Gallery, London, 1999-2000. Francblin, Catherine, '*Gary Hume. La peinture recommencée*' in *Art Press* n° 247 p. 41, periodical, Paris, June 1999. Mendes Bürgi, Bernhard, et al., *Painting on the Move,* exhibition catalogue, Kusntmuseum, Kunsthalle, Museum für Gegenwartskunst, Basel, 2002. *Gary Hume: 2002,* exhibition catalogue, White Cube, London, 2002. *Gary Hume: The Bird has a Yellow Beak,* exhibition catalogue, Kunsthaus Bregenz, Bregenz, 2004.

MUSEUMS AND GALLERIES:

DUBLIN (Irish Museum of Modern Art): *Other Men's Flowers* (1994, screenprint) - LONDON (Tate Collection): *Incubus* (1991, alkyd housepaint on Formica); *Other Men's Flowers* (1994, series of 15 screenprints); *Portraits* (1998, series of 10 screenprints); *Water Painting* (1999, household paint on aluminium panel) - LONDON (UK Government Art Collection): *Portraits* (1998, portfolio of 10 screenprints) - NEW YORK (MoMA): *Snowman* (1996, screenprint on felt).

AUCTION RECORDS:

LONDON, 27 June 1997, *Dolphin Painting Three* (1991, gloss paint/wood in two parts, 82 x 110 ins / 208.3 x 279.4 cm in all) GBP 41,100. NEW YORK, 20 Nov 1997, *Magnolia Door Three* (1989, gloss paint/canvas, 100 x 64 ins / 254 x 162.6 cm) USD 20,700. LONDON, 29 June 1999, *Magnolia Doors* (1989, gloss paint on canvas, 100 x 64 ins / 254 x 162 cm) GBP 10,000. LONDON, 10 Dec 1999, *Rome VII* (1993, pastel, 52 x 43 ins / 131 x 108 cm) GBP 11,500. LONDON, 27 June 2000, *My Guernica* (gloss household paint on canvas laid on board, 94 x 255 ins / 239 x 648 cm) GBP 50,000. NEW YORK, 14 Nov 2000, *Pauline* (1996, gloss paint on aluminium, 82 x 46 ins / 208 x 117 cm) USD 140,000. LONDON, 8 Feb 2001, *Untitled - Portrait of Zoe* (1999, enamel on aluminium, 41 x 29 ins / 104 x 73 cm) GBP 60,000. LONDON, 8 Feb 2001, *Love Loves Unlovable* (1994, gloss paint on panel, 85 x 144 ins / 216 x 366 cm) GBP 170,000. LONDON, 6 Feb 2002, *Tony Blackburn* (1993, gloss paint on MDF panel, 76 x 54 ins / 193 x 137 cm) GBP 68,000. LONDON, 22 Oct 2002, *3* (2000, enamel paint on aluminium panel, 120 x 95 ins / 305 x 241 cm) GBP 85,000. NEW YORK, 15 May 2003, *Girl Boy, Boy Girl* (1991, enamel on MDF, 82 x 56 ins / 209 x 142 cm) USD 52,000. LONDON, 25 June 2003, *Seahorse* (1997, enamel on aluminium panel, 87 x 67 ins / 221 x 170 cm) GBP 58,000. NEW YORK, 13 May 2004, *Beautiful - Kate Moss* (2002, gloss paint on aluminium) USD 35,000. NEW YORK, 13 May 2004, *Song* (1998, enamel on aluminium, 82 x 46 ins / 208 x 117 cm) USD 120,000.

HUME, J. Henry
British, 19th century.
Born c. 1858; died 25 April 1881.
Painter. Urban landscapes, landscapes.

J. Henry Hume exhibited his work at the Royal Academy and at Suffolk Street in London from 1875 to 1881 while still a young artist.

HUME, Robert
British, 19th - 20th century.
Active in Edinburgh.
Painter, watercolourist. Landscapes.

Robert Hume first exhibited in London in 1891, and was a regular exhibitor at the Royal Academy and the Suffolk Street Gallery, as well as with the Royal Institute of Painters in Watercolour.

AUCTION RECORDS:
LONDON, 21 Jan 1911, *Sunset* (1894) GBP 1.

HUME, Thomas O.
British, 19th century.
Active in London.
Painter. Landscapes.

Thomas O. Hume exhibited his work in London at Suffolk Street from 1864 and at the Royal Academy from 1871 to 1893.

HUMENOI, P.
Yugoslav, 20th century.
Painter. Landscapes.

Humenoi was one of many traditional Yugoslav naive painters who came to prominence as a result of being taken up by local associations of peasant or worker artists, and also of the considerable success of the Hlebine School and the naive artist Generalic.

His works depict the countryside of his region and are stylised and simplified in manner.

BIBLIOGRAPHY:
Gans, Louis, *Meesters der Europese naïven*, Centraal Museum, Utrecht, 1970.

HUMMEL, Carl
Austrian, 18th century.
Born c. 1769.
Active in Vienna.
Painter, lithographer.

He was the father of Eugen Hummel.

HUMMEL, Carl Maria Nicolaus
German, 19th century.
Born 31 August 1821, in Weimar; died 16 June 1907, in Weimar.
Painter, watercolourist, engraver. Landscapes.

His first study was engraving. He became a pupil of Preller, then travelled in Norway and Sicily. After returning to Germany in 1846, he became the tutor of Princess Helen of Orléans.

MUSEUMS AND GALLERIES:
LEIPZIG: *German Landscape*; *Undulating Landscape* - STUTTGART: *Mountainous Landscape*.

AUCTION RECORDS:
MUNICH, 1 Dec 1976, *Landscape* (1897, watercolour, 18 1/2 x 24 3/4 ins / 47 x 63 cm) DEM 1,350. NEW YORK, 27 May 1982, *Mediterranean Landscape* (1877, oil on canvas, 25 3/4 x 37 1/4 ins / 65.5 x 94.5 cm) USD 2,500. LONDON, 28 Nov 1985, *The Grand Ducal Palace in Weimar* (watercolour and pencil, 9 1/4 x 16 3/4 ins / 23.5 x 42.5 cm) GBP 1,300. COLOGNE, 27 June 1986, *Wooded Landscape with Figures* (1889, oil on canvas, 27 1/2 x 35 1/2 ins / 70 x 90 cm) DEM 11,000. MUNICH, 10 May 1989, *The Greek Theatre in Taormina* (watercolour, 22 x 30 1/4 ins / 55 x 77 cm) DEM 7,700. MUNICH, 21 June 1994, *Monticelli near Tivoli* (1891, oil on canvas, 32 3/4 x 46 1/2 ins / 83.5 x 118 cm) DEM 14,950. MUNICH, 27 June 1995, *View of the Valle di Cadore near Pieve di Cadore* (1902, oil on canvas, 51 1/4 x 72 3/4 ins / 130 x 185 cm) DEM 14,950. HAMBURG, 27 May 1999, *Corsican Landscape* (1872, oil on canvas, 24 x 33 ins / 60 x 83 cm) DEM 9,000. BERLIN, 26 Nov 1999, *Knarled Oak in Wood* (oil on canvas, 24 x 19 ins / 61 x 48 cm) DEM 7,500. BRUSSELS, 9 May 2000, *Wielands zimmer in neuen Flugel des residenz schlosses* (watercolour, 12 x 11 ins / 31 x 28 cm) BEF 80,000. MUNICH, 28 March 2001, *View of the Wartburg* (watercolour, 20 x 17 ins / 52 x 43 cm) DEM 3,200. ZURICH, 25 March 2002, *Portraits of Prince and Princess Schonaich Carolath* (miniature, mixed media, 4 x 3 ins / 9 x 7 cm) CHF 6,000. COPENHAGEN, 2 Dec 2002, *Landscape View of Capri* (1886, oil on canvas, 28 x 39 ins / 72 x 100 cm) DKK 115,000. MUNICH, 17 May 2003, *Ischia and Procida* (1882, oil on canvas, 44 x 59 ins / 111 x 150 cm) EUR 21,000. LONDON, 3 June 2003, *Young Lady Holding her Gauze White Dress and Light Blue Cashmere Stole* (1810, miniature, 3 x 4 ins / 7 x 9 cm) GBP 3,200.

HUMMEL, Christiane Luise.
See **DUTTENHOFER**

HUMMEL, Eugen
Austrian, 19th century.
Born 1812, in Vienna.
Painter. Genre scenes.

He exhibited in Vienna from 1834 to 1845.

MUSEUMS AND GALLERIES:
BERLIN (Nationalgal.): *The Granite Basin*; *Game of Chess*.

HUMMEL, Fritz
German, 19th century.
Born 15 April 1828, in Berlin; died 30 November 1905, in Berlin.
Painter, miniaturist. Portraits.

He was a pupil of Johann Erdmann Hummel and Karl Begas in Berlin, then of Bendemann in Dresden. In 1858, he accompanied Prince Schönaich-Carolath to Spain and South Africa, then returned to Berlin to settle, where he gained a considerable reputation as a portraitist.

AUCTION RECORDS:
PARIS, 9 June 1923, *Portrait of Mr X*; *Portrait of Mrs X* (two miniatures) FRF 1,580. AMSTERDAM, 16 Nov 1988, *Portrait of a Girl Wearing a White Dress and Holding a Book of Pictures* (oil on canvas, 34 1/4 x 25 1/2 ins / 87 x 65 cm) NLG 2,990. COLOGNE, 20 Nov 2003, *Portrait of Kaiser Friedrich III in Uniform* (oil on canvas, 54 x 36 ins / 137 x 91 cm) EUR 9,500.

HUMMEL, Johann Erdmann
German, 18th - 19th century.
Born 1 September 1769, in Kassel; died 26 August 1852, in Berlin.
Painter, engraver. Interiors with figures, landscapes with figures, landscapes.

He was a pupil of Böttner. In 1792, he set off for Italy, remaining in Rome until 1799, whereupon he returned to Germany. Thanks to the patronage of Electress Augusta of Hessen, he was appointed perspective master at the academy in Berlin in 1809.

MUSEUMS AND GALLERIES:
FRANKFURT AM MAIN: *Children in a Garden in Naples* - OSLO: *Tyrolean Landscape*.
AUCTION RECORDS:
LONDON, 10 July 1981, *Count Lamoignon with His Family in an Interior* (1789, oil on canvas, 44 1/2 x 56 1/2 ins / 113 x 143.5 cm) GBP 6,000. BERLIN, 4 June 1999, *Mausoleum of Queen Luise in Park of Castle Charlottenburg* (watercolour/ink/pen, 16 x 19 ins / 41 x 49 cm) DEM 10,000.

HUMMEL, Ludwig
German, 18th - 19th century.
Born 11 May 1770, in Naples; died 28 August 1840, in Kassel.
Painter, draughtsman.
He was on the staff of the academy in Kassel. Among other works, he did a portrait of Napoleon's brother Jérôme, King of Westphalia.

HUMMEL, Théodor
German, 19th - 20th century.
Born 15 November 1864, in Schliersee; died 1939.
Painter. Genre scenes, landscapes.
Hummel exhibited in Berlin, Munich and Paris, where he was awarded an honourable mention at the Exposition Universelle in 1900.

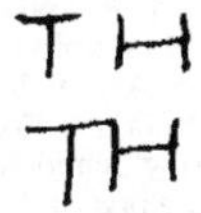

AUCTION RECORDS:
MUNICH, 14 May 1986, *Young Girl Sitting in a Field* (1906, oil on card, 12 1/2 x 17 3/4 ins / 32 x 45 cm) DEM 4,000. HAMBURG, 4 Dec 1999, *Ships in Hamburg Harbour* (oil on board, 19 x 26 ins / 47 x 66 cm) DEM 3,300. MUNICH, 25 Oct 2000, *Still-life of Flowers* (oil on panel, 22 x 24 ins / 55 x 60 cm) DEM 4,500. MUNICH, 24 Sept 2004, *Young Woman at Spinning Wheel* (oil on canvas, 24 x 25 ins / 60 x 63 cm) EUR 2,000.

HUMMEL, Willy
Swiss, 19th - 20th century.
Born 13 December 1872, in Gottlieben (Thurgau).
Painter, engraver. Portraits, landscapes.
Hummel exhibited in Zurich and Stuttgart.

HUMPHREY, Edward J.
British, 19th century.
Active in London.
Painter. Genre scenes.
Edward J. Humphrey exhibited in London at the Royal Academy between 1872 and 1889.
MUSEUMS AND GALLERIES:
SHEFFIELD: *Rest*.

HUMPHREY, Jack Weldon
Canadian, 20th century.
Born 1901, in St John (New Brunswick); died 1967, in St John.
Painter. Figures, portraits, landscapes.
Jack Weldon Humphrey studied in Boston from 1920 to 1923, then at the National Academy of Design, New York between 1924 and 1929. In 1929 he studied work of Hans Hofmann in Munich. The following year he went to the Académie de la Grande Chaumière in Paris and was impressed by Cézanne's art. He made many trips to Europe, visiting Italy, Germany, Holland and Belgium. After having spent more than a year in Paris in 1952 and two months in England, he returned for ever to Canada.

Humphrey was a founder member of the Eastern Group of Painters in 1938, and of the Contemporary Arts Society in 1939, with whom he regularly exhibited during the 1940s. He showed a female figure in the open International Exhibition in 1946 held by UNESCO at the Musée d'Art Moderne, Paris.

In his early works he painted figurative works and portraits. Later he specialised in an abstract style showing the influence of Jean Bazaine and Alfred Manessier.
MUSEUMS AND GALLERIES:
TORONTO (AG of Ontario): *Charlotte* (1959, oil).
AUCTION RECORDS:
TORONTO, 28 May 1980, *City View* (1940, watercolour, 15 x 22 ins / 38.1 x 55.6 cm) CAD 1,400. TORONTO, 1 June 1982, *Outer Harbour, Concarneau* (gouache, 18 1/4 x 23 1/2 ins / 46.3 x 60 cm) CAD 2,400. TORONTO, 28 May 1985, *Still-life* (oil on canvas, 19 3/4 x 23 1/2 ins / 50 x 60 cm) CAD 3,800. VANCOUVER, 27 May 1999, *Three Riveters* (c. 1944, oil on masonite, 16 x 12 ins / 41 x 30 cm) CAD 5,400. VANCOUVER, 10 May 2000, *Driftwood Duck* (1948, tempera on board, 28 x 36 ins / 71 x 91 cm) CAD 4,500. VANCOUVER, 8 Nov 2001, *Still-life with Violin, Gourd and Apple. Vase of Spring Flowers* (oil on canvas, double-sided, 24 x 32 ins / 61 x 81 cm) CAD 5,500. VANCOUVER, 14 Nov 2002, *Portrait of a Girl with Calendulas* (oil on canvas, double-sided, 24 x 19 ins / 60 x 49 cm) CAD 4,500. VANCOUVER, 14 Nov 2002, *Flowers and Checkerboard. Bearded Man* (oil on canvas, double-sided, 30 x 23 ins / 76 x 59 cm) CAD 4,500. VANCOUVER, 27 May 2004, *Still-life with Old Saxon Violin* (c. 1933, oil on canvas, double-sided, 24 x 30 ins / 61 x 76 cm) CAD 9,000.

HUMPHREY, Margo
American, 20th century.
Born 25 June 1942, in Oakland (California).
Painter, engraver, lithographer, monotype artist, illustrator. Figures, scenes with figures.
Margo Humphrey lived her formative years in California, studying at the California College of Arts and Crafts, Merritt College, Oakland, then Stanford University. She taught at the University of California at Santa Cruz before joining the staff of the University of Maryland. She is best known for her lithographs whose elaborate compositions are set in primary colours and which account for the artist's environment (objects, persons, vegetation, architectures). In the 1960s, she turned her attention to African history. Her stylised representation sometimes tends towards Abstraction, for instance in *Marble Box* (1977). She wrote a children's book: *The River that Gave Gifts: An Afro-American Story*. She took part in the exhibitions *Forever Free: Art by African-American Women, 1862-1980*, Center for the Visual Arts Gallery, Illinois State University, Normal, and *Through Sisters' Eyes: Children's Books Illustrated by African-American Artists*, National Museum of Women in the Arts Library and Research Center, Washington DC. She has shown her works in solo exhibitions, notably at the Museum of Modern Art, San Francisco.
BIBLIOGRAPHY:
Bontemps, Arna Alexander (ed.), *Forever Free. Art by African-American Women, 1862-1980*, group exhibition catalogue, Center for the Visual Arts Gall., Illinois State University, Normal (IL), 1980. Lewis, Samella, *African American Art and Artists*, University of California Press, Berkeley, 1990.
MUSEUMS AND GALLERIES:
LAGOS (NGA) - LONDON (Victoria and Albert Mus.) - NEW YORK (MoMA) - OAKLAND (Mus. of California) - PHILADELPHIA (MA) - RIO DE JANEIRO (MAM) - SAN FRANCISCO (California Palace of the Legion of Honor).

HUMPHREY, Ozias
British, 18th - 19th century.
Born 8 September 1742, in Honiton (Devon); died 9 March 1810, in London.
Painter, miniaturist, pastellist, draughtsman. Portraits.

Ozias Humphrey displayed a talent for drawing while still very young. He went to London and on the advice of Sir Joshua Reynolds went to study in St Martin's Lane School. The death of his father obliged him to return home after two years. He then became a pupil of the miniaturist Samuel Collins in Bath. When Collins moved to Dublin, Humphrey took over his clientele, but this did not last long as Reynolds encouraged him to go and settle in London.

His contribution to the Spring Gardens Rooms exhibition two years later gained him the King's favour, as a result of which he was commissioned to paint the Queen of England and several members of the royal family. He was admitted to the Society of Artists and enjoyed a well-deserved reputation, producing a large number of works. In 1772 a serious fall from a horse suddenly cut short his career. To combat the effects of a serious deterioration in his nervous system, which was a result of his injuries, he left for Italy in March 1773, accompanied by his great friend Romney. In Rome he studied at the Academy of France, studying the old masters and Renaissance artists. He visited Florence, Venice, Naples and Milan. After a stay of four years he returned to London with the desire to profit from his classical studies in painting. As a result his work was represented with full-length portraits at the Royal Academy in 1779, 1780 and 1783, but this did not bring him much success, even though the Academy admitted him as an associate in 1779. Humphrey was not very good at applying pressure.

At the beginning of 1785 he left for the Indies and returned to his original genre, executing a large number of miniatures of Hindu princes and Nabobs. He was unable to extend his stay for more than three years due to ill-health, even though his work brought many benefits. In 1788 he returned to London and renewed his success as a miniaturist. In 1791 he was made an Academician, and the Duke of Dorset commissioned him to decorate an office with miniatures. He had done around 50 when the extreme attention which he gave to his work caused such a deterioration in his sight that he had to give up painting and resorted to producing portraits in pencil. His success was undiminished and in 1792 he was appointed draughtsman to the king. In 1797 he executed *Portraits of the Prince and Princess of Orange*. This was his last year of exhibition. Shortly after this he became almost blind. He signed his works with his initials in capital letters placing the O inside the H.

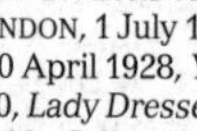

Stamp of sale

AUCTION RECORDS:

LONDON, 28 March 1908, *Lady Barbara Ashley as a Child* (pastel) GBP 210; *Georgiana, Duchess of Devonshire* (drawing) GBP 52. LONDON, 9 July 1909, *Portrait of an African Prince* (drawing) GBP 35. LONDON, July 1924, *Lady in a Blue Dress and White Hat,* GBP 27. LONDON, 8 Dec 1926, *Miss Elizabeth Paine,* GBP 50. LONDON, 1 July 1927, *Portrait of a Woman,* GBP 210. LONDON, 20 April 1928, *Young Girl Seated,* GBP 68. LONDON, 11 July 1930, *Lady Dressed as Ariadne,* GBP 231. NEW YORK, 4 March 1938, *Collector of Prints and his Wife,* USD 225. LONDON, 21 July 1944, *The Sisters,* GBP 63. LONDON, 31 May 1946, *Young People and Young Women,* GBP 42. LONDON, 18 Nov 1970, *Portrait of Frances Anne Bouverie,* GBP 350. LONDON, 22 March 1972, *Portrait of a Young Girl,* GBP 700. LONDON, 19 June 1979, *Portrait of Warren Hastings* (black, red and white chalk, 16 1/2 x 12 ins / 42 x 30.2 cm) GBP 3,800. LONDON, 10 July 1985, *Portrait of Susan, Wife of Joseph Hickey of Twickenham* (oil on canvas, 29 1/2 x 24 1/4 ins / 75 x 61.5 cm) GBP 4,000. YORK, 12 Nov 1991, *Portrait of Lady Maria Waldegrave, Head and Shoulders* (pencil heightened with white, 18 1/2 x 14 ins / 47 x 35.5 cm) GBP 2,530. LONDON, 9 April 1992, *Portrait of a Lady Seated, her Hands on her Knees* (red and black chalk, oval, 8 1/2 x 6 1/2 ins / 21.5 x 16.5 cm) GBP 880. ICKWORTH, 12 June 1996, *Portrait of Lord John Augustus Harvey* (1781, pencil, red pastel and stump, 4 x 3 1/2 ins / 10 x 9 cm) GBP 1,725. LONDON, 21 June 1999, *Mrs Crewe as the Fate Clotho* (1779, miniature, 3 x 2 ins / 8 x 6 cm) GBP 1,400. LONDON, 24 May 2000, *Indian Dignitary in White Robes* (miniature) GBP 3,500. LONDON, 21 Nov 2000, *Charles, 3rd Duke of Richmond and Lennox, in Blue Coat* (miniature) GBP 4,800. LONDON, 28 May 2002, *Haidar Beg Khan, Prime Minister to Asoph ul Dowlah* (miniature) GBP 1,700. LONDON, 5 Nov 2002, *Signor Venanzio Rauzzini with his Hand Tucked Inside his Waistcoat* (pencil and crayon on paper, miniature, h. 8 ins / 21 cm) GBP 1,700. LONDON, 3 June 2003, *Young Officer, Probably of an Indian Infantry Regiment* (1786, miniature) GBP 3,500. LONDON, 27 Nov 2003, *Portrait of George Earl Macartney, the First Ambassador to China* (pastel, 23 x 19 ins / 58 x 49 cm) GBP 9,000. DETROIT, 12 March 2004, *Mrs Sarah Hill* (miniature) USD 10,000.

HUMPHREY, Ralph

American, 20th century.
Born 1932, in Youngstown (Ohio); died 1990.
Painter.
Minimal Art.

Ralph Humphrey received a bursary from the Butler Art Gallery in Youngstown in 1948, and continued to attend the university in 1951-1952. He moved to New York in 1956. In 1959-1960 he taught at the Art Students League, New York, from 1961 to 1963 at Bennington College in Vermont, then again in New York at New School and Hunter College. In practical terms, his art belongs to the Minimal Art movement, and is specifically American. By returning deliberately to 'primary' forms and quasi-monochromaticity, often in impressive dimensions, Minimal Art tends to transmit pure sensation at its maximum intensity and by the minimum of means, and stripped of any psychological connotation. Humphrey showed paintings where monochromaticity was applied according to the 'all over' principle, and only enlivened by slight surface shakiness.

Humphrey appeared in many group exhibitions in the USA and Europe, including 1961 *American Abstract Expressionists and Imagists* held at the Solomon R. Guggenheim Museum, New York, 1967 *A Romantic Minimalism* held at the Institute of Contemporary Art (ICA), Philadelphia, 1968 *Reality Art* held at the Museum of Modern Art, New York and at the Galeries Nationales du Grand Palais, Paris, 1969 a group similar to the 'Art Fair', Cologne, and *Art about Space in American Art* held at the Kunsthaus, Zurich etc. He also showed his work in solo exhibitions, including: in New York in 1959, 1960, 1961, 1965, 1967, 1968, 1969, and in Düsseldorf in 1969.

BIBLIOGRAPHY:

L'Art du Réel, group exhibition catalogue, Galeries nationales du Grand Palais, Paris, 1968.

AUCTION RECORDS:

NEW YORK, 6 June 1974, *Sho* (1969) USD 1,100. NEW YORK, 16 May 1980, *Untitled* (1969, acrylic/canvas, 60 x 120 ins / 152.4 x 305 cm) USD 1,300. NEW YORK, 18 Nov 1981, *Untitled* (1974, wall relief with strips of canvas and acrylic/canvas, 59 x 76 x 6 ins / 150 x 193 x 15.5 cm) USD 9,000. NEW YORK, 8 May 1984, *No 9* (1978, wood relief and acrylic, 48 x 48 x 7 ins / 122 x 122 x 17.7 cm) USD 8,000. NEW YORK, 2 Nov 1984, *Warren* (1968, acrylic/canvas, 48 x 48 ins / 122 x 122 cm) USD 2,000. NEW YORK, 7 May 1986, *Untitled* (1973, acrylic/canvas, 60 x 42 ins / 152.4 x 106.7 cm) USD 3,500. NEW YORK, 9 May 1989, *Over Green* (acrylic/canvas, diam. 61 ins / 155 cm) USD 660. NEW YORK, 8 May 1990, *Transmission 5* (acrylic/shaped canvas, 48 x 69 1/2 x 6 1/2 ins / 121.9 x 176.8 x 16.5 cm) USD 24,200. NEW YORK, 4 Oct 1990, *Untitled* (1969, oil on canvas, 72 x 108 ins / 183 x 274.4 cm) USD 9,900. NEW YORK, 14 Feb 1991, *Oval*

Painting (1973, acrylic/shaped canvas, 54 x 78 ins / 137.2 x 198.1 cm) USD 13,200. NEW YORK, 2 May 1991, *Underwater Current* (casein and modelling clay on wood relief, 48 x 30 ins / 121.9 x 76.2 cm) USD 16,500. NEW YORK, 12 Nov 1991, *Van* (1980, acrylic/wood/paper, 20 x 26 ins / 50.8 x 66 cm) USD 7,150. NEW YORK, 6 Oct 1992, *Leo for Beth* (1971, acrylic/canvas, 60 1/4 x 60 1/4 ins / 153 x 153 cm) USD 3,300. NEW YORK, 19 Nov 1992, *Untitled (Number 4)* (acrylic and modelling clay/shaped canvas, 63 1/4 x 46 x 6 1/4 ins / 160.6 x 116 x 15.8 cm) USD 16,500. NEW YORK, 3 May 1994, *Untitled* (1960, oil on canvas, 48 x 36 ins / 121.9 x 91.5 cm) USD 4,370. NEW YORK, 3 May 1995, *Sinclair* (1989, casein/canvas/wood, 42 x 42 ins / 106.7 x 106.7 cm) USD 8,625. NEW YORK, 16 May 2001, *Chinatown - Tracks* (1984-1985, acrylic and modelling paste on wood, 48 x 48 ins / 122 x 122 cm) USD 13,000. NEW YORK, 12 Feb 2004, *Flick* (1979-1980, acrylic and modelling paste over wood, 9 x 11x6 ins / 24 x 28x14 cm) USD 6,000. LAMBERTVILLE, 24 April 2004, *Untitled* (oil on canvas, 14 x 14 ins / 36 x 36 cm) USD 12,000.

HUMPHREY, William
British, 18th century.
Born c. 1740; died after 1795.
Draughtsman, engraver (mezzotint).

In 1765 William Humphrey won a prize from the Society of Artists for an engraving after Rembrandt. He was an expert in mezzotint engravings and executed excellent portraits after Reynolds, Dunkarton, Kneller, Wilson and others, and genre subjects after Hoppner and Morland. His engraving *Temptation* after Morland is an excellent specimen of English engraving.

HUMPHREYS, Albert
American, 19th - 20th century.
Born in Cincinnati; died 1922, in New York.
Painter, sculptor.

Albert Humphreys was a pupil of Jean-Léon Gérôme and Tony Robert-Fleury in Paris about 1890.

HUMPHREYS, David
American, 20th century.
Born 22 July 1901, in Morristown (New Jersey).
Painter. Landscapes.

David Humphreys was a pupil of George Elmer Browne in New York and of André Lhote in Paris. He continued to pursue his career in these two cities, exhibiting in Paris at the Salon des Artistes Français and Salon d'Automne. He was a member of the Salmagundi Club and American Art Union in New York.

HUMPHREYS, F.
American, 19th century.
Active in Cincinnati.
Engraver.

HUMPHREYS, Henry Noel
British, 19th century.
Born 4 January 1810, in Birmingham; died 10 June 1879, in London.
Draughtsman, engraver, illustrator. Natural history.

Henry Humphreys worked in Italy for quite a long time. Returning to England in 1843 he devoted himself mainly to illustrating subjects from natural history.

HUMPHREYS, John. See **JOHNSTON John Humphreys**

HUMPHREYS, Malcolm
American, 20th century.
Born 7 November 1894, in Morristown (New Jersey).
Painter.

Malcolm Humphreys was perhaps related to David Humphreys. He was a member of the Salmagundi Club and American Art Union. He also appeared at the Salon des Artistes Français in Paris.

HUMPHREYS, Marie
Maiden name: Champney
American, 20th century.
Born 18 September 1876, in Deerfield; died 1 December 1906, in New Rochelle.
Miniaturist.

Marie Humphreys was the daughter of James Wells Champney. She began her training very young. She was a pupil of the Noémie Schmitt miniaturists in Paris, and Virginia Reynolds at the Art Institute of Chicago, and exhibited at the Salon des Artistes Français in Paris in 1900.

HUMPHREYS, Sallie Thomson
American, 20th century.
Born in Ohio.
Painter, watercolourist.

Sallie Thomson Humphreys was a pupil at the Art Students League, New York. She also studied in Paris and in Europe. She was a member of the Watercolorists Club of Washington and the American Art Union.

HUMPHREYS, Tom
19th century.
Painter. Landscapes.

MUSEUMS AND GALLERIES:
MELBOURNE: *Summer Sun* (1895, canvas).

HUMPHRIES, Jacqueline
American, 20th - 21st century.
Born 1960.
Painter, printmaker.
Minimal Art.

Jacqueline Humphries studied at the Parsons School of Design in New York in 1985, and with the Whitney Museum Independent Study Program in 1986. She lives in New York City, where she creates paintings and prints influenced by American abstract approaches of the 1960s, and by the work of David Salle. Techniques she has used include colour-field, dripping, over-painting, the 'non-relational' and the 'allover', as when she covers the canvas with different colours which run when the canvas is held vertically. She often works in series, such as her pattern paintings of the early 1990s, which are formed of paint spots and short brushstrokes which spread pattern-like across the painting. In the mid-1990s she engaged in her red 'poured' paintings, and later she created her horizon pictures, which were brilliantly coloured and horizontally oriented. She has since made a series of black paintings, and says that she wants her paintings to be a kind of dramatic physical event in the moment of viewing.

Humphries' exhibitions include: 1995, *A Decade of Collecting: 1985-1995/Contemporary Prints*, Hood Museum of Art, Dartmouth College; 1995, *Degrees of Abstraction*, Museum of Fine Arts, Boston; and 1990, *Cornell Collects, Johnson Museum of Art*, Ithaca, NY; 2000, *2000 Benefit Exhibition*, New Museum of Contemporary Art, New York; 2000, *Perspectives*, Foire Internationale d'Art Contemporain, Paris; 2001, *Against the Wall: Painting Against the Grid, Surface and Frame*, Institute of Contemporary Art, Philadelphia; 2002, *Jacqueline Humphries and Tony Oursler: Sleepwalk*, Newcomb Art Gallery, Tulane University, New Orleans; 2003, *The World Rehabilitation Fund's Spring Benefit*, Guggenheim Museum, New York; and 2003, *Made in California: Selections from the Frederick R. Weisman Art Foundation Collection*, Contemporary Arts Center, New Orleans.

She has received a Yale University Summer Scholarship (1984), an Edward F. Albee Foundation Fellowship, a Louis Comfort Tiffany Award (1992), a Joan Mitchell Foundation Grant (1995), a Pollack Krasner Foundation Grant (1999) and an Award in Art from the American Academy of Arts and Letters (2002).

BIBLIOGRAPHY:

Three Painters, exhibition catalogue, 470 Broome Street, New York, 1990. Good, John, *'Jacqueline Humphries'* in *Artforum* vol. XXXI n° 1, periodical, New York, September, 1992. Corn, Alfred, *'Jacqueline Humphries'* in *Art in America*, journal article, February 1996. Schmerler, Sarah, *'Jacqueline Humphries'* in *ARTnews*, journal article, March 1998. *Jacqueline Humphries: Malerei=Paintings*, exhibition catalogue, Kerber, Bielefeld, 2000 (text in German).

MUSEUMS AND GALLERIES:

BOSTON (MFA): *Antic* (1994, oil on linen) - BUFFALO (Albright-Knox AG): *Hit or Miss* (1993, oil on linen) - DARTMOUTH (Hood Mus., Dartmouth College): *Untitled (VI)* (1992, monoprint etching and mixed media) - LONDON (Saatchi Gal.) - NEW ORLÉANS (MA) - NEW ORLÉANS (Ogden Mus. of Southern Art, University of New Orleans): *Sunset (Rose)* (2000, oil) - PORTLAND (MA).

AUCTION RECORDS:

NEW YORK, 22 Feb 1993, *Untitled* (1990, oil/material, 16 x 16 ins / 40.6 x 40.6 cm) USD 1,870. NEW YORK, 3 May 1994, *95%* (1990, oil/material, 80 x 80 ins / 203.2 x 203.2 cm) USD 1,380. CHICAGO, 1 June 2003, *Four Corners* (oil on linen, 72 x 72 ins / 183 x 183 cm) USD 2,000.

HUMPHRIS, William H.

British, 19th - 20th century.
Active in Falmouth.
Painter. Genre scenes.

AUCTION RECORDS:

PARIS, 22 Nov 1946, *Spanish Mother*, FRF 2,400.

HUMPHRISS, Charles Harry

British, 19th - 20th century.
Born 1867; died 1934.
Active in the USA.
Sculptor. Genre scenes, local scenes. Statuettes, groups, equestrian groups.

Charles Harry (Henry) Humphriss settled in New York, where he specialised in representations of Native Americans, often on horseback or in groups.

AUCTION RECORDS:

NEW YORK, 14 June 1972, *Indian on Horseback* (bronze) USD 2,500. NEW YORK, 28 Sept 1973, *Indian at Prayer* (bronze) USD 4,750. NEW YORK, 29 April 1976, *Head of an Indian* (brown-patinated bronze, h. 10 3/4 ins / 27.3 cm) USD 1,900. NEW YORK, 29 Sept 1977, *Old Soldier* (brown-patinated bronze, h. 19 3/4 ins / 50.2 cm) USD 3,750. NEW YORK, 25 Oct 1979, *Dance of the Wolf Man* (brown-patinated bronze, h. 14 3/4 ins / 37.5 cm) USD 5,000. NEW YORK, 24 April 1981, *Appeal to the Great Spirit* (patinated bronze, h. 14 1/4 ins / 36.5 cm) USD 2,400. NEW YORK, 1 Dec 1989, *Indian Chief, Equestrian Group* (bronze, h. 25 1/2 ins / 64.8 cm) USD 28,600. NEW YORK, 23 May 1990, *King Arthur, Equestrian Group* (bronze, h. 34 3/4 ins / 88.4 cm) USD 7,150. NEW YORK, 31 May 1990, *Dance of the Wolf Man* (bronze, h. 15 ins / 38 cm) USD 4,950. NEW YORK, 29 Nov 1990, *Invocation to the Great Spirit* (1906, bronze, h. 30 1/2 ins / 77.5 cm) USD 6,600. NEW YORK, 27 May 1993, *Indian Chief* (bronze, h. 25 3/4 ins / 65.4 cm) USD 24,150. NEW YORK, 28 Sept 1995, *Cowboy* (bronze, h. 7 ins / 17.8 cm) USD 2,070. NEW YORK, 11 March 1999, *Appeal to the Great Spirit* (1906, brown patinated bronze, h. 30 ins / 76 cm) USD 14,000. LOS ANGELES, 29 April 1999, *Appeal to the Great Spirit* (1906, brown patinated bronze, h. 30 ins / 76 cm) USD 19,000. NEW YORK, 15 June 2000, *Bucking Bronco* (brown patinated bronze, h. 19 ins / 48 cm) USD 9,500. NEW YORK, 15 June 2000, *Appeal to Great Spirit* (1906, brown patinated bronze, a pair, h. 30 ins / 77 cm) USD 16,000. PASADENA, 13 Feb 2001, *Brave on Horseback* (1904, brown patinated bronze, h. 16 ins / 41 cm) USD 3,500. SANTA FE, 9 Nov 2002, *Sundial* (bronze, h. 19 ins / 48 cm) USD 11,000. NEW YORK, 4 Dec 2002, *Appeal to the Great Spirit* (dark brown patinated bronze, h. 31 ins / 79 cm) USD 22,500. NEW YORK, 12 Jan 2003, *Pray to the Great Spirit* (bronze) USD 2,300. NEW YORK, 5 March 2003, *Warrior* (dark reddish brown patinated bronze, h. 16 ins / 41 cm) USD 9,500. FAIRFIELD, 8 Jan 2004, *Appeal to the Great Spirit* (1906, verdigris-brown patinated bronze, h. 30 ins / 76 cm) USD 18,500. AUSTINBURG, 13 March 2004, *American Indian Astride a Horse* (bronze, h. 16 ins / 41 cm) USD 3,000.

HUMPHRISS, W.

British, 18th century.
Active in London.
Painter. Landscapes.

W. Humphriss exhibited in London at the Royal Academy and at the Society of Artists from 1791 to 1793.

HUMPHRYS

British, 18th century.
Active in London.
Painter.

Humphrys exhibited two portraits in London at the Free Society in 1771.

HUMPHRYS, William

British, 19th century.
Born 1794, in Dublin; died 21 January 1865, in Genoa.
Engraver. Banknotes.

William Humphrys went to America while still very young. He concentrated on illustration and was commissioned to engrave vignettes for banknotes. On his return to England he was commissioned to carry out the same work for English banknotes and subsequently the design and engraving of stamps. He produced some portraits and genre scenes after Reynolds, Sir Thomas Lawrence, R. Leslie and Correggio.

HUMPLIK, Josef

Austrian, 20th century.
Born 17 August 1888, in Vienna.
Sculptor, engraver. Busts.

AUCTION RECORDS:

LONDON, 15 May 1986, *Centaur* (bronze, h. total 18 1/2 ins / 47 cm) GBP 1,500.

HUNÆUS, Andreas Herman

Danish, 19th century.
Born 8 December 1814; died 15 May 1866, in Copenhagen.
Painter.

Andreas Hunæus was a pupil at the academy of Copenhagen from 1831. He painted mostly portraits and genre scenes.

HUND, Cornelius

Dutch, 20th century.
Sculptor.

Hund won the Dutch Prix de Rome in 1947.

HUNDERTPFUND, Liberat

Austrian, 19th century.
Born 11 November 1806, in Bregenz; died 28 March 1878, in Bregenz.
Painter. Portraits, genre scenes.

He showed a marked interest in art very young. He went to Vienna in 1822, then in 1832 moved on to Munich. There he gained a huge reputation as a result of his *Portrait of Johann Georg von Dilles*, director of the museum in Munich. He mostly painted portraits, but also did a number of genre paintings.

MUSEUMS AND GALLERIES:

MUNICH: *Portrait of Johann Georg von Dilles*.

HUNDERTWASSER, Friedensreich,

pseudonym of Stowasser, Friedrich or Fritz

Austrian, 20th century.
Born 15 December 1928, in Vienna; died 19 February 2000, on board the liner Queen Elizabeth II.
Active from 1953 also in France.
Painter (mixed media), watercolourist, engraver, lithographer.
Nouvelle Figuration.

From 1943, when he was 15, Friedensreich Hundertwasser produced coloured drawings of the palaces of Venice and the forest of Vienna. In 1948, he enrolled at the Akademie der Bildenden Künste in Vienna, where he remained for only four months. Visiting an exhibition of works by Egon Schiele inspired him to look into other Viennese artists of the turn of the century, art nouveau, and the Sezession artists, particularly Gustav Klimt. He was also interested in the work of Eric Kampmann, who painted trees on plates of glass in an Expressionist but populist spirit, and in the work of Paul Klee. He travelled to Italy (where he met and made friends with René Brô), to France (where he spent a very brief period at the École des Beaux-Arts in 1950), and to Tunisia and Morocco (in 1951). In 1949, he adopted the pseudonym Hundertwasser and put the finishing touches to his image as a tall, lean, red-bearded man in brightly coloured, folkloric clothing. At the same time, he was perfecting the vocabulary and syntax of the sign-based language his art would speak for the rest of his life. Hundertwasser called this language 'transautomatism' and he defined it subsequently in a number of articles on various subjects: 'Visibility in Transautomatic Creation' in the 1954 issue of the journal *Cimaise*, and 'Mould's Manifesto against Rationalism in Architecture' in 1958. In discussing the various forms of automatism in modern art, he rails against them and tries to move beyond them: these forms of automatism (including automatism based on the repetition of a single base module, and gestural automatism) reduce the artistic creative act, in his eyes, to repeated use of elementary approaches. As an alternative, he recommends a return to 'craftsmanlike' practices, which require care and time, that achieve a fullness of vision through an accumulation of detail, and that refuse to be hurried by the rush of what passes for inspiration. His designs are less ambitious and more labour-intensive.

Hundertwasser settled in France in 1953. In 1959, he was made professor at the fine arts academy in Hamburg, but released from his post immediately when he decided to paint, together with his students, a never-ending spiral that would gradually cover the city. In 1961 he spent the whole year in Japan. He then travelled to Uganda and Sudan before returning to Venice and Vienna. He began to produce engravings in 1967, and one of the fruits of this work was an album published in 1973 consisting entirely of woodcuts made in collaboration with Japanese artists. He wanted his painting to be emblematic of his stance against the inhumanity of the modern world and its environment; he sometimes expressed this stance by means of 'happenings' in which he appeared entirely naked.

Each time Hundertwasser applied the precepts that define 'transautomatism', of which he was the only advocate, he began from the same starting point, in apparent contradiction of his expressed rebuttal of modular automatism; however, his variations were ingenious in their infinite variety. Gérald Gassiot-Talabot notes his almost obsessive use of the checkerboard pattern and spirals, and his links with *Jugendstil*. Hundertwasser retained some aspects of Gustav Klimt's rich ornamental vocabulary, for example his distribution of elements across the surface of a work according to the ancient labyrinth principle, or a spiral or a mandala. Along the lines established by the labyrinth, spiral or mandala, he would position a whole range of additional motifs (small abstract medals, or sketchy elements of figurative import, such as windows or heads), from which he derived the literary and humorous titles he liked to apply to his paintings. Among these motifs are key words that form an integral part of these image-collections and echo hia personal rallying cry for a return to a natural, prelapsarian existence: drops, rain, tears, waves, fissures, entrails, gardens. He also retains Klimt's rich range of colours, as well as the harmonious combinations and extreme and striking clashes of colours reminiscent of Oriental illuminations. In his refusal to countenance quick work, which he felt would be swiftly dismissed by the viewer, he includes poetic points along his sumptuous arabesques that cannot be grasped by a swift glance. Discussing Hundertwasser's paintings, Werner Hofman calls to mind Japanese paper flowers whose multi-coloured folds only reveal themselves when the flowers are thrown into water. One thing is certain: all Hundertwasser's paintings are very beautiful, in the sense of being very pleasant to look at. With its bivalent nature as both ornament and sense-carrier, his output raises the dilemma of the work as object (responding to *a priori* aesthetic ideas), or the work as language whose function is to communicate, and which is founded on principles that are relative and no longer normative.

Work by Hundertwasser has been shown at a great many collective exhibitions, during the course of which he received a number of prizes, including a prize at the fifth São Paulo biennale (1959) and another at the 6th International Art Exhibition in Tokyo (1961). In 1962, the whole of the Austrian pavillion at the Venice biennale was given over to his work, and his work was exhibited regularly in France, at the Salon des Réalités Nouvelles and the Salon de Mai. In 2003, his work was featured posthumously at the collective exhibition *Peintres et artistes dans le Perche, 19e - 20e siècles* (*Painters and Artists in the Perche Region, 19th-20th Centuries*) at the Musée Château St-Jean in Nogent-le-Rotrou. Collections of his work have been shown in several solo exhibitions, including in Venice (1952); the Art Club in Vienna (1952, 1953); the Galerie Paul Facchetti in Paris (1954); in Milan (1955); Paris (1956, 1957, 1958, 1960); Vienna and Cannes (1957); Basel (1959); Tokyo (1961); Rome (1962); Cologne (1963); the Galerie Trigano in Paris (1999).

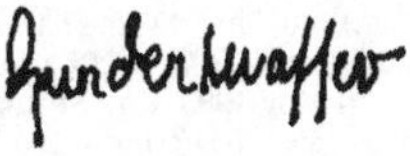

BIBLIOGRAPHY:
Pieyre de Mandiargues, André, Alain Jouffroy, '*Hundertwasser*' in *Nouvelle Revue française*, periodical, Gallimard, Paris, 1954. Hundertwasser, F., '*La Visibilité dans la création transautomatique*' in *Cimaise*, no. 6, periodical, Paris, 1956. Restany, Pierre, *Hundertwasser*, exhibition catalogue, Gal. Kamer, Paris, 1957. Jouffroy, Alain, *Hundertwasser*, Arts, New York, 1959. Restany, Pierre, '*Hundertwasser*' in *Dictionnaire des artistes contemporains*, Libraires associés, Paris, 1964. Schmied, Wieland, *Hundertwasser. Vollständiger*, Kestner-Gesellschaft, Hanover, 1964. *Hundertwasser: Recent Paintings*, exhibition catalogue, Hanover Gallery, London, 1967. *Friedensreich Hundertwasser*, exhibition catalogue, Haus der Kunst, Munich, 1975. Koschatzky, Walter, *Friedensreich Hundertwasser: das vollständige druckgraphische Werk, 1951-1986*, O. Füssli, Zurich, 1986. Koschatzky, Walter, *Friedensreich Hundertwasser: The Complete Graphic Work, 1951-86*, Alan Wofsy Fine Arts, 1986. Restany, Pierre, *Hundertwasser (Basic Art)*, Taschen, 2000. Pessey-Lux, Aude/Harel, Joram, *Hommage à Hundertwasser, 1928-2000*, exhibition catalogue, Musée des Beaux-Arts et de la Dentelle, Alençon, 2001. Schmied, Wieland, '*Hundertwasser 1928-2000*' in *2 vols.*, catalogue raisonné, Taschen, Paris, Cologne, London, 2002. *Hundertwasser*, Taschen, Sept 2002. Arpentinier, Jean, *Peintures et Artistes*

du Perche 1560-1960, Editions de la Reinette, Le Mans, 2003. Cuito, Aurora, *Friedensreich Hundertwasser*, Te Neues Publishing Company, 2003 (multilingual edition).

MUSEUMS AND GALLERIES:

AMSTERDAM (Stedelijk Mus.) - NEW YORK (Brooklyn Mus.) - PARIS (MNAM-CCI) - SÃO PAULO (MAM) - VENICE (Collezione Peggy Guggenheim): *European Man Twiddling his Moustache* (1951, watercolour) - VIENNA (Cultural Service) - VIENNA (Kunsthaus) - VIENNA (Mus. Moderner Kunst Stiftung Ludwig) - VIENNA (Österreichische Gal. Belvedere).

AUCTION RECORDS:

VIENNA, 29 May 1963, *Composition in Red and Blue* (watercolour) ATS 70,000. COLOGNE, 8-9 Dec 1966, *Styria in Green* (watercolour, egg and coloured chalks) DEM 10,000. GENEVA, 11 Nov 1967, *Garden in the Aureole*, CHF 15,000. HAMBURG, 6 June 1969, *Garden in the Aureole* (watercolour/brown paper remounted/canvas) DEM 20,000. PARIS, 3 March 1970, *Communist with Wings*, FRF 70,000. HAMBURG, 4 June 1971, *Black Tears of a Fluidoid* (watercolour, ink and oil) DEM 30,000. LONDON, 1 Dec 1971, *Egg from Ancient Japan*, GBP 9,000. VIENNA, 17 Jan 1973, *Match of the Century*, ATS 1,000,000. MUNICH, 21 March 1974, *Introverted Window* (1963) DEM 50,000. LONDON, 27 April 1976, *Composition* (lithograph, 28 1/4 x 19 1/4 ins / 71.7 x 49.2 cm) GBP 420. LONDON, 29 June 1976, *Great River of the Mountain* (1956, tempera/canvas, 33 3/4 x 46 ins / 86 x 116 cm) GBP 11,000. LONDON, 30 June 1977, *Boat and Whirlwind in a Garden* (1954, watercolour, 22 x 11 1/4 ins / 55 x 28.5 cm) GBP 4,800. NEW YORK, 9 Nov 1977, *It Hurts to Wait with Love if Love is Somewhere Else* (1971, silk screen print in colour) USD 1,000. ZURICH, 22 Nov 1978, *A Toe on Work's Foot* (1958, mixed media, 34 1/4 x 26 ins / 87 x 66 cm) GBP 55,000. ZURICH, 23 Nov 1978, *Houses* (1969, woodcut in colour, 12 1/2 x 16 1/2 ins / 32 x 42 cm) CHF 2,700. LONDON, 4 Dec 1979, *Extrovert Window* (1963, oil on canvas, 21 1/2 x 28 1/2 ins / 54.5 x 72.5 cm) GBP 8,000. LOS ANGELES, 16 June 1980, *Eyes of Macchu-Picchu* (1966, lithograph in four colours, 18 x 22 ins / 45.5 x 56 cm) USD 1,600. ZURICH, 30 Oct 1980, *Onion-Tower Soup* (1971, mixed media/aluminium card, 17 1/4 x 24 3/4 ins / 44 x 63 cm) CHF 60,000. ZURICH, 28 Oct 1981, *Three Drops of Water* (1959, mixed media/canvas, 28 1/2 x 24 ins / 72.5 x 61 cm) CHF 48,000. MUNICH, 30 June 1982, *Shadows of the Stars* (1967, coloured lithograph, 16 1/2 x 20 3/4 ins / 42 x 53 cm) DEM 4,400. PARIS, 20 May 1983, *City Seen Beyond the Sun* (1955, oil on canvas, 59 x 53 1/2 ins / 150 x 136 cm) FRF 380,000. HAMBURG, 8 June 1984, *Arab Woman* (1955, coloured lithograph) DEM 7,200. NEW YORK, 1 Nov 1984, *Consequence of a Spiral Haze* (1959, mixed media/mounted paper/canvas, 23 1/2 x 28 3/4 ins / 60 x 73 cm) USD 25,000. HAMBURG, 7 June 1985, *Green Power* (1972, silk screen print in colour) DEM 4,000. ZURICH, 8 Nov 1985, *My Knowledge of Czech* (1966, mixed media, 46 1/2 x 32 1/4 ins / 118 x 82 cm) CHF 200,000. VIENNA, 9 Dec 1987, *Portrait of Laszlo, his Head between his Knees* (1960, brush, pen and Indian ink, 11 1/2 x 8 1/2 ins / 29.5 x 21.6 cm) ATS 60,000. PARIS, 28 March 1988, *House in Bright Colours* (1952, gouache, 19 1/2 x 12 1/2 ins / 49.5 x 32 cm) FRF 90,000. PARIS, 23 June 1988, *The Pink Paths of Toggenburg* (1956, watercolour/crumpled brown paper with holes, 24 1/2 x 17 3/4 ins / 62 x 45 cm) FRF 109,000. LONDON, 30 June 1988, *Le Beau Flou Spiraloïde aux Fenêtres dans la Fente* (1957, mixed media, 19 x 22 3/4 ins / 48 x 58 cm) GBP 24,200. LONDON, 1 Dec 1988, *Green Styrias* (1958, mixed media/canvas, 23 1/2 x 20 ins / 60 x 51 cm) GBP 35,200. PARIS, 4 April 1989, *Fall in Cloud* (1979, multiple Plexiglas, 10 3/4 x 13 1/4 ins / 27.5 x 33.5 cm) FRF 9,000. PARIS, 16 April 1989, *European Man Twiddling his Moustache* (1951, watercolour/brown paper/canvas, 50 1/2 x 18 ins / 128 x 46 cm) FRF 680,000. ZURICH, 25 Oct 1989, *Mosque* (1959, mixed media/paper, 28 3/4 x 23 1/2 ins / 73 x 60 cm) CHF 110,000. LONDON, 30 Nov 1989, *Domestic Sun* (1958, egg-based distemper and ink/vinyl./canvas, 15 x 18 1/4 ins / 37.8 x 46.3 cm) GBP 28,600. LONDON, 5 April 1990, *Head from Two Viewpoints* (1954, oil/fabric and two other materials, 33 1/2 x 26 1/2 ins / 85 x 67 cm) GBP 115,500. PARIS, 29 June 1990, *Composition* (1955, gouache, 14 1/4 x 18 ins / 36 x 46 cm) FRF 200,000. ZURICH, 18 Oct 1990, *I Live Near the Main Road and the Fence of a Field* (mixed media/jute, 32 x 46 ins / 81 x 116 cm) CHF 230,000. LONDON, 6 Dec 1990, *Spiral of Gold Rain* (1961, egg tempera and gold paint/paper/sacking, 28 3/4 x 23 3/4 ins / 73 x 60.3 cm) GBP 60,500. ZURICH, 7-8 Dec 1990, *The City is a Woman's Hairdo* (1962, mixed media, watercolour and paper/canvas, 25 1/2 x 19 3/4 ins / 65 x 50 cm) CHF 135,000. LONDON, 21 March 1991, *Man Found in Zahala* (1975, watercolour, egg and oil on paper/canvas, 13 3/4 x 19 3/4 ins / 35 x 50 cm) GBP 35,200. COPENHAGEN, 30 May 1991, *Asiatic War* (1958, mixed media/silk/canvas, 46 x 34 1/4 ins / 116 x 87 cm) DKK 500,000. PARIS, 2 June 1991, *Lawn Bath for the Spiral* (oil on paper/panel, 19 x 24 1/2 ins / 48 x 62.5 cm) FRF 390,000. LONDON, 27 June 1991, *Globulant* (1956, oil on canvas, 46 x 30 1/4 ins / 117 x 77 cm) GBP 66,000. NEW YORK, 25-26 Feb 1992, *Spring Leaves (the Black Hole)* (1966, watercolour, egg, oil, polyvinyl and gold-leaf/paper/jute sacking and canvas, 20 1/2 x 28 1/4 ins / 52.1 x 71.8 cm) USD 74,250. AMSTERDAM, 19 May 1992, *Composition* (1967, watercolour/paper, 8 1/4 x 11 ins / 21 x 27 cm) NLG 8,050. MUNICH, 26 May 1992, *The Kid with Green Hair* (1967, coloured lithograph, 20 1/2 x 14 1/2 ins / 52 x 37 cm) DEM 8,280. HEIDELBERG, 9 Oct 1992, *Homo Humus Come Va, 1002 Nights* (silk screen print, 25 1/4 x 17 1/4 ins / 64 x 44 cm) DEM 2,400. NEW YORK, 4 May 1993, *Summer House* (1952, watercolour and acrylic/paper, 15 1/4 x 27 1/2 ins / 38.7 x 69.9 cm) USD 40,250. LONDON, 24 June 1993, *La Picandière* (1960, oil, gouache and gold paint/paper, 51 1/4 x 38 ins / 130.2 x 96.6 cm) GBP 71,900. PARIS, 20 Dec 1993, *Steam at Hokkaido* (1961, watercolour, 19 x 26 ins / 48 x 66 cm) FRF 205,000. PARIS, 29 June 1994, *Gas Flames together with the Flames of the Holy Spirit* (1957, egg, gold, watercolour and oil on paper/canvas, 24 3/4 x 38 1/2 ins / 63 x 97.5 cm) FRF 225,000. ZURICH, 23 June 1995, *Pacific Haze* (1985, colour woodcut/Japanese paper, 21 3/4 x 16 1/4 ins / 55.5 x 41 cm) CHF 6,500. LONDON, 26 Oct 1995, *Seven Glories* (1953, watercolour and gold leaf/paper, 14 1/2 x 19 3/4 ins / 37 x 50 cm) GBP 60,900. PARIS, 19 April 1996, *Musician* (1974, etching, 12 1/2 x 94 1/2 ins / 32 x 240 cm) FRF 18,000. NEW YORK, 9 May 1996, *Sailor Smoking at Dusk* (1968, watercolour and gold and silver paint/paper/aluminium/card, 24 1/2 x 17 1/4 ins / 62.5 x 43.8 cm) USD 54,625. LONDON, 23 May 1996, *Contracted Form with Twenty-two Interpretations* (1954, watercolour and pencil/paper, 13 3/4 ins / 35 cm, 1 1/2 x 9 3/4 ins/4 x 25 cm) GBP 17,250. BERN, 20-21 June 1996, *Nana Hyaku Mizu* (1973, woodcut in colour, 26 3/4 x 21 1/4 ins / 68 x 54 cm) CHF 34,000. PARIS, 16 Oct 1996, *Untitled* (1959, watercolour and collage/paper, 6 1/4 x 4 3/4 ins / 16 x 12 cm) FRF 12,500. LONDON, 6 Dec 1996, *The Rain is Full of Grass* (1958, egg tempera/paper/canvas, 19 3/4 x 25 1/2 ins / 50 x 65 cm) GBP 29,900. PARIS, 10 Dec 1996, *Homage to Schröder, Sonnenstein* (1972, silk screen print in colour, 33 3/4 x 25 1/4 ins / 85.7 x 64 cm) FRF 6,000. ZURICH, 8 April 1997, *Good Morning City* (1971, colour silk screen print, 33 1/2 x 21 3/4 ins / 85 x 55.5 cm) CHF 3,300. LONDON, 26 June 1997, *City in Flower* (1960, tempera, gold, ink and oil/hardboard, 19 3/4 x 39 1/2 ins / 50.2 x 100.3 cm) GBP 28,750. ZURICH, 19 Nov 1997, *Green Power* (1972, silk screen print in twenty-one colours, 32 3/4 x 25 ins / 83.5 x 63.5 cm) CHF 8,500. NEW YORK, 6 and 7 March 1998, *Shadow of the Stars* (1967, coloured lithograph, 16 1/2 x 20 3/4 ins / 42 x 53 cm) USD 4,600. PARIS, 20 March 1998, *Abstract Composition* (1966, two lithographs in colour) FRF 20,000. LONDON, 25 March 1999, *First Spiral in the Spirit of the Buddhist Sign* (1961, tempera, oil, bricks, rice on paper on jute, 35 x 46 ins / 89 x 116 cm) GBP 40,000. LONDON, 30 April 1999, *The Thirty-nine Heads* (1953, oil and pencil on canvas, 21 x 38 ins / 54 x 96 cm) GBP 36,000. LONDON, 29 June 2000, *Autofahrer in der Nacht* (1963, oil, polyvinyl, collage, 36 x 26 ins / 92 x 66 cm) GBP 130,000. ZURICH, 21 Nov 2000, *The Third Consequence of a German Earth Becoming now a Spiderweb* (mixed media, 24 x 19 ins / 62 x 48 cm) CHF 65,000. LONDON, 8 Feb 2001, *Rain of Blood Dropping into Japanese Waters in an Austrian Garden* (1961, oil, gouache, watercolour on paper on canvas, 51 x 63 ins / 130 x 161 cm) GBP 72,000. VIENNA, 26 Sept 2001, *Yellow Mould of Skyscrapers* (watercolour, casearti egg tempera, oil, gold, silver foil on paper and canvas, 21 x 27 ins / 54 x 68 cm) ATS 900,000. LONDON, 26 June 2002, *Brillen im hausrock* (1963, egg tempera, oil, tissue paper, polyvinyl, 23 x 17 ins / 59 x 42 cm) GBP 55,000. LONDON, 28 June 2002, *Rain Tree* (1959, watercolour on paper on canvas, 25 x 20 ins / 64 x 50 cm) GBP 35,000. LONDON, 22 Oct 2003, *Lauf in die Sonne* (1964, watercolour, gold paint, 14 x 39 ins / 36 x 100 cm) GBP 65,000. VIENNA, 28 Oct 2003, *Come and Go Walking with Me - Conversation* (1970, oil, colour pen, watercolour, egg, sand, polyvinyl, 20 x 29 ins / 51 x 73 cm) EUR 100,000. LONDON, 23 June 2004, *Tower of Babel* (1959, oil, egg tempera, watercolour, wrapping paper chalk, PV, 51 x 64 ins / 130 x 162 cm) GBP 240,000. PARIS, 23 Sept 2004, *Communist with Wings* (1962, tempera, oil on paper on canvas, 26 x 32 ins / 65 x 81 cm) EUR 81,500.

HUNDLEY, Philip
British, 19th century.
Active in London.
Painter. Genre scenes.

Philip Hundley exhibited his work in London at Suffolk Street from 1869 to 1880.

HUNDRIESER, Emil
German, 19th - 20th century.
Born 13 March 1846, in Königsberg (now Kaliningrad, Russia); died 30 January 1911, in Berlin.
Active in Charlottenburg.
Sculptor.

Hundrieser won the gold medal in Berlin in 1888.

MUSEUMS AND GALLERIES:
BERLIN: *Queen Louise* (statue).

HUNDT, Johann Hermann Baptist
German, 20th century.
Born 18 March 1894, in Mülheim-an-der-Ruhr.
Painter. Interiors with figures, still-lifes.
Das Junge Rheinland (Young Rhineland group).

Johann Hundt settled in Düsseldorf, where he was a student of Heinrich Nauen at the fine arts school. From 1913 to 1932 he was a member of the group Das Junge Rheinland (Young Rheinland). His work was shown at many collective exhibitions. In 1962, he was one of the artists represented in the *Düsseldorf Artists* exhibition at the fine arts museum in Ostend.

Hundt had a robust technique, his large, sensuous brush strokes underlining a liberal but determined design. He painted many still-lifes and interiors.

HUNERFAUTH, Irma
German, 20th century.
Born in Donaueschingen.
Painter.

Irma Hunerfauth was a student at the fine arts academy in Munich. In 1955, under the supervision of Conrad Westpfahl, she began to produce abstract paintings. Her work was first shown at a collective exhibition in Munich in 1958; this exhibition was followed by many others. There have also been solo exhibitions of her work; the first took place in Munich in 1960, and the second in Lausanne in the same year. Her preferred mode of expression is a series of coloured patches spread out on a white ground and linked together by a network of fine lines.

HUNG TUNG. See **HONG TONG**

HUNG WU. See **HONG WU**

HUNG-JEN. See **HONGREN**

HUNGEAR, Johann Michael
Swiss, 17th - 18th century.
Born 11 June 1634, in Rapperswil; died 21 April 1714, in Rapperswil.
Painter.

He worked initially in Italy, notably Milan. In 1654, he returned to Switzerland and did numerous paintings for various churches and abbeys.

HUNGERMUELLER, Josef
German, 19th - 20th century.
Born 10 April 1777, in Nuremberg; died 1820, in Munich.
Painter, decorative designer.

Hungermuller's works include the ceiling of the Munich Theatre, and the decoration of the cemetery church there.

HUNGLINGER, Andreas Magnus
Austrian, 18th - 19th century.
Born 19 July 1756, in Vienna; died c. 1830.
Painter. History painting, genre scenes.

Following a long period stuyding the masters, he travelled widely in Europe.

HUNIN, Mathieu Joseph Charles
Belgian, 18th - 19th century.
Born 18 September 1770, in Mechelen; died 7 November 1851, in Mechelen.
Draughtsman, engraver.

Mathieu Hunin was the father of Pierre Hunin.

HUNIN, Pierre Paul Alouis
Belgian, 19th century.
Born 8 December 1808, in Mechelen; died 27 February 1855, in Mechelen.
Painter. Portraits, genre scenes.

Pierre Hunin studied under his father and under F. de Brackelaer, Ingres and Cogniet in Paris.

MUSEUMS AND GALLERIES:
BERLIN: *The Will* - BRUSSELS: *Distribution and Alms in a Convent.*

AUCTION RECORDS:
LONDON, 19 May 1971, *Mother's Opinion,* GBP 580. AMSTERDAM, 30 Oct 1991, *Old Lady Lying against a Wall in a Town in Southern Europe* (oil on panel, 27 1/4 x 20 3/4in/69.5 x 53cm) NLG 4,830. NEW YORK, 23-24 May 1996, *The Happy Family* (oil on panel, 20 x 27in/50.8 x 68.6cm) USD 14,950. VLAAMSE KAAI, 11 Dec 2001, *Stormy Night* (oil on wood, 30 x 25 ins / 75 x 63 cm) BEF 240,000.

HUNKELER, Hans Georg
Swiss, 18th century.
Born 31 October 1682, in Altishofen; died 1740, in Lucerne.
Painter. History painting.

He was a Swiss Guard in Rome.

HUNN, Thomas H.
British, 19th - 20th century.
Active in Hackney.
Painter, watercolourist, draughtsman. Landscapes.

Thomas H. Hunn exhibited with the Royal Academy and at the Suffolk Street Gallery from 1878 to 1890.

AUCTION RECORDS:
LONDON, 4 June 1908, *Haymaking* (drawing) GBP 3. LONDON, 20 March 1909, *Mill at Mapledurham* (drawing) GBP 5. LONDON, 21 Jan 1911, *Cookham, on the Thames* (drawing) GBP 5. LONDON, 18 June 1985, *At Clandon, Surrey* (watercolour, 11 3/4 x 18 ins / 30 x 46 cm) GBP 850. LONDON, 25 Jan 1988, *Riverbank with Church* (watercolour, 10 x 14 ins / 25.5 x 35.5

cm) GBP 715. LONDON, 25-26 April 1990, *West Clandon, Surrey* (watercolour, 13 x 11 ins / 33 x 27 cm) GBP 2,640. LONDON, 5 Nov 1993, *Walled Garden at Sutton Place* (pencil and watercolour, 9½ x 13 ins / 24.4 x 32.8 cm) GBP 805.

HUNNEMAN, Christopher William

British, 18th century.
Died 21 November 1793.
Active in London.
Painter, miniaturist, draughtsman.

Christopher Hunnemann was a talented artist who exhibited portraits in crayon and miniatures at the Royal Academy in London from 1777 to 1793.

HUNOLD, Friedemann

German, 18th - 19th century.
Born 30 April 1773, in Seebergen; died 20 November 1840, in Dessau.
Sculptor, ceramicist.

He was a pupil of Schadow in Berlin.

HUNT

American, 20th century.
Born in Galena.
Engraver.

Ms Hunt lived in New York. She was the pupil of George Innes the younger and John Francis Murphy. She was an etcher and also an art critic. She taught at the American Academy of the Fine Arts, New York.

HUNT, Alfred William

British, 19th century.
Born 15 November 1830, in Liverpool; died 3 May 1896, in London.
Painter, watercolourist, draughtsman. Landscapes, still-lifes.

Alfred William Hunt was the son and pupil of Andrew Hunt, all of whose children were painters. Alfred, the only surviving son was originally destined for the clergy, and was a talented student at Oxford where he concluded his studies in 1853. However, his artistic leanings took precedence and he renounced ordination. He had not neglected drawing during his studies of the arts and theology, and from 1850 he was appointed to membership of the Liverpool Academy. He married the daughter of the Reverend Raine, a well-known antique dealer and librarian of the Deanery and Chapter of Durham, they were the reason for his frequent visits there and to the provinces of the North of England until 1870. After his marriage he lived in London. He died of a stroke, leaving his widow with three daughters. One of them, Miss Violet Hunt, was a talented writer.

Alfred Hunt applied himself to his art with a passion which was exceptional. He was directed by two main influences, namely Turner and the Pre-Raphaelites. This is understandable as he was a poet as well as a painter. He constantly endeavoured to extract the Ideal from the concrete world and impose it permanently on his canvas. Ruskin was an admirer of his landscapes and defended him passionately when Hunt's sympathies for the concepts of Rossetti and his friends brought upon him the disapprobation of the academic jury in 1856. Watercolour had become his favourite genre and he produced some first-class work.

In 1854 he exhibited his work at the Royal Academy in London for the first time and continued to make regular presentations there until 1888. In 1862 he became an associate of the Royal Society of Painters in Watercolours and a full member in 1864. His work was represented at the exhibition *Expedition Kunst. Die Entdeckung der Natur von C.D. Friedrich bis Humboldt* (*Expedition Art. The Discovery of Nature from C.D. Friedrich to Humboldt*) in the Kunsthalle in Hamburg in 2002, an exhibition which depicted the links between the natural sciences and the painted landscape.

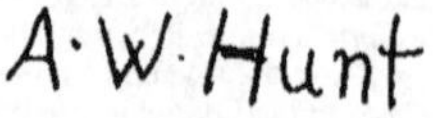

BIBLIOGRAPHY:

Secor, Robert, *John Ruskin and Alfred Hunt: new letters and the record of a friendship*, English Literary Studies, University of Victoria, 1982. *Expedition Kunst. Die Entdeckung der Natur von C.D. Friedrich bis Humboldt*, exhibition catalogue, Hamburger Kunsthalle, Hamburg, 2002.

MUSEUMS AND GALLERIES:

BIRMINGHAM: *Windsor* - BIRMINGHAM (Mus. and AG): *A Norwegian Midnight* (oil on canvas) - CARDIFF: a watercolour - GLASGOW: *Kerrera Bay* - LONDON (Tate Collection): *Cwm Trefaen* (c. 1855-1860, oil on canvas); *Windsor Castle* (1889, watercolour/paper) - LONDON (Victoria and Albert Mus.): a watercolour - MELBOURNE: *Moonrise*.

AUCTION RECORDS:

NEW YORK, 12 and 13 March 1903, *Fruit* (watercolour) USD 220. LONDON, 21 March 1908, *Styhead Pass seen from Borrowdale*, GBP 44. LONDON, 4 April 1908, *Harlech Castle*, GBP 39; *Fog Rising at Daybreak*, GBP 183. LONDON, 10 June 1909, *Drachenfels on the Rhine*, GBP 57. LONDON, 22 April 1911, *Near Loch Maree*, GBP 16. LONDON, June 1922, *Bilston Marsh near Liverpool*, GBP 10; *Harlech Castle*, GBP 33. LONDON, 8 June 1934, *Durham: Elvet Bridge* (watercolour) GBP 60. LONDON, 12 Dec 1978, *Rokeby Woods* (watercolour heightened with gouache, 9 x 19¼ ins / 23 x 49 cm) GBP 550. LONDON, 14 Dec 1979, *Blue Lights, Tynemouth Pier* (1868, watercolour, 14¼ x 20¾ ins / 36 x 53 cm) GBP 11,000. LONDON, 16 Oct 1981, *Naples, a Land of Smouldering Fire* (1871, watercolour, 19½ x 29½ ins / 49.5 x 75.2 cm) GBP 1,500. LONDON, 4 Feb 1986, *Ambleside Mill* (watercolour, 13½ x 10 ins / 34 x 25.3 cm) GBP 7,000. LONDON, 28 April 1987, *Ehrenburg an der Mosel* (watercolour and pencil, 10¼ x 13 ins / 25.8 x 33.3 cm) GBP 1,700. LONDON, 22 Sept 1988, *Boats off the Coast on a Rough Sea* (1875, oil on canvas, 12 x 18 ins / 30.3 x 45.8 cm) GBP 528. LONDON, 29 Oct 1991, *Kochem an der Mosel* (1860, pencil and watercolour, 12 x 9¾ ins / 30.5 x 25 cm) GBP 1,980. LONDON, 13 March 1992, *Patches of Mist* (1861, oil on canvas, 20 x 30 ins / 50.8 x 76.2 cm) GBP 8,800. NEW YORK, 8 Nov 1995, *Conway Lake* (watercolour heightened with white, 9½ x 14¼ ins / 24 x 36 cm) USD 3,220. LONDON, 15 July 1999, *Ullswater from Gowbarrow Park* (watercolour heightened with gouache and scratching out, 15 x 21 ins / 37 x 53 cm) GBP 7,500. LONDON, 25 Nov 1999, *Whitby, Crazy Jane in Last Berth* (1875, watercolour and pencil heightened with stopping out, 10 x 15 ins / 26 x 38 cm) GBP 2,400. LONDON, 7 April 2000, *Mist Wreaths, Scotland* (19 x 29 ins / 49 x 74 cm) GBP 26,000. LONDON, 7 April 2000, *View from Naples Across the Bay to Vesuvius in Eruption, Evening Sky* (1871, pencil, watercolour, gum arabic, gouache and scratching out, 19 x 30 ins / 49 x 75 cm) GBP 28,000. LONDON, 7 June 2001, *Whitby Harbour* (pencil and watercolour with scratching out, 11 x 16 ins / 27 x 40 cm) GBP 3,800. CARDIFF, 26 Sept 2001, *Moel Siabod in the Clwydian Range, North Wales* (1870, watercolour, 9 x 14 ins / 24 x 36 cm) GBP 1,500. LONDON, 4 July 2002, *Cochem on the Moselle* (watercolour over pencil heightened with gouache, 7 x 10 ins / 17 x 26 cm) GBP 1,650. LEWES, 15 Oct 2002, *View of Harlech Castle* (watercolour, 13 x 20 ins / 33 x 51 cm) GBP 4,400. LONDON, 5 June 2003, *Rokeby, Yorkshire* (pencil and watercolour with scratching out, 11 x 16 ins / 28 x 40 cm) GBP 2,400. LONDON, 3 June 2004, *Mill on the Coquet, Northumberland* (1887, pencil and watercolour with scratching out, 11 x 15 ins / 28 x 39 cm) GBP 4,000. LONDON, 11 June 2004, *When the Leaves Begin to Turn* (oil on canvas, 17 x 15 ins / 44 x 38 cm) GBP 44,000.

HUNT, Amy Henrietta

British, 19th century.
Active in London.
Sculptor.

Henrietta Hunt exhibited her work in London at the Royal Academy and in Suffolk Street from 1887 to 1891.

HUNT, Andrew

British, 19th century.
Born 1790, in Erdington; died 1861, in Liverpool.
Painter. Genre scenes, landscapes.

Andrew Hunt established himself in Liverpool as a landscape painter and, in particular, as a teacher. He was a member of the Liverpool Academy and took part in exhibitions. He was also to be found exhibiting genre subjects in London, at the Royal Academy and at Suffolk Street from 1852 to 1856. He had a son and four daughters who were painters.

MUSEUMS AND GALLERIES:

LIVERPOOL: *The Mersey Estuary.*

AUCTION RECORDS:

LONDON, 3 Oct 1984, *Eastham, Cheshire* (oil on canvas, 14 x 21 ins / 35.5 x 53.5 cm) GBP 1,000.

HUNT, Arthur Ackland

British, 19th century.
Active in London.
Painter. Figures.

Arthur Ackland Hunt took part in large London exhibitions from 1863 to 1887.

HUNT, Bryan

American, 20th - 21st century.
Born 7 June 1947, in Terre Haute (Indiana).
Sculptor, painter (mixed media/gouache), pastellist, printmaker.
New Image (related to).

Bryan Hunt studied at the Otis Art Institute in Los Angeles, obtaining a BFA in 1971, and participated in the Whitney Museum of American Art Independent Study Program in 1972. He travelled in Europe in 1969, and around the world from 1979-1980. He has taught at the School of Visual Arts, New York (1978). He sculpts in a variety of media including bronze and construction materials like wood cement, as in his *Hoover Dam* (1974). His sculpture *Oracle* (1988) is in the Olympic Park in Seoul, South Korea. His printmaking techniques include woodcut, etching and aquatint, as in his colour woodcut, *Window* (1986). His paintings are sometimes in mixed media, for example the watercolour, oil stick and charcoal work shown in *Autumn Falls 1* (1990).

Hunt's exhibitions include: 1983, Bryan Hunt: A Decade of Drawings, University Art Museum, California State University, Long Beach; 1983, *Gallery Six: Bryan Hunt,* Los Angeles County Museum of Art; 1986, *MATRIX: Bryan Hunt Airships,* University Art Museum, University of California, Berkeley; 1991, *Recent Work: 17 Sculptures,* Tokyo Ginza Art Center Hall, Japan; 1998, *American Abstract Art,* Ambassador's Residence, Vienna, Austria; 1992, *Sculpture and Drawings,* Aspen Art Museum, CO; 2000, *Bryan Hunt,* Indianapolis Museum of Art; 2000, *The American Century: Art and Culture 1950-2000,* Whitney Museum of American Art, New York; and 2002, *The Anderson Collection 2002: Wall Street Rising,* San Francisco Museum of Modern Art. He was awarded the Grand Prize at the International Seoul Art Festival, National Museum of Contemporary Art, Korea, in 1990.

BIBLIOGRAPHY:

Perrone, Jeff, '*Bryan Hunt: Blum Helman Gallery*' in *Artforum,* journal article, Summer 1977. Hunt, Bryan, *Conversations with Nature,* Video, Museum of Modern Art, New York, 1982. *Bryan Hunt: A Decade of Drawings,* exhibition catalogue, California State University, Long Beach, Long Beach, 1983. *Bryan Hunt,* exhibition catalogue, Blum Helman Gallery, New York, 1983. *Bryan Hunt: Sculpture and Drawing,* exhibition catalogue, Akira Ikeda Gallery, Tokyo, 1986. *Bryan Hunt: Recent Small-Scale Works,* exhibition catalogue, Blum Helman Gallery, New York, 1986. *Bryan Hunt: Falls and Figures,* exhibition catalogue, Offices of Publication Services, Cornell University, Ithaca (NY), 1988. *Drawings and Fragments of Sculpture. Bryan Hunt,* exhibition catalogue, Kyoto Sowin International, Kyoto, 1989. *Bryan Hunt: Recent Drawings,* exhibition catalogue, Blum Helman Gallery, New York, 1989. Schwartz, Marvin, *J.B. Hunt: The Long Haul to Success,* illustrated book, University of Arkansas Press, Fayetteville, 1992. Miller, Gregory Randal, '*Bryan Hunt: Sculpture and Drawing 1974-1980*' in *Art Papers,* journal article, July-August 1992. Seidel, Miriam, '*Bryan Hunt Review*' in *Art in America,* journal article, December 2002.

MUSEUMS AND GALLERIES:

AKRON (MA): *Caryatid* (1981, sculpture) - ATLANTA (High Mus. of Art) - BUFFALO (Albright-Knox AG) - CAMBRIDGE, MA (Fogg AM, Harvard University) - DALLAS (MA): *Arch Falls* (1980, sculpture) - HELSINKI (Kiasma MCA) - LOS ANGELES (County MA): *Homer 1* (1978, sculpture) - NEW YORK (Guggenheim Mus.) - NEW YORK (Lannan Foundation): *Tigress II* (1978, sculpture) - NEW YORK (Metropolitan Mus. of Art) - NEW YORK (MoMA): *Amphora* (1982, sculpture) - PORTLAND, ME (MA) - WASHINGTON DC (MAA): *Stillscape 11* (1984, sculpture) - WASHINGTON DC (NGA): *Duet: Wind and Thunder* (1982, woodcuts); *Island* (1992, etching); *Five Nights* (1988, aquatint prints); *Temple Ruins* (1988, etchings).

AUCTION RECORDS:

NEW YORK, 10 May 1984, *Cubit Quarry* (1979, bronze, 36 x 27 1/2 x 14 ins / 91.5 x 69.8 x 35.5 cm) USD 14,000. NEW YORK, 6 Nov 1985, *The Cloak of San Lorenzo* (1981, bronze, 91 x 26 x 26 ins / 231.2 x 66.1 x 66.1 cm) USD 39,000. NEW YORK, 5 May 1987, *Daphne I* (1979, bronze, 55 1/2 x 16 3/4 x 19 ins / 141 x 42.5 x 48.3 cm) USD 40,000. NEW YORK, 3 May 1988, *Lignes statiques* (1982, bronze, 37 x 41 1/2 x 23 1/2 ins / 94 x 105.4 x 59.7 cm) USD 33,000; *Metatech* (1976, copper sheets, tissue paper/balsa, diam. 7 ins / 17.8 cm) USD 82,500. NEW YORK, 8 Oct 1988, *Ritual I* (1986, bronze, h. 72 ins / 182.8 cm) USD 23,100. NEW YORK, 14 Feb 1989, *Teste* (gouache/tissue paper/wood, l. 63 1/2 ins / 161.3 cm, diam. 7 ins/17.5 cm) USD 66,000. NEW YORK, 4 May 1989, *Colossus* (bronze/limestone base, h. 59 1/4 ins / 150.5 cm) USD 11,000. NEW YORK, 5 Oct 1989, *Personnage Changeant* (1982, bronze, h. 20 1/2 ins / 52 cm) USD 27,500. NEW YORK, 23 Feb 1990, *Portrait* (1982, bronze, 56 1/4 x 21 1/4 x 12 3/4 ins / 142.8 x 54 x 32.4 cm) USD 26,400. NEW YORK, 27 Feb 1990, *Dirigeable* (1976, gold-leaf and silk/Christmas tree, 60 x 8 x 8 ins / 152.5 x 20.3 x 20.3 cm) USD 126,500. NEW YORK, 1 May 1991, *Untitled (Study for Neptune)* (1987, bronze, 30 x 8 3/4 x 8 3/4 ins / 76.2 x 22.5 x 22.5 cm) USD 16,500. NEW YORK, 7 May 1991, *Hoyle's Dream* (1976, gouache and coloured inks/paper, 6 x 6 ins / 15.2 x 15.2 cm) USD 1,980. NEW YORK, 3 Oct 1991, *Neptune* (1987, bronze and copper, 91 x 20 x 20 ins / 231.2 x 50.8 x 50.8 cm) USD 29,700. NEW YORK, 27 Feb 1992, *Double Niche* (1979, bronze, 57 x 27 x 13 ins / 144.9 x 68.6 x 33 cm) USD 30,800. NEW YORK, 4 May 1993, *Ritual II* (1986, bronze, 71 1/2 x 9 x 9 ins / 181.9 x 22.9 x 22.9 cm) USD 10,350. NEW YORK, 5 May 1993, *Airship* (silver-leaf/tissue paper around balsa wood, 7 1/4 x 7 1/4 x 59 ins / 18.4 x 18.4 x 149.9 cm) USD 51,750. PARIS, 17 March 1994, *Pilgrim* (1987, bronze, h. 63 ins / 160 cm, base 19 3/4 x 19 3/4 ins/50 x 50 cm) FRF 70,000. NEW YORK, 15 Nov 1995, *Tigress* (1979, gold-leaf and copper-leaf/tissue paper/balsa, 6 1/2 x 39 3/4 x 4 3/4 ins / 16.5 x 101 x 12 cm) USD 32,200. NEW YORK, 19 Nov 1996, *Joint Universel* (1947, graphite/vellum, 33 3/4 x 21 3/4 ins / 86 x 55.5 cm) USD 1,265. NEW YORK, 7-8 May 1997, *Reclining Figure* (1982, bronze, 59 3/4 x 20 1/2 x 11 1/4 ins / 151.7 x 52.1 x 28.3 cm) USD 20,700; *Ovid* (1980-1984, lacquered silk and gold-leaf/wood, 7 1/2 x 40 x 6 ins / 19.1 x 101.6 x 15.2 cm) USD 28,750. NEW YORK, 19 Nov 1997, *Daphne* (1979, painted bronze/limestone base, 77 x 15 x 9 ins / 195.6 x 38.2 x 22.8 cm) USD 27,600. NEW

YORK, 6 and 7 March 1998, *Ghosts* (1978, four engravings, complete series, 22 x 7 3/4 ins / 55 x 20 cm) USD 1,150. NEW YORK, 20 May 1999, *Penumbra* (1990, synthetic fibre and spruce woods, 11 x 68x8 ins / 28 x 173x20 cm) USD 17,000. LOS ANGELES, 9 June 1999, *Devil's Tub, from the Lake Quarry Series* (c. 1976, gold patinated bronze, 4 x 31x15 ins / 11 x 79x38 cm) USD 12,000. NEW YORK, 18 May 2000, *Dancers* (bronze, 58 x 26x24 ins / 148 x 66x60 cm) USD 15,000. NEW YORK, 15 Nov 2000, *Untitled: Waterfall* (1981, bronze, h. 18 ins / 46 cm, w. 13 ins/32 cm) USD 5,000. NEW YORK, 15 May 2001, *Black Falls XV* (1979, graphite and linseed oil on paper, 83 x 21 ins / 211 x 53 cm) USD 5,500. NEW YORK, 18 May 2001, *Pangaea II* (1997, bronze, 108 x 72x31 ins / 274 x 183x79 cm) USD 38,000. NEW YORK, 13 Nov 2002, *Airship* (1979, paper, oil, acrylic and wood, 8 x 41x5 ins / 20 x 103x13 cm) USD 30,000. CHICAGO, 19 Nov 2002, *Concorde Window* (oil, pastel and rag on paper, 11 x 9 ins / 29 x 22 cm) USD 2,700. NEW YORK, 13 Nov 2003, *Arch Falls* (bronze, 102 x 60x48 ins / 259 x 152x122 cm) USD 60,000. NEW YORK, 13 Nov 2003, *Shift* (bronze, h. 120 ins / 305 cm) USD 95,000. NEW YORK, 12 Feb 2004, *Separation I* (1982, pencil, conté crayon and linseed oil, 30 x 23 ins / 76 x 59 cm) USD 3,250. NEW YORK, 13 May 2004, *Daphne* (green patinated bronze, 141 x 23x21 ins / 358 x 58x53 cm) USD 80,000.

HUNT, Cecil Arthur
British, 19th - 20th century.
Born 1873, in Torquay; died 1965.
Painter (gouache), watercolourist. Landscapes, seascapes.

Cecil Arthur Hunt exhibited at the Royal Academy from 1912.

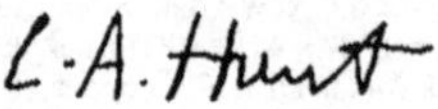

AUCTION RECORDS:

LONDON, 30 May 1985, *The Desolate Hills* (watercolour/pencil outlines heightened with gouache, 19 x 23 1/2 ins / 48 x 59.5 cm) GBP 900. LONDON, 29 July 1988, *Yachts at Sea* (oil on canvas, 23 1/2 x 31 1/2 ins / 60 x 80 cm) GBP 715. LONDON, 8 Feb 1991, *Landscape with a Distant View of the Basilica of St Julien at Brioude* (watercolour, 11 x 14 1/2 ins / 27 x 37 cm) GBP 1,045. LONDON, 25 Sept 1992, *Snow and Shadow* (pencil, watercolour and gouache, 10 1/2 x 14 3/4 ins / 26.5 x 37.5 cm) GBP 1,045. LONDON, 19 April 1999, *Alpine Lakes Scene* (watercolour, gouache and pencil, 21 x 30 ins / 54 x 77 cm) GBP 1,850. LONDON, 20 May 1999, *On the Thames Near Gravesend* (pencil and watercolour heightened with gouache, 15 x 23 ins / 39 x 59 cm) GBP 1,000. BILLINGSHURST, 1 Feb 2000, *Amalfi* (watercolour and gouache, 25 x 21 ins / 63 x 54 cm) GBP 1,650. BILLINGSHURST, 1 Feb 2000, *Dorothea Quarry, Pen y Groes* (watercolour, gouache and pencil, 10 x 14 ins / 26 x 36 cm) GBP 1,800. LONDON, 10 April 2001, *Mountain Tops on a Windy Day on the Isle of Skye* (watercolour and gouache heightened with scratching out, 13 x 19 ins / 34 x 47 cm) GBP 1,600. LONDON, 21 Nov 2001, *Demolition in the West End* (gouache, 11 x 15 ins / 28 x 38 cm) GBP 2,500. LONDON, 20 Nov 2003, *Trees by the Waters Edge* (watercolour and gouache with scratching out, 14 x 21 ins / 36 x 54 cm) GBP 2,200. LONDON, 20 Nov 2003, *Storm on Loch Awe, Argyllshire* (watercolour heightened with gouache and scratching out, 11 x 14 ins / 27 x 36 cm) GBP 2,400. LONDON, 25 March 2004, *Dunollie Castle, Oban, Argyllshire* (watercolour and gouache, 11 x 15 ins / 27 x 37 cm) GBP 1,400. LONDON, 21 July 2004, *Glen Dochart* (watercolour, 11 x 15 ins / 27 x 38 cm) GBP 1,050.

HUNT, Charles
British, 19th century.
Engraver. Sporting subjects, horse racing scenes.

Charles Hunt came from a family of engravers. He built up a considerable reputation with his excellent engravings of sport after Pollard, Jones Alken and other painters of this genre.

AUCTION RECORDS:

PARIS, 17 Oct 1997, *Goodwood Grand Stand* (coloured engraving, 19 3/4 x 29 1/4 ins / 50 x 74 cm) FRF 4,200. PARIS, 9 March 1998, *Leamington Grand Steeple Chase* (1837, coloured engraving heightened with watercolour, a pair of engravings after F. C. Turner) FRF 6,000.

HUNT, Charles
British, 19th century.
Born 1803; died 15 November 1877.
Painter. Genre scenes.
Cranbrook Artists' Colony.

Although Charles Hunt had been exhibiting his work in private galleries since 1846, it was not until he was nearly 60, in 1862, that he was able to present his works at the Royal Academy in London.

During the years which followed, he painted humorous compositions of children playing Shakespeare, which brought him quick success. The *Art Journal* also referred to him as a member of the 'Webster School', thereby inferring contact with Thomas Webster and the group of artists who gravitated round him in Cranbrook in Kent, and in every case their influence can be seen in his work.

AUCTION RECORDS:

LONDON, April 1922, *The First of April*, GBP 44. LONDON, June 1924, *A Guilty Conscience Does Not Need an Accuser*, GBP 14. LONDON, 26 Feb 1932, *Condemnation; Judgement* (a pair) GBP 36. LONDON, 29 July 1977, *Old Man Dancing a Jig* (1893, oil on canvas remounted on board, 15 1/2 x 19 1/2 ins / 39.3 x 49.5 cm) GBP 3,000. NEW YORK, 28 May 1981, *Judge and Jury* (1866, oil on canvas, 20 3/4 x 32 3/4 ins / 53 x 83 cm) USD 18,000. LONDON, 19 Oct 1983, *Make Way for the Grand Jury* (1873, oil on canvas, 30 x 50 ins / 76 x 127 cm) GBP 8,000. NEW YORK, 24 May 1985, *Ivanhoe* (1871, oil on canvas, 29 1/4 x 44 1/2 ins / 74.2 x 113.3 cm) USD 10,000. PARIS, 16 Oct 1985, *Jockey Club Prize 7000 Fr. Chantilly, May 1841.; Special prize of 5...fr Chantilly 1841* (aquatint in colour with heightenings, series of four) FRF 83,000. LONDON, 13 Feb 1987, *The Recital* (1861, oil on canvas, 11 x 16 1/4 ins / 28 x 41 cm) GBP 6,000. LONDON, 23 Sept 1988, *He Who Knows* (1875, oil on canvas, 24 1/4 x 36 1/4 ins / 61.5 x 92 cm) GBP 6,600. CHESTER, 20 July 1989, *A Fine Sunday* (1876, oil on canvas, 36 x 58 1/4 ins / 91.5 x 148 cm) GBP 4,840. LONDON, 27 Sept 1989, *The Accused* (1876, oil on canvas, 24 x 36 ins / 61 x 91.5 cm) GBP 9,900. LONDON, 13 Dec 1989, *Marriage Proposal* (1880, oil on canvas, 18 x 24 1/2 ins / 46 x 62 cm) GBP 3,300. LONDON, 9 Feb 1990, *Irish Lunch* (1870, oil on card, 8 1/2 x 11 ins / 21.6 x 28 cm) GBP 2,420. LYONS, 9 Oct 1990, *Preparations for the Carnival* (1862, oil on canvas, 12 1/4 x 18 ins / 31 x 46 cm) FRF 38,000. LONDON, 1 Nov 1990, *The Two Rivals* (1876, oil on canvas, 36 x 58 1/4 ins / 91.5 x 148 cm) GBP 5,500. NEW YORK, 22 May 1991, *The Verdict of Judges and Jury* (1866, oil on canvas, 20 3/4 x 32 1/2 ins / 52.7 x 82.6 cm) USD 27,500. LONDON, 19 Dec 1991, *The Police Tribunal* (1867, oil on canvas, 10 x 14 ins / 25.4 x 35.5 cm) GBP 3,300. LONDON, 13 March 1992, *Scene from Hamlet* (oil on canvas, 14 1/4 x 18 1/2 ins / 36.2 x 46.9 cm) GBP 2,750. NEW YORK, 13 Oct 1993, *The Tribunal* (1870, oil on canvas, 29 1/4 x 44 1/2 ins / 74.3 x 113 cm) USD 13,800. LONDON, 30 March 1994, *Ladies' Game* (oil on canvas, 24 x 36 ins / 61 x 91.5 cm)

GBP 17,825. NEW YORK, 12 Dec 1996, *The Intruder*. NEW YORK, 11 April 1997, *The Minstrels* (1873, oil on canvas, 13½ x 20 ins / 34.3 x 50.8 cm) USD 7,475. LONDON, 5 Nov 1997, *The Letter* (oil on canvas, 36 x 24 ins / 91.5 x 61 cm) GBP 11,500. LEEDS, 3 March 1999, *Flower Pickers, Two Children Collecting Flowers, Sea Beyond* (1870, oil on canvas, 13 x 11 ins / 33 x 27 cm) GBP 4,400. LONDON, 13 June 2000, *Gint who Pays Rint* (1830, oil on canvas, 37 x 28 ins / 93 x 71 cm) GBP 13,000. BILLINGSHURST, 23 Oct 2000, *Gathering Flowers* (oil on canvas, 9 x 13 ins / 24 x 34 cm) GBP 2,000. LONDON, 30 Nov 2001, *Children Playing Soldiers* (1861, oil on canvas, 22 x 30 ins / 55 x 75 cm) GBP 10,500. LONDON, 30 Nov 2001, *Wounded Soldiers* (1887, oil on canvas, 24 x 39 ins / 61 x 99 cm) GBP 15,000.

HUNT, Charles

British, 19th century.

Born 1829; died 1900.

Painter. Genre scenes, animals.

This Charles Hunt, active from 1880 to 1900, was certainly a son of Charles Hunt (1803-1877). Their styles are very similar: the pictures tell a story, the composition is often based on an interior perspective, and includes domestic animals.

BIBLIOGRAPHY:

Wood, Christopher, *The Dictionary of Victorian Painters*, Antique Collectors' Club, Woodbridge, 1971.

AUCTION RECORDS:

LONDON, 1 Nov 1990, *Game of Draughts* (1891, oil on canvas, 20 x 30 ins / 51 x 76 cm) GBP 12,650. LONDON, 14 June 1991, *The Quarrel* (1866, oil on canvas, 6½ x 9½ ins / 16.5 x 24.2 cm) GBP 1,760. NEW YORK, 30 Oct 1992, *Cluster of Puppies* (1884, oil on canvas, 25 x 28½ ins / 63.5 x 72.6 cm) USD 4,400. LONDON, 13 Nov 1992, *St Valentine's Day* (1878, oil on canvas, 26 x 23¾ ins / 66 x 60.4 cm) GBP 5,720. LONDON, 3 Nov 1993, *Country Concert* (1892, oil on canvas, 19½ x 29½ ins / 49.3 x 74.7 cm) GBP 6,325. LONDON, 29 March 1996, *Awkward Encounter* (1880, oil on canvas, 40¼ x 59¾ ins / 102.3 x 151.7 cm) GBP 13,225. LONDON, 10 July 1997, *Old Friends* (1881, oil on canvas, 16½ x 20½ ins / 42 x 52 cm) GBP 1,725. BILLINGSHURST, 18 May 1999, *Children and Animals in a Garden* (1877, oil on canvas, 23x35 ins / 59x89 cm) GBP 7,500. LONDON, 10 Nov 1999, *Rules for Paupers* (1888, oil on canvas, 36x24 ins / 92x61 cm) GBP 8,000. PARTRIDGE GREEN (WEST SUSSEX), 15 June 2000, *Study of an Itinerant Seated upon a Donkey* (oil on canvas, 17x23 ins / 44x59 cm) GBP 4,000. LONDON, 30 Nov 2000, *M. Murphy, the Clockmaker* (1899, oil on canvas, 22x36 ins / 56x91 cm) GBP 15,000. LONDON, 8 March 2001, *Retribution* (oil on canvas, 30x50 ins / 77x127 cm) GBP 16,000. BURY ST EDMUNDS, 8 March 2001, *O You April Fool* (1892, oil on canvas, 16x22 ins / 40x56 cm) GBP 10,000. SIDNEY, 3 Sept 2002, *Untitled - Gentleman Riding a Horse-pulled Cart* (1881, oil on canvas, 30x45 ins / 75x114 cm) AUD 8,500. MELBOURNE, 26 Nov 2002, *Travelling Artist* (oil on canvas, 24x36 ins / 61x91 cm) AUD 8,000. LONDON, 26 March 2003, *Suitor* (1883, oil on canvas, 18x24 ins / 46x60 cm) GBP 2,500. LONDON, 20 May 2003, *Judge and Jury* (1866, oil on canvas, 6x9 ins / 16x24 cm) GBP 2,400. CLEVEDON, 23 Sept 2004, *Group of Children Playing and Picking Flowers in a Country Lane* (1869, oil on canvas, 24x39 ins / 61x98 cm) GBP 8,000. LONDON, 13 Oct 2004, *Cottage Concert* (1892, oil on canvas, 20x30 ins / 51x76 cm) GBP 16,000.

HUNT, Charles D.

American, 19th - 20th century.

Born 1840, in Detroit; died 25 September 1914, in Brooklyn.

Painter. Genre scenes, landscapes.

Charles D. Hunt was a pupil of Wyatt and Kensett in New York.

AUCTION RECORDS:

LONDON, 20 June 1972, *Children Play-acting*, GBP 480. LONDON, 20 Nov 1973, *Before Dinner; After Dinner* (two panels) GBP 4,800. LONDON, 5 Nov 1974, *Vegetable Seller* (1873) GBP 1,300. LONDON, 6 March 1981, *Wounded Soldier* (1887, oil on canvas, 19½ x 29¼ ins / 49.5 x 74.2 cm) GBP 5,000. LONDON, 14 July 1983, *Street Fight* (1884, oil on canvas, 24 x 36 ins / 61 x 91.5 cm) GBP 8,000. LONDON, 1 Oct 1986, *Eye of the Needle* (1897, oil on canvas, 20 x 24 ins / 51 x 61 cm) GBP 5,000. NEW YORK, 9 Sept 1993, *Late Summer Landscape; Stagecoach in Winter* (oil on canvas, a pair, 11 x 17½ ins / 27.9 x 44.5 cm and 9 x 15 ins/22.9 x 38.1 cm) USD 1,725.

HUNT, Edgar

British, 19th - 20th century.

Born 1876, in the Midlands; died 1953.

Painter. Animals, birds, farmyard scenes.

Edgar Hunt was the son of the genre painter Charles Hunt, and younger brother of the animalist painter Walter Hunt, with whom he studied. He exhibited little, preferring to live quietly in the Midlands countryside. His works are characterised by his unchanging, meticulous technique and style. He specialised in farm animals: poultry, goats, ponies and donkeys.

AUCTION RECORDS:

LONDON, 16 July 1976, *Goats and Hens in a barn* (1920; *Goat and Hens in a Farmyard* (1920, two oils on canvas, 11 x 14½ ins / 27 x 37 cm) GBP 2,400. LONDON, 14 June 1977, *Farmyard Scene* (1916, oil on canvas, 22 x 29½ ins / 55 x 75 cm) GBP 5,600. LONDON, 20 March 1979, *Farm Animals* (1927, oil on canvas, 19 x 29¼ ins / 48 x 74 cm) GBP 9,500. LONDON, 20 Oct 1981, *Turkeys and Other Poultry* (1921, oil on canvas, 22 x 29¼ ins / 56 x 74 cm) GBP 6,000. LONDON, 18 Feb 1983, *Farm Animals* (1934, oil on canvas, 19½ x 29½ ins / 49.5 x 75 cm) GBP 8,500. LONDON, 11 June 1986, *Light Brahmas and Buff Cochin* (1904, oil on canvas, 24 x 36 ins / 61 x 91.5 cm) GBP 15,000. LONDON, 17 June 1987, *Farm Animals* (1907, oil on canvas, 20 x 30 ins / 51 x 76 cm) GBP 12,000. NEW YORK, 25 Feb 1988, *Calves and Poultry in a Barnyard* (oil on card, 12 x 16¼ ins / 30.5 x 41 cm) USD 10,450. LONDON, 3 June 1988, *Cockerel and Hens beside a Coop* (1914, oil on canvas, 10 x 8 ins / 25.4 x 20.3 cm) GBP 8,530. LONDON, 15 June 1988, *Farmyard Scene with a Goat and Chickens* (1924, oil on canvas, 14 x 18 ins / 35.5 x 45.5 cm) GBP 12,100. LONDON, 23 Sept 1988, *An Intruder and Fresh Fodder* (oil on card, a pair, each 10 x 7¾ ins / 25.5 x 20 cm) GBP 11,550. NEW YORK, 23 Feb 1989, *Barn Scene with Pigeons, Guinea Pigs and Lop-eared Rabbit* (1902, oil on canvas, 12¼ x 16 ins / 31.1 x 40.6 cm) USD 24,200. LONDON, 27 Sept 1989, *Chicks; Beside the Coop* (1914, oil on canvas, a pair, 7 x 6 ins / 18 x 15 cm) GBP 15,950. EDINBURGH, 22 Nov 1989, *Goat and Two Kids; Farmyard Scene with Goat* (1919, oil on canvas, a pair, 11 x 15 ins / 28 x 38.1 cm) GBP 16,500. LONDON, 13 Dec 1989, *Pigeons with a Duck and Ducklings on the Banks of a Farm Pond; Duck and Poultry beside a Farm Pond* (1922, oil on canvas, a pair, each 11 x 15 ins / 28 x 38 cm) GBP 40,700. LONDON, 9 Feb 1990, *A Family of Chicks* (1904, oil on canvas, 20 x 30 ins / 50.7 x 76.2 cm) GBP 33,000. NEW YORK, 24 Oct 1990, *Donkey and Poultry in front of a Barn Door* (1921, oil on canvas, 22½ x 30¼ ins / 57.1 x 76.8 cm) USD 13,200. NEW YORK, 28 Feb 1991, *Farmyard Scene with Poultry* (1926, oil on canvas, 14 x 12 ins / 35.6 x 30.5 cm) USD 13,200. LONDON, 5 June 1991,

Farmyard Scene (1902, oil on canvas, 30 x 50 ins / 76 x 127 cm) GBP 24,200. LONDON, 3 June 1992, *Newly-hatched Chicks; Pigeons* (1908, oil on canvas, a pair, each 12 x 10 ins / 30.5 x 25.5 cm) GBP 12,650. EDINBURGH, 13 May 1993, *Farmyard Scene with a Goat and Kids, Pigeons, a Chicken and Chicks* (1904, oil on canvas, 18 x 24 ins / 45.7 x 61 cm) GBP 9,900. LONDON, 3 Nov 1993, *Farm Friends* (1915, oil on canvas, 20 x 30 ins / 50.5 x 76 cm) GBP 28,750. LONDON, 30 March 1994, *Farmyard with Donkeys and Poultry* (1919, oil on canvas, 16 x 24 ins / 40.5 x 61 cm) GBP 20,700. LONDON, 10 March 1995, *Farm Friends* (1937, oil on canvas, 12 x 18 ins / 30.5 x 45.7 cm) GBP 14,950. LONDON, 29 March 1996, *Feeding Time* (1920, oil on canvas, 22 x 30 ins / 55.9 x 76.2 cm) GBP 18,400. LONDON, 6 Nov 1996, *Farmyard with Rabbits and Hens* (1903, oil on canvas, 18 x 24 ins / 46 x 61 cm) GBP 20,125. LONDON, 13 March 1997, *Goats in front of a Barn Door* (1903, oil on canvas, 10 x 12 ins / 25.4 x 30.4 cm) GBP 3,000. LONDON, 14 March 1997, *A New Brood* (1904, oil on canvas, 24 x 42 ins / 60.9 x 106.7 cm) GBP 38,900. LONDON, 6 June 1997, *Farmyard Friends* (1920, oil on canvas, 14 x 18 ins / 35.5 x 46 cm) GBP 11,500. LONDON, 7 Nov 1997, *The Hungry Brood* (1924, oil on canvas, 14 x 12½ ins / 35.5 x 31.5 cm) GBP 14,950. LEICESTER, 27 May 1999, *Farmyard with Ducks and Hens Eating from an Upturned Bucket* (1909, oil on canvas, 19 x 29 ins / 48 x 74 cm) GBP 30,000. LONDON, 3 June 1999, *Donkey, Hens and Chickens in Barn* (1920, oil on canvas, 22 x 30 ins / 56 x 76 cm) GBP 34,000. LEAMINGTON SPA, 12 Oct 2000, *Two Goats, Hens and Chickens in a Barn* (1909, oil on canvas, 30 x 50 ins / 75 x 126 cm) GBP 52,000. LONDON, 28 Nov 2000, *Feeding Tme* (oil on canvas, 24 x 37 ins / 61 x 94 cm) GBP 40,000. LONDON, 12 June 2001, *Cockerels, Hens and Doves in a Farmyard. Cockerels, Hens and Chicks in Farmyard* (1938, oil on canvas, a pair, 8 x 11 ins / 20 x 29 cm) GBP 27,000. SCARBOROUGH, 8 Oct 2001, *Farmyard Friends, Animals by a Barn* (1921, oil on canvas, 8 x 11 ins / 21 x 29 cm) GBP 26,500. LONDON, 26 Nov 2002, *Duck and Ducklings with Doves by Pond. Ducks and Chickens Feeding Time* (1922, oil on canvas, a pair, 11 x 15 ins / 28 x 39 cm) GBP 28,000. LONDON, 2 Dec 2002, *Corner of the Farmyard* (1916, oil on canvas, 30 x 24 ins / 76 x 61 cm) GBP 50,000. LONDON, 12 June 2003, *Visiting the New Arrivals* (1915, oil on canvas, 22 x 30 ins / 56 x 76 cm) GBP 32,000. LONDON, 19 Nov 2003, *Farmyard Scene with Donkeys and Poultry* (1925, oil on canvas, 20 x 30 ins / 51 x 76 cm) GBP 32,000. LONDON, 1 July 2004, *Farmyard Neighbours. Outside Wrld* (1926, oil on canvas, two, 14 x 12 ins / 35 x 30 cm) GBP 30,000. LONDON, 23 Nov 2004, *Hen and Chicks* (1902, oil on canvas, 24 x 36 ins / 61 x 92 cm) GBP 40,000.

HUNT, Edward Aubrey
British, 19th - 20th century.
Born 17 February 1855, in Weymouth; died 22 November 1922, in Hastings.
Painter. Genre scenes, landscapes, waterscapes.

Edward Aubrey Hunt exhibited at the Royal Academy and the Suffolk Street Gallery from 1878, and at the Paris Salon in 1888.

MUSEUMS AND GALLERIES:
LEEDS (City AG): *Embarking Cattle, Morocco* (oil on canvas) - LEICESTER: *Venice*.

AUCTION RECORDS:
LONDON, 29 Jan 1910, *Goats, Rabbits and Poultry* (1901) GBP 15. LONDON, 5 Dec 1910, *Venetian Vessel in a Storm*, GBP 8. LONDON, June 1924, *Farm Scene with a Donkey, Pony and Chickens*, GBP 25. LONDON, 10 May 1944, *Farmyard Scene*, GBP 30. LONDON, 15 Oct 1969, *Farmyard Scene*, GBP 900. SCOTLAND, 28 Aug 1970, *Farmyard Scene*, GBP 1,200. SCOTLAND, 14 Dec 1971, *Doves and Chickens*, GBP 1,500. LONDON, 28 Nov 1972, *Farm Animals* (1947) GBP 1,600. LONDON, 4 Oct 1973, *Farmyard Scene* (1925) Gns 2,600. LONDON, 8 June 1976, *Canal Scene* (oil on canvas, 19½ x 29½ ins / 49.5 x 75 cm) GBP 360. LONDON, 2 Feb 1979, *Estuary Sene* (1883, two oils on canvas, 17¼ x 25¼ ins / 43.5 x 64 cm) GBP 2,800. LONDON, 24 Nov 1982, *Fantasia in Tangiers* (oil on canvas remounted/panel, 14¾ x 22 ins / 37.5 x 56 cm) GBP 5,200. LONDON, 25 May 1983, *Portrait of Mrs Hubert Coop* (1906, oil on canvas, 31 x 26 ins / 79 x 66 cm) GBP 1,500. LONDON, 22 Feb 1985, *View of Venice* (1897, oil on canvas, 76 x 52 ins / 193 x 132 cm) GBP 3,000. LONDON, 14 Nov 1987, *St Mark's Basin, Venice* (1897, oil on canvas, 76 x 52 ins / 193 x 132 cm) GBP 9,000. LONDON, 9 June 1988, *Southampton Harbour* (oil on canvas, 18¾x23½ ins / 47.5x60 cm) GBP 3,300. LONDON, 12 May 1989, *Riverscape* (oil on panel, 6¼ x 16 ins / 15.6 x 40.7 cm) GBP 2,200. LONDON, 5 Oct 1989, *Venice* (oil on canvas, 20 x 14 ins / 51 x 35.5 cm) GBP 1,980. LONDON, 3 Nov 1989, *Threshing and Winnowing near Tangiers* (1896, oil on canvas, 48½ x 107¾ ins / 123 x 274 cm) GBP 2,750. LONDON, 7 June 1990, *Fishing on a Suffolk Estuary* (oil on canvas, 14½ x 21½ ins / 37 x 54.5 cm) GBP 1,760. LONDON, 20 May 1992, *Venice* (oil on canvas, 14½ x 22 ins / 37 x 56 cm) GBP 1,375. LONDON, 12 May 1993, *Venice* (oil on panel, a pair, each 9½ x 7¼ ins / 24 x 18.5 cm) GBP 1,840. NEW YORK, 14 Oct 1993, *Entrance to a Mosque* (oil on canvas, 20 x 24 ins / 50.8 x 61 cm) USD 6,900. LONDON, 4 Nov 1994, *Fishing-boats with the Riva degli Schiavoni, Venice, in the Background* (oil on canvas, 76 x 51¾ ins / 193 x 131.4 cm) GBP 19,550.

HUNT, F.H.
British, 19th century.
Active in London.
Sculptor.

F.H. Hunt exhibited his work at the Royal Academy in London in 1854.

HUNT, George
British, 19th century.
Active in London.
Engraver (aquatint).

HUNT, George Sidney
British, 19th - 20th century.
Active in London.
Engraver.

HUNT, H.
British, 17th century.
Active in London at the end of the 17th century.
Engraver.

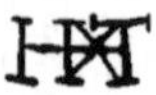

HUNT, Herbert S.
British, 19th - 20th century.
Painter. Landscapes.

Herbert S. Hunter was active in Concarneau, in Brittany.

HUNT, J. B.
British, 19th century.
Active in London c. 1850.
Engraver, illustrator.

HUNT, J.S. (Miss)
British, 19th century.

Active in Liverpool c. 1840.
Painter, watercolourist.
J.S. Hunt was the daughter and pupil of Andrew Hunt. Her work was represented in Liverpool, mainly in 1840.

HUNT, Maria or Mary (Miss)
British, 19th century.
Born in Liverpool.
Active in Liverpool.
Painter. Genre scenes, flowers, fruit.
Maria Hunt was the daughter and pupil of Andrew Hunt. She took part in Liverpool exhibitions and exhibited her work four times at the Royal Academy in London from 1856 to 1866.
AUCTION RECORDS:
LONDON, 28 July 1909, *After Work*, GBP 1.

HUNT, Richard
British, 19th century.
Active in London.
Painter. Portraits, genre scenes.
Richard Hunt exhibited his work at the Royal Academy in London from 1802 to 1842.
AUCTION RECORDS:
LONDON, 11 and 12 May 1911, *Gentleman Dressed in Black*, GBP 22.

HUNT, Richard
American, 20th century.
Born 1933.
Sculptor.
Richard Hunt is a sculptor of statuettes, creating anthropomorphic forms.
AUCTION RECORDS:
NEW YORK, 13 May 1981, *Palmate Hybrid* (1971, bronze, h. 33 ins / 84 cm) USD 1,600. CHICAGO, 11 Sept 1983, *Hybrid Head* (c. 1970, aluminium, 18 x 21 x 15 ins / 45.7 x 53.5 x 38 cm) USD 1,500. NEW YORK, 20 Feb 1988, *Untitled* (1978, bronze, 72 1/4 x 29 1/2 x 24 ins / 183.8 x 75 x 61.2 cm) USD 4,400. NEW YORK, 8 Oct 1988, *Untitled* (1968, welded steel, 7 x 16 1/2 x 9 ins / 17.8 x 41.8 x 22.8 cm) USD 2,200. NEW YORK, 12 June 1991, *Untitled* (1977, polished bronze, 10 ins / 25.4 cm) USD 2,420. NEW YORK, 26 Feb 1993, *Figurine with Stag's Head* (1981, bronze, h. 16 1/4 ins / 41.3 cm) USD 3,220. NEW YORK, 14 June 1995, *Natural Form* (bronze, h. 8 1/2 ins / 21.6 cm) USD 1,265. NEW YORK, 7 May 1996, *Untitled* (1961, bronze, 22 x 13 1/2 x 5 ins / 55.8 x 34.6 x 12.7 cm) USD 3,450. NEW YORK, 18 Nov 1997, *Sky Form, No 2* (1957, iron and welded steel, 38 x 23 1/2 x 15 1/2 ins / 95.6 x 59.4 x 39.4 cm) USD 7,475.

HUNT, Richard Howard
American, 20th century.
Born 12 September 1935, in Chicago.
Sculptor (including bronze), draughtsman, print artist, lithographer. Monuments.
Richard Howard Hunt studied at the Art Institute of Chicago. In 1957-1958 he went to Europe before being drafted into the army, where he served from 1958 to 1960. He has over a dozen honorary doctorates from schools as notable as the University of Michigan, Ann Arbor (1976) and the School of the Art Institute of Chicago (1982). He has been a member of the American Academy of Arts and Letters since 1998. He settled in Chicago.

Influenced by Julio Gonzalez, Hunt assembles pieces of recovered scrap metal, transforming them into biomorphic elements that make up huge, semi-abstract figures. He has created a number of pieces of public sculpture, such as for Roosevelt Square, Harlem, or St Matthew's Methodist Church, Chicago. His work has become more and more imposing.

Richard Hunt has taken part in various group exhibitions, including in 1957, *Recent American Acquisitions*, Museum of Modern Art, New York, and has had a number of solo exhibitions, including the Alan Gallery, New York, since 1958; 1967, Museum of Art, Cleveland; 1971, a retrospective at the Museum of Modern Art, New York and Art Institute of Chicago; 1979, Wichita Art Museum, Wichita, Kansas; Terry Dintenfass Gallery, New York since 1983; 1997, Studio Museum in Harlem, New York; and in 1998, the Museum of African-American History, Detroit.
BIBLIOGRAPHY:
39th arts festival exhibition: sculpture by Richard Hunt, paintings by Sam Middleton, exhibition catalogue, Department of Art, Fisk University, Nashville (TN), 1968. Tully, Judd, et al., *Richard Hunt*, exhibition catalogue, Dorsky Gall., New York, 1989. *Richard Hunt: public sculptures*, exhibition catalogue, Museum of African-American History, Detroit, 1991. *Richard Hunt: Affirmations*, exhibition catalogue, Museum of African-American History, Detroit, 1998.
MUSEUMS AND GALLERIES:
CHICAGO (AI): *Hero Construction* (sculpture) - CINCINNATI (AM) - CLEVELAND (MA) - JERUSALEM (National Mus. of Israel) - LOS ANGELES (County MA) - NEW YORK (Metropolitan Mus. of Art): *Arachne* (1957, sculpture) - NEW YORK (MoMA): *Construction D* (1956, sculpture) - NEW YORK (Whitney Mus. of American Art) - WASHINGTON DC (Hirshhorn Mus. and Sculpture Garden): *Construction* (1958, bronze and steel).

HUNT, Samuel Valentine
British, 19th century.
Born 14 February 1803, in Norwich; died 1892, in Bay Ridge, USA.
Painter, engraver. Landscapes.
After exhibiting his work in London Samuel Valentine Hunt moved to America.

HUNT, T.
British, 19th century.
Miniaturist.
T. Hunt exhibited at the Royal Academy in London in 1803.

HUNT, T.W.
British, 19th century.
Active in London c. 1850.
Engraver.
T.W. Hunt collaborated on various newspapers.

HUNT, Thomas
British, 19th century.
Born 1854, in Skipton; died 1929, in Glasgow.
Active in Glasgow.
Painter, watercolourist. Genre scenes.
Thomas Hunt was a pupil of Raphael Collin in Paris in 1886. He was a member of the Royal Scottish Watercolour Society and an associate of the Royal Scottish Academy. He first exhibited at the Old Cloth Hall in Leeds in 1877, then at the Royal Scottish Academy and the Royal Academy in London from 1881. He received an honourable mention in Paris in 1895.
MUSEUMS AND GALLERIES:
LEEDS (City AG): *Cattle on a Footpath* (1879, oil on canvas).
AUCTION RECORDS:
LONDON, May 1923, *A Ray of Sunshine*, GBP 7. PAISLEY, 19 March 1999, *When the Day of Work is Done* (watercolour, 24 x 35 ins / 60 x 90 cm) GBP 1,600. AUCKLAND, 29 March 1999, *Thro' the Drift* (1888, oil on canvas, 15 x 31 ins / 38 x 80 cm) NZD 5,000. LONDON, 28 Aug 2002, *When the Day of Toil is Done* (watercolour with stopping out and scratching out, 24 x 35 ins / 60 x 90 cm) GBP 2,000.

HUNT, Walter
British, 19th - 20th century.
Born 1861; died 1941.
Active in Wandsworth.

Painter, watercolourist. Genre scenes, landscapes, animals.

Walter Hunt exhibited with the Royal Academy from 1881.

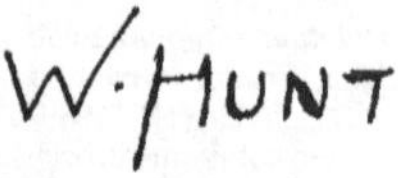

MUSEUMS AND GALLERIES:

LONDON (Tate Collection): *The Dog in the Manger* (1885, oil on canvas) - SUNDERLAND: *Babes in the Wood.*

AUCTION RECORDS:

LONDON, 30 Nov 1907, *In Search of Shelter* (1882) GBP 30. LONDON, 15 Feb 1908, *Young Boy Holding a Light* (watercolour) GBP 52. LONDON, 22 Feb 1908, *To the Rescue,* GBP 52. LONDON, 7 March 1908, *Too Hot* (watercolour) GBP 567; *Plums* (watercolour) GBP 178; *Loch Marec* (1876, watercolour) GBP 110; *Durham* (1876, watercolour) GBP 136. LONDON, 20 March 1908, *Freed Prisoners* (1882) GBP 26. LONDON, 23 May 1908, *Whitby: The Crazy Jane* (watercolour) GBP 131; *Tynemouth Harbour* (1868) GBP 152; *Bird's Nest and a Branch of Apple Blossom,* GBP 115. LONDON, 25 June 1909, *A Pot of Flowers and a Bird's Nest,* GBP 115. LONDON, 5 March 1910, *Soap Bubbles* (1892) GBP 65. LONDON, 16 March 1910, *The Dog in the Manger,* GBP 141. LONDON, Nov 1921, *The Otter Hunt,* GBP 43. LONDON, July 1922, *Left in Charge,* GBP 42. LONDON, March 1923, *Old Friends: Garden with a Horse and Goats,* GBP 21. LONDON, Nov 1924, *Frugal Repast,* GBP 75. LONDON, 19 Dec 1924, *Otter Hunt,* GBP 110. LONDON, 20 April 1925, *Baying Hounds,* GBP 120. LONDON, 31 March 1926, *Fruit* (drawing) GBP 31. LONDON, 17 Feb 1928, *Jealousy,* GBP 39. LONDON, 25 Nov 1929, *Besieged,* GBP 78. LONDON, 21 Dec 1933, *A Fly in the Milk,* GBP 39. LONDON, 3 April 1936, *Foster Mother,* GBP 37. LONDON, 22 Feb 1946, *Puppies Feeding-time,* GBP 52. LONDON, 19 June 1946, *Home after Work,* GBP 38. NEW YORK, 26 April 1967, *Foundling Puppy,* USD 700. LONDON, 20 May 1970, *Landscape,* GBP 520. LONDON, 27 March 1973, *Sleeping Shepherd-boy,* GBP 1,300. LONDON, 5 Nov 1974, *Bitch and Puppies* (1882) GBP 2,250. LONDON, 14 May 1976, *Farmyard Scene* (1908, oil on canvas, 30 1/2 x 45 1/2 ins / 77.5 x 115.5 cm) GBP 2,600. LONDON, 27 June 1978, *Summer Afternoon* (1896, oil on canvas, 29 1/4 x 41 1/2 ins / 74 x 105.5 cm) GBP 3,000. LONDON, 26 Oct 1979, *Cows in the Shade of a Tree* (1909, oil on canvas, 19 3/4 x 29 1/2 ins / 50 x 75 cm) GBP 5,000. LONDON, 20 Oct 1981, *Orphan* (1887, oil on canvas, 39 x 66 ins / 99 x 167.5 cm) GBP 9,000. LONDON, 14 July 1983, *Divided Affection* (1896, oil on canvas, 42 1/2 x 30 1/2 ins / 108 x 77.5 cm) GBP 11,000. LONDON, 1 Nov 1985, *Orphan* (1887, oil on canvas, 39 x 65 1/2 ins / 99 x 166.5 cm) GBP 16,000. LONDON, 18 March 1987, *Farmyard* (1898, oil on canvas, 30 x 41 ins / 76 x 104 cm) GBP 30,000. LONDON, 3 June 1988, *Calves and a Hen in a Barn* (1908, oil on canvas, 20 x 30 ins / 51 x 76 cm) GBP 10,450. NEW YORK, 9 June 1988, *On the Scent* (1900, oil on canvas, 30 1/4 x 45 1/4 ins / 76.8 x 114.9 cm) USD 33,000. LONDON, 17 March 1989, *An Unexpected Meal* (1890, oil on canvas, 40 1/4 x 54 1/4 ins / 102 x 138 cm) GBP 33,000. NEW YORK, 24 May 1989, *Farmyard with Two Ponies, a Calf and Chickens* (1925, oil on canvas, 20 x 30 1/4 ins / 50.9 x 76.9 cm) USD 14,300. LONDON, 2 June 1989, *Farmyard Friends* (1910, oil on canvas/panel, 18 x 24 ins / 45.7 x 61 cm) GBP 7,920. LONDON, 27 Sept 1989, *Waiting for Feeding-time* (1883, oil on canvas, 14 1/4 x 18 ins / 36 x 46 cm) GBP 7,920. LONDON, 9 Feb 1990, *Chicken-feed* (1920, oil on canvas, 8 x 10 ins / 20.3 x 25.4 cm) GBP 1,980. LONDON, 13 June 1990, *Calves by a Pond* (1919, oil on canvas, 20 x 30 ins / 51 x 76 cm) GBP 15,400. NEW YORK, 28 Feb 1991, *Horses in a Pasture* (1887, oil on canvas, 40 x 60 ins / 101.6 x 152.4 cm) USD 22,000. LONDON, 11 Oct 1991, *Chickens waiting to be Fed* (1883, oil on canvas, 14 x 18 ins / 35.5 x 45.6 cm) GBP 3,080. AMSTERDAM, 30 Oct 1991, *Dogs in a Kennel* (1883, oil on canvas, 21 1/4 x 30 ins / 54 x 76 cm) NLG 20,700. LONDON, 3 June 1992, *Eager Calves* (1890, oil on canvas, 19 3/4 x 30 ins / 50 x 76 cm) GBP 19,800. LONDON, 12 June 1992, *Playmates* (1890, oil on canvas, 35 1/2 x 48 1/4 ins / 90.2 x 122.6 cm) GBP 22,000. LONDON, 2 Nov 1994, *Calves at Feeding-time* (1911, oil on canvas, 12 x 16 ins / 30.5 x 40.5 cm) GBP 5,175. LONDON, 6 Nov 1995, *Landscape with a Cockerel and Hens* (1933, oil on panel, 7 1/4 x 9 1/4 ins / 18.5 x 23.5 cm) GBP 5,175. PERTH, 26 Aug 1996, *Otter Hunting, Hard Pressed* (1901, oil on canvas, 20 x 30 ins / 51 x 76.5 cm) GBP 5,980. LONDON, 6 Nov 1996, *Feeding-time* (1890, oil on canvas, 40 x 54 1/2 ins / 101.5 x 138.5 cm) GBP 38,900. LONDON, 6 June 1997, *A Tasty Morsel* (1908, oil on canvas, 20 x 30 ins / 50.8 x 76 cm) GBP 12,650. LONDON, 5 Nov 1997, *The New Litter* (1881, oil on canvas, 28 x 35 1/2 ins / 71 x 90 cm) GBP 13,800.

HUNT, William

British, 19th century.

Active in Greenwich.

Painter. Landscapes.

William Hunt exhibited his work in London at the Royal Academy and at Suffolk Street from 1889.

AUCTION RECORDS:

LONDON, 13 Dec 1909, *Slender Trees* (1889) GBP 6. LONDON, 5 Dec 1927, *Transhumance,* GBP 28.

HUNT, William Henry, called Bird's Nest Hunt

British, 19th century.

Born 28 March 1790, in London; died 10 February 1864, in London.

Painter, watercolourist. Genre scenes, interiors with figures, portraits, landscapes, flowers, still-lifes.

William Henry Hunt became a pupil of John Varley in about 1804 and also received tuition from Dr Thomas Munro at his academy. He frequently sketched from nature along with his fellow apprentice, John Linnell. In 1808 he was a pupil at the Royal Academy Schools. He became an associate of the Society of Painters in Watercolours in 1824 and a full member in 1826. In the early part of his career, Hunt painted many topographical views, but turned increasingly to figure subjects and still-lifes, especially of flowers, fruit and birds' nests, which earned him the nick-name 'Bird's Nest Hunt'.

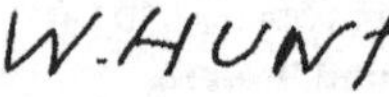

BIBLIOGRAPHY:

Lambourne, Lionel/Hamilton, Jean, *British Watercolours in the Victoria and Albert Museum,* Sotheby Parke Bernet, London, 1980. *William Henry Hunt 1790-1864,* exhibition catalogue, Wolverhampton Art Gallery, Wolverhampton, 1981. Witt, J., *William Henry Hunt (1790-1864): Life and Work,* exhibition catalogue, Barrie and Jenkins, London, 1982.

MUSEUMS AND GALLERIES:

BIRMINGHAM (Mus. and AG): *Lobster, Crab and Cucumber* (c. 1827, watercolour) - BLACKBURN (Mus. & AG): watercolours - CARDIFF: two watercolours - DUBLIN: four watercolours - LONDON (Courtauld Institute of Art): *Chaffinch Nest and May Blossom* (c. 1845, watercolour on paper) - LONDON (National Portrait Gal.): *William Henry Hunt* (oil on paper) - LONDON (Tate Collection): *Study from Nature at Twickenham* (c. 1806, oil on board); *Seascape* (watercolour on paper) - LONDON (Victoria and Albert Mus.): *Coast-guardsman* (watercolour); *Plums* (watercolour); *Hawthorn Blossoms and Bird's Nest* (watercolour); *New Court, the Temple, London* (watercolour) - MANCHESTER (City AG): *Orange and Vase* (c. 1860, watercolour); *Peach and Purple Grapes* (c. 1855, watercolour on paper); *Spring Flowers and Birds' Nests* (c. 1830, watercolour on paper) - PRESTON: twenty watercolours.

AUCTION RECORDS:

LONDON, 25 Nov 1927, *Flowers and Bird's Nest* (watercolour) GBP 48. LONDON, 28 Feb 1930, *Attack and Defeat* (two watercolours) GBP 220; *The Boy and the Cigar* (two watercolours) GBP 52. LONDON, 14 Oct 1969, *Portrait of a Little Girl* (watercolour) Gns 600. LONDON, 1 April 1976, *The Child and the Wasp* (watercolour, 16 1/2 x 12 1/4 ins / 42 x 31 cm) GBP 400. LONDON, 8 Nov 1977, *Flower Seller* (watercolour, 13 3/4 x 9 ins / 35 x 23 cm) GBP 450. LONDON, 18 March 1980, *Young Boy Picking up Dead Birds* (1827, watercolour, 10 1/4 x 7 1/2 ins / 26 x 18.8 cm) GBP 1,600. LONDON, 31 March 1981, *Green Fingers* (watercolour heightened with white, 12 1/2 x 8 1/2 ins / 32 x 21.5 cm) GBP 1,000. LONDON, 2 March 1983, *Farm Boy Stting on a Bale of Hay* (oil on panel, 12 x 10 ins / 30.5 x 25.5 cm) GBP 2,400. LONDON, 15 March 1984, *The New Red Shoes* (watercolour heightened with gouache, 13 x 8 1/4 ins / 33 x 21 cm) GBP 5,500. LONDON, 18 Dec 1984, *Portrait Head of Sir John Everett Milais as a Young Man* (pen and brown ink, 4 1/4 x 3 1/4 ins / 11 x 8.4 cm) GBP 1,500. LONDON, 18 March 1986, *Too Hot* (watercolour heightened with white/brown paper, 15 x 11 ins / 37.2 x 27 cm) GBP 8,500. LONDON, 19 Feb 1987, *Cottages at Bushey, Hertfordshire* (pen brown ink and watercolour, 14 x 10 1/4 ins / 35.5 x 26 cm) GBP 4,000. LONDON, 25 Jan 1988, *The Letter* (watercolour, 13 x 9 ins / 33 x 23 cm) GBP 3,740; *Spring Onions and Lettuce Leaves* (1827, watercolour, 6 x 7 1/2 ins / 15 x 19 cm) GBP 2,420. LONDON, 25 Jan 1989, *Young Girl Seated on a Fence* (watercolour and gouache, 9 x 6 1/4 ins / 22 x 16 cm) GBP 1,210; *Bird's Nest* (watercolour and gouache, 6 1/2 x 8 1/2 ins / 16.5 x 21.5 cm) GBP 1,650. LONDON, 25-26 April 1990, *Young Boy Holding a Candle* (watercolour, 9 3/4 x 7 3/4 ins / 25 x 20 cm) GBP 10,120. LONDON, 8 Feb 1991, *Apple Blossom and Bird's Nest on a Mossy Background* (watercolour heightened with white, oval, 8 1/2 x 12 ins / 21.6 x 30.5 cm) GBP 1,100. AMSTERDAM, 19 Oct 1993, *Little Bird's Nester* (oil on canvas/panel, 11 1/4 x 8 1/2 ins / 28.5 x 21.5 cm) NLG 3,450. ST ASAPH, 2 June 1994, *Still-life with Apples and Grapes* (watercolour, 6 x 8 ins / 15 x 20.5 cm) GBP 3,680. LONDON, 17 Nov 1994, *Interior of a Drawing Room with a Lady Writing at a Pedestal Table* (ink, watercolour and gouache, 12 1/4 x 17 1/4 ins / 31.1 x 43.5 cm) GBP 31,050. LONDON, 17 Nov 1995, *Green Drawing Room Belonging to the Earl of Essex at Cassiobury* (1823, pencil and watercolour heightened with white, 8 1/4 x 11 ins / 21.2 x 27 cm) GBP 25,300. NEW YORK, 17 Jan 1996, *Study of a Thoughtful Man* (watercolour/paper, 6 1/2 x 6 ins / 16.8 x 14.3 cm) USD 2,760. LONDON, 8 June 1999, *The Barber* (pencil, watercolour and scratching out, 18 x 13 ins / 46 x 32 cm) GBP 7,500. LONDON, 9 Nov 1999, *The Woodcutter's Breakfast* (pencil, watercolour and scratching out, 13 x 17 ins / 32 x 42 cm) GBP 13,000. LONDON, 22 March 2000, *Still-life of a Bird's Nest and Basket* (watercolour and pencil heightened with gouache scratching out and gum arabic, 7 x 11 ins / 18 x 28 cm) GBP 2,800. LONDON, 8 June 2000, *Still-life of a Pineapple and Three Plums* (1860, pencil, watercolour and gouache, 11 x 14 ins / 28 x 35 cm) GBP 5,500. LONDON, 26 June 2001, *Sunday Morning* (watercolour, gouache and gum arabic, 9 x 13 ins / 23 x 33 cm) GBP 8,000. LONDON, 26 June 2001, *Pet Lamb* (watercolour and gouache, 11 x 17 ins / 28 x 43 cm) GBP 30,000. LONDON, 6 June 2002, *Gardener in his Potting Shed* (pencil, pen, brown ink and watercolour, 12 x 13 ins / 30 x 34 cm) GBP 17,000. LONDON, 13 June 2002, *Still-life with Bird's Nest and Hawthorn on Mossy Bank* (pencil and watercolour heightened with white, 7 x 11 ins / 19 x 28 cm) GBP 5,500. LONDON, 22 Jan 2003, *Distant Shipping beneath Stormy Skies* (wash, 4 x 5 ins / 9 x 13 cm) GBP 4,000. LONDON, 20 Nov 2003, *Eavesdropper* (pencil, watercolour, gouache, gum arabic and scratching out, 29 x 22 ins / 73 x 55 cm) GBP 22,000. LONDON, 3 June 2004, *Interior of a Barn with Chickens* (pencil, watercolour and gum arabic heightened with gouache and scratching out, 12 x 18 ins / 31 x 45 cm) GBP 5,000. LONDON, 1 July 2004, *Still-life with Grapes, a Tankard and a Sprig of Holly* (watercolour and gouache, 6 x 4 ins / 15 x 11 cm) GBP 3,800.

HUNT, William Holman

British, 19th - 20th century.
Born 2 April 1827, in London; died 7 September 1910, in London.
Painter, watercolourist, draughtsman. Religious subjects, portraits, genre scenes, landscapes.
Symbolism.
Pre-Raphaelite.

William Holman Hunt worked in London as an office clerk from 1839 (when he was just 12 years old) until 1843. He entered the Royal Academy Schools on his third attempt, in 1844, and trained alongside John Everett Millais. He exhibited his first painting with the Royal Academy in 1845. Holman Hunt's earliest works announced his lifelong fascination with literary subjects, such as the *Flight of Madeline and Porphyro during the Drunkenness Attending the Revelry* of 1848 (illustrating a passage from John Keats's poem *The Eve of St Agnes*), *Rienzi Vowing to Obtain Justice for the Death of his Young Brother, Slain in a Skirmish between the Colonna and Orsini Factions*, of 1849, and *Claudio and Isabella* (1851). He discovered the Flemish Primitives during a journey through France and Belgium in 1849, and was inspired by them to paint works such as *Two Gentleman of Verona* (1851), hailed by Ruskin as the most 'fervent' and 'complete' work of art since Dürer. Visits to Egypt and Palestine in 1854 and 1892 inspired works such as *The Finding of the Saviour in the Temple* and *The Scapegoat*. The painting showing a *Converted British Family Sheltering a Christian Missionary from the Persecution of the Druids* (1850) heralded a series of religious and symbolic works: *Hireling Shepherd* (1852), *Awakening Conscience* (1854), *The Scapegoat* (1856), *The Finding of the Saviour in the Temple* (1860), *Shadow of Death* (1873). The *Triumph of the Innocents*, acquired by the Walker Art Gallery, Liverpool, was completed in 1885.

Holman Hunt's predilection for fantastical, imaginative subjects led him to Egypt and the Orient. The works inspired by his visit to Egypt in 1854 confirm his importance as an Orientalist painter. The chief purpose of the tour was a visit to the Holy Land, via Egypt, but Holman Hunt found himself spell-bound by Egypt as soon as he arrived in Cairo, in February 1854. The watercolour depicting the *Sunset over Gebel Mokattum*, in the Whitworth Art Gallery, Manchester, is a vivid record of his impressions. Holman Hunt executed numerous drawings and watercolours during his stay, often from unusual, original viewpoints (the Pyramids are relegated to the background, the Sphinx is seen from behind). This technique is further accentuated in the sketches recording his second journey to Egypt in 1892, when his reputation as the 'greatest religious painter of the age' was firmly established. Here, the archaeological relics and familiar scenes and subjects are rigourously avoided in favour of simple landscapes - an approach very much in keeping with Hunt's determination to eschew artistic precedents and break new ground. The mystical, symbolic aspect of Hunt's landscapes is equally important: the Holy Land is depicted quite explicitly as the landscape of Abraham and Sarah, the setting for the great struggle between monotheism and the gods of the pagan world. His pictures are freely scattered with Biblical references: a snake with its head crushed by a stone, or the Sphinx, facing eastwards, as if in expectation of the Messiah. Hunt saw the painter's role as comparable to that of a fearless, wandering apostle, serving a higher cause.

Early in his career, a shared concept of the Ideal sealed Hunt's friendship with his fellow students at the Royal Academy, Millais and Dante Gabriel Rossetti. The trio founded the Pre-Raphaelite Brotherhood in 1848. Aspects of the Brotherhood's style were anticipated in the mid-1840s by the painter Ford Madox Brown, who subsequently joined the group. The Brotherhood became a defining movement in modern English art; in 1886, its doctrines were expounded by Hunt in a series of articles published in the *Contemporary Review*, to coincide with his first retrospective at the Fine Art Society. The articles also sought to counter the popular identification of Rossetti (recently deceased) as the group's prime mentor, and formed the basis for Hunt's autobiographical work *Pre-Raphaelitism and the Pre-Raphaelite Brotherhood*, published in 1905. Hunt was awarded the Order of Merit in the same year. His works won him enormous popular acclaim, and his funeral cortège to St Paul's cathedral in September 1910, was attended by huge crowds. Hunt's third and final version of his celebrated painting *The Light of the World* (painted in 1900) hangs in the cathedral's north transept.

Holman Hunt's work was the subject of an important and highly successful retrospective at the Fine Art Society Rooms in 1886. He became an honorary member of the Royal Society of British Artists, and exhibited in Germany (in Berlin and Munich), notably in 1891.

Bibliography:

Stephens, F.G., *William Holman Hunt and his Works: A Memoir of the Artist's Life, with a Descripton of his Pictures*, London, 1860. Rossetti, W.M., '*Reminiscences of Holman Hunt*' in *Contemporary Review*, no. 1108, 1910 (obituary). Holman Hunt, D., *My Grandfather, his Wives and Lovers*, London, 1969. Bennett, M. (ed), *William Holman Hunt*, exhibition catalogue, Walker Art Gallery, Liverpool, 1969. Landow, G.P., *William Holman Hunt and Typological Symbolism*, New Haven, 1979. '*William Holman Hunt's 'Oriental Mania' and his Uffizi 'Self-portrait*' in *Art Bulletin*, vol 64, 1982. '*Shadows Cast by the Light of the World: William Holman Hunt's Religious Paintings, 1893-1905*' in *Art Bulletin*, vol 155, 1983. '*William Holman Hunt's Letters to Thomas Seddon*' in *Bulletin, John Rylands Library*, vol 66, 1983-1984. Errington, L., *Social and Religious Themes in English Art, 1840-1864*, New York, 1984. Parris, L. (ed.), *The Pre-Raphaelites*, exhibition catalogue, Tate Gallery, London, 1984. Bronkhurst, Judith, *An Interesting Series of Adventures to Look Back Upon: William Holman Hunt's Visit to the Dead Sea in November 1854*, Tate Gallery, London, 1984. Holman Hunt, Diana, '*The Holman Hunt Collection: A Personal Recollection*' in *Pre-Rapahelite Papers*, Tate Gallery, London, 1984. Holman Hunt, William, *Pre-Raphaelite Friendship: The Correspondence of William Holman Hunt and John Lucas Tupper*, University of Michigan Press, Ann Arbor, 1986. Bronkhurst, Judith, *William Holman Hunt: A Catalogue Raisonné of Paintings and Drawings Executed before his Departure for the Near East on 13 January 1854*, dissertation, University of London, London, 1987. Pointon, M. (ed.), *The Artist as Ethnographer: Holman Hunt and the Holy Land, Pre-Raphaelites Reviewed*, Manchester, 1989. Bronkhurst, Judith, '*William Holman Hunt's Visits to Egypt: Passion, Prejudice and Truth to Nature*' in *Apollo*, periodical, London, November, 1998.

Museums and Galleries:

Birmingham (Museum and Art Gallery): *Self Portrait* (1845, oil on canvas); act V, scene 4*The Two Gentlemen of Verona: Valentine Rescuing Sylvia from Proteus* (1851, oil on canvas); *Portrait of Dante Gabriel Rossetti* (1853, oil/panel); *The Finding of the Saviour in the Temple* (1854-1860, oil on canvas); *A Street Scene in Cairo: The Lantern Maker's Courtship* (1854-1861, oil on canvas); *May Morning on Magdalen College Tower, Oxford* (oil on canvas) - Leeds (City AG): *The Shadow of Death* (1870-1873, oil on canvas) - Liverpool (Walker AG): *The Triumph of the Innocents* (1876, oil on canvas); *Robert Braithwaite Martineau* (1860, pencil); *Edward Lear* (7 Nov 1857, pencil); *The Eve of St. Agnes* (1847-1867, oil/panel) - London (Guildhall AG): *The Eve of St. Agnes* (1848, oil on canvas) - London (Victoria and Albert Mus.): a watercolour - Manchester (City AG): *The Lantern Maker's Courtship* (c. 1854-1860, oil on panel) - Manchester (Whitworth Art Gallery): *Cairo: Sunset on the Gebel Mokattum* (1854-1857, watercolour) - Melbourne (Victoria National Gallery): *The Importunate Neighbour* - Oxford (Ashmolean Mus.): *A Converted British Family Sheltering a Christian from the Persecution of the Druids* (1850, oil on canvas); *The Schoolgirl (Miriam Wilkinson)* (1859, oil on canvas); *London Bridge at Night; Rejoicings in Honour of the Marriage of the Prince and Princess of Wales, March 10th 1863* (1863-1866, oil on canvas); *The Festival of St Swithin ('The Dovecot')* (1866-1875, oil on canvas); *Self-portrait at the Age of 14* (oil on canvas); *The Afterglow in Egypt* (oil on canvas); *Plain of Esdraelon from the Heights above Nazareth* (oil on canvas); *The Sleeping City: the Cemetry of Pera, Constantinople* (watercolour); *The Meet at Holcombe, August 1895* (watercolour) - Port Sunlight (Lady Lever Art Gal.): *The Scapegoat* - Preston (Harris Museum and Art Gallery): *The Sphinx at Gizeh Looking towards the Pyramids at Sakkarah* (1854, watercolour) - Southampton (City AG): *Afterglow in Egypt* (1854, oil on canvas) - Wilmington, DE (Delaware AM): *Isabella and the Pot of Basil* (oil on canvas).

Auction records:

London, 6 May 1889, *Morning Prayer*, FRF 5,500. London, 28 May 1908, *Study for Christ among the Doctors (The Finding of the Saviour in the Temple)* (drawing) GBP 24. London, 9 July 1909, *The Scapegoat*, GBP 2,940. London, June 1923, *The Scapegoat*, GBP 4,830. London, July 1924, *The Eve of St Agnes*, GBP 357. London, 29 Jan 1926, *After Sunset, Egypt*, GBP 682. London, 10 July 1931, *Young Girl in Tuscany*, GBP 126. London, 25 Jan 1936, *Awakening Conscience*, GBP 210. London, 3 April 1936, *Valentine Rescuing Sylvia from Proteus*, GBP 81. London, 19 March 1937, *Triumph of the Innocents*, GBP 567. London, 4 Dec 1957, *The Shepherd*, GBP 2,200. London, 22 April 1959, *Fishing Boats at Anchor* (drawing) GBP 220. London, 18 Nov 1960, *The Plain of Esdraelon Seen from the Heights above Nazareth*, GBP 189. London, 16 June 1961, *The Lady of Shallot*, GBP 9,975. London, 3 July 1964, *Young Woman and her Dog, Sitting in a Garden*, Gns 850. London, 17 June 1966, *Il dolce farniente*, Gns 2,800. London, 19 Oct 1971, *Oriana*, GBP 1,800. London, 9 Nov 1971, *The Desert at Gizeh* (watercolour) Gns 3,200. London, 27 March 1973, *Rienzi Vowing to Obtain Justice for the Death of his Young Brother, Slain in a Skirmish between the Colonna and Orsini Factions*, GBP 48,000. London, 29 June 1976, *Summer Landscape* (oil on canvas remounted/panel, 16 x 8 ins / 40.5 x 20.3 cm) GBP 750. London, 14 June 1977, *Portrait of Fanny Hunt, the Artist's First Wife*; oil on canvas, 42 x 29 ins / 106.5 x 73.5 cm) GBP 22,000. London, 9 April 1980, *Dogs (recto); Figure Studies (verso)* (oil on card, red chalk and pencil, 9 3/4 x 11 1/2 ins / 25 x 29 cm) GBP 6,000. London, 6 Oct 1980, *Marion Edith Holman Hunt* (1877, drawing in silverpoint, 10 x 7 1/2 ins / 25.5 x 19 cm) GBP 1,300. London, 10 Nov 1981, *Amaryllis, or the Shepherdess* (oil on panel, 25 1/4 x 19 3/4 ins / 64 x 50 cm) GBP 46,000. London, 18 March 1983, *Portrait of Mrs George Waugh, née Mary Walker* (1868, oil on canvas, 34 x 26 ins / 86.3 x 66 cm) GBP 18,000. London, 10 Oct 1985, *Study for The Flight of Madeleine and Porphyro during the Drunkenness Attending the Revelry* (pencil, 5 1/4 x 7 3/4 ins / 13.5 x 19.5 cm) GBP 16,000. London, 10 Oct 1985, *Study for The flight of Madeleine and Porphyro during the Drunkenness Attending the Revelry* (oil and pencil/card, 10 1/2 x 7 1/2 ins / 26.5 x 19 cm) GBP 35,000. New York, 25 Feb 1988, *Portrait of Thomas Bull, Inkeeper on the Isle of Wight* (oil on canvas, 21 1/4 x 17 1/4 ins / 54 x 43.8 cm) USD 3,300. New York, 28 Feb 1990, *Portrait of Marion Edith*

Holman Hunt (1877, silverpoint/paper, 10 x 7 3/4 ins / 25.4 x 19.7 cm) USD 17,600. London, 1 Nov 1990, *Portrait of William Etty at the 'Life School'* (ink, 4 x 4 3/4 ins / 10.4 x 12 cm) GBP 1,870. London, 28 Nov 1990, *Portrait of Fanny Hunt* (1866, coloured chalk and wash/canvas, 28 x 20 1/2 ins / 71 x 52 cm) GBP 8,800. London, 19 June 1991, *A Wadi in Palestine* (watercolour, 13 1/2 x 19 1/4 ins / 34 x 49 cm) GBP 30,800. London, 11 Oct 1991, *Bacchus and Ariadne after Titian* (oil on card/panel, 15 x 17 ins / 38 x 43 cm) GBP 1,210. London, 29 Oct 1991, *Egyptians Playing a Game of Siga in a Café at Seminood on the Nile* (1854, pencil heightened with white, 7 x 6 ins / 17.7 x 14.3 cm) GBP 2,200. London, 12 Nov 1992, *Cyril Holman Hunt* (1876, coloured chalk, 21 x 15 1/4 ins / 53.5 x 39 cm) GBP 1,650. London, 5 March 1993, *Portrait of a Young Woman, Probably Miss Isabella Waugh* (oil on canvas, 22 x 14 ins / 55.9 x 35.6 cm) GBP 5,175. London, 3 June 1994, *Master Hilary - the Draughtsman* (oil on canvas, 48 x 26 ins / 122.2 x 66 cm) GBP 969,500. London, 2 Nov 1994, *The Shadow of Death* (1873, oil on panel, 41 1/4 x 32 1/4 ins / 104.5 x 82 cm) GBP 1,871,500. London, 7 June 1995, *Morning Prayer* (1866, oil on panel, 10 x 7 1/4 ins / 25.5 x 18.5 cm) GBP 287,500. London, 7 June 1996, *Jaffa* (1855, pencil heightened with white, 7 x 10 1/4 ins / 18 x 26 cm) GBP 1,035. London, 5 Nov 1997, *Study for 'The Flight of Madeline'* (oil on panel, 10 1/2 x 7 1/2 ins / 26.5 x 19 cm) GBP 9,200; *Study 'The Flight of Madeline'* (pencil, 5 1/2 x 7 3/4 ins / 14 x 19.5 cm) GBP 6,900. London, 10 Nov 1998, *The Lost Child* (watercolour, 5 x 3 ins / 13 x 8 cm) GBP 7,100. London, 3 June 1999, *Portrait of Artist's daughter, Gladys, Aged Four* (pen and brown ink, 7 x 4 ins / 18 x 11 cm) GBP 2,000. London, 9 March 2000, *Group Portrait of Mrs Davies, of Wormbridge Court, with Four of her Clark Grandchildren* (oil on canvas, 30 x 25 ins / 76 x 63 cm) GBP 5,400. London, 26 June 2001, *The Mosque of Assakreh, Jerusalem* (watercolour heightened with bodycolour, 10 x 14 ins / 25 x 35 cm) GBP 20,000. London, 12 June 2002, *Silver Lining* (1865, pencil and watercolour heightened with bodycolour, 5 x 7 ins / 13 x 17 cm) GBP 19,000. London, 19 June 2002, *Miss Flamborough* (1882, oil on canvas, reworked by Charles Stanley Pollitt, 52 x 34 ins / 132 x 87 cm) GBP 15,500. London, 27 Nov 2003, *Piazza della Constituzione by Night, Athens* (1892, oil on paper, 15 x 20 ins / 37 x 50 cm) GBP 15,000. London, 24 Nov 2004, *Asparagus Island, Kynance, Cornwall* (pencil and watercolour heightened with scratching out, 8 x 10 ins / 20 x 26 cm) GBP 145,000. New York, 26 Oct 2004, *Portrait of Marion Edith Holman Hunt* (1877, silverpoint, 10 x 8 ins / 25 x 20 cm) USD 9,000.

HUNT, William Morris
American, 19th century.
Born 31 March 1824, in Brathleborough; died 8 September 1879, in Appledore (New Hampshire).
Painter, sculptor, draughtsman. History painting, genre scenes, landscapes.
Barbizon School.

William Morris Hunt worked initially as a sculptor. He then went to Europe where he studied painting, firstly in Düsseldorf and then in Paris in Thomas Couture's studio. He struck up a friendship with Jean-François Millet, who had some influence over his artistic development. He returned to the USA in 1865, settling in Boston after a short stay in Newport. Hunt trained a large number of pupils. Notable works include the mural decoration of the great hall of the Capitol building in Albany, in which he revealed his skill as a luminous colourist and idealist.

Auction records:
New York, 31 Jan-2 Feb 1900, *Whale*, USD 325. New York, 8-9 Jan 1903, *Mother and Child Asleep*, USD 650. New York, 20 Feb 1946, *Young Girl*, USD 300. New York, 17 May 1946, *Woman's Head*, USD 120. New York, 29 April 1976, *Waiting for Father* (oil on panel, 15 x 10 ins / 38 x 25.5 cm) USD 550. New York, 21 April 1978, *The Flight of Night* (1880, bronze with dark green patina, 19 x 28 3/4 ins / 48.5 x 73 cm) USD 9,000. New York, 28 April 1978, *Autumn Afternoon* (oil on panel, 15 x 24 ins / 38 x 61 cm) USD 7,500. New York, 20 April 1979, *Temple of Hercules, Tivoli* (oil on panel, 10 1/2 x 13 3/4 ins / 26.6 x 35 cm) USD 3,250. New York, 23 May 1979, *Fayal* (1858, pastel, 15 1/4 x 11 1/2 ins / 39 x 29.5 cm) USD 1,400. New York, 29 Jan 1981, *Portrait of a Gentleman* (charcoal, 21 1/2 x 16 1/2 ins / 54.6 x 41.9 cm) USD 4,400. Bolton, 18 Nov 1982, *Governor's Creek, Florida* (1873, oil on canvas, 10 x 16 ins / 25.3 x 40.5 cm) USD 5,000. Bolton, 12 May 1983, *Fortune* (oil on canvas, 83 3/4 x 60 ins / 213 x 152.5 cm) USD 9,250. New York, 30 May 1985, *Portrait of Agnes Elisabeth Claflin* (1875, oil on mounted canvas panel, 52 x 36 ins / 132 x 91.5 cm) USD 18,000. New York, 1 Oct 1986, *Old Man with a Derby* (charcoal, 6 3/4 x 6 3/4 ins / 17.2 x 17.2 cm) USD 1,600. New York, 29 May 1987, *Fortune, Alnay Murals* (oil on canvas, study, 87 1/4 x 60 1/4 ins / 221.7 x 152.9 cm) USD 30,000. New York, 25 May 1989, *Little Girls Playing at Injured Soldiers with a Doll* (oil on paper/card, 13 x 10 ins / 33.3 x 25.3 cm) USD 15,400. New York, 24 Jan 1990, *Head of a Woman* (charcoal/paper, 12 3/4 x 9 3/4 ins / 32.4 x 24.7 cm) USD 1,650. New York, 14 Nov 1991, *Kitchen Garden* (oil on card, 16 1/2 x 12 ins / 42 x 30.5 cm) USD 2,200. New York, 11 March 1993, *Out in a Snow-covered Forest* (1864, oil on canvas, 12 1/2 x 14 1/2 ins / 31.5 x 37 cm) USD 4,600. New York, 31 March 1994, *Tom with a Fedora* (oil on canvas, 22 x 16 ins / 55.9 x 40.6 cm) USD 1,840. New York, 9 March 1996, *Barley Field* (1866, oil on canvas, 14 x 24 ins / 35.5 x 60.9 cm) USD 6,325. New York, 4 Dec 1996, *Niagara Falls* (oil on panel, 23 1/4 x 42 1/4 ins / 59 x 107.3 cm) USD 23,000. Connecticut, 22 Feb 1999, *Young Boy* (oil on canvas, 18 x 14 ins / 46 x 36 cm) USD 3,100. Boston, 10 March 2000, *Portrait of a Woman* (oil on canvas, 22 x 18 ins / 56 x 46 cm) USD 5,000. New York, 25 May 2000, *Flight of Night* (brown patinated bronze, relief, 19 x 28x9 ins / 48 x 72x24 cm) USD 35,000. Boston, 10 May 2002, *Wooded Path* (1862, oil on canvas) USD 6,500. Boston, 22 Nov 2002, *Ophelia* (oil on canvas, 32 x 26 ins / 81 x 65 cm) USD 12,000. New York, 30 Oct 2003, *Young Girl at Table with Sculpture* (oil on canvas, 10 x 14 ins / 25 x 35 cm) USD 4,000. Maine, 3 Jan 2004, *House by the Sea* (1864, oil on panel, 5 x 11 ins / 13 x 28 cm) USD 3,600. Maine, 3 Jan 2004, *Windblown Shade Tree* (oil on canvas, 12 x 16 ins / 30 x 41 cm) USD 4,200.

HÜNTEN. See **HUENTEN**

HUNTER, Ada (Miss)
British, 19th century.
Active in London.
Miniaturist, watercolourist.

Ada Hunter exhibited at the Royal Academy in London from 1886.

Auction records:
London, 30 May 1985, *In the Gloaming* (1891, watercolour heightened with gouache, 16 x 11 3/4 ins / 40.5 x 30 cm) GBP 1,000.

HUNTER, Clementine
American, 20th century.
Born December 1886, in Cloutierville (Louisiana), or January 1887; died 1 January 1988, in Natchitoches (Louisiana).
Painter, draughtswoman. Religious subjects, scenes with figures, figure compositions, still-lifes.
Folk Art.

Clementine Hunter, of Creole origin, and daughter of a former slave, was born on Hidden Hill Plantation (now called Little Eva Plantation) in the Cane River country. The date of her birth cannot be determined, but her baptismal certificate states March 1887. From her youth until she died, she worked as a servant at the Melrose Plantation. The owners of the plantation played host to many artists and writers, and Clementine started her career as an artist in the late 1930s, using tubes of paint that had been left behind by the visitors, and encouraged by the art critic François Mignon, who was the plantation's librarian. As she was illiterate, she had to learn to sign her work using her initials, but as these were the same as those of her employer, she took to signing herself 'C'. In 1953, an article *Look Magazine* brought her to public attention, but because of racial segregation she was not allowed to attend her own first major exhibition at Natchitoches. Later, she was awarded an honorary doctorate by Northwestern Louisiana University, Natchitoches, and her house has been preserved by the Association for the Preservation of Historic Natchitoches.

Clementine Hunter's output amounts to nearly four thousand works. She painted in oils on different surfaces - card, paper bags, pieces of wood or plywood, even wine bottles. Her paintings can be divided into five main categories: cotton picking, festive scenes, religious rituals, still-lifes, and abstracts. Essentially, she painted black people going about their daily lives, using a lively palette and highly rhythmic composition but with no concern for perspective. She also transposed biblical scenes into the reality of black American life in Louisiana, as in *Nativity* (1975), where the Virgin waits beneath a palm tree, Jesus on her knees, while the Magi walk towards a chapel, above which three angels hover and in which all the figures are black.

Clementine Hunter took part in a number of group exhibitions, including in 1949, *New Orleans Arts and Crafts Show*, New Orleans; 1976, *Two Centuries of Black American Art*, Los Angeles County Museum of Art, Los Angeles and 1981, *Forever Free: Art by African American Women 1862-1980*, Illinois State University, Normal, Illinois. After she died, her work was included in thematic group exhibitions, for example, in 2000, *Narratives of African-American Art and Identity*, High Museum of Art, Atlanta. She also had a number of solo exhibitions, including in 1955, *Clementine Hunter: Primitive Painter*, Northwestern State College, Natchitoches; 1955, Delgado Art Museum, today New Orleans Museum of Art, New Orleans; 1985, *A Centennial Salute to Clementine Hunter*, New Orleans Museum of Art, New Orleans. There have also been a number of posthumous retrospectives of her work: 1993, Museum of African-American Life and Culture, Dallas; 2000, *Clementine Hunter: From Cotton Fields to Canvas*, Frederick R. Weisman Art Museum, University of Minnesota, Minneapolis and 2002, New Orleans Public Library.

Bibliography:

'*The Primitive Art of Clementine Hunter*' in *Ebony*, periodical, New York, May 1969. Wilson, James Lee, *Clementine Hunter: American Folk Artist*, Pelican Pub. Co., Gretna, 1988. Lewis, Samella, *African-American Art and Artists*, The University of California Press, Berkeley, 1990. Gilley, Shelby R., *Painting by Heart: The Life and Art of Clementine Hunter. Louisiana Folk Artist*, St Emma Press, Baton Rouge, 2000.

Museums and Galleries:

Atlanta (High Mus.) - Dallas (MA) - Minneapolis (IA) - New Orléans (Louisiana State Mus.): *Baptism* (c. 1976) - New Orléans (MA) - St Paul (Minnesota Mus. of American Art) - Washington DC (National Mus. of Women in the Arts): *Call to Church and Flowers* (1970, oil on canvas).

Auction records:

New York, 24 Sept 1992, *Still-life with Flowers* (1940, oil on paper, 14½ x 11¼ ins / 36.8 x 28.6 cm) USD 2,750. New Orleans, 24 July 1999, *Mother and Child with Birds* (oil on paper, 12 x 15 ins / 30 x 38 cm) USD 4,800. New Orleans, 30 July 1999, *Spring Fiesta at Melrose Plantation with Artist Seated to the Right* (oil on board, 24 x 30 ins / 61 x 76 cm) USD 6,500. New Orleans, 8 April 2000, *We Had a Bench to Rest on* (oil and wash on paper, 10 x 15 ins / 25 x 38 cm) USD 6,000. New Orleans, 7 Oct 2000, *Funeral* (oil on board, 19 x 24 ins / 48 x 61 cm) USD 4,500. New Orleans, 26 May 2001, *Tea Party* (c. 1940, oil on paper, 10 x 14 ins / 25 x 36 cm) USD 8,000. New Orleans, 8 Dec 2001, *What is This, Two Women After One Man* (watercolour, 10 x 14 ins / 25 x 36 cm) USD 8,250. New Orleans, 22 Feb 2002, *Cotton Pickers* (oil on board, 6 x 9 ins / 15 x 23 cm) USD 5,250. New Orleans, 13 April 2002, *Wash Day* (oil on canvas, 21 x 27 ins / 53 x 69 cm) USD 5,200. New Orleans, 22 Nov 2003, *Wash Day* (oil on board, 16 x 24 ins / 41 x 61 cm) USD 4,000. New Orleans, 22 Nov 2003, *Cotton Picking* (oil on board, 16 x 20 ins / 41 x 51 cm) USD 5,500. Buford, 24 April 2004, *Funeral* (c. 1958, oil on board, 16 x 24 ins / 41 x 61 cm) USD 9,000. Buford, 24 April 2004, *Melrose Plantation* (oil on canvasboard, 21 x 27 ins / 53 x 69 cm) USD 12,500.

HUNTER, Colin

British, 19th century.

Born 16 July 1841, in Glasgow; died 24 September 1904, in London.

Painter, engraver. Genre scenes, landscapes, seascapes. Colin Hunter was self-taught. He exhibited his work at the Royal Academy in London, of which he became an Associate in 1884, and at the Royal Scottish Academy. He also took part in the Universal Exhibitions in Berlin in 1886 and 1891, Vienna 1888, Philadelphia 1876, Paris 1878, 1889 (silver medal) and 1900 (honourable mention). He was a talented seascape painter.

Museums and Galleries:

Bristol: *London, View from Tower Bridge* - Cape Town: *The Silvery Sea* - Glasgow: *Evening on Skye; Seascape, The Dawn; Low Tide; Niagara Falls; Niagara Falls* - Hamburg: *Collecting Shells* - Leicester: *Three Fishermen* - Liverpool: *The Pool in the Forest* - London (Tate Collection): *Their Only Harvest* (1879, oil on canvas) - Melbourne (Nat. Gal. of Victoria): *Young Woman Baiting the Line* - Montreal: *Preparing the Nets*.

Auction records:

London, 30 Nov 1907, *Glasgow*, GBP 5. London, 2 Dec 1907, *Fishing Boats* (1874) GBP 6. London, 11 March 1908, *Village on the Coast of Scotland* (1878) GBP 19. London, 13 April 1908, *Fishing Village on the Coast* (1888) GBP 35. London, 24 April 1909, *Morning on the Coast* (1872) GBP 475. London, 4 Feb 1911, *Glen Ferfoch* (1869) GBP 63. London, Nov 1921, *Lake in the Scottish Highlands*, GBP 25. London, May 1923, *Salmon Fishing, Dee Falls*, GBP 63. London, 10 Dec 1926, *Trawlers*, GBP 50. London, April 1928, *The Little Fisher Girl*, GBP 37. London, 4 June 1936, *On the West Coast*, GBP 34. Scotland, 30 Aug 1974, *Lobster Fishermen* (1883) GBP 1,050. Scotland, 24 Aug 1976, *Boat off the Coast* (1903, oil on canvas, 34 x 8½ ins / 86.5 x 21.5 cm) GBP 300. Perth, 24 April 1979, *Crab Fishermen* (oil on canvas, 19¾ x 39¼ ins / 50 x 100 cm) GBP 500. Glasgow, 28 Aug 1985, *Peasants Gathering Apples at the Riverside* (1901, oil on canvas, 40 x 28 ins / 101.6 x 71.2 cm) GBP 2,600. Edinburgh, 30 Aug 1988, *Fishermen Unloading their Fish* (oil on canvas, 9½ x 14¼ ins / 24 x 36 cm) GBP 1,980. Göteborg, 18 May 1989, *Bringing in the Nets* (oil on canvas, 18½ x 26½ ins / 47 x 67 cm) SEK 4,000. South Queensferry, 1 May 1990, *Washerwoman at the Quayside* (1888, oil on canvas, 22 x 40¼ ins / 56 x 102 cm) GBP 3,300. Glasgow, 5 Feb 1991, *Emptying the Herring Nets* (1895, oil on canvas, 20 x 35¾ ins / 51 x 91 cm) GBP 1,760. South Queensferry, 23 April 1991, *Preparing the Hooks* (1889, oil on canvas, 66¼ x 49 ins / 168 x 124.5 cm) GBP 8,250. New York, 15 Oct 1991, *Fishing Boat Anchored for the Night* (oil on canvas, 16½ x 24¼ ins / 41.9 x 61.6 cm) USD 990. Perth, 30 Aug 1994, *Connemara Bay* (1894, oil on canvas, 20¼ x 36¼ ins / 51.5 x 92 cm) GBP 1,380. Glasgow, 16 April 1996, *Greenock Harbour* (1880, oil on canvas, 24 x 14¼ ins / 61 x 36 cm) GBP 1,150. London, 10 April 2000, *Pulling in the Nets* (oil on canvas, 32 x 45 ins / 81 x 114 cm) GBP 2,000. London, 26 Oct 2000, *View from Lamlash* (1882, oil on canvas, 26 x 39 ins / 67 x 99 cm) GBP 6,000. London, 8

March 2001, *Sunset over the Coast* (oil on canvas, 14 x 24 ins / 36 x 61 cm) GBP 1,100. EDINBURGH, 13 April 2001, *Give Way* (1879, oil on canvas, 35 x 62 ins / 90 x 157 cm) GBP 2,800. ANTWERP, 22 April 2002, *Fisherman Working at the Beach* (1889, oil on canvas, 25 x 74 ins / 64 x 188 cm) EUR 4,400. LONDON, 20 Feb 2003, *Fishing Boat off the Coast* (oil on canvas, 32 x 5 ins / 81 x 13 cm) GBP 4,000. LONDON, 27 Aug 2003, *Gathering Bracken* (1869, oil on canvas, 18 x 28 ins / 46 x 72 cm) GBP 2,500. BEXHILL, 3 Feb 2004, *Pennyween, Fifeshire* (1899, oil on canvasboard, 11 x 15 ins / 28 x 38 cm) GBP 1,600. LONDON, 28 Oct 2004, *Shipping in the Harbour of Oban* (1892, oil on canvas, 22 x 40 ins / 56 x 101 cm) GBP 3,800.

HUNTER, Elizabeth (Miss)
British, 19th century.
Active in London.
Painter. Genre scenes.

Elizabeth Hunter exhibited her work in London at the Royal Academy, the British Institution and Suffolk Street from 1853 to 1883.

AUCTION RECORDS:
LONDON, 7 June 1979, *In Disgrace* (oil on canvas, 20 x 16 ins / 51 x 40.5 cm) GBP 2,000.

HUNTER, George Leslie
British, 19th - 20th century.
Born 7 August 1877, in Rothesay (Isle of Bute); died 6 December 1931, in Glasgow.
Painter, watercolourist, illustrator. Portraits, genre scenes, landscapes, still-lifes, flowers.
Scottish Colourists.

George Leslie Hunter trained at Rothesay Academy. His family emigrated to California in 1892. He worked initially as a magazine illustrator and was due to hold his first exhibition in San Francisco in 1906, when his works were destroyed in a fire caused by the great earthquake that year. The family returned to Europe in 1910 and Hunter's parents died shortly afterwards. He was active in France in 1914, but was forced to return to England on the outbreak of war. In 1922 he visited Paris, the Côte d'Azur and northern Italy on a painting tour with his friend J. D. Fergusson. In 1924 he visited the USA. From 1927-1929 he was active in south-east France, principally at St-Paul-de-Vence, but also at Cassis and St-Tropez. In 1929 he travelled once again to the USA, but was brought back to Glasgow in failing health by his sister. He convalesced and began painting once more with renewed confidence (a number of still-lifes and portraits of friends date from this period). Hunter died in 1931, following a stomach operation.

Initially, he signed his paintings *George*, then *G. Leslie*, and finally *Leslie*. His drawings, watercolours and illustrations demonstrate his remarkable descriptive skill. His oil paintings are characterised by the use of thick impasto and heavy brushwork, reminiscent of early works by Cézanne (in particular the still-lifes): *Still-life with a Pot, a Vase of Roses, a Glass of Wine, Apples and Lemons on a Table Covered with a Cloth*.

His work featured in a number of group exhibitions of Scottish painters: Glasgow, 1916; London 1923, 1925, 1932 (*Paintings by Six Scottish Artists*), 1939 (*Three Scottish Painters*); Paris, 1924 (*Painters of Modern Scotland*), 1931 (*Scottish Painters*). Since his death, Hunter's work has featured in a number of group or themed exhibitions, including: 1949, Royal Scottish Academy, Edinburgh; 1952, *Four Scottish Colourists*, Edinburgh; 1961, *Scottish Painting*, Glasgow; 2000, *The Scottish Colourists 1900-1930: Peploe, Fergusson, Hunter and Cadell*, Royal Academy of Arts, London, (exhibition subsequently shown at the Scottish National Gallery of Modern Art, Edinburgh). Hunter's work was the subject of a solo exhibition in New York, in 1929.

BIBLIOGRAPHY:
Honeyman, T.J., *Introducing Leslie Hunter*, Faber and Faber, London, 1937. *Three Scottish Colorists*, exhibition catalogue, Scottish Arts Council, Edinburgh, 1970. Billcliffe, Roger, *The Scottish Colourists: Cadell, Fergusson, Hunter, Peploe*, John Murray, London, 1989. Long, Philipp/Elliot, Patrick, *The Scottish Colourists 1900-1930. Peploe, Fergusson, Hunter and Cadell*, exhibition catalogue, Royal Academy of Arts, London, 2000. Fowle, Frances, *'Three Scotish Colourists. Early patronage of Peploe, Hunter and Cadell'* in *Apollo* n° 464 p. 26, periodical, London, October 2000. Ogston, Derek, *The life and work of George Leslie Hunter, 1877-1931*, Baillieknowe Publishing, Kelso, 2002.

MUSEUMS AND GALLERIES:
EDINBURGH (Scottish Nat. Gal. of Modern Art): *Reflections, Balloch* (c. 1929-1930, oil on canvas); *Still Life* (1930, oil on canvas).

AUCTION RECORDS:
GLASGOW, 13 Oct 1943, *Still-life*, GBP 51. GLASGOW, 2 April 1969, *Fishing Village*, Gns 850. GLASGOW, 19 March 1971, *Still-life with Chrysanthemums*, Gns 1,100. GLASGOW, 19 May 1972, *Still-life with Chrysanthemums*, Gns 2,000. GLASGOW, 11 Oct 1974, *Still-life*, Gns 950. GLASGOW, 30 Nov 1976, *Venice* (oil on card, 24 1/2 x 29 1/2 ins / 62 x 75 cm) GBP 900. LONDON, 18 Nov 1977, *The Lock Gate* (oil on canvas, 40 1/4 x 50 ins / 102 x 127 cm) GBP 1,000. GLASGOW, 4 June 1979, *Still-life with Flowers and Apples* (oil on panel, 18 x 13 1/4 ins / 46 x 33.5 cm) GBP 8,000. GLASGOW, 1 Oct 1981, *In Hyde Park* (ink and colouring pencil, 16 1/4 x 22 ins / 41.5 x 55 cm) GBP 600. GLASGOW, 8 July 1982, *Still-life with Fruit* (oil on card, 15 x 14 1/2 ins / 38 x 37 cm) GBP 2,800. GLASGOW, 7 July 1983, *Still-life with Fruit Bowl* (oil on card, 22 x 17 1/2 ins / 56 x 44.5 cm) GBP 3,600. GLASGOW, 19 April 1984, *St. Monance, Fife* (watercolour, 17 x 22 ins / 43.2 x 55.9 cm) GBP 850. GLASGOW, 12 Dec 1985, *Still-life with Fruit, Glass and Roses* (oil on canvas, 14 x 16 ins / 35.6 x 40.6 cm) GBP 4,500. EDINBURGH, 30 April 1986, *Landscape in the Alpes-Maritimes* (watercolour heightened with coloured chalk, 15 x 17 1/4 ins / 38.2 x 43.8 cm) GBP 1,100. AUCHTERARDER, 1 Sept 1987, *Largo Bay, Fife* (Indian ink and coloured chalk, 13 1/2 x 16 1/4 ins / 34.5 x 41 cm) GBP 2,100. EDINBURGH, 30 Aug 1988, *Still-life with Flowers* (oil on canvas, 15 x 18 ins / 38 x 46 cm) GBP 3,520. GLASGOW, 8 Dec 1988, *Rotten Row in Hyde Park, London* (ink and pencil, 16 3/4 x 22 1/2 ins / 42.5 x 57.3 cm) GBP 6,050; *Cottages at Ceres, near Fife* (oil on panel, 8 1/2 x 11 1/2 ins / 21.6 x 29.2 cm) GBP 6,600; *Still-life with Roses in a Glass, Apples and Grapes on a Table* (oil on canvas, 27 x 22 ins / 68.5 x 55.8 cm) GBP 52,800. GLASGOW, 7 Feb 1989, *Still-life with a Bottle of Wine and Pomegranates* (oil on canvas, 13 3/4 x 11 3/4 ins / 35 x 30 cm) GBP 4,620. PERTH, 29 Aug 1989, *Vase of Flowers* (oil on card, 18 x 15 1/4 ins / 46 x 38.5 cm) GBP 13,200. EDINBURGH, 22 Nov 1989, *Kitchen Sideboard at Larkhall* (oil on card, 18 1/4 x 14 1/4 ins / 46.3 x 36.2 cm) GBP 15,400. GLASGOW, 7 Dec 1989, *Young Boy with a Cockerel* (pencil and watercolour, 26 1/2 x 21 1/2 ins / 67.2 x 54.7 cm) GBP 6,600; *Still-life with an Oriental Vase, a Box of Tea, a Fruit Bowl and Oranges on an Octagonal Table* (oil on card, 30 x 25 ins / 76.2 x 63.5 cm) GBP 39,600. GLASGOW, 6 Feb 1990, *View of Fife* (1920, oil on canvas, 22 x 27 1/4 ins / 56 x 69 cm) GBP 25,300. EDINBURGH, 26 April 1990, *Chrysanthemums in a Chinese Vase with Oranges, Apples, Pears and Grapes on a Stone Ledge* (oil on card, 27 x 22 ins / 68.6 x 55.9 cm) GBP 44,000. PERTH, 27 Aug 1990, *Roses* (oil on card, 26 3/4 x 19 3/4 ins / 68 x 50 cm) GBP 28,600. GLASGOW, 22 Nov 1990, *Young Girl before a Kitchen Table* (watercolour heightened with white, 16 1/2 x 15 ins / 41.9 x 38.2 cm) GBP 3,080. GLASGOW, 5 Feb 1991, *Black Vase* (oil on card, 27 1/4 x 30 ins / 69 x 76 cm) GBP 27,500. PERTH, 26 Aug 1991, *Village on a Hillside* (oil on card, 15 x 18 ins / 38 x 46 cm) GBP 6,600. EDINBURGH, 28 April 1992, *Riverbank at Fife* (oil on canvas, 24 x 19 ins / 61 x 48 cm)

GBP 9,900. EDINBURGH, 19 Nov 1992, *Venetian Street Scene with Figures* (ink and watercolour, 12 1/2 x 8 1/4 ins / 31.7 x 21 cm) GBP 1,650. EDINBURGH, 23 March 1993, *Mediterranean Port* (oil on canvas, 18 x 21 3/4 ins / 45.5 x 55.5 cm) GBP 14,375. GLASGOW, 1 Feb 1994, *Still-life with Fruit and Books* (oil on card, 26 3/4 x 22 1/4 ins / 68 x 56.5 cm) GBP 13,800. PERTH, 29 Aug 1995, *Anemones* (oil on canvas, 20 x 16 ins / 51 x 40.5 cm) GBP 8,050. PERTH, 26 Aug 1996, *Still-life with Fruits* (oil on card, 27 1/4 x 22 1/4 ins / 69 x 56.5 cm) GBP 45,500. EDINBURGH, 27 Nov 1996, *On the Hard, Lower Largo* (oil on panel, 16 x 20 ins / 40.6 x 50.8 cm) GBP 8,050. GLASGOW, 11 Dec 1996, *Portrait of a Young Girl* (oil on canvas, 24 x 19 3/4 ins / 61 x 50 cm) GBP 4,600. AUCHTERARDER, 26 Aug 1997, *Street Scene* (oil on canvas, 20 x 24 ins / 51 x 61 cm) GBP 24,150. GLASGOW, 20 Nov 1997, *Pomegranates and a Black Bottle* (c. 1910, oil on panel, 14 x 18 1/4 ins / 35.5 x 46.3 cm) GBP 13,800; *Rotten Row, Hyde Park, London* (1931, pastel, 13 3/4 x 16 3/4 ins / 35 x 42.5 cm) GBP 4,025. LONDON, 28 Oct 1999, *Still-life with Yellow Vase* (oil on board, 30 x 24 ins / 76 x 61 cm) GBP 32,000. EDINBURGH, 3 Dec 1999, *Still-life Roses, Fruit and Knife* (oil on board, 18 x 15 ins / 45 x 37 cm) GBP 34,000. LONDON, 10 April 2000, *Cornfield in Fife* (oil on board, 20 x 27 ins / 52 x 68 cm) GBP 47,000. EDINBURGH, 16 Dec 2000, *Still-life of Pink Roses, Fruit and Fabrics* (oil on board, 20 x 18 ins / 50 x 45 cm) GBP 48,000. LONDON, 9 April 2001, *Still-life with Flowers and Fruit* (oil on board, 27 x 22 ins / 68 x 56 cm) GBP 68,000. LONDON, 28 June 2001, *Still-life with Lemons, Grapes, Rose and Pewter Coffee Pot* (oil on canvas, 22 x 18 ins / 56 x 46 cm) GBP 74,000. LONDON, 15 April 2002, *Mill Dam, Fife. Portrait of Tom Honeyman* (1923, oil on canvas, double-sided, 25 x 30 ins / 63 x 76 cm) GBP 42,000. EDINBURGH, 22 Aug 2002, *Pink Roses in a Chinese Vase* (oil on canvas, 18 x 12 ins / 46 x 30 cm) GBP 46,000. LONDON, 27 Aug 2003, *Still-life with Apples and a Rose* (oil on canvas, 26 x 21 ins / 67 x 54 cm) GBP 40,000. LONDON, 27 Aug 2003, *Still-life with Tulips and Fruit* (oil on board, 22 x 18 ins / 56 x 46 cm) GBP 75,000. LONDON, 28 Oct 2004, *House Boats, Loch Lomond* (oil on canvas, 20 x 24 ins / 50 x 61 cm) GBP 124,000. LONDON, 19 Nov 2004, *Fruit and Pink Rose in a Blue Vase* (1931, oil on board, 18 x 15 ins / 45 x 38 cm) GBP 30,000.

HUNTER, George Sherwood

British, 19th - 20th century.
Born c. 1850, in Aberdeen; died 1919 or 1920.
Painter. Genre scenes, landscapes.
Newlyn School.

George Sherwood Hunter was an enthusiastic traveller whose artistic career flourished after 1898, when he settled in Newlyn, near Penzance in Cornwall. He became a member of the town's renowned artists' colony, and was soon asked to give painting classes by the painters Stanhope and Elizabeth Forbes. Hunter features prominently in the 1906 biography of Stanhope and Elizabeth by Mrs Lionel Birch. He was a member of the Royal Society of British Artists, and exhibited regularly with the Royal Academy and at the Suffolk Street Gallery from 1889. His paintings feature views of France, Holland, Spain, Palestine, Italy, Scotland and England. His views of Newlyn are among his finest works. Contemporary critics praised his distinctive artistic personality although today many of his pictures seem imbued with the artistic traits of the various countries in which he worked. Hunter's work featured in numerous exhibitions in Europe and Chicago, from 1882 to 1911.

AUCTION RECORDS:

LONDON, 15 Oct 1976, *Go Away* (oil on canvas, 29 1/2 x 19 1/2 ins / 75 x 49.5 cm) GBP 400. LONDON, 13 May 1977, *The Wailing Wall, Jerusalem* (1894; oil on canvas, 30 x 40 1/2 ins / 76.2 x 103 cm) GBP 5,500. LONDON, 29 Feb 1980, *Sick Child* (1891, oil on canvas, 39 3/4 x 29 3/4 ins / 101 x 75.5 cm) GBP 450. LONDON, 22 Oct 1986, *The Wailing Wall* (1894, watercolour heightened with gouache, 7 x 14 ins / 18 x 35.5 cm) GBP 1,500. LONDON, 18 Oct 1990, *Daybreak at Volendam* (1862, oil on canvas, 30 x 20 ins / 76.2 x 50.7 cm) GBP 3,080; *Aberdeen* (oil on canvas, 10 x 20 ins / 25.4 x 50.8 cm) GBP 1,100; *Breton Beach with Figures* (oil on canvas, 12 3/4 x 18 ins / 32.4 x 45.7 cm) GBP 4,400; *The Last days of Carnaval, Via Flamina, Rome* (1876, oil on canvas, 12 x 9 ins / 30.4 x 22.9 cm) GBP 1,650; *View of Jerusalem* (oil on canvas, 12 x 17 3/4 ins / 30.4 x 45.2 cm) GBP 605; *Fishermen on the Quayside* (oil on canvas, 8 1/4 x 10 1/2 ins / 20.9 x 26.7 cm) GBP 1,210; *The Waterfront, London* (1886, oil on canvas, 7 x 14 ins / 17.7 x 35.6 cm) GBP 1,870. LONDON, 3 June 1992, *Haymaking* (oil on canvas, 20 x 30 ins / 50.5 x 76 cm) GBP 880. LONDON, 8-9 June 1993, *Venice* (1887, oil on canvas, 11 1/4 x 23 3/4 ins / 28.5 x 60.5 cm) GBP 1,725. LONDON, 5 Sept 1996, *Young Dutchwoman* (oil on canvas, 18 x 12 ins / 45.8 x 30.5 cm) GBP 2,530.

HUNTER, H.C.

British, 19th century.
Sculptor.

H.C. Hunter exhibited her work at the Royal Academy in London in 1843.

HUNTER, James

British, 19th century.
Active c. 1800.
Draughtsman.

James Hunter drew the illustrations for *History of the Indies*.

HUNTER, James Brownley

British, 19th century.
Born 1855, in Edinburgh.
Engraver.

James Brownley Hunter's work includes several engravings after Velázquez.

HUNTER, John Kelso

British, 19th century.
Born 15 December 1802, in Dunkeith; died 3 February 1873, near Glasgow.
Painter. Portraits.

John Kelso Hunter was an artist of considerable repute.

HUNTER, Mason

British, 19th - 20th century.
Born 1854, in Broxburn; died 1921.
Painter. Landscapes, seascapes.

Mason Hunter trained at the Edinburgh College of Art.

AUCTION RECORDS:

EDINBURGH, 2 May 1991, *View of Edinburgh from Craigleath Quarry* (oil on card by the artist, 13 1/4 x 10 ins / 33.7 x 25.3 cm) GBP 462.

HUNTER, Matthew

Irish, 18th century.
Active in Dublin in 1779.
Pastellist, miniaturist.

HUNTER, Robert

Irish, 18th century.
Born at the beginning of the 18th century, in Ireland.
Active c. 1752-1803.
Painter.

Robert Hunter was an artist of considerable merit. He was a pupil of Pope the Elder, and in Dublin he enjoyed the reputation of being the most noteworthy portrait painter in Ireland from 1745. He was one of the founders of the school of art in Dublin.

The perfect resemblance of his models, the harmonious colours and his excellent technique earned him his reputation.

MUSEUMS AND GALLERIES:

DUBLIN (City Hall): *Portrait of the Earl of Buckinghamshire* (dated 1780).

AUCTION RECORDS:
NEW YORK, 14 and 15 April 1904, *Young Man in a Blue Suit,* USD 120. NEW YORK, 5 June 1925, *Francis Hutchinson, Esquire,* GBP 54. NEW YORK, 10 July 1931, *Portrait of a Woman,* GBP 78. NEW YORK, 3 Dec 1942, *Admiral John Macbride,* USD 700. LONDON, 11 Oct 1946, *Portrait of a Woman,* GBP 42. LONDON, 24 June 1977, *Portrait of John Conroy* (oil on canvas, 25 1/2 x 21 ins / 64.8 x 53.3 cm) GBP 700. LONDON, 21 Nov 1984, *Portrait of William Digby* (oil on canvas, 29 1/4 x 24 3/4 ins / 74.5 x 63 cm) GBP 6,800. LONDON, 15 July 1987, *Portrait of the Honorable Christopher O'Brien* (1766, oil on canvas, 58 1/2 x 44 1/2 ins / 148.5 x 113 cm) GBP 4,500. LONDON, 7 Oct 1992, *Portrait of Arthur Guinness, Founder of the Guinness Breweries in 1754* (oil on canvas, 35 1/2 x 28 1/2 ins / 90 x 72.5 cm) GBP 3,740. LONDON, 13 April 1994, *Portrait of Sarah Monck, Seated Near a Table, Wearing a Blue Dress and Holding a Book* (oil on canvas, 49 1/2 x 39 1/4 ins / 125.5 x 100 cm) GBP 2,070. LONDON, 19 May 2000, *Portrait of James Fitzgerald, Earl of Kildare Holding Tricorn with Landscape* (oil on canvas, 50 x 40 ins / 127 x 102 cm) GBP 20,000. LONDON, 17 May 2002, *Group Portrait of George Rochfort, 2nd Earl of Belvedere, and his Wife* (oil on canvas, 52 x 61 ins / 132 x 155 cm) GBP 130,000. DUBLIN, 28 May 2003, *Portrait of a Militia Officer in Uniform* (1764, oil on canvas, painted oval, 31 x 26 ins / 78 x 65 cm) EUR 8,200. LONDON, 13 May 2004, *Portrait of James Fitzgerald, 20th Earl of Kildare* (oil on canvas, 50 x 40 ins / 127 x 102 cm) GBP 25,000.

HUNTER, Robert
Australian, 20th - 21st century.
Born 1947, in Melbourne.
Painter.
Minimal Art.

Robert Hunter has been influenced by Carl André, Sol Lewitt and Robert Ryman. He has taken part in group exhibitions, including in 1968 *The Field* at the National Gallery of Victoria, Melbourne; in 1974 *Eight Contemporary Artists* at the Museum of Modern Art, New York; in 1975 at the Lisson Gallery, London; and in 1980 at the Paris Biennale.

Hunter paints on canvas, direct on to walls or on plywood. His paintings are monochrome, broken by a few sustained straight, horizontal, vertical and diagonal lines.

HUNTER, T.
British, 18th century.
Active in Armagh, Northern Ireland c. 1787.
Miniaturist, pastellist.

HUNTER, William
British, 18th century.
Active in London at the end of the 18th century.
Painter. History painting, portraits.

William Hunter painted some historical paintings after Redgrave.

HUNTER, William
British, 20th century.
Died 1967.
Painter. Animals.

William Hunter was a member of the Royal Drawing Society.

AUCTION RECORDS:
EDINBURGH, 26 April 1990, *Grey Rabbit* (oil on canvas, 14 x 18 ins / 35.5 x 45.7 cm) GBP 2,860. SAN FRANCISCO, 30 March 2004, *Morag, a Favourite Westie* (oil on canvas, 20 x 16 ins / 51 x 40 cm) USD 3,500.

HUNTINGDON, Francis H.
British, 19th century.
Active in Wanstead.
Landscape artist.

Huntingdon took part in the big London exhibitions between 1849 and 1878.

HUNTINGTON, Alonso St George
American, 19th - 20th century.
Born 2 June 1868, in Fort Leavenworth; died 3 August 1941, in Chicago.
Painter. Landscapes.

Alonso St-Georges Huntington studied in Paris under William Bouguereau and Tony Robert-Fleury. He worked in Versailles and Chicago.

HUNTINGTON, Anna Vaughan Hyatt
American, 19th - 20th century.
Born 10 March 1876, in Cambridge (Massachusetts); died 4 October 1973.
Sculptor. Animals.

Anny Hyatt Huntington studied in Boston under sculptor Henry Hudson Kittleson, and at the Art Students League in 1895 under Hermon Atkins MacNeil. She worked for sculptor Gutzon Borglum. Hyatt Huntington was the daughter of Harvard University palaeontology professor Alpheus Hyatt, who encouraged her interest in animals, which became a favourite subject of her art work, particularly wild cats - as in her bronzes *Jaguar* and *Yawning Panther* (c. 1925). Her earlier subjects were domestic animals seen on a farm at Porto Bello, Maryland, but she moved to modelling wild animals at the New York Zoological Park. Hyatt Huntington's bronze pieces were made with the lost-wax method of casting.

While best known for her animal pieces, Hyatt Huntington also made figurative statues, busts and medallions, such as *Joan of Arc* (shown at the 1910 Paris Salon), or the equestrian sculpture *El Cid Campeador* (1927), placed in Seville, Spain. She and her husband, the collector Archer Milton Huntington, established the first public outdoor sculpture garden in the USA, located on their private estate in South Carolina (now called Brookgreen Gardens). Hyatt Huntington received the Purple Rosette from the French government; a bronze medal at Saint Louis (1904); an honourable mention at the Salon des Artistes Français in Paris (1910); the Shaw Prize and the Watrous Gold Medal from the National Academy of Design, New York; a gold medal from the Pennsylvania Academy of the Fine Arts; and a gold medal from the Allied Artists of America. She was also made Chevalier of the Legion of Honour in France and was a member of the following groups and institutions: National Academy of Design, National Sculpture Society, American Federation of Arts, National Institute of Arts and Letters, National Association of Women Artists.

BIBLIOGRAPHY:
Anna Hyatt Huntington, W.W. Norton, New York, 1947. Schaub-Koch, Emile, *Hindu Art and the Art of Anna Hyatt Huntington,* Lisbon, 1958. Schaub-Koch, Emile, *Anna Hyatt-Huntington and the Hindu People,* Lisbon, 1960. Evans, Cerinda W., *Anna Hyatt Huntington,* Mariners Museum, Newport News (VA), 1965. Slate, Charles, *The Archer and Anna Hyatt Huntington Sculpture Garden,* Wyrick, Charleston (SC), 2003.

MUSEUMS AND GALLERIES:
BOSTON (MFA) - CHARLESTON (Gibbes MA): *Fawns Playing* (1934, bronze) - DENVER (AM) - JACKSON HOLE (National Mus. of Wildlife Art): *Yawning Panther* (1917, bronze) - NEW BRITAIN (New Britain Museum of American Art) - NEW YORK (Central Park): *Equestrian Statue of José Marti* (1959) - NEW YORK (Hispanic Society of America): *El Cid* - NEW YORK (Metropolitan Mus. of Art) - NEW YORK (National Academy of Design Mus.): *Diana* (1922, bronze) - ROCHESTER, NY (Memorial Art Gallery, University of Rochester): *Joan of Arc* (1915, bronze); *African Animals Medal* (bronze medal); *Joan of Arc Medal* (1919, bronze medal); *Monkey and Bird* (before 1923, bronze) - ROSLYN HARBOR, NY (Nassau County Muse-

um of Art): *Jaguar* (bronze) - SAN FRANCISCO (FAM): *Bust of Archer M. Huntington* (1927, bronze); *Yawning Tiger* (c. 1925, bronze); *Greyhounds* (1936, cast aluminium); *Collis P. Huntington* (bronze) - WASHINGTON DC (National Mus. of Women in the Arts): *Yawning Panther* (bronze).
AUCTION RECORDS:
NEW YORK, 21 April 1977, *Panther* (brownish-green patinated bronze, l. 28 ins / 71.2 cm) USD 2,000. NEW YORK, 30 April 1980, *Parrot* (1936, bluish-green patinated bronze, h. 27 1/2 ins / 69.8 cm) USD 5,000. NEW YORK, 1 July 1982, *Mountain Lion* (brownish-green patinated bronze, h. 6 1/2 ins / 16.5 cm) USD 3,500. NEW YORK, 2 June 1983, *Queen Isabella Going Through the Land of her People* (1961, brownish-green patinated bronze, h. 49 3/4 ins / 126.4 cm) USD 7,500. NEW YORK, 31 May 1985, *Yawning Tiger* (brownish-green patinated bronze, l. 28 1/4 ins / 71.8 cm) USD 9,000. NEW YORK, 4 Dec 1987, *Pair of Great Danes* (granite, h. 50 ins / 127.3 cm and 51 1/4 ins/130.2 cm) USD 100,000. NEW YORK, 17 March 1988, *Mother Bear and her Cub Playing* (brown-patinated bronze, l. 6 ins / 15 cm) USD 2,970. NEW YORK, 24 May 1990, *Three Elephants* (1902, brown-patinated bronze, h. 9 1/2 ins / 24.1 cm) USD 12,650. NEW YORK, 17 Dec 1990, *Jaguar on the Look-out* (gilded-patinated bronze, h. 6 ins / 15.2 cm) USD 2,310. NEW YORK, 14 March 1991, *Bull Charging the Cape* (reddish-brown-patinated bronze, h. 7 1/2 ins / 19.1 cm, l. 15 1/2 ins/39.4 cm) USD 3,520. NEW YORK, 15 May 1991, *Yawning Tiger* (bronze on a Verona red marble plinth, l. 13 ins / 33 cm) USD 3,850. NEW YORK, 26 Sept 1991, *Stag* (bronze, 19 ins / 48.5 cm) USD 3,300. NEW YORK, 14 Nov 1991, *Grizzly Bear* (bronze, h. 3 ins / 7.9 cm) USD 1,760. NEW YORK, 15 April 1992, *Growling Tiger* (brown-patinated bronze, l. 13 1/4 ins / 33.7 cm) USD 4,400. NEW YORK, 28 May 1992, *Get Up, Mum, I'm Hungry!* (1934, group in aluminium of a female zebra and her foal, h. 20 1/2 ins / 52 cm, l. 26 ins/66.3 cm) USD 12,100. NEW YORK, 21 Sept 1994, *Lion and Lioness* (bronze, h. 11 1/4 ins / 28.6 cm, l. 30 ins/76.2 cm) USD 25,300. NEW YORK, 23 May 1996, *Yawning Tiger* (bronze, h. 28 ins / 71.1 cm) USD 27,600. NEW YORK, 27 Sept 1996, *Yawning Tiger* (greenish-brown patinated bronze, l. 28 1/4 ins / 71.8 cm) USD 27,600. NEW YORK, 4 Dec 1996, *Yawning Tiger* (1917, bronze, h. 28 ins / 71 cm) USD 27,600. NEW YORK, 7 Oct 1997, *Winter Noon* (bronze, group, h. 7 1/4 ins / 18.4 cm) USD 10,350. NEW YORK, 3 Dec 1997, *Yawning Tiger* (green-patinated bronze, w. 28 ins / 71.1 cm) USD 28,750.

HUNTINGTON, Daniel W.
American, 19th - 20th century.
Born 14 October 1816, in New York; died 18 April 1906, in New York.
Painter. History painting, genre scenes, portraits, landscapes.

Daniel W. Huntington was a pupil of Morse and Inman. He went to Italy to work in 1839, notably in Florence and Rome. He returned to America and for a time dedicated himself to portrait painting, then went back to Rome in 1844, returning to the USA in 1850.

Huntington was elected president of the National Academy of Design, New York in 1862, having been a member since 1842. He resigned this post in 1869, but was re-elected in 1877. His painting of *Charles the Fifth in Bologna* attracted a great deal of attention at the Philadelphia Exhibition in 1876.
AUCTION RECORDS:
NEW YORK, 25-30 March 1901, *Velvet Hat*, USD 105. NEW YORK, 16-17 Feb 1911, *Landscape*, USD 200. NEW YORK, 25 March 1931, *Landscape*, USD 150. NEW YORK, 17 June 1970, *The Burgomaster of Amsterdam* (1887) USD 750. NEW YORK, 27 Jan 1972, *Young Greek Peasant Woman*, USD 1,600. NEW YORK, 17 Nov 1978, *Portrait of Dr Oliver Walcott Gibbs* (oil on canvas, 30 x 25 ins / 76.2 x 63.5 cm) USD 1,600. NEW YORK, 24 April 1981, *Ariadne* (1862, oil on canvas, 12 x 10 ins / 30.7 x 25.4 cm) USD 3,000. PORTLAND, 22 Sept 1984, *Huntsman and His Dog* (watercolour and gouache, 13 1/2 x 21 1/2 ins / 34.5 x 54.5 cm) USD 1,500. NEW YORK, 29 May 1987, *My Pleasure Ground* (oil on canvas, 18 x 14 ins / 45.7 x 35.5 cm) USD 2,600. NEW YORK, 17 March 1988, *Portrait Presumed to be of Nathaniel Platt Bailey* (1871, oil on canvas, 33 1/2 x 26 1/2 ins / 85 x 67.5 cm) USD 770. NEW YORK, 16 March 1990, *Portrait of Elizabeth Mason Turner* (oil on canvas, 27 x 22 ins / 68.5 x 56 cm) USD 2,420. NEW YORK, 6 Dec 1991, *Ruins along a River* (oil on canvas, 25 x 30 ins / 63.7 x 76 cm) USD 26,400. NEW YORK, 29 Nov 1995, *Lake Minnewaska* (1889, oil on canvas, 25 x 38 ins / 63.5 x 96.5 cm) USD 14,950.

HUNTLEY (Miss)
British, 19th century.
Active in London.
Painter. Genre scenes.

Huntley exhibited at the Royal Academy in London between 1816 and 1825.

HUNTLEY, Samantha Littlefield
British, 19th century.
Born 12 May 1865, in Watervliet.
Painter. Portraits, genre scenes.

Samantha Huntley was a pupil of Lefebvre and Grasset in Paris. She subsequently lived in Albany.

HUNTLY, J.L.
British, 19th century.
Active in Bath c. 1830.
Engraver. Ex-libris.

HUNTLY, T.D.
British, 19th century.
Active in London c. 1815.
Engraver. Ex-libris.

HUNTON, Charlotte (Miss)
British, 19th century.
Active in Torquay.
Sculptor.

Charlotte Hunton exhibited her work at the Royal Academy in London in 1892 and 1893.

HUNTON, Edith
British, 19th century.
Active in Torquay in 1889.
Sculptor.

HUNTSMAN, Maud
British, 20th century.
Active in London.
Painter.

Maud Hunstman was a member of the Royal Drawing Society.

HUNY
French, 18th century.
Active in Sèvres from 1785 to 1795.
Sculptor.

Huny worked as a sculptor at the Sèvres china works and his name figures on the records of attendance at a monthly salary of 72 francs. There is no sign of him after 1795.
MUSEUMS AND GALLERIES:
ORLÉANS: *Napoleon Bonaparte, First Consul* (bust in Sèvres porcelain bisque).

HUNYADY, Laszlo
Hungarian, 19th century.
Born 10 March 1857, in Jasz-mihalyteleh; died 1906, in Rozsahegy.
Painter.

Laszlo Hunyady studied in Budapest.

HUNZIKER, Durs
Swiss, 16th century.
Active in Aarau.
Glass painter.

HUNZIKER, Eduard
Swiss, 19th century.
Born 18 December 1827, in Biel; died 11 February 1901, in Florence.
Painter.
He worked mainly in Aarau and Bern.

HUNZIKER, Elise
Swiss, 19th century.
Born 15 March 1860, in Kulm (near Lucerne).
Painter. Still-lifes.

HUNZIKER, Frieda
Dutch, 20th century.
Born 1908, in Amsterdam; died 1966.
Painter.
Frieda Hunziker studied to be a teacher of design and taught in a school in Haarlem. She did not begin producing work of her own until 1938. After World War II, she was influenced by the activities of the CoBrA group, though she did not belong to it, and from 1945 onwards her work gradually became more abstract. She travelled to the then Dutch East Indies in 1951-52. Her work was shown at collective exhibitions of contemporary Dutch painting, and at international collective exhibitions, notably at the Salon des Réalités Nouvelles in Paris (1949 and 1950); the Carnegie International Exhibition in Pittsburgh (1952); the São Paulo Biennale (1953). A retrospective exhibition of her work was held at the Stedelijk Museum in Amsterdam in 1962.

Although she borrows themes from Informal Abstraction, Hunziker's work is nearer to the Lyrical Abstraction of Hartung or Soulages.

AUCTION RECORDS:
AMSTERDAM, 24 May 1989, *Abstract Composition* (oil on canvas, 29 1/2 x 59 ins / 75 x 150 cm) NLG 1,955. AMSTERDAM, 12 Dec 1990, *The Ghosts* (oil on canvas, 27 1/4 x 35 1/2 ins / 69.5 x 90 cm) NLG 6,325. AMSTERDAM, 8 Feb 1994, *Abstract Composition* (1951, ink and gouache/paper, 17 3/4 x 22 ins / 45 x 55 cm) NLG 4,025. AMSTERDAM, 7 Dec 1994, *Abstract Composition* (oil on canvas, 39 1/4 x 49 1/4 ins / 100 x 125 cm) NLG 5,750. AMSTERDAM, 30 May 1995, *Green Line* (oil on canvas, 35 1/2 x 47 1/4 ins / 90 x 120 cm) NLG 7,250. AMSTERDAM, 10 June 1999, *Geste 1* (oil on canvas, 18 x 22 ins / 46 x 55 cm) NLG 6,000. AMSTERDAM, 27 May 2003, *Untitled* (1950-1951, gouache, 18 x 22 ins / 45 x 55 cm) EUR 2,600.

HUNZIKER, Jean
Swiss, 19th century.
Born 1798, in Aarau; died 6 September 1868, in Rolle.
Painter, draughtsman. Portraits.

MUSEUMS AND GALLERIES:
LAUSANNE: several drawings.

HUNZIKER, Max
Swiss, 20th century.
Born 1901, in Zurich; died 1976, in Zurich.
Painter (gouache). Figures, portraits, landscapes.
Although he was not a naive artist, Hunziker's paintings have something of the freshness of vision and rendition of naive art.

AUCTION RECORDS:
BERN, 22 Oct 1976, *Dancer* (1932, oil on card, 12 1/2 x 16 ins / 31.5 x 40.5 cm) CHF 2,200. ZURICH, 30 May 1979, *Two Women* (oil on canvas, 16 1/4 x 13 ins / 41 x 33 cm) CHF 2,200. ZURICH, 13 Oct 1993, *Self-portrait* (1929, tempera, 19 x 16 1/2 ins / 48.5 x 42 cm) CHF 2,000. ZURICH, 12 June 1995, *View of the Limmatquai and Grossmunster in Zurich* (1957, tempera and casein/synthetic resin, 35 1/2 x 59 ins / 90 x 150 cm) CHF 17,250. ZURICH, 8 April 1997, *Red Wine* (1932, oil on canvas, 59 x 55 ins / 150 x 140 cm) CHF 4,600. ZURICH, 28 Nov 2000, *Artist at Easel* (oil on canvas, 38 x 51 ins / 96 x 129 cm) CHF 3,000.

HUNZIKER, Werner
Swiss, 20th century.
Born 29 June 1894, in Aarau.
Painter, decorative designer. Murals, stage sets.
Hunziker was a member of the society of Swiss painters, sculpteurs and architects. Work by him was exhibited in Paris, at the Salon de la Société Nationale des Beaux-Arts and the Salon d'Automne. He was awarded a gold medal in 1925 at the decorative arts exhibition for his decorative scheme for a theatre.

Hunziker painted several murals in Switzerland and undertook major work on decorative schemes for theatres and opera houses.

HUNZINGER, Claudie
French, 20th century.
Born 1940, in Turckheim (Haut-Rhin).
Mixed media. Artists' books.
Claudie Hunzinger is a self-taught artist. She makes sheets of paper out of herbs, berries, mosses, bark and leaves, which she gathers herself and subjects to a process of transmutation. In this way she reveals the handwriting and signs peculiar to each plant, according to its botanical family. She describes her works as 'pages of herbs', written in the 'language of herbs'.

Exhibitions of her work include: 1985, *Livres d'Artiste* (*Artists' Books*), Bibliothèque publique d'information du Centre Georges-Pompidou, Paris; 1988, *Soft Art* (*Soft Art*), Barbican Centre, London; 2002, *Retour d'exploration et spinosa/Spinoza* (*Returning from the Exploration and Spinosa/Spinoza*), FRAC Alsace, Sélestat. Her solo exhibitions have included: 1996, *49 couleurs trouvées* (*49 Colours Found*), Musée des Arts Décoratifs, Lausanne; 2003, with the photographer Françoise Saur, *V'herbe Écrire. La Recherche: l'Écriture des Plantes* (*In Search of the Handwriting of Plants*), Musée d'Art et d'Histoire, Galerie du Granit, Belfort, and Musée de la Vallée, Barcelonnette (Alpes-de-Haute-Provence).

BIBLIOGRAPHY:
Caujolle, Christian, *Image/Objet*, group exhibition catalogue, Paris, 1983. Moeglin-Delcroix, Anne, *Livres d'artistes*, group exhibition catalogue, Éd. du Centre Georges-Pompidou, Paris, 1985. Molinari, Danielle, *Soft Art*, group exhibition catalogue, Barbican Centre, London, 1989. *V'herbe*, exhibition catalogue, Musée d'Art et d'Histoire, Belfort, 2003.

MUSEUMS AND GALLERIES:
AIX-EN-PROVENCE (Mus. des Tapisseries) - LAUSANNE (MDA) - PARIS (FNAC) - ST-DIÉ (MBA).

HUNZINGER, Werner
German, 19th century.
Born 17 March 1816, in Krefeld; died in New York.
Painter. Portraits, landscapes, still-lifes.

HUOT
French, 14th century.
Active in Gray.
Glass painter.
In 1373 Huot was working at the Château de Gray.

HUOT, Adolphe Joseph
French, 19th century.
Born 15 November 1839, in Paris; died 19 February 1883, in Cannes.
Engraver.
Adolphe Huot was taught by Henriquel-Dupont and Cogniet. He entered the École des Beaux-Arts on 7 October, and

won the Prix de Rome in 1862. He was awarded a first-class medal in 1875 and a medal of honour in 1878 at the Exposition Universelle. He was also made a Chevalier of the Légion d'Honneur in 1878.

HUOT, Charles Édouard
Canadian, 19th - 20th century.
Born 1855, in Quebec; died 1930, in Quebec.
From 1874 to c. 1885 active in France.
Painter. Historical subjects, religious subjects, landscapes, self-portraits. Church decoration.

Charles Édouard Huot's talent was noticed when he was still a young man. He was granted a travelling bursary which enabled him to register at the École des Beaux-Arts, Paris, in 1874, in the studio of Alexandre Cabanel. In 1877, he took part in the Salon des Artistes Français with *The Good Samaritan*. After returning to Quebec, he continued to go on frequent study trips to Europe.

The paintings Huot produced as a young man in Quebec were pleasant landscapes, but he was ambitious to paint historical events or biblical scenes. When he was commissioned to decorate the church of St-Saviour in Quebec in 1887, he was able to devote himself entirely to the painting of historical or biblical compositions. In 1900 he executed *Battle on the Plains of Abraham*, and from 1910 to 1913 *Debate on Languages* for the Parliamentary Palace, Quebec. The style of these paintings is typical of *fin-de-siècle* official painting.

BIBLIOGRAPHY:
Ostiquy, Jean René, *Charles Huot*, National Gallery of Canada, Ottawa, 1979.

MUSEUMS AND GALLERIES:
OTTAWA (NG. of Canada) - PONTOISE: *The Good Samaritan* (1877) - QUEBEC: *Debate on Languages* (1910, sketch); other sketches.

AUCTION RECORDS:
MONTREAL, 1 Dec 1992, *Self-portrait* (oil on panel, 9 x 6 ins / 22.8 x 15.2 cm) CAD 2,100.

HUOT, E.
French, 19th century.
Lithographer.

In around 1845 this artist was working in St Petersburg, Russia.

HUOT, Eugène
French, 19th century.
Painter. History painting, portraits.

Eugène Huot exhibited at the Paris Salon between 1836 and 1841.

AUCTION RECORDS:
PARIS, 23 April 1990, *Cavalry Engagement* (oil on canvas, 27 1/4 x 32 1/4 ins / 69 x 82 cm) FRF 20,000.

HUOT, François
French, 18th century.
Active in Paris.
Draughtsman, engraver (burin). Historical portraits.

AUCTION RECORDS:
PARIS, 6 March 1942, *The Arrest*; *The Surprise* (wash) FRF 350.

HUOT, Georges Eugène
French, 19th century.
Born in the 19th century, in Paris.
Painter, engraver (etching).

George Huot's teachers were F. André, Léon Cogniet and Brunet-Debaines. He made his début at the Salon in 1875.

MUSEUMS AND GALLERIES:
LONDON (Victoria and Albert Mus.): *The Benoit-Lance Gate in Périgueux* (etching published by Cadart); *At Andresieux* (etching published by Cadart); *Kerostin, a Peninsula of Quiberon* (etching published by Cadart).

HUOT, Gustave
French, 19th century.
Active in Paris.
Engraver.

Gustave Huot was a pupil of Demangeot, and the cousin of Adolphe Huot. He was a heraldic engraver, and engraved a few burin studies between approximately 1854 and 1857.

HUOT, Hyppolyte Benoît
French, 19th century.
Born March 1795, in Paris.
Engraver.

HUOT, Louis Edmond
French, 20th century.
Born 15 October 1894, in Épinac-les-Mines (Saône-et-Loire).
Painter, designer.

Huot exhibited frequently at events in the Bourgogne region. He also showed in Paris at the Salon des Indépendants.

HUOT, Louis Eugène
French, 19th century.
Born in the 19th century, in Paris.
Painter.

Louis Huot studied with P. Delaroche and Henriquel. He started submitting charcoal drawings to the Salon in 1870.

HUOT, Robert
American, 20th century.
Born 1935, in Staten Island (New York).
Painter.
Conceptual Art, Minimal Art.

Robert Huot lives and works in New York. He took part in exhibitions dedicated to Minimal Art, notably *Reality Art* in Paris in 1968, held at the Galeries Nationales du Grand Palais, presented by E.C. Goossen.

BIBLIOGRAPHY:
L'Art du réel, U.S.A., 1948-1968, group exhibition catalogue, Galeries nationales du Grand Palais, Paris, 1968.

HUP, Aemilius
Dutch, 17th century.
Active in Dordrecht c. 1650.
Sculptor.

HUP, Samuel, or Huppe
Dutch, 17th century.
Active in Dordrecht c. 1650.
Sculptor.

Either Samuel or Aemilius Hup taught Abraham van Kalraat.

HUPÉ, Martial E. L.
French, 19th - 20th century.
Painter, sculptor. Still-lifes, flowers.

Hupé worked in St-Pierre-les-Nemours. He exhibited in Paris at the Salon des Artistes Français, of which he became a member in 1887.

AUCTION RECORDS:
NEW YORK, 19 July 1990, *Still-life with White and Purple Lilacs* (oil on canvas, 39 1/2 x 29 ins / 100.4 x 73.7 cm) USD 6,875. LONDON, 20 Nov 1996, *Bouquet of Roses* (oil on canvas, 21 1/2 x 15 1/4 ins / 54.5 x 39 cm) GBP 3,220. LONDON, 5 July 2001, *Roses in a Vase on a Mantle* (oil on canvas, 22 x 16 ins / 56 x 41 cm) GBP 2,500.

HUPET, André
Belgian, 20th century.
Born 1922, in Mons.
Sculptor, potter.

Hupet was a student of Albert Duriau, Léon Navez and Louis Buisseret at the fine arts academy in Mons. In 1947 he was awarded the Prix Godecharle. He became a professor at the

Mons academy and was a member of the (Maîtrise de Nimy).

Hupet produced monumental works for Charleroi (at the Palais des Beaux-Arts, the Palais de Justice and the Palais des Expositions), as well as for Mons, Ghlin and Tournai.

HUPPE, Henri
French, 19th century.
Born in Paris.
Sculptor.

Huppe made his Salon début in 1874.

HUPPES, Nicolas
Dutch, 20th century.
Born 21 October 1913, in Leeuwarden.
Painter.

HÜPPI, Alfonso
German, 20th century.
Born 1938, in Freiburg im Breisgau.
Sculptor.

Alfonso Hüppi was active in Baden-Baden and Düsseldorf. His work has been shown at many collective exhibitions, including the German Youth Art Prize exhibition (1966); *Directions 67* in Dortmund (1967); *Light - Movement - Colour* in Nuremberg (1967); *Young German Sculptors* in Duisburg (1968); in Norway, Finland, and Germany, *40 Germans Under 40*, (1969-70). In 1969, he won the Mogner and Soest prizes, and he has had solo exhibitions in Baden-Baden, Venice, Düsseldorf, Basel, Karlsruhe and elsewhere.

He makes reliefs from cut up and superimposed planks of wood, his motifs often reminiscent of popular ornaments.

BIBLIOGRAPHY:

IIIe Salon international des Galeries Pilotes, exhibition catalogue, Musée cantonal, Lausanne, 1970.

AUCTION RECORDS:

HEIDELBERG, 12 Oct 1991, *Pink Clouds* (1974, wooden relief in colour, 9 x 13 x 1 1/2 ins / 23 x 33 x 3.5 cm) DEM 2,500. MUNICH, 20 Nov 1999, *Wooden Object* (wood, 52 x 37x2 ins / 131 x 95x4 cm) DEM 8,300. STUTTGART, 27 Sept 2001, *Untitled* (wood, h. 62 ins / 157 cm) DEM 3,300. COLOGNE, 2 Dec 2004, *Colourful Object* (1965, casein wood, 25 x 34 ins / 63 x 87 cm) EUR 1,600.

HUQUET, Jacques Gabriel
French, 18th century.
Active in Paris in 1763.
Painter.

HUQUIER, Daniel
French, 18th century.
Active at the beginning of the 18th century.
Painter, engraver (wood).

Daniel Huquier may be the same artist as Jacques Gabriel Huquier.

HUQUIER, Gabriel, or Hucquier
French, 18th century.
Born 9 May 1695, in Orléans; died 11 June 1772, in Paris.
Painter, engraver, designer of ornamental architectural features, print dealer.

There is much confusion about the biography and whereabouts of the Huquiers, apparently because of mistakes in earlier works about Gabriel and Jacques Gabriel. Le Blanc swaps their first names around, giving the father the names of the son. Bryan's Dictionary states that Gabriel died in London, yet there is a certificate of burial drawn up in the parish of St-Benoît for the 30 June 1772 to prove the opposite. His alleged flight to England following the publication of a pamphlet attacking the Jesuits and subsequently pinned on him has not been verified and fits better with what we know of Jacques Gabriel. Because of their place in the history of French engraving, it is a matter of no small importance to get as clear a view as possible of these artists.

Gabriel Huquier was born in a well-off Orléans family (he is entered as a burgher of the city in a marriage certificate). There is no record of his apprenticeship, but by 1722 his reputation earned him work from Antoine Watteau, Claude Gillot, Aurèle Meissonnier, Gilles-Marie Oppernod, J. de La Joue, and C. Parrocel. He counts among the most considerable document engravers of his time. Of his 970 works, Watteau counts for 362 items including *Le Livre des trophées* (*The Book of Trophies*) (12 plates) *ujets divers pour mettre sur des écrans* (*Various Subjects to be Put on Screens*) (46 plates), *Les Saisons* (*The Seasons*) (3 books, 14 plates), *Études de figures et de têtes de fantaisie* (*Studies of Fanciful Figures and Heads*) (101 plates), *Études de figures* (*Studies of Figures*), *modes* (*Fashion*) (32 plates), and *Études de soldats* (*Studies of Soldiers*) (34 plates). He also treated genre subjects, and Gillot had him engrave 17 pieces for *Personnages de la Comédie italienne* (*Characters of the Commedia dell'Arte*) and ornaments and trophies (24 plates). For Meissonnier he executed plates for the *Livre d'ornements d'église* (*Book of Church Ornaments*) (6 plates) and six *Livres d' ornements* (*Books of Ornaments*). He produced 107 pieces by Oppernod for interior decoration, furniture design, keystones, chandeliers, and doors. He executed ornaments, trophies, sketches, and architectural buildings by J. de La Joue (184 plates), and produced pieces for Parrocel's *Attitudes de piquiers et de fusillers et attitudes de cavaliers et de dragons* (*Aspects of Pikemen and Fusiliers and Aspects of Horsemen and Dragoons*). This huge output suggests that Jacques Gabriel Huquier must have collaborated with his father until his marriage in 1758, and possibly later.

Gabriel Huquier married Marie-Anne Desvigne with whom he had three sons and one daughter. He lived on Rue St-Jacques and then Rue des Mathurins where he died. His funeral was conducted with much pomp and was attended by an array of clergy who sung a mass in his honour. (This does not fit with the putative exile to England for an attack on the Jesuits. However, Jacques Gabriel's failure to return from London in spite of a manageable delay between death and funeral, a delay repeated for his mother's funeral, would be consistent with his being in disgrace for the same offence.)

Though essentially an engraver and publisher, Huquier was also a painter and a member of the Académie de St-Luc.

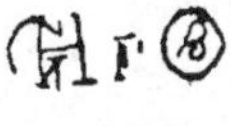

Stamp of sale

BIBLIOGRAPHY:

Bruant, Yves, '*Un grand collectionneur, marchand et graveur du XVIIIe siècle: Gabriel Huquier (1695-1772)*' in *Gazette des Beaux-Arts, p. 99-114*, periodical, April 1959. Roland Michel, Marianne, '*L'Ornement rocaile: quelques questions*' in *La Revue de l'art* n° 55, p. 66-75, periodical, 1982. Jervis, Simon, '*Huquier's Second Livre*' in *The J. Paul Getty Museum Journal* vol. XIV, p. 113-120, periodical, 1986. Brugerolles, Emmanuelle, et al., *François Boucher et l'art rocaille*, exhibition catalogue, École nationale supérieure des Beaux-Arts, Paris, 2003.

MUSEUMS AND GALLERIES:

LOS ANGELES (Getty Mus.): series of ornaments, engravings - PARIS (ENSBA).

Auction records:
Paris, 5 Dec 1941, *Flora's Head* (red chalk) FRF 525.

HUQUIER, Jacques Gabriel, or Hequier
French, 18th century.
Born 1725, in Paris; died 7 June 1805, in Shrewsbury.
Painter, draughtsman, engraver.

Jacques Gabriel Huquier was apprenticed to his father Gabriel with whom he continued working for some time. On 30 November 1758 he married Anne-Louise, daughter of the engraver Jacques Chereau, with whom he had a daughter and a son. Worth remembering among the works credited to him are the 60 plates of *Life of Our Lord Jesus Christ* after Gillot. There is good reason to believe that it was he and not his father who had to flee to London in order to escape retribution for a satirical piece attacking the Jesuits. There can be no doubt that he was in London and exhibited at the Royal Academy (from 1770 according to Redgrave, or 1771 according to Grave). It is equally clear that he no longer appears on registry documents dealing with his family, not even that recording his wife's death, which further indicates that she had not joined him abroad.

Huquier became a renowned portraitist thanks to his small portraits in pencil. He was living in Cambridge in 1783 but moved to Shrewsbury where he died.

Auction records:
Paris, 13-15 March 1905, *Apple Picking,* FRF 400.

HUQUIER, N.
French, 18th century.
Active in the middle of the 18th century.
Engraver (burin).

N. Huquier may have been related to Gabriel Huquier, though he does not appear in any official document regarding the engraver's family. Le Blanc mentions his *Animal Procession* after N. Berchem.

HUQUIER, Nicolas
French, 17th century.
Active in Orléans.
Painter.

HURANT, Claude
French, 17th century.
Active in Troyes in 1692.
Painter.

HURANT, Jacques
French, 16th - 17th century.
Active in Troyes from 1592 to 1618.
Painter.

HURANT, Jean
French, 16th - 17th century.
Active in Troyes in 1594 and 1611.
Painter.

Jean Hurant was one of those working on the church of St-Pantaleon.

HURANT, Maurice
French, 17th century.
Died c. 1627.
Active in Troyes.
Painter.

HURANT, Nicolas, the Elder
French, 16th century.
Active in Troyes.
Painter.

Nicolas Hurant the Elder married a daughter of the sculptor Domenico Fiorentino.

HURANT, Nicolas, the Younger
French, 17th century.
Active in Troyes in 1627.
Painter.

HURARD, Joseph Marius
French, 20th century.
Born 1887, in Avignon; died 1956.
Painter. Genre scenes, landscapes, still-lifes.

Joseph Marius Hurard, a student of Pierre Grivolas, painted almost exclusively landscapes of the Avignon region and of the Midi. He exhibited in Paris, in 1907 at the Salon des Indépendants, and then at the Salon of the Société Nationale des Beaux-Arts.

Museums and Galleries:
Sète: *Competitive Matches in the Martigue.*

Auction records:
Paris, 13 Dec 1937, *Old Houses in the Vaucluse; The Village of Gordes (Vaucluse), Morning,* FRF 50. Lyons, 7 Feb 1945, *Three Landscapes,* FRF 7,000, 8,000 and 10,000. Avignon, 4 March 1950, *The Martigues,* FRF 9,000. Paris, 23 Oct 1990, *The White Road* (oil on card, 18 x 24 1/2 ins / 46 x 62 cm) FRF 12,000. Paris, 29 Nov 1990, *The Charterhouse, Villeneuve-les-Avignon* (oil on card, 20 3/4 x 28 1/2 ins / 53 x 72.5 cm) FRF 9,500. Neuilly, 23 Feb 1992, *Provençal Village* (oil on card, 14 1/2 x 18 ins / 37 x 46 cm) FRF 16,800. Lyons, 9 Feb 2003, *Ribo Martiques. Burscons under Snow* (oil on panel, a pair, 10 x 21 ins / 26 x 54 cm) EUR 2,000. Marseilles, 25 Oct 2003, *Martigues* (oil on canvas, 24 x 18 ins / 61 x 46 cm) EUR 3,200. Calais, 14 March 2004, *Martigues at Sunrise* (oil on panel, 19 x 26 ins / 48 x 65 cm) EUR 1,900.

HURAULT, Charles
French, 18th century.
Active in Paris in 1719.
Painter.

HURAULT DE LIGNY
French, 19th century.
Born in the 19th century, in Rouen.
Landscape painter.

Hurault de Ligny first exhibited at the Paris Salon in 1865.

HURAUT, Nicolas. See **HURANT**

HURCK, Jan
Dutch, 17th century.
Active in Middelburg in 1660.
Painter.

HURD, Nathaniel
American, 18th century.
Born 13 February 1730, in Boston (Massachusetts); died 17 December 1770, in Boston.
Engraver.

Nathaniel Hurd is considered to be the first artist to have produced copper engravings in America. He showed great skill as a humorist.

HURD, Peter
American, 20th century.
Born 22 February 1904; died 1984.
Painter (gouache), watercolourist, illustrator. Genre scenes, landscapes.

Peter Hurd trained at the Pennsylvania Academy of the Fine Arts, Philadelphia. In 1945 he appeared at the American Art Exhibition in London. He became a member of the Pennsylvania Academy of the Fine Arts. Apart from his numerous landscapes, often executed in watercolours, he illustrated literary works, including: *The Last of the Mohicans* by Fenimore Cooper.

Museums and Galleries:
Colorado Springs (Fine Arts Center): *Portrait of Gerald Marr* (1952-1953, tempera/Masonite).

AUCTION RECORDS:
NEW YORK, 21 June 1978, *Homeward Bound* (1944, tempera/hardboard, 23¼ x 32¾ ins / 59 x 83.5 cm) USD 1,800. NEW YORK, 10 Oct 1979, *The Sapling* (oil on panel, 30 x 23 ins / 76 x 58.5 cm) USD 3,000. NEW YORK, 22 May 1980, *Windmill and Fence* (watercolour and pen, 16¾ x 23 ins / 42.5 x 58.4 cm) USD 3,800. NEW YORK, 3 Dec 1982, *Camp in the Mountains* (pen and black-brown ink/mounted paper/card, 14½ x 23 ins / 37 x 58.2 cm) USD 3,500. NEW YORK, 23 June 1983, *Adobe* (1925, watercolour, 9¼ x 7½ ins / 23.5 x 19 cm) USD 1,400. NEW YORK, 23 June 1983, *May Night, Chadds Ford, Pennsylvania* (1931, oil on canvas, 20 x 25 ins / 50.8 x 63.5 cm) USD 2,200. NEW YORK, 20 June 1985, *Mountain Landscape* (watercolour, 16 x 24 ins / 40.6 x 61 cm) GBP 5,000. NEW YORK, 20 March 1987, *La Guardia Airport at Dusk* (tempera/plastered hardboard, 36¼ x 47½ ins / 91.8 x 120.6 cm) USD 18,000. NEW YORK, 24 June 1988, *Landscape with Stream and Mountains* (watercolour, gouache and ink/paper, 11½ x 15¼ ins / 29.4 x 39 cm) USD 2,640. NEW YORK, 30 Nov 1989, *Baptising* (1969, tempera/synthetic resin, 27 x 47¼ ins / 68.5 x 120 cm) USD 28,600. NEW YORK, 24 Jan 1990, *Adobe Houses* (watercolour and ink/card, 12¼ x 14¼ ins / 31 x 36 cm) USD 2,420. NEW YORK, 31 May 1990, *Mount Blanco in the Sierra Blanco in New Mexico* (1925, oil on canvas, 25¼ x 30¼ ins / 64 x 76.9 cm) USD 5,720. NEW YORK, 27 Sept 1990, *'La Rancheria'* (egg tempera/panel, 24 x 42 ins / 61 x 106.7 cm) USD 46,200. NEW YORK, 25 Sept 1991, *Rain in the Desert* (tempera/synthetic resin, 25¼ x 42½ ins / 64.1 x 108 cm) USD 12,100. NEW YORK, 31 March 1993, *Landscape* (watercolour/paper, 14 x 20½ ins / 35.6 x 51.8 cm) USD 5,750. NEW YORK, 25 May 1995, *My Daughter Carol* (tempera/synthetic resin, 25¼ x 30¼ ins / 64.1 x 76.8 cm) USD 40,250. NEW YORK, 23 April 1997, *View from Turkey Hill* (c. 1931, oil on canvas, 18 x 25 ins / 45.7 x 63.5 cm) USD 4,600. NEW YORK, 4 Dec 1997, *The First Rider* (tempera/Masonite, 23¼ x 39¼ ins / 59 x 99.6 cm) USD 23,000. NEW YORK, 1 Dec 1999, *Rancheria* (tempera on panel, 24 x 48 ins / 61 x 122 cm) USD 42,500. NEW YORK, 24 May 2000, *The Eve of the Tobacco Auction* (tempera on masonite, 29 x 41 ins / 73 x 105 cm) USD 42,500. HOUSTON, 15 Sept 2000, *Diamond Head* (watercolour, 24 x 30 ins / 61 x 76 cm) USD 6,500. NEW YORK, 22 May 2001, *Towards a New World* (oil on canvas) USD 36,000. NEW YORK, 28 Nov 2001, *Grading Tobacco* (tempera on masonite, 37 x 48 ins / 94 x 122 cm) USD 40,000. SANTA FE, 9 Nov 2002, *Navajo Lake* (watercolour, 28 x 38 ins / 71 x 97 cm) USD 10,500. SANTA FE, 9 Nov 2002, *My Father's House* (oil on canvas, 16 x 20 ins / 41 x 51 cm) USD 11,500. SANTA FE, 23 May 2003, *New Mexico Rain* (watercolour, 24 x 28 ins / 61 x 71 cm) USD 7,500. SANTA FE, 1 Nov 2003, *An Afternoon in Summer* (watercolour, 10 x 19 ins / 25 x 48 cm) USD 5,900. DOWNINGTON, 20 March 2004, *Portrait of a Horse* (oil on panel, 21 x 26 ins / 53 x 66 cm) USD 7,500. SANTA FE, 15 May 2004, *Hondo Valley on a Hazy Afternoon* (watercolour, 11 x 17 ins / 28 x 43 cm) USD 5,800.

HURDIS, James Henry
British, 19th century.
Born 1800, in Southampton; died 30 November 1857, in Southampton.
Engraver.

James Henry Hurdis was a pupil of Heath. He executed several etchings of the Lewes area.

HURÉ, Marguerite Félicité
French, 20th century.
Born 9 December 1896, in Paris.
Stained glass painter, art restorer.

Marguerite Félicité Huré was a student at the École des Beaux-Arts in Paris, where she exhibited at the Salon d'Automne. She created numerous stained glass windows, including those of the Bourg-la-Reine church. She was also a conservator, having restored, among many others, two nineteenth-century windows at the Trinité in Fécamp.

HUREAU, Jean Baptiste Bame
French, 18th century.
Active in Paris in 1747.
Painter, sculptor.

HUREAU, Philippe, or Hurot
French, 17th century.
Died 1662.
Active in Paris.
Engraver.

HUREAU, René
French, 16th century.
Died 18 July 1574, in Le Mans.
Painter.

René Hureau was employed on the decoration of the church of the Dominicans in Le Mans.

HUREAU-BACHEVILLIER
French, 19th century.
Active in Orléans.
Lithographer.

HUREAU-NOLLEAU
French, 19th century.
Active in Orléans.
Lithographer.

HUREL
French, 17th century.
Painter, engraver.

Hurel specialised in etching. Le Blanc mentions his *St Cecilia*. He may be the same artist as Charles Hurel.

HUREL, Alexandre
French, 19th century.
Born in the 19th century, in Metz.
Engraver.

Alexandre Hurel was a pupil of Hotelin and Régnier. He made his début at the Salon of 1866.

HUREL, Charles
French, 17th century.
Active in Paris.
Painter.

Charles Hurel married one of the daughters of the painter Antoine Bornat.

HUREL, Holstein
Painter.

Holstein Hurel is listed by Ris-Paquot in his *Dictionnaire Encyclopédique des Marques et Monogrammes, Chiffres, Lettres, Initials, Signes Figuratifs*.

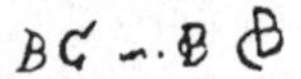

HUREL, Louis François
French, 19th century.
Born 17 June 1831, in Paris.
Sculptor.

Louis Hurel, a pupil of Feuchère, exhibited busts at the Salon in 1852 and 1857.

HUREL, Suzanne
French, 20th century.
Born 15 March 1876, in Mortagne (Orne); died 15 May 1956, in Clichy-la-Garenne.
Painter, pastellist.

Hurel was a student at the École des Beaux-Arts in Paris.

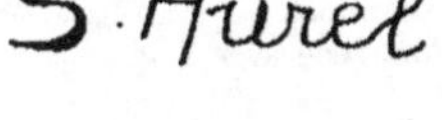

HURET, François
French, 17th century.
Active in Vicenza.
Engraver (burin), print publisher.
François Huret engraved historical portraits.

HURET, Grégoire
French, 17th century.
Baptised 24 October 1606 in Lyons; died 4 January 1670, in Paris.
Draughtsman, engraver (burin).
In Lyons in 1622-1623 Grégoire Huret engraved the plates for *The Sun in Leo* and *Reception of the Most Christian King Louis XIII... by the Canons and Counts of Lyons*. In 1626 he executed a *Portrait of L. de Serres*. He later settled in Paris where he was admitted into the Académie Royale de Peinture et de Sculpture on 7 August 1663 on presentation of his *Representation of the Passion of our Lord* (a sequence of 32 plates). A talented draughtsman, he line-engraved, very often from his own drawings, religious subjects, frontispieces and especially portraits in a pleasant if slightly bland manner. His best plates are portraits, such as: *Self-portraits, Marshal de Guébriant* (after his own drawings), *Henry IV and Louis XIII, Anne of Austria and Louis XIV, Prince of Condé, Duke of Lesdiguières, Richelieu* (after Philippe de Champaigne), *Mazarin, Séguier, Mary Stuart*, and *St Francis de Sales*. He also engraved after Rubens, Vouet, Bourdon, Dumoustier and other masters of the French School. He wrote papers on the subject of perspective and optics.
AUCTION RECORDS:
PARIS, 21 Feb 1919, *Allegorical Composition* (pencil) FRF 11. PARIS, 18 Nov 1926, *Marshal de Guébriant on Horseback* (black chalk) FRF 260.

HUREY, François
French, 19th century.
Born in Verdun-sur-Saône.
Painter, watercolourist. Landscapes, seascapes.
Hurey was taught by Van Elvin, and made his Salon début in 1881.

HURLBUT, Gertrude
German, 19th century.
Born in Germany; died 30 November 1909, in Geneva.
Painter, miniaturist, engraver. Portraits.
She lived and worked mainly in New York.

HURLEY, Edward Timothy
American, 20th century.
Born 10 October 1896, in Cincinnati; died 1950.
Painter, watercolourist, engraver, illustrator.
Edward Timothy Hurley trained in the studio of Frank Duveneck in Cincinnati. He lived in Newport. He was awarded a gold medal in St Louis in 1904.

HURLEY, Irene
Maiden name: Bishop
American, 20th century.
Born 5 December 1881, in Colorado Springs; died 1925, in Cincinnati.
Painter. Portraits.
Irene Hurley was married to Edward Hurley. She studied at the Cincinnati Art Academy.

HURLOT, Blaize
French, 17th century.
Active in Paris in 1682.
Painter, sculptor.

HURLOT, Laurent
French, 17th century.
Active in Paris in 1683.
Painter, sculptor, engraver.

HURLSTONE (Mrs)
British, 19th century.
Active in London.
Painter. Genre scenes.
Mrs Hurlstone frequently exhibited her work in London at the Royal Academy and at Suffolk Street.

HURLSTONE, F.B.
British, 19th century.
Active in London.
Painter. Genre scenes.

HURLSTONE, Frederick Yeates
British, 19th century.
Born 1801, in London; died 10 June 1869, in London.
Painter. History painting, genre scenes, portraits.
Frederick Hurlstone studied at the Royal Academy schools in London and was then a student of Beechey, Hoyson and Lawrence. He visited Italy, Spain and Morocco. Although he took part in the exhibitions of the Royal Academy and the British Institution from 1821, his artistic efforts were mainly concerned with the Society of British Artists, of which he became president in 1835. Hurlstone was an avowed opponent of the Royal Academy and his disputes with this institution had far-reaching repercussions at the time.
AUCTION RECORDS:
LONDON, 11 March 1911, *Peppino* (1837) GBP 33. LONDON, July 1922, *Little Fruit Seller*, GBP 2. LONDON, 22 July 1927, *Young Boy Eating a Pomegranate*, GBP 39. LONDON, 23 June 1939, *Two Children*, GBP 65. LONDON, 26 Nov 1982, *Queen of the Spanish Gypsies* (oil on canvas, 39 x 30 ins / 99 x 76.2 cm) GBP 2,200. LONDON, 5 June 1991, *Queen of the Gypsies at the Gate of the Alhambra Palace in Granada* (oil on canvas, 40 x 31 ins / 101.5 x 79 cm) GBP 6,380. LONDON, 9 Nov 2000, *Portrait of Lady Louisa Finch, in a Red Dress, Beside a Column* (oil on canvas, 94 x 58 ins / 239 x 147 cm) GBP 1,700.

HURLSTONE, Richard
British, 18th century.
Active in London.
Painter. Portraits.
Richard Hurlstone won an award from the Society of Arts in 1764 and took part in Royal Academy exhibitions in London from 1771 to 1780. On his return from a trip to Italy, which he made in the company of Wright, he was struck down by lightning near Salisbury.

HURLUPIN, André Carton, or Orlepin
French, 16th century.
Active in the Var.
Painter. Religious subjects.
Little is known about 'Hurlupin pintre', who is generally identified with André Carton Hurlupin, known as Orlepin, a painter in Draguignan.

In 1540 he painted a triptych for the church in Cogolin showing three saints with their attributes, *St Anthony between St Eloi and St Pons*. The three figures stand full-length against a background of azure and gold, firmly rooted in the Primitive tradition. This may have been a commission from a religious fraternity. The presence of the bishop of Cimiez, St Pons, shows that the piece originated in the Var.

Hurlupin's work was included in the collective exhibition *La Peinture en Provence au XVIe siècle* (*Provencal Painting in the 16th Century*) at the Centre de la Vieille Charité in Marseilles in 1987.
BIBLIOGRAPHY:
Honoré, L., '*Les Peintres, sculpteurs, orfèvres, doreurs, etc., en Basse-Provence du XVe au XVIIIe siècle*' in *Bulletin de la Société d'Études scientifiques et archéologiques de Draguignan et du Var, n°XXXVI, 1926-1927*, Draguignan, 1926. Laclotte, Michel/Vial, Marie-Paule/Leonelli, Marie-Claude/Pichou, Hélène, *La Peinture en Provence au XVIe siè-*

cle, exhibition catalogue, Musées de Marseille, Éd. Rivages, Marseilles, 1987.

HURNING, Hans, or Horning or Hornung
German, 15th century.
Born in Mutenau.
Engraver (wood).
Hans Hurning was in Nordlingen in 1461, where he engraved blocks after drawings by Friedrich Walter for a *Biblia Pauperum* (*Bible for the Poor*) published in 1470. The work contains scenes from the Old and New Testaments with brief comments.

HURRELL, Harold
British, 20th century.
Born 1940.
Painter (mixed media), installation artist.
Conceptual Art.
Art & Language group.
Harold Hurrell trained at the Sheffield School of Art, and in 1963 he went to London and worked as a technician at St Martin's School of Art. There he met David Bainbridge, who was studying sculpture, and with him, Terry Atkinson and Michael Baldwin he set up the group Art & Language, inspired by frustration at the lack of exposure given to their work. In 1967 he took up a teaching post at Hull College of Art, and in the same year he and Bainbridge held the exhibition *Hardware* at the Architectural Centre.

HURRY, Agnès
British, 19th - 20th century.
Active in London.
Painter.

HURRY, Leslie
British, 20th century.
Born 1909, in London; died 1978, in London.
Painter, watercolourist, draughtsman. Landscapes, portraits, decorative schemes. Stage costumes and sets.
Leslie Hurry trained at St John's Wood Art School in 1925,and studied for two years at the Royal Academy Schools. In the 1930s he travelled around Britain and Ireland, living on commissions from owners of large estates. He then travelled to France, where he wrote two books on automatic drawing (*The Journey* and *The Seven Eagles*). An exhibition at the Redfern Gallery led to a commission from Robert Helpmann, a dancer. They collaborated on the production of the ballet *Hamlet*. Hurrell became closely involved with Sadler's Wells and the world of theatre in the UK and Canada. He lived in Hundon in Suffolk.

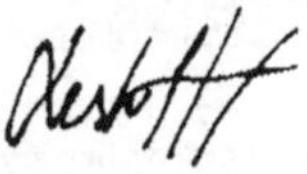

BIBLIOGRAPHY:
Hurry, Leslie/Lindsay, Jack, *Paintings and Drawings by Leslie Hurry*, The Grey Wall Press, London, 1950.
MUSEUMS AND GALLERIES:
BRIGHTON (Mus. & AG): *Landscape, Cevennes* (1950, pastel and ink) - LONDON (National Portrait Gal.) - LONDON (Tate Collection): *A Land Unvisited* (1940); *Grace Sholto* (1940); *The Courtesan* (1941); *Self-portrait* (1944); *The Extraordinary Year 1945* (1944-1945) - LONDON (Victoria And Albert Mus.).
AUCTION RECORDS:
LONDON, 9 June 1983, *'Turandot', Design for Decor* (c. 1947, watercolour heightened with gouache/pen outline, 10 3/4 x 20 1/4 ins / 27.3 x 51.5 cm) GBP 350. LONDON, 6 Feb 1985, *B58 Bombers* (1944, watercolour and pen, 16 x 15 ins / 40.5 x 38 cm) GBP 720. LONDON, 10 May 1988, *Preziosilla, a Gypsy, for 'La Forza del Destino' by Verdi* (1951, watercolour, pastel, pencil, coloured inks and brown ink pen, costume design, 17 3/4 x 10 3/4 ins / 45 x 27.6 cm) GBP 1,265. LONDON, 12 May 1989, *Two Faces* (watercolour and felt, 7 x 7 ins / 17.5 x 17.5 cm) GBP 462. LONDON, 25 Jan 1991, *Costume Design for Isolde, Covent Garden Opera Company* (1958, watercolour and ink, 18 x 11 1/2 ins / 46 x 29 cm) GBP 858; *Drawing for 'King Lear' at the Old Vic, 1958* (watercolour and ink, 11 1/2 x 15 1/4 ins / 29 x 38.5 cm) GBP 1,210. LONDON, 18 Dec 1991, *Interiors with figures* (1945, ink and watercolour, 14 x 21 1/2 ins / 35.5 x 54.5 cm) GBP 4,180. LONDON, 3 Dec 2003, *Welsh Figures* (1944, pencil, pen, black ink and watercolour, 11 x 8 ins / 27 x 21 cm) GBP 1,000.

HURRY, Lucy Washington
American, 20th century.
Born 17 October 1884, in Hagerstown; died 1950, in Mineola (New York).
Painter, draughtswoman. Genre scenes.
Lucy Washington Hurry studied in New York.

HURSON, François
French, 18th century.
Active in Angers c. 1753.
Sculptor.

HURST, Gregor
French, 20th century.
Born 13 September 1878, in Strasbourg.
Painter. Portraits, genre scenes, landscapes.
Gregor Hurst studied in Munich and then exhibited in Berlin.

HURST, Hal
British, 19th century.
Born 1865.
Active in London.
Painter, watercolourist, miniaturist.
Hal Hurst was a member of the Society of British Artists, the Royal Institute of Painters in Watercolours and the Royal Society of Miniature Painters. He took part in the Exposition Universelle of 1900 in Paris.
AUCTION RECORDS:
LONDON, 16 May 1929, *Sir John Sooclear*, GBP 36.

HURT, F. van
Dutch, 17th century.
Painter.

HURT, Louis Bosworth
British, 19th - 20th century.
Born 1856; died 1929.
Active in Ashbourne.
Painter. Animals, landscapes, mountainscapes.
Louis Bosworth Hurt exhibited at the Royal Academy and the Suffolk Street Gallery from 1881. His delicate works feature charming, poetic views of the Scottish mountains, and are highly sought-after by collectors.

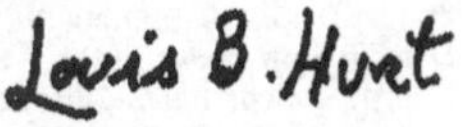

AUCTION RECORDS:
LONDON, 7 Dec 1907, *Highland Cattle*, GBP 68. LONDON, 18 Jan 1908, *Sower* (1902) GBP 86. LONDON, 13 Dec 1909, *Autumn* (1892) GBP 65. LONDON, 1 April 1911, *Misty Morning*, GBP 29. LONDON, 9 June 1911, *Glen Cannich: Rain and Sunshine* (1895) GBP 105. LONDON, Nov 1921, *Morning, Heading South*, GBP 52. LONDON, July 1922, *Loch Goilhead: Highland cattle*, GBP 27. LONDON, March 1923, *Hills of Glencoe*, GBP 63. LONDON, July 1924, *On the Banks of a Highland Stream*, GBP 105. LONDON, 26 June 1926, *On the Banks of Loch Awe*, GBP 84. LONDON, 12 March 1928, *Gleneannich*, GBP 79. LONDON, 1 March 1929, *Scottish Highland Cattle*, GBP 105. LONDON, 27 Nov 1930, *Landscape in Fog*, GBP 40. NEW YORK, 17 May 1934, *Highland Cattle*, USD 230. NEW YORK, 30 July

1936, *On the Banks of a Scottish Loch*, GBP 52. NEW YORK, 6 Nov 1936, *House on the Moors*, GBP 52. GLASGOW, 17 March 1940, *Highland Cattle*, GBP 46. GLASGOW, 12 June 1945, *Cattle Returning to the Fold*, GBP 52. LONDON, 27 June 1947, *Highland Cattle*, GBP 71. GLASGOW, 2 July 1947, *Highland Bull*, GBP 71. GLASGOW, 31 July 1973, *Landscape with Animals*, GBP 650. SCOTLAND, 24 Aug 1976, *Loch Clare, Ross-shire* (1887, oil on canvas, 23 1/2 x 35 1/2 ins / 60 x 90 cm) GBP 500. AUCHTERARDER, 30 Aug 1977, *Mountainous Landscape with Animals* (1882, oil on canvas, 23 1/4 x 35 ins / 59 x 89 cm) GBP 1,500. LONDON, 1 Nov 1979, *Highland Landscape with Animals* (1891, oil on canvas, 24 x 40 ins / 61 x 101.5 cm) GBP 2,800. AUCHTERARDER, 1 Sept 1981, *Highland Cattle Fording a River* (oil on canvas, 20 3/4 x 34 ins / 53 x 86.5 cm) GBP 3,600. GLASGOW, 7 April 1983, *Loch Cannich* (oil on canvas, 24 x 40 ins / 61 x 101.6 cm) GBP 4,600. PERTH, 26 Aug 1986, *After the Storm* (oil on canvas, 24 x 40 ins / 61 x 101.5 cm) GBP 9,200. CHESTER, 9 April 1987, *Scottish Manor House beside a Loch* (oil on canvas, 39 x 31 ins / 99 x 79 cm) GBP 9,600. ROME, 24 May 1988, *Scottish Landscape* (oil on canvas, 35 1/2 x 29 1/2 ins / 90 x 75 cm) ITL 5,000,000. LONDON, 3 June 1988, *Mountainous Landscape with Cattle on the Shore of a Loch* (oil on canvas, 20 x 30 ins / 50.8 x 76 cm) GBP 13,750; *Mountain Path* (1894, oil on canvas, 24 1/2 x 40 1/2 ins / 62 x 103 cm) GBP 19,800. LOS ANGELES, 9 June 1988, *Mountain Landscape with Cattle* (oil on canvas, 23 x 18 ins / 58.5 x 46 cm) USD 6,600. EDINBURGH, 30 Aug 1988, *Highland Bull* (oil on canvas, 24 x 40 1/4 ins / 61 x 102 cm) GBP 9,900. GLASGOW, 7 Feb 1989, *Highland Cattle in a Valley* (oil on canvas, 12 x 18 ins / 30.5 x 46 cm) GBP 1,430. PERTH, 28 Aug 1989, *Isle of Skye: The Hills of the Isle of Mist* (1885, oil on canvas, 30 x 25 ins / 76 x 63.5 cm) GBP 6,600. LONDON, 27 Sept 1989, *Morning Mist* (oil on canvas, 20 x 30 ins / 51 x 76 cm) GBP 12,650. LONDON, 3 Nov 1989, *Highand Cattle in a Mountainous Landscape* (1892, oil on canvas, 19 x 13 ins / 48 x 33 cm) GBP 2,640. EDINBURGH, 22 Nov 1989, *Misty Landscape with Highland Cattle by a Pond* (oil on canvas, 24 x 40 ins / 61 x 101.6 cm) GBP 7,150. LONDON, 9 Feb 1990, *The Countryside around Black Mount Forest near Bannock* (1901, oil on canvas, 24 1/4 x 40 1/4 ins / 61.3 x 102 cm) GBP 27,500. PERTH, 27 Aug 1990, *Showers and Sun* (1897, oil on canvas, 50 1/2 x 40 1/4 ins / 128 x 102 cm) GBP 82,500. GLASGOW, 22 Nov 1990, *Morning Mist on Loch Treachlan near Glencoe* (1907, oil on canvas, 24 x 40 ins / 61 x 101.6 cm) GBP 6,600. GLASGOW, 5 Feb 1991, *Highland Cattle in a Valley* (oil on canvas, 50 x 40 ins / 127 x 101.5 cm) GBP 22,000. LONDON, 8 Feb 1991, *Cattle Crossing a Snow-bound Valley* (oil on canvas, 24 x 40 ins / 61 x 101.6 cm) GBP 19,800. SOUTH QUEENSFERRY, 23 April 1991, *Cattle beside a Highland Stream* (1905, oil on canvas, 24 1/4 x 40 1/4 ins / 61.5 x 102 cm) GBP 12,100. PERTH, 26 Aug 1991, *Highland Cattle Drinking from a Loch* (oil on canvas, 16 x 24 ins / 40.5 x 61 cm) GBP 8,250. NEW YORK, 17 Oct 1991, *Highland Cattle in a Scottish Landscape, with a View of Glen Shiel* (oil on canvas, 24 x 40 ins / 61 x 101.6 cm) USD 15, 400. EDINBURGH, 28 April 1992, *Fog over Loch Duich* (oil on canvas, 14 1/2 x 19 ins / 37 x 48 cm) GBP 3,960. PERTH, 1 Sept 1992, *Cattle at Strathfillan in Perthshire* (1891, oil on canvas, 24 x 36 ins / 61 x 91.5 cm) GBP 11,000. PERTH, 31 Aug 1993, *Highland Cattle* (1893, oil on canvas, 35 x 59 3/4 ins / 89 x 152 cm) GBP 36,700. LONDON, 4 Nov 1994, *Countryside around Glencoe, by the Tay road* (1899, oil on canvas, 36 x 60 ins / 91.4 x 152.7 cm) GBP 31,050. GLASGOW, 14 Feb 1995, *Highland Cattle beside a Lake* (oil on canvas, 24 1/4 x 36 ins / 61.5 x 91.5 cm) GBP 11,500. NEW YORK, 16 Feb 1995, *Highland Cattle* (oil on canvas, 30 x 50 ins / 76.2 x 127 cm) USD 21,850. PERTH, 29 Aug 1995, *Highland Cattle* (1904, oil on canvas, 30 x 25 ins / 76 x 63.5 cm) GBP 14,375. NEW YORK, 12 April 1996, *Aftermath of a Storm over Glen Dochart, Perthshire* (1890, oil on canvas, 40 x 60 ins / 101.6 x 152.4 cm) USD 32,200. PERTH, 26 Aug 1996, *North Sound at Noss, Shetland* (oil on canvas, 24 x 36 1/4 ins / 61 x 92 cm) GBP 13,225. LONDON, 5 Sept 1996, *The Moors at Rannoch* (oil on canvas, 24 x 40 ins / 61 x 101.9 cm) GBP 6,440. GLASGOW, 11 Dec 1996, *Highland Cattle* (oil on canvas, 12 x 18 ins / 30.5 x 46 cm) GBP 2,300; *Highland Cattle* (1895, oil on canvas, 50 x 40 ins / 127 x 101.5 cm) GBP 23,000. LONDON, 15 April 1997, *Herd of Highland Cattle* (1905, oil on canvas, 24 x 42 1/4 ins / 61 x 107 cm) GBP 10,350. EDINBURGH, 15 May 1997, *Loch Eck* (1898, oil on canvas, 38 x 65 ins / 96.5 x 165 cm) GBP 20,700. AUCHTERARDER, 26 Aug 1997, *The Hills of Skye* (oil on canvas, 24 x 40 ins / 61 x 101.5 cm) GBP 33,350.

HURTADO, Ángel
Venezuelan, 20th century.
Born 1927, in El Tocuyo.
Painter.

Ángel Hurtado studied at the school of fine arts in Caracas. He held his first exhibition in Caracas in 1945, moving towards abstraction around 1948. Hurtado travelled in Europe, Spain and particularly France from 1954. He took part in numerous exhibitions in Latin America and he in Paris exhibited at the Salon des Réalité Nouvelles and the Salon de Mai.

Hurtado fully assimilated French lyrical abstraction with its dark drawing style, enclosed manner and backlit coloured backgrounds.

HURTADO, Francisco
Spanish, 17th - 18th century.
Born 1669, in Lucena (Cordova); died 1725, in Priego (Cordova).
Architect, sculptor.

Francisco Hurtado worked mainly as an architect and often decorated his buildings with Baroque ornaments such as plants, skulls and skeletons; a good example is the 'Camarín' at Nuestra Señora de la Victoria in Málaga.

HURTADO DE MENDOZA, Esteban.
See **MENDOZA Esteban Hurtado de**

HURTAULT, Jean Baptiste
French, 18th century.
Active in Fontenay-le-Comte.
Sculptor (wood).

HURTEAU, Alexandre Louis Marie
French, 19th century.
Active in Paris.
Painter (porcelain), draughtsman.

Hurteau exhibited flower pictures at the Salon in 1845 and 1848.

HURTEAU, Philippe
French, 20th - 21st century.
Born 1955, in Les Sables-d'Olonne.
Painter. Figures.
Computer Art (Digital Art).

Philippe Hurteau was awarded a bursary at the Villa Medicis in Rome, where he stayed from 1987 to 1989. He also went to New York, by means of the Villa Medicis fuori le Mura award, which he won in 1993. He executed a series on television presenters, plunging their faces into anonymity. To do so, he transposed the cathodic image onto a computer, which he then represented in portraits that were deliberately perturbed or altered by white bands. He used this method for a series on actors of television soap-opera, or pornographic films from cable channels. In 2002, he created another series, *XTZ*, in which he combined sports images with pornographic images, intermittently scrambled.

Hurteau has participated in collective exhibitions, including: 1995, FIAC (Foire Internationale d'Art Contemporain), Paris, presented by the Galerie Zürcher; 2002, *Le Portrait s'envisage...* (*The Portrait Visualizes Itself...*), Château de Tanlay (Yonne). He has shown his works in solo exhibitions, including: 1992, Galerie Montenay, Paris; 1996, 1998, 2002,

Galerie Zürcher, Paris; 1998, St-Croix abbey, Les Sables d'Olonne; 2002, *Visiotime 1*, with Philippe Cognée, Centre Culturel, Cesson-Sévigné.

BIBLIOGRAPHY:

Strasser, Catherine, *Philippe Hurteau*, exhibition catalogue, Gal. Charles Cartwright, Paris, 1986 (conversation with Jérôme Sans). Kaeppelin, Olivier, *'Philippe Hurteau, optique'* in *coll. Traverse Centre culturel français de Palerme et de la Sicile*, exhibition catalogue, Novecento editrice, Centre culturel français, Palermo, 1992. Aldebaran, *Ce que je fais, Philippe Hurteau*, exhibition catalogue, Espace d'art contemporain, Baillargues, 1993. Katz, Stéphanie/Ghaddab, Karim, *Personne, Philippe Hurteau*, exhibition catalogue, Abbaye Sainte-Croix, Les Sables d'Olonne, 1998 (text in French and English). Exley, Roy/Stiegler, Bernard, *Qui est là? Une proposition de Pierre Besson et Philippe Hurteau*, exhibition catalogue, Abbaye du Ronceray, Angers, 2001.

AUCTION RECORDS:

PARIS, 27 March 1996, *Study for the Messenger* (1987, acrylic/canvas, 76 3/4 x 45 ins / 195 x 114 cm) FRF 4,000.

HURTER, Carl

British, 18th century.
Active in London.
Miniaturist.

Carl Hurter exhibited his work at the Royal Academy in London in 1787 and 1789.

HURTER, Hans Kaspar von

Swiss, 17th century.
Born 3 April 1623, in Schaffhausen.
Painter.

He is documented for religious paintings.

HURTER, Johann Heinrich von

Swiss, 18th century.
Born 9 September 1734, in Schaffhausen; died 2 September 1799, in Düsseldorf.
Miniaturist, enameller. Portraits.

He worked initially in The Hague, then in 1776 in Paris. He spent from 1779 to 1784 in England, finally returning to settle in Switzerland. He did numerous copies of Sir Joshua Reynolds.

AUCTION RECORDS:

PARIS, 18 au 22 April 1910, *Portrait of Frederick II of Prussia* (miniature) FRF 420. LONDON, 30 June 1999, *Rembrandt Self-portrait wearing Black Robes and Brown Hat* (1774, miniature, oval, h. 2 ins / 5 cm) GBP 1,100. LONDON, 11 April 2002, *Young Lady called Mary Nesbitt* (1783, miniature, h. 2 ins / 6 cm) GBP 26,000.

HURTER, Johann Martin

Swiss, 18th century.
Born 27 October 1726, in Schaffhausen; died 16 March 1805, in Schaffhausen.
Painter.

HURTER, Kaspar

Swiss, 17th century.
Painter. History painting.

He worked in Schaffhausen in 1623 and Memmingen in 1627.

HURTER, Melchior

Swiss, 18th century.
Born 1 August 1686, in Schaffhausen.
Painter.

He worked in Copenhagen.

HURTER, Tobias

Swiss, 19th century.
Born 31 January 1803, in Schaffhausen; died 6 December 1889.
Engraver, lithographer.

He was a pupil of Lips.

HURTREL, Arsène Charles Narcisse

French, 19th century.
Born 25 June 1817, in Lille; died 1 December 1861, in Lille.
Painter. History painting, religious subjects, genre scenes.

After working in Armentières and Lille, in northern France, Hurtrel travelled to Paris in 1834, where he became a pupil of Ingres. He accompanied his master on a trip to Rome in 1835, and stayed there until 1840. Hurtrel exhibited at the Paris Salon from 1841 to 1861.

MUSEUMS AND GALLERIES:

DOUAI: *She is Mad* - LILLE: *St John in the Desert; The Lille National Guard in 1850; The Seated Gunners of Lille in 1851* - TOURCOING: *Torture of a Parricide in Sparta*.

AUCTION RECORDS:

PARIS, 25 Nov 1991, *Little Child Scattering Roses, Carried by Two Angels* (1850, oil on canvas, 28 3/4 x 24 1/2 ins / 73 x 62 cm) FRF 12,500.

HURTREL, Simon, or Hurtrelle

French, 17th - 18th century.
Born 1648, in Béthune (Pas-de-Calais); died 11 March 1724, in Gennevilliers.
Sculptor.

Simon Hurtrel was sent to Rome in 1676, where he figured among the most promising students. Back in France in 1682 he worked in Marly in the palace's stateroom and produced *Pomona's Attributes* (1683-1684). He was admitted into the Académie in 1690 with a bronze group of *The Holy Virgin, Christ and Three Angels* which can be seen in the Louvre. The same year he exhibited the marble statue *Saturn Devouring his Children*. He is also responsible for *The Monument to the Duke of Créqui* in the church of St-Roch; the *Tomb of Le Tellier, Chancellor of France* in the church of St-Gervais; *St Gregory of Nazianzen*, a stone statue outside the chapel in Versailles; a marble statue of *Theophrastus* on the surround of the northern flowerbed of Versailles Palace; a marble statue of a *Faun Playing the Flute* on the surround of the Latona flowerbed; and some of the statues which adorn the Œil de bœuf stateroom in Versailles Palace. He married Marie-Anne Leclerc. They had two children who died very young. Mariette indicates that Hurtrel was admitted into the Académie de St-Luc on 9 July 1678.

MUSEUMS AND GALLERIES:

NIORT: *Bacchus* - PARIS (Louvre): *Mourned Christ* - VERSAILLES (Château, Jardins): *Marble Vase; Theophrastus*.

HURTREL, Simon, or Hurtrelle or Urtrel

French, 18th century.
Draughtsman, engraver (etching). Portraits.

Simon Hurtrel was a solicitor working in Paris at the beginning of the 18th century. Le Blanc speculates that he could be the brother of the sculptor Simon Hurtrel. He made three portraits of members of his family, including his own and that of the sculptor Simon Hurtrel.

HURTRET, André
French, 20th century.
Painter. Landscapes.

HURTUBISE, Jacques
Canadian, 20th century.
Born 1939, in Montreal.
Painter.

Jacques Hurtubise trained at the École des Beaux-Arts, Montreal, between 1956 and 1960, under the guidance of Albert Dumouchel. In 1960-1961, he paid a trip to New York, and came into contact with Abstract Expressionism. Upon returning to Montreal, he contacted the Les Plasticiens group. His early works could be compared with Action Painting, then about 1964 he switched to a form of expression where marks were used to create the illusion of mobile space.

This 'space-arranging' led him in 1966 to produce painting which closely resembled Neo-Plasticism, being based on vertical and horizontal lines crossing each other at right angles. He stopped limiting himself to two colours in 1967, and at the same time introduced diagonal lines into his compositions. Pursuing his own research, he strived for a kind of appearance of spontaneity, though what appeared as spontaneous splashes of paint were in fact painted meticulously with his easel laid down flat.

Hurtubise has been exhibiting regularly several times a year in Canada since 1962. He took part in the 8th São Paulo Biennale in 1965, and was elected a member of the Canadian Royal Academy in 1971.

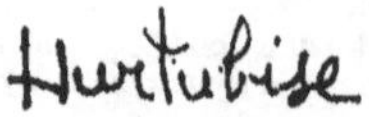

BIBLIOGRAPHY:
Shee, Mary Venner, *Jacques Hurtubise: Recent Works*, exhibition catalogue, Art Museum and Galleries, California State University, Long Beach, 1981. *Jacques Hurtubise*, exhibition catalogue, Vancouver Art Gallery, Vancouver, 1981. *Jacques Hurtubise: Four Decades, Image after Image*, exhibition catalogue, Montreal Museum of Fine Arts, Montreal, 1998.
MUSEUMS AND GALLERIES:
MONTREAL (MAC): *Tawashita* (1978).

HURTUNA GIRALT, Josep
Spanish, 20th century.
Born 1913, in Barcelona; died 1978, in Barcelona.
Painter, engraver.

Josep Hurtuna Giralt travelled in France, Italy and the Netherlands. He won a prize for engraving in Barcelona in 1951. His paintings remained figurative until 1958, after which he used effects originating in Impressionism within a Neo-Cubist system of construction.
MUSEUMS AND GALLERIES:
BARCELONA - BERN - CERBÈRE.

HURULLAH BERK
Turkish, 20th century.
Born 1904.
Painter. Landscapes, seascapes.

This artist took part in official exhibitions in Ankara. In 1946, his work was represented by the seascape *The Port* at the exhibition of modern art staged by the United Nations at the museum of modern art in Paris.

HURUM, Per
Norwegian, 20th century.
Born 1910, in Christiania (now Oslo).
Sculptor.

Hurum was a student of Wilhelm Rasmussem at the fine arts academy in Oslo. His work was shown at the São Paulo Biennale in 1953 at an exhibition at the Musée Rodin in Paris in 1956. His sculpture is figurative and very classical.

HUSAIN, Maqbool Fida
Indian, 20th century.
Born 17 September 1917, in Pandharpur, Maharashtra.
Painter, illustrator. Murals.

Maqbool Fida Husain began work as a painter of film hoardings and did not dedicate himself completely to painting until 1948, when he rapidly took a very important place in contemporary Indian art, particularly among young artists. In 1948 he was one of the founders of the Progressive Artists' Group in Bombay (now Mumbai).

Husain's work is figurative and makes use of the ethnic and artistic materials of the Indian expressionist tradition. He distances himself from everyday life in order to depict a fantastical world inhabited by beings, animals and objects that are deformed and fixed, like puppets, in anguished postures. The colours in his palette are vivid, and the robustness and diversity of his calligraphic experience is evident in his drawing.

Husain's work has been shown in several collective exhibitions in India and in shows of Indian art abroad. He has travelled frequently to Europe, the Far East and the USA. In 1995 he was awarded the Lalit Kala Academy prize in New Delhi, and subsequently became a member of the general council at the Academy. More recently, his work featured at the exhibition *Octavio Paz illustré par les peintres* (*Octavio Paz Illustrated by Painters*), Maison de l'Amérique Latine in Paris (2000). He has received Padma Vibushan, the country's highest civilian award, and other state awards.
BIBLIOGRAPHY:
Alkazi, E.F., *The Modern Artist and Tradition*, New Delhi, 1978.. *Six Indian Painters*, exhibition catalogue, Tate Gallery, 1982.
MUSEUMS AND GALLERIES:
NEW DELHI (Nat. Gal. of Modern Art, Lalit Kala Acad.): several works.
AUCTION RECORDS:
MONTREAL, 23-24 Nov 1993, *Yakka* (1961, oil on canvas, 34 x 35 ins / 86.4 x 88.9 cm) CAD 3,800. LONDON, 11 Dec 1997, *Reflection* (1954, gouache/panel, 18 x 11 1/2 ins / 45.7 x 29.3 cm) GBP 3,450. NEW YORK, 20 Sept 2000, *Musician* (oil on canvas, 30 x 36 ins / 76 x 92 cm) USD 11,000. NEW YORK, 20 Sept 2000, *They Came by a Blue Tree* (oil on canvas, 40 x 30 ins / 102 x 76 cm) USD 11,000. SINGAPORE, 1 April 2001, *Seven Nudes* (1961, oil on canvas, 22 x 52 ins / 56 x 132 cm) SGD 52,000. NEW YORK, 15 Oct 2001, *That Obscure Object of Desire. Tombstone* (oil on canvas, diptych, 67 x 134 ins / 170 x 340 cm) USD 25,000. HONG KONG, 28 April 2002, *Abduction* (oil on canvas, 36 x 36 ins / 91 x 91 cm) HKD 190,000. HONG KONG, 28 April 2002, *Farmer's Family* (acrylic on canvas, 60 x 40 ins / 152 x 102 cm) HKD 230,000. LONDON, 17 Oct 2003, *Orchestra* (1960, oil on canvas, 23 x 39 ins / 59 x 100 cm) GBP 20,000. LONDON, 17 Oct 2003, *Untitled* (1963, oil on canvas, 38 x 18 ins / 97 x 46 cm) GBP 20,000. NEW YORK, 25 March 2004, *Portrait of an Umbrella* (watercolour and black marker, a pair, 15 x 21 ins / 37 x 54 cm) USD 10,000. NEW YORK, 25 March 2004, *Ganga* (oil on canvas, 27 x 63 ins / 69 x 160 cm) USD 75,000.

HUSBAND, Dalla
Canadian, 20th century.
Born in Winnipeg.
Painter, engraver.

Dalla Husband exhibited in Canada, and also in London and Paris.

HUSDONCK, van
Painter. Fruit.

Van Husdonck is only known for the painting bearing his signature in Bourges Museum, *Dish of Figs*.
MUSEUMS AND GALLERIES:
BOURGES: *Dish of Figs*.

HUSE, Marion
American, 20th century.
Born 1896, in Lynn (Massachusetts); died 1967.
Painter, engraver, screen printer.
Marion Huse was inspired by popular imagery.

HUSER, Heinrich
Swiss, 19th century.
Born in Zurzach; died June 1820.
Painter.
He worked mainly in Lucerne.

HUSINSZUENE, Michiel
Flemish, 15th century.
Active in Bruges.
Painter.
Flemish School.

HUSKINSON, John
British, 19th century.
Active in Bingham.
Sculptor.
John Huskinson exhibited his work at the Royal Academy in London in 1886 and 1887.

HUSKINSON, L.
British, 19th century.
Active in London.
Painter. Genre scenes.
L. Huskinson exhibited his work at the Royal Academy between 1839 and 1859.

HUSKINSON, R.
British, 19th century.
Born at the beginning of the 19th century, in Langar, near Nottingham; died c. 1854, in London.
Active c. 1830.
Painter, watercolourist. Portraits, genre scenes.
The catalogue of Nottingham Museum has the letter R as the initial of the Christian name of Huskinson whilst Graves' Dictionary mentions letter H. Whichever is the case, Huskinson was a portrait painter who was still living in Nottingham in 1832 and exhibited his work at the Royal Academy in London in 1820. The Nottingham catalogue says that our artist came to London where he quickly became successful. We also find in Graves an R. Huskinson, a genre painter residing in Hammersmith. It may also be supposed that it is one and the same artist bearing both the initials R and H but only using one or the other at any one time.
MUSEUMS AND GALLERIES:
NOTTINGHAM: *David Love, the Old Ballad Singer of Nottingham* (1820, watercolour).
AUCTION RECORDS:
LONDON, 5 March 1971, *Come into These Yellow Sands,* Gns 3,600. LONDON, 8-9 June 1993, *Titania's Imps Stealing the Squirrel's Nuts* (oil on canvas, 25 3/4 x 30 1/2 ins / 65.5 x 77.5 cm) GBP 3,220.

HUSKINSON, Robert
British, 19th century.
Active in Hammersmith, between 1832 and 1854.
Painter. Figures.
R. Huskinson exhibited his work at the Royal Academy and at the British Institution in London from 1838 to 1847.

HUSLY, Hendrik
Dutch, 18th century.
Active in Amsterdam.
Sculptor.
Hendrik Husly was almost certainly the father of Jacob Otten Husly.

HUSLY, Jacob Otten
Dutch, 18th century.
Born c. 1735; died 1795, in Kampen.
Active in Amsterdam.
Draughtsman, sculptor, architect.

HUSMAN, Johan
Danish, 17th century.
Born in Copenhagen.
Active in Copenhagen from 1674 up to the end of the century.
Engraver.

HUSMANN
Swiss, 16th century.
Active at the end of the 16th century.
Painter.

HUSMANN, Heinrich
German, 15th century.
Died 1493, in Lübeck.
Active in Lübeck.
Sculptor (wood), painter.

HUSNIK, Jakob
Czech, 19th - 20th century.
Born 1837, in Vejprnice; died 1916, in Prague.
Painter, engraver.
Jakob Husnik produced genre scenes and religious paintings.

HUSON, Thomas
British, 19th - 20th century.
Born 1844, in Liverpool; died February 1920.
Painter, watercolourist, engraver. Landscapes, seascapes.
Thomas Huson made his debut exhibition in London in 1871, while living in Liverpool. He was a regular exhibitor with the Royal Academy, at the Suffolk Street Gallery, the Royal Institute of Painters in Watercolours and the Grosvenor Gallery among others. In 1909 he exhibited at the Royal Institute and the Cambrian Academy in Conway.
MUSEUMS AND GALLERIES:
LIVERPOOL: *Fire on the Landing Stage at Liverpool; A Mild Breeze on a Calm Sea; Indian Summer* - NORWICH (Castle Mus. and AG): *Changing Pastures* (watercolours); *High Life and Low Life (Stilllife)* (watercolour).
AUCTION RECORDS:
LONDON, 4 April 1908, *Low Tide* (1884, watercolour) GBP 7. LONDON, 25 Jan 1989, *When a Summer's Day is Hot and Blue...* (watercolour and gouache, 13 1/4 x 20 1/4 ins / 33.5 x 51.5 cm) GBP 792. LONDON, 25 March 1994, *Silvery Morning* (oil on canvas, 39 x 60 1/4 ins / 99.3 x 153 cm) GBP 8,970. LONDON, 2 June 1995, *Showery Weather in North Donegal* (oil on canvas, 27 1/4 x 48 ins / 69 x 122 cm) GBP 1,380.

HUSON, Thomas (Mrs)
British, 19th - 20th century.
Active in Liverpool and in Pen-y-Garth.
Painter. Landscapes.
Mrs Rhomas Huson was the wife of the landscape painter Thomas Huson. She exhibited at the Suffolk Street Gallery in 1877 and 1878. In 1909 her work featured in the autumn exhibition at the Walker Art Gallery, Liverpool.

HUSSARD, Louis Charles
French, 19th century.
Died 15 December 1857, in Paris.
Painter. Flowers, fruit.
Hussard exhibited at the Salon between 1837 and 1852.

HUSSARD, Michel Nicolas
French, 18th - 19th century.
Active in Nantes.
Painter, draughtsman.
Michel Nicolas Hussard was the head of the art school in Nantes in 1791.

Auction records:
Paris, 5 June 1935, *Bust Portraits of Claude Benoît and his Wife* (two pastels) FRF 195.

HUSSEIN GILANI
Turkish, 17th century.
Active in Constantinople.
Painter.
This artist painted miniature portraits in the courts of the Ottoman sultans.

HUSSEIN NAQQÂSCH, called Derwisch H. N.
Turkish, 17th century.
Active in the middle of the 17th century.
Painter. Portraits.
Museums and Galleries:
Boston: a portrait.

HUSSEL, Otto
German, 19th century.
Born 13 September 1833, in Munich.
Painter. Landscapes.

HUSSEM, D.
Dutch, 18th - 19th century.
Born 1772; died 1817.
Active in Amsterdam.
Engraver.
D. Hussem was a pupil of Steven Goblé.

HUSSEM, Willem or Wim
Dutch, 20th century.
Born 1900 or 1918, in Rotterdam; died 1974.
Painter.
Group: Vrij Beelden.
Hussem lived in France, both in Provence and in the Paris region, from 1919 to 1936. He began his artistic training in France and settled in The Hague in 1936. From 1930 to 1940, Hussem painted still-lifes and flowers in an Expressionist manner. He was subsequently influenced by Chagall, Picasso and then Paul Klee. His study of eastern calligraphy and Zen Buddhism directed the development of his art towards an increasingly austere version of Abstraction. In his Abstract period, he limited himself to a small number of very simple ways of indicating volume of almost monochrome tonality, which together seem to constitute a drawing of a sculpture.

His work was shown at many collective exhibitions, including at the Salon des Réalités Nouvelles in Paris (1950), and at the Venice Biennale (1960). In 2002, work by him was shown at the exhibition *Focus Paris, Bekering tot abstract* (*Focus Paris: The Turn towards Abstraction*) at the CoBrA Museum voor Moderne Kunst in Amstelveen. The exhibition was designed to recognise the work of a group of artists belonging to the *Vrij Beelden* and *Creatie* groups, who had been influenced by Abstraction in Paris. Hussem also had solo exhibitions, in London (1953); in The Hague (1960); and at the Boymans van Beuningen Museum in Rotterdam (1960).
Bibliography:
Focus Paris, die Hinwendung zum Abstrakte, exhibition catalogue, Cobra Museum voor Moderne Kunst, Amstelveen, 2002.
Auction records:
Amsterdam, 24 Oct 1983, *Composition* (1957, oil on canvas, 41¼ x 47¼ ins / 105 x 120 cm) NLG 5,600. Amsterdam, 10 April 1989, *Composition* (1956, oil on canvas, 25½ x 17¾ ins / 65 x 45 cm) NLG 9,200. Amsterdam, 22 May 1990, *Abstract Composition* (oil on canvas, 40¼ x 51½ ins / 102 x 131 cm) NLG 8,050. Amsterdam, 12 Dec 1990, *Abstract Composition* (1960, oil on canvas, 31½ x 49¼ ins / 80 x 125 cm) NLG 5,750. Amsterdam, 13 Dec 1990, *Composition* (1962, oil on canvas, 47¼ x 31½ ins / 120 x 80 cm) NLG 7,475. Amsterdam, 22 May 1991, *Abstract Composition* (1960, oil on canvas, 15¾ x 31½ ins / 40 x 80 cm) NLG 4,370. Amsterdam, 11 Dec 1991, *Abstract Composition* (1958, oil on canvas, 19¾ x 23¾ ins / 50 x 60.5 cm) NLG 8,050. Amsterdam, 21 May 1992, *Untitled* (1960, oil on sacking, 15¾ x 31½ ins / 40 x 80 cm) NLG 5,750. Amsterdam, 9 Dec 1992, *Untitled* (oil on sacking, 43¼ x 51¼ ins / 110 x 130 cm) NLG 8,050. Amsterdam, 9 Dec 1993, *Untitled* (1965, oil on sacking, 76¾ x 49¼ ins / 195 x 125 cm) NLG 13,800. Amsterdam, 6 Dec 1995, *Abstract Composition* (1957, oil on canvas, 39¼ x 47¼ ins / 100 x 120 cm) NLG 19,550. Amsterdam, 4 June 1996, *Untitled* (1965, oil/metal, 76¾ x 49¼ ins / 195 x 125 cm) NLG 18,290. Amsterdam, 3 Sept 1996, *Composition* (1960, oil on canvas, 31½ x 37½ ins / 80 x 95 cm) NLG 3,228. Amsterdam, 10 Dec 1996, *Abstract Composition* (oil on canvas, 51¼ x 39¼ ins / 130 x 100 cm) NLG 11,532. Amsterdam, 17-18 Dec 1996, *Untitled* (1954, oil on canvas, 19¾ x 24 ins / 50 x 61 cm) NLG 5,664. Amsterdam, 2-3 June 1997, *Untitled* (1965, oil on canvas, 47¼ x 31¼ ins / 120 x 79.5 cm) NLG 24,780. Amsterdam, 4 June 1997, *Composition* (1962, oil on canvas, 31½ x 47¼ ins / 80 x 120 cm) NLG 13,838. Amsterdam, 2 Dec 1997, *Abstract Composition* (1965, oil on canvas, 27½ x 22 ins / 70 x 55 cm) NLG 14,991. Gravenhage, 2 Nov 1999, *Abstract Composition* (alumimium, h. 41 ins / 104 cm) NLG 5,500. Gravenhage, 2 Nov 1999, *Abstract Composition* (1961, oil on canvas, 31 x 39 ins / 80 x 100 cm) NLG 18,000. Amsterdam, 30 Nov 2000, *Abstract Composition* (1957, oil on canvas, 30 x 35 ins / 75 x 90 cm) NLG 18,000. Amsterdam, 30 Nov 2000, *Compositie met rode en witte streep* (1963, oil on canvas, 20 x 33 ins / 50 x 85 cm) NLG 19,000. Amsterdam, 11 June 2001, *Composition* (1964, oil on canvas, 28 x 24 ins / 70 x 60 cm) NLG 15,000. Amsterdam, 4 Dec 2001, *Untitled* (1963, oil on canvas, 24 x 24 ins / 60 x 60 cm) EUR 9,000. Amsterdam, 28 May 2002, *Untitled* (1961, oil on canvas, 31 x 39 ins / 80 x 100 cm) EUR 10,000. Amsterdam, 26 Nov 2002, *Untitled* (1963, oil on canvas, 26 x 26 ins / 66 x 66 cm) EUR 11,000. Amsterdam, 27 May 2003, *Untitled* (1964, oil on canvas, 31 x 43 ins / 80 x 110 cm) EUR 14,000. Amsterdam, 2 Dec 2003, *Compositie* (1962, oil on canvas, 55 x 43 ins / 140 x 110 cm) EUR 11,000. Amsterdam, 8 June 2004, *Untitled* (oil on canvas, 59 x 79 ins / 150 x 200 cm) EUR 20,000. Amsterdam, 1 Dec 2004, *Untitled* (1962, oil on canvas, 31 x 39 ins / 80 x 100 cm) EUR 13,000.

HUSSENOT, Claude
French, 18th century.
Active in Nancy c. 1720.
Sculptor.

HUSSENOT, Jacques Marcel Auguste
French, 19th century.
Born 5 December 1799, in Courcelles; died 1885, in Metz.
Painter. Portraits.
Jacques Hussenot was awarded a bursary by the town of Metz, to go and study art in Paris. On 10 November 1823 he entered the École des Beaux-Arts, and studied in the studio of Antoine-Jean Gros. He first exhibited at the Paris Salon in 1840, and was awarded a first-class medal in 1855 at the Exposition Universelle. He was a curator at the Musée de Metz, and undertook many commissions for the churches of the town and the surrounding area. Some of his works can be seen in Metz: in the churches of Notre-Dame, St-Vincent, St-Mesmin and St Simon. Hussenot also invented an interesting procedure for fixing wall decorations in place, which proved highly lucrative for him.
Museums and Galleries:
Metz: *Portrait of Monsieur Alfred Malherbe; Portrait of the Painter Auguste Migette.*

Auction records:
Paris, 14 Feb 1920, *Portrait of a Woman in a Yellow Fur-Trimmed Dress,* FRF 380.

HUSSENOT, Joseph
French, 19th century.
Born 18 August 1827, in Metz; died 27 February 1896, in Versailles.
Painter, draughtsman. Religious subjects.

Joseph Hussenot was the son and pupil of Auguste Hussenot, and taught drawing at the military school in St-Cyr, in northwestern France.

Museums and Galleries:
Metz: *St Sebastian* - Rochefort: *Presentation of Jesus at the Temple.*

HUSSET, Henri Robert
French, 20th century.
Born 11 June 1907, in Mantes (Yvelines).
Sculptor. Animals. Statues, groups.

Henri Robert Husset studied at the École des Arts Décoratifs in Paris. His works include a statue of *St Anne* in stone, at the St-Severin church in Paris; a *Vulture,* in hard stone, at the Jardin Public in Mantes; *Amphritite,* low relief in hard stone; a monumental *Lion,* Bourgogne stone, at the Mairie in Mantes; and a *Symbolic Group,* stone, at the Mairie in Mantes. He exhibited in Paris from 1936 at the Salon des Artistes Français. In 1936 he won the silver medal, and became a member. He received a gold medal and was named *hors concours* in 1939. He was a laureate of the Institut de France in 1941, and received a travel grant from the French government in 1942.

Museums and Galleries:
Paris (MNAM-CCI): *Black Panther* (black marble).

HUSSEY, Giles
British, 18th century.
Born 10 February 1710, in Shapwich, Dorset; died June 1788, in Beeston, near Ashburton.
Painter. History painting, portraits.

Giles Hussey was born into a very old family. He began his artistic studies with Richardson and then worked with a Venetian painter, Vincenzo Domini, whom he accompanied to Italy in order to further his education. The Italian, abusing the trust of his pupil and friend, disappeared, along with everything of value which belonged to the young Englishman. Hussey, however, found friends who provided him with the necessary means for him to continue his studies in Boulogne. After following different masters, Giles Hussey eventually felt the need for his own personal aesthetic. He formulated the principle of the similitude of musical lines with the lines and harmonies of forms. After working in Rome, where his work earned him a considerable reputation, he returned to England in 1737. But his sensitivity to feeling was in advance of his time. His gracious works gave rise to envy. From 1742 he settled in London and had to resign himself to painting portraits in order to make a living. He was not cut out to fight for what he wanted, and struggled to find patrons. Discouraged, he left London to return to live in the area from which he came. The death of his elder brother made him the heir to the whole of the family inheritance in 1773, but he only enjoyed this situation for a very short time before withdrawing from the public to live his dream of the ideal in peace.

Auction records:
London, 15 June 1982, *Portrait of Prince Charles Edward Stuart, the Young Pretender* (red chalk, oval, 9 x 6¾ ins / 23 x 17 cm) GBP 1,800. London, 15 March 1984, *Profile Portrait of Prince Charles Edward Stuart, the Young Pretender* (pen and wash, oval, 9¼ x 7 ins / 23.5 x 18 cm) GBP 1,900. London, 12 March 1987, *Portraits of Edward Weld, Joseph Weld and James Weld* (three pencil drawings, oval, 9 x 7¼ ins / 23 x 18.5 cm) GBP 9,000. London, 8 April 1992, *Portrait of an Adolescent, Probably John Wolffe, Seated and Dressed in a Blue Suit Edged with Fur* (oil on canvas, 31½ x 24 ins / 80 x 61 cm) GBP 20,900. London, 31 Oct 2002, *Portrait of Prince Charles Edward Stuart* (pencil, pen, grey ink and wash, feigned oval, 10 x 7 ins / 26 x 19 cm) GBP 19,000.

HUSSEY, Henrietta
Maiden name: Grove
British, 19th century.
Born 1819, in Salisbury.
Painter, engraver. Landscapes.

Henrietta Hussey was a pupil of David Charles Read.

HUSSEY, Philip
Irish, 18th century.
Born 1713, in Cloyne; died 1782, in Dublin.
Painter. Portraits.

Philip Hussey was self-educated and enjoyed something of a reputation in Dublin, where he spent his life.

Auction records:
Stockholm, 16 May 1990, *Portrait of a Lady Dressed in Blue* (oil on canvas, 30 x 24¾ ins / 76 x 63 cm) SEK 10,000. London, 21 May 1999, *Portrait of Joseph Witheral Standing, Wearing Grey Coat* (1743, oil on canvas, 49 x 39 ins / 125 x 99 cm) GBP 3,600. London, 18 May 2001, *Portrait of Samuel Madden in Clerical Robes* (oil on canvas, painted oval, 29 x 24 ins / 73 x 60 cm) GBP 7,000.

HUSSMANN, Albert Hinrich
German, 19th - 20th century.
Born 3 March 1874, in Cuxhaven.
Sculptor. Figures, mythological figures. Equestrian groups.

Hussmann exhibited in Berlin in 1909.

Auction records:
Paris, 25 Nov 1977, *Horse's Head* (bronze, patina, medal, h. 11½ ins / 29 cm) FRF 3,100. Los Angeles, 4 March 1980, *Equestrian Group* (bronze, long. 21 ins / 53.5 cm) USD 2,000. Lokeren, 18 Oct 1986, *Rider* (brown-patinated bronze, h. 14¼ ins / 36 cm) BEF 240,000. Cologne, 15 June 1989, *Europa* (bronze, h. 11½ ins / 29.5 cm) DEM 1,600. Cologne, 28 June 1991, *Rape of Europa* (bronze, h. 19¼ ins / 49 cm) DEM 3,000. Düsseldorf, 4 March 1999, *Wounded Amazon Rider* (ivory, wood, h. 9 ins / 23 cm) DEM 4,000. Munich, 8 May 1999, *Two Jockeys* (green and black patinated bronze, 15 x 24x8 ins / 37 x 61x20 cm) DEM 4,500. Stuttgart, 22 Sept 2000, *Amazon* (brown patinated bronze, h. 29 ins / 73 cm) DEM 6,000. Billingshurst, 23 Oct 2000, *Horse* (black and green patinated bronze, h. 19 ins / 48 cm) GBP 1,850. Deauville, 24 Aug 2001, *Trotting Horse* (brown patinated bronze relief, 14 x 18 ins / 36 x 45 cm) FRF 22,000. Stuttgart, 20 Sept 2001, *Amazon on Horseback* (dark patinated bronze, h. 18 ins / 45 cm) DEM 5,000. London, 5 Nov 2002, *Dying Amazon* (brown patinated bronze, 32 x 16x15 ins / 82 x 40x38 cm) GBP 13,000. Frankfurt, 23 Nov 2002, *Amazone on Horseback* (bronze, h. 37 ins / 94 cm) EUR 9,000. Stuttgart, 27 March 2003, *Europa on Bull* (dark patinated bronze, h. 25 ins / 63 cm) EUR 1,700. Rudolstadt, 11 June 2004, *Two Jousters on Horseback* (brown patinated bronze, h. 15 ins / 37 cm) EUR 2,800. Munich, 24 Sept 2004, *The Victor* (bronze, 25 x 19 ins / 63 x 48 cm) EUR 4,000.

HUSSON
French, 15th century.
Active in Bar-le-Duc.
Sculptor, architect.

Husson was summoned to Toul in 1460 to give his opinion on plans for the cathedral doorway put forward by Tristan. He was also employed in the cathedral of Pont-à-Mousson.

HUSSON, Honoré Jean Aristide
French, 19th century.

Born 1 July 1803, in Paris; died 30 July 1864, in Belleville-Meudon (Hauts-de-Seine).
Sculptor.

Honoré Husson was a pupil of David of Angers. He came second in the Prix de Rome competition in 1827, and won it in 1830. He returned to Paris, and from 1837 began taking part in exhibitions, winning a second-class medal in 1837, and a first-class medal in 1848. Husson was a highly talented official sculptor, and received numerous state commissions. The most notable of these were: *The Guardian Angel Offering up a Repentant Sinner to God*; a bust of *Louis-Philippe* for the Rome Academy; a *Bust of Boissy d'Anglas* and a *Bust of Chancellor Dambray* at the Ministry of the Interior; *Marguerite de Provence* and *Eustache Lesueur* in the Luxembourg Gardens; *Statues of Voltaire and Bailly*, at the former Hôtel de Ville; *St Bernard*, for the church of La Madeleine; *Gouvion St-Cyr* at the Senate; *Adoring Angels* for St-Vincent-de-Paul; *Statue of Clovis*, for St-Clotilde; *Eustache Lesueur* and *Jacques Sarrazin and General Desaix* at the new Louvre; a *Statue of Coulomb the Physician* for the Conservatoire des Arts et Métiers; *Dagobert*, for the tower of St-Germain-l'Auxerrois; and statues of *St Matthias*, *St Simon* and *St Jude* for the church of St-Eustache.

MUSEUMS AND GALLERIES:
AUCH: *Fraternity* - CHARTRES: *Mucius Scævola before Porsenna*; *Bailly, Mayor of Paris* - RODEZ: *Freedom* - VERSAILLES: *Coëtivy, Admiral of France*; *Philip III the Bold*; *Jean Casini*; *Louis Suchet, Duke of Albufera*; *Jeanne de Bourbon, Queen of France*.

HUSSON, Jan
Flemish School, 17th century.
Active in Antwerp in 1668.
Miniaturist.

HUSSON, Jeanne Élisabeth. See **CHAUDET**

HUSSON, Joseph Marie
Swiss, 19th - 20th century.
Born 22 July 1864, in Pruntrut; died 26 January 1910, in Bressancourt.
Painter.

HUSSON, Paul Louis
French, 19th century.
Born 21 April 1839, in Mantes.
Painter. Portraits, genre scenes, landscapes.

Husson studied at the École des Beaux-Arts and was a pupil of Cogni and Comu. He began his career at the Salon in 1869.

HUSTENEUR, Jehan de
Flemish, 15th century.
Painter.
Flemish School.

Jehan de Husteneur painted a panorama of the town of Calais for the Duke of Burgundy in 1435.

HUSTIN, G.
French, 17th century.
Engraver.

G. Hustin is known for a *Portrait of Pope Alexander VII*.

HUSTIN, Louis Arthur
French, 19th - 20th century.
Active in Le Raincy.
Painter. Landscapes.

MUSEUMS AND GALLERIES:
ROCHEFORT: *Landscape*.

HUSUM, Peter
Danish, 17th century.
Died 1619, in Copenhagen.
Sculptor, founder.

HUSZAR, Adolf
Hungarian, 19th century.
Born in Jakabfalva; died 21 January 1885, in Budapest.
Sculptor.

Adolf Huszar studied in Vienna, then settled and worked in Budapest.

HUSZAR, Ilona von (Baroness)
Hungarian, 19th century.
Born 18 February 1865, in Szent Margila.
Painter.

Ilona von Huszar studied with Kurtz and de Marr in Munich.

HUSZAR, Vilmos
Hungarian, 20th century.
Born 1884, in Budapest; died 1960, in Hierden.
Active in the Netherlands from 1905.
Painter. Figures, landscapes, still-lifes.
Neo-Plasticism.
De Stijl.

Vilmos Huszar studied at the school of applied art in Budapest and at the Hollósy studio in Munich. Shortly after his arrival in the Netherlands in 1905, where he settled in Hierden, he met Theo van Doesburg. In 1917, with Mondrian and van Doesburg, he founded the De Stijl group and established the principles of Neo-Plasticism. Although he left De Stijl in 1923, in 1931 he still belonged to the group of abstract artists associated with Michel Seuphor and the Cercle et Carré group. He subsequently returned to figurative art.

As a figurative artist in his early years in The Hague, Huszar was influenced by the Realists, by Van Gogh and then by the artists of the Nabis group. The works of the latter led Huszar to paint works in a flatter and more simplified style. He then began to produce work seemingly influenced by Futurism. From 1917, when he met Bart van der Leck, he became a fervent follower of Mondrian. He designed the logo for the cover of the first edition of the review *De Stijl*. In this period he began to apply the principles of Neo-Plasticism to interior decoration working in collaboration with the architect Jan Wils. He also designed a number of purely abstract stained glass windows. It was not long before he departed from the strict dogma of the group - which permitted only horizontal and vertical lines - by introducing diagonals in 1922. This provoked something of a palace revolution, but nevertheless encouraged van Doesburg to follow his example. In 1922 he also began experimenting with the application of the principles of Neo-Plasticism to theatre design, although he got no further than making some models, works that can be viewed as pictures rather along the lines of Gorin's relief-pictures. Even in his most abstract works - those most obedient to the austere and strict principles of the group - Huszar succeeded in maintaining a link, however schematic and highly stylised, with a subject taken from real life. An example is his *Composition with Female Figure* (1918). Just as Mondrian arrived at his own version of abstraction through his systematic decomposition of a tree and its branches, so Huszar did something similar, taking as his point of departure the head of a woman. In 1923, he designed a multi-coloured interior for an exhibition pavilion destined to show the works of the architect Gerrit Rietveld in Berlin. In the event, this project was not carried out. In 1923 he left the Neo-Plasticist group. He collaborated for a time on the production of the review *I 10* and with the Dutch Dadists, particularly van Doesburg and Schwitters. Together, they designed the interior decoration for a room in a house in The Hague. In 1926 and 1927, he produced some typographical and advertising material and gradually returned to figurative painting, entirely so from 1935, producing many still-lifes and landscapes

His work featured in *Aspects Historiques du Constructivisme et de l'Art Concret* (*Historical Aspects of Constructivism and Concrete Art*) at the Musée d'Art Moderne in Paris (1977), and a retrospective was held at the Gemeentemuseum in The Hague (1985).

BIBLIOGRAPHY:

Seuphor, Michel, *Le Style et le Cri*, Éd. du Seuil, Paris, 1965. *I 10 et son époque*, exhibition catalogue, Institut néerlandais, Paris, 1989.

MUSEUMS AND GALLERIES:

OTTERLO (Kröller-Müller Mus.): *Boy Looking at a White Cloud* (1910); *Composition* (1924) - PARIS (MNAM-CCI): *Flowers* (1922) - THE HAGUE (Gemeentemus.): *Self-portrait with his Wife* (1910); *Composition II (Skaters)* (1917); *Hammer and Saw* (1917).

AUCTION RECORDS:

HAMBURG, 6 June 1969, *Woman*, DEM 11,000. BERN, 18 June 1970, *Carnival* (c. 1920) CHF 9,000. HAMBURG, 15 June 1973, *Still-life with Fruit*, DEM 21,000. AMSTERDAM, 24 April 1979, *Seated Nude* (oil on canvas, 35 x 27¼ ins / 89 x 69 cm) NLG 6,000. BERN, 21 June 1979, *Abstract* (c. 1922, gouache, 4¾ x 4½ ins / 12 x 11.6 cm) CHF 6,600. LONDON, 29 Nov 1982, *Abstract Composition* (c. 1918, oil on panel, 16½ x 15¼ ins / 42 x 39 cm) GBP 8,500. AMSTERDAM, 24 Nov 1986, *Landscape* (1912, oil on canvas, 23½ x 28 ins / 60 x 71 cm) NLG 48,000. HAMBURG, 12 June 1987, *Constructivist Composition* (1922, photo-collage, 7 x 5 ins / 18 x 13 cm) DEM 8,000. AMSTERDAM, 10 April 1989, *Still-life with Vegetables* (1943, oil on canvas, 14¼ x 17¼ ins / 36 x 43.5 cm) NLG 1,035. AMSTERDAM, 24 May 1989, *Farm with Haystacks* (oil on card, 15¾ x 24¾ ins / 40 x 63 cm) NLG 2,300. AMSTERDAM, 13 Dec 1990, *Still-life with Flowers in a Glass Jar* (oil on canvas, 14¾ x 11¾ ins / 37.5 x 30 cm) NLG 5,750. AMSTERDAM, 22 May 1991, *Still-life with Pear, Gourd and Wheat* (oil on canvas, 14 x 17¾ ins / 35.5 x 45 cm) NLG 3,450. AMSTERDAM, 17 Sept 1991, *Tree* (oil on canvas/panel, 19 x 15¼ ins / 48.5 x 38.5 cm) NLG 4,600. AMSTERDAM, 12 Dec 1991, *Still-life with Lemons* (oil on paper, 10¾ x 15 ins / 27.5 x 37.2 cm) NLG 3,450. AMSTERDAM, 8 Dec 1993, *Box with Abstract Geometric Design* (painted wooden box, 8½ x 5¼ x 4¼ ins / 21.5 x 135 x 10.8 cm) NLG 16,100. AMSTERDAM, 7 Dec 1994, *Vanity* (1911, oil on canvas, 13¾ x 16¼ ins / 35 x 41 cm) NLG 2,070. AMSTERDAM, 5 June 1996, *Reclining Lady* (oil on card, 26¾ x 39¼ ins / 68 x 100 cm) NLG 8,625. AMSTERDAM, 18 June 1996, *Still-life with Red Peppers in a Chinese Bowl* (1907, oil on panel, 18 x 15 ins / 46 x 38 cm) GBP 2,070. AMSTERDAM, 10 Dec 1996, *Sneeuw in't Bos* (*Snow in the Wood*) (1958, oil on card, 23½ x 19¾ ins / 60 x 50 cm) NLG 6,342. AMSTERDAM, 2 Dec 1997, *Woman, Composition* (1950, oil on canvas, 23½ x 19¾ ins / 60 x 50 cm) NLG 17,298. AMSTERDAM, 21 Jan 1998, *Still-life with Pipe and Cherries in a Jar* (c. 1910-1913, oil/hardboard, 17 x 14¼ ins / 43 x 36.5 cm) NLG 4,612.

HUTCHENS, Frank Townsend

American, 19th - 20th century.
Born 7 June 1869, in Canandaigsea; died 1937.
Painter. Figure compositions, figures.

Frank Townsend Hutchens lived in New York. He studied under Irving Wiles, Frank Du Mond, and Henry Mowbray at the Art Students League, New York, and under Benjamin Constant, and Jean-Paul Laurens at the Académie Colarossi, Paris. He was a member of the Salmagundi Club, New York, from 1900.

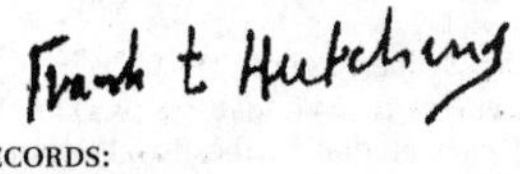

AUCTION RECORDS:

NEW ORLEANS, 13 March 1979, *Taos Pueblo* (oil on canvas, 17½ x 23½ ins / 44.5 x 60 cm) USD 1,200. NEW YORK, 27 Jan 1984, *Woman with a Mandolin* (oil on canvas, 32 x 26 ins / 81.3 x 66 cm) USD 6,000. NEW YORK, 30 May 1990, *Old Man in Interior* (1897, oil on canvas, 25½ x 21¼ ins / 64.8 x 54 cm) USD 1,100. NEW YORK, 12 Jan 1999, *Tulips* (oil on canvas, 24 x 20 ins / 61 x 51 cm) USD 4,800. MT MORRIS, 2 June 2000, *Spring Morning* (oil on canvas, 35 x 35 ins / 90 x 90 cm) USD 10,000. CINCINNATI, 10 Sept 2000, *Woman Reading* (1900, watercolour, 18 x 12 ins / 46 x 30 cm) USD 9,500. OAK PARK, 6 May 2001, *New England Landscape* (c. 1910, oil on canvas, 30 x 36 ins / 76 x 91 cm) USD 6,000. SAN FRANCISCO, 13 June 2001, *Autumn by the Sea* (oil on canvas, 40 x 40 ins / 102 x 102 cm) USD 6,500. MILFORD, 24 April 2003, *Youth* (oil on canvas, 30 x 25 ins / 76 x 64 cm) USD 60,000. GREENVILLE, 28 March 2004, *Portrait of Woman* (oil on board, 6 x 9 ins / 15 x 23 cm) USD 2,000.

HUTCHINGS, J.

British, 19th century.
Born in Blakesly, near Towcester.
Painter. History painting, landscapes.

J. Hutchings exhibited his work in London from 1859 to 1893.

HUTCHINS, Alice

American, 20th century.
Born 1916, in Los Angeles.
Active from 1950 in France.
Sculptor.
Kinetic Art.

Alice Hutchins arrived in Paris in 1950. She decided to take up painting late in life, and trained under Robert Lapoujade in 1956 and 1957. In 1967 she abandoned painting for sculpture. She often exhibited at the Salon Comparaisons and Salon de la Jeune Sculpture.

She made small adjustable sculptures. Using cylindrical or flat magnets and walls, she produced and adapted her steel sculptures, which housed circles, nails or ball bearings. These were held in place by magnetism, but were able to be moved around, which ensured spectator participation.

HUTCHINSON

British, 18th century.
Active in Cambridge.
Engraver.

HUTCHINSON, Allen

British, 19th century.
Active in Stoke-on-Trent.
Sculptor. Low reliefs.

Allen Hutchinson exhibited his work at the Royal Academy in London from 1883 to 1886.

MUSEUMS AND GALLERIES:

SYDNEY: *Sir Alfred Stephen* (marble).

HUTCHINSON, George

British, 19th century.
Miniaturist.

George Hutchinson exhibited his work at the Royal Academy in London from 1774 to 1887.

HUTCHINSON, J. W. Caldwell

British, 20th century.
Painter.

Member of the Royal Drawing Society.

HUTCHINSON, Joseph

British, 18th century.
Born in Dublin.
Miniaturist.

Joseph Hutchinson worked in London.

HUTCHINSON, M.

British, 19th century.
Active in London c. 1830.
Painter. Portraits.

HUTCHINSON, Peter

British, 20th century.

Born 1930.
Sculptor, collage artist.
Conceptual Art, Land Art.

Peter Hutchinson exhibited in Geneva in 1994. His works of Land Art are recorded in photographs. He also produces imaginary landscapes based on photo-montages and found objects, accompanied by texts. His work featured in the exhibition *Les Années 70: l'art en cause* (*The 1970s: Art in Question*) at the CAPC-Musée d'Art Contemporain in Bordeaux in 2002, and *Paysages* (*Landscapes*), a group exhibition exploring man's evolving relationship with the landscape through contemporary art - one of a number of exhibitions celebrating *Trésors publics, 20 ans de création dans les Fonds régionaux d'art contemporain(FRAC)* (*Public Treasury, 20 Years of Creation in the Regional Collection of Contemporary Art (FRAC)*), at the Centre Européen d'Actions Artistiques Contemporaines in Stasbourg.

BIBLIOGRAPHY:

Cameron, Eric, '*Peter Hutchinson: From Earth Art to Story Art*' in *Artforum*, vol 16 no. 4. Ratcliff, Carter, '*Images of Elsewhere*' in *Art in America*, vol 90 no. 12, 1939. *Peter Hutchinson: Works 1968/1974*, exhibition catalogue, Stedelijk Museum, Amsterdam, 1974. Wechsler, Jeffrey, *A Response to the Environment*, exhibition catalogue, Sarah Lawrence College Library, 1975. Tennenbaum, Judith, *Concept, Narrative, Document: Recent Photographic Works from the Morton Neumann Family Collection*, exhibition catalogue, Chicago Museum of Contemporary Art, 1979. Janin, Dorothée, '*Le Paradis d'Hutchinson*' in *Beaux-Arts Magazine* n° 130, periodical, Paris, January 1995. Fréruchet, Maurice, et al., *Les Années soixante-dix: l'art en cause*, exhibition catalogue, Capc musée d'Art contemporain, Bordeaux, 2002. Zahm, Olivier (preface), et al., *Trésors publics, 20 ans de création dans les Fonds régionaux d'art contemporain*, Flammarion, Paris, 2003 (text in French and English).

MUSEUMS AND GALLERIES:

CAEN (Basse-Normandie): *Two Chrysanthemum Pieces* (1970-1971); *Threaded Calabash* (1969); *The Paradox of the Twins II* (1974); *Paricutin Project* (1970); *Lime-Grass Piece* (1969); *Iceberg Project* (1968); *Grand Canyon Project* (1969); *Foraging* (1971); *Electric Churches* (1973); *Apple Triangle* (1970).

AUCTION RECORDS:

AMSTERDAM, 9 Dec 1988, *Panorama from my Rockery* (colouring pencil/photograph glued/paper, 11 x 13 1/2 ins / 27 x 34 cm) NLG 1,380. NEW YORK, 1 Nov 1994, *Artichoke, Blue Rose, Concentration (Alphabet series)* (1974, three coloured photographs and black felt/card, each 39 1/4 x 29 1/4 ins / 99.7 x 74.5 cm) USD 2,645.

HUTCHINSON, Samuel

British, 18th century.
Active in London.
Painter.

Samuel Hutchinson exhibited landscapes in London at the Society of Artists and at the Royal Academy in 1770 and 1802.

HUTCHISON, D.C.

American, 19th - 20th century.
Born 19 August 1869, in Arbroath, Scotland; died 1954.
Illustrator.

D.C. Hutchison was active in New York. He was a pupil of Jean-Paul Laurens at the Académie Julian in Paris.

HUTCHISON, Frederick William

Canadian, 19th - 20th century.
Born 1871, in Montreal; died 1953.
Painter. Genre scenes, landscapes with figures.

Frederick William Hutchison was a pupil of Jean-Paul Laurens and Benjamin Constant in Paris.

AUCTION RECORDS:

NEW YORK, 21 Nov 1945, *Before the St-Urban Mass*, USD 525. TORONTO, 5 Nov 1979, *Old Thatched Cottage* (oil on canvas, 25 x 30 ins / 63.5 x 76.2 cm) CAD 2,200. MONTREAL, 17 Oct 1988, *Women in front of a Porch in St-Urban* (oil on canvas, 12 1/4 x 16 1/4 ins / 31 x 41 cm) CAD 1,800. MONTREAL, 30 April 1990, *Cottage in the Laurentians* (oil on panel, 7 3/4 x 9 3/4 ins / 20 x 25 cm) CAD 1,320. MONTREAL, 17 June 1997, *Baie St-Paul, Quebec* (oil on canvas, 16 x 20 ins / 40.5 x 50.6 cm) CAD 3,200. TORONTO, 7 Dec 1999, *Rural Farm Scene with Boat and Lake* (oil on canvas, 16 x 20 ins / 40 x 50 cm) CAD 2,500. TORONTO, 15 Nov 2000, *The Old Home* (oil on canvas, 12 x 16 ins / 31 x 41 cm) CAD 2,500. TORONTO, 21 Nov 2000, *Little River* (oil on canvas, 16 x 20 ins / 40 x 50 cm) CAD 2,600. OTTAWA, 22 Nov 2001, *Winter's Glow, New York City* (c. 1925, oil on canvas, 12 x 16 ins / 30 x 41 cm) CAD 6,000. TORONTO, 3 Dec 2002, *St Urbain* (gouache, 4 x 6 ins / 9 x 15 cm) CAD 2,600. TORONTO, 3 Dec 2002, *Near Hudson Heights, Houses* (oil on canvas on board, 10 x 12 ins / 25 x 30 cm) CAD 3,000. TORONTO, 2 Dec 2003, *Home from the Village* (oil on panel, 5 x 7 ins / 12 x 18 cm) CAD 5,400. TORONTO, 2 Dec 2003, *Valley of Baie St Paul. Baie St Paul. Road to Baie St Paul* (gouache, three, 7 x 8 ins / 17 x 21 cm) CAD 9,000. TORONTO, 1 June 2004, *Old House and Poplars* (oil on canvas, 12 x 16 ins / 30 x 40 cm) CAD 3,800. TORONTO, 1 June 2004, *Quebec Village* (oil on canvas, 16 x 20 ins / 41 x 51 cm) CAD 10,500.

HUTCHISON, J.

British, 18th - 19th century.
Active in London.
Miniaturist.

J. Hutchison frequently exhibited his work at the Royal Academy in London from 1792 to 1819.

HUTCHISON, John

British, 19th - 20th century.
Born 1 June 1833, in Edinburgh; died 22 May 1910, in Edinburgh.
Sculptor. Figures. Busts.

John Hutchison was active in Edinburgh. He became a member of the Royal Scottish Academy in 1867.

MUSEUMS AND GALLERIES:

CAMBRIDGE: *Bust of William Wright* - EDINBURGH (Nat. Gal. of Scotland): *Pasquaccia, a Roman Contadina* (marble); *Robert Scott Lauder* (marble) - EDINBURGH (Royal Scottish Academy): bust*Marietta, a Roman Girl* (1860, marble).

HUTCHISON, Maud Gemmell

British, 20th century.
Painter.

Maud Gemmel Hutchison lived and worked in Musselburgh. She was a relative of the genre painter Robert Gemmel Hutchison, and exhibited with the Royal Scottish Academy in Edinburgh in 1909.

HUTCHISON, Robert Gemmell

British, 19th - 20th century.
Born 1855, in Edinburgh; died 23 August 1936, in St Abbs, Berwickshire.
Painter. Landscapes, figures, portraits.

Robert Gemmel Hutchison began his working life as a seal engraver, but later studied at the Royal Scottish Academy schools and at the Board of Manufacturers School of Art. He is well known for his paintings in watercolour and oil of children and childhood, particularly of scenes by the sea. His work is considered to be influenced by Dutch painting and by the Scottish Faed family of artists, as well as by Josef Israels and William MacTaggart. From 1878 he exhibited frequently; he was elected to the Royal Scottish Society of Painters in Watercolours in 1895, became an Associate of the Royal Scottish Academy in 1901 and a full member in 1911. He was awarded a medal for his work in 1903.

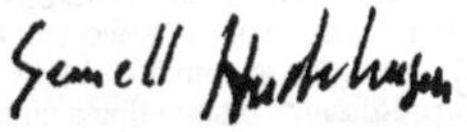

Museums and Galleries:
Edinburgh (Royal Scottish Academy): *Shifting Shadows* (1913, oil on canvas) - Liverpool: *Still-life.*
Auction records:
London, 17 Dec 1910, *Wee Jukie Daadles* (pastel) GBP 10. London, 5 Dec 1924, *The Baby,* GBP 78. London, 18 June 1926, *The Cut Joot,* GBP 29. London, 27 Oct 1928, *Mother and Child,* GBP 105. London, 12 March 1934, *Young Sailors,* GBP 30. London, 7 Oct 1937, *Children on the Seashore,* GBP 36. Glasgow, 3 March 1944, *Kite,* GBP 50; *On the Shore at Carnoustie,* GBP 70. Glasgow, 16 Nov 1945, *Sisters,* GBP 42. Glasgow, 8 Nov 1946, *Roses,* GBP 250. Glasgow, 20 Dec 1946, *Children of the Waves,* GBP 60. Glasgow, 20 Nov 1973, *Interior with Children,* GBP 1,700. Perth, 13 April 1976, *Mother and Child* (oil on canvas, 23½ x 17½ ins / 60 x 44.5 cm) GBP 700. Auchterarder, 30 Aug 1977, *Lady Golfers Looking for their Ball* (gouache, 17½ x 23½ ins / 44.5 x 60 cm) GBP 1,100; *Seashore* (oil on card, 7 x 9½ ins / 18 x 24 cm) GBP 750. London, 19 March 1979, *Young Girls on the Seashore, with Seagulls* (oil on canvas, 26¾ x 35 ins / 68 x 89 cm) GBP 5,600. Glasgow, 18 Dec 1980, *Carnoustie* (watercolour, 17¾ x 13½ ins / 45 x 34 cm) GBP 1,000. Auchterarder, 1 Sept 1981, *Washing the Creel* (oil on card, 10 x 12 ins / 24.5 x 30.5 cm) GBP 9,000. Auchterarder, 30 Aug 1983, *Sleeping Children* (oil on canvas, 15 x 14 ins / 38 x 35.5 cm) GBP 5,000. Auchterarder, 28 Aug 1984, *Young Girl on the Beach in a High Wind* (gouache and watercolour, 13¾ x 9¾ ins / 35 x 24.7 cm) GBP 1,300. Perth, 27 Aug 1985, *Two Girls in the Rain* (watercolour, 17¼ x 23½ ins / 44 x 60 cm) GBP 2,100. Glasgow, 18 Sept 1986, *Dreams* (oil on canvas, 28 x 44½ ins / 71.2 x 113 cm) GBP 18,000. Auchterarder, 1 Sept 1987, *Teatime* (oil on canvas, 20 x 27¼ ins / 51 x 69 cm) GBP 16,000. Edinburgh, 30 Aug 1988, *Sea breeze* (watercolour, 15 x 19¼ ins / 38 x 49 cm) GBP 7,700; *Mending* (oil on canvas, 20 x 16¼ ins / 51 x 41 cm) GBP 12,650. Glasgow, 7 Feb 1989, *When the Sea Rises up to the Field* (oil on canvas/card, 16¼ x 21 ins / 41 x 53.5 cm) GBP 26,400. New York, 23 May 1989, *At Glasgow Racecourse* (oil on canvas, 15 x 20 ins / 38.1 x 50.8 cm) USD 9, 350. Paris, 19 June 1989, *Children's Games on the Beach* (oil on canvas, 14¼ x 20 ins / 36.5 x 51 cm) FRF 5,500. Perth, 29 Aug 1989, *Little Girl Sitting on a Lobster Pot* (oil on canvas, 24 x 18 ins / 61 x 46 cm) GBP 22,000. Glasgow, 6 Feb 1990, *A Cheerful Greeting* (watercolour and gouache, 14 x 16 ins / 35.5 x 40.5 cm) GBP 13,200. Edinburgh, 26 April 1990, *On the Slope* (oil on canvas, 18 x 24 ins / 45.7 x 61 cm) GBP 15,400. Perth, 27 Aug 1990, *On the Clifftop* (oil on canvas, 28 x 36 ins / 71 x 91.5 cm) GBP 24,200. New York, 24 Oct 1990, *Children Looking for Seashells on a Beach* (watercolour and gouache/paper, 10 x 14 ins / 25.5 x 35.5 cm) USD 6,600. Glasgow, 22 Nov 1990, *An Attentive Reader* (oil on canvas, 25 x 30¼ ins / 63.5 x 76.8 cm) GBP 17,600. Glasgow, 5 Feb 1991, *Apple Bobbing* (oil on canvas, 43¼ x 65¼ ins / 110 x 166 cm) GBP 11,000. Edinburgh, 2 May 1991, *Sailing the Sabots, Volendam* (oil on canvas, 20 x 27 ins / 50.8 x 68.5 cm) GBP 9,020. Perth, 26 Aug 1991, *The Toy Boat* (oil on canvas/card, 9¾ x 13½ ins / 25 x 34 cm) GBP 18,700. New York, 17 Oct 1991, *Smelling the Rose* (oil on canvas, 18 x 14 ins / 45.7 x 35.6 cm) USD 11,000. Glasgow, 4 Dec 1991, *A Village Carnival: Hi! Hi!! Hi!!!* (oil on canvas, 45 x 61¾ ins / 114 x 157 cm) GBP 30,800. Edinburgh, 28 April 1992, *Little Girl Looking at a Book* (oil on canvas, 14 x 10 ins / 35.5 x 25.5 cm) GBP 5,500. New York, 27 May 1992, *After-dinner Nap* (oil on canvas, 24 x 20 ins / 61.2 x 50.8 cm) USD 4,950. Perth, 31 Aug 1993, *Dreams* (oil on canvas, 28 x 44½ ins / 71 x 113 cm) GBP 23,000. Glasgow, 14 Feb 1995, *Children Playing on a Beach* (watercolour, 9 x 11½ ins / 22 x 29.5 cm) GBP 6,210. New York, 1 Nov 1995, *The Lost Ball* (oil on canvas, 19 x 29¼ ins / 48.3 x 74.3 cm) USD 9,775. Glasgow, 16 April 1996, *The Pet Budgerigar* (oil on canvas, 12½ x 9¼ ins / 31.5 x 23.5 cm) GBP 3,680. Perth, 26 Aug 1996, *Fisherman's Daughter* (oil on canvas, 30¼ x 25½ ins / 77 x 64.5 cm) GBP 48,800. Glasgow, 11 Dec 1996, *Young `Girls' Secrets* (watercolour heightened with white, 17½ x 13¼ ins / 44.5 x 33.5 cm) GBP 19,550. London, 15 April 1997, *Mysteries of the Sea* (oil on panel, 9¼ x 12 ins / 23.5 x 30.5 cm) GBP 10, 925. Edinburgh, 15 May 1997, *Young Communicants* (oil on canvas, 45½ x 65¼ ins / 115.5 x 166 cm) GBP 9,775. Auchterarder, 26 Aug 1997, *Buckie Gatherer* (oil on panel, 18 x 14 ins / 45.5 x 35.5 cm) GBP 8,625. Haslemere, 19 May 1999, *Cup of Milk* (oil on canvas, 15 x 12 ins / 38 x 30 cm) GBP 15,500. London, 28 Oct 1999, *Among the Bents* (oil on canvas, 15 x 11 ins / 37 x 27 cm) GBP 21,000. London, 30 Aug 2000, *Best Friends* (oil on panel, 6 x 8 ins / 16 x 21 cm) GBP 20,000. London, 26 Oct 2000, *In the Dunes* (oil on canvasboard, 10 x 12 ins / 25 x 30 cm) GBP 19,500. Edinburgh, 24 Aug 2001, *Pet Rabbit* (oil on canvas, 20 x 24 ins / 50 x 60 cm) GBP 32,000. London, 5 Sept 2001, *Strawberries and Cream* (watercolour heightened with gouache, 20 x 29 ins / 51 x 74 cm) GBP 12,000. Edinburgh, 22 Aug 2002, *Doubtful Weather* (watercolour, 24 x 20 ins / 60 x 50 cm) GBP 11,500. Edinburgh, 6 Dec 2002, *Sailing the Toy Boat, Carnoustie* (oil on canvas, 16 x 20 ins / 40 x 50 cm) GBP 16,500. London, 14 April 2003, *Windy Day by the Coast* (oil on canvas, 20 x 30 ins / 51 x 76 cm) GBP 20,000. London, 27 Aug 2003, *Kitten's Milk* (oil on panel, 14 x 15 ins / 36 x 39 cm) GBP 20,000. London, 19 April 2004, *Peeling Potatoes* (oil on canvas, 24 x 20 ins / 61 x 51 cm) GBP 30,000. Hatfield, 29 Sept 2004, *Bleaching* (oil on canvas, 34 x 44 ins / 86 x 112 cm) USD 60,000.

HUTCHISSON

British, 19th century.
Active in Bath c. 1815.
Painter. Portraits.

HUTER, Andrea

Austrian, 19th - 20th century.
Born 13 November 1838, in Kannserberg; died 4 May 1910, in Kannserberg.
Sculptor.

Huter is known for his Crucifixions.

HUTER, Marie

Austrian, 18th century.
Miniaturist.

HUTER, Simon

German, 16th century.
Active c. 1560.
Engraver (wood).

Simon Huter was a gifted artist. He engraved blocks after drawings by Aman Jost, particularly for a *Neewe Biblische Figuren* (*New Bible Characters*) (Frankfurt, 1564), and in collaboration with Virgilius Solis produced a series of blocks for a *History of the Bible.*

HUTH, Carl
German, 19th century.
Active in Berlin.
Painter.
His work is genre pictures.

HUTH, Franz
German, 20th century.
Born 1876, in Thuringia; died 1970, in Weimar.
Painter, watercolourist, pastellist. Landscapes, flowers.
AUCTION RECORDS:
MUNICH, 28 Nov 1980, *Mirror* (watercolour, 27 1/2 x 19 1/2 ins / 70 x 49.5 cm) DEM 2,500. HEIDELBERG, 11 April 1981, *Pathway Bordered by Trees* (pastel, 14 1/2 x 20 ins / 37 x 50.5 cm) DEM 1,700. HEIDELBERG, 11 April 1987, *View of the Throne Room in Darmstadt Castle* (1920, watercolour, 32 1/4 x 25 1/4 ins / 82 x 64 cm) DEM 6,700. HEIDELBERG, 14 Oct 1988, *Still-life of Flowers, with Peonies and Pansies* (1942, pastel, 23 1/2 x 19 3/4 ins / 60 x 50 cm) DEM 3,400. HEIDELBERG, 12 Oct 1991, *Village by a River* (watercolour, 9 1/2 x 12 3/4 ins / 24 x 32.5 cm) DEM 1,800. HEIDELBERG, 11 April 1992, *Castle Park* (watercolour heightened with pastels, 23 1/4 x 19 1/2 ins / 58.8 x 49.5 cm) DEM 2,500; *Still-life with Roses and Other Spring Flowers* (1961, pastel, 13 3/4 x 19 1/4 ins / 35 x 49 cm) DEM 3,500. HEIDELBERG, 9 Oct 1992, *In the Garden* (watercolour, 15 3/4 x 21 ins / 40 x 53.5 cm) DEM 5,500. HEIDELBERG, 3 April 1993, *Heidelberg in Winter* (1955, pastel, 13 1/2 x 19 ins / 34.5 x 48.5 cm) DEM 5,600. HEIDELBERG, 5-13 April 1994, *The Statue of Diana in Schwetzinger Park* (pastel, 23 x 17 1/4 ins / 58.5 x 44 cm) DEM 3,800. HEIDELBERG, 12 Oct 2001, *Red and White Peonies in Blue Vase* (pastel, 26 x 20 ins / 65 x 50 cm) DEM 4,400.

HUTH, Frederick
British, 19th century.
Died before 1905.
Active in Edinburgh.
Engraver (etching).
Frederick Huth won a silver medal at the Exposition Universelle in Paris in 1900. He exhibited his work at the Royal Academy in London from 1890.

HUTH, Julius
German, 19th century.
Born 27 June 1838, in Woisenthin; died 23 July 1892, in Schöneberg.
Painter. Seascapes.
Julius Huth had been a sailor for 15 years when he was admitted to Hermann Eschke's studio.
MUSEUMS AND GALLERIES:
LEIPZIG (Mus. der Bildenden Künste): *Rough Sea*.

HUTH, Rosa
German, 19th century.
Born 6 January 1815, in Frankfurt am Main; died 28 January 1843, in Frankfurt am Main.
Painter, watercolourist. Portraits.
MUSEUMS AND GALLERIES:
MAINZ: *Portrait of Franz Anton Schick* (1841, watercolour).

HUTH, Theodor
German, 19th century.
Born 16 July 1821, in Frankfurt am Main.
Painter. Landscapes.
He was the brother of Rosa Huth.

HUTH-RÖSSLER, Waltraut
German, 20th century.
Born 1940, in Stuttgart.
Also active in Switzerland.
Painter.
From 1959 to 1963 Waltraut Huth-Rössler was a student at the fine arts academy in Stuttgart, and from 1963 to 1966 she studied philology, geography and art history at the universities of Munich and Stuttgart. From 1966 to 1969 she lived and worked as a painter in Zurich. From 1978 to 1979 she obtained an art grant from the Zurich Canton, and in 1979 she returned to live in Stuttgart. From 1981 to 1982 she held a grant from the cultural authorities of Bad-Wurttemberg. She divides her time between Zurich and Stuttgart.

She works with different materials and different supports. Her painting is purely Neo-Constructivist, with a tendency towards Minimalism that has been prevalent among Swiss artists since Max Bill, for example Gottfried Honegger, to whose work Huth-Rössler's is sometimes quite close. She divides up her surfaces with rigorously geometric, often repetitive lines. The resulting compartments are filled with different shades of grey or opposing colours.

Her work has been shown at numerous collective exhibitions, including in Zurich and Vienna (1971 onwards); Stuttgart and Karlsruhe (1973 onwards); Lugano and Schaffhausen (1977 onwards); Basel (1981 onwards); *Series, Variations, Cycles* at the Municipal Gallery in Zurich (1981); the Suzanne Bollag Gallery in Zurich (1982); the exhibition of work by Bad-Wurttemberg award-holders in Esslingen, Karlsruhe and Baden-Baden (1982-83); in Cologne (1983 onwards); the exhibition *Constructivist Trends* at the Municipal Gallery in Stuttgart, Karlsruhe, Mainz, Ulm and Munich (1984 onwards). There have been solo exhibitions of her works since 1964 in Stuttgart, and regularly since 1983 at the Suzanne Bollag Gallery in Zurich.
BIBLIOGRAPHY:
Waltraut Huth-Rössler, exhibition catalogue, Gal. Suzanne Bollag, Zurich, 1987.
MUSEUMS AND GALLERIES:
MANNHEIM (Städtische Kunsthalle) - MUNICH (Bayerische Staatsbibliothek).

HUTHSTEINER, Rudolf
German, 19th century.
Born 13 April 1855, in Düsseldorf; died 1935, in Pforzheim.
Painter. Portraits, church interiors.
He trained at the academy in Düsseldorf. In 1877, he settled in Stuttgart. He exhibited in Berlin and Munich, where he won a medal in 1905.
MUSEUMS AND GALLERIES:
DÜSSELDORF: *Mayor Wilhelm Marx* - MAINZ: *Interior of Amerbach Abbey Church* - STUTTGART: *William II of Württemberg*.
AUCTION RECORDS:
COLOGNE, 23 March 1990, *Church Interior* (1922, oil on canvas, 35 3/4 x 27 1/4 ins / 91 x 69 cm) DEM 2,600. MUNICH, 24 March 1999, *Stormy Mountain Landscape* (1909, oil on canvas, 30 x 42 ins / 75 x 106 cm) DEM 3,800. COLOGNE, 4 Dec 1999, *Concert* (1913, oil on canvas, 31 x 25 ins / 79 x 64 cm) DEM 4,000. MUNICH, 5 April 2000, *Church Interior in Furstenfeld* (1913, oil on canvas, 52 x 41 ins / 132 x 104 cm) DEM 10,000.

HUTIN, Charles
French, 19th century.
Born 1847, in Paris; died June 1898.
Painter. Genre scenes.
Hutin began his career at the Salon in 1874.
MUSEUMS AND GALLERIES:
LANGRES: *La Pâtée*.
AUCTION RECORDS:
PARIS, 20 Nov 1937, *Basket of Fruit*, FRF 135. LONDON, 16 May 1978, *Elegant Group in a Carriage with Eight Horses* (watercolour and pen heightened with white, 15 3/4 x 31 1/4in/40 x 79.5cm) GBP 500.

HUTIN, Charles François
French, 18th century.

Born 4 July 1715, in Paris; died 29 July 1776, in Dresden.
Painter, sculptor, engraver, draughtsman. Mythological subjects, genre scenes.

Charles François Hutin studied under François Le Maux. In 1736 he won the first prize for painting in the Prix de Rome and spent seven years there studying the old masters. At that time he turned his interest to sculpture. Back in Paris he was admitted into the Académie in 1746. However, he left soon afterwards for Dresden where the art academy offered him a teaching post in 1748 and the directorship in 1764. He stayed there until his death, devoting himself to painting and sculpture in equal measure. He is also remembered for some engravings such as *Actaeon Devoured by his Dogs*.

MUSEUMS AND GALLERIES:

BUDAPEST: *Hagar in the Desert* - DRESDEN: *Girl Holding a Letter* - LANGRES: *The Hotpot* - MADRID: *Man Leading a Cart; Woman Lighting a Fire* - OSLO: *An Old Man; A Beggar* - PARIS (Louvre): *Charon* (statue).

AUCTION RECORDS:

PARIS, 25 and 26 Jan 1894, *Model of a Louis XV Clock* (drawing) FRF 106. PARIS, 5 and 6 May 1898, *The Boiler* (drawing in black pencil) FRF 490; *Man with a Wheelbarrow* (drawing) FRF 530. PARIS, 1 March 1929, *Young Messenger* (drawing) FRF 3,000. NEW YORK, 17 Oct 1959, *Ballet Scene* (watercolour) USD 225. LONDON, 23 Nov 1960, *Chunk of Ham*, GBP 320. ZURICH, 15 May 1981, *Rural Festivals* (oil on canvas, a pair, 23 1/2 x 39 1/4 ins / 60 x 100 cm) CHF 46,000. MONTE CARLO, 14 Feb 1983, *Polish Interior* (oil on canvas, 36 1/2 x 24 1/2 ins / 92.5 x 62 cm) FRF 26,000. PARIS, 23 May 1986, *Tobias Burying the Dead* (grey wash/black chalk, 9 x 6 1/4 ins / 22 x 15.7 cm) FRF 15,000. MONTE CARLO, 6 Dec 1987, *Young Messenger* (1750; *Man Writing a Letter* (oil on canvas, a pair, 20 1/4 x 25 1/2 ins / 51.5 x 65 cm) FRF 580,000. PARIS, 18 Nov 1994, *Saxon Peasant Farmer Pulling a Wheelbarrow* (black and white chalk, 19 3/4 x 13 1/4 ins / 50 x 33.5 cm) FRF 5,000. LONDON, 9 April 2003, *Portrait of a Young Woman Holding a Spaniel* (1767, oil on canvas, 31 x 22 ins / 78 x 56 cm) GBP 35,000.

HUTIN, François

French, 18th century.
Born c. 1685; died August 1758.
Active in Paris.
Painter, engraver.

François Hutin was the father of Charles François, Jean Baptiste and Pierre Hutin.

HUTIN, G.W.

British, 19th century.
Active in Greenwich.
Engraver.

HUTIN, Jean Baptiste

French, 18th century.
Born c. 1725, in Paris.
Painter. Mythological subjects.

Jean Baptiste Hutin was assistant teacher at the Académie de St-Luc and featured at that society's exhibitions in 1756 and 1764.

AUCTION RECORDS:

NICE, 8 Nov 1950, *The Sacrifice*, FRF 13,000.

HUTIN, Pierre

French, 18th century.
Born c. 1720, in Paris; died 1763, in Moscow.
Sculptor, engraver (etching).

Pierre Hutin engraved religious and genre subjects. He worked in Paris and Dresden with his brother Charles François Hutin.

HUTING, Jacobus

Dutch, 18th century.
Active in Amsterdam in 1726.
Painter.

HUTINOT, Pierre

French, 17th century.
Born 1616, in Paris; died 28 September 1679, in Paris.
Sculptor.

Pierre Hutinot was apprenticed to Guillain. He was admitted into the Académie in 1667 with a marble low relief, *Painting and Sculpture Discovered by Time*, now at the Louvre. He is also remembered for the *Statue of Summer* which was in the park at Versailles.

HUTSCHENREITER, Victor Max

Austrian, 19th century.
Born 1828, in Vienna.
Painter, engraver. Hunting scenes, animals.

A pupil of Waldmüller and student at the academy in Vienna. He regularly exhibited in Vienna from 1868.

HUTSKY, Matthias

Bohemian, 16th century.
Born 1546, in Pürglitz (Krivoklat).
Painter.

Matthias Hutsky mainly worked in Prague, where he painted a number of portraits.

HUTSON, William Richard, called Bill

American, 20th century.
Born 6 September 1936, in San Marcos (Texas).
Painter (mixed media), collage artist.

Bill Hutson studied at the University of New Mexico, Albuquerque in 1956-1957; at City College, Los Angeles, in 1958-1959; at the Trade Technical College, Los Angeles, in 1959; and San Francisco Art Institute in 1960-1961. He has travelled a great deal for study purposes, work and exhibitions: from 1963 to 1970, he visited many European countries; in 1971-1972, he revisited Italy and France, and also went to Mexico and Nigeria; from 1973 to 1980, he was in France, Spain, Mexico, Venezuela and several countries in Africa; and from 1993 to 1996 he was in France, Spain, Holland and Senegal. He lives and works in Lancaster, Pennsylvania.

Hutson often paints large-scale works, including *Sasa of the First Creation Crossing a Bone Path North by Northeast*.

Hutson has participated in many group exhibitions in the USA, in the countries visited during his trips abroad, and in exhibitions dedicated to Afro-American artists. He has shown series of his works in solo exhibitions, including: 1964, H. Kikhaar Gallery, Amsterdam; 1965, Bolles Gallery, San Francisco; 1966, Stedelijk Museum, Apeldoom (Holland); 1971 Nigeria; 1978, 1991, Cinque Gallery, New York; 1979, Baton Rouge (Louisiana); 1981, 62 Gallery, New York; 1984, Onyx Art Gallery, New York; 1987, Studio Museum, Harlem, New York; 1988, California Afro-American Museum, Los Angeles; and 1990, Maryland Institute, Baltimore.

BIBLIOGRAPHY:

Honig Fine, Elsa, *The Afro-American Artist*, Holt, Rinehart and Winston, New York, 1971. *Bill Hutson: paintings, 1978-1987*, exhibition catalogue, Studio Museum in Harlem, New York, 1987.

MUSEUMS AND GALLERIES:

ADELAIDE (South Australian Mus.) - BALTIMORE (James E. Lewis Mus. of Art, Morgan State University) - COLUMBUS, OH (MA): *Broad Street Series No.4* (1988) - NEW YORK (Studio Mus. in Harlem) - NEWARK (Mus.): *Sasa of the First Creation Crossing a Bone Path North by Northeast* (1971, oil on canvas) - ROTTERDAM (Mus. Boijmans Van Beuningen) - SAN FRANCISCO (MoMA).

HUTT, John

British, 18th century.
Born in London.
Engraver.

HUTTARY, Josef
Bohemian, 19th century.
Born in Kundratice; died 1890, in Prague.
Painter.

HÜTTER, E., or Huetter
Austrian, 19th century.
Born 14 May 1835; died 21 January 1886.
Painter, watercolourist, draughtsman, engraver.
Landscapes.
He was city treasurer in Vienna. Mentioned by Lugt, he left numerous documents about the city.

Stamp of sale

Museums and Galleries:
Vienna: *Views of Vienna* (watercolour).

HUTTER, Wolfgang
Austrian, 20th century.
Born 1928.
Painter, watercolourist. Figure compositions. Murals, designs for tapestries.
Phantastischer Realismus group.
Wolfgang Hutter was a student at the arts and crafts academy and the fine arts school in Vienna, where his professor was Albert Paris Güthersloh. Güthersloh had a strong influence on Hutter, as he did on many other Austrian artists, drawing them into the realms of fantastical art he had already explored. Hutter was awarded the UNESCO prize at the Venice Biennale in 1954 and a further prize by the city of Vienna in 1958, in recognition of his ongoing work. The museum in Vienna took the step of assigning him a permanent place, thereby drawing the public's attention to this original and typically Viennese school of painting. The museum also organised exhibitions abroad, for example in Paris in 1970.

Hutter made tapestries for the Ministry of the Interior of what was West Germany; a mosaic ceiling (in collaboration with Roman Haller) for the foyer of a theatre in Vienna; and, in 1962, a mural entitled *From Night to Day* for the new festival hall in Salzburg. Within the fantastical trend, so typical of Vienna at the time, Hutter's work is distinguishable by the Rococo Baroque nature of the universe he creates, and of the creatures, fairies and demons that fill it.

Museums and Galleries:
Princeton (AM, Princeton University) - Vienna (Albertina Mus.) - Vienna (Kunsthistorisches Mus.).

Auction records:
Vienna, 20 Sept 1972, *Composition* (watercolour) ATS 80,000. Vienna, 13 March 1984, *Widow* (1962, oil on paper remounted on hardboard, 8¼ x 11½ ins / 21 x 29.5 cm) ATS 50,000. Zurich, 8 Nov 1985, *Fortune-tellers* (1972, oil on canvas, 27¾ x 39¼ ins / 70.5 x 100 cm) CHF 75,000. London, 24 June 1986, *Night Girl* (1965, tempera/card, 5¼ x 12½ ins / 13.5 x 31.6 cm) GBP 2,200. Vienna, 25 June 1986, *Heads* (pen and Indian ink, 18¼ x 23 ins / 46.5 x 57.5 cm) ATS 25,000. Munich, 1 June 1987, *Two Heads* (1951, oil on panel, 14¾ x 12¾ ins / 37.6 x 32.5 cm) DEM 15,000. London, 22 Feb 1990, *Very Tired Flowers* (1965, ink/paper, 19 x 18½ ins / 48.2 x 47 cm) GBP 660. Vienna, 19 May 1999, *The Magic Flute in Salzburg* (1956, watercolour, 17 x 10 ins / 42 x 25 cm) ATS 130,000. Vienna, 13 Oct 1999, *Dream* (1947, pencil, 24 x 20 ins / 61 x 52 cm) ATS 80,000. Vienna, 27 Nov 2002, *Summer II* (oil on masonite, 23 x 15 ins / 59 x 39 cm) EUR 9,000. Vienna, 27 Nov 2002, *Spring II* (oil on masonite, 23 x 15 ins / 59 x 39 cm) EUR 9,000.

HUTTINGER, Christian
German, 17th century.
Active in Chemnitz.
Sculptor.

HUTTMANN, Michael
German, 18th century.
Active in Würzburg.
Sculptor.

HUTTON, H. P.
19th century.
Painter. Landscapes.

Museums and Galleries:
Melbourne (Nat. Gal. of Victoria): *Halt on the Road; Seascape; Landscape.*

HUTTON, Thomas Sidney
British, 19th - 20th century.
Born c. 1865; died 1935.
Painter, watercolourist. Landscapes.

Auction records:
London, 25 Jan 1988, *The Beach in Sunderland* (1926, watercolour, 10 x 20½ ins / 25.5 x 52 cm) GBP 2,365. Edinburgh, 30 Aug 1988, *St Monance on the Fife Coast* (watercolour, 16½ x 28 ins / 42 x 71 cm) GBP 990. London, 1 Nov 1990, *Summer Evening on Holy Island with Lindisfarne Abbey in the Background* (pencil and watercolour with highlights, 12¼ x 20 ins / 31.2 x 51.1 cm) GBP 770. London, 8 Feb 1991, *Vessel in Harbour at Eyemouth, Berwickshire* (watercolour heightened with white, 9½ x 13½ ins / 24.2 x 34.4 cm) GBP 660. Edinburgh, 28 April 1992, *Windy Day at St Andrews* (watercolour, 10 x 16½ ins / 24.5 x 42 cm) GBP 550. Glasgow, 1 Feb 1994, *Loch Sligachan on the Isle of Skye* (watercolour, 10¼ x 14 ins / 26 x 35.5 cm) GBP 1,012. Newcastle, 22 June 1999, *Near St Anthony-in-Roseland, Cornwall* (watercolour, 9x13 ins / 24x34 cm) GBP 850. Newcastle, 22 June 1999, *Old Hartley, Northumberland* (watercolour, 13x25 ins / 32x63 cm) GBP 700. Newcastle, 19 Sept 2000, *Vale of Ross, Arran* (oil on canvas, 24x35 ins / 60x90 cm) GBP 780. Newcastle, 5 Dec 2000, *Whitburn Beach* (1926, watercolour, 11x20 ins / 28x52 cm) GBP 1,500. Newcastle, 13 March 2001, *Holywell Dene, Seated Sluice* (oil on canvas, 9x19 ins / 23x49 cm) GBP 940. Newcastle, 12 June 2001, *Panoramic View of the City of Durham* (1929, watercolour, 20x28 ins / 51x71 cm) GBP 780. London, 15 April 2002, *Windy Day at Eyemouth* (watercolour heightened with gouache, 20x29 ins / 50x74 cm) GBP 1,800. Whitby, 20 Sept 2002, *Staithes and Penny Nab* (watercolour, 13x10 ins / 33x25 cm) GBP 650. Newcastle, 18 March 2003, *North Coast Scene with a Castle on a Headland* (oil on canvas, 17x23 ins / 42x59 cm) GBP 920. Penzance, 144 Oct 2003, *Beach Tents* (watercolour, 10x21 ins / 25x53 cm) GBP 550. Newcastle, 23 March 2004, *Seaton Sluice, Northumberland* (watercolour, 11x20 ins / 28x51 cm) GBP 820. Leamington Spa, 29 July 2004, *View of Robin Hood's Bay* (watercolour, 13x19 ins / 32x48 cm) GBP 750.

HUTTON, Walter C. Strich
British, 19th - 20th century.
Painter. Portraits, landscapes.

Auction records:
London, 6 Nov 1995, *Sisters* (oil on canvas, 78¾ x 52 ins / 200 x 132 cm) GBP 5,750.

HUTTULA, Richard C.
British, 19th century.
Active in London.
Painter. Genre scenes.
Richard C. Huttula exhibited in London at Suffolk Street from 1866 to 1887.

HUTTY, Alfred Heber
American, 20th century.
Born 16 September 1878, in Michigan; died 1954.
Painter, engraver.

Alfred Heber Hutty was a member of the main art unions of Washington, New York and Chicago. He was awarded many prizes and distinctions.

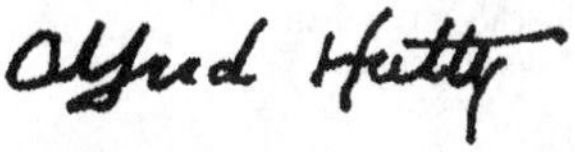

Auction records:
Washington DC, 1 Oct 1983, *Carrying the Bucket* (watercolour, 16 x 22 ins / 40.5 x 56 cm) USD 1,150. Detroit, 16 April 1999, *Autumn Landscape* (oil on canvas, 24 x 29 ins / 61 x 74 cm) USD 7,000. North Bethesda, 27 Oct 2000, *Figure and Ox Cart* (watercolour on board, 12 x 15 ins / 30 x 38 cm) USD 9,500. New Orleans, 8 Dec 2000, *St Michael's Church, Charleston* (oil on canvas, 25 x 25 ins / 64 x 64 cm) USD 30,000. New Orleans, 28 July 2001, *Birch Trees* (oil on board, 12 x 16 ins / 30 x 41 cm) USD 12,000. New Orleans, 13 Oct 2001, *Discussion Group in Carolina* (dry-point, 12 x 8 ins / 30 x 20 cm) USD 7,500. New Orleans, 22 Feb 2002, *Potato Pickers in the Low Country* (dry-point, 4 x 4 ins / 9 x 10 cm) USD 4,200. Portland, 31 July 2002, *Market Day* (watercolour, 15 x 19 ins / 38 x 48 cm) USD 13,500. New Orleans, 2 Aug 2003, *Low Country Cabin* (etching, 11 x 14 ins / 28 x 36 cm) USD 3,750. New Orleans, 2 Aug 2003, *Towards a New Day* (dry-point, 11 x 15 ins / 28 x 38 cm) USD 6,000. New Orleans, 3 April 2004, *Wash Day* (oil on canvas, 30 x 24 ins / 76 x 61 cm) USD 75,000. Boston, 14 May 2004, *Around the Campfire* (watercolour on paperboard, 11 x 13 ins / 28 x 34 cm) USD 29,000.

HUVÉ
French, 18th century.
Died 1752, in La Croix-St-Leufroy (Eure).
Active in Paris.
Glass painter.

HUVÉ, Pierre
French, 18th century.
Active in Paris in 1788.
Painter (?), sculptor (?).

HUVELLIEZ, Victor
French, 20th century.
Born in Versailles.
Watercolourist.
Victor Huvelliez worked in Paris, where he exhibited at the Salon des Artistes Français, of which he became a member in 1912.

HUVEY, Joseph
French, 19th - 20th century.
Born 1868, in Chavanes (Isère).
Painter. Portraits, landscapes, waterscapes, still-lifes.
Huvey studied at the École des Beaux-Arts in Lyons. From 1873 he exhibited in Lyons, mostly landscapes (Lyons and the Dauphiné region, views of mountains, lakes and glaciers).
Auction records:
Paris, 20 Jan 1988, *Riverbanks* (oil on canvas, 12 1/2 x 22 ins / 31.5 x 55 cm) FRF 6,000.

HUVEY, Louis
French, 19th - 20th century.
Born 4 June 1868, in St-Étienne; died 2 March 1954, in Paris.
Painter, lithographer, reproductions lithographer. Portraits.
Louis Huvey was a student at the École des Beaux-Arts in Lyons in 1885, studying with Jean-Baptiste Poncet and then Gérome. After painting and exhibiting portraits in Lyons and Paris, Huvey devoted himself to lithographs after 1895. These were either original portraits, or reproductions of works by artists such as Rembrandt, Henner, Dagnan-Bouveret and Hébert. He exhibited at the Salon in Lyons from 1889 to 1893 and in Paris at the Salon des Artistes Français from 1892 to 1908, where in 1892 he received an honourable mention for painting. At the Exposition Universelle, he received an honourable mention for engraving in 1900 and a third-class medal in 1901, as well as a second-class medal in 1902. He taught at the École des Beaux-Arts in Paris.
Auction records:
London, 28 Nov 1984, *The Libertine* (1891, oil on canvas, 28 3/4 x 23 ins / 73 x 58.5 cm) GBP 14,500.

HUVÖS DE BOTTA, László
Hungarian, 19th century.
Born in Budapest.
Sculptor.
A pupil of Raoul Verlet, he gained an honourable mention in 1910.

HUWILER, Jakob, the Elder, called Frère Niklaus
Swiss, 19th century.
Born 1822, near Lucerne; died 19 March 1902, in Munich.
Painter.
Religious paintings were his speciality. He was the father of Jakob Huwiler the Younger.

HUWILER, Jakob, the Younger
Swiss, 19th - 20th century.
Born 1867, in Sursee.
Painter.
Huwiler was son of Jakob Huwiler the Elder. He studied in Lucerne and worked a great deal in Schwyz.

HUXIAN, peasant painters of
Chinese, 20th century.
Active in Huxian (Shanxi).
Painters, engravers, illustrators. Historical subjects, genre scenes. Murals, posters.
Since ancient times, there has been a popular wood-carving and wall-painting tradition in China. Formerly, it was associated with the celebration of the lunar new year and the invocation of tutelary gods and beneficent spirits. During the Cultural Revolution, this religious-based tradition was transformed into a form of propaganda in the service of what was then called Socialist construction.

In 1975, Huxian district had some 400,000 inhabitants. It was one of the most advanced agricultural regions in China. From 1958, the year of the 'Great Leap Forward', the number of professional and amateur painters of all ages and backgrounds grew, reaching more than 700 in 1975. During that period (1958-1975) these peasant painters painted over 40,000 works - murals, traditional paintings, engravings, newspaper illustrations, and so on. In October 1973, 200 of these works were exhibited in Beijing, then all over China and abroad, notably in 1975 at the Musée d'Art Moderne in Paris. These works were also widely distributed in the form of posters, picture books, postcards and stamps. Even though Huxian did receive the most media attention, it was far from unique. During the Cultural Revolution, this sort of people's art became a means of communication and propaganda that was not just restricted to Huxian but was also to be found in Shanghai, Yangquan, Liuta, and other towns and rural districts. The main artists involved at Huxian were Guan Shanyue, Gao Ziming, Liu Zhidi, Dong Zhenyi, Wang Fulai, Li Zhenhua, Du Jilian, and Li Fenglan, at Liuta they were Zhang Diping and Chou Yurong, and in Shanghai it was Lu Mong. It is important to note that many of these artists and their works were not spontaneous, but the result of extensive training and help from professional artists sent to the countryside for thought reform, many of whom were no longer allowed to work under their own names.

For their subject matter, the peasant painters took their work in the fields and every other aspect of life in the country, their village and family histories, and the political struggle and education. The aim was not to create museum art but to paint the mass of peasants, workers and soldiers in both idealised form and as they really were, for themselves and for their own glorification. The genuinely popular origin of this way of expressing everyday life, together with its freshness, and often its naivety, to some extent saved this art from the sort of propaganda cliché that spelt the doom of Socialist Realism, whose adepts were as technically skilled as they were mentally ossified.

BIBLIOGRAPHY:

Images du peuple chinois, exhibition catalogue, Musée d'Art moderne de la Ville de Paris, Paris, 1975. Landsberger, Stefan, *Chinese Propaganda Posters: From Revolution to Modernization*, The Pepin Press, Amsterdam and Singapore, 1995.

HUXLEY, Paul
British, 20th century.
Born 1938, in London.
Painter.
Minimal Art.

Paul Huxley trained at Harrow College of Art and the Royal Academy Schools in London, from 1953 to 1960. He lived in New York from 1965 to 1967. His highly austere, Abstract-Geometric style shows the influence of Minimalism in its preference for 'primal' forms (triangles, squares) and vivid colours. His work has featured in a number of group exhibitions, including: 1959 *Young Contemporaries*, London; 1964 *The New Generation*, 3rd Tokyo Biennale, *Contemporary British Painting and Sculpture*, Buffalo; 1965 Paris Biennale, *English Eye*, New York; 1967 Pittsburgh International at the Carnegie Institute; 1968 *British Artists: Six Painters, Six Sculptors* at the Museum of Modern Art, New York. His work has also been the subject of a number of solo exhibitions, including: London, 1963, 1965, 1968; New York, 1967.

AUCTION RECORDS:

LONDON, 26 Oct 1994, *Untitled no. 141* (1974, acrylic/paper/card, 50 1/2 x 50 1/2 ins / 128 x 128 cm) GBP 920. LONDON, 16 April 2002, *Modus Operandi IV* (1988, acrylic on canvas, 60 x 60 ins / 152 x 152 cm) GBP 1,300.

HUXOLL, Anton
German, 19th century.
Born 1808, in Arnsberg; died 1840.
Painter. History painting.

He was a student at the academy in Düsseldorf.

HUY, H. M.
German, 17th century.
Active early 17th century.
Painter.

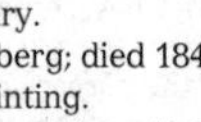

HUY, Jean Pépin de. See **PÉPIN Jean**

HUY, Nguyen Quang. See **NGUYEN QUANG HUY**

HUYBERT
17th century.
Active in Cleves in 1681.
Painter.

Huybert may have been Dutch.

HUYBERTS, Cornelis, or Huybers
Dutch, 17th - 18th century.
Born 1669, in Emmerich; died c. 1712.
Engraver (burin), draughtsman.

In 1696, Cornelis Huyberts was working in England. He made engravings after Mantegna, and worked for Lairesse.

HUYBRECHTS, called Hubert
Flemish School, 17th century.
Died 27 December 1687.
Active in Antwerp.
Engraver.

Huybrechts was the father of Gaspar Huybrechts.

HUYBRECHTS, Adrian. See also **HUBERTI**

HUYBRECHTS, Gaspar, or Huberti
Dutch, 17th century.
Born 1619; died 1684.
Engraver.

In 1652, Gerard Edelinck was a pupil of Gaspar Huybrechts in Antwerp.

HUYBRECHTS, Marten
Flemish School, 17th century.
Died 23 February 1689.
Active in Antwerp.
Painter.

HUYBRECHTS, Nicolas
Flemish School, 17th century.
Active in Antwerp in 1684.
Painter. Portraits.

HUYBRECHTS, Paul
Belgian, 20th - 21st century.
Born 1951, in Winksele.
Engraver. Medals, postage stamps, coins.

Paul Huybrechts studied at the academies in Louvain and Brussels. He completed his training at the Pforzheim art school in Germany and with Huguenin Médailleurs in Le Locle in Switzerland. He works for the Belgian postal service (25 stamps), the Royal Mint (500 Belgian Franc Piece) and issuers of medals (some 100 pieces, including Henri-Maria Thérésa of Luxembourg, the World Health Prize and the League of Arab States).

HUYBRECHTS, Peeter
Flemish School, 17th century.
Born 7 February 1614, in Antwerp; died c. 1660.
Painter.

Peeter Huybrechts is known for his *Portrait of Charles I of England*.

HUYBRECHTS, R.
French, 20th century.
Sculptor.

Huybrechts exhibited his *Thought* at the Salon des Indépendants in 1945.

HUYBREGTS, Gaspar
Flemish School, 17th century.
Born 17th century, in Antwerp.
Engraver.

HUYE, Jan van der
Flemish School, 17th century.
Born 17th century, in Brussels.
Sculptor.

In 1669, Jan van der Huye was working in The Hague. He later worked in Amsterdam.

HUYFF, Jan
Dutch, 17th century.
Born in the Netherlands.
Painter. Landscapes, seascapes.

The Valenciennes museum has a *Seascape* signed *J. Huyff*.

MUSEUMS AND GALLERIES:

VALENCIENNES: *Seascape*.

HUYGELEN, Frans
Belgian, 20th century.
Born 19 August 1878, in Antwerp; died 1940, in Ukkel.
Sculptor, painter.
Huygelen was a student at the Koninklijke Academie voor Schone Kunsten in Antwerp and of Thomas Vinçotte at the Hoger Instituut there. He won the Prix de Rome in 1900. His work was shown at the great Brussels Exhibition in 1910. During World War I, he stayed in England. He became professor at the Antwerp academy. He made several war memorials, including the medallion for the tomb of Jan Van Rijswijck in Antwerp.
BIBLIOGRAPHY:
Conrardy, Joseph, *Frans Huygelen*, Bruylant, Brussels, 1930.

HUYGENS, Chriatiaen
Flemish School, 17th century.
Born 14 April 1629, in The Hague; died 8 July 1695, in The Hague.
Draughtsman, engraver. Mythological subjects, religious subjects, portraits.
Chriatiaen Huygens was the son of Constantyn Huygens the Elder and a scholar. He mainly drew portraits, but also engraved religious and mythological subjects after Brueghel and Franz Floris.

HUYGENS, Constantyn, the Elder
Dutch, 17th century.
Born 4 September 1596, in The Hague; died 28 March 1687, in The Hague.
Draughtsman, poet.
Constantyn Huygens the Elder executed a large number of drawings.
AUCTION RECORDS:
PARIS, 4 May 1951, *Avenue Lined with Large Trees beside a Canal* (pen and wash) FRF 48,000. AMSTERDAM, 26 Nov 1984, *View of the Town of Haacht* (1675, pen and wash, 4 1/2 x 7 1/4in/11.3 x 18.4cm) NLG 17,500.

HUYGENS, Constantyn, the Younger
Dutch, 17th century.
Born 10 March 1628, in The Hague; died 2 October 1697, in The Hague.
Painter, engraver, draughtsman. Portraits, landscapes.
Constantyn Huygens the Younger was the son of Constantyn Huygens the Elder. He worked for Prince William III of Orange-Nassau as his secretary, and executed numerous drawings during the Dutch campaigns.
AUCTION RECORDS:
PARIS, 10 Feb 1926, *Portrait of a Young Girl* (pencil) FRF 170. PARIS, 13 Feb 1939, *Shady Avenue along a Canal* (pen and bistre wash) FRF 1,550. PARIS, 29 Oct 1980, *View of a Church and Village* (1675, pen and brown ink, 4 x 6 1/2in/10 x 16.5cm) FRF 17,200. AMSTERDAM, 25 Nov 1992, *Village of Beekbergen in Winter* (1675, ink, 4 1/2 x 7 1/4in/11.2 x 18.4cm) NLG 86,250. AMSTERDAM, 10 May 1994, *The Palace of Hembise at Henegouwen* (ink, 38 1/4 x 46in/97 x 116cm) NLG 12,650. NEW YORK, 9 Jan 1996, *View of Aarschot with Two Figures in the Foreground* (1675, ink, 4 1/4 x 7in/10.6 x 16.9cm) USD 25,300. AMSTERDAM, 12 Nov 1996, *Hembise Palace at Henegouwen* (pencil and brown ink, 3 3/4 x 6 1/4in/9.7 x 15.6cm) NLG 14,160. PARIS, 30 March 1998, *Village among the Trees* (1675, pen and brown ink, 4 1/4 x 6 3/4in/10.7 x 17cm) FRF 31,000. AMSTERDAM, 8 Nov 2000, *Wooden Bridge over a Stream* (1651, black pencil and brown ink, 7 x 12 ins / 19 x 30 cm) NLG 6,000. AMSTERDAM, 8 Nov 2000, *View towards the Manor at Kleef, near Haarlem* (pen and brown ink wash, 7 x 10 ins / 17 x 26 cm) NLG 78,000.

HUYGENS, François Joseph.
See **HUYGHENS François Joseph**

HUYGENS, Frédérik Lodewyn
Dutch, 19th century.
Born 3 February 1802, in The Hague; died 18 March 1887, in Leiden.
Painter, engraver.
Frédérik Huygens was a pupil of C. van Coylenbourg, A. Kransz. and G. van Os. He taught at the royal military academy in Breda. A work by him entitled *A Lion* is in the municipal museum in The Hague.

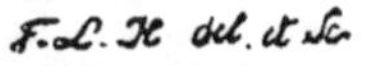

HUYGENS, Johannes
Dutch, 19th - 20th century.
Born 25 January 1833, in The Hague; died 1910.
Painter. Seascapes.
Huygens was a student of F. L. Huygens.

HUYGENS, Léon
Belgian, 20th century.
Active in Auderghem.
Engraver. Landscapes.
Work by Huygens was shown at the Brussels exhibition in 1910.

HUYGENS, Philips
Dutch, 17th century.
Born 12 October 1633, in The Hague; died in Marienburg (now Malbork, Poland).
Painter.
Philips Huygens was the son of Constantyn Huygens the Elder. He was also a statesman.

HUYGENS, Suzanna Louise
Dutch, 18th century.
Born September 1714; died 21 December 1785, in The Hague.
Painter.
Suzanna Huygens is known for her work *Card Players* after Lenain.

HUYGENSZ, Adrian, the Elder
Dutch, 17th century.
Active in The Hague c. 1600.
Glass painter.

HUYGHE, Pierre
French, 20th - 21st century.
Born 1962.
Installation artist, video artist.
Neo-Conceptual Art, Esthétique Relationnelle.
Pierre Huyghe trained at the École des Arts Décoratifs in Paris and lives and works in Paris. The Guggenheim Museum in New York awarded him the Hugo Boss Prize in 2002. He is interested in the problems of time and memory. His point of departure is often film, which he reworks in his installations. These installations lead the viewer through a new narrative circuit to discover a replay of a suspended time. The viewer must understand this suspended time as a waiting time, a reality, reactivated by the viewer. It is in this sense that *Interludes*, the title of his exhibition at Van Abbemuseum, must be understood. Among other works this exhibition included an installation based on Sidney Lumet's film *Dog Day Afternoon*. This film was in part drawn from a news item, a bank robbery, carried out by a certain John Woytowicz, which was directly recorded by television. The purpose of the video installation, entitled *Third Memory*, was simply to bring in the 'third memory' of this news item. Alongside the journalistic memories and images from Sidney Lumet's film, Pierre Huyghe shows John Woytowicz himself telling the story of the bank robbery. The result is an unusual mixture of reality and fiction. This chink of suspended time is immediately visible in the 1997 *Multi-language Version*. This installation shows German, English and

French versions of the 1929 Hollywood film of the Titanic tragedy simultaneously. Dubbing techniques did not exist at that time and each version of the film was filmed separately with native speaker actors. Although the narration is the same the versions are different in both content and form. Shot at the height of the financial crisis in the USA following the 1929 Wall Street Crash, these versions of the Titanic, and above all the economic system that brought about the crisis, symbolise for Huyghe the confusion and crisis generated by the staggering progress of the 19th century. In *Ellipse*, he reconstructs a film scene with the actor who played the same scene in the original film and shows them simultaneously. These few examples, which destroy the sacred aura of unit time, fit into the larger context of the leisure culture fed by the video game industry in particular. Pierre Huyghe also models his work on the participative aspect of the new electronic games in which the user is also the actor and presumed creator of a story. With the video *Two Minutes Out of Time*, the artist aims to interfere in the production cycle. This video portrays Ann Lee, a Manga figure developed by a Japanese agency, which was intended to be sold to the comic strip or cartoon industry. Huyghe bought the rights to this character with the artist Philippe Parreno, who also uses Ann Lee in his video creations. Inserted into Huyghe's film *Two Minutes Out of Time*, is *No Ghost, Just a Shell* (an allusion to Mamoru Oshii's 1995 Manga film Ghost in the Shell), evoking Ann Lee's status as a neglected secondary character, haunted by the voice of a little girl.

Huyghe has taken part in major collective exhibitions of contemporary art including: Lyons Biennale, with a work adapted from Pasolini's *The Hawks and the Sparrows*, 1995; *Traffic*, Capc-Musée d'Art Contemporain, Bordeaux, 1996; *Coïncidences, Coïncidences*, Cartier Foundation, Paris, with a video inspired by the story of Snow White, 1997; Manifesta 2, Luxemburg, 1998; Sydney Biennial, 1998; *Présumés Innocents: l'Art Contemporain et l'Enfance* (*Presumed Innocent: Contemporary Art and Childhood*), Capc Musée d'Art Contemporain, Bordeaux, 2000; represented France at the Venice Biennale, 2001; *Moving Pictures*, an exhibition showing the use of photography, film and video in art since the end of the 1960s, Solomon R. Guggenheim Museum, New York, 2002; *Sans Commune Mesure. Image et texte dans l'Art Actuel* (*Without Common Measure: Image and Text in Contemporary Art*), Musée d'Art Moderne, Lille Métropole, Villeneuve d'Ascq, 2002; *L'État des Choses* (*The State of Things*), a review of the status of everyday objects in contemporary art, Musée des Beaux-Arts, Nantes and *Bandes à Part: Le Cinéma dans l'Art Contemporain* (*On the Fringes: Cinema in Contemporary Art*), Musée d'Art Moderne et Contemporain, Strasbourg, two exhibitions held to mark *Trésors Public, 20 Ans de Création dans les Fonds Régionaux d'Art Contemporain (FRAC)* (*Public Treasury, 20 Years of Creation in the Regional Collection of Contemporary Art (FRAC)*), 2003; *C'est Arrivé Demain* (*It Happened Tomorrow*), Lyons Biennale, 2003.

Solo exhibitions of his work since 1995 include: *Storytellers*, Le Consortium, Dijon, 1997; Musée d'Art Moderne de la Ville de Paris, 1998; *Two Minutes Out of Time*, Musée d'Art Moderne et Contemporain, Geneva, 2000; *Interludes*, Van Abbemuseum, Eindhoven, 2001; *Multi-language Versions*, Artists' Workshops - Office de la Culture, Marseilles, 2001; Kunsthaus, Bregenz, Austria, 2002; Guggenheim Museum, New York, 2003; Dia Center for Arts, New York, 2003; Carpenter Center for the Visual Arts, Cambridge, Massachussetts, 2004.

BIBLIOGRAPHY:

Millet, Catherine, '*Pierre Huyghe*' in *Art Press* n° 227, periodical, Paris, September 1997. Bernadac, Marie-Laure/Moisdon-Tremblay, et al., *Présumés innocents: l'art contemporain et l'enfance*, exhibition catalogue, Capc musée d'Art contemporain, Bordeaux, 2000. *Pierre Huyghe*, Van Abbemuseum, Eindhoven, NAi Publishers, Rotterdam, 2001. *Moving Pictures*, exhibition catalogue, Solomon R. Guggenheim Museum, New York, 2002. '*Pierre Huyghe: rencontre avec Douglas Copland*' in *coll. Art-rencontres*, Dis Voir, Paris, 2002. Durand, Régis, et al., *Sans commune mesure. Image et texte dans l'art actuel*, exhibition catalogue, Éd. Léo Scheer, Paris, 2002. Zahm, Olivier (preface), et al., *Trésors publics, 20 ans de création dans les Fonds régionaux d'art contemporain*, Flammarion, Paris, 2003 (text in French and English).

MUSEUMS AND GALLERIES:

BORDEAUX (FRAC Aquitaine): *Versions multiples* (1997) - DIJON (FRAC Bourgogne): *Ramoner* (1994, screen-printed poster); *Untitled* (1994, screen-printed poster) - DUNKIRK (FRAC Nord-Pas de Calais): *Sans titre (le Carillon d'après 'Dream' de J. Cage)* (*Untitled (Chimes after J. Cage's 'Dream')*) (1997) - LYONS (FRAC Rhône-Alpes): *Gore* (1989) - MONTPELLIER (FRAC Languedoc-Roussillon): *Remake* (1995) - NEW YORK (Solomon R. Guggenheim Mus.): *One Million Kingdoms* (2001, video installation) - PARIS (FNAC): *Prototype of Luminary* (executed with Philippe Parreno) - PARIS (MAMVP) - PARIS (MNAM-CCI) - RHEIMS (FRAC Champagne-Ardenne).

HUYGHENS, François Joseph

Belgian, 19th century.

Born 1820, in Brussels; died 1908, in Kortenberg.

Painter. Still-lifes, flowers.

François Huyghens studied at the school of fine arts in Brussels. He exhibited at the Brussels Salon from 1842 to 1890, and at exhibitions in Paris, Ghent and Antwerp.

MUSEUMS AND GALLERIES:

BRUSSELS: *Bunch of Hawthorn*.

AUCTION RECORDS:

LOS ANGELES, 9 June 1976, *Still-life* (1848, oil on panel, 18½ x 26½in/47 x 67.5cm) USD 1,500. NEW YORK, 13 Oct 1978, *Still-life with Flowers* (1853, oil on panel, 15¼ x 12in/38.5 x 30.5cm) USD 7,000. LONDON, 28 Nov 1979, *Still-life* (1851, oil on canvas, 50½ x 39in/128 x 99cm) GBP 6,500. NEW YORK, 23 May 1985, *Still-life with Roses* (1853, oil on canvas, 28½ x 22¼in/72.5 x 56.5cm) USD 4,000. LA VARENNE-ST-HILAIRE, 12 March 1989, *Sprig of Flowers on a Hat* (oil on panel, 9¾ x 7½in/25 x 19cm) FRF 7,600. LONDON, 5 May 1989, *Basket of Fruit and Peaches on a Plate on a Draped Ledge* (1887, oil on canvas, 37¾ x 53in/96 x 134.5cm) GBP 2,200. NEW YORK, 15 Nov 1990, *Still-life with Flowers in a Basket* (1860, oil on panel, 7½ x 6in/19.1 x 14.3cm) USD 3,300. PARIS, 10 April 1991, *Still-life with Grapes in a Landscape* (1852, oil on canvas, 24 x 22in/61 x 55cm) FRF 25,000. NEW YORK, 20 Jan 1993, *Still-life with Roses in a Vase* (oil on canvas, 31 x 15½in/78.7 x 39.4cm) USD 2,300. AMSTERDAM, 19 Oct 1993, *Grapes and Strawberries on a Ledge* (oil on panel, 13 x 9½in/33 x 24cm) NLG 1,955. BRUSSELS, 11 May 1999, *Still-life with Roses* (oil on panel, 13 x 15 ins / 32 x 39 cm) BEF 240,000. AMSTERDAM, 1 Sept 1999, *Flower Still-life with Roses, Forget-me-nots and Indian Cress* (1867, oil on canvas, 15 x 19 ins / 37 x 48 cm) NLG 25,000. BRUSSELS, 14 Feb 2000, *Still-life with Flowers* (oil on canvas, 33 x 26 ins / 83 x 66 cm) BEF 440,000. BRUSSELS, 17 April 2000, *Bouquet of Flowers in a Greenhouse* (1894, oil on canvas, 44 x 30 ins / 111 x 76 cm) BEF 130,000. NEW ORLEANS, 26 May 2001, *Still-life with Fruit, Nuts, Crystal Ewer and Exotic Linen* (oil on canvas, 20 x 27 ins / 51 x 69 cm) USD 7,000. LONDON, 1 Nov 2001, *Still-life with Flowers and Berries and Butterfly on Stone Pillar* (1847, oil on panel, 19 x 15 ins / 48 x 38 cm) GBP 7,000. SAN FRANCISCO, 15 May 2002, *Still-life with Fruit, Flowers and Game* (1848, oil on panel, 22 x 17 ins / 55 x 44 cm) USD 4,250. BRUSSELS, 14 Jan 2003, *Still-life with Roses and Pansies* (1858, oil on panel, 12 x 9 ins / 31 x 24 cm) EUR 1,600. NEW YORK, 2 Dec 2003, *Vase of Flowers with Plums and Nest* (1846, oil on panel, 28 x 21 ins / 70 x 54 cm) USD 8,000. SAN FRANCISCO, 2 May 2004, *Still-life with Roses, Flowers, Butterfly and Bird's Nest* (1850, oil on canvas, 22 x 18 ins / 56 x 46 cm) USD 8,000. BRUSSELS, 7 June 2004, *Twigs in a Basket* (1891, oil on canvas, 14 x 20 ins / 36 x 52 cm) EUR 2,000.

HUYGHENS, Guillaume
Belgian, 19th century.
Died 1821, in Brussels.
Sculptor.

Guillaume Huyghens was a pupil of G. L. Godecharle. He exhibited from 1810.

HUYOT, Albert Étienne Marie
French, 19th - 20th century.
Born 8 June 1872, in Paris; died 1968.
Painter. Figures, landscapes.

Albert Étienne Marie Huyot painted a variety of subjects. After his first paintings, which were in a very general, Post-Impressionist vein, he was briefly influenced by Cubism. This left him with a solid sense of the construction of space and volume, giving his work a somewhat Neo-Classical sense that recalled the work of Cézanne. This would be succeeded by the Fauvism and Cubism of, among others, André Derain (an enduring influence) and, more briefly, Vlaminck and Friesz. He exhibited regularly in Paris, at the Salon des Indépendants, the Salon d'Automne and the Salon des Tuileries. He showed at the *Grande Exposition* in Brussels in 1910. He travelled to Russia that same year. The Galerie Berthe Weill devoted an exhibition to his paintings and drawings in 1926.

BIBLIOGRAPHY:
Albert Huyot, auction catalogue, Maître Claude Robert, Paris, 19 April 1982.

AUCTION RECORDS:
PARIS, 4 July 1928, *The Old Chestnut Tree*, FRF 300. PARIS, 13 Nov 1935, *Centenarian*, FRF 160.

HUYOT, Étienne, called Frédéric
French, 19th century.
Born 11 February 1808, in Paris.
Engraver (line-engraving).

Huyot was an engraver appointed to the Banque de France.

HUYOT, Jules Jean Marie Joseph
French, 19th century.
Born in Toulouse.
Engraver (wood).

Huyot was a pupil of his father Étienne Huyot. He exhibited regularly at the Salon from 1868, gaining a third-class medal in 1887 and a second-class one in 1894. He was also a Chevalier of the Légion d'Honneur. His illustration of *Manon Lescaut* in the style of the drawings of Maurice Leloir is particularly noteworthy.

HUYS, Baltazar
Flemish School, 17th century.
Born in Mechelen; died 1652, in Rotterdam.
Painter. Still-lifes.

Baltazar Huys studied under Jan le Saive the Elder. In 1619, he was a master artist in Mechelen.

AUCTION RECORDS:
MONTE CARLO, 6 March 1984, *Still-life with Fruit, Duck and Woodcock* (oil on canvas, 32 3/4 x 41in/83.5 x 104cm) FRF 40,000. MILAN, 10 June 1988, *Still-life with a Basket of Fruit, Poultry and Game* (1650, oil on canvas, 33 x 41 3/4in/84 x 106cm) ITL 36,000,000. MILAN, 12 Dec 1988, *Still-life with a Basket of Fruit, Poultry and Game* (oil on canvas, 33 x 41 3/4in/84 x 106cm) ITL 32,000,000. LONDON, 15 Dec 1989, *Kitchen Interior with Food on a Table and a Servant Putting a Chicken on a Spit* (1645, oil on canvas, 41 1/4 x 58 1/2in/104.5 x 148.6cm) GBP 12,650.

HUYS, Françoys
Dutch, 17th century.
Died 1661, in Amsterdam.
Active in Leiden.
Engraver.

HUYS, Franz
Dutch, 16th century.
Born 1522; died 1562.
Active in the Netherlands and Antwerp.
Engraver (burin), draughtsman.

Franz Huys engraved views, historical scenes and works by Bruegel.

HUYS, Johan Nikolas
Dutch, 19th century.
Born 5 December 1819.
Active in The Hague.
Painter.

Johan Huys was a pupil of Van der Laur and J. Moerenhout.

HUYS, Lambert de
Dutch, 17th century.
Died in Amsterdam.
Painter.

In 1664, Lambert de Huys was working in The Hague. He later settled in Amsterdam.

HUYS, Modest
Belgian, 19th - 20th century.
Born 25 October 1875, in Olsene; died 1932, in Zulte.
Painter, pastellist. Portraits, landscapes.

Modest Huys was a student at the Koninklijke Academie voor Schone Kunsten in Antwerp, but he was mainly influenced by his friend Émile Claus. His work was exhibited in several western European countries.

Huys concentrated on landscapes of the banks of the Lys and on flax cultivation scenes. He worked in the Impressionist tradition and was fond of the changing effects of light from season to season and hour to hour, though his touch was that of the Neo-Impressionists.

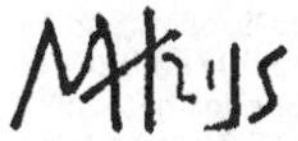

BIBLIOGRAPHY:
Chabot, G./Aconit, G., *Modest Huys*, Ghent, 1928. *Retrospectieve Modest Huys*, Museum voor schone Kunsten, Latem en Leiestree, Ghent, 1974.

AUCTION RECORDS:
ANTWERP, 13 Oct 1970, *Village in the Snow* (1923) BEF 42,000. ANTWERP, 12 Oct 1971, *September Morning*, BEF 100,000. LOKEREN, 9 Nov 1974, *The Cathedral Square* (1919) BEF 80,000. LOS ANGELES, 9 June 1976, *Landscape* (oil on canvas, 15 1/4 x 17 3/4 ins / 39 x 45 cm) BEF 75,000. LOKEREN, 5 Nov 1977, *Trees in Flower* (oil on canvas, 13 x 19 ins / 33 x 48 cm) BEF 100,000. LOKEREN, 17 Feb 1979, *Harvest Scene* (oil on canvas, 31 1/2 x 39 1/4 ins / 80 x 100 cm) BEF 180,000. ANTWERP, 27 Oct 1981, *Workers* (oil on canvas, 31 1/2 x 39 1/4 ins / 80 x 100 cm) BEF 280,000. BRUSSELS, 17 Feb 1982, *Landscape with Cattle and a Procession* (oil on panel, 13 x 17 ins / 33 x 43 cm) BEF 95,000. LOKEREN, 15 Oct 1983, *First Rays of Sun* (1915, oil on canvas, 25 1/4 x 33 ins / 64 x 84 cm) BEF

1,100,000. LONDON, 23 Oct 1985, *Little Fishermen* (oil on canvas, 35 1/2 x 43 3/4 ins / 90.2 x 111.2 cm) GBP 9,200. LONDON, 1 July 1987, *Sunny Afternoon in Summer* (1908, oil on canvas, 37 1/2 x 47 1/4 ins / 95.3 x 120.3 cm) GBP 26,000. LOKEREN, 5 March 1988, *Young Girl* (pastel, 16 1/2 x 13 3/4 ins / 42 x 35 cm) BEF 110,000. LOKEREN, 28 May 1988, *Stormy Sky over Mechelen* (oil on panel, 15 x 19 3/4 ins / 38 x 50 cm) BEF 190,000. LOKEREN, 8 Oct 1988, *The Way to School* (oil on canvas, 21 x 25 1/4 ins / 52.5 x 64 cm) BEF 2,800,000. LONDON, 29 Nov 1988, *Landscape on the Bank of a Lake* (oil on canvas, 23 1/2 x 36 ins / 60 x 91.5 cm) GBP 8,250. BRUSSELS, 27 March 1990, *September Morning* (oil on canvas, 11 3/4 x 23 1/2 ins / 30 x 60 cm) BEF 650,000. AMSTERDAM, 22 May 1991, *Autumn Evening* (oil on canvas, 19 3/4 x 23 1/2 ins / 50 x 60 cm) NLG 23,000. AMSTERDAM, 23 May 1991, *Flood* (oil on canvas, 39 x 55 1/4 ins / 99 x 140.5 cm) NLG 57,500. NEW YORK, 23 May 1991, *Midday Sun in Summer 1908* (oil on canvas, 37 3/4 x 48 ins / 96 x 121 cm) USD 24,200. AMSTERDAM, 12 Dec 1991, *Undergrowth* (oil on canvas, 35 1/2 x 43 ins / 90 x 109 cm) NLG 59,800. LOKEREN, 21 March 1992, *Bluey Dusk on the Scheldt* (1913, oil on canvas, 13 3/4 x 18 ins / 35 x 45.5 cm) BEF 650,000. LOKEREN, 5 Dec 1992, *Clear September Morning* (1908, oil on canvas, 26 x 29 1/2 ins / 66 x 75 cm) BEF 1,500,000. LOKEREN, 9 Oct 1993, *Late Autumn in St Eloois-Vijve* (1913, oil on canvas, 25 1/2 x 33 1/4 ins / 65 x 84.5 cm) BEF 1,000,000. LOKEREN, 4 Dec 1993, *Village Celebration in Flanders at Mechelen* (1906, oil on canvas, 24 x 32 ins / 61 x 81 cm) BEF 2,800,000. LOKEREN, 12 March 1994, *After the Harvest* (1908, oil on canvas, 25 1/2 x 39 3/4 ins / 65 x 101 cm) BEF 1,800,000. LOKEREN, 28 May 1994, *Sunny Afternoon in Summer* (1908, oil on canvas, 37 3/4 x 48 ins / 96 x 121 cm) BEF 2,800,000. LOKEREN, 11 March 1995, *Reading* (charcoal, 22 x 26 3/4 ins / 56 x 68 cm) BEF 55,000. LOKEREN, 18 May 1996, *Summer Morning along the Gaverbeek at Waregem* (1910, oil on canvas, 22 3/4 x 33 1/2 ins / 58 x 85 cm) BEF 1,900,000; *Landscape at Wakken* (1922, oil on canvas, 15 3/4 x 11 3/4 ins / 40 x 30 cm) BEF 110,000. AMSTERDAM, 5 June 1996, *View of Venice* (oil on canvas, 7 1/2 x 13 ins / 19 x 33 cm) NLG 4,025. LOKEREN, 5 Oct 1996, *In Spring* (1917, oil on canvas, 31 x 35 ins / 79 x 88 cm) BEF 1,400,000. LOKEREN, 7 Dec 1996, *Grey Weather on the Lys* (1922, oil on canvas, 27 1/2 x 37 1/2 ins / 70 x 95 cm) BEF 950,000. LOKEREN, 8 March 1997, *Lentedroom* (1907, oil on canvas, 25 3/4 x 34 ins / 65.4 x 85.5 cm) BEF 1,800,000. LOKEREN, 11 Oct 1997, *Barge on the Lys* (1922, oil on canvas, 27 1/2 x 37 1/2 ins / 70 x 95 cm) BEF 800,000; *Evening on the Lys* (oil on canvas, 31 1/2 x 31 1/2 ins / 80 x 80 cm) BEF 650,000. LOKEREN, 6 Dec 1997, *Heavy Snow* (1910, oil on canvas, 15 3/4 x 27 1/2 ins / 40 x 70 cm) BEF 700,000. LOKEREN, 6 March 1999, *Snow and Flood* (1910, oil on canvas, 16 x 28 ins / 40 x 70 cm) BEF 700,000. LOKEREN, 9 Oct 1999, *Midday in the Springtime* (c. 1921, oil on canvas, 24 x 30 ins / 60 x 75 cm) BEF 750,000. LOKEREN, 4 March 2000, *Field Workers* (oil on canvas, 31 x 39 ins / 80 x 100 cm) BEF 1,900,000. LOKEREN, 4 March 2000, *Poplars in the March Sunlight* (oil on canvas, 26 x 39 ins / 65 x 100 cm) BEF 2,950,000. LOKEREN, 6 Oct 2001, *Choppy Sea Flood - the Mandelvallei* (1924, oil on canvas, 30 x 42 ins / 75 x 106 cm) BEF 1,600,000. BRUSSELS, 15 Oct 2001, *Le lin le long de la Lys* (oil on canvas, 37 x 47 ins / 93 x 120 cm) BEF 2,350,000. LOKEREN, 7 Dec 2002, *Autumn in the Park* (1917, oil on canvas, 27 x 22 ins / 69 x 56 cm) EUR 23,000. VLAAMSE KAAI, 10 Dec 2002, *Paysage de la Lys* (oil on canvas, 15 x 18 ins / 37 x 45 cm) EUR 14,000. ANTWERP, 23 June 2003, *Water Rats* (1921, oil on canvas, 32 x 42 ins / 81 x 107 cm) EUR 83,000. BRUSSELS, 1 Dec 2003, *In de lente* (1910, oil on canvas, 38 x 47 ins / 96 x 120 cm) EUR 100,000. BRUSSELS, 6 Dec 2004, *Bloeiende pereboomen* (1915, oil on canvas, 26 x 20 ins / 65 x 50 cm) EUR 12,000. BRUSSELS, 6 Dec 2004, *Grey Weather on the Lys* (1922, oil on canvas, 28 x 37 ins / 70 x 95 cm) EUR 26,000.

HUYS, Pieter, or Hus
Flemish, 16th century.
Born c. 1519, in Antwerp; died 1584, in Antwerp.
Painter, engraver, illustrator. Religious subjects, genre scenes.
Antwerp School, Flemish School.

Pieter Huys was the brother of the engraver Franz Huys. He qualified as a master in Antwerp in 1545. As an engraver, he worked with Plantin and illustrated Valverda's *Judices*, Sambucus' *Emblemata Poetica*, and a *Royal Bible* in 1566. As a painter, he followed the example of Flemish artists such as Jerome Cock, Jan Mandyn and Pieter Brueghel who were returning to the themes of Hieronymus Bosch. While many of his colleagues tended to produce somewhat coarse 'devilments', Huys did not lose the pictorial qualities of works by Bosch.

MUSEUMS AND GALLERIES:
ANTWERP (Mayer Van den Bergh Mus.): *Temptation of St Anthony* - BERLIN: *Bagpipe Player* - MADRID (Prado): *The Damned* - PARIS (Louvre): *Temptation of St Anthony* - TOURNAI: *Bellows Mender.*

AUCTION RECORDS:
LONDON, 1 July 1966, *Temptation of St Anthony*, Gns 10,000. BRUSSELS, 23 March 1983, *Scenes from Dante* (oil on wood, 35 x 45 1/4 ins / 88 x 115 cm) BEF 700,000. PARIS, 26 April 1993, *David in a Fantastical Landscape* (oil on oak panel, 25 1/4 x 36 ins / 64 x 91.5 cm) FRF 90,000. LOKEREN, 4 Dec 1993, *Witches' Sabbath* (oil on panel, 22 1/4 x 34 1/4 ins / 56.6 x 87 cm) BEF 220,000. NEW YORK, 12 Jan 1996, *Temptation of St Anthony* (oil on panel, 22 1/4 x 17 1/4 ins / 56.5 x 43.8 cm) USD 27,600. PARIS, 21 March 2001, *Hell* (oil on panel, 17 x 22 ins / 44 x 55 cm) FRF 260,000. LONDON, 12 Dec 2001, *Harrowing of Hell* (oil on panel, 33 x 45 ins / 85 x 114 cm) GBP 32,000.

HUYSE, Willy van
Belgian, 20th century.
Born 1911, in Roeselare.
Sculptor.

Huyse studied at the academies in Roeselare and Ghent. In 1950, he settled in Ostend. His sculpture, with its symbols, can be seen as evocative.

MUSEUMS AND GALLERIES:
OSTEND (Mus. voor Schone Kunsten): *Herfst.*

HUYSER, Carel Jacob de
Dutch, 19th century.
Active c. 1800.
Engraver.

HUYSER, Jacob
Dutch, 16th century.
Painter.

Jacob Huyser was paid by a magistrate of Roermond for a painting in 1587.

HUYSMAN, F.
Flemish School, 18th century.
Painter. Portraits.

HUYSMANS
Flemish School, 18th century.
Born in Antwerp.
Sculptor.

HUYSMANS, Constantinus Cornelis
Dutch, 19th century.
Born 1 January 1810, in Breda; died 28 November 1886, in Breda.
Painter, engraver, lithographer. Genre scenes, landscapes.

Constantinus Huysmans studied under Van Bree in Antwerp. He went to Paris in 1833, but later returned to Holland where he was appointed as a teacher at the military academy in Breda.

AUCTION RECORDS:
COLOGNE, 25 June 1976, *River Landscape* (1841, oil on canvas, 15 1/4 x 20 1/2in/38.5 x 52cm) DEM 4,500. BRUSSELS, 13 Oct 1986, *Landscape with Figures and a Horseman in a Clearing* (oil on canvas, 88 1/2 x 78 3/4in/225 x 200cm) BEF 1,000,000. AMSTERDAM, 5 June 1990, *Kitchen Interior with Servants Preparing a Meal* (oil on panel, 20 x 25 1/2in/50.5 x 65cm) NLG 1,035. AMSTERDAM, 28 Oct 1992, *Fisherman Returning to a Village with their Catch* (oil on panel, 9 1/4 x 11 1/2in/23.5 x 29.5cm) NLG 1,725.

HUYSMANS, Cornelis, or Houseman
Flemish School, 17th - 18th century.
Born 1648, in Antwerp; died 1 June 1727, in Mechelen.
Painter, engraver. Religious subjects, figures, landscapes, landscapes with figures.

Cornelis Huysmans was the son of the architect Hendrik Huysmans. He studied under Gaspard de Witte in Antwerp and under Jacques d'Arthois in Brussels. Huysmans became the pre-eminent painter of Brabant and the forest of Soignies, which served as the subject of many of his paintings. In 1682, he spent his first period in Mechelen; in 1702, he returned to Antwerp where he became a member of the guild in 1706. By 1716, however, he had returned to Mechelen. Some biographers believe that he also worked in England for a time. One of his most highly regarded works is *The Pilgrims of Emmaus* in the church of Mechelen. A talented artist, he often painted the landscapes of works by other artists as well as painting figures for works by landscape artists. Huysmans was ranked among the best painters of the 17th and 18th-century Dutch School. He worked in the same genre as Jacques d'Arthois, but brought a livelier manner and a more poetic sense of nature to his work.

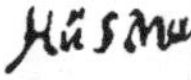

MUSEUMS AND GALLERIES:
AMIENS: *Large and Small Landscapes* - ANTWERP: *Landscape* - BREST: *Evening Light* - BRUSSELS: *Landscape* - COLOGNE: *Landscape* - COPENHAGEN (Statens Mus. for Kunst): *Landscape* - DOUAI: *Landscape* - DRESDEN: *Shepherds' Hut in a Forest Landscape* - DUBLIN: *Landscape with Figures* - FRANKFURT AM MAIN: *Two Italian Landscapes* - GLASGOW: *Two Landscapes* - HANOVER: *Italian Landscape* - KASSEL: *Ideal Landscape*; same subject - LA FÈRE: *Six Landscapes* - LE HAVRE: *Landscape with Sheep*; *Landscape with Women Bathing* - LE MANS: *Landscape* - LE PUY-EN-VELAY: *Edge of a Forest* - LIÈGE: *Two Landscapes* - LYONS: *Landscape with Animals* - MONTAUBAN: *Landscape* - MONTPELLIER: *Two Landscapes* - MUNICH: *Two Italian Landscapes* - NANTES: *Two Landscapes*; *Washerwomen*; *Cows at a Watering Place* - NEUCHÂTEL: *Ravine Road*; *Edge of the Wood* - PARIS (Louvre): *Two Forest Interiors*; *Forest Entrance*; *Edge of a Forest*; *Four Landscapes* - RENNES: *Landscape with Figures* - ROUEN: *Landscape* - ST PETERSBURG (Hermitage): *Two Landscapes* - STUTTGART: *Four Landscapes* - VALENCIENNES: *Landscape* - VIENNA: *Two Landscapes* - VIENNA (Czernin'sche Gemäldegal.): *Forest Landscape* - VIENNA (Schönborn-Buckheim): *Landscape*.

AUCTION RECORDS:
PARIS, 1865, *Landscape*, FRF 5,850. PARIS, 1873, *Landscape*, FRF 1,180. BRUSSELS, 1899, *Landscape*, FRF 4,500. LONDON, 15 May 1908, *Wooded Stream*, GBP 2. PARIS, 28 Feb 1919, *Forest Road*, FRF 450. PARIS, 12 and 13 June 1925, *Valley Road*, FRF 5,200. LONDON, 7 June 1926, *Landscape*, GBP 42. PARIS, 23 and 24 May 1927, *Pot-Holed Road*, FRF 1,600. PARIS, 15 and 16 May 1931, *Panorama of the Italian Alps*, FRF 480. PARIS, 8 May 1940, *Road in the Mountains*, FRF 500. PARIS, 7 April 1943, *Stopping beside the Water*, FRF 5,000. NEW YORK, 9 Jan 1947, *Romantic Landscape*, USD 150. VERSAILLES, 25 Nov 1968, *Shepherds*, FRF 5,000. VIENNA, 21 March 1972, *Shepherd in a Wooded Landscape*, ATS 70,000. MUNICH, 21 Sept 1978, *Landscape with Figures* (oil on canvas, 16 3/4 x 23 1/2in/42.5 x 59.5cm) DEM 6,000. LONDON, 28 March 1979, *Figures at the Foot of a Statue in a Wooded Landscape* (oil on canvas, 41 3/4 x 51 1/2in/106 x 131cm) GBP 3,200. LONDON, 10 May 1983, *The Watering Place* (oil on canvas, 34 1/4 x 41 1/4in/87 x 104.5cm) GBP 5,800. LONDON, 19 May 1989, *Wooded River Landscape with Hunters and Peasants* (oil on canvas, 23 1/4 x 26 1/2in/59.1 x 67.6cm) GBP 3,300. ROME, 23 May 1989, *Wooded Landscape with Travellers* (oil on canvas, 22 1/4 x 31 3/4in/56.5 x 80.5cm) ITL 12,000,000. NEW YORK, 10 Jan 1990, *Travellers on a Wooded Path by a River* (oil on canvas, 35 1/2 x 65in/90.2 x 165.1cm) USD 10,450. PARIS, 31 Oct 1991, *Landscape with Three Women by a Water Hole* (oil on canvas, 16 1/4 x 22in/41 x 56cm) FRF 27,000. LONDON, 18 Oct 1995, *Wooded River Landscape with Figures and Animals on the Banks* (oil on canvas, 22 1/2 x 25 1/2in/57.2 x 64.8cm) GBP 8,625. LONDON, 16 Dec 1999, *Landscape with Travellers and Drovers on Rocky Path* (oil on canvas, 54 x 76 ins / 136 x 194 cm) GBP 19,000. LONDON, 16 Dec 1999, *Hilly Wooded Landscape with Peasants and Cattle at Watering-hole* (oil on canvas, 46 x 53 ins / 117 x 135 cm) GBP 48,000. VIENNA, 7 June 2000, *Wooded Landscape with Travellers* (oil on canvas, 20 x 23 ins / 50 x 59 cm) ATS 45,000. VIENNA, 4 Oct 2000, *Wooded River Landscape with Herders and Fishermen in a Boat* (oil on canvas, 13 x 18 ins / 34 x 45 cm) ATS 45,000. LONDON, 26 April 2001, *Wooded Landscape with Figures Resting on a Path, Sheep Grazing Beyond* (oil on canvas, 31 x 31 ins / 80 x 78 cm) GBP 2,000. LONDON, 12 July 2002, *Wooded Landscape with Figures on a Track* (oil on canvas, 27 x 22 ins / 68 x 57 cm) GBP 3,600. MADRID, 7 Oct 2002, *Landscape with Classical Figures* (oil on canvas, 20 x 24 ins / 52 x 62 cm) EUR 18,000. MADRID, 21 Jan 2003, *Landscape with Classical Figures* (oil on canvas, 20 x 24 ins / 52 x 62 cm) EUR 15,000. MADRID, 30 Sept 2003, *Landscape with Classical Figures* (oil on canvas, 20 x 24 ins / 52 x 62 cm) EUR 10,000. ROME, 17 May 2004, *Landscapes with Nymphs and Shepherds* (oil on canvas, a pair, 29 x 35 ins / 74 x 90 cm) EUR 25,000.

HUYSMANS, Jacob, or Huisman or Houseman
Flemish School, 17th century.
Born c. 1633, in Antwerp; died 1680 according to Weyerman, in London, in 1696 according to Walpole.
Painter. Historical subjects, portraits.

Jacob Huysmans studied under the painter Gillis Bakhereel, and was most probably related to Cornelis Huysmans. He worked for many years in England where he became a rival of Sir Peter Lely who was then at the height of his success. He painted portraits of some of the principal members of the English aristocracy under the reign of Charles II; some of these works were featured in the exhibition *Painted Ladies. Women at the Court of Charles II*, held at the National Portrait Gallery in London in 2001.

BIBLIOGRAPHY:
MacLeod, Catharine/Marciari Alexander, Julia/Sharpe, Kevin/Dethloff, Diana/Wynne, Sonya, *Painted Ladies. Women at the Court of Charles II*, exhibition catalogue, National Portrait Gall., London, 2001.

MUSEUMS AND GALLERIES:
LONDON (National Portrait Gal.): *John Maitland, Duke of Lauderdale* (c. 1665, oil on canvas); *Catherine of Braganza* (c. 1670, oil on canvas, work of studio); *Izaak Walton* (c. 1672, oil on canvas) - LONDON (Tate Collection): *Portrait of a Lady, as Diana* (c. 1674, oil on canvas).

AUCTION RECORDS:
LONDON, 1 May 1925, *Lord O'Brien and Mary, Countess of Kildare as Children*, GBP 89. NEW YORK, 30 May 1979, *Still-life with Flowers and Fruit* (1653, oil on canvas, 46 x 67 1/2in/117 x 171.5cm) USD 8,500. LONDON, 5 March 1982, *Portrait of Sir Henry Blount* (oil on canvas, 50 x 38in/127 x

96.5cm) GBP 1,000. LONDON, 21 Sept 1983, *Portrait of Catherine of Braganza* (oil on canvas, 29 x 23 1/4in/73.5 x 59cm) GBP 850. LONDON, 13 March 1985, *Portrait of a Woman Dressed as a Shepherdess* (oil on canvas, 29 1/4 x 24 1/2in/74.5 x 62cm) GBP 1,500. LONDON, 18 Nov 1987, *Portrait of Lady Mary Johnston* (oil on canvas, 48 x 39 1/4in/122 x 100cm) GBP 8,500. LONDON, 18 Nov 1988, *Portrait of a Young Girl Dressed as Minerva in a Garden* (oil on canvas, 54 1/4 x 44 1/2in/138 x 113.2cm) GBP 19,800. NEW YORK, 1 June 1989, *Edward Henry Lee, First Count Litchfield and his Wife as Children* (oil on canvas, 74 1/4 x 69 1/2in/188.5 x 176.5cm) USD 110,000. NEW YORK, 6 Oct 1995, *Portrait of Catherine of Braganza* (oil on canvas, 48 1/2 x 37 3/4in/123.2 x 95.9cm) USD 19,550. NEW YORK, 15 May 1996, *Three-Quarter Portrait of Mary, Countess of Warrington in a Green and White Silk Dress by an Orange Tree outside an Open Window* (oil on canvas, 47 x 38in/119.4 x 96.5cm) USD 8,050. LONDON, 30 May 1997, *Portrait of Lady Cotton* (oil on canvas, 45 x 37 3/4in/114.5 x 96cm) GBP 7,130. LONDON, 31 March 1999, *Portrait of a Lady* (oil on canvas, 30 x 24 ins / 75 x 61 cm) GBP 5,500. LONDON, 14 Dec 1999, *Portrait of a Young Boy with a Quiver of Arrows and an Ostrich Feather Headdress* (oil on canvas, 67 x 43 ins / 170 x 108 cm) GBP 10,500. LONDON, 8 Feb 2000, *Portrait, believed to be Sir William Lewkner* (oil on canvas, 30 x 26 ins / 76 x 66 cm) GBP 1,200. LONDON, 8 June 2000, *Portrait of a Lady in a Gold Dress* (oil on canvas, 21 x 18 ins / 54 x 46 cm) GBP 3,500. LONDON, 15 June 2001, *Portrait of a Lady in a Grey Dress and Blue Wrap* (oil on canvas, 50 x 40 ins / 128 x 102 cm) GBP 16,000.

HUYSMANS, Jacobus Carolus
Dutch, 19th century.
Born 14 December 1776, in Breda; died 29 September 1859, in Ginneken.
Painter.

Jacobus Huysmans was a pupil of J. K. Frederiks. Between 1802 and 1804, he worked in Antwerp before returning to Breda, where he was appointed director of the military academy. He continued to hold this position until 1837, when he became blind.

HUYSMANS, Jan Baptist
Flemish School, 17th - 18th century.
Baptised on 7 October 1654 in Antwerp; died 14 July 1716.
Painter. Landscapes with figures, landscapes.

Jan Huysmans was the brother and pupil of Cornelis Huysmans. He was a member of the Antwerp guild in 1764, and in 1676 he became a master artist in the city. He is believed to have worked in Italy as well as in Mechelen.

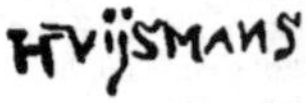

MUSEUMS AND GALLERIES:
ANTWERP: *Landscape* - BRUSSELS: *Landscape with Animals* - COLOGNE: *Three Landscapes* - KASSEL: *Ideal Landscape* - MUNICH: *Remains of a Corinthian Temple by the Sea* - STOCKHOLM: *Landscape with Pot-Holed Road.*

AUCTION RECORDS:
ZURICH, 1 June 1973, *Traveller in a Wooded Landscape,* CHF 38,000. ZURICH, 20 May 1977, *Animals at a Watering Place* (oil on canvas, 22 3/4 x 32 3/4in/58 x 83.5cm) CHF 12,500. AMSTERDAM, 12 June 1990, *Classical Landscape with Figures on a Forest Path* (oil on canvas, 35 3/4 x 30 3/4in/91 x 78cm) NLG 9,775. NEW YORK, 10 Oct 1990, *Extensive Wooded Landscape with Figures* (oil on canvas, 66 x 95in/167.6 x 241.3cm) USD 20,900. LONDON, 6 Dec 1995, *River Landscape with Figures* (oil on canvas, 35 x 39 3/4in/88 x 100.8cm) GBP 8,050. VIENNA, 6 Oct 1999, *Mountainous Coastal Landscape* (oil on canvas, 47 x 69 ins / 120 x 174 cm) ATS 180,000. LONDON, 28 Oct 1999, *Wooded Landscape with Travellers and Fortune Teller* (oil on canvas, 24 x 34 ins / 60 x 86 cm) GBP 5,500. COLOGNE, 20 May 2000, *Classical Landscape with Women by Stream* (oil on canvas, 24 x 30 ins / 60 x 75 cm) DEM 17,000. NEW YORK, 10 Oct 2001, *Wooded Landscape with Peasants and Livestock by a River* (oil on canvas, 26 x 31 ins / 65 x 79 cm) USD 9,500. LONDON, 14 Dec 2001, *Wooded Landscape with Classical Figures on a Path and by a Stream* (oil on canvas, 23 x 28 ins / 59 x 71 cm) GBP 7,000. MADRID, 25 Feb 2002, *Landscape with Figures* (oil on canvas, 23 x 28 ins / 59 x 71 cm) EUR 26,000. ANTWERP, 18 Nov 2002, *Chamber Recital* (1697, oil on panel, 19 x 15 ins / 49 x 37 cm) EUR 4,500. MADRID, 30 Sept 2003, *Landscape with Hunters* (oil on canvas, 25 x 30 ins / 64 x 76 cm) EUR 10,000.

HUYSMANS, Jan Baptist
Belgian, 19th century.
Born 25 April 1826, in Antwerp; died 1906, in Hove.
Active in France.
Painter. Historical subjects, genre scenes, local scenes. Orientalism.

Jan Baptist Huysmans studied at the Koninklijke Academie voor Schone Kunsten in Antwerp from 1843 to 1849. From 1856, he travelled in Greece, Turkey, Syria, Palestine, Egypt and Algeria and spent several years in Paris before returning to live in his native city of Antwerp. He exhibited in Antwerp in 1853, at the Glasgow Institute of Art and the Manchester City Art Gallery from 1863 to 1891, and at the Salon des Artistes Français in Paris in 1889 for the Exposition Universelle.

He produced vast religious compositions for churches in Jerusalem and is also known for his decorative panels in the church and municipal buildings of Gheel and Comines. He published his memoirs in illustrated works entitled *Travels in Italy and the Orient* in 1856-1857 and *Travels in Spain and Algeria* in 1862.

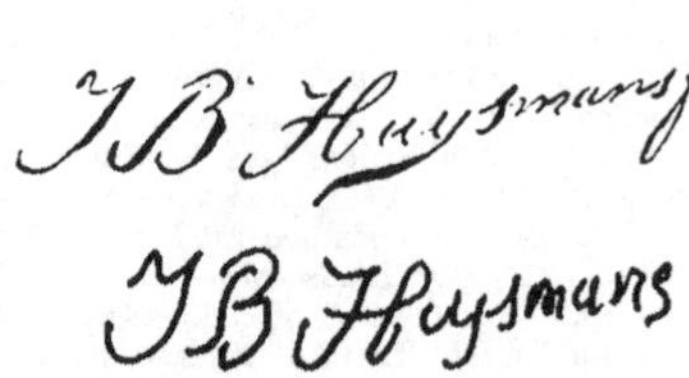

BIBLIOGRAPHY:
Thornton, Lynne, *Les Orientalistes, peintres voyageurs, 1828-1908,* ACR Édition, Paris, 1993.

MUSEUMS AND GALLERIES:
ANTWERP: *King Leopold I Lays the First Stone of the Kattendijk Reservoirs in Antwerp on 19 August 1856* (1866).

AUCTION RECORDS:
PARIS, 13-14 Jan 1926, *Travelling Entertainer at the Kaid's Palace,* FRF 680. LONDON, 19 May 1971, *The Prisoner,* GBP 180. NEW YORK, 15 Oct 1976, *Mary, Queen of Scots as a Widow* (oil on panel, 24 3/4 x 32 3/4in/63 x 83cm) USD 1,700. LONDON, 31 March 1978, *The Prisoner* (1862, oil on canvas, 34 1/2 x 52 1/2in/87.5 x 133.5cm) GBP 2,800. LONDON, 2 Nov 1979, *The Caravan Halt* (1864, oil on panel, 26 1/2 x 41 1/2in/67.2 x 105.4cm) GBP 1,400. PARIS, 21 March 1980, *The Chief of the Dervishes Blessing Children* (1885, oil on canvas, 53 1/2 x 81 1/2in/136 x 207cm) FRF 69,000. LONDON, 24 June 1981, *The Old Dervish Blessing Children* (1885, oil on canvas, 53 1/2 x 81 1/2in/136 x 207cm) GBP 9,000. LONDON, 21 March 1984, *Entertainer in the Harem* (oil on canvas, 28 1/2 x 39 1/4in/72.5 x 100cm) GBP 27,000. LONDON, 27 Feb 1985, *Café Scene in Tlemcen, Algeria* (oil on panel, 12 1/4 x 8 1/4in/31 x 21cm) GBP 4,200. LOKEREN, 28 May 1988, *Smokers* (oil on panel, 3 1/2 x 3 3/4in/8.7 x 9.5cm) BEF 44,000. MONTREAL, 30 April 1990, *The Persian Pedlar* (oil on panel, 7 1/2 x 6 1/4in/19 x 16cm) CAD 990. PARIS, 21 June 1993, *The Fortune Teller* (1875, oil on can-

vas, 19 3/4 x 29in/50 x 73.5cm) FRF 125,000. NEW YORK, 22-23 July 1993, *The Arab Carpet Merchant* (oil on panel, 7 3/4 x 6 1/2in/19.7 x 16.5cm) USD 1,150. PARIS, 22 April 1994, *Scholar* (oil on card, 8 1/4 x 5in/21 x 13cm) FRF 18,000. LONDON, 17 June 1994, *In the Harem* (1881, oil on panel, 25 1/4 x 36 1/4in/64.2 x 92.1cm) GBP 59,800. NEW YORK, 12 Oct 1994, *Interior with Moorish Women from Algeria* (1856, oil on canvas, 25 x 31 1/2in/63.5 x 80.3cm) USD 79,500. PARIS, 16 Dec 1994, *Landscape with Houses* (oil on panel, 12 1/2 x 16in/31.5 x 40.5cm) FRF 17,000. LOKEREN, 20 May 1995, *The Dance of Vesuvius* (oil on panel, 11 1/2 x 7 3/4in/29.5 x 20cm) BEF 70,000. MONTREAL, 5 Dec 1995, *Fruit Seller in the Marketplace* (oil on panel, 12 1/4 x 15 3/4in/31 x 40cm) CAD 12,000. LONDON, 15 March 1996, *The Orange Seller* (oil on panel, 12 1/4 x 15 3/4in/31.1 x 40.2cm) GBP 8,625. PARIS, 18-19 March 1996, *Dance at the Pyramids* (oil on panel, 11 1/2 x 7 3/4in/29.5 x 20cm) FRF 28,000. PARIS, 25 June 1996, *My Greetings and Respects to All Those Who Mention Me* (1861, oil on canvas, 37 1/2 x 63 1/2in/95.5 x 161cm) FRF 500,000. PARIS, 10-11 June 1997, *Street in Algiers* (1880, oil on panel, 24 x 19 3/4in/61 x 50cm) FRF 250,000. PARIS, 8 March 1999, *A Splendid Time on the Terrace* (watercolour, 11 x 7 ins / 27 x 18 cm) FRF 20,000. LONDON, 13 Oct 1999, *The Dervish Chief Blessing Children* (1885, oil on canvas, 20 x 31 ins / 52 x 80 cm) GBP 28,000. ANTWERP, 23 May 2000, *Portrait of a Lady, Zelika* (1890, oil on wood, 9 x 7 ins / 23 x 18 cm) BEF 80,000. LOKEREN, 7 Oct 2000, *Eastern Scene* (oil on panel, 4 x 4 ins / 9 x 10 cm) BEF 70,000. BRUSSELS, 12 June 2001, *The Death of Pliny the Elder in the Eruption of Vesuvius* (1867, oil on canvas, 35 x 57 ins / 89 x 146 cm) BEF 110,000. NEW YORK, 2 Nov 2001, *Captive* (1862, oil on canvas, 35 x 52 ins / 88 x 132 cm) USD 22,000. ANTWERP, 22 April 2002, *Young Girl with Flowers in a Landscape* (1851, oil on canvas, 40 x 31 ins / 102 x 79 cm) EUR 4,200. PARIS, 24 June 2002, *Portrait Artist among a Noble Family* (1861, watercolour, 6 x 7 ins / 14 x 18 cm) EUR 3,500. BATH, 7 April 2003, *Deep In Thought* (oil on panel, 9 x 16 ins / 24 x 40 cm) GBP 3,500. LUCERNE, 19 Nov 2003, *Woman Resting in Harem* (oil on panel, 8 x 11 ins / 21 x 27 cm) CHF 12,500.

HUYSMANS, Michiel
Flemish, 16th century.
Painter.
Antwerp School, Flemish School.

Michiel Huysmans studied under Jan van Hemishem. He qualified as a master in the Antwerp Guild of St Luke in 1535.

HUYSMANS, P. J.
Flemish School, 18th - 19th century.
Active c. 1790.
Painter. Landscapes.

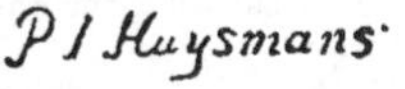

MUSEUMS AND GALLERIES:
SCHWERIN: *Landscape*.

AUCTION RECORDS:
PARIS, 12 March 1943, *Encampment; Stone Bridge* (two pendants) FRF 45,000. VERSAILLES, 6 March 1977, *Meeting near the Old Tower* (1793, wood, 11 3/4 x 15 1/4in/30 x 38.5cm) FRF 8,500. NEW YORK, 18 May 1994, *Extensive River Landscape with Peasants on the Bank and a Peasant Leading a Horse towards a Farm across a Stone Bridge* (1794, oil on panel, 19 x 26 1/4in/48.2 x 66.6cm) USD 5,750. AMSTERDAM, 7 May 1997, *Hunter in an Avenue near a Bridge* (1797, oil on panel, 27 1/4 x 38 3/4in/69.4 x 98.4cm) NLG 8,649. PARIS, 24 Oct 1997, *Landscape with Figures* (oil on panel, 12 3/4 x 19in/32.5 x 48.5cm) FRF 12,000. NEW YORK, 13 Nov 1997, *Wooded River Landscape with a Man Gathering Firewood* (1801, oil on panel, 22 1/2 x 30 1/4in/57.1 x 76.8cm) USD 3,910.

HUYSMANS, Pieter Balthazar
Flemish School, 17th century.
Born 7 January 1684, in Mechelen; died 1 November 1706, in Antwerp.
Painter. Landscapes with figures.

Pieter Huysmans was the son of Cornelis Huysmans, and studied under Peeter van Bloemen.

AUCTION RECORDS:
PARIS, 2 April 1993, *Figures and Animals in a Landscape with Ruins* (oil on oak panel, 8 1/2 x 12 1/2in/21.5 x 31.5cm) FRF 11,000.

HUYSMANS, Victor Godefridus Johannes
Dutch, 19th century.
Born 10 July 1815, in Breda; died 25 June 1856, in Paris.
Painter, watercolourist, lithographer. Genre scenes.

Victor Huysmans was the son of Jacobus-Carolus Huysmans and studied under his father. He worked in Paris.

AUCTION RECORDS:
PARIS, 9 Dec 1991, *Unloading* (watercolour, 14 1/4 x 20in/36 x 50.5cm) FRF 10,800.

HUYSON, Michiel
Flemish, 15th century.
Active in Antwerp, in 1492.
Painter.
Flemish School.

HUYSSEN, J.
17th century.
Painter. Portraits.

J. Huyssen is listed in *Art Prices Current*.

AUCTION RECORDS:
LONDON, 8 May 1908, *Portrait of a Lady* (dated 1685) GBP 12.

HUYSSEN, Margaretha
Dutch, 18th century.
Active c. 1700.
Painter. Portraits.

HUYSUM, Caspar van
Dutch, 17th century.
Active in Leeuwarden.
Painter.

On 30 May 1682, Caspar van Huysum married Cornelia van Deleen in Amsterdam.

HUYSUM, Jacob van
Dutch, 18th century.
Born c. 1686, in Amsterdam; died c. 1740, in London.
Active in England from 1721.
Painter. Flowers.

Jacob van Huysum was the son of Justus van Huysum the Elder, and the younger brother of Jan. He went to England in 1721 and lived there most of his life. He mainly painted pastiches of works by Jan van Huysum, and copies of Claude Lorraine, Caravaggio and Gaspard Dughet.

AUCTION RECORDS:
PARIS, 29 March 1960, *The Flower Basket*, FRF 16,500. LONDON, 25 Nov 1970, *Still-life with Flowers*, GBP 1,800. LONDON, 27 May 1977, *Still-life with Flowers* (1729, oil on canvas, 31 1/2 x 25in/80 x 63.5cm) GBP 9,500. LONDON, 4 May 1979, *Landscape with Still-life with Flowers on a Ledge* (oil on canvas, 25 x 34 1/4in/63.5 x 87cm) GBP 6,000. LONDON, 10 Dec 1982, *Still-life with Fruit* (oil on canvas, 16 x 13 1/4in/40.6 x 33.6cm) GBP 6,000. LONDON, 15 July 2004, *Hibiscus syriacus. Bladder-nut* (pencil and watercolour, three, 20 x 13 ins / 50 x 34 cm) GBP 4,200.

HUYSUM, Jan van, called the Elder
Dutch, 18th century.
Born 15 April 1682, in Amsterdam; died 7 or 8 February 1749, in Amsterdam.

Painter, watercolourist, draughtsman. Landscapes, still-lifes (flowers/fruit).

Amsterdam School.

Jan van Huysum the Elder was the eldest son of Justus van Huysum, a flower painter who also ran a business from his house decorating apartments and gardens. His father put Jan in charge of this enterprise and also introduced him to the art of painting. However, Jan soon tired of the more material aspects of his profession and became increasingly interested in the opportunities open to him as his talent as an artist began to develop. Various circumstances contributed to Jan van Huysum becoming a painter of flowers: his family background, the professional milieu in which he lived, and the keen interest shown by his fellow countrymen in flowers and their reproduction as decorative features. Van Huysum began to study nature, and flowers in particular, with a view to reproducing them as accurately as possible. The works of Abraham Mignon, Verelst and David de Heem helped him in this task. At the period when Van Huysum began to work as an artist, Haarlem was a town famed for its beautiful gardens. Certain flowers - tulip varieties especially - sold for very high prices. One of Van Huysum's pupils, a Miss Havermann, also excelled at painting flowers and enjoyed great success; fortunately for Van Huysum she moved to Paris.

The first person of note to purchase Van Huysum's flower paintings was the Comte de Warwick, France's envoy to Holland, who bought several paintings on behalf of the duc d'Orléans. Such noble patronage enhanced the artist's reputation, and soon the king of Poland, the king of Prussia, the elector of Saxony, the prince of Hesse and the Stadtholder had commissioned paintings from him, which he sold at very high prices. Robert Walpole, a great admirer of Van Huysum, made him well-known in England. This enduring admiration for the artist in royal circles established Van Huysum's reputation once and for all.

For Van Huysum the universe was centred upon flowers: through their study he discovered a whole world of insects and the sights and sounds associated with them - butterflies, honey bees, flying ants, beetles; he painted them all with great delicacy, conveying both their transparent qualities and their bright and motley colours. His flower arrangements, though not symmetrical, reveal a harmonious and unexpected subtlety of form. Characteristic of Van Huysum's work is the complexity he brings to the details surrounding the central motif: slender branches, capricious tendrils and graceful, flexible stems - all of which bring a sense of great lightness to the entire composition. The early skill he acquired in painting carved vases, marble consoles and low reliefs to set off his flower arrangements also came into its own.

Van Huysum's most highly regarded paintings are those of flowers and fruit rather than landscapes. With regard to price, the Louvre, which has some of the finest examples of his work, owns a *Landscape* valued at 3,000 francs under the Empire, while his paintings of flowers and fruit sold for between 4,000 and 12,000 francs. Although highly regarded during his lifetime, Van Huysum died in poverty in 1749. He had three children.

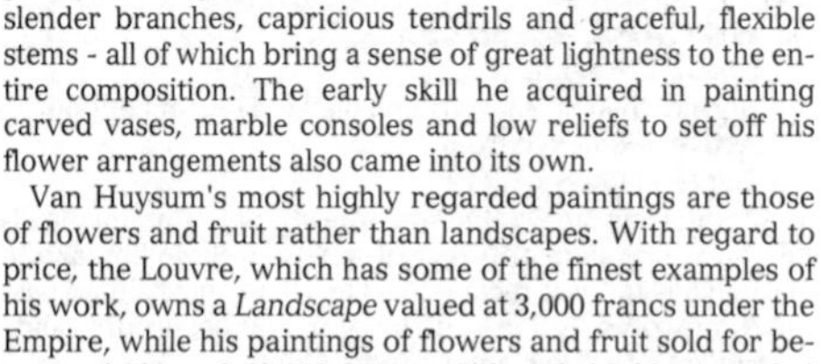

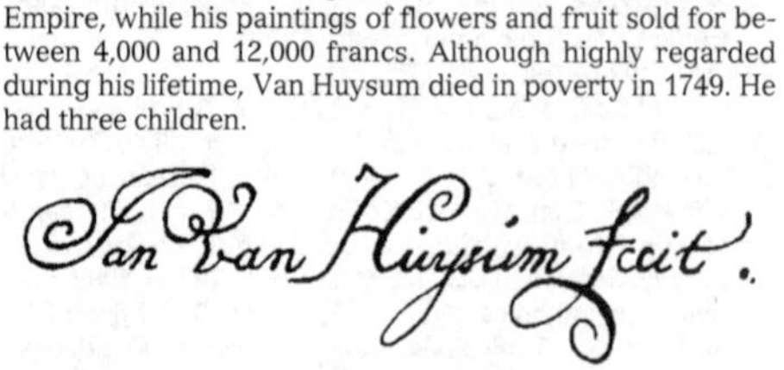

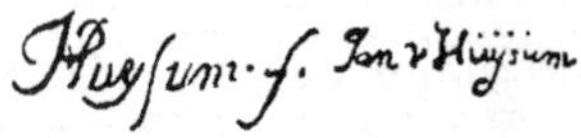

BIBLIOGRAPHY:

Grant, Maurice Harold, *Jan van Huysum, 1682-1749: Including a Catalogue Raisonné of the Artist's Fruit and Flower Paintings,* Leigh on Sea, 1954.

MUSEUMS AND GALLERIES:

AMSTERDAM: *Five Pictures of Flowers and Fruit; Arcadian Landscape; Before the Offertory* - BERLIN: *Bouquet; Spray of Flowers* - BUDAPEST: *Bouquet of Flowers in a Vase* - COLOGNE: *Flowers* - COPENHAGEN (Statens Mus. for Kunst): *Vase with Flowers* - DRESDEN: *Vase of Flowers with Orange; Flowers and Birds' Nest; Landscape with Flowers* - DUBLIN: *Bunch of Flowers Hanging from the Branch of a Tree* - FLORENCE (Palazzo Pitti): *Flowers and Fruit* - FRANKFURT AM MAIN: *Italian Landscape; Flowers* - GLASGOW: *Flowers; Flowers* - HAMBURG: *Flowers* - HANOVER: *Two Still-lifes* - LEIDEN: *Old Vase Adorned with Flowers* - LEIPZIG: *Bouquet* - LIÈGE: *Flowers and Fruit; Flowers* - LILLE: *Flowers* - LONDON (Dulwich Picture Gal.): *Vase with Flowers* (c. 1719, oil/panel) - LONDON (NG): *Hollyhocks and Other Flowers in a Vase* (1702-1720, oil on canvas); *Flowers in a Terracotta Vase* (1736, oil on canvas) - LONDON (Wallace Collection): *Flowers in a Vase* (1726, oil/panel); *Fruit and Flowers* (before 1726, oil/panel) - LOS ANGELES (Getty Mus.): *Fruit Piece* (1722, oil/panel); *Vase of Flowers* (1722, oil/panel) - LYONS: *Vase of Flowers and Birds' Nest; Flowers and Fruit on a Marble Console; Flowers in a Vase on a Marble Console* - MAINZ: *Two Landscapes* - MILAN (Ambrosiana): *Bouquet* - MONTPELLIER: *Bouquet of Flowers; Fruit* - MUNICH: *Fruit and Flowers; Fruit and Insects; Basket with Flowers* - PARIS (Louvre): *Flowers and Fruit; Vase of Flowers; Large Vase Decorated with Low-Reliefs and Filled with Flowers; Flowers in a Vase; Four Landscapes; Basket of Flowers on a Marble Table* (same subject); *Fruit and Flowers* - PARIS (Mus. Marmottan-Monet): *Flowers* - PÉRIGUEUX: *Vase of Flowers* - ROTTERDAM: *Basket of Flowers* - ST PETERSBURG (Hermitage): *Flowers and Fruit; Flowers; Site in Italy; Landscape* - STOCKHOLM: *Landscape with Archway and Ruin* - STRASBOURG: *Flowers* - STUTTGART: *Flowers* - THE HAGUE: *Fruit; Italian Landscape* - TROYES: *Vase of Flowers* - VIENNA: *Flowers; Bouquet of Flowers in a Gold Vase* - VIENNA (Czernin'sche Gemäldegal.): *Large Bouquet of Flowers in a Vase* - VIENNA (Schönborn-Buckheim): *Two Landscapes.*

AUCTION RECORDS:

PARIS, 1841, *Flowers and Fruit,* FRF 10,000. PARIS, 1854, *Flowers in a Vase,* FRF 13,000. LONDON, 1877, *Vase with Bouquet of Flowers,* FRF 8,395. PARIS, 1886, *Flowers and Birds' Nest,* FRF 10,000. LONDON, 1893, *Bouquet of Roses in a Terracotta Pot,* FRF 12,095. PARIS, 1899, *Bouquet of Flowers in a Terracotta Vase,* FRF 18,200. PARIS, 1900, *Flowers and Fruit,* FRF 2,640. PARIS, 14 Jan 1902, *Basket of Fruit on a Table,* FRF 1,205. LONDON, 29 Feb 1908, *Fruit and Flowers on a Carved Pedestal,* GBP 115. LONDON, 28 March 1908, *Flowers and Birds' Nest,* GBP 220. LONDON, 28 May 1908, *Classical Landscape* (watercolour) GBP 11. LONDON, 10 Dec 1910, *Vase of Flowers,* GBP 73. PARIS, 22 May 1919, *Vase of Flowers,* FRF 5,600. PARIS, 21 April 1921, *Vase of Flowers,* FRF 5,100. LONDON, Feb 1922, *Flowers and Birds' Nest on a Marble Slab,* GBP 42. LONDON, May 1923, *Flowers and Fruit,* GBP 399. LONDON, May 1923, *Flowers in Glass Vases* (two works) GBP

99. London, June 1923, *Fruit and Flowers on a Marble Slab,* GBP 115. London, July 1923, *Vase of Flowers,* GBP 714. London, July 1924, *Flowers in a White Vase,* GBP 50. London, 20 Feb 1925, *Flowers in a Vase,* GBP 409. London, 6 May 1926, *Flowers in a Vase,* GBP 330. London, 5 July 1926, *Still-life,* GBP 194. London, 7 Dec 1927, *Flowers,* GBP 3,800. London, 7 June 1928, *Flowers,* GBP 200. London, 7 June 1929, *Flowers in a Glass Vase,* GBP 210. London, 28 Feb 1930, *Bouquet,* GBP 892. London, 5 June 1930, *Flowers in a Terracotta Vase,* GBP 1,995. London, 25 July 1930, *Flowers in a Carved Vase.* New York, 25 March 1931, *Still-life,* USD 90. London, 20 July 1934, *Flowers in a Glass Vase,* GBP 36. Paris, 28 Nov 1934, *Spray of Flowers in a Vase* (black chalk and Indian ink wash) FRF 520. London, 22 Feb 1935, *Flowers in a Glass Vase,* GBP 367. Paris, 22 Feb 1937, *Vase of Flowers* (pen drawing, heightened with gouache) FRF 4,000. Paris, 22 Feb 1937, *Still-life,* FRF 13,900. London, 30 April 1937, *Flowers and Fruit,* GBP 315. Paris, 9 June 1937, *Vase of Flowers,* FRF 32,000. London, 27 May 1938, *Flowers,* GBP 315. London, 22 July 1938, *Flowers,* GBP 283. Paris, 13 Feb 1939, *Flowers in a Vase with Butterfly and Snails,* FRF 3,600. London, 24 Feb 1939, *Flowers in a Vase,* GBP 141. Paris, 12 and 13 Dec 1940, *Pot of Flowers* (watercolour) FRF 16,000. London, 29 July 1942, *Flowers,* GBP 95. London, 11 Dec 1942, *Basket of Flowers,* GBP 220. New York, 7 Jan 1943, *Flowers,* USD 700; *Flowers,* USD 450; *Fruit,* USD 150. Paris, 24 Feb 1943, *Vase of Flowers* (attributed) FRF 27,500. London, 1 Oct 1944, *Flowers in a Terracotta Vase,* GBP 168; *Flowers in a Vase,* GBP 336. London, 19 Jan 1945, *Flowers in a White Vase,* GBP 472. London, 12 Oct 1945, *Flowers and Birds' Nests,* GBP 672. London, 3 April 1946, *Fruit,* GBP 250. London, 31 May 1946, *Flowers in a Vase with Fruit,* GBP 168. London, 17 July 1946, *Flowers in a Vase,* GBP 380. London, 14 March 1947, *Flowers in a Vase,* GBP 630; *Flowers in a Glass Vase,* GBP 693; *Flowers in a Vase,* GBP 546. London, 3 July 1947, *Flowers in a Vase,* GBP 75. London, 9 Dec 1949, *Flowers in a Stone Basin* (watercolour heightened) GBP 220. Paris, 7 Dec 1950, *Vase of Flowers,* FRF 820,000. Paris, 7 Dec 1951, *Vase of Flowers,* FRF 830,000; *Vase of Flowers* (red chalk and wash) FRF 65,000. London, 20 Nov 1957, *Pretty Bunch of Spring Flowers with Red Poppies,* GBP 1,800. London, 2 July 1958, *Arrangement of Fruit and Flowers,* GBP 2,000. London, 23 March 1960, *Summer Flowers with Paeonies,* GBP 5,500. London, 21 June 1961, *Still-life,* GBP 1,000. London, 10 July 1963, *Bouquet of Flowers,* GBP 1,800. London, 30 June 1965, *Bouquet of Flowers,* GBP 4,000. Amsterdam, 24 Jan 1967, *Still-life with Fruit and Flowers,* NLG 56,000. London, 27 June 1969, *Flowers,* Gns 3,800. London, 27 Nov 1970, *Still-life with Flowers,* Gns 5,000. London, 23 March 1971, *Vase of Flowers* (watercolour) GBP 380. London, 23 March 1972, *Still-life with Flowers* (watercolour) GBP 1,000. Lucerne, 30 June 1973, *Still-life with Flowers,* CHF 70,000. Vienna, 3 Dec 1974, *Self-portrait,* ATS 90,000. Amsterdam, 15 Nov 1976, *Still-life with Flowers* (1932, oil on panel, 28¼ x 20in/71.5 x 51cm) NLG 34,000. Paris, 17 June 1977, *Nest with a Bouquet of Flowers* (oil on canvas, 16¼ x 13½in/41 x 34cm) FRF 562,000. London, 29 June 1979, *Still-life with Flowers and Fruit* (oil on panel, 16½ x 12½in/42 x 32cm) GBP 42,000. Amsterdam, 18 May 1981, *Vase of Flowers on a Ledge* (black chalk, 16 x 12½in/40.8 x 32cm) NLG 4,800. Zurich, 11 Nov 1982, *Italian Landscape with Horsemen* (oil on canvas, 39 x 48in/99 x 122cm) CHF 65,000. London, 9 March 1983, *Vase of Flowers* (oil/metal/panel, 19¼ x 16in/49 x 40.5cm) GBP 30,000. London, 4 July 1984, *Vase of Flowers* (black chalk and grey wash, 16 x 12¼in/40.8 x 31.4cm) GBP 3,800. London, 9 April 1986, *Figures in front of a Statue of Persephone in a Wooded Landscape* (oil on canvas, 20¼ x 28¼in/51.5 x 71.5cm) GBP 62,000. London, 14 April 1986, *Flowers in an Urn* (black chalk, 16¼ x 12¾in/41 x 32.2cm) GBP 2,000. New York, 4 June 1987, *Still-life with Vase of Flowers on a Ledge* (oil on canvas, 29¼ x 21½in/74.5 x 54.5cm) USD 360,000. New York, 11 Jan 1989, *River Landscape with Classical Constructions and Figures* (1726, chalk and ink, 11½ x 15¾in/28.9 x 40cm) USD 10,450. London, 5 July 1989, *Still-life with a Large Floral Composition and Fruit on a Ledge* (oil on canvas, 32¾ x 25¼in/83 x 64cm) GBP 396,000. Rome, 27 Nov 1989, *Vase of Flowers with Fruit* (oil on canvas, 40¼ x 33½in/102 x 85cm) ITL 46,000,000. New York, 5 April 1990, *Holy Family during the Flight into Egypt* (1727, oil on canvas, 20¼ x 28¼in/51.5 x 71.5cm) USD 192,500. New York, 17 Jan 1992, *Large Floral Composition in a Terracotta Vase with a Spray of Orange Blossom and a Nest on a Wooden Ledge* (oil on panel, 31½ x 24in/80 x 61cm) USD 3,520,000. Paris, 27 March 1992, *Arcadian Landscape* (1699, pen and grey wash, 5 x 6¾in/13 x 17cm) FRF 11,000. New York, 22 May 1992, *Arcadian Landscape with Nymphs Decorating a Bust of Hermes with Garlands of Flowers* (oil/copper, 22¼ x 34½in/56.5 x 87.6cm) USD 57,750. Paris, 14 Dec 1992, *River Landscape in the Roman Countryside* (oil on canvas, 17 x 20in/43 x 51cm) FRF 55,000. New York, 20 May 1993, *Italian Landscape with Shepherds and a Town in the Distance; Peasants by a Waterfall in a Wooded Landscape* (oil on canvas, a pair, each 17 x 20in/43.2 x 50.5cm) USD 20,700. Paris, 2 June 1993, *Bouquet of Flowers in Vase Decorated with Putti* (lead pencil and watercolour, 15¼ x 11¾in/39 x 30cm) FRF 40,000. Amsterdam, 17 Nov 1993, *Italian Landscape* (1715, ink and wash, 6¼ x 7½in/16 x 19.2cm) NLG 1,725. New York, 12 Jan 1994, *Large Composition of Flowers and Fruit on a Stone Ledge with Insects* (1730, oil on panel, 30½ x 23½in/77.5 x 59.7cm) USD 2,642,500. Amsterdam, 10 May 1994, *Basket of Flowers on a Balustrade* (black chalk and wash, 8¾ x 7¼in/22.4 x 18.6cm) NLG 4,600. London, 8 July 1994, *Roses and Other Flowers in a Basket on a Marble Ledge; Fruit, Hazelnuts and Hollyhocks on a Ledge* (oil on panel, a pair, each 15¾ x 13in/40 x 33cm) GBP 826,500. Paris, 20 Oct 1994, *Flowers in an Urn on a Ledge* (watercolour and pen, a pair, each 9¼ x 6¾in/23.3 x 17cm) FRF 48,000. London, 3 April 1995, *Study of a Vase of Flowers in a Niche* (black and white chalk/blue paper, 15 x 11½in/38 x 29cm) GBP 3,680. Milan, 3 April 1996, *Landscape with Travellers and a Bridge* (oil on canvas, 17¼ x 20in/43.5 x 51cm) ITL 13,800,000. New York, 4 Oct 1996, *Arcadian Landscape with a Shepherd Crossing a Bridge and Other Figures in the Foreground* (1723-1724, oil on canvas, 21 x 29¼in/53.3 x 74.4cm) USD 18,400. Paris, 9 Dec 1996, *Still-life with a Vase of Flowers and Fruit on a Ledge* (oil on canvas, 50½ x 40¼in/128 x 102cm) FRF 200,000. New York, 17 Oct 1997, *Italian Landscape with Shepherds in the Foreground and a Town in the Distance; Peasants by a Waterfall in a Wooded Landscape* (oil on canvas, a pair, each 17 x 20in/43.2 x 50.5cm) USD 26,450. London, 9 July 1999, *Roses, Morning Glory, Narcissi, Aster and Other Flowers in a Basket and Eggs in a Nest* (1744, oil on panel, 10 x 7 ins / 26 x 19 cm) GBP 320,000. Amsterdam, 9 Nov 1999, *Arcadian Landscape* (gouache, 7 x 7 ins / 19 x 17 cm) NLG 8,200. Paris, 25 Feb 2000, *River Landscape* (pen with ink wash, 5 x 8 ins / 13 x 21 cm) FRF 26,000. Cologne, 30 Nov 2000, *Still-life with Lobster, Oyster, Fruit and Wine Glass* (oil on canvas, 19 x 18 ins / 48 x 45 cm) DEM 14,000. New York, 23 Jan 2001, *Italianate Landscape* (watercolour and gouache over black chalk, a pair, 6 x 8 ins / 15 x 20 cm) USD 9,000. Paris, 5 Dec 2001, *Still-life with Flowers* (oil on panel, 18 x 15 ins / 46 x 38 cm) FRF 1,050,000. London, 14 June 2002, *Classical Landscape with the Worship of Bacchus* (oil on canvas, 21 x 28 ins / 54 x 72 cm) GBP 250,000. London, 11 Dec 2003, *Still-life with Flowers in a Terracotta Vase upon a Marble Ledge before a Niche* (1734, oil on panel, 32 x 24 ins / 81 x 61 cm) GBP 2,700,000. London, 11 Dec 2003, *Still-life with Fruit in a Basket with Flowers and Other Fruit all upon a Marble Ledge* (oil on panel, 31 x 24 ins / 80 x 60 cm) GBP 4,400,000. Brussels, 25 May

2004, *Vase of Flowers in a Niche* (oil on canvas, 27 x 20 ins / 69 x 50 cm) EUR 27,000. MUNICH, 30 June 2004, *Italian River Landscape* (oil on canvas, 26 x 31 ins / 65 x 79 cm) EUR 8,000.

HUYSUM, Justus van, the Elder
Dutch, 17th - 18th century.
Born 8 June 1659, in Amsterdam; died April 1716, in Amsterdam.
Painter, draughtsman. Battles, portraits, landscapes, seascapes, flowers, still-lifes (including flowers and fruit).
Amsterdam School.

In 1675, Justus van Huysum the Elder was a pupil of Nicolaes Berchem. He became a citizen of Amsterdam in 1682. He was the founding father of the Huysum dynasty of artists.

MUSEUMS AND GALLERIES:
ANTWERP: *Bouquet of Flowers* - AVIGNON: *Vase of Flowers* - MULHOUSE: *Seascapes* (two works).

AUCTION RECORDS:
PARIS, 9 and 10 March 1923, *Vase and Fruit* (pen and wash) FRF 300. PARIS, 23 March 1923, *Flowers and Fruit* (pen and wash) FRF 960. LONDON, 21 Feb 1927, *Flowers,* GBP 152. LONDON, 3 Dec 1940, *Peasant Eating among Ruins,* GBP 40. NEW YORK, 15 Jan 1947, *Flowers,* USD 525. LONDON, 26 Nov 1958, *Summer Flowers with Roses,* GBP 950. AMSTERDAM, 25 Nov 1969, *Still-life with Flowers,* NLG 11,500. COLOGNE, 26 March 1971, *Cavalry Charge,* DEM 7,000. LONDON, 1 June 1973, *Still-life with Flowers,* Gns 1,900. LONDON, 13 Dec 1978, *Vases of Flowers* (two canvases, 31 x 24¾in/79 x 63cm) GBP 13,000. NEW YORK, 11 Jan 1979, *Still-life with Flowers* (oil on panel, 30¾ x 22in/78 x 55cm) USD 16,000. ROUBAIX, 22 Feb 1981, *Vase of Flowers* (oil on canvas, 27½ x 22¾in/70 x 58cm) FRF 75,000. PARIS, 26 Nov 1986, *Still-life with Fruit and a Delft Bowl on a Ledge* (oil on canvas, 20 x 17¼in/51 x 43.5cm) FRF 290,000. DIJON, 29 Nov 1987, *Bouquet of Flowers* (oil on canvas, 29¼ x 23½in/74 x 60cm) FRF 300,000. NEW YORK, 15 Jan 1988, *Still-life with a Bunch of Paeony-Red Roses and Poppies and Other Flowers in a Glass Vase on a Carved Ledge* (oil on canvas, 32¾ x 26¼in/83 x 66.5cm) USD 13,200. PARIS, 12 Dec 1989, *Peaches and Grapes on a Ledge* (oak panel, 7¼ x 9¾in/18.5 x 25cm) FRF 350,000. NEW YORK, 10 Jan 1990, *Composition of Assorted Flowers in a Vase on a Stone Pedestal* (oil on canvas, 38¼ x 33½in/97.2 x 85.1cm) USD 66,000. PARIS, 9 April 1990, *Garland of Ivy, Tulips, Roses, Convolvulus, Narcissi, Hyacinths, Poppies, Thistles, Primulas and Lilac Supported by Two Blue Ribbons Attached to Bronze Rings* (oil on canvas, 24½ x 31¾in/62 x 80.5cm) FRF 110,000. NEW YORK, 19 July 1990, *Horseman Following a Stream* (oil on panel, 12¼ x 10½in/31.2 x 26.7cm) USD 2,090. LONDON, 3 April 1992, *Red Parrot Perched on an Urn Filled with Roses, Morning Glory, Tulips, Irises, and Other Flowers* (oil on canvas, 46½ x 42½in/118 x 107.8cm) GBP 24,200. NEW YORK, 20 May 1993, *Still-life with Paeonies, Hollyhocks, Roses, Carnations and Other Flowers in a Vase on a Stone Plinth* (oil on canvas, 37½ x 33¼in/95.3 x 84.5cm) USD 31,050. LONDON, 6 Dec 1995, *Still-life with Lilies, Roses, Carnations and Other Flowers in a Glass Vase on a Stone Ledge with a Butterfly* (oil on canvas, 25¼ x 21¼in/64 x 54cm) GBP 40,000. LONDON, 29 Oct 1999, *Roses, Lilies, Poppy, Morning Glory in Basket on a Ledge* (oil on canvas, 34 x 28 ins / 86 x 70 cm) GBP 4,800. LONDON, 29 Oct 2001, *Wooded Landscape with Hunting Party on a Path* (oil on canvas, 21 x 25 ins / 53 x 63 cm) GBP 6,500.

HUYSUM, Justus van, the Younger
Dutch, 17th century.
Born c. 1684, in Amsterdam; died 3 November 1707, in Amsterdam.
Painter. Battles.
Amsterdam School.

Justus van Huysum the Younger was the son of Justus van Huysum the Elder, and brother of Jan.

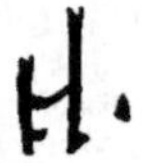

MUSEUMS AND GALLERIES:
BRUNSWICK: *Battle Scene*.

HUYSUM, Maria van
Dutch, 17th - 18th century.
Active in Amsterdam.
Draughtswoman.

Maria van Huysum was the daughter of Jan van Huysum.

HUYSUM, Michiel van
Dutch, 18th century.
Active in Amsterdam from 1729 to 1759.
Painter, watercolourist. Still-lifes (flowers, fruit).

Michiel van Huysum was the son of Justus van Huysum the Elder.

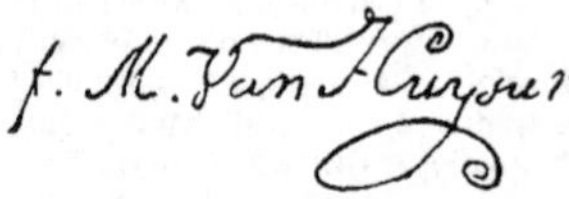

AUCTION RECORDS:
AMSTERDAM, 14 Nov 1983, *Still-life with Fruit* (watercolour, 7½ x 12¼in/18.8 x 30.9cm) NLG 9,500. PARIS, 29 April 1994, *Bouquet of Flowers with Goldfinch and Peach* (oil on panel, 17½ x 12½in/44.5 x 31.5cm) FRF 80,000.

HUYTER, C.
British, 18th century.
Active in London.
Miniaturist.

C. Huyter exhibited his work at the Royal Academy in London in 1788.

HUYTSCHOECK, Henrick Pietersz.
Dutch, 16th century.
Born c. 1553; died c. 1593.
Active in Rotterdam.
Painter.

Henrick Pietersz. Huytschoeck painted portraits and pictures inspired by mythology.

HUYTT, H. N.
Dutch.
Painter. Landscapes.

HVICMANNE
Danish.
Active in Aastrup.
Sculptor.

The signature *Hvicmanne* appears on a sculpture in the church in Aastrup.

HWA CHUN-WU. See **HUA JUNWU**

HWANG, Dennis, also known as: Huang Zhichao
Chinese, 20th - 21st century.
Born 1941, in Hunan.
Active in the USA from 1972.
Painter. Scenes with figures.

At the start of his career, Dennis Hwang used graphic techniques such as those used in batik in a so-called Abstract Surrealist style. He also wrote a book entitled *The Art of Batik*. In 1971 he was invited by the US Government to visit the USA under the auspices of the Asian Art Association, and settled in New York the following year. Hwang is influenced by Western thinking and lifestyle. He paints rather languorous, sketchy, intimate scenes in acrylics, using a broad, energetic brush. He has shown work in many group and solo exhibitions.

AUCTION RECORDS:
TAIPEI, 22 March 1992, *Young Woman in her Room* (1988, acrylic on canvas, 48 x 35 3/4 ins / 122 x 91 cm) TWD 440,000.

HWANG YOUNG SUNG
Korean, 20th century.
Born 1941, in Korea.
Active in Kwangju.
Painter.

Hwang Young Sung teaches at Chosun University in Kwangju. He initially painted landscapes with houses under moonlight or blue skies. He then moved towards a more restricted expression of reality in the form of squares and circles, culminating in a sort of demultiplication of signs symbolising certain details.

Since 1980 he has shown work in group exhibitions of the new generation of Korean artists. He has also held a number of solo exhibitions, including those at the following: the Lotte Gallery in Seoul (1980); the Shinsegae Art Center in Kwangju (1988); L'Atelier in Paris (1991); the Galerie Bernheim Jeune in Paris (1992); the Yeh Gallery in Seoul (1995); and the Musée de l'Hôtel-Dieu in Mantes-la-Jolie in France (1997).

HYACINTHE
French, 19th century.
Active c. 1800.
Miniaturist.

HYACINTHE, Flamand. See **FLAMAND**

HYAKKI, or Hyakuki, signature name: Komatsuya, popularly known as: Sanemon, pseudonyms: Fuchsoku Sanjin, Shoshoken, Komatsuken
Japanese, 19th century.
Active in the Osaka region c. 1813.
Engraver.

According to the *Kabuki Nempyo*, Hyakki made a *surimono* (limited edition print used as a greeting card, invitation or birth/death/marriage announcement) of the actor Nakamura Utamaro III.

HYAKUKOKU. See **KAISEN**

HYAKUNEN, real name: Suzuki Seiju, popularly known as: Zusho, nickname: Shiko, pseudonyms: Hyakunen, Daichino, Gasendo, Tekiseikaku, Shujin, Tokinro
Japanese, 19th century.
Born 1825; died 1891.
Active in Kyoto.
Painter.

Hyakunen trained himself and painted landscapes in the traditional Japanese style yet with his own personal touch.

HYAKUSEN, real name: Sakaki Shinen, nickname: Hyakusen, pseudonyms: Hoshu, Hassendo
Japanese, 18th century.
Born 1698, in Nagoya; died 1753.
Painter.
Nanga School.

With Nankai (1676-1751) and Kien Yanagisawa (1706-1758), Hyakusen is one of the greatest early 18th-century Nanga School painters (scholar-painters). The son of a pharmacist of probably Chinese ancestors, he was not regarded as a Confucian scholar as were Nankai and Kien. He started by learning and putting into practice the two orthodox styles of his time, from the Tosa and Kano Schools, before going on to study Chinese painting from the later Ming dynasty (1388-1644), which led him gradually towards Nanga painting. He also compiled the *Gen-min Gajinko*, a biographical dictionary of Chinese artists of the Yuan and Ming periods, which was published in 1751. A skilful *haiku* poet, he was one of the pioneers of *haiga* (*haiku* painting), which was to be a great influence on Buson (1716-1783), the great master of the Nanga School.

Hyakusen has so many different styles that it is hard to follow the growth in his work, but he may be regarded as having had a two-fold influence on the Nanga School. First, he succeeded in capturing a number of qualities in Chinese painting that had escaped Kien and Nankai, such as its sensibility, the variety of brushstrokes, its finely nuanced tone gradation and its complex but clear composition. Secondly, he succeeded in assimilating these various elements and subsuming them into the Japanese pictorial tradition in a process which Ike-no-Taiga (1723-1766) and Buson would continue and develop to a point of perfection. Hyakusen's landscapes and paintings of birds and flowers embody the first steps of the Nanga School towards independence.

BIBLIOGRAPHY:
Cahill, James, *Scholar Painters of Japan: the Nanga School*, Asia Society, New York, 1972. Guth, Christine, *Japanese Painting of the Edo Period*, Calmann & King, London, 1996.

MUSEUMS AND GALLERIES:
TOKYO (National Mus.).

HYAKUSUI. See **HIRAFUKU Hyakusui**

HYAKUTAKE, Kenko, real name: Hyakutake Kaneyuki, pseudonym: Kenko
Japanese, 19th century.
Born 1842; died 1887.
Active in Tokyo.
Painter.

Hyakutake Kenko was a diplomat and painter who worked in the Western style after training with Richardson, Léon Bonnard and Maccari.

HYARD, Hubert
Flemish School, 18th century.
Active in Liège.
Sculptor (wood).

HYATT, Anna Vaughan. See **HUNTINGTON Anna Vaughan Hyatt**

HYBERT, Fabrice
French, 20th - 21st century.
Born 1961, in Luçon.
Painter, installation artist, mixed media.
Neo-Conceptual Art, Esthétique Relationnelle.

Fabrice Hybert lives and works in Nantes, where he studied at the École des Beaux-Arts in 1984. His successive and simultaneous creations are mixed up and barely show any formal or intentional continuity. Their accidental and ill-assorted appearance is what makes them interesting. Their future unity comes about through the way his imagination works in a variety of place, time and meeting opportunities occurring in a continual process of sequences. The whole collection, which is in fact more than one, is diverse because it brings together any jumble of usually meaningful objects, as in *Fly Farm in a Bee Hive*, and even quite often in humorous drawings. The jumble of his multiple activities make the whole thing elusive and unclassifiable. The unity and coherence of his work lies merely in the diversity of the moments they comprise. However, one of his most persistent ventures is his painting moments and especially the series he calls his 'homeopathic paintings', the first of which was started in 1986 and continued for three years. In this series he takes tiny fragments of objects and shows images, which he builds up, superimposes, and thins into one another in a memorisation process, and ultimately makes a very presentable product.

Collective exhibitions in which he has participated include: *Tête à Tête*, Nantes, 1984; *Ils Créent pour Demain* (*Designers for Tomorrow*), Nantes, 1985; *Voyage aller-retour* (*Return Trip*), Montélimar and Nantes, *Ateliers internationaux des Pays de la Loire* (*International Workshops of the Loire Region*), Fontevraud, 1986; *Couverture de Première* (*First Cover*), Paris, 1987; Venice Biennale and FIAC (Foire Internationale d'Art Contemporain - International Contemporary Art Fair), Paris 1993; Lyons Biennale, 1995; Venice Biennale, where he won the prize for the best stand, 1997; *Skulptur. Projekte in Münster 1997* (*Sculpture. Projects in Münster 1997*), 1997; *Présumés Innocents: l'Art Contemporain et l'Enfance* (*Presumed Innocent: Contemporary Art and Childhood*), Capc Musée d'Art Contemporain, Bordeaux, 2000; *(O.P.E) Offre Publique d'Échange* (*Share Exchange Offer*), FRAC Poitou-Charentes collection, municipal gallery in Voûtes du Port, Royan, 2000; *Un Tableau dans le Décor. Peintures 1970-2000* (*A Painting in the Décor: Paintings 1970-2000*), Château des ducs de Bretagne, Nantes and *L'État des Choses* (*The State of Things*), a look at the status of the everyday object in contemporary art, Musée des Beaux-Arts, Nantes, two exhibitions organised under the auspices of *Trésors Publics, 20 Ans de Création dans les Fonds Régionaux d'Art Contemporain (FRAC)* (*Public Treasury, 20 Years of Creation in the Regional Collection of Contemporary Art (FRAC)*), 2003.

Hybert mainly shows the successive phases of his work in solo exhibitions, including: Nantes, 1987; Galerie Arlogos, Nantes, regularly since 1987; Ussel, 1987; (DRAC) Direction Régionale d'Art Contemporain (Regional Contemporary Art Department), Limoges; Eastman, Canada, 1988; DRAC Poitiers and the municipal theatre in Caen, 1989; Galerie Froment-Putman, Paris, 1990, 1992; Centre d'Art Contemporain, Thiers, Halle d'Art Contemporain, Rennes and Robert Walzer Gallery, St-Gall, Switzerland, 1992; Musée d'Art Contemporain, Bordeaux, 1993; Georges-Pompidou Centre, Paris, 1994; Musée d'Art Moderne de la Ville de Paris, Paris, 1995; Centre d'Art Confort Moderne, Poitiers, 1998; Galleria The Box Associati, Turin, 2002; Château Comtal, medieval city (CMN), Carcassonne.

BIBLIOGRAPHY:

Bouglé, Frédéric/Hybert, Fabrice, *1-1=2, entretiens*, Joca seria, Nantes, 1992. Froment, Jean-Louis/Giquel, Pierre/Strasser, Catherine, *Fabrice Hybert: œuvres de 1981 à 1993*, exhibition catalogue, Capc musée d'Art contemporain, Bordeaux, 1993. Frogier, Larys/Stafford, Barbara Maria/Brayer, Marie-Ange/Groys, Boris, '*Laboratoires, pour une expérience du corps. Damien Hirst, Fabrice Hybert, Kiki Smith, Patrick Van Caeckenberg*' in coll. *Métiers de l'exposition*, exhibition catalogue, Presses universitaires, Rennes, 1995. Rousseau, Pascal, *Fabrice Hybert*, Hazan, Paris, 1999 (text in French and English). Hybert, Fabrice, *POF*, Ur, 1999 (artist's book). Bernadac, Marie-Laure/Moisdon-Tremblay, et al., *Présumés innocents: l'art contemporain et l'enfance*, exhibition catalogue, Capc musée d'Art contemporain, Bordeaux, 2000. Laurent, Thierry, *Fabrice Hybert. Il est interdit de mourir: Thierry Laurent entretien*, Au même titre, Paris, 2003. Zahm, Olivier (preface), et al., *Trésors publics, 20 ans de création dans les Fonds régionaux d'art contemporain*, Flammarion, Paris, 2003 (text in French and English).

MUSEUMS AND GALLERIES:

ANGOULÊME (FRAC Poitou-Charentes): *First Insurance Company* (1989) - BORDEAUX (FRAC Aquitaine): *Sans titre* (1992); *L'Homme de Bessines, XXe s, - 1988-1995* (*Man from Bessines, 20th century, 1988-1995*) - CARQUEFOU (FRAC Pays de la Loire): *Un Mètre Carré de Rouge à Lèvres* (*A Square Metre of Lipstick*) (1981); *Programme d'Entreprise Indéterminée* (1986-1993, installation) - DUNKIRK (FRAC Nord-Pas de Calais) - LYONS (FRAC Rhône-Alpes): *Casquettes Radar* (1990-1994) - MARSEILLES (FRAC Provence-Alpes-Côte d'Azur): *Les Fondations* (1992); *Casquettes-radar* (1990-1994) - MONTPELLIER (FRAC Languedoc-Roussillon): *L'Invention de la Table* (1989) - NANTES (MBA) - PARIS (MAMVP): *P.O.F-Prototypes Objets en Fonctionnement* (*Prototypes of Working Objects*) (1992-1996) - SOTTEVILLE-LÈS-ROUEN (FRAC Haute-Normandie): *P.O.F n°6 (Peau)* (*Prototype of Working Objects no. 6 (Skin)*) (1994).

HYBON, Jan

Flemish School, 17th century.
Active in Antwerp in 1622.
Engraver.

HYBOU, Marie Anne

French, 18th century.
Active in Paris in 1749.
Painter.

HYDE, Frank

British, 19th century.
Painter. Figures, portraits, interiors.

No paintings by this artist are known other than the ones listed below.

AUCTION RECORDS:

ALNWICK, 23 Sept 1986, *The Artists's Studio; The Eton Boy* (oil on canvas, a pair, 37 1/2 x 49 1/2 ins / 95.5 x 125.5 cm) GBP 26,000.

HYDE, Helen

American, 19th - 20th century.
Born 6 April 1868, in Lima (New York); died 16 May 1919, in Pasadena (California).
Also active in Japan.
Painter, engraver (wood), illustrator. Local scenes, landscapes, genre scenes.
Japonisme.

Helen Hyde's family settled in San Francisco. From the age of 12 she studied under Ferdinand Richart in Oakland. In 1886 she enrolled at the California School of Design; from 1888 to 1894 she studied under Emil Carlsen in New York, under Skarbina in Berlin and under Felix Régamey and Raphael Collin in Paris. She lived in Japan from 1899 to 1901, where she met Ernest Fenollosa and Emil Orlik, and was a pupil of Tomanobo in Tokyo. Between 1903 to 1913, she was based in Tokyo, but travelled around the world, notably to China and Mexico. She returned to live in San Francisco in 1914, but moved to Chicago in 1916. She was awarded the bronze medal at the Panama-Pacific International Exhibition, held in San Francisco in 1915, and was a member of the Chicago Society of Etchers and California Society of Etchers.

Hyde specialised in Japanese subjects, painting and woodcuts. She faithfully imitated traditional engraving compositions, helped by the fact that she had lived in Japan. Most of the time, she portrayed children, women with children, genre scenes and landscapes. She adopted a milky-white and pinkish light, borrowed from Mannerism. Her letters have been preserved in the American Art Archives (Smithsonian Institution, Washington DC) and at the California Historical Society, San Francisco.

Hyde had solo exhibitions of her works, for example, at the Art Institute of Chicago in 1916. A posthumous retrospective of her works was organised in 1920 at the Art Institute of Chicago. In 2002, her work appeared in the exhibition entitled: *Le Japonisme en Amérique: œuvres sur papier, 1880-1930* (*Japonisme in America: Works on Paper, 1880-1930*), held at the Musée d'Art Américain/Terra Foundation for the Arts, Giverny.

BIBLIOGRAPHY:
Arnold, Edwin (Sir), *Japonica*, C. Scribner's Sons, New York, 1891. Lowell, Percival, *Occult Japan or the Way of the Gods: An Esoteric Study of Japanese Personality and Possession*, Houghton, Mifflin and Company, Boston, New York, 1895. Jaques, Bertha Evelyn Clauson, *Helen Hyde and her Work: an Appreciation*, Libby Company, New York, 1922. Peet, Phyllis, *American Women of the Etching Revival*, exhibition catalogue, High Museum of Art, Atlanta, 1988. Pollock, Griselda, *Vision and Difference: Feminity, Feminism, and Histories of Art*, Routledge, London, 1988. Meech, Julia, '*Re-inventing the Exotic Orient*' in *Japonisme comes to America: The Japanese Impact on the Graphic Arts, 1876-1925*, H.N. Abrams, New York, 1990. Acton, David, *A Spectrum of Innovation: Color in American Printmaking 1890-1960*, 1990. Mason, Tim/Mason, Lynn, *Helen Hyde*, Smithsonian Institution, Washington DC, 1991. *Le Japonisme en Amérique. œuvres sur papier 1880-1930*, exhibition catalogue, Musée d'Art américain, Giverny, Terra Foundation for the Arts, Giverny, 2002.

MUSEUMS AND GALLERIES:
ANN ARBOR (University of Michigan Mus. of Art) - BELOIT (Wright MA) - BOSTON (MFA) - CHICAGO (Terra Foundation for American Art Collection): *Moonlight on the Viga Canal* (1912, woodcut); *The Sauce-Pan Shop* (1908, woodcut) - NEW YORK (Public Library) - NEWARK (Mus.) - OAKLAND (AM, Mills College) - PARIS (BNF, Prints Collection): *Return* (c. 1907, woodcut) - SAN FRANCISCO (FAM) - TORONTO (AG of Ontario) - WASHINGTON DC (Library of Congress).

HYDE, Henry James
British, 19th century.
Active in London.
Painter, watercolourist. Genre scenes.

Henry James Hyde exhibited his work at the New Water-Colour Society from 1883.

HYDE, James
American, 20th - 21st century.
Born 1958, in Philadelphia.
Painter.

James Hyde lives and works in New York. He uses fine sheets of polystyrene or tarpaulins, and his monochrome compositions explore the concept of colour. His pictorial works also address the links between painting and sculpture (relief frescoes, glass chests filled with scraps from paintings and waste paper). Additionally he produces inflatable pillows and items of furniture. *Soak* (1994) consists of a glass box whose inner surface has been painted with grease and silicone; the piece explores the aesthetic qualities of plasticity and the tactile values essential to his work.

Hyde's work has featured in a number of solo exhibitions, including 2000, Brent Sikkema Gallery, New York; 2001, Zwemmer Gallery, London; 2002, The Box Associati, Turin; 2002, Centre d'Art d'Ivry Crédac; 2003, Parc Saint Léger - Centre d'Art Contemporain, Pouques-les-Eaux; 2004, Galerie Les Filles-du-Calvaire, Paris.

BIBLIOGRAPHY:
Masheck, Joseph/Kaufmann, David, *James Hyde*, exhibition catalogue, John Good Gall., New York, 1994. Damianovic, Maia, '*La Peinture au risque du dilemme*' in *Art Press*, vol 211, periodical, Paris, March 1996.

HYDE, Lucy
British, 20th century.
Born in Milton.
Painter.

Lucy Hyde exhibited in Paris at the Salon des Artistes Français and the Salon des Indépendants from 1913.

HYDE, William
British, 19th - 20th century.
Painter, engraver. Landscapes.

William Hyde exhibited with the Royal Academy from 1889.

HYDE, William Henry, or Hydt
American, 19th - 20th century.
Born 29 January 1858, in New York; died 1943, in Albany.
Active in New York.
Painter, illustrator. Portraits.

William Henry Hyde was a pupil of Boulanger, Lefebvre, Doucet and Alexander Harrisson in Paris. He received an honourable mention at the Exposition Universelle in Paris in 1900 and a bronze medal in Buffalo in 1901. From 1900 he was an associate of the National Academy of Design in New York.

HYDE-POWNALL, George
Australian, 19th - 20th century.
Born 1876; died 1932.
Active in London, naturalised British.
Painter, watercolourist. Landscapes, townscapes.

George Hyde-Pownall was an Australian-born artist who was also a musician and a composer. He is known for his views of London and his depictions of city life in popular urban locations such as Piccadilly Circus, the West End and Eaton Square. In his landscapes Hyde-Pownall also captured some of the most emblematic sites of London, including Hyde Park, the Embankment, the Houses of Parliament, Tower Bridge and St Paul's Cathedral. His work was influenced by the school of Impressionism and this is reflected in his use of colour and light.

MUSEUMS AND GALLERIES:
VICTORIA (Australia): *Melbourne from Victoria Gardens*.

HYE HO, or Huixu
Korean, 13th - 14th century.
Painter.

Hye Ho was a painter during the Koryo dynasty.

HYERDHAL
Dutch.
Painter. Genre scenes.

AUCTION RECORDS:
AMSTERDAM, 30 Jan 1900, *The Flower-Seller*, FRF 1,134.

HYETT, William J.
British, 19th - 20th century.
Born in Cheltenham.
Painter. Landscapes.

William J. Hyett trained under Sir Alfred East, He subsequently settled in Pittsburgh.

HYFTE, Camille van
Belgian, 20th century.
Born 1886, in Ertvelde.
Active in France.
Painter. Scenes with figures, interiors with figures, landscapes.

Camille van Hyfte was a farmer, a racing cyclist and a horse-meat butcher near Paris. He started painting in 1951, at the age of 65, when he felt the need to decorate his own home with paintings and reliefs; he modelled and then painted vases; next, with a strange effect obtained by a mirror, he painted views of the inside of his house on canvases, which he had rearranged for this purpose. Van Hyfte became a painter of interiors, which he portrayed in outdated, very rich tonal harmonies. These paintings evoke another time with the rather trivial trinkets which have accumulated in these interiors. Van Hyfte also painted landscapes with overcast skies, and funfairs. He depicted the peaceful life enjoyed by his neighbours, and the painted façades he recalled from his native Belgium. In 1955, the naive artist Anatole Jakovsky held a comprehensive exhibition of van Hyfte's works.

BIBLIOGRAPHY:

Bihalji-Merin, Oto, *Les Peintres naïfs*, Delpire, Paris, 1960.

HYGIAENON

Painter.
Ancient Greek.

Hygiaenon, one of the first painters of the Greek School, is thought to be the first to have used the technique of entirely filling an outlined space with colour.

HYGRECKOS, Hélène

French, 20th century.
Born 4 June 1919, in Paris.
Painter.

From 1945 to 1950, Hélène Hygreckos studied in the studios of Édouard Mac Avoy, Othon Friesz and Yves Brayer at the Académie de la Grande-Chaumière in Paris. She exhibited in Paris from 1954, and in Germany, the USA and Africa.

HYLLESTED, Hans Christian

Danish, 19th century.
Born 14 September 1794, in Copenhagen; died 17 March 1838, in Hamburg.
Lithographer.

Hans Hyllested is known for his *Complete Collection of Uniforms of the Danish Army and Navy*.

HYMAN, Hilda

Swedish, 19th - 20th century.
Born 1872.
Painter.

HYMAN, Miles

American, 20th - 21st century.
Born 1962, in Vermont.
Draughtsman, pastellist.

Miles Hyman studied painting at Buxton School in Williamstown, Massachusetts, then printmaking at Wesleyan University. He moved to Paris in 1985 where he studied drawing at the École des Beaux-Arts under Henri Clement. His illustrations have been published in numerous English and French magazines and newspapers (*Rolling Stone, The New Yorker, International Herald Tribune, Lire, Libération, Le Monde*...). He has produced numerous book covers for publishers including Simon & Schuster, Farrar, Straus & Giroux, Gallimard, Le Seuil, Denoël, Actes Sud and Flammarion. He has also produced a number of illustrated books (including children's books), and is the author of a significant portfolio of graphic work (advertising, packaging). He returned to the USA in 1994 and now lives and works in Vermont.

AUCTION RECORDS:

PARIS, 6 April 1991, *Manhattan Transfer* (1990, colour pastel/paper, study for cover illustration, 6 x 8 ins / 15.2 x 20.4 cm) FRF 4,000.

HYMANS, Henri

Belgian, 19th - 20th century.
Born 8 August 1836, in Antwerp; died 23 January 1912, in Brussels.
Lithographer.

Henri Hymans studied under Edward Dujardin and was an art historian.

HYMPE, Evrard

French, 15th - 16th century.
Active in Sens.
Glass painter.

Evrard Hympe was the son and pupil of Jacques Hympe.

HYMPE, Jacques

French, 15th century.
Active in Sens in 1475.
Glass painter.

Jacques Hympe was the father of Evrard Hympe and Jean Hympe the Elder.

HYMPE, Jean I, the Elder

French, 15th - 16th century.
Active in Sens.
Glass painter.

Jean Hympe the Elder made the rose window in Sens Cathedral, *Celestial Concert*.

HYMPE, Jean II

French, 16th century.
Active in Sens.
Glass painter.

Jean Hympe II was the son of Jean Hympe the Elder.

HYMPE, Jean III

French, 16th century.
Active in Sens.
Glass painter.

Jean Hympe III was the son of Jean Hympe the Elder and the brother of Jean Hympe II.

HYNAIS, Voytech

Austrian, 19th - 20th century.
Born 14 December 1854, in Vienna; died 1925.
Painter. History painting.

Voytech Hynais studied with Feuerbach in Vienna and with Baudry in Paris. He settled in Paris but often exhibited in Vienna from 1877. He received an honourable mention in 1885, gold medals in 1889 and 1900 at the Expositions Universelles in Paris and a medal in Munich in 1905. He was made Chevalier de la Légion d'Honneur.

MUSEUMS AND GALLERIES:

VIENNA: sketch for a ceiling.

AUCTION RECORDS:

NEW YORK, 23 May 1985, *Portrait of a Young Woman in a Feathered Hat* (1889, pastel, 17 1/2 x 14 1/2 ins / 44.5 x 36.9 cm) USD 4,250. PRAGUE, 18 Nov 2000, *Portrait of Mrs Hlavkova* (1894, oil on canvas, 49 x 39 ins / 124 x 99 cm) CZK 200,000. PRAGUE, 13 Oct 2001, *Nude Girl* (pencil, 18 x 11 ins / 45 x 28 cm) CZK 70,000. PRAGUE, 13 Oct 2001, *Portrait of a Young Lady* (1892, oil on board, 10 x 8 ins / 26 x 21 cm) CZK 200,000. PRAGUE, 24 May 2003, *Study of a Nude Boy* (1884, pencil, 16 x 9 ins / 40 x 22 cm) CZK 50,000.

HYNCKES, Raoul

Belgian, 20th century.
Born 1893, in Brussels; died 1973.
Active from 1914 in the Netherlands.
Painter (gouache). Interiors with figures, still-lifes, landscapes, village views.
Magical Realism.

From 1907-1912, Raoul Hynckes attended the academies in Brussels and Mechelen. In 1914 he settled in Holland, firstly in Amsterdam and then in Blaricum. He started exhibiting in 1920. In a first period of about ten years up until 1924, Hynckes painted in the spirit of the Impressionists-Expressionists with Fauve nuances and sometimes with a few constructive elements borrowed from Post-Cubism. In 1924, he destroyed almost all these paintings. This Cubist influence took shape in the subsequent period dating from 1924-1933, after the example of the later works of Spanish Cubist painter and sculptor Juan Gris, in which Hynckes analysed and produced geometrical paintings of interior scenes, which were mostly still-lifes. From 1933, alongside the Dutch painters Carel Willink and Pyke Koch, he became one of the main representatives of Dutch 'Magical Realism', the 20th-century painting movement in which a near-perfect photographic realism is achieved; sometimes combined with the fantastic through strangely-related subject matter and mysterious light effects. During this time he painted almost exclusively still-lifes, comprising mostly funereal symbols and a death skull, in the manner of the *Vanitas* of former times - a *memento mori* (*'remember death'*): a skull as part of an artwork; it could also be a clock or a similar symbol of the passing of life. Characteristically, the paintings he produced during this period demonstrate a sober technique, a synthesis of line, reduced to its essential form; plain, almost geometric, with flat colours, merely gradated from light to dark. Here, and during this same period, there was an analogy between the spirit and technique of the French painters belonging to the group known as the Forces Nouvelles (New Forces), whose members felt there was a need to return to drawing, tradition and nature, in particular still-lifes. Members of this group included Robert Humblot and Georges Rohner. Some commenttors also believe they can establish a link with the painters of the Neue Sachlichkeit (New Objectivity); however these artists primarily painted figures, which conferred another meaning, and was more involved than still-lifes - this 'cold' technique of observation. After World War II, Hynckes painted mainly fresh, poetic landscapes whilst continuing to produce still-lifes, henceforth exploring more familiar subjects.

Museums and Galleries:

Amsterdam (Stedelijk Mus.): *Still-life with Glasses* (1929); *Still-life with Skull* (1940) - Arnhem (Historisches Mus.): *Still-life with Fruits* (1928-1930) - Laren (Singer Mus.): *Church of Nieuwpoort* (c. 1912); *Still-life with Peach* (1950) - Rotterdam (Mus. Boijmans Van Beuningen): *Chains* (1934) - Utrecht (Centraal Mus.): *Hermit's Keys* (1942-1943).

Auction records:

Düsseldorf, 14 Nov 1973, *Still-life*, DEM 3,800. Amsterdam, 26 April 1977, *Still-life* (oil on canvas, 33 x 24¾ ins / 84 x 63 cm) NLG 20,000. Amsterdam, 12 June 1979, *Still-life with Flowers* (oil on canvas, 22½ x 18½ ins / 57 x 47 cm) NLG 9,200. Amsterdam, 2 Oct 1981, *Still-life* (oil on canvas, 32 x 30¾ ins / 81 x 78 cm) NLG 19,000. Amsterdam, 24 Oct 1983, *Still-life with Bottle and Mandolin* (oil on canvas, 31 x 25¼ ins / 79 x 64 cm) NLG 10,200. Amsterdam, 8 Dec 1988, *Belgian Village* (gouache/paper, 19¼ x 24½ ins / 49 x 62 cm) NLG 2,530; *Still-life with Mushrooms, Glass, Bottle and Coffeepot on a Stone Step* (oil on canvas, 14¼ x 30 ins / 36 x 76 cm) NLG 10,925. Amsterdam, 24 May 1989, *Boats aground in the Port of Rotterdam* (oil on canvas, 26 x 39¾ ins / 66 x 101 cm) NLG 10,350. Amsterdam, 13 Dec 1989, *Village Street in Beaumont, Belgium* (oil on card, 20½ x 25½ ins / 52 x 65 cm) NLG 2,990. Amsterdam, 10 April 1990, *Still-life* (oil on canvas, 19¾ x 24½ ins / 50 x 62.5 cm) NLG 14,950. Amsterdam, 22 May 1990, *Still-life with Boxes and Cylinders on a Table* (oil on canvas, 28 x 35½ ins / 71 x 90 cm) NLG 20,700. Amsterdam, 11 Sept 1990, *View of Burchtplein in Delft* (oil on card, 22 x 22 ins / 55 x 55 cm) NLG 4,370. Amsterdam, 12 Dec 1990, *Hilly Landscape around Cannes* (oil on card, 22 x 27¼ ins / 56 x 69 cm) NLG 4,600. Amsterdam, 5-6 Feb 1991, *Village Street in France* (oil on canvas, 20¼ x 25¼ ins / 51.5 x 64 cm) NLG 5,175. Amsterdam, 12 Dec 1991, *Village* (oil on canvas, 20 x 25¼ ins / 51 x 64 cm) NLG 5,290. Amsterdam, 21 May 1992, *Still-life* (oil on canvas, 31½ x 24 ins / 80 x 61 cm) NLG 52,900. Amsterdam, 31 May 1994, *Boats in a Port* (oil on card, 37½ x 38½ ins / 95 x 98 cm) NLG 14,950. Amsterdam, 5 June 1996, *View of a Village (Dt Yves Gomesez)* (oil on canvas, 20 x 25¼ ins / 51 x 64 cm) NLG 6,325. Amsterdam, 17-18 Dec 1996, *Flowers* (oil on canvas, 22 x 15¾ ins / 55 x 40 cm) NLG 28,320. Amsterdam, 2 Dec 1997, *Le Heaulme* (1939, oil on canvas, 26¾ x 37½ ins / 68 x 95 cm) NLG 132,618. Amsterdam, 10 June 1999, *Still-life with Flowers, Book and Vase on Table* (c. 1932, oil on canvas, 26 x 30 ins / 65 x 76 cm) NLG 110,000. Amsterdam, 1 Dec 1999, *Still-life and Landscape* (oil on canvas, 22 x 25 ins / 56 x 64 cm) NLG 115,000. Amsterdam, 8 June 2000, *Still-life with Fruit Bowl* (oil on canvas, 28 x 23 ins / 72 x 58 cm) NLG 80,000. Amsterdam, 30 Nov 2000, *Cigar Box* (oil on canvas, 22 x 31 ins / 55 x 80 cm) NLG 25,000. Amsterdam, 11 June 2001, *The Oil Can* (oil on canvas, 28 x 35 ins / 70 x 90 cm) NLG 24,000. Amsterdam, 3 Dec 2001, *Liggende kan* (oil on canvas, 22 x 24 ins / 55 x 60 cm) NLG 50,000. Amsterdam, 16 April 2002, *Still-life with an Old Bottle* (c. 1939, oil on canvas, 15 x 26 ins / 38 x 65 cm) EUR 24,000. Rotterdam, 23 April 2002, *Tug Boat on the River* (oil on panel, 16 x 21 ins / 40 x 53 cm) EUR 5,800. Amsterdam, 10 March 2003, *View of a River with a Moored Boat in the Distance* (oil on panel, 16 x 22 ins / 41 x 56 cm) EUR 4,200. Amsterdam, 1 July 2003, *Village Street* (oil on canvas, 19 x 24 ins / 48 x 62 cm) EUR 1,900. Amsterdam, 9 June 2004, *Friendship* (1952, oil on canvas, 26 x 35 ins / 65 x 88 cm) EUR 7,500. Amsterdam, 1 Dec 2004, *Stilleven met dode eend en snip* (oil on canvas, 30 x 39 ins / 75 x 100 cm) EUR 4,500.

HYNEMAN, Herman N.

American, 19th century.
Born 27 July 1859, in Philadelphia; died 23 December 1907, in Philadelphia.
Painter.

Herman N. Hyneman was a pupil of Bonnat in Paris and settled in Paris at the end of his career. He was a member of the Philadelphia Art Club and the Salmagundi Club in New York.

Auction records:

New York, 1 May 1947, *Snowstorm*, USD 130. Watertown, 20 June 1999, *Fifth Avenue, Winter* (oil on canvas, 30 x 20 ins / 76 x 51 cm) USD 4,500.

HYNER, Arend. See HIJNER

HYNING. See HYSING

HYON, Georges Louis

French, 19th century.
Born 1855, in Paris.
Painter. Military subjects.

Georges Hyon exhibited at the Paris Salon from 1875 to 1880.

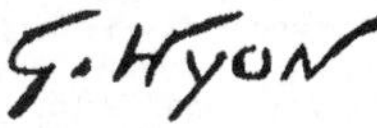

Museums and Galleries:

Le Puy-en-Velay: *The Flag of the Second Zouaves Decorated at Magenta by General de Mac-Mahon.*

Auction records:

Paris, 23 June 1943, *The Patrol*, FRF 750. New York, 4 Nov 1971, *Prisoners*, USD 2,000. New York, 14 May 1976, *Cavalry Charge* (oil on canvas, 23 x 28¼in/58.5 x 72cm) USD 1,900. New York, 14 Jan 1977, *Bonaparte at the Arcole Bridge* (oil on canvas, 25½ x 32in/65 x 81cm) USD 1,100. New York, 21 Jan 1978, *Napoleon on a Battlefield* (oil on canvas, 18½ x 24½in/47 x 62cm) USD 1,500. London, 19 June 1981, *Retreat from Russia* (oil on canvas, 25 x 31½in/63.5 x 80cm) GBP 1,900. New York, 30 Oct 1985, *Napoleon III Inspecting the Troops* (oil on canvas, 25¾ x 36¼in/65.5 x 92cm) USD 3,500. Paris, 7 Nov 1988, *Self-portrait Copying a Painting by Bouguereau* (oil on panel, 18½ x 11½in/47 x 29.5cm) FRF 14,500. Paris, 12 Dec 1990, *The Patrol* (oil on panel, 10½ x 16¼in/26.5 x 41cm) FRF 7,000. New York, 5 Oct 1999, *Self-portrait, Copying a Painting by Bouguereau* (oil on panel, 20 x 13 ins / 52 x 32 cm) USD 5,000. Copenhagen, 30 Nov 1999, *Cavalry Battle during the Franco-Prussian War* (oil on canvas, 22 x 36 ins / 57 x 91 cm) DKK 13,000. Auckland, 27 June 2000, *Meeting of Cavalry Officers in the Field during the Franco-Prussian War* (oil on canvas, 31 x 45 ins / 80 x 115 cm) NZD 15,000. Paris, 4 July 2000, *Napoleon* (oil on canvas, 26 x 21 ins / 65 x 54 cm) FRF 13,500.

HYPATODORUS
5th century BC.
Active in Thebes c. 420 BC.
Sculptor.
Ancient Greek.

Hypatodorus, with Aristogiton, made a statue of a man from Orchomenus. With Sostratus of Chios he made a colossal *Athena* that once stood at Aliphera in Arcadia.

HYPERREALISM. See for example **CLOSE Chuck, ESTES Richard, MORLEY Malcolm**

HYPPOLITE, Auguste
French, 19th century.
Active in Paris.
Miniaturist.

This artist exhibited at the Salon of 1899.

HYPPOLYTE, Hector. See **HIPPOLITE Hector**

HYPPOLYTUS, Valentin
German, 16th century.
Active in Leipzig, c. 1556.
Painter.

HYRTL, Jacob
Austrian, 19th century.
Born 23 November 1799, in Vienna; died 17 October 1868, in Vienna.
Draughtsman, engraver.

A protégé of Prince Esterházy, he was taught by Fischer. He dabbled in all genres, working from old masters and contemporaries. Notable are his views of Vienna, portraits and a number of religious subjects.

HYS, Jacques de
French, 17th century.
Active in Paris in 1662.
Engraver.

HYSBERGUE, Rémy
French, 20th - 21st century.
Born 1967, in Valenciennes.
Painter, draughtsman.

Rémy Hysbergue lives and works in Paris. He produces his works in series, applying colour with a roller onto rigid surfaces such as PVC, leaving a good deal of empty space, as in the oriental tradition. At times, he creates effects of perspective or dislocation by playing games with the roller, producing unexpected lines or structures. He uses brilliant colours, conveying a sense of poetic exuberance.

His solo shows have included: 2000 and 2002, Galerie Philippe Casini, Paris; 2001, Clermont-Ferrand; and 2001, École des Arts Décoratifs, Aubusson.

BIBLIOGRAPHY:

Dagen, Philippe, '*Les séductions de la disparition*' in *Le Monde*, periodical, Paris, Mon 16 October 2000. Suchère, Éric, *Rémy Hysbergue*, Un, Deux... Quatre Éditions, Clermont-Ferrand, 2001. Bohn, Alexandre, '*'Rémy Hysbergue*'' in *Art Press*, n° 274 p. 24, periodical, Paris, December 2001.

HYSEBRANT. See **ISENBRANT**

HYSING, Hans
Swedish, 18th century.
Born 1678, in Stockholm; died c. 1752-1753, in London.
Painter.

Hans Hysing went to London in 1700 and enjoyed much success. He was still living in 1740. Among his portraits he is known to have painted the three daughters of George II in formal dress on the occasion of their father's coronation.

BIBLIOGRAPHY:

Nisser, W., *Michael Dahl and the Contemporary Swedish School of Painting*, Almqvist & Wiksells Boktryckeri-aktiebolag, Uppsala, 1927. Einberg, E., *Manners and Morals: Hogarth and British Painting, 1700-1760*, exhibition catalogue, Tate Gallery Publishing, London, 1987.

AUCTION RECORDS:

LONDON, 21 Nov 1984, *Portrait of Colonel William Kennedy* (oil on canvas, 48 1/2 x 38 1/2 ins / 123 x 98 cm) GBP 6,000. LONDON, 19 Nov 1986, *Portrait of Sir Robert Walpole* (oil on canvas, oval, 29 1/4 x 24 ins / 74.5 x 61 cm) GBP 10,000. LONDON, 10 July 1991, *Three-quarter Portrait of Henry Howard, 4th Count of Carlisle, in Red with Green Waistcoat* (oil on canvas, 49 1/4 x 39 ins / 125 x 99 cm) GBP 11,000. LONDON, 12 July 1991, *Bust Portrait of Samuel Hughes in Brown with Blue Waistcoat* (1734, oil on canvas, 30 x 25 ins / 76 x 63.5 cm) GBP 2,750.

HYSING, Henrik
Swedish, 18th century.
Born in Stockholm; died 1723, in Stockholm.
Painter. Battles, portraits.

Henrik Hysing was a pupil of J. P. Lembke.

HYTAF
19th century.
Active in Florence.
Engraver (burin).

I

I CH'ANG-WU. See **YI CHANGWU**

I HAI. See **YI HAI**

I PING-SHOU. See **YI BINGSHOU**

I YUAN-CHI. See **YI YUANJI**

I'ANSON, Charles
British, 19th century.
Born 1848; died 1907, in London.
Active in London.
Painter. Landscapes.

Charles I'Anson exhibited his work in London, mainly at the Royal Academy, Suffolk Street, the New Water-Colour Society and the Grosvenor Gallery from 1875.

I'ANSON, F.
British, 19th century.
Active in London.
Painter. Portraits.

F. I'Anson's work was represented in London at exhibitions of the Royal Academy and the Society of British Artists in 1833, 1836 and 1837.

I'NEN. See **SOTATSU**

I-JAN. See **YIRAN**

I., Master
German, 15th century.
Born probably in Erfurt.
Sculptor.
Erfurt School.

Master I. lived in Erfurt from 1405 to 1430 and worked in Thuringia. He founded a new school which sought Realism. His earliest work was the *Christ Crucified* of St Michael's church in Erfurt, which was followed by the three statues, *Mary and the Child Jesus, St Catherine* and *St Barbara*.

I. A.
German, 16th century.
Monogram of a sculptor.

I. A. M. DE ZWOLLE, Master. See **ZWOLLE Jean de**

I. A. S.
German.
Monogram of an engraver.

I. A., MASTER OF THE INITIALS
Italian, 15th century.
Engraver.

He worked at the end of the 15th century and produced the 59 engravings that decorate the translation of the *Metamorphoses of Ovid* published by the Venetian Giovanni Rosso in 1497.

I. B., MASTER, or J. B., Master of the Initials
German, 16th century.
Active in Germany in the first half of the 16th century.
Engraver (burin).

I.B. was one of the best of the minor artists of the German School of the 16th century. Some 50 or more of his pieces are catalogued, including several copies after Albrecht Dürer, particularly *The Virgin Seated, Apollo and Diana* and *Peasants at Market*, which is dated 1523, not 1512, and does not carry Dürer's number. The original works of I.B. include figures of saints, scenes from mythology, portraits, genre scenes and, above all, ornaments. There was another engraver who used the initials I.B. with a bird, a 16th-century Italian whom some identify as Giovanni Battista del Porto, but this identification is not generally accepted.

The work of I.B. was included in the 2003 exhibition, *Les Dieux comme les Hommes. Gravures rhénanes du XVIe siècle* (*Gods as Men: Rhenish Engravings of the 16th Century*), presenting the collections held by the Prints and Drawings section of the Musée des Beaux-Arts in Strasbourg.

BIBLIOGRAPHY:
La Gravure allemande à la Renaissance, group exhibition catalogue, Musée des Beaux-Arts, Caen, 1999. Schefer, Jean Louis/Haus, Anny-Claire/Hergott, Fabrice (preface), et al., *Les Dieux comme les Hommes. Gravures rhénanes du XVIe siècle*, group exhibition catalogue, Musée des Beaux-Arts, Strasbourg, 2003. Jover, Manuel, *'Les Petits Maîtres de Nuremberg'* in *L'Œil* n° 544, periodical, Paris, February 2003.

MUSEUMS AND GALLERIES:
STRASBOURG (MBA, Prints Collection): *Combat*.

I. C., MASTER OF THE INITIALS
German, 15th century.
Active in Cologne at the end of the 15th century.
Engraver (burin).
Cologne School.

I.C. copied works by Schongauer, in particular the *Passion* series, and worked with meticulous accuracy.

I. D.
German, 16th century.
Monogram of an engraver.

I. D. is the unconfirmed monogram of an engraver working in Germany. His works include *Intemperance* (1530) and *Mars* (1530), copies of two engravings after Aldegrever.

I. D. C., MASTER OF THE INITIALS
French, 16th century.
Active in the late 16th century.
Draughtsman. Portraits.

Like many, often anonymous artists at this period, I.D.C. drew portraits in coloured chalks in the style of the Clouet father and son. Most of these portraitists focused on details of clothing, but for I.D.C. it was the face that mattered. He grasps the psychology in each face, proving himself a true heir of the Clouets, as for instance in his portrait of *Gabrielle d'Estrées* and his *Mademoiselle d'Urfé*, both in the Bibliothèque Nationale in Paris, and in the other examples attributed to him. These other drawings are dated between 1570 and 1600, and one of them bears the initials I.D.C.

Museums and Galleries:
Paris (BNF): *Gabrielle d'Estrées; Mademoiselle d'Urfé.*

I. D. R., MASTER OF THE INITIALS
Dutch, 17th century.
Painter. Portraits, figures.

The artist known by the initials I. D. R. worked during the first half of the 17th century. In 1630, he painted *Bust of an Old Man* (in The Hague). Three *Portraits of Rembrandt's Father*, one of which is in Rotterdam, have also been attributed to him.

Museums and Galleries:
Rotterdam (Mus. Boijmans Van Beuningen): *Portrait of Rembrandt's Father* - The Hague (Bredius Mus.): *Bust of an Old Man* (1630).

I. E., MASTER OF THE INITIALS, also called
Master of the Martyrdom of St Catherine
German.
Engraver (?), copyist.

A German imitator of Martin Schongauer; his most important work is the *Christ in the Wilderness with Ministering Angels.*

I. G.
German.
Monogram of an engraver.

I. H. S., MASTER OF THE INITIALS, also known as Master of the Name of Jesus
16th century.
Engraver.

I.H.S. worked in Italy from 1566 to 1572. He made burin engravings of religious and mythological subjects. 19 of his pieces are catalogued. One of his prints, *The Old Man and the Child,* is signed *Renat.* He was also a publisher.

I. I. D. G.
French.
Monogram of an engraver.

I.I.D.G. made engravings on copper representing the apostles.

I. K., MASTER OF THE INITIALS
German (?), 16th century.
Active in the first half of the 16th century.
Monogram of an engraver.
Alsace (Strasbourg) School.

I. K. is thought to have been a maker of engraved blocks in Strasbourg. The same monogram is found on a set of 144 blocks engraved with heraldic symbols for the *Wappen des Heyligen Römischen Reiches Teutscher Nation* (*Coats of Arms of the Holy Roman Empire of the German Nation*) published in Frankfurt in 1545.

Museums and Galleries:
Cologne (Wallraf-Richartz Mus.): drawing dated 1554.

Auction records:
New York, 15 Jan 1992, *Scribes' Hall with the Four Evangelists* (ink and wash, red chalk, 10 3/4 x 14 3/4 ins / 27.4 x 37.5 cm) USD 35,200.

I. M. S., MASTER OF THE INITIALS
German, 16th century.
Engraver (burin/wood).

I. M. S. is best known for two burin etchings, *The Virgin Embracing the Infant Jesus* and *The Virgin Giving Fruit to the Child Jesus*, and a wood engraving, *Hercules and Omphale.*

I. R.
Monogram of a sculptor (wood).

I. R.
French.
Monogram of a painter glassmaker.

I.R. was a master glazier working in Troyes, whose monogram appears on one of the windows of Troyes Cathedral. He is listed by Ris-Paquot.

I. S.
German.
Monogram of an engraver (wood).

I.S. made engravings after Tobias Stimmer.

I. S.
German, 16th century.
Active c. 1534.
Monogram of an engraver.

The work of I. S. includes a *Judgement of Paris.*

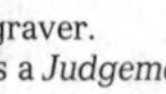

I. S., MASTER OF THE INITIALS
German, 16th century.
Active in the second third of the 16th century.
Painter. Portraits, figures.

I. S. belonged to the circle of Lucas Cranach. His work includes seven portraits of Protestant princes in Coburg, and a series of 18 bust portraits of notables kept in Gotha. These may be copies of canvases by Cranach which are now lost.

Museums and Galleries:
Gotha: *Portrait of a Prince* (18 bust portraits).

I. S., MASTER OF THE INITIALS
17th century.
Painter.

The Master of the Initials I.S. worked in the mid-17th century.

AUCTION RECORDS:
LONDON, 30 Oct 1991, *Peasants inside a Barn beside a Collection of Tools* (1639, oil on panel, 18 1/4 x 25 ins / 46.5 x 63.5 cm) GBP 3,080. LONDON, 30 Oct 1997, *Interior, Peasants beside a Fire with Numerous Pots and Pans* (1638, oil on panel, 18 3/4 x 23 3/4 ins / 47.6 x 60.6 cm) GBP 4,370.

I. V. R., MASTER OF THE INITIALS
Dutch, 17th century.
Painter. Landscapes.
The artist known by the initials I. V. R. probably worked in The Hague. There is a painting in the Munich museum attributed to Isaac Ruysdael which carries this signature. An expert at the Berlin museum, while accepting the possible connection, does not see any similarity between the style of this work and that of the artist.
MUSEUMS AND GALLERIES:
BERLIN: two landscapes - MUNICH.

I. V. S., MASTER OF THE INITIALS
Dutch, 17th century.
Painter.
The artist known by the initials I. V. S. worked during the first quarter of the 17th century. He painted a curious evocation of hell (in Gdansk), revealing a fantastical imagination. He can be compared with the Master of the Initials I. V. R..
MUSEUMS AND GALLERIES:
GDANSK (Muz. Historyczne): *Hell*.

I. V., MASTER OF THE INITIALS
French, 16th century.
Engraver.
Fontainebleau School.
The Master of the Initials I. V. worked in Fontainebleau around 1550 and engraved historical scenes from works by Primaticcio.

I. W., MASTER OF THE INITIALS
British, 17th century.
Painter. Portraits.
The Master of the Initials I.W. was mainly known for a group of portraits of personalities from Leicestershire dated 1648.
AUCTION RECORDS:
LONDON, 14 March 1990, *Portrait of Algernon Sydney Wearing a Brown Suit over a Shirt with a Collar and White Lace Cuffs* (1622, oil on panel, 32 1/2 x 23 ins / 82.5 x 58.5 cm) GBP 12,100.

IA. See also for second names starting with the letters JA and YA

IACOBELLI, Aldo
Italian, 20th century.
Sculptor of assemblages.
Iacobelli participated in the ARCO (Contemporary Art Fair), Madrid, in 1993, exhibiting oil paintings submerged in oil and contained in glass bottles.

IACOUNTCHIKOVA, Marie. See **YAKUNCHIKOVA-VEBER**

IACOVACCI, Francesco. See **JACOVACCI**

IACOVLEFF, Aleksandr Evgenevich. See **YACOVLEV**

IACURTO, Francesco
Canadian, 20th century.
Born 1908; died 2001.
Painter. Scenes with figures, landscapes, seascapes.
Francesco Iacurto handled themes typical of the Province of Quebec.
AUCTION RECORDS:
TORONTO, 14 May 1984, *Farm, Baie St-Paul* (1971, oil on canvas, 19 3/4 x 23 1/2 ins / 50 x 60 cm) CAD 1,500. MONTREAL, 24 Feb 1987, *Charlevoix* (1960, oil on canvas, 20 x 24 ins / 51 x 61 cm) CAD 2,300. MONTREAL, 1 May 1989, *Scene in Quebec* (1961, oil on canvas, 30 x 20 ins / 76 x 51 cm) CAD 2,400. MONTREAL, 30 Oct 1989, *Village on the Coast of Beaupré in the Province of Quebec* (1960, oil on canvas, 16 1/4 x 20 ins / 41 x 51 cm) CAD 1,650. MONTREAL, 5 Dec 1995, *Fishermen* (1973, oil on panel, 10 x 11 3/4 ins / 25.4 x 29.8 cm) CAD 1,200; *Quebec* (oil on canvas, 16 x 20 ins / 40.5 x 50.6 cm) CAD 1,800. MONTREAL, 17 June 1997, *By the River* (1948, oil on canvas, 16 x 20 ins / 40.5 x 50.5 cm) CAD 1,700. MONTREAL, 13 Sept 1999, *Country Landscape* (1954, oil on canvasboard, 16 x 20 ins / 40 x 50 cm) CAD 2,800. MONTREAL, 13 Sept 1999, *Wintery Scene* (1954, oil on canvasboard, 16 x 20 ins / 41 x 51 cm) CAD 3,000. MONTREAL, 22 Oct 2001, *Le temps des sucrés (Sugar Harvest)* (c. 1965, oil on canvas, 24 x 30 ins / 61 x 76 cm) CAD 6,500. MONTREAL, 12 Dec 2001, *Rue St Pierre in Quebec, Corner of Notre-Dame, Oratoires, Sault au Matelot* (1946, oil on canvas, 24 x 19 ins / 61 x 48 cm) CAD 4,500. MONTREAL, 26 June 2002, *Landscape* (1972, oil on canvas, 20 x 24 ins / 51 x 61 cm) CAD 3,500. MONTREAL, 10 Sept 2002, *Maritime Scene* (1960, oil on canvas, 20 x 24 ins / 50 x 60 cm) CAD 5,500. MONTREAL, 17 June 2003, *View of Quebec* (1963, oil on canvas, 20 x 24 ins / 51 x 61 cm) CAD 4,000. VANCOUVER, 27 Nov 2003, *Rickshaws* (1965, oil on canvas, 20 x 24 ins / 50 x 61 cm) CAD 6,000. LONDON, 19 Feb 2004, *Autumn in Canada* (1969, oil on canvas, 24 x 30 ins / 61 x 76 cm) GBP 1,000. VANCOUVER, 6 May 2004, *Under Wood, Montmorency River* (oil on canvas, 30 x 24 ins / 76 x 61 cm) CAD 6,000.

IAGODKINE, Stepan. See **YAGODKIN**

IAKIMOV, Anne Marie, or Jakimov
German, 20th century.
Born 14 March 1889, in Berlin.
Painter. Genre scenes, landscapes.
Anne Marie Iakimov was the daughter of the sculptor Max Kruse and studied under Henri Matisse in Paris. In 1912, she married Igor von Iakimov in Paris. In 1919, she contributed to a group exhibition held at the Fritz Gurlitt gallery in Berlin; 30of her oil paintings were exhibited, depicting mainly subjects brought back from a stay in Russia. Another exhibition of her works, mainly Bavarian landscapes and genre paintings, was held at the Parthenon.

IAKIMOV, Igor von. See **YAKIMOV**

IAKOFF. See **YAKOV**

IAKOUCHKA. See **YAKUSHKA**

IAKOVLEFF, Alexander Evgenevich. See **YACOVLEV Alexander**

IAKOVLEFF, Mikhail Nicolaevich. See **YAKOVLEV**

IAKOVLEV, Alexander Evgenevich. See **YACOVLEV Alexander**

IAMPOLSKY. See **JAMPOLSKY Mikhail**

IAMS, Johee Howard
American, 20th century.
Born 10 April 1897, in Washington County (Pennsylvania); died 1964, in Marion (Ohio).
Painter, draughtsman.
Johee Howard Iams was a pupil at the Carnegie Institute, Pittsburgh, and was a member of the New York Art Union and the Art Students League. He was awarded the first prize for a still-life in Washington in 1928, a first prize by the League of Artists of the Southern States in 1928, and a bronze medal for drawing in 1930.

IANCHELEVICI, Idel or Ion

Moldovan, 20th century.
Born 5 May 1909, in Leova; died 1994, in Maisons-Laffitte, France.
Active in Belgium from 1933, naturalised in 1945; also active in France from 1950.
Sculptor, engraver, draughtsman. Figures.

Idel Ianchelevici went to Liège in 1928 to complete his education. After a period of military service in Romania, he returned to Liège in 1933 to attend the Académie des Beaux-Arts, where he was awarded the first prize. He settled in Brussels. In 1950 he moved to France to Maisons-Laffitte. He was in Canada in 1952 and in Congo in 1956 with a study bursary. He made a large number of outdoor sculptures including *Woman Spitting* (1943) for the square in front of the royal residence in Brussels and a monumental frieze for the Palais des Congrès in Liège.

His sculptures are cut directly into the stone and generally represent human figures. He made many portraits of famous Belgian and French personalities and illustrated a number of books including Virgil's *Aeneid, Georgics* and *Eclogues*. Jean Cassou sees drawing as an important underlying presence in Ianchelevici's classical and figurative sculptures, a presence which he translated into mass. He was much affected by the fate of the Jewish people and his works are filled with strong emotions. His monumental works show his commitment to commemorating their history in sculpture.

Collective exhibitions include in Paris: Jeune Sculpture and Paris Biennale (from 1941); Salon des Artistes Français, Paris (winning a silver medal and the Amis de la Sculpture prize - 1951); Middelheim Biennale, Antwerp (1955, 1957, 1961 and 1975); *40 Years of Belgian Art*, New York (1960); Exposition Internationale de la Sculpture Contemporaine, Musée Rodin, Paris (1961); Sculpture Biennale, Musée Rodin, Paris (1964); Salon des Indépendants, Paris (1965). Solo exhibitions include: Amsterdam, The Hague and Rotterdam (1936); Brussels, Palais des Beaux-Arts (1935, 1939, 1945, 1956 and 1960); State Museum, Tel-Aviv (1952); Musée d'Art Wallon, Liège (1952, 1957, 1964 and 1967); Musée Royale, Congo (1956); Paris (1957); Canada (travelling exhibition, 1959); Palais des Beaux-Arts, Charleroi (1960); Musée des Beaux-Arts, Ixelles (1961); Bibliothèque Royale Albert I, Brussels (1972 and 1981); Antwerp, Hasselt and Brussels (1974); chateau, Maisons-Laffitte (1982); State Museum, Bucharest (1985). He was made an Officier de la Couronne Belge in 1966.

BIBLIOGRAPHY:
Ianchelevici, exhibition catalogue, Château de Maisons-Laffitte, Maisons-Laffitte, 1982. *Romanian Artists and the West*, American Romanian Academy of Arts and Sciences, Los Angeles, 1986.

MUSEUMS AND GALLERIES:
BRUSSELS (MBA): *Girl* (1962) - BUCHAREST (Muz. National de Arta al Românieі): *Young Woman and Child* (1952) - LA LOUVIÈRE (Mus. Ianchelevici): *Man in a Jacket* (1937) - LIÈGE: *Robert Vivier* (1934) - MAISONS-LAFFITTE (Musée Ianchelevici): around 60 sculptures, medallions, medals and drawings - PARIS (MAMVP) - THE HAGUE: *Piet Valkhoff* (1936).

IANELLI, Alfonso

Italian, 20th century.
Born 17 February 1888, in Andretta.
Active in the USA.
Painter, sculptor. Religious subjects.

Ianelli was a pupil of Gutson Borghum and simultaneously pursued careers in art and teaching.

IANELLI, Arcangelo

Brazilian, 20th century.
Born 1922, in São Paulo.
Painter.

Arcangelo Ianelli studied under Walemar da Costa from 1942 to 1944 and exhibited at the São Paulo Biennale. He also held solo exhibitions notably at the museum of modern art in São Paulo and Rio de Janeiro in 1961 and at the Lima institute of art in 1962. An important retrospective of his work took place in 1991 at the museum of modern art in Rio de Janeiro. Ianelli was awarded the Curritiba Exhibition prize in 1961 and the Salão Paulista prize in 1962.

Ianelli's rigorously abstract geometric compositions are frequently worked in two tones, plus brown. They place the artist in the strict tradition of Neoplasticism.

AUCTION RECORDS:
NEW YORK, 17 Oct 1979, *Superposed Rectangles* (1979, oil on canvas, 31 1/2 x 39 1/4 ins / 80 x 99.7 cm) USD 2,400. SÃO PAULO, 30 Nov 1981, *Carmo Church* (1946, oil on panel, 15 1/4 x 22 ins / 39 x 56 cm) BRL 400,000. NEW YORK, 22 May 1986, *Composition* (1984, oil on canvas, 51 x 41 1/4 ins / 129.5 x 105 cm) USD 6,000. NEW YORK, 21 Nov 1988, *Untitled* (1980, oil on canvas, 39 1/4 x 31 1/2 ins / 99.7 x 80 cm) USD 4,675. NEW YORK, 21 Nov 1989, *Untitled* (1982, oil and pencil/canvas, 51 x 39 1/4 ins / 129.5 x 99.5 cm) USD 5,500. NEW YORK, 1 May 1990, *Beige and Brown Geometric* (1980, oil and pencil/canvas, 39 1/4 x 31 1/2 ins / 100 x 80 cm) USD 8,800. NEW YORK, 19-20 Nov 1990, *Blue* (1976, oil on canvas, 51 x 39 1/4 ins / 129.8 x 100 cm) USD 6,050. NEW YORK, 15-16 May 1991, *Composition in Ochre* (1989, oil on canvas, 50 3/4 x 39 1/4 ins / 129 x 100 cm) USD 5,500. NEW YORK, 25 Nov 1992, *Untitled* (1980, oil on canvas, 51 x 39 1/4 ins / 129.5 x 100 cm) USD 5,500. NEW YORK, 22-23 Nov 1993, *Composition in Two Tones of Brown* (1976, oil on canvas, 70 3/4 x 51 ins / 180 x 129.5 cm) USD 26,450. RIO DE JANEIRO, 17 June 2003, *Untitled* (1977, oil on canvas, 31 x 39 ins / 80 x 100 cm) BRL 27,300. RIO DE JANEIRO, 17 June 2003, *Untitled* (1982, oil on canvas, 51 x 71 ins / 130 x 180 cm) BRL 58,800. RIO DE JANEIRO, 6 July 2004, *Untitled* (1989, oil on canvas, 51 x 39 ins / 130 x 100 cm) BRL 35,500. RIO DE JANEIRO, 14 Sept 2004, *Interior* (1955, oil on canvas, 25 x 20 ins / 63 x 50 cm) BRL 34,000.

IANELLI, Thomaz

Brazilian, 20th century.
Born 1932, in São Paulo.
Painter.

Thomaz Ianelli lived in Europe from 1961 to 1962.

He has taken part in collective exhibitions: São Paulo Biennale (1961 and 1967); Biennale des Jeunes in Paris (1963); *Brazilian Art Today* at the Royal College of Art in London, and then in London, Vienna, Bonn and Brussels (1964); *Ten Modern Brazilian Painters* at the fine arts museums of Mexico, Montevideo, Santiago and Lima (1967); the Salon d'Automne in Paris (1971); Art Gallery of the Brazilian American Cultural Institute in Washington (1976); modern art museums of Bogotá and Caracas, Tertulia de Cadi, Zea museum in Medellín, Santiago de Chile museum (1974); São Paulo museum of modern art (1977); Art Gallery of the National Museum of Singapore (1978); Latin American Engraving Triennale in Buenos Aires (1979).

Ianelli has also exhibited his work in solo exhibitions: Institute of Hispanic culture in Madrid and Brazil institute in Paris (1962); contemporary art museum in Curitiba (1979).

BIBLIOGRAPHY:
Thomaz Ianelli, exhibition catalogue, Gal. Debret, Paris, 1980.

AUCTION RECORDS:
NEW YORK, 2 May 1990, *Birds in a bath* (1977, oil on canvas, 31 1/2 x 23 1/2 ins / 80 x 60 cm) USD 3,575. RIO DE JANEIRO, 17 June 2003, *Untitled* (oil on canvas, 28 x 20 ins / 70 x 50 cm) BRL 8,400.

IANENKO. See **YANENKO**

IANIENKO. See **YANENKO**

IANKOVITZ. See **JANKOWITZ Marie Lucie de**

IANNONE, Dorothy
American, 20th century.
Born 9 August 1933, in Boston (Massachusetts).
Active since 1976 in Germany.
Painter (mixed media).

Dorothy Iannone studied at the University of Boston from 1953 to 1957. She travelled a great deal in Europe from 1961 to 1967, and settled in West Berlin in 1967. She taught at the Art Academy in Berlin and was invited to the Jan Van Eyck Academy in Maastricht in 1982 and 1983, and to the Rijksakademie in Amsterdam in 1982 and 1984. She began to study Buddhism in 1984. In order to communicate her messages better, she uses language on brightly coloured decorative paintings. She is also interested in sound and introduces it into her works. She has produced several books.

Iannone has taken part in many group exhibitions, notably, the 1975 Venice Biennale; 1980 *Écouter par les yeux* (*Listen through Your Eyes*), held at the Musée d'Art Moderne, Paris; 1985 *Livres d'artistes* (*Artists' Books*), held at the Musée National d'Art Moderne, Paris, and 1987 *Eating and Drinking*, held at the Kunstverein, Wuppertal. Her first solo exhibition took place in New York in 1967, and others followed in Europe.

MUSEUMS AND GALLERIES:
AACHEN (Ludwig Forum für Internationale Kunst) - BASEL (Kunstmus.) - BERLIN (Kunstverein) - BRUNSWICK (Kunstverein) - DÜSSELDORF (Kunstverein) - PARIS (BNF) - SAN FRANCISCO (International Mus. of Erotic Art) - TOULOUSE (Musée Municipal D'art Moderne).

IANOFF. See **YANOV**

IANUSH, Leonid
Russian, 20th century.
Born 1897; died 1978.
Painter. Interiors with figures, landscapes.

A pupil of Aleksandr Rilov at the academy of fine art in St Petersburg, Leonid Ianusch was made an Artist of the People and a member of the Union of Artists of the USSR. His paintings, realist in style and conventional in choice of subject, reveal a particular interest in the effects of light.

He exhibited both in Russia and abroad from 1928.

MUSEUMS AND GALLERIES:
MOSCOW (Ministry of Culture) - MOSCOW (Pushkin MFA) - MOSCOW (State Tretyakov Gal.) - ST PETERSBURG (Academy) - ST PETERSBURG (Gosudarstvennyj Russkij Muz.).

AUCTION RECORDS:
PARIS, 25 March 1991, *Veranda* (1976, oil on card, 23 1/2 x 31 ins / 60 x 79 cm) FRF 32,000. PARIS, 9 Dec 1991, *Sheaves of Wheat* (1940, oil on card, 13 1/2 x 17 3/4 ins / 34 x 45 cm) FRF 5,200.

IARKIN, Vladimir
Russian, 20th century.
Born 1939, in Leningrad (now St Petersburg).
Painter. Figures, landscapes, interiors.

Vladimir Iarkin studied at the Ilya Repin Institute in Leningrad and became a member of the Leningrad Association of Painters. His works are figurative, painted with confident and broad brushstrokes, and Intimist in mood.

From 1970, he took part in exhibitions both in Russia and abroad including: *Young Painters of Leningrad*, Prague (1970); *Soviet Art*, Helsinki (1974); *Soviet Painting Today*, Tokyo (1980); Autumn Salon, Moscow (1982); Autumn Salon, Leningrad (1984); *Art of Leningrad*, Madrid (1990). He held a solo exhibition in Leningrad in 1983.

BIBLIOGRAPHY:
L'École de Léningrad, auction catalogue, Drouot, Paris, 19 November 1990.

MUSEUMS AND GALLERIES:
KHABAROVSK (Mus. of Contemporary Soviet Art) - MOSCOW (Ministry of Culture) - NOVOSIBIRSK (MFA) - OSTRAVA (MCA) - ST PETERSBURG (Gosudarstvennyj Muz. Istorii) - ST PETERSBURG (MFA).

AUCTION RECORDS:
PARIS, 11 June 1990, *Schoolgirl* (oil on canvas, 25 1/4 x 43 1/4 ins / 64 x 110 cm) FRF 21,500. PARIS, 19 Nov 1990, *Summer's Day* (1970, oil on card, 13 1/2 x 19 1/4 ins / 34 x 49 cm) FRF 7,000. PARIS, 24 Sept 1991, *Before the Easel* (oil on card, 29 1/2 x 19 3/4 ins / 75 x 50 cm) FRF 5,000. PARIS, 13 March 1992, *Picking Apples* (oil on canvas, 23 1/2 x 31 3/4 ins / 60 x 80.5 cm) FRF 4,000.

IAROCHENKO, Nikolai Aleksandrovich. See **YAROSHENKO**

IARTOFF, Andrei. See **YARTOV**

IASER. See **ROUCHIER Marie Marguerite Françoise**

IASIEVICZ. See **JASIEVICZ Casimir Antonovich**

IASIKOV, Boris
Russian, 20th century.
Born 1901, in Minsk; died 1932, in Berlin.
Active in France.
Painter, newspaper cartoonist, caricaturist, decorative artist. Interiors.

By the age of 15 Boris Iasikov was already an illustrator and caricaturist for a number of St Petersburg newspapers and reviews. He fled after the Revolution, ending up in Paris where he devoted himself to painting. Two retrospectives of his work were held in 1933 and 1948.

IASOKU. See **JASOKU**

IASON, or Iasos
2nd century.
Active in Athens.
Sculptor.
Ancient Greek.

Iason's name appears on a female torso carved from pentelic marble, now in the National Museum in Athens, and on a matching piece found in 1869.

IASUS
5th century BC.
Born in the Colyttus deme (Athens).
Sculptor.
Ancient Greek.

Iasus took part in the decorating of the temple of Athena Polias in the Erechtheum at Athens. A low relief from the frieze, representing a woman and her daughter, was known to be by him.

IATRIDES, Athanasis
Greek, 19th century.
Born c. 1798, in Karpenisi; died 1866.
Draughtsman, lithographer.

Athanasis Iatrides worked in Paris in 1827 and 1828 before being attached to the Greek archaeological service as an artist from 1832 to 1844. He is known for: *Funeral of Marcos Botsaris*, *Death of Karaiskakis*, *Fall of Constantinople to the Turks in 1453* and *Ali Pasha*.

IAVLENSKI. See **JAWLENSKY Alexej Georgevich von**

IBÁÑEZ, Henri
Spanish, 20th century.
Born 6 March 1931, in Barcelona.

Active in France from 1939.
Sculptor.

Henri Ibáñez went to study at the École des Beaux-Arts in Paris in 1939. From 1958, his works appeared in group exhibitions in Paris and provincial France. His first solo exhibition was in Paris in 1952, with others in Paris and in cities in south-west France. His sculptural style is figurative, as are his occasional paintings.

IBANEZ, Manuel Ramirez. See RAMIREZ IBANEZ Manuel

IBÁÑEZ, Pablo Diego

Spanish, 18th century.
Born 1 July 1673, in Calatayud; died 10 February 1755, in Saragossa.
Sculptor.

Pablo Diego Ibáñez joined the Society of Jesus in 1710. In 1723 he collaborated on the new church buildings. From 1742 to 1750 he worked in Huesca.

IBÁÑEZ DE ALDECOA Y ARANO, Julián

Spanish, 19th - 20th century.
Born 1866, in Berriatua (Basque Country).
Painter. Figure compositions, portraits, landscapes.

Julián Ibáñez de Aldecoa y Arano began his artistic career comparatively late. After studying in Spain at the studio of Anselmo de Guinea, he went to Paris in 1910 and studied at the Académie Colarossi. He then returned to Spain, where he participated in group exhibitions, including the Exposición Nacional de Bellas Artes from 1897 onwards, and showed substantial collections of his works at the Bilbao art exhibition, 79 paintings in 1915 and 46 in 1916. He exhibited more of his most important paintings at the Salon Legorgheu in Bilbao in 1924 and 1925.

In 1926, Ibáñez de Aldecoa y Arano was responsible for the decoration of the Casino in Lequeito. He painted typical scenes of the traditional activities of the peasants and fishermen of Lequeito. His realist style, particularly incisive when he paints figures in close-up as if they were posing for group portraits, is reminiscent of the Neue Sachlichkeit (New Objectivity) period in the works of Otto Dix. He understood the farmers and fishermen he met every day, and was able to depict them with dignity.

BIBLIOGRAPHY:

Arnáiz, José Manuel/López Jiménez, Javier/Merchán Díaz, Manuel (ed.), *'Cien años de pintura en Espana y Portugal (1830-1930)'* in vol. IV, Antiqvaria, Madrid, 1990.

IBÁÑEZ MARTOS, Damian

Spanish, 19th century.
Active in Jaén.
Painter.

Damian Ibáñez Martos studied at the fine arts school in Madrid. In Jaén in 1878 he exhibited a number of paintings including portraits of *Queen Isabella II* and of *Maximilian, Emperor of Mexico*. His *Portrait of King Alfonso XII* hangs in the meeting hall of Torredonjimeno town hall.

IBARRA, José

Mexican, 18th century.
Born 1688; died 1756.
Painter. Religious subjects, portraits.

José Ibarra studied under Juan Correa. He has been called the 'Mexican Murillo' although he was in fact more influenced by the Italians, notably the Bologna school, than by the Spanish.

MUSEUMS AND GALLERIES:

MEXICO CITY (Mus. Nacional de San Carlos): *Christ and the Samaritan Woman*; *Christ and the Woman Taken in Adultery* - PUEBLA (Cathedral): *The Last Supper*; *The Assumption*; *The Washing of the Feet.*

AUCTION RECORDS:

NEW YORK, 18 May 1995, *The Annunciation* (oil/copper, 22 1/4 x 16 1/2 ins / 56.8 x 42.2 cm) USD 11,500. NEW YORK, 15 May 1996, *The Glorification of St Christina* (oil/copper, 19 1/2 x 13 3/4 ins / 49.5 x 35 cm) USD 17,250. MEXICO, 29 March 2001, *Crucifixion* (oil on canvas, 80 x 50 ins / 202 x 126 cm) MXP 200,000.

IBARROLA, Agustín

Spanish, 20th century.
Born 1930, in Dos Caminos de Besauri (Basque Country).
Painter, draughtsman, sculptor.
Equipo 57 group.

Agustín Ibarrola studied with Daniel Vázquez Díaz in Madrid. He returned to Bilbao in 1950. Between 1954 and 1961, he lived in Paris. In 1957, together with Juan Serrano, Juan Cuenca, and Angel and José Duarte, he founded the group Equipo 57, which was devoted to Geometric Abstraction and was very active until it was dissolved in 1965. He was awarded the French critics' prize in 1953. He lived in Cordova in 1960 and moved to Bilbao the following year. In 1962, he was made a political prisoner and incarcerated in Burgos prison. He lives and works in the Oma Valley in Spain.

Ibarrola was influenced by the Basque painter Aurelio Arteta and the sculptor Jorge Oteiza. While working with Equipo 57, he created flat paintings before creating figures that appear to have been sculpted on the canvas. During the 1970s, he drew inspiration from country tools or wooden beams, while continuing to explore rhythms in the space of the picture. In 1985, he used railway sleepers to create high reliefs, in which he attempted to reproduce the rhythm of the Basque musical instrument, the txalaparta, for instance in *Traviesas*, 1993. He also paints the trees of the forest of Oma, near Guernica, as if they were totem poles, by juxtaposing horizontal bands of colour, as in *Grove in the Forest of Oma*, 1983-1991. In this he is part of Land Art, exploring the interaction between art and nature, but prefers to call himself a 'traditional muralist', founded on the desire to ensure the continuity of traditional Basque culture. His works express the human condition of his people, their everyday life and craftsmanship. Ibarrola also creates sculptures from newspaper, such as *Clonar Laterales* of 1995, or metal, like the jagged iron plates of *Parque de Kantalazarra* of 1987-1988.

Ibarrola took part in all the exhibitions of Equipo 57, including those of 1957 at the Galerie Denise René, Paris; 1958 at the Salon des Réalités Nouvelles, Paris; 1958 at Thorvaldsen's Museum, Copenhagen; 1959, at Club Urbis, Madrid; 1960, *Art Construit* at the Musée d'Ixelles; the 1976 Venice Biennale and the 1993 retrospective of the group's past activities at the two Denise René Galleries in Paris. He also had solo exhibitions, including St George's Gallery, London, in 1963; the museum of fine arts in Bilbao in 1977 and 1979; the Museo San Telmo, San Sebastián, in 1991 and, with the painter Pierre Gauthier-Dubedat, at the Musée de Guéthary in 2000.

BIBLIOGRAPHY:

Equipo 57, exhibition catalogue, Museo Nacional Centro de Arte Reina Sofía, Madrid, 1993 (text in Spanish and English). Mérite, Pierre, *'Equipo 57'* in *Art Press* n° 217, periodical, Paris, October 1996. Gauthier-Dubédat, Marina/Larralde, Jean-François, *Gauthier-Dubédat, peintures. Agustín Ibarrola, sculptures*, exhibition catalogue, Musée de Guéthary, Guéthary, 2000 (text in French, Spanish and Basque).

IBBETSON, John

British, 19th century.
Active in Down Hall.
Painter. Landscapes.

John Ibbetson exhibited his work in London in 1811 and 1812. He was probably the son of Julius Caesar Ibbetson.

IBBETSON, Julius Caesar

British, 18th - 19th century.

Born 29 December 1759, in Farnley Moor, Leeds; died 13 October 1817, in Masham.

Painter, watercolourist, draughtsman, art restorer. Genre scenes, figures, landscapes, urban views, urban landscapes, landscapes with figures, seascapes, animals. Stage sets.

Julius Caesar Ibbetson was initially apprenticed to a painter of ships. He worked alone on his drawing, and at the age of 17 produced the scenery for a play enacted in Hull and in York. He went to London in 1777, carried out some restoration work on paintings and began to exhibit scenes of London suburbs at the Royal Academy from 1785. He had a very hard life, having to sell his paintings for very low prices, and in spite of a considerable output he found it very difficult to feed the many children born of his marriage. He was even arrested for debt at the very time that he gained a position as a designer in the retinue of Colonel Cathearst, the ambassador to China. He managed to obtain a delay and was able to leave, but the ambassador died en route, leaving Ibbetson to return to England as poor as when he had left. He was saved by his hard work. After a few years he managed to obtain a small amount of money thanks to the paintings he sent to exhibitions, which were highly esteemed. In 1794 the death of his wife, which preceded that of eight of his children, caused him such grief that he fell seriously ill. When he recovered to find that virtually everything he possessed had been stolen, he put his three remaining children into board and lodgings and sought to abandon himself to a life of dissipation and pleasure. His friendship with George Morland, of whom he was at one stage the faithful companion, probably influenced him in this direction. However, the debts which he incurred made the situation untenable, and in 1798 he had to flee London for Liverpool. Subsequently he visited the North of England and Edinburgh, returning to London in 1800. The following year he married for a second time, but his creditors, far from being disinterested, as he believed, attacked him. He left London once again and settled in Masham in Yorkshire where, as a result of living very frugally and carrying out many commissions, he was able to re-establish himself.

Many of Ibbetson's paintings, which depict coastal scenes, landscapes with animals and figures, are painted in very charming colours and with great precision.

Museums and Galleries:

Bristol: *View of Flamborough Head* - Bristol (City Mus. & AG): *View of Flamborough Head* (oil on canvas) - Dublin: *Landscape with Cattle* - Leeds (City AG): *Farmyard in Kent* (1793, oil on canvas); *Phaeton in a Thunderstorm* (1798, oil on canvas); *Ullswater from Gowbarrow* (1801, oil on canvas); *The Painter's Family at Masham* (1809, oil on canvas); *Grosmont Castle, Monmouthshire* (1810, oil on canvas); *River Scene with Figures* (oil on canvas); *Landscape with Figures* (oil/panel); *Gypsy Beggars* (pencil, ink and watercolour) - Leeds (Temple Newsam House): *The Market Place, Ambleside* (1817, oil on canvas); *Portrait of a Young Man* (1790, oil on canvas); *A Farmyard in Kent* (1793, oil on panel); *Portrait of the Artist's Son, J.C. Ibbetson Jnr.* (1801, oil on canvas) - Leicester: *Landscape* - London (Tate Collection): *Briton Ferry, Glamorgan* (c. 1795, oil/wood); *Smugglers on the Irish Coast* (1808, oil on canvas) - London (Victoria and Albert Mus.): *Tigers in the Jungle*; *Sailors on the Binge*; *Landscape*; *Retreat of the Siren*; *Conway Castle* - Nottingham: *Landscape with Cattle* - Washington DC (Georgetown University): *Pastoral Scene with Figures* (1799, oil on canvas).

Auction records:

Paris, 27 April 1874, *Landscape around Bocker End, Isle of Wight*, FRF 5,550. New York, 24 March 1905, *Approaching Storm*, USD 170. London, 24 Feb 1908, *Children with a Dog near a Pond* (1800, drawing) GBP 6. London, 29 Feb 1908, *Landscape*, GBP 15. London, 10 July 1908, *Rydal River* (1788) GBP 42. London, 27 May 1909, *Peasants on the Road*, GBP 21. London, 2 July 1909, *Harrow seen from Kilburn* (1787) GBP 57. London, 26 Feb 1910, *Shipwreck* (1808) GBP 54. London, 22 July 1910, *Landscape with Figures*, GBP 17; *The Calm and the Storm* (1796, two marines) GBP 73. London, 4 April 1922, *Robert Burns*, GBP 241. London, 15 June 1923, *View of Kilburn with Figures*, GBP 54. Paris, 30 April 1926, *Scissor Grinder*; *Stirrup Cup* (both) FRF 4,800. London, 2 March 1928, *Lake District*, GBP 141. London, 15 March 1929, *View of the Welsh Coast*, GBP 63. London, 11 March 1932, *Departure*, GBP 48. Paris, 23 May 1935, *Around Ventnor in the Isle of Wight*, FRF 1,000. London, 24 Feb 1939, *Conway Castle*, GBP 46. Paris, 22 Dec 1941, *Haymakers*; *Fishermen* (two watercolours) FRF 15,700. London, 16 July 1943, *Well in Knaresborough*, GBP 52; *River Scene*, GBP 294. London, 17 Dec 1945, *Landscape*, GBP 100. London, 19 March 1946, *Sailors and Dancing Girls*, GBP 40. New York, 28 March 1946, *Boy and Dog*, USD 1,800; *Children in a Landscape*, USD 1,800. Paris, 6 Dec 1946, *Fishermen Beside the Sea*, FRF 33,000. London, 18 July 1947, *Scene of the Rocky Coast*, GBP 105. London, 20 July 1951, *The Ascension of G. Biggin in the Lunardi Balloon*, GBP 399. London, 24 Oct 1958, *River Scene*, GBP 315. London, 1 May 1959, *River Landscape*, GBP 262. London, 9 Nov 1960, *Conway Castle Seen from the River*, GBP 220. London, 24 Feb 1961, *Quarry with a Cart and Labourers*, GBP 252. London, 22 Nov 1963, *View of Harrow*, Gns 1,500. London, 19 March 1968, *Beetles and Butterflies*; *Bugs and Bees* (two watercolours on pen outlines) Gns 1,500. London, 20 Nov 1968, *Landscapes with Figures*, GBP 2,400. London, 15 June 1971, *Hyde Park Teeming with Many Figures* (watercolour and pen) Gns 3,200. London, 17 Nov 1971, *Women Bathing at the Waterfall*, GBP 3,000. London, 27 June 1973, *Landscape with Bridge, Pontypridd, Glamorgan*, GBP 11,500. London, 19 July 1973, *Harvesters Taking a Break* (watercolour) GBP 1,800. London, 22 March 1974, *Wooded Landscape with Figures*, Gns 2,600. London, 26 March 1976, *The Homecoming* (oil on panel, 17 x 22 ins / 43 x 56 cm) GBP 2,800. London, 15 July 1976, *Washerwomen* (watercolour, 8 1/2 x 10 1/2 ins / 21.5 x 26.5 cm) GBP 680. London, 24 June 1977, *View of Hawthornden, Midlothian* (1814, oil on canvas, 16 1/4 x 20 3/4 ins / 41.2 x 52.7 cm) GBP 1,700. London, 22 June 1979, *Wooded Landscape with Figures* (oil on canvas, 19 1/2 x 23 1/4 ins / 49.5 x 59.1 cm) GBP 4,000. London, 19 March 1981, *View on the Serpentine Lake Looking Towards Hyde Park Corner* (1786, pen and watercolour, 9 x 12 ins / 22.5 x 30.5 cm) GBP 12,000. London, 24 March 1981, *Farm Scene* (watercolour, 6 x 9 ins / 15.2 x 22 cm) GBP 2,100. London, 28 Jan 1983, *Washerwoman near a Fountain in a Wooded Landscape* (1803, oil on canvas, 20 x 24 ins / 51 x 61 cm) GBP 6,000. London, 20 March 1984, *Java, River Inlet* (1794, watercolour and pen, 7 1/4 x 9 1/2 ins / 18.5 x 24.2 cm) GBP 3,500. London, 9 July 1985, *Fishermen Drawing in their Nets, Tenby* (1795, watercolour, pencil and pen, 13 1/2 x 19 3/4 ins / 34.5 x 50.4 cm) GBP 8,500. London, 18 April 1986, *Orchard Bay, Isle of Wight* (1796, oil on canvas, 20 x 26 1/2 ins / 51.1 x 67 cm) GBP 15,000. London, 24 March 1987, *Escort Resting his Horses near an Inn* (watercolour and pen heightened with white, 10 1/4 x 13 ins / 26 x 33 cm) GBP 1,600. London, 29 Jan 1988, *Landscape with a Cart, Harnessed, on a Path* (oil on panel, 17 1/2 x 24 ins / 44.5 x 60.9 cm) GBP 935. London, 15 April 1988, *River Through Woods with a Herd of Cattle and its Keeper on the Path* (oil on canvas, round, 12 1/4 x 15 3/4 ins / 31.4 x 40 cm) GBP 4,180. London, 21 July 1989, *Children Having Fun With Some Donkeys in the Valley* (oil on canvas, 16 3/4 x 24 ins / 42.5 x 61 cm) GBP 902. LONDON, 9 Feb 1990, *Gypsies Around a Fire near a Stream in a Wooded Landscape* (oil on panel, 17 3/4 x 24 ins / 45.4 x 61 cm) GBP 2,420. LONDON, 20 April 1990, *Portrait of Charles Knowles Robinson Wearing a Black Coat and Hat with White Trousers, Skating on Craig Lockhart Skating Pond in Edinburgh* (1813, oil on panel, 26 x 17 3/4 ins / 66 x 45 cm) GBP 26,400. LONDON, 1 March 1991, *St Mary's Abbey in York* (1793, oil on canvas, 12 x 14 ins / 30.5 x 35.6 cm) GBP 2,420. NEW YORK, 10 July 1991, *Market Day in Masham* (oil on canvas, 13 1/2 x 17 1/2 ins / 34 x 44.5 cm) USD 28,600. NEW YORK, 9 Oct 1991, *Extensive River Landscape with Fishermen Tending their Nets* (oil on canvas, 24 1/4 x 38 ins / 61.9 x 96.5 cm) USD 12,100. LONDON, 15 Nov 1991, *Woodcutter and his Family Stopping near the Ruins of Rosslyn Castle* (1801, oil on panel, 12 x 16 1/4 ins / 30.5 x 41 cm) GBP 2,750. LONDON, 10 April 1992, *View of the Old Church and the Rector at South Otterington* (oil on canvas, 12 1/4 x 16 1/2 ins / 31 x 42 cm) GBP 1,870. LONDON, 7 April 1993, *Peasants Tending a Herd of Cows in a Landscape of Woods and Valleys with Lake Windermere* (1803, oil on canvas, 27 x 36 1/4 ins / 68.6 x 91.8 cm) GBP 20,700. NEW YORK, 19 May 1993, *Milkmaid Milking a Cow Near the Ruins of an Abbey with Travellers along the Road* (oil on canvas, 28 x 35 1/2 ins / 71.4 x 90.3 cm) USD 4,600. ST ASAPH, 2 June 1994, *Italian Landscape with Figures and Livestock beside a Lake* (oil on canvas, 28 x 36 ins / 71 x 91.5 cm) GBP 14,720. LONDON, 10 July 1996, *Landscapes with Views of the Lake District* (oil on paper, a pair, each diam. 4 1/4 ins / 10.5 cm) GBP 1,150. LONDON, 13 Nov 1996, *Italian Landscape with Figures; Approaching Storm. Figures on a Path in a Wooded Landscape with a River* (1798, oil on canvas, a pair, in collaboration with John Rathborne, each 38 1/2 x 50 3/4 ins / 97.5 x 129 cm) GBP 18,400. LONDON, 9 July 1997, *Going to Market* (oil on panel, a pair, each 10 x 14 1/4 ins / 24.5 x 36.5 cm) GBP 8,625. LONDON, 31 March 1999, *Landscape with View of Temple of Maecenas and Falls of Tivoli* (1800, oil on canvas, 17 x 23 ins / 43 x 59 cm) GBP 16,000. BILLINGSHURST, 19 Oct 1999, *Vale of Glamorgan* (oil on canvas, 33 x 53 ins / 85 x 134 cm) GBP 8,000. SAN FRANCISCO, 15 Nov 2000, *Moonlit River Scene with Gypsy Figures Cooking* (oil on canvas, 25 x 30 ins / 63 x 76 cm) USD 6,000. LONDON, 1 Dec 2000, *Going to Market. Returning from Market* (1785, oil on panel, a pair, 9 x 14 ins / 24 x 36 cm) GBP 14,000. LONDON, 15 June 2001, *Children Gathering Firewood, Ox-drawn Cart Standing Beside* (1789, oil on canvas, 20 x 25 ins / 52 x 64 cm) GBP 3,800. LONDON, 30 Nov 2001, *View of Castle Campbell, Scotland, with Washerwomen on the Riverbank* (oil on panel, 13 x 18 ins / 34 x 45 cm) GBP 7,500. OXFORD, 25 June 2002, *Figures Strolling in a Mountainous River Landscape* (1810, oil on canvas, 17 x 22 ins / 43 x 56 cm) GBP 2,800. LONDON, 26 Nov 2002, *Farmyard with Cattle, Horse and Figures. Figures and Cattle by Stream* (1805, oil on panel, a pair, 11 x 15 ins / 28 x 38 cm) GBP 8,500. LONDON, 19 March 2003, *Salmon Fishery at Pont Aberglaslyn, North Wales* (oil on canvas, 39 x 48 ins / 99 x 123 cm) GBP 44,000. LONDON, 27 Nov 2003, *Two Peasants on the Bank of a Lake. Two Fishermen on the Bank of an Estuary* (oil on canvas, a pair, 10 x 12 ins / 25 x 30 cm) GBP 5,500. LONDON, 3 June 2004, *Fashionable Figures Promenading on the Mall, London* (pencil and watercolour, 7 x 10 ins / 19 x 26 cm) GBP 26,000. LONDON, 27 Oct 2004, *Figures Watering a Horse with a Mill Beyond* (1797, oil on canvas, 18 x 25 ins / 46 x 64 cm) GBP 6,000.

IBELS, Henri Gabriel

French, 19th - 20th century.

Born 30 November 1867, in Paris; died February 1936, in Paris.

Painter, pastellist, engraver, draughtsman, illustrator.

Henri Gabriel Ibels taught himself by studying nature, as well as studying at the Académie Julian and the École des Arts Décoratifs from 1886 to 1887. He belonged to the Société des Indépendants from a young age, but ceded to none of the masters who, from 1884, would affirm the freedom of art. At the Académie Julian, Sérusier, Maurice Denis and Bonnard founded the Nabis group, with whom Ibels aligned himself, inspired by the teaching of Gauguin. In 1891 he took part in the first Symbolist exhibition. He also earned a distinguished place among humourists through collaborating on the principal illustrated journals and the large dailies. With his journal *Le Sifflet* (*The Whistle*), published during the unfolding of the Dreyfus affair, he actively fought against the drawings published in *P'stt* by Forain and Caran d'Ache. Ibels was active in artistic teaching, and was associated with several universities as a professor of art history. He also staged several plays in Paris. His landscapes with shimmering colours and his pastels of soldiers, wrestlers and circus artists attracted attention. He was also prominent in an initiative to protect artists' royalties. Known for his interesting lithographs and posters, he had several exhibitions at La Bodinière (a theatre). He was decorated with the Légion d'Honneur in 1913.

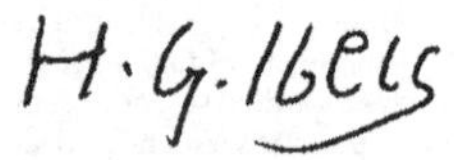

BIBLIOGRAPHY:

Osterwalder, Marcus (ed.), *Dictionnaire des illustrateurs 1800-1914*, Ides et Calendes, Neuchâtel, 1989. *Les Nabis*, exhibition catalogue, Galeries nationales du Grand Palais, Réunion des Musées nationaux, Paris, 1993.

MUSEUMS AND GALLERIES:

PARIS (BNF): *Concert and Café* (1893); *Mevisto* - ST-GERMAIN-EN-LAYE (Mus. du Prieuré-Maurice-Denis): *Circus Scene, around 1890* (fan design); *Mevisto*.

AUCTION RECORDS:

PARIS, 10 May 1900, *Fairs,* FRF 170. PARIS, 11 June 1924, *Paulus the Singer* (gouache) FRF 200. PARIS, 30 Dec 1925, *Sailors,* FRF 110. PARIS, 27 Nov 1926, *The Extras,* FRF 300. PARIS, 5-6 June 1929, *Parisian and Fishermen on the Beach,* FRF 700. PARIS, 2 Dec 1931, *The Landes,* FRF 105. PARIS, 6 March 1940, *Village Feast,* FRF 700. PARIS, 28 Jan 1942, *Pierrot* FRF 1,600. PARIS, 19 April 1943, *Pierrot's Sadness* (pastel) FRF 700. PARIS, 25 March 1944, *The Procession,* FRF 1,600. PARIS, 19 Jan 1945, *Outing Day,* FRF 3,300. PARIS, July 1946, *Seaside in Brittany,* FRF 1,400. PARIS, 25 Jan 1954, *Nude on the Grass,* FRF 3,500. LONDON, 24 April 1968, *The Circus Wings* (pastel) GBP 1,800. LONDON, 2 July 1969, *Fair,* GBP 900. LONDON, 30 Nov 1972, *Rustic Scene,* GBP 800. LONDON, 4 April 1974, *The Clown,* GBP 400. VERSAILLES, 27 June 1976, *The Clown* (oil on wood, 12 1/4 x 10 1/4 ins / 31 x 26 cm) FRF 1,800. HAMBURG, 3 June 1977, *Breton Peasant Women* (oil on canvas, 43 1/4 x 64 1/4 ins / 110 x 163 cm) DEM 8,000. PARIS, 19 March 1979, *The Road to Pont-Aven* (oil on canvas, 19 3/4 x 24 ins / 50 x 61 cm) FRF 5,200. LONDON, 25 June 1985, *The Lovers at the Table* (pastel, 10 1/2 x 6 3/4 ins / 26.7 x 17.4 cm) GBP 750. PARIS, 21 Jan 1987, *Circus Scene* (pen drawing, fan-shaped, 14 1/2 x 25 1/4 ins / 37 x 64 cm) FRF 11,500. PARIS, 10 Feb 1988, *At the Counter* (oil on panel, 8 1/2 x 10 1/4 ins / 21.5 x 26 cm) FRF 9,800. PARIS, 13 March 1989, *Siesta in a Hammock* (oil on panel, 10 1/4 x 13 3/4 ins / 26 x 35 cm) FRF 5,000; *Seated Woman* (red and blue pencil, 8 3/4 x 6 1/2 ins / 22.5 x 16.5 cm) FRF 3,800. PARIS, 26 March 1990, *The End of a Greek Artist* (watercolour and colouring pencil, 17 3/4 x 6 ins / 45 x 15 cm) FRF 9,500. PARIS, 27 Nov 1995, *At the Circus* (1893, coloured lithograph, 22 x 12 1/4 ins / 56 x 31 cm) FRF 7,000. PARIS, 7 June 1997, *At the Café-Concert* (gouache, 11 3/4 x 7 1/2 ins / 30 x 19.3 cm) FRF 41,000. PARIS, 14 April 2000, *Landscape* (oil on card, 25 x 39 ins / 64 x 100 cm) FRF 19,000. PARIS, 13 Nov 2002, *Pierrefort 12* (lithograph) EUR 10,200. BREST, 21 Dec

2003, *Landscape and Waters Edge* (oil on canvas, 11 x 18 ins / 28 x 46 cm) EUR 3,100.

IBELS, Louise Catherine
French, 20th century.
Born 11 December 1891, in Nogent-sur-Marne.
Illustrator.

Louise Catherine Ibels was a student of Bernard Naudin. She is mostly known for her illustrations for *La maternelle* (*The Nursery School*) by L. Frapié, and *Germinal* by Zola. She exhibited in Paris at the Salon des Indépendants and the Salon d'Automne.

IBERIA
French, 20th - 21st century.
Born 14 January 1956, in Amiens.
Painter. Scenes with figures.

Iberia made a wall panel for Vignacourt school, Somme, as part of the 1%. Her canvases are bathed in a strange, intimist light where dreams come alive. She has taken part in collective exhibitions in France since 1972 and at the FIAC (Foire Internationale d'Art Contemporain) in Paris since 1981.

IBI, Sinibaldo
Italian, 16th century.
Born c. 1475, in Perugia; died c. 1550.
Active probably in Gubbio at the beginning of the 16th century.
Painter. Religious subjects.
Perugian School.

Sinibaldo Ibi was a member of the guild of St Luke in Perugia in 1527. He worked in collaboration with Orlando da Perugia for the cathedral in Gubbio.

MUSEUMS AND GALLERIES:
GUBBIO: *Banner with Figure of St Ubaldo* - PERUGIA (Pinacoteca): *Annunciation*; *Virgin with Saints*; three works.

IBIA, Isabel de, called Isabelle de la Sumaya or Zumaya
Mexican, 16th - 17th century.
Born to a family originally from Zumaya; died before 1623.
Painter.

Isabel de Ibia worked in Mexico City, where she married B. de Echave.

MUSEUMS AND GALLERIES:
MEXICO CITY (Cathedral): several works.

IBING, August
German, 20th century.
Born 12 January 1878, in Westphalia.
Painter. Figures, landscapes, still-lifes.

August Ibing attended the art academy in Düsseldorf, where he lived and worked. His work appeared at the Glaspalast (Ice Palace) exhibitions in Munich, in addition to Dresden and Düsseldorf.

MUSEUMS AND GALLERIES:
DÜSSELDORF (Kunstmus.): *Young Boy Reading*.

IBN DAYA, Khodja ed Din
Egyptian, 13th century.
Active in Cairo at the end of the 13th century.
Miniaturist.

Ibn Daya was a chancellor to the Sultan Mameluk Baybar and painted several pictures representing the *Pilgrimage to Mecca*.

IBN EL AZÎZ
Egyptian, 10th century.
Active at the end of the 10th century.
Painter. Local scenes.

Ibn El Aziz was a painter at the court of the Fatimids in Cairo. He was mainly in the service of Vizir Bazuri, for whom he painted among other works a *Dancer in a Red Veil with a Yellow Background*.

BIBLIOGRAPHY:
Ettinghausen, Richard, *Arab Painting*, Geneva, 1962.

IBORRA, Lino Casimiro
Spanish, 19th - 20th century.
Born in Santoña (Cantabria).
Painter. Genre scenes, landscapes.

Lino Casimiro Iborra studied at the school of fine arts in Madrid, where he lived and worked. He exhibited there from 1882 to 1906.

IBORRA, Rosa Cabrera de
Spanish, 19th - 20th century.
Painter. Still-lifes.

Rosa Cabrera de Iborra was married to Lino Casimiro Iborra.

IBOU, Paul, pseudonym of Vermeerch, Paul Lodewijk Henry
Belgian, 20th century.
Born 1939, in Bogerhout (Antwerp).
Draughtsman, illustrator.

Paul Ibou attended the Koninklijke Academie voor Schone Kunsten in Antwerp. He produced many posters and illustrations.

IBRAHIM EL BELUTJI
Persian School, 18th century.
Miniaturist.

This artist was active in Astrabad.

IBRAHIM KAHAR
Persian School, 16th century.
Miniaturist.

Ibrahim Kahar was a painter at the court of the Indian Mughal emperor Akbar the Great (r.1556-1605).

MUSEUMS AND GALLERIES:
LONDON (British Mus.): two manuscripts.

IBRAHIM KHAN ILTJI
Persian School, 16th century.
Calligrapher, illuminator.

This artist was the Persian (Safavid) ambassador to Constantinople in 1582.

IBRAHIM TJELEBI D'AIDAR (Pasha)
Persian School, 18th century.
Calligrapher, illuminator.

This artist was a pupil of Hasan the Egyptian.

IBSEN, Henrik
Norwegian, 19th century.
Born 20 March 1828, in Skien; died 23 May 1906, in Christiania (now Oslo).
Painter, draughtsman, caricaturist, watercolourist, dramatist. Landscapes, urban landscapes. Stage costumes and sets.

During his youth, the dramatist Henrik Ibsen made drawings and painted in oil and watercolour. His subjects were landscapes and views of the region of Skien, his town of birth, and scenes from daily life. While a pharmacist in Grimstad, he continued drawing and making caricatures under which he would write humorous inscriptions in verse. While director of a theatre in Bergen, he took painting lessons and executed landscapes of the high mountains and fjords. He also sketched set decorations and costumes for the theatres in Bergen and Christiania. Several of his paintings are in the Brekke museum in Skien, and a watercolour landscape is in the Rasmus Meyer collection in Bergen.

MUSEUMS AND GALLERIES:
SKIEN (Brekke Mus.).

AUCTION RECORDS:
LONDON, 29 March 1990, *The Hardanger Fjord* (pencil and watercolour heightened with white/paper/card, 5 3/4 x 8 3/4 ins / 14.5 x 22.5 cm) GBP 13,200.

IBSEN, Immanuel
Danish, 20th century.
Born 1887; died 1944.
Painter. Interiors with figures, landscapes, waterscapes, still-lifes.

Immanuel Ibsen worked in a direct and unequivocal style, applying thick paint with sensual brushstrokes.
AUCTION RECORDS:
COPENHAGEN, 7 March 1979, *Still-life* (1942, oil on canvas, 35 x 43 1/4 ins / 88 x 110 cm) DKK 18,000. COPENHAGEN, 26 Feb 1986, *Still-life* (1943, oil on canvas, 39 1/4 x 47 1/4 ins / 100 x 120 cm) DKK 22,000. COPENHAGEN, 4 May 1988, *Still-life* (1928, 19 3/4 x 25 1/2 ins / 50 x 65 cm) DKK 9,000. COPENHAGEN, 30 Nov 1988, *Still-life with Bowl of Fruit on a Table* (1937, oil on canvas, 33 1/2 x 43 1/4 ins / 85 x 110 cm) DKK 60,000. COPENHAGEN, 9 May 1990, *Blocks of Wood in a Harbour* (1940, oil on canvas, 21 1/4 x 26 1/2 ins / 54 x 67 cm) DKK 6,000. COPENHAGEN, 31 Oct 1990, *View from Christianshavn Canal* (1938, oil on canvas, 26 x 21 1/4 ins / 66 x 54 cm) DKK 9,000. COPENHAGEN, 2 April 1992, *Interior* (1942, oil on canvas, 35 x 44 ins / 88 x 112 cm) DKK 33,000. COPENHAGEN, 13 April 1994, *Boats on Christianshavn Canal* (1917, oil on canvas, 28 3/4 x 24 3/4 ins / 73 x 63 cm) DKK 4,200. COPENHAGEN, 26 April 1995, *Still-life* (1936, oil on canvas, 19 x 23 1/4 ins / 48 x 59 cm) DKK 19,000. COPENHAGEN, 17 April 1996, *Path in a Snowy Landscape* (oil on canvas, 22 x 25 1/2 ins / 55 x 65 cm) DKK 4,800. COPENHAGEN, 12 June 2003, *Landscape, Venø 1942* (oil on canvas, 35 x 43 ins / 88 x 110 cm) DKK 20,000.

IBSEN, Niels
Danish, 17th century.
Sculptor (wood).

A coat of arms at the National Museum in Copenhagen has been attributed to Niels Ibsen.

ICARD, Honoré
French, 19th - 20th century.
Born 1845, in Tourtouse (Ariège); died April 1917, in St-Germain-en-Laye.
Sculptor.

Honoré Icard was a student of Dumont and A. Muller. He showed at the Salon from 1875 to 1882. There he received several awards, notably a second-class medal in 1890 and a first-class medal in 1892. He also received a silver medal at the 1900 Exposition Universelle. He became a member of the Société des Artistes Français in 1887.
MUSEUMS AND GALLERIES:
CAHORS: *Gilliatt, Conqueror of the Octopus* - FOIX: *St Jerome* - MARSEILLES: *The Foolish Virgins* - PARIS (Mus. Galliera): *Protection and Future* - PAU: *David before Saul* - QUIMPER: *The Spider* - TROYES: *The Foolish Virgins*.

ICARO, Paolo
Italian, 20th century.
Born 1936, in Turin.
Sculptor.

ICART, Louis
French, 20th century.
Born 1888; died 1950.
Painter, watercolourist, pastellist, engraver, draughtsman, illustrator. Nudes, portraits, genre scenes, landscapes with figures.

Louis Icart arrived in Paris in 1907 and learned engraving techniques in the postcard factory where he worked. Icart is known for his numerous colour etchings of elegant, sometimes erotic, figures, inspired by Pierre Louÿs and the Spanish women in the books of Mérimée. He also illustrated Colette's *L'Ingénue Libertine* and Goethe's two *Faust*. His prints were widely distributed in the USA between 1920 and 1940. In contrast, his painting shows an Impressionist tendency. He had a solo exhibition in Paris in 1912, and in Brussels the following year. He was named Chevalier of the Légion d'Honneur in 1927.

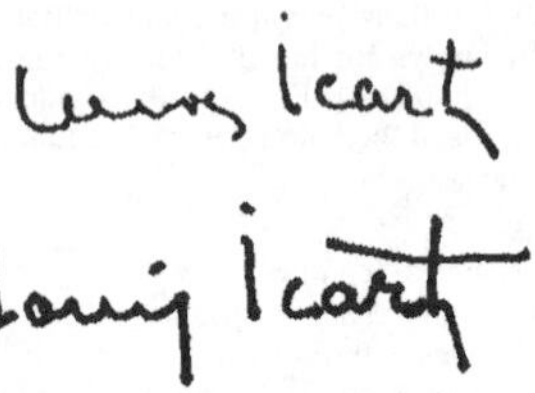

BIBLIOGRAPHY:
Schnessel, S. Michael, *Icart, The Gracious Libertine*, Studio Vista, London, 1977. Schnessel, S. Michael, *Icart*, Les Humanoïdes associés, Paris, 1978. Holland, William R., *Louis Icart Erotica*, Schiffer, Atglen, 1998.
AUCTION RECORDS:
PARIS, 12 May 1923, *The Wait* (red chalk) FRF 180. PARIS, 14 Nov 1924, *Pierrot's Kiss*, FRF 600. PARIS, 4 May 1931, *Young Blonde Woman* (drawing heightened with pastels) FRF 400. PARIS, 22-23 Dec 1941, *In the Garden*, FRF 8,500. PARIS, 11 Feb 1944, *Young Woman* (watercolour) FRF 320. PARIS, 23 April 1945, *Two Young Women in a Landscape*, FRF 550. PARIS, 27 Dec 1946, *The Broken Jug and the Bird in Flight* (two pastels, pendants) FRF 400. PARIS, 11-12 and 13 Oct 1954, *Dancer* (gouache drawing) FRF 5,200. PARIS, 16 March 1976, *Memories* (oil on card, 16 1/4 x 12 3/4 ins / 41 x 32.5 cm) FRF 3,300. NEW YORK, 31 March 1979, *Birth of Venus* (1931, etching and aquatint in colour, 19 3/4 x 15 1/4 ins / 50 x 38.6 cm) USD 1,300. LOS ANGELES, 7 Nov 1979, *China Fish* (oil on canvas, 37 1/2 x 50 3/4 ins / 95.2 x 129 cm) USD 8,000. PARIS, 19 Nov 1980, *Reflection: Young Woman with Veil* (charcoal/paper, 22 x 16 1/4 ins / 56 x 41 cm) FRF 7,800. PARIS, 19 Nov 1980, *Young Woman on a Blue Sofa* (pastel, 15 3/4 x 20 ins / 40 x 51 cm) FRF 7,500. PARIS, 14 Dec 1981, *Cottage Cheese* (oil on canvas, 28 x 41 1/4 ins / 71 x 105 cm) FRF 50,000. TOKYO, 21 Feb 1982, *Scheherazade* (1927, dry-point and aquatint in colour, 14 x 21 ins / 35.5 x 53.5 cm) JPY 605,000. NEW YORK, 15 Dec 1983, *Three Amazons* (oil on canvas, 28 1/2 x 36 1/2 ins / 72.5 x 93 cm) USD 13,000. NEW YORK, 29 March 1984, *Leda and the Swan* (1934, etching and dry-point, in colour, 31 x 21 ins / 79 x 53.5 cm) USD 3,500. NEW YORK, 29 March 1984, *Young Woman with Spanish Shawl* (1925, pastel, 47 1/4 x 36 1/4 ins / 120 x 92 cm) USD 3,400. MONTE CARLO, 6 Oct 1985, *In Costume for the Masked Ball* (c. 1925, ink and pencil, 13 x 9 ins / 33 x 22 cm) FRF 8,000. RAMBOUILLET, 20 Oct 1985, *Elegant Figures on the Beach* (oil on canvas, 19 3/4 x 24 ins / 50 x 61 cm) FRF 60,000. PARIS, 26 Nov 1987, *Prelude* (1925, dry-point and aquatint, 20 3/4 x 28 1/4 ins / 53 x 72 cm) FRF 26,000. PARIS, 20 May 1988, *Young Woman with Doves* (1924, etching, 12 1/2 x 17 1/4 ins / 32 x 44 cm) FRF 7,000; *The Puppets* (1921, oval etching, 16 1/2 x 21 1/4 ins / 42 x 54 cm) FRF 6,400. LA VARENNE-ST-HILAIRE, 29 May 1988, *The Luncheon on the Grass* (oil on canvas, 39 1/4 x 32 ins / 100 x 81 cm) FRF 12,000. LUCERNE, 30 Sept 1988, *The Ballerina* (etching, 17 x 11 ins / 43 x 28 cm) CHF 950. PARIS, 7 Oct 1988, *Elegant Figure* (oil on canvas, 22 x 15 ins / 55 x 38 cm) FRF 70,000. LONDON, 21 Oct 1988, *Mr l'Amour* (pastel and chalks/paper, 20 x 16 1/2 ins / 50.8 x 42.2 cm) GBP 880; *Leaning Female Nude* (etching, 9 x 11 ins / 22 x 28 cm) GBP 950. PARIS, 10 Nov 1988, *The Pond of Swans* (oil on canvas, 22 x 18 ins / 55 x 46 cm) FRF 95,000. PARIS, 16 Dec 1988, *Woman with Cat* (dry-point and aquatint, 20 x 16 ins / 50.5 x 40.5 cm) FRF 72,500. PARIS, 12 Feb 1989, *The Black Mask* (watercolour, 15 3/4 x 10 1/4 ins / 40 x 26 cm)

FRF 32,000. PARIS, 19 March 1989, *The Parasols* (oil on canvas, 19 3/4 x 24 ins / 50 x 61 cm) FRF 92,500. PARIS, 12 April 1989, *Young Woman by the Cradle* (oil on panel, 18 x 28 3/4 ins / 46 x 73 cm) FRF 115,000. PARIS, 22 Oct 1989, *Elegant Figure on the Sofa* (pastel, 8 3/4 x 12 1/2 ins / 22.5 x 31.5 cm) FRF 22,500. BRUSSELS, 19 Dec 1989, *Women with Swan* (drypoint, 22 x 25 1/2 ins / 55 x 65 cm) BEF 370,000. PARIS, 14 Feb 1990, *Young Woman with Flowers, Smiling* (oil on canvas, 24 x 18 ins / 61 x 46 cm) FRF 300,000. PARIS, 21 March 1990, *Tea in the Garden* (oil on canvas, 25 3/4 x 20 ins / 65.5 x 50.5 cm) FRF 420,000. BRUSSELS, 27 March 1990, *Woman with Lilies* (dry-point) BEF 190,000. MONTREAL, 30 April 1990, *The Pink Divan* (etching in colour, 9 3/4 x 13 ins / 25 x 33 cm) CAD 4,180. VERSAILLES, 27 May 1990, *Sleep* (1933, dry-point, etching, 46 x 19 1/2 ins / 117 x 49.5 cm) FRF 65,000. PARIS, 1 June 1990, *Portrait of Marcelle Ragan* (oil on canvas, 32 x 25 1/2 ins / 81 x 65 cm) FRF 330,000. LORIENT, 10 June 1990, *Nonchalance* (oil on panel, 24 1/4 x 20 ins / 61.5 x 51 cm) FRF 240,500. BRUSSELS, 12 June 1990, *Sleeping Woman* (dry-point in colour, 15 1/4 x 18 1/2 ins / 39 x 47 cm) BEF 88,000. BORDEAUX, 11 Oct 1990, *Leda and the Swan* (1934, dry-point and etching, 21 x 30 1/2 ins / 52.5 x 77.5 cm) FRF 79,500. MONTREAL, 5 Nov 1990, *Woman in the Blue Dress* (etching in colour, 23 1/4 x 19 1/4 ins / 59 x 49 cm) CAD 4,070. PARIS, 20 Nov 1990, *Youth*. PARIS, 27 Nov 1990, *The New Hairdo* (oil on panel, 13 x 16 1/4 ins / 33 x 41 cm) FRF 135,000. STOCKHOLM, 5-6 Dec 1990, *Handkissing, Interior with Couple* (1914, pastel, 17 3/4 x 23 1/2 ins / 45 x 60 cm) SEK 30,000. PARIS, 7 Dec 1990, *The Two Friends* (pastel, 19 1/4 x 24 3/4 ins / 49 x 63 cm) FRF 55,000. LYONS, 1 March 1991, *In the Boat* (oil on card, 17 3/4 x 21 1/2 ins / 45 x 54.5 cm) FRF 310,000. PARIS, 13 Nov 1991, *Young Woman with Urn* (etching in colour, 20 3/4 x 16 1/2 ins / 53 x 42 cm) FRF 4,500. PARIS, 10 June 1992, *The Afternoon Beauty* (oil on canvas, 50 1/2 x 34 1/4 ins / 128 x 87 cm) FRF 272,000. PARIS, 21 Oct 1992, *Young Woman with Trellis* (engraving in 3 colours, 22 x 14 3/4 ins / 55 x 37.5 cm) FRF 4,000. NEW YORK, 29 Oct 1992, *By the Water* (oil on canvas, 17 1/4 x 28 3/4 ins / 43.5 x 73 cm) USD 25,300. NEW YORK, 17 Feb 1993, *The Swans* (oil on panel, 24 x 19 3/4 ins / 61 x 50.2 cm) USD 19,550. LE TOUQUET, 30 May 1993, *Elegant Young Figures in a Carriage* (oil on canvas, 20 x 24 ins / 51 x 61 cm) FRF 73,000. PARIS, 24 June 1994, *Elegant Figures at the Place de la Concorde* (oil on canvas, 21 1/4 x 30 1/4 ins / 54 x 77 cm) FRF 85,000. MONTREAL, 6 Dec 1994, *Woman with Doves* (etching, 19 1/4 x 11 1/2 ins / 49.2 x 29.2 cm) CAD 1,350. PARIS, 7 Dec 1995, *End of Luncheon* (oil on canvas, 19 3/4 x 24 ins / 50 x 61 cm) FRF 50,000. MONTREAL, 18 June 1996, *Symphony in Blue* (etching, 23 x 19 ins / 58.4 x 48.2 cm) CAD 1,600. CALAIS, 7 July 1996, *Elegant Women with Puppets* (aquatint, 15 1/4 x 20 ins / 39 x 51 cm) FRF 6,800. MONTREAL, 3 Dec 1996, *Pink Beauties* (etching, 15 x 18 ins / 38 x 45.6 cm) CAD 2,100. PARIS, 10 Dec 1996, *Seated Model* (pastel and charcoal/paper, 17 1/4 x 12 3/4 ins / 44 x 32.5 cm) FRF 6,500. PARIS, 20 Dec 1996, *Smiling Buddha* (etching and aquatint) FRF 4,000. MONTREAL, 17 June 1997, *Symphony in Blue* (etching, 23 x 19 ins / 58.5 x 48.2 cm) CAD 2,200. PARIS, 4 Nov 1997, *Young Woman with Dove* (dry-point in colour, 20 3/4 x 25 1/4 ins / 53 x 64 cm) FRF 6,000. PARIS, 20 March 1998, *The Lilies* (1934, etching and aquatint) FRF 11,200. PARIS, 8 April 1998, *Des Grieux (Couple Embracing)* (1930, etching, dry-point and aquatint) FRF 4,200. PARIS, 30 April 1999, *Meeting in the Park* (1937, oil on canvas, 32 x 26 ins / 82 x 65 cm) FRF 70,000. LOS ANGELES, 14 June 1999, *Melody Hour* (1934, etching with handcoloured aquatint, 25 x 31 ins / 63 x 78 cm) USD 12,000. LONDON, 9 Feb 2000, *French Quadrille* (colour drypoint etching, 25 x 16 ins / 64 x 41 cm) GBP 6,000. LONDON, 9 Feb 2000, *Melody Hour* (colour drypoint etching, 23 x 29 ins / 59 x 74 cm) GBP 8,500. PARIS, 20 March 2001, *L'apres-midi d'un Faune* (1920, oil on canvas, 66 x 141 ins / 167 x 359 cm) FRF 510,000. PARIS, 22 April 2001, *Grand Eve* (oil on panel, 109 x 20 ins / 276 x 51 cm) FRF 75,000. LONDON, 14 May 2002, *Waltz Dream* (colour drypoint with aquatint, 21 x 27 ins / 54 x 69 cm) GBP 3,800. LONDON, 1 July 2002, *Bathers* (etching with aquatint, 26 x 20 ins / 65 x 52 cm) GBP 4,200. PARIS, 25 March 2003, *Conversation in the Salon* (oil on panel, 24 x 20 ins / 61 x 50 cm) EUR 9,100. PARIS, 5 Aug 2003, *Thoughtful Woman* (oil on canvas, 29 x 24 ins / 73 x 60 cm) EUR 9,000. NEW YORK, 11 March 2004, *Trophy* (charcoal and watercolour, 17 x 10 ins / 44 x 26 cm) USD 7,000. LYONS, 6 June 2004, *Carnival a Venice* (oil on canvas, 77 x 51 ins / 195 x 130 cm) EUR 42,000.

ICAZA, Ernesto

Mexican, 19th - 20th century.
Born 1866, in Mexico; died 1935.
Painter. Scenes with figures, local scenes.

Ernesto Icaza held his first solo exhibition in 1950 at the museum of fine arts in Mexico City. His work later came to public attention through a number of retrospectives and various publications. Icaza represented rodeos, bullfights and ranching scenes, tirelessly repeating the same, somewhat disconcerting imagery. His style remained naive throughout.

AUCTION RECORDS:
NEW YORK, 7 Nov 1980, *Mexican Cowboys* (1911, oil on canvas and oil on card, 2 1/4 x 4 ins / 6 x 10.2 cm and 4 1/4 x 6 ins/11.1 x 15.2 cm) USD 5,000. NEW YORK, 29 Nov 1983, *French Soldier Wounded in Mexico* (1918, oil on canvas, 11 1/2 x 18 1/2 ins / 29 x 46.8 cm) USD 4,000. NEW YORK, 27 Nov 1985, *Landscape with Carts* (1924, oil on canvas, 23 1/2 x 37 1/2 ins / 59.5 x 95 cm) USD 3,500. NEW YORK, 21 Nov 1988, *Bull Captured by Lasso* (oil on canvas/card, 7 3/4 x 11 1/2 ins / 19.5 x 29.4 cm) USD 7,700. NEW YORK, 20-21 Nov 1990, *The 'Los Dolores' Ranch* (1919, oil on canvas, 58 x 97 1/4 ins / 147.5 x 247 cm) USD 137,500. NEW YORK, 19-20 May 1992, *Rounding up Cattle on the San José Ranch* (1900, oil on canvas, 23 1/2 x 38 ins / 59.7 x 96.5 cm) USD 66,000. NEW YORK, 23 Nov 1992, *Bull Captured in the Countryside* (1913, oil on canvas, 29 x 39 1/2 ins / 73.7 x 100.3 cm) USD 60,500. NEW YORK, 25 Nov 1992, *Corral Entrance* (1910, oil on canvas/synthetic resin, 16 x 23 ins / 40.5 x 58.5 cm) USD 38,500. NEW YORK, 18 May 1993, *Wounded Soldier* (1918, oil on canvas, 12 1/4 x 19 ins / 31 x 48 cm) USD 23,000. NEW YORK, 18-19 May 1993, *Peasants Working a Bull with decorated Horns* (1921, oil on canvas, 23 1/2 x 38 ins / 60 x 95.6 cm) USD 34,500. NEW YORK, 16 Nov 1994, *The Arrival of the Owner and his Guests at a Corral Celebration* (1920, oil on canvas, 24 x 37 ins / 61 x 94 cm) USD 68,500. NEW YORK, 2 June 1999, *Lassoing at the Pen Gate* (oil on canvas laid on panel, 22 x 35 ins / 55 x 90 cm) USD 11,000. MEXICO, 1 July 1999, *Lassoing in the Open Field* (oil on canvas, 19 x 28 ins / 47 x 70 cm) MXP 200,000. MEXICO, 28 Sept 2000, *Tying a Bull with a Lasso* (oil on board, 3 x 5 ins / 8 x 12 cm) MXP 30,000. MEXICO, 27 June 2001, *Taming Horses* (1913, oil on panel, 12 x 19 ins / 30 x 47 cm) MXP 110,000. NEW YORK, 28 May 2003, *Preparing for the Horse Race; The Tlacuelero* (1914, oil on canvas, 40 x 60cm/16 x 24in) USD 18,000. MEXICO, 29 Oct 2003, *Waiting for the Master* (oil on canvas laid on board, 22 x 37 ins / 55 x 94 cm) MXP 150,000.

ICHANSON, Marie

French, 20th century.
Born 5 October 1889, in Albi.
Painter.

Marie Ichanson was a student of Jean-Paul Laurens. She exhibited in Paris at the Salon des Artistes Français, of which she was a member, and at which she won a silver medal.

MUSEUMS AND GALLERIES:
MULHOUSE: *Hortensias*.

ICHÉ, René

French, 20th century.
Born 1897, in Sallèles-d'Aude; died 23 December 1954, in Paris.

Sculptor, medallist. Groups, monuments.

While very young, René Iché enlisted in the army. He was made a Chevalier d'Honneur at the front in Verdun. After World War I he resumed his studies, receiving a law degree in 1921. After working in administration, he decided to devote himself to sculpture. He began with an apprenticeship in stone-cutting, working also in architecture with Auguste Perret, and in aesthetics with Henri Focillon. In 1949, he founded the sculptors' union, of which he became president. His style, similar to archaic Greek art, was initially quite heavy, but later on became more dynamic. He worked in wood and terracotta, and executed groups in the direct-cutting method, as may be seen in *Wrestlers*, 1924, and *Sweet France*, 1925, as well as in his monuments to the dead. He drew inspirations from war of 1939-1945 for various works, having been an active participant. He is also known for his *Joan of Arc* at the Boulogne-Billancourt church and for exterior frescoes decorating the Palais du Travail, des Sports et des Arts in Narbonne. Though he was not interested in Modernist preoccupations, he avoided Academicism. He expressed conflicts of solitude in his powerful masculine nudes, often in groups of wrestlers.

He exhibited regularly in Paris, at the Salon d'Automne, where the solidity of his works was always appreciated. He also showed at the Salon des Tuileries and the Salon des Indépendants. At the Exposition Universelle in Paris in 1937, he executed the façade of the Merchant Marine Pavillion and the foyer of the Palais de l'Artisanat. He also took part in decorating the streets of Paris in 1945 for the peace celebrations, receiving a second prize. In 1947, he was invited to the Biennale in Venice. He had solo exhibitions at the Galerie Zborowski in 1931. In 1967, a retrospective was organised by the municipality of St-Ouen, and in 1999 by the Musée Numismatique Joseph Puig in Perpignan. In 1953, he received the Grand Prix de Sculpture from the city of Paris.

BIBLIOGRAPHY:

René Iché et grands sculpteurs contemporains, exhibition catalogue, Palais des Archevêques, Narbonne, 1970.

MUSEUMS AND GALLERIES:

NARBONNE (MAH) - PARIS (MAMVP): *Couple* - PARIS (MNAM-CCI): *Bathers*.

ICHENHAUSER, Natalie (Mrs)
British, 19th century.
Active in London.
Painter. Portraits, figures.

Natalie Ichenhauser exhibited her figure paintings in London. From 1889, she exhibited mainly in Suffolk Street.

ICHIAN, real name: Kano Ichian
Japanese, 16th century.
Died c. 1590.
Painter.
Kano School.

Ichian is thought to have been the father of Kano Ichio. He worked as a painter in the service of Lord Hojo.

ICHIBETSUSAI. See **TOYOKUNI II**

ICHIGA, real name: Oki Tei, nicknames: Shiguo, Shikei, pseudonyms: Ichiga, Seisai, popularly known as: Tansan, Teizo
Japanese, 19th century.
Born 1830; died 1855.
Active in Edo (now Tokyo).
Painter.

The adopted son of Oki Tanchu, Ichiga was a painter in the Kano School who worked in the service of the Tottori clan.

ICHIGOOKA, Noriyoshi
Japanese, 20th century.
Painter.

Ichigooka Noriyoshi is influenced by both traditional Japanese painting and Abstract Expressionism. He creates vast calligraphic works playing on the transparency of his colours, where his gold and black respond to his red, turquoise or green. Perfectly mastered, the paint liberally covers the canvas. He showed work in a solo exhibition at the Orangerie de Bagatelle in Paris in 1992.

ICHIHARA, Arinori
Japanese, 20th century.
Born 1910, in Tokushima (Shikoku Island).
Engraver.

From 1927 Ichihara Arinori worked at the Otaru Credit Union on Hokkaido and was a member of the Otaru Art Society. He was fascinated by the play of colour when the pigment was transferred from the woodblock to the paper. His compositions, which tend towards the Abstract, are made up of small circles and irregularly intersecting vertical and horizontal lines. In 1958 and 1959 he exhibited with the Japan Print Association and with Kokugakai (the National Painting Society), and in 1962 and 1964 showed work at the Tokyo Print Biennale.

ICHIKAWA, Sadao
Japanese, 20th century.
Born 1921, in Tokyo.
Engraver, lithographer.

Ichikawa Sadao graduated from the Kawabata Art School in 1940 and until 1947 designed children's theatre décor. He exhibited with the Japan Print Association from 1951, where he was a member and was awarded a prize in 1953. He also took part in various exhibitions of Japanese art held outside Japan, including in the former Czechoslovakia, El Salvador and the USA.

ICHIKAWA, Yo
Japanese, 20th century.
Born 5 March 1929, in Hiroshima Province.
Active in Paris from 1966.
Painter.

Ichikawa Yo graduated from the art school in Kyoto. His paintings are assemblages, mobile pictures made up of interchangeable flexible forms that can be rearranged in various ways. They are placed inside Plexiglass boxes. His aim is to allow the viewer to skim through the work, rather as one would skim through a book. His work is also somewhat decorative, as the colours he uses are very refined. He held a number of solo exhibitions in Tokyo from 1963 to 1971. From 1966 he also exhibited in Paris, as well as in various other towns and cities in France.

ICHIMARU, pseudonym: Jipposha
Japanese, 19th century.
Active in Osaka during the 1820s.
Master print-maker.

ICHINOJO. See **KORIN**

ICHINOSE, Masako
Japanese, 20th century.
Born 13 December 1937.
Engraver.

Ichinose Masako graduated from the art school in Tokyo in 1960. In 1964 she left to study in Europe, spending two years at the École des Beaux-Arts in Paris (1965-1966). From 1965 she worked at S. W. Hayter's Atelier 17 in Paris. She took part in the following group exhibitions, among others: the Salon de la Société Nationale des Artistes Français at the Musée d'Art Moderne in Paris (1965); the first Cracow Print Biennale (1966); the International Print Exhibition in Oslo (1967); and in various countries in Europe.

MUSEUMS AND GALLERIES:
BRUSSELS (Bibliothèque royale Albert Ier) - LOS ANGELES (MMA) - MONTREAL (MAM) - PARIS (BNF) - PARIS (MAM) - SAN FRANCISCO (MoMA).

ICHIO. See **KANÔ Ichio**

ICHIRAKUTEI. See **EISUI**

ICHIRYUSAI. See **TOYOKUNI II**

ICHIRYUSAI. See **TOYOHIRO**

ICHIRYUSAI. See **TOYOHARU**

ICHIRYUSAI. See **HIROSHIGE I and II**

ICHIYOAN. See **SETTAN**

ICHIYOSAI. See **EINO** and **TOYOKUNI I**

ICIAR, Juan de, or Yciar
Spanish, 16th century.
Born 1525, in Durango.
Painter, calligrapher. Ornaments.
Juan de Iciar was the author of *Practical Spelling and the Art of Writing* and other publications on calligraphy.

ICKE, Hendrik Godfried
Dutch, 19th century.
Born 1855.
Draughtsman, engraver (etching).
Hendrik Icke is mentioned in the publication *Art Prices Current.*
AUCTION RECORDS:
LONDON, 14 May 1909, *Portrait of a Woman* (1892, pen and Indian ink, after Fr. Hals) GBP 14; *Near Wijk bei Duurstede* (1898, pen and Indian ink, after J. Van Ruysdael) GBP 24; *Avenue of Ash Trees* (1898, drawing, after Jan Hackaert) GBP 23; *View of Haarlem* (1898, drawing, after J. Van Ruysdael) GBP 16.

ICKE, Johannes de. See **JEKE**

ICKLER, J.
German, 19th century.
Died 1862.
Active in Kassel.
Painter, lithographer.
The city of Kassel has an oil painting by him called *The Grey Tower at Fritzlar.*

ICKOWICZ, Mayer
Polish, 20th century.
Born in Warsaw.
Painter.
Mayer Ickowicz exhibited at the Salon des Indépendants in Paris.

IDA, Shoichi
Japanese, 20th - 21st century.
Born 1940, in Kyoto.
Painter, engraver.
Ida Shoichi graduated from the Kyoto City University of Arts. He works a good deal in lithography and silk-screen printing, using contemporary photo reportage techniques. This allows him to incorporate images taken from newspapers or other facets of daily life. He has cut himself off from any ethnic roots he might have had; which makes him a perfect example of the international Pop style, no more Japanese than American. As an artist he is not lacking in humour, and using Madison Avenue's own tools creates fake publicity images that can be either funny or disturbing.

He took part in his first exhibition at the National Museum of Modern Art in Kyoto in 1967. In 1968 he won the French Government's Prize at the 3rd Contemporary Art Competition. He exhibited at the 6th Print Biennale at the Kyoto and Tokyo Museums of Modern Art in 1968. In 1969 he exhibited at the 9th Exhibition of Japanese Art at the Tokyo Fine Arts Museum. In 1972 he took part in the 4th Cracow Print Biennale and was awarded a prize at the 2nd International Exhibition of Graphic Art in Germany. In 1973 he was at the 10th Ljubljana Biennale and in 1974 participated in the exhibition *L'Art Japonais d'Aujourd'hui (Japanese Art Today)* at the Musée d'Art Contemporain in Montreal. He has also held a number of solo exhibitions.
BIBLIOGRAPHY:
IIIe Salon international des galeries Pilotes, exhibition catalogue, Musée cantonal, Lausanne, 1970.

IDANOV. See **JDANOV**

IDE-PÉREZ, María Josefa
Spanish, 20th century.
Born 1915, in Cartagena (Murcia).
Active in Belgium.
Painter.
María Josefa Ide-Pérez studied in Antwerp, at the academy and at the higher institute of fine arts. Her anguished paintings are non-figurative.

IDELER
German, 19th century.
Born 1795, in Benditsch; died 1860.
Painter.
Mentioned by Siret.

IDELSON, Nadine
Ukrainian, 20th century.
Born in Kiev.
Painter. Landscapes, Still-lifes.
Nadine Idelson exhibited her work at the Salon des Indépendants in Paris.

IDEN, Ludwig Johann Friedrich
German, 18th century.
Born c. 1770.
Active in Berlin.
Painter. Landscapes.
He exhibited drawings and paintings at the academy in Berlin.
MUSEUMS AND GALLERIES:
BERLIN (Nationalgal.): drawings.

IDOLF, Olivier
French, 16th - 17th century.
Glass painter.

IDOUX, Charles
French, 19th century.
Born 19th century, in St-Dié.
Engraver, draughtsman.
Idoux was a pupil of Hotelin, Renier, Leloir and Best. He began his career at the Salon of 1869, and collaborated on *Le Monde Illustré (Illustrated World).*

IDOUX, Claude
French, 20th century.
Born 27 February 1915, in Lyons; died 6 January 1990, in Meudon.
Painter. Designs for tapestries.
Claude Idoux studied at the École des Beaux-Arts in Lyons. At the Salon d'Automne in Lyons, the Témoignage (Testament) group of Jean Bertholle, Albert Lenormand, Claude Idoux and several others, sought out a meeting point between the unconscious and faith. This involved a synthesis between Surrealism and sacred art. Idoux and Lenormand, after studying medieval frescoes, renewed this technique, which they then taught, seeing in it a very direct language and simplifying technique. Idoux's canvases use criss-crossing lines of colour to produce complex figures. In 1950, he showed a tapestry in the same abstract spirit, the rich colour-scheme of which accentuated the splendour of the material. He exhibited in Paris at the Salon des Indépendants in

1950, and regularly at the Salon de Mai. He participated in numerous exhibitions in France, Germany, Sweden, Denmark, North America and São Paulo. He held a solo exhibition in Paris in 1951.

IDRAC, Jean Antoine Marie
French, 19th century.
Born 14 April 1849, in Toulouse; died 1884, in Paris.
Sculptor.
Idrac studied under Guillaume and Falguière at the École des Beaux-Arts. He gained his first honourable mention in the competition for the Prix de Rome in 1869. He made his debut at the Salon in 1877 and gained a first-class medal for the third time in 1879. He was also decorated in Munich in 1885.
MUSEUMS AND GALLERIES:
CHICAGO: *Salambo* - COPENHAGEN (Ny Carlsberg Glyptotek): *Salambo* - LILLE: *Wounded Love* (bronze) - PARIS (MAM): *Wounded Love* (plaster); *Mercury Inventing the Caduceus* (marble); *Salambo* (marble) - QUIMPER: *Wounded Love* (plaster) - TOULOUSE: *Salambo* (plaster); *Mercury Inventing the Caduceus* (plaster) - VERSAILLES: *Bust of Volney*.

IDROMENO, Kole
Albanian, 19th - 20th century.
Born 1860; died 1939.
Painter. Scenes with figures, landscapes.
Kole Idromeno trained in Italy but absorbed the characteristics of Albanian art, producing work that, with its mixture of romantic, ethnographic and naive elements, represented a social statement. He depicted mainly the daily life of the people of the towns and the countryside. His works include *Wedding in Shkodër*. He was also a photographer and architect.
MUSEUMS AND GALLERIES:
TIRANA (AG): *My Sister Tone; Courtyard of a House in Shkodër.*

IDSERDA, André
Dutch, 20th century.
Born 16 March 1879, in Ter Apel; died 1952.
Painter. Portraits, interiors with figures, landscapes, architectural views, flowers.
André Idserda attended the Koninklijke Academie voor Schone Kunsten in Antwerp. His architectural views incorporated old doors.
AUCTION RECORDS:
AMSTERDAM, 18 Feb 1992, *Nasturtiums in a Ginger Jar* (oil on canvas, 15 1/2 x 13 ins / 39.5 x 33 cm) NLG 1,035. AMSTERDAM, 14-15 April 1992, *View of a Church in Assen* (oil on canvas, 28 3/4 x 37 1/2 ins / 73 x 95.5 cm) NLG 1,495. AMSTERDAM, 14 Sept 1993, *Peasants in an Interior* (oil on canvas, 19 3/4 x 25 1/2 ins / 50 x 65 cm) NLG 1,265.

IDSERTS, Pieter or Pyter, or Idsertds or Idsertz
Dutch, 18th century.
Active between 1721 and 1770.
Painter, draughtsman.
Pieter Idserts painted on faïence and worked in Francker around 1727.
MUSEUMS AND GALLERIES:
VIENNA (Albertina Mus.): *Fleet in Rough Seas.*
AUCTION RECORDS:
AMSTERDAM, 16 Nov 1981, *Ships in Port* (pen and wash, 7 1/2 x 12 3/4 ins / 19.2 x 32.3 cm) NLG 2,600. AMSTERDAM, 17 Nov 1993, *Sailing Off Schellingwoude* (1741, ink, 4 x 8in/10.3 x 20.6cm) NLG 3,680. AMSTERDAM, 15 Nov 1994, *River near Durkerdam* (ink and wash, 7 3/4 x 12 3/4in/19.7 x 32.7cm) NLG 9,200.

IDSINGA, Wilhelmina-Geertruia van
Dutch, 19th century.
Born 10 November 1788, in Leeuwarden; died 9 May 1819, in Leeuwarden.
Painter, draughtswoman.
Wilhelmina-Geertruia van Idsinga was a pupil of Baar van Slangenburgh and B. W. van der Kooi.

IDYLLS, Master ot the. See **MASTERS**

IDZOWSKI, Rosette
Egyptian, 20th century.
Born in Alexandria.
Active and naturalised in France.
Painter. Landscapes.
Idzowski was a pupil of Bissière. She exhibited in Paris at the Salon des Indépendents and the Salon d'Automne.

IE. See also for second names starting with the letters JÉ and E

IEFANOV, Vassili. See **JEFIMOVIC Vassili Prokofevich**

IEFIMOFF. See **EFIMOV**

IEFREMOV, Kim, or Iefreimov
Russian, 20th century.
Born 1933, in Orenburg.
Painter. Figure compositions, figures, nudes, Still-lifes.
Kim Iefremov studied at the school of fine art in Minsk and then at the Ilya Repin Institute in Leningrad (now St Petersburg) under the direction of Viktor M. Orechnikov. His use of colour is similar to that of Intimist painters such as Bonnard. His paintings often represent delicate and almost mannerist nudes. He was a member of the Leningrad Association of Painters and the Union of Painters of the Soviet Union.

He exhibited regularly in Moscow and Leningrad and also abroad from 1960. He took part in three exhibitions of Soviet Art in Tokyo (1976 and 1982); he was one of the *Leningrad Painters* shown in Osaka (1987). His work also featured in *Art in Leningrad*, New York (1990).
BIBLIOGRAPHY:
L'École de Léningrad, auction catalogue, Drouot, Paris, 19 November 1990.
MUSEUMS AND GALLERIES:
MOSCOW (Ministry of Culture) - MOSCOW (State Tretyakov Gal.) - OMSK (Mus. of Contemporary Soviet Art) - PETROZAVODSK (MFA) - ST PETERSBURG (Academy) - ST PETERSBURG (Gosudarstvennyj Muz. Istorii) - VIBORG (Gal. of Russian Art).
AUCTION RECORDS:
PARIS, 11 June 1990, *Nude before a Mirror* (oil on canvas, 31 1/2 x 27 1/2 ins / 80 x 70 cm) FRF 4,000. PARIS, 19 Nov 1990, *First Sun* (oil on canvas, 36 1/4 x 28 3/4 ins / 92 x 73 cm) FRF 5,000. PARIS, 18 Feb 1991, *Windsurfers* (oil on canvas, 43 1/4 x 39 1/4 ins / 110 x 100 cm) FRF 5,000. PARIS, 24 Sept 1991, *Blue Vase* (oil on canvas, 32 x 25 1/2 ins / 81 x 65 cm) FRF 8,200. PARIS, 25 Nov 1991, *On the Veranda* (oil on canvas, 19 3/4 x 25 1/2 ins / 50 x 65 cm) FRF 7,500. PARIS, 13 Dec 1993, *Lilac* (oil on canvas, 23 1/2 x 19 3/4 ins / 60 x 50 cm) FRF 5,000.

IEGORNOFF, Alexander Simionovitch. See **EGOROV Andrei Simonoviev**

IEGOROFF, Alexei Yégorovitch. See **EGOROV Alexei Egorovich**

IEGOSHIN, German
Russian, 20th century.
Born 1931, in Leningrad (now St Petersburg).
Painter. Landscapes.
Iegoshin studied at the Ilya Repin Institute in Leningrad. A member of the Association of Russian Painters, he used small strokes of colour to create an atmospheric mood.

MUSEUMS AND GALLERIES:
DRESDEN (Gemäldegal.) - MOSCOW (Ministry of Culture) - MOSCOW (State Tretyakov Gal.) - ST PETERSBURG (Gosudarstvennyj Russkij Muz.).
AUCTION RECORDS:
PARIS, 31 Jan 1994, *Aquarium* (oil on canvas, 25 1/2 x 31 1/4 ins / 64.5 x 79.5 cm) FRF 7,000. PARIS, 27 March 1994, *Crimea, Gurzuf* (oil on canvas, 30 1/4 x 26 1/4 ins / 77 x 66.5 cm) FRF 4,000.

IEKIMOFF. See **EKIMOV**

IEKIMOFF. See also **IAKIMOV**

IELMONI, Charles
Italian, 19th - 20th century.
Born in Viterbo (Latium).
Sculptor. Figures.
Ielmoni showed a portrait in plaster at the exhibition of the Société Nationale des Beaux-Arts in Paris in 1910.

IEMELIANOFF, Fedossi. See **FEDOSSEEVF Ielissei Iemelianovich**

IENDOGOUROFF. See **ENDOGUROV**

IENSENN, David Ivanovitch. See **JENSEN**

IEPEREN, Johan Hendrik van
Dutch, 20th century.
Born 1909; died 1995.
Painter. Landscapes, winter landscapes, urban landscapes, still-lifes.
AUCTION RECORDS:
AMSTERDAM, 14 Sept 1993, *Landscape with Farm* (oil on card, 18 1/2 x 25 1/4 ins / 47 x 64 cm) NLG 2,530. AMSTERDAM, 18 June 1996, *Boats in the Snow* (oil on card, 12 1/4 x 21 ins / 31 x 52.5 cm) NLG 1,610. AMSTERDAM, 19-20 Feb 1997, *Rotterdam in Winter, Night on the Front; Still-life on the Back* (oil on card, 30 1/4 x 24 3/4 ins / 77 x 63 cm) NLG 4,612. AMSTERDAM, 21 Jan 1998, *Farm in a Winter Landscape* (oil on canvas, 16 x 23 3/4 ins / 40.5 x 60.5 cm) NLG 2,537. GRAVENHAGE, 31 Oct 2000, *Flowers in a White Vase* (oil on board, 35 x 25 ins / 90 x 63 cm) NLG 5,500. GRAVENHAGE, 31 Oct 2000, *White Flowers in Vase* (oil on board, 23 x 19 ins / 58 x 48 cm) NLG 6,000. AMSTERDAM, 26 Nov 2001, *Still-life with Jug and Yellow Fruit* (oil on board, 20 x 28 ins / 50 x 70 cm) NLG 4,200. AMSTERDAM, 26 May 2003, *Still-life with Flowers in a Vase* (oil on board, 25 x 19 ins / 64 x 49 cm) EUR 4,500. AMSTERDAM, 26 May 2003, *Portrait of a Lady* (oil on board, 12 x 9 ins / 31 x 24 cm) EUR 4,600. AMSTERDAM, 3 Feb 2004, *Still-life with Blue Cloth* (oil on cardboard, 16 x 24 ins / 40 x 60 cm) EUR 1,500.

IERACE, Francesco, or Jeraces
Italian, 19th century.
Born 1854, in Polistena.
Sculptor.
Francesco Ierace was a pupil of Francesco Moroni; he exhibited in Naples, Milan and, several times, in Paris. He was one of the best Italian sculptors of the 19th century. He was an honorary professor at the school of fine art, Naples, and of the academies in Milan and Bologna. He was the brother of Gaetano and Vincenzo Ierace.
MUSEUMS AND GALLERIES:
HAVANA (MMA): *Mystic* (bronze) - NAPLES (Mus. Civico): *Woman Overcome* (marble bust) - NAPLES (Mus. Civico Gaetano Filangieri): *Gaetano Filangieri* (bust); *Woman Wearing Flowers* (marble bust) - ROME (Gal. Nazionale): *Romans* (group in marble) - ROTTERDAM (Mus. Boijmans Van Beuningen): *Head of Christ* (marble relief).

IERACE, Gaetano
Italian, 19th century.
Born 1860, in Polistena.
Landscape artist.
Gaetano Ierace was the brother of Francesco and Vincenzo Ierace. He first exhibited in Rome in 1883 and subsequently in Bologna and Naples. Among his works are landscapes and seascapes, mainly of Naples.

IERACE, Severo. See **IRACE**

IERACE, Vincenzo
Italian, 19th century.
Born 1862, in Polistena.
Sculptor, painter.
Vincenzo Ierace was a brother and pupil of Gaetano Ierace and first exhibited about 1880. He showed in Naples, Bologna and Munich, mainly animal sculptures.
MUSEUMS AND GALLERIES:
BARCELONA: *Suckling Pig* (bronze) - ROME (Arcadia): *Pius X.*

IESTAFIEFF. See **EVSTAFIEV**

IFFLAND, Franz
German, 19th century.
Active in Berlin c. 1900.
Sculptor. Statues, busts, groups.
He showed bronze statuettes on mythological subjects, genre sculptures and busts in exhibitions in Berlin (academy, international exhibition, Great Exhibition of the Fine Arts).
AUCTION RECORDS:
STOCKHOLM, 29 May 1991, *Ceres as a Young Girl with a Rake* (bronze, h. incl. base 21 1/4 ins / 54 cm) SEK 5,200. NEW YORK, 4 June 1993, *Fight between Two Buffaloes* (bronze, h. 9 ins / 22.9 cm, l. 28 1/2 ins/72.4 cm) USD 2,990. STOCKHOLM, 29 Aug 2000, *Bisons Standing* (sculpture, bronze/marble, ? x 30x? ins /? x 75x? cm) SEK 14,000. MUNICH, 21 March 2001, *Listening Figure* (sculpture, dark brown patinated bronze/marble, h. 18 ins / 46 cm) DEM 4,000. BERLIN, 19 June 2004, *Young Mother with Baby* (1887, sculpture, brown patinated bronze, h. 27 ins / 69 cm) EUR 2,850.

IFOLD, Frederick
British, 19th century.
Active in London.
Painter.
Frederick Ifold exhibited his landscapes, genre and history paintings at the Royal Academy, the British Institution and the Society of British Artists from 1846 to 1867.
AUCTION RECORDS:
LONDON, 19 Oct 1971, *Children Playing Beside the Sea,* GBP 660.

IFWARSSON, Per
Swedish, 17th century.
Sculptor (wood).
In 1649 Per Ifwarsson sculpted a chair in Bracke, and in 1650 a chair in Refsund (province of Jemtland).

IGHINA-BARBANO, Mary
Italian, 19th century.
Born 1865, in Genoa.
Sculptor.
Ighina-Barbano first exhibited in Turin in 1884 with *Dante* and *Brunelleschi.*

IGIN, Fedor Ivanovich
Russian, 19th century.
Painter.
Fedor Ivanovich Igin trained at the academy of art in St Petersburg. He took part in the academy's 1842 and 1846 exhibitions, where he showed two *Portraits of Men,* while at the 1847 exhibition he showed *Old Man Reading.* All these works are still in the academy's collection, as are his portraits of *Krylov* after Brulov and of *Batyushkov* after Kriprensky.

IGLAUER. See **EGLAUER**

IGLER, Gustav
Hungarian, 19th - 20th century.
Born 15 May 1842, in Oldenburg; died 1908 or 1938.
Painter. Genre scenes.
Gustav Igler was a pupil of Waldmuller in Vienna and of Ramberg in Munich and then taught at the Stuttgart school of fine art. He exhibited in Munich from 1879.

MUSEUMS AND GALLERIES:
STUTTGART: *Monastery School; Singing Lessons.*
AUCTION RECORDS:
VIENNA, 21 Sept 1971, *Best Friend,* ATS 55,000. NEW YORK, 28 April 1977, *Dunces' Bench* (1880, oil on canvas, 26 x 74 ins / 66 x 188 cm) USD 7,000. NEW YORK, 28 May 1981, *Dolly's Bathtime* (1867, oil on canvas, 36 1/2 x 30 1/4 ins / 93 x 77 cm) USD 22,000. VIENNA, 16 Nov 1983, *Morning Prayer* (1876, oil on canvas, 24 x 17 3/4 ins / 61 x 45 cm) ATS 280,000. NEW YORK, 28 Oct 1986, *First Cigarette* (1885, oil on canvas remounted on board, 28 1/2 x 17 ins / 72.4 x 43.2 cm) USD 5,500. NEW YORK, 19 May 1987, *Children Making a Kite* (1895, oil on canvas, 31 1/4 x 47 1/4 ins / 79.4 x 120 cm) USD 26,000. NEW YORK, 22 May 1991, *Freshly-Baked Cake* (1882, oil on canvas, 41 1/4 x 47 ins / 104.8 x 119.4 cm) USD 34,100. NEW YORK, 30 Oct 1992, *Patient Companion* (1885, oil on canvas, 36 1/4 x 26 3/4 ins / 92 x 68 cm) USD 24,200. LONDON, 20 May 1993, *Unsupervised Pupils* (1881, oil on canvas, 27 1/4 x 75 ins / 69.2 x 190.6 cm) GBP 34,500. AMSTERDAM, 22 April 1997, *First Day at School* (oil on canvas, 33 3/4 x 20 3/4 ins / 86 x 53 cm) NLG 25,960. MUNICH, 2 Dec 1997, *Dunces' Bench at School* (1913, oil on canvas, 36 1/2 x 58 1/4 ins / 92.5 x 148 cm) DEM 20,700. STOCKHOLM, 28 Nov 2000, *Summer Party in the Garden* (oil on canvas, 33 x 44 ins / 85 x 112 cm) SEK 34,000. VIENNA, 28 May 2001, *Summer's Day* (oil on canvas, 33 x 44 ins / 85 x 112 cm) ATS 60,000. BUDAPEST, 11 Sept 2002, *Girl Playing By the Piano* (oil on canvas, 26 x 20 ins / 67 x 51 cm) HUF 1,200,000. TORONTO, 14 June 2004, *Playing Mother* (1887, oil on canvas, 36 x 24 ins / 91 x 61 cm) CAD 54,000.

IGLER, Johann Wolfgang
German, 19th century.
Born 20 March 1796, in Frankfurt am Main; died 16 November 1853, in Frankfurt am Main.
Engraver.

IGLESIA, Manuel de La. See **LA IGLESIA**

IGLESIAS, Ángel
Spanish, 18th century.
Active in Seville c. 1791.
Sculptor.
There is a superb life-size crucifix signed by Ángel Iglesias in the chapel of the St Philip Neri oratory in Seville.

IGLESIAS, Cristina
Spanish, 20th - 21st century.
Born 1956, in San Sebastián.
Sculptor.
Cristina Iglesias studied at the Chelsea School of Art in London, and lives near Madrid. Her sculpture, which combines different materials such as cement, iron (which she colours) and, more recently, glass, is evocative of architecture. An interplay of thrust and counter-thrust takes place between the different elements, and a relationship of force is also established with the environment, the ground on which the sculptures take shape and the walls against which they stand. Arches, curves, columns and vaulting fill the space. Some of her works are placed so that they are above the viewer and are seen from a different angle, from below, using glass to reveal the interior. She has exhibited since 1984, notably in Lisbon, Madrid, and, in 1987, at the CAPC at the Musée d'Art Contemporain in Bordeaux.
BIBLIOGRAPHY:
Grout, Catherine, '*Cristina Iglesias, Juan Munoz: sculptures*' in *Artstudio,* periodical, Gal. Templon, Paris, autumn 1989.
MUSEUMS AND GALLERIES:
NÎMES (Carré d'Art, MAC).

IGLESIAS Y ACEVEDO, Felicindo.
See **ACEVEDO Felicindo Iglesias y**

IGNACIA D'ALMEIDA. See **ALMÉIDA Ignacia d'**

IGNACIO, Francisco. See **RUIZ DE LA IGLESIA Francisco Ignacio**

IGNATI, called Zlatyi (the Golden)
Russian, 15th century.
buried in 1442.
Icon painter.
Ignati painted icons and frescoes in the Simonov Monastery Cathedral in Moscow.

IGNATI
Russian, 15th century.
Active at Pskov.
Painter.
In 1409, with his master Antoni, Ignati worked on paintings in the Cathedral of the Holy Trinity at Pskov.

IGNATIEV, Ivan
Russian, 17th century.
Active in Yaroslavl.
Icon painter.
Called to the court at Moscow, Ivan Ignatiev painted icons and murals in the Kremlin.

IGNATIEV, Vasili
Russian, 17th century.
Icon painter.
In 1643, Vasili Ignatiev executed a number of paintings in the Cathedral of the Dormition, Moscow.

IGNATIEV, Vasili Petrovich
Russian, 18th century.
Born 1698.
Painter.
In 1729, Vasili Petrovich Ignatiev worked on the Cathedral of Sts Peter and Paul in St Petersburg. He may be the same as the artist of the same name who painted four pictures for the same cathedral in 1730 (*Judas' Kiss, The Road to Golgotha, Crucifixion,* and *Entombment*). In 1740-1741, he executed paintings for Princess Anna Leopoldovna's bedroom in the Winter Palace.

IGNATIUS, Otto Friedrich
Estonian, 19th century.
Born 1794, in Haggers; died 1824, in St Petersburg.
Painter. History painting, genre scenes.
Otto Friederich Ignatius trained under K.S. Walther. He was also a poet and composer.
MUSEUMS AND GALLERIES:
ST PETERSBURG (Hermitage): *Eleonora d'Este Rewarding Tasso for his Poem.*

IGNATIV, Piotr
Russian, 20th century.
Born 1945.
Painter. Still-lifes.
Piotr Ignativ studied at the academy of fine arts in Leningrad (St Petersburg) and became a member of the association of Leningrad painters. He paints using a traditional style.
MUSEUMS AND GALLERIES:
MOSCOW (Ministry of Culture) - ST PETERSBURG (Academy of Fine Art).

IGNATSIUS, Vasili Vasilevich
Russian, 19th century.
Watercolourist.

A naval officer, Vasili Vasilevich Ignatsius had also trained at the academy of art in St Petersburg, and showed his watercolours, mostly of men o'war, at exhibitions of the Society of Russian Watercolourists.

MUSEUMS AND GALLERIES:
ST PETERSBURG (Gosudarstvennyj Russkij Muz.): *Wartime Port* (watercolour).

IGOCHEV, Vladimir
Russian, 20th century.
Born 1921, in Askino.
Painter. Figures, local scenes, interiors.

Vladimir Igochev studied at the Sukirov Art Institute in Moscow. He became a member of the Union of Painters of the USSR in 1944. He began exhibiting in 1943. Solo exhibitions include: Moscow and Leningrad (now St Petersburg) in 1964 and 1965; Tokyo (1977); Budapest (1978); Bratislava (1983). He was awarded the Russian Federation Repin State Prize in 1982.

MUSEUMS AND GALLERIES:
MOSCOW (State Tretyakov Gal.) - ST PETERSBURG (Gosudarstvennyj Russkij Muz.).

IGOE, Bert A.
American, 19th - 20th century.
Born c. 1868; died 1945, in New York.
Draughtsman.

IGON, Pierre
French, 20th century.
Born 4 August 1922, in Toulouse.
Painter.

In 1949 Pierre Igon settled in Paris, accompanied by André Marfaing and François Jousselin. His first paintings were Expressionist and figurative, close to a certain emphasis on the miserable. He depicted rocky landscapes, with animals, evoking an enclosed, frozen world. He turned to sacred art for a time, before gradually moving towards non-figurative work. He mainly uses blacks, blue-greys and earth-tones. He creates an often centrally focused or concentric space, made up of verticals and horizontals on which non-geometric graphics may be disposed. He favours a broad, gesture-oriented calligraphy, and sometimes makes use of forms and rhythms like ideograms. He began exhibiting regularly in 1959. He first showed at the Salon d'Automne in 1948, and regularly exhibited there after 1963.

IGONET, Maria Maddalena, or Igonnet
French, 18th century.
Born 18th century, in Genoa.
Active in Paris between 1752 and 1767.
Engraver (burin).

Maria Maddalena Igonet engraved genre subjects after such artists as Boucher and Jeurat.

IGORAND
French, 20th century.
Painter (mixed media). Figures, scenes with figures.

Igorand exhibited in 1986 at the Salon de Montrouge. His figurative painting is vividly coloured, with somewhat naive tonalities.

AUCTION RECORDS:
PARIS, 13 April 1988, *Head* (oil/granite, 9¾ x 11¾ ins / 25 x 30 cm) FRF 1,800.

IGOREV, Lev Stepanovich
Russian, 19th century.
Born 1823; died after 1881.
Painter.

MUSEUMS AND GALLERIES:
MOSCOW (State Tretyakov Gal.): *Chinese Beggars* - SARATOV (Radishchev Museum): *Portrait of a Man of the Church*.

IGOU, André
French, 18th century.
Active in Paris in 1752.
Painter, sculptor.

IGOUNET DE VILLERS, Charles André
French, 20th century.
Born 30 November 1881, in Paris; died 12 February 1944, in Paris.
Painter. Landscapes. Designs for tapestries.

Charles André Igounet de Villers made his début in Paris in 1902 at the Salon des Indépendants. From 1914, he showed at the Salon de la Société Nationale des Beaux-Arts and the Salon des Tuileries. It was to the Salon des Indépendants, of which he was vice-president, that he would remain the most attached, vowing to maintain its traditions of allowing artists their creative freedom while offering no material reward ('sans jury ni récompenses'). This led to his vice-presidency of the Société du Droit d'Auteur aux Artistes. He founded the Syndicat Professionnel des Arts Graphiques et Plastiques and also assumed the general secretariat of the Salon des Peintres du Paris Moderne. He produced numerous Parisian landscapes and also executed a large tapestry cartoon, *Goodbye Fortifications*, a work expressing his enduring feeling for his native city. He is also known for *Construction of the Underground* and his canvases of Belle-Île.

MUSEUMS AND GALLERIES:
PARIS (Mus. Carnavalet).

IGUAL RUIZ, Enrique
Spanish, 20th century.
Born 1896, in Valencia; died 1974.
Painter. Landscapes, still-lifes.

Enrique Igual Ruiz studied at the Academia de San Carlos in Valencia. He spent many years in Switzerland, showing his works in group and solo exhibitions in Bern, Lausanne, Paris, Barcelona and other cities. In 1926, he won the bronze medal of the National Society of Fine Arts for *Evening*, and in 1929, he exhibited at the museum of modern art in Madrid.

Igual Ruiz's chief source of inspiration was the mountainous countryside of the Madrid region, and also of Switzerland, Majorca and Granada. In his landscapes, he placed the greatest importance on effects of light.

BIBLIOGRAPHY:
Arnáiz, José Manuel/López Jiménez, Javier/Merchán Díaz, Manuel (ed.), '*Cien años de pintura en Espana y Portugal (1830-1930)*' in vol. IV, Antiqvaria, Madrid, 1990.

IGUCHI, Kashu
Japanese, 19th - 20th century.
Born 1880; died 1930.
Painter. Animals.

Iguchi Kashu essentially painted fish.

IGUEL, Auguste Vincent
French, 19th century.
Born 1830, in Paris.
Sculptor.

Auguste Iguel was a pupil of Rude. He exhibited at the Salon from 1864 to 1878, specialising in busts. He contributed to the production of the monuments erected in memory of Joseph Court in Rouen and to the monument dedicated to E.H. Langlois at the Pont de l'Arche.

MUSEUMS AND GALLERIES:
ROUEN: *Memorial of Joseph Court* (model).

IGUEL, Charles François Marie
French, 19th century.

Born 3 January 1827, in Paris; died 29 December 1897, in Geneva.
Sculptor.

The catalogue of the Rath museum in Geneva claims that Charles Iguel came from Neuchâtel and was born in 1829, but these details of his date and place of birth are merely those supplied when he was admitted to the École des Beaux-Arts in Paris, where he became a pupil in Rude's studio on 2 October 1844. His work was displayed at the Salon from 1848 to 1872, and he gained medals in 1864, 1868 and 1889, the year of the Exposition Universelle. His most important works are: *Resurrection of Christ* (low relief adorning the high altar of the church of Saint Elizabeth), *Bernard Palissy* (marble bust), *St Albert* (statue carved in stone), *The Hunter* (stone statue which stands in a courtyard of the Louvre), *Jacquard* (marble bust at the ministry of fine arts), *Ploughman* (marble statue situated in the Tuileries palace), *Commerce and Navigation* (the large frontage of the new residence of the *préfet* in Lille), *Literature, Science, the Chancellor of Montmolin, Emer de Vatel, Ostervald; the Stone Canon* (statues carved in stone at the Roman Catholic high school in Neuchâtel), *Memorial to the Duke of Brunswick* (in Geneva).

MUSEUMS AND GALLERIES:

GENEVA (MAH): *Guillaume Farel* (design); *Moses; Sesostris; Solon* - LAON: *Autumn* - NEUCHÂTEL: *Leopold Robert; Alexandre Calame; Karl Girardet; Edouard Girardet; Auguste Henri Berthoud; Auguste Bachelin; Stone Canon; Minister Osterwald; The Chancellor of Montmolin; Legal Counsel Emer de Vatel* - ROUBAIX: *Foundation of the First Charitable Organisation in Roubaix* (relief, plaster model); *Ernoult Bayard, Mayor of Roubaix* (plaster bust); *Saint Albert* (plaster model); *J.M. Jacquard* (plaster bust) - VALENCE: *Nymph* (marble bust); *General Championnet* (model) - VERSAILLES: *Houdon* (marble bust).

IHACHI, given name: Naraya
Japanese, 18th - 19th century.
Active c. 1824.
Painter.

Ihachi is recorded as a master print-maker who directed *ukiyo-e* production in Kyoto and lived and worked in Osaka.

IHLE. See also **IHLEE**

IHLE, Hans Joachim
German, 20th century.
Born 21 December 1919, in Berlin.
Sculptor. Animals.

Hans Joachim Ihle regularly held solo exhibitions in Germany, notably in 1992 at the Kunsthaus Bühler in Stuttgart. He produced animals in polished marble, using varieties of colours.

IHLE, Johann Eberhard
German, 18th - 19th century.
Born 1727, in Esslingen; died 1814, in Nuremberg.
Painter. Portraits, genre scenes, local scenes.

The son and pupil of Johann Jakob Ihle, he was director of the academy in Nuremberg in 1771. A portrait painter, he also did a number of everyday scenes.

MUSEUMS AND GALLERIES:

MUNICH (Bayerisches Nationalmus.): *C F Weisse* (miniature/wood); *M A von Thümmel* (miniature/wood); *Poet F G Klopstock* (miniature/wood) - NUREMBERG: *M Burckhardt; S Holzschuher; Paulus Pauschinger.*

AUCTION RECORDS:

PARIS, 28 Feb 1919, *Portrait of a Woman*, FRF 720. MUNICH, 27 Feb 1999, *Self-portrait* (oil on canvas, 11 x 9 ins / 27 x 23 cm) DEM 9,000. LONDON, 18 April 2000, *Chariot of Silenus* (1781, oil on canvas, 32 x 37 ins / 82 x 95 cm) GBP 11,000.

IHLE, Johann Jakob
German, 18th century.
Born 19 June 1702; died 23 April 1774.
Painter. Portraits.

He worked in Esslingen. His father and sons were likewise painters of minor importance in the same town.

IHLEE, Eduard Johann
German, 19th century.
Born 22 October 1812, in Kassel; died 15 February 1885, in Kassel.
Painter. History painting.

A pupil of Schadow in Düsseldorf and Philip Veit in Frankfurt, he travelled around Italy, notably to Rome, and did several paintings for the chapel at the Prussian embassy. On his return, he was appointed to the staff of the academy in Kassel. The museum in Kassel contains most of the copies he did of Raphael, Michelangelo, Titian, Veronese, Guido Reni etc in Italy. Probably the same artist as the history painter called Ihle (no first name) who was at work c. 1839.

MUSEUMS AND GALLERIES:

MAINZ: *St Louis Founding the Hospital in Compiègne* - STUTTGART: *Moses Saved from the Waters.*

AUCTION RECORDS:

NEW YORK, 26 May 1983, *Portrait of the Mangold Family* (1848, oil on canvas, 25 3/4 x 34 1/4 ins / 65.5 x 87 cm) USD 4,000.

IHLEE, Rudolf Ernest Charles
British, 20th century.
Born 24 January 1883, in Wimbledon; died 25 September 1968, in Peterborough.
Painter, draughtsman. Figures, scenes with figures, landscapes with figures, seascapes. Models for furniture and fabrics.

Rudolf Ernest Charles Ihlee was born into a large family that emigrated from Bismarck's Germany to England, settling in Wimbledon. Ihlee trained at the Slade School of Fine Art in London. During World War I and II he was employed as a designer in the arms industry. In the inter-war years he settled in Collioure in south-west France, but returned to England following the French defeat at the beginning of World War II. His work is a mixture of naturalism in the classical tradition and simplified forms.

He exhibited with the New English Art Club, of which he became a member in 1920, and the Salon des Indépendants in Paris. His work was also the subject of a number of solo exhibitions, including: 1912, début exhibition, Carfax Gallery, London; 1914, Carfax Gallery, London; 1921, Leicester Galleries, London; 1926, Chenil Gallery, London; 1931, 1932 Galerie Campistro, Perpignan; 1934, 1935, Salle Arago, Perpignan; 1951, St Peter's College Hall, Peterborough, an exhibition organised by the Arts Council of Great Britain; 1968, Sleaford; 1975, Rutland Sixth Form College, Oakham; 1978, double exhibition at Graves Art Gallery Sheffield and the Belgrave Gallery, London.

BIBLIOGRAPHY:

Grose, Irving, *Rudolphe Ihlee 1883-1968*, exhibition catalogue, Belgrave Gallery, London, 1978.

MUSEUMS AND GALLERIES:

GLASGOW (AG and Mus.) - LONDON (Victoria and Albert Mus.) - MANCHESTER (City AG).

AUCTION RECORDS:

LONDON, 30 April 1986, *Breton Peasants* (1913, oil on canvas, 36 x 28 ins / 91.5 x 71 cm) GBP 1,600. LONDON, 12 June 1987, *View from the Bedroom Window* (1925, oil on canvas, 25 x 30 ins / 63.5 x 76.2 cm) GBP 3,000. LONDON, 21 Sept 1989, *Sunlit Houses* (oil on card, 14 1/4 x 10 3/4 ins / 36.2 x 27.3 cm) GBP 660. LONDON, 9 March 1990, *Les Deux 'Crodeuses'* (1921, oil on canvas, 19 x 23 ins / 48.1 x 58.4 cm) GBP 3,850. LONDON, 2 May 1991, *Landscape with Cat* (1926, oil on canvas, 32 x 38 ins / 81 x 96.5 cm) GBP 1,980. LONDON, 27 Sept 1994, *Woman Knitting in a Meadow* (1913, oil on panel, 13¾ x 10 ins / 35 x 25.5 cm) GBP 747. LONDON, 5 Nov 1999, *New Shoes* (oil on canvas, 20 x 24 ins / 51 x 61 cm) GBP 1,800. LONDON, 22 Nov 2000, *Landscape, South of France* (oil on canvas, 19 x 23 ins / 48 x 59 cm) GBP 1,500. LONDON, 6 Dec 2000, *Avenue, Collioure* (1925, oil on canvas, 30 x 25 ins / 76 x 64 cm) GBP 2,200. LONDON, 22 March 2001, *Provence* (oil on canvas, 18 x 22 ins / 46 x 55 cm) GBP 2,000. LONDON, 13 June 2002, *Two Embroideresses* (oil on canvas, 20 x 24 ins / 51 x 61 cm) GBP 2,000. LONDON, 15 June 2004, *Landscape* (1925, oil on canvas, 20 x 24 ins / 51 x 61 cm) GBP 2,000. LONDON, 24 Nov 2004, *Ullapool, Seascape* (on paper, 18 x 22 ins / 46 x 55 cm) GBP 1,700.

IHLEFELD, Henry
Painter. Genre scenes.
Henry Ihlefeld is mentioned by Florence Levy.
AUCTION RECORDS:
NEW YORK, 3 March 1904, *Among the Daisies,* USD 106. LONDON, 13 Feb 1991, *Bath Time* (oil on canvas, 13¼ x 19¼ ins / 33.5 x 49 cm) GBP 2,310. ELGIN (ILLINOIS), 22 Feb 2003, *Portrait of a Young Girl* (1890, watercolour, 15x11 ins / 38x28 cm) USD 400.

IHLY, Daniel, or Jean Daniel
Swiss, 19th - 20th century.
Born 1854, in Geneva; died January 1910, in Geneva.
Active in France.
Painter. Genre scenes, landscapes, urban landscapes.
Daniel Ihly studied under Barthélemy Menn. He lived in Paris, and also visited London and Florence. Ihly exhibited at Salons held in Bern, Zurich and Paris. In 1887, he won a medal in Dijon; he also won a medal at the 1900 Exposition Universelle in Paris and in St-Étienne in 1905. He was known primarily for his Parisian landscapes, painted in grey tones.

MUSEUMS AND GALLERIES:
FRIBOURG: *Ploughing* - GENEVA (MAH): *Banks of the River Arve in Autumn; Street in Yvoire* - LA CHAUX-DE-FONDS: *Spring in Vandoeuvres* - LE LOCLE: *Pond* - NEUCHÂTEL: *Absinthe Drinker.*
AUCTION RECORDS:
BERN, 18 Nov 1972, *Village Street,* CHF 3,000. LUCERNE, 21 June 1974, *Lake Geneva,* CHF 3,600. BERN, 7 May 1976, *The Seine at Billancourt* (1889, oil on canvas, 12½ x 18 ins / 32 x 46 cm) CHF 1,000. ZURICH, 11 May 1978, *Woman Sitting on the Balcony* (oil on canvas, 23½ x 19¼ ins / 60 x 49 cm) CHF 2,400. BERN, 3 May 1979, *Geneva Landscape* (oil on canvas, 26½ x 36¼ ins / 67.5 x 92 cm) CHF 2,900. ZURICH, 14 May 1983, *Banks of the River Marne, Champigny* (oil on canvas, 16¼ x 20¾ ins / 41 x 53 cm) CHF 4,800. BERN, 25 Oct 1986, *View of Geneva* (oil on canvas, 24¾ x 36¼ ins / 63 x 92 cm) CHF 9,000.

IHRWACH, Sebastian. See **IRRWOCH**

IHWARTS
German, 19th century.
Active in Germany.
Engraver (burin).
He engraved plates for the legend of Frithiof (*Illustration zur Frithiofsage*).

IIDA, Shinshichi
Japanese, 20th century.
Born in Kyoto.
Painter (silk), mixed media artist. Waterscapes.
Iida Shinshichi took part in the 1906 exhibition in Nice. He worked on silk, embroidering his pictures.
MUSEUMS AND GALLERIES:
NICE (Mus. de la Ville): *Marsh Fowl at the Approach of a Storm.*

IIDA, Toko
Japanese, 19th century.
Active in Tokyo.
Painter (silk).
Toko Iida featured in the Exposition Universelle in Paris in 1900.

IIDA, Yoshikuni
Japanese, 20th century.
Born 1923.
Painter.
Pop Art.
Yoshikuni Iida was awarded the prize at the exhibition Contemporary Japanese Art organised by the *Mainichi* newspaper in Tokyo in 1968, and in 1969 the Grand Prix at the first Suma open air exhibition of sculpture. In 1974 he took part in the exhibition *Japanese Art of Today* in Montreal, and had a solo exhibition in New York.
BIBLIOGRAPHY:
Elliott, David/Kaido, Kazu (eds.), *Reconstructions: Avant-Garde Art in Japan 1945-1965,* Museum of Modern Art, Oxford, 1985.

IIMURA, Taka, for Takahiko
Japanese, 20th century.
Born 20 February 1937, in Tokyo.
Active from 1975 in the USA.
Painter, performance artist.
Iimura moved to New York in 1975, after numerous visits. Particularly interested in video, which enabled him to associate images and language, he took part in a large number of group exhibitions: in 1966, 1978 and 1983 at the Museum of Modern Art in New York, in 1971 at the Tokyo Biennale Arts Festival, in 1974 at the Kunsthalle in Cologne and in 1987 at the Museum of Modern Art in San Francisco. Mainly presenting films accompanied by performances, he has mounted numerous solo exhibitions: in 1969 at the ICA (Institute of Contemporary Art) in London; in 1975 and 1983 at the Museum of Modern Art in New York; in 1977 at the Stedelijk Museum in Amsterdam; in 1978 at the Carnegie Institute in Pittsburgh; in 1979 at the Whitney Museum in New York and at the Musée National d'Art Moderne in Paris; in 1980 at the Palais des Beaux-Arts in Brussels; in 1982 at the contemporary art centre in Osaka; and in 1985 at the multimedia centre in Zagreb.
MUSEUMS AND GALLERIES:
AACHEN (Ludwig Forum für Internationale Kunst) - BERLIN (Neuer Berliner Kunstverein) - PARIS (MNAM-CCI) - TOKYO (Hara MCA) - TOKYO (Metropolitan Art Mus.).

IJE. See for second names starting with the letters IYE

IJKENS, Catharina, or Eycken or Ykens
Flemish School, 17th century.
Baptised 24 February 1659 in Antwerp.
Painter. Flowers, fruit.
Catharina IJkens was the daughter of Jan IJkens and was taught by her father. Some biographers believe, incorrectly, that she was the ninth daughter of Peeter IJkens, but this is not possible as Peeter IJkens was born in 1648.
MUSEUMS AND GALLERIES:
MADRID: *Virgin and Child with St John the Baptist as a Boy; Jesus and St Theresa* - MUNICH: *Garland of Flowers around a Nativity Scene by Jan van der Hoecke.*
AUCTION RECORDS:
LONDON, 1 Nov 1996, *Bust Painting of a Lady Playing a Lute on a Box of Fruit* (oil on panel, 16¼ x 11in/41 x 27.7cm) GBP 14,950.

IJKENS, Frans, or Eyckens or Ykens
Flemish School, 17th century.
Baptised on 17 April 1601 in Antwerp; died before 27 February 1693, in Brussels.
Painter. Religious subjects, allegorical subjects, animals, still-lifes (flowers, fruit).

Frans IJkens studied under his uncle Osias Beert, and worked for a time in Aix and Marseilles. He taught Gilliam Dandoys and Hendrick de Cleys.

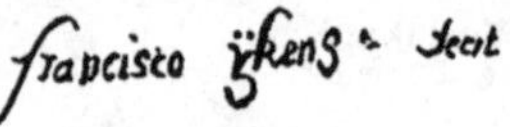

MUSEUMS AND GALLERIES:
DIEPPE: *Lady with the Attributes of Flora and Cherubs* - LEIPZIG: *Still-life* - MADRID: *Still-life* - ROHRAU (Schlossmus., Graf Harrach'sche Familiensammlung): *Still-life* - ROTTERDAM: *Garland of Flowers and Mystical Marriage of St Catherine* - VIENNA (NM): *Flowers* - VIENNA (Schönborn-Buckheim): *Flowers*.

AUCTION RECORDS:
LONDON, 12 Oct 1979, *Still-life with Flowers* (oil on canvas remounted/panel, 22 3/4 x 17in/58 x 43cm) GBP 3,800. LONDON, 11 Dec 1984, *Flowers in a Glass Vase and Butterfly on a Ledge* (oil on panel, 24 x 16 1/2in/61 x 42cm) GBP 38,000. PARIS, 8 March 1985, *Vase of Flowers and Butterflies* (oil on panel, 19 3/4 x 15 1/4in/50 x 38.5cm) FRF 300,000. MONTE CARLO, 7 Dec 1987, *Still-life with Flowers, Fruit, Sparrows and Partridges* (oil on canvas, 34 1/4 x 48 1/2in/86.7 x 123.2cm) FRF 650,000. PARIS, 14 April 1989, *Garland of Flowers and Fruit around a Central Medallion of the Virgin and Child with St John the Baptist* (oil on canvas, 45 1/4 x 38 1/4in/115 x 97cm) FRF 120,000. LONDON, 3 July 1991, *Still-life with Carnations, Roses and Other Flowers in a Glass Vase; Still-life with Roses, a Carnation, a Tulip and Other Flowers in a Glass Vase* (oil/copper, a pair, each 14 1/2 x 11 1/2in/37 x 29cm) GBP 63,800. AMSTERDAM, 14 Nov 1991, *Still-life with Shrimps, Roast Chicken and Oysters on Pewter Dishes by a Basket of Fruit and a Blue and White Faïence Ewer* (oil on canvas, 34 x 45 1/2in/85.5 x 115.5cm) NLG 87,400. PARIS, 15 April 1992, *Still-life with Oysters and Flowers in a Vase on a Table* (oil on panel, 9 1/2 x 13 1/2in/24 x 34.5cm) FRF 40,000. NEW YORK, 19 May 1993, *Roses, Carnations, Tulip and Other Flowers in a Glass Vase with a Butterfly; Carnations, Roses and Other Flowers with a Fly in a Glass Vase* (oil/copper, a pair, 16 x 12in/40.7 x 30.5cm) USD 66,300. STOCKHOLM, 30 Nov 1993, *Still-life with Oysters, Bread and a Peeled Lemon on a Table* (oil on panel, 16 1/2 x 25 1/4in/42 x 64cm) SEK 85,000. LONDON, 11 Dec 1996, *Still-life with Roses, Lilies, Tulips and Other Flowers in a Vase with a Butterfly* (oil on panel, 32 3/4 x 23 1/2in/83 x 60cm) GBP 106,000. LONDON, 2 July 1997, *St Francis and St Catherine Holding a Picture of the Virgin and Child Surrounded by Garlands of Flowers Carried by Putti* (c. 1650, oil/copper, in collaboration with Cornelis Schut, 38 1/2 x 31 1/2in/97.8 x 80cm) GBP 11,500. LONDON, 8 July 1999, *Still-life with Peaches, Grapes and Other Fruit in Bowl. Still-life with Pie and Lemon* (oil on copper, a pair, 16 x 21 ins / 41 x 54 cm) GBP 40,000. LONDON, 8 July 1999, *Still-life with Cheese in a Wicker Basket, Jug, Rummer, Figs, Plums and a Dish of Strawberries* (oil on panel, 22 x 31 ins / 57 x 80 cm) GBP 42,000. LONDON, 12 July 2001, *Virgin and Child attended by Angels, within a Cartouche adorned with Fruit and Flowers* (oil on canvas, 22 x 26 ins / 55 x 66 cm) GBP 10,500. LONDON, 13 Dec 2001, *Still-life with Garland of Fruit and Flowers around a Child* (1648, oil on panel, 35 x 28 ins / 88 x 70 cm) GBP 8,000. LONDON, 11 Dec 2002, *Grapes on the Vine and Other Fruit on a Table with Butterfly* (oil on copper, 15 x 20 ins / 37 x 50 cm) GBP 65,000. LONDON, 12 Dec 2002, *Flowers, Fruit, Baskets, Figures through a Window and a Parrot* (oil on canvas, 64 x 92 ins / 163 x 234 cm) GBP 90,000. HEIDELBERG, 10 Oct 2003, *Still-life with Flowers Including Roses, Tulips and Insects* (oil on panel, 24 x 16 ins / 62 x 40 cm) EUR 41,000. AMSTERDAM, 5 Nov 2003, *Virgin and Child with the Young St John the Baptist, surrounded by a Cartouche* (oil on panel, 29 x 22 ins / 73 x 56 cm) EUR 12,000. NEW YORK, 22 Jan 2004, *Still-life with Peaches, Grapes, Pomegranates, Figs and Wild Strawberries in a Porcelain Bowl. Still-life* (oil on copper, a pair, 16 x 21 ins / 41 x 54 cm) USD 80,000.

IJKENS, Jan, or Eyckens or Ykens
Flemish School, 17th century.
Born 19 December 1613, in Antwerp.
Sculptor, painter.

Jan IJkens studied sculpture under his father Melchior IJkens. He was a free-master sculptor and student painter from 1665 to 1668, and painted under the direction of his friend David Ryckaert. His painting *Allegory in Honour of the Birth of a Prince* is in the Antwerp museum.

IJKENS, Jan Peter, or Ykens or Eyckens
Flemish School, 17th century.
Baptised on 4 July 1673 in Antwerp
in Brussels.
Painter.

Jan Peter IJkens was the oldest son of Peter IJkens. In 1691, he won first prize for drawing at the academy.

MUSEUMS AND GALLERIES:
TOULOUSE: *Cherubs Enclosing a Landscape by P. Rysbrack.*

IJKENS, Karel, or Eyckens
Flemish School, 17th century.
Baptised on 3 February 1682 in Antwerp.
Painter.

Karel IJkens may have been the son of Peter IJkens but should not be confused with Karel Eyckens, born in 1719. He was a master artist in Brussels in 1718. One of his works is in the church of St Gudule in Brussels.

IJKENS, Melchior, or Ykens
Flemish School, 17th century.
Active in Antwerp in 1610.
Painter.

Melchior IJkens was the father of Jan IJkens.

IJKENS, Peter, or Eyckens or Ykens
Flemish School, 17th century.
Baptised on 30 January 1648 in Antwerp; died 1695, in Antwerp.
Painter. Religious subjects, mythological subjects, portraits.

Peter IJkens was taught by his father Jan IJkens, and became a free-master in 1673.

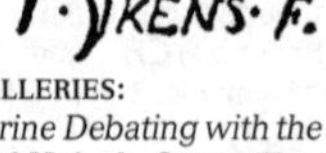

MUSEUMS AND GALLERIES:
ANTWERP: *St Catherine Debating with the Doctors; J. B. Greyns; St C. Janssen of Hujoel* - LILLE: *The Stigmatization of St Theresa* - ORLÉANS: *Diana and Apollo* - THE HAGUE: *Christ and the Roman Captain.*

IJU, real name: Konishi Mitsukore
Japanese, 18th century.
Active in Kyoto.
Painter.

Iju was a painter of the Korin School.

IKAI, Shokoku or Shikoku, real name: Ukichi Ikai
Japanese, 20th century.
Born 1881; died 1939.
Active in Japan.
Painter.

IKAM, Catherine
French, 20th - 21st century.
Born 1948, in Paris.
Sculptor, environmental artist, video artist.
Computer Art (Virtual Art).

Catherine Ikam makes sculptures and virtual environments in which she conjures up three-dimensional images. She participates in collective exhibitions. Solo exhibitions of her work include: Jesuit chapel, Nîmes, Musée des Jacobins, Morlaix, 1991; Universal Exhibition in Seville, Kunstverein, Bonn, 1992; École Nationale des Beaux-Arts, Paris, Tate Gallery, Liverpool and Wilhelm-Lehmbruck Museum, Duisberg, 1993 and Lyons Biennale, 1995, where she showed *Portraits Virtuels en Forme de Collection Particulière* (*Virtual Portraits in the Form of a Special Collection*).

BIBLIOGRAPHY:
Fargier, Jean-Paul, '*Catherine Ikam, Paul Virilio*' in *Art Press*, n° 185, periodical, Paris, November 1993.

IKEDA, Keisen, real name: Katsujiro Ikeda, pseudonym: Keisen
Japanese, 20th century.
Born 1863; died 1931.
Painter.

Keisen Ikeda featured in the exhibition *L'Art japonais*, held at the Musée du Jeu de Paume, Paris, in 1929.

IKEDA, Kotaro
Japanese, 20th century.
Painter.

Kotaro Ikeda featured in the exhibition *L'Art japonais*, held at the Musée du Jeu de Paume, Paris, in 1929.

IKEDA, Masuo
Japanese, 20th century.
Born 1934, in Mukden, Manchuria (now Shenyang, Liaoning), China; died 8 March 1997.
Engraver, writer.

Masuo Ikeda graduated with a diploma from the art school in Nagano in 1952, and then set up in Tokyo. He is a copper and wood engraver, as well as a silk-screen printer, and is considered one of the most brilliant 20th-century Japanese engravers. Having started in his youth as an oil painter in a style showing the influence of Matisse and Picasso, he then found engraving to be a more suitable medium. The technique of dry point in particular enables him to express his images and thoughts more directly, in a way that is more intimate and warm than with oils. Engraving has the further advantage of benefiting from wider exposure than a painting produced in a single copy. His figurative works are near to everyday life, out of which he produces a sort of poem in colour, drawing inspiration from both Western and Eastern traditions. There is often an underlying eroticism. He was also a writer, and his novel *Egekai ni Sasagu* (*Homage to the Aegean*) won the prestigious Akutagawa prize in 1977 and was later made into a film.

For two years (1965-1966) he lived in New York, where a solo exhibition was devoted to him at the Museum of Modern Art, and in 1967 he set up in Berlin, moving back to New York in 1972. From 1957 he featured regularly at the Biennale international print festival in Tokyo, where he won the prize awarded by the ministry of education in 1960, the prize donated by the governor of Tokyo in 1962 and the prize of the national museum of modern art in 1964. In 1963, he featured in the São Paulo Biennale, and in 1965 in the exhibition *Modern Japanese Painting*, held in Zurich. From its creation, he took part in the exhibitions of the Japan art festival association. In 1961 he won first prize at the Biennale Internationale des Jeunes in Paris, in 1965 the fourth major prize at the Ljubljana Biennale for engraving, and in 1966 the main prize at the Cracow Biennale for engraving and the engraving prize at the Venice Biennale.

MUSEUMS AND GALLERIES:
NAGANO (Masuo Ikeda museum): substantial collection.

AUCTION RECORDS:
NEW YORK, 27 April 1994, *Seven Deadly Sins* (1973, rubbing and watercolour, 9 1/2 x 9 1/4 ins / 24.1 x 23.5 cm) USD 4,370.

IKEDA, Shuzo
Japanese, 20th century.
Born 1922, in Akita Prefecture.
Engraver.

Shuzo Ikeda graduated with a diploma from the training college for art teachers in Tokyo in 1945, and then became an art teacher in Akita. He set up in Tokyo in 1955, and devoted himself to engraving, working in a figurative style. He mounted several solo exhibitions in the USA and in 1957 was awarded the Kobayashi prize at the exhibition of the Japanese printing association, of which he is a member.

IKEDA, Tatsuo
Japanese, 20th century.
Born 1928, on Kyushu.
Painter.

Tatsuo Ikeda entered the Tama school of fine art in Tokyo in 1948 and in 1949 joined the society for research into avant-garde art, founded by Taro Okamato and Abe. He exhibited in Tokyo from 1954. In 1956 he took part in the exhibition *Japanese Art of Today* in Tokyo and in 1958 in the exhibition *Satirical Art* at the museum of modern art in Tokyo. He travelled to Europe in 1967, and took part in the exhibition *Against the War in Vietnam*.

IKEDA, Yoshinobu. See **EISEN**

IKEDA, Yoshishige
Japanese, 20th century.
Born 1918, in Saitama Prefecture.
Painter.

Yoshishige Ikeda began research into painting in 1965 at the institute of contemporary art in Tokyo.

IKEDA, Yoson
Japanese, 20th century.
Born 1895.
Painter.

Yoson Ikeda featured in the exhibition *L'Art japonais*, held at the Musée du Jeu de Paume in Paris in 1929.

IKEGAMI, Shuho, real name: Kunisaburo Ikegami, pseudonym: Shuho
Japanese, 19th - 20th century.
Born 1874; died 1944.
Painter. Landscapes.

Shuho Ikegami featured in the exhibition *L'Art japonais*, held at the Musée du Jeu de Paume, Paris, in 1929. He painted in traditional style.

AUCTION RECORDS:
NEW YORK, 29 March 1990, *Rain on the Pool* (ink and diluted pigments/silk, 28 x 33 3/4 ins / 71 x 86 cm) USD 22,000.

IKEMURA, Leiko
Japanese, 20th - 21st century.
Born 1951.
Active in Germany.
Painter, sculptor, draughtswoman, watercolourist.
Figures.
Symbolism.

Leiko Ikemura lives in Cologne and Berlin, where she teaches painting at the Hochschule der Künste. She started to become known in the 1980s, notably in Switzerland. Her style, related to the new Expressionism of the beginning of the 1980s, has veered towards Symbolism. The central figures of her mythology are a little girl and a cat, and her magical universe is bathed in metamorphoses between the animal, vegetable and human kingdoms. She shows her works in solo

exhibitions, including *Leiko Ikemura: The Light Years,* held at the Musée Cantonal des Beaux-Arts in Lausanne in 2001.
BIBLIOGRAPHY:
Zenner, Roman (ed.), *Leiko Ikemura: Memory of Innocence,* exhibition catalogue, Haggerty Museum of Art, 1999. Weidle, Barbara/Drathen, Doris Van/Lepdor, Catherine/Luz, Kathrin/Nicod, Caroline, *Leiko Ikemura,* exhibition catalogue, Musée des Beaux-Arts, Lausanne, 2001 (text in German and French).
MUSEUMS AND GALLERIES:
LAUSANNE (Cantonal MFA): collection of items.

IKENO. See **TAIGA**

IKER, Alphie
French, 20th century.
Born in Paris.
Painter. Urban landscapes.
Alphie Iker exhibits in Paris at the Salon de la Société Nationale des Beaux-Arts and the Salon des Indépendants. He is known for his views of Montmartre.

IKKEI, real name: Shigenaga or Shigeyoshi Kano, nickname: Naizen
Japanese, 17th century.
Born 1599; died 1662.
Painter.
Ikkei was a disciple of Mitsunobu (1565-1608). He lived at Odawara (Kanagawa Prefecture) and worked in the service of the lord of Hojo. He was the author of a work bringing together biographies of painters, the *Tansei Jakuboku Shu,* said to be the oldest collection of biographies of Japanese artists.

IKKEI, real name: Kiminobu Ukita, original name: Yoshitame Toyotomi, nickname: Shishi, nicknames: Kuranosuke, Shume, pseudonyms: Ikkei, Sekinan Shoju, Tameushi (Igyu)
Japanese, 19th century.
Born 1795; died 1859.
Active in Kyoto.
Painter.
Ikkei was a figure painter linked to the tradition of narrative scene painting called *yamato-e* (painting in the Japanese style, that is to say traditionally), revived at the end of the Edo period, towards the middle of the 19th century, by artists in the Fukko Yamato-e (*yamato-e* revival) movement. A politically committed figure, he was imprisoned by the Shogun government after delivering a short speech on the future of Japan.

IKKI. See **FUYO**

IKKYU, real name: Sojun; nickname: Ikkyu; pseudonyms: Kyounshi, Mukei and Kokukei
Japanese, 15th century.
Born 1394; died 1481.
Painter.
Ikkyu was a monk in the Daitoku-ji temple of Murasakino in Kyoto. He was a member of the ink painting (*suiboku*) school of the Muromachi period.

IKKYU, real name: Okubo Koko; nickname: Toshio
Japanese, 19th century.
Active at the beginning of the 19th century.
Painter.
Ikkyu was a disciple of Kokan (1747-1818) and an adherent of Western painting. He was also was a samurai in the clan of the lord of Yokosuka.

IKONNIKOV, Anatoli Vasilyevich
Ukrainian, 20th century.
Born 21 June 1941, in Kiev.
Painter. Figure compositions.
Anatoli Ikonnikov graduated from the institute of art in Kiev in 1967. A figurative artist, he depicts scenes of everyday life in a naive, sometimes rather acerbic, style. He has participated in many exhibitions in Kiev and in Russia. He is also known in Japan and the USA, where his works feature in several private collections.
AUCTION RECORDS:
PARIS, 18 March 1991, *Café Strumok* (oil on canvas, 35 1/2 x 27 1/2 ins / 90 x 70 cm) FRF 4,800.

IKONNIKOV, I.
Russian, 19th century.
Reproductions engraver.
Ikonnikov is known for two etchings dated 1870: *Forest Landscape with Couple* and *Forest Landscape with Woman and Boy,* both after paintings by Shishkin. He may be the same as the painter Mikhail Yakovlevich, who was born in 1838.

IKONNIKOV, Ivan Petrovich
Russian, 18th century.
Active during the first half of the 18th century.
Painter.
Ivan Petrovich Ikonnikov frequently worked in St Petersburg for the Cabinet of Curiosities and the Senate. He is mentioned for his *Portrait of Senator Pugovishnikov.*

IKONNINOV, Vasili
Russian, 18th century.
Engraver.
Vasili Ikonnikov trained in Moscow. In 1745 he was sent by the Synod to the St Petersburg academy of sciences. He was then appointed Master of the Art of Engraving at the Synod Press in Moscow. Among his more important engravings are the *Portrait of Empress Elizaveta Petrovna,* for a Bible printed in Moscow in 1759; the *Frontispiece* of the same Bible; a *Portrait of the Empress,* dated 1762; the *Frontispiece for a Bible* printed in Moscow in 1762, with views of the Kremlin and the Peter and Paul Fortress; a *Portrait of Grand Prince Paul Petrovich;* a *Portrait of Peter I,* after Chemesov, for the book *The Glory of Russia* (Moscow, 1770); a project for a *Monument to Peter I* in Moscow; *King David,* for a 1757 Psalter; six vignettes for a Russian edition of La Fontaine; and the *Loves of Psyche,* 1769.

IKOV, Pavel Petrovich
Russian, 19th century.
Born 1828, probably in Moscow; died 18 March 1875, in St Petersburg.
Painter. History painting, portraits.
Pavel Petrovich Ikov trained first in Moscow, then at the academy of art in St Petersburg. At the same time, he drew sketches for lithographs and woodcuts for the magazine *Illyustratsiya* and illustrated the book *Costumes of the Egyptians, Jews, Greeks, Romans and Russians.* He was awarded many prizes by the academy, including the lesser gold medal in 1857 for his *Pericles Visiting Anaxagoras,* and the gold medal in 1858 for *Washing the Feet of Christ.* After spending three years in Paris and three in Italy, he returned to St Petersburg in 1867, where he exhibited oils: *Susanna; Roman Peasant Woman with Distaff; Roman Girl with Chaplet of Roses; Roman Girls; Study of Old Man; Paestum; Amalfi;* and *Villa d'Este, Tivoli;* as well as a number of drawings. While living in Paris, he painted a *Felicity of the Regency,* after Rubens. He is also known for his *Standing Portrait of Tsar Alexander I,* and *Portrait of Tsarina Maria Alexandrovna,* as well as for his *Holy Trinity,* which he painted as an altarpiece for Minsk Cathedral and his *Our Saviour,* the altarpiece in Helsinki Cathedral.
MUSEUMS AND GALLERIES:
ST PETERSBURG (Academy): *Felicity of the Regency* (after Rubens).

IKUO, Hirayama. See **HIRAYAMA Ikuo**

IKUTA, Kacho
Japanese, 20th century.
Painter.
Kacho Ikuta featured in the exhibition *L'Art japonais*, held in 1929 at the Musée du Jeu de Paume in Paris.

IL, followed by a second name. See also **LE**

ILARIO DA VITERBO
Italian, 15th century.
Active c. 1400.
Painter.
Ilario da Viterbo, who was a priest, is known only from a very long inscription on the retable of the Portioncule chapel in the church of S Maria degli Angeli, Assisi. In the museum of Viterbo there is a painting depicting *Virgin, Child and a Cardinal at Prayer* which is attributed to him.

ILARIOLI, Antonio
Italian, 19th century.
Born 25 May 1825, in Cisano.
Sculptor.
Ilarioli carved a large number of marble busts.

ILARION
Painter.
Ilarion was a monk.
MUSEUMS AND GALLERIES:
GENEVA (Mus. Ariana): *Genre Scene* (painting/wood).

ILARION
Russian, 18th century.
Active in Kiev during the second half of the 18th century.
Engraver.
A monk, Ilarion is known for the following plates: a *Holy Trinity*, the frontispiece to a *Lives of the Saints* (Kiev, 1764) showing the Ascension, the Holy Trinity and a great number of saints; *St Barba; Monk and Woman; Monk, Priest and Cross; Archpriest with His Insignia*. Four wood engravings, bearing the initial 'I', are also attributed to him.

ILENKO, Evgeni Mikhailovich
Russian, 19th century.
Sculptor.
As an extern of the academy of art in St Petersburg, Evgeni Mikhailovich Ilenko took part in the academy's annual exhibitions, in 1870 showing a bust of *Mme O. Litvinova*, in 1873 a maquette for a funerary monument to the composer *Glinka* in Smolensk, and in 1877 a *Witch*, for which he received the lesser silver medal. In 1874 he made a maquette for a *Pushkin Monument*.

ILHE, Henry
French, 20th century.
Born in Narbonne.
Painter. Designs for tapestries.
Ilhe learned the technique of tapestry drawing with Dom Robert d'Encalquat. His works include all elements of nature, fauna and flora, in compositions of subtle, shimmering colour schemes. His works are woven in Aubusson.

ILIADES, Constantin
Greek, 20th century.
Born 1903, in Athens.
Painter, sculptor. Portraits, landscapes.
Constantin Iliades studied with George Roilos at the school of fine art in Athens between 1920 and 1927; he then studied in Paris at the Académie de la Grande Chaumière in the studio of the engraver D. Galanis. He was known for the virtuosity of his technique as a portrait and landscape artist. Later he became interested in Constructivist Abstraction.

He exhibited and travelled widely in Greece, England, Germany and Italy. He participated in the Venice and São Paulo Biennales. A member of the Art group in Greece in 1934, he was the founder of the centre for fine art in Athens. He was awarded the Averoff Prize in 1929.
MUSEUMS AND GALLERIES:
ATHENS (Dimotiki Pinakothíki) - ATHENS (Ethnikí Pinakothíki).

ILIC, Theodor. See **ILLITS**

ILIESCO, Joan. See **AUREL-ILIESCO Joan** or **Jean**

ILIESCO-CALINESTI, Gheorghe, or George
Romanian, 20th century.
Born 1932, in Calinesti.
Sculptor.
Iliesco-Calinesti studied at the school of fine art in Budapest from 1953 to 1959. He started making figures of peasants carved in wood in the style of folk art in 1961. While maintaining his interest in and drawing his inspiration from the traditional arts of his country, he was also attracted to the work of the great Romanian sculptor Brancusi, seeking in the rustic objects he portrayed their essential and stripped-down formal spirit and their poetic symbolic value. He was inspired by elements of traditional furniture and by the carved uprights of balconies of peasant dwellings and produced series reminiscent of a chess game.

In 1965 he illustrated the legend of the shepherdess Dochia. In order to represent Dochia guarding her flocks he carved a series of rocks in Herastrau Park in Bucharest in the forms of animals and a human figure. Another cycle of sculptures, *Citizens of the Earth*, stands on the edge of a lake near a district of the town of Pitesti. He took part in the Paris Biennale (1967) and held his first solo exhibition in Bucharest (1966).

ILIESCU, Rodica
Romanian, 20th - 21st century.
Born 30 September 1950, in Râmnicu-Valcea.
Active in France from 1973.
Painter, draughtswoman. Portraits, urban landscapes.
Rodica Iliescu lives and works in Paris. She freely interprets the small back-streets of La Butte-Montmartre, the steps up the hill and the charms of Sacré Coeur. The emphasis is on the picturesque. She has taken part in many collective exhibitions and has had solo exhibitions in France, Italy and Yugoslavia.
BIBLIOGRAPHY:
Romanian Artists and the West, American Romanian Academy of Arts and Sciences, Los Angeles, 1986.

ILIEV, Haralampi
Bulgarian, 19th - 20th century.
Born 23 January 1873, in Vidin.
Painter. Landscapes.
Haralampi Iliev was a pupil of Jules Mark. His work was represented at the 1900 Exposition Universelle in Paris.
MUSEUMS AND GALLERIES:
SOFIA: *Roman Bridge near Sofia*.

ILIEWA, Dona
Macedonian, 20th century.
Born 16 March 1880, in Prilep.
Painter. Landscapes, portraits.
Dona Iliewa was a student at the school of art in Sofia. Her main works include: *Flowerbeds in Plewna Park; Seascapes near Burgas; Portrait of a Woman; Landscape near Burgas; My Mother*.

ILIN, Andrei
Russian, 17th century.
Active in Moscow.
Icon painter.
Andrei Ilin worked at the imperial court. In 1660 he painted murals in the Tsarina's apartments and in the Cathedral of

the Archangel. In 1664 he executed decorative paintings in the palace. He also painted icons for the imperial family. His best-known work is the painting entitled *The Capponi Saints* now in the Vatican library. These paintings, on cedar, are in the form of a Greek cross, and were presented by Peter the Great to his confessor, the Greek priest Phokas, on whose death they passed to his brother. They were then purchased by the Marchese Capponi.

MUSEUMS AND GALLERIES:

VATICAN (Biblioteca Vaticana): *The Capponi Saints.*

ILIN, Denis

Russian, 17th century.

Icon painter.

Denis Ilin was a student of Ivan Saltanov. In 1682, together with other students he painted a *Crucifixion*, a *Resurrection* (on glass), and a *St Nicholas.*

ILIN, Gerasim

Russian, 17th century.

Icon painter.

As a painter in the imperial court in Moscow, Gerasim Ilin received various commissions to paint murals in one of the churches of Our Saviour in the Kremlin.

ILIN, Polevkt

Russian, 17th century.

Icon painter.

As a painter in the imperial court in Moscow, Polevkt Ilin helped to paint the murals in one of the Kremlin court churches in 1676. In 1678 he worked on the cathedral of St Evdokia and in 1680 on the Cathedral of the Dormition.

ILIN, Vasili

Russian, 18th century.

Born to a family originally from Kostroma.

Icon painter.

As a painter in the imperial court in Moscow, Vasili Ilin helped with the paintings in the Cathedral of the Dormition, in 1642-1644, and in 1649-1650 with those in the Cloister Cathedral of Savino-Storoyev. In 1652 he worked in the Cathedral of the Archangel in Moscow and in 1655 in the Cathedral of the Trinity at Kalyasin Monastery.

ILIN, Vasili Markovich, called Markov

Russian, 18th - 19th century.

Born 6 April 1762; died after 1815.

Painter. Still-lifes.

Vasili Markovich Ilin trained at the academy of art in St Petersburg. He worked at the St Petersburg porcelain factory and received an award in 1801 for a flower painting.

ILINSKY, Konstantin

Russian, 19th century.

Painter.

Trained at the academy of art in St Petersburg, Konstantin Ilinsky took part in their annual exhibitions, showing, in 1851, a *Portrait of a Man*, and a *Study* in 1852 for which he received the silver medal, first class. In 1853 he showed a *Portrait of a Woman* and *Death of Hector.*

ILIU, Iosif or Joseph

Romanian, 20th century.

Born 1916, in the Sibiu region.

Active in France from 1951; also active and naturalised in Canada from 1956.

Painter, sculptor, illustrator, decorative artist.

Iosif Iliu qualified at the Cluj academy of fine art. He was an illustrator for a number of reviews and also designed stage sets. In 1942, he was awarded a study bursary to go to Rome where he stayed until 1949 before settling in Paris.

His abstract paintings are vast compositions in black, white and grey with smooth forms and balanced curves. He has executed more than 40 works where art is integrated into architecture and is considered one of Canada's most important designers. He seeks to give a spiritual dimension to his decorative projects made of many different types of material including ceramics, roof tiles, aluminium, glass paste, cement, brick, marble and enamel.

He has taken part in many collective exhibitions in Paris, including the Salon des Réalités Nouvelles and the Salon des Indépendants (1949 and 1950). His first solo exhibition was in Bucharest (1937) and he also showed in Montreal and Toronto.

BIBLIOGRAPHY:

Romanian Artists and the West, American Romanian Academy of Arts and Sciences, Los Angeles, 1986.

ILKKA, Elias

Finnish, 20th century.

Born 25 June 1889, in Jalasjärvi.

Sculptor.

Elias Ilkka attended the Helsinki Athenaeum, and was also active in Paris at the Académie Colarossi. He won first prize in a competition to complete the monument dedicated to the Finnish war dead. Having produced many busts, he was also proficient in working with wood, to convey a more complex composition in the form of a relief. He was prolific in producing monuments, and Ilkka's work is amongst the most prominent in contemporary Finland.

ILL, Ryckaert

Painter.

Ryckaert Ill is known for a canvas sold at auction.

AUCTION RECORDS:

PARIS, 14 Dec 1933, *Gallery of Pictures*, FRF 6,000.

ILLA, Mariano

Spanish, 17th - 18th century.

Painter. Religious subjects, portraits. Frescoes.

Mariano Illa studied at the Real Academia de San Carlos in Valencia. He became a teacher there in 1777. He also taught at the academy in Barcelona around 1800. Illa painted frescoes in the church of St Catherine in Barcelona.

MUSEUMS AND GALLERIES:

BARCELONA (Provincial Mus.): *Childhood of Mary; Portrait of J. Miguel de Yudart* (copy after Mengs) - MADRID (Real Academia de Bellas Artes de San Fernando): *Immaculate Conception.*

ILLA, Salvador

Spanish, 18th century.

Born to a family originally from Pulinia, near Barcelona; died 28 September 1730.

Sculptor (wood).

Salvador Illa was a monk at the Scala Dei monastery and executed various works for this monastery.

ILLANES, Salvador

Spanish, 18th century.

Active in Seville.

Painter.

ILLAVA, Karl

American, 20th century.

Born 1896; died 1954.

Sculptor. Monuments.

Karl Illava was a pupil of Gutzon Borglum. He lived in New York and was a member of the archaeological association of New York. He sculpted memorials.

MUSEUMS AND GALLERIES:

BUFFALO (Albright-Knox AG): *Death Mask of Katharine Cornell* (1930, plaster).

ILLE, Eduard Valentin Joseph Karl

German, 19th century.

Born 17 May 1823, in Munich; died 17 December 1900, in Munich.

Painter, watercolourist, draughtsman. Historical subjects, genre scenes.

A pupil of Schnorr and Schwind at the academy in Munich, he did drawings for *Fliegende Blätter*, which he became director of in 1863.

Museums and Galleries:

Basel: *The Thirty Years' War* (watercolour) - Munich: *Schwan Kleban; Masked Animals; The Child of God from the Cradle to the Grave.*

ILLEM, Franz Josef Georg

Austrian, 19th century.
Born 12 March 1865, in Pilsen (now Plzen, Czech Republic).
Active in Vienna.
Painter.

A pupil of the academy in Düsseldorf, he painted mostly portraits, then landscapes and seascapes with figures.

ILLER, Johann Heinrich

Russian, 18th century.
Active in St Petersburg.
Painter.

In 1740 Johann Heinrich Iller did paintings in the Tsarina's bedroom in the old Admiralty Building.

ILLÈS, Aladar Edvi, Emma Edvi, Georges Edvi. See **EDVI-ILLÈS**

ILLES, Antal

Hungarian, 19th - 20th century.
Born 1872, in Szolnok; died 11 July 1911, in Szolnok.
Painter. Portraits, scenes with figures.

Antal Illes trained at the academy of fine art in Budapest and then at the Académie Julian in Paris. He was also a pupil of his brother-in-law S. Bihari in Szolnok. He was killed in an accident and left many works unfinished.

He painted portraits of President Taft and the Mexican President Díaz while travelling in the USA, where he also made many sketches of cowboy life.

ILLESCAS BERNABÉ, Ximenes de.
See **XIMENES DE ILLESCAS Bernabé**

ILLIAN, George John

American, 20th century.
Born 29 November 1894, in Milwaukee (Wisconsin); died 1932.
Illustrator.

George John Illian was a pupil at the Art Institutes of Milwaukee and Chicago, and Art Students League, New York. He was a member of the Society of Illustrators, New York, and of the Salmagundi Club.

ILLIDGE, Thomas Henry

British, 19th century.
Born 1799, in Birmingham; died 1851, in London.
Painter. Portraits.

Thomas Henry Illidge lived for a long time in Liverpool and Manchester and then returned to London in 1842, exhibiting his work regularly at the Royal Academy. In the early days he had a marked preference for landscapes, but in order to support his large family he turned to portrait painting and also executed genre paintings.

Museums and Galleries:

Blackburn: *Portrait of James Pickup* - Liverpool (Walker AG): *The Reverend W. Shepherd* - Salford (Museum and AG): *Lord Stanley, 14th Earl of Derby.*

ILLIERS, Gaston d'

French, 20th century.
Born 26 January 1876, in Boulogne-sur-Mer; died 1952.
Sculptor. Animals. Groups.

Gaston d'Illiers studied with Count de Ruillé and G. Busson. He exhibited in Paris at the Salon des Artistes Français, beginning in 1899. He was mostly a sculptor of horses (*Horse Before the Cart, Departure for the Fair* and *Hunting Team under Louis XV*). During World War I, he executed the groups *Artillery Team, Wounded Cavalry Horse, Dead Mule* and *Group from Memory of Horses Killed in the War*. He also executed numerous 'portraits' of race horses.

Museums and Galleries:

Orléans: *Dolly.*

Auction records:

Versailles, 27 March 1977, *Return from the Wild Boar Hunt* (bronze, h. 6 ins / 15 cm, w. 18 1/2 ins/47 cm) FRF 5,100. Paris, 16 Oct 1988, *Prince* (brown-patinated bronze, h. 7 1/2 ins / 19 cm) FRF 3,000. New York, 24 May 1989, *Horse Crossing a Barrier* (bronze, h. 11 3/4 ins / 30 cm) USD 2,200. Paris, 6 July 1989, *Before the Race* (bronze, l. 10 1/4 ins / 26 cm) FRF 5,000. Paris, 8 Nov 1995, *Horse Jumping the Bars* (bronze, h. 11 ins / 27 cm) FRF 60,000. London, 13 Nov 1996, *Stallion* (dark-green-patinated bronze, h. 7 ins / 17.5 cm; l. 8 ins/20.5 cm) GBP 575. Paris, 26 May 1997, *Jack the Horse* (brown-green patinated bronze, h. 9 3/4 ins / 25 cm) FRF 4,500.

ILLIES, Arthur Karl Wilhelm

German, 19th - 20th century.
Born 9 February 1870, in Hamburg; died May 1952, in Lüneburg (Lower Saxony).
Painter, engraver (wood/etching), lithographer, draughtsman. Military subjects, religious subjects, figures, nudes, landscapes, urban landscapes, seascapes, animals. Designs (furniture).
Jugendstil.

Arthur Karl Wilhelm Illies came from a family of merchants. He trained at the Kunstgewerbeschule in Munich and the Akademie der bildenden Künste, where he was taught by Lesker and Herterich. On returning to Hamburg, where he was born, he became a founder member, in 1892, of the Hamburgischer Künstlerclub (Hamburg Artists' Club), and later president. In 1894, he moved to the Artists' Colony of Worpswede and then travelled to Paris with his friend Ernst Eitner. He taught painting at the Kunstgewerbeschule in Hamburg. At the age of 64, he settled in Lüneburg, where the town provided him with a studio. He was an artist who contributed to the renewal of art in Hamburg at the turn of the century, primarily in the area of Jugendstil. He collaborated on the Berlin magazine *Pan* in 1896, and designed the interior decoration for the Simm house in Hamburg, as well as various furnishing projects. In the sphere of painting, under the influence of Impressionism, and in particular the painting of Monet, he was one of those who tried to liberate landscape painting from its academic straitjacket, when painting *en plein air* the landscapes of North Germany, animals, Hamburg streets, or the towns of Lübeck and Braunschweig. He is known today for his series of seascapes of the Bay of Kiel, compositions with figures, and, towards the end of his life, religious subjects (*The Last Supper, The Garden of Gethsemane*). He is also remembered for his portraits of historical characters (*Siegfried; Luther; Fichte*), and Hamburg personalities. At the time of World War I, he made many sketches of military subjects. At the end of his life, he returned to landscape painting. Illies also left some poems.

In 1997, he was represented at the exhibition *Ernst Eitner, Ölgemälde und Arthur Illies, Frühe Graphik* (*Ernst Eitner, Oil Paintings, and Arthur Illies, Early Graphic Art*), at the Herold Gallery in Hamburg. In 2002, there was an exhibition to commemorate the 50th anniversary of his death at the Museum für das Fürstentum Lüneburg, organised by the Arthur and Georgie Illies Foundation (which was created in 1998).

Bibliography:

Schiefler, Gustav, *Das graphische Werk von Arthur Illies: 1894-1904*, Christians, Hamburg, 1970. Meyer-Tönnesmann, Carsten, *Arthur Illies: 1870-1952*, exhibition catalogue, Hamburgische Landesbank, Hamburg, 1988. Meyer-Tönnesmann, Carsten, et al., *Die Maler Arthur Illies, Friedrich Ahlers-Hestermann, Karl Kluth*, exhibition catalogue, Verein für Hamburgische Geschichte, Carsten, 1989. Meyer-Tönnesmann, Carsten, *Arthur Illies: der Maler des Alstertals*, exhibition catalogue, 2000.

MUSEUMS AND GALLERIES:
BERLIN (Deutsches Historisches Mus.) - BERLIN (Kupferstichkabinet) - BREMEN (Kunsthalle, Prints Collection) - COLOGNE (Wallraf-Richartz Mus.) - DRESDEN (Prints Collection) - ESSEN (Folkwang Mus.) - HAMBURG (Kunsthalle): *Regenbogen über dem Alstertal* (*Rainbow over the Alster Valley*) (1899) - HAMBURG (Kunsthalle, Prints Collection) - HAMBURG (Mus. für Hamburgische Geschichte): *Going to the Shipping Company Office* (1908, oil on canvas, permanent loan from the Wölbern Bank) - HAMBURG (Mus. für Kunst und Gewerbe) - HELSINKI (Finnish NG): *Engraving* - LEIPZIG (Mus. der Bildenden Künste) - WEIMAR (Graphische Sammlung).

AUCTION RECORDS:
HAMBURG, 11 June 1982, *Portrait of Alfred Lichtwark* (1915, oil on canvas, 39 1/4 x 23 3/4 ins / 99.5 x 60.5 cm) DEM 6,000. HAMBURG, 24 June 2000, *Houses of Fishermen in Gothmund* (1935, oil on panel, 20 x 22 ins / 50 x 56 cm) DEM 17,500. HAMBURG, 2 Dec 2000, *Lock and Bridge* (oil on canvas, 19 x 26 ins / 49 x 67 cm) DEM 8,800. HAMBURG, 25 April 2001, *Still-life of Flowers* (oil on panel, 15 x 11 ins / 37 x 29 cm) DEM 5,000. HAMBURG, 4 Dec 2003, *Female Nude* (oil on canvas, 39 x 26 ins / 100 x 65 cm) EUR 3,300. COLOGNE, 15 May 2004, *Zinnia* (oil on canvas, 28 x 45 ins / 71 x 115 cm) EUR 5,000. HAMBURG, 19 June 2004, *Autumnal Landscape* (1918, oil on cardboard, 19 x 26 ins / 49 x 67 cm) EUR 5,300.

ILLIES, Otto
German, 20th century.
Born 25 January 1881, in Yokohama, Japan.
Painter, engraver. Landscapes.

Otto Illies studied in Hummelsbüttel, Munich and Weimar. His main works include *Peasant Garden in Holstein, Fruit Tree, Quarry Covered in Snow, Beechwood* and *Hardened Snow*.

ILLIK, Martin
Hungarian, 20th century.
Born 1925, in Budapest.
Active and naturalised in Belgium.
Painter, draughtsman, sculptor. Designs for tapestries.

A self-taught artist, Martin Illik painted landscapes, nudes, still-lifes and portraits in a style characterised by its nervous gestural touch. He showed his work in Belgium, Cologne, Los Angeles, Tunis and Paris and received several prizes and distinctions.

MUSEUMS AND GALLERIES:
BRUSSELS (Bibliothèque royale Albert Ier, Prints Collection).

ILLINGWORTH, Adeline S.
British, 19th century.
Born 1858.
Active in London.
Draughtswoman, engraver (etching).

Adeline S. Illingworth exhibited her etchings of architectural scenes at the Royal Academy from 1897. They include: *Westminster Abbey, Stephen's Bridge* and *Headcorn*.

ILLINGWORTH, N.
Australian, 19th - 20th century.
Active in Sydney.
Sculptor.

MUSEUMS AND GALLERIES:
SYDNEY (AG of New South Wales): *Aboriginal Boy; Aboriginal Chief; The Father of Islam; Aboriginal Woman.*

ILLITS, Theodor, called Tchesliar
Serb, 18th century.
Born 1746, in Szoreg, near Szeged; died 3 December 1793, in Bacs-Petrovostzello.
Painter. Religious subjects, portraits.

Theodor Illits was made a freeman of in Temesvár (now Timisoara, Romania) in 1782. After painting pictures for the church in O-Kanizsa, he studied at the Akademie der Bildenden Künste in Vienna. His main work is a series of 20 paintings for the church in Bacs-Petrovostzello. Some paintings in the Greek Catholic church in Karloca are also attributed to him.

ILLITSCH, Alexander
Austrian, 19th - 20th century.
Born 23 March 1860, in Vienna.
Active in Vienna.
Sculptor.

Alexander Illitsch attended the Akademie der Bildenden Künste in Vienna and was a state scholarship holder in Rome. The following works appeared at the annual exhibition of the artists' circle: in 1889, a plaster group *Cupid and Venus*; in 1899, *Wandering Jew*, and in 1909 *Christ on the Cross*, which was produced on wood for the Christuskirche in Innsbruck. Illitsch also produced an altar group entitled *Holy Family* and three heads of *Saints* for the pulpit in the parish church of Donaufeld, near Vienna; four sandstone groups at Floridsdorf town hall, near Vienna; and the *Commemorative Monument to Zöbl* in Brünn (now Brno, Czech Republic). He produced tombs in Vienna and other places in Austria, including *Christ the Comforter*, which is to be found in Vienna Zentralfriedhof (Vienna's central cemetery, opened in 1874 and the city's largest burial ground), and also busts and statuettes.

ILLNER, Richard Carl
German, 19th century.
Born 29 March 1831, in Leipzig; died 28 June 1895, in Leipzig.
Engraver (wood).

His most notable work was woodcuts for Brehm's *Life of Animals*, but he also did illustrations for *Tonnelle* and engravings from L Richter, notably for the *Tales of Bechstein*.

ILLNER, Walther
German, 19th - 20th century.
Born 21 September 1874, in Leipzig.
Painter. Portraits, landscapes, flowers. Murals.

Walther Illner was the son of Richard Carl Illner, and attended the school of arts and crafts in Leipzig, followed by the art academy in Munich. He stayed in Amsterdam, Rotterdam and The Hague for a considerable time. In 1913, he settled in Darmstadt. Until 1911, Illner primarily produced murals such as the stairwell at the ministry of justice in Dresden and the ceiling painting in the city's new town hall. He also produced portraits, landscapes and figure paintings: *Sirens, Diana, Faun, Nymphs* and *Passing of Spring*. His portraits include the *Grand Duke Ernest Louis of Hesse, His Wife and Sons*, and *Princess J. George of Saxe*. Illner produced many portraits of children.

ILLOUSCHEG. See **JELOVSEK Franz**

ILLSPERGER, Fidelis. See **ITTELSBERGER**

ILMARI, Johannes
German, 20th century.
Born in Breslau (now Wroclaw, Poland).
Sculptor.

Johannes Ilmari exhibited in Paris at the Salon des Indépendants and the Salon d'Automne.

ILMONI, Einar
Finnish, 20th century.
Born 22 June 1880, in Lappeenranta.
Painter.

Einar Ilmoni attended the fine arts society college in Helsinki and his work featured at exhibitions in Copenhagen and St Petersburg.

MUSEUMS AND GALLERIES:
HELSINKI (Valtion Taidemus.).

ILOT, Pierre Louis
French, 18th century.
Active in Paris in 1762.
Painter, sculptor.

ILSANG, Bartholomäus
German, 17th century.
Active in Bamberg.
Sculptor.

He worked at the cathedral of St Stephen in Bamberg in 1628-1630, where he did heraldic bearings and a *Bust of St Stephen* in the choir.

ILSTED, Peter Vilhelm
Danish, 19th - 20th century.
Born 14 February 1861, in Saxkøbing; died 1933.
Painter, engraver (etching). Genre scenes, interiors with figures, street scenes, church interiors.

Peter Vilhelm Ilsted received an honourable mention and a bronze medal at the 1889 and 1900 Expositions Universelles in Paris respectively. He was the brother-in-law of Vilhelm Hammershøj and painted the same subjects in a more popular style; although he worked with a subdued palette, his colours are less monotonous.

MUSEUMS AND GALLERIES:
AALBORG: *Battle* - COPENHAGEN: *Mushrooms; Society Gathering; At the Piano* - COPENHAGEN (Den Hirschsprungske Samling): *Chemist* - KREFELD: *Interior* - PARIS (MAMVP): *Interior.*

AUCTION RECORDS:
COPENHAGEN, 9 June 1971, *Interior* (1914) DKK 3,400. COPENHAGEN, 10 May 1972, *Back View of a Woman in an Interior,* DKK 3,300. COPENHAGEN, 21 Nov 1973, *Siesta,* DKK 6,300. COPENHAGEN, 29 Aug 1978, *Young Boy Writing in an Interior* (1901, oil on canvas, 18$1/2$ x 16$1/4$ ins / 47 x 41.5 cm) DKK 10,500. STOCKHOLM, 20 April 1983, *Young Woman in an Interior* (oil on panel, 12$1/2$ x 10$1/4$ ins / 32 x 26 cm) SEK 22,400. COPENHAGEN, 16 April 1986, *Children in an Interior* (1901, oil on canvas, 22 x 22$3/4$ ins / 56 x 58 cm) DKK 520,000. LONDON, 25 March 1987, *Young Girl Sitting in a Sunny Room* (oil on panel, 23$3/4$ x 19$1/4$ ins / 60.5 x 49 cm) GBP 42,000. COPENHAGEN, 23 March 1988, *Landscape in Stormy Weather* (1924, 26 x 26$3/4$ ins / 66 x 68 cm) DKK 12,000. LONDON, 24 March 1988, *Woman in an Interior Sitting near a Window* (oil on panel, 13$3/4$ x 10$3/4$ ins / 35 x 27.4 cm) GBP 38,500. NEW YORK, 22 Feb 1989, *Interior with a Little Girl Looking through the Window* (1908, oil on canvas, 25 x 23$1/2$ ins / 63.5 x 59.7 cm) USD 63,250. LONDON, 16 March 1989, *Artist's Daughters in an Interior at Liselund* (oil on canvas, 22 x 26$3/4$ ins / 55.8 x 67.9 cm) GBP 60,500. COPENHAGEN, 21 Feb 1990, *Interior with an Old Peasant Woman Holding Her Plate on Her Knees* (1882, oil on canvas, 11 x 7$1/2$ ins / 27 x 19 cm) DKK 18,000. LONDON, 27-28 March 1990, *Young Girl Reading near a Window* (1901, oil on canvas, 29$1/2$ x 25$1/4$ ins / 75 x 64 cm) GBP 77,000. COPENHAGEN, 25-26 April 1990, *Two Young Women on a Bench in the Garden near the House* (1887, oil on canvas, 20 x 22 ins / 51 x 55 cm) DKK 320,000. STOCKHOLM, 16 May 1990, *Kitchen Interior with Bottles and Glasses on a Table* (oil on canvas, 20$1/2$ x 15$3/4$ ins / 52 x 40 cm) SEK 41,000. COPENHAGEN, 28 Aug 1991, *Interior with a Young Woman in front of a Dresser* (oil on canvas, 20$1/2$ x 15 ins / 52 x 38 cm) DKK 34,000. STOCKHOLM, 19 May 1992, *Ponds in a Park* (1895, oil on canvas, 25$1/2$ x 20 ins / 65 x 51 cm) SEK 8,000. LONDON, 22 May 1992, *In the Garden* (1913, oil on panel, 17$3/4$ x 20$3/4$ ins / 45 x 53 cm) GBP 5,500. LONDON, 17 Nov 1993, *Street Scene in Tunisia* (1891, oil on canvas, 33 x 25$1/4$ ins / 84 x 64 cm) GBP 3,680. COPENHAGEN, 2 Feb 1994, *Interior of the Duomo and the Church of S Domenico, Siena* (1905, oil on canvas, 20 x 22 ins / 51 x 56 cm) DKK 7,000. HEIDELBERG, 5-13 April 1994, *Interior* (colour etching, 12 x 10$3/4$ ins / 30.5 x 27.5 cm) DEM 1,200. COPENHAGEN, 23 Feb 1999, *Small Girl with Flat Hat* (oil on canvas, 22 x 23 ins / 57 x 59 cm) DKK 290,000. COPENHAGEN, 1 June 1999, *Young Girl Pouring Coffee in the Red Dining Room* (1887, oil on canvas, 20 x 15 ins / 50 x 39 cm) DKK 265,000. LONDON, 7 April 2000, *Young Girl in an Interior, Liselund* (1918, oil on canvas, 28 x 24 ins / 70 x 60 cm) GBP 35,000. COPENHAGEN, 30 May 2000, *Young Girl Reading by Window* (oil on canvas, 23 x 21 ins / 58 x 53 cm) DKK 350,000. COPENHAGEN, 21 March 2001, *Interior Scene with Woman Reading to a Girl* (1905, oil on canvas, 19 x 17 ins / 49 x 42 cm) DKK 295,000. COPENHAGEN, 27 Nov 2001, *Interior Scene with Young Girl Reading a Letter* (1913, oil on wood, 20 x 16 ins / 50 x 40 cm) DKK 210,000. COPENHAGEN, 27 Aug 2002, *Casual Guests* (1887, oil on canvas, 27 x 36 ins / 69 x 92 cm) DKK 310,000. NEW YORK, 30 Oct 2002, *Open Door* (1912, oil on panel, 24 x 19 ins / 61 x 49 cm) USD 40,000. NEW YORK, 23 April 2003, *Young Girls Standing by a Window in an Interior* (1906, oil on canvas, 26 x 25 ins / 66 x 64 cm) USD 42,000. LONDON, 3 June 2003, *At the Window* (oil on canvas, 23 x 23 ins / 58 x 58 cm) GBP 30,000. COPENHAGEN, 9 June 2004, *Girl Reading by Window* (1901, oil on canvas, 23 x 20 ins / 58 x 50 cm) DKK 520,000. COPENHAGEN, 8 Sept 2004, *Before Breakfast - Young Girl Reading by Table, Capri* (1891, oil on canvas, 21 x 15 ins / 53 x 38 cm) DKK 280,000.

ILYA, K.
Russian, 18th century.
Active at the beginning of the 18th century.
Engraver.

ILYA, Petrov
Bulgarian, 20th century.
Born 1903.
Painter, engraver, illustrator. History painting.

Petrov Ilya taught at the school of fine art in Sofia and worked as an official artist. His compositions, in a Realist style, are filled with figures portraying scenes from history.

MUSEUMS AND GALLERIES:
SOFIA (Nacionalna chudozestvena galerija): *Portrait of a Young Boy* (1942); *Condemned Man* (1954).

ILYS, Jacques d'
French, 17th century.
Active in Paris.
Engraver.

IMAGE, Selwyn
British, 19th - 20th century.
Born 1849, in Bodiam (Sussex); died 21 August 1930.
Painter, draughtsman, illustrator, watercolourist. Landscapes. Designs for stained glass.

Selwyn Image was educated at Marlborough College and New College, Oxford, where he studied drawing under John Ruskin. He took holy orders at the age of 24, but continued to work as a designer before abandoning the clergy in 1882. In 1883 he opened the Century Guild Workshops with Arthur Mackmurdo, the founder of the Century Guild of Artists. He was an active member of the Art Workers' Guild in London and became its master in 1900. He exhibited at the Fine Art Society, and produced a series of stained-glass windows for the Exposition Universelle of 1900 in Paris. That year he also began working for the Glasgow furniture manufacturers Wylie & Lochhead. He produced woodcut illustrations and title pages for the magazine *The Hobby Horse* (published by the Century Guild of Artists from 1884-1891). Image also produced cartoons for painted glass panels, including a window for St Luke's church in Camberwell and the parish church at Morthoe in Devon. He was the first Slade Professor of Fine Art at Oxford (appointed in 1910, his tenure ran from 1913 to 1916). He produced numerous landscape drawings and paintings.

BIBLIOGRAPHY:
Selwyn Image: Letters, Garland, New York, 1977. Osterwalder, Marcus (ed.), *Dictionnaire des illustrateurs 1800-1914*, Ides et Calendes, Neuchâtel, 1989. Price, Susan Melanie, *The Fitzroy PIcture Society: Pictures for 'Schools, Mission-rooms and Hospitals' in the 1890s*, PhD dissertation, University of London, 1996. Frost, Peter, *Selwyn Image: An Illustrated Monograph*, Eighteen Nineties Society, Bicester, 1997.

IMAI, Soho
Japanese, 20th century.
Painter.

Soho Imai featured in the exhibition *L'Art japonais*, held in 1929 at the Musée du Jeu de Paume in Paris.

IMAI, Toshimitsu
Japanese, 20th century.
Born 6 May 1928, in Arashiyara (Kyoto).
Painter, draughtsman, engraver. Murals, stage sets.
Action Painting.

Toshimitsu Imai studied literature and philosophy extensively before devoting himself to art. Staying in Paris from 1951 to 1962, he studied for a few months in 1957 at the Académie de la Grande Chaumière. In 1951, he was awarded the prize for young painters at the Tokyo salon, and in 1983 he was appointed an officer of the order of arts and letters. In 1957, Imai took part in the demonstrations Georges Mathieu organised in Paris on the anniversary of the conviction of the medieval thinker Siger de Brabant.

Toshimitsu Imai is one of the main representatives of the Japanese 'Abstract Western School'. He is adept at the gestural movements of action painting, and sees himself as continuing the style of Jackson Pollock. He practises the Classical Tachist dripping technique, but brings to it the refinements of watercolour associated with the Far East. Since the 1980s his art has evolved into 'painting poems', reconciling itself with Far Eastern decorative art. Over many years he has executed the series *Ka-Cho-Fu-Getsu* (*Flower-Bird-Wind-Moon*), inspired by traditional art, which draws its subjects from nature, generally on a gold background.

In 1958, he exhibited at the Osaka International Festival; in 1959 at the first Paris Biennale; in 1960 at the Venice Biennale, and in 1963 at the São Paulo Biennale. In 1964, he was invited to enter the Marzotto prize, and in 1986 was represented in *Japon des Avant Gardes* at the Centre Georges Pompidou in Paris. He exhibited in 1988 at the Sydney Biennial and at the arts Olympiad in Seoul. He regularly showed his works in solo exhibitions from 1952 in Tokyo, notably in 1981 at the Hara museum of contemporary art, and in 1987 at the Franco-Japanese institute. From 1957, he exhibited solo at the Galerie Stadler in Paris. In 1986, he had a solo exhibition at the Fort Mason Center in San Francisco and in 1989 at the art museum in Osaka, the Meguro museum in Tokyo and the Iwaki museum of art, as well as the museum of contemporary art in Ostend and the Franciscan abbey at Châteauroux. In 1987, he exhibited at the museum in Oita and in 1990 at the Musée d'Art Contemporain in Dunkirk.

BIBLIOGRAPHY:
Elliott, David/Kazu Kaido, eds., *Reconstructions: Avant-Garde Art in Japan 1945-1965*, Museum of Modern Art, Oxford, 1985. Restany, Pierre, *Imaï*, Paris, 1989. *Imaï*, exhibition catalogue, Gal. Urban, Paris, 1990.

MUSEUMS AND GALLERIES:
BUFFALO (Albright-Knox AG) - DUNKIRK (MAC) - FUKUOKA (AM) - HIROSHIMA (MCA) - KAMAKURA (MMA) - KITAKYUSHU (Municipal MA) - KOBE (Hyogo Prefectural MMA) - KURASHIKI (Ohara MA) - OSAKA (National MA) - OTSU (Shiga Mus. of Modern Art) - PARIS (MNAM-CCI): *Sonorous Solitude* (1956) - ROME (Gal. Nazionale d'Arte Moderna) - TAIWAN (Mus.) - TOKYO (Hara MCA) - TOKYO (MCA) - TOKYO (Metropolitan Art Mus.) - TOKYO (National MMA) - TOKYO (Sogetsu Art Mus.) - YOKOHAMA (Mus. of Art).

AUCTION RECORDS:
PARIS, 23 June 1988, *Composition with a Bird* (1955, oil on canvas, 36¼ x 28¾ ins / 92 x 73 cm) FRF 28,000. PARIS, 15 Feb 1989, *red chalk* (1974, oil on paper, 31½ x 43¼ ins / 80 x 110 cm) FRF 13,500. PARIS, 25 April 1990, *Bouquet of Flowers* (1957, mixed media/panel, 9½ x 10¼ ins / 24 x 26 cm) FRF 35,000. PARIS, 29 Oct 1990, *Work* (1959, mixed media/canvas, 46 x 35 ins / 116 x 89 cm) FRF 700,000. PARIS, 15 March 1991, *Composition* (1960, mixed media/canvas, 15¾ x 31½ ins / 40 x 80 cm) FRF 70,000. LONDON, 17 Oct 1991, *Pink Fire* (1960, oil on canvas, 54¼ x 41¼ ins / 138 x 105 cm) GBP 16,500. LOKEREN, 4 Dec 1993, *Composition* (1978, acrylic/paper, 18¾ x 18 ins / 47.5 x 45.5 cm) BEF 60,000. PARIS, 12 July 1994, *Composition in Violet* (1974, oil on canvas, 31½ x 43¾ ins / 80 x 111 cm) FRF 4,200. PARIS, 11 March 1998, *Calligraphy* (1968, Indian ink/paper, 30 x 23½ ins / 76 x 60 cm) FRF 3,800. NORWALK, 3 Jan 1999, *Abstract* (oil on canvas, 60 x 48 ins / 152 x 122 cm) USD 16,000. VENICE, 13 Nov 1999, *Paris* (1958, mixed media on card, 19 x 25 ins / 49 x 64 cm) ITL 16,800,000. ZURICH, 23 May 2000, *Composition* (1962, oil on board, 26 x 20 ins / 65 x 51 cm) CHF 4,000. ZURICH, 23 May 2000, *Composition* (1962, oil on board, 20 x 26 ins / 51 x 65 cm) CHF 4,600. LONDON, 24 July 2001, *Untitled* (1960, acrylic on canvas, 26 x 22 ins / 65 x 55 cm) GBP 1,200. LONDON, 7 Dec 2001, *Composition* (1960, oil and sand on canvas, 26 x 21 ins / 65 x 53 cm) GBP 1,700. PARIS, 23 Nov 2003, *Composition* (1958, oil on canvas, 29 x 46 ins / 73 x 116 cm) EUR 4,900. PARIS, 9 Dec 2003, *Romantic Irony* (1961, oil on canvas, 47 x 63 ins / 120 x 160 cm) EUR 9,000. PARIS, 18 June 2004, *Havana Cigars* (2001, acrylic and collage on paper, 25 x 41 ins / 64 x 104 cm) EUR 2,000.

IMAMURA, Yukio
Japanese, 20th century.
Born 1935, in Isé.
Active from 1977 in France.
Painter, draughtsman, performance artist.

Imamura works in series, the most notable of which are probably *Zenon* and *Quark*. To very fluid oils he adds raw pigments. On smooth backgrounds, in opposition to transparent effects, line drawings appear, structuring the medium and producing a microcosm. In works from the mid-1990s he has shown an interest in African art, introducing figures from the sculptures of the Mumuyés, a people of northern Nigeria.

Imamura has taken part in numerous group exhibitions since 1960: in 1962 at the museum of modern art in Tokyo; in 1971 at the museum of the city of Tokyo and the museum of modern art in Kyoto; in 1982 and 1983 at the municipal museum in Mie; in 1985 at the museum in Kaganawa; in 1986 at the Festival International de Peinture in Cagnes-sur-Mer; and in 1992 at the Miami International Art Exposition. He has shown his works in solo exhibitions since 1966 in Tokyo, since 1971 in Nagoya, and since 1984 in Paris, notably in 1990, 1992 and 1995 at the Galerie Lélia Mordoch. He has completed several public commissions in Japan.

BIBLIOGRAPHY:
Imamura - Zénon, exhibition catalogue, Gal. Christian Cheneau, Paris, 1984. *Imamura, New Works*, exhibition catalogue, Gall. Kohji Ogura, Nagoya, 1987.

IMANA, Gil
Bolivian, 20th century.
Born 1933, in Sucre.
Painter. Landscapes, figures. Murals.
From 1943 to 1948, Gil Imana studied at the school of fine arts and the Rimsa studio in Sucre.

Imana's art is very much in the tradition of the Mexican Expressionist School of the 1930s. To achieve maximum expressive effect, he brings together elements drawn from original ethnic sources with a post-Picasso expressionism. He describes Indian towns, high plateaus, ancient ruins and colonial streets with great power.

He was a funding member of the Anteo group in Sucre and taught in various schools in Bolivia and Venezuela. He took part in exhibitions of contemporary Bolivian painting: São Paulo Biennale (1957); *Five Bolivian Painters* in Lima (1959); *Bolivian Painting* in Cali, (1962); *Latin American Art Since Independence*, an exhibition that travelled to several cities in the USA (1966-1967); Lima Biennale (1968); the UNESCO gallery (1970). Since 1950 he has also held many solo exhibitions: La Paz and San Diego (1969) and Paris (1971). Imana has executed several mural decorations in Sucre and La Paz.

BIBLIOGRAPHY:
Diehl, Gaston, *Gil Imana*, exhibition catalogue, Gal. J. Massol, Paris, 1971. Lassaigne, Jacques, *Les Peintres boliviens contemporains*, exhibition catalogue, Musée d'Art moderne de la Ville de Paris, Paris, 1973.

MUSEUMS AND GALLERIES:
LA PAZ (Mus. Nacional de Arte) - QUITO (Mus. de la Casa de la Cultura Ecuatoriana) - SOFIA (Nacionalna chudozestvena galerija) - ST PETERSBURG (Hermitage) - SUCRE (Museos Universitarios Charcas) - TEL AVIV (MMA).

IMANA GARRON, Jorge
Bolivian, 20th century.
Born 1930, in Sucre.
Painter. Local scenes, landscapes. Murals.
Jorge Imana Garron taught at the fine arts academy in Sucre from 1950 to 1958. With Gil Imana and Lorgio Vaca he founded the Anteo movement. He produced many mural compositions, exalting themes specifically Bolivian such as the eternal life of the Indian.

BIBLIOGRAPHY:
Lassaigne, Jacques, *Peintres boliviens contemporains*, exhibition catalogue, Musée d'Art moderne de la Ville de Paris, Paris, 1973.

MUSEUMS AND GALLERIES:
BOGOTÁ (Mus. Nacional de Colombia) - LA PAZ (MMA) - SAN DIEGO (AI) - SUCRE (Museos Universitarios Charcas).

IMANDT, Willem
Dutch, 20th century.
Born 1882; died 1967.
Painter. Landscapes, waterscapes.

AUCTION RECORDS:
AMSTERDAM, 5 June 1990, *Village* (oil on canvas, 23 1/2 x 31 1/2 ins / 60 x 80 cm) NLG 4,025. AMSTERDAM, 21 April 1993, *Indonesian Jungle at Twilight* (oil on canvas, 24 x 32 ins / 61 x 81 cm) NLG 1,150. AMSTERDAM, 19 Oct 1993, *Coastal Landscape in Indonesia* (oil on canvas, 15 3/4 x 23 ins / 40 x 57.5 cm) NLG 690. AMSTERDAM, 23 April 1996, *Landscape at Sunset* (oil on canvas, 19 3/4 x 20 3/4 ins / 50 x 53 cm) NLG 1,888. AMSTERDAM, 5 Nov 1996, *River Landscape, Tree Reflections in the Water* (oil on canvas, 15 1/4 x 22 ins / 38.5 x 55 cm) NLG 3,068; *Rocky Bay, Capri* (oil on canvas, 30 x 40 1/2 ins / 76 x 103 cm) NLG 8,024. LOKEREN, 9 Dec 2000, *Lake in a Crater, Indonesia* (oil on canvas, 35 x 49 ins / 89 x 125 cm) BEF 110,000. AMSTERDAM, 30 Jan 2001, *Pagoda in a Mountainous Landscape at Sunset* (oil on canvas, 35 x 49 ins / 90 x 125 cm) NLG 4,500. AMSTERDAM, 4 Sept 2001, *Trees by a Lake* (oil on canvas, 32 x 35 ins / 81 x 88 cm) EUR 2,200. GRAVENHAGE, 5 Nov 2003, *Banyan-tree* (oil on canvas, 33 x 30 ins / 85 x 76 cm) EUR 7,000. AMSTERDAM, 16 March 2004, *Waringin Tree* (oil on canvas and board, 21 x 21 ins / 54 x 54 cm) EUR 4,200. BRUSSELS, 19 April 2004, *Bay in Indonesia* (oil on canvas, 19 x 30 ins / 48 x 75 cm) EUR 1,900.

IMAR, Jean
French, 20th century.
Born 25 December 1943, in Oullins.
Watercolourist, painter (gouache), draughtsman.
Jean Imar was educated at the École des Beaux-Arts in Lyons from 1961 to 1962 and the École des Beaux-Arts in Paris from 1963 to 1965, where he was taught by Legueult, and finally at the monumental art and sculpture workshop at the École des Arts Décoratifs from 1966 to 1968, where he was taught by Despierre. From 1965 he designed sets, stage devices, costumes and curtains for several theatre companies in Lyons, Paris and Brussels. He also made wall compositions for public buildings in Dijon and in Aisne at La Fère and Couvron.

After a figurative period in which he painted visually intentional and psychologically convincing portraits, he moved on to Gestural Abstraction, with generous amounts of sensual material and striking colours. This work was deliberately expressionist and apparently connected to music. He often made ink drawings, which although based on the same whirling impulses, have more sharply executed graphics as if applying the technique of drawing to copying and imitating previous paintings conferred a more marked structure on them than the Matterist-Informel process.

He has taken part in collective exhibitions since 1966 in various places in Paris, the Paris and Lyons areas, and particularly at the Paris Salons: Salon de la Jeune Peinture, Salon Jeune Expression, 1982; Salon de la Jeune Peinture, 1983; Salon Art Sacré, 1984; Salon de Figuration Critique, 1991 and Salon de Figuration Critique at the Musée de Mons, Belgium, 1992. Collections of his paintings and drawings have also been shown in solo exhibitions including: Paris, 1978; Maurice Ravel Auditorium, Lyons, 1980; Galerie Utopia, St-Étienne, 1981 and 1982; Paris 1992; Galerie Gisèle Thomas-Vitale, Lyons, 1992 and Atrium, Lyons etc.

BIBLIOGRAPHY:
Imar, exhibition catalogue, Auditorium Maurice-Ravel, Lyons, 1980.

IMBACH, Hans, or Im Bach
Swiss, 16th - 17th century.
Active in Lucerne.
Painter.

IMBAR, Lawrence. See **YMBAR**

IMBARD, Étienne F.
French, 20th century.
Born 1875.
Draughtsman, engraver (copper), lithographer.
Architectural views. Ornaments, funerary monuments.
Imbard lived and worked in Paris. He published several engraved brass plates under the titles *Tomb of Louis XII*, descriptive notice with engraved plates, Paris, 1915; *Tomb of Francis I*, drawn, published and engraved by EFI Architecte, Paris, 1917; *Tombs of Louis XII and Francis I*, drawn and etched after the marbles in the Musée des Petits Augustins, Paris, 1923; and *Ornaments and Fragments of Architecture*, lithographed, Paris, 1917.

IMBAULT
French, 18th - 19th century.
Born 18th century, in Paris.
Painter.
Imbault studied under Vincent and Vascher. He featured at the Salon from 1793 to 1810. He is remembered for *Head of*

an *Elderly Jew, A Bacchante Resting, A Threatening Cupid*, and *The Old Man and the Rose*.

IMBAULT, Léonce Édouard
French, 19th century.
Born 14 August 1845, in Orléans; died 10 February 1882, in Mustapha, Algeria.
Painter. Landscapes, ruins.

Imbault was a pupil of Chouppe. From 1872 to 1880, he exhibited landscapes at the Salon in Paris, including several watercolours. He was a Chevalier of the Légion d'Honneur.

MUSEUMS AND GALLERIES:
ORLÉANS: *Ruins of the Palais de Justice after the Fire of 24th May 1871*.

AUCTION RECORDS:
PARIS, 3 March 1926, *Waterside Landscape* (watercolour) FRF 4,250.

IMBAULT, Lucien
French, 20th century.
Born 3 April 1878, in Malakoff (Hauts-de-Seine); died 1914; on active service.
Sculptor. Figures. Busts.

Imbault exhibited busts and medallions in Paris at the Salon des Artistes Français.

IMBAULT, Paul
French, 19th century.
Died 1894.
Active in Paris.
Painter.

Paul Imbault was a member of the Société des Artistes Français. He displayed his works at the Salon as a member of this group.

IMBER, Lawrence. See **YMBAR**

IMBERCIADORI, Orazio
Italian, 19th century.
Born 17 May 1788, in Castel del Piano; died 1861, in Castel del Piano.
Painter.

Imberciadori was a pupil at the Accademia in Florence; he completed his artistic training in Rome. He received a seven-year scholarship from the Biringucci Foundation of Siena. He painted several pictures for the Foundation, mainly copies, including in 1822 *Sacred Love* after Titian's *Sacred and Profane Love*. For his native town he painted a *Madonna of the Graces* that was engraved by Domenico Monaci, and he also painted portraits and miniatures.

IMBERG
German, 20th century.
Born 1940, in Munich.
Assemblage artist, engraver, painter.

Imberg is self-taught (with the exception of engraving, which he learnt alongside Hradil, Bremer and Anderle at the summer academy in Salzburg). In 1992 he contributed works to the Salon Découvertes in Paris, but he usually avoids exhibitions. He works from objects he assembles, and creates totem sculptures and mysterious boxes.

IMBERG, Laurence
French, 20th century.
Painter.

Laurence Imberg achieves an original balance using geometrical forms. She has participated in collective exhibitions since 1981, notably at the Musée d'Art Moderne in Lyons in 1983 and the Centre Culturel in Évry in 1984. She has had solo exhibitions since 1985, notably in 1989 at the Salon de Mai in Paris.

IMBERNON, Amparo
Painter. Landscapes.

IMBERT
French, 16th century.
Active in Sens.
Sculptor, architect.

In 1551 Imbert was working on the decoration of Sens Cathedral. He was most probably a relative of Michelet Imbert, the Sens master of works who in 1513 was in charge of work connected with the portrait of Abraham.

IMBERT
French, 19th century.
Active in Paris in 1815.
Engraver.

IMBERT, Bertrand
French, 16th century.
Active in Avignon between 1550 and 1600.
Painter (?).

IMBERT, Carlos
Spanish, 19th century.
Died 1870, in Vitoria.
Active in Vitoria.
Sculptor.

Carlos Imbert collaborated on the sculptural decoration of the town halls in Vitoria and Pamplona.

IMBERT, Ch.
French, 19th century.
Painter.

AUCTION RECORDS:
PARIS, 26 Feb 1947, *Mountain Pasture* (1872) FRF 14,500.

IMBERT, Gaspard
French, 17th century.
Born c. 1628, in Blois; died 1694, in Blois.
Painter (?).

IMBERT, Henri. See **IMBERT DES MOTTELETTES Henri**

IMBERT, J. Fr.
French, 18th century.
Died 24 November 1787, in Paris.
Painter, draughtsman. Portraits.

J. Fr. Imbert featured at the Salon de la Correspondance in 1779 with two portraits, *Portrait of a Young Man in Oriental Dress* and *Portrait of a Girl*. Madame Papavoine engraved *The Hobby* and *The Cup-and-ball* after him.

IMBERT, Jean-Claude
French, 20th century.
Born 1919, in Paris.
Painter (mixed media), watercolourist, draughtsman, illustrator, sculptor. Figure compositions, figures, nudes, interiors, landscapes. Murals.

Jean-Claude Imbert lives and works in the Gard. He has exhibited since 1947. In 1948, he founded the Académie de Peinture in Marseilles. In 1950, he taught art history at the École des Beaux-Arts. He taught painting at the École des Beaux-Arts in Avignon, and in 1962 was nominated to the École des Beaux-Arts in Aix-en-Provence. He often paints in watercolour, the rapidity of the technique accommodating his elliptical strokes. He has built up a considerable body of work. Though he has treated various themes, the nude is omnipresent. He has had solo exhibitions in Paris, Marseilles, Los Angeles, Munich, Florence, Berlin, Aix-en-Provence and Cassis. He had retrospectives in 1977 in Paris and in 1985 at the École des Beaux-Arts in Aix-en-Provence.

BIBLIOGRAPHY:
Jean-Claude Imbert, auction catalogue, Drouot, Paris, 29 September 1992.

AUCTION RECORDS:
PARIS, 29 Sept 1992, *The Pecking* (1964, oil on canvas, 32 x 23½ ins / 81 x 60 cm) FRF 12,000; *On the Beach* (1974, pen

drawing and watercolour, 19¾ x 25½ ins / 50 x 65 cm) FRF 4,000; *The Bay of Cassis* (1965, oil on paper/canvas, 32 x 46 ins / 81 x 116 cm) FRF 10,000.

IMBERT, Joseph Gabriel
French, 17th - 18th century.
Born March 1666, in Marseilles; died 25 April 1749, in Villeneuve-les-Avignon.
Painter.

Joseph Gabriel Imbert was born to a dressmaker who had him apprenticed to a Marseilles painter before sending him to Paris to work first with Vermeulen and then in Charles Le Brun's studio. Through Le Brun, Imbert was taken on by the duke of Nevers who had been looking for a painter. Imbert worked for this nobleman until he moved to the South and entered the Carthusian order. He took his vows at the Charterhouse in Avignon on 29 September 1703. He worked as a painter in his convent and executed three large compositions, *The Flight into Egypt, Deposition* and *Annunciation,* after Guido Reni. Dom Berger, his prior, took him to Rome. On his return Brother Imbert produced six large paintings for the Marseilles Charterhouse, notably *Christ Dying on the Cross* which occupies the far end of the Charterhouse sanctuary and is rated as one of the artist's master works. Imbert also painted the *St Anthony* in the Grenoble Charterhouse. He trained several pupils, including his nephew Étienne, the carver Claude Imbert, Parrocel, Manglard, the sculptor Antoine Duparc, and Duplessis.

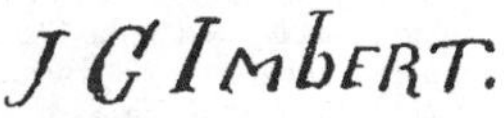

IMBERT, Louis
French, 17th century.
Active in Toulon.
Sculptor, wood carver.

Imbert was employed in the workshops of the Arsenal at Toulon. In 1685, he sculpted the arms of the city in stone for the 'Porte du Picquet Neuf', and in 1690, after the design by C. Dubreuil, he carved the doors and a lintel which still exist in the main portal of the naval hospital known as the Hôpital de la Marine in Toulon. He may also have been responsible for the similar doors in the portal of the church of La Valette (Var).

IMBERT, Michelet. See **IMBERT**

IMBERT, Pierre
French, 19th century.
Died 1867.
Painter.

Pierre Imbert exhibited portraits at the Salon in Paris from 1831 to 1836.

IMBERT DES MOTTELETTES, Henri
Flemish School, 18th - 19th century.
Born 1764, in Bruges; died 27 February 1837, in Bruges.
Painter, pastellist. Portraits, genre scenes, flowers, fruit.

Henri Imbert des Mottelettes studied under Gaeremyn. He was a member of several academies and exhibited portraits at the Paris Salons of 1831, 1833, 1834, 1835 and 1836. He lived in Paris at 56 Rue Basse-du-Rempart. The Bruges museum has three of his works.

IMBLEVAL, Jean d'
French, 20th century.
Born 1929, in Paris.
Painter, sculptor, installation artist.

After a year studying law, Jean d'Imbleval entered the studio of Lhote and Tailleux at the École des Beaux-Arts in Paris in 1949. From 1951 to 1953, he studied at the Écoles des Arts Décoratifs in Paris. He participated in collective exhibitions in 1981, 1985, 1986, 1988 (Foire Internationale d'Art Contemporain in Paris), and 1986 and 1988 (Chicago Art Fair). From 1954, he has held solo exhibitions in France and abroad. He executed several public commissions, notably a monumental sculpture in 1979 for the committee for the improvement of working conditions in the Citroën factory.

MUSEUMS AND GALLERIES:
CHOLET.

IMBRECHTS, Maerten
Dutch, 17th century.
Painter.

Maerten Imbrechts worked in Amsterdam.

IMBRECHTS, Martin. See **YMBRECHTS Marton**

IMBS, Marcel
French, 20th century.
Born 17 August 1882, in Strasbourg; died 16 June 1935, in Strasbourg.
Painter.

Marcel Imbs was a student of L.O. Merson. He exhibited regularly at the Salon des Artistes Français in Paris, where he won a silver medal in 1928.

IMELSKI, A.
Austrian, 18th century.
Active in 1728.
Miniaturist.

Son-in-law of J A Eglauer.

IMER, Berthe. See **GIRARDET**

IMER, Édouard August
French, 19th century.
Born 23 December 1820, in Avignon, to Swiss parents; died 13 or 21 June 1881, in Harlem.
Painter, watercolourist. Genre scenes, landscapes, waterscapes.

Imer studied at the castle of Lenzbourg, in Leipzig and in England. He was also a pupil of Émile Loubon. He exhibited at the Paris Salon from 1850. A biographical portrait of Imer was published in January 1882 as part of a catalogue of the works he exhibited in Paris. He is considered to be a skilful colourist.

MUSEUMS AND GALLERIES:
AVIGNON (Mus. Calvet): *Armand de Pontmartin; View of Part of the St Bénézet Bridge; View of St Honorat Island; View of St Raphael; Landscape* - GENEVA (MAH): *The Coomb of Tencisque* - GENEVA (Mus. Ariana): *Portrait of the Artist* - GUÉRET: *The Oak of Vouziers* - LA ROCHELLE: *Pond at the Fourdines* - NEUCHÂTEL: *The Pond at Soumabre; Ruins of Crozant Castle; Banks of the Creuse; Lagoon in Venice, Evening; Rocks at Port-Micou in Provence;* two watercolours.

AUCTION RECORDS:
PARIS, 1887, *Scene in Provence,* FRF 1,420. PARIS, 1898, *The Pont du Gard,* FRF 127. PARIS, 22 June 1923, *River Flowing Beneath a Ruined Viaduct,* FRF 200. PARIS, 5 April 1993, *Sultan and his Harem* (watercolour and gouache, 15¼ x 28in/39 x 71cm) FRF 23,000.

IMERVARD
German, 12th century.
Active in Brunswick, perhaps before 12th century.
Sculptor (wood).

Imervard was the creator of the triumphal cross in the crypt of Brunswick Cathedral.

IMGRABEN, Cacilie
German, 20th century.
Born 29 June 1929, in Waldshut.
Painter. Landscapes, flowers.

Cacilie Imgraben exhibited her work at the Baden-Württemberg society of artists in Karlsruhe.

IMGRABEN, Hans Jorg
Swiss, 17th century.
Born to a family originally from Sursee.
Painter.

IMHOF
Swiss, 15th century.
Born 15th century, to a family originally from Lucerne.
Painter. Religious subjects.
Imhof made several paintings for the church of St Oswald in Zug.

IMHOF, Heinrich Maximilian
Swiss, 19th century.
Born 14 May 1798, in Bürglen; died 4 May 1869, in Rome.
Sculptor.
A pupil of Franz Abart in Kerns and Dannecker in Stuttgart, he visited Greece and then Italy. He exhibited at the Royal Academy in London in 1846.
MUSEUMS AND GALLERIES:
BASEL: *Rebecca* - BERN: *Eve before the Fall* (marble); *Hagar and Ishmael* (plaster maquette); *Atalanta* (plaster maquette); *Miriam* (plaster maquette); *Ruth* (plaster maquette); *Rebecca* (plaster maquette); *David* (plaster maquette) - POTSDAM: *Miriam* - ZURICH: *Head of a Woman* (marble) - ZURICH (Zentralbibliothek): *Bust of Pestalozzi*.
AUCTION RECORDS:
ALNWICK (ENGLAND), 22 Sept 1986, *The Female Water Carrier* (1844, Carrara marble, h. 30 ins / 76 cm) GBP 13,000. COLOGNE, 30 Nov 2000, *Tambourine* (1865, sculpture, marble, h. 45 ins / 115 cm) DEM 12,000. LUCERNE, 14 Nov 2001, *Portrait of Man* (1851, sculpture, white marble, h. 19 ins / 48 cm) CHF 4,000. LUCERNE, 14 Nov 2001, *Portrait of Man* (1851, sculpture, white marble, h. 19 ins / 48 cm) CHF 4,500. STUTTGART, 5 Dec 2002, *Profile Portrait of Johann Heinrich Dannecker* (sculpture, alabaster on marble, 6 x 6x? ins / 16 x 14x? cm) EUR 10,500.

IMHOF, Joseph A.
American, 19th - 20th century.
Born 1871; died 1955.
Painter (including gouache), watercolourist. Local scenes, local figures, portraits.
Strangely, it was only after Joseph A. Imhof's return to the USA after having seen the Buffalo Bill Show in Europe that he began to study Iroquoian customs. In 1907, after several trips to Europe, he moved to Albuquerque, where he spent five years gathering information on the life of the village. In 1929 he settled permanently in Taos.
AUCTION RECORDS:
LOS ANGELES, 9 June 1976, *Portrait of Cristino Mirabal* (watercolour, 28 x 22 ins / 71.1 x 56 cm) USD 1,500. NEW YORK, 3 June 1982, *Red Willow Place, North Pueblo, Taos* (gouache and watercolour, 22 1/4 x 29 3/4 ins / 56.7 x 75.8 cm) USD 2,000. NEW YORK, 3 June 1983, *Indian Woman* (1909, watercolour and gouache, 20 3/4 x 14 3/4 ins / 52.6 x 37.5 cm) USD 5,000. NEW YORK, 31 May 1985, *Pueblo Street, Acoma* (1936, watercolour and gouache/mounted paper/card, 19 x 23 1/2 ins / 48.2 x 59.5 cm) USD 2,000. NEW YORK, 24 June 1988, *Osceola, the Rising Sun* (oil on card, 27 1/2 x 22 ins / 70 x 55 cm) USD 660. NEW YORK, 4 Dec 1992, *The Camoufleurs* (oil on canvas/card, 31 x 46 3/4 ins / 77.8 x 118.8 cm) USD 55,000. NEW YORK, 31 March 1993, *Portrait of an Indian* (watercolour/paper/card, 21 1/2 x 18 1/2 ins / 54.6 x 47 cm) USD 920. NEW YORK, 9 Sept 1993, *Potters* (oil on canvas, 30 x 36 ins / 76.22 x 91.4 cm) USD 5,463. LOS ANGELES, 3 May 2000, *Southwestern Ranch* (oil on board, 18 x 22 ins / 46 x 55 cm) USD 4,000. HATFIELD, 18 Sept 2002, *Portrait of Iron Tail Sioux, a Native American Man* (oil on board, 37 x 31 ins / 94 x 79 cm) USD 4,750. SANTA FE, 9 Nov 2002, *Ute Indians on the Warpath* (oil on canvas on board, 37 x 27 ins / 94 x 69 cm) USD 7,500. CINCINNATI, 7 Sept 2003, *Taos Pueblo* (watercolour, 20 x 26 ins / 51 x 66 cm) USD 3,000.

IMHOFF, Alexander Wilhelm, or Imhof or Imhove
German, 18th century.
Born 28 December 1689, in Westphalia; died c. 1760, in Cologne.
Sculptor (wood).
The Minorite church in Cologne has a high altar by him, while the cathedral has statues of *St Anne* and *St Barbara* by him as secondary altars.

IMHOFF, Carl C. A. von
German, 18th century.
Born in Nuremberg.
Draughtsman, engraver (etching).

IMHOFF, François
French, 20th century.
Born 1938.
Painter, pastellist.
In the tradition of the Paris school, François Imhoff creates non-figurative paintings, which are assemblages of pieces of canvas, which he then paints while flat before stretching. Over the years, his work on colour has intensified. For him, 'colour is fundamental. It is colour that imposes its limit, its place, up until the point of paradox where one forgets the colour, so that it melts into what it enables one to see.' He also produces stained glass windows, as well as stage sets and costumes. Imhoff participated in the Foire Internationale d'Art Contemporain in Paris in 1990. He has had solo exhibitions in the Galerie Clivages in Paris.

IMHOFF, Franz Xaver Bernhard
German, 18th - 19th century.
Born 14 July 1766; died 24 February 1824.
Active in Cologne.
Sculptor.
He was the son of Johann Jospeh Imhoff, and also his pupil.

IMHOFF, Johann Joseph I, or Imhof or Imhove
German, 18th century.
Born 9 April 1739; died 13 April 1802.
Active in Cologne.
Sculptor.
He was the son of Alexander Wilhelm Imhoff, and produced marble statues of *St Antony* and *St Patrocles* on side altars in Cologne Cathedral.
MUSEUMS AND GALLERIES:
DARMSTADT (Hessisches Landesmus.): *Baron Hupsch* (terracotta bust).

IMHOFF, Johann Joseph II
German, 19th century.
Died c. 1860.
Active in Cologne.
Sculptor. Religious subjects, mythological subjects.
The son and pupil of Peter Joseph Imhoff, he exhibited religiously and mythologically inspired statues and reliefs executed in marble, plaster and terracotta from 1839 to 1848.

IMHOFF, Peter Joseph
German, 18th - 19th century.
Born 13 July 1768; died 20 December 1844.
Active in Cologne.
Sculptor. Religious subjects. Statues, busts.
The son of Johann Joseph Imhoff I, he was a pupil of his father and a student at the academy in Düsseldorf. He carried out the decoration of the church of St Martin the Great in Cologne, and c. 1818 was commissioned by Baron von Stein to sculpt the patron saints of Prussia, Austria, Russia and England for his great house in Nassau - *St Adalbert, St Leopold, Alexander Nevsky* and *St George* respectively. He also

did monumental statues in sandstone relief and busts, including those of painter and modeller *K. B Hardy* and *Frederick William III of Prussia*.

IMHOFF, Wilhelm Joseph
German, 19th century.
Born 23 March 1791; died 27 February 1858.
Active in Cologne.
Sculptor. Statues, busts, monuments.

The son of Franz Xaver Bernard Imhoff, in 1822 he exhibited a plaster sculpture called *Anatomy* and an alabaster statue of *Venus Seated at Her Bath* at the academy in Berlin. He showed two busts and the maquette of a *Memorial to Beethoven* at exhibitions of the Cologne Society of Artists between 1840 and 1843.

IMHOFF ALTARPIECE, Master of the. See **MASTERS**

IMHOVE. See **IMHOFF**

IMIEN, F. S.
Painter.

F.S. Imien is known for a canvas sold at auction.

AUCTION RECORDS:
PARIS, 10 and 11 June 1929, *Allegories of Love*, FRF 2,050.

IMKAMP, Wilhelm
German, 20th century.
Born 1906, in Münster.
Painter.

From 1926-1929, Wilhelm Imkamp attended the Bauhaus and attended courses taught by the Swiss Abstract painter Paul Klee and the Russian Expressionist Wassily Kandinsky. In 1930 he stayed in Paris; from 1930-1939 in Essen; in 1940 in Giessen, where his studio was destroyed by an air raid in 1944; and from 1945-1948 in Allendorf-Lumda. In 1953, he settled in Stuttgart.

BIBLIOGRAPHY:
Leymarie, Jean/Herzogenrath, Wulf/Grote, Ludwig/Gropius, Walter, *Le Bauhaus*, exhibition catalogue, Württembergischer Kunsteverein, Stuttgart, Musée national d'Art moderne, Paris, 1969.

MUSEUMS AND GALLERIES:
ESSEN (Folkwang Mus.): *Aquatic Plants* (1952).

AUCTION RECORDS:
DÜSSELDORF, 14 Nov 1973, *Burlesque*, DEM 7,000. HEIDELBERG, 5-13 April 1994, *Abstract Composition* (1965, triptych, mixed media/three canvases, 9 1/2 x 9 ins / 24 x 23 cm and 9 1/2 x 6 ins/24 x 15 cm) DEM 6,000. COLOGNE, 2 June 2000, *Colourful Birds* (1945, oil on cloth, 12 x 16 ins / 30 x 40 cm) DEM 3,500. BERLIN, 25 Nov 2000, *Formations* (1956, oil and tempera, 11 x 17 ins / 28 x 42 cm) DEM 3,500. MUNICH, 15 Nov 2001, *Prinz Einbein* (1963, oil and sand on board, 19 x 28 ins / 49 x 70 cm) DEM 9,000. COLOGNE, 8 Dec 2001, *Boats on Beach* (1971, oil on canvas, 11 x 18 ins / 29 x 46 cm) DEM 5,000. COLOGNE, 29 May 2002, *Composition* (1949, oil on board, 17 x 13 ins / 44 x 32 cm) EUR 3,200. COLOGNE, 7 Dec 2002, *Composition* (1959, oil on board on panel, 24 x 17 ins / 62 x 43 cm) EUR 4,000. COLOGNE, 4 Dec 2003, *Abstract Composition* (1960, oil on board, 23 x 16 ins / 58 x 40 cm) EUR 5,000. MUNICH, 30 Nov 2004, *Composition* (oil on board, 12 x 25 ins / 31 x 64 cm) EUR 1,600. MUNICH, 30 Nov 2004, *Composition* (mixed media, 12 x 24 ins / 31 x 62 cm) EUR 1,900.

IMLÉ, Henri Joseph
French, 19th century.
Born 18 October 1822, in Lyons.
Painter.

Henri Joseph Imlé studied under Vibert and Bonnefond at the École des Beaux-Arts in Lyons from 1837 to 1842. He settled in Paris, where he exhibited *Annunciation* and *Nativity* and *Death of Christ* in 1865, and in 1866 *Sacré Coeur*, a drawing.

IMLER, Edgar
American, 20th century.
Born 31 January 1894, in St Clairsville (Pennsylvania); died 1973, in Altoona (Pennsylvania).
Painter, engraver.

Edgar Imler moved to New York and joined the Art Students League, New York. He worked as an etcher.

IMLER, Gert Van. See **LON**

IMMEL, Johann Sigmund. See **EMMEL**

IMMENDORF, Jörg, or Immendorf
German, 20th century.
Born 14 June 1945, in Blekede.
Painter, sculptor, installation artist. Scenes with figures.
Fluxus, New Fauves.

Jörg Immendorf studied at the Kunstakademie in Düsseldorf, at first on the theatre design course under the direction of Teo Otto and then in the studio of Joseph Beuys. He taught at the art academies in Stockholm in 1981, Hamburg in 1982, Zurich and Trondheim in 1983, Cologne and Munich in 1984 and 1985, and Frankfurt in 1989. In 1984, he opened a café, the *Paloma*, in Hamburg. He lives and works in Düsseldorf, Hamburg and Frankfurt. He has made records with the painters Martin Kippenberger and A.R. Penck.

When he made his debut in the mid-1960s, Immendorf turned to performance, like his master Joseph Beuys, and became involved in the Fluxus movement, which rejected the separation of art from life. He joined in the revolutions of that time, protesting against the Vietnam war in a collection of works entitled *Lidl* ('the term comes from baby talk - lidl, lidl, lidl and so on, the sound of a baby's rattle'). Executed between 1967 and 1970, using the Pop Art-inspired image of a chubby-cheeked Asian baby as a symbol of peace and love, this series is made up of paintings, sculptures, performances and documents couched in the subversive language of Dada and the world of childhood.

In 1970 he became a Maoist, which led him to subject his artistic production to a very severe examination of conscience, and gave rise to both writings and paintings. He then joined the Greens in order to help protect the environment. Throughout this period, though doing more and more performances, Immendorf did not stop painting, despite his 1966 work *Hört auf zu malen* (*Stop Painting*). Evidence of this is his *Selbstbildnis im Atelier* (*Self-portrait in the Studio*) of 1974, a painting within a painting about the artist's vocation, catching him in an enclosed space (in his studio, no longer out in the street) and busy painting a group of demonstrators (and excluding himself from them). This was considered absolute sacrilege at that time, when people claimed that painting was dying.

In 1976 came his crucial meeting with the East German artist Penck. Together with Penck, Immendorf signed his *Erstes Gemeininsames Kurzmanifest zur Arbeit als Kollectiv* (*First Common Manifesto for Collective Work*), to 'combine the pleasure of painting with the desire to get over the wall'. He decided to dedicate himself body and soul to the traditional medium of painting in order to try to portray the problem of the two Germanies and set up a dialogue through artistic expression. Like a film director, he chose the location for this meeting, a place where the world could be put on show, the Café Deutschland, which was to give its name to the series executed between 1976 and 1986. This symbolic space, inspired by a punk night club in Düsseldorf, is haunted by his friends and enemies, mainly from the world of art, dressed in leather and with tattoos and long hair or shaven heads. There, in an atmosphere of aggressiveness, the various artistic generations evolve: Immendorf, Penck, Beuys, Baselitz, Beuys' teacher Wilhelm Lehmbruck, Marcel Duchamp, and also writers, gallery owners, politicians, theoreticians, customs officers, policemen, soldiers, as well as allegorical symbols such as the Brandenburg Gate, the swastika, and the hammer and sickle. These abundant references invite the viewer to decipher them, even if Immendorf enjoys covering his tracks by mixing history painting with personal mythology. But as he says himself, his painting does not stand only on its iconographic content. The work can be approached without the need for identification. 'There would be no point in going through all the figures like a schoolteacher explaining their meaning and presence. Of course the choice of figures is crucial for every artist, at least at the preparatory stage. But once they are on the canvas, this is no longer important'. Drawing its elements from the history of humanity, each canvas is 'no more than a still-life, a composition put together from fragments of history which conceal within them a question on a global scale '. The fruit of an unbridled imagination, each scene is as violent as the manner in which the material is treated, both unusual and burlesque, telling of the same confrontation between the two Germanies, each one embedded in seemingly unshakeable systems, and expressing the power of painting. The way the artist treats space, with neither background nor close-ups and a very heightened perspective, which he had used previously in *Self-portrait in the Studio*, accentuates this feeling of isolation. The accumulation of details, the apparent disorder of the composition (in contradiction to the orderliness of a political system) and the way the surface breaks up, create a feeling of unease. The space seems too narrow (despite the large formats), the technique too casual, the brushwork too hasty. In this stifling world, the images emerging from the collective memory take on an air of catastrophe, reinforced by the use of colour and lighting borrowed from Fantastic art.

In the series *Lehmbrucksaga* (1987-1988) and *Café de Flore* (1987 on), which is thought to be set in France, Immendorf pursues his investigations, moving his field of intervention (to France in particular) in order to broaden his thinking and escape being labelled as a German artist by crossing borders. Bringing new protagonists together, in *Café de Flore* he invites a variety of people such as the socialist Proudhon, the German-Jewish Romantic Heinrich Heine, the Dadaist Picabia, Breton, the Surrealists, Sartre, Piero Manzoni and his *Artist's Shit*, to take part in a universal dialogue spanning the centuries. Immendorf depicts himself at the various stages of his development, as a student of Beuys, performance artist, café waiter and painter, both to confirm his position in the history of art and to distance himself from it. He reintroduces elements from previous paintings, pursues previous arguments, renewing his connection with his original choice of art form, installation. At the Musée National d'Art Moderne de Paris in 1993, he presented *Is it about a bicycle?*, which brings together paintings, sculptures, objects and sound environments created by John Cage around the paintings *Café de Flore and Gyntiana*. In this series, referring to Duchamp's bicycle wheel and a Beuys brochure, the dynamics are provided by the bicycle, which appears in several paintings, placing Immendorf's work in a historical continuity leading from ready made to performance art.

Rather than an ephemeral street art that would have a continued existence only in the form of a few photographs, tapes and articles, Immendorf chose painting. His painting is freely narrative, showing his involvement, violently revealing a perception of the world, emotions, and expressing the pleasure of painting. In this teeming universe, saturated with symbols and allegories, people with well-known faces, typecast marionettes, anything can happen. Images in perpetual evolution give birth to other scenes. The viewer becomes lost in the crowd, tossed between disgust and the burlesque, feels like a voyeur or as if 'at the theatre, where the set is outside reality' (Immendorf).

Immendorf has taken part in many group exhibitions since 1967. These have included Documenta V in Kassel in 1972, the 37th Venice Biennale in 1976, *L'Art en Allemagne Aujourd'hui* (*Art in Germany Today*) at the Musée d'Art Moderne de la Ville de Paris in 1981, Documenta VII in Kassel and the 4th Venice Biennale in 1982, the Paris Biennale in 1985, *Avant Garde in the Eighties* at the Los Angeles County Museum of Art in 1987, the National Museum of Contemporary Art in Seoul in 1988, FIAC (Foire Internationale d'Art Contemporain) in Paris in 1990 and *Painting on the Move*, which presented a century of contemporary painting, shown simultaneously at the Kunstmuseum, the Kunsthalle and the Museum für Gegenwartskunst in Basel in 2002. Since 1961, he has exhibited his works in a large number of solo shows, including 1976 at the Westfalischer Kunstverein in Münster, 1979 at the Kunstmuseum in Basel, 1980 at the Kunsthalle in Bern, 1981 and 1983 at the Stedelijk Van Abbe Museum in Eindhoven, 1982 and 1983 at the Museum of Modern Art in Oxford, 1984 at the Art Museum in Bilbao, 1991 at the Museum für Moderne Kunst in Vienna, 1992 at the Boymans van Beuningen Museum in Rotterdam, 1993 in the contemporary galleries of the Musée National d'Art Moderne in Paris, and 1994 at the Centre d'Art Contemporain in Meymac, 1994 The Barbican Art Gallery, London, 2001 Anton Kern Gallery, New York, 2004 Galerie Michael Werner. Cologne and the Arts Club of Chicago.

BIBLIOGRAPHY:

In Drawings: Baselitz, Basquiat, Brauntuch, Clemente, Cucchi, Fischl, Immendorf, Kirkeby, Lupertz, Penke, Polke, Salle, Stephan, New York, 1984. Darragon, Éric, '*Immendorf dans la nuit allemande*' in *Artstudio* n° 2, periodical, Gal. Templon, Paris, autumn 1986. Immendorf, Jörg, *In Auckland*, Auckland City Art Gallery, Auckland, 1987. Philippe, Pierre, '*La Porte de Brandebourg et quatre artistes de la mélancolie*' in *Opus international* n° 118, periodical, Paris, March-April 1990. Immendorf, Jörg, *Jörg Immendorf: I wanted to be an artist 1971-1974*, Michael Werner, New York, 1992. Millet, Catherine, '*Interview de Jörg Immendorf*' in *Art Press*, periodical, Paris, February 1993. *Jorg Immendorf*, exhibition catalogue, Centre d'Art contemporain, Meymac, 1994. Bürgi, Bernhard Mendes, et al., *Painting on the Move*, exhibition catalogue, Kunstmuseum, Kunsthalle, Museum für Gegenwartskunst, Basel, 2002.

MUSEUMS AND GALLERIES:

AACHEN (Ludwig Forum für Internationale Kunst) - EINDHOVEN (Van Abbe Mus.): *Café Deutschland Winter* - HAMBURG (Kunsthalle): *Welt der Arbeit* (*World of Work*) (1984) - ROTTERDAM (Mus. Boijmans Van Beuningen) - STRASBOURG (Mus. d'Art Moderne et Contemporain): *Kolonie Los* (1982); *Gertrude + Republik* (*Gertrude + Republic*) (1998).

AUCTION RECORDS:

HAMBURG, 8 June 1984, *Auktion Babywäsche: Baby mit Blumen* (*Babywear Auction: Baby with Flowers*) (1967, acrylic/panel, 74 1/2 x 73 1/4 ins / 189.5 x 186 cm) DEM 20,000. NEW YORK, 10 Nov 1986, *Cafe Deutschland 38: Parteitag* (*Café Deutschland 38: Party Conference*) (1983, acrylic/canvas, 79 x 119 ins / 200.6 x 302.3 cm) USD 35,000. NEW YORK, 5 May 1987, *Reichsache* (1983, oil on canvas, 98 x 98 ins / 248.8 x 248.8 cm) USD 30,000. NEW YORK, 4 May 1988, *Café Deutschland Erbe* (*The Café Deutschland Inheritance*) (1983, oil on canvas, 59 x 78 3/4 ins / 149.7 x 200.1 cm) USD 24,200. NEW YORK, 10 Nov 1988, *German Café-Concert* (1983, oil on canvas, 59 1/4 x 79 ins / 150.3 x 200.8 cm) USD 28,600. NEW YORK, 3 May 1989, *Three Party Conference* (1981, oil on paper/canvas, 40 3/4 x 36 1/4 ins / 103.5 x 92 cm) USD 17,600. NEW YORK, 8 Nov 1989, *Untitled* (oil on paper/canvas, 39 3/4 x 36 ins / 101 x 91.5 cm) USD 18,700. NEW YORK, 27 Feb 1990, *The Temptation of Saint Anthony* (1985, oil on canvas, 112 x 130 ins / 284.5 x 330.2 cm) USD 44,000. NEW YORK, 5 Oct 1990, *Untitled* (oil on paper/material, 40 x 35 1/2 ins / 101.6 x 90.2 cm)

USD 15,400. New York, 2 May 1991, *Show What You Have* (1983, oil on canvas, 98 3/4 x 98 ins / 250.8 x 249 cm) USD 28,600. London, 27 June 1991, *Show What You Have* (1983, oil on canvas, 30 x 41 3/4 ins / 76 x 106 cm) GBP 11,000. Paris, 12 Oct 1991, *Mixed Technique 2* (1981, oil on canvas, 59 x 70 3/4 ins / 150 x 180 cm) FRF 82,000. New York, 7 May 1992, *Futurologist* (1979, oil/material, 39 1/4 x 133 3/4 ins / 100 x 340 cm) USD 17,600. Frankfurt am Main, 14 June 1994, *Untitled* (1986, oil on canvas, 32 3/4 x 29 1/4 ins / 83 x 74 cm) DEM 25,000. London, 6 Dec 1996, *First Concentration* (1982, oil on canvas, 31 1/4 x 47 1/4 ins / 79.5 x 119.7 cm) GBP 12,075. Stuttgart, 30 Jan 1999, *Untitled* (1982, mixed media on canvas, 61 x 79 ins / 155 x 200 cm) DEM 18,500. Cologne, 28 May 1999, *For All the World's Loves* (1967, acrylic on canvas, 71 x 67 ins / 180 x 170 cm) DEM 84,000. Munich, 26 Nov 2000, *Untitled* (bronze, h. 22 ins / 55 cm) DEM 43,000. Munich, 26 Nov 2000, *Untitled* (oil on canvas, 47 x 39 ins / 120 x 100 cm) DEM 75,000. Munich, 19 May 2001, *Love Me* (acrylic on canvas, 18 x 18 ins / 45 x 45 cm) DEM 28,000. Cologne, 5 Dec 2001, *Each Colour Is Right - As You Know* (1981, acrylic on board on cotton, 40 x 36 ins / 101 x 92 cm) DEM 23,500. Cologne, 5 June 2002, *System from the Front* (1981, acrylic on canvas, 54 x 41 ins / 138 x 103 cm) EUR 10,000. Vienna, 27 Nov 2002, *Sons of the Sun* (1992, oil on canvas, 35 x 26 ins / 88 x 66 cm) EUR 26,000. Munich, 13 Nov 2003, *Cafe Flore, Self with Joseph Beuys* (1991, oil on canvas, 39 x 31 ins / 100 x 80 cm) EUR 13,500. Vienna, 26 Nov 2003, *Self-portrait with Nude and Rose* (1991, oil on canvas, 39 x 31 ins / 100 x 80 cm) EUR 10,000. New York, 12 Nov 2004, *Cafe Deutschland* (1984, acrylic and woodblock on canvas, 61 x 81 ins / 155 x 205 cm) USD 18,000. Vienna, 23 Nov 2004, *Babel* (1994, prints, 27, 15 x 14 ins / 39 x 35 cm) EUR 32,000.

IMMENKAMP, Wilhelm
German, 19th - 20th century.
Born 21 September 1870, in Essen.
Painter, fresco artist. Religious subjects, portraits. Murals.

Wilhelm Immenkamp attended the art academy in Munich. From 1904-1916, he exhibited frequently at the Glaspalast (Ice Palace) in Munich. His portraits include Catholic prelates and Louis III of Bavaria. Immenkamp also painted altar pictures and frescoes, representing scenes from the life of the Virgin Mary, for the church of the Ascension in Essen, and murals for the session room in the new court building there.

Museums and Galleries:
Munich (Town Hall): *Louis III of Bavaria.*

IMMENRAET, Andries, or Emmenreat or Emmelraet
Flemish School, 17th century.
Born 25 August 1662; died after 1699.
Painter. Landscapes.

Andries Immenraet was the youngest son of Philips Augustyn Immenraet and was taught by his father. In 1687, he was a master in Antwerp. He visited France, Italy and Germany.

Auction records:
Milan, 21 May 1981, *Landscape with Figures* (oil on canvas, 68 1/2 x 48in/174 x 122cm) ITL 7,500,000.

IMMENRAET, Jan Carel, or Emmereat or Immstraet
Flemish School, 17th century.
Active in Antwerp.
Painter, engraver (etching) (?). Figures, landscapes.

Jan Immenraet may have been the same person as the Etcher I. Imstraet known for a small, signed landscape etching and two other unsigned etchings: *The Shepherd and his Wife* and *Village by the Water*, the latter also being attributed to Lucas van Uden. These three plates are very similar to those of the etcher P. A. Immenraet.

IMMENRAET, Michiel Engel, or Emmelraet
Flemish School, 17th century.
Born 18 October 1621, in Antwerp; died 1683, in Utrecht.
Painter.

Michiel Immenraet was the brother of Philips Augustyn Immenraet. In 1663, he was a master in Antwerp. The municipal museum in The Hague has his *Portraits of Odile and Philippine van Wassenaer as Shepherdesses*. He died in poverty.

IMMENRAET, Philips Augustyn, the Elder, or Emelraet, Hemelraet, Immestraet, and not Emelraad
Flemish School, 17th century.
Born 21 February 1627, in Antwerp; died 25 September 1679, in Antwerp.
Painter. Landscapes with figures, waterscapes, landscapes.

Philips Immenraet the Elder studied under Lucas van Uden. As a young man he went to Italy and lived in Rome. When he returned to Antwerp he was regarded as a highly accomplished landscape artist. A master artist in Antwerp in 1655, he taught Peter Rysbrack.

Museums and Galleries:
Aix: *Italian Landscape with Waterfall* - Stuttgart: *Landscape with Lion Hunt.*

Auction records:
Amsterdam, 17 July 1709, *Landscape*, FRF 60. Monte Carlo, 5 March 1984, *River Landscape in Italy* (1671, oil on canvas, 68 3/4 x 93in/174.5 x 236cm) FRF 140,000. Lindau, 3 Dec 1999, *Southern Landscape with Figures* (oil on canvas, 15 x 17 ins / 38 x 43 cm) DEM 5,500. Lyons, 7 June 2000, *Landscape with Rocks and the Departure of a Hunt* (oil on canvas, 50 x 68 ins / 126 x 172 cm) FRF 75,000.

IMMENRAET, Philips Augustyn, the Younger
Flemish School, 17th century.
Painter.

Philips Augustyn Immenraet the Younger was the third son of Philips Augustyn Immenraet.

IMMERSEEL, Frans van
Belgian, 20th century.
Born 1909, in Borsbeek; died 1978, in Wilrijk.
Painter, engraver. Designs for stained glass.

Frans van Immerseel studied under the painter Tony van Os.

Auction records:
Lokeren, 10 Dec 1994, *Tijl and Nele* (window glass, 22 1/2 x 21 1/2 ins / 57 x 54.5 cm) BEF 24,000.

IMMERZEEL, Anne Marie
Dutch, 19th century.
Painter. Genre scenes, landscapes.

Anne Marie Immerzeel was taught by her brother Christiaan Immerzeel.

Auction records:
Amsterdam, 9 Nov 1982, *Interior Scene* (oil on panel, 15 1/4 x 19 3/4in/39 x 50cm) NLG 5,400.

IMMERZEEL, Christiaan
Dutch, 19th century.
Born 1 March 1808, in The Hague; died 13 October 1886, in Kassel.
Painter, engraver, lithographer.

Christiaan Immerzeel studied under C. Bakker and Hendrick van de Sande-Bakhuyzen.

Auction records:
Paris, 1844, *Landscape*, FRF 300. Rotterdam, 1891, *Summer Landscape with Animals*, FRF 240. New York, 4 and 5 March 1909, *View of Broderick Palace; Landscape with Animals*, USD 115. London, 20 April 1979, *Wooded River Landscape with Animals* (oil on canvas, 17¼ x 26¾in/43.8 x 68cm) GBP 950. Amsterdam, 10 Feb 1988, *Angler in a Boat in the Moonlight* (oil on panel, 13½ x 29¼in/34 x 74cm) NLG 2,760. Amsterdam, 16 Nov 1988, *Anglers by a River near a Watermill* (oil on panel, 13¾ x 18in/35 x 45.5cm) NLG 3,450; *Animals Drinking at a Pond in the Forest with Ducks Swimming* (oil on panel, 13½ x 19in/34 x 48cm) NLG 8,625. Amsterdam, 18 Feb 1992, *Winter Landscape with Peasants beside a Mill on a Frozen Canal* (oil on panel, 12 x 15¾in/30.5 x 40cm) NLG 10,350. Amsterdam, 19-20 Feb 1997, *Farms in a Wooded Landscape with Cows Grazing in the Background* (oil on panel, 6 x 10in/15 x 24.5cm) NLG 3,690. Amsterdam, 19 June 2001, *Figures in a Rowing Boat on a River Passing a Windmill* (oil on panel, 8 x 9 ins / 20 x 24 cm) NLG 4,200.

IMMINCK, B. F.
Dutch, 18th century.
Engraver, draughtsman.
In 1731, B. F. Imminck was a member of the guild of The Hague.

IMOFF
18th century.
Active in London.
Miniaturist.
Imoff exhibited at the Society of Artists in London in 1768.

IMOLA, da. See first name

IMOTO, Atsushi
Japanese, 20th century.
Born 1915, in Tokyo.
Sculptor.
Imoto graduated with a diploma from the university of fine art in Tokyo and from 1937 took part in the *Nika* salon for painting and sculpture. He became a member of the association of fine art in the army. After working for a long time in stone, he began to discover the possibilities of welded metal and produced improvisations stamped with a very Surrealist imagination. His works are presented as welded assemblages of pre-manufactured metallic forms. For example, in his series of *Flowers, Birds and Insects*, a collection of old keys bought at the Marché aux Puces flea market in Paris is used to obtain the effects of plumage, corollas and wing-cases. His art shows considerable invention, and has a mythological rather than anecdotal spirit. In 1960 he held his first solo exhibition in Tokyo, and from 1961 featured in several Parisian salons: the Salon des Indépendants from 1963, the Salon de la Jeune Sculpture at the Musée Rodin from 1963 to 1967, and in 1964 in the exhibition of the prizes for *Sculpture des quatre saisons* (*Four Seasons Sculpture*) at the Musée Rodin. In 1965 he had a solo exhibition in Paris, and others in Belgium and the USA.

IMPARATO, Francesco
Italian, 16th century.
Born c. 1530, in Naples; died 1565.
Painter. History painting.
Imparato was a pupil of Giovan Filippo Criscuola, Pierino del Vaga, and later of Titian in Venice. A *St Peter the Martyr* and an *Annunciation*, painted for the church of S Severino, are considered to be his best works. Girolamo Imparato was his son. Lanzi says he was still living in 1564. Siret gives 1565 as the date of his death, whereas other biographers say that he was still alive in this year.

IMPARATO, Giovan Tomaso
Italian, 17th century.
Active in Naples.
Sculptor (wood).
Giovan Imparato trained under Nunzio Ferraro, and worked with him on the choir stalls of the Basilica of the Abbey of S Angelo in Montescaglioso.

IMPARATO, Girolamo
Italian, 17th century.
Active from 1573 to 1621 in Naples.
Painter. Religious subjects.
Girolamo Imparato was a pupil of his father, Francesco Imparato. He worked in Rome and Venice with Tintoretto and Palma the younger. He went to Lombardy and studied the works of Correggio in Parma. It is possible to see paintings by this artist in the cell of St Thomas Aquinas and the church of SS Severinus e Sosius in Naples.
Museums and Galleries:
Naples: *Annunciation*.
Auction records:
New York, 20 May 1993, *Adoration of the Shepherds* (oil on canvas, 51 x 39 ins / 129.5 x 99.1 cm) USD 24,150. London, 18 April 2002, *Adoration of the Shepherds* (oil on canvas, 51 x 39 ins / 129 x 99 cm) GBP 8,000. Madrid, 7 Oct 2002, *Adoration of the Shepherds* (oil on canvas, 51 x 39 ins / 129 x 99 cm) EUR 12,000. Madrid, 21 Jan 2003, *Adoration of the Shepherds* (oil on canvas, 51 x 39 ins / 129 x 99 cm) EUR 12,000.

IMPENS, Josse
Belgian, 19th century.
Born 1840, in Brussels; died November 1905, in Brussels.
Painter. Genre scenes.
Josse Impens was a pupil of Portaels. From 1893, he worked in Schaerbeck.

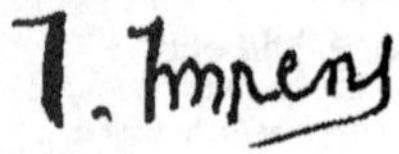

Museums and Galleries:
Brussels: *Flemish Inn*.
Auction records:
Paris, 21 Nov 1900, *Reading the Newspaper*, FRF 205. Brussels, 4 May 1976, *Fisherman* (oil on canvas, 13¾ x 11in/35 x 28cm) BEF 30,000. Lucerne, 20 May 1980, *Leaving Church in Winter* (oil on wood, 32¾ x 24¾in/83 x 63cm) CHF 4,500. Brussels, 24 March 1982, *Interior of a Tavern* (1876, oil on wood, 22½ x 29¼in/57 x 74cm) BEF 130,000. Brussels, 27 March 1985, *Market in Flanders* (oil on panel, 24 x 43¼in/61 x 110cm) BEF 150,000. Amsterdam, 30 Oct 1990, *Confidences* (oil on panel, 22 x 18½in/56 x 47cm) NLG 4,830. Lokeren, 10 Dec 1994, *In the Studio* (oil on canvas, 15¾ x 12¾in/40 x 32.5cm) BEF 26,000. Lokeren, 20 May 1995, *Small Girl Seated with a Doll* (oil on panel, 14½ x 17¾in/37 x 45cm) BEF 60,000. Lokeren, 9 March 1996, *Peasant with a Pipe* (oil on panel, 14½ x 9in/37 x 22cm) BEF 44,000. Lokeren, 6 Dec 1997, *Solitude* (oil on panel, 12½ x 9¼in/32 x 23.5cm) BEF 55,000. Antwerp, 1 Dec 1998, *Necklace* (oil on panel, 30 x 22 ins / 77 x 57 cm) BEF 200,000. Brussels, 27 Aug 2002, *Maternity* (oil on panel, 15 x 20 ins / 37 x 51 cm) EUR 2,000. Brussels, 13 Oct 2003, *Artists in a Bar* (oil on canvas, 11 x 15 ins / 29 x 38 cm) EUR 1,600. Lokeren, 13 Dec 2003, *Domestic Happiness* (oil on panel, 15 x 20 ins / 37 x 52 cm) EUR 5,500. London, 13 Oct 2004, *Print Colourer* (oil on canvas, 28 x 21 ins / 71 x 54 cm) GBP 5,000.

IMPERATO, Filippo
Italian, 19th century.
Active in Naples.
Draughtsman, engraver (burin).
Imperato engraved plates for the Royal Bourbon Museum.

IMPERATRICE, Jacopo, called Padre Umile da Messina
Italian, 17th century.

Born c. 1592; died 1680.
Active in Messina.
Painter.
Imperatrice trained under B. Rodriguez. He entered the Order of the Capuchins at the age of 40 and decorated the monastery of the church of the Capuchins in Messina with a *Transfiguration of Christ* and *Last Supper*.

IMPERIALE, Girolamo
Italian, 17th century.
Born in Genoa; died c. 1660.
Painter, engraver (etching). Religious subjects.
Imperiale learned engraving from Giulio Bensi. He worked for the cathedrals of Scala and Ravello.
AUCTION RECORDS:
LONDON, 4 Feb 1982, *Virgin and Infant with St Catherine and St Jerome* (etching, 8½ x 6½ ins / 21.3 x 16.7 cm) GBP 900.

IMPERIALI. See **FERNANDI Francesco**

IMPERIATO, Giovanni or Johannes
Italian, 14th century.
Born in Asti (Piedmont).
Painter.
In 1387, Imperiato painted a dozen banners for the duke of Orleans.

IMPO, real name: Atsuchi, later Aya or Ki Miyazaki; nicknames: Shijo, Jonoshin (or Tsunenoshin)
Japanese, 18th century.
Born 1717, in Owari (Aichi); died 1774.
Painter.
Impo was a bamboo painter of the Nanga School (scholar painting) who lived in Kyoto and is also known as a Confucianist. He is considered one of the pioneers of scholar painting in Japan.
AUCTION RECORDS:
NEW YORK, 16 April 1988, *Bamboo Leaves* (ink/panel, kakemono, a pair, 49¾ x 10½ ins / 126.5 x 26.5 cm) USD 1,210.

IMSCHOOT, A. Jules van
Flemish School, 19th century.
Born 1821; died 1884.
Painter, engraver.
According to Doctor von Wurzbach, A. Jules van Imschoot was working in 1850, which would seem to make his date of birth as given by Siret (1843) unlikely. It seems probable that this is the Brussels painter Jules von Imschoot, whose painting *Attack and Capture of Carriana* (Italian War, 1866) is in Ypres Museum.
AUCTION RECORDS:
PARIS, 17 and 18 Nov 1943, *Grenadier Loading* (1869) FRF 1,500. LOKEREN, 6 Dec 1997, *Battle of the Dunes, 14 June 1658* (1854, oil on panel, 10¾ x 16in/27.2 x 39.7cm) BEF 160,000. STOCKHOLM, 23 Nov 1999, *Horsemen Resting* (1854, oil on canvas, 21 x 25 ins / 54 x 64 cm) SEK 32,000. BRUSSELS, 7 Dec 1999, *Episode from the Battle of the Dunes, Won by the French* (1854, oil on panel, 50 x 15 ins / 127 x 39 cm) BEF 150,000. BRUSSELS, 4 April 2000, *Battle Scene* (1854, oil on panel, 11 x 15 ins / 27 x 39 cm) BEF 140,000. LONDON, 27 March 2001, *Battle Scene* (1864, oil on board, 8 x 13 ins / 21 x 32 cm) GBP 2,200. LONDON, 13 Feb 2003, *Avoiding a Live Shell. Signalling the Charge* (1864, oil on panel, a pair, 9 x 13 ins / 22 x 32 cm) GBP 1,100.

IMSLAND, Per
Norwegian, 20th century.
Draughtsman.

IMTHURM, Alexander Emil
Swiss, 19th century.
Born 2 March 1829, in Naples, grew up in Schaffhausen; died 1889, in Paris.
Painter. Portraits, genre scenes.
He began his training in Naples and completed it in Paris, but learnt drawing from Tobias Hurter in Schaffhausen. He worked in Munich, Italy and Nîmes.
MUSEUMS AND GALLERIES:
ALÈS: *Academy*.

IN TE CROON, Hendrik
Flemish, 16th century.
Active in Mechelen.
Painter.
Flemish School.

INABA, Haruo
Japanese, 20th century.
Born 1931, in Numazu (Shizuoka).
Painter.
After studying painting at the university of fine art in Tokyo, Inaba took part in numerous group exhibitions: in 1966 in the exhibition *Modern Art of the New Generation* at the Tokyo museum of modern art, and Contemporary Japanese Art under the aegis of the *Mainichi* newspaper, in 1967 in the IXth Japanese international art exhibition, as well as in a solo exhibition the same year in Tokyo.
MUSEUMS AND GALLERIES:
NUMAZU (Town Hall).

INADA, Saburo
Japanese, 20th century.
Born 1902, in Ibaraki Prefecture; died 1970.
Engraver.
Inada studied painting in oils at the art college in Taiheiyo, but he turned to copper engraving, in a more abstract style, in which he mixes many different elements. Whilst still young, he began to exhibit at the *Nika* salon for painting and sculpture and the *Shinseisaku* salon for young artists. In 1948, he became a member of the association of independent artists, which he left in 1959 to found the group called Han (engraving). He then turned to teaching engraving on copper. In 1957, 1962 and 1966 he took part in the Tokyo prints Biennale.

INAGAKI, Morio
Japanese, 20th century.
Born in Tokyo.
Painter.
Morio Inagaki exhibited in Paris at the Salon d'Automne.

INAGAKI, Tomoo
Japanese, 20th century.
Born 1902, in Tokyo; died 1980.
Draughtsman, engraver.
Tomoo Inagaki, who was a draughtsman and wood engraver, trained under the direction of Onchi Koshiro and Hiratsuka Un'ichi. He was a figurative artist with a strong decorative tendency who specialised in woodblock prints of cats. He featured from 1924 in the exhibitions of the Japanese engraving association and Kokugakai (the national painting association). He had several exhibitions in Europe and the USA.

INAMA-STERNEGG, Frantziska von
Austrian, 19th - 20th century.
Born 2 July 1870, in Innsbruck.
Painter. Religious subjects, portraits, genre scenes.
Frantziska von Inama-Sternegg studied in Vienna and Munich. Her work was featured at exhibitions held by the circle of artists in Vienna and St Louis, and at the artists' society in Munich and the Innsbruck union of artists. Her portraits were mainly of children.

INATOWIEZ-LUBIANSKY, Adolf
Polish, 20th century.
Born in Warsaw.
Painter.

Inatowiez-Lubiansky was a pupil of Noakowski and Wyerotkowski. He exhibited in France at the Salon des Artistes Français from 1927.

INCALCAVECCHIA. See **GIOVANNI DI PIETRO**

INCARDONA, Rocco

Italian, 20th century.
Born 5 August 1942, in Catania, Sicily.
Active in Spain since 1972.
Draughtsman. Figures.

Incardona was a student at the school of fine arts in Buenos Aires. In 1971, he was awarded a scholarship by the Argentinian National Fund for Contemporary Art. Since 1972, he has lived and worked in Barcelona. His works have been shown at numerous exhibitions in Buenos Aires (notably at the Museum of Modern Art, 1976), Aix-en-Provence (1974, 1976, 1980, 1982), Málaga (1978), Barcelona and Granollers (1987).

INCE, Evelyn

British, 20th century.
Born 1886; died 1941.
Painter.

MUSEUMS AND GALLERIES:

LONDON (Tate Collection): *Flower Piece* (c. 1934, tempera/wood).

INCE, J. Howard

British, 19th century.
Active in London.
Painter. Genre scenes.

The work of J. Howard Ince was represented in Paris at the Exposition Universelle of 1900.

INCE, Joseph Murray

British, 19th century.
Born 1806, in London; died 24 September 1859, in Presteigne, Wales.
Painter, watercolourist. Architectural views, landscapes.

Joseph Ince studied under David Cox in 1823; he exhibited in London, notably at the Royal Academy, at Suffolk Street, and at the New Water-Colour Society from 1826 to 1858. There are works by him, mainly architectural subjects, in the Manchester Museum and the Victoria and Albert Museum in London.

MUSEUMS AND GALLERIES:

LONDON (Victoria and Albert Mus.).

AUCTION RECORDS:

LONDON, 21 Nov 1908, *Ludlow Castle; Wooded Landscape,* GBP 7. LONDON, 29 May 1946, *Cambridge,* GBP 50. LONDON, 26 June 1968, *Port of Stockholm,* GBP 800. LONDON, 16 March 1973, *Panoramic View of the Port of Stockholm,* Gns 800. LONDON, 13 Nov 1980, *Cottage by a River* (1845, watercolour/pencil outlines, 10 x 13 3/4in/24.5 x 35cm) GBP 780. LONDON, 30 June 1981, *Crickhowell and Glan Usk; Glan Usk and Tretower* (watercolour, a pair, 8 1/2 x 13 1/2in/21.3 x 34.5cm) GBP 1,200. LONDON, 20 March 1984, *Regattas* (1842, watercolour, 8 1/4 x 13 3/4in/21 x 35cm) GBP 700. LONDON, 13 March 1985, *The High, Oxford with University College, St Mary's and Queen's College* (oil on canvas, 22 x 27 1/2in/56 x 70cm) GBP 3,200. LONDON, 29 April 1986, *Oxford* (1835, watercolour, 6 1/2 x 12in/16.5 x 30.6cm) GBP 1,800. LONDON, 25 Jan 1988, *Cows Drinking in a Bedfordshire Village* (1840, watercolour, 7 3/4 x 10 1/4in/20 x 26cm) GBP 418. LONDON, 30 Jan 1991, *Sailing in an Estuary* (1836, watercolour heightened with gouache, 7 3/4 x 12 3/4in/19.5 x 32.5cm) GBP 1,980. LONDON, 8 Nov 1995, *The High in Oxford* (1838, oil on canvas, 21 3/4 x 27 1/2in/55.5 x 70cm) GBP 3,680.

INCHBOLD, John William

British, 19th century.
Born 29 April 1830, in Leeds; died 23 January 1888, in Leeds.
Painter, watercolourist, engraver. Landscapes.
Symbolism.
Pre-Raphaelite (related to).

John William Inchbold was the son of the chief editor and proprietor of the *Leeds Intelligencer.* After studying drawing he went to live in London, working in the lithographic studio of Day and Haghe. Around 1847 he began to study watercolour with Louis Haghe. He began his career in Suffolk Street two years later with two landscapes. His name appeared in the catalogues of the London exhibitions, notably the Royal Academy from 1849 to 1887.

In the 1860s a reversal of fortune forced him to leave London in spite of the assistance of his friends Rossetti and Burne-Jones. In summer 1869 he was able to settle in the south of the Isle of Wight and in spite of his precarious financial situation, fresh landscapes renewed his creative muse. He was a poet as well as a painter and his very naturalistic work revealed a poignant poetic sentiment.

He was attracted by the pre-Raphaelites and from 1851 his works illustrated his leanings very clearly. In 1855 his painting *The Moorland* was warmly received by Ruskin. Inchbold demonstrated outstanding qualities of the observation of nature and in his skies and his far-reaching panoramas he showed his mastery as a landscape painter. He was particularly skilled at depicting large horizons, the sea, mountains and sky. He also produced many prints.

MUSEUMS AND GALLERIES:

DUBLIN: *Lake Geneva* - LEEDS (City AG): *On the Lagoon, Venice* (oil on canvas); *At Bolton (The White Doe of Rylstone)* (1855, oil/panel); *Harvest Field, Stratford upon Avon* (oil on canvas); *Scarborough* (oil on canvas); *On the Road to Sepey, Switzerland* (watercolour and gouache) - LONDON (Tate Collection): *The Moorland (Dewar-stone, Dartmoor)* (1854, oil on canvas); *Gordale Scar, Yorkshire* (exhibited in 1876, oil on canvas); around 40 drawings (pencil, watercolour and gouache/paper) - LONDON (Victoria and Albert Mus.): *View above Montreaux* (1880, watercolour) - OXFORD (Ashmolean Mus.): *Beinn Eighe.*

AUCTION RECORDS:

LONDON, 13 April 1908, *Lake Lucerne* (1857) GBP 10; *Tintagel, Cornwall* (drawing) GBP 11. LONDON, 4 June 1974, *Banks of Lake Geneva* (1888) GBP 500. LONDON, 23 Nov 1982, *Sant' Elena, Venice* (1863-1864, oil on canvas, 11 x 21 ins / 28 x 53.5 cm) GBP 950. LONDON, 10 May 1983, *Mule Drawing the Wheel of a Watermill, Algiers* (1877, watercolour heightened with white/grey-blue paper, 9 3/4 x 13 3/4 ins / 25 x 34.8 cm) GBP 800. LONDON, 15 Dec 1987, *Scarborough* (1871, watercolour and pencil heightened with gouache/grey-blue paper, 7 x 10 ins / 17.8 x 25.3 cm) GBP 1,800. LONDON, 9 Feb 1990, *Lake Geneva with the Dents du Midi in the Distance* (1863, oil on canvas, 23 1/2 x 37 1/2 ins / 60 x 95 cm) GBP 6,600. YORK, 12 Nov 1991, *Chillon Castle* (watercolour, 11 x 14 3/4 ins / 27 x 37.5 cm) GBP 2,640. LONDON, 30 March 1994, *Undercliffe in the Spring* (1870, oil on panel, 22 1/2 x 34 ins / 57 x 85.5 cm) GBP 51,000. LONDON, 14 June 2001, *Lake Geneva* (watercolour over pencil heightened with gouache, 9 x 13 ins / 24 x 34 cm) GBP 6,500. LONDON, 2 Dec 2002, *Lake Geneva from the North* (oil on canvas, 14 x 21 ins / 35 x 53 cm) GBP 3,000. LEEDS, 18 Nov 2003, *Alpine Lake Landscape* (watercolour, 9 x 14 ins / 24 x 35 cm) GBP 1,850. LONDON, 20 Nov 2003, *St Martin in the Alps* (watercolour, gouache and scratching out, 7 x 9 ins / 17 x 24 cm) GBP 2,000. LONDON, 10 March 2004, *Greenwich Park* (pencil, watercolour and gouache on paper laid on canvas, 13 x 20 ins / 34 x 52 cm) GBP 2,600. LONDON, 3 June 2004, *Swiss Mountain Scene* (pencil and watercolour heightened with touches of white, 10 x 10 ins / 26 x 25 cm) GBP 2,600.

INCHBOLD, Stanley
British, 19th century.
Born 1856.
Active in Bushey (Hertfordshire).
Painter, watercolourist.

Stanley Inchbold exhibited in London at Suffolk Street and at the New Water-Colour Society from 1884.

AUCTION RECORDS:
LONDON, 2 Nov 1979, *Palestine Landscape in Spring* (oil on canvas, 30 1/4 x 45 1/2 ins / 76.8 x 115.6 cm) GBP 800. LONDON, 12 Oct 2000, *Dome of the Rock, Mosque of Omar* (watercolour and pencil heightened with gouache and scratching out, 17 x 22 ins / 42 x 55 cm) GBP 5,800. CLEVELAND, 16 Nov 2000, *Morocco* (oil on canvas, 30 x 40 ins / 76 x 102 cm) USD 1,800. LONDON, 1 May 2002, *View of a Town in the Middle East* (oil on canvas, 30 x 50 ins / 75 x 126 cm) GBP 1,400. NOTTINGHAM, 5 Feb 2004, *Whitby at Dawn* (pencil and watercolour heightened with white, 15 x 20 ins / 37 x 50 cm) GBP 2,100.

INCISA DI CAMERANA, Vincenzo
Italian, 19th century.
Born 19th century, in Turin.
Painter. Genre scenes, landscapes.

Vincenzo Incisa di Camerana was a pupil at the Accademia Albertina in Turin. He exhibited in Naples, Milan and Rome.

INCISO, N., pseudonym of William Soncini
Italian, 20th century.
Born 1913, near Parma.
Sculptor, painter.

Inciso was born into a family of artists and studied architecture at university, but did not have any formal artistic training. He first exhibited in 1943, and since then has showed throughout Italy. His often figurative sculptures are characterised by their dynamism, floating forms and delicate elegance. He often employs a vertical, spindly structure and expresses movement and impetus using methods reminiscent of Art Nouveau. His painting shows the same concerns and the same sense of how to fill space.

INDACO, Francesco and Jacopo Dell'.
See **DELL'INDACO**

INDELLI, Giuseppe
Italian, 17th century.
Painter.

The only known work by Indelli is a painting of *St Nicholas*, which can be found in the church of S Maria del Popolo agli Incurabili in Naples.

INDENBAUM, Leon
Lithuanian, 20th century.
Born 1891, in Sevsk; died 1981.
Active from 1911 in France.
Sculptor, draughtsman. Figures.

Leon Indenbaum studied at the Odessa school of fine art before coming to Paris in 1911. He then settled in 'La Ruche' and become friendly with several of the artists who later formed the École de Paris including Soutine, Kremègne and Chagall. From 1911 to 1919, he worked in the studio of Antoine Bourdelle, becoming a friend of Modigliani. In 1913, the collector Jacques Doucet became his patron. He was a figurative artist; nevertheless he sought to capture not the outward appearance of things but their inner being.

Collective exhibitions include: Salon des Indépendants (1912); Salon des Tuileries; first exhibition of the Neuf (Nine) group of which he was a member (1964); St-Denis museum (1966); Chateau, St-Ouen (1967); the Archbishops' Palace, Narbonne (1970). The Institut de France awarded him the G. Wildenstein Prize (1968).

BIBLIOGRAPHY:
René Iché et grands sculpteurs contemporains, exhibition catalogue, Palais des Archevêques, Narbonne, 1970.

AUCTION RECORDS:
PARIS, 24 Feb 1934, *Head of a Woman* (terracotta) FRF 300; *Torso of a Girl* (marble) FRF 5,000. PARIS, 2 Dec 1976, *Head of a Young Woman* (sculpted and gilded wood, h. 12 1/2 ins / 32 cm) FRF 16,500. VERSAILLES, 2 March 1986, *Head of a Woman with Ringlets* (bronze, 12 1/4 x 7 3/4 ins / 31 x 20 cm) FRF 41,000. PARIS, 14 April 1991, *Cockerel* (c. 1930, bronze, h. 11 ins / 27 cm) FRF 10,000. PARIS, 8 July 1993, *Archaic Head* (1919, bronze, h. 9 ins / 22 cm) FRF 9,500. PARIS, 13 April 1994, *Woman with Parrot* (low relief in bronze) FRF 38,000. TEL AVIV, 25 Sept 1994, *Young Woman with Ringlets* (1913, bronze, h. 12 1/4 ins / 31 cm) USD 2,875. PARIS, 13 May 1996, *Woman with a Parrot* (c. 1920, brown-patinated bronze low relief heightened with black, 57 1/2 x 10 1/4 x 3/4 ins / 146 x 26 x 2 cm) FRF 27,000. PARIS, 25 March 2001, *Nude Model doing her Hair* (terracotta, h. 15 ins / 38 cm) FRF 18,000. CALAIS, 19 May 2002, *Beehive* (oil on canvas, 22 x 17 ins / 56 x 44 cm) EUR 2,250. PARIS, 24 Nov 2003, *Head of Woman with Headband* (black patinated bronze, h. 12 ins / 30 cm) EUR 3,500. PARIS, 25 Jan 2004, *Nude Model doing her Hair* (patinated terracotta, h. 15 ins / 39 cm) EUR 5,100.

INDERBITZI, Heinrick Dominik, or Bütziner
Swiss, 18th century.
Active in Schwyz c. 1736-1741.
Sculptor (wood).

INDEYTSEV, Dmitri
Russian, 19th century.
Born 1813.
Draughtsman.

Dmitri Indeytsev trained at the court school of architecture in Moscow, where he went on to become professor. In 1834, his *Portrait of Prince D.M. Livov* was engraved by E Skotnikov.

INDIA, Bernardino
Italian, 16th century.
Born c. 1528 or 1535, in Verona; died 1590.
Painter, fresco artist, draughtsman. Religious subjects, portraits. Murals.

India was principally a decorator and his main works, carried out between 1568 and 1584, were ceilings and frescoes for the palaces of Verona and decorations in the Casa Tierne, Vicenza. He also worked with Giulio Romano, painting religious pictures for the church of S Bernardino.

AUCTION RECORDS:
LONDON, 10 April 1985, *Entombment* (black chalk, pen and wash, 7 1/2 x 9 1/2in/18.8 x 23.9cm) GBP 1,800. NEW YORK, 10 Jan 1996, *Drawing of a Fireplace* (black chalk, ink and wash, 5 1/4 x 7 1/4in/13.6 x 18.3cm) USD 2,760. NEW YORK, 26 Jan 2000, *Mary Magdalen Washing the Feet of Christ* (pen and brown ink wash, 9 x 12 ins / 22 x 31 cm) USD 18,000. PARIS, 27 March 2003, *Wedding at Cana* (chalk, pen and ink wash, 8 x 12 ins / 20 x 31 cm) EUR 7,000. NEW YORK, 21 Jan 2004, *Design for a Ceiling Decoration with Venus and Cupid Embracing* (pen and brown ink wash, 5 x 8 ins / 12 x 20 cm) USD 4,500.

INDIA, Tullio
Italian, 16th century.
Active in Verona c. 1530.
Painter. History painting, portraits.

The nephew of Bernardino India, he was an excellent copyist of Caliari. Among his works are the frescoes in the Casa Miniscialdi and figures of saints in the church of S Giorgio, Verona.

INDIAN LEWIS. See **LEWIS Frederick Christian, the Younger**

INDIANA, Robert, pseudonym of Robert Clark
American, 20th century.
Born 13 September 1928, in New Castle (Indiana).
Painter, sculptor. Stage sets, stage costumes, posters.
Pop Art.

Robert Indiana trained at the John Herron School of Art, Indianapolis, in 1945 and 1946, then at the Munson-Williams Proctor Institute, Utica (New York), Art Institute of Chicago from 1949 to 1953, Skowhegan School of Painting (Maine), University of Edinburgh and Edinburgh College of Art, and then in London. Afterwards, he travelled to Mexico, Europe and the interior of the USA. In 1958, he moved to New York and, in 1978, settled in Vinhalven, on an island in Maine.

In 1961 Indiana featured in the exhibition *Studio of Dance*, and in 1962 in the historic exhibition *New Realists* held in New York. Contrary to the title of the latter exhibition, it effectively brought together a great proportion of international artists who could proclaim to be investigating the nature of urban popular culture, which ushered in Pop Art. He was a key artist of this movement and exhibited everywhere, taking part in every event which had Pop Art as its theme.

He joined the second wave of American Pop Art which came after Rauschenberg, Johns, Chamberlain, Stankiewicz, Kienholz and Conner. In his early works, he aimed at the objective of Pop Art as defined by Pierre Restany: 'an authentically American language which relies on the direction of modern nature. More importantly, this modern nature was conditioned by the North-American phenomenon.' He was an avid reader of Melville and Whisman, and adopted the name of the State where he was born. In reply to a survey, he stated briefly: *I would only say that I am an American.*

Like many Pop Artists, he evolved later in different directions. He followed on from Dan Flavin and Chryssa, notably using neon light tubes for their power for evoking the modern urban everyday. He was also influenced by the 'Hard Edge' artists, borrowing geometric shapes (circles, stars and pentagons) with well-defined flat-surfaced even colours. The famous *Demuth American Dream* dates from 1963. It is a composition made up of the figure five and a play of stars, as a tribute to the painter Charles Demuth. The latter was one of the precursors of the depiction of American industrialisation, whom he admired for the same reason as Edward Hopper and Charles Sheeler. Indiana was soon only using letters and numbers. Having become famous for his word *Love* with the slanting 'O', which quickly became a typical Pop-Art image, he began to elaborate on this theme and produced a great many series of it. It was an obsessional image, like Andy Warhol's *Portrait of Marilyn Monroe*, and infiltrated all levels of the American way of life, even postage stamps.

As a result of *Hermes*, Indiana extracted a monumental sculpture in welded steel sheet and recycled material collected from the port of Manhattan. It reflected the spirit of Pop Art born from the consumer society. He maintained ambiguous links to Pop Art, both denouncing and praising it. He also produced stage sets, posters and costumes for various different theatrical plays.

As a painter of his country, he selected what he considered to be its most 'natural' image: 'In Europe trees grow everywhere. In America signs grow like trees.' Working more on signs than images, Indiana borrowed the stencilling method from advertising in order to insert words into geometric structures. He inserted gaps between strongly implicit words, producing an emotional response. For example: *Love - Eat - Dead*, or extracts from Negro Spirituals and political texts. He presented them in neutral, austere, impersonal frames, and flat surfaces.

Indiana rarely exploited his fame as a Pop Artist. Around the time of his withdrawal to his island retreat, he completely stopped painting in order to devote himself exclusively to sculpture again. He also abandoned the industrial popular culture of scrap metal at the port of Manhattan. Instead, he brought back the gnarled trunks of trees on his island to the former sail-making factory which had become his studio, in order to assemble his barbaric idols. However, for the retrospective in Nice, he painted a seventh variation on the *American Dream*, dedicated to three women of America who had gone to live and die in France. Although it was a hybrid association, it was within the spirit of Pop Art and popular culture. The three women were: Isadora Duncan, the sophisticated early 20th-century dancer; Josephine Baker, the Black nude dancer of the 1930s, and Grace Kelly, the heroine of many Hitchcock films.

Indiana was invited to the great international meetings, such as the International Exhibition in Montreal in 1967; the São Paulo Biennale and Documenta IV in Kassel in 1968; *The Zero Room*, held at the Kunstmuseum, Düsseldorf, in 1973; *American Art since 1945*, held at the Museum of Modern Art, New York, in 1975; *100 Artists, 100 Years*, held at the Art Institute of Chicago in 1980; and the Foire Internationale d'Art Contemporain (FIAC), held in Paris in 1990.

He held his first solo exhibition in 1962, then: 1963 Walker Art Center, Minneapolis, and Institute of Contemporary Art (ICA), Boston; 1968 Museum of Art, Toledo; 1971 Badischer Kunstverein, Karlsruhe; 1972 Louisiana Museum, Humlebæk; 1976 and 1978 Museum of Modern Art, Indianapolis; and 1984 National Museum of American Art, Washington. Retrospectives of his work have been held in the USA, notably at the Philadelphia Museum of Art in 1968, at the Whitney Museum of American Art, New York, in 1982, and at the Musée d'Art Moderne, Nice, in 1998, and in Germany and Holland.

BIBLIOGRAPHY:

Restany, Pierre, *Les Nouveaux Réalistes*, Éd. Planète, Paris, 1968. Weinhardt, Carl J., *Robert Indiana*, Abrams, New York, 1990. Sheedan, Susan, *Robert Indiana Prints. A catalogue raisonné*, Susan Sheehan Gall., New York, 1991. *Robert Indiana. Rétrospective, 1959-1998*, exhibition catalogue, Musée d'Art moderne et d'Art contemporain, Nice, 1998. Ryan, Susan Elizabeth, *Robert Indiana, Figures of Speech*, Yale University Press, New Haven and London, 2000. Kernan, Nathan, *Robert Indiana*, Assouline Pub, New York, 2003.

MUSEUMS AND GALLERIES:

AMSTERDAM (Stedelijk Mus.): *Six* (1965); *Eight* (1965) - ANN ARBOR (University of Michigan Mus. of Art): *The American Way* (1964, pencil/paper) - BALTIMORE (MA) - BUFFALO (Albright-Knox AG) - COLOGNE (Wallraf-Richartz Mus.): *The American Gaz Works* (1961-1962) - EINDHOVEN (Van Abbe Mus.): *Red Diamond American Dream N° III* (1962) - INDIANAPOLIS (MA): *Love* (two works, a painting and a sculpture) - LOS ANGELES (County MA) - NEW YORK (Metropolitan Mus. of Art) - NEW YORK (MoMA): *American Dream* (1960) - NEW YORK (Whitney Mus. of American Art) - NICE (Mus. d'Art Moderne et d'Art Contemporain) - PORTLAND, ME (MA): *4-Star Love* (1961); *Electi* (1960-1961) - SAN FRANCISCO (MoMA): *The Fair Rebecca* (1961) - TORONTO (AG of Ontario): *The Demuth American Dream N° 5* (1963) - WASHINGTON DC (NGA): prints - WASHINGTON DC (Smithsonian American AM): *The Figure Five* (1963, oil on canvas); *Love* (1973, screenprint/paper); *Five* (1984, painted wood ceiling beam, wood dowel, wood block, and metal wheels).

AUCTION RECORDS:

NEW YORK, 18 Nov 1970, *Love* USD 19,000. NEW YORK, 17 Nov 1971, *Cuba* (wood and iron) USD 5,000. HAMBURG, 9 June 1972, *3* (1965) DEM 5,000. NEW YORK, 26 Oct 1972, *Number 10, Demeter, Decagon* (1962) USD 3,500. NEW YORK, 18 Oct 1973, *The Demuth Five* USD 19,000. NEW YORK, 3 May 1974, *Ballyhoo* (1961) USD 23,000. NEW YORK, 12 May 1977, *Love (Red, White and Black)* (1973, oil on canvas, 48 x 48 ins

/ 122 x 122 cm) USD 11,000. NEW YORK, 18 May 1979, *Self-portrait* (1971, oil on canvas, 48 x 48 ins / 121 x 121 cm) USD 18,000. NEW YORK, 13 Nov 1980, *Love* (1966, stainless steel, 11¾ x 11¾ x 6 ins / 30 x 30 x 15 cm) USD 7,000. NEW YORK, 19 Nov 1981, *The American Hug N° 1* (1964, graphite, 25 x 19 ins / 63.5 x 48 cm) USD 1,400. NEW YORK, 10 Nov 1982, *Zero* (1966, oil on canvas, 12 x 12 ins / 30.5 x 30.5 cm) USD 2,250. NEW YORK, 20 May 1983, *Spring* (1978, oil on canvas, 60 x 50 ins / 152.4 x 127 cm) USD 17,000. NEW YORK, 3 May 1985, *Love* (1966, oil on canvas, 48 x 48 ins / 122 x 122 cm) USD 19,000. NEW YORK, 20 Feb 1988, *Lillian Russell* (1966, soft chalks/paper, 25¾ x 20 ins / 65.7 x 50.8 cm) USD 1,760. ROME, 15 Nov 1988, *Mozart: A Little Night Music* (1966, acrylic/canvas, 59¾ x 50 ins / 152 x 127 cm) ITL 40,000,000. NEW YORK, 3 May 1989, *Love* (1966, oil on canvas, 48 x 48 ins / 122 x 122 cm) USD 104,500. NEW YORK, 4 Oct 1989, *Love* (1968, oil on canvas, 12¼ x 24¼ ins / 31 x 61.5 cm) USD 82,500. PARIS, 11 Oct 1989, *Love* (acrylic/canvas, 48 x 48 ins / 122 x 122 cm) FRF 910,000. NEW YORK, 7 Nov 1990, *Eat* (1962, acrylic/canvas, 12 x 12 ins / 30.5 x 30.5 cm) GBP 35,750. NEW YORK, 6 May 1992, *Love* (1974, oil on canvas, 60 x 60 ins / 152.4 x 152.4 cm) USD 44,000. MUNICH, 26 May 1992, *Picasso* (1974, colour silk screen print, 24 x 20 ins / 61 x 50.5 cm) DEM 1,667. PARIS, 26 June 1992, *Love is God* (1964, acrylic/canvas, 48 x 48 ins / 122 x 122 cm) FRF 325,000. PARIS, 11 June 1993, *The Great American Dream: San Francisco I* (1969, drawing, 40¼ x 26 ins / 102 x 66 cm) FRF 16,000. NEW YORK, 10 Nov 1993, *The Black Diamond of American Dream N° 2* (1962, oil on canvas, diagonal: 85 ins / 215 cm, 3½ x 85 ins/9 x 215.9 cm) USD 277,500. PARIS, 17 Oct 1994, *Particci Pentagon* (1962, acrylic/canvas, 24 x 22 ins / 61 x 56 cm) FRF 105,000. NEW YORK, 15 Nov 1995, *Love 4 Times* (1968, oil on canvas, assemblage of four canvases, 24 x 24 ins / 61 x 61 cm) USD 36,800. LONDON, 30 Nov 1995, *Red Sails* (1963, acrylic/canvas, 60¼ x 50 ins / 153 x 127 cm) GBP 14,950. NEW YORK, 8 May 1996, *God is a Lily of the Valley* (1962, oil on canvas, 60 x 48 ins / 152.4 x 121.9 cm) USD 57,500. LONDON, 6 Dec 1996, *USA Fun* (1964, oil on canvas, 11¾ x 11¾ ins / 30 x 30 cm) GBP 9,200. NEW YORK, 7 May 1997, *Coenties Slip 1* (c. 1964-1965, oil on canvas, 24¼ x 24 ins / 61.3 x 61 cm) USD 19,550. NEW YORK, 20 Nov 1997, *N° 3* (c. 1965, oil on canvas, 24¼ x 24¼ ins / 61.3 x 61.3 cm) USD 24,150. NEW YORK, 6 and 7 March 1998, *Decade: Self-portraits, Vinal-Haven Suite* (1980, four silk screen prints in colour, 24 x 24 ins / 61 x 61 cm) USD 3,737. NEW YORK, 7 June 1999, *One Indiana Square* (1970, acrylic on canvas, 63 x 63 ins / 160 x 160 cm) USD 48,000. NEW YORK, 16 Nov 2000, *Love* (1995, painted aluminium, 36 x 36x18 ins / 91 x 91x46 cm) USD 95,000. NEW YORK, 16 Nov 2000, *Florida - Confederacy Series* (oil on canvas, 70 x 60 ins / 178 x 152 cm) USD 125,000. NEW YORK, 17 May 2001, *Six* (1960-1962, oil on wood with metal, 23 x 18x22 ins / 58 x 46x56 cm) USD 380,000. PARIS, 20 June 2001, *One Indiana Square* (1970, acrylic on canvas, 85 x 85 ins / 216 x 216 cm) FRF 860,000. NEW YORK, 14 May 2002, *American Sweetheart* (1959, oil on canvas, 96 x 48 ins / 244 x 122 cm) USD 550,000. NEW YORK, 14 Nov 2002, *Love Wall - Black, Red and Yellow* (1968, oil on canvas, four attached, 24 x 20 ins / 60 x 50 cm) USD 260,000. NEW YORK, 15 May 2003, *Terre Haute 2* (1969, acrylic on canvas, 60 x 50 ins / 152 x 127 cm) USD 200,000. NEW YORK, 12 Nov 2003, *Love* (1966-1999, enamel on steel, 18 x 18x9 ins / 46 x 46x23 cm) USD 105,000. NEW YORK, 12 May 2004, *Love, Blue Red* (1995, painted aluminium, 72 x 72x36 ins / 183 x 183x91 cm) USD 420,000. LONDON, 24 June 2004, *Love* (1990, enamel on steel, 72 x 72x36 ins / 183 x 183x91 cm) GBP 170,000.

INDONI, Filippo

Italian, 19th century.

Born in Rome; died 1883.

Painter, watercolourist. Genre scenes.

Indoni exhibited in Rome and Turin.

AUCTION RECORDS:

LONDON, 7 Dec 1907, *Flirt*, GBP 5. LONDON, 19 May 1976, *Serenade* (oil on canvas, 32 x 25½ ins / 81.5 x 65 cm) GBP 1,400. NEW YORK, 14 Jan 1977, *Villagers* (watercolour, 30 x 21½ ins / 76 x 54.5 cm) USD 1,000. LOS ANGELES, 6 Nov 1978, *Harvesters Resting* (watercolour, 27½ x 19½ ins / 70 x 49.5 cm) USD 1,050. LONDON, 15 June 1979, *Peasant Women Going to Market* (oil on canvas, 26 x 42¾ ins / 66 x 108.6 cm) GBP 900. NEW YORK, 7 Jan 1981, *Washerwoman at the Fountain* (watercolour and pencil, 16 x 11 ins / 40.7 x 27.9 cm) USD 750. NEW YORK, 1 March 1984, *Return from Grape Harvesting* (oil on canvas, 32½ x 20½ ins / 82.5 x 52 cm) USD 1,200. LONDON, 22 March 1984, *Arab Guard* (watercolour, 20½ x 13¾ ins / 52 x 35 cm) GBP 2,400. LONDON, 25 March 1987, *Dancing Girl with Tambourine* (watercolour, 29½ x 20¾ ins / 75 x 53 cm) GBP 1,800. NEW YORK, 25 May 1988, *Arab Guard* (watercolour, 20 x 13¾ ins / 51 x 35 cm) USD 1,320. ROME, 14 Dec 1988, *Interior of an Inn* (1879, distemper/paper, 24 x 34¼ ins / 61 x 87 cm) ITL 12,500,000. LONDON, 17 Feb 1989, *Adoration of Our Lady of Pilar, Saragossa* (oil on canvas, 32½ x 22½ ins / 82.5 x 57.3 cm) GBP 2,420. MILAN, 14 March 1989, *Idyll* (watercolour/card, 21¼ x 14½ ins / 54 x 37 cm) ITL 5,500,000. LONDON, 28 March 1990, *Market Over* (aquarelle and pencil, 39¼ x 26 ins / 100 x 66 cm) GBP 5,280. ROME, 29 May 1990, *Horseman, with Peasants Collecting Sticks in a Landscape* (watercolour, 24 x 19 ins / 61 x 48 cm) ITL 11,500,000. NEW YORK, 23 Oct 1990, *In the Roman Campagna* (oil on canvas, 29¼ x 54½ ins / 74.3 x 138.4 cm) USD 13,200. LONDON, 28 Nov 1990, *Card Party* (watercolour, 30 x 21 ins / 76.5 x 53.5 cm) GBP 2,420. ROME, 28 May 1991, *Rural Kitchen* (tempera/card, 29½ x 20¾ ins / 75 x 53 cm) ITL 6,000,000. LONDON, 19 June 1991, *Happy Family of Peasants in the Roman Campagna* (oil on canvas, 28¼ x 53½ ins / 72 x 136 cm) GBP 12,100. BOLOGNA, 8-9 June 1992, *Fishermen Lazing* (watercolour, 30 x 20¾ ins / 76 x 53 cm) ITL 3,450,000. NEW YORK, 29 Oct 1992, *Peasant Woman* (watercolour/card, 19¾ x 13 ins / 50.2 x 33.3 cm) USD 990. ROME, 27 April 1993, *Spring Festival at the Sanctuary of Divine Love* (1868, oil on canvas, 33¾ x 67¾ ins / 86 x 172 cm) ITL 90,084,000. NEW YORK, 15 Feb 1994, *Domestic Tasks* (watercolour and pencil/paper/reinforced paper, 37 x 27¼ ins / 94 x 68.9 cm) USD 10,925. NEW YORK, 1 Nov 1995, *Coral Necklace* (oil on canvas, 38½ x 29½ ins / 97.8 x 74.9 cm) USD 6,900. LONDON, 11 June 1997, *Peasants in the Roman Campagna* (1877, oil on canvas, 42½ x 64¼ ins / 108 x 163 cm) GBP 29,900. NEWBURY, 17 Feb 1999, *The Wood-gatherer's Meal* (pencil and watercolour, 38 x 25 ins / 96 x 64 cm) GBP 4,000. NEW YORK, 15 June 1999, *Walk Home* (oil on canvas, 26 x 43 ins / 66 x 109 cm) USD 8,000. NEW YORK, 7 June 2000, *Hour of Idleness* (watercolour and pencil, 30 x 21 ins / 76 x 53 cm) USD 4,250. BRUSSELS, 7 Nov 2000, *Spinner and Shepherd in Roman Landscape* (Works on paper, 21 x 14 ins / 53 x 36 cm) BEF 190,000. PHILADELPHIA, 24 June 2001, *Idle Moment* (oil on canvas) USD 1,600. LONDON, 29 Nov 2001, *Courtship* (watercolour, 30 x 21 ins / 76 x 53 cm) GBP 1,800. CHESTER, 6 Nov 2002, *Courting Couple by Wayside. Young Peasant in Traditional Costume* (watercolour, two works, 21 x 14 ins / 54 x 36 cm) GBP 2,700. LONDON, 21 Nov 2002, *Source of Amusement* (1877, oil on panel, 18 x 13 ins / 46 x 34 cm) GBP 7,500. LONDON, 8 Oct 2003, *Gypsy Girl Leaning against a Wall. Gypsy Girl Carrying Wood* (pencil and watercolour, a pair, 20 x 14 ins / 51 x 36 cm) GBP 1,400. STOCKHOLM, 2 Dec 2003, *Flirting in the Countryside* (1875, oil on canvas, 63 x 49 ins / 159 x 124 cm) SEK 145,000. ROME, 10 June 2004, *Peasants in Vesta Temple* (watercolour on card, 30 x 22 ins / 75 x 55 cm) EUR

2,800. London, 13 Oct 2004, *At the Shrine. Serenade* (watercolour, a pair, 21 x 15 ins / 54 x 37 cm) GBP 1,250.

INDRA, or Yin tuo luo (in modern Chinese)
Chinese, 13th century.
Painter.

Indra was a priest in the Tien-chu-szu temple in Hangzhou, in Zhejiang Province. Several Ch'en style wash paintings are attributed to him.

INDUNI, Gottardo
Swiss, 19th century.
Born 7 October 1858, in Ligornetto near Mendrisio (Ticino).
Sculptor.

One of the best pupils of Vincenzo Vela, he exhibited at the royal academy from 1887.

INDUNO, Domenico
Italian, 19th century.
Born 1815, in Milan; died 1878, in Milan.
Painter, watercolourist. History painting, portraits, genre scenes.

Domenico Induno was a pupil of Francesco Hayez at the Accademia in Milan, and also of Sabatelli, and then continued his studies in Rome. He was active in the revolutionary movement of 1848 and had to flee to Switzerland, only returning to Milan in 1859. There he became friendly with Telemaco Signorini, who passed on his enthusiasm for Courbet. He exhibited at the Paris Exposition Universelle of 1879.

Induno belonged successively to both the Classical and Romantic Schools. In his fantasy figures he works for picturesque and brilliant effects. A contemporary of Courbet, he is not dissimilar to the painters of the Romantic School, whose brio and energetic expression give their work an attraction that may not be of the highest order, but which deserves our attention.

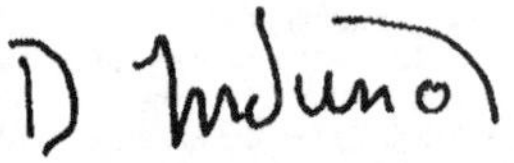

Museums and Galleries:
Boston (SFA): *Rosary* - Florence (Gal. dell'Accademia): *Antiquary* - Genoa: *Girl Considering the Price; Childhood Misfortune* - Milan (Gal. d'Arte Moderna): *Seizure; Placing of the Foundation Stone of the Victor-Emmanuel Gallery; Victor Emmanuel II on Horseback* - Milan (Mus. Poldi Pezzoli): *Sadness* (watercolour) - Milan (Pinacoteca di Brera): *Hunter's Tale* - Padua: *In Place of Mother* - Prato: *Antiquary* - Rome (Gal. Nazionale d'Arte Moderna): *Genre Painting; Portrait of a Man* - Trieste: *At the Well; Melancholy* - Vienna: *Samuel and David.*

Auction records:
Paris, 1894, *Young Girl Reading,* FRF 125. Milan, 16 March 1965, *Old Woman Seated in an Interior,* ITL 1,800,000. Milan, 25 Jan 1968, *Old Woman Knitting,* ITL 2,400,000. Milan, 16 June 1969, *Visit to the Nurse,* ITL 8,000,000. Milan, 20 Oct 1970, *Return of the Wounded Soldier,* ITL 6,000,000. Milan, 25 Nov 1971, *Chimney Sweep,* ITL 4,700,000. Milan, 29 March 1973, *Portrait of a Peasant Woman* (watercolour) ITL 1,600,000. Milan, 12 June 1973, *Young Woman Clearing a Table,* ITL 6,700,000. London, 12 June 1974, *Young Woman at her Mirror* (1865) GBP 4,400. Amsterdam, 20 Oct 1976, *The Poor* (1871, oil on canvas, 22½ x 17¼ ins / 57 x 44 cm) NLG 33,000. Milan, 26 Oct 1978, *Woman Bathing* (oil on canvas, 22 x 13 ins / 55 x 33 cm) ITL 8,500,000. Munich, 2 May 1979, *Charity* (oil on canvas, 11¾ x 14¼ ins / 30 x 36 cm) DEM 9,000. Milan, 5 Nov 1981, *Household Accounts* (oil on canvas, 13¾ x 10½ ins / 35 x 26.5 cm) ITL 6,500,000. Milan, 8 Nov 1983, *Portrait of the Countess Maffei* (oil on card, 15¾ x 13 ins / 40 x 33 cm) ITL 15,000,000. Milan, 28 Oct 1986, *Woman Musician in the Gironde* (oil on canvas, 61½ x 48 ins / 156 x 121 cm) ITL 100,000,000. Rome, 19 May 1987, *Young Peasant Girl with a Basket* (charcoal heightened with white/brown paper, 14¼ x 9 ins / 36.5 x 23 cm) ITL 5,500,000. Milan, 23 March 1988, *Wounded Man's Story* (oil on canvas, 11½ x 14¼ ins / 29 x 36 cm) ITL 19,000,000. London, 29 April 1988, *Woman Reclining on a Sofa* (9¼ x 14 ins / 23.5 x 35.5 cm) GBP 19,800. Milan, 1 June 1988, *Model Resting* (oil on canvas, oval, 9 x 7½ ins / 23 x 19 cm) ITL 8,000,000. Milan, 14 March 1989, *Portrait of a Woman Wearing a Black Mantilla* (1876, oil on canvas, 11½ x 8¼ ins / 29 x 21 cm) ITL 20,000,000. Milan, 14 June 1989, *In the Kitchen* (oil on canvas, 18 x 14¼ ins / 45.5 x 36 cm) ITL 34,000,000. Milan, 19 Oct 1989, *Broken Marriage* (1873, oil on canvas, 44½ x 63 ins / 113 x 160 cm) ITL 340,000,000. Rome, 14 Dec 1989, *Rural Landscape with Peasants and Cattle* (oil on canvas, 13½ x 17¼ ins / 34 x 44 cm) ITL 28,750,000. New York, 28 Feb 1990, *Interior of a Blacksmith's* (1865, oil on canvas, 25 x 32½ ins / 63.5 x 82.5 cm) USD 253,000. Rome, 11 Dec 1990, *Rural Scene* (oil on canvas, 10½ x 7½ ins / 26.5 x 19 cm) ITL 14,950,000. Milan, 6 June 1991, *Young Peasant Girl* (watercolour, 13¾ x 9¾ ins / 35 x 25 cm) ITL 20,000,000. Milan, 3 Dec 1992, *Memory* (oil on canvas, 20¾ x 15¾ ins / 53 x 40 cm) ITL 67,800,000. London, 16 Nov 1994, *Innocent Bystander* (1852, oil on canvas, 28¼ x 22¾ ins / 72 x 58 cm) GBP 56,500. Milan, 20 Dec 1994, *Small Girl* (pencil heightened with white, 11 x 7½ ins / 27 x 19 cm) ITL 2,990,000. Milan, 14 June 1995, *Smugglers on Lake Como* (1849, oil on canvas, 33½ x 45 ins / 85 x 114.5 cm) ITL 138,000,000. Milan, 26 March 1996, *In the Artist's Studio* (oil on canvas, 16 x 13¼ ins / 40.5 x 33.5 cm) ITL 120,750,000. Rome, 28 Nov 1996, *Waiting Bride* (1873, oil on canvas, 44½ x 63 ins / 113 x 160 cm) ITL 380,000,000. Rome, 10 Dec 1996, *Waiting Bridegroom* (oil on canvas) ITL 430,700,000. Milan, 7 Nov 2000, *Smugglers on Lake Como* (oil on canvas, 30 x 37 ins / 77 x 95 cm) ITL 150,000,000. Rome, 5 Dec 2000, *Soldier* (pencil and brush, 11 x 16 ins / 28 x 40 cm) ITL 4,500,000. Milan, 22 May 2001, *The Wounded Soldier's Tale* (1862, oil on canvas, 26 x 20 ins / 66 x 52 cm) ITL 135,000,000. Rome, 12 Dec 2001, *Peasant Woman at Mirror* (1865, oil on card, 13 x 10 ins / 33 x 25 cm) ITL 48,000,000. Vercelli, 23 Feb 2002, *Napoleonic Soldier during Battle* (oil on canvas, 17 x 12 ins / 42 x 30 cm) EUR 10,000. Milan, 22 May 2002, *Rosary* (oil on board, 12 x 9 ins / 30 x 23 cm) EUR 15,000. Milan, 29 May 2003, *Player Begging* (1878, watercolour wash on paper/cardboard, 22 x 18 ins / 55 x 46 cm) EUR 8,500. Cologne, 3 July 2003, *In Love - Girl on Sofa* (oil on canvas, 15 x 12 ins / 39 x 30 cm) EUR 10,000.

INDUNO, Girolamo
Italian, 19th century.
Born 1825 or 1827, in Milan; died December 1890, in Milan.
Painter, watercolourist, pastellist. History painting, genre scenes, landscapes.

Girolamo Induno was the brother of the painter Domenico Induno. He was a talented pastel and watercolour artist, and a member of the Accademia in Milan, where he studied. He exhibited in Turin, Naples, Milan, Rome, Venice, and Vienna, where he was awarded a medal in 1873.

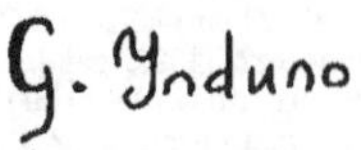

Museums and Galleries:
Genoa: *Woman Spinning* - Graz: *Lake Garda* - Milan (Ambrosiana): *St Pancras Gate, Rome; Girl at a Well; Soldiers in Camp* - Milan (Municipal Mus.): *Antiquary* - Milan (Mus. del Risorgimento): *Defending the Ship; Alpine Hunters* - Milan

(Palazzo Reale): *Street Scene* - MILAN (Pinacoteca di Brera): *Return of Garibaldi and his Troops* - NICE: *Souvenir of Rome* - ROME (Gal. Nazionale d'Arte Moderna): *Garibaldi; Landscape* - TRIESTE (Civico Mus. Revoltella): *Sentinel*.

AUCTION RECORDS:

PARIS, 1878, *Grandparents Visiting*, FRF 5,700. PARIS, 1888, *Strolling Musicians*, FRF 410. NEW YORK, 22-24 Nov 1899, *Actors in a Coach Accident*, USD 1,000. NEW YORK, 12-13 March 1903, *The Recipient* (watercolour) USD 165. NEW YORK, 6 Jan 1911, *Waiting at the Rendezvous*, GBP 130. MILAN, 16 March 1965, *Rescuing the Dog*, ITL 3,600,000. MILAN, 4 June 1970, *The Fall of Sebastopol*, ITL 2,600,000. LONDON, 4 May 1973, *View of Belgirante on Lake Maggiore*, Gns 5,500. COLOGNE, 6 June 1973, *Peasnt Women Going to Mass* (watercolour) DEM 4,800. MILAN, 28 March 1974, *Orphans*, ITL 13,500,000. NEW YORK, 14 May 1976, *The Letter* (oil on canvas, 22 x 17 3/4 ins / 56 x 45 cm) USD 3,500. MILAN, 20 Dec 1977, *Arrival in Venice of Victor Emmanuel II* (oil on canvas, 18 x 23 1/2 ins / 46 x 60 cm) ITL 6,000,000. LONDON, 23 Nov 1978, *Lake Maggiore and the Isola Bella* (watercolour and pen heightened with white, 11 x 16 1/4 ins / 27 x 41.5 cm) GBP 1,350. MILAN, 24 March 1982, *Figures in an Interior* (oil on canvas, 11 1/2 x 9 ins / 29 x 23 cm) ITL 9,500,000. MILAN, 23 March 1983, *His Country and the World* (1871, oil on canvas, 20 1/2 x 25 1/4 ins / 52 x 64 cm) ITL 75,000,000. MILAN, 13 Dec 1984, *Portrait of a Woman* (watercolour, 8 1/4 x 5 ins / 21 x 13 cm) ITL 3,800,000. NEW YORK, 28 Oct 1986, *Amorous Conversation near a Well* (oil on canvas, 38 3/4 x 55 1/2 ins / 98.4 x 141 cm) USD 93,000. MILAN, 10 Dec 1987, *Rome 1863* (1863, oil on canvas, 29 1/4 x 39 1/4 ins / 74.5 x 100 cm) ITL 180,000,000. MILAN, 23 March 1988, *Betrayed* (oil on canvas, 27 1/4 x 32 1/4 ins / 69.5 x 82 cm) ITL 310,000,000. MILAN, 1 June 1988, *A Mother's Happiness* (1871, oil on canvas, 21 x 29 1/4 ins / 53.5 x 74 cm) ITL 110,000,000. MILAN, 14 March 1989, *Faithful Nurse* (1870, oil on canvas, 30 x 41 1/2 ins / 76 x 105.5 cm) ITL 160,000,000. MILAN, 19 Oct 1989, *Departure of the Volunteer* (1870, oil on canvas, 38 1/4 x 28 1/4 ins / 97 x 72 cm) ITL 130,000,000. NEW YORK, 24 Oct 1989, *Peasant Moving Home with his Wife and Child* (pencil and watercolour/paper, 12 x 9 1/4 ins / 30.5 x 23.5 cm) USD 22,000. MILAN, 6 Dec 1989, *Seller of Religious Pictures* (1886, oil on canvas, 21 3/4 x 17 3/4 ins / 55.5 x 45 cm) ITL 120,000,000. LONDON, 30 March 1990, *An Italian Beauty* (oil on canvas, 10 1/4 x 7 1/4 ins / 26 x 18.6 cm) GBP 5,500. ROME, 29 May 1990, *Faithful Nurse* (1870, oil on canvas, 30 x 41 1/4 ins / 76 x 105 cm) ITL 184,000,000. ROME, 24 March 1992, *Battle Scene* (oil on canvas, 15 3/4 x 29 1/4 ins / 40 x 74 cm) ITL 40,250,000. MILAN, 29 Oct 1992, *Painter of Religious Pictures* (1887, oil on canvas, 21 3/4 x 18 1/2 ins / 55.5 x 47 cm) ITL 146,000,000. MILAN, 16 March 1993, *Sentinel* (1851, oil on card, 15 3/4 x 11 ins / 40 x 28 cm) ITL 40,000,000. ROME, 23 May 1996, *Charlotte Corday* (oil on canvas, 35 1/4 x 43 ins / 89.5 x 109 cm) ITL 80,400,000. VENICE, 9 March 1997, *Portrait of a Gentleman* (1865, oil on canvas, 41 1/4 x 30 3/4 ins / 105 x 78 cm) ITL 23,500,000. ROME, 2 Dec 1997, *Young Shepherd* (oil on panel, 7 x 4 1/4 ins / 17.5 x 10.5 cm) ITL 17,250,000.

INEMER, Félix Victor

French, 19th century.

Born 1801, in Paris; died 19 February 1865, in Paris.

Painter. Landscapes.

Inemer was a pupil of Lethière, Perron and Bertin. His works were exhibited at the Salon from 1831 to 1849.

INFANTE, Gaston

Brazilian, 20th century.

Born in Rio de Janeiro.

Painter, watercolourist. Landscapes.

Gaston Infante exhibited in Paris in the first half of the 20th century at the Salon des Indépendants.

AUCTION RECORDS:

PARIS, 18 May 1945, *Calvary* (watercolour) FRF 800. LONDON, 18 June 1993, *The Dressing Table* (1912, oil on canvas, 35 1/2 x 46 ins / 90 x 117 cm) GBP 4,370.

INFANTE, Scipione

Italian, 17th century.

Born 28 October 1607, in Bagnoli Irpino (Avellino); died 1657, in Bagnoli Irpino.

Sculptor (wood).

Infante contributed to the carvings of the stalls in the church of the Assunta in Bagnoli-Irpino and carved the pulpit for the cathedral in Nola.

INFANTE-ARANA, Francisco

Russian, 20th century.

Born 1943, in Vasilievka.

Installation artist.

Kinetic Art.

Dvizhenie group.

Francisco Infante-Arana is a member of the Dvizhenie group of artists, all skilled in different disciplines and led by Lev Nusberg. The group works together to create lumino-kinetic works. He was one of the founders of the ARG group with whom he has also realised several kinetic works. The cosmos has a constant presence in his work, in which he often depicts the sky and its constellations, sometimes with the aid of mirrors or photographs. In the series *Reconstruction of a Starry Sky* from 1965, which comprises 17 panels, the rigorous layout of the stars helps to counterbalance the anarchic evolution of the forest seen lower down on the panels. From the beginning of the 1960s, he exhibited in the USSR and from 1988 in western Europe. In 2003, his work featured in the panoramic *Berlin-Moscow/Moscow-Berlin 1950-2000* exhibition seen at the Martin-Gropius-Bau in Berlin and at the Tretyakov Gallery in Moscow. This exhibition followed on the heels of an earlier exhibition focusing on the years 1900-1950, which offered up for debate 50 years of German-Russian artistic and cultural relations marked by significant political transformations.

BIBLIOGRAPHY:

Popper, Frank, *Naissance de l'art cinétique*, Gauthier-Villars, Paris, 1967. *'Berlin-Moskau/Moskau-Berlin 1950-2000'* in *2 vol.*, exhibition catalogue, Martin-Gropius-Bau, Berlin, 2003 (text in German).

AUCTION RECORDS:

LONDON, 15 Oct 1992, *Reconstruction of a Starry Sky* (1965, gouache/paper, on 17 panels, each 19 1/4 x 11 3/4 ins / 49 x 30 cm) GBP 4,400.

INFORMAL. See i. e. **BRYEN Camille, FAUTRIER Jean, MATHIEU Georges, WOLS**

INGALTON, William

British, 19th century.

Born 1794, in Worplesdon; died 1866, in Clever.

Painter, architect. Genre scenes.

William Ingalton exhibited his work in London at the Royal Academy and at the British Institution from 1816 to 1823. He subsequently gave up painting for architecture and worked in Windsor.

INGANI, E.

Italian, 19th century.

Painter. Landscapes.

MUSEUMS AND GALLERIES:

SYDNEY: *Peasants of the Abruzzi* (1877, watercolour).

INGANNATI, Pietro degli

Italian, 16th century.

Active in Venice.

Painter.

Among the paintings attributed to him are *Virgin with Four Saints* (Berlin), *Virgin with St John the Baptist and a Saint* (until 1894, in the Palazzo Morosoni-Guttenburg, Venice), *Portrait of a Man* (in the Kelly Collection, Dublin), and four paintings of which one is *The Marriage of St Catherine* (Liverpool).

Museums and Galleries:

Berlin (Bodemus.): *Virgin with Four Saints* - Liverpool (Walker AG): *The Marriage of St Catherine* (three other paintings).

Auction records:

Paris, 1894, *Holy Family,* FRF 8,000. Paris, 3 May 1899, *Holy Family,* FRF 1,050. London, 12 Dec 1979, *Virgin and Child with St Peter and St Paul* (oil on panel, 12¼ x 15¾in/31 x 40cm) GBP 8,500.

INGANNI, Angelo

Italian, 19th century.
Born 1807, in Brescia; died 1880, in Milan.
Painter. Figures, portraits, genre scenes, landscapes, architectural views.

Inganni was a pupil of the Accademia in Milan, of which he was later a member. He worked in Brescia, Venice, and Milan, where he exhibited.

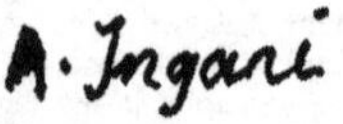

Museums and Galleries:

Bagnères-de-Bigorre: *Italian Village in Winter* - Digne-les-Bains: *Snails Roasting* - Trieste: *Porta Ticinese, Milan* - Vienna: *View of Milan Cathedral.*

Auction records:

Paris, 26 April 1898, *The Square of Milan Cathedral,* FRF 120. Milan, 8 Nov 1967, *Landscape,* ITL 900,000. Milan, 17 Oct 1972, *The Hold,* ITL 3,300,000. Milan, 29 March 1973, *Courtyard in Snow,* ITL 2,000,000. Milan, 28 Oct 1976, *Peasant* (oil on canvas, 30¾ x 24½ ins / 78 x 62 cm) ITL 3,000,000. Milan, 15 March 1977, *Market Scene* (oil on card remounted/canvas, 9 x 7½ ins / 23 x 19 cm) ITL 1,200,000. Milan, 10 Dec 1980, *Piazza della Scalla, Milan* (1850, oil on canvas, 37¾ x 30 ins / 96 x 76 cm) ITL 100,000,000. Milan, 19 March 1981, *Market Scene on the Piazza Santo Stefano* (1845, oil on canvas, 26½ x 20 ins / 67 x 50.5 cm) ITL 86,000,000. Milan, 21 April 1983, *Canal in the Fatebenefratelli, a street in Milan* (1835, oil on canvas, 18½ x 23½ ins / 47 x 60 cm) ITL 68,000,000. Milan, 18 Dec 1986, *Market Scene on a Winter's Day* (1873, oil on canvas, 20 x 22½ ins / 51 x 57 cm) ITL 155,000,000. Milan, 31 March 1987, *View of the Piazza del Teatro, Brescia* (1880, oil on canvas, 24¾ x 32¾ ins / 63 x 83.5 cm) ITL 200,000,000. Milan, 14 June 1989, *Orchards in Old Milan* (oil on canvas, 29¼ x 39¼ ins / 74.5 x 99.5 cm) ITL 400,000,000. Cologne, 23 March 1990, *Young Couple and Child in a Candlelit Kitchen* (1875, oil on canvas, 25½ x 19¾ ins / 65 x 50 cm) DEM 18,000. Milan, 19 March 1992, *Little Bird Catcher* (oil on canvas, 19 x 14¾ ins / 48.5 x 37.5 cm) ITL 17,500,000. Lugano, 16 May 1992, *The Dancer Taglioni* (oil on canvas, 29½ x 23½ ins / 75 x 60 cm) CHF 54,000. Milan, 9 Nov 1993, *Portrait of a Young Woman in Lombard Costume* (1859, oil on canvas, 23½ x 19¾ ins / 60 x 50 cm) ITL 21,850,000. Rome, 31 May 1994, *Charity* (oil on canvas/wood, 8½ x 7 ins / 21.5 x 18 cm) ITL 8,250,000. Milan, 29 March 1995, *Strolling Street Seller* (pencil and sepia/paper, 12¼ x 9¼ ins / 31 x 23.5 cm) ITL 5,980,000. Milan, 25 Oct 1995, *Woman Lit by a Lantern* (1868, oil on canvas, 32 x 25¼ ins / 81 x 64 cm) ITL 52,900,000. Rome, 23 May 1996, *Parish Priest and his Housekeeper* (oil on canvas, 27¼ x 22 ins / 69 x 56 cm) ITL 80,400,000. Milan, 20 Oct 1999, *Young Woman from Lombardy Spinning* (oil on canvas, 40 x 29 ins / 102 x 74 cm) ITL 82,000,000. Milan, 20 Oct 1999, *View of Piazza S Stefano, Milan* (1845, oil on canvas, 26 x 20 ins / 67 x 50 cm) ITL 223,217,000. Milan, 7 Nov 2000, *The Broletto Courtyard in Brescia* (oil on canvas, 13 x 15 ins / 33 x 39 cm) ITL 90,000,000. Rome, 12 Dec 2001, *Piazza del Duomo, Milan, at Night* (oil on canvas, 12 x 16 ins / 30 x 40 cm) ITL 92,000,000. Venice, 16 Dec 2001, *Intrusive Look* (oil on canvas, 16 x 12 ins / 40 x 30 cm) ITL 15,000,000. Milan, 28 Oct 2002, *Young Woman by Fire* (1880, oil on canvas, 13 x 11 ins / 33 x 27 cm) EUR 8,600. Trieste, 22 May 2003, *Giocando with Mother* (1848, oil on canvas, 20 x 26 ins / 50 x 66 cm) EUR 6,500. Milan, 10 Dec 2003, *Tamer* (1858, oil on card, 8 x 10 ins / 21 x 26 cm) EUR 5,000. Stockholm, 25 May 2004, *Interior from the Cathedral in Milan* (1843, oil on canvas) SEK 455,000. Milan, 12 Oct 2004, *Shepherds and Animals* (1850, oil on canvas, 28 x 35 ins / 70 x 90 cm) EUR 52,000.

INGANNI, Francesco

Italian, 18th - 19th century.
Born at the end of the 18th century, in Brescia; died at the age of about 80.
Active in Brescia.
Painter.

Inganni was initially a decorative painter. He then devoted himself to the painting of animals. He exhibited a large-scale painting in Milan depicting *Leaving Noah's Ark.* The Tosia Art Gallery in Brescia preserves his works.

INGEDAHL

Swiss, 20th century.
Born 1918.
Sculptor.

Since 1946, Ingedahl has lived and worked in Paris. He was advised by the French sculptors Aristide Maillol and Antoine Bourdelle. His work is based on the human form, which he portrays in a traditional style.

INGELIUS, or Ingels

Dutch, 17th century.
Active in Amsterdam.
Painter. Portraits.

Museums and Galleries:

Amsterdam (Mus. Amstelkring): *Portrait of Pastor Reynier Ingels, Brother of the Artist.*

INGELRAAM. See **ENGELRAAM Laurens**

INGELRAMS, Cornelis, the Elder, or

Engelrams, Enghelrams
Flemish, 16th century.
Born 1527, in Mechelen; died 1580, in Mechelen.
Active also in Germany.
Painter. History painting.
Mechelen School, Flemish School.

Cornelis Ingelrams the Elder lived for a long time in Germany, especially Hamburg, where he painted a *Conversion of St Paul* for St Catherine's church. There is a painting of his in Mechelen Cathedral.

INGELRAMS, Cornelis Adriaen, the Younger

Flemish, 16th century.
Died 28 February 1595.
Painter.
Mechelen School, Flemish School.

Cornelis Adriaen Ingelrams the Younger was the son of Cornelis Ingelrams the Elder. He gained his mastership in Mechelen in 1571.

INGELRANS, Paul Léon Henri

French, 19th - 20th century.
Born c. 1870, in Bully-les-Mines (Pas-de-Calais).
Painter. Genre scenes.

Paul Léon Henri Ingelrans studied with Cabanel, Delaunay and Gustave Moreau. He was curator of the Musée de Rochefort. He exhibited at the Salon des Artistes Français in Paris, of which he became a member in 1909.

Museums and Galleries:
ROCHEFORT: *Young Girl Holding a Venetian Lantern.*

INGELS, Domien
Belgian, 20th century.
Born 1881, in Ghent; died 1946, in Bachte-Maria-Leerne.
Sculptor. Animals. Busts.
Domien Ingels attended the Koninklijke Academie voor Schone Kunsten in Ghent, where he later became a teacher. He produced several commemorative monuments, and was renowned for his depiction of horses.
Auction records:
LOKEREN, 23 May 1992, *Draught Horse of the Brabant* (ceramic sculpture, h. 13¾ ins / 35 cm, l. 19 ins/48 cm) BEF 38,000.

INGELS, Frank Lee
American, 20th century.
Born 2 January 1886, in Tamora; died 1957, in Los Angeles.
Sculptor.
Frank Lee Ingels was a member of the Chicago Society of Artists. He received an honourable mention from the Art Institute of Chicago in 1915. Some agricultural colleges are decorated with sculptures by him.

INGELS, Joseph François. See **ENGELS**

INGELS-PAUWAERT, Marie
Belgian, 20th century.
Born 1884, in Ghent; died 1960.
Painter. Figures, portraits, interiors, still-lifes.
Marie Ingels-Pauwaert studied under Delvin. She taught at the Koninklijke Academie voor Schone Kunsten in Ghent. After beginning her career as a Pointillist, her work became less nebulous and more composed, but the power of light remained an essential ingredient.
Museums and Galleries:
GHENT.

INGEMANN, Lucy Marie
Maiden name: Mandix
Danish, 19th century.
Born 13 February 1792, in Copenhagen; died 15 January 1868, in Sor.
Painter.
From 1824 to 1826 Lucy Ingemann exhibited a series of flower paintings. She also executed religious paintings which may still be found in village churches.

INGEN, Hendrikus Alexander van
Dutch, 19th - 20th century.
Born 16 June 1846, in Renkum; died March 1920, in Renkum.
Painter. Animals.
Hendrikus Alexander van Ingen was active in his native country, where he painted primarily cows and horses.
Museums and Galleries:
THE HAGUE (Gemeentemus.): *Cow's Head* (study).
Auction records:
NEW YORK, 21 Oct 1983, *Livestock in a Wheatfield* (1867, oil on canvas, 40 x 66 ins / 101.6 x 167.6 cm) USD 2,500. AMSTERDAM, 5-6 Feb 1991, *Cattle in a Meadow* (oil on panel, 7¾ x 12½ ins / 19.5 x 32 cm) NLG 1,495. AMSTERDAM, 17 Sept 1991, *Cows in a Meadow* (oil on panel, 8¼ x 6¼ ins / 21 x 16 cm) NLG 1,035.

INGEN, Henry or Hendrik van
Dutch, 19th century.
Born 12 November 1833, in the Netherlands; died 17 November 1898, in America.
Painter. Genre scenes.
Henry van Ingen worked in America.
Auction records:
NEW YORK, 3 Feb 1978, *Farmyard* (1869, watercolour, 14½ x 22¼in/37 x 56.5cm) USD 1,100. NEW YORK, 30 May 1990, *The Harvesters* (1870, oil on canvas, 20 x 30in/50.8 x 76.3cm) USD 3,300. AMSTERDAM, 10 March 2003, *Resting Cows* (1915, oil on canvas, 20 x 33 ins / 50 x 85 cm) EUR 2,500. AMSTERDAM, 30 June 2003, *Resting Cows* (oil on canvas, 22 x 34 ins / 55 x 86 cm) EUR 1,600.

INGEN, Ivan
Dutch, 20th century.
Born 1918, in Surabaya, Indonesia.
Painter.
Ivan Ingen attended the art academy in The Hague. Since 1939, he has been a member of the federation of painters.

INGEN, Pieter van, or Ynghen
Dutch, 16th century.
Painter. Coats of arms.
Utrecht School.
Pieter van Ingen painted armorial bearings for an entry by the emperor. In 1521 he belonged to the guild.

INGEN, Willem or Guillelmo van
Flemish School, 17th century.
Born c. 1651; died 1708, in Amsterdam.
Active in Utrecht.
Painter. Historical subjects, portraits.
Willem van Ingen was a pupil of Antonie de Grebber and Maratti in Rome. He took inspiration from these artists.

INGEN, William Brantley van
American, 19th century.
Born 30 August 1858, in Philadelphia; died 1955.
Active in New York.
Painter.
William Brantley van Ingen was a pupil at the Pennsylvania Academy of the Fine Arts in Philadelphia, and a pupil of I. La Farge in New York and Léon Bonnat in Paris. He produced mural paintings for public buildings in the USA. His works include *Divine Law* in the Chicago Court House; *Justice and Pity* in the Indianapolis Court House; 14 paintings depicting scenes from the life of the first Pennsylvania pioneers in the Capitol building in Harrisburg; 16 paintings at the Capitol building in Trenton; and 6 paintings in the Library of Congress in Washington DC.

INGENBLEEK, Armand Joseph
French, 20th century.
Born 3 October 1896, in Mulhouse.
Painter.
Armand Joseph Ingenbleek exhibited regularly in Alsace and in Paris, particularly at the Salon d'Automne.

INGENMEY, Franz Maria
German, 19th century.
Born 1830, in Bonn; died 3 June 1878, in Düsseldorf.
Painter, lithographer. Genre scenes.
A pupil of E Correns in Munich, he established himself in Düsseldorf in 1861. He exhibited in Vienna from 1872.
Auction records:
COLOGNE, 24 Oct 1986, *Young Girl and Child in a Farmyard* (1867, oil on canvas, 17 x 19¾ ins / 43 x 50 cm) DEM 16,000. COLOGNE, 11 April 2002, *Peasants with Horse-drawn Cart by Summer Woodland* (1877, oil on canvas, 31 x 25 ins / 79 x 63 cm) EUR 3,200. COLOGNE, 20 Nov 2003, *Three Children in Park* (1863, oil on canvas, 31 x 22 ins / 79 x 57 cm) EUR 9,000.

INGENRAEM, Louweris. See **ENGELRAAM Laurens**

INGENUUS
Sculptor.
Ancient Roman.
Ingenuus' name is inscribed on the plinth of a statue of *Mercury* in the Vatican Museum.

INGERLE, Rudolph F.
Austrian, 20th century.
Born 14 April 1879, in Vienna.
Active in the USA.
Painter. Landscapes.
Rudolph F. Ingerle was a member of the Artistic Association of the Northern States of America, and in 1928 he won a gold medal in Chicago.
MUSEUMS AND GALLERIES:
CHICAGO (City Mus.): *After the Storm.*

INGERMANN, Mathäus
Flemish School, 17th century.
Born in Antwerp.
Painter.
Mathäus Ingermann studied in Rome. From 1639 to 1641, he lived in Poland where he executed paintings for the Carmelite church in Wisnicz near Cracow.

INGERSOLL, Anna Warren
American, 20th century.
Born 1887; died 1980.
Painter.
Anna Warren Ingersoll studied at the Pennsylvania Academy of the Fine Arts and in Paris. She lived and worked in Philadelphia.

INGESUATI, family of artists
German, 16th century.
Active c. 1500.
Painters. Historical subjects, portraits.
The Ingesuati family are mentioned by Siret.

INGHAM, Charles Cromwell
Irish, 19th century.
Born 1796, in Dublin; died 1863, in New York.
Painter. History painting, portraits.
Charles Cromwell Ingham was a pupil at the Dublin Academy and went to America in 1817, where he was the founder and then vice-president of the National Academy. He acquired a considerable reputation as a painter of women and children.
MUSEUMS AND GALLERIES:
NEW YORK (Historical Society): *The Black Plume; Lafayette; Gulian C. Verplanck* - NEW YORK (Metropolitan Mus. of Art): *The Little Florist; Miss Frances Wilkes; Portrait of a Man.*

INGHAM, George Bryan
British, 20th century.
Born 11 June 1936, in Preston (Lancashire); died 22 September 1997.
Painter, sculptor, graphic artist. Landscapes, portraits, still-lifes.
Bryan Ingham trained at St Martin's School of Art (1957-1961) and the Royal College of Art (1961-1964) in London, and at the British Academy in Rome (1966).

He worked in a variety of different media including sculpture, etching and graphic art. Some of his work engages with the legacy of Cubism and the influence of Picasso, Gris and Braque, but his interests were broad and not limited to this particular school. Apart from his Cubist paintings, he also produced abstract compositions. His experimentation with abstract art, however, did not lead him to abandon the representation of figurative elements, which he continued to include in his work. His intellectual and artistic interests benefited from a awards from the Leverhulme Trust, the Italian Government, and Atelier Haus in Germany.

Ingham's name is associated with the Francis Graham-Dixon gallery in London, which held exhibitions of his work in 1991 and 1995. He was an associate of the Royal College of Art.
BIBLIOGRAPHY:
Bryan Ingham: Paintings and Reliefs, exhibition catalogue, Francis Graham-Dixon Gallery, London, 1991. *Bryan Ingham: New Paintings, Collages and Assemblages*, exhibition catalogue, Francis Graham-Dixon Gallery, London, 1995. *Bryan Ingham: Sculpture and Related Prints and Drawings*, exhibition catalogue, Book Gallery St. Ives, St Ives, 1996 (Text in English and German).
AUCTION RECORDS:
PENZANCE, 28 Oct 1999, *Abstract Construction* (oil on board, 13 x 24 ins / 32 x 61 cm) GBP 1,400. LONDON, 22 Nov 2000, *Kynance Cove* (1969, mixed media, 23 x 24 ins / 58 x 61 cm) GBP 2,000. LONDON, 12 March 2002, *Yellow Jug and Lizard Point* (1986-1989, oil, collage and sand on board, 8 x 11 ins / 21 x 27 cm) GBP 3,000. PENZANCE, 16 Oct 2002, *Flower Piece, Tremayne* (1985, collage, 5 x 2 ins / 13 x 5 cm) GBP 1,150. LONDON, 25 March 2003, *Three Jugs and a Ship in Summer* (mixed media on panel, 14 x 29 ins / 35 x 74 cm) GBP 6,800. LONDON, 27 March 2003, *St Ives* (pencil, watercolour, oil and collage on board, 34 x 57 ins / 86 x 146 cm) GBP 4,000. LONDON, 15 June 2004, *Large Porthleven with Clock Tower III* (1989, oil, pencil, charcoal and collage, 70 x 15 ins / 178 x 38 cm) GBP 7,200. LONDON, 15 June 2004, *Large View of Tuscany and Pisa* (1993-1996, mixed media and collage, 53 x 47 ins / 134 x 120 cm) GBP 13,000.

INGHAM-SMITH, Elizabeth
American, 20th century.
Born in Easton (Pennsylvania).
Painter, sculptor, watercolourist.
Elizabeth Ingham-Smith studied with Henry B. Snell at the Pennsylvania Academy of the Fine Arts in Philadelphia, with Whistler in Paris and with Alex Jameson in London. She was a member of the Philadelphia and Washington Watercolor Clubs.

INGHELS, Joseph François. See **ENGELS**

INGHELSOONE, Inghels
Flemish, 16th century.
Active c. 1513.
Painter.
Flemish School.
Inghels Inghelsoone was a pupil of G. van der Weyde.

INGHERAMS, Cornelis. See **INGELRAMS**

INGHILLERI, Giuseppe
Italian, 20th century.
Sculptor.
Inghilleri's terracottas are famous. He mainly makes figures in the realist mode such as *Young Boy* and *Woman Carrying Water.*
MUSEUMS AND GALLERIES:
ROME (Gal. Nazionale): *We Reap as We Sow* (bronze).

INGHIRAMI, Francesco
Italian, 18th - 19th century.
Born 1772, in Volterra; died 17 May 1846, in La Badia di Fiesole.
Draughtsman, engraver, archaeologist. Architectural views.
MUSEUMS AND GALLERIES:
FLORENCE (Uffizi): *View of the Royal Villa in Careggi* (drawing).

INGLADA, Narciso
Spanish, 19th century.
Active in Barcelona.
Painter.

In 1854, Narciso Inglada bequeathed a number of his works, including a painting of *St Bernard*, to the monastery of Montserrat.

INGLEFIELD, E.A. (Commander)
British, 19th century.
Active in London.
Painter. Seascapes.
E.A. Inglefield exhibited his work in London at the Royal Academy and in Suffolk Street.

INGLÉS, Jorge, called El maestro Jorge
Spanish, 15th century.
Active c. 1455.
Painter. History painting, portraits.
Jorge Inglés worked in Granada, where the Marquis of Santillana commissioned him to decorate the chapel of the Buitrago hospital. The astonishingly realistic portraits of the donors are the most remarkable part of this commission. The painter has highlighted the facial features of each person and simplified the colours, the backgrounds and the furniture around them. The Marquis of Santillana and his wife are kneeling in prayer, and slightly behind them are their smaller doubles with exactly the same features, but younger. This arrangement suggests that they had decided to put the whole period of their lives under the protection of the saint. A pure and limpid landscape is visible through small openings. These realistic and psychological portraits surely owe a great deal to Northern art, and it is possible that the artist was of English origin.

Jorge Inglés was represented in the exhibition *Hispano-Flemish Gothic painting: Bartolomé Bermejo and His Time*, at the Museu Nacional d'Art de Catalunya, Barcelona, in 2003.

BIBLIOGRAPHY:

Hispano-Flemish Gothic Painting. Bartolomé Bermejo and his time, group exhibition catalogue, Museu Nacional d'Art de Catalunya, Barcelona, 2003 (Spanish, Catalan, and English edition).

INGLÉS, José
Spanish, 18th century.
Born 1718, in Valencia; died 1786, in Valencia.
Painter, miniaturist. History painting, portraits.
José Inglés was a pupil of Richarte. He became a member of the academy and was later its assistant director. Although there are some creditable religious paintings by him at the Merced monastery, the Augustinian church and the church of Campanar, he is known primarily as a portrait painter.

MUSEUMS AND GALLERIES:

VALENCIA: *St Ramon Alonso Gomez.*

INGLÉS, Vicente
Spanish, 19th century.
Died 30 August 1821, in Valencia.
Painter.
Vicente Inglés was the son and pupil of José Inglés. In Murcia in 1785 he painted part of a fresco in the S Isidoro chapel. There are two works by the artist - *The Miracle of the Loaves* and *Moses Descending from Mt Sinai* - in the communion chapel of the church of St Martin in Valencia.

MUSEUMS AND GALLERIES:

MADRID (Real Academia de Bellas Artes de San Fernando): *Scene from the Life of Jacob; Portrait of the Painter Cristobal Valero.*

INGLESI, Claudio
Italian, 17th century.
Of French origin.
Active in Perugia.
Painter.
The Perugia Art Gallery houses Inglesi's copies of paintings by Raphael depicting *Scenes from Christ's Passion.*

INGLESIS, Leonidas
Russian, 20th century.
Born 1882, in Nikolayev; died 1972, in Boulogne-Billancourt, France.
Active in France from 1928.
Painter, mosaicist. Landscapes.
A student at the academy of fine art in Moscow, Leonidas Inglesis continued his studies in the studio of Konstantin Fedorovich Yuon. On his return to Nikolayev, he was involved in the setting up of the Vereshchagin Museum of Fine Art, where he taught. He went to Paris in 1928 and worked first as a decorative artist. He exhibited some landscapes at the Salon des Indépendants.

From 1931, he began to carry out work in mosaic in the style of the 5th and 6th century mosaics in Ravenna. These were executed principally for religious buildings in Great Britain, most importantly for the Chapel of the Holy Sacrament in Westminster Cathedral in London. He is famous too for the floor mosaics in the Tate Gallery in London (Tate Britain) depicting various subjects and portraits including: *Alice in Wonderland; Mr Pickwick; Winston Churchill.*

MUSEUMS AND GALLERIES:

NIKOLAYEV (Vereshchagin Mus. of Fine Arts).

INGLIS, Esther or Hester. See **KELLO Esther**

INGLIS, Jane (Miss)
British, 19th century.
Active in London.
Painter. Genre scenes, figures.
Jane Inglis exhibited her work in London, mainly at the Royal Academy and in Suffolk Street from 1859.

INGLIS, John Johnston
Irish, 19th - 20th century.
Born 26 August 1867, in Dublin.
Painter, illustrator, sculptor. Landscapes.
John Johnston Inglis trained in Paris under Gérome, Courtois and Collin before studying and settling in London. He was a member of the Dublin Academy of Art and the Royal Hibernian Academy. He exhibited at the Royal Academy from 1890. Inglis was awarded a gold medal and a second prize for landscapes at the Rochester Art Club exhibition of 1925.

AUCTION RECORDS:

EDINBURGH, 28 April 1992, *Highland Harvest, Invernesshire* (oil on canvas, 45 x 64 ins / 114 x 162.5 cm) GBP 3,850. NEW YORK, 20 Jan 1993, *Country Lane in Spring* (oil on canvas, 24 1/4 x 20 ins / 61.6 x 50.8 cm) USD 3,738. LONDON, 5 Nov 1997, *Fishing on a Dam* (oil on canvas, 33 1/2 x 50 ins / 85 x 127 cm) GBP 8,625.

INGNERS, Joseph
Bohemian, 17th century.
Painter.
Joseph Ingners painted two pieces for the altar of St Catherine in a chapel in St Wenceslaus church in Altbunzlau (Stara Boleslav): *Virgin Seated on a Throne, with St Catherine and St Rudolph* and *Martha and Mary Worshipping Christ.* He is probably identical with the painter Ingriss, who painted a picture of the *Saviour* in 1706 for the Benedictine church of St Nicholas in Prague.

INGOBERTUS
9th century.
Calligrapher.
Ingobertus wrote and illuminated the famous Bible of San Paolo fuori le Mura in Rome. This work was dedicated to Charlemagne.

INGOLI, Matteo, called il Ravennate
Italian, 17th century.
Born 1587, in Ravenna; died 1631, in Venice, of the plague.

Painter, architect. History painting.
Ingoli went to Venice at a very young age and trained under Luigi Benfatto, known as dal Freso. He was notably inspired by Palma the younger and Caliari. His works notably include two altarpieces in the churches of S Mercedes and Corpus Christi, a *Last Supper*, a *Virgin*, in glory, and a *St Apollinarus*, preserved at the Accademia di Belle Arti of Venice.

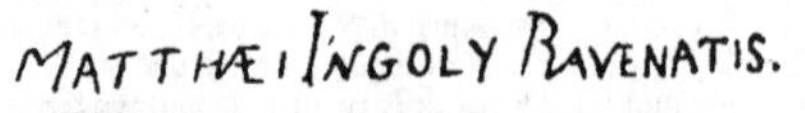

INGOMAR, Ignaz Frankel, also known as I. Ferenz
Hungarian, 19th - 20th century.
Born 1838, in Budapest; died 1924, in Budapest.
Painter. Portraits.
Ignaz Ingomar studied in Pest, Vienna and Antwerp and then settled in Paris where he lived for some 30 years. He exhibited at the Salon, showing his portraits. In about 1895, he returned to Vienna and then Budapest where he exhibited at the Salon Nemzeti in 1908.
AUCTION RECORDS:
LONDON, 19 March 1986, *Little Girl Reading* (1873, oil on canvas, 25 x 19 ins / 63.5 x 48.5 cm) GBP 3,400. MONACO, 3 Dec 1989, *Overturned Vase* (1873, oil on canvas, 34 1/4 x 25 1/2 ins / 87 x 65 cm) FRF 42,180.

INGONI, Bonnino
Italian, 16th century.
Died 1604, in Modena.
Active in Modena.
Sculptor.
Bonnino Ingoni worked for the viceroy of Naples and the king of France, and finally became cup-bearer to the grand-ducal court of Modena.

INGONI, Giovanni Battista, or Jugoni
Italian, 16th century.
Born 1528, in Modena; died 1608, in Modena.
Painter. History painting.
Vasari claims that Ingoni was a rival of Niccolò dell'Abbate. He worked in Rome, Perugia and Modena. Most of his works are now lost.

INGOUF, François Robert, called the Younger
French, 18th - 19th century.
Born 1747, in Paris; died 17 June 1812, in Paris.
Engraver (etching, burin).
François Robert Ingouf was the younger brother of Pierre-Charles Ingouf and, like his brother, was a pupil of Flippart. He holds a distinguished position among the engravers of the end of the 18th century, engraving after Raphael, Gérard Dow, Ribera, Drouais and Freudeberger. He also supplied plates for the *Musée Français*, and executed a large number of vignette portraits. He is remembered for an important and very rare print of *The Federation*, perhaps engraved together with his brother, according to M. Beraldi. He exhibited at the Salon of 1793: *The Ploughman's Return*, *The Poacher's Freedom* after Benezech, and *Canadians at their Child's Grave* after Le Barbier the Elder. François Ingouf must have had connections in Spain, because at his death he was a member of the academies in Madrid and Valencia.
AUCTION RECORDS:
PARIS, 12 and 13 March 1926, *Four Drawings for the Old Testament* (pen and wash) FRF 221.

INGOUF, Pierre Charles, called the Elder
French, 18th century.
Born 1746, in Paris; died 1800, in Paris.
Draughtsman, engraver (burin).
Pierre Charles Ingouf was a pupil of Flippart and, like his master, one of the main engravers of Greuze. He also engraved after J.G. Wille, and is particularly remembered for his engravings after S. Freudenberger of: *The Morals of Today*; *The Hawker*; *The Morning Stroll*; *The Evening Stroll* (in collaboration with Lingée); *The Winter's Evening*; and *The Soldier on Extended Leave*. He also executed some portraits.

INGPEN, A.W.
British, 19th century.
Active in Canterbury.
Painter. Animals.
The work of A.W. Ingpen was represented at the exhibitions of the Royal Academy, the British Institute and the Society of British Artists in London from 1832 to 1838.

INGRAHAM, Natalie (Mrs)
American, 19th - 20th century.
Also active in France.
Sculptor.
Natalie Ingraham was a pupil of Millet de Marcilly. She was active in New York and Paris.

INGRAM, Archibald B.
British, 19th century.
Active in Norbston.
Painter. Landscapes.
Archibald B. Ingram exhibited in London in Suffolk Street at rare intervals from 1881.

INGRAM, E.J. (Miss)
British, 19th century.
Active in Frogmore (England).
Painter. Landscapes.
E.J. Ingram exhibited her work at the British Institution in London in 1864 and 1866.

INGRAM, John
British, 18th century.
Born 1721, in London.
Active in Paris.
Engraver (burin).
After beginning his studies in London, John Ingram went to Paris in 1755 where he earned himself a distinguished position among the illustrators employed by bookshops. His works also include six plates and several prints after Boucher. He collaborated with Huquier, C. N. Cochin Tardieu and Liotard. *Subjects from Country Life* is one work he produced with Liotard.
AUCTION RECORDS:
PARIS, 8 and 9 April 1910, *Subjects from Country Life* (print, with copper border, in collaboration with Liotard) FRF 225.

INGRAM, Margaret K.
British, 19th century.
Active in London.
Painter.
Margaret K. Ingram exhibited two scenes of Venice in London at Suffolk Street in 1883.

INGRAM, Walter Rowlands
British, 19th century.
Active in Brussels and London.
Sculptor.
Walter Rowlands Ingram took part in many exhibitions in London, including the Royal Academy and the Grosvenor Gallery from 1862.

INGRAM, William Ayerst
British, 19th - 20th century.
Born 1855, in Glasgow; died 20 March 1913, in Falmouth.
Painter. Seascapes, landscapes.
William Ayerst Ingram was a pupil of John Streple and A. W. Weedon. He was a co-founder of the Anglo-Australian Society of Artists and became its president in 1888. He was a member of the Royal Institute of Oil Painters, the Royal Society of British Artists and the Ridley Art Club.

Museums and Galleries:
Bristol: *Journey's End* - Sydney: a watercolour.
Auction records:
London, 24 Feb 1908, *Newlyn Harbour* (drawing) GBP 3; *Brixham Harbour* (drawing) GBP 3. London, 14 Dec 1909, *The Red Cloud,* GBP 8.

INGRAND, Max. See **MAX-INGRAND Maurice**

INGRES, Jean Auguste Dominique
French, 19th century.
Born 29 August 1780, in Montauban; died 14 January 1867, in Paris.
Painter, draughtsman, engraver. Religious subjects, mythological subjects, nudes, portraits, landscapes. Murals, designs for stained glass.

Jean Auguste Dominique was the son of the painter, sculptor and musician Jean Marie Joseph Ingres, who, while directing him towards music, at the same time gifted him with the basic principles of drawing. Such was the potential shown by Jean Dominique for this particular artistic form that his father sent him to study in Toulouse. The young student spent time in the studios of Guillaume Joseph Roques (a pupil of Joseph Marie Vien), the sculptor Vigan and the landscape painter Briand. In 1796, Ingres went to Paris and his father found him a place in the studio of David. Since he received scarcely any money from his family, he was forced to finance himself from his musical abilities and became a violinist in the orchestra for a theatrical farce. In 1800, he competed for the Prix de Rome but gained only second place after Jean Pierre Granger, though the following year he won with *Achilles Receiving Agamemnon's Deputies in his Tent*. However, the state of the French economy at the time, and its military preoccupations, drove young artists into penurious conditions. Ingres had to wait for five years to obtain the financial resources to enable him to go to Italy. During this period he obtained a cell in the old Capuchin convent, where a number of artists lived, including Gros, Girodet, Dupaty, and Delecluze, who later became an art critic. Ingres began to move away from the influence of David. Putting some of his free time to good use in the library, he copied the drawings of the 16th-century masters and engravings in the style of their works, developing an unbounded admiration for them, especially for Raphael. Ingres' legacy from this period is a significant number of more or less authenticated drawings. In 1806, he left for Rome. He spent most of his time initially in the Raphael Rooms (Stanze di Raffaello) in the Vatican, and his admiration for Raphael only increased as a result of his constant vigil. This was where Ingres came to his own lasting vision. In 1813, he embarked upon his first marriage, to Mademoiselle Copelle. In 1820, he left Rome for Florence, where he lived before returning to Paris in 1824, bringing with him several outstanding works which he displayed in his first noteworthy exhibition at the Salon. He remained in Paris until 1834, when he was invited to succeed Horace Vernet, who wished to be relieved of his position as director of the École de Rome. During the seven years of his appointment he painted very little and became absorbed in his directorial duties. When he returned to Paris in 1841, his fellow artists gave him an enthusiastic reception and a large banquet was held in his honour. The years did not seem to have taken their toll on him, despite the fact that he was over 60; he was still as fresh, as alert and as intransigent in his ideas as he had been as a young man. His first wife died in 1849, and two years later he married Mlle Delphine Ramel, who would go on to survive him. At the beginning of 1867, he was in perfect health and even painted the portrait of Mlle Hippolyte Flandrin, his godchild, on New Year's Day. On 6 January 1867, he gathered some friends in his studio to listen to some chamber music, of which he had always been a great amateur performer with a marked preference for Mozart and Gluck. During the night following this private concert, a log fell from the fire and rolled into the bedchamber of the ageing artist. He roused himself and dealt with the log, but the room was filled with smoke and he had to open the window, as a result of which he caught a chill. A week later he was dead.

In 1802, Ingres exhibited a *Portrait of a Woman*; in 1806, the *Portrait of Napoleon I on his Throne*, intended for the legislative body, and several other portraits. Subsequently, he made occasional appearances at the Salon, which received a cool reception from the public; in 1814, *Don Pedro of Toledo, Pope Pius VII in the Sistine Chapel,* and several portraits; in 1819, *Odalisque, Philip V Giving the Order of the Golden Fleece to Marshall Berwick after the Battle of Almanza*; in 1822, *Charles V, then Regent of the Kingdom, Returning to Paris Following the Expulsion of the Duke of Burgundy*. The 1824 exhibition was a great success for Ingres: he exhibited *Louis XIII's Vow* (which is in the cathedral of Montauban), *Henry IV Playing with his Children as the Ambassador of Spain is Admitted to his Presence, Francis I Receives the Dying Breaths of Leonardo da Vinci,* and several portraits. Ingres exhibited once again in 1827, with *Portrait of a Man, Portrait of a Woman, Saint Symphorian* (in the cathedral of Autun); and in 1833, several portraits. Ingres also painted *Apotheosis of Homer* for one of the ceilings in the Louvre (since removed), which belongs to the French 19th-century School in Paris. In 1834, he sent *Martyrdom of Saint Symphorian* (ministry of public works) to the Salon, together with a portrait of a woman. Ingres received official honours over a long period: Chevalier de la Légion d'Honneur in 1824, Officier in 1826, Commandeur in 1845; as well as being elected as a member of the Insitut de France in 1825. The Exposition Universelle of 1855 marked the high point of his career. A whole room was dedicated to his works, among which were: *Jesus Christ Giving the Keys of Paradise to Saint Peter; Virgin Receiving the Host*; stained glass windows for the royal chapel of Dreux and for the chapel of St-Ferdinand; *Pope Pius VII in the Sistine Chapel; Apotheosis of Napoleon I* (ceiling painted for the old town hall and destroyed in 1871); *Portrait of Napoleon Bonaparte, 1st Consul; Apotheosis of Homer; Jupiter and Antiope; Venus Anadyomene; Oedipus and the Sphinx; Roger Delivering Angelica; Odalisque Reclining; Woman Bathing* (small study); *Odalisque* (painted in 1839, in Rome); *Francesca da Rimini; Jean Pastoret; Joan of Arc* (1854); *The Sword of Henry IV* (1832); *Aretin Receives with Disdain a Gold Chain Sent to him by Charles V; Portrait of Cherubini* (1842); *Portrait of Mme D.* (1807); *Portrait of the Countess of H.; Portrait of Mme M.* (1851); *Portrait of the Princess of B.; Portrait of Mme L.B.; Portrait of Mme G.; Portrait of Count Molé* (1832); *Portrait of the Artist's Father* (1804); and several other paintings. This was almost his total output. He was awarded an important honorary medal by the jury, and the government elevated him to the level of Grand Officier de la Légion d'Honneur. He was made a senator in 1862. Ingres was also a member of the Académie Française in Rome, and an honorary member of the academies in Berlin, Vienna, Amsterdam, Anvers, Munich, Athens, Florence and Montauban; he was also made a Knight of the Order of Civic Merit in Prussia, Commander of the Order of Leopold of Belgium, Knight of the Order of Saint Joseph in Tuscany, and was awarded a Great Cross of the Order of Guadeloupe.

His works have been shown in some thematic exhibitions such as: *Ingres et ses maîtres, de Roques à David* (*Ingres and his Masters, from Roques to David*) (1955, Augustine museum, Toulouse); *Ingres et son temps* (*Ingres and his Age*) (1967), an exhibition organised for the centenary of his death at the Ingres museum in Montauban; *Ingres e Firenze: con una sezione dedicata agli artisti toscani contemporanei di In-*

gres (*Ingres and Florence: with a Section Dedicated to the Tuscan Artists, Contemporaries of Ingres*) (1968, Centro Di, Florence); *Ingres et sa postérité: jusqu'à Matisse et Picasso* (*Ingres and his Posterity: until Matisse and Picasso*) (1980, Ingres museum, Montauban); *Les élèves d'Ingres* (*Pupils of Ingres*) (1999, Ingres museum, Montauban); and *The Triumph of French Painting: Ingres to Matisse* (2000, Baltimore Museum of Art, Baltimore).

Among solo exhibitions and retrospectives are: *Ingres Centennial Exhibition, 1867-1967: drawings, watercolours and oil sketches from American Collections* (1967, Fogg Art Museum, Harvard University, Cambridge, Mass.); *Ingres in Italia (1806-1824, 1825-1841)* (1968, Accademia di Francia, Villa Medici, Rome); 1968, museum of the Petit Palais, Paris; 1981, National Museum of Western Art, Tokyo; *Ingres, in Pursuit of Perfection: the Art of J.A.D. Ingres* (1983, Kimbell Art Museum, Fort Worth, Texas); *Les Portraits d'Ingres* (*Portraits of Ingres*) (1985, musée du Louvre, Paris); *Return to Rome of Monsieur Ingres: drawings and paintings* (1993, Villa Medici, Rome); in 2002, the Louvre presented, in the exhibition *Ingres, les cartons de vitraux* (*Ingres: Cartoons for Stained Glass*), works produced between 1842 and 1844 for the chapel of St-Ferdinand (Paris, route de Neuilly) and the basilica in Dreux, these works had already been exhibited in the Musée du Luxembourg under the Second Empire. In 2006, the Louvre organised a retrospective of his work and the Palais Rohan in Strasbourg presented 100 of his works in *Collages d'Ingres*.

Independently of his studies in the style of the ancient masters while still a student, the young Ingres was commissioned to paint the portrait of the First Consul (Napoleon) for the town of Liège. From 1806, he lived in Rome for fourteen years. Among his output during this period are: *Woman Bathing Seen from Behind* (1806), *Oedipus and the Sphinx* (1808), *Jupiter and Thetis* and *Virgil Reading the Aeneid to Augustus* at the Villa Medici; *Sleep of Ossian* and the *Temple of Romulus* at the Palazzo del Quirinale; *Roger Delivering Angelica* (1819); *Odalisque* (1819); and *Jesus Christ Giving Saint Peter the Keys of Paradise*. The same period produced about three hundred graphite portraits which he sold for 40 francs, many of which were commissions procured for him by his barber. When he first returned to Paris in 1841, the duke of Orléans commissioned his portrait. Among his final works were: *La Source* (*Spring*) (1856), *Molière and Louis XIV* and *Jesus and the Teachers*. The young Romantic School of Eugene Delacroix and Géricault monopolised public attention; Ingres opposed them with the classical tradition. In the studio where he taught, respect for tradition reigned supreme. In spite of his difficult character and uncompromising prejudice, Ingres was much-loved by his pupils. Among the painters who received their artistic education under his tutelage were, notably, Chassériau, who naturally inclined towards the Romantic ideal, and Hippolyte Flandrin, who remained a hero of Classicism right to the end.

Ingres' ambition was to attain the drawing technique and skill of Raphael. The collection of studies and the paintings which he bequeathed to the museum of his home town are evidence of this. His work as an engraver produced five pieces. One is an etching made in Rome in 1818, *Gabriel Cartois de Pressigny, Archbishop of Rennes, Ambassador of France in Rome*, reproduced as a lithograph by Mathey in 1820. Two versions of this are known: the first, the prelate's hat unfinished, the second the completed plate. His other four etchings are lithographs: *Catherine Anne (North), Lady Glenberoye* (Ingres, Rome, 1816, with lithography by C. Hulmandell), an extremely rare engraving which has been reproduced by photoengraving; *Frederick Silvester North Douglas* (Ingres, Rome, 1815); *Reclining Odalisque* (Ingres, 1825) for an album of lithography published by Delpech in 1826; *Four Magistrates who Governed Besançon when the Town was Free* (Ingres, 1825), the tailpiece of the introduction to *Journey into Franche-Comté* in the work by Baron Taylor. Ingres' paintings have also been copied by many other artsists.

Ingres saw himself as a painter of history, and throughout his life he painted many historical canvases. But also, during the course of this long life, he produced countless portraits, as paintings, drawings or sketched outlines. His early portraits are sober and dark, highlighting the face of the subject and often simply sketching in the rest of the body. The portraits of *Gilibert* (1805), *Bartolini* (1806) and *J.B. Desdéban* (around 1810) share this treatment. Others painted with the same dark background achieve great quality through the precision with which they are painted, as in the case of the portraits of *Portrait of Frédéric Desmarais* (1805), or *Doctor Defrance* (before 1815). Before embarking on a portrait, Ingres attempted several preliminary studies in which he tried to bring out the personality of the subject not only by means of physical features but by bearing, style of presentation and surrounding objects. Everything was carefully selected and positioned, nothing being left to chance. The portraits of the different members of the Rivière family are illustrations of this. The *Portrait of Mme Rivière*, for example, shows how well Ingres was able to play with intertwining folds of the shawl so as to balance the composition with the off-centre pose of Mme Rivière. The harmonious clarity of the colours brings out the eyes and the dark hair of this woman, whose whole bearing expresses a graceful nonchalance. But the most remarkable of the portraits of this family is that of *Mlle Rivière*. The face of this girl is diffused with the transparent light pervading the landscape in the background of the picture, which is reminiscent of certain Flemish landscapes. Ingres has imbued this girl with a certain ambiguity through the slightly narrowed eyes, the curve of the eyebrows precisely drawn, the high cheekbones, the full lower lip, and the shape of the head, precisely defined, following the contour of her sleek, smooth hair. The innocence of the young girl - who was then fifteen years old and died in the same year the portrait was painted - is underlined by the white of the dress and the fur, but at the same time is oddly in harmony with the red of her sensuous lips, while the fur wrap embraces with passion the arms sheathed in bright yellow gloves.

Many other skilfully executed portraits can be cited, including *François-Marius Granet* (1807), though this one is Romantic in style; or that of *Mme de Senonnes* (Musée de Beaux-Arts, Nantes), portraying an elegant woman grooming herself, the nape of her neck reflected in the mirror behind her. Even more famous is the *Portrait of M Bertin*. Here Ingres has chosen simple surroundings; there is no décor and there are no rich fabrics, and the only piece of furniture is the study chair on which the subject sits heavily, his hands on his knees. He is the incarnation of the bourgeois man of business and politics, firmly established in society, a significant figure. Perrier described this man as having, 'almost vulgar features, an obese body and squat limbs', whereas Ingres saw, 'the ardent expression of a will...the painter has drawn from his subject the general expression of his character'.

Despite his obvious skill and success as a portrait painter, Ingres demonstrated a marked preference for historical paintings, which reflect his sensitivity and his ambitions most accurately, uniting his style with the ideological content. There is, however, a difference in style between more or less recent historical scenes and subjects drawn from antiquity or from legend. The former, such as *Philip V Decorating the Marshall of Berwick with the Golden Fleece after the Battle of Almanza* (1818), or *Don Pedro of Toledo Kissing the Sword of Henry IV* (1820), or *Entry into Paris of the Dauphin, the Future Charles V*, are treated with a certain detachment, historically reconstituted down to the smallest detail, making them reminiscent of mural decorations or stained glass windows. The latter, which relate legendary tales, take on a character approaching fantasy, whether it be *Oedipus and the Sphinx* (1808), *Jupiter and Thetis* (1811), or *Roger and Angelica*. For *Jupiter and Thetis*, Ingres adopted an archaic style, painting flat and without relief, thrusting all shadows away from the body of Thetis. This emphasises the undulating curve of her body. It also exaggerates the length of her neck, which has been criticised for being anatomically incorrect but also praised for the apparently deliberate expressive boldness, its elongation being accentuated in the movement of the left arm outstretched towards Jupiter's chin, her hand seeming to brush against it. The whole thing seems to express Thetis' complete supplication to the omnipotent master of Olympus. Ingres also followed a similar style when he painted *Roger and Angelica*, which is considered to be original, but also stylised and bizarre, worthy of a Romantic artist. He imbues the naked body of Angelica with a sculpted appearance verging on the unreal, in order to remain faithful to the line from Ariosto, 'One would think oneself in the presence of a statue bound to the rock by a Florentine sculptor'. *The Dream of Ossian* in the museum of Montauban remains Ingres' truly unclassifiable work. It is not known whether, signing and dating it in 1813, he considered it complete or left it permanently unfinished. Whether completed or abandoned, it is impressive on several counts, not least for its size and its strangeness. Ossian, alone, hunched over his harp at ground level and enveloped in a huge cape, is painted in colour, while the remainder of the composition, its half-naked soldiers scattered in a rocky landscape, is painted in grisaille, signifying the absence of material existence. It is a totally dreamlike painting, very reminiscent of the pre-Romantic dream visions of Girodet-Trioson. Ingres' historical compositions, especially those with themes drawn from legend, are bold and difficult. Understanding them means moving beyond a simple stylistic interpretation of a typical 'Ingresque' style, and seeing in their contents a strangeness that is not so far removed from the ideas of the Romantics, against whom art historians have often been inclined to put Ingres in opposition.

Finally, it is the nude figure outside the constraints of any historical context which allows the art of Ingres its freest expression, though these works are often tinged with orientalism. There are three variations in his treatment of this subject: the woman bathing seen from behind, the Odalisque and the Venus Anadyomene. On all these nudes, the light, which supposedly comes from the front, throws all shadows away from the body, thereby emphasising the lithe contours of these languid bodies. He has been reproached for this absolute pursuit of the arabesque on the grounds that he deforms his nude figures, especially the *Grande Odalisque* of 1814, who like Thetis is accused of having too many vertebrae. To these accusations Ingres justified his art by saying, 'In order to express the character of the subject a certain exaggeration is allowable, sometimes necessary, even, and even more so when it is a case of emphasising and enhancing an aspect of the beautiful'. His masterpiece in this style is his last picture, *The Turkish Bath*, painted in 1862. Although Ingres is often thought of as a cold painter, devoid of sensuality if not sensitivity, the sensuality expressed in this final painting and in some of his female portraits, such as *Madame de Senonnes*, reveal him to be a dedicated lover of feminine beauty.

A relentless and dissatisfied worker, Ingres revisited the same subjects more than once, varying the compositions hardly at all. This is why several versions of the same picture can be found in the collections of different museums. Although he seemed to be specifically wedded to his era by his sometimes rather naive themes - for instance, *Oedipus and the Sphinx* or *Jupiter and Thetis* - and his Neo-Classical style, Ingres did in fact inspire painters who came after him. Manet, for one, suppressed the relief of the body, following the example of Ingres, in *Olympia*, and even Picasso was influenced by the audacity with which Ingres deliberately deformed the body for expressive purposes, to the point where one of his periods is described as 'Ingresque'.

Stamp of sale

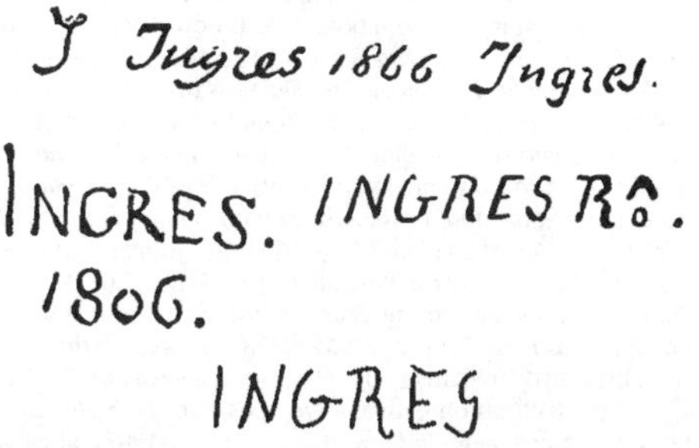

BIBLIOGRAPHY:

Ingres, Jean-Auguste-Dominique/Cognat, Raymond (preface), *Écrits sur l'art*, La Jeune Parque, Paris, 1947. Alazard, Jean, *Ingres et l'ingrisme*, Albin Michel, Paris, 1950. Wildenstein, Georges, *Ingres*, Phaidon, London, 1954. *Ingres centennial exhibition, 1867-1967: drawings, watercolors, and oil sketches from American collections*, Fogg Art Museum, Harvard University, Cambridge (MA), 1967. Rosenblum, Robert, '*Jean-Auguste-Dominique Ingres*' in *coll. Bibliothèque des Grands Peintres*, Éd. Cercle d'Art, Paris, 1967. Duclaux, L./Foucart, J./Naef, H./Serullaz, M./Ternois, D., *Ingres*, exhibition catalogue, Réunion des musées nationaux, musée du Petit Palais, Paris, 1967-1968. *Ingres et le néo-classicisme*, symposium proceedings, Les Amis du musée Ingres, Montauban, 1975. Camesasca, Ettore, et al., *Tout l'œuvre peint de Ingres*, Flammarion, Paris, 1984. Toussaint, Hélène (ed.), *Les Portraits d'Ingres: peintures des musées nationaux*, exhibition catalogue, Musée du Louvre, Paris, 1985. Goldschmidt, Ernst (ed.), *Ingres et Delacroix: dessins et aquarelles*, exhibition catalogue, Éd. Michèle Trinckvel, Paris, 1986. *Ingres et Rome*, symposium proceedings, Musée Ingres, Montauban, 1986. Picon, Gaëtan, *Ingres*, Skira, Geneva, 1991 (new edition). Vigne, Georges (ed.), *Le retour à Rome de Monsieur Ingres, dessins et peintures*, exhibition catalogue, Villa Médicis, Rome, 1993. Duval, Amaury, *L'Atelier d'Ingres*, Arthena, Paris, 1993 (reprint of the book published in 1878). Vigne, Georges, *Ingres*, Citadelles, Paris, 1995. Abe, Shigeki, '*Ingres et l'art davidien*' in *2 vol.*, dissertation, Université de Paris I Panthéon-Sorbonne, Paris, 1995 (doctorat). Vigne, Georges, *Dessins d'Ingres. Catalogue raisonné des dessins du musée de Montauban*, catalogue raisonné, Musée Ingres, Montauban, 1995. Lavallée, Marie-Hélène, *Les élèves d'Ingres*, exhibition catalogue, Musée Ingres, Montauban, 1999. *Ingres et ses élèves*, symposium proceedings, Les Amis du musée Ingres, Montauban, 2000. Flam, Jack, '*Matisse and Ingres*' in *Apollo* n° 464 p. 20, periodical, London, October 2000. Crow, Thomas, '*Ingres and David*' in *Apollo* n° 472 p. 11, periodical, Paris, June 2001. Foucart, Jacques, *Ingres. Les Cartons de vitraux des collections du Louvre*, Réunion des musées nationaux, Paris, 2002.

MUSEUMS AND GALLERIES:
AIX: *Portrait of Granet; Study of an Old Man; Jupiter and Thetis; Man's Head* - ANGERS (MBA): *Odalisque Reclining* (c. 1814, oil on canvas, sketch); *Paolo and Francesca* (1819, oil on canvas); *Oedipus and the Sphinx* (1829, oil on canvas); *Two Men's Heads* (no date, oil on canvas, study); *Greek Tragedies* (signed in 1866, oil on canvas, study) - ANTWERP: *Portrait of the Artist* - BALTIMORE (Walters AM): *L'Odalisque à l'esclave* (*Odalisque with Slave*) - BAYONNE (Mus. Bonnat): *Young Man; Charles X; Madame Devauçay; Woman Bathing; Francesca da Rimini; Study; Virgin with the Host; Woman and Child* (oil on wood); *Study for the Apotheosis of Homer; Study of Women's Hands* - BESANÇON: *Portrait of Desdéban* - BLOIS: *Madonna with Candelabra* - BOSTON: *The Marquis of Pastoret; Rosario Persico* - BRUSSELS: *Virgil Reading the Aeneid to Augustus* - CAMBRIDGE, MA (Fogg AM, Harvard University): *Odalisque with Slave* - CHANTILLY: *Artist Aged 24 Years; Madame Devançay; The Sickness of Antiochus; Venus Anadyomene; Francesca da Rimini* - CINCINNATI (Taft MA): *Mademoiselle Jeanne Gonin* (*Mademoiselle Jeanne Gonin*) (1821, oil on canvas, portrait) - COLOGNE: *Head of Athena; Head of Juno; Love; Athena with Helmet and Shield* - DIJON: *Portrait of a Woman* - DÜSSELDORF: *Marquis of Molins* - FLORENCE (Uffizi): *Portrait of the Artist* - LE MANS: *Study for Jesus among the Teachers* (oil on wood) - LIÈGE: *Bonaparte as First Consul* - LONDON (NG): *Monsieur de Norvins* (1811-1812, oil/canvas/panel); *Angelica saved by Ruggiero* (1819-1839, oil on canvas); *Oedipus and the Sphinx* (c. 1826, oil on canvas); *Pindar and Ictinus* (1830-1867, oil/canvas/panel); *The Duc d'Orléans* (after 1842, oil on canvas, in collaboration with studio); *Madame Moitessier* (1856, oil on canvas) - LONDON (Victoria and Albert Mus.): *Henry iV; Odalisque Reclining* - LONDON (Wallace Collection): *Hope and Charity* (pencil and grey wash/paper) - MONTAUBAN: *Man's Torso; Academy of Man* (same subject); *Portrait of the Artist's Father; F. Belvèze; Landscape* (same subject); *Eve; Heads of a Woman and a Child; Dream of Ossian; Alexander; Centurion's Head; Study of a Head* (same subject); *Roger delivering Angelica; Jesus among the Teachers; The Child Jesus and Two Doctors; Old Man's Arm; Study for Stratonice; Louis XIII's Vow; J.F. Gilibert; Madame Gonse* - MONTPELLIER: *Stratonice; Study for Jesus among the Teachers; Study for the Apotheosis of Homer* - MOSCOW (Pushkin MFA): *Virgin with the Host* - NANTES (MBA): *Portrait of Madame de Senonnes* - NEW YORK (Metropolitan Mus. of Art): *Joseph-Antoine Moltedo* (c. 1810); *Jacques-Louis Leblanc* (1823); *Madame Françoise Leblanc* (1823); *Edmond Cavé* (1844); *Madame Edmond Cavé* (1830) - PARIS (Louvre): *Stained-Glass Windows of the Chapel of St-Ferdinand: 'Hope'*. (1842, stained glass); *Jesus Gives St Peter the Keys of Paradise; The Virgin with the Host; Homer Challenged; Venus Anadyomene; Joan of Arc at the Coronation of Charles VII; Oedipus Explaining the Enigma; La Source* (*Spring*) (two versions); *Grande Odalisque; Woman Bathing; Sistine Chapel; Apotheosis of Napoleon I; Madame Marcotte de Ste-Marie; Turkish Bath; Monsieur Cordier; Philibert Rivière; Madame Rivière; Mademoiselle Rivière; Monsieur Bochet; Monsieur Bertin; Cherubini; Roger Delivering Angelica* - PARIS (Mus. Carnavalet): *Triumph of Napoleon I* - PARIS (Mus. de l'Armée): *Napoleon on the Throne* - PARIS (Mus. des Arts décoratifs): *The Casino of Raphael* - PHILADELPHIA (MA): *Portrait of the Countess of Tournon* (1812, oil on canvas) - POITIERS: *Study of an Arm* - RIGA: *Raphael and the Fornarina* - ROUEN: *Portrait; Woman's Head; The Beautiful Zelia; Study of Drapery* - ST PETERSBURG (Hermitage): *Count Gouriev* - STOCKHOLM: *Sketch for Achilles and the Messengers of Agamemnon* - TOULOUSE: *Virgil Reading the Aeneid to Augustus; Frederick Desmarais* - WARSAW: *Man's Torso; Portrait of Thorvaldsen* - WASHINGTON DC (NGA): *Marcotte d'Argenteuil* (1810, oil on canvas); *Pope Pius VII in the Sistine Chapel* (1814, oil on canvas); *Ulysses* (1827, oil on canvas mounted on wood); *Madame Moitessier* (1851, oil on canvas); drawings, engravings.

AUCTION RECORDS:
PARIS, 1852, *Stratonice*, FRF 63,000. PARIS, 13-16 Jan 1863, *Stratonice*, FRF 92,000. PARIS, 27 April 1867, *The Golden Age*, FRF 27,000; *Odalisque*, FRF 44,000. PARIS, 6-7 May 1867, *Angelica Bound to a Rock*, FRF 50,000. PARIS, 1868, *Turkish Bath*, FRF 20,000. PARIS, 6-9 March 1872, *Oedipus and the Sphinx*, FRF 25,600; *St Symphorian* (drawing) FRF 9,100. PARIS, 29 April 1872, *Roger Delivering Angelica*, FRF 70,000; *Apotheosis of Napoleon I* (sketch) FRF 7,200. PARIS, 28 March 1892, *Woman Bathing*, FRF 9,000. PARIS, 27 April 1897, *The Ambassador of Spain Kissing the Sword of Henry IV*, FRF 3,700. PARIS, 12 June 1900, *Tintoretto and Aretin*, FRF 2,700. NEW YORK, 8-9 Jan 1903, *Cardinal Bibienne Proposing his Niece in Marriage to Raphael*, USD 5,500. PARIS, 17 Nov 1909, *Jupiter*, FRF 2,000. PARIS, 20 April 1910, *Virgin at Prayer*, FRF 7,500. PARIS, 15 and 16 Nov 1918, *Painting* (graphite) FRF 1,000; *Group of Naked Women* (graphite, study for The Golden Age) FRF 1,020; *Study of the Child Jesus for the 'Vow of Louis XIII', Montauban Cathedral* (graphite) FRF 1,000. PARIS, 26-27 May 1919, *Portrait of Mademoiselle Nicaise-Lacroix, Cousin of the Artist* (graphite) FRF 11,000; *Portrait of M Alexandre Boyer* (graphite) FRF 19,000; *Portrait of Berlioz* (pencil) FRF 10,000; *Portrait of Madame Borel, Sister-in-Law of the Artist* (graphite) FRF 10,000; *Study of the Figure of Acron for the Painting 'Romulus Conqueror of Acron'*, FRF 19,000. PARIS, 16-19 June 1919, *Portrait of Madame Haudebourt-Lescot* (graphite) FRF 32,200; *Portrait of M de Norvins* (graphite) FRF 11,100; *Portrait of Gaspard-Bonnet* (graphite) FRF 11,000. PARIS, 6-7 May 1920, *The Odyssey*, FRF 41,000. PARIS, 17 May 1920, *Portrait of Lorenzo Bartolini*. PARIS, 27-28 May 1921, *Portrait of a Man Holding his Hat in his Left Hand* (graphite) FRF 10,000. PARIS, 26 March 1924, *Study for the Negro in the 'Odalisque'* (pencil) FRF 12,000. PARIS, 27-28 June 1924, *Death of Leonardo da Vinci*, FRF 19,500. PARIS, 23 June 1925, *Portrait of Madame Salvator Cherubini* (graphite) FRF 2,100. PARIS, 10-11 May 1926, *Portrait of Guillon-Lethière, Director of the Académie de France in Rome* (graphite) FRF 8,000. LONDON, 29 June 1926, *Study for Phidias in 'The Apotheosis of Homer'* (drawing) GBP 150; *Portrait of the Artist and His Wife* (pencil) GBP 300; *Portrait of Taurel* (pencil) GBP 310. PARIS, 25 April 1927, *Cardinal Bibienna Promises his Niece in Marriage to Raphael* (watercolour) FRF 5,050. PARIS, 2 March 1928, *Seated Figure*, FRF 8,050. PARIS, 15 Nov 1928, *Woman Bathing* (drawing) FRF 13,200; *Portrait of Madame Moitessier* (gouache) FRF 50,100; *Turkish Bath*, FRF 50,000. PARIS, 3 June 1929, *Birth of the Muses* (watercolour) FRF 143,000; *Portrait of Madame Gonse* (drawing) FRF 122,000; *Portrait Presumed to be M Lorimier* (drawing) FRF 190,000; *Portrait of Mademoiselle Louise Dubreuil* (drawing) FRF 45,100; *Portrait of a Woman* (drawing) FRF 118,000; *Portrait of the Painter Thomas Charles Naudet* (drawing) FRF 64,000; *Portraits of Mademoiselles Harvey (recto); Study of a Girl (verso)*, FRF 52,000; *Portrait of Countess Ségur-Lamoignon* (drawing) FRF 141,000; *Portrait of Madame Mottez* (drawing) FRF 165,000; *Portrait Presumed to be Lady Cavendish-Bentick* (drawing) FRF 205,000; *Portrait of Monsieur and Madame Edouard Ramel* (drawing) FRF 125,000; *Portrait of a Man* (drawing) FRF 46,000. PARIS, 21 June 1929, *Study for the Hand of Count Molé* (drawing) FRF 5,500; *Portrait of Lemasle* (drawing) FRF 10,000; *Portrait of a Man* (drawing) FRF 40,000; *Study for 'Romulus, Conqueror of Acron'* (drawing) FRF 21,000; *Portrait of Madame Madeleine Ingres*, FRF 715,000; *Portrait of the Sculptor Paul*

Lemoyne, FRF 370,000; *Francesca da Rimini and Paolo Malatesta,* FRF 78,000; *Study for Phidias,* FRF 28,000; *Study for 'The Iliad',* FRF 43,100; *Raphael, study: Arms and Hands of Racine,* FRF 33,000; *Portrait of Pierre-François Bernier,* FRF 31,000; *Portrait of Ingres at the Age of 24,* FRF 13,550. PARIS, 14 June 1930, *Bust of a Woman,* FRF 55,000. PARIS, 9 Dec 1932, *Study of a Nude for 'The Iliad'* (graphite) FRF 2,000. PARIS, 14 Dec 1933, *Angelica Bound to a Rock,* FRF 275,000. LONDON, 9 July 1936, *Doctor Defrance,* GBP 400. PARIS, 30 Nov 1936, *Portrait Presumed to be Madame de Senonnes,* FRF 72,000. PARIS, 14 Dec 1936, *Madame Ingres* (graphite) FRF 3,150. PARIS, 12 March 1937, *Young Woman Seated Seen from Behind Wearing a Feathered Hat* (pencil, and bistre wash) FRF 2,300. PARIS, 28 Feb 1938, *The Marchese Lodovico Gonzaga and his Family* (graphite, after a fresco by Mantegna in Mantua) FRF 1,080. PARIS, 13 Feb 1939, *Portrait of the Architect Alais* (graphite) FRF 4,000; *Henry IV Playing with his Children* (graphite, pen and sepia wash) FRF 3,000. PARIS, 14 March 1941, *Study for an 'Apotheosis of Homer'* (black chalk) FRF 3,800. PARIS, 21 May 1941, *Study for a 'Sleeping Woman' or for 'Jupiter and Antiope',* FRF 252,000. PARIS, 15 Dec 1941, *Portrait of the Engraver Desmarais* (1805) FRF 1,240,000. NEW YORK, 8 Jan 1942, *Martyrdom of St Symphorian,* USD 2,700; *Raphael and the Fornarina,* USD 2,200. PARIS, 24 Dec 1942, *Study of a Leg for 'The Martyrdom of St Symphorian'* (graphite) FRF 3,000. PARIS, 10 Feb 1943, *Study of Hands* (graphite) FRF 35,000. PARIS, 15 March 1944, *Study for 'The Martyrdom of St Symphorian'* (graphite heightened with gouache) FRF 14,500. PARIS, 20 March 1944, *The Virgin Wearing a Blue Veil,* FRF 300,000. PARIS, Oct 1945-July 1946, *Study for St Raphael* (pencil) FRF 14,000; *Portrait of the Architect Labrousse* (pencil) FRF 181,000. PARIS, 30 May 1949, *Francesca da Rimini and Paolo Malatesta,* FRF 400,000. PARIS, 27 June 1949, *Study of a Man's Profile,* FRF 380,000; *Martyrdom of St Symphorian* (studies) FRF 210,000; *Study for a Portrait* (graphite) FRF 40,000. PARIS, 29 June 1949, *Study of Hands for the Stained-Glass Windows of the Chapel at Dreux* (pencil) FRF 36,000. PARIS, 12 May 1950, *Stratonice, or the Sickness of Antiochus,* FRF 700,000. PARIS, 16 June 1950, *Study of Feet and Drapery,* FRF 52,000. VERSAILLES, 6 Nov 1950, *The Duke of San Pedro de Toledo Kissing the Sword of Henry IV* (pencil) FRF 28,000. PARIS, 15 March 1951, *Virgil Reading the Aeneid before Augustus* (graphite) FRF 5,500. BRUSSELS, 21 May 1951, *Hercules Chaining Cerberus,* BEF 8,000. PARIS, 28 June 1951, *Study of a Hand and Embroidery for a Woman's Portrait* (graphite) FRF 6,500; *Virgil Reading the Aeneid before Augustus* (graphite) FRF 4,200. PARIS, 10 Dec 1951, *Study for 'Roger Releasing Angelica'* (graphite) FRF 420,000; *Study for Cherubini Crowned by the Muse of Music* (graphite and pen) FRF 400,000. PARIS, 9-10 June 1953, *Portrait of a Man* (graphite) FRF 880,000. PARIS, 6 April 1954, *Portrait of Henri Lehmann* (graphite) FRF 460,000. PARIS, 15 June 1954, *Virgin Crowned,* FRF 5,500,000; *Tintoretto and Aretin,* FRF 4,700,000; *Entry of Charles V into Paris,* FRF 4,400,000. PARIS, 7-8 Dec 1954, *Allegory* (after Raphael's painting of 'The Vision of Ezekiel') FRF 205,000. PARIS, 7 March 1955, *Nude Woman Standing* (graphite) FRF 23,000. PARIS, 22 March 1955, *Study of a Woman; At Prayer; Study of Feet* (graphite) FRF 82,000; *Study of a Woman,* FRF 55,000. NEW YORK, 10 Dec 1955, *Martyrdom of St Symphorian,* USD 3,000. PARIS, 3 Dec 1957, *Portrait of Madame Borel? Sister of Madame Ingres* (pencil) FRF 1,710,000. LONDON, 26 March 1958, *St Peter,* GBP 600. PARIS, 23 June 1959, *Portrait of Madame Gallois* (pencil) FRF 6,500,000. LONDON, 4 May 1960, *Pages of Studies for a Child* (pencil and black chalk) GBP 1,000. NEW YORK, 26 Oct 1960, *Nude* (pencil) USD 1,900. LONDON, 28 June 1962, *Portrait of a Lady,* GBP 1,200. LONDON, 26 March 1963, *Profile of a Nude, Seated* (charcoal) Gns 3,000. MUNICH, 19 Oct 1965, *Portrait of Franz Liszt* (drawing) DEM 105,000. LONDON, 30 Nov 1966, *Paolo and Francesca,* GBP 16,000. PARIS, 3 Dec 1967, *Woman's Head* (pencil) FRF 19,000. LONDON, 30 April 1969, *Death of Leonardo da Vinci,* GBP 10,000. LONDON, 4 Dec 1969, *Portrait of the Countess of Castellane* (pencil) GBP 4,000. VERSAILLES, 7 June 1972, *Portrait of the Musician Victor Dourlen,* FRF 43,000. PARIS, 28 Nov 1972, *Portrait of a Young Man* (pencil) FRF 60,000. NEW YORK, 28 Nov 1973, *Portrait of Jean-Pierre Grainger* (pencil) USD 20,000. LONDON, 7 April 1976, *Francis I Witnessing the Dying Breaths of Leonardo da Vinci* (c. 1850, oil on canvas, 18 3/4 x 17 3/4in/47.5 x 45cm) GBP 16,000. VERSAILLES, 6 July 1976, *Portrait of a Woman* (graphite, 8 x 6in/20.5 x 15.5cm) FRF 6,500. NEW YORK, 28 Oct 1977, *Monsieur and Madame Ingres* (pencil, 7 1/2 x 5 1/2in/19 x 14cm) USD 55,000. LONDON, 27 June 1978, *Henry VIII of England* (c. 1806-1820, pencil, after Hans Holbein the Younger, 9 1/2 x 7in/24 x 17.5cm) GBP 26,000. PARIS, 24 Nov 1978, *Odalisque* (1825, lithograph) FRF 7,800. NEW YORK, 7 June 1979, *Portrait of Mr and Mrs Edmond Ramel* (1855, pencil heightened with white, 13 1/2 x 11in/34.3 x 27cm) USD 145,000. NEW YORK, 6 May 1980, *Odalisque* (1825, lithograph, from the album of lithographs published in 1826 by Delpech, 5 1/4 x 8 1/4in/13.2 x 21.1cm) USD 1,450. BERN, 19 June 1980, *Study for the Portrait of Madame Sigisbert Moitessier, christened Inès de Foucault* (1851-56, pencil/paper, 7 1/4 x 5 1/2 ins / 18.7 x 13.8 cm) CHF 21,000. LONDON, 30 June 1980, *Portrait of a Girl* (oil on canvas, 16 x 12 3/4in/40.5 x 32.5cm) GBP 55,000. PARIS, 30 March 1981, *Portrait of Adelaide Nicaise-Lacroix* (1813, pencil, 10 x 8in/25.5 x 20.5cm) FRF 450,000. PARIS, 22 March 1983, *Portrait of Charles Thévenin* (1817, graphite heightened with white gouache/bistre-coloured paper, 11 x 8 3/4in/28 x 22.5cm) FRF 1,520,000. PARIS, 12 Dec 1984, *Study for the Head of St John* (oil on canvas/canvas remounted on wood, irregularly shaped canvas, 15 1/2 x 11in/39.5 x 27cm) FRF 600,000. PARIS, 24 June 1985, *Portrait of the Countess of Haussonville, christened Louise de Broglie (View to the Waist)* (oil on canvas, oval, 44 x 29 3/4in/111.5 x 75.5cm) FRF 3,200,000. LONDON, 12 Dec 1985, *Portrait of the Honourable Mrs Fleetwood Pellew, later Lady Pellew* (1817, pencil, 11 3/4 x 8 3/4in/29.7 x 22.2cm) GBP 210,000. PARIS, 12 June 1986, *Reduction of the 'Grande Odalisque'* (1817, oil on canvas, 5 3/4 x 10in/14.5 x 24.5cm) FRF 1,900,000. NEW YORK, 11 May 1987, *Odalisque* (1825, lithograph, 12 1/2 x 17 3/4in/31.8 x 45.1cm) USD 9,500. LONDON, 6 July 1987, *Gatteaux Family* (1850, pencil drawing and engraving, 17 1/4 x 24in/44.1 x 60.7cm) GBP 130,000. PARIS, 20 Nov 1987, *Study for 'The Sleeping Woman'* (oil on panel, 9 x 14 1/4in/22 x 36.5cm) FRF 2,800,000. NEW YORK, 25 Feb 1988, *Woman Bathing* (pencil, 10 x 7 1/2in/24.5 x 18.8cm) USD 3,850. PARIS, 15 March 1988, *Head of a Girl in Profile from the Right, Covered by a Blue Veil* (oil on canvas, 8 1/2 x 6 1/4in/21.5 x 16cm) FRF 260,000; *Portrait of Madame Rohault de Fleury, originally named Marcotte* (1848, pencil and gouache/tinted paper, 11 1/2 x 8 3/4in/29.2 x 22.4cm) FRF 1,000,000. MONACO, 19 June 1988, *Portrait of Madame V. Baltard and her Daughter Paule at the Villa Medici in Rome* (1836, pencil, 12 x 9in/30.6 x 22.8cm) FRF 4,218,000. PARIS, 16 Dec 1988, *Portrait of the Abbé de Bonald* (1816, oil on panel, 49 1/4 x 37 1/2in/125 x 95cm) FRF 675,000. PARIS, 17 March 1989, *The Countess of Agoult and her Daughter Claire* (1849, pencil heightened with white, 19 x 15 3/4in/48.5 x 40cm) FRF 7,000,000. NEW YORK, 1 June 1989, *Raphael and the Fornarina* (oil on canvas/panel, 27 1/4 x 21 1/4in/69 x 54cm) USD 1,430,000. MONACO, 2 Dec 1989, *Man in Armour* (1799, oil on canvas, 19 x 11 1/2in/48 x 29.5cm) FRF 721,500; *Jupiter and Thetis* (oil on canvas, 32 1/4 x 25 1/2in/82 x 65cm) FRF 14,430,000. PARIS, 20 March 1990, *Portrait of Madame Godinot* (1847-1849, graphite, 9 x 6 1/2in/22 x 16.5cm) FRF 1,250,000. PARIS, 15 June 1990, *First Ideas for 'Oedipus and the Sphinx'* (lead pencil, 19 1/4 x 14 1/2in/49 x 37cm) FRF

880,000. LONDON, 19 June 1990, *Portrait of Charles Dupaty* (1810, pencil, 7 x 5 3/4in/18 x 14.5cm) GBP 110,000. NEW YORK, 23 Oct 1990, *Portrait of Madame Ingres, previously Madeleine Chapelle* (pencil/paper, 8 1/2 x 6 1/4in/21.3 x 15.9cm) USD 242,000. NEW YORK, 23 May 1991, *Portrait of a Jewish Woman* (oil on canvas/panel, 8 1/2 x 6 1/4in/21.6 x 15.9cm) USD 55,000. PARIS, 14 June 1991, *View of a Church in Rome* (graphite heightened with sepia, 7 1/4 x 9 1/2in/18.3 x 24.3cm) FRF 1,205,000; *Portrait of Madame Adèle Maizony de Lauréal* (1813, graphite, 12 x 8 3/4in/29.6 x 22.4cm) FRF 1,650,000. NEW YORK, 17 Oct 1991, *Portrait of the Architect Charles Norry* (pencil/paper, 7 3/4 x 5 3/4in/20 x 14.6cm) USD 71,500. MONACO, 7 Dec 1991, *Study of a Man's Head for 'Jesus among the Teachers'* (oil on canvas, 6 3/4 x 4 3/4in/17.2 x 12.2cm) FRF 388,500. LONDON, 17 June 1992, *Portrait of Paul Grant* (1934, graphite, 12 1/2 x 9 1/4in/31.6 x 23.8cm) GBP 66,000. NEW YORK, 17 Feb 1993, *Portrait of a Lady* (1834, graphite/white vellum paper, 12 3/4 x 9 1/4in/32.2 x 23.8cm) USD 222,500. PARIS, 11 June 1993, *Odalisque* (1825, lithograph, 5 1/4 x 8 1/4in/13.2 x 21cm) FRF 19,500. LONDON, 16 June 1993, *Don Pedro of Toledo Kissing the Sword of Henry IV* (1820, oil on panel, 19 x 15 3/4in/48 x 40cm) GBP 628,500. PARIS, 18 June 1993, *Portrait of the Engraver Auguste Gaspard Louis Boucher-Desnoyers* (1825, graphite/vellum, 14 1/4 x 11in/36 x 28cm) FRF 2,800,000. HONFLEUR, 18 July 1993, *Portrait of Gaspard Bonnet* (1812, graphite, 8 1/2 x 6 1/4in/21.7 x 15.7cm) FRF 840,000. NEW YORK, 13 Oct 1993, *Aretin and the Gift from Charles V* (1815, oil on panel, 16 3/4 x 13in/42.5 x 33cm) USD 497,500. PARIS, 5 Nov 1993, *Murat, King of Naples* (1814, lead pencil, 4 3/4 x 6 1/4in/12 x 16cm) FRF 130,000. NEW YORK, 11 Jan 1994, *The Dream of Ossian* (1811, pencil, black and white chalk/green-blue paper, 10 1/4 x 8in/26 x 20.5cm) USD 41,400. PARIS, 23 March 1994, *Venus in Paphos* (graphite, 11 1/4 x 8in/28.3 x 19.4cm) FRF 250,000. PARIS, 18 Oct 1995, *Napoleon in Coronation Robes* (graphite and black chalk/tracing paper, 8 1/4 x 4 1/2in/21 x 11.6cm) FRF 80,000. NEW YORK, 22 May 1996, *Portrait of Mademoiselle Marie Reiset, later Viscountess Adolphe Louis Edgar of Ségur-Lamoignon* (drawing) USD 345,500. LONDON, 21 Nov 1996, *Napoleon I* (graphite/brown paper, study, 13 1/2 x 7 1/2in/34.3 x 19.3cm) GBP 10,350. PARIS, 25 April 1997, *Portrait of His Lordship Gabriel Cortois de Pressigny* (1816, graphite and heightened watercolour/vellum paper/laid paper, 10 3/4 x 7 3/4in/27.5 x 19.5cm) FRF 900,000. PARIS, 21 Nov 1997, *Study for the 'Portrait of Madame Moitessier'* (pencil, 12 x 11 1/2in/30.5 x 29.5cm) FRF 160,000. PARIS, 9 March 1998, *Portrait of the Architect Antoine Marie Chenavard* (1818, graphite, 7 1/4 x 5 1/2in/18.5 x 13.7cm) FRF 590,000. PARIS, 3 April 1998, *Soldier Gathering Up the Body of Acron* (c. 1812, lead pencil, study for 'Triumph of Romulus over Acron', 5 1/4 x 7 3/4in/13.5 x 20cm) FRF 27,000. PARIS, 17 Dec 1999, *Portrait of Baron Charles-Athanase Walckenaer* (1826, graphite, 12 x 9 ins / 31 x 23 cm) FRF 1,800,000. PARIS, 17 Dec 1999, *Portrait presumed to be of Gioacchino Rossini* (1819, graphite, 11 x 8 ins / 29 x 21 cm) FRF 4,000,000. LONDON, 4 July 2000, *Young Italian Woman Turned to the Right* (pencil, 11 x 8 ins / 28 x 20 cm) GBP 18,000. LONDON, 23 Nov 2000, *Portrait of the Sculptor Henri-Joseph Rutxhiel* (1809, pencil) GBP 240,000. NEW YORK, 23 Jan 2001, *Portrait of Jean-Louis Provost* (1813, graphite heightened with white, 7 x 5 ins / 18 x 13 cm) USD 370,000. LONDON, 6 June 2001, *Odalisque* (oil on linen/board, 3 x 5 ins / 8 x 13 cm) GBP 320,000. NEW YORK, 23 Jan 2002, *Portrait of Gentleman Believed to be Charles-Bernardin-Ghislain Coppieters-Stochove* (1813, pencil, 11 x 7 ins / 27 x 19 cm) USD 140,000. PARIS, 28 Nov 2002, *Study of a Nude, Preparatory Sketch for the Upper Left-hand Angel in The Vow of Louis XIII* (black chalk, 20 x 14 ins / 51 x 35 cm) EUR 320,000. LONDON, 9 July 2003, *Portrait of the Actor, Monsieur Brochard* (1796, graphite, round, 3 x 3 ins / 8 x 8 cm) GBP 54,000. PARIS, 6 Nov 2003, *Portrait of the Emperor Napoleon* (pen and ink wash, 11 x 7 ins / 29 x 19 cm) EUR 300,000. NEW YORK, 23 April 2004, *Virgin with the Crown* (oil on panel, 28 x 20 ins / 70 x 51 cm) USD 820,000. LONDON, 8 July 2004, *Portrait of a Young Woman Wearing a Lace Bonnet* (pencil, beige and blue wash, 3 x 3 ins / 8 x 8 cm) GBP 18,000.

INGRES, Jean Marie Joseph

French, 18th - 19th century.

Born 1755, in Toulouse; died 14 March 1814, in Montauban (Tarn-et-Garonne).

Painter, sculptor, draughtsman. Portraits. Miniatures.

Jean Marie Joseph Ingres was the father of Jean Auguste Dominique Ingres. He was a pupil of Pierre Lucas at the Académie des Beaux-Arts in Toulouse, and professor of drawing at Montauban.

MUSEUMS AND GALLERIES:

MONTAUBAN: *Portrait of a Young Woman* (miniature/snuff-box) - PARIS (Louvre): *Portrait of an Unknown Man* (miniature).

INGRES, Théophile

French, 19th century.

Born 19 November 1832, in Écouen.

Sculptor.

This artist was the cousin of Jean Auguste Dominique Ingres. He was a pupil of Possot and of Jean Auguste Dominique Ingres.

INGUIMBERTY, Joseph

French, 20th century.

Born 18 January 1896, in Marseilles; died 8 October 1971, in Menton.

Painter, watercolourist, engraver. Figures, landscapes with figures, harbour scenes.

Joseph Inguimberty studied at the École des Beaux-Arts in Marseilles, and concurrently studied architecture. He went to Paris in 1913 to study at the École des Arts Décoratifs in the studio of Eugène Morand. He received several bursaries, which enabled him to travel to Holland, Italy and Spain. From 1925 to 1946, he lived and worked in Hanoi, directing the department of painting at the college of fine arts founded in 1924 by Victor Tardieu. There he created a section devoted to lacquer technique. Upon his return to France, he settled in Marseilles. In 1924, he received the Prix National de Peinture and was made Chevalier of the Légion d'Honneur in 1937. He is known for his large compositions before 1925, which were strong, structured, with a heavy social connotation. He executed numerous landscapes and figures in Vietnam, where he favoured rural themes. He also depicted his native Provence, where his use of colour and light were established.

He participated in numerous collective exhibitions, notably in the principal Parisian salons in 1927, 1929, 1932, 1934 and 1935. In 1973, he participated in the Salon de la Société Nationale des Beaux-Arts. From 1950 to 1952, then in 1955, 1958, and 1960, he participated in the Salon des Tuileries. In 1952, from 1954 to 1959, in 1962, 1963 and 1972, he participated in the Salon d'Automne as well as in 1960 at the Bibliothèque Nationale. From 1951, he participated in the Menton Biennale, of which he was a founder and a member of the jury. He had solo exhibitions in Paris, Menton and Marseilles.

BIBLIOGRAPHY:

André-Pallois, Nadine/Ménonville, Corinne de, *Paris-Hanoï-Saigon, l'aventure de l'art moderne au Viêt Nam*, exhibition catalogue, Pavillon des Arts, Paris, 1998.

MUSEUMS AND GALLERIES:
MARSEILLES (Hôtel de l'Arbois): *Marseilles* (1924).
AUCTION RECORDS:
PARIS, 26 Oct 1988, *Dockers on the Quay of Marseilles* (1924, oil on canvas, 106 1/4 x 169 1/4 ins / 270 x 430 cm) FRF 110,000. PARIS, 22 April 1998, *The Promenade* (oil on canvas). SINGAPORE, 28 March 1999, *Peasants in Ricefield, North Tonkin* (1938, oil on canvas, 28 x 35 ins / 71 x 90 cm) SGD 12,000. PARIS, 21 April 1999, *Portrait of Young Vietnamese Woman* (c. 1935, oil on canvas, 17 x 14 ins / 44 x 36 cm) FRF 18,000. SINGAPORE, 2 April 2000, *Rice Field* (oil on canvas, 29 x 46 ins / 73 x 116 cm) SGD 14,000. SINGAPORE, 1 Oct 2000, *Vietnamese Women* (1935, oil on canvas, 78 x 61 ins / 198 x 154 cm) SGD 32,000. SINGAPORE, 1 April 2001, *Return from Market* (1933, oil on canvas, 80 x 79 ins / 204 x 200 cm) SGD 65,000. SINGAPORE, 30 Sept 2001, *Studio* (1933, oil on canvas, 61 x 66 ins / 155 x 167 cm) SGD 130,000. HONG KONG, 28 April 2002, *Hammock* (1938, oil on canvas, 79 x 119 ins / 201 x 301 cm) HKD 650,000. HONG KONG, 27 Oct 2002, *Landscape and People of Tonkin* (1933, oil on canvas, 90 x 114 ins / 228 x 290 cm) HKD 700,000. SINGAPORE, 18 May 2003, *Peasants in the Rice Fields* (mixed media on paper/canvas, 79 x 118 ins / 200 x 300 cm) SGD 54,000. HONG KONG, 6 July 2003, *Vietnamese Women* (1935, oil on canvas, 78 x 61 ins / 198 x 154 cm) HKD 200,000.

INIG, Bon Lud
Italian, 18th century.
Born in Parma.
Engraver (burin).
Ingoli produced the panels for *Saggi sul ristabilimento*, a work by Don Vicenzo Requeno, published in Parma in 1787.

IÑIGO
Spanish, 15th century.
Painter. Murals.
Iñigo worked in Toledo and in 1494 painted a fresco in the cathedral there depicting the *Legend of Pilate*.

INIGO, Juan
Spanish, 17th century.
Painter.
Juan Inigo was active in Seville in the late 17th century. In 1685 he rented a house there from the cathedral chapter.

INIS, Francesco Gallo
Italian, 20th century.
Born in Ievoli (Calabria).
Active in France.
Painter, sculptor. Local scenes.
Inis was a pupil of the Accademia di Belle Arti, Naples. He lives and works in France in the Valley of the Maurienne. He has taken part in exhibitions in France and abroad: Montreal, Baden-Baden, New York. Influenced at first by Surrealism, he soon abandoned it for a purer style that is sometimes similar to Juan Gris' Cubism. His subjects are chosen by theme - clowns, music, the chapels of the Maurienne, and, in 1989, Guyana. He works in vibrant, solid colour to evoke, not depict, a jazz band, a gold-digger, a dance scene, or a cockfight.
MUSEUMS AND GALLERIES:
BAD-WILDUNGEN (Rathaus) - ST-JULIEN-MONTDENIS (Mus. ardoisien).

INJALBERT, Jean Antoine
French, 19th - 20th century.
Born 23 February 1845, in Béziers; died 3 March 1933, in Paris.
Sculptor, designer. Figures. Busts.
Jean Antoine Injalbert studied at the École des Beaux-Arts in Paris in the studio of Dumont. Of classical training, he was often inspired by mythology. He made his début in Paris with a bust of a man at the Salon des Artistes Français in 1873. The next year, he exhibited a bust of Veuve Faure, and participated in the Exposition Universelle in 1889, winning the grand prize. He won the Prix de Rome in 1874. He received a second-class medal for *The Temptation*, a plaster high-relief, and a first-class medal in 1878 at the Exposition Universelle, for *Christ* in plaster. He decorated numerous public buildings, notably the Préfecture in Montpellier, the theatre in Sète and the station in Tours. In 1900, in collaboration with the architect Victor Laloux, with whom he worked on several occasions, he executed the allegorical *Ville de Nantes* (*City of Nantes*) for the then Orsay station, now the Musée d'Orsay in Paris. He took part in numerous exhibitions abroad and received medals, notably in Munich in 1893. He was named Officier of the Légion d'Honneur in 1897, a member of the jury and *hors concours* in 1900 at the Exposition Universelle, member of the Institut de France from 1905, and Commandeur of the Légion d'Honneur in 1910.

MUSEUMS AND GALLERIES:
BÉZIERS: *Love Subduing the Lion; The Lion Subdued by Love; Singing Herder; Seated Young Man; Ermengaud the Monk; Fame; Modern Genius and the Ancient Muse; Bust of Charles Labor; Temptation; Laughing Child; Love Officiating at the Marriage; Hippomenes* - CAHORS: *Bust of Laroumet* - COPENHAGEN (Ny Carlsberg Glyptotek): *Hippomenes; Drunken Faun; Faun and Bacchant* - MONTPELLIER: *Eve and the Wrong; Study of a Head* - NANTES: *Love Subdued by Force* - NARBONNE (MAH): *Mme Nathalie Calmette* - PARIS (MAM): *Hippomenes; Bacchant with Pipes; Vase with Low Relief* - PARIS (Mus. d'Orsay) - PARIS (Mus. de la Comédie-Française): *The Republic* - PARIS (Panthéon): *Monument of Mirabeau* - TOULON: *Pierre Puget* - VERSAILLES: *Gavarni*.
AUCTION RECORDS:
COLOGNE, 20 Oct 1978, *Bust of a Young Girl* (bronze, h. 15 1/2 ins / 39.5 cm) DEM 2,800. PARIS, 17 Feb 1988, *Lion Straddled by Love* (bronze, h. 17 3/4 ins / 45 cm, w. 22 ins/55 cm) FRF 6,900. PARIS, 24 June 1994, *Young Italian Herder Singing* (bronze, h. 11 ins / 27 cm) FRF 11,000. PARIS, 18 Nov 1996, *Fame* (bronze, 21 1/4 x 10 ins / 54 x 25.5 cm) FRF 5,000.

INJO
Japanese, 11th century.
Died 1108.
Sculptor.
Injo, a Buddhist sculptor, is said to be the son of Kakujo or Chosei and the grandson of Jocho, a great sculptor who died in 1057. He was therefore part of an important line of artists who formed one of the two main currents of Buddhist art at the beginning of the Heian period. He is considered the founder of the Shichijo Omiya studio in Kyoto, where he continued to work, with his numerous assistants, in the style of Jocho. It was probably for this reason that he received the honorary title of Hogen ('eye of the law', an ecclesiastical title conferred on certain master sculptors). Nothing remains of his work.

INJO
Japanese, 13th century.
Active at the end of the 13th century.
Sculptor.
Injo was a Buddhist sculptor who received the title of Hoin (an ecclesiastical title conferred on sculptors). In 1295, he ex-

ecuted the Jizo Bosatsu (Sanskrit: Bodhisattva Ksitigarbha) of the Umegahata cemetery in Kyoto.

INKAKU

Japanese, 12th century.
Active during the first half of the 12th century.
Sculptor.

Inkaku, a Buddhist artist in the line of Jocho who died in 1057, worked in the Shichijo Omiya studio, founded in Kyoto by Injo, who died in 1108. He is said to be the sculptor of the statue of the Amida Buddha (Sanskrit: Amithaba Buddha) in the Hokongo-in monastery in Kyoto, dated 1130. The influence of Jocho can be seen in this work, although it is marked by inflexibility.

INKEI

Japanese, 12th century.
Died 1179.
Active during the second half of the 12th century.
Sculptor.

Inkei, who lived at Nishikikoji Omiya in Kyoto, was probably the son of Inkaku. He was considered a master sculptor (*dai busshi*) and like his father worked in the style of Jocho (died in 1057), with the result that he was a representative of one of the two great currents of Buddhist sculpture of the Heian period. Several of his works have been identified, notably the two statues of the Amida Buddha (Sanskrit: Amithaba Buddha) of the Shin Mido at the Sairin-ji Temple in Kyoto, one life-size, the other *joroku* size, that is to say 16 feet (4.9 metres) tall, which is the canonical height of the Sakyamuni Buddha. These two works, dated 1167, brought him the honorary title of Hokkyo ('bridge of the law', an ecclesiastical title conferred on Buddhist sculptors). In the eleventh month of 1170 he executed a statue of the Buddha for the wife of the emperor, and in 1176 he restored a statue of the Nyoin Mido in the Sairin-ji temple. He then received the honorary title of Hogen ('eye of the law', an ecclesiastical title). In 1177 he executed a triad of Sakyamuni in white sandalwood *byakudan*, and in the tenth month of 1178 a series of Go Dai Son (Sanskrit: the Five Rajas) for the wife of the emperor.

BIBLIOGRAPHY:

Kuno, Takeshi, *A Guide to Japanese Sculpture*, Mayuyama, Tokyo, 1963.

INKEN

Japanese, 13th century.
Active at the beginning of the 13th century.
Sculptor.

Inken, the son of Incho, was a Buddhist sculptor at the beginning of the Kamakura period. He was a member of the In School, founded by the sculptor Inson in Kyoto. In the twelfth month of 1200, he executed a triad of the Amida Buddha (Sanskrit: Amithaba Buddha) for the Hossho-ji temple in Kyoto, then, in the eleventh month of 1207, the 'Sanju' *bugaku* mask (the *bugaku* is a sort of imperial dance executed with a mask) for the temple of the Todai-ji in Nara. In the twelfth month of 1212, he signed the two statues of Ni-O (Sanskrit: Vajrapani - monastery doorkeepers) for the south door of the Hossho-ji temple, and in the sixth month of 1215, he signed a Jizo Bosatsu (Sanskrit: Bodhisattava Ksitigarbha) at the request of the ex-emperor Gotoba. In 1217, he executed seven statues of the Yakushi Buddha (Sanskrit: the Bhaisajyaguru Buddha - the Buddha of medicine) for the wife of the emperor. From 1199, his Shitta Taishi (Sanskrit: Siddharta, i.e. Sakyamuni) in the Ninna-ji temple in Kyoto, showed the influence of the Buddhist sculpture of the China of the Sung dynasty (960-1279), particularly in the pleating of the clothing.

BIBLIOGRAPHY:

Kuno, Takeshi, *A Guide to Japanese Sculpture*, Mayuyama, Tokyo, 1963.

INKEN

Japanese, 15th century.
Active at the beginning of the 15th century.
Sculptor.

Inken held the title of Ho-in ('seal of the law', the highest title in the ecclesiastical hierarchy, also conferred on sculptors). In the third month of 1404 he executed a statue of Shotoku Taishi (Prince Shotoku, 572-622), the first great supporter of Buddhism in Japan, for the Jodo-ji temple in Onomichi, in Hyogo Prefecture.

INKERMANN, Johann David Gottfried

German, 19th century.
Born 18 December 1791.
Lithographer.

He is recorded in Dresden from 1820 to 1829, and ran a lithography studio with J. H. D Rau.

INLANDER, Henry

Austrian, 20th century.
Born 1925, in Vienna; died 1983.
Active from 1938 in England.
Painter. Landscapes, still-lifes.

Henry Inlander attended the Slade School of Fine Art in London. Having won a scholarship to Rome, he worked in Italy from 1952-1956, then in New York from 1960-1961. From 1956, he held solo exhibitions in London, and from 1961, in New York as well as in Rome. A figurative painter, his style is free and sometimes influenced by the Expressionists.

MUSEUMS AND GALLERIES:

LONDON (Tate Collection): *Sienese Hills* (1956, oil on canvas); *Moving Surface* (1961, oil on canvas).

INMAN, Henry

American, 19th century.
Born 1801 or 1802, in Utica (New York); died 1846, in New York.
Painter. History painting, figures, portraits, genre scenes, landscapes, flowers. Miniatures.

Henry Inman was a pupil of John Wesley Jarvis in New York. He had an excellent reputation as a portraitist in New York and, later, in Philadelphia. During his stay in Europe he produced the portraits of several famous English people. Some of his works are in New York Town Hall. He was one of the founders of the National Academy of Design in New York in 1826. He exhibited in London, notably at the Royal Academy, from 1838 to 1845. An individual exhibition of his work was given at the National Portrait Gallery in Washington DC in 1987.

MUSEUMS AND GALLERIES:

BOSTON: *Mrs Buckham Wright and her Mother* - BROOKLYN, NY: *Picnic; Wooded Landscape; Rydal Water* - NEW YORK (Historical Society): *Henry Rutgers* - NEW YORK (Metropolitan Mus. of Art): *Martin van Buren; William Macready; Young Fisherman* - NEW YORK (Public Library): *Portrait of a Man* - PHILADELPHIA (Pennsylvania Academy of the Fine Arts Gal.): *Henry Pratt; Children Playing* - SALEM, MA (Essex Institute): *Portrait of the Poet Nathan* - WASHINGTON DC (NGA): *George Pope Morris* (c. 1836, oil on canvas).

AUCTION RECORDS:

NEW YORK, 12-14 April 1909, *George Washington at the Battle of Princeton*, USD 900. NEW YORK, 22-24 March 1911, *Battle of Princeton*, USD 700. NEW YORK, 14 April 1943, *Dismissal of School on an October Afternoon*, USD 1,050. NEW YORK, 24 Oct 1979, *Portrait of a Lady* (1842, oil on canvas, 10 x 8 ins / 25.5 x 20.5 cm) USD 1,500. NEW YORK, 8 Dec 1983, *Long Island* (1831, oil on panel, 12½ x 8½ ins / 31.8 x

21.6 cm) USD 10,000. NEW YORK, 20 March 1987, *Mary Mott Jones* (1845, oil on canvas, oval, 24 x 19 3/4 ins / 61 x 50.2 cm) USD 2,600. NEW YORK, 14 Nov 1991, *Peonies and Lilac in a Vase* (oil on card, 11 x 8 1/2 ins / 27.9 x 21.6 cm) USD 3,300. NEW YORK, 22 May 1996, *Children of Henry Livingston* (1827, oil on canvas, 42 1/2 x 60 1/4 ins / 108 x 153 cm) USD 26,450. SAN FRANCISCO, 14 June 2000, *Mother and Child* (oil on panel, 9 x 7 ins / 23 x 19 cm) USD 2,750. PITTSFIELD, 3 Nov 2001, *John Bishop Hall and Son* (oil on canvas, 40 x 32 ins / 102 x 81 cm) USD 2,750. MILFORD, 25 April 2002, *Mother and Child* (oil on panel, 9 x 7 ins / 23 x 18 cm) USD 8,000. NEW YORK, 27 April 2004, *Portraits of Samuel Brown and Maria Crosby Brown* (c. 1839, oil on canvas, a pair, 33 x 28 ins / 84 x 71 cm) USD 8,500. MILFORD, 21 Oct 2004, *Portrait of the Artist's Daughter Mary* (1843, oil on canvas on board, 5 x 7 ins / 13 x 18 cm) USD 10,000.

INMAN, John O'Brien
American, 19th century.
Born 1828, in New York; died 1896, in New York.
Painter. Portraits, genre scenes, flowers.

John O'Brien Inman was the son of Henry Inman. He abandoned portraiture at a very young age to paint flowers and genre scenes. He left America in 1866 and moved to Rome.

MUSEUMS AND GALLERIES:

NEW YORK (Public Library): *Young Student* - WASHINGTON DC (Smithsonian American AM): *Portrait of a Huguenot of the Time of Charles IX* (oil/wood); *Landscape* (oil/wood); *Cave Scene* (oil/wood).

AUCTION RECORDS:

NEW YORK, 21 June 1979, *The Swing* (1866, oil on card, 8 1/2 x 5 1/2 ins / 21.5 x 14 cm) USD 1,500. BOLTON, 17 Nov 1983, *New York Landscape* (1891, oil on canvas, 18 x 29 ins / 45.7 x 73.5 cm) USD 1,500. NEW YORK, 15 June 1984, *Young Boy Reading* (1863, oil on card, 10 x 12 1/4 ins / 25.5 x 31 cm) USD 4,200. NEW YORK, 31 May 1985, *Reading the News* (1863, oil on card, 10 x 12 1/4 ins / 25.5 x 31 cm) USD 4,000. NEW YORK, 28 May 1987, *Bouquet of Flowers* (1863, oil on canvas, 10 1/4 x 17 1/4 ins / 26.2 x 43.8 cm) USD 6,000. PARIS, 21 Nov 1988, *Artist's Interior* (1872, oil on panel, 14 3/4 x 22 ins / 37.5 x 56 cm) FRF 46,000. PARIS, 20 Nov 1994, *At the Folies Bergère* (oil on canvas, 32 x 23 1/2 ins / 81 x 60 cm) FRF 31,500. NEW YORK, 28 Sept 1995, *Villagers in the Street* (oil on canvas, 25 1/4 x 58 ins / 64.1 x 147.3 cm) USD 9,200. PARIS, 11 March 1999, *At the Folies Bergère* (oil on canvas, 32 x 24 ins / 81 x 60 cm) FRF 23,000. SAN FRANCISCO, 17 June 1999, *Forest Stream* (1891, oil on canvas, 20 x 30 ins / 51 x 76 cm) USD 3,250. SAN FRANCISCO, 14 June 2000, *In the Forest* (1883, watercolour, 13 x 9 ins / 32 x 23 cm) USD 1,700. NEW YORK, 18 May 2004, *Napping* (1869, oil on board, 10 x 13 ins / 26 x 34 cm) USD 24,000. CHICAGO, 23 May 2004, *Villager on the Street* (oil on canvas, 25 x 58 ins / 64 x 147 cm) USD 9,000.

INMAN, W.S.
British, 19th century.
Active in London.
Painter, architect. Architectural views.

The work of W.S. Inman was represented at the Royal Academy from 1815 to 1838 with sketches of architectural subjects.

MUSEUMS AND GALLERIES:

LONDON (British Mus.): *View of the Old Walls of London*; same subject (watercolour).

INNEGRAEVE, Jef
French, 20th century.
Born 1920, in Toulouse.
Active in Belgium.
Painter, sculptor.

Jef Innegraeve studied at the École des Beaux-Arts in Roubaix. He went on to become a filmmaker and photographer, as well as a painter and sculptor.

INNEGRAEVE, Jef
Belgian, 20th century.
Born 9 May 1936.
Sculptor.

Jef Innegraeve attended the Académie des Beaux-Arts in Bruges. He contributed works to group exhibitions in 1986 in Bruges, and in 1988 in Ostend. Since 1970, Innegraeve has produced sculptures, creating pure forms.

BIBLIOGRAPHY:

'*Jef Innegraeve*' in *Kunst Beeld Nu '88*, catalogue, Ostend, 1988.

INNERST, Mark
American, 20th - 21st century.
Born 1957.
Painter (gouache/mixed media), watercolourist, draughtsman. Figure compositions, urban landscapes.

Mark Innerst studied at Kutztown University, receiving a BFA in 1980. He is well known for his landscape paintings, which include forest and coastal scenes, the Hudson River, New York cityscapes and industrial river views. Innerst achieves his richly coloured paintings by using layers of glaze. His *Boat Launch* (2001) is an example of a river view, while *Neapolis* (2001) is taken from city life. Other works include the watercolour *Cloud and Jet Trail* (1986), the acrylic *Water Lily* (1998), and the oil *Pocket Watch* (1988).

Innerst's exhibitions include: 1984, *Current*, Institute of Contemporary Art, Boston and *An International Survey of Recent Painting and Sculpture*, Museum of Modern Art, New York; 1985, *New Horizons in American Art*, Guggenheim Museum, New York; 1986, *Au Coeur du Maelstrom* (*To the Heart of the Maelstrom*), Musées Royaux des Beaux-Arts de Belgique, Brussels; 1989, *A Certain Slant of Light*, Dayton Art Institute; the 1989 Whitney Biennial; 1989, a solo exhibition at the Museum of Contemporary Art, Houston; 1991, *Strange Vistas, Imagined Histories*, Portland Art Museum, Oregon; 1997, *Seattle Collects Paintings: Works from Private Collections*, Seattle Art Museum; 2000, *Water: A Contemporary American View*, Leigh Yawkey Woodson Art Museum, Wassau, WI; and 2005, a solo exhibition at the Museum of Art, Munson Williams Proctor Art Institute, Utica, NY.

BIBLIOGRAPHY:

Mark Innerst: Landscape and Beyond, Paintings and Works on Paper, 1981-1987, exhibition catalogue, Illinois State University Museum, Normal (IL), 1988. *Mark Innerst*, exhibition catalogue, Nelson-Atkins Museum of Art, Kansas City, 1989. *Mark Innerst*, exhibition catalogue, Curt Marcus Gallery, New York, 1990. *Mark Innerst*, exhibition catalogue, Michael Kohn Gallery, Los Angeles, 1991. Iannaccone, Carmine, '*Mark Innerst*' in *Art Issues*, journal article, January-February 1998. *Mark Innerst*, exhibition catalogue, Paul Kasmin Gallery, New York, 2000. *Mark Innerst, Paintings and Works on Paper*, exhibition catalogue, Michael Kohn Gallery, Los Angeles, 2001.

MUSEUMS AND GALLERIES:

BUFFALO (Albright-Knox AG): *A Greater Distraction* (1981, spray paint and charcoal) - CHICAGO (MCA) - LOS ANGELES (County MA) - LOS ANGELES (MCA): *Dust Storm, Australia* (1984, oil and acrylic); *Catacomb* (1985, acrylic); *Mississippi at New Orleans* (1985, oil and acrylic) - NEW YORK (Guggenheim Mus.): *Brooklyn from the East River Park* (oil).

AUCTION RECORDS:

NEW YORK, 4 May 1989, *Par une fenêtre* (spray paint and pencil/brown paper, 26 1/4 x 19 1/4 ins / 66.7 x 48.9 cm) USD 10,450. NEW YORK, 9 May 1990, *Family (Bathers)* (1983, oil/synthetic resin, 17 3/4 x 14 3/4 ins / 45 x 37.5 cm) USD 35,750. NEW YORK, 7 Nov 1990, *Used, Feared, Hated* (1983, acrylic and oil on card, 14 x 17 ins / 35.6 x 43.2 cm) USD 23,100. NEW YORK, 14 Feb 1991, *Study for The Reservoir* (1986, watercolour and pencil/paper, large version, 17 3/4 x 19 ins / 45.1 x 48.2 cm) USD 17,600. NEW YORK, 2 May 1991,

View of Brooklyn (1985, acrylic and gouache/paper, 6 1/2 x 8 1/2 ins / 16.2 x 21.9 cm) USD 9,900. NEW YORK, 13 Nov 1991, *Prewar Luxury* (1989, acrylic/panel, 19 1/2 x 15 1/2 ins / 49.6 x 39.4 cm) USD 27,500. NEW YORK, 27 Feb 1992, *Two Ships* (1983, ink, watercolour and white chalk/brown paper, study, 19 1/2 x 29 3/4 ins / 49.5 x 75.5 cm) USD 7,700. NEW YORK, 19 Nov 1992, *View of Brooklyn* (gouache and acrylic/paper, 6 1/4 x 8 1/2 ins / 15.9 x 21.6 cm) USD 7,700. NEW YORK, 5 May 1994, *The Reservoir* (1987, oil and acrylic/card, 10 x 20 1/2 ins / 25.4 x 52.1 cm) USD 23,000. NEW YORK, 7 May 1997, *Seascape Flanked by Aircraft* (1981, oil on wood, in five parts, each 8 3/4 x 5 1/2 ins / 22.5 x 13.7 cm) USD 14,950. NEW YORK, 23 Feb 2000, *Rooftop* (gouache and pencil, 13 x 11 ins / 33 x 28 cm) USD 5,000. NEW YORK, 15 May 2001, *Transformer* (1985, oil on masonite, 11 x 12 ins / 27 x 30 cm) USD 4,800. NEW YORK, 16 May 2002, *Pocket Watch* (1987, acrylic on masonite, 16 x 12 ins / 40 x 30 cm) USD 5,000.

INNES, Callum

British, 20th - 21st century.
Born 5 March 1962, in Edinburgh.
Painter.

Callum Innes studied at Gray's School of Art, Aberdeen (1980-1984), where he received an Honours BA in Fine Art, and at Edinburgh College of Art (1984-1985), obtaining an MFA. He has taught at the Glasgow School of Art. His early work contained freely painted figuration, but after a period in Amsterdam, he has concentrated on non-objective figuration since 1988. Innes' technique consists of thickly painting a canvas in sweeping left-to-right brushstrokes, then washing away the surface of the paint with turpentine in a 'deliberately accidental' process to create isolated scars of canvas, vertical lines and islands of pale colour. He is particularly known for his *Exposed* series in a vertical format, and his *Resonance* series of monochromatic paintings which explore white or near-white surfaces. Innes sees his work as a reinvigoration of traditional abstraction, and his primary subject is the act of painting itself.

Innes has had solo shows at Frith Street Gallery, London (1990, 1991, 1994, 1998, 2001); Scottish National Gallery of Modern Art, Edinburgh (1992); Institute of Contemporary Art, London (1992); Irish Museum of Modern Art, Dublin (1999); Kerlin Gallery, Dublin (2000); Pier Arts Centre, Stromness, Orkney (2000); and *Callum Innes: Resonance*, Tate St Ives (2005). Other exhibitions include *The British Art Show*, South Bank Centre (1990, tour); *Kunst Europa*, Kunstverein, Freiburg (1991); *Prospekt*, Kunstverein, Frankfurt (1993); *Paintmarks*, Southampton City Art Gallery (1994); *About Vision: New British Painting in the 1990s*, Museum of Modern Art, Oxford (1996); *Abstraction/Abstractions: Géométries Provisoires* (*Abstraction/Abstractions - Provisional Geometry*), Musée d'Art Moderne in St-Étienne (1997); *New Work: Painting Today, Recent Acquisitions*, Museum of Modern Art, San Francisco (1999); *A Century of Innocence: The Story of the White Monochrome*, Rooseum Centre for Contemporary Art, Malmø, Sweden (2000); and *Expressions: Scottish Art 1976-1989*, Dundee Contemporary Arts Centre (2000). Innes was shortlisted for the Turner Prize in 1995, and received the NatWest Art prize in 1998 and the Jerwood Painting Prize in 2002.

BIBLIOGRAPHY:

Ceysson, Bernard/Chassey, Éric de/Morineau, Camille, *Abstraction/Abstractions - Géométries provisoires*, exhibition catalogue, Musée d'Art Moderne, St-Étienne, 1997. *Callum Innes 1990-1996*, exhibition catalogue, Royal Botanic Gardens, Edinburgh, 1997. *Callum Innes*, exhibition catalogue, Irish Museum of Modern Art, Dublin, 1999. *Callum Innes: Exposed Paintings*, exhibition catalogue, C. Innes and Ingleby Gallery, Edinburgh, 2001. *Callum Innes: Resonance*, exhibition catalogue, Tate, St Ives, 2005.

MUSEUMS AND GALLERIES:

BUFFALO (Albright-Knox AG): *Exposed Painting Ivory Black, Yellow Oxide* (2000, oil on canvas) - CANBERRA (Nat. Gal. of Australia): *Exposed Painting Black Oxide* (2000, oil on gesso on linen) - DUBLIN (Irish Museum of Modern Art): *Exposed Painting, Charcoal Grey/Yellow Oxide/Asphalt* (1999, oil) - EASTBOURNE (Towner Art Gallery) - LIVERPOOL (Walker Gallery): *Exposed Painting: Cadmium Orange on White* (1997, oil) - LONDON (Contemporary Art Society) - LONDON (Tate Collection): *Three Identified Forms 1993* (1993, oil); *Exposed Painting Paynes Grey/Yellow Oxide/Red Oxide on White* (1999, oil) - LONDON (UK Government Art Collection): *Exposed Painting: Cadmium Red Deep* (1996, oil); *Exposed Painting: Cadmium Red Pale/Orange* (2000, oil) - PARIS (FNAC): *Two Identified Forms* (1994) - SOUTHAMPTON (Art Gallery): *Repetition (Grey)* (1995, oil); *Resonance XIII* (1995, oil) - SOUTHAMPTON (City AG): *Resonance* (1995, oil).

AUCTION RECORDS:

LONDON, 30 June 1994, *Six Identified Forms* (1991, oil on canvas, 86 1/2 x 74 3/4 ins / 220 x 190 cm) GBP 5,750. LONDON, 22 May 1996, *Repetition 20* (1992, oil on canvas, 29 1/2 x 25 1/2 ins / 75 x 65 cm) GBP 2,990. LONDON, 20 March 1997, *Eight Identified Pale Forms* (1990, oil on canvas, 27 1/4 x 23 1/2 ins / 69.5 x 59.5 cm) GBP 2,645. LONDON, 24 June 1999, *Exposed Painting, Olive* (1994, oil on canvas, 41 x 39 ins / 105 x 100 cm) GBP 4,000. LONDON, 29 June 1999, *Repetition* (1995, oil on canvas, 69 x 63 ins / 175 x 160 cm) GBP 9,000. LONDON, 30 March 2000, *Formed Painting* (1993, oil on canvas, 43 x 39 ins / 110 x 100 cm) GBP 6,200. LONDON, 28 June 2000, *Exposed Painting Paynes Grey - CI/C/678* (oil on canvas, 41 x 39 ins / 105 x 100 cm) GBP 13,000. LONDON, 8 Feb 2001, *Study with White* (1989, oil on paper, 50 x 38 ins / 127 x 97 cm) GBP 1,800. LONDON, 27 June 2002, *12 Identified Forms* (oil on canvas, 87 x 75 ins / 220 x 190 cm) GBP 5,000. NEW YORK, 10 June 2004, *Monologue* (oil on canvas, 90 x 80 ins / 228 x 202 cm) USD 15,000. LONDON, 20 Oct 2004, *Formed Painting in Red no. 7* (1992, oil on canvas, 65 x 69 ins / 165 x 175 cm) GBP 5,000.

INNES, James Dickson

British, 19th - 20th century.
Born 27 February 1887, in Llanelli; died 22 August 1914, in Swanley.
Painter, watercolourist. Landscapes, figures.

Born in Wales, James Innes was educated at Christ College, Brecon, at art school in Carmarthen (1904) and at the Slade School in London, where he met Augustus John. Innes' rendering of the Welsh landscape was mediated by his experience of painting in the south of France, Spain, the Canary Islands and Morocco (1908). He brought back a taste for the exotic which recalls Fauvism, while his compositions are reminiscent of Japanese art. He had a very close relationship with Arenig Fawr mountain in north Wales, at the top of which he buried his bundle of love letters; he painted its view several times, bringing to it a special colouring of luminous intensity. A memorial exhibition was held at the Chenil Gallery in London (1923).

BIBLIOGRAPHY:

Rothenstein, John, *Modern English Painters, Eyre & Spottiswoode*, exhibition catalogue, London, 1956.

MUSEUMS AND GALLERIES:

BEDFORD (Cecil Higgins Art Gallery) - BRADFORD (Cartwright Hall AG): *Town of Collioure* (1908) - CAMBRIDGE (Fitzwilliam Museum): *Arenig Fawr* (1911, oil on panel) - CARDIFF (National Museum and Galleries of Wales): *Vernet* (1912); *Canigou; The Bead Chain* (1910); *Canigou in Snow; Girl Standing by a Lake* - CARDIFF (National Museums and Galleries of Wales): *The Cathedral at Elne* (1911); *Pembroke Coast; The Girl in a Cottage* (c. 1911); *French Landscape* - LEEDS (City AG) - LLANELLI (Art Gallery): *Llanelli from Fur-*

nace Quarry - LONDON (British Mus.) - LONDON (Tate Collection): *South of France, Bozouls, near Rodez* (1908, oil on canvas); *Arenig, Sunny Evening* (c. 1911-1912, oil/wood); *Arenig, North Wales* (1913, oil/wood) - LONDON (Victoria and Albert Mus.) - MANCHESTER (City AG): *Cliff in Devon* (1907, drawing); *Bala Lake* (c. 1911) - NEWPORT (Art Gallery) - OTTAWA (Nat. Gal. of Canada): *Arenig; South Wales, Evening.*

AUCTION RECORDS:

LONDON, 3 May 1935, *Banyuls, Morning,* GBP 56. LONDON, 19 April 1940, *Wales,* GBP 71. LONDON, 9 Nov 1942, *Welsh Landscape,* GBP 120. LONDON, 8 March 1944, *The White Hind,* GBP 190. LONDON, 13 Nov 1964, *Mountain Lake,* Gns 850. LONDON, 26 Nov 1969, *Landscape,* GBP 2,000. NEW YORK, 8 April 1970, *Cactus,* USD 1,900. LONDON, 14 July 1971, *Landscape,* GBP 1,150. LONDON, 14 March 1973, *Sunset at Collioure,* GBP 6,800. LONDON, 17 March 1976, *Welsh Mountains* (oil on panel, 8 3/4 x 12 3/4 ins / 22.5 x 32.5 cm) GBP 620. LONDON, 17 June 1977, *Spanish Landscape* (c. 1911, oil on panel, 11 3/4 x 16 ins / 30 x 40.5 cm) GBP 2,600. LONDON, 13 June 1980, *Tour Madeloc* (1912-1913, oil on panel, 13 x 16 ins / 33 x 40.5 cm) GBP 5,000. LONDON, 13 March 1981, *Mountain Landscape at Sunset* (c. 1911-1912, oil on canvas, 10 x 13 3/4 ins / 25.3 x 35 cm) GBP 32,000. LONDON, 12 March 1982, *Mountain Landscape at Sunset* (c. 1911-1912, oil on canvas, 10 x 13 3/4 ins / 25.3 x 35 cm) GBP 2,400. LONDON, 15 May 1985, *Mountain Lake* (1911, oil on canvas, 14 x 10 ins / 35.5 x 25.5 cm) GBP 5,800. LONDON, 22 July 1987, *Thunder in the Mountains* (watercolour, 11 x 15 ins / 28 x 38 cm) GBP 4,000. LONDON, 5 June 1992, *Welsh Landscape* (oil on panel, 11 x 19 ins / 28 x 48 cm) GBP 2,750. LONDON, 4 June 1999, *Peasant Girl by a Jetty* (c. 1912, gouache, 49 x 30 ins / 124 x 76 cm) GBP 2,800. LONDON, 5 Nov 1999, *Fair at Perpignan* (c. 1912, oil on canvas, 11 x 15 ins / 28 x 38 cm) GBP 16,000. LONDON, 4 July 2001, *Landscape with Clouds* (c. 1911, oil on board, 10 x 12 ins / 25 x 30 cm) GBP 3,000. LONDON, 4 July 2001, *Caravan* (pen and ink on panel, 10 x 13 ins / 25 x 34 cm) GBP 5,000. BATH, 22 July 2002, *Mediterranean Coast* (1910, watercolour, 9 x 13 ins / 24 x 34 cm) GBP 1,800. LONDON, 22 Nov 2002, *Blue pool, Dorset* (1912, oil on panel, 10 x 14 ins / 25 x 35 cm) GBP 6,500. LONDON, 3 July 2003, *Mountains* (watercolour, 8 x 14 ins / 20 x 35 cm) GBP 1,700. LONDON, 16 March 2004, *Heavy Cloud, Arenig* (oil on panel, 12 x 16 ins / 30 x 40 cm) GBP 14,000. LONDON, 4 June 2004, *Collioure* (1911, oil on panel, 11 x 14 ins / 27 x 35 cm) GBP 7,500.

INNES, Robert. See **Mc INNES**

INNESS, George

American, 19th century.
Born 1 May 1825, in Newburgh (New York); died 3 August 1894, in Bridge of Allan, Scotland.
Painter. Landscapes with figures, landscapes.
Hudson River School (related to).

George Inness received some training from John Jesse Barker, a travelling artist, but was essentially self-taught by studying works of old masters while travelling in Europe. Through books, he also studied the art of Claude Lorraine. From 1841 to 1843, Inness worked as apprentice with the engraving firm of Sherman & Smith in New York. Inness made his first trip to Europe in 1851-1852, travelling particularly to Rome, followed by another trip during which he received some training from Régis François Gignoux. In 1870 he undertook a third trip, spending three years in Italy. Inness then went to paint a series of landscapes of Etretat cliffs, in 1874-1875.

Inness is considered one of the best landscape artists of the American School. He began to paint in the style of the second generation of the Hudson River School, and was then influenced by the bright naturalistic colour and informal compositions of the Barbizon painters (especially Théodore Rousseau), bringing the principle of open air painting to the USA. The influence of the Barbizon style is seen in such works as *Clearing Up* (1860). Inness preferred cultivated landscapes to wilderness subjects. His more fluid contours gave way to more atmospheric works in which he used light and colour, expressive brushwork and suppression of detail to create specific moods. Inness believed that the artist's role was to capture the spiritual and poetic qualities of nature. At the end of his life, Inness' landscapes took on a misty aspect, becoming almost unreal, such as *Hazy Morning, Montclair, New Jersey* (1893), or *Home of the Heron* (1893). He shared the mystical ideas promulgated by Swedenborg, which enhanced the romantic and pantheistic sense of landscape in his work. When Inness died, 600 completed and unfinished canvases and drawings were found in his studio, only 20 of which had been exhibited.

Inness frequently showed works at the exhibitions of the National Academy of Design in New York for 50 years, and was elected a member of the academy in 1868. He received bronze medals at the academy exhibitions, Universal Expositions in Paris in 1889 and 1900 and received a medal in Munich in 1892. His work was promoted by Crayon Gallery in New York, and he enjoyed the financial patronage of Ogden Haggerty and Reverend Henry Ward Beecher. Late in his career, Inness' work was purchased by the leading collector Thomas B. Clarke. Retrospectives of his work have been held at Montclair Art Museum, NJ (1994); and the National Academy of Design and the San Diego Museum of Art (2003-2004).

BIBLIOGRAPHY:

Le Roy Ireland, *The Works of George Inness,* Austin (TX), 1965. *Life, Art, and Letters of George Inness,* Illustrated book, Kennedy Galleries and Da Capo Press, New York, 1969. Cikovsky, Nicolai, *The Life and Work of George Inness,* Illustrated book, Garland, New York, 1977. *George Inness,* Illustrated book, Metropolitan Museum of Art, New York, 1985. Hélène Ahrweiler, Roger Mandle, D. Scott Atkinson, William H. Gerdts, Carole L. Shelby, Jochen Wierich, *Lasting Impressions: American Painters in France 1865-1915,* exhibition catalogue, Musée d'Art américain, Giverny, Terra Foundation for the Arts, Evanston (IL), 1992. *George Inness, Presence of the Unseen: A Centennial Commemoration,* Exhibition catalogue, Montclair Art Museum, Montclair (NJ), 1994. Bell, Adrienne Baxter, *George Inness and the Visionary Landscape,* Exhibition catalogue, National Academy of Design, New York, 2003. DeLue, Rachael Ziady, *George Inness and the Science of Landscape,* exhibition catalogue, Illustrated book, University of Chicago Press, Chicago, 2004.

MUSEUMS AND GALLERIES:

ANN ARBOR (University of Michigan Mus. of Art): *Figures in a Landscape with Sunset Sky* (c. 1880-1885, oil on canvas); *Sunset* (1886, oil on wood) - BALTIMORE (Peabody Art Collection): *The Storm* (oil on canvas) - BOSTON (MFA): *The Rising Storm* (1875, oil); *Blue Niagara* (1884, oil); *Lake Nemi* (1872, oil); *Eagleswood, New Jersey* (1866, oil); *Woodland Vista* (1846, oil); *The Church Spire* (1875, oil) - BUFFALO (Albright-Knox AG): *The Coming Storm* (1878, oil on canvas) - CHICAGO (AI): *Etretat, Normandy, France* (1874-1875); *Evening Landscape* - CHICAGO (Terra Foundation for American Art Collection) - CINCINNATI (AM): *Near the Village, October* (1892, painting); *Study for Landscape* (drawing); *Study for a Painting (Happy Valley of Rumley?)* (drawing) - DETROIT (IA): *Hudson River Valley* (1867, oil); *Apple Orchard* (1892, oil); *The Lonely Pine* (1893, oil) - FRANKFURT AM MAIN (Städel): *Landscape* - HARTFORD (Wadsworth Atheneum): *Etretat* (1875, oil on canvas) - LONDON (NG): *The Delaware Water Gap* (c. 1857, oil on canvas) - LOS ANGELES (County MA): *Landscape with Cattle* (1869, oil); *October* (1882 or 1886, oil)

- MONTREAL: *Moonlight in Florida* - MUNICH (Pinakothek): *Moonrise* - NEW YORK (Brooklyn Mus.): *Roman Countryside* - NEW YORK (Metropolitan Mus. of Art): *Autumn Meadows* (1869, oil); *Evening; Peace and Plenty* (1865, oil); *Pine Grove of the Barberini Villa* (1876, oil); *The Delaware Valley* (c. 1863, oil); *Evening at Medfield, Massachusetts* (1875, oil); *Spring Blossoms, Montclair, New Jersey* (c. 1891, oil); *Sunrise* (1887, oil) - NEW YORK (Public Library): *Evening* - PITTSBURGH (Carnegie MA): *The Clouded Sun* (1891, oil on canvas) - ST LOUIS (GA, Washington University): *New England Village (Catskill Cove)* (1866, oil on canvas); *Landscape* (1867, oil on canvas); *Storm on the Delaware* (1891, oil on canvas) - ST PETERSBURG (MFA): *Early Moonrise, Florida* (1893, oil on canvas) - SYRACUSE (Everson MA): *A Nook near Our Village* (1849, oil on canvas) - TOLEDO: *After a Storm in Springtime; The Tiber below Perugia; In the Adirondacks* - WASHINGTON DC (Corcoran Gal. of Art): *Sunset in the Woods* (1891, oil on canvas); *Landscape* - WASHINGTON DC (NGA): *The Lackawanna Valley* (c. 1856, oil on canvas); *Lake Albano, Sunset* (c. 1874, oil on canvas); *View of the Tiber near Perugia* (1872-1874, oil on canvas) - WILMINGTON, DE (Delaware AM): *Early Autumn, Montclair* (oil on canvas) - WASHINGTON DC (Smithsonian American AM): *September Afternoon* (1887, oil on canvas); *Niagara* (1889, oil on canvas); *Georgia Pines* (1890, oil/wood); *Sundown* (1884, oil on canvas) - WORCESTER, MA (AM): *The Meadow* (1857, oil/panel); *Late Sunset* (1857, oil/panel); *Eagleswood, New Jersey* (1868, oil/panel); *Opposite the Palisades* (1870, oil on canvas); *The Alban Hills* (1873, oil on canvas); *Landscape, A New England Valley* (1875, oil/panel); *Spring at Montclair (The Palisades, Montclair, NJ)* (1889, oil on canvas); *Pool in the Woods* (1892, oil on canvas) - YOUNGSTOWN (Butler Institute of American Art): *Hazy Morning, Montclair, New Jersey* (1893, oil).

AUCTION RECORDS:

NEW YORK, 12-14 Dec 1899, *Peaceful Afternoon*, USD 675. NEW YORK, 24 Jan 1900, *Montclair in Moonlight*, USD 1,000; *Moonlight*, USD 560; *Prairie in June*, USD 850; *Sun Setting over the Passau*, USD 2500; *Return from Pasture*, USD 980; *Georgia Pine Afternoon* (1886) USD 5900; *Winter Morning in Montclair*, USD 2,500; *Summer Morning*, USD 1200. NEW YORK, 10 April 1900, *Spring, Montclair, New Jersey*, USD 1,600. NEW YORK, 8-9 Jan 1903, *Evening, Medfield*, USD 1,500. NEW YORK, 12-14 April 1909, *Summer Leaves*, USD 1,650. NEW YORK, 19 April 1911, *Watelund the Glow*, USD 6,000. NEW YORK, 30 Oct 1929, *Sunset*, USD 1,400. NEW YORK, 15 Nov 1929, *Shower*, USD 8,100. NEW YORK, 7 Nov 1933, *Dusk in Florida*, USD 2,200. NEW YORK, 16 March 1934, *Autumn in Montclair*, USD 1,300. NEW YORK, 26 May 1943, *Sunset near Montclair*, USD 8,000; *Wood Gatherers*, USD 10,000. NEW YORK, 21 Feb 1945, *Sunset*, USD 3,250. NEW YORK, 28 March 1946, *Autumn Afternoon*, USD 13,000. NEW YORK, 10 Dec 1958, *Sacred Wood near Rome* (1872) USD 800. NEW YORK, 21 Oct 1959, *The Old Oak, Medfield*, USD 3,300. NEW YORK, 20 Nov 1960, *Sources of the Tenpon, Florida*, USD 850. NEW YORK, 9 Oct 1963, *Landscape at Sunset*, USD 7,000. NEW YORK, 27 Jan 1965, *Sunset in Virginia*, USD 10,750. NEW YORK, 22 Oct 1969, *Cliffs at Etretat*, USD 8,500. NEW YORK, 19 April 1972, *June Day*, USD 39,000. NEW YORK, 25 Oct 1973, *Landscape with People* (1866) USD 35,000. NEW YORK, 23 May 1974, *Near Eagleswood, New Jersey*, USD 23,000. NEW YORK, 18 Nov 1976, *Undergrowth* (c. 1894, oil on canvas, 27 x 41 ins / 68.5 x 104 cm) USD 4,000. LOS ANGELES, 8 Nov 1977, *Landscape* (1865, oil on panel, 22 x 36 ins / 56 x 91.5 cm) USD 16,000. NEW YORK, 20 April 1979, *Olive Grove* (c. 1872, oil on canvas, 17 3/4 x 25 3/4 ins / 45 x 65.4 cm) USD 20,000. NEW YORK, 11 Dec 1981, *Landscape with Rainbow* (oil on canvas, 16 x 24 ins / 40.6 x 61 cm) USD 55,000. NEW YORK, 3 Dec 1982, *New England Valley* (1878, oil on canvas, 30 1/2 x 45 ins / 77.2 x 114.4 cm) USD 120,000. NEW YORK, 8 Dec 1983, *Near Leeds* (1869, oil on canvas, 20 x 30 ins / 50.8 x 76.2 cm) USD 57,500. NEW YORK, 15 March 1985, *Landscape* (1870, charcoal, black ink and white chalk, 11 3/4 x 18 1/2 ins / 29.8 x 47 cm) USD 6,000. NEW YORK, 31 May 1985, *Lackawanna Valley* (watercolour and pencil, 12 1/2 x 18 1/2 ins / 31.6 x 47 cm) USD 9,500. NEW YORK, 6 Dec 1985, *Indian Summer* (1891, oil on canvas, 30 1/4 x 45 1/2 ins / 77 x 115.5 cm) USD 70,000. NEW YORK, 3 Dec 1987, *The Delaware Water Gap* (oil on panel, 8 1/2 x 13 1/4 ins / 21.6 x 33.7 cm) USD 165,000. NEW YORK, 26 May 1988, *Farmyard with a Man and a Woman* (oil on canvas, 24 1/4 x 60 ins / 61.5 x 152.7 cm) USD 11,550. NEW YORK, 30 Sept 1988, *Around Montclair in New Jersey* (oil on canvas, 19 x 28 3/4 ins / 48.1 x 73 cm) USD 5,500. NEW YORK, 24 May 1989, *Harvest Scene in the Delaware Valley* (1867, oil on canvas, 30 1/4 x 45 1/4 ins / 76.8 x 115 cm) USD 495,000; *Panorama of the Delaware River* (1857, oil on canvas, 32 x 52 ins / 81.3 x 132 cm) USD 935,000. NEW YORK, 30 Nov 1989, *Georgia Pines in the Afternoon* (1886, oil on canvas, 24 x 36 ins / 61 x 91.3 cm) USD 209,000. NEW YORK, 24 May 1990, *Country Road* (1867, oil on canvas, 10 x 14 ins / 25.4 x 35.6 cm) USD 63,250. NEW YORK, 26 Sept 1990, *Pool at Milton on the Hudson* (1880, oil on panel, 12 x 18 ins / 30.5 x 45.7 cm) USD 77,000. NEW YORK, 30 Nov 1990, *Passage of a Storm* (oil on canvas, 12 1/4 x 18 ins / 31.1 x 46 cm) USD 52,800. NEW YORK, 22 May 1991, *Through the Wood* (oil on card, 10 x 8 ins / 25.5 x 20.4 cm) USD 18,700. NEW YORK, 25 Sept 1991, *Forest at Montclair* (1889, oil on panel, 27 x 22 ins / 68.6 x 55.9 cm) USD 39,600. NEW YORK, 5 Dec 1991, *Late Afternoon at Montclair* (1876, oil on panel, 16 1/4 x 26 ins / 41.3 x 66 cm) USD 99,000. NEW YORK, 28 May 1992, *Racing of the Clouds* (1890, oil on canvas, 40 1/4 x 30 ins / 102 x 76.3 cm) USD 52,800. NEW YORK, 3 Dec 1992, *Dusk at Etretat* (1892, oil on canvas, 30 x 45 ins / 76.2 x 114.3 cm) USD 71,500. NEW YORK, 27 May 1993, *Evening* (1868, oil on canvas, 48 x 78 1/2 ins / 121.9 x 199.4 cm) USD 184,000. NEW YORK, 1 Dec 1994, *Etretat in Normandy* (1877, oil on canvas, 12 1/4 x 18 ins / 31.1 x 45.7 cm) USD 71,250. NEW YORK, 22-23 May 1996, *Valley* (oil on canvas, 15 x 26 ins / 38 x 66 cm) USD 23,000; *Evening Clouds* (c. 1883, oil on canvas, 27 x 22 ins / 68.6 x 55.9 cm) USD 310,500. NEW YORK, 26 Sept 1996, *Threatening Storm* (1893, oil on canvas, 60 x 120 ins / 152.4 x 304.8 cm) USD 34,500. NEW YORK, 27 Sept 1996, *Dusk in Italy* (oil on paper/panel, 8 1/4 x 12 1/4 ins / 21 x 31.4 cm) USD 11,500. NEW YORK, 25 March 1997, *Landscape* (oil on canvas/panel, 6 x 8 3/4 ins / 15.2 x 22.5 cm) USD 6,900. NEW YORK, 3 Dec 1997, *Landscape at Sunrise* (1870, oil on canvas, 14 x 23 ins / 35.6 x 58.4 cm) USD 27,600. WINDSOR, 1 Jan 2002, *Country Landscape with Sunset with Figure in a Field* (oil on canvas) USD 1,600. LOS ANGELES, 3 Oct 2004, *Pastoral Landscape* (1879, oil on canvas on board, 24 x 20 ins / 61 x 51 cm) USD 4,500. LOS ANGELES, 3 Oct 2004, *Autumn Pastoral Landscape* (oil on canvas, 24 x 42 ins / 61 x 107 cm) USD 13,000.

INNESS, George (Junior)

American, 19th - 20th century.

Born 4 January 1853, in Paris; died 1926.

Painter. Landscapes with figures, landscapes, animals.

George Inness Junior was the son and pupil of the landscape artist George Inness. He has an important place in the American School. He was a member of the National Academy from 1899. He won a gold medal at the Salon de Paris in 1899 and a silver medal in Buffalo in 1901.

MUSEUMS AND GALLERIES:

BOSTON: *At Lake Nemi; Shepherd with his Flock* - MONTCLAIR: *Grazing Flock* - NEW YORK (Metropolitan Mus. of Art): *The First Snow*.

AUCTION RECORDS:

NEW YORK, 1 and 2 Dec 1904, *By the Stream*, USD 450. NEW YORK, 23 and 24 Feb 1905, *The Dairymaid*, USD 290. NEW YORK, 13 Jan 1911, *Alcester Bridge, England*, USD 800. NEW YORK, 19 March 1969, *After the Storm*, USD 23,000. NEW

York, 28 Jan 1970, *Landscape with Figures,* USD 23,000. New York, 7 April 1971, *Children in a Wooded Landscape,* USD 8,500. New York, 18 Nov 1976, *The Green Wood* (oil on canvas, 36 x 48 ins / 91.5 x 122 cm) USD 800. San Francisco, 8 Oct 1980, *Shepherdess and Little Lamb* (oil on canvas, 32 x 26 ins / 81.5 x 66 cm) USD 2,750. New York, 22 June 1984, *Through the Gate* (oil on canvas, 29 x 36 1/4 ins / 73.7 x 92.1 cm) USD 5,250. Los Angeles, 9 June 1988, *Man walking along a Path* (oil on canvas, 18 x 24 ins / 46 x 61 cm) USD 4,125. New York, 31 May 1990, *Woman in a Riding Habit with her Dog* (oil on canvas, 30 x 45 ins / 76.2 x 114.3 cm) USD 8,800. New York, 3 June 1994, *Beyond the Pale* (oil on canvas, 16 x 24 ins / 40.6 x 61 cm) USD 4,025. New York, 9 March 1996, *Tivoli in Italy* (oil on canvas, 14 x 12 ins / 35.5 x 30.5 cm) USD 13,800. Boston, 8 May 1998, *After the Storm* (oil on canvas, 20 x 30 ins / 51 x 76 cm) USD 3,750. Norwalk, 3 Jan 1999, *Farmhouse Pastoral Landscape at Sunrise* (oil on canvas, 12 x 16 ins / 30 x 41 cm) USD 2,750. Downington, 23 Feb 2001, *Etretat Normandy, France, with Cottage in Woods, Sunset Landscape* (oil on canvas, 18 x 24 ins / 46 x 61 cm) USD 5,750. Oak Park, 6 May 2001, *End of the Day* (c. 1900, oil on canvas, 24 x 36 ins / 61 x 91 cm) USD 7,750. Santa Fe, 18 May 2002, *Chetolah* (oil on canvas, 2 x 4 ins / 5 x 10 cm) USD 1,800. Hatfield, 9 June 2004, *Landscape with Central Figure in Field* (oil on canvas, 16 x 24 ins / 41 x 61 cm) USD 2,500.

INNO

Japanese, 13th century.
Active during the second half of the 13th century.
Sculptor.

Inno was a Buddhist sculptor and holder of the title of Hokkyo ('bridge of the law', an ecclesiastical title conferred on sculptors). On the first day of the eleventh month of 1267 he signed an image of Jie Daishi for the Guho-ji temple in Kyoto.

INNOCENT, Ferenc

Hungarian, 19th century.
Born 28 January 1859, in Budapest.
Active in Budapest.
Painter, illustrator. Figures, portraits, genre scenes. Murals.

Ferenc Innocent studied in Budapest, Vienna, Antwerp and Munich, and spent a year each in Paris and Rome. He painted his first picture, *Medieval Knight,* in Vienna in 1879. Notable among the works which followed are *Mark Antony Looking at the Body of Caesar, Flemish Milkmaid* (Antwerp), *Pietà* (Munich), *Beatrice Cenci* (Rome), *The Kiss,* and in Paris: *In the Studio, The Dilettante* and *Miriam.* He was famous in Hungary as a portrait painter, particularly for his portraits of beautiful women, such as *Ännchen von Tharau.* He collaborated on the decoration of the abbey church of Zirc, the Cistercians' church in Eger, the monastery in Budapest and the sanctuary of the church in Gyula.

Auction records:

London, 17 March 1995, *Maternal Love* (1883, oil on canvas, 39 3/4 x 30 ins / 101 x 76 cm) GBP 17,250. Nuremberg, 6 Dec 2002, *Young Woman* (oil on board, 14x10 ins / 35x25 cm) EUR 450. Kempten, 6 Nov 2003, *Portrait of a Young Woman* (oil on canvas, 27x19 ins / 69x49 cm) EUR 900. Munich, 5 Dec 2003, *Self-portrait* (oil on canvas, 20x15 ins / 52x38 cm) EUR 3,500. Vienna, 8 April 2004, *Astrid* (oil on canvas, 27x19 ins / 69x49 cm) EUR 2,200. Vienna, 21 June 2004, *Portrait of a Young Lady with Red Hair* (oil on canvas, 19x15 ins / 48x38 cm) EUR 2,800.

INNOCENT, Franck

French, 20th century.
Born 20 November 1912, in Sahurs (Seine-Maritime); died 1983.
Painter. Landscapes, harbour scenes, still-lifes (flowers). School of Rouen.

Franck Innocent studied at the École des Beaux-Arts in Rouen, where he began exhibiting landscapes. His first landscapes of Normandy were highly constructed, with accentuated ridges and thickly impasted paint. They evolved towards a lighter, clearer art. He linked himself with what is called the School of Rouen. He regularly participated in Paris at the Salon des Indépendants, Salon d'Automne, Salon Comparaisons and Salon Peintres Témoins de Leur Temps. He also had solo exhibitions in France and abroad.

Museums and Galleries:

Honfleur - Paris (MAMVP) - Rouen.

Auction records:

Paris, 26 Feb 1973, *The Port of Honfleur,* FRF 1,900. Honfleur, 15 Feb 1976, *Norman Courtyard* (oil on canvas, 32 x 23 1/2 ins / 81 x 60 cm) FRF 2,350. Paris, 10 July 1983, *Picardie* (1961, oil on panel, 35 1/2 x 51 1/4 ins / 90 x 130 cm) FRF 11,000. Paris, 26 May 1989, *Exhibition in Guilvinec* (1961, oil on canvas, 21 1/4 x 32 ins / 54 x 81 cm) FRF 9,000. Paris, 25 Oct 1991, *Still-life with Fruit* (1959, oil on canvas, 26 x 36 1/2 ins / 66 x 93 cm) FRF 13,000. Paris, 2 June 1993, *The Bridge at Bellac* (1973, oil on canvas, 21 1/4 x 25 1/2 ins / 54 x 65 cm) FRF 5,000; *Still-life with Flowers and Fruit* (1943, oil on canvas, 28 3/4 x 23 1/2 ins / 73 x 60 cm) FRF 6,000. Paris, 3 Dec 1993, *The Village of Marebaur Ourcq* (1969, oil on canvas, 25 1/2 x 32 ins / 65 x 81 cm) FRF 6,000. Paris, 29 Nov 1994, *Fishing Boats at the Quay in Honfleur* (oil on canvas, 25 1/2 x 21 1/4 ins / 65 x 54 cm) FRF 4,800. Calais, 24 March 1996, *The Bridge at Bellac* (1973, oil on canvas, 21 1/4 x 25 1/2 ins / 54 x 65 cm) FRF 6,000. Paris, 4 April 1997, *Bouquet of Irises* (1945, oil on canvas, 21 1/4 x 25 1/2 ins / 54 x 65 cm) FRF 4,000. Neuilly, 23 Nov 1999, *Boats in the Dock, Honfleur* (1962, oil on canvas, 24 x 32 ins / 60 x 81 cm) FRF 13,500. Pont Audemer, 19 Oct 2003, *House of Paul Faure, Andelys Crossing Trees* (1964, oil on canvas, 26 x 32 ins / 65 x 81 cm) EUR 1,500.

INNOCENTI, Battista degli. See **NALDINI Giovanni Battista di Matteo**

INNOCENTI, Bruno

Italian, 20th century.
Born 1906, in Florence.
Sculptor.

Museums and Galleries:

Rome (Gal. Nazionale d'Arte Moderna).

INNOCENTI, Camillo or Camilio

Italian, 19th - 20th century.
Born 14 June 1871, in Rome; died 1961, in Rome.
Active in Egypt.
Painter, draughtsman. Genre scenes, portraits.
Group of XXV (Campagna Romana).

Camillo Innocenti was a self-taught painter. He regularly spent periods in Paris. He became the director of the École des Beaux-Arts, Cairo, where he lived for 20 years. He exhibited at the Paris Salon des Artistes Français and obtained an honourable mention in 1902. He obtained a reputation for his choice of subjects, which often contained a humorous element, and his polished technique. He conveyed marvellously the shimmer of velvets and satins.

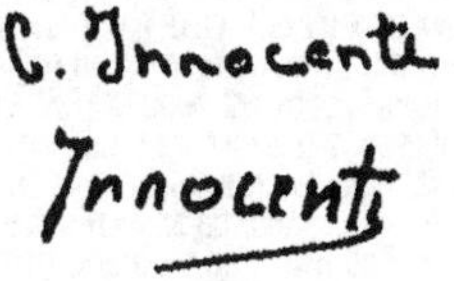

Museums and Galleries:
Melbourne: *Italian Peasants* - Nice (MBA Jules-Chéret) - Rome (Gal. Nazionale d'Arte Moderna): *Summer Evening; General Sodani; On the Square.*
Auction records:
Paris, 1881, *Bar,* FRF 1,510. Rotterdam, 1883, *Bell-ringers,* FRF 1,720. Paris, 10 April 1899, *Piquet Party,* FRF 750. Paris, 23 May 1900, *Mandolin Player,* FRF 830. New York, 19-20 March 1903, *Flirt,* USD 100. New York, 25-26 March 1909, *Woman of Rome,* USD 100. Paris, 22 Feb 1919, *Inside a Bar,* FRF 410. Paris, 9 April 1920, *Flock Returning at Sunset,* FRF 650. Paris, 28 Jan 1924, *Bourrée,* FRF 800. Paris, 20 Nov 1925, *Meal near a Farm,* FRF 2,350. Paris, 28 April 1937, *Lady in a Clearing,* FRF 750. Paris, 13 Dec 1937, *Young Guitarist,* FRF 1,180. Paris, 20 May 1942, *Card Players,* FRF 2,000. Paris, 8 Jan 1943, *Shepherdess and Sheep,* FRF 3,500. Paris, 17 Dec 1943, *Standard Bearer,* FRF 4,000. Paris, 24 April 1944, *Bar Scene; Card Players,* FRF 10,200. Paris, July 1946, *Tavern Scene,* FRF 6,200. London, 27 Sept 1946, *Meal,* GBP 52. Paris, 21 May 1947, *Cavalry Soldiers at Table,* FRF 6,100. Vienna, 30 Nov 1971, *Couple at Table,* ATS 32,000. Bern, 3 May 1974, *Amorous conversation,* CHF 7,500. Rome, 29 March 1976, *Odalisque* (oil on canvas, 47 1/4 x 63 ins / 120 x 160 cm) ITL 960,000. New York, 28 April 1977, *Card Party* (oil on panel, 12 3/4 x 16 1/4 ins / 32.5 x 41 cm) USD 1,200. London, 20 June 1979, *Flock in an Alpine Landscape* (oil on canvas, 37 1/2 x 60 1/4 ins / 95 x 153 cm) GBP 2,000. Milan, 10 Nov 1982, *Woman Reading* (1907, oil on canvas, 30 1/4 x 39 1/2 ins / 77 x 100.6 cm) ITL 5,500,000. Rome, 1 June 1983, *Portrait of a Young Girl* (oil on panel, 23 1/2 x 13 1/4 ins / 60 x 33.5 cm) ITL 4,200,000. Rome, 13 May 1986, *Guardian of the Flock* (oil on canvas, 29 1/2 x 63 ins / 75 x 160 cm) ITL 7,000,000. Rome, 19 May 1987, *Young Girl in Costume* (1924, watercolour, pencil and silver highlights, 22 x 14 1/2 ins / 56 x 37 cm) ITL 3,400,000. Paris, 30 Nov 1987, *Musketeer at Table and a Serving Girl in a Clearing* (9 1/4 x 13 ins / 23.5 x 33 cm) FRF 4,500. Bern, 30 April 1988, *Conversation* (oil on panel, 7 1/2 x 9 1/2 ins / 19 x 24 cm) CHF 4,500. Rome, 24 May 1988, *Place du Panthéon* (oil on canvas, 11 3/4 x 16 1/2 ins / 30 x 42 cm) ITL 5,000,000. Bern, 26 Oct 1988, *Young Serving Girl at an Inn Chatting with a Customer* (oil on panel, 9 x 11 ins / 22 x 27 cm) CHF 3,500. Rome, 14 Dec 1988, *Elegant Lady with a Greyhound* (1912, watercolour and white lead/paper, 18 3/4 x 12 1/4 ins / 47.5 x 31 cm) ITL 2,600,000. Monaco, 3 Dec 1989, *Card Party* (oil on panel, 10 1/2 x 13 1/2 ins / 26.5 x 34.5 cm) FRF 15,540. Monaco, 21 April 1990, *Tango* (watercolour and lead pencil, 24 1/2 x 21 ins / 62 x 53.5 cm) FRF 16,650. Amsterdam, 25 April 1990, *Unwelcome Art Lover* (oil on canvas, 18 x 28 1/4 ins / 45.5 x 72 cm) NLG 11,270. Paris, 4 March 1991, *Serving Girl and Musketeers under Trees* (oil on panel, 14 1/2 x 18 ins / 37 x 46 cm) FRF 13,000. Rome, 24 March 1992, *Portrait of a Young Woman Wearing a Large Hat* (oil on canvas, 15 3/4 x 12 1/2 ins / 40 x 32 cm) ITL 17,250,000. London, 28 Oct 1992, *Ready for Bathing* (oil on panel, 9 3/4 x 7 3/4 ins / 25 x 20 cm) GBP 825. Rome, 19 Nov 1992, *Baby* (1900, oil/plywood, 13 1/4 x 9 1/4 ins / 33.5 x 23.5 cm) ITL 3,680,000. Paris, 5 July 1993, *Musketeer* (oil on panel, 22 x 18 ins / 55 x 46 cm) FRF 6,000. Rome, 29-30 Nov 1993, *Picking Flowers in a Meadow* (oil on canvas, 30 x 35 3/4 ins / 76 x 91 cm) ITL 129,635,000. Rome, 13 Dec 1994, *Saying the Rosary* (oil on canvas, 28 x 39 3/4 ins / 71 x 101 cm) ITL 24,150,000. London, 13 March 1996, *Picnic* (oil on panel, 9 1/2 x 12 1/2 ins / 24 x 32 cm) GBP 2,300. London, 18 March 1999, *Standing Female Nude before Mirror* (oil on panel, 11 x 8 ins / 27 x 21 cm) GBP 3,000. Rome, 6 Dec 1999, *Donna di Scanno* (oil on canvas, 67 x 48 ins / 170 x 123 cm) ITL 60,000,000. Paris, 14 April 2000, *Farmer Feeding Chickens* (oil on panel, 11 x 7 ins / 27 x 17 cm) FRF 11,000. Rome, 21 Nov 2000, *In the Garden* (oil on canvas, 39 x 28 ins / 100 x 70 cm) ITL 50,000,000. Paris, 23 March 2001, *Interior Scene* (oil on canvas, 51 x 35 ins / 130 x 90 cm) FRF 185,000. London, 6 June 2001, *Leaving for the Ball* (oil on canvas, 52 x 34 ins / 131 x 87 cm) GBP 22,000. Milan, 22 May 2002, *Figures on the Seashore* (oil on canvas, 9 x 11 ins / 22 x 27 cm) EUR 2,000. Rome, 4 Dec 2002, *White Hat* (oil on canvas, 18 x 13 ins / 45 x 32 cm) EUR 3,000. Calais, 29 June 2003, *Meal next to the Hearth* (oil on panel, 8 x 11 ins / 21 x 27 cm) EUR 2,650. Ahlden, 19 Sept 2003, *Flower Seller and Suitor* (1960, oil on panel, 16 x 12 ins / 41 x 30 cm) EUR 2,500. Bern, 12 May 2004, *Farmstead with Small Girl* (oil on canvas, 26 x 33 ins / 65 x 85 cm) CHF 4,000. Cologne, 1 July 2004, *Young Girl Listening to a Story* (oil on canvas, 26 x 24 ins / 67 x 62 cm) EUR 36,000.

INNOCENZO DA IMOLA. See **FRANCUCCI Innocenzo di Piandro**

INO, Pierre, Real name: Vechegzhanin, Petr Vladimirovich
Russian, 20th century.
Born 1909.
Active in France.
Painter.

Pierre Ino encountered the Surrealist movement early in his career. He quickly perfected his technique of a highly realistic rendering of an uncompromisingly phantasmagorical vision. Like the majority of Surrealist painters, he was caught in the trap of having to depict in as photographic a way as possible a universe that, if not actually incomprehensible, is at least unusual.

Though his inspiration did not apparently impress serious collectors, the prettiness of his small and delicate compositions brought Surrealism within the reach of all. He was part of that second generation of Surrealists that was more interested in the imagery of Surrealism than in exploring the depths of the human psyche. These painters came together as the Gravitation group and were more influenced by Supervielle and Gonzague-Frick than by André Breton. They included, from 1933, Louis Cattiaux, Jean Marembert, Pierre Kino, Beothy and Jean Lafon, who supported the ideas of the *Transhylist manifesto.*

Bibliography:
Huyghe, René, *Les Contemporains*, Éd. Pierre Tisné, Paris, 1949.

Auction records:
Paris, 7 April 1943, *Woman Pouring out the Essence of Life,* FRF 20,000. Paris, 12 Dec 1946, *Composition,* FRF 5,000. Paris, 28 Sept 1993, *Portrait Turning into a Still-life or Sleeping Girl* (oil on canvas, 25 1/2 x 32 ins / 65 x 81.5 cm) FRF 4,800. Paris, 20 April 1994, *Vulcan's Daughter* (oil on canvas, 22 x 18 ins / 55 x 46 cm) FRF 6,200. Paris, 29 March 1995, *Woman in a Black Cape* (oil on canvas/panel, 32 x 25 1/2 ins / 81 x 64.5 cm) FRF 11,000.

INOKUMA, Geni'chiro
Japanese, 20th century.
Born 1902, in Kagawa Prefecture; died 1993.
Active from 1955 in the USA.
Painter. Murals.

Inokuma trained in the techniques of Western painting with Fujishima Takeji at the university of fine art in Tokyo from 1922 to 1926. His works, in an abstract style, are often full of fantasy. He became a member of the Shinseisaku (original creation) association in 1935 in Tokyo, and taught painting at the university of fine art in Tokyo until 1940. From 1940 to 1942 he travelled in Europe and in France met Matisse, who influenced his later works. In 1945 he opened his own school of painting in Tokyo which he directed until 1955, when he departed for the USA.

From 1935 Inokuma took part in the imperial exhibition (Teiten). From then on he featured in various Salons: in 1938 in the Salon des Indépendants in Paris; in 1952 in the Salon de Mai in Paris; in 1954 and 1958 in the São Paulo Biennale; in 1952, 1958, 1961 and 1964 at the Carnegie Institute in

Pittsburgh; and from 1963 to 1964 in a travelling exhibition of *Contemporary Japanese Painting and Sculpture* in the USA. From 1955 he held an annual solo exhibition in New York. He was awarded several prizes, including the prize at the International Watercolour Exhibition at the Brooklyn Museum in New York in 1955, and first prize at the exhibition *Contemporary Japanese Art* at the museum of modern art in Tokyo in 1964. In 1952 he received the prize awarded by the Mainichi newspaper for the murals he had painted in 1947 at, amongst other places, Keio university in Tokyo. He subsequently executed several other murals, notably at the central station in Tokyo, in the Takashiyama department stores in New York and the town hall of the Kanagawa Prefecture.

Museums and Galleries:
Baltimore (MA) - Boston (ICA) - San Francisco (MoMA): *Wall Street* (1964, oil on canvas) - Tokyo (National MMA).

Auction records:
New York, 12 Oct 1989, *Head of a Woman* (pencil/paper, 15 1/2 x 10 1/4 ins / 39.3 x 26 cm) USD 1,100; *Seated Nude* (oil on panel, 17 3/4 x 15 ins / 45.1 x 38 cm) USD 12,100; *Portrait of the Wife of the Artist* (1949, oil on canvas, 16 x 11 ins / 40.7 x 27 cm) USD 22,000. New York, 29 March 1990, *Woman with Her Hand in front of Her Face* (watercolour and pencil/paper, 15 x 12 ins / 38 x 30.5 cm) USD 19,800. New York, 27 April 1994, *City Composition 3* (1966, oil on canvas, 11 3/4 x 15 3/4 ins / 30 x 40 cm) USD 34,500. New York, 31 Oct 1995, *Garden* (1957, oil on canvas, 66 3/4 x 25 1/2 ins / 169.5 x 64.8 cm) USD 4,830. Philadelphia, 7 Dec 2003, *Broadway* (1966, acrylic on canvas, 47 x 48 ins / 119 x 122 cm) USD 12,000.

INOLLE, Johann Heinrich Friedrich Ludwig
19th century.
Born 1807.
Active in Milan and in Germany.
Engraver.

J.H.F.L. Inolle made engravings of religious and historical subjects.

INOSE, Tonei, real name: Jo Inose, nicknames: Joshin, Chugoro, pseudonyms: Bankado, Chokotomuro, Sensai, Tonei
Japanese, 19th century.
Born 1839; died 1910.
Active in Tokyo.
Painter (silk). Landscapes.

Inose featured in Paris at the Exposition Universelle in 1900.

INOUE, Bukichi
Japanese, 20th century.
Born 1930, in Nara Prefecture; died 1997.
Sculptor.

Bukichi Inoue was one of the central Abstract Expressionists of post-war Japan. He graduated with a diploma in 1955 from the school of fine art in Musashino near Tokyo, where he worked in the studios of Takashi Shimizu and Katsumi Kiuchi. Among other exhibitions, he featured at the museum of modern art in Tokyo in 1962 in the exhibition *The Modern School*, at the São Paulo Biennale in 1963, at the second exhibition of the Japan art festival association in 1967, and in 1968 at the third. He was also awarded several prizes, including the chief prize awarded at the exhibition *Modern Developments* in 1962 and at the 7th Tokyo Biennale.

Museums and Galleries:
Kamakura (MMA) - Tokyo (MMA).

INOUE, Hahuyo
Japanese, 20th century.
Painter.

Hahuyo Inoue featured in the exhibition *L'Art japonais*, held in Paris at the Musée du Jeu de Paume in 1929.

INOUE, Keiji
Japanese, 19th century.
Active in Tokyo.
Painter. Landscapes.

Keiji Inoue featured in the Exposition Universelle of 1900.

INOUE, Kozo, artist name Kozo
Japanese, 20th century.
Born 18 June 1937, in Osaka.
Active since 1961, also in France.
Painter, draughtsman (wash), engraver, screen printer. Nudes, still-lifes, flowers, plants. Murals.

Inoue Kozo obtained his diploma in aesthetics and art history in Tokyo in 1960. At the same time he studied painting with M. Tasaki and started to exhibit at the *I suoi kai* exhibition. That same year, he arrived in Paris, where he worked in Busse and Gillet's atelier in the Académie de la Grande Chaumière, forming a group with a number of fellow students.

In his early years in Paris, after his first studies with nudes and still-lifes, his incursion into abstraction under the direct influence of Busse, and his period in the *Ateliers*, during which he was searching for the constituent elements of Western painting, Kozo soon found that the influence of his masters was causing him to lose contact with his own nature and ethnic and cultural roots. Shutting himself away in his Paris studio in 1962, he engaged in an austere dialogue with a few simple objects, observing the passage of light over them, and tending increasingly towards the spiritual, his graphic expression becoming sharp and synthetic. He emerged from this period of self-searching with the conclusion that he could dispense with the representation of reality without impairing his self-expression, and could return to the sparse economy of means practised in the Far East, using a range of tense, full, monolithic forms from which from time to time a small spring leaf would burst forth, rendered by a few close dabs of colour, a technique particularly suited to silk-screen printing. Shortly afterwards, around 1968, he adopted the silk-screen as his favoured medium and returned to figurative art for good, giving himself up to the joyful figuration of everyday nature. His subject matter would henceforth be simple things in their myriad forms: flowers, reeds, bamboo, familiar vegetables, branches and leaves blown in the wind, the ripples on the river, the return of the seasons.

Kozo's art is based entirely on the Zen maxim that rarity - here economy of form and colour - exalts beauty. 'In the cathedrals, the accumulation of many things expresses a single thing. For us, we try to express many things through a single thing. We show one thing and the rest, we leave that for the viewer to imagine.' His prints carried his lyrical feeling and incomparable silk-screen technique of intersecting, clever colour gradations around the world. Working in the summer in his house by the Lot, Kozo also regularly produced series after series of washes of backlit leaves and the sun reflecting on the river. In this, he was rediscovering and reviving the traditional *suiboku-ga* (Indian ink painting) technique.

Though Kozo would go on to modify parts of his silk-screen technique, he never abandoned painting, keeping it for the many murals he was commissioned to do in France, Japan, Germany and the USA. These large-scale murals in public spaces allow him to come into direct contact with the people who live there or just passers-by, and give them a glimpse of his way of seeing as they relax or go to work. When carrying out a commission, he is careful to get to know and respect the natural site, its architectural space, and the psychology and sociology of those who use it. In contrast to the great solitary figures whom he respects, he fully accepts the encumbrances that accompany the principle of working to order. When conceiving a work, he takes the circumstances into account, 'as a professional'.

His murals include works for the Mash Publicity Agency, Paris; Total Oil Company, Paris; Hôtel Méridien, Paris and Nice; EDF (French Electricity Corporation) Menton; School Residence, Montereau, France; Dresdner Bank, Frankfurt; Senven City Cultural Centre, Tokyo; Villars Palace Restaurant, Paris; Dresdner Bank, Tokyo; Bretonneau Hospital, Tours, France; presidential palaces, Baghdad; Daichi Hotel, Nagoya; and the Hotel Okura, Amsterdam. Communication for Kozo is not a one-way street. His personal conception of art is that it allows the artist to find his truth in harmony and to convey it to others in order to awaken them to the marvellous in life.

Kozo has taken part in many group shows, including 1963 to 1968, Salon de Mai (Paris); 1968, Japanese Art Exhibition (International Cultural Centre, Paris), *Japan* (Maison des Siècles, Fontainebleau) and *Werngroep September* (Hilversum, The Netherlands); 1969, *Fine Arts of Japan* (Poitiers, France); 1970, *International Graphic* (Germany, Chartres Museum), *Japan Art Festival* (Tokyo, Milan, USA); and 1971, Exhibition of Contemporary Art (Japan), where he won the Prize.

He has also exhibited in numerous one-man shows, mostly of silk-screen prints with a few washes. These exhibitions include: 1960 Osaka; 1966 Tokyo; 1968 Paris; 1969 Tokyo, Paris; 1970 Paris, Marseilles, Monaco; 1971 Paris, Belgium, Kobe Museum of Contemporary Art; 1972 Tokyo, Liège, Paris; 1973 Paris, Chartres Museum, Tokyo; 1974 Paris, Tokyo, Rome, Osaka; 1975 Ostend, Bordeaux; 1976 Paris, Venice; 1978 Paris, Galerie La Hune; 1982 Paris, Artcurial; 1983 Orléans, galerie Harmonie; Limoges, Galerie d'Art Contemporain; Grenoble, Galerie J.-M. Cupillard.

Kozo has won a number of prizes, including the 1969 Grand Prize for Serigraphy, Paris; the 1971 Grand Prize, Contemporary Art Exhibition of Japan, Tokyo; and in 1980, a special jury mention in the International Painting Festival, Cagnes-sur-Mer.

BIBLIOGRAPHY:

Kozo Inoué, Nouvelles Images, Paris, 1969. Kozo, et al., *L'Été 81*, Paris, 1981 (with autobiography). Gheerbrant, Bernard/Eto, Shun, *Kozo, lavis*, Traces, Paris, 1983 (good documentation). *The Works of Kozo*, Abe, 1989 (published in Japan).

MUSEUMS AND GALLERIES:

BERLIN (National Mus.) - BRUSSELS (Bibliothèque royale Albert Ier) - CALCUTTA (MMA) - PARIS (BNF) - PARIS (MAMVP) - PARIS (Mus. Carnavalet).

INOUE, Yuichi

Japanese, 20th century.

Born 14 February 1916, in Shitaya, Tokyo; died 15 June 1985.

Painter.

Yuichi Inoue studied oil painting, then in 1941 began an eight-year study of calligraphy as the pupil of Ueda Sokyu. In 1952 he founded the society of calligraphy (Bokujin-kai). In 1976 he retired from his post of principal of the Asahi elementary school after more than 41 years as a teacher. His calligraphic style brings out the connections between Far Eastern calligraphy and certain Lyrical Abstract painters, such as Hans Hartung, Pierre Soulages and Franz Kline. He contributed essays on calligraphy to the journals *Sho no Bi* and *Hibi no Zeppitu*.

Collective exhibitions in Japan in which he participated include the Shodo Geijutsuin exhibition in 1950, the Genbi exhibition in 1954, the Japan-America abstract art exhibition in Tokyo in 1955, the first Japan Gendai exhibition at the Tokyo metropolitan art museum in 1967, *The Contemporary East-West Art Dialogue* at the museum of modern art in Tokyo in 1969, *Development of Postwar Japanese Art: Abstract and Figurative* at the same museum in 1973, *1955 and Now* at Wako hall, Ginza, Tokyo, in 1982 and *Adam in the Future* at the Seibu department store in Shibya, Tokyo, in 1985.

He participated in numerous collective exhibitions overseas. In 1954, he was represented with *Jiga-ge* and other works in the *Japanese Calligraphy* exhibition at the Museum of Modern Art in New York. In 1955-1956, he had two works in the exhibition *Indian Ink in Japanese Calligraphy and Art*, which toured western Europe. In 1957 he showed in the São Paulo Biennale, and in 1958 in the Brussels exhibition of modern art. In 1959, he was represented at *Il Documenta: Kunst nach 1945* at the Museum Fridericanium in Kassel, Germany. In 1960, he contributed to the exhibition *Pintura Japonesa Contemporanea* at the Museu de Arte Moderna in Rio de Janeiro and to *Japanische Kalligraphie* at the Museum Folkwang in Essen, Germany. In 1961 he showed again at the São Paulo Biennale, and he was represented in the Pacific Area Art Exhibition in Oakland, California, as well as the International Exhibition of Contemporary Painting and Sculpture at the Carnegie Institute in Pittsburgh. In 1962 he showed *Ko* in the travelling exhibition *Contemporary Sumie* in Canada and the USA. In 1962-1963 he participated in travelling exhibitions of Japanese calligraphy in the Netherlands and Germany. In 1966 he showed four works in the First Japanese Art Festival at the Union Carbide headquarters in New York. His work was represented in *Sho-Modern Japanische Schreibkunst*, an exhibition that travelled in Germany in 1976. In 1979, he participated in *Japan Today* at the Chicago Cultural Center. He was included postumously in the exhibition *Arbeiten auf Papier* (*Works on Paper*) at the Japan Art Gallery in Frankfurt am Main in 1993; in 1996 at the Guggenheim Museum in New York and San Francisco Museum of Art (*Japanese Art after 1945*).

Yuichi Inoue's solo exhibitions included those at the Galerie Rodolf Zwirner in Cologne in 1962 and 1965; at Wuppertal Kunst und Museumverein in 1965 (*Yuichi Kalligraphien*, more than 30 works); at the Ichibankan gallery in Tokyo in 1971 and 1972; at the Ashai gallery in Kyoto in 1980; at the UNAC Salon in Tokyo in 1984 (*Yuichi Kotoba-gaki* (*Yuichi Wordworks*)). Posthumous exhibitions were mounted in Tokyo in 1986 (*Yuichi Zeppitsu*), in 1987 (*Yuichi's Hundred Hana* at the Parco Gallery) and in 1993 (*Subarashi Hin* (*Revelation in Black on White*). In 1989 the museum of modern art in Kyoto organised the travelling exhibition *Yuichi Works 1955-1985*. Germany saw posthumous Yuichi exhibitions in 1996 at the Schirn Kunsthalle, the Galerie im Karmeliterkloster and the Museum für Kunsthandwerk in Frankfurt am Main.

BIBLIOGRAPHY:

Unagami, Masaomi, *Yuichi Catalogue Raisonné of the Works 1949-1985*, 1966-1999 (3 vols).

MUSEUMS AND GALLERIES:

KYOTO (Museum of Modern Art): 62 works.

AUCTION RECORDS:

LONDON, 22 Feb 1990, *Dragon No. 1* (1962, collage of oil/paper/canvas, 45 1/4 x 27 1/2 ins / 115 x 70 cm) GBP 3,300.

INOZEMTSEV, Vladimir

Russian, 20th century.

Born 1921.

Painter.

Vladimir Inozemtsev studied at the Ilya Repin Institute in Leningrad (now St Petersburg) and was honoured by the USSR.

AUCTION RECORDS:

PARIS, 12 Dec 1992, *Change* (1949, oil on canvas, 23 1/2 x 35 1/2 ins / 60 x 90 cm) FRF 10,500. PARIS, 4 May 1994, *Lighthouse* (oil/hardboard, 35 1/2 x 28 ins / 90 x 71 cm) FRF 4,200.

INSAM, Giovanni. See **INSOM**

INSELIN, Charles
French, 17th - 18th century.
Born c. 1673.
Active in Paris.
Engraver.

Inselin was married at St-Roch on 17 August 1702. He is also mentioned as the godfather of a daughter of the engraver Jean-Moufle.

INSHAW, David
British, 20th century.
Born 21 March 1941, in Wednesfields (Staffordshire).
Active in Devizes.
Painter, engraver, draughtsman. Figures, nudes, landscapes.
The Brotherhood of Ruralists.

David Inshaw studied painting at the Beckenham School of Painting from 1959 to 1963 and then at the Royal Academy Schools from 1963 to 1966 under the direction of P. Greenham. He received a French government bursary that enabled him to study in Paris for six months in 1964. Inshaw taught painting and engraving at the West of England College of Art in Bristol from 1966 to 1975. He was a founder member of The Brotherhood of Ruralists in 1975 with Graham and Ann Arnold. This group shared a common interest in the Romantic connotations of countryside and landscape. Inshaw left the group in 1983.

Inshaw's painting derives from a traditional vision of art. He succeeds in combining a realist representation of nature with a sensual imagination which brings a certain symbolism to his work. He has been deeply influenced by the hilly landscapes of the North Downs and Kent.

Inshaw has taken part in numerous group exhibitions, including: *Young Contemporaries*, which he organised, held at the R.B.A. Galleries in London (1966); *An Element of Landscape*, an exhibition that toured Britain (1974); *Papier sur Nature*, part of the Festival d'Automne in Paris, an exhibition conceived by Jean Clair at the height of the debate on the return to drawing and Figuration (1977); exhibitions by The Ruralists from 1976 to 1983, including those in Southampton (1977), Bristol (1980, 1981), Cambridge, Birmingham and Glasgow (1981) and the Tate Gallery in London (1983); *British Art from 1930* at the Waddington Galleries in London (1991); and *Friends and Influences* at the Royal West of England Academy in Bristol (2003). Inshaw has also shown his work in solo exhibitions, including at the following: the Arnolfini Gallery in Bristol (1969); the Waddington Galleries in London (1975, 1980, 1984); the museum of Devizes (1987); Theo Waddington Fine Art in London (1998); and the Museum of Modern Art in Machynlleth (1999).

BIBLIOGRAPHY:
Usherwood, Nicholas, *David Inshaw*, Academy Editions, London, 1978. Martin, Christopher, *The Ruralists. Art and Design*, Academy Group, London, 1991.

MUSEUMS AND GALLERIES:
BRISTOL (City Mus. & AG): *Incident in a Landscape* (oil on canvas); *Our days were a joy and our paths through flowers* (1971-1972, oil on canvas) - DEVIZES (Devizes Mus.) - LONDON (Tate Collection): *The Badminton Game* (1972-1973, oil on canvas) - SUNDERLAND (Mus. and AG).

INSHIN
Japanese, 13th century.
Active at the end of the 13th century.
Sculptor.

Inshin was considered a Buddhist master sculptor (*dai busshi*). From the twelfth month of 1251, he took part in the preparations for the assembling of the Buddhist statues in the Kofuku-ji temple in Nara. In 1283, he executed the statue of Jie Daishi for the Yakushi-do of Shiga.

INSHO, Domoto. See **DOMOTO Insho**

INSHU
Japanese, 13th century.
Active at the end of the 13th century.
Sculptor.

Inshu was considered a Buddhist master sculptor (*dai busshi*). He bore the honorary title of Ho-in ('seal of the law', the highest of the Buddhist ecclesiastical titles conferred on an artist). He took part in the restoration of the statues in the reading room of the Kofuku-ji temple in Nara. In 1294, assisted by the sculptors Intan and Inryo, he executed the Jizo Bosatsu (Sanskrit: Bodhisattva Ksitigarbha) of the Joki-in temple on Mount Koya-san, the Jizo being dated from the 24th day of the ninth month of 1294.

INSKIP, John Henry
British, 19th century.
Active in Scarborough.
Painter. Landscapes.

John Henry Inskip was a member of the Royal Society of British Artists. He exhibited his work in London from 1886, mainly at the Royal Academy and Suffolk Street.

MUSEUMS AND GALLERIES:
ROCHDALE (Art Gallery): *Walmer*; *Whitstable.*

AUCTION RECORDS:
LONDON, 4 May 1908, *Morning at Robin Hood's Bay*, GBP 15. LONDON, 4 March 1910, *Misty Autumn Morning* (1895) GBP 7. LONDON, 3 June 1992, *Nature's Garden* (1887, oil on canvas, 23 x 35 1/4 ins / 58.5 x 89.5 cm) GBP 3,520.

INSKIPP, James
British, 19th century.
Born 1790; died 1868, in Godalming.
Painter. Figures, portraits, genre scenes, landscapes.

James Inskipp began his career as a civil servant. He began exhibiting his paintings in London from 1816, but only concentrated completely on painting from 1820. He exhibited his work at the Society of British Artists until 1841.

MUSEUMS AND GALLERIES:
MONTREAL: *Return from the Market.*

AUCTION RECORDS:
PARIS, 1874, *Landscape*, FRF 2,800. NEW YORK, 7 and 8 April 1904, *Portrait of a Young Woman*, USD 226. NEW YORK, 14 and 15 Jan 1909, *Little Girl*, USD 200. LONDON, 11 Feb 1911, *Flower Seller*, GBP 33. PARIS, 5 May 1944, *Woman Breastfeeding her Child*, FRF 5,500. PARIS, 15 Dec 1944, *Motherhood*, FRF 7,500. LONDON, 1 March 1991, *Venetian Woman Carrying Water* (oil on panel, 11 1/2 x 9 1/2 ins / 28.9 x 24.4 cm) GBP 2,200. NEW YORK, 4 Oct 1996, *Portrait in the Form of a Bust of a Lady said to be Gertrude Banks Seated in front of a Landscape* (oil on canvas, 50 1/4 x 40 ins / 127.6 x 101.6 cm) USD 5,750.

INSLEY, Albert Babb
American, 19th - 20th century.
Born 1842, in New Jersey; died 1937.
Active in Nyack (New York).
Painter. Landscapes with figures, landscapes.

Albert Babb Insley, son of the pioneering photographer Henry Earle Insley, was largely self-taught. He exhibited chiefly with the National Academy of Design.

AUCTION RECORDS:
NEW YORK, 24 Jan 1973, *New York Harbour*, USD 1,300. LONDON, 2 Nov 1979, *Wooded River Landscape* (oil on canvas, 13 3/4 x 21 3/4 ins / 35 x 55.2 cm) GBP 1,100. SAN FRANCISCO, 21 Jan 1981, *Landscape with a Stream* (oil on canvas, 14 x 22 ins / 35.8 x 56 cm) USD 2,000. BOLTON, 17 Nov 1983, *Off Cape Elizabeth, Maine* (oil on canvas, 20 x 32 ins / 50.8 x 81.5 cm) USD 3,000. NEW YORK, 24 Oct 1986, *Autumn Landscape*

(1888, oil on canvas, 32 1/4 x 48 ins / 82 x 121 cm) USD 2,500. NEW YORK, 24 June 1988, *View of Clarkstown, New York* (oil on canvas, 11 3/4 x 17 3/4 ins / 30 x 45 cm) USD 880. NEW YORK, 10 June 1992, *Porcupine Island off Bar Harbor in Maine* (oil on canvas, 12 1/4 x 18 1/4 ins / 31 x 46.3 cm) USD 990. NEW YORK, 31 March 1994, *Hunter and his Dog in a Landscape* (oil on canvas, 29 x 49 1/4 ins / 73.7 x 125.1 cm) USD 2,760.

INSLEY, Will
American, 20th century.
Born 15 October 1929, in Indianapolis (Indiana).
Painter.

Will Insley graduated from the School of Design of Harvard University in Cambridge, Massachusetts. He settled in New York. He uses shaped canvases in works constructed according to strict geometrical rules. In the ensemble *Wall Fragments* of 1975, the canvases, covered in squares of black on white or white on black, are of a different shape each time and the support takes on the role of structure.

Insley has taken part in various group exhibitions, including *L'Art vivant aux États-Unis* (*Living Art in the United States*) at the Fondation St-Paul-de-Vence in 1970; Documenta in Kassel in 1972 and 1977; *Drawings-Structures* at the Institute of Contemporary Art in Boston in 1980 and *Dreams and Nightmares* at the Hirshhorn Museum in Washington in 1984. He has been showing his work in solo exhibitions since 1951, particularly at New York galleries, and the Walker Art Center, Minneapolis, in 1968; The Museum of Modern Art, New York, in 1971; the Kunstverein Stuttgart in 1974; The Museum of Contemporary Art, Chicago, in 1976 and the Guggenheim Museum, New York, in 1984.

BIBLIOGRAPHY:

Prokopoff, Stephen, *Will Insley*, exhibition catalogue, Museum of Contemporary Art, Chicago, 1976. Lippard, Lucy, *Dwellings*, exhibition catalogue, 1978. Kren, Alfred, *Drawing Distinctions: American Drawings of the Seventies*, exhibition catalogue, 1981. Kardon, Janet, *Connections: Bridges, Ladders, Ramps, Staircases, Tunnels*, exhibition catalogue, University of Pennsylvania, Institute of Contemporary Art, 1983. Shearer, Linda, *Will Insley: The Opaque Civilization*, exhibition catalogue, Guggenheim Museum, New York, 1984.

AUCTION RECORDS:

NEW YORK, 13 Nov 1986, *Building no. 42, Passage Scape Hill Slip, one point perspective, exterior view* (1975-1977, pen and black ink/card, 40 x 60 1/4 ins / 101.5 x 152.9 cm) USD 3,200.

INSOM, Giovanni, or Insam or Insamb
Italian, 19th century.
Born November 1775, in Casez; died after 1831.
Sculptor.

There are works by Insom in Trento and Rovereto (the church of S Marco). He made copies of antique works in alabaster and marble that were sold in England, France and elsewhere.

MUSEUMS AND GALLERIES:

FLORENCE (Palazzo Pitti): *Sea Nymphs* (two statues) - ST PETERSBURG (Hermitage): *Anatomical Figure* (sculpted in wood).

INSON
Japanese, 12th century.
Born 1120; died 1198.
Sculptor.

Inson was the son or disciple of Inkaky, and is the principal representative of one of the two main currents of Buddhist sculpture at the end of the Heian (or Fujiwara) period and at the beginning of the Kamakura period. He was the founder of the In, or In-pa School, known as Shichijo Omiya Bussho. He spent his life as an artist, being particularly active between 1147 and 1190-1199, working on the restoration of the statues in the great temples at Nara (including Todai-ji and Kofuku-ji). For this reason, he was the first to have conferred on him the highest honorary title in the Buddhist hierarchy, Ho-in, or 'seal of the law'. None of his works have survived, but he introduced more realistic elements into the traditional style of Jocho (died in 1057) and his descendants. This composite style was to blossom subsequently with Unkei, who was active about 1225.

INTALER, Wolfgang
Swiss, 15th - 16th century.
Active in Lucerne from 1484 to 1508.
Painter (glass).
Lucerne School.

Wolfgang Intaler painted windows for various churches in Bern, Lucerne and Gisswyl.

INTERGUGLIELMI, Elia
Italian, 18th century.
Died 1773.
Active in Palermo.
Painter.

Interguglielmi was a priest and executed the paintings for four chapels in the church of S Maria degli Agonizzanti in Palermo.

INTERLUNGO, Pietro de, or Interlegno or Interlenghi or Interlengo or Interlineo
Italian, 16th century.
Active in Morbio (Ticino).
Stucco artist.

In 1610, he collaborated with Pietro Maderno in Rome.

INTERNARI, Giovanni Battista
Italian, 18th century.
Born in Rome; died 1761, in Warsaw.
Painter.

Internari trained with Benefiali. In 1750 he went to Dresden where he executed several portraits and caricatures. In 1756 he went to Warsaw with the court of Augustus III.

MUSEUMS AND GALLERIES:

DRESDEN: *Self-portrait.*

INTINI, Paolo
Italian, 20th century.
Born 5 February 1921, in Monopoli.
Active from 1948 in France.
Painter.

In 1948 Intini settled in Paris, where he exhibited at various salons: Salon des Artistes Français, Salon d'Art Libre, Salon des Indépendants and Salon Comparaisons. He also exhibited in group exhibitions at the museums of Villeneuve-sur-Lot in 1981 and Beauvais in 1986, at the Institut de France in 1987, and at the museums of Tokyo, Osaka and Kyoto in 1986 and 1987. Since 1965 he has had solo shows in Italy, Paris and the USA. Since 1967, while remaining faithful to the demands of rigorous drawing and quality, his paintings have been in the trompe-l'oeil style of the 18th century, but have introduced contemporary elements: modern objects made of plastic or rusted material, imitations of collages and posters.

INUI, Nan Yo
Japanese, 20th century.
Painter.

Inui featured in the exhibition *L'Art japonais*, held in 1929 at the Musée du Jeu de Paume in Paris.

INUKAI, Kyohei
American, 20th century.
Born 1913; died 1985.
Painter, sculptor. Figures, portraits, landscapes with figures.

Kyohei Inukai studied art at the Chicago Art Institute, National Academy of Design and Art Students League in New York City. He lived and worked chiefly in New York City. He used steel and aluminium for his sculptural work.

AUCTION RECORDS:

NEW YORK, 26 May 1988, *Portrait of a Woman* (1932, oil on canvas, 60 x 48 ins / 152.5 x 122 cm) USD 18,700. NEW YORK, 28 Sept 1989, *The Sloping Path* (1911, oil on canvas, 42 x 57 1/4 ins / 106.5 x 145.5 cm) USD 4,400. NEW YORK, 14 March 1991, *Women Bathing in a Wood* (oil on canvas, 12 x 15 ins / 30.5 x 38.3 cm) USD 12,100. NEW YORK, 12 March 1992, *The Blue Waters* (oil on canvas, 24 x 30 ins / 61 x 76.3 cm) USD 6,600. NEW YORK, 15 Nov 1993, *Still-life with an Oriental Statuette and a Necklace on a Draped Table* (1936, oil on canvas, 27 x 21 ins / 68.5 x 53.2 cm) USD 2,300. NEW YORK, 24 Feb 1995, *Hackney Cab in a Park* (oil on canvas, 24 x 30 ins / 61 x 76.2 cm) USD 4,600. SAN FRANCISCO, 22 April 1999, *Grain Silos, Amarillo, Texas* (oil on canvas, 40 x 50 ins / 102 x 128 cm) USD 3,250. NEW YORK, 15 June 2000, *Portrait of Dorothy Hampton* (1933, oil on canvas, 36 x 30 ins / 91 x 76 cm) USD 4,000. BOLTON, 31 Jan 2002, *Along the River* (oil on canvas, 8 x 10 ins / 20 x 25 cm) USD 1,700.

INUMAKI, Kenji

Japanese, 20th century.
Born 1943, in Osaka.
Painter, engraver, sculptor.

Inumaki studied sculpture at the teacher training college in Kyoto. After completing his studies, he turned to two-dimensional art, fascinated by problems of pictorial and surface space. His art claims to be neutral in the repetition of simple forms, but proves to be quite attractive beneath an apparent dryness. Lines of movement, created from the clever play of medium on the monochrome surface, break up the austere appearance. He has taken part in numerous group exhibitions since 1967: in 1965 in the ninth exhibition of contemporary Japanese art at the metropolitan gallery in Tokyo; in 1970 in the Tokyo Biennale and in the exhibition held at the museum of modern art in Tokyo; in 1971 in the Kyoto Biennale and in *First Contemporary Japanese Graphics* at the Institute of Contemporary Art in London; in 1973 in the Paris Biennale, for which he executed an abstract work in situ; in 1974 at the Kunsthalle in Düsseldorf; in 1975 at the museum of modern art in Hyogo; and in 1976 at the municipal art museum in Tokyo. Inumaki has also displayed his works in solo exhibitions, notably in Tokyo and Kyoto since 1969 and in Osaka since 1973.

INURRIA Y LAINOSA, Mateo

Spanish, 19th - 20th century.
Born 24 March 1866, in Cordova; died 21 February 1924, in Madrid.
Sculptor. Figures. Busts.

MUSEUMS AND GALLERIES:

MADRID: *Lucius Seneca* (plaster); *Coal Mine* (plaster); *Female Torso*.

INVENTORY

British, 20th century.
Performance artists.

Inventory is a multi-disciplinary group founded in 1995 by artists, writers and theoreticians who explore contemporary urban life within a framework of what they term 'fierce sociology'.

Inventory functions on different levels. It publishes a magazine, organises events, exhibitions and performance art. In *Coagulum (Oxford Street)* they formed into a close group on London's Oxford Street, thus disrupting the flow of pedestrians, before entering a shopping centre and dancing to piped jazz music. In their exhibition *Requiem for the Empty Quarter* held at The Approach in London, they urged visitors to evacuate the city.

The group has taken part in various exhibitions, including *Beck's Futures 2003*, which presented the work of the nine artists shortlisted for the Beck's Prize, held at the ICA in London, the CCA in Glasgow and the Southampton City Art Gallery in 2003.

INVREA D'IVREA, Fabio

Italian, 20th century.
Born in Genoa.
Sculptor.

Invrea d'Ivrea has exhibited at the Paris Salon des Indépendants.

INZA, Joaquin X., or Ynza

Spanish, 18th - 19th century.
Painter. Portraits.

The academy of jurisprudence in Madrid has a *Portrait of King Charles III* by Joaquin Inxa. His *Portrait of a Woman* appeared in the retrospective portrait exhibition in Madrid in 1920. As a portraitist, he is considered to be a precursor of Goya.

IOANA

Romanian, 20th century.
Born in Bucharest.
Active in France from c. 1950.
Painter.

Ioana studied in Bucharest, partly at the French Institute. She left Romania in 1947 after publishing two slim volumes of poetry. In Stuttgart she worked in the studio of Willy Baumeister, then went to Paris to study at the Académie de la Grande Chaumière. From 1949 she spent a period of three years in Latin America, an event that had an important influence on her work.

Her artistic career has two different aspects. On the one hand, she used old pieces of specially prepared wood to create what she called 'icons', representing figures and episodes from the Bible. Although painted in an Informal Abstract style, the colours of these works evoke the sumptuous richness of Byzantine art. On the other hand in her 'profane' output, the structure and harmonies of each new work are inspired by the instinct of the moment. At first she tended to paint on a small scale, leading Ionel Jianou to describe her as 'Paul Klee's naughty little sister'. Later, she began to produce larger works, such as *Outbreaks of Joy* and *Cosmic Messages*, on canvases sometime covered in plaster into which she traced rhythmical lines enclosing fields of brilliant colour.

Ioana's work is highly expressive, relaying her moods and emotions through spontaneous action, blending lines, signs and cheerful eruptions of colour. Although geometric elements are lacking in her works, she does not belong to the Lyrical Abstract style since she is able to reconcile her spontaneous exuberance with a controlled formal structure, but one that is ever fresh and new.

Collective exhibitions include: Salon d'Automne; Salon Comparaisons; Salon des Femmes Peintres et Sculpteurs; Salon de Mai (1960); Germany; Italy; Switzerland; and the USA. Solo exhibitions include: Rome (1959); Museum of Modern Art, Caracas (1960); Milan (1961); Copenhagen (1962); Florence (1963); London (1964); Munich (1965); Brussels (1966); Luxembourg (1967); Venice (1968); Liège (1969); Galerie Jourdan, Paris and Dalles Hall, Bucharest (1970); Turin and Milan (1971); Paris (1972); Galerie Bellechasse, Paris (1973); Munich (1975); Galerie Rayomonde Cazenave, Paris (1978); Philadelphia (1983). She was awarded a number of prizes including the Valery Larbaud Prize (1968).

BIBLIOGRAPHY:

Jianou, Ionel, *Romanian Artists and the West*, American Romanian Academy of Arts and Sciences, Los Angeles, 1986.

AUCTION RECORDS:
PARIS, 23 March 1991, *Holy Week* (oil on canvas, 39 1/4 x 39 1/4 ins / 100 x 100 cm) FRF 7,000.

IOANID, Ion, or Ionid
Romanian, 20th century.
Born 1884, in Bucharest.
Painter. Genre scenes, figures.

MUSEUMS AND GALLERIES:
BUCHAREST (Muz. National de Arta al României): *Woman Reading.*

IOANN
Russian, 17th century.
Active in Vologda.
Icon painter.

Ioann painted pictures of saints for the Spaso-Nuromsky Monastery: in 1682 a *Legend of the Cross*, and in 1688 an icon of *St Sergei Obnorsky*.

IOANN
Russian, 17th century.
Engraver (wood).

Ioann is known for the following engravings: ornamental plates for a 1711 Kiev gospel book, the frontispiece for *Christ's Crown* (Kiev, 1688) representing the *Last Judgment*; a *Holy Trinity* and *Christ Distributing Crowns to Saints and Martyrs*; and *Christ and the Woman Taken in Adultery*, from the same book.

IOANN, Spassitev Fryazin
Russian, 15th century.
Icon painter.

Spassitev Fryazin Ioann was the Chaplain of the Augustinians. Certain paintings in the Cathedral of the Dormition are attributed to him.

IOANNES, Siroupolos
Russian, 15th century.
Icon painter.

An icon by Siroupolos Ioannes, in Graeco-Italian style, is in the Russian Museum, St Petersburg.

IOANNIKI
Russian, 17th century.
Active in Yaroslavl.
Icon painter.

An icon of *St Demetrius of Salonika* in the church at Yaroslavl consecrated to that saint in 1671, and a *Holy Virgin* on the outside wall of the church of St Demetrius in Smolensk are attributed to Ioanniki.

IOANOU, George
Greek, 20th century.
Born 1932, in Athens.
Painter.

Ioanou has exhibited work in Athens since 1959. He took part in the 1970 Venice Biennale.

His paintings are narratives, created by a mixture of the techniques and aesthetics of strip cartoons and cinematic images as used in Pop Art.

IOASAPH
Greek, 19th century.
Died 1882.
Painter.

Ioasaph was the head of a small school known as the 'Brothers of Ioasaph', whose aim was to preserve, as strictly as possible, the old Byzantine tradition of painting. He is probably identical to the painter of the same name who lived in the Esphigmenos Monastery on Mount Athos. He worked in the Kenasia Monastery, Mount Athos.

IOBEN. See **KOBEN**

IOCHO. See **JOCHO**

IOGANSON, Boris Vladimirovich, or Johanson
Russian, 20th century.
Born 1893, in Moscow; died 1973, in Moscow.
Painter. Stage sets.
Socialist Realism.

Boris Ioganson studied first with Petr Ivanovich Kelin before attending the institute of painting, sculpture and architecture in Moscow from 1912 to 1918

He is considered to be one of the most important representatives of Socialist Realism; the subjects and the style of his relatively few works conform to the directives of the official line. Ioganson also wrote on painting and designed a number of theatre sets. A member of the USSR Academy of Arts, he was its president from 1958 to 1962.

BIBLIOGRAPHY:
Sokoleva, Natalya, *Boris Ioganson*, Aurora Art Publishing, Leningrad, 1982.

MUSEUMS AND GALLERIES:
MOSCOW (State Tretyakov Gal.): *Interrogation of Communists* (1933).

IOHMANN. See **JOHMANN Eugène**

IOKEI. See **JOKEI**

IOKI, Bunsai
Japanese, 19th century.
Born 1863; died 1906.
Painter, watercolourist.

Ioki was born in Mita, and studied Western styles of painting in Tokyo. He was the pupil of Takahashi Yuichi, Takahashi Genkichi, Asai Chu and Koyama Shotaro. He was known as a botanical painter specialising in flora.

AUCTION RECORDS:
LONDON, 31 March 1978, *The Toshogu Temple at Nikko* (1898, oil on canvas, 26 1/2 x 35 1/2 ins / 67.2 x 90 cm) GBP 900. NEW YORK, 16 Oct 1990, *Nikko* (watercolour/paper, 19 1/4 x 13 ins / 49 x 32.8 cm) USD 12,100. LONDON, 19 Feb 2003, *Group of Figures Taking Respite in the Gardens of Nikko* (watercolour, 13 x 19 ins / 32 x 48 cm) GBP 2,200. EDINBURGH, 10 June 2004, *Outside a Japanese Temple* (watercolour, 26 x 20 ins / 66 x 50 cm) GBP 1,100.

IOLLO, Domenico. See **JOLLO**

IOMMI, Enio
Argentinian, 20th century.
Born 1926, in Rosario.
Sculptor.
Neo-Constructivism.
Arte Concreto Invención Group.

Enio Iommi trained with his father, a sculptor and engraver of Italian origin. He was one of the founders of the Arte Concreto Invención group in Buenos Aires and in 1960 took part in the international exhibition of Art Concret in Zurich. A retrospective of his work was held at the fine arts museum of Buenos Aires in 1963.

Iommi developed from constructivist figures to assemblages formed of reclaimed objects or rough stone, sometimes strongly marked by geometric form. In the early 1980s he returned to more structured works, which he integrated into urban landscapes.

MUSEUMS AND GALLERIES:
BUENOS AIRES (MAM) - GRENOBLE - RIO DE JANEIRO (MAM).

AUCTION RECORDS:
NEW YORK, 17 Nov 1994, *Construction* (1948, bronze, h. 11 ins / 27 cm) USD 9,200. NEW YORK, 25-26 Nov 1996, *Interrupted Continuity* (1946, steel and marble, h. 17 3/4 ins / 45.4 cm) USD 12,650. BUENOS AIRES, 18 Aug 2004, *Untitled* (1974, alu-

minium, h. 38 ins / 96 cm) USD 8,500. BUENOS AIRES, 5 Oct 2004, *Untitled* (1978, tin and aluminium, h. 21 ins / 54 cm) USD 5,500.

IONA
Russian, 18th century.
Active at the beginning of the 18th century.
Painter, engraver. Icons.

A monk at the Alexander Nevsky Lavra, Iona painted a canvas of *St Dimitri Rostovsky and his miracles*, and engraved a full-figure portrait of *St Alexander Nevsky holding a lance and trampling on a crown.*

IONESCO, Eugène
Romanian, 20th century.
Born 1912, in Slatina; died 1994.
Active and naturalised in France.
Painter, draughtsman.

Eugène Ionesco was the son of a Romanian father and a French mother. He lived in France until the age of 13 when he spent some time in Romania before settling permanently in France in 1938. A writer of avant-garde plays and novels that earned him both praise and scorn, his dramatic works - along with those of Samuel Beckett - marked a profound change in contemporary theatre. He was elected to the Académie Française on 22 January 1970 and was for a long time the most-performed playwright there.

He was also something of an artist and he exhibited some of his coloured drawings in 1971 in Biarritz, Paris and Stockholm. They depict figures that seem to have stepped out of his plays, or childlike outlines of hybrid beings, half-human and half-animal.

BIBLIOGRAPHY:
'Eugène Ionesco, un regard sur le monde' in *Art et Métiers du Livre* n° 178 p. 38, periodical, Paris, 1993.

IONESCO, Nicolas
Romanian, 20th century.
Born 1919, in Bucharest.
Active in France from 1946.
Painter.
Nouvelle Figuration.

After studying at the school of fine art in Bucharest, Nicolas Ionesco took part in several exhibitions in Bucharest. He went to Paris in 1946 and worked at the Académie André Lhote and then with Fernand Léger.

From 1949, his work moved increasingly towards Abstraction. He was close to Dewasne and Pillet and also knew Herbin. In the 1960s, his work underwent another change, moving closer to Pop Art.

He exhibited at the Salon des Réalités Nouvelles (1956 and 1957). Later, in 1965, his work featured in the Pop Art exhibition *La Figuration Narrative*, organised by Gérald Gassiot-Talabot. He held a solo exhibition in Paris in 1952.

IONESCU, Gina
Romanian, 20th century.
Born 28 May 1916, in Borsa (Maramures).
Active in Argentina.
Painter.
Grupo Madì.

After qualifying at the academy of fine art in Budapest in 1944, Gina Ionescu went to Paris to study at the Académie Julian from 1946 to 1947. In 1947, she moved to Buenos Aires. She belonged to the first avant-garde group in Argentina, Madí, and also to the Arte Nuevo and Arte No Figurativo groups. She produces works in cycles consisting of compositions whose strong structures are derived from the handling of the colours, the overall effect being very striking.

She has taken part in many collective exhibitions, particularly in Latin America. She has held solo exhibitions, since 1949, in Argentina, Brazil, the USA, France, Italy and Japan.

BIBLIOGRAPHY:
Romanian Artists and the West, American Romanian Academy of Arts and Sciences, Los Angeles, 1986.

IONESCU-CALINESCU, Crina
Romanian, 20th century.
Born 1939, in Bucharest.
Engraver, illustrator.

Crina Ionescu-Calinescu graduated in graphic art at the Nicolae Grigorescu Institute of Fine Arts in Bucharest in 1962. She is mainly known for her illustrations of children's books

She has taken part in several International Book Exhibitions including: Leipzig (1966); Belgrade (1969); Bologna (1970-1972). She has held exhibitions of her graphic works in Gaeta (1970) and Bucharest (1971 and 1974). She has been awarded 1st, 2nd and 3rd Prizes for her posters by the Romanian Institute of Cinematography and is a member of the Union of Fine Arts of Romania and of the UNESCO International Association of Fine Arts.

IORDAN, Fedor Ivanovich
Russian, 19th century.
Born 1800, in Pavlovsk; died 1883, in St Petersburg.
Engraver (burin).

Fedor Ivanovich Iordan's godmother, the Empress Maria Fedorovna, had him trained in the academy of arts, where in 1824 he won a medal for his plate *Mercury and Argus* and in 1829 for *Death of Abel*. The same year, he went to Paris to work with Richomme. After the July Revolution, he moved to London, where he worked under Raimbach. In 1835, he went on to Rome, working there until 1850. During his time there, he did an engraving of *Raphael's Transfiguration*. Returning to St Petersburg, he remained there for three years before returning to Italy once more, where he stayed two years. As a member of the academy of art in St Petersburg, he was Curator of prints in the Hermitage Museum. In 1871, he was appointed Rector of the academy. Iordan mainly engraved the work of Russian artists, although he is also known for a *Holy Family* (after Raphael), a *Raphael and Perugino* (after Perugino), and a *Pietà* (after Cigoli).

IORGULESCO-YAR
Romanian, 20th century.
Born 1890, in Romania; died before 1940.
Painter.

Iorgulesco-Yar was a representative of Romanian pictorial lyricism and is often referred to by Romanian critics.

IORI, Diego
Italian, 18th century.
Active in Carrara.
Sculptor.

In 1772, together with his pupil, Pompeo Franchi, Iori carved the marble statues of an *Assumption, St John the Evangelist, Holy Martyr*, and the bishops *Hugo de Lincoln* and *Anselme de Belley*. These works were undertaken in accordance with the sketches by P. Giarré and were for the façade of the Charterhouse in Calzi near Pisa. He also carved the statues of *Faith* and *Hope* with the coat of arms of the Charterhouse.

IORIS, Pio. See **JORIS**

IOSETSU. See **JOSETSU**

IOSSIF
Russian, 17th century.
Icon painter.

A monk at Makarii Unzhensky Monastery, Iossif painted an icon of the *Holy Virgin* still preserved there. He also helped with painting a number of other icons for the same monastery.

IOSTE
20th century.
Painter.
Ioste showed work at the Salon Découvertes, Discoveries, in Paris in 1992.

IOTTI, Carlo. See **JOTTI**

IOUON, Constantin Fedorovitch. See **YUON Konstantin Federovitch**

IPAS, Pascual de
Spanish, 18th century.
Sculptor.
Pascual de Ipas studied at the Real Academia de San Fernando and received a commendation from the academy for his relief of *The Entombment of Mary*. He worked on the decoration of the dome of the chapel of the Virgin at Nuestra Señora del Pilar in Saragossa. He also executed four large stucco medallions for the royal mausoleum at the church of the monastery of S Juan de la Pena near Huesca; the medallions depict the military exploits of García Jiménez, Iñigo Arista and Sancho Ramírez and the monarchs of Aragon taking the oath of loyalty.

IPEAU, Mireille
French, 20th century.
Born 7 April 1922, in Tunis.
Painter. Landscapes.
Mireille Ipeau became a member of the Salon d'Automne in Paris in 1959. Her work is figurative in the traditional sense. She exhibited at the Salon, in addition to various other art fairs in the suburbs of Paris.

IPHION OF CORINTH
Painter.
Ancient Greek.

IPOLD, Rudolf
Austrian, 19th - 20th century.
Born 23 December 1873, in Vienna.
Miniaturist.
Rudolf Ipold attended the Hochschule für Angewandte Kunst in Vienna, and also the Akademie der Bildenden Künste. In 1907, he devoted himself exclusively to painting portrait miniatures. His output comprises more than 1,000 portraits, including portraits of the Emperor Charles and the Empress Zita; Grand-Duke Frederik's family; the Grand-Duchess in coronation robes; and prominent figures from American, English, Italian, French and Austrian society.

IPOLY, Sandor
Hungarian, 19th century.
Born 1858, in Budapest; died 30 November 1902, in Budapest.
Engraver (wood), painter.
Sandor Ipoly was a student at the academy in Budapest and later at the Académie Julian and Académie Colarossi in Paris. His first large painting, *Family Happiness*, signed *Janicsek*, was shown at the Budapest exhibitions in 1891. In Budapest, he also painted the large canvases *Christ and St Thomas, Dante and Beatrice* and *The Genius of Franz Erkel*.

IPOUSTÉGUY, Jean, or Jean-Robert
French, 20th century.
Born 6 January 1920, in Dun-sur-Meuse (Meuse).
Sculptor, painter, collage artist, draughtsman, illustrator. Figures, still-lifes. Monuments, groups.
In 1938, Jean Ipoustéguy took evening classes in drawing from the city of Paris, studying in the workshop of Robert Lesbounit. He took up sculpture in 1949 and was taught by Henri Georges Adam. For a time, he was influenced by Picasso and especially by Brancusi's approach to Abstraction. In 1977, he received the Grand Prix National des Arts, and was made a Chevalier of the Légion d'Honneur in 1984. In addition to being a painter, he has also produced books, poetry and films. He has executed a variety of public commissions, most notably *Man Forcing Unity* at the Institut Langevin Max von Lave in Grenoble in 1971; *Man Building his City* in Berlin in 1980; *Le Val-de-Grâce* (*Valley of Grace*) at the Val-de-Grâce hospital in Paris in 1983; *The Part-Dieu Fountain* in Lyons in 1987; and *To the Health of the Revolution* in Bagnolet in 1988. In 1947-1948, he executed several mural frescoes, and worked on the windows, at the church of St-Jacques in Montrouge.

Ipoustéguy's sculpture is not easily accessible. It is more easily understood through psychoanalysis than aesthetics. However, in his first works, up until about 1960 (*Helmeted Head, Falcon Head* and *Du Guesclin*) he was decidedly figurative. In some cases, particularly in his portrayal of the sculptor son in *The Death of the Father*, he resorted to a highly academic representation. Yet this figurativeness occurred within the context of an accumulation of disparate elements, going far beyond the most imaginable Baroque. Such examples include his *Discourse on Mistra* of 1964-1965, in which a realistic figure delivers what is perhaps a diatribe from a pile of rocky blocks, atop which lies a great god chiselled in stone. *Death of the Father*, 1968, in addition to a great extended, convulsive form on a catafalque, includes the black steel head of the dead father under a mitre and chasuble in Carrara marble. The sculptor son, life-size, with hammer in hand, is immortalising the father as pope. There are also many other heads of popes in white marble - the real popes, their faces horribly deformed.

Ipoustéguy exhibited as a painter in Paris in 1943-1944 at the Salon des Moins de Trente Ans and in 1951 at the Salon de la Société Nationale des Beaux-Arts. As a sculptor, he exhibited in Paris at numerous salons, including: from 1943 to 1950 at the Moins de Trente Ans; in 1949 at the Salon d'Automne; from 1956 to 1957, from 1959 to 1963 and from 1965 to1967 at the Salon de Mai; in 1958 at the Salon des Réalités Nouvelles and at the Salon de la Jeune Sculpture. He also took part in the Antwerp-Middelheim Biennale in 1961; the Venice Biennale (where he received the Bright Prize) and the 1964 Documenta in Kassel and was shown at the Guggenheim Museum in New York. He participated in the Biennales in Tokyo and São Paulo; in the 1967 exhibitions at the Art Institute of Chicago and the Carnegie Institute in Pittsburgh; at the Institute of Contemporary Art in London in 1968, and in the same year at the 1st international exhibition of original drawings in Rijeka. He showed at the Fundação Calouste Gulbenkian in Lisbon in 1971 and 1979; at the 3rd international Biennale of small sculpture in Budapest in 1973; in 1976 and 1977 at the Musée d'Art Moderne and the Musée National d'Art Moderne in Paris; at the Kunstverein in Darmstadt in 1980; in 1983 at the Musée Galerie de la Seita (the tobacco museum) in Paris; at the Musée de l'Art et de l'Industrie in St-Étienne, and at the Art Fair in Chicago. He showed at the Kunsthalle in Darmstadt in 1986 and at the Musée Cantini in Marseilles in 1988.

Ipoustéguy has had solo exhibitions of his work in Paris, including: in 1954 and 1957, and from 1962, at the Galerie Claude Bernard; in 1965 at the Städtisches Museum für Moderne Kunst; in the 1970 travelling exhibition organised by the city of Darmstadt at the Badischer Kunstverein in Karlsruhe, the Von Der Heydt Museum in Wuppertal, the Kunsthalle in Basel and at the Nationalgalerie in Berlin; in 1978 at the Fondation Nationale des Arts Plastiques et

Graphiques in Paris; in 1979 at the Kunsthalle in Berlin, the Musée Ingres in Montauban and the Musée des Beaux-Arts in Pau; in 1982 at the Musée des Beaux-Arts in Lyons and the Musée d'Art Moderne in Paris; in 1989 at the Heitland Foundation in Celles; and in 2001, at the exhibition of sculpture in marble in Dun-sur-Meuse.

BIBLIOGRAPHY:

Ipoustéguy: 14 July 29 August, 1964, exhibition catalogue, Hanover Gallery, London, 1964. *Ipoustéguy*, exhibition catalogue, Galerie Claude Bernard, Paris, 1966. *Ipoustéguy, marbres*, exhibition catalogue, Galerie Claude Bernard, Paris, 1968. *Ipoustéguy; études anatomiques, dessins*, exhibition catalogue, Galerie Claude Bernard, Paris, 1969. Ipoustéguy, Jean/Glucksmann, André, *Jean Ipoustéguy*, exhibition catalogue, Gal. Claude Bernard, Paris, April 1969. *Ipousétguy: tactiles*, exhibition catalogue, Galerie Claude Bernard, Paris, 1972. *Ipoustéguy*, exhibition catalogue, Galerie Artel, Geneva, 1974. *Ipoustéguy: Suite prussienne Berlin, 1973-1974*, exhibition catalogue, Galerie Claude Bernard, Paris, 1975. *Ipoustéguy*, A. Pauli, Lausanne, 1979. *Dans le noir et sous la lune: Ipoustéguy: fusains 1978-1979*, exhibition catalogue, Gaerie Claude Bernard, Paris, 1981. Croiset-Veyre, Dominique (ed.), *Ipoustéguy. Catalogue raisonné 1938-2000*, La Différence, Paris, 2001. '*Écrire de la poésie, dessiner, voilà un amusement perpétuel. Interview*' in *Libération*, periodical, Paris, 1st July 2001.

MUSEUMS AND GALLERIES:

DARMSTADT (Kunsthalle): *The Val de Grace* - DUN-SUR-MEUSE (Church): *The Death of Bishop Neumann* - LONDON (Tate Collection): *Earth* (1962, bronze, sculpture) - MARSEILLES (Mus. Cantini): *Flayed* (1976, bronze) - NEW YORK (MoMA): *David and Goliath* (1959) - PARIS (MNAM-CCI): *Alexander Before Ecbatan* (1965) - PITTSBURGH (Carnegie MA): *David* (1959, bronze).

AUCTION RECORDS:

NEW YORK, 4 March 1972, *Sketch of Ecbatan* (bronze) USD 4,000. PARIS, 17 Nov 1972, *Mycenas* (1960) FRF 9,000. PARIS, 30 Nov 1974, *The Crab and the Bird* (1958) FRF 24,000. NEW YORK, 28 May 1976, *Forms* (black-patinated bronze, in three parts) USD 1,500. PARIS, 29 June 1977, *Du Guesclin* (1959, bronze, 9 x 24 3/4 ins / 23 x 63 cm) FRF 22,000. LONDON, 3 July 1980, *The King of the Martians* (1961, bronze, h. 10 ins / 25.5 cm) GBP 1,400. NEW YORK, 18 May 1983, *Reclining Nude Woman* (dark-brown-patinated bronze, l. 9 3/4 ins / 25 cm) USD 5,000. LONDON, 28 May 1986, *The Man Pushing the Door* (1966, bronze, 77 1/2 x 51 1/4 x 35 ins / 197 x 130 x 89 cm) GBP 41,000. PARIS, 3 Oct 1988, *The Pediment* (1962, brown-patinated bronze, 10 1/2 x 17 3/4 x 6 1/4 ins / 26.5 x 45 x 16 cm) FRF 65,000. NEW YORK, 7 May 1990, *David and Goliath* (black-patinated bronze, in four parts, 48 x 21 x 23 1/2 ins / 122 x 53.3 x 59.8 cm; 18 x 19 x 26 ins/45.6 x 48.2 x 66 cm; 18 1/2 x 17 x 20 ins/47 x 43.2 x 51 cm; 30 x 26 x 53 ins/76.2 x 66 x 134.5 cm) USD 31,900. PARIS, 2 July 1990, *Nude in the Wave* (1966, oil on canvas, 21 1/4 x 25 1/2 ins / 54 x 65 cm) FRF 18,000. LONDON, 18 Oct 1990, *Man* (1963, bronze, h. 79 ins / 200.5 cm) GBP 50,600. PARIS, 2 Dec 1991, *Du Guesclin* (1961, bronze, 9 1/2 x 12 x 12 ins / 24 x 30.5 x 30.5 cm) FRF 16 000. NEW YORK, 25-26 Feb 1992, *Head* (1958, oil and collage of paper/card, 28 1/2 x 24 ins / 72.4 x 61 cm) USD 1,650. COPENHAGEN, 20 May 1992, *Head of a Man* (1966, bronze, h. 21 1/4 ins / 54 cm) DKK 32,000. PARIS, 22 Dec 1992, *The Hand and the Colour* (1967, watercolour, 20 1/2 x 17 1/4 ins / 52.2 x 44 cm) FRF 4,600. NEW YORK, 22 Feb 1993, *Moving Shadow* (green-patinated bronze, 14 x 37 1/2 x 8 1/2 ins / 35.5 x 95.2 x 21.6 cm) USD 5,500. AMSTERDAM, 8 Dec 1993, *Abstract Composition* (lost-wax bronze, 6 1/4 x 6 1/4 x 4 1/2 ins / 16 x 16 x 11.2 cm) NLG 1,725. NEW YORK, 5 May 1994, *Helmeted Head* (1959, bronze, 14 x 11 x 19 ins / 35.6 x 27.9 x 48.3 cm) USD 2,990. ZURICH, 17-18 June 1996, *Ectaban* (1965, bronze, h. 11 3/4 ins / 30 cm, l. 22 ins/55 cm) CHF 2,800. NEW YORK, 19 Nov 1996, *Cuirassier* (bronze, 7 1/2 x 4 ins / 19 x 10 cm, 3/4 x 4 1/2 ins/2 x 11.4 cm) USD 633. PARIS, 21 Nov 1997, *Birth* (1970, marble, sculpture in three parts, 18 x 14 1/4 x 24 3/4 ins / 46 x 36 x 63 cm) FRF 39,000. PARIS, 15 Dec 1997, *Torso of a Woman* (1967, charcoal and pastel/paper, 29 1/4 x 20 3/4 ins / 74 x 53 cm) FRF 4,500. HAMBURG, 3 Dec 1999, *Mother. Of Virgin and Mother* (1958, red-brown patinated bronze) DEM 26,000. COPENHAGEN, 1 Oct 2002, *Bust Surrounded by Box* (1966, bronze, 21 x 13x12 ins / 54 x 33x30 cm) DKK 35,000. NEUILLY, 7 Nov 2002, *Nude Woman, Arms on her Bust* (patinated bronze, h. 14 ins / 36 cm) EUR 4,300. PARIS, 29 April 2003, *Breast Shadow* (bronze, 18 x 12x7 ins / 45 x 30x17 cm) EUR 1,500. NEW YORK, 12 Feb 2004, *Helmeted Head* (dark brown patinated bronze, 16 x 21 ins / 41 x 53 cm) USD 6,500. PARIS, 19 March 2004, *Mobile Mask* (1966, black patinated bronze) EUR 5,900.

IPPO, real name: Mori Keishi; nickname: Shiko, Bumpei; pseudonym: Ippo
Japanese, 19th century.
Born 1798, in Osaka; died 2 January 1871.
Painter.

Ippo was the disciple of his adoptive father Mori Tetsuzan, and followed the Realist tendency of Maruyama Okyo (1733-1795) and his school. In 1854, after the fire at the imperial palace in Kyoto, he was summoned to decorate the sliding doors (*fusuma*) in the new palace, where he depicted pines. A painter of figures, flowers and birds, he is also remembered for his *Twelve Views of Kyoto*.

MUSEUMS AND GALLERIES:

LONDON (British Mus.).

IPPOLIT
Russian, 17th century.
Monk, sculptor (wood).

Ippolit was considered one of the best sculptors in wood of his time. In 1679, he sculpted a cedar crucifix for the Voskreseniya Slovushchevo church, and did projects for the decorative ceramics for the Verkhospassky Cathedral in the Kremlin.

IPPOLITI, Maria
Italian, 19th - 20th century.
Born in Udine.
Painter, miniaturist. Landscapes.

Ippoliti was a pupil at the Accademia di Belle Arti, Venice, where she settled. Among the paintings she exhibited at various exhibitions are: *At St Mark's*, shown in Venice in 1897, *Winter Evening* in Turin in 1898, and *Evening Rest* at the Glaspalast, Munich, in 1901. She also exhibited works in Venice in 1902 and at the Paris Salon des Artistes Français in 1914.

IPPOLITO, Angelo
Italian, 20th century.
Born 1922, near Salerno; died 2001.
Active in the USA.
Painter.

Angelo Ippolito emigrated at an early age to the USA and studied at the Ozenfant School of Fine Art, New York, and the Brooklyn Museum Art School. In 1959 he was awarded a Fulbright Scholarship that enabled him to work in Rome and Florence. He taught at Yale and California universities and at the Cooper Union. He exhibited at many group exhibitions: the annual shows of the Whitney Museum, New York; the Carnegie International, Pittsburgh; the Museum of Modern Art, Rome; the Walker Art Center, Minneapolis; and others. He also gave solo shows in Bergamo, New York and at the Cleveland Art Institute.

MUSEUMS AND GALLERIES:

NEW YORK (Whitney Mus. of American Art).

IPPOLITO DA FIRENZE (Padre)
Italian, 17th century.
Active in Florence c. 1680.
Miniaturist.
Ippolito da Firenze belonged to the Order of the Capuchins.

IPPYOTEI, Yoshikuni
Japanese, 19th century.
Master engraver.
MUSEUMS AND GALLERIES:
PARIS (Mus. National des Arts asiatiques-Guimet): several works.

IPSEN, Ernest Ludwig
American, 19th - 20th century.
Born 5 September 1869, in Malden (Massachusetts); died 1951.
Painter. Portraits.
Ernest Ludwig Ipsen studied at the Museum School in Boston and the Kunstakademi in Copenhagen. He was a member of the American Arts Federation. He won a prize awarded for the best portrait by the National Academy of Design, New York, in 1921. He painted the portraits of many American personalities.
AUCTION RECORDS:
LOS ANGELES, 24 June 1980, *The Road to Ponnegannsett* (oil on canvas, 20 x 14 ins / 50.8 x 35.5 cm) USD 1,300. NEW YORK, 11 March 1993, *Still-life with Teapot* (1892, oil on canvas, 14 x 20 ins / 35.3 x 51 cm) USD 2,070. NEW YORK, 15 Nov 1993, *Landscape to the South of Dartmouth* (1907, oil on card, 10 1/2 x 14 ins / 26.5 x 35.5 cm) USD 1,725. LOS ANGELES, 9 Dec 1999, *Black Red Gold, Edith Boyden Crocker Ipsen* (1929, oil on canvas, 80 x 42 ins / 203 x 107 cm) USD 6,000. ORANGE, 11 Jan 2000, *Portrait of Young Woman Seated with Two Dogs* (1912, oil on canvas, 81 x 39 ins / 206 x 99 cm) USD 5,500. BOSTON, 12 May 2000, *Schooner in Dry Dock* (1911, oil on canvas, 30 x 20 ins / 76 x 51 cm) USD 9,500. NEW YORK, 3 Dec 2003, *Gloucester Docks* (1997, oil on canvas, 20 x 16 ins / 50 x 40 cm) USD 14,000.

IPSEN, Jacob
Danish, 18th century.
Born 24 August 1756.
Active in Flensburg.
Painter.
Jacob Ipsen is known to have painted the portraits *Princesses Meklemborg-Schwerin*. He also painted a portrait of the court preacher *Ph. E. Luder* in 1784, which was engraved by F.C. Carstens.

IPSEN, Paul
Danish, 18th century.
Born 27 August 1746 in Flensburg (then in Denmark, now in Schleswig-Holstein, Germany).
Painter, watercolourist, draughtsman. Religious subjects, portraits.
Paul Ipsen painted several religious subjects and executed numerous drawings of portraits in watercolour and red chalk. Several of his works, as well as copper engraved reproductions, are at the Kunstakademi in Copenhagen and the museum in Flensburg.
MUSEUMS AND GALLERIES:
COPENHAGEN (Kunstakademi) - HILLERØD: *C. F. Numsen; Count von Osten; Count J. Scheel; Professor C. G. Kratzenstein.*
AUCTION RECORDS:
COPENHAGEN, 25-26 April 1990, *Portrait of Joh. Nic. Wilhelm Bluhme* (1789, oil on canvas, oval, 20 x 16 1/4 ins / 51 x 41 cm) DKK 9,000.

IPSEN, Poul Janus, or Janus-Ipsen
Danish, 20th century.
Born 1936, in Copenhagen.
Painter. Scenes with figures, figures.
Poul Janus Ipsen was self-taught. In 1962, he made his painting début at the Copenhagen spring Salon held at the Charlottenborg exhibition hall. Since then, he has contributed works to group exhibitions, including: from 1962-1965, the spring and autumn Salons; in 1963, Aarhus; 1967, Oslo, Göteborg and Berlin; 1968, Stockholm; 1969, Stuttgart and London; 1973, *Art Danois 1945-1973* (*Danish Art 1945-1973*) held at the Galeries Nationales du Grand Palais in Paris. The dominant theme in his work is human solitude within the context of the modern world and its anonymity, from which sometimes featureless faces emerge, as if enveloped in mists or bandages, and figures are grabbed from behind by hostile hands.
BIBLIOGRAPHY:
Galy-Carles, Henry, *Art danois, 1945-1973*, exhibition catalogue, Galeries nationales du Grand Palais, Paris, 1973.
MUSEUMS AND GALLERIES:
COPENHAGEN (Statens Mus. for Kunst) - ODENSE - RANDERS.
AUCTION RECORDS:
COPENHAGEN, 25 Sept 1985, *Confrontation* (oil on canvas, 70 3/4 x 57 ins / 180 x 145 cm) DKK 27,000. COPENHAGEN, 4 May 1988, *Piece of Spring* (1963, 28 3/4 x 36 1/4 ins / 73 x 92 cm) DKK 8,000. COPENHAGEN, 10 May 1989, *32nd Street East, New York* (1972, oil on canvas, 39 1/4 x 59 ins / 100 x 150 cm) DKK 18,000. COPENHAGEN, 30 May 1990, *The Arrival III* (1983, acrylic/canvas, 50 1/2 x 36 1/4 ins / 128 x 92 cm) DKK 15,000. COPENHAGEN, 10 March 1993, *32nd Street East, New York* (1972, oil on canvas, 39 1/4 x 47 1/4 ins / 100 x 120 cm) DKK 9,000. COPENHAGEN, 6 Sept 1993, *Composition* (1962, ceramic relief, 34 1/4 x 25 1/2 ins / 87 x 65 cm) DKK 5,000. COPENHAGEN, 6 Dec 1994, *Forbidden Fruit VII* (1987, oil on canvas, triptych, 78 3/4 x 98 ins / 200 x 248 cm) DKK 20,000. COPENHAGEN, 6 Oct 1999, *Getting Up III - On the Way II* (1981, oil on canvas, 68 x 48 ins / 172 x 122 cm) DKK 14,000. COPENHAGEN, 17 June 2003, *They Will Not See* (oil on canvas, 57 x 57 ins / 145 x 145 cm) DKK 17,000.

IPSEN, Reinhold
Danish, 18th century.
Born 27 November 1764.
Active in Flensburg.
Painter.
Reinhold Ipsen painted landscapes and portraits. His portrait *Count W. F. of Schmettau* was engraved by H. Lips.

IPSENROD, Dietrich. See **EPSENROD**

IPSER, Hans Sigismund
Romanian, 20th century.
Born 31 August 1926, in Botosani.
Active in Italy from 1970; also active in Germany from 1976.
Painter, decorative artist. Landscapes, urban views. Stage sets.
Hans Sigismund Ipser was a student at the Bucharest academy of fine art for one year before changing direction and moving to the study of theatre design. He has worked all over Europe, designing sets for more than 100 operas, plays and shows. The theatre gave him a chance to escape from the diktats of Socialist Realism, so that, when it came to easel painting, he was able to develop his own personal style. He painted some very successful views of Rome and Venice. He exhibited his paintings for the first time in San Vito Romano in 1980.
BIBLIOGRAPHY:
Romanian Artists and the West, American Romanian Academy of Arts and Sciences, Los Angeles, 1986.

IRACE, Severo, or Jerace
Italian, 16th century.
Active in Naples.
Painter. History painting.
Irace was a pupil of Marco Calabrese and in 1534 painted a *Virgin Enthroned* for the church of S Pietro e S Paulo, Naples.

IRACEMA, pseudonym of Iracema Arditti
Brazilian, 20th century.
Born 1 February 1924, in São Paulo.
Painter. Landscapes.
Iracema Arditti originally worked in a number of different occupations including typist, journalist and air hostess. She was interested in the popular arts and encouraged naive painters she knew, before becoming a painter herself. Arditti became well known with the return of figurative expression in the 1960s.

She held her first exhibition in São Paulo and Paris in 1965. She has since taken part in several collective exhibitions devoted to naive painting and all forms of popular expression in Brazil and France.

Arditti is considered Brazil's greatest naive painter. She is a painter of vegetation rather than landscape, taking nature, foliage and birds as her theme and painting the jungle in all its luxuriance as both an Eden and a Hell. One of her favourite pieces, *Río Sobrenatural* (*Supernatural River*) is an evocation of this characteristic aspect of Brazil in which water, earth, vegetation and the animal world are intimately blended.
MUSEUMS AND GALLERIES:
LAVAL.

IRALA YUSO, Matias Antonio (Brother), or Ayuso
Spanish, 18th century.
Born 1680, in Madrid; died 1753, in Madrid.
Painter, draughtsman, engraver. History painting.
Matias Irala Yuso came from a rich family from Guipúzcoa. In 1704 he entered the Franciscan monastery in Madrid and decorated the church there. His master works are considered to be a painting of *St Thomas Aquinas* at Alcalá de Henares and one of *St Francis of Paula* in Madrid. He also made engravings and gave lessons in his cell.

IRANZO, Feliciano
Spanish, 19th century.
Born 1781.
Active in Valencia.
Sculptor.
Feliciano Iranzo exhibited in Valencia in 1798, 1801 and 1804, where his work received prizes. One of his pieces is held at the Real Academia de San Carlos.

IRAVALLS, Master of. See **DESTORRENT Ramon**

IRBACH, Sebastian. See **IRRWOCH**

IRBI, Frédéric
Draughtsman, engraver (etching).

IRDI, Salvatore
Italian, 19th century.
Active in Naples during the first half of the 19th century.
Sculptor.
Irdi was a pupil at the royal institute of fine art; he was awarded a scholarship to go to Rome in 1842. He exhibited at the fine art exhibitions of Naples with the following works: 1837, *Faun* and *Discus Thrower*; 1839, *Daedalus and Icarus*, a relief; 1841, *Hunter, Nymph, Samson and Delilah*, a group, and *The Sons of Jacob bringing to their Father the Bloody Tunic of their Brother Joseph*, a relief; 1845, *Innocence*; 1851, *Religion Triumphing over Anarchy with the Help of Pius IX and Ferdinand II*.

IRELAND, David
American, 20th century.
Born 1930, in Bellingham (Washington State).
Engraver, lithographer.
Conceptual Art.
David Ireland was one of the American artists invited to take part in the exhibition of contemporary engraving in Paris in 1995. He prints texts telling of his suspicion of images.

IRELAND, Edward A.
German, 19th century.
Born before 1830, in England; died 13 May 1896, in Düsseldorf.
Painter. Landscapes.
He painted mostly romantic landscapes. In 1861, he showed a picture called *Mill* at the great exhibition of fine arts in Copenhagen, which was bought by the local Society of Artists. In 1870 and 1880, he exhibited at the academy in Berlin, and in 1871 showed a watercolour of a *Turkey* in Munich.

IRELAND, James
British, 19th - 20th century.
Active in Liverpool.
Painter, pastellist. Genre scenes.
James Ireland exhibited in London, notably at the Royal Academy and the Royal Society of Painters in Watercolours, from 1885.
AUCTION RECORDS:
MILAN, 12 Dec 1983, *Child with cherries* (pastel, 17 3/4 x 19 3/4 ins / 45 x 50 cm) FRF 20,000.

IRELAND, Jane
British, 18th - 19th century.
Miniaturist.
Jane Ireland was the daughter of Samuel Ireland. She exhibited her work at the Royal Academy in London in 1792 and 1793.

IRELAND, Leroy
American, 20th century.
Born 24 December 1889, in Philadelphia; died 1970.
Painter. Still-lifes.
Leroy Ireland studied at the Pennsylvania Academy of the Fine Arts in Philadelphia. He lived and worked in New York and was a member of the Salmagundi Club.
MUSEUMS AND GALLERIES:
DALLAS (MA): *The Jade Bowl* (1920, oil on canvas).

IRELAND, Raymond Charley
French, 20th century.
Born 23 July 1882, in St-Cloud (Hauts-de-Seine); died 21 December 1921, in Chamalières.
Sculptor.
Raymond Charley Ireland returned from World War I in 1919. He subsequently exhibited in Paris at the Salon de la Société Nationale des Beaux-Arts and at the Salon des Artistes Français.

IRELAND, Samuel
British, 18th century.
Died 1800, in London.
Active in London.
Watercolourist, draughtsman, engraver.
Samuel Ireland exhibited a drawing and several water colour scenes at the Royal Academy in 1782. He was particularly known for his mezzotint views after various artists or his own drawings, including *A Picturesque Tour Through Holland, Brabant and Part of France* (1790) and *Picturesque*

Views of the River Thames (1792). He also published similar series on the rivers Medway, Avon, Wye and Severn. He also executed reproductions after Hogarth.

IRELAND, Thomas
British, 19th century.
Active in London between 1881 and 1903.
Painter. Landscapes.
Thomas Ireland frequently exhibited his work in London, mainly at the Royal Academy, Suffolk Street, the New Water-Colour Society and the Grosvenor Gallery from 1880.
AUCTION RECORDS:
LONDON, 3 June 1988, *River Landscape in a Silver Birch Wood* (1890, oil on canvas, 27 1/4 x 20 ins / 69.2 x 50.8 cm) GBP 605. LONDON, 18 Jan 2001, *On Margin of River* (1896, oil on panel, 12 x 8 ins / 30 x 20 cm) GBP 1,000.

IRELAND, William
British, 17th century.
Active in London.
Painter. Fruit.
William Ireland exhibited his work at the Society of Artists and the Free Society in London from 1764 to 1783.

IRENE
5th - 4th (?) century BC.
Painter.
Ancient Greek.
Irene was daughter and pupil of Cratinus (Kratinos). She painted the portrait of a young girl, seen by Pliny at Eleusis.
BIBLIOGRAPHY:
Boccacio, Giovanni, *Famous Women*, Harvard University Press, Cambridge, 2002.

IRGANG, Rainer
German, 20th century.
Sculptor.
AUCTION RECORDS:
COPENHAGEN, 20 May 1992, *Untitled* (marble, h. 19 1/4 ins / 49 cm, l. 28 1/4 ins/72 cm) DKK 10,000. COPENHAGEN, 2-3 Dec 1992, *Sculpture* (1977, bronze, h. 19 1/4 ins / 49 cm, w. 23 1/2 ins/60 cm, depth 15 3/4 ins/40 cm) DKK 8,000. COPENHAGEN, 2 March 1994, *Troubled Man* (1975, white marble, h. 9 ins / 23 cm, w. 9 ins/23 cm) DKK 4,500.

IRGENS-BERGH, Thorwald Matthias von
Danish, 19th century.
Born 3 March 1864, in Hirsholm; died 21 August 1899, in the Belgian Congo (now the Democratic Republic of the Congo).
Sculptor.
Thorwald Irgens-Bergh worked as a sculptor in Copenhagen, and in Paris in 1894. From 1893 to 1897 he exhibited in Charlottenborg, making his debut with *Naiad Playing with a Seagull*. He later sculpted busts. There is a portrait in relief by him at the city hall in Copenhagen.

IRHOVEN, H. van
Dutch, 18th century.
Active in 1787.
Draughtsman, silhouettist.

IRIARTE, Ignacio de
Spanish, 17th century.
Born 1621, in Azcoitia; died 1685, in Seville.
Painter. Landscapes.
Ignacio de Iriarte studied art in his own region before coming to Seville around 1642, where he studied under Herrera the Elder. Tradition has it that a lack of aptitude for figure painting led him to turn to landscape and genre painting and he soon acquired a considerable reputation in these fields. In 1646 he is mentioned in Aracena but soon returned to Seville where he became one of the founders of the Seville academy. In 1660 he was secretary to the academy and held this post again from 1667 to 1669. Iriarte was a friend and collaborator of Murillo; in fact Murillo rated him so highly that he often asked him to paint the backgrounds of his paintings. However, a dispute over a series of paintings of the *Life of David* brought their collaboration to an end.
Iriarte occupies an interesting place in the Spanish School and his style shows many similarities with that of Salvator Rosa.
MUSEUMS AND GALLERIES:
MADRID (Prado): *Four Landscapes* - ST PETERSBURG (Hermitage): *The Ford*.
AUCTION RECORDS:
PARIS, 22 May 1925, *Farmyard*, FRF 2,200. MADRID, 27 Feb 1985, *Fantasy Landscape* (oil on canvas, 64 3/4 x 95 1/2 ins / 164.5 x 242.5 cm) ESP 1,840,000.

IRIARTE, Valerio de (Don)
Spanish, 18th century.
Painter. Portraits.
Valerio de Iriarte was appointed as a valuer of old paintings in Madrid in 1725.
MUSEUMS AND GALLERIES:
TOLEDO (Tavera Hospital): *Portrait of Louis I*.

IRIBE, Paul
French, 20th century.
Born 8 June 1883, in Angoulême; died 21 September 1935, in Menton.
Draughtsman, caricaturist, illustrator, designer.
Designs (wallpapers/fabrics/jewels), stage costumes and sets.
Art Deco.
During World War I, Paul Iribe published a periodical entitled *Le Mot* (*The Word*), along with Dufy, Sem, Cocteau, Lhote and others. In 1906, he founded the satirical journal *Le Témoin* (*The Witness*). He later revived it at the beginning of the 1930s, taking on Bolshevism and Hitler. He was one of the chief illustrators of the iconic fashion periodical, *Gazette du Bon Ton* from 1911 to 1925. In addition to being a caricaturist and illustrator, he created jewels, fabrics, wall paper and theatre sets and costumes. He directed three comedic films.
BIBLIOGRAPHY:
Osterwalder, Marcus (ed.), *Dictionnaire des illustrateurs 1800-1914*, Ides et Calendes, Neuchâtel, 1989.
AUCTION RECORDS:
PARIS, 18 Nov 1925, *The Supper*, FRF 600. PARIS, 10 Dec 1980, *Woman at the Window* (gouache, 11 x 9 ins / 27 x 22 cm) FRF 6,200. DOUAI, 26 March 1988, *The Independents* (ink drawing, 9 1/2 x 11 3/4 ins / 24 x 30 cm) FRF 7,500. LONDON, 25 Oct 1995, *Nude Resting (Coco Chanel)* (pencil/paper, 11 x 15 3/4 ins / 28 x 40 cm) GBP 1,265.

IRIE, Hako, real name: Ikujiro Irie, pseudonym: Hako
Japanese, 20th century.
Born 1887, in Kyoto; died 1948.
Painter. Religious subjects, landscapes.
Irie, after studying at the academy of fine art in Kyoto, where he had the opportunity to make numerous copies of the works of the Japanese old masters, became an art master at a private school. In 1922 he travelled to Europe, where he was greatly impressed by the frescoes from the beginning of the Italian Renaissance. Their influence is perceptible in his paintings of mountains and water, flowers and birds and religious subjects (he worked extensively at the Horyu-ji monastery in Nara). Even so, his treatment remained near to traditional Japanese painting.

IRINARKH
Russian, 17th century.

Active in Pskov.
Icon painter.
Ipinarkh worked on the restoration of the murals in Novgorod churches and monasteries destroyed by Swedes.

IRINEI
Russian, 18th century.
Engraver (wood).
A monk at the Pecherskaya Lavra Monastery in Kiev, Irinei did five wood engravings and the frontispiece (twelve saints and a view of the Cathedral of St Sophia) for a 1784 Kiev edition of *History of the Apostles.*

IRINYI, Sandor
Hungarian, 19th century.
Born 27 January 1840, in Esztar; died 6 December 1893, in Pécs.
Painter.
Sandor Irinyi studied at the academy in Munich. He drew illustrations and painted landscapes and typical characters of the ordinary people. His paintings are in the University of Pécs.

IRION, Franz
German, 18th century.
Active in Hamburg.
Sculptor, architect.

IRIS, André
Russian, 20th century.
Painter.
André Iris featured in the first half of the 20th century at the Salon des Indépendants and the Salon d'Automne in Paris.

IRMAD, Jaimes
Bolivian, 20th century.
Born in Oruro.
Painter. Landscapes.
From 1965, Jaimes Irmad exhibited in various towns and cities in Bolivia. His landscape paintings with their black outlines extol typically Bolivian values.

IRMANN, Heinrich Otto
German, 19th - 20th century.
Born 28 May 1849, in Eipel; died 22 September 1915, in Breslau (now Wroclaw, Poland).
Painter, lithographer.
Heinrich Otto Irmann attended the art academies in Berlin and Vienna, and became a teacher at the art academy in Breslau. He painted landscapes of the Breslau region, compositions of the southern edge of the Bavarian forest, figures, interiors and still-lifes.
MUSEUMS AND GALLERIES:
WROCLAW (Muz. Narodowe): *Fürsteinstein Landscape.*

IRMER, Carl
German, 19th century.
Born 28 August 1834, in Babitz, near Wittstock; died 10 November 1900, in Düsseldorf.
Painter. Landscapes with figures, landscapes.
A pupil of court painter August Becker in Dessau and from 1855 of Gude at the academy in Düsseldorf, he also worked in Paris and Brussels. Later he was appointed court painter in Anhalt. He won medals in Vienna (1873), Düsseldorf (1880), Berlin (1880, 1881), London (1887) and Dresden (1887).

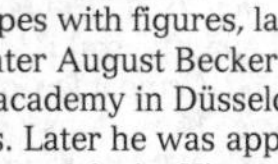

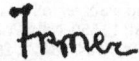

MUSEUMS AND GALLERIES:
BERLIN (Nationalgal.): *Holstein Lake* - DÜSSELDORF: *Harz Landscape; Moonrise* - HALLE: *Harz Landscape; Six landscape studies* - PRAGUE (Rudolfinum Gal.): *Evening Landscape* - ROCHDALE (Art Gallery): *The Edge of a Bavarian Forest* - STOCKHOLM: *Clearing* - STUTTGART: *Harz Landscape.*
AUCTION RECORDS:
LONDON, 7 May 1971, *Animals Grazing,* Gns 700. COLOGNE, 19 Oct 1973, *Summer Landscape,* DEM 8,500. COLOGNE, 14 June 1976, *Summer Landscape* (oil on canvas, 17¾ x 25¼ ins / 45 x 64 cm) DEM 3,400. COLOGNE, 17 March 1978, *In a Wood* (oil on canvas, 20¾ x 17 ins / 53 x 43 cm) DEM 3,300. COLOGNE, 30 March 1979, *Village Pond* (oil on canvas, 23¼ x 37¾ ins / 59 x 96 cm) DEM 14,000. BREMEN, 21 June 1980, *Harvest Scene* (9¾ x 13 ins / 25 x 33 cm) DEM 5,500. COLOGNE, 20 March 1981, *Female Water Carrier in a Landscape* (1897, oil on canvas, 39¼ x 31½ ins / 100 x 80 cm) DEM 17,000. COLOGNE, 18 March 1983, *Cows Grazing beside a Pool* (1882, oil on panel, 17¼ x 12¾ ins / 44 x 32.5 cm) DEM 11,500. COLOGNE, 21 Nov 1985, *Shepherd and Flock in a Landscape* (oil on canvas, 23½ x 31½ ins / 60 x 80 cm) DEM 12,000. MUNICH, 3 June 1987, *Landscape* (oil on canvas remounted on board, 9¾ x 12½ ins / 25 x 31.9 cm) DEM 2,600. COLOGNE, 20 Oct 1989, *Silver Birch Wood in Summer* (oil, 31½ x 25¾ ins / 80 x 65.5 cm) DEM 6,500. KEMPTEN, 27 April 2000, *Ruins in Extensive Landscape with Figures* (oil on canvas, 16 x 20 ins / 40 x 52 cm) DEM 6,000. COLOGNE, 11 April 2002, *Cows by Stream* (1882, oil on panel, 17 x 13 ins / 44 x 33 cm) EUR 4,000. STOCKHOLM, 28 May 2002, *Summer Landscape with Cattle* (1855, oil on canvas, 17 x 22 ins / 44 x 55 cm) SEK 20,000. LONDON, 16 July 2003, *Island of Rugen* (1874, oil on canvas, 24 x 34 ins / 60 x 86 cm) GBP 1,300. COLOGNE, 20 Nov 2003, *River by Full Moon* (1875, oil on canvas, 16 x 12 ins / 40 x 31 cm) EUR 1,700.

IRMINGER, Karl Friedrich
Swiss, 19th century.
Born 8 November 1813, in Aadorf (near Winterthur); died 27 March 1863, in Zurich.
Painter, engraver.
He is documented for watercolours and caricatures of Swiss military figures.
MUSEUMS AND GALLERIES:
BERN (Kunstmus.): *Portrait of S Freudenberg as a Child.*

IRMINGER, Valdemar Henrik Nicolaj
Danish, 19th - 20th century.
Born 29 December 1850, in Copenhagen; died 1938.
Painter. Genre scenes.
Valdemar Henrik Nikolaj Irminger lived in Copenhagen and Rome. From 1891-1892 he exhibited in Munich. He also exhibited at the 1889 and 1900 Expositions Universelles in Paris, where he won an honourable mention and a silver medal.
MUSEUMS AND GALLERIES:
COPENHAGEN: *Children Writing* - COPENHAGEN (Charlottenborg): *Portrait of H. O. Brasens* - COPENHAGEN (Den Hirschsprungske Samling): *Child Spirit* - COPENHAGEN (Ny Carlsberg Glyptotek): *Inn Scene* - COPENHAGEN (Statens Mus. for Kunst): *En Tilgivelse (A Pardon)* (1892); *Over Midnat (After Midnight)* (1894); *Dameportræt (Head of a Woman)* (1896); *En Ung Dame på en Altan (Young Lady on a Balcony); Børnene Siger Godnat til Deres Stjerner (The Children Saying Good Night to Their Stars)* (1898); *Hyrdedrengen Læser ABC (Little Shepherd Reading the ABC)* (1904) - HILLERØD (Frederiksborg Slot): *Portrait of Læssoe; Portrait of Holger Petersen.*
AUCTION RECORDS:
COPENHAGEN, 21 Nov 1973, *Portrait of an Italian Woman,* DKK 3,100. COPENHAGEN, 10 Feb 1976, *Summer Landscape* (oil on canvas, 16¼ x 24 ins / 41 x 61 cm) DKK 2,500. COPENHAGEN, 8 Feb 1977, *Trumpet* (1880, oil on canvas, 23½ x 15¾ ins / 60 x 40 cm) DKK 5,000. COPENHAGEN, 19 Aug 1980, *Dragoon on Horseback in a Farmyard* (1880, oil on canvas, 36½ x 45¼ ins / 93 x 115 cm) DKK 8,000. COPENHAGEN, 25 Oct 1989, *Woman and Sheep* (oil on canvas, 15¾ x 13½ ins

/ 40 x 34 cm) DKK 5,500. COPENHAGEN, 21 Feb 1990, *Horses on the Bank* (1918, oil on canvas, 22 1/2 x 27 1/4 ins / 57 x 69 cm) DKK 4,800. LONDON, 29 March 1990, *Garden Corner* (1935, oil on canvas, 26 x 30 ins / 66 x 76 cm) GBP 3,080. STOCKHOLM, 16 May 1990, *Lioness in the Amphitheatre* (oil on canvas, 40 1/2 x 54 ins / 103 x 137 cm) SEK 18,000. COPENHAGEN, 15 Nov 1993, *1881 Manoeuvre: Artillery Regiment in a Narrow Village Street* (1881, oil on canvas, 40 1/4 x 62 1/4 ins / 102 x 158 cm) DKK 22,000. LONDON, 18 Nov 1994, *Great Friends* (1873, oil on canvas, 25 1/2 x 35 ins / 65 x 89 cm) GBP 4,140. LONDON, 18 Dec 1997, *Best of Friends* (1873, oil on canvas, 25 1/2 x 35 ins / 64.8 x 88.9 cm) GBP 5,175.

IRMINSCHER, Michael
German, 17th century.
Active in Hamburg.
Painter.

In 1639, Irminscher completed the altar paintings for the church of St Catherine in Hamburg.

IROLLA, Roland
French, 20th century.
Born 29 September 1935, in Philippeville, Algeria.
Painter, draughtsman, watercolourist, engraver, medallist, illustrator. Figures, landscapes. Wall decorations, designs for stained glass, postage stamps.

Irolla's figurative painting is traditional, depicting the skies of Champagne, its valleys, vineyards, village churches and streets. He executed stained glass windows (Châlons-sur-Marne), mural decorations (Vitry-le-François, St-Memmie, Châlons-sur-Marne) and numerous postage stamps. He also illustrated several books, notably *Prestige de Paris* (*Prestige of Paris*), *Belles Églises de la Marne* (*Beautiful Churches of the Marne*) and *La Route des abbayes normandes* (*The Road to the Norman Abbeys*). Among the medals he executed is that of the inventor Nicolas Appert, which, since 1993, has been on display at Appert's studios in Massy. Irolla lives and works in Châlons-sur-Marne, where he has exhibited at the municipal museum, notably in 1959, 1963, 1967 and 1968. He also exhibited in Paris, Haguenau, Poitiers, Tours, Chinon, Sarlat and Clermont-Ferrand. His exhibition *Metz, 'la Belle'* (*Metz, the Beautiful*) was held in Metz in 1993.

IROLLI, Vincenzo
Italian, 19th - 20th century.
Born 1860, in Naples; died 1942 or 1949, in Naples.
Painter, watercolourist. History painting, figures, portraits, genre scenes, animals, landscapes.

Irolli was one of the representatives of New Neapolitan Realism and exhibited in Naples, Milan and Venice.

MUSEUMS AND GALLERIES:
FLORENCE (Gal. d'Arte Moderna): *Fish* - MULHOUSE: *Idyll*.

AUCTION RECORDS:
PARIS, 28 June 1950, *Little Fish Seller*, FRF 150,000. MILAN, 4 June 1968, *Young Girl Seated by a Window*, ITL 1,900,000. MILAN, 10 April 1969, *Young Girl Seated, Left Profile*, ITL 3,600,000. MILAN, 1 Dec 1970, *Washerwoman*, ITL 3,200,000. MILAN, 18 May 1971, *Young Girl and Cockerel* (watercolour) ITL 1,600,000. MILAN, 29 March 1973, *Motherly Love*, ITL 3,600,000. MILAN, 28 May 1974, *Child with Mandolin* (1919) ITL 5,500,000. ROME, 29 March 1976, *Landscape* (watercolour, 12 1/4 x 16 1/4 ins / 31 x 41 cm) ITL 720,000. MILAN, 14 Dec 1976, *Altar Boy* (oil on canvas, 15 x 15 ins / 38 x 38 cm) ITL 2,600,000. LONDON, 23 Feb 1977, *Market Scene* (oil on canvas, 18 1/2 x 26 1/2 ins / 47 x 67.5 cm) GBP 2,700. MILAN, 15 March 1977, *Young Girl in a Garden* (watercolour, 19 3/4 x 18 3/4 ins / 50 x 47.5 cm) ITL 2,600,000. MILAN, 14 March 1978, *Mother and Child* (watercolour, 23 1/2 x 23 1/2 ins / 60 x 60 cm) ITL 2,400,000. LONDON, 9 May 1979, *Young Girl with a Fan* (oil on canvas, 24 1/2 x 17 1/4 ins / 62 x 44 cm) GBP 4,500. LONDON, 3 Oct 1979, *Young Gardener* (watercolour, 19 x 12 ins / 48 x 30.5 cm) GBP 1,600. LOS ANGELES, 17 Nov 1980, *Portrait of an Italian Beauty* (oil on canvas, 35 x 25 ins / 89 x 63.5 cm) USD 13,000. MILAN, 10 June 1981, *Adolescent Girl* (oil on canvas, 25 1/4 x 20 ins / 64 x 50.5 cm) ITL 10,000,000. MILAN, 17 June 1982, *Figures in the Rain* (watercolour, 20 1/2 x 16 1/4 ins / 52 x 41 cm) ITL 5,800,000. NEW YORK, 26 Oct 1983, *Little Girl Selling Fruit* (oil on canvas, 44 1/4 x 24 1/2 ins / 112.5 x 62 cm) USD 29,000. LONDON, 22 March 1984, *Still-life with Fish* (watercolour, 17 3/4 x 27 ins / 45 x 68.5 cm) GBP 700. MILAN, 7 Nov 1985, *Motherly Love* (oil on canvas, 22 1/4 x 16 1/2 ins / 56.5 x 42 cm) ITL 38,000,000. MILAN, 13 Oct 1987, *The Young Bride* (oil on canvas, 39 1/4 x 26 ins / 100 x 66 cm) ITL 90,000,000. MILAN, 23 March 1988, *Young Peasant Girl with a Goose* (watercolour/paper, 18 x 12 1/4 ins / 46 x 31 cm) ITL 14,500,000. NEW YORK, 25 May 1988, *Children with Turkeys* (oil on canvas, 37 1/2 x 18 1/2 ins / 95.3 x 47 cm) USD 88,000. MILAN, 1 June 1988, *Little Girl Stretched Out in Flowers* (oil on canvas, 17 x 29 1/4 ins / 43 x 74 cm) ITL 42, 000, 000. ROME, 14 Dec 1988, *Elegant Lady and Greyhound in an Interior* (oil on canvas, 27 1/2 x 15 1/4 ins / 70 x 39 cm) ITL 13,000,000. NEW YORK, 23 Feb 1989, *Showing Off* (oil on card, 25 x 17 1/2 ins / 63.5 x 44.5 cm) USD 88,000. MILAN, 14 June 1989, *Profile of a Young Woman* (oil on canvas, 14 1/4 x 9 1/2 ins / 36 x 24 cm) ITL 2,800,000. NEW YORK, 25 Oct 1989, *Little Girl on a Terrace* (oil on canvas, 24 3/4 x 28 ins / 62.8 x 70.2 cm) USD 99,000. MILAN, 6 Dec 1989, *Meditation* (oil on canvas, 38 1/2 x 20 ins / 97.5 x 50.5 cm) ITL 68,000,000. ROME, 14 Dec 1989, *Red Carnations* (oil on canvas, 25 1/2 x 20 3/4 ins / 65 x 53 cm) ITL 27,600,000. NEW YORK, 28 Feb 1990, *The Kiss* (oil on canvas/synthetic resin, 21 1/2 x 15 3/4 ins / 54.6 x 40 cm) USD 66,000. MONACO, 21 April 1990, *Portrait of a Neapolitan Woman Wearing a Pearl Necklace* (oil on canvas, 22 1/2 x 15 ins / 57 x 38 cm) FRF 166,500. NEW YORK, 24 Oct 1990, *Dreaming* (oil on canvas, 32 1/4 x 13 1/2 ins / 81.9 x 34.6 cm) USD 82,500. MILAN, 5 Dec 1990, *Violinist and Little Girl* (watercolour/card, 35 3/4 x 22 3/4 ins / 91 x 58 cm) ITL 18,500,000. ROME, 11 Dec 1990, *Bust of a Young Girl* (oil on canvas, 20 1/2 x 14 1/4 ins / 52 x 36 cm) ITL 23,000,000. NEW YORK, 28 Feb 1991, *Elopement* (oil on canvas, 28 1/2 x 20 1/4 ins / 72.7 x 51.4 cm) USD 22,000. ROME, 16 April 1991, *Bust of a Young Girl* (oil on canvas, 20 3/4 x 13 3/4 ins / 53 x 35 cm) ITL 14,950,000. NEW YORK, 16 Oct 1991, *Returning from the Orangery* (oil on canvas, 26 1/2 x 19 ins / 67 x 48.2 cm) USD 110,000. MILAN, 7 Nov 1991, *Portrait of a Young Woman* (watercolour/paper, 11 1/2 x 9 1/2 ins / 29 x 24 cm) ITL 6,500,000. ROME, 14 Nov 1991, *The Four Dolls* (oil on canvas, 37 1/2 x 37 1/2 ins / 95 x 95 cm) ITL 63,250,000. LONDON, 29 Nov 1991, *A Loved Companion or Young Girl with a Chicken* (oil on canvas, 14 x 10 ins / 35.5 x 25.4 cm) GBP 41,800. ROME, 24 March 1992, *Sulking* (oil on canvas, 24 1/2 x 20 1/4 ins / 62 x 51.5 cm) ITL 29,900,000. MILAN, 17 Dec 1992, *Young Peasant Woman* (watercolour/paper, 18 1/2 x 12 1/4 ins / 47 x 31 cm) ITL 11,000,000. LONDON, 16 June 1993, *Little Girls Whispering a Secret* (oil on canvas, 19 1/2 x 27 1/2 ins / 49.5 x 70 cm) GBP 19,550. NEW YORK, 13 Oct 1993, *The Lesson Learnt* (oil on canvas, 36 1/2 x 28 1/2 ins / 92.7 x 72.4 cm) USD 27,600. MILAN, 22 Nov 1993, *Young Girl Seated, with Pomegranates* (oil on canvas, 29 1/2 x 23 3/4 ins / 75 x 60.5 cm) ITL 82,495,000. LONDON, 18 March 1994, *First Lesson* (oil on canvas, 15 x 22 1/2 ins / 38.1 x 57.2 cm) GBP

68,600. NEUILLY, 19 March 1994, *Face of a Child* (oil on panel, 18 x 13 ins / 46 x 33 cm) FRF 23,500. PARIS, 20 Nov 1994, *Sinina Thinking* (oil on canvas, 40 1/2 x 30 ins / 103 x 76 cm) FRF 200,000. MILAN, 14 June 1995, *Adolescent Girl with a Crucifix* (1883, oil on canvas, 45 1/4 x 19 3/4 ins / 115 x 50 cm) ITL 25,300,000. MILAN, 19 Dec 1995, *Young Girl with Binoculars* (oil on canvas, 48 1/2 x 24 3/4 ins / 123 x 63 cm) ITL 82,800,000. ROME, 23 May 1996, *Little Painter* (oil on canvas, 23 1/4 x 15 3/4 ins / 59 x 40 cm) ITL 52,900,000. NEW YORK, 23-24 May 1996, *Dreaming* (c. 1900, oil on canvas, 17 x 11 ins / 43.2 x 27.9 cm) USD 41,400. NEW YORK, 18-19 July 1996, *Aggressive Turkey* (watercolour/paper/card, 17 1/4 x 13 1/4 ins / 43.8 x 33.7 cm) USD 4,025. MILAN, 23 Oct 1996, *Young Girl in Profile* (watercolour/card, 11 3/4 x 8 ins / 30 x 20.5 cm) ITL 4,194,000; *Woman with Parasol* (watercolour/card, 13 3/4 x 9 ins / 35 x 23 cm) ITL 5,825,000. ROME, 27 May 1997, *Adolescent Girl* (c. 1911, oil on canvas, 29 1/4 x 28 ins / 74 x 71 cm) ITL 55,200,000. NEW YORK, 23 Oct 1997, *Leaving for School* (c. 1900, oil on canvas, 32 3/4 x 21 ins / 83.2 x 53.3 cm) USD 51,750. ROME, 2 Dec 1997, *Pink Shawl* (oil on canvas, 28 1/4 x 13 1/2 ins / 72 x 34 cm) ITL 78,140,000; *Young Girl* (oil on canvas, 35 1/2 x 15 3/4 ins / 90 x 40 cm) ITL 34,500,000. LONDON, 25 March 1999, *Springtime* (oil on canvas, 25 x 25 ins / 63 x 63 cm) GBP 22,000. LONDON, 26 March 1999, *At the Window* (oil on canvas, 27 x 27 ins / 68 x 68 cm) GBP 7,000. ROME, 23 May 2000, *Breakfast* (oil on canvas, 27 x 27 ins / 68 x 68 cm) ITL 78,000,000. NEW YORK, 25 Oct 2000, *Beautiful Laundress* (oil on canvas, 26 x 13 ins / 65 x 34 cm) USD 44,000. NEW YORK, 1 May 2001, *Young Girl at the Fountain* (oil on canvas, 31 x 25 ins / 80 x 63 cm) USD 32,000. NEW YORK, 1 May 2001, *In a Bed of Flowers* (oil on canvas, 11 x 15 ins / 27 x 38 cm) USD 34,000. ROME, 26 Nov 2002, *Amongst Flowers* (oil on canvas, 30 x 54 ins / 77 x 137 cm) EUR 34,000. ROME, 26 Nov 2002, *Seated Girl* (oil on canvas, 63 x 20 ins / 160 x 50 cm) EUR 54,000. MILAN, 27 May 2003, *Portrait of a Boy* (oil on canvas, 13 x 12 ins / 34 x 30 cm) EUR 9,000. MILAN, 14 Oct 2003, *Jokes* (oil on canvas, 40 x 27 ins / 101 x 68 cm) EUR 30,000. NEW YORK, 23 April 2004, *In a Bed of Flowers* (oil on canvas, 11 x 15 ins / 27 x 38 cm) USD 70,000. MILAN, 8 June 2004, *Sunday Morning* (oil on canvas, 36 x 60 ins / 91 x 152 cm) EUR 52,000.

IRONSIDE, Robin

British, 20th century.

Born 10 July 1912; died 2 November 1965.

Painter. Figures, stage sets.

Robin Ironside trained at the Courtauld Institute in London and abroad. He was a painter in gouache of Surrealist fantasies, a designer for the theatre and a writer on art. He made theatre sets, often in collaboration with his brother Christopher. These include *Der Rosenkavalier* (1948) and *Sylvia* (1952) at Covent Garden, *A Midsummer Night's Dream* for the Edinburgh Festival (1954) and *La Sylphide* for Sadler's Wells in London (1960).

He showed his work at the Redfern Gallery in London (with his brother Christopher) in 1944 and at the Durlacher Gallery in New York in 1952.

He published *Wilson Steer* (1944); *Painting since 1939* (1947); *The Pre-Raphaelites* (1948); and *David Jones* (1949). The Royal Ballet revived *Sylvia* with the Ironside brothers' original design in November 2004.

MUSEUMS AND GALLERIES:

BRISBANE (Queensland Art Gal.) - LONDON (Tate Collection): *The Somnambulist* (c. 1943, gouache/paper).

IRRWOCH, Sebastian, or Ihrwach or Irbach

Austrian, 19th century.

Born probably in Murau, Styria; died January 1813, in Rome.

Sculptor, lithographer, medallist.

Irrwoch was a boarder at the academy in Vienna. During his time there, he won a first prize in 1792 for a *Head of a Vestal* on steel, also for a *Venus Urania* modelled in wax. In 1795, he won another prize for an *Achilles* in clay.

IRURETA Y ARTOLA, Alejandrino

Spanish, 20th century.

Born in Tolosa; died 1912 or 1913, in San Sebastián.

Painter. Genre scenes.

MUSEUMS AND GALLERIES:

MADRID (Prado): *Beggar* (study).

AUCTION RECORDS:

MADRID, 8 May 1986, *Fisherwoman sitting on a Boat* (oil on canvas, 80 3/4 x 61 ins / 205 x 155 cm) ESP 425,000.

IRVIN, Albert

British, 20th century.

Born 21 August 1922, in London.

Painter.

Albert Irvin studied at the Northampton College of Art and after the World War II at Goldsmith's College in London, where he subsequently taught from 1962 to 1983. His abstract paintings explore the spatial compartmentalisation of the canvas through the use of broad bands and overlapping expanses of colour.

Irvin's work has featured in a number of group exhibitions: with the London Group from 1951 to 1953, and in 1959 and 1960; at the Hayward Gallery, London, 1974, 1980, 1982; at the Walker Art Centre, Liverpool in 1980 and 1982; at the Museo de la Ciudad, Madrid, in 1982; and the Whitechapel Art Gallery, London, in 1986. His work has also been the subject of a number of solo exhibitions since 1960: 1960, 1964, 1976 Edinburgh; 1960 Vienna; 1972, 1975, 1978 Berlin; 1961, 1963, 1965, 1967, 1971, 1973, 1976, 1980, 1982, 1984, 1986 London; 1972, 1976 Frankfurt; 1983 Glasgow and Birmingham, 1986 Dublin.

MUSEUMS AND GALLERIES:

ABERDEEN (AG): *Across* (1974, acrylic) - LINZ (Neue Gal. der Stadt) - LONDON (Contemporary Art Society) - LONDON (Royal Academy of Arts): *Blue Anchor* (1989, acrylic/canvas, competition piece) - LONDON (Tate Collection): *Empress* (1982, acrylic/canvas) - SYDNEY (AG of New South Wales).

IRVINE (Miss)

British, 19th century.

Active in London.

Painter. Landscapes.

Miss Irvine was a member of the Society of Lady Artists. She exhibited her work in London at Suffolk Street from 1863 to 1871.

IRVINE, Hugh

British, 19th century.

Active in London.

Painter. History painting.

Hugh Irvine exhibited his work in London and at the British Institution from 1808 to 1829.

IRVINE, James

British, 19th century.

Born 1833, in Scotland; died 1899.

Painter. Genre scenes, portraits.

James Irvine was a friend of George Paul Chalmers, who was assassinated in 1878. James Irvine exhibited his work at the Royal Academy in London from 1882. He was a prominent member of the young Scottish School.

IRVINE, John

British, 19th century.

Born 1805, in Lewick; died 1888, in Dunedin, Australia.

Painter. Genre scenes, figures.
John Irvine exhibited his work at the Royal Academy in London, at the British Institution and in Suffolk Street.
MUSEUMS AND GALLERIES:
DUBLIN: *Portrait of C.K. Sharpe.*

IRVINE, John or James

British, 18th century.
Painter. Genre scenes, portraits.
The work of John Irvine was represented at the Royal Academy in London in 1787 and 1794. In 1818 he worked in the USA and around 1834 in Rome.

IRVINE, Wilson Henry

American, 19th - 20th century.
Born 28 February 1869, in Byron (Illinois); died 1936.
Painter. Landscapes.
Wilson Henry Irvine studied at the Art Institute of Chicago and was a member of the Chicago Society of Artists and the Salmagundi Club. He won many prizes from the clubs to which he belonged.
BIBLIOGRAPHY:
Spencer, Harold, '*Wilson Henry Irvine*' in *American Art Review,* vol 10, no. 4, 1998.
AUCTION RECORDS:
NEW YORK, 30 Nov 1979, *Winter Landscape* (oil on canvas, 24 x 27 ins / 61 x 68.6 cm) USD 3,250. NEW YORK, 24 April 1981, *Wood in Connecticut* (oil on panel, 24 x 27 ins / 61 x 68.7 cm) USD 4,000. NEW YORK, 8 Dec 1983, *Snowbound Wooded Landscape* (oil on canvas, 29 x 36 ins / 73.7 x 91.5 cm) USD 9,000. NEW YORK, 30 May 1985, *Tea in the Garden* (oil on canvas, 36 x 40 ins / 91.5 x 101.6 cm) USD 9,000. NEW YORK, 20 March 1987, *Summer Landscape* (oil on canvas, 18 x 24 ins / 46 x 61.2 cm) USD 15,000. NEW YORK, 25 May 1989, *A Knock at the Door* (oil on canvas, 30 x 25 ins / 76.2 x 63.5 cm) USD 22,000. NEW YORK, 24 May 1990, *In the Canoe* (oil on canvas, 24 x 27 ins / 61 x 68.6 cm) USD 52,800. NEW YORK, 26 Sept 1990, *Snowbound Landscape in Connecticut* (oil on canvas, 24 x 27 ins / 61 x 68.7 cm) USD 7,700. NEW YORK, 17 Dec 1990, *Waiting for the Fog to Lift in order to put to Sea* (oil on canvas, 18 x 24 ins / 45.5 x 61 cm) USD 2,750. NEW YORK, 22 May 1991, *Spring in old Lyme* (oil on canvas, 35 x 46 ins / 89 x 117 cm) USD 12,100. NEW YORK, 26 Sept 1991, *The Coast of Monhegan in Maine* (oil on card, 11 3/4 x 16 ins / 30 x 40.4 cm) USD 4,400. NEW YORK, 23 Sept 1992, *Stream in a Snowbound Forest* (oil on canvas, 29 1/4 x 36 ins / 74 x 91.5 cm) USD 12,100. NEW YORK, 11 March 1993, *Gloucester Harbour* (oil on canvas, 24 1/4 x 27 ins / 61.6 x 68.5 cm) USD 19,550. NEW YORK, 21 Sept 1994, *November Day* (oil on canvas, 25 x 30 ins / 63.5 x 76.2 cm) USD 5,750. NEW YORK, 25 May 1995, *Riding School in Brittany* (oil on canvas, 25 x 30 ins / 63.5 x 76.2 cm) USD 20,700. NEW YORK, 27 Sept 1996, *Landscape* (oil on canvas, 24 1/4 x 27 ins / 61.5 x 68.6 cm) USD 11,500. NEW YORK, 4 Dec 1996, *Stream in the Snow* (oil on canvas, 29 1/4 x 36 ins / 74 x 91.5 cm) USD 14,950. CONNECTICUT, 24 May 1999, *Autumn Landscape* (oil on canvas, 25 x 30 ins / 64 x 76 cm) USD 8,500. SAN FRANCISCO, 17 June 1999, *Lake and Trees in Fall* (oil on canvas, 25 x 30 ins / 63 x 76 cm) USD 7,500. NEW YORK, 15 June 2000, *Summer in Lyme* (oil on masonite, 24 x 22 ins / 61 x 57 cm) USD 20,000. LOS ANGELES, 13 Dec 2000, *Trees on a Hillside Overlooking a Valley* (oil on canvas, 24 x 48 ins / 61 x 122 cm) USD 12,000. NEW YORK, 3 Oct 2001, *Widening of the river* (1919, oil on canvas, 24 x 30 ins / 62 x 77 cm) USD 7,000. NEW YORK, 28 Nov 2001, *Broken Stone Wall, Connecticut* (c. 1898, oil on canvas, 35 x 45 ins / 88 x 114 cm) USD 27,500. NEW YORK, 17 July 2002, *Teatime - Lois and Betty-June* (oil on canvas, 40 x 36 ins / 102 x 92 cm) USD 30,000. EAST DENNIS, 1 Aug 2002, *Autumn Landscape* (oil on canvas, 25 x 30 ins / 64 x 76 cm) USD 14,000. MILFORD, 23 Oct 2003, *Path to the River* (oil on canvas, 24 x 27 ins / 61 x 69 cm) USD 12,000. NEW YORK, 19 Dec 2003, *Spring Landscape* (oil on canvas, 24 x 27 ins / 61 x 68 cm) USD 16,000. NEW YORK, 11 March 2004, *Selden's Cove* (c. 1914-1918, oil on canvas, 32 x 40 ins / 82 x 102 cm) USD 50,000. NEW YORK, 27 Sept 2004, *Teatime - Lois and Betty-June* (oil on canvas, 40 x 36 ins / 102 x 92 cm) USD 38,000.

IRVING, Charles M.

British, 19th century.
Active in London.
Painter. Landscapes.
Charles M. Irving exhibited his work at the Royal Academy, the British Institution and Suffolk Street in London from 1823 to 1832.

IRVING, John Beaufain

American, 19th century.
Born 1826, in Charleston (South Carolina); died 1877, in New York.
Painter. Portraits, genre scenes.
John Beaufain Irving studied in his home town and established himself as a portrait painter there. In 1851 he went to Düsseldorf and worked with Leutz. After staying in Germany for several years he moved to New York towards the end of the American Civil War. His skills as a colourist and his careful execution rapidly gained him a reputation as a genre painter. He had great admiration for Meissonnier, who may be called his true master. Irving's painting *The Expert,* exhibited in Paris in 1878, was very successful. He exhibited for the first time at the National Academy of Design in New York in 1867, and was named an associate in 1869 and an Academician in 1872.
AUCTION RECORDS:
NEW YORK, 14 and 15 April 1909, *Horseman,* USD 230. NEW YORK, 3 Feb 1978, *Mathilda Oakley, a Rhineland Child* (1873, oil on canvas, 21 x 16 ins / 52.5 x 40.5 cm) USD 3,000. SAN FRANCISCO, 4 May 1980, *Horseman* (1875, oil on panel, 12 x 9 ins / 30.5 x 23 cm) USD 1,700. NEW YORK, 30 Sept 1985, *Little Girl Feeding a Goldfish* (1873, oil on canvas, 20 x 16 ins / 50.9 x 40.7 cm) USD 2,800.

IRVING, S. Thwaite

British, 19th century.
Active in Witley.
Painter. Landscapes.
S. Thwaite Irving exhibited his work in London from 1888, mainly at the Royal Academy, Suffolk Street and the New Water-Colour Society.
AUCTION RECORDS:
LONDON, 23 May 1984, *The End of the Day* (oil on canvas, 26 x 42 1/4 ins / 66 x 107 cm) GBP 1,000.

IRVOY, Aimé Charles

French, 19th century.
Born 25 November 1824, in Vendôme (Loir-et-Cher); died 18 March 1898, in Grenoble.
Sculptor.
A pupil of Ramey and Dumont, Aimé Irvoy was awarded the second Grand Prix de Rome in 1854. He exhibited at the Paris Salon from 1849 to 1879. In 1856, he was appointed director of the École de Sculpture in Grenoble, where he remained until his death.

His works include *Bronze Statue of Ronsard,* unveiled in Vendôme in 1872.
MUSEUMS AND GALLERIES:
GRENOBLE: *The Painter Guétal-Ronsard* (plaster model) - VENDÔME: *Hector Beseeching the Gods* (group) - VERSAILLES: *Bust of Barnave.*

IRWE, Knut

Swedish, 20th century.
Born 1912.

Painter. Portraits, scenes with figures.

Knut Irwe is more concerned with tonal relationships than with pure form.

AUCTION RECORDS:

STOCKHOLM, 28 Oct 1991, *Young Girl beneath an Apple Tree* (oil on panel, 18 x 21 1/4 ins / 46 x 54 cm) SEK 5,200. GÖTEBORG, 24 Nov 2001, *After the Summer Holiday-Makers have Left* (oil on canvas, 33 x 39 ins / 84 x 99 cm) SEK 29,000. GÖTEBORG, 25 April 2004, *Landscape with Figures on Road* (oil on canvas, 22 x 26 ins / 55 x 65 cm) SEK 14,500.

IRWIN, group

Slovene, 20th century.

Installation artists.

This group includes a number of artists: Dusan Mandic, Miran Mohar, Andrej Savski, Roman Uranjek and Borut Volguelnik. They live in Ljubljana.

The group was formed in 1984 to reclaim their Slovenian national heritage and its members take their inspiration from all arts and all countries. They use rock music, dance, theatre and architecture as well as painting and sculpture and produce eclectic and symbolic installations. Their *Still-life*, for example, consists of five panels on massive metal bases combining a photograph of Mussolini, Fontanas' technique, Malevich's cross, a Constructivist assemblage and an image of a stag (emblem of Slovenian hunters) alongside a metronome.

They exhibited first in Yugoslavia and then, from 1987, abroad including: Venice Biennale (1986); Sydney Biennial and CNAC (Centre National d'Arts Plastiques), Paris (1988); Kunstmuseum, Düsseldorf (1989); Galerie Rabouan Moussion, Paris (2000); *Berlin-Moscow/Moscow-Berlin 1950-2000*, Martin Gropius Bau, Berlin and Tretyakov Gallery, Moscow (2003), an exhibition providing an overview of 50 years of political change and artistic and cultural relations between Russia and Germany.

BIBLIOGRAPHY:

Tronche, Anne, '*Entretien: Irwin*' in *Opus international* n° 110, periodical, Paris, Sptember-October 1990. Bohn, Alexandre, '*Irwin*' in *Art Press* n° 262 p. 84, Paris, November 2000. '*Berlin-Moskau/Moskau-Berlin 1950-2000*' in *2 vol.*, exhibition catalogue, Martin-Gropius-Bau, Berlin, 2003 (text in German).

MUSEUMS AND GALLERIES:

PARIS (FNAC): *Still-life.*

IRWIN, Benoni

American, 19th century.

Born 1840, in Newmarket (Ontario); died 1896, in South Coventry (Connecticut).

Painter. Portraits.

Benoni Irwin was a pupil at the National Academy of Design in New York, and of Carolus Duran in Paris.

MUSEUMS AND GALLERIES:

NEW YORK (Metropolitan Mus. of Art): *Portrait of the Writer C. H. Farnham.*

IRWIN, Gwyther

British, 20th century.

Born 1931, in Trebetherick.

Active in the USA.

Painter, collage artist, sculptor.

Gwyther Irwin trained at the Central School in London but left London to live and work in New York. His work has featured in a number of group exhibitions: 1958, Institute of Contemporary Art (ICA), London; 1961, Museum of Modern Art, New York; 1964, Venice Biennale. One of the later generation of collage artists, Irvine's work features choreographic assemblages of different strips of paper, arranged side-by-side to resemble metal blades. Essentially abstract in character, his works nonetheless retain a figurative aspect. He also produced wooden reliefs and oil paintings, characterised by the optical play of variations in the support surface. He held his first solo exhibition in 1957 and received a number of public commissions in 1960.

MUSEUMS AND GALLERIES:

BUFFALO (Albright-Knox AG) - LONDON (Calouste Gulbenkian Foundation) - LONDON (Tate Collection): *Parade* (1961, mixed media/paper); *Forests of the Night* (1963, mixed media/board) - PITTSBURGH (Carnegie MA): two paintings - VENICE (Peggy Guggenheim Collection).

IRWIN, Madeleine (Miss)

British, 19th century.

Active in Lexdon (near Colchester).

Painter. Genre scenes, portraits.

The work of Madeleine Irwin was represented at the exhibitions of the Royal Academy in London from 1888 to 1901.

IRWIN, Robert

American, 20th century.

Born 12 September 1928, in Long Beach (California).

Painter, installation artist.

Robert Irwin studied from 1948 to 1950 at the Otis College of Art and Design in Los Angeles, in 1951 at the Jepson Art Institute and from 1952 to 1953 at the Chouinard Art Institute in Los Angeles, where he taught from 1957 to 1958. His most notable pupil was Larry Bell. He also taught at the University of California in 1968 and the University of Minnesota at Minneapolis in 1981. He settled in San Diego.

Like many American artists, Irwin first came into contact with painting around 1950 through Abstract Expressionism, but gradually moved away from it to attempts at environmental art. Around 1959, he took an important step in his painting, offering almost uniform fields of colour, with two or three parallel lines inside them making a statement about space. The colours he chose, often mixed with white, were selected for their great luminosity. From 1963, he began working on curved frames and rounded surfaces, which later, around 1966-1967, took the form of slightly curved discs, which Irwin hung a long way from the wall and lit with one or two spotlights, giving the viewer the illusion of the total integration of the surface of the disc into the surface of the wall. This is far from being just a simple optical game. Irwin symbolically reveals the deceiving mechanisms of the surface to be painted. In the 1960s, he was interested in creating environments, particularly in museums. He made use of the architecture and light of the place, inviting the spectator to penetrate a sculpture 'of space and light' that emitted physical energy. He offered a sensory experience, an exploration of the limits of the visual. He also created *Sites Projects*, placing a work of art in a natural setting, while respecting what the site had to offer. At the campus of Wellesley College, Massachusetts, he drew attention to the site by placing a band of steel around the lake and cutting outlines of maple leaves into it in a reference to the trees round about, allowing the water to be seen through it.

He has taken part in many group exhibitions, notably: 1965 São Paulo Biennale; 1968 Documenta IV in Kassel; 1970 Tate Gallery in London with Larry Bell and Douglas Wheeler; 1973 *Five Artists/Five Spaces* at the San Francisco Museum of Art; 1976 Venice Biennale; 1978 *20th-Century American Drawings* at the Whitney Museum in New York; 1981 *Seventeen Artists in the Sixties* at the Los Angeles County Museum of Art; 1982 *Form and Function* at the Academy of the Fine Arts in Philadelphia and 1990 FIAC (International Contemporary Arts Fair) in Paris. It was in Los Angeles that he first showed his work in a solo exhibition in 1957, an event that was followed by many others, including 1960 and 1968 Art museum of Pasadena; regularly at the Pace Gallery in New York since 1966; 1970-1971 at the Museum of Modern Art in New York; 1971 Walker Art Center in Minneapolis; 1977 Whitney Museum of American Art in

New York; 1982 Louisiana Museum in Humlebæk, Denmark; 1986 and 1993 Museum of Contemporary Art in Los Angeles; 1994 Kölnischer Kunstverein in Cologne and the Musée National d'Art Moderne de la Ville de Paris; 1995 Museo Nacional Centro de Arte Reina Sofia in Madrid.

BIBLIOGRAPHY:

Licht, Ira, *Robert Irwin*, exhibition catalogue, Museum of Contemporary Art, Chicago, 1976. Weschler, Lawrence, *Robert Irwin*, exhibition catalogue, University of California Art Museum, 1978. Ferguson, Russell (ed.), *Robert Irwin*, exhibition catalogue, Museum of Contemporary Art and Rizzoli, Los Angeles and New York, 1993. Sobchak, Vivian, '*From Space to Place*' in *Artform*, vol 32, no. 3, 1993. Thea, Carolee, '*Robert Irwin: de-objectifications for philosophic and actual bodies*' in *Sculpture*, vol 17, no. 8, 1998.

MUSEUMS AND GALLERIES:

CHICAGO (AI) - FORT WORTH (MMA): *Untitled* (1968, plastic, lamps) - LA JOLLA (MCA of San Diego): *Untitled* (c. 1960-1961, oil on canvas); *Untitled* (1962, oil on canvas) - LOS ANGELES (County MA) - LOS ANGELES (MCA): *Matinee Idol (Early Line Painting)* (1962, oil on canvas) - MINNEAPOLIS (Walker Art Center): *Untitled (Dot Painting)* (1963-1965); *Untitled* (1971) - NEW YORK (MoMA) - NEW YORK (Whitney Mus. of American Art) - ORLÉANS (FRAC Centre): *Lower Grand Avenue* (drawing) - PASADENA (Norton Simon Mus.): *Untitled (Late Line Painting)* (1962-1963); *Untitled (Plastic Disc)* (1967-1968) - SAN FRANCISCO (MoMA): *The Four Blues* (1961, oil on canvas).

AUCTION RECORDS:

LOS ANGELES, 27 Feb 1974, *Crazy Otto* (1962) USD 5,000. NEW YORK, 13 Nov 1980, *Untitled* (1965/66, oil on canvas, 43 x 45 1/2 ins / 109 x 115.5 cm) USD 19,000. NEW YORK, 2 May 1985, *Untitled* (painted metal disk with two lamps, diam. 60 ins / 152.5 cm) USD 45,000. NEW YORK, 22 Feb 1986, *Untitled* (1965-1966, oil on canvas remounted/panel, 82 3/4 x 84 3/4 ins / 210.3 x 215.3 cm) USD 30,000. NEW YORK, 5 May 1987, *Untitled* (1969, acrylic/canvas, diam. 54 ins / 137.2 cm) USD 48,000. NEW YORK, 3 May 1989, *Disc* (vaporised varnish/montage of aluminium discs with four spotlights, diam. 60 1/4 ins / 153 cm) USD 93,500. NEW YORK, 25-26 Feb 1992, *Untitled* (acrylic/aluminium, diam. 46 ins / 117 cm) USD 41,250. NEW YORK, 5 May 1993, *Untitled* (1971, polyester resin, 112 1/2 x 5 x 5 ins / 285.7 x 11.8 x 11.8 cm) USD 51,750. NEW YORK, 10 Nov 1993, *Untitled* (oil on canvas/wood, 82 1/4 x 2 1/4 x 84 1/2 ins / 209 x 6 x 214.6 cm) USD 222,500. NEW YORK, 18 May 1999, *Disc* (1966-1967, acrylic on aluminium) USD 120,000. MILAN, 27 March 2001, *Untitled* (wood, saucers and book, 28 x 35x5 ins / 70 x 90x12 cm) ITL 4,200,000.

IRYO. See **KORIN**

ISAAC

Spanish, 16th century.
Active in Valladolid.
Sculptor.

ISAAC

French, 17th century.
Active in Nancy in 1626.
Sculptor.

Isaac is mentioned by Jacquot in *Les Artistes Lorrains* (*The Lorraine Artists*).

ISAAC, Claude

French, 17th century.
Born in Paris; died 26 September 1672, in Paris.
Engraver, print dealer.

Claude Isaac was the son and probably a pupil of Gaspard Isaac. After the death of his father, on 23 May 1654, he must have succeeded him in the family print business because, on 21 March of the same year, he is simply described as a line-engraver on the birth certificate of a daughter of Robert Nanteuil. On subsequent certificates, particularly the marriage certificate of a daughter of Robert Nanteuil to Michel Hardouin on 29 December 1667, the profession of print dealer is added to engraver. On 3 May 1671, he married the widow of the engraver Jean Guérin, Marguerite Fremery, who, after the death of Claude, married the engraver Jean Girardin. His work is probably confused with his father's.

ISAAC, Jaspar or Gaspard de, or Isac or Isacsz.

Dutch, 17th century.
Born probably, in Amsterdam; died 23 May 1654, in Paris.
Engraver, print dealer.

Jaspar Isaac was probably the son of the painter Pieter Isaacz. and father of Claude Isaac. He went to Paris, where he married Barbe Naubert in July 1610. He produced etchings after Wierix but worked primarily as a print dealer. He appears to have been an important figure in the world of engraving, particularly through his connections with the best-known artists. On 27 June 1649, his daughter Marguerite married the engraver Nicolas Regnesson, brother-in-law of Robert de Nanteuil; his granddaughter Magdeleine Regnesson married Gerard Edelinck on 1 May 1672. He made engravings of saints, portraits and plates for booksellers, notably an illustration for Ovid's *Metamorphoses*, published in 1619.

ISAAC, John R.

British, 19th century.
Born in Liverpool; died 1871, in Liverpool.
Draughtsman, engraver, lithographer.

John R. Isaac executed sketches for applied arts, mainly for fitting out the ships of the Royal Mail Steamship Company. In 1850 he founded a lithography studio in which views of Manchester and Liverpool were displayed in chromolithography. He also engraved ex-libris.

ISAAC, Master of. See **MASTERS**

ISAACHSEN, Herman

Norwegian, 20th century.
Active c. 1937.
Painter.

ISAACHSEN, Olaf Wilhelm

Norwegian, 19th century.
Born 16 May 1835, in Mandal; died 22 September 1893, in Saetersdal.
Painter. Historical subjects, portraits, local scenes, interiors with figures, landscapes.

After having studied at the drawing school in Christiania (now Oslo), Olaf Isaachsen went to Düsseldorf in 1854 to become a pupil at the academy. He then went to Paris where he studied with Thomas Couture and Gustave Courbet. He travelled to Italy in 1863 and copied the works of Caravaggio, de Ribera and Salvator Rosa. He lived in Saetersdal from 1875 until his death.

The subjects of his works include Norwegian history, landscapes, scenes from daily life, portraits and interiors. Isaachsen had been strongly influenced by his time in Paris and he interpreted the Realism of the era through a Romantic and nostalgic perspective, as is evident in *Monks in an Evening Landscape*.

When he returned to Norway he often exhibited at the artists' society in Christiania, beginning in 1863. He also participated in the Scandinavian shows in Stockholm in 1866, and in Copenhagen in 1872. His paintings were also shown at the annual national exhibition in Oslo from 1884 to 1888, the fine arts society in 1906, and the Jubilee exhibition in 1914. In 2001 he was included in the exhibition *Da Dahl a Munch. Ro-*

manticismo, realismo e simbolismo nella pittura di paesaggio norvegese (*From Dahl to Munch: Romanticism, Realism and Symbolism in Norwegian Landscape Painting*) at the Palazzo dei Diamanti in Ferrara.

BIBLIOGRAPHY:
Willoch, Sigurd, *Olaf Isaachsen: en overgangsskikkelse i norsk malerkunst*, Aschehoug, Oslo, 1926. Boime, Albert, *Thomas Couture and the Eclectic Vision*, Yale University Press, New Haven and London, 1980. Opstad, Gunvald, *'Olaf Isaachsen'* in *coll. Norske malere*, Aschehoug, Oslo, 1993. Hjorth, Ragnhild, *'Vilhelm Krag & Olaf Isaachsen'* in *coll. Kunstgleder*, Andresen & Butenschon, Oslo, 2001. Lange, Marit (ed.), *Da Dahl a Munch. Romanticismo, realismo e simbolismo nella pittura di paesaggio norvegese*, exhibition catalogue, Palazzo dei Diamanti, Ferrara Arte editore, Ferrara, 2001.

MUSEUMS AND GALLERIES:
BERGEN (Kunstmus., Billedgal.) - OSLO (Nasjonalgal.): several works; *Monks in an Evening Landscape* (1884, oil on canvas).

ISAACS (Miss)
British, 18th century.
Active in London.
Miniaturist.
Isaacs exhibited his work at the Royal Academy in London from 1771 to 1774.

ISAACS, Walter
American, 20th century.
Born 15 July 1886, in Gillespie; died 1964.
Painter.
Walter Isaacs studied with Chase, Dumond, Guérin and Firesz. He was a member of the Association of the Artists of the West. He chaired the Department of Painting, Sculpture and Design at the University of Washington.

ISAACSON, Joseph Jacob
Dutch, 19th - 20th century.
Born 1859, in The Hague; died 1942, in Auschwitz, Poland.
Painter. Religious subjects, local scenes.
Joseph Jacob Isaacson attended the art academy in The Hague, then the École des Beaux-Arts in Paris. At that time he made friends with Theo van Gogh, who was Vincent's brother, and the French painter and writer Émile Bernard. In 1891, he returned to Amsterdam. From 1893-1904, Isaacson stayed in Egypt, and returned in 1905.

ISAACSZ., Isac or Isaac, or Isacsen or Isacsz., called Isaac Oseryn
Dutch, 17th century.
Born 1599, in Amsterdam; died after 1665, in Amsterdam.
Painter.
Isac Isaacz. was the son and pupil of Pieter Isacsz. In 1622, he was a member of the Antwerp guild. He worked in Amsterdam and Denmark.

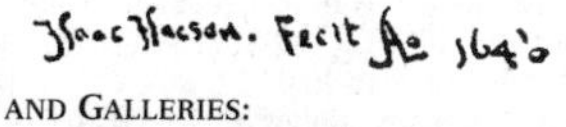

MUSEUMS AND GALLERIES:
AMSTERDAM: *Abimelech, King of Gerar, Gives Sarah to Abraham* - COPENHAGEN (Statens Mus. for Kunst): *Banquet at a Royal Wedding* - ST PETERSBURG (Hermitage): *Diana Hunting*.

AUCTION RECORDS:
LONDON, 14 Dec 1984, *Joseph Receiving the Ring of the Pharaoh* (1632, oil on panel, 17¾ x 29¾in/45 x 75.5cm) GBP 4,000. STOCKHOLM, 19 April 1989, *Queen Tomyris with Cyrus* (oil on canvas, 39¼ x 49½in/100 x 126cm) SEK 18,500. VIENNA, 27 March 2003, *Portrait of a Roman Imperial* (oil on panel, 15 x 11 ins / 37 x 28 cm) EUR 6,000.

ISAAKSZ., Pieter Franz
Dutch, 16th - 17th century.
Born 1569, in Helsingør; died 14 September 1625, in Helsingør.
Painter. History painting, portraits, group portraits.
The father of Pieter Franz Isaaksz. was a citizen of Haarlem and the Dutch consul in Helsingør, Denmark. Pieter studied in Amsterdam with Cornelis Ketel, and later worked in Munich with Johann von Aachen, whom he accompanied on journeys in Germany and Italy. In 1593 he was in Amsterdam, where on 20 November that year he married a girl from Antwerp, Susanne Craeyborn Willems. He lived in Amsterdam until 1607, then went to Denmark where he was appointed court painter. In 1614 he succeeded his father as consul, a post he held until his death. He painted scenes from history, but principally portraits.

MUSEUMS AND GALLERIES:
AMSTERDAM: *The Company of Captain Jacob Gerritz Honyck and Lieutenant Wybrand Appelman in 1596*; *The Company of Captain Gillis Jansz. Valckenier and Lieutenant Pieter Jacobsz. Bas in 1599*; *Assembly of Roman Women* - COPENHAGEN (Rosenborg Slot): *Christian IV*; *His Wife* - HILLERØD: *Christian IV Kneeling* - STEENSGAARD: *Portrait of Hendrik Holm*.

AUCTION RECORDS:
PARIS, 21 and 22 Feb 1919, *Minerva and Mercury*; *Plan for a Monument*; *Bust Portrait of a Young Man* (three drawings) FRF 50. COPENHAGEN, 23 Feb 1999, *Christian IV* (oil on canvas, 49 x 43 ins / 125 x 108 cm) DKK 160,000. LONDON, 28 Oct 1999, *Jephthah's Daughter* (oil on canvas/panel, 17 x 31 ins / 44 x 79 cm) GBP 7,000. AMSTERDAM, 14 May 2002, *Adoration of the Magi* (oil on panel, 21 x 19 ins / 54 x 47 cm) EUR 15,000. NEW YORK, 27 May 2004, *Venus and Cupid* (oil on copper, 13 x 9 ins / 32 x 24 cm) USD 22,500.

ISABEY, Eugène. See **ISABEY Louis Gabriel Eugène**

ISABEY, François Xavier
French, 18th century.
Born 1738, in Morteau (Doubs).
Painter, engraver.
François Xavier Isabey was a member of the Académie de St-Luc. He is remembered for: *Portrait of Jean-Jacques Rousseau*, *View of Rousseau's Tomb* and *Portrait of General Marquis de Montcalm de Saint-Véran*.

ISABEY, Jean Baptiste
French, 18th - 19th century.
Born 11 April 1767, in Nancy; died 18 April 1855, in Paris.
Miniaturist, painter (gouache), watercolourist, lithographer, draughtsman, caricaturist. Historical subjects, portraits.
Jean Baptiste Isabey, a member of a family of merchants, began his studies in Nancy with Jean Girardet and Jean-Baptiste Charles Claudot. He moved to Paris in 1786 and worked first with Augustin (?) Dumont, then with David. At the start, he had difficulty earning enough to live on. After obtaining the commission to paint the portraits of Marie-Antoinette, the Duc d'Angoulême and the Duc de Berry, he took a prominent place among the miniaturists

and exponents of stump and wash drawing. It is not known how he made his way through the turmoil of the Revolution, but he was subsequently the close friend of Bonaparte and Josephine, this friendship extending through the Consulate and the Empire. No courtier knew better than he did how to get the most out of the changes of regime. In 1814, having successfully flattered Napoleon I, he was taken by the Prince de Talleyrand to paint the plenipotentiaries at the Congress of Vienna, and he painted the portrait of several sovereigns. He painted Louis XVIII and Charles X, and was no less in favour with Louis-Philippe, so that he earned the nickname 'the painter of kings'. He was made Chevalier de la Légion d'Honneur in 1817, and raised to the rank of Commander in 1853. He was still active under Napoleon III, and ended his career at the Palais de l'Institut as honorary director of the imperial palaces.

He made his debut at the Salon of 1793 with several miniatures. In 1812, he exhibited portraits from life of the Imperial Family of Austria. He continued to take part in official exhibitions until 1841.

Appointed premier painter to the Empress in 1805, Isabey was not only charged with reproducing the official effigies of the Emperor and Empress, but was also the organiser of all the private and official functions at the Tuileries, St-Cloud and Malmaison in his capacity as Designer of Private and Public Ceremonies and Director of Décor for the Opera. He was the most brilliant miniaturist of his time and of the Empire. His reputation was universal.

As an engraver, Jean-Baptiste Isabey is noteworthy as one of the first painters to have done lithography, and in this genre he is remembered for the *Portrait of Prince Eugène*, with Legros, in Vienna in 1814. In 1818, Engelmann published his series of minor attempts at lithography; in 1819: *Invitation to the Masked Ball, by J. Isabey*; in 1821: *Arrival of the Duc de Bordeaux at the Château de Chambord*, dedicated to the Duchesse de Berry; in 1822, he collaborated in the work of Baron Taylor, with *Staircase of the Great Tower of the Château d'Harcourt*, and published the thirty lithographs of his journey to Italy. He also executed portraits, notably one of Eugène Isabey, with this legend: *My son, my pupil, my friend*. Isabey also produced 12 plates of caricatures signed I. I. and published by Motte, some of which are risqué or scatological.

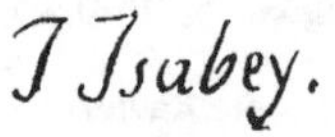

Stamp of sale

BIBLIOGRAPHY:

Wallace Osmond, Marion, *Jean Baptiste Isabey, the fortunate painter, 1767-1855*, Nicholson & Watson, London, 1947. Dagorne, Richard (dir.), *Au-delà du maître Girodet et l'atelier de David*, exhibition catalogue, Somogy, Paris, 2005 (exhibition, musée Girodet, Montargis).

MUSEUMS AND GALLERIES:

AVIGNON (Mus. Calvet): *Portrait of the Artist* - BAYONNE: *Joseph Verdier* - BERLIN: *Frederick William III* - CHANTILLY: watercolour - DRESDEN: *King Jerome* - ÉPINAL: *Portrait of a Man* - HILLERØD: *Frederick VI* - LIÈGE: *Grétry* - LONDON (Wallace Collection): *Joachim Murat; Marie-Louise and the King of Rome*; Six portraits of Napoleon I; *Marie-Louise; Jerome Bonaparte; Napoleon and Josephine; Louis XVIII; Catherine Paulowna, Queen of Wurtemberg; Augustus, Prince of Prussia; The Duke of Wellington*; same subject; *Mlle Mars; J.-B. Isabey; Louis XVIII*; numerous miniatures of women in period costume from the Restoration, the Directoire, and the First Empire - NANCY: oil portrait of Napoleon I; watercolours - PARIS (Louvre): several miniatures and drawings - PARIS (Mus. Carnavalet): *Louis XVIII; Eugène Isabey as a Child; Portrait of the Artist* - ROUEN: *M de Garcus; Girl; Napoleon* - VERSAILLES: *Napoleon Visiting the Manufacture de Jouy; Bonaparte Visiting the Factory of the Sevène Brothers in Rouen* - VIENNA (Albertina Mus.): *Princess Auersperg; Princess Bagration* - WINDSOR: *The Congress of Vienna* - ZURICH: *Napoleon I.*

AUCTION RECORDS:

PARIS, 1889, *Portrait of a General of the First Empire*, FRF 10,800. PARIS, 1891, *Portrait of the Empress Josephine* (miniature) FRF 3,050. PARIS, 1899, *Portrait of Napoleon I* (miniature) FRF 9,200. PARIS, 1899, *Portrait presumed to be of the Duchess of Abrantès* (drawing) FRF 3,300. PARIS, 3 July 1899, *Portrait of a Woman* (miniature) FRF 3,625. PARIS, 10-12 May 1900, *Portrait of Prince Eugène* (miniature) FRF 2,020. PARIS, 8 April 1919, *Portrait of a Woman* (miniature in watercolour) FRF 3,700. PARIS, 26 and 27 May 1919, *Portrait of Suzanne Lepelletier de Morfontaine* (miniature) FRF 7,000; *Portrait of Napoleon* (miniature/snuff-box) FRF 3,200. PARIS, 16-19 June 1919, *Portrait of Hubert Robert* (pencil heightened with white) FRF 9,100. PARIS, 14 and 15 June 1920, *Portrait of Dr Dubois* (miniature) FRF 1,700. PARIS, 30 Nov-2 Dec 1920, *Gaming-house at the Palais-Royal* (watercolour) FRF 6,500. PARIS, 30 Nov and 1 Dec 1923, *Portrait of a Young Woman* (miniature) FRF 4,500. PARIS, 16-18 Nov 1925, *Birth of the King of Rome* (pen and wash) FRF 7,200. PARIS, 3 and 4 June 1926, *Portrait of the Prince de Talleyrand* (drawing with watercolour wash) FRF 10,500. PARIS, 22 Jan 1927, *After the Duel* (watercolour) FRF 2,500. PARIS, 16 May 1927, *Le petit Coblentz* (pen heightened with watercolour) FRF 14,300. PARIS, 30 and 31 May 1927, *Episode from the St Barthomew's Day Massacre*, FRF 13,200. PARIS, 26 June 1928, *Portrait of Laure Roy* (miniature) FRF 20,000; *Portrait of Marquis Auguste de Talhoüet* (miniature) FRF 11,000; *Portrait of Count Antoine Roy* (miniature) FRF 16,100. PARIS, 14 Dec 1931, *Shipwreck*, FRF 3,000. PARIS, 25 Nov 1936, *Bust Portrait of a General* (large miniature) FRF 6,500. PARIS, 12 May 1939, *Portrait of the Duchess of Parma Elisa Bacciochi, Sister of Napoleon I*, FRF 4,500. PARIS, 4 Dec 1941, *Portrait of a Young Woman* (pencil and wash) FRF 1,050. LONDON, 8 Oct 1943, *Lady* (drawing) GBP 47. LONDON, 31 March 1944, *Young Man and Girl* (two drawings) GBP 115. PARIS, 26 April 1944, *Two Girls in a Park* (pencil and white gouache stump) FRF 2,650. PARIS, 29 Jan 1945, *Sketch for a Painting Depicting the Congress of Vienna* (graphite) FRF 1,500. PARIS, 24 March 1947, *General Bonaparte Dressed as First Consul* (miniature) FRF 90,000; *Napoleon I* (1814, miniature) FRF 22,000; *Portrait of the King of Rome* (miniature) FRF 21,000. PARIS, 19 May 1947, *The King of Rome, 15 August 1811* (miniature/box) FRF 197,000; *Marie-Louise in a Red Dress, Wearing a Pearl Necklace* (miniature) FRF 40,500; *Napoleon I, Emperor* (miniature) FRF 40,000. PARIS, 17 Dec 1948, *Portrait of Count J.S. Ouvarof*, FRF 40,000. PARIS, 31 March 1950, *Napoleon I in his Coronation Robes*, FRF 63,000. PARIS, 9 March 1951, *Young Woman in a Flimsy Dress*, FRF 105,000. PARIS, 27 March 1953, *Madame Campan and Isabey's Daughter* (pen drawing heightened with gouache) FRF 85,000. GENEVA, 13 June 1960, *Portrait of Hubert Robert* (stump heightened with white chalk) CHF 1,850. PARIS, 3 June 1976, *Portrait of Chenard* (1798, drawing, 22½ x 16¼in/57 x 41cm) FRF 16,500. PARIS, 24 Nov 1977, *Study for the Coronation and Anointing of Napoleon: the Holy Ampulla* (1804, graphite and wash heightened with white, 11 x 15½in/27 x 39.5cm) FRF 28,000. PARIS, 11 Dec 1978, *Draughtsman at the Entrance to a Village* (1818, pen and bistre wash, 8¼ x 10¾in/21 x 27.5cm) FRF 10,000. MONTE CARLO, 8 Feb 1981, *Portrait of Madame Tallien, Princesse de Chimay* (watercolour, oval, 9 x 6½in/23 x 16.5cm) FRF 21,000. PARIS, 23 Feb 1981, *Full-length Portrait of Empress Marie-Louise in her Coronation Robes* (pen and watercolour wash, 6 x 4¼in/15 x 10.5cm) FRF 10,500. PARIS, 29 Nov 1985, *Marquise de Rambuteau, her Son and her Dog* (1841, sepia wash, 11¼ x 6¾in/28.5 x 17.2cm) FRF 15,000. PARIS, 27 May 1987, *Man Drinking from an Antique Cup* (graphite and watercolour, 7¾ x 10¼in/20 x 26cm) FRF 11,500. PARIS, 11 March 1988, *Caricature of the Singer P.J. Garat* (drawing, pencil, pen and watercolour, 11¾ x 7¼in/30 x 18.7cm) FRF 36,500. PARIS, 22 Nov 1988, *Two Young Men Hunting* (brown pen and grey wash/beige paper, 11 x 8in/28 x 20.5cm) FRF 18,000. MONACO, 2 Dec 1988, *Portrait of the Sister of Elisabeth-Charlotte Isabey* (watercolour heightened with white, 9 x 6¼in/23 x 16cm) FRF 35,520. PARIS, 12 June 1990, *Portrait of a Young Woman* (1832, watercolour, 6 x 4½in/15.5 x 11.5cm) FRF 4,000. PARIS, 15 June 1990, *Portrait of a Woman Seated* (lead pencil, 13¼ x 9¾in/33.5 x 25cm) FRF 22,000. LONDON, 28 Nov 1990, *Portrait of Madame Fould* (1834, watercolour, 7 x 5in/18 x 13cm) GBP 4,840. LONDON, 25 Nov 1992, *The Court Dress of the Emperor* (watercolour, 10¼ x 8¼in/26 x 21cm) GBP 2,200. PARIS, 6 July 1993, *Back view of an Elegant Woman* (drawing with wash, 5¾ x 4in/14.5 x 10cm) FRF 4,200. PARIS, 29 April 1994, *Young Woman Adorned with Veils and Flowers* (watercolour/paper, large miniature, 5¼ x 3¾in/13.5 x 9.5cm) FRF 10,000; *The Baroness de Cuzieu* (miniature/ivory, diam. 3¾in/9.5cm) FRF 55,000. NEW YORK, 19 Jan 1995, *The Palazzo Labia in Venice* (watercolour/paper, 6¾ x 4½in/17.1 x 11.7cm) USD 2,300. NEW YORK, 10 Jan 1996, *Bust Portrait of a Man* (1794, black chalk and gouache, 12½ x 10in/32 x 24.5cm) USD 10,350. LONDON, 21 Nov 1996, *The Duke of Bordeaux Presented by his Mother to the Representatives of the City of Chambord* (1821, black chalk, pen, beige ink, brown and grey pastel, 8 x 12in/20.4 x 29.6cm) GBP 9,200.

ISABEY, Louis Gabriel Eugène

French, 19th century.

Born 22 July 1803, in Paris; died 27 April 1886, in Lagny.

Painter (gouache), watercolourist, lithographer, draughtsman. Genre scenes, still-lifes, seascapes, church interiors.

Honfleur (or St-Siméon) School.

Louis Gabriel Eugène Isabey was the son and pupil of the miniaturist Jean-Baptiste Isabey and was among the most admired minor masters of the 1830 school. He very quickly detached himself from the classical ideals of his father in order to follow the Romantic movement, where he came very much under the influence of Delacroix and Bonington.

He made his debut at the Salon in 1824 with seascapes and landscapes, obtaining a first-class medal. In 1827, Isabey exhibited views of Normandy, one of which belonged to the duchess of Berry. He was awarded a first-class medal once again, though the influence of his father was partly responsible for this brilliant success. He made yet another appearance at the Salon of 1831 with genre paintings and scenes of Normandy. He was made a Chevalier of the Légion d'Honneur in 1832, and on 21 January 1852 he was awarded the Croix d'Officier. Finally, he received first prize at the Exposition Universelle of 1855. Isabey continued to take part in the Paris exhibitions until 1878.

In 1830, he was appointed draughtsman for the Algiers expedition, and Isabey senior later presented Charles X with a drawing by his son representing the *Toulon Harbour on the Eve of the Departure of the Fleet*, which, according to the newspapers of the day, the Dauphin was pleased to accept. Even so, this trip to Algeria did not have a strong influence on his work. Many of Isabey's paintings date from the thirties, especially paintings of interiors with a very subtle delicate greyish tint. The colours of his most important works found their inspiration in Rubens: *Battle of Texel* (exhibited at the Salon in 1839), *Taking on Board the Body of Napoleon I* (1842), *Ceremony in a Church in Delft* (1847), and *Embarkation of Ruyter and William de Witt*. Towards the end of his career, he produced many watercolours, some of which can be said to signal the beginnings of Impressionism. He was also the master of Boudin and Jongkind. In 1997, the graphic-arts section of the Louvre acquired a collection of sketchbooks, some of which evoke the artist's sojourns in Normandy and Brittany between 1843 and 1855, or in London between 1870 and 1871. They demonstrate the rapidity and ease with which he created his works, and also his imagination.

BIBLIOGRAPHY:

Curtis, A., *Catalogue de l'œuvre lithographié de Eugène Isabey*, Prouté, Paris, 1939. Miquel, Pierre, *Eugène Isabey, 1803-1886. La Marine au XIXe siècle*, Paris, Mantes-la-Jolie, 1980. Delouche, Denise/Michaud, Jean-Marc, et al., *Bretagne, terre des peintres*, exhibition catalogue, Musée des Beaux-Arts, Vannes, 2003.

MUSEUMS AND GALLERIES:

BADEN-BADEN: *Beach* - BALTIMORE (Peabody Art Collection): *Interior of a Church* - BAYONNE (Mus. Bonnat): *Procession inside a Church; Figure in a Loose-Fitting Greatcoat and Grey Hat* - BERLIN (Gal. Ravené): *Church Interior* - BÉZIERS: *Young Woman; Fishing Boats on the Channel* - BORDEAUX: *Fire on board the Steamer 'Austria'* - BOSTON: *View of a Port* - CAEN (MBA): *Boats in a Storm; Sailors Leaving the Port of St-Valéry* (c. 1867) - CHAMBÉRY (MBA): *Landscape* - CHÂTEAUROUX: *Cavalcade* - CHICAGO: *Tempest* - DIEPPE: *Main Street in a Town on Market Day* - DOUAI: *Smugglers Loading Merchandise; Fort beside the Sea* - EDINBURGH (Nat. Gal. of Scotland, Print Room): *Fishing Boats* (watercolour) - HAMBURG: *Inshore Boats; Tempest on the Beach at Étretat* - HANOVER: *Smugglers* - KALININGRAD: *Vessel at Anchor* - LANDERNEAU (Museographic Town Collection): *Interior of the Church of St-Houardon* (1850-1851, lead pencil, watercolour and gouache on brown paper) - LAVAL: *Granville Beach* - LE MANS: *Turk on a Divan* - LILLE: *Interior of an Alchemist's Study* - LONDON (NG): *The Fish Market, Dieppe* (1845, oil/wood); *Grandfather's Birthday (The New Born)* (1866, oil/wood) - LONDON (Wallace Collection): *Court Reception at a Château* (1851, oil on canvas); *The Young Mother* (1852, oil on canvas); *A Promenade by the Sea* (1846, oil on canvas); *Boats on the Shore at Calais* (1851, oil on canvas) - MELBOURNE: *Prayer in the Chapel* - MONTPELLIER: *Seascape* - MONTREAL: *On the Beach at Fécamp* - MOSCOW (State Tretyakov Gal.): *The Dyke at Dieppe* - MULHOUSE: *Seascape* (same subject) - NANCY: *Town and Port of Dieppe* - NANTES: *Shipwreck of the Émile in 1863* - NEUCHÂTEL: *Seascape* - NEW YORK (Metropolitan Mus. of Art): *Banqueting Hall* - PARIS (Louvre): *Embarkation of Ruyter and Cornelis de Witt; Bridge; Seascape; Seaport; Wedding in the Church in Delft; Baptism in the Church at Tréport; Nobleman on the Beach at Sveningen; Duel; Visit to the Chateau; Procession; Louis XIII at the Chateau in Blois; Arrival of the Duke of Alba in Rotterdam; Imprisonment; Coming Out of Church; Royal Wedding* (collection of eighteen sketchbooks); *Small Port at the Foot of High Cliffs* (charcoal, stump, black ink wash, white gouache and scraper) - PARIS (MAM): three watercolours - PARIS (Mus. Carnavalet): *Portrait of J.-B. Isabey; Portrait of Madame E. Isabey and her Daughters* - PÉRIGUEUX: *Village beside the Sea* - PERPIGNAN: *Seascape* - POITIERS: *Seascape* - RHEIMS: *Communion* - STOCKHOLM: *Ships Attached with Grapnels; Couple in a Church* (c. 1600) - SZCZECIN: *Cathedral Entrance* - TOULOUSE: *View of Boulogne* - VERSAILLES: *Battle of Texel* (1694).

AUCTION RECORDS:

PARIS, 1863, *Gust of Wind on the Coast at St-Malo,* FRF 4,000; *Departure,* FRF 6,500. PARIS, 1870, *The Little Woodcutters,* FRF 5,000. PARIS, 1873, *Entering the Port of Varengeville in Severe Weather,* FRF 9,000. PARIS, 1875, *Procession Returning to the Sacristy,* FRF 14,600. PARIS, 1877, *Wedding in the Church at Delft,* FRF 26,000. PARIS, 1879, *Defending the Castle,* FRF 10,700; *Wedding and Baptism,* FRF 12,000. PARIS, 1883, *Hunt Meeting,* FRF 12,600. PARIS, 10 April 1884, *Hand-Kissing Ceremony,* FRF 13,500. PARIS, 1889, *Wedding in the Church at Delft,* FRF 75,100. PARIS, 1891, *Rising Tide,* FRF 12,600. PARIS, 1891, *Massacre in a Church,* FRF 24,000; *Orgy,* FRF 12,000. PARIS, 1896, *Castle Courtyard,* FRF 10,400. PARIS, 1900, *Visit to the Castle,* FRF 14,900. NEW YORK, 9-10 March 1900, *Shipwreck,* USD 875. PARIS, 11 June 1900, *Arrival of the Stagecoach,* FRF 6,200; *Tomb of the Knight,* FRF 11,800. PARIS, 11 May 1901, *Wedding at the Time of Henry II,* FRF 15,600. PARIS, 23 Dec 1901, *Boats at Low Tide,* FRF 7,000. NEW YORK, 26-28 Feb 1902, *Still-life,* USD 4,000; *Morning Call,* USD 2,350. PARIS, 22 May 1902, *The Punishment,* FRF 9,400. PARIS, 20-21 June 1902, *Blessing,* FRF 43,100; *Fabric Seller,* FRF 23,000. NEW YORK, 22 Jan 1903, *Visit to Grandfather,* USD 4,150. PARIS, 13 June 1903, *Fishing Village,* FRF 2,700. PARIS, 10 Nov 1906, *Defending the Castle,* FRF 20,000. PARIS, 1 June 1908, *Departure of the Cavaliers,* FRF 8,500. NEW YORK, 26 Feb 1909, *Returning from the Hunt,* USD 5,200. LONDON, 13 May 1909, *Fishing Village* (1852) GBP 336. LONDON, 10 June 1909, *Massacre of St Bartholomew* (1866) GBP 189; *The Trumpet* (1873) GBP 126. LONDON, 9 July 1909, *Favourite Parrot,* GBP 294. PARIS, 4-5 Dec 1918, *Fishing Boats Facing the Cliff,* FRF 4,600. PARIS, 26-27 Feb 1919, *Alchemist,* FRF 3,600. PARIS, 3 March 1919, *The Child Louis XIII Leaving Church,* FRF 8,700. PARIS, 30 June 1919, *Leaving for the Hunt in the reign of Louis XIII,* FRF 65,000. PARIS, 4-5 March 1920, *Walk on the Beach,* FRF 5,600. PARIS, 27 May 1920, *Temptation of St Anthony,* FRF 25,100; *Storm at Sea,* FRF 14,100; *Inn Courtyard,* FRF 26,000. PARIS, 29 May 1920, *Fishing Village at the Foot of the Cliff,* FRF 8,300; *Duchess of Rahar Kneeling with her Children in front of her Husband's Tomb,* FRF 5,200. PARIS, 10 Dec 1920, *Sailors Hailing Christ as they Leave the Port of St-Valéry,* FRF 12,100. PARIS, 29 April 1921, *Appeal of the Prisoners of Mont St-Michel,* FRF 7,000. PARIS, 12 May 1923, *Shooting Party,* FRF 12,100. PARIS, 8 May 1924, *Orgy,* FRF 15,100. PARIS, 19 May 1924, *Leaving for the Stroll,* FRF 13,000. PARIS, 28 Nov 1924, *Wedding in the Reign of Louis XIII; Nuptial Procession Leaving Church,* FRF 19,020. PARIS, 18 May 1925, *Trawlers in a Storm,* FRF 11,000. PARIS, 26 Feb 1926, *Returning to Port,* FRF 14,200. PARIS, 15 March 1926, *The Scuffle,* FRF 30,000; *Departure of the Stagecoach,* FRF 45,000. LONDON, 17 June 1927, *Return of the Arquebusiers,* GBP 136. LONDON, 1 July 1927, *Empress Josephine,* GBP 57. PARIS, 1 June 1928, *Young Woman in a Low-Cut Dress* (miniature) FRF 17,800; *Portrait Presumed to be the Duchess of Kent* (miniature) FRF 18, 000. PARIS, 24 May 1929, *A Street in Old Rouen,* FRF 8,200. PARIS, 27-29 May 1929, *Self-portrait* (miniature) FRF 6,300. PARIS, 1930, *The Queen of England Leaving Tréport in the King's Boat on 7 September 1843,* FRF 32,000; *Norman Seaport,* FRF 22,000; *Disembarkation of King Francis in Portsmouth on 8 October 1844,* FRF 32,000. PARIS, 11 May 1931, *Castle Staircase* (watercolour and gouache) FRF 20,800. PARIS, 15 May 1931, *Fishing Port at Low Tide* (watercolour and gouache) FRF 1,800. PARIS, 13 Oct 1933, *River Port* (watercolour) FRF 1,150. LONDON, 12 April 1935, *Birds; Still-life,* GBP 63. PARIS, 21 Oct 1935, *Prince Napoleon-Louis, Brother of Napoleon III, Dressed as a Page,* FRF 3,800. LONDON, 22 June 1938, *Baptism,* GBP 175. PARIS, 10-17 May 1939, *Shipwreck of the Austria,* FRF 6,000; *Fishing Village on the Coast,* FRF 10,000. PARIS, 24 May 1939, *Street in Old Rouen,* FRF 3,350. PARIS, 23 June 1941, *Fishing Village,* FRF 5,800. LONDON, 27 March 1942, *Interior of the Cathedral,* GBP 54. PARIS, 15 April 1942, *Port* (1863) FRF 20,000. PARIS, 11 June 1942, *Seascape, Inclement Weather* (1861) FRF 40,600. PARIS, 22 June 1942, *Steamers and Sailing Ships in a Squall,* FRF 16,000; *Church Porch* (1862) FRF 30,000. PARIS, 27 Jan 1943, *Village on the Shore,* FRF 15,500. PARIS, 22 Feb 1943, *Musketeers Handing over their Captives* (1861) FRF 50,000. PARIS, 23 June 1943, *Castle Staircase* (1868, watercolour and gouache) FRF 20,000. PARIS, 3 Feb 1944, *Fishing Village* (1854) FRF 115,000; *Old Fishing Port* (1842) FRF 20,000. PARIS, 17-18 Feb 1944, *Fishing Village* (1852) FRF 82,100. PARIS, 10 May 1944, *Alchemist's Den,* FRF 42,000. PARIS, 17 May 1944, *Meeting in the Park,* FRF 122,000; *Appeal of the prisoners of Mont St-Michel* (1870) FRF 39,000. PARIS, 2 Feb 1945, *Portrait of a Girl, Right Profile,* FRF 26,500; *Cliffs,* FRF 10,000. PARIS, 21 March 1945, *Leaving for the Stroll* (1855) FRF 51,500. NEW YORK, 18 April 1945, *French Hospitality of Yesteryear,* USD 1,400. PARIS, 20 April 1945, *Team of Horses Beside the Sea* (1825) FRF 64,000. PARIS, 24 May 1945, *Sailing Ships in Distress,* FRF 37,000. PARIS, Oct 1946-July 1946, *Seascape,* FRF 33,500; *Four Watercolours,* FRF de 2200 à 7000. LILLE, 16-20 Dec 1946, *Shipwreck,* FRF 25,000; *Episode from the History of the Stuarts* (sketch) FRF 16,600. LONDON, 20 Dec 1946, *Picnic on the Coast,* GBP 68. NEW YORK, 26 Feb 1947, *Town Beside the Sea,* USD 1,400. PARIS, 9 July 1947, *Parrots,* FRF 70,000. PARIS, 17 Nov 1948, *Landing Stage; Rowing Boat* (watercolour, matching pair) FRF 37,000. PARIS, 27 April 1951, *Leaving the Castle,* FRF 150,000. PARIS, 7 March 1955, *Fisherman's Children,* FRF 96,000. LONDON, 4 Dec 1957, *Portrait of Prince Eugène Bonaparte,* GBP 180. VIENNA, 2 Dec 1958, *Fishing Village in Brittany,* ATS 9,000. PARIS, 11 June 1959, *Normandy Seaport,* FRF 450,000. LONDON, 6 July 1960, *Seascape,* GBP 250. LONDON, 24 Nov 1964, *Apocalypse,* GBP 650. LONDON, 5 April 1968, *Mass,* Gns 1,000. PARIS, 8 Dec 1968, *Fishing Boats in a Port,* FRF 95,000. PARIS, 5 March 1970, *Fishing Village,* FRF 9,500. LONDON, 23 April 1971, *Palazzo Bergello, Florence,* Gns 650. PARIS, 17 Feb 1972, *Entering the Port of St-Malo* (watercolour and gouache) FRF 8,200. VERSAILLES, 17 Dec 1972, *Two Sailing Ships Coming Alongside Each Other in Turbulent Seas,* FRF 21,200. VERSAILLES, 18 March 1973, *Ebb Tide,* FRF 15,600. NEW YORK, 18 May 1973, *Duel,* USD 3,750. NEW YORK, 17 April 1974, *Royal Fishing Trip* (1876) USD 14,000. VERSAILLES, 2 June 1976, *Seascape* (oil on canvas remounted on hardboard, 19 1/4 x 31 1/2in/49 x 80cm) FRF 18,100. VERSAILLES, 4 Dec 1977, *Sailors Leaving the Port of St-Valéry* (1867, oil on canvas, 65 x 94 1/2in/165 x 240cm) FRF 64,000. LONDON, 23 Nov 1978, *Port in Normandy* (watercolour, 6 1/2 x 8 1/2in/16.5 x 21.5cm) GBP 2,700. PARIS, 19 June 1979, *Figures in front of a Port in Holland* (oil on panel, 12 3/4 x 18in/32.5 x 46cm) FRF 43,000. PARIS, 20 Feb 1980, *Sailing Ships in Severe Weather* (1866, watercolour and gouache, 6 1/4 x 10in/16 x 25.5cm) FRF 8,500. LONDON, 26 March 1981, *Port in Normandy* (pencil, 8 x 10 ins / 20 x 25 cm) GBP 650. NEW YORK, 25 Feb 1982, *Meal in a Convent* (1876, oil on panel, 24 1/2 x 37in/62.5 x 94cm) USD 18,000. PARIS, 11 Feb 1983, *Sailing Ships at Sea* (1866, watercolour) FRF 13,000. ROUBAIX, 27 Feb 1983, *Departure of Fishing Boats in the Channel* (1869, oil on canvas, 13 1/2 x 20 1/2in/34 x 52cm) FRF 36,000. ROUEN, 15 Dec 1985, *Boats Aground in Port* (lead pencil heightened with white, 9 x 11 3/4in/22 x 30cm) FRF 11,000. MONTE CARLO, 22 Feb 1986, *Figures in the Tempest Clinging to a Broken Mast* (1837, oil on canvas, 50½ x 76½in/128.5 x 194cm) FRF 220,000. PARIS, 27 Nov 1987, *Towpath* (oil on wood, 18 x 28in/46 x 71cm) FRF 95,000. PARIS, 11 Dec 1987, *Street in Old Rouen* (oil on paper remounted/canvas, 13 x 10¼in/33 x 26cm) FRF 13,000. NEW YORK, 24 May 1988, *Meal in a Convent* (1876, oil on panel, 24½ x 37in/62.2 x 94cm) USD 27,500. PARIS, 24 June 1988, *Sailing Ships in the Tempest* (1864, oil on canvas, 16¼ x 23¼in/41 x 59cm) FRF 50,000. PARIS, 16 Oct 1988, *Seascape* (ink, 7 x 11in/18 x 28cm) FRF 4,500. CALAIS, 13 Nov 1988, *Leaving after the Baptism* (1855, oil on canvas, 17¼ x 23¼in/44 x 59cm) FRF 42,000. STOCKHOLM, 15 Nov 1988, *Soldiers Manhandling Nuns*. MONACO, 2 Dec 1988, *Beside the Sea* (watercolour and gouache, 7¼ x 13¼in/18.2 x 33.5cm) FRF 53,280. PARIS, 9 Dec 1988, *Fisherman's Cottage Beside the Bay* (oil on canvas, 16¼ x 21¼ ins / 41 x 54 cm) FRF 51,500. CALAIS, 26 Feb 1989, *Coming out after the Baptism* (oil on canvas, 17¼ x 23½in/44 x 60cm) FRF 42,000. NEW YORK, 24 May 1989, *Gust of Wind* (oil on canvas, 16¾ x 23in/42.5 x 58.4cm) USD 10,450. NEW YORK, 25 Oct 1989, *Cardinal's Reception* (oil on canvas, 21 x 23in/53.3 x 58.5cm) USD 8,800. ZURICH, 25 Oct 1989, *Visit to a Church from the King and a Cardinal after St Bartholomew* (oil on panel, 12½ x 8¼in/32 x 21cm) CHF 4,000. PARIS, 27 Nov 1989, *Cliffs in Normandy* (oil on canvas, 11½ x 15¾in/29 x 40cm) FRF 80,000. CALAIS, 10 Dec 1989, *Family Scene* (oil on panel, 11 x 8¼in/27 x 21cm) FRF 38,000. PARIS, 4 March 1990, *Interior of a Church* (1868, oil on canvas, 32 x 23½in/81 x 60cm) FRF 45,000. NEW YORK, 23 May 1990, *Defending the Castle* (1868, oil on canvas, 33 x 22½in/83.8 x 57.2cm) USD 7,700. MONACO, 15 June 1990, *Cliffs near Étretat* (watercolour heightened with gouache, 9¾ x 13¼in/24.7 x 33.5cm) FRF 68,820. PARIS, 4 July 1990, *Shipwreck in the High Seas* (1866, oil on canvas, 26½ x 40½in/67 x 103cm) FRF 100,000. LE TOUQUET, 11 Nov 1990, *Returning to Port* (1854, oil on canvas, 22 x 32¾in/55 x 83cm) FRF 180,000. STOCKHOLM, 14 Nov 1990, *Market in a Small Town* (oil on canvas, 45¼ x 32in/115 x 81cm) SEK 65,000. LONDON, 15 Feb 1991, *Portrait of the Bust of a Lady* (oil on canvas, 28½ x 24¼in/72.4 x 61.5cm) GBP 6,050. ST-GERMAIN-EN-LAYE, 17 March 1991, *Boats in the Storm* (1866, oil on canvas, 26½ x 40½in/67 x 103cm) FRF 170,000. LONDON, 29 Nov 1991, *After the Storm* (oil on canvas, 15¼ x 11¼in/38.8 x 28.5cm) GBP 5,500. NEW YORK, 19 Feb 1992, *Approaching Storm* (oil on canvas, 22¼ x 39¼in/56.5 x 99.7cm) USD 26,400. NEW YORK, 27 May 1992, *Fishing Family* (oil on canvas, 16 x 21¼in/39.7 x 54cm) USD 4,620. MONACO, 18-19 June 1992, *Village near Dieppe* (watercolour and gouache, 10 x 13¾in/25.7 x 35cm) FRF 18,870. NEW YORK, 20 Jan 1993, *Fishing Boat Aground* (oil on canvas, 17 x 23¾in/43.2 x 60.3cm) USD 4,880. NEW YORK, 17 Feb 1993, *Mother in her Finery with Two Little Girls and a Dog under the Castle Porch* (1859, oil on canvas, 15 x 12in/38.1 x 30.5cm) USD 5,750. CALAIS, 14 March 1993, *Lady and Noblemen in Louis XV Costumes Watching the Unloading of Fish on the Shore* (oil on canvas, 13 x 20in/33 x 51cm) FRF 48,000. LONDON, 17 March 1993, *Port of Boulogne* (oil on canvas, 20½ x 15¼in/52 x 39cm) GBP 4,025. NEW YORK, 26 May 1994, *Boat in Distress near the Cliffs of Étretat* (1858, oil on panel, 19½ x 25½in/49.8 x 64.8cm) USD 11,500. PARIS, 15 Dec 1994, *Boat about to be Wrecked on the Rocks of Étretat* (1858, oil on wood, 19 x 25½in/48 x 65cm) FRF 90,200. LONDON, 10 Feb 1995, *Sailing Vessel Aground on the Shore* (oil on canvas, 12¾ x 9¾in/32.7 x 24.8cm) GBP 4,370. PARIS, 24 June 1996, *Coming out of Church* (oil on canvas, 17¾ x 19½in/45 x 49.5cm) FRF 19,000. LONDON, 21 Nov 1996, *Scene for Sir Walter Scott's Antiquary* (1821, black chalk, pen, brown ink, watercolour and gouache, 8¼ x 6¾in/20.7 x 17cm) GBP 6,900. PARIS, 29 Nov 1996, *Lords of the Manor Strolling along the Seashore* (1865, oil on canvas, 20 x 27½in/50.5 x 70cm) FRF 55,000. PARIS, 15 Dec 1996, *Seascape* (lead pencil, 9 x 10in/23 x 24.5cm) FRF 3,200. PARIS, 10 March 1997, *Young Coquette* (watercolour, 8¼ x 7in/21 x 17.5cm) FRF 7,000. PARIS, 31 March 1997, *Small Bridge in Normandy* (1841, watercolour/paper, 5 x 8¼in/12.5 x 21cm) FRF 7,500. NEW YORK, 23 May 1997, *The Love Letter (Reading in the Park)* (1853, oil on canvas, 49¾ x 35½in/126.4 x 90.2cm) USD 27,600. AMSTERDAM, 27 Oct 1997, *Coastal Scene* (oil on panel, 11¼ x 16½in/28.5 x 42cm) NLG 15,340. PARIS, 19 Dec 1997, *Boat in the Storm* (1866, canvas, 26½ x 40½in/67 x 103cm) FRF 90,000. NEW YORK, 18 March 1998, *Shipwreck* (1856, oil on canvas, 37½ x 56in/95.3 x 142.2cm) USD 34,500. PARIS, 30 April 1999, *Careening the Boats* (oil on canvas, 24 x 20 ins / 61 x 50 cm) FRF 65,000. PARIS, 18 June 1999, *Boats in the Harbour* (1839, oil on canvas, 18 x 26 ins / 46 x 65 cm) FRF 68,000. LONDON, 7 April 2000, *Lords and Ladies Attending the Arrival of the Norman Fish* (oil on canvas, 20 x 26 ins / 51 x 65 cm) GBP 12,000. PARIS, 19 June 2000, *Gale on Le Tréport Beach* (oil on canvas, 17 x 26 ins / 42 x 65 cm) FRF 75,000. LONDON, 6 June 2001, *Shipwreck* (1858, oil on canvas, 36 x 52 ins / 91 x 131 cm) GBP 15,000. LONDON, 9 Nov 2001, *Shipwreck* (oil on canvas, 25 x 38 ins / 64 x 97 cm) GBP 16,000. PARIS, 27 June 2002, *Cliff and Rocks by the Sea* (watercolour heightened with gouache, 10 x 14 ins / 26 x 35 cm) EUR 9,000. PARIS, 27 June 2002, *Album* (graphite, charcoal, pen, watercolour, gouache, set of 191, 15 x 20 ins / 37 x 51 cm) EUR 37,000. AMSTERDAM, 21 Oct 2003, *Harbour Scene in a Town* (oil on panel, 11 x 16 ins / 28 x 40 cm) EUR 12,000. LONDON, 4 Dec 2003, *Auberge de l'Ecu de France* (1857, oil on canvas, 29 x 24 ins / 74 x 60 cm) GBP 8,500. PARIS, 30 March 2004, *Brig on the Rocks* (1851, oil on panel, 17 x 23 ins / 42 x 59 cm) EUR 16,500. NEW YORK, 27 Oct 2004, *Beached Boats* (1827, oil on canvas, 29 x 36 ins / 74 x 92 cm) USD 130,000.

ISAC, Antonio
Italian, 19th century.
Born 1788, in Parma; died 1828, in Parma.
Engraver (burin).

Isac was a pupil of Bervic and Toschi; he worked in Paris and Italy. He engraved historical portraits, views and genre subjects.

MUSEUMS AND GALLERIES:
PARMA: *Theseus and the Minotaur.*

ISAC, ISACSEN, ISACSZ. See also **ISAAC, ISAACSZ**

ISACCO, or Isaach de Imbonate
Italian, 15th century.
Active at the beginning of the 15th century.
Painter.
Lombard School.

Isacco worked for the cathedral in Milan, where a fresco of 1423, *The Crucified Christ between Mary, St John and Two Saints*, is attributed to him.

ISAEV, Dmitri
Russian, 17th century.
Illuminator, draughtsman.

As a draughtsman at the Court Press in 1620, Dmitri Isaev designed vignettes and ornamental letters. He also illuminated gospel books, one of which was presented to the Tsar.

ISAGUIRRE, Manuel
Mexican, 19th century.
Painter.

Manuel Isaguirre received a commendation at the 1900 Exposition Universelle in Paris.

ISAIA DI PIPPO GHANTI DA PISA
Italian, 15th century.
Sculptor.

The son of Pippo di Giovanni di Gante, Isaia worked mainly in Rome and Naples. The tomb of Pope *Eugene IV*, sculpted in Rome in 1447, is attributed to him. He was involved in the works for the triumphal arch of Castel Nuovo, Naples, and he worked in Rome for Pope Pius II. Among his works in

Rome are: the tomb of *St Monica* in the church of S Agostino, the equestrian statues of *Nero* and *Poppea,* and a *Virgin with Child and Angels.* Also attributed to him are the tomb of *Cardinal Antonio de Chiaves of Portugal* in the cathedral of S Giovanni in Laterano, and two statuettes of apostles, probably from Pisa and now in the Kaiser Friedrich Museum, Berlin.

MUSEUMS AND GALLERIES:

BERLIN (Bodemus.): *Apostles* (two statuettes).

ISAILA, Ion

Romanian, 20th - 21st century.

Born 21 November 1953, in Sibiu.

Active in Germany from 1984.

Painter.

From 1975 to 1978, Ion Isaila studied at the N. Grigorescu institute of art in Bucharest, before moving to Düsseldorf in 1984, where he continued his training in various studios, particularly that of the engraver Rolf Sackenheim. 'I have always been fascinated by the three-dimensional expressive force of the symbol, liberated from all narration, from any Figurative element, from colour even,' Isaila has said. His spirited canvases, brimming with tension, have a pronounced dynamic. He has taken part in many group exhibitions in Romania, Germany, Switzerland, France, the Netherlands, Germany, Norway, the USA and Japan. He had his first solo exhibition in Sibiu in 1975, followed by seven others in Romania, Germany and Poland. He has been awarded many prizes and distinctions, including in 1978 the first Voronet painting prize and in 1984 a study scholarship from the academy of fine arts in Düsseldorf.

BIBLIOGRAPHY:

Romanian Artists and the West, American Romanian Academy of Arts and Sciences, Los Angeles, 1986.

ISAÏLOFF, Alexander

French, 19th - 20th century.

Born 30 December 1869, in Constantinople (Istanbul).

Painter. Landscapes, waterscapes.

Isaïloff was a pupil of Jean-Baptiste Olive. He lived and worked in Paris. He participated in the Salon des Artistes Français in Paris and was made Chevalier of the Légion d'Honneur.

MUSEUMS AND GALLERIES:

DIGNE-LES-BAINS: *View of the Esterel; St-Clair; Channel* - PARIS (Mus. de l'Armée): *View of Senones.*

ISAK, or Isaak

Swiss, 17th century.

Active in Beromünster c. 1677.

Sculptor.

ISAKA, Yasuo

Japanese, 20th century.

Born 1934.

Sculptor.

Isaka graduated with a diploma from the department of sculpture of the university of fine art in Tokyo in 1961. He featured in 1974 in the exhibition *Japanese Art of Today* held at the museum of contemporary art in Montreal.

ISAKOV, Andrei

Russian, 18th century.

Painter and decorative artist.

In 1744, Andei Isakov worked on the decoration of the Cathedral of Sts Peter and Paul, in 1745 of one of the Tsarina's palaces, in 1749 of the newly-built church at Tsarskoe-Selo, and in 1750 of the Anichkov Palace, St Petersburg.

ISAKOV, Fedor

Russian, 18th century.

Painter.

Fedor Isakov worked in St Petersburg.

ISAKOV, Filat

Russian, 17th century.

Active in Novgorod.

Icon painter.

Filat Isakov was sent to Moscow in 1660, where he helped in the painting of the Cathedral of the Dormition.

ISAKOV, Vasili Ivanovich

Russian, 19th century.

Born 1819; died 17 March 1879, in St Petersburg.

Sculptor.

In 1850, Vasili Ivanovich Isakov was awarded the title 'Free Artist' for his bust of the painter Luchaninov.

ISAKOVA, R.

Russian, 20th century.

Painter. Landscapes.

AUCTION RECORDS:

PARIS, 14 May 1990, *Mountain Stream in Summer* (1989, oil on canvas, 19 3/4 x 23 1/2 ins / 50 x 60 cm) FRF 7,000.

ISAKSON, Karl

Swedish, 20th century.

Born 1878, in Stockholm; died 1922, in Copenhagen.

Active from 1902 in Denmark.

Painter. Figures, landscapes, still-lifes, flowers.

School of Bornholm.

From 1897-1901, Karl Isakson attended the art academy in Stockholm, then made several trips to Paris, where he discovered the work of Cézanne, the Cubists, and Matisse. He studied under Zhartmann in Italy and followed Matisse's advice. He belonged to the School of Bornholm, which was formed in 1911 and was the last substantial community of Danish artists after the School of Skagen and the School of Funen in the second half of the 19th century. The School of Bornholm was fostered by new approaches to painting, with emphasis on the effects of colour and form. From the beginning of his career, Isakson explored colour and the construction of forms. He viewed his works, which were composed of plans with luminous tones, as the basis for a large Biblical project.

BIBLIOGRAPHY:

Johansen, Annette, et al., *Danske Kunstnerkolonier: Skagen, Fyn, Bornholm,* group exhibition catalogue, Aarhus Kunstmuseum, Aarhus, 2000.

MUSEUMS AND GALLERIES:

GÖTEBORG: *Raising of Lazarus* - STOCKHOLM (Moderna Mus.): *Raising of Lazarus* - STOCKHOLM (Nationalmus.).

AUCTION RECORDS:

COPENHAGEN, 20 Oct 1976, *Seated Young Woman* (oil on canvas, 38 1/4 x 26 ins / 97 x 66 cm) DKK 32,000. COPENHAGEN, 5 Oct 1977, *Still-life* (1920, oil on canvas, 24 1/2 x 18 1/2 ins / 62 x 47 cm) DKK 54,000. COPENHAGEN, 10 Oct 1979, *Still-life* (1918-1920, oil on canvas, 29 1/2 x 23 1/2 ins / 75 x 60 cm) DKK 58,000. COPENHAGEN, 13 Oct 1981, *Still-life* (1911, oil on canvas, 20 3/4 x 22 1/4 ins / 53 x 56.5 cm) DKK 92,000. STOCKHOLM, 29 Nov 1983, *Interior* (oil on canvas, 28 x 29 1/2 ins / 71 x 75 cm) SEK 75,000. COPENHAGEN, 16 Sept 1987, *Still-life* (1916-1918, oil on canvas, 20 1/2 x 25 1/4 ins / 52 x 64 cm) DKK 170,000. COPENHAGEN, 9 May 1990, *Still-life with Spring Flowers* (oil on canvas, 23 1/4 x 28 1/4 ins / 59 x 72 cm) DKK 157,000. STOCKHOLM, 5-6 Dec 1990, *Still-life with Flowers in a Vase* (oil on canvas, 26 1/2 x 20 3/4 ins / 67 x 53 cm) SEK 46,000. COPENHAGEN, 4 Dec 1991, *Still-life* (1918, oil on canvas, 25 1/2 x 29 1/4 ins / 65 x 74 cm) DKK 172,000. COPENHAGEN, 1 April 1992, *Bouquet in a Vase* (1909, oil on canvas, 23 1/2 x 26 ins / 60 x 66 cm) DKK 165,000. COPENHAGEN, 13 April 1994, *Still-life* (oil on canvas, 25 1/2 x 23 1/2 ins / 65 x 60 cm) DKK 190,000. AMSTERDAM, 31 May 1994, *Lighthouse near Christiansø* (oil on canvas, 24 1/2 x 26 1/2 ins / 62.5 x 67 cm) NLG 23,000. COPENHAGEN, 26 April 1995, *Standing Model* (oil on canvas, 38 1/2 x 26 ins / 98 x 66 cm) DKK 106,000. COPENHAGEN, 17

April 1996, *Krudttårnet på Christiansø* (*The Gunpowder Tower at Christiansø*) (1921, oil on canvas, 24½ x 26½ ins / 62 x 67 cm) DKK 103,000. STOCKHOLM, 27 April 1999, *Seated Woman Wearing Green Blouse* (c. 1920, oil on canvas, 37 x 30 ins / 95 x 77 cm) SEK 230,000. STOCKHOLM, 17 May 1999, *Still-life with Lemons, Oranges and Books* (oil on canvas, 19 x 24 ins / 49 x 61 cm) SEK 230,000. COPENHAGEN, 3 Oct 2000, *Still-life of Jugs, Books and Vase on Table* (c. 1915, oil on canvas, 22 x 25 ins / 56 x 63 cm) DKK 135,000. STOCKHOLM, 7 Nov 2000, *Standing Female Model. Interior Scene with Seated Woman* (c. 1918-1919, oil on canvas, double-sided, 37 x 25 ins / 95 x 63 cm) SEK 290,000. COPENHAGEN, 2 April 2001, *Cliffs and Green Trees, Christiansø* (c. 1920-1921, oil on canvas, 27 x 33 ins / 69 x 85 cm) DKK 200,000. COPENHAGEN, 2 Oct 2001, *Landscape with Cliffs and Sea, Christiansø* (1920-1921, oil on canvas, 26 x 30 ins / 66 x 76 cm) DKK 150,000. COPENHAGEN, 18 June 2002, *Still-life of Jugs, Books and Vase on Table* (c. 1915, oil on canvas, 22 x 25 ins / 56 x 63 cm) DKK 150,000. COPENHAGEN, 1 Oct 2002, *Still-life of Potted Plant, Orange, Jug and Books* (c. 1915, oil on canvas, 26 x 22 ins / 66 x 55 cm) DKK 300,000. COPENHAGEN, 1 April 2003, *Still-life of Green Jug, Books and Stoneware Pot* (c. 1916, oil on canvas, 27 x 21 ins / 68 x 54 cm) DKK 340,000. STOCKHOLM, 7 May 2003, *Flowers in Vase and Books on Table* (1918-1920, oil on canvas, 22 x 28 ins / 57 x 72 cm) SEK 240,000. STOCKHOLM, 27 April 2004, *Still-life of Tulips and Oranges* (oil on canvas, 27 x 20 ins / 68 x 52 cm) SEK 220,000. COPENHAGEN, 5 Oct 2004, *Model Picture. Seated Model* (1912, oil on canvas, 43 x 29 ins / 109 x 74 cm) DKK 150,000.

ISAKSON-SILLÉN, Ida
Swedish, 20th century.
Sculptor.

In 1976, Ida Isakson-Sillén contributed works to the exhibition *Street Art* in Borlänge, which brought together various contemporary Swedish sculptors.

ISAMBERT, Alphonse
French, 19th century.
Born October 1818, in Paris.
Painter. History painting, genre scenes.

Alphonse Isambert was a pupil of P. Delaroche and de Gleyre. He exhibited at the Salon from 1840 to 1867.

MUSEUMS AND GALLERIES:
AMIENS: *Diogenes*.

AUCTION RECORDS:
LONDON, 22 Nov 1990, *Tame Bird* (oil on canvas, 22 x 18in/55 x 46cm) GBP 1,650.

ISAMITT
Chilean, 20th century.
Painter.

In 1946 Isamitt exhibited at the open exhibition organised by the United Nations at the Musée d'Art Moderne in Paris, where he showed *Seals*.

ISANDRUS
Sculptor.
Ancient Greek.

Isandrus worked on the decoration of the temple of Athena Polias on the Acropolis at Athens.

ISAURE, René
French, 20th century.
Born 1929, in Vicdessos (Haute-Garonne).
Engraver.

Isaure studied at the École des Beaux-Arts in Toulouse, in the studio of Louis Louvrier. He was also a friend and pupil of Maurice Mélat. In 2002, his works were included in an exhibition in homage to Maurice Mélat, organised by the Musée Goya in Castres.

ISAYAMA, Reikichti
Japanese, 19th century.
Active in Tokyo.
Painter.

Isayama featured in the Exposition Universelle of 1900 in Paris.

ISBERG, Helena Sofia
Swedish, 19th century.
Born in Småland; died 1875, in Motala.
Sculptor (wood).

From early on Helena Isberg devoted herself to wood sculpture and executed numerous jugs, pipes and cases decorated in relief. Her works were shown at the exhibition of applied arts in Stockholm in 1847 and the International Exhibition in London in 1862. An exhibition of her work was mounted in Motala in 1925.

ISBERT, Camille Cornelia
Maiden name: Paillard
French, 19th - 20th century.
Born 20 May 1825, in Paris; died January 1911, in Paris.
Painter, miniaturist. Portraits, genre scenes, flowers.

Isbert was a pupil of Henry Scheffer. She participated in the Salon from 1845. Her membership of the Société des Artistes Français dates from 1887.

AUCTION RECORDS:
PARIS, 14 Nov 1946, *Seated Lady* (1852, miniature) FRF 14,000; *The Spinner* (miniature) FRF 16,000; *Young Woman Embroidering* (miniature after Chardin) FRF 12,500; *Couple Making Music; Love Disarmed* (two miniature pendants) FRF 14,000; *Portrait of a Young Man in Louis XVIth Dress* (miniature) FRF 10,000. COPENHAGEN, 10 Feb 1976, *Vase of Flowers* (oil on canvas, 16½ x 13 ins / 42 x 33 cm) DKK 2,700.

ISBRAND, Victor
Danish, 20th century.
Born 6 July 1897.
Painter. Figures, local figures.

Victor Isbrand attended the Kunstakademi in Copenhagen. In 1915 he exhibited in Charlottenborg, and in 1919 he won a small gold medal for his painting *Aphrodite and Eros*. Isbrand embarked on a trip to the East where, like Paul Gauguin, he explored subjects for his Primitive style of painting: *Young Malay Boy, Johore, Head of a Young Javanese Girl* and *Javanese Woman*.

AUCTION RECORDS:
COPENHAGEN, 21-22 March 1990, *Standing Model* (1934, oil on canvas, 37½ x 27½ ins / 95 x 70 cm) DKK 16,000. COPENHAGEN, 26 April 1995, *Children from Greenland* (oil on canvas, 21¼ x 25½ ins / 54 x 65 cm) DKK 4,000. COPENHAGEN, 23 March 1999, *Nude Young Girl* (1934, oil on canvas, 37 x 26 ins / 94 x 67 cm) DKK 13,000.

ISBRE, Laurent, or Ysbre
French, 15th century.
Active in Rouen.
Sculptor (wood).

Laurent Isbre did the ornamental carving of the handsome choir stalls in Rouen Cathedral on which he and Philippot Viart worked.

ISCAN, Ferit
Italian, 20th century.
Born 8 May 1931, in Trieste; died 8 March 1986, in Paris.
Active from 1938, since 1967 naturalised in France.
Painter, collage artist. Interiors with figures, still-lifes, landscapes.

Ferit Iscan was of Turkish origin and went to Paris in 1938 after travelling in childhood. He began to paint in 1948-1949 with Jean Souverbie at the École des Beaux-Arts, Paris, and in André Lhote's private workshop. He also lived in the Lot, where he was buried in Montvalent.

His discovery of the work of Paul Klee led him to investigate a language of poetic abstraction in the years 1949 to 1951. Then, after a short return to figurative painting, he adopted a style somewhere between realism and abstraction, only to move on to a neo-Cubism very much in the spirit of the Paris School. He also painted landscapes, working from photographs that he transposed, in order to achieve the 'atmospheric truth via the geological truth' by simplifying the contours imaginatively. In his search for atmosphere he often used 'chalky' paint. After 1977 there is a gradual increase in the presence of water in his painting. He also made collages. With his obvious and widely appreciated painterly gifts, he was uncomfortable working in a period when such painting was not valued, and had difficulty in choosing for himself and accepting a path that, even if he were mistaken, allowed him to be himself.

He took part in the Paris Salon de la Jeune Pinture, Salon d'Automne, Salon Comparaisons, Salon 'Schèmes 64', Salon de Mai and Salon des Réalités Nouvelles, in the Biennales of Paris, Menton and Venice 1976, and at a Royal Academy Exhibition in London. He won the Prix du Dôme in 1956 and the Prix de la Jeune Peinture in 1961. He showed in solo exhibitions in Paris in 1955, 1957, 1960, 1965, 1967, 1969, 1973, 1978, 1979, 1981; in New York in 1958; in London in 1959; in Souillac in 1960; in Toulouse in 1967; in Perpignan in 1971; in Brussels in 1975, and in Trans-en-Provence in 1979. After his death in 1997 the Galerie Taménaga organised a *Tribute to Iscan*.

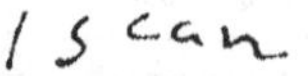

MUSEUMS AND GALLERIES:
CAEN - PARIS (FNAC) - PARIS (MAMVP) - TOULOUSE (MBA, Mus. des Augustins).

AUCTION RECORDS:
PARIS, 12 July 1988, *Composition* (1966, oil on canvas, 39 1/4 x 32 ins / 100 x 81 cm) FRF 5,500. PARIS, 15 Oct 1990, *Bombyx Moth* (1960, oil on canvas, 13 x 22 ins / 33 x 55 cm) FRF 6,000. PARIS, 8 Oct 1991, *Still-life with Pomegranate* (1983, oil on canvas, 36 1/4 x 28 3/4 ins / 92 x 73 cm) FRF 11,500. PARIS, 20 Nov 1991, *Street* (1981, oil on canvas, 20 x 20 ins / 51 x 51 cm) FRF 11,000. PARIS, 22 March 1998, *Red Paintbrushes* (oil on canvas, 36 1/4 x 28 3/4 ins / 92 x 73 cm) FRF 5,500.

ISCHER, Klara
Swiss, 19th century.
Born 19 June 1867, in Bern.
Watercolourist. Landscapes.

Ischer was a student at the École des Arts Industriels in Geneva.

ISCHI, Pierre
Swiss, 20th century.
Born 7 November 1924, in Geneva.
Active from 1948 in France.
Sculptor, engraver.

From 1939-1943, Pierre Ischi attended the École des Arts Industriels in Geneva. In 1948 he arrived in France and settled in the Alpes-Maritimes region. Since 1957 he has exhibited his engravings in Nice, Geneva and Paris. In 1969 Ischi presented a solo exhibition of his sculptures in Paris. From 1951, he has been producing sculptures, which depict unadorned forms: solids contained by parallelograms or arcs of circles, playing on a certain imbalance.

ISCHINGER, Hans
German, 20th century.
Born 7 April 1891, in Munich.
Sculptor. Animals.

In 1914, Hans Ischinger attended the art academy in Munich and exhibited animal sculptures at the Glaspalast (Ice Palace) there. His sculptures were based on the life of birds in particular.

ISEBRANT, Gérard, or Ysebrant
Dutch, 17th century.
Active in 1630.
Painter.

ISEI, real name: Eihaku
Japanese, 16th century.
Active in the middle of the 16th century.
Painter.

Isei was the pupil of Motonobu (1476-1559). He was a landscape painter living at Higo (modern Kumanoto Prefecture).

ISEK KINGELEZ, Bodys. See **KINGELEZ Bodys Isek**

ISELBURG. See also **ISSELBURG**

ISELBURG, Bartolomé
Flemish School, 17th century.
Active in Hamburg in 1650.
Engraver (burin).

Bartolomé Iselburg engraved historical portraits. He is known in particular for his *Charles I, King of England*.

ISELI, Andreas
Swiss, 16th century.
Active in Bern c. 1560.
Glass painter.

ISELI, Heinrich, or Yselin
Swiss, 16th century.
Glass painter.

Heinrich Iseli married in Bern in 1550.

ISELI, Rolf
Swiss, 20th century.
Born 22 January 1934, in Bern.
Active in France.
Painter, engraver, sculptor, mixed media.

After learning the photolithographic process as an apprentice, Rolf Iseli attended the arts and crafts school in Bern. From 1953-1954 (his training period), Iseli produced his first non-figurative pictures. In 1955, he discovered Sam Francis (1923-1994) and the other American action painters in Paris. His abstract spaces, which emerged from loose brushwork, already reflected a romantic element, with a restrained lyricism, and were more delicate than vigorous and spontaneous. As his work gradually evolved, Iseli moved on to large monochrome areas and massive polychrome spaces which characterised his abstract period, although as was the case for most painters, but particularly for Iseli, the abstract-figurative boundary was strictly meaningless. In around 1968, Iseli reintroduced figurative elements into his work, with the object as a starting point; he exploited it, saturated it with colour to express its material essence, weight and presence; he gave the object an aggressive quality, making the picture erupt in an explosion of colour. These are the series of paintings or engravings on the themes of the *Clothes Peg*, the *Wooden Cubes*, and the *Mushrooms*. Afterwards *Man-Mushroom*, *Man-Cactus* and *Earth Man* were born, in which from a photograph of his face, he tried to reach beyond the individuality of the face and find a deeper reality by transforming it into a mushroom, a cactus; by spattering it with earth, ripping it, making holes in it or covering it with informal graffiti. Here, as in the beautiful *Earth Canvases* (around 1970), he painted the earth of St-Roman, the village where he lived, conveying nature's abundance; the romantic element of nature within which its cycle, humankind and the earth are inextricably linked and where the subject matter only exists as the equivalence of an initial sensation. Primarily a painter and lithographer, in addition Iseli produced three-dimensional work, and his sculptures also seem to emerge directly from the subject matter and are more like moulds than real sculptures.

He contributed to various group exhibitions and international meetings including: 1959, 1972, the Documenta, Kassel; 1959, the Paris Biennale; 1962, the Carnegie Institute, Pittsburgh; 1963, the 7th São Paulo Biennale; 1969, the Stedelijk Museum, Amsterdam; 1970, Stuttgart; 1972, the Galerie Raeber, Lucerne; 1972, the Grand Palais, Paris; 1992, the CREDAC, Ivry-sur-Seine; 2003, with Peter Stein and Alois Lichtsteiner, the Musée des Beaux-Arts, Bern; in 1956, he held his first private exhibition in Bern, then: 1960, 1962, 1968, 1975, Basel; 1962, 1967, 1970, Solothurn; 1965, Zurich; 1965, the Kunsthalle, Bern; 1968, the Kunstmuseum, Lucerne; 1992, the Centre Culturel Suisse, Paris.

BIBLIOGRAPHY:

'Rolf Iseli, peintre-graveur' in *Art et Métiers du Livre* no. 173 p 44, periodical, Paris, 1992.

MUSEUMS AND GALLERIES:

AMSTERDAM (Stedelijk Mus.): *Stockschwamm-man* (1975); *Little Louis* (1975).

AUCTION RECORDS:

BERN, 3 May 1979, *Abstract Composition* (1961, watercolour/vellum, 24 1/2 x 19 3/4 ins / 62 x 50 cm) CHF 2,400. BERN, 25 June 1981, *Green and Blue Composition* (1962, oil on canvas, 59 x 47 1/4 ins / 150 x 120 cm) CHF 8,000. BERN, 20 June 1984, *Blue and Red* (1957-1958, oil on canvas, 25 1/2 x 19 3/4 ins / 65 x 50 cm) CHF 6,000. BERN, 18 June 1987, *Verloffene 5* (1970, watercolour and gouache/pencil outlines, 20 x 27 ins / 50.8 x 68.8 cm) CHF 10,800. ZURICH, 18 Oct 1990, *Composition* (1962, gouache, 19 1/2 x 24 1/4 ins / 49.7 x 61.5 cm) CHF 15,000. LUCERNE, 23 May 1992, *Nail Crosspieces on Watercolour* (1981, mixed media/paper, 30 3/4 x 22 1/2 ins / 78 x 57 cm) CHF 10,000. ZURICH, 14-16 Oct 1992, *Red Composition* (1965, oil on canvas, 48 x 37 1/2 ins / 122 x 95.2 cm) CHF 23,000. LUCERNE, 15 May 1993, *Untitled* (1962, watercolour/paper, 24 1/2 x 19 ins / 62 x 48 cm) CHF 8,800. ZURICH, 9 June 1993, *The 8th Stone* (1985, charcoal, watercolour and gouache/paper, 25 1/2 x 39 ins / 65 x 99 cm) CHF 10,350. ZURICH, 13 Oct 1994, *King Kong in France* (mixed media and collage, 5 1/2 x 6 1/2 ins / 14 x 16.6 cm) CHF 950. ZURICH, 7 April 1995, *Untitled* (1962, watercolour, 24 1/2 x 19 ins / 62 x 48.5 cm) CHF 10,000. LUCERNE, 23 Nov 1996, *Untitled* (1963, watercolour, 24 1/2 x 18 3/4 ins / 62.5 x 47.5 cm) CHF 4,800. ZURICH, 8 April 1997, *Put against the Wall* (mixed media/paper, sketch in relief, 20 x 26 ins / 50.5 x 66 cm) CHF 6,000. ZURICH, 19 Nov 1997, *Composition* (1975, mixed media/paper, 12 1/2 x 11 ins / 32 x 27 cm) CHF 1,900. ZURICH, 23 March 1999, *Untitled* (1976, watercolour and sand, 51 x 31 ins / 129 x 80 cm) CHF 15,500. BERN, 5 Nov 1999, *Sagorsk* (1988, acrylic, soil. graphite and powdered paint, 42 x 30 ins / 107 x 76 cm) CHF 26,000. COLOGNE, 6 June 2000, *Shadows* (1984, gouache, ink, charcoal, soil and chalk, 60 x 41 ins / 153 x 104 cm) DEM 17,000. BERN, 3 Nov 2000, *Crust at the Edge* (1979, acrylic and collage, 59 x 40 ins / 150 x 102 cm) CHF 24,000. BERN, 21 June 2001, *The Path below Roches St Romain* (acrylic, earth, watercolour, Indian ink over chalk and wash, 30 x 42 ins / 76 x 106 cm) CHF 11,000. LUCERNE, 24 Nov 2001, *Struktur des Hommes Cactusse* (1973, mixed media, tempera on paper on board, 31 x 23 ins / 79 x 59 cm) CHF 12,000. BERN, 8 Nov 2002, *Orange Composition with Feathers* (1977, feathers, soil, gouache, pastel and watercolour, 42 x 30 ins / 107 x 76 cm) CHF 18,000. ZURICH, 25 Nov 2002, *Man of the Soil* (1972, earth, watercolour, oil and pencil, 30 x 42 ins / 76 x 106 cm) CHF 13,000. LUCERNE, 22 Nov 2003, *Untitled* (1979, watercolour, sand, colour chalk, 20 x 26 ins / 52 x 66 cm) CHF 8,000. ZURICH, 25 Nov 2003, *Mushroom Man* (pencil, watercolour, earth, 26 x 19 ins / 65 x 48 cm) CHF 5,000. ZURICH, 29 Nov 2004, *Stockhorn with a Fence* (1969, pencil and watercolour, 42 x 30 ins / 106 x 76 cm) CHF 3,500.

ISELIN, Georges

French, 19th - 20th century.

Born 6 December 1874, in Claire-Goutte (Haute-Saône).

Sculptor.

Georges Iselin was a pupil of Antonin Mercié and Hector Lemaire. He exhibited in Paris at the Salon des Artistes Français, of which he became a member in 1900. He received an honourable mention in 1899 and a third-class medal in 1909.

MUSEUMS AND GALLERIES:

GRAY: *Filial Love.*

ISELIN, Henri Frédéric

French, 19th century.

Born 14 December 1825, in Claire-Goutte (Haute-Saône); died March 1905.

Sculptor.

Henri Iselin was a pupil of Rude. He began his career at the Salon in Paris in 1849, gaining third-class medals in 1852 and at the Exposition Universelle in 1855, then again in 1857, a second-class medal in 1861 and the same award again in 1863. He was made a Chevalier of the Légion d'Honneur in 1863.

Iselin's most important works are: *Jean Goujon*, a marble bust located in the ministry of the interior; *Picard, Playwright*, a marble bust in the courtroom of the of the Institut; *Count de Morny*, a marble bust; *Baron Poisson*, a marble bust at the École Normale (teacher-training college); *Lagrange*, a marble bust in the office of longitudes at the Institut, *Fire Spirit*, a group carved in stone for the new Louvre; *Napoleon III*, a marble statue for the court of the legislative body; *Donizetti*, a marble bust for the conservatory of music; and *Elegance*, a statue for the foyer of the new opera house.

MUSEUMS AND GALLERIES:

BALTIMORE (Peabody Art Collection): *Le Prince Napoléon Bonaparte* (*Prince Napoleon Bonaparte*) (1858, plaster); *Napoléon Bonaparte III* (*Napoleon Bonaparte III*) (1858, plaster); *Patterson* (bronze); *Son of Patterson* - BESANÇON: *Duke de Bauffremont* - CANNES: *Mérimée* (bronze) - ÉPINAL: *Duke de Bauffremont* (plaster) - LE HAVRE: *Abbot Cochet* (terracotta) - LURE: *P* (bronze bust) - PARIS (MAM): *President Boileau* (marble bust) - PARIS (Mus. National du Moyen Age): *Napoleon III* - ROUEN: *Abbot Cochet* (terracotta) - VERSAILLES: *King Murat* (marble); *Prince de Bauffremont; Courtenay; Duke de Morny; Marquis de Moustier; Count de Rambuteau; General de Lamorcière; Claude Bernard; The Count de Persigny* - VESOUL: *De Marmier.*

ISELIN, Louis Édouard

French, 19th century.

Born 19th century, in Claire-Goutte (Haute-Saône).

Sculptor.

Louis Iselin was a pupil of Millet, Dumont and Cordier. He exhibited at the Salon de Paris in 1873 and 1874.

MUSEUMS AND GALLERIES:

AJACCIO: *Bust of Prosper Mérimée.*

ISELLA, Louisa

American, 19th - 20th century.

Born 19th century, in Buenos Aires.

Sculptor.

Louisa Isella exhibited at the Salon des Artistes Français, where she was awarded an honourable mention in 1908.

ISELLA, Pietro

Italian, 19th century.

Born 1812, in Morcote; died 1871, in Morcote.

Sculptor.

Isella began his studies at the Accademia di Belle Arti di Brera, Milan, and then accompanied his teacher, Bianchi, to Naples and Pompeii. He was responsible for the restoration of many Italian churches and palazzi, including the cathedrals of Novara and Vercelli.

ISELLA, Pietro
Italian, 19th century.
Born 9 January 1827, in Morcote; died 1887, in Vienna.
Painter.
Isella was a pupil at the Accademia di Belle Arti di Brera, Milan. He was responsible for many decorative paintings, in the theatre of Bucharest, the Lauiger Schloss (the residence of the former Empress of Austria), the theatre and museum of Prague, and at the Paris Exposition Universelle of 1878, among others.

ISEN. See **KANO Isen**

ISENBART, Émile. See **ISENBART Marie Victor Émile**

ISENBART, Marie Victor Emile
French, 19th - 20th century.
Born 3 March 1846, in Besançon; died March 1921, in Besançon.
Painter. Mythological subjects, landscapes, mountainscapes, waterscapes.
Isenbart was a pupil of Clément Fanart. His landscapes depict the Franche-Comté region. He exhibited in Paris at the Salon, beginning in 1872, and at the Salon des Artistes Français, of which he was a member from 1888. He also exhibited in Vienna and Munich. He received various prizes, including an honourable mention in 1885, a third-class medal in 1888, a bronze medal at the Exposition Universelle in 1889, a second-class medal in 1891 and a bronze medal at the Exposition Universelle in 1900. He was named Chevalier of the Légion d'Honneur in 1897.

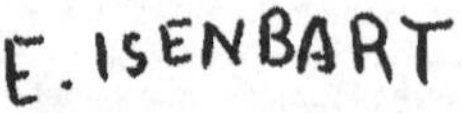

MUSEUMS AND GALLERIES:
AUTUN: *The Toilette of Venus* - BESANÇON: *The Old Chamars* - BREST: *The Banks of the Doubs; A Wood in Plougastel* - CAMBRAI: *The First Leaves* - CARPENTRAS: *Captive Love* - CHÂLONS-EN-CHAMPAGNE: *The Plateaux of the Jura* - DIJON: *Coltsfoot* - LANGRES: *Marsh in the Mountains of the Doubs* - LE MANS: *Pine Forest* - LOUVIERS (Mus. municipal): *Morning by the Doubs* - MULHOUSE: *A Branch of the Doubs* - ROUEN: *Stream of the Val-Noir* - SÈTE: *The Banks of the Doubs* - TROYES: *Evening on the Banks of the Odet.*
AUCTION RECORDS:
MARSEILLES, 1900, *Landscape,* FRF 525. MARSEILLES, 20 Nov 1925, *The Wash-house by the Bank of a Stream,* FRF 750. MARSEILLES, 9-10 May 1927, *Riverbanks,* FRF 520. MARSEILLES, 22 Feb 1928, *Harvests, Landscape,* FRF 225. MARSEILLES, 20 Nov 1942, *The Little Pool,* FRF 400. MARSEILLES, 24 May 1944, *Autumn Landscape,* FRF 2,500. MARSEILLES, 14 June 1944, *Stream in the Underbrush* (1877) FRF 17,500. MARSEILLES, 28 Jan 1949, *By the Water,* FRF 10,800. BESANÇON, 23 Feb 1951, *Underbrush Near Pontarlier,* FRF 15,000. BESANÇON, 29 June 1973, *Breton Coast,* FRF 900. VERSAILLES, 10 Dec 1978, *The Village* (oil on canvas, 19 x 25 1/2 ins / 48.5 x 65 cm) FRF 5,600. BESANÇON, 22 April 1979, *Riverbank* (oil on canvas, 46 x 31 1/2 ins / 116 x 80 cm) FRF 14,000. DIJON, 5 Dec 1982, *View of Besançon* (oil on canvas, 39 1/4 x 55 ins / 100 x 140 cm) FRF 41,000. PARIS, 24 Oct 1983, *Women by the Edge of the River* (oil on canvas, 25 1/2 x 21 1/4 ins / 65 x 54 cm) FRF 18,500. PARIS, 3 Dec 1986, *Shepherdess and Sheep by the River* (oil on canvas, 18 x 31 1/2 ins / 46 x 80 cm) FRF 35,000. PARIS, 9 March 1987, *The Laundresses* (oil on canvas, 35 3/4 x 28 1/4 ins / 91 x 72 cm) FRF 33,000. PARIS, 29 April 1988, *Underbrush* (oil on canvas, 19 3/4 x 17 3/4 ins / 50 x 45 cm) FRF 8,500. NIMES, 25 Feb 1989, *Landscape* (oil on canvas, 18 x 24 ins / 46 x 61 cm) FRF 30,000. RHEIMS, 5 March 1989, *Landscape Near a River* (oil on canvas, 49 1/4 x 74 3/4 ins / 125 x 190 cm) FRF 82,600. NEW YORK, 24 May 1989, *The Artist's Family on a Beach in Brittany Around 1890* (oil on canvas, 22 x 39 1/4 ins / 55 x 100 cm) USD 16,500. RHEIMS, 11 June 1989, *Laundress on the Banks of the Doubs* (oil on canvas, 11 x 18 ins / 28 x 46 cm) FRF 29,000. LONDON, 21 June 1989, *The Length of the River* (oil on canvas, 49 1/4 x 74 3/4 ins / 125 x 190 cm) GBP 9,350. BESANÇON, 1 April 1990, *The Banks of the Ognon in Voray* (oil on canvas, 19 1/4 x 27 1/2 ins / 49 x 70 cm) FRF 110,000. PARIS, 3 July 1991, *Maritime Landscape with Laundresses* (oil on canvas, 20 x 25 1/2 ins / 50.5 x 65 cm) FRF 57,000. PARIS, 18 Dec 1991, *The Edge of a Pond* (oil on canvas, 19 x 15 3/4 ins / 48 x 40 cm) FRF 11,000. LYONS, 8 April 1992, *River with Figures* (oil on canvas, 22 1/4 x 17 1/4 ins / 56.5 x 44 cm, 2 ins/5 cm) FRF 30,000. NEW YORK, 29 Oct 1992, *La vallée de Lion* (oil on canvas, 18 x 25 3/4 ins / 45.7 x 65.4 cm) USD 4,620. PARIS, 11 May 1993, *Livestock in the Valley* (oil on canvas, 18 x 33 1/2 ins / 46 x 85 cm) FRF 34,000. BESANÇON, 27 Feb 1994, *The Reverotte Near Gigot* (oil on canvas, 27 1/2 x 37 3/4 ins / 70 x 96 cm) FRF 83,000. PARIS, 15 June 1994, *The Quays of the Doubs in Besançon* (oil on card/canvas, 17 3/4 x 19 3/4 ins / 45 x 50 cm) FRF 8,500. BESANÇON, 8 Oct 1995, *The Banks of the Loue* (oil on canvas, 41 3/4 x 30 ins / 106 x 76 cm) FRF 80,000. PARIS, 10 April 1996, *By the Edge of a Stream* (oil on canvas, 23 3/4 x 19 1/2 ins / 60.5 x 49.5 cm) FRF 30,000. LONS-LE-SAUNIER, 27 May 1996, *Franche-Comté Landscape* (oil on canvas, 37 x 25 1/2 ins / 94 x 65 cm) FRF 73,000. PARIS, 25 May 1997, *Peasant Woman in a Clearing* (oil on canvas, 29 1/2 x 48 ins / 75 x 121 cm) FRF 34,000.

ISENBERG, Constantin Vasilievich
Russian, 19th - 20th century.
Born 25 November 1859; died September 1911.
Sculptor, silhouettist.
Isenberg was student at the St Petersburg academy in 1882. He was the sculptor of the monument placed in Alexander Square in 1910 to commemorate the torpedo boat Stereguchtchy lost on 19 March 1904 off Port-Arthur (now Lü-Shun, Manchuria) during the Russo-Japanese War.

ISENBRANT, Adriaen, or Ysenbrant, Ysenbrandt, Hysebrant, called the Pseudo-Mostaert, perhaps also the Master of the Seven Sorrows of the Virgin adored by the Van de Velde Family
Flemish, 16th century.
Born c. 1490; died July 1551, in Bruges.
Painter. Religious subjects, portraits, landscapes with figures.
Bruges School, Flemish School.
There are various theories about Adriaen Isenbrant's life. It is not known where he was born - possibly in Haarlem - or where or with whom he studied. He arrived in Bruges in 1510 and bought his citizenship there. He became a free-master of the Guild of St Luke and St Eloi on 29 November in the same year. He held 11 different posts in the corporation but never became dean. He was married twice, the first time to a daughter of the painter Pieter Grandael, and the second time, in 1547, to Clementine de Hoene. According to Sanderus he worked with Gerard David and was an excellent painter of nudes and portraits. He was buried in the church of St James in Bruges.

Van Male described Isenbrant's paintings as being works of great delicacy, executed with enormous care. His landscapes were enlivened by figures. No single painting has documentation to prove that Isenbrant produced it, but it is known that he sent work to Spain via Antwerp and Bilbao. Dr Waagen attributed to Jan Mostaert of Haarlem several paintings of Spaniards now thought to be by Isenbrant, which is why Isenbrant is sometimes referred to as the Pseudo-Mostaert of Wagen. In his critical catalogue of an exhibition of paintings in Bruges in 1902, Hulin de Loo suggested that he should be identified with the Master of the Virgin of the Seven Sorrows, a suggestion that is now generally accepted, so that Isenbrant can be credited with the other previously anonymous works of that Flemish master. It is thought that as a young man he painted the diptych *The Virgin of the Seven Sorrows Adored by the van der Velde Family*, the separated leaves of which are now in the church of Our Lady in Bruges and the Brussels museum. Various painters worked in his studio, producing Madonnas and angels which would then be attributed to him, so it is not surprising that he is thought to have had a considerable output. He may also have painted the great *Adoration of the Magi*, a triptych in Lübeck Cathedral dated to 1518, said by Wauters to be Isenbrant's greatest work, which was destroyed in World War II.

Wauters also says that work by the Master of the Virgin of the Seven Sorrows can be found in the museums of Antwerp (the catalogue attributes *Christ in the Tomb* to a pupil of Isenbrant), London, Madrid, Frankfurt, Berlin, Dresden, Aachen, and New York, in the church of St Saviour in Bruges (*The Presentation in the Temple*), and in the collections of Lord Northbrook (*The Vision of St Alfonso*), A. Valley in Munich, Prince Doria in Rome, Bussel in Aachen, Lolmar in Beme, Sir F. Cook in Richmond, van Kauffmann in Berlin, Ganz in Frankfurt, Scribe in Ghent, Visart de Brocamie in Bruges, Mayer van den Berghe in Antwerp, Paul Ollet in Brussels, and Edmond de Rothschild in Paris. All of these, therefore, could be attributed to Isenbrant. M. J. Waele says that the painting *The Wedding in Cana*, kept in the Louvre as being by Gerard David and dated to 1523, may be by Isenbrant. The *Lamentation over the Body of Christ* in Antwerp, the *Virgin and Child* in Coimbra and the *Flight into Egypt* in Vienna are also attributed to him.

Many of his works were collected together in the 1902 *L'Exposition des Primitifs flamands* (*Exhibition of Flemish Primitives*) in Bruges. His work also featured in the 1994 *Hans Memling* exhibition held in the Groeningemuseum in Bruges, in the section showing precursors, contemporaries and successors of Memling. In 1998 the Bruges exhibition *De Memling à Pourbus* (*From Memling to Pourbus*) made a central figure of Isenbrant.

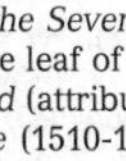

BIBLIOGRAPHY:
Friedländer, Max J., '*Die Antwerpener Manieristen, Adriaen Ysenbrant*' in *Die altniederländische Malerei*, Bruno Cassirer, Berlin, 1933. De Vos, Dirk, *Hans Memling*, exhibition catalogue, Groeningemuseum, Bruges, 1994.

MUSEUMS AND GALLERIES:
ANTWERP: *Lamentation over the Body of Christ* (attributed) - BRUSSELS: *The Virgin of the Seven Sorrows Adored by the Van der Velde Family* (one leaf of the diptych, attributed) - COIMBRA: *Virgin and Child* (attributed) - LONDON (NG): *The Magdalen in a Landscape* (1510-1525, oil/wood) - VIENNA: *Flight into Egypt* (attributed).

AUCTION RECORDS:
LONDON, 28 July 1922, *Dominican Monk at Prayer*, GBP 199. LONDON, 10 July 1925, *The Holy Family*, GBP 89. LONDON, 5 July 1929, *Nativity*, GBP 3,360. NEW YORK, 19 Dec 1929, *Adoration of the Magi; Flight into Egypt; Nativity* (triptych) USD 900. PARIS, 19 May 1933, *Saints and Donors* (two wings of a triptych) FRF 11,000. NEW YORK, 17 May 1934, *Rest on the Flight into Egypt*, USD 875. NEW YORK, 24 June 1938, *Virgin and Child*, GBP 1,050. NEW YORK, 19 Dec 1941, *Mass of St Gregory*, GBP 682. NEW YORK, 14 Sept 1942, *Triptych*, GBP 5,880. NEW YORK, 15 Nov 1945, *St John the Baptist and Donors*, USD 2,200. PARIS, 5 Dec 1951, *Virgin and Child*, FRF 3,900,000. PARIS, 20 June 1957, *The Virgin and the Child Jesus*, FRF 1,480,000. LONDON, 26 June 1957, *Madonna and Child in a Landscape*, GBP 4,200. LONDON, 8 July 1959, *Landscape and the Baptism of Christ*, GBP 1,700. LONDON, 22 June 1960, *Madonna and Child*, GBP 3,500. NEW YORK, 10 May 1961, *Portrait of a Man in a Red Tunic*, USD 2,000. LONDON, 14 June 1961, *Crucifixion* (triptych) GBP 1,400. COLOGNE, 14 Nov 1963, *Crucifixion*, DEM 46,000. COLOGNE, 11 Nov 1964, *Mary Magdalene*, DEM 40,000. LONDON, 1 July 1966, *Adoration of the Magi*, Gns 10,000. LONDON, 24 Nov 1967, *Portrait of a Lady of Quality*, Gns 5,500. COLOGNE, 29 Nov 1968, *Rest on the Flight into Egypt*, DEM 45,000. LONDON, 26 June 1970, *Virgin and Child in a Landscape*, Gns 9,000. LONDON, 14 May 1971, *Virgin and Child*, Gns 4,200. PARIS, 28 Nov 1972, *Portrait of a Young Boy*, FRF 95,000. NEW YORK, 22 Jan 1976, *St Barbara and Mary Magdalene* (two oils on panels of a triptych, 33 x 11½ ins / 84 x 29 cm) USD 100,000. LONDON, 2 July 1976, *Virgin and Child in a Landscape* (oil on panel, 19 x 13½ ins / 48.5 x 34.5 cm) GBP 19,000. AMSTERDAM, 9 June 1977, *Portrait of a Man* (oil on panel, 10¾ x 9 ins / 27.5 x 23 cm) NLG 46,000. LONDON, 13 Dec 1978, *Adoration of the Magi* (oil on panel, 16 x 11½ ins / 40.5 x 29 cm) GBP 9,500. NEW YORK, 9 Oct 1980, *Virgin and Child with St Catherine and St Agnes in a Landscape* (oil on panel, with rounded top, 36½ x 27½ ins / 93 x 70 cm) USD 100,000. LONDON, 10 July 1981, *Virgin and Child in a Landscape with a Town in the Background* (oil on panel, 32¼ x 24¼ ins / 81.8 x 61.5 cm) GBP 22,000. AMSTERDAM, 14 March 1983, *Lamentations* (oil on panel, 28¼ x 20½ ins / 71.5 x 52 cm) NLG 105,000. NEW YORK, 18 Jan 1984, *Adoration of the Magi* (oil on panel, 13¼ x 10¾ ins / 33.5 x 27.4 cm) USD 90,000. NEW YORK, 5 June 1986, *Virgin and Child* (oil on panel, 12½ x 8¾ ins / 31.5 x 22.5 cm) USD 155,000. NEW YORK, 3 June 1988, *Triptych: In the Centre the Virgin and Symbols of the Immaculate Conception, on the Sides the Flight into Egypt and the Rest during the Flight* (oil on panel, centre 38 x 21 ins / 96.5 x 53.5 cm, sides 38 x 9 ins/96.5 x 23 cm) USD 99,000. NEW YORK, 11 Jan 1991, *Rest on the Flight into Egypt* (oil on panel, 19 x 13¼ ins / 48 x 33.5 cm) USD 550,000. LONDON, 24 May 1991, *Triptych: In the Centre the Virgin and Symbols of the Immaculate Conception, on the Sides the Flight into Egypt and the Rest during the Flight* (oil on panel, centre 38 x 21 ins / 96.5 x 53.5 cm, sides 38 x 9 ins/96.5 x 23 cm) GBP 82,500. NEW YORK, 11 Jan 1995, *Virgin and Child on a Pedestal under a Renaissance Portico before a Wide Landscape* (oil on panel, 9 x 6¾ ins / 22.8 x 17.4 cm) USD 74,000. NEW YORK, 29 Jan 1998, *Crucifixion* (oil on panel, 16¾ x 12¼ ins / 42.5 x 30.8 cm) USD 145,500. LONDON, 8 July 1999, *Crucifixion. Donatrix with St James. Donatrix with St Catherine* (oil on panel, triptych, 27 x 38 ins / 69 x 97 cm) GBP 65,000. NEW YORK, 25 Jan 2001, *Portrait of a Man* (oil on panel, 9 x 6 ins / 22 x 15 cm) USD 100,000. NEW YORK, 2 Oct 2002, *St Catherine of Alexandria, with Martyrdom Scene Beyond* (oil on panel, 15 x 13 ins / 39 x 32 cm) USD 26,000.

ISENBURG, Robert

German, 19th century.

Active c. 1832.

Painter. History painting, portraits.

Isenburg is mentioned by Siret.

ISENBURGER, Eric

German, 20th century.

Born 1902, in Frankfurt am Main; died 1994, in New York.

Active then naturalised in the USA.

Painter. Portraits, figures, landscapes, still-lifes.

Eric Isenburger lived and worked in Vienna and then in Berlin. He came under attack by the Nazi authorities and was forced to flee from Germany with his wife Jula, who was a dancer. In France he was interned as a German émigré. He managed to leave Europe for the USA in 1941 thanks to the support of the Thomas Mann committee. Once there, he devoted himself entirely to art. He became a member of the National Academy of Design and taught painting. In 1947, he won the third Carnegie prize. In 2000, the Eric and Jula Isenburger Society was set up in Neuburg an der Donau in Germany.

Eric Isenburger exhibited several times in the USA. In 2001, he featured in the exhibition *Verfemt. Vergessen. Wiederentdeckt. Schickskale expressiver Bildkunst im 20. Jahrhundert* (*Condemned. Forgotten. Rediscovered. The Fate of Expressive Art in the 20th Century*), an exhibition aimed at rediscovering a generation of German and Austrian artists, who appeared during the 1920s and 1930s but suffered under the cultural and political repression of the Nazis and fell into oblivion after the war, at the Kulturgeschichtliches Museum in Osnabrück. The first European retrospective of his work took place in 1999 in Neuburg an der Donau.

BIBLIOGRAPHY:

Eric Isenburger. Ausgewählte Werke, exhibition catalogue, Städtische Galerie im Rathausfletz, Neuburg an der Donau, 1999. *Verfemt. Vergessen. Wiederentdeckt. Schicksale expressiver Bildkunst im 20. Jahrhundert. Sammlung Gerhard Schneider*, exhibition catalogue, Kulturgeschichtiches Museum, Osnabrück, 2001.

AUCTION RECORDS:

MUNICH, 29 Nov 1985, *Portrait of a Man* (1924, pen and watercolour, 12 1/4 x 7 1/2 ins / 31 x 19 cm) DEM 2,100. MUNICH, 29 May 2001, *Woman's Portrait* (oil on board, 22 x 18 ins / 55 x 46 cm) DEM 3,600. BERLIN, 26 April 2003, *Still-life with Tulips and Narcissi* (1923, oil on canvas, 33 x 27 ins / 85 x 68 cm) EUR 1,900.

ISENDOORN, Andries van, or Ysendoorn
Dutch, 17th century.
Died between 1689 and 1702.
Active in Amsterdam.
Painter.

ISENDOORN, Antony van, or Ysendorn
Dutch, 17th century.
Born c. 1625.
Active in Delft.
Painter. Still-lifes.

Anthony van Isendoorn was registered as a guild member in 1669.

ISENDOORN, Joan van, or Ysendoorn, called Schout Isendoorn
Dutch, 17th century.
Died 1684, in Wijk bij Duurstede.
Active in Utrecht.
Painter. Historical subjects, animals.

In 1637, Joan van Isendoorn was a member of the guild of Utrecht. In the Johan de Boot lottery of 1649 there were several paintings by him. In 1630, he donated a painting to the Hiobs hospital in Utrecht. He was burgomaster of Wyk, near Duurstede.

ISENDOORN DE BLOIS, Reinier Albert Lodewyk (Baron)
Dutch, 19th century.
Born 1786, at the Palace of Cannenbourg, near Vassen; died 4 March 1856, at the Palace of Cannenbourg, near Vassen.
Engraver (etching).

Reinier Isendoorn de Blois owned a large collection of old masters and made etchings of landscapes copied largely from these. The artists include E. van Drielst, A. van Erdingen, J. Hackaert, J. de Heusch, J. van Kessel, J. van der Meer, H. Meyer, P. Molyn, Frederick de Moucheron, A. van Ostade, J. Ruysdael and A. van der Velde. He also made etchings from his own drawings and those of his contemporaries. He signed his plates *R. de Blois, R. de Bl, R. B.*, and *J. de B.*. The Amsterdam engravings collection is believed to hold the artist's entire work - 71 etchings and 121 plates.

MUSEUMS AND GALLERIES:

AMSTERDAM (Rijksprentenkabinet): 71 etchings, 121 plates.

ISENDYCK, Anton van. See **YSENDYCK**

ISENHOUT
Dutch, 16th century.
Active in Gouda.
Painter (glass).

In 1580 Isenhout took over the glass-painting studio established in Gouda by the Crabeth brothers.

ISENMANN, Gaspard, Caspar or Kaspar
French, 15th century.
Died c. 1472, in Colmar (Upper Rhine).
Painter.
Colmar School.

Gaspard Isenmann worked for the church of St Martin in Colmar, where he painted six pictures on a gold background for the high altar from 1462 to 1464. He had been a citizen of Colmar since 1435. His slight, elegant figures are shown using well-observed but sometimes mannered movements. His compositions are clear and full of air, the landscapes perhaps desolate. Reality and fiction co-exist, the skies are golden, the plants and towns detailed with care. Some coarse facial types prefigure Grünewald. Isenmann chose his colours thoughtfully and achieved a certain monumentality. He was one of those of the Colmar School who, by uniting Germanic and Flemish methods, produced an international style.

MUSEUMS AND GALLERIES:

COLMAR (Mus. d'Unterlinden): *The Passion*; *Resurrection*; *Crown of Thorns*; *The Last Supper*; *Christ's Entry into Jerusalem*.

ISENRING, Johann Baptist
Swiss, 19th century.
Born 12 May 1796; died 9 April 1860, in St Gall.
Painter, engraver. Landscapes.

Johann Baptist Isenring was 24 when he enrolled at the academy in Munich. On returning home to his native town of Lütisburg near St Gall, he painted and engraved views of it. His first important work was the 20 plates of *The Thur Region*, which he published himself in 1825. In 1828, he established an art-publishing business, publishing collections of aquatints such as *A Collection of Picturesque Views of the Most Remarkable Towns and Places in Switzerland* and a *Collection of Picturesque Views of Foreign Towns*.

MUSEUMS AND GALLERIES:

ST GALL (Historisches Mus.) - ST GALL (Stiftsbibliothek) - ZURICH (ETH Graphics Collection) - ZURICH (Zentralbibliothek).

AUCTION RECORDS:

ZURICH, 15 Nov 1983, *Confederate Exercise Encampment* (1824, coloured aquatint, 7 x 10 1/4 ins / 17.5 x 26.2 cm) CHF 1,400. AMSTERDAM, 12 Sept 1985, *Hotel Loewe, Saint Gallen* (aquatint, 17 x 20 1/2 ins / 43 x 52 cm) NLG 4,800. ST GALL, 28 Nov 2000, *Christ on the Cross* (print, Prints, 22 x 17 ins / 57 x 43 cm) CHF 11,000. ST GALL, 28 Nov 2000, *Christ on the Cross* (copper print, 22 x 17 ins / 57 x 43 cm) CHF 11,000.

ISENRING, Johann Jakob
Swiss, 19th century.
Born in Lütisburg; died 16 May 1826, in Lütisburg.
Painter, sculptor. Landscapes.

Johann Jakob Isenring studied in Munich from 1820 to 1826.

ISEPP, Sebastian
Austrian, 20th century.
Born 18 February 1884, in Nötsch.
Painter. Landscapes.

Sebastian Isepp attended the Akademie der Bildenden Künste in Vienna and was active in Nötsch and Vienna. He travelled to Africa, Paris, Berlin and Rome. In 1904 his work appeared at the Vienna Hagenbund (an Austrian group of artists formed in 1900 in Vienna as 'Künstlerbund Hagen'. They took their name from Herr Hagen, the landlord of an inn which was an artists' meeting place); in 1905, 1909 and 1914 at the Secession exhibitions; in 1909, at the artists' society in Vienna; in 1912 and 1913, at the Dresden and Düsseldorf exhibitions, respectively; in addition to the international Secession exhibition in Rome in 1914. In 1915, Isepp held a solo exhibition at the Arnot gallery in Vienna. Primarily, he painted snowy landscapes: *Frost* and *Riverside in Frosty Weather*. His other landscapes include *Young Forest* and *In the Forest*.

ISER, Josif, or Iser-Josif
Romanian, 20th century.
Born 8 May 1881, in Bucharest; died 1958.
Active in France.
Painter, draughtsman.

Josif Iser studied in Rome and Paris. He settled in Neuilly-sur-Seine. He exhibited regularly in Paris at the Salon d'Automne of which he became a member. He was a friend of Derain. He returned to Bucharest in 1910, where he introduced Marcel Janco to painting.

MUSEUMS AND GALLERIES:
PARIS (MNAM-CCI).

AUCTION RECORDS:
PARIS, 29 Oct 1926, *Romanian Peasant Girl*, FRF 800.

ISERBYT, Georgina
British, 20th century.
Born 1915, in Birckington.
Active in Belgium.
Painter. Scenes with figures, portraits.

Georgina Iserbyte trained at the Académie des Beaux-Arts in Brussels. Her works feature a fantastical world of hybrid creatures, mysterious animals and plants.

MUSEUMS AND GALLERIES:
BRUSSELS - GHENT - MONTEVIDEO.

ISERENTANT, Mayou
Belgian, 20th century.
Born 1903, in Liège; died 1978, in Vaux-le-Pénil (Seine-et-Marne), France.
Active from 1938 in France.
Painter. Portraits, genre scenes, interiors, landscapes.

Mayou Iserentant attended the Académie des Beaux-Arts in Liège.

MUSEUMS AND GALLERIES:
ANTWERP - BRUSSELS - LIÈGE - TOURNAI.

AUCTION RECORDS:
ANTWERP, 8 April 1976, *Landscape* (1911, oil on panel, 22 x 29 1/4 ins / 56 x 74 cm) BEF 22,000.

ISERHJELM, Beata Maria
Maiden name: Franc
Swedish, 18th - 19th century.
Born 6 April 1739; died 2 October 1826.
Active in Stockholm.
Miniaturist.

Beata Iserhjelm painted miniature portraits and figurative paintings in small formats.

ISERMAN, François, or Ysermans
Flemish School, 17th century.
Born in Mechelen; died 1614, in Antwerp.
Painter, decorative designer.

François Iserman was made a burger of Antwerp in 1598.

ISERMANN, Jim
American, 20th - 21st century.
Born 1955.
Installation artist.

Jim Isermann lives and works in Santa Monica. Isermann's installations aim to break down the barriers between art and design, creating themed spaces incorporating elements of decorative art (floor coverings, wallpaper) and, occasionally, furniture from the 1950s and 1960s.

His work has featured in a number of group exhibitions, including: 2002, *TRESPASSING: Houses x Artists*, Bellevue Art Museum; 2002, *Deluxe*, Contemporary Art Centre, Madrid; 2002, *The Gallery Show*, Royal Academy of Art, London; 2003, *Un tableau dans le décor. Peintures 1970-2000* (*A Painting in the Décor: Paintings 1970-2000*), exhibition celebrating 20 years of the French *Fonds Régionaux pour l'Art Contemporain*, Château des Ducs de Bretagne, Nantes. His pieces have also been the subject of a number of solo exhibitions, including: 2000, Portikus, Frankfurt am Main; 2002, Corvi-Mora Gallery, London; 2002, *Hammer Projects*, UCLA Hammer Museum, Los Angeles; 2002, Galerie Praz-Delavallade, Paris.

BIBLIOGRAPHY:
Isermann, Jim, *Jim Isermann: Failed Ideas*, Metro, Los Angeles, 1995. Isermann, Jim, *Fifteen*, Institute of Visual Arts (University of Wisconsin), Milwaukee, 1998. *Jim Isermann*, exhibition catalogue, Portikus, Frankfurt am Main, 2000.

MUSEUMS AND GALLERIES:
ANGOULÊME (FRAC Poitou-Charentes): *Untitled* (1995) - DUNKIRK (FRAC Nord-Pas de Calais): *Untitled (0194)* (1994).

ISERN ALIÉ. See **YSERN Y ALIE Pedro**

ISEWYNS, Michel
Flemish School, 16th century.
Died 1532.
Sculptor.

Isewyns worked for the palace of Charles V in Mechelen in 1507.

ISEYEV, Grigori Fedorovich
Russian, 19th century.
Died 1889.
Painter.

Grigori Fedorovich Isayev was twice exhibited at the academy of art exhibition in St Petersburg, in 1872 with his canvas *Au Revoir*, for which he was named honorary member, and in 1877 with his drawing *Divine Judgement at the Time of Ivan the Terrible*.

ISGRO, Emilio
Italian, 20th century.
Born 6 October 1937, in Barcellona, Sicily.
Painter (mixed media).
Visual Poetry.

Isgro has exhibited in Italy since 1965. At first he collaborated on and contributed to various literary revues, but, as with many writers, his handwriting seemed to become a destruction of the very art of writing. Concentrating on the visual aspect of writing as the central point about it, he joined the concrete poetry movement, which, perhaps oddly, is active in all countries, whatever the language or script. Starting with 'blue-pencilling', he aims to describe the act of writing in terms of space and rhythm.

AUCTION RECORDS:
MILAN, 8 June 1988, *Stamping Error* (1971, mixed media, 16 x 23 3/4 ins / 40.5 x 60.5 cm) ITL 2,600,000. MILAN, 7 June 1989, *The Calculation and the Flower* (1987, oil and mixed media/photographic canvas, 49 x 69 ins / 124.5 x 175 cm) ITL 7,500,000. MILAN, 13 June 1990, *An Innocent Victim* (1971, book embedded in Plexiglas, 16 x 23 1/2 ins / 40.5 x 60 cm) ITL 2,600,000; *Book with Crossings Out* (pages of a book under Plexiglas, 14 1/2 x 21 1/2 ins / 37 x 54.5 cm) ITL 8,600,000. MILAN, 10 Dec 1996, *Explanation* (1972, ruled book under Plexiglas, 15 3/4 x 23 1/2 ins / 40 x 60 cm) ITL 3,000,000.

ISHAM, Samuel
American, 19th - 20th century.
Born 12 May 1855, in New York; died 1914, in East Hampton (New York).
Painter. Portraits, landscapes.

Samuel Isham went to study in Paris, where he was a pupil of Jacqueson de la Chevreuse, Boulanger and Lefebvre. He was an Associate of the National Academy from 1900 and won the silver medal at the St Louis World Fair in 1904. He wrote a *History of American Painting*.

MUSEUMS AND GALLERIES:
DETROIT: *Landscape* - NEW YORK (Metropolitan Mus. of Art): *Portrait of the Marquise de Carabas*.

AUCTION RECORDS:
NEW YORK, 15 April 1992, *The Marquise de Carabas* (1896, oil on canvas, 39$^{3/4}$ x 32 ins / 101 x 81.3 cm) USD 1,430.

ISHAM, Sheila
American, 20th century.
Born 1927, in New York.
Painter.

Sheila Isham studied in Switzerland from 1948 to 1949, in Pennsylvania in 1950, at the Berlin Academy from 1950 to 1954 and at the University of Hong Kong from 1962 to 1965. She travelled widely, especially in Asia, where she became familiar with calligraphy and oriental art. She has lived in Moscow, Hong Kong, Paris and Haiti and then in Washington and New York. Her paintings are in the form of large colourful compositions, with very subtle gradations between the various transparent colours. Her work also has an oriental side to it that is reminiscent of the world of Tobey, and often includes images of mythical animals and birds.

Isham has taken part in group exhibitions and has held solo shows since 1954, notably in Berlin in 1954; Washington in 1960-1962, 1966, 1968-1970, 1974, 1976, 1978 and 1980; Tokyo in 1964; New York in 1966, 1969-1971, 1973 and 1974; Paris in 1973, 1977 in Port-au-Prince, as well as a travelling exhibition visiting New Orleans, Panama, Peru, Bolivia, Guyana and Guatemala; 1997 in New Orleans, and 1998 and 2004 in St Petersburg.

BIBLIOGRAPHY:
Kotik, Charlotta, *Sheila Isham: Recent Work*, exhibition catalogue, Albright Knox Gallery, Buffalo, 1981. Taylor, Joshua C., *East and West: Paintings/Poems by Sheila Isham*, exhibition catalogue, 1981.

ISHCHENKOV, Filipp
Russian, 18th century.
Active in St Petersburg in 1776.
Painter.

ISHERWOOD, James Lawrence
British, 20th century.
Born 1917, in Wigan; died 1989, in Wigan.
Painter. Landscapes, seascapes, portraits, urban and industrial scenes.

James Lawrence Isherwood was a very prolific painter, often described as an eccentric and controversial artist. Inspired by the town in which he lived his whole life, Isherwood became known for his Wigan figure paintings and for what came to be described as his 'Wigan style'. He was interested in cities and produced many paintings of London as well as scenes from other European locations during his travels around the continent. He also painted many portraits of his mother Lily, to whom he was very close.

Isherwood's style is characterised by the influence of Expressionism and the use of vivid colours. His work has been compared to the compositions of L.S. Lowry because he painted industrial landscapes from the north of England. Apart from cities and landscapes, he also painted a series of portraits of celebrities. He produced some of his best-known paintings in the 1950s.

He did not receive a wide critical acclaim during his lifetime, but his work has become increasingly popular amongst art collectors. His work was included in the Northern Art Show at the Mall Galleries in 1994, and he also exhibited in Malta and Spain.

AUCTION RECORDS:
CHESTER, 24 Sept 2001, *Rain, National Gallery* (1971, oil on board, 17 x 23 ins / 44 x 59 cm) GBP 1,050.

ISHIBASHI, Wakun, or Kazukuni
Japanese, 20th century.
Born 1876, in Shimane Prefecture; died 1928.
Painter.

Ishibashi, after studying Japanese painting under the direction of Taki Katei, departed for London, where he received training in Western painting at the Royal Academy. He was an academician and a member of the Teiten (empire exhibition) jury.

ISHIDA, real name: Shuno Ishida
Japanese, 19th century.
Born in Omi (Shiga).
Painter.

Ishida is said to have been a disciple of Shirai Kayo.

ISHIGURO, Shoji
Japanese, 20th century.
Born 1935, in Nagoya (Aichi).
Sculptor.

Ishiguro completed his studies in the department of sculpture of the university of fine art in Tokyo in 1958. He has had several solo exhibitions in Tokyo.

ISHIHARA, Mikoko
Japanese, 20th century.
Born near Tokyo.
Active in Italy from 1963.
Painter.

In her painting, Mikoko Ishihara retains a nostalgia for her native country. Her works are abstract, with dark colours and forms that seem full of anguished, obsessive fear. She first exhibited in Tokyo in 1960 and 1961, before setting up in Rome in 1963, where she has exhibited since 1967. In 1968, she exhibited again in Tokyo, and then in Paris in 1970.

ISHII, Hakutei, real name: Mankichi Ishii, pseudonym: Hakutei
Japanese, 20th century.
Born 1882, in Tokyo; died 1958.
Painter, engraver.
Sosaku Hanga.

Hakutei Ishii was the son and grandson of a painter, and the elder brother of Tsuruzo Ishii. He received his initial training in traditional Japanese painting. In 1905 he returned to the school of fine art in Tokyo, and worked under the direction of Fujishima Takeji and Kuroda Kyoteru. He was obliged to interrupt his studies for health reasons. In 1921-1922 he spent a period of time in France, then in the USA until 1924. One of the founder members of the Nika association for painting and sculpture, he participated in the creation of the Assui association at the time of the dissolution of the Teiten (empire exhibition). In 1937 he was appointed a member of the academy of fine art. He was also an art critic.

Hakutei Ishii's style, which is marked by Formalism, is said to be Objectivist. In 1904 he contributed to the birth of the movement called Sosaku Hanga (Creative Prints), publishing a work by Yamamoto Kanae in the art magazine of which he was editor, *Myojo* (*New Star*). This work was a wood engraving composed of two colours, entitled *Gyofu* (*Fisherman*), engraved and printed by the artist in 1904. Depicting creative engravings in contrast to traditional engravings from everyday life (*Ukiyo-e*), the Sosaku Hanga extols the total independence of the artist. It ended in 1918 with the formation of the Nihon Sosaku Hanga Kyokai (Japanese association of printmakers), which was dissolved in 1931, to be reborn in the form of the Nihon Hanga Kyokai (Japanese engraving association). In 1905 Hakutei Ishii founded, with his brother Tsuruzo Ishii and Yamamoto Kanae, the magazine *Heitan*, inspired by the German Art nouveau magazine *Jugend* (*Youth*). In 1907, with Yamamoto Kanae and other friends, he founded another magazine, *Hosun* (*Not Much*).

BIBLIOGRAPHY:

Kawakita, Michiaki, *Contemporary Japanese Prints*, Kodansha International, Tokyo, Palo Alto (USA), 1967. Jenkins, Donald, *Images from a Changing World: Japanese Prints of the Twentieth Century*, Portland Art Museum, Portland (ME), 1983. Keyes, Roger, *Break with the Past: The Japanese Creative Print Movement, 1910-1960*, exhibition catalogue, Fine Arts Museums of San Francisco, San Francisco, 1988. Merritt, Helen, *Modern Japanese Prints: The Early Years*, University of Hawaï Press, Honolulu, 1990. *The Roy G. Cole Collection of Fine Sosaku Hanga*, auction catalogue, Sotheby's Publications, New York, June 19, 1990 (lot. 93). Merritt, Helen/Yamada, Nanako, *Guide to Modern Japanese Woodblock Prints: 1900-1975*, University of Hawaï Press, Honolulu, 1992. Reigle Stephens, Amy, *The New Wave - Twentieth Century Japanese Prints from the Robert O. Muller Collection*, Bamboo Publishing Ltd, London, 1993. Smith, Laurence, *Modern Japanese Prints 1912-1989*, exhibition catalogue, The British Museum Press, London, 1994.

MUSEUMS AND GALLERIES:

TOKYO (National MMA): *The Pont St-Michel* (1923).

ISHII, Kisaburo. See **ISHII Rinkyô**

ISHII, Rinkyo, real name: Kisaburo Ishii, pseudonyms: Tempu, Rinkyo, Daiwashi, Shokado
Japanese, 20th century.
Born 1884, in Chiba Prefecture, near Tokyo; died 1930.
Painter. Figures, landscapes.

Rinkyo Ishii was a pupil of Gaho Hashimoto. He subsequently devoted himself to scholar painting, and is known for his figures and landscapes. He refused to take part in the Teiten (empire exhibition), and founded the Josuikai group with Noda Kuyho and Shimada Bokusen. Of an independent spirit, he worked and exhibited on his own.

Rinkyo Ishii's painting *Two Country Scenes*, in black ink heightened with pointillism in gold, is characteristic of his style.

MUSEUMS AND GALLERIES:

TOKYO (National MMA).

ISHII, Tsuruzo
Japanese, 20th century.
Born 1887, in Tokyo; died 1973.
Engraver, sculptor.
First Thursday Society.

Tsuruzo Ishii was the third son of the painter Teiko Ishii and the younger brother of Hakutei Ishii. He obtained his diploma from the university of fine art in Tokyo in 1910, where he became a lecturer. In 1905 he founded a magazine, *Heitan*, with his elder brother Hakutei Ishii and the engraver Yamamoto Kanae, the founder of the movement called Sosaku Hanga (Creative Prints). He featured from 1915 in the Bunten salon sponsored by the ministry of education, and became a member of the academy of fine art (Nihon Bijutsu-in). In 1921, he returned to the association for creative Japanese prints (Nihon Sosaku Hanga Kyokai), and from 1941 he was the president of the Japanese engraving association, which succeeded it. He was also a member of Shunyokai and of the association of Japanese watercolour painters, as well as being an emeritus professor of the University of Tokyo.

Tsuruzo Ishii is well-known and well-regarded as a sculptor. There is a close interaction between his sculptures, his engravings (on wood, on copper and on stone) and his paintings. His figurative style, which is marked by the metaphysical, seeks to interpret human feelings and the conflicts they give rise to. The Tsuruzo Ishii museum is assembling his works in Ueda. In 2002 he was included in the exhibition *Japanese Prints during the Allied Occupation, 1945-1952*, held at the British Museum in London.

BIBLIOGRAPHY:

Smith, Lawrence, *Japanese Prints during the Allied Occupation, 1945-1952: Onchi Koshiro, Ernst Hacker and the First Thursday Society*, exhibition catalogue, The British Museum Press, London, 2002.

MUSEUMS AND GALLERIES:

UEDA (Tsuruzo Ishii Mus.).

ISHIKAWA, Kansai, real name: Ishikawa Ryusuke, nickname: Kojo, artist names: Kansai, Nikyo Gaishi, Shinten'o, Rokodo
Japanese, 18th century.
Born in Niigata Prefecture.
Painter.

Ishikawa Kansai was a pupil of Go Shunmei (1700-1781) and a close friend of Kameda Bosai (1752-1826) and Unzen (1759-1811). He painted landscapes and bamboo.

ISHIKAWA, Kin Itiro
Japanese, 19th century.
Active in Tokyo.
Painter. Genre scenes.

Kin Itiro Ishikawa featured in the Exposition Universelle of 1900 in Paris.

ISHIKAWA, Kin'ichiro
Chinese, 20th century.
Born 1871, in Shizuoka; died 1945.
Painter, watercolourist. Landscapes.

Kin'ichiro Ishikawa studied in England, and then became a translator in China. In 1921 the national university for teacher training invited him to teach. He played a fundamental role in the development of Western art in Taiwan, influencing the careers of several young artists. He was an accomplished artist, as well as being an eminent teacher, and was appreciated for the delicacy of his watercolours.

AUCTION RECORDS:

TAIPEI, 18 Oct 1992, *The Countryside* (watercolour/paper, 10 x 13 ins / 25.3 x 33.2 cm) TWD 770,000. TAIPEI, 10 April 1994, *Marseilles* (ink and watercolour/silk/card, 10 3/4 x 9 1/2 ins / 27.2 x 24 cm) TWD 425,000. TAIPEI, 16 Oct 1994, *The River Tamsui* (watercolour/paper, 9 x 10 3/4 ins / 22 x 27.2 cm) TWD 299,000. TAIPEI, 15 Oct 1995, *Farmhouse* (watercolour/paper, 10 1/4 x 14 1/4 ins / 26 x 36.5 cm) TWD 218,500. NEW YORK, 31 Oct 1995, *Temple beside a River* (watercolour/paper, 14 1/2 x 22 ins / 36.8 x 55.7 cm) USD 19,550. TAIPEI, 14 April 1996, *A Man Leading a Cart Drawn by a Horse* (1922, watercolour/paper, 12 3/4 x 9 1/2 ins / 32.6 x 24 cm) TWD 253,000. TAIPEI, 11 April 1999, *Venice* (1940s, watercolour, 9 x 13 ins / 24 x 33 cm) TWD 300,000. CONNECTICUT, 15 Nov 1999, *Family Life* (watercolour, 19 x 12 ins / 48 x 30 cm) USD 5,000. BILLINGSHURST, 29 Jan 2001, *Figures near an Oriental Railway* (watercolour, 13 x 20 ins / 32 x 50 cm) GBP 3,600. LONDON, 28 Sept 2001, *Japanese Landscape with Railway* (watercolour, 13 x 20 ins / 33 x 50 cm) GBP 4,500. HONG KONG, 25 April 2004, *Landscape in Paris* (watercolour on silk, 16 x 9 ins / 40 x 24 cm) HKD 30,000.

ISHIKAWA, Komei, nickname: Katsutaro
Japanese, 19th century.
Active in Tokyo.
Engraver (ivory).

Komei Ishikawa featured in the Exposition Universelle of 1900 in Paris.

ISHIKAWA, Toraji
Japanese, 19th century.
Born 1875; died 1964.
Active in Tokyo.
Painter. Landscapes.

Toraji Ishikawa featured in the Exposition Universelle of 1900 in Paris.

ISHIKAWA, Toyonobu, nicknames: Magosaburo later Nukaya Shichibe; first signature: Nishimura Shigenobu; pseudonyms: Tanjodo, Meijodo Shuha
Japanese, 18th century.
Born 1711; died 1785.
Master engraver.

Toyonobu Ishikawa was the son-in-law of Nukuya Shichihei. He was an innkeeper in the Kodemma-cho district of Edo (modern Tokyo), and the father of Masamochi Ishikawa (pen-names: Yodoya no Meshimori and Rikujuen), the famous author of *Kyoka* (a comic poem). He produced a large number of prints and portraits of women with a sensual charm. With Okumura Masanobu (1686-1764), Nishimura Shigenaga (d. 1756) and Nishikawa Sukenobu (1671-1751) he was one of the 'Primitives' of the movement depicting everyday life called *ukiyo-e*, and represented the Kyoto School. He was also a disciple of Shigenaga, and the influence of Sukenobu can be felt in his works.

Thanks to these artists, a rapid evolution can be seen in engraving technique, notably in the use of colour. To respond to the demand of the public for brilliant colouring, colours were added to the engravings, first of all by hand, and then using a new xylographic method: purple and bluish-green were added to the black engraving by superimposing the printing of each of the colours with the aid of an identifying mark (*Kento*). This technique, called *benizuri-e* (painting printed with purple) remained in fashion for almost 20 years, and Ishikawa was one of those who best exploited its possibilities. He used some rare light tones, which in their arrangement, full of fantasy, entirely harmonise with his gentle and charming style.

AUCTION RECORDS:
NEW YORK, 27 March 1991, *Woman and Her Child in an Interior* (Hosoban print, 12 x 6 ins / 30.3 x 14.3 cm) USD 1,870.

ISHIKAWA, Yoshikazu, real name: Yoshikazu Utagawa, nickname: Jirobei, Jirokichi, pseudonym: Ichijusai, Ichikawa Yoshikazu, Issen, Isshunsai
Japanese, 19th century.
Active c. 1850-1870.
Master engraver.

Yoshikazu Ishikawa executed prints, some of which are in the Musée Guimet in Paris.

MUSEUMS AND GALLERIES:
PARIS (Mus. National des Arts asiatiques-Guimet).

ISHIMURA, Nichiro. See **AI Mitsu**

ISHIZAKI, Koyo, real name: Ishiichi or Iyoichi Ishizaki, pseudonym: Koyo
Japanese, 20th century.
Born 1884; died 1947.
Painter.

Koyo Ishizaki featured in 1929 at the Salon des Tuileries in Paris.

ISHU, real name: Hideyuki Kikuta, pseudonyms: Shou and Isshu
Japanese, 19th century.
Born 1791, in Sendai; died 1852.
Painter.

Ishu was a disciple of Kano Eishin (Isen, 1775-1828)., but in other respects the influence of Buncho (1763-1840) can be seen in his works. He lived in Edo (modern Tokyo), and is said to be the great-grandson of the painter Ritsuo (1663-1747).

ISIDORE, Raymond, called Picassiette
French, 20th century.
Born 1900, in Chartres; died 1964, in Chartres.
Painter, sculptor.
Art Brut.

Raymond Isidore was a talented architect, sculptor and painter. He built his house, furniture and created numerous ornaments. He covered every surface, creating ceilings of diverse subjects in mosaics made up of multi-coloured, broken dishware. All was covered in mosaics, including chairs, beds and sewing machines, reaching even as far as the courtyard. There he created a chapel, a shelter and a garden, where a hundred pots in mosaic compete in brilliance with the natural flowers.

ISIDORO DI SER MOSCATO
Italian, 16th century.
Born to a family originally from Spoleto; died 25 August 1548.
Painter.

In 1512, in collaboration with Giovanni Brunotti, Isidoro painted frescoes in the church of Patrico, near Spoleto. These frescoes are now in the municipal art gallery of Spoleto.

ISIDORUS
Italian, 12th century.
Illuminator.

Isidorus wrote and decorated a missal in Padua in 1170.

ISIDORUS OF PAROS
Active on Paros.
Sculptor.
Ancient Greek.

Isidorus' name was discovered on a statue base found at Cumae on the site of the forum. According to Pliny, a sculptor of the same name made a statue of Hercules. It is not known if this was the same artist.

ISIDOTUS OF ATHENS
2nd century.
Active during the second half of the 2nd century AD.
Sculptor (marble).
Ancient Greek.

Isidotus worked in Crete. The lower part of a female statue, signed by the artist, was found at Gortyn. The figure holds a horn of plenty in her left arm.

ISIGONUS
3rd century BC.
Active c. 236 BC.
Sculptor.
Ancient Greek.

Isigonus is recorded by Pliny as having made made scenes showing the battles of Eumenes and Attalus I against the Gauls.

ISKE, Paul
French, 20th century.
Born 28 July 1877, in Strasbourg; died 24 April 1961, in Paris.
Painter (gouache). Portraits, landscapes, urban landscapes.

Paul Iske was a pupil of Daubner and Jordan. He spent three years at the Kunstakademie in Munich, and then studied in Florence, Rome and Naples. When he returned to Munich, he became a pupil of Franz von Stuck. In Dresden, he studied with Prell. In Strasbourg, he belonged to Henri Solveen's

ARC group, and the Barque group of Robert Heitz. He worked in several genres, including portraiture, landscapes and decoration. He preferred working in tempera and in gouache.

He had numerous exhibitions in Strasbourg between 1927 and 1932, the year he settled in Paris. He then exhibited at the Salon des Tuileries in 1932 and 1933, and at the Salon des Indépendents in 1935. He participated in the Exposition International des Arts et Techniques in 1937. A retrospective of his work was organised in Strasbourg in 1963-1964, and another in 1983.

MUSEUMS AND GALLERIES:
PARIS (MAMVP) - STRASBOURG.

ISKOWITZ, Gershom
Polish, 20th century.
Born 1921, in Kielce.
Active in Canada from 1949.
Painter.

Gershom Iskowitz had already begun to study art when he was imprisoned by the Nazis in 1939. He spent six years in the camps at Buchenwald and Auschwitz. After the war he resumed his studies, first at the Munich academy of fine art and then with Kokoschka. His painting, at first, while retaining a traditionally Jewish element, was influenced by the terrible events to which he had been a witness in the camps. More recently he has moved towards an abstract style where the canvas is scattered with fluid touches of colour in a kind of abstract and very cheerful Pointillism.

He first exhibited in Italy (1947), then in Paris and Munich. Since he moved to Canada he has mainly exhibited in Toronto.

ISKRITSKY, Maksim
Russian, 18th century.
Born 1705; died 1756.
Painter.

Maksim Iskritsky was court painter at the court of Empress Elizaveta Petrovna who raised him to the nobility.

ISLA, Juan de
Spanish, 17th century.
Active in Valladolid.
Painter.

ISLA, Simon
Spanish, 16th century.
Active in Valladolid.
Painter.

Simon Isla is referred to as having worked under Rabryate. He also did paintings for the monastery of San Francisco, Valladolid, in 1578.

ISLE, Wolfang
German, 20th century.
Painter.

In 1900, Wolfang Isle contributed works to the FIAC (Foire Internationale d'Art Contemporain) in Paris. His figurative painting has a turbulent quality.

ISLER, August
Swiss, 19th century.
Born 1857.
Active in Wädenswil.
Engraver (wood).

August Isler was a pupil of Adolf Closs in Stuttgart.

ISLER, Marie
Maiden name: Hess
Swiss, 19th century.
Born 1866.
Active in Zurich.
Engraver (wood).

Marie Isler was the wife of August Isler.

ISMAEEL, Ibraheem
Kuwaiti, 20th century.
Born 1945.
Painter.

Ibraheem Ismaeel began to paint at a very young age. He teaches at the school of fine arts, and has exhibited in more than 20 exhibitions in Kuwait and the USA.

Ismaeel's painting is influenced by the Cubist aesthetic.

ISMAIL, Abdulhamid
Kuwaiti, 20th century.
Born 1941.
Painter.

Ismail has taken part in several exhibitions in Kuwait, as well as a travelling exhibition of that country's artists, which was seen in Great Britain, Denmark, Switzerland, Austria and Spain.

ISMAN, Giovanni
Italian, 17th century.
Painter.

The Accademia Carrara di Belle Arti in Bergamo houses two battle paintings by Isman.

ISNAL
17th century.
Painter.

Isnal is mentioned by Marolles.

ISNARD
French, 18th century.
Wood carver.

Isnard was a Dominican monk who carved the organ casing in the church of La Madeleine in Aix-en-Provence.

ISNARD, Augustine Louise
French, 19th century.
Born 19th century, in Metz.
Painter (including porcelain). Portraits.

This artist was a pupil of Madame de Cool. She began her career at the Salon in 1879.

ISNARD, Jean Roch
French, 19th century.
Born 16 August 1845, in Arles.
Painter.

Jean Roche Isnard was a pupil of Gérome and of Coulanges. He was represented at the Paris Salon from 1869 to 1880. Among his works are *Washerwoman, Student's Room, The Merchant of Santibelli in Arles* and *Dévideuses*.

MUSEUMS AND GALLERIES:
BÉZIERS: *Evening in the Camargue*.

AUCTION RECORDS:
LONDON, 12 June 1997, *Woman Walking by the Riverside* (oil on canvas, 51 x 38 1/4in/129.3 x 97cm) GBP 4,600.

ISNARD, Vivien
French, 20th - 21st century.
Born 1946, in Forges-les-Eaux.
Painter, sculptor, mixed media.
Groupe 70.

Vivien Isnard studied at the École des Arts Décoratifs in Nice and then at the École des Beaux-Arts in Aix-en-Provence. He lives and works in Nice, and teaches at the École des Beaux-Arts in Tours.

After the Supports-Surfaces movement Isnard produced a series of works dealing with support as a material object. Isnard makes holes and incisions in his supports, as well as colour them, which he wants then to present both as coloured matter and as a constituent material in the painting as a whole. With the Supports-Surfaces movement, which was apparently intended to be merely analytical, one never knows how to comprehend the finished product. In Isnard's case, as with Jean-Pierre Pincemin in his ideological, or as he called it 'historical' period, the finished product, made up of fields of tangled colours following various combination systems, culminated in a recognised decorative effect. Like the majority of artists who worked in this area, Isnard progressively began carrying out work of a more personal nature and even tackled volume.

He has participated in many collective exhibitions in France, particularly the Paris Biennale in 1973 and 1975, as well as abroad. Since 1970 he has shown his work in solo exhibitions in France, Italy and Germany and in 1992 at the Musée d'Art Moderne et Contemporain in Nice.

Museums and Galleries:
Marseilles (Mus. Cantini) - Paris (CNAC) - Paris (MNAM-CCI).

Auction records:
Paris, 21 May 1990, *Maestro* (1988, patinated bronze, 19 3/4 x 7 3/4 x 5 ins / 50 x 20 x 13 cm) FRF 8,000. Paris, 26 Oct 1990, *Untitled* (1974, oil and rust/canvas, 47 1/4 x 78 3/4 ins / 120 x 200 cm) FRF 22,000. Paris, 12 Oct 1994, *Untitled* (1973, painting/unstretched stitched canvas, 82 3/4 x 61 ins / 210 x 155 cm) FRF 5,500. Versailles, 27 June 2004, *Painting S123* (1989, paint and mixed media on paper, 30 x 22 ins / 76 x 56 cm) EUR 2,000.

ISO-ISO
Swiss, 20th - 21st century.
Born 1957, in St Gall.
Painter (mixed media).

Iso-Iso is a self-taught painter. He had a solo exhibition at the Galerie Pascal Polar in Brussels in 1991. His paintings depict a kind of chaos, in which images, symbols and signs mingle with one another as if in suspense. The spontaneity of his work and the way he mixes the abstract and the figurative make the viewer question the world of the imaginary. Over the canvases of his collages, which have space but no depth, he scatters fragments of the unconscious but also of reality (man, dog, bunch of flowers), brush and pencil strokes and arabesques. Colour, opaque or brilliant and often chalky, links all these components together.

ISOBE, Yukihisa
Japanese, 20th century.
Born 1935, in Tokyo.
Active in the USA 1965-1975.
Painter, sculptor, engraver.

Isobe graduated in 1956 with a diploma from the department of Western painting at the university of fine art in Tokyo. He took up residence from 1965 for ten years in New York, where he abandoned painting and sculpture. He reappeared on the artistic scene in 1996 with two solo exhibitions in Japan. In the meantime, having presented a notable thesis on the subject of ecology and town planning at the University of Philadelphia, he became involved in research and the planning of ecological programmes in the USA and Japan, and founded his own agency.

In the first part of his artistic career, Isobe engaged in an avant-garde integration of ancient and contemporary art that treated classical subjects using contemporary elements such as Coca-Cola cans, whisky labels, different badges, textiles, etc. Using this idea as his starting point, Isobe subsequently evolved in the direction of a more abstract style in which very fine lines become infinitely entangled on more or less plain backgrounds. His *Emblems* and *Chest of Drawers* are the two series which are most well-known in Japan. A second period, some 30 years later, mixes painting and installation, integrating diagrams, tables of data, cards, matrices and ropes, symbolising surges of energy (for example, water, air, electrical networks). An ecological project and a work of art both at the same time, this unconventional aesthetic shatters the frontiers of disciplines.

Isobe featured in group exhibitions, including the Tokyo print Biennale in 1957; from 1958, exhibitions by independent artists organised by the *Yomiuri* newspaper, where he was awarded a prize in the competition for contemporary Japanese prints; in 1962, *Structures and Styles* in Turin and *Repeated Structures*; in 1963, São Paulo Biennale; 1963, Ljubljana engraving Biennale; 1965, *Modern Japanese Painting*, Zurich, *New Japanese Painting and Sculpture*, New York and *New Trends in Japanese Painting and Sculpture*, museum of modern art, Kyoto; 1981, *The 1960s: A Decade of Change in Contemporary Japanese Art*, museums of modern art, Tokyo and Kyoto; and 1992, *Repetition and Multiplication: The Shape of Contemporary Art*, metropolitan museum, Tokyo.

Isobe's first solo exhibition was in 1962 in Tokyo. He had further exhibitions in 1996, *The Ecological Context 1*, Tokyo and *The Ecological Context 2*, Kitakanto museum of fine art, Maebashi; and in 1998, *Ecological contexte* (*Ecological Context*) Centre d'Art, Ivry, France. In 1963 he was awarded first prize at the exhibition of contemporary Japanese art.

Bibliography:
Mamba, Hideo, *Yukihisa Isobe*, exhibition catalogue, Centre d'Art contemporain, Ivry-sur-Seine, 1998.

Museums and Galleries:
Nagaoka (Niigata MMA) - Tokyo (MMA).

ISODA, Koryusai. See KORYUSAI

ISOLA, Giacomo
Italian, 19th century.
Born 1840, in Parma; died 2 February 1884, in Parma.
Painter. Urban landscapes.

Museums and Galleries:
Parma: *View of the Town*.

ISOLA, Giuseppe
Italian, 19th century.
Born 1808, in Genoa; died 1893, in Genoa.
Painter. History painting.

Guiseppe Isola was a pupil of the Accademia in Genoa, of which he became a member in 1845.

Museums and Galleries:
Florence (Uffizi): *Portrait of the Artist* - Genoa (Mus. dell'Accademia Ligustica di Belle Arti): *Portrait of the Artist*; *Pius IX* - Genoa (Palazzo Bianco): *Andrea Doria Refusing the Crown* - Genoa (Palazzo Rosso): *Duke of Parma* - St Petersburg: *Resurrection* - Turin (Gal. Civica d'Arte Moderna e Contemporanea): *Temptation of St Anthony*; *Deposition* - Turin (Palazzo Reale): *Battle of Mondovi*; *Herodias*.

Auction records:
Milan, 10 March 1982, *Miracle of the Man Cured of the Palsy* (oil on canvas, 38 1/2 x 29 1/2 ins / 98 x 75 cm) ITL 2,600,000.

ISONO, Masahiko
Japanese, 20th - 21st century.
Born 1947.
Painter.

Since 1974, Masahiko Isono has featured in the 5th Warsaw poster Biennale, the 6th Brno Biennale (Czech Republic) and in the exhibition *Japanese Art Today* at the museum of contemporary art in Montreal.

ISONO, Yoshio
Japanese, 19th - 20th century.
Active in Tokyo.
Painter.

Yoshio Isono featured in the Exposition Universelle of 1900 in Paris.

ISOPI, Antonio
German, 19th century.
Born in Rome; died 2 October 1833, in Ludwigsburg.
Sculptor, plasterworker.

In 1810, Isopi was the director of the Institute of Artists at the porcelain works in Ludwigsburg. By 1823, he was a professor at the academy in Stuttgart. As a sculptor, his speciality was animals. The collection at the Ludwigsburg porcelain works has maquettes of low relief animal sculptures by him. His principal works are the Württemberg heraldic devices of the *Stag and Lion* at the entrance to the ducal *Residenz* in Stuttgart. This palace also contains alabaster and marble vases by him. It was at the suggestion of Goethe, who particularly admired his work, that he did the *cabinet rond* plasterwork at Duke Charles Augustus' palace in Weimar. The great houses at Hohenheim, Ludwigsburg, Monrepos and Stuttgart likewise have plasterwork by him.

ISORNI, Pierre
French, 20th century.
Born 1912.
Painter. Figures.

Isorni was a pupil at the École Nationale des Beaux-Arts in Paris. He exhibited at the Salon d'Automne and the Salon de Paris. He received the Blumenthal prize in 1941.

ISOU, Isidore
Romanian, 20th century.
Born 1925, in Botosani.
Active in France from 1944.
Painter.
Lettrism.

The founder of Lettrist Poetry, Painting and Music in 1946, Isodore Isou lived and worked in Paris. He put forward his ideas in the *Manifeste de la poésie lettriste* (*Manifesto of Lettrist Poetry*) and many other works. In the case of the visual arts, he used every kind of existing and invented writing to explore pictorial space, creating 'hypergraphics', a system of signs that endows letters with 'a new plastic contour' and which combines painting, sculpture and the novel. Isou sought, through his work, to show that 'Lettrist painting and hypergraphics embrace and go beyond figurative and abstract art'. Since its initial foundation, the Lettrist movement has split several times into different groups including La Lettre et le Signe and Écritures.

Apart from Apollinaire's *Calligrammes* of 1918, the use of letters in the visual arts has been explored by the first Cubists including Kurt Schwitters, Miró, Hartung and Franz Kline, revealing not only the possibilities but also the limitations and lack of expressiveness of the approach.

Isou featured in exhibitions of the Lettrist group in almost all of the official venues including the Salon d'Art Sacré. A retrospective of his work was mounted at the Galerie Weiller in Paris (1976). He also shows work at the Galerie de Paris and the Galerie Michel Broomhead in Paris.

BIBLIOGRAPHY:
'Lettrisme et hypergraphie' in *Opus international special issue*, periodical, Paris, 1971. Sabatier, Roland, *Le Lettrisme. Les créations et les créateurs*, Z'Éditions, Nice, 1989. Letaillieur, François, *Encyclopédie du lettrisme*, Paris, 1989. Donguy, Jacques, *'Isisore Isou dans l'histoire de la littérature. Interview'* in *Art Press* n° 269 p. 60, Paris, June 2001.

MUSEUMS AND GALLERIES:
PARIS (MNAM-CCI): *Swing* (1947, lettrist drawing); *Wild Signs* (1961).

AUCTION RECORDS:
PARIS, 15 Feb 1988, *Aesthetic Meditation with Soutine* (1983, oil on canvas, 22 x 18 ins / 55 x 46 cm) FRF 9,500. PARIS, 21 June 1990, *Initiation to the Pleasures of the Flesh* (1960, Indian ink on film, 6 3/4 x 5 1/4 ins / 17 x 13.5 cm) FRF 22,000. PARIS, 18 March 1992, *Actors Arrange and Dissarrange their Hair with their Fingers* (1988, print on fabric, 41 x 58 1/4 ins / 104 x 148 cm) FRF 5,500. PARIS, 6 Dec 1992, *It's the Shame of our Race* (1960, ink/tracing paper, 6 3/4 x 5 ins / 17 x 13 cm) FRF 4,100. PARIS, 17 March 1994, *Commentary on Van Gogh (5)* (1985, painting/canvas, 22 x 18 ins / 55 x 46 cm) FRF 14,000. PARIS, 2 Feb 1999, *Implied Rebus* (oil on canvas, 32 x 25 1/2 ins / 81 x 65 cm) FRF 14,100.

ISRAEL, Daniel
Austrian, 19th century.
Born 1859, in Vienna, of Hungarian parents; died 24 April 1901, in Vienna.
Painter. Figures, local scenes (harems), portraits, landscapes, urban landscapes.

Israel was a student at the academies in Vienna and Munich. He exhibited in Munich, Vienna and Budapest. His travels took him to Bosnia, Constantinople, Egypt and Palestine, where he painted small-format landscapes, views of towns and genre pictures such as *A Café in Bosnia, A Victim of Battle, Before the Party, Ball Game, A Street in Cairo, The Fortune-Teller* and *The Secret*. Also noted is a *Bust-Length Portrait of an Oriental Woman*.

MUSEUMS AND GALLERIES:
BAUTZEN (Stadtmus.): *Outside the Harem*.

AUCTION RECORDS:
NEW YORK, 30 June 1981, *Portraits of Gipsy Children* (oil on card, each 3 1/4 x 2 1/4 ins / 8.5 x 6 cm) USD 1,900. LONDON, 28 Nov 1984, *The Little Dancers* (oil on panel, 8 1/2 x 11 3/4 ins / 21.5 x 30 cm) GBP 4,500. LONDON, 27 Nov 1985, *Harem Scene* (oil on panel, 16 1/2 x 21 1/4 ins / 42 x 54 cm) GBP 15,000. LONDON, 24 June 1987, *Harem Scene* (oil on panel, 13 1/2 x 20 1/2 ins / 34.5 x 52 cm) GBP 15,000. LONDON, 17 March 1989, *In the Harem* (oil on panel, a pair, each 12 1/2 x 10 ins / 31.9 x 25.4 cm) GBP 12,100. NEW YORK, 1 March 1990, *The Beauties of the Harem* (oil on panel, 7 x 11 ins / 17.8 x 28 cm) USD 8,800. NEW YORK, 28 Feb 1991, *The Decoration of the Harem* (oil on panel, 15 x 23 3/4 ins / 37.8 x 60.3 cm) USD 44,000. NEW YORK, 29 Oct 1992, *Young Women Reading in the Harem* (oil on panel, 7 x 8 3/4 ins / 17.8 x 22.2 cm) USD 7,700. NEW YORK, 16 Feb 1993, *A Koran Lesson* (oil on card, 3 3/4 x 5 ins / 9.8 x 12.6 cm) USD 4,620. LONDON, 18 June 1993, *The Serenade* (oil on panel, 9 1/2 x 5 1/2 ins / 24 x 14 cm) GBP 5,980. PARIS, 18 June 1993, *The Lovers* (oil on canvas, 35 3/4 x 23 1/2 ins / 91 x 60 cm) FRF 60,000. LONDON, 17 June 1999, *Spoiled for Choice* (oil on panel, Oil Painting, 17 x 25 ins / 44 x 64 cm) GBP 32,000. AMSTERDAM, 26 Oct 1999, *Harem Beauties* (oil on panel, 10 x 13 ins / 25 x 33 cm) NLG 30,000. PARIS, 19 Nov 2001, *Oriental Girl at Rest* (1892, oil on panel, 4 x 6 ins / 10 x 15 cm) FRF 32,000.

ISRAËL-HENRIET. See **HENRIET Israël**

ISRAEL-SILVESTRE. See **SILVESTRE Israël**

ISRAELS, Isaac
Dutch, 19th - 20th century.
Born 1865, in Amsterdam; died 1934, in The Hague.
Painter. Military subjects, genre scenes.
Symbolism.
School of The Hague.

Isaac Israels was the son of the painter Joseph Israels. His parents settled in The Hague, where he attended the art academy. In 1885, he settled in Amsterdam. Israels was also active in Paris, where he received a mention at the Salon des Artistes Français in 1885. His father had a considerable influence on his artistic career. Israels made his painting début with military subjects, processions and a few portraits vaguely reminiscent of the work of French Realist painter Jules Bastien-Lepage (1848-1884). In 1882, his painting *Departure of the Soldiers* brought him great success. However, he often stated that 'only the modern style exists', and when artistic development took another course, he abandoned his former style to find a new and different one.

His group and thematic exhibitions are as follows: 2002, *De Haagse School: Aquarellen uit de verzameling Drucker-Fraser* (*The Hague School. Watercolours from the Drucker-*

Fraser Collection), held at the Rijksmuseum, Amsterdam; 2003, *Stad & Land. 19de-eeuwse Meesterwerken uit het Stedelijk Museum* (*Town and country: 19th-century Masterpieces from the Stedelijk Museum*), De Nieuwe Kerk, Amsterdam; 2003, *De Blijvende Verlokking: Nederlandse Kunstenaars in Italië, 1806-1940* (*Lasting Attraction: Dutch Artists in Italy, 1806-1940*), an exhibition showing the benefits of Italian travel for Dutch artists, which was held at the Kunsthal, Rotterdam. Solo shows and retrospectives are as follows: 1959, the Institut Néerlandais de Paris (Dutch institute in Paris); 1991, the Van Voorst Van Beest gallery, The Hague; and 1999, *Isaac Israels: Holland's Impressionist*, the Kunsthal, Rotterdam.

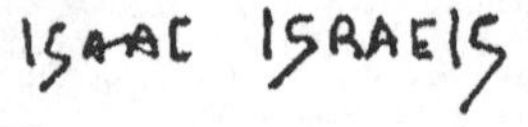

BIBLIOGRAPHY:

Welling, Dolf, *Isaac Israels: the sunny world of a Hague cosmopolitan*, exhibition catalogue, Van Voorst van Beest Gallery, The Hague, 1991. De Bodt, Saskia, *Isaac Israels: Hollands impressionist*, exhibition catalogue, Kunsthal, Rotterdam, 1999. Loos, Wiepke, *Aquarellen uit de verzameling Drucker-Fraser [The Hague School. Watercolours from the Drucker-Fraser collection]*, group exhibition catalogue, Rijksmuseum, Amsterdam, 2002. *De blijvende verlokking: Nederlandse kunstenaars in Italië, 1806-1940*, exhibition catalogue, Kunsthal, Rotterdam, 2003.

MUSEUMS AND GALLERIES:

AMSTERDAM (Rijksmus.): *Donkey Ride on the Beach; Self-portrait; Tollgate Ball* - EINDHOVEN (Van Abbe Mus.) - GRONINGEN: *Singer* - THE HAGUE (Mus. Mesdag): *Trumpet Lesson in the Barracks.*

AUCTION RECORDS:

NEW YORK, 30 April 1909, *In the Harem*, USD 65. LONDON, 16 July 1909, *Head of a Young Woman*, GBP 29 8s. LONDON, 13 Feb 1927, *Procession*, GBP 50 8s. AMSTERDAM, 18 May 1965, *Milliner's Shop*, NLG 6,600. AMSTERDAM, 25 April 1966, *Young Woman on Her Balcony*, NLG 7,800. ANTWERP, 4 and 5 Oct 1966, *Parisian Errand-boy* (pastel) BEF 95,000. AMSTERDAM, 26 May 1970, *Picnic on the Banks of the Loire*, NLG 26,000. ANTWERP, 27 April 1971, *On the Beach*, BEF 60,000. AMSTERDAM, 20 Feb 1973, *Couple in a Park*, NLG 24,500. AMSTERDAM, 18 Feb 1974, *Woman and Little Girl on a Terrace*, NLG 38,500. AMSTERDAM, 27 April 1976, *Portrait of Miss Maxa* (oil on canvas, 28 x 20 1/2 ins / 71 x 52 cm) NLG 24,500. AMSTERDAM, 25 May 1976, *Regent Street, London* (watercolour, 19 1/4 x 13 1/2 ins / 49 x 34 cm) NLG 9,000. AMSTERDAM, 26 April 1977, *Street Scene* (oil on canvas, 44 1/2 x 55 ins / 113 x 140 cm) NLG 44,000. AMSTERDAM, 31 Oct 1979, *Young Peasant Smoking a Pipe* (oil on canvas, 32 x 21 1/4 ins / 81 x 54 cm) NLG 60,000. BERN, 2 May 1980, *Reclining Nude* (charcoal and pencil highlighted with white, 8 x 11 ins / 20 x 28 cm) CHF 2,500. AMSTERDAM, 19 May 1981, *Two Women Dancing at the Cabaret, Amsterdam* (oil on canvas, 31 1/2 x 29 1/4 ins / 80 x 74 cm) NLG 50,000. AMSTERDAM, 15 March 1983, *Young Woman in a Black Hat Smoking a Cigarette* (oil on card, 31 1/4 x 21 1/2 ins / 79.2 x 54.5 cm) NLG 64,000. AMSTERDAM, 15 May 1984, *Seamstress* (pastel, 24 1/2 x 18 1/4 ins / 62.5 x 46.5 cm) NLG 22,500. AMSTERDAM, 14 April 1986, *Young Woman Sitting in a Park, Reading* (watercolour, 19 x 15 ins / 48 x 38 cm) NLG 60,000. NEW YORK, 24 Feb 1987, *Antique Dealer* (oil on canvas, 18 x 23 3/4 ins / 45.7 x 60.3 cm) USD 16,000. PARIS, 30 Nov 1987, *Washerwomen* (oil on canvas, 13 3/4 x 25 3/4 ins / 35 x 65.5 cm) FRF 4,500. NEW YORK, 25 May 1988, *New Church in Amsterdam* (oil on canvas, 38 x 31 1/4 ins / 96.5 x 79.4 cm) USD 8,250. AMSTERDAM, 16 Nov 1988, *Young Woman Sitting in an Armchair Reading a Book* (oil on canvas, 34 1/4 x 18 1/2 ins / 87 x 47 cm) NLG 86,250; *Self-portrait* (oil on panel, 22 x 15 3/4 ins / 56 x 40 cm) NLG 20,700; *Donkey Ride on Scheveningen Beach* (oil on canvas, 32 1/4 x 39 1/4 ins / 82 x 100 cm) NLG 92,000. PARIS, 13 April 1989, *Walk on the Beach* (watercolour, 20 3/4 x 26 1/2 ins / 53 x 67 cm) FRF 220,000. AMSTERDAM, 19 Sept 1989, *Portrait of Mme Kann-Polak Daniels, Sitting in a White Dress* (oil on canvas, 31 1/2 x 23 3/4 ins / 80 x 60.5 cm) NLG 11,500. NEW YORK, 24 Oct 1989, *Oosterpark* (watercolour/paper, 13 1/2 x 19 1/4 ins / 34 x 49 cm) USD 29,700. COLOGNE, 23 March 1990, *Beach Scene with Bathers and Boats* (watercolour, 13 1/2 x 19 1/4 ins / 34 x 49 cm) DEM 4,000. AMSTERDAM, 10 April 1990, *In a Park* (watercolour/paper, 14 1/2 x 11 1/2 ins / 37 x 29 cm) NLG 40,250. AMSTERDAM, 25 April 1990, *Lady at Her Washstand* (oil on canvas, 26 1/2 x 18 ins / 67 x 46 cm) NLG 126,500. AMSTERDAM, 2 May 1990, *Bois de Boulogne in Paris* (oil on canvas, 15 1/4 x 18 1/4 ins / 38.5 x 46.5 cm) NLG 276,000. NEW YORK, 23 May 1990, *Coiffer Ste-Catherine* (oil on canvas, 28 3/4 x 23 3/4 ins / 73 x 60.3 cm) USD 104,500. AMSTERDAM, 5 June 1990, *Twin Sisters* (oil on card, 26 x 21 ins / 66 x 52.5 cm) NLG 241,500. TEL AVIV, 19 June 1990, *Drummer* (charcoal, 13 3/4 x 10 3/4 ins / 35 x 27.5 cm) USD 1,210. AMSTERDAM, 30 Oct 1990, *Women Dancing in an Amsterdam Café* (oil on canvas, 31 1/2 x 29 1/2 ins / 80 x 75 cm) NLG 414,000. AMSTERDAM, 12 Dec 1990, *By the Sea: Young Girl in White on the Promenade* (black chalk and pastel/paper, 22 x 15 ins / 56 x 38 cm) NLG 92,000. AMSTERDAM, 24 April 1991, *Dinner in a Boarding House in Pontresina, Switzerland* (1915, oil on canvas, 17 3/4 x 23 1/2 ins / 45 x 60 cm) NLG 126,500; *The Dressmaker* (charcoal and pastel/paper, 25 1/2 x 19 3/4 ins / 65 x 50 cm) NLG 166,750. PARIS, 26 April 1991, *Young Woman with Mandarin* (watercolour and gouache, 13 x 8 1/4 ins / 33 x 21 cm) FRF 13,000. AMSTERDAM, 30 Oct 1991, *New Dress* (oil on canvas, 34 x 20 ins / 86.5 x 50.5 cm) NLG 218,500. AMSTERDAM, 22 April 1992, *Sunny Street in Batavia* (oil on canvas, 29 1/2 x 39 1/4 ins / 75 x 100 cm) NLG 80,500. LONDON, 30 June 1992, *At the Dressmaker's, Studio Paquin* (pastel/paper/panel, 14 x 19 ins / 35.8 x 48.4 cm) GBP 17,600. AMSTERDAM, 2-3 Nov 1992, *Portrait of a Javanese Female Dancer* (oil on canvas, 21 x 14 1/4 ins / 53.5 x 36.5 cm) NLG 23,000. AMSTERDAM, 21 April 1993, *Pony Ride on a Beach* (oil on canvas, 19 3/4 x 25 1/2 ins / 50 x 65 cm) NLG 66,700. TEL AVIV, 4 Oct 1993, *Portrait of a Woman at the Mirror* (sepia and black chalk, 16 1/4 x 9 3/4 ins / 41.5 x 25 cm) USD 4,600. AMSTERDAM, 19 April 1994, *Donkey Riding on the Beach* (oil on canvas, 21 3/4 x 27 ins / 55.5 x 68.5 cm) NLG 82,800. LONDON, 15 June 1994, *Couple in a Cart* (oil on canvas, 18 1/2 x 23 ins / 47 x 57.5 cm) GBP 9,775. AMSTERDAM, 11 April 1995, *On the Beach at Viareggio* (oil on canvas, 14 3/4 x 20 ins / 37.5 x 50.5 cm) NLG 59,000. TEL AVIV, 14 April 1996, *Bust of a Female Nude* (oil on canvas, 36 3/4 x 28 3/4 ins / 93.5 x 73 cm) USD 24,150. AMSTERDAM, 23 April 1996, *Local Orchestra* (oil on canvas, 39 1/4 x 31 1/2 ins / 100 x 80 cm) NLG 241,900. AMSTERDAM, 19-20 Feb 1997, *Head of a Woman* (pastel and black chalk/paper, 11 1/2 x 9 ins / 29.5 x 22 cm) NLG 3,459. LONDON, 26 March 1997, *Portrait of a Lady (Sophie de Vries)* (1909, oil on panel, 12 1/2 x 9 1/2 ins / 32 x 24 cm) GBP 28,750. LONDON, 11 June 1997, *A View of the Noordeinde, The Hague* (oil on canvas, 23 1/2 x 15 3/4 ins / 60 x 40 cm) GBP 42,200. AMSTERDAM, 2 July 1997, *Waspitten, Amsterdam* (c. 1892-1895, black chalk and pastel/paper, 9 x 11 ins / 22 x 28 cm) NLG 27,676. SINGAPORE, 27 Sept 1997, *Seated Figure* (oil on canvas, 21 3/4 x 13 ins / 55.5 x 33 cm) SGD 48,300. AMSTERDAM, 27 Oct 1997, *Cockney Girl* (1913-1914, oil on canvas, 30 3/4 x 22 1/4 ins / 78 x 56.5 cm) NLG 206,500; *Little Girl Riding a Donkey on the Beach* (pastel, 11 1/2 x 9 1/2 ins / 29 x 24 cm) NLG 56,640; *Young Girl with Sunhat* (watercolour, 19 3/4 x 13 1/2 ins / 50 x 34.5 cm) NLG 54,280. AMSTERDAM, 28 April 1999, *Bois de Boulogne* (oil on canvas, 23 x 17 ins / 59 x 42 cm) NLG 500,000. AMSTERDAM, 28 April 1999, *Dancing Cafe, Moulin de la Galette* (oil on canvas, 35 x 49 ins / 88 x 125 cm) NLG 850,000. AMSTERDAM, 18 April 2000, *Fair Beauty* (black chalk, pastel, 16 x 13 ins / 40 x 32 cm) NLG

410,000. AMSTERDAM, 24 Oct 2000, *Drie revuegirls van de bouwmeester revue, Scala, den Haag* (1927, oil on canvas, 39 x 28 ins / 100 x 70 cm) NLG 250,000. AMSTERDAM, 23 April 2001, *Donkey Ride on Scheveningen Beach* (c. 1900, oil on canvas, 24 x 33 ins / 60 x 83 cm) NLG 330,000. AMSTERDAM, 23 Oct 2001, *Atelier Costume Naaisters* (oil on canvas, 36 x 44 ins / 92 x 111 cm) EUR 125,000. AMSTERDAM, 23 April 2002, *Exciting Reading - Midinette in the Bois de Boulogne, Paris* (c. 1905, pastel, 24 x 19 ins / 60 x 47 cm) EUR 210,000. AMSTERDAM, 22 Oct 2002, *Revue Cirl - la Cocotte - at the Scala, The Hague* (oil on canvas, 28 x 24 ins / 70 x 60 cm) EUR 230,000. AMSTERDAM, 21 Oct 2003, *Female Nude Reading on a Bed* (oil on canvas, 22 x 32 ins / 56 x 81 cm) EUR 120,000. AMSTERDAM, 28 Oct 2003, *Busy Morning on a Canal Bridge, Amsterdam* (c. 1894, oil on canvas, 35 x 41 ins / 90 x 105 cm) EUR 140,000. AMSTERDAM, 20 April 2004, *Getting Dressed for the Show at the Scala Theatre, The Hague* (oil on canvas, 40 x 30 ins / 101 x 76 cm) EUR 180,000. AMSTERDAM, 20 April 2004, *Midinettes on the Place Vendome, Paris* (oil on canvas, 26 x 32 ins / 65 x 81 cm) EUR 370,000.

ISRAELS, Joseph

Dutch, 19th - 20th century.

Born 27 January 1824, in Groningen; died 10 August 1911, in The Hague.

Painter (gouache), watercolourist, draughtsman.

History painting, religious subjects, portraits, genre scenes, still-lifes, landscapes, seascapes.

School of The Hague.

It was not until Joseph Israels had reached the age of 16 that he achieved his wish to work in Amsterdam, where he studied under Cornelis Kruseman. In 1845 he went to Paris, where he entered the studios of the French painters Paul Delaroche and Horace Vernet and the Swiss sculptor James Pradier for three years, but his real teacher at that time was the painter François Édouard Picot. At the 1867 Paris Exposition, Israels won a third-class medal in recognition of the merit of his work and he was decorated with the cross of the Légion d'Honneur. His contribution to the 1878 Exposition in Paris firmly established his reputation. The critics were unanimous in their praise of all his pictures, notably *Alone in the World, From Darkness to Light,* and *Cobblers at Dinner.* Israels won a first-class medal and was made an Officier de la Légion d'Honneur. Subsequently, he was appointed a commander. He won two Grands Prix at the 1889 and 1900 Expositions Universelles respectively. On 3 January 1885, he had been elected as a corresponding member of the Institut de France.

The romantic influence of his artistic education can be clearly felt in his early paintings, which were often Biblical scenes. He did not free himself from this influence immediately after his return to Amsterdam in 1848, as he exhibited for the first time at the Salon de Paris in 1855 with the history painting *William 'the Silent' of Orange Bidding Defiance to King Philip II of Spain.* But Israels soon abandoned history painting in favour of genre scenes. He threw himself resolutely into the study of nature and the outdoors, and from 1857 he produced some noteworthy works. Due to illness Israels went to Zandvoort, a small fishing village, and it was here he grew to admire the sea, and he painted the lives of the fisherfolk with feeling. The following works date from this period: *Evening on the Beach* (1857); *Contented Old Age, The Peaceful House* (1861); *Shepherd* (1862); *The Eve of Separation* (1863); *Boat* (1866); and *Sleeping Women* (1868). Israels had found his vocation, and although he later dedicated himself to other genres, in particular the portrait, his best paintings remain these informal scenes depicting poor people. Until the end of his life, his powerful, varied technique was the inspiration for the Dutch painters Albert Neuhuys, Johannes Bosboom and Bloomers, and through them Van Gogh in the populist work of his first period. Israels' influence, in fact, extended beyond the Dutch School.

His work was featured at group or thematic exhibitions, including *De Haagse School: Aquarellen uit de verzameling Drucker-Fraser* (*The Hague School. Watercolours from the Drucker-Fraser Collection*) (2002), held at the Rijksmuseum in Amsterdam.

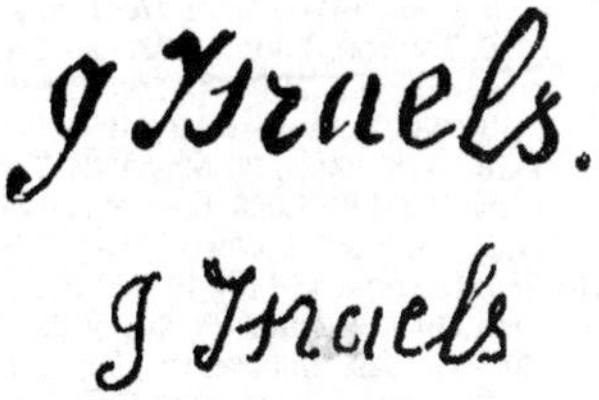

BIBLIOGRAPHY:

Loos, Wiepke, *Aquarellen uit de verzameling Drucker-Fraser [The Hague School. Watercolours from the Drucker-Fraser collection]*, group exhibition catalogue, Rijksmuseum, Amsterdam, 2002.

MUSEUMS AND GALLERIES:

AMSTERDAM (Rijksmus.): *Alone in the World; H. Holweg; Louis Jacques Veltman; Mme Sinkel; Self-portrait; Return Journey; Adam and Eve* - AMSTERDAM (Stedelijk Mus.): *Marguerite de Parme and Prince William; Study of a Head; A Son of the Ancient People; Eléazer Herschel; Eve; Path along the Cemetery; Children of the Sea; Self-portrait; Good Neighbours; After the Storm; Children of the Sea; In the Wheatfields; David before Saul* - DORDRECHT: *Peasant Interior* - GLASGOW: *Frugal Meal; Happy Family* - GRONINGEN: *Portrait of M.K. Mesdag; Poor Johannes* - LEIDEN: *Tonco Medderman* - LONDON (NG): *Fishermen carrying a Drowned Man* (1861?, oil on canvas, exhibited at the Salon in 1861) - MONTREAL: *Moonlight; Lighting his Pipe; Boats Departing* - MONTREAL (Learmont Collection): *Grace; Mme Israels; The Waders* - MOSCOW (State Tretyakov Gal.): *Dressmakers in Holland* - MUNICH: *Consolation* - ROTTERDAM: *Woman at the Window; Michel de Mouchy* - THE HAGUE (Gemeentemus.): *The Little Dressmaker; Portrait of W. Roelofs; Mlle Terlet; When One Becomes Old; Portrait of H.W. Mesdag; Alone in the World; Study of a Nude; Harp Player; Study; Courtyard; Head of a Man.*

AUCTION RECORDS:

BRUSSELS, 1875, *Prop of Old Age,* FRF 5,200. NEW YORK, 1876, *Fishing Boats in Scheveningen,* FRF 14,500. LONDON, 1879, *Untitled Picture,* FRF 40,250. LONDON, 1888, *Waiting for the Return of the Herring Fishing-Boat,* FRF 15,750. PARIS, 1891, *Rest Day,* FRF 14,410. LONDON, 1898, *Fisherman's Family in Their Cottage,* FRF 18,375; *Fisherman's Daughter on the Shore,* FRF 15,225. LONDON, 1898, *Anxious Family,* FRF 24,925; *Desolation,* FRF 5,500; *Frugal Meal* (watercolour) FRF 4,450; *Beloved Maid* (watercolour) FRF 5,250. PARIS, 30 Jan 1900, *In front of the Vast Sea,* FRF 9,665; *Woman Spinner,* FRF 6,930. PARIS, 27 June 1900, *Sewing near the Window,* FRF 8,950. NEW YORK, 26-28 Feb 1902, *Cottage Interior,* USD 8,000. NEW YORK, 8-9 Jan 1903, *Cottage,* USD 500. NEW YORK, 27 Jan 1905, *Grandfather's Consolation,* USD 18,500. LONDON, 7 Dec 1907, *Fisherwoman,* GBP 15. LONDON, 18 Jan 1908, *Rag-and-Bone Woman,* GBP 33; *Contemplation,* GBP 86. LONDON, 23 March 1908, *Prayer,* GBP 210; *Old Woman,* GBP 210. LONDON, 4 April 1908, *La Fête de Jeanne in Liverpool* (1886) GBP 1,680. LONDON, 22 May 1908, *Age,* GBP 1,417; *Children's Small Boat,* GBP 1,680; *Widow,* GBP 1,260; *Washday,* GBP 1,158. LONDON, 3 April 1909, *Murder of William 'the Silent',* GBP 567. LONDON, 13 May 1909, *Maternal Contentment,* GBP 1,134; *Woman Knitter,* GBP 441; *Laundress,* GBP 441; *Young Woman Sewing by the Window,*

GBP 546; *Mother and Child,* GBP 326; *Anxious Woman,* GBP 640. LONDON, 9 July 1909, *Your Cottage Door* (watercolour) GBP 231. LONDON, 16 July 1909, *Portrait of a Young Girl,* GBP 1,050; *The Signal,* GBP 787. LONDON, 16 July 1909, *Grace* (watercolour) GBP 430. LONDON, 3 June 1910, *Pancakes,* GBP 2,835. LONDON, 1 July 1910, *Grief,* GBP 1,470. NEW YORK, 13 Jan 1911, *The Scribe,* USD 10,000. LONDON, 30 June 1911, *Old Woman Reading the Bible near a Coffin,* GBP 1,312. PARIS, 2-4 June 1920, *Young Dutch Woman on Her Doorstep* (watercolour) FRF 1,750. LONDON, 1 June 1923, *Pancake-day,* GBP 1,942; *Drowned Fisherman,* GBP 630. LONDON, 9 May 1924, *Sewing Work,* GBP 588. LONDON, 9 May 1924, *In front of the Sea* (drawing) GBP 475. PARIS, 30 May 1924, *Portrait of an Old Man in a Black Hat,* FRF 7,000. LONDON, 20 March 1925, *An Anxious Family,* GBP 451. LONDON, 29 April 1927, *Young Mother,* GBP 756. LONDON, 15 May 1927, *Interior* (drawing) GBP 283. LONDON, 19 April 1929, *Return of the Flock,* GBP 525. LONDON, 30 May 1929, *Children Waiting for their Father* (drawing) GBP 178; *Exhausted Woman* (drawing) GBP 120; *Waiting for the Boats,* GBP 294. NEW YORK, 12 Nov 1931, *Waiting for the Fishing Boats,* USD 750. PARIS, 27 April 1932, *A Sleeping Child* (pen) FRF 200. NEW YORK, 7 Nov 1935, *Workers,* USD 1,500. PARIS, 28 April 1937, *The Little Gourmands* (watercolour highlighted with gouache) FRF 1,100. NEW YORK, 26 June 1943, *Cottage Madonna,* USD 2,000; *Maternal Care,* USD 1,400; *Road to the Village,* USD 1,200. NEW YORK, 18 April 1945, *Peasants' House,* USD 3,500. LONDON, 4 May 1945, *Young Sailor,* GBP 43; *Pancakes,* GBP 54. LONDON, 12 July 1946, *Fisherman's House,* GBP 178. LONDON, 22 Nov 1946, *Rivals,* GBP 89. AMSTERDAM, 15 April 1947, *Fisherman's Wife,* NLG 1,500. LONDON, 5 July 1950, *An Anxious Family,* GBP 300. NEW YORK, 23 Oct 1957, *Frugal Meal,* USD 1,050. NEW YORK, 21 Oct 1959, *Sun Ray,* USD 1,000. PARIS, 9 May 1960, *Harpsichord Lesson,* FRF 2,250. NEW YORK, 11 May 1960, *Prophet,* USD 625. COLOGNE, 5 May 1966, *Seated Young Woman Looking out of the Window,* DEM 13,000. NEW YORK, 13 Dec 1967, *Mother and Child* (watercolour) USD 2,500. LONDON, 4 June 1969, *Young Peasant Girl on Her Doorstep; Doing Crochet Work,* GBP 2,400. NEW YORK, 12 Feb 1970, *Seated Young Woman Sewing,* USD 4,250. LONDON, 10 Nov 1971, *Baby's Meal,* GBP 2,600. LONDON, 6 Oct 1972, *The Merchants of Bric-à-Brac,* Gns 2,500. LONDON, 30 March 1973, *Making Cakes* (watercolour) Gns 750. LONDON, 5 April 1974, *Little Girl Dragging Her Boat along a Beach,* Gns 2,100. AMSTERDAM, 27 April 1976, *Beach Scene* (oil on canvas, 20 x 27 3/4 ins / 50.5 x 70.5 cm) NLG 42,000. COLOGNE, 21 May 1976, *Park Scene* (drawing, 15 1/2 x 11 1/2 ins / 39.5 x 29 cm) DEM 1,850. AMSTERDAM, 31 Oct 1977, *Dressmaking Studio* (oil on panel, 25 x 19 ins / 63.5 x 48 cm) NLG 30,000. NEW YORK, 7 June 1979, *Self-portrait* (oil on panel, 15 1/2 x 10 3/4 ins / 39.3 x 27.4 cm) USD 12,500. AMSTERDAM, 24 March 1980, *Peasants and Children on a Country Road* (watercolour, 9 1/2 x 20 ins / 24 x 51 cm) NLG 6,000. NEW YORK, 22 Oct 1980, *Study for 'Nothing More!'* (pencil, sepia pen and gouache, 6 1/4 x 8 ins / 16 x 20.3 cm) USD 1,350. NEW YORK, 28 Oct 1982, *Returning from the Fields* (oil on canvas, 42 1/4 x 67 1/4 ins / 107 x 171 cm) USD 8,000. PARIS, 18 March 1983, *Interior Scene with Young Musician Girl* (oil on canvas, 26 3/4 x 36 1/4 ins / 68 x 92 cm) FRF 160,000. LONDON, 29 Nov 1984, *Dinner Time* (watercolour highlighted with gouache, 9 x 12 3/4 ins / 22 x 32.5 cm) GBP 2,600. NEW YORK, 31 Oct 1985, *Children Playing on a Beach* (oil on canvas, 48 x 65 1/2 ins / 122 x 166.5 cm) USD 28,000. TEL AVIV, 1 June 1987, *Beggar and His Son* (pencil, 9 3/4 x 7 1/2 ins / 25 x 19 cm) USD 2,340. BERN, 26 Oct 1988, *To Help Mother* (oil on canvas, 22 x 28 3/4 ins / 56 x 73 cm) CHF 24,000. AMSTERDAM, 16 Nov 1988, *Fisherman's Wife and Her Child Waiting for the Return of the Boats on the Beach* (oil on canvas, 26 3/4 x 35 ins / 68 x 88 cm) NLG 36,800. TEL AVIV, 2 Jan 1989, *Woman Breast-feeding Her Child in a Dutch Farm Kitchen* (oil on canvas, 28 1/4 x 24 ins / 72 x 61 cm) USD 20,350. STOCKHOLM, 19 April 1989, *Little Girl Sitting under an Open Umbrella* (oil on canvas, 26 3/4 x 20 ins / 68 x 51 cm) SEK 29,000. NEW YORK, 23 May 1989, *Mother and Infant* (oil on canvas, 23 3/4 x 19 ins / 60.4 x 48.3 cm) USD 12,100. TEL AVIV, 30 May 1989, *Family Meal in a Dutch Interior* (oil on canvas, 32 x 37 3/4 ins / 81.5 x 96 cm) USD 52,800. TEL AVIV, 3 Jan 1990, *Fisherman* (1882, print, 15 x 11 ins / 38.2 x 27.7 cm) USD 880; *Head of an Old Jew* (oil on card, 8 x 6 ins / 20.5 x 15.5 cm) USD 8,250. NEW YORK, 28 Feb 1990, *Village Path* (oil on canvas, 23 1/2 x 36 1/4 ins / 59.7 x 92 cm) USD 28,600. NEW YORK, 1 March 1990, *Woman Sewing* (oil on canvas, 35 x 45 ins / 88.8 x 114.3 cm) USD 41,800. AMSTERDAM, 2 May 1990, *Dog-Cart* (oil on panel, 10 3/4 x 19 1/4 ins / 27.5 x 49 cm) NLG 20,700. NEW YORK, 22 May 1990, *Waiting for the Fisherman's Return* (oil on canvas, 32 1/2 x 44 3/4 ins / 82.5 x 113.7 cm) USD 39,600. TEL AVIV, 31 May 1990, *Woman Sewing near a Window* (oil on canvas, 25 1/4 x 19 1/4 ins / 64 x 49 cm) USD 35,200. TEL AVIV, 19 June 1990, *Two Little Girls* (charcoal, 8 1/4 x 6 3/4 ins / 21 x 17 cm) USD 1,760. TEL AVIV, 20 June 1990, *Village Path* (oil on canvas, 23 1/2 x 36 1/4 ins / 59.7 x 92 cm) USD 46,200. NEW YORK, 23 Oct 1990, *After the Fishermen's Departure* (oil on panel, 12 3/4 x 17 1/4 ins / 32.4 x 43.8 cm) USD 17,600. NEW YORK, 24 Oct 1990, *Peasant Woman near the Hearth* (oil on canvas, 18 1/2 x 14 ins / 47 x 35.6 cm) USD 8,800. LONDON, 28 Nov 1990, *Nap in the Kitchen* (watercolour, 11 1/2 x 17 1/4 ins / 29 x 44 cm) GBP 4,400. TEL AVIV, 1 Jan 1991, *Two Little Girls Gathering Bundles of Firewood in the Snow* (oil on canvas, 18 3/4 x 16 ins / 47.6 x 40.6 cm) USD 24,200. AMSTERDAM, 24 April 1991, *Peasant Woman Washing a Child in a Kitchen* (oil on panel, 11 x 7 1/2 ins / 27 x 19 cm) NLG 15,525. NEW YORK, 22 May 1991, *Waiting for the Boats* (oil on panel, 20 x 16 3/4 ins / 50.8 x 42.5 cm) USD 16,500. TEL AVIV, 26 Sept 1991, *Woman Knitting in a Kitchen* (oil on canvas, 24 1/4 x 17 3/4 ins / 61.5 x 45 cm) USD 27,500. MUNICH, 26 May 1992, *Little Girl Peeling Potatoes in a Kitchen* (oil on wood, 15 3/4 x 11 1/2 ins / 40 x 29 cm) DEM 23,000. NEW YORK, 28 May 1992, *Children by the Sea* (oil on canvas, 24 x 20 1/2 ins / 61 x 52.1 cm) USD 44,000. AMSTERDAM, 28 Oct 1992, *Fisherman's Wife Drinking Coffee in Her Kitchen* (oil on canvas, 26 1/4 x 37 1/4 ins / 66.5 x 94.5 cm) NLG 34,500. TEL AVIV, 4 Oct 1993, *Mother's Work* (oil on canvas, 35 x 43 1/4 ins / 89 x 110 cm) USD 96,000. HEIDELBERG, 5-13 April 1994, *Woman with a Basket on Her Back, Sitting on the Shore* (1879, etching, 6 x 9 ins / 15 x 23 cm) DEM 1,200. AMSTERDAM, 8 Nov 1994, *Hannah in the Temple* (oil on canvas, 51 1/2 x 44 1/4 ins / 130.5 x 112.5 cm) NLG 126,500. LONDON, 11 April 1995, *Unloading the Fish* (oil on canvas, 16 1/2 x 27 1/2 ins / 42 x 70 cm) GBP 19,550. NEW YORK, 29 June 1995, *Children by the Sea* (oil on panel, 16 1/2 x 11 1/2 ins / 41.9 x 29.2 cm) USD 20,700. TEL AVIV, 12 Oct 1995, *Fisherman's Daughter on the Shore* (oil on panel, 15 x 11 1/2 ins / 38 x 29 cm) USD 25,300. AMSTERDAM, 16 April 1996, *Pancake-day* (oil on panel, 14 1/4 x 9 1/4 ins / 36 x 23.5 cm) NLG 34,220. AMSTERDAM, 5 Nov 1996, *Another Glass* (watercolour, 9 3/4 x 13 3/4 ins / 25 x 35 cm) NLG 17,700; *Beach Scene, Little Boy Carrying His Sister* (oil on panel, 16 1/2 x 11 ins / 42 x 28 cm) NLG 47,200. TEL AVIV, 12 Jan 1997, *Figures on the Beach* (c. 1890, oil on paper/canvas, 17 x 19 ins / 43 x 48 cm) USD 14,950. TEL AVIV, 24-26 April 1997, *Seamstresses* (watercolour/paper, 12 1/2 x 15 3/4 ins / 31.8 x 40 cm) USD 10,000; *Portrait of a Man* (oil on canvas, 22 3/4 x 17 3/4 ins / 58 x 45 cm) USD 13,800. NEW YORK, 23 Oct 1997, *Watching the Sea* (1868, oil on panel, 10 1/2 x 13 1/2 ins / 26.7 x 34.3 cm) USD 14,950. TEL AVIV, 25 Oct 1997, *Two Ladies in a Dutch Interior* (oil on canvas, 26 3/4 x 36 ins / 68 x 91.5 cm) USD 57,500. LONDON, 21 Nov 1997, *Mother of Sorrows* (oil on canvas, 35 x 24 1/2 ins / 88 x 62 cm) GBP 14,375. NEW YORK, 10 Feb 1998, *Returning to the House* (oil on panel, 11 x 14 1/4 ins / 27.9 x 36.5 cm) USD 7,475.

ISSA, real name: Kobayashi; nickname: Yataro, pseudonym: Issa
Japanese, 18th - 19th century.
Born 1763; died 1827.
Painter, poet.
Issa lived in Shinona and Tokyo, and was a poet who wrote *haikai* (*haikai*), Japanese poems of 17 syllables. He had a free and unconventional style, and left a large number of *haiga* (*haikai* pictures), including one collection, *Oraga Haru*.

ISSAEV, Nicolas, or Issaieff
Russian, 20th century.
Born 22 July 1891, in Olivia, near Odessa; died 1977.
Active in France from 1925.
Painter, draughtsman. Landscapes, Still-lifes.
Before attending the school of fine art in Odessa, Nicolas Issaev had already taken part in art exhibitions at secondary school. After World War I, he went to Belgrade with his wife where he painted and then exhibited for the first time in 1924, with some 50 paintings. In 1925 he moved to Paris and attended the Académie de la Grande Chaumière. He was friendly with Bissière and Zadkine and worked at the Académie Ranson. During World War II, he joined the Resistance, returning to Paris at the Liberation.

Originally influenced by Neo-Cubism, Issaev moved away from this style while retaining its architectural construction of space. In his rigorously composed canvases, generally predominantly blue in colour, he sought to reveal the essence of beings and objects. Still-lifes were his favourite subject. His landscapes were inspired by Paris (*La Rue St-Julien le Pauvre*) and by his travels in Spain (*Toledo* and *Spanish Landscape*), Italy and southern France. He executed some painted decorations for the theatre in Belgrade.

He showed at many of the Paris salons including the Salon d'Automne, Salon des Indépendants and Salon Comparaisons. He showed work at the Salon des Indépendants de Toulouse (1942) and at the exhibition of French painters organised by André Achard, Parke Bernet Gallery, New York (1956). His first solo exhibition was in 1929 in Paris. Other solo shows include: an exhibition to raise money for prisoners, Agen (1945); Galerie Lucy Krogh and Galerie de la Boétie (1949); Galerie Cimaise (1952); Arthur Beren Gallery, Philadelphia; André Weil Gallery; Arizona; Finland; Sweden. A retrospective was organised by Madame Paul Valéry (1954).
MUSEUMS AND GALLERIES:
BELGRADE (Mus.) - CHICAGO (Mus.) - PARIS (Mus. de la Ville).
AUCTION RECORDS:
VERSAILLES, 12 May 1976, *Portrait of Ossip Zadkine* (oil on canvas remounted on board, 18 x 13 ins / 46 x 33 cm) FRF 2,000. ZURICH, 13 Oct 1994, *Still-life with Lamp* (1973, oil on panel, 19 1/2 x 26 ins / 49.5 x 66 cm) CHF 3,000.

ISSARTI, Joachim
French, 19th century.
Born 1814, in Aurillac (Cantal); died April 1862, at the Hôpital Bicêtre in Paris.
Painter.
Issarti exhibited portraits and historical subjects at the Paris Salon from 1844 to 1848.

ISSEL, Alberto
Italian, 19th - 20th century.
Born 3 June 1848, in Genoa; died 1926.
Painter, engraver, potter. Genre scenes.
Alberto Issel exhibited from about 1872 in Naples, Turin and Milan.
AUCTION RECORDS:
MILAN, 6 Nov 1980, *Landscape with Waterfall*; *Mountain Stream* (panel, a pair, 19 3/4 x 11 3/4 ins / 50 x 30 cm) ITL 2,200,000. MILAN, 29 March 1995, *Infantry Billet* (1873, oil on panel, 5 1/2 x 12 1/2 ins / 14 x 32 cm) ITL 16,675,000.

ISSEL, Ch. van der, or Yssel
Dutch, 18th century.
Active in Utrecht in 1778.
Painter.

ISSEL, Georg Wilhelm
German, 19th century.
Born 13 October 1785, in Darmstadt; died 15 August 1870, in Heidelberg.
Painter. Landscapes.
Georg Wilhelm Issel's patron was Grand Duke Ludwig I of Hessen, who paid for him to travel. Appointed a councillor and court painter in Hessen, Issel visited virtually all the countries of Europe, either on diplomatic missions or for artistic study tours.
MUSEUMS AND GALLERIES:
DARMSTADT (Hessisches Landesmus.) - HEIDELBERG (Kurpfälzisches Mus.) - KARLSRUHE (Staatliche Kunsthalle).

ISSEL, Heinrich
German, 19th century.
Born 2 July 1854, in Rinklingen (Baden-Württemberg).
Painter. Portraits, genre scenes.
A pupil of Riefsthal, Ernst, Hildebrand and Karl Hoff in Karlsruhe, Heinrich Issel exhibited in Berlin from 1886.
AUCTION RECORDS:
VIENNA, 2 Nov 1976, *The Musketeer and the Old Lady* (1882, oil on canvas, 32 3/4 x 23 1/4 ins / 83 x 59 cm) ATS 20,000.

ISSELBURG. See also **ISELBURG**

ISSELBURG, Peter, or Yselburg, or Eisselburg
German, 16th - 17th century.
Born 1568 or 1580, in Cologne; died 1630, in Nuremberg.
Draughtsman, engraver (burin).
Isselburg was probably the student of Crispyn de Passe, although certain biographers claim he also studied under Sandrart and Gilles Sadeler. He engraved religious and genre subjects, historical portraits and landscapes. He worked in the German towns of Nuremberg, Cologne and Bamberg.

ISSELMANN, Ernst
German, 20th century.
Born 29 April 1885, in Rees-am-Rhein; died 17 March 1916, in Rees-am-Rhein.
Painter, engraver. Portraits, landscapes, still-lifes.
Ernst Isselmann studied in Düsseldorf, Dresden, Berlin, and Paris where he was influenced by Cézanne and Van Gogh. After trips to Italy and Tunis, he was primarily active in Rees-am-Rhein. Isselmann produced many landscapes of the Bas-Rhin in eastern France. He also produced etchings and lithographs.
MUSEUMS AND GALLERIES:
ESSEN (Folkwang Mus.): *Self-portrait*; *Meadow Landscape near Rees-am-Rhein*; *Industrial Port of the Ruhr*.

ISSELSTEYN, Adrianus van, or Ysselsteyn, called Losse
Dutch, 17th century.
Died 9 December 1684, in Utrecht.
Painter. Portraits, still-lifes, animals.
Adrianus van Isselsteyn is not to be confused with Adriaen van Essestevn.

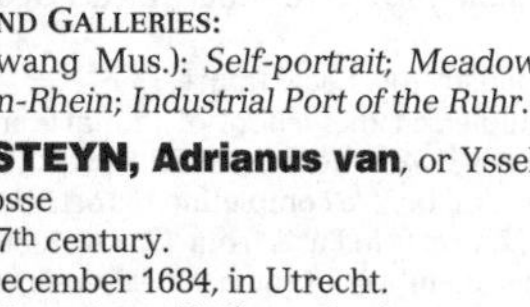

MUSEUMS AND GALLERIES:
DELFT: *Geertruida Huydecoper* - OBERSCHLEISSHEIM: *Dead Cockerel*.

AUCTION RECORDS:
NEW YORK, 10 Jan 1990, *Portrait of a Lady Dressed as Diana (perhaps the Duchess of Richmond)* (1665, oil on canvas, 45$^{1/2}$ x 35$^{3/4}$in/115.3 x 91cm) USD 9,900. AMSTERDAM, 7 May 1996, *Portrait of a Gentleman, Presumed to be a Member of the Coole Family, Dressed in Black with a White Jabot and Holding Gloves* (oil on canvas, 39$^{1/2}$ x 32$^{1/4}$in/100.1 x 82.1cm) NLG 5,175.

ISSEN, nickname: Urakawa
Japanese.
Active in Osaka.
Illustrator.

ISSER, Johanna von
Maiden name: Grossrubatscher
Austrian, 19th century.
Born 1802, in Neustift (Tyrol); died 25 May 1880, in Innsbruck.
Painter.
T. Allom drew views of the Tyrol from Isser's sketches which finished up as engravings on steel.

ISSHI, nickname: Kozasu
Japanese, 15th century.
Active at the beginning of the 15th century.
Painter.
Isshi specialised in ink painting (*suiboku*), sometimes heightened with light colours. Living in the Muromachi period (1338-1573), he is said to have lived in the Nanzen-ji temple in Kyoto.

ISSHI, real name: Fumimori Iwakura, nickname: Isshi, pseudonym: Toko
Japanese, 17th century.
Born 1608; died 1646.
Painter.
Isshi was a Zen monk who studied the Zen doctrine with Takuan. He painted portraits, and was also responsible for the restoration of the Yamagani temple at Omi (modern Shiga Prefecture).

ISSHO, pseudonym: Miyagawa Issho
Japanese, 18th century.
Master engraver.
Issho was a disciple of Choshun (1682-1752), and specialised in portraits of women.

ISSIAKHEM, Ahmed Didou. See also **DIDOU ISSIAKHEM Ahmed**

ISSIAKHEM, Mohamed Didou, or Ahmed
Algerian, 20th century.
Born 17 June 1928, in Azeffouri; died 1 December 1985, in Algiers.
Painter, illustrator. Local figures.
Issiakhem studied at the school of fine arts in Algiers between 1948 and 1952, where his teacher was the miniaturist Mohamed Racim, before completing his artistic education at the school of fine arts in Paris from 1953 to 1956. He was one of the founder members of the national union of painters in Algeria, and taught at the school of fine arts in Algiers. He was awarded the first gold Simbad in Rome in 1980. From 1951 he exhibited his works in Algeria and in other countries. His final exhibition was at the museum of Sidi Boussaid in Tunis. Mohamed Issiakhem may be related to Ahmed Didou Issiakhem, who was born in 1971.

Issiakhem's work, which is characterized by its thickly textured paint, depicts Algerian women both as a symbol of the struggle for liberation from colonialism by the Algerian people and as embodying an erotic and mythical dimension. He illustrated *Nedjima* by Kateb Yacine.

BIBLIOGRAPHY:
Tio Bellido, Ramon (ed.), *Le XXe siècle dans l'Art Algérien*, exhibition catalogue, AICA Press / AFAA, Paris, 2003.
MUSEUMS AND GALLERIES:
ALGIERS (Mus. National des Beaux-Arts): *The Beggar* (oil/plywood); *The Blinds* (oil on canvas) - ORAN (Mus. Zabana): *The Refugees* (oil on canvas).

ISSUISAI
Japanese, 19th century.
Active c. 1830.
Master engraver.
Issuisai's prints of portraits of actors were published in Kyoto.

ISTA, Auguste
French, 19th century.
Born 19th century, in Paris.
Landscape artist.
Auguste Ista was a pupil of Sauzay who began his career at the Salon in 1875.

ISTA, Ernest
French, 19th century.
Born 19th century, in Paris.
Watercolourist. Landscapes.
Ernest Ista made his debut at the Salon in 1877.

ISTLER, Josef
Czechoslovak, 20th century.
Born 13 November 1919, in Prague; died 19 June 2000, in Prague.
Painter, draughtsman.
Groups: Mánes, Ra.
From 1937 to 1939 Josef Istler studied with the Yugoslav teacher Walter Höfner. In 1946 he trained at the Prague academy of fine art with O. Spaniel. He joined the artistic group Mánes in 1945. He belonged to the Surrealist-influenced Ra group between 1946 and 1948 and, at that time, his work consisted of almost graphic signs; these seemed to develop freely across the space of the canvas and yet come together under some hidden direction to create the appearance of natural elements with forms recalling, for example, plants or trees. His work then developed towards an ever more abstract style in which the surface of the canvas was organised in geometric fields of colour. His use of inventive and abundant materials and the Informel forms that infiltrate this harmonious arrangement, however, have the effect of awakening meanings and symbols that come from the depths of the unconscious.

Istler was one of the most significant representatives of new Czechoslovak painting and his work has been shown in several important collective exhibitions including: *L'Art tchécoslovaque 1938-1946* (*Czechoslovak Art 1938-1946*), Paris (1946); *Czechoslovak Graphic Art*, Akademie der Bildenden Künste (1947); *Modern Czechoslovak Art*, Lucerne museum; *Czech Surrealism* with the Ra group, Budapest; *Czechoslovak Graphic Art*, Warsaw; *Czechoslovak Art Today*, Bochum and Baden-Baden museums (1965); *Prague Artists*, Munich; *The Transfiguration of Czech Art*, Liège and Rotterdam; *Modern Art in Czechoslovakia*, Los Angeles; *Present-Day Czechoslovak Art*, academy of fine art, Berlin (1966); *Current Czechoslovak Art*, Museo de Arte Moderno, Mexico. His work also featured in the International Surrealist Exhibition mounted in São Paulo and Rio de Janeiro (1965). His solo exhibitions include: Brno (1945); Prague (1946); Usti and Brno (1965); Prague (1966); Berlin (1967).

BIBLIOGRAPHY:
Fifty years of Czechoslovak Painting from the Collections of the Galleries, 1918-1958, exhibition catalogue, Slovenska Narodna Gal., Bratislava, 1968 (in commemoration of the 50th anniversary of the Republic of Czechoslovakia).

Auction records:
Paris, 10 May 1985, *Aquarius* (1951, oil on canvas, 63 x 47 1/4 ins / 160 x 120 cm) FRF 17,500. Amsterdam, 3 Dec 2002, *Composition* (1949, oil on board, 35 x 23 ins / 89 x 59 cm) EUR 1,900.

ISTOK, János
Hungarian, 19th - 20th century.
Born 16 June 1873, in Bacsfalu.
Sculptor.

János Istok studied in Munich and Budapest. His works include: a statue of *Count Ferenc Szechenyi* in the park of the national museum in Budapest; *Monument to M. Bartha* in Budapest; a statue of *Viktor Ramassetter* in Sümeg; reliefs of: *Rosa Szegedy; D. Szilagyi; Berzeviczy; Lukacs; Bishop Bubics; Burgomaster Gerloczy; Bokay; Hajos.*

Museums and Galleries:
Budapest (Szépmuvészeti Múz.): *David; Energy; Caesar the Dog.*

ISTOKOV, Filipp Prokhorovich
Russian, 18th - 19th century.
Born 25 July 1761; died after 1830.
Painter.

Filipp Prokhorovich Istokov trained at the academy of art in St Petersburg. He was later drawing instructor for the Second Cadet Corps.

ISTOMIN, Ivan
Russian, 19th century.
Painter. Portraits.

Ivan Istomin trained at the Moscow school of fine arts. In 1858 he was awarded the title 'Free Artist' by the academy of art in St Petersburg for his *Study of an Old Man.*

ISTOMIN, Vasili
Russian, 18th - 19th century.
Painter. Portraits.

Museums and Galleries:
Moscow (State Tretyakov Gal.): *Portrait of an Unknown Lady* - St Petersburg (Gosudarstvennyj Russkij Muz.): *Transporting an Icon to Tikhvin Cathedral.*

ISTRATI, Alexandre, real name: Istrate
Romanian, 20th century.
Born 9 March 1915, in Dorohoi; died 28 October 1991, in Paris.
Painter (gouache/mixed media).

Alexandre Istrati studied law at the same time as attending the school of fine art in Bucharest. He graduated in 1938 and remained at the school as an assistant. In 1947, he was awarded a bursary by the French Institute in Bucharest which enabled him to go to Paris where he studied at the École des Beaux-Arts and at the academy run by André Lhote. He met Brancusi who was living in a studio near his home; Istrati and his wife Natalia Dumitresco became close friends of the sculptor and, in time, the executors of his will.

Istrati's work is not easily described. It was always experimental and so always changing. In a first period, around 1950, a spontaneous and joyful Abstraction produced very free forms recalling the first Abstract or Fauve period in Kandinsky's career. In 1952-1953, colours were more controlled without losing any of their material richness, while the construction became more severely geometric in accordance with the aesthetic ideas of Magnelli or Poliakoff. From 1954, colour once again became the most important element, bright, simple and pervasive. In 1960, a desire for a more ascetic approach led Istrati to abandon the use of colour altogether. He produced works at this time in a heavy medium, much worked and almost monochrome, described by Jean-Clarence Lambert as 'a kind of vegetation of lines and forms proliferating in all directions that the painter arranges according to a number of generally sinuous lines of force. The overall effect is one of disorder, which here is richness. We seem to see the vegetation of a still-virgin wilderness in close-up'.

In around 1965, while still working in monochromes of whites, greys and blacks with only rarely a touch of colour, he returned to a tighter and more formal construction in a number of large works (as almost all his works are).

Collective exhibitions include: Carnegie Institute, Pittsburgh (1957); Turin Biennale (1951 and 1969); École de Paris, Galerie Charpentier, Paris (1962); *Une Aventure de l'art abstrait,* Musée Galliera, Paris (1967) Menton Biennale; *L'Art vivant 1965-1968 (Living Art 1965-1968),* Fondation Maeght, St-Paul-de-Vence; *L'Aventure de l'art abstrait,* Orléans museum (1968). He also exhibited regularly at the Salon des Réalités Nouvelles in Paris and fairly frequently at the Salon de Mai.

Solo exhibitions include: Bucharest (1941); Paris (1949-1952, 1956, 1960, 1964, 1968, 1976, 1983 and 1987); New York (1953 and 1958); Brussels and Caracas (1957); Milan and Washington (1959); Copenhagen and Cologne (1960); Cannes (1962, 1965, 1969 and 1976); Munich and Nantes (1962); Kunsthalle, Mannheim (1963 and 1966); Basel (1963); Grenchen (1965); Lucerne and Freiburg im Bresgau (1966); Zurich (1967); Liège (1968); Luxembourg (1969); Tokyo (1981). He received a tribute on the occasion the 10th Rencontre des artistes contemporains, Château-Musée, Cagnes-sur-Mer. He was awarded the Kandinsky Prize in 1953.

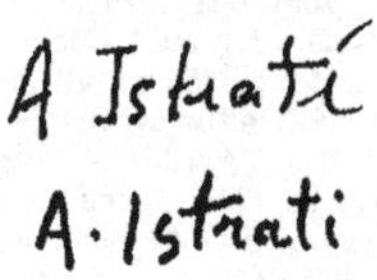

Bibliography:
Van Gindertael, Roger, *'Istrati'* in *Cimaise,* periodical, Paris, December 1953. Ionesco, Eugène, *Istrati,* exhibition catalogue, Gal. Cavalero, Cannes, 1969. *Romanian Artists and the West,* American Romanian Academy of Arts and Sciences, Los Angeles, 1986. *Alexandre Istrati, Nathalie Dumitresco,* exhibition catalogue, Musée des Arts décoratifs, Paris, 1987.

Museums and Galleries:
Antibes (Mus. Picasso) - Bucharest (Muz. National de Arta al României) - Dunkirk (MAC) - Madrid (Mus. Nacional Centro de Arte Reina Sofía) - Mannheim (Städtische Kunsthalle) - Mont-de-Marsan (Mus. Despiau-Wlérick) - Nantes (MBA) - Paris (MAMVP) - Paris (MNAM-CCI) - San Francisco (FAM) - Sofia (SM) - St Louis (GA, Washington University) - St-Étienne (Mus. d'Art et d'Industrie) - St-Paul-de-Vence (Fondation Maeght) - Washington DC (Hirshhorn Mus. and Sculpture Garden): *Blue* (1957, oil) - Zurich (Kunsthalle).

Auction records:
Paris, 17 March 1983, *Neodyne* (1964-1965, oil on paper remounted/canvas, 59 3/4 x 61 ins / 152 x 154 cm) FRF 12,500. Paris, 1 July 1987, *Compostion* (1959, watercolour and ink, 11 1/2 x 16 1/4 ins / 29 x 41.5 cm) FRF 7,000. Paris, 20 March 1988, *Composition* (c. 1954-1956, oil on canvas, 21 1/4 x 25 1/2 ins / 54 x 65 cm) FRF 25,000. Paris, 20-21 June 1988, *Blue, Green, Black* (1957, oil on canvas) FRF 16,500. Paris, 26 Oct 1988, *Harmony in Yellow* (1956-1957, oil on canvas, 36 1/4 x 28 3/4 ins / 92 x 73 cm) FRF 19,000. Paris, 12 June 1989, *Composition* (oil on canvas, 15 3/4 x 13 ins / 40 x 33 cm) FRF 14,000. Paris, 8 Oct 1989, *Solitude* (1960, 51 1/4 x 38 1/4 ins / 130 x 97 cm) FRF 220,000. Zurich, 25 Oct 1989, *Composition* (gouache/paper, 5 1/2 x 5 1/4 ins / 13.8 x 13.5 cm) CHF 1,200. Paris, 18 Feb 1990, *Composition* (oil and gouache/paper, 22 1/2 x 17 ins / 57 x 43 cm) FRF 17,000. Paris, 14 March 1990, *Composition* (oil on canvas, 19 3/4 x 24 ins / 50 x 61 cm) FRF 33,000. Paris, 10 July 1990, *Ecstasy* (oil on canvas, 25 1/4 x

21¼ ins / 64 x 54 cm) FRF 40,000. COPENHAGEN, 4 Dec 1991, *Composition* (1961, oil on canvas, 36¼ x 28¾ ins / 92 x 73 cm) DKK 20,000. PARIS, 16 Feb 1992, *Composition* (1965, oil on canvas, 36¼ x 25¾ ins / 92 x 65.5 cm) FRF 15,500. COPENHAGEN, 4 March 1992, *Initiatory Red* (1960, oil on canvas, 23½ x 31½ ins / 60 x 80 cm) DKK 13,000. COPENHAGEN, 20 May 1992, *Ecstacy* (1961, oil on canvas, 21¼ x 25½ ins / 54 x 65 cm) DKK 10,000. COPENHAGEN, 2-3 Dec 1992, *Defies All Description* (1961, oil on canvas, 15 x 18 ins / 38 x 46 cm) DKK 6,000. HEIDELBERG, 15 Oct 1994, *Abstract Composition* (1965, mixed media, 35 x 18¾ ins / 88.8 x 47.6 cm) DEM 1,000. COPENHAGEN, 7 June 1995, *Initiatory Red* (1960, oil on canvas, 23½ x 31½ ins / 60 x 80 cm) DKK 7,000. PARIS, 7 Oct 1995, *Composition* (1959, oil on canvas, 38¼ x 51¼ ins / 97 x 130 cm) FRF 23,000. PARIS, 3 June 1996, *Abstract Composition* (1959, oil on canvas, 24 x 19¾ ins / 61 x 50 cm) FRF 7,000. PARIS, 28 April 1997, *Abstract Composition* (1964, oil on paper/canvas, 37½ x 50½ ins / 95 x 128 cm) FRF 8,500. PARIS, 25 May 1997, *Composition* (1957, oil on canvas, 25½ x 18 ins / 65 x 46 cm) FRF 12,000. ZURICH, 19 Nov 1997, *Composition* (1967, mixed media/paper, 20 x 17 ins / 51 x 43 cm) CHF 800. PARIS, 9 March 1998, *Composition* (1962, mixed media/paper, 11¾ x 15¾ ins / 30 x 40 cm) FRF 2,200. PARIS, 6 July 1999, *Cycline* (1961, oil on canvas, 29 x 36 ins / 73 x 91 cm) FRF 23,000. PARIS, 15 March 2000, *Eye of the Cyclops* (1960, oil on canvas, 64 x 51 ins / 162 x 130 cm) FRF 25,000. PARIS, 13 Oct 2000, *Irony* (oil on canvas, 50 x 38 ins / 128 x 96 cm) FRF 23,000. PARIS, 6 July 2001, *Composition* (1955, oil on canvas, 57 x 45 ins / 145 x 115 cm) FRF 35,000. PARIS, 5 Dec 2001, *Composition* (1971, oil on canvas, 59 x 59 ins / 150 x 150 cm) FRF 35,000. PARIS, 16 April 2002, *Composition* (1949, oil on canvas, 51 x 63 ins / 130 x 161 cm) EUR 6,650. PARIS, 24 Nov 2002, *Grey Symphony* (1961, oil on canvas, 36 x 29 ins / 92 x 73 cm) EUR 4,800. PARIS, 26 Feb 2003, *Untitled* (1983, oil on canvas, 78 x 79 ins / 198 x 200 cm) EUR 5,400. PARIS, 26 Feb 2003, *Une Serie d'Elans Successifs* (1961, oil on canvas, 64 x 45 ins / 162 x 114 cm) EUR 6,000. PARIS, 7 April 2004, *Red Composition* (1987, oil on canvas, 77 x 69 ins / 195 x 175 cm) EUR 4,800. PARIS, 7 April 2004, *Blue Composition* (1987, oil on canvas, 77 x 51 ins / 195 x 130 cm) EUR 5,500.

ISTRIA, Veronique d'
French, 20th century.
Born in Paris.
Painter.

Istria studied art at the École Supérieure d'Arts et Techniques in 1966-1967, and at the École du Louvre in 1968-1972. She then specialised in Oriental religions and Sanskrit. She paints with a palette of evanescent and ethereal tones. Her subjects reflect upon the archaeological vestiges and books of the Orient. She has held solo exhibitions in Paris in 1977, 1984, 1985 and 1986, in Lebanon in 1979, and in Monaco in 1985.

ISTRIN, P.
Russian, 19th century.
Painter.

P. Istrin trained at the Moscow school of fine arts. His painting *At the Hunt* and a portrait were included in the school's 1886 exhibition; he also submitted *Study* for the exhibition of 1890.

ISTVANFFY, Gyula
Hungarian, 19th century.
Born 27 July 1857, in Marosujvar (Transylvania).
Active in Budapest.
Painter. Landscapes.

Gyula Istvanffy studied at the academy in Budapest and also with Ebersburger in Munich. He showed small landscapes in exhibitions in Budapest and Kolozsvar. Towards the end of 1900, he organised a collective exhibition comprising 200 of his works in his studio.

ISUPOV, Aleksei or Alessio, or Jussupoff Aleksander
Russian, 20th century.
Born 1889, in Vyatsk; died 1957, in Rome.
Active in Italy.
Painter. Figure compositions, figures, portraits, animals, landscapes with figures.

Aleksei Isupov studied at the Moscow academy of fine art between 1909 and 1913 and also at the academy in Leningrad (now St Petersburg). He travelled to The Hague in 1931 and then, from 1932, divided his time between Rome and Milan.

He specialised in painting scenes of peasant life.

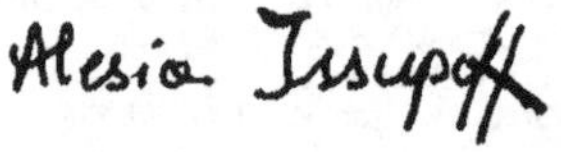

AUCTION RECORDS:
MILAN, 28 Oct 1976, *Peasants and Horses* (two oils on panel, 9¾ x 13 ins / 25 x 33 cm) ITL 3,800,000. MILAN, 5 April 1979, *Peasants* (oil on panel, 4¾ x 13¼ ins / 12 x 33.5 cm) ITL 2,000,000. MILAN, 16 June 1980, *Child with Tamburine* (oil on canvas, 39¼ x 31½ ins / 100 x 80 cm) ITL 5,000,000. NEW YORK, 28 May 1981, *Market Scene in Winter* (oil/hardboard, 33 x 35½ ins / 84 x 90 cm) USD 9,500. ROME, 15 March 1983, *Horses and Figures in a Snowy Landscape* (oil on canvas, 23½ x 31½ ins / 60 x 80 cm) ITL 7,400,000. MILAN, 28 Oct 1986, *Peasants in the Ukraine* (oil/hardboard, 28¾ x 41 ins / 73 x 104 cm) ITL 9,000,000. MILAN, 10 Dec 1987, *Winter Landscape* (oil on canvas, 15½ x 31½ ins / 39.5 x 80 cm) ITL 13,000,000. ROME, 25 May 1988, *Winter Day* (oil on canvas, 25¾ x 31¾ ins / 65.5 x 80.5 cm) ITL 13,000,000. MILAN, 14 March 1989, *The Smoker* (oil on canvas, 35½ x 23½ ins / 90 x 60 cm) ITL 15,000,000. MILAN, 14 June 1989, *Self-portrait with Guitar* (oil on canvas, 31¾ x 23¾ ins / 80.5 x 60.5 cm) ITL 3,600,000. MILAN, 6 Dec 1989, *Working in the Fields* (oil on panel, 11 x 13½ ins / 27 x 34 cm) ITL 6,000,000. NEW YORK, 17 Jan 1990, *Peasants with a Covered Wagon* (oil on card, 7¾ x 13¼ ins / 19.7 x 33.7 cm) USD 4,400. MILAN, 30 May 1990, *Friends on a Terrace with Flowers* (1927, oil on mounted card, 11 x 12½ ins / 27 x 32 cm) ITL 3,400,000. NEW YORK, 22 May 1991, *Farmyard with a Man on a White Horse* (oil on panel, 19 x 23¾ ins / 48.3 x 60.3 cm) USD 10,450. NEW YORK, 17 Oct 1991, *Stallion* (oil on reinforced canvas, 19½ x 23½ ins / 49.5 x 59.7 cm) USD 14,300. MILAN, 7 Nov 1991, *Russian Village in Winter with Peasants and a Horse* (oil on panel, 14¼ x 25¾ ins / 36 x 65.5 cm) ITL 21,500,000. ROME, 24 March 1992, *Head and Shoulders of a Girl in Pink* (oil on panel, 17¾ x 14½ ins / 45 x 37 cm) ITL 3,450,000. NEW YORK, 17 Feb 1993, *In the Garden* (oil on canvas, 40 x 27 ins / 101.6 x 68.6 cm) USD 36,800. MILAN, 8 June 1993, *Farmyard with Horses* (oil on canvas, 23¼ x 31½ ins / 59 x 80 cm) ITL 12,000,000. ROME, 31 May 1994, *White Cloak* (oil on canvas/card, 19¾ x 15 ins / 50 x 38 cm) ITL 11,785,000. LONDON, 15 June 1994, *Busy Market* (oil on panel, 11½ x 19¾ ins / 29.5 x 50 cm) GBP 5, 750. MILAN, 19 Dec 1995, *Peasants and Horses on the Russian Steppes* (oil on panel, 10 x 13¼ ins / 25.5x33.5cm) ITL 4,830,000. MILAN, 23 Oct 1996, *Figures in a Wood* (oil on canvas, 9½ x 13¾ ins / 24 x 35 cm) ITL 13,980,000. ROME, 11 Dec 1996, *Peasants and Horses* (oil on panel, 9¾ x 13½ ins / 25 x 34.5 cm) ITL 6,757. MILAN, 18 Dec 1996, *Two Peasants in a Landscape* (oil on panel, 13¾ x 22 ins / 35 x 55 cm) ITL 21,552,000. LONDON, 19 Dec 1996, *Coming Home from the Fields* (oil on panel, 11 x 17 ins / 27 x 43.2 cm) GBP 2,760. ROME, 2 Dec 1997, *Winter Landscape with Figures* (oil on canvas, 31½ x 23½ ins / 80 x 60 cm) ITL 18,400,000. ROME, 25 May 1999, *Farm Life* (oil on panel, 14 x 22 ins / 35 x 55 cm) ITL 12,000,000. MILAN, 16 June 1999, *Meal on the Terrace* (oil on canvas, 40 x 54 ins / 101 x 136 cm) ITL

54,000,000. MILAN, 28 March 2000, *Embroidery* (oil on canvas, 71 x 43 ins / 180 x 110 cm) ITL 34,000,000. TURIN, 4 Dec 2000, *A Day in the Countryside* (oil on card, 13 x 26 ins / 34 x 65 cm) ITL 14,500,000. NEW YORK, 1 May 2001, *Lilacs in Bloom* (c. 1942, oil on canvas, 43 x 54 ins / 109 x 136 cm) USD 52,500. NEW YORK, 2 Nov 2001, *Elegant Still-life* (1947, oil on panel, 20 x 28 ins / 50 x 72 cm) USD 12,000. COLOGNE, 11 April 2002, *Reclining Female Nude* (39 x 43 ins / 98 x 110 cm) EUR 9,500. ROME, 27 May 2002, *Lady* (oil on canvas, 32 x 24 ins / 82 x 61 cm) EUR 5,500. MILAN, 18 March 2003, *Reading in the Garden* (oil on canvas, 39 x 28 ins / 98 x 70 cm) EUR 15,000. ROME, 11 June 2003, *Lilac* (oil on canvas, 39 x 28 ins / 100 x 70 cm) EUR 18,000. LONDON, 26 May 2004, *Still-life with Lilacs* (1951, oil on canvas, 39 x 28 ins / 100 x 70 cm) GBP 32,000. LONDON, 26 May 2004, *Dance* (oil on panel, 24 x 31 ins / 60 x 79 cm) GBP 34,000.

ITAKURA, Kanae
Japanese, 20th century.
Born 1901, in Tokyo; died 1928.
Painter.

Itakura attended the school of fine arts in Tokyo, then worked under Okada Saburo. At the age of 26 he travelled to France, and in 1930 his work was exhibited posthumously in Paris at the Salon de la Société Nationale des Beaux-Arts, the Salon des Indépendants and the Salon d'Automne.

ITALIA, Salomon
Dutch, 17th century.
Active in Amsterdam c. 1646.
Engraver.

ITALUS. See first name

ITASONI
Swiss, 18th century.
Painter, decorative designer.

Itasoni is known solely from a signature *Itasoni pinxit 1766* on wainscoting in which individual panels are decorated with landscapes painted in blue and white. The wainscoting is now in the National Museum in Zurich.

ITASSE, Adolphe
French, 19th century.
Born 1830, in Lourmarin (Vaucluse); died 1893, in Paris.
Sculptor.

Itasse was a pupil of Belloc and Jacquot. He made his debut at the Salon in 1864 and continued to take part in exhibitions until his death. His figures were inspired by Pradier, of whom his work is often reminiscent, but he mainly achieved recognition as a portraitist.

Works often quoted include: *The Birth of Love*, a marble statue; *The Kiss*; *Dew*, a candelabra group; the bust of his master *Hilaire Belloc*, of whom the marble statue appears in the Luxembourg, and the bronze in the Père-Lachaise cemetery. *Cambert*; *Campra*; *Jean-Jacques Rousseau*; *Philidor*; *Piccini*; *Paesiello* (on the lateral façade of the new opera house); and *Astronomy*, a statue carved in plaster (in the Trocadéro) are also attributed to him.

AUCTION RECORDS:
LONDON, 6 Nov 1986, *Bust of a Child* (c. 1880, patinated bronze, h. 18 3/4in/47.5cm) GBP 900. STOCKHOLM, 16 May 2000, *Rose Bud* (marble, h. 43 ins / 108 cm) SEK 80,000.

ITASSE-BROQUET, Jeanne
French, 19th century.
Born 25 September 1867, in Paris.
Sculptor.

Jeanne Itasse-Broquet was a pupil of her father Adolphe Itasse. She made her debut at the Salon in 1881. She obtained honourable mentions in 1888 and at the Exposition Universelle in 1889, remuneration for travel in 1891, a third-class medal in 1896, and a second-prize silver medal at the 1900 Exposition Universelle. Following her father, she produced several busts for the new opera house. One of her statues can be seen in the Trocadéro palace.

ITAYA, Fusa or Foussa
Japanese, 20th century.
Born 14 October 1919, in Fukuoka.
Painter. Landscapes, flowers, animals.

Itaya studied at the school of fine art in Tokyo in 1945, before moving to France, where he lives and exhibits, as well as in Japan. As a painter of landscapes, animals and flowers, Itaya seems to have come to a certain extent under the influence of Cubism. Since 1956 he has taken part in Paris at the Salon d'Automne, and has also exhibited at the Salon des Artistes Français, where he was awarded a gold medal in 1963. He has also featured at the Salon Comparaisons and the Salon des Indépendants.

AUCTION RECORDS:
LONDON, 21 Oct 1988, *Young Girl with Dog* (oil on canvas, 11 x 9 ins / 27 x 22 cm) GBP 4,400. NEW YORK, 9 May 1989, *Woman at the Window* (1956, oil on canvas, 19 1/2 x 24 ins / 49.8 x 61 cm) USD 550. NEW YORK, 10 Oct 1990, *Madonna* (oil on canvas, 10 3/4 x 8 3/4 ins / 27.3 x 22.2 cm) USD 990. NEW YORK, 29 Sept 1993, *Chickens and Dogs* (oil on canvas, 22 x 18 1/2 ins / 55.9 x 47 cm) USD 1,610. PARIS, 29 Nov 1994, *The Castle near the Bridge* (oil on canvas, 11 x 9 ins / 27 x 22 cm) FRF 4,200. CALAIS, 24 March 1996, *Portrait of a Girl* (1971, oil on canvas, 28 3/4 x 21 1/4 ins / 73 x 54 cm) FRF 9,000.

ITAYA, Hiromasa. See **KEISHU**

ITCHKO, Sergei
Russian, 20th - 21st century.
Born 1949, in Petouchov.
Painter.

ITCHO, or Nobuka, real name: Shinko Hanabusa, original name: Taga, family name: Fujiwara; nickname: Kunju; nicknames: Sukenoshin, Jiemon, Isaburo; pseudonyms: Choko, Suisao, Kyusodo, Ippo, Kanun, Rinshoan, Rintoan, Gyoun, Kansetsu, Sessho, Wao, Kyoundo, Undo, Hokusoo, Hosho
Japanese, 17th - 18th century.
Born 1652, in Osaka; died 1724.
Painter. Genre scenes, landscapes.

Itcho, together with his contemporaries Korin (1658-1716) and Moronobu (died about 1694), was part of the most significant artistic group of the Genroku period (1688-1704), the golden age of Edo culture. Their works evoke the spirit of a period and reflect its cultural atmosphere, but in different ways. Korin represents great decorative painting, and Moronobu the popular current of the depiction of everyday life called *ukiyo-e*. Itcho, for his part, renews the academic tradition by taking up popular themes again and treating them with wit. His work has a strong national character. Born in Osaka, the son of a doctor, he lived in Edo (now Tokyo) with his family from the age of 15, and entered the studio of Yasunobu (1613-1685), the younger brother of Tan'yu (1602-1674). His artistic independence soon brought down on him the wrath of the academic school, and he pursued his career in his own way by studying, it would seem, the Tosa style and Chinese painting. The time he spent with the Kanos nonetheless affected him deeply. As a friend of Basho (1644-1694) and other poets writing *haikai*, poems of 17 syllables, Itcho gave his works a refined and often satirical tone, and he seems more at ease in these smaller formats, where he could give free rein to his fantasy and humour. He painted landscapes, but excelled particularly in scenes from popular and everyday life, which he treated simply but with great distinction, which is the reason for his success with the middle-class elite of Edo.

His rebellious spirit soon came to the attention of the rulers of the country, who were concerned to assert their authority and to stamp out any focal point of subversion. It was for this reason that an allusion adjudged irreverent to the *shogun* in one of his paintings caused him to be exiled in 1697. He spent 12 years on the island of Miyake-shima, where he retained the right to paint and to send his work to Edo. He studied the way of life of the peasants and fishermen of Miyake, reproducing it in a simple and profoundly humane style, where gentle irony often surfaces, stripped of any malice. In 1709 he returned to Edo, and at that time took the name of Itcho. It was then that the most active part of his career began: his art became more and more subtle and sophisticated. He founded a school where he taught his technique, which he perfected with perseverance, in the search for an ever more personal mode of expression. He sought to satisfy his taste for free creation, without his wit ever harming the sureness of his craftsmanship or the extraordinary vivacity of his touch. This prevented him from falling into caricature. His vision of everyday life therefore used a more refined style than the one employed by the first masters of *ukiyo-e*.

BIBLIOGRAPHY:

Akiyama, Terukazu, *La Peinture japonaise*, Skira, Geneva, 1961. Kozyreff, C., in *Encyclopædia Universalis* vol. IX, Paris, 1971. Guth, Christine, *Japanese Art of the Edo Period*, Calmann & King, London, 1996.

MUSEUMS AND GALLERIES:

TOKYO (Seikado Library and Art Mus.): *Peasant Crossing a River and Leading His Horse* (dated before 1698, colour/silk, roll opening vertically).

AUCTION RECORDS:

NEW YORK, 16 Oct 1990, *Kanzan and Jittoku* (ink and diluted pigments/paper, kakemono, 12 x 22 ins / 30.5 x 56 cm) USD 3,520.

ITEBOLDUS

French, 11th century.

Active at the beginning of the 9th century.

Miniaturist, calligrapher.

A monk from St-Vaast, Arras, Iteboldus worked with seven other monks on the writing and decoration of a manuscript richly ornamented with letters and borders that is in the library of Arras.

MUSEUMS AND GALLERIES:

ARRAS (Bibliothèque municipale): illuminated manuscript.

ITEN, Hans

Swiss, 19th - 20th century.

Born 1874; died 1930.

Painter. Landscapes, flowers.

AUCTION RECORDS:

CELBRIDGE, 29 May 1980, *Wooded Landscape by the Church* (oil on canvas, 20 3/4 x 24 3/4 ins / 52.7 x 63 cm) GBP 650. BELFAST, 28 Oct 1988, *Carpet of Bluebells* (oil on card, 15 x 18 ins / 38.2 x 46 cm) GBP 770. BELFAST, 30 May 1990, *River Valley* (oil on panel, 12 x 16 ins / 30.5 x 40.7 cm) GBP 715. LONDON, 16 June 1993, *Flower Border* (oil on canvas, 19 x 25 1/4 ins / 48 x 64 cm) GBP 4,600. SEVENOAKS, 11 Nov 1999, *Autumn Flowers* (oil on canvas, 30 x 39 ins / 75 x 100 cm) GBP 6,900. DUBLIN, 8 Dec 1999, *Cottage at Ligoniel, near Belfast* (oil on panel, 10 x 14 ins / 25 x 36 cm) IEP 4,600. DUBLIN, 29 March 2000, *Gathering Blue Bells* (oil on canvas, 17 x 24 ins / 44 x 60 cm) IEP 12,500. DUBLIN, 26 June 2000, *In the Glens of Antrim* (oil on canvas, 18 x 24 ins / 46 x 61 cm) IEP 6,500. DORCHESTER, 1 March 2001, *Roses* (oil on board, 13 x 10 ins / 33 x 25 cm) GBP 4,400. LONDON, 18 May 2001, *Cushendall, Co. Antrim* (oil on board, 9 x 13 ins / 24 x 32 cm) GBP 2,800. BELFAST, 6 Feb 2002, *Bit of Old Normandy* (oil on canvas, 24 x 28 ins / 61 x 71 cm) GBP 7,000. BELFAST, 6 Feb 2002, *In Ormeau Park* (oil on board, 10 x 12 ins / 25 x 30 cm) GBP 7,500. BELFAST, 4 June 2003, *Fair Head* (oil on board, 19 x 26 ins / 48 x 66 cm) GBP 4,500. DUBLIN, 18 Nov 2003, *Carnations* (1909, oil on canvas on board, 17 x 13 ins / 42 x 34 cm) EUR 5,000. LONDON, 13 May 2004, *Rhododendrons in a Lustre Bowl* (oil on canvas, 20 x 26 ins / 51 x 66 cm) GBP 18,000. DUBLIN, 30 Nov 2004, *Cottages on a Country Lane, County Down* (oil on canvas, 20 x 26 ins / 51 x 66 cm) EUR 13,000.

ITEN, Meinrad

Swiss, 20th century.

Born 30 June 1867, in Unter-Ageri (Zug).

Painter. Religious subjects, portraits.

Meinrad Iten painted in oils and pastels as well as red chalk. His work was featured at the Düsseldorf exhibitions in 1894 and 1896-1897. In 1897, he exhibited at the international exhibition in Berlin. In Switzerland, he exhibited portraits in Zurich, St Gall, Bern and Zug. Amongst his portraits are those of *Madame de Roll-Ritter*, exhibited in Solothurn; *Bishop Benziger*, *Abbot Fellmann* and *Abbess M. Agatha Bossard* of the monastery of Frauental, and a red chalk portrait of *Abbot J. Staub of Einsiedeln*. Amongst his religious pictures, a *Crucifixion* in Ober-Ageri is particularly notable.

ITERIUS, le clerc

French, 12th century.

Sculptor, architect.

In 1120 Iterius worked on the restoration of the abbey of St-Martin, Auxerre.

ITH, Anna Margaretha Luise

Swiss, 19th century.

Born 14 September 1849, in Bern.

Painter.

ITH, Émilie Sophie Margaritha

Swiss, 19th century.

Born 31 July 1846, in Bern; died 23 February 1904, in Zurich.

Painter.

Émilie Ith was the sister of Anna Ith.

ITHIER

French, 14th century.

Active in Troyes from 1335 to 1340.

Painter, illuminator.

ITHIER, John Robert

French, 20th century.

Born 11 September 1904, in Villemomble; died 9 March 1977, in Sevran.

Painter. Urban landscapes, landscapes.

Ithier exhibited regularly in Paris at the Salon des Indépendants. He became a member of that society in 1926, and a member of its committee in 1950. He also exhibited his landscapes in the provinces and abroad.

MUSEUMS AND GALLERIES:

PARIS (FMAC).

AUCTION RECORDS:

PARIS, Oct-July 1946, *Suburban Street* (1927) FRF 1,100. PARIS, 7 Nov 1946, *Old Houses* (1927) FRF 1,080. PARIS, 4 May 1955, *Old Houses, Rue des Reculettes*, FRF 10,000.

ITO, pseudonym of Katsu Ito

Japanese, 20th century.

Born 1938.

Active in France from 1969.

Painter, draughtsman.

Ito received a painter's training between 1956 and 1961 with Ichikawa, as well as attending courses at the art school in Osaka between 1958 and 1960. From 1974 to 1976 he attended courses in engraving at Hayter's Atelier 17 in Paris. Ito's work defies the grid as an element in perspective construction in several planes. It is no longer a question of Western Euclidian perspective organised according to static vanishing points, but of an attempt to visualise other spaces, starting from the interpenetration of straight lines, solid shapes and curves, the whole suggesting a construction of movements at different levels.

Ito has taken part in group exhibitions, including: 1965, Salon Nika, Tokyo; 1971, Salon d'Automne, Paris; 1974, Salon des Indépendants, Paris; 1980, 1981, 1983, 1985 and 1992, Salon Comparaisons, Paris; 1980, 1981 and 1982, Salon d'Art Sacré, Paris; 1980, Salon Grands et Jeunes d'Aujourd'hui, Paris; 1985, 1987 and 1989, Figuration Critique, Paris. He has shown his works in solo exhibitions, including: 1962, Osaka gallery, Osaka; 1973 and 1974, Umeda gallery, Osaka and Nagoya; 1982, 1985 and 1987, Galerie Lia Grambihler, Paris.

ITO, Ben
Japanese, 20th century.
Born 1917, in Shizuoka Prefecture.
Engraver, draughtsman.

Ben Ito was a wood engraver and abstract draughtsman who trained himself in the techniques of printmaking. In 1949 he won a prize from the Japanese engraving association, and in 1950, 1953, 1954, 1956 and 1957 he won various prizes at the salons of the Kokugakai (national academy of painting), of which he was a member. In 1958, he featured in the international print festival at Grenchen in Switzerland.

ITO, Jakuchu, real name: Shunkyo Ito or Jokin; nickname: Keiwanoms, pseudonyms: Jakuchu, Tobeian, Tomaio
Japanese, 18th century.
Born c. 1716, in Kyoto; died 1800.
Painter. Animals, flowers.

Jakuchu Ito was born into a prosperous family in Kyoto, and so was able to devote himself to painting, free of all economic and even artistic constraints. At the Zen Sokoku-ji monastery in Kyoto, where he was a frequent visitor, he had the opportunity to study the paintings of flowers and birds of the China of the Song dynasty (960-1279) and probably also of the Ming dynasty (1368-1644). An artist dissatisfied with the conventional style of the Kano School, the realism of these works probably influenced him. Like several other independent artists of his period, he created a style marked by a pervading positive spirit, in which there is a mixture of Kano elements and the teachings of Maruyama Okyo (1733-1795), the initiator of Pictorial Realism. He lived in a large house on Nishiki Street, the market area of Kyoto, and this picturesque district probably contributed to the development of his taste for the reality of the thing being painted, as did the animals and birds that he raised in his garden, including a peacock and a parrot, very rare at the period, and various sorts of cockerel. He thus had to hand a sufficiently rich cross section of nature not to be obliged to have recourse to anecdotes or poetic themes. He said: 'Many are the painters who paint, but few are those who depict true beings.' From 1758 to 1770 he executed 30 large paintings composed of flowers, birds and fish, a true natural history in colour which he offered to the Sokoku-ji monastery, and which are now in the imperial collections. The great fire which ravaged Kyoto in 1788 cost him his fortune and his home. He retired to a monastery, where continued to pursue his work. The *Cockerels with Cactus*, a vast composition which decorates the sliding doors (*fusuma*) of the Saifuku-ji temple in Osaka, are the fruit of his long labours. As an acute observer, he succeeded, by exaggerated stylisation, in giving his animals expressions full of vigour, and even majesty. The contrast of lively colours and gold is accentuated by an immense cactus, a witness to his curiosity in regard to exotic plants. Ito's realism leads to a sort of expressionism, an exceptional trait in Japanese painting, which explains the increasing interest now being shown in him.

BIBLIOGRAPHY:

Akiyama, Terukazu, *La Peinture japonaise*, Skira, Geneva, 1961.

AUCTION RECORDS:

NEW YORK, 16 April 1988, *Untitled* (ink/paper, kakemono, 44 x 11 3/4 ins / 111.5 x 29.7 cm) USD 3,300; *Cockerels, Hens and Chicks* (ink/paper, two kakemonos, each 56 1/4 x 20 3/4 ins / 143 x 53 cm) USD 4,620. NEW YORK, 29 March 1990, *Cockerels* (ink/paper, kakemono, 42 1/2 x 16 1/4 ins / 108 x 41 cm) USD 4,400; *Marrows* (ink/paper, kakemono, 39 3/4 x 10 3/4 ins / 101 x 27.5 cm) USD 4,950. NEW YORK, 26 March 1991, *Chicks* (ink/paper, kakemono, 35 3/4 x 11 1/4 ins / 91 x 28.7 cm) USD 6,050. NEW YORK, 23 Oct 1991, *Plum Blossom* (ink/paper, kakemono, 12 x 11 ins / 30.4 x 27 cm) USD 4,950.

ITO, Koun, real name: Tsunetatsu Ifo, pseudonym: Koun
Japanese, 19th century.
Born 1879; died 1939.
Active in Tokyo.
Painter. Genre scenes.

Koun Ito featured in the Exposition Universelle of 1900 and in the exhibition *L'Art japonais*, held in 1929 at the Musée du Jeu de Paume in Paris.

ITO, Kyoho
Japanese, 20th century.
Painter.

Kyoho Ito featured in the exhibition *L'Art japonais*, held in 1929 at the Musée du Jeu de Paume in Paris.

ITO, Ryugai
Japanese, 20th century.
Painter.

Ryugai Ito featured in the exhibition *L'Art japonais*, held in 1929 at the Musée du Jeu de Paume in Paris.

ITO, Saiko
Japanese, 20th century.
Painter.

Saiko Ito featured in the exhibition *L'Art japonais*, held in 1929 at the Musée du Jeu de Paume in Paris.

ITO, Shiko, or Shiko Itoh
Japanese, 20th century.
Born 14 March 1935, in Tokyo.
Painter.

Shiko Ito studied under the direction of the Chinese painter Pu Ju in 1953, obtaining a degree at Meiji University, Tokyo, in 1957. She studied under the direction of Ta-Ch'ien in 1958, and subsequently under P'u Hsin-yü in Taiwan in 1960-1962. She studied Zen with Seki Bokuö in 1965, and painting in Italy with Marino Marini in 1975. She has remained true to the ancient Oriental tradition, using Chinese ink for the execution of *Sumie* paintings. She executed her first abstract paintings in 1978. Exhibiting in Tokyo since 1957, she showed her work in Osaka in 1965 and 1969, and in Singapore and Paris in 1972. She became a full member of the Salon d'Automne in Paris in 1983.

ITO, Shinsui
Japanese, 20th century.
Born 1898, in Tokyo; died 1972.
Painter, engraver, illustrator.

Shinsui Ito, who had no financial means of support, worked in his youth in a print works. However, from the age of 14 he took courses in painting, and soon began to participate in group artistic events. He is particularly known for his very realistic portraits of women, and he executed numerous engravings and illustrations.

AUCTION RECORDS:

LONDON, 30 March 1988, *Seated Girl* (1943, oil on canvas, 46 x 31 1/2 ins / 116 x 80 cm) GBP 22,000. NEW YORK, 25 March 2003, *Snowstorm* (colour woodcut, 17 x 11 ins / 44 x 27 cm) USD 6,000. NEW YORK, 25 March 2003, *After the Bath* (colour woodcut, 18 x 12 ins / 46 x 30 cm) USD 20,000. SAN FRAN-

CISCO, 6 April 2004, *Katada Ukimido* (1918, print, 13 x 8 ins / 32 x 21 cm) USD 3,750. SAN FRANCISCO, 6 April 2004, *Snowstorm* (1932, print) USD 8,000.

ITO, Shoha, real name: Sato Ito, original name: Futami, pseudonym: Shoha
Japanese, 20th century.
Born 1877; died 1968.
Painter.

Shoha Ito was a daughter of the priest of Sarutahiko Jinja, a Shinto shrine. She painted watercolours of medieval court ladies and featured in the exhibition *L'Art japonais*, held at the Musée du Jeu de Paume in Paris in 1929.

BIBLIOGRAPHY:
The Collection of the Meito Art Museum, Museum of Modern Art, Shiga, Shiga, 1997 (text in Japanese).

MUSEUMS AND GALLERIES:
MIE (Meito Museum of Art) - MIE (Mie Prefectural Art Museum) - SHOUHA (Shouha Art Museum).

ITO, Takayuki
Japanese, 20th century.
Painter.

Takayuki Ito featured in the exhibition *L'Art japonais*, held in 1929 at the Musée du Jeu de Paume in Paris.

ITOZONO, Wasaburo
Japanese, 20th century.
Born 1911, near Oita; died 2001.
Painter.

Itozono was a student at the art academy in Kawabata. He exhibited from 1930, and featured in 1957 in the Japanese selection of works exhibited at the São Paulo Biennale.

MUSEUMS AND GALLERIES:
KITAKYUSHU (Kitakyushu Municipal Museum of Art) - TOKYO (National MMA).

ITRY, Jacob van
Dutch.
Painter. Landscapes.

MUSEUMS AND GALLERIES:
LIVERPOOL: *Landscape in Holland*.

ITSCHNER, Karl
Swiss, 19th - 20th century.
Born 5 July 1868, in Stäfa; died 1953.
Painter, draughtsman. Scenes with figures, landscapes.

MUSEUMS AND GALLERIES:
BASEL: *Autumn Holidays* - GENEVA (MAH): *Young Girls Playing*.

AUCTION RECORDS:
BERN, 1 May 1980, *Landscape* (oil on card, 14 3/4 x 22 3/4 ins / 37.5 x 58 cm) CHF 2,000. BERN, 9 May 1987, *Round Dance* (oil on panel, 23 1/2 x 31 1/2 ins / 60 x 80 cm) CHF 4,400. ZURICH, 7 Dec 2000, *Children Dancing under Birch Tree* (oil on board, 27 x 29 ins / 68 x 73 cm) CHF 5,500.

ITSUNEN. See **YIRAN**

ITSUUN, real name: Shosai Kinoshita; nicknames: Kosai, Shiganosuke; pseudonyms: Itsuun, Butsubutsushi, Yochiku Sanjin, Jora Sanjin
Japanese, 19th century.
Born 1799, in Nagasaki (Fukuoka); died 1866.
Painter.

Itsuun was a painter of the Nanga School (scholar painting), and a disciple of Yushi (1768-1846). After periods of time spent in Kyoto and Edo (now Tokyo), he set up in the town of his birth, where he was probably trained in the techniques of mainland painting in ink with the Chinese painter Jiang Jiabu (or Kokaho in Japanese), who was in Japan at that time. He painted landscapes, and was also known as a poet.

AUCTION RECORDS:
NEW YORK, 29 March 1990, *Landscape* (ink/paper, kakemono, 56 1/4 x 15 3/4 ins / 143 x 40 cm) USD 2,860.

ITTELSBERGER, Christoph
German, 19th century.
Active in Regensburg.
Sculptor (wood).

In 1809, Christoph Ittelsberger sculpted the high altar in Friesheim (Regensburg), and in 1825 three altars for the church in Brennberg (Bavaria).

ITTELSBERGER, Fidelis, or Illsperger or Ittberger
German, 18th century.
Active in Cham (Bavaria).
Sculptor.

ITTEN, Johannes
Swiss, 20th century.
Born 11 November 1888, in Süderen-Linden; died 25 March 1967, in Zurich.
Painter, sculptor, lithographer.

From 1909-1912, Johannes Itten pursued scientific studies at the University of Bern in conjunction with artistic studies at the École des Beaux-Arts in Geneva. During this period, he made trips to Paris, Munich and Cologne in 1910, 1911 and 1912 respectively. During the course of his travels, he familiarised himself with avant-garde art, particularly Cubism and the lyricism of the Blaue Reiter group. He came into contact with the Sonderbund artisans during his trip to Cologne. Itten was a science teacher at a secondary school until 1913, when he decided to pursue a career as a professional artist. He began to paint at the art academy in Stuttgart in 1913, where he remained until 1916, under the supervision of Adolf Hölzel; he was first influenced by Expressionism and Cubism, then his work rapidly moved in the direction of Abstraction. In 1916, he founded an art school in Vienna, and exhibited with the Sturm (Storm) group, and more curiously at the Dada gallery in 1917. In 1923, Itten set up a weaving studio in Switzerland. In 1919 his work was featured at an exhibition in Vienna organised by the Czech-born architect Adolf Loos, where Itten met the German architect Walter Gropius, who asked him to teach alongside him at the Bauhaus. From 1919-1923, Itten stayed there as director of the preliminary course, in addition to several studios. At the Bauhaus in 1923, Itten was overwhelmed by the trend for functionalism and constructivism introduced by the Dutch Neo-Plasticist painter Theo van Doesburg, when he endeavoured to introduce his students to 'creative automatism' and the consideration of the element of chance in creation. He spent 1923-1926 in Heidelberg near Zurich. From 1926-1934, Itten ran his own art school in Berlin, which he closed under pressure from the Nazis. From 1932-1938, he was in charge of the art school in Krefeld; then in 1938 he settled in Amsterdam before returning to Zurich, where from 1938-1954 he was the principal of the Kunstgewerbeschule (school for applied arts), the Kunstgewerbemuseum (museum of applied arts), and the Textilfachschule (technical school for textiles). He founded the Rietberg Museum in Zurich, where he subsequently remained active, having relinquished his official functions.

Itten contributed a considerable selection of his works to group exhibitions, including the Venice Biennale in 1966. In 2003, his work was featured at the group exhibition *Aux Origines de l'Abstraction (1800-1914)* (*The Origins of Abstraction (1800-1914)*), which was held at the Musée d'Orsay, Paris. His solo shows include: 1919, Vienna; 1922, Berlin; 1925, Munich. Private exhibitions and retrospectives include: 2002, *Johannes Itten. Alles in Einem - Alles im Sein*, held at the Saarland Museum, Saarbrücken; 2003, the museum of fine arts, Bern. In addition to his paintings, he notably published a series of ten lithographs in Vienna in 1919. He also produced a few sculptures and architectural designs in Weimar. From this period, his own work coincided with the implementation of his theories on art, particularly colour. A grid pattern of horizontal and vertical parallel lines acted as a support to very useful explorations of colour harmonies, often based on psychological and symbolic similarities. In 1963, Itten published *Gestaltungs- und Formenlehre. Mein Vorkurs am Bauhaus und später* (*Design and Form: The Basic Course at the Bauhaus and Later*). He recorded the key points of his theories on colour and form in *Kunst der Farbe* (*The Art of Colour*) in 1961.

BIBLIOGRAPHY:

Itten, Johannes, *Kunst der Farbe*, Ravensburg, 1961 (Eng. trans. 1961, R 1970). Wingler, H.M., *Das Bauhaus*, Bramsche and Cologne, 1962, rev. 1975 (Eng. trans. 1969, rev. 1976). Itten, Johannes, *Gestaltungs- und Formenlehre. Mein Vorkurs am Bauhaus und später*, Ravensburg, 1963, 2/1965 (Eng. trans. 1969). Roters, E., *Die Maler am Bauhaus*, Berlin, 1965 (Eng. trans. 1969). Rotzler, Willy, '*Johannes Itten*' in *Du*, periodical, Zurich, June 1966. *Itten*, exhibition catalogue, Bauhaus-Archiv, Darmstadt, 1967. Leymarie, Jean/Herzogenrath, Wulf/Grote, Ludwig/Gropius, Walter, *Le Bauhaus*, exhibition catalogue, Württembergischer Kunsteverein, Stuttgart, Musée national d'Art moderne, Paris, 1969. Itten, J., *Le Dessin et la Forme*, Dessain et Tolra, Paris, 1970. Franciscono, M., *Walter Gropius and the Creation of the Bauhaus in Weimar*, Urbana, 1971. Rotzler, Willy, *Johannes Itten - Werke und Schriffen*, Orell Füssli, Zurich, 1972. Wick, R., *Bauhauspädagogik*, Cologne, 1982. Badura-Triska, E./Bogner, D./Tietze-Conrat, E., *Johannes Itten: meine Symbole, meine Mythologien werden die Formen und Farben sein*, Museum Moderner Kunst, Vienna, 1988. Helfenstein, Josef (ed.), *Johannes Itten, Das frühwerk 1907-1919*, exhibition catalogue, descriptive catalogue, Kunstmuseum, Bern, 1992. Lemoine, Serge/Rousseau, Pascal, et al., *Aux origines de l'abstraction (1800-1914)*, exhibition catalogue, Musée d'Orsay, Paris, 2003.

MUSEUMS AND GALLERIES:

AMSTERDAM (Stedelijk Mus.) - BERLIN (Nationalgal.) - BERN (Kunstmus.): *Horizontal-Vertical* (1915) - BREMEN (Kunsthalle): *Blue-Green Resonance* (1917, oil on canvas) - GÖTEBORG: *Smoker* - VIENNA (Mus. Moderner Kunst Stiftung Ludwig) - ZURICH (Mus. Bellerive): *Encounter* (1916).

AUCTION RECORDS:

STUTTGART, 3 May 1961, *Red Tower*, DEM 19,000. STUTTGART, 3 and 4 May 1962, *House in Spring*, DEM 19,500. GENEVA, 24 April 1970, *Portrait of a Man*, CHF 26,000. HAMBURG, 15 June 1973, *Composition* (watercolour) DEM 3,800. MUNICH, 26 Nov 1976, *Houses* (1922, drawing, 10 x 12½ ins / 25.5 x 32 cm) DEM 3,800. BERN, 7 June 1978, *Composition* (1958, watercolour, 12½ x 9 ins / 31.5 x 22 cm) CHF 5,800. BERN, 19 June 1980, *Standing Nude* (c. 1918, black chalk, 18¾ x 11½ ins / 47.5 x 29 cm) CHF 11,000. BERN, 19 June 1980, *Young Girl in Red* (1936, watercolour, 10 x 6 ins / 25.4 x 15 cm) CHF 4,000. BERN, 26 June 1982, *Violet Tones* (1964, oil on canvas, 24 x 24 ins / 61 x 61 cm) CHF 46,000. MUNICH, 30 May 1983, *Autumn Structure* (1966, pastel and coloured chalks, 19¼ x 23½ ins / 49 x 60 cm) DEM 8,000. HAMBURG, 9 June 1983, *House of the White Man* (1921, lithograph) DEM 3,200. MUNICH, 29 Oct 1985, *Houses in a Tyrolean Landscape* (1918, pencil and stump highlighted with white, 7¼ x 10¼ ins / 18.5 x 26 cm) DEM 8,500. BERN, 18 June 1987, *Vase of Flowers* (1922, pencil, 10½ x 10¼ ins / 26.5 x 26.3 cm) CHF 6,600. HEIDELBERG, 15-16 Oct 1993, *Composition with Circles* (1919, lithograph, 12¾ x 12 ins / 32.3 x 30.7 cm) DEM 1,200. ZURICH, 13 Oct 1994, *Two Marks* (ink and coloured pencil, 9½ x 5¼ ins / 24.2 x 13.2 cm) CHF 800. BERN, 20-21 June 1996, *Urs* (1922, charcoal and pencil, 15 x 11¼ ins / 38 x 28.4 cm) CHF 6,000. NEW YORK, 14 Nov 1996, *Untitled* (1918, pastel/paper, 8 x 6 ins / 20.5 x 15.5 cm) USD 12,650. LUCERNE, 7 June 1997, *Untitled* (watercolour and Indian ink/Japanese paper, 10 x 4¾ ins / 25.7 x 11.9 cm) CHF 4,000. ZURICH, 23 March 1999, *Green, Blue, Red* (1967, acrylic on canvas, 31 x 16 ins / 80 x 40 cm) CHF 30,000. BERN, 25 June 1999, *Tree and Wheatfield* (1947, oil on board, 16 x 20 ins / 40 x 50 cm) CHF 38,000. ZURICH, 23 May 2000, *Standing Young Man* (c. 1919, pencil, 16 x 7 ins / 40 x 18 cm) CHF 4,600. ZURICH, 12 Dec 2000, *Fruit Trees* (1953, watercolour, 9 x 12 ins / 24 x 31 cm) CHF 5,500. ZURICH, 31 May 2001, *Mountain Landscape* (watercolour, ink, 20 x 28 ins / 50 x 71 cm) CHF 5,000. BERN, 21 June 2001, *Shepherds in the Fields* (watercolour and bodycolour over Indian ink, 13 x 9 ins / 32 x 23 cm) CHF 3,000. BERN, 20 June 2002, *Hen* (Indian ink, 12 x 8 ins / 31 x 20 cm) CHF 7,000. COLOGNE, 4 Dec 2002, *Composition* (1923, pastel on board, 11 x 15 ins / 29 x 37 cm) EUR 4,600. MUNICH, 14 May 2004, *I is Joy* (pencil, colour chalk, 11 x 8 ins / 29 x 21 cm) EUR 3,100. BERN, 12 Nov 2004, *Treasure Chest* (1959, watercolour, ink, collage, 11 x 12 ins / 28 x 30 cm) CHF 15,000.

ITTENBACH, Franz

German, 19th century.
Born 18 April 1813, in Königswinter; died 1 December 1879, in Düsseldorf.
Painter, fresco artist. Religious subjects, portraits. Murals.

Ittenbach went to Düsseldorf in 1832 and was admitted to the studio of Wilhelm Schadow there. He also worked with T. Hildebrand, but was nonetheless more influenced by Schadow, whom he accompanied to Italy in 1839, returning to Germany in 1842. After a visit to Munich, he established himself in Düsseldorf, which remained his favourite city. He had become part of a group of like-minded artists including the brothers Karl and Andreas Müller and Ernst Deger, who often went with Ittenbach on his travels.

He was primarily a religious painter, but leaving aside the ascetic coolness, his paintings have a grace and serenity. Apart from a number of portraits, his works are church decorations. His style is simple, and manifests great skill of line and profound religious sentiment. His work includes an *Enthroned Madonna* and *Assumption of the Virgin* in the church of St Remigius in Bonn, a *Holy Family* in the Prince of Liechtenstein's chapel in Vienna, four altar paintings in the church of St Remigius in Breslau (now Wroclaw, Poland), the *Baptism of Christ* in Düsseldorf, a *St Apollinaris* in Remagen and a fresco in the church of St Quirinus in Neuss.

As a protégé of the clergy, Ittenbach was also favoured with the patronage of German Catholic princes, and was awarded numerous decorations by them. He was a professor and honorary member of the academy in Vienna. *Bryan's Dictionary* mentions a *Holy Family in Egypt* by him in the Nationalgalerie in Berlin, engraved by R Stans, though the catalogue of that museum does not mention it, and the work is now in the museum in Münster.

MUSEUMS AND GALLERIES:

BERLIN (Nationalgal.): *Holy Family in Egypt* - DÜSSELDORF: *Madonna and Child* - HANOVER (Niedersächsisches Landesmus.): *Virgin Praying* - MÜNSTER: *Holy Family*.

AUCTION RECORDS:

BRUSSELS, 1875, *Madonna and Child*, FRF 2,300. PARIS, 1898, *The Countenance Divine*, FRF 1,500. NEW YORK, 8 Feb 1935, *Holy Family*, USD 1,125. NEW YORK, 23 Feb 1968, *Holy Family*, USD 2,000. LONDON, 11 Feb 1976, *St Dorothy of Cappadocia* (1853, oil on canvas rounded at the top, 15½ x 11½ ins / 39.5 x 29.5 cm) GBP 700. LONDON, 23 Feb 1977, *Madonna and Child* (1853, oil on canvas, rounded at the top, 42¼ x 32 ins

/ 107 x 81 cm) GBP 4,600. LONDON, 9 May 1979, *St Dorothy of Cappadocia* (1853, oil on canvas, rounded at the top, 15 1/4 x 11 1/4 ins / 38.5 x 28.5 cm) GBP 1,600. LONDON, 24 June 1981, *St Elizabeth with Roses* (1852, oil on canvas, rounded at the top, 33 x 18 3/4 ins / 84 x 47.5 cm) GBP 1,500. LONDON, 11 May 1984, *Christ and the Woman of Samaria* (1854, oil on canvas, 48 3/4 x 35 ins / 124 x 89 cm) GBP 2,200. COLOGNE, 25 June 1987, *St Catherine of Nivelles* (oil on canvas, 27 x 18 ins / 68.5 x 45.5 cm) DEM 5,000. NEW YORK, 31 Oct 2000, *Holy Family* (1868, oil on panel, 19 x 13 ins / 49 x 33 cm) USD 55,000.

ITTMANN, Hans
Dutch, 20th century.
Born 1914, in Waalwijk; died 1972, in Amsterdam.
Painter (including gouache).
Group: Vrij Beelden.

Hans Ittmann stayed in Paris in the 1950s. In 2002, his work was featured at the exhibition entitled *Focus Paris, Bekering tot Abstract* (*Focus Paris: The Turn towards Abstraction*) which was held at the CoBrA Museum voor Moderne Kunst in Amstelveen; it paid homage to a number of artists who were members of the groups Vrij Beelden and Creatie, influenced in Paris by the ideas of Abstraction.

BIBLIOGRAPHY:
Focus Paris, die Hinwendung zum Abstrakte, exhibition catalogue, Cobra Museum voor Moderne Kunst, Amstelveen, 2002.

AUCTION RECORDS:
AMSTERDAM, 10 April 1989, *Composition* (gouache, 17 x 24 1/4 ins / 43 x 61.5 cm) NLG 1,092. AMSTERDAM, 13 Dec 1990, *Untitled* (gouache/paper, 18 1/4 x 24 1/4 ins / 46.5 x 61.5 cm) NLG 1,840. AMSTERDAM, 21 May 1992, *Untitled* (gouache/paper, 17 x 24 ins / 43 x 61 cm) NLG 1,150. AMSTERDAM, 31 May 1994, *Composition* (oil on canvas, 19 3/4 x 27 1/2 ins / 50 x 70 cm) NLG 6,900. AMSTERDAM, 30 May 1995, *Seated Figure* (oak woodcut, h. 19 3/4 ins / 50 cm) NLG 7,250. AMSTERDAM, 28 June 2004, *Abstract Composition* (oil on canvas, 35 x 39 ins / 90 x 100 cm) EUR 3,500.

ITTOKU, real name Ittoku Tosa
Japanese, 17th century.
Active at the beginning of the 17th century.
Painter.
Tosa School.

Ittoku is known to have executed paintings of birds, especially quails, and a painting of a kind of doll for good luck called a *daruma*, dressed in a red coat.

ITURRIA, Ignacio de
Uruguayan, 20th - 21st century.
Born 1949, in Montevideo.
Painter, sculptor, engraver. Figures, genre scenes, interiors.

The son of Basque immigrant parents, Ignacio de Iturria studied design and painting. He married in 1977 and moved to Spain, living in Barcelona in 1982. He returned to live in Montevideo from 1979 to 1982 and permanently in 1984.

His works depict a sombre and oppressive space (such as theatrical scenery, bare façades) from which emerge grotesque figures. He takes scenes from everyday life and distorts them in accordance with his memory, creating an unsettling perception for the viewer and a bittersweet and profoundly nostalgic atmosphere. He also produces three-dimensional works in papier-mâché representing tables and armchairs in the form of animals, such as *Sofá Elefante* (*Elephant Couch*) of 1998.

He has taken part in collective exhibitions, including: 4th Cuenca Painting Biennale in Ecuador, where he was awarded the Grand Prix (1994); Venice Biennale where he received the Cassa di Risparmio Prize (1995); *América Latina '96* (*Latin America '96*), Museo Nacional de Bellas Artes, Buenos Aires (1996); the Havana Biennale (1997). He has also shown his work in solo exhibitions, including: Art Museum of the Americas, Washington DC (1993); Museo José Luis Cuevas, Mexico City (1994); North Dakota Museum of Art, Grand Forks, Dakota and Winnipeg Cultural Centre, Canada (1996); Museo de las Americas, San Juan, Puerto Rico (1997); Museo Nacional de Bellas Artes, Buenos Aires, Rufino Tamayo Museum, Mexico City and Museo de Monterrey, Mexico (1998); Fundación Telefónica, Madrid and the Museo de Bellas Artes, Valencia (1999); Marlborough Gallery, New York (2000). XIIIe Biennale, San Juan Puerto Rico (2001).

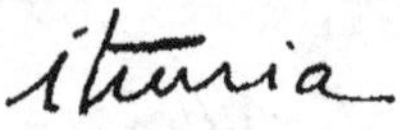

BIBLIOGRAPHY:
Diéguez Videla, Albino, *Ignacio Iturria*, exhibition catalogue, Fundación Praxis, Buenos Aires, 1990. *Iturria: Que viva la vida!*, exhibition catalogue, Museo José Luis Cuevas, Fundación Praxis, Buenos Aires, 1994. *Ignacio Iturria, XLVI Biennale di Venezia*, exhibition catalogue, Museo Nacional de Artes Visuales, Montevideo, 1995 (text in Italian, Spanish and English). *Ignacio Iturria*, exhibition catalogue, Museo Nacional de Bellas Artes, Buenos Aires, 1998 (text in Spanish and English). Jiménez, Hosé, et al., *The Loneliness of the Game. Ignacio Iturria*, exhibition catalogue, Fundacíon Telefónica, Madrid, 1999 (text in Spanish and English). *Exposicion homenaje a Ignacio Iturria. XIII Bienna de San Juan del grabado latino-americano y del Caribe*, exhibition catalogue, Museo de San Juan, San Juan (PRI), 2001.

AUCTION RECORDS:
NEW YORK, 20-21 Nov 1990, *Cupboard* (1987, oil on canvas, 51 x 39 ins / 129.5 x 99.3 cm) USD 10,450. NEW YORK, 15-16 May 1991, *Cupboard* (1988, oil on canvas, 46 3/4 x 39 ins / 119 x 99 cm) USD 11,000. NEW YORK, 20 Nov 1991, *Untitled* (1988, acrylic/canvas, 47 1/4 x 39 1/4 ins / 120 x 100 cm) USD 12,100. NEW YORK, 18-19 May 1992, *Table* (1988, oil on canvas, 51 1/4 x 63 1/2 ins / 130 x 161.5 cm) USD 13,200. NEW YORK, 24 Nov 1992, *Cadaquès* (oil on canvas, 23 1/2 x 29 ins / 60 x 73.7 cm) USD 10,450. NEW YORK, 25 Nov 1992), *Cutlery* (1990, oil on canvas, 67 x 76 3/4 ins / 170 x 195 cm) USD 13,200. NEW YORK, 18 May 1993, *The Clock* (1988, metal and oil on canvas, 76 1/2 x 51 ins / 194.5 x 129.5 cm) USD 40,250. NEW YORK, 18 May 1994, *Compartment with Elephant* (1993, oil on canvas, 71 3/4 x 89 1/2 ins / 182.2 x 227.3 cm) USD 36,800. NEW YORK, 20 Nov 1995, *Corners* (1990, oil/fabric, 72 1/2 x 92 ins / 184 x 233.7 cm) USD 63,000. NEW YORK, 25-26 Nov 1996, *Untitled* (1989, oil on canvas, 39 1/4 x 39 1/4 ins / 100 x 99.7 cm) USD 21,850. NEW YORK, 28 May 1997, *Armario* (*Cupboard*) (1993, oil on canvas, 72 x 52 ins / 182.9 x 132.1 cm) USD 63,000. NEW YORK, 24-25 Nov 1997, *Can on the Table with a Small Aeroplane* (1993, oil on canvas, 51 1/2 x 64 ins / 131 x 162.5 cm) USD 74,000. NEW YORK, 2 June 1999, *Table with Reservoir* (1991, oil on canvas, 70 x 90 ins / 178 x 229 cm) USD 82,000. NEW YORK, 22 Nov 1999, *Compartment with Two Aeroplanes* (1990, oil on canvas, 59 x 75 ins / 150 x 190 cm) USD 80,000. NEW YORK, 1 June 2000, *Many Portraits* (oil on canvas, 52 x 39 ins / 132 x 98 cm) USD 24,000. MONTEVIDEO, 17 Aug 2000, *Interior* (1994, oil on canvas, 32 x 39 ins / 82 x 100 cm) USD 25,000. NEW YORK, 30 May 2001, *Blue Plane in the Bath* (1998, oil on canvas, 39 x 51 ins / 100 x 130 cm) USD 30,000. NEW YORK, 31 May 2001, *Untitled* (1993, oil on canvas, 52 x 72 ins / 132 x 183 cm) USD 40,000. NEW YORK, 28 May 2002, *Elephant and Giraffe* (c. 1995, oil on canvas, 20 x 78 ins / 51 x 198 cm) USD 20,000. MONTEVIDEO, 10 Oct 2002, *Woman* (1980, oil on canvas, 45 x 57 ins / 114 x 146 cm) USD 10,500. NEW YORK, 19 Nov 2003, *Table with Cups* (1993, oil on canvas, 39 x 82 ins / 100 x 209 cm) USD 55,000. NEW YORK, 19 Dec 2003, *Bel Canto* (oil on canvas, 38 x 52 ins / 96 x 133 cm) USD 14,000. NEW YORK, 26 May 2004, *Field with Horse on the Table* (1990, oil on canvas, 24 x 29 ins / 60 x 73 cm) USD 18,000. MONTEVIDEO, 22 June

2004, *Houses in Cadaqués* (1978, oil on canvas, 37 x 47 ins / 93 x 120 cm) USD 9,500.

ITURRINO GONZÁLEZ, Francisco

Spanish, 19th - 20th century.

Born 1864, in Santander; died 1924, in Cagnes-sur-Mer, France.

Active in France.

Painter, engraver. Figures, genre scenes, landscapes.

Francisco Iturrino González was eight when his family settled in Bilbao, and he developed an affinity with the Basque School. After training as an engineer in Liège, he decided to earn his living exclusively by painting. In 1890, he went to Brussels to study with Henri Evenepoel at the Sint-Joost-ten-Node academy. In 1895, he settled in Paris, in the Boulevard de Clichy, where he met Evenepoel again, as well as Henri Matisse, the sculptor and ceramist Francisco Durrio, and Picasso, who was then living at 130 Boulevard de Clichy. Evenepoel painted Iturrino in *A Spaniard in Paris*, now in the museum in Ghent.

In 1911, Iturrino travelled to Morocco. A *Portrait of Iturrino*, signed by André Derain and dated 1914, is in the Musée National d'Art Moderne in Paris. The outbreak of war forced him to return to Spain, where he became well known thanks to exhibitions in Bilbao, Barcelona and Madrid. 1919 saw the painful beginnings of an attack of gangrene, resulting in the amputation of his right leg two years later. He moved to Madrid in 1920, and subsequently retired to Cagnes-sur-Mer, where he died two years later.

In Belgium, Iturrino was a member of the group Les Vingt and exhibited in 1882 at the *Libre Esthétique*. In France, he featured at the Salon des Artistes Indépendants. In 1901, he exhibited at Vollard's in company with Picasso, as he did on several other occasions, while also exhibiting at the Société Nationale des Beaux-Arts. From 1903 to 1906, he regularly sent works to the Salon d'Automne, where in 1911, 28 of his canvases were shown in a special room. He also exhibited at the modern art exhibition in Bilbao.

His French friends rallied round him in his illness. In 1922, Elie Faure organised an exhibition for his benefit at the Galerie Rosenberg in Paris, with paintings by Picasso, Derain, Matisse, Bonnard, Marquet, Dufy and others. Iturrino took part in it himself, sending a few canvases and about 50 etchings, which are sometimes considered more interesting than his paintings. In 1926, a retrospective of his works was held at the museum in Bilbao, and on the occasion of the first Hispano-American Biennale in Madrid in 1951, Juan Ramón Masoliver exhibited an important collection of his works to show one of the sources of the modern vision in Spain.

Iturrino's Belgian period was influenced by the Flemish Primitives. While in France, he was influenced by Cézanne in such works as *Nudes in a Landscape* and *Landscape* and particularly by the Fauves, including, of course, Matisse. After this he abandoned dark colours for greens and yellows, going beyond the technique of colour modulation, as in *Odalisque*. He also painted a homage to Renoir. He returned from Morocco with pictures painted in a more sober and structured style, while retaining the wonderful colours for which he was famous. It was in Salamanca and Andalusia that he found the subjects that most inspired him: beggars, gypsies, bulls, Andalusian gardens and scenes of dancing.

BIBLIOGRAPHY:

Arnáiz, José Manuel/López Jiménez, Javier/Merchán Díaz, Manuel (ed.), *Cien años de pintura en Espana y Portugal (1830-1930)*, Antiqvaria, Madrid, 1990.

MUSEUMS AND GALLERIES:

BILBAO (MBA): a collection of works - BUENOS AIRES (Mus. Nacional de Bellas Artes): *Arab Woman* - CAGNES-SUR-MER: *Washerwomen on the banks of the Cagnes* - CÓRDOBA (MBA Genaro Pérez) - IXELLES (MBA): *In the Saddle* - MADRID (Mus. Nacional Centro de Arte Reina Sofía): *Women in the Country, Collection of Works* - MENTON (MBA): *Portrait of a Woman*.

AUCTION RECORDS:

PARIS, 28 March 1919, *Malaga*, FRF 120. PARIS, 5 July 1951, *Spanish Women*, FRF 29,100. PARIS, 15 June 1970, *The Can-can*, FRF 6,500. MADRID, 13 Dec 1973, *Gypsies in a Landscape*, ESP 600,000. PARIS, 29 March 1974, *Spanish Woman with a Shawl*, FRF 17,000. VERSAILLES, 14 March 1976, *Can-can Dancers* (pastel, 15 1/4 x 11 3/4 ins / 39 x 30 cm) FRF 3,800. PARIS, 14 April 1976, *Women by the Sea* (oil on canvas, 66 1/2 x 56 3/4 ins / 169 x 144 cm) FRF 40,000. BARCELONA, 20 Oct 1982, *Fishing Scene* (oil on card, 17 3/4 x 17 3/4 ins / 45 x 45 cm) ESP 230,000. MADRID, 13 Dec 1983, *Girl in a Hat* (oil on canvas, 33 1/2 x 25 1/2 ins / 85 x 65 cm) ESP 550,000. LONDON, 20 March 1985, *Bullfight* (oil on canvas, 18 x 22 ins / 46 x 56 cm) GBP 6,000. MADRID, 27 Oct 1987, *Jerezana* (oil on canvas, 4 1/2 x 55 ins / 11.5 x 140 cm) ESP 600,000. PARIS, 7 June 1991, *Flamenco Dancers* (oil on canvas, 23 1/2 x 31 1/2 ins / 60 x 80 cm) FRF 228,000. PARIS, 19 May 1992, *Village Scene* (oil on canvas, 23 1/4 x 28 1/2 ins / 59 x 72.5 cm) FRF 95,000. PARIS, 10 June 1992, *The Bullring* (oil on canvas, 310 1/4 x 39 1/4 ins / 788 x 100 cm) FRF 168,000. MADRID, 16 June 1992, *Women* (oil on canvas, 63 3/4 x 48 3/4 ins / 162 x 124 cm) ESP 3,800,000. CALAIS, 14 March 1993, *Languid Nude* (oil on canvas, 32 3/4 x 60 1/4 ins / 83 x 153 cm) FRF 28,000. PARIS, 15 Dec 1995, *Crowd of Women* (oil on canvas, 92 x 49 1/4 ins / 233.5 x 125.3 cm) FRF 45,000. MADRID, 20 Dec 1999, *Peasants* (oil on canvas, 37 x 41 ins / 95 x 105 cm) ESP 3,750,000. MADRID, 30 Sept 2003, *Arab Street* (watercolour, 10 x 7 ins / 25 x 19 cm) EUR 1,800. MADRID, 16 Dec 2003, *Arab Street* (watercolour, 10 x 7 ins / 25 x 19 cm) EUR 3,250. MADRID, 22 June 2004, *Party in the Fields* (watercolour, 12 x 15 ins / 30 x 39 cm) EUR 8,000. MADRID, 21 Sept 2004, *Market* (oil on board, 6 x 9 ins / 16 x 22 cm) EUR 11,000.

ITZENPLITZ, Adolf

German, 19th century.

Born 1821, in Magdeburg; died 24 March 1883, in Berlin.

Sculptor.

There is a sandstone *Group of Children* by Itzenplitz in the Tiergarten in Berlin, but he also did a marble statue of *Mercury* for the Stock Exchange. He showed a *Penelope* at the Berlin academy exhibition in 1866. Numerous busts by him are known.

ITZENPLITZ, Frida von (Countess)

German, 19th - 20th century.

Born 16 September 1869; died 24 September 1921, in Danzig (now Gdansk, Poland).

Painter, watercolourist. Landscapes, urban landscapes, animals, still-lifes.

Frida von Itzenplitz studied in Berlin, Königsberg (now Kaliningrad, Russia), Munich and Paris, and travelled in Sweden, Denmark, England, Tunisia, Morocco and Italy. Her work was featured at numerous exhibitions in Gdansk; she exhibited landscapes of the town and its port, as well as watercolours of the Roman countryside, Capri, Taormino, Algiers, Tunis, still-lifes and animal pictures. Von Itzenplitz also painted a triptych for the church of Exin (in the Poznan province in Poland). Her painting *Tor zum Olivaer Schlossgarten* (*Gate to Olive Castle Garden*) was purchased by the German Emperor.

ITZFELDNER, Johann Georg, or Izfellner

Austrian, 18th century.

Born c. 1705; died 31 August 1790, in Tittmoning (Traunstein), Germany.

Active in Tittmoning.

Sculptor.

Itzfeldner is documented for a large number of altars and altar statues he made for churches either side of the German-

Austrian border, e.g. Asten (Tittmoning), St Georgen near Oberndorf (Austria), Wagrain (Austria), Arnsdorf near Laufen (Germany), Pfarrwerfen, Zederhaus, Untereching and Obereching (all Austria).

MUSEUMS AND GALLERIES:

TITTMONING (Heimathaus des Rupertiwinkels): *St Michael.*

ITZIG

German, 18th century.
Active in Berlin.
Painter. Portraits.

Itzig showed a small pastel portrait of the *Princess of Kurland*, the daughter of Count Peter of Biron, Duke of Kurland and Sagan, at the Berlin academy exhibition in 1793.

IULIANA, José. See **JULIANA Y ALBERT José**

IUNG. See **YUNG**

IUNGE. See **JUNGE**

IURASSOFF. See **YURASSOV Nikolai Ivanovich**

IUSTER, Tuvia

Romanian, 20th century.
Born 25 March 1931, in Braila.
Active in Israel from 1958.
Sculptor.
Symbolism.

A mechanic, Tuvia Iuster became interested in sculpture when posing as a model in the sculpture studio of the N. Grigorescu Institute of Fine Arts in Bucharest. He taught himself to sculpt and in 1958 entered the competition for a *Monument to the Victims of the Railwaymen's Strike* winning the fourth prize, an honour that allowed him to emigrate to Israel the same year. He lives and works in Ein Hod, the artists' village established by Marcel Iancou, who was also of Romanian origin.

He executed several works for public places: a *Low Relief* for the Maison de la Culture in Nazareth (1966); a *Funerary Stele* for the tomb of Marcel Iancou; a *Pietà* for the main square in Ein Hod; a stone sculpture entitled *Inseparable Lovers* for the Maison de la Culture in Ein Hod; a stone fountain, *Love is Life* for the Judenplatz in Vienna (1980).

The Bible and the Kabala are important sources of inspiration for his work. He sculpts in marble and stone and also makes bronzes, seeking to evoke a humanist conscience through the use of symbolic forms based principally on curves and spirals.

He has taken part in various collective exhibitions including the sculpture symposia in Vienna and in Pietrasanta, Italy. His work featured in exhibitions in the USA and other countries. After his first solo exhibition at the Katz Gallery in Tel Aviv (1961), he showed in Jerusalem and Haifa as well as again in Tel Aviv. Other solo exhibitions were held in Austria, Italy and the USA. He is a member of the Israeli Painters and Sculptors Association.

BIBLIOGRAPHY:

Jianou, Ionel/Carp, Gabriela/Covrig, Ana Maria/Scantéyé, Lionel, *Romanian Artists and the West*, American Romanian Academy of Arts and Sciences, Los Angeles, 1986.

IVACHEV, Nasar Adrianovich

Russian, 19th century.
Born 14 or 26 October 1843, in Tomsk (Siberia).
Sculptor.

Nasar Ivachev studied at the fine art academy in St Petersburg, where he was awarded a silver medal in 1868, and a gold medal in 1870 for a work entitled *Woodcutter.* In 1871, he was given the title of 'free artist' as a mark of recognition for his work, *Discus Thrower.*

IVACHEV, Pavel Adrianovich

Russian, 19th century.
Born 4 or 16 November 1844, in Tomsk (Siberia).
Painter.

Pavel Adrianovich Ivachev studied at the fine art academy in St Petersburg, where he received his diploma in 1873 after painting *David Playing the Harp before King Saul.* In 1872 he produced twelve paintings depicting *Scenes from the Life of Peter the Great.*

IVACHKIEVITCH, Clemens

Polish, 19th century.
Born 1804; died 1848, in Warsaw.
Painter.

Clemens Ivachkievitch painted a number of portraits, including one of J. Epstein.

IVACKOVIC, Djoka

Serb, 20th century.
Born 25 February 1930, in Horgoš.
Active in France from 1962.
Painter.

Djoka Ivackovic trained originally as an architect in Belgrade, qualifying in 1955. He went to Paris has lived there from 1962, exhibiting there from 1963.

His work is in an Informel and gestural Tachist style, combining graffiti and signs obtained directly from the movement of the wrist. The resulting compositions are austere and full of tension.

Collective exhibitions include: 4th Biennale des Jeunes, Musée d'Art Moderne (1965); *L'Âge du jazz* (*The Jazz Era*), Musée Galliera, Paris (1966); Salon de Mai, Paris (1970, 1972, 1973, 1975, 1977, 1978, 1985, 1986); Salon Grands et Jeunes d'Aujourd'hui, Paris (1970); *Contemporary Yugoslav Painting*, Budapest (1973); Yugoslav Cultural Centre, Paris (1975); *Art Today in France*, Piper-Heidsieck Foundation, Caracas (1978); *Exposition-hommage pour le 20e anniversaire de la révolution cubaine* (*Exhibition Marking the 20th Anniversary of the Cuban Revolution*), UNESCO, Paris (1979); *Hommage à Bela Bartok*, Galerie Nane Stern, Paris (1982); Salon de Montrouge (1978, 1980, 1981, 1983 - winning the Grand Prix - 1984); *Contemporary Yugoslavian Art*, Sarajevo and Dubrovnik (1984); Association d'Art Contemporain, Chamalières (1985). Solo exhibitions include: Galerie Nane Stern, Paris (1975, 1977, 1978, 1980 and 1982); Sebastian Gallery, Dubrovnik (1981); Cultural Centre, Belgrade (1981 and 1988); Galerie Leif Stahle, Paris (1986); Studio Kostel, Paris (1986).

BIBLIOGRAPHY:

Djoka Ivackovic, exhibition catalogue, Gal. Nane Stern, Paris, 1981.

AUCTION RECORDS:

PARIS, 20 March 1988, *Painting 25 - VI - 87/2* (oil on canvas, 39¼ x 39¼ ins / 100 x 100 cm) FRF 6,500. PARIS, 24 April 1988, *23-VI-83/1-1983* (painting/canvas, 78¾ x 78¾ ins / 200 x 200 cm) FRF 21,000. PARIS, 16 Oct 1988, *23-III-83* (1983, mixed media/canvas, 39¼ x 39¼ ins / 100 x 100 cm) FRF 13,500. PARIS, 20 Nov 1988, *Untitled* (mixed media/canvas, 31½ x 31½ ins / 80 x 80 cm) FRF 4,800. DOUAI, 2 July 1989, *Composition* (oil on canvas, 19¾ x 16½ ins / 50 x 42 cm) FRF 4,200. PARIS, 26 April 1990, *Composition* (soft pastel/paper, 24½ x 24½ ins / 62 x 62 cm) FRF 3,200. PARIS, 21 May 1990, *Painting 27-V-87* (1987, acrylic/canvas, 59 x 59 ins / 150 x 150 cm) FRF 20,000. PARIS, 18 Oct 1992, *Painting 25-3-82* (1982, acrylic/unbleached canvas, 39¼ x 39¼ ins / 100 x 100 cm) FRF 5,000. PARIS, 28 Sept 1993, *Composition* (mixed media/canvas, 78¾ x 78¾ ins / 200 x 200 cm) FRF 8,200. PARIS, 4 Oct 1997, *Painting 22.III.88* (1988, acrylic/canvas, 39¼ x 39¼ ins / 100 x 100 cm) FRF 8,500. PARIS, 15 Dec 1997, *23.IV.88* (1988, oil and graphite/unbleached canvas, 39¼ x 39¼ ins / 100 x 100 cm) FRF 6,000.

IVAL, D. J.
19th century.
Active in Paris.
Painter. Genre scenes.
D.J. Ival exhibited at the Royal Academy in London from 1855 to 1860.

IVAN
French, 20th century.
Painter.
Banlieue-Banlieue group.
Ivan is the third protagonist of the group Banlieue-Banlieue, an association of painters which also includes Alain Campoos and Kenji. Like them, he works alone. Explicit, reverential references to Picasso abound in his work. His painting is both figurative and chatty. He shows his work in solo exhibitions.

IVANCIC, Ljubo
Croat, 20th century.
Born 1925, in Split.
Painter.
Ljubo Ivancic studied at the academy of fine art in Zagreb until 1951. He began exhibiting work in 1954. He expresses himself through the material, generally in muted colours, without entirely abandoning references to a human element which survives in his work from his first, more Expressionist, period.

Ivancic took part in the first Mediterranean Biennale, Alexandria (where he received a distinction - 1955), in the International Exhibition, Bruges (1958), at the Guggenheim International Award, New York (1960) and in the 2nd Biennale des Jeunes, Paris (1961).

IVANISTKY, Valentina
Ukrainian, 20th century.
Born in Kiev.
Painter.
Her painting *Disguise* was shown at the Exposition de la Société Nationale in Paris in 1940.

IVANOFF, Boris. See **IVANOV**

IVANOFF, L.
Russian.
Painter. Genre scenes.
MUSEUMS AND GALLERIES:
MOSCOW (Rumiantsev Mus.): *In the Chapel.*

IVANOFF, Nicolai
Russian, 20th century.
Born 23 October or 3 November 1885, in Moscow.
Painter, illustrator. Landscapes.
Nicolai Ivanoff studied under Ilya Repin at the school of painting and sculpture in Moscow. He settled in Paris in 1907 and worked under the direction of Steinlein. He produced mainly illustrations for editions of works by Russian poets including Pushkin and Tolstoy and Russian folk tales. As a painter he was known for his landscapes of the Russian countryside, the outskirts of Paris and Brittany.

He exhibited in Paris at the Salon de la Société Nationale des Beaux-Arts, the Salon d'Automne and the Exposition des Artistes et Sculpteurs Russes de Paris.

IVANOFF, Sergei. See **IVANOV**

IVANOFF, Vassil
Bulgarian, 20th century.
Born 1897, in Tirnovo; died 1973.
Active in France from 1922.
Ceramicist.
Vassil Ivanoff settled in France in 1922 and started to learn the art of pottery in 1945. His ceramics are anthropomorphic. A retrospective of his work was organised by the Musée National de la Céramique at Sèvres.

IVANOV. See also **IVANOFF**

IVANOV, Afanasi
Russian, 17th century.
Active in Novgorod.
Icon painter.
Afanasi Ivanov was summoned to Moscow in 1660 to help with the painting of the Cathedral of the Archangel and with other works, including the decoration of the apartments of the imperial family. There is a mention of him in 1681.

IVANOV, Aleksandr
Russian, 20th - 21st century.
Born 1950, in Leningrad (now St Petersburg).
Painter.
Alexandr Ivanov joined the Island group in 1985 and has taken part in several of their exhibitions.
AUCTION RECORDS:
PARIS, 8 Dec 1990, *Secret Encounter* (acrylic/canvas, 27 1/2 x 27 1/2 ins / 70 x 70 cm) FRF 11,000.

IVANOV, Aleksandr Andreevich
Russian, 19th century.
Born 1806, in St Petersburg; died 1858, in St Petersburg.
Active in Italy.
Painter. History painting, religious subjects.
The Nazarenes.
Aleksandr Ivanov trained under his father Andrei and at the academy of art in St Petersburg. Aided by a grant, he went to work in Italy. His painting *The Risen Christ Appearing to Mary Magdalene* (Alexander III Museum) earned him the title of fellow of the academy. But it was not until *Ecce Homo* that he realized his own final and essentially personal shape. He was the first Russian artist to attempt to humanise the Christ figure, thereby marking an important milestone in Russian art history.

Ivanov concentrated on subjects from the Old and New Testaments. He spent most of his life in Rome, close to, if not actually one of, the Nazarenes, a group then developing a sort of German version of Pre-Raphaelitism. He sought his masterpiece in *The Appearance of Christ to the People,* on which he worked for twenty-two years, recomposing the painting as many as twenty-five times, and for which he made over 600 studies. Some of these he drew from nature. There are many of his works in Russian museums. In 2001, work by this artist was at *Un Paese incantato. Italia dipinta da Thomas Jonas a Corot,* an exhibition held in the Centro Internazionale d'Arte e di Cultura di Palazzo Te, Mantua, Italy.
BIBLIOGRAPHY:
Alpatov, Mikhail Vladimirovich, '*Aleksandr Andreevich Ivanov: zhizn i tvorchestvo*' in *2 vol.,* monograph, Russkie khudozhniki, Moscow, 1956. Allenov, Mikhail Mihailovich, *Aleksandr Andreevich Ivanov,* Izobrazitelnoe iskusstvo, Moscow, 1980. Alpatov, Mikhail Vladimirovich, *Aleksandr Andreevich Ivanov,* Khudozhnik RSFSR, Leningrad, 1983. Allenov, Mikhail Mihailovich, '*Aleksandr Ivanov*' in *ser. 'Moi muzei'*, Trilistnik, Moscow, 1997. Vinogradov, I.A., *Aleksandr Ivanov v pismakh, dokumentakh, vospominanyakh,* Izdatelskii dom "XXI vek-Soglasie", Moscow, 2001. Ottani Cavina, Anna (ed.), *Un Paese incantato. Italia dipinta da Thomas Jones a Corot,* exhibition catalogue, Electa, Milan, 2001.
MUSEUMS AND GALLERIES:
MOSCOW (State Tretyakov Gal.): *The Appearance of Christ to the People; Brothers of Joseph and Benjamin; The Risen Christ Appearing to Mary Magdalene; Pifferaro; Albanian Girl; Study of Woman; Study of Christ; Betrothed; Scene of Roman Life; Studies of Heads of Men and Women; Italian Landscapes; Annunciation; Joseph's Dream; Angel and Shepherds; Purification; Zachariah Struck Dumb; Zachariah in the Temple; Elisha Singing Psalms; Procession of the King of the Jews; Christ's Birth Foretold; Portrait of the writer NV*

Gogol; Elijah Reviving a Boy; Elijah and Elisha; Mount Savelli (oil on paper mounted/canvas).
AUCTION RECORDS:
PARIS, 21 Feb 1955, *Landscape*, FRF 19,000. NEW YORK, 27 Feb 1986, *Standing Nude from Behind* (oil on canvas, 29 1/4 x 24 1/4 ins / 74.4 x 61.5 cm) USD 6,500. PARIS, 14 May 1990, *Spring* (oil on card, 13 3/4 x 11 3/4 ins / 35 x 30 cm) FRF 5,800. LONDON, 14 Dec 1995, *Study of the Head of an Old Man* (oil on paper/canvas, 22 1/2 x 17 ins / 57 x 43 cm) GBP 54,300.

IVANOV, Andrei
Russian, 17th century.
Icon painter.
Andrei Ivanov painted decorative work in the palace of the Tsar at Kolomenskoe and murals in the Cathedral of the Dormition at Rostov. In 1686 he was summoned to the court of the Tsar, where he painted a number of works for the church of Our Saviour Nerukotvorennogo Obraza in the Kremlin. May be the same as Andreian Ivanov, who in 1670 also worked on the Cathedral of the Dormition in Rostov and who together with a number of colleagues painted eleven icons on cedar for the Tsar.

IVANOV, Andrei
Russian, 19th century.
Painter.
Andrei Ivanov trained at the academy of art in St Petersburg. In 1846 he exhibited two views of Valaam Island, *At Sunrise* and *At Sunset*.

IVANOV, Andrei Ivanovich
Russian, 18th - 19th century.
Born 1772 or 1775, in Moscow; died 1848, in St Petersburg.
Painter. History painting, religious subjects.
MUSEUMS AND GALLERIES:
MOSCOW (State Tretyakov Gal.): *Entombment of Christ; The Evangelists* - ST PETERSBURG (Gosudarstvennyj Russkij Muz.): *The Fight Between Prince Mstyslav Vladimirovich and Prince Rededeya; Episode During the Siege of Kiev in 908.*

IVANOV, Anton
Russian, 18th century.
Active in St Petersburg.
Painter.
In 1741 Anton Ivanov painted decorative paintings in the recently completed Summer Palace, in 1750 he helped with the paintings in the Anichkov Palace and in 1751 he painted the ceilings in the Peterhof church.

IVANOV, Anton Andreevich
Russian, 19th century.
Born 16 or 28 January 1815; died 3 or 15 July 1848.
Sculptor.
Anton Andreevich Ivanov trained at the academy of art in St Petersburg, which awarded him silver medals in 1832 and 1835, and a gold medal in 1835 for his low relief *St John the Baptist preaching to the People*. He is also known for: *Paris; Young Boy; Christ Healing the Blind; Healing One Possessed.*
MUSEUMS AND GALLERIES:
PARGOLOVO (church): *St Peter* - ST PETERSBURG (Academy): *Young Boy Playing*; eight low reliefs, after Hallberg's projects.

IVANOV, Anton Ivanovich
Russian, 19th century.
Born 1811; died 1868.
Painter. Landscapes.
MUSEUMS AND GALLERIES:
MOSCOW (State Tretyakov Gal.): *Gogol Crossing the Dnieper* - MOSCOW (Tsvetkov Gallery): *Small Roman Courtyards* - ST PETERSBURG (Academy): *Venice* - ST PETERSBURG (Gosudarstvennyj Russkij Muz.): *Studio of the Brothers Chernetsov.*

IVANOV, Arkip Matveevich
Russian, 18th - 19th century.
Born c. 1749, in St Petersburg; died 28 September (10 October) 1821, in St Petersburg.
Sculptor.
Arkip Matveevich Ivanov trained at the academy of art in St Petersburg, which awarded him a gold medal in 1769 for his low relief *Baptism of St Olga*. He then went to Paris on a study grant and entered the studio of A. Pajou, doing a copy of his statue of *Pluto*. Afterwards, he went to Rome, where he started his group *Victory of Russia* and *Time and History*, an allegorical low relief. He also copied the Roman bust *Young Faustina*. Returning to St Petersburg, he was recognised by the academy for his statue of *Pluto* and made a full member for *St Petersburg Triumphant*.
MUSEUMS AND GALLERIES:
ST PETERSBURG (Academy): *Baptism of St Olga*.

IVANOV, Artemi
Russian, 17th century.
Icon painter.
In 1666, Atemi Ivanov was one of the painters who worked in the Cathedral of Christ the Saviour and the Armoury in Moscow. In 1668, together with other artists, he painted a *Crucifixion* and *Prophets* and *Angels* for the Tsar's church; in 1679, he helped once more with the paintings in one of the Kremlin churches of the Saviour and in 1680 with those in the Cathedral of the Dormition.

IVANOV, Avtonom
Russian, 17th century.
Icon painter.
Avtonom Ivanov worked at the court of the Tsar in Moscow and helped paint murals and icons in various Moscow churches and palaces.

IVANOV, Boris
Russian, 17th century.
Born to a family originally from Yaroslavl.
Icon painter.
Boris Ivanoc worked at the court of the Tsar in Moscow. In 1652 he helped with the murals in the Cathedral of the Archangel and in 1667 with the decorative paintings in the Granovitaya Palace. Together with other icon painters from Kostroma, he also painted a book of images for Tsarevich Petr Alekseevich.

IVANOV, Boris
Bulgarian, 20th century.
Born 1904, in Sofia.
Painter.
Boris Ivanov's work is Port-Impressionist in style with a predilection for light colours, particularly pinks and leaf greens.
MUSEUMS AND GALLERIES:
SOFIA (Nacionalna chudozestvena galerija): *St Nicholas Square in Sofia* (1935); *Parade on 9 September* (1958).

IVANOV, Dmitri
Russian, 17th century.
Born to a family originally from Yaroslavl.
Icon painter.
In 1676 Dmitri Ivanov worked on the murals in the Tsar's chapel in the Kremlin and, in 1680, helped with the paintings in the Cathedral of the Dormition.

IVANOV, Dmitri
Russian, 19th century.
Active c. 1820.
Engraver.
Dmitri Ivanov is known for three portrait engravings: *I.I. Khemnitser*, the fable writer, in his *Fables and Stories; Count P.C. Wittgenstein* and *Prince I.P. Paskevich, Count of Erivan..*

IVANOV, Dmitri Ivanovich
Russian, 19th century.
Born 1782; died 1820.
Painter. Genre scenes.
MUSEUMS AND GALLERIES:
ST PETERSBURG (Gosudarstvennyj Russkij Muz.): *Magistrates of Russian Hanseatic Cities; Marfa Posadnitsa.*

IVANOV, Dolmat
Russian, 17th century.
Born to a family originally from Yaroslavl.
Icon painter.
In 1652, 1660 and 1666, Dolmat Ivanov was involved in painting the Cathedral of the Archangel in Moscow and in executing decorative work in various Moscow churches and palaces.

IVANOV, Efim
Russian, 17th century.
Active in Moscow.
Icon painter.
Efim Ivanov worked at the Tsar's court. In 1678 he painted saints for the church of St Evdokia in the Kremlin, in 1679 murals in one of the churches of Christ the Saviour in the Kremlin and, in 1680, he worked in the Cathedral of the Dormition.

IVANOV, Elisei
Russian, 17th century.
Active in Moscow.
Icon painter.
In 1671, Elisei Ivanov entered the Kremlin as a child to study icon painting. Subsequently he frequently worked on frescoes, icons and decorations in the Tsar's palaces and churches.

IVANOV, Fedor
Russian, 18th century.
Active in St Petersburg.
Draughtsman, engraver.
Fedor Ivanov worked for the St Petersburg academy of sciences. He produced 22 plates and several vignettes for S. Mordvinov's *On Navigation*, published by the Naval Academy, and 135 engravings for the Russian translation of Ilya Golenishchev-Kutuzov's *Art of Naval Fleets or Treatise on Naval Tactics* (St Petersburg, 1764).

IVANOV, Grigori
Russian, 17th century.
Active in Moscow.
Sculptor, sculptor (including wood).
Grigori Ivanov sculpted two lions and two eagles for the entrance to the Kremlin Palace in Moscow for the Regent Sofia.

IVANOV, Grigori
Russian, 17th century.
Active in Novgorod.
Icon painter.
Grigori Ivanov was summoned to Moscow in 1660 to assist in the painting of the Cathedral of the Archangel. Thereafter he painted many works in Moscow churches and the apartments of the Tsar, as well as in the village of Kolomenskoe.

IVANOV, Grigori Faddeevich
Russian, 18th century.
Born 1754; died 1778.
Active in Paris.
Engraver (burin).
Grigori Faddeevich Ivanov engraved religious subjects and genre pieces after Colloni, Boucher and Dietrich.

IVANOV, Ilya Nikitich
Russian, 19th century.
Born 1782.
Painter.
From 1803 to 1819 Ilya Nikitich Ivanov worked as an assistant to Fedor Shecherbakov in the decoration of various palaces in St Petersburg.

IVANOV, Ivan
Russian, 17th century.
Active in Moscow.
Icon painter.
Ivan Ivanov is frequently mentioned from 1657 to 1686 as a painter of frescoes, icons and decorations in the Tsar's palaces and churches. He also wrote a *Life of the Tsarevich Ioassaf* (1657) which he illuminated.

IVANOV, Ivan Alekseevich
Russian, 19th century.
Born 3 or 14 February 1779, in Moscow; died 25 June or 7 July 1848, in St Petersburg.
Painter, engraver.
Ivan Alekseevich Ivanov trained at the academy of art in St Petersburg, where in 1820 he exhibited *View of the New Academy Building*. He was appointed professor of drawing there and went on to be recognised and finally made a fellow. In 1827, the Tsar commissioned him to execute *Four Views of Tsarskoe-Selo*, which he later purchased. He was primarily an engraver, being known for 33 etchings, including *Scene after the Battle of Leipzig; Alexander I at Montmartre; Arrival of Alexander I at Kazan Cathedral; Return of the Civic Guard from St Petersburg; The French Retreat from Moscow, 4 October 1812; Funeral Cortège of Marshal Kutuzov.* He is also known for *Five Views of St Petersburg* and many, many caricatures of Napoleon and the French.
MUSEUMS AND GALLERIES:
ST PETERSBURG (Gosudarstvennyj Russkij Muz.): *Consecration of Kazan Cathedral.*
AUCTION RECORDS:
AMSTERDAM, 22 May 1973, *Riverscape*, NLG 3,600.

IVANOV, Ivan Ivanovich
Russian, 19th century.
Born 20 or 31 October 1791.
Engraver.
Ivan Ivanovich Ivanov trained at the academy of art in St Petersburg, which awarded him its lesser silver medal in 1809 and the greater in 1810. He may be the same as the artist who signed his engravings *I.Ivanov*, which are attributed to Ivan Alekseevich Ivanov.

IVANOV, Kiril
Russian, 17th century.
Active in Moscow.
Icon painter.
Kiril Ivanov worked at the court of the Tsar and assisted with the painting of frescoes and icons in various churches and palaces.

IVANOV, Kondrati
Russian, 17th century.
Died before 23 October 1628.
Engraver (wood), printer.
Kondrati Ivanov is mentioned in 1614 as a Master of the State Press in Moscow. Among his known woodcuts are four engravings of the *Evangelists* after drawings by P. Chirin and vignettes and ornamental letters in a 1627 Moscow edition of the *Gospels*.

IVANOV, Konstantin Matveevich
Russian, 19th century.
Born 19 September 1859, in St Petersburg.
Painter. Stage sets.
Konstantin Matveevich Ivanov trained at the academy of art in St Petersburg. He is known, among other things, for his sets for the ballet *Sleeping Beauty* and the operas *Queen of Spades* and *Boris Godunov*.

IVANOV, Leonti
Russian, 17th century.
Painter.
Leonti Ivanov worked in various Moscow churches and palaces.

IVANOV, Llya
Russian, 20th - 21st century.
Born 1952.
Painter.

IVANOV, Lyubim
Russian, 17th century.
Active in Moscow.
Icon painter.
Lyubim Ivanov is requently mentioned as a painter of frescoes, icons and decorations in Kremlin palaces and churches. He also illuminated a *Life of St Vasili*.

IVANOV, Matvei
Russian, 17th century.
Active in Moscow.
Icon painter.
Matvei Ivanov worked at the court of the Tsar. He was involved in the painting of the fresco *Vision of Emperor Constantine* in the apartments of the Polish Ambassadors.

IVANOV, Mikhail
Russian, 17th century.
Active in Moscow.
Icon painter.
Mikhail Ivanov worked at the court of the Tsar. He assisted in the painting of frescoes, icons and decorations in various churches, monasteries and palaces. In 1689 he painted a *St Peter* and a *St Natalya and the Evdokia Martyrs* on cedar wood for Tsarina Evdokia Fedorovna.

IVANOV, Mikhail
Russian, 20th century.
Born 1927, in Pushkino.
Painter.
Mikhail Ivanov lives and works in Moscow.

IVANOV, Mikhail Afanasevich
Russian, 19th century.
Born 1781; died 1839.
Active in St Petersburg.
Engraver (burin).

IVANOV, Mikhail Filippovich
Russian, 19th - 20th century.
Born 1869, in Sielo Podoutschi (Novgorod); died c. 1930.
Painter.
A student at the St Petersburg academy, Mikhail Filippovich Ivanov was awarded the academy's silver medal and made a 'free artist' for his picture entitled *A Question*.

IVANOV, Mikhail Ivanovich
Russian, 18th - 19th century.
Born 1772 or 1774; died 1847 or 1848.
Sculptor.
Mikhail Ivanovich Ivanov is known for busts that were exhibited at the Academy: *Schiller, Tsarina Maria Fedorovna, Count Stroganov* and *Bortnyansky*.

IVANOV, Mikhail Matveevich
Russian, 18th - 19th century.
Born 1748; died 1823, in St Petersburg.
Painter. Landscapes.
Mikhail Matveevich Ivanov trained at the academy of art in St Petersburg and under J.F. Grooth. Also trained in Paris under Jean-Baptiste Le Prince. He served during the Third Russo-Turkish War.
MUSEUMS AND GALLERIES:
MOSCOW (State Tretyakov Gal.): *Landscape; Views of Razumovsky Palace* - ST PETERSBURG (Academy): *Peasants Milking Cows* - ST PETERSBURG (Gosudarstvennyj Russkij Muz.): *Capture of Ochakov; On the Prut.*
AUCTION RECORDS:
NEW YORK, 1 March 1984, *View of St Petersburg* (1799, watercolour and pencil, 15 x 30 ins / 38.2 x 76.2 cm) USD 1,600.

IVANOV, Nikolai
Russian, 19th century.
Active c. 1800.
Engraver. Portraits, landscapes.
Nikolai Ivanov trained under Aleksei Osipov at the Beketov school of engraving in Moscow. He is known for *Landscape with Buildings* and a large number of portraits, including one of *Alexander I* after a drawing by Saint-Aubin.

IVANOV, Nikolai
Russian, 19th century.
Painter. Figures, portraits.
Nikolai Ivanov trained at the Moscow school of sculpture and painting. In 1839 he exhibited two studies, *Old Woman and Girl* and *Old Man Leaning on his Stick,* at the academy of fine arts. In 1849 his *Two Peasant Women of Ryazan in Local Costume* (now in the Academy Museum) was included in the academy's exhibition.
MUSEUMS AND GALLERIES:
MOSCOW (Academy Museum): *Two Peasant Women of Ryazan in Local Costume.*

IVANOV, Nikolai
Russian, 19th century.
Painter. Portraits.
As an external student at the academy of art in St Petersburg, Nikolai Ivanov was awarded the title 'free artist' in 1853 for his *Portrait of a Man.* In 1857 he exhibited a *Portrait of Count D.N. Tolstoy* at the academy.

IVANOV, Pavel Alexeevich
Russian, 19th century.
Born 1776; died 10 (22) March 1813, in St Petersburg.
Miniaturist.
Pavel Alexeevich Ivanov was recognised by the academy of art in St Petersburg in 1800 and accepted as a member in 1802 for his miniature group portraits. In 1804 he was appointed professor of miniature painting at the academy.

IVANOV, Petr
Russian, 19th century.
Active in St Petersburg.
Lithographer.
Petr Ivanov trained at the academy of art in St Petersburg. He is known for his lithographs, including the *Kutuzov Monument* and *Barclay de Tolly Monument* (both after drawings by P. Sadovnikov); *Ten views of churches* in Guillon's *L'artiste russe* (1847) as well as for *Bust and Angel* in St Isaac's Cathedral (by Vitali). The drawings for the steel engravings of Lacroix's *Mysteries of Paris,* the *Portrait of Tsarina Alexandra Fedorovna,* and the *Fustigation of Lopushina* are attributed to him.

IVANOV, Pravdolub, called Pravdo
Bulgarian, 20th - 21st century.
Born 18 February 1964, in Plovdiv.
Installation artist.
Pravdolub Ivanov studied painting at the national academy of fine arts in Sofia between 1989 and 1993 in the class of Andrei Daniel. He works exclusively in the field of installation art. His works are distinguished by their spirit of the here and now and their strongly pronounced political accent. Their interpretation pushes certain fashionable social and artistic values to the outer limits. He either uses unconventional materials such as the soil, grass, or else fabricates

strange objects. He has taken part in many collective exhibitions, including: 1990, Plovdiv, *Group Râb*, fine arts gallery; 1993, Sofia, *An Idea about Bulgarian Painting*, Ata-Ray Gallery; Sofia, *Object in the Bulgarian Style*, gallery of the union of Bulgarian painters; 1994, Sofia, *N-shapes? Reconstructions and Interpretations*, Soros arts centre, Rayko Aleksiev Gallery; Plovdiv, *In Search of my Reflected Image*, old Plovdiv exhibition rooms; Sofia, *Me, the Gods*, Galerie Art 36; Sofia, *Nail*, gallery of the union of Bulgarian painters. Solo exhibitions have included: 1993, Sofia, Studio Spectar Gallery; 1994, Zurich, *Two Paths*, Fondation Binz 39; Sofia, *Collages*, Galerie Art 36.

BIBLIOGRAPHY:

Fondation Binz 39, catalogue, Zurich, 1994. Danaïlov, Boris, '*Ivanov*' in *Plovdiv'95*, exhibition catalogue, Département de la culture de la mairie de Plovdiv, Plovdiv, 1995.

IVANOV, Semen

Russian, 17th century.
Born 17th century, in Yaroslavl.
Icon painter.

Semen Ivanov worked at the court of the Tsar in Moscow. He was sent to Rostov where in 1673 he painted a number of icons for Tsarina Natalya Kirilovna and Ilya Danilovich Miloslavsky, a rich boyar.

IVANOV, Sergei

Russian, 19th century.
Painter. Portraits, landscapes.

As an external student at the academy of art in St Petersburg, Sergei Ivanov was awarded the title 'free artist' in 1853 and was appointed member of the academy in 1854. He became subsequently professor at the Moscow school of painting, sculpture and architecture.

IVANOV, Sergei

Russian, 20th century.
Born 1893, in Moscow; died 8 February 1983.
Active in France then in the USA, from 1951 naturalised in the USA.
Painter, illustrator. Figure compositions, mythological subjects, figures, nudes, portraits, townscapes.

Sergei Ivanov's parents enrolled him at the school of fine art in Moscow when he was only 10. The Russian Revolution of 1917 obliged him and his family to move to St Petersburg where he continued his studies with Braz, conservator at the Hermitage Museum in St Petersburg. In 1922, he left Russia, travelling to France by way of Finland. He spent the next ten years travelling in Europe. From 1930, he contributed to the magazine *L'Illustration*, providing illustrated articles for many years. He executed a number of etchings to illustrate Barbey d'Aurevilly's *Les Diaboliques* He painted many portraits including one of *Mrs Eleanor Franklin Delano Roosevelt*. While working on this painting, in 1950, he decided to settle in the USA. In the late 1960s, he returned to France.

He owes his celebrity mainly to the many commissions he executed of famous people. These included portraits of church leaders including *Pope Pius XI* (1937) and the Belgian primate *Cardinal Van Roey* (1944). From the world of entertainment, he painted *Serge Peretti*, *Yvette Chauviré*, *Solange Schwartz*, *Suzanne Lorcia* and *Edwige Feuillère*, famous dancers of the Opéra, personalities from politics, ambassadors, ambassadors' wives and many celebrated Americans. Pressure of work meant that Ivanov had little time to develop a truly personal style. The quality of his portraits lies in their attention to detail and finish. By contrast, his figure compositions, nudes and erotic scenes, works in which he shows a confident ability to move from one style to another, have a greater freedom of tone and touch.

Ivanov's work was often shown at the various Paris salons and much commented on. He exhibited mainly at the Salon des Artistes Français of which he became a member in 1942.

MUSEUMS AND GALLERIES:

PARIS (Mus. Carnavalet).

AUCTION RECORDS:

PARIS, 10 March 1976, *Marianne, the Artist's Daughter* (1929, oil on canvas, 61 x 39 1/4 ins / 154 x 100 cm) FRF 4,500. PARIS, 20 April 1986, *Primavera* (oil on canvas, 25 1/2 x 21 1/4 ins / 65 x 54 cm) FRF 20,000. PARIS, 6 Nov 1989, *Bathers* (oil on canvas, 28 3/4 x 23 1/2 ins / 73 x 60 cm) FRF 7,000. NEUILLY, 27 March 1990, *Sorceresses* (oil on card, 23 1/2 x 19 3/4 ins / 60 x 50 cm) FRF 25,000. RHEIMS, 21 April 1991, *Head and Shoulders of a Nude Woman with a Red Drapery over her Shoulder* (1948, oil on canvas, 28 1/4 x 23 1/4 ins / 72 x 59 cm) FRF 9,500. PARIS, 18 Nov 1993, *Narcissus* (oil on canvas, 67 x 63 ins / 170 x 160 cm) FRF 55,500. PARIS, 4 May 1994, *Portrait of the Painter's Daughter, Student at the Conservatoire* (1929, oil on canvas, 59 3/4 x 39 ins / 152 x 99 cm) FRF 33,000. PARIS, 1 July 1994, *Shell* (1973, oil on canvas, 51 1/4 x 74 3/4 ins / 130 x 190 cm) FRF 18,000. PARIS, 1 Feb 1996, *Nude Combing Her Hair* (oil on paper, 17 x 13 3/4 ins / 43 x 35 cm) FRF 4,000.

IVANOV, Sergei Ivanovich

Russian, 19th century.
Born 1828 or 1830; died 1903.
Sculptor.

MUSEUMS AND GALLERIES:

MOSCOW (State Tretyakov Gal.): *Boy Bathing*.

IVANOV, Sergei Vasilievich

Russian, 19th - 20th century.
Born 1854 or 1864, in Ruza in the Moscow region; died 1910, in Svistukha in the Moscow region.
Painter. Genre scenes.

A pupil of Illarion Pryanishnikov and Evgraf Sorokin at the Moscow school of painting, sculpture and architecture from 1880 to 1882 and again from 1884 to 1885, S. V. Ivanov then trained at the academy. From 1900 until his death he taught at the Moscow school of painting, sculpture and architecture. He was made an academician in 1905 and was also a member of the Association of Travelling Exhibitions and of the Union of Russian Artists. He travelled widely in Russia, Italy and France.

MUSEUMS AND GALLERIES:

MOSCOW (Rumiantsev Mus.): *Emigrants* - MOSCOW (State Tretyakov Gal.): *Emigrants; Strangers Arriving in Moscow in the 17th Century* - MOSCOW (Tvietkov Gallery): *Peasant Festival* - SARATOV (Raditschev Gal.): *Scenes from Prison Life* - ST PETERSBURG (Gosudarstvennyj Russkij Muz.): *Family*.

IVANOV, Sinovi Ivanovich

Russian, 19th century.
Born 1816.
Sculptor.

Sinovi Ivanovich Ivanov is known for the following signed, dated portraits: *Professor G. Solntsev* (1838), the *Abbess Kalista* (1845, in the convent of Svyazhsk) and *Portrait of Young Boy* (1853).

IVANOV, Stepan Faddeevich

Russian, 18th - 19th century.
Born 1749; died 29 May or 10 June, in St Petersburg.
Engraver.

Stepan Faddeevich Ivanov trained at the academy of art in St Petersburg. In 1770 he went to Paris, where he trained under Louis Simon Lempereur, engraving the plates *Woman at Window* (after van Ostade) and *Portrait of a Man* (after Snyders). He also spent some time in Rome, where he engraved a *Portrait of Marshal Golytsin*. He was appointed fellow of the academy of art in St Petersburg for his *St Francis* (after G. Dou). Other works for which he is known include *En-*

graved Portrait of Count Aleksei Musin-Pushkin and *Plato,* Metropolitan of Moscow, as well as four plans, three façades and a sketch of the academy of art in St Petersburg.

IVANOV, Vasili
Russian, 17th century.
Active in Moscow.
Icon painter.
Vasili Ivanov worked at the court of the Tsar. He assisted with the frescoes in the Voznesensky-Dyevichi Monastery.

IVANOV, Vasili Ivanovich
Russian, 18th century.
Born 1773; died after 1809.
Engraver.
Vasili Ivanovich Ivanov trained at the academy of art in St Petersburg. He is known for: *Rebecca at the Well* (after Carlo Lotti); three views of *Tsarskoe-Selo* (after a drawing by Countess Eszterhazy); *Hippodrome at Constantinople* (in Reimer's *Voyage to the Ottoman Porte,* 1803); 30 copies in the Russian edition of Buffon's *Natural History* (Lepyoshin, 1806); and *engraved portraits of F. Kostsov and the sailor G.I. Shelishev.*

IVANOV, Yuri
Russian, 17th century.
Born to a family originally from Yaroslavl.
Icon painter.
Yuri Ivanov was summoned to the Tsar's court in Moscow in 1659 and worked on churches and palaces there.

IVANOV VASILEVICH, Igor
Russian, 20th century.
Born 1934, in St Petersburg.
Painter.
Igor Ivanov Vasilevich lives and works in St Petersburg.
AUCTION RECORDS:
PARIS, 7 Nov 1988, *Love* (1975, 28 1/4 x 24 1/2 ins / 72 x 62 cm) FRF 12,000. PARIS, 18 May 1990, *Two Dolls* (1982, oil on canvas, 25 1/4 x 23 1/2 ins / 64 x 60 cm) FRF 3,600.

IVANOVA, Galina Alekseevna
Russian, 20th - 21st century.
Born 1949, probably in Leningrad (now St Petersburg).
Painter.

IVANOVA, Ksenia Vasilievna
Russian, 19th century.
Painter.
Ksenia Vasilievna Ivanova trained at the Moscow school of fine arts. She took part in the academy's 1887 exhibition with portraits of the historian *E.A. Belov,* the painter *G.G. Myasoyedov* and the journalist *O.K. Notovich,* for which she was appointed honorary member of the academy. In 1888 she submitted a portrait of the writer *P.I. Weinberg* to the academy's exhibition and a watercolour, *Path in the Forest,* to the Society for the Encouragement of the Arts.

IVANOVA, Maria Ivanovna
Russian, 18th - 19th century.
Born 1760; died 1827.
Engraver.
English by birth, Maria Ivanovna Ivanova had married the Russian engraver G.I. Skorodumov, who died in 1792. She then remarried, her second husband being the landscapist M Ivanov. She is known for: *Diana's Bath* (after Carraccio); *Virgin and Child with St John the Baptist* (after F. Trevisani); *Landscape* (after a drawing by M. Ivanov).

IVANOVA-EBERLING, Elena
Russian, 20th century.
Born 1905; died 1971.
Painter. Interiors with figures, Still-lifes.
Elena Ivanova-Eberling studied at the Ilya Repin Institute at the academy in St Petersburg.
AUCTION RECORDS:
PARIS, 23 March 1992, *Still-life in the Crimea* (oil on canvas, 52 3/4 x 41 3/4 ins / 134 x 106 cm) FRF 5,000.

IVANOVA-RAEVSKAYA, Maria Dmitrevna
Russian, 19th century.
Born in Gavrilovka.
Painter.
Maria Dmitrevna Ivanova-Raevskaya trained at the academy of art in St Petersburg and under Adolf Ehrhardt in Dresden. In 1867 she exhibited *Portrait of a Woman* and *Young Peasant Woman from Saxony* at the academy of art in St Petersburg and, in 1868, *Death of a Peasant in Little Russia.* In 1869 she opened a drawing school at Kharkov, for which she was appointed honorary member of the St Petersburg academy.

IVANOVICH, Fedor
Russian, 18th - 19th century.
Born 1765; died 27 January 1832.
Painter, engraver. History painting.
Fedor Ivanovich was of Kalmyk origin and was a protégé of Catherine the Great. The Empress Catherine introduced him to Princess Amelia of Baden, who employed him as a painter and paid for his artistic training. He studied under Melling and Becker in Karlsruhe, and continued his studies in Rome, Greece and England. On his return to Karlsruhe, he became a painter at the court. Several of his works are in the Protestant church in Karlsruhe. Lord Elgin commissioned him to draw the friezes of the Parthenon. He produced several accomplished etchings, in particular the *The Doors of the church of S Giovanni in Florence,* from a work by Ghiberti (12 plates in total).

IVANOVICS, Katalin, or Ivanovits or Joannovics
Hungarian, 19th century.
Born 1817, in Székesfehérvár.
Active in Belgrade and in Agram (now Zagreb, Croatia).
Painter.
Katalin Ivanovics studied with J. Pesky in Pest and at the academies in Vienna and Munich. In exhibitions in Munich, Pest, Belgrade and Paris, she showed historical paintings such as *Storming of Belgrade by the Serbs,* genre scenes such as *Serbian Homer,* portraits and still-lifes such as *Grapes.*
MUSEUMS AND GALLERIES:
BUDAPEST (Magyar Nemzeti Múz.): *Portrait of Ferdinand V.*

IVANOVITCH, Paul. See **JOANOVITCH**

IVANOVSKY, Elisabeth
Moldovan, 20th century.
Born 1910, in Kishinev (now Chisinau).
Active in Belgium.
Painter, engraver, illustrator. Portraits. Stage sets.
Married to the poet René Meurant, Elisabeth Ivanovsky was a student at the Kishinev academy and the Académie des Beaux-Arts La Cambre in Brussels.

IVANOWSKY, Sigismund
Polish, 20th century.
Born 17 April 1874, in Poland; died 1944.
Active then naturalised in the USA.
Painter, illustrator. Portraits.
Sigismund Ivanowsky studied at the academy of fine art in St Petersburg and then in Paris with Benjamin-Constant, Jean-Paul Laurens and Cormon. He painted many portraits and also worked for magazines.
MUSEUMS AND GALLERIES:
PHILADELPHIA (Curtis Institute of Music): *Portrait of Paderewski.*
AUCTION RECORDS:
NEW YORK, 17 March 1988, *Portrait of Helen Ivanowsky, the Artist's wife* (oil on canvas, 71 1/4 x 32 ins / 181 x 81 cm) USD

11,000. NEW YORK, 30 Sept 1988, *Lady in Blue* (oil on reinforced canvas, 12 x 16 ins / 30.5 x 40.7 cm) USD 2,860. NEW YORK, 28 Sept 1989, *Window Shopping* (oil on canvas, 20 x 32 ins / 50.8 x 81.2 cm) USD 6,050.

IVANYI, Laszlo
Hungarian, 20th century.
Born 24 May 1934, in Budapest.
Painter.

Laszlo Ivanyi studied music in Budapest between 1953 and 1956 before moving to Paris where he settled and took French nationality. He studied at the École des Beaux-Arts in Paris until 1959.

His paintings express a tension between pictorial space and the figures that inhabit it. The figures, exploded, shattered or defined by small graphic signs, hatchings and flecks, seem to have sprung out of a cartoon.

IVANYI-GRÜNWALD. See **GRÜNWALD Adalbert**

IVARA. See **JUVARRA**

IVARSON, Ivan
Swedish, 20th century.
Born 1900, in Göteborg; died 1939.
Painter.

Ivan Ivarson studied under Tor Bjurström at the art academy of Valand, in Göteborg. From 1926-1927 and from 1937-1939, he travelled in Italy and France. In 1933 and 1936, he held solo exhibitions in Göteborg. His posthumous exhibitions include Göteborg (1940) and Stockholm (1946). His early works, which include many landscapes, reveal his interest in the work of the French Nabi painter Pierre Bonnard, before Ivarson turned to Expressionism.

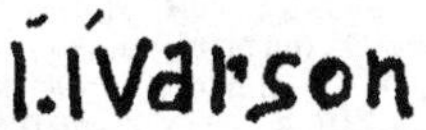

AUCTION RECORDS:
GÖTEBORG, 24 March 1976, *Figures* (oil on panel, $8\frac{1}{4}$ x 6 ins / 21 x 15 cm) SEK 3,600. GÖTEBORG, 31 March 1977, *View of Gudhjem* (oil on canvas, $19\frac{1}{4}$ x $23\frac{1}{2}$ ins / 49 x 60 cm) SEK 22,500. STOCKHOLM, 23 April 1980, *Young Girl in a Landscape* (1938, oil on canvas, $24\frac{1}{4}$ x $26\frac{1}{4}$ ins / 61.5 x 66.5 cm) SEK 50,000. STOCKHOLM, 25 Nov 1982, *Still-life with Flowers* (oil on canvas, $23\frac{1}{4}$ x $18\frac{1}{2}$ ins / 59 x 47 cm) SEK 42,500. STOCKHOLM, 29 Nov 1983, *View of Göteborg* (oil on panel, 31 x 39 ins / 79 x 99 cm) SEK 130,000. STOCKHOLM, 9 Dec 1986, *Landscape with Cypresses* (watercolour, $14\frac{1}{4}$ x $17\frac{3}{4}$ ins / 36 x 45 cm) SEK 49,000. STOCKHOLM, 26 May 1987, *Landscape with Church, St-Palais* (oil on canvas, $23\frac{1}{2}$ x $28\frac{1}{4}$ ins / 60 x 72 cm) SEK 115,000. STOCKHOLM, 5-6 Dec 1990, *Southern Landscape with Buildings* (oil on canvas, 9 x $12\frac{1}{4}$ ins / 22 x 31 cm) SEK 16,500. STOCKHOLM, 30 Nov 1993, *Woman on a Bridge at Dyrehaven, in Copenhagen* (1933, oil on canvas, $25\frac{1}{2}$ x $29\frac{1}{2}$ ins / 65 x 75 cm) SEK 115,000. STOCKHOLM, 17 May 1999, *On the Verandah* (oil on canvas, 31 x 37 ins / 79 x 93 cm) SEK 1,230,000. STOCKHOLM, 25 Nov 1999, *Woman Wearing Hat by Red Flowers* (c. 1935-1936, oil on canvas, 26 x 33 ins / 67 x 85 cm) SEK 640,000. STOCKHOLM, 2 May 2000, *Roses in Landscape* (oil on canvas, 40 x 34 ins / 102 x 86 cm) SEK 740,000. STOCKHOLM, 15 May 2000, *Woman on Balcony - Twilight* (oil on canvas, 22 x 26 ins / 56 x 67 cm) SEK 420,000. STOCKHOLM, 21 May 2001, *Villas and Summer Gardens at Hagen, Göteborg* (oil on canvas, 18 x 22 ins / 46 x 56 cm) SEK 760,000. STOCKHOLM, 27 Nov 2001, *Under the Sunroof* (oil on canvas, 23 x 28 ins / 59 x 72 cm) SEK 1,025,000. STOCKHOLM, 24 April 2002, *The Beach, St Georges* (oil on canvas, 17 x 29 ins / 44 x 73 cm) SEK 350,000. STOCKHOLM, 5 Nov 2002, *The Large Customs House, Göteborg* (oil on canvas, 26 x 26 ins / 66 x 67 cm) SEK 245,000. STOCKHOLM, 4 Nov 2003, *Girls Bathing* (oil on canvas, 20 x 18 ins / 52 x 45 cm) SEK 370,000. STOCKHOLM, 4 Nov 2003, *Mother and Child by the Sea, Stenungson* (oil on canvas, 43 x 38 ins / 110 x 96 cm) SEK 1,000,000. STOCKHOLM, 2 Nov 2004, *Still-life of Flowers* (1931, oil on canvas, 39 x 30 ins / 98 x 76 cm) SEK 240,000. STOCKHOLM, 2 Nov 2004, *Still-life of Flowers* (oil on canvas, 35 x 28 ins / 90 x 72 cm) SEK 280,000.

IVEKOVIC, Otto
Croat, 20th century.
Born 1870, in Klanjec.
Painter. Portraits.

Otto Ivekovic's work was exhibited in Paris at the 1900 Exposition Universelle.

IVEL, Karl
French, 19th century.
Born in Nancy; died 1899.
Sculptor.

Ivel was a pupil of Burdy. He exhibited busts at the Paris Salon in 1879 and 1880. He became a Chevalier of the Légion d'Honneur.

IVEN, Alexander
German, 19th century.
Born 1854, in Wegberg, near Aachen.
Active in Cologne.
Sculptor.

Iven was a pupil of Vanderlinden, de Vigne and Louis de Taye in Louvain, and gained a first-class medal at the academy in Louvain. Numerous works in churches in Berlin, Düsseldorf, Duisburg and Cologne are by him, notably a tomb of Chancellor and Archbishop Reinald von Dassel in Cologne Cathedral.

IVENITSKY, Mikhail
Russian, 20th century.
Born 1931, in St Petersburg.
Active in the USA from 1979.
Painter.

IVENS, Renaat
Belgian, 20th century.
Painter, engraver.

Renaat Ivens showed his works in group exhibitions, notably at the Foire d'Art Actuel held at the Palais des Beaux-Arts in Brussels in 1980; at the Biennale Internationale des Miniatures in Schelderode in 1983; at the Festival de Gravure in Menton in 1988; and in the selection of engravings at the Frans Masereel Centre, Georgia Museum of Art, in 1989. Ivens held solo exhibitions in Paris in 1980, in Brussels in 1984 and in Amsterdam in 1991. His works have developed a sober kind of abstraction, gently subdued by figurative elements.

MUSEUMS AND GALLERIES:
ANTWERP (Koninklijk Mus. voor Schone Kunsten) - BRUGES (Groeningemus.).

IVERNOIS, d' (Comtesse)
French, 19th century.
Died 1909.
Painter.

This artist was a member of the Société des Artistes Français, and her work is represented in the exhibition room of the same organisation.

IVERNOIS, Jean François Jules d', or Yvernois
Swiss, 19th century.
Born 29 April 1823, in Geneva; died 1884.
Painter. Seascapes.

Ivernois was a Genevan artillery officer. During his years in Paris (1848-1869), he devoted his time mainly to philanthropic institutions, and in due course he was awarded the Légion d'Honneur for his work. On his return to Switzerland, he settled in Céligny on Lake Geneva, and went over to painting full time. He exhibited in Paris and Geneva.

Museums and Galleries:

Geneva (Mus. Ariana): *Coast of Africa* - Paco da Aiuda: *Naval Battle.*

IVERNY, Jacques, or Yverni

French, 15th century.

Possibly born in the Île-de-France region; died 1435 - 1438, in the Île-de-France.

Painter.

Provencal School.

According to various archive records, Iverny worked in Avignon from 1411 to 1435 and produced the frescoes of the Palazzo de la Manta in Piedmont, which almost certainly date between 1413 and 1426. Two other, more significant, works have also been attributed to him: a triptych, now in Turin, of *The Virgin and the Holy Child, St Stephen* and *St Lucia*, and in Dublin, an *Annunciation with Donors*. These two paintings can be categorised as International Gothic, characterised by the elongation of shapes, figures, faces and hands, as well as by the 'separated' style of drawing. The latter can be seen in the folds of clothing or curtains, or in the figures, which are generally stiff, almost brittle-looking, with angular, ascetic features, conveying an impression of seriousness.

The International Gothic style was more closely associated with the Parisian School of miniaturists - which had a considerable influence on the beginnings of Italian painting - than with the Italian style of Cimabue, Duccio, and Cavallini, who were still influenced by Byzantine art. However, in the case of Jacques Iverny, International Gothic was tempered with influences from the papal Avignon School and was subject to Sienese influences, as seen in the serenity of composition, the use of gold backgrounds, and the well-balanced symmetry. These traits can be found in Provençal painting throughout the 15th, and up until the beginning of the 16th, centuries, despite the departure of the papacy from France in 1376. An example of a work of the Provençal school is the St Maximin polyptych. Along with the court of the dukes of Burgundy, the Provençal school formed the foundations of a specifically French painting. This fact, however, should not be seen to detract from the importance of the many earlier regional schools of miniaturists already mentioned.

Museums and Galleries:

Dublin: *Annunciation with Donors* - Turin (Gal. Sabauda): *The Virgin and the Holy Child, St Stephen and St Lucia* (triptych).

IVERS, Mette

Danish, 20th century.

Born in Paris.

Active in France.

Painter, draughtswoman, illustrator. Figures, scenes with figures, interiors with figures, landscapes, still-lifes.

Mette Ivers studied in France and attended the Kongelige Danske Kunstakademi in Copenhagen. She lives and works in the south of France. Mette Ivers' paintings seem to be frozen in time. Just like the work of the French painter Balthus, her views of landscapes and her interiors are composed; her figures of young girls reveal the bitter-sweetness of absence. Ivers accomplishes this with a sobriety of composition and a narrative detachment based on ochre colours, sensitively applied. She has contributed works to group exhibitions in Paris, including the Galerie Séder (1971-1972-1973); the Galerie Bateau Lavoir (1972-1973); and the Galerie Iris Clert (1974). Ivers held solo exhibitions of her work at the Galerie Philippe Frègnac in 1986 and 1988.

IVERSEN, Helen

German, 19th century.

Born 19th century, in Cismar (Holstein).

Active in Berlin.

Painter.

Iversen studied in Berlin and Antwerp, and spent some time in Paris. From 1890, she showed at exhibitions in Berlin, and from 1891 in Munich. At the Grosse Kunstausstellun in Berlin in 1898, she showed an oil painting of *Geraniums in the Window*, which was bought by the State.

IVERSEN, Kræsten

Danish, 20th century.

Born 26 January 1886, in Holsted, near Kolding; died 1955.

Painter. Portraits, landscapes, still-lifes.

Kræsten Iversen exhibited portraits, landscapes and still-lifes in Charlottenborg from 1919. In 1919, the Société des Artistes Français bought his picture *Odysseus and Nausicaa*.

Museums and Galleries:

Copenhagen (Statens Mus. for Kunst): *Self-portrait* - Göteborg: *Autumn, Still-life.*

Auction records:

Copenhagen, 28 March 1973, *Landscape*, DKK 6,700. Copenhagen, 6 April 1976, *Seaside* (oil on canvas, 22 1/2 x 33 1/2 ins / 57 x 85 cm) DKK 2,700. Copenhagen, 10 Oct 1979, *Still-life with Flowers* (1923, oil on canvas, 28 1/4 x 24 ins / 72 x 61 cm) DKK 12,600. Copenhagen, 26 May 1987, *View of Borsen* (oil on canvas, 30 3/4 x 38 1/2 ins / 78 x 98 cm) DKK 31,000. Copenhagen, 22 Nov 1989, *Rocks by the Sea in Bornholm* (oil on canvas, 26 3/4 x 37 1/2 ins / 68 x 95 cm) DKK 4,600. Copenhagen, 9 May 1990, *Still-life* (1924, oil on canvas, 22 1/2 x 30 ins / 57 x 76 cm) DKK 5,500. Copenhagen, 21 April 1993, *Blue Rocks in Svaneke* (oil on canvas, 30 1/4 x 47 1/4 ins / 77 x 120 cm) DKK 5,000. Copenhagen, 19 Oct 1994, *Still-life* (oil on canvas, 17 1/4 x 23 1/2 ins / 44 x 60 cm) DKK 4,500. Copenhagen, 26 April 1995, *Forest* (oil on canvas, 38 1/4 x 49 1/4 ins / 97 x 125 cm) DKK 7,500. Copenhagen, 1 April 2003, *Bay with Fishing Village in Background, Iceland* (oil on canvas, 42 x 70 ins / 106 x 178 cm) DKK 15,000. Copenhagen, 5 Oct 2004, *Still-life with table with Fruit, Potted Plant and Other Objects* (oil on canvas, 33 x 48 ins / 85 x 122 cm) DKK 16,000. Copenhagen, 5 Oct 2004, *Odysseus and Nausicaa* (1918, oil on canvas, 57 x 78 ins / 144 x 197 cm) DKK 42,000.

IVES, Chauncey Bradley

American, 19th century.

Born 1810, in Hamden (Connecticut); died 1894.

Active in New York 1840-1844, then in Italy.

Sculptor. Figures, mythical subjects, portraits.

Chauncey Bradley Ives lived and worked in New York City from 1840 to 1844, and then established a studio in Italy because of the easy availability of marble, where he created sculptures of idealised and classical figures, such as women in drapery like *Pandora* (1850s, three versions). The carved wet drapery of his *Undine Rising from the Waters*, a water spirit who married a human, is characteristic of the see-through illusionism popular in sculpture in the mid-19th century. Ives also chose subjects from the bible, such as *Rebecca at the Well*, which achieved widespread popularity with 25 examples being commissioned. One of his sculptures of Trumbull is situated at the New State House in Hartford. Ives' work was exhibited in *Seen But Not Heard: Images of Children from the Collection of the Boston Athenaeum* (2004).

Museums and Galleries:

Boston (Athenaeum): *Ellen Shaw* (1854, marble) - Detroit (IA): *Pandora* (1864, marble) - New Haven (Yale University): *Undine Rising from the Waters* (c. 1880-1892, marble) - New

YORK (Metropolitan Mus. of Art): *Little Florist*; *Rebecca at the Well* (1854, marble); *Winged Cupid* (graphite and grey wash on paper); *Isaac Newton Phelps* (1854, marble) - NORFOLK, VA (Chrysler Museum of Art): *Undine Rising from the Waters* (c. 1880/82, marble) - SAN MARINO (Virginia Steele Scott Gallery of American Art, Huntington Library): *Pandora* (1858, marble) - WASHINGTON DC (Corcoran Gal. of Art): *Wise Man* - WASHINGTON DC (National Statuary Hall Collection): *Roger Sherman* (marble); *Jonathan Trumbell* (marble).

AUCTION RECORDS:

SAN FRANCISCO, 3 Oct 1981, *Baby Awakes* (white marble, 12 x 10 ins / 30.5 x 25.5 cm) USD 1,200. NEW YORK, 14 March 1991, *Bust of a Boy* (white marble, h. 22 1/4 ins / 56.5 cm) USD 7,150. NEW YORK, 25 Oct 1979, *Young Shepherd* (white marble, h. 56 3/4 ins / 144.2 cm) USD 15,000. ALNWICK, ENGLAND, 22 Sept 1986, *Pandora* (1858, Carrara marble, h. 67 ins / 170 cm) GBP 22,000. NEW YORK, 14 Sept 1995, *Bust of a Woman* (1866, marble, h. 20 1/2 ins / 52.1 cm) USD 2,875. NEW YORK, 26 Sept 1996, *Rebecca* (1871, white marble, h. 50 ins / 127 cm) USD 41,400. NEW YORK, 4 Dec 1996, *Undine Receiving her Soul* (white marble, h. 49 1/4 ins / 125 cm) USD 222,500. NEW YORK, 26 May 1999, *Undine Receiving her Soul* (white marble, h. 59 ins / 150 cm) USD 140,000. NEW YORK, 30 Nov 1999, *Jephthah's Daughter* (sculpture, h. 67 ins / 170 cm) USD 38,000. NEW YORK, 13 Feb 2002, *Rebecca* (1856, white marble, h. 43 ins / 108 cm) USD 9,500. NEW YORK, 4 Dec 2002, *Ideal Figure with Harp* (white marble, h. 51 ins / 130 cm) USD 50,000. NEW YORK, 4 Dec 2003, *Ino and Bacchus* (marble, h. 54 ins / 136 cm) USD 68,000. NEW YORK, 18 May 2004, *Undine Receives her Mortal Soul* (1880-1884, marble, h. 61 ins / 154 cm) USD 240,000. GREENVILLE, 26 Sept 2004, *Classically Draped Girl* (1866, marble) USD 11,000.

IVES, Halsey Cooley

American, 19th - 20th century.

Born 27 October 1847, in Montour Falls; died 5 June 1911, in London.

Painter.

Halsey Cooley Ives was a pupil of Alexander Pratowski. He was awarded many distinctions for his services to art, including the Scandinavian honours of the Cross of a Knight of the Order of Gustavus Vasa and of the Order of the Dannebrog. He organised the art exhibitions at the World Fairs in Chicago in 1893 and in Saint Louis in 1904, and was the director of the Saint Louis Museum. He entered into the service of the American government as a draughtsman in 1864, but he was essentially an instructor.

IVES, Percy

American, 19th century.

Born 5 June 1864, in Detroit; died 1928.

Painter. Portraits.

Percy Ives was a pupil of L.T. Ives and later of Bouguereau, Gérôme, Lefebvre and Boulanger in Paris. He received an honourable mention in Buffalo in 1901.

IVKOVIC, Bogoljub

Macedonian, 20th century.

Born 1924, in Gradsko.

Active in France.

Painter.

Bogoljub Ivkovic completed his studies at the academy of fine art in Belgrade in 1957.

He seeks to recreate in his paintings the atmosphere of his place of birth. His subjects reveal a harsh and mordant fatalism. The villages of Macedonia are shown in their raw state by transposed into a massive and populist archaic vision. In his earlier works, he sought to express this rural environment and traditional feel by means of dark earthy hues relieved here and there by flashes of dramatic colour. More recent works retain these underlying tones but the general effect has changed as a result of the addition of lighter tints.

He took part in the 1st and 2nd Belgrade Triennale, the Alexandria Biennale in 1961 and in many exhibitions of Macedonian or Yugoslav art abroad. He held his first solo exhibition in Belgrade (1958), subsequently exhibiting in Skopje and Ohrid (1959), again in Belgrade (1963) and in Paris.

IVONALDO

Brazilian, 20th century.

Painter.

Although not strictly a naive painter, Ivonaldo is allied to popular art firstly through his determination to describe everyday life and through his well-defined forms recalling both the fresco and the cartoon strip. His art is also, in many ways, reminiscent of popular Haitian painting.

IVORY, pseudonym of Percy van Eman

American, 20th century.

Born 1883, in Sacramento (California); died 1960.

Illustrator.

Ivory was a pupil of Howard Pyle. He was a member of the Salmagundi Club and the New York Society of Illustrators.

IVOY, Hangest d'. See **HANGEST Egbert Marinus Frederik de**

IVRY, d' (Baron)

French, 19th century.

Active at the beginning of the 19th century.

Painter. History painting, landscapes.

D'Ivry exhibited his works at the Paris Salon between 1822 and 1823.

IVRY, Fanny d'

French, 19th century.

Painter. Portraits.

Miniatures by this artist were exhibited at the Paris Salon from 1831 to 1842.

IVSEK, Anton

Austrian, 18th century.

Active in Tüffer in Styria.

Sculptor.

Ivsek sculpted altars and statues in Tüffer and nearby places.

IWAHASHI, Eien

Japanese, 20th century.

Born 1903, in Takikawa, Hokkaido Prefecture; died 1999.

Painter.

Eien Iwahashi was one of Japan's official painters. He started exhibiting in 1934, taking part in setting up the group for the study of modern Japanese painting. He subsequently founded the Ekitiebijutsu group. He received the prize awarded by the ministry of education in 1954 and 1959.

MUSEUMS AND GALLERIES:

HOKKAIDO (Takikawa Museum of Fine Art) - TOKYO (Museum of Contemporary Art) - TOKYO (National MMA).

IWAI, Toshio

Japanese, 20th - 21st century.

Born 1962, in Kira, Aichi Prefecture.

Installation artist. Multimedia.

Iwai held a solo exhibition in 1997 to inaugurate the new intercommunication centre in Tokyo, intended to present the culture of electronic information in its relationship to art, culture, technology and science. There he presented *Seven Memories of Media Technology*, a series of interactive realisations based on objects, including a camera, a film camera and a television, designed to give an account of the evolution of picture making.

IWAMI, Reika
Japanese, 20th century.
Born 1927, in Tokyo.
Engraver, draughtsman.

Reika Iwami graduated from the Bunka Gakuin liberal arts college in 1955 and studied with three other important printmakers: Koshiro Onchi, Junichiro Sekino and Takumi Shinagawa. Her works explore nature - the flow of water in particular. Her trademark style combines printing, embossing, wood grain and applied metallic leaf. Her abstract style is characterised by lyricism and gentleness, in which the effects of nets often provide variation in the texture. She was a member of the Kokugakai, the national academy of painting, from 1954 to 1966, and she is a member of the Japanese engraving association. Her work is represented in the collections of the Museum of Modern Art in New York, the Cincinnati Art Museum, the Library of Congress, the Rockefeller Foundation, the University of California, the University of Oregon and Yale University.

From the 50s she exhibited at JPA and CWAJ shows in Tokyo, winning prizes (including the Kokuga prize in 1959) at the Salons of the Kokugakai in 1957 and 1959. In 1960, 1962 and 1964 she featured in the Tokyo print Biennale, as well as in various group artistic events for women artists. In 1960 she won a prize in the competition for contemporary Japanese prints organised by the *Yomiuri* newspaper. Overseas, she has exhibited in Düsseldorf (1977), London (1984), San Diego (1993) and Cairo (1994).

IWANOFF. See also **IVANOFF**

IWANOFF, Sergi, or Iwanov
Bulgarian, 20th century.
Born 7 May 1882, in Sofia.
Painter. Figures, portraits, landscapes, Still-lifes.

Sergi Iwanoff first exhibited at the Société des Artistes Français de Bulgarie in 1903. Thereafter, his work was shown regularly at the annual exhibitions of the Société des Artistes Indépendants from the year of its foundation in 1920. At the exhibition of the Académie des Beaux-Arts in 1921 he showed his *Portrait of a Man*, a painting entitled *Albanian Women* and several Still-lifes.

IWANOFF, Stefan, or Iwanov
Bulgarian, 20th century.
Born 25 December 1875, in Sofia.
Painter. Portraits, genre scenes, landscapes.

Stefan Iwanoff studied at art school in Sofia. He made his debut at the Salon of contemporary art in Sofia and showed work in many exhibitions both in Bulgaria and abroad including: St Louis (1904); Liège (1905); Rome (1911); Berlin (1916). A member of the Society of Art of the Fatherland in Sofia, he featured regularly in the society's exhibitions from 1920. His work was also shown at the exhibition mounted on the occasion of the jubilee of the Sofia academy in 1921.

MUSEUMS AND GALLERIES:
SOFIA (Ministry of Public Education): *The Seasons* (1912) - SOFIA (NM): *Autumn*.

IWANOFF, Todor, or Iwanov
Bulgarian, 20th century.
Born 15 August 1884, in Khaskovo.
Painter.

Todor Iwanoff was a student at art school in Sofia. His paintings of battle scenes were shown at the exhibition of the Berlin academy.

IWANOV, Sergi. See **IWANOFF**

IWANOWSKA, OR IVANOWSKA
Polish, 19th century.
Active in Warsaw.
Painter.

Iwanowska exhibited at the society of artists in Warsaw with *Dubious Question* in 1874 and *Nymphs in the Lake* in 1876. The church in Szavly in Lithuania has a painting by her, after Delaroche, *Christ on the Mount of Olives*.

IWANSOHN, Eduard Petrovitch
Estonian, 19th century.
Born 19th century, in Tartu.
Active in Tartu.
Engraver, lithographer.

Iwansohn's works include *Banquet Held for Students of the Corps Curonia*, which was lithographed by Höflinger, several plates for an album entitled *Tartu and its Surroundings*, and lithographed portraits. He is probably the artist of the same name who engraved a large number of plates in 1850 for the academy of sciences, and who exhibited a drawing entitled *The Imperial Family* at the fine arts academy in 1873.

IWASA, Katsumochi Matabei, alternate names: Katsumochi, Shoi, artist names: Doun, Un'o, Hekishokyu, nickname: Ukiyo Matabei
Japanese, 17th century.
Born 1578, in Settsu (now in Hyogo Prefecture); died 20 July 1650, in Edo (now Tokyo).
Painter.

Iwasa Matabei led a tumultuous life, surrounded by violence from the start. His father was Araki Murashige (1568-1580), who lead an unsuccessful rebellion in 1579 against his daimyo, Oda Nobunaga (1534-1582). It ended in the massacre of Araki's supporters. Matabei escaped to Kyoto where he grew up under his mother's name, Iwasa. He became a painter and drew inspiration from the Kano and Tosa Schools to illustrate scenes from classical Chinese and Japanese literature and history. He is said to have been taught painting variously by Kano Shigesato or Kano Naizen. In 1616, in Kita-no-sho in Echizen Province (now Fukui Prefecture), he went to work for Matsudaira Tadanao (1595-1650). Tadanao brought him to the attention of the shogun, Tokugawa Iemitsu (1604-1651). Tadanao was exiled in 1623 for murder and this may have inspired the realistic violence in Matabei's Yamanaka Tokiwa handscroll. In 1637, Matabei, who remained in Kita-no-sho, was commanded to produce works for the shogunate. He moved to Edo, where he produced a substantial body of work, including illustrations of scenes from classical Chinese and Japanese literature and history, such as *Genji monogatari* (*Tales of Ise and Tales of Genji*) before he died 13 years later.

Among his important works are the plaques of the *36 Poets* for the Toshogu shrine in Kawagoe, commissioned by the shogun in 1640, the *Portraits of the Poets Hitomaro and Tsurayuki* and perhaps the *Yamanaka Tokiwa emaki* (*Yamanaka Tokiwa picture scroll*), whose realistic depictions of violence may have been inspired by Matabei's tumultuous life. Matabei has long been regarded as the founder of the *ukiyo-e* style, and in fact one of the earliest *ukiyo-e* works has long been attributed to him, the *Hikone Screen* (private collection), with its sumptuous costumes, sensual lines, calm, charm and gaiety, all characteristics of the style. In one sense, this may be true; but other critics look instead to his own affiliations.

Although he trained with painters of the Kano School, he signed his *36 Poets* as: *Iwasa Matabei Katsumochi Eshi Tosa Mitsunobu matsuryu* (*Iwasa Matabei Katsumochi, descendant of Tosa Mitsunobu*). It would seem that Matabei invented his own personal style based on the practices of both schools. This can be seen to perfection in his *Daruma*, in which the broad, free Kano line and the delicate, classical Tosa line combine in a brilliant demonstration of the sheer power of ink painting.

BIBLIOGRAPHY:
Paine, Robert Treat/Soper, Alexander Coburn, *The Art and Architecture of Japan*, Penguin Books, Harmondsworth, 1955.

Kita, Sandy, *The Last Tosa: Iwasa Katsumochi Matabei, bridge to Ukiyo-e*, University of Hawaii Press, Honolulu, 1999.

MUSEUMS AND GALLERIES:

CLEVELAND (MA): *The Four Pleasures* (ink, colour and gold on paper, hanging scroll).

IWASAKI, Hajin, or Iwazaki
Japanese, 20th century.
Born 1917, in Tokyo.
Painter.

Iwazaki graduated with a diploma from the Kawabata academy in Kyoto, which teaches traditional Japanese painting. He continued to study the traditional style with Kokei Kobayashi, but also Western painting with Katsuzo Satomi. In 1937 one of his works was accepted for the exhibition of the group called 'the association of the blue dragon', and in 1938 he featured in the exhibition presented by the academy of fine art. Also in 1938 he founded and directed the school called Nihon Hyogen-ha, the Japanese school of Expressionism. In 1967 he took part in the second Japan Art Festival Association exhibition at Houston in the USA.

MUSEUMS AND GALLERIES:

KURASHIKI (Ohara MA) - MOSCOW (Mus. of Oriental Art).

IWASIUK, Mikolai
Romanian, 20th century.
Born c. 1865, in Chernovtsy.
Painter.

Iwasiuk studied at the academy in Munich. He exhibited works in Cracow between 1892 and 1894 including: *At the Well; Portrait of a Woman; Chmielnicki attacking Zbaraz.* In 1917, he exhibited two paintings in Kiev, one of which depicted *Kouban Cossacks in Lemberg (Lvov).*

IWASZKIEWICZ. See also **IVACHKIEVITCH**

IWASZKIEWICZ, Andrzej
Polish, 18th - 19th century.
Active in Grodno.
Painter, watercolourist.

A watercolour of allegorical figures and emblems by Andrzej Iwaszkiewicz, dated 1806, was included in the Warsaw retrospective exhibition of 1888.

MUSEUMS AND GALLERIES:

ST PETERSBURG (Gosudarstvennyj Russkij Muz.): *Portrait of Prince N.W. Rjepin.*

IWERKS, Ubbe
American, 20th century.
Born 24 March 1901, in Kansas City; died 1971.
Draughtsman. Comic strips.

Ubbe Iwerks spent most of his career working with Disney and the earliest Mickey Mouse cartoons were animated almost solely by him. His friendship with Disney soured and Iwerks left to work with a competitor, setting up an animation studio of his own in 1930. The Iwerks studio is known for producing Flip the Frog and Willie Whopper; however, this venture was not successful. The Disney studio suffered initially from Iwerks' departure but was able to carry on successfully with other new-found talent. Iwerks' studio by contrast was unable to compete. He lost his financial backing and had to close in 1936. Following this, Iwerks worked with Columbia Pictures until 1940 when he returned to Disney. His work was now concentrated on creating special effects (he was the special effects advisor for Hitchcock's Birds) and in combining live action with animation, as in Mary Poppins.

BIBLIOGRAPHY:

Thomas, B., *The Art of Animation: The Story of the Disney Studio Contribution to a New Art*, New York, 1966. Finch, C., *The Art of Walt Disney: From Mickey Mouse to the Magic Kingdoms*, New York, 1973. Iwerks, Leslie, director, *The Hand Behind the Mouse*, video, Walt Disney Home Video, 2001.

IWILL, pseudonym of Marie Joseph Léon Clavel
French, 19th - 20th century.
Born 1850, in Paris; died 1923, in Paris.
Painter, pastellist. Seascapes, landscapes.

At the beginning of his career, Joseph Clavel adopted the pseudonym of *IWill*, for its English meaning, in order to stress the intensity of his artistic effort. He achieved the success that he hoped for, and earned an interesting place among French landscape artists. He was named Chevalier of the Légion d'Honneur in 1894. He made his debut at the Salon in 1875, and continued showing his work in Parisian exhibitions. He became a member of the Société des Artistes Français in 1883, receiving an honourable mention in 1884. He received a silver medal at the Exposition Universelle in 1889, and a bronze at that of 1900. In 2003, his work was included in the collective exhibition *Bretagne, Terre des Peintres* (*Brittany, Land of Painters*) at the Musée des Beaux-Arts in Vannes.

BIBLIOGRAPHY:

Delouche, Denise/Michaud, Jean-Marc, et al., *Bretagne, terre des peintres*, exhibition catalogue, Musée des Beaux-Arts, Vannes, 2003.

MUSEUMS AND GALLERIES:

AMIENS: *Spaarne in Amiens* - BÉZIERS: *At The Hague* - CASTRES: *Route des Andelys* - CHÂTEAUROUX: *An Avenue in Arradan* - CHERBOURG: *A Canal in Venice* - LISIEUX: *Before the Storm* - PARIS (MAM): *Before the Storm* - PÉRIGUEUX: *Street Corner in Dinan* - RHEIMS: *The Meuse at Dordrecht, Morning* - ROCHEFORT: *The Banks of the Seine in Rouen.*

AUCTION RECORDS:

PARIS, 6 March 1893, *The Coast of Brittany, Evening,* FRF 395. PARIS, 28 April 1900, *September Morning,* FRF 280. PARIS, 25 Feb 1901, *The Pond in Montigny-sur-Loing,* FRF 180; *Moonrise,* FRF 430. NEW YORK, 1907, *Seascape,* USD 250. PARIS, 22 Feb 1919, *Evening in Venice* (pastel) FRF 400. PARIS, 18 March 1920, *La Giudecca (Venice),* FRF 210. PARIS, 28 May 1923, *Dawn in Berck,* FRF 320. PARIS, 6 Feb 1924, *The St Francis of Assisi Monastery,* FRF 920; *Venice, Dawn,* FRF 1,800; *Evening Over the Lagoon,* FRF 560; *De Panne (Belgium),* FRF 555; *Evening Storm, Venice,* FRF 850; *The Dunes at Etretat,* FRF 370; *Venice, Misty Morning,* FRF 525; *In Sologne,* FRF 610. PARIS, 23 June 1928, *Canal in Venice,* FRF 700. PARIS, 13 July 1942, *The Footpath by the Lake* (1885) FRF 600; *The Beach at Etaples* (1900) FRF 850. PARIS, 24 Dec 1942, *The Borders of Lake Annecy* (1885) FRF 3,200. PARIS, 3 Nov 1944, *Riva del Garda* (pastel) FRF 850. PARIS, 5 Feb 1945, *Views of Venice* (two canvases) FRF 7,200. PARIS, Oct 1945-July 1946, *Six Paintings,* from 850 to 2800 FRF. PARIS, 29 Nov 1946, *Seascape,* FRF 1,500. PARIS, 16 April 1947, *Landscape,* FRF 1,950. PARIS, 14 Oct 1948, *Venice,* FRF 10,200. PARIS, 10 Dec 1954, *Venice,* FRF 12,000. LONDON, 17 April 1970, *View of Venice,* Gns 900. LUCERNE, 29 June 1973, *View of Dordrecht,* CHF 3,400. PARIS, 22 June 1976, *Ambleteuse* (1898, oil on canvas, 11 x 16 1/4 ins / 27 x 41 cm) FRF 3,000. VERSAILLES, 30 Nov 1980, *On the Coast of Normandy* (oil on canvas, 11 x 16 1/4 ins / 27 x 41 cm) FRF 17,300. PARIS, 27 March 1981, *The Lagoon and the Grand Canal, Venice* (oil on canvas, 13 1/2 x 18 1/2 ins / 34 x 47 cm) FRF 15,000. PARIS, 25 Feb 1983, *St-Waast* (1886, oil on canvas, 22 x 16 1/4 ins / 55 x 41 cm) FRF 22,000. PARIS, 11 Dec 1987, *Vesuvius* (oil on canvas, 18 x 27 1/2 ins / 46 x 70 cm) FRF 12,500. PARIS, 17 June 1988, *The Sierroz*

(1898, oil on canvas, 13¼ x 19¼ ins / 33.5 x 49 cm) FRF 12,000. CALAIS, 13 Nov 1988, *Sunset in Venice* (oil on canvas) FRF 27,000. PARIS, 16 Dec 1988, *Les Lesques (Provence) Near Toulon* (oil on canvas, 12¾ x 18 ins / 32.5 x 46 cm) FRF 5,200. PARIS, 15 Feb 1989, *Riverbanks* (two pastels, pendants, 21¼ x 15¾ ins / 54 x 40 cm) FRF 7,800. PARIS, 9 March 1990, *Reeds in November* (oil on canvas, 11 x 16¼ ins / 27 x 41 cm) FRF 14,000. CALAIS, 8 July 1990, *Boats at the Quay* (oil on canvas, 19¾ x 25½ ins / 50 x 65 cm) FRF 25,000. CALAIS, 9 Dec 1990, *The Port of the City of Zaandam in Holland* (oil on canvas, 13½ x 18½ ins / 34 x 47 cm) FRF 41,500. NEW YORK, 21 May 1991, *Rural House by a the Side of a Road in the Moonlight* (oil on canvas, 13 x 19 ins / 33 x 48.3 cm) USD 1,540. MONTREAL, 4 June 1991, *Evening on the Meuse in Dordrecht* (oil on canvas, 13½ x 22 ins / 34 x 56 cm) CAD 2,500. CALAIS, 20 Oct 1991, *View of the Port of Dordrecht* (oil on canvas, 13½ x 22 ins / 34 x 56 cm) FRF 22,000. NEW YORK, 16 Feb 1993, *View of the Grand Canal in Venice* (oil on canvas, 11½ x 9½ ins / 29.3 x 24.2 cm) USD 1,650. PARIS, 23 March 1993, *Forest Path in the Snow* (pastel, 15¾ x 11 ins / 40 x 28 cm) FRF 5,200. LE TOUQUET, 30 May 1993, *The Fishing Boat on the Beach* (oil on canvas, 17 x 12½ ins / 43 x 32 cm) FRF 7,000. PARIS, 27 May 1994, *The Sea at St-Vaast* (1897, oil on canvas, 13 x 22 ins / 33 x 55 cm) FRF 5,000. PARIS, 7 July 1994, *The Seine in Paris* (1880, oil on canvas, 11 x 16 ins / 27 x 40.5 cm) FRF 10,000. PARIS, 21 Nov 1995, *Venice* (oil on canvas, 13 x 18 ins / 33 x 46 cm) FRF 17,000.

IWILL, Germaine
French, 20th century.
Born in Sèvres.
Painter, draughtswoman. Figures, portraits, still-lifes.
Iwill was the daughter of Marie Joseph Iwill. Working in Paris, she executed numerous miniature portraits. She exhibited in Paris from 1910 to 1913 at the Salon des Artistes Indépendants, in 1914 at the Salon des Artistes Français, and in 1921 and 1922 at the Société Nationale des Beaux-Arts.

IWILL, Renée
French, 20th century.
Born in Sèvres.
Painter.
Iwill was the daughter of Marie Joseph Iwill. From 1901 to 1905, she showed small landscapes inspired by Venice, Sicily and the French coast at the Exposition de la Société des Femmes Artistes, and the Salon de la Société Nationale.

IYEM, Nuri
Turkish, 20th century.
Born 1915, in Istanbul.
Painter, fresco artist.
Nuri Iyem obtained a diploma from the academy of fine arts in Istanbul in 1944, and began exhibiting in various group exhibitions in Istanbul from 1942 onwards. He took part in the exhibition of Turkish painters organised by the United Nations in Paris in 1946, an exhibition in Holland in 1948, in Venice in 1956, in *Artists of the Middle East* in the USA in 1956, and in Brazil in 1961. In addition, he has shown his work in many solo exhibitions, in Turkey from 1946 onwards, in Turkish cultural centres in the USA in 1953 and 1959, and in Germany in 1960 and 1962. Iyem has also executed several murals.
MUSEUMS AND GALLERIES:
ANKARA (National Library) - IZMIR - NEW MEXICO CITY (MMA) - SÃO PAULO (Mus. de Arte Moderna).

IYEM, Nuri
Turkish, 20th century.
Born 1915, in Istanbul.
Painter.
Nuri Iyem put forward the canvas *Blacksmith* for the Exposition Internationale d'Art Moderne set up by the United Nations at the Musée National d'Art Moderne in Paris in 1946.

IYEREMYIA
Romanian, 18th century.
Active in Bucharest.
Engraver (wood).
A *Crucifixion* by Iyeremyia appears in a 1726 edition of the Octateuch published in Bucharest.

IYEROFEI
Russian, 18th century.
Engraver (wood).
Iyerofei produced two wood engravings published in the 1784 edition of *A History of the Kiev Apostles*, called *Peter the Apostle* and *Matthew the Evangelist*.

IYEVLEV, Condrat
Russian, 17th century.
Painter.
Condrat Iyevlev worked for the Tsar in Moscow as a painter and produced a variety of work for the Imperial family between 1661 and 1675.

IYEVLEV, Nicolai Vassileevich
Russian, 19th century.
Born 1835; died 3 or 15 February 1866.
Draughtsman, caricaturist.
Nicolai Iyevlev began his career as a military officer, and lived in London for many years. He worked for various Russian satirical and humorous reviews such as *Iskra* and *Niva* from 1859, and produced illustrations for collections of poetry by Miniaev, Kolizov and N. A. Nekrassov. He published a collection of his drawings, entitled *Jokes of an Artist*, in St Petersburg in 1863.

IZARD, Edith A. (Miss)
British, 19th century.
Active in London.
Painter. Genre scenes.
Edith Izard exhibited her work in London at the Royal Academy and Suffolk Street from 1884.

IZARD, Edwin
British, 19th century.
Active in London.
Painter. Landscapes.
Edwin Izard exhibited his work at the Royal Academy and Suffolk Street from 1880 to 1885.

IZARD, Gertrude M. (Miss)
British, 19th century.
Active in London.
Painter. Flowers.
Gertrude Izard exhibited her work mainly in Suffolk Street in London from 1890.

IZARNY, François d'
French, 20th - 21st century.
Born 23 February 1952, in Paris.
Painter. Still-lifes, flowers.
François d'Izarny began his studies at the École des Beaux-Arts in Dijon in 1970. He paints masses of objects arranged on shelves with a meticulous technique and also sumptuous bouquets of all manner of flowers. He exhibited in Spain and Portugal from 1972 to 1973 and his work was shown by the Galerie Laurens-Matignon in Paris from 1975 to 1982. From 1984 to 1988 he mainly exhibited in the USA. The Galerie Alain Daune in Paris exhibited a collection of his works in 1994 and a collection of his paintings of bunches of flowers in 1996.

IZART, Marie Antoinette
French, 19th century.

Active in Roubaix.
Painter.
Izart was awarded medals in Lille, Rheims and Nantes. She was also represented at the Société des Artistes Français.

IZELLO, pseudonym of Texier, Marie Louise
French, 20th century.
Born 12 October 1909, in Clermont-Ferrand.
Painter. Nudes, flowers.
Izello was a member of the Salon des Indépendants in Paris from 1957.

IZEMBARDUS
French, 12th century.
Sculptor, architect.
Izembardus worked at the abbey of Bernay.

IZER, Zeki Faik
Turkish, 20th century.
Born 1905, in Istanbul.
Painter.
Izer studied in Paris, receiving guidance from A. Lhote, Fernand Léger and Gromaire. He began exhibiting in 1933 with Group D. He became a teacher at the school of fine arts in Istanbul. In 1946 he presented his work in the exhibition of Turkish art put on at the Cernuschi museum. In the same year, he showed *Portrait of a Man, The Garden* and *Painting and Still-life* at the exhibition of modern art staged by the United Nations at the museum of modern art in Paris.

Izer found a means of expression suited to his personality in watercolour. He brought to Turkish painting echoes of the intimacy of the Impressionist Pierre Bonnard.

IZFELLNER. See **ITZLFELDNER Johan Georg**

IZHAKEVICH, Ivan Isidorovich
Ukrainian, 19th century.
Born 18 January 1864, in Vishnepole in the Ukraine.
Painter, illustrator.
Ivan Isidorovich Izhakevich trained under Murashko and at the academy of art in St Petersburg.

IZONT, Herbert, or Izant
British, 19th century.
Active in Croydon.
Painter. Genre scenes.
Herbert Izont exhibited his work in London at the Royal Academy and Suffolk Street from 1880.

AUCTION RECORDS:
LONDON, 21 March 1910, *The Council, Mitcham,* GBP 2. LONDON, 6 Dec 2000, *Musical Friend* (oil on board, 6 x 9 ins / 16 x 23 cm) GBP 1,600.

IZQUIERDO, Cid
Spanish, 20th century.
Born 1891, in Madrid.
Painter. Landscapes.
Cid Izquierdo lived in Barcelona. He took part in group exhibitions, notably the national art exhibitions in Barcelona from 1942 to 1944, and also showed his works in solo exhibitions.

BIBLIOGRAPHY:
Arnáiz, José Manuel/López Jiménez, Javier/Merchán Díaz, Manuel (ed.), *Cien años de pintura en Espana y Portugal (1830-1930),* Antiqvaria, Madrid, 1990.

IZQUIERDO, Elena
Spanish, 19th century.
Born in Segorbe.
Active in Segorbe.
Painter.
Elena Izquierdo was the daughter and pupil of Vicente Izquierdo. From 1878 onwards, she exhibited landscapes and figure paintings.

IZQUIERDO, Maria
Mexican, 20th century.
Born 1902, in San Juan de los Lagos (Jalisco); died 1955.
Painter, watercolourist. Scenes with figures.
Maria Izquierdo was a self-taught although she did attend the school of fine arts in Mexico City. For a time she studied under Diego Rivera but in 1926 her life was disrupted by the loss of her parents and then her marriage to an older man. These events are perhaps at the root of the naive imagery drawn from her childhood which she developed in her circus scenes. Her precariously balanced circus riders appear suspended in space and free of any sense of reality or gravity. Izquierdo also received assistance from Rufino Tamayo in her gouaches and watercolours. She painted many self-portraits and portraits of children occupied in a variety of activities as well as popular scenes with figures and still-lifes on shelves. In 1929 she became the first Mexican artist to be given a solo exhibition at the New York Art Center and continued to exhibit regularly until her death, mainly in Paris, New York and Santiago de Chile. An important retrospective of her work was held at the cultural centre for art in Mexico City in 1988 or 1989. In 2001 her work featured in the *Frida Kahlo, Diego Rivera and Mexican Modernism* exhibition at the National Gallery of Australia, Canberra.

BIBLIOGRAPHY:
María Izquierdo, Departamento de Bellas Artes, Gobierno de Jalisco, Mexico, 1985. *María Izquierdo,* exhibition catalogue, Centro Cultural de Arte Contemporáneo, Mexico, 1988. *Cinco mujeres, Leonora Carrington, Maria Izquierdo, Frida Kahlo, Alice Rahon, Remedios Varo,* exhibition catalogue, Gal. Arvil, Mexico, 1995. Lozano, Luis-Martin/Conde, Teresa del, *María Izquierdo, 1902-1955,* exhibition catalogue, Mexican Fine Arts Center Museum, Chicago, 1996 (text in English and Spanish).

AUCTION RECORDS:
NEW YORK, 11 May 1979, *Peasant Couple* (1938/39, oil on canvas, 22 x 20 ins / 55 x 51 cm) USD 2,500. NEW YORK, 1 Dec 1981, *Guachinango* (1943, oil/Celotex, 24 x 24 ins / 61 x 61 cm) USD 6,000. NEW YORK, 9 June 1982, *The Tightrope Artist* (1943, gouache and pencil on paper mounted on card, 15 1/4 x 19 3/4 ins / 38.5 x 50 cm) USD 2,400. NEW YORK, 20 May 1986, *Altar de Dolores* (*Altar of Sorrows*) (1943, oil on card, 23 3/4 x 19 1/2 ins / 60.3 x 49.8 cm) USD 5,250. NEW YORK, 18 Nov 1987, *The Idyll* (1946, oil on canvas, 29 1/2 x 23 1/2 ins / 75 x 60 cm) USD 10,000. NEW YORK, 17 May 1988, *The Circus* (gouache/paper, 16 3/4 x 22 1/4 ins / 42.5 x 56.5 cm) USD 13,200. NEW YORK, 17 May 1989, *Poppies* (1945, oil on canvas, 25 1/2 x 33 1/2 ins / 65 x 85 cm) USD 46,750. NEW YORK, 21 Nov 1989, *Cows* (1959, gouache/paper, 9 1/2 x 12 1/4 ins / 24 x 31 cm) USD 16,500. NEW YORK, 1 May 1990, *Grain Silo* (1943, oil on panel, 21 1/2 x 24 ins / 54.5 x 61 cm) USD 46,200. NEW YORK, 2 May 1990, *Still-life* (1944, oil on canvas, 23 1/4 x 19 1/2 ins / 59 x 49.5 cm) USD 57,750. NEW YORK, 19-20 Nov 1990, *Portrait of Juan Soriano* (1939, oil on canvas, 27 1/4 x 23 1/4 ins / 69 x 59 cm) USD 99,000. NEW YORK, 24 Nov 1992, *Pilgrims* (1945, oil on canvas, 23 3/4 x 29 3/4 ins / 60.5 x 75.5 cm) USD 82,500. NEW YORK, 18-19 May 1993, *Self-portrait* (1940, oil/synthetic resin, 36 x 26 ins / 91.4 x 65.1 cm) USD 140,000. NEW YORK, 22-23 Nov 1993, *Slaves in a Mystic Landscape* (1936, watercolour/rice paper/card, 8 x 11 ins / 20.6 x 27 cm) USD 17,250. NEW YORK, 17 May 1994, *Tony and Teresita in their Circus Act* (1945, oil/synthetic resin, 18 1/2 x 22 1/2 ins / 46.7 x 57.2 cm) USD 68,500. NEW YORK, 25-26 Nov 1996, *Two Figures* (1937, gouache/paper, 8 x 10 3/4 ins / 20.6 x 27.3 cm) USD 8,625. NEW YORK, 20 Nov 2000, *View of Cuautla* (1943, oil on panel, 24 x 20 ins / 60 x 50 cm) USD 80,000. NEW YORK, 30 May 2001, *Pumpkins with Sweet Bread* (1947, oil on canvas, 26 x 33 ins / 65 x 85 cm) USD 120,000. NEW YORK, 29 May 2002, *Circus* (1940, watercolour, 15 x 19 ins / 38 x 49 cm) USD

on canvas, 18 x 22 ins / 45 x 55 cm) USD 170,000. MEXICO, 15 May 2003, *Gentleman with Horse* (1941, oil on board, 17 x 23 ins / 44 x 59 cm) MXP 280,000. NEW YORK, 18 Nov 2003, *Woman with Horse* (1938, gouache, 8 x 11 ins / 21 x 28 cm) USD 19,000.

IZQUIERDO, Vicente
Spanish, 19th century.
Born 19th century, in Segorbe.
Active in Segorbe.
Painter.

Vicente Izquierdo studied at the academies of Valencia and Madrid and exhibited portraits, historical paintings, genre paintings and landscapes at Madrid exhibitions from 1858 to 1881. He also carried out decorative painting for the church of Altura.

IZQUIERDO DURAN, José
Spanish, 20th century.
Born 1890, in Tuy (Pontevedra).
Active in Madrid.
Painter, draughtsman.

José Izquierdo Durán worked on a publications such as *Madrid Cómico, Ahi Va* and *El Indiscreto*. He was the artistic director of Los Contemporaneos for two years.

BIBLIOGRAPHY:
Arnáiz, José Manuel/López Jiménez, Javier/Merchán Díaz, Manuel (ed.), *Cien años de pintura en Espana y Portugal (1830-1930)*, Antiqvaria, Madrid, 1990.

IZQUIERDO VIVAS, Rafael
Spanish, 20th century.
Born 1885, in Manila, Philippines; died in Barcelona.
Painter. Scenes with figures, local scenes, landscapes.

Rafael Izquierdo Vivas studied at the school of fine art in Barcelona, and took part in group and solo exhibitions, for instance the exhibition of independent artists in Barcelona in 1936. He specialised in landscapes and scenes of working-class life.

BIBLIOGRAPHY:
Arnáiz, José Manuel/López Jiménez, Javier/Merchán Díaz, Manuel (ed.), *Cien años de pintura en Espana y Portugal (1830-1930)*, Antiqvaria, Madrid, 1990.

IZQUIERDO Y VIVAS, Mariano
Cuban, 20th century.
Born 1893, in Puerto Principe; died 1975 (?).
Active in Spain.
Painter. Figure compositions, figures, scenes with figures.

As a young man, Mariano Izquierdo y Vivas lived in Madrid and studied at the college of painting at the Academia de San Fernando. He became a teacher of drawing and an art critic.

His paintings are somewhat eclectic in their style and themes: some are classical and traditional, some more realist in approach while others are exotic representations in the Art Nouveau style.

Mariano Izquierdo y Vivas has held solo exhibitions in Madrid, La Coruña, Valencia and San Sebastián.

BIBLIOGRAPHY:
Arnáiz, José Manuel/López Jiménez, Javier/Merchán Díaz, Manuel (ed.), *Cien años de pintura en Espana y Portugal (1830-1930)*, Antiqvaria, Madrid, 1990.

IZQUIERDO-GARRIDO, Ramón José
Spanish, 20th century.
Born 1873, in Seville.
Active in France from 1898.
Painter, sculptor. Figures, scenes with figures, landscapes.

Ramón Izquierdo-Garrido first studied engineering, then sculpture. He continued his training in Paris, where he settled in 1898. He exhibited in group and solo exhibitions, including the National Fine Art Exhibition in Madrid in 1924 and the Académie Parisienne des Exposants. He was a member of the Spanish Society of Painters and from 1922 of the Société Libre des Artistes Français.

BIBLIOGRAPHY:
Arnáiz, José Manuel/López Jiménez, Javier/Merchán Díaz, Manuel (ed.), *Cien años de pintura en Espana y Portugal (1830-1930)*, Antiqvaria, Madrid, 1990.

IZQUIERDO-ORDÓÑEZ, Manuel
Spanish, 19th - 20th century.
Born 1862, in Burgos; died 1948, in Burgos.
Painter.

Manuel Izquierdo-Ordóñez studied with Marceliano Santmaria at the art school in Burgos, then with Evaristo Guerra and Isidro Giln, and with Casto Plasencia at the San Fernando special school of painting, sculpture and engraving in Madrid. He became the director of the art school in Burgos, and took part in group exhibitions, such as the 1892 Exposición Nacional de Bellas Artes.

BIBLIOGRAPHY:
Arnáiz, José Manuel/López Jiménez, Javier/Merchán Díaz, Manuel (ed.), *Cien años de pintura en Espana y Portugal (1830-1930)*, Antiqvaria, Madrid, 1990.

IZSO, Miklôs
Hungarian, 19th century.
Born 9 September 1831, in Disznoshorvat; died 29 May 1875, in Budapest.
Sculptor.

Miklôs Iszo studied with H. Gasser in Vienna and also at the academy in Munich. He mainly sculpted ordinary Hungarians, and made numerous busts. He was commissioned to carve three monuments: of the poet *Csokonai* for Debreczin, of *Dugonic* for Szeged and of *Petöfi* for Budapest. The last two were completed by Adolf Huszár.

IZUMI, Shigeru
Japanese, 20th century.
Born 1922, in Osaka; died May 1995, in Osaka.
Active in France and in the USA.
Painter, engraver, screen printer.

Izumi set up in Paris in 1963, but he also resided in New York, having been invited to the USA on a cultural exchange as a lecturer in art at the Pratt Institute in New York. His works proceed from abstract ideas using geometric methods, from pop art (by the cheerfulness of the bright colours), and from Japanese tradition (by the enigmatic symbolism of the simple forms he uses). Jean Cassou writes of him that he provides: 'the most fluid and gentle of blues, an aerial current, a celestial Gulf Stream... the profound spirit of Japanese art, [in] its script-like character'. He took part in numerous group exhibitions, including the engraving Biennale at the Tokyo museum of modern art in 1957; *Young Artists of Japan* and *Young Artists* at the Kamakura museum of modern art in 1958; the São Paulo Biennale in 1959; the Salon d'Art Sacré at the Musée d'Art Moderne in Paris and the exhibition of contemporary art in Tokyo in 1964; the Salon de Mai in Paris in 1965; *Japanese Artists Abroad* at the Tokyo museum of modern art; *The New Japanese Painting and Sculpture*, a travelling exhibition in the USA and Canada, organised by the Museum of Modern Art in New York; and the Japan Art Festival in the USA in 1966. He showed his works in numerous solo exhibitions from 1949, in Osaka, Tokyo, New York, Stockholm, Paris (1965), Switzerland and Belgium.

BIBLIOGRAPHY:
Izumi, exhibition catalogue, Gal. de Coninck, Paris, 1965. *IIIe Salon international des Galeries Pilotes*, exhibition catalogue, Musée cantonal, Lausanne, 1970.

MUSEUMS AND GALLERIES:
NEW YORK (Riverside Mus.) - NEW YORK (Rockefeller Foundation) - NEW YORK (University Mus.) - OSAKA (National MA) - PITTSBURGH (Carnegie MA): four lithographs - SAKATA (Honma Art Mus.) - TAKAMATSU (City Mus. of Art) - TOKYO (National MMA) - WAKAYAMA (Mus. of Modern Art).

IZVESSTKOV
Russian, 19th century.
Painter.

Izvesstkov showed a painting entitled *Landscape in Piedmont by Night* in the exhibition of the fine arts academy in St Petersburg in 1859.

IZVIEKOV, Ivan
Russian, 19th century.
Painter.

Ivan Izviekov studied painting at the fine art academy in St Petersburg. One of his paintings, a *Portrait of Alexander II*, is in the archives of the Ministry of Foreign Affairs in Moscow.

IZYK, Jean
Polish, 19th century.
Born 1788, in Austrian Silesia; died 1845, in Calvaria.
Painter.

IZZO, Raffaele, or Izso
Italian, 19th century.
Born 25 October 1842, in Naples.
Active in Naples.
Painter.

Raffaele Izzo was a pupil at the Accademia di Belle Arti, Naples. In 1881 the Provincial Government of Naples bought his *Palazzo of Donna Anna Carafa at Posilippo*. From 1867 to 1874 he exhibited genre paintings and views including *Port of Naples*, *Interiors* at the society for the promotion of fine art, and in 1877, he exhibited a seascape at the national exhibition of fine art.

AUCTION RECORDS:
PARIS, 27 May 1994, *Fishermen in the Bay of Naples* (oil on canvas, 18 x 30 1/4 ins / 46 x 77 cm) FRF 18,000.

J

J.
School of Champagne.
Monogram of a painter glassmaker.
J. made windows for the church of St Nizier in Troyes.

J. C. B.
Flemish School, 17th century.
Monogram of an engraver (etching).
This monogram dates back to 1687. The artist known as JCB is mentioned by Bruilliot, who refers to a study of a horse by him.

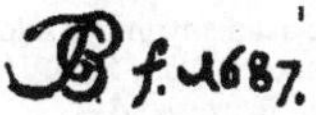

J. D.
French, 15th century.
Monogram of a painter, glassmaker.
J.D. worked in the French town of Troyes. His monogram appears on a stained glass window in Troyes Cathedral (in the first bay on entering the cathedral, yellow and blue letters on a red background). It is also found on various other stained glass windows in the cathedral (black lettering on a wine-coloured background).

J. F.
German (?).
Monogram of a painter glassmaker.
There are windows by J.F. in the choir of Troyes cathedral.

J. F.
Flemish School, 18th century.
Monogram of a painter. Religious subjects.
The artist known by this monogram was active at the beginning of the 18th century.

J. F.

MUSEUMS AND GALLERIES:
BUDAPEST: *Jesus Carrying the Cross.*

J. K.
German.
Monogram of an engraver (wood).
Ris-Paquot mentions a set of 144 engravings by J.K. representing German troops displaying flags and armorial bearings.

J. K.
German.
Monogram of an engraver (wood).
This J.K. is unidentified. He engraved *The Parable of St Matthew's Gospel.*

J. K.
17th century.
Monogram of a sculptor (ivory).
J.K. is mentioned by Ris-Paquot.

J. W., MASTER OF THE INITIALS
German, 16th century.
Painter.
Bohemian School.
He was active during the first half of the sixteenth century. He painted an altarpiece dedicated to Mary for the church of St Lawrence in Seclau in Bohemia. Two panels from this altarpiece are in Plzen and Dresden. He was influenced by L. Cranach, who lived in Saxony before settling in Bohemia in 1526.

J. W., MASTER OF THE INITIALS
17th century.
Painter.
The Master of the Initials J.W. worked in Holland at the beginning of the 17th century.
AUCTION RECORDS:
STOCKHOLM, 5 Sept 1992, *The Alchemist* (oil on canvas, 19 3/4 x 19 ins / 50 x 48 cm) SEK 14,000.

JA. See also for second names starting with the letters IA

JAAPIX, Jan, or Japiksz.
Dutch, 17th century.
Active c. 1637.
Engraver.

JAAR, Alfredo
Chilean, 20th - 21st century.
Born 1956, in Santiago.
Active in the USA from 1982.
Installation artist.
Conceptual Art.

Alfredo Jaar lives and works in New York. His approach to his work is socio-political. He sees art as having the potential for conveying meaning directly, as being almost a form of action. In his work, Jaar seeks to capture the imagination of viewers from wealthy, developed countries by representing in the most objective way the poverty born of antagonism between the countries of the northern hemisphere and those of the south. In his various installations he uses photography, often combined with mirrors and texts. From minimalism he draws a rigour that helps him to strengthen the sense of direction he gives to his works. He uses a variety of media from the picture rails of art galleries to advertising hoardings in the streets.

For a month his installation *Rushes* (1987) used the advertising spaces on the platforms at the *Spring Street* underground station in New York, situated in the heart of the artistic Soho district, but on a direct line to the commercial centre of Wall Street. Jaar covered the walls in photographic posters showing images of the appalling conditions endured at the gold mines of Serra Pelada in Brazil, making a direct connection between these and pictures showing the gold rate on Wall Street. Another installation entitled *Frame of Mind* (1987) consisted of an ornate and richly decorated mirror with a gold frame located on the wall of a museum. Opposite the wall Jaar placed a light box with a photo of a miner which, when viewed from a particular spot, was reflected in the 'mirror of opulence'. He created a work for the headquarters of the Human Rights Foundation at the Grande Arche de la Défense in Paris.

Jaar has shown his work in collective and solo exhibitions, including: *Objetos* (*Objects*), CAL gallery in Santiago (1979); New Museum of Contemporary Art, New York (1984); *Installations Projects*, Grey Art Gallery, New York (1985); *Welcome to the (Third) World*, Centre of Contemporary Art, Indianapolis (1986); *Gold in the Morning*, Venice Biennale (1986); *1+1+1*, Documenta VIII, Kassel (1987); *Frame of Mind*, Grey Art Gallery, New York (1987); Galerie Gabrielle Maubrie, Paris (1988); ARC, Musée d'Art Moderne, Paris (1988); *Effets de Miroir* (*Mirror Effects*), Centre d'Art Contemporain, Corbeil-Essonnes (1989); Anderson Gallery, Virginia (1991); Whitechapel Gallery, London (1992); *Déchirures de l'Histoire* (*Ruptures in History*), an overview of slavery and the Paris Commune at the Le 19 Regional Centre of Contemporary Art, Montbéliard (2003).

BIBLIOGRAPHY:

Vision and conscience: Ismael Frigerio, Alfredo Jaar, Pat Sheir, Steve Cagan, State University of New York, Binghamton (NY), 1984. *Alfredo Jaar: Gold in the Morning*, exhibition catalogue, Biennale de Venise, Venice, 1986. *Images critiques*, exhibition catalogue, ARC Musée d'Art moderne de la Ville de Paris, Paris, 1989. *Alfredo Jaar*, exhibition catalogue, La Jolla (CA), 1990. *Rewriting history: David Hammons, Alfredo Jaar, Sarkis, Francesc Torres*, Kettles Yard, Cambridge, 1990. Avon Drake, W., et al., *Alfrdo Jaar: geography = war Anderson Gallery, Virginia Commonwealth University*, exhibition catalogue, University Virginia Museum of Fine Arts, Richmond (VA), 1991. Bonaventura, Paul/Jaar, Alfredo/Lampert, Catherine, *Two or three things I imagine about them*, exhibition catalogue, Whitechapel Art Gallery, London, 1992. *A hundred times Nguyen*, Moderna Museet, Stockholm, 1994. Jaar, Alfredo, *Alfredo Jaar, let there be light: the Rwanda project 1994-1998*, exhibition catalogue, Actar, Barcelona, 1998 (text in English). Jaar, Alfredo, *It is difficult: ten years*, Actar, Barcelona, 1998. Bricker Balken, Debra, *Alfredo Jaar: Lament of the images*, List Visual Arts Center, M.I.T., Cambridge (MA), 1999. Cohen Hadria, Michèle, '*Alfredo Jaar. Éblouissement de l'obvie*' in *Art Press* n° 262 p. 42, periodical, Paris, October 2000. *El final del eclipse, el arte de América Latina en la transición al siglo XXI*, exhibition catalogue, Fundación Telefónica, Madrid, 2001. *Déchirures de l'histoire*, exhibition catalogue, Le 19, Centre régional d'art contemporain, Montbéliard, 2003.

MUSEUMS AND GALLERIES:

PARIS (FNAC): *Coyote* (1988).

AUCTION RECORDS:

NEW YORK, 19 Nov 1992, *Hé Ram* (1989, black and white transparencies in a light box with a mirror, 48 3/4 x 40 1/2 x 27 1/2 ins / 124.1 x 102.9 x 69.8 cm) USD 11,000. NEW YORK, 4 May 1993, *Coyote* (1988, installation with a light box and a gilt mirror, box 41 x 41 x 5 ins / 104.1 x 104.1 x 12.7 cm; mirror 16 x 16 ins/40.6 x 40.6 cm) USD 9,775.

JAARSMA, E. H.
Dutch, 20th century.
Born 1 October 1879.
Painter. Flowers.

E. H. Jaarsma studied under E. van Beever and H. Krabbe. She also attended the arts and crafts school in Amsterdam.

JABIN, Georg Ch. G.
German, 19th century.
Born 1828, in Brunswick; died 14 January 1864, in Bad Harzburg.
Landscape artist.

Jabin trained at the academy in Düsseldorf from 1850-1852, and exhibited in Munich from 1863. His favourite subject-matter was views of Switzerland.

JABIOT, Charles Édouard
French, 19th century.
Born 19th century, in Paris.
Painter, draughtsman, lithographer. Local scenes.

Jabiot exhibited at the Salon in 1879.

AUCTION RECORDS:

PARIS, 5 April 1993, *Around Medina* (1865, oil on canvas, 32 x 25 1/2in/81 x 65cm) FRF 18,000.

JABLONSKI, Martin, or Yablonsky
Polish, 19th century.
Born 1801, in Glogów; died c. 1870, in Lemberg (now Lviv, Ukraine).
Painter, lithographer. Religious subjects, portraits.

Martin Jablonski studied in Lemberg, Warsaw, Cracow and Vienna, and after 1820 worked mainly as a portrait painter. He also painted altarpieces. Notable among his lithographic works are landscapes of Galicia after B. Steczynski, which he published in 10 books of 80 views, several views of Cracow and Lemberg, a series of busts of the kings of Poland (24 plates) and a work on Polish costume.

JABOEUF, Robert A.
French, 19th - 20th century.
Sculptor.

Jaboeuf worked in Paris. There, he became a member of the Salon des Artistes Français from 1903.

JABOUIN, Bernard
French, 19th century.
Born 7 December 1810, in Bordeaux.
Sculptor, mosaicist.

Jabouin's patron was the cardinal-archbishop of Bordeaux, where he produced several altars for the church of St-Seurin as well as the mosaic for the chapel of Mount Carmel in the cathedral and many statues, confessionals, stalls and mosaics for the churches of the dioceses of Bordeaux, Auch, Agen, Cahors, Bayonne, La Rochelle, Limoges, Angoulême, Tarbes, Périgueux, Sées and Coutances. Other works include: a marble altar with a low relief depicting the *Death of Mary* at the Carmelite church in Angoulême, which was awarded a medal at the international exhibition in Paris in 1855; the baptismal fonts sculpted in marble at the church of St-Ambroise in Paris (awarded a medal at the Exposition Universelle in Paris in 1867); and mosaics in the chapel of the Virgin in the cathedral of Périgueux.

JABRE, Jacqueline
Lebanese, 20th century.
Born 1938.
Painter.

Jacqueline Jabre studied with Frick from 1960 to 1962. She began to examine the techniques of Chinese painting in Manila in 1965. Her work featured in the 1989 exhibition in Paris, *Liban - Le Regard des peintres - 200 ans de peinture libanaise* (*Lebanon as Seen by Painters - 200 Years of Lebanese Painting*). She has had solo exhibitions at the Phoenicia Hotel in Beirut, 1972, at the Kesrouan Cultural Centre in Juniye in 1978, and in 1980 at the Naaman Gallery in Juniye.

JABURG, Addig
German, 19th century.
Born 26 August 1819, in Vegesack, near Bremen; died 28 December 1875, in Vegesack.
Painter. Portraits.

Addig Jarburg worked in the Vegesack area, Bremen itself, London and Hamburg.

JABURG, Oltmann
German, 19th century.
Born 17 July 1830, in Vegesack (near Bremen); died 22 October 1908, in Vegesack.
Painter. Seascapes.

MUSEUMS AND GALLERIES:
VEGESACK (Mus.): *Portrait* (drawing).

JABVENEAU. See **LUC-LE-GAULOIS**

JAC-LEM, pseudonym of Joseph Lemonnier
French, 20th century.
Born 25 July 1914, in Le Vast (Manche); died 1995.
Painter.

Jac-Lem's painting has evolved towards Abstraction with certain decorative tendencies. He also makes reliefs. He held his first exhibition in Cherbourg, where he was living in 1946. The following year, he participated at the Salon des Artistes Français in Paris. In 1952, he had a solo exhibition in Paris.

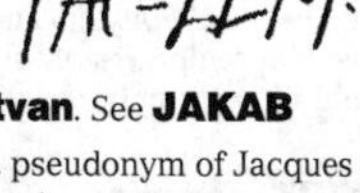

JACAB, Istvan. See **JAKAB**

JACADAM, pseudonym of Jacques Adam, called Jac
French, 20th century.
Born 1918, in Auchy-les Hesdin (Pas-de-Calais).
Painter.

Jacadam was a pupil at the École d'Art St-Luc in Tournai. He then studied at the École des Beaux-Arts in Paris, before settling in Issy-les-Moulineaux, where he set up an art school. The works of his early years were characterised by a very geometric figurative style. After working for the Resistance during the German occupation, he turned towards a more lyrical kind of Abstraction. His forms were more firmly defined in large, flat areas of vivid colour, outlined in heavy black. He executed several mural paintings, notably at the Collège des Maristes in St-Chamond, and at the Ernest Renan primary school in Issy-les-Moulineaux. He showed his work in collective exhibitions and Salons, including those of the Indépendants, Comparaisons, Montrouge, Automne and the Réalités Nouvelles. He had solo exhibitions in Paris from 1950.

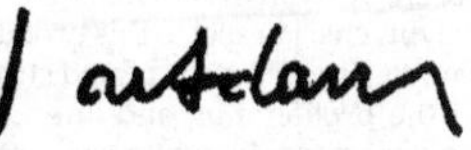

JACANO, pseudonym of Jacques Hanot
Belgian, 20th century.
Born 2 October 1923, in Brussels; died 15 April 1995, in Overijse.
Painter (including mixed media), draughtsman (including ink), watercolourist, poster artist, illustrator.
Portraits, figures, urban landscapes, scenes with figures, seascapes. Murals.

Jacques Hanot (Jacano) studied at the textile institute in Brussels and attended evening classes at the academy in Ixelles. His work was influenced by his extensive travel to places as disparate as Egypt, the Congo, Corsica, Spain, England and South America. Examples of his work were featured in the Belgian and Congolese Pavilions at the 1958 Exposition Universelle in Brussels. A foundation set up in his name exists in the Brussels district of Schaerbeck.

Jacano was primarily a designer, but his work betrays an admirable subtlety of expression and a heightened sense of fresh and vivid colour. He worked in acrylics and gold leaf or aluminium sheet and, on closer observation, his compositions evoke scenes from Africa. A favourite theme of Jacano's is the celebrated Grand Place in Brussels.

BIBLIOGRAPHY:
Hanot, Cécile, *Jacano*, monograph, Ars Libris, Brussels, 2001.

JACCARD, Christian
French, 20th century.
Born 1939, in Fontenay-sous-Bois.
Painter, engraver, sculptor, draughtsman.

Christian Jaccard studied at the École d'Art in Bourges from 1956 to 1960. Since 1976, he has taught at the École d'Art et d'Architecture de Luminy in Marseilles. From 1960, he aimed at disturbing the classical or traditional act of painting by and through printing. Freed from all structural constraint, the canvas was placed on the ground and printed upon with the aid of natural objects, such as plants and insects. From 1971, he also used rope that was knotted, twisted, plaited and coated with colour. Introduced as the 'furniture' of painting, the tools he made sustained a structural relationship with the work. From 1973 onwards, they would become a combustive material. At this time, in his *Burnt Canvasses*, Jaccard would make artistic use of combustion and burning. These extreme creative forms would recur in his later work. He progressed from plaited rope to explosive wicks, whose powder set fire to whichever material formed the support of the work, be it canvas, paper or zinc. The physical trace of the conflagration would remain on the surface.

Jaccard extended these prints of carbonised, chemical reflections of the combustion-object onto a pre-painted, strictly two-dimensional space. They were sometimes layered one upon the other, so that the whiteness of one played upon the blackness of the other. In 1977-1978, Jaccard created *Trophies*, a series of tanned skins, which he had ignited. From the enveloping of the body with skin or the victory sign, he engendered symbolic dialogues with the organic matter.

From 1979 to 1981, he created a new series called *Anonymous Burnings*. These were anonymous 17th, 18th, 19th and 20th century paintings, and later publicity banners for film, which he subjected to destructive heat. The 'cremation' attacked certain parts of the images, while leaving others more visible. Around 1983, he created his *Whites* series, in 1984, *Reds*, followed by *Brûlis* on wood, *Relief-Objects* and *Burnt Papers*. Around 1990-1991, he abandoned the lyricism of his previous works, becoming interested in the rational organisation of space, with his burnt papers in square form, arranged in polyptychs. Parallel to this production, and from the very beginning, Jaccard also created strange sculptures. They drew on the proliferation and interweaving of knots (plaits of tangled string) in white colours. They clothed structural frames, which for some, represented objects or figures. Jaccard called them *Supranodal Concepts*. At the end of the 1960s and the beginning of the 1970s, Jaccard's experimental activity helped to redefine the structural frame of the painting. He repackaged the theoretical, traditional frameworks of painting, rethinking them in a language whose syntax is fashioned by one minimal element of cohesion: fire. He turned the tools, the burnt canvases, the *Trophies*, into archaeological signs of what went before.

The collective exhibitions in which he has participated include: 1972, *Douze ans d'art contemporain 72/72* (*12 Years of Contemporary Art 72/72*), Grand Palais in Paris; 1978, *Unstretched Surfaces*, Institute of Contemporary Art, Los Angeles; 1979, *Tendances de l'Art en France 1958-1979* (*Art Trends in France, 1958-1979*), ARC (Art, Recherche, Confrontation), Musée d'Art Moderne de la Ville de Paris; 1992, *Manifeste, 30 ans de création en perspective 1960-1990* (*Manifesto: 30 Years of Creation in Perspective 1960-1990*), Musée Nationale d'Art Moderne, Centre Pompidou; 2002, *Les Années 70: l'art en cause* (*The 1970s: Art in Question*), CAPC-Musée d'Art Contemporain, Bordeaux; 2003, *Esprit des lieux* (*The Spirit of Places*), the contemporary work and its exhibited space, Palais des Papes, Avignon, and *Bandes à part: le cinéma dans l'art contemporain* (*On the Fringes: Cinema in Contemporary Art*) at the Musée d'Art Moderne et Contemporain, Strasbourg.

His solo exhibitions include: 1962, Cabinet des Estampes, Geneva; 1962, Galerie Cachet, Bern; 1963, 1966, Cercle, SMA, Geneva; 1967, Maison de la Culture, Bourges; 1972, Musée de l'Athénée, Geneva; 1974, Galerie Lucien Durand, Paris; 1975, Musée de l'Abbaye Ste-Croix, Sables d'Olonne; 1975, Centre National d'Art Contemporain, Paris; 1975, Musée des Arts Décoratifs, Nantes; 1975, Musée d'Art Moderne, Céret; 1976, Galerie Beaubourg, Paris; 1976, Musée d'Art et d'Industrie, St-Étienne; 1977, 1980, Galerie Athanor, Marseilles; 1978, Galerie La Hune, Paris; 1978, Galerie Arta, Geneva; 1979, Musée d'Art Moderne de la Ville, Paris; 1979, Galerie Sapone, Nice; 1979, Kunstsenter Sonia Henie-Niels Onstad, Oslo; 1981, Centre Culturel, *Repères 1969-79* (*Landmarks 1969-79*), Brétigny; 1982, Galerie Jean Six, Paris; 1982, Musée Cantini, Marseilles; 1983, Galerie des Ponchettes, Nice; 1984, 1986, Galerie Gilbert Brownstone et Cie, Paris; 1984, L'Autre Musée, Brussels; 1984, Artothèque, Montpellier; 1985, Centre d'Action Culturelle Pablo-Neruda, Corbeil-Essonnes; 1985, Galerie Sapone, Nice; 1987, Centro Culturale Francese, Rome; 1988, 1991, Denise Cadé Art Prospect Inc., New York; 1988, Istituto Francese di Napoli, Naples; 1989, Galerie Municipale d'Art Contemporain, Montpellier; 1990, *Christian Jaccard: les blances et les rouges 1983-1989* (*Christian Jaccard: The Whites and Reds 1983-1989*), Musée Cantini, Marseilles; 1991, *Brûlis*, 1992 *Reliefs-objets et papiers calcinés* (*Relief Objects and Charred Papers*), Galerie Louis Carré & Cie, Paris; 1996, Musée d'Art Moderne, La Terrasse, St-Étienne; 1997, Musée Montbéliard and the museum of modern art in Osaka and in Tokyo.

Bibliography:

Clair, Jean, *L'Art en France, une nouvelle génération*, Éd. du Chêne, Paris, 1972. Lamarche-Vadel, '*Christian Jaccard*' in *Opus international* n° 51, periodical, Paris, 1974. Lemaire, Gérard-Georges, *L'Œuvre en dégradé*, exhibition catalogue, ARC musée d'Art moderne de la Ville de Paris, Paris, 1979. Jaccard, Christian, '*Extrait d'un carnet 1979*' in *L'Ennemi*, periodical, Bourgois, Paris, 1980. Jaccard, Christian, '*Notes et projets, 1980*' in *Colloque de Tanger*, Bourgois, Paris, 1980. Jaccard, Christian, '*Fragments d'histoire*' in *L'Ennemi*, periodical, Bourgois, Paris, 1981. Jaccard, Christian, '*De l'iconoclastie/Manifeste*' in *L'Ennemi*, periodical, Bourgois, Paris, 1982. Hauc, Jean-Claude/Lemaire, Gérard-Georges/Laporte, D.G., *Jaccard*, exhibition catalogue, Gal. des Ponchettes, Nice, 1983. Noël, Bernard, *Christian Jaccard: le roman des nœuds*, exhibition catalogue, Maison de la culture, La Rochelle, La Différence, Paris, 1987. Jaccard, Christian, '*L'Art au nom de quoi?*' in *Opus international* n° 127, periodical, Paris, 1992. Lascault, Gilbert, *Christian Jaccard*, A. Biro, Paris, 2003.

Museums and Galleries:

Marseilles (Mus. Cantini): *Untitled* (1975, twisted rope); *Burnt Blue Canvas* (1976) - Paris (FNAC): *Supranodal Concept* (1987); *Polyptych (64 modules)* (1991) - Paris (FRAC Île-de-France): *Burnt Canvas* (1976) - Paris (MNAM-CCI) - St-Étienne (Mus. d'Art et d'Industrie) - St-Paul (FRAC Réunion): *Toile calcinée* (*Burnt Canvas*) (1985).

Auction records:

Paris, 12 June 1986, *Toile/empreinte avec échelle* (1975, 39 3/4 x 110 1/4 ins / 101 x 280 cm) FRF 18,000. Paris, 16 Oct 1988, *Toile brûlée, garance foncée* (faded green, 32 1/4 x 47 1/4 ins / 82 x 120 cm) FRF 10,100. Douai, 1 April 1990, *Composition* (1976-1979, set of nine graphite hemp tools tied up, 32 1/4 x 14 1/2 ins / 82 x 37 cm) FRF 23,000. Douai, 1 July 1990, *Composition* (1973-1974, burned canvas, 26 1/2 x 15 3/4 ins / 67 x 40 cm) FRF 15,000. Paris, 18 Oct 1992, *Pink Canvas* (1974, unstretched canvas, 86 1/2 x 70 3/4 ins / 220 x 180 cm) FRF 7,500. Versailles, 12 Dec 1999, *Burned Anonymous* (mixed media on canvas, 51 x 38 ins / 130 x 97 cm) FRF 14,000. Paris, 27 Oct 2000, *Couple* (c. 1975, painted string on canvas, a pair, 110 x 40 ins / 280 x 101 cm) FRF 17,000. Paris, 23 June 2001, *Untitled* (acrylic on canvas, 49 x 83 ins / 124 x 210 cm) FRF 13,000. Paris, 4 June 2002, *Untitled* (mixed media on canvas, 46 x 36 ins / 118 x 91 cm) EUR 2,000. Paris, 29 April 2003, *19th Century Burned Anonymous* (safety fuses on canvas laid on panel, 26 x 20 ins / 65 x 51 cm) EUR 1,800. Paris, 9 June 2004, *Couple toile/outil echelle, empreinte* (c. 1973, acrylic on canvas with book cords, 94 x 79 ins / 238 x 200 cm) EUR 2,500.

JÄCH, Gottfried, or Jeche
German, 17th - 18th century.
Born 26 February 1672, in Modlau (Modla), Silesia; died 8 November 1739, in Zittau (Saxony).
Sculptor.

Jäch worked in Breslau (now Wroclaw), Vienna, Brno, Prague, Dresden, Berlin and Potsdam, then Hamburg and Brunswick, finally settling in Zittau in 1707. Among works he did in Zittau are *The Swan Fountain* and perhaps some of the stone fountains with sculptures of men and animals set up between 1710 and 1730, a number of which are in the museum in Zittau.

JACHIMOWICZ, Theodor
Austrian, 19th century.
Born 15 March 1800, in Belzec (Galicia); died 14 April 1889, in Vienna.
Painter. Architectural views. Decorative schemes.

Jachimowicz trained at the academy in Vienna. A theatre painter, he devoted his leisure hours to painting genre pictures and architectural scenes, and every year exhibited oil paintings and watercolours at the academy in Vienna. Notable genre paintings include *The Joiner's Workshop, The Sausage Vendor, Young Girl Crying at Her Mother's Tomb, The Organ Player* and *The Invalid*. A noted landscape is *Storm at Sea*. Architectural paintings include *The Confessional, Antechamber of a Hunting Lodge* and *Interior of St Stephan's Church in Vienna*. He also painted religious scenes such as *The Generosity of David, Scene from the Magdalene Legend* and a *Baptism of Christ* for the episcopal chapel of Przemysl (Poland). In 1843, he did a *Portrait of the Emperor Ferdinand I* for the Piarists in Vienna.

JACHMANN, Friedrich, or (erroneously) Tachmann
German, 18th century.
Born 1698, in Breslau (now Wroclaw, Poland); died 1768, in Breslau.
Painter. History painting, portraits.

He painted mostly portraits of prominent Breslau personalities. The library in the city has several portraits by him.

JACHTMANN, Johann Ludwig
German, 19th century.
Born 1776, in Berlin; died 3 September 1842, in Berlin.
Sculptor, worker with precious stones, medallist, draughtsman.

Jachtmann did low reliefs in bronze, wax statues, drawings (scenes from the *Iliad*) and a large number of medals.

JACINE, Cesare
Italian, 20th century.
Painter. Portraits.

Jacine studied architecture and painting at the Accademia di Belle Arti di Brera, Milan. At the Milan Exhibition of 1922 he exhibited *Portrait of the Artist's Mother*, and in 1924 at the exhibition of portraits of women of Monza *The Yellow Dress*. He also painted a *Portrait of the Marquis Ponti, Mayor and Senator of Milan*.

JACINO, da Cividale di Aquileia. See **FABRIS Jacino**

JACINTO, Juan
Spanish, 17th century.
Born 1621, in Aracena.
Active in Seville.
Painter.

In 1685, Juan Jacinto, then aged 64, was living in Faceros street in Seville.

JACK, Richard
British, 20th century.
Born 15 February 1866, in Sunderland; died 29 June 1952 or 1959, in Montreal.
Painter. Portraits, genre scenes, architectural interiors, interiors with figures, landscapes, flowers.

Richard Jack worked initially in Paris, from where he submitted a portrait to the 1893 exhibition at the Royal Academy in London. In 1900 he won a silver medal at the Exposition Universelle in Paris. He subsequently settled in London and embarked on a career as a successful portrait painter. He became associated of the Royal Academy in 1914 and member in 1920. He moved to Canada in 1930. Jack is best-known for his portrait of King George V and Queen Mary, at Windsor Castle. He also painted a number of interiors and genre scenes, including an interior of Buckingham Palace.

MUSEUMS AND GALLERIES:

LONDON (Royal Academy of Arts): *On the Moors* (1921, oil on canvas, competition piece) - LONDON (Tate Collection): *Rehearsal with Nikisch* (1912, oil on canvas) - PITTSBURGH: *String Quartet*.

AUCTION RECORDS:

LONDON, 22 March 1946, *Waiting for Tea*, GBP 84. LONDON, 26 Sept 1984, *Portrait of Mrs Hall Hurst* (oil on canvas, 87 x 48 ins / 221 x 122 cm) GBP 1,000. LONDON, 3-4 March 1988, *Interior with Young Girl, Reading* (1916, oil on canvas, 43 1/4 x 33 1/2 ins / 110 x 85 cm) GBP 1,430. MONTREAL, 25 April 1988, *Ducks on a Pond* (1901, oil on canvas, 24 x 20 ins / 61 x 51 cm) CAD 900. MONTREAL, 17 Oct 1988, *The Kennibunk Beach Swimming Pool, Maine* (oil on panel, 20 x 24 ins / 51 x 61 cm) CAD 800; *Peonies* (oil on panel, 20 x 24 ins / 51 x 61 cm) CAD 1,500. LONDON, 7 June 1990, *Beach Huts* (1896, oil on panel, 7 3/4 x 11 1/2 ins / 20 x 29 cm) GBP 1,430. LONDON, 4 June 1997, *Portrait of Mrs C. H. B. Forth* (1900, oil on canvas, 90 1/2 x 49 1/2 ins / 230 x 126 cm) GBP 29,900.

JÄCKEL, Anton, or Jäkel or Jeckel
Bohemian, 18th century.
Born 1699, in Prague; died 7 September 1736, in Prague.
Sculptor.

Anton Jäckel was the son of Matthias Wenzel Jäckel.

JACKEL, Karl Heinrich, called Henry
German, 19th century.
Active at the end of the 19th century.
Painter. Landscapes, waterscapes.

Jackel worked in Berlin, but travelled in Italy. He exhibited in Dresden, Bremen and Berlin from 1857 to 1872.

AUCTION RECORDS:

LILLE, 24 April 1983, *View of the Borromee Islands, Lake Maggiore; View of Naples* (oil on canvas, set of two, 16 1/4 x 22 3/4 ins / 41.5 x 58 cm) FRF 81,000. COLOGNE, 22 May 1986, *Alpine Lake* (oil on canvas, 28 x 35 1/2 ins / 71 x 90 cm) DEM 4,400. LONDON, 28 Nov 1990, *Isola Bella on Lake Maggiore* (oil on canvas, 22 x 17 ins / 56 x 43 cm) GBP 2,640. ROME, 28 May 1991, *View of Lake Como* (oil on canvas, 22 3/4 x 17 1/4 ins / 58 x 44 cm) ITL 10,000,000. NEW YORK, 27 May 1992, *Panorama of the Bay of Naples* (oil on canvas, 27 1/4 x 38 ins / 68.9 x 96.5 cm) USD 12,100. MUNICH, 25 June 1992, *Nesso, on Lake Como* (1861, oil on canvas, 23 3/4 x 36 3/4 ins / 60.5 x 93.5 cm) DEM 7,910. LONDON, 11 April 1995, *Naples from Vomero* (oil on canvas, 23 3/4 x 34 ins / 60.5 x 85.5 cm) GBP 8,280. LONDON, 31 Oct 1996, *View of Varenna, Lake Como* (oil on canvas, 17 1/2 x 30 ins / 44.5 x 76 cm) GBP 4,370.

JÄCKEL, Mathias Wenzel, or Jäkel or Jeckel
Bohemian, 17th - 18th century.
Born 1655, in Prague; died 1738, in Prague.
Sculptor.

Mathias Jäckel, the father of Anton Jäckel, studied in Rome, Naples and Florence and became a master in 1699. He was one of those working on the statues on the St Charles bridge in Prague, and also on the Baroque sculptures for the church and gardens of the monastery of Marienstern.

JACKISCH, Josef
German, 19th century.
Born 25 February 1791, in Oppeln (Opole), Silesia; died 14 March 1862, in Oppeln.
Painter.

Noted works by Jackisch include several portraits of members of his family and a *Madonna* in the church of Walzen (Walce) near Oberglogau (Glogowek), Silesia.

JÄCKLI. See **JEGLI**

JACKLIN, Bill
British, 20th - 21st century.
Born 1 January 1943, in London.
Active in New York from 1985.
Painter, printmaker. Figures, still-lifes.

Bill Jacklin studied graphics at Walthamstow School of Art, London (1960-1961), worked as a graphic designer at Studio Seven in Holborn (1961-1962), returned to Walthamstow School to study painting in 1962, and studied at the Royal College of Art (1964-1967). Jacklin taught from 1967 to 1975 at the Chelsea School of Art, the Hornsey College of Art, the

Royal College of Art, and at various schools in Kent and Surrey.

Jacklin concentrated on abstraction from 1968 to 1975, as in his *Growth of Carthage* (1970, pen and ink), but moved to representation from 1976 when he began to paint still lifes, exploring the movement of light across specific objects, especially lemons and a striped vase, as in *Lemons with Vase* (1983, oil), and *Tabletop I* (1977-1978, oil and encaustic). He moved to New York City in 1985 and painted crowded interior and exterior scenes. His New York work includes two series: one of aerial views of meat packers unloading trucks on West 14th Street near the Hudson River, such as *The Meatpackers II* (1986); and another of individuals and social types in specific milieus, such as *Grand Central Station* (1988), and *Washington Square at Night* (1986, oil).

Jacklin has had solo exhibitions at Marlborough Gallery, New York (frequently since 1985); and the Museum of Modern Art, Oxford (1992-1993). Other shows include *Contemporary Drawings*, Museum of Modern Art, New York (1972); *16 Artists: The Who Album*, Tate Gallery, London (1981); *Printshops of Canada: Printmaking South of Sixty*, MacDonald Stewart Art Centre, Guelph (1987); *60 Contemporary Drawings*, Metropolitan Museum of Art (1990); the Summer Exhibitions at the Royal Academy of Art, London (1990-1994, 1997-2001, 2003); *New Acquisitions: British Drawings*, Metropolitan Museum of Art (1991); *Britain and the São Paulo Biennale 1951-1991*, British Council, London (1992); *20th Century British Art Fair*, Royal College of Art, London (1996); and *New Acquisitions*, Metropolitan Museum of Art, New York (1996-1997).

BIBLIOGRAPHY:

Lassaigne, Jacques, *Peinture anglaise aujourd'hui*, exhibition catalogue, Musée d'Art Moderne de la Ville de Paris, Paris, 1973. *Bill Jacklin: Recent Work, New York Paintings, Pastels and Drawings*, exhibition catalogue, Marlborough Gallery, New York, 1987. *Bill Jacklin: Urban Portraits*, exhibition catalogue, Marlborough Gallery, New York, 1990. *Bill Jacklin: Urban Portraits, New York 1986-1992*, exhibition catalogue, Museum of Modern Art, Oxford, 1992. Taylor, John Russell, *Bill Jacklin*, illustrated book, Phaidon Press, London, 1997. *Bill Jacklin: New York City, the Connected Image 1997-1999*, exhibition catalogue, Marlborough, New York, 1999. *Bill Jacklin: Central Park, New York City, Recent Paintings and Monoprints*, exhibition catalogue, Marlborough Gallery, New York, 2002.

MUSEUMS AND GALLERIES:

BRADFORD (City Art Gallery) - BUDAPEST (Szépmuvészeti Múz.) - CAMBRIDGE (Fitzwilliam Museum) - DUBLIN (Irish Arts Council) - GLASGOW (Hunterian Museum) - GUELPH (University of Guelph) - KANSAS CITY (Kemper MCA): *After the Dance, Great Lawn I* (2000, oil) - LEICESTER (University of Leicester) - LITTLE ROCK (Arkansas AG): *Sheep Meadow: Girl Sleeping* (1990, pastel) - LONDON (Arts Council of Great Britain): *Duet* (1971, pen and ink); *Double Buddha* (1976-1977, oil and wax on canvas) - LONDON (British Council): *First Coloured Series* (1973, oil) - LONDON (British Mus.) - LONDON (Contemporary Art Society) - LONDON (Tate Collection): *Catena* (1970, drawing); *First Light* (1974-1975, lithograph); *Northern Light* (1975, lithograph); *Ancient Light* (1975, lithograph); *Daylight* (1975, lithograph); *Sky Light* (1975, lithograph); *Night Light* (1975, lithograph); *Anemones* (1977, series of seven intaglio prints) - LONDON (UK Government Art Collection): *Coney Island* (1992, etching); *Man with a Bib* (c. 1982, etching); *Rocking my Blues Away* (1973, mezzotint); *Rocking along the Line* (1973, mezzotint); *Sun and Rain over Regent Street* (1988, oil) - LONDON (Victoria and Albert Mus.): *Car Lot* (1970, pen and ink) - MANCHESTER (Whitworth Art Gallery): *Woman in a Chair* (1987, print) - NEW BRUNSWICK, NJ (Zimmerli Art Museum, Rutgers University) - NEW HAVEN (Yale Centre for British Art) - NEW YORK (Metropolitan Mus. of Art): *Incident on 42nd Street* (1988, oil); *Chess Players: Variation* (1988) - NEW YORK (MoMA) - OXFORD (Ashmolean Mus.) - SYDNEY (AG of New South Wales) - TAMPA (Museum of Art).

AUCTION RECORDS:

LONDON, 11 June 1992, *Howley Bar and Grill* (1986, pastel, 41 x 29 1/2 ins / 104 x 75 cm) GBP 4,950. LONDON, 25 Nov 1993, *Bar and Grill* (1986, oil on canvas, 36 x 48 ins / 91.5 x 122 cm) GBP 10,350. LONDON, 6 Dec 1996, *Coffee Drinker* (1986, oil on canvas, 20 x 16 1/4 ins / 51 x 41 cm) GBP 3,680. LONDON, 4 March 1999, *The Dancers, West 42nd Street* (1984, oil on paper, 39 x 26 ins / 100 x 67 cm) GBP 3,800. LONDON, 1 March 2000, *Man with a Bib, Portrait of the Artist's Father* (1980-1981, oil on canvas, 30 x 30 ins / 76 x 77 cm) GBP 1,600. LONDON, 6 Dec 2000, *Argument* (1984, oil on paper, 40 x 26 ins / 101 x 67 cm) GBP 4,500. LONDON, 4 July 2001, *Man with a Straw Hat, No. IV* (1978, watercolour, 24 x 16 ins / 61 x 40 cm) GBP 3,000. LONDON, 3 Oct 2001, *Park II - Sheep Meadow* (1991, oil on linen, 39 x 48 ins / 99 x 122 cm) GBP 15,000. LONDON, 14 March 2002, *Argument II* (1984, oil on paper, 30 x 22 ins / 76 x 56 cm) GBP 2,800. LONDON, 3 Dec 2003, *Meatpackers, Washington Street, II* (1986, oil on canvas, 36 x 30 ins / 91 x 76 cm) GBP 10,000. LONDON, 2 June 2004, *The Bar, Coney Island* (oil on canvas, 16 x 20 ins / 40 x 51 cm) GBP 4,800.

JACKMAN, W.G.

British, 19th century.
Born 19th century, in England.
Engraver.

Around 1841 W.G. Jackman went to the USA where he worked for New York editors. He executed portraits and figure compositions in stipple and dry-point.

JACKOWSKI, Tadeusz

Polish, 20th century.
Draughtsman, engraver, illustrator.

Tadeusz Jackowski, the son of the singer Maria Modrakowska, who was famous in the 1920s, and godson of Nadia Boulanger, trained at the École Nationale des Beaux-Arts, Paris. He has taught at the Cracow and Poznan art schools. His work, which is in the Eastern European surrealist tradition, depicts the nightmare of a world gone mad. In 2002 a solo exhibition of his works *Les Aventures Graphiques avec l'Architecture* (*Graphic Adventures with Architecture*) was held at the Polish Institute, Paris.

BIBLIOGRAPHY:

Noyce, Richard, *Contemporary Graphic Art in Poland*, Craftsman House Art Books, 1997 (published in Australia).

JACKSON, Alexander Young

Canadian, 20th century.
Born 3 October 1882, in Montreal; died 5 April 1974, in Kleinburg.
Painter, illustrator, lithographer. Landscapes.
Group of Seven.

Alexander Young Jackson is famous not only for his paintings of the rugged Canadian landscape but also for his part in the Canadian art movement of the early 20th century. Born in Montreal, he also lived in England and France, showing his work in London. He first studied at the Conseil des Arts et Manufactures in Montreal with Edmond Dyonnet, then worked in Chicago as a graphic artist for a lithograph company and trained at the Art Institute of Chicago under Clute and Richardson. In 1907 he went to Paris and studied at the Acedémie Julian under Jean-Paul Laurens for six months. He also travelled to Rome, Florence and Venice. He fought in World War I in 1914; injured in 1916, he became a war artist the following year.

Returning to Canada, he joined the Group of Seven with J.E.H. MacDonald, Lawren Harris and Tom Thomson. In 1920, after a stay at Georgian Bay, Jackson exhibited in the group's first exhibition. That same year, he was elected to the Royal Canadian Academy of Arts. For almost 50 years he roamed Canada, sketching, painting and interpreting its landscape. He wanted to teach Canadians to see and appreciate the beauty of their land. Jackson went on sketching trips all over Canada for three seasons a year and painted large canvases in his Toronto studio during the winter. He travelled to the West Coast and the Arctic, capturing the landscape in every season. Jackson's travels to Quebec included trips to the Charlevoix and Lower St Lawrence region, and he also explored Canada's remote areas. He seldom used human figures in his work, and when they did appear, they were insignificant compared to the power and majesty of nature. Jackson was prolific in terms of his drawings and sketches and painted almost until the day he died.

He featured in the travelling exhibition *A.Y. Jackson paintings, 1902-1953*, Art Gallery, Toronto; National Gallery of Canada, Ottawa; The Montreal Museum of Fine Arts, 1953-1954.

BIBLIOGRAPHY:

A.Y. Jackson Paintings 1902-1953, solo exhibition catalogue, Rous & Mann Press, Toronto, 1954?. Jackson, Alexander Young, *A painter's Country; the Autobiography of A. Y. Jackson*, Clarke Irwin, Toronto, 1967 (foreword by Vincent Massey). Groves, Naomi Jackson, *A.Y.'s Canada. Pencil drawings by A.Y. Jackson.*, Clarke, Irwin, Toronto, Vancouver, 1968. Jackson, Alexander Young, *The Arctic 1927/A.Y. Jackson*, Penumbra Press, Moonbeam (Ontario), 1982 (introduction by Naomi Jackson Groves). Reid, Dennis R., *Alberta rhythm: the Later Work of A.Y. Jackson*, Art Gallery of Ontario, Toronto, c. 1982. Groves, Naomi Jackson, *One summer in Quebec: A.Y. Jackson in 1925: a Family View*, Penumbra Press, Kapuskasing, c. 1988.

MUSEUMS AND GALLERIES:

EDMONTON (AG): *The Great Lone Land* (1949) - HAMILTON, NJ (AG): *Hills at Great Bear Lake* (1953) - LONDON (Tate Collection): *The Entrance to Halifax Harbour* (1919, oil on canvas) - MONTREAL (MAC): *Road to St Tite des Caps* - MONTREAL (MBA): *Grey Day, Laurentians* (1931) - OTTAWA (NG. of Canada): *Red Maple; Frozen Lake, Early Spring, Algonquin Park* (1914); *Drought Area, Alberta* (1937); *Eldorado Mines, Labine Point* (1938); *Radium Mine, Great Bear Lake* (1938); *Camp Mile 108, west of Whitehorse* (1943); *Alaska Highway Between Watson Lake and Nelson* (1943); *Evening, Teshierpi* (1950); *Stream Bed, Lake Superior Country* (1955) - TORONTO (AG of Ontario): *Winter, Charleroix County* (1932-1933); *Lunbreck, Alberta* (1937); *Mokowan* (1937); *Blood Indian Reserve, Alberta* (1937); *Porcupine Hills, Alberta* (1938); *Great Bear Lake* (1938); *Pre-Cambrian Mountains* (1938); *South From Great Bear Lake* (c. 1939); *Monument Channel, Georgian Bay* (1953); *Country Road, Alberta* (1954) - VANCOUVER (AG): *Wild Woods* (c. 1945); *Mackintosh Bay, Lake Athabasca, Saskatchewan* (1957).

AUCTION RECORDS:

TORONTO, 14 March 1973, *Landslides*, CAD 4,400. TORONTO, 21 Oct 1974, *Caribou Country* (1947) CAD 10,000. TORONTO, 17 May 1976, *Emileville* (1913, oil on canvas, 21¼ x 26¼ ins / 54 x 66.5 cm) CAD 18,000. TORONTO, 9 May 1977, *Farm at Ripon, Quebec* (oil on canvas, 19¾ x 24½ ins / 50 x 62.5 cm) CAD 14,000. LONDON, 30 May 1979, *Forest Landscapes* (1920, oil on double-sided card, 8¼ x 10 ins / 21 x 25.5 cm) GBP 4,400. TORONTO, 26 May 1981, *Village in Nova Scotia* (oil on canvas, 25½ x 31½ ins / 65 x 80 cm) CAD 70,000. TORONTO, 8 Nov 1983, *Village by a Lake* (oil on canvas, 19¾ x 24½ ins / 50 x 62.5 cm) CAD 14,000. TORONTO, 3 June 1986, *Artillery Passing through Albert* (pencil and wash, 12 x 15 ins / 30.5 x 38.1 cm) CAD 2,100. TORONTO, 3 June 1986, *Landscape with Farmhouses in Winter* (oil on canvas, 25 x 33 ins / 63.5 x 83.8 cm) CAD 25,000. MONTREAL, 25 April 1988, *Farm at Clyde River* (1960, oil on panel, 10¼ x 13½ ins / 26 x 34 cm) CAD 5,000. MONTREAL, 1 May 1989, *Creek, Lake Millette, Quebec* (1959, oil on panel, 10¼ x 13½ ins / 26 x 34 cm) CAD 7,500. TORONTO, 12 June 1989, *Farm at Wilno, Ontario* (1966, oil on card, 10½ x 13½ ins / 26.7 x 34.3 cm) CAD 5,000; *La Cloche Hills near Algoma Lake* (1938, oil on panel, 10½ x 13 ins / 26.5 x 33 cm) CAD 12,000. MONTREAL, 30 Oct 1989, *Wrecks at Michiploten* (1959, oil on panel, 10¼ x 13½ ins / 26 x 34 cm) CAD 6,600. NEW YORK, 31 May 1990, *Around Ahmic Lake, Ontario* (1907, oil on card, 10½ x 13½ ins / 26.7 x 34 cm) USD 3,300. MONTREAL, 5 Nov 1990, *Fishermen Huts, Gaspésie* (oil on panel, 9½ x 13½ ins / 24 x 34 cm) CAD 7,700. MONTREAL, 23-24 Nov 1993, *Winter by Tadoussac* (oil on panel, 8½ x 10½ ins / 21.5 x 26.6 cm) CAD 7,000. TORONTO, 1 June 1999, *Horse and Sleigh, Lower St Lawrence* (oil on canvas, 20 x 26 ins / 52 x 65 cm) CAD 64,000. TORONTO, 2 June 1999, *Early Snow, Alberta* (1937, oil on canvas, 32 x 46 ins / 82 x 117 cm) CAD 150,000. VANCOUVER, 7 June 2000, *Overlooking Murray Bay* (oil on canvas, 20 x 47 ins / 51 x 120 cm) CAD 57,500. TORONTO, 21 Nov 2000, *Winter, La Malbaie* (oil on canvas, 20 x 26 ins / 52 x 65 cm) CAD 300,000. TORONTO, 4 Dec 2001, *The Third Row - Above St Adele* (oil on canvas, 24 x 31 ins / 62 x 80 cm) CAD 85,000. TORONTO, 4 Dec 2001, *April, Georgian Bay* (1920, oil on canvas, 24 x 31 ins / 62 x 80 cm) CAD 95,000. VANCOUVER, 2 May 2002, *Cacouna, Quebec* (1933, oil on canvas, 20 x 25 ins / 51 x 63 cm) CAD 170,000. TORONTO, 14 May 2002, *April, Les Eboulements* (1935, oil on canvas, 20 x 26 ins / 52 x 65 cm) CAD 160,000. TORONTO, 18 Nov 2003, *Quebec Village on the St Lawrence in Winter* (oil on canvas, 21 x 26 ins / 53 x 67 cm) CAD 250,000. TORONTO, 2 Dec 2003, *Encampment, Eastern Arctic* (20 x 26 ins / 50 x 65 cm) CAD 70,000. VANCOUVER, 27 May 2004, *Skeena Crossing, BC* (1926, oil on panel, 8 x 10 ins / 21 x 26 cm) CAD 110,000. TORONTO, 1 June 2004, *Deese Bay, Great Bear Lake* (oil on canvas, 26 x 30 ins / 65 x 75 cm) CAD 80,000.

JACKSON, Annie Hurlburt

American, 20th century.

Born 19 August 1877, in Minneapolis (Minnesota); died 1957, in Boston (Massachusetts).

Painter.

Annie Hurlburt Jackson was a pupil of Eric Pape, Murphy and Woodbury. She was a member of the American Federation of the Arts and the Boston Artists' Guild. She won a gold medal at the Philadelphia Exhibition in 1926. She specialised in miniatures.

JACKSON, Arthur

British, 18th century.

Active in London.

Painter.

Arthur Jackson exhibited four allegorical subjects at the Free Society in 1770.

JACKSON, Arthur, pseudonym of Hepworth Arthur J.

British, 20th century.

Born 1911; died 2003.

Painter.

Arthur Jackson (also known as Jack Hepworth) was a cousin of the sculptor Barbara Hepworth. He trained at the St Martin's School of Art in London, and later, from 1932 to 1936, as a private pupil of Ben Nicholson (Nicholson's influence is apparent in Jackson's work). He studied architecture at Hull University under Leslie Martin from 1937 and subsequently practised as a professional architect. His work featured alongside that of Mondrian, Kandinsky, Helion, Gabo, Moore, Nicholson and his cousin Barbara in the important exhibition *Abstract and Concrete*, which toured Britain in 1936.

AUCTION RECORDS:

LONDON, 22 Oct 1997, *Abstract Composition* (1936, oil on canvas remounted/panel, 20 x 24½ ins / 51 x 62 cm) GBP 11,500.

JACKSON, Charles d'O. Pilkington
British, 20th century.
Sculptor. Busts, statuettes.

Charles Jackson was active in Edinburgh. In 1913 his work featured in the annual exhibition at Edinburgh College of Art. He showed statuettes and busts at the Royal Academy from 1911.

JACKSON, Day
British, 19th century.
Painter. Landscapes.

MUSEUMS AND GALLERIES:
SALFORD (Museum and AG): *Scene on the River Irwell* (1856).

JACKSON, Emily F.
British, 19th century.
Active in Carsbalion.
Painter. Flowers.

From 1875 Emily F. Jackson frequently exhibited her work in London at the Royal Academy and Suffolk Street and also sent work to the exhibitions of the New Water-Colour Society and the Grosvenor Gallery.

JACKSON, Francis Ernest
British, 20th century.
Born 1873, in England.
Painter, watercolourist, lithographer. Portraits.

Francis Jackson was a co-founder of the Senefelder Club (a group devoted to the promotion of the art of lithography, named in honour of the great eighteenth-century German printmaker and inventor J. N. F. A. Senefelder). Jackson was himself a lithographer and painter, chiefly of portraits.

JACKSON, Franck
French, 20th century.
Painter, draughtsman, pastellist, illustrator, newspaper cartoonist. Figures.

Franck Jackson worked for the Documentation Française in Paris as an illustrator.

JACKSON, Franck G.
British, 19th century.
Born December 1831, in Birmingham; died 1 January 1905, in Birmingham.
Painter, draughtsman, professor.

Franck G. Jackson began his career as a pattern maker and studied drawing with Samuel Line. He then became a teacher of painting and drawing. He was appointed deputy head at the town's art school and held this position until his death.

MUSEUMS AND GALLERIES:
BIRMINGHAM (Mus. and AG): *William Losken Aitken* (oil on canvas).

JACKSON, Frank Henry
American, 19th century.
Born 21 September 1864, in England.
Active in Boston (Massachusetts).
Painter, architect.

JACKSON, Frederick Christian (Revd.)
British, 19th century.
Born 1825; died 1898, in Great Stanmore.
Active in London.
Painter, watercolourist. Seascapes.

Frederick C. Jackson exhibited his work in London at the Royal Academy, Suffolk Street and the Society of British Artists from 1868 to 1884.

JACKSON, Frederick Hamillon
British, 19th century.
Born 1848; died 1923.
Active in London.
Painter, illustrator. Landscapes.

Frederick Hamillon Jackson was a member of the Royal Society of British Artists and from 1870 took part in the main London exhibitions, especially at the Royal Academy and Suffolk Street.

AUCTION RECORDS:
LONDON, 14 Feb 1978, *Sir Galahad's Vision of the Holy Grail* (1893, oil on canvas, 56 x 39 ins / 142 x 99 cm) GBP 600. LONDON, 7 June 2001, *In the Garden* (1886, pencil, watercolour and gum arabic heightened with gouache, 14 x 21 ins / 35 x 53 cm) GBP 2,000. SYDNEY, 15 May 2004, *Religious Ceremony* (1888, watercolour, 15 x 27 ins / 39 x 68 cm) AUD 8,000.

JACKSON, Frederick William
British, 19th - 20th century.
Born 1859, in Middleton, near Manchester; died 1918.
Watercolourist, painter (gouache). Genre scenes, local scenes, landscapes, seascapes.

Frederick William Jackson trained in Manchester and Paris under J. Lefebvre and Boulanger. He travelled extensively in Italy (Capri, Venice, Florence and Rome), and later in Morocco. He exhibited in London at the Royal Academy and the Suffolk Street Gallery from 1909, and was a member of the Royal Society of British Artists. Jackson's delicate works are characterised by their sensitive rendering of the changing moods of nature. Several of his most important paintings were acquired by the city museums of Leeds, Oldham, Rochdale and Manchester.

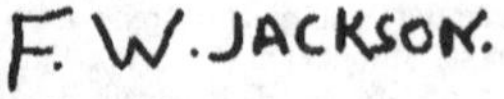

MUSEUMS AND GALLERIES:
BRADFORD (Cartwright Hall AG): *In the Springtime* (1906, oil on canvas) - MANCHESTER: *The Way Home*.

AUCTION RECORDS:
LONDON, 4 April 1910, *A Child's Boat*, GBP 7. LONDON, 23 May 1910, *The Night Coach*, GBP 16; *Ploughing in the Highlands*, GBP 16; *Fishermen, Summer*, GBP 9. CHESTER, 30 March 1984, *At the Edge of the Village* (oil on canvas, 20 x 47 ins / 51 x 119.5 cm) GBP 2,300. LONDON, 7 Nov 1985, *View of the Kremlin under Snow* (oil on canvas, 35 x 42 1/4 ins / 89 x 107 cm) GBP 4,000. LONDON, 14 Oct 1987, *The Return of the Cobles* (oil on canvas remounted on board, 16 x 24 ins / 40.5 x 61 cm) GBP 2,300. CHESTER, 20 July 1989, *Runswick Bay* (oil on canvas, 24 1/4 x 29 1/4 ins / 61.5 x 74.3 cm) GBP 3,520. LONDON, 8 Feb 1991, *A Bazaar in Tangiers* (watercolour and gouache, 10 1/2 x 14 1/2 ins / 26.7 x 37 cm) GBP 770. NEW YORK, 14 Oct 1993, *The Great Bazaar in Tangiers* (1908, watercolour and gouache/paper, 7 3/4 x 6 3/4 ins / 19.7 x 17.3 cm) USD 1,380. LONDON, 7 June 1996, *Children Playing beside a Thatched Cottage* (oil on canvas, 20 1/2 x 47 1/2 ins / 52.1 x 120.7 cm) GBP 13,800. LONDON, 5 Nov 1997, *Fishing on a River in Autumn* (oil on canvas, 35 x 49 1/4 ins / 88 x 125 cm) GBP 8,510.

JACKSON, G.
Irish, 19th century.
Miniaturist.

MUSEUMS AND GALLERIES:
DUBLIN: *Portrait of a Man* (1810, miniature on ivory, signed and dated).

JACKSON, Georges Siméon
French, 19th century.
Active in Paris.
Sculptor.

Georges Jackson was a member of the Société des Artistes Français from 1889, in whose exhibition he featured.

JACKSON, Gilbert
British, 17th century.
Active between 1622 and 1642.
Painter. Portraits.

Several collections in Oxford and Cambridge contain portraits attributed to Gilbert Jackson.

Museums and Galleries:
London (National Portrait Gal.): *John Belasyse, Baron Belasyse* (1636, oil on canvas) - London (Tate Collection): *A Lady of the Grenville Family and her Son* (1640, oil on canvas) - London (Victoria and Albert Mus.): *Portrait of Ann Clifford.*
Auction records:
London, 27 July 1984, *Portrait Presumed to be James Graham, Marquis of Montrose* (1637, oil on canvas, oval, 29 x 24 1/2 ins / 73.7 x 62.1 cm) GBP 1,600. London, 15 July 1987, *Portrait of John, Baron Belasyse* (1636, oil on canvas, 74 x 51 ins / 188 x 129.5 cm) GBP 160,000. London, 13 Nov 1996, *Portrait of Sir William Kingsmill* (1642, oil on canvas, oval, 29 x 23 1/4 ins / 73.5 x 59 cm) GBP 8,050. London, 30 Nov 2001, *Portrait of a Lady in an Embroidered Dress* (oil on canvas, feigned oval, 27 x 23 ins / 68 x 59 cm) GBP 7,000.

JACKSON, Harriet A. E. (Miss).
See **BROWNING Harriet A. E.**

JACKSON, Harry
American, 20th century.
Born 1924.
Sculptor. Local figures, portraits, animals. Monuments, groups, equestrian groups.

Harry Jackson specialised in the folklore of the Wild West, with cowboys, Native Americans and horses.
Bibliography:
Pointer, L./Goddard, D., *Harry Jackson*, New York, 1981. Pointer, Larry, *Harry Jackson*, Abrams, New York, 1981. Thornton, Gene, *Harry Jackson: A Retrospective Exhibition*, exhibition catalogue, 1981. Hassrick, Peter H., *100 Years of Western Art from the Pittsburgh Collection*, exhibition catalogue, Carnegie Institute, Museum of Art, 1982.
Museums and Galleries:
New Haven (Knights of Columbus Mus.): *Steer Roper, Hard and Fast* (bronze sculpture) - Oklahoma City (National Cowboy and Western Heritage Mus.): *Two Champions* (1974).
Auction records:
Los Angeles, 9 June 1976, *The Marshall* (1970, patinated bronze, h. 31 ins / 79 cm) USD 9,500. Los Angeles, 9 March 1977, *Cowboy on Horseback* (1973, bronze, h. 13 3/4 ins / 35 cm) USD 2,400. Los Angeles, 18 June 1979, *The Platin* (patinated bronze, h. 10 1/2 ins / 26.7 cm, w. 27 ins/68.6 cm) USD 13,500. New York, 23 April 1982, *The Marshall II* (1979, brown-patinated bronze, h. 16 1/2 ins / 42 cm, l. 17 ins/43.2 cm) USD 13,500. New York, 3 June 1983, *Sacagawea: First Working Model* (1977-1980, bronze, h. 26 3/4 ins / 68 cm) USD 5,000. New York, 4 Dec 1986, *The Marshall, polychrome* (1970, painted bronze with tempera and oil, h. 29 1/2 ins / 75 cm) USD 42,000. New York, 28 May 1988, *Algonquin Chief and Warrior* (1971, bronze, h. 31 1/2 ins / 79.8 cm) USD 12,100. Los Angeles, 9 June 1988, *Marshall II* (1979, bronze, h. 16 3/4 ins / 42.5 cm) USD 11,000. New York, 24 Jan 1989, *Self-portrait* (1955, oil on canvas, 11 3/4 x 10 ins / 30 x 25.3 cm) USD 5,500. New York, 25 May 1989, *The Rout* (1959, bronze, h. 15 ins / 38 cm, l. 60 ins/152.4 cm) USD 154,000. New York, 1 Dec 1989, *Pony Express* (1967, bronze, equestrian group, h. 18 ins / 45.5 cm) USD 29,700. New York, 16 March 1990, *Safe and Sound* (bronze, equestrian group, h. 19 ins / 48.3 cm) USD 9,350. New York, 21 May 1991, *Sacagawea II, Indian Woman with her Child* (1980, silvered bronze, h. 17 3/4 ins / 45.4 cm) USD 3,300. New York, 25 Sept 1991, *The Frontier Guard* (polychrome bronze, h. 20 1/2 ins / 52.1 cm) USD 7,700. New York, 6 Dec 1991, *John Wayne, First model for the Monument* (bronze, h. 37 1/2 ins / 95.3 cm) USD 19,800. New York, 28 May 1992, *The Cowboy's Meditation* (bronze, equestrian group, h. 22 1/4 ins / 56.8 cm) USD 11,000. New York, 2 Dec 1993, *Pony Express Rider* (1967, bronze, h. 19 ins / 48.3 cm) USD 25,300. New York, 1 Dec 1994, *Two Bits* (1974, polychrome bronze, h. 27 1/4 ins / 69.2 cm) USD 31,625. New York, 13 Sept 1995, *Washakie II, Chief of the Shoshone Indians* (bronze, equestrian group, 20 1/4 ins / 51.4 cm) USD 5,750. New York, 13 March 1996, *The Marshall* (painted bronze, h. 30 ins / 75.9 cm, l. 33 ins/83.8 cm) USD 20,700. New York, 3 Dec 1996, *The Frontier Guard* (1965, bronze, h. 21 3/4 ins / 55.3 cm) USD 6,325. New York, 25 March 1997, *Two Champions II* (1977, brown-patinated bronze, h. 21 1/2 ins / 54.6 cm) USD 10,925. Los Angeles, 28 Oct 1999, *The Flag Bearer* (1983, brown patinated bronze, h. 26 ins / 66 cm) USD 15,000. Hilton Head Island, 20 Nov 1999, *Cowboy's Meditation* (polychrome bronze, h. 22 ins / 56 cm) USD 25,000. Los Angeles, 13 Dec 2000, *Pony Express* (1983, polychrome bronze, h. 60 ins / 152 cm) USD 25,000. Los Angeles, 13 Dec 2000, *Marshal* (1980, polychrome bronze, h. 56 ins / 142 cm) USD 25,000. Santa Fe, 19 May 2001, *Flag Bearer* (bronze, h. 26 ins / 66 cm) USD 18,000. Hayden, 28 July 2001, *Algonquin Chief and Warrior* (bronze, h. 12 ins / 30 cm) USD 15,000. Santa Fe, 18 May 2002, *The Marshal Polychrome* (bronze, h. 29 ins / 74 cm) USD 55,000. Los Angeles, 20 Nov 2002, *Sacagawea, Study for the Monument* (1979, brown patinated bronze, h. 39 ins / 98 cm) USD 40,000. New York, 9 Oct 2003, *Pony Express* (1967, polychromed bronze, h. 20 ins / 52 cm) USD 19,000. New York, 9 Oct 2003, *Cowboy's Meditation* (polychromed bronze, h. 23 ins / 58 cm) USD 20,000. St Louis, 20 March 2004, *Indian Mother and Child* (1980-1981, polychrome bronze, 25 x 36 ins / 64 x 91 cm) USD 12,200. Santa Fe, 23 Oct 2004, *Ropin' a Star* (1982, bronze, h. 28/71 ins / 215 cm) USD 9,000.

JACKSON, Helen
British, 20th century.
Died 6 July 1911.
Active in London.
Painter. Genre scenes.

Helen Jackson exhibited in London at the Royal Academy, the Suffolk Street Gallery and the Royal Society of Painters in Watercolours from 1884.

JACKSON, J., the Elder
British, 19th century.
Sculptor.

J. Jackson the Elder exhibited his work at the Royal Academy in London in 1836 and 1837.

JACKSON, J., the Younger
British, 19th century.
Painter. Portraits.

J. Jackson the Younger was active in Oxford and may have been a relative of John Jackson. He exhibited his work at the Royal Academy in London from 1816 to 1835.

JACKSON, J. S.
British, 19th century.
Painter. Genre scenes.
Museums and Galleries:
Salford (Museum and AG): *Windermere.*

JACKSON, James E.
British, 19th century.
Painter. Figures.

James E. Jackson was active in Salford and also exhibited in London, mainly at the Royal Academy and in Suffolk Street from 1876.

JACKSON, James Ranalph
Australian, 20th century.
Born 3 July 1882; died 1975, in Sydney.
Painter. Landscapes with figures, landscapes, seascapes.
Auction records:
London, 22 Oct 1976, *Syndey Harbour* (oil on canvas, 21 1/2 x 27 1/2 ins / 54.5 x 70 cm) GBP 1,900. Sydney, 20 Oct 1980, *The Boatshed* (oil on canvas, 17 3/4 x 22 ins / 45 x 55 cm) AUD 1,700. Sydney, 29 June 1981, *Silvery Morning Light on Duck*

River (oil on canvas, 19¾ x 23½ ins / 50 x 60 cm) AUD 5,250. ROSEBERY, 20 June 1983, *Lavender Bay* (oil on card, 14¼ x 17 ins / 36 x 43 cm) AUD 2,400. MELBOURNE, 21 April 1986, *Evening, Spit Junction, Middle Harbour* (oil on card, 11½ x 17½ ins / 29 x 44.5 cm) AUD 17,000. MELBOURNE, 26 July 1987, *View of the Old Bridge from Seaforth* (oil on canvas, 28 x 36¼ ins / 71 x 92 cm) AUD 130,000. SYDNEY, 21 Nov 1988, *Country Road* (oil on canvas, 17¾ x 22 ins / 45 x 56 cm) AUD 4,000. SYDNEY, 20 March 1989, *The Gundagai Hills* (oil on canvas, 15 x 17¼ ins / 38 x 44 cm) AUD 4,000. SYDNEY, 3 July 1989, *Middle Harbour* (oil on card, 15¾ x 20 ins / 40 x 51 cm) AUD 10,000. SYDNEY, 16 Oct 1989, *The Crossing* (oil on card, 16¼ x 20 ins / 41 x 51 cm) AUD 9,500. LONDON, 28 Nov 1991, *Young Woman Rowing* (1917, oil on canvas, 15¾ x 31¼ ins / 40 x 79.5 cm) GBP 10,120. SYDNEY, 29-30 March 1992, *Pastureland in a Valley* (oil on card, 11¾ x 15¾ ins / 30 x 40 cm) AUD 2,600. MELBOURNE, 23 Aug 1999, *Clontarf, Middle Harbour* (oil on canvas, 22 x 28 ins / 56 x 72 cm) AUD 22,000. MELBOURNE, 23 Nov 1999, *North Sydney Harbour* (oil on canvas, 18 x 24 ins / 45 x 60 cm) AUD 19,000. MELBOURNE, 27 Nov 2000, *Bathing in the Rockpool* (oil on canvas, 15 x 19 ins / 37 x 48 cm) AUD 12,000. MELBOURNE, 28 Nov 2000, *Autumn Morning, Sydney Harbour* (oil on panel, 16 x 20 ins / 41 x 51 cm) AUD 12,000. PADDINGTON, 27 Aug 2001, *Sydney Harbour* (oil on canvas, 26 x 36 ins / 66 x 92 cm) AUD 20,000. SYDNEY, 28 Aug 2001, *Evening, Middle Harbour Sydney* (oil on canvas on board, 20 x 24 ins / 50 x 60 cm) AUD 20,000. MELBOURNE, 5 March 2002, *Spit, Middle Harbour, New South Wales* (oil on canvas, 16 x 20 ins / 40 x 51 cm) AUD 15,000. SYDNEY, 6 March 2002, *Twilight Sailing, Sydney Harbour* (oil on board, 17 x 20 ins / 43 x 52 cm) AUD 9,000. MELBOURNE, 4 June 2003, *From Above Castle Rock, Sydney* (oil on canvas, 22 x 26 ins / 56 x 66 cm) AUD 16,000. PADDINGTON, 25 Aug 2003, *Boating* (oil on canvas on board, 19 x 15 ins / 48 x 38 cm) AUD 22,000. MELBOURNE, 10 March 2004, *Spit Bridge, Sydney* (oil on canvas, 26 x 38 ins / 66 x 96 cm) AUD 18,000. PADDINGTON, 24 Aug 2004, *Crevice* (oil on canvas, 20 x 24 ins / 50 x 60 cm) AUD 38,000.

JACKSON, John
British, 18th century.
Active in Smithfield.
Engraver (wood).

John Jackson was a prolific illustrator of children's books at the end of the 18th century.

JACKSON, John
British, 19th century.
Born 31 May 1778, in Lastingham (Yorkshire); died 1 June 1831, in St John's Wood.
Painter, draughtsman, watercolourist. Portraits.

John Jackson was the son of a tailor who wanted his son to enter the same profession, but his interest in drawing took precedence, and at the age of 19 he attempted to establish himself as a painter of miniatures in York. The patronage of Lord Mulgrave, the Earl of Carlisle, and later on Sir George Beaumont ensured that his future was secure. He began with small portraits in crayon heightened with watercolour. He was permitted to copy the masters belonging to his patrons. In 1804 Sir George Beaumont gave him the means to undertake more serious studies in London. He exhibited his work at the Royal Academy and was admitted as a student there the following year. Wilkie and Haydon were his great friends. He found it easy to work and also possessed the gift of painting likenesses, enabling him to enter into active collaboration in the collection of *Portraits of Illustrious Persons of the 18th Century* by Cadell. His talent as a watercolourist stood out from his abilities as an oil painter, and it was not until much later on that he acquired an acceptable technique in oil painting. In 1815 he became an associate of the Royal Academy and visited Flanders and Holland. He became an Academician in 1817 and went to Rome two years later with Sir Francis Chantrey. He was elected to membership of the Accademia di Belle Arti di San Luca. He continued to take part in exhibitions at the Royal Academy in London until 1830, although his state of health had deteriorated considerably during the previous year. He married twice, his second wife being the daughter of the painter James Ward who was left a widow, young and penniless with three children, even though Jackson had earned large amounts of money.

His best works were his portraits of Canova, Flaxman and Lady Dover. He was an excellent colourist and his likenesses were perfect, but he did not succeed in bringing to his figures their real character or the power and grace which were the hallmarks of the great artists.

MUSEUMS AND GALLERIES:

CHICAGO: *Portrait of a Man; Portrait of the Artist* - DUBLIN (Nat.): *Thomas Moore* - LONDON (British Mus.): *Alexander I; J. Bacon; G. Colman Sen; J. Perry; J. Nollekens; William Smith; Dr. Clarke; General Phipps* - LONDON (Garrick Club): *W.C. Macready in the Role of Henry IV* - LONDON (National Portrait Gal.): *John Hunter* (1786, oil on canvas, after Joshua Reynolds); *Sir John Barrow, 1st Bt* (c. 1810, oil on canvas, attributed to John Jackson); *George Henry Harlow* (c. 1819, pencil, after George Henry Harlow); *Catherine, Countess of Essex* (c. 1822, oil on canvas); *John Jackson* (c. 1823, oil on canvas); *Sir John Soane* (1828, oil on canvas); *Arthur Wellesley, 1st Duke of Wellington* (1830-1831, oil on canvas); numerous other s, drawings - LONDON (NG): *William Seguier* (1830, oil on canvas); *Reverend William Holwell Carr* (c. 1827-1828, oil on canvas) - LONDON (Royal Academy of Arts): *A Jewish Rabbi* (c. 1817, oil on canvas, competition piece) - LONDON (Sir John Soane's Mus.): *Mrs Parry; Sir John Soane; N. Marchant* - LONDON (Tate Collection): *Sir Francis Chantrey* (c. 1830, oil/wood); other painted s; *Sir David Wilkie, R.A.* (c. 1815-1820, chalk/paper) - LONDON (Victoria and Albert Mus.): *Charles Grey; Portrait of the Artist* - MANCHESTER: *Thomas Stothard.*

AUCTION RECORDS:

PARIS, 1881, *Portrait of the English Painter Northcote,* FRF 800. NEW YORK, 10 and 11 April 1902, *Portrait of a Man,* USD 100. LONDON, 8 Feb 1908, *Portrait of George Granville, First Duke of Sutherland,* GBP 13. LONDON, 5 Dec 1908, *Portrait of Lord Howden,* GBP 11. LONDON, 7 Dec 1908, *Portrait of a Woman* (pencil heightened with watercolour) GBP 13. LONDON, 12 Dec 1908, *Macready in the Role of Macbeth,* GBP 18. LONDON, 11 Dec 1909, *Portrait of the Countess of Sheffield* (1828, watercolour) GBP 241. LONDON, 12 Dec 1910, *Sir Francis Chantrey,* GBP 9. LONDON, 24 Feb 1922, *Sir Francis Legatt Chantrey,* GBP 147. LONDON, 2 March 1923, *Robert Bertie and his Wife,* GBP 94. LONDON, 5 May 1929, *John Williams,* GBP 152. LONDON, 7 March 1930, *John Flaxman,* GBP 47. LONDON, 22 Nov 1968, *The Earl of Mulgrave with his Son,* Gns 2,400. LONDON, 14 Nov 1972, *Self-portrait* (watercolour heightened with white) Gns 380. LONDON, 28 Nov 1973, *Portrait of Antonio Canova,* GBP 600. LONDON, 10 Nov 1982, *Portrait of a Young Black Man* (oil on canvas, 23½ x 19½ ins / 59.5 x 49.5 cm) GBP 1,400. LONDON, 20 Nov 1987, *Portrait of George, First Marquis of Buckingham* (oil on canvas, 50 x 40 ins / 127 x 101.6 cm) GBP 10,000. LONDON, 31 Oct 1990, *Portrait of a Young Child with a Spaniel* (oil on canvas, 29¼ x 24¼ ins / 74.5 x 61.5 cm) GBP 1,045. NEW YORK, 14 Oct 1992, *Portrait of William Pitt the Younger* (oil on canvas, 30 x 25 ins / 76.2 x 63.5 cm) USD 2,475. LONDON, 6 April 1993, *Portrait of William Pitt the Younger in a Grey Suit* (oil on canvas, 29¼ x 24½ ins / 74.5 x 62 cm) GBP 7,130. NEW YORK, 12 April 1996, *Masters Russell, Edward and Frederick Gray* (oil on canvas, 82½ x 64½ ins / 209.6 x 163.8 cm) USD 79,500. LONDON, 9 May 1996, *Portrait of the Artist Dressed in a Blue Jacket* (oil on canvas, 29½ x 24½ ins / 75 x 62 cm) GBP 552. LONDON, 30 Nov 2001, *Cupid Asleep in a Woodland Clearing* (oil on canvas, 25 x 30 ins / 64 x 76 cm) GBP 2,000. LONDON, 30 Nov 2001, *Portrait of Captain Lyon RN, Holding a Gun* (oil on canvas, 30 x 24 ins / 77 x 61 cm) GBP 7,000. LONDON, 19 March 2003, *Portrait of Antonio Canova, Seated, View of his Studio Beyond* (oil on canvas, 50 x 40 ins / 127 x 101 cm) GBP 11,500. SHREWSBURY, 30 April 2003, *Half-length Portrait of John Flaxman* (oil on canvas, 30 x 25 ins / 76 x 64 cm) GBP 4,200.

JACKSON, John
British, 19th century.
Born 19 April 1801, in Ovingham (Northumberland); died 27 March 1848, in London.
Engraver (wood).

John Jackson was a student of Cosmo Armstrong, Bewick and W. Harvey. He worked on Knight's edition of *Shakespeare* and on Northcote's *Fables*. He also engraved the illustrations for W.A. Chatto's *Treatise on Wood Engraving, Historical and Practical* published in 1839. He is considered one of the best English wood engravers.

JACKSON, John Adams
American, 19th century.
Born 1825, in Bath (Massachusetts); died 1879, in Pracchia (Tuscany), Italy.
Sculptor, draughtsman.

John Adams Jackson has a distinguished place in American art. He studied linear and ornamental drawing in Boston and went on to produce interesting pencil portraits. He completed his art studies in Paris at the Académie Suisse, attempting to gain complete knowledge of the human anatomy. In 1851 his career in sculpture started with busts, notably that of *Webster*, produced from documents provided by the family of the celebrated philologist. He was in Florence in 1853 and, immersed in the beauties produced by Greek and Renaissance masters, he produced more remarkable busts. In 1854 he was back in Paris, where he produced the *Bust of Judge Mason*, ambassador of the USA. He went to Boston in the same year and modelled the *Portrait of Wendell Phillips* in the Boston Athenaeum.

Jackson moved to New York in 1858, and from that point no longer specialised in busts, giving his artistic expression a wider scope. In 1860 he was commissioned to produce the *Statue of Kane the Navigator*, and left for Florence for its execution. Florence was Jackson's preferred home and he sculpted his major works there, including the following: *Eve by the Body of Abel*; *Autumn*; *Cupid Drawing back his Bow*; *Titania and Bottom*; *Cupid on a Swan*; *Guilty Sprite*; *Figure of Peace* (bust); *Dawn* (bust); and *Morning Glory* (medallion).

During a journey to New York in 1867, Jackson modelled several figures to be cast in bronze for the decoration of the south gatehouse of Central Park Reservoir. His *Young Girl Reading* dates from 1869, and *Musidora*, considered his masterpiece and exhibited in Vienna, dates from 1873. His *Monument in Honour of American Soldiers, Erected in Lyons* dates from 1874, as does a composition of three large bronze figures comprising *City*, *Justice* and *War*. He also produced *Hylas*, modelled in 1875, *Il Pastorello*, an Abruzzo peasant, a goat, and around 100 busts. At the time of his death, his expression was in full force and he was working on a new group, *Eve by the Body of Abel*, with completely different attitudes.

MUSEUMS AND GALLERIES:
BOSTON (Athenaeum): *Bust of Wendell Phillips* - NEW YORK (Metropolitan Mus. of Art): *Eve by the Body of Abel*.

JACKSON, John Baptist, called Jackson of Battersea
British, 18th century.
Born 1701; died c. 1780.
Painter, engraver (wood).

John Baptist Jackson of Battersea was a student of Eckwits and Kirkal. Unable to find work in England, in or around 1726 he travelled to Paris where he was engaged by Papillon but was dismissed shortly afterwards. In about 1731, he left for Rome in the company of another painter but instead arrived in Venice where he lived until 1745, the year Pascali published 17 of Jackson's wood engravings after Titian, Veronese, Tintoretto and Jacopo Bassano. After a twenty-year absence, he returned to England where, opportunity once again lacking, he was reduced to working for a wallpaper factory in Battersea. Later he published a *Descent from the Cross* after Rembrandt, as well as a lively series of coloured landscapes. He claimed he was the first artist to use colour engraving.

MUSEUMS AND GALLERIES:
NEW HAVEN (Knights of Columbus Mus.): *Marriage at Cana* (woodcut).

AUCTION RECORDS:
PARIS, 27 Nov 1997, *Deposition in the Tomb* (engraving in chiaroscuro in the style of monochrome painting, after J. Bassano, 21 1/4 x 15 ins / 54 x 38 cm) FRF 1,400.

JACKSON, John Edwin
American, 20th century.
Born 7 November 1876, in Eagleville (Tennessee); died 1950.
Painter, illustrator. Townscapes.

John Edwin Jackson studied at the National Academy of Design in New York and the New York Art Students League. He was a member of the Salmagundi Club. He painted various districts of New York.

JACKSON, John Richardson
British, 19th century.
Born 1819, in Portsmouth; died 1877, in Southsea.
Engraver (aquatint/mezzotint).

John Richardson Jackson was the son of a Portsea banker. He trained under Robert Graves. Initially working with a burin, he successfully turned to mezzotint engraving. His work continued in the traditions set by his 18th and 19th century predecessors. A specialist in portraiture, he produced many works which were not put on the open market. These include his *Queen Victoria* after Fowler, *The Princess Royal and her Sisters* after Winterhalter, *The Duke of Edinburgh* and *The Marquis of Lansdowne* after F.R. Saye, *William Howley, Archbishop of Canterbury* after Mrs Carpenter, *John Bird Summer, Archbishop of Canterbury* also after Mrs Carpenter, *Marcus Gervais Beresford, Archbishop of Armagh*, *Archbishop Trench*, *The Duke of Buccleuch*, *The Marquis of Londonderry*, *The Earl of Radnor*, *Chancellor Hatlerby*, and *Samuel Wilberforce, Bishop of Winchester*, all after G. Richmond, *Sir Andrew Faerbairn* after G.F. Watts, and *Robert Graves* after R.W. Buss. He also engraved genre scenes and landscapes after Edward Landseer and F.D. Hardy.

JACKSON, Lesley
American, 19th - 20th century.
Born 1866, in Rochester (Minnesota); died 1958.
Painter, watercolourist, engraver.

Lesley Jackson was a student at the Art Students League in New York and a pupil of Henry B. Snell. She was active in Washington. She was a member of the American Federation of the Arts. She won the second Corcoran prize at the Watercolors Exhibition in 1905. She specialised in watercolours and engraving.

JACKSON, M.P.B.
British, 19th century.
Active in London.
Painter. Figures.

M.P.B. Jackson exhibited at the Royal Academy in London, at the Royal Institution and in Suffolk Street from 1850 to 1857.

JACKSON, Mason
British, 19th century.
Born 25 May 1819, in Ovingham (Northumberland); died 28 December 1903, in London.
Active in London.
Engraver (wood).

Mason Jackson made engravings for the *Illustrated London News* around 1839.

JACKSON, Mel
20th century.
Installation artist. Multimedia.

Mel Jackson showed work at the 1994 exhibition *Escale, Stopover, Tussenstop* at the Museum of Modern Art in Villeneuve d'Ascq.

JACKSON, Michael
British, 18th century.
Active in London.
Engraver (mezzotint).

Michael Jackson is not mentioned in biographies. In 1753 he engraved a *Portrait of Spranger Barry in the role of Warbith* after James Gwinn.

JACKSON, of Battersea. See **JACKSON John Baptist**

JACKSON, Oliver Lee
American, 20th century.
Born 1935, in St Louis.
Painter, watercolourist, sculptor (wood/marble), draughtsman, collage artist, print artist (including drypoint). Monuments.

Oliver Lee Jackson studied at Illinois Wesleyan University, Bloomington, and the University of Iowa from where he graduated with a master's degree in fine arts in 1963. During the 1960s and 1970s, he worked with the Black Artists Group (BAG), a multidisciplinary artists' group founded in 1968 to promote African-American artists in St Louis and to foster exchanges with the city's black community. He settled in California in 1971, and taught at California State University, Sacramento, from 1971 until he retired in 2003.

To serve his philosophy of an art totally integrated in the flux and transformations of the universe, Oliver Jackson uses thick impasto in luminous colours, with figures appearing out of the mesh the colours form. These deformed 'paint people', as he calls them, thus obey the movements of the paint, creating an impression of organic movement. They are not representations of people but figures that emerge from, and live in, the paint itself. His canvases are often very large, because of the need he sees for 'an expanding environment that is open enough for the figures to breathe and move in'. Similarly, he places letters of different sizes on his canvases that spell out variations and anagrams of his name, as well as recurring symbols, each with its own meaning for the artist, such as the hat (a virility symbol) or the circle (magic); all of these signs give his work its own autonomous existence and prevent it from being read as a narrative. His sculptures are powerful, incised volumes from which fragments of figures emerge. He has executed a number of monumental sculptures, including a marble for the Federal Building in Oakland.

Jackson has taken part in many group exhibitions, including in 1971, at the Oakland Museum, Oakland and the 1983, Biennale Exhibition of the Whitney Museum of Art, New York. He has had a number of solo exhibitions, including in 1964 at the Downstairs Gallery, St Louis; 1975, with Carlos Gutierrez-Solana, Museum of Modern Art, San Francisco; 1982, Seattle Art Museum and in 2002, with Marty Ehrlich, Fogg Art Museum, Harvard University, Cambridge.

BIBLIOGRAPHY:
Albright, Thomas/Butterfield, Jan, *Oliver Jackson*, exhibition catalogue, Seattle Art Museum, Seattle, 1978 (including an interview). Hackett, Regina, *Oliver Lee Jackson*, exhibition catalogue, Southeastern Center for Contemporary Art, Winston-Salem (NC), 1980. Jan, Alfred, '*Oliver Jackson*' in *Flash Art*, periodical, New York, December 1985 - January 1986. Lewis, Samella, *African-American Art and Artists*, University of California Press, Berkeley, 1990.

MUSEUMS AND GALLERIES:
SAN FRANCISCO (FAM): *Intaglio Drypoint I* (1985); *Intaglio Drypoint II* (1985); *Intaglio Drypoint III* (1985) - SAN JOSE: *Untitled* (1985).

JACKSON, Philip
British, 20th century.
Born 1944, of Scottish origin.
Sculptor. Groups, busts, low reliefs.

Philip Jackson has produced numerous private and public commissions in England, Dubai, Abu Dhabi and Jerusalem. His manner, which is technically accomplished, often takes its inspiration from the masters of the Italian Renaissance and from a 19th-century form of classicism. His low relief for Waltham Abbey is a faithful transcription of the Bayeux Tapestry.

JACKSON, Richard
American, 20th century.
Born 1939, in Sacramento (California).
Active since 1979 in Germany.
Painter (mixed media).

Richard Jackson studied in Sacramento and moved to Berlin in 1979. His early paintings tend towards the geometrical, very rigid but delicate in expression, using a scheme of line accompanied by subtle colours. He moved on to become preoccupied with performative applications of paint. Two concurrent exhibitions in New York in 2005 showed life-size decoy bears adapted.to spew paint.

He has taken part in group exhibitions and held solo shows in 1979 at the Galerie Maeght in Zurich; 1980 Galerie Maeght in Paris; 1981 Betsy Rosenfield Gallery in Chicago; 1983 Daniel Veinberg Gallery in San Francsico; 1984 Rosamund Felsen Gallery in Los Angeles; 1987 Robert Else Gallery, California State University and 1989 Galerie Tschudi in Switzerland.

JACKSON, Robert
British.
Engraver (wood/mezzotint).

Robert Jackson engraved mezzotint portraits and a wood engraving of Algernon Sidney.

JACKSON, Robert
British, 19th century.
Active in London.
Sculptor.

Robert Jackson exhibited frequently at the Royal Academy between 1850 and 1878.

JACKSON, Samuel
British, 19th century.
Born 1794, in Bristol; died December 1869, in Clifton.
Painter, watercolourist. Landscapes.

Samuel Jackson worked in his father's commercial enterprise in Bristol before travelling, for his health, to Scotland, Ireland and the West Indies. He developed such an interest in art that he became a student of Danby's and then dedicated himself to painting.

He began exhibiting in London in 1823. He became friends with Prout and Pine and, in 1832, was named an associate of the Society of Painters in Watercolours. In 1853, the two watercolour paintings which he presented at the Royal Academy were met with acclaim.

Samuel Jackson was one of the first artists to seek subject matter in the picturesque Welsh landscape. In 1848, he left the group of watercolour artists he had, up until then, been associated with. He was over 60 years of age when he made a long trip to Switzerland, memories of which were later translated into some of his best appreciated works. They marked the highpoint of his poetic interpretation of nature. Jackson is considered one of the best English watercolourists.

Museums and Galleries:
Bristol (City Mus. & AG): *View of the Avon at Hotwells* (c. 1825, oil on canvas) - London (Victoria and Albert Mus.): four watercolours.

Auction records:
London, 15 July 1976, *Mountain Landscape* (watercolour heightened with gouache, 22 1/4 x 33 ins / 56.5 x 84 cm) GBP 420. London, 14 June 1977, *City above a River* (1848, oil on canvas, 24 x 39 1/4 ins / 61 x 100 cm) GBP 700. London, 20 June 1978, *The Avon Gorge, Bristol* (watercolour and pencil, 8 3/4 x 12 1/2 ins / 22.3 x 31.5 cm) GBP 1,100. London, 13 March 1980, *River through a Wood* (watercolour heightened with gouache, 8 1/4 x 11 1/2 ins / 21 x 29 cm) GBP 460. London, 7 July 1982, *Fishermen in their boat on a River* (oil on canvas, 17 1/4 x 23 1/4 ins / 44 x 59 cm) GBP 1,400. London, 29 March 1983, *Loading up a Coach on a Stormy Evening, South Devon* (watercolour, 13 1/2 x 19 1/4 ins / 34 x 49 cm) GBP 4,000. London, 119 Nov 1985, *Putch Lake on the Island of Trinidad* (watercolour heightened with white, 6 1/2 x 9 1/2 ins / 16.2 x 24.2 cm) GBP 3,800. York, 12 Nov 1991, *Fisherman beside a Mountain Stream* (watercolour, 9 x 12 3/4 ins / 22 x 32.5 cm) GBP 1,540. London, 15 July 1999, *Caernarvon Castle* (watercolour heightened with gouache and scratching out, 11 x 9 ins / 27 x 23 cm) GBP 1,700. London, 30 Nov 2000, *Clift House on the Avon near Cumberland Basin* (watercolour over pencil heightened with gouache, 6 x 9 ins / 15 x 24 cm) GBP 4,800. Knowle, 10 Jan 2001, *Stoke Cottage, near Bristol* (c. 1826, oil on panel, 10 x 15 ins / 25 x 38 cm) GBP 2,250. London, 21 Nov 2001, *Salmon Fisherman, Probably on River Dee* (pencil, watercolour and scratching out, 8 x 11 ins / 21 x 29 cm) GBP 1,800. Godalming, 27 Nov 2002, *Happy Valley* (watercolour, 7 x 10 ins / 19 x 25 cm) GBP 1,800. London, 12 June 2003, *St Augustine's Parade, Bristol* (c. 1825, watercolour, 6 x 9 ins / 16 x 23 cm) GBP 4,300. London, 20 Nov 2003, *Porth-yr-Ogof, Ystradfellte, Vale of Neath, South Wales* (pencil, watercolour and scratching out, 11 x 15 ins / 29 x 39 cm) GBP 2,800. London, 9 March 2004, *Avon Gorge from Clifton Down, Looking Towards the Severn Estuary* (watercolour, 8 x 12 ins / 21 x 30 cm) GBP 1,300. Zurich, 26 March 2004, *View of the Eiger, Mönch and Jungfrau* (watercolour, 14 x 20 ins / 35 x 51 cm) CHF 10,000.

JACKSON, Samuel Philips
British, 19th century.
Born 4 September 1830, in Bristol; died 27 January 1904.
Painter, watercolourist. Landscapes with figures, landscapes, seascapes.

Samuel Philips Jackson was the son of Samuel Jackson. He exhibited at the Royal Academy, at the British Institution and the Society of Painters in Watercolours. Of the latter, he was elected associate in 1853 and member in 1876.

Museums and Galleries:
Bristol: *The Cornwall Coast* - Bristol (City Mus. & AG): *The Steam Packet 'Propeller'* - London (Victoria and Albert Mus.): *Morning in Cornwall; Port of Plymouth; Shipwreck; The Thames at Wargrave; Midday.*

Auction records:
London, 24 May 1910, *Shipwreck* (1851) GBP 9. London, 20 June 1978, *Fishing boats in an estuary at dusk* (1853, watercolour heightened with white, 9 3/4 x 14 1/2 ins / 25 x 37 cm) GBP 1,200. London, 30 March 1982, *On the West Coast* (1857, oil on canvas, 22 3/4 x 38 ins / 58 x 96.5 cm) GBP 1,500. London, 18 March 1986, *Emmerdale Water, Cumberland, at Evening* (1858, watercolour heightened with white, 25 1/2 x 39 1/4 ins / 64.5 x 100 cm) GBP 4,000. London, 25 Jan 1988, *Children Fishing beside a Mill* (watercolour, 9 x 12 1/4 ins / 22 x 31 cm) GBP 550; *On the Coast* (1851, oil on canvas, 12 x 16 ins / 30.5 x 40.5 cm) GBP 2,090. London, 25 Jan 1989, *People drawing in a boat in a river landscape* (watercolour and gouache, 11 1/2 x 20 3/4 ins / 29 x 53 cm) GBP 1,100; *Barge waiting by a lock* (1880, watercolour, 15 1/4 x 26 1/2 ins / 39 x 67.5 cm) GBP 2,530. London, 25-26 April 1990, *Kyance Cove in Cornwall* (watercolour, 15 1/4 x 28 1/2 ins / 38.5 x 72.5 cm) GBP 935. London, 8 Feb 1991, *A tributary of the Thames* (watercolour heightened with white, 8 x 13 1/2 ins / 20.3 x 34.4 cm) GBP 1,650. London, 6 Nov 1996, *Mont Saint-Michel* (oil on canvas, 20 x 30 1/4 ins / 51 x 77 cm) GBP 4,830. London, 9 Nov 1999, *Kynance Cove, Cornwall* (1870, pencil and watercolour heightened with white and scratching out, 17 x 25 ins / 42 x 64 cm) GBP 2,800. London, 2 Dec 1999, *View of the Port of Spain, Trinidad. View of Village by the Sea, Trinidad* (one watercolour, one pencil heightened with gouache, a pair, 11 x 24 ins / 28 x 62 cm) GBP 3,800. London, 13 Jan 2000, *Lantern Hill, Ilfracombe* (1852, oil on canvas, 9 x 13 ins / 23 x 33 cm) GBP 3,800. London, 29 Nov 2000, *Mumbles, Swansea Bay* (watercolour over pencil heightened with gouache, 9 x 13 ins / 23 x 34 cm) GBP 2,600. Salisbury, 25 April 2001, *Figures on a Beach with Shipping Beyond* (1857, watercolour, 15 x 26 ins / 38 x 67 cm) GBP 3,200. Taunton, 26 April 2001, *Sands at Ebb Tide, Possibly on the North Devon Coast* (1861, watercolour heightened with white, 15 x 27 ins / 39 x 68 cm) GBP 3,200. Godalming, 6 Feb 2002, *Clovelly Pier, North Devon* (1860, watercolour, 19 x 28 ins / 49 x 71 cm) GBP 3,000. Exeter, 26 Feb 2002, *Coastal Views* (1882, watercolour, a pair, 5 x 9 ins / 12 x 22 cm) GBP 1,050. London, 22 Jan 2003, *St Pierre Port, Guernsey* (watercolour and gouache, 4 x 6 ins / 9 x 15 cm) GBP 2,200. London, 22 Jan 2003, *Entrance to Dartmouth Harbour* (watercolour and gouache, 4 x 6 ins / 9 x 15 cm) GBP 2,300.

JACKSON, Thomas Graham (Sir)
British, 19th - 20th century.
Born 1835, in London; died 1924, in London.
Active in London.
Painter, architect. Genre scenes.

Thomas Graham Jackson who was a leading architect in his day, became an associate of the Royal Academy in 1892 and a member in 1896.

JACKSON, W.
British, 19th century.
Active in London.
Sculptor.

W. Jackson exhibited at the Royal Academy from 1848 to 1854.

JACKSON, William
British, 18th century.
Active in Liverpool.
Painter, miniaturist. Portraits, seascapes.

William Jackson showed his works at the Liverpool exhibition in 1774, 1784 and 1787.

Auction records:
Paris, 11 March 1925, *The Lovers*, FRF 165.

JACKSON, William
British, 18th century.
Born 1730, in Exeter; died 12 July 1803.
Painter, musician, art writer.

William Jackson was the son of a shopkeeper. He was dedicated to music and became well known as a music teacher. He is of interest to the art world because of his close friendship with Gainsborough about whom he wrote a small book.

He made pleasing landscapes and remarkable copies of his friend's works, more than one of which has been attributed to Gainsborough himself.

JACKSON, William (Mrs)
British, 18th century.
Active in Exeter.
Painter. Landscapes.

Mrs William Jackson was the wife of the distinguished amateur painter William Jackson. She exhibited at the Royal Academy in 1771. As her family was friendly with the great English painter, Gainsborough, it is likely that she received guidance from him.

JACKSON, William H. (Captain)
American, 19th century.
Born 15 August 1832, in Watertown (Massachusetts); died 1914.
Active in Boston (Massachusetts).
Painter.

William H. Jackson was educated in Boston while working with Grundmann, Enneking, Juglaris, Du Bois and Dr Rimmer. He specialised in religious subjects.

JACKSON-CURNOCK, James.
See **CURNOCK James Jackson**

JACKSON-RIBEIRO, Fernando
Brazilian, 20th century.
Born 1928, in Teixeira.
Sculptor.

Fernando Jackson Ribeiro was self-taught and worked in various professions before devoting himself to sculpture and painting in 1958. In 1961 he began combining ready-made mechanical elements with rough or lightly polished stone. He went on to produce contemporary totem poles using girders, rails and giant nuts assembled and soldered in simple forms. His sculptures convey a sense of monumental power.

He has exhibited at the modern art exhibition in Rio de Janeiro in 1959, 1960 and 1961. He has also taken part in various Biennale exhibitions: São Paulo (1961), and Venice (1962) and Paris (1963).

JACNO, Marcel
French, 20th century.
Engraver, graphic designer.

Marcel Jacno is best known for his production as a graphic designer, especially of posters. He is also a designer of typographical characters, and created the fonts for the Théâtre National Populaire. However, his best-known drawing is probably that for the packaging of *Gauloises* cigarettes. He also makes woodcuts and engravings.

JACOB
French, 16th century.
Active in Orléans c. 1528.
Miniaturist.

JACOB
French, 16th century.
Active in Lorraine during the 16th century.
Sculptor.

In 1531, Jacob produced sculpted coats of arms for the entrance to the main staircase at the Château de Gondreville.

JACOB
French, 18th century.
Active in Paris.
Sculptor.

Jacob was a student of the Académie. In 1793, he exhibited a model at the Salon: *Plan for a Monument Acknowledging the Supreme Being and Liberty*.

JACOB
French, 19th century.
Born in Lyons; died 26 September 1836.
Draughtsman, engraver (etching).

JACOB. See also **JACOBUS, JACOPO, JACQUES** and **JAKOB**

JACOB, Alexandre
French, 20th century.
Born 14 August 1876, in Paris; died 1972.
Painter, draughtsman. Landscapes, waterscapes, still-lifes.

Jacob was a pupil of Eugène Claude. He was noted for his effects evoking the light of dawn and dusk. From 1899, he exhibited in Paris at the Salon des Artistes Français, of which he became a member in 1902. He received an honourable mention in 1908, a gold medal *hors concours* in 1914 and a gold medal at the Exposition Internationale in 1937. He exhibited there until 1950. He also showed at the Salon d'Hiver, the Salon des Aquarellistes, as well as in private galleries.

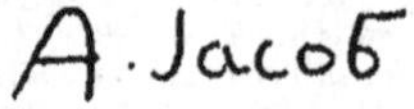

MUSEUMS AND GALLERIES:
FOUGÈRES - PARIS (MAM) - ST-QUENTIN - TROYES (Mus. d'Art, d'Archéologie et de Sciences Naturelles).

AUCTION RECORDS:
PARIS, 16 May 1924, *The Seine at Asnières and the Ile de la Jatte*, FRF 110. LONDON, 3 Oct 1979, *Thatched Cottage on the Bank of a River* (oil board, 11½ x 14½ ins / 29 x 37 cm) GBp 750. NEW YORK, 12 June 1991, *Mist on the Bogs* (oil on canvas, 32 x 25½ ins / 81.3 x 64.8 cm) USD 3,575. PARIS, 26 Feb 1992, *Farmyard in Pleaux (Cantal)* (oil on card, 12¾ x 16 ins / 32.5 x 40.5 cm) FRF 3,800. PARIS, 5 Nov 1993, *Misty Mornings on the Marne* (oil on card, 7 x 11¾ ins / 18 x 30 cm) FRF 6,000. PARIS, 19 Nov 1993, *Landscape with River and a Mill* (oil on canvas, 18 x 22 ins / 46 x 55 cm) FRF 4,000. PARIS, 17 June 1994, *Still-life with Fruit and a Copper Jug* (oil on canvas, 23½ x 29¼ ins / 60 x 74 cm) FRF 5,000. LONDON, 22 Nov 1996, *River Landscape at Dusk* (oil on canvas, 45 x 57 ins / 114.3 x 144.8 cm) GBP 1,265. BILLINGSHURST, 1 Feb 2000, *Amiens, Hautois River* (oil on board, 11 x 9 ins / 29 x 24 cm) GBP 2,200. BILLINGSHURST, 1 Feb 2000, *Winter Sun* (oil on canvas, 25 x 31 ins / 63 x 79 cm) GBP 8,500. OXFORD, 15 March 2001, *Snow on the Marshes near Amiens* (oil on panel, 11 x 10 ins / 29 x 26 cm) GBP 1,600. LONDON, 7 Feb 2002, *Woodcutters at the Bend in the River* (oil on canvas, 25 x 21 ins / 63 x 53 cm) GBP 2,800. EXETER, 15 Oct 2002, *Wildfowler* (oil on canvas, arched top, 58 x 65 ins / 148 x 165 cm) GBP 10,000. LONDON, 20 May 2003, *Sunlight on the Snow* (oil on board, 14 x 11 ins / 35 x 27 cm) GBP 4,600. CRANBROOK, 14 Dec 2003, *Farmer and Work-horses Entering Farm on Old Stone Bridge over River Marne* (oil on canvas, 21 x 21 ins / 53 x 53 cm) GBP 6,600. LONDON, 25 March 2004, *Fisherman* (oil on canvas, 11 x 12 ins / 28 x 30 cm) GBP 3,400. TORONTO, 14 June 2004, *Snow in the Ourcq Valley* (oil on canvas, 20 x 22 ins / 51 x 56 cm) CAD 18,000.

JACOB, Alexis
French, 18th century.
Active in Paris.
Painter.

Alexis Jacob was recorded as being godfather to a daughter of the painter Desacquespée on 4 December 1730.

JACOB, Alice (Mme)
French, 19th century.
Active in Paris.
Painter.

Alice Jacob was a member of the Société des Artistes Français, in whose exhibition she featured.

JACOB, Anatole
French, 19th century.
Born 19th century, in Troyes.
Sculptor.

Anatole Jacob worked with Jouffroy, and his busts appeared at the Salon de Paris from 1875.

JACOB, August
German, 19th century.
Born 28 February 1834, in Polle (Weser).
Painter, watercolourist. Landscapes, architectural views.

Jacob worked in Munich from 1855.

MUSEUMS AND GALLERIES:
MUNICH (Stadtmus., Maillinger Collection): seven watercolours with views of Munich and its environs, Bavaria and Venice.

JACOB, Charles
French, 20th century.
Born 24 October 1897, in Sedan.
Sculptor.

Jacob was a sculptor who used the direct cutting method and is known for his statues of saints. He was taught by Henri Charlier, the sculptor of religious ornaments. He showed in Paris at the Salon d'Automne and the Salon d'Art Religieux.

JACOB, Claude Antoine
French, 19th century.
Born c. 1780, in Lyons; died 26 September 1836, in Lyons.
Painter.

Claude Antoine Jacob painted landscapes, some of which were displayed at the Lyons exhibitions of 1822, 1826 and 1827. Of particular merit is *Landscape, Imitation of Constable* (1826). Jacob did etchings in the style of drawings or pictures, a noteworthy example being *View of the Entrance of the Balme Cave*.

JACOB, Cyprien Max, or Jacob, Max, pseudonym as an art critic: Léon David
French, 20th century.
Born 11 July 1876, in Quimper; died 5 March 1944, in Drancy, in the concentration camp.
Painter (gouache), watercolourist, pastellist, draughtsman, illustrator. Genre scenes, landscapes, urban landscapes.

Max Jacob made a living from writing reviews for the *Gazette des Beaux-Arts* and painting theatre decorations. He also produced works depicting Parisian cultural life in pastel and gouache, often capturing his friends in Cubist and Modernist circles. His first poems were published by the art dealer Daniel-Henry Kahnweiler and illustrated by Picasso. Jacob also illustrated his own writings and completed 40 drawings for the poetry collection *Visions des souffrances et de la mort de Jésus, fils de Dieu* (Paris, 1928). He signed a contract with the Galerie Georges Petit in Paris, lasting from 1927 to 1931. During the World War II he was arrested by the Germans because of his Jewish origins and he died in the camp at Drancy. In the French version of the Bénézit, the critic André Salmon (1889-1969) wrote the following appreciation of Jacob as an artist:

'Max Jacob's first exhibition took place before 1914, in a gallery on the Boulevard de Clichy in Paris. Later, Henri Lapauze helped him to success by organising an exhibition at the Grand Palais, which I had the honour of introducing. When he arrived in Paris from Brittany in 1894, Jacob was first a critic on the old *Gazette des Beaux-Arts* (*Fine Arts Gazette*), using the pseudonym of Léon David. At the same time, he did a little painting in oil. A self-portrait remains from this period. Later, he gave up art criticism. In 1901, he saw the first exhibition of Picasso at Ambroise Vollard's gallery. It is quite curious that the revelation of Modern art for him coincided with the arrival of the very young Picasso in Paris.... In order to help Picasso, Jacob consented to the most subordinate tasks. He devoted his nights to poetry, after evening parties dedicated to the arts. He could be spotted in the uppermost balconies in small theatres, capturing, under the footlights, the scenes that he could transform into magic. Max Jacob was thus a highly cultivated Sunday painter. His blunders were at once angelic and acutely intellectual. They corresponded to those feelings which, one day, would lead him to absolute 'mysticity' or mysticism. He painted theatre scenes before devoting himself to gouache and pastel compositions, illustrating the daily meditations of one who has been converted. He multiplied the facets of Paris and the Bois de Boulogne, with its miserable outskirts. He lived at that time from what he earned from his books, receiving payment from devotees seeking volumes of the poet illustrated by the painter. The first works of art by this fascinating man conjure up a Constantin Guys, who would have prayed in the crypt of the Sacré-Coeur. In his last years, he painted nothing that didn't seem to have been guided by the hand of his guardian angel. Max owed it to his unique painting talent to pursue his poetic work and to prolong his life as a penitent, up until the day when, on 24 February 1944, the German police dragged from his prayers the man known as 'the penitent of St-Benoît-sur-Loire'. He was interned in Orléans, and transferred on 28 February to Drancy, where he died of pneumonia on 5 March. Through the initiative of the curatorship of the Louvre, a Max Jacob room was opened in 1950, in the Musée de Quimper, in the town where he was born.'

An exhibition, *Max Jacob et Picasso* (*Max Jacob and Picasso*) was presented at the Musée Picasso in Paris in 1994-1995.

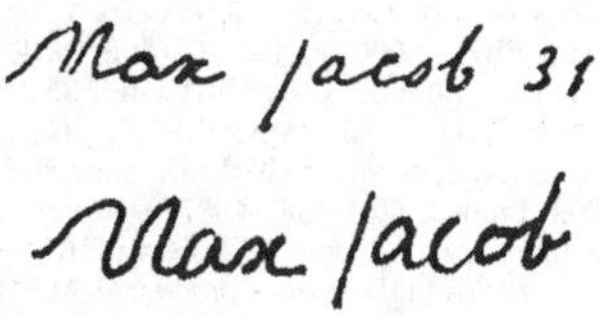

BIBLIOGRAPHY:
Jacob, Max, *Saint Matorel*, Kahnweiler, Paris, 1911. Jacob, Max, *Les Œuvres burlesques et mystiques de frère Matorel mort au couvent*, H. Kahnweiler, Paris, 1912. Jacob, Max, *Le Siège de Jérusalem; grande tentation céleste de Saint Matorel*, Henry Kahnweiler, Paris, 1914. Jacob, Max, *La Couronne de Vulcain: conte breton*, Galerie Simon, Paris, 1923. Jacob, Max, *Chemin de croix infernal*, Éditions GLM, Paris, 1936. Jacob, Max, *Drawings and Poems*, Lotus Press, Leeds, 1951. *Max Jacob: correspondance*, Editions de Paris, Paris, 1953. Palacio, J. de (ed.), '*Max Jacob*' in *Les Revues des lettres modernes, 474/478*, Ed. J. de Palacio, Paris, 1973-1981. *Max Jacob: dessins*, Shakespear & Company, Paris, 1978. Pleynet, M., *Max Jacob: Dessins*, Paris, 1978. Andreu, P., *Vie et mort de Max Jacob*, Paris, 1982. Lachgar, L., *Max Jacob*, Henri Veyrier, St-Ouen, 1984. *Max Jacob et les artistes de son temps*, exhibition catalogue, Musée des Beaux-Arts, Orléans, 1989. *Max Jacob, L'archange foudroyé*, exhibition catalogue, Museé Beaux-Arts, Orléans, 1994. *Max Jacob et Picasso*, exhibition catalogue, Museé des Beaux-Arts, Museé Picasso, Quimper, Paris, 1994. *Max Jacob: correspondance, 1917-1944*, Ripon, Paris, 2000.

MUSEUMS AND GALLERIES:
ORLÉANS (MBA): the graphic oeuvre of Max Jacob - QUIMPER (MBA): *Médrano, Acrobat and Dancer* (1909); *Old Quarter of Paris* (c. 1930-1940); *Figures of Saints* (c. 1930-1940); *Feast in Quimper* (1925).

Auction records:
Paris, 4 May 1923, *Bretons by the Seaside* (gouache) FRF 230. Paris, 2 March 1925, *Evening Gala* (gouache) FRF 1,820. Paris, 4 March 1926, *The Procession in Brittany* (watercolour) FRF 4,000. Paris, 26 Feb 1927, *Ravignan Street* (gouache) FRF 1,280. Paris, 27 Feb 1928, *Japanese Theatre* (gouache) FRF 2,000. Paris, 10 Nov 1928, *The Conjurer* (gouache) FRF 1,500. Paris, 21 May 1930, *The Circus Rehearsal*, FRF 880. Paris, 27-28 Oct 1933, *Official Funeral Procession in Quimper* (gouache) FRF 450. Paris, 10 Nov 1933, *Boating Promenade* (watercolour and gouache over pen outline) FRF 270. Paris, 30 April 1941, *Portrait of the Author* (drawing) FRF 490. Paris, 11 May 1942, *Village Street* (gouache) FRF 1,640. Paris, 11 June 1942, *Actress on Stage* (1909, gouache) FRF 950. Paris, 6 May 1943, *Place du Théâtre-Français* (watercolour and gouache) FRF 4,000. Paris, 15 June 1945, *Landscape with Old Bridge* (watercolour and gouache) FRF 2,200. Paris, Oct 1945-July 1946, *On Stage, Théâtre Montmartre* (gouache) FRF 5,500. Paris, 27 Nov 1946, *The Boats* (watercolour and gouache) FRF 7,300. Paris, 28 April 1947, *Roxane's Balcony, Scene from Cyrano de Bergerac*, FRF 7,300. Paris, 28 Nov 1949, *La Pointe du Vert Galant* (watercolour) FRF 50,000. Paris, 12 April 1954, *On Stage*; *Bathers* (two gouaches) FRF 40,000. Paris, 24 Feb 1960, *Promenade in the Wood* (gouache) FRF 1,100. Paris, 9 Dec 1969, *Breton Peasants on the Quay* (gouache) FRF 8,000. Paris, 19 Nov 1971, *Paris, Rue Ravignan* (gouache) FRF 5,800. Paris, 18 June 1973, *The Seine and the Quai des Grands-Augustins* (gouache) FRF 8,000. Versailles, 28 March 1976, *Les voiles blanches* (gouache, 6½ x 10¾ ins / 16.5 x 27.5 cm) FRF 3,800. Paris, 22 Feb 1980, *Eden* (oil on card, 8¼ x 20 ins / 21 x 51 cm) FRF 5,000. Versailles, 30 Nov 1980, *Paris, the Louvre and the Pont-Royal*. Paris, 23 May 1981, *Hackney Cabs* (1920, Indian ink, heightened with watercolour, 10¼ x 13½ ins / 26 x 34 cm) FRF 8,000. Paris, 14 May 1984, *Christ on Calvary* (oil on card, 14½ x 21¼ ins / 37 x 54 cm) FRF 14,000. Paris, 19 June 1984, *Sunday in Pont-Croix* (1919, gouache, 13¾ x 10¼ ins / 35 x 26 cm) FRF 24,000. New York, 25 April 1985, *Boxers* (1919, gouache/mounted paper/card, 10 x 13¼ ins / 25.5 x 33.6 cm) USD 2,500. Paris, 30 Nov 1987, *Breton Procession* (gouache/paper, 12¼ x 15 ins / 31 x 38 cm) FRF 23,000. Paris, 13 Dec 1987, *Promenade on Horseback, Avenue du Bois* (1918, 12¾ x 16 ins / 32.5 x 40.5 cm) FRF 40,000. Paris, 22 March 1988, *Nijinsky as a Marionnette in 'Petrouchka'*; *The Parade* (two watercolours, 9 x 11 ins / 22 x 28 cm and 5¼ x 8¾ ins/13.5 x 22.5 cm) FRF 15,000. Paris, 6 May 1988, *Portrait of Jean Cocteau* (1941, drawing, 11¾ x 9 ins / 30 x 23 cm) FRF 4,000. Paris, 12 June 1988, *The Fair* (1930, gouache, 16½ x 22 ins / 42 x 56 cm) FRF 8,500. Paris, 14 June 1988, *Ballet* (gouache, 9 x 13½ ins / 23 x 34 cm) FRF 15,000. Paris, 14 Dec 1988, *Notre Dame* (watercolour, 24 x 18 ins / 61 x 46 cm) FRF 14,000. New York, 3 May 1989, *Theatre Stage* (gouache/paper, 14 x 11¼ ins / 35.6 x 28.6 cm) USD 16,650. Paris, 18 May 1989, *Place de l'Église* (*Church Square*) (oil on canvas, 13 x 18 ins / 33 x 46 cm) FRF 26,000. Versailles, 29 Oct 1989, *Notre Dame* (gouache/card, 17½ x 14¼ ins / 44.5 x 36.5 cm) FRF 16,500. New York, 21 Feb 1990, *The Harnessing* (oil on card, 12½ x 16¼ ins / 31.8 x 41.3 cm) USD 8,250. Paris, 23 May 1990, *Outskirts of Rennes* (oil on card, 13 x 16¼ ins / 33 x 41 cm) FRF 19,000. New York, 13 Feb 1991, *Notre-Dame de Paris* (1932, ink/paper/card, 11½ x 15 ins / 28.9 x 38 cm) USD 1,430. Paris, 23 Oct 1992, *The Resurrection of Christ* (1928, pen, 10¼ x 13 ins / 26 x 33 cm) FRF 4,200. Paris, 29 March 1993, *Landscape* (1920, gouache/paper, 24 x 18 ins / 61 x 46 cm) FRF 35,000. Paris, 30 Nov 1994, *Breton Port* (gouache, 12¼ x 15¼ ins / 31 x 39 cm) FRF 14,000. Paris, 30 Jan 1995, *'Les Orientales', Nijinsky* (gouache, 8¼ x 5 ins / 21 x 13 cm) FRF 45,000. New York, 14 June 1995, *View from a Box at the Opéra* (1931, gouache/paper/card, 18½ ins / 47 cm, 2¼ x 24¾ ins/6 x 62.9 cm) USD 1,725. Paris, 27 March 1996, *He Has No Monocle, But It Is Felt, Self-portrait* (Indian ink, 9¼ x 7½ ins / 23.5 x 19 cm) FRF 9,000. Paris, 12 Dec 1996, *Paris, a Pond in the Parc Monceau* (gouache, 11 x 13¾ ins / 27 x 35 cm) FRF 6,800. Calais, 15 Dec 1996, *Paris, the Seine and Notre Dame* (1932, gouache, 11 x 14½ ins / 28 x 37 cm) FRF 9,000. Paris, 20 Nov 1997, *The Rooftops of Paris* (gouache, 9¾ x 13¼ ins / 25 x 33.5 cm) FRF 9,100. Paris, 24 March 1999, *The Seine in Paris* (1927, gouache, 12 x 19 ins / 31 x 47 cm) FRF 24,500. Paris, 21 June 1999, *Douarmenez Market* (1919, Indian ink and crayon heightened with gouache, 11 x 14 ins / 27 x 35 cm) FRF 40,000. Geneva, 13 Nov 2000, *Cubist Landscape* (1914, watercolour and Indian ink, 7 x 11 ins / 18 x 27 cm) CHF 8,500. Paris, 4 Dec 2000, *Church of Etienne du Mont* (gouache, 18 x 13 ins / 45 x 32 cm) FRF 19,000. Paris, 2 April 2001, *The Studio* (watercolour, 13 x 10 ins / 33 x 25 cm) FRF 24,000. Paris, 14 Dec 2001, *People Walking near the Place Dauphine* (1931, gouache, 17 x 21 ins / 42 x 53 cm) FRF 24,000. Paris, 17 May 2002, *Portrait of Vaslav Nijinsky* (graphite heightened with watercolour, 9 x 6 ins / 22 x 14 cm) EUR 10,000. Paris, 24 Nov 2002, *Market Scene* (1919, gouache, 11 x 14 ins / 27 x 35 cm) EUR 4,200. Brest, 11 May 2003, *The Old Bridge at Quimperle* (1927, gouache, 12 x 15 ins / 30 x 38 cm) EUR 2,100. Paris, 21 Oct 2003, *Theatrical Characters* (1917, gouache, 6 x 7 ins / 16 x 18 cm) EUR 2,800. Paris, 9 June 2004, *Orpheus and the Pelicans* (watercolour, 8 x 8 ins / 20 x 20 cm) EUR 3,200.

JACOB, d'Ancona. See **ANCONA Jacob d'**

JACOB, da Carpi. See **CARPI Jacob da**

JACOB, Denis Philippe Abraham Isaac
French, 19th century.
Born 14 June 1788, in Orléans; died 3 March 1855, in Orléans.
Draughtsman.

This artist was at one time the curator of the museum in his native town which houses one of his drawings. He exhibited genre subjects and still-lifes at the Paris Salon in 1841 and 1842, gaining a third-class medal in 1842.

Museums and Galleries:
Orléans: *View of the Port of Olivet* (pencil).

JACOB, Harro
German, 20th century.
Born 1939, in Hanover.
Sculptor.

In 1971 Harro Jacob was invited to the Biennale de Paris. Using stone, but more often polyester, he creates a morbid world. He works in a very precise, even realist, style. While the distortions he exploits can be linked to realism, above all he creates a sense of uneasiness.

JACOB, Isaak. See **JACOB Julius the Elder**

JACOB, J.P.
French, 19th century.
Painter. Still-lifes.

J.P. Jacob exhibited still-lifes at the Paris Salon in 1831 and 1833.

JACOB, Johann Wilhelm
German, 19th century.
Born 15 January 1779, in Meissen (Saxony-Anhalt).
Painter (porcelain).

Johann Wilhelm Jacob worked at the Meissen porcelain works as a painter of figurines. Works by him include a dinner plate with a *Portrait of a Blind Man* after Bigg and a plate with the *Grace*, after Teniers.

JACOB, Julius, the Younger, or Julius Jacob II
German, 19th - 20th century.
Born 26 October 1842, in Berlin; died 1929.
Painter. Portraits, landscapes.

Julius Jacob the Younger attended the art academy in Berlin. Having worked as a theatre painter, he became a landscape painter in 1870. He taught at the Technische Hochshule in Berlin. In 1881 Jacob won a medal in Berlin, and he also received an honourable mention at the 1900 Exposition Universelle in Paris. He was probably related to Julius Jacob the Elder.

MUSEUMS AND GALLERIES:

BERLIN: *The Old Cemetery; Louise; Banks of the Schöneberger.*

AUCTION RECORDS:

BERLIN, 3 July 1969, *Barge,* DEM 4,700. LONDON, 16 March 1994, *View of Rocca Sinibalda in Italy* (1876, oil on canvas, 59¼ x 39¼ ins / 150.5 x 100 cm) GBP 11,500.

JACOB, Julius, real first name Isaak, the Elder

German, 19th century.

Born 25 April 1811, in Berlin; died 20 October 1882, in Berlin.

Painter. History painting, genre scenes, portraits.

Several biographers give 1884 as the date of Julius Jacob the Elder's death, but the above date is that given by Boettichen. His training was prolonged - under Wach, at the academy in Düsseldorf, under Delaroche in Paris (he exhibited at the Salon in Paris from 1838 to 1844), continuing in Lyons and Rouen. To polish off his studies, he toured Europe, Africa and Asia Minor. He returned from his trips with over 1,200 sketches of landscapes and 300 heads copied from the masters. Medals came his way in Paris, Lyons and Rouen. In 1844, he went to London, remaining there for 11 years and charging a good price for his portraits. During this time, he exhibited at the Royal Academy (1845-1854). Around 1856, he moved to Vienna and had just as much success there. Notable personalities sat for him, including Princes Metternich, Schwarzenberg and Kinsky. He worked with such speed that he could turn out 36 portraits a year. In 1866, war prompted him to abandon Vienna for Berlin, where he remained for the rest of his life. He proved as diligent an exhibitor at the Berlin academy as previously in Paris and London.

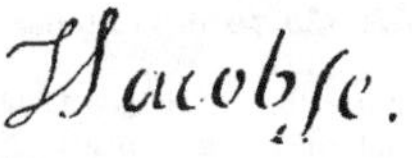

JACOB, Louis

French, 18th century.

Born 1712 or 1696, in Lisieux (Calvados).

Engraver (burin).

Louis Jacob moved to Paris whilst still very young, and was a pupil of Gérard Scotin the Younger, then of Jean Audran. He engraved several plates in the Crozat Collection, after Paolo Caliari. Hutin also commissioned him to reproduce *The Wedding Feast at Cana,* by the same master, for *The Dresden Gallery* collection. It is probable that the date 1696 suggested for his birth is nearer the truth than 1712, because his works include two engravings after François Boucher: *St Matthew* and *St Thomas,* published by Jeanrot and dated 1726.

JACOB, Marguerite Jean, Mme Bazin

French, 19th - 20th century.

Born 5 October 1867, in Paris.

Engraver.

Jacob was married to Louis Bazin. A pupil of her father, she engraved in wood. In Paris, she showed at the Salon des Artistes Français. She received an honourable mention in 1886 and in 1889 at the Exposition Universelle. She won a third-class medal in 1890, a second-class medal in 1891, a silver medal at the Exposition Universelle in 1900 and a first-class medal in 1901. Declared *hors concours* at the Salon des Artistes Français, she became a member of the jury.

JACOB, Max. See **JACOB Cyprien Max**

JACOB, Nicolas Henri (Mme). See **HUBLIER Charlotte**

JACOB, Nicolas Henri

French, 19th century.

Born 6 June 1782, in Paris; died 1871.

Painter, draughtsman, lithographer.

Nicolas Jacob was a pupil of David, Dupasquier and Morgan. His career began at the Paris Salon in 1802. In 1805, he was appointed official artist to Prince Eugène de Beauharnais, and accompanied him to Italy. Among his best works is *The Parade of the Viceroy Surrounded by his Staff,* painted in Milan in 1809. When he returned to Paris, he was appointed professor of drawing at the veterinary school of Alfort. In 1835, he opened a design school. He was decorated in 1838. His lithographs include *Marriage of Napoleon and Marie-Louise* (1853), portraits, notably *Prince Eugène, Senefelder, Mademoiselle Mars,* and various documentary plates. His work was exhibited at the Salon until 1865.

AUCTION RECORDS:

PARIS, 16 May 1924, *Bust of a Man; Portrait of a Woman Viewed from the Front* (two pencil) FRF 240. MUNICH, 17 May 2001, *Lithograph Genius* (chalk lithograph, 7 x 6 ins / 19 x 16 cm) DEM 10,000.

JACOB, Pierre. See **TAL-COAT**

JACOB, Roger

Belgian, 20th century.

Born 1924, in Arlon; died 1975, in Forêt-Trooz.

Sculptor.

Roger Jacob attended the Académie des Beaux-Arts in Brussels.

JACOB, Rudolf

German, 20th century.

Born 10 March 1888, in Kassel.

Painter, engraver.

Rudolf Jacob attended the art academy in Kassel and mainly devoted himself to colour etching.

MUSEUMS AND GALLERIES:

KASSEL: *The High Road in Kassel.*

JACOB, Stephen

French, 19th century.

Born 20 May 1846, in Baigneux (Côte-d'Or).

Painter. Portraits, genre scenes, landscapes.

Stephen Jacob was a pupil of Isidore Pils, Ange Tesser and Léon Bonnat at the École des Beaux-Arts in Paris. His work appeared at the Salon in Paris from 1868, at the salon of the Société des Artistes Français from 1883, and in Brussels in 1910. He obtained an honourable mention in 1889 and a bronze medal in 1900 for contributions to the Expositions Universelles in Paris.

He liked to draw genre scenes from the second half of the nineteenth century, which he brought to life with colourful detail. His works include: *Light-Hearted Song, Grape Picking* and *Return of the Gardener.*

AUCTION RECORDS:

NEW YORK, 29 June 1983, *Girl in Front of a Mirror* (oil on panel, 26 x 17¾in/66 x 45cm) USD 1,500. PARIS, 21 Oct 1987, *Concert of Young Musicians* (oil on canvas, 45¼ x 58¼in/115 x 148cm) FRF 52,000. PARIS, 23 Nov 2001, *Meeting* (oil on canvas, 22 x 16 ins / 55 x 40 cm) FRF 30,000.

JACOB, van Amsterdam. See **CORNELISZ Van Oostsanen Jacob**

JACOB, van Campen. See **CAMPEN Jacob van**

JACOB, van Utrecht. See **CLAESSENS Jacobus**

JACOB, von Nimburg. See **JAKOB von Olmütz**

JACOB, von Nimburg. See **JAKOB von Kuttenberg**

JACOB, Walter Friedrich Richard
German, 20th century.
Born 21 October 1893, in Altenburg; died 1964, in Hindelang.
Painter, draughtsman, illustrator, lithographer. History painting, nudes, portraits, landscapes, still-lifes (flowers), animals.

Walter Friedrich Richard Jacob attended the art academy in Dresden. He illustrated with five original lithographs *The Good Fight*, poems by Alfred Wolfenstein.

MUSEUMS AND GALLERIES:

DRESDEN (Prints Collection) - DRESDEN (Stadtmus.): 17 works.

AUCTION RECORDS:

MUNICH, 1 Dec 1980, *Self-portrait* (1921, oil on canvas, 35 x 24 1/2 ins / 89 x 62.5 cm) DEM 4,000. COLOGNE, 27 June 1986, *Still-life* (1924, oil on canvas, 35 x 29 1/2 ins / 88 x 75 cm) DEM 6,000. MUNICH, 26 May 1992, *Snowy, Wooded Mountain Landscape with Chalet* (1923, oil on canvas, 27 1/2 x 33 ins / 70 x 84 cm) DEM 23,000. MUNICH, 1-2 Dec 1992, *Church Garden* (1921, woodcut, 21 1/2 x 17 1/4 ins / 54.5 x 44 cm) DEM 1,380. BERLIN, 31 May 2003, *Self-portrait as Smoker* (1920, oil on canvas, 31 x 25 ins / 80 x 64 cm) EUR 92,000. COLOGNE, 26 Nov 2003, *Agg - Landscape* (1927, oil on canvas, 28 x 38 ins / 71 x 96 cm) EUR 8,500. MUNICH, 14 May 2004, *Lower Mountain Landscape with Farmsteads* (oil on canvas, 25 x 35 ins / 63 x 89 cm) EUR 6,300. BERLIN, 12 June 2004, *Cemetery in Eberbach* (1920, oil on canvas, 28 x 29 ins / 70 x 74 cm) EUR 27,000.

JACOB, Wendy
American, 20th - 21st century.
Born 1958, in Rochester (New York).
Installation artist.
Neo-Conceptual Art.

Wendy Jacob studied first at Yale, from 1986, and later at the Carnegie Mellon University, Pittsburgh. Her work has featured in a number of group exhibitions, notably in the USA, but also in France (1993, Galerie Jennfier Flay, Paris; *Surfaces For Projections*, Centre d'Art Contemporain La Synagogue, Delme). She has also held solo exhibitions, notably at the Andrea Rosen Gallery, New York.

MUSEUMS AND GALLERIES:

ANGOULÊME (FRAC Poitou-Charentes): *Wall* (1994, assemblage).

JACOB DE BEELDESNYDER
Dutch, 15th century.
Active in Haarlem.
Sculptor.

According to Schrevelius, Jacob sculpted the preacher's pulpit at the Groote Kerk in Haarlem in 1432.

JACOB VAN HAARLEM, also known as Master Janszen van Haarlem, or Janszen Jacob
Dutch, 15th - 16th century.
Died probably after 1509.
Painter.

According to van Mander, Jacob was the master of works in Mostaert, and produced an altarpiece, dated 1474, for a church in Haarlem. He is believed to have still been active in 1509.

JACOB VON STRASSBURG
School of Alsace, 15th - 16th century.
Born in Strasbourg.
Engraver (wood).

Jacob spent time in Venice where he produced the following works: *Triumph of Julius Caesar*, a collection of 12 engravings dated 1503; and 16 engraved plates depicting *Charles V Entering Bologna on an Official Visit*, dated 1530. He also made between 16 and 18 woodcuts of *The Life of Christ*, some of which are signed *Opus Jacobi*. According to Papillon, he produced an engraving that was part of a series of allegorical plates on the theme of the story of Rome.

JACOB-BAZIN. See **JACOB Marguerite Jeanne**

JACOB-DESMALTER, Georges Alphonse
French, 19th century.
Born 1799, in Paris; died 1870, in Paris.
Architect, painter.

From 1838 to 1866, Georges Jacob-Desmalter exhibited watercolours depicting views and factories.

JACOB-HIANS, Paul
French, 20th century.
Born 1 April 1884, in Paris; died 14 January 1967, in La Garde-Freinet (Var).
Painter, illustrator, caricaturist. Figures, portraits, landscapes. Stage sets, wall decorations.

Jacob-Hians studied at the École Estienne in Paris. He knew the Perret brothers and Picasso. He was also a close friend of Manguin. Between 1917 and 1919, he belonged to the troupe of Jacques Copeau and Louis Jouvet, creating sets for their tour in the USA. Around 1925, he painted one of the columns in the café La Coupole at Montparnasse. He divided his time between Paris and the Midi region.

JACOB-JACOBS. See **JACOBS Jakob Albrecht Michael**

JACOB-KOSSAREWSKY, Germaine
French, 19th century.
Painter.

This artist was a member of the Société des Artistes Français from 1890, in whose exhibition she featured.

JACOB-PETIT. See **PETIT Jacob**

JACOBBER, Moïse, or Jakob Ber
German, 19th century.
Born 1786, in the Rhineland; died 17 July 1863, in Paris.
Active then naturalised in France.
Painter, watercolourist. Flowers.

A pupil of Gerardus van Spaendonck, Jacobber participated in numerous French exhibitions. He was mainly a painter of flowers, and worked for the Sèvres porcelain business.

BIBLIOGRAPHY:

Les Années romantiques, la peinture française de 1815 à 1850, exhibition catalogue, Musée des Beaux-Arts, Nantes, Galeries nationales du Grand Palais, Paris, 1996.

MUSEUMS AND GALLERIES:

FONTAINEBLEAU (Mus. National du Château): *Flowers* - LYONS: *Flowers in a Vase*.

AUCTION RECORDS:

PARIS, 1887, *Flowers and Fruit*, FRF 2,850. PARIS, 19 Nov 1919, *Flowers and Fruit*, FRF 2,000. PARIS, 27 Dec 1927, *Vase of Flowers*, FRF 3,000. PARIS, 22 June 1951, *Flowers*, FRF 81,000. PARIS, 2 March 1955, *Basket of Flowers and Fruit on an Entablature*, FRF 520,000. NEW YORK, 26 Oct 1990, *Study of Pears* (watercolour/paper, 4 1/4 x 5 1/2 ins / 10.8 x 14 cm) USD 1,320. LONDON, 8 Dec 1993, *Still-life of Fruit and Flowers* (1846, oil on panel, 30 x 23 ins / 76.5 x 58.6 cm) GBP 9,775. NEW YORK, 19 May 1994, *Still-life of Flowers in an Alabaster Vase with Pineapples and a Basket of Fruit and Maize on an Entablature* (oil on canvas, 46 3/4 x 35 1/2 ins / 118.7 x 90.2 cm) USD 145,500. NEW YORK, 23 May 1997, *A Hyacinth, Poppies, a Dahlia and Other Flowers with Peaches, White and Black Grapes, a Melon and a Pineapple, All on an Entablature of Stone with Butterflies in Flight and a Wooded Landscape in the Background* (oil on canvas, 39½ x 32 ins / 100.3 x 81.3 cm) USD 51,750.

JACOBÉ, Johann
German, 18th century.
Born 1733, in Vienna; died 1797, in Vienna.
Painter, engraver (burin/mezzotint).

Initially, Jacobé trained as a painter, but then took up engraving under the direction of Schmutzer. In 1779 he went to London to finish his training, and during his time there he produced a number of engravings from Sir Joshua Reynolds and George Romney. On his return to Vienna, he produced further highly regarded engravings, notably *A Portrait of the Princess of Württemberg* (1783), *The academy of fine arts in Vienna* (Portraits of Artists, 1790), *Stag Hunting by Moonlight*, after Casanova, and *A Tiger Killed by the Prince of Nassau-Siegen* after Casanova (1797).

JACOBELLO, da Messina. See **JACOBELLO d'Antonello degli Antoni**

JACOBELLO, del Fiore. See **FIORE Jacobello del**

JACOBELLO D'ANTONELLO DEGLI ANTONI
Italian, 15th century.
Active in Messina c. 1479-1482.
Painter.

Some writers attribute to him the *Annunciation* of the Palazzo Acreide that was for a long time considered to be by his father, Antonello da Messina.

JACOBELLO DI BONOMO
Italian, 14th century.
Painter. Religious subjects.

The only painting known for certain to be his is a polyptych of 1385 now in the possession of the municipality of S Arcangelo, near Cesena. A polyptych in the church of S Maria a Mare, Torre di Palme, is attributed to him. He seems, with Paolo and Lorenzo Veneziano, to have been one of the most important Venetian painters in the period 1370-1390.

AUCTION RECORDS:
LONDON, 13 Dec 1996, *Christ Entombed, with a Dominican Monk* (tempera/panel with gilt ground, 9¼ x 7¼in/23.8 x 18.2cm) GBP 28,750.

JACOBELLUS, de Masignis. See **MASEGNE Jacobello dalle**

JACOBI. See also **JACOBY** and **JACOBSZ**

JACOBI, A.
Dutch, 19th century.
Engraver (etching). Rustic scenes.

The Amsterdam engravings collection has three small plates by A. Jacobi.

MUSEUMS AND GALLERIES:
AMSTERDAM (Rijksprentenkabinet): *Cattle in the Meadow* (after P. Potter); floor after Wouwerman; floor after Bouchez.

JACOBI, Abraham. See **JACOBSZ**

JACOBI, Armin
German, 19th century.
Born 26 April 1844, in Schwabach.
Painter, illustrator. Landscapes.

Armin Jacobi trained at the academy in Munich.

JACOBI, Bernardino. See **BUTINONE Bernardino**

JACOBI, Christian Gottfried
German, 18th - 19th century.
Born c. 1764; died 23 January 1845, in Görlitz.
Active in Görlitz.
Painter.

MUSEUMS AND GALLERIES:
GÖRLITZ (Städtische Kunstsammlungen): *View of Postplatz in Görlitz* (1806).

JACOBI, Eduard
German, 19th century.
Active in Berlin.
Painter. Genre scenes.

Eduard Jacobi exhibited in Berlin from 1864.

JACOBI, Jacques
Swiss, 20th century.
Born 3 November 1877, in Geneva.
Painter, draughtsman, designer, fresco artist.
Landscapes.

Jacques Jacobi attended the École des Beaux-Arts and the École des Arts Industriels in Geneva. He also studied in Brussels, Schaerbeek and Paris in the studio of Fernand Cormon. In 1900 he made his début at the Salon des Champs-Élysées and then worked in Liège as a draughtsman and designer. From 1909 he exhibited landscapes at the Switzerland, Paris and Brussels Expositions. Jacobi produced frescoes for chapels, castles and private houses in Switzerland, France and Belgium.

JACOBI, Johann Heinrich
German, 19th century.
Born 30 September 1803, in Hamburg; died 30 December 1859, in Hornheim, near Kiel.
Painter, miniaturist, lithographer.

Johann Heinrich Jacobi trained at the academy in Berlin and under Delaroche in Paris before settling in Hamburg, where he painted oil portraits, miniatures on ivory and genre scenes and drew portraits. He also produced lithographed portraits.

JACOBI, Marcus
Swiss, 20th century.
Born 20 August 1891, in Biel (Bern); died 1969, in Merlingen.
Painter, engraver.

Marcus Jacobi studied under H. Knirr in Munich and settled in Merlingen on Lake Thun. His works include *Morning Ride; Twilight; Holy Family; Betrayal; Solitary Ride; The Marne near Joinville-le-Pont* and portraits, including those of his parents. In 1924, he published six original etchings inspired by Lake Thun and the surrounding region.

AUCTION RECORDS:
BERN, 3 May 1979, *View of Lake Thun, in Spring* (1926, oil on canvas, 27½ x 35½ ins / 70 x 90 cm) CHF 4,300. BERN, 30 April 1988, *Niesen Mountain* (oil on canvas, 43¼ x 39 ins / 110 x 99 cm) CHF 3,800. BERN, 26 Oct 1988, *March Landscape* (oil on canvas, 30 x 28¼ ins / 76 x 72 cm) CHF 2,000. BERN, 7 May 1999, *Early Spring landscape* (oil on canvas, 32 x 44 ins / 81 x 111 cm) CHF 3,300. BERN, 11 May 2000, *Still-life of Flowers* (1942, oil on canvas, 34 x 30 ins / 87 x 76 cm) CHF 2,600. BOSTON, 14 July 2001, *Village of Shoreham, Kent. Dittisham on the Dart, Devon* (oil on canvas, a pair, 14 x 10 ins / 36 x 25 cm) USD 1,500. BERN, 13 May 2004, *Lake Thun in Autumn* (1935, oil on canvas, 30 x 36 ins / 75 x 92 cm) CHF 2,800.

JACOBI, Otto Reinhard or Reinhold
German, 19th century.
Born 1812 or 1814, in Königsberg (now Kaliningrad, Russia); died c. 1901.
Painter, engraver. Landscapes.

Otto Reinhard Jacobi trained at the academy in Düsseldorf from 1833 to 1837. After working in Wiesbaden, he set off for America in 1863.

MUSEUMS AND GALLERIES:
BERLIN: *Winter Landscape* - KALININGRAD: *View of Lake Geneva* - MONTREAL: *The Splügen Pass.*
AUCTION RECORDS:
TORONTO, 14 May 1979, *The Water Mill* (1862, oil on canvas, 26 1/4 x 36 1/4 ins / 66.5 x 92 cm) CAD 4,400. TORONTO, 26 May 1981, *The Waterfall* (1866, oil on canvas, 26 1/2 x 23 ins / 67.5 x 57.5 cm) CAD 9,000. MONTREAL, 1 May 1989, *Forest Landscape with Refuges and Mountains* (1872, watercolour, 14 1/4 x 19 1/4 ins / 36 x 49 cm) CAD 1,000. TORONTO, 12 June 1989, *Mountain Landscape with Vast Forests* (1863, oil on canvas, 17 1/2 x 15 ins / 44.5 x 38.1 cm) CAD 1,150. MONTREAL, 21 June 1994, *View of a Bend in the River* (oil on panel, 9 x 15 1/4 ins / 22.8 x 38.6 cm) CAD 1,500. TORONTO, 22 Feb 1999, *Children by River Rapids* (1850, oil on canvas, 26 x 36 ins / 66 x 91 cm) CAD 2,500. ERLANGEN, 27 Nov 1999, *Indian Boy before Canadian City* (pastel, 22 x 18 ins / 57 x 46 cm) DEM 3,300. HEIDELBERG, 14 April 2000, *Chapel by Wood* (1836, oil on canvas, 19 x 30 ins / 47 x 75 cm) DEM 11,500. TORONTO, 24 May 2000, *Sunrise. Sunset* (1877, oil on canvas, a pair, 43 x 30 ins / 110 x 76 cm) CAD 9,000. MONTREAL, 26 Feb 2001, *Couple by a Lake* (oil on canvas, 24 x 41 ins / 61 x 104 cm) CAD 3,000. TORONTO, 18 Nov 2003, *St Anne River, Quebec* (1872, oil on canvas, 29 x 41 ins / 74 x 104 cm) CAD 6,000. TORONTO, 18 Nov 2003, *Indian Encampment* (1854, oil on canvas, 26 x 41 ins / 66 x 104 cm) CAD 17,000.

JACOBI, Peter
Romanian, 20th century.
Born 1935, in Ploiesti.
Active in Germany from 1968.
Hand-weaver, sculptor, photographer.

Peter Jacobi graduated at the N. Grigorescu Institute of Fine Arts in Bucharest in 1961. That same year he met his future wife who later became known in the world of tapestry design as Ritzi Jacobi. Together they created their first three-dimensional tapestries in 1967 and their first 'textile object' in 1968, the year they left Romania for West Germany.

There are three aspects to Peter Jacobi's work: tapestry, sculpture and photography. In the area of tapestry, he worked closely with his wife Ritzi. In 1971, the two artists began to introduce drawings on rice paper into their creations which also included coconut fibre, goat's hair or horsehair. Their large tapestries include *Transylvania* (1972-1977) and *Romanica* (1978-1980). In 1975, Peter Jacobi began to turn increasingly to sculpture, an art form that he conceived more as an assemblage and a reflection of ideas and meanings, than as the creation of volumes in space. From this period his work was influenced by conceptualism.

Peter and Ritzi Jacobi have taken part in many collective exhibitions in the USA, Australia and Great Britain as well as the Venice Biennale (1970) and the São Paulo Biennale (1973). Solo exhibitions include: Städtisches Museum, Regensburg (1970); Detroit Institute of Art (1981); Chicago Museum of Contemporary Art (1981); Musée d'Art Moderne de la Ville de Paris (1984). They were awarded the Arte Communication Prize at the São Paulo Biennale and the Lewis-Tiffany Foundation Prize, New York (1974).

BIBLIOGRAPHY:
Jianou, Ionel/Carp, Gabriela/Covrig, Ana Maria/Scantéyé, Lionel, *Romanian Artists and the West*, American Romanian Academy of Arts and Sciences, Los Angeles, 1986.
MUSEUMS AND GALLERIES:
HAMBURG (Mus. für Kunst und Gewerbe) - KYOTO (National Mus. of Modern Art) - LAUSANNE (Centre international de la tapisserie ancienne et moderne) - PARIS (MAM) - PERTH (AG of Western Australia) - ROME (Gal. Nazionale d'Arte Moderna) - SYDNEY (MCA) - VIENNA (Mus. Moderner Kunst Stiftung Ludwig).

JACOBI, Ritzi
Romanian, 20th century.
Born 1943, in Bucharest.
Active since in Germany from 1968.
Sculptor.
Neo-Pop Art.

Ritzi Jacobi lives in Frankfurt am Main in Germany with her husband, Peter Jacobi. In 1973, she took part in the Paris Biennale.

JACOBI, Rudolf
German, 20th century.
Born 11 December 1889, in Mulhouse.
Painter, watercolourist. Nudes, portraits, landscapes, urban landscapes.

Rudolf Jacobi attended the art academy in Berlin. He exhibited landscapes and town views at the Grosse Berliner Ausstellung der Künste (Great Berlin Arts Exhibition). In 1912 and 1914, he exhibited at the Glaspalast in Munich. In addition, Jacobi painted portraits and nudes. His works include *Odalisque; Mediterranean Storm; Olive Trees in front of the Chiesa Nuova; Reclining Woman.*
AUCTION RECORDS:
MUNICH, 29 June 1983, *Landscape* (1924, watercolour, 21 1/4 x 26 1/2 ins / 54 x 67 cm) DEM 5,000. AMSTERDAM, 19 Sept 1989, *Village in Winter* (1914, oil on canvas, 32 x 39 1/2 ins / 81 x 100.5 cm) NLG 4,830.

JACOBI, Wilhelm
German, 19th century.
Born 6 December 1863, in Neubrandenburg.
Sculptor.

Wilhem Jacobi trained at the academy in Berlin. Among his works are the monument to *Lambert Steinwich* in Stralsund, reliefs and statues on the pulpit of St Clement's church in Berlin, a plaster *Eve*, a bronze statuette called *Reverie*, bronzes called *Flirting* and *Fivestone Players*, and a marble *Wild Rose*.

JACOBIDÈS. See **JAKOBIDES Georg**

JACOBINO
Italian, 15th century.
Painter.
Lombard School.

Jacobino was active in Brescia or Milan at the beginning of the 15th century and may be identical with Enrico da Milano; in which case he was the son of Jacobino da Papazzoni.

JACOBINO, de Papazzoni. See **PAPAZZONI Jacobino de**

JACOBINUS DA VELATE, or Jacopino da Vaulate
Italian, 15th century.
Painter. History painting.

In the choir of the church of S Maria, Selva, near Locarno, there is a *Virgin and Child in a Triumphal Arch* that is signed: *hoc opus iacobinus de vaulate pinxit* (*this work was painted by Jacobus de Velate*).

JACOBINUS DE HALACRIDIS
Swiss, 16th century.
Sculptor (wood).

Works by Jacobinus are signed *Jacobinus de Halacridis ligni faber hoc manu fecit*, and are dated from 1505.

JACOBO. See also **JACOPO**

JACOBO, Fiorentino. See **DELL'INDACO Jacopo** and **JACOPO da Firenze**

JACOBO, Parisiense. See **PARISIENSE Jacobo**

JACOBO DA FABRIANO, or Jacobus
Italian, 15th century.
Miniaturist.

Jacobo da Fabriano is referred to in 1460 as the appointed painter of miniatures to Pope Pius II. Among the manuscripts he decorated are: St Augustine's *City of God*, dated 1466, a Diodorus Siculus, several works by St Augustine and Origen, and a Virgil. Also attributed to him are a Themistius, an Isocrates and a Xenophon in the national library in Vienna, and some manuscripts in the library of the Vatican.

JACOBONI, Gioanbattista
Italian, 18th century.
Born 1728.
Active in Rome and in Florence.
Draughtsman, engraver (burin).
Jacoboni was in Florence in 1760 and engraved several panels for the *Museo Fiorentino* in the style of Raphael and A. Sacchi Sebastiano Conca.

JACOBS. See **JAKOBS Paul Émil**

JACOBS. See also **JACOBSZOON, JACOPS** and **JACOBSZ**

JACOBS, Adolphe
Belgian, 19th - 20th century.
Born 1887; died 1910.
Painter. Genre scenes, landscapes.
Adolphe Jacobs exhibited in Brussels and Munich, showing *Le Hersage (Vaches au Repos)* (*Harrowing (Cows Resting)*) at the Exposition de Bruxelles in 1910.
AUCTION RECORDS:
NEW YORK, 7 May 1909, *Entrance to the Pasture,* USD 95. LONDON, 21 April 1978, *Herd Grazing* (oil on canvas, 25 1/2 x 38 ins / 64.5 x 96.5 cm) GBP 1,200. VERSAILLES, 21 Feb 1982, *Day Labourers' Lunch in the Northern Countryside* (oil on canvas, 22 x 29 3/4 ins / 56 x 75.5 cm) FRF 14,000. BRUSSELS, 17 May 1984, *Cows Grazing* (oil on canvas, 26 x 35 ins / 66 x 89 cm) BEF 70,000. NEW YORK, 28 Feb 1990, *Haymaking* (oil on canvas, 35 x 51 ins / 88.9 x 129.5 cm) USD 52,250.

JACOBS, Andy
Belgian, 20th - 21st century.
Born 1949, in Wilrijk.
Medallist.

JACOBS, Constant
Belgian, 19th century.
Sculptor.
The Plantin-Moretus museum in Antwerp has a plaster copy of a bust of the printer *Cornelis van Kiel,* which was executed by Constant Jacobs for the meeting room at Duffel town hall. He exhibited in 1880 at the *History of Belgian Art* exhibition in Brussels.

JACOBS, Daniel, or Jacobsz.
Dutch, 17th century.
Born in The Hague; died 1691, in The Hague.
Painter. Historical subjects.
Daniel Jacobs studied under Guillaume Doudyns. He travelled in Italy and France before returning to The Hague in 1665. In 1687, he was registered as a member of the guild of The Hague. He was also senior member of the guild of St Luke. According to some biographers, he only painted as an amateur.

JACOBS, Dieudonné
Belgian, 20th century.
Born 10 June 1887, in Montegnée-les-Liège; died 1967.
Painter. History painting, portraits, landscapes.
Dieudonné Jacobs studied under A. Dewitte and J. Carpentier at the Académie des Beaux-Arts in Liège.
MUSEUMS AND GALLERIES:
BRUSSELS - LIÈGE - LYONS - SPA - TOULON.

JACOBS, Edgard Pierre
Belgian, 20th century.
Born 1904; died 1986, in Brussels.
Draughtsman, illustrator. Comic strips.
Edgard Pierre Jacobs wrote the series *Blake and Mortimer,* in which *Blake,* an officer in the intelligence service, and *Mortimer* were involved in extraordinary detective adventures. As Hergé's companion, Jacobs co-founded the comic *Tintin.* Jacobs produced simple line drawings for him and paid particular attention to details.

JACOBS, Eduard
Dutch, 19th century.
Born 1859, in Amsterdam.
Sculptor.
Eduard Jacobs studied at the Brussels academy, and in 1888 was awarded the Prix de Rome in Amsterdam. In 1909, he settled in Laren, a village in the north of Holland, where he modelled and carved genre pieces of peasants including *Peasant Woman Seated* and *Young Girl from Huizer*. He was commissioned to produce the statue *Navigation* for the Peace Palace in The Hague. He is also known for his piece *Sorrow,* a kneeling female nude, and for portraits of children and group pieces. He worked mainly in wood and clay.

JACOBS, Egidius
Flemish School, 18th century.
Born in Antwerp.
Painter.
In 1784, Egidius Jacobs was a student at the Koninklijke Academie voor Schone Kunsten in Antwerp.

JACOBS, Francis
Belgian, 20th century.
Born 1944.
Painter, engraver.
Francis Jacobs studied at the art academy in Mons.

JACOBS, Gaspar Philip, or Jacobsz.
Dutch, 18th century.
Born 1732, in Amsterdam; died 1789, in Amsterdam.
Engraver (burin).
Between 1752 and 1787, Gaspar Jacobs engraved several plates showing views of Amsterdam. He was the nephew of Jan Gaspar Jacobsz.

JACOBS, Gerard
Dutch, 18th century.
Active in Ter Vere c. 1766.
Painter.

JACOBS, Gérard
Belgian, 19th - 20th century.
Born 1865, in Antwerp; died 1958, in Flushing, the Netherlands.
Painter, draughtsman. Landscapes.
Gérard Jacobs attended the Koninklijke Academie voor Schone Kunsten in Antwerp. He exhibited paintings from drawings at the Exposition de Bruxelles in 1910.
AUCTION RECORDS:
AMSTERDAM, 3 Nov 1992, *Boat on a River in a Landscape* (1904, oil on canvas, 31 x 39 ins / 78.5 x 99 cm) NLG 1,955. LOKEREN, 15 May 1993, *Boats on the River* (oil on canvas, 10 x 14 ins / 25.5 x 35.5 cm) BEF 24,000. LOKEREN, 9 Oct 1993, *Landscape with a Harvested Field and Sheaves of Wheat near a Fortified Castle* (oil on canvas, 17 3/4 x 13 3/4 ins / 45 x 35 cm) BEF 28,000. LOKEREN, 10 March 2001, *Young Girl in a Park* (1901, oil on canvas, 20 x 28 ins / 50 x 70 cm) BEF 110,000. LOKEREN, 9 March 2002, *Fishing Boats Beached on the Schelde* (oil on canvas, 25 x 35 ins / 63 x 90 cm) EUR 2,900.

JACOBS, Harold
American, 20th century.
Born 1932, in New York.
Collage artist.

Harold Jacobs has shown his work in solo exhibitions in 1964 at the Portland Art Museum, 1973 at the American Institute of Architects in Philadelphia, 1978 at the Pennsylvania Academy of the Fine Arts in Philadelphia and 1979 at the Jack Rasmussen Gallery in Washington.

JACOBS, Henri
Belgian, 19th - 20th century.
Sculptor.

Henri Jacobs exhibited at the Exposition de Bruxelles in 1910.

AUCTION RECORDS:
LONDON, 18 April 1980, *Bust of a Young Girl* (1900, bronze and alabaster, h. 16 1/2 ins / 42 cm) GBP 1,700. TOKYO, 13 Nov 2004, *Untitled, Bust of a Woman* (gilt bronze, 20 x 11 ins / 51 x 29 cm) JPY 550,000.

JACOBS, Herman
Belgian, 20th century.
Born 13 April 1936, in Deurne, near Antwerp.
Painter.

Herman Jacobs attended the Koninklijke Academie voor Schone Kunsten and the Hoger Instituut voor Schone Kunsten in Antwerp. From 1972 he has exhibited in Belgium, and particularly in Antwerp and Brussels. From imitating anatomical plates, the silhouettes in a shadowy theatre, and transfers, his painting is subtle, often cold and ambiguous. His art has a secretive quality.

AUCTION RECORDS:
LOKEREN, 20 March 1993, *In the Classroom* (oil on canvas, 10 3/4 x 9 3/4 ins / 27.5 x 25 cm) BEF 110,000. ANTWERP, 23 Oct 2000, *Woman Sewing in Interior* (1950, oil on canvas, 10 x 13 ins / 25 x 32 cm) BEF 110,000.

JACOBS, Huybrecht, or Jacobsz., called Hubertus Grimani
Dutch, 16th century.
Born c. 1562, in Delft; died 1631; buried 11 April in Delft.
Also active in Italy.
Painter. Portraits.

After studying in Holland, Jacobs travelled to Italy and spent a long period in Venice where he was a painter for nine years to the Doge Grimani and took the name of his patron. His main influence was the work of Titian. He later went back to Holland and then spent time in England before returning once again to his home country, where he died. He taught Cornelisz. van Ryck of Delft.

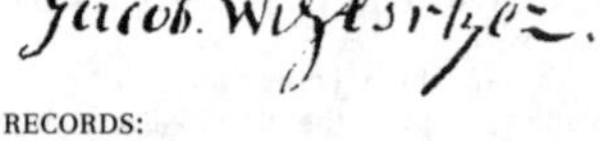

AUCTION RECORDS:
PARIS, 1 June 1901, *Portrait of a Woman.*, FRF 1,200.

JACOBS, Jakob Albrecht Michael, or Jacobsz., called Jacob Jacobs
Belgian, 19th century.
Born 19 May 1812, in Antwerp; died 9 or 10 December 1879, in Antwerp.
Painter. Historical subjects, local scenes, landscapes, seascapes.
Orientalism.

Although his family wanted him to become a printer, Jakob Jacobs pursued his passion for art. He worked in Louvain, and in 1832 became a student at the Koninklijke Academie voor Schone Kunsten in Antwerp with Ferdinand de Braekeleer. He continued his studies in Italy and Greece, and visited Russia, Scandinavia and France gathering subjects for his paintings, in particular coastal views. In 1847, he visited Germany with Wappers before returning to settle in Antwerp. He was appointed teacher of landscape art at the Koninklijke Academie voor Schone Kunsten in Antwerp in 1843 or 1849, and was made a Chevalier of the Ordre de Léopold in 1849 in recognition of his painting *Wreck of the Floridan*. In 1884, he was promoted to the rank of officer following an exhibition of his works, and was awarded medals in Brussels in 1836, 1842 and 1845.

Jakob Jacobs successfully combined the Romantic love of the Orient and historical subjects with his own genuine feeling for the sea - qualities that set him apart from the more mediocre Belgian seascape painters of the 19th century.

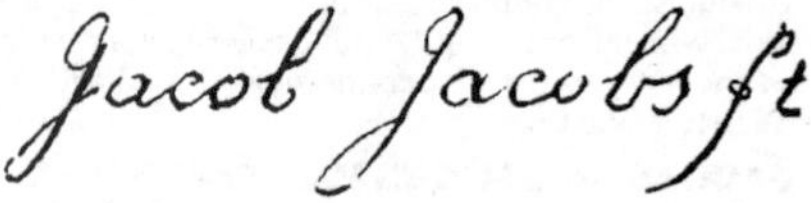

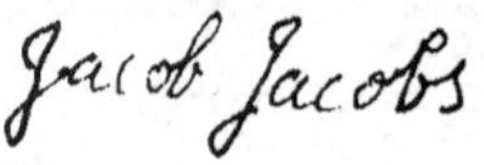

MUSEUMS AND GALLERIES:
ANTWERP: *Waterfall in Norway; Lock Gate in Étretat* - BERLIN: *Sea in Greece* - BRUSSELS: *The Sarp Falls on the River Glommen* - COURTRAI: *Waterfall in Norway* - MUNICH: *Wreck of the Floridan on the Essex Coast; In the Port of Constantinople; Sunrise in the Archipelago* - WEIMAR: *View of Cape Colonna.*

AUCTION RECORDS:
PARIS, 3 March 1902, *Storm*, FRF 100. PARIS, 12 to 15 May 1902, *Isle of Négrepont*, FRF 230. LONDON, 15 June 1960, *The Square and St Mark's Basilica, Venice*, GBP 220. MUNICH, 30 Nov 1978, *Scene in the Orient* (1856, oil on panel, 35 3/4 x 47in/91 x 118.5cm) DEM 6,500. NEW YORK, 30 June 1981, *The Bosphorus at Constantinople* (1860, oil on panel, 25 1/2 x 36 1/2in/65 x 93cm) USD 2,500. AMSTERDAM, 2 May 1990, *Camels in a Sandstorm in the Desert* (1863, oil on canvas, 16 1/2 x 23 1/4in/42 x 59cm) NLG 1,150. AMSTERDAM, 22 April 1992, *Boats Moored along the Nile near Philae with Local People* (1863, oil on panel, 32 1/2 x 46in/82.5 x 117cm) NLG 46,000. LONDON, 17 June 1994, *Ruins of the Temple of Karnak at Thebes* (1847, oil on panel, 38 1/4 x 56 1/4in/97.2 x 142.6cm) GBP 67,500. LONDON, 17 Nov 1994, *The Temple at Luxor* (1850, oil on panel, 26 3/4 x 38 1/2in/68 x 97.5cm) GBP 23,000. LONDON, 14 June 1995, *Arrival of Sultan Abdilmejid at Nusretiye with the Golden Horn in the Background* (oil on canvas, 11 x 16 1/4in/28 x 41cm) GBP 11,500. LONDON, 17 Oct 1997, *Caique on the Bosphorus* (oil on canvas, 15 x 18in/38 x 46cm) GBP 16,100. LOKEREN, 15 May 1999, *On the Bank of the Nile* (1844, oil on canvas, 24 x 30 ins / 61 x 77 cm) BEF 850,000. LONDON, 13 Oct 1999, *Shipping on the Bosphorus, overlooking Constantinople* (oil on panel, 17 x 21 ins / 44 x 54 cm) GBP 6,000. LOKEREN, 13 May 2000, *Fjord with Fishermen* (1867, oil on canvas, 32 x 46 ins / 82 x 117 cm) BEF 330,000. BRUSSELS, 19 June 2000, *Eastern Port* (1863, oil on panel, 19 x 27 ins / 49 x 69 cm) BEF 190,000. AMSTERDAM, 23 April 2001, *Sailing Vessels near the Belgian Coast* (oil on panel, 25 x 37 ins / 64 x 93 cm) NLG 15,000. PARIS, 23 April 2001, *View of the Port at Istanbul* (oil on canvas, 10 x 15 ins / 26 x 39 cm) FRF 50,000. BRUSSELS, 15 April 2002, *Caravan on the Bank of the Nile* (oil on panel, 20 x 25 ins / 51 x 63 cm) EUR 10,000. COLOGNE, 1 April 2004, *Smuggler by Racing Mountain River* (1857, oil on panel, 36 x 48 ins / 92 x 123 cm) EUR 3,000.

JACOBS, Jef
Belgian, 20th century.
Born 1905, in Mechelen.
Sculptor. Religious subjects.

Jef Jacobs studied under Tuerlinck at the Academie voor Beeldende Kunsten in Mechelen.

JACOBS, Johannes
Dutch, 20th century.
Born 15 September 1881, in Helmond.
Draughtsman.
Johannes Jacobs produced drawings and ex-libris for the magazine *Living Nature*, and sketches of the P.F. van Vlissingen textile factory in Helmond.

JACOBS, John
British, 19th century.
Active in London.
Painter. Landscapes.
John Jacobs exhibited on rare occasions at the Royal Academy, the British Institution and Suffolk Street from 1816 to 1864.

JACOBS, John Emmanuel
British, 19th century.
Born 19th century, in London.
Painter. Landscapes.
John Emmanuel Jacobs showed his work in the various London exhibitions, especially after 1878. He was a member of the Royal Society of British Artists.
MUSEUMS AND GALLERIES:
SYDNEY: *Landscape*.
AUCTION RECORDS:
LONDON, 4 Feb 1972, *River Landscape*, Gns 400.

JACOBS, Jos
Belgian, 20th - 21st century.
Born 1949, in Hasselt (Limburg).
Painter, engraver.
Jos Jacobs studied at the Koninklijke Academie voor Schone Kunsten and the Nationaal Hoger Instituut voor Schone Kunsten in Antwerp.

JACOBS, Karl
German, 19th century.
Born 28 April 1864, in Minden (Westphalia).
Active in Pasing near Munich.
Painter.
Jacobs was a student at the school of arts and crafts in Munich, and focused on decorative painting, using watercolours, oil or tempera. A published work by him is *The Decorative Painter in Modern Times*.

JACOBS, Leonebel
American, 20th century.
Born in Tacoma (Washington).
Painter. Portraits.
Leonebel Jacobs was a pupil of Brush and Hawthorne and became a member of the Pen and Brush Club and the American Federation of the Arts.

JACOBS, Lode
Belgian, 20th century.
Born 1927, in Hemiksem.
Painter.
Lode Jacobs attended the Koninklijke Academie voor Schone Kunsten and the Hoger Instituut voor Schone Kunsten in Antwerp. In 1955, he won the Prix de Rome and the Prix Verlat. From 1955-1962 he settled in Paris.
MUSEUMS AND GALLERIES:
ANTWERP.

JACOBS, Louis Adolphe
Belgian, 19th - 20th century.
Born 1855; died 1929.
Active in Brussels.
Painter. Seascapes.
Louis Adolphe Jacobs' work was featured at the Guilde de St-Luc in Mechelen, the Cercle de St-Luc in Brussels, and at the Glaspalast (Ice Palace) in Munich. He was the brother of Adolphe Jacobs.
AUCTION RECORDS:
LOKEREN, 20 May 1995, *Cove at l'Escaut, Autumn Evening* (oil on canvas, 48 1/2 x 72 1/2 ins / 123 x 184 cm) BEF 110,000. LOKEREN, 8 March 1997, *Boten op de Schelde* (*Boats on the Schelde*) (oil on panel, 10 1/2 x 14 1/4 ins / 26.5 x 36.5 cm) BEF 36,000.

JACOBS, Martin François
Flemish School, 19th century.
Died 1812.
Painter, draughtsman.
Martin Jacobs is mentioned by Nagler and Dr von Wurzbach as having worked in Brussels.

JACOBS, Michel
American, 20th century.
Born 10 September 1877, in Montreal; died 1958, in Rumson (New Jersey).
Painter, sculptor. Portraits, landscapes.
Michel Jacobs studied with Laurens in Paris. He was a member of the Salmagundi Club. He was active in Washington from 1914 to 1920, and after that in New York. He is known for his portraits of political and military figures.
AUCTION RECORDS:
MONTREAL, 18 June 1996, *Five Silver Dollars* (oil on panel, 6 1/2 x 9 ins / 16.5 x 22.8 cm) CAD 1,050. WILTON, 6 March 2000, *Snowy Brook with Trees* (oil on canvas, 12 x 16 ins / 30 x 41 cm) USD 1,600.

JACOBS, Pierre François
Flemish School, 18th century.
Born 4 October 1780, in Brussels; died 1808, in Rome.
Painter. Historical subjects.
The promising career of Pierre Jacobs was cut short by his premature death. He began his studies under A. Lens and in 1802 won a prize for drawing from nature. He went to Rome, where he was awarded a prize by the Milan academy for his painting *Theodatus Presenting the Head of Pompey to Caesar*, now in the Brussels museum. His devotion to work affected his health and he died at the early age of 28.
MUSEUMS AND GALLERIES:
BRUSSELS: *Theodatus Presenting the Head of Pompey to Caesar*.

JACOBS, Théophile
Belgian, 19th - 20th century.
Engraver.
In 1910, Théophile Jacobs exhibited at the Exposition de Bruxelles.

JACOBS, William Leroy
American, 19th - 20th century.
Born c. 1864, in Cleveland (Ohio); died 1917, in New York.
Illustrator.

JACOBSE. See **JACOBSZ**

JACOBSEN. See also **JACOBSON, JACOBSZ**

JACOBSEN, Alfred
Danish, 20th century.
Died April 1924.
Lithographer, print publisher.

JACOBSEN, Antonio Nicolo Gasparo
American (?), 19th - 20th century.
Born 1850; died 1921.
Painter. Seascapes.
Antonio Jacobsen was a painter of boats and ships.
AUCTION RECORDS:
NEW YORK, 30 Jan 1976, *The 'Helda' at Sea* (1882, oil on canvas, 12 x 20 ins / 30.5 x 51 cm) USD 1,300. NEW YORK, 18 Nov 1977, *The 'Issac Webb' at Sea* (1916, oil on card, 13 3/4 x 19 3/4 ins / 35 x 50.2 cm) USD 2,100. NEW YORK, 23 May 1979, *New York Harbour* (1884, oil on canvas, 29 x 59 ins / 73.5 x 150 cm)

USD 11,000. NEW YORK, 23 Sept 1981, *Shelter Island* (1886, oil on canvas, 22 x 36 ins / 55.9 x 91.4 cm) USD 16,500. NEW YORK, 27 Jan 1983, *Shelter Island* (1890, oil on canvas, 22 x 36 ins / 56 x 91.5 cm) USD 11,500. LONDON, 21 June 1983, *The 'Mauretania'* (1908, mixed media/card, 15 1/4 x 27 1/2 ins / 39 x 70 cm) GBP 2,400. LONDON, 5 June 1985, *The 'Grayling' Leading a Race* (1888, oil on canvas, 24 x 42 1/4 ins / 61 x 107 cm) GBP 44,000. NEW YORK, 31 Jan 1987, *The Steamer 'New York'* (1882, oil on canvas, 24 1/4 x 42 ins / 61.6 x 106.7 cm) USD 39,000. NEW YORK, 24 June 1988, *The Lifeboat* (1902, oil on canvas, 17 3/4 x 29 1/2 ins / 45 x 75 cm) USD 7,425. LONDON, 22 Sept 1988, *The 'Lusitania' at Full Steam* (1908, oil on card, 22 x 36 ins / 56 x 91.5 cm) GBP 2,750. NEW YORK, 30 Sept 1988, *The Tug 'M. Moran'* (1901, oil on canvas, 22 x 36 ins / 56 x 91.5 cm) USD 38,500. NEW YORK, 24 Jan 1989, *The Liner 'Atlanta'* (1911, oil on card, 22 x 35 ins / 55 x 88.8 cm) USD 7,700. LONDON, 31 May 1989, *The 'Greece'* (1876, oil on canvas, 22 x 36 ins / 56 x 91.5 cm) GBP 6,160. NEW YORK, 28 Sept 1989, *The Three-Master 'Great Western'* (1916, oil on card, 17 1/2 x 30 ins / 44.7 x 76.5 cm) USD 11,000. NEW YORK, 30 May 1990, *The Liner 'Olympic' guided by a Tug arriving in New York Harbour* (1914, oil on card, 20 x 36 ins / 50.8 x 91.6 cm) USD 15,950. LONDON, 30 May 1990, *The Three-Master 'Kaiser Wilhelm II'* (1889, oil on canvas, 30 x 50 ins / 76 x 127 cm) GBP 24,200. LONDON, 18 Oct 1990, *The Great Fishing Schooner 'Albertina'* (1906, oil on canvas, 22 x 36 ins / 56 x 91.5 cm) GBP 18,700. NEW YORK, 30 Nov 1990, *The 'Storm King'* (1894, oil on canvas, 22 x 36 ins / 56 x 91.5 cm) USD 14,300. AMSTERDAM, 24 April 1991, *A Tree-Master on the High Seas* (oil on canvas, 14 3/4 x 23 3/4 ins / 37.5 x 60.5 cm) NLG 9,200. LONDON, 22 May 1991, *The Steamship 'Daniel Steinmann'* (1877, oil on canvas, 22 x 35 3/4 ins / 56 x 91 cm) GBP 5, 500. LONDON, 22 Nov 1991, *The American Steamer 'City of Birmingham'* (oil on canvas, 22 x 36 ins / 55.8 x 91.4 cm) GBP 4,950. NEW YORK, 15 April 1992, *The Warship 'Dreadnought'* (1917, oil on card, 12 x 19 1/2 ins / 30.5 x 49.5 cm) USD 6,050. LONDON, 20 May 1992, *The Three-Master 'Young America'* (1916, oil on panel, 13 3/4 x 23 1/2 ins / 35 x 59.5 cm) GBP 3,520. NEW YORK, 5 June 1992, *The 'Louisiana'* (1881, oil on canvas, 21 1/2 x 35 ins / 54.6 x 88.9 cm) USD 6,600. NEW YORK, 27 May 1993, *The Three-Master 'The Amercian' leaving New York Harbour* (1884, oil on canvas, 29 x 59 ins / 73.7 x 149.9 cm) USD 43,125. LONDON, 16 July 1993, *The Steamship 'Jan Breydel'* (1882, oil on canvas, 29 1/4 x 49 ins / 74 x 124.5 cm) GBP 10,580. COPENHAGEN, 2 Feb 1994, *The Steamship 'Glenisla'* (1885, oil on canvas, 22 x 36 1/4 ins / 56 x 92 cm) DKK 21,000. NEW YORK, 21 Sept 1994, *'Gilbert M. Edgett', American Steam Tug* (1902, oil on canvas, 18 x 30 ins / 45.7 x 76.2 cm) USD 19,550. LONDON, 14 June 1995, *The Steamer 'Managua'* (1893, oil on canvas, 22 x 35 1/2 ins / 56 x 90 cm) GBP 5,750. NEW YORK, 20 March 1996, *The Pilot boat 'New Jersey'* (oil on canvas, 22 x 36 ins / 55.9 x 91.4 cm) USD 10,350. LONDON, 30 May 1996, *The Steamer 'Somerset'* (1877, oil on canvas, 22 x 36 ins / 56 x 91.5 cm) GBP 8,625. NEW YORK, 26 Sept 1996, *The Steamship 'New York'* (oil on canvas, 18 x 30 ins / 45.7 x 76.2 cm) USD 10,350; *The Paddle-Steamer 'Larchmont'* (1903, oil on canvas, 22 x 36 ins / 55.9 x 91.4 cm) USD 16,100. LONDON, 29 May 1997, *The Steamer 'Bea Bellido'* (1893, oil on canvas, 21 3/4 x 36 ins / 55.5 x 91.5 cm) GBP 7,475. NEW YORK, 16 Jan 1998, *Alaska* (oil on canvas, 30 3/4 x 51 1/4 ins / 78 x 130 cm) USD 36,800.

JACOBSEN, August
Danish, 19th century.
Born 1868, in Stavanger.
Painter. Genre scenes.

August Jacobsen won a bronze medal at the Exposition Universelle in Paris in 1900. His *Food Shop in Flekkefionel* and *Grey Weather* are at the museum in Copenhagen, and his *Dance on the Bridge* is at the museum in Oslo.

JACOBSEN, Carl Ludwig
Norwegian, 19th - 20th century.
Born 1835, in Moss; died 18 December 1923, in Christiania (now Oslo).
Sculptor.

Carl Ludwig Jacobsen was influenced by the Danish Neo-Classical sculptor Bertel Thorvaldsen. He worked for the King of Denmark.

MUSEUMS AND GALLERIES:
BERGEN: *Helberg* - COPENHAGEN: *The Minister Due; Falsen; Collett.*

JACOBSEN, Carl Ludwig
Danish, 20th century.
Born 1890, in Odense; died 1957, in Odense.
Draughtsman, illustrator.

Carl Ludwig Jacobsen was self-taught and illustrated many works published by Éditions Martin.

JACOBSEN, David Jacob
Danish, 19th century.
Born 2 July 1821, in Copenhagen; died 22 April 1871, in Florence.
Painter.

David Jacobsen was a pupil at the Kunstakademi in Copenhagen. He devoted himself almost exclusively to genre painting. Often cited is his *Patrol*, depicting a war scene in Schleswig. In 1857 he travelled to Paris, sending back to Copenhagen several genre paintings as well as a portrait of the composer *A. Hammerich*. He went to Italy for his health, and there he painted *Sleeping Savoyard* and *Card Players*.

MUSEUMS AND GALLERIES:
COPENHAGEN (Statens Mus. for Kunst): *Katten i Atelieret* (*The Cat in the Studio*) (1860); *Studie af en Siddende Pige* (*Study of a Seated Girl*); *Studie fra Pont Royal i Paris* (*Pont Royal in Paris, Sketch*) - HILLERØD: *Søren Kierkegaard* (drawing).

AUCTION RECORDS:
NEW YORK, 13 Feb 1981, *Market Scene* (1853, oil on canvas, 36 x 27 ins / 91.4 x 68.5 cm) USD 13,000. COPENHAGEN, 16 Jan 1985, *Two Italian Women with a Baby* (1846, oil on canvas, 18 x 14 1/2 ins / 46 x 37 cm) DKK 24,000. COPENHAGEN, 2 March 1999, *Woman Looking at Watercolour in French Artist's Gallery* (1864, oil on canvas, 9 x 7 ins / 24 x 19 cm) DKK 18,000. COPENHAGEN, 31 Aug 1999, *Interior of the Artist's Studio in Paris* (oil on panel, 10 x 9 ins / 26 x 22 cm) DKK 16,000. COPENHAGEN, 30 May 2000, *Outside the All Night Cafe, Paris* (oil on canvas, 13 x 10 ins / 33 x 25 cm) DKK 15,000. COPENHAGEN, 4 March 2002, *Sneak Patrol - Danish Soldiers at Dybbol during the Three Years War* (oil on canvas, 21 x 32 ins / 53 x 81 cm) DKK 21,000.

JACOBSEN, Egill
Danish, 20th century.
Born 16 December 1910, in Copenhagen.
Painter.
CoBrA Group.

In 1932 and 1933, Egill Jacobsen attended the Kongelige Danske Kunstakademi in Copenhagen. In 1933, the painter Vilhelm Bjerke-Petersen and the painter and sculptor Ejler Bille exhibited non-figurative works for the first time in Denmark. Afterwards, a journal entitled *Linier* (*Lines*) (1937) was created, which was the focal point for young Danish artists who were concerned about contemporary art forms. Also in 1937, Jacobsen painted *Ophobning* (*Accumulation*); this work is considered to mark the beginning of a new painting style, even anticipating the CoBrA movement. Influenced by fairy tales, myths and primitive art, this group encouraged spontaneous painting in order to liberate it from the norms and movements of western art. Jacobsen participated in the activities and exhibitions organised by the Linier (Lines) group, which survived during World War II and was centred around a new journal entitled *Helhesten* (*Hell Horse*), in which Jacobsen published his theoretical writings. These were the same artists who, just after the war and following the split between the Belgian and Dutch 'experimental groups' and the revolutionary Parisian Surrealist movement, would join forces with Belgian and Dutch painters to form the group CoBrA (Copenhagen-Brussels-Amsterdam: the name was formed from the first letters of the artists' hometowns), in which Egill Jacobsen would participate from 1948-1951. In 1934, Jacobsen made his first trip to Paris, where he became acquainted with Picasso's 'African period'. Between 1956 and 1958, he produced a mural for the marriage room at the town hall in Hvidovre. He was the first 'Abstract' painter to be appointed as a teacher at the Kongelige Danske Kunstakademi in Copenhagen, in 1959. Egill Jacobsen embraced wholeheartedly the experimental purpose of the CoBrA movement.

From amongst the many personalities of the flourishing Danish School Carl-Henning Pedersen is the artist with whom Egill Jacobsen showed the most affinity. They shared the same joy of painting; the paint was applied thickly and was bursting with colours; they produced masks with a full set of teeth biting the leaves of trees, and from 1935 the series known as *Masks* and *Objects*. Whatever the sources, a new form of painting appeared in Denmark, and Egill Jacobsen's painting is an essential part of this trend.

Jacobsen won prizes and distinctions, including the Eckersber medal in 1959, and the Thorvaldsen medal in 1969. In 1932, his work was featured for the first time at the autumn exhibition in Copenhagen, and subsequently at exhibitions in Denmark; then from 1945, at numerous group events: 1946, the Exposition de l'Unesco held at the Musée d'Art Moderne in Paris; 1948, 1956, the Venice Biennale; 1949, *Exposition CoBrA. La Fin et les Moyens*, the Palais des Beaux-Arts, Brussels; 1950, the Salon des Surindépendants, Paris; 1951, the CoBrA Exhibition with Dutch painter and sculptor Karel Appel (born 1921), Danish painter Mogens Balle (1921-1988), Dutch painter Cornelis van Beverloo (born 1922) and Danish painter, sculptor and writer Asger Jorn (1914-1973), held at the Galerie Pierre, Paris; 1953, the Stedelijk Museum, Amsterdam; 1953, the Palais Galliera, Paris; 1954, the Pittsburgh International; 1962, *CoBrA et Après* (*CoBrA and Beyond*) (graphic art exhibition), the Palais des Beaux-Arts, Brussels; 1963, *Visione Colore* (*Colour Visions*), the Palazzo Grassi, Venice; 1964, the Guggenheim International, New York; 1966, the CoBrA Exhibition, Boymans Van Beuningen Museum, Rotterdam; 1969, and later for a continuous period, the Galerie Ariel, Paris; 1971, the São Paulo Biennale, and others. In 1962, the Galerie Danoise held an exhibition of his works in Paris.

BIBLIOGRAPHY:

Galy-Carles, Henry, *Art danois, 1945-1973*, exhibition catalogue, Galeries nationales du Grand Palais, Paris, 1973. Hovdenakk, Per, *Egill Jacobsen*, Borgen, Oslo, 1980. Stokvis, Willemijn, *Cobra*, Gallimard, Paris, 2001.

MUSEUMS AND GALLERIES:

AALBORG (Nordjyllands Kunstmus.) - AARHUS (Kunstmus.) - COPENHAGEN (Statens Mus. for Kunst): *Pile* (1937); *Green Masks on a Green Background* (1942); *Blue Lines, Cagnes* (1947); *Catemaco I* (1971) - HUMLEBÆK (Louisiana Mus. for Moderne Kunst) - ODENSE (Fyns Kunstmus.) - PITTSBURGH (Carnegie MA): *Mask* (1947, oil on canvas) - REYKJAVIK (Listasafn Islands).

AUCTION RECORDS:

COPENHAGEN, 12 Oct 1966, *Three Green Masks*, DKK 8,600. COPENHAGEN, 28 March 1973, *Masks*, DKK 8,100. COPENHAGEN, 29 March 1974, *Figure*, DKK 30,000. COPENHAGEN, 24 Nov 1976, *Composition with Mask* (1955, oil on canvas, 28¾ x 39¼ ins / 73 x 100 cm) DKK 21,000. COPENHAGEN, 8 March 1977, *U.S.A. no. 22* (1957, oil on canvas, 39¼ x 28¾ ins / 100 x 73 cm) DKK 24,000. COPENHAGEN, 7 March 1979, *Operatic Mask* (1959, oil on canvas, 39¼ x 32 ins / 100 x 81 cm) DKK 17,500. COPENHAGEN, 27 Oct 1982, *Mask, Cagnes-sur-Mer* (1947, oil on canvas, 33½ x 27½ ins / 85 x 70 cm) DKK 31,500. LONDON, 28 June 1984, *Composition* (1947, oil on canvas, 45¼ x 35½ ins / 115 x 90 cm) GBP 4,500. COPENHAGEN, 24 Sept 1986, *Composition* (1956, oil on canvas, 51¼ x 38¼ ins / 130 x 97 cm) DKK 125,000. COPENHAGEN, 2 March 1988, *Summer* (1917, 46 x 35 ins / 116 x 89 cm) DKK 75,000. LONDON, 30 June 1988, *Untitled* (1946, oil on canvas, 25½ x 30¼ ins / 65 x 77 cm) GBP 11,000. COPENHAGEN, 8 Nov 1988, *Near the River at Pouilly in France* (1951, oil on canvas, 25½ x 20¾ ins / 65 x 53 cm) DKK 130,000. COPENHAGEN, 10 May 1989, *Green Mask* (1958, oil on canvas, 51¼ x 38¼ ins / 130 x 97 cm) DKK 200,000. AMSTERDAM, 24 May 1989, *Narrens Ridt* (1975, oil on canvas, 16¼ x 25½ ins / 41 x 65 cm) NLG 20,700. LONDON, 29 June 1989, *Operatic Mask* (1958, oil on canvas, 51½ x 38¼ ins / 130.8 x 97 cm) GBP 18,700. COPENHAGEN, 22 Nov 1989, *Dance Rhythms* (1947, oil on canvas, 46 x 59 ins / 116 x 150 cm) DKK 400,000. COPENHAGEN, 21-22 March 1990, *Yellow Mask* (1972, oil on canvas, 36½ x 25½ ins / 93 x 65 cm) DKK 90,000. COPENHAGEN, 30 May 1990, *Autumn* (1951, oil on canvas, 39¼ x 29½ ins / 100 x 75 cm) DKK 175,000. COPENHAGEN, 14-15 Nov 1990, *Masks* (1965, oil on canvas, 39¼ x 29½ ins / 100 x 75 cm) DKK 120,000. COPENHAGEN, 13-14 Feb 1991, *Composition with Masks* (1946, oil on canvas, 39¼ x 29½ ins / 100 x 75 cm) DKK 255,000. LONDON, 21 March 1991, *Composition* (1939, oil on canvas, 39¼ x 28½ ins / 100 x 72.5 cm) GBP 30,800. AMSTERDAM, 23 May 1991, *Private Eye* (1986, oil on canvas, 39¼ x 29¼ ins / 100 x 74 cm) NLG 17,250. COPENHAGEN, 29 May 1991, *Man-Bird* (1943, oil on canvas, 51¼ x 35½ ins / 130 x 90 cm) DKK 370,000. COPENHAGEN, 4 Dec 1991, *Harlequin*. AMSTERDAM, 12 Dec 1991, *Composition* (1948, oil on canvas, 31¼ x 17¼ ins / 79.5 x 44 cm) NLG 31,050. COPENHAGEN, 4 March 1992, *Cosmic Forest* (1984, oil on canvas, 39¼ x 29¼ ins / 100 x 74 cm) DKK 105,000. COPENHAGEN, 2-3 Dec 1992, *Composition* (1936, oil on canvas, 29¼ x 24 ins / 74 x 61 cm) DKK 160,000. AMSTERDAM, 9 Dec 1992, *Mask in a Blue Space* (1989, oil on canvas, 39¼ x 28¾ ins / 100 x 73 cm) NLG 20,700. COPENHAGEN, 3 June 1993, *Green Landscape with Yellow Mask* (1972, oil on canvas, 39¼ x 28¾ ins / 100 x 73 cm) DKK 85,000. COPENHAGEN, 3 Nov 1993, *Mask* (1966, oil on canvas, 18 x 25½ ins / 46 x 65 cm) DKK 52,000; *Spring* (1948, oil on canvas, 39¼ x 30 ins / 100 x 76 cm) DKK 180,000. AMSTERDAM, 8 Dec 1993, *Composition with Yellow Mask* (oil on canvas, 38½ x 31½ ins / 98 x 80 cm) NLG 23,000. COPENHAGEN, 21 Sept 1994, *Portrait of Reinhoud* (1974, oil on canvas, 36¼ x 25½ ins / 92 x 65 cm) DKK 100,000. COPENHAGEN, 7 June 1995, *Brown and Red Mask* (1969, oil on canvas, 39¼ x 29½ ins / 100 x 75 cm) DKK 110,000. COPENHAGEN, 15 March 1997, *Red Mask* (coloured lithograph) DKK 1,600. LONDON, 29 May 1997, *Untitled (on both sides)* (c. 1960, oil on canvas, 51½ x 37½ ins / 131 x 95 cm) GBP 13,800. COPENHAGEN, 22-24 Oct 1997, *Mask* (1962, oil on canvas, 27½ x 22 ins / 70 x 56 cm) DKK 46,000. COPENHAGEN, 23 March 1999, *Mask Composition* (1949, oil on canvas, 44 x 33 ins / 113 x 83 cm) DKK 410,000. COPENHAGEN, 29 Sept 1999, *Revolution's Shadow* (1975, oil on canvas, 57 x 46 ins / 146 x 116 cm) DKK 350,000. VEJLE, 7 Aug 2000, *Composition Light and Rhythms 74* (1974, oil on canvas, 35 x 46 ins / 89 x 116 cm) DKK 190,000. COPENHAGEN, 3 Oct 2000, *Mask Composition* (oil on canvas, 47 x 39 ins / 120 x 98 cm) DKK 530,000. COPENHAGEN, 2 April 2001, *Orange Market* (1960, oil on canvas, 30 x 28 ins / 75 x 70 cm) DKK 800,000. COPENHAGEN, 30 May 2001, *Mask Composition* (c. 1944, oil on canvas, 35 x 29 ins / 90 x 73 cm) DKK 248,000. COPENHAGEN, 1 Oct 2002, *Yellow Mask in Brown* (1970, oil on canvas, 45 x 57 ins / 114 x 146 cm) DKK 510,000. COPENHAGEN, 4 Dec 2002, *Dancing Mask* (1945, oil on canvas, 38 x 29 ins / 96 x 73 cm) DKK 280,000. COPENHAGEN, 26 Feb 2003, *Autumn* (oil on canvas, 44 x 33 ins / 113 x 83 cm) DKK

450,000. COPENHAGEN, 7 Oct 2003, *Masked Figure in Green* (1946, oil on canvas, 37 x 26 ins / 93 x 67 cm) DKK 400,000. COPENHAGEN, 29 March 2004, *Spring II* (1945, oil on canvas, 33 x 28 ins / 84 x 70 cm) DKK 470,000. COPENHAGEN, 5 Oct 2004, *Yellow-green Mask on Blue Background* (1970, oil on canvas, 39 x 29 ins / 100 x 73 cm) DKK 160,000.

JACOBSEN, Flora Josepha Christiane
Danish, 19th century.
Born 17 June 1863, in Frederikssund.
Sculptor.

Flora Jacobsen was a pupil at the Kunstakademi in Copenhagen. Among her works are a *Funerary Monument for Mrs J. Blicher Clausen* at the Søllerød cemetery, *Children Eating*, and a *Bust of Professor J. A. Krygell*. She showed her works from 1906 to 1920.

JACOBSEN, Georg
Danish, 20th century.
Born 17 September 1887, in Copenhagen.
Painter, architect.

Georg Jacobsen exhibited regularly in Paris at the Salon d'Automne and the Salon des Tuileries.

MUSEUMS AND GALLERIES:
COPENHAGEN - OSLO.

JACOBSEN, Jes
Danish, 19th century.
Born 6 April 1862, in Apenrade; died 12 July 1886, in Apenrade.
Active in Apenrade.
Painter.

Jes Jacobsen was a pupil at the Kunstakademi in Copenhagen from 1881 to 1884. He exhibited portraits and genre paintings, such as *Forge*, in Copenhagen.

JACOBSEN, Juriaen, or Jacobsz
German, 17th century.
Born c. 1625, in Hamburg; died 1685.
Painter. Mythological subjects, animals.

Jacobsen went to Antwerp while still very young, becoming the pupil of Frans Snyders there. Subsequently, he established himself in Amsterdam, where the skills he had learnt from his master brought him great success. He appears to have travelled widely, particularly in Switzerland.

His dates are a matter of dispute, and alternatives of 1610 and 1630 have been given for his birth and of 1664 and 1685 for his death. The dates given above are those most commonly adopted.

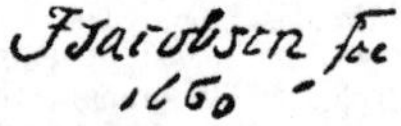

MUSEUMS AND GALLERIES:
CHAMBÉRY (MBA): *Hunting Scene* - COPENHAGEN: *Wild Boar Hunt* - DRESDEN: *Wild Boar Attacked by Dogs* (1660) - HAMBURG: *Astronomer*; *Animals*; two still-lifes; *A Side of Veal* - LILLE: *Lion Hunt*; *Stag Hunt*.

AUCTION RECORDS:
PARIS, 1747, *Jupiter in the Shape of a Boar Visiting Venus Accompanied by Cupid*, FRF 120. VIENNA, 22 May 1973, *Hounds Fighting over Game*, ATS 55,000. VIENNA, 7 June 2000, *Dogs Chasing a Bear* (oil on canvas, 47 x 67 ins / 119 x 169 cm) ATS 25,000.

JACOBSEN, Niels. See **HANSEN-JACOBSEN Niels**

JACOBSEN, Paul
20th century.
Sculptor, assemblage artist.

Paul Jacobsen exhibited at the 1993 Foire Internationale d'Art Contemporain in Paris. As well as presenting everyday objects such as chairs detached from their normal setting, he creates abstract assemblages.

JACOBSEN, Robert
Danish, 20th century.
Born 4 June 1912, in Copenhagen; died 1993.
From 1947 also active in France.
Sculptor, draughtsman, illustrator, watercolourist.
Kinetic Art.
Helhesten Group.

Robert Jacobsen came from a modest background. From 1926, after he had completed his college studies, he worked as a bar manager, a badminton and banjo player, and a sailor. He did not attend the courses run by the Kunstakademi in Copenhagen. He was self-taught in sculpture, as he only rarely received any tuition in manual work and craftsmanship, except for what he was taught by a gravestone carver from 1933-1944. His aesthetic influence stemmed from his admiration for other artists, first and foremost Auguste Rodin and Henri Laurens, and when an exhibition of German Expressionists was held in Copenhagen in 1932, for the works of Emil Nolde, Paul Klee and particularly the sculptor Ernst Barlach; and in the final period of his training - the period which led him towards Abstraction - he admired the works of Jean Arp. From 1940-1945, Jacobsen joined the ranks of the young artists who used the journal *Helhesten* (*Hell Horse*) as their focus, with which he was probably already acquainted from the time of the previous journal *Linier* (*Lines*). This was the group, organised by Asger Jorn, which would join forces with the Belgian and Dutch 'experimental groups' just after the war to form the CoBrA movement. Influenced by fairy tales, myths and primitive art, this group encouraged spontaneous painting in order to liberate it from the norms and movements of western art. At that time, Jacobsen formed friendships with Richard Mortensen and Asger Jorn. Strictly speaking, CoBrA had no aesthetic purpose, since it was supposed to be experimental, and was both anti-apriorisms and anti-aesthetic. Robert Jacobsen's work was not experimental and was clearly subject to formal constraints. Therefore, it would seem he could not be linked to CoBrA, which was also the case for two other Danish painters, Mogens Andersen and Richard Mortensen. In 1947, thanks to a grant from the French state, Jacobsen went to Paris where he shared lodgings with Mortensen, then with Jorn. In 1962, he was appointed professor at the art academy in Munich. In the 1970s he returned to Denmark, and was appointed professor at the Kongelige Danske Kunstakademi in Copenhagen in 1976.

In 1930, Jacobsen produced his first sculptures on wood without preparatory drawings and became a member of the Surrealist movement Host. A few years later, he would become interested in water as an element to work with. In 1941, he exhibited figures at the autumn exhibition in Copenhagen, which were inspired by Scandinavian mythology and produced in an Expressionist style, in granite or limestone. In this series, he gradually moved towards a sobriety of form, although not without renouncing this symbolical, native source of his art. The sculptures of this period include *Portrait of Egill Jacobsen*, dated 1944. In 1942, he was already producing abstract forms, which were solid and still organic enough to evoke life. In 1944, anthropomorphic allusions were still to be found in his forms, but in some areas he aimed at realising their geometric potential, whilst hollow, empty forms carved out a place for themselves inside the mass. Next, iron replaced stone, being more suitable for drawing straight or curved marks within the space, intertwining to define empty space with precision. It was in 1949 in Paris that Jacobsen abandoned stone to become one of the great sculptors of beaten, wrought and welded metal - and he was one of the pioneers of using scraps of rubbish: his *Dolls* are humorous figures, and the sculpture *War*, dated 1952, is made up of an old gas mask and plumbing pipes. Alongside Mortensen, his work was featured with the Neo-Plasticist group at the Galerie Denise René in 1947 in Paris. Following the period of his cube skeletons which he dismantled and reconstructed, that are sometimes referred to in terms of 'the *Boxes* period', which perhaps allowed a more imaginative approach and a greater freedom in the development of his wrought constructions, he would integrate the rough shape of a few moving parts or rather a geometric gliding of some forms into others: *Ideomotorisk Problem*, 1952. In 1962, in the *Cosmonauts* series, he added several colours to create some effects of form. Robert Jacobsen also produced engravings. He illustrated a book by Jean Laude entitled *Le Miroir Blanc* (*The White Mirror*).

Jacobsen won many prizes and distinctions: in 1952, the art prize awarded by the journal *Politiken* (*Politics*); 1966, alongside Henri Étienne-Martin (1913-1995), the grand prize for sculpture at the Venice Biennale; 1967, the Thorvaldsen medal; 1980, Chevalier de la Légion d'Honneur; 1981, he was elected honorary member of the art academies in Florence and Munich; 1983, Commander of the Danebroge. Robert Jacobsen contributed works to many group exhibitions, including: 1940, his first contribution to the autumn exhibition in Copenhagen. In the 1940s, he exhibited frequently in Scandinavia with artists such as Hansen and Mortensen, and with Serge Poliakoff at the Galerie Denise René in Paris at the beginning of the 1950s; in addition to exhibiting more recently with Jean Clarebout at the Galerie Convergence in Nantes in 1984. He contributed works regularly in Paris at the Salon de Mai, the Salon de la Jeune Sculpture and the Salon des Réalités Nouvelles. In 1966, Jacobsen participated in the International Exhibition of Sculpture at the Guggenheim Museum in New York; in 1981, his work was featured at the exhibition *Paris-Paris* held at the Centre Georges Pompidou in Paris. Jacobsen held many solo exhibitions, including: 1948, 1953, 1988, the Galerie Denise René, Paris; 1954, the Palais des Beaux-Arts, Brussels; 1954, Liège; 1955, 1960, the Stedelijk Museum, Amsterdam; 1957, 1963, the Galerie de France, Paris; 1957, the Kunsthalle, Basel; 1958, the Louisiana Museum for Moderne Kunst, Humlebæk; 1959, the Musée des Beaux-Arts, La Chaux-de-Fonds, Switzerland; 1960, the Moderna Museet, Stockholm; 1961, the Kunstnernes Kunsthandel, Copenhagen; 1962, the Kootz Gallery, New York; 1973, a retrospective at the Nordjyllands Kunstmuseum, Aalborg; 1975, the Kunstmuseum, Helsinki; 1975, the Kunsthalle, Kiel; 1978, the Kunstmuseum, Aarhus; 1979, a travelling exhibition in several American cities; 1984, a retrospective exhibition at the Musées de Toulon, Rennes and Rodin (Paris); and 1991, a retrospective at the Musée Matisse, the Palais Fénelon, Le Cateau-Cambrésis (France).

Bibliography:

Dewasne, J., *Le Sculpteur: Robert Jacobsen, sculpteur danois*, Copenhagen, 1951. Descargues, Pierre, *Entretien avec R. Jacobsen*, Gal. de France, Paris, 1963. Boesen, Anton/Johansson, Ejner, *R. Jacobsen*, Société Artistique Danoise, Copenhagen, 1965. Jensen, Christian, *Entretien avec R. Jacobsen*, Kunsthalle, Kiel, 1975. *Der Bildhauer Robert Jacobsen und seine Welt*, exhibition catalogue, Christian Albrechts-U., Kunsthalle, Kiel, 1975. *Robert Jacobsen parcours*, travelling exhibition catalogue, Musées de Toulon, Toulon, Musée des Beaux-Arts, Rennes, Musée Rodin, Paris, 1984-1985. *Robert Jacobsen/Parcours*, exhibition catalogue, Toulon, Mus. Toulon; Rennes, Mus. B.-A. & Archéol.; Paris, Mus. Rodin, 1984. *Robert Jacobsen: Raum und Zeichen Werke des Bildhauers Robert Jacobsen*, exhibition catalogue, Mannheim, Städt. Ksthalle; Marl, Skulpmus., 1987.

Museums and Galleries:

Aalborg (Nordjyllands Kunstmus.) - Aarhus (Kunstmus.) - Amsterdam (Stedelijk Mus.) - Grenoble (Mus. de Grenoble) - Høvikodden (Henie Onstad Kunstsenter) - Humlebæk (Louisiana Mus. for Moderne Kunst) - Ixelles (MBA) - Liège (Mus. de l'Art wallon) - Lund (Skissernas Mus.) - Munich (Neue Pinakothek) - Odense (Fyns Kunstmus.) - Oslo (Nasjonalgal.) - Paris (MNAM-CCI): *Iron Writing* (1950) - Pittsburgh (Carnegie MA): *The King of Hunger* (metal, sculpture) - Rennes (MBA) - São Paulo (MAM) - The Hague (Gemeentemus.) - Wuppertal (Von der Heydt Mus.).

Auction records:

Copenhagen, 1 Oct 1970, *Composition* (marble) DKK 8,000. Copenhagen, 20 Oct 1976, *Composition* (gouache, 17 3/4 x 14 1/4 ins / 45 x 36 cm) DKK 3,800. Paris, 8 Nov 1976, *Doll* (wrought iron, h. 18 1/2 ins / 47 cm) FRF 3,500. Copenhagen, 8 March 1977, *Figure* (metal, h. 12 1/4 ins / 31 cm) DKK 6,500. Paris, 14 Dec 1979, *Composition of Semi-Circles* (iron, h. 51 1/4 ins / 130 cm) FRF 35,000. London, 29 June 1982, *Untitled* (iron, h. 29 1/2 ins / 75 cm) GBP 1,900. Paris, 31 May 1983, *Farmhouse* (1952, oxidized iron) FRF 18,000. Copenhagen, 25 Sept 1985, *Composition* (coloured chalk and watercolour, 39 1/4 x 25 1/2 ins / 100 x 65 cm) DKK 10,000. Copenhagen, 26 Nov 1986, *Sculpture* (1957, wood, h. 35 1/2 ins / 90 cm) DKK 130,000. Copenhagen, 26 May 1987, *Composition* (gouache and Indian ink, 36 1/4 x 24 ins / 92 x 61 cm) DKK 20,000. Copenhagen, 2 March 1988, *Marble Sculpture* (1947, h. 13 3/4 ins / 35 cm) DKK 140,000. Copenhagen, 4 May 1988, *Composition* (35 1/2 x 24 ins / 90 x 61 cm) DKK 10,000. London, 30 June 1988, *Untitled* (1960, iron sculpture on a black wooden panel, 20 1/2 x 16 3/4 ins / 52 x 42.5 cm) GBP 14,300. Copenhagen, 30 Nov 1988, *Figure* (1940, marble, h. 19 3/4 ins / 50 cm) DKK 100,000; *Composition* (watercolour, 33 x 23 1/4 ins / 84 x 59 cm) DKK 9,000. Copenhagen, 8 Feb 1989, *Sculpture 2* (1949, black-painted iron, h. 11 1/2 ins / 29 cm) DKK 168,000. Copenhagen, 20 Sept 1989, *Figure* (limestone, h. 25 1/4 ins / 64 cm) DKK 160,000. Copenhagen, 21-22 March 1990, *Sculpture 95* (1950, black-painted iron, h. 29 1/2 ins / 75 cm) DKK 470,000. Amsterdam, 22 May 1990, *Untitled* (coloured crayon and watercolour/paper, 19 3/4 x 25 1/2 ins / 50 x 64.5 cm) NLG 11,500. Copenhagen, 30 May 1990, *Arrogant Figure* (1956, iron sculpture, h. 32 1/4 ins / 82 cm) DKK 200,000. New York, 7 Nov 1990, *Constructed Spark* (1958, welded iron, h. 35 ins / 88.9 cm) USD 63,250. Copenhagen, 14-15 Nov 1990, *Sculpture 178* (1950, iron, h. 11 3/4 ins / 30 cm) DKK 190,000. Stockholm, 5-6 Dec 1990, *Composition* (watercolour and collage, 25 1/4 x 38 1/2 ins / 64 x 98 cm) SEK 16,500; *Abstract Composition* (collage of glass and molten glass, 44 x 33 ins / 112 x 84 cm) SEK 50,000. Amsterdam, 22 May 1991, *Composition* (iron sculpture, h. 16 1/2 ins / 42 cm) NLG 31,050. Amsterdam, 23 May 1991, *Untitled* (painted metal, h. 15 1/4 ins / 39 cm) NLG 34,500. Copenhagen, 30 May 1991, *Construction* (iron sculpture, h. 20 1/2 ins / 52 cm, l. 19 3/4 ins/50 cm) DKK 125,000. Stockholm, 30 May 1991, *Composition* (red-painted iron, h. 11 1/4 ins / 28.5 cm and 11 x 7 3/4 ins/27 x 20 cm) SEK 60,000. Paris, 7 Oct 1991, *Untitled* (1988, painted steel, 18 1/2 x 13 1/2 x 11 3/4 ins / 47 x 34 x 30 cm) FRF 82,000. Copenhagen, 4 Dec 1991, *Figures* (iron sculpture, h. 12 1/4 ins / 31 cm and l. 11 ins/27 cm) DKK 28,000; *Construction* (1949, iron, h. 17 1/4 ins / 44 cm) DKK 180,000. Copenhagen, 4 March 1992, *Sculpture 101* (1950, black-painted iron, H.5 1/2 ins / 14 cm) DKK 65,000; *Construction* (1949, black-painted iron, h. 17 3/4 ins / 45 cm) DKK 180,000. Stockholm, 21 May 1992, *Cosmic Rhythm* (gouache, 14 1/2 x 17 3/4 ins / 37 x 45 cm) SEK 6,200. Copenhagen, 2-3 Dec 1992, *Composition* (soft chalk and watercolour, 14 1/4 x 11 3/4 ins / 36 x 30 cm) DKK 6,500. Copenhagen, 10 March 1993, *Non-Articulated, Immobile Construction* (1952, welded iron, h. 12 1/2 ins / 32 cm) DKK 100,000. Paris, 8 July 1993, *Untitled* (1962, iron and wood, 27 1/2 x 31 1/2 x 17 3/4 ins / 70 x 80 x 45 cm) FRF 25,000. Copenhagen, 3 Nov 1993, *Big Chief* (1955, iron, h. 16 1/2 ins / 42 cm) DKK 170,000. Stockholm, 30 Nov 1993, *Composition* (welded iron painted black, h. 18 1/2 ins / 47 cm, w. 16 1/2 ins/42 cm) SEK 64,000. London, 2 Dec 1993, *Untitled* (painted steel,

18 1/2 x 22 x 15 1/2 ins / 47 x 55.9 x 39.4 cm) GBP 6,325. AMSTERDAM, 31 May 1994, *Harlequin* (welded iron, h. 34 ins / 86.5 cm) NLG 29,900. COPENHAGEN, 14 June 1994, *Composition* (mixed media/paper/canvas, 22 x 39 1/4 ins / 55 x 100 cm) DKK 10,000. PARIS, 29 June 1994, *Untitled* (watercolour and ink/paper, 14 x 18 3/4 ins / 35.5 x 47.5 cm) FRF 12,000. COPENHAGEN, 6 Dec 1994, *Sculpture, Mobile* (1951, welded iron, h. 12 1/2 ins / 32 cm) DKK 90,000. COPENHAGEN, 8-9 March 1995, *Sculpture 68* (1951, black welded iron, h. 13 ins / 33 cm) DKK 120,000. PARIS, 1 April 1996, *Figure* (welded iron, h. 13 1/2 ins / 34 cm) FRF 43,000. AMSTERDAM, 5 June 1996, *Cat* (wrought iron, h. 12 1/2 ins / 32 cm) NLG 19,550. COPENHAGEN, 15 March 1997, *Composition* (1976, etching) DKK 5,200. COPENHAGEN, 22-24 Oct 1997, *Construction* (1980, iron painted blue and black, h. 17 3/4 ins / 45 cm) DKK 40,000. PARIS, 23 Nov 1997, *Interior* (24 x 19 3/4 ins / 61 x 50 cm) FRF 50,000. COPENHAGEN, 5 Oct 1999, *Construction* (1950, black painted metal, h. 11 ins / 27 cm) DKK 125,000. COPENHAGEN, 5 Oct 1999, *Bird Man* (patinated welded iron, h. 20 ins / 52 cm) DKK 130,000. COPENHAGEN, 9 Feb 2000, *Drawing in Iron* (1967, black painted iron, h. 16 ins / 40 cm) DKK 190,000. COPENHAGEN, 3 Oct 2000, *Doll* (patinated iron, h. 13 ins / 32 cm) DKK 96,000. COPENHAGEN, 21 Nov 2001, *The Man who Knows Everything* (1951-1952, iron, h. 36 ins / 92 cm) DKK 250,000. AMSTERDAM, 4 Dec 2001, *L'Oliver* (1955, welded metal, h. 36 ins / 92 cm) EUR 38,000. COPENHAGEN, 1 Oct 2002, *Untitled* (1951, welded patinated iron, h. 22 ins / 56 cm) DKK 145,000. COPENHAGEN, 1 Oct 2002, *The Emperor's Tailor* (1957, welded patinated iron, h. 28 ins / 70 cm) DKK 180,000. COPENHAGEN, 26 Feb 2003, *Concrete Sculpture* (1966, black painted iron, h. 18 ins / 45 cm) DKK 210,000. COPENHAGEN, 7 Oct 2003, *Jakob's Ladder* (1949-1950, black painted iron, 28 x 14x18 ins / 70 x 35x45 cm) DKK 255,000. COPENHAGEN, 29 March 2004, *Drawing in the Air - Concrete Sculpture* (1949, black painted iron, 15 x 16 ins / 37 x 40 cm) DKK 330,000. COPENHAGEN, 29 March 2004, *Construction* (c. 1950, black painted iron, 24 x 24x18 ins / 60 x 60x45 cm) DKK 580,000.

JACOBSEN, Sophus

Norwegian, 19th - 20th century.

Born 7 September 1833, in Frederikshald; died 13 May 1912, in Düsseldorf, Germany.

Painter. Genre scenes, landscapes with figures, landscapes.

Sophus Jacobsen studied under Hans Fredrik Gude. Having received a grant from the Norwegian government, he went to Düsseldorf in 1855, where he lived for the rest of his life. Jacobsen went on study trips to Norway, Germany and Italy. From 1861-1891, he exhibited in several German cities. Jacobsen excelled at painting winter scenes and he explored this theme mainly in Eifel and Westerwald. When he copied nature without looking to convey any other effects, he produced skilful work and achieved impressive results.

MUSEUMS AND GALLERIES:

DÜSSELDORF: *Landscape of the Bas-Rhin* - GÖTEBORG: *Lapps Hunting Reindeer* - HANOVER: *Fjord Landscape* - OSLO: *German Forest Setting* - STOCKHOLM: *Winter Landscape*.

AUCTION RECORDS:

PARIS, 1880, *Norwegian Fjord by Moonlight*, FRF 8,400; *Forest in Winter at Dusk*, FRF 10,500; *River and Landscape by Moonlight*, FRF 12,600. FRANKFURT AM MAIN, 19 Dec 1892, *Landscape*, FRF 862. LOS ANGELES, 6 June 1978, *Woman Gathering Bundles of Firewood* (1866, oil on canvas, 30 3/4 x 46 1/2 ins / 78.2 x 118.2 cm) USD 5,250. NEW YORK, 26 Jan 1979, *Creek by Moonlight* (oil on canvas, 22 x 33 ins / 56 x 84 cm) USD 4,000. NEW YORK, 29 May 1981, *Woman Gathering Bundles of Firewood in a Snowy Landscape* (oil on canvas, 33 x 48 1/2 ins / 84 x 123 cm) USD 7,000. COLOGNE, 30 March 1984, *View of a Fjord in Summer* (1862, oil on canvas, 26 3/4 x 79 1/2 ins / 68 x 202 cm) DEM 11,000. COLOGNE, 25 Oct 1985, *Landscape with Torrent, Norway* (1864, oil on canvas, 30 x 45 1/4 ins / 76 x 115 cm) DEM 21,000. LONDON, 23 March 1988, *Estuary by Moonlight* (oil on canvas, 31 1/4 x 47 1/4 ins / 79.5 x 120 cm) GBP 7,920. LONDON, 28 March 1990, *Woman and Child with a Dog in the Forest* (oil on canvas, 12 1/2 x 17 1/4 ins / 31.5 x 44 cm) GBP 3,520. NEW YORK, 16 July 1992, *House in the Middle of the Woods in Winter* (1866, oil on canvas, 14 1/2 x 23 ins / 36.8 x 58.4 cm) USD 2,750. AMSTERDAM, 28 Oct 1992, *Winter Landscape with a Peasant Woman and Child Bringing Back Bundles of Firewood, Crossing over a Frozen Pond at Dusk* (1881, oil on canvas, 43 1/4 x 34 ins / 110 x 85.5 cm) NLG 32,200. COPENHAGEN, 6 Sept 1993, *Winter in the Forest* (oil on canvas, 43 x 33 ins / 109 x 84 cm) DKK 39,000. LONDON, 15 June 1994, *Forest Sunset* (1878, oil on canvas, 42 x 32 ins / 106.5 x 81 cm) GBP 12,650.

JACOBSOHN, Wilhelm

German, 20th century.

Born 1895, in Berlin; died 1917.

Painter. Portraits, landscapes, landscapes with figures.

Wilhelm Jacobsohn painted a series of pictures and studies which were inspired by scenes of Berlin and its vicinity, in addition to the Baltic. He also produced portraits.

JACOBSON. See also **JACOBSZ**

JACOBSON, Albert

Danish, 19th century.

Born 1780, in Copenhagen; died 28 November 1836, in Copenhagen.

Sculptor.

Albert Jacobson was a pupil at the Kunstakademi in Copenhagen and participated in its exhibitions from 1817 to 1834. Among his works are cited *Portrait of King Frederik VI* and *Portrait of the Queen*, as well as bust and life-size medallion portraits.

JACOBSON, Dan

French, 20th century.

Born 1942, in Paris.

Painter. Figure compositions, scenes with figures, local scenes, landscapes with figures, urban landscapes.

Dan Jacobson graduated from the École des Arts Graphiques Estienne in Paris, where he studied from 1958 to 1962 and was taught by Albert Flocon and Jean Cluseau Lanauve. His painting is colourful, cheerful and unpretentious, dealing with series of themes such as markets, marine landscapes, boats, villages etc. His work sometimes leans towards fantastic realism, 'dreamed reality', which allows a steam train to be seen in the Musée d'Orsay, an old railway station, a merchant ship berthed under the arch of the Grand Palais, a liner stuck under the Alma bridge or a large sailing ship from the olden days carried up to the Panthéon by the tide.

Jacobson participates in Parisian collective exhibitions such as: Salon d'Automne, Salon des Artistes Français, Salon des Indépendants, Salon Comparaisons, Salon du Dessin et de la Peinture à l'Eau, Salon des Peintres Témoins de leur Temps. He is a member of the Critical Figuration group. Solo exhibitions of his work include: Van Gogh's house, Auvers-sur-Oise, 1975; Galerie Drouant, Paris, 1978; Galerie des Orfèvres, Paris, 1980; Monsoult Townhall, 1985; Galerie Pierre Hautot, Paris, 1988; Galerie des Îles, Paris, 1990; Galerie Fardel, Amiens, 1995; Galerie Isaac Guirgis, Paris, 1995; Centre Culturel du Panthéon, Paris, 1997.

AUCTION RECORDS:

PARIS, 14 April 1991, *C'est la Fin du Jour* (*Close of Day*) (oil on canvas, 51 1/4 x 38 1/4 ins / 130 x 97 cm) FRF 13,500.

JACOBSON, Jacob, or Jacobsohn

German, 19th century.

Born 12 February 1818, in Ludwigslust; died 18 December 1891, in Berlin.

Painter. Landscapes, architectural views.

A pupil of Volker in Berlin, Jacobson travelled around Italy and subsequently worked as a painter and draughtsman in Ludwigslust and Schwerin. In 1867, he settled in Berlin. On 15 February 1883, he celebrated the golden jubileee of his artistic career. Noted works: *Jewish Cemetery* and *Winter Paintings*. He received an honourable mention at the Universal Exhibition in 1900.

MUSEUMS AND GALLERIES:

SCHWERIN: *Breakfast*; *Jewish Cemetery*.

AUCTION RECORDS:

LONDON, 9 May 1979, *View of Amalfi* (1849, oil on canvas, 32 1/2 x 53 1/4 ins / 82.5 x 135 cm) GBP 1,000. BRUSSELS, 24 Aug 1999, *Feeding of the Five Thousand* (oil on canvas, 41 x 48 ins / 103 x 123 cm) BEF 190,000. MUNICH, 27 Sept 2000, *Civitella* (1853, oil on canvas, 20 x 24 ins / 50 x 62 cm) DEM 3,500.

JACOBSON, Lili Angelique Vilhelmine, Mrs Havell

Danish, 19th century.

Born 25 November 1859, in Copenhagen.

Sculptor.

Lili Jacobson was a pupil at the Kunstakademi in Copenhagen from 1889 to 1893 and first exhibited a bust in 1892. She married the English writer Ernest Binfield Havell and lived in London.

JACOBSON, Oscar Brousse

American, 20th century.

Born 16 May 1882, in Västervik, Sweden; died 1966.

Painter. Portraits, landscapes.

Oscar Brousse Jacobson's family left Sweden for America and settled in the Swedish Community of Lindsborg in Kansas. Jacobson studied at Bethany College, Kansas and at Yale. He established himself as a landscape artist and headed the Art department at the University of Oklahoma. He left his mark on the department by introducing new approaches to teaching, influenced by modern French painting and his interest in the utilitarian aspects of art: to this end he employed potters and those engaged in woodcraft in the department and lured John Frank from the Arts Institute in Chicago. Jacobson was a member of the American Federation of the Arts and the Society of Orientalists and Algerian Artists. He won a gold medal in 1931. He also set up his own ceramics company called Frankoma Pottery, which proved to be very successful.

Jacobson is also known for his work in establishing the Fred Jones Jr. Museum of Art In Oklahoma and for his inclusion of Native American work and his encouragement and support of Native American artists. The museum has a wide-ranging collection of Native American, Oriental and contemporary western art. Jacobson set up the museum in 1936 and directed it until 1952.

JACOBSON, Scott

American, 20th century.

Painter (mixed media), draughtsman. Figures, animals.

Scott Jacobson showed his work for the first time in a solo exhibition at the Horodner-Romley Gallery in New York in 1995. He works on glass with alternate layers of paint and resin, producing compositions with figures evoking the world of childhood and his own anxieties.

BIBLIOGRAPHY:

Harris, Susan, '*Promenade printanière*' in *Art Press* n° 204, periodical, Paris, July-August 1995.

JACOBSZ. See also **JACOBS, JACOPS** and **JAKOB**

JACOBSZ, Dirk. See also **FELAERT Dirk Jacobsz**

JACOBSZ, Jacob. See also **GEEL Jacob Jacobsz Van**

JACOBSZ, Lucas. See **LUCAS Van Leyden**

JACOBSZ., Abraham or Abrahamus, or Jacobi

Dutch, 17th century.

Active in Amsterdam.

Engraver.

JACOBSZ., Cornelis

Dutch, 16th century.

Born 16th century, in Delft, Holland.

Painter. History painting, portraits.

Jacobsz. studied under Cornelis van Haarlem. There are similarities between him and Cornelis Jacobsz. Delff.

JACOBSZ., Dirk, or Jacobszoon, also known as Dierick van Amsterdam

Dutch, 16th century.

Born 1496 - 1500, probably in Amsterdam; died before 9 September 1567, in Amsterdam, where he was buried on this date.

Painter. Figures, portraits, group portraits.

Amsterdam School.

Jacobsz. was the son of Cornelisz. Jacob van Ootsanen, who was his teacher. He also worked with Jan van Scorel. He produced the first known corporate portrait in Holland, *The Brotherhood of Arquebusiers*, in 1529, which depicted a group of civil guards. He also produced two triptychs, 15 years apart, which included the same family of donors. The first triptych shows the female donor aged about 20 and pregnant, and the second, dated 1531, shows the couple surrounded by eight children. In his portraits, the hands of his subjects are painted with fastidious attention to detail.

MUSEUMS AND GALLERIES:

AMSTERDAM (Rijksmus.): *The Brotherhood of Arquebusiers* (1529) - BESANÇON: *Portrait of a Woman* - ST PETERSBURG (Hermitage): *Group Portrait of Members of a Corporation* (1532) - STUTTGART: *Triptych: Nativity (centre), The Donors and their Children (outer panels)*.

AUCTION RECORDS:

PARIS, 29 June 1994, *Triptych: Nativity (centre), The Donors and their Children (outer panels)* (1531, oak panel, h. 25 1/4 ins / 64 cm, open: 36 1/2 ins/93 cm, closed: 18 1/2 ins/47 cm) FRF 390,000.

JACOBSZ., Foy

Dutch, 16th century.

Active in Leiden.

Painter (glass).

JACOBSZ., Jacob

Dutch, 17th century.

Painter.

A painter by the name Jacob Jacobsz. worked in Amsterdam in 1624. He may be the same as Jacobsz. Jacob van Geel.

JACOBSZ., Lambert, or Jacobs

Dutch, 17th century.

Died before October 1637, in Leeuwarden.

Painter. Religious subjects.

According to Houbraken, Lambert Jacobsz. was born before 1600 and was probably a pupil of Rubens. He was a preacher in the reformed church. His son was Abraham Lambertsz., called Van den Tempel, and his pupils included Govaert Flinck and Jac-Backer.

MUSEUMS AND GALLERIES:

AMSTERDAM: *Biblical Scene* - LEEUWARDEN: *Isaac and Rebecca*.

AUCTION RECORDS:
LONDON, 29 June 1979, *The Sacrifice* (oil on panel, 34 x 45 1/4in/86.3 x 114.9cm) GBP 2,600. LONDON, 18 May 1990, *St Paul and the Soothsayer of Philippi* (oil on canvas, 61 1/4 x 81 1/2in/155.5 x 206.7cm) GBP 5,500. NEW YORK, 10 Oct 1990, *The Good Samaritan* (oil on panel, 29 1/2 x 44in/75 x 110.9cm) USD 13,200. AMSTERDAM, 12 May 1992, *The Adulterous Woman before Christ* (oil on canvas, 41 3/4 x 55in/106 x 140cm) NLG 11,500. PARIS, 26 June 1992, *The Blessing of the Child* (oil on panel, 27 1/2 x 36 1/2in/70 x 92.5cm) FRF 35,000. NEW YORK, 27 Jan 2000, *St Paul Writing at a Desk* (1629, oil on canvas, 45 x 39 ins / 114 x 100 cm) USD 26,000. LONDON, 10 Dec 2001, *St Bartholomew* (oil on canvas, 48 x 37 ins / 121 x 94 cm) GBP 10,500. STOCKHOLM, 2 Dec 2003, *The Prophet Nathan and King David* (oil on canvas, 40 x 47 ins / 102 x 120 cm) SEK 470,000.

JACOBSZ., Simon
Dutch, 16th century.
Born 1520, in Gouda; died during the siege of Haarlem.
Painter. History painting, portraits.

Jacobsz. studied under Karel Foort van Ypern and painted in the style of Tintoretto. He tried his hand at historical painting, but success with portraiture led him to specialise in this area instead.

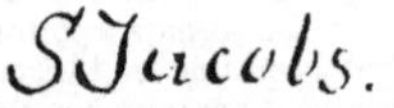

JACOBSZOON. See also **JACOBSZ**

JACOBSZOON, Hughe or Hugo
Dutch, 16th century.
Died before 16 October 1538.
Painter (glass).
Leiden School.

Jacobszoon was the father of Lucas of Leiden, and was his son's first teacher. In 1494, in Leiden, he married the daughter of the organist Dick Florisz., and was still living in 1531 at the time of his wife's death. Marc van Vaernewyck mentions a painting from the church of St Peter in Ghent, which was reportedly brought to Holland by Hughe of Leiden. None of his works have survived.

JACOBUS (Fra), or Jacopo
Italian, 13th century.
Active in Florence at the beginning of the 13th century.
Mosaicist.

A Franciscan, in 1225 he decorated with mosaic in the Byzantine style the annex tribune of the Baptistery of S Giovanni, Florence. This artist should not be confused with Jacobsz. de Turrina.

JACOBUS, also known as magister Jacobus Pictor
14th century.
Active in Chillon.
Painter.
Savoyard School.

Jacobus produced paintings of the Capella Chillonis for Amadeus V. He is mentioned in accounts belonging to Roland Garret, who was the tax collector at the Villeneuve toll gate, in 1314 and 1315.

JACOBUS
German, 15th century.
Miniaturist.

Jacobus' signature is found on the binding of a manuscript from the monastery of Boedingen, near Siegen, Germany. The binding is decorated with four medallions featuring stylised animals. Similar bindings, bearing the inscription *Jacobus illuminator*, are in the Bibliothèque de L'Arsenal in Paris, and in the British Museum in London.

MUSEUMS AND GALLERIES:
LONDON (British Mus.) - PARIS (Bibliothèque de l'Arsenal).

JACOBUS
Hungarian, 16th century.
Painter.

Jacobus was a member of the Benedictine order. He was court painter to King Louis II of Hungary.

JACOBUS. See also **JACOB, JACOPO, etc.**

JACOBUS, da Fabriano. See **JACOBO da Fabriano**

JACOBUS, van Arthois. See **ARTHOIS Jacobus van**

JACOBUS ARGENTORATENSIS. See **JACOB von Strassburg**

JACOBUS DE MONS
Flemish School, 17th century.
Engraver (copper). Religious subjects.

The Poitiers museum has a copper engraving by this artist signed *Jacobus de Mons*.

MUSEUMS AND GALLERIES:
POITIERS: *The Holy Family with the Holy Spirit Above* (engraving/copper).

JACOBUS TRAJECTENSIS.
See **CLAESSENS Jacobus**

JACOBY. See also **JACOBI**

JACOBY, Karl or Carl
German, 19th century.
Born 29 April 1853, in Berlin.
Active in Berlin.
Painter. Genre scenes.

Karl Jacoby trained in Berlin, Antwerp and Paris, exhibited in Hamburg, Berlin and Munich (1887-1891), and won a medal in Melbourne in 1881. Possibly the same Karl Jacoby won a medal in Berlin in 1900.

AUCTION RECORDS:
LONDON, 20 June 1980, *Peasants in an Interior* (oil on canvas, 49 x 65 1/2 ins / 124.5 x 166.5 cm) GBP 1,600. AMSTERDAM, 19 Oct 1993, *The Departure* (oil on canvas, 63 3/4 x 79 1/4 ins / 162 x 201.5 cm) NLG 11,500.

JACOBY, Ludwig or Louis
German, 19th - 20th century.
Born 7 June 1828, in Havelberg; died 11 November 1918, in Berlin.
Engraver (burin).

Ludwig Jacoby studied in Berlin under Mandel and Wilhelm Kaulbach, and went on to work in Rome and Paris before his appointment to a teaching post at the Academy in Vienna. In 1882 he settled in Berlin and taught there until 16 August 1898. Ludwig Jacoby was a member of the jury at the Exposition Universelle in Paris in 1900. Examples of his work include an *Emperor Franz-Joseph, Empress Elisabeth of Austria, Franz Liszt* and a *School of Athens* in the manner of Raphaël.

JACOBY, Meinhard
German, 20th century.
Born 1873, in Vienna.
Painter, sculptor, medallist. Genre scenes.

Son of Ludwig Jacoby and an exhibitor at the Berlin Exhibition of 1902.

JACOBY, Paul
German, 19th century.
Born 1844; died 2 July 1899, in Dresden.
Active in Dresden.
Landscape artist.

Paul Jacoby worked in Dessau, Munich and Italy, and between 1874 and 1881 exhibited in Berlin several times.
MUSEUMS AND GALLERIES:
DRESDEN: *View of Hohnstein Castle in Switzerland.*

JACOBY, Valeri Ivanovitch. See **YACOBY**

JACOBY, Zahavit
Israeli, 20th century.
Born 1900, in Lódz; died 1975.
Painter. Scenes with figures.
Zahavit Jacoby emigrated to Palestine in 1914. She studied applied art and watercolours in the Reimann school, Berlin (1927). In 1954 she left for Montevideo, staying until 1957, when she went to study in Paris (1957) and started to paint. In 1969 she returned to Israel. Zahavit took her inspiration from the Bible, sometimes even from the Gospels, and sometimes from myths and legends. Speaking of her work, Waldemar-George talked of 'flamboyant gardens like the paradises of Persian miniatures, flower-carpeted backgrounds like Gothic tapestries'.

JACOMA, Giacomo della. See **GIACOMA Giacomo della**

JACOMART. See **BAÇO Jaime**, called Jacomart

JACOMB-HOOD, George Percy
British, 19th - 20th century.
Born 1857, in Redhill; died 1929.
Painter, engraver. Portraits, allegorical subjects, figures, genre scenes, landscapes.
George Percy Jacomb-Hood trained at the Slade School under Legros, and in Paris with Jean-Paul Laurens. He also travelled to Madrid to study the works of Velazquez. He exhibited in London at the Royal Academy and the Suffolk Street Gallery from 1877, and at the Grosvenor Gallery. In 1887 he exhibited at the Salon des Artistes Français, winning a jury commendation. Jacomb-Hood won a bronze medal for printmaking at the Exposition Universelle of 1900 in Paris. He was a member of the Royal Institute of Oil Painters and of the New English Art Club. He also worked as an illustrator, and in this capacity travelled to Greece in 1896 and to India in 1902, 1905 and 1911.
MUSEUMS AND GALLERIES:
LONDON (National Portrait Gal.) - MANCHESTER (City AG) - SYDNEY: *Triumph of Spring.*
AUCTION RECORDS:
LONDON, 3 June 1988, *The Nymphs* (1909, oil on canvas, 36 x 28 1/2 ins / 91.5 x 72.4 cm) GBP 2,090. LONDON, 21 Sept 1989, *West of the Palace Pier, Brighton* (oil on panel, 8 3/4 x 12 1/4 ins / 22.2 x 31.1 cm) GBP 2,420. LONDON, 21 March 1990, *Mermaids* (1909, oil on canvas, 36 1/4 x 28 1/4 ins / 92 x 72 cm) GBP 2,750.

JACOME
Spanish, 16th century.
Active in Valladolid in 1548.
Sculptor.

JACOMELLO. See also **JACOPO**

JACOMELLO DI BARTOLO
Italian, 15th century.
Sculptor.

JACOMETTI, Fabio, or Giacometti
Italian, 16th - 17th century.
Active in Urbino during the 16th and 17th centuries.
Sculptor.
Between 1597 and 1646, Jacometti made fonts, cupboards, and other items for the cathedral and churches of Urbino.

JACOMETTI, Ignazio
Italian, 19th century.
Born 1819, in Rome; died 22 April 1883.
Sculptor.
Jacometti became a member of the Accademia di San Luca in Rome in 1855 and in 1870 was appointed director of the papal art collections. Among his works are the marble groups *The Kiss of Judas* and *Ecce Homo* in the church of S Salvatore alla Scala Santa, Rome. He carved many statues for the churches of Rome, including *St Peter* for the church of S Paulo, *Pope Pius IX Kneeling* for S Maria Maggiore, the funerary monument of *Cardinal Gaspare B. Pianetti*, the funerary monuments of the *Abbot Figiani* and the *Countess Piccolomini* in S Maria Sopra Minerva, and an *Immaculate Conception* for the church of the Immacolata Concezione. Outside Rome he carved the funerary monuments of *Cardinal Altieri* in Albano Cathedral and the *Countess Bardi* in Pau, a *Virgin with Four Angels* for Santiago, Chile, and the monument of *Count Luigi Pelagello* in the church S Bartolomeo della Pietà, Fermo.

JACOMETTI, Pietro Paolo
Italian, 17th century.
Born 1580, in Recanati; died 1655.
Painter, sculptor, founder, architect.
Jacometti belonged to a noble family, but his liking for the arts led him to train under Pomarancio. He subsequently became the latter's assistant. He worked notably with him on frescoes for the dome of the church in Lorette. He executed only one *Assumption of the Virgin.*

JACOMETTI, Tarquinio
Italian, 16th century.
Born 16th century, in Recanati.
Sculptor, architect.

JACOMETTO
Italian, 15th century.
Born in Venice; died 1472, in Venice.
Active in Venice.
Painter, miniaturist. Portraits.
In his time, Jacometto enjoyed a considerable reputation.

JACOMETTO
Italian, 16th century.
Active in Venice.
Miniaturist.
Jacometto painted four miniatures in a service book and four others in an *Officiolo.*

JACOMIN
Spanish, 15th century.
Active in Seville in 1429.
Painter.
In 1429, he appears in a list of various artists and artisans.

JACOMIN, Alfred Louis, also known as Jacomin-Vigny
French, 19th - 20th century.
Born 3 January 1842, in Paris; died c. 1913.
Painter, watercolourist. Genre scenes, landscapes.
Jacomin studied with his father, Jean-Marie Jacomin, and then at the Académie Suisse and the École des Beaux-Arts. He made his debut in 1864, with a canvas entitled *Hamlet.* He also executed numerous watercolours. From 1867, he exhibited at the Salon de la Société des Artistes Français, of which he became a member in 1883. He exhibited his work and was awarded medals in London, Philadelphia, Barcelona and Lyons.

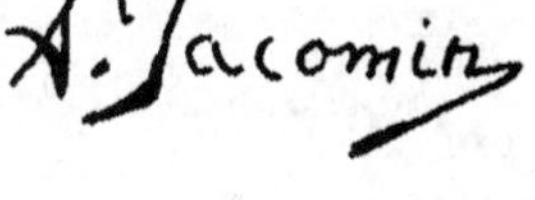

Auction records:
Paris, 1869, *The Narration*, FRF 950. Rotterdam, 1883, *Forges* FRF 3,990. New York, 1889, *Faust and Mephistopheles*, FRF 4,750. New York, 22-24 Nov 1899, *At the Astrologer's*, USD 250; *Friendly Critique*, USD 450. Paris, 16-19 Dec 1901, *At the Gunsmith's*, FRF 300. New York, 20 April 1905, *At the Gunsmith's*, USD 105. Paris, 9 March 1951, *Two Devotees of Painting*, FRF 19,000. Los Angeles, 28 Feb 1972, *At the Blacksmith's*, USD 650. New York, 12 Oct 1978, *Faust and Mephisto* (1869, oil on panel, 38 x 31 ins / 96.5 x 79 cm) USD 5,000. Paris, 6 March 1979, *Woodsman's Cabin in the Barbizon Forest* (oil on canvas, 22 x 25 1/2 ins / 55 x 65 cm) FRF 7,000. New York, 19 Oct 1984, *Hamlet: Act 3, Scene 4* (1869, oil on panel, 37 3/4 x 51 ins / 96 x 129.5 cm) USD 3,250. New York, 13 Feb 1985, *The Dessert* (1873, oil on panel, 25 1/2 x 21 ins / 64.8 x 53.4 cm) USD 2,750. New York, 30 Oct 1985, *The Woman at Fault* (oil on panel, 7 1/4 x 23 3/4 ins / 18.2 x 60.3 cm) USD 2,000. Copenhagen, 23 April 1987, *Interior with a Flirt Standing Before a Seated Man* (oil on canvas, 39 1/4 x 30 3/4 ins / 100 x 78 cm) DKK 90,000. London, 7 June 1989, *Sunday Afternoon in the Luxembourg Gardens in Paris* (oil on panel, 18 x 15 ins / 45.5 x 38 cm) GBP 5,500. New York, 19 July 1990, *The Flirt* (1873, oil on panel, 25 1/2 x 20 3/4 ins / 64.8 x 52.7 cm) USD 3,850. Versailles, 25 Nov 1990, *At the Gunsmith's* (oil on panel, 18 x 15 ins / 46 x 38 cm) FRF 20,000. New York, 15 Oct 1993, *The Forge* (1871, oil on panel, 18 x 14 3/4 ins / 45.7 x 37.5 cm) USD 6,900.

JACOMIN, Jean Marie
French, 19th century.
Born 1789, in Lyons; died May 1858, in Lyons.
Painter, draughtsman, engraver (etching), lithographer. Military subjects, portraits, genre scenes, interiors with figures, architectural interiors.

Jean-Marie Jacomin studied at the École de Dessin in Lyons and, from 1807 to 1813, with Revoil at the École des Beaux-Arts in the same city. He exhibited in Paris from 1819 to 1824, and in Lyons from 1821, many portraits drawn or painted in a precise and true-to-life manner, a few interiors, and military or genre subjects. Among these are: *Sculptor's Studio* and *Interior of a Cloister* (Paris, 1819), *Wounded Soldier Recounting his Campaigns* (Paris, 1822), *Departure for the Hospital* (Paris, 1824), and *Girl Saddened by a Bird Escaping* (Lyons, 1827). In Lyons, he exhibited the portraits of *Abbot Rozier*, of the *Author*, and the painters *Revoil*, *Berjon*, *Richard* and *Thierrat*. Several of his portraits have been engraved or lithographed. He himself etched and lithographed *Portrait of the Author*, *Eight Heads of Artists from Lyons*, *The Good Samaritan* and others.

Bibliography:
Les Années romantiques, la peinture française de 1815 à 1850, exhibition catalogue, Musée des Beaux-Arts, Nantes, Galeries nationales du Grand Palais, Paris, 1996.

Museums and Galleries:
Avignon: *Potrait of A.M.F. Artaud, Director of the Lyons Museum* - Lons-le-Saunier: *Portrait of Chabanne* - Lyons (MBA): *Self-portrait* (1832); *The Good Mother* (1824); four portraits.

Auction records:
Paris, 16 May 1925, *Jockey Racing* (watercolour) FRF 125. Paris, 14 June 1955, *Hussars at a Table Teasing a Child*, FRF 36,000. London, 14 June 1972, *Officers at a Table in an Interior*, GBP 380. Paris, 18 March 1980, *Soldier Recounting his Campaigns* (oil on canvas, 30 1/2 x 23 3/4in/77.5 x 60.5cm) FRF 21,000. Paris, 2 Dec 1994, *Portrait of a Young Woman* (1819, oil on canvas/panel, 10 1/2 x 7 3/4in/26.5 x 20cm) FRF 15,000. Paris, 14 June 2002, *Painting Class at the Fine Arts School in Lyons* (oil on canvas, 39 x 50 ins / 100 x 126 cm) EUR 15,000. Antwerp, 21 Oct 2002, *Bully* (oil on canvas, 37 x 30 ins / 93 x 75 cm) EUR 9,000.

JACOMIN, Marie Ferdinand
French, 19th century.
Born 1843 or 1848, in Paris; died 1902, in St-Germain-en-Laye (Yvelines).
Painter. Landscapes.

Marie Ferdinand Jacomin studied at the Swiss free academy and then at the École des Beaux-Arts in Paris. He contributed works to the Paris Salon from 1870 and exhibited at the Exposition Universelle of 1889.

His landscapes of forests, undergrowth and glades have much in common with the art of the Barbizon painters.

Museums and Galleries:
Dieppe: *The Seine at Poissy* - Paris (MAM): *Hornbeams in Montchevreuil* - St-Omer: *Landscape*.

Auction records:
Paris, 1898, *The Seine at Poissy*, FRF 400. New York, 17 Jan 1902, *Hundred-Year-Old Tree (Forest of Marly)*, USD 475. New York, 12-14 March 1906, *Forest of Rambouillet*, USD 100. Paris, 11 March 1909, *The Glade*, FRF 90. Paris, 7 July 1932, *Forest Glade*, FRF 70. Bern, 3 May 1979, *Three Cows in a Glade* (oil on panel, 28 3/4 x 36 1/4in/73 x 92cm) CHF 4,300. Bern, 23 Oct 1982, *Painter at his Easel in a Mountainous Landscape* (oil on canvas, 15 x 18in/38 x 46cm) CHF 3,600. Paris, 4 March 1991, *Riverside* (oil on canvas, 25 1/2 x 32in/65 x 81cm) FRF 4,800. Stuttgart, 24 Sept 1999, *Village Square* (oil on canvas, 15 x 18 ins / 39 x 46 cm) DEM 3,600.

JACOMIN, Suzanne Angélique
French, 19th century.
Born 19th century, in Chatou.
Painter. Genre scenes.

Suzanne Jacomin was a pupil of her father Alfred-Louis Jacomin. She obtained an honourable mention at the salon of the Société des Artistes Français in 1905.

JACOMINI, Antonio
Italian, 18th century.
Born in Ancona; died c. 1750, probably in Rome.
Painter.

An oil painting by Jacomini entitled *Christ Crucified with St Francis de Sales and Two Franciscan Saints* can be found in the church of S Francesco in Ancona.

JACOMINO. See also **JACOPO**

JACOMO, or Jacopo
Italian, 16th century.
Born 1515; died 24 January 1560.
Miniaturist.

Jacomo was a pupil of Giulio Romano, but his surname is not known.

JACOMO, da Treviso. See **DESTRE Jacomo dalle**

JACOMO, de Valenza. See **VALENCIA Jacoppo**

JACOMO, di Guglielmo di Ser Gherardo da Città della Pieve. See **GIACOMO DI GUGLIELMO**

JACOMO, di Onofrio. See **JACOMO DI GIOVANNI**

JACOMO DAVALENSO. See **VALENCIA Jacoppo**

JACOMO DI GIOVANNI, or Jacomo di Onofrio
Italian, 16th century.
Active in Spoleto (Umbria).
Painter.

In the municipal gallery of Spoleto there is an *Annunciation* by him that is copied from a painting by Spagna.

JACOMO DI LORENZO DA BOLOGNA, or
Jacopo da Bologna, Giacomo da Bologna
Italian, 15th century.
Painter, mosaicist.
Between 1487 and 1492, he worked on the mosaic decorations of the façade of the cathedral in Orvieto and, in 1494, refurbished its Corporale chapel.

JACOMO DI SER MICHELE DA CITTA DI CASTELLO
Italian, 15th century.
Painter.
Sienese School.
He was a member of the painters' guild of Siena and painted a retable for the cathedral of Città di Castello.

JACOMUCCIO, or Giacomuccio di Guarneri, called Muccio
14th century.
Active in Siena.
Painter.
School of Siena.

JACONE. See **JACOPO DI SANDRO I**

JACONISSA, Francesco
Italian, 18th century.
Active in Messina, during the first half of the 18th century.
Painter. Portraits.
Jaconissa mainly painted miniature portraits.

JACOPELLO D'ANTONIO
Italian, 15th century.
Painter. History painting.
It is possible that Jacopello d'Antonio, referred to by Siret, could have been identical with Jacopo (or Jacomo) de Antonio Negreto Palma.

JACOPI, Bernardino. See **BUTINONE**

JACOPINO, known as Jacopo da Tradate
Italian, 15th century.
Sculptor.
Jacopino worked from 1401 to 1425 in the cathedral in Milan.

JACOPINO. See also **JACOPO**

JACOPINO, da Vaulate. See **JACOBINUS DA VELATE**

JACOPINO D'AREZZO
Italian, 15th century.
Miniaturist.
In 1435, Jacopino d'Arezzo illustrated a prayer book for the Marquis of Ferrara and, a little later, *The Commentaries of Caesar*, *Theseus* by Albert the Great, a *Psalter* and a book of *Love Lyrics*.

JACOPINO DA REGGIO
Italian, 15th (?) century.
Active in Reggio Emilia and Bologna between 1461 and 1477.
Painter.
In collaboration with his brother Bartolomeo da Reggio, he painted a Gothic retable in several sections that is now in the Pinacoteca di Brera in Milan. This bears the signature *Hanc Tabulam Fecerunt Bartholomeus et Jacopinus de Regio*.
MUSEUMS AND GALLERIES:
MILAN (Pinacoteca di Brera): *Crucifixion; Annunciation; Vision of St Joachim and Various Saints.*

JACOPO (Fra), or Giacomo
Italian, 14th century.
Died August 1369, in Viterbo.
Sculptor (including wood).
Jacopo was a lay brother in the Dominican order.

JACOPO
Italian, 15th century.
Active c. 1400.
Painter.
Jacopo was involved in the fresco decorations of the Mazzarata church, Bologna, where there are still several works in the 14th-century Bolognese style that are signed by him.

JACOPO, or Giacomo
Italian, 15th century.
Active in Venice.
Painter.
Jacopo took part in the exhibition of the frescoes of the S Tarasio chapel in the church of S Zaccaria.

JACOPO
Italian, 15th century.
Died 1447.
Active in Padua.
Painter.

JACOPO
Italian, 16th century.
Painter. History painting.
According to Siret, Jacopo was a pupil of Leonardo da Vinci.

JACOPO (Fra)
Italian, 17th - 18th century.
Active in Florence.
Painter.
Jacopo was a member of the Order of the Carmelites. He painted two large-scale paintings depicting the *Conversion* and *Beheading of St Paul* for the chancel of the church of S Paolo dei Teresiani in Florence.

JACOPO. See also **GIACOMO, JACOMO, JACOBUS**

JACOPO , Boni. See **BONI Giacomo Antonio**

JACOPO, d'Antonello. See **JACOBELLO D'ANTONELLO DEGLI ANTONI**

JACOPO, da Bologna. See **JACOMO di Lorenzo da Bologna**

JACOPO, da Bologna. See also **RIPANDA Jacopo**

JACOPO, da Empoli. See **CHIMENTI Jacopo**

JACOPO, da Faenza. See also **BERTUCCI Jacopo**

JACOPO, da Firenze. See also **DELL'INDACO**

JACOPO, da Montagna. See **MONTAGNANA Jacopo di Paride Parisati da**

JACOPO, da Parma. See also **CARAGLIO Giovanni Jacopo**

JACOPO, da Pietrasanta. See **PIETRASANTA Jacopo**

JACOPO, da Prato Vecchio. See **VIGNALI** and **LANDINI Jacopo**

JACOPO , da Siena. See **JACOPO della Quercia**

JACOPO, da Soncino. See **SAGRAMORO Jacopo**

JACOPO, da Trezzo. See **TREZO Jacopo da**

JACOPO, da Ulma. See **GRIESINGER Jakob**

JACOPO, da Urbino. See **JACOPO DI PIANDRO BERARDUCCI DA GAIFA**

JACOPO, da Valencia. See **VALENCIA Jacoppo**

JACOPO, da Villa. See **JACOPO DI MARCO DA VILLA**

JACOPO, del Casentino. See **LANDINI Jacopo**

JACOPO, del Conte. See **CONTE Jacopo del**

JACOPO, del Corso. See **JACOPO D'ANTONIO**

JACOPO, del Maza. See **JACOPO DI ANDREA DI MATTEO**

JACOPO, del Sellaio. See **SELLAIO Jacopo del**

JACOPO, dell'Indaco. See **DELL'INDACO**

JACOPO, di Alemannia. See **GRIESINGER Jakob**

JACOPO, di Cosma. See **JACOPO DI LORENZO DI TEBALDO**

JACOPO, di Giovanni di Francesco. See **JACOPO DI SANDRO I**

JACOPO, di Mino. See **PELLICCIAIO Giacomo di Mino del**

JACOPO, di Nerito. See **NERITO Jacopo di**

JACOPO, di Paride Parisatida. See **MONTAGNANA Jacopo di Paride Parisati da**

JACOPO, di Pietro d'Angelo. See **JACOPO DELLA QUERCIA**

JACOPO, di Pietro della Fonte. See **JACOPO DELLA QUERCIA**

JACOPO, di Rossello. See **FRANCHI Rossello di Jacopo**

JACOPO, Fiorentino. See **JACOPO D'ANTONIO DI JACOPO** and **FIORENTINO Jacopo**

JACOPO ANDREA DA FERRARA, or Giacomo Andrea da Ferrara
Italian, 16th century.
Active in Bologna.
Sculptor.
He collaborated in carving the sculptures of the porch of the monastery church of S Michele in Bosco, Bologna.

JACOPO ANTONIO DA TRENTO
Italian, 16th century.
Painter.

JACOPO D'ANDREA DA FIRENZE
Italian, 15th century.
Active in Rome.
Sculptor.
He carved the marble tomb of Marco Albertoni in the church of S Maria del Popolo, Rome.

JACOPO D'ANTONIO, called Jacopo del Corso
Italian, 15th century.
Died 1453.
Painter.
Jacopo d'Antonio painted a retable for the high altar of the Badia, Florence.

JACOPO D'ANTONIO DA POLI, or Giacomo d'Antonio da Poli
Italian, 15th century.
Painter. Religious subjects.
He was a pupil of Fra Angelico and worked under his direction in the chapel of the Virgin of S Brizio in the cathedral in Orvieto, and in the chapel of Nicholas V in the Vatican.

JACOPO D'ANTONIO DI JACOPO, called Jacopo Fiorentino
Italian, 16th century.
Sculptor (wood).
He worked in Perugia, where with Ercole Ricci in 1576 he finished the fine stalls of the St Bernard chapel in the cathedral.

JACOPO DA BOLOGNA, or Jacopino da Bologna
Italian, 14th century.
Painter.
He managed to balance the teaching of his master, Vitale da Bologna, with that of the Rimini School.

JACOPO DA CAMPIONE
Italian, 13th century.
Sculptor, architect.

JACOPO DA CAMPIONE, or Giacomo da Campione
Italian, 16th century.
Active in Genoa.
Sculptor.
Jacopo da Campione worked with a fellow native of Lombardy on a marble altar for the All Saints' chapel of the church of S Maria di Castello, Genoa.

JACOPO DA CAMPLI
Italian, 15th century.
Born to a family originally from Campli (Abruzzo).
Painter.
Jacopo da Campli worked in Ripatransone, near Fermo (Marche). The remains of the frescoes in the church of S Francesco, Ripatransone, are attributed to him, as are the frescoes of the town's Palazzo Communale and those in the church of SS Giacomo e Filippo. Also attributed to him are the mural paintings in a chapel near the church of S Vittorio, Matteano, and some frescoes in Offida, Teramo and Campli (Abruzzo).

JACOPO DA CARRARA, or Giacomo da Carrara
Italian, 15th century.
Active in Rome.
Sculptor.
Jacopo da Carrara worked in 1472 with the Florentine Antonio Lori on the Trevi Fountain in Rome.

JACOPO DA FAENZA
Italian, 15th century.
Sculptor (wood).
He carved the frame containing B. Vivarini's altar painting *St Ambrose, St Louis and St Sebastian*, which is now in the possession of the art gallery in Vienna.

JACOPO DA FIRENZE
Italian, 15th century.
Active in Pistoia.
Illuminator.
He was a Franciscan monk and in 1470 illuminated two missals that are now in the chapter archives in Pistoia.

JACOPO DA FIRENZE, also known as Jacobo Fiorentino
Italian, 16th century.
Born 16th century, of Florentine origin.
Active in Spain.
Sculptor, painter, architect.
Jacopo da Firenze went to Spain in 1520 and died somewhere in Murcia. He worked as an architect, sculptor and painter in Murcia, Granada and Seville.

JACOPO DA MILANO
Italian, 15th century.
Painter.
Jacopo di Milano worked in Corsica, where he is referred to as having painted in the council room of Bastia, the governor's palace in the same town (coat of arms of the republic of Genoa), and in the antechamber of the Palazzo di Terranuova.

JACOPO DA MONSELICE
Italian, 14th - 15th century.
Active at the end of the 14th and at the beginning of the 15th century.
Painter.

JACOPO DA NAPOLI, or Jacopo Giovanni da Napoli, also known as Giovanni Jacopo da Pollonia
Italian, 15th century.
Active in Naples.
Sculptor. Monuments.
In 1549, he carved the marble tomb of *Baldassare Ricca* in the church of S Pietro ad Aram, Naples.

JACOPO DA PADOVA, or Giacomo da Padova
Italian, 15th century.
Active in Venice.
Sculptor. Statues.
In the church of the Frari, there is a marble statue by him, *Angel Holding a Scrolled Document.*

JACOPO DA PARMA
Italian, 15th century.
Sculptor.

JACOPO DA RIVA
Italian, 15th century.
Born to a family originally from Riva da Trento.
Painter.
His signature appears on a very damaged fresco depicting a *Virgin and Child* that was discovered on a choir pillar in the church of S Stefano, Verona, during restoration in 1843. It is probable that he also painted other frescoes in the same style both in this church and in S Zeno, Verona.

JACOPO DA VENEZIA
Italian, 15th century.
Sculptor.
In 1465, he carved an *Annunciation* for the main porch of the cathedral of Cividade (Friuli).

JACOPO DA VERONA
Italian, 15th century.
Calligrapher, miniaturist.
In 1460, he wrote two manuscripts of *The Triumph of Petrarch* for Borso d'Este. These are now, respectively, in the library in Vienna and the national library in Dresden. The first is decorated with seven miniatures, the second with six, all probably his work.

JACOPO DALLA CHIESA, or Jacobello, or Giacomo dal Musaico
Italian, 15th century.
Painter, mosaicist.
Jacopo dalla Chiesa was active in Venice, where he worked for St Mark's in 1414.

JACOPO DEL VASTO AIMONE, or Giacomo
Italian, 12th century.
Sculptor.
This artist was active about 1190. There are many works by him in the church of S Giovanni, Venere (Abruzzo).

JACOPO DELLA QUERCIA, also known as Jacopo di Pietro d'Angelo
Italian, 14th - 15th century.
Born c. 1374, in Siena; died 1438, in Siena or in Bologna.
Sculptor. Statues, monuments, funerary monuments (recumbent statues).
Sienese School.
In 1401, Jacopo della Quercia unsuccessfully entered the competition to make the second door for the baptistery of Florence. In 1406, he sculpted a *Virgin and Child* for the cathedral in Ferrara, and for Lucca cathedral the *Tomb of Ilaria del Carretto*, the restoration of which in the 1980s caused a great deal of controversy. The part of this tomb that has recumbent figures leads one to believe that Jacopo must have been acquainted with the similar sculptures of Claus Slutter, especially the recumbent effigies of the dukes of Burgundy. He drew the plans for a public fountain in Siena, the *Fonte Gaia* (*Fountain of Joy*), which was built between 1414 and 1422, and of which only a few fragments in an antique style remain. Between 1416 and 1422, he sculpted the tombs and altar in the Trenta chapel of S Frediano, Lucca. He decorated the baptismal fonts of Siena with gilt bronze in a realist style, using a play of high and low relief to create perspective effects. Finally, in 1425, he began the decoration of the main porch of S Petronio, Bologna, in which his style foreshadows that of the young Michelangelo, a point that has also been made in connection with the recumbent figure of Ilaria.

Jacopo della Quercia represents a fusion of styles: sometimes derived from the ancient past, or from the 14th century, sometimes turned towards the 15th century, or even beyond. He still has certain ties to Northern Gothic, accompanied by reminiscences of the antique, but to this are added an acquaintance with Burgundian sculpture, especially that of Claus Slutter, and a taste for naturalism suggestive of the innovations of Donatello and Ghiberti.

JACOPO DI ANDREA DI MATTEO, called del Maza
Italian, 15th century.
Sculptor.
Working with Andrea Ferucci, and on the basis of their own design, he carved the altar of the Holy Sacrament in the cathedral in Fiesole. This altar includes statues and reliefs.

JACOPO DI BARTOLOMEO DA SETTIGNANO
Italian, 15th century.
Active in Florence.
Sculptor.
He was commissioned to make a marble tabernacle to be part of a triptych painted by Fra Angelico; this triptych is now in St Mark's, Venice. He may be identical with Jacopo di Bartolomeo of Florence, who collaborated in providing a marble facing for the tomb of the bishop from Pistoia, Ubertino degli Albizzi.

JACOPO DI BEDO DI BENEDETTO DA GUBBIO
Italian, 15th century.
Painter.
He painted the frescoes of the chapel of S Sebastian of the cemetery of S Secondo, near Gubbio. There is another fresco by this artist in the former monastery of S Benedetto. He also worked in the church of S Domenico, Gubbio, where a fresco by him has recently been discovered.

JACOPO DI BENEDETTO, or Giacomo di Benedetto
Italian, 15th century.
Active in Palermo.
Sculptor.

JACOPO DI CASTELLO DI MINO DI MARTINELLO
Italian, 15th century.
Born in Siena.
Active c. 1400.
Painter (including glass). History painting.

JACOPO DI CINO ARRIGHI, or Jacopo di Cione
Italian, 14th century.
Active in Siena.
Painter.
Jacopo di Cino Arrighi worked in the cathedral in Siena, where he painted frescoes in 1362. He is perhaps identical with a Florentine painter of the same name who was commissioned to paint for the Florence mint a *Coronation of the Virgin* that is now in the Uffizi gallery.
AUCTION RECORDS:
NEW YORK, 17 Jan 1985, *Virgin and Child Surrounded by Sacred Figures* (tempera/panel, gold background, $63\frac{1}{2}$ x 27in/161 x 68.5cm) USD 40,000. NEW YORK, 15 Jan 1987, *Virgin and Child Surrounded by Sacred Figures* (1367, oil on panel, gold backgound curved at the top, 22 x $11\frac{1}{2}$in/56 x 29.5cm) USD 300,000.

JACOPO DI CORSO, called Papi
Italian, 15th century.
Born c. 1382.
Active in Florence.
Painter.
Jacopo di Corso worked in 1416 in the baptistery of Siena, and is perhaps identical with Jacopo d'Antonio.

JACOPO DI DOMENICO DA MILANO, or Giacomo di Domenico da Milano
Italian, 16th century.
Of Lombard origin.
Painter. Religious subjects.
He worked in Perugia. The art gallery of Città di Castello owns a *Martyrdom of St Sebastian* by him.

JACOPO DI FRANCESCO (Don)
Italian, 14th century.
Born c. 1337; died 1396, in Florence.
Active in Florence.
Miniaturist.
Jacopo di Francesco was a monk at the Monastero degli Angeli. He left a large number of works, many of them in the monastery of S Michele, Murano.

JACOPO DI LAZZARO DA VENEZIA, or Giacomo di Lazzaro da Venezia
Italian, 15th century.
Died 23 April 1475, in Venice.
Active in Venice.
Sculptor, architect.

JACOPO DI LORENZO DI TEBALDO
Italian, 13th century.
Sculptor (marble), mosaicist.
Cosmati School.
This artist was responsible for mosaic decoration in the church of S Paulo fuori le Mura and the S Giovanni in Laterano, Rome. He was a member of the Cosmati School.

JACOPO DI LOTTO, or Giacomo di Lotto
Italian, 14th century.
Active in Orvieto.
Sculptor (wood).
From 1325 to 1368, Jacopo di Lotto he worked in the cathedral of Orvieto, where he carved stalls that were partly of his own design.

JACOPO DI MARCO DA VILLA, or da Lucca
Italian, 15th century.
Active in Lucca.
Sculptor (wood).
He was probably a pupil of Matteo Civitali. In 1462, he carved in the Charterhouse of Pisa stalls, consisting of 36 seats, for the monks' choir, and he also worked on the canopy for the stalls of the cathedral in Pisa. Among his still extant works is the middle door of the façade of the cathedral in Lucca, and the side doors are also attributed to him. The museum of Lucca has an inlay depicting *St Martin* that was once part of the bishop's throne in the cathedral in Lucca. This throne was carved by him but no longer exists.

JACOPO DI MICHELE, called il Gera
Italian, 14th century.
Active in Pisa during the second half of the 14th century.
Painter. History painting.
The son of Jacopo di Niccolo, known as Gera di Pisa, in 1390, Jacopo di Michele painted 30 fresco figures in the cupola of the cathedral in Pisa. In collaboration with Turino Vanni he decorated the tabernacle of the same church, and he painted a *Crucifix* on the door of the Campo Santo (Porta del Leone), for which he was paid 24 pounds and 10 soldi. In the archives in Pisa, he is mentioned as having painted a banner. The museum in Pisa owns two of his works: *Virgin on a Throne Holding the Child Jesus on her Knee, with St Margaret and St Mary Magdalene*, a painting on wood signed *Iachobus. Dictus. Gera. Me. Pinxit (Jacopo Known As Gera Painted Me)*, and *Virgin on a Throne with the Child Jesus, St Anthony and St Francis*, a painting on wood with a gold background signed *Iacopo Dimiselc Dipiture Ditto Gerad Pisa Mi Dipinse (Jacopo Dimiselc Painter Known As Gerad Pisa Painted Me)*. In his *History of Painting in Italy* Cavalcaselle refers to a work by this artist in the Chiesa d'Annunziata, Palermo.
MUSEUMS AND GALLERIES:
PISA (Mus. Civico): *Virgin on a Throne Holding the Child Jesus on her Knee, with St Margaret and St Mary Magdalene* (painting/wood); *Virgin on a Throne with the Child Jesus, St Anthony and St Francis* (painting/wood).

JACOPO DI PAOLO
Italian, 14th - 15th century.
Painter.
Four small paintings in the art gallery of Bologna and two more in the Stefano museum are attributed to him. The municipal museum has an *Annunciation* by him. One of his main works is the predella of the Bolognini altar in S Petronio, Bologna.
AUCTION RECORDS:
LONDON, 6 July 1983, *St Francis of Assisi; St John the Baptist* (oil on panel with gold background, a pair, $35\frac{1}{2}$ x $14\frac{1}{4}$in/90 x 36cm) GBP 8,500.

JACOPO DI PERCOSSA
Italian, 15th century.
Painter.

JACOPO DI PIERO GUIDI, or Jacopo di Guido
Italian, 14th - 15th century.
Active in Florence at the end of the 14th century and at the beginning of the 15th century.
Sculptor, architect.
Florentine School.
His main sculptural works were carried out for the loggia of lances and the former façade of the Duomo in Florence.

JACOPO DI PIETRO
Italian, 15th century.
Active in Florence.
Sculptor (wood).
Jacopo di Pietro is perhaps identical with Jacopo di Papino di Pietro, who, like him, worked for the haberdashers' guild.

JACOPO DI PIETRO
Italian, 16th century.
Active in Venice.
Sculptor (wood).
Working to sketches by Veronese, Jacopo di Pietro carved the organ case of the church of S Sebastiano.

JACOPO DI PIETRO BERARDUCCI DA GAIFA, or Giacomo, called Giacomo da Urbino
Italian, 15th century.
Active in Urbino and Fano.
Painter.
He is referred to as painting several works for the society of St Anthony the Abbot, Urbino.

JACOPO DI PIETRO DA CITTA DI CASTELLO, or Giacomo, also known as Fra Beato Giacomo
Italian, 13th century.
Born in Città di Castello; died 1292, in Città di Castello.
Sculptor.
Pietro di Jacopo was a Franciscan friar.

JACOPO DI PIETRO DA VENEZIA
Italian, 15th century.
Active in Florence.
Painter.

JACOPO DI SANDRO I, or Jacopo di Giovanni di Francesco, called Jacone
Italian, 16th century.
Died 1553.
Active in Florence.
Painter. History painting, portraits.
A pupil of, friend and assistant to Andrea del Sarto, he is said to have been very lazy, and this may explain the paucity of paintings by him. He is known to have decorated the Palazzo Buondelmonti. Attributed to him are a *Madonna* in the church of Gesu, Cortone, and a *St Lucy* in the church of this saint in Florence. He died in penury. Although Lanzi distinguishes between two artists, Jacone and Jacopo di Sandro, the similarities between the works referred to establish that they are by the same painter, who must have been a pupil of Andrea del Sarto.
AUCTION RECORDS:
MONTE CARLO, 20 June 1987, *Rear View of a Man with Cupids* (pen and brown ink, 11 1/2 x 8 1/4in/29 x 21cm) FRF 20,000.

JACOPO DI SANDRO II
Italian, 16th century.
Active in Florence c. 1500.
Painter.
He may be identical with Jacopo del Tedesco, and he may have been one of the painters Michelangelo called upon for the ceiling works of the Sistine Chapel. He may also have contributed to the decorations for the visit of Leo X to Florence.

JACOPO DI TADDEO D'AREZZO, or Giacomo di Taddeo d'Arezzo
Italian, 14th century.
Illuminator.
He was a monk, who in 1371 wrote and illuminated the large antiphonaries of the church of S Niccolo, Foligno.

JACOPO DI TOMME, or Giacomo di Tommè
Italian, 14th century.
Active in Siena.
Painter. Religious subjects.
He worked in the chapel of S Jacopo in the cathedral in Siena.

JACOPO DI VENCIOLO DA SPOLETO
Italian, 15th century.
Painter.

JACOPO FILIPPO DA BRESCIA
Italian, 15th century.
Of Lombard origin.
Active c. 1480.
Sculptor.
He carved the porch of the monastery church of Barbarano.

JACOPO FILIPPO DA MILANO
Italian, 15th - 16th century.
Illuminator.
There are manuscripts from the monastery of S Salvatore, Bologna that are signed by him: *Psalterium nocturnam* in two volumes, dated 1490 and 1491, now in the possession of the municipal museum of Bologna, and a *Diurnium, festivum*, dated 1507.

JACOPO GIOVANNI DA NAPOLI. See **JACOPO da Napoli**

JACOPO SICULO. See **SICULO Jacopo**

JACOPO SPAGNOLO
Italian, 16th century.
Active in Spello (Umbria).
Illuminator.
In 1519, Jacopo Spagnolo, a Benedictine monk, illuminated with miniatures a book on the chapter house of the church of S Maria Maggiore.

JACOPO ZABOLINO. See **ZABOLINO Giacomo** or **Jacopo**

JACOPONE DA FAENZA. See **BERTUCCI Jacopo**

JACOPS, Cornelis. See **ZEEU Cornelis de**

JACOPS, Gérard
Flemish School, 17th century.
Painter.
Gerard Jacops lived in Amsterdam. He was registered as a member of the guild of St Luke in 1621.

JACOPS, Joseph
Belgian, 19th century.
Born 1 March 1808, in Antwerp.
Painter. Historical subjects, battles, hunting scenes, seascapes.
Joseph Jacops was a pupil of Carpentero and Herreyns at the academy in Antwerp.
AUCTION RECORDS:
LONDON, 28 Feb 1973, *Hunting Scene*, GBP 1,200.

JACOPS, Roland
Flemish School, 17th century.
Died c. 1632.
Active in Antwerp.
Painter.
Roland Jacops was senior member of the guild of St Luke in 1625.

JACOPSEN, H.
Flemish School, 17th century.
Active in Flanders c. 1620.
Engraver, illustrator.
H. Jacopsen engraved a number of plates, particularly portraits, for a *History of the Low Countries*, published in 1620.

JACORIS, Colard
Flemish, 14th century.
Painter, engraver.
Flemish School.
Jacoris is recorded as being an 'engraver of pictures' in 1395 at the Grands Malades hospital in Namur.

JACOT, Daniel
Dutch, 17th century.
Painter.

Daniel Jacot studied under Doudyns. He was a member of the guild of The Hague in 1685.

JACOT, Henry
Swiss, 20th century.
Born 16 March 1928, in Le Locle.
Engraver (burin), medallist, draughtsman.
Henry Jacot studied engraving at the art college in La Chaux-de-Fonds and went on to complete his studies in Zurich, at the fine arts academy in Stuttgart (1950-1952) and under H. Dropsy at the École Nationale des Beaux-Arts in Paris (1952-1955). He works as a cold-chisel engraver, executing commissions for medals and other more personal and more original pieces. His style encompasses both the figurative and the abstract.

Examples of his work featured at the International Triennale of Colour Printing in 1979. In 2003, the Numismatics Collection and the Department of Graphic Arts of the Museum of Art and History in Neuchâtel mounted a Henry Jacot retrospective featuring a selection of his medals, sepia engravings and post-1950 drawings.

BIBLIOGRAPHY:
Henry Jacot, exhibition catalogue, Galerie Numaga, Auvernier, 1978. Liègme, Bernard/Perret, Gilles/Girardin-Cestone, Lucie, *Henry Jacot. Dessins, médailles et gravures au burin*, Éditions Gilles Attinger, Hauterive (CHE), 2003.

JACOT, Pierre Martin
Swiss, 20th century.
Born 10 April 1941, in Diegten.
Active in France since 1962.
Painter, sculptor, engraver.
Pierre Martin Jacot studied at the Basel Art School from 1957 to 1962, then settled in France, where he has been living since 1962. In both his sculptures and his paintings and engravings, he uses simple geometric shapes that could be said to bring him close to the Minimalists, from whom he has learned without adopting their neutrality. The final aim of this geometric abstraction tends towards the monumental, and this tendency is reinforced by his use of polychromy. He has taken part in various group exhibitions, including the Salon de la Jeune Sculpture in 1968 and 1969, the 1969 Salon de Mai and the Paris Biennale.

JACOT-GUILLARMOD, Jules Jacques
Swiss, 19th century.
Born 20 July 1828, in La Chaux-de-Fonds; died 5 August 1889, in St Blaise (Lake Neuchâtel).
Painter. Landscapes, animals.
Jacot-Guillarmod was a pupil of Barthélemy Menn in Geneva, and later of Gleyre and Couture in Paris. On his return to Switzerland from Paris, he worked in La Cibourg (Jura), then the Erlach-Cerlier area, where he painted canvases for the Salons in Neuchâtel from 1853 on. In 1863 and 1864, he travelled to Transylvania and Wallachia. On his return, he was appointed drawing master at the college in La-Chaux-de-Fonds. He attracted attention chiefly as a painter of horses.

MUSEUMS AND GALLERIES:
GENEVA (MAH): *Cows Grazing* - NEUCHÂTEL: *The Special Effort; Wallachian Transport; Train of Horses Crossing the Tisza; St Blaise Mill in 1875*; various studies.

JACOTIN D'AVIGNON. See **PAPEROCHA Jacotin**

JACOTT, Henriette
Maiden name: Cappelaere
French, 19th century.
Born 19th century, in Paris.
Painter.
Henriette Jacott worked in Paris, where she was a pupil of Léon Cogniet. She was represented at the Salon from 1846 to 1877 with portraits, landscapes and genre paintings, subjects for which she found inspiration in Brittany and Normandy.

MUSEUMS AND GALLERIES:
RHEIMS: *Evening Bells*.

JACOTT, Jean Julien
French, 19th century.
Born 19th century, in Metz.
Lithographer.
Jean Julien Jacott was a pupil of Maréchal and began his career at the Salon in 1845. Prior to this he had collaborated on various publications: *The Mirror, La France Littéraire* (*Literary France*), *Musée Pittoresque* (*Picturesque Museum*), *Galerie Pittoresque* (*Picturesque Gallery*) (1840), *Poetic Revue at the Salon of 1840, Museum Omnibus* and *Gallery Omnibus*. He painted portraits but dedicated his talent mainly to religious engravings in publications such as: *Christian Masters, Religious and Moral Gallery* and others.

JACOTTET, Jean
Swiss, 19th century.
Born 1806, in Echallens.
Painter, engraver, lithographer. Landscapes.
There is confusion between this Jean Jacottet, the Swiss Julien (sometimes called Julien Louis Jacottet) and Frenchman Louis Julien Jacottet. All three appear to have been born in 1806, according to different sources. The two Swiss seem to have come from Echallens and lived in Bonneval (Savoy), where Julien died.

This Jean Jacottet sent work to the Swiss Society of Fine Arts. Like the others, he made lithographs depicting mountain landscapes.

AUCTION RECORDS:
LONDON, 3 Oct 1983, *Lausanne - View from the Asile des Aveugles* (tinted lithograph, 17 1/4 x 24 ins / 44 x 61 cm) GBP 520.

JACOTTET, Julien or Louis Julien
Swiss, 19th century.
Born 1806, in Echallens; died in Bonneval (Savoy).
Painter, engraver, lithographer. Landscapes.
This Julien Jacottet, sometimes called Louis Julien Jacottet, is sometimes confused with his French counterpart Louis Julien Jacottet, born the same year, also a painter and lithographer and treating similar themes. He is equally confused with Jean Jacottet, who was also born in 1806, in Echallens.

Is this the man mentioned in a work by Dr Brun in connection with an exhibition in Lucerne in 1874? His main subject-matter was mountains and views of spas (which were very fashionable at the time), of which he produced lithographs that allowed him to sell his pictures widely like picture postcards. He gives his views of mountains a dramatic, romantic character, with strong light contrasts. His favourite mountains were those in Switzerland, Baden and even the Pyrenées, where he went several times in 1834, 1835 and probably 1841. He called in Adolphe Bayot and Victor Adam for help with figures.

MUSEUMS AND GALLERIES:
PAU (MBA): *Hourat Madonna, Pyrénées Atlantiques* (lithograph).

JACOTTET, Louis
French, 19th century.
Born 1843, in Paris.
Painter. Landscapes.
Louis Jacottet was a pupil of his father Louis Julien Jacottet and of Gleyre. He made his debut at the Salon in 1865 and continued to exhibit there, in particular with views of the *département* of Eure-et-Loir and of Switzerland. So great is the similarity of subject matter between his works and those of the painter Louis Jean Jacottet, who exhibited his works

during the same period, that they could easily be mistaken for each other. If they are indeed two different people, then they must be related.

AUCTION RECORDS:

PARIS, 16 Dec 1925, *The Area around Tours*, FRF 300.

JACOTTET, Louis Jean

French, 19th century.
Born 19th century, in Paris.
Painter.

This artist exhibited landscapes at the Salon from 1861 to 1870.

JACOTTET, Louis Julien

French, 19th century.
Born 1806, in Paris; died 1880.
Painter, engraver, lithographer. Landscapes.

There is some confusion between this Louis Julien Jacottet and the Swiss artist Julien Jacottet. The works of these two men, especially the lithographs depicting the same subjects, namely mountain scenes, bear such a striking resemblance to each other that they have often been mistaken.

This Jacottet seems to have contributed works to the Paris Salon from 1827 to 1839.

Above all, he specialised in producing for commercial gain *Landscape Series*, engravings intended to popularise spas, which were sold in those places before postcards were invented. His works include: *Walks in Paris and its Surroundings - Views of Switzerland - Banks of the Rhine - Scandinavia - St Petersburg and Moscow* in the style of Charlemagne, *Cracow* in the style of Clowak, and *Album of Wilna - Spain - Rome - Cuba - Jamaica - The Orient, Italy as the Crow Flies* by Guesdon, and part of *Monuments of Italy* by Benoist.

JACOULET, Paul

French, 20th century.
Born 1902, in Paris; died 1960, in Kauizawa.
Active in Japan.
Engraver, draughtsman, photographer. Scenes with figures, landscapes with figures, fish.
Sosaku Hanga.

Paul Jacoulet went to Japan with his parents in 1906, and began to study painting from the age of 11. His father taught at the University of Tokyo. He lived in Japan all his life, and followed the teachings of Seiki Kuroda, Takeji Fujishima and Terukata Ikeda. He worked as an interpreter at the French Embassy in Japan. A violinist and collector of butterflies, he made numerous voyages in the South Seas. In 1934, he worked with the engraver Kazuo Yamagishi. In 1941, he left Tokyo to settle in Karuizawa, where he later died. He had adopted a Japanese lifestyle, which gave him a reputation as an eccentric amongst westerners. Jacoulet achieved mastery of traditional Japanese techniques, and figured within the domain of the *sosaku hanga*, founded by Yamamoto Kanae. He used a special, hand-made paper of precious materials (gold, silver, platinum), as well as opal and the dust of semi-precious stones. He depicted figures of the South Seas, of Japan and Asia, in portraits combining the traditional Japanese style with that of Art Nouveau, resulting in decorative, picturesque works.

BIBLIOGRAPHY:

Miles, Richard, *The Prints of Paul Jacoulet*, R.G. Sawers, London-Pacific Asia Museum, Pasadena (CA), 1982.

AUCTION RECORDS:

LONDON, 16 April 1988, *The Mysterious Pacific: South Seas* (print, 18 3/4 x 14 1/4 ins / 47.5 x 36 cm) GBP 4,180. LONDON, 16 June 1988, *The Pearls: Mandchoucuo, from the Fishing Series* (print, 17 1/2 x 13 3/4 ins / 44.5 x 34.8 cm) GBP 1,210. LONDON, 9 Nov 1988, *The Tragic Actor Mandchoukuo, from the Peonies Series* (print, 18 1/2 x 14 1/4 ins / 47.1 x 36 cm) GBP 1,760; *The Song of the Spinners, Mongolia* (print, 18 1/2 x 14 ins / 47.3 x 35.6 cm) GBP 1,650. NEW YORK, 20 April 1989, *Mandchoukuo Sandalwood Smoke* (Dai Oban ukiyo-e print, 14 x 18 1/2 ins / 35.7 x 47.3 cm) USD 1,540. LONDON, 13 Nov 1989, *A Korean Bride Sitting on the Ground* (Dai Oban Tatee print, 18 1/2 x 14 ins / 47 x 35.5 cm) GBP 2,420. LONDON, 6 June 1990, *Evening Flowers, Truck-Toloas* (Dai Oban ukiyo-e print, 18 1/2 x 14 ins / 47.1 x 35.8 cm) GBP 1,760. NEW YORK, 15 June 1990, *Evening Flowers, Truck-Toloas* (Oban Tatee print, 18 1/2 x 14 ins / 46.7 x 35.8 cm) USD 4,180; *Tatooed Woman of Falalap Quest Carolines* (Dai Oban Tatee print, 18 3/4 x 14 1/4 ins / 47.5 x 36.5 cm) USD 7,150. NEW YORK, 27 March 1991, *Snowflakes in Pengyong in Korea* (Dai Oban Tatee print, 18 1/2 x 14 ins / 47.2 x 35.7 cm) USD 4,620. NEW YORK, 23 Oct 1991, *The Goldfish Bowl* (Dai Oban Tatee print, 18 3/4 x 14 1/4 ins / 47.9 x 36 cm) USD 4,400. MUNICH, 1-2 Dec 1992, *The Song of the Waves* (woodcut in colour, oban tate-e) DEM 1,058. PARIS, 5 Dec 1997, *Three Japanese* (wood printed in colour, 15 1/4 x 11 3/4 ins / 39 x 30 cm) FRF 2,200. EAST DENNIS, 23 Aug 2000, *Young Girl of Polowat* (print) USD 5,000. EAST DENNIS, 23 Aug 2000, *Korean with Crossed Arms, Tokyo* (1939, watercolour) USD 8,000. PARIS, 26 June 2001, *Parisian Woman* (print, 15 x 12 ins / 39 x 30 cm) FRF 28,500. EAST DENNIS, 21 Aug 2002, *Song of Waves* (mural of 80 tiles with border tiles, 60 x 48 ins / 152 x 122 cm) USD 5,600. EAST DENNIS, 21 Aug 2002, *Mysterious Pacific* (coloured print) USD 7,100. EAST DENNIS, 20 Aug 2003, *Modern Japanese Beauty* (print) USD 12,000. EAST DENNIS, 20 Aug 2003, *Parisian Lady* (print) USD 12,000. LOS ANGELES, 2 May 2004, *Portrait of Ramon* (1940, mixed media on paper, 20 x 14 ins / 50 x 36 cm) USD 3,500.

JACOULOV

Russian, 20th century.
Born between 1885 and 1890, in the Caucasus; died c. 1930, in Paris.
Painter.

Jacoulov's brightly coloured abstract works show the influence of Delaunay whom he encountered while staying in Paris in 1912-1913 and again around 1926.

JACOUNTCHIKOVA, Marie.
See **YAKUNCHIKOVA-VEBER**

JACOUTY, Georges, or George

French, 19th - 20th century.
Landscape artist.

AUCTION RECORDS:

PARIS, 2 July 1926, *Il Tago in Toledo*, FRF 580; *The Cattle Market in Saulieu (Côte-'Or)*, FRF 250.

JACOVACCI, Domenico

Italian, 17th century.
Born c. 1624, in Rome; died 1701, in Rome.
Painter.

Jacovacci was a member of the Accademia di San Luca. One of the two paintings of the *Baptism of Christ*, which can be found in the chapel of Baptisms in the church of S Andrea delle Fratte in Rome, is by him.

JACOVACCI, Francesco, or Iacovacci

Italian, 19th century.
Born 30 January 1838, in Rome; died 26 June 1908.
Painter. History painting, genre scenes.

Jacovacci was a pupil of Alessandro Marini and Capolti. He then went to Paris where he worked with the Spanish painter Fortuny. He exhibited in Rome and Turin, and, in 1891, in Berlin *Vittoria Colonna on the Stretcher*, for which he was awarded an honourable mention.

MUSEUMS AND GALLERIES:
NAPLES (Mus. di Capodimonte): *Michelangelo by the Body of Vittoria Colonna; Bernini Working on his Own Bust* - ROME (Gal. Nazionale d'Arte Moderna): *Alexander VI and the Venetian Ambassadors.*
AUCTION RECORDS:
PARIS, 14 April 1891, *First Arrivals,* FRF 1,963. NEW YORK, 29 Oct 1992, *Last Day of the Venetian Republic* (1888, oil on canvas, 51 x 115 ins / 129.5 x 292.1 cm) USD 13,200. AMSTERDAM, 20 April 1993, *Morning Visit* (1877, oil on panel, 14¾ x 18 ins / 37.5 x 46 cm) NLG 7,130. LONDON, 17 June 1999, *Arriving by Gondola* (oil on canvas, 18 x 21 ins / 46 x 54 cm) GBP 2,400. SAN FRANCISCO, 17 May 2000, *Reading the Love Letter* (1867, oil on panel, 17 x 13 ins / 42 x 32 cm) USD 6,000. CLEVELAND, 16 Nov 2000, *Interior Scene with Mother, Baby and Nurse* (1876, oil on panel, 14 x 10 ins / 36 x 25 cm) USD 7,600.

JACOVETTI, Rinaldo, called Rinaldo da Calvi
Italian, 16th century.
Painter, sculptor, architect.

Jacovetti's earliest known work, finished in 1521, was the painting and the chapel of St Anthony of Padua in the monastery of S Bernardo, Calvi. Also by him is a well-preserved altar painting bearing his signature and depicting the coronation of the Virgin. This is in the sacristy of the church of S Niccolo, Stroncone, near Terni.

JACOVLEFF, Aleksandr Evgenevich.
See **YACOVLEV**

JACQMOTTE, Georges Philippe
Belgian, 19th - 20th century.
Active in Brussels.
Painter. Flowers.

Showed his *Amethyst* at the Brussels Exhibition of 1910.
AUCTION RECORDS:
BRUSSELS, 19 Dec 1989, *Vase of Flowers* (oil on canvas, 31½ x 39¼ ins / 80 x 100 cm) BEF 22,000.

JACQUAND
French, 19th century.
Active at the beginning of the 19th century.
Miniaturist.
MUSEUMS AND GALLERIES:
LONDON (Wallace Collection): *Portrait of a Man in Civil Dress* (1818, signed and dated).

JACQUAND, Claude, called Claudius
French, 19th century.
Born 16 December 1804, in Lyons; died 2 April 1878, in Paris.
Painter, watercolourist, lithographer. Religious subjects, portraits, genre scenes. Murals.

Claude Jacquand was a pupil of Fleury Richard at the École des Beaux-Arts in Lyons and won the first prize for painting in 1821. He took part in the Lyons Salon from 1822 and the Paris Salon from 1824. His work was much admired by Louis Philippe, who in 1834 bought *Louise Labbé presented to François I,* following which Jacquand received an official commission for seven paintings for the museum at Versailles. He settled in Paris in 1836 and was decorated with the Légion d'Honneur in 1839. After living the high life and enjoying brief success in his career, he fell into financial decline and obscurity. He was forced to sell his own residence to pay off his debts. He left Paris and went to live in Boulogne-sur-Mer between 1852 and 1855, where he was commissioned to undertake the decoration of the town hall. In 1857, he was further commissioned by the authorities to create *Coronation of the Virgin,* which was painted on a gold background.

His historical and genre paintings were skilfully composed and painted, and beautifully finished, but they are sometimes thought to be lacking in realism and rather pompous. According to the rather spiteful words of Baudelaire in the Salon of 1848, he 'produces twentieth-class Delaroche'. In his large compositions, the figures are sometimes sacrificed for the décor and the accessories, whilst his portraits are dark but natural. His works include charcoal drawings and watercolours, and he left several lithographs in the style of his own drawings: *Little Girl Asleep on a Staircase, Portrait of Monseigneur Pins, The Strolling Fiddler, The Beggar Lady of Chazottes.*

BIBLIOGRAPHY:
Boyer, Sylvain, *Les Années romantiques, la peinture française de 1815 à 1850,* exhibition catalogue, Musée des Beaux-Arts, Nantes, Galeries nationales du Grand Palais, Paris, 1996.
MUSEUMS AND GALLERIES:
AMIENS: *Sentencing in Galilee* - AMSTERDAM (Stedelijk Mus.): *Soap Bubbles* - ARRAS: *The Maidservant of Palaiseau* - AUTUN (Mus. Rolin): *Gaston, Known as the Angel of Foix, Leaving his Mother to Return to the Chateau of Foix* - BAGNÈRES-DE-BIGORRE: *Consolatrix Afflictorum* - BAYONNE: *Anne of Austria and Chancellor Séguier* - BOURG-EN-BRESSE: *Greenish Green; By the Road from the Saône to the Loire* (1840) - CAMBRAI: *The Virgin at Work* - DIJON (Mus. Magnin): *Monk Meditating; Pietro Vannucci Painting among the Monks of Perugia* - DÔLE: *Death of Adelaide of Comminges* (1831) - LE HAVRE: *Christopher Columbus* - LEIPZIG: *Death of Gaston de Foix* - LILLE (MBA): *Interior of the Sacristy of the Convent* - LYONS (MBA): *Thomas More in Prison* (1827); *Parting Kiss* (1836); *Comminges Acknowledging Adelaide in the Habit of the Trappist Monks at the Moment of her Burial; The Confession* (1840); *Making Amends; Portraits of the Artist and Madame Jacquand* - MONTARGIS: *The Rhône in Flood* - MOREZ: *The Lady of the Manor and her Son* (1843); *Meditation* - MUNICH: *Group of Gypsies before the Judge* - NANTES (MBA): *Ribera in Naples* (1839); *Maria de Medici at the Home of Rubens* (1839) - NEUCHÂTEL: *Voltaire Arrested in Frankfurt; Jean-Jacques Rousseau Ordered by Parliament to be Arrested* - NICE (MBA Jules-Chéret): *Main Staircase* - PROVINS: *Muslim; Mater Dolorosa* - QUIMPER (MBA): *An Episode Drawn in Greenish Green* - RENNES (MBA): *The Count de Comminges Acknowledging Adelaide* (1836) - ROUBAIX: *Two Misers* - ROUEN: *The Rebuke* - ST-ÉTIENNE: *The Invalid's Prayer* (1836) - STRASBOURG: study - TOUL: *View of an Interior during the Time of Henry II* - VERSAILLES: *James Molloy Takes Jerusalem; Congress of Munster; Henry of Burgundy Welcomes the Appointment of the Count of Portugal;* same subject; *Charlemagne Crowned King of Italy; General Chapter of St John of Jerusalem* - YPRES: *The Sleeper.*
AUCTION RECORDS:
PARIS, 1850, *William the Silent Selling Jewellery,* FRF 5,000. PARIS, 1876, *Gaston de Foix,* FRF 7,200. PARIS, 9 March 1891, *The Way to Calvary,* FRF 500. PARIS, 22 Dec 1920, *Charles I in Captivity,* FRF 200. PARIS, Oct 1945-July 1946, *Place Vendôme (17th August 1859), Return of the Troops from Italy,* FRF 7,500. PARIS, 17 Nov 1948, *Place Vendôme, Return of the Troops from Italy,* FRF 40,000. LONDON, 22 Jan 1971, *The Zingeri Arrested and Tried in 1650,* Gns 480. LONDON, 28 Feb 1973, *Destitution,* GBP 750. NEW YORK, 19 Oct 1984, *The Painter and his Disciples* (oil on canvas, 28 x 39¼in/71 x 99.5cm) USD 4,000. MONTE CARLO, 29 Nov 1986, *Place Vendôme, 14th August 1859, Return of the Troops from Italy* (oil on canvas, 16½ x 23½in/42 x 59.5cm) FRF 60,000. PARIS, 31 March 1999, *The Parrot Vert-Vert Shocking the Nuns of Nantes* (oil on canvas, 24 x 19 ins / 61 x 49 cm) FRF 29,000. MELBOURNE, 22 Nov 1999, *Louis XI of France Surprising the*

Queen Instructing the Dauphin (oil on canvas, 47 x 71 ins / 120 x 180 cm) AUD 16,000. LYONS, 19 Nov 2000, *Visit of Marie de Médicis to Rubens' Workshop* (oil on panel, 4 x 6 ins / 11 x 16 cm) FRF 12,000.

JACQUARD, Anthoine
French, 17th century.
Died c. 1640, in Poitiers.
Draughtsman, engraver (burin).

Anthoine Jacquard engraved *Portraits* and *Allegories,* as well as several sets of embellishments for jewellery and vignettes. He often signed himself *A.D.J.F.*

JACQUARD, Claude
French, 17th century.
Active in Nancy.
Sculptor.

Claude Jacquard was the grandfather of the Lorraine painter Claude Jacquard.

JACQUARD, Claude
French, 18th century.
Born 1686, in Nancy; died 1736, in Nancy.
Painter. Historical subjects.

Claude Jacquard was a pupil of Claude Charles. He worked for Charles V, Duke of Lorraine, and there are frescoes by him in the cupola of the cathedral church at Nancy. He may be the same artist as the painter Jacquard mentioned by de Marolles.

MUSEUMS AND GALLERIES:
AACHEN (Suermondt-Ludwig Mus.): *Massacre of the Innocents* (1716, oil on canvas) - NANCY (Cathédrale): frescoes.

AUCTION RECORDS:
PARIS, 7 Dec 1981, *The Mystical Marriage of St Catherine; Glorification of St Theresa* (oil on canvas, two pendants with contorted views, each $44\frac{3}{4}$ x $18\frac{1}{4}$in/113.5 x 46.5cm) FRF 58,000.

JACQUART, Demange
French, 17th century.
Active in Nancy.
Painter.

JACQUART, Lucie
Belgian, 20th century.
Born 22 July 1882, in Etterbeek (Brussels); died 1956, in Ghent.
Painter. Still-lifes, fruit, flowers.

A pupil of P. Host, she made her debut at the Brussels Triennale of 1907 and went on to exhibit in Charleroi in 1911 and the 1914 Salon des Artistes Français in Paris. From 1919 Lucie Jacquart was a regular exhibitor at the Brussels Triennale, the Ghent Artists' Circle and the Flanders Artists' Circle. Her work, preserved in various collections in Ghent and Antwerp, includes *Twilight; Pink Azaleas; White Bouquet; Interior with Bouquet of Flowers.*

AUCTION RECORDS:
LOKEREN, 21 March 1992, *Crystal Bowls* (1928, oil on canvas, $30\frac{3}{4}$ x 33 ins / 78 x 84 cm) BEF 80,000. PARIS, 3 Feb 1993, *Still-life with Spectacles* (oil on canvas, $13\frac{3}{4}$ x $11\frac{1}{2}$ ins / 35 x 29 cm) FRF 8,800.

JACQUE, Charles Émile
French, 19th century.
Born 23 May 1813, in Paris; died 7 May 1894, in Paris.
Painter, engraver, draughtsman. Interiors with figures, landscapes with figures, animals, farmyard scenes.
Barbizon School.

Charles Jacque's early years were difficult. At 17 years old, he was apprenticed to an engraver of geographical maps. But, from the very beginning, he had artistic leanings and produced his first etching, *Woman's Head,* in the style of Rembrandt. Soon after this, disillusioned with the engraving trade in the conditions in which he practised it, he joined the army for seven years, during which time he took part in the siege of Anvers in Belgium, the result of which was a drawing depicting the environs of *Anvers* which was later engraved in dry-point. When he had completed his military service, Jacque travelled to England, where he spent two years working on wood carvings for the illustration of Shakespeare's works and for a *History of Greece.* When he returned to France, he travelled in Burgundy, where his family settled from 1830, after which he settled in Paris. But his best work was produced in the forest of Fontainebleau in Barbizon, because Charles Jacque, like Rousseau, was essentially a painter of the Barbizon School and could even be said to have been its last surviving artist. In 1867, he was decorated with the Légion d'Honneur.

He began his career by showing etchings at the Salon in 1845. In subsequent years he also exhibited engravings. His first Salon painting was in 1848, so it follows that he first acquired a much-deserved reputation for his etchings, then as a painter. It was not long before he gained official recognition. As an engraver, he obtained a third-class medal in 1851, two rappels in 1861 and 1863, a second-class medal in 1867 and a major prize in 1889. For his paintings he was awarded a third-class medal in 1861, a second-class medal in 1864 and a gold medal at the Exposition Universelle of 1889. Charles Jacque continued to exhibit at the Paris Salons, with the exception of the years from 1870 to 1888. Indeed, his return in 1888 was accompanied by the triumphant appearance of *The Large Herd,* one of his most masterly canvases. In 2001, his works were featured in the exhibition devoted to *Paysages de Bourgogne, de Corot à Laronze* (*Burgundy Landscapes from Corot to Laronze*) in the Musée de Beaux-Arts in Dijon.

The talent of Charles Jacque offers a reasonable summary of the Barbizon School, containing all its qualities and few of its weaknesses. The sheep he painted are perhaps rather conventional, like the oak trees of Théodore Rousseau, but, this aside, the transparent effects of the skies even in dull weather, the impression of energy, the breadth of composition are notable. Jacque was a painter who drew his inspiration from pastoral scenes - not the artificial pastoral scenes of the 18th century, but sweaty stalls inside which the sheep crowd together in a confused mass. Domestic fowl in their surroundings was also a subject which featured in Jacque's repertoire, and he excelled perhaps more than any other artist in conveying the nervous gestures of these birds. He was their amused and conscientious recorder, and this meticulous attention to detail is evident in the strange work which he wrote and illustrated himself in 1869, *Domestic Fowl.* But as well as being a fine painter, he also had great talent in etching, which always remained his preferred medium and to which he owed his most resounding successes and greatest acclaim. Two quite distinctive periods of etching can be observed in Jacque's work. From his early days through to around 1860, he seemed to aim for a graceful effect in portraying his subject matter. His peasants, shepherdesses, even the animals, displayed a prettiness which could be said to be a little too refined. During the second part of his career, perhaps under the influence of Millet, his style became more defined, more energetic and more realist. This later work contains a sense that he has studied paintings such as Millet's *Shepherdess* and *Water-carrier.*

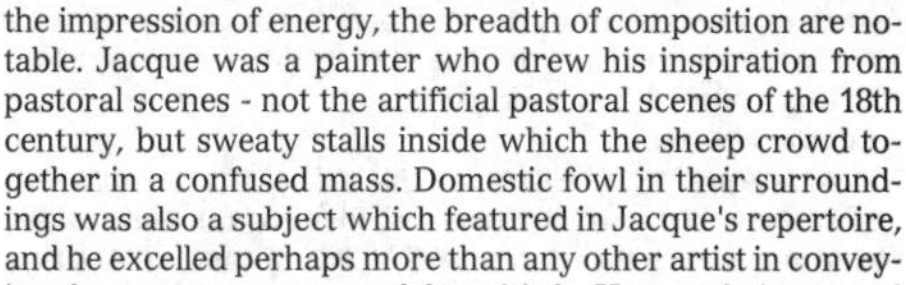

Stamp of sale

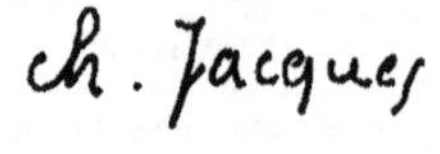

Bibliography:

Fanica, Pierre-Olivier, *Charles Jacque (1813-1894): graveur original et peintre animalier*, Montigny-sur-Loing, 1995. Barthélémy, Sophie/Tran, Catherine, *Paysages de Bourgogne, de Corot à Laronze*, exhibition catalogue, Musée des Beaux-Arts, Dijon, 2001.

Museums and Galleries:

Amsterdam (Stedelijk Mus.): *Hens; Sheep* - Angers (MBA): *Oxen at the Drinking Trough* - Béziers: *Farmyard* - Bucharest: *Hen* - Chambéry (MBA): *Landscape* - Glasgow: *Close of Day* - La Rochelle: *Return to the Sheepfold* - Montreal: *Sheep; Under Cover* - Montreal (Learmont Collection): *Sheep* - Mulhouse: *Hens and Cockerel* - Nantes: *Inside a Sheepfold* - Paris (Chauchard): *Sheep Grazing; Small Sheepfold; Large Sheepfold* - Paris (Mus. d'Orsay): *Troupeau de moutons dans un paysage (ou Berger conduisant un troupeau de montons en plaine)* (*Flock of Sheep in a Landscape (or Shepherd Leading a Flock of Sheep on the Plain)*) (oil on canvas) - Rheims: *Sheep in the Pasture* - Rouen: *Three Children and Two Ewes* - Sheffield: *The Flock; Forest Scene* - St-Étienne: *Sheep in the Pasture* - The Hague (Mus. Mesdag): *Stable; Landscape; Animals Drinking.*

Auction records:

Paris, 9 April 1874, *Sheep at the Edge of a Wood,* FRF 10,080. New York, 1886, *Cowshed,* FRF 16,200. Paris, 1892, *Returning Before the Storm,* FRF 10,305. Paris, 1894, *Large Flock (or Herd),* FRF 30,000; *The Knoll,* FRF 15,000. Paris, 1898, *Time to Return,* FRF 7,140. New York, 1899, *Sheep Grazing,* FRF 10,250. New York, 1899, *Landscape with Sheep,* FRF 14,250. Paris, 1899, *Shepherdess,* FRF 11,000. Paris, 1900, *Stag in the Forest,* FRF 13,500; *Sheepfold,* FRF 15,700. Paris, 1900, *Near the Fence,* FRF 9,600. Paris, 17 Dec 1900, *Shepherdess,* FRF 5,200. New York, 1 Feb 1901, *Interior of a Cowshed,* USD 2,000; *Shepherdess and her Flock,* USD 4,600. Paris, 7 May 1901, *The Flock Returning,* FRF 37,500. Brussels, 11 May 1901, *Sheep in the Pasture,* FRF 12,800. New York, 30 Jan 1902, *Sheep at the Drinking Trough,* USD 3,500. Paris, 6-7 Feb 1902, *Sheep at the Edge of a Wood; Sheep in the Forest* (two pendants) FRF 50,000. New York, 26-28 Feb 1902, *Sheep at the Drinking Trough,* USD 4,000; *Shepherd and his Flock,* USD 8,100. New York, 1 Feb 1903, *Landscape and Sheep,* USD 5,050. Paris, 8 June 1903, *Spring,* FRF 18,050; *Oak Trees,* FRF 24,000; *Sheep Grazing,* FRF 13,500. New York, 1-2 Dec 1904, *Landscape and Sheep,* USD 6,500. Paris, 1905, *Sheepfold,* FRF 40,800. New York, 15-16 March 1906, *Shepherdess and her Flock,* USD 9,100. Paris, 4 May 1906, *Sheep in the Forest,* FRF 31,000; *King Cockerel,* FRF 8,100. Paris, 11 and 12 March 1908, *Sheep in the Pasture,* FRF 12,200; *Shepherd Tending his Sheep,* FRF 30,000. London, 22 May 1908, *The Flock,* GBP 2,625; *Horses at the Drinking Trough,* GBP 567; *Shepherd Bringing Home his Flock.* London, 29 June 1908, *Wooded Pasture,* GBP 924; *Flock at the Drinking Trough,* GBP 1312. London, 10 July 1908, *Landscape,* GBP 1,102. New York, 26 Feb 1909, *Shepherd and Flock,* USD 1,900. London, 13 May 1909, *Shepherdess,* GBP 1,764; *Chickens,* GBP 52; *Sheep Grazing,* GBP 210. London, 21 May 1909, *The Flock,* GBP 3,360; *The Shepherdess* (1883) GBP 2205. London, 10 June 1909, *Shepherdess,* GBP 1,732. London, 3 June 1910, *Shepherd and Flock on a Hill,* GBP 441. London, 30 June 1910, *Shepherd and his Flock,* GBP 945. New York, 6 Jan 1911, *Return of the Flock,* USD 2,800. New York, 13 Jan 1911, *Sheepfold,* USD 5,100. New York, 14-17 March 1911, *Farmyard,* USD 2,700. Paris, 31 March 1911, *Shepherd Grazing his Sheep,* FRF 20,000; *The Flock Returning,* FRF 15,600. London, 30 June 1911, *Forest Pasture,* GBP 1,356. Paris, 6 Dec 1911, *In the Sheepfold,* FRF 15,000. Paris, 4-5 Dec 1918, *Shepherd Leading his Flock,* FRF 19,600. Paris, 7 Dec 1918, *Inside a Sheepfold,* FRF 19,000. Paris, 26 Nov 1919, *Woman Guarding Sheep,* FRF 27,000. Paris, 4-5 March 1920, *Shepherdess and her Flock,* FRF 41,800. Paris, 27 May 1920, *Cows at the Drinking Trough* (drawing) FRF 3,000. London, 26 May 1922, *Shepherd and his Flock,* GBP 588. Paris, 5 March 1923, *A Farm,* FRF 6,100. London, 22 June 1923, *Abating Storm,* GBP 546. Paris, 8 May 1924, *Inside a Sheepfold,* FRF 23,000. Paris, 19 May 1924, *Sheep in the Pasture,* FRF 43,000. Paris, 23 Feb 1925, *The Flock Returning, Evening Time,* FRF 15,000. Paris, 10 June 1925, *Sheep in the Pasture at the Edge of a Wood,* FRF 40,120. Paris, 1 March 1926, *Feeding the Hens,* FRF 16,000. London, 29 April 1927, *The Flock,* GBP 1,837. London, 13 May 1927, *Sheepfold,* GBP 577. Paris, 20 June 1928, *Sheep and Hens in a Sheepfold,* FRF 12,000. Paris, 16 Nov 1928, *Interior of a Stable,* FRF 11,100. London, 19 April 1929, *Inside a Sheepfold,* GBP 504. New York, 30 Jan 1930, *Landscape with Sheep and a Shepherd,* USD 1,000. Paris, 18 May 1934, *Flock of Sheep on the Chailly Plain,* FRF 16,600. Paris, 7 June 1935, *Sheep in a Pasture near a Clump of Oak Trees with a Stormy Sun,* FRF 16,000; *Flock of Sheep Returning from the Pasture in the Evening,* FRF 14,100. New York, 4 March 1937, *Shepherd and Sheep,* USD 1,550. Paris, 13 March 1942, *Sheep in the Fold,* FRF 5,000. London, 27 March 1942, *Leaving the Stable,* GBP 168. Paris, 18 May 1942, *Pigs Resting,* FRF 6,500. Paris, 29 May 1942, *Flock Returning,* FRF 10,000. Paris, 23 Dec 1942, *Cows at the Drinking Trough* (charcoal) FRF 16,000; *Pigsty,* FRF 15,100. Paris, 22 Feb 1943, *Cockerel and Hens,* FRF 21,000. Paris, 7 May 1943, *Shepherd and his Flock,* FRF 36,000. New York, 15 Jan 1944, *Sheepfold,* USD 1,250. Paris, 3 Feb 1944, *Farmyard,* FRF 65,000. Paris, 17 May 1944, *Shepherdess and her Flock,* FRF 101,000; *Inside the Sheepfold* (1874) FRF 101,000. New York, 24 May 1944, *Sheep in a Wood near a Pond,* USD 1,700. Nice, 2 June 1945, *Sheep in a Landscape,* FRF 40,000. Paris, Oct 1945-July 1946, *Shepherd and his Flock near a Pond,* FRF 36,000; *Inside a Sheepfold,* FRF 70,000. New York, 20 Feb 1946, *Mealtime,* USD 1,700. Paris, 8 Dec 1948, *Sheep, Cockerel and Hens in a Farmyard,* FRF 46,000. Paris, 17 March 1950, *Shepherd,* FRF 88,000. Paris, 20 June 1951, *Sheepfold,* FRF 110,000. Paris, 15 June 1954, *Sheep in a Cowshed,* FRF 180,000. New York, 23 Oct 1957, *At the Edge of the Wood,* USD 750. New York, 21 Oct 1959, *Going into the Pasture,* USD 850. Paris, 5 Feb 1960, *Inside a Sheepfold,* FRF 900. New York, 24 Nov 1965, *Flock of Sheep,* USD 1,300. New York, 12 March 1969, *Flock of Sheep in a Landscape,* USD 2,250. Bern, 7 May 1971, *Stable,* CHF 5,500. Cologne, 6 June 1973, *Flock of Sheep in a Landscape,* DEM 6,000. London, 6 March 1974, *Flock of Sheep in a Landscape,* GBP 1,100. Paris, 26 Oct 1976, *Inside the Sheepfold* (oil on panel, 9½ x 12¾in/24 x 32.5cm) FRF 7,000. New York, 7 Oct 1977, *Shepherd and Flock in a Wooded Landscape* (1879, oil on canvas, 29 x 40in/73.5 x 101.5cm) USD 9,500. New York, 3 May 1979, *Flock Return-*

ing (oil on canvas, 32 x 26in/81 x 66cm) USD 19,000. LONDON, 29 Nov 1979, *Sheep in the Cowshed* (charcoal heightened with white, 10 1/2 x 16 1/4in/26.5 x 41cm) GBP 2,100. LONDON, 16 March 1983, *In the Cowshed* (1845, charcoal, 17 3/4 x 13 1/4in/45 x 33.5cm) GBP 1,250. NEW YORK, 27 Oct 1983, *Flock Returning* (oil on panel, 12 1/2 x 18in/31.7 x 45.7cm) USD 5,500. NEW YORK, 27 Feb 1986, *Flock of Sheep at the Drinking Trough* (oil on canvas, 32 x 26in/81.2 x 66cm) USD 21,000. LONDON, 24 June 1987, *Shepherdess and Flock of Sheep* (1893, charcoal heightened with white, 18 1/4 x 15in/46.5 x 38cm) GBP 1,800. PARIS, 5 Feb 1988, *Sheep in the Pasture* (oil on panel, 9 x 6in/22 x 15cm) FRF 6,900. NEW YORK, 25 Feb 1988, *Flock of Sheep near a Wood* (oil on canvas, 21 1/4 x 28 1/2in/54 x 72.7cm) USD 12,100. NEW YORK, 25 May 1988, *Guiding his Flock* (oil on panel, 9 1/2 x 16in/24.2 x 39.7cm) USD 10,450. PARIS, 27 May 1988, *Shepherdess and Sheep* (1879, charcoal and white chalk, 11 3/4 x 16 1/2in/30 x 42cm) FRF 125,000. LOS ANGELES, 9 June 1988, *Couple of Shepherds Watching Over their Flock* (oil on canvas, 30 1/4 x 25 3/4in/77 x 65.5cm) USD 22, 000. PARIS, 4-6 July 1988, *Farmyard* (oil on panel, 7 3/4 x 8 1/4in/19.5 x 21cm) FRF 14,500. NEW YORK, 23 Feb 1989, *End of the Day* (oil on canvas, 21 3/4 x 18 1/4in/55.3 x 46.4cm) USD 38,500. PARIS, 20 March 1989, *Sheepfold* (1887, oil on panel, 11 x 16 1/4in/28 x 41cm) FRF 9,000. LONDON, 21 June 1989, *Horses and Domestic Fowl inside a Stable* (oil on canvas, 19 3/4 x 29 1/2in/50 x 75cm) GBP 7,700. NEW YORK, 24 Oct 1989, *Shepherdess* (oil on canvas, 25 1/2 x 32in/65 x 81cm) USD 40,700. VERSAILLES, 19 Nov 1989, *Pigs Feeding* (oil on panel, 5 3/4 x 8in/14.5 x 20.5cm) FRF 13,500. PARIS, 21 March 1990, *Animals* (oil on panel, 5 3/4 x 8 1/4in/14.5 x 21cm) FRF 22,000. PARIS, 10 April 1990, *Inside the Cowshed* (oil on canvas, 18 x 15in/46 x 38cm) FRF 45,000. NEW YORK, 22 May 1990, *Shepherdess and her Flock* (oil on canvas, 26 x 22in/66 x 55.8cm) USD 39,600. PARIS, 12 Oct 1990, *Woman Tending her Sheep* (1892, drawing, charcoal/mounted paper/canvas, 32 x 25 1/2in/81 x 65cm) FRF 27,000. NEW YORK, 23 Oct 1990, *Returning to the Sheepfold by Moonlight* (oil on canvas, 28 x 39 1/2in/71.1 x 100.3cm) USD 44,000. AMSTERDAM, 30 Oct 1990, *Domestic Fowl in a Barn* (oil on panel, 7 1/2 x 8 1/4in/19 x 21cm) NLG 5,750. NEW YORK, 28 Feb 1991, *Shepherdess Resting* (oil on canvas, 32 x 39 1/2in/81.4 x 100.3cm) USD 6,600. PARIS, 12 April 1991, *Forest Clearing* (oil on canvas, 25 1/2 x 38 1/2in/65 x 98cm) FRF 81,000. AMSTERDAM, 23 April 1991, *Sheep on the Cliff* (1875, oil on canvas, 40 1/2 x 55 3/4in/103 x 141.5cm) NLG 12,650. NEW YORK, 21 May 1991, *Hens and Chickens Pecking* (oil on panel, 5 x 8 1/2in/12.8 x 21.5cm) USD 7,700. NEW YORK, 23 May 1991, *Sheep Coming out of the Fold, Morning* (1878, oil on canvas, 21 3/4 x 18 1/4in/55.5 x 46.4cm) USD 26,400. PARIS, 29 Nov 1991, *Interior of a Peasant's Dwelling* (lead pencil, 2 3/4 x 4in/7.3 x 10.4cm) FRF 3,800. VICHY, 23 May 1992, *Sheep* (oil on canvas, 25 1/2 x 32in/65 x 81cm) FRF 140,000. NEW YORK, 28 May 1992, *The Flock* (oil on canvas, 28 3/4 x 39 1/2in/73 x 100.3cm) USD 33,000. LONDON, 17 June 1992, *Sheep in the Forest in Fontainebleau* (oil on canvas). PARIS, 7 July 1992, *Shepherdess and her Sheep* (oil on canvas, 32 1/4 ins / 82 cm, 2 x 26 1/4in/5 x 66.5cm) FRF 96,000. EDINBURGH, 19 Nov 1992, *Flock of Sheep Grazing on the Banks of a River with a Shepherd and his Dog* (oil on canvas, 28 x 47 1/2in/71.4 x 120.6cm) GBP 3,720. AMSTERDAM, 20 April 1993, *Sheep in a Barn* (oil on canvas, 17 x 14 1/2in/43 x 37cm) NLG 12,650. BARBIZON, 13 June 1993, *Towhorses* (oil on canvas, 25 1/2 x 32in/65 x 81cm) FRF 163,000. NEW YORK, 12 Oct 1993, *Shepherd and his Flock* (oil on canvas, 42 1/2 x 30 1/4in/108 x 76.8cm) USD 68,500. PARIS, 21 March 1994, *Two Hens* (oil on panel, 8 1/2 x 6 1/2in/21.5 x 16.5cm) FRF 15,500. PARIS, 25 March 1994, *Child with Hen* (oil on panel, 6 x 9 1/2in/15 x 24cm) FRF 27,000. LYONS, 18 May 1994, *Sheepfold* (oil on canvas, 9 3/4 x 13 3/4in/25 x 35cm) FRF 50,000. MONACO, 19 June 1994, *Inside the Sheepfold with Ewes, Lambs and Domestic Fowl* (oil on canvas, 36 3/4 x 53 1/2in/93.6 x 136cm) FRF 105,450. PARIS, 29 June 1994, *Card Game* (oil on panel, 4 1/4 x 3 1/2in/11 x 9cm) FRF 6,000. NEW YORK, 16 Feb 1995, *Shepherd with his Flock* (oil on canvas, 32 3/4 x 26in/83.2 x 66cm) USD 46,000. LONDON, 11 April 1995, *Shepherd Leading his Flock* (charcoal and white chalk, 10 x 15in/25.5 x 38cm) GBP 1,495. BARBIZON, 21 May 1995, *Shepherdess and Her Sheep* (oil on canvas, 28 3/4 x 48in/73 x 121cm) FRF 132,000. PARIS, 7 June 1995, *Herd of Pigs* (charcoal, stump heightened with white/beige paper, 7 x 9 1/2in/17.5 x 24cm) FRF 7,500. PARIS, 28 Feb 1996, *Woman Guarding Sheep* (oil on canvas, 36 1/2 x 59 3/4in/93 x 152cm) FRF 112,000. NEW YORK, 23-24 May 1996, *Sheep Grazing near an Old Tree* (1869, oil on canvas, 30 x 25in/76.2 x 63.5cm) USD 20,700. PARIS, 7 June 1996, *Country Scenes and Landscapes* (etchings and dry-points, set of 55 items) FRF 5,300. NEW YORK, 18-19 July 1996, *Sheep in the Fold* (oil on canvas, 18 x 15in/45.7 x 38.1cm) USD 7,475. LONDON, 21 Nov 1996, *Shepherd and his Flock* (oil on panel, 10 1/2 x 17 3/4in/26.5 x 45cm) GBP 5,750. PARIS, 12 Dec 1997, *On the Farm* (oil on panel, 4 1/4 x 3 1/2in/11 x 9cm) FRF 11,500. NEW YORK, 18 March 1998, *Shepherd Tending his Flock by Moonlight* (oil on canvas, 27 x 36 1/2in/68.6 x 93cm, 1 1/4in/3cm) USD 20,700. NEW YORK, 2 Nov 1999, *Approaching Storm* (1868, oil on canvas, 17 x 27 ins / 43 x 69 cm) USD 47,500. NEW YORK, 3 Nov 1999, *Shepherdess and her Flock* (oil on canvas, 27 x 39 ins / 69 x 100 cm) USD 52,500. NEW YORK, 8 March 2000, *Sheepfold* (1880, oil on canvas, 29 x 39 ins / 73 x 100 cm) USD 21,000. NEW YORK, 1 May 2000, *Shepherd with his Flock* (oil on canvas, 26 x 39 ins / 67 x 99 cm) USD 36,000. NEW YORK, 2 May 2001, *Shepherdess with her Flock near a Stream* (oil on canvas, 32 x 26 ins / 81 x 66 cm) USD 90,000. ZURICH, 5 Oct 2001, *Shepherdess with Flock* (1882, oil on canvas, 37 x 60 ins / 93 x 152 cm) CHF 42,000. MUNICH, 26 June 2002, *Shepherd with Flock in Barn* (oil on canvas, 18 x 26 ins / 46 x 67 cm) EUR 11,000. LONDON, 19 Nov 2002, *Landscape with Cows and Sheep* (oil on canvas, 18 x 28 ins / 46 x 70 cm) GBP 6,000. MELUN, 15 June 2003, *Cock and Hens* (oil on canvas, 18 x 26 ins / 46 x 67 cm) EUR 10,000. LONDON, 4 Dec 2003, *Shepherd and his Dog with Cattle and Sheep in a Field* (oil on canvas, 30 x 39 ins / 75 x 100 cm) GBP 9,000. NEW YORK, 22 April 2004, *Shepherd Resting with his Sheep* (oil on canvas, 32 x 43 ins / 81 x 110 cm) USD 60,000. NEW YORK, 23 April 2004, *Spring* (1859, oil on canvas, 42 x 30 ins / 107 x 77 cm) USD 95,000.

JACQUE, Emile

French, 19th - 20th century.

Born 1848, in Epervans (Saône-et-Loire); died 1912, in Paris.

Painter. Scenes with figures, still-lifes, animals.

Émile Jacque was the elder son of the painter Charles Émile Jacque. He studied with Gérome and took up many of the same themes of his father, but specialised in horses. He received an honourable mention at the Exposition Universelle in 1889, and a third-class medal in 1901.

AUCTION RECORDS:

PARIS, 11 Feb 1904, *Horses at the Plough*, FRF 191. PARIS, 21 Jan 1924, *Sheep in the Sheep Pen*, FRF 710. PARIS, 4 Nov 1924, *Still-life: Vegetables and Kitchen Utensils*, FRF 400. PARIS, 10 Dec 1926, *Pulling Horses*, FRF 360. PARIS, 27 Nov 1944, *Horses*, FRF 4,400. PARIS, 22 June 1945, *Horses Drinking*, FRF 2,600. NEW YORK, 12 May 1978, *The Farmyard* (oil on panel, 13 3/4 x 10 1/2 ins / 35 x 26.5 cm) USD 1,700. PARIS, 20 Nov 1991, *Horses at the Ford* (oil on canvas, 13 x 10 ins / 33 x 24.5 cm) FRF 8,000. NEW YORK, 16 July 1992, *Horses Quenching Their Thirst at Dusk* (oil on canvas, 10 x 13 ins / 25.4 x 33 cm) USD 1,980. LONDON, 16 June 1993, *The Break During the Harvest* (oil on canvas, 19 x 28 ins / 48 x 71 cm) GBP 4,140. LONDON, 27 Oct 1993, *Four Sheep and Two Chick-*

ens in a Barn (oil on panel, 8 1/4 x 6 3/4 ins / 21 x 17 cm) GBP 690. AMSTERDAM, 21 April 1994, *Horses Quenching Their Thirst in the Midst of the Ford* (oil on canvas, 22 x 29 1/2 ins / 55 x 75 cm) NLG 19,550. PARIS, 27 Jan 1995, *Pulling Horses* (oil on canvas, 20 3/4 x 17 1/4 ins / 53 x 44 cm) FRF 4,000. PARIS, 16 March 1998, *Farmyard in Bordes* (oil on panel, 7 3/4 x 11 3/4 ins / 20 x 30 cm) FRF 6,500.

JACQUE, Frédéric
French, 19th century.
Born 1859, in Paris.
Painter, engraver (including etching). Landscapes.

Frédéric Jacque, son of the painter Charles, studied under Cabanel. He featured mainly as an engraver at the Salon of French Artists and was awarded an honourable mention in 1888 and a third class medal at the 1900 Exposition Universelle.

Like his father, he painted landscapes dotted with herds of cows, but also views of the outskirts of Fontainebleau, and riverside scenes, all with an impressionist flavour.

AUCTION RECORDS:
PARIS, 11 Feb 1944, *Cows at Pasture*, FRF 780. PARIS, 22 Nov 1944, *Cows at Pasture*, FRF 4,800.

JACQUE, Léon
French, 19th century.
Born 1828, in Paris.
Painter, engraver (including etching). Landscapes with figures.

Léon Jacque, brother of the painter Charles, featured at the Paris Salon from 1864 to 1866.

As well as his engravings reproducing his brother's compositions, Léon painted pasture scenes with landscapes dotted with sheep, herds of cows etc.

MUSEUMS AND GALLERIES:
LONDON (Victoria and Albert Mus.): *Farm Interior* (engraving); *Cottage* (engraving); *Countryside* (engraving); *Charenton Mill* (engraving); *After the War* (engraving); *Duck Shoot* (engraving); *Galette Mill* (engraving); *Ile de Billancourt after the War* (engraving); *At Barbizon* (engraving).

JACQUE, Louis
French, 19th century.
Painter.

Louis Jacque exhibited scenes of the Doubs region of France at the 1836 and 1837 Paris Salons.

JACQUE, Louis
Canadian, 20th century.
Born 1919, in Montreal.
Painter.

Louis Jacque was a pupil of the painters Jean-Pierre Lemieux and Borduas. He took part in the Montreal Salon du Printemps from 1956 to 1960. He had solo exhibitions in Montreal in 1958, 1960 and 1963-1964. His abstract paintings, consisting of large symbolic forms in graduated shades of colour, featured in the group exhibition Six Montreal Painters in Paris in 1964.

JACQUE, Louis Gaston. See **JACQUES Louis Gaston**

JACQUE, Maurice
French, 19th century.
Born during the second half of the 19th century.
Painter.

Maurice Jacque, son of the painter Charles, owned an inn in Barbizon - the Auberge Ganne - where painters from the so-called Barbizon school used to stay.

JACQUELART, Lambert
Dutch, 19th century.
Born 10 March 1820, in Diekirch.
Painter, engraver.

Lambert Jacquelart worked in Luxembourg.

JACQUELIN
French, 19th century.
Died before 1878.
Active in Tournus.
Goldsmith, sculptor.

Tournus museum holds an ivory statuette of the painter *Greuze* by Jacquelin, which reproduces Rougelet's statue and pedestal, and was donated by Mme Jacquelin-Lefebvre in 1878.

MUSEUMS AND GALLERIES:
TOURNUS: *Greuze* (ivory, after Rougelet).

JACQUELIN, Marguerite
French, 19th century.
Born 19th century, in Bordeaux.
Painter. Flowers.

Marguerite Jacquelin was a pupil of Auguin, Lalanne, Robert Fleury and Bonnat and made her debut at the 1879 Paris Salon.

JACQUELIN DE MONTLUÇON, or Molisson
French, 15th century.
Died 1505.
Active in Bourges (Cher).
Painter.

Records place Jacquelin de Montluçon in Bourges between 1487 and 1504. His name appears almost every year in documents relating to ornamental paintings, coats of arms and glass paintings.

JACQUELINE-HUBERT, Madeleine Suzanne
French, 20th century.
Born 30 November 1883, in Paris.
Miniaturist.

Jacqueline-Hubert was a pupil of Laforge, Baschet and Schommer. In Paris, she exhibited at the Salon des Artistes Français and became a member in 1907.

JACQUELOTTE
French, 15th century.
Painter.

According to Siret, Jacquelotte undertook work relating to the 'entremets' festival in Bruges in 1468.

JACQUEMAIN, P. L., or Jaquemain
French, 19th century.
Engraver.

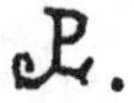

AUCTION RECORDS:
NEW YORK, 22-23 July 1993, *Landscape with River and Woods* (oil on canvas, pair, each 12 1/2 x 18 ins / 31.8 x 45.7 cm) USD 2,185.

JACQUEMARD, Jean Amédée
French, 14th century.
Active in Lyons.
Sculptor.

Jacquemard worked at the Château de Pont-d'Ain near Bourg-en-Bresse from 1342 to 1346. He could possibly be the artist named Jacquemet who was recorded in Lyons in 1363.

JACQUEMART, called Jakeme de Mons
Flemish, 14th century.
Painter, sculptor.
Flemish School.

Jacquemart is recorded as producing numerous decorative paintings in Mons from 1352 to 1376, notably for the church of St-Waudru.

JACQUEMART, called le Ghistreneur
French, 14th century.
Active in Cambrai.
Sculptor.
Of Flemish origin, Jacquemart worked on the decoration of the spire of Cambrai Cathedral in 1398 and 1399.

JACQUEMART, or Jaquemin, called Jacques de Mons
Flemish, 15th century.
Active in Tournai.
Painter, illuminator.
Flemish School.
Jacquemart painted a fresco in 1455, depicting the jurymen of Tournai, in the former 'Hall of the Gentleman Counsellors' in Tournai.

JACQUEMART, Albert
French, 19th century.
Born 1808, in Paris; died 1875.
Painter, draughtsman. Botanical subjects, flowers.
Albert Jacquemart was a pupil at the College of Fine Arts in Paris, where he first devoted himself to drawing, then changed the course of his studies towards the reproduction of plants, insects and shellfish.

He made his debut at the Paris Salon in 1835. For Jacqumart, art was, above all, an accomplishment, not a raison d'être. He entered the civil service and became head clerk at the Ministry of Finance.

In 1840, he published *A Plant Guide for Women* followed, the following year, by a new *Language of Flowers*. He also collaborated on a variety of botanical works. In 1861 and 1862 he published, in collaboration with Le Blant, *A History of Porcelain* completed, in 1873, by *A History of Ceramics*.

Albert Jacquemart played an important part in the development of decorative art and in organising French exhibitions.

JACQUEMART, Alexander, or Zackeimar
16th century.
Painter, decorative designer. Banners.
Passing through Freiburg with his wife at some date between 1511 and 1515, Alexander Jacquemart painted arquebus dragons, a banner, standards, flag-staffs, shields and so on.

JACQUEMART, Henri Alfred Marie
French, 19th century.
Born 22 February 1824, in Paris; died 4 January 1896, in Paris.
Sculptor. Animals.
Henri Alfred Marie Jacquemart began at the College of Fine Arts in Paris on 22 September 1845 and spent time in the studios of Paul Delaroche and de Klagmann. He was awarded medals in 1857 and 1865 and was made Chevalier of the Légion d'Honneur in 1870. He featured at the Paris Salon from 1847 to 1879, with animal figures.

Jacquemart's pieces include *Two Griffins* on the fountain at St-Michel, two stone *Symbolic Figures* at the church of St Augustin, the low relief at Compiègne's town hall showing *Louis XII on Horseback*, and bronze statues of *Suleyman-Pacha* and *Mohammed Bey-Lazzogloer* for two Cairo squares.

BIBLIOGRAPHY:
Kjellberg, Pierre, *Les Bronzes du XIXe siècle dans le Dictionnaire des sculpteurs*, Éd. de l'Amateur, Paris, 1987.

MUSEUMS AND GALLERIES:
AIX-LES-BAINS: *Antelope and Snake* (bronze, group) - BERGUES: *Lioness* (bronze) - CHAMBÉRY: *Roe Deer* (bronze) - METZ: bust*C H de Lacretelle* (bronze) - NANTES: *Field Marshal Ney* (plaster); *Camel Driver from Asia Minor* (bronze).

AUCTION RECORDS:
OSSAGES, 23 July 1984, *Kennel Attendant* (bronze, h. 67 ins / 170 cm) FRF 210,000. ENGHIEN-LES-BAINS, 6 Oct 1985, *Horse and Hound* (brown patinated bronze, h. 9 ins / 22 cm) FRF 12,000. PARIS, 22 Nov 1987, *Horseback Portrait of the General in Chief of the Italian Army in 1796* (patinated bronze, h. 56 3/4 ins / 144 cm) FRF 200,000. PERTH, 30 Aug 1994, *Deer* (bronze, h. 7 1/2 ins / 19 cm) GBP 1,035. NEW YORK, 19 Jan 1995, *Horse and Hound* (bronze, h. 8 1/2 ins / 21.9 cm) USD 3,680. PERTH, 29 Aug 1995, *Standing Herons with Frogs in their Beaks* (bronze, a pair, 12 1/4 x 9 ins / 31 x 22 cm) GBP 2,990. LONDON, 19 April 2000, *Bloodhound Studying a Tortoise* (brown patinated bronze, 6 x 7 ins / 15 x 18 cm) GBP 1,400. BRUSSELS, 16 May 2000, *Hounds* (a pair, 37 ins / 95 cm) BEF 140,000. NEW YORK, 12 Feb 2002, *Tortoise and the Hound* (bronze, 6 x 7 ins / 15 x 18 cm) USD 2,250. CIRENCESTER, 4 Oct 2002, *Bloodhound Studying a Tortoise* (bronze, 6 x 7 ins / 15 x 17 cm) GBP 3,200. LONDON, 22 July 2003, *Head of a Hound* (cast iron, 16 x 16 ins / 41 x 41 cm) GBP 5,000. NEW YORK, 28 Oct 2003, *Bloodhound Studying Tortoise* (patinated bronze, 6 ins / 14 cm) USD 3,500. NEW YORK, 10 Feb 2004, *Standing Hound* (brown patinated bronze, 7 x 8x11 ins / 18 x 20x28 cm) USD 2,800.

JACQUEMART, Jules Ferdinand
French, 19th century.
Born 1837, in Paris; died 26 September 1880, in Paris, in Nice according to Brian's Dictionary.
Watercolourist, engraver.
Jules Ferdinand, son of Albert Jacquemart, was also his pupil - although Jules trained himself, discovering engraving procedures and creating his own, particular techinque. He had a delicate nature and was extremely refined; his father's position in society giving him the ideal boost to his fledgling career. He was a considerable success - indeed, crowned a 'great' - from the very beginning.

He has since suffered a possibly unfair counter-reaction, at least in his capacity as an aquafortist, and his works are rarely studied. Jules Jacquemart made his debut in 1859 when he carried out some engravings for the *Fine Art Gazette*. In 1862, he provided 26 plates for his father's: *A History of Porcelain*. That same year, Cadart published his most remarkable original plates: *Compositions of Flowers*. His reproductions of bindings for *A History of the Techener Bibliography* are also worthy of mention.

In 1864, M Barbet de Jouy commissioned him to illustrate *The Crown Gems and Jewels*: 60 plates, which were highly successful and 12 plates for *M de Nieuwerkerke's Armament Collection* followed this.

Also of note are 12 plates for *A History of Ceramics* by Albert Jacquemart, *A History of America in Medals*, 12 plates for the New York Museum and numerous reproductions of paintings - all in all, a body of work of close on 400 pieces.

A chest infection, contracted in Vienna in 1873, forced Jacquemart to pass his winters in Menton, on the south west coast. Contrary to the version published in *Brian's Dictionary*, Jacquemart did indeed continue to engrave, as is proved by his submissions to the Paris Salon (he exhibited *The Mona Lisa*, after da Vinci in 1879) and he continued his collaboration with the *Fine Arts Gazette* almost up to his death.

He made his debut at the Paris Salon in 1861 and was awarded medals in 1864, 1866, 1867 and 1878 (medal of honour). He was also made a Chevalier of the Légion d'Honneur on 11 August 1869.

Jacquemart was one of the founders of the Société des Aquarellistes and displayed interesting drawing and colouring skills in this genre, several of his works being held by the

Louvre. He was art master to the Baroness Nathaniel de Rothschild.

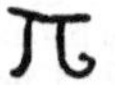

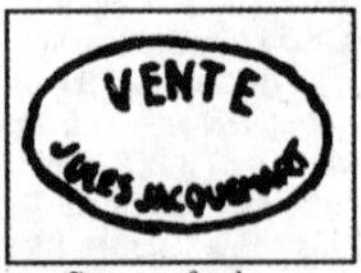

Stamp of sale

AUCTION RECORDS:

PARIS, 1880, *Stormy Sea,* FRF 1,000. PARIS, 1881, *Young Woman* (watercolour) FRF 1,000. PARIS, 12-15 April 1899, *Carei Bridge at Menton* (watercolour) FRF 3,900. PARIS, 26 April 1899, *Bazaar at Menton* (watercolour) FRF 8,250. PARIS, 16-19 June 1919, *View of a Port* (watercolour) FRF 4,500; *Cape Martin-Menton* (watercolour) FRF 1,100. PARIS, 2-4 June 1920, *Road next to the Stream* (pen) FRF 560. PARIS, 3 and 4 Dec 1923, *Port of Marseilles, Sunny Effect* (watercolour) FRF 7,000; *Menton's Old Port* (watercolour) FRF 3,750; *Pool at Marseilles* (watercolour) FRF 4,200. PARIS, 15 Dec 1927, *Marseilles' Old Port* (watercolour) FRF 2,450. PARIS, 19 Jan 1945, *Cape Martin* (watercolour) FRF 1,000. PARIS, 2 Dec 1946, *Southern French Villa* (1879, watercolour) FRF 1,460.

JACQUEMART, Nelie Barbe Hyacinthe, later Mme Edward André
French, 19th - 20th century.
Born 25 July 1841, in Paris; died 14 May 1912, in Paris.
Painter. Portraits, genre scenes, still-lifes.

Jacquemart studied with Léon Cogniet. She made her debut at the Salon de Paris in 1863. She received medals in 1868, 1869, 1870, and in 1878 at the Exposition Universelle. She was married to the banker and collector Édouard André, and bequeathed her mansion on Boulevard Haussmann to the Institut de France. It became the Musée Jacquemart-André. A member of Parisian high society, she drew many of her models from amongst them, including *M Thiers, Marshall Canrobert* and *General Palikao.* Her success was due not only to her social ties, but also to her power and firmness of touch, as much for her portraits as for her genre subjects and still-lifes.

MUSEUMS AND GALLERIES:

PARIS (Mus. Jacquemart-André): *Portrait of M Edward André* (1872).

AUCTION RECORDS:

NEW YORK, 21 May 1987, *Molière at the Barber's* (1863, oil on canvas, 42 3/4 x 61 1/4 ins / 108.5 x 155.5 cm) USD 4,500.

JACQUEMART, Nicolas
French, 19th century.
Sculptor.

Nicolas Jacquemart exhibited statuettes and medallions at the Paris Salon in 1849 and 1850.

JACQUEMART DE HESDIN, or Esdin or Odin
Flemish, 14th - 15th century.
Active 1380 to 1410 or 1411 in France.
Painter, illuminator, draughtsman.
Flemish School.

Jacquemart de Hesdin was of Flemish origin and was probably born in Hesdin, which is now in the Pas-de-Calais region of France. Active at the end of the 14th, and the beginning of the 15th, centuries, he belonged to the Flemish-Parisian strain in art. This movement had not yet come into contact with Italian influences, and would, during the course of the 15th century, establish itself around the court of the dukes of Burgundy, representing, along with the Provençal School based at the papal court in Avignon, one of the two sources of French painting.

He is believed to have worked as a miniaturist in Paris and, in 1384, allegedly painted several miniatures for the Book of Hours of John, Duke of Burgundy. However, he is also known to have worked for John, Duke de Berry, in Poitiers from 1384 until his death - a fact that would seem to cast doubt on the previous assertion.

Two of his works, the *Très Belles Heures de Notre Dame* of c. 1402, and the *Grandes Heures,* completed in 1409, have been attributed to him on the basis of evidence found in documents. Another work, the *Petites Heures du Duc de Berry,* c. 1385, has been attributed on the basis of comparison with the *Grandes Heures.* He is thought to have worked on the decoration of the Château de Poitiers in 1384, and on decorations in Bourges in 1400. It seems possible that he also worked in Valencia.

Jacquemart de Hesdin elevated the art of illumination to new heights: decorating margins with graceful foliage and realistic birds, developing and refining a naturalist style of landscape, and employing a colourful, subtly nuanced palette that included pinks, pale greens and lilacs. The style of his work falls into the category of International Gothic, and provides a missing link between the refinement of Jean Pucelle (the influence of Pucelle's *Breviary of Belleville* can be seen in the drawing and themes used for the illustrations) and the more humanist art of the Limbourg brothers who succeeded him in working for the Duke de Berry.

BIBLIOGRAPHY:

Dupont, Jacques/Gnudi, Cesare, *Les Grands Siècles de la Peinture. La Peinture gothique,* Skira, Geneva, 1990.

MUSEUMS AND GALLERIES:

BRUSSELS (Bibliothèque royale Albert Ier): n° 11060*Très Belles Heures de Notre Dame* - NEW YORK (Pierpont Morgan Library): *Boxwood sketchbook* (silverpoint drawing, attributed) - PARIS (BNF): B.N. latin 919*Grandes Heures du Duc de Berry;* B.N. MS. latin 18014*Petites Heures du Duc de Berry* - PARIS (Louvre): *The Bearing of the Cross* (attributed).

JACQUEMART DU BOS
Flemish, 15th century.
Died 1467.
Active in Tournai.
Sculptor.
Flemish School.

JACQUEMART-ANDRÉ, Nélie.
See **JACQUEMART Nelie Barbe Hyacinthe**

JACQUEMENT, Edmond
French, 20th century.
Born 5 November 1906, in Limoges.
Painter, enameller.

Jacquement exhibited in Paris at the Salon des Indépendants.

JACQUEMET, Simonet
French, 15th century.
Active in Grenoble.
Painter.

Jacquemet is recorded as having painted coats of arms in 1409.

JACQUEMIN, called Sauvaje
French, 14th century.
Active in Troyes 1382-1388.
Painter (glass).

Siret mentions a glass painter of this name, active at a similar time, who worked on Troyes Cathedral. They could be one and the same artist.

JACQUEMIN, André
French, 20th century.

Born 3 September 1904, in Épinal.
Painter, pastellist, watercolourist, draughtsman, engraver, illustrator, fresco artist, designer. Figures, nudes, portraits, landscapes, animals.

André Jacquemin entered the École des Beaux-Arts in 1922, where he worked in the studio of Charles Waltner. He was also a pupil of the painter Ernest Laurent. He was a founding member of Jeune Gravure Contemporaine (young contemporary engraving) in 1929 with Guastalla, Yves Alix, Cochet, Lotiron and La Patelière. He received the Franco-American Foundation's Florence Blumenthal Prize for *La Pensée et l'Art Français* (*French Art and Thought*) (1930), and travelled in Spain and Morocco.

Jacquemin participated in numerous exhibitions in France and abroad. He was included in the French engraving section in the Biennale in Venice in 1937. He was a member of the Peintres-Graveurs Français from 1931. He was curator at the Musée Départemental des Vosges and the Musée International de l'Imagerie in Épinal (1953 to 1974). André Jacquemin was named Chevalier of the Légion d'Honneur, Officier des Arts et Lettres and Chevalier du Mérite Postal. A solo exhibition of his works was presented at the Musée de la Monnaie in Paris in 1982. In collaboration with J. Bersier, he wrote a treaty on the technique of engraving.

Though Jacquemin was also a fresco artist, drawing remained his predominant passion. He executed an ensemble of several thousand graphic works on the landscapes of France, Italy, Greece and Portugal, on railways, restaurants, dance and concerts. He also worked in pastel, watercolour, as well as painting in oil, and he recreated the engraved and drawn portrait. He also worked in etching and dry point. His engraved subjects include mountain landscapes and nocturnal views of Paris evoking a nostalgic poetry; landscapes of Lorraine, Seine-et-Marne, Ile-de-France, Velay and other regions of France; animals, figures and nudes. His engraved work includes more than 800 plates, of which a catalogue was compiled by the Bibliothèque Nationale in Paris. Jacquemin executed mural decorations for the state. He illustrated numerous books, by Colette, Montherlant, Gide, Bosco, Suarès, Malraux, Brillat-Savarin and Barrès (*La Colline inspirée* (*The Inspired Hill*)).

BIBLIOGRAPHY:
Dehaye, Pierre, *André Jacquemin*, Éd. Serpenoise, Metz, Presse Universitaire de Nancy, Nancy, 1986. '*André Jacquemin*' in *Art et Métiers du Livre* n° 172 p. 53, periodical, Paris, 1991.

MUSEUMS AND GALLERIES:
PARIS (MAMVP).

AUCTION RECORDS:
PARIS, 2 April 1990, *Memory of Foix* (1982, oil on canvas, 37 1/2 x 43 1/4 ins / 95 x 110 cm) FRF 4,000.

JACQUEMIN, Clair
French, 18th century.
Active in Grenoble in 1721 and 1725.
Engraver.

JACQUEMIN, Cyprien
French, 19th century.
Born 19th century, in Thonnance-les-Joinville (Haute-Marne).
Engraver (burin).

Cyprien Jacquemin studied under Thouvenin and exhibited at the Paris Salon from 1836 to 1852. His works include *The Last Supper* after da Vinci, portraits and various historical and genre subjects.

JACQUEMIN, Étienne
French, 19th century.
Born 6 August 1823, in Trois-Fontaines-la-Ville (Haute Marne); died 1897.
Active in Joinville (Haute-Marne).
Sculptor (plaster/bronze), medallist. Busts.

Étienne Jacquemin studied under Brion and was a member of the Société des Artistes Français.

MUSEUMS AND GALLERIES:
ALBI: *Voltaire* (wax) - ÉPINAL: *Bust of Claude Gellée* (plaster) - NANCY: *Bust of Claude Lorraine* (bronze) - ST-DIZIER: *Voltaire* (bronze); *Bust of the Artist* (plaster).

JACQUEMIN, François
French, 18th century.
Active in Toulouse.
Painter.

François Jacquemin won first prize as a pupil of the Académie de Paris in 1787. He may be identical to the painter Jacquemin or Jaquemin, curator of the museum at Toulouse from 1828 to 1836, who painted a *Descent from the Cross* for the cathedral.

JACQUEMIN, François
French, 20th century.
Born 1923, in Paris.
Painter.

Jacquemin exhibited *The Septet*, a work of not unskilled composition, at the Salon de Mai in Paris in 1950.

JACQUEMIN, Gérard
French, 15th century.
Active in Nancy c. 1480.
Painter.

Jacquemin is thought to be the same artist as the sculptor Gérard Jacquemin.

JACQUEMIN, Gérard
French, 15th century.
Born in Commercy; died 1491.
Sculptor, architect.

Jacquemin was the son of the architect Rogier Jacquemin. In 1460, Duke René commissioned him to sculpt a chimney at the Château de Joinville, and in the same year, he began sculpting the main portal of the church in Toul, which would not be completed until 1547. In 1474, he built the portal of the church of Pont-à-Mousson, and, in 1480, he worked at the chapel of the ducal palace in Nancy. Before his death, he completed plans for the new chapel of the church of St-Jacques, the building of which was completed in 1492.

JACQUEMIN, Jeanne
French, 19th century.
Born c. 1845, in the Côte d'Or.
Painter. Portraits, genre scenes.

Jeanne Jacquemin studied under Pils and Bonnat and took part in the Paris Salon from 1868 onwards. Her paintings often depict dreamy, melancholy women drawn very precisely and painted in a style reminiscent of Puvis de Chavannes.

AUCTION RECORDS:
PARIS, 30 April 1945, *Interior Scene* (1854) FRF 6,000.

JACQUEMIN, Raphaël
French, 19th century.
Born 1821, in Paris; died 1881, in Paris.
Painter, engraver (etching).

Raphaël Jacquemin studied under Mondain and in various Italian academies. He made his debut at the Salon in 1851 and his works include: *General and Methodical Iconography of Attire from the 4th to the 14th Century*, 200 coloured plates (1863) and *A General History of Clothes* (1876).

JACQUEMIN, Rogier, also called Jean de Commercy
French, 14th - 15th century.
Born c. 1371, in Commercy; died 11 February 1446, in Toul.
Sculptor, architect.

Jacquemin decorated the portal of Toul Cathedral in 1436. The bishop of Metz, Conrard Bayer de Bompart, commissioned him to produce the bishops' chapel in the cathedral in 1443. He also took part in work on the town's fortifications.

JACQUEMIN DE BAR
French, 15th century.
Painter.
Jacquemin de Bar produced decorative paintings in 1458, and painted coats of arms at the Château de Louppy, and for the churches of Louppy, Villette, and Dieu-en-Sorbonne.

JACQUEMON, or Jakemon, or Jaqkemon de Fives
French, 14th century.
Active in Lille (Nord).
Sculptor, painter.
Jacquemon may be the same artist as Jacquemon Creste.

JACQUEMON, Pierre, or Peter
French, 20th century.
Born 6 August 1936, in Lyons.
Active in the USA.
Painter.
Nuagisme.
Jacquemon lives and works in New York and Paris. He is self-taught. His painting can be likened to the 'nuagisme' of Lyrical Abstraction. It demonstrates much tenderness and refinement. He has participated in exhibitions in France, including *Antagonismes* (*Antagonisms*) at the Musée des Arts Décoratifs in Paris, as well as exhibitions at the Musée d'Art Moderne de la Ville de Paris and at the Musée des Beaux-Arts in Lyons. His work was included in exhibitions at the Musée de Charleroi in Belgium and at the Institute of Contemporary Art in Chicago. He has had solo exhibitions at the Galerie de Beaune in Paris; at the Abreu Gallery in New York; at the Galerie Bernard Letu in Geneva; at the Weeden Gallery in Boston, and at the Old Jail Foundation in Texas.
AUCTION RECORDS:
LYONS, 4 Dec 1985, *Untitled* (oil on canvas, 30 3/4 x 26 3/4 ins / 78 x 68 cm) FRF 21,000. LYONS, 1 Dec 1987, *Untitled* (oil on canvas, 26 3/4 x 30 3/4 ins / 68 x 78 cm) FRF 55,000. PARIS, 12 July 1988, *Brown Composition* (oil on canvas, 40 1/2 x 13 3/4 ins / 103 x 35 cm) FRF 5,200. LYONS, 27 April 1989, *Hostages Series* (oil on canvas, 29 1/4 x 19 3/4 ins / 74 x 50 cm) FRF 8,000. NEW YORK, 7 May 1990, *Untitled* (oil on card, 9 x 11 3/4 ins / 22.8 x 29.8 cm) USD 1,100.

JACQUEMOND, Nicolas
French, 18th century.
Active in Arras.
Painter. Historical subjects.
Jacquemond painted *The Calvary* in 1743 for the sacristy of the cathedral at Arras.

JACQUEMONT, Victor
French, 19th century.
Born 8 August 1801, in Paris; died 7 December 1832, in Bombay.
Draughtsman.
Victor Jacquemont was an explorer and sketched his own illustrations for the diary he kept of his travels to India and Central Asia. These sketches included landscapes, types of people, animals and studies of various plants. After his death, a six-volume edition of his diary was published (*Travels in India*), with 300 plates.
MUSEUMS AND GALLERIES:
SEMUR: *Hindu* (1832, study, watercolour).

JACQUEMOT
French, 19th century.
Active in Dieppe.
Painter.
Jacquemot exhibited at the Paris Salon in 1831 and 1833.
MUSEUMS AND GALLERIES:
DIEPPE: *Portrait of the Lawyer Jacques Delamare; Portrait of an officer; Landscape, Depicting the Artist Walking in the Background.*

JACQUEMOT, Charles
French, 20th century.
Born 31 July 1879, in Tours; died 1946.
Painter, engraver (wood). Landscapes, still-lifes.
Charles Jacquemot abandoned his studies in science to devote himself to painting in 1903. He first attracted attention with his Impressionist tendencies, before producing canvases of a more structured Realism. His still-lifes are particularly noted for their beautiful texture. In 1911, he founded the Groupe Libre (Free Group), which included Desnoyer, Rivera, Peské and Mathieu Verdilhan. He was briefly a secretary of the committee of the Salon des Indépendants, and was invited to the Salon des Tuileries in Paris. He participated in exhibitions in Düsseldorf, Amsterdam, Stockholm, Brussels and Tokyo.
MUSEUMS AND GALLERIES:
HONFLEUR - LE HAVRE - OTTAWA - TOURS - TUNIS.
AUCTION RECORDS:
PARIS, 31 May 1943, *Vase of Nasturtiums,* FRF 350; *Landscape in Provence,* FRF 520. PARIS, 9 March 1945, *Landscape,* FRF 1,000.

JACQUEMYNS, Sébastien
Belgian, 20th century.
Died 6 July 1965, in Ukkel.
Painter, sculptor.

JACQUES
French, 14th century.
Active in Lille.
Sculptor.
Jacques worked at the collegiate church of St-Pierre in Lille in 1387 and 1388.

JACQUES, called des Stalles
French, 14th century.
Sculptor (wood).
Burgundy School.
A member of the Burgundy School, Jacques sculpted the stalls of the Chapelle St-Laurent in the archbishop's palace in Sens in 1370.

JACQUES (Maestro)
Spanish, 14th - 15th century.
Painter. History painting. Miniatures.
Jacques worked in Portugal during the reign of John I and also lived in Italy. There are references to him between 1385 and 1433.

JACQUES
15th century.
Illuminator.
The name of Jacques appears on the lists published by De Laborde for the year 1462.

JACQUES, also known as Master Jacques
French, 16th century.
Died 1547.
Painter.
Jacques worked at Auch Cathedral.

JACQUES, called Nantelle
French, 16th century.
Painter.
Jacques lived in Lyons in 1574.

JACQUES
French, 18th century.
Active c. 1756.

Painter. Flowers.
Jacques was a member of the Académie de St-Luc in Paris.

JACQUES, André
French, 20th century.
Born 31 May 1880, in Paris.
Painter, sculptor, engraver, watercolourist, illustrator.
André Jacques studied with his father and with Jean Esroula. He worked in Chambéry, Annecy, Geneva, Paris and London. He is particularly known for his prints and illustrated works on the Savoy region.
MUSEUMS AND GALLERIES:
ARRAS: *Rest.*

JACQUES, Charles Symphorien
French, 18th century.
Died 1799.
Active in Paris.
Sculptor.
Charles Symphorien Jacques was the son-in-law of Nicolas Félix Adam (or Adan). He worked in particular as a porcelain modeller.

JACQUES, E. F.
French, 19th - 20th century.
Sculptor.
Jacques exhibited statues, busts and medallions in the Salon de la Société des Artistes Français from 1889 to 1894, 1897 to 1899 and in 1905.

JACQUES, Émile
Belgian, 20th century.
Born 1874, in Moorslede; died 1937, in Chicago.
Active from 1918 in the USA.
Painter. Figures, portraits, landscapes.
Émile Jacques studied at high school in Antwerp and at the colleges of fine arts in Roulers and Antwerp. His work was influenced by that of Franz Courtens.

JACQUES, François
French, 17th century.
Born 1628, in Rheims; died 20 July 1664.
Sculptor.
François Jacques was the son of Nicolas Jacques. In 1659, with Henri Gentillastre, he decorated the north portico of the church of St-Rémi in Rheims, and died from a fall that he sustained in the course of this work.

JACQUES, Georges or Jehan
French, 17th century.
Active in Le Puy-en-Velay (Haute-Loire) in 1653.
Painter.

JACQUES, Jean I
French, 17th century.
Active in Toulon.
Painter, wood carver.
Jean Jacques I is remembered for a portrait of *Count Alais,* Governor of Provence, and frescoes for the cathedral at Toulon, now Ste-Marie Majeure, and for the chapel of the Château de Grenouille (Gard).

JACQUES, Jean II
French, 18th century.
Active in Toulon.
Wood carver.
Jean Jacques II was the son of Thomas Jacques.

JACQUES, Jean Pierre
Swiss, 20th century.
Born 1913, in Yverdon.
Painter. Landscapes.
Jean Pierre Jacques studied under Alexandre Blanchet and went on to live and work in Geneva.
AUCTION RECORDS:
ZURICH, 23 Nov 1977, *Spring Landscape* (1973, oil on canvas, 18 x 24 ins / 46 x 61 cm) CHF 2,800. BERN, 7 May 1982, *View of Grand-Saconnex in the Jura* (1956) CHF 7,000.

JACQUES, Laurent
French, 17th - 18th century.
Active in Toulon during the 17th and 18th centuries.
Painter.
Laurent Jacques was the son of Jean Jacques I, and is mentioned from 1681 to 1790.

JACQUES, Louis Gaston
French, 20th century.
Born 14 November 1878, in Paris.
Engraver (wood).
Louis Gaston Jacques was a pupil of Georges Aubert, and a member of the Salon des Artistes Français in Paris, where he won a bronze medal.

JACQUES, Lucien, or Lucian
French, 20th century.
Born 20 October 1891, in Varennes-en-Argonne (Meuse); died 11 April 1961, in Nice.
Painter, engraver (wood), poet.
Jacques was also a translator.

JACQUES, Marcel. See **MARCEL-JACQUES Alphonse**

JACQUES, Marie. See **JACQUES-MARY**

JACQUES, Maurice
French, 18th century.
Born c. 1712, in Paris; died 26 March 1784, in Paris.
Painter, draughtsman.
Maurice Jacques was a pupil at the Académie de St-Luc. He exhibited three paintings of flowers at the Salon of 1756. He was a painter and designer of patterns at the tapestry workshops known as the Manufacture des Gobelins, and also executed designs for embroidery, in part after F. Boucher. He published several series of compositions for ornamentation: vases, trophies, flowers and fruit. The Louvre has some works executed after his sketches, and the Musée des Arts Décoratifs has a sketch by him for a folding-screen in Gobelins embroidery, dated 1764.

JACQUES, Nicolas
French, 17th century.
Born c. 1578, in Rheims; died 1649, in Rheims.
Sculptor.
Nicolas Jacques was the son of Pierre Jacques. In 1610, he executed a larger than life statue of Louis XIII for his coronation and anointing. In 1626, he executed a tabernacle for the church of the Carmelite Monastery, and sculpted the equestrian statue of Louis XIII on the pediment of the town hall in 1635. In 1636, he executed six life-size statues of apostles for the pillars of the choir of the church of St-Maurice, and in 1648 he sculpted the rood screen, porticos and choir screens of the church of St-Rémi. He had one son and one grandson, both sculptors like him.

JACQUES, Nicolas
French, 17th - 18th century.
Born 1654, in Rheims; died January 1726.
Sculptor.
Nicolas Jacques was the son of François Jacques. He worked with his father on the north portico of the church of St-Rémi in Rheims, and executed a terracotta group depicting a boy and girl dancing, which is now in the museum at Rheims.
MUSEUMS AND GALLERIES:
RHEIMS: *Boy and Girl Dancing.*

JACQUES, Nicolas
French, 19th century.

Born 1780, in Jarville-la-Malgrange (Meurthe-et-Moselle); died 21 March 1844, in Paris.

Painter, miniaturist. History painting, portraits.

Nicolas Jacques came to Paris to study under David and initially devoted himself to painting historical subjects. However, he became extremely poor when he found it difficult to sell his work and switched to miniatures, probably on the advice of his compatriot from Lorraine, J B Isabey.

The latter gave him lessons and Jacques soon became one of the better miniaturists of the early 19th century. He exhibited for the first time at the 1804 Paris Salon with his *Brother of the Artist Surrounded by his Family* and regularly took part in Parisian Exhibitions until 1840.

Among his more notable works are portraits of the Imperial Family (maybe due to Isabey's support), particularly *Queen Hortense, Bernadotte, Joséphine* and *Princess Borghese*.

After the Restoration, the Duke of Orlean's patronage, which continued after his accession to the throne, gave Jacques the opportunity to paint several official effigies: *The Royal Family, Cherubini, Cuvier, Benjamin Constant, Léopold 1st; King of Belgium* and *Mme de Lavalette*. He also painted portraits of artists: *Mlle Mars, Mlle Rose Dupuis* and *Mme Gévaudan*.

MUSEUMS AND GALLERIES:

MOSCOW (Rumiantsev Mus.): *Forge*.

AUCTION RECORDS:

PARIS, 1844, *Portrait of the Duke of Orleans*. PARIS, 28 Nov 1898, *Portrait of a Young Woman* (miniature) FRF 180. PARIS, 23 June 1926, *Portrait of a Young Woman* (miniature) FRF 20,000; *Portrait of an Officer of the Hussars* (miniature) FRF 11,000. PARIS, 24 Feb 1939, *Woman with Red Scarf* (miniature) FRF 2,500. PARIS, 8 Dec 1989, *Young Woman with Ringlets Wearing a White, Flounced Dress with Lace Collar* (1815, oval miniature, h. 3 ins / 6.7 cm) FRF 13,000. LONDON, 6 Nov 2001, *Young Girl Holding a Porcelain Doll* (1823, miniature, 3 ins / 7 cm) GBP 2,200. LONDON, 9 Dec 2003, *Comte de Flahaut in Blue Coat with Black Collar* (miniature, 2 x 2 ins / 6 x 5 cm) GBP 5,500. LONDON, 9 Dec 2003, *Louis Philippe of Orleans, King of the French. Madame Adelaide* (1818, pair of miniatures, 3 ins / 7 cm) GBP 12,000.

JACQUES, Noël

Belgian, 20th century.

Born 1937, in Etterbeek (Brussels).

Potter.

Noël Jacques studied at art colleges in Maredsous and La Cambre.

JACQUES, Pierre, called Jacques d'Angoulême

French, 16th century.

Born c. 1520, in Rheims; died 1596, in Rheims.

Sculptor. Statues, monuments.

Jacques completed his studies in Rome, where he had been sent by the archbishop Robert de Lenoncourt. On returning to France, he spent time in Angoulême and was named after the town. In Rheims he produced the *Tomb of St Remi*, which was destroyed in 1793 during the French Revolution and rebuilt behind the altar of the church of St-Rémi, along with the 12 ecclesiastical pairs of statues that had survived destruction. In 1540, he sculpted the small side portal of the former church of Épernay, and in 1541, produced the figures for the altar of the Apostles, or of the Resurrection, which today is in Rheims Cathedral.

He returned to Rome in 1549 with Cardinal Charles of Lorraine, where he earned himself a good reputation. There he produced a marble statue, *Autumn*, in 1552, for the Château de la Grotte in Meudon, which was being built by the Cardinal. On his return to the Champagne region of France, he directed the building of the chapel of St-André in the church of St-Alpin in Châlons-sur-Marne in 1553. In 1565, he sculpted the *Tomb of the Mother of Mary Stuart, Mary of Guise* for the church of St-Pierre les Dames in Rheims. He also produced a statue, dated 1586, which is now on the altar of the chapel next to the main portal of the new church of St-André in Rheims.

Dussieux mentions an important event in Jacques' life that took place during his stay in Rome: he produced a model for a statue of *St Peter* at the same time as Michelangelo, which was selected in preference to the work of the great master.

AUCTION RECORDS:

PARIS, 29 April 1942, *St Luke* (pen and wash) FRF 750.

JACQUES, Pierre

French, 17th century.

Active in Toulon.

Painter.

Pierre Jacques was the son of Jean Jacques I, and is mentioned from 1665 to 1691.

JACQUES, Pierre Narcisse

French, 19th century.

Born 29 October 1849, in Consenvoyes (Meuse); died 17 December 1904, in Geneva.

Painter, sculptor.

Pierre Jacques was a pupil of Carpeaux and exhibited in Geneva in 1896. He became Professor of sculpture in stone and wood at Geneva's College of Industrial Arts and exhibited at the Paris Salon in 1875.

JACQUES, Raphael

French, 20th century.

Born 1882, in Nancy; died 7 September 1914, in Nancy.

Painter, engraver.

Raphael Jacques was a pupil at the École des Beaux-Arts in Nancy and at the École Nationale des Beaux-Arts in Paris. He exhibited landscapes in the Salon de la Société Nationale des Beaux-Arts in Paris from 1906 to 1908. In 1913, he exhibited a portrait. He worked in etching.

JACQUES, Théodore Joseph Napoléon

French, 19th century.

Born 12 May 1804, in Paris; died before 30 March 1876.

Sculptor.

Théodore Jacques began at the College of Fine Arts in Paris on 24 August 1818 and studied under Cartelli and Cortot. He was awarded second place in the 1828 Prix de Rome for his *Death of Hercules*. He exhibited at the Paris Salon from 1831 and 1875 and his works include: *Neva*, a huge, bronze statue made in St Petersburg, *Jean Cousin*, a stone statue for the Louvre, *Peter the Great*, a statue erected in Kronstadt's Arsenal Square - and finally two enormous caryatids made out of porphyry for the Hermitage's peristyle.

JACQUES, Thomas

French, 17th century.

Active in Toulon.

Wood carver.

Thomas Jacques was the son of Jean Jacques I, and is mentioned from 1668 to 1703.

JACQUES ALMAND. See **GRIESINGER Jakob**

JACQUES D'ANGOULEME. See **JACQUES Pierre**

JACQUES D'ARTHOIS. See **ARTHOIS**

JACQUES D'AUVERGNE, real name Jacques Meignem or Meignant

French, 16th century.

Born in Bourges; died 1523.

Painter. Religious subjects. Ornaments.

According to Siret, Jacques d'Auvergne painted a *Christ on the Cross*, which was much admired in its time.

JACQUES D'ESCAMAING. See **ESCAMAING**

JACQUES DE BESANÇON
French, 15th century.
Active in Paris.
Illuminator.
MUSEUMS AND GALLERIES:
PARIS (Bibliothèque Mazarine): *Prayer Book* (illuminations, attributed).

JACQUES DE BOULOGNE, or Jake, Jakemes
French, 13th century.
Painter, fresco artist. Religious subjects.
Jacques de Boulogne was a painter in the service of the Countess Mahaut of Artois at the château of Hesdin (Pas-de-Calais). Among his works is *The Count of Artois on Horseback* in the cathedral of Notre Dame, Boulogne, and the altar panes for the château of Hesdin and the 'Maison du Marais' that formed part of it.

JACQUES DE BRABANT
French, 14th century.
Died 1400, in Cambrai.
Active in Tournai.
Sculptor (including wood), painter.
References place Jacques de Brabant in Cambrai from 1370. He took part in work on the church of St-Jacques, including the belfry, and on Notre-Dame Cathedral. He also worked in Douai at the church of St-Amé.

JACQUES DE HERDE. See **HERDE**

JACQUES DE LÜBECK, or Jacob von Lübeck
German, 16th century.
Born in Lübeck.
Painter. History painting, portraits.
Jacques de Lübeck was a member of the Roggendorf family of painters, who were in the service of Charles V.

JACQUES DE MONS. See **JACQUEMART**

JACQUES DE PARIS
French, 16th century.
Of Parisian origin.
Sculptor.
Jacques de Paris was invited to work in Auch, in the Gers region of France, by Jean de Beaujeu, where he produced a series of sculptures for the cathedral from 1560 to 1567. He is recorded as being a bourgeois citizen of Auch in 1574.

JACQUES DE TOUL
French, 15th century.
Sculptor.
Jacques de Toul produced a crucifix for the brotherhood of St Nicholas-des-Clercs in 1487, which was placed in the church of St-Vast.

JACQUES DE TROYES
French, 15th - 16th century.
Active in Spain.
Painter (glass).

JACQUES DE TROYES. See also **JACQUES le Peintre**

JACQUES LE BOUC
French, 16th century.
Active in Paris c. 1540.
Painter.
Jacques le Bouc was a genealogist, who was known as the French L'Appelles (Names). There is no known work by him, but taking into account the artistic standards of the time, he may well have been an artist of some merit.

JACQUES LE CATELAN, called the Catalan
15th century.
Painter.
Jacques the Catalan was employed in Lyons in 1490 on preparations for the ceremonial entry of Charles VIII.

JACQUES LE PEINTRE, called Jacques de Troyes
French, 14th century.
Born in Bar-sur-Aube.
Painter.
Jacques le Peintre decorated the Château de Germoles in 1320, where his paintings were much admired.

JACQUES-CHARLES, J.
French, 20th century.
Born 14 February 1882, in Paris.
Draughtsman, illustrator.
Beginning in 1900, Jacques-Charles illustrated Parisian figures from cafés, theatres and race-tracks in the reviews *Le Sourire* (*The Smile*), *Le Clou* (*The Nail*), *Le Rire* (*Laughter*), *Frou-Frou* (*Rustle*), *Pêle-Mêle* (*Higgeldy-Piggeldy*), *Le Bon Vivant, La Caricature, L'Indiscret, Le Journal*. He also executed the original lithographs and illustrations for *Chez Nous* (*In Our Home*) by H. Frémont, and for *Cloches de Potin-ville* (*Bells of Potin-ville*) by R. Valdens. He specialised in portraits of actresses.

JACQUES-MARY, pseudonym of Jacques, Marie
French, 19th - 20th century.
Born 5 March 1868, in Paris.
Painter. Genre scenes.
Jacques-Mary was a pupil of Albert Goisselin. She exhibited in Paris at the Salon des Artistes Français, and became a member in 1899. She received an honourable mention in 1898, and a third-class medal in 1900 at the Exposition Universelle in Paris.
MUSEUMS AND GALLERIES:
PARIS (MAM): *Old Bridge in Dinan*.
AUCTION RECORDS:
PARIS, 14-15 Dec 1925, *Street Leading up Montigny-sur-Loing*, FRF 610. PARIS, 15 May 1944, *Path by the Side of a River*, FRF 480. PARIS, 11 Dec 1946, *Landscape and Village Street* (two canvases) FRF 10,000. LOS ANGELES, 17 March 1980, *Moret Bridge* (oil on canvas, 13 1/4 x 18 1/4 ins / 33.5 x 46.5 cm) USD 1,400.

JACQUESME
French, 19th century.
Painter.
MUSEUMS AND GALLERIES:
BERNAY: *Full-length Portrait of Louis-Philippe*.

JACQUESSON DE LA CHEVREUSE, Louis Marie François
French, 19th century.
Born 5 November 1839, in Toulouse; died 1903, in Paris.
Painter, musician. History painting, portraits, genre scenes. Designs for stained glass.
Louis Jacquesson de la Chevreuse achieved first place at the College of Fine Arts in Paris, having studied under Flandrin, Ingres and Gérome. He also won the Grand Prix de Rome in 1865.

He then set up numerous painting and drawing studios and devoted himself to his professorship until 1880, when he started exhibiting at the Paris Salon again. He bequeathed his fortune to the Société des Artistes Français and the College of Fine Arts in Paris.

Jacquesson de la Chevreuse's coolly accurate drawing style and his skills as a colourist marked him out as a true leader of a school. In addition to his numerous paintings, he is also credited with cartoons for the stained glass windows at the cathedrals of Bordeaux and Lyons and at the churches of Beaufort, Neuchâtel and Poligny. He also made a name for himself as a musical composer.

Museums and Galleries:
Avignon: *Recumbent Martyr; In Front of the Mirror; Mme Jacquesson de la Chevreuse* - Gray: *Awakening* - Toulouse: *Orpheus in the Underworld.*
Auction records:
Paris, 5 Nov 1971, *Sweet Idleness* (oil on canvas, 6 1/4 x 17 3/4 ins / 16 x 45 cm) FRF 1,200.

JACQUET
French, 14th - 15th century.
Sculptor.
Jacquet was active in Troyes.

JACQUET, Achille
French, 19th century.
Born 28 July 1846, in Courbevoie (Hauts-de-Seine); died 30 October 1908, in Paris.
Engraver (burin /etching).
Achille Jacquet, younger brother of Jules, studied at the College of Fine Arts in Paris under Henriquel-Dupont, Pils and Laemlin. He was awarded the Grand Prix de Rome in 1870, and regularly participated in the Société des Artistes Français' Salons, where he received medals in 1877, 1881 and 1884.

He also won a medal of honour and the Grand Prix at the 1889 and 1900 Expositions Universelles, respectively, and was made a member of the Légion d'Honneur in 1889. Achille Jacquet also became a member of the Institut de France, as a replacement for Henriquel-Dupont, on 19 March 1892.

His engravings borrowed from the old masters, notably Daniel de Volterre, Palma Vacchio and Lesueur and from the new masters, notably Bouguereau, Cabanel, Meissonier and Detaille. He is also credited with a large number of original portraits.

JACQUET, Alain
French, 20th century.
Born 22 July 1939, in Neuilly-sur-Seine.
Active in the USA from 1964.
Painter (mixed media), sculptor, engraver.
Mec Art, Nouvelle Figuration, Figuration Narrative.
Alain Jacquet began his studies in the dramatic arts, attending the University of Grenoble. He then studied architecture at the École des Beaux-Arts. After travelling, he settled in Paris in 1959, and devoted himself to painting. In 1960-1961, he met the artists of the New Realism movement, and in 1964 and 1965, he met the American Pop artists Andy Warhol, Roy Lichtenstein and Robert Rauschenberg in New York. In 1968, he became interested in esoteric trends of thought. In 1974, he travelled to Morocco, before settling in St-Martin in the French Antilles in 1978. He returned to New York in 1980, regularly visiting the Antilles until 1988-1989, when he returned to Paris to work in a studio loaned to him by the Musée National d'Art Moderne in Beaubourg. Since 1989, he has been an associate of a programme devoted to new technologies, attached to the Délégation aux Arts Plastiques.

As a young artist, Alain Jacquet began by painting a series of canvases playing on the theme of the game of Jacquet (a kind of backgammon). He drew inspiration from the six colours of the rainbow, juxtaposing rather than mixing them, and the corresponding form (*Game of Jacquet*, 1961; *Puzzle*, 1962). Beyond the homonyms - the game of jacquet, Jacquet bread - this common proper name puts the elementary concepts of singularity within multiplicity into play. These are two ideas which would be found in his subsequent work. With *Camouflages*, the series to follow, the canvases represent scenes taken from ancient and modern art history while concealing or veiling another image. This embedding of an image within an image might be the pretext for Pop-Art-influenced compositions such as *Michelangelo Camouflage, Leda*, in which a triangular road sign depicts a roughly painted cow over a plaster representation of Leda.

The themes of decomposition and the distortion of representation continue with *Luncheon on the Grass* (1964), a key work. It is derived from Manet's painting, which itself was painted after Giorgione's *Le Concert champêtre* (*Pastoral Concert*). It is presented as a silkscreen in three primary colours, produced from a photo by Jacques Montagnac, and according to Jacquet's own instructions. Other than the profoundly thought-out composition of the image, Jacquet's intervention focused on enlarging the fragmented points of the photographic texture that entirely break up the original image. To enlarge the image so seemingly true to reality reveals a hidden surface (or interior) to us, fulfilling a function of 'disinformation' and a dematerialisation of the image. This work, which did not require painting, also falls under the banner of Mechanical Art, which appeared in 1965 in Paris, during a collective exhibition presented by Pierre Restany at the Galerie 'J'. There are 95 versions of *Luncheon on the Grass*. Jacquet insisted upon the play of colours or reworking of the interior of the image through texture. The point, or the dot, is interpreted in its materiality and symbolic meaning, and will acquire its full importance later on.

Jacquet also pursued the effects of lined texture, as in *Olympia* (1965), *Bengali Fires* (1966), or of concentric texture, as in *Zebra* (1967). Similarly, he created woven textures on woven materials. At the beginning of the 1970s, his work led him to the Braille point, which he would subject to enlargements. Moving from the visual to the tactile, Alain Jacquet sought out correspondences between these two modes of perception. He integrated them into a system of alphabetical and numerical signs in *La Grande Gaufre* (1973); a work in circular form, synthesizing the correspondences between Braille writing, binary notation and the hexagrams of the *I-Ching*, the Chinese book of divination. At this time, he also created a series of 'topological' sculptures, functioning on the principle of the Mobius strip, in which objects having two surfaces, are shown in a uniform manner on one side only: *The Watering Can* (1972-1975), *Mâ coco* (1977).

With *First Breakfast* (1972-1978), Jacquet inaugurated a series of silkscreens between 1978 and 1983, entitled *Visions*, which marked his return to painting and to the principle of camouflage, but a new manner. In 1969, the Apollo space mission brought back views of the Earth. Jacquet chose one and printed several versions of it. He reworked them by means of concentric patterns, and enlarged specific areas such as clouds or continents, which he then painted. *Truth Coming Out of the Well* (1983) is a work that, in this series, transforms itself into a coitus between a man and a woman, through a poetic transformation of the continents. There are numerous versions of this single image, including *Après-midi à la grande chatte* (1987), mixing sexual and religious images. Others, such as *Dolphin* (1985), restore familiar animals. In more recent works, Jacquet has used any photo of the earth in order to create an image. For several years, he has pursued original figurative works. He has created computer-assisted 'paintings', which he has then repainted by hand. They are a testament to the fact that the interplay between mind and matter lies elsewhere than in the simple, artificial illusion.

Jacquet has taken part in numerous collective exhibitions, most notably: 1961, the Biennale in Paris; 1962, the Salon des Réalités Nouvelles at the Musée d'Art Moderne in Paris; 1962, the Salon International des Galeries Pilotes, at the Musée Cantonal in Lausanne; 1964, the Salon Comparaisons, at the Musée National d'Art Moderne in Paris; 1965, the Salon de Mai at the Musée National d'Art Moderne in Paris; 1965, the International Award exhibition at the Guggenheim Museum in New York; 1966, the Biennale in São Paulo; 1968, Documenta 3 in Kassel; 1969, *Quand les attitudes deviennent formes* (*When Attitudes Become Form*), at the Kunsthalle in Bern; 1976, the Biennale in Venice; 1978,

Mechanised Image (*Mechanised Image*) at the British Arts Council in London; 1983, *Bonjour monsieur Manet* (*Hello, Mr. Manet*) at the Musée National d'Art Moderne in Paris; 1985, *Ripe Fruit* at PS1 in New York; 1989, *De l'instabilité* (*On Instability*) at the Centre National des Arts Plastiques in Paris; 1989, the Biennale in São Paulo; 1991, at the Royal Academy of Arts in London; 1992, at the Centro de Arte Reina Sofia in Madrid; 1993, at the Montreal Museum of Fine Arts in Montreal; 2003, *Phantom der Lust: Visionen des Machochismus in der Kunst* (*Phantom of Desire. Visions of Masochism in Art*), at the Neue Galerie am Ladesmuseum, Graz.

Jacquet's solo exhibitions include: 1961, 1963, Galerie Breteau, Paris; 1962, Galerie Aujourd'hui, Brussels; 1963, Robert Fraser Gallery, London; 1964, Alexandre Iolas Gallery, New York; 1965, Museo de Arte Moderna, Rio de Janeiro; 1966, Gallery 20, Amsterdam; 1967, Galerie Heiner Friedrich, Munich; 1968, Museum of Contemporary Art, Chicago; 1968, 1971, Galerie Yvon Lambert, Paris; 1970, 1971, Galerie Der Spiegel, Cologne; 1971, Galleria La Salita, Rome; 1972, Galerie Block, Berlin; 1973, Galerie Bama, Paris; 1974, Centre National d'Art Contemporain, Paris; 1977, Jacobson Gallery, Stockholm; 1978, Musée d'Art Moderne de la Ville de Paris; 1978, Musée d'Art et d'Histoire, Geneva; 1981, Galerie de France, Paris; 1985, 1986, Patrick Fox Gallery, New York; 1987, Galerie Michel Vidal, Paris; 1988, Musée de Nîmes, Galerie des Arènes, Nimes; 1990, Galerie Beaubourg, Paris; 1996, Galerie Daniel Templon, Paris; 1998, Musée de Picardi, Amiens; 2002, *Alain Jacquet, Camouflages (1961-1964)*, Cordeliers, Châteauroux.

Bibliography:

'*Alain Jacquet invente l'anti-ready made*' in *Art Press* n° 57, periodical, Paris, March 1982. Restany, Pierre, *Le Déjeuner sur l'herbe, 1964-1989, 25e anniversaire*, La Différence, Paris, 1989. Smith, Duncan, '*Alain Jacquet*' in *Art Press*, periodical, Paris, 1989. Millet, Catherine, '*Voyage à la surface de la Terre*' in *Art Press*, periodical, Paris, 1990. *Alain Jacquet*, exhibition leaflet, Gal. Artmeudon, Gal. Jousse Seguin, Paris, 1991. Scarpetta, Guy, *Alain Jacquet. Camouflages 1961-1964*, Éd. Cercle d'Art, Paris, 2002. Weibel, Peter (ed.), '*Phantom der Lust. Visionen des Masochismus in der Kunst*' in *2 vol.*, exhibition catalogue, Neue Galerie am Landesmuseum, Graz, Belleville Verlag, Munich, 2003.

Museums and Galleries:

Marseilles (Mus. Cantini): *Jumping Rope* (1984); *Florence* (1969) - Paris (FNAC): *The Egg* (1988); *Meatloaf Saucer, the Great Corrida* (1983).

Auction records:

Paris, 2 Dec 1976, *Thomas Eakins' 'Swimming Hole'* (1967, painting/plexiglas, 47 1/4 x 72 ins / 120 x 182 cm) FRF 8,000. Paris, 31 May 1978, *Luncheon on the Grass* (1964, mec-art/joined canvases, 61 x 76 3/4 ins / 155 x 195 cm) FRF 13,000. Paris, 21 June 1979, *Luncheon on the Grass* (1954, silk screen print/canvas, two panels, each 76 3/4 x 38 1/4 ins / 195 x 97 cm) FRF 9,000. Paris, 23 Oct 1981, *The Siesta* (1966, mec-art/waxed canvas, 44 1/2 x 63 3/4 ins / 113 x 162 cm) FRF 13,500. Paris, 1 June 1983, *Gabrielle d'Estrée* (1965, silk screen print/canvas, 63 3/4 x 45 ins / 162 x 114 cm) FRF 5,100. Paris, 6 Dec 1985, *Luncheon on the Grass* (1964, silk screen print/canvas, diptych, 70 3/4 x 78 3/4 ins / 180 x 200 cm) FRF 29,000. Paris, 15 Oct 1987, *Flooring* (1968, silk screen print/hardboard, 78 3/4 x 48 1/4 ins / 200 x 122.5 cm) FRF 25,000. Paris, 3 Dec 1987, *Landscape* (painting and silk screen print/canvas, 38 1/4 x 62 1/2 ins / 97 x 159 cm) FRF 13,000. Paris, 24 April 1988, *Walt Disney Camouflage* (1963, oil on canvas, 39 1/4 x 32 ins / 100 x 81 cm) FRF 13,000; *Luncheon on the Grass* (1964, silk screen print/paper/canvas, diptych, 69 x 39 1/4 ins / 175 x 100 cm) FRF 50,000. Paris, 20 Nov 1988, *Luncehon on the Grass* (1964, acrylic and silk screen print/canvas) FRF 190,000. Paris, 12 Feb 1989, *Luncheon on the Grass* (1964, 70 x 77 1/4 ins / 178 x 196 cm) FRF 17,500. Paris, 6 March 1989, *Survival of the Planet Depends on Humanity Evolving to a New Level of Consciousness* (silk screen print/paper 58/150, 35 1/2 x 22 ins / 90 x 56 cm) FRF 14,000. Paris, 23 March 1989, *The Battle of the Pyramids, Images of Épinal* (1962, acrylic/canvas, 75 1/2 x 81 ins / 192 x 206 cm) FRF 85,000. Paris, 6 April 1989, *Marbles* (1970, acrylic/canvas, 39 1/4 x 63 3/4 ins / 100 x 162 cm) FRF 88,000. Paris, 12 June 1989, *Portrait of a Man* (1964, acrylic/canvas, 63 3/4 x 44 ins / 162 x 112 cm) FRF 60,000. Paris, 8 Oct 1989, *The Egg* (1987, photosensitive canvas, 33 3/4 x 26 3/4 ins / 86 x 68 cm) FRF 41,000. Paris, 11 Oct 1989, *Luncheon on the Grass: Portrait of Jeanine* (sized paper/card, tondo, diam. 27 1/2 ins / 70 cm) FRF 90,000. Paris, 13 Dec 1989, *Lounging Woman* (silk screen print/hardboard, 12 1/2 x 18 ins / 32 x 46 cm) FRF 18,000. Paris, 17 Dec 1989, *Portrait of a Little Girl* (1966, acrylic/canvas, 29 1/4 x 23 ins / 74 x 57.5 cm) FRF 29,000. Paris, 18 Feb 1990, *Luncheon on the Grass* (1964, silk screen print/paper/canvas, diptych, 69 1/4 x 39 1/4 ins / 176 x 100 cm) FRF 185,000. Paris, 7 March 1990, *Gabrielle d'Estrée* (1968, 38 1/4 x 63 3/4 ins / 97 x 162 cm) FRF 90,000. Paris, 11 June 1990, *Swimming Hole* (1966-1968, silk screen print/hardboard, 40 1/4 x 59 3/4 ins / 102 x 152 cm) FRF 50,000. Paris, 2 June 1991, *Luncheon on the Grass* (1968, silk screen print/canvas, 31 1/2 x 20 1/4 ins / 80 x 51.5 cm) FRF 26,000. Paris, 30 Nov 1991, *The Luncheon on the Grass* (1964, cellulose on canvas, four-colour printing process, diptych, 70 3/4 x 78 3/4 ins / 180 x 200 cm) FRF 95,000. Paris, 30 June 1992, *Bat Girl* (1966, silk screen print on plexiglas, 41 x 30 3/4 ins / 104 x 78 cm) FRF 30,000. Stockholm, 10-12 May 1993, *Head of a Goat* (1984, oil on canvas, 55 x 33 3/4 ins / 140 x 86 cm) SEK 14,500. New York, 8 Nov 1993, *Mondrian Camouflage* (1963, acrylic/canvas, 59 x 59 ins / 150 x 150 cm) USD 20,700. Paris, 17 March 1994, *Birth of Venus III Camouflage* (1964, oil on canvas, 86 1/2 x 41 1/4 ins / 220 x 105 cm) FRF 82,000. Paris, 16 March 1995, *Portrait of a Man* (1964, silk screen print and acrylic/canvas, 63 3/4 x 45 1/4 ins / 162 x 115 cm) FRF 27,000. Paris, 13 June 1995, *Frontier Earth Water* (acrylic/canvas, 63 3/4 x 45 ins / 162 x 114 cm) FRF 35,000. Paris, 8 March 1996, *Reclining Nude* (1969, silk screen print/hardboard, 12 1/2 x 18 ins / 32 x 46 cm) FRF 8,000. Paris, 19 June 1996, *The Egg* (1987, silk screen print/canvas, 33 3/4 x 27 1/2 ins / 86 x 70 cm) FRF 6,500; *Botticelli Birth of Venus II Camouflage* (1962-1964, oil on canvas, 90 1/2 x 55 ins / 230 x 140 cm) FRF 102,000. Paris, 5 Oct 1996, *Portrait of a Man* (1964, silk screen print/canvas, 63 1/2 x 44 3/4 ins / 161 x 113.5 cm) FRF 28,000. Paris, 28 April 1997, *Portrait of a Man (Black, Purple, Green)* (1964, acrylic and silk screen print/canvas, 63 3/4 x 45 ins / 162 x 114 cm) FRF 22,000; *The First Breakfast* (1972-1978, acrylic and silk screen print/canvas, 46 3/4 x 64 1/2 ins / 119 x 164 cm) FRF 11,000. Paris, 26 Jan 1998, *Thomas Eakins' 'Swimming Hole'* (1966-1968, silk screen print/hardboard, 41 1/4 x 61 ins / 105 x 155 cm) FRF 21,000. Paris, 22 March 1998, *Portrait of a Man* (1964, four-colour printing process cellulose/canvas, 63 3/4 x 45 ins / 162 x 114 cm) FRF 22,000. Paris, 3 April 1998, *Luncheon on the Grass* (1964, four-colour printing process cellulose/mounted paper/canvas, diptych, 63 x 76 1/2 ins / 160 x 194 cm) FRF 48,000. Versailles, 11 April 1999, *The Tub* (1965, silk screen print, 51 x 38 ins / 130 x 97 cm) FRF 25,000. Paris, 15 June 2000, *Déjeuner sur l'Herbe* (*Luncheon on the Grass*) (coloured silk screen print, 69 x 75 ins / 175 x 190 cm) FRF 95,000. Paris, 28 Oct 2000, *Detail of 'Déjeuner sur l'Herbe'* (silk screen print on canvas, 64 x 45 ins / 162 x 114 cm) FRF 50,000. Paris, 20 June 2001, *Rolls Royce Engine* (silk screen print on plexiglas, 74 x 50 ins / 187 x 127 cm) FRF 90,000. Paris, 29 Oct 2001, *Portrait of Martial Raysse* (cellulosique, 64 x 45 ins / 162 x 114 cm) FRF 45,000. Paris, 4 Feb 2002, *Déjeuner sur l'Herbe* (1964, coloured silk screen print, diptych, 69 x 38 ins / 175 x 97 cm) EUR 35,000. Paris, 27 Nov 2002, *Déjeuner sur l'Herbe* (1964, silk screen print on canvas, diptych, 69 x 77 ins / 175 x 196 cm) EUR 27,000. Paris, 25 Nov

2003, *Déjeuner sur l'Herbe* (1964, acrylic on panel, diptych, 69 x 76 ins / 174 x 194 cm) EUR 24,000. PARIS, 9 Dec 2003, *Cranes* (1967, silk screen print on plexiglas, 72 x 48 ins / 183 x 122 cm) EUR 40,150. PARIS, 18 May 2004, *Gabrielle d'Estrée* (1965, silk screen print, 45 x 64 ins / 115 x 162 cm) EUR 11,500. PARIS, 8 June 2004, *Camouflage: Print of a Gondola in Venice* (1962, acrylic on canvas, 76 x 75 ins / 192 x 190 cm) EUR 13,500.

JACQUET, Antoine, called Jacquet de Grenoble
French, 16th century.
Born in Grenoble; died after 1590, in Avon.
Sculptor. Religious subjects. Low reliefs.
Fontainebleau School.

Jacquet worked on the construction of a chimney in a room at the Château de Fontainebleau from 1550 to 1555. The room was named 'Salle de la belle cheminée' (room of the beautiful chimney) in homage to his work, and several marble low reliefs from the chimney are now owned by the Louvre.

MUSEUMS AND GALLERIES:
PARIS (Louvre): *Victory of Henri IV at Ivry* (low relief); *Victory* (low relief); *Spirits* (low relief).

JACQUET, Baptistin Clement
French, 20th century.
Born 31 July 1895, in Marseilles.
Painter.

Jacquet exhibited mostly in salons in the south of France.

JACQUET, Claude. See **DELSAULT**

JACQUET, Constance
Maiden name: de Valmont
Belgian, 19th century.
Born 1805, in Liège.
Painter. Historical subjects, portraits, genre scenes.

Constance Jacquet was a pupil of Girodet. She exhibited at the Paris Salon from 1831 to 1848.

JACQUET, Edmond
French, 19th century.
Born in Guichen (Ille-et-Vilaine).
Painter.

Edmond Jacquet was a pupil of M Carpentier and exhibited the following in Angers in 1886: *Magdalene at Prayer in her Grotto, Meadows of Varade* and *Chrysanthemums*.

JACQUET, François Romain
French, 19th century.
Born 1788, in Limoges.
Active in Paris.
Lithographer.

JACQUET, Germain, called Jacquet de Grenoble
French, 17th century.
Died after 1636, in Paris.
Sculptor.

Germain Jacquet was the son of Mathieu Jacquet, and in 1610 was appointed Sculptor to the King's Household and Keeper of Antiquities. Jacquet and Guillaume Dupré were each commissioned to model a wax effigy of Henri IV which was to be used at his funeral; Jacquet's was chosen, and Dupré's is now in the museum at the Château de Chantilly. Jacquet remained Sculptor to the King until 1636. He had one son, Alexandre Jacquet, called 'de Grenoble', born about 1614, who had the double title of Sculptor to the King and Keeper of Antiquities.

JACQUET, Gustave Jean
French, 19th - 20th century.
Born 25 May 1846, in Paris; died 1909, in Paris.
Painter, watercolourist. Nudes, portraits, genre scenes.

Jacquet was a pupil of Bouguereau. He began exhibiting at the Salon de Paris in 1865, receiving a third-class medal in 1868 with his *Army Outing in the 16th Century*, and a first-class medal in 1875. He was decorated with the Légion d'Honneur in 1879. Jacquet's Salon debut, *The Reverie*, was painted in the style of Bouguereau. In his small canvases depicting genre subjects, he evoked the elegance of the 16th, 17th and 18th centuries, with a conscientious attention to detail. In his portraits, he sometimes preferred to redress his models in the shimmering costumes of the 16th century. He worked tirelessly, producing many paintings, imbuing them with a sometimes exaggerated minuteness.

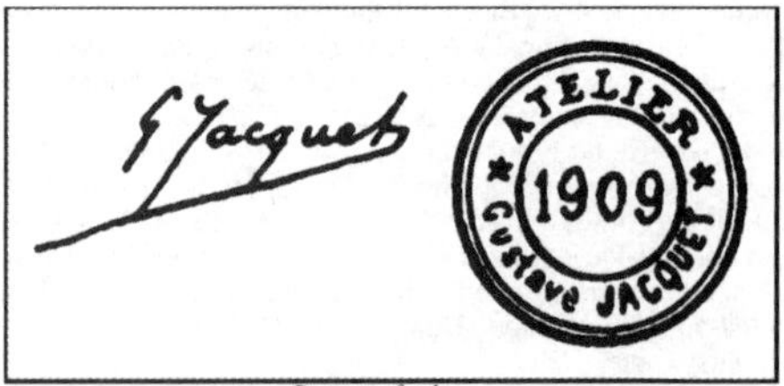

Stamps of sale

MUSEUMS AND GALLERIES:
BLOIS: *Army Outing* - BROOKLYN, NY: *Head of a Young Girl* - CHÂTEAU-THIERRY: *Cavalier* - CHICAGO (AI): *The Queen of the Camp; Young Woman* - LA ROCHELLE: watercolour - NEW YORK (Metropolitan Mus. of Art): *The Reverie* - PARIS (MAM): *Young Girl with the Lizard* - ROUEN: *Woman in a Bonnet* (watercolour, miniature) - SHEFFIELD (AG): *Sport, Music and Good News*.

AUCTION RECORDS:
PARIS, 1880, *Head of a Woman*, FRF 4,350. NEW YORK, 13-14 Feb 1900, *Head of a Young Girl*, USD 1,100. NEW YORK, 9-11 March 1904, *The Pavane*, USD 5,425. LONDON, 29 June 1908, *A Woman of the World* (1886) GBP 63. PARIS, 4 Dec 1944, *The Mandolin Player* (watercolour) FRF 1,700. PARIS, 9 July 1945, *Head of a Woman with a Lace Bonnet*, FRF 5,900. PARIS, 28 May 1951, *Young Serving Girl with Book*, FRF 50,500. NEW YORK, 6 Oct 1966, *Bust Portrait of a Young Woman*, USD 1,100. LONDON, 12 July 1968, *The Dance at Kerduel Castle*, Gns 750. LOS ANGELES, 9 April 1973, *Portrait of a Young Woman*, USD 2,500. NEW YORK, 2 April 1976, *Portrait of a Young Girl* (oil on canvas, 14 x 10 1/2 ins / 35.5 x 26.5 cm) USD 950. NEW YORK, 7 Oct 1977, *Pandora* (oil on canvas, 39 3/4 x 30 1/2 ins / 101 x 77.5 cm) USD 10,000. LONDON, 15 June 1979, *Love Letter* (1883, oil on canvas, 39 1/2 x 29 1/4 ins / 100.5 x 74 cm) GBP 5,500. LOS ANGELES, 5 Oct 1981, *Desire* (oil on canvas, 28 1/2 x 23 3/4 ins / 72.5 x 60.5 cm) USD 9,000. LONDON, 21 Oct 1983, *The Hurdy-Gurdy Player* (oil on canvas, 35 1/2 x 28 1/4 ins / 90 x 71.6 cm) GBP 4,000. NEW YORK, 20 Sept 1986, *A Beauty with a Crown of Flowers* (oil on canvas, 29 1/2 x 25 1/2 ins / 74.9 x 64.8 cm) USD 8,000. NEW YORK, 19 May 1987, *Portrait of a Young Girl in a White Dress* (oil on canvas, 21 3/4 x 18 1/4 ins / 55.5 x 46.4 cm) USD 19,000. NEW YORK, 24 May 1988, *The Red Dress* (oil on panel, 12 3/4 x 9 1/2 ins / 32.4 x 24 cm) USD 4,125. MONACO, 17 June 1988, *Elegant Woman with Feather Hat* (oil on canvas, 18 x 14 3/4 ins / 45.5 x 37.5 cm) FRF 28,860. STOCKHOLM, 15 Nov 1988, *Young Girl Reading in a Chair* (oil, 26 x 22 ins / 66 x 55 cm) SEK 125,000. NEUILLY, 22 Nov 1988, *Portrait of an Elegant Young Woman* (oil on panel, 12 1/2 x 9 1/2 ins / 32 x 24 cm) FRF 17,000. NEUILLY-SUR-SEINE,

16 March 1989, *Portrait of Mrs Chabod* (oil on canvas) FRF 12,000. PARIS, 12 May 1989, *Portrait of a Young Woman* (oil on panel, 10 x 7½ ins / 24.5 x 19 cm) FRF 29,000. NEW YORK, 23 May 1989, *Portrait of a Woman* (oil on panel, 12½ x 9¼ ins / 32 x 23.5 cm) USD 5,500. NEW YORK, 25 Oct 1989, *Young Elegant Woman with the Black Hat* (1878, oil on panel, 42¼ x 28¼ ins / 107.3 x 71.7 cm) USD 13,200. LONDON, 16 Feb 1990, *A Lady with a Parasol* (oil on canvas, 36¼ x 24¼ ins / 92.1 x 61.8 cm) GBP 8,800. NEW YORK, 24 Oct 1990, *Young Woman with Pearl Necklace* (oil on canvas, 16½ x 12¾ ins / 42 x 32.4 cm) USD 7,700. NEW YORK, 22 May 1991, *Portrait of a Young Woman* (oil on canvas, 22 x 18 ins / 55.9 x 45.7 cm) USD 10,450. PARIS, 24 May 1991, *Madame Valtesse de la Bigne* (1879, oil on canvas, 24 x 19¾ ins / 61 x 50 cm) FRF 14,000. LONDON, 19 June 1991, *Portrait of a Young Woman with Blue Ribbon* (oil on panel, 12½ x 10 ins / 32 x 25.5 cm) GBP 8,250. NEW YORK, 17 Oct 1991, *The Coquette* (oil on canvas, 24 x 20 ins / 61 x 50.8 cm) USD 13,200. PARIS, 22 May 1992, *Young Woman* (oil on panel, 13¾ x 10¼ ins / 35 x 26 cm) FRF 13,000. NEW YORK, 20 Jan 1993, *Lady Holding a Carafe* (watercolour and pencil/paper, 20 x 14 ins / 50.5 x 35.6 cm) USD 1,380. LONDON, 12 Feb 1993, *The Belle Epoque* (oil on canvas, 24 x 19¾ ins / 61 x 50.2 cm) GBP 2,750. CALAIS, 14 March 1993, *Portrait of a Young Woman* (oil on panel, 13¾ x 11 ins / 35 x 27 cm) FRF 15,000. NEW YORK, 12 Oct 1993, *Portrait of Marie-Ann Piret* (1900, oil on panel, 11 x 9 ins / 27 x 22 cm) USD 13,800. NEW YORK, 15 Oct 1993, *A Glance* (oil on canvas, 12 x 9¾ ins / 30.5 x 24.8 cm) USD 17,250. NEW YORK, 20 July 1994, *Portrait of a Young Woman* (oil on panel, 16 x 12¾ ins / 40.6 x 32.4 cm) USD 3,450. LONDON, 15 March 1996, *Letter* (oil on panel, 12½ x 15¾ ins / 31.8 x 40 cm) USD 5,175. NEW YORK, 23 May 1996, *Portrait of a Beautiful Woman* (oil on panel, 16 x 12½ ins / 40.6 x 31.8 cm) USD 5,750. LONDON, 13 March 1997, *Portrait of a Seated Lady* (1879, oil on panel, study, 28¼ x 21¾ ins / 71.8 x 55.2 cm) GBP 4,600. LONDON, 21 March 1997, *The Card Seller* (oil on panel, 13 x 8¼ ins / 33 x 21 cm) GBP 4,830. NEW YORK, 10 Feb 1998, *Young Girl* (oil on panel, 12¾ x 9¾ ins / 32.4 x 24.8 cm) USD 23,000. PARIS, 1 April 1998, *Bust of a Young Blond Girl* (1880, oil on panel, 12½ x 9½ ins / 32 x 24 cm) FRF 43,000.

JACQUET, Hélène
Belgian, 20th century.
Born 1912, in Tirlement (Brabant); died 1949, in La Louvière.
Painter.

MUSEUMS AND GALLERIES:
LA LOUVIÈRE (Mus. Ianchelevici).

JACQUET, Henriette
French, 19th century.
Born 19th century, in Narbonne (Aude).
Painter. Flowers.

Henriette Jacquet was a pupil of Marie Euphrosine Jacquet and exhibited in Angers in 1886.

JACQUET, Henry Léon
French, 19th century.
Born 1856, in Anzin.
Painter. Genre scenes.

Henry Jacquet studied under Cabanel. He featured at the Paris Salon, receiving an honourable mention in 1894 and a third class medal in 1906. He was also a member of the Société des Artistes Français and a qualified art teacher.

MUSEUMS AND GALLERIES:
CHÂTEAUROUX: *Election Time* - TOURCOING: *Druid Sacrifice*.

AUCTION RECORDS:
LONDON, 9 Oct 1985, *Encounter in the Village Street* (oil on canvas, 84¾ x 68¼ ins / 215.5 x 173.5 cm) GBP 4,500. MILFORD, 25 Oct 2001, *Reading by the Window* (oil on panel, 15 x 18 ins / 38 x 46 cm) USD 6,000.

JACQUET, Jean
French, 16th century.
Active in Rheims.
Sculptor (including wood).

JACQUET, Jean or Jehan
French, 16th century.
Painter.

Jacquet is recorded working in Lyons, in 1548, on preparations for the official visit of Henri II.

JACQUET, Jules
French, 19th - 20th century.
Born 1 December 1841, in Paris; died 4 March 1913, in Paris.
Engraver (burin/etching).

Jules Jacquet was a pupil of Henriquel-Dupont, Pils and Laemlin at the École des Beaux-Arts. He won the Prix de Rome in 1866. He exhibited regularly at the Salon de Paris, receiving a second-class medal in 1875, a first-class medal in 1882 and a gold medal at the Exposition Universelle in 1889. He was named Chevalier of the Légion d'Honneur in 1883, and Officier in 1895. Upon the death of Ferdinand Gaillard in 1883, he was elected president of the Société des Graveurs au Burin (society of burin engravers). He engraved after old masters such as Titian, Raphael, Michelangelo and Le Sueur. Of the modern masters, he engraved after the works of Meissonier, Millet, Chaplin, Cabanel and Bonnat. He also executed original engravings, his *Portraits* in particular.

JACQUET, Jules Léon Édouard
French, 19th century.
Born 19th century, in Féole.
Painter.

Jules Jacquet exhibited portraits at the Paris Salon from 1879 onwards and was a member of the Société des Artistes Français from 1889.

AUCTION RECORDS:
LONDON, 5 Oct 1990, *Woman with Black Hat* (oil on panel, 18 x 14½ ins / 45.8 x 36.8 cm) GBP 1,320.

JACQUET, Marie Euphrosine
French, 19th century.
Painter.

Marie Jacquet exhibited portraits and still-lifes at the Paris Salon between 1839 and 1950.

JACQUET, Marie Zélie. See **GUILLOT**

JACQUET, Mathieu, called Jacquet de Grenoble
French, 17th century.
Born before 1610, in Avon (Seine-et-Marne).
Sculptor.
Second School of Fontainebleau.

Mathieu Jacquet was the son and pupil of Antoine Jacquet. He worked with his father at the Palais de Fontainebleau and on the pendentives in the church of St-Gervais in Paris. He was Sculptor to the King.

MUSEUMS AND GALLERIES:
PARIS (Louvre): *Victory* (marble, low relief); *Four Children Carrying the Letter H* (marble, low relief); *Battle of Ivry and Surrender of Mantes* (marble, low relief).

JACQUET, Maurice
French, 20th century.
Born 9 February 1877, in Paris.
Painter. Portraits, genre scenes.

Maurice Jacquet was a pupil of Bonnat and Jules Lefebvre. In Paris, he exhibited at the Salon des Artistes Français, of which he became a member in 1903.

AUCTION RECORDS:
NEW YORK, 23-24 Feb 1906, *An Interesting Chapter,* USD 1,100. LONDON, 21 July 1911, *The Coquette,* GBP 21.

JACQUET, Nicolas
French, 16th century.
Active in Lyons.
Sculptor (wood).
Jacquet was the brother of Pierre Jacquet, and worked on preparing the celebrations for the official visit of Henri II and Catherine de' Medici to Lyons in 1548.

JACQUET, Perrin
French, 16th century.
Active in Lyons.
Sculptor (wood), carver.
Jacquet was a master sculptor who took part in preparing the celebrations for the official visit of Queen Éléonore and King Henri II to Lyons in 1548.

JACQUET, Pierre
French, 16th century.
Active in Lyons.
Sculptor (wood).
Pierre Jacquet was the son of Perrin Jacquet, and took part in preparing the decorations commissioned by the town for the official visits of Queen Éléonore, King Henri II and King Charles IX in 1548.

JACQUET D'ANGOULEME. See **JACQUES Pierre**

JACQUET D'ANVERS
Flemish School, 15th - 16th century.
Illuminator.
Jacquet d'Anvers was the manservant of the painter Jean Bellegambe, and illuminated a Mass book for the abbey at Flines. The book is now in the library in Douai.
MUSEUMS AND GALLERIES:
DOUAI (Library): illuminations of a Mass book.

JACQUET DE LA BOUTICLE
French, 15th - 16th century.
Active in Troyes.
Sculptor, architect.
Jacquet de la Bouticle worked at the cathedral of St-Pierre, as well as at the churches of St-Étienne and St-Urbain in Troyes between 1468 and 1500.

JACQUET DE VALENCIENNES
French, 15th century.
Active in Troyes.
Painter.
Jacquet de Valenciennes produced an altarpiece for the high altar of the church of Ste-Madeleine in Troyes. He may be the same artist as Jacquet Cordonnier I.

JACQUETTE, Julia
American, 20th - 21st century.
Born 1964, in New York.
Painter.
Julia Jacquette studied at the Skowhegan School of Painting and Sculpture until 1985, after which she went on to study for a BA at Skidmore College. In 1992 she graduated with a MFA from Hunter College. Soon after graduating, she won the Marie Walsh Sharpe Art Foundation Studio Grant (1993) and in 1994 she became a Fellow at the Virginia Center for the Creative Arts. This was followed by fellowships at the MacDowell Colony (1995-1996) and at Yaddo (1997-1998). In 1998 she also won the Pollock/Krasner Grant. She is a lecturer in the Council of the Humanities and Visual Arts and also teaches at the Rhode Island School of Design. In 2000 she designed a series of paper plates, cups and napkins for the *Projects 69* exhibition at the Museum of Modern Art in New York, which are used in the visitors' cafe there.

Jacquette's works explore issues of gender, sexuality, desire and eating, often depicting American-style desserts and cakes such as brownies and ice-cream sundaes in great detail. Many of her works also include text. For the series *White Paintings* (2004), Jacquette produced several large-scale oils showing details of 1950s wedding dresses, wedding cakes, and wedding flowers. The series also included a number of small-scale Abstract works.

Jacquette has showed her work at numerous exhibitions since the early 1990s, including *Women's Art/Lives/Issues* at the Tweed Gallery in New York (1993); *Domestic Bliss* at the Margarete Roader Gallery in New York (1995); *Hearts Desire* at the Judy Ann Goldman Fine Art in Boston (1996); *Eat!* at the Museum of Contemporary Art in Sydney (1998); *Food for Thought* at the New Jersey Center for Visual Arts in New Jersey (1998); *Food Matters* at the E. S. Vandam Gallery in New York (1998); *The Likeness of Being* at the D.C. Moore Gallery in New York (1999); *Projects 69: Julia Jacquette,* MoMA, New York (1999); *Smoking* at the Galerie Oliver Schweden in Munich (2000); *Virtues and Vices* at the Judy Ann Goldman Fine Art in Boston (2001); *Subject Matters* at the Kravets/Wehby Gallery in New York (2002); *The Burbs* at the DFN Gallery in New York (2003); and *White Paintings* at the Michael Steinberg Fine Art in New York (2004).
MUSEUMS AND GALLERIES:
ALBUQUERQUE (Art Mus., University of New Mexico) - NEW YORK (MoMA) - SARATOGA SPRINGS, NY (Skidmore College) - SYDNEY (MCA) - TUCSON (University of Arizona Museum of Art).

JACQUIAU, Ponce. See **PONCE Jacquio** or **Jacquiou** or **Jacquieu** or **Jacquin**

JACQUIER, Alphonse
French, 19th century.
Active in Paris.
Painter, decorative designer.
Alphonse Jacquier painted frescoes for the churches of St Ambroise (with F Perrodin), St Georges de la Villette and St François de Sales, in Paris, in 1870 or around then. The paintings on the high altar of Angers' Church of the Trinity are also his work.

JACQUIER, Charles François Marie
French, 20th century.
Born in St-Loup-sur-Semouse (Haute-Saône).
Sculptor.
Jacquier was a pupil of Dumont and Perraud. In Paris, he was a member of the Salon des Artistes Français from 1908.
MUSEUMS AND GALLERIES:
CAEN: bust*Christ* (plaster).

JACQUIER, Fanny
French, 19th century.
Born 19th century, in Paris.
Painter.
Fanny Jacquier was a pupil of Flandrin and Pommeyrac and exhibited miniature portraits at the Paris Salon from 1868 to 1902.

JACQUIER, Georges
Italian, 15th century.
Active in Turin.
Painter.
Georges Jacquier is referred to in 1484-1485 as painter of decorations to the duke of Savoy.

JACQUIER, Guillaume
French, 16th century.
Active in Paris.
Painter.
Jacquier produced decorations for the official visit of King Charles IX to Paris in 1561, working in partnership with Pas-

quier Desjardins. In 1566, he made copies of portraits of the mother and wife of François I for Claude Gouffier de Boisy.

JACQUIER, Henry
French, 19th - 20th century.
Born 20 November 1878, in St-Étienne; died 1921, in Cannes.
Painter. Military subjects, genre scenes, portraits.
Jacquier was a pupil of Fernand Cormon, Aimé Morot, François Flameng and Paul Sain. Though he began his career depicting battle themes, he eschewed these for portraiture, becoming sought-after for his easy, elegant and natural style. He also painted anecdotal scenes, skilfully rendering the atmosphere of interiors. He was a member of the Salon des Artistes Français in Paris. He received an honourable mention in 1900 at the Exposition Universelle in Paris, a third-class medal in 1906, a travel grant in 1906, a second-class medal in 1907 and the national prize in 1909.
MUSEUMS AND GALLERIES:
MONTPELLIER (Mus. Fabre): *Fabre de l'Hérault* - NÎMES: *They Burn the Flags* - ROUEN (MBA): *The Shroud of a Hero* - VIENNA: *The Pont St-Martin.*
AUCTION RECORDS:
PARIS, 6-8 Dec 1926, *Christ Child,* FRF 220. PARIS, 5 April 1943, *Portrait of a Woman,* FRF 3,200. LYONS, 28 Nov 1999, *Studio Interior, Portrait of Mr P.S.* (1898, oil on canvas, 27 x 31 ins / 68 x 80 cm) FRF 32,000. MADRID, 8 May 2002, *Arab Riders* (oil on canvas, 39 x 32 ins / 100 x 81 cm) EUR 4,000.

JACQUIER, Marcel J. L.
French, 20th century.
Born 1 November 1877, in Paris.
Painter, engraver, watercolourist.
Jacquier was a pupil of L.O. Merson. He exhibited at the Salon of the Société des Artistes Français, of which he became a member in 1909.

JACQUIN, Antoine
French, 17th - 18th century.
Active in Nancy.
Sculptor.
Antoine Jacquin worked in 1719 on the new ducal palace at Nancy.

JACQUIN, Christophe, or Jaquin
French, 17th century.
Active in Paris c. 1656.
Painter.
Christophe Jacquin was the son of Pierre Jacquin.

JACQUIN, François
French, 17th century.
Born 1631; died 1708, in Paris.
Architect, sculptor.
François Jacquin was Architect and Engineer to the King and Principal Sculptor to Monsieur, the younger brother of Louis XIV. He married on 12 January 1687.

JACQUIN, François Xavier Joseph
Flemish School, 18th - 19th century.
Born 1756, in Brussels; died 1 November 1826, in Louvain.
Painter. Portraits.
François Jacquin studied at the academies of Brussels and Antwerp. He worked in Louvain, painting still-lifes, historical subjects and a large number of portraits of high-ranking ecclesiastical dignitaries. In 1792, he painted a portrait of *Francis II* for Louvain town hall; the painting was later engraved by A. Cardon. There are works by Jacquin in the churches, town hall and university of Louvain, and in the church of St Rombaut in Mechelen.

JACQUIN, Gabriel
French, 17th - 18th century.
Active at the end of the 17th and at the beginning of the 18th century.
Sculptor.
Gabriel Jacquin worked in Grenoble, and married for the second time in 1707.

JACQUIN, Georges Arthur
French, 19th century.
Born 1851, in La Fère-Champenoise (Marne).
Painter, sculptor, engraver, potter. Landscapes.
Georges Jacquin studied under Gérome and made his debut at the Paris Salon in 1877. He was an associate of the National College of Fine Arts from 1905. While better known for his works of decorative art such as jewellery, enamels and ceramics, he also did etchings and dry-point engravings, and was even a chemist. The Museum of Decorative Arts in Paris holds some of his works.
AUCTION RECORDS:
NEW YORK, 28 Oct 1982, *Shepherd and Sheep* (oil on canvas, 25 x 37 ins / 63.5 x 94 cm) USD 4,250. NEW YORK, 30 Oct 2001, *Going Out to Pasture* (oil on canvas, 26 x 37 ins / 65 x 93 cm) USD 8,000.

JACQUIN, Jean, or Jaquin
French, 17th century.
Sculptor, painter.
Jean Jacquin was the father of François Jacquin.

JACQUIN, Joseph
French, 17th century.
Active in Paris during the 17th century.
Sculptor.
Joseph Jacquin received a pension from the King of Sweden, for whom he worked in 1690. He also worked at Versailles for the Trianon and the Château de Clagny.

JACQUIN, Marc Edmond
French, 20th century.
Born 28 February 1901, in Paris.
Sculptor.
Marc Edmond Jacquin studied in the studio of Injalbert at the École des Beaux-Arts in Paris. His sculpture is traditionally classic, and he often represented religious subjects. In 1903, he received a bursary from the City of Paris, enabling him to settle in North Africa. He exhibited in Paris at the Salon des Artistes Français from 1926 to 1937. From 1948 to 1962, he exhibited in Paris at the Salon de la France d'Outre-Mer. He received several public commissions in Chartres, St-Dié, Vernon and Paris.
MUSEUMS AND GALLERIES:
DREUX - PARIS (Mus. des Arts d'Afrique et d'Océanie).

JACQUIN, Mathieu, or Jaquin
French, 17th century.
Active in Nancy between 1614 and 1656.
Sculptor.

JACQUIN, Nicolas, or Jaquin
French, 17th century.
Born 1625, in Neufchâteau.
Sculptor.

JACQUIN, Pierre, or Jaquin
French, 17th century.
Active in Paris.
Painter, sculptor.
Pierre Jacquin became a widower in 1654, and remarried in 1656. Originally from Lorraine, he also worked at Châlons-sur-Marne and Neufchâteau.

JACQUIN DE MARGERIE, Ch.
French, 19th century.
Born 16 January 1855, in Paris.
Sculptor.

Jacquin de Margerie studied under D Puech. He was a member of the Société dzes Artistes Français from 1888 and exhibited at their Salon.

JACQUINET
French, 19th century.
Active in Tours.
Portrait painter.

Jacquinet exhibited at the Paris Salon from 1833 to 1838.
MUSEUMS AND GALLERIES:
TOURS: *Portrait of the Artist's Mother.*

JACQUINET, C.
French, 17th century.
Active in Paris c. 1657.
Engraver.

JACQUINET, Nicolas
French, 18th century.
Painter.

Nicolas Jacquinet was admitted to the Académie de St-Luc in Paris on 5 May 1753.

JACQUINOT, Louise Françoise
French, 19th century.
Born 19th century, in Paris.
Engraver.

Louise Jacquinot featured at the 1800 Salon and engraved portraits.

JACQUIO, Ponce. See **PONCE Jacquio** or **Jacquiou** or **Jacquieu** or **Jacquin**

JACQUISE, Gabriel
French, 17th - 18th century.
Active in Grenoble at the end of the 17th century and at the beginning of the 18th century.
Sculptor.

Gabriel Jacquise sculpted the ceiling of the office of the Chambre des Comptes in 1663.

JACQUOS
French, 15th century.
Born 15th century, in La Mothe.
Painter (glass).

JACQUOT
French, 14th century.
Active in Toul.
Painter (glass).

Jacquot worked on the stained glass windows of Toul Cathedral in 1353.

JACQUOT
French, 15th century.
Born to a family originally from Bar (Bas-Rhin).
Painter (glass).

JACQUOT, Charles
French, 19th - 20th century.
Born 12 January 1865, in Bains (Vosges); died 1930.
Sculptor.

Charles Jacquot was a pupil of Falguière and Aubé. In Paris, he was a member of the Salon des Artistes Français from 1890. He received an honourable mention in 1887, a third-class medal in 1888, a silver medal in 1889 at the Exposition Universelle in Paris, a travel grant in 1893, a silver medal at the Exposition Universelle in 1900 and a first-class medal in 1905.
MUSEUMS AND GALLERIES:
ÉPINAL: *The Prayer in the Fields* - NANCY: *Joan of Arc Before Battle* - PARIS (MNAM-CCI): drawing - PÉRIGUEUX: *Nymph and Satyr.*

JACQUOT, Clément
French, 17th century.
Active in Nancy.
Sculptor.

JACQUOT, Denis
French, 18th - 19th century.
Born 1737, in Parcey, near Dôle (Jura); died 6 April 1816, in Dôle.
Miniaturist.

MUSEUMS AND GALLERIES:
DÔLE: two miniatures.

JACQUOT, Georges
French, 19th century.
Born 15 February 1794, in Nancy; died 25 November 1874, in Paris.
Sculptor.

Georges Jacquot was a pupil of Bosio from 1813 and studied at Paris' College of Fine Arts. In 1817 he came second in the Prix de Rome and in 1820 was awarded first prize.

He featured at the Paris Salon from 1817 to 1857. His most significant works are: *Bust of Louis XVII; Daphne Gazing at her Reflection in the Waters of the Peneus,* marble; *St Joseph,* statue at the church of St Médard; *Cupid on a Dolphin,* marble statue; *Young Fawn and Bacchante,* marble group; *Colossal Bronze Statue of King Stanislas,* made for the town of Nancy; *The Rule of Grace,* bronze statue; and *Sermon on the Mount,* bronze low relief.
MUSEUMS AND GALLERIES:
AMIENS: *Nicolas Berchem* - BOURGES: *Odalisque* - LISIEUX: *Plaster Model of the Arc de Triomphe's Motif* - NANCY: *Cupid and Dove; Accursed Cain; Death of Epaminondas; Paris and Helen; The Apollino in Florence* - VERSAILLES: *Paris; Mercury Separating Two Snakes with his Rod; Duke of Frioul; Colonel Philippe Strozzi; Cupid with Gold and Bronze Arrows; General Duroc.*

JACQUOT, Jacques
French, 18th century.
Born 1760, in Raon-l'Étape (Vosges); died in Nancy.
Sculptor.

Jacques Jacquot was living in Nancy in 1785.

JACQUOT DE FLORANGES
French, 15th century.
Painter (glass).

Jacquot de Floranges produced three windows for the Château de Sancy in c. 1458.

JACQUOT-DEFRANCE, Laurent, called Gaston
French, 19th century.
Born 1874, in Perthus (Pyrénées-Orientales); died 1902, in Rome.
Painter.

Laurent Jacquot-Defrance studied at Nancy's College of Fine Arts and was a pupil of Bonnat and Maignan in Paris. He won the 1901 Prix de Rome and exhibited outside the competition at the Paris Salon that same year.
MUSEUMS AND GALLERIES:
NANCY: *Cattle.*
AUCTION RECORDS:
PARIS, 15 May 1944, *Profile of a Woman* (pastel) FRF 300; *On the Terrace* (1901) FRF 2,550.

JACQUOTOT, Marie Victoire.
See **JAQUOTOT**

JACTA, Lucie Alexandrine
French, 19th century.
Born 19th century, in Paris.
Painter.

Lucie Jacta exhibited miniatures at the Paris Salon from 1875 to 1880.

JACTA, Suzanne
French, 19th - 20th century.
Painter.
Suzanne Jacta was a member of the Salon des Artistes Français in Paris from 1909.

JACUS, Jean Theobald
French, 20th century.
Born 21 April 1924, in Paris.
Painter.
Jacus first studied commerce, before attending the École des Beaux-Arts in Rheims and in Paris. He received a travel grant to go to Holland, and also travelled in Italy, England, Switzerland and the USA. Though he is a figurative painter, the fantastic often permeates his still-lifes and landscapes, especially his landscapes of industrial civilisation. In 1954, he was classed *hors concours* for the Prix de la Jeune Peinture. He showed in numerous collective exhibitions, notably at the Salon des Peintres Témoins de leur Temps in Paris. He has also had solo exhibitions, including at the Galerie St-Hubert in Lyons in 2003.

AUCTION RECORDS:
PARIS, 15 March 1988, *Fireworks Music* (23 1/2 x 28 1/4 ins / 60 x 72 cm, 2 ins/5 cm) FRF 4,100. VERSAILLES, 28 Jan 1990, *The Apple Trees* (oil on canvas, 21 1/4 x 28 3/4 ins / 54 x 73 cm) FRF 4,800. PARIS, 18 Nov 1997, *Rotterdam* (1958, oil on canvas, 28 1/4 x 39 ins / 72 x 99 cm) FRF 1,950.

JACYSZYN, Andrezj
Polish, 20th - 21st century.
Born 1950, in Warsaw.
Painter.
Andrezj Jacyszyn trained at the academy of fine arts in Warsaw under the direction of Henryk Tomaszewski. He has taken part in several collective exhibitions, notably the 1981 young painters' salon.

JADAM VON ZADOR. See **GORCZYNSKI Adam**

JADDOULLE, Marin Nicolas, or Jadouille
French, 18th century.
Born 16 April 1736, in Rouen; died 22 March 1805, in Rouen.
Sculptor.
Jaddoulle became a professor at the Académie de Rouen in 1770. He moved to Paris in 1793, where he was appointed a member of the 'Commission des Arts'. He executed numerous works in Rouen and the surrounding area, of which only a few have survived, including the low relief of *Charity* on the gable of the church of Ste-Madeleine in Rouen. On his death, his estate included, amongst other works, two small terracotta groups: *Abduction of Proserpine* and *Pygmalion and Galatea*.

JADELOT, Jean
French, 20th century.
Born 1875; died 1944.
Painter. Landscapes.
Jadelot painted mostly landscapes and scenes of forests. He collaborated on the journal *Crapouillot* (*Mob*), edited by Jean Galtier-Boissière. An exhibition of his works was presented in Paris in 1944.

JADELOT, Sophie
Maiden name: Weyer
French, 19th century.
Born 1820, in Metz.
Painter.
Sophie Jadelot exhibited subjects in the style of masters at the Paris Salon from 1848 to 1857.

JADIN, Charles Emmanuel
French, 19th century.
Born c. 1845, in Paris.
Painter. History painting, genre scenes, local scenes, still-lifes, animals.
Charles Emmanuel Jadin, son of the painter Louis Godefroy, studied initially under his father and then attended Cabanel's studio. He made his debut at the Paris Salon in 1868 and was a member of the Société des Artistes Français from 1885. He was awarded a medal in Philadelphia.

Jadin's taste for authenticity is reflected in the details within his genre and historical subjects.

MUSEUMS AND GALLERIES:
DIEPPE: *Musical Attributes*.

AUCTION RECORDS:
PARIS, 3-4 May 1923, *Stag Fight, Evening Effects* (pastel) FRF 240; *Two Mice*, FRF 340. PARIS, 13 Oct 1944, *Ensnared Stag Next to a Doe*, FRF 300. PARIS, 29 March 1979, *Nomadic Encampment at Biskra* (1874, oil on canvas, 50 3/4 x 86 1/2 ins / 129 x 220 cm) FRF 15,000. NEUILLY, 15 Nov 1988, *Pair of Greyhounds* (oil on canvas, 52 3/4 x 83 1/2 ins / 134 x 212 cm) FRF 38,000. PARIS, 5 July 1994, *Stag Kill* (pastel, 20 3/4 x 29 1/4 ins / 53 x 74 cm) FRF 5,000. PARIS, 16 Nov 1999, *Young Married Woman and her Sisters* (1873, oil on canvas, 66 x 50 ins / 167 x 127 cm) FRF 200,000. PARIS, 28 June 2000, *Arrival of the Caravanserai* (oil on canvas, 56 x 43 ins / 143 x 108 cm) FRF 118,000.

JADIN, François Léonard
French, 17th century.
Active in Nancy in 1658.
Sculptor.

JADIN, Louis Godefroy
French, 19th century.
Born 30 June 1805, in Paris; died 1882, in Paris.
Painter, watercolourist, engraver. Landscapes, still-lifes, animals.
Barbizon School.
Louis Jadin was a pupil of Hersent, Abel de Pujol, Paul Huet, Bonington and Decamps. He made his debut at the Paris Salon in 1831 and won medals in 1840 and 1855 (first class at the Exposition Universelle). He was made a member of the Légion d'Honneur on 5 April 1854.

Jadin began by painting hunts, still-lifes and finally landscapes. He was a personal friend of Alexandre Dumas and travelled with him on several occasions.

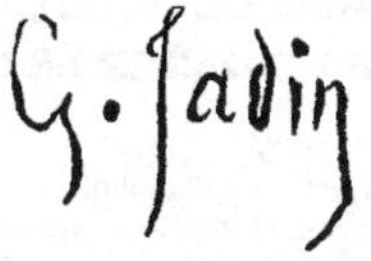

BIBLIOGRAPHY:
Les Années romantiques, la peinture française de 1815 à 1850, exhibition catalogue, Musée des Beaux-Arts, Nantes, Galeries nationales du Grand Palais, Paris, 1996.

MUSEUMS AND GALLERIES:
ANTWERP: *Two Dogs* - ARRAS: *Dog Relay* - BLOIS: *Dogs' Heads* - CHANTILLY: *Stag Kill* - COMPIÈGNE: *Fox Terrier* - DUNKIRK: *Boar Kill* - FONTAINE-CHAALIS (Mus. Jacquemart-André): *Pack, - 1840; Kill on the Hoof* (1841); *Boar's Restart, - 1841* - LONDON (Victoria and Albert Mus.): *Greyhound Study* - NARBONNE: *The Kill* - PARIS (Mus. Carnavalet): *Corner of St Pierre de Montmartre* - RENNES: *Hunt Relay* - STRASBOURG: *Greyhound Study*.

Auction records:
Paris, 1873, *Greyhound Head,* FRF 1,900; *Head of Griffon Dog,* FRF 1,880; *Russian Greyhounds,* FRF 3,800. Paris, 27 Feb 1893, *Russian Greyhounds,* FRF 460. Paris, 21 au 23 May 1902, *The Frolics, The Restart, The Kill, The Scramble for the Spoils* (four compositions) FRF 7,400; *Portrait of Griffon Dog,* FRF 170. Paris, 17 au 21 May 1904, *Portrait of Dogs,* FRF 205. Paris, 20-22 May 1920, *Pond* (watercolour) FRF 200. Paris, 18 March 1921, *Two Coupled Dogs Running* (pencil) FRF 100. Paris, 14 Dec 1933, *Head of Basset Dog,* FRF 500. Paris, 16 and 17 May 1945, *At Rest in the Countryside* (watercolour) FRF 3,200. New York, 5 June 1986, *Relay of Dogs on the Scent at Milly's Rock, Fontainebleau Forest* (1855, oil on canvas, 49 x 74 ins / 124.5 x 188 cm) USD 62,000. London, 22 Sept 2000, *Dog's Dinner* (oil on canvas, oval, 18 x 15 ins / 46 x 38 cm) GBP 1,000. Lille, 20 Oct 2002, *The Grande Allée, Rambouillet* (1832, oil on canvas) EUR 2,100. Fontainebleau, 7 Dec 2003, *The Grande Allée, Rambouillet* (1832, oil on canvas, 56 x 42 ins / 141 x 106 cm) EUR 2,800.

JADKO-BAZILIEVICH, Ludmilia
Russian, 20th century.
Born 1931, in Leningrad (now St Petersburg).
Painter. Still-lifes.

Ludmilia Jadko-Bazilievich studied at the academy of fine art in Leningrad. She was a member of the Union of Painters of Leningrad.

Museums and Galleries:
Moscow (Ministry of Culture) - St Petersburg (MFA).

Auction records:
Paris, 29 May 1991, *Still-life with Flowers* (oil on canvas, 31 1/2 x 23 1/2 ins / 80 x 60 cm) FRF 4,000. Paris, 24 Sept 1991, *The Orange Room* (oil on canvas, 23 1/2 x 20 1/2 ins / 60 x 52 cm) FRF 10,000.

JADOT, Maurice
Belgian, 20th century.
Born 1892, in Brussels; died November 1983, in London.
Active from 1918 in England.
Painter, sculptor.

Maurice Jadot studied architecture at the Académie Royale des Beaux Arts in Brussels. As a painter, he was self-taught. From 1950 he worked as a sculptor, incorporating aluminium, bronze and Plexiglas elements into his work.

JADOUIN, Eugène Paul
French, 19th century.
Born 1 September 1856, in Paris.
Sculptor.

Eugène Jadouin was a member of the Société des Artistes Français from 1896 and featured at its Salon.

JADRAQUE Y SÁNCHEZ DE OCANA, Miguel
Spanish, 19th century.
Born 19th century, in Valladolid.
Painter. History painting, genre scenes.

Miguel Jadraque y Sánchez de Ocana studied under Agapito López Sanromán and Joaquín Espalter at the Valladolid academy and later at the Real Academia de San Fernando in Madrid. He first exhibited in Madrid around 1864. He was awarded bronze medals at the exhibition of the national fine arts society of Madrid in 1871 and 1876 and also won a medal in Vienna in 1873. He exhibited at the Exposition Universelle in Paris in 1878.

Museums and Galleries:
Madrid: *An Interesting Reading; St Theresa in Ecstasy; An Argument; Tavera Visiting Berruguete.*

JAECKEL, Lotte
German, 20th century.
Born 22 July 1889, in Neusalz an der Oder (now Nowa Sól, Poland).
Draughtsman, engraver (wood). Portraits, landscapes, architectural views.

Lotte Jaeckel is noted for her pen-and-ink landscapes and architectural drawings. She also produced woodcut engravings of landscapes and female portraits.

JAECKEL, Willy
German, 20th century.
Born 10 February 1888, in Breslau (now Wroclaw, Poland); died 1944.
Painter, engraver.

Willy Jaeckel studied at the college of fine arts in Breslau and at the academy in Dresden. His body of work includes (in chronological order): *Bridge,* a landscape dated 1911; monumental canvases depicting heroes and their deeds (notably *Fight for Existence,* painted in 1912-1913); *Loving Couple* and *Family* (1913); *Birth* and a *Medea* (1914) and *Separation* (1915). In 1916-1917, Jaeckel started painting frescoes, notably four large murals (*Traveller; Tenderness; Meditation and Contemplation; Motherhood*), a *Crucifixion* and a *Sacred and Profane Love* (1919); he painted a mystical 'theosophical' composition in 1920 (*Cosmic Love*).

Willy Jaeckel was a prolific engraver, notably with *Memento,* a series of lithographs on the subject of war (1914-1915), 234 etchings entitled *Man-God, God-Man,* six original etchings for *St Paul's Epistle to the Romans,* twenty-eight original etchings illustrating Goethe's *Faust* and twelve further engravings for the *Songs of Bilitis.* Additional single engravings include two etchings of self-portraits, together with other original etchings (*Loving Couple; Adoration; Eros; Saint Sebastian*), lithographs (*Man and Woman; Love; Samson*) and a number of woodcut engravings.

Bibliography:
Friedemann, Berger/Jahn, Beate, *Die Schaffenden. Eine Auswahl der Jahrgänge I bis III. Katalog des Mappenwerkes,* Gustav Kiepenheuer Verlag, Leipzig, Weimar, 1984. Stilijanov-Nedo, Ingrid, *Willy Jaeckel 1888-1944. Das druckgraphische Werk,* Museum Ostdeutsche, Gal. Regensburg, Regensburg, 1987. Klein, Dagmar, *Der Expressionist Willi Jaeckel: Gemälde, Biographie, Künstlerbriefe,* Müller-Botermann Verlag, Cologne, 1990.

Museums and Galleries:
Berlin (Nationalgal.): *Sand Quarry* - Chemnitz: *Halt during the Flight into Egypt* - Hamburg (Kunsthalle): *St Sebastian* - Wroclaw: *Female Portrait* - Wuppertal (Ruhmeshalle): *Portrait of the Artist's Wife.*

Auction records:
London, 26 Nov 1973, *Portrait of a Young Woman,* DEM 2,700. Munich, 25 May 1976, *Portrait of the Artist's Wife* (1923, oil on canvas, 32 x 27 1/2 ins / 81 x 70 cm) DEM 3,800. London, 30 June 1978, *Bouquet of Flowers* (1935, oil on canvas, 36 x 31 3/4 ins / 90.5 x 80.5 cm) GBP 700. Lindau, 9 May 1979, *Self-portrait* (1919, oil on canvas, 47 1/4 x 39 1/4 ins / 120 x 100 cm) DEM 17,000. Cologne, 20 March 1981, *Male Portrait* (oil on card, 28 x 28 ins / 71 x 71 cm) DEM 11,000. Munich, 30 June 1982, *Canal Scene, Berlin* (1913, oil on card, 20 x 27 3/4 ins / 51 x 70.5 cm) DEM 6,000. Cologne, 4 June 1983, *Mountain Lake* (oil on canvas, 27 1/2 x 39 1/4 ins / 70 x 100 cm) DEM 4,800. Munich, 29 June 1983, *Reclining Nude* (pastel, 18 1/2 x 26 ins / 47 x 66 cm) DEM 2,500. Berlin, 23 May 1987, *Mountain Landscape* (oil on canvas, 27 3/4 x 31 3/4 ins / 70.5 x 80.5 cm) DEM 3,500. Amsterdam, 27-28 May 1993, *Port of Hamburg* (Indian ink/rice paper, 14 1/2 x 19 1/2 ins / 37 x 49.5 cm) NLG 1,265. Lucerne, 26 Nov 1994, *Roses in a Jug* (oil on canvas, 19 3/4 x 15 3/4 ins / 50 x 40 cm) CHF 1,500. Stuttgart, 30 Jan 1999, *Seated Female Nude* (1926, oil on canvas, 35 x 31 ins / 90 x 80 cm) DEM 11,000. Cologne, 10 Nov 1999, *Still-life with Cactus and Blue African Sculpture* (oil on canvas, 47 x 31 ins / 120 x 80 cm) DEM 17,000. London, 18 Oct 2000, *Battle in*

the Trench (pen and ink wash, 17 x 16 ins / 43 x 41 cm) GBP 4,500. LONDON, 18 Oct 2000, *Thinker* (c. 1916, gouache on vellum, 13 x 12 ins / 33 x 30 cm) GBP 8,000. STUTTGART, 10 May 2001, *Female Nude* (1926, oil on canvas, 35 x 31 ins / 90 x 80 cm) DEM 10,000. AHLDEN, 28 Sept 2001, *Storm Clouds over Hiddensee Beach* (pastel on board, 19 x 25 ins / 48 x 64 cm) DEM 3,800. COLOGNE, 29 May 2003, *Still-life with Flowers in a Vase in front of a Red Cloth* (1919, oil on canvas, 22 x 29 ins / 55 x 74 cm) EUR 6,000. BERLIN, 29 Nov 2003, *Reclining Nude* (oil on canvas, 39 x 57 ins / 98 x 146 cm) EUR 20,000. COLOGNE, 5 June 2004, *Dancer in Red* (1929, oil on canvas, 46 x 47 ins / 118 x 119 cm) EUR 30,000. AHLDEN, 17 Sept 2004, *Still-life with Lilies* (oil on canvas, 32 x 28 ins / 81 x 70 cm) EUR 9,500.

JAECKLE, Charles
French, 19th - 20th century.
Born 26 April 1872, in Serienz (Alsace); died 15 February 1923, in Basel.
Sculptor. Busts, statues.

Charles Jaeckle studied at the Kunstgewerbe Schule in Munich. His works include female busts, two busts of his wife, and the statue *The Song*. He worked in Munich, where, from 1896 to 1923, he exhibited busts in bronze and marble at the GlasPalast. He also exhibited in Berlin, Dresden and Düsseldorf, and in Paris at the Salon de la Société des Artistes Français in 1905, 1906 and 1912. He exhibited at the international fine arts exhibition in Venice in 1909.

JAECKLIN, Just
British, 20th century.
Painter, film maker.

Just Jaecklin's work has featured in a number of Paris exhibitions. In 1975 his first feature film, *Emmanuelle*, based on an erotic novel, won him worldwide fame. Later films included an adaptation of Pauline Réage's *The Story of O*. His artworks draw on his earlier experience as a fashion photographer: sophisticated fashion shots are dissected and reassembled in collage reliefs, often with striking Op-Art style effects.

JAEGER. See also **JÄGER**

JAEGER, Albert de
French, 20th century.
Born 28 October 1908, in Roubaix.
Sculptor, medallist.

Albert de Jaeger first studied at the École des Arts et Métiers in Roubaix, and patented inventions in domains as varied as electronics, foundry work, furniture and construction. Nevertheless, he also learned sculpture at the École des Beaux-Arts in Tourcoing, and at the École des Beaux-Arts in Paris, in the studio of Despiau. In Paris, he exhibited at the Salon des Artistes Français, the Salon d'Automne and the Salon des Artistes Indépendants. In 1933, he received the first prize in sculpture at the École des Arts Décoratifs, and in 1935, the first Grand Prix de Rome.

JAEGER, Anna
German, 19th century.
Born 24 September 1849.
Active in Berlin.
Painter. Genre scenes, portraits.

Anna Jaeger trained at the Düsseldorf academy, and exhibited her genre paintings, landscapes and portraits (including those of the physician *F. Clausius* and the theologian *F. Fabri*), at the academy and the Grosse Kunstausstellun in Berlin.

JAEGER, August
French, 20th century.
Born 14 December 1881, in Metz.
Active in Switzerland.
Painter, engraver. Interiors, village scenes, landscapes, seascapes.

Jaeger was a pupil at the École des Arts et Métiers in Strasbourg and at the Kunstakademie in Munich. He made a study trip to Paris. He participated in exhibitions in Strasbourg, Bern and Zurich with landscapes, village interiors and seascapes. He worked in Twann, in the Bern district.

JAEGER, Bernhard
German, 20th century.
Born 1882.
Painter (including glass), watercolourist. Religious subjects, historical subjects, scenes with figures, landscapes. Church decoration.

Bernhard Jaeger studied at the college of fine arts in Weimar and at the Munich academy. He lived and worked in Munich and featured at the Munich Secession exhibition with oil and watercolour landscapes, together with religious compositions, projects for frescoes and paintings on glass. Prime examples of his work include war memorials in the parish church of Bad Tölz (*Landscape with Pietà*) and paintings on glass for the evangelical church in Solin, in the form of 12 windows representing the Christmas and Easter festivals.

JAEGER, Carl
German, 19th century.
Born 1833, in Nuremberg; died 5 December 1887, in Nuremberg.
Painter, engraver. Historical subjects, portraits.

Carl Jaeger trained with Reindel and Kreling in Nuremberg and at the academy in Munich. He was an honorary member of the Hochstift in Frankfurt.

MUSEUMS AND GALLERIES:
NUREMBERG (Germanisches Nationalmus.): *Portrait of A von Essenwein* - NUREMBERG (Municipal Mus.): *Maximilian I Visiting Albrecht Dürer; Portrait of Lothar, Freiherr von Faker.*

AUCTION RECORDS:
NEW YORK, 29 June 1983, *Portrait of Mozart* (1870, oil on canvas, 24¾ x 18 ins / 63 x 46 cm) USD 1,500.

JAEGER, Ernst Gustav
German, 20th century.
Born 3 May 1880.
Sculptor, engraver, illustrator. Nudes, portraits, genre scenes, interiors with figures, landscapes with figures, animals. Busts.

Ernst Gustav Jaeger's sculpture includes young male nudes, busts and animals (monkeys, horses, bulls, stags, dogs). He was steeped in the study of prehistory and so fascinated by the excavations of sites in the Dordogne that he attempted a sculpture of 'Primeval Man', copies of which are now preserved in the museums of Hamburg and Hanover. As a painter, Jaeger is remembered for landscapes with figures, genre compositions, interiors and portraits, including a self-portrait and a portrait of his father; as an engraver, he illustrated the *March to the East* calendar of 1922 and provided drawings for satirical journals.

MUSEUMS AND GALLERIES:
HANOVER: copies - MAGDEBURG: copies.

JAEGER, Gotthilf
German, 20th century.
Born 29 June 1871, in Cologne.
Sculptor.

Gotthilf Jaeger studied at the schools of arts and crafts in Iserlohn and Karlsruhe, at the Karlsruhe academy and at the Städel Institute in Frankfurt am Main before going on to live and work in Berlin. His sculptures include a *Battle of the Centaurs and Lapiths* for the gable end of the Victoria Insurance Company building in Berlin, allegorical reliefs of *War and Peace* for the War Ministry building, the *Austro-German War Memorial* in Lokov Cemetery (Poland), the *Monument to Ramirez* in Santiago de Chile, and a group entitled *Christ*

Befriending the Children for the House of Deaconesses in The Hague, and a number of bronzes (*Woman Playing Bowls; Centaurs; Recovering from Battle; Wrestler*).

JAEGER, Gustav Maria
Austrian, 19th century.
Born 1835, in Vienna; died 1861, in Vienna.
Engraver. Landscapes.
Gustav Maria Jaeger trained at the academy in Vienna. His subject-matter was principally views of the area around Meran (Merano) and the Tyrol.

JAEGER, Herbert de. See **JAGER**

JAEGER, István
Hungarian, 20th century.
Born 1877, in Cseve.
Painter. History painting, religious subjects.
István Jaeger studied at the Budapest academy. He painted altarpieces for Jázova and Arad as well as an historical composition entitled *German Settlers in Hungary*

JAEGER, Martha
German, 19th - 20th century.
Born 19 June 1867, in Elberfeld.
Painter, watercolourist, draughtsman, engraver (etching/wood), lithographer. Interiors, landscapes with figures, landscapes, urban landscapes, flowers.
Martha Jaeger studied in Düsseldorf and Munich, and went on to exhibit from 1908 to 1920 at the Glaspalast in Munich, showing coloured drawings, woodcut engravings, etchings, lithographs, oils and watercolours of landscapes, cityscapes, village scenes and flowers. She also exhibited in Berlin, Dessau, Dresden, Düsseldorf and Leipzig.

JAEGERHUBER, Herbert A.
Haitian, 20th century.
Born 4 April 1892, in Port-au-Prince.
Painter, draughtsman, engraver.
Herbert Jaegerhuber studied in Hamburg, Altona and Munich. Etchings and wash drawings by him can be found in the Brown Robertson Galleries.
MUSEUMS AND GALLERIES:
HAMBURG (Altonaer Mus.): woodcuts and drawings - HAMBURG (Kunsthalle): woodcuts and drawings.

JAEGERS, Albert
German, 19th - 20th century.
Born 28 March 1868, in Elberfeld.
Sculptor.
Self-taught sculptor Albert Jaegers was awarded a bronze medal at the St Louis Exhibition of 1904. He lived mainly in America.

JAEGERS, Augustine
German, 20th century.
Born 31 March 1878, in Barmen.
Sculptor.
Augustine Jaegers studied at the Art Students' League and the National Academy of Design in New York and also under Mercié at the École des Beaux-Arts in Paris.

JAEGHER, Luc de
Belgian, 20th century.
Born 1912, in Borgerhout (near Antwerp).
Painter.
Luc de Jaegher studied at the Academie and at the Hoger Instituut voor Schone Kunsten in Antwerp. He was awarded the Grand Prix de Rome in 1940.
MUSEUMS AND GALLERIES:
BRUGES (Prints Collection).

JAEGLI. See **JEGLI**

JAELET, Andrée
French, 20th century.
Painter.
MUSEUMS AND GALLERIES:
ÉPINAL (Mus. départemental d'Art ancien et contemporain): *The Parrot without a Beak* (1965).

JAENISCH, Hans
German, 20th century.
Born 1907, in Eilenstedt (near Halberstadt).
Painter, sculptor.
Hans Jaenisch was a member of the Berlin *Sturm* (Storm) Gallery group. He moved to Berlin in 1923 and returned there in 1946 after military service during World War II. He was awarded the City of Berlin Prize in 1950 and, in 1952, the Hallmark Art Prize. From 1953, Jaenisch taught at the academy in Berlin. He took part in numerous group exhibitions of contemporary German painting and exhibited solo in New York (1960 and 1962), Paris, St Gall and Düsseldorf (1961).

Hans Jaenisch worked in the semi-abstract manner of Paul Klee, evoking human figures, animals and décors using a repertoire of rune-like symbols, often etched into the paint surface.
MUSEUMS AND GALLERIES:
PITTSBURGH (Carnegie MA): *Scorpion* (1951, mixed media on board) - RICHMOND (Virginia MFA): *Sunset* (oil/card).
AUCTION RECORDS:
NEW YORK, 23 March 1961, *Island*, USD 550. COLOGNE, 21 May 1976, *Icarus* (1956, oil on canvas, 13 3/4 x 19 3/4 ins / 35 x 50 cm) DEM 1,400. HAMBURG, 12 June 1981, *Recumbent Ox* (1952, bronze, h. 8 1/4 ins / 20.8 cm) DEM 2,800. COLOGNE, 2 June 1984, *Horse and Rider* (green-patinated bronze, h. 7 3/4 ins / 19.5 cm) DEM 3,500. NEW YORK, 7 May 1990, *Horseman* (oil/synthetic resin, 59 1/2 x 39 1/2 ins / 151 x 100.5 cm) USD 16,500. AMSTERDAM, 11 Dec 1991, *Erdfisch* (1956, oil on canvas, 17 3/4 x 23 1/2 ins / 45 x 60 cm) NLG 4,600. AMSTERDAM, 9 Dec 1992, *Untitled* (gouache/paper, 18 x 13 1/2 ins / 46 x 34 cm) NLG 1,380. STUTTGART, 23 Oct 1999, *Angelic Musician* (mixed media on board, 28 x 40 ins / 71 x 101 cm) DEM 3,500. BERLIN, 27 Nov 1999, *Blue Fish* (c. 1955, egg tempera and oil on paper on board, double-sided, 28 x 39 ins / 70 x 100 cm) DEM 6,000. MUNICH, 6 May 2000, *Abstract Composition* (oil on board laid on panel, 28 x 39 ins / 70 x 100 cm) DEM 10,500. BERLIN, 27 May 2000, *Homecoming* (tempera over gypsum relief on panel, 26 x 42 ins / 67 x 106 cm) DEM 5,000. HAMBURG, 28 Sept 2002, *May Landscape* (1954, oil on paper on panel, 28 x 39 ins / 70 x 100 cm) EUR 3,800. HAMBURG, 7 Dec 2002, *Mother and Child* (bronze, 15 x 2x2 ins / 37 x 6x6 cm) EUR 2,800. HAMBURG, 11 June 2004, *African Cow* (bronze, 5 x 6x5 ins / 12 x 14x12 cm) EUR 2,200. DÜSSELDORF, 25 Sept 2004, *Aerodrome* (mixed media on panel, 39 x 28 ins / 99 x 70 cm) EUR 2,300.

JAENSSON, Carl Vilhelm
Swedish, 19th - 20th century.
Born 1853, in Sweden; died 1931.
Painter. Genre scenes, landscapes.
MUSEUMS AND GALLERIES:
STOCKHOLM: *Evening by the Seaside*.
AUCTION RECORDS:
STOCKHOLM, 28 Oct 1980, *Landscape* (1889, oil on canvas, 38 x 61 1/2 ins / 96.5 x 156 cm) SEK 10,500. STOCKHOLM, 5 Sept 1992, *Harvest Scene at Nightfall with a Lake in the Background* (oil on canvas, 38 1/4 x 61 3/4 ins / 97 x 157 cm) SEK 25,000.

JAERN, Albert
Norwegian, 20th century.
Active c. 1937.
Draughtsman.

JAERNEFELT, Eero Nikolai or Father. See **JÄRNEFELT**

JAESPAERT, or Jasper
Flemish, 15th century.
Born in Louvain.
Painter.
Flemish School.
Jaespaert worked for the festival of entremets in Bruges in 1468.

JAFÉ, Myriam
French, 20th century.
Born 17 December 1920, in Paris.
Painter, lithographer. Landscapes, flowers.
Myriam Jafé was first self-taught, and then studied with Jules Cavaillès. The expressiveness of her work is rendered by using thickly textured paint. Since 1970, she has been a member of the Salon d'Automne, the Salon de la Société Nationale des Beaux-Arts, the Salon Comparaisons, and the Salon Gemmail in Tours. Her solo exhibitions include: 1967, Galerie Bernheim; 1978, Galerie Emma, Paris; 1988, Banque Hervet, Paris; 1991, the French Embassy in Washington DC; and 1992, Galerie Colette Dubois.
MUSEUMS AND GALLERIES:
PARIS (FMAC) - PARIS (FNAC).

JAFFART, Charles
French, 19th century.
Active in Le Mans.
Painter, decorative designer.
Charles Jaffart painted some decorative pieces in 1863 for the church of Notre-Dame du Pré in Mans, including two frescoes depicting *The Annunciation* and *Coronation of the Virgin*.
MUSEUMS AND GALLERIES:
LE MANS: *Portrait of the Artist*.

JAFFÉ, Franz
German, 19th century.
Born 5 September 1855, in Berlin.
Painter, decorative designer, architect.
Notable among Jaffé's decorative works were those he did for the German section at exhibitions in Melbourne (1888-1889), Chicago (1893) and Paris (1900). For exhibitions, he painted: *Tent of Ptolemy II Philadelphus in Alexandria in 270 BC*, *The Baths of Caracalla* and *The Funeral Pyre of Hephæstion in Babylon in 326 BC*.

JAFFE, Lee
American, 20th - 21st century.
Born 1950, in New York.
Painter, draughtsman, installation artist. Multimedia.
Lee Jaffe lives in Venice California. His work is composed of various types of materials, he uses aesthetic images that reference different cultures or sub-cultures with socio-political connotations. His installation *Birth of the nation* shows a woman standing in the middle of Jamaican slums imitating the Statue of Liberty. Jaffe has also taken inspiration from African-American Jazz musicians for his installations. The Galerie Georges Lavrov in Paris showed his work in 1989.
BIBLIOGRAPHY:
Golstenne, Laurence, '*Lee Jaffe*' in *Art Press*, periodical, Paris, 1989.
AUCTION RECORDS:
STOCKHOLM, 21 May 1992, *Composition* (mixed media) SEK 7,000.

JAFFE, Shirley
American, 20th century.
Born 1923, in New Jersey.
Active from 1950 in France.
Painter, draughtswoman.
Shirley Jaffe studied at the Cooper Union Art School in New York, then at the Phillips Art School in Washington. In 1949, she went to Paris, where she finally settled in 1954. She began exhibiting in Paris in 1951. She was funded by the association *La Peau de l'Ours* of Basel, founded in 1955, which also helped to promote Chillida, Nay, Poliakoff, Riopelle, Held, Sam Francis and Davis, among others. She spent the year of 1963-1964 in Berlin on a grant from the Ford Foundation. In 1981, she produced a decorative piece for the Direction Régionale des Télécommunications de Bourgogne in Dijon.

Starting out from Abstract Expressionism, her painting is an odd combination of Constructivism and a technique that is almost reminiscent of certain forms of Lyrical Abstraction. Her use of bright colours on a geometrical canvas suggests the term 'Geometrical Expressionism'. In conversation with Yves Michaud, reported in the catalogue for the exhibition at the Château de Jau in 1989, she stated '... It was only when I saw Matisse's paper-cuts that I saw something that impressed me.' Her later works - elements of colour and shape cleanly cut out and arranged in a two-dimensional structure in a space with a white background - may be compared to those of Stuart Davis. She told Catherine Lawless in 1991: 'The town meets my needs. The dispersion I see in the town and which I put into my paintings has no central object. The forms as a whole have broken out on the surface in an organised jolt, like a complex visual game.'

Jaffe has taken part in many group exhibitions in the USA and Japan, including *Un Tableau dans le Décor. Peintures 1970-2000* (*A Painting in the Décor: Paintings 1970-2000*), and exhibition presented in 2003 to mark 20 years of the FRAC at the Château des Ducs de Bretagne in Nantes. She has also had solo shows, the first in 1959 at the Kornfeld and Klipstein Gallery in Bern, followed by regular shows at the Galerie Jean Fournier in Paris since 1980; 1981 at the Musée de Chambéry; 1987 at the Fondation Cartier, Jouy-en-Josas; 1989 at the Fondation de Château de Jau; 1991, a big exhibition organised by the Fonds Régional d'Art Contemporain de Limousin at the Musée de Valence; 1994 at the École Régionale des Beaux-Arts in Le Mans; 1994 at the Musée Matisse in Nice; 1995 at the Foire Internationale d'Art Contemporain, presented by the Galerie Jean Fournier of Paris, and 2004 at the Centre d'Art d'Ivry Galerie Fernand Léger, Ivry-sur-Seine.
BIBLIOGRAPHY:
Schipper, Merle, *American in Paris: the 50s*, exhibition catalogue, California State University Fine Arts Gallery, 1979. Boudou, Dominique, '*Shirley Jaffe à la lisière du signe*' in *Beaux-Arts Magazine* n° 128, periodical, Paris, November 1994. Rubinstein, Raphael, '*An Eye in the City*' in *Art in America*, vol 83, no. 1, periodical, 1995. Rosenthal, Deborah, '*Border Crossings: Shirley Jaffe, Painting and Stained Glass*' in *Modern Painters*, vol 13, no. 1, periodical, 2000. Rubinstein, Raphael, '*Consecrated by Color*' in *Art in America*, vol 88, no. 5, periodical, 2000.
MUSEUMS AND GALLERIES:
CLERMONT-FERRAND (FRAC Auvergne): *Remembering Whistler* (1999) - PARIS (MNAM-CCI).
AUCTION RECORDS:
PARIS, 8 Oct 1989, *Four Corners with White Lines* (1975, oil on canvas, 29 3/4 x 23 1/2 ins / 75.5 x 60 cm) FRF 19,000. LONDON, 22 Feb 1990, *The Circus* (oil on canvas, 70 1/2 x 114 1/4 ins / 179 x 290 cm) GBP 8,250. PARIS, 28 March 1991, *Composition* (1977, oil on canvas, 18 x 13 ins / 46 x 33 cm) FRF 9,500. PARIS, 7 June 2000, *Pandora's Box* (1980, oil on canvas, 16 x 13 ins / 41 x 33 cm) FRF 16,000. PARIS, 7 June 2000, *Witch's Brother* (1982, oil on canvas, 46 x 22 ins / 117 x 56 cm) FRF 33,000. PARIS, 29 Oct 2001, *The White Middle* (1983, oil on canvas) FRF 13,000. PARIS, 18 Dec 2001, *Tulip Time* (1985, oil on canvas, 55 x 47 ins / 140 x 120 cm) FRF 65,800. PARIS, 9 Dec 2003, *Poste Restante* (gouache and watercolour, 13 x 10 ins / 33 x 25 cm) EUR 1,500. ZURICH, 8 June 2004, *Untitled* (gouache, 30 x 21 ins / 75 x 54 cm) CHF 2,800.

JAFFRÉ, Marc
French, 20th century.
Born 26 December 1908, in Courbevoie; died 1 March 1987, in Courbevoie.
Painter. Landscapes, landscapes with figures.
Marc Jaffré worked in a fabric design studio. He began by painting landscapes of Brittany and the Creuse region. Around 1975, he painted landscapes of the Midi, using a palette of ochres and browns in definite tones, and with a perceptible brushstroke. He sought less to put the landscape views into perspective, than to render the density of colour in the fore- and middle grounds of the composition. He participated in collective exhibitions in Paris, including the Salon des Artistes Indépendants (1931, 1952, 1953, 1954), the Salon des Artistes Français (1952, 1953, 1954, 1955, 1956), and the Salon d'Automne (1975). A solo exhibition of his paintings was organised by the Galerie Bernheim-Jeune in Paris in 1957, with a preface by Maximilien Gauthier. The Galerie Alexander in Paris also exhibited his works in 1976 and 1977.

JAGAN, or Iaganath
Indian, 16th century.
Miniaturist.
Jagan worked at the court of Emperor Akbar the Great (1556 to 1605) and was named as the eleventh out of the 17 painters listed in the *Ayin-i Akbari*.
MUSEUMS AND GALLERIES:
LONDON (British Mus.) - LONDON (India Mus.).

JAGEMANN, Anna von
Maiden name: Kolb, or Anna von Kettenacker
German, 19th century.
Born 17 November 1816, in Freiburg im Brisgau; died 9 March 1905, in Mannheim.
Painter, lithographer.
Anna von Jagemann was the wife of the painter Karl von Jagemann. She divorced him in 1869. Her half-length portrait of *Frau Henriette Wertheimer* dating from 1840 was shown at the portraits exhibition at the academy in Berlin in 1920. Another noted work was a lithographed portrait of *Gustav Barth*, choirmaster of the Viennese Sängerverein.

JAGEMANN, Ferdinand
German, 19th - 20th century.
Born 24 August 1780, in Weimar; died 9 January 1820, in Weimar.
Painter. History painting, portraits.
Son of Chr. Jagemann and brother of the actress Caroline Jagemann of Weimar, he worked as a librarian in the service of the Duchess Anna-Amalia. Fedinand Jagemann studied at the College of Art in Weimar under Georg-Melchior Krauss and under Füger in Vienna. He also studied in both Paris and Rome before going on to teach in Weimar. Jagemann is noted for *Martin Luther at the Diet of Worms* (1817), and for his portraits (*Goethe; Wieland; Schiller; Gall*), most notably that of *Graf Karl August von Sachsen-Weimar*.
MUSEUMS AND GALLERIES:
WEIMAR (Bibl.): *Portrait of Graf Karl August von Sachsen-Weimar*.

JAGEMANN, Karl von
German, 19th century.
Born 1819, in Wertheim; died 1883, in Vienna.
Painter. Portraits.
Karl von Jagemann trained in Munich and Vienna. At an exhibition of master portraits from private collections in Heidelberg, there was a portrait of *Councillor Franz von Jagemann* by him.

JAGEN, Cornelis van
Dutch, 18th century.
Active in Amsterdam.
Engraver.
Cornelis van Jagen worked for Lairesse.

JAGEN, Jan van
Dutch, 18th century.
Born 1709, in Amsterdam.
Engraver.
Jan van Jagen engraved geographical maps of Palestine, Holland and France. He is also known for his book illustrations, including a *View of Jerusalem*.

JAGENDEUBEL, Joseph
German, 19th century.
Born 1792, in Salzburg; died 15 June 1857, in Munich.
Painter. Landscapes. Decorative schemes.
Jagendeubel was a pupil of the academy in Munich.
MUSEUMS AND GALLERIES:
MUNICH (Stadtmus., Maillinger Collection): two landscapes (wash).

JÄGER. See also **JAEGER**

JÄGER, Anton
Austrian, 18th century.
Born 1731, in Graun (Curon Venosta), South Tyrol; died 1802.
Painter.
Anton Jäger did ceiling paintings and altars in the Tyrol.

JÄGER, Carl August
German, 20th century.
Born 27 January 1879, in Völkingen.
Painter. Portraits, landscapes, still-lifes, flowers.
Carl (Karl) August Jäger lived and worked in Munich. From 1919, he took part in annual Secession group exhibitions at the Glaspalast in Munich, showing Impressionist-style portraits, still-lifes (flowers) and landscapes.

JÄGER, Derick, or Jeger
German, 15th - 16th century.
Sculptor (wood).
Jäger produced some of the sculptures for the high altar of the parish church in Kalker.

JÄGER, Franz Xaver
Austrian, 19th century.
Born 19 July 1816; died 19 March 1862, in Alberschwende, near Bregenz.
Painter.
MUSEUMS AND GALLERIES:
BREGENZ (Voralberger Landesmus.): collection of ten drawings (portraits, genre pictures and landscapes) (pencil).

JÄGER, Friedrich Wilhelm Johannes
German, 19th century.
Born 24 June 1833, in Schlitz (near Fulda); died 21 September 1888, in Munich.
Painter. Landscapes, horses.
Friedrich Jäger was a pupil of the court painter Lucas and of Paul Weber in Darmstadt. From 1865, he trained at the academy in Munich and later with Raupp in Nuremberg. He exhibited in Vienna (1869) and Munich (1878-1879). Noted works include *Evening Return* and *On the Move*. A collection of 28 of his works, pen drawings, watercolours, landscapes, hunting scenes, military exercises etc. were sold in Munich in 1892.
AUCTION RECORDS:
LUCERNE, 21 June 1974, *Bavarian Landscape*, CHF 20,000.
MUNICH, 24 Sept 2003, *Peasant on Horseback by Water Pump with Peasant Girl and Dog* (oil on canvas, 26 x 37 ins / 67 x 93 cm) EUR 2,400.

JAGER, Gérard de
Flemish School, 17th century.

Born in Dordrecht; died c. 1679.
Painter. Seascapes.
In 1646, Gerard de Jager joined the guild of St Luke in Dordrecht.

MUSEUMS AND GALLERIES:
DORDRECHT: *Port in the Orient; Rotterdam (Mus. Boymans): View of Algiers.*

JÄGER, Gustav
German, 19th century.
Born 12 July 1808, in Leipzig; died 19 April 1871, in Leipzig.
Painter, fresco artist. Religious subjects. Murals.
Gustav Jäger trained at the academies in Leipzig and Dresden and later (1830) with Julius Schnorr in Munich. He first exhibited publicly in Dresden in 1832, and subsequently showed works in Munich, Berlin and Vienna. Eventually he became the director of the academy in Leipzig.

In 1836 and 1837, he was working in Rome. In 1850, he completed Schnorr's frescoes for the Nibelung Room at the Neue Residenz in Munich. One of his more outstanding commissions was the decoration of the palace in Weimar.
MUSEUMS AND GALLERIES:
LEIPZIG: *The Burial of Christ.*

JAGER, H. de
Dutch, 17th century.
Portrait artist.
H. de Jager probably worked in Utrecht, and is almost certainly the same artist as Herbert de Jager.
AUCTION RECORDS:
PARIS, 8 March 1937, *Portrait of a Young Woman,* FRF 220.

JÄGER, Hans
Bohemian, 19th century.
Born 19 August 1844, in Tetschen (now Decín, Czech Republic).
Active in Aussig (Bohemia).
Sculptor.
In 1911-1912, Hans Jäger worked on the sculptures for the central station in Leipzig (statues on the pillars and coats of arms from Prussia and Saxony), from his own designs. From 1918, he worked mainly for the industrialist Georg Schicht in Aussig, making busts, plaques, statuettes, ceramics and interior decorations.

JAGER, Herbert de
Dutch, 17th century.
Born 1642, in Zwammerdam; died 1705.
Draughtsman.
Herbert de Jager spent some time in the Dutch Indies and in Persia. During one of his stays in Persia, he drew two views of the *Ruins of Persepolis* that were published by the Royal Society of London in its *Philosophical Transactions* of May 1694.

JAGER, J. de
Dutch, 17th century.
Active c. 1671.
Painter. Portraits.
J. de Jager is mentioned by Siret as probably being related to H. de Jager; he may even be the same person.

JÄGER, Jean
French, 20th century.
Painter.
Jäger has exhibited his work in collective exhibitions, including the Parisian Salons, the Salon d'Hiver and the Salon des Artistes Français, in addition to regional exhibitions. He has had solo exhibitions in Switzerland. He is an associate member of the Société des Artistes Français.

JÄGER, Joseph
Hungarian, 18th century.
Active in Prague and Tyrnau (now Trnava, Slovakia).
Engraver.
Joseph Jäger's engravings include *St John Nepomucenek,* after the statue by J. Brokoff on the St Charles bridge in Prague, *Arms of the Family of Baron von Wunschwitz, Full-length Portrait of the Grandfather of Baron von Wunschwitz* and *Altarpiece for Maria Thal.*

JÄGER, Julius
19th century.
Died 1887, in Paris.
Landscape artist.
Julius Jäger travelled through Bregenz to visit Italy.

JAGER, Michel de
Dutch, 17th century.
Died 1684, in Paris.
Engraver (line-engraving).
Michel de Jager may have been a pupil of P. van Gust.

JAGER, R.
Dutch (?).
Engraver (etching).
R. Jager produced an etching of *The Spanish and Dutch Fleets.*

JAGERSPACHER, Gustav
German, 20th century.
Painter. Figure compositions, figures, nudes, portraits, scenes with figures.
Gustav Jagerspacher was a pupil of Simon Hollosy in Munich before spending some time studying in Paris. He exhibited in Munich, Berlin, Dresden, Düsseldorf and Wiesbaden. A full-scale exhibition of his work, including a self-portrait, was held at the Salon Caspari in Munich in 1914. Jagerspacher painted first and foremost scenes from working-class life and the lives of the poor and downtrodden (*Prisoner; Fusillade; Accident; Beggars; Gypsy Children*), but he also produced portraits and female nudes.

JAGERSPACHER, Hélène
Maiden name: Hafliger
Swiss, 20th century.
Born 16 November 1885, in Lausanne.
Painter. Figures, portraits, interiors with figures, landscapes.
Hélène Jagerspacher studied in Bern, then under Simon Hollosy in Munich. She continued to study under her husband Gustav Jagerspracher. She spent a study year in Paris before going on to exhibit in Bern and Munich, showing principally group studies, landscapes, interiors and occasional portraits.

JAGGER, Charles
British, 18th - 19th century.
Born c. 1770, probably in Bath; died 1827, in Bath.
Miniaturist.
Charles Jagger appears not to have exhibited his work in London, in spite of his notable talent. His miniatures were finely coloured and showed much character. A portrait he made of the Duke of Clarence later provided a source for an engraving.

JAGGER, Charles Sargeant
British, 20th century.
Born 1885, in London; died 1934, in London.
Sculptor, draughtsman. Allegorical subjects, mythological subjects, figures, nudes.
Charles Sargeant Jagger studied at the Royal College of Art in London from 1908 to 1911. He was a laureate of the Prix de Rome, and studied in Rome and Venice before enlisting in the army at the outbreak of war in 1914. In 1913 he present-

ed a relief to the Royal Academy based on a series of works by Rossetti. He taught drawing at Sheffield College of Art, where he produced works such as *Man and the Abyss* and *Prometheus*. His models for public memorials were regularly exhibited at the Royal Academy in London - the Royal Artillery memorial, on London's Hyde Park Corner, is one of his best-known works. Jagger's work includes historical, Biblical, mythological and allegorical figures; marble and plaster reliefs featuring Bacchic scenes; and male and female nudes. After World War I he executed *No Man's Land*, an immense relief depicting the horrors of war for the British School in Rome.

BIBLIOGRAPHY:

Penny, N., '*English Sculpture and the First World War*' in *Oxford Art Journal IV/2*, November 1981. *Charles Sargeant Jagger: War and Peace Sculpture*, Imperial War Museum, London, 1985. Bonaventura, Paul, '*Framed: Charles Sargeant Jagger*' in *Tate*, no. 4, Winter 1994.

MUSEUMS AND GALLERIES:

LONDON (Tate Collection): *No Man's Land* (bronze, relief) - LONDON (Victoria and Albert Mus.): *Cathal and the Woodfolk* (1914, bronze).

AUCTION RECORDS:

LONDON, 7 June 1972, *The Weary Cavalryman*, GBP 750. LONDON, 14 March 1973, *H. R. H. The Duke of Winsdor* (bronze) GBP 700. LONDON, 28 Feb 1979, *The Kiss* (c. 1965, bronze, low relief, green patina, h. 63 1/2 ins / 161 cm) GBP 7,000. LONDON, 29 March 1983, *Cathal and the Woodfolk* (c. 1920, brown-patinated bronze plaque, 19 3/4 x 25 1/2 ins / 50 x 65 cm) GBP 950. LONDON, 3 April 1985, *The Infantryman (Commemoration of the Battle of Ypres)* (bronze, h. 24 1/2 ins / 62 cm) GBP 4,500. LONDON, 25 Nov 1987, *The Sentinel* (dark-brown-patinated bronze, h. 28 ins / 71 cm) GBP 26,000. LONDON, 8 March 1991, *Soldier Mourning the Death of a Friend* (brown-patinated bronze, l. 17 3/4 ins / 45 cm) GBP 6,380. LONDON, 26 June 2001, *Wipers* (dark brown patinated bronze, 18 x ?x? ins / 46 x ?x? cm) GBP 34,000.

JAGGER, J.
British, 18th century.
Architect, architectural draughtsman. Urban landscapes.

J. Jagger exhibited a painting featuring the town hall and the market place of an English town at the Free Society in London in 1774. In 1784, he exhibited drawings, plans and projects at the Royal Academy.

JAGGI, Luc
Sculptor. Figures.

MUSEUMS AND GALLERIES:

LAUSANNE (Cantonal MFA): *Seated Woman*.

JÄGGLI. See also **JEGLI**

JÄGGLI, Hermann Walter, or Jäggli-Fröhlich
Swiss, 19th - 20th century.
Born 17 June 1862, in Winterthur; died 1925, in Brugg.
Painter (glass).

Hermann Walter Jäggli studied under Seder and Petua in Winterthur, and under Gebhart in Munich. He lived and worked in both Vienna and Paris before settling in Zurich. An example of his work is his *Allegory on the Theme of President Kruger*.

MUSEUMS AND GALLERIES:

ZURICH: *Jacob's Dream*.

JAGGLI, Karl August
Swiss, 19th century.
Born 24 February 1824, in Winterthur; died 19 April 1879, in Winterthur.
Painter, decorative designer.

Jaggli visited Strasbourg, Augsburg, Mannheim, Vienna, Budapest and Paris. On his return to Switzerland, he specialised in church commissions, and worked for churches in Zug, Montreux, Herdern and Chur.

JÄGGLI, Margrit
Swiss, 20th century.
Born 1941, in Bern; died July 2003.
Painter. Figures, portraits, nudes.

From the start of her career in 1968, Margrit Jäggli pursued an extremely intensive, even aggressive, realism and took part in Swiss exhibitions dedicated to the renewal of realism that had emerged in Europe. The success of the American Hyperrealists invites comparison, and it is evident that in her choice of portraits, whose subjects are often nude, Jäggli shared the same spirit that can be seen in the sculptures of J. de Andrea. Adopting the technique of painting on mirrors previously used by the Italian artist Pistoletto in the 1960s, like him she succeeded in integrating the painting and the viewer into the same image. However, where Pistoletto used subtlety, Jäggli preferred the effect of shock. She exhibited in Switzerland and Belgium and featured in many group exhibitions

JAGODKINE, Stepan. See **YAGODKIN**

JAGT, Martinus van der
Dutch, 18th century.
Born 3 November 1747, in Haarlem; died 3 September 1805, in Zeist.
Painter, watercolourist. Seascapes.

Martinus van der Jagt studied under J. H. Jelgersma and Jan Punt in Amsterdam.

MUSEUMS AND GALLERIES:

HAARLEM (Teylers Mus.): *Italian Landscape* (drawing).

JAGUER, Édouard
French, 20th century.
Born 1924, in Paris.
Painter, writer, art critic.
Phases group.

Édouard Jaguer is best known for his activities as a man of letters and as a tireless defender of the Surrealist cause. He participated in the activities of La Main à Plume (1943 to 1945), of the Cobra movement (1948 to 1951), the International Surrealist Movement (1949 to 1951), and of Phases, of which he has since coordinated the activities.

BIBLIOGRAPHY:

Durozoi, Gérard, '*Ceux qui n'ont pas la mémoire trop courte...*' in *Le Mouvement Phases de 1952 à l'horizon 2001*, exhibition catalogue, Centre Noroit, Arras, 2000.

JAHANDIER, Étienne. See **DESROCHERS Étienne Jehandier**

JAHANDIEZ, Albert
French, 19th - 20th century.
Died 1938, in Hyères.
Painter. Rustic scenes.

Jahandiez is from Mortagne.

MUSEUMS AND GALLERIES:

VIRE: *Harvest in the Perche*.

JAHL, Ladislas
Polish, 20th century.
Born 10 August 1886, in Jaroslaw.
Active in France from 1912.
Painter, engraver. Stage sets, stage costumes.

Ladislas Jahl exhibited in Paris at the Salon des Indépendants (1921), Salon d'Automne (1922), Salon des Tuileries (1937-1938), Salon des Peintres et Graveurs Français (1937), Exposition Universelle (1937), Exposition de l'Art Sacré (1937), in the Marsan Pavillion, at the Madrid autumn salon (1926), at the Warsaw Winter Salon (1935-1936) and at the New York International Exhibition (1939-1940). He designed sets and costumes for the Odeon Theatre in Madrid (1926)

and for the Ballets Karnecki in Lyons. In 1926, the French State acquired his *Polish Household Cavalry* for the Elysée Palace.
MUSEUMS AND GALLERIES:
WARSAW (Mus.) - WARSAW (Prints Collection).
AUCTION RECORDS:
PARIS, 17 June 1991, *Landscape* (oil on canvas, 23 1/2 x 35 3/4 ins / 60 x 91 cm) FRF 5,500. PARIS, 25 June 2001, *Don Quixote* (c. 1930, oil on canvas, 20 x 26 ins / 50 x 65 cm) FRF 16,000.

JAHN
German, 18th century.
Born to a family originally from Meissen.
Painter (porcelain).
MUSEUMS AND GALLERIES:
FLENSBURG (Museumsberg) - HAMBURG (Mus. für Kunst und Gewerbe) - OLDENBURG (Landesmus. für Kunst und Kulturgeschichte) - SCHLESWIG (Thaulow-Mus.).

JAHN, Adolf
German, 19th century.
Born 17 December 1858, in Stettin (now Szczecin, Poland).
Active in Berlin.
Sculptor.
Adolf Jahn trained at the academies in Berlin and Vienna. He worked in Berlin, and showed numerous statues, groups, busts and reliefs in bronze, marble and plasters at the academy (from 1881) and the Great Arts Exhibitions of 1891 to 1918. They included statuettes of *Wilhelm II as a Crusader, Shylock, Othello, Dante* and *Alfred Krupp* and busts of *Wilhelm I* and *Kristeller*. Among works of his in public possession, mention should be made of two allegorical figures of the universities of *Marburg* and *Greifswald* and busts of *Leibnitz, Goethe, Kant* and *W. von Humboldt* at the Municipal Library in Berlin; a bust of Reichstag deputy *Karl Schrader* at the National Museum in Brunswick; female allegorical figures at the Reichsbank and Fulda Bank in Danzig (now Gdansk), and a monument of Kaiser Wilhelm I in Lüben (now Lubin) in Lower Silesia.
MUSEUMS AND GALLERIES:
BERLIN (Stadtbibliothek) - BRUNSWICK (Herzog Anton Ulrich-Mus.).

JAHN, Adolf Moritz
Danish, 19th century.
Born 25 July 1803, in Kiel; died 24 September 1881, in Copenhagen.
Sculptor.
Adolf Jahn was a pupil at the academies in Copenhagen and Berlin. Bertel Thorvaldsen summoned him to Rome to execute the statue of *The Apostle Thomas*. Upon his return to Denmark he worked at Frederiksborg castle. In 1826 he exhibited a low relief in Copenhagen, *Odysseus and Tyresias*, and busts from 1838 to 1845.

JAHN, Albert Karl Alexander
Swiss, 19th century.
Born 16 June 1841, in Bern; died 11 June 1886, in Bern.
Watercolourist, draughtsman, architect. Landscapes, architectural views.
The Kunstmuseum in Bern has several landscapes, architectural views and sketches by Albert Jahn.
MUSEUMS AND GALLERIES:
BERN (Kunstmus.): 26 watercolours; two drawings.

JAHN, Andreas
Bohemian, 17th century.
Born 7 November 1653, in Ossek.
Painter.
Andreas Jahn often worked for the Cistercian monastery in Ossek. He drew the sketches for the copper engravings in A. Sartorius' *Cistercium bistercium* (Prague 1708), with views of the monastery of Citeaux near Nuits, allegorical figures for the frontispiece and views of the monastery of Ossek and the church of Maria Radice.

JAHN, Anton
German, 19th century.
Born 1810; died 1841.
Active in Koblenz.
Painter. Portraits, genre scenes, animals.
Anton Jahn showed a painting of the *Dance of the Monkeys* at the academy exhibition in Berlin in 1842.
MUSEUMS AND GALLERIES:
KOBLENZ (Mittelrhein Mus.): *Portrait of the Artist by Himself.*

JAHN, Carl Ernst Albrecht
German, 19th - 20th century.
Born 27 January 1844, in Berlin; died 9 January 1912, in Helsinki.
Sculptor, medallist.
Carl Jahn studied at the academy in Berlin and worked in Dresden and then in London, where he exhibited portrait medallions at the Royal Academy from 1868 to 1873, notably of *Luther, Beethoven, Dickens, Tennyson* and *Kaiser Wilhelm I.*
MUSEUMS AND GALLERIES:
HELSINKI (Ateneumin Taidemus.): four models for medals (wax).

JAHN, Elias. See **JOHN Elias**

JAHN, Georg
German, 19th - 20th century.
Born 1869, in Meissen.
Painter. Portraits.
Georg Jahn exhibited in Berlin in 1909, and in Dresden from 1897 to 1914.
MUSEUMS AND GALLERIES:
CHEMNITZ: *Head Study* (chalk drawing).

JAHN, Gustav
Austrian, 19th century.
Born 22 August 1850, in Kreutzen (Moravia); died 26 September 1904, in Vienna.
Sculptor.
A student at the academy in Vienna, Gustav Jahn did decorative sculpture, including a fountain for Sturany. He restored the *Holy Trinity Column* in the Graben in Vienna.

JAHN, Gustav
Austrian, 20th century.
Born 1879, in Vienna; died August 1919, in Vienna.
Painter, lithographer.
Gustav Jahn was a well-known Alpiniste who painted landscapes and genre compositions in Alpine and Adriatic settings. His lithographs include *Mariazell; Vlosterneuburg; Springtime.*
AUCTION RECORDS:
VIENNA, 18 Nov 1981, *Rose Garden* (oil on canvas, 27 1/4 x 33 3/4 ins / 69 x 86 cm) ATS 55,000. VIENNA, 11 Sept 1984, *Landscape in the Dolomites* (watercolour and gouache, 6 x 9 1/4 ins / 15 x 23.5 cm) ATS 20,000. VIENNA, 28 Sept 2004, *Climbers on a Rockface* (mixed media, 13 x 8 ins / 32 x 20 cm) EUR 1,800. VIENNA, 28 Sept 2004, *Mountaineers on a Glacier* (mixed media, 13 x 7 ins / 33 x 17 cm) EUR 1,900.

JAHN, Hans Emil
Norwegian, 19th century.
Born 1834, in Drontheim; died 1902, in Drontheim.
Painter. Seascapes.
Hans Jahn received an honourable citation at the Exposition des Beaux-Arts in Rouen in 1860. His *Yachts in the North* are in a private collection in Drontheim.

JAHN, Heinrich
Bohemian, 17th - 18th century.

Born 17 April 1672, in Ossek; died 1712, in Ossek.
Painter.

Heinrich Jahn was the official painter for the Cistercian monastery of Ossek. He painted many frescoes and altarpieces, both for the monastery and for the parish church of Maria Radice.

JAHN, Jakob Lorenz
Bohemian, 18th century.
Born 10 August 1706, in Ossek; died 21 May 1767, in Prague.
Painter.

Jakob Lorenz Jahn painted a number of historical scenes, flower paintings and portraits for the monastery of Ossek.

JAHN, Johann Quirin
Bohemian, 18th century.
Born 1739, in Prague; died 1802, in Prague.
Painter, art writer. History painting.

Johann Quirin Jahn was the son of Jakob Lorenz Jahn, and probably received his first lessons from him. He then worked as assistant to Palko. He travelled in the Netherlands and France, and finally settled in Vienna, where he was appointed a member of the academy. He decorated a number of churches in Bohemia, Silesia and various towns in Austria, his works including a copy of *Night* by Correggio in the church at Liebesnitz, and *St Philip Neri* in St Vitus Cathedral in Prague. He also wrote on artistic topics.

JAHN, Rudolf Friedrich
Swiss, 19th century.
Born 16 January 1844, in Bern; died 29 January 1883, in Bern.
Painter, art restorer.

JAHNCKE, Karl
German, 19th - 20th century.
Born 20 April 1860.
Engraver (etching), painter. Portraits, genre scenes.

Karl Jahncke studied at the Berlin and Munich academies and exhibited at the Glaspalast in Munich from 1888 to 1895 and in Berlin, showing etchings from originals by H. von Bartel, Wilhelm von Diez, Otto Friedrich Gebler and August von Kreling, together with etchings from his own originals. Jahncke also produced oil portraits and genre compositions.

JAHNS, Maximilien
German, 20th century.
Born 23 October 1887, in Hamburg; died 1957.
Painter. Landscapes.

As of 1919 he is on record as a landscape painter.

MUSEUMS AND GALLERIES:
HAMBURG (Kunsthalle): *Nervi Harbour, Landscape near Arosa.*

JAHNS, Rudolf
German, 20th century.
Born 1896, in Wolfenbüttel; died 1983, in Holzminden.
Painter.
Constructivism.
Die Abstrakten Hannover group.

Rudolf Jahns studied in Brunswick prior to being drafted into military service. In co-operation with other artists, including Kurt Schwitters and Carl Buchheister, Jahns founded the D.A.H. Group (*Die Abstrakten Hannover* ('The Hannoverian Abstracts') in 1927. One of Jahns' compositions is in the 'Abstract Collection' set up in 1927 by Lissitsky in Hanover's Provincial Museum. Jahns was banned by the National Socialist Party in 1933.

Rudolf Jahns exhibited at the *Der Sturm* (Storm) Gallery in Berlin in 1924. A retrospective (*Notturno: Works 1919-1976*) was held in 2001 under the auspices of the Sprengel Museum in Hanover.

Jahns' body of work is similar to that of the Constructivists in that he works in verticals and horizontals, and flatly-applied blocks of colour.

BIBLIOGRAPHY:
Büchner, Joachim, *Rudolf Jahns: Retrospektive 1919-1980*, exhibition catalogue, catalogue raisonné, Kunstmuseum, Hanover, 1981. *Rudolf Jahns. Malen ist Leben: Tagebücher, Briefe, Texte*, Westfälisches Landesmuseum, Münster, 1988. Volkwein, Peter, *Rudolf Jahns. Linien-Spiele*, exhibition catalogue, Museum für Konkrete Kunst, Éd. Braus, Heidelberg, 1997.

MUSEUMS AND GALLERIES:
HANOVER (Sprengel Mus.): *Nudes in Space.*

AUCTION RECORDS:
COLOGNE, 28 Nov 1987, *Geometric Composition* (1927, watercolour and chalk/pencil outlines/paper, 19 3/4 x 15 1/4 ins / 50.2 x 38.5 cm) DEM 8,200. COLOGNE, 29 May 1999, *Untitled* (1928, watercolour over pencil, 11 x 8 ins / 28 x 21 cm) DEM 9,000. COLOGNE, 7 June 2000, *Composition* (1920, charcoal and pastel, 17 x 24 ins / 44 x 62 cm) DEM 6,000. COLOGNE, 7 June 2000, *Improvisation* (1922, watercolour and ink, 9 x 11 ins / 22 x 27 cm) DEM 64,000. MUNICH, 25 May 2004, *Composition R 9* (1928, tempera on canvas, 10 x 8 ins / 25 x 20 cm) EUR 16,000. BERLIN, 26 Nov 2004, *Construction* (1928, tempera on canvas, 18 x 24 ins / 45 x 62 cm) EUR 1,900.

JÄHRIG, Karl Gustav
German, 19th century.
Born 12 August 1819, in Meissen (Saxony-Anhalt); died 21 February 1899, in Dresden.
Painter, lithographer, copyist. Genre scenes, figures.

Karl Gustav Jährig trained in the art school of the Meissen porcelain works, then at the academy in Dresden. Noted among his lithographic works is *Childish Desire*, after Edlinger. He was very active copying paintings in the Dresden gallery, and painted mainly in pastels.

JÄHRIG, Richard Hermann
German, 19th century.
Born 14 November 1859, in Meissen (Saxony-Anhalt).
Active in Dresden.
Painter.

Richard Hermann Jährig trained at the academy in Dresden, and painted mostly portraits of members of the families of Saxony, Brunswick and Hanover.

JAHRIG-LOHR, Mathilde or Tilla
German, 20th century.
Born 1870, in Hanover.
Painter, pastellist. Portraits, landscapes, interiors with figures, flowers.

Mathilde Lohr studied art in Hanover, Berlin and Paris, and subsequently married the painter Richard Jährig. She produced oil and pastel portraits, some landscapes, a number of interiors and still-life (floral) compositions.

JAHYER, Octave Édouard Jean
French, 19th century.
Born 26 November 1826, in Paris.
Engraver (wood).

Octave Jahyer was a pupil at Paris' College of Fine Arts.

JAILLANT, Lydia
French, 20th century.
Born 29 April 1937.
Painter. Figures, landscapes with figures.

Jaillant began painting in 1978. She exhibited at the Salon International d'Art Naïf in Paris.

She expressly positions her figures in front of long, broad stretches of landscape. Her rendering of both figures and nature evokes a great serenity.

JAILLOT, Alexis Hubert, or Jailloteau
French, 17th - 18th century.

Died 2 November 1712.
Sculptor, engraver, geographer.
Alexis Hubert Jaillot was the brother of Pierre Jaillot, with whom he worked at first, but he soon abandoned the arts for geography. He was Sculptor and Geographer in Ordinary to the King.

JAILLOT, Pierre Simon, or Jailloteau
French, 17th century.
Born c. 1631, in St-Oyan-en-Joux (Saône-et-Loire); died 1681, in Paris.
Sculptor (ivory).
Pierre Simon Jaillot came to Paris with his brother in 1657, and was admitted to the Académie in 1661 on submission of an ivory of *Christ Dying on the Cross*, but was expelled in 1673 for 'insults and calumnies'. The work on the basis of which he was admitted was offered by the Académie to the Hôpital St-Germain-des-Prés. The Abbé de Marolles mentions his beautiful Christs in ivory.

JAIME. See **BAÇO Jaime called Jacomart**

JAIME, Ernest
French, 19th century.
Born 1802, in Paris; died June 1884, in Versailles.
Painter, engraver, caricaturist, dramatist. Landscapes.
Ernest Jaime contributed to The *Figaro* and *La Caricature*, and was the author of *Life of a Journalist, Complete Course in Art* and *A Museum of Caricature*.

From 1825 onwards, he made numerous engravings after H Vernet, Gudin, Gérard, Jacottet, Destouche, Thomas, X Leprince, Ciceri, Grenier, Decamp and de Dreux, amongst others - notably in the *Painters' Review* and the 1838 *Cosmopolitan Album*. He also painted small landscapes in the 19th Century English style.

JAIME, Gérardo. See **STARNINA Gherardo di Jacopo**

JAIME, Jean François
French, 19th century.
Born 1804, in Paris.
Painter, watercolourist. Scenes with figures, harbour views, urban landscapes, landscapes.
Jean François Jaime exhibited his *Views* at the Paris Salon from 1831 to 1864, winning a second class medal in 1831. He staged several plays at the Vaudeville Theatre, the dramatist Adolphe Jaime is his son.

MUSEUMS AND GALLERIES:
COMPIÈGNE: *Paris Street* - PARIS (Louvre): *Débarquement (Disembarkation)* (1859, oil on canvas).

JAIME SÁNCHEZ, Humberto
Venezuelan, 20th century.
Born 1930, in San Cristóbal.
Painter.
Humberto Jaime Sánchez attended the Caracas school of fine arts from 1947 to 1950 and still lives in the city. He later studied at the École des Beaux-Arts in Paris. His early works display the influence of Pre-Colombian art but during his time in Paris he developed towards a more abstract form of art, using Expressionism and colour.

He exhibited in Washington in 1957 and 1958, in New York the same year and in 1959 in Lima and Caracas.

JAIMES-ZUNA, Humberto
Bolivian, 20th century.
Born 1926, in Oruro; died 1975, in La Paz.
Painter. Figures. Murals.
Humberto Jaimes Zuna's painting expresses the isolation of the individual within society, together with a feeling of national identity, in a plastic language related to abstract art. He received commissions for various public monuments in Oruro and was awarded the grand prix at the National Murillo Exhibition of 1970.

BIBLIOGRAPHY:
Lassaigne, Jacques, *Peintres boliviens contemporains*, exhibition catalogue, Musée d'Art moderne de la Ville de Paris, Paris, 1973.

MUSEUMS AND GALLERIES:
LA PAZ (Mus. Nacional de Arte).

JAIS, Josef
Austrian, 18th century.
Born 1716, in Imst (Tyrol).
Sculptor, painter.
Joseph Jais painted ceilings and frescoes in Dormitz, near Nassereith (Inn Valley), in Arzl, near Imst, and in Kronburg, near Zams.

MUSEUMS AND GALLERIES:
BAMBERG (Municipal Mus.): *Judith with the Head of Holofernes; Jael and Sisera.*

JAIS-NIELSEN, Henrik
Danish, 20th century.
Born 1885; died 1961.
Painter. Historical subjects, figures, nudes, scenes with figures, landscapes with figures, seascapes, still-lifes.

AUCTION RECORDS:
COPENHAGEN, 29 April 1976, *Beach Scene* (1923, oil on canvas, 25 1/2 x 29 1/2 ins / 65 x 75 cm) DKK 3,600. COPENHAGEN, 10 May 1989, *Composition with Figure* (oil on canvas, 28 3/4 x 25 1/4 ins / 73 x 64 cm) DKK 7,000. COPENHAGEN, 20 Sept 1989, *Frederik VIII and Countess Danner at Jaegerspris Castle* (1918, oil on canvas, 25 1/4 x 25 1/2 ins / 64 x 65 cm) DKK 84,000. LONDON, 27-28 March 1990, *Bottles on a Table* (oil on canvas, 19 1/4 x 25 1/4 ins / 49 x 64 cm) GBP 5,500. COPENHAGEN, 9 May 1990, *Paris Cafe c. 1916* (1916, oil on canvas, 19 1/4 x 22 3/4 ins / 49 x 58 cm) DKK 52,000. COPENHAGEN, 31 Oct 1990, *Jar with Varnished Ceramic Lid Decorated with Two Figures* (1916, h. 16 1/2 ins / 42 cm) DKK 7,000. COPENHAGEN, 1 April 1992, *Still-life* (1922, oil on canvas, 23 1/2 x 22 1/2 ins / 60 x 57 cm) DKK 14,000. PARIS, 16 April 1992, *Still-life* (1914, oil on canvas, 30 x 28 3/4 ins / 76.5 x 73 cm) FRF 10,000. LE TOUQUET, 8 June 1992, *Reclining Nude* (1917, oil on canvas, 25 1/4 x 29 1/2 ins / 64 x 75 cm) FRF 8,000. COPENHAGEN, 13 April 1994, *Young Woman Putting on Her Stockings* (1913, oil on canvas, 25 1/2 x 20 ins / 65 x 51 cm) DKK 39,000.

JAKAB. See also **JACOB** and **JACOBUS**

JAKAB, Istvan
Hungarian, 19th century.
Born 1798; died 1876, in Budapest.
Painter.

JAKABCIC, Michal
Czechoslovak, 20th century.
Born 14 September 1930, in Klenovci.
Painter. Figures.
Michal Jakabcic studied with Mudroch in Bratislava from 1950 to 1955, and settled in that city. He paints strange dolls or idols in a style where the strongly emphasised modelling of the forms almost gives the impression of a traditional trompe l'oeil work. These figures, inspired by primitive folk art, are placed in a rigorously defined geometric space containing cubes and other very precisely rendered geometrical forms.

He participated in collective exhibitions from 1957 including Havana (1964), Cracow (1966), Düsseldorf (1967) and Antwerp (1967). Two of his works also featured in the exhibition of Czechoslovak art organised on the occasion of the 50th anniversary of the founding of the Republic in 1968.

Bibliography:
Fifty years of Czechoslovak Painting from the Collections of the Galleries, 1918-1958, exhibition catalogue, Slovenska Narodna Gal., Bratislava, 1968 (in commemoration of the 50th anniversary of the Republic of Czechoslovakia).

JAKAC, Bozidar
Slovene, 20th century.
Born 16 July 1899; died 1965.
Painter, pastellist, engraver, illustrator. Figure compositions, portraits.

Bozidar Jakac studied at the Prague academy of fine art, also spending time in Berlin and Paris. After World War II he became professor of drawing and engraving at the newly-founded Ljubljana academy of fine art. As a result, he was one of those involved in the setting up of the Ljubljana Engraving Biennale, an event that gained an international reputation.

Jakac started by working in pastel, producing landscapes and portraits including one of the Norwegian composer Serverund and one of the violinist Kurent. His main area of activity, however, was in printmaking - woodcuts, etchings and lithographs. His subjects include scenes in dancehalls, cafés and theatres and also portraits. He illustrated the anthology *Letters* by the Slovene poet H. Gradnik. His work was to remain strictly figurative throughout his career and much influenced by the Expressionists and Edvard Munch in particular, especially in his woodcuts.

He has taken part in a large number of collective exhibitions, from 1918, and solo shows from 1923, when he exhibited in Prague. His third exhibition, in 1925, was in Paris. He received many distinctions including: bronze medal (Exposition des Arts Décoratifs in Paris - 1925); Presern Prize (Ljubljana - 1947, 1948 and 1949); 1st place in the national prize for engraving (1950); a prize at the exhibition *Xylon*, Zurich (1954); a prize for his illustrations to A. Gradnik's book *Eros Tanatos*; City of Zagreb Prize (1965).

Bibliography:
Cosic, Bozica, *Bozidar Jakac,* exhibition catalogue, Salon moderne galerije, Beograd, 1965 (text in serbo-croat). Krzisnik, Zoran, *Bozidar Jakac,* exhibition catalogue, Moderna Galerija, Ljubljana, 1979 (text in serbo-croat). *Bozidar Jakac,* exhibition catalogue, Narodni Muzej, Beograd, 1986 (text in Bulgarian).

JAKEME DE MONS. See **JACQUEMART**

JAKEMES DE BOULOGNE. See **JACQUES de Boulogne**

JAKEMON DE FIVES. See **JACQUEMON**

JAKESCH, Alexander
Czech, 19th - 20th century.
Born 9 June 1862, in Prague.
Painter, engraver, sculptor. Historical subjects, portraits, genre scenes, landscapes.

Alexander Jakesch studied at the Prague and Munich academies of fine art. He became a professor at the Munich academy in around 1908.

Museums and Galleries:
Prague (Národní Gal.): *An Old Song.*

JAKESCH, Heinrich
Czech, 19th - 20th century.
Born 8 January 1867, in Prague; died 19 November 1909, in Prague.
Painter, pastellist, engraver. History painting, figures, portraits, landscapes, urban landscapes.

Heinrich Jakesch was the pupil of his brother Alexander and also trained at the academy of fine art in Munich. He settled in Prague where, from 1892, he exhibited regularly at the Spring Exhibition of Fine Art.

He originally produced small works in oil and pastel. Later he exhibited only drypoint engravings and etchings. He painted some portraits as well as compositions with figures situated in landscapes, such as his *Pyramus and Thisbe,* and seascapes like his *Calm Sea.* He is particularly known for his historically valuable depictions of Prague at the turn of the century.

Museums and Galleries:
Prague (Národní Gal.): most of his works.

JAKIC, Richard, or Jakitsch
Austrian, 19th - 20th century.
Born 2 March 1872, in Graz.
Sculptor.

Richard Jakic studied under Kundmann and went on to receive an honourable mention at the Exposition Universelle in Paris in 1900. He worked principally on commissions from Prague and Vienna.

JAKIC, Vojislav
Macedonian, 20th century.
Born 1 December 1932, in Radobiljici.
Painter, draughtsman, sculptor.
Art Brut.

Vojislav Jakic, the son of an Orthodox priest, went to Belgrade in 1952 to learn drawing and painting. A gifted draughtsman, Jakic would draw the likenesses of deceased relatives of villagers from the photographs on their identity cards. He started as a painter, but from 1960 drew scenes with figures, sometimes using a number of sheets, so that the finished work was very large (up to 16 feet (5 metres)). His pictures show grotesque figures, which are repeated over and over. They are drawn in minute detail using a ballpoint pen, which heightens the disquieting effect. He describes one of his works as 'the sedimentation of pain'.

An exhibition of his work was held in the Collection de l'Art Brut, Lausanne, in 2000.

Bibliography:
Jakic, Vojislav, *Nemanikuce ('sans domicile fixe'),* autobiography, Éditions Demoures, Essertines-sur-Rolle, 2000.

Museums and Galleries:
Lausanne (Collection de l'Art Brut): several works.

JAKIMOV. See **IAKIMOV**

JAKIMOWICZ
Polish, 19th century.
Painter. Landscapes.

JAKIROF, Sebastian. See **ZAKIROV**

JAKISCH, Josef. See **JACKISCH**

JAKITSCH, Richard. See **JAKIC**

JAKOB, called le Prédicateur
Swiss, 16th century.
Painter.

Jakob was a monk of the Dominican order, and produced a painting entitled *Die Rosen im Rathaussaale* in Lucerne in 1525.

JAKOB. See also **JACOB** and **JACOBUS**

JAKOB, Ernst
German, 19th century.
Born 22 March 1869, in Frankfurt am Main.
Painter, engraver (etching).

Ernst Jakob painted mostly landscapes. From 1906, he went over almost entirely to engraving.

JAKOB, Ignaz
Swiss, 18th century.
Active 1758-1787.
Painter.

JAKOB DE LÜBECK. See **CLAESSENS Jacobus**

JAKOB DER DEUTSCHE. See **GRIESINGER Jakob**

JAKOB DER NIEDERLÄNDER. See **ROMENT Jakob**

JAKOB VAN OOSTSANEN. See **CORNELISZ. VAN OOSTSANEN Jacob**

JAKOB VON KUTTENBERG
Bohemian, 16th century.
Died 1546, in Prague.
Active in Kuttenberg (now Kutná Hora, Czech Republic).
Sculptor (including wood).

Among the surviving works of Jakob von Kuttenberg are a figure of Christ and a bench in low relief in Kuttenberg, which were saved from the fire in the town hall in 1770, and sculptures on the altar of St James church and the pulpit of the church of the Assumption. There are also busts on the town hall in Tabor and statues in the chapel of Pürglitz castle (Krivoklat).

JAKOB VON OLMÜTZ
Moravian, 16th century.
Miniaturist.

In the Kunsthistorische Museum in Vienna is a two-volume gradual dating from 1499-1500, which Jakob von Olmütz wrote and illuminated with 17 ornamented capitals representing Biblical scenes, and 22 smaller ones. He carried out this work in the monastery of Bechyne for Laslav of Sternberg. In the marginal decorations are ten small figures surrounded by foliage. Gold and intense colours are used abundantly in these miniatures.

JAKOB VON ULM. See **GRIESINGER Jakob**

JAKOBE, Johann. See **JACOBÉ**

JAKOBER, Ben
20th century.
Born 1930.
Sculptor.

Ben Jakober was born in Vienna. A British subject, he lives and works in Majorca and Paris. His steel sculpture *La Copa de Paolo Uccello*, commissioned by the Spanish state, was installed in 1994 at an intersection on the motorway leading to Palma which was built in the early 1990s. This work was formed by computer-transposition of the angles of a polygonal panel of Uccello's drawings, so placed that they produce a crested shape.

In 1993, he co-founded the Fundación Yannick y Ben Jakober in Alcúdia, Majorca, which houses a collection of Spanish art, Old Master portraits of children and the sculptures jointly created by Jakober and his wife, Yannick Vu.

Exhibitions of his work include: 1984, Galerie Littmann, Basel, Switzerland; 1987, Galerie Eric Franck, Genebra, Switzerland; 1990, Galerie Montenav, Paris; 1991, Centro Cultural de la Misericordia, Palma de Mallorca; 1993, Arnolfini, Bristol; Museum Moderner Kunst Stiftung Ludwig Palais, Liechtenstein; Il Cavallo di Leonardo, XLV Venice Biennale; 1994, Istituto Italiano di Cultura, Madrid, Spain; Centre Cultural Contemporani Pelaires, Palma de Mallorca; 1995, Galerie Montenay, Paris and 1996, Istituto Italiano di Cultura, Paris.

MUSEUMS AND GALLERIES:
ARLES (Fondation Vincent van Gogh) - BREMEN (Kunsthalle) - BRUSSELS (MAM) - FLORENCE (Uffizi, Drawings and Prints Collection) - HAMBURG (Kunsthalle) - MADRID (Mus. Nacional Centro de Arte Reina Sofía) - SCHEVENINGEN (Museum Beelden aan Zee) - VIENNA (Mus. Moderner Kunst, Liechtenstein Palace).

AUCTION RECORDS:
PARIS, 13 Dec 1989, *Cumulus Vulgaris* (expanding foam suspension, sculpture, 78 3/4 x 59 x 39 1/4 ins / 200 x 150 x 100 cm) FRF 9,000. PARIS, 7 Oct 1996, *Mask* (1986, bronze, mask, 23 1/2 x 11 x 9 ins / 60 x 28 x 22 cm) FRF 10,000.

JAKOBEY, Karoly
19th century.
Born 1826; died 14 July 1891, in Budapest, Hungary.
Painter.

Karoly Jakobey trained in Pest and in Vienna. He settled in Pest, where he painted numerous portraits and a large number of retables for local churches.

MUSEUMS AND GALLERIES:
BUDAPEST (Magyar Nemzeti Múz.): *Portrait of Franz Liszt; Portrait of Count Szechenyi; Portrait of Paul Zichy.*

JAKOBI. See **JACOBI**

JAKOBIDES, Georg, or Jacobidès ou Iakovidis Georgios
Greek, 19th - 20th century.
Born 11 January 1853, in Mitilíni, Lesbos; died 1932, in Athens.
Painter. History painting, mythological subjects, genre scenes.

A pupil of Nikiforos Lytras at the Athens academy of fine art and of Gabriel von Max and Ludwig von Löfftz at the Munich academy, Georg Jakobides settled in Munich. He painted mainly mythological subjects and compositions with children.

He took part in a number of exhibitions including the Munich International Exhibition (1883) and the exhibition of the Dresden academy (1889). He received several distinctions including a bronze medal at the Paris 1889 Exposition Universelle, an honourable mention in Berlin (1891), a medal in Munich (1893) and a gold medal at the 1900 Exposition Universelle in Paris. When he returned to Greece he became the first director of the national art gallery from 1910 to 1918 and also the director of the fine arts school from 1910 to 1930.

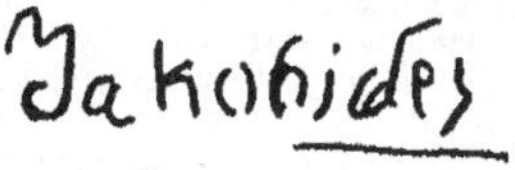

MUSEUMS AND GALLERIES:
ATHENS: *Improvised Concert* - ATHENS (Ethnikí Pinakothíki): *Paul Melas; First Steps* (1892, oil on canvas) - WIESBADEN: *Mischievous Grandson* - ZURICH: *Grandmother and her Granddaughter.*

AUCTION RECORDS:
PARIS, 23 April 1897, *A Mother's Love*, FRF 390. LONDON, 28 Nov 1984, *Grandfather and Granddaughter* (oil on card, 10 1/4 x 8 1/4 ins / 26 x 21 cm) GBP 16,000. LONDON, 26 Nov 1985, *Grandmother with her Grandchildren* (oil on canvas, 16 1/4 x 24 1/2 ins / 41 x 62 cm) GBP 17,000. LONDON, 25 Nov 1987, *Noisy Trio* (oil on canvas, 37 1/2 x 51 1/4 ins / 95 x 130 cm) GBP 65,000. LONDON, 25 March 1988, *Wilful Child* (oil on canvas, 12 1/2 x 10 ins / 32 x 25.5 cm) GBP 17,050. LONDON, 5 Oct 1990, *Storybook* (ink, 12 x 10 1/4 ins / 30.5 x 26 cm) GBP 2,200. LONDON, 27 Nov 1992, *Bath* (oil on canvas, 12 1/2 x 14 1/4 ins / 31.8 x 36.2 cm) GBP 27,500. LONDON, 17 March 1993, *Smoker* (oil on canvas, 35 3/4 x 25 1/4 ins / 91 x 64 cm) GBP 58,700. LONDON, 19 March 1993, *Little Girl Knitting* (oil on canvas, 13 1/4 x 9 1/4 ins / 33.5 x 23.5 cm) GBP 34,500. NEW YORK, 15 Feb 1994, *Grandmother's Story* (oil on panel, 10 x 7 1/4 ins / 25.7 x 18.1 cm) USD 46,000. LONDON, 14 June 1995, *Girl with a Fan* (oil on card, 13 3/4 x 11 1/2 ins / 35 x 29 cm) GBP 10,925. ATHENS, 9 Dec 1996, *Grandmother's Darling* (oil on canvas) GRD 66,500,000.

JAKOBS, Jeanine
French, 20th century.
Born 1932.
Painter.
AUCTION RECORDS:
PARIS, 9 April 1989, *Orion* (oil on canvas, 40 1/4 x 29 1/4 ins / 102 x 74 cm) FRF 5,000. PARIS, 8 Oct 1989, *The Temple of Solomon* (oil on canvas) FRF 6,800. LES ANDELYS, 19 Nov 1989, *RER* (acrylic/canvas, 39 1/4 x 29 ins / 100 x 73.5 cm) FRF 4,600. PARIS, 26 April 1990, *Labyrinth* (oil on canvas, 39 1/4 x 32 ins / 100 x 81 cm) FRF 8,200. PARIS, 10 June 1990, *Le Billard* (oil on canvas, 39 1/4 x 32 ins / 100 x 81 cm) FRF 6,500. PARIS, 28 Oct 1990, *Boomerang* (oil on canvas, 39 1/4 x 32 ins / 100 x 81 cm) FRF 10,500.

JAKOBS, Paul Emil, or Jacobs
German, 19th century.
Born 18 August 1802, in Gotha; died 6 January 1866, in Gotha.
Painter, art restorer. Mythological subjects, portraits, genre scenes.
Jakobs trained initially under Peter and Robert Langer in Munich. From 1818 to 1825, he continued his studies in Rome. He worked as a portrait painter in Frankfurt, then moved to St Petersburg, where he became a member of the academy. He travelled widely in Greece and Italy. Among noted commissions was restoration work in various rooms at the palace in Hanover. A member of the academy in Berlin and court painter in Gotha, he exhibited widely, especially in Germany, from 1823 until his death. He won awards in Manchester (1842) and Philadelphia (1850).
MUSEUMS AND GALLERIES:
ALTENBURG: *Holy Family with St John as a Child* - GDANSK: *Antigone* - GOTHA: *Venus and Cupid; Head of an Old Man; Portrait of J. von Plänkner; Ecce Homo; Roman Woman* - KALININGRAD: *Sheherazade Telling the Caliph a Thousand and One Stories* - PHILADELPHIA (Pennsylvania Academy of the Fine Arts Gal.): *Judith and Holofernes.*
AUCTION RECORDS:
NEW YORK, 11 Feb 1981, *Judith and Holofernes* (1848, oil on canvas, 60 x 48 ins / 152.5 x 122 cm) USD 5,500. LONDON, 26 Nov 1986, *Greek Women on a Balcony* (1863, oil on canvas, 45 x 37 1/4 ins / 114 x 94.5 cm) GBP 8,000. NEW YORK, 21 May 1987, *View of Constantinople* (1849, oil on panel, 26 3/4 x 38 1/4 ins / 68 x 97 cm) GBP 32,000. NEW YORK, 24 Oct 1989, *Young Woman of the Harem at Her Toilette* (1839, oil on canvas, 50 1/4 x 38 3/4 ins / 127.6 x 98.4 cm) USD 88,000. LONDON, 12 Feb 1993, *Diana and Nymphs Bathing* (1846, oil on canvas, 61 x 79 3/4 ins / 154.9 x 202.6 cm) GBP 17,050. NEW YORK, 1 Nov 1995, *Judith and Holofernes* (1848, oil on canvas, 58 3/4 x 47 3/4 ins / 149.2 x 121.3 cm) USD 31,625. LONDON, 11 Oct 1996, *Women in Oriental Dress Making Music* (1850, oil on canvas, 49 1/2 x 40 1/4 ins / 126 x 102 cm) GBP 23,000.

JAKOBS, JAKOBSZ., JAKOBUS. See **JACOBS, JACOBSZ., JACOBUS**

JAKOBY, Julius
Slovak, 20th century.
Born 28 March 1903, in Kosiciach.
Painter.
Julius Jakoby studied in Kosiciach between 1923 and 1926 and then became a pupil of István Reti at the academy of fine art in Budapest in 1927-1928. He began to exhibit in Kosiciach in 1929, going on to exhibit in cities including Bratislava and Budapest.
He works in an Expressionist graphism related to the 'automatic writing' practised by the artists of the CoBrA group after World War II.
BIBLIOGRAPHY:
Fifty years of Czechoslovak Painting from the Collections of the Galleries, 1918-1958, exhibition catalogue, Slovenska Narodna Gal., Bratislava, 1968 (in commemoration of the 50th anniversary of the Republic of Czechoslovakia).

JAKOFF. See **JACOB** and **YAKOV**

JAKOPIC, Richard
Slovene, 19th - 20th century.
Born 12 April 1869, in Ljubljana; died 1943, in Ljubljana.
Painter. Figures, landscapes.
Richard Jakopic studied at the Vienna academy of fine art in 1887 and, the following year, at the Munich academy. Remaining in Munich, he encouraged his compatriot Anton Azbé to open a school of painting there in 1890, a school that gained a considerable reputation. Jakopic worked with Azbé in Munich and spent his summers in the Slovenian countryside painting out of doors.
Jakopic, Sternen and Matija Jama were, from 1900, the champions of Slovenian Post-Impressionism. Jakopic remained loyal to this style until 1906, returning to a more Realist style thereafter. From 1914, he began to produce works that were highly Expressionist in the use of colour but which continued his interest, dating from his Impressionist period, in the changing effects of light according to the time of day or the season of the year.
Nadezda Petrovic, Richard Jakopic and a number of his fellow artists from the Impressionist period can be said to have laid the foundations of modern art in Yugoslavia.
MUSEUMS AND GALLERIES:
BELGRADE (Narodni Muzej): *Birch Trees* (1910) - LJUBLJANA (Moderna Gal.): *Bather* (1910); *Orchard* (1913); *The River Sava* (1922); *In the Blue Room* (1923); *Evening on the Sava River* (1926) - LJUBLJANA (Narodna Galerija): *The Green Veil* (undated); *Birch Trees in Autumn* (1902); *Winter* (1905); *Krizani Monastery* (1909); *Memories* (1912).

JAKOUCHKA. See **YAKUSHKA**

JAKOULOFF, Gueorgui Bogdanovitch. See **YAKULOV**

JAKOVITS, Jozef Szobrai
Hungarian, 20th century.
Born 1909, in Budapest.
Active in the USA from 1965 to 1980.
Sculptor, painter, photomontage artist.
European School group.
Jozef Jakovits was a worker until World War II when he taught himself sculpture and then, from 1945, painting. His sculptures suggest imaginary animals, portrayed in a style influenced more by primitive art than by the work of Victor Brauner with whom they are often compared. During his period in America he produced a number of paintings with a graphism inspired by Hebrew script.
Jakovits was not able to show his work until 1962, when he exhibited some photomontages at the National Gallery in Budapest. On his return from the USA, the National Gallery organised a second exhibition, this time of all aspects of his work.

JAKOWLEFF, Mikhail Nicolaevich. See **YAKOVLEV**

JAKSIC, Jura
Serb, 19th century.
Born 1832, in Srpska Crnja; died 1878, in Belgrade.
Painter, poet, dramatist.
Jaksic painted in the Romantic style. He earned a meagre living as a schoolteacher, travelling from town to town. He painted heroes from Slav legends, portraits and religious and historical subjects.

JAKUBONIS, Gediminas or Gedimius
Lithuanian, 20th century.
Born 8 March 1927, in Kupiskis.

Sculptor. Low reliefs, monuments, medals.
Gediminas Jakubonis went to Kaunas Seminary before going to the State Institute of Applied and Decorative Art in Kaunas, where he studied under Viktoras Polis. He created decorative low reliefs for public buildings. His war memorial in the village of Purcipius (1961) is his best known work, for which he was awarded the Lenin Prize. His colleague, the sculptor Antanas Kmieliauskas, has revealed that Jakubonis drew his inspiration from the little statuettes of Christ of the Holy Virgin on Lithuanian country crosses.

JAKUBOWICZ, Michel
French, 20th century.
Born c. 1940, in Paris.
Painter.
In his paintings, as much through his lacquered colours as by his drawing, Jakubowicz seeks above all to achieve an economy of message. He creates a strange universe, where the figures are neither entirely man or animal, but 'deformed humanoids interpenetrating each other in postures evoking ecstasy as much as torture'.

JAKUCHU, Ito. See **ITO Jakuchu**

JAKUSAI. See **NOBUZANE**

JAKUSAI, real name Rokkaku Jakusai
Japanese, 14th - 15th century.
Born 1348; died 1424.
Painter.
Jakusai was a painter of the Tosa School, and worked in the studio of the imperial court (*e-dokoro*). He later became a priest. In 1414 he collaborated with Yukihiro (working at the beginning of the 15th century) on the horizontally opening roll *Yuzu Nembutsu Engi* (*Legends of the Yuzu Sect*), still kept at the Seiryoji temple in Kyoto. It relates the ascendancy of the Amidist sect Yuzu Nembutsu, and the life of its founder Ryoshim (1072-1132). Even though the grand tradition of these rolls had long since passed its peak, the *Yuzu Nembutsu Engi* remains a living painting in the classical tradition. Several xylographic reproductions of it are in existence.

JAKUSHO SHUJIN. See **GESSEN**

JALABERT, Charles François
French, 19th century.
Born 1 January 1819, in Nîmes; died 1901, in Paris.
Painter. Portraits, genre scenes.
Charles François Jalabert began at Paris' College of Fine Arts on 9 October 1839 and studied under Paul Delaroche. He came second in the 1841 Prix de Rome, was made a Chevalier of the Légion d'Honneur in 1855, rising to Officer in 1867. He featured at the Paris Salon from 1847 to 1882. See Jean Jalabert.

Museums and Galleries:
Alençon: *M Rattier* - Amsterdam (Stedelijk Mus.): *Faith and Hope* - Carcassonne: *Gamelin; Thieving Magpie; M. Coste and His Mother* - Chantilly: *Portrait of the Duke of Guise; Two Portraits of the Prince of Condé; Portrait of Queen Marie-Amélie* - Montpellier: *Italian Woman* (watercolour) - Nîmes: *Oedipus and Antigone; Marie des Abruzzes* - Paris (MAM): *Portrait of Mme Rattier; Virgil, Horace and Varius at the House of Maecenas* - Paris (Mus. National de Céramique Sèvres): *Saints; Louis-Napoleon, King of Holland.*

Auction records:
Paris, 1863, *Nymphs Listening to Orpheus*, FRF 8,900. Paris, 1873, *Golden Fleece*, FRF 1,080. Paris, 1890, *Christ Walking on Water*, FRF 2,000. Paris, 25 Feb 1926, *Maternal Affection* (pencil) FRF 190. Paris, 18 June 1930, *Young Mother and her Two Children*, FRF 1,350. Paris, 25 June 1931, *Portrait of Mme Sabatier* (pencil) FRF 1,700. Paris, 1 July 1932, *Mother and Child*, FRF 800. Paris, 17 Dec 1984, *Young Woman Standing in a Red Carpeted Interior* (1872, oil on canvas, 28¾ x 23¼ ins / 73 x 59 cm) FRF 48,000. London, 24 June 1987, *Samuel Blessing David* (1842, oil on canvas, 43½ x 57½ ins / 110.5 x 146 cm) GBP 4,500. Monaco, 14-15 Dec 1996, *Portrait of the Count of Paris; Portrait of the Countess of Paris* (1865, oil on canvas, a pair, 30 x 23¾ ins / 76.5 x 60.5 cm) FRF 102,960. Paris, 20 Oct 1997, *Christ Walking on Water* (oil on panel, 7½ x 10½ ins / 19 x 26.5 cm) FRF 4,600. New York, 22 Oct 1997, 1850, oil on canvas, 13¼ x 10 ins / 33.7 x 25.1 cm) USD 9,775. Paris, 10 Dec 1999, *Portrait de Louis-Marie de Belleyme in Magistrate's Dress* (1857, oil on canvas, 83 x 53 ins / 210 x 135 cm) FRF 22,000. Zofingen, 29 Nov 2002, *Chiara - Young Roman on a Terrace with View of the Campagna* (1747-1850, oil on parquet) CHF 3,800.

JALABERT, Dominique
French, 20th century.
Born 21 July 1945, in Bordeaux.
Painter.
Dominique Jalabert studied at the École des Beaux-Arts in Bordeaux and Paris. He quickly progressed from Lyrical Abstraction to Realism based on political themes, developed from photographic documents.

JALABERT, Jean
French, 19th century.
Born 11 July 1815, in Carcassonne; died 1900.
Painter. History painting, portraits, genre scenes.
Jean Jalabert began at Paris' College of Fine Arts in 1840 and studied under Paul Delaroche. He featured at the Paris Salon from 1842 to 1849.

His *Magdalene*, held at Carcassonne Museum, is reminiscent of Manet's *Olympia*. In general, he combined the line of Ingres with the colours of Delacroix.

Bibliography:
Les Années romantiques, la peinture française de 1815 à 1850, exhibition catalogue, Musée des Beaux-Arts, Nantes, Galeries nationales du Grand Palais, Paris, 1996.

Museums and Galleries:
Carcassonne: *Odalisque* (1842); *Magdalene in the Desert* (1843); *Portrait of François Bosque; Thieving Magpie* (1848); *Portrait of Jacques Gamelin* - Marseilles (MBA): *Plague of Thebes, or Oedipus and Antigone* (1842, sketch); *Oedipus and Antigone Fleeing Thebes* (1843) - Nîmes: *Virgil, Horace and Varius at the House of Maecenas* (1847).

Auction records:
Paris, 8 Dec 1949, *Romeo and Juliet*, FRF 11,600.

JALABERT-EDON, Eliane
French, 20th century.
Born 21 November 1904, in St-Quentin (Aisne).
Active from 1930 to 1956 in Morocco.
Painter. Figures, landscapes.
In 1920, Jalabert-Édon studied at the École d'Art in Valenciennes. In 1922, she entered the Atelier Fernand Humbert at the École des Beaux-Arts in Paris. She was especially attentive to the teachings of the animal painter Jouve, whom she met in the Jardin des Plantes in Paris. She also studied wood engraving with Stéphane Pannemaker. She began exhibiting in 1926, at the Salon des Artistes Français in Paris. In 1927, a travel grant enabled her to make a first trip to Morocco, where she settled in 1930. In 1935, she married Félix Édon, an officer, who was killed in Dong Hoï in 1950. Having returned to France in 1956, she settled in Angers, and later, near Mans. A first retrospective of her work was organised in Valenciennes in 1983. Though she remained true to the spirit of the light of the North, the most important part of her work is that produced during her extended stay in Morocco. There she accumulated a large number of drawings. She published three catalogues of drawings in Rabat, *Itinéraire au Maroc* (*Moroccan Itinerary*), *Artisans du Vieux Maroc* (*Craftsmen of Old Morocco*) and *Marrakech*. She illustrated several works, including Henri Bosco's *L'Enfant et le Rivière* (*The Boy and the River*).

BIBLIOGRAPHY:
Ponsignon, J.C., *Éliane Jalabert-Édon*, 1983.
MUSEUMS AND GALLERIES:
VALENCIENNES: *The Silence*.

JALAL, Ibrahim

Syrian, 20th - 21st century.
Born 8 December 1947, near Maaret-al-Nouman.
Active in France since 1973.
Painter.

Ibrahim Jalal studied at the school of fine art in Damascus, gaining a diploma in 1972, and subsequently at the school of fine arts in Paris under Gustave Singier, where he was awarded a diploma with merit in 1978. In Paris he exhibited his work in the 1974 Salon de Automne, the Salon de Mai 1988-1990, and regularly at the Salon des Nouvelles Realities since 1988. Since its inception in 1939, this latter Salon has promoted international abstract art, and it is here that Jalal found the context best suited to the personal expression of his art. He also participated in other group exhibitions in Paris, such as *Arab Art of Today* at the Espace Cardin in 1978 and *Syrian Artists in France* at UNESCO in 1979, as well as collective exhibitions in many surrounding areas, notably Marne-la-Vallée, where he lives and works on his boat *Studio Atys*. His work has also been seen in other French towns, including Cagnes-sur-Mer, Toulon, and Tours, and abroad. From the early days of his career Jalal has also mounted solo exhibitions: 1971 in Darnas, 1976 in Paris, 1985 in Konstanz, Germany, 1987 at the Syrian cultural centre in Paris, 1993 in Lagny, and in 1993 at the Norestrean gallery in Sandnes, Norway. In 1989 he created murals at the Paris Metro station Abbesses, together with two at Sandnes in Norway in 1991.

Jalal's work is symptomatic of a reaction against the ephemeral values of passing fashions. In other words, he is too enamoured of sinuous line and enchanting colour to be tempted by any simplistic minimalism, and is adamant that he wishes to stay in touch with observable reality. Moreover, his work encompasses both Islamic and European influences; having studied in Paris, the points of reference in his form of 'lyrical abstraction' are typically French - Bazaine, Manessier or Singier. On the other hand, his painting recalls the decorative patterns and calligraphic signs of Islamic art. These are very freely interpreted in harmonies of shimmering colour, and Jalal is concerned to preserve the cultural roots of every individual against an anonymous universalism.

Painting on his houseboat at Marne-la-Vallée, Ibrahim Jalal combines the present - in the form of the dull blue-green of the river and the gentle greens of the leaves shot through with a few pale rays of Île de France sunshine - with distant memories of his homeland, such as the red terracotta brick of villages harmonising with the blues of the cool decorated interiors, and the yellows of sun and sand.

MUSEUMS AND GALLERIES:
DAMASCUS (Ministry of Culture).
AUCTION RECORDS:
PARIS, 10 June 1990, *No title* (mixed media/mounted paper, 39 1/4 x 59 ins / 100 x 150 cm) FRF 9,500. PARIS, 7 Feb 1991, *No title* (mixed media/canvas, 57 1/2 x 38 1/4 ins / 146 x 97 cm) FRF 10,500. PARIS, 17 Nov 1991, *Composition* (oil on canvas, 57 1/2 x 45 ins / 146 x 114 cm) FRF 5,000.

JALEA, Joan

Romanian, 20th century.
Born 1887, in Bucharest.
Active in France.
Sculptor. Mythological subjects. Monuments.

Joan Jalea first studied in Bucharest before going to Paris where he studied at the Académie Julian and settled permanently. He executed the war memorial in Dieuze near Nancy and is also remembered particularly for a group representing *Hercules Fighting the Centaurs* and a *Faun Playing a Flute*.

JALEY, Jean Louis Nicolas, or Léon

French, 19th century.
Born 27 January 1802, in Paris; died 30 May 1866, in Neuilly (Hauts-de-Seine).
Sculptor. Allegorical subjects, portraits.

Jean Jaley's parents were from St Etienne. He studied under monument and portrait sculptor Pierre Cartellier, and began at Paris' College of Fine Arts in 1820.

In 1824, he came second in the Prix de Rome for sculpture but carried off the first prize in 1827. He exhibited works at the Paris Salon, official and unique as it then was, regularly from 1824 to 1863. He was made a member of the Légion d'Honneur in 1837 and of the Institut de France in 1857.

His principal works include: *Modesty*, marble statue at the Palais de Luxembourg; *François Miron*, stone statue at Paris' Hôtel de Ville; *Fountain*, stone statue at the new Louvre; *Painting*, stone statue at the new Louvre; *Strength and Justice*, stone statues at Paris' law courts; *London Town*, stone statue at the Gare du Nord; *Marble Bust of Ganneron*, at the 2nd arrondissement's town hall; *Virgin and Infant Jesus*, marble group for the church of Trouville; *Bronze Statue of Duke Decazes*, at Liboume; and *Napoleon III*, marble statue at the Senate Palace. These statues of allegorical figures are generally full-scale.

MUSEUMS AND GALLERIES:
BAYONNE (Mus. Bonnat): *Mirabeau; Louis XI; Bailly* - CHANTILLY: *Duke of Bourbon*; second version of the same - COMPIÈGNE: *Revelation* - FONTAINEBLEAU: *Memory of Pompeii* - MARSEILLES: *Melancholy* - NANTES: *A Clarke; Edgar Clarke; Count Alphonse de Feltre* - PARIS (former Mus. du Luxembourg): *Golden Age* - PARIS (Louvre): *Prayer; Louis XI; Duke of Orleans; Spring, Painting and Assyrian Art* - PARIS (National Archives): *J A Letronne* - ST-ÉTIENNE: *Louis XI; Danadïes; Prayer; Revelation; Augustin Dupré* - TROYES: *Memory of Pompeii* - VERSAILLES: *Étienne Gérard, Marshal of France; Georges Lobau, Marshal of France; General of Hautpoul; André de Montalambert; Louis XI; Philippe Auguste Ferdinand, Duke of Orleans; Marshal Ney*.

JALI-BORY

French, 20th century.
Born in Bourges.
Painter.

Jali-Bory trained as a biologist and took a science degree, then studied painting with Yves Brayer and Edward MacAvoy. She began by working on the composition of paintings, then on the use of space and colour, both in her pictures and in university theses. In 1970 she settled in Paris, where she showed work at the Salon des Artistes Français, Salon des Indépendants and Salon d'Automne.

JALICA, pseudonym of Ogonowska, Alicia

Maiden name: Biskupska
Polish, 20th century.
Born 29 June 1929, in Kielce.
Active in the USA and in France from 1961.
Painter, pastellist.

Jalica, as she was known, left Poland for New York, later moving to Paris.

Her work is abstract but retains some connections with reality; it is executed in a thick impasto with a palette knife and a good feel for colour. The universe she depicts can be compared to that of Poliakoff or Klee.

She has taken part in various collective exhibitions including: Salon des Artistes Français, Paris (1969); Galerie Soleil, Paris (1969 and 1972); Salon des Artistes Indépendants, Paris (1970); Galerie Robert Faure in Lyons (1974); American Art Center, Monaco (1984). Solo exhibitions include: at the Palace St Moritz, Switzerland (1972, 1973, 1974 and 1977);

Galerie G. R., Paris (1976); Galerie Méridien, Paris (1978); Café de la Paix, Paris (1980).
MUSEUMS AND GALLERIES:
LUDWIGSHAFEN - PARIS (FMAC): *Landscape* - PARIS (FNAC).

JALIFIÉ, Félix Émile
French, 20th century.
Born 4 April 1882, in Marseilles.
Painter. Portraits, landscapes.
Félix Émile Jalifié worked in museums, copying Dutch artists. He also painted portraits and landscapes.
AUCTION RECORDS:
LONDON, 9 Oct 1997, *Interior of Marseilles Museum* (oil on canvas, 18 x 24 ins / 45.7 x 61 cm) GBP 977.

JALLAND, H. G.
Watercolourist. Sporting subjects.
H.G. Jalland is mentioned in *Art Prices Current*.

JALLIER, Claude Jean-Baptiste, or Jallier de Savault
French, 18th century.
Born 1738; died 1807, in Paris.
Watercolourist, painter (gouache). Genre scenes, landscapes, architectural views.
Works by Jallier were shown in the Paris exhibition *Exposition des Petits-Maîtres du XVIIIe Siècle (Exhibition of the Minor Masters of the 18th Century)* in June, 1920.
AUCTION RECORDS:
PARIS, 27 March 1919, *Traces of a Triumphal Arch; The Great Rock* (two red chalks) FRF 700. PARIS, 7 and 8 May 1923, *The Collation* (watercolour heightened with gouache) FRF 1,050. PARIS, 4 May 1955, *Plan for the Construction of a Discount House Seen from the Angle of the Rue Ste-Anne and a New Road* (pen and watercolour) FRF 15,100. PARIS, 6 Nov 1986, *Perspective View of the Discount House Taken from the Angle of the Rue Ste-Anne and a New Road* (pen and watercolour, 7 3/4 x 13 1/4in/20 x 33.5cm) FRF 51,000. PARIS, 4 Dec 1987, *Chinese Pavilion* (1775, watercolour heightened with gouache, 10 3/4 x 7 3/4in/27.5 x 20cm) FRF 36,000. PARIS, 4 Dec 1987, *Chinese Pavilion* (1775, watercolour heightened with white gouache, 10 3/4 x 7 3/4in/27.5 x 20cm) FRF 36,000.

JALLOIS, Claire
French, 20th century.
Painter, sculptor, lithographer, illustrator.
Claire Jallois moved easily from one kind of subject or style to another, sometimes bordering on fantasy. She sold illustrations to newspapers and magazines, and produced lithographs to illustrate works by Balzac, Stendhal and Flaubert. In 1957, she began to show work in collective exhibitions, mainly in the south of France. She also had solo shows there as well as several in Paris, including one in 1996 in the Espace Quartier Latin.

JALLOT. See **DUMONT Pierre**

JALLOT, Marcel Édouard
French, 20th century.
Born 17 March 1904, in Paris.
Painter. Landscapes, flowers.
Marcel Édouard Jallot received a diploma and a grant from the French Institute in London. He did most of his work in Haute-Provence, and in Manosque (Basses-Alpes) to which he retired. His work was included in many collective exhibitions in France and elsewhere. In Paris he exhibited at the Salon d'Automne, Salon des Tuileries and Salon des Artistes Décorateurs, and at the Salon des Indépendants, to which he belonged.
AUCTION RECORDS:
PARIS, 12 Dec 1946, *Flowers*, FRF 1,300.

JALLU, Jean
French, 19th century.
Born in Paris; died 21 December 1887.
Painter, draughtsman.
Jean Jallu was one of the founders of the Académie de Dessin in Grenoble, where he settled.

JALÓN, Nicolás, or Xalón
Spanish, 16th century.
Active in Huesca.
Painter, sculptor.

JALVO, Juan
Spanish, 19th century.
Painter.
Juan Jalvo is known mainly as a decorative artist.

JAMA, Luise
Maiden name: Van Raders
Dutch, 19th - 20th century.
Born 1871, in Batavia, now Jakarta.
Painter, engraver.
The wife of Matija Jama, Luise Jama worked in The Hague, Amsterdam and Munich.

JAMA, Matija
Slovene, 19th - 20th century.
Born 4 January 1872, in Ljubljana.
Active in the Netherlands.
Painter. Landscapes.
Matija Jama studied in Munich. He exhibited in Vienna, Belgrade, London, Sofia and in the Netherlands.

JAMAIN, Émile Théodore
French, 19th century.
Born 19th century, in Fumay (Ardennes).
Sculptor (including ivory), medallist.
Émile Jamain featured at the Salon of the Société des Artistes Français, receiving an honourable mention in 1890 and a third class medal in 1907.

JAMAL, Ghada
Lebanese, 20th - 21st century.
Born 1956.
Active in the USA.
Painter, pastellist.
In 1978 Ghada Jamal received a diploma from the Santa Anna College in California. She studied from 1981 to 1985 at New York University and in the Beirut College for Women. Her work was included in the 1984 *Annual Student Art Exhibition* in Beirut, and in the *Beit Eddine Festival* in 1985.

JAMAR, Armand Gustave Gérard
Belgian, 19th - 20th century.
Born 18 April 1870, in Liège; died 1946, in St-Gilles (Brussels).
Painter, watercolourist. Figure compositions, figures, portraits, local scenes (Kermesses), interiors with figures, landscapes, urban landscapes, architectural views, harbour scenes, seascapes.
Armand Gustave Gérard Jamar studied law before enrolling at the college of fine arts in Liège, where he studied under Evariste Carpentier and Adrien de Witte. Jamar travelled extensively in Europe and North Africa, returning to exhibit first in Liège, then at various official Salons in Antwerp, Ghent and Brussels. From 1900 he was invited to exhibit at the Paris Salon des Artistes Français. He received an honourable mention at the 1904 Salon and a gold medal in 1907. Jamar's work featured at the Brussels Exposition Universelle of 1910 and he went on to exhibit solo almost annually thereafter. In 1974, the Belgian Postal Administration issued a stamp bearing a picture of Jamar's. After a succession of retrospectives during his lifetime, others were held from 1970 at various venues in Belgium, notably at Deurle Museum in 1974, the Museum of Walloon Art in Liège in 1975, the Palace of Congress in Liège in 1977, the Hôtel de

Ville in Brussels in 1980, and in 1993 at a private gallery in Liège, which exhibited about 100 of his paintings.

Even in his early canvases, it was evident that Jamar's landscapes and seascapes owed a considerable debt to the Pre-Impressionist works of J.M.W. Turner and Eugène Boudin; by contrast, Jamar's interiors were indebted to the Flemish tradition. In these early paintings, he worked using a classic technique of lightly-applied paint for clear colours and transparent brushwork to produce shadow effects. According to Jamar himself, his style evolved from Post-Impressionism style towards a more Expressionist approach after 1918, a fact borne out by his vigorous use of the palette knife. From 1930 to around 1939, he started to paint again using brushes, capturing succinctly the lush pastures and heavy clouds that dominate the Flemish landscape and city views of Bruges, his two favourite themes. In the latter years of his life he drew inspiration from the legend of *Till Eulenspiegel*, from the *Apocalypse* and from Dante's *Divine Comedy*. In his cycle entitled *Creation*, Armand Jamar came his closest to non-figurative painting as an expression of what art historian Michel de Ghelderode has termed 'Jamar's visionary approach to art'.

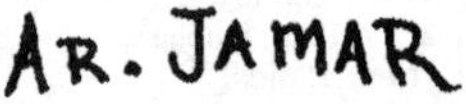

BIBLIOGRAPHY:
Retrospectieve Armand Jamar, exhibition catalogue, Museum Roerick-Tulpinck, Presses de la Sabip, Bruges. Cayman, H., *Le Postimpressionnisme de Armand Jamar*, Bruges, 1939. De Ghelderode, Michel, *Armand Jamar, 1870-1946, son œuvre brugeois*, Bruges, c. 1956. Delmelle, Joseph/Muls, Jozef/De Ghelderode, Michel, *Armand Jamar*, Arcade, Brussels, 1972. Gérard, F., *'Armand Jamar'* in *Coll. La Mémoire de l'Art*, Les Éditeurs d'Art Associés, Brussels, 1988.
MUSEUMS AND GALLERIES:
BRUSSELS (MAM) - LIÈGE: *Farm Interior, Holland* - ROUEN: *Portrait of Géricault.*
AUCTION RECORDS:
PARIS, 18 March 1920, *River adjacent to a Park*, FRF 330. PARIS, 28 April 1937, *Dutch Interior*, FRF 320. ANTWERP, 6 April 1976, *Fair in Bruges* (1933, oil on panel, 18 x 13¾ ins / 46 x 35 cm) BEF 20,000. BRUSSELS, 28 March 1984, *North Sea Storm* (oil on canvas, 39¼ x 59 ins / 100 x 150 cm) BEF 38,000. LOKEREN, 5 March 1988, *Young Woman with a Parasol* (oil on panel, 23 x 19 ins / 57.5 x 48 cm) BEF 70,000. BRUSSELS, 19 Dec 1989, *Oriental Scene* (1924, oil on canvas, 15 x 11 ins / 38 x 28 cm) BEF 36,000. LOKEREN, 17 March 1990, *Evening on the Lagoon, Venice* (1926, oil on panel, 22 x 29½ ins / 55 x 75 cm) BEF 145,000. BRUSSELS, 19 March 1990, *La Rochelle* (oil on canvas, 29½ x 22 ins / 75 x 55 cm) BEF 270,000; *Mouth of the Canche at Paris-Plage* (1921, oil on canvas, 14¼ x 19¾ ins / 36 x 50 cm) BEF 110,000. BRUSSELS, 27 March 1990, *Seascape* (oil on panel, 8¼ x 11 ins / 21 x 27 cm) BEF 32,000. BRUSSELS, 23 April 1990, *Fishermen at Low Tide at Oostduinkerke* (1900, oil on canvas, 39¼ x 59 ins / 100 x 150 cm) BEF 290,000; *Young Women Fishing at Vlissingen* (1926, oil on canvas, 28 x 18 ins / 71 x 46 cm) BEF 170,000. TONGEREN (BELGIUM), 9 May 1990, *Claes en Soetkin at Damme* (1940, oil on canvas, 59 x 39¼ ins / 150 x 100 cm) BEF 140,000. BRUSSELS, 12 June 1990, *Interior* (oil on canvas, 22 x 29½ ins / 55 x 75 cm) BEF 38,000. LIÈGE, 13 July 1990, *Near Montreux* (1928, oil on canvas, 22 x 29½ ins / 55 x 75 cm) BEF 140,000. BRUSSELS, 18 July 1990, *Washerwoman, Verona* (1928, oil on canvas, 29½ x 22 ins / 75 x 55 cm) BEF 230,000; *Breton Coast* (1906, oil on panel, 14¼ x 19¾ ins / 36 x 50 cm) BEF 105,000. LIÈGE, 26 Sept 1990, *Seascape* (1935, oil on canvas, 59 x 39¼ ins / 150 x 100 cm) BEF 150,000. BRUSSELS, 13 Oct 1990, *Venice* (1930, oil on panel, 25½ x 19¾ ins / 65 x 50 cm) BEF 230,000. TONGEREN (BELGIUM), 6-7 Feb 1991, *Winter Landscape* (oil on canvas, 27½ x 39¼ ins / 70 x 100 cm) BEF 150,000. LIÈGE, 27 March 1991, *Venice Lagoon* (1930, oil on panel, 11½ x 14½ ins / 29 x 37 cm) BEF 85,000. BRUSSELS, 27 May 1991, *Estuary, Algiers* (1922, oil on panel, 17¾ x 17¼ ins / 45 x 44 cm) BEF 150,000. BRUSSELS, 7 Oct 1991, *Breton Harbour* (1905, oil on panel, 7¼ x 11 ins / 18.5 x 27 cm) BEF 50,000. LIÈGE, 11 Dec 1991, *Estuary View, Venice* (1921, oil on panel, 19¾ x 23½ ins / 50 x 60 cm) BEF 100,000. BRUSSELS, 14-16 April 1992, *Doges' Palace, Venice* (1921, oil on canvas, 22 x 29¼ ins / 55 x 74 cm) BEF 170,000. LOKEREN, 23 May 1992, *Brewery, Bruges* (1934, oil on canvas, 39¼ x 59 ins / 100 x 150 cm) BEF 70,000. AMSTERDAM, 3 Nov 1992, *Belgian Coast* (1903, oil on canvas, 39 x 58¼ ins / 99 x 148 cm) NLG 3,910. LOKEREN, 5 Dec 1992, *Stable* (1929, oil on canvas, 22 x 29½ ins / 55 x 75 cm) BEF 30,000. PARIS, 3 Feb 1993, *Last Refuge* (1942, oil on canvas, 22 x 29½ ins / 55 x 75 cm) FRF 19,000. LOKEREN, 11 March 1995, *Gondola near the Accademia, Venice* (1933, oil on canvas, 29½ x 22 ins / 75 x 55 cm) BEF 95,000. AMSTERDAM, 2 Sept 1997, *La Rochelle* (1927, oil on canvas, 14½ x 11½ ins / 37 x 29 cm) NLG 1,153. BRUSSELS, 22 Feb 1999, *Venice* (1921, oil on canvas, 30 x 22 ins / 75 x 55 cm) BEF 210,000. BRUSSELS, 28 Sept 1999, *Seascape* (1890, oil on canvas, 39 x 60 ins / 100 x 152 cm) BEF 120,000. BRUSSELS, 29 Feb 2000, *Doge's Palace, Venice* (1933, oil on canvas, 22 x 30 ins / 55 x 76 cm) BEF 150,000. BRUSSELS, 13 Dec 2000, *River Landscape* (1902, oil on canvas, 28 x 39 ins / 70 x 100 cm) BEF 130,000. BRUSSELS, 19 March 2001, *Lagoon in Venice* (1933, oil on canvas, 22 x 30 ins / 55 x 75 cm) BEF 210,000. BRUSSELS, 17 Sept 2001, *Grand Canal in Venice* (1922, oil on canvas, 19 x 28 ins / 47 x 70 cm) BEF 120,000. BRUSSELS, 19 March 2002, *Lagoon in Venice* (1932, oil on canvas, 20 x 24 ins / 50 x 60 cm) EUR 3,800. BRUSSELS, 19 March 2002, *Bridge in Venice, by the Church of S Giovanni e Paolo* (1925, oil on canvas, 22 x 30 ins / 55 x 75 cm) EUR 4,600. ANTWERP, 21 Oct 2003, *Venice* (1928, oil on canvas, 30 x 22 ins / 75 x 55 cm) EUR 2,400. VIENNA, 19 Dec 2003, *Doge's Palace in Venice* (1933, oil on canvas, 22 x 30 ins / 55 x 75 cm) EUR 3,000. ANTWERP, 27 April 2004, *Bridge in Venice* (1924, oil on canvas, 22 x 30 ins / 55 x 75 cm) EUR 2,400. BRUSSELS, 6 Dec 2004, *Landscapes* (1931, double-sided, 18 x 24 ins / 46 x 60 cm) EUR 1,600.

JAMAR, Louis Alexis

French, 19th century.
Painter.

Louis Jamar exhibited paintings with a variety of subjects at the Paris Salon, from 1842 to 1850.

JAMAR, Pauline

Belgian, 19th - 20th century.
Born 1850 or 1859, in Liège; died 1911.
Painter. Landscapes, still-lifes, flowers.

MUSEUMS AND GALLERIES:
LIÈGE.
AUCTION RECORDS:
LONDON, 21 Nov 1997, *Hollyhocks in a Basket* (oil on canvas, 51¾ x 35½ ins / 131.5 x 90.2 cm) GBP 4,600.

JAMART, Louis François

French, 17th century.
Born c. 1644; died 12 January 1694, in Laon.
Painter.

Jamart executed paintings for the church of St-Jean in Laon which have not survived. He also painted coats-of-arms for that city.

JAMAS, Abel or Albert

French, 19th century.
Born 23 June 1862, in Cramant (Meuse).
Engraver (burin).

Abel or Albert Jamas studied under Lamatte and Cormon and featured at the Salon of the Société des Artistes Français. He was awarded an honourable mention in 1897, a third class medal in 1898, a second class medal in 1908 and a first class medal in 1910. He was an Officer of the Légion d'Honneur. His works are exhibited in various museums.

JAMBELLE, Dimanche
French, 17th century.
Died before 1649.
Active in Paris.
Painter.

JAMBERS, Theodorus or Thierry
Belgian, 19th century.
Born 1804, in Brussels; died after 1842.
Painter. Historical subjects, genre scenes.

The Flight of Henrietta Maria, Wife of Charles I is known as one of the best works of Theodorus Jambers.

MUSEUMS AND GALLERIES:
COURTRAI: *The Smokers*.

AUCTION RECORDS:
AMSTERDAM, 11 May 1982, *Grace* (1840, oil on canvas, 20 x 23 1/2in/50.7 x 60cm) NLG 6,800.

JAMBON, Marcel
French, 19th century.
Born 19 October 1848, in Barbézieux (Charente); died 1 October 1908, in Paris.
Painter, decorative designer.

Marcel Jambon was, from 1884, a stage designer for the Comédie Française, and the Odéon, Opéra-Comique and Opéra theatres. He also did paintings for the French State.

JAMBOR, Louis
American, 20th century.
Born 1884, in Hungary; died 1955.
Painter, illustrator. Genre scenes, figures, still-lifes, flowers.

AUCTION RECORDS:
LOS ANGELES, 9 June 1988, *The Picnic* (oil on canvas, 55 x 43 1/2 ins / 140 x 110.5 cm) USD 20,900. NEW YORK, 28 Sept 1995, *Still-life with Begonia* (oil on canvas, 30 1/2 x 36 1/2 ins / 77.2 x 92.4 cm) USD 3,220. SAUGERTIES, 13 March 1999, *Woman in the Field* (oil on canvas, 30 x 25 ins / 76 x 64 cm) USD 6,500. LONDON, 17 June 1999, *Pink Parasol* (oil on canvas, 31 x 24 ins / 79 x 61 cm) GBP 1,100. LONDON, 23 Nov 2000, *Ladies Enjoying a Picnic* (oil on canvas, 38 x 33 ins / 96 x 85 cm) GBP 1,500. SAN FRANCISCO, 9 June 2002, *Picking Fruit in the Afternoon* (oil on canvas, 37 x 31 ins / 95 x 79 cm) USD 1,800. BUDAPEST, 6 Dec 2002, *Afternoon Tea in the Garden* (oil on canvas, 39 x 29 ins / 98 x 74 cm) HUF 700,000. OAKLAND, 18 Oct 2003, *Travellers by Moonlight* (oil on canvas) USD 15,000. OAKLAND, 18 Oct 2003, *Remembrance* (oil on canvas) USD 16,000.

JAMBU, Marie-Thérèse
French, 20th century.
Born 1923, in Rennes.
Painter, watercolourist. Nudes, portraits, landscapes, seascapes, still-lifes.

Marie-Thérèse Jambu studied at the art college in Nantes, and then at free schools in Paris, attending the Post-Fauvist studios of Freisz and MacAvoy. After some 10 years she was more strongly influenced by André Lhote and Gromaire. Her paintings are strong and firmly constructed, and treat a wide range of subjects, including most notably the landscapes and seascapes of Normandy. She exhibited in Paris at the Salon d'Automne and Salon des Indépendants, and in collective exhibitions in Honfleur and Rouen. In 1948 she began to have solo shows in Nantes, Rouen, Le Havre and elsewhere, including Paris in 1950.

JAMBURINI, J.M.
Spanish, 20th century.
Active in Paseo de Graci.
Painter.

Works by J.M. Jamburini were included in the 1910 Exposition de Bruxelles.

JAME, Alphonse
French, 19th century.
Born in Lyons.
Painter.

Alphonse Jame studied at the École des Beaux-Arts in Lyons and exhibited portraits and miniatures in Paris in 1839. He went on to exhibit *Hammock* (1843), *She-wolf* (1846), *Flowers and Fruit* and *Bowl of Strawberries* (1880).

JAMES (Miss)
British, 18th century.
Born 1759, in London.
Painter. Flowers.

Miss James exhibited a painting of flowers at the Society of Artists in 1773 when she was just 14 years old.

JAMES
British, 18th century.
Painter. Landscapes.

James was active in St Petersburg. He exhibited at the Free Society in London between 1773 and 1783.

JAMES, Alexander R.
American, 20th century.
Born 1890, in Cambridge (Massachusetts); died 1946.
Painter. Portraits.

Alexander James studied at the Boston Museum of Fine Arts School. He was active in Dublin, New Jersey.

MUSEUMS AND GALLERIES:
BOSTON (MFA): *Portrait of a Girl*.

AUCTION RECORDS:
NEW YORK, 21 May 1991, *Portrait of a Man* (oil on panel, 11 x 7 1/4 ins / 28 x 18.4 cm) USD 880.

JAMES, Alice (Miss)
British, 19th century.
Active in Bath.
Miniaturist.

Miss Alice James exhibited frequently at the Royal Academy after 1887.

JAMES, Alice
Maiden name: Archer Sewall
American, 19th - 20th century.
Born 23 August 1870, in Glendale (Ohio); died 1955, in Ohio.
Painter.

Alice James studied at the Glasgow School of Art, then with Howard Helmick in Washington. She won the second Corcoran Prize in Washington in 1902. She was active in Urbana.

JAMES, David
British, 19th - 20th century.
Died 1913.
Painter. Seascapes.

David James lived in London, where he was active from 1881 to 1898. His seascapes frequently depict stormy scenes on the high seas or waves crashing against rocky outcrops. His favourite subject was the sea in all its power and fury, and his pictures only occasionally feature boats. He exhibited at the Royal Academy from 1881.

AUCTION RECORDS:
NEW YORK, 19 Jan 1905, *The Ocean*, USD 205. LONDON, 7 Dec 1907, *The Raging Sea* (1900) GBP 18. LONDON, 5 March 1910, *Leaving Yarmouth* (1880) GBP 9. LONDON, 5 Oct 1945, *Breakers on the High Seas*, GBP 57. LONDON, 27 June 1947, *Cornish Breakers*, GBP 105. LONDON, 20 Nov 1973, *Waves*, GBP 1,500. LONDON, 16 Nov 1976, *Incoming Tide, Devon* (1891, oil on canvas, 24 1/2 x 49 1/4 ins / 62 x 125 cm) GBP 2,200. LONDON, 6 Dec 1977, *Seascape* (1892, oil on canvas, 25 x 50 1/4 ins / 63.5

x 127.5 cm) GBP 1,000. LONDON, 20 March 1979, *A Sunlit Sea* (1897, oil on canvas, 24 x 49½ ins / 61 x 126 cm) GBP 6,500. NEW YORK, 29 May 1981, *The Waves* (oil on canvas, 30¼ x 50 ins / 76.8 x 127 cm) USD 5,500. LONDON, 19 Oct 1983, *Rising Tide* (1892, oil on canvas, 30 x 50 ins / 76 x 127 cm) GBP 2,200. LONDON, 22 Feb 1985, *Cornish Breakers* (1889, oil on canvas, 24 x 49¼ ins / 61 x 125 cm) GBP 2,200. LONDON, 3 June 1987, *Time and Tide* (1898, oil on canvas, 25 x 50 ins / 63.5 x 127 cm) GBP 6,800. NEW YORK, 25 May 1988, *A Rocky Coastline* (1884, oil on canvas, 25¼ x 42¼ ins / 64.1 x 107.4 cm) USD 3,520. LONDON, 23 Sept 1988, *Cornish Breakers* (1892, oil on canvas, 19¼ x 28 ins / 49 x 71 cm) GBP 1,980. LONDON, 2 June 1989, *Low tide at Pimm Bay, Cornwall* (oil on canvas, 24¾ x 50¼ ins / 63 x 127.5 cm) GBP 3,960. LONDON, 21 March 1990, *Boats Returning on the Incoming Tide, Scilly Isles* (1892, oil on canvas, 20¾ x 30¾ ins / 53 x 78 cm) GBP 2,200. LONDON, 15 June 1990, *Atlantic Rollers* (1895, oil on canvas, 25 x 50 ins / 63.5 x 127 cm) GBP 15,400. LONDON, 22 May 1991, *The Penzance Fishing Fleet on the High Seas* (1889, oil on canvas, 25 x 50 ins / 63.5 x 127 cm) GBP 3,300. LONDON, 14 June 1991, *Breakers* (1893, oil on canvas, 25 x 50 ins / 63.5 x 127 cm) GBP 6,050. NEW YORK, 17 Oct 1991, *In the Hollow of the Waves* (1894, oil on canvas, 25¼ x 50 ins / 64.1 x 127 cm) USD 24,200. YORK, 12 Nov 1991, *Breakers* (oil on canvas, 25 x 30 ins / 63.5 x 76 cm) GBP 2,860. NEW YORK, 28 May 1992, *Manorbier Bay, South Wales* (1888, oil on canvas, 25 x 50 ins / 63.5 x 127 cm) USD 17,600. LONDON, 3 June 1992, *Falmouth* (1884, oil on canvas, 25¼ x 50 ins / 64 x 127 cm) GBP 2,200. LONDON, 3 Feb 1993, *Cornish Coast* (oil on canvas, 25¼ x 50 ins / 64 x 127 cm) GBP 2,300. LONDON, 11 May 1994, *Portsmouth Harbour* (1886, oil on canvas, 30 x 50 ins / 76 x 127 cm) GBP 12,650. LONDON, 6 Nov 1995, *Atlantic Breakers* (1895, oil on canvas, 25¼ x 50 ins / 64 x 127 cm) GBP 24,150. LONDON, 27 March 1996, *Morning Tide* (1898, oil on canvas, 24¾ x 49¾ ins / 63 x 126.5 cm) GBP 27,600. LONDON, 14 March 1997, *Wave* (1897, oil on canvas, 25 x 50 ins / 63.5 x 127.3 cm) GBP 34,500. LONDON, 5 Nov 1997, *Waves off a Rocky Coastline, Cornwall* (1889, oil on canvas, 25 x 50 ins / 63.5 x 127 cm) GBP 9,200. LONDON, 7 Nov 1997, *Time and Tide* (1896, oil on canvas, 25 x 49¾ ins / 63.5 x 126.4 cm) GBP 38,900. EDINBURGH, 26 Nov 1997, *The Undertow* (1898, oil on canvas, 25 x 50 ins / 63.5 x 127 cm) GBP 34,500.

JAMES, E. d'O. (Miss)
British, 19th century.
Painter, watercolourist. Landscapes.

Miss E. d'O James showed her work at the Society of Female Artists.

MUSEUMS AND GALLERIES:
DUBLIN: *Windsor Forest* (1869).

JAMES, Edith
French, 20th century.
Born 29 June 1928, in Mont-St-Aignan.
Painter, engraver, watercolourist, mosaicist.
Landscapes, landscapes with figures. Stage sets.

Edith James trained in Paris at the École Nationale Supérieure des Beaux-Arts, and then travelled to study in Spain, the Netherlands and Morocco. Working within the Post-Impressionist tradition, she liked to create extensive landscapes with wide views. In 1962, she was awarded the Antal prize. She showed her work in many group exhibitions., particularly at the Musée Galliera in Paris in 1963, 1965 and 1967, when the salons were showing work by laureates of the City of Paris.

She also exhibited regularly at the main Paris salons: Salon de Jeune Peinture 1955-1959; Salon d'Automne from 1957; Salon des Terres Latines, 1964-1966; Salon Comparaisons from 1984; the Salon de la Société Nationale des Beaux-Arts, to which she belonged from 1956; Salon des Indépendants, to which she belonged from 1957 to 1960, and the Salon des Artistes Français, to which she also belonged from 1981. Her solo shows in Paris, across France and abroad included: 1960-1968, at the Galerie Dauphine in Paris; 1971-1982, Morocco; 1983, the Galerie Colette Bletel, Paris; 1989, the Orangery in the Luxembourg Palace, Paris, and 1995, at the Goldsmiths' Gallery in Paris.

BIBLIOGRAPHY:
Vignoht, Guy, *La Jeune Peinture, 1941-1961*, Terre des peintres, Paris, 1985.

MUSEUMS AND GALLERIES:
PARIS (MAMVP).

JAMES, Edith Augusta
British, 19th century.
Born 24 January 1857, in Eton; died 31 December 1898, in Tunbridge Wells.
Painter, watercolourist, pastellist. Portraits, church interiors, flowers.

Edith Augusta James trained in Paris with Chaplin and Luminais. She frequently exhibited in London and Paris, from 1884 to 1896, especially at the Salon des Femmes Peintres (exhibition of women painters).

She is known in particular for her portraits and paintings of flowers; however, she dedicated the last three years of her life to painting the interior of St Paul's cathedral in London.

MUSEUMS AND GALLERIES:
LONDON (Victoria and Albert Mus.): *Interior of St Paul's Cathedral, London* (watercolour).

AUCTION RECORDS:
LONDON, 7 April 1993, *Children in Church* (1890, pastel, 31 x 24¾ ins / 79 x 63 cm) GBP 3,220.

JAMES, Francis
British, 19th century.
Active in Florence.
Painter. Landscapes.

Francis James exhibited in London from 1832 until 1845, especially at the Royal Academy, the British Institution and at Suffolk Street.

JAMES, Francis Edward
British, 19th century.
Born 1849, in Willington; died 1920, in Great Torrington (Devon).
Painter, watercolourist. Landscapes.

Francis Edward James was a member of the Society of British Artists and an associate of the Royal Society of Painters in Watercolours. As of 1884, he was a frequent exhibitor at Suffolk Street.

AUCTION RECORDS:
LONDON, 24 July 1911, *Port of Harwich* (watercolour) GBP 1.

JAMES, Frederick
American, 19th century.
Born 1845; died August 1907, in Peru, Canada.
Painter.

Frederick James first studied art in Philadelphia, and then went to work in Paris with Gérôme. When he returned to America he settled in New York where he lived for many years. He exhibited frequently at the National Academy of Design in New York.

AUCTION RECORDS:
NEW YORK, 1 and 2 March 1906, *Franklin and General Braddock*, USD 450. NEW YORK, 21 June 1979, *Presentation* (oil on mounted canvas on board, 13 x 16 ins / 33 x 40.5 cm) USD 3,000.

JAMES, G. (Mrs)
American, 19th century.
Active in Canterbury (Connecticut).
Miniaturist.

G. James exhibited in Suffolk Street in London from 1826 to 1828.

JAMES, George
British, 18th century.
Born in London; died probably in 1795, in Nice according to Brian's Dictionary, in Boulogne-sur-Mer according to some sources.
Painter. History painting, portraits.

George James studied in Rome before settling in Bath and then in London. He joined the Society of Artists, where he exhibited history paintings from 1762 and portraits from 1768. In 1770 he was made an Associate of the Royal Academy, at whose exhibitions he showed only portraits. He returned to Bath in 1780, by which time his grandfather's inheritance and an advantageous marriage assured him a high position in society. He moved to Boulogne-sur-Mer in France, where he was imprisoned during the Revolution, and it is to this imprisonment that his death is attributed. James was a meticulous painter, though one of somewhat mediocre talent.

AUCTION RECORDS:
LONDON, 18 March 1970, *Portraits of the Three Misses Walpole,* GBP 4,500. PARIS, 6 April 1973, *First Baptist Buses* (gouache) FRF 7,000. LONDON, 19 Nov 1976, *Portrait of Emily and Georgiana Mason* (oil on canvas, 35 1/2 x 35 1/2 ins / 90 x 90 cm) GBP 3,000. LONDON, 15 Nov 1991, *Portrait of a Young Girl Wearing a Pink Dress and a Lace Bonnet, Playing the Lute* (oil on canvas, 30 x 24 3/4 ins / 76.2 x 62.8 cm) GBP 3,520. LONDON, 9 July 2002, *Portrait of Emily and Georgina Mason* (oil on canvas, 50 x 40 ins / 127 x 102 cm) GBP 4,500. GODALMING, 20 Oct 2004, *Portrait of a Lady, Full-length, Seated, Holding a Parasol* (oil on canvas, 76 x 59 ins / 193 x 151 cm) GBP 15,000. GODALMING, 20 Oct 2004, *Portrait of a Lady, Full-length, Italian Costume, Basket of Fruit and Dog at her Side* (oil on canvas, 76 x 59 ins / 193 x 151 cm) GBP 16,000.

JAMES, Harold Francis
British, 20th century.
Born 9 November 1881, in Drayton.
Active in the USA.
Painter.

Harold James trained under Jean-Paul Laurens in Paris. He was a member of the Chicago and Prairie Watercolours Clubs. He exhibited at Southern States Art League and taught at Illinois State Normal School and Kansas State Technical College.

JAMES, J.
British, 18th century.
Active during the second half of the 18th century.
Engraver.

J. James is mentioned as having produced two mezzotints in the style of R.P. Pine: *Portrait of Mrs Pine as Calliope* and the portrait of a *Lady J.D.*

JAMES, J. T.
British.
Draughtsman. Figures, landscapes.

J.T. James is listed in *Art Prices Current.*

AUCTION RECORDS:
LONDON, 18 July 1910, *Landscape* (charcoal); *Figures in a Vault; Two Children in a Landscape* (drawing, after Gainsborough) GBP 4.

JAMES, John
British, 20th - 21st century.
Born 1947.
Painter. Urban landscapes, landscapes.

In 1968, John James studied at the Ravensbourne School of Art. He has taken part in group exhibitions, notably in 1987 at the Maclean Gallery, London. During the 1970s he painted panoramic landscapes of Scotland and Wales. He later moved to London and painted mainly views of the Thames.

JAMES, John Wells
American, 19th - 20th century.
Born 22 February 1873, in Brooklyn (New York City); died 1951, in France.
Painter.

John Wells James was a pupil of James Knox. He was a member of the Salmagundi Club and the American Artists' Federation.

JAMES, Louis Robert
Australian, 20th century.
Born 1920, in Adelaide; died 1996.
Painter. Figures, urban landscapes.

Louis James served in the Australian forces during World War II, and then became interested in painting. Having exhibited for the first time in Adelaide, he moved to London in 1950 where he worked until the early 1960s. He returned to Australia and exhibited regularly throughout the 1970s.

AUCTION RECORDS:
PARIS, 26 Oct 1988, *G. Garouste Meeting Dorian Gray* (1985, photograph in colour heightened with paint, 49 1/4 x 49 1/4 ins / 125 x 125 cm) FRF 10,500. SYDNEY, 16 Oct 1989, *Mother and Child* (oil on card, 16 1/4 x 18 ins / 41 x 46 cm) AUD 2,300. LONDON, 30 Nov 1989, *Still-life* (1951, oil on card, 7 x 9 3/4 ins / 17.5 x 25 cm) GBP 825. SYDNEY, 2 July 1990, *Urban Roofscape* (oil on canvas, 11 3/4 x 16 1/4 ins / 30 x 41 cm) AUD 2,000. PARIS, 5 Oct 1996, *Townscape* (1960, oil on canvas, 24 3/4 x 30 ins / 63 x 76.5 cm) FRF 6,000. MELBOURNE, 27 April 1999, *Yellow Lndscape* (oil on canvas, 13 x 30 ins / 34 x 75 cm) AUD 3,500. MELBOURNE, 28 June 2000, *Red Night* (oil on canvas, 39 x 50 ins / 100 x 126 cm) AUD 12,000. MELBOURNE, 28 June 2000, *Don't Walk* (oil on board, 71 x 50 ins / 181 x 126 cm) AUD 32,000. PADDINGTON, 27 Aug 2001, *Spy Hole No.9* (oil on composition board, 37 x 38 ins / 93 x 97 cm) AUD 4,000. PADDINGTON, 27 Aug 2001, *Passers-by* (oil on composition board, 40 x 40 ins / 101 x 101 cm) AUD 6,000. MELBOURNE, 30 April 2002, *Midsummer Night* (oil on canvas, 30 x 40 ins / 76 x 101 cm) AUD 5,250. MELBOURNE, 27 Aug 2002, *Red Night* (oil on canvas, 39 x 50 ins / 100 x 126 cm) AUD 10,000. MELBOURNE, 6 May 2003, *Drift 12* (acrylic and oil on canvas, triptych, 96 x 96 ins / 243 x 243 cm) AUD 6,000. SYDNEY, 10 June 2003, *Yellow Interior* (oil on masonite on board, 40 x 40 ins / 101 x 101 cm) AUD 3,000. MELBOURNE, 10 March 2004, *Landscape, Village* (oil on canvas, 30 x 45 ins / 76 x 114 cm) AUD 5,500. MELBOURNE, 3 May 2004, *Terra Nova, 2* (oil on canvas, 40 x 50 ins / 101 x 127 cm) AUD 6,500.

JAMES, M. E. (Miss)
British, 18th - 19th century.
Painter.

M.E. James worked in London where she exhibited at the Royal Academy in 1804.

JAMES, Merlin
British, 20th - 21st century.
Born 1960, in Cardiff.
Active in London.
Painter.

From 1978 to 1979, Merlin James studied at the Cardiff College of Art, from 1979 to 1982 at the Central School of Art in London, and from 1983 to 1986 at the Royal College of Art in London. In 1995 he spent a year as art critic in residence at Kingston University. James is an editor of *The Burlington Magazine*.

The subjects of his paintings appear to be less important than the simplified and sometimes spare geometric form he gives them. Whether painting a sheep or signs of urban landscapes and architectural views, James resists categorisation. He appears to take pleasure in making his subjects emerge through colour and matter. He aspires to the middle ground between the Traditional and the Post-Modern and it is not difficult to see why he should have taken Jean Hélion as a role model.

James has exhibited regularly in the UK at the following: the Albemarle Gallery in London (1991); the National Museum of Wales (1995); Kettle's Yard in Cambridge (1996); the Edinburgh College of Art (1997); and the Hoffmann Gallery in London (2001).

BIBLIOGRAPHY:

Merlin James, exhibition catalogue, Albemarle Gallery, London, 1990. *British Art in the 90s: The Saatchi Decade*, Booth-Clibborn Editions, London, 1999. Bonacossa, Ilaria, *Merlin James. Pictures*, Lubrina Editore, Bergamo, 2002.

JAMES, René

French, 20th century.
Born 1935, in Clichy.
Painter. Landscapes, seascapes.

A self-taught artist, René James began painting when he was 45. He painted landscapes in Provence and Normandy, and views of Paris, at first in a Fauvist manner and later in a style of restrained Pointillism. He showed work regularly at collective exhibitions in the Paris salons, beginning in 1981 at the Salon des Indépendants, to which he belonged, and also at the Salon d'Automne and the Salon des Artistes Français.

JAMES, Richard S.

British, 19th century.
Active in London.
Painter. Genre scenes.

Richard S. James exhibited his work very frequently at the Royal Academy and the British Institution.

AUCTION RECORDS:

LONDON, 17 June 1910, *Palmist; Sword Throwers*, GBP 2. LONDON, 26 Oct 1979, *My Lord's Luggage* (oil on canvas, 15 1/4 x 19 1/2 ins / 39 x 49.5 cm) GBP 1,500.

JAMES, S. Berthe

Maiden name: Rous
French, 19th century.
Active in Paris.
Engraver.

S. Berthe James was a member of the Société des Artistes Français from 1892 and featured at its Salon.

JAMES, W.

British, 18th century.
Active towards the middle of the 18th century.
Engraver (copper).

W. James signed a mezzotint plaque entitled *Portrait of Charles Spencer, third Duke of Malborough*, after J.-B. Van Loo.

JAMES, Walter Charles

British, 19th century.
Born in London.
Painter, engraver (etching). Landscapes.

Sir Walter Charles James exhibited at the Royal Academy and the Royal Institution from 1849 to 1853.

JAMES, Walter John (Baron Northbourne)

British, 19th - 20th century.
Born 2 September 1869, in London; died 22 December 1932.
Painter, watercolourist, etcher. Landscapes.

Walter John James was the son of Walter Henry James, 2nd Baron Northbourne. He married Laura Gwenllian Rice in 1894, and lived in Kent and Otterburn in Northumberland. Lord Walter John James was a member of the Royal Society of British Artists. He exhibited at the Dowdeswell Galleries, London in 1910 and 1913, and at the Fine Art Society in London in 1920.

BIBLIOGRAPHY:

Catalogue of an Exhibition of Landscapes by the Hon. Walter J. James, R.E., exhibition catalogue, Dowdeswell Galleries, London, 1913. *Catalogue of Landscape paintings by the Hon. Walter J. James*, exhibition catalogue, Fine Art Society, London, 1920. James, Walter J./Clausen, George, et al., *Charlton Lectures on Art*, Clarendon Press, Oxford, 1925.

MUSEUMS AND GALLERIES:

NEWCASTLE UPON TYNE (Laing Art Gallery): *Cheviots - Clouds Passing Away* (1924, gouache, pencil and watercolour on board); *Evening* (1913, oil and pastel) - SOUTHAMPTON (Southampton City Art Gallery): *Valley of the Rede* (oil on Canvas).

JAMES, William

British, 18th century.
Born 1754; died 1771, in London.
Active in London.
Painter. Urban landscapes.

William James exhibited his work in London from 1761 to 1771 at the Society of Artists and at the Royal Academy. In 1766, as a member of the Society of Artists, he was charged with selling paintings. When Canaletto went to London, William James became his pupil and assistant.

Clearly, James sought to imitate Canaletto; however, the results were literal rather than stylistic as can be seen in his views in the gallery in Hampton Court.

AUCTION RECORDS:

LONDON, 25 June 1931, *Westminster Cathedral*, GBP 82. LONDON, 16 Dec 1942, *Garden at Somerset House*, GBP 140. LONDON, 22 April 1959, *View of the Square Looking towards the Grand Canal*, GBP 900. NEW YORK, 21 April 1961, *Westminster Bridge*, USD 800. LONDON, 10 July 1963, *View of the Grand Canal lin Venice*, GBP 2,200. LONDON, 24 March 1965, *Venice, the entrance to the Grand Canal*, GBP 3,500. LONDON, 26 June 1968, *Riva degli Schiavoni in Venice*, GBP 5,500. LONDON, 17 June 1970, *Westminster Bridge over the Thames*, GBP 5,400. LONDON, 10 Dec 1971, *Grand Canal in Venice*, Gns 5,000. LONDON, 13 Dec 1972, *View of Venice*, GBP 7,200. LONDON, 4 April 1973, *View of Venice*, GBP 19,000. LONDON, 30 May 1974, *Thames at London*, Gns 7,000. LONDON, 26 March 1976, *Grand Canal, Venice* (oil on canvas, 29 x 49 ins / 73.5 x 124.5 cm) GBP 3,200. LONDON, 18 March 1977, *Grand Canal, Venice* (oil on canvas, 31 x 49 ins / 79 x 124.5 cm) GBP 6,000. LONDON, 23 March 1979, *View of Venice* (oil on canvas, 31 x 51 ins / 79 x 129.5 cm) GBP 9,000. LONDON, 8 April 1981, *Venice, View of the Grand Canal* (oil on canvas, 27 1/2 x 46 ins / 70 x 116 cm) GBP 8,000. NEW YORK, 20 Jan 1983, *Savoy Palace, Savoy Church and Somerset House on the Thames; Lambeth Palace, Westminster Hall and Westminster Bridge on the Thames* (oil on canvas, a pair, 29 1/2 x 49 1/4 ins / 75 x 125 cm) USD 82,500. LONDON, 19 July 1985, *Port of London* (oil on canvas, 29 1/4 x 49 1/4 ins / 74.3 x 125 cm) GBP 32,000. LONDON, 24 April 1987, *Thames at York Steps with boats in the foreground and Westminster Abbey in the background* (oil on canvas, 30 ins / 76 cm, x 50 ins/127 cm) GBP 52,000. NEW YORK, 11 Jan 1989, *Ducal Procession entering the Church of Santa Maria della Salute from the Grand Canal in Venice* (oil on canvas, 30 x 50 ins / 76.2 x 127 cm) USD 93,500. NEW YORK, 2 June 1989, *The Bucintoro returning to the Molo on Ascension Day* (oil on canvas, 37 x 60 ins / 94 x 152.5 cm) USD 110,000. LONDON, 14 July 1989, *Grand Canal in Venice from the Church of Santa Croce* (oil on canvas, 41 x 59 ins / 104 x 150 cm) GBP 52,800. LONDON, 15 Nov 1989, *View of Thames with St Paul's Cathedral in the background* (oil on canvas, 29 1/4 x 49 1/2 ins / 74 x 126 cm) GBP 57,200. NEW YORK, 10 Jan 1990, *View of Riva degli Schiavoni in Venice* (oil on canvas, 37 1/4 x 60 ins / 94.6 x 152.4 cm) USD 110,000. LONDON, 12 July 1990, *Regatta on the Grand Canal in Venice* (oil on canvas, 29 1/2 x 50 ins / 75 x 127 cm) GBP 35,200. LONDON, 14 Nov 1990, *Doge going to the Church of Santa Maria della*

Salute along the Grand Canal in Venice (oil on canvas, 35 3/4 x 60 ins / 91 x 152.5 cm) GBP 63,800. LONDON, 15 Nov 1991, *The Bacino Orseolo in Venice* (oil on canvas, 29 3/4 x 50 ins / 75.6 x 127 cm) GBP 26,400. PARIS, 15 Dec 1991, *Grand Canal with the Church of Santa Maria della Salute* (oil on canvas, 31 1/2 x 52 ins / 80 x 132 cm) FRF 240,000. LONDON, 8 April 1992, *View of Westminster from Adelphi Terrace showing the Royal Barge and other boats* (oil on canvas, 28 1/2 x 48 1/2 ins / 72.5 x 123 cm) GBP 22,000. NEW YORK, 14 Oct 1992, *Grand Canal in Venice with the church of Santa Maria della Salute and the Dogana seen from Santa Maria Zobenigo* (oil on canvas, 22 3/4 x 38 ins / 57.8 x 96.5 cm) USD 38,500. NEW YORK, 20 May 1993, *Riva degli Schiavoni in Venice* (oil on canvas, 29 x 49 ins / 73.7 x 124.5 cm) USD 79,500. LONDON, 13 July 1994, *Grand Canal and Doge's Palace in Venice* (oil on canvas, 31 3/4 x 51 3/4 ins / 80.5 x 131.5 cm) GBP 37,800. NEW YORK, 11 Jan 1995, *Grand Canal in Venice with S Geremia, Palazzo Labia and entrance to the Cannaregio Canal* (oil on canvas, 27 x 41 ins / 68.5 x 104 cm) USD 32,200. LONDON, 3 April 1996, *St Paul's Cathedral seen from the terrace of Somerset House* (oil on canvas, 29 1/4 x 49 ins / 74 x 124.5 cm) GBP 34,500. NEW YORK, 15 May 1996, *Molo in Venice looking towards the Column of S Teodoro* (oil on canvas, 30 x 50 1/2 ins / 76.2 x 128.3 cm) USD 59,700. LONDON, 12 Nov 1997, *Doge's Palace on the left at the entrance of the Grand Canal, Venice* (oil on canvas, 39 1/4 x 58 1/4 ins / 100 x 148 cm) GBP 33,350. PARIS, 16 Dec 1997, *View of Grand Canal, Venice* (canvas, 21 1/4 x 36 1/2 ins / 54 x 93 cm) FFR 115,000. LONDON, 14 July 1999, *Entrance to Grand Canal, Venice, with Dogana and Santa Maria della Salute* (oil on canvas, 28 x 48 ins / 71 x 121 cm) GBP 45,000. NEW YORK, 27 Jan 2000, *Riva degli Schiavoni Looking Towards the Entry of the Grand Canal* (oil on canvas, 30 x 50 ins / 76 x 128 cm) USD 75,000. LONDON, 15 June 2000, *View of Santa Maria della Salute with Doge's Palace Beyond* (oil on canvas, 30 x 49 ins / 75 x 125 cm) GBP 44,000. LONDON, 4 July 2001, *View on the Grand Canal, Venice with Church of S Geremia* (oil on canvas, 29 x 49 ins / 73 x 124 cm) GBP 56,000. NEW YORK, 5 June 2002, *View of the Riva degli Schiavoni, Venice* (oil on canvas, 29 x 46 ins / 74 x 117 cm) USD 190,000. LONDON, 9 July 2002, *Riva degli Schiavoni, Looking South-West Towards the Entry to the Grand Canal* (oil on canvas, 30 x 50 ins / 76 x 126 cm) GBP 55,000. LONDON, 12 June 2003, *Venice, the Entrance to the Grand Canal Looking East* (oil on canvas, 39 x 65 ins / 98 x 165 cm) GBP 82,000. LONDON, 10 Dec 2003, *Thames at Westminster with Old Westminster Bridge and the Shot Tower, Somerset House, London* (oil on canvas, 30 x 50 ins / 76 x 127 cm) GBP 56,000. VENICE, 4 July 2004, *Grand Canal, Venice* (oil on canvas, 15 x 25 ins / 38 x 63 cm) EUR 100,000. LONDON, 25 Nov 2004, *Procession of the Doge, Venice* (oil on canvas, 29 x 50 ins / 74 x 126 cm) GBP 90,000.

JAMES, William

American, 20th century.

Born 17 June 1882, in Cambridge (Massachusetts); died 1961.

Painter. Portraits.

William James was a pupil of Frank Benson and Edmund Tarbell at the Boston Museum of Fine Arts School. He was a member of the Boston Artists' Guild. At the Academy of the Fine Arts in Philadelphia, he won a silver medal in 1915 and a gold medal in 1925.

AUCTION RECORDS:

NEW YORK, 23 March 1984, *Portrait of a Girl* (1919, oil on canvas, 26 1/4 x 21 ins / 66.5 x 53.5 cm) USD 1,500. NEW YORK, 4 June 1986, *The Grand Canal, Venice* (oil on canvas, 27 1/4 x 45 ins / 69 x 114 cm) USD 35,000.

JAMES, Willy, pseudonym of Willy Rochat

Swiss, 20th century.

Born 2 June 1920, in Echallens.

Painter, pastellist. Urban landscapes.

Willy James studied under the painter René Auberjonois and exhibited solo in Lausanne in 1944, showing landscapes from his native Vaud. He moved to Paris and started painted typical street scenes around places such as Montmartre and Notre-Dame. These scenes are often identical with those favoured by Maurice Utrillo, but James adopts a different approach to them, painting in a highly personal style - often in pastel - and achieving a sense of lightness and joie de vivre. His human figures are sketch-like silhouettes seen from a considerable distance: archetypes almost of crowd scenes.

AUCTION RECORDS:

ZURICH, 6 June 1980, *Winter Fun with Snowman* (oil on canvas, 19 3/4 x 25 1/2 ins / 50 x 65 cm) CHF 3,400. ZURICH, 27 May 1982, *Fairground Frolics* (oil on canvas, 21 1/4 x 26 ins / 54 x 66 cm) CHF 9,000. ZURICH, 14 May 1983, *Rue Balande, Paris* (pastel, 21 1/4 x 14 1/2 ins / 54 x 37 cm) CHF 2,900. ZURICH, 14 May 1983, *Springtime on Lake Geneva* (watercolour, 22 x 29 1/2 ins / 56 x 75 cm) CHF 2,200. ZURICH, 29 Oct 1983, *Breton Port in the Snow* (oil on canvas, 28 1/4 x 35 3/4 ins / 72 x 91 cm) CHF 2,800. LYONS, 3 Dec 1986, *Théâtre de l'Atelier* (pastel, 15 1/4 x 16 1/2 ins / 39 x 42 cm) FRF 10,000. LONDON, 21 Feb 1989, *Street with Demolished House* (pastel/paper, 19 3/4 x 25 1/2 ins / 50 x 65 cm) GBP 3,520. PARIS, 13 April 1989, *Rue de l'Abreuvoir* (pastel, 20 x 24 3/4 ins / 51 x 63 cm) FRF 28,000. PARIS, 6 June 1990, *Moulin de la Galette in the Snow* (pastel, 15 x 19 ins / 38 x 48.5 cm) FRF 9,000. LE TOUQUET, 11 Nov 1990, *Farm at Céligny* (1971, pastel, 13 x 16 1/4 ins / 33 x 41 cm) FRF 12,000. MADRID, 24 Jan 1991, *Place du Tertre, Paris* (pastel, 18 x 24 1/2 ins / 46 x 62 cm) ESP 392,000. PARIS, 4 March 1991, *Paris Street Scene* (pastel, 13 1/2 x 15 1/4 ins / 34 x 39 cm) FRF 4,500. PARIS, 6 Dec 1991, *Garden Flowers* (pastel, 15 3/4 x 12 1/2 ins / 40 x 32 cm) FRF 10,000. LONDON, 24 March 1992, *Fairground with Blue Trees* (oil on canvas, 20 3/4 x 32 ins / 53 x 81 cm) GBP 2,750. PARIS, 18 Nov 1992, *La Petite Place in the Snow* (oil on canvas, 21 1/4 x 25 1/2 ins / 54 x 65 cm) FRF 28,000. LONDON, 24-25 March 1993, *Fairground with Rose Trees* (oil on canvas, 25 1/4 x 31 1/2 ins / 64 x 80 cm) GBP 4,830. PARIS, 8 April 1993, *Canal in Autumn* (oil on canvas, 25 1/2 x 32 ins / 65 x 81 cm) FRF 18,000. NEW YORK, 2 Nov 1993, *River Seine at the Pont de la Concorde* (pastel/paper, 22 x 29 1/4 ins / 55 x 74 cm) USD 4,025. PARIS, 20 Nov 1994, *Paris Street in the Snow* (oil on canvas, 22 1/2 x 30 ins / 57 x 76 cm) FRF 16,000. LUCERNE, 26 Nov 1994, *Yachts* (1960, oil on canvas, 22 x 15 ins / 55 x 38 cm) CHF 2,900. PARIS, 26 March 1995, *Moulin de la Galette, Montmartre* (pastel, 19 3/4 x 24 ins / 50 x 61 cm) FRF 5,000. PARIS, 13 June 1996, *Montmartre: Hôtel de la Tourelle* (oil on canvas, 23 1/2 x 28 3/4 ins / 60 x 73 cm) FRF 24,000. PARIS, 13 Nov 1996, *Champs-Elysées* (oil on canvas, 36 1/4 x 28 3/4 ins / 92 x 73 cm) FRF 18,000. PARIS, 11 June 1997, *July 14 at Belleville* (oil on canvas, 25 1/2 x 43 1/4 ins / 65 x 110 cm) FRF 35,000. LONDON, 22 Oct 1997, *Porte de Brancion, Paris* (pastel/paper).

JAMESON, Gabrielle, later Mme Robert

French, 19th - 20th century.

Born 8 May 1864, in Tonneins (Lot-et-Garonne).

Engraver (etching).

Gabrielle Robert Jameson became a member of the Société des Artistes Français in 1906. She showed work at the society's salon, winning an honourable mention in 1902.

JAMESON, Middleton

British, 19th - 20th century.

Died 1918.

Painter. Genre scenes.

Middleton Jameson exhibited at the Salon des Artistes Français in Paris in 1888, winning a jury commendation.

Auction records:
Edinburgh, 27 March 1984, *Peasant Woman and Child in the Fields* (1883, oil on canvas, 28 x 20$3/4$ ins / 71 x 53 cm) GBP 1,200. Glasgow, 4 Feb 1987, *Young Woman beside a Pond* (1880, oil on canvas, 32 x 24 ins / 81 x 61 cm) GBP 3,800. New York, 16 Oct 1991, *A Meeting with her First Love* (1881, oil on canvas, 23$1/2$ x 32$1/4$ ins / 59.7 x 81.9 cm) USD 11,000. New York, 26 May 1993, *The Fsherman's Daughter* (1887, oil on canvas, 48 x 73$3/4$ ins / 121.9 x 187.3 cm) USD 18,400. London, 30 March 1994, *Gathering Reeds* (1881, oil on canvas, 32 x 23$1/2$ ins / 81 x 60 cm) GBP 5,750.

JAMESON, Rosa
British, 19th century.
Active in London.
Painter, watercolourist. Genre scenes.

Rosa Jameson exhibited her works, starting in 1886, in London at the Royal Academy, at Suffolk Street and at the New Water-Colour Society.

Auction records:
London, 23 Sept 1988, *Fight for a Scrap* (oil on canvas, 12 x 26 ins / 30.5 x 66 cm) GBP 2,970. London, 11 June 2002, *Narrow Escape* (oil on canvas, 15 x 21 ins / 37 x 54 cm) GBP 4,500. London, 17 Sept 2002, *Squirrels Eating Berries* (watercolour, 20 x 17 ins / 51 x 43 cm) GBP 1,100.

JAMESONE, Anna
Maiden name: Murphy
Irish, 19th century.
Born 1794, in Dublin; died 1860, in Ealing.
Draughtswoman, art critic.

Anna Jamesone was the daughter of miniaturist painter, Dennis Brownell Murphy. In 1823, she married a public attorney in Canada. Between 1834 and 1860, she published several works of art and criticism which she illustrated with her own drawings.

JAMESONE, George
British, 17th century.
Born c. 1587, in Aberdeen; died 1644, in Edinburgh.
Painter, miniaturist. Historical painting, portraits, landscapes.
Scottish School.

George Jamesone is one of the first important artists of the Scottish school. The son of an architect, in 1612 he was apprenticed for eight years to John Anderson, a painter and his maternal uncle, in Edinburgh; however, in 1616 he returned to Aberdeen. Between 1616 and 1620, tradition has it that he went to Antwerp as a student of Rubens' and became friends with Van Dyck. Indeed, Rubens was in Antwerp during this period and Van Dyck attended his academy from 1615 to 1620. In 1620, Jamesone painted *Portrait of Sir Paul Menzies, Provost of Aberdeen* in a style which corroborates the tradition.

In 1633, Charles I called the Scottish parliament in Edinburgh. The magistrates, aware of the king's artistic taste, borrowed portraits by Jamesone and placed them along the royal route. Impressed, the king paused to look at several of them and, in a mark of admiration for the artist, allowed himself to be painted standing. Shortly afterwards, Jamesone travelled to Italy with his principal patron, Sir Colin Campbell of Glenorchy. His fame as a portrait artist led him in 1630 to Edinburgh where he would finally establish himself in 1635. He would later be cited as a burgher of the city. About 1623 he is thought to have married Isabel Tosh: biographies mention a family portrait including his wife and son around that date. His will of 1641, however, only mentions a daughter, also an artist, and who embroidered biblical subjects for the church of St Nicholas in Aberdeen.

Jamesone's style bears the clear imprint of the 17th century Flemish school and earned him the nickname of the Scottish Van Dyck. Although he painted historical subjects, landscapes and miniatures, it was the portrait which he had to rely upon for his living. In his monograph of Jamesone, M. Bulloch catalogues 186 works, most of which are kept in private collections or housed in the College of Aberdeen. The majority are busts 'to the vest' as Jamesone designated them. The most illustrious Scots were painted by him.

Museums and Galleries:
Dublin: *Lady Alexander* - Edinburgh (Scottish National Portrait Gallery): *Campbells of Glenorchy Family Tree* (1635, oil on canvas); *Anne Erskine, Countess of Rothes, with her daughters* (oil on canvas).

Auction records:
London, 30 March 1908, *Portrait of Lord Cobham,* GBP 7. London, 25 and 26 May 1911, *Portrait of Charles I* (1633) GBP 147. London, 1 May 1925, *James I,* GBP 63. London, 23 April 1926, *Portrait of a Young Man,* GBP 92. London, 8 June 1928, *Sir William Drummond,* GBP 546. London, 1 March 1946, *Lady Dundas,* GBP 42. London, 22 June 1973, *Portrait of Lady Anne Erskine with her two children,* Gns 2,200. London, 19 Nov 1976, *Portrait of Sir George Hay, Earl of Kinnoul* (1625, oil on canvas, 43$1/2$ x 33$1/2$ ins / 110.5 x 85 cm) GBP 900. London, 5 May 1978, *Portrait of John Leslie, 6th Earl of Rothes* (1625, oil on canvas, 85 x 51 ins / 215.8 x 129.4 cm) GBP 1,000. Haddington, 21-22 May 1990, *Portrait of a Gentleman, presumed to be John Sinclair* (oil on canvas, 25 x 21 ins / 63.5 x 53.5 cm) GBP 660. London, 4 July 2001, *Portrait of Sir John Henderson of Fordel in a Black Tunic, a Galley Beyond* (oil on canvas, 24 x 22 ins / 62 x 55 cm) GBP 4,800.

JAMET. See **HANARD François**

JAMET, Alain
French, 20th century.
Painter.

Alain Jamet trained in Paris at the École des Beaux-Arts. He showed work at various Paris salons including the Salon d'Automne, Salon des Indépendants and Salon Comparaisons.

JAMET, Henri Pierre
French, 19th century.
Born 25 September 1858, in Gien (Loiret).
Painter. Genre scenes.

Henri Jamet studied under Gérome, Albert Maignan and Harpignies. He became a member of the Société des Artistes Français in 1890 and featured at its Salon, winning an honourable mention in 1897, a bronze medal in 1900 (Exposition Universelle) and a third class medal in 1906.

Museums and Galleries:
Bourges: *Berry Interior; Village Slope* (watercolour) - Châteauroux: *Two Nannies; Noir-Goû, Near to Gargilesse; Peasant; Old Wine Growers* - Moscow (Rumiantsev Mus.): several landscapes - Orléans: *Change of Life.*

Auction records:
London, 17 Feb 1939, *Ladies and Gentlemen,* GBP 52. Copenhagen, 3 Sept 2001, *Interior Scene with Small Girl Seated by Window* (1912, oil on canvas, 22 x 18 ins / 55 x 46 cm) DKK 13,000.

JAMET, Pauline
Maiden name: Allain
French, 19th century.
Born in Paris.
Painter.

Pauline Jamet studied under Lesourd, Beauregard and Rosa Bonheur. From 1848 to 1880 she exhibited, under her maiden name, still-lifes - fruit, flowers and game - at the Paris Salon. She received an honourable mention in 1859.

Museums and Galleries:
Orléans: *Still-life.*

Auction records:
Paris, 28 Oct 1938, *Flowers and Fruit,* FRF 5,350.

JAMETE, or Xamete
Spanish, 16th century.
Active in Toledo.
Sculptor, architect.

Jamete carved sculptures of his own design for the transept of the cathedral in Toledo and also worked in the cathedral of Cuenca for Bishop S. Ramirez.

JAMI, Domenico de. See **AIMO Domenico**

JAMIESON, Alexander
British, 19th - 20th century.
Born 1873, in Glasgow; died 1937.
Painter. Figures, portraits, landscapes, architectural views. Murals.

Alexander Jamieson travelled and lived in France from 1898. He made a number of open-air studies in Paris and copied works of art in the Louvre. He exhibited with the Société Nationale des Beaux-Arts in 1898, and was a frequent exhibitor with other group exhibitions in many cities, including Paris, London, Glasgow, Berlin, Dresden, Düsseldorf, Munich, Amsterdam, Venice and Helsingfors. Jamieson's 1898 submission to the Société Nationale des Beaux-Arts consisted of two paintings: *The Little Dancer* and *The Dwarf*, both of which show the influence of Manet and Degas. His *Portrait of the Artist's Father* marked the beginning of a successful career as a portrait painter - he exhibited a number of female portraits at the Salon des Artistes Français. Scenes painted during his stay in France include a *View of Moret, near Fontainebleau*, street scenes in Versailles and Blois, and harbour scenes at Dieppe and Le Tréport. Oil sketches made during a journey to Spain include *Gibraltar* and *The Mosque at Cordoba*. Jamieson also travelled and painted in Belgium (notably the city of Bruges), Sweden, and Stockholm. He also executed a number of decorative wall-paintings, including a mural at the London townhouse of the English aristocrat Count Ellesmere.

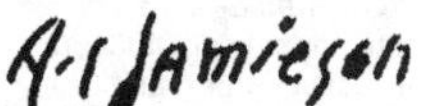

MUSEUMS AND GALLERIES:
BRADFORD (Cartwright Hall AG): *Barges on the Seine*.

AUCTION RECORDS:
PERTH, 24 April 1979, *On the Quayside, Paris* (1902, oil on canvas, 23 x 31 ins / 58.5 x 78.5 cm) GBP 1,500. LONDON, 10 June 1981, *May Tree, Weston Turville* (1914, oil on canvas, 38 1/2 x 29 1/2 ins / 98 x 75 cm) GBP 6,200. EDINBURGH, 30 April 1986, *Still-life with Flowers* (1921, oil on canvas, 31 x 26 1/2 ins / 78.8 x 67 cm) GBP 5,800. SOUTH QUEENSFERRY, 29 April 1987, *The Bouquet and the Glove* (oil on card, 23 1/2 x 19 ins / 60 x 48.5 cm) GBP 1,800. EDINBURGH, 30 Aug 1988, *French Garden* (1910, oil on canvas, 25 x 30 ins / 63.5 x 76 cm) GBP 2,310. EDINBURGH, 22 Nov 1988, *The Bruges Canal* (oil on panel, 14 3/4 x 18 ins / 37.5 x 45.7 cm) GBP 4,500. GLASGOW, 7 Feb 1989, *Stockholm* (1930, oil on canvas, 34 x 44 ins / 86.5 x 112 cm) GBP 3,520. LONDON, 2 March 1989, *The Palace of Versailles* (1907, oil on canvas, 39 3/4 x 39 1/4 ins / 101.2 x 100 cm) GBP 5,500. PERTH, 29 Aug 1989, *Dieppe Harbour* (1904, oil on canvas, 39 x 55 ins / 99 x 140 cm) GBP 10,450. LONDON, 21 Sept 1989, *Notre-Dame* (1910, oil on panel, 12 1/2 x 15 3/4 ins / 31.8 x 40.1 cm) GBP 1,650. LONDON, 21 March 1990, *The Chateau at Blois* (1910, oil on panel, 12 1/2 x 15 3/4 ins / 32 x 40 cm) GBP 2,310. EDINBURGH, 26 April 1990, *Canal scene, Bruges* (oil on panel, 14 3/4 x 18 ins / 37.5 x 45.7 cm) GBP 5,500. PERTH, 27 Aug 1990, *Fontainebleau* (1911, oil on panel, 12 1/2 x 16 1/4 ins / 32 x 41 cm) GBP 2,200. GLASGOW, 1 Feb 1994, *Siesta in the Shade of the Trees* (1927, oil on canvas, 44 x 60 ins / 112 x 152.5 cm) GBP 1,150. PERTH, 29 Aug 1995, *Still-life with a Bouquet and Gloves* (oil on card, 25 x 20 1/2 ins / 63.5 x 52 cm) GBP 1,092. PERTH, 26 Aug 1996, *Stockholm Harbour* (1930, oil on canvas, 34 x 44 ins / 86.5 x 112 cm) GBP 4,600. GLASGOW, 25 Aug 1997, *Reflections, San Valery* (1903, oil on panel, 5 x 7 ins / 12.7 x 17.8 cm) GBP 414. LONDON, 28 Oct 1999, *View of St Marks, Venice. View of Dieppe* (oil on panel, a pair, 9 x 11 ins / 22 x 27 cm) GBP 2,600. LONDON, 10 April 2000, *Basin des Cascades, Fontainebleu* (oil on board, 18 x 15 ins / 45 x 38 cm) GBP 2,600. LONDON, 28 June 2000, *Figures on Beach, Beer, Devon* (1911, oil on panel, 13 x 16 ins / 33 x 41 cm) GBP 2,200. LONDON, 8 March 2001, *On the River, Quimperle, Brittany* (1925, oil on panel, 15 x 18 ins / 37 x 46 cm) GBP 3,000. LONDON, 5 Sept 2001, *On the Clyde* (oil on panel, 11 x 16 ins / 29 x 40 cm) GBP 2,600. EDINBURGH, 11 April 2002, *Tuileries, Paris* (1897, oil on canvas, 28 x 36 ins / 72 x 91 cm) GBP 4,200. BATH, 22 July 2002, *Midsummer* (oil on canvas, 33 x 43 ins / 85 x 110 cm) GBP 1,850. LONDON, 10 Sept 2003, *Spring in Weston Turville* (1929, oil on canvas, 35 x 50 ins / 89 x 128 cm) GBP 4,000. LONDON, 30 Oct 2003, *Rosaire Quay, Bruges* (1921, oil on canvas, 30 x 24 ins / 76 x 61 cm) GBP 5,200. LONDON, 4 March 2004, *Laburnum, the Old Mill, Weston Turville, Buckinghamshire* (oil on board, 13 x 16 ins / 32 x 41 cm) GBP 1,000. LONDON, 4 March 2004, *Autumn Landscape* (1932, oil on canvas, 34 x 44 ins / 86 x 112 cm) GBP 1,800.

JAMIN
French, 18th century.
Active in Le Mans (Sarthe) in 1776.
Sculptor.

JAMIN, Diederik Franciscus
Dutch, 19th century.
Born 23 January 1838, in Amsterdam; died 7 January 1865, in Amsterdam.
Painter. Genre scenes.

Diederik Jamin was a pupil of P. F. Greive.

MUSEUMS AND GALLERIES:
AMSTERDAM: *Prayer for the Deceased; The Tearful Widow*.

AUCTION RECORDS:
AMSTERDAM, 15 Nov 1976, *The Art Lover* (1857?, oil on panel, 8 1/2 x 6 1/2in/21.5 x 16.5cm) NLG 4,600. COLOGNE, 21 March 1980, *At the Hairdresser's* (1862, oil on panel, 30 x 23 1/2in/76 x 60cm) DEM 11,000. AMSTERDAM, 23 April 1991, *Children in a Cornfield* (1859, oil on panel, 6 3/4 x 7 3/4in/17 x 20cm) NLG 3,450. AMSTERDAM, 8 Nov 1994, *The Necklace* (oil on panel, 16 3/4 x 12 1/4in/42.5 x 31cm) NLG 9,200. AMSTERDAM, 16 April 1996, *In the Park* (1863, oil on panel, 14 1/2 x 19 1/4in/37 x 49cm) NLG 14,780. AMSTERDAM, 5 Nov 1996, *Small Girl Sitting in the Shade of a Tree* (oil on panel, 10 x 12 1/2in/25.5 x 31.5cm) NLG 2,360.

JAMIN, Léon
Belgian, 19th - 20th century.
Born 1872, in Liège; died 1944.
Painter. Landscapes.

Léon Jamin painted predominantly landscapes in the Ardennes and La Campine in Belgium.

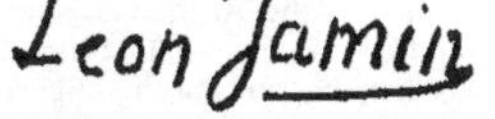

MUSEUMS AND GALLERIES:
LIÈGE (Mus. de l'Art wallon).

JAMIN, Paul
Belgian, 20th century.
Born 1939, in Brussels.
Painter, watercolourist. Landscapes.

Paul Jamin studied in Brussels at St Luke's Academy and the Académie Royale des Beaux Arts. He worked predominantly in the Ardennes and Walloon Bravantia.

JAMIN, Paul Joseph
French, 19th century.

Born 9 February 1853, in Paris; died 10 July 1903, in Paris.
Painter. History painting, portraits, genre scenes. Murals.

Paul Joseph Jamin, son of the physicist Jules, gave up the École Polytechnique and devoted himself to painting. He studied under Boulanger and Jules Lefebvre at Paris' College of Fine Arts and took part in the Paris Salon from 1879 to 1903.He was a member of the Société des Artistes Français from 1883 onwards and was awarded an honourable mention and a second class medal at its 1892 and 1898 Salons, respectively. He also won a bronze medal at the 1889 Exposition Universelle.

Jamin featured in the 2003 collective themed exhibition at the museum of Aquitaine, Bordeaux: *Vénus et Caïn. Figures de la préhistoire 1830-1930* (*Venus and Cain. Prehistoric Figures 1830-1930*), an exhibition charting the emergence of prehistory as a scientific discipline and source of artistic inspiration.

Jamin painted *The Men's Return is Announced* for the decoration of the new Sorbonne.

He came to particular attention for his paintings depicting the lives of pre-historic and medieval men, with, sometimes insidiously erotic, scenes painted in sickly sweet tonalities.

BIBLIOGRAPHY:
Lafont-Couturier, Hélène/Dagen, Philippe/Loizeau, Sigolène, *Vénus et Caïn. Figures de la préhistoire 1830-1930*, exhibition catalogue, Musée d'Aquitaine, Bordeaux, 2003.

MUSEUMS AND GALLERIES:
FÉCAMP: *Face of a Young Man* - GRAY: *Last Prisoner of the Bastille* - LA ROCHELLE (MBA): *Gallic Chief and his Spoils* - RHEIMS: *Abduction, Stone Age.*

AUCTION RECORDS:
PARIS, 23 Feb 1901, *Caesar and Alexander's Tomb*, FRF 100. LOS ANGELES, 13 Nov 1972, *Moorish Conqueror*, USD 1,500. ÉVREUX, 16 Dec 1975, *Woman in Antiquity* (oil on panel, 13 3/4 x 10 1/4 ins / 35 x 26 cm) FRF 500. ST. LOUIS, 8 June 2002, *Dramatic Scene of a Man and Woman Fighting an Eagle* (oil on canvas, 30 x 20 ins / 77 x 51 cm) USD 7,000. PARIS, 19 June 2003, *Le Brenn in Rome* (oil on canvas, 44 x 57 ins / 113 x 145 cm) EUR 9,000.

JAMINET, Philippe
French, 20th century.
Installation artist.
Conceptual Art.

Philippe Jaminet collects natural materials from particular places and sets them in ephemeral installations. In 1992, the Musée St-Jacques in Béziers put on a solo exhibition of his work.

JAMINS, François. See **FAMINS**

JAMIS, Fayad
Cuban, 20th century.
Born 1930, in Palma-Soriano; died 1988.
Painter, collage artist.

Fayad Jamis studied at the Academia Nacional de Bellas Artes San Alejandro and began exhibiting in 1951. In 1954 he went to Paris where he took part in numerous exhibitions with the Surrealist group. In 1959, after the revolution, he returned to Cuba and blossomed as both a poet and an artist. He was awarded the Casa de las Americas poetry prize in 1962 and first prize for painting at the fine arts exhibition of 1967. He exhibited at the Museo Nacional in 1977 and in 1977-1978 took part in the *Cuba - Peintres d'aujourd'hui* (*Cuba - Painters of Today*) exhibition at the Musée d'Art Moderne in Paris. Jamis was cultural advisor to the Cuban embassy in Mexico City.

From lyrical abstraction Fayad Jamis developed a kind of magic realism which may be considered similar to the work of Wilfredo Lam.

BIBLIOGRAPHY:
Carpentier, Alejo, *Cuba, peintres d'aujourd'hui*, exhibition catalogue, Musée d'Art moderne de la Ville de Paris, Paris, 1977-1978.

JAMISON, Archer Isabel (Mrs)
British, 19th century.
Active in St Helena.
Painter, watercolourist. Flowers.

Mrs Jamison began exhibiting her work in London in 1877 at the Royal Academy, Suffolk Street and at the New Water-Colour Society.

JAMME, Édouard
Belgian, 19th century.
Painter. Historical subjects.

Édouard Jamme worked around 1843.

JAMMES, Louis
French, 20th - 21st century.
Born 1958, in Carcassonne.
Painter (mixed media).
Figuration Libre.

Louis Jammes studied in Paris from 1979 to 1980. He first became known for painting portraits of figuration libre artists such as Combas, the Di Rosa brothers, Jean-Charles Blais, Jean-Michel Basquiat and Andy Warhol. In a subsequent series entitled *Bag People*, he photographed anonymous immigrants in street settings. He went on to juxtapose and superimpose photographs of people and painted scenery. He experimented increasingly with the film itself and during shooting, as well as on supports such as metal plates, mirrors or silkscreen prints on canvas. During the war in Bosnia, he worked in Sarajevo hanging silkscreen prints based on photographs of children in the town.

He has taken part in collective exhibitions including: *Douceur de l'Avant-garde* (*Mildness of the Avant-garde*), Rennes, 1983; *Figuration libre 5: 5*, Musée d'Art Moderne de la Ville de Paris, 1984; *New Attitudes: Paris/New York*, Pittsburgh Centre for the Arts, Pittsburgh, 1984; *Sur les Murs* (*On the Walls*), Fondation Cartier, Jouy-en-Josas, 1986; Centre National d'Art Contemporain (CNAP), Paris and the Musée d'Art Contemporain, Bordeaux, 1987. Since 1983 he has held solo exhibitions in Villeurbanne, Amsterdam and New York, Other solo exhibitions of his work include shows at the Musée de Nice and at the Palais des Beaux-Arts, Charleroi in 1986; in Chicago in 1987 and at the Musée des Beaux-Arts in Carcassonne in 1988.

BIBLIOGRAPHY:
Girard, X./Jammes, L., *Bag People - Louis Jammes 88*, exhibition catalogue, Musée des Beaux-Arts, Carcassonne, 1988.

MUSEUMS AND GALLERIES:
LYONS (MAC).

AUCTION RECORDS:
PARIS, 13 April 1988, *Portrait of Hervé di Rosa* (1982, painting/photograph in four parts, 41 3/4 x 41 3/4 ins / 106 x 106 cm) FRF 11,000. PARIS, 25 May 1994, *Portrait of Miguel Barcelo* (1985, painting/photograph, 56 x 49 1/2 ins / 142 x 126 cm) FRF 6,500. PARIS, 21 June 1999, *Shipwreck* (1985, photo heightened with gouache, 56 x 50 ins / 143 x 126 cm) FRF 12,100. PARIS, 2 May 2000, *Untitled* (serigraph, diptych, 94 x 94 ins / 240 x 240 cm) FRF 25,000. PARIS, 29 Oct 2001, *Untitled* (1989-1990, serigraph, 94 x 94 ins / 240 x 240 cm) FRF 25,000.

JAMNITZER, or Jamister or Gamiczer
German, 16th century.
Born in Vienna; died 1590, probably in Nuremberg.
Engraver, goldsmith.

Jamnitzer was the brother of Wenzel Jamnitzer, and most of his work was undertaken in partnership with him.

JAMNITZER, Christoph, or Jamitzer or Gamiczer
Dutch, 16th - 17th century.

Born 1563, in Nuremberg; died 1618, in Nuremberg.
Goldsmith, engraver (burin).
Jamnitzer was a student and nephew of Wenzel, and probably the son of Albrecht Jamnitzer. In 1600, he published a series of three books, each containing 21 prints, entitled *Arabesque Figures and Other Decorations*.
AUCTION RECORDS:
PARIS, 28 Nov 1928, *Goblet of Jasper and Marble, Decorated with Enamelwork and Small Stones* (watercolour) FRF 7,500.

JAMNITZER, Wenzel, or Jamitzer or Gamiczer
Austrian, 16th century.
Born 1508, in Vienna; died 1585, in Nuremberg.
Engraver, goldsmith.
A master in Nuremberg in 1534, where he had settled as a young man with his brother Albrecht, Jamnitzer worked for Charles V and other noblemen. The Berlin Museum owns a series of etchings by him, and notably a *Triumphal Arch*, along with 40 other etchings of various objects, including goblets and jugs. He also produced the drawing of *The Glory of Maximillian II*, which was engraved by Jost Amman.
MUSEUMS AND GALLERIES:
BASEL: *Untitled* (watercolour) - BERLIN: series of etchings including 'Triumphal Arch' - PRAGUE: *Etchings*.

JAMOIS, Charlotte
Maiden name: Bud
German, 20th century.
Born 26 March 1899, in Berlin.
Active from 1933.
Painter, potter. Figures.
Charlotte Jamois studied at the National College of Applied Arts in Berlin. Up to 1930 she worked as a ceramicist. After moving to France in 1933, she met and married the painter Edmond Jamois and took French citizenship. Her painting is in the classic mould and is principally preoccupied with the land and the peasants who work it.

JAMOIS, Edmond V.
French, 20th century.
Born 1 April 1876, in Lille.
Painter. Genre scenes.
Edmond V. Jamois studied with Paul Sinibaldi. He exhibited in Paris at the Salon des Artistes Français, of which he became a member, winning a third-class medal in 1907.
MUSEUMS AND GALLERIES:
PARIS (Mus. du Petit Palais): *Gathering outside a Northern Church*.

JAMONT
French, 19th century.
Engraver.
Jamont exhibited at the 1819 Paris Salon.

JAMONTT, Bronislaw
Polish, 20th century.
Painter. Landscapes.
Bronislaw Jamontt's work was shown in the Polish section of the Salon d'Automne organised by the Société d'Échanges littéraires et artistiques entre la France et la Pologne (Society for Literary and Artistic Exchanges between France and Poland) and by the Cercle des Artistes Polonais de Paris (Circle of Polish Artists in Paris).

JAMPOLSKY, Mikhail, or Iampolsky
Ukrainian, 19th - 20th century.
Born 13 December 1874, in Kiev.
Active and naturalised in France.
Sculptor, medallist.
A pupil of Daniel Dupuis, Hubert Ponscarme and Félix Rasumny, Mikhail Jampolsky exhibited regularly at the Salon des Artistes Français in Paris of which he became a member in 1908. He received honourable mentions at the Expositions Universelles of 1897 and 1900.

JAMRATH, J. F.
German, 19th century.
Active in Berlin.
Painter. Portraits.
Jamrath featured at exhibitions at the academy in Berlin from 1826 to 1846, showing flower paintings in oils and watercolours and portraits, mostly on porcelain.

JAMSIN, Michel
Belgian, 20th century.
Born 1941, in Fléron.
Painter, sculptor.
Michel Jamsin studied at the Mons academy and later taught there. He has won a number of prizes including the 1971 Prix de la Province du Hainault. He was one of the founder members of the Maka group. Mention has been made of a Hyperrealist aspect to certain of his works.

JAN. See **MERETTE DE GAND**

JAN. See **JUAN Flamenco**

JAN, or Jean, called le Brabançon or Johannes von Brabant
Flemish School, 13th century.
Sculptor.
The *Statue of Wenzel III of Bohemia* is by Jan.

JAN, or Jean or Johann or Hans
Dutch, 15th century.
Painter.
Jan was a painter to the court of the Great Elector, Frederick the Wise of Saxony, and accompanied him on a trip to Jerusalem in 1493, and to the towns of Mechelen and Antwerp in 1494. Frederick also commissioned him to travel to Cracow and Venice. In 1494, he produced nine paintings, which included *Annunciation, Adoration of the Shepherds, The Madonna, St Anne and St Christopher*, and *St George*. In 1493 he is recorded as having made five oil paintings and one painting on wood. A *Portrait of Frederick the Wise*, in the art gallery in Gotha, has also been attributed to him.

JAN (Meister), called Meister Johann de Munich
Dutch, 15th - 16th century.
Active in Germany.
Painter.
Munich School.
Jan worked in Munich and produced decorative paintings, trophies and banners, among other items, for Albert IV of Bavaria. He became a guild member in 1502.

JAN (Maître or Meester), or Jean
French, 15th - 16th century.
Died 1528.
Glass painter.
Jan is recorded as working in Bathala between 1489 and 1528.

JAN, or Jean, called Jean de Bruxelles, Jan de Rome or Jan van Room
Dutch, 15th - 16th century.
Painter, draughtsman. Designs for tapestries.
Jan was a painter at the Dutch court, and worked for the Countess Margaret, who was the daughter of the Emperor Maximillian and the wife of the governor of Holland. He was commissioned by her to decorate Brou cathedral. His name appears on the list of painters employed by the brotherhood of the Holy Sacrament in louvain, for whom he designed tapestries.
A figure marked twice with the name *Jan de Ron* appears on a tapestry of the story of David in the royal museum in Brussels. It is possible that a painter called Jan de Bruxelles

or Jan de Rome did exist at that time, but the reference most likely concerns Jan Gossaert-Mabuse or Jan Mostaert.

JAN. See also **JEAN, JOHANN, JUAN**

JAN, Elvire, or Elvire-Jan, pseudonym of Kuyumdjian
Bulgarian, 20th century.
Born 1 May 1904, in Rustchuk; died 19 January 1996, in Paris.
Active in France from 1926.
Painter, watercolourist. Designs for stained glass.

Born in Bulgaria, Elvire Jan lived in Switzerland, spent a year in the USA studying with Max Weber and then went to France, studying at the Académie Julian in Paris.

Until 1949, Elvire Jan's works were allusively figurative in the style of the École de Paris. Later works are typical of post-war French Abstraction. Her strictly abstract work falls into several periods: between 1950 and 1955 a light and warm chromaticism is contained within a supple linear network; between 1955 and 1960 more muted colours predominate; from 1960 to 1970 her work once again becomes fluid, particularly - and not surprisingly - in her watercolours, where bright flashes of colour stand out against dark backgrounds; from 1970 her works become increasingly monochromatic.

Seen in its entirety, her work can best be described as Abstract Impressionist. Elvire Jan succeeds in combining the best of the Cubism of the inter-war period with her own poetic sensibility derived from her observation and memory of reality. Her limpid canvases are imbued with a strong sense of serene spirituality.

As well as painting, Elvire Jan designed stained glass windows including those for the Villa de la Réunion in Paris, the Franciscan chapel in Boulogne-sur-Mer and for the following churches: Ézy-sur-Eure, Notre-Dame de Beligny in Villefranche-sur-Saône, Ste-Bernadette in Robertsau, St-Servan-sur-Oust, Notre-Dame de Tours near Payern in Switzerland, Le Bizot in Besançon, St-Pierre-St-Paul in Levier and the abbey church of Ottmarsheim.

Collective exhibitions include: Salon des Indépendants, Paris (1932); Salon de Mai, Paris (from 1945); Salon des Réalités Nouvelles, Paris (1959 and 1961); Salon d'Automne, Paris (1961); Salon de l'Art Sacré and Salon Comparaisons, Paris (1962); Groupe 109, Paris (in the 1980s). Her work has also often appeared alongside other artists including Bazaine, Le Moal, Bertholle, Seiler and Vulliamy.

Solo exhibitions include: Galerie Van Leer, Paris (1933); Galerie Jeanne Castel, Paris (1942); Galerie Mouradian-Vallotton, Paris (1947 and 1969); Lille (1953); Galerie Roque, Paris (1954, 1957, 1969 and 1983); Blanche Gallery, Stockholm (1955 and 1962); Galerie Bénador, Geneva (1955); Lyons Museum (1955); Zurich (1956 and 1961); Galerie Le Zodiaque, Brussels (1957); Basel (1957, 1960 and 1988); Cannes (1959); Galerie de Varenne, Paris (1959); Galerie Numaga, La Chaux-de-Fonds (1960); Musée d'Art Moderne, Paris (1962); Galerie Marbach, Bern (1963); Maison de la Culture, Orléans (1970); Galerie Kaganovitch, Paris (1979, 1981 and 1982); Esch-sur-Alzette (1980); Luxembourg (1983); St-Dié Cathedral (1987); Galerie La Pochade, Paris (1988). Posthumous exhibitions: Galerie du Port and Chapelle des Pénitents Bleus, La Ciotat.

BIBLIOGRAPHY:
Guichard-Meili, J., *Regarder la peinture*, Éd. du Seuil, Paris, 1960. Bourniquel, Camille, *Elvire Jan: histoire d'une amitié*, Guitardes, Paris, 1984. Bourniquel, Camille, *Elvire Jan*, exhibition catalogue, Gal. La Pochade, Paris, 1988.

MUSEUMS AND GALLERIES:
BERGEN (Kunstmus.) - DIJON (MBA) - DUBLIN (MFA) - LUND (Konsthall) - LUXEMBOURG (Mus. national d'histoire et d'art) - LYONS (MBA) - METZ (La Cour D'or) - PARIS (MNAM-CCI) - TOURCOING (MBA).

AUCTION RECORDS:
PARIS, 20-21 June 1988, *Composition in Blue* (oil on canvas, 28 3/4 x 36 1/4 ins / 73 x 92 cm) FRF 15,000. NEUILLY-SUR-SEINE, 22 Nov 1988, *Spring* (1960, oil on canvas, 13 x 16 1/4 ins / 33 x 41 cm) FRF 14,000. NEUILLY-SUR-SEINE, 16 March 1989, *Composition* (15 x 18 ins / 38 x 46 cm) FRF 65,000. PARIS, 26 May 1989, *Composition* (1967, oil on canvas, 37 3/4 x 57 1/2 ins / 96 x 146 cm) FRF 7,500. NEUILLY-SUR-SEINE, 6 June 1989, *Composition* (1957, oil on canvas, 35 x 45 1/4 ins / 88 x 115 cm) FRF 143,000. DOUAI, 2 July 1989, *Composition* (1977, watercolour, 25 1/2 x 19 3/4 ins / 65 x 50 cm) FRF 3,500. PARIS, 29 Nov 1989, *Composition* (1976, oil on canvas, 13 x 16 1/4 ins / 33 x 41 cm) FRF 10,000. DOUAI, 3 Dec 1989, *Study in Blue* (1978, oil on canvas, 15 x 18 ins / 38 x 45.5 cm) FRF 27,000. NEUILLY, 7 Feb 1990, *Composition* (1956, oil on canvas, 46 x 35 ins / 116 x 89 cm) FRF 160,000. PARIS, 21 May 1990, *Composition* (1970, watercolour and ink, 9 x 13 3/4 ins / 23 x 35 cm) FRF 4,000. PARIS, 30 May 1990, *Composition* (oil on canvas, 45 1/4 x 35 ins / 115 x 88 cm) FRF 155,000. DOUAI, 1 July 1990, *Composition* (1954, oil on canvas, 9 1/2 x 7 1/2 ins / 24 x 19 cm) FRF 20,000. PARIS, 6 Nov 1990, *Composition* (1959, oil on canvas, 23 1/2 x 32 ins / 60 x 81 cm) FRF 48,000. CALAIS, 7 July 1991, *Composition* (1964, watercolour, 19 1/4 x 25 1/4 ins / 49 x 64 cm) FRF 6,000. PARIS, 1 July 1992, *Composition* (1958, oil on canvas, 15 3/4 x 31 1/2 ins / 40 x 80 cm) FRF 18,000. PARIS, 5 July 1994, *Composition* (1957, oil on canvas, 35 x 45 1/4 ins / 88 x 115 cm) FRF 20,000. PARIS, 30 Sept 1994, *Untitled* (1947, oil on canvas, 15 x 18 ins / 38 x 46 cm) FRF 21,000. PARIS, 15 May 1995, *Composition* (1957, oil on canvas, 18 x 25 1/2 ins / 46 x 65 cm) FRF 10,500. ZURICH, 14 Nov 1995, *Return from Alba* (1956, oil on canvas, 28 3/4 x 39 1/4 ins / 73 x 100 cm) CHF 4,400. LONDON, 23 May 1996, *Autumn* (1961, oil on canvas, 25 1/4 x 31 1/2 ins / 64 x 80 cm) GBP 690. PARIS, 5 Oct 1996, *Composition* (1958, oil on canvas, 15 3/4 x 31 1/2 ins / 40 x 80 cm) FRF 12,000. VERSAILLES, 12 Dec 1999, *Composition* (1960, oil on canvas, 38 x 50 ins / 97 x 128 cm) FRF 40,000. VERSAILLES, 12 Dec 1999, *Composition* (1959, oil on canvas, 35 x 51 ins / 89 x 130 cm) FRF 45,000. VERSAILLES, 2 April 2000, *Valley* (1963, oil on canvas, 26 x 37 ins / 66 x 93 cm) FRF 27,000. VERSAILLES, 2 April 2000, *Composition* (1958, oil on canvas, 38 x 51 ins / 97 x 130 cm) FRF 51,500. PARIS, 28 Jan 2001, *Composition* (oil on canvas, 51 x 35 ins / 130 x 89 cm) FRF 26,000. VERSAILLES, 1 April 2001, *Composition* (1959, oil on canvas, 26 x 36 ins / 65 x 92 cm) FRF 25,000. PARIS, 27 Jan 2002, *Composition* (1965, oil on canvas, 15 x 18 ins / 38 x 46 cm) EUR 2,300. PARIS, 19 June 2002, *Forest in the Sun* (1958, oil on canvas, 20 x 26 ins / 50 x 65 cm) EUR 2,900. VERSAILLES, 14 Dec 2003, *Untitled* (oil on canvas, 13 x 16 ins / 32 x 40 cm) EUR 2,600. VERSAILLES, 14 Dec 2003, *Composition* (1958, oil on canvas, 29 x 36 ins / 73 x 92 cm) EUR 5,200. VERSAILLES, 27 June 2004, *Composition* (1949, oil on canvas, 18 x 15 ins / 46 x 38 cm) EUR 3,000. VERSAILLES, 27 June 2004, *Composition* (1952, oil on canvas, 46 x 57 ins / 117 x 145 cm) EUR 9,000.

JAN, Fiammingo, or Giovanni Fiammingo
Dutch, 15th - 16th century.
Active in Italy.
Painter.

Jan painted flowers, fruit, festoons and garlands, among other subjects, for Raphael, and was the teacher of Giovanni da Udine. He seems not to have been one of the artists named Giovanni Fiammingo.

JAN, Georges
French, 19th century.
Died 1907.
Active in Paris.
Painter.
Georges Jan was a member of the Société des Artistes Français and featured at its Salon.

JAN, Jules
French, 19th century.
Born in Valenciennes.
Painter.
Jules Jan studied at Rennes College and was a pupil of Drolling.
MUSEUMS AND GALLERIES:
RENNES: *Portrait of Leperdit, Mayor of Rennes.*

JAN ALLEMAN, or Allemans
Flemish, 16th century.
Painter (?), sculptor (?).
Antwerp School.
Jan Alleman is recorded as being a master of the Guild of St Luke in 1502.

JAN ALLEMAN, or Allemans
Flemish, 16th century.
Active during the second half of the 16th century in Antwerp.
Painter (?), sculptor (?).
Antwerp School.
Jan Alleman is recorded as being a master of the Guild of St Luke in Antwerp on 3 January 1589.

JAN DE BISSCHOP. See **EPISCOPIUS Johannes**

JAN DE HOLLANDE
French, 14th century.
Active in Poitiers c. 1398.
Painter.
According to Bouchot, Jan de Hollande could be the same person as Jean Malouel.

JAN DE L'ARC, or Jean de L'Arc, Hans in den Booghe
Flemish, 16th century.
Died 1585.
Painter.
Flemish School.
Jan de L'Arc worked in Antwerp. According to van Mander, he went to Rome with Pieter Ulrick.

JAN JOEST VON KALKAR. See **JOOST Jan**

JAN VAN AMSTEL. See **AMSTEL Jan van**

JAN VAN ANTWERPEN, Hans. See **KNIEPER Hans**

JAN VAN BASTEL. See **BATTEL Jan van**

JAN VAN BRÜGGE. See **JEAN de Bondolf**

JAN VAN DER ASSELT. See **ASSELT Jan van der**

JAN VAN GENT. See **JUAN de Gante**

JAN VAN HALDERN
German, 15th - 16th century.
Sculptor (wood).
Jan van Haldern worked in the studio of the sculptor Arnold in Zwolle from 1491. He produced a small altar that is now in the Badois museum in Karlsruhe.

JAN VAN LEYDEN. See **LEYDEN Jan van**

JAN VAN MEMMINGEN. See **HANS VAN MEMMINGEN**

JAN VAN OOSENBRUGGHE
Belgian, 15th century.
Painter, sculptor.
Jan van Oosenbrugghe painted panels at the palace of the prince in 1428, and produced six of the statues for the façade of the town hall in Bruges.

JAN VAN SAINT-OMAERS. See **JEAN de Saint-Omer**

JAN VAN WOLUWE. See **WOLUWE**

JAN-DAY. See **DAY Jan**

JAN-MONCHABLON, Ferdinand. See **MONCHABLON Jean Ferdinand**

JAN-PENNINGH, Heinrich. See **PENNINGH Harry John**

JANACOPOULOS, Adrienne
Argentinian, 20th century.
Born in Buenos Aires.
Sculptor.
Adrienne Janacopoulos exhibited at the Salon d'Automne in Paris.

JANCE, Paul Claude
French, 19th century.
Born 5 July 1840, in Lyons.
Painter. Portraits, genre scenes, landscapes, still-lifes, flowers.
Paul Jance was a pupil at the École des Beaux-Arts in Lyons from 1855 to 1861 and studied under Gleyre. From 1863, he exhibited, in both Lyons and Paris, still-lifes, flowers, portraits, miniatures, and several landscapes and genre paintings. In Paris, he was awarded an honourable mention in 1884 for his portrait miniatures.
AUCTION RECORDS:
PARIS, 27 June 1983, *Vase of Peonies* (1883, oil on canvas, 36 1/4 x 28 3/4 ins / 92 x 73 cm) FRF 14,000. PARIS, 4 March 1992, *Still-life with Hare* (1862, oil on canvas, 35 3/4 x 28 1/4 ins / 91 x 72 cm) FRF 9,000. NEW YORK, 16 July 1992, *Little Gardeners* (oil on canvas, 19 3/4 x 24 ins / 50.2 x 61 cm) USD 5,500. LONDON, 31 Oct 1996, *Bouquet of Roses* (oil on canvas, 10 x 13 ins / 25.5 x 33 cm) GBP 1,495. NEW YORK, 9 Feb 1999, *Still-life of Roses with Two Books on Table* (oil on canvas, 36 x 26 ins / 92 x 67 cm) USD 8,500. BERN, 6 Nov 2002, *Still-life of Roses* (oil on canvas, 16 x 11 ins / 40 x 27 cm) CHF 3,600. BEAUNE, 25 April 2004, *Family Portraits* (1875/1877, oil on canvas, two, 19 x 15 ins / 47 x 39 cm) EUR 3,000.

JANCEL, Dominique
French, 20th - 21st century.
Born 19 May 1946, in Paris.
Painter (mixed media), lithographer. Figures.
Dominique Jancel was awarded distinctions at the Concours General de Dessin d'Art de la Ville de Paris in 1961 and 1962. Like many painters she works while listening to music, classical and contemporary, and may be inspired by it. With a deliberately furious technique she creates apparently human figures and expresses suffering and drama. Her themes and the expression emanating from them resemble the Expressionism of Bacon or Rebeyrolle and the Abstract Expressionism of De Kooning. She has participated in many collective exhibitions in France and abroad since 1975, notably: Salon de la Jeune Peinture, 1986 and 1987; *IVe Rencontre des Artistes Contemporains à Cannes* (*4th Meeting of Contemporary Artists in Cannes*), 1986; she was selected for the exhibition *Revolution, Violence and Passion*, 1988-89 in Paris, Toulouse, New York, Tokyo and Beijing and at the White Penitent's Chapel in Gordes, 1991. Solo exhibitions include shows at the Opera House in Cairo in 1989 and the Galerie Éocène, Paris in 1991. She has also painted in public, such as at the Auvers-sur-Oise Festival in 1989.

JANCIC, Olga
Macedonian, 20th century.
Born 1929, in Bitola.
Sculptor. Figures.

Olga Jancic studied at the Belgrade academy of fine art until 1947 and then worked for five years with Toma Rosandic.

Her works take reality as their point of departure, but a reality stripped of all detail with inward-turning forms that resemble bubbling pools of petrified lava. Typical subjects are mothers and children, weeping women and torsos.

BIBLIOGRAPHY:
Protic, Miodrag B., *Skulptura XX veka*, Umetnost na tlu Jugoslavije, Beograd, 1982.

JANCK, Angelo. See **JANK**

JANCKE, Auguste Martin Heinrich
German, 19th century.
Born 29 July 1810, in Hamburg; died 3 November 1840, in Hamburg.
Painter, lithographer.

Jancke's principal subject-matter was moonlight. He lithographed two plates after C. F. Schulz depicting stags.

MUSEUMS AND GALLERIES:
HAMBURG (Kunsthalle): *View of the Old Monastery and Church of St John in Hamburg* (several); *View of Uhlenhorst, Hamburg*.

JANCO, Marcel
Romanian, 20th century.
Born 24 May 1895, in Bucharest, born Marcel Iancu; died 21 April 1984, in Tel Aviv.
Active in Switzerland from 1915 to c. 1922, active then naturalised in Israel from 1942.
Painter, sculptor, engraver, illustrator, architect. Dadaism.
Zurich Dadaist, Artistes Radicaux, Das Neue Leben, New Horizons. Ein Hod Artists' Village.

Marcel Janco studied painting with Josif Iser, who had been a friend of Derain in Paris, from 1910 to around 1913. He exhibited at the official salon in Bucharest. From 1912 he contributed to the review *Simbolul* edited by Tristan Tzara. In 1913 or 1915 until 1916 he was in Zurich where he attended classes in architecture at the polytechnic. Here he met Tzara again and got to know Arp and Huelsenbeck with whom he collaborated in the setting up and organising of Hugo Ball's Cabaret Voltaire, where the aims of the Zurich Dadaists were formulated. This group differed radically from the Berlin Dadaist group who were motivated by a violently political and anarchistic ideology. As a member of the Zurich Dadaists, Janco became involved in designing and making costumes and particularly masks for the Dadaist performances held at the Cabaret Voltaire. He also contributed to the group's review *Dada*, designing the cover for the first issue. From 1917 to 1919, he continued to take part in Dadist events, making scenery and masks, and collective exhibitions for which he designed the posters. In 1919, Arp and Augusto Giacometti and Janco set up the Artistes Radicaux in Basel. This group expressed clearly its faith in a socially just future where art would be integrated into, and contribute to the improvement of the lives of, ordinary people. Abstract art would participate 'in the ideological evolution of the State'. With the artists of the Basel group and with those of another new group, Das neue Leben (New Life), which he set up in 1920, Janco began to exhibit with Klee, Eggeling, Richter, Arp, Sophie Taeuber and other emerging abstract artists. From 1921 to 1923 he was in Paris where he met Picabia, Ernst and Dalí. During this period in which he was drawn to the work of the Cubists, particularly that of Marcoussis and Henri Laurens, Janco adopted some of the principles of Cubism, adapting them to his own increasing interest in Abstraction. It was also at this time that he severed his links with the Dadaists, writing: 'A vast gulf divides us from the Dadaist poets who continue in their mystification and jokes for the pure pleasure of non-sense'. He decided to return to Romania: 'I decided to forge my own way and spread the word of the new art in my native land'. In 1923, in Bucharest, he founded the group Contimporanul and the review of the same name. Through these, he was able to mobilise various avant-garde movements. In 1940, after the establishing of a Fascist government, or perhaps in 1942, he fled to Israel where he settled permanently. Here he provided an important impetus to the cultural life of the newly-created country through his activities as a teacher and organiser of exhibitions. In 1948, he set up the New Horizons group and, in 1953, founded an artists' community in the ruined village of Ein Hod near Haifa on the slopes of Mount Carmel.

Janco's paintings of 1916-1917, including *Cabaret Voltaire* and *Ball in Zurich*, still betray the influence of Expressionism, but belong more to the style of the Futurists or even Picasso's Cubist-Expressionism. At this time he provided coloured woodcuts to illustrate Tzara's first book, *La premiere aventure céleste de Monsieur Antipyrine* (*The First Celestial Adventure of Monsieur Antipyrine*) and a series of eight woodcuts illustrating a poem by Tzara. Other work produced by Janco at this time, often consisting of very austere still-lifes, is characterised by the combined influences of Futurism and Cubism with a leaning towards the kind of formal Abstraction espoused by his close friend Arp. From 1917 to 1919 he began producing works in relief using white or coloured plaster. These used two of the ideas of the Zurich Dadaists: unusual materials in architectural projects, and a formal vocabulary with non-figurative elements. These abstract reliefs and sculptures, such as *Evening Prayer-Flash* and *Small Architecture-Light*, were followed in 1918-1920 by paintings on sacking or plaster of geometric forms in subdued colours of ochre and blue. Some of these works, such as *Jazz 333* (1918), have a strong sense of rhythm. In the years that followed, Janco used a combination of all these techniques. After the Israeli War of Independence of 1948 he began to introduce military themes into his compositions. Avram Kampf has written of this aspect of his work: 'Even though he was the painter of an army of partisans, Maccabees fighting for their existence, wounded soldiers resting on their guns, he did not glorify war. He felt it, rather, as a daily reality that could not be ignored.' His response to contact with this new world, in a country drawing together Jews from all over the world, was to paint its landscapes, still-lifes of daily objects, figures and typical scenes with a touch of humour, symbolic of his contented later years. Nevertheless, in a final change of direction in 1965, he returned to many of the artistic ideas and aesthetic and civic enthusiasms of his youth.

His work featured at the exhibition *Jawlensky in Switzerland*, Fondation de l'Hermitage, Lausanne (2000). Retrospectives were mounted by the museum in Tel Aviv in 1968 and 1972 and the centenary of his birth was marked by *Centenar Marcel Iancu 1895-1995*, National Museum of Art of Romania, Bucharest (1996).

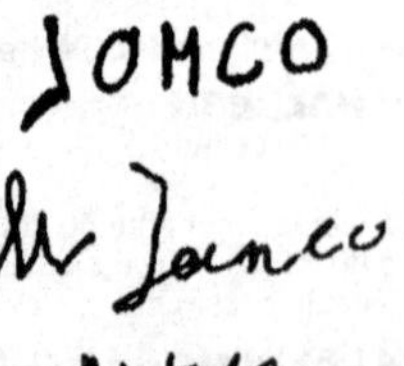

BIBLIOGRAPHY:

Motherwell, Robert (ed.), *The Dada Painters and Poets, an Anthology*, Wittenborn, New York, 1951. Seuphor, Michel, *Le Style et le Cri*, Éd. du Seuil, Paris, 1965. Dorival, Bernard/Hoog, Michel, *Dada*, exhibition catalogue, Musée national d'Art moderne, Paris, 1966. Kampf, Avram, *Jewish Experience in 20th Century Art*, Barbican Art Gall., London, 1990. *Centenar Marcel Iancu, 1895-1995*, exhibition catalogue, National museum of Art of Romania, Bucharest, 1996 (bilingual edition in English and Romanian). Machedon, Luminita/Scoffham, Ernie, '*Marcel Janco as architect*' in *Architectura* vol. 29, n° 2, 1999 (text in German).

MUSEUMS AND GALLERIES:

CHICAGO (AI) - JERUSALEM (Israel Mus.): *Ball in Zurich, 1916*; *Landscape* (1963) - PARIS (MNAM-CCI): *Flower-Geometry* (1917); *Jazz 333* (1918, oil and collages) - TEL AVIV.

AUCTION RECORDS:

PARIS, 18 March 1972, *Composition* (painted plaster/wood) FRF 10,500. MILAN, 24 Oct 1972, *Desolation* (mixed media/hardboard) ITL 2,800,000. HAMBURG, 3 June 1977, *Relief* (1915-1950, copper, aluminium and steel on a black metal plaque, 13 3/4 x 9 ins / 35 x 22 cm) DEM 3,100. MUNICH, 27 Nov 1981, *Portrait of a Man* (oil on canvas, 25 3/4 x 22 1/2 ins / 65.5 x 57 cm) DEM 17,000. TEL AVIV, 16 May 1983, *Nude Couple* (1922, oil on canvas, 23 1/2 x 15 3/4 ins / 59.5 x 40 cm) ILS 284,100. LONDON, 4 Dec 1985, *Dadaga* (1920, oil on card, 19 x 27 1/4 ins / 48.5 x 69.5 cm) GBP 20,000. LONDON, 25 Feb 1987, *Spanish Civil War* (c. 1939-1940, oil on card, 19 3/4 x 27 1/2 ins / 50 x 70 cm) GBP 4,500. TEL AVIV, 26 May 1988, *Jaffa* (oil on card, 19 3/4 x 27 1/2 ins / 50 x 70 cm) USD 18,700. PARIS, 20 Nov 1988, *Life's Journey* (1921-1924, oil on canvas, 23 1/2 x 35 1/2 ins / 60 x 90 cm) FRF 340,000. TEL AVIV, 2 Jan 1989, *Aqueduct in the Mountains of Galilee* (oil/synthetic resin, 18 1/2 x 26 1/4 ins / 47 x 66.5 cm) USD 9,350. PARIS, 16 April 1989, *Composition* (oil on canvas, 15 3/4 x 22 ins / 40 x 55 cm) FRF 18,000. TEL AVIV, 30 May 1989, *Refugees Leaving Spain* (oil on panel, 20 x 28 ins / 51 x 71 cm) USD 14,300. PARIS, 19 Nov 1989, *Little Ball in Zurich* (1916, oil on card, 23 1/2 x 17 3/4 ins / 60 x 45 cm) FRF 900,000. TEL AVIV, 3 Jan 1990, *Nudes* (oil on card, 19 1/4 x 27 ins / 49 x 68.5 cm) USD 13,750; *Figures by the Walls of a Village* (oil on canvas, 20 x 27 3/4 ins / 50.5 x 70.5 cm) USD 27,500. PARIS, 4 Feb 1990, *Tablets* (1960, sculpture in thick Perspex, 18 1/2 x 13 1/2 ins / 47 x 34.2 cm) FRF 45,000. PARIS, 8 April 1990, *Abstract Composition* (oil on card, 13 1/2 x 19 1/4 ins / 34 x 49 cm) FRF 28,000. TEL AVIV, 31 May 1990, *Way of the Heroes* (1950, oil on canvas, 32 x 39 1/4 ins / 81 x 100 cm) USD 44,000. TEL AVIV, 19 June 1990, *Port on the Black Sea* (oil on card, 19 1/2 x 26 1/2 ins / 49.5 x 67 cm) USD 27,500. NEW YORK, 10 Oct 1990, *Still-life* (oil on card, 13 3/4 x 19 3/4 ins / 35 x 50 cm) USD 6,600. PARIS, 26 Nov 1990, *Still-life* (mixed media and plaster/jute sacking, 10 1/4 x 17 ins / 26 x 43 cm) FRF 240,000. TEL AVIV, 1 Jan 1991, *Throwing the Dice* (1920, relief-collage, 18 x 13 1/2 ins / 45.5 x 34 cm) USD 28,600. PARIS, 17 March 1991, *Rusty Trophy* (painted plaster/jute sacking/card, 23 x 15 1/2 ins / 58.5 x 39.5 cm) FRF 190,000. NEW YORK, 7 May 1991, *Tents in Jaffa (recto)*; *Walking in Jaffa (verso)* (watercolour, ink and pencil/paper, 8 x 12 1/2 ins / 20.3 x 31.7 cm) USD 2,200. TEL AVIV, 12 June 1991, *Don Quixote* (1955, oil on canvas, 24 3/4 x 36 1/4 ins / 63 x 92 cm) USD 26,400. TEL AVIV, 26 Sept 1991, *Composition* (collage, mixed media and oil on canvas, 27 1/2 x 19 ins / 70 x 48 cm) USD 37,400; *Dock* (1931, oil on card, 19 1/4 x 27 1/4 ins / 49 x 69 cm) USD 18,150. TEL AVIV, 20 Oct 1992, *Composition with Owl* (oil on canvas, 21 1/4 x 28 3/4 ins / 54 x 73 cm) USD 8,140; *Studio* (1945, oil on card, 19 3/4 x 27 1/2 ins / 50 x 70 cm) USD 18,700. PARIS, 4 April 1993, *Arab Coffee House* (1950, watercolour and Indian ink, 9 x 13 1/4 ins / 22 x 33.8 cm) FRF 3,000. TEL AVIV, 27 Sept 1994, *Romanian Peasant Women at the Market* (oil on card, 19 1/2 x 27 1/4 ins / 49.3 x 68.9 cm) USD 41,400. TEL AVIV, 11 April 1996, *Arab Coffee House in Majdal* (oil on card, 41 1/4 x 30 ins / 105 x 76 cm) USD 60,800. BERN, 20-21 June 1996, *Dada on Cahiers d'Art* (1950, watercolour, pen and collage, 8 x 9 1/2 ins / 20.5 x 24.4 cm) CHF 2,600. TEL AVIV, 30 Sept 1996, *White Mandolin* (c. 1921, plaster painting/sacking/canvas, 17 3/4 x 23 1/2 ins / 45 x 59.5 cm) USD 50,600. TEL AVIV, 7 Oct 1996, *Vault of Heaven* (oil on card, 13 3/4 x 19 3/4 ins / 35 x 50 cm) USD 19,550. TEL AVIV, 12 Jan 1997, *Peaches* (c. 1920, oil, collage and mixed media/panel, 27 1/2 x 19 ins / 70 x 48 cm) USD 60,650; *Ruins in Jaffa* (1949, pen and ink, 16 1/4 x 12 ins / 41.5 x 30.5 cm) USD 2,530. TEL AVIV, 26 April 1997, *Arabs in the Marketplace* (c. 1948, oil on panel, 19 x 26 ins / 48 x 66 cm) USD 20,700. TEL AVIV, 23 Oct 1997, *Green Landscape* (1955, oil on canvas, 21 1/4 x 28 3/4 ins / 54 x 73 cm) USD 13,800. TEL AVIV, 25 Oct 1997, *Sun on the Port* (oil on panel, 29 1/4 x 46 ins / 74.3 x 117 cm) USD 13,800. TEL AVIV, 5 Jan 1999, *Acre and the Bay* (1948, oil on canvas, 29x36 ins / 73x92 cm) USD 84,000. TEL AVIV, 8 April 1999, *Mediterranean Scene. Cafe Scene* (oil on board, double-sided, 20x27 ins / 50x69 cm) USD 44,000. TEL AVIV, 16 Jan 2000, *Acre and Gulf* (oil on board, 19x27 ins / 48x68 cm) USD 32,000. TEL AVIV, 29 April 2000, *Sha'ar Hagai* (oil on board, 19x27 ins / 49x69 cm) USD 27,000. TEL AVIV, 16 April 2001, *Composition with Owl* (oil on canvas, 21x29 ins / 54x73 cm) USD 7,000. TEL AVIV, 12 June 2001, *Acrobat* (oil on board, 20x16 ins / 52x41 cm) USD 52,000. NORTH BETHESDA, 19 July 2002, *Village Scenes* (ink and watercolour, a pair, 13x19 ins / 32x47 cm) USD 3,300. PARIS, 29 April 2003, *Self-portrait* (1922, Indian ink, 8x6 ins / 20x14 cm) EUR 6,300. TEL AVIV, 2 Oct 2003, *Cubes Dominos* (oil on canvas laid on masonite, 20x28 ins / 50x70 cm) USD 6,500. TEL AVIV, 1 March 2004, *Abstract Composition* (c. 1950, oil on canvas laid on board, 13x19 ins / 34x49 cm) USD 2,700. TEL AVIV, 1 April 2004, *Parisian Street Lamp with a Bouquet of Flowers* (c. 1950, oil on card laid on board, 13x19 ins / 34x49 cm) USD 2,950.

JANDA, Hermine von

Austrian, 19th - 20th century.
Born 30 August 1854, in Klosterbruck; died 1925.
Painter. Architectural views, landscapes, urban landscapes, still-lifes (including flowers).

Hermine von Janda studied in Vienna and spent some time in Munich before returning to Vienna to show her still-lifes and Austrian and North Italian landscapes and cityscapes at Circle of Artists exhibitions. Her paintings of the Offensee and Lanbathsee hunting lodges in Austria were acquired in 1890 by Emperor Franz Joseph.

MUSEUMS AND GALLERIES:

BRNO (Moravské zemské Muz.): *Farm at Klosterneuburg.*

AUCTION RECORDS:

VIENNA, 10 Dec 1987, *View of Salzburg* (1914, oil on canvas, 15 1/4 x 19 1/4 ins / 39 x 49 cm) ATS 30,000. NEW YORK, 20 Jan 1993, *Still-life with Spring Flowers* (1895, oil on panel, 14 1/2 x 18 1/2 ins / 36.8 x 47 cm) USD 4,888.

JANDA, Johannes

German, 19th century.
Born 3 January 1827; died 14 November 1875, in Berlin.
Sculptor (including wood).

Janda studied at the school of fine arts in Breslau (now Wroclaw, Poland), and in 1867 made a trip to Rome. From 1852 to 1874 he showed a large number of works at academy exhibitions in Berlin, carved wooden and ivory crucifixes being the most frequently mentioned items. Other pieces were statues of saints for a Catholic hospital in Berlin, busts and statuettes. A notable work was a monumental *St Hubert* group in the 1860s for the hunting lodge of Jan Hochberg, Prince of Pless, at Promnitz (Kobiór-Promnice) near Pless (Pszczyna), Silesia. He did two lifesize reclining stags for the same prince which were exhibited in Paris in 1867 and often copied for sale. He frequently did sculptures of horses and hunting hounds. Other works that attracted attention were a marble statue of a kneeling bishop for the parish church of Glatz (Klodzko), Silesia, a large relief of *Mary Giving the Rosary to St Dominic* for the church of St Paul in Moabit (Berlin) and a group of children for the Königsbrücke bridge in Berlin (1872).

JANDAY. See **DAY Jan**

JANDELLE, Eugène Claude

French, 19th century.

Born c. 1825, in Paris.

Painter, engraver, lithographer. History painting, portraits, genre scenes, landscapes.

Eugène Jandelle was a pupil of Paul Delaroche and Diaz and took part in the Paris Salon from 1848 to 1870.

After the 1848 Revolution, he dealt with subjects depicting his radical republican opinions, for example *Liberty, Equality and Fraternity Bringing the Spirit of Revolution to the People*, 1849; *Stocks, 25 April 1849; Proceedings of 13 June 1849, Accused Present at the High Court of Versailles; Guignard and Huber,Sentenced to Deportation; Eugène Sue, 19 April 1850* and *The Future will Compensate us for the Present.*

He lithographed portraits of the leading lights of the Socialist Party: *Albert, Barbès, Louis Blanc, Boichot, Cadet, de Flotte, Greppo, Joigneaux, Lachambaudie, Legrange, Pierre Leroux, Madier de Montjau, Proud'hon, Félix Piat* and *Rattier*. Jandelle's genre scenes and historical subjects are influenced by Cabanel, whilst his landscapes echo Diaz's art.

AUCTION RECORDS:

PARIS, 16 June 1899, *Nymphs and Cupids,* FRF 260. RHEIMS, 18 March 1990, *Venus and Cupids* (oil on panel, 21 1/4 x 11 3/4 ins / 54 x 30 cm) FRF 10,500.

JANDL, Anton

Austrian, 18th century.

Born 1723, in Graz; died 1805, in Graz.

Painter. History painting, portraits.

Jandl began his training in his home town and continued in Vienna, Salzburg, Munich and Brno, where Palko put him to work. On his return to Graz, he was appointed municipal painter. He did numerous altar paintings for churches in the area.

JANDRON, Françoise

French, 19th - 20th century.

Born 19 December 1857, in Lyons.

Painter.

Françoise Jandron studied with Jean-Paul Laurens and Royer. She painted portraits, landscapes, interiors and still-lifes. She exhibited at the Salon des Artistes Français and Salon des Indépendants and won a silver medal from the Salon des Arts Décoratifs in 1925.

JANE-HENRY, pseudonym of Georgette Ghosson

French, 20th century.

Born 2 January 1924, in Annecy.

Painter. Landscapes, flowers. Decorative work on silk.

Jane-Henry studied at the art college in Lyons from 1939 to 1943. She exhibited in Paris, showing work from 1965 to1970 at the Salon des Artistes Français, Salon d'Automne and Salon des Indépendants. Her solo exhibitions took place mainly in St-Étienne.

JANEBÉ, pseudonym of Barraud-Pellet, Jeanne

Swiss, 20th century.

Born 1907, in Vully.

Painter. Figures.

AUCTION RECORDS:

BERN, 12 May 1990, *Young Peasant Woman wearing a Straw Hat* (1955, oil/synthetic resin, 29 1/4 x 27 1/4 ins / 74 x 69 cm) CHF 2,200. ZURICH, 13 Oct 1993, *Young Girl* (1969, oil on panel, 27 1/2 x 19 3/4 ins / 70 x 50 cm) CHF 3,600. ZURICH, 15 June 1999, *Portrait of Young Woman in Headscarf* (1958, oil on board, 25 x 23 ins / 64 x 59 cm) CHF 2,800. BERN, 5 Nov 1999, *Young Man Sitting on a Chest* (1964, oil on board, 35 x 26 ins / 90 x 66 cm) CHF 5,500. BERN, 11 May 2000, *Still-life with Fruit* (1977, oil on pavatex, 18 x 29 ins / 45 x 73 cm) CHF 3,600. ZURICH, 15 May 2001, *Female Nude* (1950, oil on board, 36 x 26 ins / 91 x 65 cm) CHF 6,500. BERN, 9 Nov 2001, *Girl playing a Mandolin* (1959, oil on panel, 31 x 20 ins / 78 x 50 cm) CHF 4,400. BERN, 16 May 2002, *Female Nude* (1946, oil on pavatex, 46 x 32 ins / 118 x 82 cm) CHF 3,000. BERN, 14 May 2004, *Young Woman Pouring Water from a Jug* (oil on panel, 43 x 26 ins / 108 x 65 cm) CHF 5,000. BERN, 12 Nov 2004, *Girl of the House* (1956, oil on panel, 33 x 22 ins / 84 x 57 cm) CHF 4,400.

JANECEK, Ota

Czechoslovak, 20th century.

Born 1919, in Pardubicky; died 1 July 1996.

Painter, engraver, illustrator. Figures, landscapes.

Ota Janecek first studied at the school of architecture in Prague from 1937 to 1939 and then, turning to painting in 1940, at the school of applied arts in 1941 and 1942. In 1956 he studied in Paris. While in Prague he apparently came into contact with Jiri Trnka a designer and creator of animated films, and his influence, combined with that of the narrative and decorative spirit of Persian miniatures and Chinese brush drawings, is apparent in Janecek's many illustrations for works of poetry.

During his career Janecek was influenced by a number of different artistic movements. His landscapes and townscapes painted in the early years of his career, observed with intimist detail and highly sensitive to the inner life of things, are in a late-Cubist style typical of many young artists of his generation in many countries. These works are also solidly anchored in the traditions of Bohemian art. The other major influence, and one that dominated in Central Europe, was Expressionism. Its influence on Janecek's second period has led his work to be compared with that of Rouault. He then went on the paint an important series of works based on the observation and interpretation of plants including the series entitled *Grasses* of 1950 where we see traces or echoes of the humour so frequently encountered in the imagination, themes and variations of Paul Klee's work. Indeed, one of the preoccupations of both artists was the expression of elemental signifiers. In addition to this series of plant paintings, Janecek also produced portraits and drawings of nudes in a more realist style. His visit to Paris in 1956 prompted a return to his earlier interest in townscapes, now reduced to a network of coloured squares crossed by a number of curves. In his series *Forms* of the 1960s he was again drawn towards Abstraction, perhaps because he wished to dissociate himself from the official Realism of the Eastern bloc or perhaps because he finally found the courage to abandon any idea of representation in an outpouring of coloured forms and planes of colour against a black background.

Janecek has taken part in many collective exhibitions of contemporary Czechoslovak art in his country and abroad.

BIBLIOGRAPHY:

Fifty years of Czechoslovak Painting from the Collections of the Galleries, 1918-1958, exhibition catalogue, Slovenska Narodna Gal., Bratislava, 1968 (in commemoration of the 50th anniversary of the Republic of Czechoslovakia).

AUCTION RECORDS:

LONDON, 29 June 1972, *Village,* GBP 500. LONDON, 5 July 1973, *Townscape,* GBP 480. MUNICH, 25 May 1976, *Landscape with Houses* (1955, oil on canvas, 23 1/2 x 29 1/2 ins / 60 x 75 cm) DEM 1,200. PARIS, 26 Oct 1988, *Ecce Homo* (1964, oil on canvas, 22 x 17 ins / 55 x 43 cm) FRF 4,500. PRAGUE, 12 Oct 2002, *Sun and Earth* (1985, oil on canvas, 30 x 21 ins / 75 x 54 cm) CZK 65,000. PRAGUE, 12 Oct 2002, *Form* (1964, oil on canvas, 28 x 24 ins / 72 x 60 cm) CZK 70,000.

JANECK, Franz Christoph. See **JANNECK**

JANEL
French, 18th century.
Draughtsman.
Janel is known to have drawn four series of six plates of sketches of carriages which were engraved by Choffard: *Sketchbook of Six English Berlin Coaches, Carriages in the New Style from Paris* and *Stagecoaches in the French Style*. The collection of ornaments from Berlin has a series of four plates engraved by J.T. Hauer.

JANELLA, Ottaviano. See **JANNELLA**

JANENSCH, Gerhard Adolf
German, 19th - 20th century.
Born 24 April 1860; died 1933.
Sculptor. Figures. Busts.
Gerhard Janensch lived and exhibited in Berlin, where he was awarded a gold medal in 1892.
MUSEUMS AND GALLERIES:
BERLIN (Nationalgal.): *Bust of Frieda Mitscherlich, Sculptress.*
AUCTION RECORDS:
COLOGNE, 22 Oct 1977, *Stonemason* (1920, bronze, h. 41 ins / 104 cm) DEM 1,800. LOKEREN, 20 Oct 1984, *Casting Bronze* (1918, brown-patinated bronze, h. 16½ ins / 42 cm) BEF 48,000. STUTTGART, 8 Dec 2000, *Girl with Satchel* (patinated bronze, h. 22 ins / 56 cm) DEM 3,600. AMSTERDAM, 16 May 2001, *Diana Holding a Bow and Deer* (gold-brown-patinated bronze, h. 37 ins / 93 cm) NLG 4,500. VIENNA, 29 Oct 2001, *Hunter with Chamois* (brown-patinated bronze, h. 17 ins / 42 cm) ATS 35,000. BRUSSELS, 15 Oct 2003, *Blacksmith* (1897, brown-patinated bronze, h. 38 ins / 97 cm) EUR 3,200.

JANER
Spanish, 16th century.
Active in Palma (Majorca).
Sculptor (including wood).
The Franciscan monastery of Palma, Majorca, has two life-size crucifixes by Janer which he carved for the now-destroyed Dominican church. He also carved a large crucifix in 1586 for the Privilegio chapel of the Dominican church of Valencia.

JANES. See **JOHANNES**

JANESCH, Albert
Austrian, 20th century.
Born 12 June 1889, in Vienna; died 1973.
Painter. Figure compositions, landscapes.
Albert Janesch studied at the Akademie der bildenden Künste in Vienna and was awarded a Prix de Rome in 1912. He was enlisted as an official war artist during the war of 1914-1918 and served on the Isonzo and Eastern Fronts. Janesch brought back numerous paintings from the battlefields and, although less well-known than Ivo Saliger, he was nonetheless one of the painters the National Socialists subsequently held up as a shining example of 'official' Nazi art (as opposed to the then proscribed avant-garde) in the deplorable Adolf Hitler-endorsed *Entartete Kunst* ('Degenerate Art') exhibition in Munich in 1937. An exhibition held at the Goethe Institute in Paris in 1989 reflected to a degree the disparity between 'offical' and 'proscribed' art under the Hitler regime. The exhibits included a composition by Albert Janesch featuring rowers straining at their oars, the well-muscled athletes painted in a highly-stylised quasi-Arts Deco style, epitomising the Aryan ideal.
MUSEUMS AND GALLERIES:
VIENNA (Heeresgeschichtliches Mus.): several paintings from World War I.
AUCTION RECORDS:
VIENNA, 14 March 1980, *Autumn Fruits* (1933, oil on panel, 18 x 16¼ ins / 46 x 41 cm) ATS 30,000. NEW YORK, 22 May 1985, *Market, Aleppo* (c. 1914-1918, oil on panel, 30 x 24¾ ins / 76.2 x 62.8 cm) USD 5,500. NEW YORK, 23 Feb 1989, *Peonies and Poppies* (1923, oil on panel, 34¼ x 28¾ ins / 87 x 73 cm) USD 5,280. LINDAU, 3 May 2000, *Portrait of a Young Woman in a Blue Velvet Dress* (1924, oil on panel, 47 x 38 ins / 120 x 97 cm) DEM 3,500.

JANET. See also **CLOUET François** and **Jean**

JANET, Adèle
French, 19th century.
Died 1877, in Paris.
Painter. Flowers.
From 1833 to 1834, Adèle Janet exhibited floral subjects at the Paris Salon and was awarded a third class medal in 1838.
AUCTION RECORDS:
PARIS, 26 June 1991, *Vase of Anemones* (watercolour, 12¼ x 9 ins / 31 x 23 cm) FRF 14,000.

JANET, François
French, 19th century.
Active in Paris in 1824.
Engraver (burin).

JANET, Gustave
French, 19th century.
Born 1829, in Paris.
Draughtsman, lithographer.
Gustave Janet was a brother of Ange-Louis Janet-Lange and is known for his *Political Caricatures, Memories of the Opera Theatre* and various musical titles.

In 1868 he published *Artistic Fashion: Compendium of New Fashions, Coloured and Touched Up in Watercolours.*

He was also a founding contributor to the *Illustrated World* and to the *Fashion Review.*

JANET, Henri Auguste
French, 19th century.
Born 19th century, in Paris.
Painter.
Henri Janet studied under Cabanel and Allongé. From 1874 to 1882 he exhibited portraits and landscapes at the Paris Salon.

JANET, Jean-Claude
French, 20th century.
Born 27 May 1918, in Paris.
Painter. Portraits.
Jean-Claude Janet studied in Paris at the private school of André Lhote.

JANET-LANGE, Ange-Louis
French, 19th century.
Born 26 November 1815, in Paris; died November 1872, in Paris.
Painter, engraver, lithographer, illustrator. History painting, portraits, genre scenes.
Ange-Louis Janet-Lange began at Paris' College of Fine Arts in 1833 and studied under Ingres, Alexandre Collin and Horace Vernet. He took part in the Paris Salon from 1836 to 1970.

Janet-Lange painted hunting scenes, and episodes from the Crimean, Italian and Mexican wars.

In 1846, he was commissioned by Marshal Soult to paint a series of military uniforms. He contributed for a long time to *Illustration, Comical Digest* and *Tour of the World.*

He produced a certain number of lithographies, notably, several pieces on Louis-Napoleon Bonaparte, when collaborating with Horace Vernet on the illustrations for *A History of Napoleon.* He illustrated La Fontaine's *Tales and Short Stories* and Balzac's *Shagreen.* He also provided illustrations for several popular publications.

MUSEUMS AND GALLERIES:
AJACCIO: *Sentry* - CARPENTRAS: *Ambush in Algeria* - CHAMBÉRY (MBA): *Nero at the Circus* - ÉPINAL: *Episode in the Battle of Kranghil* - ROCHEFORT: *Cavalryman* (watercolour) - TOURS: *Napoleon Abdicating at Fontainebleau.*

JANETSCHEK, Hans
Austrian, 20th century.
Born 27 January 1892, in Salzburg.
Active in Germany.
Sculptor. Figures, animals. Busts.
Hans Janetschek studied initially in Salzburg, then at the Institute of the Arts and Crafts Conservatory in Berlin. His sculpture features predominantly heads and animals carved in wood.

JANETTE, or Gemett or Jennett
British, 17th century.
Painter. Portraits.
This artist may never have existed. Although cited by Siret as having painted a *Portrait of Mary, Queen of Scots* kept at the British Museum in London, the artist does not appear in any English biography, which seems improbable for an artist important enough to have painted royal portraits. The mistake may be due to the fact that the painting, which has been housed at the National Portrait Gallery since 1879, is an old copy of another conserved at Windsor Castle and attributed to François Clouet, also called Janet. The English pronunciation of the name could have caused the confusion.

JANETZKY, Luc
Belgian, 20th century.
Born 1938, in Tirlement.
Painter.
Luc Janetzky studied at the École de la Cambre in Brussels and went on to collaborate with the architects Gio Ponti and Busiri Vici in Milan (1964) and Rome (1965) respectively. Janetzky's work is abstract on the surface but not without figurative allusions, which can be interpreted in a number of ways: for examaple, as stellar nebulae or harmoniously intertwined bodies.

JANG, Seung-up, Ohwon
Korean, 19th century.
Born 1843; died 1897.
Painter.
A Chosun-period (1392-1910) painter, Jang Seung-up came from a poor background but enjoyed great fame during the 19th century as much for the quality of his work as for his eccentric, libertine lifestyle. In 1897 he disappeared in mysterious circumstances. Chosun painting incorporates the three basic elements of native Korean (*Chuche*) art: realism, ideology and tradition. Jang, however, introduced colour along Western lines while still painting using traditional Korean ink techniques. In 2001, the South Korean director Im Kwontaek made a film about his life, *Che-hwa-seon* (*Drunk on Women and Poetry*) (Che-hwa-seon).

JANI, Diego, or Gani
Spanish, 16th century.
Active in Valladolid.
Sculptor.
Diego Jani worked with Berruguete.

JANICOT, Françoise
French, 20th century.
Born in Paris.
Painter.
Françoise Janicot creates works which are deliberately nonrepresentational, using the immediate language of pure colour and matter where subtle irregularities fascinate the eye, drawing the viewer into contemplation of the monochrome. Her work has featured in such collective exhibitions as: from 1961, the Salon Comparaisons in Paris; 1961, the 2nd Biennale des Jeunes Artistes in the Musée d'Art Moderne de la Ville de Paris, as a guest of the judges; 1962, *Donner à Voir II* (*Let it be Seen II*), Paris; 1963, *Poésie Objective* (*Objective Poetry*) in Antwerp, Brussels and Bruges; 1963, *La Boîte et son Contenu* (*Container and Content*), Paris; 1964, *Sept Peintres de Paris* (*Seven Painters in Paris*) subtitled *Du Vide à l'immatériel* (*From the Void to the Immaterial*), with Degottex, Jean Dupuy, Yves Klein, Georges Mathieu, Henri Michaux and Sima; at the Madrid Ateneo, in Barcelona and elsewhere. She has had solo shows in Paris in 1959 and 1965; in Duisburg in 1966; at the Madrid Ateneo in 1967; at the Rouen *Festival of Contemporary Art*, 1967, and at other venues.

JANICSEK, Sandor. See **IPOLY**

JANIENKO. See **YANENKO**

JANIKOWSKY, Mieczyslaw Tadeusz
Polish, 20th century.
Born 13 January 1912, in Zalishchyky; died 14 December 1968, in Cracow.
Active in France from 1947 to 1968.
Painter, collage artist.
Janikowsky studied law at Cracow University in 1933-1934 before enrolling at the Cracow academy of fine art from 1934 until 1939 when he obtained a diploma and a number of awards. He joined the army in 1939 and was active in Poland, France, England, France, Belgium and Holland where he was wounded in September 1944 and evacuated. From 1945 to 1947 he studied at the Edinburgh College of Art, where he obtained a diploma and a travel bursary. He settled in Paris, living at the artists' colony 'La Ruche', staying there until he returned to Cracow where he died the same year.

Collective exhibitions include: Annual Exhibition of the Society of Scottish Artists, Edinburgh (1945 and 1946); Royal Scottish Academy, Edinburgh (1946); Salon d'Automne, Paris (1948 and 1949); Salon des Réalités Nouvelles, Paris (regularly from 1955); Salon des Réalités Nouvelles, Musée des Beaux-Arts, Nantes (1957); *Mesure*, Musée des Beaux-Arts, Rennes (1961); *Cinquante ans de Collages* (*Fifty Years of Collage*), Musée d'Art et d'Industrie, St-Étienne (1964); *La Ruche Aujourd'hui* (*La Ruche Today*), Paris (1966).

Solo exhibitions include: Galerie Colette Allendy, Paris and New Vision Gallery, London (1956) and Cracow (1962). Posthumous retrospective include: Salon d'Automne (1969); Cologne (1972); Museum of Contemporary Art, Lódz and private galleries, Cracow and Warsaw (1974); Paris (1977); Drian Galleries, London and Cracow (1979); Historical Museum, Sanok and Bibliothèque Polonaise, Paris (1983); *Autour de Janikowski*, Galerie Darial, Paris (1983).

JANIN. See also **JEAN**

JANIN, Fernand
French, 20th century.
Born 1880, in Nîmes; died 1912, in Toulouse.
Painter, watercolourist. Landscapes.
Fernand Janin enrolled to study architecture at the École des Beaux-Arts in Paris, and he travelled widely in Spain, Italy, North Africa and the USA. In 1909 he won the Prix de Rome and set off for the Villa Medici, but ill health forced him to return to Toulouse, where he died at the age of 32. On his travels he painted a number of watercolours, views of towns, landscapes, figures and local scenes.
MUSEUMS AND GALLERIES:
NÎMES: *Landscapes* (watercolour).

JANIN, Jean
French, 20th century.
Born 1898, in Geneva, to French parents; died 1970.
Painter, designer. Scenes with figures, figures. Stage sets, wall decorations.

Jean Janin trained at the art school in Geneva, then at the Académie Ranson in Paris, and in 1923 began to exhibit in Paris at the main annual salons. In 1929, he and the American William Gwinn founded the *Children's Travelling Theatre*. He did a great deal of decorative work and produced screens, lacquer panels and mosaics for Poissy town hall. He belonged, like Pierre Ino and Lucien Coutaud, to a second generation of Surrealist painters. He did not pay much attention to previous Surrealist trends such as automatic writing, the release of the unconscious or the use of dreams; he kept only the unfamiliar imagery. Later his painting developed into a more Expressionist style.

Museums and Galleries:
Chicago - Cincinnati - Los Angeles - Paris (MNAM-CCI).

Auction records:
Paris, 3 July 1981, *Les Travestis* (1927, oil on canvas, 54 1/4 x 38 1/4 ins / 138 x 97 cm) FRF 16,000. Paris, 10 June 1987, *Underwater City* (oil on canvas, 51 1/2 x 76 3/4 ins / 131 x 195 cm) FRF 37,500. Paris, 12 Feb 1989, *Hunters' Halt* (1927, oil on canvas, 31 1/2 x 33 3/4 ins / 80 x 86 cm) FRF 11,000. New York, 12 June 1991, *Les Travestis* (1927, oil on canvas, 54 1/4 x 38 1/4 ins / 138 x 97 cm) USD 1,980. Paris, 20 May 1992, *Les Travestis* (1927, oil on canvas, 54 1/4 x 38 1/4 ins / 138 x 97 cm) FRF 6,000. Paris, 27 May 1994, *Flowers in a Park* (oil on canvas, 15 x 18 ins / 38 x 46 cm) FRF 5,000. Paris, 25 Nov 1999, *Hunters' Rest* (1927, oil on canvas, 31 x 34 ins / 80 x 86 cm) FRF 15,000.

JANIN, Louise

American, 20th century.
Born in Durham (New Hampshire); died 1997, in France.
From 1924 also active in France.
Painter.
Symbolism, Musicalism (the attempt to interpret music in painting).
Les Artistes Musicalistes.

Louise Janin spent the early part of her life in San Francisco surrounded by the rich collection of Chinese art put together by her father. A long trip through Asia also played a part in determining the future direction of her work. She then moved to New York, and in 1924 went to Paris. Her earliest pictures are variations on themes from Hinduism, Taoism and Buddhism. During her New York period, her works, for instance *The Virgin of the Bamboo Forest*, are full of symbolism that is often esoteric. When she arrived in France, she exhibited the *Virgin of the Bamboo Forest* in her 1924 solo show, which also featured the *Dragon above Kwen Lun*, which was acquired by the former Musée du Luxembourg. During the years 1925-1932, probably while she was still in Paris, her work was influenced by her research into decorative art from diverse sources - the Near, Middle and Far East, Mayas, Celts, Guinea and Oceania. At the same time, the profuse ornamentation in the paintings of Gustav Klimt seems to have led her towards relative, then total, abstraction. This was not a current trend at the time, and in her case, it is proof of her aesthetic and ethnological curiosity. In 1926, she became acquainted with Franz Kupka and Henri Valensi, and when the latter founded the Association des Artistes Musicalistes (Association of Musicalist Artists) in 1932, Louise Janin played and active role, taking part in the Salons Musicalistes, while continuing to feature in some other exhibitions. Her work gradually evolved from very transposed figuration to almost total abstraction, though an interpretation of vegetable motifs can be seen in the carefully coloured whorls and spirals that recur so frequently in her paintings. Immediately after the war, she took part in the Salon des Réalités Nouvelles when it was founded as an association for the purpose of showing international abstract art. In 1950, she began experimenting with a more automatist technique and the possibilities of osmosis in her series *Cosmogrammes*. In this fantastical representation of the universe and a more 'classic' version of abstraction, she was one of the first, in around 1945, to become interested in the extraterrestrial world and to choose cosmic, interplanetary subjects.

Janin had her first solo exhibition in New York in 1921. In 1924, she went to France, where she took part in the major annual Paris Salons - Artistes Français, Indépendants, Automne and Tuileries. As soon as she arrived, she also had a solo show at the Galerie Bernheim-Jeune, with a catalogue preface written by Édouard Schuré, the chronicler of Esotericism. In 1925, she took part in five sections of the International Exhibition of Decorative Arts, with works using many different techniques, most notably a design for a tapestry entitled *L'Après-midi d'un Faune* (*The Afternoon of a Faun*). In 1926, her painting *Mandara* was bought for the lecture hall of the Theosophical Society of France. In 1927, she painted panels for the Grands Magasins du Louvre, which were shown at the Exhibition of Decorative Arts in Madrid. In 1928, the Galerie Georges Petit showed an important collection of her works. At the 1931 Colonial Exhibition in Paris, a group of her paintings featured in the Hindustan pavilion. She spent the years of 1938-1945 in Corsica. After World War II, she exhibited at the Salon des Réalités Nouvelles from 1946 to 1954, then returned to the Salon des Artistes Indépendants.

Auction records:
Paris, 14 June 1978, *Underwater Fantasy* (oil on canvas, 51 1/4 x 76 3/4 ins / 130 x 195 cm) FRF 19,500. Paris, 22 Nov 1989, *Linking* (oil on canvas remounted/panel, 39 1/4 x 39 1/4 ins / 100 x 100 cm) FRF 65,000; *Musicalist Composition* (oil on panel, 31 x 23 1/2 ins / 79 x 60 cm) FRF 32,000; *Solo in three Movements* (oil on panel, 42 1/4 x 20 ins / 107 x 51 cm) FRF 32,000; *Modulations on the Sign of Grace* (oil on panel, 22 x 18 ins / 55 x 46 cm) FRF 42,000; *Isabella of Castille* (1949, oil on card, 48 x 36 1/2 ins / 121 x 93 cm) FRF 120,000. Paris, 23 April 1993, *Living* (oil on card, 16 x 12 3/4 ins / 40.8 x 32.5 cm) FRF 7,000.

JANIN, Louise Sophie Jeanne

Maiden name: Delarue
Swiss, 19th century.
Born 28 December 1781, in Geneva; died 18 May 1842, in Plainpalais, Geneva.
Miniaturist.

In 1821, Janin exhibited her works in Zurich. In 1826, she featured in an exhibition at the Musée Rath in Geneva. A portrait of a woman by her was included in an exhibition of miniatures by Friedmann & Weber in Berlin in 1906.

JANIN-PELTIER, Suzanne

French, 20th century.
Painter (gouache), watercolourist, designer.
Landscapes with figures.

Suzanne Janin-Peltier, wife of Jean Peltier, painted landscapes in Brittany, Provence and Savoy, as well as views and picturesque village scenes. She also created fabrics for the fashion industry. She exhibited in Paris at the Salon des Artistes Français, Salon de la Société Nationale des Beaux-Arts, Salon d'Automne, Salon des Indépendants and Salon des Artistes Décorateurs. In 1954 she had a solo exhibition of gouaches and small watercolours.

JANINET, Jean François

French, 18th - 19th century.
Born 1752, in Paris; died 1 November 1814, in Paris.
Engraver (mezzotint, aquatint), reproductions engraver, illustrator. Mythological subjects, genre scenes, portraits, landscapes, animals.

Jean-François Janinet, the son of an engraver of semi-precious stones who lived in the Rue St-Germain, near the Grenier à Sel, probably started to study drawing with his father.

He then became a pupil of Bachelier, and entered the École de l'Académie Royale in March 1772, as a student of painting. The Académie's registers mention his change of domicile to the house of the Abbé Lucas in September 1773. He therefore trained himself to be an engraver, without outside assistance. He married Marie-Madeleine-Françoise Poumentin and had one daughter, who became a painter and engraver, and probably had to help her father in his work. Janinet always felt himself attracted to science, and became a physicist; on his death certificate he is described as an engraver and chemist. In 1784, ballooning was very much in fashion. Janinet became sufficiently seriously involved to construct, assisted by Abbé Miollan, a lighter-than-air craft exceeding the dimensions of what had been achieved at that time. J.G. Wille recounts in his memoirs the sad outcome of this attempt. The 110 foot high balloon, inflated with 'inflammable air', was due to depart from the Palais du Luxembourg on 11 July 1784, to where it had been transported the previous day. It was to have carried Janinet, Abbé Miollan, the Marquis d'Arlande and a fireman, but the balloon caught fire as it was being inflated. Miollan and Janinet fled, protected by guards, because the spectators, who had paid three *livres*, tore down the barriers and threw them on the fire, which burnt for 24 hours. Janinet was for a time the laughing stock of Paris, cruelly ridiculed by songs and caricatures. He died at 5, Rue Poliveau.

The *Portrait of Marie-Antoinette*, dating from 1774, shows Janinet, at barely 22, in full possession of his art. The variety in his uses of colour shows an enquiring mind. Baron Portalis and H. Béraldi place at the start of his career the pieces after Philippe Caresme: *The Shepherd Crowned, The Shepherdess Crowned, The Drunken Bacchante, The Impatient Satyr* and *Unconditional Worship*; and after Louis Doublet: *The Kiss of Love* and *The Kiss of Friendship*. These engravings, or at least the first, are said to have appeared shortly after September 1773. Janinet's success seems to have been considerable, because his reproductions after the most fashionable masters multiplied. He showed the same skill in his landscapes after Hubert Robert, notably in: *Ruins of the Palace of Pope Jules II* (1775), *Villa Madama, Villa Sachetta* and *Column and Garden of the Medici Palace*. In 1777, he engraved after H. Fragonard: *Love - Madness*. Mention should also be made of the following: after the well-known miniaturist Charlier: *Ariadne Asleep, Venus Thinking* and *Venus Disarming Love*; after Charles Eisen the Younger: *Tarquin and Lucretia*; after Baudouin: *The Pleasant One Neglected*; after Freudeberg: *Childish Fear* and *Childish Confidence*; after St-Quentin: *The Aimiable Peasant Woman*; after Antoine Watteau: *The Actors* and *The Comic Meeting*; after P.A. Wille the Younger: *The Village Wedding* and *The Reapers' Meal*; after Jean Houel: *Landscape with Figures*; after Bouchardon: *Galatea on the Waters*; after Greuze, four plates: *Heads of Men, Women and Children*; after Clerisseau: *Remains of an Ancient Temple near Pozzuoli*; after de Machy: *Two Views of Paris*; and after Wolff: *The Staubbach Falls in the Lauterbrunnen Valley*. He also engraved portraits: *Mlle Duthé*, after Lemoine; *Mlle Bertin*, Marie-Antoinette's milliner, considered one of his masterpieces; *Henri IV*; *The Duc de Sully*, after Pourbus; and *Loménie de Brienne*.The enlightened amateur collector Basan was impressed by the remarkable results obtained by Janinet, and commissioned him to reproduce several watercolours by Adrina Van Ostade to decorate his private rooms in the Rue Serpente: *The Dutch Tobacconist's* (1778); *The Rustic Hut*; *The Flemish Cottage* and *The Dutch Fair* (1779). Janinet executed them using a raised etched line and flat tints to give the appearance of watercolours. He engraved for the same publisher: *Remains of a Temple in Greece*, after Pannini. The Le Campion brothers, engravers and print dealers, had him execute, in collaboration with Guyot, Mlle Guyot, Capuy and themselves, the series of small round views of the monuments of Paris, after the drawings by Durand: *Ste-Geneviève*, interior and exterior; *Notre-Dame*, interior and exterior; *St-Eustache*; *St-Sulpice*; *The Place Dauphine*; *Le Collège des Quatre Nations*; *Le Théâtre de l'Ambigu-Comique*; *The Halle au Blé (Corn Market)*; *Le Palais de Justice (Law Courts)*; *The Houses of M. de Marigny, M. Demonville, M. Rousseau, M. de Ste-Foix* and *M. de Sinety*. In 1781, Janinet executed an engraving on the occasion of the birth of the king's eldest son, the Dauphin, with the title: *Sentiments of the Nation*, after J.-B. Huet, depicting Marie-Antoinette seated in front of Louis XVI and holding the Dauphin in her arms. *The Three Graces*, after Pellegrini, and *The Toilette of Venus*, after F. Boucher, appeared during the same period (1783). Janinet had found in Nicolas Lavreince a gouachist capable of giving to the colour print all its delicacy. *The Comparison* (1786); *The Difficult Confession* (1787); *Oh! Let Me Have a Look*; *The Little Piece of Advice*; *Oh! What a Pretty Little Dog*; *The Discreet Pupil*; *Poor Pussy, How I Feel for You* and *Indiscretion* were successful pieces. Levachez and Charnois, when founding the weekly publication *Costumes and Annals of the Great Theatres of Paris*, entrusted the illustrations to Janinet. Examples of these illustrations that are especially worth mentioning are: *Mme Dugazon, in Nina or Maddened by Love*, after Hoin; *Mlle Contat* in the role of Suzanna in the *Marriage of Figaro*, after Duplessi Bertaux; *Mlle Olivier* as Cherubino, in the same play; *Mlle Vestris*, in the role of Gabrielle de Vergy; *Mme St-Huberti*, after Lemoine; *Mme Favart* in the *Three Sultanas*; *Mme Dugazon* in the role of Robert, and a second time as Nina; *Michu*, in the role of Blaise; *Mlle Guimard*, in the *Ballet of the Seafarers*; *The Dancer*; *Gardel the Younger*; *Mlle Colombe the Elder*; *Sophie Arnould*, in *Iphigenia in Aulis*; *Caillot*; *Mlle Raucourt*; *Mlle Dumesnil*; *Lekain*; *Lainez*; *Rousseau*; *Adrienne Lecouvreur*; *Molé*; *Mlle Renaud the Younger*; *Garrick*; *Brizard*; *Préville*, in the role of *La Rissole*; *Benjamin Franklin* (1789); *Janinet*. In 1791, he appeared for the first time at the Salon with *View of the Champ de Mars at the Moment of the Delivery of the Civil Oath* and a *Frieze in the Classical Style* after Moitte. At the Salon in 1793, he also exhibited: *The Catilina Conspiracy* and *The Death of Lucretia*, after Moitte. By the same artist, Janinet also engraved: *The Muses Presented to Minerva*; *Hercules Presented to Jupiter and Juno*; *The Virtue of Lucretia*; *The Last Moments of Demosthenes*; *The Constancy of Coriolanus*. He also engraved after Le Barbier the Elder: *The Creation*; *Adam and Eve*; *The Death of Abel*; *The Death of Cain*; *Fight of the Horaces and the Curiaces*, and after A. Panier: *Liberty, Equality*, two plates, a *Collection of Different Vases*, two sketchbooks of four plates, as well as: *Rose Windows*, two sketchbooks of four plates; a *Seascape* after Alkins, and *Charlotte Corday*.

Janinet was an innovator in colour engraving and he created the process by which Debucourt later became famous. Engraving in mezzotint, inaugurated about 1610 by Prince Rupert, had allowed Leblond of Frankfurt to produce coloured prints using three superimposed plates, engraved with a 'rocker', or scraper, and which, when covered with one of the three primary colours of blue, yellow or red, produced intermediate colours when mixed. It was using this method that Jacques-Christophe Leblond produced, about 1719, the *Portrait of Prince Eugène*. After a period in London, where Janinet executed different interesting pieces in colour, and published a book in 1730 entitled *Il Coloristo or Harmony of Colour through Printing, Reduced to Mechanical Processes, according to Simple Precepts and Infallible Rules*, printed in English and French, he moved to Paris, where he published a *Portrait of Louis XV*.

Janinet had as a pupil Gautier Dagoty, who, after the death of his master, claimed to be the inventor of the printing process with four plates, the first in black, giving the drawing and shadows (See *Letter on the New Art of Printing Paintings in Four Colours*, 1749), a process of which Leblond had claimed paternity before his death (1741). François de Nancy, in 1756, devised *engraving in the style of pencil drawing*, which is done using the roulette. Demarteau brought this process to perfection. Bonnet created engraving in the style of a pastel. Jean-Baptiste Le Prince, by his invention of *wash, or aquatint engraving*, in which a layer of sifted resin is baked in an oven, allowing the biting of the acid to be perfectly controlled. It was this process, giving the suppleness to Le Prince's aquatints, which Janinet used in the preparation of his colour plates. He produced his line using acid, added his aquatint grain and superimposed his colours. The first application of the process seems to be a small round piece entitled *The Operator*, bearing this comment: 'Engraved in imitation of wash, in colour, by F. Janinet, the only person to have discovered this technique: at the artist's, Abbé Lucas's house, Rue du Plâtre-St-Jacques'.

Janinet, as a reproductions engraver, could not escape the fashion which, at the time of the Revolution, substituted the Neo-Classicism of the David School for the graciousness of the minor masters of the 18th century. He became the interpreter of Le Barbier and Moitte, the sculptor of the draughtsman Devarenne, after whom he executed *Plan of a Monument to be Erected for the King*.

AUCTION RECORDS:
PARIS, 1896, *Portrait of Marie-Antoinette* (drawing) FRF 1,070. PARIS, 30 March 1925, *Palace in Rome with Figures* (watercolour) FRF 420. LONDON, 28 Nov 1979, *Marie-Antoinette* (1777, etching and aquatint in colour, oval, with gold printed oval border, 16 1/4 x 12 1/2in/41.5 x 31.5cm; 15 1/4 x 11 1/2in/38.8 x 29.5cm) GBP 500. PARIS, 22 Oct 1982, *Marie-Antoinette of Austria* (1777, tinted engraving, after J.-B. A. Gautier Dagoty) FRF 19,000. HEIDELBERG, 22 April 1983, *Offering to Love* (colour-tinted engraving, after Lagrenée, 12 3/4 x 16in/32.4 x 40.9cm) DEM 2,100. PARIS, 22 May 1985, *The Kiss of Friendship; The Kiss of Love* (tinted engraving printed in colour, two pendants) FRF 42,000. PARIS, 2 Dec 1987, *The Toilette of Venus* (print, after Boucher, 19 3/4 x 15 1/4in/50 x 39cm) FRF 42,000. PARIS, 7 July 1992, *Bacchus Presides at the Festival; Unconditional Worship* (coloured engraving, two pendants) FRF 5,000. PARIS, 3 Feb 1993, *The Three Graces* (tinted engraving, 14 x 10 3/4in/35.5 x 27.5cm) FRF 6,000. PARIS, 16 June 1993, *The Comparison* (1786, tooled engraving, colour tinted, 14 1/4 x 11in/36 x 28.2cm) FRF 18,000. PARIS, 21 Dec 1993, *Villa Sacchetti* (1778, colour-tinted engraving) FRF 10,800. PARIS, 17 June 1994, *The Toilette of Venus* (1783, tinted engraving, after Boucher, 14 3/4 x 11 1/2in/37.5 x 29.3cm) FRF 6,200. PARIS, 10 May 1995, *Portrait of Marie-Antoinette* (tooled engraving, stippled in colour, 15 x 11 3/4in/38 x 30cm) FRF 12,000. PARIS, 26 March 1996, *Portrait of Marie-Sophie-Frédérique, Wife of Frederick VI, Queen of Denmark* (tinted engraving) FRF 7,500. PARIS, 29 May 1996, *Ruins of a Greek Temple; Ruins of an Egyptian Palace* (coloured engraving, two pendants) FRF 4,800. PARIS, 27 Nov 1997, *Bacchanale* (colour-printed engraving, after Caresme, 9 1/4 x 12 1/2in/23.8 x 32cm) FRF 3,200. PARIS, 13 March 1998, *Ruins of an Egyptian Palace; Remains of a Temple in Greece* (coloured engraving, 12 1/2 x 10in/31.5 x 24.5cm) FRF 13,200. PARIS, 27 June 2000, *Villa Sacchetti* (engraving, 13 x 18 ins / 34 x 46 cm) FRF 20,000. LONDON, 8 Nov 2001, *Toilette of Venus* (colour etching/engraving, 19 x 15 ins / 49 x 38 cm) GBP 3,400. STOCKHOLM, 25 May 2004, *Toilette of Venus* (1783, colour engraving, 15 x 134 ins / 38 x 340 cm) SEK 62,000.

JANINET, Nicolas
French, 17th century.
Died 1612; buried on 16 October in Paris.
Painter.

JANINET, Sophie, later Mme Giacomelli
French, 19th century.
Born c. 1786, in Paris.
Painter, engraver.
Sophie Janinet, daughter and pupil of Jean-François Janinet, made her debut at the Paris Salon in 1799 with an Indian ink picture entitled: *Death of Lucretia*. In 1800, she exhibited a bronze-style engraving - *Abundance* - after Sauvage, and *Portrait of First Consul Bonaparte*, a wash drawing. She first exhibited at the Paris Salon in 1804 with *View of the New Theatre at Nîmes*, after pictures by the architect, Meunier. Then, under her married name, she exhibited mythological subjects until 1814.

JANISCH, Albert
German, 20th century.
Painter. Figures, sporting subjects.

JANISS, Johann
Austrian, 19th century.
Born 8 May 1808; died 15 February 1851, in Bad Aussee (Styria).
Active in Bad Aussee.
Painter.
Janiss painted mainly landscapes in oils and watercolours.
MUSEUMS AND GALLERIES:
GRAZ (Landesmus. Joanneum): *Self-portrait; Bad Aussee Landscape* (three).

JANISZEWSKI, Martin
Polish, 19th century.
Born 1788, in Warsaw; died 28 April 1823, in Warsaw.
Draughtsman.
Martin Janiszewski studied with Bacciarelli. He was appointed drawing master at the lyceum in Warsaw.

JANIT, Antonio, or Xanit
Spanish, 16th century.
Active in Valladolid.
Sculptor.
Antonio Janit worked with Pompego Lioni, the sculptor to the Escorial court.

JANK, Angelo, or Janck
German, 19th - 20th century.
Born 30 October 1868, in Munich; died 9 October 1940, in Munich, in 1956 according to some sources.
Painter, draughtsman, illustrator. Military subjects, horse racing scenes, animals.
Die Scholle group.
Angelo Jank studied under Ludwig von Loefftz and Paul Höcker at the college of fine arts in Munich. He joined the Scholle group in 1895 and exhibited alongside the Secession Group artists in 1898. He also exhibited at the Salon des Artistes Français at the Exposition Universelle of 1900, where he received an honourable mention. Jank secured further medals in Munich in 1901 and 1905. From 1899 to 1907, he taught at the Munich-based academy of women art teachers, then at the fine arts academy, also in Munich.

As an illustrator, Jank contributed to the periodicals *Jugend* ('Youth') and *Simplicissimus* in 1896. From 1910 he illustrated works on military subjects. He specialised in painting horses and racing or hunting scenes.

BIBLIOGRAPHY:
Osterwalder, Marcus (ed.), *Dictionnaire des illustrateurs 1800-1914*, Ides et Calendes, Neuchâtel, 1989.
MUSEUMS AND GALLERIES:
ELBERFELD: *Obstacle Race* - GENEVA (MAH): a drawing - GOTHA: *In the Rain* - HANOVER (Kestner-Mus.): *Horsewoman* - MUNICH (Army Mus.): designs for uniforms - MUNICH (Neue Pinakothek): *Reburial of F. von Uhde* - MUNICH (Stadtmus.): *In the Pack; View Halloo!* - OPAVA: *Nostalgia* - VENICE (Mus. d'Arte Moderna): *Iron Army*.

AUCTION RECORDS:
MUNICH, 24 Nov 1978, *Foxhunt* (oil on canvas, 27 1/4 x 35 1/4 ins / 69 x 89.5 cm) DEM 4,000. COLOGNE, 21 March 1980, *Patrol* (1913, oil on canvas, 22 x 19 3/4 ins / 55 x 50 cm) DEM 2,400. STUTTGART, 6 March 1981, *Clearing an Obstacle* (oil on canvas, 27 1/2 x 35 1/2 ins / 70 x 90 cm) DEM 4,000. NEW YORK, 10 June 1983, *Horse Race* (oil on canvas, 16 3/4 x 24 1/2 ins / 42.6 x 62.2 cm) USD 4,200. LONDON, 27 Nov 1985, *Horse Race* (oil on canvas, 19 3/4 x 27 1/2 ins / 50 x 70 cm) GBP 2,800. BERN, 30 April 1988, *Jockey on a White Horse Clearing a Hurdle* (1917, oil on canvas, 38 1/2 x 47 1/4 ins / 98 x 120 cm) CHF 2,000. AMSTERDAM, 2 May 1990, *Horse Race* (oil on canvas, 27 3/4 x 36 ins / 70.5 x 90.5 cm) NLG 6,900. AMSTERDAM, 18 Feb 1992, *Hunting Party* (oil on canvas, 22 x 29 1/2 ins / 55 x 75 cm) NLG 4,370. KEMPTEN, 8 April 1999, *Hussar on Horseback* (oil on canvas, 22 x 15 ins / 56 x 38 cm) DEM 4,000. AHLDEN, 17 Sept 1999, *At the Water Hurdle* (oil on canvas, 28 x 35 ins / 70 x 90 cm) DEM 3,500. MUNICH, 29 June 2000, *Horseman of the Ulans* (1912, oil on canvas, 28 x 28 ins / 70 x 70 cm) DEM 3,800. KÖNIGSTEIN, 25 Nov 2000, *Party of Horsewomen and Men* (1910, oil on canvas, 29 x 27 ins / 73 x 68 cm) DEM 7,000. MUNICH, 2 July 2003, *Horse Racing* (oil on canvas, 16 x 19 ins / 41 x 47 cm) EUR 3,300. MUNICH, 3 Dec 2003, *Woman Riding a Horse in the Hall at a Riding School* (oil on canvas, 20 x 12 ins / 50 x 30 cm) EUR 2,600. MUNICH, 4 Feb 2004, *Woman on a Horse Jumping a Fence* (oil on canvas, 29 x 23 ins / 73 x 58 cm) EUR 1,800. WARSAW, 20 June 2004, *Horse Race* (1930, oil on canvas, 22 x 30 ins / 55 x 76 cm) PLN 9,000.

JANK, Christian
German, 19th century.
Born 15 July 1833, in Munich; died 25 November 1888, in Munich.
Painter, watercolourist, engraver. Landscapes, architectural views.

A pupil of Emil Kirchner in Munich, Jank was a painter at the court theatre there. He exhibited in Munich in 1858. A noted work was *Burgos Cathedral*.

AUCTION RECORDS:
VIENNA, 18 Sept 1973, *View of a Town*, ATS 45,000. ZURICH, 16 May 1980, *Portrait of Bourges Cathedral* (1863, oil on canvas, 26 x 19 1/2 ins / 66 x 49.5 cm) CHF 3,000. LONDON, 25 June 1981, *Pompeii-Style Drawing Room* (1883, gouache and ink, 11 3/4 x 18 1/4 ins / 30 x 46.5 cm) GBP 4,400. ZURICH, 18 March 2002, *Lively Street in Rouen with Cathedral* (oil on canvas, 33 x 28 ins / 85 x 70 cm) CHF 9,500.

JANKES, Karl Emil
Finnish, 20th century.
Born 16 March 1884, in Helsinki.
Painter, watercolourist. Portraits.

Karl Jankes studied at the fine arts society in Helsinki and then spent several years completing his studies in Paris. He exhibited at the 1911 and 1912 Salon des Artistes Indépendants and went on to show his work in Helsinki from 1912 to 1922.

JANKO
French, 20th century.
Painter. Figures, seascapes, still-lifes.

Janko uses traditional subjects which suggest absence or the beauty of the world, and treats them in a stylised, strongly coloured and to some extent eclectic manner. He first exhibited at the Galerie Vendôme in 1999.

JANKÓ, Elemér
Hungarian, 19th century.
Born 1872, in Budapest; died 27 February 1892, in Munich.
Painter, caricaturist.

Elemér Jankó, son of Janos Jankó, studied first with his father, and then in Munich. There he drew a large number of sketches and caricatures for the *Fliegende Blätter*. Cartoons from his estate were published in Budapest in 1895.

JANKÓ, Janos
Hungarian, 19th century.
Born 1 November 1833; died 29 March 1896, in Budapest.
Active in Budapest.
Painter. Genre scenes.

MUSEUMS AND GALLERIES:
BUDAPEST (Szépmuvészeti Múz.): *Tragedy at the Wedding*.

JANKOVIC, Jozef
Czechoslovak, 20th century.
Born November 1937, in Bratislava.
Sculptor of assemblages.
Conceptual Art.

Jozef Jankovic was a student at the school of fine art in Bratislava from 1956 to 1962.

From 1964, Jankovic has concentrated on disturbing representations of the torture and massacres that have taken place in so many parts of the modern world. Using a technique often similar to the multiple images of Arman and borrowing elements from reality in the style of Pierre Restany and the 'New Realists', he assembles mangled and torn body parts, arms, legs, hands, sometimes parcelled up into sinister packages or strapped to a bed or a chair.

Since 1961, he has exhibited work in many collective exhibitions in Czechoslovakia, Hungary, Poland, Italy (particularly at the 1995 Venice Biennale) and France. Solo exhibitions include: Bratislava (1965), Brno (1966), Budapest (1966), Vienna (1967), Prague (1968), Bratislava (1968); Düsseldorf and Cologne (1969).

JANKOVICH, Theodor
Yugoslav, 20th century.
Born in Karlovel.
Painter.

Theodor Jankovich exhibited in Paris from 1926.

JANKOVICS VON JESZENICZE, Vincenz
Hungarian, 19th century.
Born 1820, in Hungary; died 1880, in Besançon, France.
Painter.

Vincenz Jankovics von Jeszenicze arrived in France in 1838. He painted landscapes around Paris and Versailles, and in the regions of Jura and Doubs, as well as the Pyrenées, Algeria, Italy and Hungary. He also painted still-lifes, which he exhibited in Budapest in 1840 and Besançon in 1862 and 1872. One of his paintings, *Route de Consolation, Doubs*, can be seen in the castle of Deschaux.

JANKOVITS, Gyula
Hungarian, 19th - 20th century.
Born 1865, in Budapest.
Sculptor. Historical subjects, religious subjects, mythological subjects, genre scenes. Monuments, groups.

A student at the school of arts and crafts in Budapest, Gyula Jankovits then trained in Munich and at the Vienna academy of fine art where he stayed for six years.

While in Munich, he carved statues of the *Virgin* and *Penitent Magdalene* for which he was awarded the Franz-Joseph Prize in 1888. In Vienna, he received several awards for his works including *Amazons in Battle*, *Goose Thief* and *Flood* as well as the Court Prize for a relief depicting *Jacob and Joseph*. He executed many commemorative monuments in Budapest.

JANKOWITZ, Marie Lucie de, or Iankovitz
French, 19th century.
Born 24 April 1778, in St Petersburg; died 1 January 1866, in Paris.
Lithographer.

Marie Lucie de Jankowitz was the daughter of the painter E Falconnet and was brought up in Paris. She is credited with a lithograph of the monument to Peter the Great in St Petersburg, the work of her grandfather, Étienne Falconnet, and a portrait of her mother, Marie Anne Collet, after a picture by her father.

AUCTION RECORDS:

BERN, 2 May 1986, *Village in Normandy* (oil on canvas, 17 x 24 3/4 ins / 43 x 63 cm) CHF 5,500.

JANKOWSKI, J. Wilhem or Friedrich Wilhelm

Polish, 19th century.
Born 1825; died 1870.
Painter. Landscapes, urban landscapes, seascapes.

AUCTION RECORDS:

VIENNA, 15 May 1979, *View of Bad Ischl* (oil on canvas, 22 x 26 3/4 ins / 55 x 68 cm) ATS 15,000. VIENNA, 17 March 1982, *View of Gmunden* (c. 1860, oil on canvas, 12 1/2 x 15 1/2 ins / 31.5 x 39.5 cm) ATS 50,000. LUCERNE, 19 May 1983, *View of Lucerne* (oil on canvas, 19 x 36 1/2 ins / 48 x 92.5 cm) CHF 11,000. PARIS, 16 June 1987, *View of La Salute* (oil on canvas, oval, 20 1/4 x 16 1/2 ins / 51.5 x 42 cm) FRF 28,000. PARIS, 17 Feb 1988, *Seascape* (oil on card, 12 1/2 x 16 1/4 ins / 32 x 41 cm) FRF 3,000. PARIS, 18 Dec 1991, *View of La Salute* (oil on canvas, oval, 20 1/4 x 16 1/2 ins / 51.5 x 42 cm) FRF 30,000. PARIS, 2 Dec 1994, *View of a Canal in a Dutch Town* (oil on canvas, 18 1/2 x 37 1/2 ins / 47 x 95 cm) FRF 15,500. LONDON, 22 Feb 1995, *View of the Rhine* (oil on canvas, 20 3/4 x 26 ins / 53 x 66 cm) GBP 805. NEW YORK, 20 July 1995, *Venice* (oil on canvas, 20 3/4 x 16 1/2 ins / 52.7 x 41.9 cm) USD 3,335. PARIS, 21 Jan 1998, *Bringing in the Nets* (1909, oil on canvas, 79 1/2 x 39 1/4 ins / 202 x 100 cm) FRF 30,000. LONDON, 18 March 1999, *Venetian Capriccio. Roman Capriccio* (oil on panel, a pair, 11x19 ins / 27x48 cm) GBP 2,200. DUBLIN, 31 May 1999, *Bird's Eye View of Venice with Doge's Palace and Piazza S Marco* (1871, oil on canvas, 33x51 ins / 84x130 cm) IEP 5,500. ROTTERDAM, 9 May 2000, *View of Venice* (oil on canvas, 18x36 ins / 46x91 cm) NLG 11,000. LUCERNE, 8 Nov 2000, *View of Lucerne* (oil on canvas, 27x41 ins / 68x105 cm) CHF 4,000. VIENNA, 13 June 2001, *View of Melk* (oil on canvas, 17x21 ins / 42x53 cm) ATS 32,000. PARIS, 23 Nov 2001, *Town by River* (oil on canvas, 19x36 ins / 47x92 cm) FFR 38,000. LONDON, 25 April 2002, *Venetian Capriccio* (oil on canvas, 27x25 ins / 68x63 cm) GBP 550. ERLANGEN, 12 July 2003, *Old City of Lucerne* (oil on canvas, a pair, 42x53 ins / 107x135 cm) EUR 3,400. AHLDEN, 19 Sept 2003, *Venice* (oil on canvas, 19x37 ins / 48x93 cm) EUR 4,000. LONDON, 6 July 2004, *Doge's Palace, Venice, the Grand Canal Beyond* (oil on canvas, 18x35 ins / 46x90 cm) GBP 1,800.

JANLET, Henry

Belgian, 19th - 20th century.
Born November 1857, in Brussels; died 1935, in Ukkel.
Painter. Landscapes.

Henry Janlet was a pupil of Joseph van Severdonck at the Académie Royale des Beaux Arts in Brussels and subsequently of Artan de St-Martin and Franz Courtens. He worked predominantly in Flanders and exhibited on a regular basis in Brussels, Ghent and Antwerp.

AUCTION RECORDS:

PARIS, 29 Nov 1992, *Windmills* (oil on panel, 10 x 14 1/4 ins / 24.5 x 36 cm) FRF 3,800.

JANMOT, Anne François Louis, called Jean-Louis or Louis

French, 19th century.
Born 21 May 1814, in Lyons; died 1 June 1892 or 1894, in Lyons.
Painter, fresco artist, draughtsman. Religious subjects, portraits. Murals.
Lyons School (French Nazarenes).

A fellow student of F Ozanam at Lyons' Collège Royal, Jean-Louis Janmot began at the College of Fine Arts, working in Bonnefond's studio and won the Golden Laurel in 1832 with his *Self-portrait*. He then moved to Paris and worked under Ingres and, in 1834, Orsel. In 1835-36, he rejoined Ingres and Flandrin in Rome.

Upon his return to Lyons, he had some success with: *Raising the Son of the Widow of Naim* (1839), *Christ in the Tomb* (1840, church of Pugetville), and *Christ in the Olive Grove* (1840). He then painted an *Assumption* (1844) and portraits of Blanc-St-Bonnet and Laprade, which feature with his group of wise men from Lyons on the fresco at the Antiquaille Hospice (1846). His *Wild Flower*, which earned him a third class medal at the 1845 Paris Salon. This also drew the attention of Baudelaire's, but the latter thought little of his *Christ Carrying His Cross* in 1846.

Janmot returned from a stay in Chalais with two portraits of Lacordaire (1846, le Saulchoir-Etiolles). An abrupt change of style, in terms of smoothness, is then apparent in 1850, with his *Triptych of St John* (Lyons Cathedral). The same style pervades numerous studies for his *Poem of the Soul*, which was only finished in 1854, and which is made up of 18 paintings telling the story of the Soul and his companion. A booklet of verse accompanies the paintings without describing them: a succession of mysticism and strange poetry, which was described well by the writer and art critic Théophile Gautier, but which achieved no success at the 1855 Exposition Universelle despite the opinion of Delacroix. In Lyons, Janmot decorated three important edifices: the church of St Polycarpe (*The Last Supper*, 1856, destroyed around 1960), the church of St François-des-Sales (Dome, wax painting) and the Town Hall (Ceiling of the Emperor's Salon, which dates from improvements to the city under Vaïsse, 1861).

Janmot then settled in Paris, where the architect Victor Baltard commissioned him to paint a picture of St Augustine, but the commission was then withdrawn in favour of Bouguereau and Janmot was relegated to a gloomy chapel of St Étienne-du-Mont (*Life of St Etienne*, 1866). This failure redoubled the artist's natural pessimism, which had been apparent in the drawings and verse of the second part of the *Poem of the Soul*, in a way slightly reminiscent of his friend Chenavard. He created a fine fresco on the subject of the family in his house in Bagneux, but it was damaged by the Prussians during the Franco-Prussian war. After 1871, he attracted the interest of Charles Blanc, who commissioned, amongst others, a copy of a Naples fresco (College of Fine Arts, Paris, 1872. His final State-commissioned work was for the chapel of the Franciscans of the Holy Land: a beautiful fresco (1878-79, partly exposed).

Janmot moved to Toulon, where family problems prevented him painting. Apart from his *Rosary* (St Germain-en-Laye, 1880) and *Martyrdom of St Christine* (Solliès-Pont, 1883), all the works towards the end of his life were drawings: *Purgatory* (1885, Thiollier), *End of Time* (1888, destroyed in 1960) and *Final Judgement* (1891, sketch at the Museum of St Étienne), three large, very freely drawn sketches, full of vision and turbulence.

Janmot's body of pictures is enormous and consists of preparatory sketches, which have been signed and dated. Some fine pastel pieces of children still survive. His paintings, imbued with vigour in his youth, have dulled, but there are still some fine portraits, fragments and frescoes of interest. Finally, his literary works (verses from his *Poem of the Soul*, published thanks to Félix Thiollier in 1881, *An Artist's Opinion on Art*, Paris, Lecoffre 1887, plus letters and articles) is a source of knowledge rendered all the more valuable due to Janmot's acquaintances with Ozanam, Lacordaire, Father Captier, Montalembert, Laprade, Delacroix, Rvier, Chenavard, etc...

His *Nightmare,* held at the Museum of Lyons, adds a curious facet to the otherwise conventional personality of Louis Janmot. Spied upon by four identical old men, and clutching a semi-conscious girl while chasing another petrified child on the point of throwing himself into a sheer tunnel at his feet, what could that seemingly mad woman want? The picture's technique is classically italianate, its composition is reminiscent of Paolo Uccello's *Desecration of the Host,* but its theme is evocative, above all, of Füssli, from whom the fainting girl in the long white robe seems to have been directly borrowed. But Janmot was an idealist, a romantic and a Pre-Raphaelite in his own, very personal manner and always in defiance of fashion.

Bibliography:

Baudelaire, Charles, *Salon de 1845,* J. Labitte, Paris, 1845. Thiollier, *L. Janmot et son œuvre,* periodical, 1893. Denis, Maurice, *Théories, 1890-1910. Du symbolisme et de Gauguin vers un nouvel ordre classique,* periodical, Bibliothèque de l'Occident, Paris, 1913. Audin, Mariu/Vial, Eugène, '*Dictionnaire des artistes et ouvriers d'art du Lyonnais*' in vol. I, periodical, Bibliothèque d'Art et d'Archéologie, Paris, 1918-1919. Delacroix, '*22-24 mars et 17 juin 1855*' in *Journal,* periodical, Plon, Paris, 1996. Baudelaire, Charles/Moulinat, Francis (presentation), *Écrits sur l'art,* periodical, Le Livre de poche, Paris, 1999.

Museums and Galleries:

Bagnols-sur-Cèze: drawings - Blois: *St Cecilia* (1869) - Lyons (MBA): *Wild Flowers* (1845); *General Gémeau* (1851); *Ceiling of the Emperor's Salon* (1861); *Nightmare* - Lyons (Mus. des Hospices civils): *Sketch of the Antiquaille Hospice* (1845) - Lyons (Mus. Gadagna): *Blanc-St-Bonnet* (1844) - Paris (Louvre): drawings - Périgueux (Mus. du Périgord): drawings; *Woman's Head* (1860) - St-Étienne: *Assumption* (1844); *Final Judgement* (1891, sketch) - Versailles: *Father Lacordaire* (1878 replica of the 1846 painting).

Auction records:

Paris, 4 Dec 1985, *Study for the Poem of the Soul* (1867, lead pencil heightened with white, 18 x 13 1/2 ins / 45.5 x 34 cm) FRF 8,000. Paris, 20 Jan 1988, *Study for poem of the Soul* (1877, lead pencil drawing heightened with white/beige paper, 9 x 11 3/4 ins / 23 x 30 cm) FRF 2,200. Paris, 31 March 2000, *Cartoon for the Poem of the Soul, Second Cycle* (black crayon/stump, 45 x 56 ins / 114 x 142 cm) FRF 170,000. Toulouse, 3 Oct 2000, *Allegory of Sleep* (1866, oil on canvas, 79 x 55 ins / 200 x 139 cm) FRF 240,000. Lyons, 17 Oct 2004, *Eve* (1866, charcoal/stump, 40 x 26 ins / 102 x 65 cm) EUR 2,400.

JANNECK, Franz Christoph

Austrian, 18th century.
Born 3 October 1703, in Graz; died 13 January 1761, in Vienna.
Painter. Religious subjects, portraits, genre scenes, landscapes, interiors with figures.

A pupil of Mathieu Vangus in Graz, Janneck continued his training in Frankfurt and Vienna. In 1740, he was appointed to the staff of the Akademie der bildenden Künste in Vienna. He was proficient and successful in all genres. His works are generally small-scale, but manifest expert handling.

Museums and Galleries:

Bordeaux: *Interior Scene* - Graz: *Visitation of the Virgin; Holy Family* - Rohrau (Schlossmus., Graf Harrach'sche Familiensammlung): *Bay* - Vienna: *Society Gathering; Landscape with Forest; Wood with Hunters; Gathering.*

Auction records:

Paris, 27 March 1893, *The Minuet,* FRF 780. Paris, 9 May 1898, *People Meeting in a Park* (set of two) FRF 2,250. Paris, 28-29 Nov 1923, *The Celebrations at the Great House; The Music Party* (for both) FRF 9,500. Paris, 24 March 1924, *The Raising of Lazarus,* FRF 2,000. Paris, 12 June 1936, *Diana Resting; Diana and Endymion* (for both) FRF 1,800. London, 17 Feb 1939, *Ladies and Gentlemen,* GBP 52. London, 21 Dec 1953, *Interior Scene,* FRF 44,000. Vienna, 4 Dec 1962, *The Visit to the Mill* (oil/copper) ATS 45,000. Vienna, 23 March 1965, *Merry Company Resting in the Woods,* ATS 140,000. New York, 17 Dec 1969, *Rural Celebrations* (copper, forming sets of two) USD 5,500. London, 24 Nov 1971, *The Sculptor's Studio, the Painter's Studio* (set of two) GBP 6,400. London, 17 Nov 1972, *Soldiers Drinking in a Tavern; Soldiers Playing Cards* (two paintings) Gns 4,500. Vienna, 4 Dec 1973, *Merry Company Dancing in the Park of a Great House,* ATS 700,000. London, 2 Dec 1977, *Elegant Company Feasting in an Interior* (oil/copper, 16 1/2 x 23 1/2 ins / 42 x 59.7 cm) GBP 22,000. New York, 31 May 1979, *The Departure of the Prodigal Son; The Dissolute Life of the Prodigal Son* (oil/copper, a pair, 12 x 17 1/2 ins / 30.5 x 44.5 cm) USD 26,000. New York, 11 June 1981, *Jesus Preaching* (1739, oil/metal, 20 1/2 x 29 1/2 ins / 52 x 75 cm) USD 21,000. Munich, 20 Oct 1983, *Elegant Company Feasting in an Interior* (oil/copper, 16 1/2 x 23 1/2 ins / 42 x 59.7 cm) DEM 60,000. London, 11 Dec 1985, *Portrait of M. Mathieu Chandelle of Bischoffsheim* (1729, oil on canvas, 32 1/2 x 26 3/4 ins / 82.5 x 68 cm) GBP 4,000. London, 10 April 1987, *Jesus Feeding the Five Thousand* (1739, oil/copper, 21 x 29 1/2 ins / 53.5 x 75 cm) GBP 26,000. London, 3 July 1991, *Celebrations in a Palace* (1752, oil/copper, a pair, each 25 3/4 x 32 1/4 ins / 65.5 x 82 cm) GBP 82,500. London, 13 Dec 1991, *Bacchus and Ariadne on Naxos; King Oeneus Rendering Allegiance to Bacchus* (oil/copper, 16 x 19 1/2 ins / 40.6 x 49.5 cm) GBP 33,000. London, 7 July 1993, *Trio of Musicians in an Elegant Baroque Interior* (oil/copper, 10 3/4 x 8 1/2 ins / 27.5 x 21.7 cm) GBP 14,950. London, 20 April 1994, *The Miracle of the Loaves* (1739, oil/copper, 21 1/4 x 29 3/4 ins / 53.8 x 75.4 cm) GBP 43,300. London, 5 July 1996, *Bacchanal* (oil/copper, 22 1/4 x 31 1/4 ins / 56.5 x 79.2 cm) GBP 38,000. London, 11 Dec 1996, *Assumption of the Virgin* (1748, oil on canvas, 42 x 49 ins / 106.6 x 123.6 cm) GBP 13,800. London, 13 Dec 1996, *Allegories of Love in Wooded Landscapes* (oil on panel, 9 1/2 x 13 ins / 24.3 x 33 cm) GBP 38,900. London, 30 Oct 1997, *Venus and Adonis; Diana Resting with Her Nymphs* (oil on panel, a pair, each 10 1/4 x 14 ins / 26 x 35.8 cm) GBP 17,250. London, 3 Dec 1997, *Elegant Assembly Feasting in a Wood* (oil/copper, 21 1/2 x 31 ins / 54.6 x 78.7 cm) GBP 89,500. New York, 25 May 1999, *Nativity* (1741, oil on copper, 26 x 20 ins / 66 x 51 cm) USD 150,000. Vienna, 6 Oct 1999, *Mountain Village with Mill and Figures* (oil on copper, 14 x 20 ins / 35 x 51 cm) ATS 1,200,000. New York, 25 May 2000, *Mary Magdalene Washing the Feet of Christ* (oil on copper, 14 x 19 ins / 36 x 47 cm) USD 50,000. London, 7 July 2000, *Italianate River Landscape with Figures by a Ruin* (1759, oil on canvas, 41 x 59 ins / 103 x 150 cm) GBP 25,000. Vienna, 22 March 2001, *Extensive River Landscape with Ruins and Many Figures* (1759, oil on canvas, 41 x 60 ins / 103 x 152 cm) ATS 1,000,000. London, 11 July 2001, *Village Market in an Extensive Mountain Landscape. Kermesse in an Extensive River Landscape* (1729, oil on copper, a pair, 11 x 13 ins / 27 x 33 cm) GBP 60,000. Vienna, 5 June 2002, *Mountainous Wooded Landscape with Resting Figures* (oil on canvas, 20 x 27 ins / 51 x 68 cm) EUR 7,000. Zurich, 3 Oct 2002, *Festivities in the Castle* (oil on copper, 13 x 17 ins / 34 x 42 cm) CHF 41,000. Cologne, 15 Nov 2003, *Old Testament Scenes* (oil on copper, a pair, 5 x 7 ins / 13 x 19 cm) EUR 19,000. London, 22 April 2004, *Elegant Company with Musicians* (oil on copper, 16 x 23 ins / 40 x 58 cm) GBP 230,000. Paris, 25 June 2004, *Departure of the Prodigal Son. Prodigal Son in the Girls' House* (oil on panel, a pair, 15 x 21 ins / 39 x 54 cm) EUR 58,000.

JANNEL

Dutch, 20th century.
Born 23 January 1943.
Painter, potter.

Jannel studied at the Academie Beeldende Kunsten in Maastricht, the Nationaal Hoger Instituut voor Schone Kunsten in Antwerp and the Institute of Art for Ceramics in Faenza. He has won prizes, notably a gold medal at the 28th International Competition for Ceramic Arts in Faenza. His ceramics, in particular, were influenced by a visit to Japan. He lives and works in Maastricht. He has taken part in group exhibitions in Holland, Belgium, the Czechoslovakia, Italy, France, Germany, the USA, Japan and England, and in the exhibition *Maastricht Artists Now* at the Ostend Museum in 1991.

JANNEL, Jean
French, 20th century.
Born 20 April 1894, in Paris.
Painter. Portraits.

Jean Jannel was a pupil of Luc-Olivier Merson. He exhibited in Paris at the Salon des Artistes Français and Salon des Indépendants.

JANNELLA, Ottaviano, or Janella
Italian, 17th century.
Born 23 December 1635, in Ascoli Piceno; died 10 December 1661, in Ascoli Piceno.
Sculptor (wood), painter. Religious subjects. Miniatures.

Jannella's works notably include small carvings the size of a nut, depicting biblical scenes, hunting scenes and battle scenes. A miniature painting by this artist, depicting a *Descent from the Cross*, in the style of Tintoretto, is also worthy of a mention.

JANNELLI, Filippo
Sicilian School, 17th century.
Active in Castroreale (Messina).
Painter.

An altarpiece in the church of Castroreale, depicting *St Cosmas and St Damian*, is attributed to Jannelli, as is an *Immaculate Conception of Mary*, 1676, in the cathedral of S Lucia del Mela.

JANNEMANS
Dutch, 18th century.
Sculptor (wood).

In 1702, Jannemans executed elaborate carvings for the organ chest of the new church in The Hague.

JANNERET
French, 18th century.
Draughtsman, designer of ornamental architectural features.

Janneret is known to have executed the *New Collection of Arabesques*, by La Vallée Poussin, engraved by Guyot.

JANNI. See **GIOVANNI**

JANNI, Guglielmo
Italian, 19th - 20th century.
Born 1872, in Rome; died 1958, in Rome.
Painter. Figures.

AUCTION RECORDS:
ROME, 20 May 1986, *Training* (oil on panel, 29 1/2 x 25 1/2 ins / 75 x 65 cm) ITL 22,000,000. ROME, 7 April 1988, *Figure* (1930, oil on canvas, study of a David, 63 1/2 x 24 1/2 ins / 161 x 62.5 cm) ITL 27,000,000. ROME, 15 Nov 1988, *Daniel or the Young Prophet* (1937, oil on panel, 24 1/2 x 16 1/4 ins / 62 x 41 cm) ITL 14,000,000. ROME, 21 March 1989, *Fever* (1933, oil/plywood, 14 1/2 x 9 ins / 37 x 22 cm) ITL 11,000,000. ROME, 28 Nov 1989, *Head of a Boxer* (1936, oil on panel, 12 1/4 x 7 3/4 ins / 31 x 20 cm) ITL 13,000,000. ROME, 9 April 1991, *Head of a Man* (1937, oil on panel, 14 3/4 x 8 1/4 ins / 37.5 x 21 cm) ITL 11,000,000. ROME, 28 March 1995, *Woman in Grey* (1933, oil on canvas, 61 x 28 3/4 ins / 155 x 73 cm) ITL 27,600,000. ROME, 27 April 1999, *Self-portrait* (1933, oil on canvas/panel, 23 x 19 ins / 58 x 47 cm) ITL 12,000,000. ROME, 25 Nov 1999, *Sleeping Youth* (1936, oil on canvas/panel, 15 x 36 ins / 37 x 92 cm) ITL 28,500,000. ROME, 18 April 2000, *Athlete* (oil on panel, 13 x 9 ins / 33 x 23 cm) ITL 6,000,000.

JANNIER, Pierre
French, 17th century.
Died 1666; buried on 18 September in Paris.
Painter.

Jannier was Painter to Monsieur, the younger brother of Louis XIV.

JANNIN, Dany
Belgian, 20th century.
Born 1919, in Forêt; died 1980.
Painter. Figures.

Dany Jannin studied in Brussels at the academies of St-Gilles, the Fine Arts and St Luke. He went on to teach at St Luke's academy from 1957 to 1965. The bulk of Dannin's work focuses on portraits of his wife.

JANNIN, Émile Louis
French, 19th century.
Born 19th century, in Paris.
Sculptor.

Émile Jannin exhibited plaster subjects of fantasy at the Paris Salon from 1873 to 1877.

JANNIN DE TOURNAY. See **LOMME Janin**

JANNIN-OMS, Patrick
French, 20th century.
Born 1944.
Engraver.

Patrick Jannin-Oms trained at the École des Beaux-Arts, Paris, between 1961 and 1967. Since 1973 his favourite form of expression has been engraving. He has taken part in many collective exhibitions and has also held solo exhibitions including: Galerie Arcadia, Paris, 1978 and New Gallery, Nîmes, 1979.

MUSEUMS AND GALLERIES:
CAEN (MBA) - MALMÖ (Konstmus.) - PARIS (BNF).

JANNINI. See **GIANNINI**

JANNIOT, Alfred Auguste
French, 20th century.
Born 13 June 1889, in Paris; died 18 July 1969, in Neuilly-sur-Seine.
Sculptor. Figure compositions. Monuments, groups, statues.
Art Deco.

Alfred Auguste Janniot studied under Antoine Injalbert at the École des Beaux-Arts in Paris and won the Grand Prix de Rome for sculpture in 1919. He taught at the École from 1945 to 1959 and was made a Chevalier of the Légion d'Honneur and elected to membership of the Institut de France. He collaborated on the decoration of the liners *Normandie* and *Île-de-France*, and is best known for his huge stone relief, 325 x 27 feet (100 x 13 metres), *L'Apport des territoires d'outre-mer à la mère patrie et à la civilisation* (*Contribution of the Overseas Territories to the Mother Country and to Civilisation*). This covers the whole exterior of the former Colonial Museum at Vincennes, built by Laprade and Jaussely for the 1931 Exposition Coloniale and which is now the museum of African and South Sea Art. In 1932, he worked with others on the decoration of Puteaux town hall. For the 1937 Exposition Internationale, he made the decorative reliefs for the south face of the Musée d'Art Moderne de la Ville de Paris (Palais de Tokyo): *Legend of the Earth* and *Legend of the Sea*. He also created the decoration of the French House in the Rockefeller Center in New York, the memorial at Mont Valérien and the monument to the fallen in Nice. He exhibited regularly at the Salon des Artistes Français, winning an honourable mention in 1910, and also showed work at the Salon des Tuileries. In 1925, his work was included in the Ruhlmann pavilion of the Exposition des Arts Décoratifs, where he showed a group of three women in honour of Jean Goujon. His work was exhibited in 2003 in a solo show at the Musée

Antoine Lécuyer in St-Quentin, and again the same year in Paris at the Galerie Michel Giraud.

BIBLIOGRAPHY:

Alfred Janniot 1889-1969: sculpteur Art déco, exhibition catalogue, Musée Antoine-Lécuyer, St-Quentin, 2003.

MUSEUMS AND GALLERIES:

PARIS (BNF) - PARIS (MNAM-CCI) - VENICE (Mus.).

AUCTION RECORDS:

PARIS, 20 Jan 1939, *Spring, Three Young Women Nude and Clothed, a Hind and Birds,* FRF 26,000. MONTE CARLO, 6 Dec 1987, *Fontainebleau Nymoh* (white stone lightly heightened with natural tones and gilding, h. 70 ins / 178 cm) FRF 800,000. PARIS, 22 Oct 1989, *The Three Graces* (bronze) FRF 70,000. PARIS, 11 May 1990, *Head and Shoulders of a Woman* (patinated bronze, h. 35 3/4 ins / 91 cm) FRF 29,000. PARIS, 15 Oct 1990, *Seated Model* (red chalk, 18 1/2 x 14 1/4 ins / 47 x 36 cm) FRF 23,000. PARIS, 21 June 1993, *Woman of Dahomey in Profile* (bronze, low relief, 19 1/4 x 16 1/4 ins / 49.2 x 41.5 cm) FRF 15,500. PARIS, 13 May 1996, *Nude* (c. 1930, brown-patinated bronze, h. 35 1/2 ins / 90 cm) FRF 37,000. PARIS, 26 June 1996, *Nymph* (c. 1925, reformed stone, sculpture, 67 x 17 1/4 x 22 ins / 170 x 44 x 56 cm) FRF 128,000. PARIS, 19 Oct 1997, *Reclining Nude* (red chalk, pen and charcoal/paper, 13 3/4 x 18 1/2 ins / 35 x 47 cm) FRF 16,000. PARIS, 22 March 1998, *Eros* (1920, low relief in plaster, 37 x 35 x 9 ins / 94 x 88 x 22 cm) FRF 35,000. PARIS, 11 June 1999, *Seated Nude, Face in Profile* (colour ink, colour wash and red chalk, 13 x 19 ins / 34 x 47 cm) FRF 35,000. PARIS, 11 June 1999, *Europa* (terracotta heightened with gold, 17 x 24x15 ins / 43 x 61x37 cm) FRF 140,000. PARIS, 19 Dec 2000, *Queen of the Fields, Queen of the Woods* (on canvas) FRF 38,000. PARIS, 19 Dec 2000, *Draped Woman* (white stone, h. 53 ins / 134 cm) FRF 140,000. PARIS, 28 March 2001, *Seated Nude seen from behind* (1943, red chalk, 13 x 7 ins / 34 x 19 cm) FRF 19,000. PARIS, 6 April 2001, *Head of a Woman* (marble, 14 x 6x8 ins / 36 x 16x20 cm) FRF 128,000. PARIS, 28 May 2002, *Head of a Muse* (patinated plaster, h. 15 ins / 37 cm) EUR 22,000. PARIS, 28 May 2002, *Leda* (colour pencil, 73 x 47 ins / 185 x 120 cm) EUR 180,000. PARIS, 26 Nov 2003, *Untitled* (crayon, 55 x 32 ins / 140 x 82 cm) EUR 8,500. PONTOISE, 13 Dec 2003, *Antelope* (gold patinated bronze, h. 28 ins / 70 cm, w. 28 ins/70 cm) EUR 8,800.

JANNOIS, André

French, 19th century.
Active in Versailles.
Landscape painter.

André Jannois exhibited at the Paris Salon from 1845 to 1849.

JANNOT, Henri

French, 20th century.
Born 27 January 1909, in Paris.
Painter. Figure compositions, figures, portraits, landscapes, still-lifes.
Group Forces Nouvelles.

Jannot began by painting still-lifes influenced by those of Baschenis and Baugin, then moved on to serious and almost geometrical portraits, and after that to landscapes in the Vexin, seascapes in Brittany and compositions with figures. A solemn style and essential gravity typifies all his work. He trained from 1926 to 1932 in the studio of Lucien Simon at the École des Beaux-Arts in Paris, where he met Robert Humblot. Later, like Georges Rohner and Pierre Tal-Coat, he was more impressed by certain exhibitions than by the teaching in the school. These exhibitions were *Les Maîtres de la Réalité en France au XVIIe siècle* (*Masters of Realism in 17th Century France*) at the Orangery Museum in 1934, *Les Le Nain* (*The Le Nain Brothers*) at the Petit-Palais in the same year and in 1935 the great exhibition of Italian art where they saw works by Masaccio, Piero della Francesca and Paolo Uccello. Together in 1935, they formed the group Forces Nouvelles, aiming at a return to the objective, the real, in reaction against what they felt to be risky experiments. The works they had seen in the three exhibitions of 1934 and 1935 encouraged them in their attempt to grasp reality by using simple spaces and creating form by the effect of light.

Jannot's work was shown in the exhibitions of this group until it was dissolved in 1939, and in retrospectives, concluding with the 1980 *Forces Nouvelles 1935-1939* at the Musée d'Art Moderne de la Ville de Paris, later shown also in Orléans and Strasbourg. His work was also featured in numerous collective exhibitions in France, the USA, London, Australia, Switzerland and elsewhere. He showed work in Paris at the Salon d'Automne from 1931, Salon des Moins de Trente Ans in 1932, Salon des Tuileries from 1935, at Salon de la Nouvelle Génération in 1937, Salon des Indépendants in 1945 and Salon des Peintres Témoins de leur Temps in 1973. He won a gold medal at the Salon des Artistes Français in 1969, the Taylor prize in 1973, the Salon's first prize in 1976 and the medal of honour in 1982. He was invited to the São Paulo *Biennale* in 1951. His solo exhibitions began in 1938 with the first of many in Paris at the Galerie Billiet-Vorms, and included: 1946, Galerie Hermann; 1960, Galerie Tonalités; 1962, Galerie du Roy; 1973, Galerie Cardo-Matignon; 1977, Galerie de Lutèce; 1983, a retrospective at the Salon des Artistes Français; 1986, Galerie Taylor; 1994, retrospective at the museum in Issoire; and an exhibition of work done in the 1930s at the Galerie Callu Mérite in Paris.

BIBLIOGRAPHY:

Diehl, Gaston, *L'Échappée belle. Henri Jannot, période forces nouvelles, et Rohner, Humblot, Pellan, Tal Coat, Moisset, Lautrec*, exhibition catalogue, Gal. Callu Mérite, Paris, 1994.

AUCTION RECORDS:

PARIS, Oct 1945-July 1946, *Still-life,* FRF 32,000. PARIS, 14 March 1990, *Still-life* (1943, oil on canvas, 23 1/2 x 28 3/4 ins / 60 x 73 cm) FRF 18,000. PARIS, 30 April 1993, *Still-life with Bottle of Cognac* (oil on canvas, 28 3/4 x 46 ins / 73 x 117 cm) FRF 3,800.

JANNOT-PINET, Marie

French, 19th - 20th century.
Born 20 January 1874, in Lyons.
Painter. Scenes with figures.

Marie Jannot-Pinet won a third-class medal in Lyons and a second-class in Toulon.

MUSEUMS AND GALLERIES:

LYONS (MBA): *La collation.*

JANNOTTA, Michele

Italian, 19th - 20th century.
Born 6 September 1866, in Casapulla (Caserta).
Painter. Genre scenes, landscapes with figures.

Jannotta was a pupil of his father, the painter Pasquale Jannotta, and at the Accademia di Belle Arti, Naples. Among his works are: *Morning Prayer; Cloister Bells; Washerwomen of Lauria; First Evening of Snow*

JANNOTTA, Pasquale

Italian, 19th century.
Painter.

MUSEUMS AND GALLERIES:

NAPLES (Mus. di Capodimonte): *Buosa da Duero.*

JANOFF. See **YANOV**

JANOIR, Jean

French, 20th century.
Born 26 October 1929, in Mâcon.
Painter.

Jean Janoir studied at the art college in Lyons, where he has lived and exhibited since 1957. His work has also been shown in Paris at the Salon d'Automne and the Salon Comparaisons.

JANOS. See **JOHANNES**

JANOSIK, Fabrice
Hungarian, 20th - 21st century.
Born 1968.
Active in France.
Painter (mixed media).
Fabrice Janosik lives and works in Paris. He has taken part in many group exhibitions held at galleries in Geneva.
AUCTION RECORDS:
PARIS, 14 Oct 1991, *Alphabétique barbare* (1991, mixed media, 39¼ x 61 ins / 100 x 155 cm) FRF 20,000. PARIS, 21 March 1992, *Ethnic Shadows* (1992, mixed media/canvas, 57½ x 45 ins / 146 x 114 cm) FRF 14,000.

JANOT, Jean Rainaut
French, 20th century.
Born 18 June 1913, in Beausoleil.
Painter. Landscapes.
Jean Rainaut Janot, a professional cook and restaurant owner, painted landscapes of the south of France in his spare time.

JANOTA, Johann Georg
Austrian, 18th century.
Born 1747, in Bohemia; died 1780 or 1800, in Vienna.
Engraver (burin).
The Prince of Liechtenstein took Janota under his wing very young and sent him to Italy to continue his studies. Janota subsequently settled in Vienna, where he was elected a member of the academy. He engraved numerous plates, particularly from works in his patron's collection.

JANOWSKI, Fritz
German, 20th century.
Born 22 February 1884, in Prenzlau.
Engraver.
Exhibited in Berlin in 1909.
AUCTION RECORDS:
HANOVER, 19 May 1984, *Carriage* (oil on card, 29½ x 39¼ ins / 75 x 100 cm) DEM 5,500.

JANOWSKI, Ludomir
Polish, 20th century.
Painter. Still-lifes.
Ludomir Janowski's work featured in the Polish section of the Salon d'Automne, organised by the Société d'Échanges Littéraires et Artistiques entre la France et la Pologne and the Cercle des Artistes Polonais de Paris (1928).

JANOWSKI, Mikolaj
Polish, 18th century.
Born 18th century, in Cracow.
Painter.
Mikolaj Janowski was a pupil of Konitch. He decorated several monasteries in his native city of Cracow, notably those of the Capucins and the Reformers.

JANOWSKI, Valentin
Polish, 18th century.
Born 18th century, in Cracow.
Painter.
Valentin Janowski was the brother of Mikolaj and a pupil of Molitor. His painting *Birth of Jesus* can be seen in Cracow Cathedral.

JANOWSKY-ROMANENKO, Michael
German, 20th - 21st century.
Born 12 December 1972, in Boulogne-Billancourt, France, to a German mother and a Russian father.
Active in France.
Painter.
Michael Janowsky-Romanenko studied in Paris at the Académie Julian from 1989 to 1991 and at the École des Beaux-Arts in 1992-1993. He seems to have opted for the abstract route, where his personality expresses itself in the deliberate pursuit of sober line and colour. He has shown his works in solo exhibitions at the Galerie Tachelles in Berlin in 1993 and the Galerie des Beaux-Arts in Paris in 1996.

JANS. See also **JANSZ, JANSEN, JANSON, JANSS, JANSSENS, JOHANN, JOHANSEN**

JANS, Edouard de
Belgian, 19th - 20th century.
Born 1855, in St-André-les-Bruges; died 1919.
Active in Antwerp.
Painter. Portraits, genre scenes.
Edouard de Jans was a Premier Prix de Rome laureate who subsequently featured at the Salon des Artistes Français, securing an honourable mention in 1884.
MUSEUMS AND GALLERIES:
BUCHAREST (Muz. National de Arta al României): *Interior, Rocca di Papa; Italian Smoking.*
AUCTION RECORDS:
AMSTERDAM, 23 April 1991, *Woman Adjusting her Stockings* (1914, oil on canvas, 17¾ x 21 ins / 45 x 53.5 cm) NLG 3,450. LOKEREN, 9 March 1996, *Portrait of a Young Girl* (1877, oil on canvas, 14¼ x 11¾ ins / 36 x 30 cm) BEF 30,000.

JANS, Hendrik. See **JANSENS**

JANS, Jos
Belgian, 20th century.
Born 1933, in Achel.
Painter, potter.
Neo-Constructivism, Conceptual Art.
Research Group.
Jos Jans was educated at the provincial institute of architecture and the applied arts in Hasselt. He was a founder member of the Research Group. Jans was awarded the Limbourg fine arts prize in 1968 and the young Belgian painters' prize in 1971.

JANS, Werner Ignaz
Swiss (?), 20th century.
Sculptor.
MUSEUMS AND GALLERIES:
LAUSANNE (Cantonal MFA): *Blue Tango* (1985).

JANSA, Vaclav
Austrian, 19th - 20th century.
Born 22 October 1859; died 29 June 1913, in Prague.
Painter. Landscapes, architectural views.

MUSEUMS AND GALLERIES:
PRAGUE: *Viper's Bugloss in Blossom.*

JANSCHA, Laurens or Lorenz
Hungarian, 18th - 19th century.
Born 1749, in Krain; died 1 April 1812, in Vienna.
Painter, draughtsman. Landscapes, urban landscapes.
Laurens Janscha studied at the Akademie der Bildenden Künste in Vienna with Weirotter and Christian Brand, and became a professor at the academy in 1801. His best-known work is *Panorama of Vienna.*

JANSE. See **JANSZ, JANSEN, JANSSON, etc.**

JANSEM, Jean
Armenian, 20th century.
Born 9 March 1920, in the Bursa region, Turkey.
Active in France.
Painter, lithographer, sculptor. Figures, nudes, landscapes, still-lifes.

Jean Jansem's family settled in Paris in 1931. In 1938, he was a student at the École des Arts Décoratifs. Little affected by the experimentations of his contemporaries in the artistic world, he belongs to the so-called *Misérabliste* group of painters. He produced work in series which depicted the poor and sickly, gipsies and shepherds in sombre colours emphasised by dry, hatched lines. From 1970, he began to represent more optimistic subjects, particularly nudes, mothers and children and dancers.

Living and working in Paris, he took part in a number of collective exhibitions including the Salon des Artistes Témoins de leur Temps. He has held many solo exhibitions, particularly in Paris where he showed regularly at the Galerie Matignon

BIBLIOGRAPHY:

Sorlier, Ch./Berger, Y., *Jansem lithographe. Catalogue raisonné des lithographies 1954-1983*, Nice, 1984. *L'Œuvre graphique de Jansem, 1984-1993*, Éd. Flora, Paris, 1994.

AUCTION RECORDS:

PARIS, 8 Jan 1960, *Girl with Bundle of Firewood*, FRF 2,350. PARIS, 2 Dec 1963, *Children's Weddings*, FRF 11,800. NEW YORK, 8 Oct 1969, *Still-life with Jug*, USD 3,500. VERSAILLES, 20 Dec 1970, *Italian Landscape*, FRF 9,000. GENEVA, 8 Dec 1973, *Girl with Jug*, CHF 11,000. PARIS, 30 March 1976, *Seated Nude* (oil on canvas, 12 1/2 x 18 ins / 32 x 46 cm) FRF 2,500. LONDON, 9 Feb 1977, *Washerwoman* (oil on canvas, 28 3/4 x 36 1/4 ins / 73 x 92 cm) GBP 650. PARIS, 17 Oct 1978, *Seated Woman* (patinated bronze, h. 10 3/4 ins / 27.5 cm) FRF 4,500. NEW YORK, 19 Jan 1979, *Domestic Scene* (oil on canvas, 102 1/2 x 55 1/2 ins / 260.3 x 141 cm) USD 6,500. NEW YORK, 17 July 1980, *Seated Young Man* (Indian ink wash, 25 x 19 ins / 63.8 x 48.3 cm) USD 1,100. VERSAILLES, 14 Dec 1980, *Girl Undressing* (gouache, oil and pastel, 25 1/2 x 19 ins / 64.5 x 48.5 cm) FRF 7,100. NEW YORK, 17 July 1981, *Head of a Woman* (pen and wash, 26 x 20 ins / 66 x 51 cm) USD 1,000. PARIS, 26 Nov 1982, *Girl Lying on a Bed* (1970, oil on canvas, 32 x 39 1/4 ins / 81 x 100 cm) FRF 21,000. NEW YORK, 22 June 1983, *Mother and Child* (1961, oil on canvas, 76 3/4 x 38 1/4 ins / 195 x 97 cm) USD 2,900. LONDON, 27 March 1984, *Seated Dancer seen from Behind* (pen wash and colouring pencil, 25 1/2 x 19 1/2 ins / 65 x 49.5 cm) GBP 1,600. NEW YORK, 30 May 1985, *Dancer* (Indian ink/watercolour, 19 3/4 x 25 3/4 ins / 50 x 65.5 cm) USD 1,700. PARIS, 26 June 1986, *Procession (Praying Woman)* (oil on canvas, 63 1/2 x 51 1/4 ins / 161 x 130 cm) FRF 52,000. PARIS, 11 Feb 1987, *Dancer seen from Behind* (drawing in watercolour, 26 x 19 1/2 ins / 66 x 49.5 cm) FRF 17,500. PARIS, 27 Nov 1987, *Returning from the Market* (1964, oil on canvas, 51 1/4 x 38 1/4 ins / 130 x 97 cm) FRF 75,000. PARIS, 10-11 Dec 1987, *Village Women* (oil on canvas, 9 1/2 x 7 1/2 ins / 24 x 19 cm) FRF 5,000; *Recumbent Woman* (pen, 25 1/4 x 19 ins / 64 x 48 cm) FRF 6,000. VERSAILLES, 15 May 1988, *Nude Woman and Masks* (Indian ink, 19 x 10 3/4 ins / 48.5 x 27.5 cm) FRF 5,200. PARIS, 7 Oct 1988, *Crouching Female Nude* (Indian ink wash, 25 1/4 x 19 1/4 ins / 64 x 49 cm) FRF 15,000. PARIS, 27 Oct 1988, *Still-life with Lamp* (oil on canvas) FRF 52,000. PARIS, 24 May 1989, *Provencal Landscape* (ink/paper, 18 1/2 x 25 1/2 ins / 47 x 65 cm) FRF 12,000. PARIS, 31 Jan 1990, *Still-life with Bottles* (oil on canvas, 24 1/2 x 19 3/4 ins / 62 x 50 cm) FRF 163,000. PARIS, 21 June 1990, *Two Children* (oil on canvas, 46 x 32 ins / 116 x 81.5 cm) FRF 360,000. NEUILLY, 26 June 1990, *Woman Spinning* (oil on canvas, 15 1/4 x 12 1/4 ins / 39 x 31 cm) FRF 20,000. NEW YORK, 10 Oct 1990, *Two Women and a Child* (1959, oil on canvas, 102 1/4 x 55 ins / 259.5 x 139.7 cm) USD 115,500. PARIS, 5 Dec 1990, *Woman Selling Vegetables* (watercolour, Indian ink and pastel, 6 3/4 x 7 1/2 ins / 17 x 19 cm) FRF 7,600. NEW YORK, 13 Feb 1991, *Three Figures* (oil on canvas, 14 x 9 1/2 ins / 35.5 x 24 cm) USD 7,700. PARIS, 16 March 1991, *Seated Boy* (oil on canvas, 39 1/4 x 23 1/2 ins / 100 x 60 cm) FRF 160,000. NEW YORK, 7 May 1991, *Girls* (oil on canvas, 39 1/4 x 19 1/2 ins / 99.5 x 49.5 cm) USD 28,600. NEW YORK, 12 June 1991, *Motherhood* (oil on canvas, 38 1/4 x 51 1/4 ins / 97.2 x 130.2 cm) USD 13,200. PARIS, 9 July 1992, *Seated Boy* (1953, oil on canvas, 18 x 13 ins / 46 x 33 cm) FRF 28,000. NEW YORK, 10 Nov 1992, *Dancer with a White Headband* (oil on canvas, 28 3/4 x 36 1/4 ins / 73 x 92 cm) USD 18,700. PARIS, 21 Dec 1992, *Four Musicians* (oil on canvas, 11 x 16 1/4 ins / 27 x 41 cm) FRF 53,000. LE TOUQUET, 30 May 1993, *Seated Peasant Woman* (oil on canvas, watercolour and Indian ink wash, 25 1/2 x 19 1/4 ins / 65 x 49 cm) FRF 17,000. NEW YORK, 30 June 1993, *Still-life* (oil on canvas, 51 x 76 1/2 ins / 129.5 x 194.3 cm) USD 28,750. LONDON, 13 Oct 1993, *Still-life with Shells* (gouache and ink, 15 3/4 x 20 1/4 ins / 40 x 51.5 cm) GBP 1,840. PARIS, 6 Feb 1994, *Harlequin* (watercolour and Indian ink, 25 x 19 ins / 63.5 x 48.5 cm) FRF 30,000. NEW YORK, 23 Feb 1994, *Harlequin's Wedding* (oil on canvas, 45 x 57 1/2 ins / 114.3 x 146 cm) USD 25,300. PARIS, 14 June 1994, *Carnival* (oil on canvas, 45 x 57 1/2 ins / 114 x 146 cm) FRF 150,000. CALAIS, 3 July 1994, *Seated Dancer* (bronze, h. 8 1/4 ins / 21 cm) FRF 29,000. LONDON, 14 March 1995, *Girl with Bunch of Flowers* (oil on canvas, 25 3/4 x 32 ins / 65.4 x 81 cm) GBP 10,925. NEW YORK, 14 June 1995, *Three Children* (oil on canvas, 28 1/2 x 39 ins / 72.7 x 99.1 cm) USD 24,150. PARIS, 27 March 1996, *Carnival* (51 x 77in/130x196cm) FRF 140,000. CALAIS, 7 July 1996, *Flower Seller* (oil on canvas, 25 1/2 x 19 3/4 ins / 65 x 50 cm) FRF 62,000. NEW YORK, 10 Oct 1996, *Procession* (1962, oil on canvas, 89 x 138 ins / 226.1 x 350.5 cm) USD 24,150. NEW YORK, 12 Nov 1996, *Peasant Women and Children* (oil on canvas, 51 1/4 x 64 ins / 130 x 162.5 cm) USD 19,550. PARIS, 8 Dec 1996, *Women in a Studio* (1956, oil on canvas, 75 1/2 x 45 ins / 191.8 x 114.3 cm) FRF 96,000. PARIS, 26 May 1997, *Dancer Resting* (coloured lithograph, 17 1/4 x 24 1/4 ins / 44 x 61.5 cm) FRF 4,800. PARIS, 4 March 1998, *Spectators* (1970-1971, oil on canvas, 51 1/4 x 63 3/4 ins / 130 x 162 cm) FRF 85,000. PARIS, 22 March 1998, *Woman Resting on a Chair* (oil on canvas, 18 1/4 x 13 ins / 46.5 x 33 cm) FRF 40,000. PARIS, 1 April 1999, *Village in Italy* (1964, oil on canvas, 45 x 64 ins / 114 x 162 cm) FRF 150,000. CALAIS, 12 Dec 1999, *Still-life with Pitcher and Jug* (oil on canvas, 28 x 39 ins / 72 x 100 cm) FRF 125,000. CALAIS, 5 Nov 2000, *Women and Children* (oil on canvas, 57 x 77 ins / 145 x 196 cm) FRF 200,000. CALAIS, 5 Nov 2000, *Eve of the Festival* (oil on canvas, 77 x 57 ins / 196 x 145 cm) FRF 201,000. NEW YORK, 8 May 2001, *Little Tray* (oil on canvas, 51 x 76 ins / 129 x 194 cm) USD 38,000. NEW YORK, 6 Nov 2001, *Still-life with Basket* (oil on canvas, 29 x 39 ins / 73 x 100 cm) USD 15,000. SAN FRANCISCO, 14 Oct 2002, *Exercises, Three Ballerinas* (1969, oil on canvas, 64 x 51 ins / 163 x 129 cm) USD 17,000. PARIS, 19 Dec 2002, *Women Crouching* (oil on canvas, 51 x 64 ins / 130 x 162 cm) EUR 20,000. SAN FRANCISCO, 22 April 2003, *Fisherman* (oil on canvas, 52 x 64 ins / 131 x 162 cm) USD 13,000. PARIS, 25 June 2003, *Still-life with Blue Vase* (oil on canvas, 51 x 64 ins / 130 x 162 cm) EUR 29,000. NEW YORK, 25 Feb 2004, *Street Scene with Children* (c. 1957, oil on canvas, 41 x 55 ins / 104 x 140 cm) USD 15,000. NEW YORK, 29 Sept 2004, *Dancer in Red Leotard* (oil on canvas, w. 24 ins / 60 cm) USD 22,000.

JANSEN. See also **JAN, JANS, JANSON, JANSZ, JOHANSEN**

JANSEN, Cornelis, or Janssen

Engraver.

Cornelis Jansen produced two plates after Le Blanc, listed in the Reness-Breitach catalogue.

JANSEN, Dirk

Dutch, 19th - 20th century.

Active in Tangiers.

Painter. Figures, landscapes, seascapes, architectural views.

Dirk Jansen was taken prisoner in the Transvaal during the Boer War and incarcerated for two years on St Helena. His paintings drew inspiration from his native Holland and from the various countries he had visited, notably southern France and Spain.
Auction records:
Paris, 28 May 1991, *Sailing Ships on the Bosphorus* (oil on canvas, 23 1/2 x 35 3/4 ins / 60 x 91 cm) FRF 85,000.

JANSEN, F.
Dutch, 19th - 20th century.
Painter (gouache), watercolourist, pastellist.
Active in The Hague and an exhibitor at the 1910 Brussels Exposition Universelle.
Auction records:
Versailles, 17 March 1985, *Horse Show, Paris* (1892, gouache and watercolour, 22 x 29 1/2 ins / 55 x 75 cm) FRF 21,500.

JANSEN, F. or P.
Dutch, 17th century.
Painter.
F. Jansen worked in Haarlem.

Museums and Galleries:
Amsterdam: *Guardhouse*.

JANSEN, Ferdinand
German, 18th - 19th century.
Born 1758; died 1834.
Active in Aachen.
Painter, poet.
Ferdinand Jansen painted views of Aachen and the surrounding area in oils and watercolours. He also painted portraits, including a self-portrait, and religious works. In 1825, he restored paintings in the vault of the cathedral and furnished the west vault with a painting.
Museums and Galleries:
Aachen (Burg Frankenberg): several views of Aachen and region.

JANSEN, Franz Maria or Franck
German, 20th century.
Born 4 February 1885, in Cologne; died 1958, in Büchel.
Painter, engraver. Figures, portraits, landscapes.
Franz Maria Jansen was a self-taught artist who travelled extensively in Hungary, Italy and Dalmatia before settling first in Cologne in 1909 and then moving to Winterscheid. He took part in Secession Group exhibitions from 1911 to 1920 and, in 1929, his work featured at an exhibition in Paris of German painters and engravers. By 1910 Jansen had already organised a solo exhibition of his work in Cologne, where he showed landscapes and figures inspired by Van Gogh. In 1912 he turned definitively to etchings and woodcut engraving. That year he produced six woodcuts (*Six Days in a Young Boy's Life*. In 1913 came his series entitled *Black Gondolas of Venice*. This was followed by *Harvest* (1914), a series of 22 engravings entitled *War* (1915-1916), 15 etchings in 1917 (*A Prophet*), *Rhine Landscapes* (1919) and, in 1920, *Industry*.

JANSEN, Gerhard, or Janssen
Dutch, 17th - 18th century.
Born 1636, in Utrecht; died 1725, in Vienna.
Painter (glass), engraver.
Gerhard Jansen was attached to the court, and was working in Vienna in 1622.

JANSEN, Heinrich, or Jansonius or Janssonius
Danish, 17th century.
Born 14 April 1625, in Flensburg (then in Denmark, now in Schleswig-Holstein, Germany); died 1667, in Flensburg.
Painter. History painting, animals.
Heinrich Jansen first served as a secretary to the king in Copenhagen. He then went to Holland where he was a pupil of Rembrandt for three years. It is probably there that he was referred to as Jansonius. After travelling throughout Spain and Italy he became court painter to Frederik III in Copenhagen in 1659.
Museums and Galleries:
Copenhagen (Statens Mus. for Kunst): *Jesus the Gardener* (after Rembrandt) - Hillerød (Frederiksborg Slot): *Hunting Scene*.

JANSEN, Hendricus W., or Henricus
Dutch, 19th - 20th century.
Born 2 January 1867, in The Hague; died February 1901, in The Hague.
Painter, engraver.
Hendricus Jansen studied at the academy in The Hague. He lived in Paris from 1887 to 1892 and from 1899 to 1901 in Tunis, a city that inspired him to paint compositions in the Dutch Impressionist mould. He subsequently turned to decorative compositions and illustration work, and contributed caricatures to a Dutch weekly. Major decorative compositions by Hendricus Jansen are to be found in the royal theatre in The Hague and the town hall in Rotterdam.

JANSEN, Hendrik Willebrord
Dutch, 19th century.
Born 12 December 1855, in Nijmegen; died 4 November 1908, in Zeist.
Painter.
Hendrik Jansen worked at the fine arts academy in Amsterdam under the direction of Auguste Allebé and Wynveld. He later lived in Arnhem before moving to Dœsburg, where he studied landscape. In 1888, he visited Amsterdam and began to paint the city's port, boats, squares and canals, and became highly regarded in this field. He exhibited at the Salon des Artistes Français and received a commendation in 1899. He was awarded medals in Munich in 1891 and 1893.
Museums and Galleries:
Amsterdam (Stedelijk Mus.): *Moonlight*; *Canal Lock* - Munich: *Horn Bridge* - The Hague (Mus. Mesdag): *In the Shipyard*; *Amsterdam Bridge*.
Auction records:
Amsterdam, 7 Sept 1976, *Landscape with River* (oil on canvas, 15 1/4 x 23in/39 x 58.5cm) NLG 2,400. Vienna, 14 June 1977, *Summer in Holland* (1898, oil on canvas, 15 3/4 x 23 1/2in/40 x 60cm) ATS 100,000. Amsterdam, 19 Sept 1989, *Young Dairymaid on a Forest Road* (oil on panel, 7 1/4 x 10 1/2in/18.7 x 26.7cm) NLG 1,150. Amsterdam, 2 May 1990, *Fishwives Talking on the Loggerstraat in Katwijk* (oil on canvas, 16 x 23 1/2in/40.5 x 60cm) NLG 6,900. Stockholm, 16 May 1990, *Threemaster in the Moonlight* (oil on canvas, 24 x 36 1/4in/61 x 92cm) SEK 37,000. Amsterdam, 5 June 1990, *Peasant Woman in a Kitchen Garden* (oil on canvas/card, 16 1/4 x 23 1/2in/41 x 60cm) NLG 1,150. London, 4 Oct 1991, *The Scuola Grande di S Marco, now the Civil Hospital in Venice* (oil on canvas, 15 3/4 x 23 1/2in/40 x 60cm) GBP 1,760. Amsterdam, 9 Nov 1993, *The Venice Lagoon with S Maria della Salute* (oil on canvas, 24 1/2 x 32 1/4in/62 x 82cm) NLG 2,300. Amsterdam, 21 April 1994, *Port with Sailing Ships Pulled Up by a Lift Bridge with a Church Tower in the Background* (oil on canvas, 11 3/4 x 22 3/4in/30 x 58cm) NLG 4,025. Amsterdam, 11 April 1995, *View of Prins Hendrikkade at the Corner of Kalkmarkt in Amsterdam* (oil on canvas, 24 x 16 1/4in/61 x 41cm) NLG 2,360. Amsterdam, 18 Jan 2000, *Child Playing in*

Yard (oil on canvas, 25 x 32 ins / 63 x 82 cm) NLG 12,000. AMSTERDAM, 20 March 2001, *View of Katwijk* (oil on panel, 9 x 14 ins / 23 x 35 cm) NLG 3,800. BERN, 7 May 2003, *Fishermen on River* (oil on canvas, 33 x 51 ins / 85 x 130 cm) CHF 3,600. AMSTERDAM, 1 July 2003, *Sailing Barges in a Breeze* (oil on canvas, 31 x 24 ins / 80 x 60 cm) EUR 3,000.

JANSEN, Johann Filips
Flemish School, 17th century.
Draughtsman, engraver.
Johann Jansen worked for almost half the 17th century in Madrid.

JANSEN, Johannes Mauritz or Maurisz.
Dutch, 19th century.
Born 1812, probably in Amsterdam; died 25 March 1857, in Utrecht.
Painter. Landscapes with figures.
AUCTION RECORDS:
LONDON, 28 Feb 1973, *Wooded Landscapes with Figures* (two pendants, pair) GBP 2,000. AMSTERDAM, 16 Nov 1988, *Shepherd Lying under a Tree Watching his Flock* (oil on canvas, 26¾ x 22in/68 x 56cm) NLG 3,450. AMSTERDAM, 19 Sept 1989, *Travellers Resting by a Bridge in a Wooded River Landscape* (oil on canvas/panel, 24½ x 30¼in/62 x 77cm) NLG 5,175. AMSTERDAM, 19 Jan 1999, *Wooded River Landscape with Cattle Drivers on Sandy Track* (oil on panel, 9 x 11 ins / 23 x 29 cm) NLG 4,000. COLOGNE, 6 April 2000, *Wooded Landscape with Farmer* (1843, oil on panel, 19 x 24 ins / 48 x 60 cm) DEM 3,600. AMSTERDAM, 4 July 2000, *Peasants on a Sandy Trail in a Wooded Landscape* (1843, oil on panel, 19 x 24 ins / 48 x 60 cm) NLG 6,500. AMSTERDAM, 15 April 2003, *Extensive Landscape with Shepherd and Travellers on a Sandy Trail* (1842, oil on panel, 10 x 14 ins / 26 x 35 cm) EUR 1,800.

JANSEN, Joseph
German, 19th century.
Born 20 July 1829, in Aachen; died 5 February 1905, in Düsseldorf.
Painter. Landscapes.
Joseph Jansen trained at the academy in Düsseldorf and exhibited in Vienna in 1872. He painted numerous views of the Alps, Switzerland, the Rhine and the Moselle.
MUSEUMS AND GALLERIES:
CINCINNATI: *The Jungfrau.*
AUCTION RECORDS:
NEW YORK, 1899, *The Sea of Ice,* FRF 1,400. COLOGNE, 22 Oct 1971, *Landscape with Waterfall,* DEM 3,000. NEW YORK, 13 May 1978, *The Entrance to the Farm* (oil on canvas, 25 x 37 ins / 63.5 x 94 cm) USD 2,400. COLOGNE, 12 June 1980, *The Water Mill* (1896, oil on canvas, 37 x 51¼ ins / 94 x 130 cm) DEM 11,000. NEW YORK, 29 May 1981, *An Alpine Village* (1895, oil on canvas, 36½ x 51 ins / 92.7 x 129.5 cm) USD 7,000. LONDON, 18 June 1986, *Mountain Lake* (oil on canvas, 36 x 54¼ ins / 91.5 x 138 cm) GBP 5,500. NEW YORK, 23 May 1989, *End of the Day on a Lake* (oil on canvas, 37½ x 11½ ins / 95.3 x 29.5 cm) USD 11,000. COLOGNE, 6 April 2000, *Man Crossing a Bridge* (1876, oil on canvas) DEM 6,000. TOESTORF, 26 Aug 2000, *Mountain Landscape with Waterfall* (1851, oil on canvas, 52 x 42 ins / 131 x 106 cm) DEM 6,000. VIENNA, 30 Nov 2000, *Mountain Landscape* (1876, oil on canvas, 48 x 39 ins / 121 x 100 cm) ATS 250,000. ZURICH, 2 May 2001, *Landscape with Mill and Figures* (1901, oil on canvas/masonite, 37 x 40 ins / 95 x 101 cm) CHF 3,500. COLOGNE, 15 May 2002, *Storm Brewing in the Mountains* (oil on canvas, 23 x 37 ins / 58 x 95 cm) EUR 4,800.

JANSEN, Louise
Maiden name: Siebke
German, 19th - 20th century.
Born 28 January 1835; died 16 January 1912.
Active in Düsseldorf.
Painter. Landscapes with figures, landscapes.
Louise Jansen exhibited in Germany between 1867 and 1888.
AUCTION RECORDS:
COLOGNE, 22 Nov 1973, *Landscape with Church,* DEM 5,000. COLOGNE, 1 June 1978, *Castle on the Banks of the Moselle River* (1879, oil on canvas, 18¾ x 26 ins / 47.5 x 66 cm) DEM 6,500. NEUILLY, 25 Nov 1987, *Rhineland Castle with Figures* (oil on canvas) FRF 9,000. CALAIS, 28 Feb 1988, *Near Düsseldorf* (oil on canvas, 12½ x 18 ins / 32 x 46 cm) FRF 20,000. CALAIS, 3 July 1988, *Near Düsseldorf* (oil on canvas, 12½ x 18 ins / 32 x 46 cm) FRF 20,000.

JANSEN, P.. See **JANSEN F.**

JANSEN, Willem
Dutch, 19th - 20th century.
Born 1892.
Painter. Landscapes, flowers.
Noted for paintings of typical Dutch landscapes.
AUCTION RECORDS:
AMSTERDAM, 19 Sept 1989, *Sunflowers* (1923, oil on canvas, 34 x 27¾ ins / 85.5 x 70.5 cm) NLG 2,300. AMSTERDAM, 30 Oct 1990, *Vast Polder Landscape* (oil on canvas, 23½ x 31½ ins / 60 x 80 cm) NLG 1,380. LOKEREN, 28 May 1994, *Near Zaandam* (1937, oil on canvas, 15¾ x 23½ ins / 40 x 60 cm) BEF 28,000. AMSTERDAM, 19 April 2000, *Farm under the Trees* (oil on panel, 10 x 14 ins / 25 x 35 cm) NLG 4,200. AMSTERDAM, 19 April 2000, *Figures Working by a Sandpit* (oil on canvas, 12 x 18 ins / 30 x 46 cm) NLG 5,500.

JANSEN, Willem George Frederik
Dutch, 19th - 20th century.
Born 25 December 1871, in Harlingen; died 1949.
Painter, watercolourist. Landscapes with figures, seascapes. Panoramas.
Willem George Frederik Jansen worked initially in the applied arts, producing ceramics, models and projects for the Rozenburg and Distel factories. He was also responsible for the background landscape in the diorama in Amsterdam's Botanical Gardens. As a painter, he focused on typical Dutch scenes: people gathering shellfish or seaweed on the beaches, navigating the network of polder canals, fishing in the harbours or tending their livestock.
AUCTION RECORDS:
AMSTERDAM, 27 April 1976, *Canal Scene* (oil on canvas, 23½ x 15¾ ins / 60 x 40 cm) NLG 14,500. LONDON, 19 Oct 1976, *View of Amsterdam* (watercolour heightened with white, 11½ x 21½ ins / 29.5 x 54.3 cm) GBP 500. AMSTERDAM, 25 Jan 1977, *Mill by the Sea* (oil on canvas, 15¼ x 23½ ins / 38.5 x 60 cm) NLG 5,000. AMSTERDAM, 27 June 1977, *Wooded Landscape* (watercolour, 20¾ x 15¼ ins / 53 x 38.5 cm) NLG 4,600. AMSTERDAM, 24 April 1979, *Gathering Wrack* (oil on canvas, 16¼ x 26¾ ins / 41 x 68 cm) NLG 5,800. AMSTERDAM, 11 May 1982, *View of Enkhuizen Harbour* (oil on canvas, 27½ x 38½ ins / 70 x 98 cm) NLG 4,600. NEW YORK, 24 May 1984, *Returning with the Catch* (oil on canvas, 40 x 32½ ins / 101.5 x 82.5 cm) USD 3,000. AMSTERDAM, 10 Feb 1988, *Gathering Shellfish at the Coast with a Horse-Drawn Cart* (oil on canvas, 20 x 30 ins / 51 x 76 cm) NLG 2,070. AMSTERDAM, 23 April 1988, *Gathering shellfish on the Beach* (oil on canvas, 20½ x 26 ins / 52 x 66 cm) NLG 6,350. AMSTERDAM, 30 Aug 1988, *Near the Cowshed* (oil on canvas, 36¾ x 30¼ ins / 93.5 x 77 cm) NLG 6,325. AMSTERDAM, 16 Nov 1988, *Boats Moored on the River near a Village* (oil on canvas, 15¾ x 23½ ins / 40 x 60 cm) NLG 8,625. LONDON, 6 June 1990, *Mending the Nets* (oil on canvas, 19¼ x 15¼ ins / 49 x 39 cm) GBP 4,180. AMSTERDAM, 30 Oct 1990, *Gathering Seaweed on the Beach at Scheveningen, Holland* (oil on canvas, 18 x 29¾ ins / 45.5 x 75.5 cm) NLG 10,350. LONDON, 22 Nov 1990, *Pastoral Scene* (oil on canvas, 28 x 22½ ins / 71.2 x 57.3 cm) GBP 1,210. AMSTERDAM, 24 April 1991, *Harvesting Shell-*

fish on the Incoming Tide (oil on canvas, 25 x 40¼ ins / 63.5 x 102.5 cm) NLG 6,900. AMSTERDAM, 5-6 Nov 1991, *Landscape with River* (oil on canvas, 13½ x 19¼ ins / 34 x 49 cm) NLG 2,300. AMSTERDAM, 18 Feb 1992, *Vast Polder Landscape with Yachts Moored in a Canal* (oil on canvas, 24 x 39¾ ins / 61 x 101 cm) NLG 4,600. AMSTERDAM, 14-15 April 1992, *Shepherd and Flock Leaving the Fold* (oil on canvas, 11½ x 15¼ ins / 29 x 39 cm) NLG 4,025. AMSTERDAM, 2-3 Nov 1992, *Gathering Shellfish* (oil on canvas, 17¼ x 28¼ ins / 44 x 72 cm) NLG 10,120. AMSTERDAM, 11 Feb 1993, *View of Enkhuizen Harbour* (oil on canvas, 13¾ x 19¾ ins / 35 x 50 cm) NLG 5,405. NEW YORK, 22-23 July 1993, *On the Way Home* (oil on canvas, 39½ x 31¾ ins / 100.3 x 80.6 cm) USD 2,875. AMSTERDAM, 19 Oct 1993, *Gathering Shellfish on the Incoming Tide* (oil on canvas, 39¾ x 31¾ ins / 101 x 80.5 cm) NLG 14,950. AMSTERDAM, 8 Nov 1994, *On the Way to Market* (oil on canvas, 17¼ x 28¼ ins / 43.5 x 72 cm) NLG 9,200. AMSTERDAM, 11 April 1995, *View of Oud den Bosch* (oil on canvas, 16¼ x 20 ins / 41 x 51 cm) NLG 4,720. AMSTERDAM, 16 April 1996, *Fieldworkers* (oil on canvas, 23½ x 39¼ ins / 60 x 100 cm) NLG 6,136. AMSTERDAM, 5 Nov 1996, *Elburg Harbour* (oil on canvas, 19¾ x 27½ ins / 50 x 70 cm) NLG 6,490. AMSTERDAM, 19-20 Feb 1997, *Harlingen Harbour* (oil on canvas, 11¾ x 15¾ ins / 30 x 40 cm) NLG 16,144. AMSTERDAM, 27 Oct 1997, *Ferryboat* (oil on canvas, 20½ x 26½ ins / 52 x 67 cm) NLG 9,440. AMSTERDAM, 21 Jan 1998, *Wooded Landscape with Woodcutter Carrying a Tree Trunk* (oil on canvas, 23¾ x 31¾ ins / 60.5 x 80.5 cm) NLG 9,802. AMSTERDAM, 27 April 1999, *On the Waal* (oil on canvas, 24 x 20 ins / 60 x 50 cm) NLG 16,000. AMSTERDAM, 27 April 1999, *Ships on the Waal at Woudrichem, Loevenstein Castle beyond* (oil on canvas, 30 x 49 ins / 76 x 125 cm) NLG 48,000. AMSTERDAM, 18 April 2000, *Ferry in Wessem, Limburg* (oil on canvas, 39 x 51 ins / 100 x 129 cm) NLG 16,000. AMSTERDAM, 4 July 2000, *Bomschuit on the Beach* (oil on canvas, 16 x 24 ins / 40 x 60 cm) NLG 12,000. AMSTERDAM, 23 April 2001, *Summer Landscape with Farm* (oil on canvas, 20 x 28 ins / 50 x 70 cm) NLG 17,000. AMSTERDAM, 23 April 2001, *Shell Fisher on the Beach* (oil on canvas, 24 x 41 ins / 60 x 105 cm) NLG 20,000. AMSTERDAM, 22 Jan 2002, *View of Harlingen* (oil on panel, 10 x 14 ins / 25 x 35 cm) EUR 7,000. AMSTERDAM, 4 March 2002, *Winter Scene in Amsterdam* (oil on canvas, 20 x 30 ins / 50 x 75 cm) EUR 8,500. AMSTERDAM, 29 April 2003, *Shellgatherer on the Beach* (oil on canvas, 20 x 26 ins / 50 x 65 cm) EUR 4,000. AMSTERDAM, 21 Oct 2003, *View of the Prinsengracht with the Westerkerk, Amsterdam* (oil on canvas, 24 x 39 ins / 60 x 100 cm) EUR 15,000. AMSTERDAM, 20 April 2004, *View of Haelingen Harbour* (oil on canvas, 12 x 16 ins / 30 x 40 cm) EUR 6,500. NEW YORK, 29 June 2004, *Shrimper* (oil on canvas, 15 x 25 ins / 37 x 63 cm) USD 11,000.

JANSENIUS, Michiel van Aelst
Dutch, 17th century.
Active in 1619.
Draughtsman.

JANSENS. See also **JANS, JANSEN, JANSS, JANSSEN, JANSSENS, JANSSON, JANSZ, JOHANSEN**

JANSENS, Ann Veronica. See **JANSSENS**

JANSENS, Hendrik, or Jans
Dutch, 17th century.
Painter (?), engraver (line-engraving). Portraits.

Hendrik Jansens studied in Paris under Largillière, and engraved portraits after Largillière and Hyacinthe Rigaud. He married Marguerite Petit, the widow of Redouté, on 20 April 1682. He may be the same as Hendrik Jans, mentioned by Siret as a portrait painter.

JANSER, Joseph Anton
Swiss, 18th century.
Born 1740; died 30 January 1808.
Active in Schwyz.
Sculptor.

Janser was a monumental mason in Schwyz.

JANSON. See also **JANSENS, JANSZ, JOHANSEN**

JANSON, Andrew
American, 20th century.
Born 18 November 1900, in New York.
Painter, illustrator.

Andrew Janson studied at the École des Beaux-Arts in Paris. He was a member of the Art Students League of New York. He was awarded the John Alexander medal.

AUCTION RECORDS:
PARIS, 29 April 1991, *Abstract Composition* (1960, oil on canvas, 39¼ x 39¼ ins / 100 x 100 cm) FRF 4,100.

JANSON, Bernard. See **JANSSEN**

JANSON, Cornelis. See **CEULEN**

JANSON, Gunnar
Norwegian, 20th century.
Born 1901.
Sculptor.

JANSON, Jacques. See **JANSON Johannes**

JANSON, Jean
Swedish, 17th century.
Active in Stockholm.
Engraver, printer.

Jean Janson engraved portraits.

JANSON, Johann Mathias
German, 18th century.
Born 1751, in Potsdam; died 1794, in Königsberg (now Kaliningrad, Russia).
Painter, decorative designer. Historical subjects, portraits.

Janson began his training with Krüger in Potsdam, but in 1770 went to Vienna. The following year he was in Rome. In 1774, he went to Paris. On his return to Germany, he was much in demand as a painter of decorations and portraits, but he also did a number of history paintings. There are works by him in the gallery in Brunswick.

AUCTION RECORDS:
MONTE CARLO, 23 June 1976, *The Falconer, The Gardener* (c. 1780, two oils/copper with mother-of-pearl and shell highlights, 34½ x 26¾ ins / 87.6 x 68 cm) FRF 90,000.

JANSON, Johannes and not Jacobus nor Jacques, the Elder
Dutch, 18th century.
Born 17 April 1729, in Amboine, The Moluccas; died 1 April 1784, in Leiden.
Painter, watercolourist, engraver. Portraits, landscapes, animals.

Johannes Janson the Elder was brought to Holland at the age of eight. He became a military engineer, and on leaving the army settled in Leiden. He was registered as a member of the Leiden guild in December 1671 with the forename Jacobus. Janson worked mainly as a painter of landscapes and animals. He copied several paintings by Paul Potter and made some etchings of landscapes copied from his own drawings.

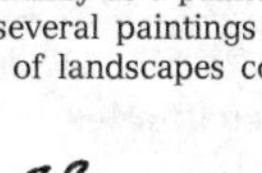

MUSEUMS AND GALLERIES:
AMSTERDAM: *Heemstede Castle* - CAMBRIDGE (Fitzwilliam Mus.): *Cattle-Piece* (1779, oil on canvas) - HAARLEM (Teylers

Mus.): three watercolours - KASSEL: *Dutch Town*; same subject - LEIDEN: *View of Koeport*; *View of the White Gate in Leiden*; *Mountain Landscape*; same subject; *City Gate in Leiden* - STOCKHOLM: *River View*.

AUCTION RECORDS:

PARIS, 1777, *Two Landscapes*, FRF 1,060. PARIS, Oct 1945-July 1946, *Mill by a River*, FRF 6,500. PARIS, 9 and 10 Nov 1953, *River Landscape*, FRF 14,000. LONDON, 24 March 1961, *Frozen Canal in Winter*, GBP 315. LONDON, 29 March 1968, *The Joys of Winter*, Gns 480. VIENNA, 6 June 1972, *Pastoral*, ATS 45,000. MUNICH, 23 Nov 1978, *Animals in a Landscape* (1768, oil on panel, 15 1/4 x 12in/39 x 30.5cm) DEM 2,800. LOS ANGELES, 18 June 1979, *Animals Grazing* (1779, oil on panel, 9 1/2 x 12in/24.2 x 30.5cm) USD 1,900. AMSTERDAM, 24 March 1980, *River Landscape* (oil on panel, 14 1/4 x 18 1/2in/36 x 47cm) NLG 4,500. PARIS, 7 Dec 1981, *The Watering Place* (1778, oil on wood, 16 3/4 x 21 1/4in/42.5 x 54cm) FRF 35,000. LONDON, 9 Dec 1992, *Winter Landscape with Skaters and a Herdsman Leading his Animals* (1783, oil on panel, 16 1/2 x 22in/41.7 x 55.8cm) GBP 6,820. AMSTERDAM, 6 May 1993, *View of Muidepoort in Amsterdam with Elegant Figures Walking in Summer* (oil on panel, 22 1/2 x 30 3/4in/57.2 x 78cm) NLG 23,000. LONDON, 27 Oct 1993, *Shepherds with their Animals in Classical Landscapes* (oil on panel, a pair, each 8 1/4 x 11 1/2in/21 x 29.3cm) GBP 4,830. PENRITH (CUMBRIA), 13 Sept 1994, *Cattle in a Meadow* (1768, oil on panel, 14 x 11 1/2in/35.5 x 29cm) GBP 2,875. LONDON, 17 April 1996, *Winter Landscape with Skaters* (oil on panel, 12 1/4 x 16 1/2in/31 x 41.6cm) GBP 9,775. AMSTERDAM, 11 Nov 1997, *Amsterdam: View of Muiderpoort in Winter with Skaters on the Frozen Singelgracht and a Horse-Drawn Carriage alongside on the Road* (1779, oil on panel, 11 1/2 x 14in/29.4 x 35.8cm) NLG 6,342. DORCHESTER, 11 March 1999, *Figures on Track by Canal* (oil on panel, 8 x 11 ins / 20 x 28 cm) GBP 2,600. LONDON, 15 April 1999, *Dune Landscapes, with Figure Herding and Travellers* (oil on panel, a pair, 9 x 8 ins / 24 x 21 cm) GBP 4,000. BILLINGSHURST, 24 July 2000, *Cattle and Sheep in a Landscape* (1779, oil on panel, 9 x 12 ins / 23 x 30 cm) GBP 1,200. COLOGNE, 16 Nov 2002, *Southern Landscapes with Figures* (1775, watercolour, a pair, 9 x 8 ins / 23 x 21 cm) EUR 1,600. YORKSHIRE, 7 May 2004, *Dutch Landscape with Figures and Cattle on a Canal Towpath* (oil on panel, 12 x 16 ins / 30 x 41 cm) GBP 1,300. NEW YORK, 27 May 2004, *Winter Landscape with Skaters* (oil on panel, 10 x 14 ins / 26 x 35 cm) USD 9,000.

JANSON, Johannes Christiaan

Dutch, 18th - 19th century.

Born 1763, in Leiden; died 17 October 1823, in The Hague.

Painter, engraver.

Johannes Christiaan Janson was the son and pupil of Johannes Janson. He joined the army in 1795 and, as an officer, took part in several campaigns in Germany. When Holland and France were reunited, he left the army and began to work as a painter in The Hague.

MUSEUMS AND GALLERIES:

AMSTERDAM: *Mother Cutting Bread*; *Two Neighbours* - LISBON (Museu Nacional): *Landscape with Figures*.

AUCTION RECORDS:

PARIS, 1822, *Interior with Two Female Figures*, FRF 168. LONDON, 13 Dec 2000, *Boy Buying Cherries. Woman Talking to Man* (oil on panel, 8 x 7 ins / 20 x 18 cm) GBP 1,800.

JANSON, Louis Charles

French, 19th century.

Born 4 November 1823, in Arcis-sur-Aube; died 26 March 1881, in Paris.

Sculptor. Statues, groups.

Louis Janson worked with Ramey and Dumont and featured at the Paris Salon from 1850 to 1880. He is particularly known for his: *Comedy and Tragedy*, a stone low relief on the staircase of the Louvre's library; and *Volition*, a decorative statue in the foyer of the new Opera House.

MUSEUMS AND GALLERIES:

BERGUES: *Grief* - COGNAC: *Timon of Athens* - ÉPINAL: *Grief* - LYONS: *Bacchus and Cupid* - PARIS (ENSBA): *Death of Narcissus* - TOULOUSE: *Molière* (plaster); *Mozart* (plaster) - TROYES: *Attila Halted at the Gates of Troy by St Lupus*; *Defeat of Attila's Army*; *Dawn*; *The Republic*; *Diogenes*; *Salome*; *City of Troy*; *Mgr de Séguin des Hons*; *Saint*; *Meditation* - VERSAILLES: *Louis Partonneaux, lieutenant général*.

AUCTION RECORDS:

ROME, 24 Oct 1995, *Diana the Hunter* (bronze, h. 20 3/4 ins / 53 cm) ITL 1,840,000.

JANSON, Marc

French, 20th century.

Born 21 January 1930, in Ukkel, near Brussels, to French parents.

Painter (including gouache). Landscapes with figures.

Marc Janson was born in Belgium to parents from Marthemont (Meurthe-et-Moselle), and as a child lived in Italy and in Switzerland. He went to Paris in 1948, spent two years studying at the École du Louvre and began painting in 1950. As a young man, he had been influenced by those great visionaries of space, Claude Lorraine and Turner, and his early paintings of 1954-1958 bear witness to the attraction that drew him to the twilight or monochrome distances of Patinir, Guardi or Whistler. Then his empty spaces acquire figures, and gather ruins, ghosts and shadows. Echoes of the Settecento, *capricci*, waves, labyrinths and illusory lagoons occupy a space which is here turbulent, marked by lightning flashes, and there swept by mist and gloom. His technique became light-handed and his landscapes fantastic; mountains, clouds and architectural shapes in airy forms seem to emerge as if shaken out of the canvas, revealing patches of background. As it developed, his painting continued to explore distance, empty or peopled, dream landscapes where winged creatures flit among strange plants and the viewer can hardly tell which is creature, which plant. His gentle colours, sweet and sharp like acid drops, can be compared to those of Fra Angelico.

His work appeared in such collective exhibitions as: 1964, *Le Surréalisme, histoire,sources, affinités* (*Surrealism, Its History, Origins and Connections*), staged by Patrick Waldberg at the Galerie Charpentier in Paris; 1967, *Surrealist Exhibition*, in galleries in England; 1968, *Art actuel* (*Art Now*), at the Fondation Maeght in St-Paul-de-Vence; 1969, *Signes d'un renouveau surréaliste* (*Signs of a Surrealist Revival*), at the Galerie Isy Brachot in Brussels; 1970, *Résonances surréalistes* (*Surrealist Echoes*), at the Galerie A. Zerbib in Paris; 1971, *D'après* (*According to*), in Lugano; 1973-1974 *Surrealismo ancora i sempre* (*Surrealism Now and Always*), in Milan, Turin, Bologna and Rome; 1976, *Les Demeures d'Hypnos* in Paris, Brussels and Milan; 1976, *Contemporains IV* at the Musée National d'Art Moderne de Paris, and in other venues. Solo exhibitions of his paintings included: 1956, 1958, 1960, Galerie François Petit, Paris; 1957, London; 1961, Brussels; 1965, 1971, 1973, Galerie Armand Zerbib, Paris; 1966, Brussels; 1972, Sweden; 1973, Milan; 1976, Galerie Attali, Paris; 1986, in Chamalières.

BIBLIOGRAPHY:

Courthion, Pierre, '*Marc Janson, l'univers de l'insinuation*' in *L'Œil*, periodical, Paris, December 1975. Waldberg, Patrick, '*Marc Janson, le paysage irradié*' in *Les Demeures d'Hypnos*, periodical, La Différence, Paris, 1976. Pieyre de Mandiargues, André, *Janson*, exhibition catalogue, Gal. Attali, Paris, 1977 (good documentation). '*Marc Janson*' in *Cimaise*, periodical, Paris, December 1987. Barthes, Roland/Pieyre de Mandiargues, André/Waldberg, Patrick, *Janson*, Altamira, Paris, 1999.

MUSEUMS AND GALLERIES:
PARIS (FNAC).
AUCTION RECORDS:
DOUAI, 26 March 1988, *Dans les traîtres filets de l'herbe* (1985, oil on canvas, 32 x 39 1/4 ins / 81 x 100 cm) FRF 10,000. NEUILLY, 22 Nov 1988, *The Sky and its Tortured Life* (oil on canvas, 21 1/4 x 25 1/2 ins / 54 x 65 cm) FRF 6,000. PARIS, 8 Oct 1989, *And the Great River at Last Is Quiet* (oil on canvas, 13 x 16 1/4 ins / 33 x 41 cm) FRF 4,900. PARIS, 8 Nov 1989, *Touch in a Wave* (oil on canvas, 25 1/2 x 32 ins / 65 x 81 cm) FRF 11,000. DOUAI, 1 April 1990, *Nautilus* (1956, oil on canvas, 28 1/4 x 45 ins / 72 x 114 cm) FRF 10,000. PARIS, 6 June 1990, *Shifting Sands* (oil on canvas, 19 3/4 x 39 1/4 ins / 50 x 100 cm) FRF 6,200. DOUAI, 11 Nov 1990, *Shells, Armour, a Disturbed World* (1989, oil on canvas, 35 x 51 1/4 ins / 89 x 130 cm) FRF 18,500. NEUILLY, 16 April 1991, *Leaves, a Cloud* (oil on canvas, 32 x 39 1/4 ins / 81 x 100 cm) FRF 10,500. PARIS, 3 June 1992, *Sybre* (oil on canvas, 32 x 23 1/2 ins / 81 x 60 cm) FRF 6,500. PARIS, 16 Oct 1994, *Dying Day in Shock* (1984, oil on canvas, 39 1/4 x 28 3/4 ins / 100 x 73 cm) FRF 5,000. PARIS, 27 Nov 2003, *Midday and Midnight* (oil on canvas, 29 x 39 ins / 73 x 100 cm) EUR 1,500. VERSAILLES, 25 April 2004, *All the Knives in the World* (1965, oil on canvas, 45 x 57 ins / 114 x 146 cm) EUR 1,800. VERSAILLES, 25 April 2004, *Composition* (1956, oil on canvas, 11 x 16 ins / 27 x 41 cm) EUR 2,800.

JANSON, Pieter
Dutch, 18th - 19th century.
Born 1768, in Leiden; died 1851, in Arnhem.
Painter, engraver (etching). Landscapes with figures, animals.

Pieter Janson was the son and pupil of Johannes Janson the Elder, and brother of Johannes Christiaan Janson. He too was a military officer but a serious injury forced him to leave the army. He settled in Arnhem, remaining there until at least 1820. He painted landscapes with figures and animals.
AUCTION RECORDS:
LONDON, 29 Oct 1976, *Animals Grazing* (oil on panel, 12 x 15in/30.5 x 38cm) GBP 350. LONDON, 28 Oct 1992, *Milking Cows by a Cottage* (oil on panel, 24 x 31in/61 x 78.5cm) GBP 2,970.

JANSON VAN CEULEN, Cornelis.
See **CEULEN**

JANSONIUS. See also **JANSEN Heinrich**

JANSONIUS, Wilhelmus, or Janssonius
Dutch, 17th century.
Active in Amsterdam in 1616-1620.
Engraver.

JANSONS, Karlis
Latvian, 20th century.
Born 1896, in Nitaure.
Sculptor. Portraits. Monuments.

Karlis Jansons studied at the academy of fine art in Riga until 1925 and then taught there. He executed several monuments in Riga and other parts of Latvia.

In 1929, he was awarded a prize by the Cultural Fund. His work featured in *Exposition de l'Art de la Lettonie* (*Exhibition of Latvian Art*), Paris (1939).
MUSEUMS AND GALLERIES:
RIGA.

JANSS. See also **JANS, JANSEN, JANSSENS, JANSZ, JANSON, JOHANSEN, etc.**

JANSS, Dominicus
Dutch, 17th century.
Died 7 June 1636, in Haarlem.
Sculptor, metal worker.

JANSS, Jacob
Dutch, 18th century.
Painter.

Jacob Janss was a member of the Haarlem guild in 1732. From the difference between the dates of registration in the Haarlem guild, it would seem unlikely that Jacob Janss is the same artist as Jacob Jansz.

JANSS, Jacob. See also **JANSZ. Jacob**

JANSSAUD, Mathurin, and perhaps **Jacques** or **Jacquin**
French, 19th - 20th century.
Born 30 March 1857, in Manosque (Alpes-de-Haute-Provence); died 1940.
Painter, watercolourist, pastellist. Local figures, fishing scenes, harbour views, interiors with figures, landscapes with figures, landscapes, urban landscapes, seascapes, boats.

Mathurin Janssaud seems to have had no connection with the annual Paris salons. He worked in pastels and occasionally in watercolours. Using an effective if facile technique, he became popular for his Breton harbour scenes depicting a time when fishing boats had sails and peasant women wore coiffes. His output was considerable, and the lists of auction sales show how well he could produce variations on the theme of Breton women waiting for the boats to come home. At first his pastels sold almost exclusively in Brittany, then they became known in France and abroad. His success is confirmed by the number of fakes that seem to have appeared since his death. Suspect pictures have been examined for anachronistic details, such as buildings or other elements that did not exist in his lifetime.

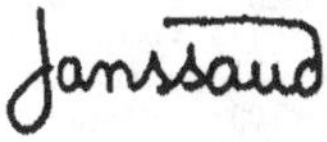

AUCTION RECORDS:
PARIS, 23-24 April 1920, *The Seine by the Trocadero* (watercolour) FRF 275. PARIS, 21 Feb 1921, *Setting Sun* (pastel) FRF 300. PARIS, 17 Dec 1931, *Breton Interior* (pastel) FRF 130; *Neighbourhood of Concarneau* (pastel) FRF 230. PARIS, 2 June 1943, *Twilight in Concarneau* (pastel) FRF 500. PARIS, 29 Jan 1945, *The Fish Market* (pastel) FRF 1,300. PARIS, 4 Nov 1946, *Fishing Boats Return to Concarneau* (pastel) FRF 3,500. PARIS, 22 Nov 1946, *Breton Harbour* (pastel) FRF 2,600. BREST, 6 June 1976, *Breton Women Waiting for the Boats to Return* (pastel, 18 x 22 ins / 46 x 56 cm) FRF 2,200. LONDON, 9 Feb 1977, *Concarneau, the Fishing Fleet Comes Home* (pastel and charcoal, 19 3/4 x 28 3/4 ins / 50 x 73 cm) GBP 340. BREST, 17 Dec 1978, *The Boats Coming Home, Evening* (pastel, 14 1/2 x 11 3/4 ins / 37 x 30 cm) FRF 2,700. ST-BRIEUC, 8 April 1979, *Sailing Vessels Return to Harbour* (pastel, 10 x 15 1/2 ins / 25.5 x 39.5 cm) FRF 2,400. BREST, 16 Dec 1979, *Vessels Return to the Lanriec Passage, Concarneau* (pastel, 25 1/4 x 19 ins / 64 x 48 cm) FRF 12,500. BREST, 16 Dec 1979, *Vessels Return to the Lanriec Passage, Concarneau* (pastel, 25 1/4 x 19 ins / 64 x 48 cm) FRF 12,500. BREST, 13 Dec 1981, *Sailing Vessels at Anchor, Concarneau* (pastel, 17 3/4 x 25 1/4 ins / 45 x 64 cm) FRF 9,500. BREST, 16 May 1982, *Sardine Boats Return* (pastel, 12 1/2 x 16 1/4 ins / 32 x 41 cm) FRF 6,100. BREST, 12 Dec 1982, *The Pardon of Our Lady of Joy at St-Guénolé* (pastel, 17 x 24 3/4 ins / 43 x 63 cm) FRF 6,200. DOUARNENEZ, 12 Aug 1983, *Cottage at Ker Embrase Cove* (pastel, 22 x 16 1/2 ins / 55 x 42 cm) FRF 8,200; *Return from Fishing* (pastel) FRF 19,000. DOUARNENEZ, 12 Aug 1983, *Return from Fishing* (pastel) FRF 19,000. DOUARNENEZ, 10 Aug 1984, *Concarneau Harbour* (pastel, 14 1/4 x 21 1/4 ins / 36 x 54 cm) FRF 14,000. PARIS, 16 Nov 1984, *Le Gardien de troupeau* (pastel, 16 1/2 x 22 1/2 ins / 42 x 57 cm) FRF 5,500. LONDON, 8 May 1985, *In Harbour, End of the Day* (pastel, 13 x 16 1/4 ins / 33 x 41 cm) GBP 500. ENGHIEN-LES-BAINS, 1 Dec 1985, *Sunrise over a Breton Port* (pastel, 11 1/2 x 15 ins / 29 x 38 cm) FRF 15,000. RAMBOUILLET,

23 Feb 1986, *Pardon in Ste-Anne-La-Palud* (pastel, 22 x 17 1/4 ins / 56 x 44 cm) FRF 36,000. RAMBOUILLET, 23 Feb 1986, *Pardon at Ste-Anne-La-Palud* (pastel, 22 x 17 1/4 ins / 56 x 44 cm) FRF 36,000. GRANDVILLE, 9 Nov 1986, *Fishermen Return* (pastel, 12 1/4 x 15 1/4 ins / 31 x 39 cm) FRF 13,100. DOUARNENEZ, 25 July 1987, *Return from Fishing* (pastel, 12 1/2 x 9 ins / 32 x 23 cm) FRF 9,000; *Vessels Return to Concarneau* (pastel, 15 x 23 1/2 ins / 38 x 60 cm) FRF 22,500. BREST, 13 Dec 1987, *Fishing Boats, Breton Women Seated by the Ville Close* (pastel, 13 3/4 x 20 3/4 ins / 35 x 53 cm) FRF 30,000. BREST, 13 Dec 1987, *Fishing Boats, Breton Women Seated by the Ville Close, Concarneau* (pastel, 13 3/4 x 20 3/4 ins / 35 x 53 cm) FRF 30,000. PARIS, 30 May 1988, *Drinking Trough* (pastel, 18 x 22 ins / 46 x 55 cm) FRF 13,500. GRANDVILLE, 16-17 July 1988, *Fishing Boats Return to Concarneau* (12 1/2 x 15 3/4 ins / 32 x 40 cm) FRF 21,000. RHEIMS, 23 Oct 1988, *Fishing Boats Return in Brittany, Evening* (pastel, 19 3/4 x 25 1/2 ins / 50 x 65 cm) FRF 37,000. PARIS, 14 Dec 1988, *Sailing Vessels at Concarneau* (pastel, 12 3/4 x 16 3/4 ins / 32.5 x 42.5 cm) FRF 26,500. COPENHAGEN, 5 April 1989, *Breton Fishing Harbour* (pastel, 17 3/4 x 22 1/2 ins / 45 x 57 cm) DKK 22,000. LA VARENNE-ST-HILAIRE, 3 Dec 1989, *The Harbour at Sunset* (pastel, 19 1/4 x 22 3/4 ins / 49 x 58 cm) FRF 20,000. MONACO, 15 June 1990, *Lanrioc Banks* (pastel, 20 x 29 1/4 ins / 51 x 74 cm) FRF 27,750. RHEIMS, 17 June 1990, *Fishing Boats in Harbour* (pastel, 12 1/4 x 16 1/4 ins / 31 x 41 cm) FRF 17,000. NEUILLY, 3 Feb 1991, *Concarneau, the Ville Close* (pastel, 8 1/4 x 13 1/2 ins / 21 x 34 cm) FRF 17,000. CALAIS, 26 May 1991, *Breton Kermesse* (pastel, 12 1/4 x 15 3/4 ins / 31 x 40 cm) FRF 20,000. LE TOUQUET, 10 Nov 1991, *Boats at Sunset* (pastel, 17 1/4 x 21 1/4 ins / 44 x 54 cm) FRF 22,000. PARIS, 5 Feb 1992, *Breton Women at Prayer* (oil and pastel/paper, 15 1/4 x 19 3/4 ins / 39 x 50 cm) FRF 6,000. LE TOUQUET, 8 Nov 1992, *Fishermen Return* (pastel, 17 1/4 x 20 3/4 ins / 44 x 53 cm) FRF 20,000. COPENHAGEN, 18 Nov 1992, *Breton Harbour* (pastel, 17 3/4 x 22 1/2 ins / 45 x 57 cm) DKK 13,000. PARIS, 25 March 1994, *Return from Fishing* (pastel, 10 3/4 x 14 ins / 27.5 x 35.5 cm) FRF 12,000. LORIENT, 19 June 1994, *Fishing Boats Return to Concarneau Harbour* (pastel, 12 1/4 x 15 3/4 ins / 31 x 40 cm) FRF 15,000. PARIS, 11 July 1994, *Return from Fishing* (pastel, 17 3/4 x 22 ins / 45 x 55 cm) FRF 26,000. LORIENT, 30 April 1995, *Boat Crossing at Concarneau* (pastel, 13 x 16 1/4 ins / 33 x 41 cm) FRF 15,000. CALAIS, 24 March 1996, *Concarneau Sardine Boats Return* (pastel, 17 3/4 x 14 1/4 ins / 45 x 36 cm) FRF 25,500. CALAIS, 7 July 1996, *Breton Holiday* (pastel, 7 x 9 ins / 18 x 23 cm) FRF 15,500. PARIS, 29 Nov 1996, *Pottery Sellers at Concarneau* (pastel, 17 1/4 x 22 ins / 44 x 56 cm) FRF 36,000. PARIS, 2 April 1997, *Afternoon at the Luxembourg* (pastel, 9 x 12 3/4 ins / 23 x 32.5 cm) FRF 8,500. PARIS, 25 May 1997, *Breton Women at Prayer, the Chapel of the Virgins, Trémorzennes, Finistère* (pastel/paper, 16 1/2 x 22 ins / 42 x 56 cm) FRF 15,000. PARIS, 23 June 1997, *Concarneau, the Quays, Return from Fishing* (pastel, 16 3/4 x 24 1/2 ins / 42.5 x 62 cm) FRF 24,500. PARIS, 27 Oct 1997, *Fishing Boats on Shore in Brittany* (oil on canvas, 18 x 22 ins / 46 x 55 cm) FRF 12,000. NEUILLY, 27 Nov 1997, *Fishing Boats Set Sail, and Return* (two pastels, 12 1/2 x 15 3/4 ins / 32 x 40 cm) FRF 30,000.

JANSSEN. See also **JANSZ, JANSEN, JANSS, JANSON, JOHANSEN**

JANSSEN, Bernard, or Janson

British, 17th century.

Active in London at the beginning of the 17th century.

Architect, sculptor.

Bernard Janssen or Janson was of Dutch origin. He was known mostly for his architecture.

JANSSEN, Evelien

Dutch, 20th - 21st century.

Born 1956.

Assemblage artist, installation artist.

Evelien Janssen lives and works in Rotterdam. From the consumer society he takes toys, vases, bottles, sweet wrappers, cigarette packets, and integrates them in an original manner into his installations, the aim of which is to restore order and meaning to these harmless objects. He exhibits regularly in solo shows in Amsterdam.

JANSSEN, Geraert. See **JOHNSON Gerard**

JANSSEN, Gerhard

German, 19th - 20th century.

Born 26 September 1863, in Kalkar; died 1931, in Düsseldorf.

Painter. Genre scenes.

Gerhard Jansen exhibited at the Salon des Artistes Français in Paris within the framework of the Exposition Universelle of 1900, where he was awarded a bronze medal. He drew his inspiration first and foremost from Dutch genre painting of the 17th century.

MUSEUMS AND GALLERIES:

DÜSSELDORF: *Singer by the Rhine*; *Gathering of Old Women*; *Bendemann, a Friend of the Artist*; *Bockhalle* - ELBERFELD: *Tippler* - WIESBADEN: *Drinking Companions*; *Fairground Singers*.

AUCTION RECORDS:

COLOGNE, 23 March 1973, *Toast*, DEM 5,000. COLOGNE, 26 March 1976, *Portrait of an Old Woman* (oil on panel, 18 x 14 1/2 ins / 46 x 37 cm) DEM 1,000. COLOGNE, 21 May 1984, *Card Players* (1912, oil on canvas, 39 3/4 x 57 1/2 ins / 101 x 146 cm) DEM 14,000. COLOGNE, 21 Nov 1985, *Cabaret Act* (oil on canvas, 31 1/2 x 28 1/4 ins / 80 x 72 cm) DEM 5,000. COLOGNE, 28 June 1991, *Laughing Couple* (oil on canvas, 25 1/4 x 17 3/4 ins / 64 x 45 cm) DEM 2,200. COLOGNE, 4 Dec 1999, *Making Merry* (oil on panel, 11 x 12 ins / 29 x 31 cm) DEM 3,400. COLOGNE, 4 Dec 1999, *In the Coffee House* (oil on canvas, 14 x 11 ins / 35 x 28 cm) DEM 3,900. BREMEN, 29 June 2001, *Wine Tasting* (1916, oil on canvas, 36 x 47 ins / 91 x 120 cm) DEM 3,800.

JANSSEN, Gerhard. See also **JANSEN**

JANSSEN, Hans

Dutch, 17th century.

Born 31 July 1605, in Amsterdam.

Engraver, draughtsman.

Hans Janssen worked in Amsterdam. He is known for his many biblical scenes including: *The Wedding at Canaan*; *Esther and Ahasuerus*; and *Belshazzar's Feast*.

JANSSEN, Horst

German, 20th century.

Born 14 November 1928, in Hamburg; died 31 August 1995, in Hamburg.

Painter, engraver (wood/etching), draughtsman.

Figures, portraits, self-portraits, flowers.

Horst Janssen was educated at Hamburg Art College from 1946 to 1951 and, at the age of sixteen years, was the youngest-ever student to be admitted. Janssen was the recipient of numerous awards and distinctions, including the Hamburg Lichtwart Prize (1952), the City of Darmstadt Prize (1964), the Edwin-Scharff Prize (Hamburg, 1965), the Venice Biennale Prize (1968), the City of Mannheim Schiller Prize (1975) and the City of Oldenburg Prize (1990).

Horst Janssen ranks as one of the most accomplished draughtsmen in post-war Germany. He drew chiefly in colour pencil and was an etchings and woodcut engraver. Both his drawings and engravings are characterised by a cruel yet lucid sarcasm that attests to Janssen's acute sense of the absurd, the grotesque and the macabre. His work also develops on another dimension, namely that of the surreal and fantastic, reminiscent of a Füssli or a James Ensor. His self-portraits are nothing short of monstrous and his eroticism vacillates between hallucination and sexual depravity. His style emerged over time as allusive rather than realist, but always obsessive. He is noted particularly for two series: *Hokusai's Spaziergang* ('Hokusai's Walks') and *Carnival in Venice*.

During his lifetime, examples of Janssen's work featured at a large number of exhibitions. Among the more recent are those at the Berggruen Gallery in Paris (1986); the Galerie Jacques Benadot in Geneva (1987); the Sursock Museum in Beirut (1987); the National Gallery of Tirana (1988); the Foreign Cultural Relations Institute in Stuttgart (1990); the Galerie Claude Bernard in Paris (1990); the Deichtorhallen in Hamburg and the Albertinum in Dresden (both 1991); the Fine Arts Museum in Leipzig (1993); the Taipei Fine Arts Museum (1993); and the Kunsthalle in Hamburg (1994). To date, posthumous exhibitions of Horst Janssen's works have been held at the Käthe Kollwitz Museum in Berlin (1996); at the Bavarian fine arts academy in Munich in 1996 (*Horst Janssen: A Retrospective*); and at the Kunsthalle in Hamburg in 1999 (*Horst Janssen: Early Works*) and 2003 (*Horst Janssen: Caspar David Friedrich and I - Etchings 1973-1974* and *Horst Janssen and his Publisher Hartmut Freilinghaus*).

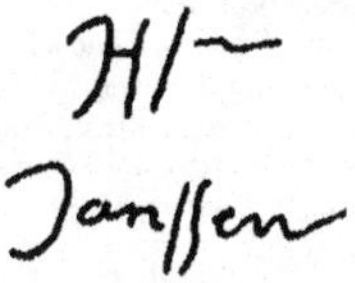

BIBLIOGRAPHY:

Brockstedt, Hans, *Horst Janssen: Farbholzschnitte. Werkverzeichnis 1957-1961*, catalogue raisonné, Gal. Brockstedt, Hamburg, 1987. *Horst Janssen, Radierungen 1957-1969*, catalogue raisonné, Gal. Brockstedt, Hamburg, 1989. Frielinghaus, Hartmut, *Verzeichnis aller Janssen Radierungen Zusammengefasst in Jahrgangsheften*, catalogue raisonné, Dornbusch, Hamburg, 1991. Blessin, Stefan, *Horst Janssen: aus dem Dunkel ins Licht*, Steidl, Göttingen, 1992. *Horst Janssen. Ich bin dir ganz Auge, Zeichnungen, Ragierungen 1957-1991*, exhibition catalogue, Käthe-Kollwitz Museum, Berlin, 1996. *Horst Janssen. Retrospektive*, exhibition catalogue, Bayerische Akademie der Schönen Künste, Munich, 1996. Spielmann, Heinz, *Horst Janssen - Farbradierungen 1958 bis 1995*, catalogue raisonné, St. Gertrude, Hamburg, 1997. Meyer-Schomann, Helga/Döring, Jürgen, *Horst Janssen - Das Plakat, eine Auswahl aus den Jahren 1957-1994*, catalogue raisonné, St. Gertrude, Hamburg, 1999. *Horst Janssen und Sein Drucker Hartmut Frielinghaus*, exhibition catalogue, Hamburger Kunsthalle, Hamburg, 2003.

MUSEUMS AND GALLERIES:

HAMBURG (Kunsthalle) - OLDENBURG (Horst-Janssen Mus.).

AUCTION RECORDS:

HAMBURG, 3 June 1976, *Head* (1965, drawing, 18¼ x 16½ ins / 46.3 x 42.1 cm) DEM 3,000. HAMBURG, 3 June 1977, *Rain II* (1961, coloured woodcut) DEM 2,800. HAMBURG, 2 June 1978, *Bartered Bride* (1962, pencil, 25 x 18¼ ins / 63.5 x 46.2 cm) DEM 11,500. HAMBURG, 8 June 1979, *Town with Bridge* (1958, woodcut in colour) DEM 2,800. COLOGNE, 5 Dec 1979, *Self-portrait* (1971, pencil, 10 x 8¼ ins / 24.5 x 21.2 cm) DEM 7,500. HAMBURG, 5 June 1980, *Young Girls with Umbrellas* (1962, watercolour and pencil, 24½ x 19¼ ins / 62.5 x 49 cm) DEM 10,500. HAMBURG, 12 June 1981, *Schleswig Railway Station No Less* (1970, watercolour and pen, 10¾ x 13¼ ins / 27.4 x 33.8 cm) DEM 13,000. HAMBURG, 9 June 1983, *Large Crab* (woodcut in colour, 31½ x 15 ins / 80 x 37.8 cm) DEM 10,500. HAMBURG, 9 June 1983, *At Remo's in Locarno* (1972, pencil and chalk, 8¾ x 14¼ ins / 22.4 x 36.5 cm) DEM 16,500. COLOGNE, 1 June 1984, *Stephen Lüsers' Dream* (1982, watercolour and pen, 6¼ x 7¾ ins / 16 x 20 cm) DEM 3,000. HAMBURG, 7 June 1985, *Large Steamer* (1957, coloured woodcut) DEM 18,000. HAMBURG, 5 Dec 1985, *Self-portrait* (1982, pastel/pencil outlines, 13 x 11½ ins / 33 x 29 cm) DEM 38,000. HAMBURG, 11 June 1987, *Proper Gentlemen* (1963, graphite and colouring pencil, 21½ x 17¾ ins / 54.5 x 45 cm) DEM 32,000. HAMBURG, 12 June 1987, *Phyllis* (1984, gouache/pencil outlines, 11 x 16½ ins / 28.1 x 41.6 cm) DEM 20,000. HEIDELBERG, 12 Oct 1991, *Nuns* (1957, coloured woodcut, 18¾ x 25 ins / 47.7 x 63.5 cm) DEM 11,000. MUNICH, 26-27 Nov 1991, *Throwing Dice* (1966, pencil, 11¾ x 8¼ ins / 30 x 21 cm) DEM 1,495. HEIDELBERG, 11 April 1992, *Cat and Bird* (1959, etching, 12 x 16 ins / 30.5 x 39.7 cm) DEM 2,200. HEIDELBERG, 9 Oct 1992, *Late in the Evening II* (1956, lithograph, 25½ x 36 ins / 65 x 91.3 cm) DEM 1,500. MUNICH, 1-2 Dec 1992, *Young Girl Seated* (1971, graphite and colouring pencil, 16 x 10¼ ins / 40.5 x 26 cm) DEM 12,420. HEIDELBERG, 15-16 Oct 1993, *Self Sketching a Beach Scene* (pencil, 9¼ x 9¼ ins / 23.2 x 23.5 cm) DEM 2,800. HEIDELBERG, 8 April 1995, *Don Quixote* (1958, etching, 23½ x 16 ins / 59.7 x 39.7 cm) DEM 2,300. ZURICH, 23 June 1995, *Self-portrait: My Compliments to Sunday* (white pencil and pastel, 11 x 9 ins / 28 x 22 cm) CHF 3,500. LONDON, 15 March 1996, *Bouquet in a Vase* (1975, pencil/paper, 17¾ x 11½ ins / 45 x 29 cm) GBP 13,800. LONDON, 5 Dec 1996, *Traffic Jam in Svanshall: Diary Entry No. 17* (1986, watercolour and ink, 6¾ x 10¼ ins / 17.2 x 26 cm) GBP 2,415. HEIDELBERG, 11-12 April 1997, *Fire Brigade* (1957, coloured engraving/wood, 31½ x 19¾ ins / 80.3 x 50.4 cm) DEM 15,100. LONDON, 26 June 1997, *Heinz Adler* (1978, watercolour, black ink and wash/paper, 17½ x 10¼ ins / 44.5 x 26 cm) GBP 3,450. HAMBURG, 11 June 1999, *Eiderland* (1985, etching and ink, album, 21 x 15 ins / 54 x 37 cm) DEM 43,000. HAMBURG, 3 Dec 1999, *Self-portrait* (1979, gouache and pencil on paper on board, 17 x 9 ins / 42 x 24 cm) DEM 40,000. HAMBURG, 8 June 2000, *Landscape, Fleien* (1970, colour pencil, 13 x 19 ins / 33 x 49 cm) DEM 46,000. HAMBURG, 1 Dec 2000, *Gesche* (1971, 26 x 20 ins / 65 x 50 cm) DEM 38,000. HAMBURG, 8 June 2001, *Snow White* (1978, watercolour, pen and pencil, 15 x 22 ins / 39 x 57 cm) DEM 60,000. HAMBURG, 7 Dec 2001, *Birgit Dreaming - Botticelli, Slander of Apelles* (1974, pencil and chalk, 17 x 13 ins / 43 x 32 cm) DEM 46,000. HAMBURG, 14 June 2002, *Arsenic and Old Lace* (Indian ink, brush and ink, 31 x 22 ins / 80 x 55 cm) EUR 16,000. BERLIN, 30 Nov 2002, *2. Advent* (1980, pencil, pen and bodycolour, 21 x 16 ins / 53 x 40 cm) EUR 12,000. HAMBURG, 3 Dec 2003, *Self-portrait* (watercolour on pencil, 17 x 13 ins / 43 x 33 cm) EUR 16,500. HAMBURG, 3 Dec 2003, *Self-portrait* (pencil and colour, pen double-sided, 19 x 12 ins / 47 x 30 cm) EUR 23,000. HAMBURG, 11 June 2004, *Bobethanien, 19 September 1990* (Indian ink and watercolour, 13 x 17 ins / 32 x 43 cm) EUR 25,000. HAMBURG, 3 Dec 2004, *Poster Design ' Berggruen, Paris'* (colour pen and pencil, 26 x 17 ins / 65 x 43 cm) EUR 50,000.

JANSSEN, Jan or John. See **JOHNSON**

JANSSEN, Karl

German, 19th century.
Born 29 May 1855, in Düsseldorf.
Sculptor.

The younger brother of painter Peter Johann Theodor Janssen, Karl Janssen studied at the academy in Düsseldorf and went to Rome in 1881. Later he taught at the academy in Düsseldorf, but regularly exhibited in Berlin, where he won a medal in 1902.

MUSEUMS AND GALLERIES:

BERLIN: *Woman Breaking Stones* (bronze) - DÜSSELDORF: *Woman Breaking Stones* (marble); *Battle of the Centaurs and Sea Serpents*.

JANSSEN, Ludovic

Belgian, 20th century.
Born 1888, in Liège; died 1954.

Painter, draughtsman, humorist, engraver, illustrator. Landscapes.
Ludovic Janssen studied at the fine arts academy in Liège. His body of work most notably features La Campine, Flanders and the Belgian coast. He is noted principally for his rendering of clouds and skies.
AUCTION RECORDS:
LIÈGE, 11 Dec 1991, *Woods at Laplanche* (oil on canvas, 25 3/4 x 31 3/4 ins / 65.5 x 80.5 cm) BEF 35,000.

JANSSEN, Luplau Johan
Danish, 19th - 20th century.
Born 15 June 1869.
Painter, engraver, decorative artist. Figures, portraits, landscapes.
Luplau Janssen studied at the Kongelige Danske Kunstakademi in Copenhagen and went on to be an accomplished painter of children's portraits. He is noted in particular for a *Portrait of M. Lendrop in 'Carmen'* and a *Self-portrait with Family*.
MUSEUMS AND GALLERIES:
HILLERØD (Frederiksborg Slot): *Funeral of Christian IX; Posthumous Portrait of Søren Kierkegaard; Posthumous Portrait of Peter Faber.*

JANSSEN, Marie Hermine
German, 20th century.
Born 30 January 1876, in Paris, to German parents.
Sculptor, potter. Statues, busts, low reliefs, medallions, marionettes.
Marie Hermine Janssen exhibited her work in Munich, Nuremberg, Ghent and Brazil. She most notably produced busts and statues for fountains. She also devised a puppet show that she personally carved and decorated. In her later years, she turned increasingly to ceramics.

JANSSEN, Nicholas. See **JOHNSON**

JANSSEN, Peter Johann Theodor
German, 19th century.
Born 12 December 1844, in Düsseldorf; died 19 February 1908, in Düsseldorf.
Painter (gouache). History painting, religious subjects, mythological subjects, portraits, genre scenes. Murals.
The elder son of engraver Theodor Janssen, Peter Johann Theodor Janssen was a pupil of his father and student at the academy in Düsseldorf, where he worked under the direction of Bendemann and Karl Sohn. He was strongly influenced by the works of Cornelius and Alfred Rethel. On 14 April 1877, he was appointed to the staff of the academy in Berlin and in 1885 the academy in Berlin. The sculptor Karl Janssen was his younger brother. He first exhibited in Munich in 1869, but also exhibited in Berlin, Dresden, Düsseldorf and Vienna. He did a large amount of decorative painting, notably in the Festsaal at Erfurt Town Hall and the academy in Düsseldorf.
MUSEUMS AND GALLERIES:
BERLIN: *Field Marshal Herwarth von Bittenfeld; Portrait of a Man; The Legend of Prometheus* (frieze mural) - DÜSSELDORF: *Andreas Achenbach; Monk Walther; They All Followed the Star; Large Portrait; The Battle of Worringen; Fritz Roeber with His Assistants* - PHILADELPHIA (Pennsylvania Academy of the Fine Arts Gal.): *St Peter's Denial.*
AUCTION RECORDS:
COLOGNE, 18 March 1989, *Young Girl with a Pail of Water* (gouache, 38 1/2 x 24 3/4 ins / 98 x 63 cm) DEM 2,400. BERLIN, 12 June 2004, *Figures on Bicycles* (1861, oil on canvas, 35 x 39 ins / 90 x 100 cm) EUR 2,000.

JANSSEN, Pieter
Dutch, 17th century.
Active between 1621 and 1640.
Painter. Flowers.
Pieter Janssen worked in the style of B. van der Ast and Boschaert.

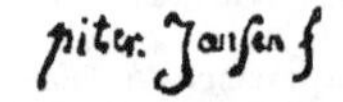

JANSSEN, Pieter, or Janssens or Janszen
Dutch, 17th century.
Born 1612, in Amsterdam or in Haarlem; died 8 April 1672, in Amsterdam or in Haarlem.
Painter, glass painter, engraver. Historical subjects, figures.
Pieter Janssen was a pupil of Jan van Boekhorst. He worked for the military court and received the sum of 248 florins for this work in 1663. His pupils included Jan Pietersz. Zopner.
AUCTION RECORDS:
LONDON, 16-17 April 1997, *Figures* (pen, brown ink and grey and brown wash, study, 7 3/4 x 12 1/2in/19.5 x 31.5cm) GBP 690.

JANSSEN, Stephan Theodor
British, 18th century.
Active in Battersea (London).
Enameller. Portraits, genre scenes, landscapes.
Stephan Theodor Janssen produced small enamelled objects such as boxes, vials and vases which he decorated with portraits, genre scenes and etched landscapes. A series of these is kept at the Victoria and Albert Museum in London.
MUSEUMS AND GALLERIES:
LONDON (Victoria and Albert Mus.).

JANSSEN, Theodor Tamme Weyerd
German, 19th century.
Born 21 June 1816; died 21 June 1894, in Düsseldorf.
Painter, engraver.
Theodor Janssen trained at the academy in Düsseldorf. He did several history paintings, including *Huss at the Stake, Jairus's Daughter* and *Virgins*, also a large watercolour of *The Birth of Christ*. He subsequently took up engraving, even though still continuing to paint a large number of portraits and genre pictures. Among his engravings are *Saved from Shipwreck*, after R. Jordan, *Luther Burns the Papal Bull*, after Lessing, *A Child is Born to Us*, after F. Deger and *The Shepherds on Christmas Eve*, after A. Scheffer.

JANSSEN, Ulfert
German, 20th century.
Born 11 December 1878, in Silesia.
Sculptor. Statues, busts, monuments.
Ulfert Janssen studied at the fine arts academy in Munich. He settled in Stuttgart and exhibited in Baden-Baden, Berlin, Darmstadt, Dresden, Düsseldorf, Munich and Stuttgart. Ulfert Janssen produced a large number of monumental works, among them a *Fountain for the Century* in Essen; sculptures for the façade of the town hall in Apolda; gable statues and a fountain for the Sparkasse (savings bank) building in Mülheim; statues of *Prometheus* and *Heraclitus* for Munich University; busts of philosophers and poets for the library building at Tübingen University; the funerary sculptures of *Wagner* in Zweibrücken and *Ludwig Knaus* at Berlin-Dahlem. Janssen also sculpted a very large number of portrait busts in marble, granite, basalt, bronze, iron and lost-wax, including those of *Friedrich Schiller*, the designer *Erich Wilke*, the painter *W. Köppen*, the Norwegian educator *Axel Helst* and the actress *Grete Lorma*, together with busts of his sister, wife and daughter.

JANSSEN, Victor Emile
German, 19th century.
Born 1807, in Hamburg; died 23 September 1845, in Hamburg.
Painter.

Victor Emile Janssen was a pupil of Cornelius. Apart from a few drawings and portraits, the greater part of his work has disappeared. He is said to have destroyed them himself. An exhibition based on a self-portrait at the easel (*Selbstbildnis vor der Staffelei*) was put on at the Kunsthalle in Hamburg in 2001.

MUSEUMS AND GALLERIES:

HAMBURG (Kunsthalle): *Self-portrait at the Easel* (c. 1829); *The Good Shepherd.*

JANSSENO, René
Belgian, 19th - 20th century.
Born 1870; died 1936.
Painter, lithographer.

JANSSENS. See also **JANSZ, JANOS, JANSON, JANSEN, JOHANSEN, etc.**

JANSSENS, Abraham, the Elder, or van Nuyssen
Flemish, 16th - 17th century.
Born c. 1575, in Antwerp; died 25 January 1632, in Antwerp.
Painter. Religious and allegorical subjects.
Antwerp School.

Janssens studied under Jan Snellinck in 1585 and is recorded as having been a master painter in Antwerp in 1601. He was made a dean of the guild on 23 September 1606, and in 1610 entered the brotherhood of Romanists. His students included Geerard Zegers and Theodor Rombouts. According to Houbraken, Janssens was openly hostile to Rubens, but this claim, like many others made by the Dutch biographer, has been disputed by critics.

Janssens produced many works for churches in Flanders, especially in Antwerp, where his *Entombment*, and *The Virgin and Child with St Catherine and St Cecilia* is in the Carmelite church. He also produced a *Descent from the Cross*, for Ghent Cathedral. His subjects were often taken from antique sculpture and the paintings of masters such as Michelangelo and Raphael, but he created an individual style that combined these influences with Antwerpian mannerism.

MUSEUMS AND GALLERIES:

ANTWERP: *The Holy Family; Scaldis and Antverpia; Adoration of the Kings* - AUGSBURG: *Olympus* - BERLIN: *Vertumnus and Pomona; Meleager and Atalanta* - BRUNSWICK: *Tobias and the Angel; Tobias and the Angel* (same subject) - BRUSSELS: *Allegory* - BUDAPEST: *St Jerome* - COLOGNE: *St Cecilia; Church Elders; Repentant Sinners* - DUNKIRK: *Woman Forced into Being Sacrified to the Idols* - KASSEL: *Diana and her Nymphs Caught Unawares by Satyrs* - LILLE: *Mary Magdalene Repenting* - MUNICH: *The Deification of Aeneas; Death of Acis* - POTSDAM (Schloss Sanssouci): *Adoration of the Kings* - ROUBAIX: *Entombment* - SEATTLE: *The Origin of the Cornucopia* (c. 1619, oil on canvas) - SIBIU (Nom All. de Sibiu): *Venus, Bacchus and Ceres* - TOULOUSE: *Crown of Thorns* - VALENCIA: *Bird-Catcher* - VALENCIENNES: *The Passion of Christ; Strength in Unity* - VIENNA: *Venus and Adonis* - WÜRZBURG: *Eos.*

AUCTION RECORDS:

PARIS, 1769, *Old Men*, FRF 147. COLOGNE, 1862, *A Sibyl Contemplating the Resurrection*, FRF 337. PARIS, 8 Dec 1893, *Ball*, FRF 560. LONDON, 20 Dec 1929, *Adoration of the Kings*, GBP 110. LONDON, 12 June 1968, *Winter Allegory*, GBP 1,500. LONDON, 17 Nov 1982, *Assembly of the Gods* (oil on canvas, 76 1/2 x 91 1/4 ins / 194 x 232 cm) GBP 36,000. NEW YORK, 20 Jan 1983, *Death of Mary Magdalene* (oil on canvas, 47 1/4 x 65 1/4 ins / 120 x 166 cm) USD 26,000. MADRID, 20 June 1985, *The Three Ages of Woman* (oil on canvas, 66 1/4 x 46 ins / 168 x 117 cm) ESP 805,000. LONDON, 31 March 1989, *St Catherine of Alexandria* (oil on canvas, 43 3/4 x 32 1/4 ins / 111.2 x 82 cm) GBP 6,050. LONDON, 7 July 1989, *Adoration of the Kings* (1605, oil on panel, 42 1/4 x 83 1/4 ins / 107.5 x 211.3 cm) GBP 154,000. NEW YORK, 11 Jan 1991, *Peace and Abundance Tying up the Arrows of War* (1622, oil on canvas, 59 x 46 1/2 ins / 150 x 118 cm) USD 66,000. PARIS, 5 April 1991, *Suzanne the Chaste Bathing* (oil on canvas, 65 3/4 x 85 3/4 ins / 167 x 218 cm) FRF 960,000. NEW YORK, 31 May 1991, *Allegory of Autumn: Young Woman Holding a Sickle and a Cornucopia filled with Fruit by a Harvested Field* (oil on panel, 48 1/4 x 35 3/4 ins / 122.6 x 90.8 cm) USD 71,500. LONDON, 9 Dec 1992, *The Virgin, the Holy Child and St John the Baptist* (oil on canvas, 56 x 47 3/4 ins / 142 x 121.2 cm) GBP 38,500. LONDON, 5 July 1995, *The Virgin, the Holy Child and St John the Baptist* (oil on canvas, 56 3/4 x 43 1/4 ins / 144 x 110 cm) GBP 45,500. NEW YORK, 31 Jan 1997, *Allegory of Vanity* (oil on canvas, 47 1/4 x 40 ins / 120 x 101.6 cm) USD 43,700. NEW YORK, 23 May 1997, *Death of Procris* (c. 1606, oil on canvas, 49 1/4 x 41 3/4 ins / 125 x 106 cm) USD 68,500. LONDON, 4 July 1997, *Constance* (oil on panel, 41 1/4 x 28 1/2 ins / 104.8 x 72.4 cm) GBP 25,300. NEW YORK, 29 Jan 1998, *Atalanta and Meleager* (oil on panel, 48 x 37 1/2 ins / 122 x 95.3 cm) USD 27,600. LONDON, 15 April 1999, *Virgin and Child with Infant St John the Baptist* (oil on panel, oval, 34 x 27 ins / 86 x 69 cm) GBP 32,000. NEW YORK, 26 Jan 2001, *Lascivia* (oil on canvas, 46 x 39 ins / 118 x 99 cm) USD 150,000. COLOGNE, 5 April 2001, *Mary Magdalene* (oil on canvas, 40 x 50 ins / 102 x 128 cm) DEM 17,000.

JANSSENS, Abraham, the Younger
Flemish School, 18th century.
Born c. 1719, probably in Ghent.
Engraver.

JANSSENS, Ann Veronica
Belgian, 20th - 21st century.
Born 1956, in Folkestone, England, to Belgian parents.
Installation artist.

Ann Veronica Janssens lives and works in Brussels. She creates interventions in a wide variety of places, including Venice, Rome, Madrid, Ghent, Antwerp, Bruges and Dijon. Apart from sheets of fibreboard, glass balls, aquariums and glass cases, her favourite materials are sheets of glass and concrete blocks, which she arranges in the places that have been allocated to her. The basis of her strategy is to make people see these spaces in a new way by alternating effects. Sheets of glass piled in layers one on top of the other make the transparency of a window or the reflection in a mirror translucent, while concrete blocks give a tactile opacity to an interior space.

She has participated in group exhibitions, including *Inside the Visible* in 1996 at the Whitechapel Art Gallery, London, which was devoted to the work of women artists; *Coconut Tour* in 2003 at the Centre Régional d'Art Contemporain Languedoc-Roussillon in Sète and *Perception of Space* in 2004 at the Museum Boymans van Beuningen in Rotterdam. She has also shown in solo exhibitions, including 1989 at the Villa Gillet in Lyons and the Galerie Alice in Rome, 1990 at the Galerie Micheline Swajcer in Antwerp, 1992 at the Galerie Jennifer Flay in Paris, 1999, when she represented Belgium at the Venice Biennale, 2001 *Sculpture of Smoke* at the Centre d'Art Contemporain la Synagogue in Delme in Lorraine and 2002 *Surfaces for Projections* at the same venue.

BIBLIOGRAPHY:

Brayer, Marie-Ange, '*Ann Veronica Janssens - L'Espacement du regard*' in *Art Press* n° 175, periodical, Paris, December 1992. Ergino, Nathalie (ed.), *Ann Veronica Janssens*, exhibition catalogue, Musée d'Art contemporain, Marseilles, 2004. Rousseau, Pascal, '*Light Games*' in *Art Press* n° 299, periodical, Paris, March 2004.

MUSEUMS AND GALLERIES:
BRUSSELS (MAM): *L'Espace infini* (*Infinite Space*) (1999, metal structure with plaster and wood, design for an installation) - METZ (FRAC Lorraine) - PARIS (FNAC).

JANSSENS, Bernard

Belgian, 20th century.
Born 1887, in Lier.
Also active in the Netherlands.
Painter, copyist, art restorer. Religious subjects, portraits, landscapes, urban landscapes.

Bernard Janssens was educated at the fine arts academy in Lier. He was also recognised as a copyist and restorer of Old Dutch and Flemish Masters.

JANSSENS, Cornelis. See CEULEN

JANSSENS, Daniel

Flemish School, 17th century.
Born 1636, in Mechelen; died 1682, in Mechelen.
Painter. Architectural views. Decorative schemes, designs for tapestries (?).

Daniel Janssens was a pupil of Jac van Hornes and was a master artist in Mechelen in 1660. His pupils included Gillis Vermeulen in Antwerp in 1667. In 1680, he painted a triumphal arch for the town of Mechelen.

JANSSENS, François Joseph

Belgian, 18th - 19th century.
Born 1744, in Brussels; died 22 December 1816, in Brussels.
Sculptor.

François Janssens studied in Italy and Brussels.

MUSEUMS AND GALLERIES:
BRUSSELS: *Philoctetes* (clay, statuette); *Hercules* (clay, statuette); *Hebe* (clay, statuette); *Primavera* (clay, statuette); *St Luke* (clay, model) - BRUSSELS (Beaux-Arts): *David* (clay, model).

JANSSENS, Hendric

Flemish School, 17th century.
Engraver, draughtsman.

Hendric Janssens is believed to have worked in Amsterdam around 1630. He produced mainly engravings for decorative plates for goldsmiths, often after his own drawings. He also created frontispieces. Janssens signed himself *HI in, H Jans fecit, H Janss Inv*. He may be the same person as the artist Hans Janssen or, less likely, Hendrik Jansens.

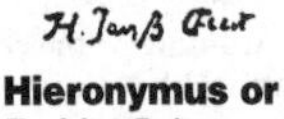

JANSSENS, Hieronymus or Jeroom, called The Dancer and The Fashion Painter

Flemish School, 17th century.
Born 1624; died 1693.
Painter. Genre scenes.

Hieronymus Janssens was baptised in Antwerp on 1 October 1624. He studied under Christophe van der Laemen and in 1644 was made a free master of the guild of St Luke in Antwerp. In 1650 he married Catharina van Dooren and they had a daughter.

Janssens, who worked for Don John of Austria, painted mainly scenes of balls and celebrations. He also painted the figures on architectural paintings by other artists, in particular Van Ehrenberg and Jan Gherinx. For many years his work was confused with that of Victor Honoré Janssens and was attributed by some experts to an artist by the name of Gonzalez Coques.

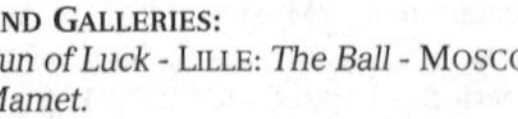

MUSEUMS AND GALLERIES:
BRUSSELS: *Run of Luck* - LILLE: *The Ball* - MOSCOW (Rumiantsev Mus.): *Mamet*.

AUCTION RECORDS:
PARIS, 28 Nov 1904, *Dutch Interior*, FRF 7,500. PARIS, 28 May 1907, *Run of Luck*, FRF 7,100. LONDON, 14 Dec 1907, *Ladies and Gentlemen*, GBP 15. LONDON, 2 July 1909, *Interior with a Group of Ladies and Children*, GBP 157. LONDON, 10 April 1911, *Portraits of a Gentleman and a Lady*, GBP 31. PARIS, 30 April 1924, *The Ball*, FRF 6,100. LONDON, 17 Dec 1924, *A Light Meal*, GBP 44. LONDON, 6 May 1927, *Minuet*, GBP 451. LONDON, 28 June 1935, *Terrace of a Private House*, GBP 57. LONDON, 3 July 1937, *Ladies and Gentlemen*, GBP 46. LONDON, 14 Feb 1947, *Ballroom Interior*, GBP 315. PARIS, 12 June 1950, *Run of Luck*, FRF 182,000. PARIS, 15 June 1954, *Light Meal on the Terrace*, FRF 180,000. VIENNA, 2 June 1964, *Merry Company in a Park*, ATS 20,000. LONDON, 14 May 1965, *Merry Company Carousing in a Garden*, Gns 950. VERSAILLES, 8 June 1967, *The Ball*, FRF 17,000. LONDON, 5 March 1969, *Celebration in a Garden*, GBP 2,100. LONDON, 27 Nov 1970, *Several Figures*, Gns 950. AMSTERDAM, 23 Nov 1971, *Merry Company on a Terrace*, NLG 21,500. LONDON, 9 Feb 1973, *Merry Company Carousing in a Park*, Gns 4,000. PARIS, 8 Dec 1974, *An Intimate Concert*, FRF 16,500. LONDON, 7 July 1976, *Interior with Family Group* (oil on canvas, 26¼ x 35½ ins / 66.5 x 90 cm) GBP 5,000. LONDON, 2 Dec 1977, *Interior with Family Group* (oil on canvas, 25½ x 34¾ ins / 64.8 x 88.2 cm) GBP 6,500. MONTE CARLO, 27 May 1984, *Run of Luck* (1655, oil on canvas, 28¾ x 39¾ ins / 73 x 101 cm) FRF 110,000. MONTE CARLO, 6 Dec 1987, *Romantic Scene in an Interior* (1648, oil on panel, 22½ x 32 ins / 57 x 81 cm) FRF 120,000. LONDON, 17 June 1988, *Run of Luck* (oil on canvas, 18½ x 25 ins / 47.3 x 63.8 cm) GBP 2,200. MILAN, 25 Oct 1988, *Run of Luck* (oil on canvas, 18½ x 25¼ ins / 47 x 64 cm) ITL 13,000,000. AMSTERDAM, 29 Nov 1988, *Host Interrupting the Quadrille to Welcome New Guests* (oil on canvas, 47¼ x 60¼ ins / 120 x 153 cm) NLG 19,550. PARIS, 12 Dec 1988, *Opening of the Ball* (oil on canvas, 17 x 24 ins / 43 x 61 cm) FRF 95,000. NEW YORK, 7 April 1989, *Elegant Company Gathered for a Banquet with Musicians Playing for a Couple to Dance* (oil on canvas, 23½ x 36¼ ins / 59.5 x 92 cm) USD 15,400. COLOGNE, 23 March 1990, *Interior with Elegant Company Having Dinner* (oil on canvas, 14 x 17¼ ins / 35.5 x 44 cm) DEM 6,000. NEW YORK, 31 May 1990, *Women Celebrating a Churching with Two Men Spying from behind a Screen* (oil on canvas, 31½ x 46¾ ins / 79.8 x 118.8 cm) USD 28,600. AMSTERDAM, 10 Nov 1992, *Elegant Company Leaving for a Country Outing* (oil on canvas, 24¼ x 35 ins / 61.6 x 88 cm) NLG 69,000. LONDON, 11 Dec 1992, *Interior with Elegant Company Dancing, Playing Cards and Conversing* (oil on canvas, 23¼ x 33½ ins / 59 x 85.3 cm) GBP 8,250. LONDON, 21 April 1993, *Elegant Company on a Terrace with a Couple Dancing* (oil on canvas, 46 x 33½ ins / 116 x 85 cm) GBP 16,100. AMSTERDAM, 10 May 1994, *Soldier and Horseman in a Barn* (oil on panel, 24 x 27¾ ins / 61 x 70.5 cm) NLG 20,700. LONDON, 9 Dec 1994, *The Parable of the Prodigal Son. The Prodigal Son Driven from the House. The Return of the Prodigal Son* (oil on canvas, collection, 19¼ x 23¼ ins / 48.8 x 58.8 cm) GBP 78,500. LONDON, 3 July 1996, *Elegant Company Carousing, Making Music and Dancing in a Palace Loggia* (oil on canvas, 43¾ x 64 ins / 111 x 162.7 cm) GBP 14,950. LONDON, 1 Nov 1996, *Elegant Lady with Two Musicians in an Interior* (oil on panel, 13 x 12½ ins / 33 x 31.8 cm) GBP 8,970. NEWMARKET, 24 Feb 1999, *Festive Gathering of Elegant Company Before Country House* (oil on canvas, 45 x 66 ins / 114 x 167 cm) GBP 24,000. LONDON, 16 Dec 1999, *Scene on the Terrace of Palace with Elegant Company Feasting* (oil on panel, 25 x 19 ins / 64 x 48 cm) GBP 36,000. VIENNA, 30 March 2000, *Elegant Party in a Palace* (oil on canvas, 24 x 33 ins / 61 x 85 cm) ATS 160,000. LONDON, 6 July 2000, *Elegant Figures Dancing on the Terrace of a Country Villa* (1656, oil on canvas, 44 x 65 ins / 113 x 164 cm) GBP 38,000. NEW YORK, 7 June 2002, *Ladies Celebrating the Birth of a Child, with Gentlemen*

Looking on from Behind a Screen (oil on canvas, 30 x 46 ins / 77 x 117 cm) USD 19,000. MUNICH, 6 Dec 2002, *Elegant Circle Dance* (oil on canvas, 46 x 76 ins / 116 x 192 cm) EUR 17,000. LILLE, 23 March 2003, *Beginning of the Ball* (oil on canvas, 22 x 32 ins / 57 x 81 cm) EUR 34,000. PARIS, 25 June 2004, *Interior Scene with Dancers* (oil on canvas, 22 x 31 ins / 56 x 80 cm) EUR 17,500. LONDON, 8 July 2004, *Interior with Elegant Company* (oil on canvas, 23 x 33 ins / 59 x 85 cm) GBP 15,000.

JANSSENS, J. Alexander
Dutch, 18th century.
Active c. 1700.
Engraver (etching).
J. Alexander Janssens is known for a series of 13 plates and frontispieces depicting the *Life of Achilles* after drafts by the painter Victor H. Jansen and also a pastoral piece entitled *Love and the Shepherdess*.

JANSSENS, Jan. See **JANSSENS Joannes** or **Jan**

JANSSENS, Jan
Flemish School, 18th century.
Painter. Portraits.
The son of Victor-Honoré Janssens, he died soon after his father.

JANSSENS, Jean-Martin
Belgian, 18th - 19th century.
Born 1764, in Geel (Flanders); died 11 February 1856.
Sculptor.
He worked for churches in the Campine region.

JANSSENS, Joannes or **Jan**
Flemish School, 17th century.
Born c. 1592, in Ghent.
Painter. History painting.
Joannes Janssens was an imitator of Caravaggio. He became a master of the guild in 1621 and senior guild member in 1646.
MUSEUMS AND GALLERIES:
GHENT: *Annunciation.*

JANSSENS, Johan
Belgian, 19th century.
Born 1809, in Antwerp.
Painter. Genre scenes.
A pupil of F de Braekelaer, he started exhibiting in 1838.
AUCTION RECORDS:
PARIS, 30 Nov 1984, *Raphael Drawing* (1847, oil on panel, 40 3/4 x 30 1/2 ins / 103.5 x 77.5 cm) FRF 28,000. COPENHAGEN, 5 March 2001, *Fishermen Selling the Day's Catch* (1839, oil on canvas, 28 x 34 ins / 70 x 87 cm) DKK 50,000. BRUSSELS, 28 May 2002, *Fishermen Returning* (1839, oil on canvas, 28 x 34 ins / 70 x 87 cm) EUR 6,500. AMSTERDAM, 1 Sept 2004, *Secret Letter* (1847, oil on panel, 29 x 21 ins / 73 x 53 cm) EUR 3,800.

JANSSENS, Joseph Marie Louis
Belgian, 19th - 20th century.
Born 1854, in St Niklaas; died 1930, in Antwerp.
Painter. Historical subjects, religious subjects, portraits. Church decoration.
Symbolism.
Joseph Janssens studied under Jan Swerts in Antwerp, under Franz Ittenbach in Düsseldorf, and under Godefroid Guffens at the Académie Royale des Beaux Arts in Brussels. Examples of his work were shown at the Brussels Exposition Universelle of 1910. Godefroid Guffens introduced Janssens to the work of the German Brotherhood of St Luke (the so-called 'Nazarenes'), which had a considerable influence on Janssens' own work. Joseph Janssens built his reputation on a remarkable number of portraits - over 400 - and on his decorative murals with religious themes, notably for the Brussels church of St Joseph and the Cathedral of Our Lady in Antwerp.
MUSEUMS AND GALLERIES:
ANTWERP - GHENT.
AUCTION RECORDS:
LONDON, 22 Nov 1989, *Presentation to the Temple* (oil on canvas, 70 3/4 x 47 1/4 ins / 180 x 120 cm) GBP 14,300.

JANSSENS, Josette
Belgian, 20th century.
Born 1949, in Schoten; died 1985, in Antwerp.
Sculptor, watercolourist.
Josette Janssens was active in a variety of areas, as a jewellery designer, a designer of film scenarios and a maker of animated films.

JANSSENS, Laurent
Flemish School, 18th century.
Painter. Landscapes, architectural views.
He was the son and pupil of Victor-Honoré Janssens, and often assisted his father by painting the landscapes and architectural features of his father's portraits.

JANSSENS, Michel
Flemish, 16th century.
Born in Antwerp.
Active c. 1548.
Painter.
Flemish School.
Janssens was made a bourgeois citizen of Antwerp in 1548.

JANSSENS, Pieter Elinga
Dutch, 17th century.
Painter. Genre scenes, interiors, still-lifes.
Pieter Janssens is believed to have been a pupil of Pieter de Hoog and was such an accomplished imitator of his style that his work is often confused with that of his teacher.

MUSEUMS AND GALLERIES:
BRUSSELS: *Lady at her Toilette* (1670, signature erased) - FRANKFURT AM MAIN: *Dutch Interior.*
AUCTION RECORDS:
ANTWERP, 1853, *Interiors with figures, Fruit and Shells,* FRF 200. LONDON, 11 Dec 1925, *The Queen of Bohemia,* GBP 90. PARIS, 25 May 1949, *The Letter,* FRF 250,000. PARIS, 28 May 1951, *Genre Scenes* (pair) FRF 100,000. LONDON, 12 Dec 1984, *Interior of a Dutch House* (oil on canvas, 19 x 23 1/2 ins / 48 x 60 cm) GBP 14,000. AMSTERDAM, 29 May 1986, *Still-life with Oranges, Lemons and a Pewter Plate* (oil on canvas, 31 3/4 x 25 3/4 ins / 80.8 x 65.4 cm) NLG 40,000.

JANSSENS, René or **Emmanuel J. René**
Belgian, 19th - 20th century.
Born 1869 or 1870, in Brussels; died 1936.
Painter, watercolourist, draughtsman, lithographer.
Interiors with figures, landscapes, still-lifes, flowers.
René Janssens studied under Jean-François Portaels at the Académie Royale des Beaux Arts in Brussels and also received instruction from Pierre Victor Galland at the École des Beaux-Arts in Paris. He was a co-founder and member of the group of artists known as Le Sillon (The Furrow), and he exhibited on a regular basis in Brussels, notably at the Salon du Sillon and at a number of institutional exhibitions in Brussels, Antwerp, Ghent and Liège. He also exhibited in Paris at the Salon de la Société Nationale des Beaux-Arts, where he received an honourable mention in 1900 at that year's Exposition Universelle. In 1934 René Janssens published a work entitled *Painters of Intimacy*. This was followed in 1935 by his *Leading Art Critics in France and Belgium*.

René Janssens' own early work was in the Symbolist vein but he subsequently painted more in the Flemish tradition, producing, above all, interiors and still-lifes.

Bibliography:

Jottrand, Lucien, *'René Janssens'* in *coll. Peintres et Sculpteurs belges*, Dietrich, Brussels, 1938. *René Janssens 1870-1936: dessins, aquarelles*, Goossens, Brussels, 1940.

Museums and Galleries:

Antwerp - Brussels (Mus. Communal): *Staircase* - Ghent: *Red Drawing Room* - Paris (Mus. d'Orsay): several drawings.

Auction records:

Amsterdam, 14-15 April 1992, *Still-life with Flowers* (1931, oil on card, 17¼ x 19¾ ins / 44 x 50 cm) NLG 2,070. Brussels, 20 Nov 2001, *In the Studio* (1897, oil on canvas on panel, 42 x 28 ins / 106 x 71 cm) BEF 66,000.

JANSSENS, Victor Honoré

Flemish School, 17th - 18th century.
Born 1658, in Brussels; died 1736 or 1738, in Brussels.
Painter. Religious subjects, mythological subjects, figures, portraits, genre scenes. Designs for tapestries.

Victor Honoré Janssens was the son of a tailor and destined to take up the same profession, but his artistic inclinations took him in a different direction. In 1675 he was sent to study under the painter Lancelot Volders and remained working with him for seven years. In 1689 he was made a master artist in Brussels. The duke of Holstein summoned him to his court, where, over a period of four years, he produced some excellent small portraits. His patron provided him with the means to go to Italy and Janssens remained there for 11 years. In Italy he became friends with Domenico Marchi Tempesta and often painted the figures for his landscapes. He returned to Brussels in 1711; there he painted a ceiling at the city hall and also created a large number of tapestry designs. In 1718 he was invited to go to Vienna to give lessons to the Empress Eleanor and was appointed painter to the court. After spending three years in Vienna he went to London before returning to Brussels, his native city, where he eventually died. His daughter married the painter Duchâtel.

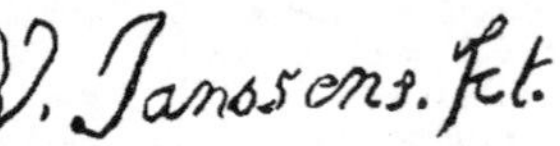

Museums and Galleries:

Brussels: *Virgin Appearing to St Bruno* - Caen: *Aeneas Hears of the Murder of Polydorus* - Douai: *Transfer of the Body of St Vaast* - Dunkirk: *Jesus Receiving the Children*; *Gathering outside a Palace* - Paris (Louvre): *Run of Luck* - Stockholm: *Moses and the Rock* - Valenciennes: *Strength through Unity* - Vienna: *Venus and Adonis.*

Auction records:

Paris, 1777, *Women Bathing* (pair) FRF 203. Brussels, 1865, *Portrait of Louis XIV*; *Portrait of Condé* (pair) FRF 2,100. Paris, 1890, *Tending the Newborn,* FRF 850. New York, 4 Nov 1971, *Rustic Interior,* USD 1,000. Versailles, 5 March 1978, *The Feast* (oil on canvas, 41¾ x 30¾ ins / 106 x 78 cm) FRF 14,500. Paris, 18 March 1981, *Equestrian Portrait of Maximilian of Bavaria* (oil on metal, 14¼ x 11 ins / 36.5 x 28 cm) FRF 45,500. London, 22 July 1983, *The Feeding of the Five Thousand* (oil on canvas, 108¼ x 76½ ins / 275 x 194.2 cm) GBP 1,700. New York, 15 Oct 1992, *Venus Reclining Surrounded by her Servants and Putti with a Temple in the Distance* (oil on panel, 11½ x 17¼ ins / 29.5 x 44.1 cm) USD 4,950. London, 3-4 Dec 1997, *Diana and her Servants Resting in a Wooded Landscape* (oil on panel, 11 x 16¼ ins / 28.2 x 41 cm) GBP 13,800. Amsterdam, 13 May 2003, *Death of Caesar* (oil on canvas, 24 x 35 ins / 60 x 90 cm) EUR 5,500.

JANSSENS VAN CEULEN, Cornelis. See **CEULEN**

JANSSOENS. See **JANSZ, JANS, JANSEN, JOHANSEN**

JANSSON. See also **JANSON, JANSZ, JANS, JANSEN, JANSS, JANSSENS, JOHANSEN**

JANSSON, Alfred

Swedish, 19th - 20th century.
Born 1863, in Sweden; died 1931.
Painter.

Alfred Jansson studied in Stockholm and Paris. He was a member of the Palette and Chisel Club in Chicago.

Auction records:

New York, 20 April 1979, *Snowy Landscape* (1926, oil on canvas, 30 x 25 ins / 76.2 x 63.5 cm) USD 1,700. San Francisco, 21 June 1984, *Winter Landscape* (1919, oil on canvas, 32¼ x 38¼ ins / 82 x 97 cm) USD 2,500.

JANSSON, Eugène Fredrik

Swedish, 19th - 20th century.
Born 18 March 1862, in Stockholm; died 15 June 1915, in Stockholm.
Painter, pastellist. Nudes, genre scenes, landscapes, seascapes.

Eugène Fredrik Jansson came from a modest family background. Poor health as a child persisted into adulthood and affected him for the rest of his life. Jansson was admitted to the Swedish royal academy of fine arts but left without graduating. His distaste for academism was already pronounced and this became stronger as he grew older. As a militant socialist and a declared homosexual, Jansson was already on the margins of society. On the death of his father, he was forced to provide for the material needs of his family. Although he was not accepted into 'official' art circles, he was admired by King Oscar II and the banking magnate Ernest Thiel, both of whom acquired some of his paintings. He was ultimately accepted into the Association of Swedish Artists and duly showed examples of his work at the group's exhibitions in Sweden and abroad. In 1900, Jansson spent some time in Paris, where he received an honourable mention at that year's Exposition Universelle. He also travelled in Italy. His health deteriorated rapidly, however, and he died in Stockholm in 1915 when he was 53 years old.

Jansson was unpopular in his native Sweden and remained largely unknown outside his own country until a comprehensive exhibition of his work was held at the Musée d'Orsay in Paris in 1999. In terms of technique, Eugène Jansson's work is in a Post-Impressionist/Neo-Impressionist mode, with sweeping strokes reminiscent of Edvard Munch. In his earlier work, Jansson painted Stockholm street scenes and cityscapes and favoured populist themes: sailors scrubbing themselves clean on the beach after work or the working-class suburbs of the Swedish capital. He soon began to focus exclusively on nocturnal cityscapes, however, painted predominantly in a range of sombre dark blues punctuated by watery lights, such as a solitary bicycle lamp or the reflection of a train's headlights on metal rails. Here, the fluid blues alternate with sporadic daubs of paint applied with a palette knife. Again like Munch, Jansson adopts the leitmotif of a long vertical shaft of light from a sun setting over the sea. These *Nocturnes* have the haziness and fog-like penumbra familiar from the work of British Impressionists or that of Turner and Whistler. In his final years, Eugène Jansson reverted to daylight scenes. A casually elegant full-length self-portrait is painted against the unusual backdrop of groups of nude male bathers - an allusion perhaps to his own sexual preferences but also to the naturist tradition in Scandinavia. The male nude theme may be considered audacious - even innovative - but from a technical standpoint at least, Jansson seems distinctly less at ease than in his benchmark *Nocturnes*.

Bibliography:
Eugène Jansson, nocturnes suédois, exhibition catalogue, Musée d'Orsay, Paris, 1999. Dagen, Philippe, '*Eugène Jansson, artiste maudit, provocateur méconnu*' in *Le Monde,* periodical, Paris, 20 May 1999.

Museums and Galleries:
Göteborg: *Five Landscapes* - Stockholm (Nationalmus.): *Acrobats; September Evening; Evening at Kornhamn* - Stockholm (Thielska Gal.): *Nocturne; Hornsgatan; Baths.*

Auction records:
Stockholm, 31 Jan 1947, *Dusk,* SEK 5,550. Stockholm, 30 Oct 1984, *November Sun* (1898, oil on canvas, 61 x 91 1/4 ins / 155 x 232 cm) SEK 300,000. Göteborg, 9 April 1986, *Summer Landscape* (oil on canvas, 17 3/4 x 11 1/2 ins / 45 x 29 cm) SEK 25,000. Stockholm, 19 Oct 1987, *Landscape* (1893, oil on canvas, 24 x 35 3/4 ins / 61 x 91 cm) SEK 290,000. New York, 23 Oct 1990, *Stockholm by Feburary Moonlight* (oil on canvas, 29 x 21 3/4 ins / 73.7 x 55.2 cm) USD 55,000. Stockholm, 29 May 1991, *Road in Holland in the Evening* (oil on canvas, 24 x 35 3/4 ins / 61 x 91 cm) SEK 240,000. Stockholm, 30 Nov 1993, *Near Djurgarden in Autumn: Landscape with a Fenced Meadow and a Tree beside a Lake* (oil on canvas, 20 x 30 3/4 ins / 51 x 78 cm) SEK 20,000. London, 12 June 1996, *Male Nudes* (chalk/paper, five studies) GBP 2,070. Stockholm, 25 Nov 1998, *Evening, Landscape from Arstaviken* (1894, oil on canvas, 41 x 30 ins / 104 x 76 cm) SEK 1,550,000. Stockholm, 26 May 1999, *Moonlit Night - from Studio in Stockholm* (1896, oil on canvas, 34 x 48 ins / 87 x 122 cm) SEK 1,200,000. Stockholm, 24 Nov 1999, *View from Skeppsholmen* (wash heightened with white, 13 x 20 ins / 33 x 51 cm) SEK 38,000. London, 7 April 2000, *Varkvall - Spring Evening* (oil on canvas, 29 x 24 ins / 73 x 60 cm) GBP 168,500. London, 6 June 2001, *Evening Mood* (c. 1896, oil on canvas, 19 x 27 ins / 49 x 68 cm) GBP 68,000. Stockholm, 4 Dec 2001, *Towards Sunset* (oil on canvas, 21 x 17 ins / 53 x 42 cm) SEK 305,000. Stockholm, 28 May 2002, *Evening Landscape* (oil on canvas, 32 x 26 ins / 81 x 67 cm) SEK 59,000. Stockholm, 26 May 2003, *Summer Evening, Aarsta bay* (oil on canvas, 33 x 53 ins / 84 x 135 cm) SEK 190,000.

JANSSON, Karl Emmanuel

Finnish, 19th century.
Born 7 July 1846, near Finström; died 1874.
Painter. Genre scenes, landscapes.

Museums and Galleries:
Helsinki: *Fishermen Holding their Nets; Peasants; Bride from the Åland Province; Danish Sailors Playing Cards; The First Lesson; A Farm; At the Door of the Vestry; The Church Collection; Portrait of a Friend of the Painter; The Marriage Proposal.*

Auction records:
London, 16 March 1989, *The Watch in the Evening* (1865, oil on canvas, 21 3/4 x 29 3/4 ins / 55.5 x 75.5 cm) GBP 187,000. Helsinki, 24 April 1999, *Landscape* (watercolour, 3 x 5 ins / 8 x 12 cm) FIM 12,500. Helsinki, 25 April 1999, *By the Window* (oil on canvas/board, 9 x 7 ins / 23 x 19 cm) FIM 18,000. Helsinki, 17 May 2003, *Interior, Jomala* (oil on canvas/board, 11 x 13 ins / 27 x 34 cm) EUR 10,000.

JANSSON, Rune

Swedish, 20th century.
Born 1918.
Painter (mixed media). Allegorical subjects.

Auction records:
Stockholm, 26 May 1987, *Composition* (1961, oil on canvas, 18 1/2 x 38 1/2 ins / 47 x 98 cm) SEK 20,500. Stockholm, 6 June 1988, *Composition* (1986, oil, 24 1/2 x 36 1/2 ins / 62 x 93 cm) SEK 16,000. Stockholm, 21 Nov 1988, *Red Sea* (distemper and coloured chalks, 9 x 12 1/2 ins / 23 x 31.5 cm) SEK 4,100. Stockholm, 22 May 1989, *Still-life* (1946, oil on panel, 18 x 15 ins / 46 x 38 cm) SEK 8,000. Stockholm, 14 June 1990, *Cross on Rattan Branches* (1959, oil on canvas, 19 1/4 x 21 1/4 ins / 49 x 54 cm) SEK 12,500. Stockholm, 5-6 Dec 1990, *Valley in Summer* (1959, oil on canvas, 16 1/4 x 13 3/4 ins / 41 x 35 cm) SEK 9,200. Stockholm, 28 Oct 1991, *Archipelago* (1986, oil on canvas, 11 x 20 ins / 27 x 51 cm) SEK 4,600. Stockholm, 21 May 1992, *Prehistoric Creature* (1957, oil on canvas, 24 3/4 x 31 ins / 63 x 79 cm) SEK 15,000. Stockholm, 30 Nov 1993, *Impressions in Black* (oil on canvas, 17 1/4 x 54 ins / 44 x 137 cm) SEK 15,000. Stockholm, 17 May 1999, *Red Sea* (1965, oil on canvas, 20 x 54 ins / 51 x 138 cm) SEK 16,000. Stockholm, 22 Nov 1999, *Disolving Surface and Red* (1961, oil on canvas, 32 x 54 ins / 81 x 138 cm) SEK 16,000. Stockholm, 22 Nov 1999, *Lion* (1957, oil on canvas, 35 x 46 ins / 88 x 116 cm) SEK 16,000. Stockholm, 27 Nov 2000, *Green Sea* (1988, oil on canvas, 23 x 43 ins / 58 x 108 cm) SEK 15,000. Stockholm, 28 Aug 2001, *Composition* (1961, oil on canvas, 45 x 53 ins / 115 x 135 cm) SEK 25,500. Stockholm, 3 Nov 2004, *Green and Pink* (1963, mixed media, 22 x 54 ins / 55 x 137 cm) SEK 25,000.

JANSSON, Thorolf

Swedish, 20th century.
Born 3 March 1877, in Stockholm.
Painter. Stage sets.

Thorolf Jansson studied in Germany and went on to paint numerous decorative compositions for opera sets in the royal theatre in Stockholm (*Carmen, Don Giovanni, Orpheus in the Underworld, The Magic Flute, Tosca*), together with sets for a range of Wagnerian operas.

JANSSON, Viktor Bernhard

Finnish, 20th century.
Born 1 March 1886, in Helsinki.
Sculptor. Statues, busts, monuments.

Viktor Jansson studied at the fine arts society in Helsinki; he spent three years in Paris, where he was a pupil of Antoine Injalbert. In Helsinki, Jansson sculpted a granite *Athlete* and commemorative bronzes of *Tammerfors* and *Lahtis*.

Museums and Galleries:
Helsinki (Valtion Taidemus.): *Robert Stigell, Sculptor* (bronze bust); *Toivo Juula, Composer* (bronze mask).

JANSSON-BLOMMER, Edla

Finnish, 19th century.
Born 10 May 1817, in Helsinki; died 19 December 1908, in Helsinki.
Painter.

Edla Jansson-Blommer's *Woman at the Spinning-wheel* and *Portrait of Mrs Sarah Waklin* are in the Helsinki museum.

JANSSON-HAMMARSTEN, Signe

Swedish, 20th century.
Born 1 June 1882, in Hannäs.
Humorist artist.

Signe Jansson-Hammarsten studied at the technical high school in Stockholm before spending two years in Paris, where she studied under Guérin. She is noted for her caricatures in the periodical *Lucifer* contributed between 1916 and 1924. She married the sculptor Viktor Jansson.

JANSSONIUS. See **JANSONIUS Wilhelmus** and **JANSEN Heinrich**

JANSSZ. See also **JANS, JANSS, JANSEN, JANSON, JANSSENS, JANSZ, JOHANSEN**

JANSSZ., Jacob, or Jansz.

Dutch, 16th century.
Active in Haarlem.
Painter.

Janssz. restored the 12 portraits of the counts of Holland at the town hall of Haarlem in 1578. He should not be confused with Jacob of Haarlem.

JANSZ. See also **JANS, JANSEN, JANSON, JANSS, JANSSEN, JANSSENS, JOHANSEN**

JANSZ, Egbert
German, 17th century.
Active in Germany c. 1600.
Engraver (burin).

Egbert Jansz is credited with a series of small prints called *Icons of Venantium* (1598) from A. Tempesta, engraved after Crispyn de Passe.

JANSZ, Filips
German, 17th century.
Active in Danzig (now Gdansk, Poland).
Engraver.

Filips Jansz is known for portraits of Danzig notables and for engravings showing the catafalque of King Sigismund III of Poland, dated 1632. He also did an engraved portrait of the king.

JANSZ, Jacob. See also **JACOB van Haarlem**

JANSZ., Antonis
German, 16th century.
Active in Utrecht c. 1561.
Painter (glass).

JANSZ., Claes
Flemish School, 17th century.
Active in Rotterdam c. 1600 and in Amsterdam c. 1606.
Painter (glass).

JANSZ., Cornelis
Dutch, 17th century.
Active in Groningen.
Engraver (line-engraving).

Cornelis Jansz. married Catharina Cornelisz. Hellemans in The Hague on 10 November 1647.

JANSZ., Dirck
Dutch, 16th century.
Died 1603, in Delft.
Active in Delft.
Painter (glass).

JANSZ., Govert, called Mynheer
Flemish School, 17th century.
Born 1578; died before 1619.
Painter.

Govert Jansz. was a pupil of Cornelis Cornelissen. In 1603 he married the sister of the painter Cornelis van der Voort.

JANSZ., Henri
Dutch, 16th century.
Active c. 1518.
Painter. History painting.

According to Siret, Jansz.' name is listed in the old accounts of the church in Utrecht.

JANSZ., Herman
German, 16th century.
Active c. 1518.
Painter. History painting.

According to Siret, Jansz. painted a *Last Judgement* in Utrecht for the house of Hazenberg, which is today in the town hall.

JANSZ., Jacob
Dutch, 17th century.
Born in Haarlem.
Painter.

Jacob Jansz. was working successfully in 1670 and is still shown as a member of the guild of St Luke in 1732.

JANSZ., Jan
Flemish School, 17th century.
Painter.

Jan Jansz. was the son of Willem Jansz. and was from Casselbergh. He worked in The Hague in 1605.

JANSZ., Nicolas
Dutch, 17th century.
Active in Rotterdam c. 1600.
Glass painter.

JANSZ., R.
Dutch, 17th century.
Painter. Battles.

R. Jansz. may be identical with Reynier Jansz. who was married in The Hague in 1668 at the age of 44. He may also be the same as Ritgart Jansen who was a member of the Dordrecht guild in 1622. He worked in the style of Palamedes.

JANSZ., Symon, or Janz
Dutch, 15th century.
Painter.

Records place Symon Jansz. in Leiden in 1464, where he is recorded as having painted portraits of *The Duke of Burgundy, The Wife of the Duke of Burgundy* and *The Count of Charolais.*

JANSZ., Tierry
Dutch, 16th century.
Painter.

The name of Tierry Jansz. appears in a document dating from about 1520, which belongs to the town of Utrecht.

JANSZ., Willem
Dutch, 17th century.
Painter.

Willem Jansz. worked in Jisp in 1658, and is thought to have produced a painting of *Adam and Eve.*

JANSZON. See **JANSZ, JANS, JANSS, JANSEN, JANSON, JANSSEN, JOHANSEN**

JANTHUR, Richard
German, 20th century.
Born 12 April 1883, in Zerbst.
Painter, engraver, lithographer, illustrator. Scenes with figures, still-lifes.

Richard Janthur studied at the college of fine arts in Breslau (now Wroclaw, Poland). He settled in Berlin in 1908 and in the same year became a member of the Secession Group. He also exhibited at the fine arts exhibition from 1919. His *Company by the Sea*, exhibited at the Secession, was a critical success. His style tended towards Expressionism, notably in his still-lifes. Above all, Janthur was an etcher and a lithographer. Among the literary works he illustrated were Swift's *Gulliver's Travels*, Defoe's *Robinson Crusoe*, Kipling's *Jungle Book*, and *Roses of Chiraz, Travels in Greece*. He also published an *Exotic Album* comprising eleven lithographs, and a *Men and Beasts* portfolio of nine etchings. In his later years, he was active in the applied arts.

JANTL, Anton. See **JANDL**

JANTSCH, Carl Paul
German, 19th - 20th century.
Born 1 June 1871, in Görlitz.
Painter, art restorer.

Carl Paul Jantsch studied at the fine arts academy in Dresden, and lived and worked in Dresden-Loschwitz. He is remembered as a painter and restorer.

MUSEUMS AND GALLERIES:
DRESDEN (Stadtmus.) - GÖRLITZ (Städtische Kunstsammlungen).

JANTSCHA, Laurens or Lorenz.
See **JANSCHA**

JANTUNEN, Antti
Finnish, 20th century.
Born 1944, in Hollola.
Painter.

Antii Jantunen studied at the Finnish academy of art from 1963 to 1968. Rather than being descriptive, his painting is a reflection on forms taken from the technological world of contemporary reality. His subjects are trucks, columns and various constructions.

JANTYIK, Matyas
Hungarian, 19th century.
Born 10 May 1864, in Békés; died 16 October 1903, in Békés.
Painter.

Matyas Jantyik studied in Budapest, Rome, and at the Académie Julian in Paris. In 1885 he sent his first work, *Noon*, back from Paris to the Budapest exhibition. *Laocoon* in 1886 and *Beggar* in 1887 were exhibited at the Paris Salons. When he returned to Budapest, he spent several years drawing illustrations and painted his historical composition *Maria Theresa Transforming the Village of Szabadka into a Town*. In 1899, he exhibited a large open-air painting *Corpus Christi*. There are two frescoes by him in the meeting hall of the palace in Budapest.

JANTZEN, David
Livonian, 19th century.
Active in Riga.
Draughtsman, lithographer, illustrator. Portraits, landscapes, urban views.
Baltic School.

K.F. Hauswald used David Jantzen's drawings for his lithographs of a portrait of the Mayor J.J. Rolssen and 12 plates of *Picturesque Views of Riga and its Surroundings*. Jantzen drew 600 illustrations for the *History of Peter the Great* by N.P. Lambin.

JANTZEN, Hans Henrik
Danish, 19th century.
Born 14 February 1857, in Vesterladen, near Aalborg; died 15 February 1897, in New York.
Painter, engraver.

Hans Jantzen was a pupil at the Kunstakademi in Copenhagen and exhibited a *Portrait*, several landscapes in oil and pastel, and an etching between 1885 and 1889. From 1891 onwards he worked in New York as a portrait artist.

JANTZEN, Horace, or Janzen
German, 19th century.
Painter. Genre scenes, landscapes.

Jantzen work in Dresden, Berlin and Stuttgart in about 1870, and exhibited in Vienna in 1871.

JANUARIO. See **GENNARO Gaetano de**

JANULA, Frantisek
Czechoslovak, 20th century.
Born 1932.
Active in France from 1967.
Collage artist, assemblage artist, mixed media, sculptor, engraver, illustrator.

Frantisek Janula studied at the school of decorative art in Prague from 1949 to 1955 and later, in 1967-1968, at the École Supérieure des Beaux-Arts in Paris.

Janula's works are created out of anything and everything that comes to hand which he takes, cuts and assembles, adding colour - white, ochre, brown, yellow, blue and mauve. Jean Orizet has described him as a 'painter and craftsman, a handyman of genius, gorging on material, an insatiable collector of everyday objects and scraps, scavenging the refuse abandoned on our polluted shores by a consumerist society'. In 1993 the Galerie Jean-Claude Riedel showed his 'picture-sculptures' created on door panels. These are 6 feet (2 metres) high works in which Janula recreated the surface of the wood, inserting various disparate objects - car hubcaps, jam pot lids, metal blades from a fridge - which he carefully painted. Janula also made engravings and has illustrated poems by Jean Orizet, Joseph Paul Schneider, André Simoncini, François Lescun, Jean-Luc Signaux, Ahmed Boulahfa and Michel de Smet.

He has exhibited since 1957, taking part in collective exhibitions since 1959 including: Salon of Young Painters, Brno (1967); Cabinet des Estampes, Bibliothèque Nationale, Paris (1979); Salon Comparaisons (1983 and 1986); Salon de la Jeune Peinture, Paris (1986); Foire Internationale d'Art Contemporain, Luxembourg (1988); Art Fair, Stockholm (1989); 24th Prix International d'Art Contemporain in Monte Carlo (1990); Galerie Horizon in Marseilles (1991 and 1993); Galerie Jean-Claude Riedel in Paris (1993).

Solo exhibitions include: Mlada Fronta Gallery, Prague (1957); Galerie Paul Facchetti, Paris (1973); Galerie Biren, Paris (1976); Galerie Septentrion, Marcq-en-Barœul (1980); Amsterdam and Rotterdam (1982); at the Galerie Simoncini, Luxembourg (1983, 1984, 1987 and 1990); Galerie Arkadia, Paris (1983 and 1986); Galerie Bosquet, Paris (1987); Bibliothèque Henri Michaux, Aubervilliers (1991); Galerie Jean-Claude Riedel, Paris (1993).

BIBLIOGRAPHY:

Orizet, Jean (preface), *Portes en abîme*, exhibition catalogue, Gal. Jean-Claude Riedel, Paris, 1993.

JANUS-IPSEN, Poul. See **IPSEN Poul Janus**

JANUSCH. See **JOHANNES**

JANUSEK, Frantisek
Czech, 20th century.
Born 1890, in Jesené, near Semily; died 1943, in Prague.
Painter. Scenes with figures.
Mánes Group.

Frantisek Janusek was briefly a school teacher before attending the Prague academy of fine art from 1918 to 1922. From 1923, having decided to devote himself to painting, he became a member of the Mánes Association of Artists. In 1926, he went to Paris and, in 1929, to Italy.

The main influence on his work was Surrealism. From a sort of Cubist-Expressionism that became progressively more detached from the natural appearance of things, he developed his work through a series of different periods. Around 1933, vague vegetable or animal forms placed here and there in barren landscapes bring to mind the work of Tanguy and Dalí. From 1935, these forms, sometimes soft, sometimes sharp, blend into one another in tightly composed pictures reminiscent of Brauner and Dominguez. The mood of his paintings after 1937 where vague beings seems to wander in the darkness, takes on a tragic note. From 1938 to his death in 1943, his figures seem to have been consumed by the heat of the Apocalypse into fused forms that have lost all appearance of humanity.

Frantisek Janusek took part in many collective exhibitions and a retrospective devoted to him was held in 1965. He featured in the 1968 exhibition *Fifty years of Czechoslovak Painting from the Collections of the Galleries, 1918-1958*, a touring exhibition commemorating the foundation of the Republic in 1918.

BIBLIOGRAPHY:

Fifty years of Czechoslovak Painting from the Collections of the Galleries, 1918-1958, exhibition catalogue, Slovenska Narodna Gal., Bratislava, 1968 (in commemoration of the 50th anniversary of the Republic of Czechoslovakia).

AUCTION RECORDS:

PARIS, 22 June 1984, *The Sculptor* (1932, oil on canvas, 38 1/2 x 49 1/4 ins / 98 x 125 cm) FRF 30,000. PRAGUE, 13 Oct 2001, *Still-life with Bread* (oil on canvas, 20 x 26 ins / 50 x 65 cm)

CZK 100,000. PRAGUE, 13 Oct 2001, *Abortionist* (1936, oil on canvas, 28 x 37 ins / 70 x 93 cm) CZK 700,000.

JANUSEK, Vladimir
Czechoslovak, 20th century.
Born 30 January 1922, in Zdirnice.
Sculptor.

Vladimir Janusek first studied at the school of arts and crafts in Brno and then, from 1945 to 1950, at the school of decorative arts in Prague.

After a period during which he made many portrait sculptures, he began to work in cut and welded metal often combining it with cement to create forms recalling human bodies or strange animals with spindly extremities. He executed a number of monumental sculptures for the crematorium in Ostrava and for the nautical stadium in Prague.

He has taken part in international collective exhibitions, including: 1954 Venice Biennale; Czechoslovak Pavilion, Exposition Internationale, Brussels (1958); 2nd Biennale of Sculpture, Carrara (1959); 2nd Exposition Internationale de Sculpture Contemporaine, Musée Rodin, Paris (1961); exhibition of Czechoslovak art, Bochum museum (1965); Essen museum (1966).

JANUSKOVA, Vera
Czechoslovak, 20th century.
Born 25 June 1922, in Ubislavice, near Nová Paka.
Sculptor.

Vera Januskova was a student at the school of decorative arts in Prague from 1942 to 1948. After a first period influenced by Cubist ideas of volume and construction, in around 1960 she began to produce works using items of the refuse of today's consumer society first by mounting them in concrete and later by welding them together in such a way as to exploit the garish colours of their painted metal surfaces.

She has taken part in many collective exhibitions in Czechoslovakia and also abroad including in Bochum and Genoa (1965) and Berlin (1966). She held solo exhibitions in Prague (1960 and 1965).

JANVIER, Hortense
French, 20th century.
Born 20 May 1896, in Le Perreux (Val-de-Marne).
Painter.

Hortense Janvier studied with Paul-Albert Laurens. She exhibited in Paris at the Salon des Artistes Français, of which she was a member.

JANVIER, Jehan
French, 16th century.
Active in Le Mans.
Sculptor (wood).

Janvier produced a statue of *St Nicholas* for the chapel of St-Nicolas in the church of Notre Dame in Alençon.

JANVIER, Jules Louis
French, 19th century.
Born 12 March 1824, in Toulon; died 16 January 1871, in Toulon.
Painter, watercolourist, draughtsman. Landscapes.

Jules Janvier was an engineer and sub-director of the Marine's hydraulic works at the port of Toulon, while also a keen painter and watercolourist, taking advice from his friend, the painter Vincent Courdouan.

His landscapes are constructed using very assured compositions, based on his topographical knowledge of the location, yet they retain touches of sensitivity and emotion.

MUSEUMS AND GALLERIES:
TOULON: *Var Coast* (pencil).

JANVIER, Lucien Joseph René
French, 20th century.
Born 17 August 1878, in Paris.
Sculptor, medallist.

L. J. R. Janvier was a pupil of Denis Puech. He exhibited in Paris at the Salon des Artistes Français, of which he became a member, with an honourable mention, in 1898.

JANVIER, Victor
French, 19th century.
Active in Paris.
Sculptor, medallist.

Victor Janvier was a member of the Société des Artistes Français from 1893 and featured at that society's Salon, receiving an honourable mention in 1892. He was made a Chevalier of the Légion d'Honneur in 1901.

JANYN, Anthoine
French, 16th century.
Painter.

Janyn was a painter and card maker, and produced escutcheons and cartouches for the official visit of a dignitary to Lyons in 1516.

JANZ, Philipp
German, 19th century.
Born 1813, in Mainz; died 1885, in Mainz.
Painter.

Janz was also a restorer of paintings.

MUSEUMS AND GALLERIES:
MAINZ: *Part of the Hallgarter Zange*; *The Writer* (sketch).

AUCTION RECORDS:
PARIS, 28-29 Nov 1923, *Landscape Crossed by a River, Figures and Animals*, FRF 880. PARIS, 4 March 1925, *Crossing the Ford*, FRF 610. COLOGNE, 20 May 1985, *Winter Landscape, Holland* (1860, oil on panel, 7 3/4 x 10 1/2 ins / 19.5 x 26.5 cm) DEM 5,400.

JAO CHING. See **RAO JING**

JAO KING. See **RAO JING**

JAOUEN, Théophile
French, 19th century.
Active in Brittany.
Painter. Landscapes.

Théophile Jaouen is known for his typically regionalist works, held in the Museum of Brest since 1895.

MUSEUMS AND GALLERIES:
BREST: several works.

JAPHET, Alexandre Jean Louis. See **JAZET**

JAPIKSZ., Jan. See **JAAPIX**

JAPPÉ, Jean Paul
French, 20th century.
Born 21 August 1936, in Lorient.
Painter.

Jean Paul Jappé scrapes, crosshatches, scars and lacerates his canvases in pitiless battles between sea and land, wind and plants, joy and anguish. He showed work in various collective exhibitions, including the 1965 Paris Biennale des Jeunes Artistes and the 1981 Paris FIAC (Foire Internationale d'Art Contemporain). He had solo shows at the Galerie Nane Stern in Paris from 1977.

BIBLIOGRAPHY:
Jean Paul Jappé, exhibition catalogue, Gal. Nane Stern, Paris, 1981.

JAPY, Louis Aimé
French, 19th - 20th century.
Born 1840, in Berne (Doubs); died 17 January 1916, in Paris.
Painter. Genre scenes, landscapes.

Louis Aimé Japy studied under Français and under Corot. Early in his career he painted subjects in Italy, but he mostly painted scenes in France, especially in the Jura and the Doubs. He began to show work at the Paris Salon in 1864, and won a medal in 1870 and a second-class medal in 1873.

He became a member of the Société des Artistes Français in 1883, won silver medals at the Exposiitions Universelles in Paris in 1889 and 1900 and was made a Chevalier of the Légion d'Honneur in 1906.

Museums and Galleries:
Amsterdam: *Landscape* - Budapest: *Shepherd* - Langres: *Dusk in Brittany; Evening Landscape* - Limoux: *Moonrise* - Morlaix: *Brittany, Flock Resting* - Roanne: *Marshland in Picardy* - Salford (Museum and AG): *Spring in the Valley of the Somme* - St-Étienne: *Field Labours in the Ain* - Washington DC: *Spring in the Mountains; Dusk in Brittany*.
Auction records:
Paris, 27 March 1897, *Mill in Normandy,* FRF 305. Paris, 21 June 1902, *Fisherman,* FRF 480. Paris, 14 Feb 1927, *Riverbank Landscape,* FRF 3,200. Paris, 20 March 1944, *Sheep in the Hills, Riverbanks* (two pendants) FRF 12,500. Paris, 18 March 1955, *Woodland,* FRF 13,000. Tokyo, 27 May 1969, *Beside a Pool,* GBP 1,150. Versailles, 16 March 1972, *Solitary Horseman* (oil on canvas, 18 x 22 ins / 46 x 55 cm) FRF 1,500. Lucerne, 28 June 1973, *River Landscape,* CHF 4,200. Bern, 22 Oct 1976, *Ferry* (1891, oil on canvas, 18 x 22 ins / 46 x 55 cm) CHF 7,000. Bern, 21 Oct 1977, *Shepherdess and Sheep by Water* (1883, oil on canvas, 32 x 39¼ ins / 81 x 100 cm) CHF 8,000. London, 6 April 1979, *Sunset* (1873, oil on canvas, 40¼ x 63¾ ins / 102.2 x 162 cm) GBP 1,500. Stuttgart, 6 March 1981, *Landscape with Birch Trees* (oil on canvas, 22 x 18 ins / 55 x 46 cm) DEM 9,500. Barbizon, 27 Feb 1983, *Shepherdess and Flock near Woodland* (1886, oil on canvas, 25¾ x 32 ins / 65.5 x 81 cm) FRF 32,000. New York, 26 Feb 1986, *Landscape, Pool at Nightfall* (oil on canvas, 35 x 46 ins / 89 x 117 cm) USD 7,000. St-Maur-des-Fossés, 18 Oct 1987, *Watermill* (oil on canvas, 25½ x 32 ins / 65 x 81 cm) FRF 54,000. New York, 25 Feb 1988, *River Landscape with Shepherdess and Flock* (oil on canvas, 26 x 32¼ ins / 66 x 81.8 cm) USD 7,700. London, 25 March 1988, *Shepherd and Flock Crossing a Bridge* (1893, oil on canvas, 25½ x 31½ ins / 65 x 80 cm) GBP 6,380. Paris, 13 April 1988, *Sheep Coming Home* (oil on canvas, 20 x 25½ ins / 51 x 65 cm) FRF 7,500. Paris, 29 April 1988, *Landscape, Pool at Nightfall* (oil on canvas, 19¾ x 25½ ins / 50 x 65 cm) FRF 14,000. Monaco, 17 June 1988, *Oak Trees in Meadowland* (oil on canvas, 18½ x 22 ins / 47 x 55 cm) FRF 7,770. Bern, 26 Oct 1988, *Landscape, Fishermen beside a Calm River near a Road.* (1870, oil on canvas, 38¼ x 51¼ ins / 97 x 130 cm) CHF 5,800. Versailles, 5 March 1989, *Shepherdess and Flock on a River Bank* (oil on canvas, 13 x 16¼ ins / 33 x 41 cm) FRF 20,500. Paris, 27 April 1990, *Shepherd and Flock by a Pool* (oil on canvas, 26 x 32 ins / 66 x 81 cm) FRF 58,500. London, 11 May 1990, *On the Way to the Farm* (1888, oil on canvas, 20 x 24½ ins / 50.5 x 62 cm) GBP 4,180. Bern, 12 May 1990, *River Landscape near Barbizon* (oil on panel, 12½ x 16 ins / 32 x 40.5 cm) CHF 10,000. Paris, 5 July 1990, *Sheep* (oil on card, 9¾ x 12¼ ins / 25 x 31 cm) FRF 6,500. London, 5 Oct 1990, *Cattle Drinking at a Stream near Trees* (1884, oil on canvas, 32¾ x 39¼ ins / 83 x 100 cm) GBP 6,820. New York, 21 May 1991, *End of the Day* (oil on canvas, 15¼ x 18¼ ins / 38.8 x 46.3 cm) USD 4,400. Paris, 22 June 1992, *Girl Keeping Cattle* (1884, oil on canvas, 26 x 32¼ ins / 66 x 82 cm) FRF 42,000. London, 1 Oct 1993, *Ferryman* (oil on canvas, 26 x 22 ins / 66 x 55 cm) GBP 3,680. New York, 15 Feb 1994, *Cattle Drinking in a Wooded Landscape* (oil on canvas, 25¾ x 32¼ ins / 65.4 x 82.2 cm) USD 9,200. Barbizon, 29 May 1994, *Keeping the Flock* (oil on canvas, 39¾ x 32 ins / 101 x 81 cm) FRF 113,000. Paris, 2 Dec 1994, *Pastoral Scene in an Orchard in Flower* (1891, oil on canvas, 27¼ x 36 ins / 69 x 90.5 cm) FRF 58,000. London, 12 June 1996, *Figures in a Clearing* (oil on canvas, 21½ x 17¾ ins / 54.5 x 45 cm) GBP 2,300. New York, 18-19 July 1996, *Landscape* (oil on canvas, 29 x 36½ ins / 73.7 x 92.7 cm) USD 2,300. New York, 24 Oct 1996, *Returning Flock* (1884, oil on canvas, 57½ x 45¾ ins / 146.1 x 116.1 cm) USD 34,500. Paris, 22 Nov 1996, *Silhouettes by a Pool* (oil on canvas, 15¼ x 22 ins / 38.5 x 56 cm) FRF 28,000. London, 26 March 1997, *Flock beside a River in Spring* (1896, oil on canvas, 26 x 32 ins / 66 x 81.5 cm) GBP 4,600. Paris, 16 March 1998, *Sheep* (oil on panel, 11 x 13¾ ins / 28 x 35 cm) FRF 4,200.

JAQKEMON DE FIVES. See **JACQUEMON**

JAQUAND, Claude. See **JACQUAND**

JAQUE, or Jacques
French, 15th century.
Painter.

Jaque was a master card maker in Lyons in 1472 and 1475 and almost certainly produced a set of wooden moulds (in the form of engraved slabs) for a pack of cards, which are decorated with sure, elegant figure drawing. A Jack in this pack of cards is decorated with the caption 'Iaque', which Rondot claims to be the name of the model used for the design. No names appear beside other figures in the pack.

JAQUE, Louis
Canadian, 20th century.
Born 1919.
Painter.

Louis Jaque was active in Canada. In 1971, he showed a collection of his works in Paris. From the age of twenty-five, he always pursued the same direction of research into abstract space, corresponding to what are known as ambiguous structures. The shapes are bounded by bands in the colours of the spectrum, which fade into one another with subtle gradations.
Auction records:
Montreal, 1 May 1989, *Impact - Momentium 5* (1966, oil on canvas, 50¾ x 38¼ ins / 129 x 97 cm) CAD 950.

JAQUELIN
French, 17th century.
Active in Avignon in 1623.
Painter.

JAQUEMART, or Jaquorart
French, 15th century.
Active in Paris.
Miniaturist.

Jaquemart worked at the French court at the beginning of the 15th century.

JAQUEMART. See also **JACQUEMART, JACQUEMIN** and **JACQUEMON**

JAQUEMET, Marguerite
Swiss, 19th century.
Born 1859, in Geneva.
Painter, watercolourist, decorative designer.

At the exhibition in Geneva in 1896, Jaquemet received a bronze medal on behalf of herself and her pupils.

JAQUEMIN
French, 20th century.
Sculptor. Statuettes.
Auction records:
Paris, 4 Dec 1987, *Skier Sets Off* (chryselephantine sculpture, ivory head with polychrome brown and gilt patinate, h. 11¾ ins / 30 cm) FRF 7,500.

JAQUEMIN DE MONS. See **JACQUEMART**

JAQUEMOT, Georges François Louis
Swiss, 19th century.
Born 19 May 1806, in Valangin (Neuchâtel); died 15 February 1880, in Pforzheim (Germany).
Engraver.

Jaquemot trained in Germany, but exhibited at the Société des Amis des Arts in Neuchâtel and at the Salon in Paris, where he won a third-class medal in 1875.

JAQUERIO, Giovanni
Italian, 14th - 15th century.
Active in Turin.
Painter.

JAQUERO, Matteo
Italian, 15th century.
Painter, fresco artist. Religious subjects, figures.
Matteo Jaquero was active in Piedmont between 1429 and 1440.

He worked for Prince Louis d'Achaja in the château of Pinerole and for Duke Amadeus VIII of Savoy in the chapel of the château of Thonon on Lake Geneva. He painted *Crucifixion* and *Saints* in the château of Fénis (Val d'Aosta); and *Fountain of Youth* and *Knights and Ladies* in the château of Manta (Piedmont). Attributed to him are *Prophets, Climb to Calvary* and several scenes from the *Life of St Anthony*, frescoes discovered during restoration in the abbey church of S Antonio, Ranverso, near Turin.

JAQUES. See also **JACQUES**

JAQUES, Bertha E.
Maiden name: Clauson
American, 19th century.
Born 24 October 1863, in Covington (Illinois); died 1941.
Painter, engraver, illustrator writer, teacher.
Bertha E. Jaques studied in Chicago, where she settled. She founded the Chicago Society of Etchers in 1910.
BIBLIOGRAPHY:
Patterson, Joby, *Bertha E. Jaques and the Chicago Society of Etchers*, FDU Press, Madison (NJ), 2002.

JAQUES, Francis Lee
American, 20th century.
Born 28 September 1887, in Geneseo (Illinois); died 1969, in St Paul (Minnesota).
Painter. Animals, wildlife.
Francis Lee Jaques was a member of the Salmagundi Club.

JAQUES, Jules
British, 19th century.
Painter.
Jules Jaques exhibited a landscape at the Society of British Artists in London in 1882. Two landscapes signed J. Jaques were exhibited in 1914 at the New Orleans Museum of Art. They came from private collections.

JAQUES, Julia (Miss)
British, 19th century.
Active in London.
Painter. Portraits.
Julia Jaques exhibited in London, notably at the Royal Academy and Suffolk Street from 1826 to 1836.

JAQUET, called Giaquetto and il Francioso
French, 15th century.
Active in Italy.
Painter.
Jaquet worked in Rome and painted a *Portrait of Pope Eugene IV*, which is in the sacristy of the church of S Maria sopra Minerva.

JAQUET
French, 19th century.
Active in Poitiers.
Painter, watercolourist.
Jaquet received a bronze medal in 1876.

JAQUET, Adèle
Maiden name: Bouvier
Swiss, 19th century.
Born 24 August 1828, in Geneva; died 28 November 1899, in Geneva.
Watercolourist, pastellist, miniaturist. Portraits.
Adèle Jaquet was a pupil of Mesdames Munier-Romilly and Hardy-Dufour.

JAQUET, Désiré Alfred
French, 19th - 20th century.
Born 28 June 1873, in Paris.
Sculptor.
Désiré Alfred Jaquet was a pupil of Alexandre Falguière and Ernest Guilbert. He exhibited in Paris at the Salon des Artistes Français, of which he became a member in 1904, winning an honourable mention in 1905.

JAQUET, Jacques
Belgian, 19th century.
Born 1830, in Antwerp; died July 1898.
Sculptor.
Jacques Jaquet was one of the most distinguished members of the Belgian School of Sculpture and studied under Geefs. As a young man he was appointed to teach modelling at the fine arts academy in Brussels, and he held this post for almost 40 years. He received some important official commissions, including the *Fountain in Memory of Burgomaster Rouppe* and an *Equestrian Statue of Charles de Lorraine de Grand Marche*. His *Medallion of Deputy Delfosse* is in the Ypres museum.

JAQUET, Jan Jozef
Belgian, 19th century.
Born 1822, in Antwerp; died 9 June 1898, in Brussels.
Sculptor. Figures. Groups, busts.
A pupil of Geefs, he taught at the Brussels academy.
MUSEUMS AND GALLERIES:
BRUSSELS: *The Golden Age* (marble, group); *Bust of General Anoul* (marble).

JAQUET, Jean
Swiss, 18th - 19th century.
Born 1765; died 1839.
Sculptor.
Jean Jaquet lived and worked in Geneva.
MUSEUMS AND GALLERIES:
GENEVA (MAH): *Bust of C. Bonnet.*

JAQUET, Jean-Michel
Swiss, 20th - 21st century.
Born 8 November 1950, in La Chaux-de-Fonds.
Draughtsman.
Jean-Michel Jaquet studied at the École des Art Décoratifs in Geneva. He exhibited for the first time in Auvernier-Neuchâtel in 1973. Without being Surrealist, his drawings have the same freedom of invention, the same taste for puns and disrespect. In 1974, he exhibited at the Maison de Culture de St-Étienne and in 1975 he again exhibited in Auvernier-Neuchâtel. He shows his work in solo exhibitions, such as the one in 2002 at the Galerie Jörg Stummer in Zurich under the title *Neue Bilder auf Papier oder Leinwand* (*New Pictures on Paper or Canvas*).
BIBLIOGRAPHY:
Jaquet, Jean-Michel, *Euphorie*, Buchet Chastel, Paris, 2003.

JAQUET, Louis
French, 20th century.
Born 27 March 1944, in Paris.
Since 1973 also active in Italy.
Painter, draughtsman.
Louis Jaquet comes from a family of antique dealers and sculptors. He began working as a cabinetmaker in his father's workshops in 1954. In 1964 he studied at the Atelier de la Ville de Paris, Place des Vosges, in 1965 at the Académie de la Grande Chaumière, in 1966 at the Académie Julian and

in 1967 he entered the École Supérieure des Beaux-Arts de Paris, where he gained his degree in 1972. In 1973 he settled in Italy, where he met the American painter William Congdon.

Jaquet has taken part in various collective exhibitions including: International Biennale of Contemporary Art, Salsomaggiore-Terme, 1982; International Biennale of Graphic Arts, Tokyo, 1983; International Biennale of Contemporary Art, Los Angeles, 1984; Royal Academy, London, 1984 and the Biennale of Contemporary Art, Palazzo Corsini, Rome, 1984. Solo exhibitions of his work include: Galerie Karl Flinker, Paris, 1973 and 1974; San Bartolomeo Cultural Centre, Bergamo, 1976; Galeria Asinelli, Bologna, 1978; Galeria Il Navila, Bologna, 1980; French Cultural Centre, Tel-Aviv, 1983 and S. Ilario Cultural Centre, Reggio Emilia, 1984.

BIBLIOGRAPHY:

Biennale d'Art contemporain, exhibition catalogue, Palazzo Corsini, Rome, 1984.

JAQUET, Lucy

Swiss, 19th century.

Born 23 June 1849, in Geneva; died 23 December 1893, in Geneva.

Painter. Portraits, landscapes.

A pupil of B. Menn in Geneva, Lucy Jaquet also trained in Paris and exhibited at the Salon in 1880 and 1881.

JAQUET, JAQUIN, JAQUOT. See also **JACQUET, JACQUIN, JACQUOT**

JAQUINTO

10th century.

Calligrapher, illuminator.

In 949 the scribe Jaquinto copied and illuminated a missal now at Monte Cassino. His illustrations include many pictures of dogs, birds and fish.

JAQUORART. See **JAQUEMART**

JAQUOTOT, Marie Victoire, or Jacquotot

French, 18th - 19th century.

Born 15 January 1772, in Paris; died 27 April 1855, in Toulouse.

Painter (porcelain).

Marie Victoire Jaquotot was a pupil of Leguay, and subsequently Painter to the King and to the royal porcelain factory known as the Manufacture de Sèvres. From 1790 to 1836, she exhibited at the Salon subjects from life and after the masters. In 1807, after the Peace of Tilsit, Napoleon I commissioned her to paint a dessert service which was presented by him to the Emperor of Russia. The museum at Montpellier has *Danaë*, a painting signed: *Victoire Jaquetot*, after Girodet, 1827, which cost M. Valedau 10,000 francs.

BIBLIOGRAPHY:

Guillon-Lajoix, Anne-Mauricette, *Marie-Victoire Jaquotot (1772-1855), peintre sur plaque pour porcelaines*, Paris, 1992.

MUSEUMS AND GALLERIES:

ANGERS: *Portrait of a Woman* - MONTPELLIER (Mus. Fabre): *Danaë* - VATICAN: *The Virgin of Loreto, after Raphael* - VIENNA (Österreichisches Mus. für Angewandte Kunst): *Portrait of Marie-Louise, after Isabey*.

AUCTION RECORDS:

PARIS, 1861, *The Holy Family after Raphael* (painting/porcelain) FRF 11,400. PARIS, 1872, *Bouquet of Flowers* (painting/porcelain) FRF 10,000. PARIS, 14 and 15 April 1924, *Thel Blacksmith's Beautiful Wife* (painting/porcelain) FRF 500.

JARA, Antonio de La. See **LA JARA**

JARA, José

Mexican, 19th - 20th century.

Born 1867, in Tecamachalco; died 1939.

Painter, watercolourist. Genre scenes.

José Jara studied in the classical style with José Maria Velasco at the Academia de San Carlos. He was appointed to teach painting and drawing at the college of San Nicolas by the government of Michoacán. His paintings show scenes of daily life in Mexico.

MUSEUMS AND GALLERIES:

TOLUCA (Mus. José María Velasco): several works.

AUCTION RECORDS:

LONDON, 18 Jan 1980, *Landscape with Gypsies* (oil on canvas, 16 3/4 x 20 3/4 ins / 42.5 x 52.7 cm) GBP 480. NEW YORK, 22-23 Nov 1993, *Man with Hens*; *Urchins Playing* (watercolour/paper, 13 1/2 x 9 1/2 ins / 34.4 x 24.4 cm and 14 3/4 x 9 1/4 ins/37.5 x 23.7 cm) USD 18,400. LYONS, 10 Feb 2002, *Portraits of Mexicans* (oil on skin, a pair, 33 x 44 ins / 83 x 113 cm) EUR 9,300.

JARABA Y JIMENEZ, Enrique

Spanish, 19th - 20th century.

Born 7 January 1872, in Málaga, in 1876 according to some sources; died 1926, in Málaga.

Painter. Religious subjects, figures, portraits, interiors with figures, landscapes.

Enrique Jaraba y Jiménez studied at the school of fine arts in Málaga. He continued his studies abroad, particularly in Stockholm. He took part in group exhibitions, including the Exposición Nacional de Bellas Artes in Madrid from 1892 to 1910, winning a bronze medal in 1892 and in 1901. His works also appeared occasionally in the Málaga regional exhibitions between 1899 and 1920, and he held solo exhibitions of collections of his paintings. He became a teacher at the school of applied arts of Seville and Málaga.

Typical of Jaraba y Jiménez's subjects are *The Guitar Lesson* and *A Girl from Málaga*. He also painted religious subjects such as *The Flight into Egypt* and *St Peter and St John*, portraits and views of the city of Málaga.

BIBLIOGRAPHY:

Arnáiz, José Manuel/López Jiménez, Javier/Merchán Díaz, Manuel (ed.), *Cien años de pintura en Espana y Portugal (1830-1930)*, Antiqvaria, Madrid, 1990.

MUSEUMS AND GALLERIES:

STOCKHOLM: *Head of an Old Spanish Woman*.

JARAMILLO, Alipio

Colombian, 20th century.

Born 1913.

Painter. Murals.

Alipio Jaramillo collaborated with Siqueiros in Chillán, Chile. In his own right he executed mural compositions with social content at the University of Manizales.

Jaramillo's didactic concerns as a painter kept him apart from the aesthetic movements of the West.

JARAMILLO, Ignacio Gómez

Colombian, 20th century.

Born 1900 or 1910; died 1970.

Painter. Murals.

After spending time in Mexico, Ignacio Gómez Jaramillo turned his hand to producing work with a strong social message in a style displaying the influence of European Cubism and Abstraction.

AUCTION RECORDS:

NEW YORK, 13 May 1983, *Portrait of a Man* (oil on canvas, 63 1/4 x 47 1/4 ins / 160.6 x 120 cm) USD 1,500.

JARAMILLO, María de La Paz

Colombian, 20th - 21st century.

Born 1948, in Manizales.

Painter (gouache), engraver. Figures.

María de La Paz Jaramillo's works represent exclusively figures from the nightlife of bars and dancehalls, with the raw artificial light erasing the details of their natural features and emphasising the make-up on their eyes and mouths. From 1970 to about 1980, she exhibited mainly engravings and paintings on paper; she then began to produce large-format paintings. She has shown her work in collective exhibitions and in solo exhibitions including: Panarte (Panama) and Medellín (Colombia) (1980); various towns and cities in Colombia (1981); Bogotá (1982); Colombia, Panama and New York (1983); Germany and Monterrey Museum in Mexico (1984).

BIBLIOGRAPHY:

Stringer, John, *Nouvelle Biennale de Paris*, exhibition catalogue, Electa, Le Moniteur, Paris, 1985.

JARAY, Sandor

Hungarian, 19th - 20th century.
Born 11 January 1870, in Timisoara.
Sculptor.

Sandor Jaray exhibited in Berlin in 1909.

JARAY, Tess

British, 20th century.
Born 31 December 1937, in Vienna, to British parents.
Painter, etcher, environmental artist.

Tess Jaray trained at the St Martin's School of Art (1954-1957) and at the Slade School in London (1957-1960). She taught at the Slade School until 1999. Her paintings are in a strict abstract style with suggestive interactions of colour and form in complex patterns. As an environmentalist artist, she has carried out several commissions including a floor for Victoria Station in London, Centenary Square in Birmingham, Cathedral Precinct in Wakefield, Jubilee Square, Leeds General Infirmary and the forecourt to the new British Embassy in Moscow. She is married to the artist Mark Vaux and lives in London.

She has held solo exhibitions at the Whitworth Gallery, Manchester (1984); the Ashmolean Museum, Oxford; the Serpentine Gallery, London (1988); and the Purdy Hicks Gallery (2001). She participated in the third Salon des Galeries Pilotes in Lausanne in 1970.

BIBLIOGRAPHY:

IIIe Salon international des Galeries Pilotes, exhibition catalogue, Musée cantonal, Lausanne, 1970.

MUSEUMS AND GALLERIES:

AMSTERDAM (Peter Stuyvesant Foundation): *St Stephen Green* (1984, oil on canvas); *Capital Blue* (1965, oil on canvas) - CAMBRIDGE (New Hall Art Collection): *Vault* (1991) - LEVERKUSEN (Stadtisches Museum) - LIVERPOOL (Walker AG) - LONDON (Tate Collection): *P.P.* (1991, on paper, print); *Fifteen* (1969) - WARWICK (University Art Gallery).

JARDEL, Bernard

French, 20th century.
Born 23 September 1932, in Paris.
Painter.

Bernard Jardel studied architecture in Paris at the École des Beaux-Arts, which he left to manage a building firm. Later, he devoted himself to painting. His interest in architecture is clear in his work. Regular geometric planes, nuanced tones and kaleidoscopic effects bring his painting close to Op Art, though with an added effect of strangeness. He exhibited in Paris at the Salon de Mai and at the Salon des Grands et Jeunes d'Aujourd'hui.

AUCTION RECORDS:

BRUSSELS, 27 Oct 1976, *Composition 73 212* (oil on canvas, 9½ x 13 ins / 24 x 33 cm) BEF 17,000.

JARDELLA, Aristide

Dutch, 19th century.
Born 19th century, in Carrara.
Sculptor.

Aristide Jardella was a pupil of Alfred Boucher. He exhibited at the Salon des Artistes Français and received a bronze medal in 1906.

JARDIM, Manuel de Azambuja Pereira

Portuguese, 20th century.
Born 1884, in Meas-do-Campo, near Montemor-o-Velho; died 1923, in Coimbra.
Painter.

Manuel de Azambuja Pereira Jardim studied in Coimbra, then from 1903 to 1905 at the school of fine arts in Lisbon. Later, he studied with Jean-Paul Laurens at the Académie Julian in Paris, living there until 1914. He visited Germany in 1906 and Italy in 1908. He exhibited at the Salon des Artistes Français in 1911, the Salon d'Automne in 1913, and the Salon des Artistes Décorateurs in 1914. After returning to Portugal in 1915, he exhibited at the National Society of Fine Arts and was one of the co-founders of the Portuguese Society of Modern Art. He admired many different artists, including Van Gogh, Puvis de Chavannes, Eugène Carrière, Steinlen and Derain, but his own work retained close links with Post-Impressionism.

BIBLIOGRAPHY:

Arnáiz, José Manuel/López Jiménez, Javier/Merchán Díaz, Manuel (ed.), *Cien años de pintura en Espana y Portugal (1830-1930)*, Antiqvaria, Madrid, 1990.

JARDIN

French, 19th century.
Active c. 1844.
Painter. Landscapes.

Jardin is credited by Siret with an 1844 painting: *Roman Countryside*.

JARDIN. See also **DUJARDIN**

JARDIN, E.

French, 19th century.
Active in Paris.
Draughtsman.

Young Girl Jesting with Cupid, a coloured picture signed *E Jardin*, Paris, 1832, was sold under auction at Helbing, Munich, in 1910.

JARDIN, H.

French, 18th century.
Active in Rome.
Engraver (etching).

Jardin executed a *Plan of a Triumphal Arch* (1748).

JARDIN, Jacques and Pierre

French, 16th century.
Active in Laval.
Sculptors.

The Jardin brothers produced decorative sculptures for several altars in Laval Cathedral, and sculpted four statues for the old portal of the cathedral in 1552.

JARDIN, Nicolas. See **DESJARDINS**

JARDIN, Pierre. See **JARDIN Jacques** and **Pierre**

JARDIN, Pierre Charles

French, 19th century.
Born 19th century, in Paris.
Engraver.

Pierre Jardin exhibited at the 1850 and 1853 Paris Salons.

JARDINES, Antonio

Spanish, 20th century.
Born 1898, in Paris, to Spanish parents.
Painter. Landscapes, seascapes.

Antonio Jardines was the son and pupil of José María Jardines, who lived in Paris. He later studied at the Real Academia de Bellas Artes de San Fernando in Madrid, after which he returned to Paris to complete his training. He took part in group exhibitions and also exhibited collections of his works in solo shows.

Jardines painted mainly landscapes and seascapes, expressing a feeling for nature reminiscent of Corot.

Bibliography:

Arnáiz, José Manuel/López Jiménez, Javier/Merchán Díaz, Manuel (ed.), *Cien años de pintura en Espana y Portugal (1830-1930)*, Antiqvaria, Madrid, 1990.

Auction records:

Rome, 26 May 1993, *Town seen through Trees* (oil on canvas, 39 1/4 x 15 3/4 ins / 100 x 40 cm) ITL 1,700,000.

JARDINES, José María

Spanish, 19th - 20th century.
Born 26 January 1862, in Cádiz.
Painter. Genre scenes, figures, landscapes.

José María Jardines studied at the academy of fine arts in Cádiz, then at the Real Academia de Bellas Artes de San Fernando in Madrid. He lived in Paris for many years, returning to Spain in 1914, after which he became a teacher at the academy in Cádiz. He exhibited in Cádiz, Madrid, Paris and Latin America in both group and solo exhibitions.

Jardines was a sensitive and talented landscape painter in the Romantic tradition. His landscapes with figures at the edge of a wood or on a riverbank are reminiscent of Corot. He also painted local people and characters, possibly inspired by Manet, as in his elegant portrait of a *Woman on a Balcony*, in beautiful Spanish costume, with a lace mantilla and a fan.

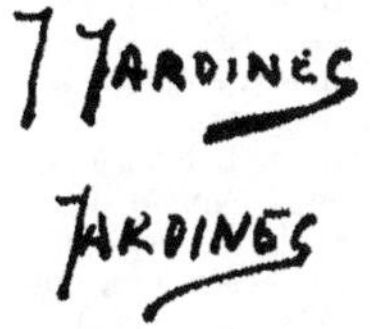

Bibliography:

Arnáiz, José Manuel/López Jiménez, Javier/Merchán Díaz, Manuel (ed.), *Cien años de pintura en Espana y Portugal (1830-1930)*, Antiqvaria, Madrid, 1990.

Auction records:

Paris, 22-23 Dec 1920, *Seascape*, FRF 610. Paris, 15 April 1924, *The Lake in Springtime*, FRF 135. New York, 12 May 1978, *Sunlit Street* (oil on canvas, 25 3/4 x 36 1/2 ins / 65.5 x 92.5 cm) USD 1,600. Washington DC, 25 Feb 1979, *Sunlit Street* (oil on canvas, 13 x 21 1/2 ins / 33 x 54.5 cm) USD 1,400. New York, 18 June 1982, *River Landscape in Summer* (oil on canvas, 21 1/4 x 25 3/4 ins / 54 x 65.5 cm) USD 2,300. London, 29 May 1985, *Women Harvesting* (oil on canvas, 21 1/4 x 14 1/2 ins / 54 x 37 cm) GBP 2,200. Madrid, 27 Oct 1987, *Harvesters at Rest* (oil on canvas, 28 3/4 x 36 1/2 ins / 73 x 92.5 cm) ESP 1,200,000. Bern, 30 April 1988, *Herdswoman with her Herd of Cows at the Edge of a Wood* (oil on canvas, 25 1/2 x 32 ins / 65 x 81 cm) CHF 3,100. Paris, 15 Feb 1989, *Rustic Scene* (oil on panel, 16 1/4 x 12 3/4 ins / 41 x 32.5 cm) FRF 6,200. New York, 17 Jan 1990, *Two Peasant Girls in a Landscape* (oil on card, 12 x 15 1/4 ins / 30.5 x 38.8 cm) USD 3,960. New York, 15 Oct 1991, *Break during the Harvest* (oil on canvas, 22 x 15 1/4 ins / 55.9 x 38.7 cm) USD 2,420. London, 16 June 1993, *Peasants Harvesting in a Field* (oil on panel, 12 1/2 x 15 1/4 ins / 32 x 39 cm) GBP 2,300. New York, 19 Jan 1994, *Mediterranean Villa* (oil on canvas, 22 x 13 ins / 55.9 x 33 cm) USD 2,070. Paris, 4 Dec 1995, *Flower-bedecked House in Seville* (oil on canvas, 18 x 15 ins / 46 x 38 cm) FRF 5,500. New York, 17 Jan 1996, *Women Potato Pickers* (oil on canvas, 26 x 32 ins / 66 x 81.3 cm) USD 3,450.

JARDINES, Manuel

Spanish, 20th century.
Born 24 December 1910, in Garches, France, to Spanish parents.
Painter. Genre scenes.

Manuel Jardines was the son and pupil of José María Jardines.

Auction records:

Paris, 28 Sept 1984, *Paris Street Scene* (oil on panel, 13 3/4 x 11 ins / 35 x 27 cm) FRF 16,000.

JARDINIER, Claude Donat

French, 18th century.
Born 1726, in Paris; died before 14 April 1771.
Engraver (burin).

Jardinier was a pupil of Nicolas Dupuis and J.-P. Le Bas, also working with Laurent Cars. He engraved religious subjects and scenes from everyday life, notably after C. Maratti, A. Carracci, Valentin, Jeaurat, and after Greuze: *Three Women and a Child, Silence* and *Woman Knitting*.

JARDINS. See **DESJARDINS**

JARDON, L. E.

French, 19th - 20th century.
Active in Paris.
Painter. Portraits, genre scenes.

L. E. Jardon exhibited at the Salon of the Société des Artistes Français from 1888 to 1890 and in 1905.

Museums and Galleries:

Saratov (Raditschev Gal.): *Portrait of the Physician Jablochkov in his Paris Laboratory*.

Auction records:

Paris, 4 March 1991, *Bathers on a Beach* (1890, oil on canvas, after Virginie Demont-Breton, 28 3/4 x 51 1/4 ins / 73 x 130 cm) FRF 30,000.

JAREMA, Jozef

Polish, 20th century.
Born 1900.
Painter.
Neo-Plasticism.

Jozef Jarema studied at the academy of fine art in Cracow, also spending some time in Paris and Egypt. In 1933, he founded the avant-garde Cricot theatre in Cracow in collaboration with his younger sister Maria Jarema.

He took part in a number of collective exhibitions in Poland, Paris, the Middle East and also in Italy where he founded and became president of the Italian Art Club in Rome.

While in Italy, he met Prampolini and Soldati and under their influence he began, from 1948, to move towards a more abstract style. He settled in Nice in 1951 where he got to know Jean Gorin, the friend and disciple of Mondrian. The result for Jarema was that his Abstraction moved closer to Neo-Plasticism, particularly in relation to his search for universal principles on which to base his art.

Auction records:

Paris, 14 March 1990, *Composition* (1957, oil on panel, 10 1/4 x 19 1/4 ins / 26 x 49 cm) FRF 4,000.

JAREMA, Maria

Polish, 20th century.
Born 1908, in Staryy Sambir; died 1958, in Cracow.
Painter, sculptor, monotype artist. Stage sets.
Cracow Group.

The younger sister of Josef Jarema, Maria Jarema soon became known as one of the most active representatives of the artistic milieu in Cracow. From 1930, while she was also studying sculpture at the school of fine art with Xavier Dunikowsky, she was involved in the left-wing artistic movement associated with the Cracow Group founded that year. She began exhibiting work in 1933. From 1933 to 1939, she contributed to the work of the avant-garde Cricot Theatre, founded by her brother Jozef Jarema, both as an actress and a designer of sets, costumes and masks. In the later 1930s she was involved with the anti-Fascist movement in Poland. While visiting Paris in 1937 she came into contact with Surrealist art. After World War II she took part in a number of important exhibitions of Polish art. She re-joined the Cracow Group that was revived in 1957, and also executed sets and costumes for the experimental theatre in Cracow revived by Tadeusz Kantor under the name of Cricot 2.

Her first sculptures, dating from the late 1930s, are typically Cubist-Expressionist in conception with a rhythmical organisation of organic volumes opposing convex and concave surfaces. From the beginning of the war she devoted herself mainly to painting. Her encounter with Surrealism on the occasion of her visit to Paris led to a series of works in gouache evoking movement. From 1950 she began to make monotypes as well as continuing to work in oils. Created in combination with tempera, her monotypes are characterised by their summary line, the limpid fluidity of the fields of colour and their rhythmical clarity and simplicity. In the later part of her career she produced a number of cycles, at first including allusively human forms, as in the series *Figures* and *Heads* or *Expressions* (1954), and later becoming entirely abstract with the three series *Rhythms; Filters* and *Penetrations*. This succession of cycles went from the dreamlike poetry of Surrealism to an abstract style where a few simple interpenetrating or superimposed transparent planes are rendered in ever-new subtly coloured variations.

She was awarded the City of Cracow Prize in 1957. In the year of her death, 1958, she represented Poland at the 29th Venice Biennale. Her work also featured at the 6th São Paulo Biennale (1961). A retrospective was mounted by the Krzysztofory Gallery in 1988.

BIBLIOGRAPHY:

Peinture moderne polonaise, exhibition catalogue, Musée Galliera, Paris, 1969.

MUSEUMS AND GALLERIES:

WARSAW (Muz. Narodowe): *Expressions* (1954).

JARENUS

German, 15th - 16th century.
Painter. Religious subjects.
Westphalian School.

This is the fictitious name of a painter who was believed to have worked in Westphalia from 1450 to 1500. Passavant discovered what he thought was a signature, *Jarenus P*, on a painting of *Pietà* (*The Body of Christ*), which belonged to the collection of the count of Pembroke. Waagen believed that this artist also produced an altarpiece owned by the Berlin museum, depicting the *Crucifixion* and other scenes from the life of Christ. The name of Jarenus was listed in artistic directories, in particular Siret, as an 'historical painter who lived in Westphalia from 1450 to 1500'. It has since been established by Woltmann that the signature on *Pietà* was, in fact, part of an inscription that should have read *Jesus Nazarenus Rex Judacoruni*. The painting owned by the Berlin museum was listed as the work of an unknown artist of the Westphalian School in Soest at the end of the 15th century. The side panels of the painting are on show at the museum in Münster.

JARESCH, Johann

Hungarian, 19th century.
Active in Budapest.
Engraver (copper/wood).

Johann Jaresch showed two of his works at the academy exhibition in Vienna in 1820. His works include *Holy Virgin*, 1824, after F. Penni, *Dying Magdalene*, after Ch. Lebrun, and among his portraits, *Beatrice d'Este*, widow of the Grand Duke Ferdinand. He later devoted himself to wood engraving.

JARIE, Maurice La. See **LAJARIE**

JARKI, Yuri Aleskandrovich, or Jarkikh

Russian, 20th century.
Born 16 July 1938, in Tikhoretz.
Active in Germany in 1977 then in Paris from 1978.
Painter. Figures.

Jarki attended the naval school in Leningrad (now St Petersburg) from 1958 to 1961 before studying at the Mukhina School of Arts and Industry in the same city, from 1961 to 1967. In 1977, he emigrated to Germany and obtained political asylum in France in 1978. He founded the *Eidos Group* in 1984.

His compositions depict, in an Expressionistic style, schematic or distorted figures, alone or in groups engaged in activities that clearly have a symbolic intent. He executed a fresco and a sculpture for the town of Combs-la-Ville in 1984.

A member of the younger generation of Russian artists, he has taken part in many collective exhibitions since 1971 including: *Peinture Russe Contemporaine* (*Contemporary Russian Painting*), Palais des Congrès, Paris (1976); Institute of Contemporary Arts, London (1977); Venice Biennale (1977); *L'Art russe non-officiel* (*Unofficial Russian Art*), Musée des Beaux-Arts in Chartres, subsequently Musée des Beaux-Arts, Tours and Musée du Vieux Château, Laval (1978); *Group Eidos* (*The Eidos Group*), Grand Palais, Paris (1985); Galerie Présence, Brussels (1986); Musée des Beaux-Arts, Fribourg (1993). Solo exhibitions include: exhibition of portraits at the premises of the newspaper *Aurora*, Leningrad (1973); Galerie Schèmes, Lille (1981 and 1983-1985); Musée des Beaux-Arts, Belfort (1983); *Jeux du Hazard* (*Games of Chance*), Musée Toulouse-Lautrec, Albi (1983); Worpswede Gallery, Bonn (1985); Galerie du Vieux Moulin, Rouen (1988); National Galleries of Leningrad, Kubishev and Yerevan (1989); Galerie St-Aubin, Toulouse (2000); Fondation Taylor, Paris (2002). Jarki was awarded the gold medal of the Belgian Académie des Sciences Humanitaires.

BIBLIOGRAPHY:

Crispolti, Enrico/Moncada, Gabriella, *La nuova arte sovietica*, La Biennale di Venezia, Marsilio Editori, Venice, 1978. Gagnebin, Murielle, *Jarki*, exhibition catalogue, Palais de la Berbie, Albi, 1981. Castel, Michel/Devoisins, Jean, *Jarki*, exhibition catalogue, Musée Toulouse-Lautrec, Albi, 1983. Xuriguera, Gérard, *Jarki*, exhibition catalogue, Gal. d'Art de la Place Beauvau, Paris, 1990. Gagnebin, Murielle, et al., *Jarki*, Fragments, Paris, 2003.

MUSEUMS AND GALLERIES:

ALBI (Mus. Toulouse-Lautrec) - BITBURG (German Mus., Béda House of Culture) - ST PETERSBURG (Gosudarstvennyj Russkij Muz.) - YEREVAN (Nat. Mus. of Armenia).

AUCTION RECORDS:

LILLE, 12 Dec 1989, *The Virgin and St Mary Magdalene* (oil and tempera/canvas, 78 3/4 x 39 1/4 ins / 200 x 100 cm) FRF 19,000; *The Four Elements* (39 1/4 x 39 1/4 ins / 100 x 100 cm) FRF 19,100.

JARKOV, Piotr Gerassimovich, or Jarkoi, Jerkov

Russian, 18th century.
Born 1742; died 8 or le 20 July 1802.
Miniaturist.

Jarkov studied at the fine art academy in St Petersburg and joined its teaching staff in 1779.

JARL, Axel

Danish, 19th - 20th century.
Born 28 May 1871, in Copenhagen.
Painter. Figure compositions, religious subjects, figures, portraits, landscapes.

Axel Jarl studied at the Académie Julian in Paris and travelled in Italy and India. A special exhibition of his work was held in Paris from 1910 to 1913. He also exhibited in Naples in 1921. During his travels in India, he painted numerous landscapes and portrait studies. His style is an unusual mixture of Indian art and that found in the wall paintings in Pompeii. A number of biblical subjects painted by Jarl are preserved in the YMCA building in Copenhagen.

JARL, Otto
Swedish, 19th - 20th century.
Born 10 April 1856, in Uppsala; died 16 November 1915, in Dornbach, near Vienna.
Active in Austria.
Sculptor. Animals.
Jugendstil.

Otto Jarl trained at technical college in Stockholm as protégé of Björnstjerne Björnson, then attended the Akademie der Bildenden Künste in Vienna, and subsequently worked in Vienna. He was the son-in-law of the sculptor and architect Friedrich Schmidt. His wife, Karin, was also an artist. He began by making sculptures from portraits and then devoted himself exclusively to animal sculpture. Among the works for which he is well known are *Polar Bear* and *Seal*, which he executed for the Meissen porcelain factory. This firm was the first to produce these wholly original animal figures, from Otto Jarl's *The Polar Bear* of 1903 right through to the 1920s, following stylistic innovation from Copenhagen. *Tiere aus Meissener Porzellan* (*Animals in Meissen Porcelain*), at the Naturmuseum Senckenberg, Frankfurt-on-Main. Otto Jarl also made a *Lion* for the Hackher monument in Graz.

He was represented at the exhibition *Traumwelten. Porzellanfiguren zwischen Jugendstil und Art deco* (*Dream Worlds: German Porcelain Figures from Jugendstil to Art Deco*), at the Huelsman Museum in Bielefeld, 1999. The products of the Meissen factory were the subject of a retrospective exhibition in 1996.

Bibliography:
Franzke, Irmela, *Jugendstil. Glas, Graphik, Keramik, Metall, Möbel, Skulpturen und Textilien von 1880 bis 1915*, exhibition catalogue, Badisches Landesmuseum, Karlsruhe, 1987.

Museums and Galleries:
Berlin (Bröhan-Mus.) - Stockholm (Nationalmus.): statuette of an animal - Vienna (Fire Fighters Mus.): *Group of Fire Fighters*.

Auction records:
New York, 17 May 1983, *Hippopotamus Family* (reddish-brown-patinated bronze with grey tones, h. 7 3/4 ins / 19.5 cm) USD 1,500.

JARL, Viggo Hieronimus, or Jörgensen
Danish, 20th century.
Born 28 November 1879, in Copenhagen; died March 1965, in Cannes, France.
Also active in France.
Painter. Scenes with figures.
Symbolism.

Viggo Jarl studied in Paris under Victor Ségoffin and exhibited at the Paris Salon des Artistes Français, receiving an honourable mention in 1905.

Museums and Galleries:
Copenhagen: *Broken Wings; Evil Thoughts*.

JARMAN, Derek
British, 20th century.
Born 31 January 1942, in Northwood (Middlesex); died 19 February 1994.
Active in London and Dungeness.
Painter, film maker, designer. Landscapes, townscapes. Designs for stage sets, films, gardens.

Derek Jarman studied English, History and Art History at King's College in London before going on to fulfil his desire to study fine art at the Slade School of Art in London (1963-1967). In 1968 he was asked to produce the set designs for the ballet *Jazz Calendar* for the Royal Ballet in Covent Garden in London. Jarman continued in this mode as a prolific and versatile painter and stage-set designer, eventually also becoming an equally prolific and successful film maker and author.

In the 1960s the body of paintings Jarman produced of landscapes and townscapes were usually black and white, and sparse and linear. In the 1970s he also produced a series etched on slate called *Archeologies* (1977). He had a strong interest in Egyptian culture and history and this is evident both in his paintings and in his garden designs, which included obelisks and pyramids, as seen in his 1972 film *A Garden in Luxor*. His interest in garden design culminated in the design of his own, much celebrated garden at his Prospect Cottage in Dungeness by the sea. In the 1970s Jarman also produced a series of transparent plastic capes decorated with dollar bills, symbols associated with alchemy, and debris from the river Thames. During this time he produced fewer paintings and devoted more energy to stage-set design, including a design for Ken Russell for the production of Stravinsky's *Rake's Progress* at the Pergola Theatre in Florence (1982). During the 1980s Jarman produced a series of abstact works using gold leaf, gold paint and black paint, covering the gold leaf and paint with black paint and then scratching the black paint to reveal the gold beneath, as in *Silence* (1986).

From the late 1970s he increasingly spent time making films. His films are unlike conventional commercial feature films and are frequently described as 'painterly'. Roger Wollen (in *Derek Jarman: A Portrait*, London, 1996) refers to a 'flow of imagery' in Jarman's films, and likens them to paintings and collages as 'a series of two-dimensional compositions'. His most acclaimed films include *The Tempest* (1979), *Sebastiane* (1976), *Jubilee* (1978) and *Caravaggio* (1986).

In 1986, the year he was nominated for the Turner Prize, Jarman was also diagnosed as HIV positive, and both his sexuality and the illnesses he subsequently suffered became a source and focus of his creative energies. He returned to painting, creating intense, rich and energetic landscapes in bright primary colours, and continued his film-making. Admirers, reviewers and writers on Jarman all comment on his extraordinary energy. Gray Watson (see Wollen, 1996) comments that in the final seven years of his life, despite debilitating and painful illnesses, he produced and directed six feature films, wrote five books, 'painted as many pictures as some painters would in an entire lifetime, and created a garden whose originality has earned it a place in gardening history'. Jarman is famous as a tireless campaigner of gay rights.

He held his first solo exhibition in 1960 at the True Lovers' Knot Pub in Northwood. In 1961 he was joint amateur winner of the university of London and *Daily Express* art exhibition for his painting *We Wait and Wait* (1960-1961). In 1967 he was a prize winner at the *Young Contemporaries* exhibition at the Tate Gallery. The same year he also took part in an exhibition at the Lisson Gallery in London, the *John Moores Exhibition* in Liverpool, and the 5th Biennale des Jeunes Artistes at the Musee d'Art Moderne in Paris.

Bibliography:
The Complete Derek Jarman, exhibition catalogue, Stuttgart, 1988. Lippard, Chris, *By Angels Driven: The Films of Derek Jarman*, Flick books, Trowbridge, 1996. O'Pray, Michael, *Derek Jarman: Dreams of England*, British Film Institute, London, 1996. Wollen, Roger, *Derek Jarman: A Portrait*, London, 1996. Peake, Tony, *Derek Jarman: A Biography*, Overlook Press, Woodstock, 2000.

Museums and Galleries:
London (Tate Collection): *Ataxia* (1993, oil on canvas).

JARMORINI, Giuseppe, or Armorini
Italian, 18th - 19th century.
Born 1732, in Bologna; died 1816, in Bologna.
Painter, architect. Ornaments.
Jarmorini trained under P. Scandellari. His reputation is based on his skill with ornaments.

JARMUSIEWICZ, Jan X
Polish, 19th century.
Born 1781; died 5 August 1844, in Zaczernia.
Painter.
Jan Jarmusiewicz studied at the University of Lemberg (now Lviv, Ukraine) and took holy orders in 1807. He painted many pictures, including a large altarpiece representing the *Birth of Mary* in the church in Zaczernia.

JARNAC, Constantin de. See **CONSTANTIN,** or Constantinus of Jarnac

JÄRNEFELT, Eero, or Jaernefelt (Father)
Finnish, 19th - 20th century.
Born 8 November 1863, in Viborg; died 1937.
Painter (gouache). Portraits, landscapes.
Eero Järnefelt became a member of the association of Finnish artists when he was 11 years old. He went on to study in St Petersburg, Paris, Germany and Italy. He was a medal winner at the Expositions Universelles in Paris in both 1889 and 1900.

Järnefelt was clearly influenced by Bastien-Lepage, and his work exhibits Bastien-Lepage's realist tendencies. Even so, Järnefelt's landscapes dating from the 1890s are remarkable in both composition and style (one example is his *Flowers in the Water* of 1895 now in Helsinki. His style may perhaps best be described as 'bucolic realism'.

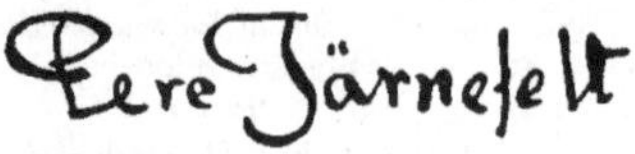

MUSEUMS AND GALLERIES:
HELSINKI (Ateneumin Taidemus.): *Flowers in the Water* (1895); *Landscape Study*; *Autumn at Prelisjarvi*; *Portrait of Miss Matilda Wrede* (gouache); *Landscape* (gouache).
AUCTION RECORDS:
LONDON, 25 March 1987, *Pine Tree by the Sea* (1894, watercolour heightened with gouache, 9 x 7 ins / 23 x 18 cm) GBP 4,000. LONDON, 27-28 March 1990, *Sunset over a Lake* (1894, mixed media and gold paint/paper, 29 1/4 x 18 1/2 ins / 74 x 47 cm) GBP 79,200. LONDON, 11 April 1995, *View of Lago di Garda* (oil on canvas, 26 1/2 x 41 1/4 ins / 67 x 105 cm) GBP 3,680. HELSINKI, 11 Dec 1999, *Marshall C.G. Mannerheim* (1922, pastel, 24 x 19 ins / 61 x 47 cm) FIM 104,000. HELSINKI, 11 Dec 1999, *Autumnal Shore* (1912, oil on canvas, 18 x 23 ins / 45 x 58 cm) FIM 125,000. HELSINKI, 13 May 2000, *Lady by Lamp* (1910, pastel, 24 x 18 ins / 61 x 45 cm) FIM 80,000. HELSINKI, 13 May 2000, *Seascape from Porkala Skerries* (1895, oil on canvas, 18 x 26 ins / 46 x 66 cm) FIM 410,000. HELSINKI, 1 Dec 2001, *Boat on the Shore* (1889, oil on canvas, 11 x 9 ins / 28 x 22 cm) EUR 14,295. HELSINKI, 2 Dec 2001, *Coastal Landscape with Breakers* (1896, oil on canvas, 18 x 26 ins / 45 x 65 cm) FIM 230,000. HELSINKI, 27 April 2002, *Marsh Marigolds at Tusby Beach* (1929, oil on canvas, 17 x 12 ins / 42 x 30 cm) EUR 32,000. HELSINKI, 28 April 2002, *Landscape from Lapland* (1929, gouache, 15 x 22 ins / 39 x 56 cm) EUR 16,000. HELSINKI, 29 Nov 2003, *Leda and the Swan* (1926, pastel, 18 x 25 ins / 46 x 63 cm) EUR 11,500. HELSINKI, 29 Nov 2003, *Winter Landscape with Silver Birch Trunks* (1905, oil on canvas, 19 x 13 ins / 48 x 33 cm) EUR 25,000. HELSINKI, 15 May 2004, *Larin Paraske* (1893, oil on canvas, 17 x 19 ins / 44 x 48 cm) EUR 70,000. HELSINKI, 15 May 2004, *Nelma Sibelius* (1899, oil on canvas, 9 x 11 ins / 22 x 29 cm) EUR 80,000.

JAROCKI, Wladyslaw
Polish, 20th century.
Born 1879, in Podhajczyki.
Painter. Figures, local figures, scenes with figures, genre scenes.
Jarocki was a student at the polytechnic in Lemberg (now Lviv, Ukraine), the Cracow academy of fine art and, in 1906, of Jean-Paul Laurens at the Académie Julian in Paris.

His paintings were inspired by the landscapes and people of the Carpathians. One of his works, *Peasants in a Village Church*, shown in Venice in 1911 was much acclaimed. In Vienna in 1912 he exhibited *Blind Beggars, Skiers, Village Church in the Carpathians* and *Study of Peasants*. In 1914 he exhibited *Village Beauty* and *Ave Maria*. In Paris in 1921 he showed *Coming Home from Church*.

His work featured at the International Exhibition of Fine Art, Venice (1911), in Vienna (1912 and 1914) and also in Düsseldorf. In 1921, he took part in the exhibition of Polish art held at the Salon de la Société Nationale des Beaux-Arts in Paris.
MUSEUMS AND GALLERIES:
LVIV: *Water Festival in Poland; Laughing Landowner* - ROME (Gal. Nazionale d'Arte Moderna): *Carpathian Peasants in the Village Church* - VIENNA (Österreichische Gal. Belvedere): *Village Church in Tararow*.
AUCTION RECORDS:
VIENNA, 18 June 1985, *Portrait of a Peasant* (1941, oil on canvas, 33 3/4 x 32 1/4 ins / 86 x 82 cm) ATS 18,000. WARSAW, 5 Dec 1999, *Girl in Snowy Landscape* (1913, oil on canvas, 40 x 36 ins / 101 x 92 cm) PLZ 19,000. VIENNA, 18 April 2001, *Woman in Traditional Costume* (oil on canvas, 38 x 39 ins / 96 x 98 cm) ATS 38,000.

JAROCZYNSKI, Marianus Jakob Ignaz
Polish, 19th century.
Born 1819, in Posen (now Poznan).
Painter, engraver.
The Mielzynski gallery in Poznan has five oil paintings by Marianus Jaroczynski, one of which is a *Self-portrait*. He mainly worked as an engraver. Six plates by him are known: a plate for the Merzbach edition of the Bible of 1858; a *Portrait of a Man Wearing a Fur Coat* of 1857; three engravings after drawings by Zaleski in an 1867 edition of Marja by Malcewski and the *Portrait of the Poet Jan Kochanowski* in the 1867 edition of the *Psalms of David*. In the retrospective exhibition of Polish art in Lemberg (now Lviv in Ukraine) in 1894, there were two plates by him: *Woman's Head* and two *Beggars' Heads* after Plonski, and five *Peasants' Heads* and a *Bust of a Peasant Woman*.

JARONEK, Bohumir
Czech, 19th - 20th century.
Born 1866, in Zlín.
Painter, watercolourist, engraver. Landscapes.
Bohumir Jaronek studied at the Budapest academy of fine art. He spent five years in Egypt, Palestine, Syria, Constantinople and Italy. He stayed in Paris where he exhibited his watercolours of the Middle East. He also exhibited work in Prague, at the watercolour exhibition in Dresden in 1909 and at the exhibition of the Artists' Circle held in Hodonín near Brno in 1913. Bohumir Jaronek settled in Moravia and painted many landscapes of the countryside and particularly of the small town of Stramberg. He also made woodcuts.

JAROS, Peter J.
Bohemian, 19th century.
Born 29 June 1859, in Prague.
Painter. Landscapes.

JAROSCHENKO, Nikolai Aleksandrovich. See **YAROSHENKO**

JAROSSLAWZEFF, Ivan. See **FILATEEV**

JAROSZ, Romain
French, 20th century.
Born 29 January 1889; died 1932.
Painter. Nudes, scenes with figures, landscapes, flowers.

Romain Jarosz was a pupil of Charles Guérin. He began as a landscape and flower painter, then became known as a painter of scenes at fairs and of well-built male nudes.

AUCTION RECORDS:
PARIS, 27 Dec 1926, *Flowers*, FRF 250. PARIS, 21 Nov 1928, *Reclining Nude*, FRF 500. PARIS, 10 Nov 1943, *Circus Scene* (charcoal and red chalk) FRF 240. LUCERNE, 8 Nov 2000, *Reclining Female Nude* (1927, oil on canvas, 18 x 24 ins / 46 x 60 cm) CHF 4,200.

JAROVA, Aleksandra Aleksandrovna, or Jarovova
Russian, 19th century.
Born 1853.
Painter.

Aleksandra Jarova studied at the fine art academy in St Petersburg from 1873 to 1878.

JARPA, Onofre
Chilean, 19th century.
Active in Santiago.
Painter. Landscapes.

Onofre Jarpa received a number of awards in Santiago from 1875 to 1893 and in Buffalo (New York State) in 1901.

JARRAUD, Léonard
French, 19th - 20th century.
Born 24 February 1848, in La Couronne; died 1926.
Painter. Religious subjects, genre scenes.

Léonard Jarraud was a pupil of Gérome. Some of his peasant scenes are treated in the style of Millet. Others are nearer to the Symbolists. He occasionally painted a canvas in delicate shades of grey, as with his *Railway* in the Limoges museum. He showed work at the Paris Salon from 1873 to 1876, then at the Salon of the Société Nationale des Beaux-Arts, of which he became a member in 1891.

MUSEUMS AND GALLERIES:
COGNAC: *Dream of a Tramp* - LIMOGES: *Railway*.

JARRAUD, Léonard Antoine
French, 19th century.
Born 5 August 1867, in St-Léonard (Haute-Vienne).
Painter (?), engraver (wood).

Léonard Jarraud studied under Brabant and Rousseau. He was a member of the Société des Artistes Français from 1907 and featured at its Salons, receiving an honourable mention in 1897, a third class medal in 1899 and a second class medal in 1904. He was a member of the Committee and of the Panel of Judges and was a Chevalier of the Légion d'Honneur.

JARRELL, Wadsworth A.
American, 20th century.
Born 1929, in Albany (Georgia).
Painter, lithographer. Portraits. Murals.
AfriCobra Group.

Wadsworth Jarrell moved to Chicago, where he studied at the Art Institute (1954-1958), after serving in the US Army. In 1962, he and Jeff Donaldson founded the Organization of Black American Culture (OBAC), which in 1968 became AfriCobra (the African Commune of Bad Relevant Artists). He taught at Howard University, Washington DC, from 1971 to 1988, and settled in New York.

Jarrell took part in the painting of the mural *The Wall of Respect* in Chicago (1967), which was painted on the outside wall of a building in Chicago's South Side by professional painters and ordinary citizens living in the neighbourhood, under the direction of the mural artist William Walker. It depicted African-American heroes such as Mohammed Ali and Malcolm X. Destroyed in 1971, the *Wall of Respect* marks the birth of a mural art movement, which gave rise to the creation of 1500 murals in US cities between 1967 and 1972. Jarrell continues to work in the Africa-centred approach of AfriCobra, drawing inspiration from jazz music for his brightly coloured, explosively composed portraits such as *Jazz Giants* (1987), which depicts five famous musicians. His work is resolutely figurative, always conscious of the need to speak positively and accessibly to his ethnic community. Consequently, even though his work tends now rather to celebrate the African-American identity, it has not lost the revolutionary aesthetic of the 1960s and 1970s.

Jarrell took part in various group exhibitions, including in 1970, *AfriCobra I* and in 1972, *AfriCobra II*, Howard University, Washington DC. He also had a number of solo exhibitions, including in 2002, Hammond's House, Atlanta College of Art, Atlanta.

BIBLIOGRAPHY:
Coalition of Black Revolutionary Artists, *An AFRI-COBRA artist, Wadsworth Jarrell - painter. AfriCobra I*, group exhibition catalogue, Howard University, Washington DC, 1970. *AfriCobra II*, group exhibition catalogue, Howard University, Washington DC, 1972. Douglas, Robert, *Wadsworth Jarrell: Artist as Revolutionary*, Pomegranate Art Books, San Francisco, 1996. Douglas, Robert L., in *American Visions*, October-November 1996.

JARRIN, Élise Sophie
French, 19th century.
Born 19th century, in Besançon.
Painter.

Élise Jarrin featured at the Salons of the Société des Artistes Français, and was awarded an honourable mention in 1886.

JARRY, Alfred
French, 19th - 20th century.
Born 1873, in Laval (Mayenne); died 1907, in Paris.
Draughtsman, engraver, lithographer, illustrator.

Alfred Jarry, the well-known writer who created the character of Le Père Ubu, also produced prints and paintings. His first wood engraving was *This is the Centaur* (c.1890). His engravings, made to illustrate his writings, show the influence of Gauguin and the Post-Impressionist Nabis. He used lithography to produce the cover for his 1898 *Puppets' Repertory*, in the review *Mercure de France*, and for posters and programmes for his theatrical pieces. He also collaborated on the illustration of the *Ballades* by Paul Fort in 1896, and on other publications such as the *Revue Blanche* (*White Review*). the *Mercure de France, L'Ymagier*. His own illustrations fixed the appearance of Le Père Ubu and his fellow actors. At Le Pouldu in Brittany in 1894, he met Charles Filiger, about whom he wrote a study for the *Mercure de France*. He also became a friend of the Nabis painters Paul Sérusier, Édouard Vuillard and Pierre Bonnard and of Toulouse-Lautrec and Félix Vallotton. By his writing as well as his illustrations he contributed greatly to the spirit of his times.

BIBLIOGRAPHY:
Osterwalder, Marcus (ed.), *Dictionnaire des illustrateurs 1800-1914*, Ides et Calendes, Neuchâtel, 1989.

JARRY, Jacques
French, 18th century.
Painter (porcelain).

Jacques Jarry worked at the porcelain factories known as the Manufacture d'Aprey (Haute-Marne) and the Manufacture de Sceaux. His speciality was painting flowers and birds.

MUSEUMS AND GALLERIES:
NARBONNE: five items.

JARRY, Joseph
French, 19th century.
Active in Avignon at the beginning of the 19th century.
Draughtsman, watercolourist.
Joseph Jarry drew pictures of the town of Avignon.

JARRY, Nicolas
French, 17th century.
Born 1620, in Paris; died 1670.
Miniaturist, calligrapher.
Nicolas Jarry was the most well-known calligrapher of his time and was called as much by Louis XIII. He is known for certain to have executed 107 works, and a large number of others are attributed to him. His first written work for the Bishop of Meaux, *Preparatio ad Missam* (*Preparation for the Letter*), is dated 1633, whilst his last work, *Devices for the King's Tapestries*, is dated 1668. His most well-known work is the *Julie's Garland*, containing 61 madrigals, composed by members of high society, and which he wrote for Charles de Sainte Maure Montausier and decorated in collaboration with the flower painter Nicolas Robert. Among his famous manuscripts are: a *Psalter* of 1640, for Nicole de Lorraine, *The Adoration of Jesus* of 1643, the *Temple of Glory*, of 1647, these last written for the queen mother, Anne of Austria, the *Book of Prayers by François de Beauvilliers* of 1647 and *Adonis*, by La Fontaine, of 1658. He confined himself mostly to the calligraphy of these manuscripts and commissioned the most well-known miniaturists of the 17th century to execute the miniatures.

JARRY DE MANCY, Adèle
Maiden name: Lebreton
French, 19th century.
Born in Paris; died 1854, in Paris.
Painter.
Adèle Jarry de Mancy was a pupil of her father, J. F. Lebreton, a decorator in a factory in Aprey.

JARSAILLON, Georges
French, 15th century.
Born 15th century, in Ambert.
Illuminator.
Jarsaillon was recorded as living in Lyons in 1475 and 1503 and was known as 'Master George the Writer'. His wife, Jeanne Dedorin, worked with him from 1493 to 1503.

JARSAILLON, Jeanne. See **JARSAILLON Georges**

JARTOFF, Andrei. See **YARTOV**

JARVIS, John
British, 18th century.
Born c. 1749, in Dublin; died 1804, in London.
Stained glass painter.
John Jarvis is believed to be the brother of Thomas Jarvis to whom he was assistant and heir. He was in turn assisted in his chemical research in Dublin by Dr Cunningham. Jarvis came to London at an early age and was renowned until his death.

JARVIS, John Wesley
American, 18th - 19th century.
Born 1780, in South Shields (Tyneside), England; died 1839 or 1840, in New York.
Painter. Portraits.
John Wesley Jarvis was a nephew of John Wesley, who brought him up until he was five years of age and then sent him to his father, who had emigrated to Philadelphia. He soon became a brilliant portraitist. Unfortunately, his liking for pleasure often impeded his work and, despite his fame, he died in complete poverty. Many of his paintings are in American museums.

AUCTION RECORDS:
NEW YORK, 1903, *Portrait of Daniel Tompthurs*, USD 300. NEW YORK, 22 Oct 1969, *Portraits of Jacob and Mary Ricketts* (paintings/panel, two) USD 2,500. NEW YORK, 7 April 1971, *Portrait of Judge Josiah Ogden Hoffman*, USD 2,100. NEW YORK, 17 Nov 1978, *Portrait of Henry Clay* (oil on panel, 32 x 23 ins / 81.3 x 58.5 cm) USD 9,500. NEW YORK, 24 April 1981, *Portrait of Commodore Oliver Hazard Perry* (oil on panel, 29 x 21 ins / 73.8 x 53.3 cm) USD 27,500. WASHINGTON DC, 2 Oct 1983, *Portrait of Henry Clay* (oil on panel, 32 x 23 1/2 ins / 81.5 x 59.5 cm) USD 3,000. NEW YORK, 5 Dec 1986, *Portrait of Major Richard Wisner Thor of New York City* (oil on canvas, 30 x 25 ins / 75.9 x 63.7 cm) USD 2,600. NEW YORK, 24 Jan 1990, *Portrait of Mr Nixon* (1807, watercolour and gouache/paper, 5 x 3 3/4 ins / 11.8 x 9.8 cm) USD 528. NEW YORK, 18 Dec 1991, *Portrait of Dr Samuel Latham Mitchell* (oil on canvas, 30 x 24 1/2 ins / 76.2 x 62.2 cm) USD 1,650. NEW YORK, 16 Jan 1998, *Portrait of General Jacob Brown* (oil on canvas, 43 x 36 ins / 109.2 x 91.5 cm) USD 11,500. NEW ORLEANS, 13 Oct 2001, *Louisiana Governor Joshua Baker* (oil on canvas, 34 x 27 ins / 86 x 69 cm) USD 7,000. BOSTON, 22 March 2002, *Portrait of Col James Burn* (oil on canvas) USD 1,500.

JARVIS, Thomas, or Jervis
Irish, 18th century.
Born in Dublin; died 29 August 1799, in Windsor.
Stained glass painter.
Thomas Jarvis began practicing his art as a stained glass painter in his home town of Dublin. Success took him to London where the protection of Lord Cremorne assured his favour in the English capital. Jarvis made stained glass windows for his patron's house in Chelsea. In 1776, he held an exhibition of his work showing himself to be a daring innovator, leaving behind centuries of tradition in favour of the grand works of nature: moonlight, the glow of fire and the effects of snow and ice. In his work, Jarvis drew upon the natural English genius for landscape; however, he did not limit himself merely to that: in 1777, he began work on the stained glass west window in New College, Oxford, reproducing the cartoons of Raphael, adapting Reynolds' *Nativity* as well as adding numerous allegorical figures. For the chapel at Windsor, he reproduced West's *Resurrection*, a work which has since been moved but for which Jarvis was harshly criticised by classicists and traditionalists. Nevertheless, for his discoveries and his innovation in the field, Jarvis should be counted one of the pioneers in the new school of stained glass artists.

JARWART, Sixtus Heinrich
German, 19th century.
Born 20 January 1813, in Nuremberg; died 22 February 1865, in Bayreuth.
Active in Bayreuth.
Painter, lithographer.
A student at the school of fine arts in Nuremberg and the academy in Munich, in 1853 Jarwart was appointed court painter by Frederick William IV of Prussia, and was commissioned to copy monuments relating to the Hohenzollern dynasty. In watercolours and gouache, these works came to rest in the Hohenzollern archives in Berlin. Some of them were lithographed by A. Klaus for the *Antiquities and Monuments of the House of Hohenzollern* published in Berlin and Stuttgart. Jarwart lithographed seven plates for *Slav Costumes in the Bayreuth Region*. He did sketches, of which A. Fleischmann did etchings, for Uhland's *Ballads and Romances*, and lithographed portraits. He also did the drawings from which A. F. Schultheiss engraved the coat of arms of the Emperor of Austria.

JAS
Dutch, 20th century.
Born 1945, in Hillegom.
Painter.

In 1967, Jas spent some time in Sweden and Finland, and in 1982, he travelled through Australia and the USA. In 1984-1985, he worked in Miami and New York, visiting Willem de Kooning on Long Island. In 1985, he settled permanently in Belgium. In his early period, his painting was gestural, lyrical abstract and sometimes, starting with Expressionist nudes, in large formats. From 1989, because of his past as a grower and seller of tulips, he made this multicoloured flower into a kind of repetitive module, multiplying the variations from canvas to canvas, rather like Claude Viallat's knucklebone, except that he treats it both gesturally and in a sensually generous manner, using a knife to add accents.

He has taken part in group exhibitions, including the 1987 Salon des Indépendants in Paris; a group consisting of himself and Bram van Velde, Sonia Delaunay and Kees van Bohemen at the Groot Schermer Museum in the Netherlands; *Lineart* in Ghent in 1988; at the Hillegom Cultural Centre in 1989; the Ostend Casino in 1991, and others. He has shown collections of paintings in solo exhibitions in 1985 and 1986 at the Galerie Catharina in Holland and in 1990 and 1991 at exhibitions presented by the Galerie Catharina at *Lineart* in Ghent.

JASCARD

French, 17th century.
Painter.

Jascard is mentioned by de Marolles.

JASCHKE, Franz

Austrian, 19th century.
Born 1775, in Rosenthal (Bohemia); died 6 November 1842, in Vienna.
Active in Vienna.
Painter, engraver (etching). Landscapes.

Jaschke trained at the academy in Vienna, and won several awards. After accompanying Archduke Ludwig to the Turkish frontier and Archduke Rainer across Bukovina, part of Galicia, Transylvania and Hungary, he brought back drawings, watercolours, oil and gouache paintings depicting the landscapes and popular costumes he saw. Some of these he turned into etchings. Other noted works include a *Panorama of Milan*, the *Ruins of Catullus's Villa on Sirmione/Garda*, *Petrarch's House* and the *Tomb of Petrarch*, plus a series of little watercolours with views of the Salzburg area. The castle of Grafenegg has a watercolour by him called *A View of Grafenegg Castle and Its Park*.

AUCTION RECORDS:

LONDON, 22 Nov 1996, *Budapest* (pencil and watercolour, 10 3/4 x 16 ins / 27.3 x 40.6 cm) GBP 2,760.

JASCHKE, Franz

Austrian, 19th - 20th century.
Born 19 June 1862, in Vienna; died December 1910, in Vienna.
Painter.

Franz Jaschke studied at the Akademie der bildenden Künste in Vienna and went on to paint portraits, historical subjects and landscapes. His children's portraits and floral-patterned borders were particularly well received.

JASER, Marie Marguerite Françoise.
See **ROUCHIER**

JASIEVICZ, Casimir Antonovich

Lithuanian, 19th century.
Born 1812 or 1813, in Vilnius; died 28 January 1888, in St Petersburg.
Painter. Religious subjects, portraits, landscapes.

Casimir Jasievicz studied at the fine art academy in St Petersburg and became a teacher there in 1849. He became a fellow of the academy in 1859 for his *Portrait of the Count of Osten-Sacken*. He painted landscapes, notably *By the Sea*, *Moonlit Night*, *Startled Bird* and many pictures of saints for Russian churches.

MUSEUMS AND GALLERIES:

MOSCOW (State Tretyakov Gal.): *Portrait of General Jerkov*; *Portrait of a Hussar*; other portraits.

JASIEWO, K.

Polish, 19th century.
Active at the beginning of the 19th century.
Miniaturist.

In the 1912 exhibition of Polish miniatures in Lemberg (now Lviv in Ukraine), there was a miniature portrait by Jasiewo of *Princess Natalia Galicyn*.

JASINSKI

Polish, 18th century.
Born 18th century, in Warsaw.
Painter.

Jasinski was the painter and decorator of the Warsaw theatre in the time of Stanislas Augustus.

JASINSKI, Félix Stanislas

Polish, 19th century.
Born 1862, in Poland; died 8 August 1901, in Puteaux.
Draughtsman, engraver, reproductions engraver.
Religious subjects, figures, portraits, self-portraits.

Félix Jasinski first settled in Paris, where his reproductions of the old and modern masters were highly rated, notably *Portrait of Mme Molé Raymond*, after Mme Vigée-Lebrun; *Portrait of Cardinal Lavigerie* (1888) after Bonnat; *William Warbam* after Holbein; *Head of a Child* after Fragonard, for a work by Baron Portalis; *Madonna and Child*, after Della Robbia, and *Portrait of a Man* after Quentin Metsys. He also reproduced works by Marius Roy, Alfred Stevens, Montegut, Jules Lefebvre and Fantin Latour. Jasinski also worked in London and seems to have become very fond of reproducing the Pre-Raphaelites, especially Burne-Jones.

BIBLIOGRAPHY:

Wellisz, Léopold, *Jasinski, graveur. Sa vie, son œuvre*, Van Oest, Paris, 1934.

MUSEUMS AND GALLERIES:

MANCHESTER: *Love among the Ruins* (engraving after Burne Jones).

AUCTION RECORDS:

PARIS, 31 Oct 1991, *Self-portrait* (1887, lead pencil, 5 3/4 x 3 3/4 ins / 14.5 x 9.5 cm) FRF 3,500. WARSAW, 7 Sept 2000, *Primavera* (engraving, after Botticelli, 17x24 ins / 43x60 cm) PLZ 2,500. LONDON, 6 July 2001, *Golden Stairs* (etching, after Burne-Jones, 28x13 ins / 70x33 cm) GBP 1,900. SYDNEY, 15 May 2004, *Golden Stairs* (engraving, after Burne-Jones, 24x11 ins / 62x27 cm) AUD 7,000.

JASINSKI, Michel

French, 20th - 21st century.
Born 1951.
Painter, pastellist, draughtsman. Figures.

Michel Jasinski attended a provincial art school and then the École des Arts Décoratifs in Paris where he studied engraving until 1978. He was of Polish origin and while working as an artist for the major French newspapers such as *Témoignage Chrétien*, *Le Point*, *L'Express* and *Le Figaro*, he was able to comment through his drawings on the events that culminated in the liberalisation of Poland in the 1980s. He paints in acrylics and draws in pastels and coloured pencils, charcoal and Indian ink. He only draws and paints figures and faces, with violently and expressively deformed postures and facial expressions, bulging eyes and howling mouths. Through successive periods all his work takes on a strong religious connotation: *Expression d'Amour* (*Expression of Love*), *Violence d'Amour* (*Violence of Love*), from 1980 to 1990 and *Rencontre et Transfiguration* (*Meeting and Transfiguration*), since 1991.

He set up his own gallery where he exhibited until 1981. Since then he has exhibited in hotels in Paris and the Paris area as well as the Salon d'Automne in 1981 and the Salon des Indépendants since 1982.

BIBLIOGRAPHY:

Jasinski, auction catalogue, Drouot, Paris, January 1985.

AUCTION RECORDS:

PARIS, 24 Jan 1994, *Allons-y Ensemble* (*Let's Go Together*) (wash and pen, Indian ink and acrylic wash, 6 1/2 x 9 3/4 ins / 16.6 x 24.6 cm) FRF 3,000; *Le Choix de la Paix* (*Choice of Peace*) (1989, drawing) FRF 5,000.

JASINSKI, Zdzislaw
Polish, 19th century.
Born 19th century, in Warsaw.
Painter. Portraits, genre scenes.

Zdzislaw Jasinski studied at the academy in Munich. He won a gold medal in Berlin in 1891 and a bronze medal at the 1900 Exposition Universelle in Paris. He was thought of as the painter of peasant life around Cracow.

AUCTION RECORDS:

NEW YORK, 28 May 1980, *The Picture Book* (oil on canvas, 15 3/4 x 30 ins / 40 x 76 cm) USD 2,700. LONDON, 6 Oct 1989, *Old Priest Lecturing Two Revellers* (oil on canvas, 14 1/4 x 20 3/4 ins / 36.2 x 52.6 cm) GBP 2,200. MADRID, 3 April 2000, *Allegory of the Republic* (1922, oil on canvas/cardboard, 30x43 ins / 75x110 cm) ESP 1,200,000.

JASOKU, or Dasoku, real name: Soyo Soga, nickname: Shikibu, monastic name: Fusen, Sojo
Japanese, 15th century.
Died 1483.
Active during the second half of the 15th century.
Painter.

Jasoku was a Zen monk, and successor to Hyobu-bokkei. His pen-and-ink paintings in the spirit of Shubun (working 1425-1450) are characterised by sharp ink marks. At the beginning of the 17th century, the founder of the Soga School Soga Chokuan (working about 1596-1610) and his son Chokuan II traced the origins of their family back to Josaku, in order to increase its prestige. This kind of genealogical fantasy was current in the 17th century, and it is for this reason that Jasoku is often portrayed as the founder of this Soga School.

JASOKUKEN. See **KANO Sansetsu**

JASON. See **IASON, IASUS**

JASPAR, Guy
Belgian, 20th century.
Born 1943.
Painter, screen printer, illustrator.

Guy Jaspar lives and works in Brussels. His paintings are made up of broad zones breaking up the space of the canvas from bottom to top, rather like Rothko's 'colour-field painting'. He is well versed in contemporary music and has established a relationship between his painting and music. Because he is also a poet, he writes parts of his own texts in beautiful handwriting on one of the fields of the composition. In addition to his paintings with spiritualistic intentions, he has illustrated the works of St John of the Cross. In 1992, the Fondation pour l'Art Belge Contemporain mounted a solo exhibition of his paintings; in 2003 his work was shown at the Edouard Roch gallery in Ballens, Switzerland, and in 2004 by the Gallery Saoh and Tomos in Tokyo.

MUSEUMS AND GALLERIES:

BRUSSELS (Bibliothèque royale Albert Ier).

JASPAR, Marcel
Belgian, 20th century.
Born 1886, in Liège; died 1952.
Painter. Landscapes, still-lifes. Murals.
Symbolism.

Marcel Jaspar was a pupil of Auguste Donnay at the college of fine arts in Liège. He perfected his studies at the Académie Julian in Paris.

JASPARD, or Gaspard
French, 16th century.
Active in Paris.
Sculptor.

Jaspard produced a clay model in 1548 featuring a *Crucifix*, the *Four Evangelists*, and the *Magdalene* which were then cast in bronze and used to decorate the fountain in the middle of the Celestine cloister built by Pierre Hanon.

JASPE Y MOSCOSO, Antonio
Spanish, 19th century.
Born 19th century, in La Coruña (Galicia).
Painter. Portraits, genre scenes.

Antonio Jaspe y Moscoso studied at the college of painting, sculpture and engraving and under Ign Suarez Llanas. He first exhibited in Madrid in 1875 and was awarded a medal. In 1880 he was accepted at the school of fine arts in Rome. Jaspe y Moscoso was decorated with the order of Charles III for his *Portraits of King Alfonso XII* and *Queen Cristina*.

AUCTION RECORDS:

PARIS, 1 July 1992, *Young Woman Harvester* (1883, oil on canvas, 32 x 24 1/2 ins / 81 x 62 cm) FRF 40,000.

JASPER, Johns. See **JOHNS Jasper**

JASPER, Théodore
German, 19th century.
Born 19th century, in Atendorf.
Painter.

Théodore Jasper is mentioned by Siret.

JASPER, Victor
Austrian, 19th century.
Born 30 March 1848, in Vienna.
Active in Vienna.
Engraver, painter, art restorer. Religious subjects, portraits, figures. Vignettes.

Victor Jasper studied at the academy in Vienna and became one of the most important engravers of his time. Initially, he engraved sculptures for the academy of sciences and archaeological reviews. He also did a frontispiece vignette for Thausing's monograph of Dürer, *All Saints* and the *Portrait of Emperor Maximilian I* after Dürer. Other principal works mentioned include *St Sebastian* after Mantegna, a *Portrait of an Old Woman* after Waldmüller and a *Portrait of Archduke Albert* after E. von Engerth. More than 50 of his portraits of contemporaries are known, including quite a few artists. As a painter, he did some inspired landscapes of the Vienna Woods and a *Holy Trinity* for the Gnaden Church in Mariazell.

JASPERS, Jan Baptist. See **GASPERS**

JASSAUD, de (Baron)
French, 19th century.
Painter. Portraits, landscapes.

De Jassaud exhibited at the Paris Salon from 1834 to 1839.

JASSAUD, Gervais
French, 20th century.
Born 15 May 1944, in Colombes.
Painter.

Gervais Jassaud was firstly a poet and his work as a writer led him to express himself in painting. In 1969 he created an editorial organisation, *Génération*, around the magazine *Génération - Cahier Littéraire*, with the purpose of making books on artists. He was a member of the Textruction group from 1971 to 1974. When he gave up painting the majority of his time was taken up with editorial work on the artists' books for which he developed a unique and original approach. Through this project he worked with Buren, Viallat,

Dezeuze, Sol Lewitt and other artists as well as a number of writers.

In his writing his intention was to grasp the word as a material or even materialistic component. He combined collages and deletions with fragmented writing on the page of a book, and from this he moved on to pictorial techniques. From a painted text which had been made illegible, he tried to highlight the body of the text, compare it with the texture of the canvas that served him as a support and comprehend it as space and as material evidence. In his 'caviardages', erasing parts of text by overwriting in blue or black ink, he superimposed the same text or texts in different characters, such as Latin or Far Eastern languages, and crumpled the canvas or hid part of the text within the canvas by adding in a new untouched piece of canvas, concealing the original text and destroying it in order to remove any meaning from it, but keeping just the signifier. While not consciously looking for a visual gesture, this nonetheless remains an underlying component, revealing an unconscious mind that no longer expresses itself beyond words but in words. While this painting has some similarity with the studies of other painters, such as Viallat or members of the Supports-Surfaces movement, the integration of text as a component of consciousness is a characteristic feature of Jassaud's work.

When he was a member of the Textruction group he took part in collective exhibitions including: Montreal, 1971, with Viallat, Dolla, Saytour and Valensi; École Spéciale d'Architecture, Paris, 1972; Mons, 1973; *Hors langage*, Nice, 1973; *En Marge de `Réalités Nouvelles'* (*On the Fringe of `Réalités Nouvelles'*), Paris, 1973; Galerie Rencontres, 1974. Solo exhibitions of his work include: Maison des Jeunes, Lorient, 1971; Culture Centre, Aubernas, 1972; Institute of Contemporary Arts, London, 1973; Galerie Rencontre, Paris, 1973; Descartes' House, Amsterdam, 1974 and Studio F 4, Bordeaux, 1974.

BIBLIOGRAPHY:

Textruction, exhibition catalogue, Gal. Rencontres, Paris, 1973. *Textruction*, exhibition catalogue, Institut Français des Pays-Bas, Maison Descartes, Amsterdam, 1974. *Livres d'artistes de collectif Génération*, Association française d'action artistique, 1991.

JASSE, Guillaume, or Josse

French, 15th century.

Active in Paris.

Sculptor.

Jasse produced statues of Charles VI and Charles VII in 1438, working in partnership with Philippe de Foncières. The statues were placed in niches decorating the main entrance to the Louvre.

JASSOGNE, Louis

French, 19th century.

Portrait painter.

Louis Jassogne exhibited at the Paris Salon from 1839 to 1844 and is known for his: *St Perpetua in Her Prison, Morning Prayer* and *Backwards Glance*.

JASSON, Émile Louis Ernest

French, 19th century.

Died 1901.

Active in Paris.

Painter.

Émile Jasson was a member of the Société des Artistes Français and featured at its Salon.

JASSON, Joséphine

French, 19th century.

Painter.

Joséphine Jasson featured at the 1845 and 1847 Paris Salons with her views.

JASSUSCH, Anton

Slovak, 20th century.

Born 25 April 1882, in Kosiciach; died 3 July 1965.

Painter.

Anton Jassusch studied in Budapest, Munich and Paris. His paintings show the inspiration of natural elements such as the sun, waves expressed in abstract rhythmical and gestural compositions.

He took part in many collective exhibitions of contemporary Czechoslovak painting, most importantly *Fifty years of Czechoslovak Painting from the Collections of the Galleries, 1918-1958* held in various national museums in Czechoslovakia to commemorate the 50th anniversary of the founding of the Republic in 1968. Solo exhibitions included: Kosiciach (1912, 1958 and 1962), Bratislava (1924 and 1962), and Berlin (1965).

JASTER, Joachim

German, 17th century.

Active in Celle.

Painter.

JASTRAU, Gudrun

Danish, 20th century.

Draughtsman.

Gudrun Jastrau - the daughter of Viggo Jastrau - exhibited her work in Charlottenburg in 1920 and 1921. She is noted for having designed frescoes represent episodes from Danish history for a school in Halskov-Korsør.

JASTRAU, Viggo

Danish, 19th century.

Born 29 March 1857, in Flensburg (then in Denmark, now in Schleswig-Holstein, Germany).

Illustrator.

Viggo Jastrau studied in Copenhagen and also worked in Paris. He produced illustrations, notably for *Aucassin and Nicolette* translated by S. Michaelis, and *The Fables of La Fontaine* translated by Prahl. Both works were published in Copenhagen.

JASTREBZOFF, Serge. See **FÉRAT Serge**

JASZAI, Jozsef

Hungarian, 19th - 20th century.

Born 17 March 1869.

Painter. Religious subjects, genre scenes.

Jozsef Jaszai studied in Budapest, Munich and at the Académie Julian in Paris.

He first exhibited work in Budapest in 1893. His paintings include: *Outside the Factory* exhibited in Budapest in 1893; *Hate, Thwarted Flight, After the Battle of Tapio-Bicske, The Flag Saved* and *Hunter*. He painted an altarpiece for the church at Ruttka depicting *Christ on the Mount of Olives*.

JASZCZEWSKI

Polish, 19th century.

Born in Warsaw; died c. 1820.

Painter. Religious subjects, figures.

Jaszczewski studied with Bacciarelli. He mainly painted religious subjects.

MUSEUMS AND GALLERIES:

POZNAN: *Study of a Head* (red chalk).

JASZCZOLD, Wojciech

Polish, 18th - 19th century.

Born 1763; died 22 March 1821, in Warsaw.

Painter, draughtsman, sculptor.

Wojciech Jaszczold studied with Bacciarelli and Smuglevitch, and completed his studies in Italy and France. On his return to Poland, he was invited to the Czatoryski palace in Poulavej, where he produced a number of works. In 1813, he went to the castle of Count Potocki at Wilanow, near Warsaw. He also painted for churches and his *St Anthony* is in the Reformers' church in Kasimierz.

JATIVA, Master. See **MASTERS**

JATIVA MASTER, or Master of the Seven Sorrows of the Virgin
Spanish, 16th century.
Painter. Religious subjects.

The Jativa Master was active in Catalonia at the beginning of the 16th century. He was named after Jativa, near Valencia, where most of his works may be found. The painting, *Seven Sorrows of the Virgin*, is in the church of S Francisco in Jativa. The figures in his work are quite rigid.

MUSEUMS AND GALLERIES:
BARCELONA (Mus. Nacional d'Art de Catalunya): seven panels for an altar to Mary - TOLEDO: *Adoration of the Magi* - VALENCIA (MBA San Pío V): *Pietà with St John and Mary Magdalene.*

AUCTION RECORDS:
MONACO, 17 June 1988, *Crucifixion* (oil on panel, 34¼ x 33½in/87 x 85cm) FRF 155,400.

JATON, Henri
Swiss, 19th century.
Born 23 June 1850, in Villars-Mendraz (Vaud).
Painter, draughtsman.

Jaton was a pupil of Bocion in Lausanne and Mayor, Menn and Salmson in Geneva.

JATTIOT, Charles
French, 19th century.
Born 19th century, in Chartres.
Engraver.

Charles Jattiot exhibited at the Paris Salon in 1853.

JÄTTNIG, Ernst
German, 19th century.
Active in Berlin.
Engraver. Architectural views, anatomical subjects, natural history.

Ernst Jättnig engraved archaeological, natural history, anatomical and architectural subjects.

JÄTTNIG, Ferdinand
German, 19th century.
Active in Berlin.
Engraver.

Ferdinand Jättnig engraved mainly mythological, architectural and ornamental subjects.

JÄTTNIG, Theodor
German, 19th century.
Active in Berlin.
Engraver.

Theodor Jättnig did engravings from C. Kretschmar and N. Verkolje, but also original portraits.

JAUBERT, Alfred de
French, 19th century.
Born 19th century, in Metz.
Painter.

Alfred de Jaubert worked in Hersent's studio and exhibited *Le Giaour* and *Suzanne* at the 1841 and 1852 Paris Salons, respectively.

MUSEUMS AND GALLERIES:
METZ: *Old Man in Front of a Table Laden with Books and a Map of the World* - VERSAILLES (Mus.): *Full-length Portrait of General du Teil.*

JAUBERT, Henri Auguste
French, 19th - 20th century.
Born 21 May 1860, in Digne (Alpes-de-Haute-Provence); died 1936, in Périgueux.
Painter. Landscapes, still-lifes.

Henri Auguste Jaubert, a brother of Melchior Jaubert, who was his first teacher, mainly painted strong and sincere landscapes of Digne and its neighbourhood. He began to exhibit at the Paris Salon in 1884.

MUSEUMS AND GALLERIES:
ALÈS: *Skinned Ox Head*; three watercolours - DIGNE-LES-BAINS: *St-Dommin, Digne, in Autumn*; *Hot Water in the Thermal Baths*; *Banks of the Mardaric in Digne*; *View of Digne*; *Flowers.*

AUCTION RECORDS:
VERSAILLES, 27 Jan 1980, *Landscape* (watercolour, 17 x 23½ ins / 43 x 60 cm) FRF 880.

JAUBERT, Melchior Antoine
French, 19th century.
Born 5 January 1848, in Digne (Alpes-de-Haute-Provence); died 1913, in Grenoble.
Painter, watercolourist. Landscapes.

Melchior Jaubert was a Catholic secondary school teacher, then moved to Digne's Municipal College of Art before teaching at Vaucansson College in Grenoble.

Like his brother, Henri Jaubert, he painted scenes from his native region, but concentrated on markets, fairs and the streets of Digne, Bourg-d'Oisans and Grenoble. His landscapes are painted with swift strokes, which deftly pepper them with luminous specks.

MUSEUMS AND GALLERIES:
DIGNE-LES-BAINS: *Market in Grenoble.*

JAUBERT DE BECQUE. See **BECQUE Maurice Jaubert de**

JAUD, Benedikt
Austrian, 19th century.
Born 27 July 1800.
Painter.

Benedikt Jaud was the son of Sebastian Jaud.

JAUD, Isfried
Austrian, 19th century.
Born c. 1792, in Wessobrunn (Germany); died 7 May 1865, in Salzburg.
Active in Salzburg.
Painter.

The parish church of Grödig (near Salzburg) has 14 paintings of the Stations of the Cross by Isfried Jaud, while the church of nearby Siezenheim has a *Christ with a Crown of Thorns* and the collegiate church of St Peter in Salzburg has a *St Maximus* by him.

MUSEUMS AND GALLERIES:
SALZBURG (Carolino Augusteum Mus.): *Death of St Joseph*; *Ave Maria.*

JAUD, Josef
Austrian, 19th century.
Born c. 1833; died 28 June 1864.
Painter.

Josef Jaud was the son of Isfried Jaud. The church of St Blaise in Siezenheim (Salzburg) has a *St Blaise* by him, while the cemetery chapel in the same town has a *Resurrection* on the high altar.

JAUD, Sebastian
Austrian, 18th century.
Born 11 November 1751, in Wessobrunn (Germany).
Painter.

Several self-portraits are known by Sebastian Jaud.

MUSEUMS AND GALLERIES:
SALZBURG: *Death of St Joseph* - WEILHEIM (Stadtmus.): several sketches and studies.

JAUDIN, Henri Laurent
French, 19th - 20th century.
Born in Paris.

Painter. Landscapes.
Henri Laurent Jaudin exhibited in Paris at the Salon des Indépendants from its foundation in 1884.

JAUDON, René
French, 20th century.
Born 18 March 1889, in Marvejols (Lozère).
Painter.
René Jaudon studied with Gabriel Ferrier and Paul-Albert Laurens and was manager of a lithographical workshop. In Paris, he exhibited at the Salon des Artistes Français and at the Salon des Indépendants, winning prizes in 1925, 1926 and 1927.

JAUDON, Valerie
American, 20th century.
Born 6 August 1945.
Painter (mixed media). Landscapes.
Valerie Jaudon studied at the Mississippi State College for Women, Columbus (1963-1966), the Memphis Academy of Art, Tennessee (1965), the University of the Americas, Mexico City (1966-1967) and St Martin's School of Art, London (1968-1969). During her time in Mexico she was inspired by Mayan architecture, and she also cites Matisse as an inspiration. She moved to New York City in 1969 and married the artist Richard Kalina. She has stated that her goal is to prove that abstraction can speak in a representational way.

Jaudon's paintings comprise bands and curves in a limited colour range. Her early works were on grids with repeating patterns. In 1973, she created *Toomsuba*, an acrylic painting in which she drew concentric circles with a compass and overlapped them with diagonal and rectilinear grids. She then painted the shapes created with more than two hundred colours. She has continued to use the patterns generated in this work for other paintings. In the 1980s she began to separate and enlarge the interlaced shapes, as in her painting *Tallahatchee* (1984), which she created with gold leaf and a limited palette. Later in that decade, she began to use geometric shapes on monochrome backgrounds with a double-banded grid. In the 1990s she arranged her interlaces into sinuous figures, as in *Concordance* (1992) or the oil painting *Back Street* (1995).

Jaudon has also designed public art, such as her *Long Division* (1988), a steel security fence decorated with her trademark patterns in an IRT Subway in New York City, or *Reunion* (1989), which is a brick and granite paving plan in the Police Plaza Civic Center, Manhattan.

Her exhibitions include: 1979, *Patterning, Painting*, Musées Royaux des Beaux-Arts de Belgique, Brussels; 1982, *A Look Back, A Look Forward*, Aldrich Museum of Contemporary Art, Ridgefield, CT; 1985, *American Art: American Women*, Stamford Museum, CT; 1987, *Generations of Geometry*, Whitney Museum of American Art at the Equitable Center, New York; and 1989, *Making their Mark*, Cincinnati Arts Museum.

She has received a Creative Artists Public Service Grant (1980), a Mississippi Institute of Art and Letters Art Award (1981), a National Endowment for the Arts Fellowship (1988), an Art Award for Excellence in Design, Art Committee, New York (1988), a New York State Fellowship in Painting (1992) and a Merit Award from the American Society of Landscape Architects (1992).

BIBLIOGRAPHY:
Mallison, Constance, '*Valerie Jaudon at James Corcoran*' in *Images and Issues*, journal article, Summer 1981. Perreault, John, '*Allusive Depths: Valerie Jaudon*' in *Art in America*, journal article, October 1983. *Valerie Joudon*, exhibition catalogue, Sidney Janis Gallery, New York, 1990. Welish, Marjorie, '*Valerie Joudon*' in *Tema Celeste*, journal article, Winter 1993. Barilleaux, René Paul, *Valerie Jaudon*, exhibition catalogue, Mississippi Art Museum, Jackson, 1996.

MUSEUMS AND GALLERIES:
AACHEN (Neue Galerie-Sammlung Ludwig) - BIRMINGHAM, AL (MA) - BUFFALO (Albright-Knox AG): *Sound* (1986, painting); *Constant* (1986, painting) - CAMBRIDGE, MA (Fogg AM, Harvard University) - CAMBRIDGE, MA (Harvard University) - DAYTON (AI) - NEW YORK (MoMA) - RIDGEFIELD (Aldrich MCA): *Yazoo City* (1975, oil) - WASHINGTON DC (Hirshhorn Mus. and Sculpture Garden): *Jackson* (1976, metallic pigment and pencil) - WASHINGTON DC (National Mus. of Women in the Arts): *Avalon* (1976, oil and metallic paint); *Ingomar* (1979, oil and metallic paint).

AUCTION RECORDS:
NEW YORK, 3 May 1985, *Vicksburg* (1980, oil on canvas, 84 x 120 ins / 213.4 x 304.8 cm) USD 14,000. NEW YORK, 20 Feb 1988, *Avalon* (1976, oil and metallic paint/canvas, 72 x 68 1/2 ins / 183 x 174.3 cm) USD 7,700. NEW YORK, 4 May 1989, *Sartartia* (oil/material, 88 1/2 x 135 3/4 ins / 225 x 345 cm) USD 28,600. NEW YORK, 5 Oct 1989, *Montrose* (1983, oil on canvas, 94 x 116 ins / 238.7 x 294.7 cm) USD 37,400. NEW YORK, 9 Nov 1989, *Bay Springs* (1976, oil on canvas, 72 x 72 ins / 183 x 183 cm) USD 41,800. NEW YORK, 27 Feb 1990, *Locopolis* (1977, oil on canvas, 72 x 72 ins / 183 x 183 cm) USD 34,100. NEW YORK, 7 Nov 1990, *Prairie Point* (1977, oil on canvas, 72 x 72 ins / 182 x 182 cm) USD 24,200. NEW YORK, 14 Feb 1991, *Martinsville* (1980, oil and copper pigment/canvas, 36 x 36 ins / 91.3 x 91.3 cm) USD 6,050. NEW YORK, 7 May 1991, *Brazil* (1982, oil on canvas, 36 x 36 ins / 91.4 x 91.4 cm) USD 5,500. NEW YORK, 17 Nov 1992, *Untitled* (1976, graphite/paper, 25 1/4 x 25 ins / 64.1 x 63.8 cm) USD 1,100. NEW YORK, 4 May 1993, *Egypt River* (1980, oil and metallic pigments/canvas, 90 x 98 ins / 228.6 x 248.9 cm) USD 11,500. NEW YORK, 7 May 1996, *Homewood* (1976, oil on canvas, 48 x 48 ins / 121.9 x 121.9 cm) USD 8,050. LOS ANGELES, 7 June 2000, *Osaka* (1978, oil on canvas, 36 x 36 ins / 91 x 91 cm) USD 3,200. CHICAGO, 15 Dec 2003, *Kosciusko* (oil on canvas, 72 x 72 ins / 183 x 183 cm) USD 12,000.

JAUFFROY. See **JOUFFROY**

JAUGE, Charles or Jean Charles
French, 19th century.
Born 1820, in Paris; died 17 April 1852.
Painter.
Charles or Jean Charles Jauge completed a training course in a bank in London but illness forced him to return to France, which he then left for Rome. He worked in Rome for four years as a painter, producing views of the city, notably *The Coliseum* and *Castel Gandolfo*.

He featured at the Paris Salon from 1846 to 1852. Obsessed by the uselessness of his existence however, he descended into madness and killed himself.

JAUGEY, Daniel
French, 20th century.
Born 21 January 1929, in Lyons.
Painter, watercolourist, draughtsman. Figure compositions, landscapes, seascapes, still-lifes, flowers.
Daniel Jaugey, a self-taught artist, discovered painting in 1956 and was able to devote himself to it full time from 1965. He began by painting landscapes in a Post-Impressionist style. Later, he invented a style of his own, characterised by blurred lines and delicate tones of grey. He retained the landscapes - the harbour at Nice, canals in Venice, public gardens in Paris - but only as evocative backgrounds, while he focused his compositions on figures of dreamers, buffoons, lovers and children. He travelled in Italy, Spain, Portugal, Sweden and Morocco, showing work and winning prizes and distinctions in numerous collective exhibitions across France and abroad, especially in Germany, Belgium, the USA, Canada and Africa and also in Paris at the Salon des Indépendants, Salon d'Automne and Salon de Dessin et de la Peinture à l'Eau. After his first solo show in Cannes in 1957 he had solo exhibitions almost annually, and frequently

several times a year, in many cities in France as well as in Sweden, Portugal, often in Canada, Italy, Hong Kong, Morocco, Switzerland and Egypt, and regularly in Paris at the Galerie Vendôme.

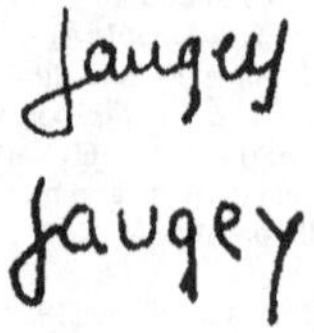

BIBLIOGRAPHY:
'Daniel Jaugey' in *coll. Art-Documents*, Éd. Pierre Cailler, Geneva, 1966. *'Daniel Jaugey'* in *coll. Chronique des Arts*, Éd. L'Archipel, Paris, 1976. *Jaugey*, Éd. Triangle, Paris, 1987. Igulay, Jean de, et al., *Jaugey*, Edisud, Aix-en-Provence, 1993 (extensive documentation).
AUCTION RECORDS:
VERSAILLES, 26 Nov 1989, *Fishermen's Bay* (oil on canvas, 28¾ x 36¼ ins / 73 x 92 cm) FRF 20,000. PARIS, 17 June 1991, *Harbour* (oil on canvas) FRF 7,000. NEW YORK, 9 May 1994, *Group of Mountebanks* (1970, oil on canvas, 32 x 39¼ ins / 81.3 x 99.5 cm) USD 805.

JAULIN, Gérard
French, 20th century.
Painter, pastellist.
Gérard Jaulin exhibited pastel drawings in 1988 at the Musée de Libourne. His style has affinities with Expressionism.

JAULMES, Gustave Louis
French, 20th century.
Born 14 April 1873, in Lausanne, Switzerland; died 1959.
Active in France.
Painter, designer. Allegorical subjects, figures, portraits, interiors with figures, still-lifes, landscapes. Murals, designs for tapestries.
Art Deco.
Gustave Louis Jaulmes was a son of a French pastor who ministered in Lausanne. When he came of age, the young man chose France, and did his military service in Nîmes. He studied in Paris in the Jean-Paul Laurens studio and at the Académie Julian. In 1913 he helped to found the French Studio created by Louis Süe, which in 1919 became the Compagnie des Arts Français, Süe et Mare. In 1918 he received his first official commissions from the French government, the decoration of the Hall of the Kiss in the Musée Rodin in Paris, and the cartoon for the tapestry *The Americans Go to War* woven at the Gobelins factory. In 1919, he exhibited a plan for a tapestry woven by the Gobelins which the French government presented to the city of Philadelphia. In 1922, he painted a curtain for the city theatre in Lyons, in 1927 the decoration of the Pleyel Hall which a few months later was destroyed by fire, in 1932 the decorations of the town hall in Arras, and of the Fifth Arrondissement in Paris, in 1934 the decor of the theatre in Carcassonne, in 1937 the decor in the main foyer of the theatre of the Palais de Chaillot, and a picture, *The Arms of France*, ordered by the government for the city of Strasbourg. He saw painting as an extension and a complement of architecture. Influenced at first by the Impressionists and the Nabis, he later returned to a more classical concept, giving pride of place to monumentality, harmony and simplicity.

He showed work in collective exhibitions in Paris - at the Société Nationale des Beaux-Arts from 1906 to 1922, at the Salon d'Automne from 1908 to 1919 and at the Salon des Indépendants from 1909 to 1912. His solo shows in Paris during his lifetime include: Galerie Druet, 1909, 1911, 1914, 1920, 1926; Galerie Charpentier, 1928; Galerie Durand-Ruel, 1947; Paul Ambroise, 1954; and after his death at the town hall of the Fifth Arrondissement in Paris. In 1983, the Annonciade Museum in St-Tropez showed a series of his paintings of Provence.
BIBLIOGRAPHY:
Child, Eric/Guttinter-Mettetal, Christiane, *La Provence de Gustace Jaulmes*, exhibition catalogue, Musée de l'Annonciade, St-Tropez, 1983.
MUSEUMS AND GALLERIES:
LE HAVRE (Mus. Malraux) - PARIS (Mus. des Arts décoratifs): wall decorations; sketches for tapestries - PARIS (Mus. Rodin): wall decorations - ST-TROPEZ (Mus. de l'Annonciade): *Sunset over the Harbour at Cannes; St-Tropez, the Annonciade Museum* (1958).
AUCTION RECORDS:
PARIS, 21 Feb 1920, *Plenty*, FRF 800. PARIS, 15 Jan 1945, *Woman and Children in a Park*, FRF 1,100. PARIS, 18 May 1945, *Autumn*, FRF 2,700. PARIS, 30 March 1984, *Flora's Toilette* (oil on canvas, 50½ x 61 ins / 128 x 155 cm) FRF 30,000. PARIS, 6 March 1987, *Young Woman by a Pool* (oil on canvas) FRF 23,000. LONDON, 24 Feb 1988, *Still-life with Dish* (oil on card, 30 x 39¼ ins / 76 x 100 cm) GBP 2,310. VERSAILLES, 29 Oct 1989, *Bouquet of Flowers* (oil on panel, 13 x 16¼ ins / 33 x 41 cm) FRF 6,000. PARIS, 6 Feb 1991, *Round the Pool in the Garden at Versailles* (oil on card, 14½ x 20½ ins / 37 x 52 cm) FRF 4,500. PARIS, 4 March 1991, *Women and Children in a Garden* (oil on panel, 14¾ x 18 ins / 37.5 x 46 cm) FRF 5,000. PARIS, 16 Dec 1992, *Bacchantes* (oil on canvas, 24 x 19¾ ins / 61 x 50 cm) FRF 4,500. PARIS, 22 March 1993, *St-Tropez* (oil on card, 13 x 18 ins / 33 x 46 cm) FRF 3,800. PARIS, 5 Dec 1997, *Village in the Midi* (oil on canvas, 27½ x 22¾ ins / 70 x 58 cm) FRF 2,200.

JAULMES, Marc
French, 20th century.
Born 1928.
Painter.
Marc Jaulmes studied from 1953 to 1955 at the art college in Montpellier. He became a medical ophthalmologist, and collected works by painters of the group Support/Surface, which included the two Montpellier artists, Bioulès and Dezeuze. In Montpellier in 1968 he organised their first exhibition. He continued to paint in the spirit of the group, working on experimental analysis of the original components of the objects depicted.
AUCTION RECORDS:
PARIS, 19 Nov 1995, *Untitled* (1994, acrylic/canvas, 57½ x 45 ins / 146 x 114 cm) FRF 7,000.

JAUMANN, Rudolf Alfred
German, 19th century.
Born 1 May 1859, in Pilsen (now Plzen, Czech Republic).
Painter. Genre scenes.
A pupil of Lofftz in Munich and Makart in Vienna, Jaumann settled in Munich, exhibiting there from 1888.
AUCTION RECORDS:
LONDON, 6 Oct 1989, *The Trophy* (1887, oil on canvas, 17¼ x 14 ins / 44 x 35.5 cm) GBP 1,650. AMSTERDAM, 25 April 1990, *Man Talking to a Crow by a Table* (1885, oil on panel, 9 x 6¾ ins / 23 x 17 cm) NLG 2,990.

JAUME. See also **JAIME**

JAUME, Antoinette, or Jaume-Boyé
French, 20th century.
Born in Tarn-et-Garonne.
Painter.
Antoinette Jaume settled in Montgeron (Essonne). She published collections of her poetry, then became interested in artistic bookbinding. In 1970, with help from Claude Schurr,

she began to paint. Her painting is abstract and to some extent constructed but never rigid. Delicately coloured planes, worked in superimposed touches, succeed one another into the imagined depths of the canvas. Her work was shown in Paris in various salons - Salon des Beaux-Arts, Salon des Artistes Français, Salon d'Automne and Salon d'Art Sacré. She also exhibited in collectives in the Paris neighbourhood, such as Essonne and the Montauban region. In 1981 she had a solo show in Paris.

JAUME, Gerardo. See **STARNINA Gherardo di Jacopo**

JAUMOTTE, Gaston
Belgian, 20th century.
Born 15 November 1926, in Orp-le-Grand.
Painter, potter. Figures, portraits, landscapes, still-lifes.
Gaston Jaumotte studied under Léon Devos and others at the Académie Royale des Beaux Arts in Brussels, and went on to teach drawing and composition. His body of work is distinguished by its gravitas: a portrait of his grandmother painted in 1953 immediately recalls the stern hospice matrons portrayed by Frans Hals. Jaumotte's landscapes and seascapes are somewhat conventional, but he demonstrates a keen feeling for composition in his still-lifes of fruit and vegetables painted around 1957, and his shellfish studies of 1996.
AUCTION RECORDS:
LOKEREN, 17 May 1997, *Pitcher* (1956, oil on canvas, 27¾ x 35½ ins / 70.5 x 90 cm) BEF 55,000. LOKEREN, 6 Dec 1997, *Country Bread* (1949, oil on canvas, 23½ x 31½ ins / 60 x 80 cm) BEF 50,000.

JAUNÂTRE, Jacques
French, 20th century.
Born 5 April 1939, in Nantes.
Painter.
After getting to know Gen-Paul and Lorjou, Jacques Jaunâtre developed a post-Pollock Tachist and paint-dripping technique. His work has featured in collective exhibitions, including the Salon des Artistes Français (honourable mention 1967) and the Salon des Indépendants.

JAUNEZ, Lina
French, 19th century.
Painter.
Lina Jaunez exhibited views at the Paris Salon in 1833 and 1834.
MUSEUMS AND GALLERIES:
PARIS (Mus. Carnavalet): *Ruins of the Church of St Thomas du Louvre.*

JAURAN, pseudonym of Repentigny, Rodolphe de
Canadian, 20th century.
Born 1926, in Quebec; died 1959, in the Rocky Mountains, as the result of an accident.
Painter.
Groupe des Plasticiens.
Jauran took an early interest in painting, but nevertheless began by studying mathematics. He went to France in 1949 and studied philosophy at the Sorbonne, but also discovered French painting of the period. He then worked in London and went on a walking tour of Italy, before returning to Montreal. Matching words to deeds, he also became a critic and theoretician, publishing many articles in the magazines of the time, notably, in 1955, the *Manifeste des Plasticiens* (*Plasticians' Manifesto*), in which, on the occasion of an exhibition by a group of artists he belonged to, he detailed their Neo-Constructivist principles in opposition to the Neo-Romantic expressionism of the Automatists of the preceding generation. His career was cut short by a fatal climbing accident.
His own paintings, though very rigorously constructed, do not have a geometrical rigidity, and their sober, muted colour combinations give them an air of dignity.
MUSEUMS AND GALLERIES:
MONTREAL (MAC): *No. 197, Greys and Yellows* (c. 1955).

JAUREGUIZCAR, Eliezer
Spanish, 19th century.
Born 19th century, in Santander; died September 1880, in Santander.
Painter. History painting, portraits, seascapes.
Eliezer Jaureguizcar studied at the Cádiz fine arts academy. He first exhibited in Cádiz in 1870 and in Madrid in 1871.

JAUREGUY Y AGUILAR, Juan de
Spanish, 16th - 17th century.
Born c. 1570, in Biscay; died 1641, in Madrid.
Painter, poet.
Juan de Jaureguy y Aguilar came from an aristocratic family and was a knight of the order of Calatrava and an equerry to Elizabeth of Bourbon, the wife of Philip IV. He took up painting as a recreation, visited Rome and there studied the Renaissance masters. He returned to Spain and painted some excellent portraits, including one of *Cervantes*. In 1619, he supplied drawings for the engravings in Luis Alcazar's *Investigatio arcani Sensus in Apocalypsi*. He also wrote a dialogue in verse, *Dialogue on Art and Nature* and translated Tasso's *Anunta*.

AUCTION RECORDS:
PARIS, 1843, *Portrait*, FRF 200.

JAURES, Jean Émile
French, 20th century.
Born 24 March 1932, in Paris.
Painter.
Nouvelle Figuration.
Jean Émile Jaures trained in Paris under Robert Humblot and Jean Aujame. He lives and works in Toulouse. The figurative style he learned from his teachers is connected to the method described by Gérald Gassiot-Talabot as narrative figuration.

JAUSLIN, Karl
Swiss, 19th century.
Born 21 May 1842, in Muttenz (Basel); died 13 October 1904, in Muttenz.
Painter.
The son of a quarryman, Jauslin worked without a teacher until 1871, when he went to Stuttgart and attended courses at the school of fine arts there. He was mainly a decorative painter.
MUSEUMS AND GALLERIES:
BASEL - BERN - LUCERNE: *The Battle of Grandson; The Death of Charles the Bold* - ST LOUIS.
AUCTION RECORDS:
LUCERNE, 4 Oct 1986, *The Return of Duke Leopold I to Winterthur after the Battle of Morgarten* (1897, watercolour, 25¼ x 33 ins / 64 x 84 cm) CHF 5,000. BERN, 13 May 2004, *Napoleon Receiving Oberst von Affri* (oil on canvas, 25 x 33 ins / 64 x 85 cm) CHF 6,000.

JAUSS, Georg
German, 19th century.
Born 15 March 1867, in Hattenhofen.
Active in Munich.
Painter. Genre scenes.
Jauss exhibited in Munich from 1889 and in Berlin in 1909.

JAUVAU DE CRUSEN. See **CRUSEN**

JAUVELLE
French, 18th century.
Active in Paris.
Engraver (burin).
Jauvelle is mentioned by Le Blanc as having engraved: *Old Peter's Mare*, after Vleughel.

JAUVIN, Aline
French, 19th century.
Born 19th century, in Tours.
Painter.
Aline Jauvin was a pupil of Lazerges. She exhibited *Italian Bandit* and *Basket of Grapes* at the 1859 and 1861 Paris Salons respectively.

JAUVIN, Jules
French, 19th century.
Painter.
Jules Jauvin exhibited landscapes at the Paris Salon from 1831 to 1835. Among his works are: *Evening, Genoese River; Fog, Amsterdam Suburbs; Naples Viewed from Santa Lucia; Salt Barges on the Laguna* and *Fishing by Torchlight.*

JAUZION, Aline
French, 19th century.
Died 1862.
Painter.
MUSEUMS AND GALLERIES:
DIJON (Mus. Magnin): *Portrait of Mme Magnin.*

JAUZION, Jeanne
French, 19th century.
Born 19 April 1851, in Paris.
Sculptor.
Jeanne Jauzion studied under Rouland, Rolard and Inkalbert. She was a member of the Société des Artistes Français from 1894 and received an honourable mention in 1907.
MUSEUMS AND GALLERIES:
LE MANS (Mus. de Tessé): *Bust of the Painter Coypel; Inspiration.*

JAVACHEV. See **CHRISTO**

JAVAUX, Ginette
Belgian, 20th century.
Painter. Nudes, landscapes.
Ginette Javaux studied under Léon Devos at the Académie Royale des Beaux Arts in Brussels, where she was a prize winner. Her style is particularly vigorous, with a confident and well-constructed draughtsmanship, and a series of contrasting browns.

JAVOR, Pal
Hungarian, 20th century.
Born 13 November 1880, in Budapest; died 1923, in Budapest.
Painter. Figure compositions, figures, portraits. Murals.
Pal Javor studied at the Budapest academy of fine art and at the Académie Julian in Paris. He took part in a number of exhibitions and received a number of awards. He painted a mural for the Ken-Ucca School in Budapest depicting *Traditional Folk Tales.*
MUSEUMS AND GALLERIES:
BUDAPEST (Szépmuvészeti Múz.): *Reverie.*
AUCTION RECORDS:
LONDON, 14 Feb 1990, *Sleeping Girl* (oil on canvas, 33 1/2 x 41 1/4 ins / 85 x 105 cm) GBP 3,850. LONDON, 15 Jan 2004, *Sweet Dreams* (oil on canvas, 33 x 41 ins / 84 x 105 cm) GBP 2,200.

JAVORSKA, Tamara
Russian, 20th century.
Born 1926, in Arkhangel.
Active in Canada.
Hand-weaver.
Tamara Javorska graduated at the Lódz academy of fine art in Poland in 1950; she then enrolled in the textile department of the academy, qualifying in weaving in 1952.

She has taken part in various collective exhibitions including: *Experimental Three-Dimensional Tapestries*, Museum of Fine Art in Ontario (1973); travelling exhibition *Contemporary Canadian Tapestry* organised by the Canadian Ministry of Foreign Affairs (1980).

Solo exhibitions include: Museum of Fine Art, Warsaw (1965); Radom Museum, Poland (1966); Pushkin Museum (1966); Scottish Woollen Art Gallery in Galashiels, Scotland (1968); Merton Gallery, Toronto (1970); Glendon Gallery, Toronto (1972); Galerie Inard, Paris (1984).
MUSEUMS AND GALLERIES:
LÓDZ (Centralne Muzeum Wlokiennictwa/Museum of Textiles) - MOSCOW (Pushkin MFA) - WARSAW (Muz. Narodowe).

JAVUREK, Karel
Bohemian, 19th century.
Born 1815, in Prague; died 24 March 1909, in Prague.
Painter.
Karel Javurek was a student at the academy in Prague and also studied in Vienna, Antwerp, Brussels and Paris, where he was taught by Th. Couture. He painted historical scenes, choosing subjects from the history of his own country: *Jan Huss Saying Farewell to his Compatriots, Death of John of Luxembourg, Frederick V at the Battle of the White Mountain, Murder of Wallenstein's Officers* and *Count Chotek Leaving his Native Land in 1621.* He also painted subjects from religious history and genre scenes.
MUSEUMS AND GALLERIES:
PRAGUE (Rudolfinum Gal.): *No Mercy; Portrait of the Painter J. Cermak.*
AUCTION RECORDS:
ENGHIEN-LES-BAINS, 24 Feb 1980, *Market Scene* (oil on canvas, 11 x 14 1/2 ins / 28 x 37 cm) FRF 6,600. LONDON, 12 Oct 2000, *Card Players* (1867, oil on canvas, 26x32 ins / 67x81 cm) GBP 3,200. KEMPTEN, 6 Nov 2003, *Academic in Study* (1901, oil on canvas, 19x13 ins / 47x34 cm) EUR 650.

JAWLENSKY, Alexej Georgevich von, or Iavlenski or Yavlensky, A.G.
Russian, 19th - 20th century.
Born 13 or 26 March 1864, in Torzhok, or in Tver according to some sources; died 15 March 1941, in Wiesbaden.
Active in Germany from 1921.
Painter. Figures, landscapes, still-lifes.
Groups: Der Blaue Reiter, Die Blauen Vier.
The son of an aristocratic landowner, Jawlensky entered military school in Moscow in 1877. His first contact with painting was in 1880 at the time of the Universal Exhibition in Moscow. From that time he began to visit the Tretiakov Gallery every Sunday and to make sketches. In 1884, he was appointed an officer of the Imperial Guard in Moscow and also began to discover French art in the home of the Botkin family. He obtained a transfer to St Petersburg in 1889 so that he could attend classes at the academy of fine art there, studying particularly with Repin who introduced him into artistic circles. In 1891 he met Marianne von Werefkin. Unsatisfied with the teaching that he was receiving, he resigned from the army and left for Munich in 1896 where he was joined by Marianne von Werefkin and her lady companion. They enrolled in the private academy set up by Anton Azbé, and were joined there by Kandinsky the following year. In 1902 Jawlensky decided to work on his own. He exhibited for the first time at the Berlin Secession in 1902 and, according to some accounts, at the Munich Secession of 1903 and at the Berlin Secession in 1905. In 1903 he visited

Paris with Marianne von Werefkin, meeting Kubin there and also visiting Normandy. It was in 1904 that he first saw a painting by Gauguin. In 1905 he returned to Paris on the occasion of the exhibition of Russian artists organised by Serge Diaghilev as part of the Salon d'Automne. From Paris, he extended his travels to Pont-Aven in Brittany and to Provence where he was particularly affected by the brilliant colours and a decisive meeting with Matisse. On his return home he passed through Geneva where he visited Hodler. The following year he returned again to Paris for the Gauguin retrospective at the Salon d'Automne. The same year, Diaghilev organised a solo exhibition of his work in St Petersburg. In 1907 he again visited Paris, this time for the Cézanne retrospective at the Salon d'Automne. He spent the summers of 1907, 1908 and 1909 in Murnau in the Bavarian alps with Marianne von Werefkin, Kandinsky and Gabriele Münter. In 1908 he bought Van Gogh's painting *House of Père Pilon*. In 1909, with Kandinsky, Kubin, Gabriele Münter and others, he was involved in setting up the NKVM (New Association of Munich Artists) and the organisation of the group's first exhibition at the Thannhauser Gallery. This was followed by a second exhibition in 1910 which included some French artists. In 1910 he met Franz Marc and exhibited at the Sonderbund. In 1911, he spent the summer at Prerow on the Baltic and went again to Paris where he met Matisse and Van Dongen. In 1911, the NKVM split, mainly because of Kandinsky's adoption of Abstraction. Jawlensky remained a member, but left the association in 1912. Kandinsky's departure had been followed by the defection of the Burlyuk brothers, Campendonk, August Macke, Franz Marc and Gabriele Münter who left to set up - with a number of other artists - the Blaue Reiter group. Jawlensky refused the invitation of the new group to take part in their first exhibition in December 1911 but, with Marianne von Werefkin, Klee and Nolde, joined them in 1912. In 1913, when the Blaue Reiter held its last exhibition as a group, Jawlensky took part in the *Futurist and Expressionist Exhibition* in Budapest and in the first Deutscher Herbstsalon (German Autumn Salon) at the Sturm Gallery in Berlin. In 1914, he spent the spring in Bordighera and visited Russia. Expelled from Germany in August 1914, he spent the period of World War I in Switzerland in St-Prex near Zurich and in Ascona. Travelling exhibitions of his paintings was mounted in a series of German towns in 1920 and 1923 and in 1921, the year when Jawlensky's relationship with Marianne von Werefkin ended. He settled in Wiesbaden. In 1924, with Kandinsky, Klee and Feininger, he founded a new group, Die blauen Vier (The Blue Four). They exhibited in Dresden, Wiesbaden and in the USA until 1934. In 1927, Jawlensky began to experience the first signs of a deforming, ultimately paralysing, arthritis that gradually and cruelly took over his life, making painting and his material situation became ever more difficult. Eventually, like Renoir, he had to have his paintbrushes tied to his hands. In 1929 he was invited to teach at the Bauhaus, but the proposal was not followed up. When the Nazis took over Germany in 1933, Jawlensky's work, along with the rest of contemporary avant-garde art, was condemned as ' *entartete Kunst* ' (degenerate art) and he was banned from exhibiting it. In 1935 he joined Klee in Bern. In 1937, 72 of Jawlensky's paintings were removed from German museums, some being exhibited in the exhibition *Entartete Kunst* (*Degenerate Art*) held first in Munich and then in other German towns. By 1938 he was totally paralysed and had to abandon painting all together and died in 1941. After World War II Jawlensky's work did not at first receive the attention it deserved, mainly because it was somewhat overshadowed by the rediscovery of the great abstract painters Kandinsky, Klee and Mondrian. He was, however, eventually rediscovered; scholars see him as something of a special case, closer to the Die Brücke group although he never took part in that group's exhibitions than to the Blaue Reiter group with whom he associated and exhibited.

In the early years of his career, when he studied with Anton Azbé in Munich, Jawlensky's work was still influenced by Impressionism. However, when he came into contact with the art of Western Europe and, particularly, that of Van Gogh and Cézanne, his own style began to establish itself, becoming simplified and more expressive. In 1907, when he met Jan Verkade and Sérusier, the influence of Symbolism and of Gauguin replaced that of Cézanne. After his encounter with Matisse, his paintings of 1905 to 1910, characterised by the use of areas of pure colour, show the influence of the French Fauves. In 1911 he painted landscapes of the North Sea. Until 1913 his work - landscapes, still-lifes and figures - continued to show the influence of both the Fauves and most of the German Expressionists of his time. A personal element in his work, however, is derived from Russian folk icons where simplified forms, often outlined with a heavy black or blue line, are flatly painted in bright colours. His daring juxtapositions of colours have been described as 'barbaric'. While most of the members of the Blaue Reiter group were seeking a new kind of innocence in their work - looking at folk art, Gothic art and the painting of children and naive artists - Jawlensky was more interested in investigating the relationships between colours and music. He was, in fact, a talented musician, composing fugues for the organ. During the period he spent in Murnau with Marianne von Werefkin, Kandinsky and Kandinsky's companion and fellow-artist Gabriele Münter and then again during World War I, Jawlensky came under the influence of Cubism. His bright colours became more muted, his reds, blues and greens now balanced by darker tones, and the construction of the works more geometrical. At the time he wrote: 'I had understood that I needed to paint not what I saw but only what I felt living within me in my soul'. In 1914, he began to paint works in series, the first of which was *Variations on a Landscape near St-Prex*. He also began, in 1913, a series of faces in close-up. These oval, mainly female, faces with elongated necks and noses and huge eyes are simplified in a typically Cubist manner but may refer also to the faces of Byzantine art. The paintings of faces from the period 1918-1921 take this simplification to its furthest extreme and express a deep sense of mysticism. They are all constructed in the same way: two lines, horizontal or curved, for the eyes, a long vertical line for the nose, a horizontal or a curved line, or the two together, for the mouth, an oval for the chin. It is only the colour that distinguishes these works from one another. Their titles are evocative: *Mystic Heads* (1917), *Visions of the Saviour* (1919) and then *Abstract Heads*. Jawlensky's apparent indifference to the graphic structure of these stereotyped faces is indicative of what was, throughout his career, most important for him: the expressive force of colour. These unidentified faces, which he described as 'songs without words', could have led to pure Abstraction. The series *Abstract Heads*, which he continued to produce until 1933, preserve nothing more of a face than the oval form, the line of the nose and the curve of the lower lip, while all the other elements in the paintings belong to a style close to Neo-Constructivism. The austerity of his simplified, iconic faces became yet more marked after Jawlensky settled in Wiesbaden in 1921. Thereafter they varied on only minute details. He gave up painting landscapes at this period. The mystical character of his works also became more pronounced, his series of *Meditations* (1934-1937) suggest versions of the *Ecce Homo*, with images clearly intended to suggest Christ, full of sorrow and resignation, painted in warm, deep colours. From 1934, the style of these *Meditations* becomes freer and less geometric, perhaps as a result of the ever-increasing difficulty he found in the physical activity of painting. The faces are more expressive and seem to echo the deeply-felt belief underlying all Jawlensky's work after 1920: 'A work of art is God made visible and art is our longing for Him'.

Jawlensky's work has often featured in thematic collective exhibitions including: *Die Blaue Vier: Feininger, Jawlensky, Kandinsky, Klee in der Neuen Welt* (*The Blue Four: Feininger, Jawlensky, Kandinsky and Klee in the New World*), Kunstmuseum, Bern (1991); *Jawlensky - Werefkin*, Musée-Galerie de la Seita, Paris (1999); *Der Sturm* (*The Storm*), Städtische Galerie Haus Coburg, Delmenhorst (2000); *Jawlensky en Suisse 1914-1921* (*Jawlensky in Switzerland 1914-1921*), Fondation de l'Hermitage, Lausanne (2001); *Under the Spell of the Modern: Picasso, Chagall, Jawlensky*, BA-CA Kunstforum, Vienna (2003).

Retrospective exhibitions include: Kunsthalle, Bern (1957); Musée des Beaux-Arts, Lyons (1970); Lehnbachhaus, Munich (1983); Musée Rath, Geneva Palazzo Reale, Milan (1995); *Alexej von Jawlensky, Reisen, Freunde, Wandlungen* (*Alexej von Jawlensky, Travels, Friends and Walks*), Museum am Hostwall, Dortmund (1998).

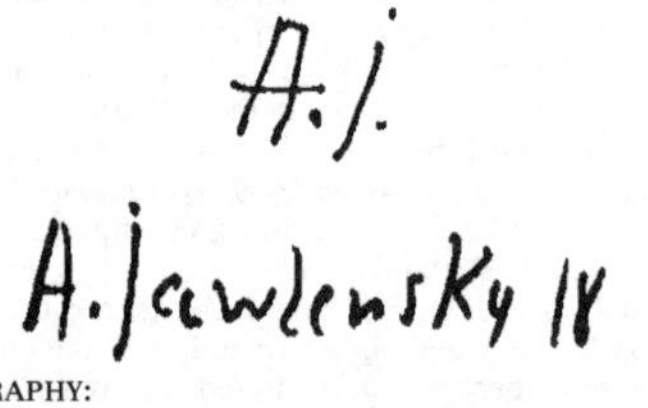

BIBLIOGRAPHY:

Grohmann, Will, '*Alexej von Jawlensky*' in *Cahiers d'Art*, periodical, Paris, 1943. Weiler, Clemens, *Alexej von Jawlensky*, DuMont Schauberg, Cologne, 1959. Weiler, Ch., *Alexej von Jawlensky, Der Maler und Mensch*, Limes Verlag, Cologne, 1959. Read, Herbert, *Histoire de la peinture moderne*, Somogy, Paris, 1960. Fricker, Jacques, et al., *Alexej Jawlensky*, exhibition catalogue, Musée des Beaux-Arts, Lyons, 1970. Weiler, Clemens, *Alexej von Jawlensky. Köpfe, Gesichte, Meditationen*, H. Peters, Hanau, 1970. *Alexej Jawlensky*, exhibition catalogue, Städtische Gal. im Lenbachhaus, Munich, 1983. Rosenbach, Detlev, *Alexej von Jawlensky. Leben und druckgraphisches Werk*, Rosenbach, Hanover, 1985. *Alexej Jawlensky*, exhibition catalogue, Locarno, 1989. Jawlensky, Maria/Pieroni-Jawlensky, Lucia/Jawlensky, Angelica, '*Alexej von Jawlensky, Catalogue Raisonné of the Oil Paintings*' in vol. 1 1890-1914, Sotheby's Publications, London, 1991. Jawlensky, Maria, et al., '*Alexej von Jawlensky, Catalogue Raisonné of the Oil Paintings*' in vol. 2 1914-1933, Sotheby's Publications, London, 1992. Jawlensky, Maria, et al., '*Alexej von Jawlensky, Catalogue Raisonné of the Oil Paintings*' in vol. 3 1934-1937, Sotheby's Publications, London, 1993. Endicott Barnett, Vivian/Helfenstein, Josef, *The Blue Four: Feininger, Jawlensky, Kandinsky, and Klee in the New World*, Yale University Press, London, 1998. Belgin, Tayfun, *Alexej von Jawlensky: eine Künstlerbiographie*, Umschau/Braus, Heidelberg, 1998. Goldberg, Itzhak, *Jawlenski ou le visage promis*, L'Harmattan, Paris, 2000. *Jawlensky en Suisse 1914-1921*, exhibition catalogue, Fondation de l'Hermitage, Lausanne, 2001. *Im Bann der Moderne: Picasso/Chagall/Jawlensly*, group exhibition catalogue, BA-CA Kunstforum, Vienna, 2003.

MUSEUMS AND GALLERIES:

BASEL (Kunsthalle): *Harsh Winter* (1916); *Senecio* (1922) - BIELEFELD: *Russia* (1911) - COLOGNE (Wallraf-Richartz Mus.): *Vase and Jug* (1909); *Red Lips*; *Variation* - DORTMUND: *Solitude* (1912) - DÜREN (Leopold-Hoesch Mus.): *Girl with a Red Veil* (c. 1913) - DÜSSELDORF (Kunstmus.) - ELBERFELD (Kaiser Friedrich Mus.): *Bunch of Flowers* - ESSEN (Folkwang Mus.): *Peonies*; *Mediterranean near Marseilles* (1907) - LYONS (MBA): *Medusa* (1923) - MÖNCHENGLADBACH (Mus. Abteiberg): *Woman with a Blue Hat* (1912-1913) - MUNICH (Städtische Gal. im Lenbachhaus) - MÜNSTER (Westfälisches Landesmus.): *Head of a Woman* (1910) - NEW YORK (MoMA): *With Open Eyes* (1923) - PARIS (MNAM-CCI) - ROTTERDAM (Mus. Boijmans Van Beuningen): *Study of a Partially-Clothed woman* (1913) - SAN DIEGO (MA): *Red Blossom* (1910, oil/panel); *Large Variation, Autumn* (1915, oil on canvas/panel); *Abstract Head, Inner Vision* (1923, oil/panel); *Meditation* (February 1935, oil/paper/panel); *Large Still-life, Roses II* (1937, oil/paper/panel) - STUTTGART (Kunstkabinett): *Head of a Saint* (1919) - STUTTGART (Staatsgal.): *White Feather* (1909) - THE HAGUE (Gemeentemus.): *Murnau Landscape* (1910); *Head of a Woman* (1911) - WIESBADEN (Wiesbaden Mus.): *Lady with a Fan* (1909); *Nikita* (1910); *Woman with a Fringe* (1913); *Large Meditation (St John the Baptist)* (1936); *Meditation (Winter's Night when the Wolves are Howling)* (1936, 27 paintings in total) - WUPPERTAL (Von der Heydt Mus.): *Girl with Peonies* (1909).

AUCTION RECORDS:

STUTTGART, 26 Nov 1957, *Winter Fairy Stories* (oil on remounted paper) DEM 4,200. NEW YORK, 15 Jan 1958, *Green Trees* (oil on card) USD 3,000. COLOGNE, 28 Oct 1958, *Vase of Red Flowers*, DEM 7,500. NEW YORK, 27 April 1960, *Japanese Flowers* (oil on card) USD 7,500. STUTTGART, 20 May 1960, *Garden in Carento*, DEM 41,500; *Variation* (oil on card) DEM 12,000. STUTTGART, 3 May 1961, *Saracen Woman* (oil on card) DEM 34,500. COLOGNE, 20 May 1965, *Girl with a Black Fan*, DEM 74,750. GENEVA, 17 June 1966, *Woman with Plaits*, CHF 49,000. LONDON, 26 April 1967, *Pensive Woman*, GBP 8,000. HAMBURG, 4 June 1971, *Head of a Woman*, DEM 78,000. LONDON, 4 July 1973, *Murnau Landscape*, GBP 30,000. LONDON, 3 April 1974, *Head of a Woman* (1912) GBP 22,000. NEW YORK, 26 May 1976, *Green Trees* (1906, oil on card, $20\frac{3}{4}$ x 19 ins / 53 x 48.2 cm) USD 15,000. HAMBURG, 3 June 1976, *Vase of Flowers* (watercolour and pencil, $6\frac{1}{2}$ x 4 ins / 16.4 x 10.4 cm) DEM 8,400. MUNICH, 29 Nov 1976, *Head* (1922, lithograph, $6\frac{3}{4}$ x $4\frac{3}{4}$ ins / 17.2 x 12.3 cm) DEM 1,850. HAMBURG, 3 June 1977, *Tragic Mask* (1932, oil on card, 14 x $9\frac{3}{4}$ ins / 35.5 x 25 cm) DEM 47,000. COLOGNE, 19 May 1979, *Head of a Girl* (c. 1922, lithograph, $17\frac{3}{4}$ x $15\frac{1}{4}$ ins / 45 x 39 cm; 21 x $16\frac{1}{2}$ ins/53.5 x 42 cm) DEM 4,200. MUNICH, 28 May 1979, *Seated Nude* (c. 1912, pencil, $11\frac{1}{2}$ x 9 ins / 29 x 22 cm) DEM 8,200. HAMBURG, 8 June 1979, *Head* (c. 1920, watercolour, $8\frac{3}{4}$ x $6\frac{1}{2}$ ins / 22.2 x 16.5 cm) DEM 24,000. HAMBURG, 8 June 1979, *Greek* (1931, oil on card, $16\frac{3}{4}$ x 13 ins / 42.5 x 33 cm) DEM 65,000. MUNICH, 1 June 1981, *View from the Hotel Window* (1933, watercolour, 6 x $3\frac{3}{4}$ ins / 15 x 9.5 cm) DEM 8,000. BERN, 26 June 1981, *Morning* (oil on canvas remounted on board, 14 x $10\frac{3}{4}$ ins / 35.5 x 27.2 cm) CHF 90,000. NEW YORK, 20 May 1982, *Nudes* (1912, black chalk/paper, two drawings. NEW YORK, 3 Nov 1982, *Girl in a Turban* (1910, oil on card, 27 x $19\frac{1}{2}$ ins / 68.5 x 49.5 cm) USD 200,000. NEW YORK, 17 May 1983, *Head (portrait of Klamm)* (1913, oil on card, 21 x $19\frac{1}{2}$ ins / 53.3 x 49.5 cm) USD 270,000. MUNICH, 25 Nov 1983, *Bunch of Flowers in a Violet Vase* (c. 1925-1930, watercolour and pencil, $6\frac{1}{2}$ x $4\frac{1}{4}$ ins / 16.5 x 10.5 cm) DEM 20,000. MUNICH, 26 Nov 1984, *Head of a Woman* (1919, lithograph, $11\frac{1}{2}$ x 9 ins / 29 x 23 cm) DEM 8,000. BERN, 18 June 1986, *Recumbent Nude* (1912, brush and Indian ink, $9\frac{3}{4}$ x $12\frac{3}{4}$ ins / 24.8 x 32.5 cm) CHF 17,000. PARIS, 27 June 1986, *Enthusiast in the Sunlight* (1922, oil on canvas, $14\frac{1}{4}$ x 11 ins / 36 x 28 cm) FRF 700,000. VIENNA, 9 Sept 1986, *Two Brushes in a Glass* (watercolour and pen, $5\frac{1}{2}$ x $4\frac{1}{2}$ ins / 14.2 x 11.5 cm) ATS 140,000. NEW YORK, 19 Nov 1986, *October* (1928, oil on card, $17\frac{1}{4}$ x $12\frac{3}{4}$ ins / 43.8 x 32.5 cm) USD 165,000. LONDON, 31 March 1987, *Nude on a Couch* (1910, soft chalk, $11\frac{3}{4}$ x $9\frac{3}{4}$ ins / 30 x 24.7 cm) GBP 3,000. LONDON, 30 March 1988, *Flowers in a Blue Vase and Apples in a Blue Bowl* (oil on card, $19\frac{1}{2}$ x $15\frac{1}{2}$ ins / 49.5 x 39.2 cm) GBP 79,200. NEW YORK, 12 May 1988, *Fe-*

male Nude (pencil and watercolour/paper, 11 1/2 x 7 1/2 ins / 29.2 x 19.3 cm) USD 9,350. MUNICH, 8 June 1988, *Variation No. 39* (1917, oil on card, 14 x 11 ins / 35.5 x 27 cm) DEM 165,000; *Abstract Head* (1925, oil on card, 16 3/4 x 12 3/4 ins / 42.5 x 32.5 cm) DEM 451,000; *Meditation* (oil on canvas, 9 3/4 x 6 1/4 ins / 25 x 16 cm) DEM 90,200. LONDON, 28 June 1988, *Red Feather* (1912, oil on card, 21 x 19 1/4 ins / 53.5 x 49 cm) GBP 539,000. MUNICH, 26 Oct 1988, *Mountain* (1912, oil on card, 12 1/2 x 17 1/4 ins / 32 x 44 cm) DEM 550,000; *White Office* (1918, oil on canvas, 14 1/4 x 11 ins / 36.2 x 27 cm) DEM 187,000. PARIS, 21 Nov 1988, *Meditation* (c. 1936, oil on canvas, 10 x 7 ins / 25.1 x 17.8 cm) FRF 220,000. LONDON, 3 April 1989, *Dark Blue Head* (1913, oil on card, 19 3/4 x 14 ins / 50.2 x 35.6 cm) GBP 352,000. NEW YORK, 11 May 1989, *Large Variation: the Red Path* (1916, oil on canvas/card, 21 1/2 x 14 1/4 ins / 54.6 x 36.2 cm) USD 187,000. MUNICH, 7 June 1989, *Meditation* (1935, oil on paper/card, 7 1/2 x 5 1/4 ins / 18.9 x 13.6 cm) DEM 88,000. LONDON, 27 June 1989, *Mantilla (Green and Wine-Coloured Head)* (1913, oil on card, 26 3/4 x 19 1/2 ins / 68 x 49.3 cm) GBP 550,000. NEW YORK, 13 Nov 1989, *Girl with Blue Eyes* (1912, oil on card, 20 3/4 x 19 1/4 ins / 53 x 49 cm) USD 748,000. LONDON, 28 Nov 1989, *Still-life with Utensils, Fruit and a Statuette* (oil on card, 21 3/4 x 22 3/4 ins / 55.4 x 57.7 cm) GBP 121,000. MUNICH, 13 Dec 1989, *Abstract Head* (oil on thick paper/card, 14 1/4 x 11 ins / 36 x 27 cm) DEM 418,000. LONDON, 3 April 1990, *Abstract Head* (1929, oil on card, 16 3/4 x 12 3/4 ins / 42.5 x 32.5 cm) GBP 154,000. NEW YORK, 16 May 1990, *Head* (oil on card, 13 3/4 x 9 3/4 ins / 35 x 24.8 cm) USD 286,000; *Sleep* (1912, oil on card, 19 1/2 x 21 ins / 49.4 x 53.6 cm) USD 286,000. MUNICH, 31 May 1990, *Red Roofs* (1907, oil on card, 15 x 21 1/4 ins / 38 x 54 cm) DEM 550,000. LONDON, 26 June 1990, *Meditation* (1934, oil on woven paper/card, 7 x 4 3/4 ins / 17.7 x 12.3 cm) GBP 41,800. NEW YORK, 2 Oct 1990, *Meditation* (1935, oil on canvas/card, 8 x 6 1/4 ins / 20.3 x 15.9 cm) USD 35,200. LONDON, 17 Oct 1990, *Meditation* (1935, oil on paper/card, 6 x 4 3/4 ins / 15.3 x 12 cm) GBP 44,000. NEW YORK, 14 Nov 1990, *Earth* (1918, oil on card, 21 x 19 1/4 ins / 53.3 x 49 cm) USD 440,000. LONDON, 5 Dec 1990, *Head* (1928, oil on card, 11 1/2 x 8 ins / 29 x 20.5 cm) GBP 79,200. NEW YORK, 14 Feb 1991, *Still-life with Apples* (oil on card, 18 3/4 x 21 ins / 47.6 x 53.3 cm) USD 187,000. NEW YORK, 15 Feb 1991, *Meditation* (1936, oil on tissue paper/card, 7 x 4 3/4 ins / 17.5 x 12 cm) USD 44,000. PARIS, 9 March 1991, *Sunday Morning Dreamer - Variation No. 122* (oil on paper/card, 15 3/4 x 11 1/4 ins / 40 x 28.5 cm) FRF 410,000. AMSTERDAM, 22 May 1991, *Face* (1929, oil on card, 9 1/4 x 6 3/4 ins / 23.5 x 17 cm) NLG 345,000. BERLIN, 30 May 1991, *Wooded Landscape near Wasserburg* (1907, oil on card, 21 x 18 1/2 ins / 53.5 x 46.8 cm) DEM 577,200. LONDON, 24 June 1991, *View of the Baltic* (1911, oil on card, 24 x 24 ins / 61 x 61 cm) GBP 231,000. NEW YORK, 7 Nov 1991, *Head* (oil on card, 12 x 15 3/4 ins / 30.4 x 40 cm) USD 297,000. NEW YORK, 12 May 1992, *Summer Evening* (1916, oil/paper fabric/card, 14 x 10 3/4 ins / 35.5 x 27.3 cm) USD 154,000. BERLIN, 29 May 1992, *Head of the Saviour* (oil on card, 14 1/4 x 11 ins / 36 x 27 cm) DEM 372,900. PARIS, 24 Nov 1992, *Face* (1917, oil on card on canvas, 15 1/4 x 11 ins / 39 x 28 cm) FRF 880,000. LONDON, 30 Nov 1992, *Still-life with Jug* (oil on card/panel, 26 1/2 x 19 1/4 ins / 67.4 x 48.6 cm) GBP 286,000. NEW YORK, 3 Nov 1993, *Mosaic* (1913, oil on card/synthetic resin, 21 1/4 x 19 3/4 ins / 53.7 x 50.2 cm) USD 310,500. NEW YORK, 12 May 1994, *Mountainous Landscape with Houses* (1912, oil on canvas, 18 x 21 3/4 ins / 46 x 55.2 cm) USD 123,500. LONDON, 13 Oct 1994, *Spanish Woman in a Red Shawl* (oil on card, 25 1/4 x 18 1/4 ins / 64.4 x 46.3 cm) GBP 595,500. NEW YORK, 10 Nov 1994, *Woman in a Yellow Armchair* (1907, oil on card/canvas, 25 x 20 ins / 63.6 x 50.8 cm) USD 200,500. LONDON, 27 June 1995, *Princess with a White Flower* (1913, oil on card, 26 3/4 x 19 1/4 ins / 68 x 49 cm) GBP 606,500. NEW YORK, 8 Nov 1995, *Looking Inwards* (1928, oil on card, 16 1/2 x 12 1/4 ins / 42 x 31 cm) USD 310,500. NEW YORK, 14 Nov 1996, *Abstract Head, The Cup Passed before Me* (1929, oil on linen paper/panel, 13 3/4 x 9 3/4 ins / 35 x 25 cm) USD 288,500. LONDON, 2 Dec 1996, *Envious Face* (1923, oil on card, 13 3/4 x 9 3/4 ins / 35 x 25 cm) GBP 199,500. LONDON, 4 Dec 1996, *Variation* (1915, oil on lined paper/card, 17 1/4 x 13 1/2 ins / 43.5 x 34 cm) GBP 51,000; *Goddess Dusy* (1924, watercolour and pencil/paper, 6 x 5 1/4 ins / 15.5 x 13.5 cm) GBP 16,100. LONDON, 24 June 1997, *Still-life with Cake* (1905, oil on panel, 30 x 28 ins / 76 x 71 cm) GBP 1,211,500; *Farmer* (c. 1912, oil on panel, 20 3/4 x 19 1/4 ins / 53 x 49 cm) GBP 573,500. LONDON, 25 June 1997, *Abstract Head: wintery, red and orange* (1932, oil on paper/panel, 16 1/4 x 13 1/2 ins / 41.5 x 34.5 cm) GBP 128,000. LONDON, 9 Dec 1997, *Abstract Head: Composition No. 2 Winter* (c. 1924, oil on paper remounted/canvas, 16 3/4 x 12 3/4 ins / 42.5 x 32.3 cm) GBP 161,000. LONDON, 7 Oct 1999, *Girl Wearing Purple Blouse* (c. 1912, oil on thin card laid on canvas, 21 x 19 ins / 53 x 48 cm) GBP 550,000. LONDON, 7 Dec 1999, *Berggipfel (Mountain Peak)* (1912, oil on card, 13 x 17 ins / 32 x 44 cm) GBP 320,000. HAMBURG, 9 June 2000, *Head Blue-Brown* (c. 1913, oil on card, 20 x 14 ins / 50 x 35 cm) DEM 1,100,000. LONDON, 17 Oct 2000, *Face of the Saviour, Distance - Buddha II* (c. 1921, oil and pencil on paper laid on board, 14 x 11 ins / 36 x 27 cm) GBP 455,000. LONDON, 25 June 2001, *Lowered Head* (1909, oil on board, 26 x 20 ins / 65 x 51 cm) GBP 1,300,000. LONDON, 11 Oct 2001, *Dark Eyes* (1912, oil on board, 27 x 20 ins / 68 x 50 cm) GBP 700,000. LONDON, 8 Oct 2002, *Nude Half Figure* (c. 1912, oil on board, 29 x 20 ins / 73 x 52 cm) EUR 2,200,000. NEW YORK, 6 Nov 2002, *Young Girl with Green Eyes* (c. 1910, oil on board, 21 x 19 ins / 53 x 49 cm) USD 3,000,000. LONDON, 3 Feb 2003, *Blue Vase with Oranges* (c. 1907, oil on canvas, 18 x 22 ins / 45 x 56 cm) GBP 400,000. NEW YORK, 5 Nov 2003, *Schokko - Schokko mit Tellerhut* (1910, oil on card laid on canvas, 30 x 26 ins / 76 x 65 cm) USD 7,400,000. LONDON, 3 Feb 2004, *Mystical Head of a Girl* (c. 1918, oil on board, 11 x 9 ins / 27 x 24 cm) GBP 170,000.

JAY, Cecil, married name: Hitchcock
American, 20th century.
Born 1884, in London; died 1930.
Also active in France.
Painter, miniaturist.

Cecil Jay studied at the South Kensington School of Art under Sir Hubert von Herkomer and George Hitchcock, whom she married. She was a member of the Royal Miniature Society, London and the New York Watercolor Club. She painted portraits, but is best known for her miniatures, and won the silver medal for miniatures at the *Panama Pacific International Exposition*, San Francisco, in 1915.

AUCTION RECORDS:
LONDON, 4 Oct 1989, *Letter* (oil on canvas, 26 x 17 ins / 66 x 43 cm) GBP 8,800. NEW YORK, 21 Sept 1994, *Miniature* (oil on canvas, 24 x 17 3/4 ins / 61 x 45.1 cm) USD 36,800.

JAY, Hamilton
British, 19th century.
Active in London.
Painter. Genre scenes.

Jay Hamilton exhibited in London starting in 1875, regularly at Suffolk Street and more rarely at the Royal Academy.

JAY, Isabella Lee
British, 19th century.
Active in London.
Painter, watercolourist.

Isabella Lee Jay, under the direction of John Ruskin, dedicated herself to making copies of Turner's works. A certain number of these were exhibited at the Sussex Galleries, the Fine Arts Society and the Society of British Artists. In 1896, she showed some compositions including *St David's Cathedral* and *South Wales* at the Royal Academy.

JAY, Louis-Joseph
French, 18th - 19th century.
Born 8 March 1755, in St-Hilaire-de-la-Côte (Isère); died 7 July 1836, in Vienne (Isère).
Painter. Historical subjects, portraits.

Jay started working in Montpellier, but rapidly returned to his native area and set up in Grenoble. He opened a public studio and, after some years of private teaching, was appointed lecturer in drawing at the École Centrale de l'Isère. As François Devosge had done for Dijon following the Revolution, Jay conceived the idea of creating a museum at Grenoble. He spent several years achieving his ends, and was then appointed curator of the new museum, inaugurated in 1800. The imperial government gave him an artistic mission in Italy, so it is reasonable to suspect that this was not unconnected with the numerous levies made under the title of conqueror on the Italian artistic heritage. Perhaps his official role was the reason that in 1815 he was stripped of his functions, after which he retired to Vienna.

MUSEUMS AND GALLERIES:
GRENOBLE (Mus. de Grenoble): *Portrait of Abbot Gattel.*

AUCTION RECORDS:
PARIS, 31 March 1943, *Portrait of a Man* (1783, drawing) FRF 260.

JAY, William Samuel
British, 19th century.
Born 1843; died 1933.
Active in London.
Painter. Landscapes.

William Samuel Jay was a member of the Society of British Artists. He exhibited regularly at the Royal Academy and Suffolk Street, beginning in 1868. He combined his deep feelings with a scientific understanding of nature to produce landscapes of a wide variety.

MUSEUMS AND GALLERIES:
NOTTINGHAM (Castle Mus. & AG): *Falling of the Leaves* (1883).

JAYAT, Sandra
French, 20th century.
Born 13 May 1939, in Moulins (Allier).
Painter, watercolourist, writer, poet.

Sandra Jayat, a gypsy by birth, is a self-taught painter, given help and encouragement by Jean Cocteau. She has published collections of poetry, including *Herbes manouches* (*Manou Plants*), La Colombe, 1961; *Lunes Nomades* (*Nomadic Moons*), Seghers, 1963; and *Moudravi où va l'amitié?* (*Moudravi, Where Does Friendship Go?*) in 1966. She has produced discs of verse and stories for children set to her own music (Django Reinhardt, Manistas de Plata and others). In 1978, she published *La Longue route d'une Zingarina*, Éditions Bordas, Paris. She creates a picture by cutting into planes of gay, brilliant colours, producing part abstract, part figurative images connected with music, with travel and with the fortunes of her own Romany people. Over these she scatters a variety of signs and symbols. In 1992 she designed a postage stamp in honour of 'travelling people' which was issued by the French Post Office. She was awarded a silver medal by the City of Paris in 1984 and a silver-gilt medal in 1992.

Her work has been shown in collective exhibitions, including: 1983, and regularly after that, the Paris Biennale des Beaux-Arts; and in 1985, the Salon of Contemporary Art in Antwerp. Her solo exhibitions began in 1964 and among them were: 1971, 1972, 1973 and 1977 Galerie Ades, Paris; 1978 and 1980, Galerie Castiglione-Vendôme, Paris; 1982, Galerie Scribe, Paris; 1984, Galerie Jacqueline Lemaire, Paris; 1985, Galerie des Muses, Paris; 1988, Galerie Herouet, Paris; 1991, the museum in Trouville; 1991, museum of Sacred Art, Venice; 1992, Liehrmann Gallery in Liège; and 1992 the Bourdelle Museum in Paris.

BIBLIOGRAPHY:
Sandra Jayat, exhibition catalogue, Musée Bourdelle, Paris, 1992.

JAYET, Clément, called Clément
French, 18th century.
Born 27 February 1731, in Langres; died 1804, in Lyons.
Sculptor. Figures.

Jayet was a lecturer at the École des Beaux-Arts in Lyons in 1780.

MUSEUMS AND GALLERIES:
LYONS: *Bust of Antoine Berjon.*

AUCTION RECORDS:
LONDON, 29 April 1980, *Bust of an Aristocrat* (terracotta, h. 28in/71cm) GBP 2,800. PARIS, 18 March 1985, *Bust of a Man Wearing a Hat Decorated with Fur* (1773, lacquered terracotta, h. 31in/79cm) FRF 45,000.

JAYEZ, Léon
French, 20th century.
Born 1 May 1878, in Besançon.
Sculptor.

JAYNE, Charles
British, 19th century.
Active in London.
Painter. Landscapes.

Charles Jayne exhibited on different occasions from 1838 to 1879, at the Royal Academy, Suffolk Street and the British Institution.

JAYNE, Mary
British, 19th century.
Active in London.
Painter. Landscapes.

Mary Jayne was the wife of the painter Charles Jayne. Like him, she exhibited regularly from 1846 to 1878 at the Royal Academy, Suffolk Street and the British Institution.

JAZET, Alexandre Jean Louis, or Japhet
French, 19th century.
Born 10 May 1814, in Paris.
Engraver.

Alexandre Jazet was initially a pupil of his father, Jean Pierre Marie Jazet, before working with Léon Cogniet. He made his debut at the Paris Salon in 1839, and continued to feature there until 1864. His engravings were after H. Vernet, H Bellangé, Le Poitevin and Paul Delaroche but he most closely reproduced Faustin Besson.

JAZET, Eugène Pontus
French, 19th century.
Born 1 May 1815, in Paris; died 6 April 1856, in Paris.
Engraver.

Eugène Jazet studied under his father, Jean Pierre Marie Jazet and also Léon Cogniet. He began at Paris' College of Fine Arts on 2 April 1834, and featured at the Paris Salon from 1838 to 1845, winning a third class medal in 1842. He engraved after H Vernet, Gosse, Paul Delaroche, Biard, Steuben and above all Schopin.

JAZET, Jean Pierre Marie
French, 19th century.
Born 31 July 1788, in Paris; died 1871, in Yerres (Essonne), buried the 18 August in Paris.
Engraver (aquatint/mezzotint), engraver of reproductions.

Jean Pierre Marie Jazet lost his father at a very early age. in 1793, his father, a royal buildings inspector, was killed by an exploding cannon whilst serving in the National Guard. Jazet was taken in by his uncle on his mother's side, the engraver Debucourt, who passed on his trade to him. Initially,

Jazet copied the subjects which had built his uncle's reputation: morality scenes, hunting scenes and landscapes, before the latter became more or less exclusively Carle Vernet's engraver. Unlike Debucourt, who produced his own works, however, Jazet was happy to be a reproductive engraver.

He made his debut at the Paris Salon in 1817 and made his mark in 1819, notably exhibiting his *Full-length portrait of General Lasalle* after Grosa and *Colonel Loncey's Bivouac*, after H Vernet, which together earned him a second class medal. He was from then on, and for some time to come, considered to be one of France's best reproductive engravers. He was made a member of the Légion d'Honneur in 1846.

Jazet was an excellent engraver of Horace Vernet's works, just as his uncle Debucourt had been of Carle Vernet's. He popularised his paintings showing the splendour of the First Empire. He also reproduced paintings by David, Gué, Steuben, Bellangé, Gosse, Vigneron, Destouches, Briard, Brion, Faustin Besson, G Vibert and Rigo - a list demonstrating the mixed quality of his sources.

He exhibited for the last time at the 1865 Paris Salon. Jazet's body of work is considerable and executed mainly in aquatint. He developed this procedure to a remarkable degree of perfection, but the mediocrity of some of the works he reproduced, later aided by his two sons, Alexandre and Eugène, has somewhat compromised his reputation.

AUCTION RECORDS:
PARIS, 10 May 1995, *Walk in the Turkish Garden* (aquatint print in colour, 11 3/4 x 21 1/2 ins / 30 x 54.5 cm) FRF 5,000.

JAZET, Paul Léon Jean
French, 19th century.
Born 13 June 1848, in Paris.
Painter. Military subjects, genre scenes, portraits.

Paul Jazet studied under Barrias and made his debut at the Paris Salon in 1869, becoming a member of the society in 1886.

He is certainly the same P Jazet, who contributed 10 illustrations to an 1891 edition of Musset's *The Confession of a Child of the Century*

MUSEUMS AND GALLERIES:
MINNEAPOLIS (Walker Art Center): *Death of Nelson*.

AUCTION RECORDS:
LONDON, 12 March 1943, *French Outposts*, GBP 48. PARIS, 4 July 1947, *A Queen's Entourage*, FRF 30,000. NEW YORK, 4 June 1971, *Death of Lord Nelson*, USD 2,200. LOS ANGELES, 9 April 1973, *Return of the Sailor*, USD 1,100. AMSTERDAM, 27 April 1976, *Reception* (1878, oil on canvas, 21 1/4 x 28 3/4 ins / 54 x 73 cm) NLG 19,500. LONDON, 4 Nov 1977, *Charge of the Armoured Cavalry* (1881, oil on canvas, 29 x 21 1/2 ins / 73.7 x 54.6 cm) GBP 1,100. LONDON, 18 Jan 1980, *Charge of the Armoured Cavalry* (1881, oil on canvas, 29 x 21 1/2 ins / 73.7 x 54.6 cm) GBP 750. NEW YORK, 26 May 1993, *French Cavalry Bugle* (1879, oil on panel, 10 1/2 x 6 3/4 ins / 26.7 x 17.1 cm) USD 2,875. NEW YORK, 13 Oct 1993, *Death of Lord Nelson* (1882, oil on canvas, 42 x 61 1/2 ins / 106.7 x 156.2 cm) USD 48,875. NEW YORK, 19 Jan 1995, *Soldiers* (1878, oil on panel, a pair, 11 x 7 1/4 ins / 27 x 18.7 cm) USD 3,450. MELBOURNE, 27 April 1999, *Charge of the Curassiers* (1881, oil on canvas, 29 x 21 ins / 74 x 54 cm) AUD 10,000. SANDWICH, 14 July 1999, *Lady and Gentleman Having Tea* (oil on panel, 17 x 13 ins / 43 x 33 cm) USD 4,500. LONDON, 14 June 2000, *French Cavalry Trumpeteer* (1879, oil on panel, 9 x 6 ins / 23 x 16 cm) GBP 2,800. LONDON, 26 Sept 2001, *French Cavalry and Austrian Volunteers Skirmishing in Mexico. Mexican Prisoners* (1887, oil on canvas, a pair, 20 x 30 ins / 50 x 75 cm) GBP 11,500.

JAZINSKI, Félix Stanislas. See **JASINSKI**

JAZWINSKI, Joseph
Austrian, 19th century.
Born in Lemberg (now Lviv, Ukraine); died 1818 or 1819, in Lemberg.
Painter. History painting, portraits.

Joseph Jazwinski studied under Stroinski. He worked mainly for churches, but did produce some portraits: *Portrait of Kraniski* and *Portrait of King Jan III Sobieski*.

JDANOV, Andrei Ossipovich, or Idanov, Shdanov
Russian, 19th century.
Born 1775; died 2 or le 14 April 1811.
Painter. Portraits.

Jdanov studied at the fine art academy in St Petersburg.

MUSEUMS AND GALLERIES:
ST PETERSBURG (Gosudarstvennyj Russkij Muz.): *Portrait of a Woman*.

JEAKES, J.
British, 18th - 19th century.
Painter, engraver. Landscapes.

J. Jeakes worked in London where he exhibited eleven landscapes at the Royal Academy between 1796 and 1809.

JEAN, or Johannes
10th - 11th century.
Born between 960 and 970, in Italy or in Greece; died 1016, in Liège.
Painter, sculptor, architect. Religious subjects. Church decoration.

Jean was employed by the emperor Otto III in 980 and 1002. He was rewarded for work on the chapel of Charlemagne by the gift of a bishopric in Italy. He returned to Germany, then went to Liège where he became a friend of the bishop Baldéric II, who encouraged him to decorate the choir of St James' Abbey. He built the church of St Andrew in Liège. This may be the same man as the painter Johannes who was working at this period at Nepi.

JEAN
12th century.
Miniaturist.

Jean was active in 1146. He illustrated *Gospels* in Liessies Abbey (Metz, Salis Collection).

JEAN
12th century.
Miniaturist, monk. Religious subjects.

Jean, active before 1165, was a Benedictine monk of St Sauveur d'Anchin, who worked on St Augustine's book on the *Trinity*, now in the library at Douai.

MUSEUMS AND GALLERIES:
DOUAI (Library): miniatures for The Trinity of St Augustine.

JEAN, or Jehan d'Orléans
French, 14th century.
Died after 1408.
Painter.

Jean was a painter to King Charles V and a valet to Charles VI, and worked at the Château de St-Germain and painted an *Annunciation* for the Dauphin in 1392. His name appears in the royal accounts in 1408. In 1292, another artist of the name of Jehan d'Orléans was quoted in the tallage of Paris. An altar facing and a *Entombment*, attributed to a Jean of Orléans and dated 1374, featured in an exhibition of primitive artists.

JEAN, called Jehan d'Avesnes
French, 15th century.
Painter.

Jehan d'Avesnes worked in Gray, and in 1432 and 1433, for the Duke of Burgundy in Dole.

JEAN, called Le Maçon
French, 15th century.
Sculptor, architect.
Jean Le Maçon was master of works at the Château de Josselin in Brittany, and is believed to have produced the tomb of Olivier de Clisson, who died in 1406, as well as that of his wife, Marguerite de Rohan. The tomb itself was destroyed; the current tomb is a restoration.

JEAN, also known as Master Jean
French, 15th century.
Sculptor.
Master Jean was probably the sculptor who was recorded as living in Rome in the 16th century, working at the Vatican in 1462 and 1463, and at the French church of S Luigi dei Francesi. He may also be the master named Jean who was invited to work in Rome in 1575 by the Duke of Ribera, Viceroy of Naples.

JEAN
French, 15th - 16th century.
Painters.
There were several painters named Jean working in Lyons from the 14th to the 16th centuries. One of them is mentioned in records in 1471, and again in 1494, when he took part in preparations for the official visit of Charles VIII and Anne of Brittany. Another artist named Jean is recorded in 1499 and 1500 as having worked on preparations for the visit of Louis XII and Anne of Brittany.

JEAN
French, 15th - 16th century.
Painter (glass).
Jean was a curate who worked in Mont, near Lunéville. He worked for various churches, particularly the church of Cordeliers in Nancy.

JEAN, also known as Maistre Jean
French, 16th century.
Died 1540.
Painter, miniaturist. History painting.
Maistre Jean was a miniaturist in Avignon. He visited Italy and painted a *Christ* in Arezzo.

JEAN (Maître)
French, 16th century.
Sculptor.
The journal of Albert Dürer contains a reference to this artist in Metz.

JEAN, pseudonym of Jean Dandleuf
French, 19th century.
Born 29 March 1840, in Segré (Maine-et-Loire); died 19 April 1878, in Vic-sur-Aisne, drowned.
Painter, decorative designer. Still-lifes.
Jean was a decorative artist in Soissons. Following a sudden disappearance, he was found dead in the river of Vic-sur-Aisne, on 19 April 1878. In 1877, Soissons museum had bought a small panel from him entitled: *Dead Birds*.
Museums and Galleries:
Soissons: *Dead Birds*.

JEAN
French, 19th century.
Born 19th century, in Paris.
Painter, watercolourist, miniaturist, potter. Portraits, still-lifes.
Jean studied under Braquemond, Quost, Belloc and Chaplin. He exhibited miniature portraits at the Paris Salon in 1868, 1869 and 1870. Later, he devoted himself to watercolours and ceramics.
Museums and Galleries:
Limoges: *Peaches and Grapes* (watercolour).

JEAN. See also **GIOVANNI, JAN, JEHAN, JOAN, JOHANN, JOHANNES, JOHN, JUAN**

JEAN, Amand Edmond. See **AMAN-JEAN Edmond**

JEAN, André
French, 20th century.
Born 7 March 1913, in Le Havre; died 5 October 1998.
Painter. Landscapes.
André Jean studied in the art college at Le Havre. At first he painted in the Normandy countryside, then he settled near Bordeaux.

JEAN, Antoine
Italian, 18th century.
Born c. 1690, in Ascoli.
Painter, engraver. History painting, landscapes.
Antoine Jean is mentioned by Ris Paquot.

JEAN, Auguste Émile
French, 19th century.
Born 4 January 1869, in the Aisne.
Painter.
Auguste Jean was a pupil of Gustave Moreau and exhibited from 1895 onwards at the Salons of the Société des Artistes Français.

JEAN, Auguste Toussaint
French, 19th century.
Born 19th century, in Rocanval-Amencourt.
Sculptor.
Auguste Jean studied under Dubray and Lebourg. He exhibited a plaster medallion at the 1861 Paris Salon and, in 1863, a marble bust entitled: *Faith*.

JEAN, Fernand
French, 20th - 21st century.
Born 19 November 1948, in Orly.
Painter. Scenes with figures.
Fernand Jean's paintings feature fantastic moon-like or extra-terrestrial and often strangely coloured landscapes peopled with figures, painted in the photographic realist technique and in poses that often have erotic connotations. He has taken part in various collective exhibitions such as those at the Galerie Ror Volmar in Paris and Vichy, as well as the Salon des Indépendants where he has exhibited since 1970. He also holds solo exhibitions of his paintings.

JEAN, Georges
French, 19th century.
Born 19th century, in Paris.
Enameller.
Georges Jean exhibited at the Paris Salon from 1879 onwards.

JEAN, Louis. See **BRUGGEN Louis van der**

JEAN, Marcel, also called Marcel-Jean
French, 20th century.
Born 1900, in La Charité-sur-Loire (Nièvre); died 1994.
Painter (mixed media), watercolourist, draughtsman, engraver, medallist.
Surrealist group.
Marcel Jean studied at the Paris École des Arts Décoratifs from 1919 to 1921. He did a number of different things until 1924 and then went to the USA to work as an industrial draughtsman. He must have returned to France in the early 1930s, when he was involved in the Surrealist movement. From 1938 to 1945 he lived in Hungary, working mainly as a writer and publishing an essay called *Mnésiques* (*Memory*) and other essays on the early Surrealists and on Surrealist

poets. He returned to Paris, gave up Surrealism and moved on to abstract work.

He showed work in collective exhibitions, including: 1930, the Salon d'Automne in Paris; 1933-1952, regularly with the Surrealist group on Paris, and in New York, particularly the 1968 *Dada, Surrealism and their Heritage* at the Museum of Modern Art; in London *Dada and Surrealism Reviewed* at the Hayward Gallery; in Tokyo and Brussels; also at the Salon des Surindépendants in Paris; 1977, *Paris-New York* at the Pompidou Centre in Paris; and in 1989 the Venice *Biennale.* His work has also been shown since his death in collective exhibitions, such as the 2002 *La Révolution Surréaliste* (*The Surrealist Revolution*) in Paris at the Pompidou Centre. He began solo shows in Paris in 1946 and in New York in 1947. Others were in 1981, at the Kölnischer Kunstverein in Cologne, in 1984, at the French Institute in Hamburg, and in 1987 at the Galerie 1900-2000 in Paris.

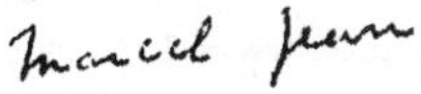

BIBLIOGRAPHY:

Marcel Jean, exhibition catalogue, Gal. 1900-2000, Paris, 1987. Spies, Werner (ed.), *La Révolution surréaliste*, exhibition catalogue, Éd. du Centre Georges-Pompidou, Paris, 2002.

AUCTION RECORDS:

LONDON, 4 July 1974, *Ghost with Gardenia* (1936, plaster) GBP 950. NEW YORK, 27 Feb 1976, *Black Mirror* (1973, oil and gouache/panel, 11 1/2 x 9 1/2 ins / 29.2 x 24 cm) USD 1,100. NEW YORK, 22 Oct 1976, *Enchantress* (1973, gouache, 12 1/2 x 19 1/2 ins / 32 x 49.5 cm) USD 750. NEW YORK, 6 Oct 1988, *Décalcomania* (1936, gouache/paper, 12 3/4 x 9 3/4 ins / 32.6 x 25 cm) USD 2,420. LONDON, 29 Nov 1989, *Pearl and Rose* (1945, oil on canvas, 15 x 22 ins / 38 x 55 cm) GBP 16,500. PARIS, 31 Oct 1990, *Backlighting* (1930, pencil and watercolour/paper, 12 1/4 x 9 1/2 ins / 31 x 24 cm) FRF 4,000. PARIS, 4 May 1993, *Still Water* (1925, charcoal, black ink and watercolour, 12 1/2 x 9 1/2 ins / 31.5 x 24 cm) FRF 7,200. PARIS, 20 May 1994, *Untitled, Decalcomania-Stencil* (1936, gouache/paper, 20 1/2 x 12 1/2 ins / 52 x 32 cm) FRF 13,000. PARIS, 21 Dec 2001, *Moraine* (gouache and pencil, 24 x 19 ins / 61 x 48 cm) FRF 20,000. PARIS, 21 Dec 2001, *Clearing* (1945, oil on canvas, 21 x 29 ins / 54 x 74 cm) FRF 32,000. NEW YORK, 6 March 2002, *On the Open Sea* (gouache and watercolour on board, 13 x 9 ins / 32 x 24 cm) USD 2,600.

JEAN, Maria

French, 19th - 20th century.

Painter.

Maria Jean exhibited regularly in Paris at the Salon des Artistes Français, of which she became a member in 1897.

JEAN, Philip

British, 18th century.

Born 1755, in St-Ouen (Jersey), Channel Islands; died 1802, in Hempstead.

Active in London.

Miniaturist.

Philip Jean started out as a sailor. Between 1787 and 1802, he exhibited 118 miniatures at the Royal Academy.

MUSEUMS AND GALLERIES:

JERSEY: *Major Francis Pierson* (miniature) - LONDON (National Portrait Gal.): *Dominic Serres* (1788, watercolour and gouache on ivory, medallion, miniature); *James Saumarez, 1st Baron of Saumarez* (1801, watercolour and gouache on ivory, miniature) - LONDON (Victoria and Albert Mus.): *Portrait of an unknown man.*

JEAN, R.

British, 19th century.

Active in London.

Miniaturist.

R. Jean exhibited at the Royal Academy from 1801 to 1803.

JEAN CHARLES DE LAON. See **DELAON**

JEAN D'AIRE

French, 14th century.

Sculptor, designer of ornamental architectural features.

Jean d'Aire worked at the charterhouse in Gosnay, Artois, in 1324.

JEAN D'AIX-LA-CHAPELLE

French, 15th century.

Sculptor.

School of Alsace.

Jean d'Aix-la-Chapelle was made a citizen of Strasbourg in 1493, where he produced the large statues for the north portal of the cathedral (also known as the St Lawrence door) for the architect Jacob de Landshut.

JEAN D'ALVERCA

Portuguese, 15th century.

Died before 1466.

Active during the first half of the 15th century.

Sculptor.

JEAN D'AMBOISE

French, 15th century.

Painter. History painting, portraits.

According to Jean Fouquet, Jean d'Amboise was a successful painter in Tours.

JEAN D'AMIENS

French, 14th century.

Jean d'Amiens was active in Beauvais in 1316.

Painter.

JEAN D'ANGERS

French, 16th century.

Born in Angers.

Active at the beginning of the 16th century.

Sculptor, designer of ornamental architectural features.

Jean d'Angers produced a large pall for the guardroom at the state palace in Dijon in 1504, which is now in the town's museum.

MUSEUMS AND GALLERIES:

DIJON: *Pall of the Guardroom.*

JEAN D'ARBOIS

French, 14th century.

Painter.

Jean d'Arbois was invited to work for Philip the Bold, Duke of Burgundy, in a letter dated 21 June 1373. The letter has survived, as has the record of fees paid to him on various dates. He travelled with the duke to Paris and Bruges, and also spent time in Italy, where he introduced the Franco-Flemish style of paintings of the Virgin. Examples of this style can be found in the work of Michelino de Besozzo. He taught Melchior Broederlam.

JEAN D'ARCY

French, 14th - 15th century.

Active in Paris.

Illuminator.

JEAN D'ARRAS

French, 13th century.

Active at the end of the 13th century.

Sculptor. Funerary monuments (recumbent statues).

Jean d'Arras worked with Pierre de Chelles on the tomb of Philippe III, le Hardi, the recumbent figure of which is in St-Denis. It is the first such figure to be a realistic portrait, showing the king with thin lips, a straight nose and a flattened chin.

JEAN D'ASSELT. See **ASSELT Jan van der**

JEAN D'AUBONNE

French, 15th - 16th century.

Born in Tournus; died before 8 April 1520.

Sculptor.
Jean d'Aubonne was a stonemason and sculptor who worked on the stone wall of the chapel of Gendret, or of the Passion, in the cathedral of St-Vincent in Chalon in 1499. A sketch of these sculptures, which were destroyed in 1788, is in the regional archives of Saône-et-Loire.

JEAN D'AUTEUIL
French, 14th century.
Active in Paris c. 1325.
Painter. Wall decorations.

JEAN D'AVESNES
Dutch, 14th century.
Architect, sculptor.
Jean d'Avesnes worked for the church of St-Pierre in Lille in 1387. His name appears in records for the last time in 1399.

JEAN D'ESCAMAING. See **ESCAMAING**

JEAN D'ORLÉANS. See **POTIN Jean,** and **MASTER of the NARBONNE FRONTAL**

JEAN DE AQUIS. See **AQUIS Jean de**

JEAN DE BADE
French, 15th century.
Of German origin.
Sculptor.
Jean de Bade was recorded as a citizen of Strasbourg in 1479.

JEAN DE BANDOL. See **JEAN de Bondolf**

JEAN DE BASTEL. See **BATTEL Jan van**

JEAN DE BAVIÈRE
French, 16th century.
Painter.
Jean de Bavière was a member of the Corneille de Bavière family who worked in Lyons in 1533.

JEAN DE BEAUMES. See **BEAUMETZ Jean de**

JEAN DE BIAUMEZ. See **BEAUMETZ Jean de**

JEAN DE BOIS-LE-DUC
Flemish, 16th century.
Painter. History painting.
Flemish School.
Jean de Bois-le-Duc worked for Margaret of Austria around 1500.

JEAN DE BOLOGNE. See **BOLOGNE Jean de** and **VALENTIN Jean**

JEAN DE BONDOLF, or Bondol, Bandol, called Jean or Hennequin de Bruges, Johann von Brügge, and other names
Franco-Flemish, 14th century.
Illuminator, painter. Designs for tapestries.
Franco-Flemish School.
Jean de Bondolf is best known for having produced the sketches for the *Apocalypse* tapestry of Angers, which was commissioned for the chapel of the Château d'Angers by Louis I of Anjou. It was produced by Nicolas Bataille between 1375 and 1381, using vertical stitching. Despite the grandeur of the work, its style is close to that of an illumination. Jean had been strongly influenced by the illuminations of the Fons Salin manuscript (no. 30) in the Metz library, as well as by a northern French manuscript dating to the beginning of the 14th century in the Museum in Namur, and especially by another manuscript (no. 482), dating to the end of the 12th century, which belonged to the Cambrai library. He also produced an original miniature that headed a translation of the Vulgate, which is masterful in its accuracy and looseness of form. It was given as a present to King Charles V of France by Jehan Vandetor or Jean de Vaudétour in 1371, and is now in The Hague Museum.

The suppleness and skill of the miniature is also apparent in the *Apocalypse* tapestry, which is a monumental composition, remarkable for the sobriety of its palette: a deep blue background, alternating with red (now slightly faded), a grey monochrome for the buildings, and various shades of green for the rest of the landscape. His backgrounds are decorative, often using flowers, and his mountains artificial-looking - a trait that is typical of Gothic art. His drawings of figures show remarkable ease and grace, especially in the folds of clothing that reflect the movements of the body. Jean's mastery of perspective, however, was often shaky, as can be seen from the canopies covering the prophets; but he must have made a considerable effort in his drawing of the fragment of Gothic gallery, under which sits a bishop from the church of Asia.

BIBLIOGRAPHY:
Dupont, Jacques/Gnudi, Cesare, *La Peinture gothique*, Skira, Geneva, 1954.

MUSEUMS AND GALLERIES:
THE HAGUE: *Miniature* (miniature heading the translation of La Vulgate).

JEAN DE BOULLONGNE. See **BOLOGNE Jean de** and **VALENTIN Jean**

JEAN DE BOURGES
French, 15th century.
Active in Lyons.
Painter, carver.
Jean de Bourges lived in Lyons from 1489 to 1491, and took part in the preparations for Charles VIII's official visit there in 1490.

JEAN DE BOURGOGNE
15th century.
Sculptor.
In 1485 Jean de Bourgogne began work on the rood screen of St John's church in Bourbourg (Nord) jointly with Matthias Keldermans. Jean died in 1490 and the work was completed by Keldermans in 1491. The church was demolished in 1784.

JEAN DE BOURGOGNE
French, 16th century.
Born in Mâcon.
Also active in Spain and Italy.
Painter. History painting.
Jean de Bourgogne was active around 1514. He travelled to Spain, possibly with his brother, and then went to live in Bologna, where several of his frescoes and paintings remain. There are similarities between him and Juan de Borgona.

JEAN DE BOURGOGNE. See also **JUAN de Borgoña**

JEAN DE BRUGES. See **JEAN de Bondolf**

JEAN DE BRUXELLES. See **JUAN de Bruxelas**

JEAN DE CAMBRAI
French, 15th century.
Born in Roupy-en-Picardie; died 1438, in Bourges.
Sculptor. Funerary monuments (recumbent statues).

JEAN DE CAUMONT. See **CAUMONT Jean de**

JEAN DE CHALONS
French, 16th century.
Sculptor (wood).
Fontainebleau School.

Jean de Chalons worked at the Château de Fontainebleau from 1540 to 1550 where he sculpted a large wooden statue representing *Faith*.

JEAN DE CHARTRES
French, 16th century.
Died between 1511 and 1515.
Sculptor.
Jean de Chartres worked with his teacher, Michel Colombe, on most of the latter's works, in particular, on the tomb of François II of Brittany, which was produced in partnership with Guillaume Regnault.
MUSEUMS AND GALLERIES:
PARIS (Louvre): *St Anne with the Virgin as a Child* (statue).

JEAN DE CHELLES
French, 13th century.
Died 1270.
Active in Paris.
Sculptor, architect.
Bishop Regnault of Corbeil commissioned Jean de Chelles to direct the works of Notre-Dame. In 1257 he built the south porch, which is decorated with *The Birth of Jesus, The Adoration of the Magi, The Flight into Egypt, The Massacre of the Innocents,* and *The History of Saint Stephen*. Most famously, he created the model of the lateral façade with a rose window, which was copied almost universally.

JEAN DE COLOGNE. See **ZWOLLE Jean de**

JEAN DE COLOGNE, or Jean de Coulongne
French, 15th century.
Sculptor (wood).
Jean de Cologne worked on the archiepiscopal pulpit of Rouen Cathedral from 1465 to 1469, under the direction of Laurent-Adam.

JEAN DE COLOGNE. See also **COLART Jean**

JEAN DE COMMERCY. See **JACQUEMIN Rogier**

JEAN DE CONNET. See **CONNET**

JEAN DE DIJON
French, 14th century.
Active in Troyes c. 1385.
Painter.
Jean de Dijon worked at Troyes Cathedral in 1383 and 1384, and at the church of St-Urbain in 1384 and 1385.

JEAN DE DIJON
French, 15th century.
Sculptor, architect.
Jean de Dijon was from Rheims, where he worked on the cathedral. He was invited to Troyes to visit the church of St-Étienne.

JEAN DE DINANT
French, 14th century.
Active in Béthune c. 1372.
Sculptor, founder.
Jean de Dinant was of Flemish origin and sculpted the lectern of Tongeren Cathedral, which bears the inscription *Jehans Joses de Dinant 1372*.

JEAN DE EYCHUISE. See **EYCHUISE**

JEAN DE FÉVIN
French, 14th century.
Designer of ornamental architectural features.
Jean de Févin produced several decorative motifs for the chapel at the Château d'Hesdin in the Pas-de-Calais region of France, in 1380.

JEAN DE FRIBOURG. See **JEHAN le Peintre**

JEAN DE GAND
Flemish, 14th century.
Illuminator.
Flemish School.
Jean de Grand worked for Mahaut d'Artois in Paris in 1328.

JEAN DE GASCOIGNE
French, 16th century.
Active in Lyons in 1533.
Painter.

JEAN DE GORZE. See **GORZE Jean de**

JEAN DE GRISE
Spanish, 14th century.
Illuminator.
In 1344, Jean de Grise illuminated *The Romance of King Alexander*.

JEAN DE HASSET. See **ASSELT Jan van der**

JEAN DE HOLLANDE
Flemish School, 15th - 16th century.
Painter.
Jean de Hollande was of Flemish origin, and is recorded as living in Lyons in 1492 and 1507.

JEAN DE HONET, or Jehennin
French, 14th - 15th century.
Sculptor.
Burgundy School.
Jean de Honet worked on the portal of the charterhouse church of Champmol in Dijon from 1399 to 1401, under the direction of Claus Sluter.

JEAN DE HUY. See **PÉPIN Jean**

JEAN DE JOUY. See **JEHAN de Jouy**

JEAN DE JUVIA. See **JUVIA** and **JUVIAC**

JEAN DE JUYS. See **JUYS**

JEAN DE KELY. See **KELY**

JEAN DE L'ARC. See **JAN de L'ARC**

JEAN DE LA CROIX DE LIÈGE. See **JEAN de Liège**

JEAN DE LA HUERTA, or Juan
Spanish, 15th century.
Born in Daroca (Aragon); died after 1462.
Sculptor.
Jean de la Huerta was of Spanish origin, but the only known works by him are in France, mostly in Burgundy. In 1443 he was summoned to Dijon by Philip the Good, Duke of Burgundy, to sculpt a tomb for his parents John the Fearless and Margaret of Bavaria. Philip wanted a tomb similar in style to the famous one created for John's father Philip the Bold under the direction of Claus Sluter, without being a crude imitation. We do not know on what basis Jean de la Huerta was chosen since we know nothing of his earlier work, but he evidently had a good reputation. On 23 March 1443 he was contracted to make the tomb of John the Fearless and Margaret of Bavaria over the course of the next four years. However, by 1449 he had only completed a third of the work, while a large part of the money allocated to the monument's construction had been spent. In 1456 he left Dijon under some unknown pretext; the Duke's accountants tried to persuade him to return in 1461, without success. In 1462 he was in Mâcon, and there is no further record of him.

The overall layout of Jean de la Huerta's unfinished work, which was completed by Le Moiturier, followed exactly that of Philip the Bold's tomb. Jean had completed the pillars, angels, cherubs, weeping figures, and the helmet of John's effigy. His non-completion of the work could be explained by the fact that he received other important commissions during the same period, although these also often went unfinished. In 1448 Louis de Chalon ordered him to sculpt three tombs for the abbey of Mont-Ste-Marie, from which the figure of an *Abbess* is now in the Louvre. Jean de la Huerta was called before the ecclesiastical court of Besançon in 1457 because these tombs were still not finished. The bulk of Jean's output, however, consists of medium-sized free-standing statues. The church of Rouvres-en-Plaine contains a *Virgin and Child* and *St John the Baptist* attributed to him. Jean Chevrot, the Bishop of Tournai, commissioned images of the *Virgin* and *St Anthony* from him to decorate his chapel in the church of St-Hippolyte in Poligny. Around 1447 he sculpted a *Virgin* for the town gate in Auxonne, which resembles other statues of the *Virgin* attributed to him in Sully, Pluvault and Autun. He did a considerable amount of work in Autun, especially for the Bishop (later Cardinal) Jean Rolin. Jean de la Huerta renewed the art of Claus Sluter, made his mark on the artistic life of Dijon and gave an impulse to the studios of Autun.

BIBLIOGRAPHY:

Quarre, P., *Jean de la Huerta et la sculpture bourguignonne au milieu du XVe siècle*, exhibition catalogue, Palais des ducs de Bourgogne, Musée de Dijon, Dijon, 1972.

MUSEUMS AND GALLERIES:

ANGERS (Mus. St-Jean): *St Margaret* - ARGUEL (Church): *St Genoux* - AUTUN (Cathedral of St-Lazare): *Virgin and Child* - AUTUN (Mus. Rolin): *St Margaret; St Catherine; Bishop St; Head of a Prophet; Angel Lectern* - AUXONNE (Collegiate Church): *Virgin and Child* - AVIGNON (Mus. Calvet): *St Lazarus* - BAR-LE-RÉGULIER (Church): *St John the Evangelist* - BEAUMONT-SUR-VINGEANNE (Church): *St Barbara* - BESANÇON: *Sleeping Lion* - BUCEY-LES-GY: *Virgin and Child* - CHALON-SUR-SAÔNE (Mus. Vivant-Denon): *Heads of St John the Baptist and a Female St* - DIJON (MBA): *Angels on the Tomb of John the Fearless and Margaret of Bavaria; St Reading; Virgin and Child; Virgin and Child* - ÉPOISSES (Church): *Virgin of Pity* - LAIZY (Church): *Virgin and Child* - MOULINS: *Crowned St* - PARIS (Louvre): *Abbess* - PESMES (Church): *Virgin and Child* - PLOMBIÈRES (Church): *Virgin and Child* - PLUVAULT (Church): *Virgin and Child* - POLIGNY (Church of Moutier-Vieillard): *St Anthony* - ROUVRES-EN-PLAINE (Church): *Virgin and Child; St John the Baptist* - SAULIEU: *Virgin of Mercy* - SAVOISY (Church): *Virgin and Child; St Catherine* - SEURRE (Hôtel-Dieu): *St Barbara* - SULLY (Church): *Virgin and Child.*

JEAN DE LIÈGE, or Jehan, also known as Hennequin de Liège, also called de La Croix de Liège
Flemish School, 14th century.
Born in Liège; died 1382, in Paris.
Sculptor. Funerary monuments (recumbent statues).
Flemish School.

Jean de Liège worked for the counts of Flanders and for King Charles V of France. His works include two statues of *Charles IV the Handsome, and his Wife Jeanne of Évreux,* which are in the Louvre, a monument (previously in Rouen Cathedral, but which was destroyed) to the heart of King Charles V, who died in 1368, and the *Tomb of Thévenin of St-Léger*, the King's Jester, who died in 1340. He may have been the student of Jean Pépin de Huy, and went to England to sculpt a statue of the wife of King Edward III, *Philippa of Hainaut.* He also produced a recumbent figure of *Blanche of France*, the daughter of Charles IV who was born after the latter's death, for St-Denis Cathedral. According to Dr von Wurzbach, Dehaisnes mistook him for another sculptor of the same name.

MUSEUMS AND GALLERIES:

PARIS (Louvre): *Charles IV the Handsome and his Wife Jeanne of Évreux* (two statues).

JEAN DE LIÈGE
French, 16th century.
Active in Paris in the 16th century.
Sculptor.

Jean de Liège was a master carpenter who was invited to work in Dijon in 1390 by Philip the Bold, Duke of Burgundy, in order to take part in work on the charterhouse of Champmol. He produced the large wooden church doors and decorated them with four escutcheons showing the arms of both the duke and duchess of Burgundy, and of John, Count of Nevers. These doors are now at the entrance to the chapel of the 'refuge for outcasts' in Dijon. He also sculpted stalls with a decorative canopy for the charterhouse in 1399, a fragment of which is in the museum in Dijon. On his return to Paris, he produced an alabaster statue of Our Lady in 1401, which was given to the Celestine convent by Louis of Orléans. He participated in the production of various works in the church of St-Paul.

MUSEUMS AND GALLERIES:

DIJON: *Piece of a Church Stall* (fragment of a stall).

JEAN DE LILLE. See **JEAN Le Cybouleur**

JEAN DE LIMOGES. See **LIMOSIN Jehan**

JEAN DE LOOZ. See **PEECKS Jan**

JEAN DE LORRAINE. See **TABOURIN Jean**

JEAN DE LUXEMBOURG
French, 15th century.
Active in Metz.
Sculptor, founder.

Jean de Luxembourg cast the main bell, known as the 'Mutte', for Metz Cathedral in 1428, working with Jean of Guerle. He then went to Avignon, where he produced a glazed cross for the cemetery of St-Didier in 1451.

JEAN DE LYON, or Giovanni dal Lione
French, 16th century.
Painter.

Jean de Lyon worked in Rome under Giulio Romano. A reference to him is dated 1524. Jean de Luxembourg was one of his most active employees.

JEAN DE LYON
French, 16th century.
Painter.
Rouen School.

Originally from Lyons, Jean de Lyon settled in Rouen and produced decorative paintings and coats of arms. References to him are dated 1506 and 1510.

JEAN DE MAISONCELLES. See **MAISONCELLES**

JEAN DE MALINES
Flemish, 16th century.
Active in Lyons.
Painter.
Flemish School.

Jean de Malines was of Flemish origin, and is recorded as living in Lyons in 1528 and 1534.

JEAN DE MALINES. See also **JUAN de Malinas**

JEAN DE MARVILLE. See **HENNEQUIN DE MERVILLE**

JEAN DE MERTENS, Fernande. See **MERTENS**

JEAN DE MONTLUÇON, or Molisson
French, 15th century.
Active in Bourges.
Painter.

JEAN DE NANCY, called Le Lorrain
French, 16th century.
Active c. 1590-1592.

Painter, glassmaker. History painting, portraits.
Siret lists two different names for this artist: Jean de Nancy and Jean le Lorrain, and he may also have been known as Jean de Wayembourg, who was a painter who worked for the court of Duke Charles III in Nancy in 1599. Jean de Nancy produced several paintings for the ducal palace. Works attributed to him include *The Virgin with Rosary* in Nancy Cathedral, and decorations for the church in Minimes.

JEAN DE NOGENT
French, 14th century.
Medallist.
Jean de Nogent worked for Philip the Reckless in 1384.

JEAN DE PARIS. See **PERRÉAL Jean** and **LAVENIER Jean**

JEAN DE PARIS
French, 16th century.
Active in Troyes.
Painter, sculptor.
Jean de Paris produced the main altar for the church of St-Nicolas in Troyes. An artist named Jehan de Paris is recorded as living in Amiens and working for the church of Notre-Dame du Puy in 1581.

JEAN DE PIMONT. See **GRASSI Giovanni**

JEAN DE PRINDALLES. See **PRINDAL Jean**

JEAN DE REIMS
French, 14th century.
Sculptor (?), architect (?).
Jean de Reims worked on the rebuilding of the abbey of Monte Cassino in 1370.

JEAN DE RENTY
French, 16th century.
Active in Orléans c. 1555.
Painter. History painting.
Jean de Renty worked at Orléans Cathedral. He may also have been known by the name of Jean de Connet.

JEAN DE ROUEN
French, 16th century.
Active between 1510 and 1572.
Sculptor, architect.
Jean de Rouen is believed to have worked in Gisors between 1510 and 1512. In 1517, he produced the funerary monument for Cardinal George I of Amboise in Rouen Cathedral. He settled in Coimbra in 1530, and produced the altarpiece of Varziela, which is, without doubt, his masterpiece, possessing a charm that is lacking from the altarpiece he produced in Guarda from 1540 to 1553.

JEAN DE ROUPY. See **JEAN de Cambrai**

JEAN DE RUE. See **RUE**

JEAN DE SAINT-OMER, or Jan van Saint-Omaers
Dutch, 17th century.
Painter.
Jean de Saint Omer is mentioned by Siret in 1631 in Utrecht as being commissioned to decorate the chapel of Schoonhoven palace.

JEAN DE SAINT-ROMAIN
French, 14th century.
Active in Paris.
Painter, sculptor, architect.
Jean de St-Romain worked for the Louvre, from 1365 to 1370, with Raymond du Temple. His works include statues of *Charles V the Wise, The Duke of Anjou, St John the Baptist* and a *Virgin*.

JEAN DE SAINT-YORE, or Saint-Jore, or Saint-Joire
French, 16th century.
Sculptor. Monuments.
MUSEUMS AND GALLERIES:
BAR-LE-DUC: *Tomb of Guy de Sailly*.

JEAN DE SALINS. See **JEAN de Selles**

JEAN DE SANHOLIS
French, 14th century.
Sculptor.
Avignon School.
Jean de Sanholis worked as a sculptor at the Chaise-Dieu abbey, in 1351, on the tomb of *Clement VI*. He probably also worked at the Château des Papes (Papal Castle) in Avignon in 1360.

JEAN DE SELLES
French, 14th century.
Active in Dijon in 1390.
Sculptor.
Jean de Selles worked at the charterhouse of Champmol on the tomb of Philip the Reckless. He was probably also known by the name of Jean de Salins, who is recorded as working on the same tomb in 1398 and 1399.

JEAN DE SOIGNOLES
French, 14th century.
Active in Paris in 1358.
Sculptor.
Jean de Soignoles worked for Queen Jeanne on the tomb of *Philip of Burgundy*.

JEAN DE STAVELOT, also known as Joannes de Stabulis
Flemish, 15th century.
Born 5 June 1388, in Stavelot; died 1449.
Miniaturist.
Flemish School.
Jean de Stavelot was the son of a country magistrate, and became a monk at the age of 14 at the Benedictine abbey of St Lawrence under the name of Dom Jean de Stavelot, receiving orders in 1414. In 1411, he had probably begun producing illuminations of manuscripts, several of which have survived. He is generally known as the author of a *Chronicle*, which bears his name. Some of his illuminated manuscripts can be found in the royal library in Brussels.

JEAN DE TOULOUSE
French, 14th century.
Active in Avignon at the end of the 14th century.
Miniaturist.
Avignon School.
A missal belonging to Pope Clement VII, previously attributed to Niccolo da Bologna, has now been attributed to Jean de Toulouse.
MUSEUMS AND GALLERIES:
AVIGNON (Bibliothèque Calvet): *Missal Belonging to Pope Clement VII*.

JEAN DE TROYES. See **CORDONNIER Jean** and **JEANNIN**

JEAN DE VALENCIENNES
Flemish, 14th century.
Died c. 1401.
Active in Bruges.
Sculptor.
Flemish School.
Jean de Valenciennes worked for the towns of Bruges and Cambrai. He may also have worked in Palma, Majorca, under the name of Juan de Valencines.
MUSEUMS AND GALLERIES:
BRUGES: *Remains of Sculptures for the Town Hall*.

JEAN DE VALENCIENNES
Flemish, 15th - 16th century.

Active in Cambrai in 1480 and 1517.
Sculptor (wood).
Flemish School.

JEAN DE VIENNE
French, 15th century.
Painter.

Jean de Vienne was a painter and sculptor, originally from Vienne in Dauphiné. He is recorded as living in Lyons in 1490 and 1492, and took part in preparations for the official visit of Charles VIII to the town in 1490.

JEAN DE VILLIERS, or Jeannin
French, 15th century.
Active in Troyes 1440-1455.
Painter.

JEAN DE WAYEMBOURG. See **JEAN de Nancy**

JEAN DES PORTES. See **DES PORTES**

JEAN DU PARKET
French, 13th century.
Painter.

Jean du Parket worked on the residence of the Count of Artois in Arras.

JEAN FRANÇOIS. See **FRANÇOIS Jean I**

JEAN GRANDSON. See **GRANDSON Jean**

JEAN L'ESPAGNOL
French, 15th century.
Painter, decorative artist.

Jean l'Espagnol is recorded as living in Lyons in 1494 and 1499. He produced carved mermaids' scales, which he painted silver, for the official visit of Anne of Brittany to Lyons in 1494. His life shows similarities to that of Giovanni Spagna.

JEAN LE BOUCHER
French, 15th century.
Born to a family originally from Mechelen.
Sculptor.

Born in Mechelen, Jean le Boucher produced statues of *St Christopher* and *St Nicholas* for the northern portal of Troyes Cathedral in 1463, with his cousin, Petit Jean, who was also a Belgian.

JEAN LE BOUTELLIER. See **LE BOUTELLIER**

JEAN LE CYBOULEUR
French, 14th century.
Active in Lille.
Sculptor.

Jean le Cybouleur produced a tabernacle, in 1342, for the church of St-Pierre in Lille, and in 1349, decorated a picture containing saints' relics in the county magistrates' hall, which was used for making oaths. He also made decorations for the portal of the church of St-Pierre in 1369, which had been built by Liotard de Biauvoir. The following year, he sculpted an eagle and low reliefs for the jube, and in 1380 and 1381, he worked on the chancel.

JEAN LE FLAMAND
15th century.
Active in Cambrai.
Sculptor.

In 1459 Jean le Flamand repaired the sculptures on the clock of Cambrai Cathedral.

JEAN LE MUET
Flemish, 15th century.
Miniaturist.
Flemish School.

Jean le Muet worked for Charles the Reckless in Mechelen in 1473.

JEAN LE NOIR. See **LE NOIR**

JEAN LE PAINTRE. See **LE PAINTRE**

JEAN LE PEINTRE. See **JEHAN le Peintre**

JEAN LE SAUVAGE
French, 14th century.
Active in Arras between 1323 and 1343.
Painter (glass).

Jean le Sauvage worked at the Château de la Buissière.

JEAN LOMBART. See **LOMBART**

JEAN PÉPIN DE HUY. See **PÉPIN Jean**

JEAN PETIT. See **PETIT Jean**

JEAN SCRIVERE. See **SCRIVERE**

JEAN VAN KESSEL. See **KESSEL Jean Thomas or Nicolas van**

JEAN-BOUCHER. See **BOUCHER Jean**

JEAN-HAFFEN, Yvonne
French, 20th century.
Born 1895; died 1993.
Painter, engraver, illustrator, designer, potter.
Landscapes, still-lifes (flowers/fruit).

Yvonne Jean-Haffen, a pupil of Mathurin Méheut, began her career as a painter on wood and as a potter in Quimper. Later she continued training in the Sèvres National Factory. She did a great deal of decorative work on the vessels of the General Transatlantic Company and of the shipping line Messageries Maritimes. Among the books she illustrated are *En dérive* (*Adrift*) by Roger Vercel, *En parcourant la Normandie* (*Exploring Normandy*) by La Varende, and *Les Champignons* (*Mushrooms*) by Roger Heim. In honour of her former teacher, she became secretary of the Society of Friends of M. Méheut, and was also director of Lamballe Museum.

She exhibited in 1924 at the Salon des Artistes Français and later at the Société Nationale des Beaux-Arts, of which she became a member. She also showed work at the Salon des Artistes Décorateurs, Salon de la Marine, Salon des Femmes Peintres et Sculpteurs and Salon de Dessin et de la Peinture a l'Eau. Solo exhibitions were held in Paris, Brest, St-Brieuc, Rennes, Dinan and Nancy, and posthumously in 1997 at the Musée des Jacobins in Morlaix and at the Maison d'Artiste de la Grande Vigne in Dinan.

BIBLIOGRAPHY:
Puget, François, *Yvonne Jean-Haffen, 1895-1993*, Le Télégramme, Morlaix, 2001.

MUSEUMS AND GALLERIES:
DINAN (Maison d'Artiste de la Grande Vigne): numerous works.

JEAN-JOVENEAU. See **JOVENAU Jean**

JEAN-LOUP
French, 20th century.
Painter.

Jean-Loup was a son of Forain.

JEAN-MARTIN
French, 20th century.
Born 1911, in Lyons; died 1996.
Painter. Religious subjects, scenes with figures.

Jean-Martin lived in Lyons until 1945, when he moved to Paris. He studied Byzantine art and from 1953 to 1967 concentrated exclusively on sacred art, subsequently returning to secular art. He began exhibiting in 1933, showing work at various collectives in Lyons until 1940, and in Paris at the Salon des Indépendants.

JEAN-ROBERT, André
French, 20th century.

Born 25 October 1921, in Chantemerle-les-Blés (Drôme).

Painter.

André Jean-Robert trained at the art college in Geneva. In 1946, he studied the techniques for making painted glass. His paintings tend to the non-representational and to fantasy.

He showed work in collective exhibitions in Paris, Germany, Austria, Pittsburgh, Barcelona and elsewhere, also in regional salons such as the Salon des Surindépendants, Salon Comparaisons and Salon d'Art Sacré in Paris, and also at the Salon d'Art Fantastique. He had the first of many solo shows of his paintings in 1954, to be followed among others by: 1955, at the Musée Lorrain in Bar-le-Duc; 1956, at the Galerie Creuze in Paris, founded by Philippe Soupault; several shows from 1962 at the Galerie Valérie Schmidt, Paris; 1974 in Valence museum; 1979, in the museum at Forcalquier; 1980, in the centre for contemporary art in Grignan; 1984, the Musée Denon in Chalon-sur-Saône; 1990 at a private gallery in Grenoble; 1994, at St-Péray (Ardèche).

BIBLIOGRAPHY:

Soupault, Philippe (preface), *Jean-Robert*, exhibition catalogue, Gal. Creuse, Paris, 1958.

MUSEUMS AND GALLERIES:

BAR-LE-DUC (Mus. Barrois) - CHALON-SUR-SAÔNE (Mus. Vivant-Denon) - LE HAVRE (Mus. Malraux) - PARIS (MAMVP) - PARIS (MNAM-CCI) - VALENCIA (MBA) - YVERDON-LES-BAINS (Maison d'Ailleurs).

JEAN-ROGER, pseudonym of Roger, Jean

French, 20th century.

Born 30 August 1924, in Nîmes.

Painter. Figure compositions, landscapes.

Jean-Roger, a grandson of Nicodème Reboul, studied at the school of decorative art in Nice under André Maillart for painting and Jules Lengrand for drawing. In his figure compositions and some of his landscapes he tends towards Fauvism, both in the balanced drawing and in the very strong use of colour. He showed work in collective exhibitions in the regions and in Paris, both at the Salon des Artistes Français and from 1958 at the Salon des Indépendants, of which he became a member in 1961. His solo exhibitions have included: 1955, Nice; 1961, 1963, Banyuls-sur-Mer; 1976, Villefranche-sur-Mer; and 1977, Falicon.

JEANCLERC

French, 18th century.

Active in Gray in 1764.

Sculptor.

JEANCLOS, Georges, or Jeankelowitch or Jeanclos-Mossé

French, 20th century.

Born 9 April 1933, in Paris; died 30 March 1997, in Paris.

Sculptor. Figures. Monuments, statuettes.

Georges Jeanclos enrolled at the École des Beaux-Arts in Paris in 1952, and in 1959 he won the Prix de Rome for sculpture. He spent the years 1960-1963 at the Villa Medici, working under Balthus, who was then its director and had great influence on many of his students. Jeanclos studied classical antiquity, especially the art of the Etruscans. In 1976 he was appointed to teach as the head of a studio in the École des Beaux-Arts in Paris, and in 1982 he set up the Research and Creation workshop in the Sèvres factory. He travelled widely in the East, the Far East and Africa, increasing his knowledge of classical sculpture and ancient rituals, and devoting much of his time to drawing.

From 1975 onwards, he produced almost nothing but terracotta shapes, hollow, finely detailed and very brittle. He built them up using multiple projections of 'slices of clay', soft, damp layers as thin as cloth. He remained faithful to the theme of *Dormeurs (Sleepers)*, couples reclining or sometimes emerging painfully from the clay of which they were made, and the *Kamakura* series he produced after his 1984 journey to Japan. Alongside his *Sleepers* and similar works he produced in 1984 the *Monument to Jean Moulin*, five bronze stele erected in the Champs-Élysées. In 1985-1989, he produced a new tympanum for the 12th century church of St-Ayoul de Provins, which includes a mandorla with Christ in Majesty, two apostles, a lintel and a pier. During the same period he made his 23 x 23ft (7 x 7 metre) monumental *Grand Entrance* of the new Finance Ministry at the Quai de Bercy, on the theme of *Fruits of the Earth*. In this sometimes mannerist repetition of subjects, styles and techniques, his figures - with angelic faces, bandaged like mummies, tucked into cradles like the basket in which Moses floated on the Nile - seem to echo the emblems, ornaments and objects of the Jewish tradition of his childhood in the St-Paul quarter of Paris. Commissions for monumental works compelled him to move away from reclining figures and create upright forms, a change that made him abandon his habitual methods, especially that of working hollowed-out forms, so that now he had to use armatures. This produced a renewal of subjects, if not of style, in the *Monument to Jean Moulin*, the *Adam and Eve* series and the *Dormition* planned for the Provins tympanum. In these the *Sleepers* awake, stand up, talk to each other and suffer. The basic constant of his work, transcending the renewal of themes demanded by commissions for monuments, is the hieratic and mysterious impassibility of sleep, or of its close neighbour, interior recollection. Sleep exposes the fragility of life, as does the fragility of his terracotta with its chiselled layers, as brittle as glass.

He did not show much work in collective exhibitions, as his pieces were too fragile, but he exhibited at the Salon de Mai from 1966, and in 1979 at the Budapest *Biennale*, where he was awarded a prize. Mainly, he showed his work in solo exhibitions both abroad and in Paris. These shows included; 1960, 1961, Rome; 1964, 1965, Paris; 1966, Oslo, Cologne; 1974, 1975, Paris; 1977, Marseilles, Brussels, the Botrop and Essen museums in Germany and Paris at the exhibition *Ateliers d'aujourd'hui* (*Studios Today*) at the Pompidou Centre; 1978, Brussels; 1979, 1980, 1981 and subsequently at the Galerie Albert Loeb, Paris; 1980, New York; 1981, Washington, Brussels; 1983 a large exhibition in the museum at Troyes; 1986, La Rochelle; 1988, the Herzliya Museum in Israel, and the Cambrai Museum. In 1990, the Galerie Gilbert Trigano exhibited a collection of his works at the Paris FIAC (Foire Internationale d'Art Contemporain). In 1993, the Tessé museum in Le Mans put on a display of his sculptures and drawings. One of the posthumous exhibitions of his work was a show in 2001 at the Paris Museum of Jewish Art and History.

BIBLIOGRAPHY:

Clair, Jean, *Ateliers d'aujourd'hui*, exhibition catalogue, Éd. du Centre Georges-Pompidou, Paris, 1977. Chabert, P./Pleynet, Marcelin/Lascault, Gilbert, *Jeanclos*, exhibition catalogue, Musée d'Art moderne, Troyes, 1983. *Jeanclos-Mossé: terres cuites et dessins*, exhibition catalogue, Musée d'Art Moderne, Troyes, 1983. This, Bernard, *Jeanclos*, exhibition catalogue, Gal. Albert Loeb, Paris, 1984. Lascault, Gilbert, *Jeanclos*, exhibition catalogue, Centre culturel de l'Yonne, Avallon, 1985. Mollard, Claude/Foucart, Bruno/Pleynet, Marcelin, *Jeanclos. Le tympan de Saint-Ayoul*, exhibition catalogue, Maison de la Culture, La Rochelle, La Différence, Paris, 1986. Le Bot, Marc, *Jeanclos*, exhibition catalogue, Gal. Albert Loeb, Paris, 1987. Chabla, Katherine, *Jeanclos: recent sculpture: October 14 - Novemeber 14, 1987*, exhibition catalogue, Claude Bernard Gallery, New York, 1987. Foucart, Bruno/Jeanclos, '*Entretien: la gloire du tympan*' in *Beaux-Arts Magazine*, periodical, Paris, 1987. *Georges Jean-*

clos: Musée de Cambrai, 27 novembre 1988-27 février 1989, exhibition catalogue, Musée de Cambrai, 1988. *Georges Jeanclos - Terres-cuites 1988*, exhibition catalogue, Gal. Albert Loeb, Paris, 1988 (good documentation). *L'Art Moderne à Marseille. La Collection du Musée Cantini*, exhibition catalogue, Musée Cantini, Marseilles, 1988. *Terres*, École Nationale Supériere des Beaux-Arts, Paris, 1991. *Georges Jeanclos*, exhibition catalogue, Musée de Tessé, Le Mans, 1993 (extensive documentation, artist's comments).

MUSEUMS AND GALLERIES:

LYONS (MBA) - MARSEILLES (Mus. Cantini): *Adama* (c. 1981) - NEW YORK (Jewish Mus.) - PARIS (FNAC) - PARIS (MAH du Judaïsme) - PARIS (MAMVP) - RHEIMS (FRAC Champagne-Ardenne) - SÉLESTAT (FRAC Alsace).

AUCTION RECORDS:

PARIS, 14 April 1986, *Figures in a Bed* (terracotta, 11¾ x 17¼ ins / 30 x 44 cm) FRF 11,000. PARIS, 15 June 1988, *Cécile* (1983, brown-patinated bronze, h. 16½ ins / 42 cm) FRF 17,000. PARIS, 20 Nov 1988, *Two Sleepers* (c. 1980-1981, terracotta, 9 x 19¾ x 11 ins / 22 x 50 x 28 cm) FRF 32,000. PARIS, 30 Jan 1989, *Kamakura* (1984, terracotta, 11 x 21¼ x 12½ ins / 27 x 54 x 32 cm) FRF 33,000. PARIS, 22 May 1989, *Sleeping Child* (terracotta, 17¼ x 11¾ ins / 44 x 30 cm) FRF 36,000. PARIS, 26 Sept 1989, *Couple* (1989, terracotta, 17¾ x 9 x 14¼ ins / 45 x 23 x 36 cm) FRF 32,000. PARIS, 22 Dec 1992, *Children* (terracotta, h. 29 ins / 73.5 cm) FRF 31,000. PARIS, 25 June 1993, *Two Sleepers* (terracotta, 9¼ x 17 x 8¼ ins / 23.5 x 43 x 21 cm) FRF 15,500. PARIS, 26 June 1995, *Jacob Wrestling with the Angel* (1990, terracotta, 22 x 19 x 5½ ins / 55 x 48 x 14 cm) FRF 20,000. PARIS, 29-30 June 1995, *Meditation* (terracotta, h. 98½ ins / 250 cm, diam. 17¾ ins/45 cm) FRF 32,000. PARIS, 29 April 1997, *Couple* (1994, terracotta, h. 9½ ins / 24 cm) FRF 16,000. PARIS, 22 March 1998, *Sleeper* (1973, terracotta, 7¾ x 18 x 9 ins / 20 x 46 x 23 cm) FRF 18,000. PARIS, 23 June 1999, *Untitled* (terracotta, 24 x 26x18 ins / 62 x 65x45 cm) FRF 29,000. PARIS, 27 Oct 2000, *Sabra and Chatilla* (terracotta, 33 x 15x14 ins / 85 x 38x35 cm) FRF 71,000. PARIS, 3 Dec 2001, *Kamakura* (brown and black patinated bronze, 21 x 20x12 ins / 54 x 51x30 cm) FRF 62,000. PARIS, 17 June 2002, *Traveller's Tree* (1990, black patinated bronze, h. 26 ins / 64 cm) EUR 9,000. PARIS, 17 June 2002, *Tree of Life* (1987, black patinated bronze, h. 23 ins / 58 cm, w. 24 ins/61 cm) EUR 10,000. PARIS, 9 Dec 2003, *Cecile* (bronze, 17 x 8x5 ins / 42 x 20x13 cm) EUR 5,200. PARIS, 9 Dec 2003, *Untitled* (c. 1980, terracotta, 24 x 20x18 ins / 62 x 52x45 cm) EUR 6,000. PARIS, 4 Aug 2004, *Kamakura* (patinated bronze, h. 12 ins / 31 cm, w. 24 ins/70 cm) EUR 12,000.

JEANDEL, Charles François

French, 19th century.

Born 9 September 1859, in Limoges.

Painter.

Charles Jeandel was a pupil of Maignan and a member of the Société des Artistes Français from 1889 onwards, featuring at its Salon.

JEANDEL, F. A.

French, 18th century.

Active in Sens in 1790.

Engraver.

Jeandel engraved the *Coat-of-Arms* and cipher of the Marquis de Chambonas.

JEANDON, Jean Jacques Adolphe

French, 19th century.

Portrait painter.

Jean Jeandon exhibited portraits at the Paris Salon in 1831 and 1849.

JEANDOT, René

French, 20th century.

Painter. Landscapes.

AUCTION RECORDS:

PARIS, 5 June 1944, *Landscape*, FRF 1,600; *Flowers*, FRF 3,000.

JEANÈS, Sigismond Jean Ernest

French, 19th - 20th century.

Born 1863, in Nancy.

Painter, watercolourist. Landscapes.

S. J. E. Jeanès, a self-taught painter, studied the great masters in Italian museums. His watercolours and light-coloured tempera paintings were inspired by the Alps, especially the Dolomites, and by Venice. In about 1925 he painted one of the columns of the brasserie *La Coupole* in Montparnasse. In 1906, he began to exhibit work in the Salon d'Automne and Salon des Indépendants and in solo shows.

AUCTION RECORDS:

PARIS, 28 March 1919, *The Cathedral* (watercolour) FRF 800. PARIS, 8 March 1943, *Croda di Lago* (watercolour) FRF 260. PARIS, 27 Nov 1946, *Valley at Longueil*, FRF 600. PARIS, 28 Nov 1995, *Snow at Night in the Tyrol* (watercolour, 23½ x 15¾ ins / 60 x 40 cm) FRF 9,500; *Beautiful Mountains* (oil on panel, 46 x 31½ ins / 116 x 80 cm) FRF 6,200.

JEANJEAN, Marcel

French, 20th century.

Born 31 January 1893, in Sète.

Painter, humorist artist, illustrator.

In 1915, during World War I, Marcel Jeanjean created the first newspaper of the trenches, *Le Canard poilu* (*Other Ranks' Rag*). In 1919, he published a book of pictures, *Sous les cocardes* (*Wearing the Cockade*), reissued in 1964. He collaborated on an illustrated edition of the complete works of Rabelais, and also illustrated the poems of François Villon, Daudet's *Lettres de mon Moulin* and various lively medieval works. Many of his paintings deal with the subject of aviation.

MUSEUMS AND GALLERIES:

LE BOURGET (Mus. de l'Air et de l'Espace): several paintings.

JEANKELOWITCH. See **JEANCLOS Georges**

JEANLIN, Micheline

French, 20th century.

Born 6 July 1929, in Herblay (Val-d'Oise).

Painter, illustrator.

Micheline Jeanlin gained her diploma in drawing in Paris in 1948, and in 1949 began to work at the Académie Julian. From 1948 to 1953 she exhibited in Paris at the Salon des Artistes Français and the Salon d'Hiver, and then until 1974 in salons in the outskirts of the city. Later, she retired to the Côte d'Azur, and showed work in Cannes and Antibes. She illustrated documentary works, and as a specialist in archaeology she was curator of the archaeological museum in Dijon.

JEANMAIRE, Édouard, or Jeanmarie

Swiss, 19th - 20th century.

Born 1847, in La Chaux-de-Fonds; died 13 April 1916, in La Chaux-de-Fonds.

Painter, engraver. Genre scenes, landscapes, animals.

Edouard Jeanmaire's body of work is generally regarded as belonging to the artists around Geneva and Neuchâtel. He received an honourable mention at the Exposition Universelle in Paris in 1900.

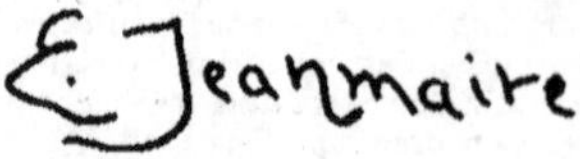

MUSEUMS AND GALLERIES:

BERN: *Forest Interior, La Joux-Perret; Late Autumn in Chasseral* - GENEVA (MAH): *Spring in Hermance; Fir Tree Wood* - NEUCHÂTEL: *Pastures at La Joux-Perret; Thonon; Street in Old*

Sion; Pastoral Calm; Alone in the Forest of La Joux-Perret - SOLOTHURN: *View of La Joux-Perret.*
AUCTION RECORDS:
COLOGNE, 24 March 1972, *View of Lake Neuchâtel*, DEM 4,400. BERN, 22 Oct 1976, *Coming out of Church* (1908, oil on canvas, 31 x 19 1/4 ins / 79 x 49 cm) CHF 2,000. LONDON, 20 March 1981, *Landscape of Combe-Varin, Sagne Valley* (1886, oil on canvas, 15 x 23 ins / 38 x 58.5 cm) GBP 1,900. LONDON, 10 Oct 1986, *Livestock in an Alpine Landscape* (oil on canvas, 27 1/4 x 39 ins / 69.2 x 99 cm) GBP 2,800. LONDON, 17 March 1993, *Cows Grazing* (oil on canvas, 27 1/2 x 39 1/4 ins / 70 x 100 cm) GBP 3,220.

JEANMOUGIN, Alfred Pierre Joseph
French, 19th century.
Born 19th century, in Lure (Haute-Saône).
Painter. Genre scenes, landscapes.
Alfred Jeanmougin studied under Gérôme and Petitjean and featured at the Salon of the Société des Artistes Français.
MUSEUMS AND GALLERIES:
CHARTRES: *View of a Church* - GRAY: *Street in Chaudefontaine.*
AUCTION RECORDS:
PARIS, 23 April 1945, *Mountain Torrent*, FRF 450. NEW YORK, 17 Jan 1990, *Conscripts* (1887, oil on canvas, 47 3/4 x 79 1/2 ins / 121.3 x 201.9 cm) USD 6,600. NEW YORK, 21 May 1991, *Farm Surroundings* (oil on canvas, 44 1/2 x 64 1/2 ins / 113 x 164 cm) USD 1,980.

JEANNE, Alain
French, 20th century.
Born 24 June 1945, in Falaise.
Engraver.
Alain Jeanne studied at the École des Beaux-Arts in Caen and at the engraving workshop at the École des Beaux-Arts in Paris. He mainly does burin engravings or etchings. He exhibits at the Salon de la Gravure (Engraving Exhibition) in Bayeux, where he has been a prize-winner.

JEANNE, Roger
French, 20th century.
Died June 1986.
Painter. Still-lifes.
Roger Jeanne studied classical art and painted nothing but still-lifes, with objects, fruit and so on, using exact and meticulous traditionalist methods. He showed work in numerous suburban Paris salons, where he won prizes and awards, as well as in salons in Paris - Salon des Artistes Français, the Salon de l'École Française and Salon d'Hiver, to all of which he belonged.

JEANNE-DENISE
French, 19th century.
Active in Paris.
Painter. Animals.
Jeanne-Denise was an associate of and featured at the Salon of the Société Nationale des Beaux-Arts.

JEANNE-JULIEN, Henry
French, 19th century.
Painter.
Henry Jeanne-Julien exhibited religious and genre subjects, notably sourced in Brittany, at the 1843, 1845 and 1848 Paris Salons.

JEANNENEY, François Victor
French, 19th century.
Born 9 April 1832, in Besançon; died 22 December 1885, in Vesoul (Haute-Saône).
Painter. Landscapes.
Jeanneney worked with Gleyre and featured at the Paris Salon from 1855 to 1867. He founded the Georges Garret museum at Vesoul.
MUSEUMS AND GALLERIES:
BESANÇON: *Right Bank of the Doubs Before the Construction of the Strasbourg Bridge* - VESOUL (Mus. Georges-Garret).
AUCTION RECORDS:
PARIS, 20 May 1980, *Anglers on the Bank of the Canal* (oil on canvas, 37 x 65 1/4 ins / 94 x 166 cm) FRF 17,000. ZURICH, 14 May 1983, *Hunting* (1866, oil on card, 31 1/2 x 22 3/4 ins / 80 x 58 cm) CHF 2,800. LONDON, 7 April 2000, *La Pharmacie de l'Abbeye* (oil on canvas, 31 x 42 ins / 80 x 106 cm) GBP 3,000.

JEANNEQUIN DE LIMBOURG.
See **LIMBOURG Pol**

JEANNERAT, Carlo
Italian, 20th century.
Born 25 June 1875, in Bologna.
Painter, miniaturist. Portraits.
Jeannerat studied in Bologna and Vienna and worked in Berlin and Paris.

JEANNERET, Blaise
Swiss, 20th century.
Born 12 July 1897, in Cressier (Neuchâtel); died November 1988, in Cressier.
Painter.
Blaise Jeanneret, son of the painter Gustave Jeanneret, studied architecture at the federal institute of technology in Zurich, completing his studies in 1922. He moved to France, first to Arras and St-Quentin, and later to Paris, where he remained until the outbreak of World War II. While continuing to practice as an architect, he followed courses under Roger Bissière at the Académie Ranson, and it was there that in 1925 he first exhibited. Jeanneret soon became firm friends with Bissière. He returned to Switzerland and in 1951 he moved into the house he had lived in as a child and took over the studio formerly occupied by his father.

From a very early age, Blaise Jeanneret built a personal vision of the world around him, searching for the reality behind appearances and exploring his own deepest emotions in a bid to convey them on canvas. His technique favours permutation after permutation of dots, lines, networks and interlocking puzzle-like patterns, which are assembled to create dream-like and frequently amusing harmonies. His painting is so facile that it takes on a child-like quality. Indeed, throughout his life, Blaise Jeanneret retained this ability to live his life and paint his paintings with all the composure and easy grace that typifies an enduring sense of childhood.

Jeanneret exhibited solo on numerous occasions at various venues in Switzerland, Italy and France. The Musée des Beaux-Arts in Neuchâtel mounted a tribute exhibition in 1985
BIBLIOGRAPHY:
Kuenzi, André, *'Jeanneret'* in *Gazette de Lausanne*, periodical, Lausanne, 1953. Delessert, Étienne, *'Blaise Jeanneret'* in *Ecritures 14*, Éd. Bertil Galland, Lausanne, 1978. Allmen, Pierre von, *Hommage à Blaise Jeanneret - soixante années de peinture*, Musée des Beaux-Arts, Neuchâtel, 1985. Monnier-Raball, Jacques, *'Blaise Jeanneret ou l'Enfance retrouvée'* in *Cahiers protestants* no. 3, periodical, Lausanne, June 1985.

JEANNERET, Charles Édouard. See **LE CORBUSIER**

JEANNERET, Claude
Swiss, 20th century.
Born 1886, in La Chaux-de-Fonds.
Engraver. Ex-libris plates.
Claude Jeanneret lived and worked in Biel in the canton of Bern. From 1912 he produced wood and linoleum engravings, and numerous hand-coloured ex libris devices.

JEANNERET, Frédéric
Swiss, 19th century.

Born 1793, in Travers; died February 1849, in Neuchâtel.
Painter, draughtsman.

Though his own artistic ability was small and he was principally a drawing master, Jeanneret deserves much credit for his efforts to popularise artistic ideas in Switzerland. He was the promoter of the first exhibitions in Neuchâtel, and contributed to the establishment of a large number of museums.

MUSEUMS AND GALLERIES:
NEUCHÂTEL: *Portrait* (drawing); *Same subject* (drawing).

JEANNERET, Gustave
Swiss, 19th - 20th century.
Born 1847, in Môtiers; died 1927.
Painter, potter. Mountainscapes.

Gustave Jeanneret studied initially in Switzerland before moving in 1867 to Paris, where he worked as a furniture designer in order to earn a living. At the same time, he studied painting as and when he could, and was particularly drawn to the socially-conscious Realists of the 19th century such as Millet, Courbet and Bastien-Lepage. He then returned to Switzerland and began painting landscapes, rapidly emerging as the leading painter of this type of painting in the Neuchâtel/Fribourg region. He exhibited in Neuchâtel.

Gustave Jeanneret was entrusted with supervision of the Swiss fine arts section at the Exposition Universelle in Paris in 1889. He was awarded a bronze medal at the Exposition Universelle of 1900. Although Jeanneret had visited Venice in 1884 there is little evidence of a Venetian influence in his work. He finally retired to the Swiss Alps, where he painted a large number of the region's most spectacular glacial landscapes.

MUSEUMS AND GALLERIES:
GENEVA (MAH): *First Ray of Sun*; *Vintners* - GRESSIER: *Wine Press* - LA CHAUX-DE-FONDS: *Lauterbrunnen Valley* - NEUCHÂTEL: *Last Blooms*; *Little Glass*; *Pastoral Calm*; *Seasons of the Vine*; *Melancholy*; *Madame Guillou*; *Young Girl* - SOLOTHURN: *Working the Vineyard*.

AUCTION RECORDS:
BERN, 25 Nov 1976, *View of Fribourg* (oil on canvas, 30 1/4 x 46 ins / 77 x 117 cm) CHF 1,700. ZURICH, 6 June 1980, *Peasant Woman in a Wooded Landscape* (oil on canvas, 30 x 45 1/2 ins / 76.5 x 115.5 cm) CHF 2,000.

JEANNES, Michel
French, 20th - 21st century.
Born 1958, in Casablanca.
Engraver.

Michel Jeannes has taken part in collective exhibitions, including: *Le Bois Gravé en Chine et en Occident* (*Wood Carving in China and the West*), at the Cultural Centre in Boulogne-Billancourt, 1987 and *Gravures Contemporaines en Relief* (*Contemporary Relief Engravings*), at the Musée du Dessin et de l'Estampe Originale, Gravelines, 1987.

BIBLIOGRAPHY:
Jean-François Blanc, Michel Jeannes, Charles Pouderoux, exhibition catalogue, Fonds régional d'Art contemporain d'Auvergne, Clermont-Ferrand, 1988.

JEANNEST, Emile
British, 19th century.
Born 1813, in Paris; died 1857, in Birmingham.
Draughtsman, modeller.

Emile Jeannest was the son of Louis Jeannest. After training under Delacroix, he left for England in or about 1845 or 1846. He spent two years in London before working for Herbert Mireton in Stoke on Trent and for the Fine Art Department of Elkington's Works in Birmingham where he created many interesting models.

JEANNEST, Louis François
French, 19th century.
Born 19th century, in Paris.
Sculptor.

Louis François Jeannest studied under Rolland. Between 1812 and 1815 he exhibited medallions, wax models, ivories and bronze reproductions at the Paris Salon. He appears to have worked in industry.

MUSEUMS AND GALLERIES:
ANGERS: *Henri IV on Horseback* (bronze, after M. Brunot).

JEANNET. See **GIOVANNI da Milano**

JEANNIN, also called Jean de Troyes
French, 14th century.
Sculptor (wood).

Jeannin worked in Troyes from 1345 to 1370. Another sculptor of this name is recorded as working at Troyes cathedral between 1420 and 1428. He produced a wooden sculpture of an angel under the organ, and repaired the statues of St Peter and St Paul on the old portal. He also worked for the churches of Ste-Madeleine and St-Urbain.

JEANNIN, Blanche
French, 20th century.
Born 1929.
Painter. Figures, portraits, scenes with figures.

Blanche Jeannin studied with Maurice Denis and Georges Desvallières and then at the École des Beaux-Arts in Paris. She painted events in Parisian life and portraits of numerous personalities. In 1947 she began exhibiting in Paris at the Salon des Indépendants and the Salon des Artistes Français, where she won a gold medal in 1950. In 1958, she began putting on solo exhibitions of her paintings in the Galerie Marcel Bernheim in Paris.

JEANNIN, Frédéric Émile
French, 19th - 20th century.
Born 29 December 1859, in Paris; died 10 February 1925, in Paris.
Engraver (etching).

Jeannin, a pupil of Champollion and Boilvin, became a member of the Société des Artistes Français in 1887 and showed his work in the society's salon. He won an honourable mention in 1887, a third-class medal in 1895, an honourable mention at the 1900 Exposition Universelle, second-class in 1905, and first-class in 1909. He also served on the panel of judges for engraving and showed work at the 1910 exhibition in Brussels.

JEANNIN, Georges
French, 19th - 20th century.
Born 1841, in Paris; died 10 December 1925.
Painter. Still-lifes (flowers/fruit).

Georges Jeannin painted bouquets of flowers with sweeping brush strokes and rich, thick impasto. He exhibited regularly at the Paris Salon from 1868. He became a member of the Société des Artistes Français in 1878 and won a third-class medal in the same year, a second-class medal in 1888 and a bronze at the 1889 Exposition Universelle in Paris. He was president of the Society of Flower Painters and was made a Chevalier of the Légion d'Honneur in 1903.

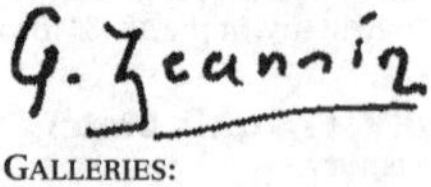

MUSEUMS AND GALLERIES:
BÉZIERS: *Grapes and Poppies*; *Reliefs of the Feast of Samson and Delilah* - ÉPINAL: *Basket of Flowers* - MULHOUSE: *Bunch of Red Roses* - NANCY: *Apples* - PARIS (Mus. du Petit Palais): *Flowers* - ROCHEFORT: *Basket of Flowers* - ROUEN: *Flowers* - THE HAGUE (Mus. Mesdag): *Basket of Grapes* - VALENCIENNES: *Apples and Pears*.

AUCTION RECORDS:
PARIS, 25 June 1896, *Gladioli*, FRF 250. NEW YORK, 1900-1903, *Choice Fruit*, USD 145. PARIS, 27 Jan 1943, *Roses*, FRF 9,300. PARIS, 10 Dec 1954, *Basket of Flowers*, FRF 37,500. PARIS, 5 Nov 1971, *Still-life* (oil on canvas, 44 1/2 x 57 ins / 113 x 145 cm) FRF 3,500. VIENNA, 19 Sept 1972, *Bunch of Flowers*, ATS 15,000. ZURICH, 8 Nov 1974, *Garden in Bloom* (1916) CHF 5,800. BERN, 22 Oct 1976, *Still-life with Flowers* (oil on canvas, 22 x 17 ins / 55 x 43 cm) CHF 4,000. HEIDELBERG, 21 Oct 1977, *Bunch of Roses* (oil on panel, 14 3/4 x 18 ins / 37.5 x 46 cm) DEM 2,800. LE HAVRE, 20 June 1980, *Still-life with Flowers and Fruit* (oil on canvas, 28 3/4 x 23 1/2 ins / 73 x 60 cm) FRF 20,000. PARIS, 27 June 1983, *Flowered Throw* (oil on canvas, 22 x 32 3/4 ins / 56 x 83 cm) FRF 18,000. LONDON, 10 Oct 1986, *Still-life with Flowers and Fruit* (oil on canvas, 15 1/2 x 33 1/2 ins / 39.5 x 85 cm) GBP 5,500. COLOGNE, 27 March 1987, *Still-life with Bunch of Flowers* (oil on canvas, 16 1/4 x 13 ins / 41 x 33 cm) DEM 12,000. CALAIS, 8 Nov 1987, *Still-life with Fruit* (oil on canvas, 14 1/2 x 22 ins / 37 x 56 cm) FRF 20,000. CALAIS, 28 Feb 1988, *Bunch of Roses* (oil on canvas, 22 x 18 ins / 55 x 46 cm) FRF 42,000. MORLAIX, 25 April 1988, *Bunch of Flowers* (oil on canvas, 24 x 18 ins / 61 x 46 cm) FRF 8,000. CALAIS, 3 July 1988, *Bunch of Flowers* (oil on canvas, 18 x 22 ins / 46 x 55 cm) FRF 35,000. PARIS, 18 April 1989, *Tall Vase of Dahlias* (two oils on canvas, 46 x 32 ins / 116 x 81 cm) FRF 33,000. PARIS, 5 June 1989, *Rose Throw* (oil on canvas, 21 3/4 x 32 1/2 ins / 55.5 x 82.5 cm) FRF 22,000. COLOGNE, 20 Oct 1989, *Still-life with Flowers* (oil on canvas, 25 1/2 x 21 1/4 ins / 65 x 54 cm) DEM 5,500. MONACO, 3 Dec 1989, *Still-life with Flowers and Fruit* (1911, oil on canvas, 19 1/4 x 23 1/2 ins / 49 x 60 cm) FRF 27,750. LA FLÈCHE, 24 June 1990, *The Gardener's Place* (oil on canvas, 45 1/4 x 57 3/4 ins / 115 x 147 cm) FRF 132,000. PARIS, 14 July 1990, *Little Girl with Basket* (oil on canvas, 13 3/4 x 9 ins / 35 x 22 cm) FRF 95,000. PARIS, 12 Oct 1990, *Still-life with Apples* (oil on canvas, 25 1/2 x 32 ins / 65 x 81 cm) FRF 32,000. VERSAILLES, 25 Nov 1990, *Bunch of Roses* (1910, oil on canvas, 22 x 18 ins / 55 x 46 cm) FRF 39,000. CALAIS, 20 Oct 1991, *Still-life with Peaches and Grapes* (1920, oil on canvas, 25 1/2 x 36 1/4 ins / 65 x 92 cm) FRF 23,000. PARIS, 5 Nov 1991, *Basket of Roses* (oil on canvas, 28 3/4 x 35 ins / 73 x 89 cm) FRF 27,000. CALAIS, 5 April 1992, *Vase of Roses* (1919, oil on canvas, 18 x 15 ins / 46 x 38 cm) FRF 11,200. PARIS, 10 Feb 1993, *Bunch of Flowers* (oil on canvas, 35 1/2 x 45 3/4 ins / 90 x 116.5 cm) FRF 22,000. LE TOUQUET, 14 Nov 1993, *Branches of Lilac* (oil on canvas, 16 1/4 x 22 ins / 41 x 55 cm) FRF 15,500. NEW YORK, 16 Feb 1994, *Still-life with Dahlias* (oil on canvas/synthetic resin, 35 x 45 1/2 ins / 88.9 x 115.6 cm) USD 9,200. PARIS, 17 June 1994, *Vase of Roses* (oil on canvas, 15 x 18 1/2 ins / 38 x 47 cm) FRF 12,000. CALAIS, 11 Dec 1994, *Basket of Pansies* (oil on canvas, 19 3/4 x 24 ins / 50 x 61 cm) FRF 27,000. NEW YORK, 16 Feb 1995, *Barrowful of Flowers* (1878, oil on canvas, 55 x 71 ins / 139.7 x 180.3 cm) USD 59,700. LONDON, 12 June 1996, *Basket of Flowers* (oil on canvas, 23 1/2 x 28 3/4 ins / 59.5 x 73 cm) GBP 8,050. PARIS, 26 June 1996, *Still-life with Basket of Apples* (oil on canvas, 25 1/2 x 32 ins / 65 x 81.5 cm) FRF 22,000. NEW YORK, 18-19 July 1996, *Vase of Flowers* (oil on canvas, 21 1/4 x 32 ins / 54 x 81 cm) USD 4,600. NEW YORK, 9 Jan 1997, *Basket of Apples* (oil on canvas, 26 x 32 ins / 65.1 x 81 cm) USD 10,062. PARIS, 27 May 1997, *Bunch of Flowers* (oil on canvas, 28 3/4 x 23 1/2 ins / 73 x 60 cm) FRF 56,000.

JEANNIN, Maurice

French, 19th century.
Born in Paris; died 1907, in Paris.
Portrait painter.

Maurice Jeannin studied under Tony Robert-Fleury, Bouguereau and Jules Lefebvre, and featured at the Salon of the Société des Artistes Français. He was awarded an honourable mention in 1895, a third class medal in 1898 and an honourable mention in 1900 (Exposition Universelle).

AUCTION RECORDS:
PARIS, 14 March 1931, *Portrait of an Engraver*, FRF 250.

JEANNIN, René Félicien

French, 19th century.
Born 19th century, in Paris.
Sculptor.

René Félicien Jeannin featured at the Salon of the Société des Artistes Français, receiving an honourable mention in 1898.

JEANNIOT, Pierre Alexandre

French, 19th century.
Born 28 May 1826, in Champlitte (Haute-Saône); died 1892, in Vesoul (Haute-Saône).
Painter, pastellist. Portraits, genre scenes, landscapes.

Pierre Alexandre Jeanniot studied under Diday and Calame in Geneva from 1847 to 1849. He was a professor of art and painting and then head of Dijon's École des Beaux-Arts.

From 1852 to 1973 he exhibited scenes and portraits at the Paris Salon. He also contributed pieces of his own to exhibitions in Dijon in 1849 and 1858, in Besançon in 1862, 1868, 1870 and 1877 and in Lons-le-Saunier in 1876. His works have been included in collective, posthumous exhibitions, including, in 1996: *Les Années romantiques, la peinture française de 1815 à 1850* (*The Romantic Era: French Painting from 1815 to 1850*) at the Musée des Beaux-Arts in Nantes and the Galeries Nationales of the Grand Palais in Paris; and in 2001: *Paysages de Bourgogne, de Corot à Laronze* (*Burgundian Landscapes, from Corot to Laronze*), at the Musée des Beaux-Arts in Dijon.

Jeanniot painted numerous views of Switzerland, of Savoy and of Burgundy. He is also credited with pastels, notably portraits, and a series of plant and animal studies. Possessed with a thorough knowledge of nature, he excelled at the realistic depiction of plants, trees and foliage.

BIBLIOGRAPHY:
Les Années romantiques, la peinture française de 1815 à 1850, exhibition catalogue, Musée des Beaux-Arts, Nantes, Galeries nationales du Grand Palais, Paris, 1996. Barthélémy, Sophie/Tran, Catherine, *Paysages de Bourgogne, de Corot à Laronze*, exhibition catalogue, Musée des Beaux-Arts, Dijon, 2001.

MUSEUMS AND GALLERIES:
DIJON (MBA): *Landscape*; *Countryside Around Geneva* (1849); *View of Dijon Castle: St Bénigne Tower* (c. 1860, drawing); *View of Dijon Castle: St Bénigne Tower* (1862, oil on canvas); *Entrance to Dijon Castle* (1862, oil on canvas); *View of Dijon Castle-Safety Gate* (1862, oil on canvas) - NANCY: *Annecy Lake* - TOUL: *Plain of Dammartin-les-Toul*.

AUCTION RECORDS:
PARIS, 1882, *Reservists*, FRF 3,000. ZURICH, 5 May 1972, *Wooded Countryside*, CHF 4,600. LONDON, 1 Feb 1979, *Landscape of Switzerland* (1853, oil on canvas, 14 x 13 ins / 35.5 x 33 cm) GBP 900. NEW YORK, 18 Sept 1981, *Alpine Lake* (1873, oil on canvas, 32 x 48 ins / 81 x 121 cm) USD 2,200. LINDAU, 4 May 1983, *Still-life with Flowers* (oil on canvas, 27 1/2 x 33 1/2 ins / 70 x 85 cm) DEM 4,200. ZURICH, 14 June 2004, *Landscape* (oil on canvas, 30 x 46 ins / 75 x 117 cm) CHF 4,800.

JEANNIOT, Pierre Georges

French, 19th - 20th century.
Born 2 July 1848, in Geneva, to French parents; died 1934.
Painter, watercolourist, draughtsman, illustrator. Portraits, genre scenes, landscapes.

Pierre Georges Jeanniot was taught by his father Pierre-Alexandre Jeanniot, who for a long time was director of the art college in Dijon. He embarked on a military career, but exhibited watercolours as early as 1872 at the Paris Salon. In 1873, he exhibited his first oil painting there, *Le Vernan at Nass-sous-Ste-Anne*, and continued to show work there regularly. In 1881, having reached the rank of captain, he left the army in order to work full time as an artist. He settled in Paris, where he won an honourable mention in the Salon of 1882, a third-class medal in 1884 and a silver in 1889 and 1900. His was an assured and independent mind, and so he joined the Société Nationale des Beaux-Arts as soon as it was set up in 1890. He was made a Chevalier of the Légion d'Honneur.

The earliest works he sent in consisted mainly of scenes of military life. Later he was best known for his scenes of fashionable women in Paris at the time of the Belle Époque and on the beaches of the then very new seaside resorts, and for his views of race-meetings, all of these providing valuable sociological evidence. He also illustrated many literary works, among them Maupassant's *Contes choisis* (1886), *Germinie Lacerteux* (1886), Goncourt's *La fille Élisa* (1895), and Daudet's *Tartarin de Tarascon* (1887). He collaborated on the illustration of Victor Hugo's *Les Misérables* in 1887 and also illustrated Zola's *La Débâcle* and *La Curée* (*The Rat-Race*) of 1893-1894, Octave Mirbeau's *Le Calvaire* (*Calvary*) of 1901, Molière's *Le Misanthrope* in 1907, Balzac's *Les Paysans* (*The Peasants*) in 1911, *Les Liaisons dangereuses* by Laclos in 1917, as well as Voltaire's *Candide* and the *Voyage à St-Cloud* and other works. He was one of those who launched *La Vie Moderne* (*Modern Life*), and later he directed the *Journal amusant*. His drawing is vigorous and expressive, and his great strength lay in his brilliant depictions of the comedy of contemporary life.

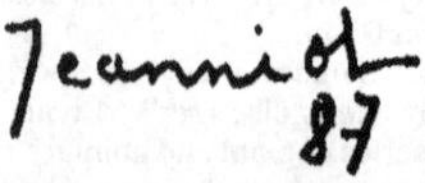

Bibliography:
Osterwalder, Marcus (ed.), *Dictionnaire des illustrateurs 1800-1914*, Ides et Calendes, Neuchâtel, 1989. Robichon, François, *L'Armée française vue par les peintres - 1870-1914*, Herscher, Paris, ministère de la Défense, Paris, 2000.

Museums and Galleries:
Alès: *An Old Couple* - Buenos Aires: *Woman Leaning on Her Elbows* - Nancy: *View near Diénay* - Oslo: *Water in a Garden* - Paris (MAMVP): *Air* (sketch) - Paris (MNAM-CCI): *Woman at Prayer; Five O'Clock; La Fallé; Portrait of the Artist* - Paris (Mus. Carnavalet): *Paris under the Commune*; four watercolours.

Auction records:
Versailles, 13 Feb 1977, *Polo Players* (1887, oil on canvas, 24$^{3}/_{4}$ x 31 ins / 63 x 79 cm) FRF 5,000. London, 23 June 1983, *The Place de la Concorde in Snow* (1888, watercolour heightened with gouache, 14$^{1}/_{4}$ x 17$^{3}/_{4}$ ins / 36 x 45 cm) GBP 500. London, 28 Nov 1985, *Café Scene* (1892, watercolour and pencil heightened with gouache, 19 x 23$^{1}/_{4}$ ins / 48 x 59 cm) GBP 2,800. New York, 21 May 1987, *At the Dressmaker's* (1901, oil on canvas, 20$^{3}/_{4}$ x 33 ins / 53 x 84 cm) USD 8,000. Paris, 22 June 1989, *Racing* (oil on panel, 11$^{3}/_{4}$ x 12$^{1}/_{4}$ ins / 30 x 31 cm) FRF 9,500. Paris, 30 Nov 1990, *Reading* (1906, oil on paper remounted on panel, 15$^{3}/_{4}$ x 17$^{1}/_{4}$ ins / 40 x 44 cm) FRF 6,800. New York, 15 Oct 1993, *Woman on a River Bank* (1908, oil on canvas, 28 x 36$^{1}/_{4}$ ins / 71 x 92 cm) USD 6,325. Paris, 9 Dec 1994, *Portrait of Edgar Degas* (1891, etching) FRF 3,500. Paris, 26 June 1995, *Polo Match* (1887, oil on canvas, 25$^{1}/_{4}$ x 31$^{1}/_{2}$ ins / 64 x 80 cm) FRF 100,000. Paris, 20 Nov 1995, *Galloping on the Racecourse* (oil on panel, 19$^{1}/_{4}$ x 25$^{1}/_{2}$ ins / 49 x 65 cm) FRF 35,000. Paris, 5 June 1997, *Polo Players* (1920, oil on canvas, 28$^{3}/_{4}$ x 36$^{1}/_{4}$ ins / 73 x 92 cm) FRF 40,000.

JEANNOT. See also **JEAN**

JEANNOT, Alfred
French, 19th century.
Born 19th century, in Paris.
Engraver (wood).
Alfred Jeannot studied under H Delaville. He was a member of the Société des Artistes Français from 1886 and featured at its Salons.

JEANNOT, Joseph Clément Maxime
French, 19th century.
Born 5 January 1855, in Ornans.
Painter, watercolourist. Landscapes.
Joseph Jeannot featured at the Salon of the Société des Artistes Français, receiving an honourable mention in 1905.

Museums and Galleries:
Paris (MAM): *Frozen Fairy Pool.*

Auction records:
Paris, 1898, *Landscape: Fontainebleau Forest*, FRF 200. Paris, 5 May 1927, *Undergrowth in Fontainebleau Forest* (watercolour) FRF 150.

JEANNOT DE TOUL. See **JEHAN de Toul**

JEANPIERRE, Auguste
French, 19th century.
Born 19th century, in Changy.
Engraver.
Auguste Jeanpierre studied under Bouchu and featured at the 1879 Paris Salon with an engraving entitled *Landscape*.

JEANRON, André
French, 19th century.
Born 19th century, in Paris.
Painter, engraver. Genre scenes, landscapes.
André Jeanron was the son and pupil of Philippe-Auguste. He also worked with Forster. He made his debut at the Paris Salon in 1864 and continued to feature there until 1870, exhibiting an etching entitled *Mills at Montmartre*, that final year.

JEANRON, Désirée Angéline
Maiden name: Sirey
French, 19th century.
Active in Paris.
Painter. History painting.
Désirée Angéline Jeanron exhibited *St Catherine of Alexandria* and *St John* at the 1844 and 1850 Paris Salons, respectively.

JEANRON, Philippe Auguste
French, 19th century.
Born 10 May 1809, in Boulogne; died 8 April 1877, in Comborn (Corrèze).
Painter, illustrator, art writer. Historical subjects, religious subjects, military subjects, portraits, genre scenes, scenes with figures, rustic scenes, landscapes, harbour scenes. Church decoration.
Philippe Auguste Jeanron studied under Souchon in Lille and then Sigalon in Paris. He made his debut at the Paris Salon in 1831, was awarded a second class medal in 1833 and exhibited further in 1848, 1850, 1852, 1853 and 1855.

Jeanron affiliated himself with the republican camp very early on and took part in the so-called 'trois Glorieuses' (Three Days of Revolution in July 1830, which put an end to Charles X's reign). However he was quickly disappointed by the regime that followed, opposed its institutions and founded, with Didron, *Liberty: Bulletin of the Arts*, which campaigned for freedom of the arts, but which folded in 1833.

He was a friend of Ledru-Rollin, whom he hid for 12 days at the Louvre during the aftermath of the radical republican protests of 13 June 1848. In turn, Ledru-Rollin made Jeanron director of the national museums, a post he retained until December 1850, when Ledru-Rollin was made minister within the provisional government of the Republic.

Jeanron was astutely active in his post, founding the Open Exhibition, which gave orders to previously snubbed artists such as Millet, Tassaert and Charles Jacque. He persuaded the Constituent Assembly to vote through a sum of two million francs for the decoration of the Apollo Gallery and repairs to other galleries within the Louvre and he commissioned Delacroix to decorate the ceiling of the Apollo. When he lost his post, he returned to the area where he was born around 1853-1855, then moved to Corrèze around 1859, just as he had done during the unrest of 1834, returning there for a third time, later in life, to die. He was made a member of the Légion d'Honneur in 1855 and became, from 1863 to 1869, director of the museum of Marseilles.

A republican by conviction, Jeanron exhibited *Young Patriots* at his first Paris Salon in 1831: it was a piece symbolising a populace which has been liberated as a result of the July 1830 uprising, but whose hopes are swiftly dashed. His 1833 piece on the same theme, *Paris Scene*, is not only a scene of misery, but also depicts the despair of the veterans of 1830 at seeing their victory snatched from them by the bourgeoisie. These pictures, with their sombre, dramatic tones clashing with lighter hues, take on a realist, romantic character, sometimes close in style to Delacroix.

Jeanron is also credited with the main decorations to the Chapel of the Virgin at the church of Chaillot, the restoration of the Chapel of the Virgin at St Sulpice, the Chapel of St Vincent-de-Paul at St Louis-en-l'Ile and *Christ the Consoler* at Ensisheim remand prison, in Alsace. He also illustrated Louis Blanc's *History of Ten Years*.

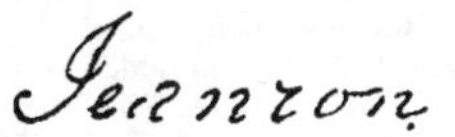

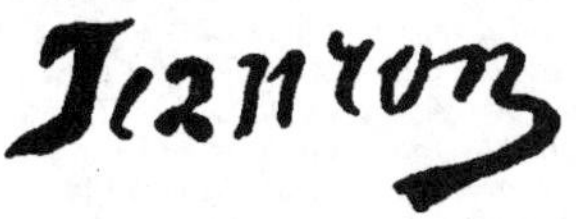

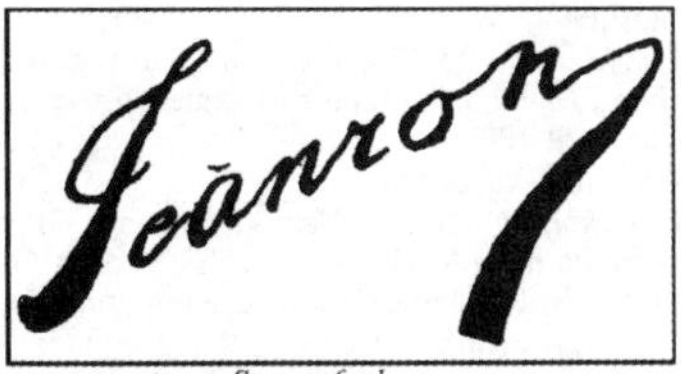

Stamp of sale

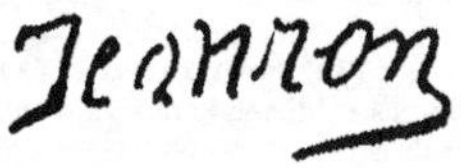

Bibliography:

Chaudonneret, Marie-Claude, *Les Années romantiques, la peinture française de 1815 à 1850*, exhibition catalogue, Musée des Beaux-Arts, Nantes, Galeries nationales du Grand Palais, Paris, 1996.

Museums and Galleries:

Aix-en-Provence: *At Ambleteuse Camp, August 1854* - Arras: *View of the Dam at Bezons* - Bagnères-de-Bigorre: *Marseilles Lighthouse* - Bayeux: *Island of Calypso* - Bayonne: *White Horse* - Caen (MBA): *Young Patriots* (1831); *Death of a Child* - Chalon-sur-Saône: *Ambleteuse Camp* - Chambéry: *Sestri, Near to Genoa* - Chartres: *Équilhem Camp, September 1854*; *Paris Scene* (1833) - Cherbourg: *View of Ambleteuse* - Douai: *Neap-tide at the Fort of Adreselles* - Le Mans: *Tintoretto and his Daughter* - Lille (MBA): *Peasants Listening to an Accordian Player an the Banks of the Great Lake of Aigue-Perse* (1834) - Montargis: *At the Seaside* - Roanne: *Maidservant in the Pigsty* - Rochefort: *Ambleteuse Coast* - Rouen: *Beheading of John the Baptist* (1846) - St-Étienne: *Zouaves at Melegnano* - St-Lô: *Notre Dame de la Garde at Marseilles* - Tours: *Location near Comborn* - Valence: *Catalans* - Versailles: *Mirabeau.*

Auction Records:

Paris, 12 May 1923, *Fishermen's Wives Gathering Wood on the Beach,* FRF 130. Paris, 24 Feb 1943, *Portrait of Buonarotti: Conspirator,* FRF 12,000. Paris, 14 June 1944, *Bacchanalia,* FRF 1,700. Paris, 18 March 1983, *Paris Scene: a July Hero* (oil on canvas, $38\frac{1}{2}$ x $51\frac{1}{2}$ ins / 98 x 130.5 cm) FRF 28,000. New York, 19 Jan 1995, *Penitent Magdalene* (watercolour/paper/paper, $8\frac{3}{4}$ x $11\frac{1}{2}$ ins / 22.2 x 29.2 cm) USD 2,587.

JEANS

British, 18th century.
Active in Edinburgh.
Sculptor.

Jeans exhibited at the Royal Academy in London from 1769 to 1771.

JEANSON, Alfred de

French, 19th century.
Active in Paris.
Painter.

Alfred de Jeanson was a member of the Société des Artistes Françaises from 1885 onwards and featured at its Salon.

JEANSON, Louise Esther J.

French, 19th century.
Born 19th century, in Paris.
Miniaturist.

Louise Esther J. Jeanson studied under Mme Latruffe-Colomb, Delattre, Humbert and Cuyer. She was a member of the Société des Artistes Français from 1909 onwards, receiving an honourable mention in 1910.

JEANSON, Marguerite Cécile Marie

French, 19th century.
Born 19th century, in Paris.
Miniaturist.

Marguerite Cécile Marie Jeanson studied under Thoret and Mme Debillemont-Chardon and featured at the Salon of the Société des Artistes Français.

JEANSSON, Carl

Swedish, 18th century.
Born to a family originally from Stockholm.
Active in Ystad and Göteborg.
Miniaturist.

JEANTET, Catherine

French, 20th - 21st century.
Born 1959, in Nîmes.
Engraver.

Catherine Jeantet was selected for the Grav'X prize at the Michèle Brouta Gallery, Paris in 1991.

JEANTET, Philippe

French, 20th century.
Painter (mixed media).
Kinetic Art, Cyber Art, Copy Art.

Philippe Jeantet produces abstract-kinetic numerical images on video screens.

Auction Records:

Paris, 13 April 1988, *Numerical Kinetic Image/Video Screen in a Metallic Structure* ($27\frac{1}{2}$ x 17 x $14\frac{1}{2}$ ins / 70 x 43 x 37 cm) FRF 17,000.

JEANTET, Pierre

French, 19th century.
Born 1807; died 1882.
Painter.

BIBLIOGRAPHY:
Les Années romantiques, la peinture française de 1815 à 1850, exhibition catalogue, Musée des Beaux-Arts, Nantes, Galeries nationales du Grand Palais, Paris, 1996.
MUSEUMS AND GALLERIES:
DIJON (MBA): *Self-portrait* (1848).

JEAUGON, Charles A.
French, 19th century.
Born 19th century, in Paris.
Engraver (wood).
Charles A Jeaugon was a member of the Société des Artistes Français and featured at its Salon, receiving a third class medal in 1884 and an honourable mention in 1900 (Exposition Universelle).

JEAURAT, Edme
French, 18th century.
Born 1688, in Vermenton (Yonne); died 1738, in Paris.
Engraver (burin).
Edme Jeaurat was the Elder brother of Étienne Jeaurat. He moved to Paris with his father, who is thought also to have been an engraver. Edme Jeaurat was apprenticed to Bernard Picart, whose style he adopted. In 1708, he published a small plate after Poussin: *Venus* and *Love*, followed by the *Abduction of Europa*, after Caliari, in 1709. At the age of 25 he departed for Holland, and devoted himself to a conscientious study of Vosterman the Elder and P. de Jode the Younger. On his return to Paris in 1715, he was the equal of the best burinists of his time, and M. Crozat employed him to engrave several paintings in his collection. Edme Jeaurat married Charlotte Le Clerc, the daughter of Sébastien Le Clerc the Elder and sister of Sébastien Le Clerc the Younger. Although he engraved a certain amount after the main masters, he devoted himself mainly to reproducing the works of his close friend Nicolas Vleughel, as well as of his father-in-law and his brother-in-law, and later, those of his brother Étienne. His work is considerable and includes more than 150 pieces, in all genres, which deserve to be collected together.

AUCTION RECORDS:
PARIS, 10 Dec 1923, *The Charlatan* (red chalk, heightened with white) FRF 3,900.

JEAURAT, Étienne, or Joras
French, 18th century.
Born 9 February 1699, in Vermenton, near Auxerre; died 14 December 1789, in Versailles.
Painter, draughtsman, illustrator. Mythological subjects, portraits, genre scenes, interiors with figures.
Étienne Jeaurat was orphaned very young. His brother, the engraver Edme Jeaurat, who was 10 years older, entrusted him to Nicolas Vleughel, a friend of Watteau. The latter's influence can be detected in several of Jeaurat's works. In 1724, Vleughel was appointed director of the Académie de Rome and took his pupil with him. After executing some amusing subjects from everyday life, Jeaurat turned his attention to historical subjects, and was admitted as an academician on 24 July 1733 with *Pyramus and Thisbe*. He exhibited for the first time at the Louvre in 1737, and continued to feature quite regularly at the Salon until 1769. In 1782, he also exhibited at the Salon de la Correspondance. Apart from director, he occupied all the posts in the Académie: assistant professor on 2 July 1737; professor, 6 July 1743; assistant education officer, 7 March 1761; chief education officer, 23 August 1765; chancellor, 24 February 1781. He was Painter to the King and, from 1767, Keeper of the King's Paintings at Versailles.

His success was considerable. Dating from the beginning of his career, several subjects after La Fontaine are worthy of mention: *Love and Folly* (1732), *The Ass Carrying Relics* (1736), *The Astrologer Who Fell into a Well*, *The Child and the Schoolmaster*, *The Drowned Woman* (1736), *Fortune and the Young Child*, *The Oyster and the Two Litigants* (1733), *The Mountain Which Gives Birth to a Mouse* (1736), *The Cobbler and the Financier* (1732). There are also compositions that his brother Edme engraved, such as: *Flirtatious Love* (1732), *Love, the Petty Master* (1732). Louis XV commissioned four paintings from him of the *Loves of Daphnis and Chloë*, which appeared at the Salon of 1745. He also executed for the tapestry works known as the Manufacture des Gobelins *A Village Wedding* (Salon of 1753), which Cozette and Audran executed and which Jeaurat painted in the style of Watteau, as also the *Love of Hunting* and *The Love of Wine* (1741), and *A Village Fair* (1755). Jeaurat enjoyed good living, and was a great friend of Piron, Panard, Collé and Vadé. One of his best works was a group portrait of the first three.

Jeaurat painted accurately, in the style of the period. It is only in giving full rein to his vigour as a painter of manners that he showed himself to be a real artist. He certainly did not possess the power of expression of Chardin, and there is nothing special about his interiors, such as: *The Woman Who Has Recently Given Birth*, *The Convalescent*, *The Gout Sufferer* (Salon of 1743) and *A Convalescent Woman* (1769). Chardin easily eclipses him in this area. However, his charm and skill come to the fore when he paints the picturesque aspects of Paris street life of the period, his paintings amounting to precious social documents. *The Place Maubert* (1753), *The Police Raid*, *Moving House* (1755), *Carnival in the Streets of Paris*, *The Taking Good-time Girls to the Salpétrière, as They Pass through the Porte St-Bernard*, *The Pea-shellers at la Halle (the Paris Vegetable Market)* (1757) and *The Central Paris Markets* (1761), to mention just a few, each deserve special study. Jeaurat is the equal of the wittiest of the Dutch and Flemish painters.

BIBLIOGRAPHY:
Sahut, Marie-Christine, '*Étienne Jeaurat*' in *Diderot et l'Art de Boucher à David*, exhibition catalogue, Hôtel de la Monnaie, Paris, 1984-1985.
MUSEUMS AND GALLERIES:
AUXERRE: *Grandma's Lesson*; *Venus and Cupid* - BESANÇON: *Cook Returning from Market* - BLOIS: *The Broken Contract* - CAEN (Église Notre-Dame-de-la-Gloriette): *Annunciation* - CAMBRAI (MBA): *Achilles Departing to Avenge the Death of Patroclus* - COMPIÈGNE: *Pyramus and Thisbe* - DUBLIN: *Little Girl Making Chocolate* (pencil) - FONTAINEBLEAU: *Diogenes Breaks His Bowl* - LA FÈRE: *The Picnic*; *The Charlatan* - MÂCON (Mus. des Ursulines): *Royal Tennis in a Meadow* (1789) - MOSCOW (Rumiantsev Mus.): *Venus Restraining Adonis as He is about to Set Off Hunting* - NANTES: *Portrait of a Young Boy* - ORLÉANS: *Jesus Giving the Keys to St Peter*; *Kitchen Interior* - OXFORD (Ashmolean Mus.): *Interior with Two Women* (oil on canvas) - PARIS (Church of St-Bernard de la Chapelle): *Six Cathusian Monks in Meditation* - PARIS (Louvre): *Portrait of N. Dorigny* (red chalk) - PARIS (Mus. Carnavalet): *View of the Pont-Neuf and the Place Dauphine*; *Bringing Good-time Girls to the Police Lieutenant*; *Armed Confrontation at the Fountain* - ROANNE (Mus. Joseph-Déchelette): *Pyramus and Thisbe* (1733, oil on canvas, competition piece for the Academy) - ST PETERSBURG (Hermitage): *The Convalescent* - VALENCIENNES (MBA): *Les Oies du Frère Philippe* (*Brother Philip's Geese*).
AUCTION RECORDS:
PARIS, 14 May 1891, *Portrait of a Noble Lady in Disguise*, FRF 2,200. PARIS, 4 June 1891, *The Caged Bird*, FRF 2,550. PARIS, 30 and 31 Jan 1894, *The Amorous Turk*; *The Favourite Sultana*, FRF 885. PARIS, 15-17 Feb 1897, *Man and Woman of the People Dancing*, FRF 195; *Three Women from Les Halles (the Cen-*

tral Parisian Markets), FRF 195; *Man Harnessed to a Cart*, FRF 105; *Woman in an Armchair*, FRF 305; *The Sick Woman*, FRF 530. PARIS, 10 and 11 May 1897, *Tavern Interior*, FRF 872. PARIS, 12 and 13 Dec 1899, *Rustic Meal*, FRF 2,050. PARIS, 13-15 May 1903, *Portrait of a Hunter*, FRF 1,000. PARIS, 21 and 22 March 1905, *The Family Meal*, FRF 1,150. PARIS, 21 June 1920, *Awakening*, FRF 1,500. PARIS, 7 and 8 May 1923, *The Fountain from the Parched Tree* (wash and pen) FRF 2,120. PARIS, 17 July 1925, *The Cook; The Little Tinker* (pair) FRF 8,600. PARIS, 23 June 1926, *The Dance; Hunting; Love; Wine* (set of four) FRF 38,000. PARIS, 21 March 1927, *Study of a Young Woman Seated* (heightened pencil) FRF 8,600. PARIS, 28 Nov 1928, *The Three Friends* (drawing) FRF 14,200. PARIS, 13-15 May 1929, *Woman Playing a Hurdy-gurdy* (drawing) FRF 40,000. PARIS, 31 March 1938, *The Blue Dress*, FRF 7,300. PARIS, 18 Nov 1942, *Street Scene* (attributed) FRF 54,000. PARIS, 6 Dec 1944, *Young Man with a Tricorn Hat* (red chalk) FRF 2,000. PARIS, 5 Feb 1947, *Woman modelling a headscarf* (attributed) FRF 48,000. PARIS, 4 Dec 1950, *The Amateur Collector of Statues* (bistre wash) FRF 40,000. PARIS, 24 June 1954, *The Carefree Age: Children's Games*, FRF 300,000. PARIS, 10 Dec 1959, *The Vigil*, FRF 280,000. VERSAILLES, 28 May 1963, *The Village Fair*, FRF 8,000. VERSAILLES, 16 May 1971, *Charlatans; Paris Streets* (two pendants) FRF 11,600. PARIS, 19 May 1972, *The Painter's Studio*, FRF 81,000. LONDON, 8 July 1974, *Children's Games*, Gns 7,000. NEUILLY-SUR-SEINE, 23 Nov 1978, *The Cleaner* (oil on canvas, 17 1/4 x 13 3/4in/44 x 35cm) FRF 18,000. PARIS, 15 Dec 1980, *The Milliner* (oil on canvas, 16 x 12 3/4in/40.5 x 32.5cm) FRF 21,500. LILLE, 12 Dec 1982, *The Money Changer* (oil on canvas, 32 x 39 1/4in/81 x 100cm) FRF 46,000. MILAN, 27 Nov 1984, *The Gentleman and the Coachman* (oil on canvas, 16 x 12 3/4in/40.5 x 32.5cm) ITL 8,500,000. PARIS, 16 Dec 1987, *Study of Three Figures* (black chalk heightened with white/blue paper, 8 3/4 x 11in/22.5 x 28cm) FRF 21,500. PARIS, 16 Dec 1987, *Study of Three Figures* (black chalk heightened with white/blue paper, 8 3/4 x 11in/22.5 x 28cm) FRF 21,500. MONACO, 19 June 1988, *Two Girls Sorting Flowers under a Tree* (oil on canvas, 43 3/4 x 36 1/2in/111 x 92.8cm) FRF 133,200. MILAN, 24 Oct 1989, *The Coachman's Complaint* (oil on canvas, 16 x 12 3/4in/40.5 x 32.5cm) ITL 15,000,000. PARIS, 13 Dec 1989, *Group of Guests round a Table* (oil on canvas, 37 x 46 1/2in/94 x 118cm) FRF 64,000. LONDON, 2 July 1990, *View of the Banks of the Tiber with a Boat in the Foreground* (black and white chalk/grey paper, 12 1/2 x 19 1/4in/31.8 x 48.7cm) GBP 4,180. LONDON, 17 April 1991, *Brother Philip's Geese* (1734, oil on canvas, 25 1/4 x 31 1/4in/64 x 79.5cm) GBP 20,900. NEW YORK, 17 Jan 1992, *Market Scenes with Peasants Drinking in front of a Tavern; Two Women Arguing and Dropping a Basket of Eggs* (oil on canvas, a pair, each 23 3/4 x 21in/60.3 x 53.3cm) USD 22,000. PARIS, 15 May 1992, *View of a Village on the Side of a Mountain* (brown wash heightened with white/blue paper, 12 1/2 x 17 1/2in/31.5 x 44.5cm) FRF 16,000. STOCKHOLM, 19 May 1992, *Couple near a Table inside an Inn* (oil on panel, 13 3/4 x 11 1/2in/35 x 29cm) SEK 25,000. MONACO, 18-19 June 1992, *The Drinker* (oil on canvas, 31 1/2 x 26in/80 x 66cm) FRF 49,950. PARIS, 7 July 1992, *Diana and Actaeon* (1752, oil on canvas, 24 3/4 ins / 63 cm, 2 x 31 1/2in/5 x 80cm) FRF 180,000. PARIS, 4 Dec 1992, *Scene from Family Life* (black and red chalk heightened with white, 19 x 25 1/4in/48 x 64cm) FRF 325,000. NEW YORK, 15 Jan 1993, *The Modest Woman; The Frivolous Woman* (oil on panel, a pair, 11 1/2 x 9 1/4in/29.2 x 23.2cm) USD 46,000. PARIS, 31 March 1993, *Study of Two Women* (black chalk heightened with white, 8 1/2 x 13 1/2in/21.5 x 34cm) FRF 15,000. MONACO, 2 July 1993, *Three Nymphs Bathing* (red and white chalk/beige paper, 15 1/4 x 10 1/2in/38.5 x 26.7cm) FRF 66,600. PARIS, 6 May 1994, *The Assumption* (black chalk and white chalk, 14 1/4 x 9in/36.2 x 23.1cm) FRF 20,000. LONDON, 7 Dec 1994, *Market Scene in a Town with Oriental Travellers on Horseback and Girls Dancing in a Circle* (1748, oil on canvas, 23 1/4 x 42 1/4in/59.3 x 107.5cm) GBP 47,700. LONDON, 5 April 1995, *Jupiter and Semele; An Angel with Cherubs* (1766, oil on canvas, a pair, each 21 1/4 x 15 3/4in/54 x 40cm) GBP 8,625. NEW YORK, 10 Jan 1996, *The Convalescent Woman* (black, red and white chalk, 15 1/4 x 19in/39 x 47.4cm) USD 8,050. LONDON, 2 July 1996, *The Finding of Moses* (1779, black and white chalk/grey paper, 14 1/4 x 19 3/4in/36.5 x 50cm) GBP 1,725. PARIS, 18 May 1999, *Study of Couple Dancing for the 'Marché des Innocents'* (black crayon/white chalk, 9 x 11 ins / 23 x 27 cm) FRF 52,000. PARIS, 25 June 1999, *Meal by the Mill* (oil on canvas, 26 x 40 ins / 65 x 102 cm) FRF 46,000. PARIS, 30 June 2000, *Cup of Tea* (c.1740, oil on canvas, 31 x 28 ins / 80 x 71 cm) FRF 20,000. UPPSALA, 10 Dec 2000, *The Jealous Husband - Interior with Man and Woman* (oil on canvas, 18 x 15 ins / 45 x 37 cm) SEK 57,000. PARIS, 6 July 2001, *Public Fountain* (pen/ink wash, 8 x 7 ins / 20 x 18 cm) FRF 18,000. PARIS, 21 Nov 2001, *Evening Gathering of Peasant Women* (oil on canvas, 18 x 13 ins / 46 x 34 cm) FRF 40,000. PARIS, 25 April 2003, *Erigone* (1763, oil on canvas, 28 x 35 ins / 71 x 89 cm) EUR 9,000.

JEAURAT DE BERTRY, Nicolas Henry, or Bertrix
French, 18th century.
Born 28 July 1728, in Paris; died after 1796, in Vermenton.
Painter, decorative designer. Allegorical subjects, figures, portraits, genre scenes, landscapes, urban views, still-lifes.

Jeaurat de Bertry was the son of Edme Jeaurat and a pupil of Étienne Jeaurat. He was admitted as an academician on 31 January 1756 on the basis of *Kitchen Utensils*. The following year, he exhibited three paintings depicting *Instruments used for Music, War and Science*. He was appointed painter to Marie Leczinska. He exhibited again at the Salon in 1796, but was no longer at that time the painter of the queen and noble lords. He exhibited: *Portrait of Citizen J. Gelé Receiving the Warrant as Printer to the National Constabulary* and *View of the Collegiate Church and Bridge at Corbeil*, with the water bus going under the bridge.

MUSEUMS AND GALLERIES:
AUXERRE: *Still-life, Vegetables with Kitchen Utensils* - FONTAINEBLEAU: *Still-life* - NANTES: *Memento Mori* - NARBONNE: *An Old Man Surrounded by His Family* (watercolour).

AUCTION RECORDS:
PARIS, 10 March 1877, *The Milkmaid*, FRF 1,000; *The Egg Seller*, FRF 460. PARIS, 24 and 25 Feb 1910, *Portrait of a Young Female Artist*, FRF 650. PARIS, 27 Jan 1921, *Portrait of a Man*, FRF 300. PARIS, 6 May 1925, *Books and Astronomical Instruments*, FRF 1,700. PARIS, 20 Nov 1953, *The Attributes of Painting*, FRF 40,000. PARIS, 23 March 1968, *Still-life with Brioche*, FRF 25,000. PARIS, 7 Dec 1979, *The Kitchen Table* (oil on canvas, 37 x 54in/94 x 137cm) FRF 119,000. MONTE CARLO, 13 June 1982, *Still-life with Mallard* (1757, oil on canvas, 17 1/2 x 23 1/2in/44.5 x 59.5cm) FRF 20,00. MONTE CARLO, 8 Dec 1984, *The Instruments of the Arts* (oil on canvas, 33 1/2 x 42 1/2in/85 x 108cm) FRF 70,000. PARIS, 8 Dec 1989, *Still-life of Fruit and Game* (oil on canvas, 28 1/4 x 35 1/2in/72 x 90cm) FRF 80,000. MONACO, 5-6 Dec 1991, *Fruit in a Landscape* (1765, oil/vellum, a pair, 10 1/4 x 15 1/4in/26 x 39cm) FRF 31,080. LUGANO, 16 May 1992, *Still-life with Fish and a Chicken in a Basket* (oil on canvas, 11 x 15in/28 x 38cm) CHF 18,000. PARIS, 3 June 1999, *Kitchen Table* (oil on canvas, 36 x 53 ins / 92 x 135 cm) FRF 300,000. LONDON, 8 July 1999, *Still-life of Pipes, Globe, Musical Score and Violin on Table Draped with Red Cloth* (oil on canvas, 32 x 39 ins / 81 x 100 cm) GBP 30,000.

JEAUSENNE
French, 19th century.
Active in Avignon c. 1860.
Sculptor.

JEAVONS, Thomas
British, 19th century.

Born probably at the beginning of the 19th century
26 January 1867, in Welshpool.
Engraver (burin).

Thomas Jeavons dedicated himself to reproducing landscapes painted by watercolour artists including Samuel Prout, J.D. Harding, Clarkson Stanfield, David Robert, W.H. Bertlet, W. Brockedon and E. Cook. There are also two plates after J.P. Neale signed by Jeavons in *Views of the Seats of Noblemen and Gentlemen in England, Wales. Scotland and Ireland*, a six-volume work published in London in 1822. Jeavons collaborated on *The Landscape Annual* of London in 1830, 1831, 1832, 1838. His date of birth cited in Redgrave and Bryan's Dictionary as 1816 is probably wrong unless there were two burin engravers of the same name. If he had been born in 1816, he would have started working at the age of six.

JEAY, Jean le. See **LEGEAY Jean Laurent**

JEAY, Lucien
French, 20th century.
Born 5 March 1911, in Bordeaux; died 4 June 1997, in Bordeaux.
Painter. Religious subjects, figures, landscapes, seascapes. Designs for tapestries.

Lucien Jeay studied at the Bordeaux art college from 1928 to 1933, leaving as victor in the competition, and then from 1935 to 1937 in Paris, where he settled and worked. As a devout Christian, Jeay served religious art, and was a highly productive painter. He created frescoes or paintings on wooden panels using bases of casein and pure wax, techniques he had learnt after the war. His figurative paintings, partly Expressionist and Symbolist, have echoes of primitive Roman and Byzantine work.

His works include: 1948, a retable showing *St Bonaventure and his Disciples* for the Franciscan house in Paris; 1949, a mural in the chapel of the Sacred Heart in St Helen's church, Paris; a fresco of *Christ Pantocrator* in the church in Vandy (Ardennes); 1953, a fresco in the church in Givry-sur-Aisne (Ardennes); 1954, a *Way of the Cross* for the church in Cherval (Dordgone); another for the collegiate church in St-Lô (Manche); 1963, a fresco of the *Blessed Virgin* in St-Malo church; a *Way of the Cross* for the Sanatorium at Chantoiseau, Briançon (Hautes-Alpes); and a retable of the *Assumption of the Blessed Virgin* at the same Sanatorium. He also painted landscapes and seascapes.

He exhibited in Paris at the Salon d'Automne and in 1963 at the Salon Comparaisons. His solo shows included: in 1959 Galerie M. Bernheim, Paris, and in 1960 Galerie Yves Michel, Paris. In 1962, his *Way of the Cross* for the church in Périers (Manche) was exhibited in Paris in the church of St-Germain-des-Prés.

BIBLIOGRAPHY:
Vauthier, Jean, '*Lucien Jeay, peintre*' in *L'Art d'église* n° 3, periodical, 1955.

JEBENS, Adolf
German, 19th century.
Born 19 March 1819, in Elbing (now Elblag, Poland); died 8 May 1888, in Berlin.
Painter. Genre scenes, portraits.

Jebens began his training in Berlin, but then went to Paris to have lessons with Delaroche. He was portrait painter to the imperial court in St Petersburg in 1845.

MUSEUMS AND GALLERIES:
BERLIN (Society of Artists): *Painter E Hildebrandt* - COLOGNE: *The Lady with the Mask* - GDANSK: *Baron von Weichmann; Mayor von Winter; Friedrich Hennings.*

JEBSEN, Johann. See **JEPSEN**

JECHE, Gottfried. See **JÄCH**

JECHIMOFF. See **EKIMOV**

JECKEL. See also **JÂCKEL**

JECKEL, Bernhard Maria
German, 19th century.
Born c. 1824; died 19 May 1884, in Lima, Mexico.
Painter, engraver.

A Capuchin monk, Jeckel came from Munich, and was a member of the Emperor Maxmimilian's retinue when he arrived in Mexico in 1863. Jeckel worked as a sculptor and architect there. Noted among his engravings are *SS Antony and Benedict* after A.M. Seitz, a *Holy Family* after F.V. Rohden (altar painting in the church of S Alfonso di Ligori in Rome), a *St Birgitta* (drawing) after E. von Steinle, and several *Scenes from the Life of St Margaret of Cortona*. Also by him are a *Portrait of the Artist by Himself*, a *St Crispin of Viterbo* and a *St Ludovico di Gonzago* based on his own drawings.

JECKEL, Mathias Wenzel. See **JÄCKEL**

JECKLIN, André
Swiss, 19th century.
Born 1823, in Schiers (near Chur); died 1895, in Rongellen (Graubünden).
Landscape artist.

MUSEUMS AND GALLERIES:
NEUCHÂTEL (MAH): *View of the Alps.*

JEDROYTZ. See **GJEDROYTZ**

JEDRZEJOWSKI, Pawel Josef
Polish, 18th century.
Active in Warsaw and Zamosc.
Engraver.

Eleven plates by Pawel Josef Jedrzejowski are known, mostly portraits of clergymen and figures of saints.

JEE, Horace
British, 19th century.
Active in England.
Painter.

AUCTION RECORDS:
LONDON, 25 June 1908, *Waterloo Bridge*, GBP 1.

JEENS, Charles Henry
British, 19th century.
Born 1827, in Uley; died 1879.
Engraver (burin).

Charles Henry Jeens was a student of Brain and Greatbach. His first work was dated 1848. He made engravings of historical subjects and genre scenes after Millais, Armitage and Romney, among others. He also designed stamps for the British colonies.

JEFFEREYS, James. See **JEFFERYS**

JEFFERSON, Joseph
American, 19th century.
Born 20 February 1829, in Philadelphia; died 23 April 1905, in Palm Beach (Florida).
Painter, dramatic artist.

Joseph Jefferson was very well known as an actor in America, but also as a landscape artist. Several of his works are in various American museums. He owned a large collection of paintings which was sold in New York on 27 April 1907 for $228,120. The collection included very fine modern Dutch paintings (a Mauve sold for $42,550 and a Joseph Israël for $19,500) and works by the principal masters of the Barbizon School.

MUSEUMS AND GALLERIES:
NEW YORK (Metropolitan Mus. of Art): one work.

AUCTION RECORDS:
NEW YORK, 2 Feb 1911, *Old Mill*, USD 120; *Old Beech Tree*, USD 80; *Cannon*, USD 100. LOS ANGELES, 15 Oct 1979, *Fish-*

ing in the Bayous (1898, oil on paper, 23 1/2 x 18 1/2 ins / 59.6 x 47 cm) USD 1,600. NORTH BETHESDA, 22 July 2000, *Along Key Marsh* (oil on canvas, 20 x 17 ins / 51 x 43 cm) USD 2,400. NEW ORLEANS, 7 Oct 2000, *Palm and Mangrove Trees along Water* (1904, oil on canvas, 19 x 29 ins / 48 x 74 cm) USD 4,500. NEW ORLEANS, 3 Feb 2001, *Louisana Landscape* (1902, oil on canvas, 20 x 30 ins / 51 x 76 cm) USD 4,000. NEW ORLEANS, 7 April 2001, *Louisiana Landscape* (oil on board, 36 x 28 ins / 91 x 71 cm) USD 2,400. BOSTON, 22 March 2002, *Birch Woods* (1895, oil on canvas) USD 2,600. PORTSMOUTH, 2 Nov 2002, *Moonrise, Louisiana* (oil on canvas, 20 x 30 ins / 51 x 76 cm) USD 5,000.

JEFFERSON, Robert
British, 19th century.
Died 1870.
Active in London.
Sculptor.

Robert Jefferson exhibited between 1853 and 1860 at the Royal Academy and the Society of British Artists. His cited works include: *Wellington's Entry into Madrid*, a sculpture in high relief and *The First Prince of Wales*.

JEFFERYS, Charles William
Canadian, 19th - 20th century.
Born 25 August 1869, in Rochester, England; died 8 October 1951, in Toronto.
Painter, watercolourist, illustrator, caricaturist. Landscapes. Murals.

Charles William Jefferys emigrated with his family from England to Philadelphia in 1875, then to Ontario in around 1878, and settled in Toronto in 1881.

He began work as a newspaper illustrator in Toronto in 1889, notably for the *Herald* and then the *Globe*. He was also a caricaturist. He was an open-air painter, producing a number of watercolours. He painted mainly scenes of the Canadian prairies, with a preference for the vast undulating stretches of Saskatchewan, normally only visited by those passing through on their way to the Rocky Mountains, often painted by Canadian artists and especially by the Group of Seven. In 1920, he was invited to join this group, but he refused. He experimented with the abstract, inspired by Richard Strauss' symphonic poem *Death and Transfiguration*.

BIBLIOGRAPHY:
Stacey, Robert, *Charles Williams Jefferys 1869-1951*, exhibition catalogue, 1976. Stacey, Robert, *C. W. Jefferys*, National Museums of Canada, Ottawa, 1985.

MUSEUMS AND GALLERIES:
CALGARY (Glenbow Mus.): *Appelle Valley* (1911) - EDMONTON (AG): *Rain in the Foothills, Alberta* (1924) - OTTAWA (NG. of Canada): *Flying Blossoms, New Jersey Garden* (1897); *Western Sunlight, Last Mountain Lake* (1911); *Winter Afternoon* (1914); *Rocks of Georgian Bay* (1917); *Time* (1921) - TORONTO (AG of Ontario): *A Prairie Trail* (1912); *Wheatfield on the Prairie* (1910-1911); *Sunset on the Prairie* (1915); *Woodland Interior* (1921); *Near Bobcaygeon* (1924); *Death and Transfiguration* (1934-1937).

AUCTION RECORDS:
TORONTO, 17 May 1976, *Ocean Shore* (1931, watercolour, 12 1/2 x 21 1/4 ins / 32 x 54 cm) CAD 1,800. TORONTO, 27 May 1980, *The Waterfall* (watercolour, 14 x 19 1/2 ins / 35.6 x 49.4 cm) CAD 4,000. TORONTO, 27 May 1980, *The St. Maurice River, Quebec* (oil on panel, 36 3/4 x 19 3/4 ins / 93.3 x 50 cm) CAD 3,400. TORONTO, 3 May 1983, *Landscape, Oakville* (1905, oil on mounted card, 8 1/2 x 11 1/4 ins / 21.9 x 28.8 cm) CAD 1,800.

JEFFERYS, Jack, or Jeffreys
Belgian, 20th century.
Born 1896, in Ixelles (Brussels); died 1961.
Painter, watercolourist, potter.

Jack Jeffreys gave up painting after 1944 to concentrate on his sculpture and ceramic work.

BIBLIOGRAPHY:
Geerts, Robert, *Jack Jefferys*, Elsevier, Brussels, 1959.

AUCTION RECORDS:
LOKEREN, 23 May 1992, *Turkey* (1954, ceramic sculpture, h. 10 3/4 ins / 27.5 cm, l. 22 3/4 ins/58 cm) BEF 85,000.

JEFFERYS, James, or Jeffereys
British, 18th century.
Born c. 1757, in Maidstone; died 31 January 1784, in London.
Painter. Seascapes.

James Jefferys was the son of a carriage painter. He trained under the engraver Woollett before turning to painting and enrolling at the Royal Academy. In 1773, he began exhibiting at the Society of Artists. In 1774, he won a gold medal. After a four-year stay in Rome, he returned and exhibited one of his best works at the Royal Academy, *Destruction of the Spanish Batteries in front of Gibraltar* engraved by Woollett.

AUCTION RECORDS:
LONDON, 23 Nov 1973, *Spanish Fleet off Gibraltar*, Gns 700. LONDON, 21 March 2002, *Study of a Man Carrying a Woman* (1779, pen, ink and wash, 21 x 14 ins / 53 x 36 cm) GBP 5,600.

JEFFERYS, Marcel
Belgian, 19th - 20th century.
Born 9 August 1872, in Milan, to Belgian parents; died 14 May 1924, in Brussels.
Painter, watercolourist. Landscapes, landscapes with figures, seascapes, still-lifes, flowers.

Milan-born Marcel Jefferys returned with his family to Brussels in 1880 and studied under Henriette Ronner and her son Alfred. He made his exhibition debut in 1892 and went on to exhibit in Ghent, Brussels, Munich, Berlin, Glasgow, Prague and Bordeaux. Jefferys spent long periods in Paris and London but also travelled elsewhere in Europe. In Paris, he was a regular exhibitor at the Salon de la Société des Beaux-Arts, becoming a member of the Society in 1908. He was also a member of the artistic circle Pour l'Art.

Like Whistler and Monet before him, Marcel Jefferys found inspiration in the fogs that swirled about the Thames in London, but he was equally at home painting clear and shimmering landscapes in and around the Paris region.

BIBLIOGRAPHY:
Bendère, Robert de, *Marcel Jefferys*, Vermaut, Paris, c. 1929.

MUSEUMS AND GALLERIES:
BRUSSELS (MAM): *View of the Seine at Pont-Royal* - GHENT - LIÈGE.

AUCTION RECORDS:
BRUSSELS, 21 Oct 1950, *Hills of St-Germain*, BEF 5,500. ANTWERP, 18 April 1972, *Nocturnal Festival*, BEF 32,000. BRUSSELS, 26 Feb 1974, *Flowers and Objects* (1917) BEF 38,000. BRUSSELS, 24 March 1976, *River Thames* (oil on canvas, 19 3/4 x 23 1/2 ins / 50 x 60 cm) BEF 44,000. BREDA, 26 April 1977, *River Thames seen from a Window* (oil on canvas, 24 3/4 x 30 1/4 ins / 63 x 77 cm) NLG 5,200. BRUSSELS, 28 March 1979, *Valley* (oil on panel, 10 1/4 x 12 1/2 ins / 26 x 32 cm) BEF 75,000. BRUSSELS, 29 Oct 1986, *Olive Trees near Florence* (oil remounted on canvas, 20 3/4 x 26 1/2 ins / 53 x 67 cm) BEF 280,000. LOKEREN, 16 May 1987, *Park* (1910, oil on canvas remounted on panel, 11 3/4 x 15 3/4 ins / 30 x 40 cm) BEF 170,000. LOKEREN, 23 May 1992, *Landscape* (oil on canvas/card, 14 1/4 x 18 ins / 36.5 x 45.5 cm) BEF 50,000. ANTWERP, 27 April 1999, *Harbour at Ostend* (oil on canvas, 20 x 27 ins / 50 x 68 cm) BEF 220,000. ANTWERP, 24 Oct 2000, *S Giorgio, Grey Weather in Venice* (oil on canvas) BEF 700,000.

BRUSSELS, 7 Nov 2000, *Still-life with White Vase* (oil on canvas, 20 x 24 ins / 50 x 60 cm) BEF 110,000. BRUSSELS, 10 Dec 2001, *Garden in Summer* (oil on canvas, 17 x 20 ins / 43 x 50 cm) BEF 110,000. LOKEREN, 9 March 2002, *In the Garden* (oil on canvas on board, 15 x 18 ins / 38 x 45 cm) EUR 10,000. LOKEREN, 5 Oct 2002, *Interior of St Mark's Bascilica in Venice* (watercolour and pastel, 19 x 15 ins / 48 x 38 cm) EUR 2,000. ANTWERP, 21 Oct 2003, *Island Poppies* (oil on canvas, 26 x 30 ins / 65 x 77 cm) EUR 3,400. LOKEREN, 13 Dec 2003, *Clothes* (watercolour and gouache, 13 x 15 ins / 34 x 37 cm) EUR 3,300. BRUSSELS, 13 Jan 2004, *Parisian Restaurant Interior* (1912, charcoal, watercolour and gouache, 10 x 10 ins / 25 x 25 cm) EUR 2,700. BRUSSELS, 13 Jan 2004, *Bowl of Poppies* (1918, oil on canvas, 25 x 30 ins / 63 x 76 cm) EUR 7,400.

JEFFERYS, T.
British, 19th century.
Engraver.

T. Jefferys made an engraving entitled *A South View of the City of Genoa*.

JEFFERYS, William
British, 18th century.
Died 1805.
Active in Maidstone.
Painter. Fruit.

William Jefferys exhibited at the Society of Artists from 1766 to 1775. He was the father of James Jefferys.

JEFFRAY, A. Edgar
British, 19th century.
Active in London.
Painter. Landscapes.

A. Edgar Jeffray exhibited his works in London between 1833 and 1848, in particular at the Royal Academy, the British Institution and at Suffolk Street.

JEFFRAY, Richard
British, 19th century.
Active in London.
Painter. Religious subjects.

Richard Jeffray exhibited at the Royal Academy, the British Institution and at Suffolk Street from 1835 and 1854.

JEFFRAY, W.
British, 18th century.
Active in London.
Painter. Portraits.

W. Jeffray exhibited at the Royal Academy in 1788 and 1789.

JEFFREY, James, or Jeffray
British, 19th century.
Active in London.
Painter. Animals.

James Jeffrey exhibited at the Royal Academy, the British Institution and at Suffolk Street from 1833 to 1853.

JEFFREYS, Lee
American, 20th century.
Born 24 January 1901, in New York.
Painter.

Lee Jeffreys studied at the Art Students League of New York and the Académie Julian in Paris. He was a member of the National Art Club of New York. He became a teacher.

JEFIMOFF. See **EFIMOV**

JEFIMOVIC, Vassili Prokofevich, or Iefanov Vasilii
Russian, 20th century.
Born 1900, in Samara; died 1978, in Moscow.
Painter.

Jefimovic's work featured at the collective exhibition, *Traumfabrik Kommunismus - die Visuelle Kultur der Stalinzeit* (*Dream Factory Communism, the Visual Culture of the Stalin Period*), Schirn Kunsthalle, Frankfurt (2003). He is known for his *Portrait of Gorky*.

BIBLIOGRAPHY:
Hollein, Max, et al., *Dream Factory Communism, the Visual Culture of the Stalin Period*, exhibition catalogue, Schirn Kunsthalle, Frankfurt, 2003 (text in English and German).

JEGER, Derick. See **JÄGER**

JEGER, Fridolin
Swiss, 17th century.
Active in Lucerne 1613-1634.
Sculptor (wood).

JEGERLEHNER, Hans
Swiss, 20th century.
Born 24 November 1906, in Bern; died 1974, in Bressonaz.
Painter.

Hans Jegerlehner, son of the writer Johannes Jegerlehner, studied privately in Paris under André Lhote, Roger Bissière and Othon Friesz. His painting was influenced by Fauvism in general and by the work of Kees van Dongen in particular.

AUCTION RECORDS:
BERN, 3 May 1979, *Studio Interior* (oil on canvas, 33 1/2 x 49 1/4 ins / 85 x 125 cm) CHF 5,000. BERN, 26 Oct 1988, *Still-life with Flowers in a Pitcher* (oil on panel, 23 1/2 x 17 1/4 ins / 60 x 44 cm) CHF 1,400. BERN, 12 May 1990, *Chamber Orchestra* (tempera/canvas, 25 1/2 x 29 1/2 ins / 65 x 75 cm) CHF 2,300. BERN, 5 Nov 2003, *Svajatoslav Richter at Piano* (oil on canvas, 24 x 28 ins / 60 x 72 cm) CHF 3,000.

JEGHER, Christophe or Christoffel, or Jeghers or Jegers or Jaegher
German, 17th century.
Born between 1578 and 1590, in Germany; died 1660 or 1670, in Antwerp, in 1652 according to some sources, between 1660 and 1670 according to Bryan's Dictionary.
Engraver (metal/wood).

Jegher qualified as a master in Antwerp in 1627. He worked extensively for Rubens, engraving on wood several important works that the Flemish master proposed to publish. Produced under the latter's watchful eye, they are executed with great virtuosity and create an illusion of pen drawing. After Rubens died, Jegher bought back his engravings and exploited them for his own benefit. He also reproduced drawings by F. Franck (1637) and other masters.

AUCTION RECORDS:
LONDON, 18 June 1982, *Bust Portrait of a Bearded Man* (wood engraving in several shades of brown, after Rubens, 11 1/4 x 8 1/2 ins / 28.8 x 21.7 cm) GBP 1,800. LONDON, 9 Dec 1983, *Hercules Fighting Rage and Discord* (wood engraving, after P. P. Rubens, 24 x 14 1/4 ins / 60.8 x 36.5 cm) GBP 1,000. LONDON, 26 June 1985, *Susanna and the Elders* (wood engraving, 17 1/2 x 22 3/4 ins / 44.4 x 57.7 cm) GBP 2,800. PARIS, 8 April 1998, *Resting on the Flight into Egypt* (after Rubens) FRF 9,000. LONDON, 22 June 1999, *Susannah and the Elders* (c. 1635, woodcut, 17 x 22 ins / 44 x 57 cm) GBP 7,000. COLOGNE, 23 March 2001, *Hercules Fighting Anger and Discord* (woodcut, 24 x 14 ins / 60 x 36 cm) DEM 15,000. BERLIN, 30 Nov 2001, *Resting on the Flight into Egypt* (woodcut, 18 x 24 ins / 46 x 60 cm) DEM 16,000.

JEGHER, Jan. See **JEGHERS**

JEGHERS, Christophe or Christoffel. See **JEGHER**

JEGHERS, Henri
Belgian, 19th century.
Born 25 October 1848, in Antwerp.
Engraver.

JEGHERS, Jan
Flemish School, 17th century.

Baptised 3 November 1618 in Antwerp; died c. 1667.
Carver.
Jan Jeghers was the son of Christophe Jegher. He was registered as a member of the Antwerp guild in 1643.

JEGLI, Hans, or Jaggli or Jaegli or Heggli
Swiss, 16th century.
Painter (glass).
Jegli worked for a convent in 1514.

JEGLI, Hans, or Jäggli or Jaeglj or Heggli
Swiss, 17th century.
Born 1580; died 15 February 1643.
Active in Winterthur.
Painter (glass).
Jegli is documented on 27June 1598 as a pupil of a Schaffhausen glass painter called Hans-Friedrich Kolmann. His real identity is somewhat obscure. It is not known if the painter born in 1580 and deceased in 1643 is the same as the one mentioned between these two dates.

JEGLI, Hans Ulrich, or Jäckli or Jäglj or Heggli
Swiss, 17th century.
Born 30 August 1604; died 30 April 1654.
Active in Winterthur.
Painter (glass).
Hans Ulrich Jegli was probably a pupil of Gotthard Ringgli. He signed: HI.

JEGOROFF. See **EGOROV**

JÉGOU, Jean
French, 20th century.
Born 14 February 1899, in Paris.
Sculptor, pastellist.
Jean Jégou won a travel grant in 1924.
AUCTION RECORDS:
PARIS, 27 Nov 1925, *Les Chalands* (pastel) FRF 135.

JEHAN. See **MERETTE DE GAND**

JEHAN. See **JEHAN de Toul**

JEHAN
French, 14th century.
Active in Château-Gontier in 1379.
Painter. History painting, portraits.

JEHAN. See also **JEAN, JEANNOT, JEANNIN, JAN, JOHANN**

JEHAN, Jean-Luc
French, 20th century.
Sculptor (mixed media).
Jean-Luc Jehan lives and works in Paris. To a base of laminated, cut and worked wood, he adds fragments of material, varied but ordinary - rusty sheet metal, wire netting, splinters of mirrors, and so on - and then paints the piece in ochres and browns.

His sculptures have been included in collective exhibitions such as: 1983, at the Paris Salon Grands et Jeunes d'Aujourd'hui and at Figuration Critique; 1986, New York, *Young Artists from Europe*; 1988, 1989, in Paris at the FIAC (Foire Internationale d'Art Contemporain); 1990 at the Salon in Montrouge and in Lódz (Poland), *Construction in Process*. In Paris a solo exhibition of his sculptures was shown in 1990 at the Galerie Françoise Palluel and in 1995 at the Galerie Jacques Elbaz.
BIBLIOGRAPHY:
Andrade, Marie-Odile, '*Jean-Luc Jehan - La terre et les rêveries de la volonté*' in *Artension* n° 18, periodical, Rouen, autumn 1990.

JEHAN, Sire
French, 13th century.
Illuminator.
His name occurs in a list drawn up in Paris in 1292.

JEHAN D'ASSELT. See **ASSELT Jan van der**

JEHAN D'ASSONVILLE. See **ASSONVILLE**

JEHAN D'AVESNES. See **JEAN d'Avesnes**

JEHAN D'ORLEANS. See **POTIN Jean,** and **MASTER of the NARBONNE FRONTAL**

JEHAN DE BOULOGNE, or Jehan de Lachenel
French, 15th century.
Painter.
Jehan de Boulogne was the eldest son of Hugues de Boulogne, and like him, was a valet and a painter. References to him are dated 1427 and 1451.

JEHAN DE COUILLY
French, 14th century.
Combmaker/ivory worker.
Jehan de Couilly was almost certainly also known as Jehan de l'Imaige, or may have been the son of a man of this name. He worked for Philip the Bold, Duke of Burgundy, from 1367 to 1387, and produced ivory combs.

JEHAN DE HONGRIE. See **HONGRIE**

JEHAN DE JOUY, also known as Jean de Jouy
French, 14th century.
Active in Paris.
Miniaturist.
Jehan de Jouy worked for Isabeau de Bavière in 1387.

JEHAN DE L'IMAIGE
French, 14th century.
Active in Paris in 1319 and 1320.
Painter, decorative artist, combmaker/ivory worker.

JEHAN DE LAUNAY. See **DELAUNAY Jehan**

JEHAN DE LIÈGE. See **JEAN de Liège**

JEHAN DE LIGNIEU
French, 14th century.
Painter. History painting.
Jehan de Lignieu produced paintings on parchment for the library of King Charles V of France.

JEHAN DE MONTMARTRE
French, 14th century.
Illuminator.
Jean de Montmartre worked on the missal of King John of France in 1351.

JEHAN DE PARIS. See **JEAN de Paris** and **PERRÉAL Jean**

JEHAN DE SAINT-ELOY. See **SAINT-ELOY**

JEHAN DE SAINT-PRIEST. See **SAINT-PRIEST Jehan de**

JEHAN DE SAINTE-CATHERINE.
See **SAINTE-CATHERINE Jehan de**

JEHAN DE SENLIS
French, 15th century.
Born 15th century, in Senlis.
Painter (glass). History painting.
One of Jehan de Senlis' works, *Life of Lazarus*, is in the church of St-Maclou in Rouen. He also worked for Rouen Cathedral and for the town of Vernon in 1435.

JEHAN DE SENLIS
French, 16th century.
Active in Nancy 1521-1530.
Sculptor.
Jehan de Senlis worked for Anthony, Duke of Lorraine.

JEHAN DE SOLESMES (Dom).
See **GOURBEILLON Eugène**

JEHAN DE TOUL
French, 15th century.
Born 15th century, in Toul.
Painter (glass).
Jehan de Toul produced a stained glass window in 1483 for the church of St-Vast in Toul, and may have been the artist known as Jehan recorded as working in Nancy in 1463 as a painter to René de Lorraine, and as a stained glass artist at the ducal palace. A Jeannot de Toul worked for the Ste-Chapelle in Dijon in 1424.

JEHAN DE VITRY
French, 14th - 15th century.
Born at the end of the 14th century, in Pontverre.
Sculptor (wood).
Jehan de Vitry worked in Geneva in 1445, and in St-Claude in 1465. The Victoria and Albert Museum owns a relief by him, which was formerly in the church of St-Pierre in St-Claude.
MUSEUMS AND GALLERIES:
LONDON (Victoria and Albert Mus.): *Relief* (relief).

JEHAN DEL URBINA
Spanish, 16th century.
Active in Castile.
Painter.
Jehan del Urbina lived in Madrid and was considered one of the best painters of his time. He collaborated a great deal with Martinez Sanz and painted mainly in the Escorial during the reign of Philip II. He was probably a relation of Diego de Urbino.

JEHAN DES PINS
French, 15th century.
Born in Troyes.
Painter (glass).
Jehan des Pins worked at Troyes Cathedral.

JEHAN DU BOS. See **DU BOS**

JEHAN LE PEINTRE, or Jean de Fribourg
Swiss, 15th century.
Active in Fribourg in 1453 and 1454.
Painter, decorative artist.
Jehan le Peintre was commissioned by the town authorities in Fribourg to replace the coat of arms of the House of Austria on the Jacquemart tower with that of the House of Savoy, following the voluntary surrender of the town to Louis I, Duke of Savoy in 1452. The true identity of this painter is not known.

JEHAN SAMSON
French, 16th century.
Born in Tours.
Painter.
The name of Samson Jehan appears in accounts dated 1519, concerning parchments and escutcheons. He may also have been known by the name Samson Jean.

JEHAN VAN DER HASSELT. See **ASSELT Jan van der**

JEHANDIER, Étienne. See **DESROCHERS Étienne Jehandier**

JEHANNET DE MILAN. See **GIOVANNI da Milano** and **BUGATTI Zanetto**

JEHANNIN. See **JEAN**

JEHANNOT LE FLAMENT. See **DREUX Jehan**

JEHIN, Henri
Belgian, 19th century.
Died 14 June 1880, in Spa.
Painter, musician. Flowers.
He exhibited in Paris and London.

JEHLE, Caspar. See **JELE Kaspar**

JEHLE, Jacob, or Jele or Jelle or Yelle
German, 16th century.
Died 2 February 1602, in Regensburg.
Painter.
Jehle painted portraits, and historical and religious scenes.

JEHLY, Jakob
Austrian, 19th century.
Born 17 April 1854, in Bludenz; died 27 March 1897, in Bludenz.
Painter.
After training at the academy in Munich, Jehly worked for a while in Karlsruhe, where he did numerous sketches and studies, principally landscapes. Subsequently he did ceiling paintings for Schloss Au near Landshut and a *Descent from the Cross* for the Franciscan church in Feldkirch. Paintings of his exhibited at the National Exhibition in Bregenz in 1887 were *The Potato Harvest*, *Little Grandmother* and *Lansquenet*. After trips to Italy, France and England in 1893, he painted *When the Trees Blossom* and *Young Girl Praying beneath the Cross*.
MUSEUMS AND GALLERIES:
BREGENZ (Voralberger Landesmus.): *Birth of Christ*; *Self-portrait* (copy).
AUCTION RECORDS:
VIENNA, 14 March 1978, *The Potato Harvest* (1895, oil on canvas, 18 x 29 1/4 ins / 46 x 74 cm) ATS 100,000.

JEHNER, Isaac, or Jenner
British, 18th century.
Born 1750, in Westminster; died after 1806.
Painter, draughtsman, watercolourist, engraver (mezzotint).
Isaac Jehner or Jenner was the son of a German goldsmith who sold silver-plated tableware in England. Following an accident, Isaac became severely deformed. At the age of 20, he was apprenticed to an engraver and around 1775, became an assistant to William Pether. In 1777, he made an engraving of Sir Joshua Reynolds' *Young Girl with a Muff*. In 1791, under the name of Jenner, he exhibited five prints at the Society of Artists. Jehner also made his name with portraits executed in pencil, watercolour and oil, especially on silk. He worked in Exeter and Plymouth. In 1806, the last year in which he is mentioned, he published an autobiography under the title of *Fortune's Football* where he presented himself under the name of Jenner. He made engravings of works by Rubens, Correggio, Hogarth, Cosway, Bruegel and Morland, as well as of his own drawings.

JÉHOTTE, Arnold
Flemish School, 19th century.
Born 1789, in Herstal; died 1836, in Paris.
Engraver.
Arnold Jéhotte studied under his brother Léonard Jéhotte, and worked for booksellers in Paris. He is especially known for his vignettes after Desenne and for his portraits of *Grétry*, after Lefebvre, and *Napoleon I*, as well as for his costumes for the coronation of Charles X.

JÉHOTTE, Léonard
Flemish School, 18th - 19th century.
Born 1 August 1772, in Herstal; died 1 August 1851, in Maastricht.
Active in Liège.
Engraver (burin), medallist.
Léonard Jéhotte was engraver to the Prince Bishop of Liège. He is known for the following engravings: *Napoleon Visits*

and Relieves the Amercoeur District in Liège, 14 Thermidor Year XII; Hubert Goffin and His Son in the Beaujone Colliery, 28 February 1812 (devotional piece) after Johns; and *Portrait of Hubert Goffin, Chevalier de la Légion d'Honneur, and his Son Mathieu.*

JÉHOTTE, Louis
Belgian, 19th century.
Born 7 November 1803 or 1804, in Liège; died 3 February 1884, in Brussels.
Sculptor.

Louis Jéhotte was the son of the medallist Léonard Jéhotte, and studied under Kessel and Thorvaldsen in Rome. He worked in Brussels in 1830. Jéhotte exhibited *Child Holding a Spaniel* (marble group) at the Salon of 1844, *Cain* (plaster statue) in 1850, *Madonna* (marble statue) in 1852 and *Mater Dolorosa* (marble figure), also in 1852. He is also known for his *Statue of Charlemagne* in Liège.

MUSEUMS AND GALLERIES:

AMIENS (Mus. de Picardie): *General F. A. Desprez* (plaster, bust) - BRUSSELS (Beaux-Arts): *Baron Surlet de Chokier* (plaster); *King Leopold I* (plaster); *The Painter H. van Assche* (marble); *The Artist's Wife* (marble) - IXELLES (MBA): *Baron Stassart* (plaster, bust).

AUCTION RECORDS:

LOKEREN, 5 Oct 1996, *The Emperor Charles Hunting on Horseback* (bronze, 16¼ x 16½ ins / 41 x 42 cm) BEF 75,000.

JEIDELS, Charles Henry
German, 19th century.
Born 20 June 1862, in Frankfurt am Main; died 12 December 1900, in Hyères (France).
Painter.

Jeidels trained at the academies in Düsseldorf, Munich and Paris, settling in Pais, where he showed genre paintings, portraits and landscapes at the Salon (Société des Artistes Français in 1887, Société Nationale in 1890 and 1899). The Städelsches Institut in Frankfurt acquired a landscape by him.

JEJAR, Anatoli
Russian, 20th century.
Born in Dneprodzerzhinsk.
Painter. Still-lifes.

Anatoli Jejar studied at the school of fine art in Dniepropetrovsk from 1955 to 1961. He became a member of the Union of Painters of the Ukraine in 1979.

AUCTION RECORDS:

PARIS, 13 March 1992, *Apples* (oil on canvas, 27¼ x 31¼ ins / 69.5 x 79.5 cm) FRF 7,000. PARIS, 7 Oct 1992, *Children* (oil on canvas, 31 x 42¾ ins / 79 x 108.8 cm) FRF 6,500. PARIS, 31 Jan 1994, *Spring* (oil on canvas, 23½ x 31½ ins / 60 x 80 cm) FRF 4,000.

JEKE, Johannes de, also known as Icke
Flemish, 15th century.
Active in Cambrai in 1423.
Painter.
Flemish School.

Jeke has been wrongly confused with Jan van Eyck.

JEKEL, Juliette von, pseudonym of Balint
Hungarian, 20th century.
Born 7 May 1936, in Budapest.
Naturalised in Brazil, active in France.
Sculptor, ceramicist.

Juliette von Jekel studied at the Accademia di Belle Arti in Florence. She then went to Paris where she studied with Volti. Her sculptures, in polished copper, stone or clay, are austere, the dominant form being the curve.

She has taken part in several Paris salons including the Salon d'Automne, Salon de Mai and Salon Comparaisons and also in two sculpture exhibitions at the Musée Rodin. She showed work at the São Paulo Biennale (1964).

JEKER, Melchior Karl
Swiss, 19th century.
Born 30 April 1834; died c. 29 March 1868, in Bern.
Engraver (wood).

A citizen of Erschwil (Solothurn), Jeker was a collaborator and brother-in-law of Rudolf Buri.

JEKIMOFF. See **EKIMOV**

JEKLIN, Andreas
Swiss, 19th century.
Born 1823, in Schiers; died 1895.
Painter, draughtsman, miniaturist. Landscapes.

A pupil of Frizzoni, Jeklin continued his studies in Zurich, Munich and Geneva (with A. Calame). His works are in private collections in Chur, nearby Thusis and Andeer, Celerina (St Moritz) and Berlin.

MUSEUMS AND GALLERIES:

NEUCHÂTEL: *Landscape.*

AUCTION RECORDS:

VIENNA, 20 May 1987, *View of Lake Geneva with the Dents du Midi* (1873, oil on canvas, 18½ x 29½ ins / 47 x 75 cm) ATS 45,000.

JEKULINA, Olga
Russian, 20th century.
Born 1900, in Kherson; died 1973, in Moscow.
Painter. Historical subjects, landscapes, interiors with figures, still-lifes. Stage sets.

Olga Jekulina lived all her life in Moscow. She worked at the Higher State Artistic and Technical Workshops or Vkhutemas as a pupil of konstantin Korovin. In 1920-1930, she worked with propaganda teams and then, after 1944, in puppet theatres. She was a member of the Jar-Tsvet Association, taking part in its exhibitions in 1926, 1928 and 1929. She became a member of the Union of Painters of the USSR in 1940. During World War II, she designed some theatre sets for the army. After 1950, she was able to return to painting full time.

Olga Jekulina preferred to paint out of doors. Before the war her painting was influenced by modernist trends in post-Revolutionary Russia. After the war, her work became more picturesque and her palette brighter. From 1960 to 1970, she painted a cycle of works inspired by the historic landscapes of Krasnaia Presnia. A retrospective exhibition of her work was held in 1977.

BIBLIOGRAPHY:

Tableaux soviétiques, auction catalogue, Drouot, Paris, 3 October 1990.

JELE. See also **JEHLE**

JELE, Kaspar
Austrian, 19th century.
Born 5 January 1814, in Ried; died 17 December 1893, in Innsbruck.
Painter, engraver. History painting.

A pupil of Gebhard Flatz, then Johann Ender and Joseph Redl at the academy in Vienna, Jele worked in the studios of Kupelweiser and Frehrich. In 1842, he settled in Innsbruck, and from 1856 to 1884 taught at the academy there. He decorated a large number of churches, including Dominican churches in Innsbruck and Linz and the Lady Chapel in the church at Konstanz, the latter being executed at the orders of Franz Joseph I.

MUSEUMS AND GALLERIES:

INNSBRUCK (Tiroler Landesmus. Ferdinandeum): *The Distribution; The Poachers* - VIENNA (Kunsthistorisches Mus.): *Biblical Scene* (watercolour); sketches for the Lady Chapel in Konstanz Church.

JELENKIEWICZ, Christophe
Polish, 20th century.
Born 1931, in Warsaw.
Active in Switzerland from 1961.
Painter, watercolourist, draughtsman.

At the same time as pursuing his own career as a painter, from 1951 to 1957 Christophe Jelenkiewicz set up and ran his own art school. The Polish Ministry of Fine Art in Warsaw commissioned him to produce several drawings and watercolours. He left Poland for France in 1957 and settled in Switzerland in 1961. Many of his works are watercolours in which he conveys an abstract moving space and fantastical atmosphere hinting at some kind of plant life.

JELEZNOV, Mikhaïl
Russian, 20th century.
Born 1912; died 1978.
Painter. Figure compositions, figures, landscapes with figures.

Mikhaïl Jeleznov studied at the Ilya Repin Academy in Leningrad (now St Petersburg) under the direction of Aleksandr Osmerkin. An Artist of the People, he was also a member of the Union of Artists of the USSR. From 1942, his work was regularly exhibited in Leningrad and Moscow.

BIBLIOGRAPHY:
L'École de Léningrad, auction catalogue, Drouot, Paris, 19 November 1990.

MUSEUMS AND GALLERIES:
DRESDEN (Gemäldegal.) - MOSCOW (Ministry of Culture) - MOSCOW (Pushkin MFA) - MOSCOW (State Tretyakov Gal.) - NOVGOROD (MFA) - ST PETERSBURG (Gosudarstvennyj Muz. Istorii) - ST PETERSBURG (Gosudarstvennyj Russkij Muz.).

AUCTION RECORDS:
PARIS, 19 Nov 1990, *Games on the Beach* (1953, oil on card, 17 3/4 x 19 ins / 45 x 48 cm) FRF 25,000. PARIS, 4 March 1991, *Children* (1957, oil on card, 14 1/4 x 17 ins / 36 x 43 cm) FRF 5,800. PARIS, 25 March 1991, *Children* (1954, oil on card, 18 1/2 x 23 1/4 ins / 47 x 59 cm) FRF 10,500; *Reading Lesson* (1951, oil on card, 15 3/4 x 19 ins / 40 x 48 cm) FRF 15,000. PARIS, 25 Nov 1991, *Children of the Beach* (1965, oil on card, 13 x 17 3/4 ins / 33 x 45 cm) FRF 5,000.

JELGERHUIS, Johannes, or Jergerhuis
Dutch, 18th - 19th century.
Born 24 September 1770, in Leeuwarden; died 6 October 1836, in Amsterdam.
Painter. Portraits, scenes with figures, genre scenes, church interiors, landscapes, urban landscapes.

Johannes Jelgerhuis studied under his father Rienk Jelgerhuis and P. Barbiers. He became an actor in 1806 but also continued to paint. He is known for his church interiors and views of Leiden, Amsterdam and Delft, and also painted many portraits.

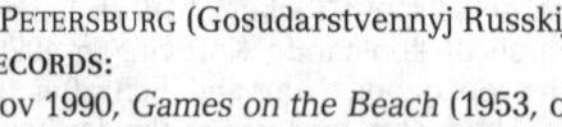

MUSEUMS AND GALLERIES:
AMSTERDAM: *A. d'Ailly's Laboratory in 1818; Same Subject; Pieter Mayer's Books; The Leiden Gate in Amsterdam; Corner of Delft; The Small Fish Market in Amsterdam.*

AUCTION RECORDS:
PARIS, 16-18 Feb 1931, *Dutch Skaters* (drawing with wash) FRF 220. PARIS, 19 March 1987, *View of Amsterdam in the Snow* (oil on canvas, 14 1/4 x 17 3/4 ins / 36.5 x 45 cm) FRF 28,000. AMSTERDAM, 11 April 1995, *Woman Embroidering* (oil on panel, 7 1/2 x 6 3/4 ins / 19 x 17 cm) NLG 4,838. GRAVENHAGE, 27 April 1998, *The Great Church, Zutphen* (1825, watercolour, 15 x 13 ins / 37 x 33 cm) NLG 3,800.

JELGERHUIS, Rienk
Dutch, 18th century.
Born 13 April 1729, in Leeuwarden; died 17 April 1806, in Amsterdam.
Painter, draughtsman, engraver.

Who taught Rienk Jelgerhuis is not known. He painted in oils, drew and made mezzotint engravings, mainly of portraits. He is believed to have produced 7,763 of these. He also made some fine drawings for a *Story of Joseph*. Jelgerhuis was highly regarded for his excellent painting of musical instruments. The Leiden museum has five portraits by him and there are three pastels at the municipal museum in The Hague. He also invented some special glasses which he used when drawing.

JELGERSMA, Tako or Jako Hajo
Dutch, 18th century.
Born 24 October 1702, in Harlingen; died 18 March 1795, in Haarlem.
Painter, watercolourist, pastellist, draughtsman.
Allegorical subjects, portraits, seascapes.

Tako Jelgersma was a pupil of W. Vitringa. He settled in Haarlem and was made a member of the guild in 1752. He produced many very fine sepia and bistre seascapes and also produced grisaille pieces in the style of Jan de Wit.

MUSEUMS AND GALLERIES:
BRUSSELS: *Allegory* (red chalk); *Cupids and Birds* (Indian ink) - HAARLEM (Teylers Mus.): *Angel's Head* (watercolour); *Drawings* - LONDON (British Mus.): *Seascape* (drawing) - VIENNA (Albertina Mus.): *Seascape* (drawing).

AUCTION RECORDS:
PARIS, 22 March 1991, *Fishermen's Boats in Holland* (1774, pen and brown wash, 6 x 8 3/4 ins / 15 x 22.5 cm) FRF 4,000. AMSTERDAM, 20 April 1993, *Family Portrait* (1833, pastel, 14 1/4 x 19 3/4 ins / 36.5 x 50 cm) NLG 3,680.

JELIAN DE BAUME
French, 14th century.
Painter. History painting.

Jelian de Baume was a valet to the Duke of Burgundy. He worked at the Château d'Argilly.

JELIESNOV, Michail Ivanovich, or Jeleznov, or Sheljesnov
Russian, 19th century.
Born 17 (29) February 1825.
Painter, engraver.

Michail Jeliesnov studied under Karl Bryulov at the fine art academy in St Petersburg.

JELIN, Christoph, or Yelin
German, 17th century.
Died 1610, in Tübingen.
Sculptor.

There are a number of memorials by Jelin in Tübingen Cathedral, but his principal work is considered to be the lower doorway of the Schloss in Tübingen. The alabaster surround of a door in the old castle in Stuttgart is also attributed to him.

JELINEK, Ernestine
German, 20th century.
Born 1884, in Berg-Reichenstein.
Painter. Portraits.

Ernestine Jelinek lived and worked in Märisch-Ostrau, where the local conservatory of arts and crafts still houses her *Portrait of G. Fielder*.

JELINEK, Jiri
Czech, 20th century.

Born 1901, in Dvur Králové, near Beroun; died 1941, in Mauthausen, where he had been deported.
Painter.

Jiri Jelinek studied in Paris where he was close to the Abstraction-Création group. During the 1930s, he painted abstract compositions influenced by the Cubism of Juan Gris.

He exhibited in Beroun in 1931. A posthumous exhibition of his work was mounted at the Mánes Hall in Prague in 1945.

BIBLIOGRAPHY:
Fifty years of Czechoslovak Painting from the Collections of the Galleries, 1918-1958, exhibition catalogue, Slovenska Narodna Gal., Bratislava, 1968 (in commemoration of the 50th anniversary of the Republic of Czechoslovakia).

JELÍNEK, Jirí Josef
Bohemian, 18th century.
Born 1697, in Kosmanos; died 1776.
Active in Kuttenberg (now Kutná Hora, Czech Republic).
Sculptor, engraver.
Bohemian School.

In 1747, Jirí Jelínek made the decorative ornaments and figures for an altar consecrated to the *Virgin with the Rosary* in the church of St Anne at the Parists' college in Beneschau (Benesov).

Jelínek was represented in the exhibition *Lumière et ténèbres, art et civilisation du Baroque en Bohême* (*Light and Darkness. Baroque Art and Civilisation in Bohemia*) at the Palais des Beaux-Arts in Lille in 2002.

BIBLIOGRAPHY:
Hladík, Tomás, *Josef Jirí Jelínek (1697 - 1776). barokní socharská dílna z kosmonos*, exhibition catalogue, Národní galerie, Prague, 1997. Vlnas, Vit (ed.), *Lumière et ténèbres, art et civilisation du Baroque en Bohême*, exhibition catalogue, Palais des Beaux-Arts, Lille, Réunion des musées nationaux, Paris, 2002.

JELINK, Hendricus Johannes K.
Dutch, 19th century.
Born 1808; died 1846 or 1847, in Nykerk.
Active in Nykerk.
Painter. Animals, landscapes.

AUCTION RECORDS:
AMSTERDAM, 7 Nov 1995, *River Landscape with Cows Drinking and a Woman in a Boat* (1836, oil on canvas, 17 x 20¼ ins / 43 x 51.5 cm) NLG 1,770.

JELISSEN, Meynert
Dutch, 18th century.
Engraver.

Worked in Amsterdam.

JELLE, Jacob. See **JEHLE**

JELLET, Mainie Harriet, or Jellett
Irish, 20th century.
Born 1897, in Dublin; died 1944, in Dublin.
Painter.

Manie (Mary Harriet) Jellett trained at the Metropolitan School of Art in Dublin, and under Walter Sickert at the Westminster School in London, from 1917. In 1920 she attended the studio of André Lhôte in Paris. In 1921 she became a follower of the French artist and writer Albert Gleizes. She exhibited with the Salon des Surindépendants from 1930 to 1938, and her work was featured in the exhibition *1940*, in 1931. Jellett was a member of the group Abstraction-Création from 1931-1936. In 1943, together with Evie Hone (another disciple of Gleizes), she founded the *Irish Exhibition of Living Art*, an annual show that sought to mark a break with the academic tradition.

Jellett and Hone were the first Irish artists to explore purely abstract painting. Jellett, in particular, is often hailed as the founder, in the 1920s, of the Irish contemporary art scene when she began publishing articles and lecturing on abstract art (especially its relationship to traditional Celtic decorative styles). Her later, large-scale canvases used colour, rhythm and Cubist-inspired forms to render recognisable Christian symbols.

In 1978 her work featured in the exhibition *Abstraction-Création 1931-1936* at Münster City Mmuseum, and the Musée d'Art Moderne de la Ville de Paris. Her work has featured in three posthumous exhibitions: in 1962, at the Dublin Municipal Art Gallery; 1974, Neptune Gallery, Dublin; 1991-1992, Irish Museum of Modern Art, Dublin. Jellett's work was strongly influenced by 'Orphic' abstraction and the spiritual ideas of Albert Gleizes.

AUCTION RECORDS:
LONDON, 2 Nov 1983, *Abstraction* (oil on card, 36 x 28¾ ins / 91.5 x 73 cm) GBP 3,000. DUBLIN, 12 Dec 1990, *Figure* (1925, gouache, 10½ x 4¾ ins / 26.7 x 12.1 cm) IEP 1,000. DUBLIN, 26 May 1993, *Nude Model* (oil on canvas/card, 12¾ x 10 ins / 32.4 x 25.4 cm) IEP 6,600. LONDON, 21 May 1999, *Abstract Composition* (1926, oil on canvas, 72 x 36 ins / 183 x 92 cm) GBP 24,000. LONDON, 21 May 1999, *Composition* (oil on canvas, 24 x 36 ins / 61 x 91 cm) GBP 35,000. LONDON, 18 May 2000, *Abstract Composition* (pencil and gouache, 10 x 7 ins / 25 x 18 cm) GBP 6,500. LONDON, 18 May 2000, *Abstract Composition* (1927, oil on canvas, 72 x 36 ins / 183 x 91 cm) GBP 20,000. DUBLIN, 6 March 2001, *Madonna and Child* (1930, watercolour and gouche, 19 x 9 ins / 47 x 24 cm) IEP 10,000. DUBLIN, 28 March 2001, *Still-life Study of a Vase of Flowers* (oil on canvasboard, 12 x 15 ins / 30 x 39 cm) IEP 5,000. DUBLIN, 17 Sept 2002, *Abstract* (1927, silkscreen and gouache, 15 x 12 ins / 39 x 30 cm) EUR 3,600. DUBLIN, 19 Nov 2002, *Abstract with Stepped Composition* (gouache over pencil on card, 7 x 6 ins / 17 x 16 cm) EUR 3,200. DUBLIN, 15 April 2003, *Female Nude* (gouache, 8 x 11 ins / 21 x 28 cm) EUR 7,000. DUBLIN, 25 Nov 2003, *Babbin and Betty at Home in Fitzwilliam Square* (1918, gouache, 9 x 8 ins / 24 x 21 cm) EUR 6,000. LONDON, 13 May 2004, *Three Elements* (oil on canvas, 36 x 28 ins / 91 x 71 cm) GBP 19,000. LONDON, 13 May 2004, *Abstract Composition* (1926, oil on canvas, 72 x 36 ins / 183 x 92 cm) GBP 20,000.

JELLEY, James Valentine
British, 19th - 20th century.
Born 1856, in Lincoln; died 1943.
Painter, watercolourist. Landscapes, flowers.

James Valentine Jelley worked in Birmingham and at Hampton in Arden in Warwickshire. He exhibited in the main London Galleries.

MUSEUMS AND GALLERIES:
BIRMINGHAM (Museum and Art Gallery): *River Scene; The Lily Garden\.*

JELLEY, William
Belgian, 19th - 20th century.
Born 1856, in Brussels; died 1932.
Painter. Landscapes with figures, harbour scenes, still-lifes.

William Jelley studied at the Académie Royale des Beaux Arts in Brussels and was a co-founder of various artistic groups, including *L'Effort and Pour l'Art* and, in 1903, Les Indépendants.

AUCTION RECORDS:
AMSTERDAM, 17 Sept 1991, *Capriccio: Harbour with Various Dignitaries on the Quayside* (oil on canvas, 24½ x 31¼ ins / 62 x 79.5 cm) NLG 3,450. AMSTERDAM, 3 Nov 1992, *Port of Antwerp* (oil on canvas, 23½ x 30¾ ins / 60 x 78 cm) NLG 4,600.

JELLOUSCHEKH, Franz. See **JELOVSEK**

JELOVSEK, David
Croat, 20th century.

Born 25 December 1879, in Zagreb.
Active in Germany.
Sculptor. Busts, monuments.

David Jelovsek studied at the academy of arts and crafts and the academy of fine art in Munich where he then settled. He executed monuments and decorative reliefs including a *St George* for Prince Fugger's residence of Babenhausen, busts including one of *Prince Philip Ernest of Hohenlohe* and relief portraits including one of *Princess Bariatinsky*.

JELOVSEK, Franz, or Illouscheg or Jellouschekh
Italian, 18th century.
Born 4 October 1700, in Carniole; died 1764; buried 2 January in Ljubljana, Slovenia.
Painter, fresco artist. Religious subjects.

Jelovsek painted frescoes and paintings on canvas, including a *Holy Family* in the church of St Peter in Ljubljana. Some of his frescoes are preserved in Kamnik, Slovenia (in the church of St Joseph), in the church of St Peter in Ljubljana (in the dome, the main nave and the chancel), in the churches of Vesela Gora and Zalostna Gora in Basse-Carniole, and in the parish churches of Nevlje and Celje.

JELTOV, Yuri
Russian, 20th century.
Born c. 1943.
Painter.
Neo-Constructivism.

Yuri Jeltov lives and works in Moscow. Following an Expressionist period, he looked to the Russian Constructivists of the 1920s, especially Malevich and El Lissitzky. He was able to find new ways of articulating squares and rectangles by means of refined chromic aberrations. He pays particularly close attention to the borders of his compositions, emulating the way that icons are set into precious frames. The Galerie Denise René in Paris held a solo exhibition of his works in 1990.

JELTSEMA, Frederik Engel
Dutch, 20th century.
Born 4 October 1879, in Uithuizen, near Groningen.
Sculptor. Statues, busts, monuments.

Frederik Jeltsema studied at the Amsterdam Hogeschool voor de Kunsten, where he was a Prix de Rome laureate in 1903. He went on to study in Rome and, for a period of four years, in Paris, where he was a pupil of Jules-Clément Chaplain. Jeltsema subsequently settled in The Hague.

Examples of Seltsema's work include: *Monument to J. de Witt* (The Hague), an allegorical statue of a seated young man (*Morning*), a marble *Bacchante*, and busts of the sculptor *F. Leenhoff* (in bronze) and of the Dutch cabinet minister *Kraus* (in marble).

JEMANTZOON, Maur., or Jemantsz.oen
Dutch, 15th century.
Active in Delft c. 1477.
Engraver, printer.

JEMEC, Andrej
Slovene, 20th century.
Born 1934, in Ljubljana.
Painter, engraver.

Andrej Jemec studied at the academy of fine art in Ljubljana. From the outset, he adopted the Informal Abstraction style, exploring the effects of different materials. His works feature broad patches of bright colour tending towards a monochrome effect, alternating smooth surfaces with areas of impasto with clearly defined edges. His work has also been interpreted as evoking fantasy worlds or abstract landscapism.

He exhibited for the first time in 1959. He has taken part in various collective exhibitions of young Yugoslav painters. He won the prize for engraving at the 1964 Tokyo Biennale. He has also held many solo exhibitions in Yugoslavia and abroad.

BIBLIOGRAPHY:
IIIe Salon international des Galeries Pilotes, exhibition catalogue, Musée cantonal, Lausanne, 1970.

JEMERIKINE, Wieceslav
Russian, 20th century.
Born 1942.
Painter. Landscapes with figures, still-lifes.

Wieceslav Jemerikine studied at the Repin Institute of the academy of fine arts in Leningrad and was the pupil of Ievsei Moisseenko. He became a Painter Emritus of the USSR.

AUCTION RECORDS:
PARIS, 23 March 1992, *Three Apples and Daisies* (oil on canvas, 31 1/2 x 23 1/2 ins / 80 x 60 cm) FRF 12,500. PARIS, 12 Dec 1992, *Lilac Blossoms* (oil on canvas, 29 1/2 x 25 1/2 ins / 75 x 65 cm) FRF 8,500.

JEMOLI, Achille
Italian, 19th - 20th century.
Born 1878, in Lecco, on Lake Como; died 1960.
Painter. Religious subjects, genre scenes, portraits, landscapes.

Jemoli was a pupil at the Accademia in Milan. His first exhibited painting was historical, *The Death of Nero*, and he later participated in many exhibitions in Milan, Turin, Genoa and Naples. Among his works are *When Night Falls*, *Portrait of a Woman*, *Lombard Costumes*, *Classical Spring* and *St John the Baptist*.

AUCTION RECORDS:
MILAN, 14 June 1989, *Garden near a Lake* (1940, oil on panel, 19 x 23 1/2 ins / 48.5 x 60 cm) ITL 1,000,000.

JEMTCHUNIKOV, Lev Mikhailovich
Russian, 19th - 20th century.
Born 2 November 1823, in the Orel region; died 1912.
Painter, engraver (etching).

After studying at the St Petersburg academy, Jemtchunikov continued his studies in Paris with A. Glaize and A. Delâtre in 1956. He worked in St Petersburg, in the Ukraine and in Moscow. He produced a series of etchings of *Picturesque Ukraine*.

JEN CHE-TCHONG. See **REN SHIZHONG**

JEN HIONG. See **REN XIONG**

JEN HSIUN. See **REN XUN**

JEN HSIUNG. See **REN XIONG**

JEN I. See **REN YI**

JEN JEN-FA. See **REN RENFA**

JEN K'ANG-MIN. See **REN KANGMIN**

JEN PO-NIEN. See **REN YI**

JEN SHIH-CHUNG. See **REN SHIZHONG**

JEN SIUN. See **REN XUN**

JEN TSEU-CHAO. See **REN ZIZHAO**

JEN TZU-CHAO. See **REN ZIZHAO**

JENCE, Henri
French, 17th century.
Active in Paris.
Engraver (line-engraving).

Jence's son was buried on 10 July 1680.

JENDOGOUROFF. See **ENDOGUROV**

JENDRASSIK, Jenô or Eugen, or Jendrassiz
Austrian, 19th - 20th century.
Born 30 October 1860, in Budapest; died December 1919.
Painter. Genre scenes.

Jenô Jendrassik studied under Löfftz in Munich and Aimé Morot in Paris. He returned to Budapest, where he was awarded a prize in 1891. Jendrassik also received an honourable mention at the Exposition Universelle of 1900 in Paris.

Museums and Galleries:

Budapest: *Nightmare*; *Misery*; *The End*.

Auction records:

Vienna, 17 March 1982, *Young Girl with a Dog* (1911, oil on canvas, 46 1/2 x 33 ins / 118 x 84 cm) ATS 25,000. Paris, 27 Feb 1984, *Young Girl with a King Charles Spaniel* (1911, oil on canvas, 46 x 33 ins / 117 x 84 cm) FRF 15,000. London, 24 June 1988, *Close Friends* (1911, oil on canvas, 43 x 33 1/4 ins / 109 x 84.5 cm) GBP 5,280.

JENDRITZKO, Guido

German, 20th century.

Born 1925, in Kirchhain.

Sculptor.

Guido Jendritzko studied from 1950 to 1956 under Karl Hartung at the college of fine arts in Berlin and was awarded the 1956 Berlin Critics' Prize. He was introduced by Uhlmann to the art of sheet metalworking, but Jendritzko soon returned to sculpting in stone and bronze. He took part in Documenta 1959 in Kassel, the Antwerp-Middelheim Biennale and other exhibitions by young German sculptors. In 1958, he exhibited solo in both Berlin and Frankfurt.

Early in his career, Jendritzko's marble sculptures were very much in the mould of his mentor Karl Hartung and, by extension, of Jean (Hans) Arp. He went on to produce a series of curvilinear and angular reliefs that could be incorporated into a building design. In the 1960s he began to work with slate, producing vacillating vegetable-like sculptures curiously disembodied in space.

JENÉ, Edgar

German, 20th century.

Born 1904, in Saarbrücken; died 1984, in La Chapelle-St-André (Nièvre), France.

From 1952 active in France.

Painter, draughtsman.

Novembergruppe.

Edgar Jené began to draw and paint in the 1920s. His early influences were post-Cézanne, but once he had been exposed in the 1930s to the writings and collages of André Breton and Max Ernst, Jené worked resolutely within the context of Surrealism, where his primary influences were Dali, Ernst and Tanguy.

Edgar Jené studied from 1922 to around 1925 at the fine arts academy in Munich; he completed his studies in Munich by 1928, including a study year spent in Paris. Between 1928 and 1935, he worked in Saarbrücken, although he visited Paris on a very frequent basis. The award of the Prix de Rome in 1931-1932 enabled him to spend nine months at the Villa Massimo in Rome. Jené took out Austrian nationality in Vienna in 1935, and spent time between 1938 and 1940 in Switzerland, Italy and the former Yugoslavia. He served in the Wehrmacht from 1940 to 1945, acting as an interpreter in a prisoner-of-war camp in Krems an der Donau. He returned to Vienna in 1945, and spent his time between 1950 and 1952 in Vienna, Saarbrücken and Paris. He settled permanently in France in 1952, living first near Sancerre and then moving in 1965 to La Chapelle-St-André.

Edgar Jené participated in a number of group exhibitions, notably in Paris at the 1928 Salon des Artistes Indépendants and the 1929 Salon des Surindépendants, and in Berlin at the Secession exhibition of 1930 and the Novembergrupppe exhibition of 1931. He also showed his work at a number of Surrealist exhibitions from 1952: at the Salon de Mai in Paris (1954, 1956 and 1962) and at the Salon Comparaisons (1957-1963). Solo exhibitions by Edgar Jené include those in at the Saarbrücken Museum in 1929, 1930-1931, 1932, 1951, 1964 and 1974; Kaiserslautern, (at the Pflaz Crafts Museum in 1929); Vienna (at the Volkstheater in 1945); Paris (at the Galerie du Dragon in 1948); New York (at the Artist's Gallery in 1949); Heidelberg (at the Kunstverein in 1950); Kaiserslautern (at the Pflazgalerie, 1950 and 1965); Paris (at the Galerie Furstemberg in 1954, 1957, 1959 and 1960); Bourges (at the Maison de la Culture in 1968); Paris (at the Coard Gallery in 1968); and in Saarbrücken (at the Saarland Museum in 1974).

Bibliography:

Bugs, Monica, *La Vie et l'Œuvre du peintre Edgar Jené (1904-1984)*, dissertation. Költzsch, Georg-W., *Schön ist nur das Wunderbare - Leben, Werke, Begegnungen des Malers Edgar Jené*, Die Mitte, Saarbrücken, 1984 (texts taken from André Breton/Paul Celan/Julien Gracq/Maurice Nadeau).

Museums and Galleries:

Heidelberg (Kunstverein) - Kaiserslautern (Pfalzgal.) - Mannheim (Städtische Kunsthalle) - Paris (MAMVP) - Rouen (MBA) - Saarbrücken (Saarlandmus.) - St-Étienne (Mus. d'Art et d'Industrie).

JENER. See **GENER**

JENERE, Pierre Jean Philippe

French, 20th century.

Born 12 July 1934, in Pontalier.

Painter, sculptor, burin engraver, lithographer. Local scenes.

A self-taught artist, Pierre Jean Philippe Jenere has done several kinds of work including photographic modelling and film acting in Italy and has spent time in Tahiti. He has exhibited his work in numerous solo shows in France and abroad, often in tourist hotels. One of his favourite subjects is the world of the circus, which he illustrates graphically. He has produced many postcards and greeting cards on copper, tin, aluminium and other metal. He engraves and carves glass, rare woods, stone, marble and bronze.

JENET, Johann, or Gennet

German, 17th century.

Active in Munich and perhaps in Venice at the beginning of the 17th century.

Engraver (burin).

Noted works by Johann Jenet include a *Christ on the Cross* (after J. Robusti), 1621, a *St John in the Desert*, 1621, *Venus and Adonis* after Jacopo Palma Giovanne, a *St George and the Dragon* after B.S. Reiter, and *Zara (Antonios) Episcopos Petinensis* after Titian.

JENET, Sebastian, or Jennet

Austrian, 17th century.

Engraver (burin), draughtsman.

Sebastian Jenet engraved plates for *Philippo Friderico episcopo Viennensi*, for *La Gara, Opera dramatica da Alberto Vimina*, and numerous portraits.

JENEVIÈRE. See **JENNEVIÈRE**

JENEWEIN, Felix

Bohemian, 19th century.

Born 4 August 1857, in Kuttenberg (now Kutná Hora); died 3 January 1905, in Brno.

Painter.

Felix Jenewein's first compositions were *Melody*, eight plates, and *Blood Tax*. In 1889, he made sketches for *St Gilbert, St Adalbert, and Mary on the Road to Golgotha*, then *Lamentations of Jeremiah* and *Good Friday Morning*. In 1896 came the large triptych *Judas*, and in 1900 the cycle of six plates entitled *Plague*.

Also worthy of mention are the altarpiece *St Francis Preaching*, *Death of St James* and *St Vincent Consoling the Prisoners*. He also designed some stained glass windows. Jenewein's estate, which included most of the original sketches for his works, was left to the gallery of modern art in Prague.

BIBLIOGRAPHY:
Felix Jenewein, exhibition catalogue, National Gall., Prague, 1996-1997.

JENICHEN, Balthasar, or Jenitch or Jenisch
17th century.
Died before 1621.
Active in Nuremberg.
Engraver (burin/wood), printer.

The dates of Balthasar Jenichen's period of active work are disputed, but there are certainly a number of dated pieces produced between 1560 and 1577. His portraits are interesting, especially those of the Protestant reformers: *Martin Bucer; Calvin; Camerarius; Erasmus; Huss; Luther; Melanchthon; Paracelsus; Zwingli; Solis* and others, 37 plates. He also issued 25 plates of notable individuals and 16 of the *Dukes of Saxony*. 24 *Scenes of the Life of Christ* are also recorded, 25 of the *Apostles*, 15 of the *Life of the Virgin*, 14 *Saints*, 12 *Labours of Hercules, The Seasons, The Elements*, and *The Senses*.

JENICHEN, Ernst
German, 19th century.
Born 8 April 1822, in Gotha; died 8 October 1874, in Gotha.
Painter, lithographer.

Ernst Jenichen studied in Munich and Antwerp before settling in Gotha, where he painted genre pictures such as *Children at Prayer* and portraits of notable figures in the town.

JENICKOVA, Jana
Czechoslovak, 20th century.
Born 3 July 1941, in Prague.
Painter (mixed media), mosaicist.

Jana Jenickova studied first at the school of decorative arts and then at the academy of fine arts in Prague until 1968. During this time, she visited several Mediterranean and North African countries. She later studied mosaics in Ravenna. Painting in oils, she also uses synthetic materials. Her style is abstract, although her shapes are nonetheless figurative.

JENISCH, Balthasar. See **JENICHEN**

JENKENSON, Anthony
British, 16th century.
Born c. 1560, in England.
Engraver.

Jenkenson produced maps and plans.

JENKIN, Bernard (Mrs). See **GILES Margaret M.**

JENKINGS, George
British, 20th century.
Born in London.
Active in the USA from 1922.
Sculptor.

George Jenkings settled in the USA in 1922 and trained at the Art Students League in New York. He subsequently embarked on a three-year collaboration with the Hispanic-American sculptor José de Creeft before settling in Florida, where he taught painting at Palm Beach. His abstract sculptures in wood or marble are characterised by their use of curvaceous lines and forms.

JENKINS, Anne
British, 18th - 19th century.
Active in London.
Painter. Flowers.

Anne Jenkins exhibited at the Royal Academy and Suffolk Street from 1786.

JENKINS, Blanche
British, 19th century.
Painter. Genre scenes.

Blanche Jenkins was a member of the Society of Lady Artists. She exhibited very frequently in London after 1872, notably at the Royal Academy and Suffolk Street.

AUCTION RECORDS:
LONDON, 17 June 1987, *Hush* (oil on canvas, 30 x 25 ins / 76 x 63.5 cm) GBP 2,800. BILLINGSHURST, 26 Jan 1999, *Little Apple Blossoms* (1910, oil on canvas, 14 x 16 ins / 36 x 40 cm) GBP 2,800. JERSEY, 21 April 1999, *Young Girl Sitting on Tree Branch Holding Flowers in Air* (1899, oil on canvas, 50 x 35 ins / 128 x 90 cm) GBP 10,000.

JENKINS, D.
British, 18th century.
Active in London c. 1780.
Engraver (burin).

D. Jenkins made engravings of the works of Angelica Kauffmann and Reynolds. There is also mention of two plates entitled *Horse Races* dated 1786.

JENKINS, David C.
British, 19th - 20th century.
Painter. Landscapes.

David C. Jenkins was active in Nottingham and Liverpool. In 1884 his work featured in an exhibition by the Royal Society of British Artists. He also exhibited with the Royal Academy from 1885 to 1891 and again in 1910. His bucolic paintings feature views that include village scenes, landscapes and riverscapes, and animals at pasture.

AUCTION RECORDS:
LONDON, 11 Nov 1981, *Spring landscape* (1891, oil on canvas, 43 1/4 x 33 1/4 ins / 110 x 84.5 cm) GBP 1,300. LONDON, 25 May 1983, *Spring* (oil on canvas, 49 3/4 x 88 1/2 ins / 126.5 x 224.5 cm) GBP 1,900.

JENKINS, Frank Lynn
British, 19th - 20th century.
Born 1870; died 1927.
Sculptor. Figures, nudes.

Frank Lynn Jenkins was a member of the Society of British Sculptors.

MUSEUMS AND GALLERIES:
NEW YORK (Metropolitan Mus. of Art): *Diana* (bronze).

AUCTION RECORDS:
NEW YORK, 22 May 1980, *Diana the Huntress* (1921, patinated bronze, h. 18 ins / 46 cm) USD 1,500. NEW YORK, 27 Sept 1990, *Young Woman Removing her Bathrobe* (bronze, h. 16 1/4 ins / 41 cm) USD 2,420. NEW YORK, 15 April 1992, *Torso of a Standing Female Figure* (brown-patinated bronze, h. 9 1/4 ins / 23.5 cm) USD 990.

JENKINS, George W.
American, 19th century.
Painter. Portraits.

George W. Jenkins was referred to by Florence Levy.

AUCTION RECORDS:
NEW YORK, 1902, *Portrait of George Washington*, USD 125.

JENKINS, Hannah Tempest
American, 20th century.
Born in Philadelphia; died 1927, in Claremont (in California).
Painter. Landscapes, still-lifes, portraits.

Hannah Tempest Jenkins studied at the Pennsylvania Academy of the Fine Arts in Philadelphia, and in Paris with Tony Robert-Fleury and Benjamin-Constant. She travelled to Japan. She taught at various institutions, including Pomona College, and founded the Rembrandt Club.

AUCTION RECORDS:
VERSAILLES, 18 March 1990, *The Market* (watercolour, 13¾ x 11 ins / 35 x 27 cm) FRF 8,000.

JENKINS, J.
British, 19th century.
Active in London.
Engraver (burin).
J. Jenkins may be Joseph John Jenkins. Noteworthy engravings by him include *Susanna and the Elders* after P.F. Mola, and *Holy Family* after Poussin (1844).

JENKINS, John Eliot
American, 19th - 20th century.
Born 1868, in Onaga (Kansas); died 1937, in Eastland (Texas).
Painter.
John Eliot Jenkins studied in Paris with Benjamin-Constant and Jules Lefebvre and was advised by Claude Monet. He exhibited mainly in Texas and Virginia.

JENKINS, Joseph John
British, 19th century.
Born 1811, in London; died 9 March 1885, in London.
Painter, watercolourist, engraver. Genre scenes, landscapes.
Joseph John Jenkins was trained by his father, D. Jenkins; however, he soon left engraving to turn to watercolour. He exhibited in London from 1829 to 1881. He became a member of the New Water-Colour Society in 1842, and was later admitted to the Society of Painters in Watercolours, of which he was secretary from 1854 to 1864. He collected documents with a view to writing a history of the latter society, but his death prevented him from finishing it.
MUSEUMS AND GALLERIES:
LONDON (Victoria and Albert Mus.): *Watercolour Paintings.*
AUCTION RECORDS:
PARIS, 1861, *Story of a Soldier* (watercolour) FRF 3,400. LONDON, 4 June 1909, *Summer Rain* (1873, watercolour) GBP 7; *Haymaking* (1872, watercolour) GBP 7. LONDON, 24 July 1911, *Games* (1852, watercolour) GBP 8. LONDON, 6 Nov 1995, *Country Holiday* (1862, watercolour with touches of white, 26¼ x 18¾ ins / 66.7 x 47.5 cm) GBP 1,840. LONDON, 17 March 1999, *Towing Path, Boys Fishing at Lock at Dusk* (1867, watercolour and gouache, 9 x 15 ins / 22 x 38 cm) GBP 3,200. LEWES, 5 Sept 2000, *Wedding Party Gathering Outside a Parish Church* (1863, Works on paper, 12 x 19 ins / 30 x 48 cm) GBP 1,900. STOCKHOLM, 8 March 2004, *Fishergirls* (oil on canvas, 34 x 43 ins / 87 x 110 cm) SEK 18,500. LONDON, 13 Oct 2004, *Sorting the Catch* (oil on canvas, 34 x 44 ins / 86 x 112 cm) GBP 2,300.

JENKINS, Lynn. See **JENKINS Frank Lynn**

JENKINS, Michael
American, 20th - 21st century.
Born 1957, in Savannah (Georgia).
Sculptor, draughtsman, installation artist.
Michael Jenkins lives and works in New York. His work has featured in a number of group exhibitions: 1987, Nexus Contemporary Arts Center, Atlanta; 1988, Nova Scotia College of Art and Design, Halifax; 1989, University Art Museum, Berkeley; 1990, Wadsworth Atheneum, Hartford; 1992, Art Museum, Portland. He has exhibited regularly in New York since 1988, notably in 1991 at Whitney Museum of American Art. Jenkins' work has also been the subject of a number of solo exhibitions, including: 1986, Atlanta; 1987, University of Georgia School of Art and Design, Atlanta; 1988, 1990, 1991, New York; 1991, Brussels and Santa Monica; 1992 San Francisco and Chicago.
BIBLIOGRAPHY:
Saltz, Jerry, '*Michael Jenkins Raft of Tender Mercies*' in *Arts Magazine*, periodical, New York, February, 1991.
AUCTION RECORDS:
NEW YORK, 11 Nov 1993, *Cabinet #2* (1989, construction using mixed media, 73 x 17 x 7 ins / 185.4 x 43.2 x 17.8 cm) USD 2,300.

JENKINS, Paul, pseudonym of William Paul
American, 20th century.
Born 12 July 1923, in Kansas City (Missouri); died 1980.
From 1953 also active in France.
Environmental artist, watercolourist.
Paul Jenkins studied at the Kansas City Art Institute from 1938 to 1941, then continued his training at Struthers in Ohio, before working as an apprentice in a ceramics factory. He was called up and fought in the American army from 1944 to 1946. After his demobilisation, he became a pupil of Morris Kantor and Yasuho Kuniyoshi at the Art Students League in New York from 1948 to 1951. He travelled to Sicily and Spain. After 1953, he divided his time between Paris and New York.

His earliest works, in the Abstract-Expressionist idiom, had names from Hermann Melville, such as *To Queequeg* of 1957, evoking the fury of the elements in a vast movement of thickly applied paints or Captain Ahab's blind search for the absolute. He then developed a more serene version of Tachism in paintings he often called *Phenomena*, in which only fleeting traces of the shadows of Plato's 'Myth of the Cavern' appear in a misty atmosphere with vague lighting. He himself commented: 'What is left in silence completes the expression and makes the unknown visible and perceptible.' Though he remained faithful to the title *Phenomena*, the appearance of his work continued to evolve, coming closer to that of the American painters Mark Rothko, Morris Louis and Kenneth Noland, for whom colour was becoming the dominant means of expression. During the 1980s, Jenkins more or less abandoned the flow technique in order to have greater control over the structure of his paintings in respect of the way things or non-things are seen through a prism.

Although his process, which can be compared to the ancient craft of marbling - making coloured paper in a tank in which liquid paints have been poured into the water - or to paintings from after 1980 with kaleidoscopic effects, is repeated indefinitely, it continues to give rise to new outbursts of more or less controlled tricks and chances, endlessly generating the unexpected and forcing one to pay attention. In 1988, moving on from the multiple to extension, he produced an environment of 11,000 square metres (13,000 square yards) of painted silks for the Peking Opera House.

Jenkins took part in a very large number of international group exhibitions of contemporary art and young American painters in the USA, Europe and Japan. These include the Venice, São Paulo and Tokyo Biennales, the Carnegie international in Pittsburgh and the Whitney International in New York. He showed collections of his paintings in countless solo exhibitions. The major ones from the first 25 years of his career are: 1954 Galerie Paul Facchetti, Paris; 1956 Martha Jackson Gallery, New York; 1957 Galerie Stadler, Paris; 1958 Martha Jackson Gallery, New York and Arthur Tooth and Sons Gallery, London, Los Angeles and Taos (New Mexico); 1960 Galerie Karl Flinker, Paris; 1962 Galerie Karl Flinker, Paris; 1962 Zurich; 1962 Kunstverein, Cologne; 1962 Milan; 1963 Galerie Karl Flinker, Paris; 1963 Stockholm; 1964 Tokyo Gallery, New Delhi, Kestner Gesellschaft, Hanover; 1965 Galerie Karl Flinker, Paris; 1965 Detroit; 1966 Montreal; 1968 Galerie Daniel Gervis, Paris; 1968 Martha Jackson Gallery, New York; 1968 Toronto; 1971 Martha Jackson gallery, New York; 1971 Chicago, Houston Museum of Fine Arts; 1972 Museum of Art, San Francisco; 1972 Gimpel Fils, London; 1972 Corcoran Gallery of Art, Washington; 1973 Galerie Karl Flinker, Paris; 1974 Palais des Beaux-Arts, Charleroi; 1974 Cologne; 1974 Gimpel-Weitzenhoffer Gallery, New

York; 1975 Munich, Brussels, Vienna; 1975 Art Fair, Basel; 1975 Gimpel-Weitzenhoffer Gallery, New York; 1976 Galerie Karl Flinker, Paris; 1977 Copenhagen, Teheran, Athens; 1977 Galerie Gimpel-Hanover, Zurich; 1977 Galerie Balcon des Arts, Paris and Gimpel-Weitzenhoffer Gallery, New York; 1978 Turin; 1981 Palm Springs Desert Museum; and a posthumous exhibition in 2001 at the Bouvet Ladubay Centre d'Art Contemporain, Saumur.

BIBLIOGRAPHY:

Sawyer, Kenneth B./Restany, Pierre, *The Painting of Paul Jenkins*, Éd. Two Cities, Paris, 1961. Cassou, Jean, *Paul Jenkins*, Gal. Karl Flinker, Paris, 1963. *Paul Jenkins*, exhibition catalogue, Gal. Karl Flinker, Paris, 1973. Elsen, Albert, *Paul Jenkins*, Abrams, New York, 1973. Restany, Pierre, '*Paul Jenkins - Un prisme brisé comme une table de poker*' in *Cimaise* n° 206-207, periodical, Paris, June-August 1990.

MUSEUMS AND GALLERIES:

AMSTERDAM (Stedelijk Mus.) - ANN ARBOR (University of Michigan Mus. of Art) - BERKELEY (AM, University of California) - BUFFALO (Albright-Knox AG) - DALLAS (MA): *Phenomena Franklin's Kite* (lithograph) - DUNKIRK (MAC): *Phenomena Wind Pool* (1977) - HOUSTON (MFA) - JERUSALEM (Israel Mus.) - LIVERPOOL (Walker AG) - LONDON (Tate Collection): *Phenomena, Yonder Near* (1964, acrylic/canvas) - MINNEAPOLIS (IA): *Phenomena Bite Metal* (1975, watercolour) - NEW YORK (MoMA) - NEW YORK (Solomon R. Guggenheim Mus.) - NEW YORK (Whitney Mus. of American Art) - PARIS (MAMVP) - PARIS (MNAM-CCI): *Phenomena Wakiyashi* (1961) - PHOENIX (AM): *Nile Guardian* (1957, oil); *Phenomena-Good Omen* (oil on canvas) - SAN FRANCISCO (California Palace of the Legion of Honor): *Celestial Phenomena Stanchion* (c. 1969-1970, watercolour) - SAN FRANCISCO (MoMA): *Phenomenom with Inviolate Cadmium Red* (1965, oil on canvas) - STANFORD (Iris and B. Gerald Cantor Center For Visual Arts, University) - STUTTGART (Staatsgal.) - TEHRAN (Honarhaye Moaser/MAC) - TORONTO (AG of Ontario) - WASHINGTON DC (Hirshhorn Mus. and Sculpture Garden) - WASHINGTON DC (Smithsonian American AM): *Phenomena Ring Rang Rung* (1961, oil on canvas); *Phenomena: Sun Over the Hour Glass* (1966, synthetic polymer/acrylic on fabric/canvas).

AUCTION RECORDS:

COLOGNE, 4 Dec 1969, *Phenomena Violet,* DEM 8,000. NEW YORK, 14 May 1970, *Phenomena over Chalice* (watercolour) USD 2,750. NEW YORK, 17 Nov 1971, *Phenomena Spectrum Sundance,* USD 3,000. PARIS, 12 June 1974, *Phenomena Highwater,* FRF 18,000. NEW YORK, 14 Dec 1976, *Phenomena Telling Green* (acrylic, 25 1/2 x 21 ins / 65 x 53.5 cm) USD 1,200. NEW YORK, 17 Nov 1977, *Phenomena High Vortex* (1966, oil on canvas, 48 x 50 ins / 122 x 127 cm) USD 4,000. NEW YORK, 19 Oct 1979, *Phenomena Salt on Mantle* (1967, watercolour, 74 3/4 x 39 1/4 ins / 189.8 x 99.7 cm) USD 3,600. NEW YORK, 19 Oct 1979, *Dory's Locker* (1962, oil on canvas, 64 x 116 ins / 162.5 x 294.5 cm) USD 7,500. NEW YORK, 3 Oct 1980, *Sanctuary Light Graphic* (1972, coloured lithograph, 38 1/4 x 53 3/4 ins / 97.2 x 136.8 cm) USD 1,400. NEW YORK, 12 May 1981, *Phenomena Anvil Still Anvil* (1974, acrylic/canvas, 50 x 80 ins / 127 x 203.2 cm) USD 20,000. NEW YORK, 13 May 1981, *Phenomena Voice of Hamlet* (1967, watercolour, 30 1/2 x 22 ins / 77.5 x 56 cm) USD 2,200. NEW YORK, 21 May 1983, *Phenomena Turning Pillar* (1962, watercolour, 30 1/4 x 22 1/4 ins / 76.9 x 56.5 cm) USD 2,200. NEW YORK, 10 Nov 1983, *Phenomena Warlock* (1963-1964, oil on canvas, 72 x 48 ins / 182.9 x 121.9 cm) USD 18,000. NEW YORK, 27 Feb 1985, *Phenomena Anvil Still Anvil* (1974, acrylic/canvas, two panels, 50 x 80 ins / 127 x 203.2 cm) USD 25,000. GENEVA, 24 Nov 1987, *Phenomena Heaven, Heaven, Heaven* (watercolour, 30 x 22 ins / 75.3 x 55.7 cm) CHF 7,500. NEW YORK, 20 Feb 1988, *Remarkable Éminence Grise* (1962, acrylic/canvas, 76 3/4 x 51 1/4 ins / 195 x 129.9 cm) USD 9,900; *Remarkable Curtain of Fire* (1986, acrylic/canvas, 38 3/4 x 120 ins / 98.7 x 305 cm) USD 19,800. PARIS, 20 March 1988, *Phenomena St Elmo's Fire* (1960, acrylic/canvas, 38 1/4 x 51 1/4 ins / 97 x 130 cm) FRF 35,000. LONDON, 29 March 1988, *Fall of the Sunfish* (1958, oil on canvas, 39 1/4 x 33 1/4 ins / 99.7 x 84.5 cm) GBP 2,200. NEW YORK, 4 May 1988, *Samothrace* (1967, oil on canvas, 71 1/2 x 48 ins / 181.6 x 122 cm) USD 9,350. NEW YORK, 8 Oct 1988, *Phenomena Draught* (1978, acrylic/canvas, 77 x 115 3/4 ins / 195.6 x 294 cm) USD 23,100. LONDON, 20 Oct 1988, *Phenomena to Shade the Gaze* (1965, watercolour/paper, 30 3/4 x 23 ins / 78 x 57.5 cm) GBP 2,310. PARIS, 12 Dec 1988, *Phenomena. The Long Run* (1982, coloured ink, 43 1/4 x 31 1/2 ins / 110 x 80 cm) FRF 13,000. MILAN, 14 Dec 1988, *Phenomena invoking the Solstice* (1970, oil on canvas, 38 1/4 x 76 3/4 ins / 97 x 195 cm) ITL 19,000,000. LONDON, 23 Feb 1989, *Phenomena of the 14 July* (watercolour/paper, 29 1/2 x 23 3/4 ins / 75 x 60.5 cm) GBP 2,200. ROME, 17 April 1989, *Untitled* (gouache/paper, 29 1/2 x 22 ins / 75 x 55 cm) ITL 5,200,000. NEW YORK, 4 May 1989, *Phenomena of the Wind in the Burning Fog* (1979, acrylic/canvas, 76 3/4 x 41 ins / 195 x 104.2 cm) USD 19,250. PEKING, 6 May 1989, *Phenomena Magnetic Arch* (1984-1987, acrylic and collage/canvas, 65 1/4 x 38 ins / 166 x 96.5 cm) FRF 102,080. PARIS, 21 June 1989, *Phenomena with Light* (1961, oil on canvas, 39 1/4 x 25 1/2 ins / 100 x 64.5 cm) FRF 110,000. NEW YORK, 5 Oct 1989, *Phenomena Spiral of the Sun* (1981, acrylic/canvas, 78 x 67 ins / 198 x 170 cm) USD 25,300. LONDON, 26 Oct 1989, *Phenomena of the Right Corner* (1963, acrylic/canvas, 25 1/4 x 20 3/4 ins / 64 x 53 cm) GBP 4,620. MILAN, 8 Nov 1989, *Phenomena of Veils at Vespers* (1970, acrylic/canvas, 61 x 55 ins / 155 x 140 cm) ITL 34,000,000. PARIS, 18 Feb 1990, *Composition* (acrylic/paper, 29 1/4 x 22 ins / 74.5 x 56 cm) FRF 35,000. NEW YORK, 21 Feb 1990, *Phenomena Anvil Still Anvil* (1974, acrylic/canvas, two panels, 50 x 80 1/2 ins / 127 x 204.7 cm) USD 28,600. PARIS, 3 May 1990, *Composition* (acrylic/paper, 6 x 9 3/4 ins / 15 x 25 cm) FRF 24,000. NEW YORK, 7 May 1990, *Phenomena Maize Bringer* (1960, oil on canvas, 77 3/4 x 62 ins / 197.5 x 157.5 cm) USD 55,000. PARIS, 18 June 1990, *Phenomena Near Gander* (1965, acrylic/canvas, 35 1/2 x 39 3/4 ins / 90 x 101 cm) FRF 100,000. PARIS, 2 July 1990, *Phenomena Prims Reach* (1988, acrylic/canvas, 28 1/4 x 45 ins / 72 x 114 cm) FRF 60,000. VERSAILLES, 16 Dec 1990, *Phenomena Maize Bringer* (1960, oil on canvas, 78 x 61 3/4 ins / 198 x 157 cm) FRF 300,000. NEW YORK, 13 Feb 1991, *Phenomena when I was Looking into the Distance* (1960, oil and chrysochrome/canvas, 78 x 62 ins / 198.1 x 157.5 cm) USD 37,400. PARIS, 19 April 1991, *Phenomena Cast a Spell* (1963, oil on canvas, 59 x 39 1/4 ins / 150 x 100 cm) FRF 72,000. COPENHAGEN, 4 March 1992, *Composition* (watercolour, 29 1/2 x 22 ins / 75 x 55 cm) DKK 15,000. PARIS, 15 June 1992, *Phenomena Early Omens* (1982, acrylic/canvas, 50 x 59 3/4 ins / 127 x 152 cm) FRF 42,000. NEW YORK, 6 Oct 1992, *Phenomena The Wheel of Fortune* (1967, acrylic/canvas, 63 3/4 x 47 3/4 ins / 161.9 x 121.3 cm) USD 14,300. NEW YORK, 23-25 Feb 1993, *Phenomena of the Site of Comstock II* (1974, acrylic/canvas, 77 x 160 ins / 195.6 x 406.4 cm) USD 46,000. LONDON, 25 March 1993, *Phenomena of the Yellow Edge* (1962, watercolour/paper, 30 x 21 3/4 ins / 75.3 x 55.4 cm) GBP 805. STOCKHOLM, 10-12 May 1993, *Phenomena Crossing the Sun's Anvil* (mixed media/canvas, triptych, 32 x 70 1/2 ins / 81 x 179 cm) SEK 66,000. LE TOUQUET, 30 May 1993, *Phenomena Orange Profile* (1987, watercolour, 42 1/4 x 30 ins / 107 x 76 cm) FRF 22,000. PARIS, 23 June 1993, *Phenomena to Remember* (acrylic/canvas, 39 1/4 x 31 1/2 ins / 100 x 80 cm) FRF 45,000. STOCKHOLM, 30 Nov 1993, *Phenomena the Throneroom of Heaven* (acrylic/canvas, 70 3/4 x 76 3/4 ins / 180 x 195 cm) SEK 130,000. LONDON, 26 May 1994, *Phenomena the Limit of the Earth* (1984, acrylic/canvas, 29 1/4 x 24 ins / 74 x 61 cm) GBP 3,680. ZURICH, 2 Dec 1994, *Phenomena Blue Ash* (1979, watercolour, 31 x 43 ins / 78.7 x 109.2 cm) CHF 9,000. AMSTERDAM, 8 Dec 1994, *Untitled* (watercolour/paper, 31 x 43 1/4 ins

/ 79 x 110 cm) NLG 3,450. PARIS, 5 April 1995, *Phenomena Overseer* (1989, acrylic/canvas, 45 x 57 1/2 ins / 114 x 146 cm) FRF 30,000. NEW YORK, 7 May 1996, *Phenomena over the Face of the Dials* (1966, acrylic/canvas, 96 x 72 ins / 243.9 x 182.9 cm) USD 11,500. MILAN, 20 May 1996, *Untitled* (watercolour/paper, 43 1/4 x 30 3/4 ins / 110 x 78 cm) ITL 2,070,000. LONDON, 23 May 1996, *Phenomena, Prism, Aurora* (1989, acrylic/canvas, 31 3/4 x 39 1/4 ins / 80.7 x 100 cm) GBP 5,175. PARIS, 28 June 1996, *Untitled* (watercolour, 22 x 30 ins / 56 x 76 cm) FRF 5,000. PARIS, 7 Oct 1996, *Phenomena Elliptical* (1985-1986, acrylic/canvas, 96 x 77 1/4 ins / 244 x 196 cm) FRF 55,000. PARIS, 23 Feb 1997, *Phenomena Prism Entry* (1987, watercolour/paper, 42 1/2 x 30 1/4 ins / 108 x 77 cm) FRF 12,000. PARIS, 28 April 1997, *Phenomena Winston Signal* (1975, watercolour/paper, 29 1/2 x 22 ins / 75 x 55 cm) FRF 7,000. ZURICH, 18 Nov 1997, *Phenomena Walk with Red* (1962, watercolour, 29 3/4 x 22 ins / 75.5 x 55 cm) CHF 4,000. PARIS, 23 March 1998, *Phenomena Angel of the Part* (1990, watercolour/paper, 22 x 29 1/2 ins / 55 x 75 cm) FRF 6,000. PARIS, 23 June 1999, *Phenomena Declension of Light* (1985, oil on canvas, 81 x 78 ins / 205 x 198 cm) FRF 50,000. NEW YORK, 10 Nov 1999, *Phenomina* (1965, oil on canvas, 68 x 38 ins / 173 x 97 cm) USD 7,500. HAMBURG, 8 June 2000, *Phenomena Antler Path* (oil on canvas, 36 x 20 ins / 91 x 51 cm) DEM 14,000. LOS ANGELES, 5 Dec 2000, *Phenomena Blue Greets Cardinal* (oil on canvas, 77 x 74 ins / 196 x 188 cm) USD 8,000. NEW YORK, 15 May 2001, *Phenomenon Seventh Undertow* (1971, oil on canvas, 63 x 116 ins / 161 x 295 cm) USD 11,000. MONTREAL, 22 Oct 2001, *Phenomena Dylan's Host* (oil on canvas, 64 x 48 ins / 163 x 122 cm) CAD 12,000. NEW YORK, 20 Feb 2002, *Phenomena Neanderthal Burn* (1973, watercolour, 72 x 36 ins / 183 x 91 cm) USD 7,500. NEW YORK, 17 April 2002, *Phenomena Feel the Helm* (1979, oil on canvas, 68 x 65 ins / 173 x 165 cm) USD 9,500. NEW YORK, 7 Oct 2003, *Phenomena Katherine's Guardian* (oil on canvas, 63 x 37 ins / 161 x 94 cm) USD 6,000. NEW YORK, 3 Dec 2003, *Phenomena Veronica* (1968, oil on canvas, 63 x 38 ins / 161 x 97 cm) USD 7,500. NEW YORK, 13 July 2004, *Phenomena Port of Call* (1984, oil on canvas, 77 x 128 ins / 196 x 325 cm) USD 19,000. NEW YORK, 13 July 2004, *Phenomena 190 Degree Prism* (1985, oil on canvas, 77 x 131 ins / 196 x 332 cm) USD 26,000.

JENKINS, Thomas
British, 18th century.
Born c. 1722, in Sidbury; died 1798, in Yarmouth.
Painter. History painting, portraits.

Thomas Jenkins was a history and portrait painter before becoming a dealer and important figure in British artistic circles in Rome. He studied in London under Hudson. By 1753, he was living in the same house as Richard Wilson in Rome and became an honorary member of the Accademia di San Luca in 1761.

AUCTION RECORDS:
LONDON, 18 June 1976, *Portrait of Thomas Brand* (1753, oil on canvas, 45 1/2 x 36 ins / 115.5 x 91.5 cm) GBP 1,400. LONDON, 6 Nov 1995, *Portrait of Sir William Morice, Bt., Standing in a Landscape Wearing a Grey Coat and Red Breeches* (oil on canvas, 19 3/4 x 16 ins / 50 x 40.5 cm) GBP 1,150.

JENKS, Col. Albert
American, 19th century.
Born c. 1824, in New York; died 22 July 1901, in Los Angeles.
Painter. Portraits.

JENKS, Phoebe A.
Maiden name: Pickering Hoyt
American, 19th century.
Born 28 July 1847, in Portsmouth (Massachusetts); died 1907, in New York.
Painter. Portraits.

Phoebe A. Jenks studied in Boston with B.C. Porter and D.T. Kendrick, and settled in that city, where she continued to exercise her talent. She was known mainly for her portraits of women and children. She was married to Lewis E. Jenks.

AUCTION RECORDS:
NEW YORK, 18 March 1998, *Portrait of a Gentleman* (oil on canvas, 48 x 35 1/4 ins / 121.9 x 89.5 cm) USD 6,900. PARIS, 16 Nov 2001, *Boy in a Velvet Suit* (1878, oil on canvas, 50 x 27 ins / 127 x 69 cm) FRF 55,000.

JENLIS, Édouard
French, 19th century.
Born 19th century, in Fontaines-Montdidier.
Sculptor.

Édouard Jenlis featured at the Salon of the Société des Artistes Français and was awarded an honourable mention in 1896.

JENNER, Anton Detlef
German, 18th century.
Died 26 June 1732.
Active in Brunswick.
Sculptor (including wood).

The Catholic church of St Nicholas in Brunswick contains statues of St Peter and St Paul by Anton Jenner, also a Baroque canopy on the pulpit. Also by him is the marble and alabaster high altar at the church of St Martin in the same city.

JENNER, Eduard
Swiss, 19th century.
Born 27 January 1830, in Bern.
Miniaturist, copyist.

JENNER, Emanuel
Swiss, 18th - 19th century.
Baptised 4 March 1756 in Ammerswil (Aargau canton); died 31 March 1813, in Bern.
Painter, watercolourist, draughtsman. Military subjects.

Emanuel Jenner spent 20 years or so in Holland as an officer of the Wattenwyl company. On his return to Switzerland in 1795, he took up painting, mainly watercolours.

JENNER, Enno Alexander
German, 20th century.
Born 9 October 1878, in Bautzen.
Painter.

Studied at the academies of Karlsruhe and Dresden.

AUCTION RECORDS:
PARIS, 13 Nov 1922, *Capuchin Cloister in Belp* (watercolour) FRF 200.

JENNER, Isaac. See **JEHNER Isaac**

JENNER, Johann Niklaus
French, 18th - 19th century.
Born 23 November 1743, in La Rochelle; died 16 August 1817, in Muri.
Watercolourist, miniaturist.

Johann Niklaus Jenner was an officer in the French army. He submitted works for exhibition in Bern in 1810.

JENNER, Samuel
Swiss, 17th - 18th century.
Born 1653; died 6 March 1720.
Architect.

Of Bernese origins, Samuel Jenner was said at the time to be a 'foreman' or 'site supervisor'.

JENNER, Thomas
British, 17th century.
Active c. 1650.
Engraver.

Thomas Jenner engraved portraits including *Olivier Cromwell, Earl of Rutland* and *Sir William Wadd*. There is mention of an engraving entitled *Soverayne of the Seas*. He was also a dealer in engravings.

JENNET, Eugène
French, 19th century.
Born 1828.
Painter. Landscapes.
MUSEUMS AND GALLERIES:
CHERBOURG: *Kelp Fishers on the Normandy Coast.*
AUCTION RECORDS:
LONDON, 21 Nov 1997, *Stockholm* (oil on panel, 18 1/2 x 24 1/2 ins / 47.2 x 62 cm) GBP 5,175.

JENNET, Sebastian. See **JENET**

JENNETER, Lukas. See **GMÜNDER**

JENNETT. See **JANETTE**

JENNEVIÈRE, Jacques, or Gennevière or Yennevière
Flemish School, 17th century.
Died after 1676.
Active in Tournai.
Painter.
The son of Jean Jennevière, he was registered as a guild member in 1659.

JENNEVIÈRE, Jean, or Gennevière or Yennevière
Flemish School, 17th century.
Born in St-Amand (Cher); died after 1643.
Painter.
Jean Jennevière was made a master of the Tournai guild in 1626. He was paid 98 *livres* for a *Nativity* he painted for a church in Ramelies.

JENNEVIÈRE, Jean Baptiste, or Gennevière
Flemish School, 17th century.
Active in Tournai.
Painter.
The son of Jacques Jennevière.

JENNEWEIN, Carl Paul
German, 20th century.
Born 2 December 1890, in Stuttgart; died 1978.
Sculptor. Architectural integration, monuments.
Carl Paul Jennewein was a member of the National Academy of Design in New York and the Alumni Academy in Rome - he received awards from both institutions. His sculptures decorate a number of theatres, stores and hotels in New York City. Jennewein also sculpted a number of memorials.
AUCTION RECORDS:
NEW YORK, 29 Sept 1977, *Golden Diana* (gilded bronze, h. 18 1/4 ins / 46.3 cm) USD 2,750. NEW YORK, 5 Dec 1980, *Diana* (patinated bronze, h. 18 1/4 ins / 46.4 cm) USD 2,600. NEW YORK, 26 June 1981, *Rest* (1920, black-patinated bronze, l. 19 1/4 ins / 48.9 cm) USD 2,000. NEW YORK, 18 Dec 1991, *At Rest: Reclining Female Nude, Draped* (1920, brown-patinated bronze, h. 12 ins / 30.5 cm) USD 4,400. NEW YORK, 26 May 1993, *Greek Dance* (bronze, h. 18 1/4 ins / 46.4 cm) USD 9,775. NEW YORK, 4 Dec 1996, *Cupid and Psyche* (1926, bronze, group, h. 12 1/2 ins / 32 cm) USD 6,325.

JENNEWEIN, Felix. See **JENEWEIN**

JENNEY, Edgar Whitfield
American, 19th - 20th century.
Born 11 December 1869, in New Bedford (Massachusetts); died 1939.
Painter, decorative designer. Murals.
Edgar Whitfield Jenney was a pupil of Laurens in Paris. He was a member of the American Federation of the Arts. He specialised in painting murals.

JENNEY, Neil
American, 20th century.
Born 1945, in Torrington (Connecticut).
Painter, sculptor, mixed media.
Bad Painting, New Image.
Neil Jenney studied at the Massachusetts College of Art in Boston, where he encountered Abstract Expressionism, which became an important influence on his early work. He lives and works in New York.

Jenney's earliest paintings date from the late 1950s. Later he created sculptures using tree branches, metal wire and neon, in a style closely similar to that of Arte Povera. He quickly turned to the creation of Conceptual Art installations using everyday objects, as in *The Press Piece* (1969), which consists of two storeys featuring words in neon (on the first level) and yellowed newspaper cuttings in frames (on the second level). His work has always positioned itself at the forefront of the avant-garde, although he freely admitted that Abstract Expressionism and Minimalism constituted a 'point of no return'. His perception that art had 'done abstraction' and demanded a return to realism inspired him (from 1969) to create paintings challenging specific types of imagery. During the same period he became a pioneer of so-called 'Bad Painting', an American movement that began as a reaction to the abstract tendency in art in the 1970s, but which sought to differentiate itself from the other anti-Abstract movements of the time (including Conceptual Art, the 'pretty', highly-finished works of the Hyperrealists, and Pop Art). Jenney's works during this period depict his immediate environment, using plain, roughly-applied colours, clearly visible brushwork, drips and streaks. His adoption of so-called Bad Painting was reflected in the choice of subject-matter - banal narrative scenes reminiscent of children's drawings. *Them and Us* (1969) is an implicit comment on the Cold War, showing two planes in a blue sky; *Aggressor and Possessor* (1969) depicts a young man and his dog. His colour palette remains similarly childlike and reductive: green for landscape, blue for sky and water, and brown for the earth or floor. In the latter painting, the grass is green, the man's clothing is blue and red, and the dog is black. There are no extraneous details or ornamentation to detract from the main image. In 1971, reacting to the prevailing tendency to classify his work as Punk Art, Jenney adopted a more refined approach that emphasised his accomplished technique. He abandoned acrylics in favour of highly finished oil paintings on panels, evocative of 19th-century art. Numerous subsequent works have focused on landscape, addressing important environmental issues. His works are characterised by the use of prominent, window-like frames incorporated into the composition and often bearing the picture's title. The *North America* series depicts tree motifs on narrow, elongated canvases (vertical and horizontal) set within broad frames of painted wood, featuring the title of the work in large letters (*Meltdown Morning - North America Abstracted - Venus from N.A.*). The viewer's attention is inevitably drawn first to these highly prominent inscriptions rather than to the work itself. Jenney's work has embraced successive movements but remains characterised by its highly personal, essentially figurative slant, and by an emphasis on technique. Great artists, he has said, are never content to explore art for art's sake; rather, art should address social issues and aim to foster a more humane society.

His work has featured in a number of group exhibitions: 1970 *When Attitudes Become Form*, Kunsthalle, Bern (one of the first exhibitions of Conceptual Art); 1972, Documenta V, Kassel (Hyperrealism section); 1978 *Bad Painting*, New Museum, New York; 1979 *New Image Painting*, Whitney Museum of American Art, New York. His rare solo exhibitions include: 1968, Cologne; 1970, New York; 1981-1982, University Art Museum, Berkeley, Stedelijk Museum in Amsterdam, Louisiana Museum in Humlebaek (Denmark), and Contemporary Art Museum, Houston; 1991, Museum of Modern Art, New York; 1994, Whitney Museum of American Art, New York.

BIBLIOGRAPHY:

Rosenthal, M., *Neil Jenney: Paintings and Sculpture 1967-1980*, University Art Museum, Berkeley (California), Berkeley, 1981. Jenney, Neil,, *Neil Jenney: The Bad Years 1969-1970*, Gagosian Gallery, New York, 2001.

MUSEUMS AND GALLERIES:

LOS ANGELES (County MA): *Acid Story* (1983-1984) - NEW YORK (MoMA): *Them and Us* (1969) - NEW YORK (Whitney Mus. of American Art): *Saw and Sawed* (1969); *North American Abstracted* (1978-1980) - PHILADELPHIA (MA): *Meltdown Morning* (1975).

AUCTION RECORDS:

LONDON, 6 Dec 1983, *Angles and Curves* (1971, oil on canvas, 54 x 52 ins / 137 x 132 cm) GBP 17,000. NEW YORK, 11 Nov 1986, *Row and Row* (1968, acrylic/canvas, 54 1/2 x 72 1/4 ins / 138.5 x 183.5 cm) USD 130,000. NEW YORK, 3 May 1988, *Angles and Curves* (1971, oil and graphite/canvas, 58 x 56 1/4 ins / 147.3 x 142.9 cm) USD 165,000. NEW YORK, 9 Nov 1988, *Man+Thing* (1969, oil on canvas, 71 1/4 x 44 1/4 ins / 181.2 x 112.6 cm) USD 242,000. NEW YORK, 3 May 1989, *Schmuck and Schlemiel* (1969, oil on canvas, 59 x 77 ins / 149.8 x 194.7 cm) USD 264,000. NEW YORK, 5 Oct 1989, *Felis Catus* (acrylic/canvas, 18 x 66 1/2 ins / 45.5 x 169 cm) USD 198,000. NEW YORK, 1 May 1991, *Love and Joy* (1969, acrylic/canvas, 59 3/4 x 76 ins / 151.8 x 193.3 cm) USD 231,000. NEW YORK, 12 Nov 1991, *Schmuck and Schlemiel* (1969, acrylic and graphite/canvas, 59 x 76 3/4 ins / 149.8 x 195 cm) USD 170,500. NEW YORK, 5 May 1992, *Saw and Sawed* (1969, acrylic/canvas, 60 x 65 ins / 151.5 x 165 cm) USD 198,000. NEW YORK, 6 Oct 1992, *Man and Beast* (1970, oil on canvas, 60 1/2 x 85 1/4 ins / 153.7 x 216.5 cm) USD 115,500. NEW YORK, 8 Oct 1992, *Shepherd and Sheep* (1969, acrylic/canvas, 58 x 58 ins / 147.3 x 147.3 cm) USD 82,500. NEW YORK, 18 Nov 1992, *Stop and Spades* (1970, acrylic and graphite/canvas, 58 1/2 x 83 1/4 ins / 148.6 x 211.5 cm) USD 176,000. NEW YORK, 4 May 1994, *Paint and Painted* (1970, acrylic and graphite/canvas, 48 x 48 1/4 x 3 1/2 ins / 122.2 x 122.6 x 8.9 cm) USD 151,000. NEW YORK, 22 Feb 1995, *Vexation and Rapture* (1969, oil on canvas, 62 1/2 x 96 ins / 159 x 244 cm) USD 85,000. NEW YORK, 9 May 1996, *Shepherd and Sheep* (1969, acrylic/canvas, 57 3/4 x 58 ins / 147 x 147.3 cm) USD 57,500. NEW YORK, 7 May 1997, *Man and Beast* (1970, oil on canvas, 61 x 51 ins / 154.9 x 129.5 cm) USD 57,500. NEW YORK, 19 May 1999, *Dog and Food* (1969, graphite and oil on paper, 55 x 76 ins / 140 x 192 cm) USD 75,000. NEW YORK, 18 Nov 1999, *Atmosphere* (oil on panel, 33 x 80 ins / 84 x 202 cm) USD 35,000. LOS ANGELES, 7 June 2000, *Forest and Lumber* (acrylic on canvas, 58 x 68 ins / 148 x 173 cm) USD 175,000. NEW YORK, 15 Nov 2000, *Piano Pianist* (oil on canvas, 58 x 76 ins / 147 x 193 cm) USD 95,000. NEW YORK, 16 May 2001, *Scent and Pup* (1970, acrylic on canvas, 32 x 48 ins / 81 x 123 cm) USD 75,000. LOS ANGELES, 6 June 2001, *North America* (1978-1990, acrylic on panel, 26 x 113 ins / 65 x 287 cm) USD 70,000. NEW YORK, 15 May 2002, *Rake and Leaves* (1969, acrylic on canvas, 58 x 78 ins / 148 x 199 cm) USD 120,000. NEW YORK, 13 Nov 2002, *Sawn and Saw* (1970, oil on canvas, 39 x 61 ins / 99 x 156 cm) USD 100,000. NEW YORK, 14 May 2003, *Atmosphere* (1988-1991, oil on panel, 33 x 80 ins / 84 x 202 cm) USD 57,500. NEW YORK, 14 May 2003, *Angled Wood and Angled Wood* (1969, acrylic and pencil on canvas, 59 x 76 ins / 149 x 194 cm) USD 90,000. NEW YORK, 12 May 2004, *Intercoastal* (1983, oil on canvasboard, 49 x 29 ins / 125 x 74 cm) USD 20,000.

JENNI, Christian Albrecht

Swiss, 19th century.
Born 1786; died 19 June 1861, in Bern.
Active in Eggiwil.
Lithographer, engraver, printer.

JENNI, Friedrich

Swiss, 19th century.
Born 14 May 1825, in Eggiwil (Bern canton); died 9 October 1878, in Solothurn.
Draughtsman, calligrapher, illustrator.

Friedrich Jenni did illustrations for the *Solothurner Volksalmanach* from 1850 to 1866.

MUSEUMS AND GALLERIES:

OLTEN (Kunstmus.): *Portrait of Dr Aquinoll.*

JENNINGS, Benjamin

British, 19th century.
Active in Rome.
Sculptor.

Benjamin Jennings exhibited at the Royal Academy in 1849 and 1850. His exhibited works were a marble bust entitled *Thomas Elliotson* a marble statuette, *Birth of the Rose* and a *Virgin*.

JENNINGS, Humphrey

British, 20th century.
Born 1907, in Walberswick; died 1950, in Poros, Greece.
Painter (mixed media).
English Surrealist group.

Humphrey Jennings was a noted English film-maker and photographer. He was active with the English Surrealists until 1938, and helped organised the first International Surrealist Exhibition in London in 1936, featuring works by Dali and Max Ernst. His own painting is characterised by its markedly elegant, almost Mannerist, style and by the introduction of absurd elements into otherwise highly realistic settings. *Flaming Woman* of 1934 is one of his best-known works.

AUCTION RECORDS:

LIMOGES, 4 Dec 1983, *England's Story* (oil on canvas, 11 3/4 x 15 3/4 ins / 30 x 40 cm) FRF 11,000. LONDON, 26 Sept 1985, *The Silent Village* (c. 1938, oil on canvas, 30 x 36 ins / 76 x 91.5 cm) GBP 950. LONDON, 9 June 1989, *St Paul's Cathedral* (oil on canvas, 20 x 24 1/2 ins / 50.8 x 62.3 cm) GBP 2,090. PARIS, 15 April 2003, *Perfume Factory* (oil on canvas, 9 x 12 ins / 23 x 31 cm) EUR 9,500.

JENNINGS, James

British, 18th century.
Active in London.
Miniaturist.

James Jennings was a member of the Free Society of Artists. Between 1763 and 1793, he exhibited 40 miniatures at the Society of Artists and one at the Royal Academy.

JENNINGS, Leonard

British, 20th century.
Born 1877.
Sculptor.

Leonard Jennings was a member of the Society of British Sculptors. He worked in India.

JENNINGS, Louise

American, 19th - 20th century.
Born 6 November 1870, in Tecumseh (Michigan).
Painter.

Louise Jennings was a pupil of William Chase. She was a member of the Society of Independent Artists and the American Federation of the Arts.

JENNINGS, Mary

British, 19th century.
Active in Brighton.
Miniaturist.

Mary Jennings exhibited miniatures at the Royal Academy in London after 1885.

JENNINGS, R.

British, 19th century.
Active in London.
Engraver.

R. Jennings is cited in *Art Prices Current*. He may have been the same artist as Reginald George Jennings (born 13 July 1872, died 1 October 1930), who painted in oils and watercolours.

JENNINGS, S.
British, 19th century.
Active in London.
Painter. History painting.
S. Jennings painted religious subjects. He exhibited in London from 1798 to 1834, in particular, at the Royal Academy and the British Institution.

JENNINGS, W. G.
British, 18th - 19th century.
Painter. Landscapes.
W.G. Jennings was a member of the Society of British Artists. He worked in London where he exhibited between 1797 and 1830, particularly at the Royal Academy.

JENNY, Arnold
Swiss, 19th century.
Born 20 July 1831, in Langenbruck (Basel canton); died 16 August 1881.
Painter, watercolourist. Mountainscapes, landscapes.
Orphaned very young, Arnold Jenny worked without a teacher, initially as an industrial painter, but then took up painting the mountains and plains of Switzerland. He also established a reputation as a watercolourist. He worked in Langenbruck until 1854 then moved to the Lausitz region of Saxony and Bohemia.

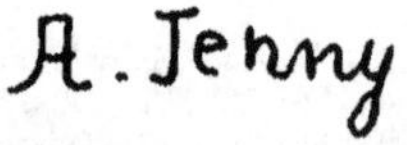

MUSEUMS AND GALLERIES:
BASEL: *Rosenlau Glacier*.
AUCTION RECORDS:
BERN, 22 Oct 1971, *Landscape*, CHF 3,800. BERN, 18 May 1973, *View of the Jungfrau*, CHF 9,000. LUCERNE, 25 June 1976, *Bernese Oberland Landscape* (1864, oil on canvas, 39 1/4 x 52 1/4 ins / 100 x 133 cm) CHF 2,000. BERN, 25 June 1982, *General View of the City of Lucerne* (1859, gouache, 17 1/2 x 23 1/2 ins / 44.5 x 59.4 cm) CHF 26,000. LONDON, 19 June 1985, *View of an Alpine Lake* (1868, oil on canvas, 39 1/4 x 51 1/2 ins / 99.5 x 130.5 cm) GBP 1,500. ZURICH, 3 Dec 1987, *The Rhine Falls in the Moonlight* (1876, oil on canvas, 19 3/4 x 27 1/2 ins / 50 x 70 cm) CHF 5,500. ZURICH, 14 Sept 1999, *Rheinfall by Moonlight* (1873, oil on canvas/panel, 23 x 28 ins / 58 x 72 cm) CHF 3,000. WASHINGTON, 28 April 2001, *Alpine Landscape* (1862, oil on canvas, 39 x 30 ins / 98 x 77 cm) USD 2,200.

JENNY, Fanny
Swiss, 19th century.
Born 3 October 1867, in Zurich.
Active in Chur.
Painter. Flowers.
Fanny Jenny did flower paintings.
MUSEUMS AND GALLERIES:
CHUR.

JENNY, Hans
Swiss, 19th century.
Born 21 November 1866, in Churwalden.
Active in Chur.
Painter. Landscapes.
Hans Jenny painted landscapes.
MUSEUMS AND GALLERIES:
CHUR: *Landscape*.

JENNY, Heinrich
Swiss, 19th century.
Born 2 July 1824, in Langenbruck (Basel canton); died 13 August 1891, in Solothurn.
Painter, illustrator. History painting, portraits.
Like many itinerant portrait painters, Heinrich Jenny moved from area to area in Switzerland from 1843 on. In Soloturn, he did illustrations for Almanachs and drawings for a *History of Switzerland in Pictures* and Schiller's play *Wilhelm Tell*. In 1865, he went to Germany and acted as a painter of battles during the campaign of 1866. Noted works include portraits of *Wilhelm I, Crown Prince Friedrich, Prince Friedrich Karl, Bismarck* and *Von Moltke*. The town hall in Solothurn has a painting of the *The Admission of Fribourg and Solothurn to the Swiss Confederation*.
MUSEUMS AND GALLERIES:
SOLOTHURN: *Lenore* (from the ballad by Gottfried Bürger); *In the Alps* (watercolour).

JENNY, Johann Heinrich
Swiss, 19th century.
Born 4 January 1786, in Ennenda (Glarus canton); died 23 February 1854, in Ennenda.
Painter. Portraits, landscapes.
In his youth, Johann Heinrich Jenny worked in St Petersburg, but left it for Paris in 1814, moving on to England and Spain. Then he set off for Chile, where he established a good reputation (1822-1828). After that he spent time in North America before settling in his home town, where he mainly painted portraits.
AUCTION RECORDS:
COLOGNE, 22 Nov 1979, *Winter Landscape* (1850, oil on panel, 12 x 18 ins / 30.2 x 45.8 cm) DEM 4,400.

JENOUDET, Paul Louis Séraphin
French, 19th century.
Born 21 March 1853, in Lyons; died 1886, in Paris.
Painter. Portraits, genre scenes.
Paul Louis Séraphin Jenoudet studied under J. A. Clément at Lyons' College of Fine Arts, which he joined in 1871. He then studied under Jules Lefebvre and Gustave Boulanger at Paris' College of Fine Arts. He exhibited at the Lyons Salon from 1876 and at the Paris Salon from 1878 to 1885, receiving a third class medal in 1883.

His genre scenes are tinted with a certain maudlin sentimentality, fashionable in the 1880s.
MUSEUMS AND GALLERIES:
LYONS: *November*.

JENOUR, C.
British, 19th century.
Active in London.
Painter.
C. Jenour exhibited at the Royal Academy from 1825 to 1832.

JENSEN, Agnes Emma Sofie
Danish, 19th century.
Born 4 December 1854, in Nykøbing (Seeland).
Painter.
Agnes Jensen studied in Copenhagen. From 1887 to 1892 she exhibited portraits and figurative paintings. She then devoted herself to the applied arts.

JENSEN, Agnes Louise Agnete
Danish, 20th century.
Born 7 April 1878, in Copenhagen.
Painter. Figures.
From 1907, Agnes Jensen exhibited predominantly tableaux of figures. She was awarded several scholarships and spent some time in Brittany with the support of the fine arts academy.

JENSEN, Alfred
Danish, 19th century.
Born 16 November 1859, in Randers.
Painter. Seascapes.

Alfred Jensen travelled on the seas for many years. He studied in Hamburg and then at the academy in Kassel. He received a gold medal in Lyons in 1901.

Auction records:

Cologne, 15 June 1989, *Seascape* (oil on canvas, 27½ x 39¼ ins / 70 x 100 cm) DEM 1,300. Cologne, 29 June 1990, *The South of Helsingør* (oil on canvas, 25¼ x 39¼ ins / 64 x 100 cm) DEM 1,400. Amsterdam, 28 Oct 1992, *A Four-mast Ship and Other Crafts in the Port of Hamburg* (oil on canvas, 31½ x 47½ ins / 80 x 120.5 cm) NLG 1,955. Bremen, 23 Oct 1999, *The Petroleum Steamer Prometheus* (1906, oil on canvas, 35 x 59 ins / 90 x 150 cm) DEM 6,200. Havnen, 30 Oct 1999, *Ships's Portrait of the Chilean Steamer Rancagua* (1903, oil on canvas, 34 x 67 ins / 87 x 170 cm) DKK 15,000. Hamburg, 1 April 2000, *Harbour of Hamburg* (oil on canvas, 31 x 47 ins / 80 x 120 cm) DEM 7,000. Hamburg, 7 Oct 2000, *View of Harbour in Hamburg* (oil on canvas, 63 x 83 ins / 160 x 210 cm) DEM 18,000. Helsinki, 12 May 2001, *Hamburg Harbour* (oil on canvas, 31 x 47 ins / 80 x 120 cm) FIM 35,000. Hamburg, 8 Dec 2001, *Bark and Other Sailing Ships off Cuxhaven* (1902, oil on canvas, 19 x 29 ins / 48 x 73 cm) DEM 7,000. Hamburg, 8 May 2002, *Hamburg Harbour in 1880* (1910, oil on canvas, 21 x 79 ins / 53 x 201 cm) EUR 2,500. Bremen, 29 June 2002, *Ships in Øresund near Kronborg Castle* (1906, oil on canvas, 36 x 59 ins / 91 x 150 cm) EUR 1,800. Hamburg, 10 April 2003, *Passenger Ship* (1903, oil on canvas, 31 x 85 ins / 80 x 215 cm) EUR 8,000. Warsaw, 19 Oct 2003, *Sailing Vessel on the Open Seas* (c. 1910, oil on canvas, 21 x 32 ins / 54 x 81 cm) PLN 14,000.

JENSEN, Alfred, called Al

Guatemalan, 20th century.
Born 1903, in Guatemala; died 1981, in Livingston (New Jersey), USA.
Active in the USA.
Painter.

Alfred Jensen spent his childhood between Guatemala and Denmark. In 1925-1926 he studied at the San Diego school of fine arts in California and later in Munich with Hans Hoffman and in Paris at the Scandinavian academy. On his return to the USA he became a teacher and worked in this profession from 1929 to 1951 in Baltimore and in 1958 at the Maryland Institute in Baltimore. He travelled in Africa and Spain and lived and worked in New York from 1951. Jensen produced constructivist sculptures before turning to a form of figurative painting which remained close to abstract expressionism. He then moved on to a form of abstraction consisting of geometric forms. He was influenced by Goethe's theories on colour, oriental philosophy and Peruvian calendars. He called his abstract paintings 'Diagrams'.

Jensen took part in many group exhibitions: Mexico City Biennale (1960); Art Institute of Chicago and 2001, *Abstracción - El Paradigma Amerindio* (*Abstraction - The Amerindian Paradigm*), Julio González centre, Valencia (1961). He has also exhibited his work in solo exhibitions: in New York (1952, 1955, 1957, 1959 and 1961); Stedelijk Museum, Amsterdam (1964); Kunsthalle, Baden-Baden (1973); Albright-Knox Gallery, Buffalo (1977); Max Protech Gallery, New York (2001); Dia Center, New York (2002).

Bibliography:

Cathcart, Linda L./Tucker, Marcia, *Alfred Jensen, paintings and diagrams from the years 1957-1977*, exhibition catalogue, Albright-Knox Art Gall., Fine Arts Academy, Buffalo (NY), 1978. Messer, Thomas M./Reidelbach, M./Schjeldahl, Peter, *Alfred Jensen. Paintings and Works on paper*, exhibition catalogue, Solomon R. Guggenheim Museum, New York, 1985. *Alfred Jensen. Paintings*, exhibition catalogue, Pace Gall., New York, 1991 (including texts by the artist). *Alfred Jensen. The Relationship between structure and function*, exhibition catalogue, Buchmann Gal., Cologne, 1997. Paternosto, César/Frame, Mary/Lippard, Lucy R., et al., *Abstracción: El paradigma amerindio*, exhibition catalogue, Instituto Valenciano de Arte Moderno (IVAM), Valencia, 2001.

Museums and Galleries:

Buffalo (Albright-Knox AG): *The Great Mystery II* (1960) - Dayton (AI) - New York (MoMA): *Clockwork in the Sky* (1959) - New York (Solomon R. Guggenheim Mus.): *Uaxactun* (1964) - Pittsburgh (Carnegie MA): *The Doric Order* (1972, oil on canvas).

Auction records:

Bern, 18 June 1965, *The Blessing*, CHF 11,000. Los Angeles, 27 Feb 1974, *Systole and Diastole* (1962) USD 3,300. Bern, 9 June 1976, *Black Rain* (1959, oil on canvas, 21¼ x 17 ins / 53.7 x 43.2 cm) CHF 6,800. New York, 30 March 1978, *The Acrobatic Rectangle - Per VII* (1967, oil on canvas, 64½ x 40¾ ins / 163.7 x 103.5 cm) USD 6,750. New York, 19 Oct 1979, *God and Man* (1959, oil on card, 10 x 15 ins / 25.3 x 38 cm) USD 1,800. New York, 12 Nov 1980, *Mayan Temple, Per I - Tikal* (1962, oil on canvas, 76 x 50 ins / 193 x 127 cm) USD 21,000. New York, 18 Nov 1981, *The Nine Cauldrons, Per I - Yü the Great* (1958, oil on canvas, 83¾ x 52 ins / 213 x 132 cm) USD 40,000. New York, 1 Nov 1984, *The Acrobatic Rectangle - Per VII* (1967, oil on canvas, 64½ x 40¾ ins / 164 x 103.5 cm) USD 35,000. New York, 2 May 1985, *Mayan Mat Patterns Number Structures* (1974, oil on canvas, 72 x 72 ins / 182.8 x 182.8 cm) USD 55,000. New York, 20 Feb 1987, *Two Resolute Diagrams, Per I and II* (1978, oil on canvas, diptych, 78 x 96 ins / 198.3 x 244 cm) USD 51,000. New York, 4 May 1988, *Portrait of the Moon* (oil on canvas, 54 x 5 ins / 137.2 x 11.8 cm) USD 38,500. New York, 8 Oct 1988, *The Acrobatic Rectangle, Per VIII* (1967, oil on canvas, 69½ x 44¼ ins / 176.5 x 112.5 cm) USD 41,250. New York, 9 Nov 1988, *Recalling the Soul* (1960, oil on panel, 76 x 50¼ ins / 193 x 127.4 cm) USD 49,500. New York, 3 May 1989, *Homage to the Nobel Prize for Peace* (1947, ink and oil on card, 30 x 20 ins / 76.2 x 50.8 cm) USD 22,000. New York, 9 Nov 1989, *Atlantis, Per II* (1965, oil on canvas, 50 x 50 ins / 127 x 127 cm) USD 66,000. New York, 8 May 1990, *Doric Order* (1962, oil/material, 54 x 54 ins / 137.2 x 137.2 cm) USD 77,000. New York, 7 Nov 1990, *The Marriage of Odd and Even Numbers - Per I, Per II* (1964, oil on canvas, two panels, en tout 72 x 100 ins / 183 x 254 cm) USD 88,000. New York, 14 Feb 1991, *The Goddess Iris* (1968, oil on canvas, 52 x 40 ins / 132 x 101.6 cm) USD 30,800. New York, 15 Feb 1991, *Humab Ku* (1962, oil on canvas, 48 x 32 ins / 122 x 81.2 cm) USD 33,000. New York, 13 Nov 1991, *Amphitrite Above, Poseidon Below* (oil on canvas, 60¼ x 41 ins / 153 x 104.1 cm) USD 33, 000. New York, 27 Feb 1992, *Untitled* (1958, oil on paper/synthetic resin, 12¼ x 12 ins / 31.1 x 30.5 cm) USD 6,600. New York, 6 May 1992, *Direction of Colour* (1962, oil on canvas, 64½ x 54 ins / 163.8 x 137.2 cm) USD 28,600. New York, 18 Nov 1992, *Model of a Numbered Mayan Drawing* (1974, oil on canvas, 72 x 72 ins / 182.9 x 182.9 cm) USD 71,500. New York, 19 Nov 1992, *Earth, Moon, Sun and Venus* (oil on canvas, en tout 50 x 72¼ ins / 127 x 183.5 cm) USD 30,800. London, 25 March 1993, *The Acrobatic Rectangle* (1967, oil on canvas, 64¼ x 32¼ ins / 163 x 81.8 cm) GBP 24,150. New York, 4 May 1993, *Male and Female Circular Structures* (1963, oil on canvas, 50 x 46 ins / 127 x 116.8 cm) USD 26,450. New York, 3 May 1994, *Homage to the Nobel Prize* (1947, black ink and oil on card, 30 x 20 ins / 76.2 x 50.8 cm) USD 9,200. New York, 4 May 1994, *The Great Occupation - Per II* (1973, oil on canvas, in three parts, 48 x 108 ins / 121.9 x 274.3 cm) USD 31,625. New York, 9 May 1996, *The Marriage of Odd and Even Numbers, Per III* (1964, oil on canvas, 72 x 50 ins / 182.9 x 127 cm) USD 24,150. New York, 19 Nov 1996, *Thirteenth of Time Inc.s Project Diagram* (1959, oil on canvas, 31 x 22½ ins / 78.8 x 57.2 cm) USD 14,950. New York, 20 Nov 1996, *Portrait of the Moon* (1961, oil on canvas, 54 x 44 ins / 137.2 x 111.8 cm) USD 15,525. New York, 21 Nov 1996, *Squaring the 260-Day Calendar* (1966, oil on canvas, diptych, 84 x 84 ins / 213.4 x 213.4 cm) USD

34,500. NEW YORK, 7 May 1997, *Dielectric Absorption Spectrum, Per I* (1975, oil on canvas, 37 1/4 x 37 ins / 94.3 x 94 cm) USD 12,650. NEW YORK, 13 May 1998, *Greece* (1970, oil on canvas, 52 x 52 ins / 131 x 131 cm) USD 24,000. NEW YORK, 14 May 1999, *The Integer Rules the Universe, Windows in Heaven* (1960, oil on canvas, 76 x 50 ins / 193 x 127 cm) USD 35,000. BERN, 25 June 1999, *Strange Start* (1966, oil on canvas, 43 x 36 ins / 108 x 91 cm) CHF 40,000. NEW YORK, 16 Nov 2000, *Integer Rules the Universe* (1960, oil on canvas, 75 x 49 ins / 190 x 124 cm) USD 38,000. NEW YORK, 17 May 2001, *The Earthly Plate* (1973, oil, ball pen, felt pen and board, 40 x 30 ins / 102 x 76 cm) USD 10,000. NEW YORK, 15 May 2002, *Mayan Mat Patterns* (1974, oil on canvas, 72 x 72 ins / 183 x 183 cm) USD 45,000. NEW YORK, 14 Nov 2002, *King Yu's Odd Progression and King Yu's Even Progression* (1971, oil on canvas, diptych, 48 x 40 ins / 122 x 102 cm) USD 32,000. BERN, 20 June 2003, *Pyramid Study* (oil on canvas, 28 x 35 ins / 70 x 90 cm) CHF 42,000. NEW YORK, 12 Nov 2003, *Earth, Moon, Sun and Venus* (1968, oil on canvas, two attached canvases, 50 x 72 ins / 127 x 183 cm) USD 45,000. NEW YORK, 12 Feb 2004, *God and Man* (1959, oil on panel, 10 x 15 ins / 25 x 38 cm) USD 8,000.

JENSEN, Arthur
German, 19th century.
Active in Danzig (Gdansk).
Painter. Portraits, seascapes.

Arthur Jensen worked in Berlin from 1891. A noted work is *Beach Scene near Danzig*.

JENSEN, Axel P.
Danish, 20th century.
Born 1885; died 1972.
Painter. Landscapes.

AUCTION RECORDS:
COPENHAGEN, 29 Oct 1957, *Landscape*, DKK 2,300. COPENHAGEN, 26 Feb 1959, *Landscape*, DKK 1,900. COPENHAGEN, 11 Oct 1960, *Flat Landscape with a House*, DKK 3,450. COPENHAGEN, 28 April 1976, *Two Figures on a Road in the Snow* (oil on canvas, 45 1/4 x 65 ins / 115 x 165 cm) DKK 8,300. COPENHAGEN, 14 March 1978, *Winter Landscape* (1940, oil on canvas, 45 x 63 ins / 114 x 160 cm) DKK 10,000. COPENHAGEN, 23 Jan 1979, *By the Sea* (1942, oil on canvas, 58 1/4 x 82 3/4 ins / 148 x 210 cm) DKK 9,500. STOCKHOLM, 7 Dec 1987, *Still-life* (oil on panel, 26 1/2 x 26 3/4 ins / 67 x 68 cm) SEK 12,500. COPENHAGEN, 30 Nov 1988, *Firs behind the Dunes* (oil on canvas, 25 1/2 x 36 1/4 ins / 65 x 92 cm) DKK 4,200. COPENHAGEN, 22 Nov 1989, *Autumn Landscape with Leafless Trees* (oil on canvas, 32 x 39 1/4 ins / 81 x 100 cm) DKK 5,600. COPENHAGEN, 21-22 March 1990, *Undulating Landscape with a Farm Building* (oil on canvas, 45 1/4 x 63 3/4 ins / 115 x 162 cm) DKK 11,000. COPENHAGEN, 31 Oct 1990, *Still-life* (oil on canvas, 19 3/4 x 24 ins / 50 x 61 cm) DKK 6,800. COPENHAGEN, 13-14 Feb 1991, *Summer Landscape* (oil on canvas, 25 1/2 x 39 1/4 ins / 65 x 100 cm) DKK 4,200. COPENHAGEN, 1 April 1992, *Summer's Day in Town* (1933, 25 1/4 x 35 1/2 ins / 64 x 90 cm) DKK 3,000. COPENHAGEN, 21 April 1993, *Landscape with Henne Church* (1947, oil on canvas, 45 1/4 x 61 1/2 ins / 115 x 156 cm) DKK 8,500. COPENHAGEN, 19 Oct 1994, *Autumn Day by the Sea* (oil on canvas, 45 1/4 x 63 3/4 ins / 115 x 162 cm) DKK 4,500. COPENHAGEN, 26 April 1995, *View of Amagertorv* (1957, oil on canvas, 46 x 59 ins / 116 x 150 cm) DKK 6,000.

JENSEN, Bill
American, 20th century.
Born 26 November 1945.
Painter (mixed media).

Bill Jensen studied at the University of Minnesota, where he obtained a BFA in 1968 and an MFA in 1970, and taught from 1965 to 1970. He has also taught at the Brooklyn Museum Art School (1971-1975) and York College, Queens, New York City (1972-1973). He first came to prominence in 1980 for a group of labour-intensive paintings of spirals, pod shapes and ellipses made with a palette knife, for example *Crown of Thorns* (1979) and *Ryder's Eye* (1978-1979). Since then he has exchanged the palette knife for the brush and shifted from dark tones to bold, rich colours, as in *Bright Moments* (1992). His paintings from the 1990s, such as *Winter Light* (1994) and *Colossus* (1993-1994), are typically divided horizontally into two distinct zones representing sky and earth.

Jensen's exhibitions include: 1983, *Content in Abstraction: The Use of Nature*, High Museum, Atlanta; 1986, *Major Acquisitions since 1980*, Whitney Museum of American Art, New York; *An International Survey of Recent Paintings and Sculpture*, Museum of Modern Art, New York; 1996, a solo exhibition at the Museum of Modern Art; 1987, the Biennial Exhibition at the Corcoran Gallery Art, Washington DC; 1997, Newhouse Center for Contemporary Art, Staten Island, NY; and 2000, *Celebrating Modern Art: The Anderson Collection*, San Francisco Museum of Modern Art.

He has received a National Endowment for the Arts Fellowship (1985), an American Academy of Arts and Letters Award (1997) and a Guggenheim Fellowship (1998).

BIBLIOGRAPHY:
Bill Jensen: First Etchings, exhibition catalogue, Museum of Modern Art, New York, 1986. Rathbone, E.E., *Bill Jensen*, exhibition catalogue, The Phillips Collection, Washington DC, 1987. Gibson, Eric, *'Bill Jensen'* in *Art News*, journal article, January 1996. Yau, John, *'Epiphany and Surrender: The Recent Paintings of Bill Jensen'* in *LINGO*, journal article, March 1996. Breidenbach, Tom, *'Bill Jensen'* in *Artforum*, journal article, December 1998. Westfall, Stephen, *'Bill Jensen at Mary Boone'* in *Art in America*, journal article, July 2003.

MUSEUMS AND GALLERIES:
BOSTON (MFA): *Untitled (XXIV)* (1992, brush and ink); *Drawing for 'Guy and the Loon'* (1985, pastel, charcoal, gouache) - CAMBRIDGE, MA (Fogg AM, Harvard University) - LONDON (Tate Collection): *Lie-Light* (1989-1990, etching); *Deadhead* (1991-1992, etching) - LOS ANGELES (County MA) - MINNEAPOLIS (Walker Art Center): *XVII* (1975, plaster, charcoal, lead on canvas); *Red Passion* (1977) - NEW YORK (Metropolitan Mus. of Art) - NEW YORK (MoMA) - WASHINGTON DC (Hirshhorn Mus. and Sculpture Garden): *Lie-Light* (1989-1990, oil on linen); *Study for Lie-Light* (1988, watercolour) - WASHINGTON DC (Smithsonian American AM): *Drawing for Legion* (1983-1984, charcoal) - WICHITA (AM): *Voodoo* (1976-1977); *April 1977* (1977) - WORCESTER, MA (AM).

AUCTION RECORDS:
NEW YORK, 13 Nov 1986, *Untitled* (1973, oil and sand/canvas, 96 1/2 x 77 1/4 ins / 244.8 x 196.5 cm) USD 5,000. NEW YORK, 10 Nov 1988, *Untitled* (1978, charcoal/vellum, 15 3/4 x 16 ins / 40.3 x 39.8 cm) USD 3,520. NEW YORK, 1 May 1991, *Fragil* (oil on canvas, 32 x 24 1/4 ins / 81.3 x 61.3 cm) USD 28,600. NEW YORK, 13 Nov 1991, *Dolphie* (oil/material, 15 x 13 3/4 ins / 38.1 x 35 cm) USD 13,200. NEW YORK, 25-26 Feb 1994, *Drawing for Ribbons for Harriet* (pastel, gouache and charcoal/paper, 23 1/2 x 17 3/4 ins / 59.7 x 45.1 cm) USD 9,200. NEW YORK, 22 Feb 1995, *White Heat* (1977, oil/material, 25 x 17 1/2 ins / 63.5 x 44.2 cm) USD 18,400. NEW YORK, 19 Nov 1996, *Desire* (1981-1982, oil/linen, 30 x 21 1/4 ins / 76.5 x 54 cm) USD 3,450. NEW YORK, 20 Nov 1996, *Greek Gardens* (1993, tempera and gouache/paper/linen, 27 1/4 x 35 ins / 69.2 x 88.9 cm) USD 9,200. NEW YORK, 16 May 2001, *Garden of Affliction* (1983, oil on linen, 22 x 16 ins / 56 x 41 cm) USD 3,000. NEW YORK, 13 Nov 2002, *Divers Ferry* (1983, oil on linen, 36 x 24 ins / 91 x 61 cm) USD 12,000. NEW YORK, 12 Feb 2004, *Untitled* (1973, oil and sand on canvas, 96 x 78 ins / 245 x 197 cm) USD 8,500. LAMBERTVILLE, 24 April 2004, *Untitled* (1975, graphite on vellum, 9 x 7 ins / 23 x 19 cm) USD 3,250.

JENSEN, Carl Andreas
Danish, 19th century.
Born 13 July 1844, in Ordrup, near Copenhagen.
Painter, lithographer.

Carl Jensen initially studied lithography. He was a pupil at the Kunstakademi in Copenhagen and devoted himself to landscape painting. He exhibited *Leaving for Dyrehaven* in 1871. He worked as a lithographer and master of drawing in Copenhagen and Malmö.

JENSEN, Carl Martin. See **SOYA-JENSEN**

JENSEN, Carlo Christoffer Hornung
Danish, 20th century.
Born 1882; died 1960.
Painter. Portraits, interiors with figures, landscapes with figures, landscapes, seascapes.

AUCTION RECORDS:
NEW YORK, 26 Feb 1986, *Picnic* (oil on canvas, 463/4 x 633/4 ins / 118.8 x 161.9 cm) USD 7,500. LONDON, 16 March 1989, *Dining Room* (1911, oil on canvas, 20 x 24 ins / 51 x 61 cm) GBP 9,350. LONDON, 17 May 1991, *Water Gardens* (1939, oil on canvas, 28 x 321/4 ins / 71 x 82.2 cm) GBP 4,400. LONDON, 22 May 1992, *Beach at Hornbæk* (1925, oil on canvas, 24 x 37 ins / 61 x 94 cm) GBP 3,080. LONDON, 18 June 1993, *At the Window* (oil on canvas, 193/4 x 233/4 ins / 50 x 60.5 cm) GBP 2,300. COPENHAGEN, 15 Nov 1993, *Carl Pedersen the Painter at Dyrehaven, Summer of 1925* (oil on canvas, 91/2 x 13 ins / 24 x 33 cm) DKK 4,000.

JENSEN, Christian Albrecht
Danish, 19th century.
Born 1792, in Bredsted; died 1870, in Copenhagen.
Painter.

Christian Jensen was a pupil at the Kunstakademi in Copenhagen. He became a member in 1824 and then curator of engravings. He visited Rome and Venice around 1818. He was included in the exhibition *Twee gouden eeuwen: schilderkunst uit Nederland en Denemarken* (*Two Golden Ages: Masterpieces of Dutch and Danish Painting*) at the Rijksmuseum in Amsterdam in 2001.

MUSEUMS AND GALLERIES:
COPENHAGEN (Statens Mus. for Kunst): *The Artist's Mother; Hjört-Lorentzen; The Sculptor; Portrait of Hermann Ernst Freund; D.J. Rawert; Chamberlain Irgens-Berg; Mrs Irgens-Berg; The Painter Troels Lund; Eckersberg; Portrait of the Artist; Portrait of the Artist's Son; The Theologian Andreas Gottlob Rudelsbach* (1858); *Ole Jorgen Rawert* (1839) - COPENHAGEN (Thorvaldsens Mus.): *Portrait of Cl. D. Fritzsch* - HILLERØD (Frederiksborg): *The Artist's Wife; Self-portrait; Self-portrait* - ODENSE (Andersen Mus.): *Portrait of Andersen.*

AUCTION RECORDS:
COPENHAGEN, 21 March 1957, *Bust of Hans Puggaard,* DKK 2,725. COPENHAGEN, 19 March 1969, *Portrait of Prof. B. Borgen,* DKK 10,000. COPENHAGEN, 9 June 1971, *Portraits of George Gordon McDougall and his Wife Julie* (two canvases, a pair) DKK 7,000. COPENHAGEN, 11 April 1972, *Portrait of Sophie Hansen,* DKK 12,000. COPENHAGEN, 4 May 1976, *Portrait of a Man* (1829, oil on canvas, 161/4 x 121/4 ins / 41 x 31 cm) DKK 11,200. COPENHAGEN, 5 Dec 1978, *Portrait of Baron Gustav Blücher-Altona* (1826, oil on canvas, 91/2 x 71/2 ins / 24 x 19 cm) DKK 16,000. COPENHAGEN, 30 April 1981, *Portrait of a Young Woman* (1824, oil on canvas, 93/4 x 8 ins / 25 x 20.5 cm) DKK 26,000. COPENHAGEN, 27 Sept 1983, *Portrait of Wilhelmina Lowenstern* (1826, oil on canvas, 9 x 71/2 ins / 23 x 19 cm) DKK 25,000. COPENHAGEN, 12 Nov 1986, *Portrait of Brigitte Sobotker Hohlenberg, née Malling* (1826, oil on canvas, 251/4 x 20 ins / 64 x 51 cm) DKK 900,000. COPENHAGEN, 23 April 1987, *Portrait of the Painter J. P. Möller; Portrait of his Wife Anna Catherine Margrethe Haase* (1827, oil on canvas, pair, 91/4 x 71/4 ins / 23.5 x 18.5 cm) DKK 310,000. LONDON, 24 March 1988, *Bust Portrait of a Lady in Black* (1828, oil on canvas, 91/4 x 71/2 ins / 23.5 x 18.8 cm) GBP 3,850. COPENHAGEN, 25 Oct 1989, *Portrait of Andreas Peter Thomsen; Portrait of his Wife Anna Sabine* (1833 and 1837, oil on canvas, a pair, each 11 x 9 ins / 27 x 22 cm) DKK 52,000. COPENHAGEN, 29 Aug 1990, *Portrait of Hanna Marie Schmidt* (1827, oil on canvas, 91/2 x 71/2 ins / 24 x 19 cm) DKK 30,000. COPENHAGEN, 28 Aug 1991, *Portrait of a Man* (oil on canvas, 91/4 x 71/2 ins / 23.5 x 19 cm) DKK 12,800. COPENHAGEN, 14 Feb 1996, *Portrait of the History and Genre Painter Ferdinand Flachner* (oil on canvas, 171/4 x 133/4 ins / 44 x 35 cm) DKK 21,000. COPENHAGEN, 31 Aug 1999, *Portrait of a Lady in a Low-cut Dress* (1827, oil on canvas, 9 x 7 ins / 23 x 18 cm) DKK 28,000. COPENHAGEN, 4 Sept 2000, *Madonna and Child with Infant St John* (oil on canvas) DKK 50,000. COPENHAGEN, 6 Sept 2000, *Portrait of Professor Hans Christian Orsted* (c. 1832-1833, oil on canvas, 26 x 20 ins / 67 x 50 cm) DKK 520,000. COPENHAGEN, 27 Nov 2001, *Portraits of Landowner Daniel Isaksen and his Wife Johanne Henriette* (1836, oil on canvas, a pair, 9 x 8 ins / 24 x 20 cm) DKK 240,000. COPENHAGEN, 27 Aug 2002, *Portrait of Levin Jorgen Rohde in Blue Uniform* (1828, oil on canvas, 26 x 20 ins / 66 x 51 cm) DKK 80,000. VEJLE, 5 May 2003, *Portraits of Hans Staal and Anne Sophie Hagen* (1820, oil on canvas, a pair, 25 x 20 ins / 64 x 50 cm) DKK 41,000. COPENHAGEN, 2 Sept 2003, *Bertel Thorvaldsen Seated in a Chair* (oil on panel, 11 x 9 ins / 29 x 23 cm) DKK 70,000.

JENSEN, David Ivanovitch, or Iensenn
Danish, 19th century.
Born 9 November 1816, in Copenhagen; died 1902, in St Petersburg.
Sculptor.

From 1832 to 1841 David Jensen studied at the Kunstakademi in Copenhagen, receiving the silver medal in 1841 and a gold medal for *Jesus with Martha and Mary.* He was summoned to St Petersburg by Princess Maria Nicolaïevna. Remaining there until his death, he executed numerous decorative sculptures for the imperial palace, public buildings and private palaces. Among his most often cited works are his low reliefs *Chiron the Centaur Teaching Achilles the Bow and Arrow, Achilles Dragging the Body of Hector* and *Diana.* He won several titles for these at the academy. In Riga he executed several decorative sculptures for the exchange and for the Romanoff house in Moscow. In 1845 he founded the first and only terracotta factory in St Petersburg, producing numerous low reliefs, busts, statues and vases. He executed a great quantity of decorative sculptures, notably for the palaces of Princes Nicolaï Nicolaïevitch, Michaïl Nicolaïevitch, and Serge and Paul Alexandrovitch in St Petersburg, a theatre in Helsinki, the seminary in Riga, a palace in Kiev, and a church in Kronstadt. He also executed works in the applied arts.

JENSEN, Edvard Michael
Danish, 19th - 20th century.
Born 2 November 1822, in Copenhagen; died 30 December 1915.
Painter. Landscapes with figures, landscapes.

Edvard Michael Jensen moved to England in 1863 and exhibited at the British Institution, at the Scandinavian Gallery in London, and in Manchester and Dublin. He exhibited in Denmark in 1864 and thereafter almost every year until 1878, showing Danish and English landscapes. Examples of his work include *Lake in the Zoo* (1872), *Forest Path* and *Sunset over the Thames.*

AUCTION RECORDS:
LONDON, 28 Nov 1984, *Does in a Wood* (oil on canvas, 20 x 18 ins / 50.5 x 46 cm) GBP 2,000. LONDON, 10 Oct 1986, *Does in a Wooded Landscape* (oil on canvas, 201/2 x 183/4 ins / 52 x 47.6 cm) GBP 1,500. GIEN, 20 June 1988, *River View near Manchester* (oil on canvas, 111/2 x 141/2 ins / 29 x 37 cm) FRF

6,000. COPENHAGEN, 25 Oct 1989, *Old Man and Little Girl Walking in the Winter near Sollerod* (oil on canvas, 15¾ x 13¾ ins / 40 x 35 cm) DKK 11,000. STOCKHOLM, 29 May 1991, *Figures on the Foreshore near Øresund* (oil on canvas, 24¾ x 37½ ins / 63 x 95 cm) SEK 12,000.

JENSEN, Frederik Nicolai
Norwegian, 19th century.
Born 21 June 1818, in Bergen; died 28 November 1870, in Steigen.
Painter.

Frederik Jensen was a pupil of the landscapist H. L. Reusch in Bergen and studied history painting in Düsseldorf. In 1841 he executed the large painting, *Marguerite in Prison*, as well as numerous portraits in Bergen. Many of his portraits and paintings are in the Bergen gallery, including *Ingeborg by the Sea* and *Viking Abducting a Southern Woman*.

JENSEN, Gabriel Olouf
Danish, 19th - 20th century.
Born 7 July 1862, in Copenhagen; died 1930.
Painter. Genre scenes, landscapes.

Awarded a bronze medal at the Exposition Universelle in Paris in 1900.

AUCTION RECORDS:
LONDON, 16 March 1989, *Erik, Else, Ove and Birthe Schultz on the Beach* (1919, oil on canvas, 39 x 27¾ ins / 99 x 70.5 cm) GBP 2,200. COPENHAGEN, 25 Oct 1989, *Daydreaming* (1893, oil on canvas, 24½ x 20½ ins / 62 x 52 cm) DKK 5,200. LONDON, 18 Oct 1990, *Brig Entering Copenhagen Harbour* (oil on canvas, 40¼ x 56 ins / 102 x 142 cm) GBP 1,430.

JENSEN, Georg Arthur
Danish, 19th - 20th century.
Born 31 August 1866, in Raavad, near Copenhagen; died 1935.
Painter. Local scenes, landscapes.

Georg Jensen studied at the Kongelige Danske Kunstakademi in Copenhagen from 1887 to 1892. In 1889 he exhibited a bust and came to public notice with his *Reaper* (1892), *Hunting Boar* and *Springtime* (both 1894). He exhibited at the 1913 Paris Autumn Salon with 49 pieces of jewellery and went on to show his creations at the 1915 International Exhibition in San Francisco, where he was awarded a first prize. Jensen immediately started producing silverware and jewellery and set up a highly successful business marketing his products.

AUCTION RECORDS:
PARIS, 10 Dec 1997, *Belt Buckle decorated with a Bird, Fruit and Leaves* (silver, 3 x 6 ins / 6.7 x 15 cm) FRF 4,000.

JENSEN, Hans Christian
Danish, 19th century.
Born 1 February 1836, in Copenhagen; died 9 September 1903.
Painter.

Hans Jensen executed a series of portraits of the Danish royal family, nobility and aristocracy.

MUSEUMS AND GALLERIES:
HILLERØD: *Portrait of Christian IX*; *Portrait of J. J. Worsaaes*.

AUCTION RECORDS:
LONDON, 21 June 1984, *Children in a Wooded Landscape* (1867, oil on canvas, 12¼ x 17½ ins / 31 x 44.5 cm) GBP 1,300. COPENHAGEN, 17 Nov 1987, *Portrait of Anne Sophie Hagen* (oil on canvas, 11 x 9¾ ins / 27 x 25 cm) DKK 40,000. COPENHAGEN, 5 March 2001, *Portrait of a Highly Decorated Gentleman. Portrait of his Wife* (1891, oil on canvas, a pair, 36 x 26 ins / 92 x 65 cm) DKK 13,000. COPENHAGEN, 5 March 2003, *Portrait of Agnes Drake, Married to William Wain* (oil on canvas, 44 x 38 ins / 111 x 97 cm) DKK 16,000.

JENSEN, Harald Christian
Danish, 19th - 20th century.
Born 5 August 1834, in Copenhagen; died 27 March 1913.
Lithographer.

Harald Christian Jensen studied in Vienna and Paris before going to work in Copenhagen for the Baerentzen Institute and the Hoffenberg Institute. He became self-employed in 1887 and started turning out reproductions of well-known paintings and portraits, including Købke's *Frederiksborg Castle*, and Bloch's *Two Monks* and *Card Players*. Harald Jensen's *Self-portrait* was subsequently reproduced by A. Londborg.

JENSEN, Herman
Danish, 20th century.
Born 1893; died 1941.
Painter. Local scenes, landscapes.

AUCTION RECORDS:
STOCKHOLM, 6 June 1988, *Terrace Café under the Trees in Summer* (oil, 14½ x 19¼ ins / 37 x 49 cm) SEK 3,000. VEJLE, 13 Aug 1998, *Street Scene with Figures and Tram, Copenhagen* (1915, oil on canvas, 34 x 39 ins / 86 x 100 cm) DKK 13,000.

JENSEN, Ida Marie Juliane. See **SCHIÖTTZ-JENSEN**

JENSEN, Jens Thomsen
Danish, 19th century.
Born 29 December 1862, in Skanderborg.
Painter. Landscapes.

From 1883 onwards Jens Jensen showed landscapes of his birthplace almost every year. He also painted portraits and figurative works. His *Winter Morning* was acquired by the royal collection in 1891.

JENSEN, Johan Laurents, Laurentz or Laurits, or I. L.
Danish, 19th century.
Born 1800, in Gjentofte, near Copenhagen; died 1856, in Gjentofte.
Painter. Still-lifes (flowers/fruit).

Johan Jensen studied with Fritz at the Kunstakademi in Copenhagen. He went to Paris in 1822 and studied painting on porcelain in Sèvres. He then travelled to Rome and Naples. He became a member of the Kunstakademi in Copenhagen in 1825 and became first painter of the royal Copenhagen porcelain factory.

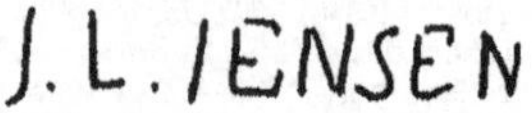

MUSEUMS AND GALLERIES:
ALTONA: *Flowers* - MONTPELLIER: *Flowers*.

AUCTION RECORDS:
PARIS, 21 Oct 1943, *Roses and Orange Blossoms*, FRF 4,500. LONDON, 19 May 1971, *Still-life with Fruit and Flowers*, GBP 400. LONDON, 19 April 1978, *Still-life with Flowers* (1826, oil on canvas, 13½ x 16½ ins / 34 x 42 cm) GBP 3,200. LONDON, 15 June 1979, *Flower Basket* (1829, oil on canvas, 40 x 32½ ins / 101.6 x 82.5 cm) GBP 1,800. COPENHAGEN, 19 Aug 1980, *Vase of Flowers* (1835, oil on canvas, 27¼ x 23¼ ins / 69 x 59 cm) DKK 42,000. COPENHAGEN, 30 April 1981, *Still-life with Flowers* (1830, oil on canvas, 35¾ x 29¼ ins / 91 x 74 cm) DKK 100,000. MUNICH, 30 June 1983, *Still-life* (1830, oil on canvas, 24½ x 30¾ ins / 62 x 78 cm) DEM 11,500. COPENHAGEN, 16 April 1986, *Still-life with Fruit and Flowers* (1833, oil on canvas, 28¾ x 36¼ ins / 73 x 92 cm) DKK 300,000. NEW YORK, 29 Oct 1987, *Still-life of Flowers in a Greek Vase with Shells* (oil on canvas, 32 x 25¼ ins / 81.2 x 64.2 cm) USD 110,000. NEW YORK, 25 Feb 1988, *Still-life of Flowers in a Glass Vase* (oil on panel, 13 x 9¾ ins / 33.3 x 25 cm) USD 13,200. LONDON, 24 March 1988, *Roses in a Basket* (1842, oil on panel, 15 x 19¼ ins / 38 x 49 cm) GBP 22,000. STOCKHOLM,

15 Nov 1988, *Still-life with Spring Flowers and Oak Leaves* (oil, 11 1/2 x 15 ins / 29 x 38 cm) SEK 200,000. NEW YORK, 22 Feb 1989, *Still-life with Poppies* (oil on canvas, 19 1/2 x 14 1/2 ins / 49.8 x 36.8 cm) USD 63,250. LONDON, 16 March 1989, *Vase of Roses on an Entablature* (oil on canvas, 31 1/2 x 23 ins / 80 x 58.4 cm) GBP 154,000. COPENHAGEN, 5 April 1989, *Still-life of Flowers and Fruit in an Antique Dish on a Marble Entablature* (1838, oil on canvas, 22 3/4 x 27 1/4 ins / 58 x 69 cm) DKK 630,000. STOCKHOLM, 19 April 1989, *Still-life with Melon, Peaches and Nuts on an Entablature* (oil on canvas, 18 1/2 x 22 3/4 ins / 47 x 58 cm) SEK 105,000. COPENHAGEN, 25 Oct 1989, *Camellia* (oil on canvas, 11 x 7 ins / 28 x 18 cm) DKK 64,000. STOCKHOLM, 15 Nov 1989, *Crown of Roses* (oil on panel, 5 x 6 3/4 ins / 13 x 17 cm) SEK 65,000. LONDON, 21 Nov 1989, *Still-life with Flowers in Greek Vase* (1848, oil on panel, 30 3/4 x 23 1/4 ins / 78 x 59 cm) GBP 187,000. COPENHAGEN, 21 Feb 1990, *Still-life with Game* (painting/wood, 9 x 6 3/4 ins / 22 x 17 cm) DKK 40,000. NEW YORK, 28 Feb 1990, *Still-life with Alpine Periwinkles* (1845, oil on panel, 6 1/4 x 8 ins / 16 x 19.4 cm) USD 27,500. LONDON, 29 March 1990, *Hortensia in an Urn behind a Basket of Fruit and a Branch of Magnolia* (1834, oil on canvas, 29 1/4 x 34 1/2 ins / 74.4 x 87.6 cm) GBP 242,000. COPENHAGEN, 25-26 April 1990, *Anemones* (oil on canvas, 7 3/4 x 5 1/2 ins / 20 x 14 cm) DKK 36,000. STOCKHOLM, 16 May 1990, *Still-life with Anemones and Stock in a Vase* (oil on panel, 13 3/4 x 10 1/4 ins / 35 x 26 cm) SEK 77,000. NEW YORK, 23 May 1990, *Poppies* (oil on panel, 14 3/4 x 12 1/4 ins / 37.5 x 31.1 cm) USD 30,800. COPENHAGEN, 29 Aug 1990, *Roses in Crystal Vase* (painting/mahogany, 13 3/4 x 10 1/4 ins / 35 x 26 cm) DKK 230,000. STOCKHOLM, 14 Nov 1990, *Still-life with Branches of Orange Blossom, Flowers and Almonds* (oil on panel, 20 x 15 ins / 51 x 38 cm) SEK 78,000. LONDON, 28 Nov 1990, *Still-life with Lillies and Roses* (oil on panel, 19 1/4 x 14 1/2 ins / 49 x 37 cm) GBP 13,200. COPENHAGEN, 6 Dec 1990, *Vase of Roses* (1843, oil on canvas, 17 x 9 1/2 ins / 43 x 24 cm) DKK 130,000. COPENHAGEN, 1 May 1991, *Red and White Roses* (painting/mahogany, 8 1/4 x 11 3/4 ins / 21 x 30 cm) DKK 46,000. LONDON, 17 May 1991, *Pink Roses* (oil on panel, 5 1/2 x 4 1/4 ins / 14 x 10.5 cm) GBP 13,200. STOCKHOLM, 29 May 1991, *Still-life with Nasturtiums and Phlox* (oil on panel, 20 x 15 ins / 51 x 38 cm) SEK 72,000. LONDON, 4 Oct 1991, *White and Pink Roses* (oil on panel, 10 1/2 x 14 1/4 ins / 26.6 x 36.2 cm) GBP 15,950. NEW YORK, 20 Feb 1992, *Still-life with Pink Roses and Camellias* (oil on panel, 17 1/2 x 13 1/2 ins / 44.5 x 34.6 cm) USD 30,800. PARIS, 11 April 1992, *Still-life With Grapes Arranged on an Entablature* (oil on canvas/card, 10 x 12 3/4 ins / 24.5 x 32.5 cm) FRF 23,000. STOCKHOLM, 19 May 1992, *Still-life with Apples, Flowers and Nuts* (oil on panel, 20 x 15 ins / 51 x 38 cm) SEK 50,000. AMSTERDAM, 28 Oct 1992, *Mixed Flowers in a Greek Dish on a Marble Entablature* (1844, oil on panel, 9 1/4 x 12 1/2 ins / 23.5 x 32 cm) NLG 25,300. COPENHAGEN, 18 Nov 1992, *Pink Roses* (oil on wood, 10 1/4 x 8 1/4 ins / 26 x 21 cm) DKK 10,500. LONDON, 19 March 1993, *Roses, Forget-me-nots and Hawthorn on an Entablature* (oil on panel, 5 1/2 x 7 1/2 ins / 14 x 19 cm) GBP 8,280. NEW YORK, 28 May 1993, *Still-life with Carafe and Glass of Wine, with Grapes and an Ivy Crown* (1834, oil on canvas, 17 x 20 ins / 43.2 x 50.7 cm) USD 5,750. COPENHAGEN, 15 Nov 1993, *Bouquet of Flowers in a Glass Vase on a Stone Entablature* (1851, painting/mahogany, 15 1/4 x 11 1/2 ins / 39 x 29 cm) DKK 110,000. NEW YORK, 16 Feb 1994, *Bird of Paradise* (1835, oil on canvas, 18 1/4 x 15 ins / 46.5 x 38.1 cm) USD 25,875. COPENHAGEN, 7 Sept 1994, *Violets* (1848, painting/mahogany, 4 1/4 x 6 3/4 ins / 11 x 17 cm) DKK 17,000. LONDON, 17 Nov 1995, *Roses, Morning Glories and Honeysuckle* (1854, oil on canvas, 21 3/4 x 28 1/2 ins / 55.2 x 72.5 cm) GBP 52,100. COPENHAGEN, 14 Feb 1996, *White and Pink Lillies* (oil on mahogany panel, 7 x 5 1/4 ins / 18 x 13.5 cm) DKK 33,000. NEW YORK, 23-24 May 1996, *Still-life with Peaches, Grapes, Corn, Nuts, Melon and Chestnuts* (oil on canvas, 19 x 23 ins / 48.3 x 58.4 cm) USD 18,400. NEW YORK, 18 March 1998, *Still-life with Flowers on a Ledge* (1843, oil on panel, 8 3/4 x 12 1/2 ins / 22.2 x 31.8 cm) USD 24,150. COPENHAGEN, 23 Feb 1999, *Basket of Pink Roses on Ledge, Bush with Elderflowers behind* (1855, oil on canvas, 29 x 37 ins / 73 x 93 cm) DKK 250,000. LONDON, 26 March 1999, *Grapes and Strawberries in a Bowl. Lilacs and Beech Leaves on a Ledge* (1840, 1841, oil on panel, a pair, 10 x 14 ins / 26 x 36 cm) GBP 18,000. COPENHAGEN, 6 Sept 2000, *Basket with Roses, Auriculars and Pansies on Stone in Woodland* (1846, oil on canvas, 24 x 32 ins / 62 x 82 cm) DKK 660,000. NEW YORK, 18 Oct 2000, *Thistle, Echinops and Myrtle in a Glass Vase with Oranges, Blackberries and a Butterfly* (1834, oil on canvas, 14 x 18 ins / 35 x 46 cm) USD 55,000. COPENHAGEN, 27 Nov 2001, *Garland of Flowers and Fruit* (1839, oil on canvas, 37 x 51 ins / 94 x 130 cm) DKK 800,000. COPENHAGEN, 27 Nov 2001, *Garland of Flowers and Fruit* (1839, oil on canvas, 37 x 51 ins / 94 x 130 cm) DKK 800,000. NEW YORK, 24 April 2002, *Red and Pink, White Primroses in an Etruscan Vase on a Marble Base* (1841, oil on canvas, 31 x 23 ins / 79 x 58 cm) USD 94,000. COPENHAGEN, 3 June 2002, *Roses, Poppies and Other Flowers in a Basket* (1853, oil on canvas, 28 x 35 ins / 70 x 90 cm) DKK 600,000. COPENHAGEN, 2 Dec 2002, *Hollyhocks and Dahlias in a Garden* (1853, oil on canvas, 63 x 43 ins / 160 x 108 cm) DKK 950,000. LONDON, 3 June 2003, *Still-life with Dahlias* (1842, oil on canvas, 37 x 27 ins / 94 x 69 cm) GBP 48,000.

JENSEN, Johannes

Danish, 19th century.
Born 1818, in Copenhagen; died 23 May 1873, in Copenhagen.
Painter, draughtsman. Portraits, genre scenes, landscapes with figures.

Johannes Jensen was a pupil at the academy. He exhibited portraits and genre paintings from 1843 to 1869. He then went to the USA where he lived until 1872. Several of his paintings and drawings were reproduced as lithographs.

AUCTION RECORDS:

STOCKHOLM, 19 May 1992, *Landscape with Young Vagabond* (1859, oil on canvas, 22 1/2 x 17 3/4 ins / 57 x 45 cm) SEK 6,200.

JENSEN, Karl George

Danish, 19th - 20th century.
Born 22 November 1851, in Holstebro; died 1933.
Active in Copenhagen.
Painter. Interiors with figures, church interiors, landscapes, architectural views.

Received an honourable mention at the Exposition Universelle in Paris in 1889.

MUSEUMS AND GALLERIES:

COPENHAGEN (Den Hirschsprungske Samling): *Landscape near Næstved* - COPENHAGEN (Statens Mus. for Kunst): *Landskab fra Næstvedegnen* (1884); *Audienssalen på Rosenborg* (1889).

AUCTION RECORDS:

COPENHAGEN, 4 May 1976, *Wooded Landscape* (1890, oil on canvas, 23 1/4 x 39 ins / 59 x 99 cm) DKK 4,500. COPENHAGEN, 25-26 April 1990, *Interior of St. Mary's Church, Elsinore* (oil on canvas, 20 x 16 1/4 ins / 51 x 41 cm) DKK 38,000. COPENHAGEN, 5 Feb 1992, *Frederiksborg Castle (from an original by Christen Købke)* (1912, oil on canvas, 23 1/2 x 24 3/4 ins / 60 x 63 cm) DKK 16,000. COPENHAGEN, 7 Sept 1994, *Interior, Château de l'Ermitage* (1899, oil on canvas, 19 1/4 x 15 1/4 ins / 49 x 39 cm) DKK 11,000.

JENSEN, Laurits

Danish, 19th century.
Born 22 August 1859, in Viborg.
Sculptor. Figures, historical figures.

Museums and Galleries:
Copenhagen: several gun-dogs - Hillerød (Frederiksborg): *Christian IX on Horseback* (statuette); *Frederik VIII on Horseback* (statuette) - Randers: *Two Christians in the Arena*.
Auction records:
Chester, 5 May 1983, *Scenting of Panther* (1896, gilt bronze, h. 17 ins / 43 cm) GBP 820. Copenhagen, 6 Oct 1986, *Christian IV on Horseback* (1901, bronze, h. 18 ins / 46 cm) DKK 8,000.

JENSEN, Louis Isak Napoleon
Danish, 19th century.
Born 15 August 1858, in Copenhagen; died 21 May 1908.
Landscape artist.
Museums and Galleries:
Aalborg - Copenhagen (Statens Mus. for Kunst): *The Little Vallø River* (1907) - Randers.

JENSEN, Marius Carl Wilhelm
Danish, 19th century.
Born 12 June 1819, in Ringsted; died 13 August 1882, in Liliedal, near Assens.
Painter.
Marius Jensen was a pupil at the Kunstakademi in Copenhagen. He exhibited several landscapes and drawings of portraits between 1839 and 1842.
Museums and Galleries:
Copenhagen (Statens Mus. for Kunst): *Monastery in Gisselgeld* - Copenhagen (Thorvaldsens Mus.): *Garden in Gisselgeld (Seeland).*

JENSEN, Max
German, 19th century.
Active in Berlin c. 1887.
Painter. Seascapes.

JENSEN, Milton Carl
Danish, 19th - 20th century.
Born 16 June 1855, in Slagelse; died 1928.
Painter. Religious subjects, landscapes.
Milton Carl Jensen worked initially as a painter and interior decorative artist. He studied at the Kunstakademi in Copenhagen from 1874 to 1880, but he had already started to exhibit in 1879. He continued to exhibit virtually every year until his death in 1928. Jensen was awarded the Sødring Prize in 1892 for his *Sunny Spring Day*. He settled in Aarhus in 1893 and went on to paint landscapes of the region, which he exhibited in Aarhus galleries.
Museums and Galleries:
Thorsted (Church): *Christ Calming the Storm* (oil on canvas).
Auction records:
Copenhagen, 25 Feb 1976, *Winter Landscape* (1891, oil on canvas, 13½ x 11 ins / 34 x 28 cm) DKK 1,500. Copenhagen, 27 Feb 1985, *Street Scene* (1892, oil on canvas, 22 x 27¼ ins / 56 x 69 cm) DKK 40,000. Copenhagen, 5 April 1989, *Landscape near Helgenæs* (1928, oil on canvas, 31½ x 51¼ ins / 80 x 130 cm) DKK 5,200. London, 5 May 1989, *Wooded Coastal Landscape* (1886, oil on canvas, 15¾ x 22½ ins / 40 x 57 cm) GBP 605. Copenhagen, 29 Aug 1990, *Summer's Day near Silkeborgsoerne* (1895, oil on canvas, 33¾ x 49½ ins / 86 x 126 cm) DKK 6,000. Copenhagen, 1 May 1991, *Landscape with Cattle in a Meadow* (1907, oil on canvas, 39¼ x 63 ins / 100 x 160 cm) DKK 9,500. Copenhagen, 15 Nov 1993, *Summer's Day near Silkeborgsoene* (1913, oil on canvas, 30¼ x 43¼ ins / 77 x 110 cm) DKK 4,000. Copenhagen, 8 Feb 1995, *Peasant Woman Knitting in front of her House* (1886, oil on canvas, 16¼ x 24¾ ins / 41 x 63 cm) DKK 6,200.

JENSEN, Ole
Swedish, 20th century.
Born 1926.
Painter.
Ole Jensen's body of work went through a number of different periods but it was characterised by squared and hatched links juxtaposed to create a mesh that delineated and highlighted curves and spatial volumes. His work is reminiscent of that of Oscar Dominguez.
Auction records:
Stockholm, 6 June 1988, *Street with Figures and a Tree* (oil, 24 x 30¼ ins / 61 x 77 cm) SEK 7,000. Stockholm, 5-6 Dec 1990, *Emperor* (oil on canvas, 39¼ x 27½ ins / 100 x 70 cm) SEK 5,000.

JENSEN, Olga Wilhelmine
Maiden name: Meissner
Danish, 20th century.
Born 12 February 1877.
Painter. Portraits, flowers.
Olga Jensen studied at the fine arts academy and, in 1910, in Paris. She is remembered for numerous paintings of children.

JENSEN, Oluf Carl Christian
Danish, 19th - 20th century.
Born 17 February 1871.
Painter, watercolourist. Landscapes, flowers.
Oluf Jensen was retained by the Royal Copenhagen porcelain factory. Away from work, he produced a number of watercolours.

JENSEN, Oluf Simony
Danish, 19th - 20th century.
Born 1871; died 1934.
Painter. Local scenes, interiors with figures.
Auction records:
London, 27-28 March 1990, *Interior with Men Drinking Tea* (1901, oil on canvas, 30¼ x 41¼ ins / 77 x 105 cm) GBP 2,420. London, 29 March 1990, *Café Scene* (oil on canvas, 27 x 38¼ ins / 68.5 x 97 cm) GBP 3,520.

JENSEN, P. Marius
Danish, 20th century.
Born 8 February 1883, in Fredericia.
Sculptor. Scenes with figures.
Marius Jensen moved to Germany in 1901, working initially in Dresden and then in Berlin, where he worked alongside the sculptor C. Bernewitz. He produced various pieces, among them a number of bronzes (*Icarus and Psyche, Warriors after Battle*). In 1902, Marius Jensen sculpted a sandstone statue (*Education*) and a sandstone relief for the city of Kassel.

JENSEN, Peder, also known as Kolding or Peder Jensson
Danish, 17th century.
Born to a family originally from Kolding.
Sculptor (wood).
Peder Jensen executed his first works in the region of Kolding. His richly sculpted, painted and gilded altarpiece depicting *The Last Communion* (1648) is in the church in Jannerup (Jutland). He executed altars in 1654 for a church in Glud and a church in Skødstrup near Randers. He later worked in the region of Horsens.

JENSEN, Peder Vilhelm. See **JENSEN-KLINT**

JENSEN, Søren Christian
Danish, 19th - 20th century.
Born 6 October 1870, in Træløse.
Painter. Portraits.
Søren Christian Jensen studied at the Kongelige Danske Kunstakademi in Copenhagen and exhibited portraits from 1892.

JENSEN, Søren Georg
Danish, 20th century.

Born 1917, in Copenhagen.
Sculptor. Monuments.

Søren Georg Jensen was the son of Georg Arthur Jensen. He was apprenticed to his silversmith father from 1931 to 1936, prior to enrolling at the Kongelige Danske Kunstakademi in Copenhagen. He spent a period in Paris, where he was greatly influenced by the sculpture of Aristide Maillol. He then worked for a short time in the studio of Ossip Zadkine, whose influence was also immense. In 1959, Søren Jensen aligned himself with the Den Frie group.

Jensen sculpted a number of pieces in the manner of Maillol but his work then evolved towards the radically abstract. He produced monumental pieces for public squares and schools for example. His sculpture comprises straightforward or articulated assemblies where flat and convex surfaces are juxtaposed to produce pure form. Søren Georg Jensen was fully aware that his sculptures were conceptually and structurally dependent on the base material employed. Accordingly, his style varies as a function of that material, be it metal, ceramic or bronze.

He started showing his work at group exhibitions in Copenhagen as of 1940, and examples of his work featured at the *Art Danois* (*Danish Art*) exhibition held in the Galeries Nationales du Grand Palais in Paris in 1973.

BIBLIOGRAPHY:
Galy-Carles, Henry, *Art danois, 1945-1973*, exhibition catalogue, Galeries nationales du Grand Palais, Paris, 1973.

MUSEUMS AND GALLERIES:
COPENHAGEN (Statens Mus. for Kunst): *Monument for Aalborg (preparatory study)* (bronze) - HUMLEBÆK (Louisiana Mus. for Moderne Kunst): *Air* (1953-1960, iron).

AUCTION RECORDS:
COPENHAGEN, 2 March 1994, *Tragikos Johannes; Tragikos Bertel* (two aluminium sculptures painted white, each h. 53 1/4 ins / 135 cm) DKK 12,200. COPENHAGEN, 23 March 1999, *Untitled* (1979, brown-patinated bronze, h. 14 ins / 35 cm) DKK 17,000. COPENHAGEN, 30 Aug 2000, *Construction* (c. 1960, art stone, h. 8 ins / 27 cm, w. 19 ins/47 cm) DKK 18,500. COPENHAGEN, 29 Nov 2000, *Bird* (patinated bronze, h. 17 ins / 43 cm) DKK 38,000. COPENHAGEN, 7 Oct 2003, *Constructive Sculpture* (c. 1955, stoneware, h. 9 ins / 24 cm, w. 20 ins/52 cm) DKK 30,000. COPENHAGEN, 29 March 2004, *Untitled* (black and green-patinated bronze, h. 8 ins / 21 cm) DKK 16,000. COPENHAGEN, 29 March 2004, *Untitled* (brown-patinated bronze, h. 8 ins / 21 cm) DKK 18,000.

JENSEN, Theodor
British, 19th century.
Active in London.
Painter.

Theodor Jensen showed his genre paintings between 1854 and 1864 in exhibitions held at the Royal Academy, the British Institution and the Suffolk Street Gallery. In 1864, he exhibited his portraits of the *Prince and Princess of Wales*.

AUCTION RECORDS:
LONDON, 26 Oct 1979, *Portrait of a Young Girl* (1853, oil on canvas, oval, 35 x 27 ins / 89 x 68.5 cm) GBP 1,100. LONDON, 9 Dec 1980, *Floral Abundance* (1853, oil on canvas, oval, 35 x 27 ins / 88 x 68.5 cm) GBP 820. LONDON, 11 June 2002, *Farmer's Daughter* (oil on canvas, 23 x 19 ins / 59 x 49 cm) GBP 1,800.

JENSEN, Thomas Martin
Danish, 19th - 20th century.
Born 20 May 1831, in Apenrade; died 1916, in New York.
Painter. Religious subjects, genre scenes, landscapes, landscapes with figures, flowers.

Thomas Martin Jensen was awarded second and first class silver medals at the Kongelige Danske Kunstakademi in Copenhagen in 1855 and 1856 respectively. As of 1858, he started to exhibit genre compositions and landscapes with figures (*Hunters Lying in Wait, Home Life in Fanø*). He also painted still-lifes of flowers, together with a number of altarpieces for various churches in Frijsenborg. He moved to New York City in 1869, settling in Brooklyn. Paintings by Thomas Martin Jensen are preserved in Brooklyn Museum and in New York City Hall.

MUSEUMS AND GALLERIES:
NEW YORK (Brooklyn Mus.).

AUCTION RECORDS:
LONDON, 7 May 1971, *Selling Cherries*, Gns 600. NEW YORK, 2 May 1979, *Ships off the Port of New York* (1903, oil on canvas, 27 x 47 1/2 ins / 68.6 x 120.6 cm) USD 2,250. COPENHAGEN, 15 Nov 1993, *Children Sitting on a Stone Wall surrounding a Village* (oil on canvas, 15 x 20 ins / 38 x 51 cm) DKK 17,000. NEW YORK, 12 Sept 1994, *Ships off the Port of New York with the Statue of Liberty in the Background* (oil on canvas, 27 1/2 x 43 1/2 ins / 69.9 x 110.5 cm) USD 3,737.

JENSEN, Ulf Valde
Norwegian, 20th century.
Born 27 April 1945, in Lillehammer.
Engraver, painter.

Ulf Valde Jensen studied first in Stockholm, then at the École des Beaux-Arts in Paris and finally with Friedlaender. From 1966, he has made regular stays in Paris. His canvases present a small, humorous world with a hint of Surrealism, certain aspects of which are reminiscent of the world of Klee. He produces narrative sequences that are theatrical and eccentric. He participated in the Biennale de l'Estampe in Paris in 1970, the Salon de Mai in 1972 and the Salon des Réalités Nouvelles in 1972 and 1973. He exhibited in Oslo in 1970 and since then has shown in Göteborg and Stockholm.

MUSEUMS AND GALLERIES:
PARIS (Prints Collection): *The Fat Girl* (1980, etching).

JENSEN-EGEBERG, Jens Jorgen
Danish, 19th - 20th century.
Born 26 April 1848; died 20 September 1922.
Painter.

Jens Jensen-Egeberg studied at the Kongelige Danske Kunstakademi in Copenhagen and from 1881 started exhibiting his landscapes and portraits, including portraits of his parents (1885) and his wife (1892). He is also credited with an altarpiece entitled *Suffer the Little Children to Come unto Me*.

JENSEN-KLINT, Peder Vilhelm
Danish, 19th century.
Born 21 June 1853, near Skelskr.
Painter, architect.

Peder Jensen-Klint first studied engineering, and then studied painting at the academy from 1878 to 1885. He began to exhibit his landscapes in 1883 under the name P. V. Jensen. For a time he engaged in sculpture, executing models for fountains and decorative vases, and then devoted himself exclusively to architecture.

JENSSEN, Olav Christopher
Norwegian, 20th - 21st century.
Born 1954, in Sortland (Vesterålen Islands).
Active since 1985 in Germany.
Painter.

Olav Christopher Jenssen lives and works in Berlin and Bastad. He composes his pictures by superimposition, creating a network of bands and outlines which he covers with dots and geometric shapes. His abstracts, which are bathed in Nordic light - from white to black - may evoke silent landscapes. Since 1986, he has participated in many group exhibitions including 1987 at the Konsthall in Malmö, 1989 at the Nordiskt Konstcentrum in Helsinki, 1990 at the Museum of Modern Art in Oxford, 1991 at the Museu de Arte de São Paulo and Moderna Museet in Stockholm, 1992 at the Barbican Centre in London and Documenta in Kassel, 1993 at the Copenhagen Kunstforening, 1994 at the Oslo Museum of Modern Art, 1995 at the Düsseldorf Kunsthalle and 1996 at the Museo Nacional Centro de Arte Reina Sofia in Madrid. He has also held solo shows in 1979, 1983, 1985, 1987, 1989, 1990, 1992 and 1995 in Oslo; 1987 and 1990 in Stockholm; 1988, 1991 and 1993 in Helsinki; 1992 in Copenhagen; 1992 and 1993 in Berlin; 1993 at the Neue Galerie in Kassel; 1994 in Paris, Bremen and Hanover; 1996 in Ghent and Düsseldorf and 1996 at the Musée des Beaux-Arts in Nantes.

BIBLIOGRAPHY:

Storsve, Jonas, *Olav Christopher Jenssen*, exhibition catalogue, Musée des Beaux-Arts, Nantes, 1996.

MUSEUMS AND GALLERIES:

NANTES (MBA) - PARIS (FNAC).

JENSSON, Peder. See **JENSEN Peder**

JENTSCH, Adolph Friedrich Stephan

German, 20th century.

Born 29 December 1888, in Deuben.

Painter, draughtsman, engraver.

Adolph Jentsch studied at the fine arts academy in Dresden between 1905 and 1914. He is noted for numerous lithographs of Dresden and the surrounding area.

AUCTION RECORDS:

JOHANNESBURG, 17 March 1976, *Bome, Southwest Africa* (1967, watercolour, 14 3/4 x 23 1/2 ins / 37.5 x 59.5 cm) ZAR 900. JOHANNESBURG, 26 April 1978, *Landscape with Large Tree* (1943, oil on canvas, 18 1/2 x 27 1/4 ins / 47 x 69 cm) ZAR 1,500. LONDON, 17 Sept 1999, *Karakoelkraal* (oil on canvas, 27 x 39 ins / 69 x 100 cm) GBP 22,000. JOHANNESBURG, 8 Nov 1999, *Landscape, Namibia* (1943, oil on canvas, 27 x 39 ins / 68 x 99 cm) ZAR 160,000. LONDON, 18 April 2000, *Windhoek* (oil on canvas, 24 x 31 ins / 60 x 80 cm) GBP 10,000. LONDON, 18 April 2000, *Bush Landscape* (1940, oil on canvas, 28 x 39 ins / 70 x 100 cm) GBP 16,000. JOHANNESBURG, 12 Nov 2001, *Southern Nambian Landscape* (1939, oil on canvas on board, 23 x 31 ins / 58 x 78 cm) ZAR 45,000. JOHANNESBURG, 3 Dec 2003, *Extensive Landscape, Namibia* (1943, oil on canvas, 27 x 39 ins / 69 x 99 cm) ZAR 110,000. JOHANNESBURG, 30 March 2004, *South West Africa* (1950, watercolour, 11 x 7 ins / 27 x 19 cm) ZAR 130,000. JOHANNESBURG, 31 May 2004, *Namibian Landscape* (1940, oil on canvas, 27 x 39 ins / 68 x 98 cm) ZAR 100,000.

JENTZEN, Friedrich

German, 19th century.

Born 24 May 1804, in Berlin; died 25 August 1875, in Weimar.

Active in Berlin.

Lithographer.

The lithographer Friedrich Jentzen trained at the academy in Berlin. In 1824, he showed a *Portrait of a Woman* in oils at the academy exhibition, but subsequently took up lithography to the exclusion of all else, and did reproductions of paintings and drawings by Kruger. In 1828 he exhibited his first portrait lithographs, all taken from Kruger. Noted portraits include *Friedrich Wilhelm IV on Horseback, Princes Waldemar and Adalbert of Prussia, Princess Elizabeth of Prussia*, the *Duke of Coburg* and painter *Horace Vernet*. Further works lithographed include Wach's *Portrait of the King*, Bendemann's *The Arts at the Source of Poetry* and Pistorius's *Summer Afternoon*. He also did a number of lithographs from old masters such as Correggio (*Io and Jupiter*) and *Christ and the Woman Taken in Adultery* after Pordenone.

JENTZEN, Friedrich

German, 19th century.

Born 13 June 1815, in Schwerin; died 17 May 1901, in Schwerin.

Painter. Landscapes, architectural views.

The patronage of Duchess Helen of Orléans enabled the painter Friedrich Jentzen to attend classes at the academy in Berlin, where his teachers were K. Gropius and W. Kranse. Subsequently he went to Munich to study architecture, was later appointed court painter in Mecklenburg, and won gold and silver medals. He exhibited in Paris in 1867.

AUCTION RECORDS:

NEW YORK, 4 May 1979, *The Foro Romano* (oil on canvas, 46 x 68 3/4 ins / 117 x 174.5 cm) USD 5,250.

JENTZSCH, Johann Moritz Gottfried

German, 18th - 19th century.

Born 1759, in Hinter-Jessen (Pirna), Saxony; died 1826, in Dresden.

Painter, draughtsman, engraver.

Johann Jentzsch learned to paint very young, secretly, then went to work at the Meissen porcelain works. By 1780, he was considered a skilled landscape painter. In 1800, he was painter to the court theatre in Dresden, and the Saxon Elector subsequently sent him to Italy. In 1824, he became a member of the academy in Dresden. As an engraver, he reproduced mainly views of the Sächsische Schweiz hills near Dresden after Aberli.

JENTZSCH, Johannes Gabriel

German, 19th century.

Born 1862, in Dresden.

Painter. Genre scenes.

Johannes Jentzsch trained at the academy in Dresden and under Pauwels in Dresden. He won a medal in 1886, and exhibited in Munich from 1890.

JENTZSCH, Moritz Gottfried

German, 18th century.

Born 7 December 1770, in Dresden.

Painter, engraver (etching). Landscapes, architectural views.

Noted works by Moritz Jentzsch include two drawn views of gates of the city of Dresden, a panoramic view of the city, a number of watercolour interiors and two small landscape etchings.

JENYNS, Lorraine

Australian, 20th century.

Born 1945.

Sculptor, potter.

Lorraine Jenyns creates ceramic vases in violent colours, decorated with figures and animals depicted with populist humour. These bear a certain similarity with Egyptian urns used to store the mummified internal organs of the dead.

JEOFFROY. See **GEOFFROY** and **JOFFROY**

JEPES, Tomás. See **HIEPES**

JEPSEN, Johann, or Jebsen

Danish, 17th century.

Died 1 February 1700.

Active in Copenhagen.

Painter.

JEPSEN, Morten

Danish, 19th century.

Born 24 July 1826, in Strandby, near Frederikshavn; died 21 July 1903.

Painter. Portraits, architectural views, church interiors.

Morten Jepsen was a pupil at the Kunstakademi in Copenhagen. From 1869 he showed his work almost every year. These were architectural paintings either from Denmark, Sweden, Prague, Rome or Paris, such as *Hôtel de Cluny* and *Interior of Notre-Dame During a Morning Mass*.

MUSEUMS AND GALLERIES:

HILLERØD: *Church Interior in Prague*; *Portrait of the Writer Krossing*.

JEQUEL, Christian
French, 20th century.
Born 16 January 1935, in Ganges (Hérault).
Painter. Scenes with figures, landscapes, animals.
Christian Jequel exhibits regularly in France and in New York, Los Angeles, Abidjan and Barcelona. He depicts the everyday, painting with a full brush.

JEQUIER, Jules
Swiss, 19th century.
Born 14 July 1834, in Geneva; died 24 August 1898, in Montreux.
Painter, engraver (etching). Landscapes.
Works by Jequier include original etchings, notably *Pointe du Raz, near Douarnenez, Étang du Carré, Evening* and *Morning in Bellerive* (1882).
MUSEUMS AND GALLERIES:
AARAU: *Brittany Coast* - BASEL: *Pointe du Raz; Belle Isle Reefs* - GENEVA: *Mont Blanc Seen from the Garden* - ST GALL: *Oak Pool* - WINTERTHUR: *Cap St Mathieu.*
AUCTION RECORDS:
LUCERNE, 8 Nov 1984, *View of Lake Lucerne* (oil on canvas, 14 x 21 ins / 35.5 x 52.5 cm) CHF 5,000. BERN, 26 Oct 1988, *Mountain Village* (oil on card, 10 1/2 x 15 1/2 ins / 26.5 x 39.5 cm) CHF 2,700. ZURICH, 25 Nov 2002, *St Gingolph at Lake Leman* (oil on canvas, 13 x 19 ins / 34 x 49 cm) CHF 3,200.

JERACE, Severo. See **IRACE**

JERACES, Francesco. See **IERACE**

JÉRAMEC, Gabriel
French, 19th century.
Born 19th century, in Paris.
Sculptor.
Gabriel Jéramec studied under Marc Robert and featured at the Salon of the Société des Artistes Français, receiving an honourable mention in 1910.

JERANIAN, Richard
French, 20th century.
Born 17 July 1921, in Sebaste, Armenia.
Painter, draughtsman. Figures, landscapes, still-lifes.
Richard Jeranian studied in Marseilles and in Paris, and then took painting courses at the Académie Julian and the Grande Chaumière. He served in the French Air Force from 1944 to 1946. He painted with confidence, producing landscapes of Armenia and France, still-lifes, nudes, figures, religious subjects such as the 1981 *Christ's Entry into Ani*, mythological subjects such as the 1976 *Myth of Sisyphus*, everyday subjects such as the 1980 *Girl Ironing*, Surrealist subjects such as the 1982 *Times, Civilisations*, and musical subjects such as the 1972 *Homage to Mozart*. He varied his subjects and he also varied his styles, moving from figurative to the surreal and then through Cubism to the Abstract. He painted his figurative works with a full brush, broad strokes and strong colours. He also did a great deal of drawing in tinted Indian ink, using a technique of surface lines that produce an effect of striped planes not unlike engraving. This is the method he used for musical subjects such as his *Bach Fugues* and the 1972 *Homage to Tchaikovsky*, in which the abstract style is in natural harmony with the music, and where the artist's musical awareness is expressed in a dynamic construction allowing the levels of sound to be visually perceived.

He exhibited regularly in Paris at various salons - Salon d'Automne, Salon des Artistes Indépendants and Salon des Artistes Français, and occasionally at the Salon des Terres Latines and Salon Peintres Témoins de Leur Temps. He had work shown abroad in group exhibitions: 1960, Los Angeles; 1964, Brussels; 1971, Beirut; 1974, New York; and 1982, New Jersey. His first solo show took place in Paris in 1953 and was followed by many others: 1957, 1959, 1961, 1963, 1971, 1988 and 1990. Others were in Beirut in 1958, 1960, 1964, 1965, 1972 and 1974; in Geneva in 1961, 1963 and 1973; in New York in 1964 and 1977, in Washington in 1965 and 1977; in Bordeaux in 1971 and 1984. He was awarded the City of Paris silver medal in 1955 and the first prize in Europe for drawing at Monaco in 1966.
MUSEUMS AND GALLERIES:
AVIGNON (Mus. Calvet) - MOSCOW (Pushkin MFA) - PARIS (BNF) - PARIS (MAMVP).
AUCTION RECORDS:
ROMANS-SUR-ISÈRE, 3 Feb 1989, *Seated Nude* (Indian ink, 22 3/4 x 23 1/2 ins / 58 x 60 cm) FRF 12,000. PARIS, 10 April 1989, *Landscape* (oil on canvas, 32 x 25 1/2 ins / 81 x 65 cm) FRF 25,000. PARIS, 29 March 1990, *Inwardness* (Indian ink, 17 3/4 x 19 3/4 ins / 45 x 50 cm) FRF 7,500.

JEREBTSOV, Anna
Russian, 20th century.
Born 18 October 1885.
Painter, engraver. Portraits, landscapes, still-lifes.
Anna Jerebtsov exhibited portraits, landscapes and still-lifes at the Salon des Indépendants and the Salon d'Automne in Paris.

JERGEN, Johann Joseph
Swiss, 19th century.
Born 10 April 1810; died 28 July 1873.
Sculptor.
The church in Brig contains four busts of the Fathers of the Church by Johann Jergen.

JERIC-DUCHAL, pseudonym of Dupuy, Éric
French, 20th century.
Born 5 April 1942, in Paris.
Sculptor.
Jeric-Duchal trained with Stahly whose influence can still be felt in his own work. He has taken part in the Salon de la Jeune Sculpture since 1966 and exhibited at the Salon de Mai in 1972.

JERICHAU, Harald Adolf Nikolaj, or Jerikau
Danish, 19th century.
Born 17 August 1851, in Copenhagen; died 6 March 1878, in Rome.
Painter. Landscapes.
Harald Jerichau was the son of Jens Adolf Jerichau and Anna Jerichau-Baumann. He began his artistic education at the age of six and then became a pupil of Jean-Achille Benouville in Paris. In 1870 he had already produced several paintings, such as *Ponte Mollé* and *View of Velletri*. He travelled to Switzerland, Greece, Asia Minor and Turkey, and worked in Paris, Rome and Denmark. Among his best works are *The Shore in Sorrente* and *Caravan in Sardara*.
MUSEUMS AND GALLERIES:
COPENHAGEN (Ny Carlsberg Glyptotek): *Mosque in Constantinople; The Coast of Sorrento* - COPENHAGEN (Statens Mus. for Kunst): *Caravan in Sardara* (1878) - GDANSK: *View of Constantinople* - GÖTEBORG: *The Coast of Capri.*
AUCTION RECORDS:
LONDON, 14 April 1976, *Roman Ruins in Tunisia* (1875, oil on canvas, 11 x 15 1/2 ins / 27 x 39.5 cm) GBP 300. COPENHAGEN, 21 Feb 1990, *The Ass in front of his Shed* (oil on canvas, 14 1/2 x 20 ins / 37 x 51 cm) DKK 4,500. LONDON, 30 March 1990, *View of Constantinople from Bosphorus* (oil on canvas, 31 x 61 1/2 ins / 78.7 x 156.3 cm) GBP 10,450. LONDON, 14 June 1995, *View of Istanbul* (1871, oil on canvas, 14 x 22 ins / 35.5 x 56 cm) GBP 5,175. COPENHAGEN, 1 Dec 1998, *View towards Istanbul* (oil on canvas, 24 x 38 ins / 61 x 96 cm) DKK 17,000. STOCKHOLM, 25 Jan 1999, *River Landscape with View of Town* (1871, oil on canvas, 13 x 22 ins / 32 x 57 cm) SEK 17,500. COPENHAGEN, 6 Sept 2000, *Fishing Boats in the Gulf near Naples* (oil on canvas, 9 x 15 ins / 23 x 37 cm) DKK

19,000. AARHUS, 12 June 2001, *Red Evening Sky over Constantinople* (oil on canvas, 12 x 21 ins / 30 x 53 cm) DKK 20,000. VEJLE, 23 Sept 2002, *Parthenon in Athens* (oil on canvas, 16 x 21 ins / 40 x 54 cm) DKK 70,000. VEJLE, 10 Nov 2003, *River Landscape with Boats and Figures, Constantinople in Background* (oil on canvas, 10 x 21 ins / 25 x 54 cm) DKK 31,000. LONDON, 18 Nov 2003, *Overlooking the Acropolis* (1873, oil on canvas, 16 x 21 ins / 40 x 54 cm) GBP 7,500. COPENHAGEN, 2 March 2004, *View of Constantinople from the Graveyard outside Town* (oil on canvas, 16 x 23 ins / 41 x 58 cm) DKK 150,000.

JERICHAU, Holger Hvitfeldt

Danish, 19th century.

Born 29 April 1861, in Copenhagen; died 26 December 1900, in Copenhagen.

Painter. Genre scenes, landscapes.

Holger Jerichau painted several landscapes in the Horsholm region in Seeland.

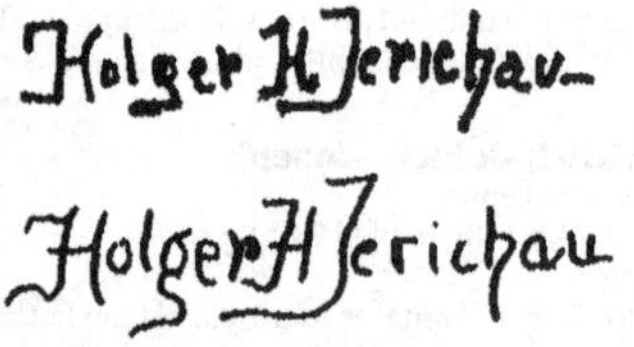

AUCTION RECORDS:

LONDON, 5 Oct 1983, *View of Château de Chillon* (1897, oil on canvas, 32 1/2 x 48 1/4 ins / 82.5 x 122.5 cm) GBP 900. LONDON, 6 Feb 1987, *Capri* (oil on canvas, 41 1/4 x 28 ins / 105 x 71 cm) GBP 7,500. STOCKHOLM, 15 Nov 1988, *Coastline of the Bay of Naples with Two Female Figures* (oil, 9 x 15 1/4 ins / 23 x 38.5 cm) SEK 9,500. STOCKHOLM, 19 April 1989, *Italian Landscape with Mountain Road* (oil on canvas, 9 3/4 x 15 1/4 ins / 25 x 39 cm) SEK 8,200. NEW YORK, 17 Jan 1990, *Promenade on a Hilly Road* (oil on canvas, 24 1/4 x 16 1/4 ins / 61.6 x 41.3 cm) USD 1,320. COPENHAGEN, 25-26 April 1990, *Monk and Fisherman on a Terrace* (1894, oil on canvas, 27 1/2 x 19 ins / 70 x 48 cm) DKK 9,000. STOCKHOLM, 16 May 1990, *Marina Grande in Capri* (oil on panel, 13 x 17 1/4 ins / 33 x 44 cm) SEK 6,700. NEW YORK, 19 July 1990, *Young Couple Conversing near a Wall with Capri in the Background* (oil on canvas, 16 1/2 x 30 1/4 ins / 41.6 x 76.6 cm) USD 3,575. ROME, 28 May 1991, *Fishing Village in Capri* (oil on canvas, 16 1/2 x 25 1/4 ins / 42 x 64 cm) ITL 9,000,000. COPENHAGEN, 16 May 1994, *Sloping Landscape near Naples* (oil on canvas, 15 x 24 3/4 ins / 38 x 63 cm) DKK 8,000. LONDON, 17 June 1994, *The Gulf of Naples* (oil on panel, 6 3/4 x 12 1/4 ins / 17.4 x 31.4 cm) USD 1,380. COPENHAGEN, 16 Nov 1994, *View of the Sea with Large Rock in Foreground* (oil on canvas, 39 1/4 x 64 1/4 ins / 100 x 163 cm) DKK 4,400. LONDON, 15 Nov 1995, *Peasants in Southern Italy* (oil on canvas, 28 1/4 x 22 ins / 72 x 56 cm) GBP 3,105. COPENHAGEN, 1 June 1999, *Italian Pergola with Man Carrying Watermelon* (oil on canvas, 41 x 27 ins / 105 x 69 cm) DKK 14,000. VIENNA, 2 Dec 1999, *Peasant Holding Melon on Shoulder under Grape Arbour, Capri* (oil on canvas, 41 x 27 ins / 105 x 69 cm) ATS 50,000. LONDON, 22 June 2000, *State Elephant at the Raja, Benares* (oil on canvas, 16 x 25 ins / 41 x 64 cm) GBP 3,000. COPENHAGEN, 4 Dec 2000, *Bay of Naples* (1889, oil on canvas, 18 x 26 ins / 45 x 65 cm) DKK 30,000. PARIS, 18 June 2001, *Bank of the Ganges at Benares* (oil on canvas, 21 x 30 ins / 54 x 75 cm) FRF 39,000. COPENHAGEN, 3 Sept 2001, *Busy Street Market by Italian Town Gate at Sunset* (oil on canvas, 22 x 38 ins / 55 x 96 cm) DKK 36,000. COPENHAGEN, 27 Aug 2002, *Coastal Landscape with Beached Boats, Capri* (oil on canvas, 13 x 19 ins / 32 x 47 cm) DKK 19,000. HAVNEN, 30 Nov 2002, *Italian Coastal Landscape with Sailing Boats and Fishermen Mending Nets on a Beach* (oil on canvas, 28 x 44 ins / 71 x 112 cm) DKK 20,000. COPENHAGEN, 21 May 2003, *View towards Sorrento from Capri* (oil on canvas, 28 x 44 ins / 71 x 112 cm) DKK 33,000. COPENHAGEN, 9 Dec 2003, *Meeting in an Italian Pergola* (oil on canvas, 20 x 30 ins / 52 x 77 cm) DKK 29,000.

JERICHAU, Jens Adolf

Danish, 19th century.

Born 17 April 1816, in Assens; died 24 July 1883, in Neder Draaby.

Sculptor.

After beginning his artistic education in Copenhagen, Jens Jerichau went to Rome where he became one of Thorvaldsen's best pupils. Upon his return to Copenhagen he rose to prominence as a proponent of the Danish School. He received several important commissions, including the Œrsted and Andersen monument in Copenhagen, *The Marriage of Alexander and Roxanne* (a low relief for the royal palace) and the group *Hercules and Hebe*. *Penelope* is considered to be a masterpiece. He also executed *The Creation of Eve* and *Adam and Eve after the Fall*. He is considered to be a Classical artist in every sense of the word. He received a gold medal in Berlin in 1868, and exhibited at the Royal Academy in London from 1858 to 1868.

MUSEUMS AND GALLERIES:

AALBORG: *Young Girls Bathing; The Angel of Peace; The Panther Hunters; Flora; Sleeping Child with Dog; Sleeping Cupid* - AARHUS: *Slave; Christ* - COPENHAGEN: *Thorvaldsen; Pastoral Scene; Children Playing with a Goat; Sleeping Dog; Goat; Hercules and Hebe; The Panther Hunter; Cupid in Victory with the Arms of Mars; The Female Slave; The Reaper; Queen Alexandra; Young Girls Bathing; Adam and Eve; The Alma Goethe Mausoleum; Flora; Young Girl with Kittens; Colonel A. F. Tscherning* - COPENHAGEN (Den Hirschsprungske Samling): *Leda* - COPENHAGEN (Ny Carlsberg Glyptotek): *Sleeping Child with Dog; Donar; Penelope; Slave; Hercules and Hebe; Ulysses and Nausicaa; Hector and Ajax; Orpheus* - HILLERØD: *Andersen* - ODENSE: *The Angel of Death; Resurrection; C. J. Thomsen; Lieutenant Laessoe; Sleeping Reaper* - STOCKHOLM: *The Panther Hunter* - WEIMAR (Goethe-Nationalmus.): *The Alma Goethe Mausoleum.*

AUCTION RECORDS:

COPENHAGEN, 12-14 Nov 1997, *Head of a Man* (1913, sculpture, 7 1/2 x 9 ins / 19 x 22 cm) DKK 15,000. COPENHAGEN, 26 Nov 2002, *The Panther Hunter* (patinated bronze, h. 28ins / 70cm) DKK 12,500. VEJLE, 15 March 2004, *The Panther Hunter* (patinated bronze, h. 28ins / 70cm) DKK 16,500.

JERICHAU, Jens Adolf Emil

Danish, 20th century.

Born 11 December 1890, in Roskilde; died 16 August 1916, in Paris.

Painter. Figures, local scenes, landscapes.

Jens Jerichau was the son of the painter Holger Jerichau; he studied at the Kongelige Danske Kunstakademi in Copenhagen and exhibited to considerable acclaim in the Danish capital.

AUCTION RECORDS:

COPENHAGEN, 10 Oct 1963, *Suzanne Bathing*, DKK 11,000. COPENHAGEN, 1 April 1981, *Composition* (oil on canvas, 51 1/4 x 63 ins / 130 x 160 cm) DKK 22,000. COPENHAGEN, 9 May 1984, *Cardinal, Opus III, Madrid* (1915, oil on canvas, 51 1/4 x 45 ins / 130 x 114 cm) DKK 90,000. COPENHAGEN, 24 April 1985, *Landscape near Toledo* (1915, oil on canvas, 19 3/4 x 23 1/2 ins / 50 x 60 cm) DKK 92,000. COPENHAGEN, 25 Feb 1987, *Under the Plane Trees* (1915, oil on canvas, 23 1/4 x 28 1/4 ins / 59 x 72 cm) DKK 175,000. COPENHAGEN, 9 May 1990, *The Magi* (1916, oil on canvas, 55 x 67 ins / 140 x 170 cm) DKK 250,000. COPENHAGEN, 31 Oct 1990, *Hessel's House* (1909, oil on canvas, 11 1/2 x 17 1/4 ins / 29 x 44 cm) DKK 4,000. COPENHAGEN, 1 April 1992, *Man and Woman* (1913, bronze, h. 9 ins / 23 cm) DKK 27,000. COPENHAGEN, 21 Oct 1992, *Fishermen in Provence* (1912, oil on canvas, 30 3/4 x 38 1/2 ins / 78 x 98 cm) DKK 60,000. COPENHAGEN, 20 Oct 1993, *Landscape with Seated Figures* (1916, oil on canvas, 25 1/2 x 32 ins / 65 x 81 cm) DKK 50,000. COPENHAGEN, 13 April 1994, *The Magi* (1916, oil on canvas, 55 x 67 ins / 140 x 170 cm) DKK 140,000. COPENHAGEN, 17 April 1997, *Composition with Figures* (1914, oil on canvas, 46 x 53 1/2 ins / 116 x 136 cm) DKK 55,000. COPENHAGEN, 23 March 1999, *Dante. Prophets, Opus I* (1913, oil on canvas, 76 x 53 ins / 192 x 135 cm) DKK 105,000. COPENHAGEN, 20 Oct 1999, *Landscape from the South of France* (watercolour, 17 x 24 ins / 44 x 61 cm) DKK 12,000. VEJLE, 19 Nov 1999, *Lions Fighting* (oil on canvas, 41 x 44 ins / 103 x 112 cm) DKK 15,000. VEJLE, 15 March 2000, *Three Holy Kings and the Whore of Babylon* (oil on cardboard on canvas, 46 x 54 ins / 116 x 136 cm) DKK 45,000. COPENHAGEN, 3 Oct 2000, *Dante* (oil on canvas, 61 x 52 ins / 155 x 132 cm) DKK 460,000. COPENHAGEN, 2 April 2001, *Sacrifice: Figures Seeking Warnings, Opus II* (oil on canvas, 57 x 64 ins / 146 x 162 cm) DKK 1,600,000. COPENHAGEN, 2 Oct 2001, *Christopherus* (c. 1915, watercolour, gouache and pencil, 14 x 10 ins / 35 x 25 cm) DKK 15,000. COPENHAGEN, 20 Feb 2002, *Head Portrait* (clay, 8 x 6x7 ins / 21 x 16x19 cm) DKK 15,000. COPENHAGEN, 10 April 2002, *Gods of the Sea, Opus I* (oil on canvas, 55 x 57 ins / 140 x 144 cm) DKK 500,000. COPENHAGEN, 1 April 2003, *School in Athens* (c. 1914, oil on canvas, 22 x 32 ins / 55 x 81 cm) DKK 40,000. COPENHAGEN, 29 March 2004, *Girls Bathing* (1916, oil on canvas, 26 x 31 ins / 65 x 80 cm) DKK 200,000.

JERICHAU-BAUMANN, Anna Maria Elisabeth

Danish, 19th century.

Born 27 November 1819, in Warsaw; died 11 July 1881, in Copenhagen.

Painter. Religious subjects, figures, portraits, genre scenes.

Anna Jerichau-Baumann was the daughter of a map manufacturer. In 1835 she became a pupil of K. Sohn in Düsseldorf, where she would live for three years. She also received instruction from Lessing, Hildebrand and Schadow. Her first painting, *Young Girl Making her Way to the Church*, was highly successful. In 1845 she went to Rome where she married the sculptor Jens Adolf Jerichau the following year. She also visited England, where she exhibited from 1859 to 1869, as well as Greece, France, Asia Minor and Egypt. She won a gold medal in 1866 in Berlin and, according to some sources, a posthumous prize in Amsterdam in 1886.

A member of the Kunstakademi in Copenhagen, she enjoyed considerable renown in Denmark, and appears to have had the status of official portrait artist. Often cited works include *The Princess of Wales (later Queen of England) in her Wedding Dress* and *Frederik VII, King of Denmark*. Napoleon III commissioned her to paint *Reading of the Bible*. Her works were executed in a careful but rather heavy style. She painted religious subjects in particular. In addition to being an accomplished musician she also wrote several works, either by herself or in collaboration with her son Harald Jerichau.

MUSEUMS AND GALLERIES:

BERLIN: *Jacob and Wilhelm Grimm* - COPENHAGEN (Ny Carlsberg Glyptotek): *Denmark* - COPENHAGEN (Statens Mus. for Kunst): *Wounded Soldier* (1865); *The Sculptor Jerichau* (1846) - LEIPZIG: *Head of a Young Girl* - STOCKHOLM: *Italian Hotel.*

AUCTION RECORDS:

LONDON, 4 May 1922, *The Engagement of the Danish Fisherman*, GBP 44. COPENHAGEN, 30 Oct 1974, *Young Girl at her Mirror* (1855) DKK 12,500. COPENHAGEN, 31 Aug 1976, *Little Girl with Lambs* (1865, oil on canvas, 18 1/2 x 22 ins / 47 x 56 cm) DKK 9,000. COPENHAGEN, 16 March 1977, *Young Girls Fishing with a Net* (1877, oil on canvas, 43 1/4 x 30 ins / 110 x 76 cm) DKK 15,500. COPENHAGEN, 25 April 1979, *The Storyteller* (oil on canvas, 61 x 50 ins / 155 x 127 cm) DKK 9,000. LONDON, 30 May 1986, *Concubine* (oil on canvas, 39 x 29 1/4 ins / 99 x 74.2 cm) GBP 1,600. COPENHAGEN, 17 Nov 1987, *Princess Naxili Hanum, Daughter of Prince Mustafa Fazil Pacha* (1875, oil on canvas, 52 x 62 1/4 ins / 132 x 158 cm) DKK 500,000. LONDON, 24 March 1988, *Young Girl in Red Bonnet Reading near a Table* (1863, oil on canvas, 4 1/4 x 31 3/4 ins / 11 x 80.6 cm) GBP 3,080. COPENHAGEN, 5 April 1989, *Siren* (oil on canvas, 7 1/2 x 9 1/2 ins / 19 x 24 cm) DKK 5,200. LONDON, 5 Oct 1990, *The Water Carrier* (oil on canvas, 22 1/2 x 18 1/2 ins / 57.2 x 47.3 cm) GBP 3,300. COPENHAGEN, 6 March 1991, *Lady on a White Balcony* (oil on canvas, 14 1/4 x 11 ins / 36 x 28 cm) DKK 5,500. COPENHAGEN, 28 Aug 1991, *Interior of Italian Country House with Women and Children* (oil on canvas, 24 x 17 ins / 61 x 43 cm) DKK 6,000. AMSTERDAM, 14-15 April 1992, *Oriental Beauty* (oil on canvas, 38 1/4 x 28 1/2 ins / 97 x 72.5 cm) NLG 9,200. COPENHAGEN, 15 Nov 1993, *Little Girl in a White Dress* (1860, oil on canvas, 11 3/4 x 11 3/4 ins / 30 x 30 cm) DKK 4,000. COPENHAGEN, 14 Feb 1996, *Little Girl in a White Dress* (oil on canvas, 49 1/4 x 37 1/2 ins / 125 x 95 cm) DKK 48,000. VEJLE, 22 Jan 1999, *Mermaid* (1863, oil on canvas, 37 x 53 ins / 95 x 135 cm) DKK 53,000. VEJLE, 11 Aug 1999, *Denmark - Allegorical Female Figure* (oil on canvas, 20 x 15 ins / 51 x 37 cm) DKK 30,000. COPENHAGEN, 4 Dec 2000, *Egyptian Woman Putting her Baby in the Shade by the Nile* (oil on canvas, 39 x 54 ins / 98 x 138 cm) DKK 70,000. COPENHAGEN, 4 Dec 2000, *Italian Girl in the Roman Campagna at Sunset* (1877, oil on canvas, 66 x 42 ins / 167 x 107 cm) DKK 84,000. HASLEMERE, 21 Feb 2001, *Bible Reading* (1880, oil on canvas, 56 x 76 ins / 142 x 193 cm) GBP 20,000. COPENHAGEN, 1 March 2001, *Portrait of the Swedish Opera Singer Jenny Lind* (1845, pencil and chalk, 7 x 8 ins / 19 x 21 cm) DKK 16,500. COPENHAGEN, 4 March 2002, *Peasant Children and Sheep* (oil on canvas, 46 x 54 ins / 116 x 137 cm) DKK 42,000. COPENHAGEN, 28 Aug 2002, *Portrait of the Young Archaeologist Conrad Engelhardt* (oil on canvas, 24 x 19 ins / 62 x 49 cm) DKK 74,000. COPENHAGEN, 26 May 2003, *Mother and Child* (1852, oil on canvas, oval, 22 x 19 ins / 57 x 47 cm) DKK 33,000. COPENHAGEN, 9 Dec 2003, *Mother and Baby* (1852, oil on canvas, 32 x 36 ins / 82 x 92 cm) DKK 46,000. VEJLE, 15 March 2004, *Turkish Pipe Boy, Tschibuktschi* (oil on canvas, 24 x 20 ins / 62 x 50 cm) DKK 100,000.

JERIGH, E.. See **JERRIGH**

JERIKAU. See **JERICHAU**

JERKEN, Erik

Swedish, 20th century.

Born 1898; died 1947.

Painter. Landscapes, still-lifes, flowers, landscapes.

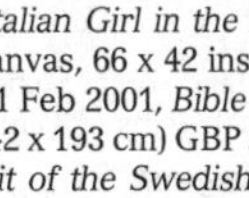

AUCTION RECORDS:

STOCKHOLM, 7 Dec 1987, *Still-life with a Vase of Flowers* (oil on canvas, 28 1/4 x 19 1/4 ins / 72 x 49 cm) SEK 30,000. STOCKHOLM, 6 June 1988, *Winter Landscape with a Green House* (oil, 11 3/4 x 15 3/4 ins / 30 x 40 cm) SEK 4,200. STOCKHOLM, 22 May 1989, *Interior with a Bouquet of Summer Flowers on a Low Table* (oil on canvas, 32 x 23 1/2 ins / 81 x 60 cm) SEK 30,000. STOCKHOLM, 6 Dec 1989, *Still-life with Wild Flowers in a Blue Basket in front of a Blue Curtain* (oil on canvas, 23 1/2 x 19 1/4 ins / 60 x 49 cm) SEK 38,000. STOCKHOLM, 13 April 1992, *Anemones in a Pitcher on a Table* (1940, oil on panel, 15 3/4 x 12 1/4 ins / 40 x 31 cm) SEK 3,600.

JERLI, Hans, or Jerlin, Jôrlin, Gerli

Swiss, 16th century.

Died 1565.

Painter (glass).
Fribourg School.
Jerli was a member of the council between 1551 and 1557, and of the 'council of the sixty' from 1557 until his death. He was made a bourgeois citizen of Fribourg on 18 May 1558.

JERLI, Lienhard or Léonard, or Jerlin, Jôrlin, Gerli
Swiss, 16th century.
Died 1565.
Painter (glass).
Fribourg School.
Jerli was made a bourgeois citizen of Fribourg on the same day as his brother Hans. He was a member of the council of Fribourg from 1558 to 1562, and then of the 'council of the sixty' from 1562 to 1565.

JERMAN, Karl
German, 19th century.
Born 29 December 1868, in Berlin.
Sculptor.
Karl Jerman exhibited in Berlin from 1892 to 1915.
MUSEUMS AND GALLERIES:
DRESDEN (Albertinum): *The Torments of Death.*

JERN, Knut
Swedish, 20th century.
Born 1885; died 1948.
Sculptor. Figures.
AUCTION RECORDS:
STOCKHOLM, 22 May 1989, *Young Female Nude Kneeling in a Dancer's Pose* (bronze, h. 9 ins / 23 cm) SEK 4,500.

JERNBERG, August
Swedish, 19th century.
Born 16 September 1826, in Stockholm; died 1896, in Düsseldorf.
Painter. Figures, religious subjects, genre scenes, interiors with figures, still-lifes.
August Jernberg was a pupil at the academy in Stockholm. He later became a member. He also studied in Düsseldorf and Paris, and received medals in Vienna and Philadelphia.
MUSEUMS AND GALLERIES:
GÖTEBORG: *Still-life; Jesus Chasing the Shopkeepers from the Temple; A Young Talent; Bubbles of Soap; A Studio* - HELSINKI: *Nymph* - NORRKÖPING: *Marcus Larsson; Interior* - STOCKHOLM: *The Dance of the Bear; Child Playing with Cat; The Broken Pipe; Fruit; Village Fair in Westphalia.*
AUCTION RECORDS:
STOCKHOLM, 22 April 1958, *Farm Interior,* SEK 1,825. STOCKHOLM, 8 Nov 1972, *Still-life with Fruit,* SEK 10,000. STOCKHOLM, 26 April 1982, *The First Day of School* (oil on canvas, 31 1/2 x 39 ins / 80 x 99 cm) SEK 81,100. STOCKHOLM, 20 April 1983, *Still-life with Fruit* (oil on panel, 10 1/4 x 13 1/2 ins / 26 x 34.5 cm) SEK 15,900. STOCKHOLM, 22 April 1986, *Interiors with figures Watching a Painter at his Easel* (1868, oil on canvas, 25 1/2 x 31 1/2 ins / 65 x 80 cm) SEK 110,000. MUNICH, 21 Oct 1987, *Young Boys Smoking their First Pipe* (oil on canvas, a pair, 16 1/4 x 12 1/2 ins / 41 x 32 cm) DEM 14,300. LONDON, 16 March 1989, *Kitchen Interior* (oil on canvas/card, 23 1/2 x 28 3/4 ins / 59.8 x 73.3 cm) GBP 4,950. LONDON, 28 Nov 1990, *Beauty* (1854, oil on canvas, 23 1/2 x 49 1/4 ins / 60 x 125 cm) GBP 8,800. STOCKHOLM, 29 May 1991, *Kitchen Interior with Young Woman by a Stair* (oil on panel, 11 x 16 1/4 ins / 28 x 41 cm) SEK 13,500. STOCKHOLM, 19 May 1992, *Village Reception Hall with Dancers and Musicians on a Platform* (oil on canvas, 47 1/4 x 77 1/4 ins / 120 x 196 cm) SEK 175,000. STOCKHOLM, 30 Nov 1993, *Beware of Strangers!* (oil on panel, 13 3/4 x 11 ins / 35 x 28 cm) SEK 25,000. STOCKHOLM, 24 Nov 1999, *Fruit in Vase and Fallen Fruit* (oil on canvas, 29 x 24 ins / 73 x 60 cm) SEK 38,000. UPPSALA, 5 Dec 1999, *Kitchen Interior with Women and Child* (oil on canvas, 26 x 32 ins / 65 x 81 cm) SEK 38,000. STOCKHOLM, 16 May 2000, *Still-life with Grapes and Apple* (oil on panel, 9 x 13 ins / 23 x 32 cm) SEK 32,000. STOCKHOLM, 5 Dec 2000, *Interior Scene with Lovers* (oil on canvas, 19 x 15 ins / 47 x 39 cm) SEK 26,000. STOCKHOLM, 29 May 2001, *Still-life with Pears and Plums* (oil on panel, 14 x 11 ins / 35 x 28 cm) SEK 25,000. COPENHAGEN, 27 Nov 2001, *Italian Woman Carrying Flowers - Allegory of Summer* (1852, oil on canvas, 48 x 37 ins / 123 x 93 cm) DKK 18,000. STOCKHOLM, 3 March 2003, *Basket of Flowers* (oil on canvas, 17 x 20 ins / 43 x 52 cm) SEK 28,000. STOCKHOLM, 2 Dec 2003, *Still-life with Fruit* (oil on canvas, 24 x 20 ins / 62 x 50 cm) SEK 44,000.

JERNBERG, Olof August Andreas
German, 19th - 20th century.
Born 23 May 1855, in Düsseldorf; died 1935, in Düsseldorf.
Painter. Landscapes, seascapes.
Olof Jernberg studied under Dücker at the fine arts academy in Düsseldorf, and subsequently in Paris. He was awarded medals in London (1878 and 1879), Berlin (1891) and Munich (1892). Jernberg went on to teach at the Düsseldorf academy.

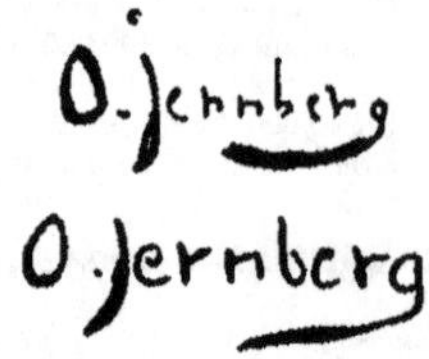

MUSEUMS AND GALLERIES:
BERLIN: *Harvest Time* - DÜSSELDORF: *Dutch Landscape; Angermund in the Snow* - KALININGRAD: *Leaving Church on Sunday; Old Bridge* - MAGDEBURG (Kulturhistorisches Mus.): *Golden Autumn* - MUNICH: *In the Fields.*
AUCTION RECORDS:
COLOGNE, 23 March 1973, *Autumn Landscape,* DEM 3,800. COLOGNE, 17 March 1978, *Landscape* (oil on canvas, 13 x 18 1/4 ins / 33 x 46.5 cm) DEM 2,400. COLOGNE, 11 June 1979, *Winter Landscape* (oil on canvas, 46 x 69 ins / 116 x 175.5 cm) DEM 13,000. COPENHAGEN, 22 April 1982, *Landscape with River* (oil on canvas, 18 x 26 ins / 46 x 66 cm) DKK 18,000. COLOGNE, 18 March 1983, *Landscape with River and Houses* (oil on canvas remounted on board, 9 3/4 x 12 3/4 ins / 25 x 32.5 cm) DEM 4,600. LONDON, 19 March 1986, *Children in a Forest* (1881, oil on canvas, 26 x 39 3/4 ins / 66 x 101 cm) GBP 3,600. LONDON, 6 Feb 1987, *Wooded Landscape with Shepherd and Flock and a Farm* (oil on canvas, 69 1/4 x 57 1/2 ins / 176 x 146 cm) GBP 5,500. STOCKHOLM, 27 April 1988, *Rocky Coast Panorama* (oil on panel, 13 1/2 x 21 1/4 ins / 34 x 54 cm) SEK 7,200. COLOGNE, 15 Oct 1988, *Summer Landscape with Young Girl* (oil on canvas, 11 x 19 3/4 ins / 28 x 50 cm) DEM 2,000. COLOGNE, 28 June 1991, *Landscape with River* (oil on panel, 17 3/4 x 19 3/4 ins / 45 x 50 cm) DEM 3,000. LONDON, 22 May 1992, *In the Fields* (oil on canvas, 51 1/2 x 76 1/2 ins / 130.8 x 194.4 cm) GBP 7,700. STOCKHOLM, 30 Nov 1993, *Vast Rocky Landscape with a Fir Forest and a Watercourse* (oil on panel, 14 1/4 x 23 1/2 ins / 36 x 60 cm) SEK 19,000.

JERNDAHL, Aron
Swedish, 19th century.
Born 1858.
Sculptor.
Aron Jerndahl's bronze with green patina, *Mask of the Carnival of Life,* is in the National Museum in Stockholm, and his *Young Peasant Girl* is in the Göteborg museum.

JERNDORFF, August Andreas
Danish, 19th century.

Born 26 January 1846, in Oldenburg; died 28 July 1906, in Copenhagen.
Painter, illustrator. Portraits, genre scenes, landscapes.
August Jerndorff was a pupil at the Kunstakademi in Copenhagen. He received silver medals at the Exposition Universelle in Paris in both 1889 and 1900.
MUSEUMS AND GALLERIES:
COPENHAGEN: *The Organist Matthisson-Hansen; Mrs Hellesen, née Top; The Beach in Vedbak; Portrait of a Child; Mrs J. D. F. Andersen; The Wife of the Artist* - COPENHAGEN (Den Hirschsprungske Samling): *Young Girl Leaning on a Pillar; Landscapes* - HILLERØD: *J. C. Jacobsen; Portrait of Claude du Plat; General Bülow; General Rye* - OSLO: *Fifteen Illustrations for The Witches' Tricks by Holger Drachman.*
AUCTION RECORDS:
COPENHAGEN, 16 March 1982, *The Israelites in the Desert* (1880, oil on canvas, 67 1/4 x 92 1/4 ins / 171 x 234 cm) DKK 25,000. LONDON, 27-28 March 1990, *The Duo* (1890, oil on panel, 19 3/4 x 15 1/4 ins / 50 x 39 cm) GBP 2,970. NEW YORK, 16 Feb 1994, *The Israelites Crossing the Desert* (1886, oil on canvas, 67 1/4 x 92 1/4 ins / 170.8 x 234 cm) USD 57,500. COPENHAGEN, 14 Feb 1996, *View from Veytaux with Genfersoen* (1887, oil on canvas, 9 x 13 ins / 22 x 33 cm) DKK 5,000. COPENHAGEN, 30 May 2000, *Portrait of Theodora Jacobsen, Seated in Ny Carlsberg Glypotek* (1885, oil on canvas, 22 x 17 ins / 56 x 42 cm) DKK 80,000. COPENHAGEN, 9 Dec 2003, *Gerda and Elin in the Garden* (1898, oil on canvas, 67 x 48 ins / 169 x 123 cm) DKK 75,000.

JERNDORFF, Just Ulrik
Danish, 19th century.
Born 1806, in Copenhagen; died 1847, in Oldenburg.
Painter, art restorer.
Just Jerndorff was a pupil of Möller in Oldenburg. A travel grant enabled him to visit Germany and Italy. He was named court painter in 1839 by the Duke of Oldenburg.

JERNDORFF, Povl
Danish, 20th century.
Born 31 December 1885, in Copenhagen.
Painter. Mythological subjects, figure compositions, portraits, landscapes.
Povl Jerndorff, son of August Andreas Jerndorff, studied at the Kongelige Danske Kunstakademi in Copenhagen. He is noted for having worked on frescoes in Viborg Cathedral. Jerndorff first exhibited in Charlottenburg in 1910 and was awarded a medal in 1914 for his *Loki and Sygin*. He painted portraits, landscapes and group figures, and his work betrays the occasional influence of Cubism.
AUCTION RECORDS:
COPENHAGEN, 20 Oct 1993, *Episode from Homer's 'Iliad'* (1920, oil on canvas, 53 1/4 x 61 ins / 135 x 155 cm) DKK 10,000.

JERNMARK, Sigge
Swedish, 20th century.
Born 1887; died 1982.
Painter. Local scenes, landscapes.
AUCTION RECORDS:
GÖTEBORG, 17 Oct 1989, *Farmyard at Dusk* (oil on canvas, 2 1/4 ins / 6 cm-20 3/4 x 24 3/4 ins/53 x 63 cm) SEK 3,600.

JÉROME. See **MAGAGNI**

JERÔME
French, 17th century.
Active in Lorraine.
Painter.
Jerôme is mentioned as the master of J. Courtois the Burgundian.

JEROME, Ambrosini, pseudonym of James Parker Jerome
British, 19th century.
Born 8 August 1810; died April 1883, in London.
Active in London.
Painter, illustrator. History painting, portraits.
James Parker Jerome spent some time in Italy, where he probably acquired the name Ambrosini. Between 1871 to 1884 he exhibited his work at the Royal Academy (where he was awarded a gold medal), the British Institution and the Suffolk Street Gallery. He was appointed portrait painter to the Duchess of Kent.
AUCTION RECORDS:
NEW YORK, 26 and 27 Feb 1903, *Queen Victoria's Children*, USD 225. LONDON, 1 Nov 1990, *Fleur de Marie at the Bouqueval Farm* (1844, oil on canvas, illustration of the 'Mysteries of Paris', 30 x 24 3/4 ins / 76 x 63 cm) GBP 2,200. SEVENOAKS, 10 Feb 2000, *Portrait of Edwin Collins* (oil on canvas, sold with another by same hand, 23 x 19 ins / 59 x 49 cm) GBP 1,000.

JEROME, Jean Pierre
Canadian, 20th century.
Painter (mixed media).
Jean Pierre Jerome began his artistic career in about 1954 after an academic training lasting ten years and was part of the Plastician movement. While in Paris from 1956 to 1958, he discovered French painting and made the acquaintance of Atlan. He then abandoned Plastician rigor and painted rhythms, which he recorded and translated by means of pencil and brush.

JÉRÔME, Pierre
French, 20th century.
Born 20 January 1905, in Dunkirk.
Painter. Figures, nudes, portraits.
Pierre Jérôme taught at the Académie Julian in Paris. He was declared hors concours at the Salon des Artistes Français in 1931 and in 1934 was awarded the Prix de Rome. He became a member of the Salon d'Automne in 1954.

JEROME DE BRESCIA (Fra)
Italian, 16th century.
Born in Brescia.
Active c. 1519.
Painter. History painting.
He was a friend and pupil of Giovannaria or Giovanni Maria da Brescia and, like him, a Carmelite monk. He may be identical with Fra Girolamo da Brescia.

JÉROME DE BRESCIA. See also **MUZIANO, ROMANINO Girolamo Romani,** and **SAVOLDO**

JEROME DE FIESOLE, or Pacherot Jerome, Passerot, Pacchiarotti
Italian, 15th - 16th century.
Born c. 1463, in Florence; died c. 1543, in Florence.
Sculptor, designer of ornamental architectural features.
Originating from Fiesole, or more probably working there, he was from 1497 in the service of Charles VIII in France. He worked in the Château de Gaillon, Amboise, where he made the fountain of the great courtyard. Among the works attributed to him, or in which he is thought to have collaborated, are the carving (in the workshop of Michel Colombe?) of the tomb of Francis II, duke of Brittany, and Marguerite de Foix for the cathedral in Nantes; those of the children of Charles VIII in the cathedral in Tours (of which there is a cast in the Musée des Monuments français); the decoration of the tomb of Cardinal Amboise in the cathedral in Rouen; and the *Entombement* group in the abbey of Solesmes. Some churches in the Loire valley certainly have works by him: holy water stoups and fonts decorated in the Italian style. He was one of the first to introduce Italian motifs into the decoration of French monuments.

Museums and Galleries:
Paris (Mus. des Monuments Français): one casting.

JERONIMA DA SALAMANCA.
See **JERONIMO da Salamanca**

JERONIMO. See **GIROLAMO, JEROME** and **JÉRÔME**

JERONIMO
Spanish, 16th century.
Active in Valladolid.
Sculptor (?), painter (?).
In about 1543, Jeronimo collaborated in the works carried out for the reception of Philip II's third wife.

JERONIMO, called the Neapolitan
Spanish, 16th century.
Active in Valladolid.
Painter.
It is not known where the surname Neapolitan comes from. In the monastic church of Notre-Dame de la Viel, there is a very fine retable, the Gospel side of which is the work of Jeronimo and carries the date 1592.

JERONIMO DA SALAMANCA
Spanish, 16th century.
Active from 1593 to 1594.
Painter.
Jeronimo da Salamanca made the Easter monument in the cathedral in Seville.

JERONIMO DE VALENCIA
Spanish, 16th century.
Sculptor.
He was a pupil of Al. Berruguete in Valladolid, carved some of the stalls of the Charterhouse of Jeréz de la Frontera, and worked in the cathedral in Badajoz.

JERONIMUS. See also **GIROLAMO, HIÉRONIMUS** and **ROSENBAUM Hieronimus**

JERRIÈRE
Swiss, 18th century.
Born in Geneva.
Painter.

JERRIGH, E.
German, 16th - 17th century.
Active probably in Germany during the 16th and 17th centuries.
Painter. History painting, portraits.
According to van Mander, Jerrigh was from Wallonia, and taught Jan van Achen in 1568. He was probably still working in Cologne in 1601. He could have been the painter George, who was also known as Jerrigh. The museum in Cologne had a work by him entitled *Annunciation*.

JERRY, Sylvester
American, 20th century.
Born 20 September 1904, in Woodville.
Painter.
Sylvester Jerry studied at the Layton Art School and the Art Students League of New York, where he became a member. He received an award from the Art Institute of Milwaukee.

JERVAS, Charles
Irish, 17th - 18th century.
Born c. 1675, in Ireland; died 2 November 1739, in London.
Painter, draughtsman. Portraits.
Charles Jervas was a student of Kneller's in London. According to Walpole, Norris, the keeper of King William and Queen Anne's paintings allowed Jervas to make numerous copies of works in the royal collection. Jervas then sold these to Dr Clark of Oxford and used the proceeds to travel to Paris and Italy. On his return, he met with success and made an advantageous marriage to a rich widow which allowed him to establish himself well in London.

Jervas was appointed first painter to George I and later to George II. He was an intimate friend of Pope, Addison and Swift and was considered the best portrait painter of his time. Posterity has not, however, shared this opinion and later criticism has been somewhat harsh considering that Jervas was not without merit. Of late, his work has been seen in a more favourable light.

In 1738, Jervas travelled to Italy a second time, for his health; however, he did not remain there preferring to return to London where he died.

Jervas possessed a remarkable collection of objets d'art. It took nine days to sell his paintings, statues, porcelain items and other effects, while his drawings, divided into 2,275 lots, required 25 days of auctions. He also made a translation of Cervantes' *Don Quixote*, which was published posthumously in 1742 under the name Jarvis.

Museums and Galleries:
London (National Portrait Gal.): *Alexander Pope* (1713-1715, oil on canvas, attributed); *Jonathan Swift* (c. 1718, oil on canvas); *Caroline Wilhelmina of Brandenburg-Ansbach, Princess of Wales* (1727, oil on canvas, studio work); *William Augustus, Duke of Cumberland as a child* (c. 1728, oil on canvas).

Auction Records:
Paris, 1842, *Portrait of Pope*, FRF 3,565. London, 29 Feb 1908, *Portrait of the Duchess of Berwick*, GBP 9. London, 14 June 1911, *Young Boys with Bows and Arrows*, GBP 4; *Portrait of the Duchess of Newcastle* (1716) GBP 16. London, 1 May 1925, *Dean Jonathan Swift*, GBP 73. London, 15 June 1928, *Henry, Duke of Kent*, GBP 99. London, 1 Feb 1929, *Captain Robert Chadwick*, GBP 65. London, 27 June 1973, *Portrait of a Lady*, GBP 2,200. London, 18 June 1976, *Portrait of a Lady* (oil on canvas, 53 x 61 1/2 ins / 134.5 x 156 cm) GBP 2,600. London, 27 April 1983, *Portrait of Colonel Smith* (oil on canvas, 29 1/4 x 24 1/4 ins / 74 x 61.5 cm) GBP 1,000. London, 20 Nov 1985, *Portrait of Elizabeth Cosby* (*Portrait of Elizabeth Cosby*) (oil on canvas, 39 3/4 x 40 1/4 ins / 101 x 102 cm) GBP 7,500. London, 24 April 1987, *Children of Charles, Second Viscount Townsend* (oil on canvas, 71 x 104 ins / 180.3 x 264.2 cm) GBP 20,000. London, 12 July 1989, *Portrait of Thomas Pelham Holles, First Duke of Newcastle standing and wearing the Order of the Garter* (oil on canvas, 80 1/4 x 57 ins / 204 x 145 cm) GBP 6,050. London, 14 March 1990, *Portrait of General William Cosby, Governor of New York and Jersey wearing a red robe over an armoured breastplate* (oil on canvas, 29 1/2 x 24 1/2 ins / 75 x 62 cm) GBP 18,150. London, 14 Nov 1990, *Portrait of William Pulteney, Earl of Bath, standing wearing a blue indoor coat* (oil on canvas, 93 1/4 x 56 1/4 ins / 237 x 143 cm) GBP 17,600. London, 10 April 1991, *Portrait of Elizabeth Cosby of Stradbally Hall in Ireland, wearing a black, fur-trimmed cloak and a red and white bonnet* (oil on canvas, 38 1/4 x 29 1/4 ins / 97 x 74 cm) GBP 7,700. London, 8 April 1992, *Portrait of Charles I and Lord Hamilton, his page* (oil on canvas, after Van Dyck, 87 x 75 1/4 ins / 221 x 191 cm) GBP 18,700. London, 7 Oct 1992, *Portrait of a Young Girl* (oil on canvas, 53 x 39 ins / 134.5 x 99 cm) GBP 3,080. London, 6 April 1993, *Portrait of General William Cosby, Governor of New York and Jersey wearing a red robe over an armoured breast piece*. London, 15 Dec 1993, *Three-Quarters Portrait of Colonel William Forward wearing a red coat over a white shirt* (oil on canvas, 49 3/4 x 40 ins / 126.4 x 101.6 cm) GBP 9,200. London, 12 April 1995, *Portrait of Lady Mary Wortley Montagu* (oil on canvas, 29 3/4 x 24 3/4 ins / 75.5 x 63 cm) GBP 11,500. London, 13 Nov 1996, *Portrait of Lady Mary Wortley Montagu* (oil on canvas, 47 x 37 1/2 ins / 119.5 x 95.5 cm) GBP 11,500. Billingshurst, 14 Sept 1999, *Portrait of Lady Elizabeth Howard* (oil on canvas, 49 x 39 ins / 125 x 100 cm) GBP

10,000. LONDON, 14 Dec 1999, *Family Portrait with Four Sisters and their Brother* (oil on canvas, 68 x 57 ins / 173 x 146 cm) GBP 21,000. LONDON, 22 March 2000, *Portrait of a Lady Wearing a Blue Dress* (oil on canvas, 49 x 39 ins / 125 x 99 cm) GBP 6,500. LONDON, 30 Nov 2000, *Portrait of Wearing a Blue Coat Dress and Holding a Basket of Flowers* (oil on canvas, 50 x 41 ins / 126 x 103 cm) GBP 6,500. NEW YORK, 16 May 2001, *Portrait of a Lady with a Straw Hat* (oil on canvas, 50 x 40 ins / 127 x 102 cm) USD 4,500. DUBLIN, 28 May 2001, *Portrait of Mrs Trevor, Seated in a Wooded Landscape* (oil on canvas, 18 x 15 ins / 45 x 38 cm) IEP 24,000. LONDON, 11 June 2002, *Portrait of a Lady, Identified as Elizabeth Felton* (oil on canvas, 50 x 41 ins / 126 x 103 cm) GBP 38,000. LONDON, 9 July 2002, *Portrait of a Gentleman, Seated in a Dark Blue Coat and Burgundy Gown, at a Table* (1725, oil on canvas, 50 x 40 ins / 127 x 102 cm) GBP 15,000. LONDON, 10 June 2003, *Portrait of the Hon. Mary Digby in a Maroon Dress and Blue Wrap, Holding a Basket of Oranges* (oil on canvas, 50 x 41 ins / 128 x 103 cm) GBP 5,500. LONDON, 2 July 2003, *Portrait of a Lady* (oil on canvas on panel, 45 x 39 ins / 115 x 99 cm) GBP 5,500. STOCKHOLM, 25 May 2004, *Portrait of Lady Wearing Blue* (oil on canvas, oval, 30 x 25 ins / 77 x 64 cm) SEK 15,000.

JERVUD, Vladimir Ossipivich
Russian, 19th century.
Born 1832, in Isleievo; died 9 July 1897, in Moscow.
Painter, sculptor, architect. Portraits, genre scenes.

JESCHKE, Richard
German, 19th - 20th century.
Born 24 September 1871, in Jüterbog; died 2 March 1924, in Kassel.
Painter, draughtsman.

JESI, Samuel
Italian, 19th century.
Born 4 September 1788, in Correggio; died 4 September 1853, in Florence.
Engraver (burin).

Jesi was a pupil of Giuseppe Longhi. He engraved *Abraham Rejecting Hagar, Leo X* (1840) and *Virgin of the Palazzo Tempi*, after Raphael, *Portrait of Benvenuto Cellini* after G. Vasari, *Virgin and Child* after Baccio della Porta (1834), *Motherly Love* after Cipriani, and *Virgin of the Vine* after Paul Delaroche (1847).

MUSEUMS AND GALLERIES:
MONTPELLIER: *Dog* (charcoal).

JESPERS, Émile Louis
Belgian, 19th - 20th century.
Born 1862, in Deurne or Antwerp; died 1918.
Sculptor. Figures, nudes.

Émile Jespers exhibited in Paris, with an honourable mention at the 1893 Paris Salon, and at the Brussels Exposition Universelle of 1910.

MUSEUMS AND GALLERIES:
ANTWERP: *Daybreak* - BUCHAREST (Muz. National de Arta al României): *Bust of a Worker*.

AUCTION RECORDS:
LOKEREN, 5 March 1988, *Young Girl* (bronze, h. 16 1/4 ins / 41 cm) BEF 60,000. LOKEREN, 28 May 1988, *Adolescent* (bronze, h. 16 1/4 ins / 41 cm) BEF 40,000. LOKEREN, 20 May 1995, *Stevedore* (bronze on a wooden plinth, h. 10 3/4 ins / 27.5 cm, w. 12 3/4 ins/32.5 cm) BEF 33,000.

JESPERS, Floris
Belgian, 20th century.
Born 1889, in Antwerp; died 16 April 1965, in Antwerp.
Painter, decorative artist, sculptor. Figures, portraits, landscapes.

Floris Jespers was the son of the sculptor Émile Jespers and the younger brother of the sculptor Oscar Jespers. Floris initially studied music and subsequently was able to make a living playing in a theatre orchestra. He attended the Academie and the Hoger Instituut voor Schone Kunsten in Antwerp, studying under Frans Courtens and was a frequent exhibitor at the Centaure Gallery in Brussels. Three tapestries exhibited by Jespers at the Exposition Universelle in Paris in 1937 secured him the Grand Prix award.

Jespers went through a short period as an Impressionist before being exposed to the Cubists of the Paris School and to the work of the German Expressionists. As a result, his canvases between 1920 and 1930 may be regarded as Flemish Expressionist, despite the fact that he was experimenting at the time with various techniques and continuing to develop as a painter. He tackled a broad variety of subject matter - landscapes, interiors, figures, genre compositions - and also produced murals, tapestries and painting on glass.

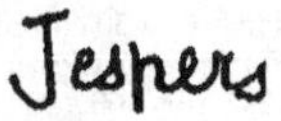

MUSEUMS AND GALLERIES:
ANTWERP (Koninklijk Mus. voor Schone Kunsten): *Fortress* (1935) - GRENOBLE (Mus. de Grenoble).

AUCTION RECORDS:
ANTWERP, 13 and 15 Oct 1964, *Madman*, BEF 56,000. ANTWERP, 26 April 1966, *Clown*, BEF 54,000. ANTWERP, 23-24 April 1968, *Seated Clown*, BEF 70,000. ANTWERP, 27 April 1971, *Honfleur Harbour*, BEF 70,000. ANTWERP, 10 Oct 1972, *Clown*, BEF 160,000. ANTWERP, 23 Oct 1973, *Portrait of the Artist's Wife Olympe* (watercolour) BEF 60,000. ANTWERP, 2 April 1974, *Lovers* (1875) BEF 260,000. ANTWERP, 6 April 1976, *Chaste Suzanne* (1926, oil/hardboard, 36 1/4 x 32 3/4 ins / 92 x 83 cm) BEF 750,000. LOKEREN, 1 May 1976, *Still-life with Guitar* (gouache, 22 x 28 1/4 ins / 55 x 72 cm) BEF 55,000. BREDA, 26 April 1977, *Aquarium* (oil on canvas, 51 1/2 x 43 3/4 ins / 131 x 111 cm) NLG 15,000. ANTWERP, 8 May 1979, *Clowns* (1927, oil/hardboard, 25 1/2 x 22 1/2 ins / 65 x 57 cm) BEF 160,000. LOKEREN, 13 Oct 1979, *Standing Nude* (1949, gouache, 72 3/4 x 32 1/4 ins / 185 x 82 cm) BEF 80,000. ANTWERP, 27 Oct 1981, *Fortune-Teller* (oil/hardboard, 11 3/4 x 15 ins / 30 x 38 cm) BEF 200,000. ANTWERP, 26 April 1983, *Circus* (oil/hardboard, 19 3/4 x 23 1/2 ins / 50 x 60 cm) BEF 400,000. ANTWERP, 22 Oct 1985, *Sailors on Shore* (1921, oil on canvas, 29 1/4 x 42 1/2 ins / 74 x 108 cm) BEF 500,000. BRUSSELS, 7 Dec 1987, *Seated Nubian* (gouache) BEF 110,000. LOKEREN, 5 March 1988, *Landscape with Potato Field* (oil on canvas, 35 1/2 x 44 ins / 90 x 112 cm) BEF 180,000. LOKEREN, 28 May 1988, *Young Peasant in the Studio* (oil on canvas, 23 1/2 x 16 1/4 ins / 60 x 41.5 cm) BEF 100,000. LOKEREN, 8 Oct 1988, *Interior* (1959, oil on canvas, 40 3/4 x 69 ins / 103.5 x 175 cm) BEF 300,000. AMSTERDAM, 10 April 1989, *Cityscape* (1925, oil on panel, 10 x 24 ins / 25.5 x 61 cm) NLG 11,500. LONDON, 19 Oct 1989, *Green Mirror* (1917, oil on canvas, 47 1/4 x 35 1/4 ins / 120 x 89.5 cm) GBP 66,000. PARIS, 13 Dec 1989, *Clown with Accordion* (oil on canvas, 52 x 40 1/4 ins / 132 x 102 cm) FRF 330,000. AMSTERDAM, 13 Dec 1989, *Branches with Flowers* (oil on canvas, 15 1/4 x 12 1/4 ins / 38.5 x 31 cm) NLG 8,050. PARIS, 13 Dec 1989, *Seated Clown* (oil on canvas, 52 x 40 1/4 ins / 132 x 102.5 cm) FRF 320,000. AMSTERDAM, 10 April 1990, *Abstract Composition* (oil on sacking/panel). PARIS, 19 June 1990, *Clowns* (19 1/4 x 25 1/4 ins / 49 x 64 cm) FRF 43,000. AMSTERDAM, 13 Dec 1990, *Plums* (1915, oil on canvas, 31 1/2 x 43 1/4 ins / 80 x 110 cm) NLG 126,500. AMSTERDAM, 22 May 1991, *Clown* (1933, oil/glass, 25 x 20 3/4 ins / 63.5 x 53 cm) NLG 41,400. AMSTERDAM, 17 Sept 1991, *Village Scene in the Belgian Congo* (oil/gilded glass, 23 x 20 1/4 ins / 57.5 x 51.5 cm) NLG 8,970. AMSTERDAM, 11 Dec 1991, *Shaman* (iron sculpture and various materials on a cement base, total height 19 ins / 48.5 cm) NLG 5,175. AMSTERDAM, 12 Dec 1991, *Ass* (oil on card, 27 3/4 x 36 1/4 ins / 70.5 x 92 cm) NLG 6,900. LOKEREN, 21 March 1992, *Sailing Ship* (1928, oil on canvas,

16 1/2 x 20 1/4 ins / 42 x 51.5 cm) BEF 260,000. AMSTERDAM, 21 May 1992, *Clown* (gilded glass, 45 x 27 3/4 ins / 114 x 70.5 cm) NLG 48,300. LOKEREN, 23 May 1992, *Female Head* (gilded glass, 8 1/4 x 6 1/2 ins / 21 x 16.5 cm) BEF 120,000; *Clown* (1932, oil on canvas, 23 1/2 x 19 3/4 ins / 60 x 50 cm) BEF 260,000. LOKEREN, 10 Oct 1992, *Portrait of Jean Cocteau* (painting/triplex, 48 x 36 1/2 ins / 122 x 92.5 cm) BEF 750,000. AMSTERDAM, 9 Dec 1992, *Near Knokke* (oil on canvas, 37 3/4 x 57 3/4 ins / 96 x 147 cm) NLG 17,250. LOKEREN, 20 March 1993, *Young Girl with Palette* (1930, oil on canvas, 37 1/2 x 29 1/2 ins / 95 x 75 cm) BEF 1,300,000. PARIS, 19 March 1994, *Composition* (1920, watercolour and gouache/paper, 7 1/2 x 5 1/2 ins / 19 x 14 cm) FRF 4,000. PARIS, 25 March 1994, *Clown* (gilded glass, 22 x 19 3/4 ins / 56 x 50 cm) FRF 58,000. AMSTERDAM, 31 May 1994, *Red Cow* (oil on canvas, 22 1/2 x 31 3/4 ins / 57 x 80.5 cm) NLG 74,750. LOKEREN, 8 Oct 1994, *Clowns in the Greenery* (gilding on glass, 23 1/2 x 19 3/4 ins / 60 x 50 cm) BEF 650,000. AMSTERDAM, 7 Dec 1994, *Woman and Clown on a Beige Ground* (oil/gilded glass, 26 x 23 1/2 ins / 66 x 60 cm) NLG 27,600. LOKEREN, 11 March 1995, *Bouquet of Flowers* (1939, oil on canvas, 55 x 47 1/4 ins / 140 x 120 cm) BEF 260,000. AMSTERDAM, 31 May 1995, *Clown on Horseback* (gilded glass, 28 x 24 ins / 71 x 61 cm) NLG 59,000. LOKEREN, 9 Dec 1995, *Going Aboard* (oil on canvas, 39 1/4 x 49 1/4 ins / 100 x 125 cm) BEF 750,000. LOKEREN, 9 March 1996, *Landscape with Mill* (1921, oil on canvas, 33 1/2 x 33 3/4 ins / 85 x 86 cm) BEF 650,000. LOKEREN, 18 May 1996, *Golgotha* (c. 1927-1930, gilded glass, 20 x 24 1/4 ins / 51 x 61.5 cm) BEF 100,000; *Congo Craft* (oil on canvas, 31 1/2 x 41 ins / 80 x 104 cm) BEF 100,000. AMSTERDAM, 4 June 1996, *Cattle at Pasture* (c. 1935, oil on canvas, 21 3/4 x 29 3/4 ins / 55.5 x 75.5 cm) NLG 5,428. LOKEREN, 8 March 1997, *Landscape with Farm* (oil on canvas, 23 1/2 x 32 1/4 ins / 60 x 82 cm) BEF 200,000. LOKEREN, 11 Oct 1997, *Seated Woman* (1915, wash, 20 x 19 ins / 51 x 48 cm) BEF 105,000; *Interior with Standing Woman* (1914, watercolour, 16 1/2 x 13 ins / 42 x 33 cm) BEF 120,000. AMSTERDAM, 1 Dec 1997, *Still-life with Bowl of Fruit* (oil on canvas, 20 3/4 x 25 1/2 ins / 53 x 65 cm) NLG 10,384. AMSTERDAM, 2 Dec 1997, *Woman under a Banana Tree* (1955, oil on canvas, 45 1/4 x 26 1/2 ins / 115 x 67 cm) NLG 13,838. LOKEREN, 6 Dec 1997, *Thérèse at Table* (1916, wash and Indian ink, 20 x 14 3/4 ins / 51 x 37.5 cm) BEF 110,000. AMSTERDAM, 25 Oct 1999, *Birdcage* (oil on canvas, 35 x 28 ins / 89 x 70 cm) NLG 38,000. AMSTERDAM, 25 Oct 1999, *Portrait of Mme. X* (1931, oil on canvas, 30 x 22 ins / 75 x 55 cm) NLG 118,000. ANTWERP, 4 April 2000, *Young Girl* (1928, drawing, 33 x 22 ins / 85 x 56 cm) BEF 400,000. PARIS, 14 April 2000, *Ferry* (1926, oil on canvas, 24 x 33 ins / 60 x 85 cm) FRF 380,000. BRUSSELS, 5 Nov 2001, *Gardens on the Edge of the Town* (1929, oil on panel, 19 x 24 ins / 49 x 61 cm) BEF 460,000. BRUSSELS, 24 Sept 2002, *Harlequin* (oil on glass, 17 x 10 ins / 44 x 26 cm) EUR 12,000. LONDON, 5 Feb 2003, *Masquerade of Clowns* (oil on board, 37 x 42 ins / 93 x 107 cm) GBP 100,000. LOKEREN, 15 March 2003, *Clown* (c. 1957, eglomise, 18 x 16 ins / 46 x 40 cm) EUR 4,500. ANTWERP, 23 June 2003, *Circus Scene* (oil on glass, 35 x 26 ins / 88 x 67 cm) EUR 25,000. BRUSSELS, 10 May 2004, *Married Couple* (1926, oil on canvas, 52 x 42 ins / 133 x 106 cm) EUR 95,000. AMSTERDAM, 1 Dec 2004, *Still-life with Apples* (1916, oil on canvas, 31 x 37 ins / 78 x 94 cm) EUR 55,000.

JESPERS, Oscar

Belgian, 20th century.

Born 1887, in Bogerhout (Antwerp); died 1970, in Woluwe-St-Lambert.

Sculptor. Figures. Architectural integration.

Oscar Jespers was the son of Émile Jespers and brother of Floris Jespers. He studied initially under his sculptor father, then at the Academie and Hoger Instituut voor Schone Kunsten in Antwerp, where he was a pupil of Thomas Vinçotte. After World War I Oscar Jespers aligned himself with Selection, an artistic movement that promoted the Expressionist tenets that influenced Belgian art. In 1977, an Oscar Jespers retrospective was held at the Rodin Museum in Paris.

Oscar Jespers' early work was influenced by that of Rik Wouters, but Jespers soon became attracted to Neo-Cubism and proceeded to simplify and 'geometricise' his formal approach. In this respect, he was a genuine innovator on the Belgian scene. His massive (not to say ponderous) sculptures of the 1920s are starkly monolithic and reminiscent of primitive sculpture. As such, they are readily incorporated into large public buildings. Examples include a granite *Torso* (sculpted around 1921); a towering polychrome wooden *Relief* for the new Brussels railway station built to accommodate visitors to the Exposition Universelle of 1935; a *Low-Relief* in copper for the Belgian Pavilion at the Exposition Universelle in Paris 1937; and two large stone *Reliefs* for the Office des Chèques Postaux in Brussels.

As of 1937, Oscar Jespers' sculpture increasingly took on the sweeping curvature of the female form and, as a result, is perhaps both more conventional and more accessible. Jespers worked in a variety of materials, including beaten copper and modelling clay, but he consistently favoured working directly on wood or stone.

MUSEUMS AND GALLERIES:

ANTWERP (Koninklijk Mus. voor Schone Kunsten): *Brother and Sister* (1934); *Prisoner* - NEW YORK (MoMA): *St Anthony* (1934) - OSTEND (Mus. voor Schone Kunsten): *Hands of Léon Spillaert* (1928); *The Four Elements* (1954, bronze) - OTTERLO (Kröller-Müller Mus.): *Torso* (1921).

AUCTION RECORDS:

ANTWERP, 27 April 1971, *Shepherdess* (patinated bronze) BEF 180,000. ANTWERP, 19 Oct 1976, *Nude (rear view)* (drawing, 42 1/4 x 28 ins / 107 x 71 cm) BEF 28,000. BRUSSELS, 26 Oct 1977, *Crouching Woman* (stone, h. 9 ins / 23 cm) BEF 38,000. LOKEREN, 17 Oct 1981, *Head* (bronze, h. 9 ins / 23 cm) BEF 75,000. PARIS, 22 June 1984, *Child's Head* (c. 1925, bronze, 6 x 6 ins / 15 x 15 cm) FRF 11,000. LOKEREN, 16 Feb 1985, *New-Born* (stone, h. relief 37 x 43 1/4 ins / 94 x 110 cm) BEF 360,000. ANTWERP, 21 Oct 1986, *Seated Nude* (drawing, 23 1/4 x 17 ins / 59 x 43 cm) BEF 36,000. LOKEREN, 5 March 1988, *Child's Head* (1925, bronze, h. 9 ins / 23 cm) BEF 240,000. LOKEREN, 8 Oct 1988, *Dutchman from the North* (terracotta, h. 15 ins / 38 cm) BEF 85,000. LONDON, 19 Oct 1989, *Fallen Soldier* (bronze, h. 37 1/2 ins / 95 cm) GBP 6,600. PARIS, 13 Dec 1989, *Female Nude Cubist-Style* (1921, glazed chamois earthenware, h. 12 1/4 ins / 31 cm) FRF 80,000. NEUILLY, 3 Feb 1991, *Child's Head* (bronze) FRF 20,500. AMSTERDAM, 12 Dec 1991, *Nude Study* (1914, red chalk/paper, 10 3/4 x 6 1/2 ins / 27.6 x 16.5 cm) NLG 2,300. NEW YORK, 10 Nov 1992, *Full-length Female Nude* (brown-patinated bronze, h. 18 ins / 46 cm) USD 2,860. LOKEREN, 12 March 1994, *Female Head* (terracotta, h. 6 3/4 ins / 17 cm, w. 5 1/2 ins/14 cm) BEF 75,000. LOKEREN, 8 Oct 1994, *Man in a Singlet (Floris Jespers)* (1917, bronze, h. 44 1/4 ins / 112.5 cm) BEF 500,000. AMSTERDAM, 12 Oct 1999, *Dialogue* (1939, welded relief, 28 x 28x59 ins / 72 x 72x150 cm) NLG 15,000. LOKEREN, 11 Dec 1999, *Head of a Baby* (plaster, h. 5 ins / 13 cm, w. 6 ins/14 cm) BEF 230,000. ANTWERP, 24 Oct 2000, *Dying Soldier* (plaster, h. 36 ins / 92 cm) BEF 550,000. COLOGNE, 11 Nov 2000, *Bird* (plaster, h. 11 ins / 29 cm) DEM 17,000. ANTWERP, 23 April 2002, *Head of a Woman* (1929, ceramic, h. 13 ins / 32 cm) EUR 3,600. AMSTERDAM, 3 Dec 2002, *Head of a woman* (1933, enamelled earthenware, h. 7 ins / 17 cm) EUR 3,200. AMSTERDAM, 3 June 2003, *Young Girl* (1930, limestone, h. 17 ins / 43 cm) EUR 19,000. LOKEREN, 15 May 2004, *Baby's Head* (light brown-patinated bronze, h. 5 ins / 13 cm, w. 6 ins/14 cm) EUR 2,400.

JESPERSEN, Henrik Gamst

Danish, 19th - 20th century.

Born 1853, in Holbæk; died 1936.

Painter. Landscapes.

Museums and Galleries:
Bucharest (Muz. National de Arta al României): *Sunset* - Copenhagen (Den Hirschsprungske Samling): *Autumn Day* - Innsbruck: *Waterfall* - Stockholm: *Roman Evening.*
Auction records:
Copenhagen, 25 Feb 1976, *By the Sea* (oil on canvas, 21 1/4 x 37 1/2 ins / 54 x 95 cm) DKK 2,600. London, 8 Feb 1985, *Landscapes with Farm Buildings* (oil on canvas, 14 1/2 x 24 ins / 37 x 61 cm) GBP 1,500. London, 9 Oct 1987, *Palatine Hill, Rome* (1897-1911, oil on canvas, 22 1/2 x 39 1/4 ins / 57 x 100 cm) GBP 3,600. Stockholm, 15 Nov 1988, *Spring Day on Lake Maribo* (oil, 11 3/4 x 17 1/4 ins / 30 x 44 cm) SEK 26,000. Stockholm, 14 Nov 1990, *Landscape with Lake Maribo* (oil on canvas, 11 3/4 x 17 1/4 ins / 30 x 44 cm) SEK 5,200. Copenhagen, 6 Dec 1990, *Garden with Poppies and Lupins* (oil on canvas, 27 1/4 x 39 ins / 69 x 99 cm) DKK 7,000. London, 17 May 1991, *Summer Garden with Delphiniums and Tiger Lilies* (oil on canvas, 26 3/4 x 39 ins / 68 x 99 cm) GBP 1,650. London, 19 June 1991, *Lily Pond* (oil on canvas, 23 1/2 x 41 ins / 60 x 104 cm) GBP 4,180. London, 22 May 1992, *Garden with Rhododendrons* (oil on canvas, 24 3/4 x 38 1/2 ins / 63 x 98 cm) GBP 1,760. New York, 16 July 1992, *Mountain Village and Stream* (1902, oil on canvas, 24 x 18 ins / 61 x 45.7 cm) USD 1,540. London, 16 Nov 1994, *Rose Garden* (oil on canvas, 27 1/4 x 35 ins / 69 x 89 cm) GBP 2,760. London, 20 Nov 1996, *Rhododendrons with a Snow-Capped Mountain in the Background* (oil on canvas, 16 1/4 x 26 1/2 ins / 41 x 67 cm) GBP 2,990.

JESS, pseudonym of Collins, Jess
American, 20th century.
Born 6 August 1923, in Long Beach (California); died 2 January 2004, in San Francisco.
Painter, collage and assemblage artist, sculptor. Figure compositions, scenes with figures.

Jess (the artist's first name) was a nuclear chemist during World War II, working on the atomic bomb in the Manhattan Project. After dreaming in 1949 that the world would end in 1975, he became an artist, studying at the California School of Fine Arts under Clyfford Still and David Park. His partner, poet and writer Robert Duncan often collaborated in his work.

At the beginning of the 1950s, Jess painted with an abstract tendency, yet with a narrative strand. In the 1960s, he did a series, *Translations*, in which he did paintings based on the enlargement of photographs, interpreted in a personal manner and accompanied by captions, resulting in surrealist associations. Jess was best known for his paste-up work from the 1950s to the 1990s, which were collages of magazine images assembled to create a unified work, somewhat in the pointillist technique, such as *The Mouse's Tale* (1951-1954). From the 1970s, his paste-ups became complicated works, including images from Dick Tracy comics and tarot cards, and a huge work begun in 1976 based on the Narcissus myth was left unfinished. Jess also created assemblage art of cast-off material made into light stands and table decorations, such as *St Nick* (1962), in which Santa Claus holds an object resembling a brain or a cloud. Although considered a precursor of Pop Art, his work differed from this movement in his loving and unironic treatment of his subjects in his collages. His work has been exhibited at the Museum of Modern Art, New York (1974); *Translations, Salvages, Paste-Ups*, Dallas Museum of Fine Arts (1977); *Jess, Paste Ups (and Assemblies), 1951-1983*, Ringling Museum of Art, Sarasota, Florida (1983); and a solo at the Whitney Museum of American Art (1994, tour).
Bibliography:
Translations, Salvages, Paste-Ups by Jess, exhibition catalogue, Dallas Museum of Fine Arts, Dallas (TX), 1977. Auping, Michael, *Jess, Paste Ups (and Assemblies), 1951-1983*, exhibition catalogue, John and Mable Ringling Museum of Art, Sarasota (FL), 1983. *Jess*, exhibition catalogue, Whitney Museum of American Art, New York, 1994.
Museums and Galleries:
Boston (MFA): *Cross Purposes* (1974, collage) - Fort Worth (MAM): *Montana Xibalba: Translation #2* (1963, oil) - Minneapolis (Walker Art Center): *A Universe* (1961, mixed media sculpture) - New York (MoMA): *Trinity's Trine: Translation no. 5* - San Francisco (MoMA): *The Mouse's Tale* (1951-1954, mixed media); *Narkissos* (1976-1979, pencil on paper and paste-up); *Fig. 4 - Far and Few...* (1965, oil) - Washington DC (Hirshhorn Mus. and Sculpture Garden): *Tricky Cad: Case V* (1958, mixed media); *A Western Prospect of Egg and Dart* (1988, mixed media); *Will Wonders Never Cease: Translation No. 21* (1969, oil).
Auction records:
New York, 10 Nov 1993, *Picture of Flowers near the End of the Mantle* (1960, collage of paper/card, 34 1/2 x 29 ins / 87.6 x 73.7 cm) USD 96,000. New York, 5 May 1994, *Chiron's Souvenir from the Arco's Crew* (1960, collage of paper on a black and white photograph in a frame by the artist, 24 x 28 ins / 61 x 71.1 cm) USD 57,500. New York, 22 Feb 1995, *Goddess Because is Falling Asleep* (1954, print on paper collage/card, 15 1/4 x 11 1/2 ins / 38.6 x 29.2 cm) USD 11,500. New York, 21 Nov 1996, *Cover Design for A Lesbian Estate by Lynn Lonidier* (1977, paper collage and graphite/paper/panel, 16 1/2 x 23 1/2 ins / 41.9 x 59.4 cm) USD 24,150. New York, 23 Feb 2000, *Cover Design for A Lesbian Estate by Lynn Lonidier* (1977, printed paper collage and graphite on board, 17 x 23 ins / 42 x 59 cm) USD 12,000. New York, 23 Feb 2000, *Passage of the Black Dove from Thebes to Dodane* (1960, printed paper collage on board, 17 x 21 ins / 44 x 53 cm) USD 25,000. San Francisco, 14 Oct 2002, *Untitled, Tribute to Edward Kitson* (collage on paper, 22 x 33 ins / 57 x 84 cm) USD 12,000.

JESSÉ. See also **GISSEY** and **GESSE**

JESSÉ, Gaston
French, 19th century.
Painter. Landscapes.

Gaston Jessé exhibited at the Paris Salon from 1838 to 1844. His paintings depict views of the French regions of Dauphiné, Savoy and Provence, and also Switzerland.
Bibliography:
Les Années romantiques, la peinture française de 1815 à 1850, exhibition catalogue, Musée des Beaux-Arts, Nantes, Galeries nationales du Grand Palais, Paris, 1996.
Museums and Galleries:
Poitiers: *Landscape* (around 1838).

JESSEN, Georges
Belgian, 20th century.
Born 30 March 1893, in La Louvière; died 21 April 1963, in Ukkel.
Painter.

JESSEN, Heinrich
German, 19th century.
Born 19th century, in Altona (Hamburg).
Draughtsman, lithographer.

Jessen worked in Copenhagen and Hamburg.

JESSEN, Jes
Danish, 18th century.
Born 14 August 1743, in Apenrade; died 9 April 1807, in Apenrade.
Painter.

Jes Jessen's works are in several churches in Pleswig.
Museums and Galleries:
Schleswig (Thaulow-Mus.): *Claus Hess.*

JESSEN, Karl Ludwig
German, 19th - 20th century.
Born 22 February 1833, in Deetzbüll; died 4 January 1917, in Deetzbüll.

Painter. Portraits, genre scenes.

Karl Ludwig Jessen was a student at the Kongelige Danske Kunstakademi in Copenhagen from 1854 to 1856. He worked at various times in Paris, Italy, Hamburg and Deetzbüll.

MUSEUMS AND GALLERIES:

FLENSBURG: *Self-portrait; Same subject; Same subject; Studies* - HAMBURG: *Sunday Morning in front of the Church in Deetzbüll; Girl on Her Deathbed* - HAMBURG (Altonaer Mus.): *Burial* - KIEL: *The Judgement; Smoker; In the Frisian Islands* - NUREMBERG: *Peterswarf.*

AUCTION RECORDS:

COPENHAGEN, 12 Nov 1986, *Family in an Interior* (1897, oil on canvas, 35 3/4 x 59 1/2 ins / 91 x 151 cm) DKK 310,000.

JESSEN, Tycho Vilhelm Carl

Danish, 19th - 20th century.

Born 21 March 1870, in Copenhagen; died 18 April 1921.

Painter. Portraits.

MUSEUMS AND GALLERIES:

COPENHAGEN: *Portrait of a Woman; Portrait of Professor C.J. Salomonsen.*

JESSOP, Anne Phyllis (Lady). See BEECHEY

JESSOP, W.

British, 19th century.

Active in London.

Painter.

W. Jessop exhibited at the Royal Academy in 1802 and 1808.

JESSUP, Frederick Arthur

Australian, 20th century.

Born 1920, in Talbot, Victoria.

Painter. Interiors, still-lifes, flowers.

Frederick Arthur Jessup won a travel bursary in 1944, enabling him to travel from his native Australia to study in Europe. In 1948 he travelled to London, where he trained under the painter and printmaker Victor Pasmore. In 1949 he settled in Paris, where he attended Macavoy's sudio at the Académie de la Grande Chaumière. He has lived and worked in Languedoc since 1956. Jessup's paintings are characterised by a graceful, naive quality. His work has been the subject of a number of solo exhibitions, notably in the USA.

AUCTION RECORDS:

PARIS, 10 Oct 1990, *Bangkok Batik* (oil on canvas, 19 3/4 x 25 1/2 ins / 50 x 65 cm) FRF 10,000. NEW YORK, 12 June 1991, *Sunflowers* (oil on canvas, 25 1/2 x 30 1/2 ins / 64.8 x 77.5 cm) USD 935. PARIS, 29 March 2000, *Mr H. and his Dogs* (mixed media and ink on paper on canvas, 37 x 49 ins / 95 x 125 cm) FRF 27,000. SYDNEY, 28 Aug 2001, *Cassis, France* (oil on canvas, 20 x 23 ins / 51 x 58 cm) AUD 3,800. MELBOURNE, 25 Nov 2002, *Still-life* (oil on canvas, 16 x 37 ins / 40 x 94 cm) AUD 3,000. SYDNEY, 29 Oct 2003, *Schizophrenic Coming Out of Insulin Coma* (c. 1943, oil on board, 15 x 11 ins / 39 x 29 cm) AUD 3,200.

JETOT, Ernest Charles Molière

French, 19th century.

Born 16 January 1845, in Paris.

Sculptor.

Ernest Charles Molière Jetot exhibited bronze medals at the 1870, 1872 and 1873 Paris Salons.

JETOT, Ernestine

French, 19th - 20th century.

Born 19th century, in Paris.

Painter.

Ernestine Jetot studied with Pereyron and Toller in Lyons, and in 1890 began to exhibit portraits, figure and flower paintings in both oils and pastels in the Lyons Salon. In 1903, she won a second-class medal.

JETTEL, Eugen

Austrian, 19th century.

Born 1845, in Johnsdorf (Janovice), Moravia; died August 1901, in Lussingrande (Mali Lošinj), Croatia.

Painter (gouache), draughtsman. Landscapes.

Barbizon School.

Eugen Jettel started his training at the academy in Vienna with Albert Zimmermann, but dissatisfaction with his teacher drove him to Paris in 1866. There he took up with painters of the Barbizon School such as Corot, Dupré, Daubigny and Theodore Rousseau, who gave him useful advice. He established his own style after going on study tours of Hungary, Italy and Holland, returning eventually to Paris. His successes there attracted the attention of the Austrian government, and he was called home to take up an official position.

He won a major gold medal in Munich in 1869, while his contribution to the Universal Exhibition in 1889 won him the cross of the Légion d'Honneur. In 1900, he exhibited two works that were much admired - *Dutch Landscape* and *The Duckpond.* Some of his works were on show at the exhibition *Masterpieces from the Belvedere in Vienna* at the Musée Marmottan in Paris in 1994.

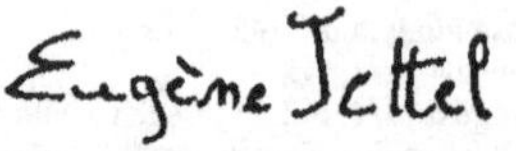

MUSEUMS AND GALLERIES:

ABBEVILLE: *Landscape* - AMSTERDAM: *Bend in a River* - BERLIN: *Hungarian Landscape* - VIENNA (Österreichische Gal. Belvedere): *Sunken Road*; two gouaches.

AUCTION RECORDS:

VIENNA, 3 Dec 1957, *Windmill,* ATS 11,000. VIENNA, 3 Dec 1959, *Village Street in Holland,* ATS 20,000. VIENNA, 22 March 1966, *Landscape,* ATS 100,000. VIENNA, 13 Sept 1966, *Autumn Morning near Fontainebleau,* ATS 20,000. VIENNA, 7 Nov 1972, *Landscape* (tempera) ATS 25,000. LONDON, 10 Nov 1972, *The Tiller,* Gns 1,500. LUCERNE, 26 June 1976, *The Meadow* (oil on canvas, 17 1/4 x 25 3/4 ins / 44 x 65.5 cm) CHF 6,500. NEW YORK, 13 Oct 1978, *Children Bathing in a River* (oil on panel, 26 x 40 1/2 ins / 66 x 103 cm) USD 11,000. VIENNA, 12 Dec 1978, *Washerwomen beside the River* (mixed media, 17 3/4 x 24 ins / 45 x 61 cm) ATS 35,000. NEW YORK, 4 May 1979, *Flock Grazing beside a Canal* (1888, oil on canvas, 23 x 33 ins / 58.5 x 84 cm) USD 23,000. VIENNA, 18 Sept 1979, *The Village Church* (1901, mixed media, 22 x 17 ins / 55 x 43 cm) ATS 30,000. VIENNA, 15 Sept 1981, *Seashore* (1883, 34 x 47 1/2 ins / 85.5 x 120.5 cm) ATS 380,000. VIENNA, 17 March 1982, *Broom in Flower* (watercolour, 17 x 24 1/2 ins / 43 x 62 cm) ATS 70,000. LONDON, 23 June 1983, *Banks of the River* (gouache, 21 1/4 x 30 3/4 ins / 54 x 78 cm) GBP 3,000. NEW YORK, 26 Oct 1983, *After the Storm* (1884, oil on canvas, 35 1/2 x 49 ins / 90 x 124.5 cm) USD 13,000. VIENNA, 19 June 1985, *Landscape with Pool* (oil on canvas, 23 1/2 x 30 ins / 60 x 76 cm) ATS 300,000. VIENNA, 27 June 1986, *View of a Village* (pastel/canvas, 17 3/4 x 21 1/4 ins / 45 x 54 cm) ATS 100,000. VIENNA, 10 Dec 1987, *Washerwomen beside a Stream* (1892, oil on canvas, 26 x 36 1/4 ins / 66 x 92 cm) ATS 380,000. MUNICH, 10 Dec 1992, *Marshlandscape with Herdsman and Cows* (1866, pencil/paper, 9 x 12 1/2 ins / 23 x 32 cm) DEM 2,034. LONDON, 16 March 1994, *Marshy Landscape* (oil on panel, 22 1/2 x 34 1/4 ins / 57 x 87 cm) GBP 10,120. MUNICH, 25 June 1996, *Flock of Sheep* (1886, oil on card, 9 3/4 x 18 3/4 ins / 25 x 47.5 cm) FRF 4,800. VIENNA, 23 March 1999, *Dutch Meadow Landscape with Cows* (oil on canvas, 16 x 10 ins / 40 x 25 cm) ATS 38,000. NEW YORK, 15 June 1999, *Horses Watering in*

Country Village (oil on panel, 20 x 31 ins / 51 x 79 cm) USD 28,000. DÜSSELDORF, 31 Jan 2000, *Village Street* (oil on panel, 30 x 46 ins / 77 x 116 cm) DEM 70,000. VIENNA, 9 May 2000, *Landscape near Cayeux* (pastel on paper/board, 16 x 23 ins / 40 x 59 cm) ATS 30,000. VIENNA, 15 May 2001, *Village Road with Horses* (1879, oil on panel, 20 x 31 ins / 51 x 79 cm) ATS 820,000. WEST TWO, 27 Nov 2001, *Potted Flowers on a Garden Path* (1896, gouache over pencil on paper/board, 15 x 11 ins / 38 x 29 cm) GBP 3,800. LONDON, 9 April 2002, *Water Meadow* (1882, oil on board, 16 x 24 ins / 40 x 61 cm) GBP 13,000. PRAGUE, 12 Oct 2002, *Landscape at Sunset* (1880, oil on panel, 22 x 28 ins / 55 x 71 cm) CZK 380,000. VIENNA, 28 Oct 2003, *Dutch River Landscape with Farmsteads* (oil on panel, 17 x 24 ins / 42 x 60 cm) EUR 24,000. NEW YORK, 3 Dec 2003, *An der kuste, 1899* (oil on board, 13 x 17 ins / 33 x 44 cm) USD 2,750. LONDON, 16 June 2004, *Normandy Landscape* (oil on panel, 17 x 36 ins / 44 x 92 cm) GBP 8,500. AMSTERDAM, 7 Sept 2004, *Cows Near the Waterfront* (oil on canvas, 14 x 23 ins / 36 x 58 cm) EUR 15,000.

JETTEL, Wladimir
Austrian, 19th century.
Born 18 July 1843, in Janowitz (Janovice).
Watercolourist. Landscapes.
Wladimir Jettel trained at the academy in Dresden and with Ferdinand Pauwels, subsequently working in Dresden and Berlin and passing the summer in Garmisch. He exhibited in Germany from 1878.
MUSEUMS AND GALLERIES:
ALTENBURG: *In the Dunes* - BERLIN: *Landscape* (watercolour); *Landscape* (watercolour) - CHEMNITZ: *Wildbach*.

JETTER, Frances
American, 20th - 21st century.
Born 1951, in New York.
Engraver.
Frances Jetter lives and works in New York. In 1995 she was among the American artists invited to exhibit in Paris at the Salon de la Jeune Gravure Contemporaine. Her prints explore human relationships in a markedly socio-political context.

JETTMAR, Rudolf
Polish, 19th - 20th century.
Born 10 September 1869, in Zawodzie; died 21 September 1939, in Vienna.
Active in Austria.
Painter, engraver, decorative artist, draughtsman, illustrator. Scenes with figures.
Rudolf Jettmar studied at the Vienna academy of fine art from 1886 and then at the Karlsruhe academy in 1892. He travelled in Italy and Germany. In 1896 he was awarded a bursary enabling him to return to Italy. He was a member of the Vienna Secession in 1898. He painted easel paintings, some very large works and also designed posters. He was appointed director and taught at an art school in Vienna. He received an honourable mention at the 1900 Exposition Universelle in Paris.
BIBLIOGRAPHY:
Osterwalder, Marcus (ed.), *Dictionnaire des illustrateurs 1800-1914*, Ides et Calendes, Neuchâtel, 1989.
MUSEUMS AND GALLERIES:
PARIS (Prints Collection): *Lovers* (1904, etching) - PRAGUE: *Monsters and Dragons*; *Storm*.
AUCTION RECORDS:
LONDON, 27 Nov 1984, *Fall of Phebus* (1905, oil on canvas, 32 1/4 x 60 3/4 ins / 82 x 154.5 cm) GBP 36,000. LONDON, 8 Oct 1986, *Victims of War* (1918, oil on canvas, 49 3/4 x 104 1/4 ins / 126.5 x 264.5 cm) GBP 18,000. ENGHIEN-LES-BAINS, 25 Oct 1987, *Perseus and Andromeda* (oil on canvas, 32 1/4 x 44 1/2 ins / 82 x 113 cm) FRF 50,000. NEW YORK, 22 May 1991, *Evening Reverie* (1924, oil on canvas, 24 x 39 1/2 ins / 61 x 100.3 cm) USD 8,800.

JETZELLER. See **JEZLER**

JETZLER, Karl Ferdinand
Swiss, 19th century.
Born 20 May 1866, in Basel.
Active in Schaffhausen.
Draughtsman.
Jetzler was a drawing master.

JEU-KOUAN. See **WEN RIGUAN**

JEUDY, Pierre
French, 20th century.
Born 19 November 1935, in Vouziers (Ardennes).
Painter, draughtsman.
Partly self-taught, Pierre Jeudy studied drawing at City of Paris evening classes and took courses in the history of contemporary art. He worked in several fields which he attempted to link together into a synthesis - the creation of a 'Surrealising' world by means of a sometimes abstract Expressionism, coloured planes in a balanced drawing heavily outlined in black, elements of a 'concrete' universe, places and people hinted at, in a universe of the imagination. In 1971 he began to concentrate more on the technique of ink on paper, which allowed him to do fresh experimental work, nearer to Abstract Lyricism, to action and chance. In 1964, he began to show his work in group exhibitions in France and abroad, including Paris salons: 1965 at the Salon des Indépendants; 1970-1972 at the Salon des Surindépendants; 1981, 1982, 1985 and 1990-1992, at the Salon d'Automne; and 1987 and 1989 at Figuration Critique. He also had solo shows in Paris and the regions.
MUSEUMS AND GALLERIES:
PARIS (Mus. de la Ville).
AUCTION RECORDS:
PARIS, 26 April 1990, *Changing Landscape 1* (oil on canvas, 46 x 33 3/4 ins / 116 x 86 cm) FRF 3,200.

JEUFFRAIN, Pierre
French, 18th century.
Born 1772, in Tours; died 1802, in Tours.
Painter. Portraits, rustic scenes.
Jeuffrain was a pupil of David. He exhibited two portraits of women at the Salon de Paris in 1801.
MUSEUMS AND GALLERIES:
TOURS: *Reaper Bringing Down a Lynx with a Fork*.

JEUGHT, Jan Josef van der
Flemish School, 18th century.
Painter. History painting, portraits.
In 1767, he was appointed assistant director of the academy in Antwerp and was made director in 1770.

JEUNE, Jean-Baptiste Ibert
Haitian, 20th - 21st century.
Born 1959.
Sculptor.
At the age of 18, Jean-Baptiste Jeune began studying sculpture with Boss Narcisse and Sanon. In 1985 he formed a studio with Jean Sonson Beaujour.

Jeune works mainly in mahogany and in different works leaves this in its natural colour or tints it with vegetable or spice dyes. 'My dream,' he said, 'would be to sculpt an entire forest of mahogany trees to immortalise life on Haiti'.
AUCTION RECORDS:
PARIS, 14 Dec 1992, *The Farmer* (1991, mahogany sculpture, h. 37 1/2 ins / 95 cm) FRF 3,500.

JEUNE, le. See **LEJEUNE**

JEUNE CŒUR, François Le. See **FRANÇOIS** called **Le Jeune Cœur ('the Young Heart')**

JEUNET, Charles
Swiss, 19th century.
Born 1836, in Vevey; died 18 May 1888, in Estavayer-le-Lac.
Sculptor (including wood).
Charles Jeunet trained in Lons-le-Saunier (Jura) and Paris. He worked mainly for churches. Also noted as by him is a *Monument to Dead French Internees in Estavayer*.

JEUNET, Louis François Victor
French, 19th - 20th century.
Born 8 August 1866, in Voiteur (Jura); died 21 April 1920, in Paris.
Miniaturist.
L.F.V. Jeunet, a pupil of Jean Gigoux and Paul Sain, exhibited in Paris at the Salon des Artistes Français. He was made a Chevalier of the Légion d'Honneur.
MUSEUMS AND GALLERIES:
PARIS (Mus. d'Orsay).

JEURDIGUE, or Yeurdigue
French, 17th century.
Painter.
Jeurdigue, who is mentioned by Descamps, was a pupil of Philippe de Corbehem. He was a deaf-mute, and executed two landscapes in the church of the Jesuits at Dunkirk.

JEVONS, Louisa E. (Mrs)
British, 19th century.
Active in Durham.
Miniaturist.
Mrs Louisa E. Jevons exhibited at the Royal Academy in 1893.

JEVRIC, Olga
Serb, 20th century.
Born 29 September 1922, in Belgrade.
Sculptor.
Olga Jevric studied music at the Belgrade conservatoire from 1946 to 1949 at the same time as studying sculpture at the academy of fine art. She also studied art history. She travelled in France, Italy, Greece, England, Switzerland, Poland, Belgium and Holland.

She began her career by painting portraits but, in 1964, she turned to an uncompromising abstraction producing a series of *Designs for Monuments* in metal and cement. These rough assemblages of raw materials impaled on metal rods take their inspiration from medieval tombstones of her country. Jesa Denegri has written of her work: 'These concrete masses and iron rods do not contain within them the transposed characteristics of some other object. They are, rather, pure matter, tamed and modelled by the creative strength of humankind and thus made eternal and permanent'.

She has taken part in many collective exhibitions since 1948 both at home and abroad including: Musée Rodi, Paris (1956); Paris (1959); Tate Gallery, London (1961). She showed work at the Venice Biennale (1958) and at the Antwerp-Middelheim Biennale (1959). Solo exhibitions include: Belgrade (1957); Turin (1959); Sremska-Mitrovica (1960); London (1962); Zagreb (1964). A retrospective was held in Belgrade (1981).
BIBLIOGRAPHY:
Horvat-Pintaric, Vera, *Olga Jevric*, exhibition catalogue, Gal. Grada Zagreba, Zagreb, 1964 (text in Serbo-Croat). Denegri, Jesa, *Olga Jevric, retrospektivna izlozba, 1948-1981*, Muzej savremene umetnosti (musée d'Art moderne), Beograd, 1981 (text in Serbo-Croat).

JEWEL
British, 18th century.
Active in London.
Painter. Portraits.
Jewel exhibited at the Royal Academy in 1793.

JEWETT, Maud Sherwood
American, 19th - 20th century.
Born 6 June 1873, in Englewood (New Jersey); died 1953.
Sculptor. Monuments.
Maud Sherwood Jewett studied at the Art Students League in New York. She became a member of the American Federation of the Arts and the American Artists Professional League. She sculpted memorials and specialised in carving sundials.
AUCTION RECORDS:
NEW YORK, 22 May 1980, *Flower Holder* (dark red patinated bronze, h. 11 ins / 27 cm) USD 2,400. NEW YORK, 26 June 1986, *Male and Female: a Flower Holder* (1924, bronze, h. 11 ins / 27 cm) USD 6,750. LOS ANGELES, 9 June 1988, *Male and Female: a Flower Holder* (bronze, h. 10 ins / 25.5 cm) USD 2,475. NEW YORK, 28 Sept 1989, *Dancers* (1924, bronze flower-holder, h. 10 1/2 ins / 26.7 cm) USD 3,850. NEW YORK, 16 March 1990, *Flower Holder, Group of Two Dancers* (1924, bronze, h. 10 1/2 ins / 26.7 cm) USD 8,250. NEW YORK, 28 May 1992, *Flower Holder, Group of Two Dancers* (1928, bronze, h. 10 1/2 ins / 26.7 cm) USD 6,050. NEW YORK, 4 Dec 1992, *Flower Holder, Group of Two Dancers* (1924, bronze, h. 10 1/4 ins / 26 cm) USD 5,500. NEW YORK, 12 Sept 1994, *Pretty Young Woman with Grapes* (bronze, h. 16 ins / 40.6 cm) USD 1,380. NEW YORK, 20 March 1996, *Flower Holders, Group of Two Dancers* (1924, bronze, h. 10 1/2 ins / 26.7 cm) USD 5,750. NEW YORK, 13 June 2001, *Flower Holder* (brown patinated bronze, h. 11 ins / 27 cm) USD 7,000.

JEWETT, William
American, 19th century.
Born 1795, in East Haddam (Connecticut); died 1873, in Bayonne (New Jersey).
Painter. Portraits.
William Jewett was initially a farm worker, and then became apprenticed to a carriage manufacturer in New London. He left his master because of his love of art and went to New York where he was initially employed by Waldo, before becoming his pupil and finally his assistant. He set up in business on his own and was named an associate of the National Academy of Design in New York in 1847.
MUSEUMS AND GALLERIES:
NEW YORK (Metropolitan Mus. of Art): several works.

JEWETT, William Danbar
British, 20th century.
Born in England.
Active in the USA.
Sculptor.

JEWITT, Llewellyn Frederick William, or Jewett
British, 19th century.
Born 24 November 1816, in Kimberworth (Yorkshire); died 5 June 1886, in Duffield (Derbyshire).
Draughtsman, engraver (includ.ing wood).
Llewellyn Frederick William Jewitt made nearly all the illustrations for *London Interiors*, the *Pictorial Times* and the *Illustrated London News* around the year 1838. In about 1846, he worked with his brother, Orlando on different illustrations including those for Parker's *Glossary*. In London, he was in charge of the illustrations for *Punch*. He was also active writing about local English history and archaeology.

JEWITT, Thomas Orlando Sheldon, or Jewett
British, 19th century.
Born 1799; died 30 May 1869, in London.
Painter, illustrator, engraver (wood/etching/aquatint). Architectural views, natural history.
Thomas Jewitt was self-taught. By the age of 16, he had made wood engravings for a work of his brother's entitled

Wandering of Memory. Two years later saw him working for his father's newspaper, *The Northern Star*, producing woodcuts, etchings and aquatints. He made the illustrations for the architectural publications produced by John Henry Parker of Oxford, including *Memorials of Oxford - Domestic Architecture of England*, *Glossary of Architecture* and other works. In 1838, he established himself in Oxford but would later move back to London. He made illustrations for *Murray's Cathedrals* and Scott's *Westminster Abbey*. He also illustrated numerous works on natural history.
MUSEUMS AND GALLERIES:
MANCHESTER: a watercolour.

JEWRIN
Swiss (?).
Pastellist.
MUSEUMS AND GALLERIES:
GENEVA (Mus. Ariana): *Portrait of a Young Woman Dressed for a Ball* (pastel).

JEX, Garnet W.
American, 20th century.
Born 1895; died 1979.
Painter.
Garnet Jex was a member of the American Federation of the Arts and the Southern States Art League.

JÉZÉQUEL, Claire-Jeanne
French, 20th - 21st century.
Born 1965, in Fontenay-aux-Roses.
Installation artist, sculptor.
Claire-Jeanne Jézéquel studied at the École des Beaux-Arts in Grenoble and from 1988 to 1989 at the Institut des Hautes Etudes en Arts Plastiques in Paris, run by Pontus Hulten. She graduated with a degree in visual arts from Villa Arson, Nice. She was a resident at the Villa Médici in Rome between 1991 and 1992. She was a prizewinner in the XIII Ivry-sur-Seine Monumental Art Grant in 2001. She lives and works in Paris.

One of her first works consisted of superimposing sheets of white paper coated with white paint on the wall. She then turned to the use of raw materials. She places basic shapes, cubes, parallepipeds and arcs, on the ground, against the wall. She builds these components herself out of Formica ('fake wood' as she likes to say), and chipboard, which she then paints white to base them on the environment, and just keep the line emerging from the wall. Into these pre-established structures she sometimes inserts elements like black and white photographs. At the beginning of the twenty-first century she started working in soft plywood and painting the back of her sculptures. She has also created works in ceramics and cast aluminium, while retaining the flowing lines of wood creations.

Claire-Jeanne Jézéquel has participated in group exhibitions since 1987, including: Villa Arson, Nice, 1987 and 1988; *Germinations V*, in Lyons, Bonn, Glasgow and Breda, 1990; *Mouvements II*, Musée National d'Art Moderne de Paris, 1991 *The Big Nothing*, the New Museum, New York, 1992; *Nouvelles Acquisitions* (*New Acquisitions*), FRAC Marseilles; *Mouvements 2*, Geroges-Pompidou Centre, Paris; *Nouvelles Augures* (*New Omens*), FRAC Languedoc-Roussillon, Sète, 1993; *En Regard* (*In Parallel*), FRAC Franche-Compté, Musée de Lons-Le-Saulnier, 1994; *Echanges d'Espaces* (*Space Exchanges*), FRAC Franche-Compté, Musée Arlaud, Lausanne; *Morceaux Choisis du Fonds National d'Art Contemporain* (*Selected Pieces from the Fonds National d'Art Contemporain (Regional Collection of Contemporary Art)*), Le Magasin, Grenoble, 1995; *Couleurs et Construction* (*Colour and Construction*), Musée de Grenoble, 1996; *L'Utopie, L'Auberge Espagnole* (*Utopia, Spanish Inn*), Rueil-Malmaison Centre for Contemporary Art, 1997; *Transit*, FNAC collection, Ensb-a, Paris; *Les États de la Sculpture* (*The States of Sculpture*), Centre Régional d'Art Contemporain, Montbéliard, 1998-1999; *Ad Libitum, Artistes du XXIème siècle* (*Ad Libitum, Twenty-First Century Artists*), Palais des Congrès, Paris, 2000; *Que Saurions-nous Construire d'Autre?* (*What Else Would We Be Able To Build?*), Musée Ziem, Martigues.

Claire-Jeanne Jézéquet's solo exhibitions include: Galerie de l'École, Villa Arson, Nice, 1990; Galerie Nikki Diana Marquardt, Paris, 1990; Galerie Gilles Peyroulet, Paris, 1994 and 1995; *Quoi, N'est-ce ça?* (*What, Isn't That It?*), Nouvelle Galerie, Grenoble, 1996; Vassivière Centre for Contemporary Art, 1998; Galerie Renos Xippas, Paris, 1999; *Bilan/Actualité* (*Outcome/Topicality*), Vassivière Centre for Contemporary Art; FRAC, Corsica, Corte; Centre for Contemporary Art, Georges-Pompidou Art Centre, Carjac; *Prélèvements d'espace* (*Space Samples*), Galerie de la Friche Belle de Mai, FRAC Provence-Alpes-Côtes d'Azur, Marseilles; *XIIIe bourse d'art monumental d'Ivry* (*Thirteenth Ivry Monumental Art Grant*), Galerie Fernand Léger, Ivry-sur-Seine, 2001; *Ça s'Organise* (*It's Getting Organised*), Crédac, Centre d'Art, Ivry-sur-Seine, 2002; Galerie Fernand Léger, Ivry-sur-Seine, 2002; Galerie Xippas, Paris, 2002.
BIBLIOGRAPHY:
Giquel, Pierre, '*Claire-Jeanne Jézéquel, Galerie Nikki Diana Marquardt*' in *Art Press*, n° 152, periodical, Paris, November 1990. Bozo, Dominique/Bordaz, Jean-Pierre, *Mouvements I-II*, exhibition catalogue, Éd. du Centre Georges-Pompidou, Paris, 1991. Perrodin, François, '*C. J. Jézéquel*' in *Le Journal des Expositions*, periodical, March 1994 (conversation with the artist). Bellet, Harry, '*C. J. Jézéquel*' in *Le Monde*, periodical, Paris, 10 March 1994. Michaud, Yves, '*C. J. Jézéquel, en situation d'étrangeté*' in *Les Marges de la vision*, Jacqueline Chambon, Paris, 1996 (collection of critical textes). Pittolo, Véronique, '*Claire-Jeanne Jézéquel, In Praise of Discretion*' in *Katalogs*, 1997. Drathen, Doris von/Kobry, Yves/Partridge, Matthew, *Claire-Jeanne Jézéquel. Soulever les problèmes, aplanir les difficultés*, travelling exhibition catalogue, Centre d'Art contemporain de Vassivière en Limousin, Beaumont-du-Lac, Gal. Xippas, Paris, 1999 (text in French and English). Le Thorel-Daviot, Pascale, '*Claire-Jeanne Jézéquel, Galerie Xippas*' in *Art Press*, n° 253, periodical, January 2000. Régnier, Philippe, '*Claire-Jeanne Jézéquel*' in *Le Journal des Arts, n°110*, periodical, Paris, 8-20 September 2000.
MUSEUMS AND GALLERIES:
DÔLE (FRAC Franche-Comté): *Face no Face* (1993) - LIMOGES (FRAC Limousin) - MARSEILLES (FRAC Provence-Alpes-Côte d'Azur) - MONTPELLIER (FRAC Languedoc-Roussillon) - PARIS (FNAC) - PARIS (FRAC Île-de-France).

JEZIERSKI, Anton
Polish.
Painter. History painting.
Anton Jezierski studied at the art college in Cracow and at the Maseyko school of composition.
MUSEUMS AND GALLERIES:
CRACOW: *The Christening*.

JEZLER, Hans Heinrich, or Jetzeller
Swiss, 17th century.
Born 3 July 1606; died 1629, in Pest, Hungary.
Active in Schaffhausen.
Painter (glass).
The son of Hans Wilhelm Jezler and pupil of Konrad Stör, Hans Heinrich Jezler gained his master status on 11 December 1626.

JEZLER, Hans Wilhelm, or Jetzeller
Swiss, 16th - 17th century.
Born 4 February 1571; died 26 October 1611, in Pest.
Active in Schaffhausen.
Painter (glass).

Jezler studied under Jakob Pläpp in Basel, and Marx Grimm in Schaffhausen.

JI KANG, or Chi K'ang or Ki K'ang
Chinese, 20th century.
Born in Shigu (Zhejiang).
Painter. Flowers, animals.

Ji Kang was a painter of the traditional Chinese School. He studied in Shanghai and then lived in Beijing. He painted insects and crabs as well as flowers.

JI ZHEN, or Chi Chen
Chinese, 15th century.
Active towards the middle of the 15th century.
Painter.

Ji Zhen is not mentioned in the biographies of artists. He was a painter of the Ming Imperial Academy. One work known to be his is *Dog with her Two Puppies in a Garden*.

JIA QUAN, or Chia Ch'uan
Chinese, 18th century.
Active during the reign of the Qing emperor Qianlong (1736-1796).
Painter.

Jia Quan was a court painter specialising in figure painting. He is known for a signed painting of the *The Eighteen Scholars*.

JIA SHIGU, or Chia Shih-ku
Chinese, 12th century.
Born in Kaifeng (Henan).
Active during the reign of the Song emperor Shaoxing (1131-1161).
Painter. Religious subjects, figures, landscapes.

Jia Shigu was a painter of the Imperial Academy of Painting at Hangzhou, specialising in Buddhist and Taoist figures in the style of Li Gonglin (1040-1106), and landscapes in the style of Li Tang (c.1050-1130).

MUSEUMS AND GALLERIES:
TAIPEI (National Palace Mus.): *Temple near a Mountain Pass* (ink and colours on silk, signed, album leaf).

JIA YOUFU
Chinese, 20th century.
Born 1942, in Ningxin (Hebei).
Painter. Local scenes, landscapes.

Jia Youfu's highly original work stands at the forefront of modern Chinese landscape painting, but is firmly rooted in the ancient tradition of Chinese landscape art. From a peasant family in Hebei province, he graduated from Beijing Central Institute of Fine Arts in 1965. He was a teacher of traditional painting at the Central Institute of Fine Arts where he began his painting career. He paints in ink, using traditional techniques together with his own very personal styles of ink-accumulating, ink-splashing and ink-splitting. He has specialised in landscapes since 1976, incorporating a knowledge of Chinese philosophy into paintings inspired by the Taihang mountains. He has travelled to the mountains many times to observe and study them.

His work appeared in solo exhibitions between 1986 and 1997 at the CIFA, the Lion Gallery in Taipei, the Municipal Council of Macau, the Yokohama Art Museum, the Kyoto National Museum for Contemporary Art, the Singapore Art Museum, the Caves Art Center in Taiwan, and Trésors 97.

AUCTION RECORDS:
HONG KONG, 2 May 1991, *Mount Taiheng* (ink and colour on paper, 87 1/2 x 50 1/2 ins / 222.4 x 128.2 cm) HKD 242,000. HONG KONG, 30 March 1992, *Clouds on the Mountains* (ink and colour on paper, mounted handscroll, 38 x 37 1/2 ins / 96.5 x 95.4 cm) HKD 187,000. NEW YORK, 1 June 1992, *Tea by Moonlight* (ink and colours on paper, 81,3x52,7) USD 3,025. HONG KONG, 28 Sept 1992, *Landscape of the Yellow Earth Plateau* (ink and colours on paper, 38 x 70 1/2 ins / 96.4 x 179 cm) HKD 187,000. HONG KONG, 22 March 1993, *Sunlit Clouds above the High Mountains* (ink and colours on paper, 16 1/2 x 38 1/4 ins / 42 x 97 cm) HKD 78,200. HONG KONG, 25 April 2004, *Returning in the Sunset* (1984, ink and colour, scroll, 11 x 36 ins / 27 x 92 cm) HKD 26,000.

JIA YUQIAN. See **XIE YUQIAN**

JIANG AI, or Chiang Ai or Tsiang Ai, nickname: Zhihe
Chinese, 17th century.
Born in Huating (Jiangsu).
Active c. 1620.
Painter.

Jiang Ai painted landscapes in the style of Shen Shichong, who was working 1611-1640. He is known to have painted several signed and dated works: *Landscape after Dong Yuan*, dated 1604, *Sheer Green Cliffs*, dated 1614, and *Sheer Cliffs and Trees in Leaf on the Rocky Bank of a River*, a leaf of an album dated 1616.

JIANG BAOHUA, or Chiang Pao-hua or Tsiang Pao-houa, nickname: Ziying
Chinese, 18th (?) century.
Born in Xushui (Zhejiang).
Painter.

Jiang Baohua, according to his painter's inscription, considered his *Blue Phoenix in a Magnolia* to be in the style of Yi Yuanji, who was working in the second half of the 19th century.

MUSEUMS AND GALLERIES:
NEW YORK (Metropolitan Mus. of Art): *Blue Phoenix in a Magnolia*.

JIANG BAOLIN, or Chiang Pao-lin or Tsiang Pao-lin, nickname: Ziyan, pseudonym: Xiazhu
Chinese, 19th century.
Born in Zhaowen, near Suzhou (Jiangsu).
Painter.

Jiang Baolin was working in Shanghai about 1830-1850. A painter of landscapes, he began by working in the style of Wen Zhengming (1470-1559), then of Dong Yann (died in 962) and finally of Juran (working about 960-980). He was the author of a treatise on landscape entitled *Molin Jinhua*. He is known to have painted a roll, *Mountain Landscape*, signed and dated 1832, as well as an album of 16 landscapes, each having a colophon and a poem, the last of which is dated 1832.

JIANG CAN, or Chiang Ts'an or Kiang Ts'an, nickname: Guandao
Chinese, 12th century.
Born in Wuxing (Zhejiang).
Active during the first half of the 12th century.
Painter. Landscapes.

Jiang Can was a painter of landscapes in the tradition of Dong Yuan (died in 962) and Juran (working about 960-980). There exists by him a leaf of an album, *A Grove in the Mountains, with Small Houses beside a Stream*, as well as a roll, *Lu Mountain, after Fan Guan*, inscribed with the name of the painter, and which is probably a work from the Southern Song dynasty (1127-1279) after an earlier model.

JIANG CHANGYI
Chinese, 20th century.
Born 1943, in Xiangxiang (Hunan).
Painter. Figures, local scenes.

Jiang Changyi graduated with a diploma from the academy of fine art in Nanjing in 1966, and since 1988 has been the president of the Shanghai oil painting and sculpture research institute. He has shown his works in numerous exhibitions in China and abroad. In his realistic works, which are filled with a certain softness, Jiang Changyi often depicts South China and its inhabitants.

AUCTION RECORDS:

HONG KONG, 30 March 1992, *April* (1990, oil on canvas, 31 3/4 x 25 1/2 ins / 80.8 x 65 cm) HKD 231,000. HONG KONG, 28 Sept 1992, *The Silk Flower* (1992, oil on canvas, 39 1/4 x 32 ins / 100 x 81 cm) HKD 154,000.

JIANG CHENGZONG, or Chiang Ch'eng-tsung or Kiang Tch'eng-tsong
Chinese, 14th - 17th century.
Active at the end of the Ming dynasty (1368-1644).
Painter.

Jiang Chengzong is not mentioned in the biographies of artists. He is known, however, to have painted *Landscape with Bare Trees*, a large leaf of an album, signed and dated 1635, which had been attributed by mistake to Zong Hao, a painter of the Qing dynasty (1644-1911).

JIANG DALAI, or Chiang Talai or Kiang Talai, nicknames: Lianshan and Jiapu
Chinese, 19th century.
Active during the first half of the 19th century.
Painter.

Jiang Dalai was a painter of landscapes who is known to have moved to Nagasaki, Japan, in 1804. There remains by him a *Landscape after Shen Zhou*, signed and executed in Nagasaki, as well as two other landscapes which are signed and accompanied by poems.

JIANG DING, or Chiang Ting or Tsiang Ting, nickname: Zuomei
Chinese, 18th century.
Active in the middle of the 18th century.
Painter.

Jiang Ding was the grandson of the painter Jiang Tingxi (1669-1732). He painted flowers in the family tradition, and executed *Crows in a Weeping Willow*, a signed fan painting.

JIANG ERSHI, or Chiang Er-Shih or Kiang Eui-Che
Chinese, 20th century.
Born 1910.
Painter. Landscapes, animals.

Jiang Ershi was a lecturer in the school of fine art of the province of Guangxi, and curator of the museum of fine art in Nanning, the provincial capital. He painted landscapes and birds, combining the Chinese technique of drawing and Western chromatic richness.

JIANG FENG, or Chiang Feng or Kiang Feng
Chinese, 20th century.
Born 1910, in Jiangsu; died 1982.
Painter, engraver.

Jiang Feng was one of the young artists of the Realist School of the 1930s, whose art was closely associated with the Chinese Communist movement. Political commitment is especially perceptible in their wood engravings, stamped with a profound awareness of the poor conditions of the Chinese masses at the time. Although these works take their inspiration from Soviet Realism, they demonstrate more freedom, invention and vitality than their models. The works of Jiang Feng, in an Expressionist style with black predominating, celebrate political struggle.

In 1930, the writer Lu Xun (1881-1936) created an apprentice class in Shanghai, with a Japanese lecturer. He enjoined the young engravers to choose what suited them in the Chinese artistic heritage, and to adopt what is best in foreign art so as to establish a new national style of art in accordance with the taste of the masses. Numerous groups of engravers were formed, including the One-eight group in Shanghai in 1930, of which Jiang Feng was a member. This movement incurred the hostility of the government, and a number of young artists were arrested, including Jiang Feng. He later rejoined the Communist revolutionaries in Yanan. He was appointed director of the fine art department of the Luxun academy in Yanan in 1942, which had been the centre of Communist agitation in 1939, and was director of the national academy of fine art in Hangzhou, Zhejiang province, from 1949. He was a directing member of the association of the artists of China, as well as of the national association of engravers.

BIBLIOGRAPHY:

Andrews, Julia F., *Painters and Politics in the People's Republic of China: 1949-1979*, University of California Press, Berkeley, 1994. Clunas, Craig, *Art in China*, Oxford University Press, Oxford and New York, 1997.

JIANG GAN, or Chiang Kan or Tsiang Kan
Chinese, 16th century.
Active during the second half of the 16th century.
Painter.

Jiang Gan was the son of a painter, and worked in the tradition of Wu Wei (1459-1508). He led a solitary existence.

JIANG GUFENG
Chinese, 20th century.
Born 1930.
Engraver.

Jiang Gufeng took part in the exhibition *De Bonnard à Baselitz - Dix ans d'enrichissements du cabinet des estampes 1978-1988* (*From Bonnard to Baselitz: A Decade of Acquisitions by the Prints Collection 1978-1988*) at the Bibliothèque Nationale in Paris in 1992.

JIANG HAN, or Chiang Han or Tsiang Han, nickname: Chengchuan, pseudonym: Luyun
Chinese, 17th (?) century.
Painter.

Jiang Han is not mentioned in the biographies of artists, but he is known to have executed *Girl at a Table, Seen through a Circular Window*, a painting he accompanied with a colophon and a poem.

JIANG HANTING, or Jiang Handing
Chinese, 20th century.
Born 1903; died 1963.
Painter.

AUCTION RECORDS:

HONG KONG, 30 April 1992, *Legend of the Seventh Lunar Month* (1963, ink and pigments/paper, kakemono, 23 1/2 x 36 3/4 ins / 59.5 x 93.5 cm) HKD 18,700. HONG KONG, 22 March 1993, *Chickens* (1958, ink and pigments/paper, kakemono, 53 x 26 1/2 ins / 134.5 x 67 cm) HKD 43,700. NEW YORK, 29 Nov 1993, *Pheasant in a Garden* (1949, ink and pigments/paper, kakemono, 54 x 26 ins / 137.2 x 66 cm) USD 2,300. HONG KONG, 5 May 1994, *White Parrots* (1937, ink and pigments/paper, kakemono, 50 1/4 x 25 1/4 ins / 127.5 x 64 cm) HKD 28,750. HONG KONG, 30 Oct 1995, *Two Birds on a Branch of Bamboo* (ink and pigments/paper, kakemono, 57 1/2 x 12 1/2 ins / 145.8 x 32 cm) HKD 32,200. HONG KONG, 28 Oct 2001, *Nature* (ink and colour, album of sixteen, 5 x 6 ins / 12 x 14 cm) HKD 110,000. STUTTGART, 30 May 2003, *Lotus and Insects* (seal, Indian ink and colour, hanging scroll, 40 x 19 ins / 101 x 49 cm) EUR 1,600. HONG KONG, 27 Oct 2003, *Lotus and Dragonfly* (ink and colour, hanging scroll, 39 x 19 ins / 100 x 49 cm) HKD 30,000. LONDON, 6 May 2004, *Bird Perched among Prunus and Magnolia* (1943, colour ink, hanging scroll, 44 x 19 ins / 112 x 48 cm) GBP 3,000.

JIANG HENG, or Chiang Heng or Kiang Heng, nicknames: Weinan and Huinan, pseudonym: Yanqi
Chinese, 18th century.
Born in Changshu (Jiangsu).
Active during the reign of the Qing emperor Qianlong (1736-1796).
Painter.

Jiang Heng lived in Yangzhou (Jiangsu), and painted landscapes in the style of the masters of the Yuan dynasty (1279-1368). He executed two signed album leaves: *Five Pines near a Stream* and *Studio in the Cassia Trees*

JIANG HONGWEI
Chinese, 20th - 21st century.
Born 1957, in Wuxi (Jiangsu).
Painter. Birds, flowers.

Jiang Hongwei has taught at the Nanjing fine arts institute since his graduation there in 1977. He has exhibited widely in Asia and won several domestic painting awards.

AUCTION RECORDS:
HONG KONG, 30 March 1992, *Birds Resting on a Sandbank* (ink and pigments/paper, mounted makemono, 26 1/4 x 26 1/2 ins / 66.5 x 67 cm) HKD 28,600. HONG KONG, 28 Sept 1992, *Flowers and Bird* (ink and pigments/paper, 25 1/2 x 25 3/4 ins / 65 x 65.5 cm) HKD 41,800.

JIANG JI, or Chiang Chi or Tsiang Ki or Tsiang Tsi
Chinese, 18th century.
Active during the first half of the 18th century.
Painter. Portraits.

Jiang Ji was the author of the second of two treatises on portrait painting in a collection entitled *Chuanshen Miyao*. The first treatise, *Xiexiang Mijue* is from the Yuan period (1279-1368) and is less extensive, but that by Jiang Ji is very well-developed. It is largely a manual intended for the practitioner, divided into 27 short chapters systematically covering the various problems of expression and technique. The account is remarkably complete, clear and precise.

In China, portrait painting is a very specialised field, on the margins of the great pictorial trends. Since the Song dynasty (960-1279), when painting became a form of spiritual expression for the scholarly elite, portraiture has remained a craft discipline, with its own rules. This explains the extreme rarity of writings on this technique, which was only passed down from master to disciple, and thus indicates the significance of Jiang Ji.

BIBLIOGRAPHY:
Ryckmans, Pierre, *Les 'Propos sur la peinture' de Shitao. Traduction et commentaires pour servir de contribution à l'étude terminologique et esthétique des théories chinoises de la peinture*, Institut belge des hautes études chinoises, Brussels, 1970.

JIANG JIE, or Chiang Chieh or Kiang Kiai, real name: Jiang Jian, nickname: Shiru
Chinese, 19th century.
Born in Hangzhou (Zhejiang).
Active c. 1800-1830.
Painter.

After studying figure painting, Jiang Jie turned to flower painting in the style of Chen Shun, who was working in the mid-17th century. He painted several signed and dated works, including *Chrysanthemums*, after Yun Shouping, dated 1817; *Four Paintings of Flowers Depicting the Four Seasons*, including two after Yun Shouping, dated 1831; *Tao Yuanming Gathering Chrysanthemums*, dated 1831; *Peonies and Magnolias*, after Yun Shouping, accompanied by two lines of poetry; and *Old Plum Tree in Flower*.

JIANG JING, or Chiang Ching or Tsiang King, nickname: Jing Zhi, pseudonyms: Zhi Zhou, Yunshan and Caizhisheng
Chinese, 19th century.
Born in Qiantang (Zhejiang).
Active c. 1800.
Painter.

Jiang Jing painted landscapes after Li Liufang (1575-1626), but also figures, flowers and pine trees. He painted *Branches of Plum in Flower*, signed and dated 1804.

JIANG LIGANG, or Chiang Li-kang or Kiang Li-kang, nickname: Tingxian, pseudonym: Dongqi
Chinese, 15th century.
Born in Yongjia (Zhejiang).
Active during the reign of the Ming emperor Tianshun (1457-1464).
Painter, calligrapher.

Jiang Ligang was a famous calligrapher who invented the Jiang style in calligraphy. He is also known as a painter of landscapes in the styles of Huang Gongwang (1269-1354) and Wang Meng (1298-1385). He is known to have painted *Landscape with Two Men and a Boy Standing on a Bridge*, a work he also signed.

MUSEUMS AND GALLERIES:
LONDON (British Mus.): *Flowers and Birds*.

JIANG LINGJIAN, or Chiang Ling-Chien or Kiang Ling-Kien
Chinese, 20th century.
Died before 1934.
Painter.

Jiang Lingjian belonged to the scholarly traditional school. He worked in the first half of the 20th century.

JIANG MINGXIAN, or Chiang Ming-hsien
Chinese, 20th century.
Born 1942, in Taichung.
Painter. Landscapes.

Jiang obtained a diploma at the national university of fine art in 1968, and competed his training at the Spanish teacher-training college for the fine arts in 1974. He then moved to the University of New York, and became a lecturer in Chinese painting at the University of St John. On returning to Taiwan in 1979, he was appointed director of the national academy of fine art.

AUCTION RECORDS:
HONG KONG, 30 March 1992, *The Bridge at Lugou* (ink and pigments/paper, mounted makemono, 16 1/4 x 59 3/4 ins / 41.4 x 152 cm) HKD 71,500. HONG KONG, 30 April 1992, *Fishing Boats* (1990, ink and pigments/paper, kakemono, 53 1/4 x 13 1/2 ins / 135.5 x 34.5 cm) HKD 44,000. HONG KONG, 28 Sept 1992, *Waterfall High in the Mountains* (ink and pigments/paper, kakemono, 47 1/4 x 23 3/4 ins / 120.2 x 60.2 cm) HKD 88,000. TAIPEI, 18 Oct 1992, *Xian Revisited* (1992, ink and pigments/paper, 18 3/4 x 113 ins / 47.8 x 287 cm) TWD 572,000. HONG KONG, 22 March 1993, *The Tower at Hugiu* (1992, ink and pigments/paper, kakemono, 39 1/2 x 27 1/4 ins / 100.5 x 69 cm) HKD 69,000. TAIPEI, 18 April 1993, *Listening to the Falling Rain* (1981, ink and pigments/paper, 27 x 53 ins / 68.5 x 134.5 cm) TWD 253,000. NEW YORK, 28 Nov 1994, *Garden in Suzhou* (ink and pigments/paper, 26 3/4 x 18 ins / 67.9 x 45.7 cm) USD 2,990.

JIANG PU, or Chiang P'u or Tsiang P'ou, nickname: Zhifu, pseudonym: Hengxuan
Chinese, 18th century.
Born 1708, in Changshu (Jiangsu); died 1761.
Painter.

Jiang Pu was the son of the painter Jiang Tingxi (1669-1732), and executed flowers in the style of his father. Several signed works by him are still in existence, including *Magnolias* (after Wen Zhengming, dated 1753), *Pines, Bamboos and Plum Blossom, Cassia Blossom and Rabbits* (accompanied by a poem), *Orchids and Bamboos* (a horizontal roll), *Bamboo Thicket near a Stream* (accompanied by an inscription).

JIANG QIAN, or Chiang Ch'ien or Tsiang K'ien, nickname: Zijian, pseudonym: Hongqiao
Chinese, 16th century.
Born in Nanjing.
Active c. 1540-1560.
Painter.

Jiang Qian was the son of the painter Jiang Song, who was working about 1500. He lived in Suzhou, in the province of Jiangsu, and painted landscapes. Several signed and dated works by him are still in existence, including *Old Trees by a River* (dated 1541? and accompanied by a poem by Wang Zhideng dated 1607), *Hills and Water* (a roll opening horizontally, dated 1548), *Thatched Cottage at the Foot of a High Wooded Mountain* (after Wang Meng, dated 1563 and accompanied by a poem by Jiang Qian) and landscape paintings on fans.

JIANG SHEN, or Chiang Shen or Kiang Chen
Chinese, 12th century.
Born in the region of Jiangnan (Zhejiang and Jiangsu).
Active during the first half of the 12th century.
Painter. Landscapes.

Jiang Shen was a distinguished artist from the end of the Northern Song dynasty (960-1127), and a disciple of the monk and painter Juran, who was working from about 960 to about 980. According to the painter and critic Dong Quichang (1555-1636), he was one of the few painters to have understood the essence of the work of his master, and the only one to have continued in that tradition.

MUSEUMS AND GALLERIES:
KANSAS CITY (Nelson-Atkins MA): *Verdant Mountains* (dated 1785, ink and light colours/silk, signed, roll opening horizontally, 22 seals from the Qing emperor Qianlong (reigned 1736-1796)) - TAIPEI (National Palace Mus.): *One Thousand Miles of Rivers and Mountains* (roll opening horizontally, ink/silk, with several colophons including a Lushan landscape by the painter Dong Qichang, after Fan Kuan).

JIANG SHIJIE, or Chiang Shih-chieh or Kiang Chetsie, nickname: Xuezai, pseudonyms: Haojian, Siwei, etc, posthumous name: Xiaozheng
Chinese, 17th century.
Born 1647, in Laiyang (Shandong); died 1709.
Painter. Figures, landscapes, flowers.

Jiang Shijie lived in Suzhou, in the province of Jiangsu, and painted landscapes in the style of Ni Zan (1301-1374). Several of his signed and dated works are still in existence, including *Branch of Plum in Flower* (dated 1698), *Man Resting on a Bench* (dated 1700), *Visit to a Friend on the Mountain* (after Tang Yin, with a poem and colophon by Jiang Shijie, dated 1705), *Mountain Peaks and Waterfalls* (a roll opening horizontally, accompanied by five poems by Jiang Shijie, dated 1707), *River in Autumn, in the Style of Ni Zan* (accompanied by two poems, one by Jiang Shijie and the other by Zhi Yicun), and *Riverscape in Autumn* (after Jing Hao, with a colophon).

MUSEUMS AND GALLERIES:
BEIJING (Palace Mus.): *Small House in the Mountains in Autumn* (poems by Jiang Shijie).

AUCTION RECORDS:
NEW YORK, 31 May 1990, *Landscape* (ink/paper, kakemono, 37 3/4 x 17 ins / 95.8 x 42.3 cm) USD 3,850. NEW YORK, 1 June 1992, *Landscapes* (ink/paper, collection of 4 makemono sketchbooks, each sheet 10 3/4 x 14 1/4 ins / 27.3 x 36.2 cm) USD 2,475. NEW YORK, 29 Nov 1993, *Landscape* (ink/paper, kakemono, 37 3/4 x 16 1/2 ins / 95.9 x 42.2 cm) USD 2,875.

JIANG SIZHOU, or Chiang Ssu-chou or Kiang Sseutcheou, nickname: Zhouchen, pseudonym: Huajiu Toutuo
Chinese, 17th century.
Born in Qiantang (Zhejiang).
Active c. 1620.
Painter.

Jiang Sizhou was a disciple of the painter Guangxi, who was working 1590-1630, and a friend of the painter Lan Ying (1585-after 1660). He painted landscapes and flowers after Shen Zhou (1427-1509). He painted a horizontally opening roll, *Mountains as far as the Eye Can See, beside a Wide River*, in the style of Mi Fu (1051-1107), with an inscription dated 1621, a colophon and biographical notes.

JIANG SONG, or Chiang Sung or Tsiang Song, nickname: Sansong
Chinese, 16th century.
Born in Nanjing.
Active c. 1500.
Painter.

Jiang Song was a painter of landscapes and figures, in the style of Wu Wei (1459-1508). He had a rather coarse style, with a dry brush, just like Zhang Lu (from about 1464 to about 1538) and his friends. He painted and signed *Man in a Boat, Playing the Flute* (on a fan), *River with Fishing Boats, a Fisherman in a Boat at the Foot of High Mountains*, and others.

MUSEUMS AND GALLERIES:
BERLIN: *Four Views of Rivers in Valleys* (together in a single roll).

JIANG TIEFENG
Chinese, 20th century.
Born 1938, in Ningbo (Zhejiang).
Engraver.

In 1959, Jiang Tiefeng was admitted to the central academy of fine arts in Beijing, where he graduated in 1964 (in the last class before the Cultural Revolution). He then settled in Yunnan province. Between 1966 and 1973, he was commissioned to produce propagandist Socialist Realist posters and sculpture for the Chinese government. During this time he co-founded the Yunnan School, and from 1978 to 1983 he was an associate professor at the Yunnan art academy. In 1979, he was commissioned by the government to paint a mural depicting Yunnan province for the Great Hall of the People in Beijing. It came to be known as the 'stone forest' mural. In the late 1970s and early 1980s, he worked predominantly as an illustrator. He then fell out of favour with the government in the early 1980s, and his works were condemned and publicly criticised. In 1983 he went to the USA on a cultural exchange as visiting professor of art at the University of Southern California, and he later moved to Minnesota. He took part in the exhibition *De Bonnard à Baselitz - Dix ans d'enrichissements du cabinet des estampes 1978-1988* (*From Bonnard to Baselitz: A Decade of Acquisitions by the Prints Collection 1978-1988*), held at the Bibliothèque Nationale in Paris in 1992. His works have been widely exhibited in the USA.

BIBLIOGRAPHY:
Andrews, Julia F., *Painters and Politics in the People's Republic of China: 1949-1979*, University of California Press, Berkeley, 1994.

MUSEUMS AND GALLERIES:
PARIS (BNF, Prints Collection): *Happy Childhood* (1975, engraving/wood).

JIANG TINGXI, or Chiang T'ing-hsi or Ts'iang T'ing-si, nickname: Yangsun, pseudonyms: Youjun, Xigu and Nansha
Chinese, 17th - 18th century.
Born 1669, in Jiang-su (Jiangsu); died 1732.
Painter. Flowers.

Jiang Tingxi was a writer and famous flower painter. Following his appointment to an important post in the imperial civil service about 1703, he ceased his artistic activity, only painting very occasionally for the emperor. The majority of his works are therefore kept in the imperial collections. For private individuals, he had his paintings executed by his pupil Ma Yi.

Museums and Galleries:
Boston (MFA): *Lotus and Seaweed* (poem by Jiang Tingxi) - London (British Mus.): *Lotus* (dated 1730, after Xu Wei, signed); *Peonies, Magnolias and Peach Blossom* (signed) - New York (Metropolitan Mus. of Art): *Tree in Flower, Peony and White Heron* (dated 1724, after Zhao Mengfu, signed) - Shanghai: *Daffodils, Lingzhi and Bamboo near a Rock* (dated 1723, signed) - Taipei (National Palace Mus.): *Two Peonies* (ink/silk, roll opening vertically); *New Year's Day* (ink and colour/paper, roll opening vertically); *Cassia Flowers* (ink and colour/silk, inscription, roll opening vertically).
Auction records:
New York, 31 May 1990, *Peonies* (ink/silk, kakemono, 42 1/4 x 17 3/4 ins / 107 x 45.1 cm) USD 2,475. New York, 25 Nov 1991, *Flowers from the Four Seasons* (ink and pigments/silk, collection of four paintings, 33 3/4 x 7 1/2 ins / 85.7 x 19 cm) USD 25,300.

JIANG WENZHAN
Chinese, 20th century.
Born 1940, in Shandong.
Painter. Landscapes.
A traditional *guohua* ink painter, Jiang Wenzhan studied at the Xian Institute of Fine Arts.

JIANG XIAOJIAN, or Jiang Xin, Chiang Hsiao-Chien, Chiang Siao-Kien
Chinese, 20th century.
Born 1893, in Wuxing (Jiangsu); died before 1937.
Sculptor.
Modern school.
Jiang Xiaojian was active in Shanghai in the first half of the 20th century and spent two years in France in the 1930s. He made the Sun Yat-Sen memorial statue that was erected in Shanghai in 1925.

JIANG XUN, or Chiang Hsun, sobriquets: Yuanyang tingzhang, etc., style name: Xiaoquan
Chinese, 18th - 19th century.
Born 1764, in Songjiang (Jiangsu); died 1821 or 1834.
Painter.
Jiang Xun painted birds and flowers in the style of Yun Shouping (1633-1690) as well as figures. Several of his works are known, including *Portrait of Su Dongpo* (signed and dated 1806, in the style of a painting by Li Longmian), *Lady near a Pond with Lotus* (signed and acccompanied by a poem): *Portrait of Lady Qiongxian* (signed); *Lady Beneath the Bamboos* (signed), *Flowers and Trees* (painted in collaboration with Wang Xuehao, Zhu Angzhi, Zhai Jichang and Zhou Li) and *Chrysanthemums*.

JIANG YIN, or Chiang Yin, style name: Zhouzuo
Chinese, 16th century.
Born in Huangxian (Shandong).
Painter.
Jiang Yin painted figures, flowers and fruit. Among his signed works is *The Emperor Muwang Visiting Xi Wangmu*.

JIANG YU, or Chiang Yu, style name: Liren
Chinese, 19th century.
Born in Chaoxian (Anhui).
Active in Jiangsu c. 1800-1820.
Painter.
Jiang Yu was a pupil of Zhang Yu (1734-1803) and painted flowers and birds. He also worked in the styles of Chen Shun (1483-1544) and Xu Wei (1521-1593). Among his works are: *Epidendrums and Lilies near a Rock* (signed and dated 1817) and *Plum Blossom and Bamboos in a Vase, Two Birds* (signed and accompanied by a colophon).

JIANG YUJIAN, or Chiang Yu-chien, style name: Juting
Chinese, 19th century.
Born in Suizhou (Henan).
Active during the first half of the 19th century.
Painter.
Jiang Yujian specialised in painting Epidendrum orchids. He sat the provincial civil service examinations in 1822. His works include *Epidendrums and Jujube* (in the style of Zhao Mengfu, accompanied by his own poem) and an *Album of Epidendrum Flowers*.
Museums and Galleries:
Berlin (Museum für Ostasiatische Kunst): *Album of Epidendrum Flowers*.

JIANG ZHANG, or Chiang Chang, style name: Tieqin
Chinese, 18th century.
Born in Danyang (Jiangsu).
Active during the first half of the 18th century in Nanjing, Shanghai, Beijing.
Painter. Human Figures.
Jiang Zhang was a rival of the painter Huang Shen (1687-after 1768). He founded the Jiang School and specialised in figure painting. Among his works is a series of 'broken ink' (*pomo*) paintings signed and dated 1737: *The Twelve Animals of the Zodiac*.

JIANG ZHAOHE, or Chiang Chao-Ho
Chinese, 20th century.
Born 1904, in Luzhou; died 1986.
Active in Nanjing, Shanghai, Beijing.
Painter. Human figures.
Jiang Zhaohe was orphaned as a young boy and experienced poverty firsthand. After studying calligraphy and painting, he attended courses in Western art and sculpture. He taught decorative arts at National Central University, Nanjing, in 1928, at the Shanghai School of Fine Arts in 1930 and in the studio which he opened in Beijing in 1935. He was strongly influenced by the style of Xu Beihong, who asked him in 1940 to teach at the Beijing National Art College. After 1949, he was professor at the Central Institute of Fine Arts in Beijing, where he taught until his death. He painted contemporary figures on the bottom rung of society - often homeless beggars. He is quoted as saying, 'It's only through realistic art that we can expose the miserable fate and aching hearts of the labouring poor.' He mixed traditional techniques using ink painting with Western naturalism. His legacy is his monumental work *Refugees*, completed in 1943 in Beijing. It depicts Chinese refugees during the Sino-Japanese war.
Bibliography:
Weihe Chen/Pratt, Keith, '*Chinese Figure Painter Jiang Zhaohe*' in *Arts of Asia*, vol 23, no. 4, July-August 1993. Andrews, Julia F., *Painters and Politics in the People's Republic of China: 1949-1979*, University of California Press, Berkeley, 1994. Yang Xin and others, *Three Thousand Years of Chinese Painting*, Yale University Press, 1997.

JIANG ZHAOSHEN, or Chiang Chaoshen
Chinese, 20th century.
Born 1925, in Anhui; died 1996.
Active in Taiwan.
Painter. Landscapes.
Chiang Chaoshen did not fit in at primary school and was educated at home. He left for Taiwan in 1949 and the following year began studying painting with Pu Ru. He was engaged at the National Palace Museum in Taipei and published many articles on the history of Chinese painting. He relinquished this post in 1991 to devote himself to painting.

BIBLIOGRAPHY:
Chiang Chao-shen: Selections of His Works of Art, National Palace Museum, Taipei, 1974 (text in Chinese with summary in English).
AUCTION RECORDS:
HONG KONG, 16 Jan 1989, *Temple at the Foot of the Mountains* (1987, ink and colour on paper, 24 1/2 x 39 ins / 62.3 x 99.1 cm) HKD 66,000. HONG KONG, 15 Nov 1989, *Landscape* (1981, ink and colour on paper, hanging scroll, 24 1/2 x 38 1/2 ins / 62.5 x 98 cm) HKD 66,000. TAIPEI, 18 Oct 1992, *Landscape* (1992, ink and colour on paper, 36 3/4 x 72 3/4 ins / 93.5 x 184.8 cm) TWD 1,100,000. TAIPEI, 10 April 1994, *Summerhouse in a Landscape* (ink and colour on paper, hanging scroll, 37 3/4 x 12 1/2 ins / 96 x 32 cm) TWD 207,000. HONG KONG, 27 Oct 2003, *Hermitage* (1988, ink and colour, handscroll, 12 x 39 ins / 30 x 98 cm) HKD 35,000.

JIANG ZHU, or Chiang Chu, style name: Yunning
Chinese, 17th century.
Born in Xixian (Anhui).
Active during the second half of the 17th century.
Painter.
Jiang Zhu was a poet and painter and a pupil of Hongren (1610-1664). Among his signed works is *Fantastic Rocks and Twisted Pines*.

JIANG ZICHENG, or Chiang Tzu-ch'eng
Chinese, 15th century.
Born in Yixing (Jiangsu).
Active at the imperial court during the reign of the Ming emperor Yongle (1403-1424).
Painter.
Although he began as a landscape painter, Jiang Zicheng subsequently painted only figures. He worked at court with Bian Wenjin and Zhao Lian, where they formed a group called 'The Three Excellents'. Among the works attributed to him is a hanging scroll with a portrait of Marshal Wen in ink and colours on silk (Museum of Fine Arts, Boston).

JIAO BINGZHEN, or Chiao Ping-chen
Chinese, 17th - 18th century.
Born in Jining (Shandong).
Painter. Figures, animals, landscapes, flowers.
Jiao Bingzhen was active around 1680-1720 in the reign of the Qing Emperor Kangxi (1662-1722). He worked as a court painter and held a post as an official on the Imperial Board of Astronomy. His known works include: *Two Girls in a Garden* (signed and dated 1721), *Mountain Landscape with Pavilions and Figures* (a signed hanging scroll), *The Emperor Kangxi on the Southern Tour of his Temporary Palace of Huqiu* and a leaf from the album *General Su Wu as a Hun shepherd*.
MUSEUMS AND GALLERIES:
LONDON (British Mus.): *Journey of a Government Official* (handscroll, signed) - STOCKHOLM (Nationalmus.): *Lady in a Summerhouse* (signed).
AUCTION RECORDS:
NEW YORK, 1 June 1989, *Horse Tethered to a Willow Tree* (ink and colours on silk, hanging scroll, 53 1/2 x 27 1/4 ins / 136 x 69 cm) USD 38,500. NEW YORK, 31 May 1990, *Lake Tai in Suzhou* (ink on paper, 23 1/2 x 13 1/2 ins / 59.4 x 34.3 cm) USD 7,700.

JIAO KEQUN
Chinese, 20th century.
Born 1930, in Xian (Shanxi).
Painter. Flowers, animals.
A traditional ink painter, Jiao Kequn studied at the Central Institute of Fine Arts, where he went on to teach.

JIAO XUN, or Chiao Hsun
Chinese, 19th century.
Born 1763; died 1820(?).
Active during the first half of the 19th century.
Painter.
Jiao Xun was a scholar, mathematician and literary theorist during the Qing dynasty. He is not mentioned in the biographies of artists but is known for his *Branch of Plum Blossom* (signed and dated 1822).

JIBOKU. See **SOTAN**

JICHÔSAI. See **NICHOSAI**

JICINSKA, Vera
Czech, 20th century.
Born 3 July 1898, in Petrokocice.
Painter.
Vera Jicinska exhibited in Budapest, where she received an honourable mention in 1928, Prague and Paris at the Salon des Indépendants and the Salon d'Automne.

JIE JISI. See **JIE XISI**

JIE XISI, or Chieh Hsih-Ssu, sobriquet: Manshi
Chinese, 13th - 14th century.
Born 1274, in Longxing (Jiangxi); died 1344.
Painter.
Jie Xisi (Jie Manshi) was a Yuan dynasty scholar and poet, a member of the Hanlin Academy, known for its historic writings, and one of the *Four Leading Confucian Figures*. The only painting known by him is *Cow Standing and Facing Inside*, signed and dated 1341.
AUCTION RECORDS:
NEW YORK, 31 May 1990, *Prose Poem 'Ocean' in running script* (ink/paper, handscroll, 8 1/4 x 101 ins / 20.8 x 255.7 cm) USD 26,400.

JIEGER, D.
Painter. Figures.
D.Jieger is mentioned in *Art Prices Current*.
AUCTION RECORDS:
LONDON, 30 April 1909, *Head of a Boy*, GBP 1.

JIEJING, or Chieh-ching
Chinese, 10th century.
Active during the second half of the 10th century.
Painter (silk).
Jiejing was a Buddhist nun, to whom a Guanyin as Saviour from Perils in the Boston Museum was formerly attributed.
MUSEUMS AND GALLERIES:
BOSTON (MFA): *Guanyin* (dated 975, hanging scroll, colour on silk, formerly attributed).

JIGALOV, Anatoli
Russian, 20th century.
Born 1941, in Caraamas.
Painter.
Anatoli Jigalov lives and works in Moscow.

JIH-KUAN. See **WEN RIGUAN**

JIHEL, Elisabeth
French, 20th century.
Born 12 May 1931, in Rouen.
Painter, watercolourist, draughtsman. Landscapes.
Elisabeth Jihel followed the examples of Chardin and Cézanne, specialising in the depiction of space and light. From 1978 onwards her principal subject was Mount Ventoux. She showed work in collective exhibitions, mainly in Paris at the Salon des Indépendants, of which she became a member in 1973. Her solo exhibitions include one at the Musée Comtadin in Carpentras in 1982.
BIBLIOGRAPHY:
Présence du mont Ventoux. Elisabeth Jihel, exhibition catalogue, Bibliothèque Inguimbertine, musée Comtadin, Carpentras, 1982.

JIHUI, or Chi-hui, sobriquets: Jingsun, Xuezhou, style name: Jingsheng
Chinese, 18th century.

Born 1723; died 1799.
Painter.
Jihui was a priest and a painter. His birthplace is not known. He painted landscapes, of which one, signed and dated 1751, has been preserved.

JIJE, pseudonym of Gillain, Joseph
Belgian, 20th century.
Born 1914, in Gedinne (Wallonia); died 1980, in Paris.
Painter, draughtsman.
Jije was a student at the École des Beaux-Arts La Cambre in Brussels.
He executed numerous humorous drawings.

JILINSKY, Dimitri
Russian, 20th century.
Born 1927, in Sochi.
Active in France.
Painter.
Socialist Realism.
Dimitri Jilinsky lived and worked in Paris and was a member of the Union of Painters of the USSR. The exhibition *L'Art russe des Scythes à nos jours* (*Russian Art from the Scythians to Today*) mounted at the Grand Palais, Paris (1967) featured one of his works, *The Family*, a characteristic example of official Soviet art.

JILL, Rome
Painter. Landscapes.
Rome Jill is mentioned in *Art Prices Current*.
AUCTION RECORDS:
LONDON, 20 March 1911, *Ferry Boat*, GBP 31. LONDON, 5 July 1978, *Herding Turkeys* (oil on canvas, 31 x 19¼ ins / 79 x 49 cm) GBP 850.

JILLINA, Natalia Vladimirovna
Russian, 20th century.
Born 1933, in Leningrad (?) (now St Petersburg).
Painter.

JIMENES. See also **XIMENES**

JIMÉNEZ, Carmen
Spanish, 19th century.
Painter. Genre scenes.
Carmen Jiménez exhibited in Cádiz in 1879.

JIMÉNEZ, Eugenio, or Ximenes De Cisneros
Spanish, 18th - 19th century.
Born in Valdecracete; died 1828.
Active probably c. 1757.
Painter, miniaturist.

JIMÉNEZ, F. F., or Ximenes
Spanish, 17th century.
Painter. Still-lifes.
F.F. Jiménez is mentioned by Siret.

JIMÉNEZ, Guillermo
Spanish, 19th century.
Painter. Genre scenes.

JIMÉNEZ, José
Spanish, 19th century.
Engraver.
José Jiménez was a pupil of Vicente Castrello. He worked for various Spanish periodicals.

JIMÉNEZ, Pedro
Spanish, 15th century.
Active in Seville in 1423.
Painter.
Pedro Jiménez painted palace interiors.

JIMÉNEZ ASTORGA, Gumersindo
Spanish, 19th century.
Sculptor.
Gumersindo Jiménez Astorga first exhibited in Seville in 1858. His works include *Monument to Murillo* (1861).

JIMÉNEZ COSTA, José
Spanish, 19th century.
Painter. Genre scenes.
José Jiménez Costa first exhibited in Cádiz in 1882.

JIMENEZ DONOSO, José. See **DONOSO José Jimenez**

JIMÉNEZ HERRAIZ, Ángel
Spanish, 20th century.
Born 31 March 1900, in Madrid; died 11 February 1980.
Painter, decorative designer, illustrator. Portraits, scenes with figures.
Ángel Jiménez Herraiz spent a number of years in Paris, completing his artistic training there before settling permanently in Madrid. He was a member of the Spanish association of painters and sculptors and of the union of Spanish draughtsmen. He participated in many exhibitions in Madrid, notably the National Society of Fine Arts Autumn exhibitions, where he won a bronze medal for his project for a mural *Returning from the Hunt*. He also mounted solo exhibitions of his works.
BIBLIOGRAPHY:
Arnáiz, José Manuel/López Jiménez, Javier/Merchán Díaz, Manuel (ed.), '*Cien años de pintura en Espana y Portugal (1830-1930)*' in vol. IV, Antiqvaria, Madrid, 1990.

JIMÉNEZ LINDE, Genaro
Spanish, 19th century.
Born 19th century, in Jaén.
Painter. Genre scenes, landscapes, seascapes.
Genaro Jiménez Linde was a pupil of Ignacio Montalvo. He first exhibited in Madrid in 1878.

JIMÉNEZ NICANOR, Federico
Spanish, 19th century.
Born 19th century, in Madrid.
Painter. Genre scenes, still-lifes.
Federico Jiménez Nicanor studied at the school of fine arts in Madrid and under Francisco Jover. He first exhibited in 1881.

JIMÉNEZ PRIETO, Manuel
Spanish, 19th century.
Active in Paris.
Painter. Genre scenes.
Manuel Jiménez Prieto is known for his painting *The Guitar Lesson*.
AUCTION RECORDS:
NEW YORK, 6 and 7 April 1904, *The Violin Lesson*, USD 100. LONDON, 18 June 1980, *Transcribing Telegrams* (1886, oil on panel, 17¾ x 26 ins / 45 x 66 cm) GBP 1,600.

JIMÉNEZ SARABIA, Rafael
Spanish, 19th century.
Active in Cordova.
Sculptor.
Rafael Jiménez Sarabia first exhibited at the Madrid exhibition of 1878.

JIMÉNEZ Y ARANDA, José
Spanish, 19th - 20th century.
Born 7 February 1837, in Seville; died 6 May 1903, in Seville.
Painter (including gouache), draughtsman, illustrator.
Religious subjects, genre scenes, landscapes, landscapes with figures.
José Jiménez y Aranda, brother of Luis Jiménez y Aranda, studied at the academy of fine arts in Seville. He began exhibiting in Paris in 1864 and was awarded an honourable mention at the exhibition of the National Society of Fine Arts in Madrid in 1866. He participated in all the Spanish exhibi-

tions and also showed in London, Munich, Berlin and Chicago. He worked in Rome from 1872 to 1875, then moved to Paris, before finally settling in Seville, where he was appointed professor. He won a gold medal, first class, at the 1900 Exposition Universelle in Paris. He was a member of the Royal Academies of Madrid and Seville, the Royal Academy in London and the Berlin academy.

Jiménez y Aranda's genre scenes are often set in the 18th century and are clever imitations of that rather precious style. He was also an illustrator, producing vigorous, witty drawings for editions of *Don Quixote*, *La visión de Fray Martín* (*The Vision of Brother Martin*) by Gaspar Núñez de Arce and *Tartarin in the Alps*. He occasionally worked for French magazines including *La Revue Illustrée* (*The Illustrated Review*) and *Paris Illustrated* (*Paris Illustré*).

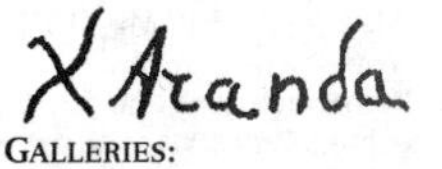

MUSEUMS AND GALLERIES:
CÁDIZ: *Goodnight* - NEW YORK: *Interior of a Spanish Barber's Shop* - NEW YORK (Public Library): *The Presentation* - PHILADELPHIA: *A Joyful Hour* - SEVILLE: *Portrait of Eduardo Cano.*
AUCTION RECORDS:
NEW YORK, 22-23 Feb 1907, *Spanish Pharmacy,* USD 1,400. NEW YORK, 15-16 April 1909, *Gossip,* USD 3,900. LONDON, 30 April 1910, *Little Grandfather,* GBP 42. NEW YORK, 13 Nov 1936, *Overloud Serenade,* USD 340. NEW YORK, 4 Nov 1971, *Baby's First Steps,* USD 2,600. MADRID, 13 Dec 1973, *The Violinist,* ESP 200,000. NEW YORK, 25 Oct 1977, *The Fiancé's Visit* (1884, oil on panel, 18 1/2 x 24 1/2 ins / 47 x 62.5 cm) USD 23,000. MADRID, 28 Oct 1980, *The Connoisseur of Engravings* (1879, oil on panel, 12 1/2 x 8 1/4 ins / 32 x 21 cm) ESP 1,000,000. LONDON, 19 June 1981, *Latest News* (1884, oil on panel, 20 3/4 x 27 1/4 ins / 53 x 69 cm) GBP 10,000. LONDON, 21 June 1983, *At the Apothecary's* (1882, oil on panel, 22 1/2 x 36 ins / 57 x 91.5 cm) GBP 20,000. NEW YORK, 30 Oct 1985, *Open in the King's Name!* (1887, oil on canvas, 38 1/4 x 63 1/4 ins / 97.3 x 160.7 cm) USD 65,000. MADRID, 15 Oct 1986, *Don Quixote* (watercolour, 12 1/4 x 9 ins / 31 x 22 cm) ESP 225,000. MADRID, 26 May 1987, *The Painter Ayxela* (1876, oil on panel, 11 x 8 1/2 ins / 27 x 21.5 cm) ESP 2,750,000. LONDON, 22 June 1988, *Hide and Seek* (1895, oil on canvas, 30 3/4 x 39 3/4 ins / 78 x 101 cm) GBP 39,600. NEW YORK, 24 Oct 1989, *The Two Painters* (1886, gouache/paper, 11 1/2 x 17 1/4 ins / 29.2 x 43.8 cm) USD 29,700. NEW YORK, 28 Feb 1990, *The Bull-ring in Seville* (1870, oil on panel, 20 1/4 x 18 ins / 51.7 x 46 cm) USD 99,000. LONDON, 19 June 1991, *Reading the Gazette 'La Esperanza'* (1870, oil on canvas, 17 1/4 x 24 1/2 ins / 44 x 62 cm) GBP 11,000. LONDON, 29 May 1992, *The Lace-Seller* (1869, oil on canvas, 22 x 28 1/4 ins / 56 x 71.7 cm) GBP 16,500. NEW YORK, 26 May 1993, *Good Friday, the Penitents* (1874, oil on canvas/synthetic resin, 20 1/4 x 30 3/4 ins / 51.4 x 78.1 cm) USD 60,250. PARIS, 8 Nov 1993, *The Arrest of Christ* (oil on canvas, 30 1/4 x 20 3/4 ins / 77 x 53 cm) FRF 38,000. NEW YORK, 19 Jan 1994, *Farmer's Wife with her Chickens* (oil on canvas, 32 x 21 1/2 ins / 81 x 54.9 cm) USD 4,600. LONDON, 17 Nov 1995, *Street leading to the Bull-ring in Málaga* (1860, oil on canvas, 24 1/2 x 32 3/4 ins / 62.2 x 83.2 cm) GBP 8,280. LONDON, 20 Oct 1998, *The Go-between* (1882, oil on panel, 18 x 22 ins / 45 x 56 cm) GBP 32,000. LONDON, 1 Dec 1999, *Pause for Reflection* (1886, oil on panel, 13 x 9 ins / 32 x 24 cm) GBP 10,000. LONDON, 6 April 2000, *Bird Fancier* (1878, oil on panel, 11 x 8 ins / 28 x 20 cm) GBP 26,000. MADRID, 20 June 2000, *Bookworms* (1879, oil on panel, 14 x 20 ins / 36 x 51 cm) ESP 24,000,000. NEW YORK, 1 May 2000, *Bookworms* (1879, oil on panel, 14 x 20 ins / 36 x 51 cm) USD 75,000. LONDON, 19 Nov 2002, *Sketches for Don Quijote* (pen and ink wash heightened with white) GBP 14,000. MADRID, 18 Dec 2002, *Lace Sellers* (1869, oil on canvas, 22 x 28 ins / 56 x 72 cm) EUR 85,000. NEW YORK, 29 Oct 2003, *Don Quixote and Sancho Panza* (oil on canvas, 22 x 17 ins / 56 x 42 cm) USD 12,000. SEVILLE, 19 May 2004, *Shepherdess* (oil on canvas, 50 x 34 ins / 126 x 86 cm) EUR 40,800.

JIMÉNEZ Y ARANDA, Luis

Spanish, 19th - 20th century.
Born 21 June 1845, in Seville; died 1928, in Pontoise (Val-d'Oise), France.
Active in France from 1875.
Painter. Genre scenes.

Luis Jiménez y Aranda, brother of José Jiménez y Aranda, studied with Eduardo Cano at the academy of fine arts in Seville. A grant from a rich patron enabled him to go to Rome, where he stayed for almost 10 years. He moved to Paris in 1875, and settled in Pontoise the following year. He won medals at the Paris Exposition Universelle in 1889 and in Munich in 1890, and received an honourable mention in Berlin in 1891. His genre paintings, such as *Village Idyll, The Tailor's Shop* and *The Fishmonger* depict scenes of Spanish life.

MUSEUMS AND GALLERIES:
COLOGNE: *The Guardroom* - DALLAS (Meadows Mus.): *Dama en la Exposición de Paris* (*Lady at the Paris Exposition*) (1889, oil on canvas) - NEW YORK (Library): *The Poet* - PHILADELPHIA: *The Music Lesson; Tavern in Spain* - PONTOISE (Mus. Tavet-Delacour): a watercolour; *Corner of the Town Park; Portraits of M. and Mme. Tavet.*
AUCTION RECORDS:
PARIS, 1868, *Mandrin's Weapon,* FRF 2,000. NEW YORK, 13-14 Feb 1900, *Music Critics,* USD 925. LONDON, 15 May 1911, *The Sculpture Gallery,* GBP 33. PARIS, 3 Feb 1919, *The Ferryman,* FRF 550. LONDON, 13 June 1973, *Resting in the Garden,* GBP 350. NEW YORK, 12 May 1978, *The Suitors* (oil on canvas, 29 1/4 x 24 1/2 ins / 74 x 62 cm) USD 8,250. PARIS, 28 Nov 1979, *Little Girl Drawing* (oil on panel, 17 3/4 x 22 ins / 45 x 55 cm) FRF 57,000. LONDON, 22 June 1983, *Figures on a Patio* (oil on canvas, 30 x 44 1/2 ins / 76 x 113 cm) GBP 15,000. NEW YORK, 28 Oct 1986, *The Audition* (oil on canvas, 18 1/2 x 30 1/2 ins / 47 x 77.4 cm) USD 27,000. LONDON, 23 Nov 1988, *Woman playing the Harp* (1886, oil on canvas, 74 3/4 x 38 ins / 190 x 96.5 cm) GBP 35,200. LONDON, 17 Feb 1989, *Little Girl Feeding the Ducks* (oil on canvas, 23 3/4 x 18 3/4 ins / 60.5 x 47.5 cm) GBP 14,300. NEW YORK, 23 May 1989, *Coming Home from Market* (1890, oil on panel, 18 x 12 1/4 ins / 46 x 30.9 cm) USD 8,250. LONDON, 21 June 1989, *Waiting for an Audience* (1880, oil on canvas, 28 3/4 x 47 ins / 73 x 118.5 cm) GBP 71,500. LONDON, 15 Feb 1990, *The Sculptor* (1882, oil on panel, 9 1/4 x 12 1/2 ins / 23.7 x 32 cm) GBP 7,700. LONDON, 19 June 1990, *Potato Pickers at Pontoise* (1895, oil on canvas, 34 1/4 x 48 1/2 ins / 87 x 123 cm) GBP 49,500. AMSTERDAM, 6 Nov 1990, *Two Women in a Meadow* (oil on canvas, 17 1/4 x 25 1/2 ins / 43.5 x 64.5 cm) NLG 17,250. LONDON, 30 Nov 1990, *Reunion with Grandmother* (oil on canvas, 30 x 46 1/4 ins / 76.2 x 117.5 cm) GBP 27,500. LE TOUQUET, 19 May 1991, *Women near the Parapet* (oil on panel, 9 x 5 ins / 22 x 13 cm) FRF 16,000. NEW YORK, 22 May 1991, *The Presbytery Garden* (1922, oil on canvas, 34 1/4 x 49 1/2 ins / 87 x 125.7 cm) USD 15,400. NEW YORK, 20 Feb 1992, *In the Poppy Field* (1895, oil on canvas, 25 x 38 3/4 ins / 63.5 x 98.4 cm) USD 159,500. PARIS, 18 March 1992, *Lady of Fashion on a Balcony* (oil on panel, 8 1/2 x 5 ins / 21.5 x 13 cm)

FRF 22,000. New York, 17 Feb 1993, *Chicken Feed* (oil on canvas, 32 x 21½ ins / 81 x 54.9 cm) USD 8,913. New York, 16 Feb 1995, *The Cradle* (oil on canvas, 32½ x 23 ins / 82.6 x 58.4 cm) USD 19, 550. London, 17 March 1995, *The Wigmaker* (1889, oil on panel, 13 x 9½ ins / 33 x 24 cm) GBP 3,220. Paris, 14 June 1995, *Potato Pickers* (oil on canvas, 23½ x 37 ins / 60 x 94 cm) FRF 75,000. New York, 23 May 1996, *Afternoon Pleasure* (1912, oil on canvas, 23½ x 33½ ins / 59.7 x 85 cm) USD 18,400. Paris, 16 March 1998, *Interior of the Church of St Médard in Paris* (1914, watercolour, 11½ x 8 ins / 29 x 20.5 cm) FRF 2,500. Madrid, 24 March 1998, *On the Bank of the Oise, Pontoise* (oil on panel, 16 x 13 ins / 41 x 33 cm) ESP 1,200,000. St Louis, 8 May 1999, *Figures Picnicking on Sunlit Path* (oil on canvas, 24 x 36 ins / 61 x 91 cm) USD 36,000. London, 28 June 1999, *Violin Audition* (1878, oil on canvas, 20 x 37 ins / 51 x 93 cm) GBP 69,000. New York, 8 March 2000, *Picking Wildflowers* (oil on panel, 17 x 12 ins / 44 x 30 cm) USD 10,000. London, 22 June 2000, *A Moment of Reflection* (1876, oil on panel, 14 x 10 ins / 36 x 26 cm) GBP 10,000. Boston, 11 May 2001, *Watched on her Way from Market* (oil on canvas, 18 x 13 ins / 46 x 32 cm) USD 8,000. San Francisco, 15 May 2002, *Young Girl with a Goat by a Field of Flowers* (1890, oil on panel, 13 x 8 ins / 33 x 20 cm) USD 6,000. London, 17 July 2002, *Goat Herd* (oil on canvas, 49 x 33 ins / 124 x 85 cm) GBP 5,500. Cologne, 15 Nov 2003, *Conversation in the Park* (1879, oil on panel, 13 x 9 ins / 32 x 24 cm) EUR 50,000. New York, 29 Oct 2003, *Dancing Lesson* (1888, oil on canvas, 29 x 39 ins / 73 x 99 cm) USD 45,000. Madrid, 14 Jan 2004, *The Painter's Study* (oil on canvas, 13 x 10 ins / 34 x 26 cm) EUR 6,000. Madrid, 26 Jan 2004, *Goat Keeper* (1890, oil on canvas, 13 x 8 ins / 33 x 20 cm) EUR 7,000.

JIMÉNEZ Y ARANDA, Manuel

Spanish, 19th century.
Born 1848, in Seville.
Painter. History painting, genre scenes.

Manuel Jiménez y Aranda was the brother of José and Luis Jiménez y Aranda. He first exhibited in 1874 and was awarded a medal in 1880 at the Cádiz exhibition.

Auction records:
London, 12 Feb 1910, *Writing the Dispatches* (1886) GBP 65.

JIMÉNEZ Y CARRA, Vicente

Spanish, 19th century.
Born 18 January 1796, in Madrid; died 9 November 1857.
Painter. History painting.

Vicente Jiménez y Carra was the son of the painter José Antonio Carra. He studied under Maella and also Vicente; he joined the Real Academia de San Fernando and in 1819 received a royal bursary to study in Rome. Jiménez y Carra was a prolific painter of historical subjects and was one of the most highly regarded Spanish artists of the first half of the 19th century.

JIMÉNEZ Y FERNANDEZ, Federico

Spanish, 19th century.
Born 1841, in Madrid.
Painter. Genre scenes, still-lifes, animals.

Federico Jiménez y Fernandez studied at the school of fine arts in Madrid and at the studio of José Gonzalez Bande. He first exhibited in 1858 at the age of 17 and received a commendation; the following year he was awarded a bronze medal. His reputation soon grew and in 1862 his painting *The Dead House*, exhibited at the Madrid exhibition, was purchased by the national museum. He also exhibited in Germany from 1871 onwards and in Paris on a number of occasions.

Museums and Galleries:
Madrid: *A 'Gargotte'*; *Fruit*; *Eagle and Scarab Beetle*; *Mother and Children*; *Two Ducks and a Fox*; *The Dead House*.

Auction records:
Versailles, 19 March 1989, *Birds of Prey* (two oils on canvas, in pairs, 26 x 21½ ins / 66 x 54.5 cm) FRF 40,000. New York, 28 May 1992, *Ducks; Cockerel and Hens* (oil on panel, a pair, each 9 x 14 ins / 22.9 x 35.6 cm) USD 8,800. New York, 22-23 July 1993, *The Connoisseurs* (oil on canvas/card, 24 x 35 ins / 61 x 88.9 cm) USD 5,463. New York, 17 Feb 1994, *Odalisques on a Terrrace* (oil on canvas, 91¾ x 11 ins / 233 x 28 cm) USD 6,325. New York, 3 June 1994, *Family of Ducks* (oil on canvas, 34 x 47 ins / 86.4 x 119.4 cm) USD 6,325. Madrid, 23 Sept 2002, *Unexpected* (oil on canvas, 16 x 30 ins / 40 x 75 cm) EUR 4,500. Madrid, 23 Sept 2002, *Good Mother* (oil on canvas, 30 x 20 ins / 75 x 52 cm) EUR 4,500. Madrid, 27 May 2003, *Unexpected* (oil on canvas, 16 x 30 ins / 40 x 75 cm) EUR 3,250. Madrid, 22 March 2004, *Hens* (oil on canvas, 28 x 38 ins / 70 x 96 cm) EUR 7,500. Madrid, 30 March 2004, *Still-life with Rabbit, Lobster and Turkeys* (oil on canvas, 44 x 30 ins / 113 x 76 cm) EUR 7,590.

JIMÉNEZ Y FERNANDEZ, José

Spanish, 19th century.
Born 1846, in Madrid; died 16 May 1873, in Madrid.
Painter. Landscapes.

José Jiménez y Fernandez was the brother of Federico Jiménez. He first exhibited in 1864 with as much success as his brother. One of his paintings was purchased for the national museum of cultural development. In 1882 the artist moved to Paris and exhibited regularly at Paris exhibitions. He was a talented landscape artist.

Museums and Galleries:
Madrid: twelve landscapes.

JIMÉNEZ Y GARCIA, Miguel

Spanish, 19th century.
Born 19th century, in Madrid.
Painter. History painting.

Miguel Jiménez y Garcia was a pupil of Bernardino Montanes. He first exhibited in 1858 at the Madrid exhibition.

Auction records:
New York, 16 June 1977, *The Crucifixion* (oil on panel, 60½ x 50¾ ins / 153.5 x 129 cm) USD 23,000.

JIMÉNEZ Y MARTÍN, Juan, erroneously known as Jiminez

Spanish, 19th - 20th century.
Born 27 May 1858, in Ávila; died 1901.
Painter. Genre scenes, local scenes (harems).
Orientalism.

Juan Jiménez y Martín studied at the Real Academia de Bellas Artes de San Fernando in Madrid, and first exhibited at the national exhibitions in Madrid in 1876. He specialised in Roman and Oriental genre scenes.

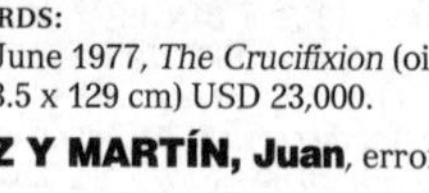

Museums and Galleries:
Madrid: *The Farewell*; *Roman Lady's Bathroom*.

Auction records:
London, 23 March 1984, *The Harem* (oil on panel, 11½ x 17 ins / 29 x 43 cm) GBP 16,000. London, 7 Oct 1987, *Choosing a Concubine* (oil on canvas, 15½ x 23 ins / 39.5 x 58.5 cm) GBP 9,500. New York, 22 May 1991, *The Sultana* (oil on canvas, 23½ x 15¾ ins / 59.7 x 40 cm) USD 7,975. New York, 19 Feb 1992, *The Sultan's Favourite* (oil on panel, 9½ x 15½ ins / 24.2 x 39.4 cm) USD 22,000. New York, 30 Oct 1992, *In the Harem* (oil on panel, 9¼ x 15½ ins / 23.8 x 39.4 cm) USD 18,700. New York, 12 Oct 1993, *The Favourite* (oil on panel, 9½ x 15½ ins / 24.2 x 39.4 cm) USD 23,000. New York, 24 May 1995, *In the Harem* (oil on canvas, 25½ x 14½ ins / 64.8

x 36.8 cm) USD 20,700. LONDON, 11 June 1997, *In the Harem* (oil on canvas, 22 x 15 1/4 ins / 56 x 39 cm) GBP 35,600.

JIMÉNEZ-BALAGUER, Laurent
Spanish, 20th century.
Born 1938, in Barcelona.
Active in France from 1957.
Painter, sculptor, mixed media.

Laurent Jiménez-Balaguer studied at the La Lonja art school in Barcelona and won a bursary to the academy of fine arts in Madrid. He lived and worked in Paris from 1957. He exhibited in solo shows in France and Spain, including the Centre for Catalan Studies in Paris in 2002.

From 1957, Jiménez-Balaguer incorporated nails, ropes, wood and pieces of fabric into his canvases, which are thickly covered in paint. He also uses these materials in his sculptures, and generally paints them, often in klein blue. Abstract without being strictly geometric, his art is built on a free construction of space, structured by a tormented graphic network. During the 1980s, he introduced wire netting into his works.

BIBLIOGRAPHY:
Jiménez-Balaguer, exhibition catalogue, Gal. Viener, Paris, 1980.

AUCTION RECORDS:
PARIS, 18 Feb 1976, *Untitled* (1959, mixed media, 57 x 44 1/2 ins / 145 x 113 cm) FRF 20,000. PARIS, 29 April 1991, *Composition* (mixed media/canvas, 45 x 57 1/2 ins / 114 x 146 cm) FRF 5,600. PARIS, 7 Oct 1991, *Fragile Parallelism* (1983, mixed media/canvas, 51 1/4 x 38 1/4 ins / 130 x 97 cm) FRF 9,000. PARIS, 21 May 1992, *Women* (1959, acrylic and sand on canvas, 45 x 57 1/2 ins / 114 x 146 cm) FRF 11,000. ZURICH, 13 Oct 1994, *Composition* (1992, mixed media, 34 3/4 x 46 ins / 88.5 x 116 cm) CHF 4,000. ZURICH, 14 Nov 1995, *Meeting Point* (1993, construction, 57 x 44 3/4 ins / 145 x 113.5 cm) CHF 3,000.

JIMENO, Agustin, or Gimeno y Bartual
Spanish, 19th century.
Born 1798, in Valencia; died 6 March 1853, in Rome.
Painter. History painting.

Agustin Jimeno studied at the Real Academia de San Carlos in Valencia.

MUSEUMS AND GALLERIES:
VALENCIA: *Judith*.

JIMENO, Eduardo, or Gimeno y Canancia
Spanish, 19th century.
Born 1838, in Madrid; died 18 August 1868, in Madrid.
Painter. History painting.

Eduardo Jimeno was the son and pupil of a painter and taught at the school of fine arts in Madrid. He was also a student at the Real Academia de San Fernando. Jimeno was an artist of considerable talent who unfortunately died young.

JIMENO, Eugenio, or Gimeno Reguier
Spanish, 19th century.
Born 19th century, in Játiva.
Painter, illustrator. Genre scenes.

Eugenio Jimeno studied at the school of fine arts in Valencia. He first exhibited in Madrid in 1876.

JIMENO, José Antonio, or Gimeno y Carrera
Spanish, 18th - 19th century.
Born 1757, in Valencia; died after 1807.
Painter, engraver.

José Antonio Jimeno was a member of the Real Academia de San Fernando. He illustrated *Don Quixote* and the *Novelas* of Cervantes.

JIMINEZ, Luis
American, 20th - 21st century.
Born 30 July 1940, in El Paso (Texas).
Sculptor, printmaker, graphic artist. Figures.

As a child, Luis Jiminez learned welding and spray-painting in his father's sign shop. He studied at the University of Texas in Austin, obtaining a BS in art and architecture in 1964, and at Ciudad University in Mexico City in 1964. He worked as an assistant to Seymour Lipton when living in New York City in 1966, where he was exposed to the Pop Art movement. He returned to the southwest USA in 1971. He is professor of sculpture and painting at the University of Texas in Houston, but lives in New Mexico.

He is best known for his fibreglass sculptures, but he also works in a variety of media, including neon and lights, coloured pencil drawings and lithographs. He is inspired by Pop Art and European baroque art, and particularly by the folk art tradition in his childhood home of El Paso, and Chicano culture and mythology. Jiminez seeks to make his sculptures an integral part of the space and society they inhabit. His colourful sculptures have a bright metal-flake epoxy finish, as in his *Southwest Pietà*, and may incorporate lighting, as in *End of The Trail (with Electric Sunset)*. Jiminez's public commissioned sculptures stand in El Paso (*Plaza de los Largatos*), Pittsburgh, Oklahoma City, Houston, Albuquerque, Fargo (*Sodbuster*) and Washington DC.

Jiminez has participated in many exhibitions, including: *Myth of the Cowboy* at the Library of Congress in Washington DC (1983); *Source and Vision* at the New Museum of Contemporary Art in New York (1983); *Automobile and Culture* at the Museum of Contemporary Art in Los Angeles (1984); *Hispanic Art in the USA* at the Houston Museum of Fine Art (1987); *Different Drummers* at the Hirshhorn Museum and Sculpture Garden in Washington DC (1988); and at the El Paso Museum of Art (2001). Solo exhibitions include those at the Contemporary Arts Museum in Houston (a retrospective, 1975); the Museum of Modern Art in New York (1983); the Dallas Museum of Art (1983); and *Luis Jimenez: Man on Fire* at the Albuquerque Museum of Art (a retrospective, 1994).

He has received numerous awards, including the Skowhegan Medal for Sculpture (1989); fellowships from the National Endowment for the Arts (1997, 1990); the Hasson Ford Purchase Award from the American Academy of the Arts and Letters in New York (1997); a Distinguished Alumnus Award from the University of Texas in Austin (1998); and the Artist of the Year Award from the Art League of Texas (1998).

BIBLIOGRAPHY:
Luis Jiminez, exhibition catalogue, Graham Gallery, New York, 1970. *Luis Jiminez: Progress 1*, exhibition catalogue, Contemporary Arts Museum, Houston, 1974. *Luis Jiminez*, exhibition catalogue, Laguna Gloria Art Museum, Austin (TX), 1983. *Luis Jiminez*, exhibition catalogue, Alternative Museum, New York, 1984. Fores-Turney, Camille, *Howl: The Artwork of Luis Jimenez*, Illustrated book, New Mexico Magazine, Santa Fe, 1997. *Luis Jiminez: Working-Class Heroes, Images from Popular Culture*, exhibition catalogue, Exhibits USA, Mid-America Arts Alliance, Kansas City, 1997.

MUSEUMS AND GALLERIES:
ALBUQUERQUE (Mus.): *North Dakota Proposal* (coloured pencil) - BUFFALO (Albright-Knox AG): *Study for Sculpture: Buffalo* (1980, coloured pencil) - EL PASO (El Paso MA): *Barfly: Statue of Liberty* (fibreglass sculpture with electric lighting) - NEW ORLÉANS (Mus.) - NEW YORK (Metropolitan Mus. of Art) - NEW YORK (Rockefeller Foundation) - ROSWELL (Mus. and Art Center) - WASHINGTON DC (Hirshhorn Mus. and Sculpture Garden): *American Dream* (1967/1990, acrylic urethane on fibreglass) - WASHINGTON DC (National Collection of Fine Art) - WASHINGTON DC (Smithsonian American AM): *Reclin-*

ing Nude (1967, coloured pencil); *Vaquero* (fibreglass sculpture).

JIN CHENG
Chinese, 20th century.
Born 1878; died 1926.
Painter. Landscapes, flowers.

In 1918 Jin Cheng helped set up the Research Society for Chinese Painting with several other renowned Beijing painters (including Zhou Zhaoxiang and Chen Shizeng) in reaction to modern and Western influences. The society had as its goal the preservation of national tradition.

BIBLIOGRAPHY:
Yang Xin and others, *Three Thousand Years of Chinese Painting*, Yale University Press, 1997.

AUCTION RECORDS:
HONG KONG, 15 Nov 1989, *Green Mountains in the South* (1926, ink and colour on paper, hanging scroll, 43 x 18 1/4 ins / 109.5 x 46.5 cm) HKD 14,300. HONG KONG, 30 March 1992, *Yellow Plum Blossom* (ink and colour on paper, hanging scroll, 59 1/4 x 16 1/4 ins / 150.6 x 41.4 cm) HKD 33,000. HONG KONG, 5 May 1994, *River Landscape in Autumn* (ink and colours on silk, hanging scroll, after Tang Yin, 12 3/4 x 129 1/4 ins / 32.3 x 328 cm) HKD 69,000. HONG KONG, 29 April 1996, *Landscapes* (ink/paper, sixteen-leaf album, copied after various masters, each 117 3/4 x 13 1/2 ins / 299.3 x 34.5 cm) HKD 28,750. HONG KONG, 2 Nov 1997, *Landscape in the Style of the Ancients* (1908, ink and colour on paper, handscroll, 14 x 107 3/4 ins / 35.5 x 274 cm) HKD 71,300. HONG KONG, 26 April 1999, *Lotus* (1917, seals, ink and colour, folding fan, 7 x 20 ins / 17 x 51 cm) HKD 15,000. HONG KONG, 26 April 1999, *Village in Snow* (1924, seal, ink and colour, hanging scroll, 43 x 20 ins / 109 x 51 cm) HKD 26,000. HONG KONG, 27 Oct 2003, *Corn and Pea* (1922, ink and colour, fan, 9 x 27 ins / 23 x 69 cm) HKD 40,000.

JIN CHENG, or Chin Ch'eng, sobriquets: Jin Shaocheng, Beilou, Ouchao, style names: Gongbei, Gongbo, also known as Qing Gongba (Ching Kung-pa)
Chinese, 20th century.
Born 1878; died 1926.
Painter.

The scion of a rich Beijing family, Jin Shaocheng was a member of the academic school and like all painters of that tradition worked in the style of the ancient masters. Jin was a member of the National Essence group, which sought a way to face the challenge posed by Western art within the tradition of Chinese painting itself, and regarded defending the tradition of Chinese painting as their inescapable responsibility. In 1918 he co-founded the Research Society of Chinese Painting. He also opened a school in Beijing where it was compulsory to copy the great works of the past.

JIN DASHOU, or Chin Ta-shou
Chinese.
Active in the 13th century.
Painter (silk).

Jin Dashou was a painter of the Song dynasty (960-1279).

MUSEUMS AND GALLERIES:
TAIPEI (National Palace Mus.): *Sixteen Arhats* (colour/silk, set of ten hanging scrolls).

JIN GAO
Chinese, 20th century.
Born 1933, in Beijing.
Painter. Figure compositions, local scenes, landscapes.

Jin Gao studied in the oil painting department of the Central Academy of Fine Arts, Beijing, from 1949 to 1952. She then moved to Inner Mongolia, where she lived until 1983, working at the National Museum and as an art editor. She was also a teacher, actively contributing to the discovery of young talent in this remote province. Since 1983, she has travelled and participated in exhibitions in the USA. She displayed her works in a solo exhibition in New York in 1989. With her inspiration coming from her daily surroundings, she has painted landscapes and other realistic works depicting the inhabitants of Mongolia and their way of life.

AUCTION RECORDS:
HONG KONG, 30 March 1992, *Haymaking with Camel Carts* (1991, oil on fabric, 22 x 28 ins / 55.9 x 71.1 cm) HKD 49,500; *Hanging Cradle* (1990, oil on fabric, 22 x 28 ins / 55.9 x 71.1 cm) HKD 82,500.

JIN GONGBEI. See **JIN CHENG**

JIN HONGGU
Chinese, 20th century.
Born 1937, in Beijing.
Painter. Flowers, animals.

Jin Honggu studied in the department of traditional painting at the Central Academy of Fine Arts and went on to teach there. Remaining faithful to tradition, he works in ink and is a talented colourist.

JIN JUNMING, or Chin Chun-ming, sobriquets: Gengan, Bumeitaoren, style names: Qiuzhang, later Xiaozhang
Chinese, 17th century.
Born 1602, in Suzhou (Jiangsu); died 1675.
Painter.

Jin Junming painted landscapes, bamboo and plum blossom. After 1644, he retired and continued to paint in solitude. Several of his works have survived, among which are: *Album of Eighteen Paintings of Plum Blossoms*, one of which is signed and dated 1662, *Landscape* in the style of Guo Xi, signed and dated 1666, *Plum Tree in Flower, Bamboos and Orchids*, signed and dated 1667, *Pine Branches*, album leaf, accompanied by a poem, signed and dated 1669, *Album of Plum Blossom*, signed and dated 1670, *Branches of a Flowering Plum Tree*, an album leaf signed and dated 1672.

MUSEUMS AND GALLERIES:
SHANGHAI: *Plum Blossoms, Bamboos and Orchids* (ink on paper, hanging scroll painted by Jin Junming, Gui Zhuang and Chen Mai).

JIN KAN, or Chin K'an, sobriquets: Lian, Litao, style name: Yitao
Chinese, 17th century.
Born in Suzhou (Jiangsu); died 1703.
Painter.

Jin Kan was the son of Jin Junming (1602-1675). He painted plum blossom in the style of his father and also landscapes in colour. Among his known works are: *Two Men Seated beneath a Pine Tree*, an album page signed and dated 1675 and *Flowering Plum Tree*, an album leaf, signed and accompanied by a poem.

JIN KUN, or Chin K'un
Chinese, 17th - 18th century.
Active during the reign of the Qing emperor Kangxi (1662-1722).
Painter.

Jin Kun was a court painter. The former Imperial collections used to contain a small *Album of twelve leaves* signed by Jin Kun illustrating various episodes in Chinese history.

JIN LIYING, or Chin Li-ying, sobriquets: Wuyun, Zhao mingge nei-shi, style name: Yunmen
Chinese, 18th century.
Born 1772, in Shanyin (Zhejiang); died 1807.
Painter. Figures, portraits, landscapes, still-lifes, flowers.

Jin Liying was the wife of the painter Wang Tan (style name Zhongqu). She lived in Qiantang (Zheijiang), where she painted Buddhist and other figures, landscapes and flowers, and plum blossom. One signed work by her is known: *Plum*

Blossoms in a Vase, Teapot and Dish of Green Shoots, a copy of a painting from the Song dynasty (960-1279).

AUCTION RECORDS:

NEW YORK, 1 June 1993, *Portrait of a Lady* (ink and colour on paper, hanging scroll, 38 3/4 x 13 3/4 ins / 98.4 x 34.9 cm) USD 2,070.

JIN LONGGUI
Chinese, 20th century.
Born 1942, in Liaoning Province.
Painter (gouache), illustrator. Figures.

Jin Longgui has diplomas in different artistic techniques, such as painting, gouache and illustration. He is an active member of the Chinese National Association of Artists and director of the Association of Artists of Jilin Province.

AUCTION RECORDS:

HONG KONG, 30 April 1996, *Little Girl Alone* (oil on canvas, 31 x 24 3/4 ins / 78.7 x 62.9 cm) HKD 34,500.

JIN NONG, or Chin Nung or Kin Nong, sobriquets: Dongxin, Guquan, Laoding, Sinong, Jijing, Jiujiang, Waishi, Sijing, etc, style name: Shoumen
Chinese, 18th century.
Born 1687, in Renhe (Zhejiang); died after 1764.
Painter, calligrapher. Figures, animals, landscapes, flowers.

Jin Nong became a painter only at the age of 50 and is the incarnation of the distinguished amateurism of the Yangzhou Baguai (Eight Eccentrics of Yangzhou). Together with Hua Yan (1682-1765) and Luo Ping (1733-1799), Jin Nong is one of the three great artists of this group, if not the most eminent. After some years travelling he settled in Yangzhou in 1748. Yangzhou was a town of traders who had become rich in the trading of salt and other produce and who voluntarily became patrons of the arts and letters and supported many scholars, poets and painters. It enjoyed a special cultural climate which allowed artists complete freedom to create.

In Jin Nong's work can be found a subtle mixture of an intentional awkwardness and genuine lack of skill which betrays the amateur but which he monitored carefully, since for a scholar the slightest technical refinement is suspect. The original clumsiness, once eliminated, would never reappear. Although he appealed to the great Song masters of 960-1279 as his authorities, it is difficult to discern their influence in the bamboo paintings, the plum blossom, horses or Buddhist figures of Jin Nong. His pictorial technique, which comes from his unorthodox and archaic calligraphy, has a rough aspect. His design is ponderous and expresses a certain insolence in the face of tradition. He has great freedom of composition, flattening his forms and arranging them according to a system of proportions which is unique to him, as are the faltering lines of construction and the settings which are as colourful as they are abundant. Jin appears to be very comfortable with his subjects, his only purpose to convey a simple message - for example, the warm atmosphere of a summer's day. He does this with boundless assurance and tranquillity.

BIBLIOGRAPHY:

Cahill, James, *Chinese Painting*, Skira, Geneva, 1960. Cahill, James, *Fantastics and Eccentrics in Chinese Painting*, Asia Society, New York, 1972. Van Der Meyden, Hans, *'Jin Nong - The Life of an Eccentric Scholar and Artist'* in *Oriental Art*, vol 31, no. 2 (Summer 1985). Yang Xin and others, *Three Thousand Years of Chinese Painting*, Yale University Press, New Haven and London, 1997. Fahr-Becker, Gabriele (ed.), *The Art of East Asia*, Könemann, Cologne, 1998 (vol 1).

MUSEUMS AND GALLERIES:

BEIJING (Palace Mus.): *Top of a Flowering Plum Tree* (1756, painted after Wang Mian when Jin Nong was 70); *Plum Blossom* (four album leaves) - HONOLULU (Academy of Arts): *Album of Figures and Landscapes* (dated 1759, 10 or 12 leaves, ink on paper, a poem by the artist on each leaf) - KYOTO (Yurinkan): *Young Monk Seated Beneath the Trees* - PARIS (Mus. National des Arts asiatiques-Guimet): *Plum Blossom* (dated 1733, ink on paper, signed with two other names, Jiujiang and Jin Jijing) - SHENYANG (Liaoning Mus.): *Narcissi* (album of flowering plants, colour on paper).

AUCTION RECORDS:

NEW YORK, 4 Dec 1989, *Verse in clerical script* (ink on paper, a pair of hanging scrolls, each 55 x 13 ins / 140 x 33 cm) USD 19,800. NEW YORK, 6 Dec 1989, *Japanese Flowering Cherry* (ink on paper, 52 1/2 x 17 1/2 ins / 133.3 x 44.7 cm) USD 66,000. NEW YORK, 31 May 1990, *Flowers, Plants and Trees* (ink on paper, 12 album leaves, each 9 3/4 x 11 1/2 ins / 24.8 x 29.2 cm) USD 203,500. NEW YORK, 26 Nov 1990, *Poems in clerical script* (ink on paper, a pair of hanging scrolls, each 66 1/4 x 17 ins / 168.2 x 43.2 cm) USD 16,500. NEW YORK, 29 May 1991, *Calligraphy in clerical script* (ink on paper, hanging scroll, 50 x 20 ins / 127.3 x 50.8 cm) USD 33,000. NEW YORK, 25 Nov 1991, *Guanyin in a Bamboo Plantation, in the Style of Li Gonglin* (ink heightened with colour on paper, hanging scroll, 44 3/4 x 18 ins / 113.7 x 45.8 cm) USD 33,000. NEW YORK, 1 June 1992, *Calligraphy in clerical script* (ink on paper, handscroll, 13 3/4 x 91 1/2 ins / 34.9 x 232.4 cm) USD 35,200. NEW YORK, 28 Nov 1994, *Calligraphy in li shu (clerical script)* (ink on silk, handscroll, 12 3/4 x 59 1/4 ins / 32.7 x 150.5 cm) USD 13,800. NEW YORK, 27 March 1996, *Calligraphy in li shu (clerical script)* (ink on silk, hanging scroll, 49 1/4 x 19 1/2 ins / 125.1 x 49.5 cm) USD 41,400. HONG KONG, 30 Oct 2000, *Plum Blossoms* (ink, hanging scroll, 56 x 12 ins / 143 x 31 cm) HKD 70,000. HONG KONG, 28 Oct 2001, *Studio of Jin and Tang Mirrors in Li Shu* (ink, 7 x 31 ins / 19 x 78 cm) HKD 48,000. HONG KONG, 25 April 2004, *Sixteen Arhats* (1759, ink and colour on silk, album of sixteen, 15 x 11 ins / 39 x 27 cm) HKD 1,400,000.

JIN SHENG, or Chin Sheng, sobriquet: Zheng Xi
Chinese, 17th century.
Born 1598, in Xiuning (Anhui); died 1645.
Painter.

Jin Sheng was not mentioned in the biographies of painters but one of his works is known: *Seated Buddha*, signed and dated 1619.

JIN SHI, or Chin Shih, sobriquets: Taishousheng, Xiumu Jushi, style name: Benqing
Chinese, 15th century.
Born in Ningbo (Zhejiang).
Active towards the middle of the 15th century.
Painter.

Jin Shi sat his triennial civil service examinations in the provincial capital in 1441 and became secretary of the Grand Council. He was a calligrapher and painter of bamboos and rocks. His known works are *Bamboos near a Rockery* signed and accompanied by a poem, and *Two Bamboos Growing near a Rock* with an inscription by the artist and another by Zhang Bangqi (1484-1544).

JIN SHI, or Chin Shih, style name: Guliang
Chinese, 17th century.
Born in Shanxi (Zhejiang).
Active during the second half of the 17th century.
Painter.

Jin Shi was a figure painter who worked in the style of Chen Hongshou (1768-1822).

MUSEUMS AND GALLERIES:

LONDON (British Mus.): *The Accomplishments* (signed).

JIN TINGBIAO, or Chin T'ing-piao, style name: Shikui
Chinese, 18th century.
Born in Wucheng (Zhejiang).
Active c. 1720-1760.
Painter.

Jin Tingbiao painted figures, flowers and portraits. It appears that while the Qing emperor Qianlong, who reigned from 1736 to 1796, was travelling in the south of China, Jin Tingbiao offered him an album of portraits of Arhats (disciples of the Buddha) in black with white outlines. The emperor was so impressed that he made Jin a court painter. He left many signed works and one dated 1761: *Guanyin*.

MUSEUMS AND GALLERIES:

TAIPEI (National Palace Mus.): *Transplanting a Peach Tree* (hanging scroll, ink and colour on paper); *Scholar's House in Autumn* (hanging scroll, ink and colour on paper).

AUCTION RECORDS:

NEW YORK, 22 Sept 1997, *Portrait of a School Master* (72½ x 38½ ins / 184 x 97.8 cm) USD 14,950.

JIN WENJIN, or Chin Wen-chin, sobriquet: Yunshi, style name: Yanhui
Chinese, 15th century.
Born in Suzhou (Jiangsu).
Active c. 1400-1450.
Painter. Flowers.

Jin Wenjin was first and foremost a bamboo painter.

MUSEUMS AND GALLERIES:

CAMBRIDGE, MA (Fogg AM, Harvard University): *Ten Thousand Bamboos* (signed and dated 1438, ink on paper, small handscroll, 14 colophons (including one by the artist) and 44 seals).

JIN YUE, or Chin Yueh, sobriquet: Yuanyu, style name: Xiaozhu
Chinese, 17th century.
Born in Kunshan (Jiangsu).
Active during the second half of the 17th century.
Painter.

Jin Yue specialised in painting flowers and landscapes. In 1667 she became the mistress of the famous poet Mao Xiang (Mao Pijiang) (1611-1693). Among her known works are: *Landscape in the Style of Mi Fei: Wooded Mountains and Leafy Trees* (hanging scroll with a colophon by Mao Xiang, dated 1675) and *Autumn Flowers and Butterfies* (with the painter Cai Han, inscribed and signed).

JIN ZHEN. See **JIN CHENG**

JIN ZHENGHUI
Chinese, 20th century.
Born 1940, in Zhejiang.
Painter. Flowers, animals.

Jin Zhenghui studied traditional painting at the Zhejiang Institute of Fine Arts and remains faithful to the tradition.

JIN ZUNNIAN, or Chin Tsun-nien, style name: Guchen
Chinese, 18th century.
Born in Shangyuan (Jiangsu).
Active towards the middle of the 18th century.
Painter.

MUSEUMS AND GALLERIES:

NEW YORK (Metropolitan Mus. of Art): *Yellow Parrot on the Branch of a Flowering Tree* (1732, signed and dated).

JINEZ, Gaspard de
Spanish, 17th century.
Active in Seville.
Sculptor, architect.

Gaspard de Jinez is on record as taking an unidentified pupil, aged 12, on 21 July 1638.

JING HAO, or Ching Hao, sobriquet: Hongguzi, style name: Haoran
Chinese, 9th - 10th century.
Born in Henan.
Active at the end of the 9th and beginning of the 10th century.
Painter.

Jing Hao (c. 855-915) was one of the most important painters of an era which itself marked a turning point in the history of Chinese painting. Virtually nothing is known about him other than that he was extremely cultured and a scholar of sophistication. In order to escape the troubles which followed the fall of the Tang dynasty (906) he took refuge in a hermitage in the Taihang Mountains where he lived in solitude, painting for pleasure. The north of China was at the time under the short-lived Liang dynasty (907-923)and did not benefit from the enlightened patronage of the Shu court in Sichuan, or the court of the later Tangs in the region of Jiangnan. Jing Hao worked in the utmost solitude and only had one direct follower, Guan Tong. The works which are attributed to him are too rare and of uncertain origin to undertake a serious stylistic analysis. The success of his work (and Guan Tong's) lies in the great maturity evident in those artists who came after him, in particular Fan Kuan (after 1025). The profound nature of his art is also encapsulated in his theoretical treatise the *Bifaji* (*Notes on Painting*) (also known as *Pi-fa Chi* or *Pi-fa Ki*). Although the copies of this short work that have come down to us are all to some extent corrupted and have given rise to much debate, there is sufficient evidence to justify attributing it to the time of Jing Hao. As P. Ryckmans points out the treatise is noteworthy on several levels. First, the philosophical views it expresses have a depth rarely equalled in China's very extensive literature on aethestics. Second, because the book is organised systematically and its contents presented in condensed form, the author can discuss each problem in turn, be it philosophical (the nature and significance of the art of painting), critical (classifications and faults), technical (observations on design) and historical (the book includes a brief history of painting in the form of a series of critical judgements of the most characteristic artists). The entire work is skilfully composed, taking the form of a conversation between a mysterious old man and a young painter, the former replying to the latter with marked authority. Even though the concepts that Jing Hao uses to establish laws of pictorial creation are not original to him but date from an earlier time, he was the first to deduce a genuine system of art criticism from them.

The ultimate goal of painting is not 'ornamental beauty' but 'truth'; not 'formal likeness', which represents only the outward appearance of things, but the truth, which grasps their profound essence. Jing Hao lists the 'six essential points' of painting, the qualities that constitute its triple essence: spiritual (spirit, harmony and thought), natural (effect of scenery), and plastic (brush and ink). He then goes on to offer a four-level classification of painters (divine, wonderful, clever, skilful), before proposing a theory of faults, of which there are two kinds, those dependent on shapes, and those independent of shapes, the former being of lesser importance than the latter, which cannot be corrected. Finally, Jing Hao gives a practical demonstration of these concepts by applying them to the works of the great masters of the past. At this point he introduces a famous distinction between painters who wield the paintbrush and not the ink and those who wield the ink and not the paintbrush. In Jing Hao's view, the ink and paintbrush are complementary: the brush conveys the 'bones' by creating the form, and the ink provides the 'flesh' by apprehending the essence of the form. Guo Ruoxo (active around 1070-1080) would take up these principles and all the other themes in his turn.

The Bifaji illustrates the new direction taken by the painting of the Five Dynasties and reflects the preference given thereafter to landscape over portraiture, to ink over colour, and to the expression of 'spirit resonance' over the old demand for formal likeness. It would remain one of the richest Chinese sources for all later theoreticians and was to become the royal route of Chinese art criticism.

BIBLIOGRAPHY:

Sakanishi, Shio, *The Spirit of the Brush: Being the Outlook of Chinese Painters on Nature, from Eastern Chin to Five Dynasties, A.D. 317-960*, John Murray, London, 1957. Cahill, James, *Chinese Painting*, Skira, Geneva, 1960. Ryckmans, Pierre, *Les `Propos sur la peinture' de Shitao. Traduction et commentaires pour servir de contribution à l'étude terminologique et esthétique des théories chinoises de la peinture*, Institut belge des hautes études chinoises, Brussels, 1970. Ryckmans, P., in *Encyclopædia Universalis* vol. IX, Paris, 1971. Yang Xin and others, *Three Thousand Years of Chinese Painting*, Yale University Press, New Haven and London, 1997. Lawton, Thomas/Lentz, Thomas W., *Beyond the Legacy: Anniversary Acquisitions for the Freer Gallery of Art and the Arthur M. Sackler Gallery*, Smithsonian Institution, Washington, 1998 (mentioned briefly in relation to an unattributed album leaf in The Freer Gallery).

MUSEUMS AND GALLERIES:

BEIJING (Palace Mus.): *Mount Kuanglu* (c. 900, title inscribed by the Song emperor Gaozong) - KANSAS CITY (Nelson-Atkins MA): *Winter Landscape* (ink and light colours on silk, signed Hongguzi, probably copied from a design) - TAIPEI (National Palace Mus.): *Mount Kuanglu* (c. 900, hanging scroll) - WASHINGTON DC (Freer Gal. of Art): *Deep Gorges in the Mountains and Travellers* (probably from the Yuan period).

JING HENGYI, or Zihan, Sichan, later Yiyuan
Chinese, 20th century.
Born 1877, in Shanyu (Zhejiang); died 1938.
Painter.

Jing Hengyi was a prominent educationalist during the Nationalist era. His most important work was Collected Works of Inscriptions, Poems, Calligraphic Works and Paintings.

JING JIANMING
Chinese, 20th century.
Born 1942, in Wujin (Jiangsu).
Painter. Landscapes.

Jing Jianming is a traditional ink painter who has developed his own personal style while remaining faithful to tradition. He works at the Jiangsu Institute of Traditional Painting.

JIRA, Josef
Czechoslovak, 20th century.
Born 1929, in Male Skale, near Turnova.
Painter, draughtsman. Local scenes.

Josef Jira studied at the academy of fine art from 1947 to 1951. His well-crafted paintings depict scenes of everyday life.

He has taken part in collective exhibitions in Moscow and London, at the 1961 Paris Biennale and the 1963 São Paulo Biennale. He has held solo exhibitions in Prague (1958 and 1965) and in Litomerice (1967).

BIBLIOGRAPHY:

Fifty years of Czechoslovak Painting from the Collections of the Galleries, 1918-1958, exhibition catalogue, Slovenska Narodna Gal., Bratislava, 1968 (in commemoration of the 50th anniversary of the Republic of Czechoslovakia).

JIRAK, Ivan
American, 20th century.
Born 5 November 1893, in Allegheny (Pennsylvania).
Painter.

Ivan Jirak was a pupil of Christian Walter. He was a member of the American Arts Federation and the Art Association of Pittsburgh. In 1922, he won a prize of 100 dollars awarded by the Art Association of Pittsburgh.

JIRANEK, Milos
Czech, 20th century.
Born 1875, in Luznice nad Vltavou; died 1911.
Painter, engraver. Genre scenes, landscapes.

Milos Jiranek studied for a time at the academy of fine art in Prague before going to Munich where he learned engraving, and then to Italy and France.

As an artist working under the influence of Impressionism, he is considered one of the inventors of modern art in Czechoslovakia. Interested, like the Impressionists, in capturing the effects of light, he sought in his painting to convey not so much the decorative aspect of a landscape or a scene from daily life as its construction.

MUSEUMS AND GALLERIES:

PRAGUE (Národní Gal.).

JIRLOW, Lennart
Swedish, 20th century.
Born 1936, in Stockholm.
Active since 1965 in France.
Painter (including gouache). Figures, scenes with figures, interiors with figures, still-lifes.

Lennart Jirlow executes interchangeable naive pictures, indistinguishable from each other. Characterising them as 'international naive' is not intended to detract from their easy charm.

MUSEUMS AND GALLERIES:

PARIS (Prints Collection): *The Gourmet* (1980, lithograph).

AUCTION RECORDS:

STOCKHOLM, 23 April 1980, *Woman Seated in an Interior* (oil on panel, 8¼ x 10¼ ins / 21 x 26 cm) SEK 9,700. STOCKHOLM, 26 Nov 1981, *Painter and Model* (oil on canvas, 44½ x 40¼ ins / 113 x 102 cm) SEK 48,000. STOCKHOLM, 27 April 1983, *Still-life with Flowers* (gouache, a pair, 8¼ x 4 ins / 21 x 10 cm and 7½ x 3¼ ins/19 x 8 cm) SEK 13,100. STOCKHOLM, 29 Nov 1983, *Gardener in His Garden* (oil on canvas, 34¼ x 45¼ ins / 87 x 115 cm) SEK 77,000. STOCKHOLM, 30 Nov 1983, *Sculptor* (1977, bronze, h. 23¼ ins / 59 cm) SEK 25,000. STOCKHOLM, 18 Nov 1984, *Still-life with Flowers* (pencil, 20¾ x 17 ins / 53 x 43 cm) SEK 15,000. STOCKHOLM, 9 Dec 1986, *Cafè Scene, Paris* (oil on canvas, 21¼ x 31½ ins / 54 x 80 cm) SEK 150,000. STOCKHOLM, 7 Dec 1987, *Couple in a Cafè* (tempera, 15¾ x 12¼ ins / 40 x 31 cm) SEK 30,000. STOCKHOLM, 22 May 1989, *Blue Door* (1975, oil on canvas, 14½ x 18 ins / 37 x 46 cm) SEK 72,000. STOCKHOLM, 5-6 Dec 1990, *Interior of a Cafè in France* (oil on canvas, 19¾ x 23½ ins / 50 x 60 cm) SEK 140,000. STOCKHOLM, 30 May 1991, *Cafè Terrace with Figures in the Evening in France* (oil on panel, 18 x 15 ins / 46 x 38 cm) SEK 35,000. STOCKHOLM, 21 May 1992, *'Le Figaro'* (1990, page of hand-coloured newspaper, 19 x 14¼ ins / 48 x 36 cm) SEK 26,000. STOCKHOLM, 10-12 May 1993, *Dance, Couple in an Interior* (gouache, 25½ x 21¼ ins / 65 x 54 cm) SEK 39,000. STOCKHOLM, 22 Nov 1999, *Model in the Studio* (oil on canvas, 26 x 32 ins / 65 x 81 cm) SEK 205,000. STOCKHOLM, 22 Nov 1999, *On the Terrace* (oil on canvas, 38 x 51 ins / 97 x 130 cm) SEK 630,000. STOCKHOLM, 7 Nov 2000, *Greenhouse in the Town* (oil on canvas, 60 x 73 ins / 152 x 185 cm) SEK 300,000. STOCKHOLM, 27 Nov 2000, *In the Wine Cellar* (oil on canvas, 21 x 25 ins / 53 x 64 cm) SEK 165,000. STOCKHOLM, 2 May 2001, *The Artist* (oil on canvas, 19 x 15 ins / 47 x 38 cm) SEK 150,000. STOCKHOLM, 27 Nov 2001, *French Bistro Interior with the Chef* (oil on canvas, 32 x 39 ins / 81 x 100 cm) SEK 205,000. STOCKHOLM, 24 April 2002, *Walking in the Park* (oil on canvas, 39 x 52 ins / 100 x 133 cm) SEK 250,000. STOCKHOLM, 24 April 2002, *French Restaurant* (oil on canvas, 26 x 36 ins / 66 x 92 cm) SEK 260,000. STOCKHOLM, 7 May 2003, *Picnic in the Country* (oil on canvas, 26 x 32 ins / 65 x 81 cm) SEK 190,000. STOCKHOLM, 4 Nov 2003, *Man with Parrots* (oil on canvas, 35 x 46 ins / 90 x

117 cm) SEK 155,000. STOCKHOLM, 26 April 2004, *Restaurant's Kitchen* (oil on canvas, 21 x 29 ins / 54 x 73 cm) SEK 265,000. STOCKHOLM, 26 April 2004, *Grand Hotel des Palmiers* (oil on canvas, 45 x 89 ins / 115 x 225 cm) SEK 460,000.

JIROUCH, Frank Louis
American, 20th century.
Born 3 March 1878, in Cleveland (Oklahoma); died 1970.
Painter, sculptor. Monuments.

Frank Louis Jirouch studied with Garber, Pearson, Landowski and Bouchard. He was a member of the National Sculpture Society of New York. He sculpted a number of memorials.

AUCTION RECORDS:
NEW YORK, 3 Dec 1996, *Draped Woman* (1930, bronze, h. 27 3/4 ins / 70.5 cm) USD 2,760.

JIRUDEK, Frantisek
Czech, 20th century.
Born 1915, in Lhota.
Painter. Allegorical subjects, local scenes, landscapes.

A student from 1935 to 1939 at the Prague academy of fine art, Frantisek Jirudek taught there from 1961.

His subjects are often drawn from the world of theatre, both on-stage and behind the scenes, and he also paints landscapes of an Expressionist type. After World War II, he painted a series of allegorical and dramatic compositions inspired by the horrific events of the period. In 1946, while in France, he visited the retrospective exhibition of *Pierre Bonnard* whose works influenced some of his, particularly in terms of a greater clarity and serenity of mood. After 1960, he returned to painting large landscapes, monumental and dramatic in expression. Frantisek Jirudek lived and worked in Prague, but has visited France, Russia, Germany, Yugoslavia and Italy.

From 1940, he took part in the exhibitions of the October Seven group. He also participated in many collective exhibitions abroad including: Naples, Paris, Brussels, Antwerp, Lucerne, Moscow and São Paulo for the 1957 Biennale. Solo exhibitions include: Prague (1943, 1947, 1959 and 1965) and Brno (1957 and 1960).

BIBLIOGRAPHY:
Fifty years of Czechoslovak Painting from the Collections of the Galleries, 1918-1958, exhibition catalogue, Slovenska Narodna Gal., Bratislava, 1968 (in commemoration of the 50th anniversary of the Republic of Czechoslovakia).

JISSÉ, Germain. See **GISSEY**

JITEKISAI. See **NAONOBU**

JITNEV, Evgeni Ivanovich
Russian, 19th century.
Born 1809; died 24 April 1860.
Painter, miniaturist, lithographer. Portraits.

JIVAGO, Semion Afanasseevich
Russian, 19th century.
Born 1812; died 27 March 1863.
Painter. History painting.

MUSEUMS AND GALLERIES:
MOSCOW (State Tretyakov Gal.): *Last Supper.*

JIVKO
Bulgarian, 20th - 21st century.
Born 14 February 1963.
Active in France from 1990.
Sculptor (bronze). Figures, animals. Groups.

Jivko first studied at the school of fine arts in Prague. In 1990, he was invited to enrol at the École des Beaux-Arts in Paris, and he moved to France. Jivko is drawn to the world of the figure, which he deals with in a Symbolist style. His subjects often stem from anthropomorphist mythology. The subject-matter is carefully interrogated, the kernel clearly and cleanly revealed, the shapes restructured into an articulation made up of small planes, full and empty spaces. He had his first solo exhibition in Prague in 1986. In 1992, he won the Association Renoir prize. He has regularly exhibited at the Paris salons, and the Fonderie Suisse awarded him its prize in 1993. He showed a series of works at the Univers du Bronze exhibition in Paris in 2002.

BIBLIOGRAPHY:
Harambourg, Lydia, *Jivko*, exhibition leaflet, Univers du bronze, Paris, 2002.

JO. See **SAN'YO**

JOACHIM, pseudonym of Serge Joachim Jean Bredeche
French, 20th century.
Born 25 April 1921, in Orléans.
Painter.

Joachim studied at the art college in Orléans and in the Othon Friesz studio in the Académie de la Grande Chaumière in Paris. He began exhibiting with the Société des Artistes de l'Orléanais in 1943, and also showed work at the Salon de l'École Française in 1942 and 1943 and at the Salon des Surindépendants in 1947. He had a solo exhibition in Orléans in 1957.

JOACHIM, Christian Hans
Danish, 19th - 20th century.
Born 30 October 1870.
Painter, potter. Portraits.

Christian Joachim was a student at the Kongelige Danske Kunstakademi in Copenhagen. From 1893 he exhibited a few portraits, including a self-portrait. He then devoted himself to ceramics and executed a series of models for the Aluminia porcelain factory in Copenhagen. He became artistic director of that factory as well as of the Royal Copenhagen porcelain factory.

JOACHIM, Ferenc
Hungarian, 20th century.
Born 21 May 1882, in Szeged.
Painter.

Ferenc Joachim studied at the Budapest academy of fine art and then in Munich and Paris. He exhibited frequently at the Salon Nemzeti in Budapest and has participated in the Salon d'Automne (1911) and the Salon des Indépendants in Paris (1913).

JOACHIM, Joseph, pseudonym Superi
French, 19th - 20th century.
Active in Paris.
Sculptor.

Joseph Joachim became a member of the Société des Artistes Français in 1906, and showed his work at the society's salon.

JOACHIMS, Jeronimus, or Joachimus, Jochmuss
Dutch, 17th century.
Painter.

AUCTION RECORDS:
COLOGNE, 26 March 1971, *Diana Resting,* DEM 5,300.

JOAN
Albanian, 16th century.
Painter, icon painter.

Joan collaborated with Nicolas Onuphre on the decoration of the church of St George in Arbanas in Bulgaria.

JOAN. See also **JOHANN, JUAN, JEAN**

JOANE
Spanish, 15th century.
Painter.

A pupil of Gonzalo Gomez, Joane is referred to by Siret.

JOANES. See also **JEAN, JOHANN, JUAN** and **JUANES**

JOANES, Juan de. See **MASIP Vicente Juan**

JOANID, Gheorghe
Romanian, 19th - 20th century.
Born 1836, in Bucharest; died 1920, in Bucharest.
Painter. Church decoration.

JOANISSE, André
French, 17th century.
Active in Blesle (Haute-Loire) in 1618.
Painter.

JOANNE
French, 16th century.
Born in Le Plessis-Donat; died 12 November 1586, in Montmirail.
Painter (glass).

JOANNES. See **JEAN de Stavelot**

JOANNIN, Georges
French, 19th century.
Born 19th century, in Lyons.
Painter.

Georges Joannin exhibited landscapes and seascapes in Lyons from 1857 and in Paris from 1861 onwards. His most notable works are: *Woodland Pool* (Béziers Museum); *Thuille Valley, Near to Morestel* and *Pond Near Crest* (Paris 1861, honourable mention); *High Tide at St Malo* (Lyons, 1876); and *Canal* (Lyons, 1870).

MUSEUMS AND GALLERIES:
BÉZIERS: *Woodland Pool.*

JOANNIS, Alexandrine
French, 19th century.
Born 1831, in Paris.
Active in Paris.
Painter.

Alexandrine Joannis was probably the daughter of Louis Alexandre, studied under Léon Cogniet. She featured at the Paris Salon from 1859 to 1883, exhibiting portraits and sometimes landscapes and genre paintings.

JOANNIS, Antonio. See **ANTONIO Joannis**

JOANNIS, Léon de
French, 19th century.
Engraver.

Léon de Joannis was a marine lieutenant and is credited with *Picturesque Countryside of Luxor* (1835).

JOANNIS, Louis Alexandre
French, 19th century.
Born in Paris.
Painter. Landscapes.

Louis Alexandre Joannis exhibited at the Paris Salon from 1808 to 1850.

BIBLIOGRAPHY:
Les Années romantiques, la peinture française de 1815 à 1850, exhibition catalogue, Musée des Beaux-Arts, Nantes, Galeries nationales du Grand Palais, Paris, 1996.

MUSEUMS AND GALLERIES:
LILLE (MBA): *Landscape.*

JOANNIS, Pauline. See **GIRARDIN Pauline**

JOANNIS, Virginie. See **MÉDARD Virginie**

JOANNON, Étienne Albert Eugène,
pseudonym Joannon-Navier
French, 19th - 20th century.
Born 24 December 1857, in Lyons.
Painter, watercolourist, pastellist. Figures, nudes, portraits, genre scenes, landscapes.

Joannon was a pupil of Danguin and Clément in the art college in Lyons, which he entered in 1873, and then in Paris of Cabanel. He began to exhibit in Lyons in 1878 and in Paris in 1884, showing portraits, figures, genre scenes and landscapes in oils, watercolours and pastels. The works shown in Paris included the 1886 *Wife of Ephraim the Levite*; the 1892 *Leaving Church*, which won him a third-class medal; in 1898, *The Fitting*; in 1902, *Tender Awakening*; 1906, *The Last Veil*; 1907, *Rolla*; and in 1910, *The Cat Turned into a Woman*. He became a member of the Société des Artistes Français in 1892, and won a bronze medal at the Exposition Universelle in 1900.

AUCTION RECORDS:
PARIS, 25-26 June 1928, *Woman at a Mirror* (life study) FRF 150. PARIS, 16 June 1955, *The Cab*, FRF 32,000. COPENHAGEN, 7 Dec 1976, *Getting Up* (1901, oil on canvas, oval, 69 1/4 x 46 ins / 176 x 117 cm) DKK 8,500. NEW YORK, 19 May 1987, *Rainy Day* (1890, oil on panel, 12 1/2 x 16 1/4 ins / 31.5 x 41 cm) USD 3,000.

JOANNOVICS, Katalin. See **IVANOVICS**

JOANNY. See **DOMER Jean Barthélemy**

JOANNY, Michel
French, 17th century.
Active in Paris in 1615.
Painter.

JOANNY-DURAND. See **DURAND Joanny**

JOANOVITCH, Paul, or Joannovics or Ivanovits or Ivanovitch or Joanovits
Serb, 19th - 20th century.
Born 16 June 1859, in Vrsac, to Serbian parents; died after 1913.
Active in Vienna.
Painter. Genre scenes, animals.

Paul Joanovitch was a pupil of C.L. Muller. He was awarded medals in Berlin in 1900 and Munich in 1905.

MUSEUMS AND GALLERIES:
MELBOURNE: *The Traitor* - MUNICH: *Study of a Head.*

AUCTION RECORDS:
LONDON, 3 April 1909, *In Pursuit of the Traitor* (1887) GBP 204; *Greek Peasant Smoking*, GBP 18. LONDON, 5 March 1910, *Tavern Interior*, GBP 57. LONDON, 23 March 1925, *The Winning Card*, GBP 110. LONDON, 29 Jan 1926, *Cockfight*, GBP 262. LONDON, 30 July 1936, *Fight with a Sword and a Dagger*, GBP 141. LONDON, 20 Feb 1976, *Peasants in an Interior* (1890, oil on canvas, 37 x 55 ins / 94 x 139.5 cm) GBP 5,500. LONDON, 20 June 1979, *Cockfight* (1902, oil on panel, 22 1/2 x 30 ins / 57 x 76 cm) GBP 5,000. LONDON, 18 March 1983, *Guard* (oil on canvas, 25 x 17 ins / 63.5 x 43 cm) GBP 6,000. ROME, 17 Oct 1985, *Return of the Victors* (oil on panel, 7 x 9 1/2 ins / 18 x 24 cm) ITL 7,000,000. LONDON, 27 Nov 1985, *Bairam Dance* (1890, oil on canvas, 38 1/2 x 58 1/4 ins / 97.5 x 148 cm) GBP 18,000. NEW YORK, 24 Oct 1989, *Serbian Bard* (1891, oil on canvas, 39 1/2 x 59 3/4 ins / 100.3 x 151.8 cm) USD 8,800. NEW YORK, 22 May 1990, *Sword Dance* (oil on canvas, 35 x 52 3/4 ins / 88.9 x 134 cm) USD 41,800. NEW YORK, 27 May 1993, *The Old, Old Story* (1894, oil on canvas, 38 x 56 1/2 ins / 96.5 x 143.5 cm) USD 60,800. LONDON, 18 March 1994, *Oriental Warrior* (oil on panel, 16 x 12 3/4 ins / 40.6 x 32.4 cm) GBP 23,000. LONDON, 20 Nov 1996, *Comely Servant* (oil on panel, 11 1/2 x 15 1/4 ins / 29 x 39 cm) GBP 16,100.

JOANS, Ted
American, 20th century.
Born 1928, in Illinois; died 2003.
Painter.

Ted Joans travelled widely in Europe and Africa. He lived in Timbuktu and then in Tangier. He held a number of solo exhibitions of his work.

The only true black Surrealist, he found out about this movement from magazines at a very early age. He was also influenced by jazz, Abstract Expressionism and the rhinoceros figure that haunts his creations. He made collages, wrote and played the trumpet, announcing the 'odious end of a world that petrifies black laughter' (Benayoum).

BIBLIOGRAPHY:

'Ted Joans: I, Black Surrealist' in *Opus international* n° 123-124, periodical, Paris, April-May 1991.

JOANSUINI, Giacomo
Italian.
Painter, engraver.

Giacomo Joansuini produced a *Presentation in the Temple* signed *Jacobue Joansuinus pictor et incisor*. See also Giovannini.

JOAÕ. See also **JUAN**

JOAO DA BELIDA. See **DOMINGUES de Campos Dias João**

JOAS, Joseph
Austrian, 19th century.
Born c. 1807, in Gais (Pustertal), South Tyrol; died 1857, in Vienna.
Sculptor.
Tyrolean School.

Joas' plaster models of a *Greek Bowman* and a *Paris*, also some reliefs of *Marshal Prince Windischgratz on Horseback* and *St George Fighting the Dragon* were bought by the Ferdinandeum museum in Innsbruck.

JOB, pseudonym of Jacques Marie Gaston Onfray de Bréville
French, 19th - 20th century.
Born 25 November 1858, in Bar-le-Duc; died 15 September 1931, in L'Aigle (Orne).
Painter, draughtsman, illustrator.

After his military service, Job worked from 1882 to 1885 under the direction of Luminais. From 1886 to 1892, he exhibited military paintings at the Salon des Artistes Français in Paris under the name of Bréville. He went on to concentrate exclusively on humorous drawings. He was made a Chevalier of the Légion d'Honneur. A witty writer and amusing draughtsman, Job is known mainly for his whimsical sketches of the French army, in which the depiction of the uniforms is extremely skilful and artistic. He illustrated numerous publications for young people and collaborated on most of the major magazines in France and abroad, including *L'Illustration, Le Monde Illustré, Le Figaro Illustré, La Caricature, St-Paul,* as well as *Pick-Me-Up* - a London publication - and *Scribners Magazine* published in New York.

BIBLIOGRAPHY:

Osterwalder, Marcus (ed.), *Dictionnaire des illustrateurs 1800-1914*, Ides et Calendes, Neuchâtel, 1989.

AUCTION RECORDS:

PARIS, 4 Dec 1918, *Napoleon I on Horseback* (pen drawing) FRF 75. PARIS, 22 May 1920, *Two Little Drummers before the Battle* (watercolour) FRF 160.

JOB, Alice
American, 20th century.
Born in Alton (Illinois).
Painter.

Alice Job was a pupil of Lefebvre, Constant and Puvis de Chavannes in Paris.

JOB, Henri. See **JOBARD Hippolyte Henri**

JOB, Ignjat
Croat, 20th century.
Born 1895, in Dubrovnik; died 1936.
Painter. Local scenes.

After studying at the Zagreb school of arts and crafts, Ignjat Job travelled in Italy. His pictures of scenes from daily life in Galicia are painted in warm tones and an Expressionist style.

MUSEUMS AND GALLERIES:

BELGRADE (Narodni Muz.): *Women Bathing*.

JOB, Matee
Spanish, 15th century.
Sculptor.

There is reference to the works of Job in the cathedral in Valencia.

JOB, Salomon Gottfried
Czech, 17th century.
Born to a family originally from Rudolfstadt.
Painter.
Bohemian School.

JOB-VERNET, Léon
French, 19th century.
Born 19th century, in Paris.
Painter.

Léon Job-Vernet exhibited portraits and genre subjects from 1849 to 1870.

MUSEUMS AND GALLERIES:

RHEIMS: *Portrait of Baron P J Nicolas Ponsardin*.

JOBARD, A. M.
Flemish School, 19th century.
Active in Brussels c. 1825.
Draughtsman, lithographer, engraver.

JOBARD, Clémence Jeanne
French, 19th century.
Born 19th century, in Précy-sous-Thyl (Côte-d'Or).
Painter (porcelain), miniaturist.

Clémence Jeanne Jobard, sister of Hippolyte, studied under Mme Cool. She exhibited portraits on porcelain, miniatures and copies - notably after Bouguereau - at the Paris Salon from 1878 to 1884.

JOBARD, Hippolyte Henri, pseudonym Henri Job
French, 19th century.
Born 1857, in Vierzon (Cher); died 5 January 1885, in Ville-d'Avray (Val-d'Oise).
Painter (including glazed earthenware), watercolourist, potter. Landscapes, animals.

Hippolyte Henri Jobard studied under Pils and Maillart. He featured at the Paris Salon from 1877 onwards, exhibiting landscapes - frequently of Parisian suburbs - watercolours and glazed earthenware.

MUSEUMS AND GALLERIES:

BOURGES: *Farmyard* - GUÉRET: *Séville, Near Crozant*.

JOBARD, J.
French.
Painter. Genre scenes.

MUSEUMS AND GALLERIES:

GRAY: *Portrait of Miss Grace; Slave Girl; Resignation; Bohemian Woman*.

AUCTION RECORDS:

PARIS, 5 Feb 1923, *Atalanta*, FRF 250.

JOBBAGY DE TUR, Miklos
Hungarian, 20th century.
Born 13 May 1882, in Budapest.
Sculptor. Busts.

Miklos Jobbagy de Tur exhibited his first sculptures in 1907 at the Glaspalast in Munich and at the International Exhibition of Fine Art in Mannheim.

His works include two bronze statues representing *Hungarian Man Harvesting* and *Hungarian Woman Harvesting*.

In 1910, he executed the monumental bust of *Archduke Joseph* for the new polytechnic in Budapest.

JOBBÉ-DUVAL, Félix Armand Marie
French, 19th century.
Born 17 July 1821, in Carhaix (Finistère); died 1889, in Paris.
Painter. Portraits, genre scenes. Murals.

Félix Armand Marie Jobbé-Duval studied under Paul Delaroche and M Gleyre from 1840 at Paris' College of Fine Arts and featured at the Paris Salon from 1841 to 1882. He was made a member of the Légion d'Honneur in 1861.

Jobbé-Duval completed a number of murals for churches and chapels, notably five of the tympans for the great nave of Paris' Church of the Trinity. His compositions, mainly reminiscent of Ingres, are often neo-classical in nature.

Museums and Galleries:
Brest: *Mysteries of Bacchus* - Chartres: *Consciousness Supports Duty* - Le Mans: *Harvest* - Lyons: *Bride at her Toilette* - Rennes: *Corinthe's Fiancée* - Rheims: *Flowers* - Rochefort: *Joseph-René Bellot.*

Auction records:
Paris, 30 Jan 1947, *Outing in the Country,* FRF 1,550. Monte Carlo, 23 Feb 1986, *Bacchanalia* (oil on canvas, 42 1/4 x 64 1/4 ins / 107 x 163.5 cm) FRF 120,000. Paris, 28 March 1988, *Working in the Fields at Sunset* (oil on panel, 13 3/4 x 22 3/4 ins / 35 x 58 cm) FRF 11,500. Paris, 29 June 1988, *Lock* (oil on canvas, 25 1/4 x 31 1/2 ins / 64 x 80 cm) FRF 12,000. Calais, 10 Dec 1989, *Washerwomen* (oil on canvas, 13 1/2 x 22 3/4 ins / 34 x 58 cm) FRF 33,000. New York, 10 Feb 1998, *On the Beach* (oil on canvas, 18 x 25 1/2 ins / 45.8 x 65 cm) USD 10,350.

JOBBÉ-DUVAL, Gaston
French, 20th century.
Painter.

Gaston Jobbé-Duval lived and worked in Paris, and showed his paintings at the Salon d'Automne, of which he became a member in 1906.

JOBBINS, William H.
British, 19th century.
Active in Nottingham.
Painter. Landscapes.

William H. Jobbins exhibited his work in London at the Royal Academy, the Suffolk Street Gallery and the New Water-Colour Society from 1872 onwards.

Museums and Galleries:
Nottingham (Castle Mus. & AG): *Fish Market in Venice.*

Auction records:
London, 20 March 1911, *Water Carrier in a Street in Venice* (1885) GBP 1. London, 12 May 1999, *The Ferry of S Maria Zobenigo, Venice* (oil on panel, 9 x 6 ins / 22 x 15 cm) GBP 1,300. London, 4 March 2004, *Time for Supper* (1883, oil on canvas, 16 x 23 ins / 41 x 58 cm) GBP 1,000.

JOBERT, Fernand
French, 20th century.
Born 9 May 1876, in Paris; died 12 November 1949, in Paris.
Painter, watercolourist, engraver. Nudes, landscapes, seascapes, still-lifes.

Fernand Jobert bought Gauguin's house near Belon and was a friend of the Pont-Aven group (Moret, Maufra, Sérusier and Jourdain). His landscapes and seascapes were inspired by scenes in France, especially Brittany, and in Algeria. His palette was similar to that of Maurice Denis, with mauve, grey and pink tones. He also made etchings.

He showed work in the principal Paris salons: 1901, Salon des Artistes Français; 1908-1911, Salon des Beaux-Arts; 1906, 1908 and 1910-1913, Salon d'Automne; 1907 and 1909-1913, Salon des Indépendants. Some of his pieces were shown at the Galerie Philippe Delarue in Paris in 1996.

JOBERT, Paul C. F.
French, 19th - 20th century.
Born 19 August 1863, in Tlemcen, Algeria; died 1942.
Painter. Seascapes.

Paul C.F. Jobert was a pupil of Bastien-Lepage, Jules Lefebvre and Benjamin Constant. A painter of the navy and vice-president of the national society of marine art, he used generous brush strokes to depict coastal scenes and storms, as well as harbours under a setting sun, given rhythmic form by judicious light effects.

He exhibited at the Salon des Artistes Français, of which he became a member in 1886, and where he won a third-class medal in 1893 and a second-class medal in 1897. He showed work at the Paris Salon from 1888 to 1914 and again from 1920 to 1924. He won an honourable mention at the Exposition Universelle in 1889 and a bronze medal in 1900. His work was very popular in the USA, where he had solo shows in New York in 1896 and 1897 and another in Philadelphia in 1897. In 1908 he was made a Chevalier of the Légion d'Honneur, and later an Officer.

Museums and Galleries:
Cherbourg: *The French Fleet on Manoeuvres* - Dieppe: *Sunset over the Atlantic; Folliers et Lamaneurs* - Honfleur: *In the Bay* - Paris (Louvre): *Fog in the Atlantic* - Philadelphia: *Fishing Boats off Dieppe* - Valenciennes: *A Good Haul* - Versailles: *Arrival of the Russian Fleet.*

Auction records:
Paris, 16 Oct 1946, *Gaud Seated at the Foot of the Cross or Island Fisherman,* FRF 4,000. New York, 2 April 1996, *The Berigny Basin, Dieppe* (oil on card, 9 1/4 x 13 ins / 23.8 x 33 cm) USD 2,530. New York, 15 June 1999, *Boats in Harbour* (oil on canvas, 15 x 18 ins / 38 x 46 cm) USD 3,500. Neuilly, 10 Dec 2000, *Fishing Boats and the Admiralty Harbour in Algiers* (oil on canvas, 24 x 29 ins / 60 x 73 cm) FRF 35,800. St Louis, 15 Sept 2001, *Harbour Scene at La Rochelle* (1918, oil on canvas, 28 x 23 ins / 71 x 58 cm) USD 3,000. New York, 2 Oct 2002, *Sailing Ship at Sea* (oil on canvas, 24 x 29 ins / 60 x 73 cm) USD 1,700. Paris, 23 Oct 2002, *Port at Philippeville* (oil on canvas, 24 x 29 ins / 60 x 74 cm) EUR 3,300. Paris, 3 June 2004, *Biskra* (oil on canvas, 28 x 35 ins / 70 x 90 cm) EUR 3,800.

JOBERT, Sophie
French, 19th century.
Born 19th century, in Paris.
Painter.

Sophie Jobert was a pupil of Léon Cogniet and exhibited genre paintings and several portraits at the Paris Salon from 1839 to 1870.

JOBERT, Yves
French, 20th century.
Born 1930, in Paris.
Sculptor, draughtsman, engraver, illustrator. Figures.

Yves Jobert studied engraving and lithography at the École des Beaux-Arts in Paris. He lives and works in Paris. Jobert's engravings and drawings show misshapen figures, without faces, executed in a complex and swirling hatching system that suggests movement, as in *Getting Lost in Venice*. He has also produced line engravings as book illustrations. Examples include Jean Pothier's *Tarots* and Ionesco's *The Colonel's Photograph.* He has exhibited at group exhibitions in Paris, including the Paris Biennale, the Salon de la Jeune Gravure Contemporaine, the Salon de Mai and the Salon des Réalités Nouvelles. In 1992, he showed in the exhibition *De Bonnard à Baselitz - Dix Ans d'enrichissements du cabinet des estampes 1978-1988* (*From Bonnard to Baselitz: A Decade of Acquisitions by the Prints Collection 1978-1988*) at the Bibliothèque Nationale. In 2001, he showed at the Fondation Taylor in Paris. He has also shown his work in solo exhibitions, notably at the Paul Ambroise Gallery in Paris.

Museums and Galleries:
Paris (BNF): *Éducation nationale* (*The State Education System*) (1979, engraving).

JOBI
Japanese.
Sculptor.
Museums and Galleries:
Bucharest (Muz. National de Arta al României): (bronze).

JOBIN, Arthur
Swiss, 20th century.
Born 1927, in Yverdon (Vaud).
Painter.
Neo-Plasticism.
Jobin was a student at the school of applied art in Lausanne and paid frequent visits to Paris. He showed his works in solo exhibitions in Lausanne in 1952 and 1954. His art developed towards the Abstract from 1949, and specifically towards Neo-Plasticism from 1953.

JOBIN, Bernard
French, 20th century.
Born 1945, in Arc-en-Senans.
Sculptor, draughtsman, engraver.
Bernard Jobin has made monumental sculptures in Lons, Besançon and Villeneuve-St-Georges, often in beaten copper. He took part in the exhibition *Formes Humaines* (*Human Forms*), at the Rodin Museum and at the Salon Comparaisons, Paris, in 1974. He also shows his work at solo exhibitions in Paris.
Museums and Galleries:
Paris (Prints Collection): *Danseuse Bleue* (*Blue Dancer*) (1981, lithograph).

JOBIN, Bernhard
Alsatian, 16th century.
Active in Strasbourg from 1562 to 1577.
Engraver (wood), print publisher, printer.
Strasbourg School.
Jobin engraved portraits, notably that of Coligny, and views of Strasbourg.

JOBLING, Robert
British, 19th - 20th century.
Born 1841; died 1923 or 1926.
Active in Newcastle.
Painter, watercolourist. Genre scenes, seascapes.
Robert Jobling exhibited in London at the Royal Academy and the Suffolk Street Gallery from 1878.
Museums and Galleries:
Sunderland: *The Mouth of the Tyne by Moonlight.*
Auction records:
London, 4 Dec 1909, *Seascape* (1881) GBP 4. London, 6 June 1984, *Setting her Course* (1922, oil on canvas, 35 1/2 x 51 1/2 ins / 90 x 131 cm) GBP 1,900. London, 13 Dec 1989, *Old Friends* (oil on canvas, 36 x 24 ins / 91.5 x 61 cm) GBP 3,520. York, 12 Nov 1991, *Women Working in an Alleyway* (watercolour, 11 x 17 3/4 ins / 28 x 45 cm) GBP 1,430. London, 3 May 1995, *Low Tide, Tyneside* (1875, oil on canvas, 16 x 26 ins / 40.5 x 66 cm) GBP 2,070. London, 5 Nov 1997, *The Vale of Rothbury* (1879, oil on canvas, 54 x 36 ins / 137 x 91.5 cm) GBP 6,900.

JOBST, Christoph
German, 16th - 17th century.
Born 1557, in Dippoldiswalde, near Dresden; died May 1630, in Dippoldiswalde.
Painter.
Dresden School.
Jobst's works include portraits produced for the court in Nassau and the design for a carpet (with the German town of Hersfeld as a background), which is now in the national library in Kassel. He also worked on the decoration of the chapel of Bückebourg castle.

JOBST, Franz
Austrian, 19th century.
Born 30 November 1840, in Hallein (near Salzburg); died 23 June 1890, in Speising (Vienna).
Painter. History painting.
Franz Jobst went to the preparatory school of the Akademie der bildenden Künste in Vienna, studying under Wurzinger and Karl Mayer there, and later F. von Schmidt.

JOBST, Heinrich
German, 19th - 20th century.
Born 6 October 1874, in Schönlind (Bavaria).
Sculptor. Busts, monuments.
Jobst was a student at the academy of fine art in Munich. He featured in exhibitions at Darmstadt, the Munich and Berlin Secessions, the exhibition in Cologne in 1907 and the international exhibition in Munich in 1909, where he was awarded a gold medal.

In Munich he executed the monumental fountains *Day, The Hour, Victor* and *Dancer*, as well as the monument to the composer J. Rheinberger. Summoned in 1906 by Grand Duke Ernst-Ludwig to Darmstadt, he created numerous works there, including: the Ernst-Ludwig Fountain, the Benecke Fountain, the Liebig Monument and the two lions in bronze in front of the national museum. He is also remembered for numerous busts, including those of *Grand Duke Ernst Ludwig of Hesse* and his wife *Leonora*.

JOBST, Heinrich
German, 19th - 20th century.
Born 6 October 1874, in Schönlind (Bavaria); died 10 February 1943, in Darmstadt.
Sculptor. Busts, medals, monuments.
Darmstadt Artists' Colony.
Heinrich Jobst did his first apprenticeship in sculpture in Munich with J. Hartmann. Following this, he trained at the academy in Munich from 1896 to 1898, then studied under Georg Wrba. From 1901, he taught sculpture at the Kunstgewerbeschule in Munich. In Munich, he created the monumental fountains: *Day, Time, Conqueror* and *Dancer*, and the commemorative monument to the composer *J. Rheinberger*. Summoned by Grand Duke Ernst Ludwig of Hesse to Darmstadt in 1906, he created numerous works there, including: the *Ernst Ludwig Fountain*, the fountain in honour of the philosopher Friedrich Eduard Beneke, the commemorative monument to *Justus Liebig*, the relief on the door of the *Marriage Tower* (Hochzeitturm), erected by Joseph Maria Olbrich to celebrate the union of the Grand Duke and his wife, and the *Two Lions* in bronze in front of the National Museum. One could also mention many busts, including those of the *Grand Duke Ernst Ludwig of Hesse* and of his wife *Eleonore*.

His work was shown at exhibitions in Darmstadt, at Secession exhibitions in Munich and Berlin, at the Cologne exhibition of 1907, and at the Munich International Exhibition in 1909, where he was awarded a Gold Medal.
Bibliography:
Umelecka Kolonie Darmstadt, 1899-1914, exhibition catalogue, Narodni Galerie, Prague, 1989.

JOBST, Johann Christoph
German, 17th century.
Born 1599, in Kassel; died 1657; buried 6 June in Kassel.
Painter.
The son of Christoph Jobst, Johann Jobst qualified as a guild master in 1640.
Museums and Galleries:
Kassel (Hessisches Landesmus.): *Portrait of Landgrave William V; Portrait of the Wife of William V.*

JOBST, Karl
Austrian, 19th century.

Born 8 September 1835; died 16 December 1907, in Vienna.
Painter. History painting.
The brother of Franz Jobst, Karl Jobst is credited with numerous paintings for churches and public monuments in Vienna.

JOBST, Melchior, or Jost or Juste
German, 16th century.
Sculptor.

JOCELIN
French, 20th century.
Painter. Figures.
Nouvelle Figuration.
Jocelin's acrylic paintings are action-based and primitive in style. He has exhibited at numerous group exhibitions in Paris: in 1983 at the Musée National d'Art Moderne and the Musée d'Art Moderne de la Ville; in 1985 at the Musée des Arts Décoratifs; and in East Berlin in 1986 at the centre for fine arts.

JOCELYN, Nathanael, or Joscelyn
American, 19th century.
Born 31 January 1796, in New Haven (Connecticut); died 31 January 1881, in New Haven.
Engraver, painter, miniaturist. Portraits.
Nathanael Jocelyn was an associate of Hartford Graphic and Bank Note Engraving Company, and founded the National Bank Note Company. In 1820 he dedicated himself to painting portraits and miniatures. Several of his works featured in the exhibition of the National Academy of Design in New York in 1826.

JOCELYN, Simeon Smith
American, 19th century.
Born 21 November 1799, in New Haven (Connecticut); died 17 August 1879, in Tarrytown (New York).
Engraver. Banknotes.
Simeon Smith Jocelyn engraved portraits after drawings by Nathanael Jocelyn in New Haven in 1824. He produced the engraved ex-libris of *Brothers in Unity* after a drawing by E. Tisdale, now held at Yale University. He was also an illustrator of books, and engraved bank notes.
MUSEUMS AND GALLERIES:
NEW HAVEN (Yale University): ex-libris.

JOCH, Leonhard Johannes
German, 19th century.
Born 1831, in Nuremberg; died 1874, in Munich.
Active in Leipzig.
Engraver (wood).
Joch engraved plates for the *Richter Album* and illustrations from Richter, Pletsch and Schnorr von Carolsfeld.

JOCH, Peter Johann
School of Alsace, 17th century.
Active in Strasbourg c. 1670.
Engraver (burin).
Joch was a pupil of Peter Aubry, his uncle.

JOCHAMS, Hyacinth
Belgian, 19th century.
Active in Brussels.
Painter. Landscapes with figures, animals.
Hyacinth Jochams showed his paintings of animals at exhibitions in Belgium and abroad: in 1875 at the Salon Triennal in Brussels; in 1877 at the Brussels *Cercle des Artistes* exhibition; in 1855 at the Universal Exhibition in Antwerp and at the Salon des Artistes Français in Paris; and in 1886 at the Namur Salon and the academy exhibition in Berlin.
AUCTION RECORDS:
LONDON, 15 June 1994, *Return from the Fields* (oil on panel, 29 1/2 x 46 ins / 75 x 116 cm) GBP 3,450. NEW YORK, 11 April 1997, *Horse Dressage* (oil on canvas, 25 x 39 1/2 ins / 63.5 x 100.3 cm) USD 24,150. CLWYD, 27 March 2001, *Cattle on a Polder with Other Cattle* (oil on canvas, 25 x 31 ins / 64 x 79 cm) GBP 3,400.

JOCHEMS, François or Frans
Belgian, 20th century.
Born 1880, in Antwerp; died 1949.
Sculptor. Animals.
François Jochems was a pupil at the Académie and Institut des Beaux-Arts in Antwerp, where his teacher was T. Vinçotte. He featured at the 1910 Exposition Universelle in Brussels.
BIBLIOGRAPHY:
Turkry, René, *Langs beelden lopen. Frans Jochems 1881-1949 [Au fil des portraits]*, Edicon, Antwerp, 1987.
MUSEUMS AND GALLERIES:
ANTWERP (Koninklijk Mus. voor Schone Kunsten).
AUCTION RECORDS:
LOKEREN, 7 Oct 1995, *Small Monkey Playing with a Frog* (bronze, h. 12 1/4 ins / 31 cm, w. 8 1/4 ins/21 cm) BEF 95,000. BRUSSELS, 6 Dec 1999, *Petit lama* (bronze, 16 x 16 ins / 41 x 41 cm) BEF 120,000. ANTWERP, 20 Oct 2003, *Art Deco Figure of a Bowman* (brown patinated bronze, h. 26 ins / 67 cm) EUR 1,900. ANTWERP, 21 Oct 2003, *Golden Pheasant* (patinated plaster, h. 18 ins / 46 cm) EUR 1,800.

JOCHI
Japanese, 12th century.
Active in the mid-12th century.
Painter.
Jochi was a Buddhist priest and painter who lived in one of the monasteries of Mount Koya. He decorated the pillars of the Daidempo-in Temple in 1147.

JOCHIMS, Raimer
German, 20th century.
Born 1935, in Kiel.
Painter.
Raimer Jochims lives and works in Frankfurt am Main.
AUCTION RECORDS:
FRANKFURT AM MAIN, 14 June 1994, *Simurgh 1* (1990, acrylic/shaped panel, 35 1/2 x 11 ins / 90 x 27 cm) DEM 5,000. COLOGNE, 12 Nov 1999, *Miniature Brown Grey* (1966, mixed media on wood, 11 x 11 ins / 28 x 28 cm) DEM 3,800. COLOGNE, 6 June 2000, *Black Light Number 8* (1966, acrylic on panel, 14 x 14 ins / 35 x 35 cm) DEM 5,000.

JOCHMUS, Harry
German, 19th - 20th century.
Born 28 April 1855, in Harburg (Bavaria); died 22 January 1915, in Lüneburg (Lower Saxony).
Painter. Portraits, genre scenes, animals.
Harry Jochmus was a student at the academy in Düsseldorf, and a pupil of W. Sohn. He travelled to Italy and, in 1886, set up in Munich, where he painted portraits.
MUSEUMS AND GALLERIES:
COLOGNE: *Outside the Village Smithy* - DÜREN: *Flood*.
AUCTION RECORDS:
NEW YORK, 25 May 1988, *At the Door of the Posting House* (oil on canvas, 44 1/4 x 55 1/4 ins / 112.2 x 140.6 cm) USD 24,200. NEW YORK, 25 Oct 1989, *Feed of Oats* (oil on canvas, 40 x 48 1/4 ins / 101.6 x 122.5 cm) USD 11,000.

JOCHMUSS, Jeronimus. See **JOACHIMS Jeronimus**

JOCHO
Japanese, 11th century.
Died 1057.

Active in Kyoto.
Sculptor.
At the end of the 9th century Japan was distancing itself from the influences of the Chinese Tang dynasty (618-906) and creating its own national art (*wa-yo*).

Tradition places the sculptor Jocho at the origin of profound changes which would transform the style of sculpture and the social status of the artist. He can be traced back to 1022 but his date of birth is unknown. He belongs to the fifth generation after the emperor Koko (885-888). His ancestors were probably governors of the central provinces. He was probably the son or the adopted son - in any case the pupil - of the sculptor Kosho (active 990-1020) from whom no works survive but who remains famous for the nine statues of Buddha in the Muryoju-in of the Hojo-ji temple in Kyoto. The first mention of the name of Jocho was also made in connection with this temple where he seems to have been Kosho's assistant.

An artist of outstanding merit, Jocho was honoured with the title of Hokkyo (bridge of law, a Buddhist ecclesiastical title conferred on sculptors) in 1022 at the time of the inauguration of the Kondo (Gold Pavilion) and Godai-do of the Hojo-ji, in recognition of his outstanding service in executing the statues for these two pavilions. He was the first sculptor to be awarded such an honour. In 1023, he was made responsible for the triad of the Buddha Yakushi (Sanskrit: Bhaisajyaguru) and the six Kannons (Sanskrit: bodhisattva Avalokitesvara) for the pavilion of Yakushi in the same temple. In 1026 he made 27 life-size statues for the greatly welcomed childbirth of Iko, wife of the emperor Ichijo. On the death of Ichijo in 1036, Jocho also created images for his funeral, such as a one-foot-high (30 cm) silver statuette of Yakushi, which was destined to become the protector icon of the emperor Go-Shujaku (1037-1045). In 1048, in recognition for his labours on the Kofuku-ji of Nara he was promoted to the rank of Hogen (eye of the law). In 1053 he executed a monumental statue of Amida Buddha (Sanskrit: Amithaba) for the Hoodo (Phoenix Pavilion) of Byodo-in of Uji, near Nara, by order of Fujiwara-no-Yorimichi. The statue is still preserved there and remains Jocho's most celebrated work.

Finally, his last sculpture, which has long since disappeared, was probably an Amida of *joruku* size (16 feet or 4.8 metres), which was made in 1054 for the private chapel of the courtesan Kunitsume-no-Ason, in the Nishino-in, Kyoto. This work of art bears witness to the genius of Jocho. It was greatly appreciated by his contemporaries and is evoked in the texts of the era: 'His face full of grace as beautiful as the full moon should be the ideal model for all Buddhist images'. This, and the work that went before, would effectively provide the canon for Japanese Buddhist sculpture for several centuries. In fact the Amida of the Phoenix Pavilion, in lacquered and gilded wood, has remained the classic example of the national style *wa-yo*. As the culmination of a centuries-old process that arrived at a point of perfect balance and synthesis, this statue marks the complete assimilation of the Chinese influences of the preceding three centuries.

The name of Jocho is linked to the birth of the style *wa-yù*, or national style, and also to a technique called *yosegi*, or 'pieced together'. In fact, the growing demand for Buddhist images following the spread of religious establishments could no longer be met by the *khiboku* (one single operation) technique, the only one practised into the tenth century. This procedure required that the head and the body at least be sculpted in a single operation or by one sculptor only. It was for this reason that workshops on *bussho* slowly developed and the practitioners of *sho busshi* were in the charge of a master sculptor *dai busshi*. Although these corporations of sculptors already existed in the time of Jocho, as did the *yosegi* technique which they practised, it was he who rationalised and organised them in such a way that several practitioners could work together. Following this technique, the different parts of the statue were worked on separately and then assembled, which demanded extensive but well-ordered collaboration in order to obtain a homegeneous result. The Amida of the Byodo-in, executed under the supervision of Jocho in his Kyoto workshop is a dazzling example of this method. This technique would prodominate well beyond the middle of the 9th century and would prepare the way for the arrival on a grand scale of sculpture in wood in the 13th century. Jocho was then the precursor of a whole line of sculptors, among them his son Kakujo (died in 1077) and his grandson Raijo (1054-1119). Notwithstanding the divisions between different tendencies (the School of the 17th Street, Schihijo Bussh, active particularly in Nara, and the School of the 3rd Street, Sanjo Bussho, which was less important, in Kyoto), they represent the main trend in sculpture until the close of the Heian period.

Bibliography:
'Pageant of Japanese Art' in vol. III Sculptures, Toto Bunka Co., Tokyo, 1954. Kidder, Jonathan Edward, *Sculptures japonaises*, Bijutsu Shuppan-Sha, Tokyo, Office du livre, Fribourg, 1961. Kuno, Takeshi, *A Guide to Japanese Sculpture*, Mayuyama, Tokyo, 1963. Mathelin, Marie, *'Jôchô'* in *Encyclopaedia Universalis* vol. IX, Paris, 1971.

JOCHUMSEN, Peter
Danish, 17th century.
Born c. 1661; died 1711; buried on 8 November.
Active in Copenhagen.
Painter.
Peter Jochumsen was probably the first teacher of Ismael Meng.

JOCHUMSEN, Peter Niels
Danish, 19th century.
Born 1 November 1795, in Copenhagen; died 2 February 1866.
Sculptor.
Peter Jochumsen was a pupil at the Kunstakademi in Copenhagen where he received silver medals in 1817 and 1820. After the death of his teacher Nicolai Dajon, he worked at Fredriksborg castle. In 1825 he exhibited the relief *The Redemption of Peter* and in 1835 the marble relief *Activity*.

JOCINO, Antonino
Italian, 17th century.
Born 17th century, in Messina.
Painter. Seascapes, landscapes.
Jocino is mentioned by Siret.

JOCK, W. See **WILSON John**

JOCQUE, Willy
Belgian, 20th century.
Born 30 September 1900, in Eeklo (Flanders); died 1 April 1960, in The Hague.
Active in France and the Netherlands.
Painter. Figures, genre scenes, landscapes, seascapes.
Willy Jocque was a student at the Académie des Beaux-Arts St-Luc in Ghent. Having spent some time in Holland, he was mainly influenced by Van Gogh.

JOCZ, Pawel
Polish, 20th century.
Born 1943.
Sculptor, draughtsman. Figures.
Pawel Jocz's preferred subject-matter is figures, which he produces with fervour, the workings of his fingers remaining visible on the finished product. In 1982, he created *The Bedouin* in tinted cement, the mouth open, a haggard look on his face. He showed in exhibitions in Stockholm in 1967, in Paris in 1968 and 1976, in Lódz museum, Poland, in 1984 and in Belgium in 1984 and 1985.

JODE, Arnold de
Flemish School, 17th century.
Born 1638, probably in Antwerp.
Engraver (line-engraving).
Arnold de Jode studied under his father, Peter de Jode. He was a master artist in Antwerp in 1658 and worked in England in 1666. He made engravings of historical subjects, portraits and landscapes.

JODE, Cornelis de
Flemish, 16th century.
Born c. 1568, probably in Antwerp; died 1600, in Mons.
Also active in Spain.
Engraver (line-engraving), geographer.
Antwerp School.
Jode entered the Guild of Antwerp in 1595.

JODE, Egide de
Flemish School, 17th century.
Painter (?).
Egide de Jode, a free master in 1653, is mentioned by Siret.

JODE, Gerhard de
Flemish, 16th century.
Born 1509, in Nijmegen; died 5 February 1591, in Nijmegen.
Engraver.
Antwerp School.
According to certain biographers, Jode was born in Antwerp, but more recent accounts of his life have claimed his birthplace to be Nijmegen. Gerhard de Jode was the first in a long line of artists and seems to have been a wealthy man. He was both an artist and a trader in prints, and engraved religious subjects and portraits in the style of Cornelis Cort. His works are dated between 1565 and 1585, and include, notably, a series of 29 portraits of popes bearing the date 1585. He became a member of the *Liggeren* artist's guild in 1547. Records of membership of the *Liggeren* in 1568 include a certain Gerardus de Jode Neomagensis. This could be a reference to this artist, although Dr von Wurzbach believes that it could be his son, who shared his father's name.

JODE, Hans de
Flemish School, 17th century.
Born c. 1630, in The Hague; died after 1662, in The Hague.
Painter. Landscapes.
Hans de Jode married on 8 January 1662 in Vienna. In around 1659, he worked in The Hague, Constantinople and then Vienna.
MUSEUMS AND GALLERIES:
FRANKFURT AM MAIN (Städel): *Southern Landscape.*
AUCTION RECORDS:
NEW YORK, 23 Feb 1968, *River Landscape,* USD 1,000. VIENNA, 1 Dec 1970, *Landscape with Bridge,* ATS 50,000. VIENNA, 20 March 1973, *The Sultan's Palace on the Golden Horn,* ATS 90,000. VIENNA, 14 June 1977, *Hilly Landscape* (oil on canvas, 18 1/4 x 23 ins / 46.5 x 58.5 cm) ATS 35,000. COLOGNE, 9 May 1983, *Turkish Encampment* (oil on canvas, 33 3/4 x 44 1/2 ins / 86 x 113 cm) DEM 11,000. VIENNA, 29-30 Oct 1996, *Italian River Landscape with Figures Going towards a Villa* (oil on canvas, 14 x 19 1/4 ins / 35.5 x 49 cm) ATS 80,500. LONDON, 3-4 Dec 1997, *Italian River Landscape at Sunset with Figures on a Road* (oil on canvas, 42 x 61 1/2 ins / 106.5 x 156 cm) GBP 12,650. AMSTERDAM, 12 March 2002, *Italianate Landscape with Peasants and Fishermen, Evening* (oil on canvas, 37 x 56 ins / 95 x 142 cm) EUR 4,000.

JODE, Paul de
Flemish School, 17th century.
Painter, engraver.
He is mentioned by Siret.

JODE, Peeter I de, or Iode or Oude
Belgian, 16th - 17th century.
Born c. 1570, in Antwerp; died 9 August 1634, in Antwerp.
Draughtsman, engraver. Historical subjects, religious subjects, portraits, local scenes (carnival).
Jode probably studied under H. Goltzius. He became a member of the guild of Antwerp in 1600, and was made a dean of the guild in 1608. He worked in Italy and Paris and was the brother-in-law of Jan 'Velvet' Bruegel.

MUSEUMS AND GALLERIES:
LONDON (National Portrait Gal.): engravings.
AUCTION RECORDS:
LONDON, 18 June 1982, *Carnival Scene in Venice* (engraving/copper, after Pozzoserrato, 14 1/2 x 19 3/4 ins / 37.1 x 50.2 cm) GBP 880. LONDON, 3 July 1989, *Roman Victory* (ink and brown and blue wash/black chalk, 7 1/2 x 9 1/4 ins / 19.3 x 23.4 cm) GBP 4,400. NEW YORK, 15 Jan 1992, *Eli Riding her Chariot of Fire and the River of Jordan Opening before Elisha* (black chalk, ink and wash, 8 x 11 ins / 19.4 x 28.2 cm) USD 5,280. AMSTERDAM, 11 Nov 1997, *Parable of the Rich Man* (pen, brown ink and wax heightened with white, 7 3/4 x 10 ins / 19.8 x 25.7 cm) NLG 10,856. AMSTERDAM, 6 Nov 2001, *Judgement of Paris* (pen and ink wash heightened with white chalk) NLG 45,000.

JODE, Peeter II de, or de Jonghe
Flemish School, 17th century.
Born 22 November 1606, in Antwerp; died after 1674.
Engraver.
The son and pupil of Peeter de Jode I, in 1628 he was registered as a member of the Antwerp guild. In 1632 he worked in Paris, and in 1641 he had Mathias Borekens as his pupil. He married twice. There are two drawings by him in the Musée Royal in Brussels.

JODE, Peeter III de
Dutch, 17th century.
Born 1648.
Active in Amsterdam in 1667.
Engraver (line-engraving).

JODEIKO, Leonid Florianovich
Russian, 19th century.
Born 1826; died 20 November 1878.
Painter. Figures, portraits, perspectives.
MUSEUMS AND GALLERIES:
MOSCOW (State Tretyakov Gal.): *Head of a Woman.*

JODELET, Emmanuel Charles
French, 20th century.
Born 24 December 1883, in Augerans (Jura); died 3 January 1973, in Paris, in 1969 according to Le Mayer.
Painter, draughtsman, illustrator, watercolourist.
Scenes with figures, portraits, figures, landscapes, flowers, fruit.
Emmanuel Charles Jodelet studied under Bernard Naudin at the Académie Colarossi in Paris and also under Charles Guérin. He worked initially as a lithographer, drawing only in his spare time. Then, in the tradition of Degas, he painted graceful dancers in the wings and greenroom of the Opéra. These are suggestive of movement and 'seek to show subtle and delicate harmonies'. He exhibited in Paris at the Salon d'Automne, of which he became a member, at the Société Nationale des Beaux-Arts and at the Salon des Tuileries, as well as in the provinces in Strasbourg, Mulhouse, Nantes,

Lille and Besançon. In 1918, he showed his work in a solo exhibition for the first time at the Galerie Georges Petit.

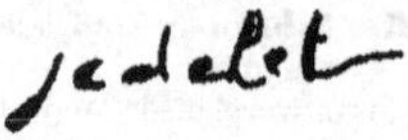

MUSEUMS AND GALLERIES:
BESANÇON - CHICAGO - DÔLE - LE HAVRE - NEW YORK - PARIS (Hôtel de Ville) - PARIS (Mus. de l'Armée) - ST LOUIS - ST-ÉTIENNE - STRASBOURG.
AUCTION RECORDS:
PARIS, 29 June 1927, *In Rossignolet Wood* (drawing) FRF 900. PARIS, 29 April 1933, *Rats*, FRF 720. PARIS, 22 Feb 1936, *Young Woman in Bed Reading*, FRF 220. PARIS, 20 March 1944, *The Mistletoe Seller* (1927, watercolour) FRF 480. PARIS, 25 June 1945, *Little Rats*, FRF 10,000. PARIS, 9 Dec 1985, *Dancer at the Barre* (1921, charcoal, 18 x 17 ins / 46 x 43 cm) FRF 13,000. PARIS, 9 Dec 1985, *Dancers in the Wings* (1937, oil on canvas, 44 x 56 3/4 ins / 112 x 144 cm) FRF 25,000. PARIS, 7 Nov 1988, *Reading by a River* (oil on canvas, 13 x 16 1/4 ins / 33 x 41 cm) FRF 3,800. RHEIMS, 11 June 1989, *By the River* (oil on canvas, 16 1/4 x 13 ins / 41 x 33 cm) FRF 9,000. AMSTERDAM, 19 Oct 1993, *The Guitar Lesson* (oil on canvas, 18 1/4 x 21 3/4 ins / 46.5 x 55.5 cm) NLG 4,600.

JODELET DE LA BOISSIERE. See **LA BOISSIÈRE Gilles Jodelet de**

JODIN, Anne Charlotte
French, 19th century.
Painter.
Anne Charlotte Jodin exhibited the following at the 1844 Paris Salon: *Anne Boleyn Being Embraced by her Daughter Elizabeth on the Day Before her Execution; Young Girl; Portrait of a Woman; Portrait of Doctor Thierry-Valdajou;* and *Young Spaniard* (pastel study).

JODL, Ferdinand
German, 19th century.
Born 1805, in Munich; died 1882, in Munich.
Painter, architect. Architectural views.
Bavarian School.
Jodl trained at the academy in Munich. Probably he is the same artist as the one mentioned by Siret under the name of F. Judl.
MUSEUMS AND GALLERIES:
MUNICH: *Hohenschwangau Castle; Auer Church in Munich; Inn near Munich; The Old Ministry of War in Munich.*

JODOCUS VON GENT. See **JUSTE de Gand**

JODOCY, Hubert
German, 20th century.
Born 1943, in Frankfurt am Main.
Active in Belgium, also active in France.
Painter.
Hubert Jodocy studied at the art academy in St Joost-ten-Node, where he was taught by J. Maes. His work was first Expressionist, then abstract, before he returned to figurative painting with symbolist tendencies.

JODOIGNE, Gilles de, or Jourdogne
French, 14th century.
Active in Cambrai.
Sculptor.
Jodoigne worked on the decoration of the Château d'Escaudoeuvres, near Cambrai, in 1356 and 1357.

JOE-DESCOMPS. See **CORMIER Joseph J. Emmanuel**

JOEDEN, Frieda Blanca von
German, 20th century.
Born 23 April 1878.
Active in Frankfurt am Main.
Painter, engraver. Flowers.
Frieda Blanca von Joeden featured in exhibitions at Darmstadt and Munich, and was awarded a medal by the City of Leipzig in 1913. Her original works include: *Bridge over the Rhine* and *Haywain*.

JOEL, Robert
Swiss, 20th century.
Born 31 October 1894, in Lausanne; died 2 February 1974.
Active in France.
Painter, engraver, illustrator.
Robert Joel was a pupil of Laverrière and of Héraud, both architects. He illustrated texts by Charles Maurras, Kessel, Simenon and Marguerite Audoux.

JOEN, real name: Okamato, given name: Rozen, priest name: Joen, artist names: Gengenshi, Gengen'o
Japanese, 17th century.
Born 1628, in Osaka; died 1673.
Painter.
Joen lived in Kyoto and painted flowers and birds as well as figures in the style of Shojo (1584-1639).

JOER, Pieter
Dutch, 18th century.
Active in Amsterdam c. 1730-1788.
Engraver.
Studied under B. Picart.

JOERBRANDT, Adriaen
Flemish School.
Active in Bruges.
Painter.
MUSEUMS AND GALLERIES:
BERGAMO (Accademia Carrara): *The Virgin and the Infant Jesus.*

JOERDENS, Gerhard Anton
German, 19th century.
Born 9 March or 29 May 1828, in Muskau (Silesia, now Saxony-Anhalt).
Painter, draughtsman, engraver.
Gerhard Joerdens worked in Dresden. The Prints Room there has a drawn portrait of the actress Sophie Albrecht by him. He did engravings on wood from L. Richter and J. Schnorr von Carolsfeld.

JOERDENS, J. G.
German, 18th century.
Active in Nuremberg.
Draughtsman.
J. G. Joerdens did sketches for engraved frontispieces in two works by G. A. Will: *History and Description of the University of Altdorf* (1795) and *History and Description of the Landscape of Altdorf, Nuremberg* (1796).

JOERG. See **JORG** and **JORGEN**

JOERGENSEN. See also **JORGENSEN**

JOERGER, Johann Septimes von (Count)
German, 17th century.
Born 1594; died 1662, in Nuremberg.
Draughtsman, engraver (etching).
Count von Joerger engraved his portrait and landscapes.

JOES, Arnoldus Gérardi
Flemish School, 17th century.
Painter. History painting.
Mentioned by Marolles and Siret.

JOEST, Jan. See **JOOST Jan**

JOËTS, Jules Arthur
French, 20th century.
Born 1 September 1884, in St-Omer; died 1959.

Painter, watercolourist. Figure compositions, portraits. After completing his education, Jules Arthur Joëts studied at evening classes run by the fine arts academy in St-Omer, and was then accepted as a student at the École des Arts Décoratifs in Paris. He travelled in England, Belgium, Holland and Italy. Joëts was a conscientous and skilful painter, and his work is striking for its strength of vision and touch. A friend of Paul Fort and Georges Rouault, he was influenced by them in his use of light and materials and in his spiritual intent. He also produced light-handed, spontaneous watercolours. Joëts showed his work at the Salon des Artistes Français in Paris, where he received a silver medal, the Bashkirtseff prize in 1913, a travel bursary, the Prix National and a gold medal in 1914. In 1923, again in Paris, he joined the Salon des Indépendants and soon became a committee member. He was selected by the Académie des Beaux-Arts as a jury member for the Prix de Rome and was also a jury member of the Exposition Internationale in Parais in 1937.

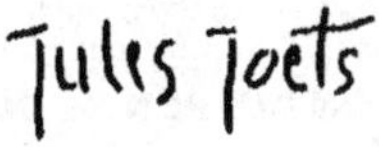

Museums and Galleries:
Arras: *Still-life* - Douai: *Landscape* - Glasgow: *Portrait of Field Marshal Douglas Haig* - Lille: *Portrait of Georges Rouault* - Paris (MAM): *Portrait of Georges Rouault; The Hare; Flowers* - Pau: *Hommage to the Le Nains* - Roubaix: *Landscape* - St-Omer: *The Burial; The Orchestra* - Valenciennes: *Grace*.
Auction records:
Paris, 27 Dec 1926, *Celebration at Roubaix* (watercolour) FRF 220. Paris, 24 Feb 1936, *Still-life with Blue Pot and Fruit*, FRF 150. Paris, 11 May 1942, *Les enfants de Marie* FRF 1,400. Paris, 14 May 1943, *Landscape at Bray-Dunes* (1939, watercolour) FRF 4,100. Paris, 28 June 1968, *Pont Royal*, FRF 11,000. Versailles, 5 Dec 1971, *Barns Concealed by Bushes at Tilques*, FRF 5,000. Versailles, 13 June 1972, *Landscape at Tilques*, FRF 7,600. Paris, 13 June 1974, *Yellow Farm at Tilques*, FRF 7,000. Paris, 15 Dec 1976, *In the Marshes at Tilques* (oil on canvas, 23 1/2 x 31 1/2 ins / 60 x 80 cm) FRF 10,500. Zurich, 23 Nov 1977, *Day's End at Tilque* (oil on canvas, 25 1/2 x 32 ins / 65 x 81 cm) CHF 9,000. Paris, 24 June 1988, *Lelatre Farm* (oil on canvas, 28 3/4 x 36 1/4 ins / 73 x 92 cm) FRF 32,000. Paris, 21 Nov 1989, *Young Girl in a White Dress* (oil on canvas, 25 1/2 x 21 1/4 ins / 65 x 54 cm) FRF 12,500. Paris, 27 April 1990, *Teacup* (oil on canvas, 29 1/2 x 23 1/2 ins / 75 x 60 cm) FRF 42,500. Chaumont, 7 April 1991, *Pont-Neuf, Paris* (oil on canvas, 25 1/2 x 32 ins / 65 x 81 cm) FRF 38,500. St-Jean-Cap-Ferrat, 16 March 1993, *Pont Royal, Paris* (oil on canvas, 25 1/2 x 32 ins / 65 x 81 cm) FRF 14,000. Paris, 30 June 1995, *Kitchen Corner* (oil on canvas, 29 1/4 x 36 1/4 ins / 74 x 92 cm) FRF 6,500. Paris, 7 June 2002, *Provincial Concert Audience* (oil on canvas, 95 x 98 ins / 242 x 250 cm) EUR 30,000.

JOFFRE, Félix
French, 20th century.
Born 26 March 1903, in Marcille-la-Ville (Mayenne); died 1982.
Sculptor.

Félix Joffre studied under Jean Boucher. He received the Grand Prix de Rome in 1929 for *Summer*.

JOFFRIN, Guily, also called Guily-Joffrin
French, 20th century.
Born 30 July 1909, in Paris.
Painter, watercolourist, illustrator. Designs for stained glass.

Guily Joffrin studied at the Lucine Simon studio at the École des Beaux-Arts in Paris and was a fellow student of Humblot, Rohner, Fontanarosa and Despierre. At the same time, she studied to become a drawing teacher, and from 1939 to 1945 she taught at the Lycée in Aurillac. When she returned to Paris she concentrated exclusively on her own art. She exhibited regularly at and became a member of the Salon d'Automne, the Salon of the Société Nationale des Beaux-Arts (where she received several prizes), the Salon des Indépendants and the Salon du Dessin et de la Peinture à l'Eau. She also exhibited at the Salon Comparaisons and from 1961 at the Salon des Peintres Témoins de leur Temps. Joffrin exhibited at regional salons and group exhibitions abroad, including in London, New York, Los Angeles and Philadelphia. She received various awards, including the Prix Chenavard; a travel bursary awarded by the Ville de Paris; a gold medal at the Salon de Montrouge; and a prize at the Salon d'Asnières. She also showed collections of her work at some 30 solo exhibitions in France, Switzerland, the USA and Japan. Joffrin illustrated literary works by Francis James, Pierre Louÿs, Daphne du Maurier, Gilbert Cesbron and Henri Troyat. She also designed stained glass windows for churches in Brittany.
Museums and Galleries:
Paris (Prints Collection): *Solange* (1979, lithograph).

JOFFRIN, Pierre
School of Lorraine, 18th century.
Active in Nancy c. 1728.
Sculptor.

JOFFROY. See also **GEOFFROY**

JOFFROY, Henri
French, 19th century.
Born 19th century, in Paris.
Engraver (wood).

Henri Joffroy studied under Yon and Perrichon. He was a member of the Société des Artistes Français from 1889 and featured at that society's Salon.

JOFFROY, Jean Barthélemy
Flemish School, 17th century.
Born 27 June 1669, in Mechelen; died 1740; buried the 13 March in Mechelen.
Painter, engraver, writer.

Jean Joffroy was more an art enthusiast and scholar than an artist in the true sense of the term. He began to paint at around the age of 40 and mainly made copies of nudes and carried out restorations. In 1721 he published a book on Mechelen.

JOFFROY, Marc
French, 20th century.
Born 28 June 1925, in Rheims.
Sculptor. Monuments.

Marc Joffroy lives and works in Aix-en-Provence. In Paris, he exhibited at the Salon de la Jeune Sculpture and the Salon des Indépendants and received various awards, particularly in the Mediterranean region. His sculptures are abstract and through the purity of his forms and soaring lines he instills them with a certain symbolism. Joffroy executed monuments at various sites, including the church in Tallard, Châtel-Guyon, the Palais des Congrès in Marseilles and the Palais des Congrès in Aix-en-Provence.

JOGA
Japanese, 13th century.
Died 1295.
Active before 1295.
Painter.

Joga was a priest at the Koraku-ji Temple in Shinano (Nagano district) who specialised in painting Buddhist themes. The scroll *Biography of the Priest Shinran* is attributed to him.

JOGEN, real name: Araki Jogen, original name: Ichinose, nicknames: Zenjuro, Zenjito
Japanese, 18th - 19th century.
Born 1765, in Nagasaki (Fukuoka); died 1824, in Nagasaki (Fukuoka).
Painter.

Jogen was a disciple of his father-in-law, the painter Genyu (1733-1799). He painted in Western style subjects in oils and was also known as a prolific collector.

JOGUES, Jean Louis Laurent
French, 19th century.
Born 23 June 1818, in Bourg (Ain).
Painter.

Jean Louis Laurent Jogues began at Marseilles' College of Fine Art in 1836 and studied under Grobon and Bonnefond. He then moved to Lyons and studied under St Jean. He exhibited watercolour and pencil landscapes at the Lyons Salon from 1857 to 1873 and became professor of art at Lyons.

JOHAN. See also **JAN, JOHANNES, JUAN, JEAN, HANS, HANUS**

JOHANN, also known as Hans von Trarbach or Drorbach
German, 16th century.
Born 1530; died 15 November 1586, in Simmern (Rheinland).
Sculptor.

Johann produced a large number of funerary monuments in the German towns of Simmern, Erbach, Hanau, Öhringen, Baden-Baden, Meisenheim and Pforzheim.

JOHANN. See also **HANS, ANS, HANSE, HANUS, JOHANNES, JAN, JEAN, GIOVANNI, JOAO, JOHN, JUÄN**

JOHANN, Hans
German, 16th century.
Died between 1544 and 1550, in Dresden.
Active in Dresden.
Painter.

A series of ten paintings by Hans Johann of the *Ten Commandments* are owned by the municipal museum in Dresden. He also produced paintings for the church of das Kreuze in Dresden in 1531 and 1532, and painted the vault of the church in 1543 and 1544.

JOHANN, Hermann
German, 19th century.
Born 1821, in Berlin; died 1884, in Bad Landeck (Ladek Zdroj), Silesia.
Draughtsman. Landscapes.

MUSEUMS AND GALLERIES:
BERLIN (Nationalgal.): drawings.

JOHANN DE CUMIS
German.
Miniaturist.

Johann de Cumis painted the miniatures in the Duchess Blanca's *Book of Prayers* now kept in Munich library.

MUSEUMS AND GALLERIES:
MUNICH (Bayerische Staatsbibliothek).

JOHANN DE MUNICH. See **JAN, called Meister Johann de Munich**

JOHANN DE SABAC, or Sabatiis or Sabaria
Bavarian, 15th century.
Active in Eichstätt.
Sculptor.

The historical society museum in Eichstätt owns a commemorative monument of *Sophie von Hirschberg*, with a red marble plaque, produced by Johann de Sabac.

JOHANN GEORG II OF SAXONY (Great Elector)
German, 17th century.
Born 31 May 1613; died 22 August 1680, in Freiberg (Saxony).
Sculptor (ivory).

MUSEUMS AND GALLERIES:
DRESDEN (Historisches Mus.): *Allegory of the Past* (ivory); *Scenes from the Legend of Actæon* (trunk in ivory).

JOHANN VON BRÜGGE. See **JEAN de Bondolf**

JOHANN VON DER LYNEN
Livonian, 16th century.
Died before 15 September 1522.
Painter.
Baltic School.

In 1466-1467, Johann von der Lynen painted a *Virgin* on the outer wall of the town hall in Riga, and in 1470-1471, a decoration for the church of St Peter in the same city.

JOHANN VON DUYREN. See **DÜREN Johann von**

JOHANN VON ESSEN. See **LADENSPELDER Johann**

JOHANN VON FREIBURG. See **JEHAN le Peintre** and **GEILER Hans**

JOHANN VON KAADEN, or Hans von Kaaden, also known as Franck or Rörich
German, 16th century.
Painter.

Johann von Kaaden worked in Annaberg, Silesia, from 1515 to 1524, where he painted 100 reliefs on panels in the gallery of the church of St Anne.

JOHANN VON KÖLN, or Hans von Köln
German, 16th century.
Painter.

Johann von Köln lived in Chemnitz from 1501 to 1503, and then in Annaberg, and is thought to be the Hans von Clalent who is mentioned in the Annaberg town chronicles. He produced a *Virgin*, painted on copper, in the former vestry of the church at Annaberg. He also produced the altarpieces of the church at Einsiedel, near Chemnitz, in about 1515, and eight pictures for the altar of the church at Ehrenfriedersdorf.

JOHANN VON SOEST
German, 15th century.
Painter.

Johann von Soest produced mural paintings for the old cathedral in Münster in 1485 and 1486.

JOHANN VON TROPPAU, also known as Johannes de Oppavia
Moravian, 14th century.
Calligrapher, miniaturist.

The national library in Vienna has a *Gospel* written by Johann von Troppau in gold lettering on parchment for Duke Albert of Austria. He was a priest in Landskron (Lanskroun) and a canon in Brno.

JOHANNES. See the entry **ANGELUS**

JOHANNES, erroneously known as Eposius
Italian, 11th century.
Calligrapher, illuminator.

According to D'Agincourt, Johannes was a priest who wrote and illuminated an *Exultet*, a missal in two volumes in the possession of the Barberini Library, Rome. We know that he was a priest from an inscription on the side of the second volume. *Exultet*, the name of the work, is the first word of the hymn. Doubts have been raised about whether such a person ever existed.

JOHANNES
13th century.
Born to a family originally from Constantinople.
Painter. Religious subjects.
Johannes worked in Italy. There is an *Adoration* signed by him in the Vatican Museum.
MUSEUMS AND GALLERIES:
VATICAN (Mus. Vaticani): *Adoration*.

JOHANNES
German, 13th - 14th century.
Illuminator.
The name of Johannes, and that of his wife, Hilda, appear in the *Cölner Schreinbücher*, dated 1301.

JOHANNES
French (?), 14th century.
Illuminator.
Johannes produced illuminations in Paris commissioned by John the Good.

JOHANNES, called Jan von Prag, known as Aliapers or Aliaps
Czech, 15th century.
Miniaturist, illustrator, calligrapher.
Bohemian School.
The national library in Vienna has a Bible, copied and illuminated by Johannes between 1432 and 1435 for the governor of Ostromec, Philipp von Paderow.

JOHANNES. See also **JEAN, JOHANNES**

JOHANNES
9th century.
Calligrapher, illuminator.
Johannes wrote and illuminated a work called *Gregori Moraha, libre 28-35*, now in Monte Cassino.

JOHANNES, Godefridus
16th century.
Active probably c. 1585 in the Netherlands.
Painter.

JOHANNES ALAMANUS. See **GIOVANNI d'Alamagna**

JOHANNES AQUILA. See **AQUILA Johannes**

JOHANNES DE ALIGHERIO. See **ALIGHIERI Giovanni**

JOHANNES DE CASTRO
German, 15th century.
Sculptor. Religious subjects, figures.
MUSEUMS AND GALLERIES:
HANOVER (Niedersächsisches Landesmus.): *Baptismal Fonts* (1490, with sculpted figures).

JOHANNES DE LAYBACE, or Laybach
15th century.
Painter.
Balkan School.
The son and pupil of Frederick of Villach, Johannes de Laybace worked in Carniola. In 1443, he painted the frescoes in the chapel of St Ernest in Millstadt (Carinthia) and in the church of Visiko to the south of Laybach. In 1456, he painted the frescoes in the church at Muljava in Lower Carniola.

JOHANNES DE OPPAVIA. See **JOHANN von Troppau**

JOHANNES DE THOLOSA. See **JEAN de Toulouse**

JOHANNES HISPANUS. See **GIOVANNI Lo Spagna**

JOHANNES PARISIENSIS. See **PERRÉAL Jean**

JOHANNES VON BRABANT. See **JAN, called the Brabançon**

JOHANNES VON MORCOTE?
16th century.
Painter.
There is a fresco signed *Op' Joanes* in the chapel of St Anthony of Padua in the church of S Maria del Sasso in Morcote.

JOHANNES VON VALKENBURG
German, 13th century.
Active in Cologne.
Calligrapher, miniaturist.
Cologne School.
Johannes von Valkenburg was a monk. The Library of the University of Bonn has a missal by him, and the Cologne Museum a gradual, both of which came from the monastery of the Friars Minor in Cologne.

JOHANNESSEN, Kare Jens
Norwegian, 20th century.
Born 1934, in Trondheim.
Painter, sculptor, engraver, lithographer. Figures.
Kare Jens Johannessen featured in the 1992 exhibition: *De Bonnard à Baselitz - Dix ans d'enrichissements du cabinet des estampes 1978-1988* (*From Bonnard to Baselitz: A Decade of Acquisitions by the Prints Collection 1978-1988*) at the Bibliothèque Nationale in Paris.
MUSEUMS AND GALLERIES:
PARIS (Prints Collection): *Bathers* (1986, lithograph).

JOHANNIS. See also **JOHANN**

JOHANNIS, Alexandrine. See **JOANNIS**

JOHANNOT, Alfred
French, 19th century.
Born 21 March 1800, in Offenbach, of French parents; died 7 December 1837, in Paris.
Painter, watercolourist, engraver. Religious subjects, military subjects, genre scenes.
Alfred Johannot came to Paris with his father in 1806 and began by studying at the Louvre. He learned engraving with his brother, Charles, made his debut at the Paris Salon in 1831 and was decorated by the King. He continued exhibiting until his death from a chest infection.

He is known for the following paintings: *Haïdé Finding a Shipwrecked Don Juan; Execution of Cinq-Mars; Arrest of Jean de Crespierre; Mlle de Montpensier Entering Orleans During the Fronde Revolt*; and *Henri II, King of France, and his Family*. He is credited with two scenes from the *Life of St Hyacinth* for the church of Notre Dame de Lorette in Paris.

Johannot, a charming artist whose lightness of touch is evident even in the humblest of his pieces, worked in constant collaboration with his brother Tony and a number of their works are signed *Johannot Brothers*. Alfred's personal body of engraved work is of little importance and is mainly made up of vignettes. Two engravings only are worthy of mention: *Lost Children*, after Ary Scheffer, and *Duke of Anjou Proclaimed King of Spain*, after Gérard.
BIBLIOGRAPHY:
Les Années romantiques, la peinture française de 1815 à 1850, exhibition catalogue, Musée des Beaux-Arts, Nantes, Galeries nationales du Grand Palais, Paris, 1996.
MUSEUMS AND GALLERIES:
BESANÇON: *Lord Byron's Don Juan* - NICE (MBA Jules-Chéret): *Presentation of the Duke of Guise's Son to the Future Henri III* (1837) - ORLÉANS (MBA): *Mlle Montpensier Entering*

Orleans During the Fronde Revolt (1833) - VERSAILLES: *Battle of Rosebecque in 1382; Battle of Brattelen on 26 August 1444; Funeral Rites at the Invalides for the Victims of the Attack of 28 July 1835.*

AUCTION RECORDS:

PARIS, 1852, *Duchess of Orleans Reading,* FRF 1,300. PARIS, 1876, *Queen Elizabeth and Walter Raleigh,* FRF 1,700. PARIS, 27 au 29 May 1880, *Ten Watercolours for Tom Jones,* FRF 600. PARIS, 10 and 11 May 1897, *Mounted Hussar* (watercolour) FRF 40; *Matching Piece For the Previous Work* (watercolour) FRF 35. LONDON, 29 June 1908, *Arrest* (watercolour) GBP 9. PARIS, 9 and 10 May 1911, *Game of Chess* (watercolour) FRF 155; *Family Scene* (watercolour) FRF 165. PARIS, 2-4 June 1920, *In Prison* (watercolour) FRF 410. PARIS, 10 April 1924, *Massacre Under Charles IX* (watercolour) FRF 320. PARIS, 23 April 1928, *Romantic Scenes* (two watercolours) FRF 1,300. PARIS, 22 Jan 1943, *Marie Stuart's Embarkation* (1835, watercolour) FRF 3,600; *Arrest Warrant* (watercolour) FRF 3,200. PARIS, 8 March 1943, *Scene Taken from the Story of Charles the Bold,* FRF 1,200. PARIS, 10 Feb 1950, *Manon and Knight Des Grieux,* FRF 9,500. PARIS, 22 Jan 1988, *Arrest* (watercolour and gouache, 13 1/4 x 9 1/2 ins / 33.7 x 24.2 cm) FRF 6,500. PARIS, 2 Dec 2002, *Francois I and Charles V* (watercolour heightened with gouache, 19 x 27 ins / 48 x 68 cm) EUR 7,100.

JOHANNOT, Charles

French, 19th century.

Born 1798, in Offenbach, to French parents; died 1825, in Paris.

Engraver.

Charles Johannot was the eldest son of François and a descendant of the French family established in Hesse after the 1685 Revocation of the Edict of Nantes (whereby Louis XIV suppressed all the rights previously granted to French protestants by Henri IV). The family founded the Annonay paperworks. Johannot senior had become, in Lyons, a silk weaver and he set up a silk factory in Offenbach.

He painted flowers and was the first to use a stone press for music printing and the first to introduce lithography to France, after a reverse of fortune had forced him to leave Germany in 1806. He seems not have had more success in France. He was made an inspector of the Hombourg and then the Lyons book trade. When the collapse of the Empire led to him losing his post, he settled in St Maur in 1817, where the family appears to have lived on Charles' earnings as an engraver. From 1813, the latter engraved vignettes after Desenne: Torquato Tasso's *Aminta, L'Hermite de la Chausée d'Antin* and *Paul and Virginia.* Two other engravings are of importance: *Orphans,* after Ary Scheffer and *Injured Bugler,* after H Vernet. He died of angina.

JOHANNOT, Charles Émile

French, 19th century.

Painter.

Charles Émile Johannot exhibited military pieces at the 1838 Paris Salon.

JOHANNOT, Tony

French, 19th century.

Born 9 November 1803, in Offenbach; died 4 August 1852, in Paris.

Painter, watercolourist, pastellist, illustrator, engraver. Military subjects, genre scenes.

Johannot hailed from the French family which had settled in Hesse after the 1685 Revocation of the Edict of Nantes (whereby Louis XIV suppressed all the rights previously granted to French protestants by Henri IV). The youngest of François Johannot's three sons, he benefitted from the family's renown. Young, intelligent and spiritual, Tony Johannot was the blue-eyed boy of the Romantic School and a regular at Charles Nodier's Salon at Paris' Bibliothèque de l'Arsenal.

He made his debut at the Paris Salon in 1827 with an engraving and began exhibiting paintings there from 1831, continuing, until his death from apoplexy, to take part in Parisian Exhibitions. He was a keen collaborator on the magazine *Artist.* He received medals in 1831 and 1848 and was decorated in 1840.

Johannot was principally a vignettist, displaying within this modest genre a first class talent. His charming illustrations are worthy of being set alongside the best engravings of the eighteenth century. He illustrated more than one hundred and fifty publications from a body of more than three thousand engravings. His most noteworthy works include the extremely spiritual *Molière*; the 1836 edition of *Don Quixote,* containing seven hundred and sixty five wood engravings; *Paul and Virginie,* published by Curmer in 1838; *Manon Lescaut; Werther; Songs of Béranger; The Vicar of Wakefield; The Lame Devil; The Sentimental Journey; The Journey to Wherever You Please; My Prisons; Tales* by Charles Nodier; *Jérôme Paturot in Search of the Ideal Republic*; Goethe's *Faust*; George Sand's *Complete Works* etc.

BIBLIOGRAPHY:

Les Années romantiques, la peinture française de 1815 à 1850, exhibition catalogue, Musée des Beaux-Arts, Nantes, Galeries nationales du Grand Palais, Paris, 1996.

MUSEUMS AND GALLERIES:

ANGOULÊME: *Return of Charles VII to Paris After the Retreat of the Duke of Bedford: 1437* (around 1843) - LONDON (Wallace Collection): *Minna and Brenda* (c. 1827-1840, pencil, water and bodycolour/paper); *The Fair Sleeper* (pencil and watercolour/paper) - ROUEN: *Seated Woman* - VERSAILLES: *Louis VII Crosses the Menderes River in 1148; Battle of Fontanet: 25 June 1841.*

AUCTION RECORDS:

PARIS, 13 au 16 Jan 1863, *Death of Duguesclin,* FRF 1,500. PARIS, 27 au 29 May 1880, *Marriage of Figaro* (43 pictures and watercolours) FRF 3,800. PARIS, 23 Nov 1907, *Count Douglas,* FRF 150. PARIS, 8 au 10 May 1911, *Sleeping Child* (watercolour) FRF 375; *Woman Dressed in her Finery* (watercolour) FRF 210. PARIS, 29 Nov 1920, *Marriage of Figaro,* FRF 485. PARIS, 4 April 1924, *The Letter* (watercolour) FRF 825. PARIS, 12 June 1926, *Italian Pastors,* FRF 500. PARIS, 17 Dec 1941, *Maid Attending to her Mistress' hair* (graphite) FRF 280. PARIS, 12 Feb 1945, *Moroccan Cavalrymen and Spahi Officers,* FRF 2,600. BRUSSELS, 18 Nov 1946, *Brawl,* BEF 14000. PARIS, 27 March 1947, *In Algeria,* FRF 1,300. PARIS, 19 March 1976, *Embarkation* (1837, oil on canvas, 19 1/4 x 26 3/4 ins / 49 x 68 cm) FRF 2,500. PARIS, 5 April 1991, *Young Woman in Oriental dress* (pastel, 17 3/4 x 13 1/2 ins / 45 x 34 cm) FRF 5,500. PARIS, 28 May 1993, *Two Young Women Daydreaming by a Cliff* (watercolour and gouache, 16 3/4 x 14 ins / 42.5 x 35.5 cm) FRF 6,300. PARIS, 29 Nov 1994, *Return of the Falcon Hunt* (charcoal and wash heightened with white gouache, 17 x 22 1/2 ins / 43 x 57 cm) FRF 4,900. PARIS, 17 March 1999, *Portrait of Alfred Johannot at the Age of 22* (1822, pencil, 7 x 8 ins / 17 x 21 cm) FRF 30,000.

JOHANNSEN. See also **JOHANSEN, JOHANSON, JOHANSSON**

JOHANNSEN, Theodor

German, 19th - 20th century.

Born 27 December 1868.

Painter, illustrator. Portraits, landscapes.

Theodor Johannsen was a student at the academy of fine art in Berlin and specialised in painting landscapes inspired by the Marches and Schleswig-Holstein, and also portraits. He published *Education in Nostalgia by Word and Image,* which he illustrated himself.

JOHANSEN

German, 19th century.

Miniaturist.

Museums and Galleries:
Berlin (Mus. Hohenzollern): *Portrait of Louisa, Princess Frederick of Prussia, née Princess of Anhalt-Bernburg* (miniature).

JOHANSEN. See also **JOHANNSEN, JOHANSON, JOHANSSON**

JOHANSEN, Fridolin Hans
Danish, 20th century.
Born 21 August 1888, in Copenhagen; died 13 July 1908.
Painter. Scenes with figures, local scenes.
Fridolin Hans Johansen is best known for his paintings of Dyrehaven, Allberg and other leisure destinations.
Auction records:
Copenhagen, 4 May 1976, *Peasant Cleaning out a Byre* (1893, oil on canvas, 12¾ x 15¼ ins / 32.5 x 39 cm) DKK 3,200. Copenhagen, 28 Aug 1991, *Landscape with the Mill at Dronningens and the Ramparts of Copenhagen* (oil on canvas, 14¼ x 11 ins / 36 x 28 cm) DKK 4,000. Copenhagen, 8 Feb 1995, *Farmyard in Autumn* (1905, oil on canvas, 13 x 15 ins / 33 x 38 cm) DKK 5,000.

JOHANSEN, Jean Myrtle
Maiden name: Maclane
American, 20th century.
Born 14 September 1878, in Chicago; died 1964.
Painter.
Jean Myrtle Johansen was a pupil of Franck Duveneck and William Chase. She married John Christen Johansen in 1905. She won a bronze medal in Saint Louis in 1904 and the Burgess Prize at the New York Women's Arts Club.
Museums and Galleries:
Chicago (AI) - Syracuse - Toledo, OH - Washington DC (National Portrait Gal.).
Auction records:
New York, 4 Dec 1986, *Young Girls by Lamplight* (oil on canvas remounted on hardboard, 27¾ x 36 ins / 70.5 x 91.4 cm) USD 24,000.

JOHANSEN, John Christian
Swedish, 20th century.
Born 25 November 1876, in Copenhagen; died 1964.
Active in the USA.
Painter. Landscapes, portraits.
John Christian Johansen began his studies in Chicago, with Duveneck, and moved to Paris to work in the Académie Julian. He won several prizes in Chicago and was awarded a bronze medal in St Louis in 1904. He was a member from 1906 of the Salmagundi Club in New York, and was elected an associate of the National Academy of Design in 1911.
Museums and Galleries:
Chicago (AI): *St Mark's Square in Venice* - Richmond: *Fiesole* - Syracuse (Everson MA): *Sunrise over the Grand Canal* (oil on canvas); *Cafè* (oil on canvas) - Washington DC (National Portrait Gal.): *General Joffre*; *General Haig*; *Signing of the Treaty of Versailles* (1919, oil on canvas); *General Diaz*; *Minister Orlando*.
Auction records:
New York, 23 May 1979, *Borderland* (1923, oil on canvas, 40 x 50 ins / 101.5 x 127 cm) USD 1,800. New York, 10 March 1993, *St Mark's Square in Venice* (1908, oil on canvas, 29½ x 39½ ins / 74.9 x 100.3 cm) USD 8,625.

JOHANSEN, Nanna Viga
Danish, 20th century.
Born 2 May 1888, in Copenhagen.
Sculptor. Religious subjects, mythological subjects. Busts.
Nanna Viga Johansen was a student at the Kongelige Danske Kunstakademi in Copenhagen from 1912 to 1914. In 1916 she was awarded the small gold medal for her relief *The Finding of Moses*. She exhibited from 1911; works include *Tobias and the Fish*, *Venus and Cupid* and a *Bust of Dr J.F. Fischer*.

JOHANSEN, Otto Emil
Norwegian, 20th century.
Born 14 July 1886, in Holmestrand.
Painter. Landscapes.
Otto Emil Johansen studied in Oslo and then Paris. He specialised in landscapes, and sometimes paintings of figures. From 1909 he often showed his work at the national exhibition in Oslo, and later in the Jubilee Exhibition there in 1914, in the San Francisco Panama-Pacific Exhibition, the exhibition of fine art in Göteborg in 1913 and the Salon des Indépendants in Paris in 1919 and 1921. Group exhibitions of his work were held in Oslo in 1913, 1918 and 1922.
Museums and Galleries:
Oslo (Nasjonalgal.).

JOHANSEN, Peter
Danish, 19th century.
Born 7 June 1858, in Copenhagen.
Painter.
From 1884 to 1891 Peter Johansen exhibited interiors and landscapes. He then devoted himself to art history. In 1901 he became professor of art history and librarian at the Kunstakademi in Copenhagen. He published a series of art history works.

JOHANSEN, Viggo
Danish, 19th - 20th century.
Born 3 January 1851, in Copenhagen; died 1935.
Painter. Genre scenes, animals, landscapes.
Skagen Artists' Colony.
Viggo Johansen was a student for seven years at the Kongelige Danske Kunstakademi in Copenhagen. He was awarded an honourable mention at the Salon de Paris in 1887, a medal in Munich in 1889 and in Berlin in 1891, as well as a gold medal at the Exposition Universelle in Paris in 1889 and 1900.

He was a member of the Skagen Group of painters, named after a small town in the north of Jutland which was home to a colony of artists, the main representatives being Michael Ancher, his wife Anna Ancher and Paul Severin Kroyer. They practised open air painting and prolonged the quest for a Danish national identity begun at the beginning of the 19th century with the painters of the so-called Golden Age. Johansen was particularly interested in the problems of light, especially in interiors, giving an expressive value to aspects by merging individual lines.

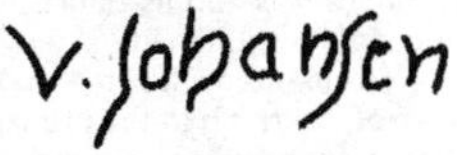

Bibliography:
Johansen, Annette, et al., *Danske Kunstnerkolonier: Skagen, Fyn, Bornholm*, group exhibition catalogue, Aarhus Kunstmuseum, Aarhus, 2000.
Museums and Galleries:
Budapest: *My Wife and My Daughter* - Copenhagen: *Evening Chat*; *Town Meadow*; *Mother Is Going to Read*; *Geese and Sheep*; *Cow Byre*; *Storm Approaches*; *Evening Entertainment*; *Sister of the Artist*; *Dusk*; *Self-portrait*; *Moonrise over Lake Tyre*; *Council Meeting of the Academy in 1904* - Copenhagen (Den Hirschsprungske Samling): *Meal*; *Winter Evening* - Göteborg: *At Sunset* - Hamburg: *Confirmation Day in Dragor* - Hillerød (Frederiksbörg Slot): *J.C. Hostrup*; *H. Hoffding* - Munich: *My Friends near Me in the Evening* - Stockholm: *Laying the Table*; *Between Artists*.

AUCTION RECORDS:
COPENHAGEN, 10 May 1973, *Fishwife*, DKK 10,000. COPENHAGEN, 9 Nov 1976, *Boat on the Beach* (1890, oil on canvas, 16 1/2 x 32 3/4 ins / 42 x 83 cm) DKK 13,500. COPENHAGEN, 20 Feb 1979, *Young Woman Writing in an Interior* (1891, oil on canvas, 24 3/4 x 22 3/4 ins / 63 x 58 cm) DKK 29,000. COPENHAGEN, 19 Jan 1983, *Boats on the Beach* (1887, oil on canvas, 16 1/4 x 24 ins / 41 x 61 cm) DKK 27,000. COPENHAGEN, 12 Aug 1985, *Village Pond* (1892, oil on canvas, 25 1/4 x 33 ins / 64 x 84 cm) DKK 30,000. COPENHAGEN, 17 Nov 1987, *Geese by a Pond* (1904, oil on canvas, 33 3/4 x 37 3/4 ins / 86 x 96 cm) DKK 65,000. COPENHAGEN, 23 March 1988, *Boys Playing Cards on the Beach* (1885, oil on canvas, 15 3/4 x 20 3/4 ins / 40 x 53 cm) DKK 14,000. LONDON, 16 March 1989, *The Artist's Family in the Evening in Skagen* (1886, oil on canvas, 16 3/4 x 23 ins / 42.5 x 58.3 cm) GBP 4,620. COPENHAGEN, 5 April 1989, *Beach to the North Seen from Skagen* (1890, oil on canvas, 15 3/4 x 22 3/4 ins / 40 x 58 cm) DKK 36,000. COPENHAGEN, 21 Feb 1990, *Breakers on the Coast* (1910, oil on canvas, 17 x 28 ins / 43 x 71 cm) DKK 17,000. STOCKHOLM, 16 May 1990, *Rocky Coast in Summer* (1905, oil on canvas, 26 3/4 x 35 3/4 ins / 68 x 91 cm) SEK 16,500. COPENHAGEN, 29 Aug 1990, *Goose Girl with Her Flock* (1901, oil on canvas, 27 1/2 x 34 1/4 ins / 70 x 87 cm) DKK 20,000. COPENHAGEN, 6 March 1991, *Seated Model* (1904, oil on canvas, 32 1/4 x 23 1/4 ins / 82 x 59 cm) DKK 28,000. COPENHAGEN, 6 May 1992, *September Evening in Skagen* (1889, oil on canvas, 25 1/4 x 33 1/2 ins / 64 x 85 cm) DKK 30,000. STOCKHOLM, 5 Sept 1992, *Interior with Two Little Girls* (oil on canvas, 11 3/4 x 18 1/4 ins / 30 x 46.5 cm) SEK 9,000. COPENHAGEN, 10 Feb 1993, *On the Coast at Skagen* (1889, oil on canvas, 17 x 22 3/4 ins / 43 x 58 cm) DKK 11,500. COPENHAGEN, 14 Feb 1996, *Two Women Seated in an Interior with a Loom* (oil on canvas, 30 1/4 x 24 ins / 77 x 61 cm) DKK 25,000.

JOHANSON. See also **JOHANNSEN, JOHANSEN** and **JOHANSSON**

JOHANSON, Patricia
American, 20th century.
Born 1940, in New York.
Painter, draughtsman.
Minimal Art.

Patricia Johanson lives and works in New York, where she also exhibits. In her minimalist paintings, you are expected to take in at a single glance a simple, narrow, thirty-foot (nine metre) long monochrome strip, running across the middle of an otherwise empty unprepared canvas approximately 30 feet x 6ft 6 in (9 metres long x about 2 metres high). In this minimalist project, you should benefit from the perception of the colour of the strip, the length and narrowness, the emptiness of the canvas and its dimensions, under the most favourable conditions, that is to say by being offered the minimum of perceptions within the maximum dimensions. It is a matter of returning to the primary perceptions of three-dimensional language, as a reaction against the degenerations of Lyrical Abstraction. The intention of the Minimalist artists is lofty, even puritanical, but not without historical basis. However bulky their works may be by definition, they appear to arouse only intellectual, very 'sophisticated' enthusiasm. M. Goosen notes that 'Such paintings remind us that painting had reached the *minimum* twice in this century - in the *Blue Lines* of Georgia O'Keeffe and in *White on White* by Malevitch in 1918 - but in Johanson's work, the facts are irreducible, physically rather than mentally.' She has also created many drawings of a labyrinthine world, landscapes or architecture, in which we lose ourselves amid words and phrases.

Johanson has taken part in minimalist group exhibitions in the USA and elsewhere, notably in *L'Art du Réel U.S.A. 1948-1968* (*The Art of the Real, USA, 1948-1968*), organised by the Centre National d'Art Contemporain at the Grand Palais in Paris in 1968.

BIBLIOGRAPHY:
Geburd, Gail, *The Transparent thread: Asian Philosphy in Recent American Art*, exhibition catalogue, Distributed by the University of Pennsylvania press, 1990. Johanson, Patricia, '*Art and Survival: Creative Solutions to Environmental Problems*' in *Gallerie*, no. 8, periodical, 1992. Matilsky, Barbara C., *Fragile Ecologies: Contemporary Artists' Interpretations and Solutions*, exhibition catalogue, periodical, Rizzoli in association with Queens Museum of Art, New York, 1992. Scrupe, Mara Adamitz, '*Environment, Audience, and Public Art in the New World (Order)*' in *Sculpture*, vol 19, no. 2, Washington DC, 2000.

JOHANSSEN. See **JOHANNSEN, JOHANSEN, JOHANSON** and **JOHANSSON**

JOHANSSON. See also **JOHANNSEN, JOHANSEN** and **JOHANSON**

JOHANSSON, Albert
Swedish, 20th century.
Born 1926.
Active in Nordmaling.
Painter.

Albert Johansson has featured on several occasions, notably in 1953, at the Salon des Réalités Nouvelles in Paris.

AUCTION RECORDS:
STOCKHOLM, 14 April 1984, *Composition* (1983, oil on panel, 23 1/2 x 28 3/4 ins / 60 x 73 cm) SEK 10,500. STOCKHOLM, 20 April 1985, *Durot* (1957, pencil, 39 1/4 x 39 1/4 ins / 100 x 100 cm) SEK 12,000. STOCKHOLM, 20 April 1985, *Sedimentation* (oil on canvas, 35 3/4 x 48 ins / 91 x 122 cm) SEK 15,200. STOCKHOLM, 9 Dec 1986, *Composition* (oil on panel, 35 3/4 x 48 ins / 91 x 122 cm) SEK 22,000. STOCKHOLM, 6 June 1988, *Physiognomies* (1965, mixed media, 33 1/2 x 27 1/2 ins / 85 x 70 cm) SEK 30,500. STOCKHOLM, 22 May 1989, *Composition* (oil on panel, 36 1/4 x 48 ins / 92 x 122 cm) SEK 29,000. STOCKHOLM, 6 Dec 1989, *Fata Morgana XIII* (oil on panel, 35 3/4 x 48 ins / 91 x 122 cm) SEK 45,000. STOCKHOLM, 14 June 1990, *June with Two Trees* (1977, oil on panel, 36 1/4 x 48 ins / 92 x 122 cm) SEK 27,000. STOCKHOLM, 30 May 1991, *Vertical Red* (1988, oil on panel, 35 3/4 x 48 ins / 91 x 122 cm) SEK 20,000. STOCKHOLM, 21 May 1992, *Painting* (oil on panel, 35 3/4 x 48 ins / 91 x 122 cm) SEK 16,000. STOCKHOLM, 10-12 May 1993, *Internal Spaces VI* (1979, oil on paper, 48 x 35 3/4 ins / 122 x 91 cm) SEK 5,000. STOCKHOLM, 30 Nov 1993, *Design* (oil on canvas, 36 1/4 x 48 ins / 92 x 122 cm) SEK 12,000. STOCKHOLM, 28 Feb 2000, *Conception O* (oil on panel, 35 x 48 ins / 90 x 122 cm) SEK 17,000. MALMÖ, 7 May 2000, *Composition* (oil on panel, 35 x 48 ins / 90 x 122 cm) SEK 19,000. STOCKHOLM, 27 Nov 2001, *Laila - Composition* (1958, oil and mixed media on panel, 48 x 33 ins / 122 x 85 cm) SEK 24,000. STOCKHOLM, 27 Nov 2001, *Essau - Composition* (1958, oil and mixed media on panel, 48 x 33 ins / 122 x 85 cm) SEK 24,000. STOCKHOLM, 24 April 2002, *Indra - Composition* (1957, oil on panel, 41 x 30 ins / 105 x 75 cm) SEK 31,000. STOCKHOLM, 6 Nov 2002, *Ra - Composition* (1959, oil on panel, 39 x 78 ins / 100 x 199 cm) SEK 23,000. STOCKHOLM, 7 May 2003, *Boys' Choir* (1962, mixed media, 20 x 24 ins / 50 x 60 cm) SEK 14,000. STOCKHOLM, 7 May 2003, *Gront Jaglosa I - Green Mask Composition* (1965, mixed media, 24 x 30 ins / 60 x 75 cm) SEK 15,500. STOCKHOLM, 27 April 2004, *Aniara II - Homage a Harry Martinson* (1959, mixed media on panel, 39 x 79 ins / 100 x 200 cm) SEK 16,000. STOCKHOLM, 27 April 2004, *Indra II* (1959, mixed media on panel, 39 x 39 ins / 100 x 100 cm) SEK 16,000.

JOHANSSON, Arvid Claes William
Swedish, 19th - 20th century.
Born 29 May 1862, in Stockholm; died March 1923, in Paris.

Painter. Seascapes.

Arvid Claes William Johansson was awarded a bronze medal at the Exposition Universelle in Paris in 1889 and a silver medal in 1900. He was made a Chevalier of the Légion d'Honneur in 1889.

Museums and Galleries:

Mulhouse: *Torpedo Boat; Night Effect near Berck* - St-Brieuc: *Arrival of the Tsar in Cherbourg in 1898.*

Auction records:

Paris, 17 May 1900, *Seascape,* FRF 130. Paris, 30 March 1925, *Fisherfolk Shrimping,* FRF 1,250. Paris, 27 Dec 1926, *Fishing Boat at Sea,* FRF 200. Paris, 7 March 1947, *Marseille la Cannebière under Snow,* FRF 7,800. Paris, 25 June 1951, *Return of the Fishermen,* FRF 20,000. Göteborg, 24 March 1976, *Fishing Boats* (oil on canvas, 25 1/2 x 41 1/4 ins / 65 x 105 cm) SEK 3,300. Stockholm, 27 April 1988, *Seascape with Warships on a Large Lake* (oil on canvas, 28 x 38 1/2 ins / 71 x 98 cm) SEK 6,000. Versailles, 15 May 1988, *Fishermen* (oil on canvas, 32 x 46 ins / 81 x 116 cm) FRF 5,000. Paris, 22 Nov 1988, *Fishermen by Moonlight* (oil on canvas, 32 1/4 x 46 ins / 82 x 116 cm) FRF 10,000. Göteborg, 18 May 1989, *Fishermen in France* (oil on canvas, 39 1/4 x 31 1/2 ins / 100 x 80 cm) SEK 8,800. London, 18 Oct 1990, *French Yacht in Sight of a Port* (1886, oil on canvas, 32 x 39 ins / 81 x 99 cm) GBP 1,100. Paris, 31 May 1991, *Fishing Boats* (oil on canvas, 21 1/4 x 32 ins / 54 x 81 cm) FRF 13,500. Malmö, 8 April 2000, *Entrance to Gothenburg, Alvsborg Fort in Background* (oil on canvas, 35 x 56 ins / 90 x 141 cm) SEK 14,500. Zurich, 19 Sept 2003, *Sailing Ship on the High Seas* (1890, oil on canvas, 32 x 39 ins / 81 x 100 cm) CHF 3,000.

JOHANSSON, Erling

Swedish, 20th century.
Born 1934.
Painter.

Auction records:

Stockholm, 5-6 Dec 1990, *Model with Birds* (1969, oil on canvas, 26 x 47 1/4 ins / 66 x 120 cm) SEK 10,500. Neuilly, 4 Oct 2001, *Magda, Lady from Prague* (acrylic on canvas, 51 x 35 ins / 130 x 90 cm) FRF 15,500.

JOHANSSON, Jert

Norwegian, 20th century.
Born 1942, in Orkdal.
Painter, sculptor, engraver.

Jert Johansson took part in the exhibition *De Bonnard à Baselitz - Dix ans d'enrichissements du cabinet des estampes 1978-1988* (*From Bonnard to Baselitz: A Decade of Acquisitions by the Prints Collection 1978-1988*) at the Bibliothèque Nationale in Paris in 1992.

JOHANSSON, Johan Albin

Swedish, 20th century.
Born 1 March 1897, in Lund.
Painter. Figures, portraits.

Johan Albin Johansson studied at the school of art and design in Strasbourg and at the academy of fine art in Dresden. He painted and drew portraits, including one of the painter *Claus* and a *Self-portrait,* as well as paintings of figures: *Woman at a Garden Table; Dressmaker; Woman Knitting; Woman Reading; The Harmonica Player,* and a few landscapes in pastel, inspired by his mother country.

Museums and Galleries:

Malmö: *Portrait of Anders Osterling* - Stockholm (Nationalmus.): *Midsummer.*

JOHANSSON, Karl A. or Carl A.

Swedish, 19th - 20th century.
Born 1863, in Hernösand; died 1944.
Painter. Genre scenes, landscapes.

Museums and Galleries:

Stockholm: *December Day.*

Auction records:

Stockholm, 23 April 1980, *Summer Landscape* (1886, oil on canvas, 30 x 48 ins / 76 x 121 cm) SEK 31,000. Stockholm, 22 April 1981, *Landscape with Lake* (1888, oil on canvas, 25 1/2 x 35 1/2 ins / 65 x 90 cm) SEK 29,000. Stockholm, 1 Nov 1983, *Summer Landscape* (1890, oil on canvas, 12 1/4 x 17 3/4 ins / 31 x 45 cm) SEK 14,000. Stockholm, 10 Dec 1986, *Winter Landscape* (1913, oil on canvas, 26 x 36 1/4 ins / 66 x 92 cm) SEK 20,000. Stockholm, 20 Oct 1987, *Landscape with Lake* (1888, oil on canvas, 25 1/2 x 35 1/2 ins / 65 x 90 cm) SEK 260,000. Stockholm, 27 April 1988, *Mountain Landscape with Lake* (oil on panel, 11 x 11 3/4 ins / 27 x 30 cm) SEK 21,000. Stockholm, 15 Nov 1988, *River Landscape with Birches in Summer* (1888, oil, 6 x 9 1/2 ins / 15 x 24 cm) SEK 30,000. Stockholm, 19 April 1989, *Summer at Afton near Faxelfven* (oil on panel, 13 x 17 ins / 33 x 43 cm) SEK 26,000. Göteborg, 18 May 1989, *Small Houses in the Country* (oil on canvas, 7 3/4 x 5 ins / 20 x 13 cm) SEK 4,100. Stockholm, 15 Nov 1989, *Nordic Coast with Tree-covered Mountains, Fishing Boats and Fishermen's Huts* (oil, 24 x 31 1/2 ins / 61 x 80 cm) SEK 26,000. Stockholm, 16 May 1990, *Track across Fields in Summer* (oil on canvas, 9 3/4 x 13 ins / 25 x 33 cm) SEK 15,500. Stockholm, 14 Nov 1990, *Spring Landscape beside a Pool* (oil on panel, 11 x 15 3/4 ins / 27 x 40 cm) SEK 67,000. Stockholm, 29 May 1991, *Extensive Nordic Summer Landscape with Trees* (oil on canvas, 20 x 32 ins / 51 x 81 cm) SEK 19,000. Stockholm, 13 April 1992, *View of Borgsjön in Winter* (1923, oil on canvas, 19 1/4 x 28 1/4 ins / 49 x 72 cm) SEK 10,000. Stockholm, 19 May 1992, *Winter's Day in Medelpad* (oil on canvas, 19 3/4 x 25 1/4 ins / 50 x 64 cm) SEK 16,500.

JOHANSSON, Lasse

Swedish, 20th century.
Born 1899.
Painter. Seascapes.

Auction records:

Stockholm, 13 April 1992, *Seascape with Sailing Boats* (1933, oil on canvas, 25 1/4 x 31 1/2 ins / 64 x 80 cm) SEK 6,300.

JOHANSSON, Natan

Swedish, 20th century.
Born 1893; died 1951.
Painter. Landscapes.

Auction records:

Stockholm, 28 Oct 1991, *View of Riddarfjärden in Stockholm* (oil on canvas, 35 x 67 1/4 ins / 89 x 171 cm) SEK 14,000.

JOHANSSON, Stefan

Swedish, 20th century.
Born 1876, in Filipstad; died 1955.
Painter. Figures, portraits, interiors.

Stefan Johansson featured at the Baltic exhibition in 1914 in Malmö with eight portraits and studies of heads. Very limited in his choice of subjects, he specialised in painting interiors and the effects of artificial light. His paintings are empty of human presence and possess an unnatural calm. He painted on a specially prepared support, repainting constantly until the canvas had completely absorbed the pigments.

Museums and Galleries:

Malmö: *Portrait of the Artist's Mother* (watercolour).

Auction records:

London, 16 March 1989, *Lamp-globe in the Evening* (1926, oil on canvas, 15 3/4 x 15 ins / 40 x 38 cm) GBP 52,800. New York, 23 Oct 1990, *Shadows in a Corner of a Bedroom* (1944, watercolour/canvas/card, 25 1/2 x 23 1/2 ins / 64.8 x 59.7 cm) USD 55,000; *Moonlit Dawn in May* (1942, watercolour/canvas/card, 28 1/2 x 22 ins / 72.4 x 55.9 cm) USD 77,000. Stockholm, 14 Nov 1990, *Light through a Green Screen* (watercolour, 29 1/2 x 23 1/4 ins / 75 x 59 cm) SEK 200,000. STOCKHOLM, 5-6 Dec 1990, *Sky Study* (watercolour/canvas, 11 x 9 3/4 ins / 27 x 25 cm) SEK 8,200. STOCKHOLM, 21 May 1992, *Landscape Reflected in Water in the Evening* (watercolour/canvas, 18 1/2 x 14 1/4 ins / 47 x 36 cm) SEK 14,000. STOCKHOLM, 30 Nov 1993, *Green Transparency* (watercolour, 29 1/2 x 23 1/4 ins / 75 x 59 cm) SEK 85,000. GÖTEBORG, 24 May 2000, *Hazy Rain* (watercolour, 10 x 11 ins / 25 x 28 cm) SEK 25,000. STOCKHOLM, 29 May 2000, *View from a Window* (oil on canvas, 16 x 12 ins / 40 x 30 cm) SEK 45,000. AMSTERDAM, 11 June 2001, *Interior* (oil on canvas on board, 25 x 19 ins / 64 x 48 cm) NLG 11,000. STOCKHOLM, 4 Dec 2001, *In the Light of the Night Lamp* (watercolour, 25 x 20 ins / 64 x 50 cm) SEK 135,000. LONDON, 13 June 2002, *Evening Globe* (tempera on canvas on board, 16 x 15 ins / 40 x 38 cm) GBP 20,000. LONDON, 13 June 2002, *Shadows in the Bedroom Corner* (tempera on canvas on board, 26 x 23 ins / 65 x 59 cm) GBP 23,000. STOCKHOLM, 26 May 2003, *Study of Lamp* (watercolour, 9 x 6 ins / 23 x 16 cm) SEK 33,000. STOCKHOLM, 2 Dec 2003, *Street Lights* (watercolour, 15 x 13 ins / 37 x 32 cm) SEK 100,000. STOCKHOLM, 25 May 2004, *Summer Night - Landscape from Eksharad, Varmland* (mixed media, 14 x 20 ins / 36 x 50 cm) SEK 50,000.

JOHANSSON, Sven Erik
Swedish, 20th century.
Born 1925, in Borås.
Painter.

Sven Erik Johansson studied at the Valand school of fine art in Göteborg from 1951 to 1955, under the direction of Endre Nemes. He took part in group exhibitions in Lübeck, Bochum and Amsterdam in 1956, and in Oslo in 1959. In Göteborg, the artistic centre of the west coast, he is a member of 54 Group, with which he exhibited in Paris in 1962. He showed his works in solo exhibitions in Borås in 1956, Göteborg in 1959 and Uppsala in 1962.

BIBLIOGRAPHY:
Aspects de la jeune peinture suédoise, exhibition catalogue, Gal. Massol, Paris, 1962.

MUSEUMS AND GALLERIES:
GÖTEBORG (Konstmus.) - STOCKHOLM (Moderna Mus.).

AUCTION RECORDS:
STOCKHOLM, 14 June 1990, *Landscape of Death* (1974, acrylic/panel, 48 x 70 1/2 ins / 122 x 179 cm) SEK 26,000. STOCKHOLM, 26 Oct 1999, *Vertical Carnival* (oil on canvas, 39 x 27 ins / 99 x 69 cm) SEK 15,000. GÖTEBORG, 1 Dec 1999, *Composition* (1962, oil on panel, 23 x 48 ins / 58 x 122 cm) SEK 22,000. GÖTEBORG, 6 May 2000, *Occurrence by White Column* (1964, mixed media, 27 x 35 ins / 69 x 90 cm) SEK 15,500. STOCKHOLM, 21 May 2001, *Vertical Carnival* (1958, oil on canvas, 39 x 27 ins / 99 x 68 cm) SEK 22,000. LUND, 4 May 2002, *Something of a Horse* (1985, oil on panel, 47 x 63 ins / 120 x 160 cm) SEK 42,000. LUND, 4 May 2002, *House of Intrigue* (1978-1980, oil on canvas, 63 x 87 ins / 161 x 220 cm) SEK 50,000. STOCKHOLM, 5 Nov 2003, *Fairytale of the Wheel* (1959, oil on panel, 24 x 47 ins / 60 x 120 cm) SEK 15,000. STOCKHOLM, 3 Nov 2004, *Fantasy with Grey Background* (1964, oil on panel, 25 x 29 ins / 64 x 74 cm) SEK 22,000. STOCKHOLM, 3 Nov 2004, *Towards Unknown Goal* (1977, oil on panel, 63 x 47 ins / 160 x 120 cm) SEK 30,000.

JOHANSSON, Yo
Danish, 20th century.
Born 1897; died 1963.
Painter. Seascapes.

AUCTION RECORDS:
GÖTEBORG, 18 Oct 1988, *Boats on Their Fishing Grounds* (1931, oil on canvas, 25 1/4 x 37 ins / 64 x 94 cm) SEK 3,800. GÖTEBORG, 17 Oct 1989, *Fishing Grounds* (oil on canvas, 22 x 25 1/2 ins / 55 x 65 cm) SEK 4,200.

JOHANSSON-THOR, Emil
Swedish, 20th century.
Born 20 March 1889, in Landskrona; died 1958.
Painter, engraver.

Emil Johansson-Thor was a student at the school of fine art in Stockholm, subsequently studying in England, Germany and Paris, where he exhibited in 1929. He then became director of engraving at the school of fine art in Stockholm.

MUSEUMS AND GALLERIES:
MALMÖ (Konstmus.) - STOCKHOLM (Nationalmus.).

AUCTION RECORDS:
STOCKHOLM, 30 Oct 1979, *Winter Landscape* (1930, oil on canvas, 23 x 17 3/4 ins / 58.5 x 45 cm) SEK 8,000. STOCKHOLM, 16 May 1984, *Landscape* (1939, oil on canvas, 16 1/2 x 23 1/2 ins / 42 x 60 cm) SEK 6,500.

JOHFRA, pseudonym of Franciscus Johannes Gijsbertus van den Berg
Dutch, 20th century.
Born 1919, in Rotterdam.
From 1962 to 1972 active in France.
Painter. Figures, landscapes, architectural views.

Johfra was a student at the academy of fine art in The Hague. Subsequently he studied astronomy, and built telescopes. After 1941 he devoted himself to painting, but in 1945 all his works were destroyed during an air raid. After the war, he travelled to Italy and France and devoted himself to speleology and archaeology. He also drew up a map of the moon.

In 1959 Johfra met Salvador Dalí. From 1962 he was based in Aspremont (Alpes-Maritimes), where he built his house himself. He exhibited in Holland, England and France. In 1972 he returned to Holland, where he had several solo exhibitions, in Zandvoort and Amsterdam, and, in 1973, in The Hague.

Following the example of Dalí, he mastered an academic technique and applied it to fantasy images, desert landscapes bristling with monstrous anthropomorphic constructions, or based on the myth of Hell.

AUCTION RECORDS:
AMSTERDAM, 20 March 1978, *Pierrot Seated in a Desolate Landscape* (1961, oil on canvas, 25 1/2 x 37 1/2 ins / 64.8 x 95.4 cm) NLG 15,000. AMSTERDAM, 24 Oct 1983, *Pan* (1979, painting, triptych, 75 x 118 ins / 190.5 x 300 cm) NLG 15,000. AMSTERDAM, 10 April 1989, *Amazon* (1952, oil on card) NLG 2,300. PARIS, 14 Oct 1989, *Hell* (oil on canvas, 30 x 26 3/4 ins / 76 x 68 cm) FRF 80,000. AMSTERDAM, 21 May 1992, *Dedication of Mercury* (1951, oil on canvas, 17 1/4 x 37 3/4 ins / 44 x 96 cm) NLG 5,750. AMSTERDAM, 24 Sept 1992, *Oriental Beauty* (1957, oil on card, 15 3/4 x 11 3/4 ins / 40 x 30 cm) NLG 1,265. AMSTERDAM, 9 Dec 1993, *Landscape I* (1966, oil on card, 14 x 17 3/4 ins / 35.5 x 45 cm) NLG 5,175. AMSTERDAM, 19-20 Feb 1997, *Dedication of Mercury* (1995, oil on canvas, 17 x 37 1/2 ins / 43 x 95 cm) NLG 2,998. ZURICH, 7 June 2000, *Genesis* (1967, oil on panel, 19 x 26 ins / 49 x 66 cm) CHF 10,000. AMSTERDAM, 4 July 2000, *Nymph* (1949, crayon, 19 x 13 ins / 47 x 33 cm) NLG 4,500. AMSTERDAM, 26 Nov 2001, *Cyclops* (1955, gouache, 13 x 9 ins / 32 x 24 cm) NLG 4,200.

JOHMANN, Eugène, called Félix, or Iohmann
French, 19th century.
Born 1852, in Nancy; died 1884, in Nancy.
Sculptor.

Nancy Museum has a work by Johmann entitled *Sleeping Child*. The artist signed himself *Iohmann*, but exhibited at the Salon of the Société des Artistes Français under the name of Johmann and was awarded an honourable mention in 1883.

JOHN, Alfred
German, 20th century.
Born 22 August 1886, in Magdeburg (Saxony-Anhalt).
Painter, engraver.

Alfred John was a student at the school of fine art in Magdeburg from 1909 to 1913. He featured in local exhibitions and the Grosse Kunstausstellung in Berlin, in 1919 and 1920. He is remembered for *The Mother, Man at the Window* and *Magdeburg Landscape.*

JOHN, August Wilhelm
German, 19th century.
Born 1813, in Templin (Uckermark).
Landscape artist.

August Wilhelm John trained at the academy in Düsseldorf, and worked there and in Berlin.

MUSEUMS AND GALLERIES:
MAINZ: *Rhine Landscape.*

JOHN, Augustin
German, 17th century.
Born 1602, in Dresden.
Active still living in Hamburg in 1678.
Painter, engraver, medallist.

Augustin John was painter to the courts of Prussia and Poland.

JOHN, Augustus Edwin (Sir)
British, 20th century.
Born 4 January 1878, in Tenby, Wales; died 31 October 1961, in Fordingbridge (Hampshire).
Painter. Figures, portraits, landscapes, still-lifes.
Murals.

Augustus Edwin John who was the brother of the British painter Gwen John, trained at the Slade School of Fine Art from 1894 to 1898, where he won numerous prizes and awards. He became a member of the New English Art Club in 1903, and was Professor of Painting at the University of Liverpool from 1901 to 1904. He travelled throughout Europe (his first visit was to Paris in 1900) and he was a regular visitor to the USA. Before World War I John lived as a traveller with his family, in caravans in England and Wales. During World War I he was attached to the Canadian forces as a war artist. John was made a member of the Royal Academy in 1928; he resigned in 1928; but he was re-appointed in 1940. He was a president of the Society of Mural Painters. He was a member of the Camden Town Group in 1911 and a member of the London Group from 1940 to 1961. He was awarded the Order of Merit in 1942.

John quickly earned a reputation as one of England's foremost painters. His earliest works combine the poetic sentiment of the Pre-Raphaelites with a broadly Impressionist technique. Numerous works (of variable quality) illustrate aspects of Roman life, to which John was introduced by his friend John Sampson, University Librarian at Liverpool. His mural paintings showed remarkable talent, but his work in this area was curtailed by his numerous portrait commissions - by turns intimate or grand and sumptuous in character, and often strikingly composed - undertaken to support his large family and notoriously bohemian lifestyle. These include: *Madame Suggia, Joseph Widener, G.B. Shaw* and *Dylan Thomas*. Some of the best portraits are of his two wives and his many children.

He first exhibited with the New English Art Club in 1900. Numerous exhibitions followed. In 1946 portraits and a figure composition by John featured prominently at the exhibition *Peinture anglaise du XXe siècle* (*Twentieth century English painting*) at the Musée du Jeu de Paume in Paris. A retrospective exhibition of his drawings was held at the National Gallery in 1940, and of his drawings and paintings at Temple Newsam, Leeds, in 1946; at Scott and Fowles, New York, in 1949; at the Royal Academy in 1954; and at the Graves Art Gallery, Sheffield, in 1956.

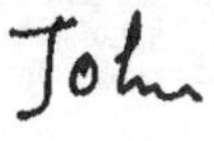

BIBLIOGRAPHY:
Rothenstein, John, *Augustus John*, Phaidon, Oxford, 1946. Easton, M./Holroyd, M., *The Art of Augustus John*, London, 1974. Holroyd, M., *Augustus John: A Biography, 2 vols*, 1974-1975. Easton, M./John, R., *Augustus John*, exhibition catalogue, National Portrait Gallery, London, 1976. Fraser Jenkins, A. D., '*Augustus John: Studies for Compositions*' in *Centenary Exhibition*, exhibition catalogue, 1978. Rowan, Eric, *Some Miraculous Promised Land: J.D. Innes, Augustus John and Derwent Lees in North Wales,1910-1913*, exhibition catalogue, 1982. John, Rebecca/Evans, Mark, *Themes and Variations: The Drawings of Augustus John 1901-1931*, Lund Humphries, 1996 (introduction by Michael Holroyd). Holroyd, M., *Augustus John: The New Biography*, London, 1996. *Gwen John and Augustus John*, exhibition catalogue, Tate Gallery, London, 2004.

MUSEUMS AND GALLERIES:
CAMBRIDGE (Fitzwilliam Mus.): *George Bernard Shaw* (1915, oil on canvas) - CARDIFF (National Museum and Gallery): *Portrait of Dylan Thomas* (c. 1938) - LONDON (Royal Academy of Arts): *Portrait of a Young Man* (c. 1928, oil on canvas, competition piece) - LONDON (Tate Collection): *Woman Smiling* (1908-1909, oil on canvas); *W.B. Yeats* (1907, oil on canvas); *Llyn Treweryn* (1911-1912, oil/wood); *Robin* (c. 1912, oil/wood); *Lyric Fantasy* (c. 1913-1914, oil and pencil/canvas); *Washing Day* (c. 1915, oil/wood); *Galway* (1916 and 1920, oil on canvas); *Colonel T.E. Lawrence* (1919, oil on canvas); *Madame Suggia* (1920-1923, oil on canvas) - WASHINGTON DC (NGA): *Joseph E. Widener* (1921, oil on canvas); *Mrs. Alexander H. McLanahan* (c. 1927, oil on canvas).

AUCTION RECORDS:
LONDON, 29 April 1927, *Portrait of a Young Girl*, GBP 630. LONDON, 6 July 1928, *Miss Pettigrow*, GBP 304 10s. LONDON, 28 March 1930, *Beside the Sea*, GBP 262. LONDON, 13 July 1934, *Little Spanish Girl*, GBP 168. LONDON, 20 Dec 1935, *Blue Cineraria in a Vase*, GBP 252. LONDON, 20 March 1936, *Mother and Child*, GBP 173. LONDON, 15 July 1938, *Princess Bibosco in a Pink Dress*, GBP 588. LONDON, 8 July 1940, *The Red Dress*, GBP 357. LONDON, 19 Dec 1941, *Three Children*, GBP 220. NEW YORK, 8 Jan 1942, *Trelawny*, USD 1,600. LONDON, 20 Dec 1944, *Nirvana*, GBP 580. LONDON, 11 July 1951, *Vase of Flowers*, GBP 280. LONDON, 17 July 1959, *Dorelia with Earrings* (red chalk) GBP 682. LONDON, 6 April 1960, *Little Kalmukh*, GBP 550. LONDON, 12 July 1961, *Woman with a Plumed Hat*, GBP 3,800. LONDON, 20 June 1962, *Portrait of W. B. Yeats as a Young Man*, GBP 6,500. LONDON, 21 June 1963, *Portrait of David*, Gns 3,200. LONDON, 13 Nov 1964, *Young Peasant Girl with a Jug*, Gns 3,400. NEW YORK, 17 April 1969, *Portrait of Tallulah Bankhead*, USD 19,000. NEW YORK, 7 Oct 1970, *Standing Nude*, USD 3,750. LONDON, 15 Dec 1971, *Woman sitting beneath an Olive Tree*, GBP 1,100. LONDON, 26 April 1972, *Landscape with Dorelia*, GBP 4,500. LONDON, 11 May 1973, *The Blue Shawl* (watercolour and pencil) Gns 1,200. LONDON, 13 March 1974, *Sunflowers*, GBP 3,200. LONDON, 16 June 1976, *Dorelia and Child* (1924, oil on card, 15 x 18 ins / 38 x 45.5 cm) GBP 800. NEW YORK, 9 Oct 1976, *Portrait of Dorelia* (drawing, 16 1/4 x 9 ins / 41 x 23 cm) USD 1,300. LONDON, 17 June 1977, *Ivy* (1937, oil on canvas, 16 x 13 1/2 ins / 40.5 x 34.5 cm) GBP 950. NEW YORK, 9 June 1979, *Self-portrait* (c. 1901, pencil, 4 1/4 x 3 3/4 ins / 10.8 x 9.5 cm) USD 4,000. NEW YORK, 9 June 1979, *Lady Ottoline Morrell* (c. 1908, gouache and pencil, 14 1/4 x 11 1/2 ins / 36.5 x 29.5 cm) USD 19,000. NEW YORK, 9 June 1979, *Self-portrait* (c. 1923, oil on panel, 36 x 24 1/2 ins / 90.5 x 62.2 cm) USD 36,000. LONDON, 14 Nov 1980, *Portrait of a Man Wearing a Turban* (dry-point retouched with wash, 4 1/4 x 2 3/4 ins / 10.7 x 7 cm) GBP 520. LONDON, 12 June 1981, *Magnolia* (oil on canvas, 24 x 24 ins / 61 x 61 cm) GBP 6,800. LONDON, 4 March 1983, *Seated portrait of Gwen John* (c. 1897, pencil, 9 x 6 1/2 ins / 22.8 x 16.5 cm) GBP 7,500. LONDON, 4 March 1983, *Self-portrait with*

Pipe (1923, oil on panel, 34 3/4 x 23 3/4 ins / 88.5 x 60.5 cm) GBP 16,000. LONDON, 4 Nov 1983, *Dorelia, Standing* (c. 1907-1908, watercolour and pencil, 21 x 10 3/4 ins / 53.5 x 27.3 cm) GBP 7,800. LONDON, 15 March 1985, *Portrait of Henry* (oil on canvas, 29 1/2 x 23 1/2 ins / 75 x 59.6 cm) GBP 11,000. LONDON, 21 May 1986, *Dorelia* (red and black chalks/grey paper, 12 x 9 ins / 30.5 x 23 cm) GBP 6,500. LONDON, 2 Dec 1986, *Dorelia, Standing, in a Blue Smock* (c. 1905-1910, watercolour and pencil/paper, 11 1/2 x 6 1/2 ins / 29.2 x 16.5 cm) GBP 9,000. ORCHARDLEIGH PARK (SOMERSET), 21 Sept 1987, *Study of Dorelia* (pencil, 17 1/4 x 12 ins / 43.5 x 30.5 cm) GBP 8,000. LONDON, 3-4 March 1988, *Head of a Gypsy Woman* (pencil, 11 1/4 x 7 3/4 ins / 28.7 x 19.6 cm) GBP 3,520. LONDON, 9 June 1988, *Study for a Nude Fgure of a Little Boy, Walking* (pencil, 11 1/4 x 7 3/4 ins / 28.8 x 19.5 cm) GBP 1,870; *Portrait of Poppet, the Artist's Daughter* (oil on canvas, 28 x 23 ins / 71.3 x 58.7 cm) GBP 7,700; *Self-portrait* (oil on panel, 10 x 8 ins / 24.5 x 19.4 cm) GBP 17,600. LONDON, 29 July 1988, *Little Girl with a Large Hat* (pencil, 11 1/4 x 8 3/4 ins / 28.8 x 22.5 cm) GBP 4,620. LONDON, 9 June 1989, *Profile Portrait of David* (1906, pencil, 10 3/4 x 8 3/4 ins / 27.6 x 22.5 cm) GBP 8,800; *Winter Morning, Martigues* (oil on canvas, 18 1/4 x 21 3/4 ins / 46.1 x 55.2 cm) GBP 7,150. LONDON, 10 Nov 1989, *Study of a Young Woman* (1907, pencil, 10 x 14 ins / 25.4 x 35.6 cm) GBP 8,800. LONDON, 9 March 1990, *Self-portrait* (1946, oil on canvas, 30 x 25 ins / 76.3 x 63.5 cm) GBP 28,600. CALAIS, 8 July 1990, *Portrait of a Young Girl* (oil on canvas/panel, 27 1/2 x 23 1/2 ins / 70 x 60 cm) FRF 23,000. NEW YORK, 19 July 1990, *Dorelia* (pencil and watercolour/paper, 21 1/2 x 12 3/4 ins / 54.8 x 32.4 cm) USD 2,475. LONDON, 20 Sept 1990, *Nude Study of a Young Boy* (charcoal, 24 x 19 ins / 61 x 48.5 cm) GBP 5,500. LONDON, 8 Nov 1990, *Head study of Dorelia* (1909, watercolour and lead pencil, 14 1/4 x 10 ins / 36 x 25.5 cm) GBP 34,100. LONDON, 25 Jan 1991, *Coastal landscape, Dorset* (oil on panel, 11 1/4 x 15 1/4 ins / 28.5 x 38.5 cm) GBP 2,420. LONDON, 7 March 1991, *Ursula Nettleship* (lead pencil, 5 1/2 x 5 1/2 ins / 14 x 14 cm) GBP 5,500. LONDON, 6 March 1992, *Female Nude Seen from the Back* (pencil, 16 x 6 3/4 ins / 40.5 x 17 cm) GBP 3,740. LONDON, 14 May 1992, *Portrait of Reresby Sitwell* (pencil, 14 1/4 x 9 3/4 ins / 36 x 25 cm) GBP 5,500. LONDON, 6 Nov 1992, *Portrait of a Young Mulatto Girl* (1937, oil on canvas, 28 1/4 x 20 ins / 71.5 x 51 cm) GBP 17,600. LONDON, 12 March 1993, *Young Girl with a Bobble Hat* (oil on canvas, 19 x 14 1/2 ins / 48 x 37 cm) GBP 6,325. ST ASAPH, 2 June 1994, *Sierra de Gabor* (oil on canvas, 20 3/4 x 24 ins / 53 x 61 cm) GBP 13,225. LONDON, 2 June 1995, *Portrait of William Butler Yeats* (oil on canvas in grisaille, 24 x 18 ins / 61 x 45.5 cm) GBP 62,000. LONDON, 5 March 1999, *Portrait of David, the Artist's Son, Aged Four* (pencil, 14 x 11 ins / 36 x 29 cm) GBP 24,000. LONDON, 23 June 1999, *Portrait of the Artist's Son David, in Uniform* (oil on canvas, 29 x 21 ins / 73 x 54 cm) GBP 15,000. LONDON, 24 Nov 2000, *In Memorium Amadeo Modigliani* (c. 1920, oil on canvas, 50 x 40 ins / 127 x 102 cm) GBP 20,000. LONDON, 24 Nov 2000, *Edwin, the Artist's Son* (c. 1930, oil on canvas, 19 x 15 ins / 47 x 37 cm) GBP 38,000. LONDON, 23 Nov 2001, *Portrait of Miss Dorothy Duveen* (c. 1950, oil on canvas, 22 x 18 ins / 55 x 46 cm) GBP 35,000. LONDON, 4 Dec 2001, *Girl Leaning on a Stick* (1910, oil on board, 13 x 9 ins / 33 x 23 cm) GBP 44,000. LONDON, 4 July 2002, *Women at Cork* (pen, black ink, watercolour and gouache, 17 x 12 ins / 44 x 30 cm) GBP 13,000. LONDON, 21 Nov 2002, *Head of Edie McNeill* (c. 1906, pencil, 13 x 9 ins / 34 x 23 cm) GBP 55,000. LONDON, 6 June 2003, *Dorelia in a Red Dress* (c. 1906, oil on canvas, 72 x 32 ins / 183 x 82 cm) GBP 110,000. LONDON, 21 Nov 2003, *Portrait of Mrs Eve Fleming* (c. 1922, oil on canvas, 42 x 34 ins / 107 x 86 cm) GBP 26,000. LONDON, 13 May 2004, *Shawled Girls, Galway* (pen, black ink and watercolour, 17 x 12 ins / 44 x 30 cm) GBP 8,000. LONDON, 24 Nov 2004, *Dorelia Standing* (c. 1905-1910, on paper, 18 x 10 ins / 46 x 25 cm) GBP 9,500.

JOHN, Elias, or Jahn
German, 17th century.
Died 1628, in Freiberg (Saxony).
Painter.

Elias John painted portraits of *Luther* and *Melanchthon* (1592), also of *Great Elector Christian I* (1595) and a painting of the *Saviour* (1599) for the Council of Freiberg. Other works of his mentioned include a portrait of the *Emperor Ferdinand II* (1621) and a painting of the *Fall of Man* (1622), also for the Council of Freiberg.

JOHN, Eugen
German, 19th - 20th century.
Born 1 July 1863, in Berlin.
Landscape artist.

Eugen John exhibited in Berlin in 1909.

JOHN, Friedrich
German, 18th - 19th century.
Born 1769, in Marienburg (now Malbork, Poland); died 1843, in Marburg.
Engraver (stippling).

Friedrich John worked in Warsaw, England and finally in Vienna. During his long term in Poland, he did portraits of *Bredezki, Kosciuzko* (after Grassi), *Prince Lubomiesky as a Child*, and *Prince Joseph Poniatowski*. Other works of his mentioned include 20 plates for the illustrated edition of Klopstock's *Messias*, and four plates on subjects from the same work after Fuger (1798). He also engraved history and genre subjects, plus portraits of rulers and celebrities, including *Thirty Portraits of Celebrated Men of Bavaria*, after Edlinger.

JOHN, Gwen for Gwendolen Mary
British, 20th century.
Born 22 June 1876, in Haverfordwest, Wales; died 18 September 1939, in Dieppe, France.
Painter (gouache), watercolourist. Figures, portraits, interiors with figures, cats.

Gwen John was the elder sister of Augustus Edwin John. She studied at the Slade School of Fine Art from 1895 to 1898 under Henry Tonks, a staunch advocate of the importance of a thorough grounding in the art of drawing. In 1898 she travelled to Paris and studied at the Académie Carmen, under James Abbott McNeill Whistler (whose teaching concentrated on painting techniques). She returned to England in 1899 but finally settled in France once again, in 1904. Initially based in Montparnasse, she supported herself by working as an artist's model for English and American women painters, and for Auguste Rodin, who became her lover. In 1914 she moved to the Paris suburb of Meudon, where Rodin had established a studio and 'held court' at the Villa des Brillants. Gwen was also an associate of the poet Rainer Maria Rilke.

In 1913 she followed Rodin's long-time lover Camille Claudel and converted to Catholicism. She corresponded with the Jesuit father Martin D'Arcy, and sought the spiritual counsel of the French Catholic philosopher Jacques Maritain and his wife Raïssa. Her passionate attachment to Raïssa's sister, Vera Oumançoff, was not reciprocated and the Maritains sought to curb Gwen's obsessive attentions. Her devout faith seems to have encouraged her increasingly reclusive and ascetic lifestyle (acquaintances observed her 'passionate violence that caused her suffering'). She remained in Meudon until shortly before her death, eventually building a chalet studio on Rue Babie. The nuns of the town's Dominican convent were among her sitters, together with members of her church congregation. On the eve of war in September 1939, at the age of 63, Gwen travelled to the French channel port of Dieppe, carrying only an official copy of her will and instructions for her burial. She collapsed and died in the town's public hospital on 18 September.

Her works are Intimist in character: small-scale portraits, quiet interiors, her cats or a familiar sitter (*The Convalescent*) in a frequently-recurring setting. In recent decades, increasing critical and popular appreciation of her work has gone some way towards realising her brother Augustus's prediction that he would ultimately be remembered as 'Gwen John's brother'.

BIBLIOGRAPHY:

Chitty, Susan, *Gwen John*, Hodder and Stoughton, London, 1981. Taubman, M., *Gwen John*, London, 1985. *Gwen John: An Interior Life*, exhibition catalogue, Barbican Art Gallery, London, 1985 (introduction by A.A. Fraser, essay by C. Langdale). Langdale, Cecily, *Gwen John: with a Catalogue Raisonné and a Selection of the Drawings*, Paul Mellon Centre for Studies in British Art, New Haven and London, 1987. Langdale, Cecily, *Gwen John*, New Haven and London, 1987. *Gwen John, 1876-1939*, exhibition catalogue, Browse and Farby, London, 1998. Roe, Sue, *Gwen John: A Life*, London, 2001. Roe, Sue, *Gwen John. A Life*, Chatto & Windus, London, 2001. *Gwen John and Augustus John*, exhibition catalogue, Tate Gallery, London, 2004.

MUSEUMS AND GALLERIES:

CAMBRIDGE (Fitzwilliam Mus.): *The Convalescent* (c. 1923-1924, oil on canvas) - LONDON (Tate Collection): *The Nun* (c. 1915-1921, oil/board); *Dorelia in a Black Dress* (c. 1903-1904, oil on canvas); *Self-portrait* (1902, oil on canvas) - MANCHESTER (City AG).

AUCTION RECORDS:

LONDON, 5 May 1943, *Sister Marie Céline*, GBP 100. LONDON, 11 Dec 1968, *Sleeping Cat* (watercolour/pencil outline) GBP 1,050. LONDON, 26 Nov 1969, *Profile of a Little Girl* (watercolour and gouache) GBP 1,450. LONDON, 29 Oct 1971, *Study of a Young girl in a Blue Dress*, Gns 2,800. LONDON, 21 Nov 1973, *Woman in a Green Coat, from Behind* (watercolour, pencil and gouache) GBP 1,300. LONDON, 11 Oct 1974, *Young Girl holding a Rose* (1922) Gns 3,700. PARIS, 16 June 1976, *Reclining Woman, Reading* (gouache, 13 x 20 ins / 33 x 50.5 cm) FRF 6,200. LONDON, 7 June 1978, *Vase of Flowers* (watercolour and pencil heightened with gouache, 8 3/4 x 7 3/4 ins / 22.5 x 19.8 cm) GBP 1,700. NEW YORK, 9 June 1979, *Portrait of Arthur Symons* (charcoal, 10 1/2 x 10 ins / 26.4 x 25.4 cm) USD 3,000. LONDON, 27 June 1979, *Two Young Girls Wearing Hats* (watercolour heightened with gouache, 6 x 4 3/4 ins / 15.5 x 12 cm) GBP 1,900. LONDON, 11 Nov 1981, *Standing Figure of a Young Girl in a Church, Meudon* (gouache, 6 1/2 x 5 ins / 16.5 x 12.5 cm) GBP 1,700. LONDON, 4 Nov 1983, *Rue Terre-Neuve, Meudon* (watercolour, 8 1/4 x 8 3/4 ins / 21 x 22.3 cm) GBP 1,700. LONDON, 8 Oct 1985, *Self-portrait* (pencil and grey wash, heightened with white, 9 x 6 ins / 22 x 15 cm) GBP 3,600. LONDON, 14 Nov 1986, *Little Girl* (1916, watercolour, gouache and pencil/beige paper, 8 1/2 x 6 3/4 ins / 21.3 x 17 cm) GBP 13,000. LONDON, 12 June 1987, *Study for 'The Convalescent'* (wax crayon/grey-brown paper, 13 x 11 ins / 33.3 x 27.8 cm) GBP 2,600. LONDON, 10 June 1988, *Black cat, Resting* (watercolour and gouache, 6 1/2 x 8 1/2 ins / 16.3 x 21.4 cm) GBP 14,850; *The Precious Book* (oil on canvas, 10 1/4 x 9 ins / 26.3 x 22 cm) GBP 176,000. LONDON, 21 Sept 1989, *Study for a Young Girl Wearing an Apron* (charcoal, 7 1/2 x 6 1/2 ins / 19.1 x 16.5 cm) GBP 2,640. LONDON, 10 Nov 1989, *Head of a Young Girl* (pencil, 9 x 6 ins / 22.9 x 15.2 cm) GBP 4,950. LONDON, 9 March 1990, *Seated Woman* (oil on canvas, 10 1/2 x 8 1/2 ins / 26.7 x 21.6 cm) GBP 181,500. LONDON, 3 May 1990, *Two Nuns* (watercolour and ink heightened with white, 3 3/4 x 2 3/4 ins / 9.5 x 7 cm) GBP 3,300. LONDON, 8 Nov 1990, *Seated Figure of a Young Servant Girl, Sewing* (oil on canvas, 17 1/4 x 14 1/4 ins / 43.8 x 36.2 cm) GBP 44,000. LONDON, 7 Nov 1991, *Small Profile Portrait* (watercolour and gouache, 6 1/2 x 6 ins / 16.5 x 15 cm) GBP 6,050. LONDON, 6 March 1992, *Old Woman with a Black Shawl* (watercolour and gouache/beige paper, 6 x 4 1/2 ins / 15.5 x 11.5 cm) GBP 4,620. LONDON, 5 June 1992, *Study of a Sleeping Cat* (pencil and wash/brown paper, 4 3/4 x 6 ins / 12 x 15 cm) GBP 6,050. LONDON, 12 March 1993, *Old Woman with a Black Shawl* (watercolour, gouache and lead pencil/beige paper, 6 x 4 1/2 ins / 15.5 x 11.5 cm) GBP 4,370. LONDON, 5 March 1999, *Portrait of Girl with Clasped Hands* (c. 1918-1919, pencil, 9 x 6 ins / 22 x 15 cm) GBP 7,500. LONDON, 2 Nov 1999, *Tree-tops in Twilight* (gouache, 9 x 8 ins / 22 x 21 cm) GBP 3,200. LONDON, 21 Nov 2000, *Black Cat on Blue and Pink* (watercolour and pencil, 7 x 9 ins / 17 x 22 cm) GBP 6,000. LONDON, 6 Dec 2000, *Study of a Girl's Head* (charcoal, 8 x 8 ins / 21 x 20 cm) GBP 10,000. LONDON, 5 Dec 2001, *Young Woman Holding a Piece of Sewing* (oil on canvas, 18 x 15 ins / 46 x 38 cm) GBP 65,000. LONDON, 5 Dec 2001, *Girl Posing in a Hat with Tassels* (oil on canvas, 18 x 15 ins / 46 x 38 cm) GBP 74,000. LONDON, 21 Nov 2002, *Portrait of Lady Reclining* (c. 1910, pencil and grey wash, 7 x 10 ins / 19 x 25 cm) GBP 12,000. LONDON, 4 Dec 2002, *Portrait of a Girl in Grey* (1910-1920, oil on canvas, 10 x 8 ins / 25 x 20 cm) GBP 54,000. NEW YORK, 3 March 2003, *Seated Cat Washing* (c. 1905, brush, ink, wash and pencil, 7 x 6 ins / 17 x 14 cm) USD 4,000. LONDON, 3 Dec 2003, *Seated Girl* (pencil, 6 x 5 ins / 15 x 12 cm) GBP 3,200. LONDON, 14 Oct 2004, *Children in Church at Meudon* (c. 1917-1920, gouache, 6 x 4 ins / 14 x 11 cm) GBP 5,500. LONDON, 18 Nov 2004, *Girl in a Blue Hat* (watercolour and gum arabic, 3 x 4 ins / 8 x 10 cm) GBP 4,000.

JOHN, J. H.

British, 19th century.

Active in London.

Painter. Portraits.

J.H. John exhibited his work at the Royal Academy from 1828 to 1833.

JOHN, Jiri

Czechoslovak, 20th century.

Born 6 November 1923, in Trešt; died June 1972, in Prague.

Painter, engraver.

Jiri John studied at the school of graphic arts in Prague in 1945-1946 and then at the school of applied arts from 1946 to 1951. From 1963 until his death, he taught at the academy of fine art in Prague.

After an initial period when his work showed the influence of Cubism and Neo-Constructivism, he gradually moved away from the figurative representation of things, whether objects in a still-life or elements of landscape, arriving in around 1963 at an abstract organisation of calm surfaces and restrained colours. This restraint in both form and tone is even more marked in his engravings where delicate greys are arranged in alternating plank-like bands.

Collective exhibitions include: São Paulo Biennale (1963, winning a silver medal for engraving); *Czechoslovak Art Today*, Bochum; 16th Salon de la Jeune Peinture, Musée d'Art Moderne de la Ville de Paris; *New Reality in Contemporary Czechoslovak Art*, Genoa; and 5th Biennale of Contemporary Art, San Marino where he was awarded a prize (1965); *Czechoslovak Printmakers*, Rome; *Prague Printmakers*, Stedelijk Museum, Amsterdam; and *Contemporary Czechoslovak Art*, Academy of Fine Art, Berlin (1966); *Contemporary Czechoslovak Art*, Stockholm (1967). He has held several solo exhibitions since 1960, particularly in Prague. His monumental works include the memorial to the Jewish victims of Nazi persecution in Prague.

BIBLIOGRAPHY:

Fifty years of Czechoslovak Painting from the Collections of the Galleries, 1918-1958, exhibition catalogue, Slovenska Narodna Gal., Bratislava, 1968 (in commemoration of the 50th anniversary of the Republic of Czechoslovakia).

JOHN, Wilhelm. See **JOHN August Wilhelm**

JOHN, William Goscombe (Sir)
British, 19th - 20th century.
Born 21 February 1860, in Cardiff; died 15 December 1952, in London.
Sculptor. Monuments.

William Goscombe John trained at the Royal Academy in London. He lived and worked in London, and was a member of the Royal Society of British Sculptors. He was made a member of the Royal Academy in 1909 (where he had exhibited from 1886). He also exhibited at the Salon des Artistes Français in Paris, winning a jury commendation in 1892. He won a gold medal at the Exposition Universelle in Paris in 1900, and a second medal in 1901. He executed numerous public monuments for towns throughout Britain.

MUSEUMS AND GALLERIES:
CARDIFF: *Alderman Taylor; Morpheus* (bronze) - GLASGOW: *Elf* - LONDON (Tate Collection): *A Boy at Play* (c. 1895, bronze).

AUCTION RECORDS:
LONDON, 12 June 1985, *The Drummer Boy* (brown-patinated bronze, h. 17¼ ins / 44 cm) GBP 3,800. LONDON, 26 Nov 1986, *The Elf* (brown-patinated bronze, h. 23¼ ins / 59 cm) GBP 5,000. LONDON, 13 May 1987, *Bouquet of Flowers* (gouache and watercolour, 5½ x 5¾ ins / 14 x 14.5 cm) GBP 2,800. BILLINGSHURST, 19 Oct 1999, *Elf* (dark brown patinated bronze, h. 23 ins / 59 cm) GBP 7,500. LONDON, 26 June 2001, *Bust of Eliza Hulme Lady Lever* (1916, white marble on green marble column, h. 76 ins / 192 cm) GBP 8,000. LONDON, 26 June 2001, *Bust of Sir William Hesketh Lever* (1915, white marble on green marble column, h. 70 ins / 179 cm) GBP 10,000.

JOHN OF LIMOGES. See **LIMOSIN Jehan I**

JOHN OF LIUBLJANA, or Johannes de Laybaco
Slovene, 15th century.
Active in the middle of the 15th century.
Painter.

John of Liubljana produced decorations for several churches, including those in Visoko, Kameni Vrh, and Muljava. His figures have gentle, sentimental and idealised expressions, in contract to the realist painting of Flemish gothic.

JOHN THE PAINTER
Irish, 20th century.
Painter, draughtsman. Figures, urban views.
Art Brut.

John the Painter spent 30 years of his life in a psychiatric hospital. In the 1990s, encouraged by art therapists working for the association Artlink, he began to paint. A self-taught artist, he painted scenes from the neighbourhood of his home town of Cork. His paintings are unconventional, using lines and diagrams and displaying an intuitive use of colour.

In 2003 an exhibition of his work was shown at the Irish Museum of Modern Art in Dublin.

MUSEUMS AND GALLERIES:
DUBLIN (Irish Museum of Modern Art): collection of works, gift.

JOHNNY DE ROLA, real name: Rola Janicki de Janice John or Janusz
Polish, 20th century.
Born 1 June 1910, in Lviv.
Active in France.
Painter. Portraits.

Johnny de Rola studied in Liège. He worked with the painter Sylvain Vigny between about 1940 and 1950. His exhibitions have mainly been held in towns on the Mediterranean coast. He lived and worked in Nice.

JOHNS, Ambrose Bodwen
British, 19th century.
Born c. 1776, in Plymouth; died 10 December 1858, in Plymouth.
Painter. Landscapes.

Ambrose Bodwen Johns started out as a bookseller; however, his paintings were sought after to the point that he was able to dedicate himself totally to his art. Much of his work was painted in the county of Derby. He exhibited in London from 1814 to 1846, especially at the Royal Academy, the British Institution and the Suffolk Street Gallery.

JOHNS, H.
Dutch, 18th century.
Active c. 1791.
Miniaturist, watercolourist. Portraits, historical figures.

MUSEUMS AND GALLERIES:
BERLIN: *Portrait of a Prince* - VIENNA (Albertina Mus.): *Leopold II* (watercolour) - WASHINGTON DC (National Portrait Gal.): *Portrait of James Smithson* (miniature).

JOHNS, Jasper
American, 20th century.
Born 15 May 1930, in Allendale (South Carolina) or Augusta (Georgia).
Painter, sculptor, draughtsman, engraver, mixed media.
Neo-Dadaism, Pop Art.

Jasper Johns grew up in South Carolina. He followed courses in art and painting at the University of South Carolina, and enrolled in a commercial art school for two semesters in New York City. He was enlisted in World War II, but was able to resume his studies at the City College in New York in 1950-1951 thanks to a G.I Bill (an ex-combatants' bursary). It was at this time that he met Rauschenberg, the composer John Cage, and the dancer Merce Cunningham. He acted as artistic adviser for John Cage and Merce Cunningham's Dance Company until 1972, collaborating with painters such as Robert Morris, Frank Stella, Bruce Naumann and Andy Warhol. He lives and works in New York State and St Martin in the French West Indies. He has been a member of the New York Academy of Arts and Letters since 1988.

Together with Rauschenberg, who once lived in the neighbouring apartment, Jasper Johns belongs to the third generation of Modern American artists. Both artists reacted against the effusions of Lyrical Abstraction and Abstract Expressionism, and were responsible for launching the various processes of appropriating everyday urban reality that characterise Pop Art. However, they remained faithful to a certain aestheticism of mind and formulation that make them direct heirs of Dada and Duchamp.

Johns initially created assemblages inspired by Cornell and Schwitters, which he later destroyed precisely because they were imitation. In 1955 he produced his first original works in which he respected a formal, geometrical and minimalist vocabulary applied to elements of the everyday. He took very common, depersonalised, devalued images such as the American flag and the shooting target, reduced them to bands and concentric rings, and carefully removed any visual cultural references, subjecting them instead to expressive ends. This was often achieved through a delicate blending of wax crayons, creating sumptuous monochromes with the subtlest greys. The ancient encaustic or hot wax process also enables the introduction of depth.

In 1959, with *False Start* (in colour) and *Jubilee* (black and white), he introduced words, recalling his earlier assemblages featuring letters and numbers. There is a marked discordance between the meaning of the words and the actual colours. The words 'red, yellow and blue', in stencilled characters, appear alongside gestural, abstract fields of colour, inspired by Expressionism, and lozenges of colour which evoke the chromatic circle or the paint-merchant's palette. According to Johns, 'the idea is to scatter the names of the colours across the canvas on more or less the same scale; so this canvas will bring together all the colours, but by their names rather than on the level of visual sensations'. By dissociating things from their names, assembling a diverse collection of words and objects, spots and monochromes, and by using aggressive brush strokes, Johns strikes a balance between the figurative and the hard-edged abstract. He also creates sculptures such as the series of torches and Ballantine's beer cans in papier maché, plaster and glass or in bronze. In the early 1960s, his works are marked by the use of hinged sections, signs and labels, and a bleaker palette. The use of his own body in his work introduces a sensual dimension and merges the limits between creation and creator (*Studies for Skin*, 1962). Johns perfected a technique for representing human skin; he spread graphite powder over oil paint, smeared himself with it and then pressed his features or body against the paper or the canvas.

Johns recycled key themes and images, such as the motif of the map of the United States (first used in 1966). He also introduced the technique of collage into his work. Newspapers camouflaged under paint and real objects appeared first in the margins and then directly in the centre of the image, as with the broom in *Fools House*, or with, handprints and footprints, the pieces of a chair and a wax mould of a leg in *According to What*, 1964. At the same time he experimented with hatched surfaces, tangled lines, strokes and slab motifs on abstract canvases in which he restricted himself to a few colours. These compositions still find inspiration in the everyday. Although far-removed from his Pop Art flags and targets, the flatness that reigns throughout, where volume is only created by either sculpture or the use of real objects, is a constant feature in his work. The decorative aspect is predominant, rather like a kaleidoscope that produces a new and unexpected pattern each time it is moved. The absence of subject matter becomes the object of his paintings. Johns plays with shapes in an infinite variety of structures, as apparent in the monumental *Untitled* of 1972 (183 x 487,5 cm/72 x 191 ins) which combines an assemblage of wooden battens and wax moulds of the human body in the tradition of his previous work. In collages, screenprints and various media such as neon, photoreproductions or metal, the real constantly emerges from the abstract. A tireless experimenter, he draws his inspiration from sources as varied as Duchamp's 'ready-mades' and Grünewald's altar; Munch's self-portrait and Cezanne's skull. His painting is impulsive, rich with impasto and, for over a decade, applied in a cross-hatched pattern. New motifs evolve around three-dimensional objects, or literal depictions of them, and optical illusions. Painting is, for Johns, a subject in itself. He continually makes reference to his own pictorial past, aserting that 'my work feeds on itself'. In the 1980s his concern for autobiography led him to develop the theme of the painter and his studio. Inspired by Picasso, he felt the need to narrate the various phases of his life through painting as with *Seasons* (1985-86). For the first time, he uses the full human figure, treated as an outline whose spirit hovers over the canvas. A naked grey man (the shadow of the artist) stands surrounded by his personal effects: a silk-screen print of the Mona Lisa (reference to Duchamp and Warhol), earlier works such as *Double Flags* and a field of coloured hatchings, ceramics by Georges Ohr (whose work he collected), fragments of the Grünewald altar and a road sign warning of the risk of avalanches. Later, he tried to blur his own recognisable style by incorporating tracings from an unknown source (*Green Angel*, 1990). For Johns, the 1990s represent a period of synthesis, a reflexion on picture-making and memory.

Johns produced numerous prints on the same subjects as his paintings using a variety of techniques. 'Prints', he said, 'allow the artist to satisfy all his curiosity. And that nourishes painting: the elements that are essential to the print become interesting in themselves and are subsequently used as ideas in painting. In this sense, my work with prints has greatly influenced my painting.' He also produced stage sets for Merce Cunningham and 33 engraved illustrations for a work by Samuel Beckett, *Foirades/Fizzles*.

Johns' art unites a methodical working process with experimentation and craft which quotes and appropriates art history as it sees fit. It goes beyond definite boundaries or categorisations and combines simplicity with mystery. His early style engendered many subsequent art movements (Pop Art, Minimal Art and Conceptual Art) transforming well-known images into cultural icons. Working in extensive series, he explored new motifs as well as a multiplicity of techniques and gradually moved away from the anonimity of his early works both by his gestual and physical involvement and by incorporating images with autobiographical significance.

He has participated in countless group exhibitions, including: 1958, Venice Biennale, International Young Artists Section; 1958, Pittsburgh International Biennale, Carnegie Institute, Pittsburgh (International Prize); 1959, *Sixteen Americans*, Museum of Modern Art, New York; 1959, 1965, 1974, 1978 and 1981, Whitney Museum of American Art, New York; 1960, Salon de Mai, Paris; 1960, Museum of Art, Columbus, Ohio; 1961, Galerie Rive Droite, Paris; 1961, Art Institute of Chicago; 1961, 1963, 1964, 1965 and 1976, Solomon R. Guggenheim Museum, New York; 1962, Moderna Museet, Stockholm; 1963, Institute of Contemporary Art, London; 1964, Musée d'Art Moderne de la Ville de Paris; 1964, 1972, Documenta, Kassel; 1965, 1966, 1968, 1971, 1976, 1980, 1986 and 1987, Museum of Modern Art, New York; 1964, 1978, 1988, Venice Biennale (Grand Prize in 1988); 1965, 6th International Exhibition of Graphic Art, Ljubljana, Yugoslavia (prize); 1966, *Three Centuries of American Art*, Whitney Museum of American Art, New York; 1967, 9th São Paulo Biennale; 1968, Carnegie Institute, Pittsburgh; 1968, *L'Art du Réel U.S.A., 1948-1968* (*The Art of the Real, USA, 1948-1968*) at the Centre National d'Art Contemporain, Paris; 1969, Metropolitan Museum of Art, New York; 1982, 1984 and 1985, Stedelijk Museum, Amsterdam; 1986, Whitechapel Art Gallery, London; 1988, Ludwig Museum, Cologne, CAPC Musée d'Art Contemporain, Bordeaux; 1990, *L'Art Conceptuel, une Perspective* (*Conceptual Art: A Perspective*) at the Musée d'Art Moderne de la Ville de Paris; 2002, *The Big Americans*, National Gallery of Australia, Canberra.

His work has been the subject of a great many solo exhibitions in galleries and museums in America and Europe, starting in 1958 at the Leo Castelli Gallery in New York. Others include: 1960, *Jasper Johns 1855-1960*, Columbia Museum of Art, Columbia, S.C.; 1962, *Jasper Johns: Retrospective Exhibition*, Everett Ellin Gallery, Los Angeles; 1964, Jewish Museum, New York and Whitechapel Art Gallery, London; 1965, Minami Gallery, Tokyo; 1965, Pasadena Art Museum, California; 1966, *The Drawings of Jasper Johns*, National Collection of Fine Arts, Washington DC; 1968, travelling exhibition organised by the New York Museum of Modern Art; 1969, *Jasper Johns: 30 Lithographien 1960-1968*, Kunstmuseum, Basel; 1970, *Jasper Johns: Prints 1960-70*, Philadelphia Museum of Art, Philadelphia; 1970, *Jasper Johns Litografie*, Museum of Modern Art, New York; 1971, travelling exhibition organised by the Kunsthalle, Bern; 1974, travelling exhibition organised by the Museum of Modern Art in Oxford and the Arts Council of Great Britain; 1977, travelling exhibition organised by the Whitney Museum of American Art, New York, shown at Hayward Gallery in London, Seibu Museum of Art in Tokyo, and the Museum Ludwig in Cologne; 1978, Centre Georges Pompidou, Paris; 1979, *Jasper Johns: Working Proofs*, travelling exhibition in Europe, organised by the Kunstmuseum Basel; 1986, *Jasper Johns: L'oeuvre gravé*, Fondation Maeght, St-Paul-de-Vence; 1986, *A Print Retrospective*, Museum of Modern Art, New York; 1988, *Jas-*

per Johns: Works since 1974, Philadelphia Museum of Art, Philadelphia; 1988, *Jasper Johns: A Print Retrospective*, National Musem of Art, Osaka; 1990, *The Drawings of Jasper Johns*, Hayward Gallery, London; 1990-1991, travelling exhibition in the USA in Houston, San Francisco, St Louis etc; 1992, Fondation Van Gogh, Arles; 1996, *Jasper Johns: A Retrospective*, Museum of Modern Art, New York then Ludwig Museum, Cologne and Museum of Contemporary Art, Tokyo; 1996, *Jasper Johns: The Sculptures*, Centre for the Study of Sculpture, Henry Moore Institute, Leeds; 2002, *L'Œuvre gravé, 1960-2000* (*Prints, 1960-2000*), Musée d'Art Américain, Giverny.

BIBLIOGRAPHY:

Rosenblum, Robert, '*Jasper Johns*' in *Art International*, periodical, Zurich, September 1960. Steinberg, Leo, *Jasper Johns*, Wittenborn, New York, 1963. Tillim, Sidney, '*Ten Years of Jasper Johns*' in *Arts Magazine*, periodical, New York, April, 1964. Crichton, Michael, *Jasper Johns*, exhibition catalogue, Whitney Museum of American Art, New York, 1977. Field, Richard S., *Jasper Johns: Prints 1970-1977*, exhibition catalogue, 1978. Burks, Nan, in *Jasper Johns: 'False Start' and His Painting before 1964*, Ph.D. dissertation, 1979 (Massachusetts Institute of Technology, Cambridge, mass.). Shapiro, David, *Jasper Johns. Drawings 1954-1984*, Abrams, New York, 1984. Francis, Richard, *Jasper Johns*, Abbeville Press, New York, 1984. Bernstein, Roberta, in *Jasper Johns' Paintings and Sculptures 1954-1974: 'The Changing Focus of the Eye'*, UMI Research Press, Ann Arbor, 1985 (Ph.D dissertation, Columbia University, New York, 1975). Castelman, Riva, *Jasper Johns, A Print Retrospective*, Museum of Modern Art, New York, 1986. Gilbert, Gregory, in *American Neo-Dada and the Problematic of Collage*, Ph. D. dissertation, 1990 (Rutgers University, Camdem, N.J.). Naumann, Francis M., *Jasper Johns: According to What and Watchman*, Gagosian Gallery, New York, 1992. Bernstein, Roberta, in *Jasper Johns*, Rizzoli, New York, 1992. Crichton, Michael, *Jasper Johns*, Harryr N. Abrams, Whitney Museum of American Art, New York, 1994 (revised and expanded edition of exhibition catalogue at Whitney Museum of American Art). Field, Richard, in *The Prints of Jasper Johns: 1960-1993, A Catalogue Raisonné*, catalogue raisonné, Universal Limited Art Editions, West Islip, NY, 1994. Orton, Fred, *Figuring Jasper Johns*, Reaktion, London, 1994. Varnedoe, Kirk/Bernstein, Roberta, *Jasper Johns*, retrospective exhibition catalogue, Museum of Modern Art, New York, 1996. Curtis, Penelope/Orton, Fred, *Jasper Johns, the sculptures*, exhibition catalogue, Henry Moore Institute, Centre for the Study of Sculpture, Leeds, 1996. Varnedoe, Kirk (ed.), *Jasper Johns, writings, sketchbook notes, interviews*, The Museum of Modern Art, New York, 1996. *Jasper Johns Flags, 1955-1994*, exhibition catalogue, A. d'Offay Gallery, London, 1996. Yau, John, *The United States of Jasper Johns*, Zoland, Cambridge (MA), 1996. Johnston, Jill, in *Jasper Johns: Privileged Information*, Thames and Hudston, New York, 1997. Rosenthal, Mark, in *Jasper Johns: drawings: the Menil Collection*, Menil Foundation, Houston, 2003. Bernstein, Roberta/Foster, Carter E., in *Jasper Johns: numbers*, exhibition catalogue, Cleveland Museum of Art, Cleveland, 2003. Rothfuss, Joan, in *Past things and present: Jasper Johns since 1983*, Walker Art Center, Minneapolis, 2003.

MUSEUMS AND GALLERIES:

AACHEN (Ludwig Forum für Internationale Kunst): *0-9* (1959) - AMSTERDAM (Stedelijk Mus.): *Untitled* (1964-1965) - BALTIMORE (MA) - BASEL (Kunstmus.): *Céline* (1978, oil on canvas); *Figure 2* (1962); *Flag over White Collage* (1955, encaustic and collage on canvas); *Out of the Window Number 2* (1962, oil and canvas with objects); *The Bath* (1988, encaustic and canvas); *Voice 2* (1971, oil and collage on canvas) - BOSTON (MFA) - BUFFALO (Albright-Knox AG): *Numbers in Colour* (1958-1959) - CHICAGO (AI): *Near the Lagoon* (encaustic on canvas and wooden boards, hinges and string); *0-9* (1967, lithograph on paper) - CLEVELAND (MA): 21 works - COLOGNE (Mus. Ludwig): *Flag on Orange Field* (1957); *Painted Bronze* (1960, oil on bronze); *Passage* (1962); *Eddingsville* (1965); *Untitled* (1972, oil, encaustic, and collage on canvas with objects) - COLOGNE (Wallraf-Richartz Mus.) - DALLAS (MA): *Device* (1961-1962, mixed media) - DETROIT (IA): *Figure 1* (1966, lithograph); *Green Angel 2* (1997, intaglio); *Hand* (1963, lithograph) - FORT WORTH (MAM): *Target* (1958, pencil, wash, and collage on paper mounted on cardboard) - HOUSTON (MFA): *Ventriloquist* (1983, encaustic on canvas); *Map* (1961, oil on canvas); *Untitled* (1991, etching and aquatint with scraping and burnishing); *Untitled (Red, Yellow, Blue)* (1984, encaustic on three canvas panels) - LONDON (Arts Council Collection, Hayward Gal.) - LONDON (Tate Collection): *0 through 9* (1961, oil on canvas); *Dancers on a Plane* (1980-1981, oil and acrylic on canvas with painted bronze frame) - LONDON (Victoria and Albert Mus.): *Three Flags* (1959) - LOS ANGELES (County MA): *Figure 0* (1969) - LOS ANGELES (MOCA): *Dutch Wives I* (1977, silkscreen, edition 23/70); *Map* (1962, encaustic and collage on canvas); *Light Bulb* (1967, line etching with photo engraving); *Paint Brushes* (1967, print) - MINNEAPOLIS (Walker Art Center): *Green Angel* (1990, encaustic and sand on canvas); *Flag* (1969, embossed lead); *High School Days* (1969, embossed lead, glass mirror); *Light Bulb* (1969, embossed lead); several lithographs - NEW YORK (Metropolitan Mus. of Art): *White Flag* (1955, encaustic, oil, newsprint, and charcoal on canvas); *Usuyuki* (1981, screenprint) - NEW YORK (MoMA): *Two Flags* (1954); *Target with Four Faces* (1955); *White Numbers* (1957); *Jubilee* (1960, graphite on paper); *Numbers* (1966); *Flag* (1954-55, encaustic, oil and collage on fabric mounted on plywood) - NEW YORK (Whitney Mus. of American Art): *Three Flags* (1958, encaustic on canvas); *Racing Thoughts* (1983, encaustic and collage on canvas) - PARIS (MNAM-CCI): *The Big Five or Black Figure 5* (1960); sixteen works - PARIS (Prints Collection): *Two Maps II* (1966, lithograph) - PHILADELPHIA (MA): *Savarin Can* (1960); *Painted Bronze* (1960) - RICHMOND (Virginia MFA): *Between the clock on the bed* (1982-1983, encaustic/panel) - SAN FRANCISCO (Achenbach Foundation for Graphic Arts): numerous books illustrations - SAN FRANCISCO (FAM): *Two Maps, 1* (1966); *Target* (1971) - SAN FRANCISCO (MoMA): *Land's End* (1963, oil on canvas with stick) - STOCKHOLM (Moderna Mus.) - TEHRAN (Museum of Contemporary Art): *Pinion* (1963-66, lithograph); *Passage 1* - TOKYO (Seibu MA) - TOYAMA (MMA): *Disappearance II* (1961) - WASHINGTON DC (Hirshhorn Mus. and Sculpture Garden): *Untitled* (1954, painted wood, painted plaster cast, photomechanical reproductions on canvas, glass and nails); *Untitled* (1897, oil, encaustic, and charcoal on linen) - WASHINGTON DC (NGA): *False Start I, II, III* (1962, multicolour lithographs, three works); *Perilous Night* (1982, encaustic/canvas with objects) - WASHINGTON DC (Smithsonian American AM): *Corpse and Mirror II* (1976, colour lithograph/paper); *Gray Alphabets* (1968, color lithograph on paper); *Souvenir* (1970, color lithograph on paper); *First Etchings, Second State* (1967-69, etching and drypoint on paper on paper, 13 prints); numerous prints; *Dancers on a Plane* (1980-81, oil and acrylic on canvas); *Numerals* (1970, lead relief) - ZURICH (Kunsthaus): *Zone* (1962).

AUCTION RECORDS:

NEW YORK, 18 Nov 1970, *Tennyson* (encaustic/canvas) USD 70,000. NEW YORK, 3 Feb 1971, *The Critic Smiles* (lead relief) USD 2,900. NEW YORK, 18 Oct 1973, *Double White Map* (encaustic and collage/canvas) USD 240,000. MILAN, 16 Nov 1976, *Good Time Charley* (1972, $4\frac{1}{4}$ x $28\frac{3}{4}$ ins / 11 x 73 cm)

ITL 700,000. Los Angeles, 6 March 1977, *Figure 7 (Gemini 94)* (1968, black and brown lithograph) USD 3,500. New York, 12 May 1977, *Bronze Flag* (1960, bronze, 12 1/4 x 18 3/4 ins / 31 x 47.5 cm) USD 14,000. New York, 17 May 1979, *Number 2* (encaustic and collage/canvas, 3 x 2 1/2 ins / 7.5 x 6.5 cm) USD 19,000. New York, 19 Oct 1979, *Flag II* (1960, white lithograph, 17 1/2 x 27 ins / 44.5 x 68.3 cm) USD 6,000. New York, 16 May 1980, *The Critic Smiles* (1969, lead relief, 23 x 17 ins / 58.5 x 43 cm) USD 6,200. New York, 12 Nov 1980, *Study for Watchman* (1964, graphite and oil on paper, 26 1/2 x 19 1/2 ins / 67 x 49.5 cm) USD 16,000. New York, 4 Nov 1982, *Light Bulb* (1960, brown-patinated gilded bronze, l. 6 ins / 15 cm) USD 35,000. New York, 2 May 1983, *False Start I* (1962, coloured lithograph, 18 x 13 3/4 ins / 44.8 x 34.9 cm) USD 10,000. New York, 20 May 1983, *In Memory of my Feelings - Frank O'Hara* (1961, oil on canvas and objects, 40 x 60 ins / 101.6 x 152.4 cm) USD 330,000. New York, 9 Nov 1983, *Untitled* (1969, pastel and gouache, 29 3/4 x 41 1/2 ins / 75.5 x 105.7 cm) USD 55,000. New York, 18 April 1985, *Study for Recent Still-life* (1965, gouache and lead pencil, 31 1/4 x 19 ins / 79.4 x 48.2 cm) USD 60,000. New York, 10 Nov 1986, *Construction with Toy Piano* (1954, graphite and collage of remounted newspaper/toy piano, 11 1/2 x 9 1/4 x 2 1/4 ins / 29.3 x 23.2 x 5.6 cm) USD 160,000. New York, 10 Nov 1986, *Out the Window* (1959, encaustic and collage of newspaper/canvas, 54 1/2 x 40 1/4 ins / 138.5 x 102 cm) USD 3,300,000. New York, 11 Nov 1986, *Flag* (1959, liquid graphite/paper, 12 x 16 ins / 30.5 x 40.6 cm) USD 320,000. New York, 4 Nov 1987, *Figure 3* (1962-1967, charcoal and chalk/grey paper, 28 x 21 1/2 ins / 71 x 54.8 cm) USD 130,000. New York, 3 May 1988, *Diver* (1962, oil on canvas, 90 x 170 ins / 228.6 x 432 cm) USD 4,180,000. New York, 9 Nov 1988, *Form 3* (1961, metal and paper collage/canvas, 26 x 20 ins / 66.3 x 50.8 cm) USD 825,000. New York, 10 Nov 1988, *False Start* (1959, oil on canvas, 67 1/2 x 53 ins / 171.5 x 134.7 cm) USD 15,500,000. New York, 2 May 1989, *Alphabets* (1968, oil on canvas, 50 3/4 x 34 ins / 128.8 x 86.5 cm) USD 2,860,000. New York, 3 May 1989, *Coloured Alphabet* (1959, encaustic oil and paper collage/panel, 12 x 10 1/2 ins / 30.5 x 26.7 cm) USD 3,520,000. New York, 7 Nov 1989, *0 through 9* (1960, oil and collage of paper/paper/synthetic resin, 30 x 22 1/4 ins / 75.9 x 56.5 cm) USD 2,970,000. New York, 8 Nov 1989, *Two Flags (of the United States)* (1973, oil on canvas and encaustic/canvas, three panels, each 52 1/4 x 69 1/2 ins / 132.7 x 176.5 cm) USD 12,100,000. New York, 23 Feb 1990, *Alphabet* (1959, oil pencil and black chalk/paper, 12 3/4 x 12 ins / 32.4 x 30.5 cm) USD 572,000. New York, 12 Nov 1991, *Device Circle* (1959, encaustic, collage of newspaper, wooden stick and oil on canvas, 40 x 40 ins / 101.7 x 101.7 cm) USD 4,400,000. New York, 13 Nov 1991, *Jubilee* (collage of packaging and oil on canvas, 60 x 44 ins / 152.3 x 111.7 cm) USD 4,950,000. New York, 18 Nov 1992, *0 through 9* (1961, oil on canvas, 54 x 45 ins / 137.1 x 114.3 cm) USD 2,310,000. New York, 4 May 1993, *Untitled* (1980, acrylic/plastic/canvas, 30 1/2 x 54 1/2 ins / 77.5 x 138.2 cm) USD 607,500. New York, 3 May 1994, *Desert I* (1963, wooden ruler, polyester, wire, brush, charcoal and pencil/paper, 42 x 26 x 2 1/2 ins / 106.6 x 66 x 6.6 cm) USD 266,500. New York, 4 May 1994, *Untitled* (1983, encaustic and collage/canvas with objects, 48 x 75 ins / 122.2 x 190.8 cm) USD 1,432,500. London, 29 June 1994, *Green Target* (encaustic and collage/panel, 8 1/2 x 8 1/2 ins / 21.5 x 21.5 cm) GBP 253,000. Paris, 17 Oct 1994, *Savarin Coffee* (1978, print, 26 x 20 1/4 ins / 66 x 51.5 cm) FRF 25,000. New York, 15 Nov 1995, *Winter* (1986, encaustic/canvas, 75 x 50 ins / 190.5 x 127 cm) USD 3,082,500. New York, 5 May 1996, *Beer Cans* (1964, coloured lithograph, 14 1/4 x 11 ins / 36 x 28 cm) USD 101,500. New York, 9 Nov 1996, *Flags I* (1973, coloured lithograph, 28 x 35 1/2 ins / 70.2 x 90 cm) USD 233,500. New York, 7 May 1997, *1 through 9* (c. 1958, charcoal and pencil/paper, 16 x 12 ins / 40.6 x 30.5 cm) USD 68,500. New York, 7 May 1997, *Target* (1958, encaustic, oil, soft pastel and collage/panel, 14 x 14 ins / 35.6 x 35.6 cm) USD 937,000. New York, 10 Nov 1997, *Body and Mirror* (1974, encaustic, rolls of newsprint, fragments of paper, pencil and oil on canvas, 50 x 68 ins / 127 x 172.7 cm) USD 8,362,500; *White Numbers* (1959, encaustic/canvas, 53 1/4 x 40 1/4 ins / 135.3 x 102 cm) USD 7,922,500; *Decoy* (1971, ink and oil on canvas with copper ring, 72 x 50 1/4 ins / 183 x 127.6 cm) USD 4,402,500. New York, 6 and 7 March 1998, *Cup 2 Picasso* (1973, coloured lithograph, 15 1/4 x 10 1/2 ins / 39 x 26.5 cm) USD 1,610. Paris, 23 March 1998, *Composition* (1976, coloured lithograph, 30 x 29 3/4 ins / 76 x 75.5 cm) FRF 10,500. New York, 13 May 1999, *Two Flags* (1973, oil and encausted on canvas, 52 x 69 ins / 133 x 176 cm) USD 6,500,000. New York, 17 Nov 1999, *Flag* (graphite and wash, 12 x 16 ins / 30 x 41 cm) USD 1,600,000. New York, 14 Nov 2000, *Green Flag* (1956, graphite, colour wax crayon and paper collage, 8 x 10 ins / 20 x 25 cm) USD 600,000. New York, 15 Nov 2000, *Untitled* (1983, monotype, 37 x 96 ins / 94 x 244 cm) USD 550,000. New York, 8 May 2001, *Coloured Alphabet* (1959, oil, encausted on paper collage on panel, 12 x 11 ins / 30 x 27 cm) USD 3,400,000. New York, 14 Nov 2001, *Montez Singing* (1989, encaustic and sand on canvas, 75 x 50 ins / 191 x 128 cm) USD 3,400,000. New York, 12 Nov 2002, *Untitled* (1995, encaustic on canvas, 66 x 44 ins / 168 x 112 cm) USD 1,800,000. New York, 13 Nov 2002, *0 Through 9* (1961, oil on canvas, 54 x 41 ins / 137 x 105 cm) USD 9,000,000. New York, 11 Nov 2003, *Figure 3* (1961, sculptmetal and collage on canvas, 26 x 20 ins / 66 x 51 cm) USD 1,100,000. New York, 11 Nov 2003, *Grey Numbers* (1957, encaustic on canvas, 28 x 22 ins / 71 x 56 cm) USD 4,700,000. New York, 11 May 2004, *Map* (1971, graphite and wash, 19 x 24 ins / 49 x 62 cm) USD 950,000. New York, 12 May 2004, *Corpse and Mirror* (1975-1976, watercolour, 17 x 21 ins / 43 x 54 cm) USD 2,800,000.

JOHNSEN, Alfhild Borsum

Norwegian, 20th century.

Born 5 August 1882, in Lillehammer.

Engraver.

Alfhild Borsum Johnsen was the wife of the sculptor Sverre Johnsen. She studied in Oslo, and for a time also in Copenhagen. She produced etchings and aquatints. Group exhibitions of her works were organised in Oslo in 1913, 1914 and 1921. She featured in the Jubilee Exhibition in Oslo in 1914 and the Norwegian exhibition of engraving in 1922, and exhibited etchings in Oslo and Stockholm in 1924.

JOHNSEN, Birger

Norwegian, 20th century.

Born 8 December 1888, in Larvik.

Active in Moss, near Oslo.

Painter, draughtsman. Landscapes.

Birger Johnsen studied at the academy of fine art in Oslo. He specialised in painting landscapes, and produced drawings for an Oslo newspaper, *Morgenposten*. He featured in the annual national exhibition in Oslo from 1911 and the Jubilee Exhibition in Oslo in 1914. In 1915 an exhibition of his works was organised in Oslo and Geneva.

JOHNSEN, Erik William

Danish, 20th century.

Born 1 January 1886, in Hillerød.

Painter. Figures, portraits, landscapes, flowers.

Erik William Johnsen painted landscapes (*Bornholm, The Area around Copenhagen*), as well as paintings of flowers and figures, and portraits, including a self-portrait. He had a group exhibition of his works organised for him by the society of fine art in Copenhagen in 1920 and a solo exhibition in Charlottenborg in 1922.

JOHNSEN, Hjalmar

Norwegian, 19th century.

Born 25 June 1852, in Stavanger; died 28 November 1901.
Painter. Seascapes.
First a sailor, Hjalmar Johnsen turned to painting at the age of 30. He executed seascapes and especially motifs depicting the southern coastline of Norway. Among his works is the large painting *The Bay of Bergen* (1887). He exhibited at the annual national exhibition in Christiania (now Oslo) between 1884 and 1901. He also exhibited at the Exposition Décannale in Paris in 1900 and the Jubilee exhibition in Christiania in 1914.

JOHNSEN, Johann
17th century.
Born after 1650; died c. 1705.
Painter. Flowers.
Johann Johnsen lived many years in Sweden.
MUSEUMS AND GALLERIES:
STOCKHOLM (Nationalmus.): *Bouquet Tied with Red Ribbon.*
AUCTION RECORDS:
LONDON, 19 July 1973, *Still-life with Flowers and Fruit* (two canvases) Gns 4,800. LONDON, 24 Feb 1984, *Still-lifes with Fruit and Flowers* (oil on canvas remounted on board, a pair, 21 1/2 x 17 ins / 54.6 x 43.1 cm) GBP 13,000. NEW YORK, 17 Jan 1985, *Still-lifes with Fruit and Flowers* (oil on canvas, a pair of ovals, 21 1/2 x 17 ins / 54.5 x 43 cm) USD 26,000. STOCKHOLM, 26 May 2003, *Flowers in Vase. Landscape with Cockatoos* (c. 1700, gouache, a pair, 5x4 ins / 12x10 cm) SEK 66,000.

JOHNSEN, Sverre
Norwegian, 20th century.
Born 19 December 1884, in Christiania (now Oslo).
Painter, engraver, sculptor. Religious subjects, portraits, landscapes.
Sverre Johnsen was a student at the academy of fine art in Christiania in the department of painting, working from 1912 mainly on humorous and decorative woodcuts. He studied ancient Japanese woodcuts in particular. He executed a series of sculpted and painted decorative panels, as well as an altarpiece for the Methodist church in Frederikstad.

He featured in the Norwegian exhibition of engraving in Christiania and in the exhibitions of Nordic engraving in Stockholm and Christiania in 1924. He showed his work in the annual national exhibition in Christiania from 1911.

JOHNSON
19th century.
Engraver.
Johnson made an engraving, *Edinburgh,* after Ewbonk.

JOHNSON
Maiden name: Content
American, 20th century.
Born in Bloomington (Illinois).
Painter.
Mrs Johnson studied under W. Chase and Jean-Paul Laurens in Paris. She lived and worked in New York and was a member of the Pen and Brush Club.

JOHNSON, A.
British, 19th century.
Active in London.
Sculptor.
A. Johnson exhibited busts at the Royal Academy in 1848, 1849, 1850 and 1852.

JOHNSON, Adelaide
American, 20th century.
Born 1859, in Plymouth (Illinois); died 1955, in Washington DC.
Active in Washington.
Sculptor. Busts.
Adelaide Johnson was a pupil of G. Monteverde and Falbi-Altini in Rome. The Capitol in Washington has a memorial by her to Lucrecia Mott, E. Cady Stanton and Susan B. Anthony.
MUSEUMS AND GALLERIES:
CHICAGO (Historical Society): busts - NEW YORK (Metropolitan Mus. of Art): busts.

JOHNSON, Alfred George
Irish, 19th - 20th century.
Painter.
Alfred Johnson exhibited oil paintings and watercolours at the Dublin Academy from 1846 to 1850. He was the brother of Blucher Johnson.

JOHNSON, Arthur
American, 19th - 20th century.
Born 7 August 1874, in Cincinnati; died 1954.
Active in Germany.
Painter, draughtsman. Portraits, genre scenes, landscapes.
Arthur Johnson studied in Germany, where his parents settled. He was active in Berlin. He made his début in 1898 at the Grosse Kunstausstellung in Berlin with a study for a portrait of the poet Peter Hille. He also exhibited paintings and drawings there in 1900, 1904, 1914 and 1924. Among his works mention may be made of *Play of Sunlight, Day of Dreaming, Silence, Romantic Landscape, Children Bathing.* His caricatures appeared in the *Kladderadatsch,* to which he was a regular contributor.
AUCTION RECORDS:
NEW YORK, 4 June 1982, *Silence* (1902, oil on canvas, 59 1/2 x 69 1/4 ins / 151.1 x 175.9 cm) USD 9,500. MUNICH, 5 June 1984, *Wooded Landscape* (oil on canvas, 35 3/4 x 36 1/2 ins / 91 x 93 cm) DEM 6,000. NEW YORK, 20 June 1985, *Wading* (oil on canvas, 36 1/4 x 37 1/4 ins / 92.1 x 94.6 cm) USD 4,000.

JOHNSON, Ben
American, 20th century.
Born 1902; died 1967.
Painter. Nudes, architectural views.
AUCTION RECORDS:
NEW YORK, 22 March 1979, *Nude with Pear* (oil on canvas, 34 1/4 x 36 1/2 ins / 87 x 92.5 cm) USD 1,700. LONDON, 22 Feb 1990, *Spiral Staircase* (acrylic/card, 59 3/4 x 63 1/2 ins / 151.7 x 161 cm) GBP 1,430.

JOHNSON, Bessie Basil
Maiden name: Percival
British, 19th - 20th century.
Painter. Genre scenes, landscapes.
Bessie Johnson was active in Oxford and Eton. Her best-known works show views of Taormina, in Sicily, and Egyptian landscapes. She exhibited at the Royal Academy in 1885, 1889, 1891, 1893, 1896, 1897 and 1914.

JOHNSON, Blucher
Irish, 19th century.
Born 1816, in Dublin; died October 1872, in Dublin.
Sculptor, draughtsman.

JOHNSON, Buffie
American, 20th century.
Born 1912, in New York.
Painter.
Buffie Johnson studied in New York, Los Angeles, then at the Art Students League in New York. Michel Seuphor said of her painting, 'On a bed of colour, often monochrome, scraps of calligraphy swim, float and dissolve into one another.' The poet Pierre Emmanuel has likened her work to the music of Mozart.

Johnson made long stays in Paris, where she took part in the Salon des Réalités Nouvelles in 1949, 1950 and 1957. She has had solo exhibitions in Paris and the USA, notably on several occasions in New York.

Bibliography:
Ratcliff, Carter, '*Buffie Johnson*' in *Arts Magazine*, vol 51, no. 2. Seuphor, Michel, *Buffie Johnson et Alcopley*, Gal. Bing, Paris, 1956. Kinglsey, April, '*The Primal Plants of Buffie Johnson*' in *Women's Art Journal*, vol 3, no. 1, spring-summer 1982.

JOHNSON, C.
British, 17th century.
Engraver.

C. Johnson was one of the first English engravers. Amongst his works is a *Head of the Queen, Wife of James I.*

JOHNSON, Cécile
German, 20th century.
Active in England.
Sculptor.

Cécile Johnson lived and worked in London, where she showed her works for the first time in a solo exhibition at the Nicolas Jacobs Gallery. She produced receptacles whose openings were obstructed so as to leave the interior hidden. She used terracotta, a traditional material, which she treated using industrial methods to obtain a perfectly smooth surface and give a contrast between the antique forms of her pieces and their flawless finish.

JOHNSON, Charles Edward
British, 19th - 20th century.
Born 1832, in Stockport; died 1913, in Richmond (Surrey).
Painter, watercolourist, engraver. Landscapes, landscapes with figures, animals.

Charles Johnson was a member of the Royal Society of Painters in Watercolours and the Institute of Oil Painters. He was a frequent exhibitor in London from 1885, particularly at the Royal Academy, and won a bronze medal at the Exposition Universelle in Paris in 1889.

Museums and Galleries:
Derby: *In Sherwood Forest* - London (Tate Collection): *The Swineherd: Gurth, Son of Beowulph* (1879, oil on canvas) - Rochdale (Art Gallery): *Cub Hunting in the Midlands* - Sheffield: *Part of the Invincible Armada, off the Scottish coast.*

Auction records:
London, 12 June 1908, *Waes Me for Prince Charlie* (1885) GBP 99. London, 6 Feb 1909, *Isleworth Church*, GBP 16. London, 5 April 1909, *Evening* (1878) GBP 23. London, 9 April 1910, *Hampstead Heath* (1875) GBP 27. London, 26 Nov 1910, *A Watering Hole, Evening* (1893) GBP 10; *A Welsh Bridge* (1890) GBP 6. London, 17 Dec 1910, *Scottish Landscape* (Royal Academy, 1883) GBP 25. London, 14 July 1972, *Salisbury Cathedral*, Gns 770. London, 29 June 1976, *Thatched Cottages on the Banks of a River* (1899, oil on canvas, 33½ x 48 ins / 85 x 122 cm) GBP 1,400. London, 20 March 1979, *Rustic Scene* (1887, oil on canvas, 31½ x 47 ins / 80 x 119.5 cm) GBP 750. New York, 27 May 1983, *Knaresborough* (1902, oil on canvas, 47 x 60½ ins / 119.1 x 153.5 cm) USD 2,500. Chester, 22 July 1983, *Lago di Guarda* (1864, heightened with gouache, 12 x 27 ins / 30.5 x 68.5 cm) GBP 550. Glasgow, 7 Feb 1989, *Herd of Cattle Crossing a Stone Bridge* (1870, oil on canvas, 32 x 53¼ ins / 81 x 135 cm) GBP 1,870. Perth, 28 Aug 1989, *Herd of Highland Cattle* (1904, oil on canvas, 24 x 36 ins / 61 x 91.5 cm) GBP 1,595. London, 13 Dec 1989, *Peasant on Horseback, Galloping along a Beach* (1881, oil on canvas, 24 x 36 ins / 61 x 91.5 cm) GBP 1,980. London, 21 March 1990, *Village Street* (1888, oil on canvas, 24 x 36 ins / 61 x 91.5 cm) GBP 1,540. Glasgow, 4 Dec 1991, *Hunstman Bringing Home a Stag on the Back of his Horse* (1890, oil on canvas, 39½ x 27½ ins / 100.5 x 70 cm) GBP 4,950. New York, 26 May 1992, *Mosque Beside a Lake* (1884, oil on canvas, 14 x 25 ins / 35.6 x 63.5 cm) USD 1,100. Perth, 30 Aug 1994, *On the Moors* (1889, oil on canvas, 14 x 24 ins / 35.5 x 61 cm) GBP 460.

JOHNSON, Clarence Raymond
American, 20th century.
Born 1894; died 1981.
Painter. Landscapes.

Auction records:
New York, 1 Dec 1988, *Autumn Colours* (oil on canvas, 22 x 24 ins / 55.9 x 61 cm) USD 31,900. New York, 18 Oct 1989, *Summer Landscape* (oil on canvas, 36 x 40 ins / 91.4 x 101.5 cm) USD 121,000. New York, 30 Nov 1990, *Hills of Pennsylvania* (oil on canvas, 19¾ x 24 ins / 50 x 61 cm) USD 22,000. New York, 1 Dec 1994, *New Hope in Pennsylvania, by the River* (oil on canvas, 28¼ x 30 ins / 71.8 x 76.2 cm) USD 71,250. New York, 26 May 1999, *Pennsylvania Landscape* (oil on canvas, 30 x 30 ins / 76 x 76 cm) USD 48,000. New York, 29 Sept 1999, *Spring Trees* (oil on canvas, 34 x 39 ins / 86 x 100 cm) USD 9,000. New York, 28 Nov 2001, *Springtime* (oil on canvas, 30 x 30 ins / 76 x 76 cm) USD 75,000.

JOHNSON, Cornelius, the Elder, or Cornelis Janssens, Janson, Johnson or Jonson van or Johnson Cornelius Ceulen
Dutch, 17th century.
Baptised 14 October 1593 in London; died c. 1664, in Amsterdam or Utrecht.
Painter. Portraits.

Cornelis Janssens Ceulen worked in England from 1618 to 1643, was married there and had a son, Cornelis. He only left, it is said, out of disgust at the fame of Van Dyck (though it was perhaps simply because of the civil war). He entered the guild at Middelburg in 1643, and in 1650 he painted the portraits of the commanders of the crossbowmen there. In 1646 he was in Amsterdam and in 1647 at The Hague, where he painted the portrait of the *Council*. Some authors state that he remained in England until 1648.

He painted most of his portraits as head-and-shoulders studies within an oval in a trompe l'oeil setting, concentrating all the interest on the subjects' faces.

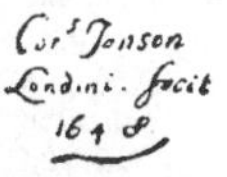

Museums and Galleries:
Aachen: *Young Man* - Amsterdam: *Burgomaster Geelvinck* - Bath (Holburne Mus. of Art): *Portrait of a young gentleman* (oil on canvas); *Portrait of a gentleman* (oil on canvas) - Berlin: *Old Man* - Brunswick: *Portrait of a Man* - Brussels: *Portrait of a Woman* - Cologne: *Two Portraits, a Man and a Woman; Two Portraits* - Dresden: *Man with His Gloves in His Hand; Lady with Her Fan in Her Hand* - Frankfurt am Main: *Portrait of a Woman* - Karlsruhe: *Elisabeth van Essen; Old Lady* - Lille: *Portrait of a Woman* - London (Dulwich Picture Gal.): *Lady in White* (oil on canvas); *Lady in Blue* (oil on canvas) - London (National Portrait Gal.): *Unknown man, formerly known as Richard Weston, 1st Earl of Portland* (1627, oil on canvas); *Unknown man, formerly known as Cornelius Johnson* (1636, oil on canvas); *King Charles II* (1639, oil/wood, full-length portrait); *Mary, Princess of Orange* (1639, oil/wood, full-length portrait); *King James II* (1639, oil/wood, full-length portrait); *Thomas Coventry, 1st Baron Coventry* (1639, oil on canvas); *The Capel Family* (c. 1640, oil on canvas, group portrait) - London (Royal Collection): *Portrait of a Lady; William III as a Child* - London (Tate Collection): *Portrait of Susanna Temple, Later Lady Lister* (1620, oil/wood) - Lyons: *Portrait of a Lady* - Middelburg: *Arquebusiers* - Milan: *Old Lady* - Naples: *Portrait of a Magistrate* - Oldenburg: *Old Man* - Rotterdam: *Nobleman; Young Lady with a Veil* - Schwerin: *Man at a Desk; Old Man; Duke Adolf*

Friedrich and his Wife - ST PETERSBURG (Hermitage): *Man in a Black Cloak; Lady in Black with Pearls* - THE HAGUE: *Council of The Hague* - UTRECHT: *Young Nobleman; Antonie van Hilten, Secretary of Utrecht Council.*

AUCTION RECORDS:

BRUSSELS, 1882, *Portrait of a Man,* FRF 760. PARIS, 1889, *Portrait of a Nobleman,* FRF 1,600; *Portrait of a Lady of Quality,* FRF 2,450; *Supposed Portrait of Henrietta of France,* FRF 3,400. PARIS, 1899, *Head and Shoulders Portrait of a Man,* FRF 2,100. PARIS, 9-10 and 11 April 1902, *Portrait of a Man,* FRF 1,450. PARIS, 16 May 1904, *Portrait of M. Neudigate,* FRF 1,350. PARIS, 10 June 1904, *Portrait of a Man,* FRF 2,200. PARIS, 8 May 1906, *Portrait of a Nobleman,* FRF 920. PARIS, 20 April 1907, *Head and Shoulders Portrait of a Man,* FRF 630. PARIS, 21-22 June 1920, *Portrait of a Woman,* FRF 12,500. PARIS, 4 Dec 1920, *Portrait of a Man,* FRF 2,300. PARIS, 22 Dec 1920, *Portrait of a Lord; Portrait of a Lady* (two pencil drawings) FRF 510. PARIS, 18 and 19 May 1922, *Portrait of an Officer in Armour,* FRF 1,000; *Portrait of Sir John Cage,* FRF 745. PARIS, 16 May 1924, *Portrait of a Magistrate,* FRF 900. PARIS, 18 March 1929, *Portrait of a Woman,* FRF 300. LONDON, 24 Oct 1929, *Lady in a Black Dress,* GBP 29. NEW YORK, 4 and 5 Feb 1932, *Lady with a Fan,* USD 170. NEW YORK, 7 and 8 Dec 1933, *Portrait of a Woman,* USD 650. GENEVA, 23 March 1937, *Portrait of Charles I,* CHF 4,200. COLOGNE, 4 May 1937, *Henrietta of Orléans,* DEM 5,000; *Lady Warwick,* DEM 5,000. NEW YORK, 16 Jan 1942, *Portrait of a Lady,* USD 190. PARIS, 6 March 1942, *Portrait of a Man,* FRF 80,000. NEW YORK, 29 April 1965, *Portrait of a Man in a Ruff,* USD 350. PARIS, 10 June 1966, *Portrait of a Man,* FRF 8,500. BRUSSELS, 19 Oct 1968, *Portrait of Lady Laetitia, Viscountess Falkland,* BEF 60,000. VIENNA, 16 March 1971, *Portrait of Margaret, Lady Hungerford,* ATS 160,000. LONDON, 8 Dec 1971, *Sir William Godolphin; Lady Godolphin* (two canvases) GBP 1,300. PARIS, 23 Nov 1972, *Portrait of a Man,* FRF 23,000. LONDON, 26 March 1976, *Portrait of a Nobleman* (oil on card, 12 x 9 ins / 30.5 x 23 cm) GBP 1,500. LONDON, 24 June 1977, *Portrait of Dorothy Lee* (1623, oil on oval panel, 26 1/2 x 20 ins / 67.4 x 51 cm) GBP 1,200. LONDON, 17 March 1978, *Portrait of a Nobleman in Armour* (1659, oil on canvas, 49 x 39 ins / 124.4 x 99 cm) GBP 2,600. PARIS, 15 June 1978, *Portrait of a Man* (oil on wood, 28 1/4 x 23 1/4 ins / 72 x 59 cm) FRF 10,000. LONDON, 22 June 1979, *Portrait of Lady Hunsdon* (1628, oil on panel, 30 x 24 1/2 ins / 76.2 x 62.2 cm) GBP 2,600. LONDON, 18 March 1981, *Portrait of Elizabeth Petre* (1620, oil on panel, oval, 26 1/2 x 24 ins / 67 x 61 cm) GBP 11,500. PARIS, 2 April 1981, *Lady with a Fan* (oil on canvas, 47 1/4 x 35 1/2 ins / 120 x 90 cm) FRF 21,000. NEW YORK, 25 March 1983, *Portrait of Lady Wilhelmina Shelley* (1633, oil on canvas, 29 1/2 x 24 1/4 ins / 75 x 61.5 cm) USD 4,500. LONDON, 13 July 1984, *Portrait of Elizabeth, Daughter of Sir Thomas Norris* (1624, oil on canvas, 79 x 50 ins / 200.5 x 126.9 cm) GBP 24,000. LONDON, 16 Dec 1986, *Portrait of Laetitia, Viscountess Falkland* (oil on canvas, 30 1/4 x 25 1/4 ins / 77 x 64 cm) GBP 13,000. LONDON, 11 March 1987, *Portrait of a Young Boy* (oil on panel, oval, 29 1/4 x 24 1/2 ins / 74 x 62 cm) GBP 5,200. NEW YORK, 7 April 1988, *Head and Shoulders Portrait Thought To Be of Edward Cornewall* (oil on canvas, 29 1/2 x 24 1/4 ins / 75 x 61.5 cm) USD 6,875. LONDON, 18 Nov 1988, *Head and Shoulders Portrait of a Lady in a Brocade Dress with a Lace Collar* (1624, oil on panel, 26 x 19 1/4 ins / 66.1 x 49 cm) GBP 13,200. NEW YORK, 12 Jan 1989, *Portrait of a Nobleman* (oil on canvas, 28 3/4 x 21 3/4 ins / 73 x 55.5 cm) USD 11,000. NEW YORK, 2 June 1989, *Portrait of a Little Girl in a Pink Dress with Her Little Pet Dog* (1652, oil on canvas, 43 x 35 ins / 109 x 89 cm) USD 143,000. LONDON, 14 July 1989, *Portrait of a Seated Nobleman Wearing Black with White Collar and Cuffs* (oil on canvas, 50 x 39 3/4 ins / 127 x 101 cm) GBP 8,800. NEW YORK, 12 Oct 1989, *Head and Shoulders Portrait of Queen Henrietta Maria in a Yellow Satin Gown with Lace and a Set of Pearls* (oil on canvas, 29 x 24 1/2 ins / 73.6 x 62.2 cm) USD 41,800. LONDON, 17 Nov 1989, *Portrait of Dorothy Wylde in a Pink Gown with Silver Embroidery and a Lace Collar* (1636, oil on canvas, oval, 31 1/4 x 25 1/2 ins / 79.5 x 65 cm) GBP 18,700. NEW YORK, 10 Jan 1990, *Portrait of Sir Christopher Nevill in Black with a Lace Collar, and a Red Cord across His Chest; Portrait of Lady Nevill in a State Gown with Coral Beads and a Lace Collar* (1627, oil on canvas, a pair, 31 x 24 1/2 ins / 78.8 x 62.2 cm) USD 41,800. NEW YORK, 5 April 1990, *Portrait of an Elegant Lady in a Yellow Gown with a Lace Collar, and Two Roses in Her Hair* (1635, oil on canvas, 29 1/2 x 24 1/2 ins / 75 x 62 cm) USD 9,350. LONDON, 11 July 1990, *Portrait of Sir Richard Fanshawe in a Black Doublet with a White Ruff* (1632, oil on panel, 31 x 24 3/4 ins / 79 x 63 cm) GBP 11,550. LONDON, 10 April 1991, *Portrait of Edward Sackville, Fourth Earl of Dorset, in a Black and White Doublet with a Lace Collar, Wearing the Order of the Garter* (oil on panel, 31 x 23 3/4 ins / 79 x 60.5 cm) GBP 22,000. LONDON, 17 July 1992, *Portrait of a Nobleman Standing, Wearing a Blue Coat* (oil/copper, 12 1/2 x 9 1/2 ins / 32 x 24 cm) GBP 11,000. LONDON, 7 April 1993, *Portrait of Two Children Standing Dressed in White, with a Greyhound* (1648, oil on canvas, 52 1/2 x 46 1/2 ins / 133.4 x 118.2 cm) GBP 14,950. PARIS, 26 April 1993, *Portrait of a Young Woman* (1654, oil on canvas, 41 x 32 3/4 ins / 103.3 x 83.2 cm) FRF 70,000. LONDON, 10 Nov 1993, *Portrait of Sir John Finch wearing his Coat and Chain of Office* (oil on canvas, 23 1/2 x 19 3/4 ins / 60 x 50 cm) GBP 7,130. LONDON, 13 April 1994, *Head and Shoulders Portrait of Henry Oxenden of Kent* (oil on canvas, 29 1/4 x 24 1/4 ins / 74.5 x 61.5 cm) GBP 8,970. NEW YORK, 18 May 1994, *Head and Shoulders Portrait of George Villiers, Duke of Buckingham* (oil on canvas, 30 1/2 x 25 ins / 77.5 x 63.5 cm) USD 11,500. LONDON, 6 Nov 1995, *Portrait of a Lady* (oil on canvas, oval, 29 x 24 ins / 73.5 x 61 cm) GBP 4,830. LONDON, 13 Nov 1996, *Portrait of a Nobleman with a Child* (oil on canvas, 50 x 38 1/4 ins / 127 x 97 cm) GBP 8,050. PARIS, 20 June 1997, *Portrait of a Nobleman* (canvas, 44 x 31 ins / 112 x 79 cm) FRF 80,000. AMSTERDAM, 11 Nov 1997, *Head and Shoulders Portrait of a Nobleman* (oil on panel, 25 x 21 1/4 ins / 63.5 x 54 cm) NLG 7,080. AMSTERDAM, 11 Nov 1997, *Head and Shoulders Portrait of Anna Reesen, née Van der Stringe, in a Black Silk Gown with Slashed Sleeves, a Lace Chemise, a Brooch, a Pearl Collar, Earrings and Pearls in her Hair; her Coat of Arms Placed High on the Right* (oil on panel, a fragment, 28 1/2 x 30 ins / 72.3 x 76.2 cm) NLG 23,064.

JOHNSON, Cornelius, or Cornelis.
See **CEULEN Cornelis Janssens Van**

JOHNSON, Cyrus

British, 19th - 20th century.

Born 1 January 1848; died 1925.

Painter, watercolourist. Genre scenes.

Cyrus Johnson was a member of the Royal Institute of Oil Painters and the Royal Society of Painters in Watercolours. He exhibited numerous works from 1872 onwards, at the Royal Academy and the Suffolk Street Gallery.

AUCTION RECORDS:

LONDON, 13 May 1977, *Simple Lessons* (oil on canvas, 24 1/2 x 23 1/2 ins / 62.2 x 59.7 cm) GBP 1,500. LONDON, 27 Nov 1987, *Simple Lessons* (oil on canvas, 25 x 24 ins / 63.5 x 61 cm) GBP 8,500.

JOHNSON, David

American, 19th - 20th century.

Born 10 May 1827, in New York; died 30 January 1908, in Walden (New York).

Painter, draughtsman. Landscapes.

David Johnson taught himself through the study of nature, apart from a few lessons with Jasper F. Cropsey. He was one of the founders and last survivors of what was known as the Hudson River School. He never visited Europe but was the perfect example of an American landscape painter. He was elected a member of the National Academy in 1861. He won medals at various American exhibitions, notably at Philadelphia in 1876. He exhibited at the Salon de Paris in 1877.

AUCTION RECORDS:

NEW YORK, 25-26 Jan 1900, *Cool Retreat,* USD 250. NEW YORK, 10 Feb 1903, *Study from Nature,* USD 825; *Landscape,* USD 1,200. NEW YORK, 24-26 Feb 1904, *Near Chapinville,* USD 220; *Dresden, Lake George,* USD 250. NEW YORK, 19 March 1969, *View of the Hudson from Fort Montgomery,* USD 10,000. NEW YORK, 28 Oct 1971, *Banks of the Hudson,* USD 6,500. NEW YORK, 28 Sept 1973, *Lancaster, New Hampshire,* USD 4,500. NEW YORK, 29 April 1976, *Landscape in Connecticut* (1883, oil on canvas, 12 1/4 x 15 ins / 31 x 38 cm) USD 2,000. LOS ANGELES, 8 Nov 1977, *River Landscape at Sunset* (1858) USD 3,400. NEW YORK, 21 June 1979, *Near Warwick, New York* (1873, oil on canvas, 14 1/4 x 12 1/4 ins / 36.2 x 31.1 cm) USD 8,750. NEW YORK, 23 April 1981, *Androscoggin River, Maine* (1869-1870, oil on canvas, 28 x 40 ins / 71.2 x 101.7 cm) USD 20,000. NEW YORK, 8 Dec 1983, *Pear Tree in Blossom* (1874, oil on canvas, 20 x 13 1/2 ins / 50.8 x 34.3 cm) USD 7,000. NEW YORK, 15 March 1985, *Boating on Lake George* (1870, oil on canvas remounted on board, 16 1/4 x 26 1/4 ins / 41 x 66.5 cm) USD 26,000. NEW YORK, 29 May 1987, *Apples and Quinces* (oil on canvas remounted on board, 10 1/4 ins / 26.31.7 cm) USD 58,000. NEW YORK, 26 May 1988, *Marlborough* (1870, oil on canvas, 11 1/4 x 18 1/2 ins / 28.6 x 47 cm) USD 13,200. NEW YORK, 24 May 1989, *The Coast near Noroton in Connecticut* (1875, oil on canvas, 16 x 23 ins / 40.6 x 58.4 cm) USD 132,000. NEW YORK, 24 May 1990, *West Cornwall in Connecticut* (1875, oil on canvas, 17 1/4 x 13 1/2 ins / 43.8 x 34.3 cm) USD 67,100. NEW YORK, 30 May 1990, *On the 'Wallkill'* (1894, pencil heightened with white/paper, 11 3/4 x 17 3/4 ins / 30 x 45.2 cm) USD 1,870. NEW YORK, 26 Sept 1990, *The Pink House in Kingston* (1858, oil on canvas, 11 x 16 ins / 27.9 x 40.6 cm) USD 9,900. NEW YORK, 22 May 1991, *Mount Lafayette in New Hampshire* (oil on canvas, 17 x 14 ins / 43.3 x 35.7 cm) USD 22,000. NEW YORK, 25 Sept 1991, *Landscape in Essex County* (1859, oil on canvas, 12 x 20 ins / 30.5 x 50.8 cm) USD 12,100. NEW YORK, 6 Dec 1991, *Panorama looking westward from Dollar Island to Lake George* (1879, oil on card, 13 3/4 x 20 ins / 35 x 50.5 cm) USD 60,500. NEW YORK, 12 March 1992, *Spring, Study of the Bronx River* (1873, oil on canvas, 16 1/4 x 26 1/4 ins / 41 x 66.4 cm) USD 16,500. NEW YORK, 27 May 1992, *The Hudson from Fort Montgomery* (1870, oil on canvas, 38 1/2 x 60 ins / 97.8 x 152.4 cm) USD 209,000. NEW YORK, 27 May 1993, *Lake George* (1870, oil on canvas, 157 3/4 x 26 ins / 400.6 x 66 cm) USD 40,250. NEW YORK, 25 May 1995, *Mount Star King at Lancaster in New Hampshire* (1869, oil on canvas, 12 x 20 ins / 30.5 x 50.8 cm) USD 14,950. NEW YORK, 21 May 1996, *Landscape with a Bridge* (oil on canvas, 9 1/2 x 14 ins / 24 x 35.5 cm) USD 3,680. NEW YORK, 26 Sept 1996, *Lake Mohonk* (1858, oil on canvas, 17 x 23 ins / 43.2 x 58.4 cm) USD 19,550. NEW YORK, 4 Dec 1996, *Landscape at Hurley* (1859, oil on canvas, 10 x 28 ins / 25.7 x 71.4 cm) USD 11,500. PARIS, 9 March 1998, *The Flock by the Pond* (1885, oil, 10 x 14 ins / 25.5 x 35.5 cm) FRF 7,000.

JOHNSON, Douglas J.

American, 20th century.
Born 1940, in Coldwater (Michigan).
Active in France.
Painter, draughtsman.
Neo-Pop Art.

Douglas J. Johnson was influenced by David Hockney. He has exhibited mainly in Germany and Holland in 1976, 1977, 1980, 1981 and 1983. He had a solo exhibition in 1975 at the Galerie Flinker in Paris.

JOHNSON, Eastman

American, 19th century.
Born 29 July 1824, in Lovell (Maine); died 5 April 1906, in New York.
Painter, draughtsman. Portraits, genre scenes, landscapes.

Eastman Johnson was a pupil of Lentye. He started his career by producing portraits in pencil. He went to Europe in 1849 and produced oil paintings in Düsseldorf for two years. He then travelled to Italy, Paris, The Netherlands and The Hague, where he lived for four years. In 1855 he was in America again, and became established in New York as a genre painter. He became a member of the National Academy of Design in New York in 1860.

He was highly successful, especially with his picturesque scenes from the lives of black Americans. After painting scenes from the Civil War, he produced highly coloured canvases of rural life and then of landscapes. He also produced portraits.

Johnson exhibited in Paris, receiving a bronze medal at the Exposition Universelle in 1889 and a silver medal at the exhibition of 1900. His work featured in *L'Héroïque et le Quotidien: Les Artistes Américains, 1820-1920* (*The Heroic and the Everyday: American Artists, 1820-1920*) at the Musée d'Art Américain in Giverny in 2001.

BIBLIOGRAPHY:

Hills, Patricia, *The Genre painting of Eastman Johnson: the sources and development of his style and themes,* dissertation, Garland, New York, 1977 (New York University, 1973). Marc Simpson, Sally Mills, Patricia Hills, *Eastman Jonhson: The cranberry harvest, Island of Nantucket,* exhibition catalogue, Timken Art Gall., San Diego (CA), 1990. Carbone, Teresa A./Hills, Patricia/Weiss, Jane/Burns, Sarah/Rose, Anne C., *Eastman Johnson: painting America,* travelling exhibition catalogue, Art Museum, Seattle, Brooklyn Museum of Art, Rizzoli, New York, 1999.

MUSEUMS AND GALLERIES:

BROOKLYN, NY: *Savoyard* - CHICAGO (Terra Foundation for American Art Collection): *Travelling Violin Player* (1866, oil on panel) - COLUMBUS, GA (Columbus Mus.): *Earnest Pupil (The Fifers)* (1881, oil on canvas) - FORT WORTH (Amon Carter Mus.): *Bo-Peep* (1872, oil/panel) - NEW YORK: *Portrait of S.G. Cleveland* - NEW YORK (Metropolitan Mus. of Art): *S.R. Gifford; Two Men; Husking Corn in Nantucket* - PHOENIX (AM): *Portrait of Clara Hall* (1873, oil/panel); *Tea Party* (1873, oil on canvas) - PITTSBURGH (Carnegie MA): *My Jew Boy* (1852, crayon and white chalk/paper); two paintings - RICHMOND (Virginia MFA): *A Ride for Liberty: The Fugitive Slaves, March 2, 1862* (1862, oil on panel) - SAN DIEGO (MA) - WASHINGTON DC (Georgetown University): *Hannah Amidst the Vines* (c. 1860, oil on canvas).

AUCTION RECORDS:

NEW YORK, 1880, *Chimney Sweep,* FRF 3,125. NEW YORK, 1899, *Reprimand,* FRF 3,850. NEW YORK, 8-9 Jan 1903, *Guilty,* USD 700. NEW YORK, 26-27 Feb 1907, *Embers,* USD 810; *A Glass with the Squire,* USD 305; *The Fabulous Dolly Madison,* USD 810; *Corn Husking,* USD 800. NEW YORK, 2 Feb 1911, *Self-portrait,* USD 55. NEW YORK, 16-17 Feb 1911, *Sunday,* USD 250. NEW YORK, 18 April 1945, *Horse Trading,* USD 1,400. NEW YORK, 17 June 1964, *Portrait of a Little Girl,* USD 1,600. NEW YORK, 18 Nov 1965, *Down East Court Ship,* USD 4,000. NEW YORK, 19 March 1969, *Interesting News,* USD 25,000. NEW YORK, 28 Oct 1971, *Confidence and Admiration,* USD 28,000. NEW YORK, 25 Oct 1973, *Washington Crossing the Delaware,* USD 260,000. NEW YORK, 18 Nov 1976, *Portrait of James Garfield* (1884, oil on canvas, 30 x 25 ins / 76.2 x 63.5 cm) USD 2,800. NEW YORK, 29 April 1977, *Master Trask Holding a Football* (oil on canvas, 18 x 14 ins / 45.7 x 35.6 cm) USD 1,800. NEW YORK, 20 April 1979, *Little Girl with Skates* (1880, oil on canvas, 52 1/2 x 30 ins / 133.3 x 76.2 cm) USD 31,000. NEW YORK, 23 April 1982, *Child with Bare Feet* (1860, oil on card, 12 3/4 x 9 1/2 ins / 32.4 x 24.1 cm) USD 59,000. NEW YORK,

4 Dec 1986, *Street Musicians* (1861, oil on canvas, 11 1/4 x 9 ins / 28.5 x 22.8 cm) USD 31,000. NEW YORK, 4 Dec 1987, *Wigwams* (1869, oil on card, 8 3/4 x 10 3/4 ins / 22.2 x 27.3 cm) USD 30,000. NEW YORK, 24 June 1988, *Portrait of Mrs Cross of Milford in Pennsylvania* (oil on card, 15 x 13 1/4 ins / 38.4 x 33.5 cm) USD 1,870. NEW YORK, 1 Dec 1988, *Self-portrait with Bottle of Champagne* (1863, oil on card, 15 1/2 x 12 ins / 39.4 x 30.5 cm) USD 8,800. NEW YORK, 28 Sept 1989, *Edwin Booth as Hamlet* (1845, charcoal and white chalk/tinted paper, 19 3/4 x 14 3/4 ins / 50.2 x 37.5 cm) USD 8,250. NEW YORK, 24 May 1990, *It is Not Cold* (1876, oil on card, 21 x 17 ins / 53.3 x 43.2 cm) USD 46,750. NEW YORK, 27 Sept 1990, *Study for 'Banter'* (oil on card, 20 x 9 ins / 50.9 x 22.8 cm) USD 24,200. NEW YORK, 22 May 1991, *Naughty Rascal* (oil on card, 11 1/2 x 6 1/2 ins / 29 x 16.2 cm) USD 30,800. NEW YORK, 26 Sept 1991, *Little Girl Warming her Hands* (1862, oil on canvas, 12 1/2 x 9 1/2 ins / 31.5 x 24.3 cm) USD 55,000. NEW YORK, 14 Nov 1991, *Medieval Man* (charcoal and white chalk/grey paper, 10 1/2 x 8 ins / 26.8 x 20.6 cm) USD 1,100. NEW YORK, 6 Dec 1991, *Colloquium* (oil on card, 22 x 12 1/4 ins / 55.9 x 31 cm) USD 66,000. NEW YORK, 12 March 1992, *Bohemian Girl* (oil on canvas, 9 1/2 x 7 1/4 ins / 24.2 x 18.3 cm) USD 8,800. NEW YORK, 27 May 1992, *Children Reading* (oil on canvas, 12 x 9 ins / 30.5 x 22.9 cm) USD 17,600. AMSTERDAM, 28 Oct 1992, *Portrait of Professor W. Hendricksz., Standing, Wearing Black and Leaning on a Table before a Red Curtain* (1853, oil on canvas, 59 3/4 x 44 1/2 ins / 152 x 113 cm) NLG 14,950. NEW YORK, 3 Dec 1992, *Young Boy in a Maine Forest in Winter* (oil on canvas, 12 x 20 ins / 30.5 x 50.8 cm) USD 93,500. NEW YORK, 26 May 1993, *Little Chimney Sweep* (1863, oil on card, 12 1/4 x 9 1/2 ins / 31 x 24 cm) USD 145,500. NEW YORK, 25 May 1994, *Self-portrait* (oil on canvas, 10 x 8 ins / 25.4 x 20.6 cm) USD 48,300. NEW YORK, 25 May 1995, *Little Commander* (1853, charcoal/paper heightened with white, 23 x 18 1/2 ins / 58.4 x 47 cm) USD 11,500. AMSTERDAM, 7 Nov 1995, *Portrait of Mr Kooman* (1853, oil on canvas, 13 1/2 x 11 3/4 ins / 34 x 30 cm) NLG 4,720. NEW YORK, 29 Nov 1995, *Precocious Pupil (Flute Player)* (1881, oil on card, 26 1/4 x 22 1/4 ins / 66.7 x 56.5 cm) USD 145,500. NEW YORK, 26 Sept 1996, *Return Journey* (oil on panel, 9 1/4 x 7 ins / 23.5 x 17.8 cm) USD 13,800. NEW YORK, 4 Dec 1996, *Hiding Place* (oil on panel, 6 1/4 x 8 1/2 ins / 15.8 x 21.9 cm) USD 41,400. NEW YORK, 5 June 1997, *Maple Sugar Camp Fête* (oil on canvas, 30 1/4 x 40 1/4 ins / 76.8 x 102.2 cm) USD 211,500; *Self-portrait* (oil on card, 29 1/2 x 22 3/4 ins / 75 x 57.8 cm) USD 25,300. NEW YORK, 7 Dec 1999, *John Philip Kemble as Hamlet* (1845, black chalk, 20 x 14 ins / 51 x 36 cm) USD 3,500. NEW YORK, 7 Dec 1999, *Little Soldier* (1864, oil on board, 14 x 11 ins / 36 x 28 cm) USD 550,000. NEW YORK, 23 May 2000, *Man with a Hat, Self-portrait* (1853, oil on canvas, 28 x 21 ins / 70 x 53 cm) USD 58,000. BOSTON, 9 March 2001, *Falling Market* (c. 1873, oil on canvas, 17 x 13 ins / 43 x 33 cm) USD 30,000. NEW YORK, 22 May 2001, *Feeding the Lamb* (oil on canvas) USD 75,000. NEW YORK, 13 Feb 2002, *Portrait of a Young Boy with a Hoop and Stick* (1857, charcoal and gouache on paper on board, 33 x 24 ins / 84 x 62 cm) USD 5,000. NEW YORK, 5 Dec 2002, *Study for Wounded Drummer Boy* (c. 1871, oil on board, 10 x 9 ins / 25 x 22 cm) USD 85,000. NEW YORK, 22 May 2003, *Ojibwe Encampment* (oil on canvas, 10 x 22 ins / 25 x 57 cm) USD 520,000. NEW YORK, 4 Dec 2003, *Little Soldier* (oil on board, 15 x 13 ins / 39 x 32 cm) USD 200,000. PORTSMOUTH, 6 March 2004, *Embers* (1879, oil on board, 17 x 14 ins / 43 x 36 cm) USD 215,000.

JOHNSON, Edward Killingworth

British, 19th century.

Born 1825, in Stratford-le-Bow; died 7 April 1896 or 1923.

Active in Wembly.

Watercolourist, painter (gouache). Genre scenes, landscapes.

Edward Killingworth Johnson showed a very precocious talent for art. He trained himself through acute observation of nature but would only dedicate himself exclusively to painting in 1863. In 1871, he left London to establish himself in a family property he owned in Essex. An active participant in the exhibitions of the Society of Painters in Watercolours from 1848 onwards, he became an associate in 1866 and a member in 1876. He also exhibited at the Royal Academy and the Suffolk Street Gallery. In 1873, he showed his work in New York, in 1874, in London, in 1875, in Birmingham, in Philadelphia in 1976, and at the Exposition Universelle in Paris in 1878.

BIBLIOGRAPHY:

Wood, Christopher, *The Dictionary of Victorian Painters*, Antique Collectors' Club, Woodbridge, 1971.

AUCTION RECORDS:

LONDON, 21 Dec 1907, *Ducks' Feeding Time* (watercolour) GBP 4. LONDON, 17 Feb 1908, *Little Girl putting on her Shoes* (1865, watercolour) GBP 8. LONDON, 21 Nov 1908, *Old Home* (1878, watercolour) GBP 9. LONDON, 11 July 1972, *Fly Butterfly* (watercolour heightened with white) Gns 260. LONDON, 22 May 1979, *Young Woman sitting under a Tree* (watercolour heightened with gouache, 30 x 20 1/2 ins / 76 x 52 cm) GBP 1,200. LONDON, 23 Nov 1982, *Young Girl Picking Flowers* (watercolour heightened with gouache, 37 x 19 ins / 94 x 48 cm) GBP 2,500. LONDON, 27 Oct 1983, *Catching the Pony* (1879, watercolour/pencil outlines heightened with gouache, 20 x 30 ins / 51 x 76 cm) GBP 8,500. NEW YORK, 26 Feb 1986, *Little Girl Feeding Ducks* (1883, watercolour and gouache, 16 x 29 ins / 40.6 x 73.6 cm) USD 16,000. LONDON, 29 April 1987, *Bird's Nest* (1878, watercolour/pencil outlines heightened with gouache, 27 x 18 1/2 ins / 68.5 x 47 cm) GBP 9,500. LONDON, 25 Jan 1989, *The Pet Bird* (1869, watercolour and gouache, 12 1/4 x 8 1/2 ins / 31 x 21.5 cm) GBP 2,860. LONDON, 8-9 June 1993, *Happy as Day is Long* (1881, gouache and watercolour, 16 3/4 x 21 1/4 ins / 42.5 x 54 cm) GBP 8,050. LONDON, 30 March 1994, *Summer's Day* (1884, watercolour and gouache, 8 1/2 x 7 ins / 21.5 x 17.5 cm) GBP 3,680. LONDON, 6 Nov 1995, *In a Summer's Garden* (pencil, watercolour and gouache, 17 1/2 x 23 1/2 ins / 44.5 x 59.7 cm) GBP 17,250. NEW YORK, 23 May 1996, *Happy as Day is Long* (1881, gouache/pencil outlines/paper, 17 1/2 x 22 ins / 44.5 x 55.9 cm) USD 27,600. LONDON, 5 June 1996, *The Scent of Summer* (1877, watercolour and gouache, 17 1/4 x 26 ins / 44 x 66 cm) GBP 3,795. CREWKERNE, 21 May 1999, *Sunflowers* (1881, watercolour, 27 x 19 ins / 69 x 48 cm) GBP 3,400. LEYBURN, 25 Nov 1999, *Calling Down the Bees* (1877, watercolour and gouache, 31 x 53 ins / 78 x 135 cm) GBP 20,000. LONDON, 22 March 2000, *Dandelion Clocks* (watercolour heightened with gouache, 29 x 19 ins / 74 x 47 cm) GBP 4,300. LONDON, 15 June 2000, *Day Dreams* (1882, watercolour heightened with gouache, 21 x 11 ins / 54 x 28 cm) GBP 4,600. LONDON, 10 April 2001, *Expectations* (1873, watercolour and gouache, 26 x 17 ins / 66 x 42 cm) GBP 3,200. LONDON, 3 Dec 2002, *Breton Fisher Girl* (1864, watercolour heightened with gouache, 6 x 8 ins / 15 x 20 cm) GBP 1,400. SALISBURY, 26 March 2003, *Lady and her Daughter Looking at Butterflies on Sunflowers* (1881, watercolour, 27 x 19 ins / 69 x 48 cm) GBP 3,200. LONDON, 3 Dec 2003, *Watching the Butterflies* (1881, pencil, watercolour and gouache, 26 x 19 ins / 67 x 47 cm) GBP 2,400. LONDON, 10 March 2004, *Pet Bird* (1864, watercolour, 12 x 8 ins / 31 x 21 cm) GBP 1,800. LONDON, 25 Nov 2004, *Hammock* (1881, watercolour, 16 x 19 ins / 40 x 49 cm) GBP 21,000.

JOHNSON, Elena Mix

American, 20th century.

Born 19 August 1889, in Nogales (Arizona); died 1939, in Raleigh (North Carolina).

Painter.

Elena Johnson studied at the Pennsylvania Academy of the Fine Arts on a fellowship and was a pupil of Daniel Garber.

She was a member of the American Arts Federation and the American Artists Professional League.

JOHNSON, Eli
British, 19th century.
Born c. 1850; died 14 January 1881, in Northampton.
Sculptor.
Eli Johnson showed marble and terracotta busts at the Royal Academy in 1878 and 1880.

JOHNSON, Ernest and Esther Borough.
See **BOROUGH-JOHNSON**

JOHNSON, F.
British, 18th century.
Active in Croydon.
Painter. Sporting subjects.
F. Johnson exhibited at the Society of Artists and the Royal Academy from 1791 to 1797.

JOHNSON, Frank Tenney
American, 19th - 20th century.
Born 26 June 1874, in Big Grove (Iowa); died 1939, in New York.
Painter, watercolourist, illustrator. Local scenes.
Frank Tenney Johnson studied with Lorenz and at the Art Students League in New York. He became a member of the Salmagundi Club in 1912 and belonged to the American Arts Federation and the New York Society of Painters. He won many awards for his work: one from the Salmagundi Club in 1923, an Edgar B. Davis prize of 1250 dollars and a silver medal from the Painters of the West. His favourite subjects were cowboys and Native Americans in the wide open spaces of the American West.
AUCTION RECORDS:
NEW YORK, 27 Jan 1965, *In the Night,* USD 1,900. NEW YORK, 15 Nov 1967, *Cowboy and his Horse,* USD 3,500. NEW YORK, 19 March 1969, *Three Indians in a Cart,* USD 15,000. NEW YORK, 7 April 1971, *Cowboy with his Rifle in his Hand,* USD 10,500. NEW YORK, 11 April 1973, *Apache Indians,* USD 27,000. LOS ANGELES, 4 March 1974, *Camp of the Blackfeet* (1938) USD 55,000. LOS ANGELES, 9 June 1976, *Horseman* (1938, oil on canvas, 20 x 24 ins / 51 x 61 cm) USD 2,000. LOS ANGELES, 9 March 1977, *Cowboy on Horseback* (1925, oil on canvas, 19 x 25 ins / 48 x 63.5 cm) USD 8,500. NEW YORK, 20 April 1979, *Horseman and Horsewoman* (1906, watercolour, 20 3/4 x 14 1/2 ins / 52.7 x 36.8 cm) USD 2,250. NEW YORK, 25 Oct 1979, *Camp of the Paleface* (1917, oil on canvas, 32 1/4 x 42 1/4 ins / 82 x 107.3 cm) USD 62,500. LOS ANGELES, 16 March 1981, *Black-Hawk* (polychrome wood, h. 12 ins / 30.5 cm) USD 1,100. NEW YORK, 23 April 1981, *Scout and Covered Wagon* (1914, oil on canvas, 36 x 24 ins / 91.5 x 61 cm) USD 87,500. SAN FRANCISCO, 21 June 1984, *Beehive, Chippewa* (polychrome wood, h. 12 ins / 30.5 cm) USD 900. NEW YORK, 5 Dec 1985, *Portrait of a Cowboy* (watercolour, 14 1/4 x 10 1/2 ins / 36.2 x 26.7 cm) USD 3,500. NEW YORK, 5 Dec 1986, *Lovers of the Desert* (oil on canvas, 36 x 28 ins / 91.5 x 71 cm) USD 34,000. NEW YORK, 4 Dec 1987, *A Brush with the Posse* (oil on canvas, 16 1/4 x 12 1/4 ins / 41 x 30.8 cm) USD 11,000. NEW YORK, 1 Dec 1988, *The District Sheriff* (1929, oil on canvas, 24 x 18 ins / 61 x 45.7 cm) USD 31,900. NEW YORK, 24 Jan 1989, *Forest Landscape* (watercolour/paper, 28 1/2 x 21 ins / 72.5 x 52.5 cm) USD 2,750. NEW YORK, 1 Dec 1989, *Mountain Hunter* (1917, oil on canvas, 36 x 24 ins / 91.4 x 60.9 cm) USD 33,000. NEW YORK, 14 Feb 1990, *Herdsman on Horseback* (watercolour/paper, 12 x 9 ins / 30.5 x 22.8 cm) USD 2,750. NEW YORK, 23 May 1990, *Sunset Glows* (oil on canvas, 20 x 16 ins / 50.8 x 40.7 cm) USD 16,500. NEW YORK, 26 Sept 1990, *The Lone Cowboy* (1937, oil on canvas, 20 x 24 ins / 50.8 x 60.9 cm) USD 16,500. LOS ANGELES-SAN FRANCISCO, 10 Oct 1990, *A Pacific Island* (1912, oil on canvas mounted on card, 7 3/4 x 6 ins / 20 x 15 cm) USD 3,025. NEW YORK, 30 Nov 1990, *The Night Bird* (1936, oil on canvas, 24 x 30 ins / 61 x 76.5 cm) USD 28,600. NEW YORK, 14 March 1991, *The Meeting* (1931, oil on canvas, 20 x 24 ins / 51 x 61 cm) USD 18,700. NEW YORK, 22 May 1991, *Canyon by Moonlight* (1928, oil on canvas, 22 1/4 x 16 1/4 ins / 56.3 x 41.2 cm) USD 41,800. NEW YORK, 27 May 1992, *Reflections* (1936, oil on canvas, 24 x 30 1/4 ins / 61 x 76.8 cm) USD 46,750. NEW YORK, 3 Dec 1992, *A Bad Omen* (1930, oil on canvas, 25 x 18 1/2 ins / 63.5 x 47 cm) USD 38,500. NEW YORK, 27 May 1993, *Evening* (1933, oil/synthetic resin, 11 1/2 x 8 1/2 ins / 29.2 x 21.6 cm) USD 13,800. NEW YORK, 2 Dec 1993, *Returning from the Hunt* (1934, oil on canvas, 25 x 30 ins / 63.5 x 76.2 cm) USD 57,500. NEW YORK, 1 Dec 1994, *Changing Horses* (1932, oil on canvas, 36 1/4 x 46 ins / 92.1 x 116.8 cm) USD 101,500. NEW YORK, 14 March 1996, *Summer Night* (1929, oil on canvas, 24 x 18 ins / 61 x 45.7 cm) USD 32,200. NEW YORK, 4 Dec 1996, *Moose Hunting* (watercolour/paper, 18 1/2 x 12 ins / 47 x 30.5 cm) USD 9,200. NEW YORK, 3 Dec 1997, *The Night Watch* (1936, oil on canvas, 30 x 40 1/2 ins / 76.2 x 102.9 cm) USD 134,500. NEW YORK, 27 May 1999, *Two Figures at Dusk* (1929, oil on canvas, 37 x 28 ins / 93 x 72 cm) USD 170,000. NEW YORK, 27 May 1999, *Twilight Rendezvous* (1934, oil on canvas, 40 x 50 ins / 102 x 127 cm) USD 310,000. SANTA FE, 3 June 2000, *Home of the Navajo* (oil on canvas, 16 x 20 ins / 41 x 51 cm) USD 90,000. HAYDEN, 29 July 2000, *The Stillness of Night* (watercolour, 10 x 6 ins / 26 x 16 cm) USD 55,000. DALLAS, 13 Oct 2001, *Hasty Departure* (oil on masonite, 24 x 30 ins / 61 x 76 cm) USD 135,000. LOS ANGELES, 7 Nov 2001, *Horse Thief* (1925, oil on canvas on masonite, 26 x 38 ins / 66 x 96 cm) USD 100,000. SANTA FE, 9 Nov 2002, *Navajo Shepherdess* (1914, watercolour, 29 x 20 ins / 74 x 51 cm) USD 140,000. SANTA FE, 9 Nov 2002, *Somewhere on the Range* (oil on canvas, 24 x 30 ins / 61 x 76 cm) USD 155,000. NEW YORK, 22 May 2003, *Nocturne* (1915, watercolour on board, 26 x 17 ins / 67 x 42 cm) USD 50,000. NEW YORK, 22 May 2003, *Voices in the Night* (oil on canvas, 28 x 36 ins / 71 x 91 cm) USD 110,000. SAN FRANCISCO, 8 June 2004, *On the Drive* (1938, oil on canvas, 30 x 40 ins / 76 x 101 cm) USD 180,000. HAYDEN, 24 July 2004, *Moonbathed Night* (oil on board, 16 x 12 ins / 41 x 30 cm) USD 170,000.

JOHNSON, Frost
American, 19th century.
Born 1835, in New York.
Painter. Genre scenes.
Frost Johnson was a pupil of Cummings in New York and of Édouard Frère in Écouen, and also studied at the academy in Düsseldorf, the Académie St-Luc in Anvers, and the École des Beaux-Arts in Paris. He worked in London and then returned to New York and to Philadelphia in 1876. He produced *Bouquet, Last and Best,* and *Love Me, Love Me Not.*

JOHNSON, G.
British, 18th century.
Active c. 1744.
Painter, engraver. Portraits.

JOHNSON, Gerard, or Janssen
British, 17th century.
Active in London.
Modeller.
Gerard Johnson or Janssen is known for the monument to Shakespeare in Stratford-upon-Avon.

JOHNSON, Grace Mott
American, 20th century.
Born 28 July 1882, in New York; died 1967.
Sculptor, draughtswoman, engraver (wood). Animals.
Grace Mott Johnson studied in New York under the direction of Hermon Atkins MacNeil and Gutzon Borglum, after spending her childhood on a farm. She exhibited a *Percheron Horse* in 1910 at the Salon de la Société des Artistes

Français in Paris and a *Group of Chimpanzees* in San Francisco in 1915. In a solo exhibition at the Whitney Studio Club in 1922, she showed an orang-utan, dogs and elephants. She also produced drawings and engravings in relief on wood of giraffes, circus horses and kangaroos.

AUCTION RECORDS:
NEW YORK, 14 Nov 1991, *Lamb* (bronze, h. 11 1/2 ins / 29.2 cm) USD 2,420.

JOHNSON, Guy
American, 20th century.
Born 1927, in Fort Wayne (Indiana).
Painter.

Guy Johnson exhibited regularly in Houston from 1960 to 1970. In 1972, he took part in *Sharp Focus Realism* in New York, an event that later became famous and marked the birth of photo-realism. His work has also been seen in group exhibitions in Paris in 1972 and Brussels in 1973. He had a solo exhibition in New York in 1971.

AUCTION RECORDS:
NEW YORK, 7 June 1984, *Passenger Plane* (1928-1974, mixed media and photograph, 14 1/2 x 23 3/4 ins / 36.8 x 60.4 cm) USD 1,600. COPENHAGEN, 2 March 1994, *Grandmother's House* (1928, oil on canvas, 10 1/4 x 18 ins / 26 x 46 cm) DKK 4,500. PARIS, 27 May 2004, *Watching TV* (oil on paper on card, 17 x 23 ins / 42 x 59 cm) EUR 3,400. PARIS, 27 May 2004, *California Moon* (oil on paper on aluminium, 25 x 27 ins / 63 x 69 cm) EUR 4,800.

JOHNSON, Harry John
British, 19th century.
Born April 1826, in Birmingham; died 31 December 1884, in St John's Wood, London.
Painter, watercolourist. Genre scenes, landscapes, architectural views.

Harry John Johnson was the son of W.B. Johnson. He trained with S. Lines and W.J. Muller, accompanying the latter to the Levant. He began exhibiting at the Royal Academy in 1845. In 1868, he was an associate of the Royal Institute and he became a member in 1870.

MUSEUMS AND GALLERIES:
LONDON (Victoria and Albert Mus.): several watercolours (views of ancient buildings in England and views of Switzerland and Italy).

AUCTION RECORDS:
LONDON, 21 Nov 1908, *Ruins of the Temple of Minerva in Sunium*, GBP 5. LONDON, 13 Feb 1909, *Mont Saint-Michel*, GBP 7. LONDON, 3 May 1909, *Ruins of Selinessus, Asia Minor* (1856) GBP 1. LONDON, 8 May 1980, *Temple of Minerva* (1864, oil on canvas, 22 x 40 1/4 ins / 55 x 102.5 cm) GBP 1,700. LONDON, 30 June 1981, *Head of a Young Girl* (1846, watercolour and pencil, 11 x 20 ins / 28 x 51 cm) GBP 650. LONDON, 17 Nov 1989, *Harvesters Resting with Edinburgh in the distance* (1847, oil on card, 12 x 18 ins / 30.5 x 45.5 cm) GBP 3,080. LONDON, 15 Nov 1991, *Temple of Poseidon at Sunion* (oil on canvas, 12 1/2 x 24 ins / 31.6 x 61.2 cm) GBP 1,320. PENZANCE, 18 Feb 1999, *Barge on River, Windsor* (oil on board, 9 x 14 ins / 23 x 36 cm) GBP 1,250. LONDON, 9 Nov 1999, *View of Kenilworth Castle, Warwickshire* (pencil and watercolour with scratching out, 12 x 20 ins / 31 x 50 cm) GBP 1,100. LONDON, 29 Nov 2000, *Melrose Abbey Looking Towards Glendearg, the Borders* (1846, watercolour heightened with white, 13 x 20 ins / 34 x 51 cm) GBP 1,000. LEEDS, 13 March 2001, *Lake Thun* (1852, oil on canvas, 24 x 36 ins / 61 x 91 cm) GBP 1,200. BATH, 18 March 2002, *Pella - Lago d'Orta, with the Isola S Guilio* (1854, oil on canvas, 24 x 35 ins / 60 x 88 cm) GBP 2,800. LONDON, 15 Oct 2002, *Temple of Aphaea, Aegina, Greece* (oil on canvas, 22 x 40 ins / 55 x 102 cm) GBP 58,000.

JOHNSON, Harry Leroy
American, 20th century.
Born 1876, in Philadelphia.
Painter, miniaturist. Figures, landscapes.

Harry Leroy Johnson studied and exhibited at the Pennsylvania Academy of the Fine Arts. In 1915, he showed seven miniatures of figures and landscapes in the exhibition *Panama Pacific International Exposition* in San Francisco. He was a member of the Pennsylvania Society of Miniature Painters.

JOHNSON, Helen Mary
British, 19th century.
Active in London.
Painter. Landscapes.

Mary Helen Johnson exhibited in London from 1865 to 1881, notably at the British Institution and at Suffolk Street Gallery.

JOHNSON, Henry
British, 19th century.
Active in London.
Painter. Figures.

Henry Johnson exhibited at the Royal Academy, the British Institution and at Suffolk Street Gallery from 1824 to 1847.

JOHNSON, Herbert
British, 19th century.
Born 1848; died 1906.
Active in London.
Painter. Genre scenes.

Herbert Johnson exhibited at the Royal Academy and at Suffolk Street Gallery after 1868.

JOHNSON, Horace C.
American, 19th century.
Born 1820, in Oxford (Connecticut); died 1890.
Painter. Genre scenes, portraits.

Horace C. Johnson was a pupil of Morse in New York and of William Page in Rome. He produced a lot of work in Italy. Many of his portraits were procured by families in Connecticut.

JOHNSON, Isaac
British, 18th - 19th century.
Active in Woodbridge between 1799 and 1816.
Architectural draughtsman.

Isaac Johnson specialised in producing views of old buildings.

JOHNSON, J. Theodore
American, 20th century.
Born 7 November 1902, in Oregon (Illinois); died 1963.
Painter. Portraits.

J. Theodore Johnson was a pupil of Leon Kroll and André Lhote. He won a gold medal and a prize of 2500 dollars from the Art Institute of Chicago in 1928.

JOHNSON, James
British, 18th century.
Active in London.
Engraver (mezzotint).

James Johnson made mezzotint engravings of historical subjects, genre scenes and portraits after Andrews, C. Coypel, Rubens, Allegri, Lebrun, N.Fouché, Page and F. Lemoine.

JOHNSON, James
British, 19th century.
Born 1803, in Bristol; died 1834.
Painter, watercolourist. Landscapes, interiors.
Bristol School.

James Johnson was influenced by Henry Nelson O'Neill and Francis Denby, and was probably their pupil. His earliest drawings date from 1819. He moved to London and returned to the West Country to teach in Bath in 1827. By 1829 signs of mental illness were becoming apparent and Johnson made plans to go to Jamaica to recover his health, but it appears that these plans never materialised. He painted poetic landscapes in oils close to Denby. He is also the author of detailed architectural views and interiors in watercolour, especially of churches, and of topographical works.

Museums and Galleries:

Bristol (City Art Gallery): *Radcliffe Street, Bristol* (c. 1821, oil on canvas) - Hull (City Museum and Art Gallery): *Romantic Landscape* (1820, oil on canvas).

Auction records:

London, 7 Nov 2001, *Montacute House, Somerset* (1825, watercolour heightened with white, 9 x 17 ins / 23 x 42 cm) GBP 3,800.

JOHNSON, James C.
American, 20th century.
Born 20th century, in the USA.
Sculptor.

James C. Johnson was a pupil of Ossip Zadkine.

JOHNSON, Jan or John, or Janssen
British, 17th century.
Sculptor.

Jan or John Johnson or Janssen was probably the son of Nicholas Johnson the Elder.

JOHNSON, Jeanne Payne
American, 20th century.
Born 14 April 1887, in Danville (Oklahoma); died 1958.
Miniaturist.

Jeanne Payne Johnson studied at the Art Students League in New York, and with Richard Miller and Lucien Simon in Paris. She was a member of the Brooklyn Society of Miniaturist Painters.

JOHNSON, John
British, 18th century.
Died c. 1797, in Newcastle.
Engraver (wood), draughtsman.

John Johnson was the cousin of Robert Johnson and student of Bewich. He died young. There is mention of two plates for *The Beauties of Cambria*.

JOHNSON, Joshua or William, or Johnston
American, 18th - 19th century.
Born 1762 or 1763, in Maryland; died around 1830.
Active in Baltimore, 1793-1824.
Painter. Portraits, compositions with figures.

There is not very much information on the life of Johnson. His mother was a slave and his father was probably the white painter George Johnson. He was liberated from slavery at age 19, thanks to a law in Maryland in 1790 that allowed children from mixed unions to be free. It is said that his father bought him when he was one and a half from his mothers' slave master. Or that he was a slave worker for Colonel John Moale or the Charles Willson Pale family, where numerous artists lived. However it is sure that he was an aprentice blacksmith in Baltimore and that he signed his works 'Johnson', a name that was often used among the Afro-Amercan population during that time. The name 'Johnson' often appeared in the registers next to the name 'Johnston' which might have been a spelling mistake. His fair skin sometimes made him pass for a white man. He may have taken painting classes from the painter Charles Peale Polk, because their style and subject of portraits is very similar. He was active in Baltimore possibly up until 1832 and might have also been a building decorator.

Johnson is the oldest known black portrait painter in America. During his life he acquired a certain amount of fame and recognition in Maryland and Virginia. Eighty works of art are attributed to him, of which only two are portraits of black people: *Portrait of a Cleric* (around 1805-1910) and *Portrait of a Gentleman* (1805-1810). Johnsons clients were mostly white, and like his fellow artists he wanted to integrate into a professional career. Johnson followed a painting aprenticeship to become a portraitist, which was common for slaves during his time. Portraits were still considered a craft art form. His work was naive but had a realistic representation. He painted detailed rendition of the clothes of his subjects and numerous portraits of children. He was rediscovered in the 1930s.

His work has been part of many thematic 20th century exhibition such as: *Two Centuries of Black American Art*, Los Angeles County Museum of Art 1976; *American Folk Art in the Metropolitan Museum of Art*, Metroploitan Museum of Art New York 2000; *Sankofa: A Century of African American Expression in the Decorative Arts*, Harriet Tubman Museum, Macon Georgia 2000; and at the *Maryland Artists from the Collection, 1890-1970*, Baltimore Museum 2002. Retrospectives of his work have been at the Peale Museum in Baltimore in 1948 and at the Seattle Art Museum in 1986.

Bibliography:

Hall Pleasants, J., '*Joshua Johnston: The First American Negro Portrait Painter*' in *The Maryland Historical Magazine* n° 2, periodical, June 1942. Hall Pleasants, J., *An Exhibition of Portraits by Joshua Johnston*, exhibition catalogue, Peale Museum, Baltimore, 1948. Porter, James A., *Modern Negro Art*, Arno Press, The New York Times, New York, 1969. Bearden, Romare / Henderson, *Six Black Masters in American Art*, Zenith Books, New York, 1972. Driskell, David, *Two Centuries of Black American Art*, collective exhibition catalogue, Los Angeles County Museum of Art, Los Angeles, Alfred A. Knopf, New York, 1976. Hartigan, Lynda Roscoe, *Sharing Traditions: Five Black Artists in Nineteenth Century America*, collective exhibition catalogue, National Museum of American Art, Smithsonian Institution Press, Washington DC, 1985. Weekley, Carolyn / Hayward, Graham, *Joshua Johnson: Freeman and Early American Portrait Painter*, Maryland Historical Society, Baltimore, 1987.

Museums and Galleries:

Baltimore (Maryland Historical Society): *The James McCormick Family* (c. 1804, oil on canvas) - Brunswick, ME (Bowdoin College Museum of Art): *Portrait of a Cleric* (c. 1805-1810, oil on canvas) - New York (Metropolitan Mus. of Art): *Edward and Sarah Rutter* (c. 1805, oil on canvas) - Washington DC (NGA): *Family Group* (1800, oil on canvas); *Mr. Baylor* (c. 1805, oil on canvas); *Sarah Ogden Gustin* (c. 1805, oil on canvas); *The Westwood Children* (c. 1807, oil on canvas); *Adelina Morton* (c. 1810, oil on canvas) - Washington DC (Smithsonian American AM): *Portrait of Mrs Barbara Baker Murphy (wife of Sea Captain)* (c. 1810, oil on canvas); *Portrait of Sea Captain John Murphy* (c. 1810, oil on canvas).

Auction records:

New York, 26 Oct 1985, *Portrait of a Young Woman Seated* (c. 1810, oil on canvas, 30 1/4 x 25 1/2 ins / 77 x 65 cm) USD 42,500.

JOHNSON, Lawrence
British, 17th century.
Engraver (etching).

Lawrence Johnson worked on the illustrations for *The General History of the Turks*. He also engraved a very rare *Portrait of King James I*.

JOHNSON, Lester
American, 20th century.
Born 1919, in Minneapolis (Minnesota).
Painter. Figures.

Lester Johnson studied at the Minneapolis School of Art, then at the Art Institute of Chicago from 1942 to 1947. He taught in Newhaven. Though his painting is figurative, it cannot be described as Expressionist as one might say of De Kooning, for example, with whom he often exhibits. It borrows many if its techniques from Gestural Abstraction, with strange human forms emerging from the substance of the picture.

Though not well known in Europe, he has taken part in many group exhibitions in Philadelphia; in New York, notably at the Whitney Museum of American Art in 1958, 1967, 1968 and 1973; the Museum of Modern Art in 1961 and 1968; the Solomon R. Guggenheim Museum in 1964 and 1972 and at the Metropolitan Museum in 1984 and 1985; in Minneapolis at the Institute of Art in1957; in Boston at the Institute of Contemporary Art in 1959 and 1960; in Los Angeles; in Chicago, notably at the Institute of Arts in 1962 and 1972; In Pittsburgh at the Carnegie Institute in 1961, 1964, 1967 and 1970; in Madrid in 1969 and in St-Paul-de-Vence at the Fondation Maeght in 1970. He has had a great many solo shows, mainly in the USA.

BIBLIOGRAPHY:

Premier Salon international des Galeries Pilotes, exhibition catalogue, Musée cantonal, Lausanne, 1963. Sandler, Irving, *The New York School: The Painters and the Sculptors of the Fifties,* Harper and Row, New York, 1978. Kunitz, Daniel, '*Out of the Fifties - into the Sixties: Six Figurative expressionists at Michael Rosenfield Gallery, New York*' in *New Criterion,* vol 19, no. 9, periodical, 2001.

MUSEUMS AND GALLERIES:

BALTIMORE (MA) - BUFFALO (Albright-Knox AG) - DETROIT (IA) - NEW YORK (Metropolitan Mus. of Art) - NEW YORK (MoMA) - NEW YORK (Solomon R. Guggenheim Mus.) - PHOENIX (AM): *Dark Man* (1963, oil on canvas) - PITTSBURGH (Carnegie MA): *Three Men, Green Writing* (1962, oil on coloured canvas) - WASHINGTON DC (Hirshhorn Mus. and Sculpture Garden).

AUCTION RECORDS:

NEW YORK, 20 Oct 1978, *Five Figures with Hats, Seated* (1969, oil on canvas, 22 x 22 ins / 56 x 56 cm) USD 1,300. NEW YORK, 22 March 1979, *Grand Street* (1963, oil on canvas, 66 1/4 x 44 ins / 168 x 112 cm) USD 2,400. NEW YORK, 27 Feb 1980, *Street Scene* (charcoal, 29 x 23 ins / 73.7 x 58.4 cm) USD 2,400. NEW YORK, 2 Oct 1980, *Untitled* (1975, mixed media, 30 x 22 ins / 76.2 x 55.8 cm) USD 2,900. NEW YORK, 12 May 1981, *Early Arrival Blue* (1970, oil on canvas, 80 1/4 x 90 ins / 204 x 228.5 cm) USD 13,000. NEW YORK, 11 May 1983, *Grand Central* (oil on canvas, 40 x 40 ins / 101.5 x 101.5 cm) USD 4,800. NEW YORK, 16 Feb 1984, *City Women II* (1974, coloured chalk, 29 1/2 x 21 1/4 ins / 75 x 54 cm) USD 1,400. NEW YORK, 23 Feb 1985, *Untitled* (watercolour, 27 3/4 x 21 3/4 ins / 70.5 x 55.5 cm) USD 1,800. NEW YORK, 27 Feb 1985, *The Crowd* (1971, charcoal and coloured chalk, 23 x 29 ins / 58.5 x 73.6 cm) USD 1,400. NEW YORK, 11 Nov 1986, *Tip of Broadway* (1972, oil on canvas, 80 x 89 1/2 ins / 203.3 x 227.4 cm) USD 21,000. NEW YORK, 20 Feb 1988, *A Green Man* (1963, oil on panel, 46 3/4 x 42 1/2 ins / 118.8 x 108 cm) USD 15,400. NEW YORK, 4 May 1988, *Promenade* (1965, oil on canvas, 34 x 22 ins / 86.4 x 55.9 cm) USD 4,620. NEW YORK, 8 Oct 1988, *Untitled* (oil on canvas, 40 x 50 ins / 101.6 x 127 cm) USD 27,500. NEW YORK, 3 May 1989, *Three Men* (1960, oil on canvas, 53 1/2 x 68 ins / 136 x 173 cm) USD 18,700. NEW YORK, 5 Oct 1989, *Two Women with Men* (1974, oil on canvas, 50 x 40 ins / 127 x 101.7 cm) USD 16,500. NEW YORK, 9 Nov 1989, *Street Scene - Strollers no. 5* (1978, oil on canvas, 60 x 50 ins / 152.5 x 127 cm) USD 19,800. NEW YORK, 23 Feb 1990, *Street Scene* (coloured chalk/paper, 29 3/4 x 21 1/4 ins / 75.5 x 54 cm) USD 5,500. NEW YORK, 27 Feb 1990, *City Women* (1974, oil on canvas, 40 x 30 ins / 101.5 x 76 cm) USD 15,400. NEW YORK, 4 Oct 1990, *Man with the Letter N* (1965, oil on canvas, 68 x 47 3/4 ins / 172.7 x 121.3 cm) USD 14,300. NEW YORK, 7 Nov 1990, *Untitled (Six Characters)* (oil on canvas, 60 x 50 ins / 152.4 x 127 cm) USD 15,400. NEW YORK, 13 Feb 1991, *The Girls of the Town* (1986, oil on panel, 24 x 17 3/4 ins / 61 x 45.4 cm) USD 6,050. NEW YORK, 17 Nov 1992, *The Women's Quarter* (oil on canvas, 60 x 50 ins / 152.4 x 127 cm) USD 9,900. NEW YORK, 23-25 Feb 1993, *Emerging from the Crowd* (1970, oil on canvas, 68 x 60 ins / 172.7 x 152.4 cm) USD 14,950. NEW YORK, 14 June 1995, *Portrait of a Man* (1965, oil on canvas, 24 x 24 ins / 61 x 61 cm) USD 2,587. NEW YORK, 7 Nov 2000, *Man with Plant, Blue* (oil on canvas, 52 x 60 ins / 132 x 152 cm) USD 4,000. NEW YORK, 7 Nov 2000, *City Scene* (oil on canvas, 18 x 22 ins / 46 x 55 cm) USD 5,000. BOSTON, 7 Sept 2001, *Portrait of a Man* (1961, watercolour, 40 x 26 ins / 101 x 66 cm) USD 2,000. BOSTON, 7 Sept 2001, *Silhouette* (1964, oil on canvas, 30 x 25 ins / 77 x 64 cm) USD 5,000. NEW YORK, 20 Feb 2002, *Bathers in Milford Number 2* (oil on canvas, 76 x 96 ins / 193 x 244 cm) USD 14,000. DETROIT, 17 May 2002, *Street Scene Peugeot* (oil on canvas, 50 x 40 ins / 127 x 102 cm) USD 12,000. CHICAGO, 9 Nov 2003, *Untitled - Still-life. Untitled - Portrait* (ink and oil on paper, 11 x 17 ins / 28 x 43 cm) USD 3,250.

JOHNSON, M. H. (Miss)

British, 19th century.
Active in London.
Painter.

M.H. Johnson exhibited very often between 1843 and 1852 at the Suffolk Street gallery and also at the Royal Academy and the British Institution.

JOHNSON, Malvin Gray

American, 20th century.
Born 28 January 1896, in Greensboro (North Carolina); died 4 October 1934.
Painter, draughtsman, watercolourist. Portraits, street scenes, still-lifes.
Harlem Renaissance.

Malvin Gray Johnson studied under F.C. Jones and at the National Academy of Design in New York in 1916. He was a member of the Society of Independent Artists, working as a commercial artist. He took part in the Public Works of Art Project, a New Deal governmental programme which employed artists during the 1930s. He was party to the Harlem Renaissance.

He drew his inspiration from Afro-American music and Negro Spirituals, as well as Harlem life for his genre scenes in dark, warm tonalities, but he is better known for his expressionist portraits. He also executed abstract paintings in a post-Cubist style where he introduced formal elements of African art. Art historian James A. Porter chose his painting *Roll, Jordan, Roll* (1930) to illustrate the cover of his famous work, *Modern Negro Art* (Howard University Press, Washington, 1943).

He took part in collective exhibitions in the early 1930s at the Harmon Foundation, New York then notably: 1976, *Two Centuries of Black American Art,* Los Angeles; 1987, *Harlem Renaissance: Art of Black America,* Studio Museum in Harlem, New York; 1999, *To Conserve a Legacy. American Art from Historically Black Colleges and Universities,* Andover (Massachusetts). Posthumous retrospectives of his work were set up, notably in 2002, by the North Carolina Central University, Durham.

BIBLIOGRAPHY:

Driskell, David C., *Two Centuries of Black American Art,* group exhibition catalogue, Los Angeles County Museum of Art, Los Angeles, 1976. Powell, Richard/Reynolds, Jock, *To conserve a Legacy: American Art from Historically Black Colleges and Universities,* group exhibition catalogue, Addison Gall. of American Art, Phillips Academy, Andover, 1999. Rodgers, Kenneth G./Francis, Jacquelyn/Hurt, Perry, *Climbing Up the Mountain: The Modern Art of Malvin Gray Johnson,* exhibition catalogue, North Carolina Central University Art Museum, Durham (NC), 2002.

MUSEUMS AND GALLERIES:

HAMPTON (Hampton University Mus.) - NASHVILLE (Aaron Douglas Gallery, Fisk University) - NEW YORK (Whitney Mus. of American Art) - OAKLAND (Mus. of California) - WASHING-

TON DC (GA, Howard University) - WASHINGTON DC (Smithsonian American AM): *Brothers* (1934, oil on canvas); *Self-portrait* (1934, oil on canvas).

JOHNSON, Mary (Mrs)
19th century.
Active in London.
Painter. Landscapes.

Mary Johnson exhibited at the Royal Academy, at the British Institution and in Suffolk Street from 1814 to 1827.

JOHNSON, Michael
Australian, 20th century.
Born 1938, in Sydney.
Painter.

Michael Johnson received a grant from the Joye Art Foundation of Australia. He trained at the Julian Ashton Art School in Sydney and subsequently lived abroad at regular intervals, notably in London and New York. His early work was influenced by the 1960s Hard-edge painters of the American West Coast. Later works reflect a more personal style, which feature landscape references comprising thickly-applied impasto grounds superposed with lighter, dancing signs. His work has featured in a number of group exhibitions, including the Galerie Baudoin Lebon, Paris, in 1989.

AUCTION RECORDS:
MELBOURNE, 29 April 1997, *Vina* (1994, oil on Belgian linen, 72 x 60 ins / 183 x 152.5 cm) AUD 21,850. SYDNEY, 17 Aug 1999, *Yuin* (1991-1992, oil on canvas, 83 x 60 ins / 212 x 152 cm) AUD 39,000. MELBOURNE, 23 Nov 1999, *Italian Yellow* (1984-1985, oil on Belgian linen, 96 x 83 ins / 243 x 212 cm) AUD 35,000. MELBOURNE, 1 May 2000, *Balmoral* (1989, oil on linen, 48 x 144 ins / 121 x 366 cm) AUD 47,000. MELBOURNE, 3 May 2000, *avr-86* (1986, oil on canvas, 96 x 82 ins / 243 x 208 cm) AUD 45,000. MELBOURNE, 8 May 2001, *Freer* (1982, acrylic on canvas, 84 x 66 ins / 213 x 167 cm) AUD 30,000. SYDNEY, 28 Aug 2001, *Untitled* (1987, oil on canvas, 48 x 144 ins / 121 x 366 cm) AUD 26,000. MELBOURNE, 2 May 2002, *Black Water* (1991, oil on linen, 48 x 144 ins / 122 x 367 cm) AUD 50,000. MELBOURNE, 25 Nov 2002, *Under and Over* (1992, linen on canvas, 96 x 84 ins / 243 x 213 cm) AUD 48,000. PADDINGTON, 25 Aug 2003, *Inuit* (1999, oil on canvas, 60 x 48 ins / 153 x 122 cm) AUD 35,000. MELBOURNE, 24 Nov 2003, *Untitled* (oil on canvas, 48 x 144 ins / 122 x 366 cm) AUD 62,500. PADDINGTON, 24 Aug 2004, *Earth Line* (1997-1998, oil on canvas, 48 x 144 ins / 122 x 365 cm) AUD 62,500. MELBOURNE, 8 Sept 2004, *Yuzen* (1989-1990, oil on canvas, 48 x 144 ins / 121 x 366 cm) AUD 48,000.

JOHNSON, Nicholas, the Elder, or Janssen
Dutch, 16th century.
Born 16th century, in Amsterdam.
Sculptor.

Johnson worked in England where he settled in about 1567 and became a bourgeois citizen of London.

JOHNSON, Nicholas, the Younger
British, 16th - 17th century.
Sculptor.

Johnson was probably the youngest son of Nicholas the Elder and worked in Southwark in Surrey. He took part in work on the tombs of the third and fourth counts of Rutland in the church of Bottesford, and produced those of the fifth count of Rutland and his wife. The latter was the daughter and heiress of Sir Philip Spencer.

JOHNSON, Pattie or Patty
Maiden name: Townsend
British, 19th - 20th century.
Painter. Genre scenes, landscapes.

Patty Townsend was active in Nuneaton, Leicestershire. She exhibited under her maiden name at the Royal Academy in 1881 and 1892, and as Mrs Patty Townsend-Johnson in 1897, 1900 and 1904.

AUCTION RECORDS:
LONDON, 25 Jan 1988, *House at Newdigate in Surrey* (1896, watercolour, 9 1/2 x 12 3/4 ins / 24 x 32.5 cm) GBP 858.

JOHNSON, Ray
American, 20th century.
Born 1927, in Detroit (Michigan); found dead 13 January 1995 in Sag Harbor (New York).
Painter (mixed media).
Visual Poetry, Fluxus, Mail Art.

Ray Johnson studied under Josef Albers, at Black Mountain College, then under Robert Motherwell, Mary Callery and Ossip Zadkine from 1945 to 1948. In the 1960s, he subscribed to Fluxus' outlook. Along with Dick Higgins, he published in 1965 *The Paper Snake*, a collection of letters, poems and drawings. As the founder of the New York Correspondence School, he played an important part in the multiplication of mailings as an artistic channel which became so prevalent in the 1970s as to generate the name Mail Art for the movement which bypassed the galleries network. Often indefinable, alluding as it does to notions external to the piece on show, stemming from the range of potential gaps within language and images, Ray Johnson's work is not easily described. A collage by Ray Johnson tends to account for one random moment in an ongoing information handling process, achieved at that stage but arbitrary in the greater scheme of things.

From 1949 to 1952, he belonged to the American Abstract Artists Group, in New York, with whom he exhibited. From 1959, he took part in numerous group exhibitions, notably in 1967, *Pictures to be Read, Poetry to be Seen*; he also put forward a collage-painting revolving around *Marianne Moore's Hat* for *Art Process* at Finch College, New York. In 1970, he set up the important mail art operation whereby 106 artists sent the curator of the Whitney Museum a 'work of art'. On account of this movement, the 1971 Biennale de Paris chose postage as one of its themes; Johnson was in attendance. In 1965, he had his first solo show in New York, followed by many others in that city and in Chicago, Philadelphia.

AUCTION RECORDS:
LONDON, 5 July 1973, *Jacqueline Kennedy Onassis Dollar Bill* (collage and mixed media) GBP 900. LONDON, 30 April 1976, *Massage Ball* (1967, collage, 14 1/2 x 16 1/2 ins / 37 x 42 cm) GBP 800. NEW YORK, 6 May 1982, *Untitled* (c. 1965, collage and gouache/hardboard, 26 1/2 x 24 1/4 ins / 67 x 61.5 cm) USD 1,600. NEUILLY, 20 June 1988, *Untitled* (1972, gouache, 24 3/4 x 19 ins / 63 x 48 cm) FRF 8,000. PARIS, 16 Oct 1988, *Interview* (1967, collage and text/panel, 19 3/4 x 19 3/4 ins / 50 x 50 cm) FRF 12,000. PARIS, 12 Feb 1989, *Cupid with Pipe II* (1973, tempera and collage/card, 19 x 14 1/4 ins / 48.5 x 36 cm) FRF 17,000. NEW YORK, 8 Nov 1993, *Gustave Eiffel* (black and white photograph, painted wood, ink and gouache/panel/panel, 17 x 17 ins / 43 x 43 cm) USD 3,910. NEW YORK, 3 May 1994, *Spiral Staircase* (collage of paper and oil on card, 30 1/2 x 30 1/2 ins / 77.5 x 77.5 cm) USD 1,725. PARIS, 17 Oct 1994, *Americano-Japanese Flags - Are you Cross Jasper Johns* (1959, assemblage of wooden bars and collage, 11 x 14 ins / 27 x 35.5 cm) FRF 44,000. NEW YORK, 10 Nov 1999, *Ancient Ladder* (1965, acrylic, wax crayon and collage on card on board, 18 x 22 ins / 45 x 55 cm) USD 6,000. NEW YORK, 17 Nov 1999, *Untitled* (collage and gouache on card, 9 x 7 ins / 23 x 18 cm) USD 5,500. COPENHAGEN, 2 April 2001, *Black Swan* (1979, mixed media on paper, 14 x 20 ins / 36 x 50 cm) DKK 13,000. COPENHAGEN, 1 Oct 2002, *Buddha Urinating* (1979, collage on paper, 12 x 5 ins / 30 x 12 cm) DKK 15,000. COPENHAGEN, 1 April 2003, *Mirojoan* (1979-1986, collage on paper, 14 x 7 ins / 35 x 19 cm) DKK 16,000. NEW YORK, 23 Sept 2003, *Kiss the Lotus* (1969, ink, watercolour and collage on card on board, 17 x 15 ins / 42 x 39 cm) USD 12,000. COPEN-

HAGEN, 5 Oct 2004, *Rimbeaud Birds* (1979-1986, collage on card and paper, 11 x 5 ins / 29 x 12 cm) DKK 48,000.

JOHNSON, Robert

British, 18th century.
Born 1770, in Shortley; died 26 October 1796, in Kenmore.
Watercolourist, engraver (wood).

Robert Johnson learned engraving from Bewick but was not successful in this medium. On the other hand, his watercolours were much admired and several of them were made into engravings by Bewick.

JOHNSON, Robert

British, 18th century.
Active in London at the end of the 18th century.
Engraver (burin).

Robert Johnson was cited by Nagler.

JOHNSON, Robert

Australian, 19th - 20th century.
Born 1890; died 1964.
Painter. Landscapes.

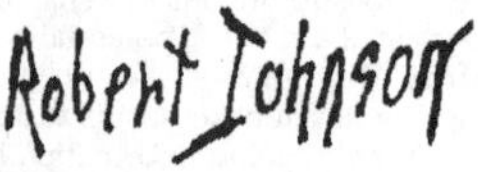

AUCTION RECORDS:

LONDON, 30 April 1976, *Landscape* (1927, oil on canvas remounted on board, 14½ x 17½ ins / 37 x 44.5 cm) GBP 1,100. WOLLAHRA, 26 Sept 1977, *Riverscape* (oil on canvas, 18 x 21¾ ins / 46 x 55.5 cm) AUD 3,000. SYDNEY, 21 March 1979, *North Ryde* (oil on card, 14¼ x 17¼ ins / 36 x 44 cm) AUD 1,800. SYDNEY, 29 June 1981, *In the McDonalds Ranges* (oil on canvas, 46½ x 67 ins / 118 x 170 cm) AUD 2,800. ARMADALE, 11 April 1984, *Old farm, Ryde, New South Wales* (oil on canvas remounted on board, 14½ x 17¼ ins / 37 x 44 cm) AUD 7,000. MELBOURNE, 21 April 1986, *Milton River, Victoria* (oil on canvas, 27¼ x 35½ ins / 69 x 90 cm) AUD 30,000. MELBOURNE, 26 July 1987, *Hawkesbury River* (1929, oil on canvas, 28¼ x 36 ins / 71.5 x 91.5 cm) AUD 95,000. SYDNEY, 17 April 1988, *The Red Centre* (oil on card, 15 x 17¾ ins / 38 x 45 cm) AUD 5,500. SYDNEY, 3 July 1989, *Old Cedar Mill near Cairns* (oil on card, 16½ x 22 ins / 42 x 55 cm) AUD 11,000. SYDNEY, 26 March 1990, *Bilgola Beach* (oil on card, 17¾ x 22 ins / 45 x 55 cm) AUD 14,000. SYDNEY, 2 July 1990, *The Edward River, Deniliquib* (oil on card, 14½ x 17¾ ins / 37 x 45 cm) AUD 3,500. NEW YORK, 19 July 1990, *Harbour Panorama* (oil on card, 15 x 18 ins / 38.2 x 45.5 cm) USD 4,950. MELBOURNE, 29 April 1997, *Milton River* (oil on canvas, 28 x 36 ins / 71 x 91.5 cm) AUD 18,400. SYDNEY, 20 April 1999, *Road Through the Capertee Valley* (oil on canvas, 24 x 30 ins / 61 x 76 cm) AUD 5,800. PHILADELPHIA, 12 Dec 1999, *Landscape, Australia* (oil on masonite, 18 x 20 ins / 46 x 52 cm) USD 4,200. VICTORIA, 4 April 2000, *Clareville, Pittwater* (oil on canvas, 21 x 25 ins / 54 x 64 cm) AUD 11,000. MELBOURNE, 15 Aug 2000, *Pittwater* (oil on canvas, 27 x 35 ins / 69 x 89 cm) AUD 24,000. MELBOURNE, 7 May 2001, *Bush Road* (1927, oil on canvas on panel, 15 x 17 ins / 37 x 44 cm) AUD 5,040. PADDINGTON, 3 June 2001, *Berry's Bay* (oil on canvas on board, 14 x 17 ins / 36 x 44 cm) AUD 13,000. MELBOURNE, 2 May 2002, *Morning, Kanimbla Valley* (1950, oil on canvas, 28 x 36 ins / 71 x 92 cm) AUD 5,500. VICTORIA, 6 May 2002, *Mount Stegg* (oil on canvas, 21 x 25 ins / 54 x 64 cm) AUD 9,500. SYDNEY, 15 April 2003, *Jugiong Landscape* (oil on canvas on board, 17 x 21 ins / 44 x 53 cm) AUD 6,500. MELBOURNE, 26 Nov 2003, *Whale Beach* (c. 1940, oil on canvas on board, 15 x 18 ins / 38 x 45 cm) AUD 6,500. VICTORIA, 10 May 2004, *Valley of the Hawkesbury* (1928, oil on canvas, 27 x 35 ins / 69 x 89 cm) AUD 19,500. MELBOURNE, 8 Sept 2004, *Waterwheel* (oil on canvas on board, 17 x 21 ins / 44 x 54 cm) AUD 7,000.

JOHNSON, Robert Ward

American, 20th century.
Painter.

Robert Ward Johnson featured at the Salon des Indépendants and the Salon d'Automne in Paris.

JOHNSON, Sargent Claude

American, 20th century.
Born 7 October 1887, in Boston; died 10 October 1967, in San Francisco.
Sculptor (including wood), draughtsman, watercolourist, print artist, lithographer, ceramicist.
Murals, mosaics.

Sargent Claude Johnson had an unsettled childhood. He lost his father at age ten, his mother at age fifteen, and was raised first by an uncle, then by his grandparents, and finally in an orphanage in Worcester, Massachusetts. He moved to the Bay area in 1915. He studied with Beniamino Bufano and Ralph Stackpole at the California School of Fine Arts, San Francisco (1919-1923). During the 1930s he served as a supervisor on the Work Progress Administration's Federal Arts Project. Between 1945 and 1965 he travelled frequently to Mexico, being fascinated with that country's pre-Columbian sites. He visited Japan in 1958.

In his desire to return to the sources of African-American culture, Johnson drew his inspiration from African and pre-Columbian art and adopted a syncretistic neo-primitive style. He also applied colour to his statues in exactly the same way as in the ancient tradition. His best-known work is probably *Forever Free* (1940), a maternal figure, her head turned to one side, her arms held rigid against her cylindrical body, with the silhouettes of two children incised into her skirt. Carved of sequoia wood, the piece is covered by lacquered fabric that divides her body in two: her body is white and her skirt black. Johnson also made bronze masks that are freely inspired by original art of the Baule people of Ivory Coast, and lithographs that clearly testify to his love of music, such as *Singing Saints* (1940). He also produced a number of monumental works, such as the mosaic murals for the Maritime Museum of Aquatic Park, San Francisco, in which he used stylisations typical of Art Deco; the cast-stone frieze made for the George Washington High School Athletic Field; and the sculptures of Inca Indians seated on llamas for the Court of Pacifica at the 1939-1940 Golden Gate International Exposition. Sargent Johnson drew freely on the early art of Africa and the Americas, combining with it elements of synthetic Cubism and Art Deco yet without ever sacrificing his expressive power or falling into the trap of imitation. He is a central figure in the Harlem Renaissance.

Johnson took part in various group exhibitions, including the Harmon Foundation, New York (regularly from 1926 to 1935) as well as in 1933 at the Harlem Art Center, New York. He exhibited in 1935, with Malvin Gray Johnson and Richmond Barthe, at the Harmon Foundation, Delphic Studios, New York; in 1939, Golden Gate International Exhibition, San Francisco. After he died, his work was included in thematic group exhibitions such as 1997, *Rhapsodies in Black: Art of the Harlem Renaissance*, Hayward Gallery, Institute of International Visual Arts, London, and California Palace of the Legion of Honor, San Francisco. Retrospective exhibitions were held in 1971 at the Oakland Museum, Oakland and in 1998 at the Museum of Modern Art, San Francisco.

BIBLIOGRAPHY:

Porter, James A., *Modern Negro Art*, Arno Press, New York Times, New York, 1943. Lewis, Samella, *African-American Art and Artists*, University of California Press, Berkeley, 1990. Powell, Richard J, et al., *Rhapsodies in Black: Art of the Harlem Renaissance*, group exhibition catalogue, Hayward Gallery, Institute of International Visual Arts, London, University of California Press, Berkeley, 1997. Lefalle-Collins, Lizzetta/Wilson, Judith, *Sargent Johnson African-American*

Modernist, exhibition catalogue, San Francisco Museum of Modern Art, San Francisco, 1998.
Museums and Galleries:
Oakland (Mus. of California): *Singing Saints* (1940, lithograph) - San Francisco (MoMA): *Forever Free* (1933, wood with lacquer on cloth); *Woman's Head* (c. 1940, cast stone).

JOHNSON, Thomas
British, 17th century.
Painter, draughtsman. Religious subjects, genre scenes, landscapes, architectural views.
Thomas Johnson is mentioned from 1651 to 1685. Works by him which have survived are: *Choir of Canterbury, Christ at the Home of Martha and Mary* and *St Jerome in a Church*.
Museums and Galleries:
London (British Mus.): *King's and Queen's Baths in Bath* (wash drawing).

JOHNSON, Thomas
British, 18th century.
Active in London.
Draughtsman, engraver (mezzotint/burin). Portraits.
Thomas Johnson worked in London and produced portraits among other subjects, many of which were based on his own compositions. These included portraits of the comedian *W. Bullock, Edward Ward, The Seasons* and four plates. He also made engravings of works by G. Kneller and Rubens.

JOHNSON, Thomas
British, 18th century.
Active in London.
Sculptor (wood), engraver, draughtsman, designer of ornamental architectural features.
Thomas Johnson is mentioned in the period covering 1755-1761. An etching of a landscape showing ruins, animals and shepherds, one of a series of 12 plates, is kept at the British Museum.
Museums and Galleries:
London (British Mus.): *Landscape* (etching).

JOHNSON, Thomas
British, 19th century.
Born 19th century, in London.
Engraver (including etching).
Thomas Johnson trained with F. Williams. He worked in Brooklyn, New York. Among his works are a portrait of the American philanthropist *Peter Cooper*, the poet *Henry Wadsworth Longfellow* engraved on wood, and etched portraits of *Abraham Lincoln, Franz Liszt* and *Walt W. Whitman*. There are also engravings of *Daubigny* and *Paderewski* as well as a *Portrait of a Child* after John W. Alexander and a *Portrait of a Man* after Rembrandt.

JOHNSON, Thomas. See also **JOHNSTON**

JOHNSON, Thomas Crosham
British, 19th century.
Active in London.
Painter. Landscapes.
Thomas Crosham Johnson exhibited in London from 1852 to 1880, especially at the Suffolk Street Gallery; his name also appears in the catalogues of the Royal Academy and the British Institution.

JOHNSON, V.
British, 18th - 19th century.
Active in Nottingham.
Painter. Portraits.
V. Johnson exhibited at the Royal Academy in 1802 and 1803.

JOHNSON, W. Noel
British, 19th - 20th century.
Painter, watercolourist. Landscapes.
Noel W. Johnson made his début at the Suffolk Street Gallery in 1892. He went on to become a regular exhibitor in London and other British towns, including Bowdon in Wales.
Museums and Galleries:
Manchester: *Evening Calm, Lake Rauza* (watercolour); *Isle of Arran* (watercolour); *The Tide and the Davon River, Anglesey*.

JOHNSON, William Henry
American, 20th century.
Born 18 March 1901, in Florence (South Carolina); died 13 April 1970, on Long Island.
Also active in France, Denmark and Norway.
Painter (including gouache), draughtsman, watercolourist, print artist (woodcuts), screen printer. Figures, portraits, nudes, genre scenes, sporting subjects, landscapes, still-lifes. Murals.
William Henry Johnson came to New York in 1918 with an uncle who was looking for work. He worked for a few years himself before going to study at the National Academy of Design. Afterwards he studied with Charles Hawthorne at the Cape Cod School of Art, Provincetown, Massachusetts. He went to Paris in 1926, visited the South of France and travelled around Europe. In 1929 he returned to New York but travelled to Denmark the following year, where he married the weaver and ceramicist Holcha Krake. In 1932 the couple travelled around Europe and North Africa. In 1935 they settled in Volda, Norway, before fleeing to New York in 1938 to escape the Nazi threat. Johnson taught at the Harlem Art Center, New York, under the Federal Arts Project, the Work Progress Administration (WPA) programme set up by President Roosevelt in 1934 to promote art and education in the USA while helping artists who were threatened by the Depression. In 1943 his wife died. In 1946 he returned once more to Denmark. In 1947 he was found wandering the streets of Oslo and was repatriated. Confined to a psychiatric hospital at Central Islip, Long Island, he died without ever being able to paint again.

While in Europe, Johnson devoted himself almost entirely to landscapes, painting in an expressionist style close to that of Soutine. After returning to the USA, he concentrated on figures whose outsize presence fills his canvases. He also changed his palette, applying bright colours in flat areas in compositions full of powerful contrasts, simplifying his forms in a clear desire to return to the primitive values he so admired. He became involved in telling the story of the rural South and the black urban communities of the North, taking as his themes passages from the Gospels or other biblical episodes. Between 1939 and 1943 he executed a number of murals for the WPA. Johnson brought to his depiction of this rural and cultural reality a new pictorial language. He was thoroughly imbued with European modernist ideas and defined himself as a primitivist. He made a major contribution to the aesthetic development of the Harlem Renaissance, the first black art movement in America, which promoted the representation of African-American life and culture.

William Johnson took part in various group exhibitions, including in 1931, *Travelling Art Exhibit of Paintings by Negro Artists*, Capetown; 1933, with fabrics and ceramics by his wife Holcha, Christian Larsen Gallery, Copenhagen; 1942, travelling exhibition, *American Artists' Record of War and Defense*, National Gallery of Art, Washington DC and in 1968, *Invisible Americans: Black Artists of the 30s*, Studio Museum in Harlem, New York. Among his solo exhibitions were 1928, Galerie Alban, Nice; 1939, Artists' Gallery, New York; 1941, Alma Reed Gallery, New York; 1946, New York Public Library, New York; 1947, Kunsthallen, Copenhagen; 1968, College Museum, Hampton Institute, Hampton, Virginia); 1970, Spellman College, Atlanta. Posthumous retrospectives of his work included in 1982, *William H. Johnson: The Scandinavian Years*, National Museum of American Art, Smithsonian Institution, Washington DC and in 1991, *Homecoming: William H. Johnson and Afro-America, 1938-1946*, National Museum of American Art, Smithsonian Institution, Washington DC.

Bibliography:

Lowe, Jeannette, '*Paintings by William H. Johnson. Arts and crafts by Holcha Krake*' in *Art News* n° 37, periodical, 25 February 1939. *Paintings: William H. Johnson*, exhibition catalogue, Alma Reed Gall., New York, 1941. *William H. Johnson, Afro-American Painter*, exhibition catalogue, Spellman College, Atlanta, 1970. Breeskin, Adelyn D., *William H. Johnson, 1901-1970*, exhibition catalogue, National Collection of Fine Arts, Smithsonian Institution Press, Washington DC, 1971. Powell, Richard J., *William H. Johnson: Expressionist and Artist of the Blues Aesthetic*, dissertation, 1988 (Yale University, New Haven, Connecticut). Powell, Richard J./Puryear, Martin (introduction), *Homecoming. The Art and Life of William H. Johnson*, exhibition catalogue, National Museum of American Art, Smithsonian Institution, Washington, DC, Rizzoli, New York, 1991.

Museums and Galleries:

Chicago (DuSable Mus. of African-American History) - Columbia, SC (Columbia Mus. of Art) - Florence, SC (Florence Mus.) - Gävle, Sweden (Länsmuseet) - Keterminde, Denmark (Keterminde Mus.) - Los Angeles (California African American Mus.) - New York (Metropolitan Mus. of Art): *Three Children* (1940) - Newark, NJ (Newark Mus.) - Oakland (Mus. of California) - Stockholm (Moderna Mus.) - Washington DC (Library of Congress) - Washington DC (Smithsonian American AM): *Still-life* (c. 1923-1926, oil on canvas); *Farm Couple at Well* (c. 1939-1940, oil/plywood); large collection.

Auction records:

North Bethesda, 19 May 2002, *Deep South* (colour screenprint, 18 x 14 ins / 45 x 35 cm) USD 23,000. North Bethesda, 19 May 2002, *Training for War* (colour screenprint, 11 x 18 ins / 29 x 46 cm) USD 35,000. Copenhagen, 29 March 2004, *Portrait of the Artist Regner Lange* (oil on canvas, 14 x 14 ins / 35 x 35 cm) DKK 34,000.

JOHNSON NATIVITY, Master of the.

See **MASTERS**

JOHNSON VAN CEULEN, Cornelis.

See **CEULEN**

JOHNSSON, Ivar Viktor

Swedish, 20th century.

Born 12 February 1885, in Skåne; died 1970.

Sculptor. Mythological subjects. Monuments.

Ivar Viktor Johnsson was a student at the academy of fine art in Stockholm and travelled to France and Italy before setting up in Helsinki. In 1922 he became a member of the academy of fine art in Stockholm.

Among his first works are his decorative sculptures for the technical college in Stockholm, as well as a bronze statue of *David* and, later, *Aphrodite* and *Adonis Dying*.

Auction records:

Stockholm, 26 Nov 1982, *Fountain* (green-patinated bronze, h. 40 1/2 ins / 103 cm) SEK 16,500. Stockholm, 26 May 1999, *Female Model* (sandstone, h. 22 ins / 55 cm) SEK 18,000.

JOHNSTON, Alexander

British, 19th century.

Born 1815, in Scotland; died March 1891.

Painter. History painting, portraits, genre scenes.

Alexander Johnston was taught at the Edinburgh Academy and then at the Royal Academy. He began exhibiting at the latter in 1835 or 1836 and continued to do so until his death. He exhibited in Paris in 1878 with great success. With his fine drawings and intelligent compositions, Johnston takes his place among the most notable historical painters in the English school.

Museums and Galleries:

London (Tate Collection): *Lord Russel receiving the Last Rites in the Tower of London* - Sheffield: *Robin Adair; Flora MacDonald being taken to Bonnie Prince Charlie* - Sunderland: *Scene from 'The Lady of the Lake'* - Sydney: *A Wreck.*

Auction records:

London, 4 June 1908, *Lady Teazle*, GBP 5. London, 6 Feb 1909, *Poet*, GBP 7. London, 18 June 1909, *Leaving the Presbytery* (1852) GBP 3. London, 5 March 1910, *Flight of James II of England's Wife*, GBP 21. Paris, 25 June 1951, *Gallant Officer*, FRF 45,000. London, 14 July 1972, *Girl Queen*, Gns 600. Perth, 11 April 1978, *The Altercation* (oil on canvas, 24 1/4 x 19 ins / 61.5 x 48 cm) GBP 1,900. Cologne, 26 June 1981, *John Brown's Arrest* (1856, oil on canvas, 46 1/2 x 67 ins / 118 x 170 cm) DEM 11,000. London, 25 July 1983, *The Jilted Suitor* (oil on canvas, 39 3/4 x 50 1/4 ins / 101 x 127.5 cm) GBP 2,000. London, 8 Feb 1991, *The Flirt* (oil on canvas, 36 1/4 x 27 3/4 ins / 92.1 x 70.5 cm) GBP 5,280. New York, 26 May 1992, *The Abduction* (1871, oil on canvas, 48 x 36 ins / 121.9 x 91.4 cm) USD 4,620. Perth, 31 Aug 1993, *O'Gowrie's Daughter* (oil on canvas, 26 x 20 1/2 ins / 66 x 52 cm) GBP 1,495. London, 10 March 1995, *Too Tired* (oil on canvas, 43 x 32 1/4 ins / 109.2 x 81.6 cm) GBP 5,750. Göteborg, 2 June 1999, *Reading Aloud - Interior Scene with Family* (1851, oil on canvas, 34 x 45 ins / 86 x 114 cm) SEK 40,000. London, 16 March 2000, *Painful Necessity* (1872, oil on canvas, 36 x 30 ins / 91 x 76 cm) GBP 20,000. Edinburgh, 24 Aug 2001, *Cotter's Saturday Night* (1863, oil on canvas, 27 x 37 ins / 68 x 93 cm) GBP 20,000. London, 27 Sept 2001, *Winter* (1861, oil on canvas, 37 x 26 ins / 94 x 66 cm) GBP 14,000. London, 6 March 2003, *Winning Hand* (oil on board, 11 x 16 ins / 29 x 40 cm) GBP 1,500. London, 4 March 2004, *Highland Jennie* (1840, oil on canvas, 28 x 36 ins / 71 x 91 cm) GBP 1,800.

JOHNSTON, Andrew

British, 17th century.

Engraver (mezzotint).

Andrew Johnston made the two engravings: *The Earl of Cromartie with Two Women* and *The Earl of Cromartie with his Wife*.

JOHNSTON, David Claypoole

American, 19th century.

Born March 1797 or 1799, in Philadelphia; died 8 November 1865, in Dorchester (Massachusetts).

Engraver, draughtsman.

David Claypoole Johnston engraved some portraits and book illustrations for publishers. He became famous mainly for etchings of caricatures which he produced for the collection *Scraps*, which contained caricatures of politicians and personalities of the time. He also engraved on wood and produced drawings for lithographs.

Auction records:

New York, 24 April 1981, *Fur Hat* (oil on panel, 11 x 9 ins / 28 x 22.8 cm) USD 1,800. New York, 11 March 1999, *Bee Catching* (c. 1818, watercolour, 10 x 13 ins / 25 x 34 cm) USD 14,000. New York, 4 Oct 2000, *Self-portrait* (oil on paper on board, 28 x 20 ins / 71 x 51 cm) USD 3,500.

JOHNSTON, Duncan

American, 20th century.

Born 1924.

Sculptor.

Duncan Johnston's figurative sculptures, symbolist in shape, combine lyricism with dynamism.

JOHNSTON, Francis Hans or Franz or Frank

Canadian, 20th century.

Born 19 June 1888, in Toronto; died 9 July 1949, in Toronto.

Illustrator, painter (gouache), watercolourist. Scenes with figures, landscapes.

Group of Seven.

Franz Johnston trained in Toronto at the Central Technical School under Gustav Hahn and at the Ontario School of Art under William Cruikshank and George Agnew Reid. He worked briefly at Grip Ltd. in 1908 and then moved on to work for Rous and Mann Printing House. In 1910 he went to the USA; he first studied art in Philadelphia and then did commercial work in New York. He returned to Canada just before World War I. All along he had been involved in the activities of the Group of Seven. A member of the Arts and Letters Club, he was a friend of both MacDonald and Harris. During 1917-1918 he had been commissioned by the Canadian War Memorials project to depict Canadian air force personnel in training. His work, completed in canvases such as *Beamsville* (1918-1919), probably includes the first Canadian views painted from an aircraft. The majority of Johnston's works from the air use a mixture of watercolour, gouache and some pastel. What distinguishes them is their often dazzling colour, and the artist's obvious delight in the spectacular viewpoint. At the same time Johnston depicted the aircrafts as accurately as possible, resulting in a certain static model-like quality. Accidents provided an opportunity for dramatic compositions, as in *A Tragic Incident* where an aircraft is depicted being struck by lightning. Johnston's contribution to the depiction of Canada at war remains unique.

After the war Johnston was closely involved in the development of the new style of landscape painting identified with the Group of Seven; he went on almost all the Algoma trips during which the group's members painted the Canadian wilderness. In the 1919 *Algoma* show he contributed 60 works, more than any other artist. A few months later, he extended his independence even more, having a large solo show of 200 paintings at the T. Eaton Company Galleries. In 1921, Johnston left Toronto to accept the position of principal of the School of Art in Winnipeg. He had been slowly moving away from the Group of Seven, and now the break was complete. In 1924 he announced his official resignation, claiming that he had no disagreement with the group, only that he wanted to go his own way with regards to exhibitions. When Johnston left the Group of Seven, he turned more to working for commercial purposes; unfortunately his work lost its earlier fresh vitality and became more decorative. An excellent craftsman, he became mainly concerned with ornamental effects, which he consciously sought out. After the war, Johnston became curator of the Art Gallery of Winnipeg. Later he returned to Toronto to teach at the Ontario College of Art and established a summer school at Tondakea on Georgian Bay. He lived and painted there for a large part of his remaining life.

Bibliography:

Johnston, Francis Hans, *Western Sketchbook - 1924*, White Briar Publications, Annan, Ontario, 1970 (text by Paul Rodrik).

Museums and Galleries:

Kleinburg (Ontario) (McMichael Canadian Art Collection): *Sunset in the Bush* (c. 1918, oil on canvas) - Ottawa (Canadian War Mus.): *Beamsville* (1918-1919); *Flying Over the Sky and Seas* - Ottawa (Nat. Gal. of Canada): *The Fire Ranger* (1921, oil on canvas) - Owen Sound (Ontario) (Thomson Memorial Gallery): *Untitled* (oil on panel); *Hills, Great Bear Lake* (oil on canvas and panel) - Owen Sound (Ontario) (Thomsonn Memorial Gallery): *Spring Snow* (oil on panel).

Auction records:

Toronto, 19 Oct 1976, *Indian Summer* (oil on card, 15 3/4 x 19 3/4 ins / 40 x 50 cm) CAD 2,600. Toronto, 9 May 1977, *Wooden Landscape* (tempera, 20 1/4 x 23 1/4 ins / 51.3 x 58.8 cm) CAD 2,400. Toronto, 9 May 1977, *Mountain Landscape* (oil on card, 19 3/4 x 41 1/4 ins / 50 x 105 cm) CAD 4,400. Toronto, 5 Nov 1979, *Shooting the Rapids* (oil on card, 19 3/4 x 23 1/2 ins / 50 x 60 cm) CAD 6,500. Toronto, 26 May 1981, *Nordic Town* (oil on card, 23 1/2 x 29 1/2 ins / 60 x 75 cm) CAD 23,000. Toronto, 3 May 1983, *On the Lost River 89 Miles West of Cochrane, on Foot* (c. 1922, tempera, 9 1/4 x 14 1/4 ins / 23.8 x 36.3 cm) CAD 3,000. London, 1 June 1983, *Ontario Side Road* (oil on card, 18 x 30 ins / 46 x 76 cm) GBP 1,800. Toronto, 18 Nov 1986, *Easy Going* (oil on card, 13 1/2 x 19 1/2 ins / 34.4 x 49.4 cm) CAD 6,000. Toronto, 28 May 1987, *Algonkins Park* (1928, tempera, 39 x 29 ins / 99 x 73.6 cm) CAD 14,000. Montreal, 25 April 1988, *Beginning of Spring* (oil on panel, 15 x 18 ins / 38 x 46 cm) CAD 3,200. Toronto, 12 June 1989, *Fraser River Canyon* (distemper, 39 1/4 x 29 1/2 ins / 99.8 x 74.9 cm) CAD 7,500. Montreal, 30 Oct 1989, *In the Woods* (oil on panel, 14 1/4 x 9 3/4 ins / 36 x 25 cm) CAD 3,080. Vancouver, 18 Nov 1999, *Silver Birch Grove* (1928, oil on board, 40 x 30 ins / 102 x 76 cm) CAD 40,000. Toronto, 7 Dec 1999, *Autumn, Algoma* (oil on canvas, 59 x 52 ins / 151 x 131 cm) CAD 72,000. Toronto, 23 May 2000, *Miracle of Moonlight* (oil on board, 30 x 39 ins / 75 x 100 cm) CAD 13,000. Toronto, 21 Nov 2000, *Near Beaver Meadows, Algoma* (1919, oil on canvas, 19 x 13 ins / 47 x 34 cm) CAD 22,000. Vancouver, 8 Nov 2001, *The Hemlock Grove* (c. 1922, oil on board, 20 x 16 ins / 51 x 41 cm) CAD 16,000. Toronto, 4 Dec 2001, *Waking Waters* (oil on board, 22 x 28 ins / 55 x 70 cm) CAD 22,000. Toronto, 14 May 2002, *Lichen, Lake of the Woods* (oil on board, 13 x 10 ins / 33 x 26 cm) CAD 38,000. Vancouver, 14 Nov 2002, *Algoma, Heavy Morning Mist* (1918, oil on board, 10 x 13 ins / 26 x 34 cm) CAD 20,000. Vancouver, 15 May 2003, *Midsummer - Northern Lake* (1922, oil on canvas, 40 x 32 ins / 102 x 82 cm) CAD 150,000. Toronto, 2 Dec 2003, *Autumn, Algoma* (oil on canvas, 59 x 52 ins / 151 x 131 cm) CAD 230,000. Vancouver, 27 May 2004, *Orient Bay, Lake Nipigon* (1933, oil on board, 30 x 40 ins / 76 x 101 cm) CAD 45,000. Toronto, 1 June 2004, *Northern Lake* (1932, oil on board, 30 x 39 ins / 75 x 100 cm) CAD 40,000.

JOHNSTON, H. J.

British, 19th - 20th century.

Born in Marlow.

Painter, watercolourist, draughtsman. Genre scenes, landscapes.

H. J. Johnston is noted for a number of watercolours executed during a tour of Australia. He was a member of the Royal Society of British Artists and exhibited at the Royal Academy and the Suffolk Street Gallery from 1884. The catalogue of the Australian Museum in Sydney gives his nationality as Australian.

Museums and Galleries:

Sydney: *A Billabong on the Gulbourn River, Victoria.*

Auction records:

New York, 19 Jan 1906, *On the Fulbourn River, Australia* (watercolour) USD 225. New York, 12 June 1908, *Fisherwoman* (watercolour) USD 500. London, 5 March 1910, *The Favourite Lamb* (watercolour) GBP 15. London, 12 May 1922, *Friends* (drawing) GBP 44. London, 23 March 1928, *Waiting for Papa*, GBP 44.

JOHNSTON, Harry Hamilton (Sir)

British, 19th century.

Born 12 June 1858, in London.

Painter, writer.

Sir Harry Hamilton first showed his work at the Royal Academy in 1879 with the study for a portrait. He continued to exhibit there until 1914, showing landscapes, paintings of animals and so on.

AUCTION RECORDS:

LONDON, 29 March 1983, *Nature's Mirror* (1881, oil on canvas, 50 x 40 ins / 127 x 101.5 cm) GBP 3,000. LONDON, 17 March 1999, *Garden of the British Consulate, Tunis, La Villa Marsa* (oil on canvas, 21 x 8 ins / 53 x 21 cm) GBP 6,500.

JOHNSTON, Henrietta
American, 18th century.
Active 1708-1729.
Painter, pastellist.

Henrietta Johnston produced mainly small Baroque pastels. She worked in Charleston in South Carolina.

AUCTION RECORDS:

NEW YORK, 27 April 1978, *Portrait of Colonel John Moore* (c. 1725, pastel, 11¼ x 8¾ ins / 28.3 x 22.2 cm) USD 3,500.

JOHNSTON, Henry
British, 19th century.
Active in London.
Painter, watercolourist.

Henry Johnston was a member of the New Water-Colour Society. He exhibited his work in London at the Society, as well as at the Royal Academy.

JOHNSTON, John
American, 18th - 19th century.
Born 1752 or 1753, in Boston (Massachusetts); died 1812 or 1818, in Boston.
Painter. Portraits.

John Johnston painted portraits of famous Americans, including *Samuel Adam* and *Governor Philipp with his Family*.

MUSEUMS AND GALLERIES:

BOSTON: *Portrait of Sally Bass*.

AUCTION RECORDS:

NEW YORK, 10 June 1976, *Mr and Mrs Benjamin Williams* (1808, oils on panel, two, 29¼ x 22¼ ins / 74 x 56.5 cm) USD 1,100.

JOHNSTON, John Humphreys
American, 19th - 20th century.
Born 2 November 1857, in New York; died 1941.
Active in Venice and in Paris.
Painter. Figures, portraits, landscapes, seascapes.

John Humphreys Johnston worked in New York with John La Farge, then in Paris with J. Lefebvre and Doucet. He ranked among the best American painters and had a distinguished career, gaining medals in Paris for the 1900 Exposition Universelle and Munich in 1901. He was made a Chevalier de la Légion d'Honneur in 1901, became an associate member of the Société des Beaux-Arts in Paris, a member of the Society of Miniature Painters, Sculptors and Gravers in London and other Americans and Europeans artistic associations. He settled in Venice.

MUSEUMS AND GALLERIES:

PARIS (MAM): *The Artist's Mother; Seascape, Night Effect.*

AUCTION RECORDS:

NEW YORK, 30 and 31 March 1911, *Seascape*, USD 425. PARIS, 22 May 1919, *Cheval Glass*, FRF 280. NEW YORK, 30 May 1990, *Twilight in the Garden* (oil on canvas, 33 x 24½ ins / 83.9 x 62.3 cm) USD 2,420.

JOHNSTON, Joshua. See **JOHNSON Johshua**

JOHNSTON, Reuben le Grande
American, 19th - 20th century.
Born 27 July 1850, in Alexandria (Virginia); died 1918.
Active in Belleville (Maryland).
Painter. Landscapes, animals.

Reuben le Grande Johnston exhibited at the Royal Academy exhibition in 1882.

JOHNSTON, Robert E.
Canadian, 20th century.
Born 14 September 1885, in Toronto; died 1933.
Illustrator.

Robert E. Johnston studied under Harvey Dunn and Walter Sickert in London. He was a member of the Salmagundi Club.

JOHNSTON, Roy
British, 20th century.
Born 1936, in Pomeroy, Northern Ireland.
Painter (mixed media).

Roy Johnston trained at Belfast College of Art and at Cardiff College of Art. He received a grant from the Arts Council of Northern Ireland in 1966, and was the winner of a special prize at the *Belfast Open Painting Exhibition* of 1970. His essentially monochrome canvases are characterised by the play of areas of relief, sometimes underscored with aluminium sheets. His work has featured in a number of group exhibitions in Ireland, Scotland, the USA and France, including: *Irish Imagination*, Dublin, Philadelphia, Boston and Washington; and *Art Irlandais Actuel* (*Contemporary Irish Art*) at the Musée d'Art Moderne de la Ville de Paris in 1973. His work has also been the subject of a number of solo exhibitions, including shows in Dublin, Belfast and Edinburgh.

BIBLIOGRAPHY:

Art irlandais actuel, exhibition catalogue, Musée d'Art moderne de la Ville de Paris, Paris, 1973.

MUSEUMS AND GALLERIES:

BELFAST (Ulster Mus.): *Over View* (*Over View*) (1971, acrylic/canvas); *Study for a Painting* (*Study for a Painting*) (1984) - DUBLIN (Municipal Museum of Modern Art): *Summary for P.B.* (1971).

JOHNSTON, Thomas, or Johnson
American, 18th century.
Born 1708, in Boston (Massachusetts); died 8 May 1767, in Boston.
Engraver, painter.

Thomas Johnston produced many ex-libris and architectural drawings.

JOHNSTON, Thomas
20th century.
Painter.

Thomas Johnston had a solo exhibition at the Galerie Jean Claude Riedel in Paris in 1989.

JOHNSTON, Thomas. See also **JOHNSON**

JOHNSTON, Thomas Alix
American, 20th century.
Born 1941, in Oklahoma City.
Engraver, lithographer.

Thomas Alix Johnston trained under Stanley William Hayter (1901-1988) in Paris and Rudolf Broulim in Antwerp. He lives and works in Bellingham, in the state of Washington. In 1995 he was among the American artists invited to exhibit at the Salon de la Jeune Gravure Contemporaine. His prints are abstract in style and yet present figurative images in a markedly individual approach.

JOHNSTON, Tim
Australian, 20th - 21st century.
Born 1947.
Painter.

Tim Johnston's painting *After Canaletto*, executed in acrylics, is an abstract mosaic composed of small white circles on which are planted floating signs, like the scraps of some unknown calligraphy.

BIBLIOGRAPHY:

Creating Australia: 200 Years of Art 1788-1988, exhibition catalogue, Art Gall. Board of South Australia, Adelaide, 1988.

JOHNSTON, W. Herbert

British, 19th century.
Painter.

W. Herbert Johnston painted portraits.

MUSEUMS AND GALLERIES:

BLACKBURN: *Portrait of W.M. Billington* - WARRINGTON: *Portrait.*

JOHNSTON, William M.

American, 19th century.
Born 1821, in New York; died 30 April 1907, in Brookline (Boston).
Painter. Portraits.

JOHNSTONE, George Whitton

British, 19th century.
Born 3 May 1849, in Glamis (Angus), Scotland; died 22 October 1901, in Edinburgh.
Painter, watercolourist. Religious subjects, portraits, genre scenes, landscapes.

George Whitton Johnstone worked initially as a cabinet maker; however, his serious interest in drawing led to his enrolling at the Royal Scottish Academy. Beginning in 1872, he exhibited his work at the Royal Scottish Academy of which he became an associate in 1883 and member in 1895. He was also a member of the Royal Scottish Watercolour Society. In 1885, he began to exhibit at the Royal Academy in London.

Johnstone made a name for himself as a painter of portraits, of genre scenes and of landscapes in oil as well as in watercolours. In the end, he dedicated himself to the landscape.

MUSEUMS AND GALLERIES:

EDINBURGH (Royal Scottish Academy): *'Where the Burnie Runs into the Sea'* (c. 1895, oil on canvas) - LONDON (Victoria and Albert Mus.): *St Monance.*

AUCTION RECORDS:

LONDON, 21 July 1978, *On the Lunan Burn, near Blairgowrie* (1879, oil on canvas, 24 1/2 x 39 1/2 ins / 62.5 x 100.2 cm) GBP 850. PERTH, 31 Aug 1993, *Playing by the Stream* (oil on canvas, 25 1/4 x 36 1/2 ins / 64 x 93 cm) GBP 1,700. LONDON, 11 Nov 1999, *Tents Muir, Scotland* (1886, oil on canvas, 25 x 36 ins / 63 x 91 cm) GBP 1,300. LONDON, 14 April 2003, *Leuchars Church* (oil on canvas, 20 x 31 ins / 52 x 78 cm) GBP 2,000.

JOHNSTONE, Henry James

British, 19th - 20th century.
Born 1835; died 1907.
Painter, watercolourist. Genre scenes, landscapes.

Henry James Johnstone lived and worked in Marlow. He was a member of the Royal Society of British Artists, and exhibited in London at the Royal Academy and the Suffolk Street Gallery from 1884. He is noted for his numerous watercolours executed during a tour in Australia.

AUCTION RECORDS:

NEW YORK, 19 Jan 1906, *The Fulbourn River, Australia* (watercolour) USD 225. LONDON, 12 June 1908, *Fisherwoman* (watercolour) GBP 21. LONDON, 18 Dec 1908, *Tired* (1892, watercolour) GBP 13. LONDON, 5 March 1910, *The Favourite Lamb* (watercolour) GBP 15. LONDON, 12 May 1922, *Friends* (drawing) GBP 44. LONDON, 23 March 1928, *Waiting for Papa*, GBP 44. SYDNEY, 21 March 1979, *Brownhill Creek, Mitcham, South Australia* (oil on canvas, 14 1/4 x 10 1/4 ins / 36 x 26 cm) AUD 2,800. LONDON, 17 Oct 1984, *The Little Sweeper* (watercolour, 7 x 5 ins / 17.8 x 12.7 cm) GBP 1,100. LONDON, 27 Feb 1985, *Shepherdess* (watercolour, 10 x 6 3/4 ins / 24.5 x 17 cm) GBP 1,500. MELBOURNE, 21 April 1986, *Forest Stream* (oil on panel, 6 x 9 ins / 15 x 22 cm) AUD 3,000. NEW YORK, 25 Oct 1989, *Backwater on the Murray River, South Australia* (oil on canvas, 24 x 36 ins / 61 x 91.4 cm) USD 19,800. LONDON, 12 June 1992, *Fisherman's Daughter Sitting on a Rock Holding a Basket of Mussels* (watercolour, 10 x 6 3/4 ins / 25.2 x 17.4 cm) GBP 2,860. LONDON, 11 June 1993, *Resting beside a Gate* (pencil and watercolour, 9 3/4 x 6 3/4 ins / 24.8 x 17.1 cm) GBP 2,012. NEW YORK, 20 July 1994, *Shepherd and his Flock* (1877, oil on canvas, 24 x 18 ins / 61 x 45.7 cm) USD 2,070. LONDON, 29 March 1995, *Fisherman's Daughter* (watercolour, 9 3/4 x 7 ins / 25 x 17.5 cm) GBP 2,185.

JOHNSTONE, James

British, 18th century.
Active in London.
Painter. Portraits.

James Johnstone exhibited at the Free Society in 1783.

JOHNSTONE, John Young

Canadian, 20th century.
Born 12 November 1897, in Montreal; died 13 February 1930, in Havana.
Painter. Landscapes.

AUCTION RECORDS:

TORONTO, 5 Nov 1979, *St Joachim Road, P. Quebec* (oil on card, 11 x 20 1/4 ins / 28 x 51.5 cm) CAD 2,400. TORONTO, 3 May 1983, *Old Barns, Beaupré* (oil on panel, 4 3/4 x 7 ins / 11.9 x 17.5 cm) CAD 2,000. MONTREAL, 30 April 1990, *Old Barns at Beaupré* (oil on panel, 4 3/4 x 7 ins / 12 x 18 cm) CAD 2,640. NEW YORK, 2 Dec 1992, *Snowy Street* (oil on reinforced canvas, 4 3/4 x 7 ins / 12 x 17.8 cm) USD 1,430. MONTREAL, 17 June 1997, *The Milk Maid* (oil on panel, 6 3/4 x 8 3/4 ins / 17 x 22.1 cm) CAD 3,800. TORONTO, 16 May 2001, *Back River, P.Q* (1917, oil on panel, 9 x 13 ins / 24 x 33 cm) CAD 4,750. TORONTO, 4 Dec 2001, *St Joachim, PQ* (oil on panel, 9 x 13 ins / 23 x 34 cm) CAD 6,500. TORONTO, 3 Dec 2002, *White Farmhouse, Summer* (oil on panel, 5 x 7 ins / 12 x 17 cm) CAD 2,800. TORONTO, 3 Dec 2002, *Return to the Fields* (1914, oil on canvas, 12 x 15 ins / 30 x 37 cm) CAD 5,000. MONTREAL, 25 March 2003, *Old Church, Pointe aux Trembles* (oil on board, 5 x 7 ins / 12 x 18 cm) CAD 5,400. TORONTO, 3 June 2003, *Old Farmhouse, St Joachim* (oil on board, 8 x 12 ins / 21 x 30 cm) CAD 9,500. TORONTO, 31 May 2004, *White Farmhouse, Summer* (oil on canvas, 5 x 7 ins / 12 x 17 cm) CAD 4,000.

JOHNSTONE, William

British, 20th century.
Born 1897, in Denholm, Scotland; died 1981.
Painter, watercolourist, sculptor. Portraits, landscapes.

William Johnstone was encouraged to take up an artistic career by the painter Tom Scott (the Elder). He trained at Edinburgh College of Art and spent time in Paris. He was Director of Camberwell College of Art in London from 1938 to 1946, and of the Central School of Art and Design from 1947 to 1960. Johnstone was one of the first members of the English art establishment to recognise the work of the Surrealists in Paris. His own paintings were inspired by Surrealism and by American art of the 1920s. His distinctive Abstract Expressionist works have sometimes been compared to those of Jackson Pollock.

AUCTION RECORDS:

SOUTH QUEENSFERRY, 29 April 1987, *Composition* (1959, oil on canvas, 36 x 48 ins / 91.5 x 122 cm) GBP 3,400. LONDON, 12 May 1989, *Wooded Landscape* (oil on card, 29 1/2 x 35 1/2 ins / 75 x 90 cm) GBP 1,100. PERTH, 27 Aug 1990, *Oil Composition* (oil on canvas, 16 x 20 ins / 40.5 x 51 cm) GBP 1,870. SOUTH QUEENSFERRY, 23 April 1991, *Abstraction* (watercolour, 7 3/4 x 12 ins / 20 x 30.5 cm) GBP 682. GLASGOW, 1 Feb

1994, *Field in Autumn* (oil on canvas, 36 x 28 ins / 91.5 x 71 cm) GBP 3,450. GLASGOW, 18 June 1996, *Countryside in Time of War, Broomhill* (1923, oil on card, 29 x 25 ins / 73.7 x 63.4 cm) GBP 5,500; *The Folies Bergère* (1926, oil on panel, 30 x 30 ins / 76.2 x 76.2 cm) GBP 6,900. GODALMING, 29 Sept 1999, *Moving Earth* (c. 1963, oil on canvas, 22 x 34 ins / 56 x 86 cm) GBP 1,500. LONDON, 2 Nov 1999, *Forest Scene* (oil on board, 31 x 24 ins / 80 x 61 cm) GBP 2,200. LONDON, 26 Oct 2000, *Irregular Forms* (1969, oil on canvas, 25 x 30 ins / 63 x 76 cm) GBP 3,800. LONDON, 26 Oct 2000, *Portrait of Mary, the Artist's Wife* (1944, oil on canvas, 28 x 24 ins / 71 x 61 cm) GBP 5,500. LONDON, 7 March 2002, *red chalk* (1963, oil on canvas, 25 x 30 ins / 63 x 76 cm) GBP 1,300. LONDON, 10 Sept 2003, *Blue Composition* (oil on canvas, 28 x 36 ins / 71 x 91 cm) GBP 1,100. LONDON, 24 Nov 2004, *Window Lights, Bird* (oil on canvas, two, 54 x 96 ins / 137 x 244 cm) GBP 4,500. LONDON, 24 Nov 2004, *Red Spot. Rebus* (1979, oil on canvas, two, 54 x 88 ins / 137 x 224 cm) GBP 7,000.

JOHNSTONE, William Borthwick
British, 19th century.
Born 21 July 1804, in Edinburgh; died 5 June 1868, in Edinburgh.
Painter, miniaturist, writer. Historical subjects, figures, portraits, landscapes with figures.

William Borthwick Johnstone was a lawyer; however, his love of drawing from a very early age eventually led him to leave the bar for painting. In 1836, he showed his work for the first time at the Scottish Academy. His early work shows the clear influence of Wilkie. In 1843, he went to Rome where his appreciation of the Italian primitives caused him to change his style. After his return from Italy, Johnstone turned to painting miniatures, a genre in which he excelled. In 1840, he had become an associate of the Royal Scottish Academy. In 1848, he was elected a full member. When the National Gallery of Scotland was founded, he was named director and his vast knowledge of art and archaeology rendered his service invaluable. The gallery houses one of his finer works, *The Murder of Rizzo in 1566*. Although his work was principally exhibited in Scotland, it also featured in exhibitions at the Royal Academy in London from 1848 to 1853. In addition, he was a distinguished writer.

MUSEUMS AND GALLERIES:
LONDON (Victoria and Albert Mus.): *Young Country Women in a Landscape* (watercolour).

JOHO, Bert
German, 20th century.
Born 23 February 1877, in Bruchsal (Karlsruhe).
Painter. Figures, scenes with figures.

Bert Joho featured with decorative figure compositions, small plaques, etc. in numerous exhibitions in Germany, including the national society of fine art in Baden, and other exhibitions in Karlsruhe in 1920-1921, Frankfurt am Main in 1916, Baden-Baden in 1919 and 1923, as well as in Elberfeld, Düsseldorf and Pforzheim. He was married to Vera Joho.

JOHO, Vera
Maiden name: Fahrner
German, 20th century.
Born 23 January 1895, in Pforzheim.
Painter, draughtswoman.

Vera Joho, like her painter husband Bert Joho, featured in numerous exhibitions in Germany: 1914, Munich; 1915, Berlin; 1916, Frankfurt am Main; 1919 and 1923, Baden-Baden; 1920, Pforzheim; 1923, Karlsruhe and 1924, Düsseldorf.

JOHS, Pieter Josselin de. See **JOSSELIN DE JONG Pieter**

JOIGNEAU, Pierre
French, 16th century.
Sculptor.
Fontainebleau School.

Joigneau worked on the decoration of the Château de Fontainebleau from 1540 to 1550.

JOIGNY, G. de
French, 19th century.
Painter. Flowers.

This is perhaps Grenet de Joigny (Dominique Adolphe).

MUSEUMS AND GALLERIES:
TROYES: *Flowers and Fruit*.

JOIGNY, Jean de. See **JUNI Juan de**

JOINDY, Joseph François
French, 19th century.
Born 1832, in Paris; died 1906.
Sculptor.

Joseph François Joindy was made a Chevalier of the Légion d'Honneur in 1900. Paris' Museum of Decorative Arts holds some of his works.

JOINER, Harvey
American, 19th century.
Born 1852, in Charlestown (Indiana); died 1932.
Active in Louisville (Kentucky).
Painter. Landscapes.

Harvey Joiner gained a reputation with his views of beech forests.

AUCTION RECORDS:
WASHINGTON DC, 10 June 1984, *Cherokee Park, Louisville, Kentucky* (oil on canvas, 18 x 30 ins / 45.7 x 76.2 cm) USD 1,200. CINCINNATI, 23 May 1999, *Sisters* (1885, oil on canvas, 51 x 40 ins / 130 x 102 cm) USD 4,500. OAK PARK, 6 May 2001, *Forest Interior* (c. 1900, oil on canvas, 20 x 40 ins / 51 x 102 cm) USD 3,750. OAKLAND, 21 Sept 2002, *Autumn Landscape* (oil on canvas) USD 2,250. OAKLAND, 16 Nov 2002, *Road Home* (oil on board, 10 x 20 ins / 25 x 51 cm) USD 4,250. FLORIDA, 19 Jan 2003, *Tree Lined Country Path in the Early Morning Light* (oil on canvasboard, 10 x 20 ins / 25 x 51 cm) USD 4,000.

JOINER, Luther E. de
American, 20th century.
Born 9 October 1886, in Switzer (Kentucky).
Painter. Landscapes.

Luther E. de Joiner specialised in Californian landscapes.

JOINET
French, 18th - 19th century.
Watercolourist, architect.

Joinet was established in London at the beginning of the 19th century, and exhibited at the Royal Academy in 1804. He seems to have been more an architect than an artist.

MUSEUMS AND GALLERIES:
LONDON (Victoria and Albert Mus.): *Country House* (watercolour).

JOING, Jean
French, 16th century.
Born in Bourges.
Active c. 1507.
Painter (glass).

JOINVILLE, Antoine Victor Edmond Madeleine
French, 19th century.
Born 23 September 1801, in Paris; died 1849.
Painter, draughtsman. Local scenes, landscapes. Orientalism.

Antoine Victor Edmond Madeleine Joinville began at Paris' College of Fine Arts in 1818 and studied under Hersent. From 1831 to 1848, he exhibited scenes of Italy, where he had stayed for some time, and Algeria at the Paris Salon. He was an excellent draughtsman.

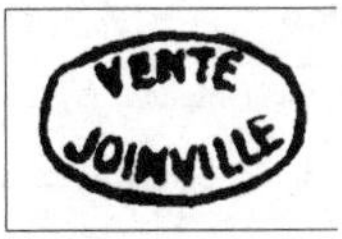

Cachet de vente

Bibliography:
Les Années romantiques, la peinture française de 1815 à 1850, exhibition catalogue, Musée des Beaux-Arts, Nantes, Galeries nationales du Grand Palais, Paris, 1996.
Museums and Galleries:
Chartres: *Campo Vaccino in Rome* (1836) - Honfleur: *Honfleur's Powder Keg* (1827) - Troyes (Mus. d'Art, d'Archéologie et de Sciences Naturelles): *Roman Forum*.
Auction records:
Los Angeles, 17 March 1980, *People in a Pavilion* (oil on panel, 8 1/4 x 11 ins / 21 x 27 cm) USD 1,500. Enghien-les-Bains, 26 June 1983, *Harem* (oil on panel, 11 1/2 x 15 3/4 ins / 29.5 x 40 cm) FRF 25,500. Rome, 21 March 1985, *Italian Landscape* (1839, oil on panel, 7 3/4 x 11 ins / 19.5 x 27 cm) ITL 3,200,000. Paris, 8 Nov 1993, *Scenes of Entertainment in the Harem* (oil on panel, a pair, 13 3/4 x 11 ins / 35 x 27 cm) FRF 35,000. Paris, 20 Nov 2000, *Women of Algiers in the Garden* (oil on canvas, 13 x 9 ins / 32 x 23 cm) FRF 40,000. Heidelberg, 17 Feb 2001, *Sunset in Italian Landscape* (1845, oil on canvas, 10 x 14 ins / 26 x 35 cm) DEM 3,500. Cologne, 5 April 2001, *Allegory of Summer. Allegory of Winter* (oil on panel, two, 9 x 16 ins / 24 x 40 cm) DEM 4,400. Paris, 10 Dec 2003, *View of the Campo Vaccino in Rome* (1827, oil on canvas, 16 x 22 ins / 41 x 57 cm) EUR 4,000.

JOINVILLE, François d'Orléans (Prince de)
French, 19th century.
Born 14 August 1818, in Neuilly; died 16 June 1900, in Paris.
Painter (gouache), watercolourist, engraver.
Landscapes.

François d'Orléans, the Prince de Joinville and son of Louis-Philippe, studied watercolours with William Callow and was Théodore Gudin's pupil, but the person he considered to be his 'true master' was Ary Scheffer. Beraldi credits him with a lithograph entitled *Battle of Gaine's Mill, Virginia, 27 June 1862*.

François d'Orléans painted the landscapes and people that he encountered in his travels all over Europe, always combining observational accuracy with sensitivity.

Bibliography:
Orléans, François d', prince de Joinville, *Vieux Souvenirs, 1818-1848*, Calmann-Lévy, Paris, 1894. *Le Prince de Joinville et la Marine de son temps*, exhibition catalogue, Musée de la Marine, Paris, 1953-1954.
Museums and Galleries:
Amboise (Fondation St-Louis): a series of watercolours.
Auction records:
Monaco, 14-15 Dec 1996, *Grenada, Sierra Nevada* (watercolour, 10 x 19 1/4 ins / 25.5 x 48.8 cm) FRF 37,440; *Seville, view of Guadalquivir* (watercolour and gouache, 12 x 21 1/4 ins / 30.5 x 54 cm) FRF 25,740.

JOIRE, Jean
French, 19th - 20th century.
Born 5 September 1862, in Lille; died 1950.
Sculptor. Animals.

Jean Joire exhibited in Paris at the Salon des Artistes Français, of which he became a member in 1906. In 1907 he received a commendation and in 1909 a bronze medal.

Auction records:
New York, 1 March 1980, *Two Wolfhounds* (patinated bronze, l. 27 ins / 68.6 cm) USD 1,300. London, 7 June 1984, *Horse Trotting* (brown-patinated bronze, h. 18 3/4 ins / 47.5 cm) GBP 1,500. London, 25 Sept 1986, *Two German Shepherd Dogs* (greenish-patinated bronze, h. 19 1/4 ins / 49 cm) GBP 1,400. Perth, 29 Aug 1995, *Alsatian at Dead Set* (lost-wax bronze, 9 3/4 x 18 1/2 ins / 24.7 x 47 cm) GBP 1,035. Paris, 8 Nov 1995, *Mail Coach Equipage* (bronze, h. 18 ins / 45.5 cm, l. 41 3/4 ins/106 cm) FRF 100,000.

JOISTENS, Bernard
French, 20th - 21st century.
Born 1962.
Painter.
Neo-Conceptual Art, Esthétique Relationnelle.

Bernard Joistens was a student at the École d'Art in Grenoble, where he lives and works. Taking his inspiration from advertising images, he parodies cinema posters, appropriates Warhol's *Marilyn Monroe* using computer generated images and cuts up, frames and mounts his pictures as in the cinema. He belongs to the new generation who borrow their forms from advertising, video, cinema and information technology. His work has been shown in the Galleria Carrieri in Rome. He appeared at the exhibition *The Köln Show*, at the Esther Gallery in Cologne alongside Philippe Parreno, Pierre Joseph and Dominique Gonzalez-Foerster.

JOKE, pseudonym of Lagrillière, Jo
Belgian, 20th century.
Born 1934, in Bruges; died 1982.
Draughtsman.

Joke was a student at the Académie and Institut Supérieur des Beaux-Arts in Antwerp.

JOKEI, or Echizen no Hokkyo
Japanese, 12th - 13th century.
Born 1246; died after 1283.
Active during the Kamakura Period (1185-1337).
Sculptor.

Jokei, the name of three sculptors from the Kamakura period (1185-1337).

Jokei I (Daibusshi Jokei) was a member of the Kei school and may have been Unkei's son Koun, working under an assumed name. He is known for an unusual Bugaku mask (dated 1184), a statue of Nio in Kofuku-ji, Nara (between 1190 and 1198), and possibly a statue of *Yuima Koji* in Kofuku-ji, Nara (1196). Between 1201 and 1202 he also carved for Kofuku-ji a *Bon Ten* (Sanskrit: Brahma Deva) and *Taishaku Ten* (Sanskrit: Sakradevanam Indra), both of which show a fine sense of realism in the Song style, and in particular the naturalism of the hangings.

Jokei II, who may or may not have been related to Jokei I, was born in 1184, and was also a master (busshi) of the Kei school. At first steward of Higo province (Higo betto), he later received the honorific titles hoggyo and hogen, which he added to his name. Consequently he is known variously as Higo Betto Jokei, Higo Hokkyo Jokei and Higo Hogen Jokei. Among his known works are the six Kannon figures in Daihoon-ji and the statue of *Bishamon-Ten* (Sanskrit: Vaisravana) (Tokyo National University of Fine Arts and Music), both from 1224, and the *Shokannon* (Sanskrit: Aryavalokitesvara) in the Kurama-dera (1226). This work is also clearly influenced by the Chinese style of the Song dynasty (960-1279) in the treatment of the folds and the way the hair is gathered into a chignon on top of the head. Later in his career, he carved the *Kongo Rikishi* in the Ozo-ji in Gifu Prefecture (1256).

Jokei III worked later in the century. According to the inscriptions on the works, in June 1283 he restored the halo of the *Yashuki nyorai (Bhaisajaguru)* of the Saiendo and in August 1284 he restored the *Nikkö bosatsu (Suryaprabha) and*

Gakko bosatsu (Candraprabha) of the Shindo, both in Horyu-ji, Nara.

Bibliography:
Kanamori, Jun, *Busshi Jôkei ni oite*, Tôyôbijutsu, 1950. Kuno, Takeshi, *A Guide to Japanese Sculpture*, Mayuyama, Tokyo, 1963.

JOKEI. See also **RYUKOSAI**

JOKI, or Jozen
Japanese, 14th century.
Active at the end of Kamakura era (beginning of the 14th century).
Sculptor.

In the sixth month of 1302, Joki executed a relief image of Kobo Daishi (778-835) for the Jingo-ji, Kyoto, in the manner of the prototype in the Kongocho-ji, Kochi (Tosa). He was granted the title Hogen (eye of the law, a religious title conferred on artists).

JOKISCH, Eduard
German, 19th century.
Born 13 October 1867.
Active in Berlin.
Painter, engraver (etching).

Jokisch painted portraits and landscapes. Noted among his etchings are four plates of *Conversations about Love* and six plates for Shakespeare's *Tempest*.

JOLAGE, Louis Charles
French, 18th century.
Active in Brioude (Haute-Loire) in 1733.
Painter.

JOLAIN, Louis
French, 20th century.
Born 27 August 1909, in Paris; died 4 December 1982, in Paris.
Painter, designer, mixed media.
Kinetic Art.

Louis Jolain studied at the École Boulle from 1922 to 1936. He specialised in the decorative arts and was awarded a silver medal at the International Exhibition of 1937 in Paris. In addition to his decorative work, he produced paintings, collages and reliefs based on abstract and later on kinetic concepts.

JOLE, Jef van
Dutch, 20th century.
Born 1905; died 1961.
Painter. Landscapes.

Auction records:
Amsterdam, 20 April 1993, *Polder Landscape with a Mill* (oil on canvas/card, 13 1/2 x 19 1/4 ins / 34 x 49 cm) NLG 1,725.

JOLE, Joseph Gerardus van
Dutch, 20th century.
Born 19 March 1877, in Hontenisse; died 21 February 1919, in The Hague.
Painter. Landscapes.

Joseph Gerardus van Jole painted small Dutch landscapes.

Museums and Galleries:
The Hague (Gemeentemus.).

Auction records:
Amsterdam, 23 April 1980, *Reading* (oil on canvas, 14 x 11 1/2 ins / 35.5 x 29.2 cm) NLG 2,500. Amsterdam, 5 June 1990, *Farmers Working beside the River* (oil on canvas, 11 3/4 x 16 1/4 ins / 30 x 41 cm) NLG 1,840. Amsterdam, 11 Sept 1990, *Farmyard in Winter* (oil on canvas, 11 x 14 1/4 ins / 27 x 36 cm) NLG 1,725. Amsterdam, 30 Oct 1990, *House beside a Frozen River* (oil on canvas/panel, 5 x 8 1/2 ins / 12.5 x 21.5 cm) NLG 1,495. Amsterdam, 14 June 1994, *Winter Landscape with Boats near a Bridge over a Canal* (oil on canvas, 16 x 23 3/4 ins / 40.5 x 60.5 cm) NLG 1,840.

JOLI. See also **JOLLY** and **JOLY**

JOLI, Antonio. See **JOLI DE DIPI Antonio**

JOLI, Faustino
Italian, 19th century.
Born 1814, in Brescia; died 22 September 1876, in Brescia.
Painter, draughtsman. Landscapes, landscapes with figures, animals.

Faustino Joli was the son of Girolamo Joli. He studied at the Accademia in Brescia and first exhibited at the city's annual exhibition in 1832 with two animal drawings; thereafter he was represented regularly at this exhibition.

Museums and Galleries:
Bologna (Pinacoteca Nazionale): *Mountain Landscapes in Winter* - Brescia (Municipal Mus.).

Auction records:
Milan, 23 March 1983, *Shepherd with his Flock* (oil on canvas, 35 1/2 x 51 1/4 ins / 90 x 130 cm) ITL 3,600,000. Rome, 27 April 1993, *Peasant Women and their Cattle in a Landscape* (oil on panel, 26 1/4 x 40 3/4 ins / 66.5 x 103.5 cm) ITL 29,277,300.

JOLI, Gabriel. See **JOLY**

JOLI, Girolamo
Italian, 19th century.
Born 20 July 1780, in Brescia; died 2 August 1855, in Brescia, of cholera.
Painter. Landscapes.

Girolamo Joli was represented in the annual exhibition of the Atheneum, Brescia, in 1830 by two landscapes. He was also a coin-collector and an archaeologist. He was the father of Faustino Joli.

JOLI DE DIPI, Antonio
Italian, 18th century.
Born c. 1700, in Modena; died 1777, in Naples.
Painter, decorative designer. Historical subjects, landscapes, urban landscapes, urban views, harbour scenes, ruins, architectural views. Stage sets.

Joli de Dipi trained under Pannini and worked for theatres in Germany, England and Spain. Charles III, king of Naples, appointed him court painter.

Museums and Galleries:
Madrid (Prado): *Charles III Leaving Naples; Same Subject* - Venice (Gal. Nazionale): *Imaginary Architecture.*

Auction records:
London, 28 May 1941, *Forum Campo Vaccino* GBP 40. Paris, 13 June 1949, *Two Views of the Thames near Richmond* (two pendants) FRF 40,000. London, 25 Oct 1957, *View of the Thames near Richmond,* GBP 1,470. London, 2 July 1958, *View in Madrid,* GBP 600. London, 29 June 1960, *View of Horseguards Parade, Whitehall,* GBP 6,000. London, 14 June 1961, *View of Bacino with San Giorgio Maggiore,* GBP 2,100. London, 2 July 1965, *View of Rome with San Angelo Palace,* Gns 6,000. London, 30 Nov 1966, *Embarkation of Charles III in Naples,* GBP 4,200. London, 7 July 1967, *View of London,* Gns 12,000. London, 3 April 1968, *Thames at Richmond* (two pendants) GBP 12,000. London, 8 Dec 1971, *View of Rome,* GBP 23,000. London, 29 June 1973, *Ruins of Roman Thermal Baths,* Gns 18,000. London, 21 June 1974, *View of the Thames in London,* Gns 24,000. London, 12 July 1978, *View of Naples* (oil on canvas, 34 1/4 x 59 3/4 ins / 87 x 152 cm) GBP 12,000. Rome, 4 April 1979, *St Peter's Square* (oil on canvas, 29 1/4 x 39 ins / 74 x 99 cm) ITL 2,800,000. London, 26 June 1981, *Thames Seen from the Terrace of Somerset House* (c. 1750, oil on canvas, a pair, each 39 x 49 ins / 99 x 124.5 cm) GBP 48,000. New York, 10 June 1983, *View of Venice from a Portico* (oil on canvas, 40 1/2 x 45 1/2 ins / 103 x 115.5 cm) USD 70,000. London, 13 Dec 1985, *Campo Vicino, Rome* (oil on canvas, 36 x 44 1/2 ins / 91.5 x 113 cm) GBP 50,000. London, 9

Dec 1987, *Views of Venice; Doge's Palace and Rialto Bridge* (oil on canvas, a pair, 18 1/2 x 29 ins / 47 x 73.5 cm) GBP 82,000. NEW YORK, 14 Jan 1988, *Bay of Naples Seen from the South, with a Bourbon King in the Foreground* (oil on canvas, 30 x 42 1/4 ins / 76 x 107 cm) USD 57,750. PARIS, 28 June 1988, *Imaginary Chinese Landscape* (oil on canvas, 44 x 58 1/4 ins / 112 x 148 cm) FRF 650,000. LONDON, 21 April 1989, *St Mark's Square in Venice* (oil on canvas, 15 1/2 x 28 ins / 39.2 x 71.2 cm) GBP 24,200. ROME, 23 May 1989, *General View of the Palace in Naples* (oil on canvas, 16 1/4 x 33 1/4 ins / 41.5 x 84.5 cm) ITL 90,000,000. NEW YORK, 1 June 1989, *St Mark's Square in Venice Seen from the South* (oil on canvas, 20 3/4 x 37 3/4 ins / 52.8 x 96 cm) USD 176,000. MILAN, 12 June 1989, *St Mark's Basin and the Island of San Giorgio in Venice* (oil on canvas, 22 x 37 3/4 ins / 55 x 96 cm) ITL 115,000,000. LONDON, 7 July 1989, *Royal Palace of Aranjuez with Kind Ferdinand VI of Spain and Queen Maria Barbara of Braganza in the Royal Barge on the Tagus, with Soldiers and Courtiers on the Banks; Square and Church of St Anthony of Aranjuez with the Royal Barouche Approaching the Palace Gates* (oil on canvas, a pair, 30 1/4 x 49 1/2 ins / 77 x 125.5 cm and 29 1/2 x 48 1/2 ins/75 x 123.5 cm) GBP 506,000. LONDON, 28 Feb 1990, *Panorama of the Bay of Naples* (oil on canvas, 25 1/4 x 65 3/4 ins / 64 x 167 cm) GBP 46,200. ROME, 8 March 1990, *St Mark's Basin in Venice with the Ducal Palace* (oil on canvas, 22 x 38 1/2 ins / 56 x 98 cm) ITL 290,000,000. LONDON, 9 April 1990, *Vast Panorama of Rome, with the Sant'Angelo Palace and Bridge, St Peter's and the Vatican, and Barges on the Tiber in the Foreground* (oil on canvas, 30 x 43 1/2 ins / 76 x 110.5 cm) GBP 352,000. ROME, 8 May 1990, *View of the Piazza Navona* (oil on canvas, 41 x 31 1/2 ins / 104 x 80 cm) ITL 260,000,000. NEW YORK, 31 May 1990, *Capriccio with Classical Ruins, a Pyramid and Figures* (oil on canvas, 18 1/2 x 15 ins / 46.8 x 38 cm) USD 17,600. LONDON, 24 May 1991, *Campo Vaccino in Rome with the Arch of Titus from the Temple of Saturn* (oil on canvas, 37 3/4 x 54 ins / 96 x 137 cm) GBP 231,000. NEW YORK, 31 May 1991, *Embarcation of King Charles III in Naples* (oil on canvas, 30 x 67 1/4 ins / 76.2 x 170.8 cm) USD 638,000. LONDON, 11 Dec 1991, *Roman Forum with Campo Vaccino, S Francesca Romana, Arch of Titus and the Colosseum* (oil on canvas, 36 x 44 1/2 ins / 91.5 x 113 cm) GBP 34,100. NEW YORK, 16 Jan 1992, *Thames in London with Westminster Abbey and Bridge under Construction, and Other Monuments* (oil on canvas, 34 x 50 1/2 ins / 86.3 x 128.3 cm) USD 286,000. MADRID, 20 Feb 1992, *Two Views of Aranjuez* (oil on canvas, a pair, each 16 1/2 x 30 1/4 ins / 42 x 77 cm) ESP 61,600,000. LONDON, 9 Dec 1992, *Fair Seen from the Balcony of the Royal Palace in Naples* (1763, oil on canvas, 30 x 50 ins / 76 x 127 cm) GBP 253,000. NEW YORK, 15 Jan 1993, *View of Messina from the Sea with an English Boat in the Foreground* (oil on canvas, 9 1/2 x 30 ins / 24.1 x 76.5 cm) USD 54,625. LONDON, 9 July 1993, *Madrid and the Royal Palace from the West Bank of the Manzanares* (oil on canvas, 59 x 88 1/2 ins / 150 x 224.5 cm) GBP 397,500. NEW YORK, 7 Oct 1994, *View of Paestum* (oil on canvas, 29 3/4 x 50 1/4 ins / 75.6 x 127.6 cm) USD 206,000. PARIS, 20 Dec 1994, *View of Naples from Santa Lucia* (oil on canvas, 29 3/4 x 49 1/2 ins / 75.5 x 125.5 cm) FRF 470,000. ROME, 9 May 1995, *View of Marsala* (oil on canvas, 10 x 40 1/4 ins / 24.5 x 102 cm) ITL 64,400,000. LONDON, 6 Dec 1995, *Rome Seen from the Campo Vaccino with the Colosseum in the Distance* (oil on canvas, 46 x 61 ins / 117 x 154 cm) GBP 89,500. LONDON, 9 July 1997, *Thames, Looking Towards the City* (1746, oil on canvas, 43 x 68 ins / 109 x 173 cm) GBP 826,500; *Thames, Looking Towards Westminster* (oil on canvas, 43 x 68 ins / 109 x 173 cm) GBP 969,500. LONDON, 16 Dec 1999, *Rome, View of the Tiber Looking Downstream* (oil on canvas, 25 x 35 ins / 63 x 90 cm) GBP 240,000. LONDON, 17 Dec 1999, *King Ferdinand IV, Queen Caroline of Naples at Game of Palla a Bracciale* (oil on canvas, 30 x 50 ins / 75 x 128 cm) GBP 250,000. NEW YORK, 28 Jan 2000, *Rome, View of the Campo Vaccino* (oil on canvas, 36 x 54 ins / 92 x 138 cm) USD 240,000. LONDON, 30 Nov 2000, *View of London and the Thames with St. Paul's and Somerset House* (oil on canvas, 15 x 28 ins / 38 x 71 cm) GBP 220,000. LONDON, 13 Dec 2001, *Rome, Campo Vaccino* (oil on canvas, 15 x 28 ins / 37 x 71 cm) GBP 100,000. LONDON, 13 Dec 2001, *Venice, with the Bacino di San Marco* (oil on canvas, 51 x 45 ins / 129 x 114 cm) GBP 750,000. LONDON, 13 June 2002, *Thames Looking Towards the City. Thames Looking Towards Westminster* (oil on copper, a pair, 13 x 18 ins / 32 x 46 cm) GBP 600,000. LONDON, 28 Nov 2002, *Thames Looking Towards the City. Thames Looking Towards Westminster* (oil on canvas, a pair, 18 x 35 ins / 45 x 90 cm) GBP 500,000. NEW YORK, 24 Jan 2003, *Rome, view of the Tiber Looking Downstream with the Castle and Ponte Sant' Angelo* (oil on canvas, 35 x 49 ins / 88 x 125 cm) USD 920,000. LONDON, 10 Dec 2003, *Calle de Alcala, Madrid* (oil on canvas, 30 x 47 ins / 77 x 120 cm) GBP 900,000. NEW YORK, 22 Jan 2004, *Cappriccio of Roman Ruins with Classical Figures* (oil on canvas, 41 x 45 ins / 104 x 114 cm) USD 65,000.

JOLICLERCQ, Philippe
French, 20th - 21st century.
Born 4 February 1950, in Soissons.
Painter.

Philippe Joliclercq teaches in Charleville-Mézières where he lives and works. In 1986 he was involved in the creation of the Kaliko group, which works pictorially on the theme of Jazz, with Y. Saillard, Ch. Boisson and A. Baudry. In his abstract works and action paintings a few bits and pieces of reality still show through, a guitar perhaps, or the silhouette of a musician. He has participated in collective exhibitions including: Salon Figuration-Critique, Paris, 1987 and 1988; Musée Rimbaud, Charleville-Mézières, 1989. Solo exhibitions include Charleville-Mézières, 1977.

JOLIET, Auguste
French, 19th century.
Born 19th century, in Paris.
Engraver (wood).

Auguste Joliet exhibited at the Paris Salon from 1861 to 1878 and was awarded a medal in 1870.

JOLIMONT, Théodore Basset de, or Joilmond
French, 19th century.
Born 1787, in Rouen.
Painter, watercolourist, lithographer, writer.
Landscapes.

Théodore Basset de Jolimont featured at the Paris Salon from 1822 to 1827. He mainly did lithographs of views of buildings in Rouen.

MUSEUMS AND GALLERIES:
DIJON: *Portrait of Chancellor Rollin; Portrait of Guignone de Salins; Group of Portraits of the Duke of Burgundy Philippe the Good, Pope Eugene IV and the Painter J Van Eyck* (watercolour, after an altarpiece by Van der Weyden); *Sitting of the Burgundy Parliament, with Charles the Bold Presiding.*

AUCTION RECORDS:
PARIS, 3-4 July 1941, *Expiatory Fountain* (1826; *Ruins of the Tower Where Joan of Arc was Imprisoned, in Rouen* (two pictures in pairs) FRF 230.

JOLIN. See also **JOLLAIN**

JOLIN, Édouard
French, 19th century.
Born 1817, in Nantes.
Painter. Religious subjects, genre scenes.

Édouard Jolin featured at the Paris Salon from 1844 to 1869, showing genre and religious subjects.

MUSEUMS AND GALLERIES:
RENNES: *Aftermath of the Battle of Auray.*

Auction records:
Paris, 30 June 1993, *Monks in a Library* (oil on canvas, 39¼ x 32¾ ins / 100 x 83 cm) FRF 3,000.

JOLIN, Einar
Swedish, 20th century.
Born 7 August 1890, in Stockholm; died 1976.
Painter, watercolourist. Figures, portraits, landscapes, still-lifes.

Einar Jolin studied in Stockholm, and then in Paris with Henri Matisse, coming under his influence. In his own country he was a member of the group Eight and took part in the Phalange group during the 1920s. He featured in exhibitions in Stockholm, at the Salon d'Automne in Paris in 1913 and in Berlin, Copenhagen, Helsinki and Malmö.

He painted in oils and watercolour, and was one of the representatives of Swedish Expressionism. He practised drawing with a simplified outline in open compositions. He often painted townscapes, and certain views of Stockholm traversed by the port are reminiscent of Marquet. He was also influenced by Oriental art.

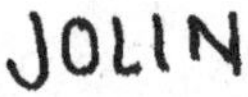

Museums and Galleries:
Copenhagen - Göteborg - Helsinki (Ateneumin Taidemus.) - Stockholm.

Auction records:
Stockholm, 24 April 1947, *Model*, SEK 1,800. Stockholm, 23 April 1980, *View of Stockholm* (1967, oil on canvas, 23¼ x 35¾ ins / 59 x 91 cm) SEK 20,000. Stockholm, 15 Nov 1981, *Corrida* (oil on canvas, 35 x 42½ ins / 89 x 108 cm) SEK 16,500. Stockholm, 26 April 1982, *Street Scene, Venice* (1920) SEK 5,000. Stockholm, 23 April 1983, *View of Stockholm* (1930, watercolour, 13½ x 19¾ ins / 34.5 x 50 cm) SEK 8,000. Stockholm, 29 Nov 1983, *Boats in Port* (1914, oil on canvas, 39¼ x 46 ins / 100 x 116 cm) SEK 305,000. Stockholm, 16 Nov 1985, *View of Stockholm* (oil on canvas, 25½ x 18 ins / 65 x 46 cm) SEK 96,000. Stockholm, 26 May 1987, *View of Stockholm* (oil on canvas, 20¾ x 25¼ ins / 53 x 64 cm) SEK 67,000. Stockholm, 6 June 1988, *Sitting Room with Window onto Stockholm* (oil, 32 x 39 ins / 81 x 99 cm) SEK 82,000. Stockholm, 22 May 1989, *View of Stockholm Palace* (1964, oil on canvas, 19¾ x 24 ins / 50 x 61 cm) SEK 45,000. Stockholm, 6 Dec 1989, *Aerial View of Visby with the Dome of the Church* (oil on canvas, 14½ x 17¾ ins / 37 x 45 cm) SEK 26,000. Stockholm, 14 June 1990, *Young Woman under Trees* (1937, oil on panel, 16¼ x 12½ ins / 41 x 32 cm) SEK 16,000. Stockholm, 5-6 Dec 1990, *View of Stockholm from Skinnarviksparken in Winter* (oil on canvas, 32¾ x 46 ins / 83 x 116 cm) SEK 150,000. Stockholm, 13 April 1992, *Still-life with Potplant, Statuette, Framed Photograph and other objects on a Table* (1951, oil on canvas, 14½ x 17¾ ins / 37 x 45 cm) SEK 13,000. Stockholm, 21 May 1992, *Elk in the Snow* (1941, oil on panel, 23½ x 28¾ ins / 60 x 73 cm) SEK 20,000. Stockholm, 30 Nov 1993, *Interior with a Small Boy Standing* (oil on canvas, 28¾ x 23½ ins / 73 x 60 cm) SEK 19,000. Stockholm, 27 April 1999, *View towards Gamle Stan, Stockholm* (1969, oil on canvas, 26 x 39 ins / 66 x 100 cm) SEK 145,000. Stockholm, 26 Oct 1999, *View of Stockholm from the South* (1971, oil on canvas, 39 x 79 ins / 100 x 200 cm) SEK 230,000. Stockholm, 2 May 2000, *Primavera Mariagraete* (1916, oil on canvas, 41 x 32 ins / 103 x 82 cm) SEK 90,000. Stockholm, 11 Nov 2000, *Female Nude with Long Hair* (1915, oil on canvas, 67 x 43 ins / 169 x 108 cm) SEK 110,000. Stockholm, 2 May 2001, *Oriental Still-life* (1941, oil on canvas, 39 x 31 ins / 100 x 80 cm) SEK 70,000. Stockholm, 6 Nov 2001, *Interior Scene with Female Model* (1915, oil on canvas, 46 x 32 ins / 117 x 81 cm) SEK 310,000. Stockholm, 5 Nov 2002, *Seated Model with Dog and Parrot* (1918, oil on canvas, 30 x 25 ins / 75 x 63 cm) SEK 210,000. Stockholm, 5 Nov 2002, *Model in a Black Fur Coat* (1916, oil on canvas, 46 x 32 ins / 116 x 81 cm) SEK 350,000. Stockholm, 4 Nov 2003, *View of Riddarholmen and the Old Town* (1941, oil on panel, 24 x 20 ins / 61 x 51 cm) SEK 62,000. Stockholm, 4 Nov 2003, *Riddarholmen's Church* (1931, oil on canvas, 39 x 29 ins / 100 x 73 cm) SEK 105,000. Stockholm, 2 Nov 2004, *View from the South towards Town Hall, Stockholm* (1937, oil on canvas, 33 x 45 ins / 85 x 115 cm) SEK 210,000. Stockholm, 3 Nov 2004, *In a Green Suit* (1914, oil on canvas, 51 x 32 ins / 130 x 81 cm) SEK 150,000.

JOLIN, François Gérard, the Elder, or Jollain
French, 17th century.
Born 1641; died 18 April 1704.
Engraver (burin).

François Gérard Jolin the Elder was the son of Gérard Jolin. He engraved portraits, and is mentioned in February 1697 as a dealer, engraver, juror and wood moulder.

JOLIN, Gérard, or Jollain
French, 17th century.
Died 1683; buried on 28 May.
Engraver.

Gérard Jolin was the father of François Gérard Jolin. He lived in the Rue St-Jacques at the sign of the *City of Cologne*

JOLIN, Jacques, the Younger, or Jollain
French, 17th - 18th century.
Engraver (burin).

Jacques Jolin the Younger engraved portraits, and was also a print seller.

JOLINON, M.
French, 20th century.
Painter.

M. Jolinon was active in Lyons.

JOLIVARD, André
French, 19th century.
Born 15 September 1787, in Le Mans (Sarthe); died 8 December 1851, in Paris.
Painter, engraver. Landscapes.

André Jolivard was apprenticed to Bertin's studio, which he joined in 1816, having finished his law studies. Encouraged by his teacher, he succumbed to his taste for painting and gave himself entirely to it. He made his debut at the Paris Salon in 1819 and continued to feature there more or less regularly until 1850.In 1827 he was awarded a first class medal and was made a member of the Légion d'Honneur in 1835. At the beginning of the 19th century, when art was still bogged down by the hotchpotch of moralising sentimentality inherited from the previous century, Jolivard set himself apart with the simple frankness of his genuine awareness of nature and the countryside. He is also credited with seven landscape etchings.

In 2001, he was included in the exhibition entitled *Les Peintres et la Sarthe* (*Painters and the Sarthe Region*) held at Le Mans in the Queen Bérengère Museum (19th century artists) and at the Abbaye de l'Épau (20th century artists).

Bibliography:
Les Années romantiques, la peinture française de 1815 à 1850, exhibition catalogue, Musée des Beaux-Arts, Nantes, Galeries nationales du Grand Palais, Paris, 1996. Arpentinier, Jean, *Sarthe, terre d'artistes*, exhibition catalogue, Éd. de la Reinette, Le Mans, 2001.

Museums and Galleries:
Aix-en-Provence: *Landscape* - Angoulême: *Forest Interior* (1834) - Bordeaux: *Landscape* - Compiègne: *Landscape; Forest Interior* - Le Mans: *Landscape with Ford; View from Above Sillé-le-Guillaume; Mill; Landscape with Pool; Les Coëvrons Seen from the Heights of Sillé-Le Guillaume* (oil on canvas) - Le Puy-en-Velay: *Breton Scene* (1846) - Lisieux: *Landscape Seen from the Hills of St Cloud* (1838) - Pont-Au-

DEMER: *View of Mountainous Countryside on a Morning in Autumn* (1836) - ROUEN (MBA): *View from the Heights of St Cloud* (1840) - VERSAILLES (Mus. Lambinet): *Donkey Farm* (1835).
AUCTION RECORDS:
PARIS, 1851, *Forest,* FRF 825. PARIS, 1869, *Landscape with Waterfall,* FRF 800. PARIS, 2 May 1900, *Bathing,* FRF 102. BERN, 6 May 1972, *Herd in the Undergrowth,* CHF 5,500. BERN, 3 May 1979, *Wooded Landscape with Small Bridge* (oil on canvas, 15 x 18 ins / 38 x 46 cm) CHF 4,500. BERN, 26 Oct 1988, *Rural Scene at the Edge of an Oak Wood* (1832, oil on panel, 20 x 26¾ ins / 50.5 x 68 cm) CHF 6,000. MELUN, 20 May 2001, *Scene of Country Life, with Paris in the Distance* (1840, oil on canvas, 20 x 24 ins / 50 x 61 cm) FRF 24,000.

JOLIVET, or Jollivet
French, 18th century.
Died July 1726, in Paris.
Wood carver.

Jolivet worked from 1699 to 1713 in the Châteaux of Marly, Meudon and Versailles. From 1705 to 1708, he took part in the sculptural decoration of the dome of Les Invalides. In about 1709, he was working for the chapel of the Château de Versailles, on the confessionals and friezes.

JOLIVET. See also **JOLLIVET**

JOLIVET, François
French, 20th century.
Born 11 November 1931, in Chalon-sur-Saône.
Painter.

François Jolivet was an architect by trade but also trained as a painter at Legueult's studio at the École des Beaux-Arts in Paris from 1958 to 1962. He made several study visits to Latin America.

His painting is visionary, showing large, dark spaces filled with mineral forms. Its violence speaks eloquently of bodies and mutilated flesh and of life and death. In Paris he exhibits at the Salon d'Automne, the Salon de la Jeune Peinture, the Salon Comparaisons and the Salon des Artistes Français. He also shows his work in solo exhibitions, notably in 1990 at the Espace Latino-Américain in Paris.
MUSEUMS AND GALLERIES:
PARIS (CNAC).

JOLIVET, Henri
French, 19th century.
Born in Dijon; died c. 1825, in London.
Painter.

Henri Jolivet studied under Anatole Devosge.
BIBLIOGRAPHY:
Les Années romantiques, la peinture française de 1815 à 1850, exhibition catalogue, Musée des Beaux-Arts, Nantes, Galeries nationales du Grand Palais, Paris, 1996.
MUSEUMS AND GALLERIES:
BESANÇON: *Portrait of Ethis* - DIJON (MBA): *Portrait of Women* (1825).

JOLIVET, Louis
French, 18th century.
Engraver (burin).

Louis Jolivet engraved figures and subjects from everyday life. He is particularly remembered for two pieces, both entitled: *Firework Let off at Dijon in 1757.*

JOLIVET, Merri
French (?), 20th century.
Painter, mixed media, collage artist, draughtsman, illustrator.

In 1968, Merri Jolivet ran the Atelier Populaire at the École des Beaux-Arts in Paris. He shows his work in solo exhibitions, notably in 1990 at the Galerie Jacqueline Felman in Paris. Jolivet works in series. In 1992 he produced canvases consisting of four horizontal, superposed bands of different colours, each independent of the other. He mixes collage, frottage, superposed pale and dark tones, drawing and painting. Jolivet illustrated *Méditerranée* (*Mediterranean*).

JOLIVET, Yves
French (?), 20th century.
Painter.

Yves Jolivet's paintings are neutral, white or almost bare and convey a sense of mysticism.

JOLLAIN. See also **JOLIN**

JOLLAIN, Nicolas René, the Elder, or Joullain
French, 18th century.
Active in Paris.
Painter.

Nicolas René Jollain the Elder is mentioned as Painter to the King on the birth certificate of his daughter Jeanne-Marie, dated 5 March 1698. He was probably the father of the painters Pierre and Nicolas René Jollain.

JOLLAIN, Nicolas René, the Younger, or Joullain
French, 18th century.
Born 1732, in Paris; died 1804.
Painter. Historical subjects.

Nicolas René Jollain the Younger, who was probably the son of Nicolas René the Elder, studied at the schools of the Académie Royale, as the pupil of Jean-Baptiste Pierre. There he obtained a third class medal in July 1747, a second class medal in April 1748, and was second in the Prix de Rome in 1754, which Chardin's son won. He was elected to the Académie on 31 December 1765, and was made an academician on 3 July 1773, with *The Good Samaritan* (in the church of St-Nicolas at Le Chardonnet), and Keeper of the King's Museum in 1788. Jollain exhibited for the first time at the Salon of 1767 and continued to do so regularly until 1791. He was a productive artist, and each exhibition had several submissions from him. He specialised in painting historical subjects, allegories and religious subjects, notably *Jesus Entering Jerusalem,* for the Carthusian monastery known as the Chartreuse de Paris (Salon of 1771), *Jesus with the Teachers,* for the Chapelle de Fontainebleau (Salon of 1781), and *Striking the Rock,* for the king's household (Salon of 1783). However, he was also responsible for subjects from high society and everyday life, as well as some portraits and landscapes. Jollain has a respected place in the 18th Century School, and deserves to be better known.

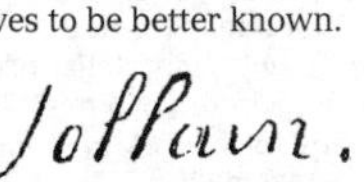

MUSEUMS AND GALLERIES:
ALENÇON: *Moses on Mount Sinai; The Holy Spirit Descending on the Evangelists; Pierre de Valois; Rotrou III Plans to Found the Chartreuse du Val-Dieu* - ANGERS: *Arethusa, Pursued by the River Alpheus, is Saved by Diana* - CALAIS: *Apotheosis of De Belloy* - FONTAINEBLEAU: *Clytie Changed into the Sun* - LONDON (Wallace Collection): *Sleeping Child or Sleeping Cupid* (oil on canvas) - MONTAUBAN: *The Tarn Bursts its Banks.*
AUCTION RECORDS:
PARIS, 1873, *The Toilette,* FRF 1,020. PARIS, 15 May 1903, *A Bacchante,* FRF 8,000. NEW YORK, 22-24 March 1911, *Cupid Holding a Bow and Arrows,* USD 55; *Cupid Holding a Dove,* USD 55. LUCERNE, 20 May 1980, *Rest during the Flight into Egypt* (1778, oil on canvas, 10 x 19¾in/25.5 x 50cm) CHF 1,600. PARIS, 10 Dec 1999, *Young Women Bathing* (oil on canvas, 26 x 56 ins / 66 x 142 cm) FRF 40,000. PARIS, 27 June 2002, *Paul and Virginie by the Cradle* (oil on canvas, 24 x 30 ins / 60 x 75 cm) EUR 9,500. PARIS, 28 June 2002, *Entry of Christ in Jerusalem* (oil on canvas, 13 x 25 ins / 33 x 64 cm) EUR 11,500. PARIS, 25 June 2003, *Venus and Cupid* (oil on panel, 15 x 21 ins / 39 x 54 cm) EUR 11,000.

JOLLAIN, Pierre, or Joullain
French, 18th century.
Born 1720, in Paris; died 1762.
Painter. Religious subjects, allegorical subjects, mythological subjects, portraits, genre scenes. Decorative schemes.

No trace has yet been found of a connection between the Jollain or Jolin family of engravers and the Jollain family of painters; Pierre and Nicolas René the Younger seem to have been the sons of Nicolas René Jollain the Elder and his wife Christine Benoist. Pierre studied at the École de l'Académie Royale, where he obtained a second class medal in January 1743, and the same year was second in the Prix de Rome, the prize itself being awarded to Vien. The subject was: *The Angel Strikes the House of David with the Plague.* On 2 December 1744, he married Jeanne-Louise-Thérèse Duportail. Pierre Jollain was a member of the Académie de St-Luc in Paris, and an assistant professor. He took part in its exhibitions of 1751, 1752, 1753, 1756 and 1762, with paintings of historical and religious subjects, portraits and *sopraporte*

AUCTION RECORDS:
ROME, 7 March 1989, *Sculpture and Poetry* (1753, oil on canvas, a pair, each 24 1/2 x 56in/62 x 142cm) ITL 68,000,000. ROME, 28 April 1992, *The Concert* (oil on canvas, 24 1/2 x 56in/62 x 142cm) ITL 16,500,000. PARIS, 2 Dec 1994, *Vertumnus and Pomona* (1779, oil on panel, 19 x 23 1/2in/48.5 x 60cm) FRF 27,000. NEW YORK, Jan 1998, *Allegory of the Birth of a Noble Child* (oil on paper/canvas, attributed, 10 1/4 x 13in/26 x 33cm) USD 9,200. LONDON, 18 April 2000, *Diana and Endymion. The Education of Cupid* (1744, oil on card, a pair, 5 x 6 ins / 13 x 16 cm) GBP 3,000. NEW YORK, 10 Oct 2001, *Cupid on a Cloud Holding a Bow and Arrow, and with a Torch and Doves* (2 May 1768, oil on canvas, a pair, 21 x 30 ins / 53 x 75 cm) USD 5,000. VIENNA, 21 March 2002, *Venus Breaking Cupid's Arrow* (1784, oil on panel, 9 x 13 ins / 24 x 32 cm) EUR 5,500.

JOLLAT
French, 15th - 16th century.
Active in Paris 1490-1550.
Engraver (wood).

References to the name of Jollat are found preceded by the initial J, or by the first names François and Mercure. Papillon, who is an authority on French wood engravers, treats these references as referring to one artist. It is possible that the differences in first name are due to Jollat having had a son who was also an engraver. Jollat produced decorative woodcarvings for the borders of a missal printed in Paris in 1490, and engravings for a work on anatomy published by Charles Estienne in 1530-1532.

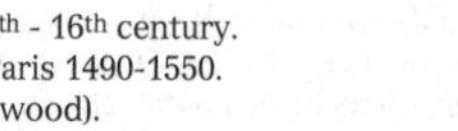

JOLLER, M.
19th century.
Active in Italy.
Engraver (burin).

M. Joller engraved the plates for the *Opera Ornementale di Giuseppe Borsatto* (Milan, 1831).

JOLLEY, Martin, or Gwilt-Jolley
British, 19th century.
Born 1859, in Croydon.
Painter.

Martin Jolley worked in France, Italy and England.

AUCTION RECORDS:
LONDON, 22 April 1911, *Courtyard in Anacapri*, GBP 4. LONDON, 2 Feb 1984, *Aestas* (oil on canvas, 20 1/2 x 26 1/2 ins / 52 x 67 cm) GBP 2,000. LONDON, 12 Oct 1987, *Sea Story* (oil on panel, 9 1/2 x 6 1/4 ins / 24 x 16 cm) GBP 1,300. LONDON, 12 Nov 1987, *Hilda, the General, Lodgings in Pimlico* (gouache, 23 1/2 x 9 ins / 60 x 23.1 cm) GBP 4,800. BILLINGSHURST, 23 Oct 2000, *Sunshine and Blossom* (oil on canvas, 28 x 37 ins / 72 x 93 cm) GBP 6,000. SEVENOAKS, 11 July 2001, *Locomotive, St Ives* (oil on canvas, 49 x 35 ins / 124 x 89 cm) GBP 5,200. LONDON, 15 Jan 2004, *Serenada Above the Bay of Naples* (oil on canvas, 16 x 28 ins / 41 x 70 cm) GBP 3,000. LONDON, 23 March 2004, *Campania, Summer Morning* (oil on canvas, 21 x 14 ins / 53 x 35 cm) GBP 3,500.

JOLLI DE DIPI, Antonio. See **JOLI DE DIPI**

JOLLIET, Auguste. See **JOLIET**

JOLLIFFE, Michael
British, 20th century.
Born 1945, in Darlington.
Active in Canada from c. 1970.
Painter (mixed media). Scenes with figures, landscapes.

Michael Jolliffe graduated from Concordia University. He began exhibiting in 1974 and exhibited at the fine arts museums of Montreal and New York in 1986. Jolliffe paints biblical and mythical scenes. He interprets then freely, simplifying highly evocative figurative motifs such as landscapes and figures and organising them in sections of colour. His work combines traditional references with contemporary formal preoccupations and his use of colour and materials makes his work decorative.

MUSEUMS AND GALLERIES:
MONTREAL (MAC): *Crowned* (1981) - MONTREAL (MBA) - TORONTO (AG of Ontario).

AUCTION RECORDS:
PARIS, 24 May 1992, *Sabina* (1991, oil on canvas, 48 x 36 1/4 ins / 122 x 92 cm) FRF 15,500.

JOLLIVET. See also **JOLIVET**

JOLLIVET, Pierre Jules
French, 19th century.
Born 26 June 1794, in Paris; died 1871, in Paris.
Painter. History painting, genre scenes, still-lifes.

Pierre Jules Jollivet began at Paris' College of Fine Arts in 1822 and studied under Gros and Depeine. He participated in the Paris Salon from 1831 to 1880. He was awarded a second class medal in 1833, a first class medal in 1835 and the cross of the Légion d'Honneur in 1851.

Jollivet was fond of medieval historical subjects, such as *Louis VI Taking the Standard to St Denis.*

BIBLIOGRAPHY:
Les Années romantiques, la peinture française de 1815 à 1850, exhibition catalogue, Musée des Beaux-Arts, Nantes, Galeries nationales du Grand Palais, Paris, 1996.

MUSEUMS AND GALLERIES:
AJACCIO: *Holy Family and St Simeon* - AUTUN: *Gypsies Resting in the Ronda Mountains* (1832) - METZ: *Perseus, Son of Jupiter* - MONTPELLIER: a study; *Christ Being Tried* (study) - PARIS (Louvre): *Lara* - ROUEN (MBA): *Massacre of the Innocents* (1845) - SOISSONS: *Death of Philippe II* - VALENCIENNES: *Bandits From the Kingdom of Valence* (1833) - VERSAILLES: *Battle of Hooglède: 13 June 1794; Louis XII at the battle of Agnadel; Louis VI Takes the Standard to St Denis; Philippe III the Bold, King of France; Capture of Foix Castle; Battle of Tourcoing; Godefroy de Bouillon Holds the Assizes of the Kingdom of Jerusalem; Battle of Aïcha in 1805.*

AUCTION RECORDS:
PARIS, 1876, *Museum Interior*, FRF 800. PARIS, 18 March 1920, *Albanian Women Bathing in a Fountain*, FRF 190. PAR-

IS, 2 June 1971, *Cross-examination of the Smugglers* (1831, oil on canvas, 23 1/4 x 30 ins / 59 x 76 cm) FRF 1,250. PARIS, 23 April 1986, *Painter and his Models* (1867, oil on panel, 14 1/2 x 18 ins / 37 x 46 cm) FRF 34,000. MONACO, 17 June 1988, *Young Woman and her Child Hiding Behind a Rock* (1834, oil on canvas, 14 1/2 x 17 3/4 ins / 37 x 45 cm) FRF 24,420. BRUSSELS, 21 March 2000, *Smugglers* (1831, oil on canvas, 24 x 30 ins / 60 x 75 cm) BEF 130,000.

JOLLO, Domenico, or Iollo
Italian, 20th century.
Sculptor.
Jollo lived and worked in Naples. He was awarded an honourable mention in Paris in 1892 and a bronze medal at the Exposition Universelle of 1900.
MUSEUMS AND GALLERIES:
BUCHAREST (Muz. National de Arta al României).

JOLLOT, André
French, 19th century.
Born 19th century, in Paris.
Landscape painter.
André Jollot studied under Joaquin, Sorolla y Bastida and Dagnaux and featured at the Salon of the Société des Artistes Français.

JOLLY, A. E.
Flemish School, 19th century.
Born in Brussels.
Active c. 1835.
Painter. History painting, genre scenes.
A. E. Jolly was a colonel in the Engineers and later a general in the Belgian army. Dr von Wurzbach mentions him only as an art lover.

JOLLY, Adolphe Gustave
French, 19th century.
Born 26 September 1826, in Paris.
Sculptor.
Adolphe Gustave Jolly studied under Dantan senior and featured at the Paris Salon from 1848 to 1870. He made a marble vase and a statue of *Ganymede* for the gardens of the Palace of Versailles.
MUSEUMS AND GALLERIES:
COMPIÈGNE (Mus. Antoine Vivenel): *Monument to Pierre d'Ailly*.

JOLLY, André
French, 20th century.
Born 1882, in Charleville (Marne); died 1969.
Painter. Scenes with figures, landscapes.
André Jolly was a self-taught artist who trained by studying the works of his contemporaries such as Cézanne, Monet, Gauguin and Van Gogh displayed in galleries. He began exhibiting at the Salon des Indépendants in 1906. An admirer of Gauguin, he went to Pont-Aven and eventually settled there. While his early landscapes, in their light tones, show signs of Impressionism, other pieces are in very rich colours, applied in flat, outlined tints in the style of the Nabis. From 1910, he tended towards the latter style.
MUSEUMS AND GALLERIES:
CHARLEVILLE-MÉZIÈRES: *The Bread Oven* (c. 1905) - NANTES (MBA).
AUCTION RECORDS:
PARIS, 4 June 1926, *Bellflowers and Wildflowers*, FRF 55; *Pharmacy Pot*, FRF 55. PARIS, 9 July 1942, *Landscape*, FRF 230. PARIS, 22 Oct 2000, *Tremorvezen Chapel, Brittany* (oil on canvas, 24 x 31 ins / 62 x 78 cm) FRF 15,000. BREST, 10 Dec 2000, *Tuna Boats at Anchor at Kerdruc sur l'Aven. Garden Scene* (1911, oil on canvas, double-sided, 39 x 51 ins / 100 x 130 cm) FRF 100,000. BREST, 16 Dec 2001, *Still-life with Apples and Quimper Pottery* (oil on canvas, 20 x 24 ins / 51 x 61 cm) FRF 50,000. BREST, 12 May 2002, *Forest of Love* (oil on canvas, 18 x 22 ins / 45 x 55 cm) EUR 2,900.

JOLLY, Charles
French, 17th century.
Died before 1698.
Painter.
Jolly is mentioned in a civil status certificate as living at the Pont au Change.

JOLLY, Fanny C. (Miss)
British, 19th century.
Active in Bath.
Painter. Landscapes.
Fanny C. Jolly exhibited in London, notably at the Royal Academy, the Suffolk Street Gallery and at the British Institution.

JOLLY, Ferdinand Louis
French, 19th century.
Born 1801, in Charonne (Seine); died 1861.
Painter. Military subjects.
Ferdinand Louis Jolly was an officer in the chasseurs' regiment in Africa and was made a Chevalier of the Légion d'Honneur.
MUSEUMS AND GALLERIES:
DIJON: two watercolours.

JOLLY, Henri Jean Baptiste, or Joly
Belgian, 19th century.
Born 21 July 1812, in Antwerp; died 9 January 1853, in Amsterdam.
Painter. Portraits, genre scenes.
Henri Jolly travelled in Holland, France and Germany. His *Portrait of Dr Mergell* is in the municipal museum in The Hague. He exhibited at the Paris Salons of 1847 and 1848.
AUCTION RECORDS:
NEW YORK, 26 May 1983, *The Letter* (oil on panel, 29 1/2 x 23 1/2 ins / 75 x 60 cm) USD 1,300.

JOLLY, Paul
French, 20th century.
Born in Toulon; died April 1911, in Toulon.
Lithographer, watercolourist.
The Musée de Toulon has some works by Paul Jolly.

JOLLY, Paulus
Dutch, 19th century.
Born 1805, in Amsterdam.
Painter. Portraits.
Pupil of F. Montauban van Swyndregt and W. van Leen.

JOLY, real name: Adrien Jean Baptiste Muffat
French, 18th - 19th century.
Born 1772; died 1839, in Grand-Pré, near Lormes (Nièvre).
Lithographer, draughtsman, watercolourist.
Joly was also an actor. Worthy of mention are his drawings for the *Theatre Gallery* by Martinet.
AUCTION RECORDS:
PARIS, 30 Oct 1928, *Joly in the Role of Darmancé* (watercolour) FRF 170.

JOLY. See also **JOLLY**

JOLY, Alexis Victor
French, 19th century.
Born 1 May 1798, in Paris; died 1874, in Paris.
Painter, watercolourist, lithographer. Landscapes, landscapes with figures, architectural views.
Alexis Victor Joly studied with Mougin and exhibited landscapes and watercolours at the Paris Salon from 1817 to 1870. He engraved landscapes and architectural views.
MUSEUMS AND GALLERIES:
BALTIMORE (Peabody Art Collection): *Landscape*.

Auction records:
Paris, 4 April 1925, *Place de la Concorde Before the Obelisk was Installed,* FRF 240. Paris, 2 Dec 1994, *Landscape with Bridge; Landscape with Large Trees* (oil on canvas, a pair, each 6 1/4 x 8 1/2 ins / 16 x 21.5 cm) FRF 13,000. Paris, 22 March 1995, *Wooded Landscape with Villagers Resting Near a Spring* (oil on canvas, 6 1/2 x 8 1/2 ins / 16.5 x 21.5 cm; *Wooded Landscape with Two Young Women Resting Near a Fountain* (oil on canvas, 6 1/2 x 9 ins / 16.5 x 22 cm) FRF 15,000.

JOLY, Alexis Victor
French, 19th century.
Painter.
Mme Alexis Victor Joly was a pupil of her husband and exhibited views at the Paris Salon from 1833 to 1889.

JOLY, André, or Jolly
French, 18th century.
Born 1706, in St-Nicolas-du-Port (Meurthe).
Painter. Urban landscapes.
André Joly painted a *View of Nancy and the Surrounding Area* which hangs in the museum at Nancy. He was Painter to the King of Poland, and exhibited at the Salon de la Correspondance in 1780 and 1781.

JOLY, Charles. See **MONTLEVAULT**

JOLY, François
French, 16th century.
Painter.
Joly worked in Lyons in 1548 on preparations for the official visit of Henri II.

JOLY, François, or Jolly
French, 17th century.
Active in Nantes in 1655.
Glass painter.

JOLY, Gabriel, or Joli
French, 16th century.
Died 1538, in Teruel.
Sculptor.
Joly travelled to Italy and then to Spain, where he settled. In 1536, he produced a large altarpiece featuring ten low reliefs from the *Life of Christ*, an *Assumption of the Virgin*, and 30 statues of saints for the niches of the church at Teruel. He also produced an altarpiece for the church of St-Pierre in Teruel, and another for the church in Cella.

JOLY, Henri
French, 20th century.
Painter.
Henri Joly exhibited in Paris at the Salon des Indépendants from 1909 and also at the Salon d'Automne.

JOLY, J. N.
French, 19th century.
Active c. 1820.
Engraver (stippling).
J. N. Joly engraved portraits.

JOLY, Jean
French, 17th - 18th century.
Born 1654, in Troyes; died 24 December 1740, in Montpellier.
Sculptor.
Jean Joly was sent to Rome as a boarder at the Académie. He worked from 1687 to 1699 for Versailles, Marly and the church of Les Invalides.

JOLY, Jean Michel
French, 20th century.
Painter, sculptor. Landscapes.
Jean Michel Joly conceives landscapes of other planets in the universe, taking his inspiration from scientific data.

JOLY, Jeanne
French, 20th century.
Born in Marcigny (Saône-et-Loire).
Painter, pastellist. Portraits.
Jeanne Joly began working in 1910. She exhibited in Paris at the Salon des Indépendants and the Salon d'Automne. She is known for her *Portrait of Madame Raoul Dufy*.

JOLY, Jules
French, 19th century.
Born 19th century, in Amiens.
Painter, pastellist. Portraits, landscapes.
Jules Joly studied under Léon Cogniet and Debras. He exhibited portraits in pastel at the Paris Salon from 1849 to 1882 and is also credited with several landscapes, again in pastel.
Auction records:
London, 4 April 1910, *Young Girls' Heads* (two pastels in pairs) GBP 6; *Portrait of a Woman* (pastel) GBP 2. London, 31 Oct 1996, *Young Woman with a Dog* (pastel, 32 3/4 x 23 1/2 ins / 83 x 60 cm) GBP 1,150.

JOLY, Laurent. See **LOLLI Lorenzo**

JOLY, Louis
French, 20th century.
Born 15 April 1908, in Paris; died 1990.
Painter, draughtsman, illustrator. Humorous cartoons.
Louis Joly was first and foremost a mathematician. As an illustrator he produced numerous caricatures under the pseudonym of Yjo. He was also influenced by Constructivism and appears to have been particularly interested in the possibilities of optical effects. He produced paintings and drawings based on mathematical formulas. He was a member of the Mesure group founded by Georges Folmer, with whom he exhibited in German museums. He also exhibited at the Salon des Réalités Nouvelles in Paris. In 1994, the Musée de Toul mounted an exhibition of the collection of works he bequeathed to the museum.

JOLY, Luc
Swiss (?), 20th century.
Sculptor.
Museums and Galleries:
Lausanne (Cantonal MFA): *Wood Shape* (1971).

JOLY, Maurice
Belgian, 20th century.
Born 1941, in Wasmes.
Sculptor.
Maurice Joly teaches ceramics at the Académie des Beaux-Arts de la Cambre in Brussels. In his sculptures and ceramics, he favours the geometry and harmony of forms.

JOLY, N.
French, 19th century.
Active c. 1822.
Landscape painter.
N. Joly is mentioned by Siret.

JOLY, Paul Antoine
French, 19th century.
Born 16 April 1786, in Soissons (Aisne); died 30 May 1861, in Soissons (Aisne).
Painter, gilder, watercolourist. Landscapes.
Museums and Galleries:
Soissons: 5 watercolours.

JOLY, René Charles Paul
French, 20th century.
Born 10 June 1885, in Courbevoie.
Sculptor, medallist, engraver.
René Charles Paul Joly lived and worked in Choisy-le-Roi. He exhibited sculptures, medals and lithographs in Paris at

the Salon des Artistes Français in 1912, 1920 and 1921, receiving a commendation in 1921.

JOLY, Victorine
French, 19th century.
Miniaturist.

Victorine Joly exhibited miniature portraits at the 1822 and 1824 Paris Salons.

JOLY DE BEINAC, René
French, 20th century.
Born 1876.
Painter. Landscapes.

René Joly de Beinac studied under J. Lefebvre and T.R. Fleury. He exhibited landscapes of the Dordogne and the Pyrenées at the Salon des Artistes Français in Paris.

AUCTION RECORDS:
VERSAILLES, 23 Sept 1990, *The Mediterranean Coast* (oil on card, 13 x 15 3/4 ins / 33 x 40 cm) FRF 6,500. VERSAILLES, 21 Oct 1990, *The Small Fishing Port of Les Martigues* (oil on mounted card, 21 x 25 1/2 ins / 53.5 x 64.5 cm) FRF 9,500.

JOLY DE LA VAUBIGNON, Adrien
French, 19th century.
Born in Paris.
Painter. Landscapes.

Adrien Joly de la Vaubignon exhibited at the Paris Salon between 1822 and 1846.

His landscapes mainly offer views of Fontainebleau, Switzerland and the Dauphiné.

BIBLIOGRAPHY:
Les Années romantiques, la peinture française de 1815 à 1850, exhibition catalogue, Musée des Beaux-Arts, Nantes, Galeries nationales du Grand Palais, Paris, 1996.

MUSEUMS AND GALLERIES:
GUÉRET: *View of Vaubignon Castle and the Bridge over the Beaume* (about 1822).

JOLY DUEZ, Chris
French, 20th century.
Born in the Pas-de-Calais.
Painter. Still-lifes.

Chris Joly Duez studied at the École des Beaux-Arts in Versailles. He lives and works in Élancourt. He has exhibited at exhibitions in France and received various prizes. Joly Duez's still-lifes are stripped bare, with plain backgrounds, and are reminiscent of Morandi's work. The objects shown - bottles, jugs and pots discreetly outlined in black - are arranged frontally, in an atmosphere of silence with muted tones.

JOLYET, Philippe
French, 19th century.
Born 11 November 1832, in Pierre-en-Bresse (Saône-et-Loire); died 1908, in Nay (Lower Pyrenées).
Painter. Portraits, genre scenes.

Philippe Jolyet began at Paris' College of Fine Arts in 1854, in the studio of Léon Cogniet. He made his debut at the Paris Salon in 1863 and was awarded an honourable mention in 1885. He also won a bronze medal at the 1889 Exposition Universelle in Paris.

Aside from his somewhat theatrical scenes of monks, he painted portraits of women in a style reminiscent of Corot, although the chromatic refinement of his compositions brings Raffaëlli to mind.

MUSEUMS AND GALLERIES:
BAYONNE: *Skittles; Saturday Round at Bayonne; Portrait of M H Durand* - CHALON-SUR-SAÔNE: *The Young Pud'hon, Taken in and brought up by the Monks of Cluny, is Caught Copying the Abbey's Paintings* - DIJON: *Cornmeal in Burgundy* - MÂCON - PARIS (Louvre): *Young Soldiers* - ROUEN: *Indiscretion* - TOURNUS: *Reading.*

AUCTION RECORDS:
LONDON, 19 Nov 1993, *Reading the Paper* (1889, oil on canvas, 39 x 51 3/4 ins / 99 x 131.5 cm) GBP 9,200. NEW YORK, 12 Feb 1997, *Two Young Girls Posting a Letter* (1904, oil on canvas, 56 x 27 1/2 ins / 142.2 x 69.8 cm) USD 57,500. PARIS, 16 Dec 1998, *Street Cries* (oil on paper mounted on board, 7 x 10 ins / 17 x 25 cm) FRF 10,000.

JOMBERT
French, 17th century.
Engraver (burin).

Jombert engraved portraits and subjects from architecture. He may be the same artist as one Charles Antoine Jombert, a bookseller and engraver, living in the Rue St-Jacques, who is mentioned in a civil status certificate on 14 August 1730.

JOMBERT, Pierre Charles
French, 18th century.
Born 1748 or 1749, in Paris.
Painter.

Pierre Charles Jombert was a student at the Académie Royale. He received a second class medal in 1767, a first class medal in 1769, and won the Grand Prix in 1770 for his diploma work: *Niobe's Children Killed by Apollo and Diana*. In 1773, he received his diploma as a boarder at the Académie de France in Rome.

AUCTION RECORDS:
PARIS, 28 Nov 1978, *Niobe's Children Killed by Apollo and Diana* (oil on canvas, 56 1/2 x 44 1/4in/143.5 x 112.5cm) FRF 30,000.

JOME, Jean le. See **LE JOME**

JOMEAU, Louis
French, 19th century.
Born 19th century, in Paris.
Painter.

Louis Jomeau studied under Guérin and exhibited pen and ink drawings at the Paris Salon in 1870 and 1879.

JOMET, Jean
French, 17th century.
Painter.

JOMOUTON, Frédéric
Belgian, 19th - 20th century.
Born 5 May 1858, in Namur.
Painter. Landscapes.

Frédéric Jomouton was a student at the Académie in Namur. He made his debut in 1886 at the Exposition Triennale in Namur, and subsequently featured in the main Belgian exhibitions (including 1911 in Charleroi). A special exhibition in Namur in November 1921 brought together 54 of his oil paintings and 25 watercolours.

MUSEUMS AND GALLERIES:
NAMUR: painting.

JON-AND, John Erik Algot
Swedish, 20th century.
Born 8 March 1889, in Göteborg.
Draughtsman, painter.

John Erik Algot Jon-And studied in Göteborg, and in Paris with Le Fauconnier. A group exhibition of his works was organised in 1916 by the Olsen house of art in Göteborg. He worked as an illustrator for the press and as a scene painter for the Lorensberg theatre in Göteborg and variety shows in Stockholm.

JONAERT, Philippe
French, 18th century.
Born c. 1691, in Dunkirk; died 6 September 1734.
Painter. Military subjects.

For his painting depicting the *Bombardment of Dunkirk in 1695* (Dunkirk Museum), Jonaert copied a composition on

the same subject made up of 150 Delft pottery tiles, also in that museum. His painting was given to the town in 1793.
Museums and Galleries:
Dunkirk: *Bombardment of Dunkirk in 1695* (after a ceramic composition).

JONAS
German, 17th century.
Active in Kassel.
Sculptor.

The Hessisches Landesmuseum in Kassel possesses a round relief portrait of *Landgrave Frederick II* on mother-of-pearl, signed by Jonas. The landgrave is wearing armour and a wig.
Museums and Galleries:
Kassel (Hessisches Landesmus.): *Portrait of Landgrave Frederick II.*

JÓNÁS
Hungarian, 19th century.
Active in Besztercebánya.
Painter.

The museum in Besztercebánya has a *Portrait of Madame Daniel Huszag* by Jónás.

JONAS, B.
German, 18th - 19th century.
Born to a family originally from Meiningen.
Draughtsman, painter.

B. Jonas trained at the academy in Berlin, and showed works in exhibitions there. In 1788, he exhibited two drawings of *The Facade and Rear of the Belvedere.* In 1793 he presented two pencil drawings of *St Cecilia* (after Domenichino) and *Mary Magdalene* (after A. Carracci). In 1794 he showed a pencil drawing of a *Bacchant* (after Frisch) and in 1806 a pastel portrait of the dean, *Dr Spalding*, and court preacher *A. F. W. Sack*, after Graff.

JONAS, Joan
American, 20th century.
Born 1936, in New York.
Sculptor, draughtswoman, performance artist, video artist, installation artist.

Joan Jonas settled in New York. She has travelled a great deal, and lived in Japan in 1970. She has taught at the Stuttgart Kunstakademie and at the Massachusetts Institute of Technology, Cambridge (Mass.). Her art springs from a dramatic approach announced by Dada and resumed notably by Fluxus, more significantly in the person of John Cage. Combining happening and behavioural art, Joan Jonas' concerts/actions aim at redefining the body as a means of expression. In 1968, she executed her first piece with a mirror, in which space is broken and the audience's presence is reflected and its involvement in the process stated. In 1970, with Susan Rothenberg among others, she executed *Jones Beach Piece - Mirror Peace* and *Underneath* before taking up video performance. Starting from tales and legends, she develops graphic representations which bring familiar objects into highly personal pieces. Drawings, prepared before or during the performances, play an important role in her videos, and she sees them as art works in their own right. She also acted in a Chekhov play in order to experience performance in the theatrical framework, 'when voice has a major part'. In the 1980s and 1990s she created electronic performances and films. She plays on digital technology, looks to contemporary choreographers like Ann Halprin and Lucinda Childs, dancing herself in some of her works, for instance *Volcano Saga* (1985). Through a poetic and critical approach she investigates the image of seductress forced on women by the media, exposing the weight of culture and image.

She has taken part in collective exhibitions including, in 1972, Documenta V in Kassel, in 1995, the Lyons Biennale, in 2002 *Video Acts* among others in New York. She has shown her work in solo exhibitions or performances, in the USA and in Europe: in the 1990s in New York, Paris, Berlin; including retrospectives at the Stedelijk Museum, Amsterdam and at the Galerie der Stadt in Stuttgart (1968-2000).
Bibliography:
Joan Jonas: Scripts and Description 1968-1982, University Art Museum, Berkeley, 1983. *Joan Jonas, Works 1968-1994*, exhibition catalogue, Stedelijk Museum, Amsterdam, 1994. *Joan Jonas*, exhibition catalogue, Neue Gesellschaft für Bildende Künste, Berlin, 2001 (texts in German and English). Nabakowski, Gislind, '*Joan Jonas*' in *Art Press* n° 266, periodical, Paris, March 2001. *Joan Jonas: Five Works*, exhibition catalogue, Queens Museum of Art, New York, 2003.
Museums and Galleries:
Paris (Prints Collection).

JONAS, Karl Rudolf Hugo
German, 19th century.
Born 1822, in Goldapp (Goldap), East Prussia; died 1888, in Berlin.
Painter. Landscapes.

Karl Jonas was a pupil of Behrendsen at the academy in Königsberg (now Kaliningrad), Prussia. In 1851, he was in Munich. From 1852 to 1854 he taught in Danzig (now Gdansk, Poland). He subsequently settled in Munich and later (1860) Berlin. Jonas visited the Alps, Upper Italy and Corsica. A favourite theme was evening pictures.

JONAS, Lucien Hector
French, 20th century.
Born 8 April 1880, in Anzin; died 20 September 1947, in Paris.
Painter, draughtsman (charcoal), engraver, lithographer, illustrator, designer. Historical subjects, military subjects, religious subjects, sporting subjects, figures, portraits, historical portraits, scenes with figures, local scenes, genre scenes, street scenes, interiors with figures, church interiors, landscapes, waterscapes, seascapes, gardens, panoramas. Church decoration, wall decorations, posters, banknotes. Japonisme.

Lucien Jonas was born in the industrial basin of the Nord region of France, where his father had founded an essential oils distillery. He began studying in Valenciennes under Layraud before going to Paris to study at the École des Beaux-Arts under the guidance of Albert Maignan, Léon Bonnat and Henri Harpignies. When his father died in 1902, Jonas abandoned his studies and ran the family business until 1903. In 1915, he enlisted as a 'military painter attached to the Musée de l'Armée' and was sent to the Front. He began travelling in 1932 and visited Italy, Savoy, Nice and Algeria. In 1939 and 1940 he worked his way along the Maginot Line, executing drawings.

Jonas focused on realist subjects, and often depicted the life of miners, the mining country and domestic scenes, sometimes caricaturing provincial worthies. During his time on the Front during World War I, he painted 800 panels in oil and produced almost 4,000 drawings that were reproduced in various papers and magazines, including *L'Illustration* and in collections such as *La Guerre racontée par nos généraux* (*The War Recounted by our Generals*) (published by Fayolle, Paris in 1920). He also produced portraits of the principal military leaders, including Foch. Immediately after the end of the war he produced notices for loans for reconstruction work. He also painted religious compositions, including 28 Ways of the Cross for ruined churches in the Nord region between 1920 and 1925, and in 1944 a series of 17 major compositions showing the *Life of the Virgin* for the Spanish church in Paris.

Work by Jonas taking its inspiration from the war and also from street scenes was later used to decorate various public buildings, including the Maison des Centraux in Paris; the Café Bellevue in Lille; the casino at Pougues-les-Eaux; the theatre, fine arts museum (1922), chamber of commerce (1922) and station buffet at Valenciennes; and the town hall (1935), theatre and church of Anzin. Some of these works have since disappeared but the preparatory drawings have been preserved. In 1943, he produced ten views of Paris hospitals. Works illustrated by Jonas include *La Belle au Bois et le Prince Charmant* by Gaston-Charles, *César Birotteau* by Balzac, Molière's *Tartuffe*, Daudet's *L'Arlésienne* and *Daphnis et Chloé* by Longus. Jonas also illustrated menus, and designed numerous banknotes for the Bank of France. In 1933 he was asked by the Bank to produce designs for the 100-franc note showing Sully and a Loire landscape, then the image of Jacques Cœur and the Berry region and finally Descartes. He also designed banknotes issued by the Bank of Syria, the Bank of Lebanon, the Bank of Indochina and the Bank of Djibouti.

As a mural artist, Jonas produced friezes and pageants, often turning allegory into mockery. He also worked regularly as a portrait artist and his paintings include some of the famous actors of the Comédie Française, including André Brunot (1932). Although trained in an academic style, he quickly developed his own approach in every area, showing a vigorous drawing technique, a psychological awareness of his many portrait subjects and a luminosity in his landscapes and domestic interiors. He remains a true master of line and his work continues to serve as a reference for many artists. Although he did not belong to any 20th-century avant-garde movement, Jonas's work displays an understanding of Japonism, Impressionism and Fauvism in the use of broad brushstrokes in beach and street scenes and even portraits, and a fondness of luminous colours.

Jonas was awarded numerous official prizes: a silver medal at the Salon and the second Grand Prix de Rome in 1905; a gold medal and a travel bursary in 1907; the Prix National du Salon in 1911; the medal of honour for engraving in 1935; and the medal of honour for painting in 1945. He became a member of the engraving jury and later the painting jury and was made a Chevalier of the Légion d'Honneur in 1929. Jonas exhibited at the Salon des Artistes Français in Paris from 1901 until his death, having become a member in 1904 and being declared *hors concours* in 1907. He also received commissions for temporary decorative work at the International Exhibition in Brussels in 1935 and at the International Exhibition in Paris in 1937. In 2003 his work was featured at the group exhibition *Lumineuse Algérie, sous le regard des peintres de marines (1830-1960)* (*Luminous Algeria, Through the Eyes of Seascape Painters (1830-1960)*) at the Musée Nationale de la Marine in Toulon. His solo exhibitions include: 1943, Art Français, Paris; and posthumously in 1992 a retrospective exhibition in Paris; 1993 at the Musée Municipal, Hazebrouck; 1999 at the Musée Faure, Aix-les-Bains; and 2003, *Lucien Jonas et le Décor Mural des Années 30 à Paris* (*Lucien Jonas and Mural Painting of the 1930s in Paris*) at the Musée Carnavalet, Paris.

BIBLIOGRAPHY:

Jonas, Lucien, *Les armées de l'Est: mars-avril 1915*, Librairie Dorbon-ainé, Paris, 1915 (artist's sketch book). Poiteau, Emile, *Lucien Jonas*, exhibition catalogue, Gal. Dujardin, Roubaix, 1926. Westover, Wendell, *Suicide Btallions*, G. P. Putnam's Sons, New York and London, 1929 (Illustrated by the artist). *Exposition Lucien Jonas*, exhibition catalogue, Art français, Paris, 1943. Magny, Françoise, *Lucien Jonas, 1880-1947*, exhibition catalogue, Mairie du XVIe arrondissement, Ville de Paris, Paris, 1992. *Lucien Jonas: le Chemin de Croix de l'église Saint-Éloi d'Hazebrouck et autres oeuvres*, exhibition catalogue, Musée municipal, Hazebrouck, 1993. *Lucien Jonas*, exhibition catalogue, Musée Faure, Aix-les-Bains, 1999. Descamps, Patrick, '*La Chute du Tyran de Lucien Jonas au musée d'Hazebrouck*' in *Revue du Louvre* n° 3 p. 65, periodical, Paris, June 2001. Leribault, Christophe, *Lucien Jonas et le décor mural des années 30 à Paris*, exhibition catalogue, Musée Carnavalet, Éd. Paris-Musées, Paris, 2003. Mourot, Marjolaine/Vidal-Bué, Marion/Cazenave, Elisabeth, et al., *Lumineuse Algérie, sous le regard des peintres de marines (1830-1960)*, exhibition catalogue, Musée national de la Marine, Toulon, 2003.

MUSEUMS AND GALLERIES:

AMIENS (Mus. de Picardie): *The Final Rush at Parc des Princes* (1905, sketch) - ANZIN (Mus. Théophile-Jouglet): *Miners, Metallurgy; Le Coron* (1909) - BOCHUM (Deutsches Bergbau-Mus.) - CAMBRAI (MBA): *The Churchwardens* (1906) - DIJON: *The Boarding School* - DOUAI: *The Deliberation or The Magistrates* - GRENOBLE (Mus. de Grenoble): *Olive Trees at Cap Martin* - HAZEBROUCK (Municipal Mus.): *Consultation* (1911); *The Tyrant's Fall; Portrait of Abbé Lemire* - LILLE (MBA): *Anzin: Les hommes, les femmes, les enfants (Les Mineurs, les Ramasseuses de gaillette, le Café au coron)* (*Anzin: Men, Women, Children (Miners, Small Coal Gatherers, Mining Village Café)*) (1906) - MONTREAL: *Les Débuts dans le monde* - NEW YORK (Metropolitan Mus. of Art): *Portrait of General Pershing* - PARIS (Mus. Carnavalet): Jonas donation; *Cour du Dragon* - PARIS (Mus. de l'Armée): 150 profiles and portraits - PARIS (Mus. du Petit Palais): *The Consultation; Les Vieilles Fées* (1911, charcoal); *La Malade malgré elle* (1911, charcoal) - PÉRIGUEUX: *The Beggar; Lady in Blue; At the Velodrome* - PÉRONNE: 40 sketches and posters - ROUBAIX (La Piscine, Mus. d'Art et d'Industrie): *The Final Rush at Parc des Princes* (1905, three sketches) - VALENCIENNES (MBA): *Consolations* (1905); *Portrait of Harpignies*; bequest of over 100 works - VERSAILLES (Château): *Portrait of Admiral Germinet; Portrait of Marshal Fayrolle*.

AUCTION RECORDS:

PARIS, 27 Oct 1922, *Church Interior*, FRF 90. PARIS, 16 Nov 1923, *Attack on a Trench* (watercolour) FRF 200. PARIS, 12 April 1943, *Priest Presenting the Host* (charcoal) FRF 300. PARIS, July 1946, *Place de la Concorde* (1943) FRF 1,800. PARIS, 17 March 1947, *Interiors with figures*, FRF 850. LONDON, 23 Oct 1985, *Lunch in the Garden*, GBP 1,500. NEW YORK, 31 Oct 1985, *Return of the Victors*, USD 8,000. NEW YORK, 31 Oct 1985, *Return of the Victors* (1908, oil on canvas, 53 1/4 x 61 ins / 135.5 x 154 cm) USD 8,000. PARIS, 4 Dec 1986, *The Beach at Dinard* (18 x 22 ins / 46 x 55 cm) FRF 34,000. LONDON, 20 May 1987, *Beach Scene* (c. 1930, oil on canvas, 18 x 21 3/4 ins / 46 x 55.5 cm) GBP 10,000. PARIS, 14 June 1988, *Young Woman Sewing beside the Water* (oil on canvas, 18 x 24 ins / 46 x 61 cm) FRF 10,000. PARIS, 14 Oct 1988, *Fisherman near the Pont-Neuf* (1941, oil on canvas, 25 1/2 x 36 1/4 ins / 65 x 92 cm) FRF 13,000. RHEIMS, 23 Oct 1988, *The Pont de Sospel* (1936, oil on canvas, 19 3/4 x 26 ins / 50 x 66 cm) FRF 8,500. PARIS, 14 June 1989, *Beach* (1922, oil on panel, 12 3/4 x 15 3/4 ins / 32.5 x 40 cm) FRF 57,000. VERSAILLES, 29 Oct 1989, *Rue Norvins, Montmartre* (1945, oil on paper, 25 1/2 x 19 3/4 ins / 65 x 50 cm) FRF 18,500. VERSAILLES, 25 March 1990, *Washsheds on the Seine, Paris* (oil on panel, 20 x 28 3/4 ins / 50.5 x 73 cm) FRF 46,000. PARIS, 22 June 1990, *On Dinard Beach* (1920, oil on canvas, 19 3/4 x 25 1/2 ins / 50 x 65 cm) FRF 72,000. DOUAI, 30 June 1991, *Boules Players* (1923, oil on canvas, 23 1/4 x 31 1/2 ins / 59 x 80 cm) FRF 66,000. LONDON, 24 March 1992, *Two Figures on a Beach* (oil on card, 11 x 15 1/4 ins / 28.2 x 38.7 cm) GBP 2,530. LOKEREN, 10 Oct 1992, *View of the Rialto Bridge and Grand Canal, Venice* (1935, oil on canvas, 25 1/2 x 32 ins / 65 x 81 cm) BEF 75,000. CALAIS, 13 Dec 1992, *Fisherman by a River* (oil on canvas, 19 3/4 x 25 1/2 ins / 50 x 65 cm) FRF 12,500. CALAIS, 4 July 1993, *Fisherman by a River* (oil on canvas, 19 3/4 x 25 1/2 ins / 50 x 65 cm) FRF 13,500. PARIS, 24 March 1996, *The Jardin de Bagatelle* (1905, oil on canvas, 17 3/4 x

23½ ins / 45 x 60 cm) FRF 6,200. PARIS, 12 Dec 1996, *Canal* (1943, oil on canvas, 23½ x 32 ins / 60 x 81 cm) FRF 5,600. VALENCIENNES, 21 Sept 1997, *Panoramic View of Valenciennes* (oil on canvas, 25½ x 32 ins / 65 x 81 cm) FRF 16,500. PARIS, 6 April 1998, *The Château de Bonport* (1923, oil on canvas, 25¼ x 32 ins / 64 x 81 cm) FRF 3,500. PARIS, 29 Nov 1999, *Woman with Tambourine* (1930, oil on canvas, 32 x 26 ins / 81 x 65 cm) FRF 31,000. PARIS, 12 Dec 1999, *St Jean Cap Ferrat* (1938, oil on canvas, 26 x 32 ins / 65 x 81 cm) FRF 12,000. PARIS, 21 June 2001, *Canal in Venice* (1935, oil on canvas, 26 x 32 ins / 65 x 81 cm) FRF 31,000. NEUILLY, 25 Oct 2001, *Annecy* (c. 1932, oil on canvas, 26 x 32 ins / 65 x 81 cm) FRF 23,000. PARIS, 15 Dec 2003, *Muezzin at Bou-Saada* (1934, oil on canvas, 15 x 22 ins / 38 x 55 cm) EUR 2,800.

JONAS, Margarethe J.
German, 19th century.
Born 1783, in Brunswick; died 1858, in Berlin.
Painter.

Margarethe Jonas painted portraits, landscapes and genre paintings. She exhibited a *Landscape with Nymphs* and a *Landscape* scene from Sir Walter Scott's *Ivanhoe* at the academy in Berlin in 1824. In 1826, she showed a copy of a Rubens painting, and in 1832 two portraits. In 1834, she returned with a *Landscape with Mill*, a *Winter Landscape* and a *Portrait*.

JONAS, Martin
Serb, 20th century.
Born 1924, in Kovacica.
Painter. Landscapes.

A self-taught artist, Martin Jonas was a peasant who produced paintings of country life with the energetic charm typical of the naive painters of the Hlebine School.

BIBLIOGRAPHY:
Gans, Louis, *Meesters der Europese naïven*, exhibition catalogue, Centraal Museum, Utrecht, 1970.

JONAS, Siegfried
Swiss, 20th century.
Born 8 October 1909, in Geneva, to Russian parents.
Active from 1949 and from 1959 naturalised in France.
Sculptor.

Siegfried Jonas spent his childhood in Russia from 1910 to 1920, in Moscow and the provinces, then returned to Switzerland with his parents. From 1925-1926 and 1929-1930 he was a student at the École des Beaux-Arts in Geneva, where he had James Vibert as his professor of sculpture. He returned to Paris in 1931 for two years, discovering the works of Picasso, Henri Laurens, Lipchitz and archaic art, Roman sculpture and the Negro primitives. Returning to Switzerland in 1933 and obliged to earn his living, he abandoned artistic activity until 1940. In 1946 he set up in Paris for good, occupying a studio on a housing estate on the Rue de la Tombe-Issoire from 1947 to 1963. On being expelled from that studio, he set up in Plessis-St-Jean (Yonne), where he converted an old farm.

After a number of trial and error works from nature from 1940 to 1945, such as bust portraits and nudes in clay and plaster, Jonas moved resolutely in the direction of Abstraction. At that time his sculptures were made up of simple shapes, carefully conceived and executed works, in general from original plaster casts, welded sheet metal, rough-hewn stone or polished marble and bronze, which can be situated between Duchamp-Villon and (more clearly) Arp and Gilioli. Around 1956, after some study maquettes, he produced a *Major Symbolic Cross-bearer*, 120 feet (37 metres) high in concrete, for the church of Sacré-Coeur in Mulhouse. Around 1960 he began to design more complex works, less withdrawn into themselves. He produced welded iron gates in 1964, a mural for a block of flats in Geneva in 1965, a large bronze sculpture, *The Siren of Lake Geneva*, for a private garden in 1966-1967 and sculptures in welded tubes. In the 1970s he evolved towards an Expressionism inspired by organic forms.

During the evolution of his successive periods, and although he remained resolutely attached to his fundamental option of Abstraction, Jonas sometimes gave his sculptures titles, for example: 1951, *Waiting*; 1953, *The Song of the Hours*; 1954, *Bestiary*; 1959, *The Dead on Holiday*; 1962, *Genesis*; and 1964, *The Challenge*, no doubt intended to bear witness to his original emotion, and to assist the perception of the public.

He exhibited in the annual Paris salons, notably in 1948 at the Salon des Indépendants; from 1950 at the Salon des Réalités Nouvelles and the Salon de la Jeune Sculpture; and in 1959 at the Salon de Mai. He took part in group exhibitions, including: 1949 and 1950, Paris, Galerie René Breteau; 1953 and 1955, Paris, Galerie Arnaud; 1956 and 1957, Paris, Galerie Colette Allendy; 1958, Charleroi, Paris des Expositions, and Göteborg, Lorenzberg gallery; 1958 and 1959, Paris, Galerie Claude Bernard; 1959, Lunds (Sweden), Kunsthalle; 1960, St-Étienne, Musée d'Art et d'Industrie; 1962, Musée du Havre and Paris, *Small Bronzes*, Musée National d'Art Moderne. His first solo exhibitions took place in Paris, in 1953 at the Galerie Arnaud and 1958-1959 at the Galerie René Breteau.

BIBLIOGRAPHY:
Van Gindertael, Roger, *Jonas*, Éd. Anthropos, Paris, 1969.

AUCTION RECORDS:
PARIS, 17 Dec 1984, *Nude* (1950, gilt-patinated bronze, 28¼ x 9 ins / 72 x 22 cm) FRF 20,000.

JONAS, Suzanne
French, 20th century.
Born 1 October 1885, in Paris; died 28 December 1928.
Engraver.

Suzanne Jonas was the wife of Lucien Jonas and a line engraver.

JONAS, Walter Hermann
Swiss, 20th century.
Born 1910, in Oberursel; died 1979, in Zurich.
Painter (including gouache). Figures, landscapes, urban landscapes.

AUCTION RECORDS:
ZURICH, 30 Oct 1980, *Tessin Landscape* (1944, oil on canvas, 31¾ x 39¾ ins / 80.5 x 101 cm) CHF 23,000. ZURICH, 14 May 1983, *Three Figures in the Night* (1953, oil on canvas, 28¾ x 19¾ ins / 73 x 50 cm) CHF 3,800. ZURICH, 5 June 1986, *Piazza di Castagnola* (1945, oil on canvas, 32 x 39¼ ins / 81.5 x 100 cm) CHF 7,000. BERN, 9 May 1987, *Rio under a Starlit Night* (1951, oil on canvas, 38¼ x 51¼ ins / 97 x 130 cm) CHF 8,500. LUCERNE, 24 Nov 1990, *Abstract Composition* (1953, gouache/paper, 13¾ x 19¾ ins / 35 x 50 cm) CHF 1,700. ZURICH, 14-16 Oct 1992, *The Dalmatian Coast* (oil on canvas, 21½ x 25¾ ins / 54.5 x 65.5 cm) CHF 2,600. ZURICH, 24 Nov 1993, *Colourful Houses* (oil on card, 12½ x 15¼ ins / 31.5 x 39 cm) CHF 1,725.

JONASSEN, Jonas Balju van Schiedam, or Jonasz.
Dutch, 17th century.
Born 1625; died 1667 or 1668, in Schiedam.
Active in Utrecht.
Landscape artist.

Worked in Italy.

JONAVILLE, Pierre
French, 19th century.
Born 1827, in Metz.
Painter.

Pierre Jonaville studied under Léon Cogniet. He exhibited *Broken Jug* and *Medieval Hunt* at the 1849 and 1868 Paris Salons, respectively.

JONCHEER, Jacobus de. See **JONCKHEER**

JONCHÈRE, Évariste

French, 20th century.

Born 8 July 1892, in Les Hérolles (Vienne); died 1956, in Paris.

Sculptor, painter, designer. Mythological subjects. Monuments.

At the age of 16, Évariste Jonchère was accepted as a student at the École des Beaux-Arts in Paris. He studied first at the studio of Jean Antonin Mercié and then worked under the direction of the sculptor Boucher. He was awarded the Prix de Rome in 1925 for *Grape Harvest*. Jonchère taught at the École des Beaux-Arts in Le Havre and, after winning the Indochina Prize in 1932, spent two years in Vietnam. When he eventually returned to France after travelling extensively all over the world, he exhibited as a sculptor at the Paris Exposition Universelle of 1937. Jonchère produced decorative work for the colonial exhibition of 1931 and for the Exposition Universelle in Paris in 1937. He also worked on the Palais d'Élysée. In 1938, he succeeded Victor Tardieu as director of the Indochina school of fine arts where he made a considerable contribution before leaving in 1944. In 1952, he was appointed director of the school of fine arts in Brazzaville in the Congo. In 1996 an exhibition of his work was held in a museum in Vauban.

BIBLIOGRAPHY:

André-Pallois, Nadine/Ménonville, Corinne de, *Paris-Hanoï-Saigon, l'aventure de l'art moderne au Viêt Nam*, exhibition catalogue, Pavillon des Arts, Paris, 1998.

MUSEUMS AND GALLERIES:

VAUBAN (Mus. de la Citadelle): *Pasiphaë and the White Bull* (1926).

AUCTION RECORDS:

PARIS, 19 Oct 1997, *African Dancer* (1950, patinated polychrome bronze, 10 1/2 x 10 1/4 x 2 ins / 26.8 x 25.9 x 5 cm) FRF 8,500. PARIS, 25 Nov 1999, *Maori Woman* (black patinated bronze, h. 20 ins / 52 cm) FRF 38,000.

JONCHERIE, Gabriel Germain

French, 19th century.

Painter. Genre scenes, interiors, still-lifes.

Gabriel Germain Joncherie featured at the Paris Salon from 1831 to 1844.

AUCTION RECORDS:

NEW YORK, 14 May 1976, *Suppertime* (oil on canvas, 21 1/4 x 26 ins / 54 x 66 cm) USD 1,200. MONTE CARLO, 22 June 1985, *Tea Tray* (1832, oil on canvas, 17 1/4 x 21 1/4 ins / 43.5 x 54 cm) FRF 48,000. MONACO, 17 June 1988, *Baskets of Fruit and Vegetables* (1840, oil on canvas, 19 3/4 x 23 1/2 ins / 50 x 60 cm) FRF 27,750. PARIS, 26 March 1999, *Kitchen Interior* (1821, oil on canvas laid on panel, 20 x 25 ins / 52 x 63 cm) FRF 27,000. PARIS, 3 June 1999, *Bank Teller's Window* (1829, oil on canvas, 17 x 14 ins / 44 x 35 cm) FRF 105,000. PARIS, 23 March 2000, *Still-life with Kitchen Dishes, Brazier and Cat* (oil on canvas, 20 x 24 ins / 50 x 61 cm) FRF 35,000. NEW YORK, 30 Oct 2001, *Breakfast Tray* (1832, oil on canvas, 18 x 22 ins / 46 x 56 cm) USD 2,000. LUCERNE, 14 Nov 2001, *Still-life with Fruit* (1831, oil on canvas, 20 x 24 ins / 51 x 61 cm) CHF 4,000. PARIS, 24 June 2004, *Still-life with Basket of Eggs* (oil on canvas, 25 x 30 ins / 64 x 77 cm) EUR 8,000.

JONCHERIE, Hector François

French, 19th century.

Born 6 August 1824, in Paris.

Painter. Still-lifes.

Hector François Joncherie studied initially under his father, Gabriel Germain, before beginning at the College of Fine Arts on 7 October 1846. He exhibited still-lifes at the Paris Salon from 1842 to 1868.

AUCTION RECORDS:

MONTE CARLO, 6 March 1984, *Kitchen Interior* (1843, oil on canvas, 14 1/4 x 17 3/4 ins / 36.5 x 45 cm) FRF 14,000.

JONCHERY, Charles Émile

French, 19th - 20th century.

Born 27 June 1873, in Paris; died 1 February 1937, in Issy-les-Moulineaux.

Sculptor.

Charles Émile Jonchery was the son of the sculptor Émile Jonchery and worked in Paris at Rodin's studio. He exhibited in Paris at the Salon des Artistes Français and the Salon des Indépendants.

Jonchery is known for *The Seven Deadly Sins; Humanity Vomiting Up its Vices; The Curse; Man with Claw; Our Victory*. He also produced numerous bronze statuettes, notably *Polar* in *Claudine at School* and *Little Fisher on the Rocks*, as well as a series of low relief war scenes.

JONCHERY, Émile

French, 19th century.

Sculptor.

Émile Jonchery came from Autun, but was trained in Paris, in Carpeaux's studio.

Apart from his statues, he carried out numerous restoration works.

JONCHET, Louis

French, 16th century.

Sculptor, architect.

Jonchet worked in Lyons from 1517 to 1520. In 1518, he sculpted an escutcheon featuring the coat of arms of Lyons, which decorated the chimney of the main hall of the town hall.

JONCIÈRES, Léonce J. V. de

French, 19th - 20th century.

Born 14 February 1871, in Dompierre (Allier); died 1947.

Painter. Genre scenes.

Léonce J.V. de Joncières studied under Gérome, Bouguereau and L.O. Merson. Joncières' landscapes are lit by gentle sunlight, conveying a sense of calm. He exhibited in Paris at the Salon des Artistes Français, becoming a member of the society in 1902. In 1897, he received a commendation, in 1907 a bronze medal and later a gold medal. He was made a Chevalier of the Légion d'Honneur.

AUCTION RECORDS:

PARIS, 8-9 Dec 1933, *Madame J. Massenet's Small Hallway in Versailles*, FRF 250. PARIS, 21 Oct 1946, *Long Live Spain (Dancer on Stage)*, FRF 650. PARIS, 1 March 1978, *A Walk in the Gardens* (oil on canvas, 13 x 17 1/4 ins / 33 x 44 cm) FRF 2,100. ENGHIEN-LES-BAINS, 24 March 1985, *Blue Alcove* (1930, oil on card, 15 x 18 ins / 38 x 46 cm) FRF 30,000. PARIS, 13 Nov 1992, *Sunny Patio* (1943, oil on paper, 17 1/4 x 14 ins / 44 x 35.5 cm) FRF 4,200. PARIS, 8 April 2002, *View of the El Kettar Cemetery* (1930, oil on canvas, 18 x 22 ins / 46 x 55 cm) EUR 1,700.

JONCKERS, Jodocus or Joost

Dutch, 16th century.

Active in 's Hertogenbosch.

Sculptor (wood).

In 1529, Jonckers produced four statuettes of emperors for the town hall of 's Hertogenbosch.

JONCKHEER, Jacobus de, or Jonkheer or Joncheer
Flemish School, 17th century.
Painter, engraver. Animals.

In 1668, Jacobus de Jonckheer was registered in the Antwerp guild. He made engravings of dogs and is also believed to have worked as a painter, though his output was small.

AUCTION RECORDS:
LONDON, 28 Nov 1962, *View of the Piazetta in Venice,* GBP 480.

JONCKHEERE, Robert de
Belgian, 20th century.
Born 31 December 1882, in Ypres.
Painter. Portraits.

Robert de Jonckheere was a pupil of Philippe de Winter. He made his debut in 1905 in Paris at the Salon des Artistes Français.

JONCKMAN, Wilhelm. See **JONGMAN Wouter**

JONCOURT, Roger
French, 20th century.
Born 4 July 1932, in Moëlan-sur-Mer (Finistère).
Sculptor.

Roger Joncourt first studied from 1947 to 1952 at the royal fine arts academy in Antwerp; he then went to Paris and studied at Zadkine's studio and finally in London at the Royal College of Arts.

Joncourt's stone and metal sculptures are abstract. He seems to be interested in large, rather flat, geometric surfaces which he assembles in rigorous constructions. He also produces reliefs.

AUCTION RECORDS:
PARIS, 3 June 1991, *Élan* (patinated brass, 16 1/2 x 11 ins / 42 x 28 cm) FRF 7,000.

JONDET, Henri Michel
French, 19th - 20th century.
Born 1862, in Rouen; died 20 March 1922, in Paris.
Sculptor.

Henri Michel Jondet exhibited in Paris at the Salon des Artistes Français, receiving a commendation in 1892. He became a member of the Society in 1893.

MUSEUMS AND GALLERIES:
ROUEN: *Death of a Tramp.*

JONES, A. Garth
British, 19th century.
Painter, illustrator.

A. Garth Jones trained in Manchester and, towards 1893, in Paris with J.P. Laurens and Benjamin Constant. He made pen drawings for Contes de Haute-Lisse and Contes de la Fileuse which appeared in the *Revue Illustrée* in Paris. He also designed the frontispieces for editions of works by Goldsmith, Coleridge, Swift, Keats, and Marco Polo, all of which met with success with book lovers.

JONES, Adolphe. See **JONES Daniel Adolphe Robert**

JONES, Adrian
British, 19th - 20th century.
Born 9 February 1845, in Ludlow; died 1938.
Active in London.
Sculptor, watercolourist.

Adrian Jones exhibited at the Royal Academy and the Grosvenor Gallery from 1884.

AUCTION RECORDS:
LONDON, 30 Oct 1973, *The Racehorse Amphion with his Jockey,* GBP 520. LONDON, 26 Jan 1984, *Arab Thoroughbred* (oil on canvas, 20 x 16 ins / 51 x 40.5 cm) GBP 3,000. LONDON, 8 March 1984, *Gone Away* (1880, bronze, h. 20 ins / 51 cm) GBP 3,400. LONDON, 12 April 1985, *Cloister with Jockey up* (1893, oil on canvas, 27 1/2 x 35 1/2 ins / 70 x 90 cm) GBP 4,500. LONDON, 29 April 1987, *Workhorse* (1901, watercolour heightened with white, 29 1/4 x 42 1/2 ins / 74 x 108 cm) GBP 3,200.

JONES, Albertus E.
American, 20th century.
Born 31 October 1882, in South Windsor (Connecticut); died 1957.
Painter.

Albertus Jones studied under Charles Noel Flagg and belonged to the Salmagundi Club.

JONES, Alfred
American, 19th century.
Born 7 April 1819, in Liverpool, England; died 28 April 1900, in New York.
Engraver.

Alfred Jones went to New York in 1834. He was apprenticed in a workshop and engraved bank notes, an industry in which he would occupy a prime place. He later gave up industry for art and was much employed by American publishers. In 1839 he won first prize at the National Academy of Design in New York. In 1846 he went to Europe to complete his art studies. He was elected a member of the National Academy in 1851, and was secretary and treasurer for many years.

He reproduced many paintings by American artists, and also engraved postage stamps. His last works were an important *Portrait of Washington* after the most authentic documents, and two portraits of *Carlyle.*

JONES, Allen
British, 20th century.
Born 1937, in Southampton.
Painter, sculptor, draughtsman. Scenes with figures, figures. Stage sets, stage costumes.
Pop Art.

Allen Jones studied painting at Hornsey College of Art from 1955 to 1959, and from 1960 to 1961 (the intervening year was spent at the Royal College of Art in London). He travelled to Paris in 1958, where he discovered the work of Robert Delaunay. He taught in the USA in the mid-1960s, and then returned to live and work in London. Allen's earliest sculptural compositions feature warm colours and forms circled with haloes of paler tints. Initially reminiscent of Braque, his work later evolved in the direction of Pop Art, using vivid colours applied to everyday subjects such as a representation of a 'bus together with its speed', sometimes defined by drawing from the repertory of Conceptual Art. In 1964 he adopted a range of subjects drawn from erotic reviews, magazines and comics. These have constituted his distinctive artistic vocabulary ever since: figures of women, couples and hermaphrodites, depicted in close detail (with underwear, stockings, high heels) and articulating a view of the female body and its component parts (breasts, legs) as idealised objects of desire; or 'off-the-shelf' consumer items.

In 1969 he began using moulded forms in his paintings, and embarked on a series of pieces of furniture incorporating female figures in fetish garb. The resulting tables, coat stands, chairs, etc. provided him with a fresh iconographical repertory that was subsequently exploited in a later series of paintings. During the 1980s Allen produced large-scale canvases and sculptures based on assemblages of fluid, cut-out forms in painted or enamelled wood, metal and fibreglass. In 1970 he produced designs for the erotic stage musical *Oh, Calcutta!,* produced in London by the theatre critic Kenneth Tynan. His essentially formalist approach focuses on form as the instigator of subject matter in art, rather than subject matter as the 'creator' of form. His characteristically violent colour palette articulates the underlying aggression and obsessive quality of his work.

Allen's work has featured in a number of group exhibitions by British Pop artists, including a début show in 1961 with Derek Boshier, David Hockney and Peter Phillips. Subsequent shows include: 1961, 1963, 1965, 1971, Paris Biennale; 1962, Institute of Contemporary Art, London and Museum of Art, San Francisco; 1963, 1964, Whitechapel Gallery, London; 1964, Tate Gallery, London; 1964, 1968, Documenta, Kassel; 1966, 1971, Palais des Beaux-Arts, Brussels; 1968, Fondation Maeght, St-Paul-de-Vence; 1969, National Museum of Art, Tokyo; 1970, National Gallery, Washington; 1971, Palazzo Reale, Milan; 1972, Museum of Modern Art, New York; 2003, *Phantom der Lust. Visionen des Machochismus in der Kunst* (*Phantom of Desire. Visions of Masochism in Art*), exhibition dedicated to Sacher-Masoch, the 'founder' of masochism, Neue Galerie, Ladesmuseum, Graz. Allen's work has also been the subject of a number of solo exhibitions since 1963, in Britain and internationally: 1963, 1964, 1967, 1968, 1970, 1971, 1972, 1976, 1979, London; 1964, 1965, 1970, New York; 1965, Chicago; 1965, 1977, Los Angeles; 1965, Biennale de Dessin, Paris; 1967, 1970, 1971, Cologne; 1978, 1998, Galerie Patrice Trigano, Paris; 1978, Montreal; 1978, retrospective, Institute of Contemporary Art (I.C.A.), London; 1979, Wallraf-Richartz Museum, Cologne and Walker Art Centre, Liverpool; 2001, Alan Cristea Gallery, London.

BIBLIOGRAPHY:

Allen Jones: Gemälde 1957-1978, exhibition catalogue, 1970. Peters, Hans Albert, *Allen Jones: Retrospective of Paintings 1957-1978*, exhibition catalogue, Staatliche Kunsthalle, Baden-Baden, Walker Art Gall., Liverpool, 1979 (text in English and German). Livingstone, Marco, *Allen Jones: Sheer Magic*, Thames and Hudson, London, 1979. Wheeler, Daniel, *L'Art du XXe siècle*, Flammarion, Paris, 1991. *Allen Jones: Sculpture*, exhibition catalogue, Glynn Vivian Art Gallery, Swansea, 1992. Hodges, Nicola/Robertson, Natasha, *'Allen Jones'* in *coll. Art and design monographs*, Academy Editions, London, 1993. Livingstone, Marco/Lloyd, Richard, *Allen Jones Prints*, catalogue raisonné, Prestel, Munich, 1995. Restany, Pierre, *Allen Jones*, exhibition catalogue, Gal. Patrice Trigano, Paris, 1998. Weibel, Peter (ed.), *'Phantom der Lust. Visionen des Masochismus in der Kunst'* in *2 vol.*, exhibition catalogue, Neue Galerie am Landesmuseum, Graz, Belleville Verlag, Munich, 2003.

MUSEUMS AND GALLERIES:

AMSTERDAM (Stedelijk Mus.) - BOCHUM (Kunstverein Mus.) - CAMBRIDGE, MA (Fogg AM, Harvard University) - CHICAGO (MA) - COLOGNE (Wallraf-Richartz Mus.): *Perfect assortment* (1966-1967); *Free-fall* (1966-1967) - GÖTEBORG (Konstmus.) - HAMBURG (Kunsthalle) - LIVERPOOL (Walker AG) - LONDON (Tate Collection): *Chair* (1969, plastic and mixed media) - LONDON (Victoria and Albert Mus.) - NEW YORK (MoMA) - ROTTERDAM (Mus. Boijmans Van Beuningen) - SUNDERLAND: *Sunplane* - VIENNA (Mus. of 20th Century Art).

AUCTION RECORDS:

LONDON, 1 July 1976, *Veiled woman* (1969, oil/photograph and collage, 30¾ x 18¾ ins / 78 x 47.5 cm) GBP 850. LONDON, 7 Dec 1977, *Red latex suit* (1973, oil and latex/canvas, 48 x 48 ins / 122 x 122 cm) GBP 3,000. LONDON, 7 Dec 1977, *Red, white and blue shoe* (1966, oil on canvas, shoe on presentation box, 11 x 7¾ x 4 ins / 27 x 20 x 10 cm) GBP 680. LONDON, 3 July 1979, *Red latex suit* (1973, oil and latex/canvas, 48 x 48 ins / 122 x 122 cm) GBP 2,200. NEW YORK, 6 Nov 1979, *Green Bosom (Chest)* (1964-1965, oil on canvas with plaster and lace, 20 x 14 x 4¼ ins / 51 x 35.5 x 11 cm) USD 1,500. LONDON, 2 Dec 1982, *Table sculpture* (1969, fibreglass, resin, glass, leather and mixed media, 26 x 50¾ x 30 ins / 66 x 129 x 76.5 cm) GBP 6,000. LONDON, 6 Dec 1983, *Gallery Gasper* (1966-1967, oil on canvas and plastic panel, 36¼ x 36¼ ins / 92 x 92 cm) GBP 6,000. NEW YORK, 10 May 1984, *Green table* (1972, fibreglass, resin, leather, glass and mixed media, 24 x 33 x 57 ins / 61 x 83.8 x 144.8 cm) USD 11,000. LONDON, 25 June 1985, *Untitled* (1981, pencil, 60 x 40 ins / 152.4 x 101.6 cm) GBP 2,500. LONDON, 5 Dec 1986, *Red dancer* (1982, painted steel, h. 74 ins / 188 cm) GBP 3,800. MILAN, 11 Dec 1986, *Sheer* (1968, acrylic/canvas, aluminium and plastic stairs, t. 72 x 59¾ ins / 183 x 152 cm and staircase 18 x 59¾ ins/46 x 152 cm) ITL 22,000,000. NEW YORK, 20 Feb 1987, *Curious man* (1964, pencil and oil on wood with wooden relief, 47 x 38 x 24 ins / 119.5 x 96.6 x 60.7 cm) USD 12,000. LONDON, 8 Sept 1988, *Green table* (1972, sculpture in painted fibreglass, glass and leather, 24 x 33 x 57 ins / 61 x 83.8 x 144.8 cm) GBP 20,900. NEW YORK, 8 Oct 1988, *Table (crouching figure of a woman serving as the support for a glass table-top)* (1969, fibreglass resin and black leather, 25 x 52 x 30 ins / 63.5 x 132.3 x 76.5 cm) USD 28,600. LONDON, 20 Oct 1988, *Two figures* (1964, oil on canvas, 8 x 8 ins / 20.5 x 20.5 cm) GBP 2,530. ROME, 21 March 1989, *Untitled* (1978, watercolour/paper, 10¼ x 14½ ins / 26 x 37 cm) ITL 5,500,000. LONDON, 6 April 1989, *Untitled* (1973, chalk, collage and varnish/paper, 30 x 22¼ ins / 76.5 x 56.5 cm) GBP 1,540. NEW YORK, 3 May 1989, *Black shadow* (1964, oil on canvas, 48 x 84 ins / 122 x 213.3 cm) USD 22,000. PARIS, 4 June 1989, *Untitled* (1973, enamel, collage, chalks and watercolour/paper, 22¼ x 30 ins / 56.5 x 76.5 cm) FRF 33,000. LONDON, 18 Oct 1990, *The Fourth Man* (1964, painted wood and plastic, h. 29¼ ins / 74 cm) GBP 3,300. LONDON, 9 Nov 1990, *Gallery Gasper* (oil on canvas, 36¼ x 36¼ ins / 92 x 92 cm) GBP 25,300. LONDON, 8 March 1991, *Sculpted legs* (1972, leather/fibreglass and metal, h. 42¼ ins / 107 cm) GBP 6,380. NEW YORK, 3 Oct 1991, *Headstand* (1988, painted steel, 97 x 48 x 43 ins / 246.4 x 121.9 x 109.2 cm) USD 17,600. LONDON, 8 Nov 1991, *L.A. Sheer* (1969, oil on canvas with plastic steps, 90¼ x 59¾ ins / 229 x 152 cm) GBP 13,200. ZURICH, 4 Dec 1991, *Magic moment* (1981, coloured lithograph, 30¼ x 22 ins / 77 x 56 cm) CHF 800. PARIS, 30 June 1992, *A pigment in pigment* (1969, acrylic/canvas, 83¾ x 120 ins / 213 x 305 cm) FRF 115,000. LONDON, 2 July 1992, *Girl in red* (oil on canvas, 60 x 72 ins / 152.5 x 183 cm) GBP 17,600. LONDON, 15 Oct 1992, *Maid to order II* (1971, acrylic/canvas, 72 x 59¾ ins / 183 x 152 cm) GBP 18,700. PARIS, 9 June 1994, *Frieze* (1985, oil on canvas, 72 x 72 ins / 183 x 183 cm) FRF 60,000. LONDON, 23 Oct 1996, *Male and female composition* (1964-1965, oil on canvas, 114 x 132 ins / 289.6 x 335.3 cm) GBP 11,500. NEW YORK, 6 and 7 March 1998, *Composition* (1964, coloured lithograph, 29¾ x 22 ins / 75.5 x 55.8 cm) USD 345. LONDON, 28 April 1999, *Rhapsody* (oil on canvas, two, 72 x 96 ins / 183 x 245 cm) GBP 5,500. LONDON, 10 Dec 1999, *Thais* (oil on canvas, 83 x 60 ins / 211 x 152 cm) GBP 14,000. HELSINKI, 6 May 2000, *The Music of Time II* (1985, lithograph, 34 x 43 ins / 87 x 108 cm) FIM 30,000. PARIS, 9 Dec 2000, *Danseuse* (watercolour, 29 x 20 ins / 73 x 52 cm) FRF 23,000. PARIS, 23 April 2001, *Danseuse* (watercolour, 29 x 20 ins / 73 x 52 cm) FRF 24,000. AMSTERDAM, 3 Dec 2001, *Swing Low* (oil on canvas, 68 x 52 ins / 172 x 132 cm) NLG 45,000. LONDON, 8 Feb 2002, *Hats Off* (waxed, rusted steel with painted elements, 46 x 11x11 ins / 118 x 27x27 cm) GBP 2,800. LONDON, 22 Nov 2002, *Portrait - Flower* (1966, oil on canvas, 48 x 48 ins / 122 x 122 cm) GBP 29,000. LONDON, 6 June 2003, *General and his Girl* (1961, acrylic on canvas, 48 x 36 ins / 122 x 91 cm) GBP 61,000. LONDON, 3 July 2003, *Green Table* (1972, fibreglass, leather and glass, 29 x 44x29 ins / 74 x 112x74 cm) GBP 32,000. LONDON, 17 Nov 2004, *Dancing Couple* (painted steel, h. 90 ins / 229 cm) GBP 21,000. LONDON, 19 Nov 2004, *Cleavage* (1964, oil on canvas, 11 x 9 ins / 27 x 22 cm) GBP 23,000.

JONES, Anna M.

British, 19th century.

Active in Guernsey.

Painter, watercolourist. Landscapes.

Anna M. Jones exhibited in London from 1868, mostly at the Royal Academy.

Auction records:

London, 23 May 1910, *Windsor Castle from the Thames* (1869, watercolour) GBP 5.

JONES, Annie Weaver

American, 20th century.

Painter, illustrator.

Annie Weaver Jones studied under Lazar and in Paris with R. Collin and Merson. She lived and worked in Chicago.

JONES, Arne

Swedish, 20th century.

Born 1914, in Borgsjö (Medelpad); died 1976.

Sculptor.

Konkretisterna (Concretists) group.

Arne Jones worked first in the studio of a stone sculptor and then took courses for five years in Stockholm at the technical school and, until 1947, at the school of fine art. After a figurative period concerned with the human body, he moved on to abstract spatial structures, frames making full use of space and reminiscent of Gothic buildings, and then to monolithic structures. The titles of his works clearly show their inspiration: *Cathedral* of 1948, *Spiral Space* of 1953, and *Inside and Out* of 1959.

Museums and Galleries:

Norrköping: *Cathedral* (1948).

Auction records:

Stockholm, 6 June 1988, *Graphic Construction* (copper blades, h. 20 ins / 51 cm) SEK 33,000. Stockholm, 30 May 1991, *Composition* (copper, h. 5¾ ins / 14.5 cm) SEK 8,000. Stockholm, 19 May 1992, *Composition* (1960, metal on a black wooded plinth, h. 7¼ ins / 18.5 cm) SEK 8,700. Stockholm, 10-12 May 1993, *Spiral* (polished copper, h. 7¼ ins / 18.5 cm) SEK 8,000. Stockholm, 27 April 1999, *Graphic Building* (copper, h. 20 ins / 51 cm) SEK 22,000. Stockholm, 7 Nov 2000, *Triad* (patinated bronze, h. 11 ins / 28 cm) SEK 18,000. Stockholm, 6 Nov 2001, *The Cyclist* (brown patinated bronze, 19 x 28 ins / 48 x 70 cm) SEK 54,000. Stockholm, 5 Nov 2002, *Pirouette* (1958, dark patinated bronze, h. 41 ins / 104 cm) SEK 35,000. Stockholm, 5 Nov 2003, *Fly* (brass and pewter, 18 x 18 ins / 46 x 45 cm) SEK 20,000.

JONES, Benjamin or Ben

American, 20th century.

Born 1942, in Paterson (New Jersey).

Painter, sculptor, installation artist.

Ben Jones studied at Paterson State College, Wayne (New Jersey), at the Pratt Institute in New York and at New York University. He has taught at Jersey City College. In 1967, he founded, with like-minded artists, the Nyumba ya Sanaa Gallery in Harlem with a view to offer an exhibition space to Afro-American artists. From 1967 to 1982, he was a dancer in the Chuck Davis Dance Company in New York. He upholds the Afro-centric principles expounded by 1960s Afro-Americans artists' groups, taking a particular interest in the representation of the black body, for instance in *Black Face and Arm Unit*, a trophy-like display of faces and arms cast in plaster and decorated in traditional ethnic patterns (1971). He has produced groups of decorated masks, arms and legs and installations in which he inscribes frescoes of black bodies, for instance the *Shango Wall Installation* (1994), which illustrates the rites surrounding the Voodoo god, Shango. In his abstract compositions, his own face may appear amid geometric symbols and African attributes such as shells. He took part in the exhibition *Three Generations of Black Art: Amiri Baraka, Ben Jones, and Mansa Mussa*, Brothers Art Exhibition, New Jersey City University, Montclair. He has shown his works in solo exhibitions in New York and Atlanta.

Bibliography:

Fine, Elsa Honig, *The Afro-American Artist*, Holt, Rinehart and Winston, New York, 1971. Powell, Richard J., *Black Art and Culture in the 20th Century*, Thames and Hudson, London, 1997. Patton, Sharon, *African-American Art*, Oxford University Press, Oxford, 1998.

Museums and Galleries:

Montclair (AM): *Juxtaposition #11* (1989, acrylic on canvas) - Newark (Mus.): *High Priestess of Soul* (1970, mixed media) - Trenton (New Jersey State Mus.) - Washington DC (GA, Howard University).

JONES, Charles

British, 19th century.

Born 1836; died 1892.

Active in Barnham.

Painter, watercolourist. Animals.

Charles Jones was a member of the Royal Cambrian Academy and an associate of the Royal Scottish Academy. After 1860, he exhibited in London, notably at the Royal Academy, the British Institution, the New Water-Colour Society and, especially, at the Suffolk Street Gallery.

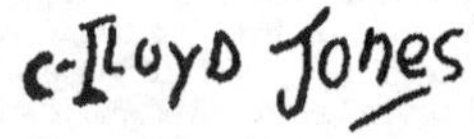

Museums and Galleries:

Cardiff: *Rest* - Sydney: *A Corner of the Farm.*

Auction records:

London, 25 April 1908, *The Eve of Hungerford Fair*, GBP 51. London, 8 May 1908, *Sheep in Scotland* (1873) GBP 44. London, 21 March 1910, *Sheep*, GBP 42. London, 2 April 1910, *On the Hampshire Hills*, GBP 31. London, 17 Dec 1910, *Flock of Sheep beside a Scottish Lake*, GBP 24. London, 4 Feb 1911, *Sussex Landscape*, GBP 16. London, 30 Jan 1925, *Sheep in the Snow*, GBP 47. London, 27 July 1976, *Shepherd and Flock in a Landscape* (1869, oil on canvas, 25½ x 21 ins / 65 x 53.5 cm) GBP 450. London, 26 Oct 1979, *Hunters' Rest* (1870, oil on canvas, 35¼ x 67 ins / 89.5 x 170.2 cm) GBP 2,600. London, 23 June 1981, *Flock of Sheep in a Woody Lane* (1875, oil on canvas, 50 x 40 ins / 127 x 101.5 cm) GBP 2,600. London, 25 July 1983, *Sheep in a Landscape* (oil on canvas, 23¾ x 35¾ ins / 60.5 x 91 cm) GBP 1,400. London, 17 Dec 1986, *Flock of Sheep in a River Valley* (1891, oil on canvas, 24 x 42 ins / 61 x 106.5 cm) GBP 6,000. Lucerne, 30 Sept 1988, *Flock of Sheep Resting by a River* (oil on canvas, 23½ x 41¼ ins / 60 x 105 cm) CHF 1,100. Perth, 28 Aug 1989, *Cattle and Sheep* (1856, oil on canvas, 17 x 25 ins / 43 x 63.5 cm) GBP 2,090. London, 3 Nov 1989, *Donkeys and Sheep among the Dunes* (1866, oil on canvas, 14 x 20 ins / 35.5 x 51 cm) GBP 2,200. Perth, 27 Aug 1990, *Shepherds in the Highlands* (oil on canvas, a pair, each 24 x 35¾ ins / 61 x 91 cm) GBP 7,700. London, 26 Sept 1990, *Spring* (1877, oil on canvas, 36 x 59¾ ins / 91.5 x 152 cm) GBP 6,600. London, 8 Feb 1991, *Sheep at the top of a Hill* (1890, oil on canvas, 12¼ x 20¼ ins / 31.2 x 51.5 cm) GBP 2,530. London, 3 June 1992, *Summer*; *Winter* (1876, oil on canvas, each 7 x 9 ins / 18 x 23 cm) GBP 1,980. London, 12 Nov 1992, *Sheep Grazing* (1891, oil on canvas, 24 x 42¼ ins / 61 x 107 cm) GBP 4,950. Perth, 30 Aug 1994, *Highland Cattle in Winter*; *Sheep by a Loch* (oil on panel, a pair, each 8¾ x 6¾ ins / 22.5 x 17 cm) GBP 2,645. London, 2 Nov 1994, *Sheep in a Pasture* (1891, oil on canvas, 24¼ x 42 ins / 61.5 x 106.5 cm) GBP 5,520. London, 27 March 1996, *Sheep in the Snow* (1873, oil on panel, 11 x 15 ins / 28 x 38 cm) GBP 6,900. London, 18 Dec 1997, *The Keeper is Coming* (1879, oil on canvas, 30¼ x 25¼ ins / 76.6 x 64.3 cm) GBP 3,220. Billingshurst, 19 Oct 1999, *Sheep in a Meadow* (1863, oil on canvas, 24 x 36 ins / 60 x 91 cm) GBP 7,000. London, 26 Nov 1999, *Waiting for Master* (oil on canvas, 30 x 44 ins / 76 x 112 cm) GBP 6,000. London, 15 June

2000, *Highland Flock* (1875, oil on canvas, 30 x 44 ins / 76 x 112 cm) GBP 10,500. ZURICH, 22 Sept 2000, *Sheep* (oil on canvas, 24 x 42 ins / 61 x 107 cm) CHF 24,000. CREWKERNE, 18 Oct 2001, *Highland Shepherd* (1868, oil on canvas, 21 x 37 ins / 54 x 95 cm) GBP 15,000. LONDON, 1 Nov 2001, *Sheep in Valley* (1870, oil on canvas, 28 x 40 ins / 71 x 102 cm) GBP 11,000. LEYBURN, 25 April 2002, *Morning in the Highlands* (1868, oil on canvas, 56 x 41 ins / 142 x 104 cm) GBP 8,500. EDINBURGH, 22 Aug 2002, *Highland Cattle and Black-faced Sheep on a Snowy Mountainside* (1874, oil on canvas, arched top, 33 x 24 ins / 83 x 62 cm) GBP 10,800. KNOWLE, 11 Feb 2003, *Sheep on a Hillside Overlooking an Open Vista* (1881, oil on canvas, 24 x 40 ins / 61 x 102 cm) GBP 8,500. LONDON, 10 June 2003, *Morning Visit* (1878, oil on canvas, 36 x 60 ins / 91 x 153 cm) GBP 14,000. AMSTERDAM, 20 April 2004, *Resting Cattle, Sheep and Deer, a Farm Beyond* (1871, oil on canvas, 30 x 50 ins / 77 x 127 cm) EUR 10,000. LONDON, 1 Sept 2004, *Grazing in the Highlands* (1876, oil on canvas, 41 x 56 ins / 104 x 142 cm) GBP 15,000.

JONES, Charlotte

British, 19th century.
Died 21 September 1847, in London.
Miniaturist.

Charlotte Jones exhibited regularly at the Royal Academy between 1801 and 1823. She painted miniatures for the Princess of Wales. Her best-known works are a *Portrait* of 1805, *George IV, Queen Caroline*, and twelve miniatures of *Princess Charlotte*.

JONES, Conway Lloyd

British, 19th century.
Active in Wimborne.
Painter. Landscapes.

Conway Lloyd Jones exhibited at the Suffolk Street Gallery in London after 1871.

AUCTION RECORDS:

LONDON, 30 March 1908, *In the New Forest; Mist Effect*, GBP 1.

JONES, Cora Ellis

American, 20th century.
Born 14 May 1875, in Aurora (Illinois); died 1932, in Birmingham (Alabama).
Painter. Landscapes.

Cora Ellis Jones studied under Roderick Mackenzie. She was a member of the American Federation of Arts.

JONES, Daniel Adolphe Robert

Belgian, 19th century.
Born 14 November 1806, in Brussels; died 1874, in Schaerbeek.
Painter. Animals, landscapes.

Pupil of Eug Verboeckhoven.

MUSEUMS AND GALLERIES:

MAINZ: *Cow in a Cattle Shed* - SYDNEY: *Cowshed*.

AUCTION RECORDS:

PARIS, 1844, *Cowshed Interior*, FRF 220. LONDON, 19 April 1978, *Landscape with Sheep and Horse* (oil on canvas, 19$1/4$ x 26$1/2$ ins / 49 x 67.5 cm) GBP 1,300. LINDAU, 5 May 1982, *Mountainous Landscape* (oil on panel, 15$1/4$ x 19$1/2$ ins / 39 x 49.5 cm) DEM 4,800. COLOGNE, 23 March 1990, *Ewe and Lambs* (oil on canvas, 7$3/4$ x 9$3/4$ ins / 20 x 25 cm) DEM 2,500. LONDON, 16 March 1994, *Shepherd and Flock* (oil on canvas, 43 x 59 ins / 109 x 149 cm) GBP 3,680.

JONES, David Michael

British, 20th century.
Born 1895, in Brockley; died 28 October 1974.
Painter, engraver (wood/etching), watercolourist, illustrator. Scenes with figures, landscapes, still-lifes, portraits.

David Jones trained at the Camberwell school under Archibald Hartrick, Walter Bayes and Bernard Meninsky from 1909 and 1914 and at the Westminster Art School in London in 1919. He knew Eric Gill, the engraver, letterer and sculptor; in 1921 he converted to Roman Catholicism and joined the community of craftsmen living according to religious and medieval principles that had built itself around Gill at Ditchling in Kent. In 1924 he left it and founded his own community in a very isolated location in an old monastery at Capel-y-ffin in the Vale of Ewyas in Wales, where he produced his most mature work.

Jones had an intense feeling for the Welsh ancient past which he expressed in his art and writings. His work can be seen at Capel-y-ffin, where he painted the tabernacle in the newly built chapel and a *Crucifixion* in the long room of the monastery. He was also a prolific illustrator, producing etchings for *The Deluge* (1927), *The Ancient Mariner* (1929) and *Arthurian Legends* (for which he borrowed the Capel-y-ffin landscape). His refined style belongs to the visionary tradition of Blake and Cecil Collins.

After 1947 he mainly focused on writing. His first and most famous written work, *In Parenthesis*, published in 1937, provides a vivid portrait of the experiences of a number of ordinary World War I soldiers between December 1915 and July 1916, ending with their tragic slaughter at Mametz Wood. Exhibitions of Jones' work were held at the Tate Gallery, London (1981) and the Brewhouse Theatre and Art Centre, Taunton (1998).

BIBLIOGRAPHY:

Ironside, Robin, *David Jones*, Penguin; the Modern Painter Series, London, 1949. Blamires, David, *David Jones: Artist and Writer*, Toronto University Press, Toronto, 1972.

MUSEUMS AND GALLERIES:

CAMBRIDGE (Kettle's Yard): *Vexilla Regis* (1948, pencil and watercolour); *Flora in Calix-Light* (1950, pencil and watercolour) - LEEDS (City AG): *The Open Bay* (1931, watercolour and gouache) - LONDON (British Mus.): *Resting Deer* (etching) - LONDON (Tate Collection): *Aphrodite in Aulis* (1940-1941, pencil, pen and ink and watercolour/paper); *The Garden Enclosed* (1924, oil/wood).

AUCTION RECORDS:

LONDON, 9 April 1895, *The Orchard's Hedge*, GBP 52. LONDON, 7 April 1971, *Red Jar* (watercolour) GBP 400. LONDON, 18 July 1973, *Sheep in a Landscape* (watercolour, gouache and pencil) GBP 2,800. LONDON, 16 March 1977, *Low Tide* (1931, oil on card, 20 x 24 ins / 51 x 61 cm) GBP 2,100. LONDON, 27 June 1979, *No. 2 Illustration to 'The Winter Solstice'* (1928, pen and colour wash, 14$1/4$ x 10$3/4$ ins / 36 x 27.5 cm) GBP 1,200. LONDON, 10 March 1982, *Out Tide* (1931, oil on canvas, 20 x 24 ins / 51 x 61 cm) GBP 2,500. LONDON, 9 March 1984, *Church Street, Kensington* (1946, pencil coloured chalk and red wash, 12$3/4$ x 8 ins / 32.5 x 20.3 cm) GBP 3,200. LONDON, 23 May 1984, *Trees* (1930, watercolour/pencil outlines, 19 x 24 ins / 48 x 61 cm) GBP 3,800. LONDON, 10 Dec 1985, *Illustrations for the 'Rhyme of the Ancient Mariner'* (1929, drypoint, series of eight, 7 x 5$1/4$ ins / 17.5 x 13.4 cm) GBP 550. LONDON, 21 May 1986, *Mr Gill's Hay Harvest* (1926, watercolour/pencil outlines, 22$3/4$ x 15$1/4$ ins / 58 x 39 cm) GBP 11,500. LONDON, 13 Nov 1987, *Still-life: Hierarchy* (1932, watercolour, ink and pencil, 29$1/4$ x 21$1/2$ ins / 74.1 x 54.7 cm) GBP 3,600. LONDON, 29 July 1988, *Young Girl with a Knot* (pencil, 12$1/2$ x 8 ins / 32 x 19.4 cm) GBP 1,155. ST-DIÉ, 11 Feb 1990, *Panther Licking its Paw* (dark-patinated bronze, 6 x 13$1/4$ ins / 15 x 33.5 cm) FRF 12,500. LONDON, 3 May 1990, *Edward, King of England by the Grace of God* (ink, 12$1/4$ x 7$3/4$ ins / 31 x 20 cm) GBP 715. LONDON, 26 Oct 1994, *Merlin's Tree* (1947, watercolour, gouache, pencil and coloured chalk, 24 x 19 ins / 61 x 48.5 cm) GBP 7,475. LONDON, 23 June 1999, *Blaeu Bwch* (1926, pencil and watercolour, 22 x 15 ins / 56 x 39 cm) GBP 16,500. LONDON, 1 Dec 1999, *Cattle Home* (1932, watercolour and pencil, 31 x 23 ins / 79 x 58 cm) GBP 15,000. LONDON, 28 April 2000, *The Cricket Match* (1937, pencil, watercolour and gouache, 19 x 24 ins / 48 x 61 cm) GBP 16,000. LONDON, 8 June 2000, *Brockley Gardens, Summer* (1925, pencil, watercolour and coloured chalks, 20 x 15 ins / 51 x 39 cm) GBP 11,000. LONDON, 7 June 2001, *Cat at 1 Victoria Square* (1947, pencil, 11 x 9 ins / 29 x 23 cm) GBP 5,000. LONDON, 4 July 2001, *Farm through Trees* (gouache, watercolour, colour chalk and pencil, 18 x 15 ins / 45 x 38 cm) GBP 6,000. LONDON, 7 June 2002, *Elephant* (1928, oil on canvas, 20 x 27 ins / 51 x 69 cm) GBP 11,000. LONDON, 5 Sept 2002, *Town Gardens, Brockley* (1926, watercolour, 22 x 15 ins / 56 x 38 cm) GBP 11,500. LONDON, 6 June 2003, *Dusk is Growing* (1947, pencil, colour chalk, watercolour and gouache, 30 x 22 ins / 75 x 55 cm) GBP 9,000. LONDON, 6 June 2003, *Portslade* (1929, pencil, watercolour and gouache, 24 x 19 ins / 62 x 49 cm) GBP 14,000. LONDON, 2 June 2004, *Dusk is Growing* (1947, gouache, chalk and pencil, 30 x 22 ins / 75 x 55 cm) GBP 12,000. LONDON, 19 Nov 2004, *Rebecca Rose* (1957, pencil, watercolour and brown ink, 7 x 9 ins / 17 x 22 cm) GBP 1,400.

JONES, E. F.
British, 19th century.
Painter, watercolourist. Landscapes.

MUSEUMS AND GALLERIES:
CAPE TOWN (Museum): *Ben Lomond* (watercolour).

JONES, E. Nora (Miss)
British, 19th century.
Active in London.
Miniaturist.

Nora Jones began exhibiting at the Royal Academy in 1890.

JONES, Edward
British, 19th century.
Born c. 1775, of Scottish origin; died 17 February 1862, in Dublin.
Miniaturist.

Edward Jones trained in Dublin and exhibited there for the first time in 1800 with seven drawings of portraits. A series of preachers and ecclesiastical figures was engraved by Maguire for the *Methodist Magazine*.

JONES, Eliza
British, 19th century.
Active in London.
Miniaturist, watercolourist. Natural history (birds).

Eliza Jones was a regular exhibitor at the Royal Academy, the British Institution and the Society of Painters in Watercolours between 1807 and 1852.

JONES, Emma E.. See **SOYER, Mrs**

JONES, Eugene Arthur
American, 20th century.
Born 1881, in Brooklyn; died 1965.
Painter. Landscapes.

Eugene Arthur Jones studied under J.H. Boston. He was a member of the Salmagundi Club.

JONES, Fitzedward
American, 19th century.
Engraver.

Fitzedward Jones produced dry-point and copper engravings of portraits and genre scenes. He was a printer and worked in Carlisle in Pennsylvania, and in Cincinnati in 1854.

JONES, Francis Coates
American, 19th - 20th century.
Born 25 July 1857, in Baltimore (Maryland); died 27 May 1932, in New York.
Illustrator, painter (gouache). Figures, interiors with figures, landscapes.

Francis Coates Jones studied under Boulanger and J. Lefebvre in Paris then at the École des Beaux-Arts. He became a member of the National Academy of Design in 1894. He was awarded medals in 1901 in Buffalo, and in 1904 in Saint Louis. He belonged to many of the most significant American artistic associations.

MUSEUMS AND GALLERIES:
CHICAGO: *Fishing in Alaska* (gouache); *The Four o'Clock Club* (gouache); *Interior in Alaska* - CHICAGO (Terra Foundation for American Art Collection): *Mother and Child* (c. 1885, oil on canvas).

AUCTION RECORDS:
NEW YORK, 24 Jan-2 Feb 1900, *A Young Visitor,* USD 270. NEW YORK, 23-24 Jan 1901, *Spring,* USD 330. NEW YORK, 17 Jan 1911, *Preparing the Feast,* USD 85; *Chloe,* USD 67. NEW YORK, 20 April 1979, *Lady and Lyre* (pastel, 12½ x 15 ins / 31.7 x 38.1 cm) USD 2,750. NEW YORK, 21 June 1979, *The Song* (oil on canvas, 24¼ x 40 ins / 61.5 x 101.6 cm) USD 9,750. NEW YORK, 3 June 1982, *Friends* (oil on canvas, 36¼ x 30¼ ins / 92 x 77 cm) USD 12,000. NEW YORK, 18 March 1983, *Girl Picking Wild Flowers* (oil on canvas, 26½ x 19½ ins / 67.2 x 49.3 cm) USD 15,000. NEW YORK, 30 Sept 1985, *Sunny Day* (oil on canvas, 36¼ x 30 ins / 92 x 76.5 cm) USD 3,500. NEW YORK, 20 March 1987, *Sunny Window* (oil on canvas, 27¼ x 22¼ ins / 69.2 x 56.8 cm) USD 20,000. NEW YORK, 1 Dec 1988, *Mother and Daughter Playing Checkers* (oil on canvas, 22 x 32 ins / 55.9 x 81.4 cm) USD 47,300. NEW YORK, 30 Nov 1989, *Candlelight Romance* (oil on canvas, 21¾ x 29¾ ins / 55.2 x 75.6 cm) USD 27,500. NEW YORK, 1 Dec 1989, *Baiting the Line* (oil on canvas, 19 x 26 ins / 48.2 x 66 cm) USD 41,800. NEW YORK, 12 April 1991, *The Water Carrier* (oil on canvas, 20 x 14 ins / 50.8 x 35.6 cm) USD 7,700. NEW YORK, 28 May 1992, *An Interesting Story* (oil on canvas, 27¼ x 22¼ ins / 69.2 x 56.5 cm) USD 49,500. NEW YORK, 4 Dec 1992, *Friends* (oil on canvas, 36 x 30 ins / 91.5 x 76.5 cm) USD 38,500. NEW YORK, 11 March 1993, *Lady and Lyre* (pastel/paper/card, 13 x 15½ ins / 33 x 39.5 cm) USD 13,800. NEW YORK, 23 Sept 1993, *Exchanging Confidences* (oil on canvas, 18½ x 20½ ins / 47 x 52.1 cm) USD 27,600. NEW YORK, 13 Sept 1995, *Women in a Rowing Boat* (oil on canvas, 21¼ x 31 ins / 54 x 78.8 cm) USD 64,100. NEW YORK, 30 Nov 1995, *Moments of Peace* (oil on canvas, 19 x 26¼ ins / 48.3 x 66.7 cm) USD 48,300. NEW YORK, 26 Sept 1996, *The Floral Bonnet* (oil on canvas, 10¼ x 14 ins / 26 x 35.6 cm) USD 5,462. NEW YORK, 27 Sept 1996, *Ponds and Rocks* (oil on canvas, 30 x 36 ins / 76.2 x 91.7 cm) USD 6,900.

JONES, Gaston
Belgian, 20th century.
Born 1891, in Merksem (Antwerp).
Painter. Military subjects, figures, portraits, interiors, still-lifes.

Gaston Jones was a pupil of Jean Mayné and Jos Dierickx at the Institut des Arts Décoratifs in Ixelles. He painted numerous scenes of life at the Front during World War I.

JONES, George
British, 19th century.
Born 1786, in London; died 1869.
Painter, draughtsman. Historical subjects, battles, figures, scenes with figures, genre scenes, interiors with figures, landscapes, urban landscapes, architectural views.

George Jones was the son of John Jones. He trained at the Royal Academy in 1801, became an associate in 1822 and a member in 1824. He followed Wellington in 1815. For his painting entitled *Waterloo* he received a payment of 200 pounds from the British Institute in 1820. During the wars of the Empire, he served in the English army and accompanied the troops who occupied Paris. He was one of the executors of Turner's will.

MUSEUMS AND GALLERIES:
BRISTOL: *Drawbridge* - GLASGOW: *The Relief of Lucknow; Fire of Magdala; Crossing the Ganges at Cawnpore* - LONDON (Victoria and Albert Mus.): *John Newton* - NOTTINGHAM (Castle Mus. & AG): *Napoleon Leaving Waterloo; Audernach, Prussia; Edinburgh Castle; Views of Nuremburg and Rome; Battle of Borodino; Scene in a Frankfurt Street* - SYDNEY: *Battle of Joppa.*
AUCTION RECORDS:
LONDON, 1872, *View of Strasbourg,* FRF 7,200. LONDON, 25 June 1908, *View of Abbeville* (1819) GBP 63. LONDON, 19 April 1909, *View of Inverness,* GBP 6. LONDON, 8 Feb 1946, *Market in Prague,* GBP 48. LONDON, 18 April 1978, *Town in Westphalia* (oil on panel, 35 1/4 x 27 1/2 ins / 89.5 x 70 cm) GBP 900. LONDON, 26 May 1989, *Interior Scenes: People with Marchal Ferrant - Women doing Laundry, others sitting in front of a fire* (oil on canvas, a pair, each 13 x 18 ins / 33.2 x 45.7 cm) GBP 3,080. LONDON, 11 July 1990, *Wellington and Napoleon at the Battle of Waterloo* (oil on canvas, a pair, each 23 x 35 ins / 58.5 x 89 cm) GBP 15,400. YORK, 12 Nov 1991, *People near a cottage on the Isle of Wight* (oil on canvas, 13 x 11 ins / 33 x 28 cm) GBP 1,430. PARIS, 8 June 1994, *Cavalrymen in Combat* (pen, ink and wash, 9 x 14 1/4 ins / 23 x 36.2 cm) FRF 6,200. LONDON, 16 May 1996, *Views of Cork: South Mall from Nelson's Quay; Parliament Bridge* (1813, brown and blue wash/greyish-blue paper, a pair, 5 x 7 1/4 ins / 12.5 x 18.5 cm and 5 1/4 x 7 ins/13.5 x 17.5 cm) GBP 5,060. LONDON, 4 March 2004, *Bristol Harbour. Pont Royal, Paris* (1825, oil on paper on canvas, a pair, 7 x 9 ins / 17 x 22 cm) GBP 3,000.

JONES, Glyn
British, 20th century.
Born 1920.
Painter. Scenes with figures.

Glyn Jones trained at the St Martin's School of Art in London and the École des Beaux-Arts in Paris. He lived in Colombia, Peru and Mexico after the end of World War II. Jones's painting features imagery drawn from the legends and mythology of South America. His characteristic scenes of musicians playing are notable for their magical atmosphere. His work has featured in a number of group exhibitions and one-man shows since 1954: Havana, Miami, Palm Beach, Barcelona, Madrid, Grenoble and St-Étienne.

JONES, Grace Church
American, 20th century.
Born 1868, in West Falls (New York); died 1959.
Painter.

Grace Church Jones studied in Paris at the Académie Colarossi and the Grande Chaumière. She was a member of the American Federation of Arts.

JONES, Hugh Bolton, or Bolton-Jones
American, 19th - 20th century.
Born 20 October 1848, in Baltimore; died 1927.
Painter. Landscapes.

Hugh Bolton Jones studied in Baltimore. He painted mostly spring and summer landscapes. After a study tour in France and Italy, he moved to New York in 1881. From 1873 to 1883, he exhibited landscapes at the Royal Academy and Suffolk Street in London. He was awarded medals at World fairs in Paris, Chicago, Saint Louis (gold) and also a silver medal at the Panama-Pacific exhibition in San Francisco in 1915.
MUSEUMS AND GALLERIES:
ALBANY (Institute of History and Art): *Early Spring* - BALTIMORE (Peabody Art Collection): *A Quiet Morning* (1872, oil on canvas); *Near Union Bridge, Maryland* (1873, oil on canvas) - CHICAGO (AI): *Oasis in Tunis* - LIVERPOOL (Walker AG): *Falling Leaves* - MINNEAPOLIS (Walker Art Center): *Geneva* - NEW YORK (Brooklyn Mus.): *Landscape* - NEW YORK (Metropolitan Mus. of Art): *Spring; Autumn* - PHILADELPHIA (Pennsylvania Academy of the Fine Arts Gal.): *Meadow* - PORTAVON - WASHINGTON DC (Corcoran Gal. of Art): *Diverse Pieces.*
AUCTION RECORDS:
NEW YORK, 1901, *Landscape,* USD 390. NEW YORK, 29 April 1977, *River Port* (oil on canvas, 18 x 30 ins / 45.7 x 76.2 cm) USD 1,600. NEW YORK, 21 June 1978, *The Old Mill* (1872, oil on canvas, 30 x 54 1/4 ins / 76 x 137.5 cm) USD 11,000. NEW YORK, 25 Oct 1979, *South End of Wooded Island* (1893, oil on canvas, 20 1/4 x 28 1/4 ins / 51.5 x 71.7 cm) USD 11,500. NEW YORK, 30 Sept 1982, *Riverscape in the Spring* (oil on canvas, 16 x 24 ins / 40.8 x 61.1 cm) USD 8,500. NEW YORK, 30 May 1985, *Village Road* (oil on canvas, 18 x 30 ins / 45.7 x 76.2 cm) USD 16,000. NEW YORK, 28 May 1987, *Winter Landscape* (oil on canvas, 14 x 22 1/2 ins / 35.5 x 57.2 cm) USD 12,500. NEW YORK, 26 May 1988, *Early Spring* (oil on canvas, 16 x 24 ins / 40.8 x 61.1 cm) USD 30,800. NEW YORK, 30 Sept 1988, *Lush Spring* (oil on canvas, 14 x 20 ins / 35.5 x 50.8 cm) USD 4,400. NEW YORK, 24 May 1989, *Wooded Stream in the Morning* (oil on canvas, 29 3/4 x 36 ins / 75.5 x 91.5 cm) USD 13,200. NEW YORK, 28 Sept 1989, *Landscape with Ducks* (1868, oil on canvas, 18 1/4 x 36 1/4 ins / 46.3 x 92 cm) USD 24,200. NEW YORK, 14 Feb 1990, *New Jersey Landscape* (oil on canvas, 18 x 24 ins / 46 x 61.2 cm) USD 3,300. NEW YORK, 26 Sept 1990, *Spring Landscape* (oil on canvas, 20 x 24 ins / 50.8 x 61 cm) USD 13,200. NEW YORK, 30 Nov 1990, *Rocky Wooded Landscape* (oil on canvas, 24 x 39 3/4 ins / 61 x 101.2 cm) USD 19,800. NEW YORK, 14 March 1991, *The Lily Pond* (oil on canvas, 18 x 26 ins / 45.9 x 66 cm) USD 14,300. NEW YORK, 26 Sept 1991, *The Cumberland Valley* (1873, oil on canvas, 30 1/4 x 54 ins / 77 x 137 cm) USD 28,600. NEW YORK, 14 Nov 1991, *Near Stockbridge* (oil on canvas, 30 x 36 1/4 ins / 76.5 x 92 cm) USD 2,640. NEW YORK, 5 Dec 1991, *Autumn Landscape* (oil on canvas, 15 1/2 x 23 1/2 ins / 39.4 x 59.7 cm) USD 9,900. NEW YORK, 12 March 1992, *The Susquehanna River* (1873, oil on canvas, 16 1/4 x 26 ins / 41 x 66 cm) USD 33,000. NEW YORK, 28 May 1992, *Autumn Reflections* (oil on canvas, 16 x 24 ins / 40.8 x 61.2 cm) USD 26,400. NEW YORK, 10 March 1993, *Landscape with Cows by a Stream* (oil on canvas, 12 x 23 ins / 30.5 x 58.4 cm) USD 10,925. NEW YORK, 1 Dec 1994, *Old Foundry* (1870, oil on canvas, 30 1/4 x 54 1/4 ins / 76.8 x 137.8 cm) USD 18,400. PARIS, 19 Feb 1996, *Cows at the Trough* (oil on canvas, 15 3/4 x 19 3/4 ins / 40 x 50 cm) FRF 8,500. NEW YORK, 23 May 1996, *Meadow Crossing* (oil on canvas, 30 x 36 ins / 76.2 x 91.5 cm) USD 32,200. NEW YORK, 27 Sept 1996, *Gathering Leaves* (1878, oil on canvas, 22 x 16 ins / 55.9 x 40.6 cm) USD 16,100. NEW YORK, 4 Dec 1996, *Early Spring near Sheffield, Massashussetts* (oil on canvas, 24 x 37 1/2 ins / 61 x 95.3 cm) USD 37,950. NEW YORK, 3 Dec 1997, *Maples in Spring.*

JONES, Ignatius or Inigo
British, 16th - 17th century.
Born 15 July 1573, in London; died 21 June 1652, in London.
Draughtsman, architect. Figures, architectural views.

Inigo Jones was sponsored by Charles I to work in England, Italy, and Denmark and is best known for his architectural work.
MUSEUMS AND GALLERIES:
LONDON (British Architectural Library): numerous drawings.
AUCTION RECORDS:
LONDON, 20 March 1979, *Two Heads of Bearded Men* (pen, 3 1/4 x 3 1/2 ins / 8 x 8.7 cm) GBP 800.

JONES, J.
British, 18th century.
Active in England at the beginning of the 18th century.
Painter. Portraits.

AUCTION RECORDS:
LONDON, 5 May 1911, *Portraits of a Gentleman and a Lady* (two pendants signed and dated 1720) GBP 15; *Portraits of Ladies* (two pendants dated and signed 1720) GBP 4. PARIS, 23 Feb 1920, *Young Girl Holding a Garland of Roses* (pastel) FRF 650. LONDON, 30 Jan 1985, *Portrait of a Boy and a Little Girl* (1713, oil on canvas, a pair, 29 1/2 x 24 1/2 ins / 75 x 62 cm) GBP 6,000.

JONES, Joe
British, 20th century.
Born 1909; died 1963.
Painter, watercolourist. Landscapes, still-lifes.

Joe Jones's watercolours are characterised by their use of 'spiritual' signs, reminiscent of notation. His style shows the influence of Dufy and John Marin.

AUCTION RECORDS:
NEW YORK, 30 Jan 1980, *Cornfield* (1941, oil on canvas, 30 x 40 ins / 76.2 x 101.6 cm) USD 3,750. NEW YORK, 16 March 1990, *Hope and Hard Times* (1939, oil on canvas, 72 x 36 1/2 ins / 183 x 92.4 cm) USD 14,300. NEW YORK, 27 Sept 1990, *Harvest* (1935, oil/synthetic resin, 36 3/4 x 48 3/4 ins / 93.5 x 124 cm) USD 66,000. NEW YORK, 31 March 1994, *Industrial City* (oil on canvas, 26 x 30 ins / 66 x 76.2 cm) USD 6,325. NEW YORK, 21 Sept 1994, *Rye Harvest* (oil on canvas, 24 x 36 ins / 61 x 91.4 cm) USD 6,900.

JONES, John
British, 18th century.
Born c. 1745; died 1797.
Engraver (mezzotint/stippling).

John Jones was one of the finest of the English school. He worked in London where he met with considerable success reproducing the best of the masters: Reynolds, Romney, Gainsborough, Hone, Mortimer, Bigg, Singleton, Bartolozzi and Downman, among others. His work, which appeared between 1774 and 1791 was carried out in mezzotint and stippling and, for the most part, handled historical subjects and portraits. He was nominated engraver to the Prince of Wales and the Duke of York.

JONES, John
British, 18th century.
Painter. Portraits.

John Jones was registered in the guild in the Hague.

BIBLIOGRAPHY:
Smith, John, *A Catalogue Raisonné of the Works of the Most Eminent Dutch, Flemish and French Painters*, Smith and Son, London, 1829-1942.

JONES, John Edward
Irish, 19th century.
Born 1806, in Dublin; died July 1862, in Dublin.
Active in London.
Sculptor. Figures, historical figures. Busts.

John Edward Jones exhibited at the Royal Academy between 1842 and 1862. He sculpted busts of Queen Victoria, the Prince Consort, Napoleon III, Louis-Philippe, the King of Holland and Wellington, among others.

MUSEUMS AND GALLERIES:
BIRMINGHAM: *Sir Robert Peel* - DUBLIN: *William Dargan; Daniel O'Connell; Queen Victoria* - VERSAILLES: *Lord Mayor Charles Magnay*.

JONES, Josiah Clinton
British, 19th - 20th century.
Born 1848; died 1936.
Active in Conway.
Painter. Landscapes with figures, landscapes.

Josiah Clinton Jones was a member of the Royal Cambrian Academy. He exhibited in London, notably at the Royal Academy, from 1885.

MUSEUMS AND GALLERIES:
BLACKBURN (Mus. & AG): *Blakey Moor, Blackburn* (watercolour, urban landscape); *Dinckley Passage* - LIVERPOOL (Walker AG): *Moel Siabod; October Morning; View of Snowdon from Anglesey*.

AUCTION RECORDS:
MONTREAL, 6 Dec 1994, *Young Boys Fishing from a Stone Bridge* (oil on canvas, 20 1/2 x 16 1/4 ins / 52 x 41 cm) CAD 1,100.

JONES, Kim
American, 20th century.
Born 1944, in San Bernardino (California).
Performance artist, installation artist.

Kim Jones is the creator numerous performance works, including: 1981, Art Institute of Chicago; 1982, in Brooklyn, New York; 1985, at the Paris Biennale. His work has also been the subject of a number of solo exhibitions, notably in New York in 1982, and Los Angeles in 1980. One performance featured the artist carrying an eclectic assortment of objects on his back, such as wooden framework structures, string, rolls of paper, metal bars and sticks.

JONES, Leon Forster
British, 19th - 20th century.
Born 18 October 1871, in Manchester.
Active in the USA.
Painter. Landscapes.

Leon Forster Jones studied in Boston and settled in New York. He was a member of the Salmagundi Club. In 1915 he exhibited two paintings in the *Panama-Pacific International Exhibition* in San Francisco, and was awarded a silver medal.

MUSEUMS AND GALLERIES:
BOSTON (MFA): *Winter landscape; Suncook River (New Hampshire)*.

JONES, Lois Mailou
American, 20th century.
Born 3 November 1905, in Boston; died 9 June 1998, in Washington DC.
Painter, draughtswoman, illustrator, watercolourist, textile artist. Figures, nudes, portraits, genre scenes, street scenes, landscapes, still-lifes.

Lois Mailou Jones graduated in textile design from the School of the Museum of Fine Arts, Boston, and went on to study further at the Designers Art School, Boston, Columbia University Teachers College, New York, and Howard University, Washington DC. In 1937 she went to Paris, where she studied at the Académie Julian and the Académie de la Grande Chaumière. She worked as a textile designer with the F.A. Foster Company in Boston and the Schumacher Company in New York, and taught at Howard University, Washington DC, from 1930 to 1977, where she ended her career as professor emeritus. She married the Haitian painter Louis Vergniaud Pierre-Noel in 1953.

At the beginning of her career, Lois Mailou Jones painted in the Impressionist tradition. From 1939 to 1945, her attention turned to the condition of Black Americans, as in *Mob Victim* (1944), in which an old man, his hands tied, his face tired and resigned, waits to be lynched. She then enlarged her vocabulary, adding formal African symbolism. Her work may be classified by geography: her American period, her French period (she produced some forty works in Paris), her Haitian period (she lived in Haiti) and her African period (she visited a dozen African countries). She also designed textiles. In addition, she illustrated many books, such as Eloise Culver Crosby's *Great American Negroes in Verse, 1723-1965* (Associated Publishers, Washington DC, 1966), and children's books such as Jane Dabney Shackelford's *The Child's Story of the Negro* (Associated Publishers, Washington DC, 1956).

Lois Jones took part in many group exhibitions, such as in 1930 at the Harmon Foundation, New York; 1937, Exposition des Beaux-Arts et Arts Décoratifs, Asnières; 1938, 1966, Société des Artistes Français, Paris; 1944, National Academy of Design, New York; 1976, *Two Centuries of Black American Art*, Los Angeles County Museum of Art; 1980, *Forever Free, Art by African-American Women, 1862-1980*, Center for the Visual Arts Gallery, Illinois State University, Normal and 1996, *Exploration of the City of Light: African-American Artists in Paris, 1945-1960*, Studio Museum in Harlem, New York. After her death, her work was included in thematic group exhibitions, including in 1999, *To Conserve a Legacy. American Art from Historically Black Colleges and Universities*, Addison Gallery of American Art, Phillips Academy, Andover, Massachusetts and 2003, *African-American Artists, 1929-1945. Prints, Drawings and Paintings in the Metropolitan Museum of Art*, Metropolitan Museum of Art, New York.

Among her solo exhibitions were, 1944, Vose Art Gallery, Boston; 1972, Howard University Gallery of Art, Washington DC and 1973, Museum of Fine Arts and National Center of Afro-American Artists, Boston. In 1983, she exhibited with her husband Vergniaud Pierre-Noël, *Lois & Pierre: two master artists*, National Center of Afro-American Artists, Boston. Posthumous retrospectives of her work included *Lois Mailou Jones and Her Former Students: An American Legacy*, Mint Museum of Art and Afro-American Cultural Center, Charlotte, 1999.

Jones received honorary doctorates from Suffolk University, Boston; Colorado State Christian University, Evergreen, in 1972; Massachusetts College of Art, North Adams; and Howard University, Washington DC. In 1962, she was also elected to the Royal Society of Arts of London. She won numerous awards, notably for her part in founding the art departments of Palmer Art Institute, Sedalia, North Carolina, and Howard University, as well as for promoting the work of African-American artists.

BIBLIOGRAPHY:

Lois Mailou Jones - Peintures, 1937-1951, exhibition catalogue, Presses Georges Frères, Tourcoing, 1952 (text in English and French). *Lois Mailou Jones. Reflective Moment*, exhibition catalogue, Museum of the National Center of Afro-American Artists, Museum of Fine Arts, Boston, 1973. Driskell, David C., *Two Centuries of Black American Art*, group exhibition catalogue, Los Angeles County Museum of Art, Los Angeles, 1976. Tritobia Hayes, Benjamin, *The Life and Art of Lois Mailou Jones*, Pomegranate Artbooks, San Francisco, 1994. Powell, Richard J./Reynolds, Jock, *To Conserve a Legacy. American Art from Historically Black Colleges and Universities*, group exhibition catalogue, Addison Gall. of American Art, Phillips Academy, Andover (MA), 1999. Mintz Messinger, Lisa, et al., *African-American Artists, 1929-1945. Prints, Drawings and Paintings in the Metropolitan Museum of Art*, Metropolitan Museum of Art, New York, 2003.

MUSEUMS AND GALLERIES:

BOSTON (MFA): *Ubi Girl from Tai Region* (1972, oil on canvas) - BOSTON (Mus. of the National Center of Afro-American Artists) - NEW YORK (Metropolitan Mus. of Art): *Cauliflower and Pumpkin* (1938) - PORT-AU-PRINCE (Palais national) - WASHINGTON DC (GA, Howard University): *Jennie* (1943, oil on canvas) - WASHINGTON DC (Hirshhorn Mus. and Sculpture Garden): *Challenge-America* (1964, mixed media/canvas) - WASHINGTON DC (National Mus. of Women In the Arts): *Sketch for Ode to Kinshasa* (1972); *Ode to Kinshasa* (1972, mixed media on canvas) - WASHINGTON DC (National Portrait Gal.) - WASHINGTON DC (Smithsonian American AM): *Les Fétiches (Fetishes)* (1938, oil/linen); *Jardin du Luxembourg* (c. 1948, oil on canvas).

AUCTION RECORDS:

NORTH BETHESDA, 19 May 2002, *Canal Scene* (1952, oil on canvas, 21 x 26 ins / 54 x 65 cm) USD 14,500. WASHINGTON, 14 Dec 2002, *Canal, Georgetown* (1939, oil on canvas, 20 x 24 ins / 50 x 61 cm) USD 16,000. WASHINGTON, 13 Dec 2003, *Voodoo* (oil and gold leaf on canvas, 24 x 30 ins / 62 x 75 cm) USD 14,000.

JONES, Lonie Johnson

British, 19th century.

Born 1856, in Holywell, Wales.

Painter. Animals.

Lonie Johnson Jones trained in London. From 1807 to 1810, she painted murals for the church of Holywell, her home town in Wales. She also painted a long frieze of horses in a landscape for Cheadle Royal in Cheshire. Three exhibitions of her work were organized in London by the Colnaghi house of art.

AUCTION RECORDS:

LONDON, 15 May 1987, *Spaniel* (oil on canvas, 20 x 24 ins / 50.8 x 61 cm) GBP 1,800. NEW YORK, 12 Feb 2002, *Study of a Hound* (1917, oil on canvas, 18 x 16 ins / 46 x 40 cm) USD 3,000. DUBLIN, 14 April 2003, *Study of a Horse in a Stable* (oil on canvas, 17 x 20 ins / 42 x 52 cm) GBP 4,500.

JONES, Louis Edward

American, 20th century.

Born 7 March 1878, in Rushville (Pennsylvania).

Painter.

Louis Jones studied at the Academy of Fine Arts in Philadelphia. He was a member of the Salmagundi Club and of the American Federation of Arts.

JONES, Marion

Australian, 19th - 20th century.

Born in Bendigo.

Painter. Portraits, flowers.

Marion Jones exhibited in Sydney, with the Royal Academy in London, and in Liverpool. She may be the artist also known as Marion Alexandra Clayton-Jones.

MUSEUMS AND GALLERIES:

MELBOURNE - SYDNEY (National Academy).

JONES, Maud Raphael

British, 19th - 20th century.

Painter, watercolourist. Landscapes.

MUSEUMS AND GALLERIES:

BRADFORD (Cartwright Hall AG): *February* (1898).

AUCTION RECORDS:

LONDON, 21 May 1986, *Young Boy beside a Stream* (1894, oil on canvas, 13 x 20 ins / 33 x 51 cm) GBP 4,500.

JONES, Nancy Christine

American, 20th century.

Born 7 May 1888, in Providence (Rhode Island).

Painter.

Nancy Jones studied at the École des Beaux-Arts in Paris and often worked in Fontainebleau. She was a member of the American Federation of Arts.

JONES, Owen

British, 19th century.

Born 1809, in London; died 1874, in London.

Draughtsman, architect, designer. Ornaments.

Owen Jones was more of an architect than an artist; however, his work in decoration was important enough for it to be recognised. After he had completed his training at the Royal Academy, he travelled in Europe and the Orient. In 1834, he visited Granada where the Alhambra became the focus of his attention to the point that he made 101 coloured plates of it (1845). In 1851 he was made Superintendant of Works for the Great Exhibition in London, and was responsible for the decoration of the Crystal Palace. He also wrote several pieces on decoration, including *The Grammar of Ornament* (1856).

MUSEUMS AND GALLERIES:

LONDON (Victoria and Albert Mus.): *Decoration for the transept of the Crystal Palace.* (watercolour).

JONES, Paul

British, 19th century.
Active from 1856 to 1888.
Painter. Genre scenes, animals.

AUCTION RECORDS:

LONDON, 14 Dec 1976, *Rough Shooting* (1877, two oils on card, $7\frac{3}{4}$ x $5\frac{1}{2}$ ins / 20 x 14 cm) GBP 660. LONDON, 2 Feb 1979, *Hunting Scenes* (1873, two oils on canvas, $7\frac{1}{2}$ x $11\frac{3}{4}$ ins / 19 x 29.8 cm) GBP 1,000. AUCHTERARDER, 1 Sept 1981, *Hunters in Landscapes* (1873, oil on canvas, a pair, each $7\frac{3}{4}$ x 12 ins / 20 x 30.5 cm) GBP 1,900. LONDON, 3 Nov 1989, *Hunter; Near a Stream* (1879, oil on canvas, a pair, 12 x 18 ins / 30.5 x 45.8 cm) GBP 8,800. LONDON, 14 Feb 1990, *Young boy feeding terriers scraps before the hearth* (1856, oil on canvas, 10 x 13 ins / 25.3 x 33 cm) GBP 1,210. LONDON, 13 June 1990, *Norfolk Terriers* (1880, oil on canvas, a pair, each $8\frac{1}{4}$ x 14 ins / 21 x 35.5 cm) GBP 1,650. NEW YORK, 7 June 1991, *Work: Flushing a Mallard; Leisure: End of the Day* (oil on canvas, a pair, each 8 x 10 ins / 20.3 x 25.4 cm) USD 4,950. PERTH, 26 Aug 1991, *Young Hunter* (1883, oil on canvas, 12 x 18 ins / 30.5 x 46 cm) GBP 4,400. LONDON, 11 Oct 1991, *Day's End* (1883, oil on canvas, 12 x 18 ins / 30.5 x 45.5 cm) GBP 1,540. PERTH, 31 Aug 1993, *After the Deer Hunt* (1876, oil on canvas, $7\frac{3}{4}$ x 12 ins / 20 x 30.5 cm) GBP 2,070. PERTH, 29 Aug 1995, *Spaniels Pointing a Wild Duck* (1857, oil on canvas, a pair, each 8 x 10 ins / 20.5 x 25.5 cm) GBP 2,300. LONDON, 5 Sept 1996, *Terriers Hunting Rats; Terriers Hunting Rabbits* (1857, oil on canvas, a pair, each 8 x 10 ins / 20.3 x 25.4 cm) GBP 1,035. LONDON, 10 July 1997, *After the Deer Hunt* (1876, oil on canvas, $7\frac{1}{2}$ x $11\frac{1}{2}$ ins / 19 x 29.2 cm) GBP 4,830. CAMBRIDGE, 25 March 1999, *Dogs Stalking and Retrieving* (1858, oil on canvas, set of four, 8 x 10 ins / 20 x 25 cm) GBP 4,000. CHESTER, 10 June 1999, *Terriers at Rabbit Hole, Pointers Picking up Scent* (1872, oil on canvas, a pair, 8 x 12 ins / 20 x 30 cm) GBP 2,500. LONDON, 21 June 2000, *Putting up Duck. Terriers by a Burrow* (1868, oil on canvas, a pair, 7 x 10 ins / 18 x 25 cm) GBP 2,700. BISHOPS STORTFORD, 1 Aug 2000, *Pony and Dogs by Mountain Lake* (1871, oil on canvas, 7 x 11 ins / 19 x 29 cm) GBP 2,600. NEW YORK, 13 Feb 2001, *Terriers* (1860, oil on canvas, 8 x 10 ins / 20 x 25 cm) USD 4,250. LONDON, 14 June 2001, *Terriers with Rabbit. Terriers at Rabbit Hole. Terriers with Rat. Terriers with a Caged Rat* (1859, oil on canvas, set of four, 8 x 10 ins / 20 x 25 cm) GBP 3,400. NEW YORK, 12 Feb 2002, *Terriers Ratting* (1857, oil on canvas, a pair, 8 x 10 ins / 20 x 25 cm) USD 2,300. NEW YORK, 12 Feb 2002, *Terriers Hunting* (1882, oil on canvas, a pair, 8 x 12 ins / 20 x 30 cm) USD 4,250. CANTERBURY, 12 Aug 2003, *Scottish Highland Scenes* (1868, oil on canvas, a pair, 8 x 12 ins / 20 x 30 cm) GBP 5,200. LONDON, 3 Dec 2003, *Waiting for Master. Fallen Stag* (oil on canvas, a pair, 8 x 12 ins / 20 x 30 cm) GBP 3,200. LONDON, 4 March 2004, *Rest at the Fence. The Day's Bag* (1873, oil on panel, a pair, 7 x 5 ins / 19 x 13 cm) GBP 2,800. SAN FRANCISCO, 30 March 2004, *Setters in a Landscape. Terriers* (1872, 1873, oil on canvas, a pair, 8 x 12 ins / 20 x 30 cm) USD 6,500.

JONES, Paul

American, 19th century.
Born 9 June 1860, in Harrodsburg (Kentucky).
Painter. Portraits.

Paul Jones was a pupil of Flameng, Courtois and Laurens in Paris. He specialised in portraits.

JONES, R.

British, 18th - 19th century.
Active in London.
Painter.

R. Jones, as an honorary exhibitor, exhibited the following works at the Royal Academy between 1780 and 1812: *Head of an Old Man, Portrait of a Woman, Plan for the Transformation of a House, Ajax* and *Bard.*

JONES, R.

British, 19th century.
Active in Reading and London.
Painter. Sporting subjects.

R. Jones exhibited at the Royal Academy from 1818 to 1820.

AUCTION RECORDS:

LONDON, 25 Nov 1977, *Horse and Dog in a Landscape* (oil on canvas, $27\frac{1}{2}$ x $35\frac{1}{4}$ ins / 70 x 89.5 cm) GBP 1,400.

JONES, Reginald

British, 19th century.
Born 1857, in Old Charlton (Kent).
Painter, watercolourist.

Reginald Jones exhibited in London, notably at the Royal Academy, the Suffolk Street Gallery and at the New Water-Colour Society after 1880. He also exhibited at the Salon des Artistes Français where he received a honourable mention in 1904.

MUSEUMS AND GALLERIES:

MONTREAL: *In the Virgin Forest.*

JONES, Ronald

American, 20th - 21st century.
Born 1952.
Sculptor, installation artist, mixed media.

Ronald Jones lives and works in New York. He has exhibited in the USA from the early 1980s, and held his first exhibition in France in 1992. His work is steeped in art historical references, from Surrealism to classical art, and also reveals a strong commitment to socio-political and historical issues. His sculptures, which use realistic albeit simplified forms, are accompanied by texts calculated to provoke, thereby allowing the viewer to penetrate to the heart of the work.

JONES, S. (Mrs)

British, 18th - 19th century.
Miniaturist.

Mrs S. Jones worked in London where she frequently exhibited at the Royal Academy between 1797 and 1812.

JONES, Samuel John Egbert

British, 19th century.
Active from 1820 to 1849 in London.
Painter. Sporting subjects.

Samuel John Egbert Jones frequently exhibited in London, notably at the Royal Academy, the British Institution and the Suffolk Street Gallery between 1820 and 1845.

AUCTION RECORDS:

LONDON, 21 June 1926, *The Meet,* GBP 136. LONDON, 26 June 1929, *Fox Hunting Scene,* GBP 700. LONDON, 18 June 1931, *Landscape with Men Fishing,* GBP 100. LONDON, 25 May 1934, *Duck Shoot* (four paintings) GBP 399. LONDON, 17 May 1946, *Pheasant Shoot,* GBP 47; *Pheasant Shoot,* GBP 84. LONDON, 25 April 1969, *Hunting Scenes* (two pendants) Gns 5,500. NEW YORK, 7 Oct 1977, *Hunting Scenes* (two pendants, 14 x 18 ins / 35.5 x 46 cm) USD 5,000. LONDON, 27 June 1980, *Horse in a Landscape* (1827, oil on canvas, 41 x 59 ins / 104.1 x 149.8 cm) GBP 2,800. LONDON, 16 July 1982, *Hunt Scenes* (two oils on canvas, $19\frac{3}{4}$ x $23\frac{1}{2}$ ins / 50.2 x 59.6 cm) GBP 4,800. NEW YORK, 10 June 1983, *Trout Fishermen* (oil on canvas, $14\frac{3}{4}$ x 18 ins / 37.5 x 45.8 cm) USD 4,000. NEW YORK, 29 Oct 1986, *Hunting Scenes* (oil on canvas, a pair, 20 x 24 ins / 50.8 x 61 cm) USD 16,000. LONDON, 16 Oct 1987, *Wooded Landscapes* (1830, oil on canvas, a pair, 20 x $24\frac{1}{4}$ ins / 50.8 x 61.3 cm) GBP 6,000. LONDON, 17 Nov 1989, *Gentleman Hunting with his Dogs* (oil on canvas, a pair, $19\frac{3}{4}$ x 24 ins / 50 x 61 cm) GBP 33,000. LONDON, 15 Nov 1991, *Partridge Shoot; Woodgrouse Shoot* (oil on canvas, a pair, each 23 x 29 ins /

58.4 x 73.6 cm) GBP 22,000. NEW YORK, 5 June 1992, *Dogs Flushing a Pheasant* (oil on canvas, 17 3/4 x 24 ins / 45.1 x 61 cm) USD 7,425. LONDON, 15 Dec 1993, *Pheasant Shoot; Hare Hunt* (oil on canvas, each 10 x 11 3/4 ins / 25.4 x 29.8 cm) GBP 9,200. LONDON, 9 March 2000, *Gypsy Encampment* (1813, oil on canvas, 28 x 36 ins / 71 x 91 cm) GBP 3,800. CLEVELAND, 14 Sept 2000, *Huntsmen and Dogs* (oil on canvas, a pair, 10 x 12 ins / 25 x 30 cm) USD 3,400. LONDON, 5 Sept 2001, *Shooting on a Heath* (oil on canvas on panel, 9 x 11 ins / 22 x 28 cm) GBP 3,800. MELBOURNE, 27 Nov 2002, *English River Scene* (1851, oil on canvas, 24 x 36 ins / 61 x 91 cm) AUD 5,000.

JONES, Sophia
British, 18th century.
Active in London.
Miniaturist.

Sophia Jones exhibited at the Royal Academy from 1798 to 1796.

JONES, Susan
American, 20th century.
Born 12 December 1897, in Philadelphia.
Painter. Portraits, still-lifes.

Susan Jones Studied at the Pennsylvania Academy of Fine Arts of which she was a member.

JONES, Sydney Robert
British, 20th century.
Born 1881.
Painter, engraver, watercolourist, illustrator.
Landscapes.

Sydney Robert Jones trained at Birmingham College of Art, and travelled throughout France, Belgium and Holland studying architectural and landscape drawing. In 1907 he exhibited with the Royal Academy in London; his etchings, watercolours and drawings subsequently featured in numerous exhibitions throughout the British Isles. He won a jury commendation at the Paris Salon des Artistes Français in 1922. Jones is noted for his numerous book illustrations, including plates for Charles Vince's work *England in France*. His best-known etchings include: *Magnus Martyr, London Bridge, Harvard House, Stratford-upon-Avon, Village Church.*

JONES, T.
British, 19th century.
Active c. 1820.
Engraver (aquatint).

T. Jones produced engravings including: *Portrait of the Conjurer, Henry,* based on the artist's own drawing, two portraits of *The Singer Hughes* in Weber's *Oberon* after W. McCall, as well as some plates for *London Singer Magazine*.

JONES, T. H.
British, 19th century.
Active in London.
Draughtsman. Figures, urban landscapes, architectural views.

MUSEUMS AND GALLERIES:
LONDON (British Mus.): *George; Nell Gwyn's House; St James's Square; Hyde Park Gate.*

JONES, T. Hampson
British, 19th - 20th century.
Active in Liverpool.
Painter, watercolourist. Genre scenes, landscapes, seascapes.

T. Hampson Jones exhibited regularly at the Royal Academy from 1874, as well as with the Royal Society of Painters in Watercolours and the Grosvenor Gallery.

MUSEUMS AND GALLERIES:
LIVERPOOL: *Summer in Sussex.*

AUCTION RECORDS:
LONDON, 25 June 1909, *Sussex Village* (1883) GBP 11. CHESTER, 20 July 1989, *Small Messengers* (1892, watercolour and gouache, 7 1/4 x 13 3/4 ins / 18.5 x 35 cm) GBP 748.

JONES, T. L.
Australian.
Active in Melbourne.
Landscape artist.

MUSEUMS AND GALLERIES:
SYDNEY: *A Dry Season.*

JONES, T.W.
British, 19th century.
Active in London.
Painter. History painting.

T.W. Jones exhibited in London, notably at the Royal Academy, the British Institution and at the Suffolk Street Gallery from 1832 to 1871.

JONES, Thomas
British, 19th century.
Born 1742, in Llandrindod Wells; died 29 April 1803, in Llandrindod Wells.
Active in London.
Painter, watercolourist. Landscapes.

Thomas Jones was the second son of a Welsh landowner. He left his career in the church to devote himself to painting. In London, he was a student of Henry Pars and became connected with the landscape artist, Richard Wilson. His *Memoirs* were published in 1951.

Jones exhibited in 1769 at the Society of Artists; from 1806 to 1835, he showed his work at the British Institution and the New Water-Colour Society in London. He was rediscovered in 1970 when his landscapes were put on exhibition in Marble Hill in London. In 2001, his works were included in the exhibition *Un Paese incantato. Italia dipinta da Thomas Jones a Corot* (*An Enchanted Countryside. Italy painted by Thomas Jones and Corot*) held at Palazzo Te, the international centre of art and culture in Mantua, Italy. In 2003, on the occasion of the bicentenary of his death, the National Museum and Gallery in Cardiff organized a retrospective.

Jones began by painting landscapes featuring mythological figures. His *Landscape with Dido and Aeneas* with figures painted by John Mortimer was purchased by Catherine II about the year 1785. Following this period, Jones left his studio to paint the landscapes of Wales in the open air. His stay in Italy, which started in 1776, allowed him to perfect his oil on paper technique in a series of views of Naples which were remarkable for the simplicity of the subjects chosen, his interest in light and his viewpoint. Nowadays, he is considered to be one of the precursers of the modern landscape, joining the English painters Wright of Derby and Cozens and the French Valenciennes, Michallon and, naturally, Corot. In 1783, he returned to England, easy success having eluded him.

BIBLIOGRAPHY:
Thomas Jones, 1742-1803, exhibition catalogue, Marble Hill House, Twickenham, 1970. Gowing, Lawrence, *The Originality of Thomas Jones*, Thames and Hudson, London, 1985. Ottani Cavina, Anna (ed.), *Un Paese incantato. Italia dipinta da Thomas Jones a Corot*, exhibition catalogue, Electa, Milan, 2001. Sumner, Anne, et al., *Thomas Jones (1742-1803) An Artist Rediscovered*, exhibition catalogue, National Museum and Gall., Cardiff, 2003. Egerton, Judy, '*Thomas Jones*' in *Burlington Magazine* vol. CXLV n° 1205, periodical, London, August 2003.

MUSEUMS AND GALLERIES:
BIRMINGHAM (Mus. and AG): *Cupola on the Hill of Naples* (oil on paper) - CARDIFF (National Mus. and Gal.): *Houses in Naples* (oil on paper) - DUBLIN (NG of Ireland): *View over the Rooftops* - LONDON (Tate Collection): *Wall in Naples* (oil on

canvas); *Posillipo Grotto* (oil on paper); *Capella Nuova seen beyond the Chiaia Gate* (oil on paper); *Excavating a bulding from antiquity in a cave at Villa Negroni* (oil on paper); *Houses built on Rocks in Naples* (oil on paper) - SWANSEA (Glynn Vivian Art Gallery and Mus.): *Ruined House in Naples* (oil on paper).

AUCTION RECORDS:

LONDON, 26 July 1961, *View of Tivoli* (drawing) GBP 420. LONDON, 4 April 1973, *Traveller in a Wooded Landscape with Naples in the Background,* GBP 1,900. LONDON, 23 March 1979, *Façade of a House in Naples* (1782, oil on paper remounted on board, 4 1/2 x 6 ins / 11.3 x 15.2 cm) GBP 5,500. LONDON, 7 July 1982, *A storm: Prospero, Miranda and Caliban espying the shipwrecked 'Ferdinand'* (1778, oil on canvas, 46 3/4 x 59 1/2 ins / 119 x 151 cm) GBP 8,500. LONDON, 21 Nov 1984, *Piperno* (heightened watercolour, 9 x 12 3/4 ins / 23 x 32.5 cm) GBP 1,700. LONDON, 11 March 1987, *River Landscape with Figures Beside a Dam* (1775, oil on canvas, 17 x 23 1/4 ins / 43 x 59 cm) GBP 5,000. LONDON, 14 March 1990, *Landscape with Figures Overlooking a River Valley; Elegant Company on a Hill Overlooking Rome* (oil on canvas, a pair, each 18 x 25 1/4 ins / 45.5 x 64 cm) GBP 44,000. ROME, 19 Nov 1991, *River Landscape with Figures* (1775, oil on canvas, 33 x 47 1/4 ins / 84 x 120 cm) ITL 38,000,000. LONDON, 9 April 1997, *Landscape with View of Lake Avernus with the Island of Ischia in the Distance.* (oil on canvas, 48 x 67 ins / 121 x 170 cm) GBP 53,200. LONDON, 12 Nov 1997, *Landscape with view over the River Wye* (oil on canvas, 17 x 22 3/4 ins / 43 x 58 cm) GBP 17,250. LONDON, 31 March 1999, *Lerici from Convent of Galoro* (1777, watercolour over pencil heightened with gum arabic, 11 x 16 ins / 27 x 41 cm) GBP 45,000. LONDON, 10 June 1999, *View from Ponte Loreto, near Nettuno* (oil on paper on canvas, 14 x 21 ins / 35 x 53 cm) GBP 65,000. LONDON, 22 March 2000, *Coast Scene with Approaching Storm* (1771, oil on canvas, 24 x 29 ins / 61 x 74 cm) GBP 9,000. LONDON, 5 Nov 2001, *A Classical Scholar Instructing his Apprentice* (graphite, 6 x 10 ins / 15 x 26 cm) GBP 1,300. LONDON, 11 June 2004, *Wooded River Landscape with Figures by a Ford* (oil on panel, 11 x 16 ins / 29 x 40 cm) GBP 9,500.

JONES, Thomas Alfred (Sir)
Irish, 19th century.
Born 1823, in Dublin; died 10 May 1893, in Dublin.
Painter. Figures, portraits, genre scenes.

Thomas Alfred Jones was a student at the Royal Dublin Society. He became a member of the Royal Hibernian Academy in 1861 and its president in 1869, at which point he was knighted.

MUSEUMS AND GALLERIES:

DUBLIN: *Portrait of Sir Magiere Brady Bart.*

AUCTION RECORDS:

LONDON, 8 May 1908, *Departure of the Immigrants,* GBP 5. LONDON, 18 March 1983, *Portrait of Miss Mary Banks* (c. 1868, oil on canvas, 50 1/4 x 40 1/4 ins / 127.6 x 102 cm) GBP 1,900. DUBLIN, 24 Oct 1988, *Gallant Conversation in Ireland* (oil on canvas, 43 x 33 1/2 ins / 109.3 x 85 cm) IEP 8,250. DUBLIN, 31 May 2000, *I'm Sitting on Stile, Mary* (oil on canvas, 21 x 16 ins / 53 x 41 cm) IEP 2,800. LONDON, 7 March 2002, *Portrait of Sir Clement Wolseley, Bt.; Portrait of Lady Wolseley in a White Dress* (1874, oil on canvas, a pair, 30 x 25 ins / 76 x 63 cm) GBP 1,600.

JONES, Thomas Dempster
British, 20th century.
Born in Harlech, North Wales.
Painter. Landscapes, still-lifes.

Thomas Dempster Jones studied photography in 1943. He received numerous awards and honours. His best-known works include *Still-life with a Chinese Horse, Winter Prelude* and *Gypsy and Bird*. He also worked as restorer of paintings. His work was exhibited at the Royal Academy and the Royal Society of British Artists in London, and in Paris with the Société des Artistes Français (of which he was a member).

JONES, Thomas Dow
American, 19th century.
Born 1808 or 1811; died 1881.
Sculptor. Historical figures. Busts.

Thomas Dow Jones was an associate of the National Academy of Design in New York in 1853. He produced the busts of many American personalities.

AUCTION RECORDS:

NEW YORK, 25 March 1997, *Bust of Lincoln* (1861, green-patinated bronze, h. 32 1/2 ins / 82.6 cm) USD 6,325.

JONES, W.
British, 19th century.
Active in London.
Sculptor.

W. Jones exhibited at the Royal Academy from 1843 to 1853.

JONES, W.H.H.
British, 19th century.
Active in London.
Painter. Landscapes.

W.H.H. Jones exhibited at the Royal Academy and at the Suffolk Street Gallery from 1845 to 1878.

JONES, Watkin D.
British, 19th century.
Born in Merthyr Tydfil, Wales.
Active in London.
Sculptor.

Watkin D. Jones was the brother of William Jones. He exhibited at the Royal Academy and the British Institution from 1846 to 1861.

JONES, William
Irish, 18th century.
Born in Ireland; died 1747.
Active during the first half of the 18th century.
Painter. Landscapes.

William Jones is known especially for the engravings made from his works painted around Dublin. The most important of these was *Salmon Leap, of Wicklow*.

BIBLIOGRAPHY:

Crookshank, Anne, *Painters of Ireland, c.1660-1920,* Barrie and Jenkins, London, 1979.

AUCTION RECORDS:

LONDON, 25 April 1940, *Fisherman,* GBP 52; *Fishing for Pike,* GBP 189. LONDON, 15 Dec 1993, *View of Leixlip with the River Liffey in County Kildare* (oil on canvas, 17 x 25 ins / 43.2 x 63.2 cm) GBP 5,750. LONDON, 16 May 1996, *Dublin Bay with a view over Howth Hill* (oil on canvas, 29 x 45 ins / 73.5 x 114 cm) GBP 37,800.

JONES, William, called of Bath
British, 18th century.
Active in Bath.
Painter. Fruit.

William Jones exhibited at the Society of Artists, the Free Society and at the Royal Academy from 1764 to 1771.

AUCTION RECORDS:

LONDON, 31 March 1976, *Still-life with Fruit* (oil on canvas, two pendants, 16 1/2 x 20 1/2 ins / 42 x 52 cm) GBP 700. LONDON, 12 March 1980, *Still-life with Peaches* (1774, oil on canvas, 17 x 14 1/2 ins / 43 x 37 cm) GBP 620. LONDON, 14 March 1984, *Still-life with Fruit in a Landscape* (oil on canvas, 35 x 29 1/4 ins / 89 x 74 cm) GBP 2,000. LONDON, 20 July 1987, *Still-lifes with Fruit* (oil on canvas, a pair, 8 3/4 x 11 ins / 22.5 x 28 cm) GBP 3,200. LONDON, 18 Oct 1989, *Still-life with Fruit on a Pewter Plate with a Glass; Still-life with Fruit and a bird on a Pewter Plate* (oil on panel, a pair, each 10 x 12 ins / 24.5 x 30.5 cm) GBP 1,980. LONDON, 28 Feb 1990, *Basket of Strawberries with a Jay and a Bluetit* (oil on canvas, 25 1/2 x 19 1/2 ins / 65 x

49.5 cm) GBP 3,300. LONDON, 20 Nov 1992, *Still-life With Fruit, Grapes, Peach, Gooseberries and nuts with a Squirrel on a Stone Entablature* (oil on canvas, 19 1/2 x 25 3/4 ins / 49.8 x 65.4 cm) GBP 3,520. LONDON, 6 April 1993, *Still-life with Fruit on an Entablature* (oil on canvas, 24 1/2 x 29 1/4 ins / 62 x 74.5 cm) GBP 3,450. LONDON, 8 Nov 1995, *Still-life with Fruit and a Bullfinch in a Landscape* (1779, oil on canvas, a pair, each 20 1/4 x 26 1/2 ins / 51.5 x 67.5 cm) GBP 11,500. LONDON, 7 June 2001, *Basket of Strawberries with a Bluetit and Butterfly on a Rocky Bank* (oil on canvas, 20 x 25 ins / 51 x 63 cm) GBP 2,800.

JONES, William
British, 18th century.
Active c. 1780.
Engraver.
William Jones made an engraving of *The Three Kings* after John Philips.

JONES, William
British, 19th century.
Active in Chester.
Painter. Portraits, genre scenes, animals.
William Jones exhibited in London, at the Royal Academy, the British Institution and at the Suffolk Street Gallery from 1834 to 1836.
AUCTION RECORDS:
LONDON, 9 July 1980, *Woodgrouse Shoot* (oil on canvas, 18 1/2 x 22 1/2 ins / 47 x 57 cm) GBP 750. NEW YORK, 10 June 1983, *Hunting Scene* (oil on canvas, 18 x 24 ins / 45.7 x 60.9 cm) USD 3,000. LONDON, 13 March 1985, *Fishing the Pool; A Good Cast* (oil on canvas, a pair, 11 x 14 3/4 ins / 28 x 37.5 cm) GBP 9,500. LONDON, 14 Nov 1990, *Gentlemen Hunting* (oil on canvas, 17 1/4 x 23 1/4 ins / 43.5 x 59 cm) GBP 6,050; *Gentlemen Shooting Woodgrouse* (oil on canvas, 19 1/2 x 23 1/4 ins / 49.5 x 59 cm) GBP 6,600. LONDON, 10 April 1991, *Hounds Flushing a Pheasant; Hound chasing a Hare* (oil on canvas, each 19 1/2 x 23 1/2 ins / 49.5 x 59.5 cm) GBP 8,250.

JONES, William
British, 19th century.
Born 19th century, in Merthyr Tydfil, Wales.
Sculptor.
William Jones worked in London. He began exhibiting at the Royal Academy in 1843 with a bust entitled *Caswallon*. In 1845, he exhibited a relief entitled *Jacob's Dream*, a statue and three busts. In 1847, he showed four busts.

JONES, William E.
British, 19th century.
Active in Bristol.
Painter. Landscapes.
William E. Jones exhibited in London, notably at the Royal Academy, the British Institution and at the Suffolk Street Gallery from 1849 to 1871.
AUCTION RECORDS:
TOKYO, 15 Feb 1980, *Christmas Evening* (oil on canvas, 27 1/2 x 48 ins / 69.8 x 122 cm) JPY 1,700,000. NEWBURY, 16 May 2001, *South Luffingham, Rutland* (oil on canvas, 16 x 20 ins / 40 x 51 cm) GBP 1,400. LONDON, 21 Jan 2004, *Resting on a Woodland Track* (1875, oil on canvas, 19 x 30 ins / 49 x 75 cm) GBP 1,300.

JONES, William R.
American, 19th century.
Active in Philadelphia 1811-1824.
Reproductions engraver.
William R. Jones engraved numerous portraits.

JONES, Zebedee
British, 20th - 21st century.
Born 1970.
Painter.
Zebedee Jones lives and works in London. Jones is part of the Real Art - A New Modernism movement which emerged in England in the 1980s and which focuses on the process of painting itself. Brian Muller describes these artists as creating non-figurative objects which are entirely self-referential and revealing a structural and analytical approach to paint as a material. In these works, the physical process of the act of painting and the materiality of the paint put in check the viewer's customary references and associations. Jones works in series, applying various colours in thick layers which then combine to produce a bluish-grey or greenish-grey surface, which he then scrapes with a wooden scraper to enhance the effects of material and volume. His works are a combination of painting and sculpture and, like Process Art, which they resemble, focus on the realisation process. In 1995, he took part in the exhibition *Real Art - A New Modernism: British Reflexive Painters in the 1990s* at Southampton City Art Gallery; in 1995 and 1996 in exhibitions at various regional museums in the UK and later in London. He showed his work solo in 1997 at the Waddington Galleries, London.
BIBLIOGRAPHY:
Muller, Brian, '*Real Art - Un nouveau modernisme: les reflexive painters des années 90*' in *Art Press* n° 202, periodical, Paris, May 1995. Rondi, Joëlle, '*Zebedee Jones*' in *Art Press* n° 223, periodical, Paris, April 1997.

JONET, Nestor
Belgian, 19th - 20th century.
Active in Brussels.
Painter. Landscapes.
Nestor Jonet featured in the Exposition de Bruxelles of 1910.

JONG. See also **JONGH** and **JONGE**

JONG, Betty de
French, 20th century.
Born 25 March 1881, in Paris; died 20 January 1916, in San Francisco.
Active in the USA.
Painter. Figures, portraits, landscapes.
Betty de Jong studied at the Académie Julian in Paris and made study trips to Brittany, Holland and Granada. She lived first in Paris and moved to San Francisco where she became a portrait painter. Works by de Jong exhibited at French exhibitions include *Old Woman of Greenland, Breton Woman* (study), *Dutch Woman* (study); *View of Meaux, Old Garden, Little Girl with a Doll, Japanese Dolls, Study of a Nude, The Red Stockings, Woman from Plomarch, Port of Dourdanez.*
AUCTION RECORDS:
NEW YORK, 16 July 1992, *Dutch Peasant Woman* (oil on canvas, 32 x 25 1/2 ins / 81.3 x 64.8 cm) USD 1,100.

JONG, Daniel de
Dutch, 18th - 19th century.
Active in Rotterdam during the 18th and 19th centuries.
Engraver, draughtsman.
On 26 March 1810, drawings and engravings by Daniel de Jong were sold in Rotterdam.

JONG, Dirk de
Dutch, 18th century.
Active at the end of the 18th century.
Engraver (line-engraving).
He made engravings from drawings by Cornelis Pronk, J. Versteegh, and so on.

JONG, Frans de, or Jongh
Dutch, 17th century.
Died 15 January 1705, in Haarlem.
Active in Haarlem.
Painter. History painting.

Frans de Jong was the nephew and pupil of Adriaen van Ostade. Houbraken mentions him as the teacher of Jan de Groot. The museum in Copenhagen has his paintings *Jason Killing the Dragon* and *Cadmus in Fear of Hearing the Voice Telling Him that He Is To Be Transformed into a Serpent*.

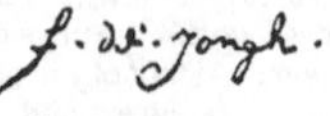

JONG, Germ.-Gerin de

Dutch, 20th century.

Born 8 March 1886, in St-Jocibi Parochie; died 1967.

Painter, draughtsman, illustrator. Portraits, landscapes, still-lifes, flowers.

Germ.-Gerin de Jong was a student at the academy of fine art in Amsterdam and then Rotterdam, and also worked in Berlin and Düsseldorf. From 1926 he exhibited at the Salon d'Automne in Paris, showing views of Morocco and landscapes of the area around Paris. He featured in *Lasting Attraction: Dutch Artists in Italy, 1806-1940* at the Kunsthal, Rotterdam, in 2003.

Bibliography:

De blijvende verlokking: Nederlandse kunstenaars in Italië, 1806-1940, exhibition catalogue, Kunsthal, Rotterdam, 2003.

Auction records:

AMSTERDAM, 25 April 1978, *Landscape in Algeria* (1937, oil on canvas, 25½ x 31¾ ins / 64.7 x 80.7 cm) NLG 4,600. AMSTERDAM, 18 Sept 1979, *Flowers* (1958, oil on canvas, 29¼ x 23¼ ins / 74 x 59 cm) NLG 3,400. AMSTERDAM, 18 March 1985, *Mountain Village* (1924, oil on canvas, 34¾ x 27 ins / 88.5 x 68.5 cm) NLG 4,000. AMSTERDAM, 24 May 1989, *Still-life of Summer Flowers in a Vase on a Cloth* (1964, oil on canvas, 57¾ x 33¾ ins / 147 x 86 cm) NLG 3,680. AMSTERDAM, 22 May 1990, *Dunes* (oil on canvas, 19¾ x 27½ ins / 50 x 70 cm) NLG 2,300. AMSTERDAM, 22 May 1991, *Hillside in Corsica* (1958, oil on canvas, 25½ x 21¼ ins / 65 x 54 cm) NLG 8,625. AMSTERDAM, 11 Dec 1991, *Landscape in Algeria* (1939, oil on canvas, 25¾ x 32 ins / 65.5 x 81 cm) NLG 10,350. AMSTERDAM, 19 May 1992, *Landscape with a Mountain Village* (1945, oil on canvas, 19¾ x 28¾ ins / 50 x 73 cm) NLG 5,520. AMSTERDAM, 21 May 1992, *Still-life of Flowers* (1951, oil on canvas, 17¾ x 14¼ ins / 45 x 36 cm) NLG 4,600. AMSTERDAM, 26 May 1993, *Still-life of Flowers in a Glass Vase* (1945, oil on canvas, 28 x 24½ ins / 71 x 62 cm) NLG 6,325. AMSTERDAM, 31 May 1994, *Daffodils* (1924, oil on canvas, 27½ x 21¾ ins / 70 x 55.5 cm) NLG 8,625. AMSTERDAM, 31 May 1995, *Landscape* (oil on canvas, 13¾ x 17¾ ins / 35 x 45 cm) NLG 1,770. AMSTERDAM, 4 June 1996, *Still-life with Flowers* (1949, oil on canvas, 32 x 25½ ins / 81 x 65 cm) NLG 8,496. AMSTERDAM, 2 Dec 1997, *Still-life of Flowers* (1951, oil on canvas, 32¾ x 25½ ins / 83 x 65 cm) NLG 12,685. AMSTERDAM, 10 June 1999, *Azaleas in Decorated Pot* (1952, oil on canvas, 26 x 21 ins / 65 x 54 cm) NLG 10,000. AMSTERDAM, 7 June 2000, *Still-life of Flowers* (1945, pastel, 22 x 17 ins / 57 x 43 cm) NLG 6,000. AMSTERDAM, 28 Nov 2000, *Autrans* (1951, oil on canvas, 20 x 24 ins / 51 x 62 cm) NLG 7,200. AMSTERDAM, 20 March 2001, *Bouquet, Still-life with Amaryllis and Tulips in a Vase* (1952, oil on canvas, 35 x 29 ins / 88 x 73 cm) NLG 10,000. AMSTERDAM, 12 June 2001, *Still-life with Flowers and Red Cloth* (1930, oil on canvas, 39 x 39 ins / 100 x 100 cm) NLG 28,000. AMSTERDAM, 22 Jan 2002, *Still-life with an Oil Lamp, Flowers, Plate and Rooster* (1945, oil on canvas, 37 x 29 ins / 93 x 74 cm) EUR 2,200. AMSTERDAM, 3 Sept 2002, *Still-life with Lillies and Gladioli* (1946, oil on canvas, 26 x 21 ins / 65 x 54 cm) EUR 4,500. AMSTERDAM, 2 Dec 2003, *Mountain Village* (1929, oil on canvas, 24 x 32 ins / 60 x 81 cm) EUR 1,800. AMSTERDAM, 9 June 2004, *Still-life with Sunflowers in a Blue Vase* (1921, oil on canvas, 39 x 31 ins / 99 x 79 cm) EUR 4,500. AMSTERDAM, 21 Dec 2004, *Still-life with Flowers* (1929, oil on canvas, 18 x 14 ins / 45 x 35 cm) EUR 2,600.

JONG, Gerrit Pietersz. de

Dutch, 17th century.

Died 17 May 1642, in Alkmaar.

Painter. Genre scenes, landscapes.

Gerrit de Jong was registered as a member of the Alkmaar guild in 1631. He taught Jan Teunisz. Blanckhof.

Museums and Galleries:

UTRECHT (Mus. Catharijneconvent): *Ruins of the Chapel of the Virgin at Runxputte*.

Auction records:

AMSTERDAM, 17 Nov 1993, *Portrait of a Small Girl with a Goat* (1647, oil on panel, 48 x 34½ ins / 122 x 87.5 cm) NLG 28,750. AMSTERDAM, 16 Nov 1994, *Sailing off a Rocky Coast* (oil on canvas, 15¼ x 26¼ ins / 38.5 x 66.5 cm) NLG 10,350.

JONG, Jacqueline de

Dutch, 20th century.

Born 1939, in Hengelo.

Painter, engraver.

Pop Art.

Jacqueline de Jong lives in Amsterdam and exhibited in Amsterdam and Rotterdam from 1962. She also exhibited in France and Germany. She took part in the Salon de Mai in Paris in 1963, 1964 and 1965; the Salon

Grands et Jeunes d'Aujourd'hui in 1966 and 1967, and, as an engraver, in the Grenehen triennial engraving festival in 1970 and 1973.

Auction records:

COPENHAGEN, 10 May 1989, *Phenomena Subject to Local Modification* (1966, acrylic and ink/paper, 51¼ x 38¼ ins / 130 x 97 cm) DKK 17,000. AMSTERDAM, 13 Dec 1989, *Head of a Monkey* (1962, oil on canvas, 18 x 22 ins / 46 x 55 cm) NLG 4,830. AMSTERDAM, 11 Dec 1991, *Improvised Baseball* (1965, oil on canvas, 32 x 23½ ins / 81 x 60 cm) NLG 4,600. COPENHAGEN, 21 Sept 1994, *At the Mercy of the Waves* (1960, oil on canvas, 19¾ x 25½ ins / 50 x 65 cm) DKK 6,500. AMSTERDAM, 7 Dec 1994, *Suicide No IV* (1965, oil on canvas, 39 x 39¼ ins / 99 x 100 cm) NLG 3,450. COPENHAGEN, 17 May 2000, *Molto rustico* (oil on canvas, 38 x 51 ins / 97 x 130 cm) DKK 20,000.

JONG, Jan de

Dutch, 19th century.

Born 1863 or 1864, in Rotterdam; died 1901, in Rotterdam.

Painter, engraver (etching). Figures, portraits, genre scenes, landscapes.

Jan de Jong studied at the Rotterdam academy and later became a teacher there.

Museums and Galleries:

AMSTERDAM (Rijksprentenkabinet): etching - ROTTERDAM (Mus. Boijmans Van Beuningen): watercolour.

Auction records:

AMSTERDAM, 10 Feb 1988, *Young Boy* (1891, oil on canvas, 27½ x 18 ins / 70 x 46 cm) NLG 1,035. AMSTERDAM, 19 Sept 1989, *Interior with a Peasant Family Seated around a Table* (oil on canvas, 22 x 17¼ ins / 56 x 44 cm) NLG 2,760. AMSTERDAM, 20 April 1993, *Bacchante* (oil on canvas, 65 x 40¼ ins / 165 x 102 cm) NLG 11,500. AMSTERDAM, 22 April 1997, *Townspeople by a Town Gate on a Sunny Day* (1884, oil on canvas, 12¼ x 19¾ ins / 31 x 50 cm) NLG 15,930. GRAVENHAGE, 28 April 1999, *Barmaid with Pitchers* (1891, oil on canvas, 27 x 17 ins / 69 x 44 cm) NLG 3,800. GRAVENHAGE, 31 Oct 2000, *Drowning Person* (oil on canvas, 29 x 48 ins / 74 x 121 cm) NLG 5,500.

JONG, Jean de
French (?), 20th century.
Born 1929.
Painter. Landscapes.

Jean de Jong exhibited in France and abroad. Many of his works are kept in Strasbourg. A self-taught artist, he painted in a naive style. In his landscapes, the sense of freshness compensates for what can be a somewhat basic technique.

JONG, Jurjen de
Dutch, 19th century.
Born 7 October 1807, in Harlingen; died 7 May 1890, in Harlingen.
Painter. Portraits, genre scenes.

Pupil of Otto de Boer.

MUSEUMS AND GALLERIES:
AMSTERDAM: *Portrait of J. D. B. Wilkens.*

AUCTION RECORDS:
AMSTERDAM, 10 Feb 1988, *The Newborn: Peasant Woman Watching a Young Girl Taking Care of her Baby* (oil on canvas, 23 1/4 x 31 ins / 59 x 79 cm) NLG 1,955. COLOGNE, 18 March 1989, *Family Scene in a Dutch Interior* (oil on panel, 9 1/4 x 13 ins / 23.5 x 33 cm) DEM 1,600.

JONG, M. de
Dutch, 17th century.
Painter. Military subjects, battles.

MUSEUMS AND GALLERIES:
AVIGNON: *Attack on a Convoy.*

AUCTION RECORDS:
PARIS, 1 June 1927, *Troops Resting,* FRF 3,500. LONDON, 8 Dec 1930, *Battle Scene* (1634) GBP 16. LONDON, 13 Feb 1946, *Battle,* GBP 52. PARIS, 12 Dec 1988, *Clash of Cavalry* (oil on copper, oval, 6 1/4 x 8 1/2 ins / 16 x 21.5 cm) FRF 38,000.

JONG, Servaas de
Dutch, 19th century.
Born 1808, in Leeuwarden.
Painter, writer. History painting, portraits.

Pupil of W. B. van der Kooi.

JONG, Synco Schram de
20th century.
Born 1910; died 1984.
Painter, watercolourist, pastellist, draughtsman.
Figures, portraits, genre scenes, landscapes.

Synco Schram de Jong, an official in Java from 1947 to 1950, specialised in Indonesian subjects.

AUCTION RECORDS:
AMSTERDAM, 23 April 1996, *Portrait of an Adolescent Bedja* (1948, black chalk, 27 1/2 x 17 3/4 ins / 70 x 45 cm) NLG 2,360. AMSTERDAM, 5 Nov 1996, *Indonesian Subjects* (watercolour and pastel, complete series of 45 works) NLG 4,720.

JONG, Toon or Antoon J. de
Dutch, 20th century.
Born 14 August 1879, in Laren.
Engraver, draughtsman.

Toon de Jong, an etcher, featured at the Exposition de Bruxelles.

JONG, W. de
Dutch, 19th century.
Painter. Landscapes.

Mentioned in *Art Prices Current.*

AUCTION RECORDS:
LONDON, 18 Dec 1909, *Two Landscapes,* GBP 9. AMSTERDAM, 17 May 2004, *Italian Landscape with Hunting Scene. Italian Landscape with Riders* (oil on canvas, two, 12 x 14 ins / 30 x 36 cm) EUR 4,400.

JONG SANG LEE. See **LEE Jong Sang**

JONGBLOET, Hendrick Hendricksz.
Dutch, 17th century.
Born c. 1614; died c. 1655, in Amsterdam.
Painter.

In 1637, he obtained burgher's rights in Rotterdam.

JONGE. See also **JONG** and **JONGH**

JONGE, Esaias de
Dutch, 17th century.
Active in Rotterdam.
Painter.

JONGE, Eva Maria Alida de
Dutch, 19th - 20th century.
Born 24 December 1872, in Amersfoort.
Painter. Still-lifes.

Eva Maria Alida de Jonge was a student at the academy of fine art in Amsterdam in 1900, and director of the International Studio in the same city.

JONGE, Geert Kiwiet de
Dutch, 19th century.
Born 1801, in Finster Wolde, near Groningen.
Landscape artist.

JONGE, J. D.
Dutch, 18th century.
Active in Amsterdam at the beginning of the 18th century.
Engraver.

JONGE, Jakob Jakobsz. de
Dutch, 17th century.
Sculptor (wood).

JONGE, Jan Martszen de. See **MARTSZEN Jan** or **Jacob**

JONGE, Jaques de. See **JONGHELINCK Jacques**

JONGE, Johan Antonio de
Dutch, 19th century.
Born 7 November 1864, in Rotterdam.
Active in The Hague.
Painter.

Johan Antonio de Jonge painted figures, still-lifes, interiors, winter landscapes and coastal scenes. He exhibited from time to time at exhibitions in Germany: *Young Jewish Girl* (Berlin, Great Fine Arts Exhibition 1897); *Young Girl with Music Score* (Berlin, 1901); and *Still-life with Pheasants* (Munich, Ice Palace exhibition, 1901).

JONGE, Johan Karel Jacob de
Dutch, 19th century.
Born 17 June 1828, in The Hague; died 15 March 1880, in The Hague.
Painter, engraver.

JONGE, Lucas de. See **JONGH**

JONGE DE. See **JONG de**

JONGELINCX, Antoine
Flemish School, 18th century.
Born 18th century, in Flanders.
Active in England.
Engraver. Natural history (fish).

Antoine Jongelincx was known as an engraver. In England he produced natural history plates (of fish) after Arnout van Aken.

JONGELINX, Jan Baptist, or Jongelinck
Flemish School, 18th century.
Born 27 July 1689, in Antwerp.
Engraver (burin).

He engraved portraits for Andreas Foppens' *Bibliotheca Belgica* (1739).

JONGEN, Christine
20th century.
Sculptor, draughtswoman.
As a sculptor Christine Jongen kept to representational and classical themes. Her drawings in coloured inks tend towards geometric abstraction.

JONGERE DE. See **DRULMAN Marinus Johannes**

JONGERING, H. F.
Dutch, 19th century.
Born 16 October 1778, in Amsterdam; died 9 March 1808, in Amsterdam.
Painter. Landscapes.
A colour drawing entitled *Landscape with Sheep Returning to the Fold* and two other landscapes signed *N. F. Jongeving* have been attributed to H.F. Jongering.

JONGERS, Alphonse
American, 19th - 20th century.
Born 17 November 1872; died 1945 or 1964.
Active in the USA from 1897.
Painter.
Alphonse Jongers' parents were Dutch. He studied at the École des Beaux-Arts in Paris with Delaunay and Gustave Moreau. He later went to work in Spain for two years before moving to New York. Jongers became an associate member of the National Academy in 1906. He exhibited in Paris at the Salon des Artistes Français, receiving a commendation in 1909. His portraits are highly regarded.
MUSEUMS AND GALLERIES:
NEW YORK (Metropolitan Mus. of Art): *Arthur H. Hearn; Harpist; Louise* - WASHINGTON DC (NGA): *William T. Evans* (no dated, oil on canvas).

JONGH. See also **JONG** and **JONGE**

JONGH, Claude de
Dutch, 17th century.
Died 16 March 1663, in Utrecht.
Painter. Aquatic landscapes, urban landscapes.
Claude de Jongh was a member of the Utrecht guild in 1626 or 1633. He worked for many years in England and married there. After returning to Utrecht he remarried on 18 July 1643; his new wife was Juliana van Pisa.

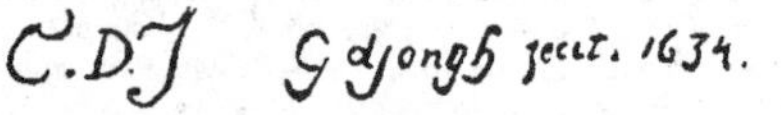

MUSEUMS AND GALLERIES:
AMSTERDAM: *River and Castle* - LONDON (Victoria and Albert Mus.): *The Thames*.
AUCTION RECORDS:
LONDON, 1878, *View of London Bridge*, FRF 19,687. PARIS, 1888, *View of the Old London Bridge*, FRF 13,120. LONDON, 14 Dec 1928, *Old London Bridge*, GBP 1,732. LONDON, 11 June 1969, *Mill on the Walls of a Town*, GBP 950. NEW YORK, 15 Jan 1993, *Figures in a Ferryboat on a Small River* (1634, oil on panel, 7 x 9 1/4 ins / 17.8 x 23.2 cm) USD 10,925. NEW YORK, 11 Jan 1996, *View of the Tiber with the Tiberine Island on the Left and the Fabrizio Bridge* (1634, oil on panel, 10 x 13 1/2 ins / 25.4 x 34.6 cm) USD 19,550. LONDON, 10 Dec 2001, *Extensive Landscape with a Monastery above a River* (1632, oil on panel, 13 x 20 ins / 32 x 51 cm) GBP 3,000.

JONGH, Cornelis Barends de
Dutch, 17th century.
Born 17th century, in Haarlem; died before 1702.
Painter. Portraits, landscapes.
Cornelis de Jongh was admitted to the guild of The Hague in 1618. He is mentioned by Siret.

JONGH, Frans de. See **JONG**

JONGH, Germ.-Gerin de. See **JONG Germ.-Gerin de**

JONGH, Hendrick de, or Jong
Dutch, 17th - 18th century.
Died before 22 June 1708.
Active in The Hague c. 1667.
Sculptor.

JONGH, Jan de
Dutch, 17th century.
Painter. Group portraits, portraits.
Jan de Jongh was a member of the Haarlem guild in 1664. He collaborated with Jan de Bray on *The Administrators of the Guild of St Luke in Haarlem, 1675* (Amsterdam museum).
MUSEUMS AND GALLERIES:
AMSTERDAM: *The Administrators of the Guild of St Luke in Haarlem, 1675* (in collaboration with Jan de Bray).

JONGH, Joannes de, or Johann van
Dutch, 17th century.
Probably active in Middelburg.
Engraver.
Joannes de Jongh worked in Batavia in 1684.

JONGH, L. de
Dutch, 19th century.
Painter. Genre scenes.
AUCTION RECORDS:
AMSTERDAM, 9 Nov 1993, *Fishing Party* (oil on panel, 16 1/2 x 20 1/2 ins / 42 x 52 cm) NLG 1,725.

JONGH, Lucas de, or Jonge
Dutch, 17th century.
Born c. 1646, in Amsterdam.
Painter.

JONGH, Ludolf, Leuff or Lendertsz., also called Lieve de Jongh
Dutch, 17th century.
Born 1616, in Overschie; died 1679, in Hillegesberg.
Painter. Religious subjects, military subjects, portraits, genre scenes, landscapes.
Ludolf Jongh was the son of a Rotterdam shoemaker who for many years remained opposed to his son's vocation. He studied under Cornelius Saftleven in Rotterdam, A. Palamedes in Delft and Jan van Bylert in Utrecht. In 1635 he went to France with Bacon and remained there until 1642. In 1646, after his return to Holland, he married the daughter of Pierre Montagne. He lived in both Rotterdam and Hillelgesberg - in the latter between May and September 1679. He collaborated on a number of paintings with Joris van der Hagen and has often been confused with Lievens.

MUSEUMS AND GALLERIES:
AMSTERDAM: *Jan van Nes; Wife of Jan van Nes; Aletta van Ravensberg; Family Scene* - AMSTERDAM (Rijksmus.): *Fox Hunt* - ANGERS: *Portrait of a Woman* - BONN: *Wine Merchant and his Wife* - DRESDEN: *Portrait of a Young Woman* - DUBLIN: *Canal in Holland; Hunting Party* - GENEVA: *Halt at an Inn* - GENEVA (Mus. Ariana): *Landscape with Hunters and Dogs* - HAARLEM: *Portrait of a Woman* - HELSINKI: *Card Players* - LEIPZIG: *Society at Table* - MOSCOW (Rumiantsev Mus.): *Attack by Brigands; The Old Folk; Landscape with Animals; Virgin and Child; Young Girl Sleeping in the Grass* - NEW YORK (Metropolitan Mus. of Art): *Boar Hunt* - NUREMBERG: *Evening Landscape* - OLDENBURG: *Guardroom* - OSNABRÜCK: *Landscape with Figures* - ST PETERSBURG (Hermitage): *Con-*

cert; *Hunting Scene* - THE HAGUE: *Jacob Cats* - THE HAGUE (Mauritshuis): *Hunting Scene* - WÜRZBURG: *Mountain Landscape with Cattle.*

AUCTION RECORDS:

PARIS, 22-24 April 1901, *A Bite to Eat,* FRF 250; *Young Mother,* FRF 370; *Two Friends Take a Siesta,* FRF 360. LONDON, 12 Dec 1908, *Mountain Landscape,* GBP 10. LONDON, 25 Feb 1911, *Stag Hunt,* GBP 12; *Portrait of a Gentleman* (1650) GBP 304. PARIS, 1 June 1911, *Portrait of a Woman,* FRF 300. LONDON, 16 April 1926, *Standard Bearer,* GBP 92. LONDON, 13 Dec 1933, *Dutch Priest,* GBP 42. LONDON, 20 April 1934, *Lady in Blue,* GBP 99. LONDON, 1 Feb 1946, *Falcon Hunting,* GBP 52. PARIS, 25 April 1951, *The Reprimand,* FRF 220,000. PARIS, 24 March 1952, *The Reprimand,* FRF 320,000. LONDON, 29 Oct 1965, *Portrait of a Gentleman, Three-quarter Left View,* Gns 7,000. VIENNA, 29 Nov 1966, *Horsemen Resting,* ATS 90,000. NEW YORK, 23 Feb 1968, *Hunting Scene,* USD 3,100. LONDON, 11 June 1971, *Huntsman on Horseback Sounding the Horn,* Gns 1,400. NEW YORK, 15 June 1977, *Portrait of a Young Girl* (oil on canvas, 27 1/4 x 23 1/2 ins / 69 x 60 cm) USD 6,000. NEW YORK, 9 Oct 1980, *Game of Backgammon* (oil on panel, 25 x 18 ins / 63.5 x 45.5 cm) USD 17,000. NEW YORK, 15 Jan 1988, *Portrait of a Man Dressed in Black with a Lace Collar* (oil on canvas, 28 1/4 x 25 ins / 71.6 x 63.5 cm) USD 6,600. PARIS, 22 June 1990, *Horsemen in Engagement; After the Battle* (panel, a pair, 6 3/4 x 10 1/2 ins / 17 x 26.5 cm) FRF 70,000. NEW YORK, 19 July 1990, *Couple in an Interior with a Greyhound* (oil on panel, 21 1/2 x 20 1/4 ins / 54.6 x 51.4 cm) USD 1,870. PARIS, 28 Sept 1990, *Young Woman Seated by a Piece of Furniture Decorated in the Chinese Style Writing a Letter* (oil on panel, 14 3/4 x 11 ins / 37.5 x 27 cm) FRF 55,000. LONDON, 16 April 1997, *Landscape with a Huntsman,his Servant and Pack of Hounds* (oil on panel, 20 1/4 x 24 1/4 ins / 51.5 x 61.5 cm) GBP 9,430. NEW YORK, 23 May 1997, *Reprimand: Guardroom Interior with Peasants Smoking and Drinking and a Woman Scolding a Child* (oil on panel, 19 3/4 x 17 1/4 ins / 50.2 x 43.8 cm) USD 32,200. LONDON, 3 July 1997, *Three-quarter Portrait of an Officer Dressed in Yellow Chamois Leather with an Orange Sash, Holding a Whip in his Hand* (oil on canvas, 40 1/2 x 33 1/4 ins / 102.6 x 84.4 cm) GBP 41,100. HAMBURG, 10 June 1999, *Hunting Party by a River* (oil on panel, 28 x 41 ins / 72 x 104 cm) DEM 15,000. NEW YORK, 28 Jan 2000, *Paying the Hostess* (oil on panel, 26 x 26 ins / 66 x 65 cm) USD 140,000. LONDON, 5 July 2000, *Beach at Scheveningen, with Fisherfolk Displaying their Catch* (oil on canvas, 26 x 42 ins / 66 x 107 cm) GBP 5,200. COLOGNE, 19 May 2001, *Horseman and Beggar Woman before Tavern* (oil on panel, 18 x 12 ins / 46 x 30 cm) DEM 7,500. VIENNA, 21 March 2002, *Huntsmen Resting in Wooded Landscape* (oil on panel, 37 x 28 ins / 94 x 71 cm) EUR 19,000. AMSTERDAM, 3 Feb 2004, *Portrait of a Vicar, Aged 34, in a Black Costume* (1667, oil on canvas, 28 x 24 ins / 70 x 61 cm) EUR 1,500.

JONGH, Oene Romkes de

Dutch, 19th century.
Born 1812; died 1896.
Painter. Landscapes with figures, urban landscapes, seascapes.

AUCTION RECORDS:

NEW YORK, 15 Oct 1976, *Street Scene* (oil on canvas, 26 3/4 x 21 1/2 ins / 68 x 54.5 cm) USD 950. LONDON, 12 Oct 1977, *Town in Holland in Winter* (oil on canvas, 25 3/4 x 20 1/2 ins / 65.5 x 52 cm) GBP 1,200. NEW YORK, 28 May 1980, *View of a Town in Holland in the Snow* (oil on canvas, 21 1/4 x 17 1/2 ins / 54 x 44.5 cm) USD 3,200. AMSTERDAM, 16 Nov 1988, *Sailing Ships Moored to a Quay with Numerous Figures in Calm Weather* (oil on canvas, 18 1/4 x 26 1/2 ins / 46.5 x 67 cm) NLG 3,680. AMSTERDAM, 2 May 1990, *Figure in a Village Street under Snow* (oil on canvas, 26 1/4 x 21 1/2 ins / 66.5 x 54.5 cm) NLG 8,050. AMSTERDAM, 30 Oct 1990, *Village Street in Winter* (oil on canvas, 21 1/4 x 26 1/2 ins / 54 x 67 cm) NLG 5,520. LONDON, 22 Nov 1990, *Dutch Village in Winter* (oil on canvas, 25 x 30 ins / 63.5 x 76.2 cm) GBP 3,080. AMSTERDAM, 23 April 1991, *View of Delft* (oil on canvas/panel, 14 x 18 ins / 35.5 x 46 cm) NLG 5,750. AMSTERDAM, 17 Sept 1991, *Het Kolkje in Amsterdam* (oil on canvas, 26 1/2 x 21 1/4 ins / 67 x 54 cm) NLG 3,680. AMSTERDAM, 14-15 April 1992, *Street in a Dutch Town with Figures* (oil on canvas, 24 1/2 x 19 ins / 62 x 48 cm) NLG 4,600. AMSTERDAM, 2-3 Nov 1992, *Villagers in a Small Market Town by a Canal* (oil on canvas, 14 1/4 x 19 1/2 ins / 36.5 x 49.5 cm) NLG 4,600. AMSTERDAM, 20 April 1993, *Urban Scene* (oil on canvas, 13 x 11 ins / 33 x 28 cm) NLG 2,990. NEW YORK, 17 Feb 1994, *Dutch Village with Canal, in Winter* (oil on canvas, 19 1/2 x 27 1/2 ins / 49.5 x 70 cm) USD 6,325. AMSTERDAM, 2 July 1997, *The Port of Amsterdam, Haarlem* (oil on canvas, 20 x 28 ins / 51 x 71 cm) NLG 7,495. AMSTERDAM, 27 Oct 1997, *Figures in a Snowy Street* (oil on canvas, 24 1/2 x 32 3/4 ins / 62 x 83 cm) NLG 14,160. AMSTERDAM, 1 Sept 1999, *Kolkje, Amsterdam, in Winter* (oil on canvas, 26 x 21 ins / 67 x 54 cm) NLG 7,500. AMSTERDAM, 1 Sept 1999, *View of Delft with Oude Kerk on Sunny Day* (oil on canvas, 26 x 21 ins / 67 x 54 cm) NLG 13,000. AMSTERDAM, 19 April 2000, *City View in Winter* (oil on canvas, 21 x 26 ins / 53 x 66 cm) NLG 8,000. AMSTERDAM, 5 Sept 2000, *Numerous Townsfolk in City in Winter* (oil on canvas, 26 x 21 ins / 67 x 54 cm) NLG 17,000. AMSTERDAM, 23 April 2001, *View of Utrecht in Winter* (oil on canvas, 26 x 21 ins / 67 x 54 cm) NLG 16,000. BOSTON, 7 Sept 2001, *Skating Party* (oil on canvas, 28 x 34 ins / 70 x 86 cm) USD 3,000. AMSTERDAM, 22 Jan 2002, *Town View in Winter with Figures* (oil on canvas, 26 x 21 ins / 67 x 54 cm) EUR 2,800. AMSTERDAM, 23 April 2002, *View of a Dutch town with Skaters on a Frozen Canal* (oil on canvas, 26 x 21 ins / 67 x 54 cm) EUR 3,300. AHLDEN, 9 May 2003, *Dutch Town in Winter* (oil on canvas, 17 x 14 ins / 44 x 35 cm) EUR 4,400. AMSTERDAM, 1 July 2003, *Dutch Town on a Sunny Day in Winter* (oil on canvas, 26 x 21 ins / 67 x 54 cm) EUR 5,500. AMSTERDAM, 20 April 2004, *View of the Brouwersgracht in Amsterdam on a Winter Day* (oil on canvas, 28 x 34 ins / 70 x 87 cm) EUR 15,000. AMSTERDAM, 21 April 2004, *Dutch Canal Scene in Summer. Figures on a Frozen Canal in a Dutch Town* (oil on canvas, a pair, 26 x 22 ins / 67 x 55 cm) EUR 8,000.

JONGH, Tinus de

Dutch, 20th century.
Born 1879 or 1885; died 1942.
Painter. Landscapes.

AUCTION RECORDS:

LONDON, 11 May 1976, *View of Constantia* (c. 1923, oil on canvas, 12 3/4 x 19 ins / 32.5 x 48 cm) GBP 550. JOHANNESBURG, 26 April 1978, *Mountains of the Cape of Good Hope at Dusk* (oil on canvas, 27 1/4 x 39 3/4 ins / 69 x 101 cm) ZAR 2,800. LONDON, 6 Feb 1980, *Table Mountain* (oil on canvas, 12 x 19 1/4 ins / 30.5 x 49 cm) GBP 600. JOHANNESBURG, 21 June 1983, *Farm Gate* (oil on canvas, 14 1/2 x 10 3/4 ins / 37 x 27.5 cm) ZAR 2,600. LONDON, 22 Oct 1986, *Hout Bay and Chapman's Peak Drive, Cape Province* (1934, oil on canvas, 35 x 65 ins / 88 x 165 cm) GBP 3,400. AMSTERDAM, 28 Feb 1989, *Country Road in a Wooded Landscape* (oil on canvas, 32 1/2 x 41 3/4 ins / 82.5 x 106 cm) NLG 4,140. AMSTERDAM, 25 April 1990, *Peasant Woman with Cows on a Path* (oil on canvas, 11 1/2 x 15 1/4 ins / 29 x 39 cm) NLG 2,300. AMSTERDAM, 2 May 1990, *Summer - Road beside a Canal; Winter - Farm on a Path under Snow* (oil on canvas, a pair, each 23 3/4 x 18 ins / 60.5 x 45.5 cm) NLG 10,350. AMSTERDAM, 24 Sept 1992, *View of the Dam at Amsterdam with Numerous Figures* (ink/paper, 15 3/4 x 24 1/2 ins / 40 x 62 cm) NLG 1,725. AMSTERDAM, 21 April 1994, *Trees in Bloom in Spring* (oil on canvas, 17 3/4 x 23 1/2 ins / 45 x 60 cm) NLG 2,530. AMSTERDAM, 30 May 1995, *Traffic on the Dam* (1912, oil on canvas, 24 1/2 x 31 ins / 62 x 78.5 cm) NLG 6,875. JOHANNESBURG, 17 May 1999, *Wilderness, George* (oil on canvas, 28 x 42 ins / 72 x 106 cm) ZAR 30,000. JOHANNESBURG, 17 May 1999, *Sunlight on Mountains, Re-*

flecting River (oil on canvas, 24 x 39 ins / 60 x 99 cm) ZAR 32,000. JOHANNESBURG, 8 May 2000, *Valley of a Thousand Hills, Natal* (oil on canvas, 26 x 39 ins / 66 x 99 cm) ZAR 44,000. LONDON, 14 Dec 2000, *Mountainous Landscape in the Cape* (oil on canvas, 28 x 40 ins / 70 x 102 cm) GBP 2,800. JOHANNESBURG, 7 May 2001, *Mountainous Landscape with House and Figure in Sunlight* (oil on canvas, 33 x 47 ins / 83 x 120 cm) ZAR 32,000. JOHANNESBURG, 7 May 2001, *Cloud Burst - Orange Free State* (oil on canvas, 35 x 30 ins / 89 x 77 cm) ZAR 38,000. JOHANNESBURG, 13 May 2002, *Cape Dutch House* (oil on canvas, 12 x 19 ins / 30 x 49 cm) ZAR 17,000. JOHANNESBURG, 12 May 2003, *House in a Mountainous Landscape* (1934, oil on canvas, 26 x 39 ins / 65 x 99 cm) ZAR 26,000. JOHANNESBURG, 3 Dec 2003, *Cape Cottages in the Late Afternoon* (oil on canvas, 13 x 19 ins / 32 x 47 cm) ZAR 24,000. JOHANNESBURG, 15 Nov 2004, *Winter Sunshine in a Valley* (oil on canvas on board, 25 x 39 ins / 64 x 98 cm) ZAR 35,000. JOHANNESBURG, 15 Nov 2004, *Dry Riverbed* (oil on canvas, 25 x 38 ins / 64 x 97 cm) ZAR 45,000.

JONGHE, Clement de

Dutch, 17th century.
Active in Amsterdam.
Engraver.

Clement de Jonghe appears to have worked mainly as a printer. He was a friend of Rembrandt, who engraved his portrait. De Jonghe is mentioned between 1640 and 1670. His most important works include an equestrian portrait of *Frederick III, King of Norway*. He also produced an engraving of the port of Dieppe entitled *Urbs Diepa Nobilis Galliae Portus*, which appears to be part of a series.

MUSEUMS AND GALLERIES:
DIEPPE: *Urbs Diepa Nobilis Galliae Portus* (engraving).

JONGHE, François de

Flemish, 16th century.
Painter.

According to Siret, Jonghe was a follower of the Lutheran faith.

JONGHE, Gustave Leonhard de

Belgian, 19th century.
Born 4 February 1829, in Courtrai; died January 1893, in Antwerp.
Painter. Genre scenes.

Gustave de Jonghe was the son of the landscape artist Jan Baptiste de Jonghe. He studied first under his father before following classes by Louis Gallait and François Jozef Navez. Having settled in Paris around 1850, he exhibited at the Paris Salon and was awarded a bronze medal there in 1863. The same year he also received a medal in Amsterdam and again in Brussels in 1864. He was a Chevalier of the Ordre de Léopold.

The pleasant subjects of his paintings and their harmonious and refined use of colour made them popular among the bourgeoisie of the Second Empire.

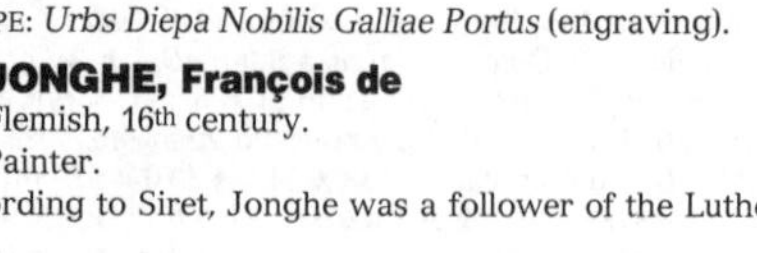

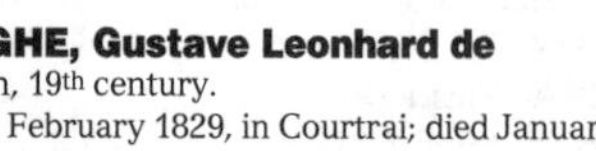

MUSEUMS AND GALLERIES:
ANTWERP: *At the Mirror* - BRUSSELS (MAM): *The Pilgrims; Visiting Baby* - COURTRAI: *Devotion* - GHENT: *The Beggar Girl* - IXELLES: *Interior of the Madeleine; Louis XV Salon.*

AUCTION RECORDS:
PARIS, Dec 1883, *The Bath,* FRF 1,500. PARIS, 21 Nov 1900, *Forbidden Fruit,* FRF 1,200. LONDON, 25 Feb 1927, *A Difficult Lesson,* GBP 39. BRUSSELS, 21 Feb 1938, *Young Woman with a Cup of Tea,* BEF 800. PARIS, 8 March 1943, *Young Woman with Blonde Hair* (1867) FRF 3,000. LONDON, 12 Oct 1945, *Coquette,* GBP 50. PARIS, 18 June 1951, *The Lesson,* FRF 72,000. LONDON, 9 May 1979, *Young Woman and Girl Playing with a Parrot* (oil on panel, 30¼ x 23½ ins / 77 x 60 cm) GBP 5,700. LONDON, 24 Nov 1982, *Beach Scene in Normandy* (oil on panel, 30 x 39¼ ins / 76 x 100 cm) GBP 17,500. NEW YORK, 29 Feb 1984, *The Visit* (oil on panel, 31¼ x 39 ins / 79.5 x 99 cm) USD 50,000. LONDON, 26 Nov 1986, *Siesta* (oil on panel, 35¼ x 28¼ ins / 89.5 x 72 cm) GBP 20,000. NEW YORK, 29 Oct 1987, *Young Woman at Her Toilette* (oil on panel, 30½ x 23¼ ins / 77.7 x 59 cm) USD 12,500. NEW YORK, 24 May 1988, *An Admirer of Japan* (oil on canvas, 44¼ x 34 ins / 112.7 x 86.6 cm) USD 63,250. LONDON, 24 Nov 1989, *The Letter of Condolence* (1867, oil on panel, 22 x 18 ins / 55 x 46 cm) GBP 15,400. NEW YORK, 1 March 1990, *Moments of Relaxation* (oil on panel, 21 x 25¾ ins / 53.3 x 65.4 cm) USD 60,500. NEW YORK, 22 May 1990, *Exercises on the Piano* (oil on canvas, 21 x 25½ ins / 53.3 x 64.8 cm) USD 26,400. PARIS, 13 June 1990, *The Conversation* (oil on panel, 22 x 18 ins / 55 x 46 cm) FRF 80,000. NEW YORK, 22 May 1991, oil on panel, 31 x 23 ins / 77.8 x 58.4 cm) USD 23,100. LONDON, 18 March 1992, *The Secret Drawer* (oil on panel, 28¾ x 21¼ ins / 73 x 54 cm) GBP 12,100. NEW YORK, 27 May 1992, *Peek-a-Boo!* (oil on panel, 21¾ x 18 ins / 55.5 x 45.7 cm) USD 17,600. NEW YORK, 13 Oct 1993, *Family Prayers* (1864, oil on panel, 22 x 17¾ ins / 55.6 x 45.1 cm) USD 21,850. LONDON, 18 March 1994, *The Confidant* (oil on canvas, 15 x 11½ ins / 38 x 29 cm) GBP 8,625. AMSTERDAM, 19 April 1994, *Pet Cat* (oil on panel, 23¾ x 19 ins / 60.5 x 48 cm) NLG 8,050. LOKEREN, 8 Oct 1994, *Interior with a Lady and Cat* (oil on panel, 24 x 18¾ ins / 61 x 47.5 cm) BEF 140,000. NEW YORK, 16 Feb 1995, *Itinerant Vegetable Seller in a Town in Holland* (oil on canvas, 27½ x 33½ ins / 69.9 x 85.1 cm) USD 17,250. LOKEREN, 8 March 1997, *Artist's Wife in a Kimono* (oil on panel, 18 x 14¾ ins / 46 x 37.5 cm) BEF 380,000. NEW YORK, 10 Feb 1998, *A Lovable Heart* (oil on canvas, 34 x 25¾ ins / 86.4 x 65.4 cm) USD 13,800. NEW YORK, 18 March 1998, *The Visit* (oil on panel, 32¾ x 25 ins / 83.2 x 63.8 cm) USD 20,700. NEW YORK, 9 Feb 1999, *Afternoon in the Park* (oil on panel, 16 x 12 ins / 41 x 30 cm) USD 7,000. LONDON, 23 March 1999, *First Steps* (1864, oil on panel, 18 x 22 ins / 46 x 56 cm) GBP 18,500. LONDON, 21 June 2000, *Afternoon Siesta* (oil on panel, 18 x 24 ins / 46 x 61 cm) GBP 14,000. NEW YORK, 18 Oct 2000, *Vanity* (oil on panel, 26 x 19 ins / 65 x 48 cm) USD 28,000. NEW YORK, 1 Nov 2001, *Afternoon Visit* (oil on panel, 31 x 39 ins / 80 x 100 cm) USD 95,000. BRUSSELS, 5 Nov 2001, *Reading* (oil on panel, 16 x 14 ins / 40 x 36 cm) BEF 750,000. NEW YORK, 29 Oct 2002, *Sunday Morning* (1864, oil on panel, 22 x 18 ins / 56 x 45 cm) USD 15,000. BRUSSELS, 18 Nov 2003, *Young Woman in the Harem* (oil on panel, 18 x 15 ins / 46 x 38 cm) EUR 5,000. LONDON, 3 Dec 2003, *Secret Whisper* (oil on canvas, 32 x 26 ins / 81 x 65 cm) GBP 12,000. LONDON, 15 June 2004, *The Kiss* (oil on panel, 24 x 19 ins / 61 x 49 cm) GBP 27,000. AMSTERDAM, 1 Sept 2004, *Deep Devotion* (oil on panel, 24 x 20 ins / 62 x 50 cm) EUR 4,800.

JONGHE, Jacques de

Belgian, 20th century.
Born 1941, in Brussels.
Painter, draughtsman.

Jacques de Jonghe studied at the academy in Brussels for a year, then worked in the studio of Charles Philippe Schott. After devoting some 10 years to the theatre, he returned to painting. The works he creates, using first oils, then later exclusively acrylic on panel, are often considered macabre. Inspired by Satan, he plunges us into a world haunted by evil, with references to Hoffmann, Edgar Allan Poe, Bram Stoker, and also to Hieronymus Bosch. With bats, moonlight, a giant spider, ruins, a skeleton, black and red, de Jonghe offers us a descent into Hell, inviting us to penetrate the heart of darkness. He signs his work *DE JONGHE V*. He has taken part in group exhibitions in Belgium and had solo shows in Brussels in 1980, 1982 and 1983, Ostend in 1980, Paris in 1982, as well as Antwerp and Amsterdam.

JONGHE, Jan Baptiste de
Flemish School, 19th century.
Born 8 January 1785, in Courtrai; died 14 October 1844, in Brussels.
Painter, watercolourist, engraver. Genre scenes, landscapes, landscapes with figures.

Jan Baptiste de Jonghe was a pupil of P. van Reable and P. Omneganck. He travelled in France, Holland and England.

MUSEUMS AND GALLERIES:
AMSTERDAM: *Market Day in Courtrai* - ANGERS: *Ardennes Landscape* - BRUSSELS: *Outskirts of Tournai* - COURTRAI: *Landscape with Horseman; Landscape with Animals; Flemish Farm; Forest Entrance.*

AUCTION RECORDS:
GHENT, 1856, *Landscape with Animals,* FRF 250. PARIS, 1895, *Landscape* (watercolour) FRF 95. BRUSSELS, 5 Oct 1971, *Landscape with Figures,* BEF 80,000. LONDON, 28 Feb 1973, *Wooded Landscape,* GBP 700. LOS ANGELES, 15 Oct 1979, *Travellers in a Wooded Landscape* (oil on panel, 10 1/2 x 12 ins / 26.5 x 30.5 cm) USD 1,600. BERN, 6 May 1983, *Animals in a Wooded River Landscape* (oil on canvas, 30 1/4 x 39 ins / 77 x 99 cm) CHF 40,000. AMSTERDAM, 22 April 1992, *Vast Undulating Landscape with a Peasant Woman Leading her Animals along a Path* (oil on panel, 14 1/4 x 19 3/4 ins / 36.5 x 50 cm) NLG 5,750. AMSTERDAM, 11 April 1995, *Summer Landscape with Travellers* (oil on canvas, 24 3/4 x 35 ins / 63 x 89 cm) NLG 12,980. VIENNA, 6 Oct 1999, *River Landscape with Travellers Resting* (oil on panel, 11 x 15 ins / 29 x 39 cm) ATS 50,000. VIENNA, 6 Oct 1999, *Wooded River Landscape with Figures on Path* (oil on panel, 11 x 15 ins / 29 x 39 cm) ATS 60,000. BRUSSELS, 12 Nov 2001, *Crossing the Ford Near the Farm* (oil on panel, 20 x 26 ins / 50 x 66 cm) BEF 170,000. NEW YORK, 4 June 2003, *Deer in a Wooded Landscape* (oil on panel, 8 x 12 ins / 21 x 30 cm) USD 2,800.

JONGHE, Luc de
Belgian, 20th - 21st century.
Born 1959, in Nieuport.
Painter.

Luc de Jonghe studied at the academy in Brussels, winning the Prix Godecharle in 1980.

JONGHE, Lucas François de
Flemish School, 17th century.
Born 1615, in Mechelen; died 1660.
Portrait artist.

Lucas de Jonghe is mentioned by Siret.

JONGHE, Peeter de. See **JODE Peeter II de**

JONGHELINCK, Jacques, or Jongelincx, called Jaques de Jonge
Flemish, 16th century.
Born 21 October 1530, in Antwerp; died 31 March 1606, in Antwerp.
Sculptor, medallist, engraver. Seals.
Antwerp School.

After a stay in Rome, Jonghelinck returned to Antwerp, where he was appointed sculptor to Philip I in 1563. The tomb of Charles the Reckless, which was constructed in the church of Notre-Dame in Bruges, is considered to be his masterpiece. He also produced a statue of the Duke of Alba.

BIBLIOGRAPHY:
Smolderen, Luc, *Jacques Jonghelinck: sculpteur, médailler et graveur de sceaux (1530-1606)*, Université catholique de Louvain, Louvain-la-Neuve, 1996.

JONGKIND, Johan or Jean Barthold
Dutch, 19th century.
Born 3 June 1819, in Latrop, near Rotterdam; died 9 February 1891, in the lunatic asylum in Grenoble, France.
Painter (gouache), watercolourist, engraver, draughtsman. Portraits, landscapes, urban landscapes, waterscapes, seascapes.
Honfleur (or St-Siméon) School, The Hague School.

Johan Barthold Jongkind was initially taught by Schelfhout. In 1845, at the inauguration of the statue of William the Conqueror, he was introduced to Eugène Isabey and in 1846 began to frequent his studio. Isabey became an important influence on the artist's early career. Jongkind divided his time between France and Holland. He was awarded a silver medal at the Salon of 1852; his *Clairs de Lune* (*Moonlight Pieces*), *Views of Paris* and *Skaters* established his reputation among art enthusiasts. In 1856, to pay off debts, Jongkind arranged for the Paris art dealer Firmin Martin to auction his work. In 1860 he was living in poverty when his friends Corot, Isabey, Rousseau and Bonvin organised another sale of his work on his behalf. He fled to Holland but the painter Cals sought him out and brought him back to Paris. Jongkind exhibited at the Salon des Refusés (exhibition of rejected work) in 1863, alongside Fantin La Tour, Whistler and Manet. From 1860, free now from the influence of both Isabey and Schelfhout, he began to develop a personal style and started to produce his best work. Around this time he began what was to be a lifelong relationship with Madame Fesser, whom he referred to as his 'good angel' and who became his pupil. During his visits to Honfleur (1862 to 1865) Jongkind met Claude Monet, Boudin and Charles Baudelaire. His notebooks show that in the company of Madame Fesser he travelled around France - to Nièvre in the Burgundy region and to the south of France - to Belgium, to the shores of Lake Geneva and to Isère, where he eventually settled in 1880, although he continued to visit Paris from time to time.

During his lifetime Jongkind did not enjoy the same success in Holland as the Maris brothers or Mauve. He was not unknown - the Goncourts and Roger-Marx favoured him - but he was still considered a minor artist. It was not until Manet and Cézanne became critically acclaimed that Jongkind too was taken up by art enthusiasts and impassioned artists such as Signac. In 1997, the Musée Mainssieux in Voiron (Isère) devoted an exhibition to Jongkind's work.

He merits comparison with Van Goyen, Ruysdael and in particular Rembrandt, indeed his etchings are often reminiscent of Rembrandt. His work has more in common with these artists than it does with the friends in Paris and Honfleur whom he influenced, but was not influenced by. Jongkind's draughtsmanship is the key to his concise and shimmering style. What makes his painting great (like Lautrec) is his adherence to the essential qualities of his own artistry. Jongkind was blessed with a marvellous visual memory and back in his studio, away from the scenes he had observed, he was able to recreate them.

He excelled as both a watercolourist and an oil painter. From 1863 he began to paint some fine views of Honfleur and Paris (notably his views of Notre-Dame) which equal Corot's best and are reminiscent of Vermeer's *View of Delft*. Although, as a body, his oil paintings remain uneven (lesser works are usually commissions or painted as a matter of routine), his watercolours by contrast display the same authority and potential throughout his career. Jongkind remained faithful to the same ports and villages and his work lost nothing through repetition; as he grew older he felt less bound by convention and more open to new approaches. The Isère watercolours, often executed with a trembling hand, are quite astounding (in particular certain *Snow Scenes*) for the conciseness with which each thing is suggested, for the warmth of the energy they convey, for the transposition of colour - bolder still than that of the Impressionists or Cézanne - and for his yet greater natural sense of the organisation of space and light. Jongkind was in many ways an ingenuous, somewhat primitive artist who worked from instinct rather than theory, but who was capable of translating his emotions visually, and went on producing numerous small masterpieces consigned to his sketchbooks until they were removed and signed by the artist. Generous donations from Camondo and Moreau-Nélaton have provided the Louvre with a particularly fine collection of Jongkind watercolours, while the Netherlands, slower off the mark, is still trying to fill the gaps in its collections.

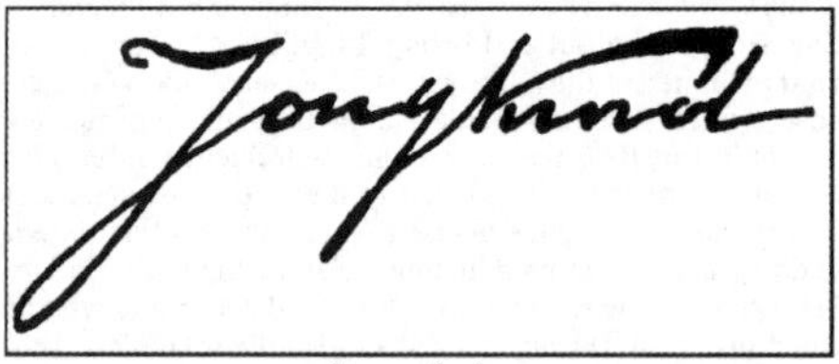

Stamp of sale

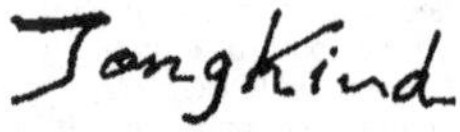

BIBLIOGRAPHY:

Moreau-Nélaton, *Jongkind raconté par lui-même*, Laurens, Paris, 1918. Hefting, Victorine, *J. B. Jongkind*, J. M. Meulenhoff, Amsterdam, 1960. Hefting, Victorine, *Jongkind. Sa vie, son œuvre, son époque*, Arts et Métiers Graphiques, Paris, 1975. Bionda, R. and others, eds., *The Age of Van Gogh: Dutch Painting, 1880-1895*, exhibition catalogue, Burrell Collection, Glasgow, 1990-1991. Lorenceau, Bernard, *Jongkind 1819-1891*, Gal. Brame et Lorenceau, Paris, 1996.

MUSEUMS AND GALLERIES:

AMIENS: *Seascape* - AMSTERDAM: *Mill by the Water; Rotterdam in the Moonlight* - AMSTERDAM (Stedelijk Mus.): *The Port at Rotterdam* - ANGERS: *The Seine in Paris* - BAGNÈRES-DE-BIGORRE: *Dutch Mill; The Tuileries and the Pont Royal; The Factory, Moonlight Study* - BAYONNE: *Seascape; View of Maaslins* - BRUSSELS: *The Port* - CHARTRES: *Landscape* - DÔLE: *Mill in Holland* - ELBERFELD: *Winter Landscape* - IXELLES: *Portrait of the Artist* - LE HAVRE: *L'Aube* - PARIS (Louvre, Camondo Collection): *The Mill* (1858); *Barge on the Canal* (1858); *Leaving Honfleur* (1864); *Pier on the River Escaut* (1866); *Fishing Boats on the River Escaut at Sunset* (1866); *Boats at the Mouth of the River Escaut* (1866); *Flotilla of Boats at the Entrance to Antwerp* (1866); *The Brussels Canal* (c. 1866); *Village of Overschie in Holland* (1866); *Mill by a Canal in Holland* (1867); *Boat Wash-houses at Notre Dame Bridge* (1868); *Outskirts of The Hague* (1868); *In Holland* (c. 1866); *The Seine at Argenteuil* (1869); *Brig on the River Meuse at Dordrecht* (1869); *Hay Boat on the River Meuse at Dordrecht* (1869); *Fishing Boats in Dordrecht* (1869); *Canal in Rotterdam* (1869); *Bridge on the Canal* (1869); *Village Pond* (c. 1869-1872); *Tree-Lined Road at Magny-Cours near Nevers* (1871); *The St-Parize-le-Chatel Road, Nièvre* (1872); *The Port of Marseilles* (1873); *Road at St-Éloy-sur-Loire, Nièvre* (1873); *Hardware Store in Rouen* (c. 1875-1880); *The Isère at Grenoble* (1877); *Winter Morning* (1880); *Chuzeau, Isère in Snowy Weather* (1880); *Col de Balbins and the Ornacieux Mountain, Isère* (1880); *Tower in Narbonne* (1880); *Ciotat* (1880); *The Roads, Toulon* (1880); *Banks of the Isère at Grenoble* (1883); *The Lesdiguières Bridge near Grenoble* (1883); *The Lyons Road at Côte-St-André* (1883) - PARIS (Louvre, Moreau Collection): *Ruins of Rosemont Château* - RHEIMS: *Canal in Holland; Dutch Canal; Village* - ROTTERDAM: *View of Overschie* - SAINTES: *Snow Scene.*

AUCTION RECORDS:

PARIS, March 1891, *Entrance to a Village in Le Nivernais,* FRF 805. PARIS, 6 May 1891, *Bridge on a Canal,* FRF 3,000; *Canal in Holland,* FRF 5,200. PARIS, 10 June 1891, *Main Road on the Outskirts of Paris,* FRF 2,600. PARIS, 28 Jan 1892, *Village in Brittany,* FRF 2,225. PARIS, 25 March 1892, *Port of Rotterdam,* FRF 4,100. PARIS, 20 May 1892, *Port-Royal Boulevard, Paris,* FRF 3,300. PARIS, 30-31 May 1892, *Skaters in Holland,* FRF 3,200; *The Hôtel-Dieu and Notre-Dame,* FRF 3,100. PARIS, 27 Feb 1893, *Canal in Holland,* FRF 2,500. PARIS, 10 June 1893, *Bridge on a Canal,* FRF 3,300. PARIS, 4 May 1896, *View of the Ile St-Louis,* FRF 3,450. PARIS, 9 March 1897, *Castle in the Nivernais,* FRF 1,730; *Rotterdam in Moonlight,* FRF 2,000. PARIS, 2 April 1897, *Canal,* FRF 3,250. PARIS, 7 Feb 1898, *Canal at Montaignac,* FRF 4,255; *Moonlight,* FRF 4,100; *Castle Entrance,* FRF 1,400; *View of Holland,* FRF 7,000. PARIS, 30 March 1898, *The Skaters,* FRF 6,700. PARIS, 20-21 June 1898, *The Towpath,* FRF 3,450. PARIS, 20-21 March 1899, *View of Dordrecht* (watercolour) FRF 1,020. PARIS, 11 April 1899, *Canal in Holland,* FRF 4,400. PARIS, 6 March 1900, *Sunset at Dordrecht,* FRF 4,700; *Rotterdam* (watercolour) FRF 1,680; *The River Drac at Grenoble,* FRF 4,454. PARIS, 8 May 1900, *Moonrise in Holland,* FRF 5,650; *Boulevard Montparnasse,* FRF 2,000; *Rue du Faubourg-St-Jacques,* FRF 2,400. PARIS, 11 June 1900, *The Seine at Quai d'Anjou,* FRF 15,000; *Sudden Wind on the River Escaut* (drawing) FRF 500. PARIS, 7 Feb 1901, *The Mill,* FRF 7,900; *Quai de la Tournelle,* FRF 6,125; *Rue de l'Abbé-de-l'Épée,* FRF 6, 000. PARIS, 11 March 1901, *Canal in Holland,* FRF 8,310; *Rue de l'Abbé-de-l'Épée,* FRF 9,050. PARIS, 11 March 1901, *Skaters in Holland,* FRF 19,100; *Port of Marseilles,* FRF 10,000; *Notre-Dame de Paris,* FRF 7,000. PARIS, 22-23 March 1901, *The Mulberry Tree* (watercolour) FRF 2,100. PARIS, 7 May 1901, *The Canal by Moonlight,* FRF 9,500. NEW YORK, 26-28 Feb 1902, *Pont-Royal Boulevard,* USD 950; *Canal in Holland,* USD 950; *At the Foot of the Staircase,* USD 1,250. PARIS, 7 May 1902, *Boats at Rest,* FRF 3,000. PARIS, 26-27 May 1902, *The River Meuse,* FRF 42,000; *The Port of Rotterdam,* FRF 27,000; *Skaters,* FRF 14,500; *Spring, Canal at Dordrecht,* FRF 17,000. NEW YORK, 8-9 Jan 1903, *Near Dordrecht,* USD 2,500. NEW YORK, 23 Jan 1903, *The Lazy Schoolboy,* USD 450. PARIS, 8 June 1903, *The Canal at Dordrecht,* FRF 10,000; *Winter on the Canal,* FRF 14,300. NEW YORK, 3 Feb 1905, *Canal in Holland,* USD 1,900. PARIS, 27 May 1905, *Nyons,* FRF 10,000. NEW YORK, 12-14 March 1906, *Ships,* USD 1,900; *Canal near Rotterdam by Moonlight,* USD 1,750. PARIS, 4 May 1906, *Port of Marseilles,* FRF 14,100. PARIS, 4 March 1907, *The Seine at Rouen* (watercolour) FRF 850. PARIS, 15 April 1907, *The Ourcq Canal,* FRF 4,600; *The Quay at Honfleur,* FRF 8,500. PARIS, 10 May 1907, *Canal at Rotterdam by Moonlight,* FRF 13,300. PARIS, 11-12 March 1908, *Old Woman,* FRF 6,050; *Pont de Bercy,* FRF 6,400; *Windmills in Holland,* FRF 5,800; *Moonlight on a Canal,* FRF

5,200. New York, 2 April 1909, *Canal near Rotterdam in Moonlight*, USD 1,550. London, 30 April 1909, *Port of Rotterdam* (1876) GBP 399; *Rotterdam* (1885) GBP 63. London, 27 Nov 1909, *Port* (1856) GBP 56. Paris, 30 May 1910, *Averchies Canal*, FRF 9,000. New York, 6 Jan 1911, *Dutch Canal by Moonlight*, USD 2,000. London, 18 Feb 1911, *Honfleur* (1863, watercolour) GBP 34. New York, 14-17 March 1911, *Pont Royal in Paris*, USD 1,000. Paris, 22 March 1911, *Winter in Holland*, FRF 8,000; *Road on the Côte St-André*, FRF 3,000. Paris, 31 March 1911, *Port Royal Boulevard*, FRF 6,500. London, 29 April 1911, *Coppet, Lake Geneva* (1876) GBP 46. Paris, 18 May 1911, *Twilight*, FRF 15,500; *The Mill*, FRF 6,480. Paris, 22 June 1911, *Skaters*, FRF 6,200; *The Mill*, FRF 5,500. Paris, 25 Nov 1918, *Skaters*, FRF 83,100. Paris, 2 Dec 1918, *Winter in Holland*, FRF 16,000. Paris, 24 Feb 1919, *Mulberry Tree* (watercolour) FRF 750. Paris, 26 Feb 1919, *Skaters*, FRF 17,000. Paris, 16-19 June 1919, *Ste-Adresse*, FRF 9,000. Paris, 26 Nov 1919, *View of the Canal on the Ourcq*, FRF 9,000. Paris, 1-3 Dec 1919, *Port Exit*, FRF 33,000; *Skaters in Holland*, FRF 21,000; *Canal in Holland* (watercolour) FRF 2,050. Paris, 1-2 March 1920, *Skaters at Overshie*, FRF 39,000; *Boulevard des Invalides in Snow*, FRF 17,500. Paris, 6-7 May 1920, *Quay at Honfleur*, FRF 25,200; *Canal near Leeden*, FRF 15,100. Paris, 27 May 1920, *Rotterdam Sunset*, FRF 20,000. Paris, 10 Dec 1920, *River Meuse at Dordrecht*, FRF 11,100. Paris, 4-5 March 1921, *Fort Rabot and Porte de France at Grenoble on the Banks of the River Isère*, FRF 10,450; *Sailing Ship Leaving Port, Antwerp*, FRF 12,000. Paris, 18 April 1921, *Canal in Rotterdam; Sunset*, FRF 14,000. Paris, 7 Dec 1922, *Port of Dordrecht in Foggy Weather*, FRF 30,500. Paris, 25 May 1923, *Skaters*, FRF 32,000; *Steam Boat*, FRF 8,500. Paris, 8 May 1924, *The Petit Bras of the Seine: View from the Quai St-Michel*, FRF 14,220. Paris, 28 Nov 1924, *Church of St-Germain-des-Près, View from the School of Medicine*, FRF 30,600. Paris, 17-18 June 1925, *Canal in Holland* (watercolour) FRF 9,100. Paris, 15 March 1926, *Skaters*, FRF 74,000; *View of Notre-Dame de Paris from the Bank near Pont St-Michel*, FRF 56,000; *Beside the Canal*, FRF 38,000. Paris, 18 March 1926, *River Banks*, FRF 30,000. Paris, 15 June 1926, *Moonlight in Holland*, FRF 40,000. Paris, 20 May 1927, *Brig and Boats at the Mouth of a River in Cloudy Weather*, FRF 42,100. Paris, 16-17 June 1927, *The Ourcq Canal at Pantin*, FRF 11,200. Paris, 17-18 June 1927, *The Towpath (Holland)*, FRF 18,100. Paris, 3 Dec 1927, *The Seine and Ile St-Louis*, FRF 16,200. Paris, 16 Dec 1927, *Kooswyk near Rotterdam*, FRF 16,600. Paris, 26 June 1928, *Large Sailing Ships*, FRF 61,000. Paris, 16 Nov 1928, *Demolition for the New Port-Royal Boulevard*, FRF 19,200. Paris, 26-27 Nov 1928, *Ships Alongside in the Port of Honfleur*, FRF 57,500. Paris, 28 Nov 1928, *The Lighthouse, View from Honfleur* (watercolour) FRF 8,500. Paris, 3-4 June 1929, *Vieille Rue, Rouen* (watercolour) FRF 25,200. Paris, 26 June 1929, *Fishing Port*, FRF 24,100. Paris, 6 Feb 1930, *The New Port-Royal Boulevard in Snow*, FRF 45,000. Paris, 28 May 1930, *Farm at the Foot of a Hill* (watercolour) FRF 4,600. Paris, 6 Dec 1930, *Antwerp* (watercolour) FRF 3,000. Paris, 15 May 1931, *Overschie Church*. Paris, 15 June 1931, *The New Port-Royal Boulevard Seen from the Place de l'Observatoire*, FRF 37,000. Paris, 14 Dec 1931, *The Hôtel de Ville Quay in Paris*, FRF 32,900; *The River Isère at Grenoble*, FRF 40,500. Paris, 2 June 1932, *Dordrecht*, FRF 40,000; *Road on the Outskirts of Honfleur*, FRF 40,100. Paris, 27 June 1932, *The Grenoble High Road* (watercolour) FRF 7,000. Paris, 17 Nov 1932, *Road Lined by Five Poplar Trees* (drawing pencil and wash) FRF 920; *Farm at the Foot of a Hill* (watercolour) FRF 1,160. Paris, 15 Dec 1932, *Canal in Holland* (watercolour) FRF 8,200. Paris, 3 April 1933, *Sailing Ship Leaving the Port of Antwerp*, FRF 13,500. Paris, 2 June 1933, *The Hackney Carriage*, FRF 11,000. Paris, 16 Dec 1933, *Virieu Mill*, FRF 4,500. Paris, 20 March 1935, *Skaters at Overschie*, FRF 40,000. Paris, 28 May 1935, *River Meuse at Dordrecht*, FRF 13,100. Paris, 7 June 1935, *The Old Tower at the Entrance to the Port of Rotterdam in Moonlight*, FRF 17,100. Paris, 28 June 1935, *Barges on a Canal in Brussels* (watercolour) FRF 5,010; *Dock in Brussels* (watercolour) FRF 4,020. Paris, 10 Feb 1936, *Canal on the Outskirts of Rotterdam*, FRF 12,450. Paris, 17 March 1936, *Village Street*, FRF 4,300. Paris, 6 March 1937, *Interior of the Port of Dordrecht*, FRF 25,000. Paris, 28 Feb 1938, *Landscape with a Large Tree* (watercolour and pencil outlines) FRF 4,100. Paris, 1 June 1938, *River in Holland*, FRF 18,600; *Moonrise over a River in Holland*, FRF 14,000. Paris, 15 June 1938, *The River Isère outside Grenoble*, FRF 32,600. Paris, 17 June 1938, *Road in Autumn* (watercolour) FRF 8,000; *Alleyway* (watercolour) FRF 14,000. Paris, 18 Feb 1939, *Café Courbet* (watercolour) FRF 3,750; *Sailing Ships at Honfleur* (watercolour) FRF 9,000; *Clump of Trees* (watercolour) FRF 5,000. Paris, 13 March 1939, *Place du Vieux Marché, Bruges*, FRF 16,500; *River in Holland*, FRF 17,000. Paris, 19 Jan 1940, *Waterscape*, FRF 26,600. Paris, 8 Nov 1940, *Charité-sur-Loire* (1872, watercolour, recto-verso) FRF 16,000; *The Suburbs of Paris* (1865) FRF 26,000. Paris, 5 Dec 1940, *Mill by a Canal in Holland* (watercolour) FRF 14,000. Paris, 14 March 1941, *Washerwomen* (1856) FRF 18,020; *The Port*, FRF 18,500; *Boats in the Moonlight* (1855) FRF 9,500. Paris, 11 May 1942, *House by a Stream* (1846) FRF 51,000. Paris, 18 May 1942, *Village Street* (watercolour) FRF 45,500; *Sandieu near Côte St-André* (1890) FRF 75,100. Paris, 14 Dec 1942, *Skaters on a Canal* (1873) FRF 88,000. Paris, 10 Feb 1943, *Street in Abbé-de-l'Épée* (1877) FRF 82,100; *Boats at Sea* (1870) FRF 250,000. Paris, 3 May 1944, *Low Tide at Honfleur* (watercolour) FRF 45,000. Paris, 17 May 1944, *The Omnibus in the Suburb of St-Jacques* (1875, watercolour and gouache) FRF 38,000; *River Drac near Grenoble* (1883, watercolour and gouache) FRF 85,000. Paris, 13 April 1945, *Women Bathing by a River*, FRF 131,000. Paris, 15 June 1945, *Sailing Ships in Port, Antwerp* (1866, watercolour) FRF 62,100. Paris, 22 June 1945, *Canal in Holland* (1868) FRF 118,000; *Course of the Isère* (1888, watercolour and gouache) FRF 39,500. Paris, July 1946, *Canal in Holland* (1873) FRF 150,000; *Banks of the River Meuse in Holland* (lead pencil) FRF 15,100. Paris, 14 Feb 1947, *Mills* (watercolour) FRF 115,000. Paris, 24 May 1955, *Skaters on a Canal in Holland* (1863, watercolour) FRF 2,200,000. Paris, 21 May 1957, *View of Dordrecht, Holland*, FRF 425,000. Paris, 3 Dec 1957, *The River Escaut near Antwerp* (watercolour) FRF 1,180,000. Paris, 19 March 1958, *The River Escaut near Antwerp* (watercolour) FRF 720,000. New York, 23 April 1958, *View near Delft*, USD 1,250. Paris, 4 June 1958, *Lake Geneva at Nyon* (1875) FRF 4,300,000. Paris, 11 June 1958, *Port and Canal in Holland* (watercolour and wash) FRF 700,000. Versailles, 16 March 1959, *Skaters in Holland* (1875) FRF 5,060,000. London, 6 May 1959, *Notre-Dame de Paris*, GBP 1,500. London, 25 Nov 1959, *View of Grenoble*, GBP 7,200. Paris, 14 March 1960, *Côte St-André, Isère*, FRF 27,500. London, 4 May 1960, *Port in Holland, View of a Church* (watercolour) GBP 2,000. London, 20 May 1960, *Skaters on a Canal in Holland*, GBP 2,100. Paris, 21 June 1960, *Fishermen's Return*, FRF 7,000. New York, 16 Feb 1961, *Quai d'Austerlitz, Paris* (watercolour and lead pencil) USD 950. Paris, 21 June 1961, *Skaters in Holland*, FRF 105,000. London, 28 June 1961, *Trouville at Low Tide*, GBP 2,000. London, 11 April 1962, *Port-Royal Boulevard in Snow* (watercolour) GBP 1,700; *Skaters at Overschie*, GBP 13,500. Paris, 23 March 1963, *At the King of the Desert*, FRF 100,000. London, 1 July 1964, *The Towpath*, GBP 17,800. London, 30 March 1966, *Côte St-André, Isère* (gouache) GBP 1,700. London, 24 June 1966, *The Seine at Rouen*, Gns 12,500. London, 26 April 1967, *Landscape in Bas-Meudon*, GBP 21,000. Paris, 10 Dec 1968, *The River Drac at Grenoble* (watercolour) FRF 23,000. Paris, 14 March 1969, *Nyon, Switzerland*, FRF 205,000. Geneva, 28 June 1969, *Winter in Côte St-André* (watercolour) CHF 29,500. GENEVA, 14 June 1970, *Bend in the Road*. LONDON, 2 Dec 1970, *Barge on a Canal outside Paris*, GBP 20,000. LONDON, 7 July 1971, *Pont-Neuf and the Statue of Henry IV*, GBP 13,500. VERSAILLES, 5 Dec 1971, *Port of Marseilles* (watercolour) FRF 23,000. NEW YORK, 17 Oct 1973, *Village Street* (watercolour and pencil) USD 15,000. NEW YORK, 28 Nov 1973, *Notre-Dame de Paris Seen from the Pont de l'Archevêché*, USD 80,000. LONDON, 2 April 1974, *The Port, Honfleur* (1865) Gns 12,000. PARIS, 17 June 1976, *Sailing Ship at Low Tide* (watercolour, 8 1/4 x 11 1/2 ins / 21 x 29 cm) FRF 30,000. LONDON, 30 June 1976, *Seascape at Antwerp* (1867, oil on canvas, 13 x 17 ins / 33 x 43 cm) GBP 18,000. NEW YORK, 11 May 1977, *View of Rouen* (1865, oil on canvas, 16 1/2 x 22 1/4 ins / 42 x 56.2 cm) USD 70,000. PARIS, 23 Nov 1978, *Exit from the Port of Honfleur* (1864, etching) FRF 13,000. NEW YORK, 7 Nov 1979, *Skaters in Holland* (1863, oil on canvas, 33 3/4 x 46 ins / 86 x 116 cm) USD 130,000. LONDON, 4 Dec 1979, *Côte St-André* (watercolour and pencil, 5 3/4 x 9 1/4 ins / 14.5 x 23.5 cm) GBP 1,300. BREST, 16 Dec 1979, *Beau Séjour, the Jongkind House at Ste-Adresse* (1884, watercolour and gouache, 4 3/4 x 7 3/4 ins / 12 x 20 cm) FRF 35,000. PARIS, 13 June 1980, *Sunset, Port of Antwerp* (etching/paper) FRF 6,300. AMSTERDAM, 2 Oct 1981, *Skaters* (1866, oil on canvas, 23 x 28 1/4 ins / 58.5 x 72 cm) NLG 330,000. PARIS, 16 Dec 1981, *Clamart* (1864, watercolour, 7 x 11 3/4 ins / 18 x 30 cm) FRF 42,000. PARIS, 7 June 1983, *Sunset, Port of Antwerp* (1868, etching) FRF 8,000. VERSAILLES, 27 Nov 1983, *Rue Méchain* (1874, watercolour, 6 x 9 1/2 ins / 15 x 24 cm) FRF 60,000. NEW YORK, 25 May 1984, *The Towpath* (1858, oil on canvas, 16 3/4 x 22 1/4 ins / 42.5 x 56.5 cm) USD 50,000. PARIS, 14 Dec 1984, *Skaters at Overshie* (1867, pen, 7 1/2 x 11 3/4 ins / 19 x 30 cm) FRF 47,000. LONDON, 26 June 1985, *Honfleur* (1866, watercolour heightened with gouache/pencil outlines, 10 x 18 1/4 ins / 25.5 x 46.5 cm) GBP 11,000. NEW YORK, 22 May 1986, *Mill beside a Canal* (1860, oil on canvas, 16 1/2 x 22 1/4 ins / 42 x 56.5 cm) USD 41,000. PARIS, 16 Dec 1987, *Entrance to the Port of Honfleur* (1863, etching) FRF 40,500. LONDON, 24 Feb 1988, *Peasant on Horseback* (charcoal and Indian ink, 10 x 17 1/4 ins / 24.5 x 43.5 cm) GBP 2,200; *Moonlight in Paris* (oil on canvas, 20 3/4 x 32 ins / 53 x 81 cm) GBP 14,300. PARIS, 26 Feb 1988, *Around the Tree* (1871, watercolour and charcoal, 8 1/4 x 11 1/2 ins / 21 x 29.5 cm) FRF 22,000. PARIS, 11 March 1988, *Sailing Ships and Boats near the Coast* (1866, oil on canvas, 23 1/4 x 32 ins / 59 x 81 cm) FRF 830,000. PARIS, 23 June 1988, *Young Girl with Sunshade* (1855, 8 1/2 x 6 1/4 ins / 21.5 x 16 cm) FRF 48,000. PARIS, 29 June 1988, *Exit from the Port of Honfleur* (watercolour, 5 1/4 x 11 1/4 ins / 13.5 x 28.5 cm) FRF 119,000. PARIS, 5 July 1988, *Thatched Cottage at Equemonville* (1865, charcoal, 5 1/2 x 9 ins / 14.2 x 22.7 cm) FRF 16,000. PARIS, 21 Nov 1988, *Landscape near Virieu Château (Isère)* (1877, watercolour, 8 x 16 1/4 ins / 20.5 x 41 cm) FRF 180,000. PARIS, 24 Nov 1988, *Outskirts of Honfleur* (1868, oil on canvas, 17 1/4 x 13 1/4 ins / 43.5 x 33.5 cm) FRF 205,000. LONDON, 21 Feb 1989, *Grenoble Landscape* (1884, watercolour/paper, 6 1/2 x 10 ins / 16.2 x 25.4 cm) GBP 7,150. CALAIS, 26 Feb 1989, *Landscape near Nevers* (drawing and watercolour, 6 1/4 x 11 ins / 16 x 27 cm) FRF 40,000. PARIS, 3 March 1989, *Landscape with Mill* (1962, watercolour, 6 x 9 1/2 ins / 15.5 x 24 cm) FRF 28,000. LONDON, 4 April 1989, *The Port of Rotterdam* (1857, oil on panel, 8 1/2 x 11 ins / 21.5 x 27 cm) GBP 52,800. NEW YORK, 18 Oct 1989, *The Ourcq Canal in the Aisne* (1872, oil on canvas, 10 3/4 x 15 1/4 ins / 27.3 x 38.7 cm) USD 66,000. VERSAILLES, 19 Nov 1989, *Mill in Holland* (charcoal, 7 3/4 x 10 ins / 20 x 25.5 cm) FRF 6,500. PARIS, 24 Nov 1989, *Dutch Port* (watercolour, 10 3/4 x 17 1/4 ins / 27.5 x 43.5 cm) FRF 53,000. AMSTERDAM, 13 Dec 1989, *Mill near Overschie at Sunset* (1872, oil on canvas, 13 x 18 1/2 ins / 33 x 47 cm) NLG 97,750. ST-DIÉ, 11 Feb 1990, *Mills* (graphite drawing, 5 1/2 x 10 1/2 ins / 14 x 26.5 cm) FRF 6,500. PARIS, 27 March 1990, *Canal in the Moonlight* (1868, 13 1/4 x 16 3/4 ins / 33.5 x 42.5 cm) FRF 150,000. LONDON, 2 April 1990, *Barge on the Canal outside Paris* (1870, oil on canvas, 16 1/4 x 25 3/4 ins / 41 x 65.5 cm) GBP 88,000. LYONS, 15 May 1990, *Vines at Côte St-André* (1883, watercolour, 7 x 10 1/2 ins / 17.5 x 26.5 cm) FRF 60,000. NEW YORK, 22 May 1990, *The Seine at Charenton* (1868, oil on canvas, 9 3/4 x 13 ins / 24.8 x 33 cm) USD 44,000. PARIS, 15 June 1990, *Roadside House* (watercolour, 8 1/2 x 18 1/4 ins / 21.5 x 46.5 cm) FRF 56,000. PARIS, 12 Oct 1990, *The Hamlet* (1883, watercolour and gouache, 6 1/2 x 10 ins / 16.5 x 24.5 cm) FRF 50,000. LONDON, 17 Oct 1990, *St Catherine's Church, Honfleur - The Market* (1865, oil on canvas, 16 1/2 x 26 1/4 ins / 42 x 66.5 cm) GBP 41,800. ZURICH, 18 Oct 1990, *Landscape on the Dauphiné Plain* (1885, watercolour and charcoal heightened with white, 6 3/4 x 10 ins / 17 x 25.5 cm) CHF 3,000. PARIS, 25 Nov 1990, *Notre-Dame de Paris from the Pont de l'Archevêché* (1849, oil on canvas, 13 3/4 x 23 3/4 ins / 35 x 60.5 cm) FRF 900,000. NEW YORK, 28 Feb 1991, *The Port of Rotterdam* (1856, oil on canvas, 17 x 22 ins / 43.2 x 55.9 cm) USD 71,500. AMSTERDAM, 23 April 1991, *On the Mountain* (1885, watercolour, 5 3/4 x 10 ins / 14.5 x 24.5 cm) NLG 11,500. AMSTERDAM, 14-15 April 1992, *View of Delft with Ducks on a Canal* (1859, oil on canvas, 17 1/4 x 13 ins / 44 x 33 cm) NLG 69,000. PARIS, 7 July 1992, *Banks of the Seine at Argenteuil* (1864, oil on canvas, 14 1/4 x 18 ins / 36 x 46 cm) FRF 360,000. LONDON, 1 Dec 1992, *The Port of Rotterdam* (1869, oil on canvas, 20 3/4 x 32 1/4 ins / 53 x 82 cm) GBP 74,800. NEW YORK, 17 Feb 1993, *Sailing Ships in the Mouth of a River with a Mill in the Distance* (1862, oil on canvas, 12 1/4 x 9 ins / 31.1 x 22.9 cm) USD 16,100. PARIS, 2 April 1993, *The Mountains of Grenoble* (watercolour, 6 3/4 x 20 ins / 17 x 51 cm) FRF 110,000. MONTREAL, 23-24 Nov 1993, *Sailing Ships Leaving Port* (1880, watercolour, 4 3/4 x 8 ins / 12 x 20.3 cm) CAD 1,500. PARIS, 26 Nov 1993, *Street in Avignon* (1880, watercolour and charcoal, 9 x 6 ins / 23 x 15 cm) FRF 64,000. PARIS, 9 March 1994, *Wooden Jetty in the Port of Honfleur* (etching) FRF 6,000. HEIDELBERG, 5-13 April 1994, *Entrance to the Port of Honfleur* (1863, etching, 9 1/2 x 12 1/2 ins / 24 x 32 cm) DEM 1,800. AMSTERDAM, 31 May 1994, *View of Dordrecht in the Moonlight* (1969, oil on canvas, 20 3/4 x 32 1/2 ins / 53 x 82.5 cm) NLG 126,500. LONDON, 29 June 1994, *Sailing Ships near the Coast* (1885, oil on canvas, 11 x 15 1/4 ins / 28 x 39 cm) GBP 12,420. PARIS, 16 Dec 1994, *Sailing Ship at the Mouth of the Seine* (1863, painting/paper/canvas, 9 3/4 x 13 3/4 ins / 25 x 35 cm) FRF 215,000. NEW YORK, 16 Feb 1995, *Canal in the Moonlight* (oil on canvas, 17 1/4 x 21 ins / 43.8 x 53.3 cm) USD 24,150. PARIS, 13 Dec 1995, *Canal near Rotterdam* (1867, oil on canvas, 13 1/4 x 22 ins / 33.4 x 56 cm) FRF 440,000. TOURCOING, 12 May 1996, *The Holie River at Rotterdam* (1868, oil on canvas, 9 3/4 x 13 ins / 25 x 33 cm) FRF 205,000. NEW YORK, 23-24 May 1996, *Windmill near Delft* (1857, oil on canvas, 22 x 16 1/2 ins / 55.9 x 41.9 cm) USD 85,000. PARIS, 7 June 1996, *Entrance to the Port of Honfleur* (1863, etching, 9 x 12 1/4 ins / 23 x 31.3 cm) FRF 6,000. LONDON, 21 Nov 1996, *View of Dordrecht by Moonlight* (1869, oil on canvas, 21 x 32 1/2 ins / 53.4 x 82.5 cm) GBP 63,100. PARIS, 4 Dec 1996, *Departure from the Port of Honfleur* (1864, etching, 9 1/4 x 12 1/2 ins / 23.5 x 31.5 cm) FRF 4,200. PARIS, 17 Dec 1996, *The Nevers Road* (drawing, 10 x 16 1/4 ins / 24.5 x 41 cm) FRF 6,000. NEW YORK, 12 Feb 1997, *Mill beside the Water* (1844, oil on panel, 17 1/2 x 20 ins / 44.5 x 50.8 cm) USD 43,700. CALAIS, 23 March 1997, *Sailing Ship in a Bay, Holland* (oil on canvas, 15 x 17 ins / 38 x 43 cm) FRF 220,000. PARIS, 16 June 1997, *Landscape* (watercolour and charcoal, a pair, 4 1/2 x 5 1/2 ins / 11.5 x 14 cm and 4 1/4 x 2 ins/11 x 5 cm) FRF 10,200. LONDON, 22 Oct 1997, *Canal in Holland by Moonlight* (1867, oil on canvas, 13 1/4 x 18 ins / 33.5 x 46 cm) GBP 11,500. PARIS, 1 April 1998, *Women Washing Clothes by a River* (oil on panel, 11 x 16 1/4 ins / 27 x 41 cm) FRF 180,000. PARIS, 8 April 1998, *Antwerp* (1866, watercolour and charcoal, 9 1/4 x 22 ins / 23.5 x 55 cm) FRF 29,500.

New York, 6 May 1999, *The River* (1857, oil on canvas, 17 x 22 ins / 43 x 56 cm) USD 90,000. London, 30 June 1999, *Winter Scene* (1871, oil on canvas, 9 x 13 ins / 22 x 32 cm) GBP 66,000. New York, 3 May 2000, *Dutch Landscape* (1865, oil on canvas, 17 x 22 ins / 42 x 56 cm) USD 240,000. Neuilly, 19 June 2000, *Three Skaters by a Windmill* (oil on canvas, 13 x 17 ins / 33 x 43 cm) FRF 810,000. London, 7 Feb 2001, *Boats by the Quay* (1855, oil on canvas, 16 x 13 ins / 41 x 32 cm) GBP 42,000. Paris, 19 Dec 2001, *The Merwede with Dordrecht Behind* (1878, oil on canvas, 9 x 13 ins / 24 x 32 cm) FRF 360,000. London, 7 Feb 2002, *Road in Nevers* (1872, gouache, watercolour and charcoal, 11 x 17 ins / 29 x 42 cm) GBP 19,000. New York, 23 April 2002, *In the Dauphiné* (1874, oil on canvas, 17 x 22 ins / 42 x 56 cm) USD 55,000. Calais, 18 May 2003, *The Old Dock, Brussels Entrepot* (oil on canvas, 10 x 13 ins / 25 x 33 cm) EUR 50,000. Amsterdam, 21 Oct 2003, *View of the Hoofdpoort, Rotterdam* (1878, oil on canvas, 13 x 20 ins / 33 x 52 cm) EUR 85,000. London, 3 Feb 2004, *Norwegian Ship Leaving Honfleur Harbour* (1865, oil on canvas, 13 x 19 ins / 33 x 47 cm) GBP 72,000. Amsterdam, 21 April 2004, *Winter Scene in Holland* (1878, oil on canvas, 9 x 13 ins / 23 x 32 cm) EUR 60,000.

JONGMAN, Dirk, or Jonkman
18th century.
Born c. 1684, in Amsterdam.
Draughtsman, engraver.

Dirk Jongman, a contemporary of Houbraken, made illustrations for the Hoets *Bible* and other works.

JONGMAN, Wouter
Dutch, 17th century.
Active at the end of the 17th century.
Engraver, draughtsman.

Wouter Jongman is known for 169 engravings he produced for the *History of the Military Orders*, published in Amsterdam in 1721.

JONGSMA, Jac
20th century.
Born 1893; died 1926.
Painter. Local scenes, landscapes.

Auction records:
Amsterdam, 11 Feb 1993, *Peasant Woman in a Farm Garden* (oil on canvas, 15¾ x 23½ ins / 40 x 60 cm) NLG 1,150. Gravenhage, 9 May 2000, *Lamb in Pasture by Small Farm* (oil on board, 17x13 ins / 44x33 cm) NLG 1,200. Gravenhage, 12 May 2004, *Farm* (oil on canvas, 10x13 ins / 25x34 cm) EUR 500. Gravenhage, 30 June 2004, *House of Hoorn, Ryswyk* (oil on canvas, 15x23 ins / 38x58 cm) EUR 900.

JONIC, Milos
French, 20th century.
Born 1916, in Paris.
Active in Venezuela from c. 1960.
Painter, watercolourist.

Milos Jonic studied at the fine arts academy in Munich and exhibited there in 1955. He also exhibited his work in 1959 and 1961 in Caracas, in 1960 in Maracaibo and in 1962 in New York.

JONIN, or Seinin, artist name: Enichibo
Japanese, 13th century.
Active in Kyoto during the first half of the 13th century.
Painter. Portraits, figures.

The beginning of the Kamakura period (from the late 12th century to the early 13th century) was a disrupted period from the religious point of view. Several new movements animated Buddhism and painting was called on to play an important role in spreading their doctrines in the form of illuminated scrolls. These explained to the faithful the origin of a sect as well as the life of its venerable founder. A group of artists was attached to each monastery. One of the most noteworthy temples from this point of view was the Kozan-ji in Kyoto established in 1206 by the monk Myoe Shonin (1173-1232) of the Kegon sect. Among the treasures of this temple is a series of six handscrolls *Kegonshu-soshi-e-den* or *Kegon-engi-emaki* (History of the Kegon Sect). The treatment using natural flowing lines and the use of thin colour, which allows the movement of the design to show through, are typical of a new style, influenced by Chinese painting of the Song dynasty (960-1279). This work is attributed to Myoe's favorite artist, Enichibo Jonin, to whom we also owe several portraits, of which one remains in Kozan-ji. This is a long hanging scroll, drawn in Indian ink heightened with colour, of the monk Myoe in solitary meditation in the mountains. Even though Chinese elements are still present in this picture, nonetheless it has a very Japanese feeling for nature and is a typical example of the realistic art of the period, which is deeply imbued with humanity.

Museums and Galleries:
Kyoto (Kozan-Ji Temple): *History of the Kegon Sect* (from the first half of the 13th century, colour on paper, handscroll, attributed); *Portrait of Myoe Meditating* (from the first half of the 13th century, ink and colour on silk, hanging scroll, listed on the register of important cultural properties).

JONJO, Henri Alphonse Joseph
French, 20th century.
Born 1907 and 1912.
Active in Paris between 1907 and 1912.
Painter. Genre scenes, landscapes.

Henri Alphonse Joseph Jonjo lived alternately in Paris and St-Leu-Taverny. He exhibited in Paris in 1908, 1910 and 1912 at the Salon des Artistes Français and in 1907 and from 1909 to 1912 at the Salon des Indépendants.

JONK, Nic
Dutch, 20th century.
Born 1928, in Shermerhorn; died 11 October 1995.
Sculptor. Mythological subjects, animals.

Auction records:
Siren (1974, bronze, h. 34¼ ins / 87 cm) NLG 31,860. Amsterdam, 15 Nov 1976, *Figure* (1968, bronze, h. 37½ ins / 95 cm) NLG 13,000. Amsterdam, 24 March 1986, *Woman Seated* (bronze, h. 10 ins / 24.5 cm) NLG 2,600. Amsterdam, 10 April 1989, *Sea II* (1980, bronze, h. 10¼ ins / 26 cm) NLG 2,875. Amsterdam, 24 May 1989, *Eve and the Serpent* (1966, bronze, h. 17¼ ins / 44 cm) NLG 17,250. Amsterdam, 22 May 1990, *Nereus on a Sea Horse* (1961, bronze, h. 24 ins / 61 cm) NLG 20,700. Amsterdam, 9 Dec 1992, *Two Horses* (1990, oil on canvas, 39¼ x 47¼ ins / 100 x 120 cm) NLG 4,140. Amsterdam, 10 Dec 1992, *Mother and Child* (1962, bronze, h. 9¾ ins / 24.8 cm) NLG 5,750. Amsterdam, 26 May 1993, *Nereid on a Triton III* (1962, bronze, h. 9 ins / 23 cm) NLG 5,175. Amsterdam, 14 June 1994, *Nereid on a Triton* (bronze, h. 5¼ ins / 13.5 cm) NLG 2,300. Amsterdam, 8 Dec 1994, *Female Figure* (1964, bronze, h. 10¼ ins / 26 cm) NLG 4,485. Amsterdam, 7 Dec 1995, *Sea* (1976, bronze, h. 11 ins / 27 cm) NLG 3,540. Amsterdam, 17-18 Dec 1996, *Vrouw met gele boa* (*Woman with a Yellow Boa*) (1988, acrylic/canvas, 65 x 39¼ ins / 165 x 100 cm) NLG 19,470. Amsterdam, 2-3 June 1997, *Untitled* (1980-1985, bronze, h. 30¾ ins / 78 cm) NLG 49,560. Amsterdam, 1 Dec 1999, *Jacob and the Angel* (1964, bronze, h. 13 ins / 32 cm) NLG 4,000. Amsterdam, 13 June 2001, *Watchman* (1973, bronze, 41 x 31x24 ins / 103 x 80x60 cm) NLG 48,000. Amsterdam, 25 Nov 2002, *Dawn* (1973, bronze, h. 8 ins / 21 cm) EUR 2,000. Amsterdam, 3 June 2003, *Nereid on a Triton II* (1964, bronze, h. 30 ins / 75 cm) EUR 13,000. Amsterdam, 25 Nov 2003, *Nereid on a Triton II*

(bronze, h. 30 ins / 75 cm) EUR 18,000. AMSTERDAM, 7 June 2004, *Nereid on a Triton II* (1981, silver, h. 5 ins / 13 cm) EUR 2,400. AMSTERDAM, 2 Dec 2004, *Europa and the Bull* (bronze, h. 9 ins / 23 cm) EUR 2,500.

JONKER, C. de
Dutch, 18th century.
Active c. 1791.
Draughtsman, engraver.

JONKHEER. See **JONCKHEER**

JONKHER, Joseph
School of Lorraine, 18th century.
Sculptor.
Jonkher executed sculptures for the cathedrals at Toul and Verdun.

JONKMAN
Belgian, 20th century.
Born in Brussels.
Painter. Landscapes.
AUCTION RECORDS:
BRUSSELS, 19 Dec 1989, *Garden in Bloom* (oil on canvas, 28 3/4 x 23 1/2 ins / 73 x 60 cm) BEF 20,000.

JONKMAN, Dirk. See **JONGMAN**

JONNAERT, Clémence
Belgian, 19th - 20th century.
Born 1866, in Ghent; died 1941, in Brussels.
Painter. Still-lifes, flowers.
Clémence Jonnaert was a student at the Académie des Beaux-Arts in Ghent, where she had as teachers Jules de Keghel and Jean Delvin. She featured in the Exposition de Bruxelles of 1910.
AUCTION RECORDS:
PARIS, 9 Dec 1988, *Flowers* (oil on canvas, 31 x 22 1/2 ins / 78.5 x 57 cm) FRF 5,800. BRUSSELS, 19 Dec 1989, *Flowers* (oil on canvas, 39 1/4 x 25 1/2 ins / 100 x 65 cm) BEF 250,000; *Flowers* (oil on canvas, 26 x 23 1/2 ins / 66 x 60 cm) BEF 45,000. LOKEREN, 21 March 1992, *Still-life of Flowers* (oil on canvas, 25 1/2 x 31 1/2 ins / 65 x 80 cm) BEF 55,000. LOKEREN, 8 Oct 1994, *Still-life with Dahlias* (oil on canvas, 23 1/2 x 19 3/4 ins / 60 x 50 cm) BEF 30,000. LOKEREN, 10 March 2001, *Rhododendrons* (oil on canvas, 31 x 35 ins / 78 x 88 cm) BEF 160,000.

JONNARD-PACEL, Paul
French, 19th century.
Born in Paris; died 1902, in Paris.
Engraver.
Paul Jonnard-Pacel studied under Trichon. He exhibited at the Paris Salon in 1863 and 1866 and was a member of the Société des Artistes Français.

JONNÈS, A. de
French, 19th century.
Painter. History painting, genre scenes.
A. de Jonnès exhibited historical subjects and portraits at the Paris Salon from 1831 to 1843. He is known for: *Scene of the Execution of Charles Ist*, *Last Moments of Charles IX*, *Holy Water: Scene from the Time of Louis XIII*, *Claire Varsen* and *Lady Jane Grey Praying Before Her Verdict*.

JONNIAUX, Alfred
Belgian, 20th century.
Born 21 November 1882, in Brussels; died 4 February 1974.
Painter. Portraits.
Alfred Jonniaux was a student at the Académie des Beaux-Arts in Brussels, and a member of the Société Royale des Beaux-Arts there. He spent periods of time in England, Italy, the USA and France as an official or society portrait painter in the grand manner.

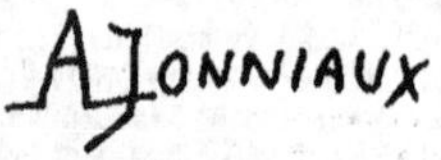

JONQUIÈRES, Eduardo
Argentinian, 20th century.
Born 27 February 1918, in Buenos Aires.
Active in France from 1959.
Painter.
Eduardo Jonquières studied at the Buenos Aires fine arts academy from 1932 to 1936 and taught history of art at the University of La Plata. He lived and worked in Paris from 1959.

His painting is abstract with a geometric tendency, sometimes using curved forms.

Jonquières has participated in a large number of collective exhibitions including: Grands et Jeunes d'Aujourd'hui, Paris (1966, 1968 to 1974, 1976, 1978 and 1980 to 1988); Salon Comparaisons, Paris (1967, 1969 to 1972 and 1976); Salon d'Automne (1976 and from 1981 onwards); Salon des Réalités Nouvelles, Paris (1971 to 1974, 1976 and from 1983 onwards); 4th São Paulo Biennale (1956); Universal Exhibition, Brussels (1958 winning a bronze medal); Musée d'Art Moderne, Paris (1962, 1964 and 1965); national fine arts museum, Santiago (1970); Espace Latino-Américain in Paris (1981, 1986, 1988 and 1990); Havana Biennale (1984); Orangerie du Luxembourg, Paris (1985); Basel Exhibition (1988); *Abstraction-Intégration* touring exhibition in Essonne (1977).

Jonquières has also shown his work at solo exhibitions in Buenos Aires (1951, 1954, 1956, 1958, 1960, 1964 and 1974); in Paris (1964 and 1986); in São Paulo (1974); in Genoa (1977); Madrid (1980); Valencia (1981); Rome (1982), and Saarlouis (1982). He was made Chevalier des Arts et des Lettres.
MUSEUMS AND GALLERIES:
BUENOS AIRES (MA Plásticas Eduardo Sívori) - BUENOS AIRES (MAM) - BUENOS AIRES (Mus. Nacional de Bellas Artes) - HAVANA (Casa de Las Americas) - MANAGUA (MCA) - PARIS (BNF) - SAN MARTINO DI LUPARI (Mus. d'umbro Appollonio) - SÃO PAULO (MAC) - VILLAFAMÉS (Mus. Popular de Arte Contemporáneo).

JONQUIÈRES, Victor Philippe Auguste de
French, 19th century.
Born 19th century, in Paris.
Painter. History painting, portraits, genre scenes.
Victor Philippe Auguste de Jonquières studied under Blondel and Horace Vernet. He exhibited portraits and genre subjects at the Paris Salon from 1838 to 1870.
AUCTION RECORDS:
VERSAILLES, 13 May 1984, *(Allegorical) Victory Procession after the Coup d'État of 2 December 1851; 1865* (oil on canvas, 63 1/2 x 89 3/4 ins / 161 x 228 cm) FRF 102,000. MONACO, 17 June 1989, *The Dividing Up of France* (1879, oil on canvas, 28 1/4 x 35 3/4 ins / 71.5 x 91 cm) FRF 28,860. LYONS, 17 Oct 2004, *La Créole* (1848, oil on canvas, 44 x 55 ins / 113 x 140 cm) EUR 44,000.

JONSDOTTIR, Kristin, or also Stefansson Jonsdottir
Icelandic, 20th century.
Born 25 January 1888, in Arnarnes; died 1959.
Painter. Figures, landscapes.
Kristin Jonsdottir lived and worked in Reykjavik.
MUSEUMS AND GALLERIES:
COPENHAGEN (Nationalmus.).
AUCTION RECORDS:
COPENHAGEN, 8 March 1977, *Landscape* (oil on canvas, 35 x 50 3/4 ins / 89 x 129 cm) DKK 14,000.

JØNSEN-MIKINES, Samuel
Danish, 20th century.
Born 1906; died 1979.
Painter. Landscapes, seascapes, fishing scenes, harbour views.

AUCTION RECORDS:
COPENHAGEN, 29 April 1976, *View of a Port* (1962, oil on canvas, 29½ x 39¼ ins / 75 x 100 cm) DKK 8,800. COPENHAGEN, 3 May 1977, *Beside the Sea* (1937, oil on canvas, 45¼ x 61 ins / 115 x 154 cm) DKK 20,000. COPENHAGEN, 30 May 1979, *View of a Fjord* (1954, oil on canvas, 35¾ x 51¼ ins / 91 x 130 cm) DKK 31,000. COPENHAGEN, 9 April 1981, *Seaside Landscape, The Faeroe Islands* (1964, oil on canvas, 41¼ x 49¼ ins / 105 x 125 cm) DKK 27,000. COPENHAGEN, 2 June 1983, *The Faeroe Islands* (1964, oil on canvas, 33½ x 39¼ ins / 85 x 100 cm) DKK 28,800. COPENHAGEN, 13 Feb 1985, *Sunset* (1968, oil on canvas, 33½ x 39¼ ins / 85 x 100 cm) DKK 63,000. COPENHAGEN, 25 Feb 1987, *Two Men beside the Sea* (1959, oil on canvas, 39¼ x 47¼ ins / 100 x 120 cm) DKK 46,000. COPENHAGEN, 2 March 1988, *Harpoon Fishing* (25½ x 31½ ins / 65 x 80 cm) DKK 4,900. COPENHAGEN, 4 May 1988, *Buildings at Mykenes* (1957, 33½ x 39¼ ins / 85 x 100 cm) DKK 51,000. COPENHAGEN, 10 May 1989, *Whaling* (1956, oil on canvas, 39¼ x 53¼ ins / 100 x 135 cm) DKK 50,000. COPENHAGEN, 20 Sept 1989, *Ascetics* (1937, oil on canvas, 43¼ x 31½ ins / 110 x 80 cm) DKK 65,000. COPENHAGEN, 22 Nov 1989, *Waves Breaking on the Shore* (1961, oil on canvas, 41¼ x 49¼ ins / 105 x 125 cm) DKK 40,000. COPENHAGEN, 21-22 March 1990, *Village beside the Sea* (1953, oil on canvas, 23½ x 31½ ins / 60 x 80 cm) DKK 25,000. COPENHAGEN, 30 May 1990, *Whaling* (1970, oil on canvas, 33¾ x 53½ ins / 86 x 136 cm) DKK 47,000. COPENHAGEN, 31 Oct 1990, *The House near the Sea* (1964, oil on canvas, 35½ x 43¼ ins / 90 x 110 cm) DKK 46,000. COPENHAGEN, 14-15 Nov 1990, *Sun Setting over a Fishing Port* (1962, oil on canvas, 26 x 31½ ins / 66 x 80 cm) DKK 20,000. COPENHAGEN, 13-14 Feb 1991, *Houses by the Sea in the Faeroe Islands* (1943, oil on canvas, 38¼ x 49½ ins / 97 x 126 cm) DKK 76,000. COPENHAGEN, 2 April 1992, *Whale Fishing* (1964, oil on canvas, 25½ x 32 ins / 65 x 81 cm) DKK 32,000. COPENHAGEN, 21 April 1993, *View of Gudhjem* (oil on canvas, 43¼ x 47¼ ins / 110 x 120 cm) DKK 35,000. COPENHAGEN, 20 Oct 1993, *The Storm is Gathering in the Faeroe Islands* (1962, oil on canvas, 33½ x 39¼ ins / 85 x 100 cm) DKK 39,000. COPENHAGEN, 19 Oct 1994, *Village* (1940, oil on canvas, 24½ x 32¼ ins / 62 x 82 cm) DKK 30,000. COPENHAGEN, 17 April 1996, *View of a Village* (1940, oil on canvas, 31½ x 39¼ ins / 80 x 100 cm) DKK 23,000. COPENHAGEN, 17 April 1997, *View of the Port* (oil on canvas, 25¼ x 30¾ ins / 64 x 78 cm) DKK 21,000. COPENHAGEN, 12-14 Nov 1997, *Summer's Day, Houses beside the Sea* (1955, oil on canvas, 25½ x 31½ ins / 65 x 80 cm) DKK 20,000. COPENHAGEN, 22 June 1999, *Vessels by Coast* (1940, oil on canvas, 39 x 53 ins / 100 x 134 cm) DKK 46,000. COPENHAGEN, 5 Oct 1999, *Evening* (1939, oil on canvas, h. 69 ins / 175 cm) DKK 80,000. COPENHAGEN, 28 March 2000, *Men Looking Out at Breakers* (1961, oil on canvas, 35 x 43 ins / 90 x 110 cm) DKK 46,000. COPENHAGEN, 3 Oct 2000, *Fishermen by the Sea, Faroe Islands* (1958, oil on canvas, 39 x 49 ins / 100 x 125 cm) DKK 42,000. COPENHAGEN, 2 April 2001, *Killing of Whale* (1944, oil on canvas, 57 x 75 ins / 146 x 190 cm) DKK 160,000. COPENHAGEN, 10 Oct 2001, *Landscape from the Island of Myggenaes with Vaago, Sorvagsfjord* (1954, oil on canvas, 40 x 52 ins / 102 x 132 cm) DKK 85,000. COPENHAGEN, 10 April 2002, *Killing of Whales* (oil on canvas, 31 x 39 ins / 80 x 100 cm) DKK 52,000. VEJLE, 11 Nov 2002, *Killing of Whales, Faroe Islands with Figures and Boats* (1964, oil on canvas, 33 x 39 ins / 85 x 100 cm) DKK 56,000. COPENHAGEN, 26 Feb 2003, *Killing of Whale* (1942, oil on canvas, 39 x 51 ins / 100 x 130 cm) DKK 75,000. COPENHAGEN, 1 April 2003, *Green Cliff Formation* (1960, oil on canvas, 42 x 49 ins / 106 x 125 cm) DKK 72,000. COPENHAGEN, 29 March 2004, *View from Mykines with Figures in Foreground* (1961, oil on canvas, 42 x 50 ins / 106 x 126 cm) DKK 75,000. COPENHAGEN, 29 March 2004, *Evening* (1939, oil on canvas, 69 x 55 ins / 175 x 139 cm) DKK 120,000.

JONSON, Raymond
American, 20th century.
Born 1891, in Chariton (Iowa); died 1982, in Albuquerque (New Mexico).
Active in Chicago and New Mexico.
Painter, lithographer. Landscapes.

Raymond Jonson grew up in Portland, Oregon, before moving to Chicago with a few savings. He studied at the Chicago Art Institute and at the Academy of Fine Arts where he met painter B.J.O. Nordfeldt. On the occasion of the 1913 Armory Show, held in Chicago, Raymond Jonson discovered Kandinsky and the Expressionist movement. In the 1920s, he moved to Santa Fe and, enthralled by the majesty of the landscapes, he began painting in a Cubist style (*Grand Canyon Trilogy*, 1923). In Santa Fe, he later founded the Transcendental Painting Group which enabled its nine members to explore all aspects of abstraction as well as to promote it to an unreceptive public. From 1934 to 1954, he taught at the University of New Mexico.

Already in his 1924-1927 New Mexico landscapes, Raymond Jonson's style tended towards stylisation. He projected abstraction on Nature's geometries with great coloured flat tints. His painting was still realist in that an outward reality was being suggested. He was giving a free account of the vastness of the mountains, much as Cézanne or Picabia would have. After 1927, he was fully engaged in abstraction. The sets *Universe* and *Cosmic Theme*, begun in 1935 and 1936, were a turning point in the artist's production. He left landscapes behind for a more mysterious painting, airy and punctuated with light effects. Jonson would explain that *Cosmic Theme no. 3* represented essentially a structural research, a quest for pure sensations as opposed to any imitation of nature or vision of it. In 1938, he started to paint with a spray gun. This modern technique released in him unbound creativity with a new freedom of expression leading to optical illusion created by the superposition and juxtaposition of colours.

He took part in collective exhibitions in Chicago, many venues in New York, Los Angeles, Cincinnati, Philadelphia and San Francisco. He has shown his works in solo exhibitions in Santa Fe, Minneapolis and Houston.

BIBLIOGRAPHY:
Garman, Ed, *The Art of Raymond Jonson*, University of New Mexico Press, Albuquerque, 1976. Rohlfsen Udall, Sharin, *Modernist Painting in New Mexico 1913-1935*, University of New Mexico Press, Albuquerque, 1984. *The Raymond Jonson Centennial Retrospective*, exhibition catalogue, University of New Mexico, Albuquerque, 1991. *Raymond Jonson: Late Abstractions*, exhibition catalogue, Gerald Peters Gallery, Santa Fe, 1992. Chassey, Éric de (ed.), *Made in USA. L'art américain de 1908 à 1947*, exhibition catalogue, Musée des beaux-arts, Bordeaux, Réunion des musées nationaux, Paris, 2001.

MUSEUMS AND GALLERIES:
DALLAS (MA): *Polymer No. 17* (1960); *Composition 7, Snow*; *Variations on Rythm P.*; *Watercolor No. 25* - DENVER (AM) - MINNEAPOLIS (Frederick R. Weisman AM, University of Minnesota) - NEW MEXICO CITY (University of New Mexico, Fine Arts Center, Jonson Gal.) - PHOENIX (AM) - PORTLAND, OR (AM): *City Perspectives* (1932, oil on canvas) - SAN FRANCISCO (MoMA): *Growth Variant No. VII* (1931, oil on canvas) - SANTA FE (MFA) - WASHINGTON DC (NGA): *Variations on a Rhythm-U* (1933, oil on canvas) - WASHINGTON DC (Smithso-

nian American AM): *Josephine White* (1921, charcoal/paper); *Arroyo (2)* (1922, oil/paperboard); *Composition Four - Melancholia* (1925, oil on canvas); *Variations on a Rhythm-H* (1931, oil on canvas); *Monument to Sound* (1936, pencil/paper/fiberboard).

AUCTION RECORDS:

NEW YORK, 26 June 1985, *Eclipse* (1933, pencil, 15 x 11 ins / 38 x 28 cm) USD 1,300. NEW YORK, 26 June 1985, *Watercolor No. 18* (1939, watercolour, 22 x 35 ins / 56 x 89 cm) USD 2,400. NEW YORK, 23 May 1990, *Eclipse - Universe Series* (1935, oil on canvas, 40 x 41 ins / 101.3 x 104 cm) USD 38,500. NEW YORK, 4 Dec 1992, *Houses in the Hill No. 4* (1928, oil on canvas, 35 x 40 1/2 ins / 88.9 x 102.9 cm) USD 88,000. NEW YORK, 27 May 1993, *Chelly Canyon* (1928, oil on canvas, 23 x 31 ins / 58.4 x 78.7 cm) USD 63,000. NEW YORK, 30 Nov 1999, *Oil No. 10* (1946, oil on canvas, 40 x 40 ins / 102 x 102 cm) USD 22,000. LOS ANGELES, 9 Dec 1999, *Oil No. 16* (1954, oil on canvas, 28 x 40 ins / 71 x 102 cm) USD 5,000. LOS ANGELES, 3 May 2000, *Prismatic Figuration* (1934, oil on canvas, 20 x 15 ins / 51 x 38 cm) USD 32,000. VANCOUVER, 4 April 2002, *Dragon Fly Fantasy, Fifth Fantasy* (1919, oil on canvas, 30 x 33 ins / 76 x 84 cm) CAD 45,000. LOS ANGELES, 19 June 2002, *Variations on a Rhythm-E* (1931, oil on canvas, 33 x 29 ins / 84 x 74 cm) USD 36,000. CHICAGO, 9 Nov 2003, *Oil No.4, 1942* (oil on linen, 40 x 40 ins / 102 x 102 cm) USD 22,000. NEW YORK, 3 Dec 2003, *Growth Variant No. V* (1929, oil on canvas, 38 x 27 ins / 96 x 69 cm) USD 27,500. LOS ANGELES, 28 April 2004, *Oil No. 3* (1946, oil on canvas, 20 x 14 ins / 50 x 35 cm) USD 7,500. CHICAGO, 16 May 2004, *Chromatic Contrasts No. 23, Oil No. 15* (1947, oil on canvas, 40 x 40 ins / 102 x 102 cm) USD 16,000.

JONSON, Sven

Swedish, 20th century.
Born 1902, in Halmstad; died 1981.
Painter. Scenes with figures, sporting subjects, architectural views.
Purism.
Halmstad Group.

Sven Jonson studied at the Wilhelmson academy of painting in Stockholm, and then in Paris, and was a member of the Halmstad group from 1930. His style recalls the Purism of Ozenfant and Jeanneret. He painted ambitious architectural views in refined colour harmonies, with restrained but imposing forms which are to a certain extent geometric. Their grandiose scale is confirmed by the small size of the few figures positioned at the entrances. He subsequently developed in the direction of Surrealism.

Jonson took part in the group exhibitions *Concrete Art* in Stockholm in 1930 and *Surrealism Cubism* in Copenhagen in 1935, and in the Surrealist exhibitions in London in 1936, Lund in 1937 and Paris in 1938.

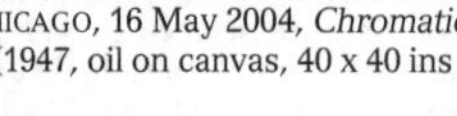

BIBLIOGRAPHY:

Pagé, Suzanne/Winock, Michel/Michaud, Éric/Vidal, Aline, *Les Années trente en Europe. Le Temps menaçant*, exhibition catalogue, Musée d'Art moderne de la Ville de Paris, Paris musées, Flammarion, Paris, 1997.

AUCTION RECORDS:

STOCKHOLM, 22 April 1981, *Vertical Composition* (1957, oil on canvas, 38 1/2 x 16 1/4 ins / 98 x 41 cm) SEK 19,000. STOCKHOLM, 29 Nov 1983, *Off the Port* (oil on canvas, 31 1/2 x 25 1/4 ins / 80 x 64 cm) SEK 90,000. STOCKHOLM, 20 April 1985, *Break-up* (1937, oil on panel, 35 3/4 x 23 1/4 ins / 91 x 59 cm) SEK 45,000. STOCKHOLM, 7 Dec 1987, *Dark Ruin* (1951, oil on canvas, 9 x 11 ins / 22 x 27 cm) SEK 49,000. STOCKHOLM, 6 June 1988, *Vertical Fault* (oil, 17 3/4 x 21 1/4 ins / 45 x 54 cm) SEK 81,000. STOCKHOLM, 6 Dec 1989, *Sunbeams* (1955, oil on canvas, 8 1/4 x 10 1/4 ins / 21 x 26 cm) SEK 43,000. STOCKHOLM, 14 June 1990, *Girl at Dusk* (oil on canvas, 10 1/4 x 13 1/2 ins / 26 x 34 cm) SEK 30,000. STOCKHOLM, 5-6 Dec 1990, *Nocturn* (oil on canvas, 15 x 18 ins / 38 x 46 cm) SEK 40,000. STOCKHOLM, 21 May 1992, *Fragment* (oil on canvas, 16 1/4 x 28 ins / 41 x 71 cm) SEK 45,000. STOCKHOLM, 10-12 May 1993, *Women in a Landscape* (oil on canvas, 9 x 11 ins / 22 x 27 cm) SEK 21,500. STOCKHOLM, 30 Nov 1993, *Spring Morning* (oil on canvas, 18 x 22 ins / 46 x 55 cm) SEK 46,000. STOCKHOLM, 27 April 1999, *Return* (1972, oil on canvas, 26 x 31 ins / 66 x 80 cm) SEK 96,000. STOCKHOLM, 27 April 1999, *Dawn* (1935, oil on canvas, 30 x 33 ins / 75 x 85 cm) SEK 108,000. STOCKHOLM, 7 Nov 2000, *Harbour Scene, Possibly Halmstad* (1928, oil on canvas, 26 x 22 ins / 66 x 56 cm) SEK 94,000. STOCKHOLM, 7 Nov 2000, *Still-life of Mug, Jug and Fruit* (1925, oil on canvas, 22 x 18 ins / 55 x 46 cm) SEK 130,000. STOCKHOLM, 21 May 2001, *Nocturn* (oil on canvas, 13 x 17 ins / 34 x 42 cm) SEK 39,000. STOCKHOLM, 6 Nov 2001, *Elegy* (oil on canvas, 26 x 31 ins / 65 x 80 cm) SEK 78,000. STOCKHOLM, 23 April 2002, *Night's Horizon* (oil on canvas, 26 x 33 ins / 65 x 83 cm) SEK 94,000. STOCKHOLM, 23 April 2002, *In the Making* (1935, oil on canvas, 21 x 27 ins / 53 x 69 cm) SEK 145,000. STOCKHOLM, 28 April 2003, *Hurdlers* (1929, oil on canvas, 22 x 30 ins / 55 x 75 cm) SEK 280,000. STOCKHOLM, 4 Nov 2003, *Cathedral* (1951, oil on canvas, 52 x 64 ins / 133 x 163 cm) SEK 120,000. STOCKHOLM, 27 April 2004, *Light Night* (oil on canvas, 26 x 31 ins / 65 x 80 cm) SEK 100,000. STOCKHOLM, 27 April 2004, *Statue in a Landscape* (1932, oil on canvas, 16 x 20 ins / 40 x 50 cm) SEK 115,000.

JONSON VAN CEULEN, Cornelis.

See **CEULEN**

JONSRUD, Ole

Norwegian, 20th century.
Born 14 May 1875, in Christiania (now Oslo).
Painter. Landscapes.

Ole Jonsrud was a student at the school of fine art in Christiania, and studied the nude at the institute of fine art in Florence. He continued his studies in Copenhagen, France, Brittany and in Paris in the studio of Othon Friesz. From 1895 he often featured in the annual national exhibition in Christiania, as well as at the Exposition Universelle in Paris in 1900, at the Krystallpalast in Munich in 1913, and the Nordic Exhibition of Fine Art in Brighton in 1913. He painted landscapes of Norway.

JONSSON, Adolf Sven August

Swedish, 19th - 20th century.
Born 7 July 1872, in Småland.
Sculptor. Busts.

Adolf Sven August Jonsson was a pupil of Injalbert and Rolland in Paris and a student at the Académie Colarossi. He lived from in Rome 1904 to 1914 and featured in numerous exhibitions in Paris, Rome and Stockholm.

He is remembered in particular for busts of the sculptor Bissen, of Hjalmar Branting and of the painter Axel Holmström, a statue of *Misery* (exhibited at the Salon de Paris in 1900), the group *The Power of Thought* and the statues *Morning, Christ in the Garden of Gethsemane* and *Young Boy*.

JØNSSON, Anders

Swedish, 20th century.
Born 30 December 1883, in Malmö.
Sculptor. Busts.

Anders Jønsson studied in Munich and Paris. He featured at the Salon des Artistes Français in Paris, where he was awarded an honourable mention in 1909, and at the Musée du Jeu de Paume in 1929.

MUSEUMS AND GALLERIES:

MALMÖ: *Female Torso* - STOCKHOLM: *Sten Selander* (bust); *Abyssinian* (blue marble bust).

JONSSON, Asgrimur
Icelandic, 20th century.
Born 4 March 1876, in Rutsstadahjaleigu; died 1958.
Painter. Landscapes.

Asgrimur Jonsson was a student at the Kongelige Danske Kunstakademi in Copenhagen, and exhibited his works in Charlottenborg from 1904 to 1912. He featured in an Icelandic exhibition in Copenhagen in March 1920 with a landscape.

MUSEUMS AND GALLERIES:
REYKJAVIK (Listasafn Islands): *Self-portrait c. 1900.*

AUCTION RECORDS:
COPENHAGEN, 8 March 1977, *Landscape in Iceland* (oil on canvas, 29 1/2 x 37 1/2 ins / 75 x 95 cm) DKK 32,000. COPENHAGEN, 11 May 1983, *Mountainscape with Houses* (oil on canvas, 16 1/4 x 28 3/4 ins / 41 x 73 cm) DKK 54,000. COPENHAGEN, 1 June 1983, *Landscape in Iceland* (watercolour, 20 x 26 ins / 51 x 66 cm) DKK 29,000. COPENHAGEN, 24 April 1985, *Seaside Landscape* (oil on canvas, 30 x 37 1/2 ins / 76 x 95 cm) DKK 86,000. COPENHAGEN, 26 Nov 1986, *Landscape in Iceland* (watercolour, 11 x 40 1/2 ins / 27 x 103 cm) DKK 26,000. COPENHAGEN, 16 Sept 1987, *Landscape in Iceland* (oil on canvas, 21 1/4 x 25 1/2 ins / 54 x 65 cm) DKK 50,000. COPENHAGEN, 30 May 1990, *View of a Fjord with Snow Covered Mountains in Iceland* (oil on canvas, 20 3/4 x 24 1/2 ins / 53 x 62 cm) DKK 68,000. COPENHAGEN, 26 April 1995, *Fjord Landscape at Thingvalla in Iceland* (oil on canvas, 43 1/4 x 49 1/4 ins / 110 x 125 cm) DKK 76,000. COPENHAGEN, 17 April 1997, *Fjord at Thingvalla* (1948-1949, oil on canvas, 27 1/2 x 39 1/4 ins / 70 x 100 cm) DKK 17,000. COPENHAGEN, 6 Oct 1999, *Mountain Landscape* (oil on canvas, 13 x 18 ins / 34 x 45 cm) DKK 14,000. COPENHAGEN, 7 Oct 2003, *View towards Tingvalla and Aimannagja* (1903, oil on canvas, 10 x 13 ins / 26 x 34 cm) DKK 24,000. COPENHAGEN, 29 March 2004, *Sketch from Tjorsa* (1904, oil on board, 9 x 14 ins / 23 x 36 cm) DKK 24,000. COPENHAGEN, 29 March 2004, *Cattle Grazing at Stigagil near Hornafjorthur, Iceland* (oil on canvas, 37 x 50 ins / 94 x 128 cm) DKK 75,000.

JONSSON, Einar
Icelandic, 19th - 20th century.
Born 11 May 1874; died 18 October 1954.
Sculptor. Statues, busts, monuments.

Einar Jonsson studied in Copenhagen and began to exhibit in Charlottenborg in 1901. His work *The Outlaw* brought him a travelling bursary which enabled him to go to Italy and Germany. From 1905 to 1907 he exhibited *Antiquity, The Typhoon* and *Dawn*, abstract works which brought him interest from America, where in 1915-1919 he produced the monument *Thorfinn Karlefsen*, to the first immigrant in Philadelphia.

In Winnipeg Jonsson was commissioned to sculpt a monument to those who had died in World War I. In 1914 he donated a large number of his works to the city of Reykjavik. In Reykjavik are his statues of *Christian IX, Jon Sigurdson, Jonas Hallgrimsson* and *Ingolf Anarson*, the first colonist in Iceland. He is also remembered for *Evolution, New Times, Night* and *The Birth of Psyche*.

MUSEUMS AND GALLERIES:
REYKJAVIK (Einarr Jonsson Mus.).

JONSSON, Lars
Swedish, 20th - 21st century.
Born 1952.
Painter, watercolourist, illustrator, ornithologist.
Landscapes, birds.

Lars Jonsson lives on the island of Gotland. He is widely respected in the ornithological world as a painter of birds. His style is characterised by its unforced realism. He has also published illustrated books and ornithological guides, notably *Birds of Europe with North Africa and the Middle East*. He has featured in many group exhibitions in the USA and throughout Europe. In 1995, he held a solo show of his works at the art museum in Visby, Gotland.

BIBLIOGRAPHY:
Jonsson, Lars/Brummer, Hans Henrik, *Lars Jonsson. La Lumière et les oiseaux*, Nathan, Paris, 2002.

AUCTION RECORDS:
STOCKHOLM, 21 May 1992, *Sunny Shore* (watercolour, 17 1/4 x 26 1/2 ins / 44 x 67 cm) SEK 14,000.

JONVAL, Fernand
French, 20th century.
Painter. Local scenes, urban landscapes.

Fernand Jonval exhibited in Paris at the Salon des Indépendants from 1907. He painted the streets of Montmartre.

JONVAUX
British, 19th century.
Active in London.
Miniaturist.

Jonvaux exhibited three miniatures at the Royal Academy in 1831.

JONXIS, Jan Lodewyk
Dutch, 19th century.
Born 9 April 1789, in Utrecht; died 17 February 1867, in Utrecht.
Painter, lithographer. Portraits, genre scenes, interiors with figures.

Jan Jonxis was the son of Pieter Hendrik Jonxis and a pupil of Ander Puyll. He was still working in 1859. He was a talented painter of Dutch interiors and taught at the Utrecht academy.

MUSEUMS AND GALLERIES:
UTRECHT: *Inspiration.*

AUCTION RECORDS:
LONDON, 24 June 1987, *Young Woman and Children in an Interior Looking at a Bird in a Cage* (oil on panel, 16 1/2 x 14 1/2 ins / 42 x 37 cm) GBP 3,000. GRAVENHAGE, 3 Nov 1998, *Smithy, Evening* (oil on canvas, 31 x 36 ins / 78 x 92 cm) NLG 7,500.

JONXIS, Pierre Etienne Lambert
Dutch, 19th century.
Born 1787, in Utrecht.
Engraver.

Son and pupil of Pieter Hendrik Jonxis.

JONXIS, Pieter Hendrik
Dutch, 18th - 19th century.
Born 1757, in Utrecht; died 30 May 1843, in Utrecht.
Engraver.

Registered as a member of the Utrecht guild in 1804, he made engravings of historical and mythological subjects after Giordano, J. Raoux and A. Pujos.

JONXIS, Pieter Hendrik Lodewyk
Dutch, 19th century.
Born 5 October 1815, in Utrecht; died 17 June 1852, in Brussels.
Painter. Landscapes with figures, landscapes.

The son and pupil of Jan Lodewyk Jonxis, he settled and worked in Brussels.

MUSEUMS AND GALLERIES:
UTRECHT: *River in the Moonlight.*

AUCTION RECORDS:
AMSTERDAM, 14-15 April 1992, *People around a Hole in the Ice on a Frozen Canal* (oil on canvas, 17 1/4 x 22 1/4 ins / 43.5 x 56.75 cm) NLG 8,280. GRAVENHAGE, 28 April 1999, *Harbour Landscape at Moonlight* (oil on canvas, 20 x 28 ins / 50 x 72 cm) NLG 12,000. LONDON, 3 Dec 2002, *Frozen River* (1842, oil on canvas, 24 x 28 ins / 60 x 72 cm) GBP 2,000.

JONZEN, Karin
British, 20th century.
Born 22 December 1914, in London, to Swedish parents; died 29 January 1998.
Sculptor (terracotta/bronze). Figures, portraits.

Karin Jonzen was a figurative sculptor who trained in Stockholm (where she received the Prix de Rome in 1939) and at the Slade School of Fine Art in London. Her work was exhibited at the Royal Academy, the Royal Society of British Artists and the New English Art Club, and was also included in exhibitions by the London Group. Her work was bought by important British collectors, including Robert Sainsbury and Kenneth Clark. In the early 1950s Jonzen was commissioned by the Arts Council to produce a sculpture for the South Bank, which was being developed as part of the Festival of Britain in 1951. One of her sculptures, *Beyond Tomorrow* (1972), has been placed at the Guildhall Plaza in London. In 1994 the David Messum Fine Art Gallery in London organised a solo exhibition of her work.

BIBLIOGRAPHY:
Karin Jonzen: Sculptor, exhibition catalogue, David Messum Fine Art, London, 1994.

MUSEUMS AND GALLERIES:
LONDON (National Portrait Gal.): *Learie Nicholas Constantine* (1971, bronze bust) - LONDON (Tate Collection): *Head of a Youth* (cast).

AUCTION RECORDS:
LONDON, 13 June 2002, *Girl Tying Her Hair* (terracotta, h. 11 ins / 27 cm) GBP 3,000. LONDON, 13 June 2002, *Female Nude with Raised Arms* (terracotta, h. 28 ins / 71 cm) GBP 3,800. LONDON, 27 March 2003, *Seated Female Nude* (green patinated bronze, h. 19 ins / 49 cm) GBP 7,000. LONDON, 19 May 2004, *Seated Female Nude* (green patinated bronze, h. 19 ins / 49 cm) GBP 5,500.

JOÓ, Bela
Hungarian, 19th - 20th century.
Born 27 November 1874, in Szentes; died 27 November 1909, in Szentes.
Painter. Landscapes.

Bela Joó studied in Munich before settling in Szentes. He exhibited a portrait at the Society of Artists of Budapest in 1901.

MUSEUMS AND GALLERIES:
SZEGED: painting.

JOONG, Kim En. See **KIM EN JOONG**

JOORIS DE SCHILDERE. See **CUPERE Jooris de**

JOORS, Eugène
Belgian, 19th - 20th century.
Born 1850, in Borgerhout near Antwerp; died 1910, in Berchem (Antwerp).
Painter. Portraits, landscapes, still-lifes, animals.

Eugène Joors was a student at the Koninklijke Academie voor Schone Kunsten in Antwerp under the direction of Professors Polydore Beaufaux, Nicaise de Keyser and Joseph van Lerius. He was a remarkable colourist.

AUCTION RECORDS:
AMSTERDAM, 6 March 1984, *Still-life with Fruit* (oil on canvas, 28 1/4 x 66 1/2 ins / 72 x 169 cm) NLG 4,000. NEW YORK, 26 Feb 1986, *Children Feeding Pigeons* (1887, oil on canvas, 47 1/2 x 32 3/4 ins / 120.6 x 83.3 cm) USD 8,000. LONDON, 17 April 1996, *Lady on a Bench* (oil on panel, 4 3/4 x 7 3/4 ins / 12 x 20 cm) GBP 805.

JOOS. See also **JOES, JOSSE, JOST**

JOOS, Henri
Belgian, 20th century.
Born 1880, in Schaerbeek (Brussels); died 1951, in Brussels.
Sculptor. Portraits. Busts.

Henri Joos was a student at the Académie des Beaux-Arts in Brussels, and a pupil of Julien Dillens. He was the sculptor of the statue of St Albert of Louvain in the church of Le Sablon in Brussels and also the founder of the École de Musique Instrumentale in Schaerbeek. He featured in the Exposition de Bruxelles of 1910.

JOOS, Julien
Belgian, 19th century.
Born in Bruges.
Painter. Interiors with figures.

Worked in Brussels from 1832.

MUSEUMS AND GALLERIES:
COURTRAI: *Kitchen Interior*.

JOOS, Peter
Swiss, 19th century.
Born 1857, in Niederumen (Glarus); died 17 January 1894, in Netstal (Glarus).
Painter. Figures, landscapes.

Peter Joos trained in Munich and completed a large number of decorative paintings, especially for concert rooms.

JOOS, Zimprecht
Swiss, 17th century.
Probably active in Schaffhausen c.1641.
Painter.

JOOS VAN DER BEKE. See **CLEVE**

JOOS VAN WASSENHOVE. See **JUSTE de Gand**

JOOSS, George
Dutch, 19th century.
Born 30 April 1799, in Brielle; died 20 March 1845, in 's Hertogenbosch.
Engraver (etching), lithographer.

MUSEUMS AND GALLERIES:
AMSTERDAM (Rijksprentenkabinet): portrait (lithograph); ten etchings, dated from 1828 to 1834.

JOOST. See also **JOST**

JOOST, Jan, or Joest, Joesten, or Jan Joest Calcar, Calcker, van Harlem or von Kalkar
Dutch, 15th - 16th century.
Born 1460, in Kalkar; died 1519, in Haarlem.
Painter. History painting.
Cologne School, Haarlem School.

Joost was unknown until the research of Weale, Eisemann and Wolf cast light on his work. His name was recorded in the archives of the town of Kalkar before 1500, and was mentioned again in 1505 and 1508, when he was busy on a major work: a painting showing scenes from the life of Jesus for the high altar of the church of St Nicolas in Kalkar, which was first attributed to him by James Weale. In 1515, he worked in Cologne for the Hackeneq family, returning to Haarlem soon after, and he also worked in Italy, leaving works in Genoa and Naples. The cathedral in Palencia has a *St John* by him. His work forged a link between the expressionism of Gérard de St-Jean, and the mannerism of Scorel and Heemsberck. He has also been identified with the Master of the *Death of Mary Magdalene*.

Museums and Galleries:
Brussels (Mus. Fetis): *The Holy Family* - Munich (Pinakothek): two small portraits.

Auction records:
London, 28 May 1937, *The Virgin and Child*, GBP 294. New York, 2 March 1950, *Hunting with a Falcon*, USD 900. London, 29 Nov 1961, *The Holy Family*, GBP 12,000. Lucerne, 2 Dec 1967, *The Virgin and Child*, CHF 22,500. London, 26 June 1970, *Lamentation*, Gns 22,000. Amsterdam, 18 Feb 1974, *Still-life of Fruit and Flowers*, NLG 33,000. New York, 22 Jan 1976, *Hunting with a Falcon* (oil on panel, 38 x 17¼ ins / 96.5 x 44 cm) USD 20,000.

JOOST, Jansz. See **BILHAMER Joost Jansz**

JOOST VON GENT. See **JUSTE de Gand**

JOOSTEN, Dirk Jan Henrik
Dutch, 19th century.
Born 25 September 1818, in Haarlem; died 7 June 1882, in Haarlem.
Painter, watercolourist. Still-lifes.

Pupil of G. J. J. van Os.

Museums and Galleries:
Haarlem (Teylers Mus.): *Still-life*.

Auction records:
Paris, 22 June 1945, *Still-life*, FRF 4,100. Amsterdam, 8 March 1978, *Still-life* (1850, oil on panel, 11½ x 9½ ins / 29.3 x 24.3 cm) NLG 4,200. Amsterdam, 24 April 1979, *Still-life* (1850, oil on panel, 11½ x 10 ins / 29.5 x 24.5 cm) NLG 5,600. Roubaix, 13 Dec 1981, *Thrush and Snipe* (oil on wood, 14½ x 11½ ins / 37 x 29 cm) FRF 40,000. Amsterdam, 30 Oct 1990, *Still-life with Peeled Lemons, Orange, Primulas and a Dead Bird on an Entablature* (1845, oil on panel, 6 x 7¾ ins / 15 x 19.5 cm) NLG 5,175. Amsterdam, 5 Nov 1996, *Still-life with Kingfisher* (oil on panel, 6 x 8¼ ins / 15.5 x 21 cm) NLG 3,068. Amsterdam, 27 April 1999, *Still-life with Roses and Other Flowers in Ornamental Vase* (oil on panel, 11 x 9 ins / 29 x 22 cm) NLG 48,000. Gravenhage, 31 Oct 2000, *Still-life with Flowers and Butterfly* (1856, oil on panel, 19 x 15 ins / 47 x 37 cm) NLG 36,000. Amsterdam, 22 Oct 2002, *Still-life with Flowers, Lace and Jewellery* (oil on panel, 26 x 20 ins / 65 x 50 cm) EUR 25,000.

JOOSTENS, Antoon L.
Flemish School, 19th century.
Died 25 February 1886.
Painter. Genre scenes.

Taught at the Bruges academy.

JOOSTENS, Paul
Belgian, 20th century.
Born 18 June 1889, in Antwerp; died 24 March 1960, in Antwerp.
Painter (including mixed media), collage artist, photomontage artist, illustrator. Figure compositions, figures.

Paul Joostens studied architecture, and then fine art at the Koninklijke Academie voor Schone Kunsten in Antwerp from 1909 to 1913. His first drawings bear witness to his admiration for the Flemish Primitives. Starting with Impressionism, he tried his hand at all the avant-garde styles of his time. About 1914 he came under the influence of Ferdinand Khnopff and James Ensor, and produced works which were Neo-Impressionist, then Fauvist and Expressionist. He then detached himself resolutely from all Realism, saying 'The sight of a tree makes me sick'. He tried his hand at Cubism, Futurism, abstract collages and Constructivist assemblages.

Joostens' horror of Realism and rationality brought him close to the spirit of *Dada*, and he was influenced by the different activities of the movement, experimenting with various materials and practising collage and photomontage following Kurt Schwitters. He was also a poet. At the same time he drew erotic figures under the pseudonyms Duco and Malibot, and published a collection *Sluts, The Quarter Hour of Madness or The Sun without a Hat*. He collaborated on the magazines *Selection; That Will Do; The Overview* and *The New Spirit*. About 1927, he again came under the influence of the Flemish Primitives and Mysticism, and shortly before World War II fantasy is the dominating element in his compositions. After the war, he pursued the techniques of assemblage and photomontage which he had never really given up, pursuing his creations in the last five years of his life in a Dadaist spirit (*My Soliloquies*, 1957).

He began to exhibit in 1917, at the Artists' Circle of Antwerp and in Brussels, and featured in the exhibition devoted to Belgian art at the Musée d'Art Moderne in Paris in 1991. He showed his works in a first solo exhibition in Antwerp, at the artistic centre, and in a second at the Galerie Giroux, also in Antwerp. His work was the subject of a retrospective in 1976 at the international cultural centre in Antwerp.

Bibliography:
Marlier, Georges, *L'Œuvre plastique de Paul Joostens*, Ça ira, Antwerp, 1923. Neuhuys, P., *Paul Joostens*, Elsevier, Brussels, 1961. Dorival, Bernard/Hoog, Michel, *Dada*, group exhibition catalogue, Musée national d'Art moderne, Paris, 1966.

Museums and Galleries:
Antwerp: *Nordic Madonna* (1930) - Brussels (MAM): *Object*.

Auction records:
Antwerp, 18 April 1972, *Purgatory*, BEF 40,000. Antwerp, 22 Oct 1974, *Christ The King* (1935) BEF 110,000. Lokeren, 13 March 1976, *Surrealist Composition* (1940, oil on panel, 37¾ x 37¾ ins / 96 x 96 cm) BEF 100,000. Breda, 26 April 1977, *Poezeloesen* (1945, oil on panel, 23½ x 19¾ ins / 60 x 50 cm) NLG 3,600. Antwerp, 22 April 1980, *Abundance* (1917, oil on canvas, 35½ x 43¾ ins / 90 x 111 cm) BEF 200,000. Antwerp, 29 April 1981, *Notre-Dame-de-la-Garde* (1929, oil on canvas, 47¼ x 57½ ins / 120 x 146 cm) BEF 90,000. London, 23 Feb 1983, *Composition* (c. 1924, watercolour and collage/pencil outlines, 10 x 7 ins / 24.5 x 18 cm) GBP 600. Lokeren, 23 April 1983, *Neo-Gothic Girl* (1939, oil on panel, 47¼ x 24¾ ins / 120 x 63 cm) BEF 90,000. London, 4 Dec 1985, *The Ultimate Distiller* (1923, pen, 15 x 19¼ ins / 38 x 49 cm) GBP 2,000. Cologne, 4 Dec 1985, *Dadaist Object* (1926-1927, wooden relief, 17 x 19¾ ins / 43 x 50 cm) DEM 3,500. London, 2 Dec 1986, *Dadaist Collage* (1919, collage paper, 17¾ x 11½ ins / 45 x 29 cm) GBP 2,600. Lokeren, 10 Oct 1987, *Damper* (1945, oil on panel, 49½ x 37½ ins / 125.5 x 95 cm) BEF 220,000. Lokeren, 5 March 1988, *Casserole Dish* (oil on canvas, 33½ x 26 ins / 85 x 66 cm) BEF 420,000. Lokeren, 28 May 1988, *The First Living Thing* (1931, oil on canvas, 43¼ x 27¼ ins / 110 x 69 cm) BEF 180,000. New York, 6 Oct 1988, *Untitled* (collage/card, 12½ x 11½ ins / 31.9 x 29 cm) USD 6,380. Lokeren, 8 Oct 1988, *Fortune-teller* (1938, oil on panel, 23½ x 19¼ ins / 60 x 49 cm) BEF 70,000. Paris, 8 Nov 1989, *Altar* (mixed media, 28¾ x 20¾ ins / 73 x 53 cm) FRF 20,000. Amsterdam, 12 Dec 1990, *Choirboy* (1927, oil on panel, 24½ x 16½ ins / 62 x 42 cm) NLG 3,450.

LOKEREN, 9 Oct 1993, *Primavera (Marlène Dietrich)* (1949, oil on panel, 23 1/2 x 18 1/2 ins / 60 x 47 cm) BEF 130,000; *Arrest of St Ursula* (1930, oil on canvas/panel, 35 1/2 x 27 1/4 ins / 90 x 69.5 cm) BEF 180,000. LOKEREN, 11 March 1995, *Seated Woman* (oil on canvas/panel, 30 x 22 ins / 76 x 56 cm) BEF 150,000. AMSTERDAM, 10 Dec 1996, *Resounding Success* (collage/paper, 13 1/4 x 10 ins / 33.5 x 25.5 cm) NLG 2,306. VLAAMSE KAAI, 27 April 1999, *Good Angel, Bad Angel* (1925, oil on panel, 21 x 28 ins / 54 x 70 cm) BEF 200,000. COLOGNE, 13 Nov 1999, *Untitled* (panel, brass, wire, metal, h. 9 ins / 24 cm) DEM 8,000. ANTWERP, 27 March 2000, *Two Women* (oil on panel, 22 x 26 ins / 57 x 65 cm) BEF 240,000. ANTWERP, 27 March 2000, *Brugge* (oil on canvas, 25 x 25 ins / 63 x 64 cm) BEF 260,000. BERN, 21 June 2001, *Dada Collage* (collage, 18 x 12 ins / 46 x 30 cm) CHF 11,000. ANTWERP, 15 Oct 2001, *Fulminante* (oil on cardboard, 20 x 13 ins / 52 x 34 cm) BEF 70,000. VLAAMSE KAAI, 23 April 2002, *Aztec Figure* (1919, oil on canvas, 31 x 25 ins / 79 x 64 cm) EUR 15,000. VLAAMSE KAAI, 22 Oct 2002, *Composition with Figures* (colour drawing, 30 x 28 ins / 76 x 71 cm) EUR 1,800. ANTWERP, 29 April 2003, *La scala* (1916, oil on canvas, 31 x 24 ins / 80 x 60 cm) EUR 1,500. BRUSSELS, 7 June 2004, *Figure* (1957, collage, 13 x 7 ins / 34 x 18 cm) EUR 1,500.

JOPLÈRE, Georges Pierre
French, 18th - 19th century.
Born 18th century.
Sculptor (ivory).

Joplère was a pupil of Berruer. He exhibited at the Salon de Paris in 1796 and 1808. He is remembered for: *The Death of Arria-Poetus* (ivory), *Herodias* (ivory) and *Cleobes and Biton* (ivory).

JOPLING, Joseph Middleton
British, 19th century.
Born 1831, in London; died 1884, in Chelsea.
Painter, watercolourist. History painting, genre scenes, flowers.

Joseph Middleton Jopling, a self-taught painter, worked at the War Ministry. In 1848, he began to exhibit his work in London, at the Royal Academy and at the Suffolk Street Gallery. This was followed by a study tour of Rome. Elected an associate of the New Water-Colour Society in 1859, he left the society in 1876. He was awarded a medal at the Crystal Palace and in Philadelphia the same year. In 1874, he married Louise Goode, the widow of Romer and a talented painter in her own right.

MUSEUMS AND GALLERIES:
LIVERPOOL: *See the Star* - LONDON (British Mus.): *Queen Victoria Reviewing the Troops* (drawing).

AUCTION RECORDS:
LONDON, 24 March 1981, *Dream in a Dream* (1876, watercolour heightened with white, 38 1/2 x 25 ins / 98 x 63.5 cm) GBP 600. LONDON, 11 June 1993, *Azalea* (1883, watercolour and gouache, 26 1/4 x 18 1/4 ins / 66.7 x 46.4 cm) GBP 1,725.

JOPLING, Louise
Maiden name: Goode
British, 19th - 20th century.
Born 1843, in Manchester; died 1933.
Active in London.
Painter. Portraits, landscapes.

Louise Goode was widowed following her first marriage to Frank Romer; she subsequently married J. M. Jopling, a pupil of Chaplin and Alfred Stevens, in Paris. She exhibited in London, chiefly at the Royal Academy, the Suffolk Street Gallery and the Grosvenor Gallery, from 1874. Her work was also shown in Philadelphia in 1876 and at the Exposition Universelle in Paris in 1878. She was a member of the Royal Society of British Artists.

AUCTION RECORDS:
LONDON, 30 Nov 1907, *Lorraine* (1876) GBP 5. LONDON, 30 Sept 1987, *Dear Miss Disdain* (oil on canvas, 50 x 29 1/2 ins / 127 x 75 cm) GBP 9,000. LONDON, 13 Feb 1991, *Portrait of a Woman* (1878, oil on canvas, 47 3/4 x 37 1/4 ins / 121.5 x 94.5 cm) GBP 4,400.

JOQUE, Charles
French, 18th century.
Painter.

Joque was Painter in Ordinary to the King at the tapestry workshops known as the Manufacture des Gobelins, and is mentioned in a civil status certificate dated 27 July 1749.

JORA SANJIN. See **ITSUUN**

JORAN, Michel
French, 17th century.
Active in Paris in 1685.
Engraver (line-engraving).

JORAND, Jean Baptiste Joseph
French, 19th century.
Born 1788, in Paris; died April 1850, in Eu (Seine-Maritime).
Painter, lithographer, archaeologist.

Jean Baptiste Joseph Jorand was a pupil of Fragonard the Younger, Baron Gros and Pillement. His genre subjects were exhibited at the Salon from 1810 to 1849.

MUSEUMS AND GALLERIES:
ROUEN (MBA): *Woman Going out a Fortress*.

JORAS, Étienne. See **JEAURAT**

JORDA Y CANTO, Vicente
Spanish, 19th century.
Painter. Portraits.

Vicente Jorda y Canto received a commendation at Jerez de la Frontera in 1858.

JORDAENS, Aart
Dutch, 15th century.
Carver.

Jordaens worked for the church of St John in 's Hertogenbosch from 1478 to 1494.

JORDAENS, Abraham
Flemish, 15th century.
Born 15th century, probably in Antwerp.
Painter.

Abraham Jordaens studied under Hans Jordaens the Elder.

JORDAENS, Arnold
Flemish School, 17th century.
Born 1636, in Antwerp.
Painter.

The son of Isaac Jordaens, in 1652 he studied under his uncle Jacob Jordaens. In 1664 he was a master artist in Antwerp.

JORDAENS, Hans I, the Elder
Flemish, 16th - 17th century.
Born c. 1539, according to Siret; died 1630, in Delft, Holland.
Painter. History painting, religious subjects, genre scenes, landscapes.
Antwerp School.

Hans Jordaens was the son of Simon Jordaens. In 1572, he was studying under Martin de Cleef or Noe de Noewiele, and in 1581 was recorded as a member of the guild of Antwerp. On 19 June 1582, he married the widow of François Pourbus, who had died in 1580. He lived in Delft until his death, the date of which varies between biographical accounts.

MUSEUMS AND GALLERIES:
DRESDEN: *Men and Woman at a Feast* - KIEV: *The Beach and a Whale with Figures*.

Auction records:
London, 11 July 1980, *Rebus* (oil on panel, diamond-shaped, 26 1/2 x 26 1/4 ins / 67.3 x 66.7 cm) GBP 5,000. Paris, 26 April 1991, *Salomé with the Head of John the Baptist* (oil on panel, oval, 20 1/2 x 27 1/2 ins / 52 x 70 cm) FRF 34,000. London, 20 April 1994, *Sermon of St John the Baptist* (1598, oil on canvas, 28 3/4 x 38 1/4 ins / 73 x 97.3 cm) GBP 6,900. London, 7 Dec 1994, *Siege of Weinberg* (oil on canvas, 58 x 80 1/2 ins / 147.5 x 204.5 cm) GBP 25,300.

JORDAENS, Hans II
Flemish School, 17th century.
Born 1581, in Antwerp; died 1653, in Antwerp.
Painter. Religious subjects, mythological subjects, genre scenes.

In 1600, Hans Jordaens II was a member of the Antwerp guild. He may have been the father of Hans Jordaens III, but if so 1581 cannot be correct as the year of his birth. He died in poverty.

Museums and Galleries:
Dresden: *A Meal* - Dunkirk: *Amazons Fighting; Noah's Ark.*

JORDAENS, Hans III, called le Long Jordaens or le Long Jan
Flemish School, 17th century.
Born c. 1595, in Antwerp; died between 14 July 1643 and le 21 March 1644, in Antwerp, in 1643 according to Dr von Wurzbach.
Painter. Religious subjects, mythological subjects, landscapes with figures.

According to Van Mander, Hans Jordaens III was a pupil of Cornelis Cornelissen, but it seems likely that he was both the son and pupil of Hans Jordaens II, who died in Antwerp in 1653. If we assume this relationship to be true, it follows that the date of birth given for Hans Jordaens II must be incorrect. On 26 November 1617 he married Maria van Dyck, daughter of Siger van Dyck. His widow died in Antwerp in 1652. In 1620 he was registered as a member of the guild of St Luke in Antwerp.

Museums and Galleries:
Antwerp: *Death of Pharaoh* - Budapest: *The Jews Crossing the River Jordan* - St Petersburg (Hermitage): *The Crossing of the Red Sea* - The Hague: *The Crossing of the Red Sea* - Vienna: *Art Collection.*

Auction records:
Paris, 10 June 1942, *The Animals Entering the Ark,* FRF 43,000. Vienna, 16 Nov 1983, *Allegory of Charity* (oil on wood, 27 1/2 x 36 ins / 70 x 91.3 cm) ATS 180,000. London, 21 July 1989, *Solomon and the Queen of Sheba* (oil on panel, 11 x 16 ins / 28 x 40.4 cm) GBP 4,180. London, 8 Dec 1989, *The Abduction of Helen* (oil on panel, 23 1/4 x 33 ins / 59.2 x 83.8 cm) GBP 17,600. New York, 10 Jan 1990, *David and Abigail* (oil on canvas, 30 x 51 3/4 ins / 76.2 x 131.4 cm) USD 13,200. Paris, 16 Nov 1990, *Preaching of St John the Baptist* (oil on canvas, 32 x 41 ins / 81 x 104 cm) FRF 108,000. London, 23 April 1993, *Taste Crowned by Venus, Bacchus and Ceres and Celebrated by Apollo, Diana and the Four Seasons* (oil on panel, 27 1/2 x 35 3/4 ins / 70.1 x 91.1 cm) GBP 23,000. London, 9 Dec 1994, *Wooded River Landscape with Jacob Fighting the Angel; Landscape with Christ Curing a Blind Man* (oil on canvas, a pair, 46 3/4 x 61 3/4 ins / 119 x 157 cm) GBP 21,850. Paris, 13 June 1997, *Neptune's Banquet* (oak panel, 20 1/2 x 37 ins / 52 x 94 cm) FRF 115,000. Rome, 1 June 1999, *Crossing of the Red Sea* (oil on panel, 23 x 36 ins / 58 x 91 cm) ITL 66,000,000. London, 17 Dec 1999, *Apollo Enthroned, Presented with the Gifts of the Continents and Oceans* (oil on canvas, 47 x 79 ins / 119 x 200 cm) GBP 15,000. Vienna, 4 Oct 2000, *Meeting of Jacob and Joseph* (oil on panel, 35 x 50 ins / 90 x 128 cm) ATS 300,000. Bremen, 8 Dec 2000, *Crucifixion* (oil on panel, 16 x 22 ins / 40 x 55 cm) DEM 20,000. Vienna, 3 Oct 2001, *Susanna and the Elders* (oil on canvas, 20 x 16 ins / 52 x 41 cm) ATS 280,000. Paris, 25 Oct 2002, *Suffer the Little Children to Come Unto Me* (oil on copper, 17 x 22 ins / 43 x 57 cm) EUR 6,500. Paris, 26 March 2003, *Adoration of the Magi* (oil on panel, 12 x 10 ins / 31 x 25 cm) EUR 2,800. London, 12 Dec 2003, *Israelites Worshipping the Golden Calf* (oil on canvas, 50 x 93 ins / 127 x 236 cm) GBP 9,500.

JORDAENS, Hans IV, also known as Potlepel or Brypotlepel
Dutch, 17th century.
Born 1616, in Delft; died 1680 or 1681, in Delft.
Painter. History painting, landscapes, seascapes.

For many years, Hans Jordaens IV worked in Italy. This gave credence to the hypothesis that the painter Luca Giordano, born in Naples in 1632 and son of a Dutch painter called Hans Jordaens, from Delft, was in fact his son; this has not, however, been proved. In 1650 Hans Jordaens was still in Rome, but by 1654 he had returned to Holland and was working in Leiden and, in 1657, in Delft, where he became a member of the guild. Houbraken attributes *The Death of Pharaoh in the Red Sea* to Jordaens, although it is usually considered to be the work of Hans Jordaens the Long (1595-1657) and appears under the latter's name in the museum of The Hague.

JORDAENS, Jacob
Flemish School, 17th century.
Born 19 May 1593, in Antwerp; died 18 October 1678, in Antwerp.
Painter (including gouache), watercolourist, engraver, draughtsman. Historical subjects, religious subjects, mythological subjects, allegorical subjects, genre scenes, portraits, interiors. Wall decorations, designs for tapestries.

Jacob Jordaens was the eldest of the eleven children of Jacques Jordaens, a cloth merchant in Antwerp, with a factory in Mechelen that produced wall hangings in imitation of Cordoban leather. Jacob worked there in close collaboration with his father and may have provided the designs. The relationship between Jacob Jordaens and the various painters who shared his surname living in Antwerp at that period has not been clearly established; it seems likely, however, that he was the nephew of Hans Jordaens the Elder, who was almost certainly the brother of Jacques Jordaens. In 1616 Simon Jordaens, son of Hans the Elder, was a witness at the marriage of Jacob Jordaens; Abraham, Jacob's younger brother, who later took holy orders, is mentioned as a pupil of Hans the Elder.

In 1607, Jacob Jordaens was apprenticed to Adam van Noort. It has been claimed that he was a fellow student of Rubens, but this cannot be true since Rubens was admitted as a free master in 1598 and had left for Italy by 9 May 1600. At one time Adam van Noort was a very important figure in the Antwerp art world, having no fewer than 32 pupils. However, it seems that towards the end of his life - perhaps because he was a member of the reformed church and close to many Calvinists - he was shunned by the Spanish aristocracy. According to some biographers he was embroiled in religious and political disputes. In this milieu, Jordaens was able to develop an independent spirit quite different from the temperaments of the other members of his family: Abraham became prior of a monastic order and three of his sisters became nuns.

In 1615 Jordaens was admitted to the guild as a free master specialising in distemper-painting, and on 15 May 1616 he married Catarina van Noort, daughter of his former teacher. In order to marry her, Jacob had abandoned a study trip to Italy; she appears to have become his favourite model. The young couple lived with Van Noort and from 1617 onwards Jordaens did a considerable amount of work for churches and, while collaborating with Rubens, also continued to work on his own projects. By 1626 he no longer took students himself but directed those studying under Rubens. In 1632 he accompanied his father-in-law to Holland. It is generally thought that it was during the course of this trip that Jordaens adopted the reformed religion, although no precise date is known. In 1630 the artist had become sufficiently wealthy to buy the Turnhout hall in Antwerp, under demolition at the time, and to have a house built on the site, completed in 1641. He decorated the house with paintings and collected many works by the great artists. Charles I of England commissioned him to decorate the queen's drawing room at Greenwich. Jordaens painted the ceiling, completed in 1641 and was paid 690 pounds sterling. However, political troubles in England prevented the artist from completing the series.

In 1644 Rubens, having received a commission from the king of Spain for tapestries for the royal palace, entrusted the execution of the designs to Jordaens. He painted watercolour originals that were then worked up to scale by his pupils. Jordaens appears to have enjoyed a considerable reputation as a watercolourist and received important commissions from abroad, notably from the king of Sweden and Princess Amelia of Orange. For the Swedish king he painted a number of works, ceilings in particular. However, it would seem that more work has been attributed to Jordaens than he actually executed. His undisputed works include *The Story of Psyche* and twelve scenes from the *Life of Christ*. In 1649 he painted *Triumph of the Prince of Nassau* for the Princess of Orange - considered to be one of his best works - and another decorative piece, for the price of 3,000 guilders. Other important works by the artist include 35 large compositions executed for Silvercroon and Hondius in The Hague, for which he was paid 28,000 Flanders pounds.

Jordaens had three children from his marriage: Jan Jordaens, who died in Denmark, Anna Catarina, who married the civil servant Johan Wierts, and another daughter, Elisabeth, who lived with her father after the death of his wife in 1659. Jordaens and Elisabeth both died of the plague that devastated Antwerp in 1678. Some biographers date his abjuration of the Catholic religion around 1671 but it seems likely that it was earlier than this, since works such as *Truth Before Time*, executed around 1655 (the drawing for which is in the museum of Grenoble), show him as opposed to the Catholic Church.

In 1708 his grandchildren sold his house in the Rue Haute in Antwerp, along with 111 pictures, including 44 by Jordaens, that were kept there; these were resold in The Hague on 22 March 1734.Jordaens was undeniably influenced by Rubens, but mainly in his love of powerful forms. Resolutely realist, Jordaens was far more Dutch than Rubens. He adopted only the unavoidable elements of Italian ornamentation; if his work does display an Italian influence it is that of Venice, Giorgione and Titian.

Besides his decorative work, Jordaens created compositions around three main subjects: *The Satyr and the Peasant*; *The Family Concert* or *As the Old Sing, so the Young Twitter*; and *The King Drinks*. After becoming a Calvinist Jordaens turned to themes relating to the land of his birth and produced the work that is without doubt his masterpiece: *Allegory of Fecundity*. His paintings also became more boisterous and disorderly, conveying a sense of movement.

There have been thematic exhibitions featuring the work of Jacob Jordaens including, in 2000, *Dans la lumière de Rubens. Peintres Baroques des Pays-Bas du Sud* (*In the Light of Rubens. Baroque Painters of the Southern Netherlands*) at the Musée des Beaux-Arts in Valenciennes, which aimed to do justice to some of those talented artists often eclipsed by the great Flemish masters of the Baroque, including Jordaens; and, in 2002, *Around Jordaens. Flemish Masters in the Rijksmuseum*, Amsterdam.

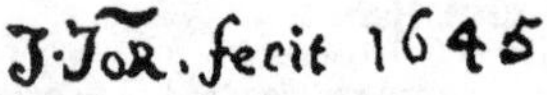

BIBLIOGRAPHY:

Devisscher, Hans/De Poorter, Nora/D'Hulst, R.A., et al., '*Jacob Jordaens (1593-1678)*' in vol. 1: Paintings and tapestries, exhibition catalogue, Koninklijk Museum voor Schone Kunsten, Antwerpen, Gemeentekredit van Belgie, Brussels, 1993. Limousin, Isabelle/Ramade, Patrick/Cordier, Gaëlle, *Dans la lumière de Rubens: peintres baroques des Pays-Bas du Sud*, exhibition catalogue, Musée des Beaux-Arts, Valenciennes, 2000.

MUSEUMS AND GALLERIES:

AIX: *Man's Head; The Return of Ulysses* - AJACCIO: *Satyr and Passer-by* - AMIENS: *Appearance of Jesus to Mary Magdalene; The Poultry Seller; Two Heads of Old Men; Portrait of a Man* - AMSTERDAM: *Satyr; St Peter Finding Money in the Mouth of a Fish; Marsyas Ill-treated by the Muses* - ANGERS: *St Sebastian; François Flamand; Self-portrait* (c. 1650) - ANTWERP: *The Last Supper; The Sisters of Mercy; Christ Entombed; Pegasus; Allegory; Human Law Founded on Divine Law; Adoration of the Shepherds; Family Concert; St Yves; Studies of Heads; The Daughters of Cecrops Discovering Erichthonius; Atalanta and Meleager* - ANTWERP (Church of St James): *St Charles Borromeus* - ANTWERP (Church of St Paul): *Christ on the Cross* - ANTWERP (St Augustine's Church): *Martyrdom of St Apollinus* - ARRAS: *Bacchanal* - BAGNÈRES-DE-BIGORRE: *Il Bambino* - BASEL (Öffentliche Kunstsammlung): *Odysseus bedroht Circe* (*Ulysses Threatens Circe*) - BAYONNE (Mus. Bonnat): *Isaac Blessing Jacob* (sketch) - BERGUES: *Man Drinking* - BERLIN: *Merry Company* - BESANÇON: *Heads of Old Men; Young People Singing; Diana and Actaeon; The Painter and his Wife; The Head of St John the Baptist Brought before Herod; The Wrath of Juno* - BÉZIERS: *Woman and Child* - BORDEAUX: *Head of a Young Boy; Portrait of a Child* - BORDEAUX (Cathedral of St-André): *Calvary* - BRUSSELS: *St Martin; Abundance; The Satyr and the Peasant; Eliezer and Rebecca; Pan and Syrinx; Susanna Bathing; The King Drinks; St Yves; Portrait of a Lady; The King Drinks; Triumph of Bacchus; The Food Merchant* - BUDAPEST: *Portrait of a Man; The Peasant and the Satyr* - CAEN: *Beggar; Bust of a Man Praying* - CARCASSONNE: *Temptation* - CHÂTEAUROUX: *Caesar's Penny; The Adulteress* - CHAUMONT: *Man's Head; Susanna Bathing* - CHERBOURG: *Adoration of the Magi* - COLOGNE: *Portraits; Prometheus in Chains* - COPENHAGEN (Statens Mus. for Kunst): *Hercules overcoming Achelous. Allegory on Fruitfulness. The Origin of Cornucopia (Ovid: Metamorphoses IX, 80-88); Christ Blessing the Little Children; Susanna and the Elders; The Betrayal and Arrest of Christ in Gethsemane* - CORAL GABLES (Lowe AM, University of Miami): *The Judgement of Paris* (c. 1620-1625, oil on canvas) - DARMSTADT: *Virtue Tempted by the Demon and Supported by the Angel* - DOUAI: *Portraits* - DRESDEN: *Ariadne and Bacchus; Diogenes and his Lantern; The Prodigal Son Guarding the Swine; Presentation at the Temple; Family Concert* - DUBLIN: *Allegory; The Supper at Emmaus; The Triumph of the Eucharist* - FLORENCE (NG): *Self-portrait; Venus at her Mirror; Neptune* - FRANKFURT AM MAIN: *Adoration of the Shepherds* - GHENT: *Reconciliation; The Judgement of Midas; Offering to Ceres* - GLASGOW: *The Fruit Seller* - GRENOBLE: *Adoration of the Shepherds; The Sleep of Antiope; Truth be-*

fore Time (a watercolour) - HAMBURG: *Abraham and Isaac* - HELSINKI: *Jupiter and Mercury at the House of Philemon and Baucis* - KALININGRAD: *Faun* - KASSEL: *Moor Presenting a Stallion to his Master; Family Group; The Feast of the Bean King; Triumph of Bacchus; Moses Striking the Rock; Family; The Satyr and the Peasant; Same Subject; The Child Bacchus; Jupiter and the Goat Amalthea* (two) - LA FÈRE: *The Disciples at Emmaus* - LANGRES: *Christ at the Column* - LEIDEN (Universiteit Leiden): *Isaac Blessing Jacob* (study drawing) - LILLE (MBA): *The Rape of Europa* (1643); *Christ and the Pharisees; The Prodigal Son in Distress; The Apostles; The King Drinks; Susanna Bathing; Huntsman with Hounds; Isaac Blessing Jacob; Temptation* - LONDON: *Interior of an Art Gallery; Baron Waha de Luiter* - LONDON (Courtauld Institute of Art): *Isaac Blessing Jacob* (c. 1660, chalk (black and red), pen and ink, watercolour (brown-grey)/paper, draught study) - LONDON (NG): *The Virgin and Child with Saints Zacharias, Elizabeth and John the Baptist* (c. 1620, oil on canvas); *The Holy Family and Saint John the Baptist* (c. 1620-1625?, oil/wood); *Portrait of Govaert van Surpele (?) and his Wife* (c. 1636-1638, oil on canvas) - LONDON (Wallace Collection): *An Allegory of Fruitfulness (Homage to Pomona)* (c. 1620-1640, oil on canvas) - LYONS: *Visitation of the Virgin; Adoration of the Shepherds; Mercury and Argus; The Drunkenness of Silenus* - MADRID (Prado): *Judgement of Solomon; Betrothal of St Catherine; Jesus and St John as Children; Meleager and Atalanta; Offering to Pomona; Diana Bathing; Scene in a Garden; Travelling Musicians* - MAINZ: *Jesus in the Temple at the Age of Twelve; Adoration of the Shepherds* - MILAN (Pinacoteca di Brera): *Abraham's Sacrifice* - MONTAUBAN: *Silenus and the Four Seasons; Faun's Head* - MOSCOW (Rumiantsev Mus.): *Judgement of Paris; St Paul; Cherubs and Garland of Flowers* - MUNICH: *Satyr at Table; As the Old Sing, so the Young Twitter; Christ at the Temple at the Age of Twelve* - NANCY: *Heads of Two Old Women* - NAPLES: *Jesus Taken to Execution* - NARBONNE: *Drunkenness of Silenus; The Family of Darius before Alexander; Triumph of Silenus; Bacchanal* - OSLO: *Man's Head; Allegory* - PARIS (ENSBA): *Isaac Blessing Jacob* (study drawing) - PARIS (Louvre): *Jesus Driving the Merchants from the Temple; The Four Evangelists; Childhood ofJupiter; The King Drinks; The Concert; Admiral Michel Adrien Ruyter; Mythological Meal* - RENNES: *Christ* - ROHRAU (Schlossmus., Graf Harrach'sche Familiensammlung): *St Christopher and the Christ Child* - ROUEN: *Head of an Old Man; Jesus at the House of Martha and Mary* - ST PETERSBURG (Hermitage): three heads of children; *Diana Resting; The Satyr and the Peasant; Family Portrait; Family Meal* (three portraits of men); *Head of an Old Man, Head of an Old Woman* - ST-BRIEUC: *Know Thyself* - STOCKHOLM: *Candaules Showing his Wife to Gyges; Adoration of the Shepherds; Old Satyr* - STRASBOURG: *Peasants' Bacchanal* - STUTTGART: *Daedalus and Icarus; Bacchus and Ceres; Sacrifice of Isaac* - THE HAGUE (Mauritshuis): *Marsyas Ill-treated by the Muses* - TOULOUSE: *River and Naiad* - TOURNAI: *Child's Head* - VALENCIENNES: *The King Drinks; Children in the Cradle; Judgement of Midas* - VIENNA (Kunsthistorisches Mus.): *The Feast of the Bean King* - VIENNA (Schönborn-Buckheim): *River Gods* - WARRINGTON: *Abbess* - WROCLAW: *Begging for Protection in the Prince's Palace* - YPRES: *Bacchus.*

AUCTION RECORDS:

PARIS, 1793, *The Bean King,* FRF 6,020. PARIS, 1881, *Huntsman and his Hounds,* FRF 11,100. PARIS, 1881, *The Fool,* FRF 1,075. PARIS, 26 Feb 1892, *Travelling Musicians,* FRF 2,350; *Satyr* (after Rubens) FRF 2,350. PARIS, 10 June 1893, *Family Concert,* FRF 11,500. PARIS, 2 Dec 1896, *Portrait Assumed to be of Catarina van Noort,* FRF 4,550. PARIS, 30 April 1900, *Triumphal Entry of Prince Henry of Orange Nassau,* FRF 2,400. PARIS, 18-24 May 1903, *The Feast of the Bean King,* FRF 800. PARIS, 12-13 March 1906, *Satyr and Bacchant,* FRF 4,000. BRUSSELS, 26 March 1906, *Flemish Idyll,* FRF 4,000. PARIS, 24-25 April 1907, *The Happy Family,* FRF 14,000. LONDON, 27 Jan 1908, *Man and Satyr,* GBP 10. LONDON, 27 May 1908, *Interior* (drawing heightened with watercolour) GBP 38; *Study for Leda and the Swan* (drawing) GBP 5. LONDON, 12 Dec 1908, *Portrait of a Gentleman,* GBP 39. LONDON, 7 Feb 1910, *Christ in the House of Martha,* GBP 48. PARIS, 22 May 1919, *Diana and Actaeon,* FRF 5,500. PARIS, 17-19 Nov 1919, *Presentation at the Temple,* FRF 4,800. PARIS, 3 June 1921, *Nymphs and Satyrs,* FRF 10,000. LONDON, 24 Nov 1922, *The Feast of the Bean King,* GBP 399. LONDON, 25 July 1924, *The Triumph of Neptune,* GBP 220. PARIS, 6 Dec 1924, *Bacchus and his Followers,* FRF 4,250. LONDON, 1 May 1925, *The Artist and his Wife,* GBP 3,990. LONDON, 5 June 1925, *Holy Family and St John,* GBP 152. PARIS, 17-18 June 1925, *Study: Heads of Two Old Women* (black chalk, red chalk heightened with white) FRF 7,100. PARIS, 10-11 May 1926, *People Blowing a Seashell* (black chalk and sepia) FRF 7,000. LONDON, 16 April 1928, *The Flute Player,* GBP 131. LONDON, 20 April 1928, *The Miraculous Catch.* PARIS, 28 June 1928, *Concert after the Meal,* FRF 72,100. PARIS, 15 Nov 1928, *Adoration of the Shepherds* (drawing) FRF 4,000. LONDON, 12 July 1929, *Three Musicians,* GBP 735. LONDON, 31 Jan 1930, *Lady at a Balustrade,* GBP 2,625. PARIS, 28 Nov 1934, *Christ before Pilate* (black chalk, red chalk and watercolour) FRF 3,800. PARIS, 3 Dec 1935, *Diana's Meal,* FRF 30,000. PARIS, 14 Dec 1936, *Merry Meal* (pen and wash heightened with white) FRF 2,550. PARIS, 26 May 1937, *Jesus Driving Merchants from the Temple* (watercolour) FRF 4,900. PARIS, 8 Dec 1938, *Nymphs and Satyrs* (watercolour, heightened with white gouache) FRF 11,500. BRUSSELS, 15 April 1939, *Descent from the Cross,* BEF 17,000. LONDON, 19 July 1946, *Mercury and Argus,* GBP 273. PARIS, 19 March 1947, *Christ at the House of Martha and Mary* (bistre wash) FRF 47,000. PARIS, 24 Feb 1949, *Sleeping Faun Dreaming of his Youth,* FRF 270,000. BRUSSELS, 30 Jan 1950, *Fruitfulness,* BEF 67,000. PARIS, 5 Dec 1951, *Young Girl,* FRF 1,900,000. NEW YORK, 18 April 1956, *The Visitation,* USD 1,750. LONDON, 1 April 1960, *The Miraculous Catch,* GBP 1,785. PARIS, 20 June 1961, *Golgotha* (mounted paper) FRF 16,000. VIENNA, 4 Dec 1962, *Young Girl, Scholar and Fool,* ATS 55,000. LONDON, 28 May 1965, *Education of a Young Prince,* Gns 65,000. BRUSSELS, 8 Dec 1966, *St Yves, Patron Saint of Lawyers,* BEF 300,000. BERN, 12 June 1968, *The Wife of Jeroboam at the House of the Prophet Ahia* (watercolour and gouache) CHF 16,500. LONDON, 10 July 1968, *Judas' Betrayal of Christ,* GBP 25,000. LONDON, 26 March 1969, *As the Old Sing, so the Young Twitter,* GBP 79,000. LONDON, 26 March 1971, *The Rape of Europa,* Gns 42,000. LONDON, 12 Dec 1973, *Diana and Callisto,* GBP 30,000. LONDON, 29 March 1974, *Mount Calvary,* Gns 46,000. AMSTERDAM, 4 May 1976, *Jeroboam and the Prophet* (drawing, 12 3/4 x 10 ins / 32.5 x 25.2 cm) NLG 15,000. LONDON, 7 July 1976, *Ulysses and Nausicaa* (oil on canvas, 43 1/4 x 61 1/4 ins / 110 x 155.5 cm) GBP 12,000. AMSTERDAM, 9 June 1977, *Meleager and Atalanta* (oil on panel, 28 3/4 x 38 1/2 ins / 73 x 98 cm) NLG 200,000. PARIS, 28 Nov 1978, *Supplicants before the High Priest* (1670, black chalk, pen and wash, red chalk and white, 10 x 13 1/2 ins / 25.5 x 34.5 cm) FRF 38,000. NEW YORK, 5 June 1979, *Two Satyr's Heads* (black chalk heightened with red chalk, 8 3/4 x 13 ins / 22.5 x 33 cm) USD 3,800. PARIS, 28-29 Jan 1980, *Coronation of the Virgin* (watercolour, gouache and black chalkheightened with oil, 18 1/4 x 15 1/4 ins / 46.5 x 38.5 cm) FRF 231,500. LONDON, 18 April 1980, *St Simon (?)* (oil on panel, 26 x 20 ins / 66 x 51 cm) GBP 9,500. LONDON, 8 April 1981, *The King Drinks* (oil on canvas, 66 1/4 x 95 ins / 168 x 241 cm) GBP 65,000. MONTE CARLO, 5 March 1984, *Christ and the Repentant Sinners* (oil on canvas, 39 x 52 1/4 ins / 99 x 133 cm) FRF 650,000. LONDON, 4 July 1984, *Woman's Head* (black and red chalk with brown wash, heightened with white, 9 1/4 x 7 1/4 ins / 23.7 x 18.7 cm) GBP 60,000. PARIS, 19 June 1986, *Man Kneeling Facing towards the right* (lead pencil, brown wash and coloured gouache, 14 1/2 x 13 ins / 37 x 33 cm) FRF 720,000. LONDON, 2 July 1986, *Hippomenes and Atalanta* (1646, oil on canvas, 43 3/4 x 34 3/4 ins / 111 x 88.5 cm) GBP 30,000. BERN, 17 June 1987, *Head of a Young Woman* (c. 1645, black chalk and red chalk lightly heightened with white, 7 1/4 x 5 1/2 ins / 18.3 x 14.2 cm) CHF 52,000. PARIS, 27 May 1988, *Christ and the Pilgrims of Emmaus* (ink, black chalk and watercolour, 9 1/2 x 12 ins / 24 x 30.5 cm) FRF 100,000. LONDON, 31 March 1989, *Bust Study of a Man with his Hand Raised* (oil on panel, 25 x 18 ins / 63.5 x 46 cm) GBP 24,200. LONDON, 21 April 1989, *Adoration of the Shepherds* (oil on canvas, 58 x 46 1/4 ins / 147.5 x 117.5 cm) GBP 440,000. MONACO, 16 June 1989, *Silenus* (oil on canvas, 46 1/2 x 57 3/4 ins / 118 x 147 cm) FRF 466,200. LONDON, 18 May 1990, *Moses and the Israelites Gathering Manna* (oil on panel, 49 3/4 x 83 1/2 ins / 126.5 x 212 cm) GBP 22,000. PARIS, 22 June 1990, *As the Old Sing, so the Young Twitter* (oil on canvas, 83 x 74 1/2 ins / 211 x 189 cm) FRF 4,200,000. NEW YORK, 9 Jan 1991, *Bust Study of a Cleric* (coloured chalks, 6 3/4 x 5 1/2 ins / 17.2 x 14.2 cm) USD 3,520. PARIS, 9 April 1991, *Adoration of the Magi* (oil/different sheets of paper assembled and stuck on wood, 20 3/4 x 26 ins / 53 x 66 cm) FRF 200,000. LONDON, 19 April 1991, *Head of an Old Woman* (oil on paper/panel, sketch, 9 1/2 x 7 1/4 ins / 24.4 x 18.2 cm) GBP 9,350. LONDON, 2 July 1991, *Diana and Callisto* (graphite, black chalk and ink, diam. 4 ins / 10.2 cm) GBP 10,450. NEW YORK, 15 Jan 1992, *Head of a Bearded Man, Left Profile* (black and white chalk, red chalk and ink/paper, 11 x 8 ins / 27 x 20.3 cm) USD 22,000. NEW YORK, 17 Jan 1992, *Triumph of the Eucharist* (oil on canvas, 47 1/4 x 31 3/4 ins / 120 x 80.6 cm) USD 24,200. AMSTERDAM, 25 Nov 1992, *Studies of Heads: Two Old, Grotesque Men, Two Gossips and a Young Woman* (1664, red and black chalk, ink and wash, 8 1/2 x 6 ins / 21.6 x 14.3 cm) NLG 32,200. STOCKHOLM, 10-12 May 1993, *Satyr with a Family of Peasants* (oil on canvas, 46 1/2 x 59 ins / 118 x 150 cm) SEK 240,000. LONDON, 9 Dec 1994, *Three Musicians* (oil on canvas, 43 1/2 x 42 ins / 110.3 x 106.7 cm) GBP 62,000. AMSTERDAM, 15 Nov 1995, *Family Concert* (ink/black chalk, 7 1/2 x 10 1/2 ins / 18.9 x 26.5 cm) NLG 68,440. PARIS, 12 April 1996, *The Bearing of the Cross* (black chalk and red chalk, 13 1/2 x 11 ins / 34.5 x 27 cm) FRF 23,000. LONDON, 13 Dec 1996, *Doctors of the Church* (oil on canvas, 82 x 98 3/4 ins / 208 x 250.8 cm) GBP 771,500. NEW YORK, 31 Jan 1997, *Four Studies of Male Heads* (oil on panel, 20 x 25 1/2 ins / 51 x 65 cm) USD 156,500. LONDON, 18 April 1997, *Holy Family* (c. 1616, oil on panel, 24 1/2 x 19 1/4 ins / 62.2 x 48.8 cm) GBP 43,300. LONDON, 2 July 1997, *Bust of an Old Man Singing* (red and black chalk, study, 9 1/4 x 7 3/4 ins / 23.5 x 20 cm) GBP 25,300. NEW YORK, 28 May 1999, *The Woman, the Fool and his Cat* (oil on canvas, 44 x 46 ins / 111 x 116 cm) USD 100,000. AMSTERDAM, 9 Nov 1999, *Merry Company Around Table Outside Inn* (black chalk/watercolour heightened with white, 9 x 9 ins / 22 x 24 cm) NLG 380,000. NEW YORK, 28 Jan 2000, *Christ and the Pharisees* (oil on canvas, 55 x 83 ins / 140 x 212 cm) USD 240,000. LONDON, 7 July 2000, *Head Studies of Two African Men* (oil on canvas, 13 x 19 ins / 32 x 47 cm) GBP 190,000. LONDON, 12 July 2001, *Portrait of Magdalena de Cuyper, Seated Wearing Black Dress with Fur Trimmed Coat* (oil on canvas, 60 x 46 ins / 152 x 118 cm) GBP 850,000. LONDON, 12 July 2001, *Portrait of Rogier le Witer. Portrait of his Wife Catharine* (1635, oil on canvas, a pair, 60 x 46 ins / 152 x 118 cm) GBP 2,000,000. LONDON, 10 July 2002, *Portrait of the Infanta Isabella Clara Eugenia as a Nun* (oil on canvas, 50 x 40 ins / 127 x 101 cm) GBP 85,000. AMSTERDAM, 5 Nov 2002, *Merry Company, Allegory of Integrity* (1668, pen/brown ink/watercolour/gouache/colour chalk, 8 x 12 ins / 21 x 30 cm) EUR 80,000. OAKLAND, 20 Sept 2003, *Study of an Evangelist* (oil on canvas) USD 7,000. VIENNA, 1 Oct 2003, *Painter and his Model* (oil on canvas, 46 x 38 ins / 117 x 96 cm) EUR 55,000. LONDON, 7 July 2004, *Portrait of the Artist's Daughter* (oil on canvas, 29 x 23 ins / 74 x 59 cm) GBP 100,000. VIENNA, 29 Sept 2004, *Flora, Silenus and Zephyr* (oil on canvas, 56 x 49 ins / 141 x 125 cm) EUR 140,000.

JORDAENS, Jacobus or Jan, the Younger
Flemish School, 17th century.
Born 2 July 1625, in Antwerp; died probably in Denmark.
Painter.

The son and pupil of the celebrated painter Jacob Jordaens.

JORDAENS, L.
Dutch, 17th century.
Active in the Netherlands c. 1650.
Draughtsman.

JORDAENS, Symon or Simon
Flemish School, 17th century.
Born c. 1590, in Antwerp; died 23 March 1640, in Delft.
Active in Antwerp.
Painter. Genre scenes.

Symon Jordaens was the son of Hans Jordaens the Elder. In 1612 he was a citizen of Delft and on 15 May 1616 acted as a witness at the marriage of the painter Jacob Jordaens in Antwerp. His sister married a painter named Goetkint. There is another painter by the name of Symon Jordaens who was a master artist in Leiden in 1648.

AUCTION RECORDS:

VIENNA, 22 May 1973, *Spring*, ATS 150,000. AMSTERDAM, 28 Nov 1989, *Men at Arms Taking a Peasant along a Frozen Path by a River* (1624, oil on copper, 6 x 11 1/4 ins / 14.4 x 28.8 cm) NLG 17,250. VIENNA, 4 Oct 2000, *Mountainous River Landscape with Stone Bridge and Figures* (oil on panel, 17 x 27 ins / 42 x 69 cm) ATS 80,000.

JORDAN, André
French, 20th century.
Born 9 July 1908, in Paris.
Painter, engraver, sculptor, lithographer, illustrator.

Though figurative in his early career, André Jordan moved on to abstraction and began to work sculpturally. His approach is usually to explore the geometric possibilities of a single unit. He exhibited at the Salon des Tuileries in Paris after World War II and also at the Salon des Indépendants, where in 1950 he showed a landscape bold with rhythm and harmony. He was also invited to exhibit at the Salon de Mai. Jordan showned his work in solo exhibitions from 1935 in Paris, Rouen, Marseilles, Aix-en-Provence, Mannheim, Stuttgart and Lausanne. He was a member of the Comité Nationale du Livre Gravé (national committee of engraved books). He illustrated numerous works, including: *Présent de la Beauce* by Péguy (1946); *La Vie d'un simple* by Guillaumin (1946) and several texts he wrote himself. He also produced monumental low reliefs in glass blocks for secondary schools and high schools. In 1978, he received a commission from the faculty of human sciences in Avignon.

MUSEUMS AND GALLERIES:

ÉPINAL (Mus. départemental d'Art ancien et contemporain): *St-Jacques Hill* (1965).

JORDAN, Carl
German, 19th century.
Born 14 February 1826; died 5 January 1907.
Active in Ballenstedt (Harz).
Painter. Landscapes.

A noted work by Karl Jordan of Ballenstedt is a *Harz Landscape*.

JORDAN, Carl
Austrian, 19th century.
Born 19 May 1863, in Bozen, South Tyrol (now Bolzano, Italy).
Painter. History painting, portraits.

A pupil of Defregger in Munich, the Austrian Carl Jordan taught at the school of fine arts in Strasbourg from 1891, and exhibited in Munich from 1890.

MUSEUMS AND GALLERIES:

COLOGNE: *Emperor Sigismund in Strasbourg* - STRASBOURG: *Walthari*.

AUCTION RECORDS:

MUNICH, 21 June 1994, *The Claimant* (oil on canvas, 19 1/4 x 23 1/4 ins / 49 x 59 cm) DEM 13,800.

JORDAN, César

Bolivian, 20th - 21st century.
Born 1947.
Painter.
Op Art, Kinetic Art.

César Jordan studied at the Accademia di Belle Arti in Rome. In 1971 he was awarded the prize for kinetic art at the Salon Nacional Murillo in La Paz. In 1973 he took part in a collective exhibition at the Musée Municipal d'Art Moderne in Paris.

His works, which are close to Pop Art, lean towards kinetics.

BIBLIOGRAPHY:

Lassaigne, Jacques, *Peintres boliviens contemporains*, exhibition catalogue, Musée d'Art moderne de la Ville de Paris, Paris, 1973.

AUCTION RECORDS:

PARIS, 7 Oct 1996, *Homo Volens* (1982, oil on canvas, 25 1/2 x 27 1/2 ins / 65 x 70 cm) FRF 6,000.

JORDAN, David Wilson

American, 19th century.
Born 2 June 1859, in Harrisburg (Pennsylvania); died 1935.
Painter. Landscapes.

David Wilson Jordan studied with Schussele and Eakins at the Pennsylvania Academy of the Fine Arts in Philadelphia. He belonged to the major art groups in Philadelphia.

JORDAN, Edouard

German, 19th century.
Born in Berlin.
Active c. 1830.
Painter. History painting.

Edouard Jordan was a pupil of Wach.

JORDAN, Esteban

Spanish, 16th century.
Born c. 1534; died 1600.
Active in Valladolid.
Sculptor, painter.

Esteban Jordan married a niece of Berruguete and worked in Valladolid, where he made a retable and finished that of *St Eulalia* which Berruguete had begun. He worked not only with Berruguete, but with the other masters of the period. One of Jordan's finest works is the retable he made for the church of the Pardo monastery in 1567. In Medina del Rioseco, he carved many magnificent sculptures and finished a retable started by Juni. Notable among his works is the retable of Sta Maria Magdalena, but the funerary monument of D.P. Gasca in the same church, the retable of Monserrate and most certainly many other works are either lost or not yet recognised as being his. His work made him fairly rich and he bought buildings in Valladolid or León. He is one of the best Castilian sculptors of the second half of the 16th century.

JORDAN, Fédor Ivanovitch or Théodor. See **IORDAN**

JORDAN, Francisco

Spanish, 19th century.
Born c. 1778, in Muro; died 1832, in Porta Coeli Convent.
Engraver.

JORDAN, Julius Gotsch

German, 19th - 20th century.
Born 28 March 1864, in Bloemfontein (Orange Free State), South Africa; died 9 August 1907, in Germany.
Sculptor.

Julius Gotsch Jordan studied in Hanover and Berlin as well as at the Académie in Brussels. He set up in Munich in 1891, and in Frankfurt am Main in 1900. He featured in the exhibition at the Krystalpalast in Munich from 1890 to 1899, sometimes in the Grosse Kunstausstellung in Berlin, and at the Salon de la Société des Artistes Français in Paris in 1895. He is remembered for *Pygmalion*, a marble group, *Murmurs of Love*, a bronze group, *The Artist and Life*, a plaster group, busts including those of the sculptor Schlöth, the painter H. von Zügel, the chemist Keim, and statuettes (*David*, *Faun and Sparrows*, and *Two Golfers*).

JORDAN, Lucas. See **GIORDANO Luca**

JORDAN, Ludwig Heinrich Ernst Erdmann von

German, 19th century.
Born 15 May 1849, in Pawlau (Pawlow), near Ratibor (Racibórz), Upper Silesia.
Painter, illustrator, writer.

Ludwig Jordan studied at the academy in Dresden, then in Munich and Weimar, finally settling in Weimar. He painted landscapes, portraits, still-lifes in oils, watercolours and pastels, and did book illustrations. From 1893 to 1896 he showed at the Grosse Kunstausstellung in Berlin, and in 1912 at the Great Exhibition in Hanover.

JORDAN, Rudolf

German, 19th century.
Born 4 May 1810, in Berlin; died 26 March 1887, in Düsseldorf.
Painter, engraver. Genre scenes, landscapes.

Rudolf Jordan began his career as a self-taught painter at an early age, but then attended the academy from 1833 to 1840, where his teachers were Schadow and Sohn. He subsequently travelled to Holland, Belgium, France and Italy to study the art of these countries. He became a member of and teacher at the academies in Berlin, Dresden and Amsterdam. Mentioned among his pupils were H. Ritter, B. Vautier, A. Kindler and J. Geertz. In 1830, he first showed in a public exhibition in Berlin, and also featured in exhibitions in Cologne, Düsseldorf, Hamburg, Vienna and Philadelphia. He won gold medals in Berlin in 1866 and Vienna in 1873. He engraved genre scenes both of his own and from modern masters.

MUSEUMS AND GALLERIES:

BERLIN: *Marriage Proposal in Heligoland*; *The Widow's Consolation* - BREMEN: *The Clumsy Dentist* - COLOGNE: *Soup Time at the Convent* - DÜSSELDORF: *The Newborn*; *The Wait* - KALININGRAD: *The House of Old Men* - LEIPZIG: *The First Wedding Call* - OSLO: *Worship at a Boarding School* - STUTTGART: *Shipwreck on the Coast of Normandy* - WROCLAW: *The Return of the Daughter*.

AUCTION RECORDS:

PARIS, 1880, *Sunday Morning of the Island of Marken*, FRF 2,050. NEW YORK, 1-2 Dec 1904, *Meditation*, USD 105. COLOGNE, 14 June 1976, *The Navigation Lesson* (oil/zinc, 15 x 13 1/4 ins / 38 x 33.5 cm) DEM 5,800. COLOGNE, 1 June 1978, *The Wait* (oil on canvas, 30 x 33 ins / 76 x 84 cm) DEM 12,000. LONDON, 18 June 1980, *Marriage Proposal in Heligoland* (oil on canvas, 34 1/4 x 53 3/4 ins / 87 x 136.5 cm) GBP 11,000. Co-

LOGNE, 18 Nov 1982, *The Invalid Woman's Meal* (1862, oil on canvas, 24 3/4 x 28 1/4 ins / 63 x 71.5 cm) DEM 14,000. COLOGNE, 22 Nov 1984, *Fishermen on the Beach* (oil on canvas, 13 3/4 x 17 3/4 ins / 35 x 45 cm) DEM 8,000. DÜSSELDORF, 1 April 1987, *Old Heligoland Fishing Couple* (1875, oil on canvas, 29 1/4 x 31 1/2 ins / 74 x 80 cm) DEM 15,000. COLOGNE, 20 Oct 1989, *Wedding of Common People in an Interior* (1855, oil on canvas, 49 1/4 x 69 ins / 125 x 175 cm) DEM 60,000. AMSTERDAM, 5-6 Nov 1991, *Flirtatious Words* (1852, oil on canvas, 13 3/4 x 17 ins / 35 x 43 cm) NLG 28,750. MUNICH, 21 June 1994, *Marriage Proposal in Heligoland* (oil on canvas, 34 1/4 x 53 3/4 ins / 87 x 136.5 cm) DEM 51,750. AMSTERDAM, 27 April 1999, *Precious Moment* (1855, oil on canvas, 7 x 8 ins / 19 x 20 cm) NLG 5,000. COLOGNE, 11 April 2002, *Old Fishing Couple* (1869, oil on canvas, 26 x 21 ins / 65 x 53 cm) EUR 2,000. NEW YORK, 21 Jan 2003, *Sailing Class* (oil on tin, 17 x 21 ins / 43 x 53 cm) USD 4,000. NEW ORLEANS, 5 April 2003, *Sailor's Wife with Her Sleeping Baby* (1853, oil on canvas, 13 x 16 ins / 33 x 41 cm) USD 4,500.

JORDAN, Samuel

17th century.

Active in Seville at the end of the 17th century.

Engraver.

This may be the same Samuel Jordan as the engraver known to be in Bern at this period.

JORDAN, Sauveur or Salvador

Spanish, 18th century.

Active c. 1736.

Portrait artist.

Sauveur Jordan is mentioned by Siret.

JORDAN, Vasilije

Croat, 20th century.

Born 1934, in Zagreb.

Painter.

Vasilije Jordan studied at the school of applied arts and the academy of fine art in Zagreb.

Patrick Waldberg has written of his work: 'We are confronted with some kind of post-Freudian Monsu Desiderio, the red glows of the dramatic lighting seeming to illuminate the rubble of humanity in a landscape of ruins... Scarcely distinguishable one from the other, objects and human beings appear struck by hypnosis'. The magical and the fantastic, children's reveries and dreams of the childhood of humanity come together in these paintings arousing a strange mixture of delight and fear. Vasilije Jordan lives in Zagreb.

Collective exhibitions include: Sopot (Poland), Zurich, Lausanne, São Paulo, San Marino, Lisbon. Solo exhibitions include: in Zagreb, Belgrade, Split, Skopje, Novi Sad, Antwerp, Dubrovnik and Paris (1966). He has received a number of prizes including the painting prize at the 2nd Belgrade Triennale (1964); the 3rd prize for painting at the exhibition *The Struggle for Liberation in Yugoslav Art*, Belgrade (1961); 1st prize for painting at the 1962 Biennale of Young Artists, Rijeka.

BIBLIOGRAPHY:

Waldberg, Patrick, *Vasilije Jordan*, exhibition catalogue, Gal. Lambert, Paris, 1966.

JORDAN, Wilhelm

German, 20th century.

Born 25 May 1871, in Stargard (Pomerania).

Painter, draughtsman, illustrator, lithographer.

Wilhelm Jordan studied in Breslau (now Wroclaw, Poland), Berlin and Munich. From 1899 he often featured in the exhibition of the Berlin Secession and in the Gross Kunstausstellung. Amongst his works are three portraits of the governors of the province of Posen (now Poznan, Poland), illustrations, bookplates and original lithographs.

MUSEUMS AND GALLERIES:

LEIPZIG (Mus. der Bildenden Künste): *Portrait of the Art Writer Franz Servaes* (pastel); *Portrait of Privy Councillor Max Jordan* (pastel).

JORDAN-ROMAN, Véronique

French, 20th century.

Painter, engraver, watercolourist, draughtswoman.

Véronique Jordan-Roman has provided twelve watercolours as illustrations for *Amours de Marie. Sonnets pour Hélène* (*The Loves of Marie. Sonnets for Helen*) by Pierre de Ronsard (Imprimerie Nationale, 1985), and has also illustrated the literary anthology *Instant d'après* (*The Moment After*).

Her work has featured in group exhibitions, including *Le Désespoir du peintre* (*The Painter's Despair*), in 1975, at the Salle du Vieux Marché, Jouy-en-Josas. Her solo shows have included one in 2003, at the Galerie Jacques Elbaz, Paris.

JORDANESCU, Joan

Romanian, 20th century.

Born 1881, in Bucharest.

Sculptor.

Joan Jordanescu studied in Bucharest, Paris and Naples. His works include: *Maternal Happiness*, *Blind People* and *Unease*. He also executed some commemorative monuments.

JORDANUS. See **JORDAN, JORDAENS** and **GIORDANO**

JORDE, Lars

Norwegian, 19th century.

Born 22 July 1865, in Vang.

Active in Christiania (now Oslo).

Painter. Genre scenes.

Lars Jorde received a silver medal at the Exposition Universelle in Paris in 1900. He was best known for his Norwegian landscapes.

JORDEN, G.

British, 19th century.

Active in London.

Sculptor.

G. Jorden exhibited in London at the Royal Academy and at the Suffolk Street Gallery from 1835 to 1842.

JORDI, pseudonym of Jorge Mercade-Farres

Spanish, 20th century.

Born 21 December 1923, in Barcelona.

Also active in France after 1948.

Painter. Figures, landscapes with figures.

Jordi was the son of the painter Jaime Mercade-Queralt. He lived in Paris from 1948 to 1954 and later travelled widely. He trained in various groups and schools in Barcelona.

Jordi exhibited for the first time in 1946, and was one of the founders of the Spanish October Salon. His works have featured in many collective exhibitions of Catalan art, for instance in St Étienne in 1977. He has exhibited in solo shows in Paris, at the Galerie St-Placide in 1951 and the Galerie Cimaise in 1953. He has also had solo exhibitions in Barcelona in 1954, 1957, 1959, 1965 and 1973; in Madrid in 1955, 1961 and 1966; in Palma de Majorca in 1967 and in the USA in 1962.

Jordi's painting was first influenced by Cubism, but at the time of his stay in Paris the traces of Expressionism became more marked in the way he depicted sad figures. As his work evolved, he wavered between a rather informal style based on richness of materials and a figurative representation of reality using the range of sombre tones that traditionally characterise Spanish painting. From 1972, he painted austere and mysterious landscapes in blue tones using broad brush-strokes, sometimes adding a cottage or a boat, abandoned to the rebellious forces of nature.

Museums and Galleries:
Barcelona (MAC) - Madrid (Mus. Nacional Centro de Arte Reina Sofía).
Auction records:
Madrid, 27 June 1974, *House in the Trees,* ESP 280,000. Zurich, 14 May 1983, *Still-life with Melons and Grapes* (1952, oil on canvas, 28 3/4 x 37 1/2 ins / 73 x 95 cm) CHF 3,800.

JORDI DE DEU, Juan
Spanish, 14th - 15th century.
Sculptor.
He was the father of Juan Pedro or Johan Pere. A pupil of and collaborator with Jaime Castayls, he took part in the carving of several tombs commissioned by Pedro IV for the monastery of Poblet (Tarragona). The *St Lawrence* retable of 1362 in Santa Coloma, Queralt, is attributed to him. In 1400, he undertook the sculptures for the main porch of the home of the municipal council of Barcelona. The tomb of the painter P. Serra in the church of Santa Maria, Cervera, is also attributed to him.

JORDIC-PIGNON, Georges
French, 20th century.
Born 5 January 1876, in Philippeville, Algeria; died 28 November 1915; on the battlefield.
Painter.
Georges Jordic-Pignon became a member of the Salon des Artistes Français in Paris in 1907.

JORDOT, Jérôme
French, 17th century.
Born 17th century, in Lyons.
Goldsmith, engraver.
Jordot was established in Grenoble in 1658, where he engraved colophons for printers and booksellers. An engraver of the name of Jordot engraved tokens towards the middle of the 17th century.

JOREL, Alfred
French, 19th - 20th century.
Died 3 April 1927.
Active in Paris.
Sculptor.
Alfred Jorel became a member of the Société des Artistes Français in 1896 and exhibited at the Society's salons. He was awarded a bronze medal in 1907.

JOREL, Alfred
French, 20th century.
Painter. Urban landscapes.
Alfred Jorel was the son of the sculptor Alfred Jorel. He exhibited in Paris at the Salon des Indépendants during the 20th century. He painted the sights of Paris.

JORELLE, Jules Émile
French, 20th century.
Painter.
Museums and Galleries:
Pontoise: *Inferior* (1907).

JORET, Louis Justin Prosper
French, 19th century.
Born 19th century, in Paris.
Painter, miniaturist.
Louis Justin Prosper Joret's work appeared at the Salon from 1874 to 1880, represented by portraits in miniature.

JÖRG (Meister)
Painter.
Meister Jörg may be identical with Georg Kattler.

JÖRG. See also **GEORG**

JORG VAN DELFFS. See **DELFFS Jorigen van**

JORGE, Affonso
Portuguese, 16th century.
Died before 1552.
Active in Lisbon.
Painter.
He was appointed court painter by King Manuel I in 1508 and in 1529 became court painter to King João III. The art museum in Lisbon owns several paintings by Affonso Jorge.

JORGE, Aleman. See **FERNANDEZ Jorge**

JORGE, Inglès. See **INGLÈS**

JORGEN, or Jørgen Danus
Danish, 17th century.
Born to a family originally from Helsingør.
Painter. Self-portraits.
In the 1608 almanac of Christian IV, Jørgen is named Jørgen Danus. The king acquired two of his paintings.
Museums and Galleries:
Hillerød: *Self-portrait* (wood).

JØRGENSEN, Aksel Karl
Danish, 20th century.
Born 3 February 1883.
Painter, engraver, illustrator.
Aksel Karl Jørgensen painted in Copenhagen. In 1919 he featured in the Aarhus exhibition with his monumental *Ironmaster at Work.* From 1911 to 1913 he executed a series of paintings on the life of the poet H. Drachmann. He was one of the founders of and collaborators on the magazine *L'Ètincelle* (*The Spark*), for which he did the illustrations. He also illustrated books, working on the woodcuts for *The Gods of the North* by Oehlenschlaeger.
Museums and Galleries:
Copenhagen (Statens Mus. for Kunst): *Portrait of Two Children; Portrait of a Man.*
Auction records:
Copenhagen, 21 Nov 1973, *View of a Port,* DKK 6,200. Copenhagen, 20 Oct 1976, *The Painter at His Easel* (1913, oil on canvas, 35 3/4 x 31 1/2 ins / 91 x 80 cm) DKK 7,100. London, 24 March 1988, *The Christiansborg Palace, Copenhagen* (1908, oil on canvas, 33 x 36 1/4 ins / 84 x 92 cm) GBP 1,980. Copenhagen, 9 May 1990, *Philosopher* (1908, oil on canvas, 22 x 9 ins / 56 x 23 cm) DKK 4,500. Copenhagen, 6 March 1991, *Self-portrait* (1907, oil on canvas, 15 3/4 x 9 1/2 ins / 40 x 24 cm) DKK 6,500. Copenhagen, 18 Nov 1992, *View from Amaliegade* (1907, oil on canvas, 18 x 22 3/4 ins / 46 x 58 cm) DKK 5,500. Copenhagen, 20 Oct 1993, *Townscape in Dybensgade* (oil on canvas, 27 1/2 x 33 ins / 70 x 84 cm) DKK 21,000. Copenhagen, 26 April 1995, *Master Craftsman* (1903, oil on canvas, 49 1/2 x 25 1/2 ins / 126 x 65 cm) DKK 6,500. Copenhagen, 12-14 Nov 1997, *Dance Hall* (1908, oil on canvas, 41 1/4 x 49 1/4 ins / 105 x 125 cm) DKK 90,000. Vejle, 20 May 1999, *Summer Landscape with Man on Bench Reading Newspaper* (1910, oil on canvas, 37 x 51 ins / 93 x 130 cm) DKK 18,500. Aarhus, 11 Sept 1999, *Market Day in Copenhagen* (1921, oil on canvas, 22 x 24 ins / 57 x 61 cm) DKK 19,000. Copenhagen, 2 April 2001, *The Candidate for Confirmation* (1908, oil on canvas, 62 x 34 ins / 158 x 87 cm) DKK 32,000. Copenhagen, 10 April 2002, *Self-portrait* (1916, oil on canvas, 34 x 25 ins / 87 x 64 cm) DKK 13,000. Copenhagen, 5 March 2003, *Woman Rolling Cigar with the Artist in Background* (1916, oil on canvas, 31 x 26 ins / 80 x 65 cm) DKK 15,000. Lysaker, 27 Sept 2004, *The Post-boat* (oil on canvas, 22 x 31 ins / 56 x 78 cm) NOK 16,500. Copenhagen, 5 Oct 2004, *Composition with Flowers* (1917, oil on canvas, 26 x 23 ins / 65 x 58 cm) DKK 13,000.

JØRGENSEN, Anita
Danish, 20th century.
Born 1942, in Copenhagen.
Sculptor, installation artist.

Anita Jørgensen lives and works in Copenhagen. Her sculptures appear massive, sometimes huge volumes of iron that have been hollowed out in certain places, which she calls 'walls', or crates in the form of rectangular solids or are even made of corrugated iron. This formal 'minimalism' is almost virtual, since the artist's intention is not only to strive to denude it and make it impersonal, but also to insist on reminding us that the light that is part of the way we perceive our environment is also one of the factors defining it. Anita Jørgensen captures this light, 'desires' it by occasionally inserting strips of glass into the spaces in her materials, playing with it by bringing it into confrontation with different textures such as rubber, lead or iron.

She has taken part in group exhibitions, including exhibitions in 1982, 1983 and 1984 in Copenhagen, 1985 at Nordjyllands Kunstmuseum in Aalborg, 1986 in Odense, *K 18* in 1987 in Kassel, *Danemark 88, Ateliers en Liberté* (*Denmark 88, Studios at Liberty*) at the Fondation Cartier in Jouy-en-Josas, the 1988 Salon de la Jeune Sculpture in Paris, *Le Gabut* in 1989 in La Rochelle, at the Museo d'Arte Moderna e Contemporanea in Bolzano in 1990 and *Questions de Sens - huit artistes danois* (*Questions of Meaning - Eight Danish Artists*) in 1991 at the Centre d'Art Contemporain in Ivry and the Centre d'Art Contemporain in Corbeil-Essonnes.

She has also shown her work in solo exhibitions, including those at the Kunstmuseum in Randers in 1985, the Galerie Keller in Paris in 1988 and 1991, the Maison de la Culture in Amiens in 1989 and the Kunstmuseum in Esbjerg in 2001.

BIBLIOGRAPHY:

Töjner, Poul Erik, *Questions de sens - huit artistes danois*, exhibition catalogue, Centre d'Art contemporain, Corbeil-Essonnes, Centre d'Art d'Ivry, Ivry-sur-Seine, 1991.

MUSEUMS AND GALLERIES:

AALBORG (Nordjyllands Kunstmus.) - COPENHAGEN (Statens Mus. for Kunst) - RANDERS (Kunstmus.).

JØRGENSEN, Børge

Danish, 20th century.
Born 1926, in Rudkøbing.
Sculptor. Monuments.

Børge Jørgensen is self-taught. He worked in iron, polishing the metal and playing with the reflection of light. His works do not lack humour. Sometimes imposing, they have often been associated with images of plant growth. He produced a homage to Egill Jacobsen as well as monumental sculptures for public squares in Denmark, Germany and the USA.

He participated in the following group exhibitions: 1947, Fyn exhibition in Odense; spring salon in Copenhagen; 1956, autumn salon in Charlottenborg; 1963, Musée Rodin, Paris; 1964, Göteborg; 1973, *Danish Art 1945-1973*, Galeries Nationales du Grand Palais, Paris; 1979, Middelheim Biennale; 1983, listed at the Foire Internationale d'Art Contemporain, Paris; 1984, IIe Biennale de Sculpture de Normandie, Centre d'Art Contemporain in Jouy-sur-Eure. He also showed his works in solo exhibitions from 1952, and was a member of the *Groningen* group from 1962.

MUSEUMS AND GALLERIES:

AARHUS (Kunstmus.) - CHICAGO (AI) - COPENHAGEN (Statens Mus. for Kunst) - DENVER (MMA) - ESBJERG (Kunstpavilionen) - GÖTEBORG (Konstmus.) - HJØRRING (Vendyssel Kunstmus.) - JERNING (Kunstmus.) - ODENSE (Fyns Kunstmus.) - RANDERS (Kunstmus.) - SKIVE (Kunstmus.) - TØNDER (Sønderjyllands Kunstmus.) - VEJLE (Kunstmus.) - WASHINGTON DC (MMA).

AUCTION RECORDS:

COPENHAGEN, 28 April 1976, *Sculpture* (1975, h. 31 1/2 ins / 80 cm) DKK 2,800. COPENHAGEN, 1 April 1981, *Sculpture* (1960, wood and glass, h. 70 3/4 ins / 180 cm, w. 33 1/2 ins/85 cm) DKK 7,000. COPENHAGEN, 9 May 1984, *Sculpture* (1976, stainless steel, h. 20 3/4 ins / 53 cm) DKK 8,000. COPENHAGEN, 26 Nov 1986, *Sculpture* (stainless steel, h. 22 1/2 ins / 57 cm) DKK 6,500. COPENHAGEN, 2 March 1988, *Sculpture* (iron and glass, h. 12 1/2 ins / 32 cm) DKK 6,000. COPENHAGEN, 30 Nov 1988, *Sculpture* (1972, stainless steel, h. 14 1/2 ins / 37 cm) DKK 6,800. COPENHAGEN, 4 Dec 1991, *Sculpture* (1982, stainless steel, h. 19 3/4 ins / 50 cm) DKK 25,000. NEW YORK, 27 Feb 1992, *Abstract Shape* (1971, welded iron and glass, 54 1/2 x 16 3/4 x 6 3/4 ins / 138.4 x 42.5 x 17.2 cm) USD 1,760. COPENHAGEN, 4 March 1992, *Relief* (1973, stainless steel, 25 1/4 x 23 1/2 x 4 3/4 ins / 64 x 60 x 12 cm) DKK 13,000. COPENHAGEN, 2-3 Dec 1992, *Relief* (black-painted iron and glass, h. 30 3/4 ins / 78 cm, l. 19 ins/48 cm) DKK 6,000. COPENHAGEN, 10 March 1993, *Sculpture* (1983, rusted steel, h. 18 1/2 ins / 47 cm) DKK 8,500. COPENHAGEN, 6 Sept 1993, *Sculpture* (stainless steel and white acrylic, h. 40 1/4 ins / 102 cm) DKK 20,000. COPENHAGEN, 15 June 1994, *Lifelines* (1977, stainless steel, h. 85 ins / 215 cm) DKK 16,000. COPENHAGEN, 8-9 March 1995, *Joie de Vivre* (1973, stainless steel, h. 24 3/4 ins / 63 cm) DKK 8,500. COPENHAGEN, 24 Feb 1999, *Untitled* (1978, stainless steel, h. 69 ins / 175 cm) DKK 65,000. COPENHAGEN, 23 March 1999, *Untitled* (1970, iron, clear coloured glass, h. 40 ins / 102 cm) DKK 14,000. COPENHAGEN, 28 March 2000, *Untitled* (1976, polished matted steel, h. 81 ins / 205 cm) DKK 57,000. COPENHAGEN, 3 Oct 2000, *Woman and Man* (1988, polished steel, h. 81 ins / 205 cm) DKK 55,000. COPENHAGEN, 2 April 2001, *Untitled* (1986, polished steel, h. 23 ins / 58 cm) DKK 20,000. COPENHAGEN, 2 Oct 2001, *Untitled* (1976, polished matt steel, h. 81 ins / 205 cm) DKK 46,000. COPENHAGEN, 10 April 2002, *Untitled* (steel, h. 23 ins / 59 cm) DKK 13,000. COPENHAGEN, 10 April 2002, *Gate to Heaven* (steel on stone, h. 18 ins / 45 cm) DKK 14,000. COPENHAGEN, 1 April 2003, *Staning Figure* (1979, corten steel, h. 46 ins / 116 cm) DKK 25,000. COPENHAGEN, 7 Oct 2003, *Untitled* (1979, stainless steel, h. 19 ins / 48 cm) DKK 18,000. COPENHAGEN, 5 Oct 2004, *Figures* (polished stainless steel, h. 16 ins / 40 cm) DKK 14,000.

JORGENSEN, Christian A., called Chris

American, 19th - 20th century.
Born 1860, in Norway; died 24 June,1935, in Oakland (California).
Painter. Mountainscapes, seascapes, landscapes.

Christian Jorgensen came to San Francisco with his mother in 1870, and was one of the first pupils at the School of Design when it opened. He later taught at the School of Design. He travelled to Italy and Mexico, but spent most of his time in the countryside of California, especially in Yosemite.

AUCTION RECORDS:

LOS ANGELES-SAN FRANCISCO, 7 Feb 1990, *Mount Donner from Sugar Bowl* (watercolour/paper, 14 1/2 x 10 1/4 ins / 37 x 26 cm) USD 1,320. LOS ANGELES-SAN FRANCISCO, 12 July 1990, *Monterey Bay* (1888, watercolour/paper, 9 x 31 1/2 ins / 23 x 80 cm) USD 2,750. NEW YORK, 15 April 1992, *Yosemite* (oil on reinforced canvas, 8 x 10 ins / 20.3 x 25.4 cm) USD 1,760. NEW YORK, 25 Sept 1992, *Mariposa Grove, California* (watercolour/paper/card, 15 x 10 1/2 ins / 38.1 x 26.7 cm) USD 990. NEW YORK, 9 Sept 1993, *Snow-capped Mountains* (1918, oil on canvas, 21 x 27 ins / 53.3 x 68.6 cm) USD 2,530. LOS ANGELES, 9 Dec 1999, *Chilnualna Falls Wawona* (1900, watercolour on board, 17 x 9 ins / 42 x 23 cm) USD 2,750. LOS ANGELES, 9 Dec 1999, *Stairway Leading to Choir, San Gabriel Mission* (1903, watercolour, 13 x 9 ins / 32 x 23 cm) USD 3,500. SAN FRANCISCO, 14 June 2000, *Carmel* (1923, oil on canvas, 17 x 30 ins / 44 x 76 cm) USD 6,500. SAN FRANCISCO, 13 June 2001, *Yosemite Woodland* (watercolour on paper on paperboard, 9 x 31 ins / 22 x 78 cm) USD 7,500. SAN FRANCISCO, 13 June 2001, *Vernal Falls, Yosemite* (1900, watercolour and pencil on paper on board, 19 x 13 ins / 48 x 32 cm) USD 7,500. SAN FRANCISCO, 19 Nov 2002, *Adobe Mission* (1903, watercolour on paperboard, 10 x 15 ins / 25 x 38 cm) USD 5,500. SAN FRANCISCO, 19 Nov 2002, *Bridalveil Falls and El Capitan, Yosemite Valley* (watercolour, 13 x 19 ins / 34 x 48 cm) USD 7,000. PASADENA, 18 Nov 2003, *High Sierra Land-*

scape (watercolour, 18 x 11 ins / 46 x 28 cm) USD 6,000. PASADENA, 18 Nov 2003, *Cypress near Blue Water, Point Lobos* (1929, oil on canvas, 26 x 40 ins / 66 x 102 cm) USD 9,000. SAN FRANCISCO, 8 June 2004, *Vernal Falls, Yosemite* (1900, pencil and watercolour, 19 x 12 ins / 48 x 31 cm) USD 4,000. SAN FRANCISCO, 8 June 2004, *Woodlands with a Stream* (1916, pencil and watercolour, 15 x 10 ins / 37 x 26 cm) USD 5,000.

JØRGENSEN, Claus Rohland
Danish, 20th century.
Painter.
Claus Jørgensen lived and worked in Copenhagen. He featured in the exhibition *De Bonnard à Baselitz - Dix ans d'enrichissements du cabinet des estampes 1978-1988* (*From Bonnard to Baselitz: A Decade of Acquisitions by the Prints Collection 1978-1988*) at the Bibliothèque Nationale in Paris in 1992.

JØRGENSEN, Ejler Andreas Christoffer
Danish, 19th century.
Born 16 July 1838, in Roskilde; died 17 December 1876, in Oakland (California), USA.
Painter.
Ejler Jørgensen studied at the Kunstakademi in Copenhagen. From 1865 to 1871 he exhibited portraits, including that of *Magdelene Thoresen*, in addition to a painting with figures. In 1873 he went to San Francisco and the Sandwich Islands, where he painted numerous portraits.

JØRGENSEN, Erling
Danish, 20th century.
Born 1905; died 1977.
Painter.
AUCTION RECORDS:
COPENHAGEN, 20 Sept 1989, *Composition* (1943, oil on canvas, 17¼ x 24 ins / 44 x 61 cm) DKK 5,000. COPENHAGEN, 22 Nov 1989, *Rome* (1962, oil on canvas, 29½ x 39¼ ins / 75 x 100 cm) DKK 8,500. COPENHAGEN, 30 May 1990, *Composition* (1962, oil on canvas, 18½ x 12½ ins / 47 x 32 cm) DKK 9,000. COPENHAGEN, 13-14 Feb 1991, *Composition* (oil on canvas, 15¾ x 19¾ ins / 40 x 50 cm) DKK 4,000. COPENHAGEN, 20 May 1992, *Composition* (1954, oil on canvas, 19¾ x 22½ ins / 50 x 57 cm) DKK 3,200. COPENHAGEN, 1 Dec 1993, *Composition* (1942, oil on canvas, 19¾ x 28¼ ins / 50 x 72 cm) DKK 4,000. COPENHAGEN, 15 June 1994, *Composition* (1942, oil on canvas, 29¼ x 19¾ ins / 74 x 50 cm) DKK 4,800. COPENHAGEN, 26 May 1999, *Composition* (1962, oil on canvas, 30 x 39 ins / 75 x 100 cm) DKK 16,000. COPENHAGEN, 29 Sept 1999, *Composition* (1957, oil on canvas, 29 x 39 ins / 73 x 100 cm) DKK 12,000.

JØRGENSEN, Hans Peter Sigismund
Danish, 19th century.
Born 25 July 1806, in Copenhagen; died 12 May 1887.
Painter. Portraits.
Hans Jørgensen was a pupil at the Kunstakademi in Copenhagen. Some of his works were exhibited from 1823 to 1831, and from 1855 to 1866.

JØRGENSEN, Jørgen
Danish, 20th century.
Born 6 December 1871, in Denmark.
Active in the USA.
Painter, sculptor.
Jørgen Jørgensen was a member of the American Artists Professional League.

JØRGENSEN, Lorents, or Jories
Danish, 17th century.
Died after 1679.
Sculptor (wood).
Most of Lorents Jørgensen's work is in the Holbaek region. Among his most important works are the altars in Kallundborg, Asminderod, Koge and Helsingør. Three of his statues sculpted in oak and originating from a church altar in Holbaek are now in the museum in Frederiksborg.

JØRGENSEN, Magnus, or Jurgensen
Danish, 17th century.
Born 1638, in Randers.
Painter.
Magnus Jørgensen painted the portraits *Frederik III, Christian V* and *Frederik IV on Horseback* for Frederiksborg castle. His painting *Old Man During a Funerary Speech* is mentioned as being in Randers, and his *Allegory* in Fredensborg.

JØRGENSEN, Marius Erik Jakob
Danish, 20th century.
Born 18 July 1870, in Copenhagen.
Sculptor.
Marius Erik Jakob Jørgensen was a student at the Kongelige Danske Kunstakademi in Copenhagen from 1889 to 1907, and began to exhibit in 1906. In 1911 he received the Neuhausen Prize for his *Wrestlers*, and 1913 he was awarded a travelling bursary. He is noted for a bust of H. Schwanenflügel.

JORGENSEN, Monique
French, 20th century.
Painter, illustrator. Local scenes.
Monique Jorgensen painted picturesque views of old Paris and provided illustrations for two books on historic houses prefaced by J.L. Vaudoyer.

JØRGENSEN, Robert Frederik
Danish, 20th century.
Born 15 July 1887, in Copenhagen.
Painter. Mythological subjects, figures, landscapes, flowers.
Robert Frederik Jørgensen was a student at the Kongelige Danske Kunstakademi in Copenhagen from 1908 to 1915, and in 1919 was awarded a prize, the Neuhausen Bequest, for his architectural paintings. He exhibited in Charlottenborg with *Open Windows*. He also produced landscapes, flower paintings and figure paintings such as *Dianas with Nymphs*.

JØRGENSEN, Søren Møller
Danish, 19th century.
Born 28 January 1791, in Rosenholm, near Aarhus; died 30 November 1873, in Aalborg.
Painter.
Søren Jørgensen studied at the Kunstakademi in Copenhagen and exhibited copies of an historical painting, *Coriolanus*, between 1809 and 1811. He was a drawing master in Aarhus.

JØRGENSEN, Sven
Norwegian, 19th century.
Born 23 February 1861, in Drammen.
Painter.
Sven Jørgensen trained in Christiania (now Oslo), and from 1884 to 1914 he showed at French, German, Belgian and Norwegian exhibitions. He was awarded a bronze medal at the Exposition Universelle in Paris in 1889. His works are inspired by the life of Norwegian peasants.
MUSEUMS AND GALLERIES:
OSLO: *The Son; Without Work; The Goodbye.*

JÖRGENSEN, Viggo Hieronimus. See **JARL**

JØRGENSEN, Waldemar
Danish, 19th - 20th century.
Born in Svendborg.
Painter.
Waldemar Jørgensen featured at the Salon d'Automne, in Paris, at the beginning of the 20th century.

AUCTION RECORDS:
PARIS, 29 Oct 1946, *The Black Dress*, FRF 2,100.

JORGES, Alexandre
French, 19th century.
Active in Paris.
Sculptor.
Alexandre Jorges was a member of the Société des Artistes Français from 1892 and exhibited at the Salon as part of this group.

JORGI, Melchior. See **GORGI**

JORHAN, Christian Franz Xaver, the Younger
German, 18th - 19th century.
Born 6 August 1758, in Landshut; died 14 July 1844, in Passau.
Sculptor.
Bavarian School.
Christian Jorhan the Younger was a son of Christian Jorhan the Elder and also his pupil. Noted works in Passau include tomb monuments and a marble tabernacle in the Cathedral, a crucifix and tabernacle in St Gertraud's church, and a miniature monument with the apotheosis of Prince Bishop Thomas von Thun at the bishop's palace. He also sculpted a large number of altars and memorials in the Passau region (e.g. Hengersberg, Wegscheid and Ruhmannsfelden), Regensburg and Schärding (Austria).

JORHAN, Christian Johann Wenzeslaus, the Elder, or Johrhann or Jordan
German, 18th century.
Born 1727, in Griesbach (Bavaria); died 8 October 1804, in Landshut.
Sculptor.
Bavarian School.
Christian Jorhan the Elder made altar statues, tabernacles, pulpits, confessionals and groups for several churches and chapels in Landshut, also other nearby towns in Bavaria such as Altenerding, Altheim, Dingolfing, Gars and Kötzling.
MUSEUMS AND GALLERIES:
BERLIN (Bodemus.) - DARMSTADT (Hessisches Landesmus.).

JORHAN, Thomas Johann Nepomuk
German, 18th - 19th century.
Born 21 December 1761, in Landshut; died 22 January 1837, in Landshut.
Sculptor.
Bavarian School.
A son of Christian Jorhan the Elder, Thomas Jorhan was granted civic rights in Landshut on 9 September 1826.

JORHAN, Zacharias Joseph, or Johrhann or Jordan
German, 18th century.
Born 19 October 1766; died 12 December 1798.
Painter.
Bavarian School.
Zacharias Jorhan was a son of Christian Jorhan the Elder.

JORI. See **GORGI**

JORI LLOBET, Roman
Spanish, 20th century.
Born 1877, in Camp de Tarragona; died 1921, in Barcelona.
Draughtsman.
Roman Jori Llobet was also an art critic, the director of the magazine *Vell i Nou* (*Old and New*) and author of a biography of the sculptor Clara.
BIBLIOGRAPHY:
Arnáiz, José Manuel/López Jiménez, Javier/Merchán Díaz, Manuel (ed.), *Cien años de pintura en Espana y Portugal (1830-1930)*, Antiqvaria, Madrid, 1990.

JORI ROIG, Ramón
Spanish, 20th century.
Born 1888, in Lérida (Lleida).
Draughtsman.
Ramón Jori Roig studied at the academy of fine arts in Barcelona. He was forced to work mainly on industrial design in order to make a living, but nevertheless made a few purely artistic drawings.
BIBLIOGRAPHY:
Arnáiz, José Manuel/López Jiménez, Javier/Merchán Díaz, Manuel (ed.), *Cien años de pintura en Espana y Portugal (1830-1930)*, Antiqvaria, Madrid, 1990.

JORIES, Lorentz or Lars. See **JORGENSEN**

JORIGEN VAN DELFFS. See **DELFFS**

JÖRIN, Jean
Swiss, 20th century.
Born 5 August 1888, in Basel.
Sculptor. Busts, statuettes.
Jean Jörin exhibited statuettes and busts in Switzerland and Paris, notably at the Salon d'Automne.

JORINGHEM, Arthur Van. See **GORINCHEM**

JORIS, Edgard
Belgian, 20th century.
Born 1885, in Antwerp; died 1916, in Antwerp.
Sculptor. Animals.
Edgard Joris was a pupil of his father Frans, and a student at the Koninklijke Academie voor Schone Kunsten in Antwerp. He specialised in exotic animals.

JORIS, Fernand
Belgian, 20th century.
Born 1885, in Anderlues; died 1966, in Anderlues.
Painter.
Fernand Joris had a variety of trades, including being a pitface worker. He took evening classes at the Institut des Arts et Métiers in La Louvrière.

JORIS, Frans Joseph or Franz Josef
Belgian, 19th - 20th century.
Born 1851, in Deurne; died 23 October 1914, in Antwerp.
Active in Antwerp.
Sculptor. Portraits, figures. Busts.
Frans Joseph Joris, father of the Edgard Joris, was a student at the Koninklijke Academie voor Schone Kunsten in Antwerp and a pupil of Jos Geefs. He was awarded the Prix de Rome in 1914. He sculpted numerous busts and portraits, including one of Léopold de Waele, now in Antwerp, as well as figures of children.
MUSEUMS AND GALLERIES:
ANTWERP: *The Missus* - BRUSSELS: *My Beau*.

JORIS, Paul
Belgian, 20th century.
Born 1887, in Molenbeek-St-Jean.
Sculptor. Portraits.
Paul Joris was a lecturer at the Institut des Arts et Métiers in St-Ghislain.

JORIS, Pio, or Ioris
Italian, 19th - 20th century.
Born 6 June 1843, in Rome; died 6 March 1921, in Rome.
Painter (gouache), watercolourist, pastellist. Figures, genre scenes, landscapes.

Pio Joris was a pupil of Vertumni at the Accademia in Rome and of the Spanish painter Fortuny. He first exhibited in Rome about 1869. He travelled in France, Spain, Germany and England. He exhibited in Suffolk Street, London, in 1879; in Munich; very frequently in Berlin after 1873; and in Vienna and Brussels. He participated in the Paris Exposition Universelle of 1900, when he was awarded a gold medal, and won a medal in Munich in 1869 and an honourable mention in 1876. He was made a knight of the Order of the Italian Crown in 1876.

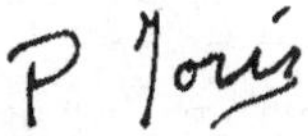

Museums and Galleries:
Bucharest (Muz. National de Arta al Românie): *Market at Campo Fiori* - Budapest: *Public Scribe; In the Garden* - Groningen: *City of Rome* - New York: *Courtyard of an Italian House* (watercolour) - Rome (Gal. Nazionale d'Arte Moderna): *Watercolour* - Stuttgart: *Under Octavian's Portico*.
Auction records:
Paris, 3 Feb 1919, *Gypsies*, FRF 50. Milan, 16 March 1971, *Garden Festival*, ITL 850,000. Milan, 17 Oct 1973, *Washerwomen*, ITL 3,400,000. Rome, 29 March 1976, *The Marriage* (oil on canvas, 21 1/4 x 16 1/2 ins / 54 x 42 cm) ITL 890,000. New York, 21 Jan 1978, *Walking* (oil on canvas, 33 1/4 x 25 1/2 ins / 84.5 x 65 cm) USD 2,900. New York, 26 Jan 1979, *Market Street* (oil on canvas, 32 3/4 x 69 ins / 83 x 175 cm) USD 9,500. Milan, 19 March 1981, *Elevation* (1913, oil on canvas, 26 x 44 1/2 ins / 66 x 113 cm) ITL 4,500,000. Milan, 23 March 1983, *Interior of a Church* (oil on canvas, 46 1/2 x 64 1/2 ins / 118 x 164 cm) ITL 9,000,000. Milan, 30 Oct 1984, *Via Flaminia, Rome* (watercolour, 21 1/4 x 19 3/4 ins / 54 x 50 cm) ITL 2,200,000. London, 30 May 1986, *Holiday in Naples* (oil on canvas, 36 3/4 x 63 ins / 93.2 x 160 cm) GBP 13,000. Rome, 16 Dec 1987, *Flower Seller* (watercolour, 16 1/4 x 11 3/4 ins / 41 x 30 cm) ITL 3,000,000. Milan, 1 June 1988, *Lemon Tree in a Pot* (1890, oil on panel, 13 1/2 x 8 ins / 34 x 20.5 cm) ITL 7,000,000. Monaco, 2 Dec 1988, *Encampment Scene* (1883, ink, 11 1/2 x 17 1/4 ins / 29.5 x 44 cm) FRF 11,100. Rome, 14 Dec 1988, *Women in an Alley* (oil on panel, 3 1/2 x 7 ins / 9 x 17.8 cm) ITL 1,900,000. London, 6 Oct 1989, *Flower Seller* (oil on canvas, 9 x 6 1/4 ins / 22 x 16 cm) GBP 3,080. Paris, 28 Nov 1989, *Lovers' Roundabout* (oil on canvas, 31 1/2 x 22 1/2 ins / 80 x 57 cm) FRF 19,000. Rome, 14 Dec 1989, *Fishing Boats at Sunset* (oil/plywood, 7 x 4 ins / 18 x 10 cm) ITL 1,380,000. Amsterdam, 10 April 1990, *Little Girl Selling Water* (1871, pencil, watercolour and gouache/paper, 5 1/2 x 8 3/4 ins / 13.8 x 22.5 cm) NLG 2,300. Rome, 29 May 1990, *Young Women Spinning* (1890, oil on panel, 12 1/2 x 9 1/2 ins / 32 x 24 cm) ITL 17,250,000. Rome, 31 May 1990, *Village Women Doing Washing* (oil on canvas, 39 x 56 3/4 ins / 99 x 144 cm) ITL 46,000,000. Rome, 14 Nov 1991, *Young Peasant Girl Sewing* (1903, watercolour, 22 1/2 x 14 1/2 ins / 56.9 x 37 cm) ITL 2,760,000. New York, 20 Feb 1992, *Distaff* (1888, oil on canvas, 63 1/2 x 38 3/4 ins / 161.3 x 98.4 cm) USD 25,300. Rome, 9 June 1992, *Bust of a Young Girl* (oil on panel, 17 x 11 3/4 ins / 43 x 30 cm) ITL 4,000, 000. Rome, 19 Nov 1992, *On the Edge of a Lake* (oil on canvas, 29 1/4 x 18 1/4 ins / 74 x 46.5 cm) ITL 34,500,000. Milan, 16 March 1993, *Garden* (oil on panel, 6 3/4 x 11 ins / 17 x 28 cm) ITL 6,000,000. Rome, 6 Dec 1994, *Gathering* (1887, oil on panel, 10 1/4 x 6 1/4 ins / 26 x 16 cm) ITL 7,660,000. London, 10 Feb 1995, *Tivoli* (1861, oil on canvas, 23 x 28 3/4 ins / 58.4 x 73 cm) GBP 6,900. Milan, 14 June 1995, *Rural Houses in Subiaco* (oil on canvas, 22 1/4 x 13 1/2 ins / 56.5 x 34 cm) ITL 2,990,000. Rome, 23 May 1996, *Young Girl at a Fountain* (oil on canvas, 19 3/4 x 15 3/4 ins / 50 x 40 cm) ITL 9,200,000. Munich, 23 June 1999, *Italian Women on Road* (oil on canvas, 31 x 22 ins / 80 x 57 cm) DEM 11,000. New York, 2 May 2000, *The Proposal* (oil on canvas, 40 x 26 ins / 102 x 66 cm) USD 9,500. Rome, 23 May 2000, *Young Girl* (1870, oil on canvas, 28 x 19 ins / 70 x 49 cm) ITL 22,000,000. Bern, 10 May 2001, *Fishermen in Boat Fishing* (oil on canvas, 42 x 72 ins / 107 x 182 cm) CHF 14,000. Florence, 12 Dec 2001, *Yard Scene* (oil on board, 6 x 11 ins / 16 x 28 cm) ITL 3,200,000. Rome, 5 June 2002, *Rain on the Flaminia* (watercolour, 21 x 14 ins / 54 x 35 cm) EUR 2,600. Hatfield, 4 June 2003, *Italian Woman in Yard Feeding Chickens* (oil on canvas, 14 x 22 ins / 36 x 56 cm) USD 6,000. Rome, 11 Dec 2003, *Path in the Park* (watercolour on card, 12 x 18 ins / 30 x 45 cm) EUR 1,600.

JORISSEN, Antoine
Belgian, 20th century.
Born 1884, in Louvain; died 1962, in Herent.
Sculptor, medallist.

Antoine Jorissen was a lecturer at the Académie des Beaux-Arts in Louvain.

JORISSEN, Madeleine
Belgian, 20th century.
Born 1944, in Tongeren (Limburg).
Painter.

Madeleine Jorissen studied at the academies of Art in Liège, Antwerp and La Cambre. Some of her works have been acquired by the Belgian State and the Province of Limburg.
Museums and Galleries:
Antwerp (Prentenkabinet).

JORISSEN, Willem
Dutch, 19th century.
Active in the Netherlands.
Painter, watercolourist. Genre scenes.

Mentioned by Florence Lévy.
Auction records:
New York, 11 March 1909, *Pet Bird*, USD 140. New York, 27 Jan 1911, *Young Woman Spinning*, USD 175. Amsterdam, 10 Feb 1988, *Young Woman Cutting Bread by her Child Seated at Table* (watercolour on paper, 18 x 14 1/2 ins / 46 x 37 cm) NLG 1,265.

JORISZ, Augustin. See **VERBURCHT**

JORISZ., Jan, also known as David
Flemish, 16th century.
Born c. 1500, probably in Bruges; died 25 August 1556, in Basel, Switzerland.
Painter (glass).

Jorisz. worked in Holland, France and England as a stained glass artist under the name of Jean van Brugge, Jan van Broeck, or Jan van Burg. In 1522 he produced a stained glass window for the church of St Gommers in Enkhuizen. He played an active role in the religious unrest of his time. His mother was accused of being a heretic and beheaded in Delft in 1537, and he himself was forced into exile in 1544 on account of his beliefs.

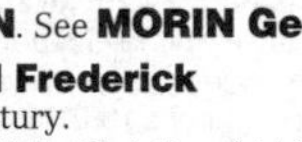

JORJ-MORIN. See **MORIN Georges**

JORKO, Carl Frederick
Danish, 19th century.
Born 1 June 1800, in Christiansfeld (Schleswig); died 2 January 1876, in Dijon.
Painter.

Carl Jorko arrived in Sweden when very young and entered the army, rising quickly through the ranks. A squadron leader in 1829, he became captain of the cavalry in 1837. In 1838 he left the army to become a painter of sporting subjects, not without success. He visited Berlin and Paris, where he won a third-class medal at the Salon in 1844 and a second-class in 1844. He was decorated by the Légion d'Honneur in 1860. He painted horses, dogs, foxes and hunting scenes with great mastery. His most famous painting is *Flood*, in which a dog with a sled, on the roof of its kennel, looks on helplessly as its offspring are swept away in the water. In 1858 he was accepted into the Swedish academy. He nevertheless continued to live in France, remaining even during the siege of 1870. He later retired to Dijon where he lived until his death.

JORLET, Bastien, or Sorlet
French, 16th century.
Sculptor.

Jorlet took part in preparations for the celebrations to mark the official visit of Henri II and Catherine de' Medici to Lyons in 1548.

JÖRLIN. See **JERLI**

JORN, Asger, pseudonym of Oluf AsgerJørgensen
Danish, 20th century.
Born 3 April 1914, in Veirum or Vejrum (Jutland); died 1 May 1973, in Aarhus.
Also active in France.
Painter (including gouache/mixed media), watercolourist, collage artist, sculptor, lithographer, potter, draughtsman. Designs for tapestries.
Groups: International Situationist, CoBrA, International Movement for an Imaginist Bauhaus.

Asger Jorn's father died in 1924, after which the family lived in Silkeborg in Jutland. During World War II he lived in Denmark and participated in the review *Helbesten* (*Horse from Hell*) with Bille, Pedersen and Jacobsen, which continued the work of the review *Linien* (*Lines*), produced in Copenhagen by a group of young artists, admirers of the creators of non-representational art. Jorn published an article in it supporting kitsch art, texts presenting Kafka to Danish readers, and philosophical reflections. He took a prominent part in the intense artistic activity organised around the review.

In 1945 he changed his name from Jørgensen to Jorn. In 1946 he painted in Lapland, and in 1947 he produced tapestries with Pierre Wemaere in Normandy. In 1947-1948 he painted in Tunisia, at Djerba (possibly imitating the work of Paul Klee at Kairouan). In 1951 he contracted tuberculosis, which led him to Switzerland in 1953. In 1956 he rented a flat in Paris. In 1958, in Paris, he published *For Form: A Draft Methodology of the Arts*, a collection of his aesthetic aims which put human beings at the centre of his preoccupations. There followed *Time for a snifter, signs carved on the churches of Eure and Calvados* (1964); a pamphlet, written with Noël Arnaud and denouncing the freedom adopted by Structuralism: *Rich Language and Drunkenness* (1968); and *Backs to the Wall*, with Noël Arnaud and François Dufrêne.

At the beginning of the 1960s Jorn played an important part in the International Situationist movement, which he left in 1962. He also took the initiative, after CoBrA, in the creation of the Movement for an Imaginative Bauhaus (1953-1957) and, in 1961, founded the Dano-French Experimental Film Company and became the promoter of the Scandinavian Institute of Comparative Vandalism. From the 1960s he travelled in Europe in search of Scandinavian art from the Prehistoric era to the middle of the Middle Ages and collected numerous photographs. In 1967 he visited Cuba, and in 1970 he travelled to the USA for an exhibition, then set up a studio in Colombes, near Paris.

Jorn is undeniably the contemporary Scandinavian artist with the most important place at world level. Conscious of what he represented, he devoted a part of his activity to making contemporary Danish and Scandinavian painting, as well as the popular art of these countries, better known in the world. The meeting, of which he was one of the principal architects, of Danish artists with their counterparts in Belgium and Holland, in the CoBrA movement, opened up a wider audience to him.

In 1936 Jorn travelled to Paris on a motorbike to work in the studio of Kandinsky, whose ideas and works he knew from the review *Linien* (*Lines*). What the young Dane did not imagine was that though Kandinsky was indeed living in Paris, not only did he not have any pupils, but he was completely unknown in that city and no gallery was showing his works. Luckily Fernand Léger kept a studio open for young artists from everywhere, the Académie Contemporaine, which Jorn attended regularly, and if Léger's artistic ideas were not those of Jorn, Jorn had great respect for his master, and was happy to be tied down to the discipline of his teaching. He collaborated with Fernand Léger on vast decorations, including *Transfer of Forces*, for the *Palace of Modern Times* in the Exposition Universelle of 1937 and, on that occasion, found himself under the direction of Le Corbusier. This was much harder for him. Léger was able to forge Jorn's character, if not his taste. Le Corbusier inspired in him an enduring animosity against what he called 'Functionalist-Calvinist architecture, that mother of all the arts who strangles her children'. He later turned to Mirò, Klee and children's drawings.

It is difficult to define periods in Jorn's work. For example, from 1936 to 1953, it is estimated that he painted about 700 canvases, not including watercolours and drawings, and it is natural that styles are intermingled. At best one can try to highlight some reference dates. After studying Chinese calligraphy to rid himself, by the liberation of the graphic gesture for its own sake and its detachment from any perceptible reality, of the formalism acquired with Léger, Jorn considered his *Blue Painting* of 1940 to be important in his development, because from that moment he took account of the fertility of a certain automatism in artistic creation, giving him access to a more primitive reality. 1944-1945 was the year of the *Didaska* series of watercolours. The works of 1946-1948 constitute a separate group, where an equilibrium is established between the formal knowledge he had acquired and spontaneous creative instincts. As in all his work, the problem of representative painting and abstraction is disdainfully put to one side as being an academic problem, while the only goal of the creative artist is to express something. Here, however, creative spontaneity is backed up by graphic support which is almost ornamental, as happens in popular art.

After the war, the Danes, Dutch, Belgians and French made contact again, but the French in the revolutionary Surrealist movement could not get their dogmatic position accepted by their contacts, who decided to cement their split with Paris by the creation, in 1948, of the CoBrA movement (COpenhagen-BRussels-Amsterdam). CoBrA claimed to be collective and experimental. By collective (and this is why it is a waste of time to look for the influence of one or other of these artists on the rest) they meant that they pooled their creative potential, as the Analytical Cubists had done. Being experimental, they rejected the bourgeois formalism of the Paris School, believing that what was important for artists was to catch the reality of human beings in their primitive manifestations, without censure of any sort, and not to compose poems or paintings as objects for aesthetic purposes.

From 1948 to 1951 Jorn participated totally in the CoBrA movement with, among other works, the series *The Right of the Eagle* (1949). In 1950 he had an internal crisis: he had always broadly called on a personal bestiary, generally of animals from Hell, confused, rightly or wrongly, with Scandinavian mythology. He had glorified *Aganak*, a hybrid beetle and crocodile. He now wanted to exorcise himself of this fantastic menagerie, but his efforts were futile. He therefore took up these familiar monsters a second time, in 1951, the year of the celebration of the Danish mythology. In 1950-1951 he executed two series of paintings: The Seasons and *On Silent Myth*. Later he divided his time between Switzerland, Paris and Albisola in Italy, where he produced a large ceramic mural, completed in 1959, which would be transported to Denmark for a school at Aarhus. He worked on this ceramic with Appel, Enrico Baj, Corneille, Lucio Fontana and Matta.

1957 is considered to have been a year of very important works, including *Stalingrad*. It was the period where Jorn's art reached maturity. Other reference dates are: the *Modifications* of 1959, old paintings bought in second-hand dealers, which he repainted, a series which he was to continue until 1963 with *New Modifications* or *Distortions* and the *Luxury Paintings* of 1961 which use dribble techniques. At this period he also produced collages and décollages. In 1962 he abandoned the black and white rings around shapes, which had always accentuated his dream-like figures, a typically characteristic graphic aspect of CoBrA art, where painting is closely linked to signs. From 1950 he engraved, and in 1970 he produced colour woodcuts in Munich: *Studies and Surprises* (1970-1971). During the last period of his life, Jorn devoted himself to sculpture, bronzes and figures in Carrara marble.

Jorn never looked for material success; he considered the act of painting a necessity for the painter, and that he should be shielded from the temptations of material fame and fortune. He refused to exhibit at the Venice Biennale. He contributed to the enrichment of the collections of contemporary art at the Silkeborg Museum, where he wanted only paintings totally independent of official and bourgeois 'good taste' to be displayed; apart from his work, works by Saura, Dubuffet and Matta are on show there. Jorn the man is clearly inseparable from Jorn the artist. He had a mission and devoted himself to it totally. Paraphrasing Christian Dotremont, who devoted a monograph to him in the *CoBrA Library*, one can say that he springs from original states of chaos which have a harmony of their own, whereas our organising era ends in chaos. He is raw freedom, but he has the organic coherence of a tree or a scream.

He took part in numerous group exhibitions from the end of the 1930s. In 1937 he featured for the first time in *Linien* (*Lines*) in Copenhagen, which, that year, had invited Kandinsky, Klee, Ernst, Tanguy, Arp and Mirò, his masters, in whom he found the example of emancipated artistic creation. From 1948 he featured in all the CoBrA exhibitions, notably in 1949 at the Stedelijk Museum in Amsterdam. In 1958 he took part, with his painting *Letter to My Son*, in the exhibition *50 Years of Modern Art*, in Brussels, the starting point for his international recognition, and in the following year important exhibitions of his work were organised in Europe and America. He was represented in other themed exhibitions, including: 2001, *Primary Vision*, an exhibition on the influence of a child's vision in the work of artists of the 20th century, at the Tate Liverpool.

He exhibited in numerous solo exhibitions, including: 1938, his first, in Copenhagen; between 1941 and 1944, Copenhagen; 1948, his first exhibition in Paris; 1962, his first exhibition in New York; 1964, a retrospective at the Kunsthalle in Basel and at the Stedelijk Museum in Amsterdam; 1965, a retrospective at the Louisiana Foundation in Humlabaek (Denmark); 1973, a retrospective at the Kestner-Gesellschaft in Hanover, also shown in Berlin, Brussels and in Denmark at the Louisiana Foundation; 1994, a vast retrospective of about 100 paintings and numerous drawings at the Stedelijk Museum in Amsterdam, subsequently shown at the Louisiana Foundation; 2001-2002, *Planet Jorn*, Musée d'art Moderne et Contemporain, Strasbourg, and Fundació Antoni Tàpies, Barcelona.

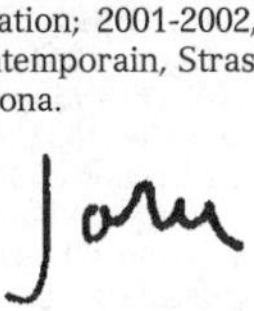

Bibliography:
Atkins, Guy, '*Jorn. Catalogue Raisonné*' in *4* vol. vol. I: Jorn in Scandinavia (1930-1953) vol. II: The Crucial Years (1954-1964) vol. III: The Final Years (1965-1973) vol. IV: Paintings (1930-1973), catalogue raisonné, Lund and Humphries, London, 1968 (Borgen Forlag, København [Copenhague], 1977, Yves Rivières Éd., Paris, 1980, Asger Jorn Foundation, London, Wittenborn, New York, 1986). Weihrauch, Jürgen, *Asger Jorn, Werkverzeichnis Druckgrafik,* catalogue raisonné, Gal. van de Loo, Munich, 1976 (graphic works 1932-1972). Atkins, Guy, *Asger Jorn,* Solomon R. Guggenheim Museum, New York, 1982. Zweite, Armin, *Asger Jorn, 1914-1973: Gemälde, Zeichnungen, Aquarelle, Gouachen, Skulpturen,* exhibition catalogue, Städtische Gal. im Lenbachhaus, Munich, 1987. *Baj-Jorn, lettres 1953-1961,* Musée d'Art moderne, St-Étienne, 1989. Fuchs, Rudi/Andersen, Troels/Birtwistle, Graham, et al., *Asger Jorn 1914-1973,* exhibition catalogue, Asger Jorn Foundation, Stedelijk Museum, Amsterdam, 1994 (text in Dutch and French). Van de Loo, Otto, *Asger Jorn in München,* Boer, Munich, 1996. Caprile, Luciano/Lehmann-Brockhaus, Ursula/Larese, Franz/Baj, Enrico, '*Asger Jorn*' in *2 vol.,* exhibition catalogue, Pinacoteca comunale Casa Rusca, Locarno, Skira, Milan, 1996 (text in Italian, German and English). Hobolth, Nina, *Jorn til Folket, Jorn for the people, udvalgte vaerke 1935-1972: selected works 1935-1972,* exhibition catalogue, Nordjyllands Kunstmuseum, Aalborg, 1997 (text in Danish and English). Andersen, Troels/Asger, Jorn, *Peinture détournée (articles, essais, lettres),* École nationale des beaux-arts, Paris, 2001. Gervereau, Laurent, *Asger Jorn. Critique de l'image quotidienne,* Éd. Cercle d'Art, Paris, 2001. Parsy, Paul-Hervé/Gervereau, Laurent/Caprile, Luciano, et al., *La Planète Jorn,* exhibition catalogue, Musée d'Art moderne et contemporain, Strasbourg, Adam Biro, Paris, 2001. Jorn, Asger, *Discours aux pingouins et autres écrits,* École nationale supérieure des beaux-arts, Paris, 2001. Stokvis, Willemijn, *Cobra,* Gallimard, Paris, 2001.

Museums and Galleries:
Aalborg: *Right of the Eagle* (1950) - Aarhus (Kunstmus.): *Feast of St John II* (1952) - Amsterdam (Stedelijk Mus.): *Guillaume Appolinaire* (1956); *L'Énigme de l'eau glassée* (1970); *In the Wing Beat of the Swans* (1963) - Boston (MFA) - Buffalo (Albright-Knox AG) - Cincinnati (AM): numerous works on paper - Copenhagen (Statens Mus. for Kunst): *Det store tog* (*The Big Procession*) (1948-1950); *Undselig hyrdescene* (*Bashful Pastoral*) (1952); *Livshjulet. Januarbilledet af årstidssuiten* (*The Wheel of Life. January Picture from the Suite of Seasons*) (1952-1953) - Eindhoven (Van Abbe Mus.): *Hooking up* (1958); *Hunger* (1960); *Lost World* (1960) - Ghent (Stedelijk Mus. voor Actuele Kunst): *Loss of the Middle* (1958) - Høvikodden (Henie Onstad Kunstsenter): *Untitled* (1951); *Festival of Fish* (1956); *Poetic Gratification* (1956); *Attention Danger* (1957); *They Must Be Kept* (1958); *Disturbing Perspective* (1960); *The Scream* (1960, oil on canvas); *Yellow Sky* (1961); *Lucid Lewdness of Hyperaesthesia* (1970); *Cabaret Voltaire* (1971-1972) - Humlebæk (Louisiana Mus. for Moderne Kunst): *On the Silent Myth, op. 5* (1952-1953); *Untitled* (1959); *Red Meadows, Green Boys* (1966-1968); *In the Beginning was the Image* (1965) - Ljubljana (Moderna Gal.) - London (Tate Collection): *The Timid Proud One* (1957, oil/board); *Letter to my Son* (1956-1957, oil on canvas) - Montreal (MAC): *Whispering* (1965); *Untitled* (1972) - Munich (Staatsgal. Moderne Kunst): *Albisola* (1955, oil on canvas) - Munich (Städtische Gal. im Lenbachhaus): *They Never Came Back* (1958) - New York (MoMA) - New York (Solomon R. Guggenheim Mus.): *Ballet Gren* (1960) - Paris

(MNAM-CCI): *Woman of 5 October* (1958); *Head of a Turk* (1967) - PITTSBURGH (Carnegie MA): *Incredible Energy* (1957, oil on canvas); *Dead Spot* (lithograph); *Untitled* (1965, paper collage); *Winter* (1953, etching) - SILKEBORG (Kunstmus.): *Green Beard* (1939); *One Gets Out of It Thus* (1962); *Euphorism* (1970); *Right of the Eagle* (1951); *Stalingrad, the Non-place or the Mad Guffaws of Courage* (1957-1960); *Wounded Beast, II* (1951); *Bridal Couple* (1953); *Lapdog* (1955); *Choreography of the Moment* (1958); *Memories Go Past* (1971) - STOCKHOLM (Nationalmus.) - THE HAGUE (Gemeentemus.).

AUCTION RECORDS:

LONDON, 6 July 1960, *Terrifying Fable* (oil on card) GBP 600. MILAN, 28 March 1962, *Polemicists and Witnesses*, ITL 2,600,000. HAMBURG, 7 June 1969, *Composition* (gouache) DEM 4,200. GENEVA, 9 Dec 1970, *Wings at Rest*, CHF 20,000. MILAN, 2 Dec 1971, *Anthropomorphic Landscape*, ITL 1,700,000. NEW YORK, 24 Oct 1974, *Nocturne* (1959) USD 12,000. COPENHAGEN, 28 April 1976, *Buttadeo, the Eternal Traveller* (1951, oil on canvas, 35 1/2 x 46 3/4 ins / 90 x 119 cm) DKK 85,000. MUNICH, 29 Nov 1976, *Composition* (1960, gouache, 19 x 15 1/4 ins / 48 x 38.5 cm) DEM 3,050. COPENHAGEN, 8 March 1977, *Spanish Composition* (1954, oil on canvas, 48 3/4 x 36 1/4 ins / 124 x 92 cm) DKK 120,000. COPENHAGEN, 8 March 1979, *The Two Elements* (1970, coloured lithograph, 82 3/4 x 56 ins / 210 x 142 cm) DKK 6,500. LONDON, 5 Dec 1979, *The Only Property* (1960, oil on canvas, 39 1/4 x 32 ins / 100 x 81 cm) GBP 7,800. LONDON, 1 July 1980, *Head* (1961, gouache and watercolour, 22 x 18 ins / 55 x 46 cm) GBP 1,250. PARIS, 27 Oct 1980, *Dog* (1956, painted ceramic, 7 x 11 3/4 x 5 ins / 17.5 x 30 x 13 cm) FRF 5,800. LONDON, 2 Dec 1980, *Two Figures* (black chalk, 11 1/4 x 8 3/4 ins / 28.5 x 22.5 cm) GBP 900. ZURICH, 26 March 1981, *Composition* (1962, gouache, 17 3/4 x 20 3/4 ins / 45 x 53 cm) CHF 15,000. NEW YORK, 18 Nov 1981, *Homage to Baudelaire* (1942, oil on canvas, 32 1/4 x 38 ins / 82 x 96.5 cm) USD 36,000. LONDON, 24 March 1983, *Suresnes* (1950, brush and Indian ink, 15 3/4 x 13 ins / 40 x 33 cm) GBP 1,400. NEW YORK, 10 May 1983, *Den reflekterende Nystamand (Thoughtful Nystamand)* (1964, oil on canvas, 42 1/4 x 31 ins / 107.5 x 79 cm) USD 28,000. COPENHAGEN, 11 May 1983, *Composition* (1962, gouache, 12 x 18 ins / 30.5 x 45.5 cm) DKK 18,700. COPENHAGEN, 2 June 1983, *Red Earth* (1953, coloured lithograph, 38 1/4 x 53 1/2 ins / 97 x 136 cm) DKK 41,000. COPENHAGEN, 15 Oct 1985, *Composition* (1967, gouache, 16 1/4 x 13 ins / 41 x 33 cm) DKK 95,000. MILAN, 27 Oct 1986, *Through the Ages* (1972, bronze, h. 23 1/2 ins / 60 cm) ITL 66,000,000. LONDON, 4 Dec 1986, *Untitled* (1946, oil on canvas, 26 3/4 ins / 68 cm, 2 3/4 x 36 ins/7 x 91.5 cm) GBP 40,000. COPENHAGEN, 7 May 1987, *Composition* (1953, coloured lithograph, 38 1/4 x 53 1/2 ins / 97 x 136 cm) DKK 51,000. PARIS, 24 Nov 1987, *Composition* (1961, gouache, 21 1/4 x 17 3/4 ins / 54 x 45 cm) FRF 60,000. COPENHAGEN, 24 Feb 1988, *Composition* (1941, oil on canvas, 20 x 15 3/4 ins / 51 x 40 cm) DKK 300,000; *Snowstorm* (1958, 31 1/2 x 25 1/2 ins / 80 x 65 cm) DKK 410,000; *Exhaustion* (1964, 46 x 35 ins / 116 x 89 cm) DKK 890,000. LONDON, 25 Feb 1988, *Untitled* (1965, gouache/paper, 15 3/4 x 12 1/4 ins / 40 x 31 cm) GBP 6,380. COPENHAGEN, 2 March 1988, *Composition* (coloured lithograph) DKK 16,000. COPENHAGEN, 4 May 1988, *Return* (1967, lithograph) DKK 15,000; *Barbary by Moonlight* (1970, silk screen print) DKK 7,000. MILAN, 8 June 1988, *Untitled* (1966, mixed media/paper, 9 3/4 x 7 3/4 ins / 25 x 20 cm) ITL 13,500,000. LONDON, 30 June 1988, *Birds* (watercolour and gouache, 21 1/4 x 17 3/4 ins / 54 x 45 cm) GBP 15,400. LONDON, 20 Oct 1988, *Untitled* (1958, gouache/paper/canvas, 14 x 17 3/4 ins / 35.5 x 45 cm) GBP 6,820. COPENHAGEN, 8 Nov 1988, *Sabbath Witches* (1944, oil on canvas, 20 x 30 3/4 ins / 51 x 78 cm) DKK 330,000; *Festival of the Imps* (1970, oil on canvas, 51 1/4 x 38 1/4 ins / 130 x 97 cm) DKK 1,050,000. STOCKHOLM, 21 Nov 1988, *Composition* (1965, watercolour, 18 x 14 ins / 45.5 x 35.5 cm) SEK 42,000. LONDON, 1 Dec 1988, *Falbo II* (1951, oil on card, 29 1/4 x 23 3/4 ins / 74.5 x 60.5 cm) GBP 77,000. AMSTERDAM, 8 Dec 1988, *Figure* (1967, acrylic/paper/canvas, 15 3/4 x 11 3/4 ins / 40 x 30 cm) NLG 29,900. VERSAILLES, 18 Dec 1988, *Composition* (1947, oil on card, 23 1/4 x 17 ins / 59 x 43 cm) FRF 400,000. COPENHAGEN, 8 Feb 1989, *Come into the World, Spontaneous Birth* (1963, oil on canvas, 39 3/4 x 59 3/4 ins / 101 x 152 cm) DKK 710,000. LONDON, 23 Feb 1989, *Untitled* (1945, oil on canvas, 22 x 27 1/4 ins / 55 x 69 cm) GBP 26,400. MILAN, 20 March 1989, *In the Shade* (oil on canvas, 10 3/4 x 13 3/4 ins / 27.5 x 35 cm) ITL 50,000,000. AMSTERDAM, 10 April 1989, *Untitled* (1965, oil on canvas, 16 1/4 x 13 ins / 41 x 33 cm) NLG 63,250. LONDON, 29 June 1989, *Beaches* (1964, oil on canvas, 43 1/4 x 55 ins / 110 x 140 cm) GBP 82,500. COPENHAGEN, 20 Sept 1989, *Blue Ardour*. LONDON, 26 Oct 1989, *Admiration of a Super-Donna* (1954, oil on canvas, 20 3/4 x 17 1/4 ins / 53 x 44 cm) GBP 28,600. MILAN, 8 Nov 1989, *Portrait of a Human Angel* (1959, oil on canvas, 30 1/4 x 24 3/4 ins / 77 x 63 cm) ITL 175,000,000. PARIS, 18 Feb 1990, *The Infuriated Boat* (oil on canvas, 31 1/2 x 39 1/4 ins / 80 x 100 cm) FRF 700,000. COPENHAGEN, 21-22 March 1990, *Composition with Fabulous Birds and Animals* (painting/synthetic resin, 35 x 24 ins / 88 x 61 cm) DKK 620,000. LONDON, 5 April 1990, *Running Waters* (1962, oil on canvas, 31 3/4 x 43 1/2 ins / 80.6 x 110.5 cm) GBP 82,500. AMSTERDAM, 10 April 1990, *Head* (1955, terracotta, 13 x 9 x 8 1/2 ins / 33 x 23 x 21.5 cm) NLG 33,350. PARIS, 3 May 1990, *Cosmic Stanism on the Lowest Level* (1966, gouache/paper, 15 x 11 ins / 38 x 28 cm) FRF 85,000. AMSTERDAM, 22 May 1990, *Ridicule* (1954, oil on card, 19 1/2 x 24 1/4 ins / 49.5 x 61.5 cm) NLG 149,500. PARIS, 11 June 1990, *Fanatic* (oil on panel, 18 3/4 x 23 3/4 ins / 47.5 x 60.5 cm) FRF 480,000. NEW YORK, 5 Oct 1990, *Untitled* (1964, collage of ripped paper/card, 13 3/4 x 10 ins / 34.9 x 24.5 cm) USD 15,400. LONDON, 18 Oct 1990, *Underdeveloped Insult* (1961, oil on canvas, 25 1/2 x 33 ins / 65 x 84 cm) GBP 39,600. COPENHAGEN, 14-15 Nov 1990, *Mask* (1941, painting/wood, 14 1/4 x 12 1/4 ins / 36 x 31 cm) DKK 75,000. LONDON, 6 Dec 1990, *Albisola* (1955, oil on canvas, 26 3/4 x 22 ins / 68 x 55 cm) GBP 41,800. STOCKHOLM, 5-6 Dec 1990, *Untitled* (1971, watercolour, 19 x 15 1/4 ins / 48.5 x 39 cm) SEK 36,000. AMSTERDAM, 12 Dec 1990, *The Escape* (1959, oil on canvas, 38 1/4 x 51 1/4 ins / 97 x 130 cm) NLG 155,250. COPENHAGEN, 13-14 Feb 1991, *Composition with Figure* (1949, soft chalk, 9 x 7 ins / 23 x 18 cm) DKK 27,000. LONDON, 21 March 1991, *Poor You* (1958, oil on canvas, 38 1/4 x 51 1/4 ins / 97 x 130 cm) GBP 90,200. AMSTERDAM, 23 May 1991, *Two Animals* (1951, ink/paper, 12 1/2 x 15 1/2 ins / 32 x 39.5 cm) NLG 27,600. COPENHAGEN, 29 May 1991, *They Are Not Listening* (1970, oil on canvas, 38 1/4 x 51 1/4 ins / 97 x 130 cm) DKK 1,400,000. LONDON, 17 Oct 1991, *The Prophecy* (1951, oil on panel, 18 x 23 1/2 ins / 46 x 59.7 cm) GBP 26,400. COPENHAGEN, 4 Dec 1991, *Titio* (1943, oil on canvas, 33 x 39 1/4 ins / 84 x 100 cm) DKK 265,000. LONDON, 5 Dec 1991, *Untitled* (1945, oil on canvas, 30 1/2 x 39 1/4 ins / 77.5 x 100 cm) GBP 27,500. AMSTERDAM, 11 Dec 1991, *Torch* (1962, oil on canvas, 19 x 15 ins / 48 x 38 cm) NLG 80,500. MILAN, 14 April 1992, *Spring* (1971, oil on canvas, 20 x 15 ins / 51 x 38 cm) ITL 36,000,000. AMSTERDAM, 19 May 1992, *Extraordinary Garden* (oil on canvas, 25 1/2 x 32 ins / 65 x 81.2 cm) NLG 155,250. PARIS, 21 May 1992, *The Stranger* (1953, Indian ink wash, 11 1/2 x 8 ins / 29.5 x 20.5 cm) FRF 21,000. MUNICH, 26 May 1992, *Two Heads* (1960, watercolour, 19 1/4 x 25 1/4 ins / 49 x 64 cm) DEM 41,400. LONDON, 15 Oct 1992, *Bird Figure* (1956, oil and sand/canvas, 23 3/4 x 17 1/2 ins / 60.5 x 44.5 cm) GBP 22,000. COPENHAGEN, 2-3 Dec 1992, *Ardour of the Impassioned Flemish* (1967, oil on canvas, 39 1/4 x 32 ins / 100 x 81 cm) DKK 360,000. AMSTERDAM, 27-28 May 1993, *Awakening II* (1953, oil/synthetic resin, 60 x 47 3/4 ins / 152.5 x 121.5 cm) NLG 155,250. LONDON, 23 June 1993, *Indian* (1956, soft chalk and pencil, 27½ x 19¾ ins / 70 x 50.3 cm) GBP 6,500. Copenhagen, 3 Nov 1993, *Fabulous Animal* (1945, watercolour, 11½ x 9 ins / 29 x 23 cm) DKK 52,000. London, 2 Dec 1993, *Burning City II* (oil/synthetic resin, 24 x 29¼ ins / 61 x 74.5 cm) GBP 49,900. New York, 24 Feb 1994, *Composition* (watercolour/paper, 17¾ x 21½ ins / 45.4 x 54.9 cm) USD 7,475. London, 23-24 March 1994, *Half Servant* (1959, oil on canvas, 51¼ x 38¼ ins / 130 x 97 cm) GBP 128,000. Copenhagen, 14 June 1994, *Green Market* (1944, oil on canvas, 29¼ x 39¼ ins / 74 x 100 cm) DKK 725,000. Copenhagen, 6 Dec 1994, *Composition with Figures* (1945, oil on canvas, 39¼ x 35½ ins / 100 x 90 cm) DKK 900,000. Amsterdam, 8 Dec 1994, *Untitled* (1945, oil on canvas, 30 x 35¾ ins / 76 x 91 cm) NLG 161,000. Lokeren, 11 March 1995, *Fabulous Animal* (1951, watercolour and gouache, 11 x 8¼ ins / 27 x 21 cm) BEF 200,000. London, 28 June 1995, *Untitled* (1948, oil on sacking, 39¼ x 37½ ins / 100 x 95 cm) GBP 67,500. Paris, 29-30 June 1995, *Figure* (1951, oil on hardboard, 24 x 18½ ins / 61 x 47 cm) FRF 109,000. London, 30 Nov 1995, *Rest* (oil on card, 59½ x 47¼ ins / 151 x 120.3 cm) GBP 144,500. Amsterdam, 6 Dec 1995, *Untitled* (1945, oil on card, 28¼ x 24½ ins / 72 x 62 cm) NLG 184,000. Copenhagen, 12 March 1996, *Festival of the Imps* (1970, oil on canvas, 51¼ x 38¼ ins / 130 x 97 cm) DKK 750,000. Paris, 1 July 1996, *Figure* (1972, acrylic/panel canvas, 19½ x 15¾ ins / 49.5 x 40 cm) FRF 33,000. London, 24 Oct 1996, *Storm* (1971, oil on canvas, 32 x 39¼ ins / 81 x 100 cm) GBP 60,900. Milan, 25 Nov 1996, *Animal* (terracotta, 9 x 9½ x 7 ins / 22 x 24 x 18 cm) ITL 10,350,000. Amsterdam, 10 Dec 1996, *Untitled* (1953, oil on panel/card, 24½ x 34 ins / 62.5 x 85.5 cm) NLG 40,362. Copenhagen, 29 Jan 1997, *Didaska IV* (1945, oil on canvas, 16¼ x 11½ ins / 41 x 29 cm) DKK 195,000. Copenhagen, 15 March 1997, *Diplomatic Confusion* (1969, coloured lithograph) DKK 8,000. London, 20 March 1997, *Study* (1951, gouache, watercolour and pencil/paper, 13¾ x 12½ ins / 35 x 32 cm) GBP 2,990. Rome, 8 April 1997, *Illegal Questionaire* (1960, oil on canvas, 21¼ x 25½ ins / 54 x 65 cm) ITL 69,900,000. London, 29 May 1997, *Untitled* (1967, oil on canvas, 15¾ x 12 ins / 40 x 30.5 cm) GBP 12,650. Amsterdam, 2-3 June 1997, *Untitled* (1958, gouache and soft pastel/paper/canvas, 43 x 38 ins / 109 x 96.5 cm) NLG 43,660. Paris, 18 June 1997, *Composition* (1961, gouache/paper, 21¼ x 17¾ ins / 54 x 45 cm) FRF 38,000. London, 25 June 1997, *Mobile Immobilisation* (1966, oil on canvas, 38¼ x 51¼ ins / 97 x 130 cm) GBP 199,500. Paris, 27 June 1997, *Composition* (1956, oil on canvas, 15¾ x 18½ ins / 40 x 47 cm) FRF 95,000. Paris, 3 Oct 1997, *Composition with Two Figures* (1956, oil on canvas, 20 x 25½ ins / 50.5 x 65 cm) FRF 240,000. London, 23 Oct 1997, *Dawn* (1960, oil on canvas, 25½ x 32 ins / 65 x 81 cm) GBP 32,200. Copenhagen, 22-24 Oct 1997, *Composition with Figures* (1942, oil on glued paper/support, 20¾ x 26½ ins / 53 x 67 cm) DKK 115,000. London, 30 April 1999, *The Future Passes* (1962, oil on canvas, 57 x 38 ins / 145 x 96 cm) GBP 90,000. London, 23 June 1999, *Fabeldyr* (*Composition with Figures*) (1945, oil on canvas, 38 x 50 ins / 96 x 127 cm) GBP 120,000. Copenhagen, 27 Sept 2000, *Composition* (c. 1972, oil on canvas, 31 x 39 ins / 80 x 100 cm) DKK 1,000,000. Copenhagen, 27 Sept 2000, *Composition* (oil on masonite, 36 x 48 ins / 91 x 122 cm) DKK 1,500,000. Copenhagen, 2 April 2001, *Le bateau enrage* (1957, oil on canvas, 31 x 39 ins / 80 x 100 cm) DKK 725,000. Copenhagen, 2 April 2001, *Didaska - Composition, Midsummer Night Fun* (1944 or 1945, oil on canvas, 46 x 36 ins / 116 x 91 cm) DKK 780,000. New York, 14 May 2002, *In the Beginning Was the Image* (1965, acrylic on canvas, 79 x 118 ins / 200 x 300 cm) USD 1,900,000. London, 27 June 2002, *Allegretto furbo* (1964, oil on canvas, 64 x 51 ins / 162 x 130 cm) GBP 210,000. Copenhagen, 17 Sept 2003, *Titania I* (1940, oil on canvas, 39 x 49 ins / 100 x 125 cm) DKK 4,600,000. Copenhagen, 7 Oct 2003, *That's Obvious* (1971, oil on canvas, 46 x 35 ins / 116 x 89 cm) DKK 3,400,000. Copenhagen, 29 March 2004, *Summer Land - Didaska Figure Composition* (1944, oil on canvas, 38 x 51 ins / 97 x 130 cm) DKK 2,500,000. Copenhagen, 5 Oct 2004, *Drakabygget* (1961, oil on canvas, 47 x 39 ins / 120 x 100 cm) DKK 2,900,000.

JORON, Auguste
French, 19th century.
Painter, draughtsman. Allegorical subjects, architectural views.

Auguste Joron exhibited drawings of churches at the Salon in 1836 and 1838.

AUCTION RECORDS:
Amsterdam, 10 Nov 1992, *Allegory of Death: Man on his Death Bed with Time Seated on a Funeral Monument* (oil on panel, 17¼ x 14¼ ins / 44 x 36 cm) NLG 2,760.

JORON, Maurice Paul
French, 20th century.
Born 18 January 1883, in Paris.
Painter, sculptor. Figures, portraits, genre scenes, interiors with figures.

Maurice Paul Joron studied under Cormon. He became a member of the Salon des Artistes Français in Paris in 1908. He received a commendation in 1905, a bronze medal in 1907 and a silver medal *hors concours* in 1909.

AUCTION RECORDS:
Paris, 22 Dec 1924, *Interior*, FRF 555. London, 27 July 1973, *A Delicate Question*, Gns 1,100. London, 12 Feb 1986, *Portrait of the Cardinal* (oil on canvas, 25 x 31¼ ins / 63.5 x 79.5 cm) GBP 1,800. Paris, 10-11 June 1997, *Idleness* (1916, oil on canvas, 21¼ x 28¾ ins / 54 x 73 cm) FRF 38,000. Paris, 30 March 2001, *Winter Day near the Chimney* (oil on canvas, 24 x 29 ins / 60 x 73 cm) FRF 30,000. San Francisco, 16 May 2001, *After Dinner* (oil on canvas, 26 x 32 ins / 65 x 81 cm) USD 3,000. Lund, 15 Nov 2003, *Cardinals around Coffee Table* (1926, oil on canvas, 25 x 31 ins / 63 x 78 cm) SEK 20,000. Munich, 17 March 2004, *Tempting Offer* (oil on canvas, 21 x 25 ins / 54 x 64 cm) EUR 5,500. London, 23 March 2004, *Funny Story* (1926, oil on canvas, 26 x 32 ins / 66 x 81 cm) GBP 4,000.

JORRAND, Antoine M.
French, 19th century.
Born in Aubusson (Creuse).
Active in Paris.
Painter. Landscapes.

Antoine M. Jorrand was a member of the Société des Artistes Français in Paris from 1891 and exhibited at the Salon as part of this group.

JORRETO Y MADROGA, Manuel
Spanish, 20th century.
Born in Madrid.
Painter.

Manuel Jorreto y Madroga studied at the Real Academia de Bellas Artes de San Fernando in Madrid, where he was taught by the painter Luis Álvarez Català. He took part in the Exposición Nacional de Bellas Artes in Madrid in 1910.

BIBLIOGRAPHY:
Arnáiz, José Manuel/López Jiménez, Javier/Merchán Díaz, Manuel (ed.), *Cien años de pintura en Espana y Portugal (1830-1930)*, Antiqvaria, Madrid, 1990.

JORRETO Y PANIAGUA, Manuel
Spanish, 19th century.
Draughtsman, writer.

JORRO, José
Spanish, 19th century.
Engraver.

José Jorro made engravings after Rubens, Wouwermans and Veronese.

JORZIG, Ewald
German, 20th century.
Born 1905, in Lütgen-Dortmund (North Rhine-Westphalia).
Painter. Scenes with figures.
Ewald Jorzig studied at the school of fine art in Düsseldorf with Professor Ederer. He featured in numerous exhibitions. His figurative painting mingles the influences of Post-Impressionism and Cubism.

JOSCELYN, Nathanael. See **JOCELYN**

JOSCHKO, Karl Heinz
German, 20th century.
Born 15 June 1941, in Ratibor (now Racibórz, Poland).
Painter. Landscapes.
Karl Heinz Joschko has lived in Australia, South Africa, the USA and Brazil. He returned from his travels with a number of sketches and notes that enabled him to paint landscapes, often bathed in sunshine, but always underpinned by very precise draughtsmanship.

JOSE, F. C.
British, 19th century.
Painter. Animals.
MUSEUMS AND GALLERIES:
CAPE TOWN (museum): *Grey Horse; Arab Horse.*

JOSÉ-JULIO
Portuguese, 20th century.
Born 1916, in Lisbon; died 1963, in Lisbon.
Painter, engraver.
José-Julio was a mathematics teacher and art critic, and a self-taught painter and engraver. He started exhibiting in 1949 and participated in group exhibitions in Paris for engraving, Brussels, Venezuela, and at the São Paulo Biennale. He also held solo shows, particularly in Germany. He was at first influenced by Cézanne, from whom he obtained a varied palette of blues, but his work became progressively less figurative.

JOSEF, Carl
Austrian, 20th century.
Born 5 May 1877, in Vienna.
Painter, draughtsman, illustrator. Portraits.
Carl Josef studied portrait painting at the academies in Vienna and Prague. He specialised in illustrations for the Vienna daily newspapers and for humorous publications like *Le Mousquet* (*The Mosquito*), in which his political caricatures were published.

JOSEPH (Frère)
French, 17th century.
Born c. 1650; died before 1688.
Painter. Landscapes.
Joseph is mentioned by Siret.

JOSEPH, real name: Hope, Miss
Indian, 20th century.
Born in Ajmeet.
Active in England.
Painter.
Joseph's work was shown at the Salon des Indépendants from 1905 onwards.

JOSEPH, Albert
French, 20th century.
Born June 1868, in Auteuil; died 1952.
Painter. Landscapes.
Albert Joseph began painting around 1900 after long visits to England, Italy and Algeria, although he did not return with any paintings from these trips. From 1900, he lived alternately in Paris, Barbizon and Moret and made frequent trips to Brittany, particularly to Pont Aven and Pouldu. In 1901, he exhibited for the first time at the Salon des Artistes Français in Paris and from 1905 on several occasions at the Salon des Indépendants and the Salon d'Automne. At this period he also painted on the Mediterranean coast at Banyuls-sur-Mer, Cassis and Collioure. These places are represented in his work, which displays an Impressionist influence in his study of light on water and snow. Around 1925, Joseph moved to the Creuse in Limousin. His painting then became tighter and more austere as he increased the rigour of his composition. He became increasingly withdrawn, neither socialising nor selling his works, though he continued painting until the end of his life.
AUCTION RECORDS:
PARIS, 14 June 1977, *Brittany Landscape* (oil on canvas, 21 1/4 x 28 3/4 ins / 54 x 73 cm) FRF 1,500. LIMOGES, 19 Oct 1986, *The Mill* (oil on canvas, 18 x 22 ins / 46 x 55 cm) FRF 34,000. LA LOGGIA (TURIN), 21 Sept 1987, *The Fisherman's House* (oil on canvas, 20 3/4 x 25 1/4 ins / 53 x 64 cm) FRF 16,000. VERSAILLES, 20 March 1988, *Landscape at Crozant* (oil on canvas, 18 x 32 ins / 45.5 x 81 cm) FRF 8,800. PARIS, 5 July 1990, *Spring* (oil on canvas, 18 1/4 x 25 3/4 ins / 46.5 x 65.5 cm) FRF 12,500. NEUILLY, 20 May 1992, *Sailing Boats at Anchor* (oil on canvas, 19 3/4 x 24 ins / 50 x 61 cm) FRF 9,000. NEW YORK, 10 Nov 1992, *Winter Landscape in the Creuse* (1905, oil on canvas, 19 1/4 x 25 3/4 ins / 49 x 65.5 cm) USD 2,200. CALAIS, 11 Nov 2001, *Little Path in the Normandy Countryside* (oil on canvas, 20 x 26 ins / 50 x 65 cm) FRF 14,000. NEW YORK, 25 Sept 2003, *Spring in Bougogne* (oil on canvas, 18 x 24 ins / 46 x 61 cm) USD 6,500.

JOSEPH, Antonio
Dominican, 20th century.
Born 1921, in the Dominican Republic.
Painter.
Antonio Joseph was an admirable watercolourist and produced a large body of work. He exhibited his piece *Two Children* in the West Indian section of the open exhibition organised by the United Nations in Paris in 1946.

JOSEPH, Cliff
American, 20th century.
Born 1922, in Panama.
Painter, draughtsman.
Cliff Joseph studied at the Pratt Institute, New York. He was co-director of the Black Emergency Cultural Coalition (BECC), an artists' organisation whose aim was to fight racism and sexism in the art world. He ran the Westbeth Gallery, New York. He condemned the injustices in American society, as in *My Country Right or Wrong* (1968), in which both black and white figures wander across a land littered with bones and upside-down crosses and flags, their eyes blindfolded with strips of the American flag. In connection with his work as an art therapist he also wrote books on the relationship between art and psychology.

Joseph took part in a number of group exhibitions, including in 1969, Hunter College, New York and in 1972, Pratt Institute, New York, and had various solo exhibitions in African-American churches.
BIBLIOGRAPHY:
Honig Fine, Elsa, *The Afro-American Artist*, Holt, Rinehart and Winston, New York, 1973. Lewis, Samella, *African-American Art and Artists*, University of California Press, Berkeley, 1990.

JOSEPH, Francisco
Portuguese, 19th century.
Active c. 1843.
Landscape artist.
Francisco Joseph was probably the same person as the artist José Francisco. He is mentioned by Siret.

JOSEPH, George Francis
British, 18th - 19th century.

Born probably in 1764, in Dublin; died 1846, in Cambridge.
Painter. History painting, portraits.

George Francis Joseph began his training at the Royal Academy in 1784. He started to exhibit there in 1788 and was elected an associate in 1813. Until his death, he continued to show his historical paintings in the important London exhibitions. These works included *Priam Bringing Back the Body of Hector* and *The Procession to Calvary*, which earned him recognition from the British Institution. Joseph was, however, primarily a portrait painter.

MUSEUMS AND GALLERIES:

DUBLIN: *Sir John Stevenson* - LONDON (National Portrait Gal.): *Spencer Perceval* (1812, oil on canvas, two portraits); *Sir Thomas Stamford Bingley Raffles* (1817, oil on canvas).

AUCTION RECORDS:

LONDON, 12 Dec 1930, *Boy, supposedly George James, 6th Count of Egmont*, GBP 78. LONDON, 1 Feb 1980, *Portrait of the Right Hon. John Robinson, Surveyor General of Works* (oil on canvas, 54 3/4 x 43 ins / 139 x 109.2 cm) GBP 3,500. LONDON, 30 Jan 1985, *Sentimental Meeting* (oil on panel, 24 x 20 ins / 61 x 51 cm) GBP 1,900. LONDON, 12 Sept 2000, *John Boydell in Blue Coat* (1795, miniature, oval) GBP 3,200. LONDON, 21 March 2001, *Portrait of Spencer Percival, Wearing a Dark Blue Coat and White Stock* (oil on canvas, 24 x 20 ins / 60 x 50 cm) GBP 3,500. SAVANNAH, 16 Nov 2003, *Portrait of an Officer in Dress Uniform* (oil on canvas, 35 x 28 ins / 89 x 71 cm) USD 2,700.

JOSEPH, Germain

French, 16th century.
Active in Bourges.
Sculptor.

Joseph took part in decoration work in Bourges Cathedral in 1513.

JOSEPH, Henri Jules

French, 20th century.
Born in Dampierre-sur-Salon (Haute-Saône).
Painter. Portraits.

Henri Jules Joseph exhibited at the Salon of the Société Nationale des Beaux-Arts in Paris.

JOSEPH, Jasmin

Haitian, 20th century.
Born 1923.
Painter. Figures, still-lifes.

Jasmin Joseph has taken part in collective exhibitions including: *Three Generations of Haitian Art*, Allentown Art Museum (1982); *Haitian Art in the Angela Gross Collection*, Woodmere Art Museum, Philadelphia (1984-1985).

BIBLIOGRAPHY:

Rodman, S., *When Art is Joy*, New York, 1988.

AUCTION RECORDS:

NEW YORK, 29 Nov 1984, *Cérémonie Mappoux Lindilotte Pour Les Enfants Gravement Malades* (*Mappoux Lindilotte Ceremony for Seriously Ill Children*) (c. 1947, oil on card, 19 1/4 x 24 1/4 ins / 49 x 61.3 cm) USD 1,500. NEW YORK, 15 May 1991, *St John the Baptist* (oil/synthetic resin, 48 1/2 x 19 1/2 ins / 123 x 49.5 cm) USD 3,520. NEW YORK, 21 Nov 1995, *Fruits of Haiti* (oil/synthetic resin, 39 1/4 x 31 1/2 ins / 100 x 80 cm) USD 5,175.

JOSEPH, Lily Delissa

British, 19th - 20th century.
Born 24 June 1863, in Bermondsey; died 24 July 1940, in London.
Painter. Portraits, interiors, landscapes.

Lily Delissa Joseph was the sister of the painter Solomon J. Solomon. She exhibited at the Royal Academy and the New English Art Club in London, as well as at the Paris Salons, where she won a silver medal in 1929.

MUSEUMS AND GALLERIES:

LONDON (Tate Collection): *Roofs, High Holborn* (c. 1937, oil on canvas).

JOSEPH, Lucien

French, 20th century.
Born 30 September 1903, in Le Havre.
Painter. Portraits.

Lucien Joseph studied at the École des Beaux-Arts in Le Havre. He was awarded a gold medal and is known for his character heads.

JOSEPH, Lucy (Mme)

French, 19th - 20th century.
Born 13 April 1869.
Painter.

Lucy Joseph studied under Benjamin-Constant. She became a member of the Salon des Artistes Français in Paris and exhibited there.

JOSEPH, Marguerite

French, 19th - 20th century.
Born 1856, in Rixheim (Haut-Rhin); died 1905, in Paris.
Painter. Flowers, landscapes.

MUSEUMS AND GALLERIES:

BASEL: *Bunch of Roses* - MULHOUSE: *Cornfields in Alsace*.

JOSEPH, Mely

German, 20th century.
Born 6 March 1886, in Pforzheim; died 14 January 1920, in Berlin.
Painter, sculptor, lithographer.

Mely Joseph produced the following works which featured in the exhibition organised by the Nassau Society of Artists in Wiesbaden in May-June 1920: the sculpture *Mother and Child*, fifteen lithographs and the paintings *Seated Girl, Finnish Landscape, Crucifixion, Nudes, Arabian Landscape, Jews on the Way to the Wailing Wall in Jerusalem, Rhenish Landscape, Annunciation, Tales from the Thousand and One Nights* and a copy after Gauguin: *The Birth*.

JOSEPH, Peter

British, 20th century.
Born 1929, in London.
Painter, environmental artist.
Minimal Art.

Peter Joseph is a self-taught painter who worked initially in advertising. Joseph's painting shows the influence of the American Abstract Expressionists - notably Newman, Rothko and Kelly; his work is also comparable in effect to Minimalist art. His canvases play on colour tonalities, and feature a sensitive use of light, sometimes heightened by 'all-over' painting techniques (*Colour continuum*, 1966). Traditional picture formats are sometimes challenged, as in the *Yellow Painting* of 1969, in which the support has been cut into a triangular shape and displayed as if balanced on one point. Joseph has also executed a number of public commissions. His trademark motif (a coloured rectangle within another coloured rectangle) first appeared in works of the early 1970s. These paintings-within-paintings use flat expanses of colour, strict symmetry and pre-defined proportions to induce a kind of phenomenological experience beyond the effects obtainable through conventional compositional means. As such, they strive to instil a sense of classicism, even catharsis, in the viewer - a means of reconciliation between oneself and the surrounding world. Joseph's work featured in the exhibition *Post-minimal Paintings* in Edinburgh (1974). His work has also been the subject of a number of solo exhibitions, including: 1983, Museum of Contemporary Art, Chicago; 1988, Flanders Gallery, Minneapolis; 1989, 1992, Galerie Laage-Salomon, Paris; 1989, Lisson Gallery, London.

Bibliography:
Peter Joseph, exhibition catalogue, Museum of Contemporary Art, Chicago, 1983. Hallmark Neff, J./Ward, D./Clark, T.A., *Peter Joseph - Paintings 1973-1983,* Museum of Modern Art, New York, 1986. Morgan, Stuart, '*Peter Joseph - de la tonalité*' in *Art Press* n° 169, periodical, Paris, May 1992.

Museums and Galleries:
Dunkirk (FRAC Nord-Pas de Calais).

JOSEPH, Pierre
French, 20th - 21st century.
Born 1965, in Caen.
Environmental artist. Multimedia.
Esthétique Relationnelle.

Pierre Joseph is active in Paris and sometimes works with Philippe Parreno. He does not use traditional art materials in his environments. The use of photography appears to be fundamental to his technique which operates on the fashion of taking quotations from the individual and collective memory and portraying them in an interactive world fed by science fiction, video games, cinema and advertising. At the preview of the Villa Arson exhibition *Man's Time* in Nice in 1991 he presented extras dressed as characters such as *Bloody Mary, Cat Woman, Cupid, Fairy,* creatures that artists reactivate from time to time and which have been immortalised by film sequences. One such creation is *Paintballers,* soldiers with weapons loaded with paint who threaten the integrity of works of art hanging in art galleries. In 1996 he was commissioned by the French Ministry of Culture and the Public Investment Organisation in Paris to create *Recherches Histoires.*

He has taken part in collective exhibitions including: *Nouvelle Vague* (*New Wave*), Musée d'Art Contemporain, Nice, 1994; *Transit - 60 Artistes Nés Après 60 - Œuvres du Fonds National d'Art Contemporain* (*Transit - 60 Artists Born After 60 - Works from the National Collection of Contemporary Art*), École des Beaux-Arts, Paris, 1997; *(O.P.E) Offre Publique d'Échange* (*Share Exchange Offer*), FRAC Poitou-Charante collection, Galerie Municipale des Voûtes du Port, Royan, 2000; *Présumés Innocents: l'Art Contemporain et l'Enfance* (*Presumed Innocent: Contemporary Art and Childhood*), Capc Musée d'Art Contemporain, Bordeaux, 2000; *L'Altro Mondo,* FRAC Poitou-Charentes, Château d'Oiron, Deux-Sèvres, 2002; *No Ghost, Just a Shell,* Van Abbemuseum, Eindhoven, Netherlands and SFMOMA, San Francisco, 2003; *Bandes à Part: le Cinéma dans l'Art Contemporain* (*On the Fringes: Cinema in Contemporary Art*), an exhibition for the *Trésors Public, 20 Ans de Création dans les Fonds Régionaux d'Art Contemporain (FRAC)* (*Public Treasury, 20 Years of Creation in the Regional Collection of Contemporary Art (FRAC)*), Musée d'Art Moderne et Contemporain, Strasbourg.

Joseph's work has also been shown in solo exhibitions such as: FRAC (Fonds Regional d'Art Contemporain - Regional Contemporary Art Funds), Champagne-Ardenne, Rheims, 1995 and Palais de Tokyo, Paris, 2003.

Bibliography:
Bourriaud, Nicolas/Perreau, David/Troncy, Éric, *Personnages à réactiver,* Éd. Le collège, Fonds régional d'Art contemporain de Champagne-Ardenne, Reims, centre d'Art contemporain Le Parvis, Tarbes, Fonds régional d'Art contemporain du Languedoc-Roussillon, Montpellier, 1995. Bernadac, Marie-Laure/Moisdon-Tremblay, et al., *Présumés innocents: l'art contemporain et l'enfance,* exhibition catalogue, Capc musée d'Art contemporain, Bordeaux, 2000. Moisdon Trembley, Stéphanie, '*Pierre Joseph, ce que montrer veut dire*' in *Beaux-Arts Magazine,* n° 234 p. 54, Paris, November 2003.

Museums and Galleries:
Angoulême (FRAC Poitou-Charentes): *Purgatory (2 Characters to Reactivate)* (1991) - Marseilles (FRAC Provence-Alpes-Côte d'Azur): *Great Blue* (1993, triptych with three characters to reactivate) - Paris (FNAC): *Paintballers 1 & 2* (1992) - Rheims (FRAC Champagne-Ardenne): *Oogie the Ectoplasme* (1995, Cibachrome and costume).

JOSEPH, Samuel
British, 19th century.
Born 1791; died 1850, in Edinburgh.
Active in Edinburgh and in London.
Sculptor.

Samuel Joseph was a cousin of George Francis Joseph. He was the son of the bursar of St John's College in Cambridge. A student at the Royal Academy, he began exhibiting there in 1811 and was awarded a medal in 1815. After having worked as an artist in London for some time, he moved to Edinburgh in 1823. He met with considerable success and was named a member of the Royal Scottish Academy. When he was recalled to London in 1828, his earlier success eluded him and he rarely sent work to the exhibitions at the Royal Academy and to Suffolk Street. In 1848, he stopped sending work to them altogether. His most important works are in London, and include a *Bust of George IV* commissioned in 1830, a *Statue of Wilberforce* in Westminster Abbey and a *Statue of David Wilkie* in the National Gallery. His effigies were extremely life-like.

Museums and Galleries:
Edinburgh (Royal Scottish Academy): *Lord Brougham* (1835, marble, bust); *Bust of Dugard Stewart* - Edinburgh (Scottish National Portrait Gallery): *Reverand Archibald Alison* (marble, bust); *Sir David Wilkie* (marble, bust) - London (NG): *Statue of David Wilkie.*

JOSEPH OF MELITENE
Turkish, 13th century.
Active in Melitene (now Malatya on the River Euphrates).
Miniaturist.

A work by this artist, who was a deacon, can be found in the Bibliothèque Nationale in Paris.

JOSEPH-RIGNAULT, Émile
French, 20th century.
Born 1874, in Varzy (Nièvre).
Painter. Genre scenes, landscapes.

Émile Joseph-Rignault worked in Paris. He studied under Gustave Moreau at the École des Beaux-Arts. He became a member of the Salon d'Automne in Paris and exhibited there frequently from 1905 onwards and also at the Salon des Indépendants.

JOSEPHI, Isaac A.
American, 20th century.
Born in New York; died 1954.
Miniaturist.

Isaac Josephi started his art education at the Art Students League of New York, later studying under Léon Bonnat in Paris. He gained distinctions at the Paris Exposition Universelle in 1900 and in Charleston. He was a member of the Royal Society of Miniatures Painters in London, and one of the founders of the American Society of Miniature Painters.

JOSEPHSON, Ernst
Swedish, 19th century.
Born 1851, in Stockholm; died 1906, in Stockholm.
Painter. Portraits, genre scenes, landscapes.

Ernst Josephson studied at the fine arts academy in Stockholm between 1851 and 1875. He then travelled throughout Norway, Holland, Germany, France, Italy and Spain. He stayed in France in 1875, entering the École des Beaux-Arts in Paris. After a two-year stay in Italy, he returned to Paris in 1878 and became prominent among the Swedish painters then in the city. He travelled to Spain in 1881 and was deeply impressed both by the paintings of Velázquez and by the people whom he met and painted. Rembrandt would also be a powerful influence in his work. Between 1883 and 1886 he lived between France and Sweden. During this time his works were refused by the Salon de Paris, and in 1885 he founded an independent artists' union. He would resign, however, in 1887, having lost the support of his fellow painters due to his philosophical views which were deemed too revolutionary. He retreated to Brittany, remaining there until the spring of 1888, where he withdrew into an irrational and imaginary world, allowing spirituality and the occult sciences to transform his mind to the point of dementia. He was sent to a psychiatric hospital in Uppsala where he remained until 1891. Encouraged by his physician, he devoted himself intensively to painting. It was during this period that he treated subjects inspired from history, the Bible, literature and Nordic mythology. Once he had recovered from his illness he returned to Stockholm, where he lived in solitude until his death.

Josephson's work seeks to reconcile two opposing movements; plein-airism (open air painting), through which he showed his debt to Impressionism, and Realism, by which he aligned himself with the work of Manet. Portraits such as *Renholm, Journalist and Art Critic* or *Mrs Gelly Marcus in the Forest* are examples of this attempt between 1878 and 1880 to integrate the two tendencies. Josephson freed himself from conventional subjects and thereby enabled his technique to better reflect his thought processes. During his period of mental illness he adopted a style approaching Expressionism, manifested in his broad brushstrokes and combining these with large unpainted zones, giving an impression of lightness. The latter technique contributes to a spiritual effect in his work. The forms of his figures are often elongated, if not tormented, recalling the influence of El Greco's studies during his trip to Spain in 1881. A retrospective exhibition of his work at the Berlin Secession in 1909 expanded his own influence, and his portraits certainly had an impact on the German Expressionists as well as on Emil Nolde. Josephson favoured the use of colour over line to express emotion, affirming his admiration of Delacroix, whom he called 'the father of the school of colour'. His portraits may be divided into three groups. In the first, the composition is at its most simple and the brushstrokes are broad and impetuous. In the second, the setting takes prominence over the figures, who are evoked with less definition. In the third group, the setting continues to play an important role but the individual features of his figures are more clearly represented.

In 2001 Prince Eugens Waldemarsudde of Stockholm presented an exhibition devoted entirely to his works.

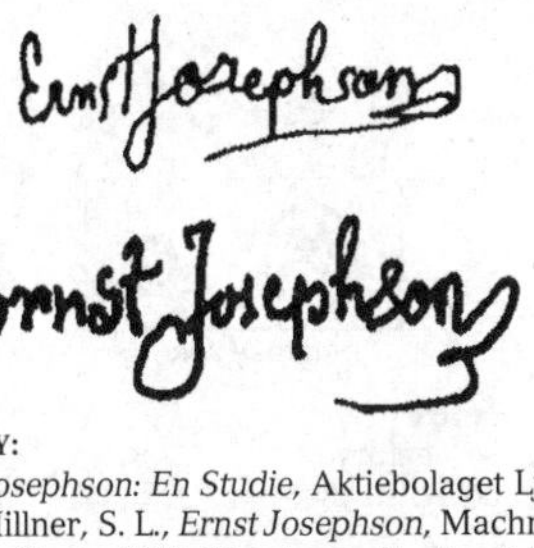

Bibliography:
Pauli, G., *E. Josephson: En Studie*, Aktiebolaget Ljus, Stockholm, 1902. Millner, S. L., *Ernst Josephson*, Machmadim Art Editions, New York, 1948. Blomberg, E., *Ernst Josephson: Hans liv*, Wahlström & Widstrand, Stockholm, 1951. Mesterton, I., *Vägen till Försoning: En Konstpsykologisk Studie i Ernst Josephsons Religiôsa Fantasivärld (The Road to Reconciliation: An Art Psychological Study of the Religious Fantasy World of Ernst Josephson)*, Wettergren & Kerbers Förlag, Göteborg, 1957. *Ernst Josephson*, exhibition catalogue, Nationalmuseum, Stockholm, 1979.

Museums and Galleries:
Göteborg (Konstmus.): *Young Spanish Girl; Portrait of Jeanette Rubenson* (1883); *The Convalescent; Diana; The Footpath; The Water Trick or Narcissus; Norwegian Interior; Interior of Gripsholm Castle* - Stockholm (Moderna Mus.): *The Holy Sacrament* - Stockholm (Nationalmus.): *Portrait of Renholm, Journalist and Art Critic; Boy with a Wheel-barrow; The Dwarf; Portrait of Ludwig Josephson; Spanish Blacksmiths; Portrait of Caroline Schloss* (1885); *Portrait of Louise Breslau* (1885).

Auction records:
Stockholm, 24 April 1947, *Rustic Interior*, SEK 3,255. Stockholm, 29 Oct 1958, *Interior with Man*, SEK 62,000. Stockholm, 19 April 1961, *Nude Woman*, SEK 17,500. Göteborg, 8 Nov 1973, *Standing Figure*, SEK 32,800. New York, 8 Nov 1979, *Portrait of the Journalist Spada* (oil on panel, 14 3/4 x 11 1/2 ins / 37.5 x 29 cm) USD 4,200. Stockholm, 8 April 1981, *The Torrent* (oil on panel, 9 x 13 ins / 23 x 33 cm) SEK 49,000. Stockholm, 26 April 1982, *Josephina* (pen, 12 1/4 x 9 1/2 ins / 31 x 24 cm) SEK 5,700. Stockholm, 27 April 1983, *Portrait of Georg Pauli* (watercolour, chalk and pencil, 12 x 9 ins / 30.5 x 23 cm) SEK 58,000. Göteborg, 9 Nov 1983, *Sleeping Nude with Red Drapery in Landscape* (oil on canvas, 28 1/4 x 35 3/4 ins / 72 x 91 cm) SEK 70,000. Stockholm, 28 Oct 1985, *Landscape with Nude* (oil on panel, 20 1/2 x 13 1/2 ins / 52 x 34 cm) SEK 305,000. London, 25 March 1987, *Forward!* (pen, 14 1/4 x 8 3/4 ins / 36.5 x 22.5 cm) GBP 1,500. London, 24 March 1988, *Self-portrait with Diary* (ink/paper, 13 3/4 x 8 1/4 ins / 35 x 21 cm) GBP 1,650. London, 29 March 1990, *Tha Water Trick or Spiritual Self-portrait or Narcissus* (oil and watercolour/card) GBP 154,000. Stockholm, 5 Sept 1992, *Salon* (watercolour, 35 x 24 1/2 ins / 89 x 62 cm) SEK 16,000. Copenhagen, 21 April 1993, *Painters II* (pencil, 9 3/4 x 8 1/4 ins / 25 x 21 cm) DKK 10,000. Stockholm, 30 Nov 1993, *Nollfallet* (oil on canvas, 10 1/4 x 13 1/2 ins / 26 x 34 cm) SEK 24,000. Stockholm, 27 May 1999, *Lady Dressed in Black* (1881, oil on panel, 13 x 9 ins / 33 x 24 cm) SEK 175,000. Stockholm, 23 Nov 1999, *Riccio's Murder* (c. 1890, oil on panel, 11 x 17 ins / 28 x 44 cm) SEK 2,000,000. Stockholm, 29 May 2000, *The Judgement of Paris* (mixed media, 12 x 16 ins / 31 x 40 cm) SEK 1,025,000. Stockholm, 5 Dec 2000, *Scholander's Song* (Indian ink, four, 13 x 9 ins / 33 x 22 cm) SEK 155,000. Stockholm, 22 May 2001, *Young Female Nude with her Hair Hanging Loose by the Sea* (watercolour and Indian ink, 12 x 9 ins / 30 x 23 cm) SEK 755,000. Stockholm, 29 May 2001, *David and Saul* (oil on panel, 6 x 9 ins / 15 x 23 cm) SEK 410,000. Stockholm, 29 May 2002, *Landscape with Brook* (1876, gouache, 10 x 7 ins / 26 x 17 cm) SEK 110,000. Stockholm, 3 Dec 2002, *Old Man and Girl* (c. 1888, oil on panel, 17 x 14 ins / 43 x 36 cm) SEK 580,000. Stockholm, 26 May 2003, *The Old Telephone Exchange at Malmskillnads Street* (Indian ink, 9 x 15 ins / 22 x 38 cm) SEK 36,000. Stockholm, 3 Dec 2003, *Portrait of the Artist Severin Nilson* (oil on canvas, 19 x 15 ins / 49 x 39 cm) SEK 140,000.

JOSEPHSON, James

American, 20th century.
Painter. Figures, portraits.
Conceptual Art.

James Josephson settled in Florida. He frequently associates text and image. In his series *All Eight of Me* (1991), *Jan van Eyck was Here* (1992) and *Terra Incognita* (1993) he presented images associated with text.

Bibliography:
Josephson, James, *All Eight of me*, 1991. Josephson, James, *Jan van Eyck was here*, 1992. Josephson, James, *James Josephson: terra incognita*, 1993. Josephson, James, *Winter Scenes*, 1993.

JOSETSU

Japanese, 15th century.

Active at the beginning of the 15th century.
Monk-painter. Landscapes, figures, genre scenes.

During the Muromachi period (1338-1573), the economic and social situation of Japan under the Ashikaga shogunate favoured contact with China. Zen monks played an important role as diplomats and intermediaries, and it was through the Zen temples that Chinese culture continued to infiltrate Japan. The Japanese, however, respected the Song and Yuan traditions in preference to the Ming culture then flourishing on the mainland.

In painting, the taste for ink and wash spread, in religious milieux and then in the secular domain. Song and Yuan ink monochrome landscapes were found in the form of screens and sliding doors in interior decoration, and soon after a new format appeared, the small hanging scroll, which demanded a much stricter and more meticulous composition. The upper part of the picture was reserved for poems in the Chinese style which the landscape painters among the monks required their fellow monks to write, in praise of their communion with nature.

Three works are attributed to him. *Hyonen-zu* was executed before 1415 for the shogun Ashikaga Yoshimochi (1386-1428). It illustrates the parable of the old fisherman who wanted to catch a catfish with a gourd. Several features are close to the Song style but the lines lack strength and the features are too strong to be Chinese. The upper part is covered with around 30 inscriptions by Zen monks. The *Three Teachers* is an imaginary portrait of Confucius, Laozi and Sakyamuni, the founders of Confucianism, Taoism and Buddhism. The message is the transcendental unity of these three philosophies. One of the inscriptions on the scroll tells how the painter Josetsu received his name from Zekkai Chushin, priest of the Zen temple Nanzen-ji in Kyoto. (The name Josetsu means like clumsiness, the implication being that great skill or intelligence is similar to clumsiness.) The final work *Illustrated Fan of Wang Xizhi* shows the great Chinese calligrapher Wang Xizhi (321-379) writing calligraphy on old fans for a destitute fan vendor, with some children looking on. The figures on the two final scrolls are derived from the Southern Song master Liang Kai (active mid-13th century). In the decades that followed his death the most important representatives of monochrome painting would all take their inspiration from Josetsu.

Bibliography:
Akiyama, Terukazu, *La Peinture japonaise*, Skira, Geneva, 1961. Tanaka, Ichimatsu, *Japanese Ink Painting: Shubun to Sesshu*, Weatherhill, New York, 1972.

Museums and Galleries:
Kyoto (National Museum): *Illustrated Fan of Wang Xizhi* (hanging scroll, light colour on paper, Important Cultural Property) - Kyoto (Taizo-In, Myoshin-Ji): *Hyonen-zu* (*Catching a Catfish with a Gourd*) (hanging scroll, colour on paper).

JOSEY, John William
British, 19th century.
Active in London.
Engraver.

John William Josey exhibited at the Royal Academy in London, starting in 1891.

JOSEY, Richard
British, 19th century.
Born 1840 or 1841; died February 1906.
Active in London.
Engraver.

Richard Josey exhibited at the Royal Academy in London, from 1876 to 1887.

JOSHIN
Japanese, 14th century.
Active during the first half of the 14th century.
Sculptor.

Joshin was a Kamakura period *dai busshi* (master sculptor) who held the rank of Hogen (eye of the law, a religious title bestowed on artists). It is known that in 1308 he worked as an assistant on the standing statue of *Shaka Nyorai* (the Buddha Sakyamuni) in the Shomyo-ji temple in Kamakura, completed on the 26th day of the second month of 1308. As a *dai busshi* he carved the *Shingon Hasso* (the eight patriarchs of Shingon Buddhism) for the Kongocho-ji of Kochi (Tosa).

JOSHO. See MITSUOKI

JOSI, Charles
British, 19th century.
Active in London.
Painter. Sporting subjects, landscapes.

Charles Josi was a member of the Society of British Artists. He exhibited in London between 1827 and 1851 at the Royal Academy, the British Institution and especially at the Suffolk Street Gallery.

Auction records:
New York, 4 June 1987, *Feeding the Team* (oil on canvas, 49 1/4 x 68 ins / 125.1 x 172.7 cm) USD 22,000.

JOSI, Christian
Dutch, 18th - 19th century.
Born in Utrecht; died November 1828, in Ramsgate, England.
Engraver.

Christian Josi first studied at the art institute of his native city of Utrecht before going to London in 1791 to complete his studies under the direction of Raphael Smith. According to some biographers he also worked with Barlolozzi. He returned to Holland in 1795 and began working as an engraver, specialising in colour engraving. Ill health forced him to abandon this trade and he became a dealer in engravings and paintings, developing a considerable reputation in this field. In 1808 he was a member of the Maler Kollegium in Utrecht; he also worked in Amsterdam. In 1818 or 1819 he moved permanently to London with his family. In 1821 he published the remarkable *Collection of Imitations after the Principal Dutch and Flemish Masters* which had been started by his relative Ploos van Amstel in 1765 and to which Josi added a further 59 illustrations, bringing the total to 105. One of the most interesting items in the series is a portrait of Rembrandt executed by Josi himself in stippled engraving so that it could be printed in colour. Josi amassed a remarkable collection of etchings and engravings which were put on sale at auction in 1829, the auction lasting some fifteen days.

Stamp of sale

JOSI, Henri
British, 19th century.
Born c. 1802; died 1845.
Engraver.

Henri Josi was the son of Christian Josi. He was the curator of drawings and engravings in the British Museum.

JOSIC, Mladen
Yugoslav, 20th century.
Painter.

Mladen Josic founded the Belgrade School of Fine Art in 1936.

It is likely that his painting style changed during the course of his career. By 1970, his paintings are abstract in style with highly structured and interlinked geometric forms.

JOSIMOVICH, Georg
Slovene, 20th century.
Born 3 May 1894, in Sremska Mitrovica.
Active in the USA.
Painter.
Georg Josimovich studied at the Art Institute in Chicago and was later a member of the Society of Independent Artists. He received a medal in Chicago in 1929.

JOSINALDO
Brazilian, 20th century.
Painter. Scenes with figures.
Josinaldo's paintings evoke his memories of childhood on the banks of the São Francisco river.

JOSQUIN, Alexandre
French, 19th century.
Painter, watercolourist, draughtsman. Mythological subjects, portraits, genre scenes.
Alexandre Josquin was a painter and water colourist. He also drew mythological scenes, portraits and genre scenes.
AUCTION RECORDS:
PARIS, 23 Dec 1918, *Leda,* FRF 110. PARIS, 12 June 1929, *Departure for the Hunt,* FRF 650. PARIS, 1 June 1931, *Hunt Meeting Chantilly Forest,* FRF 810. LOS ANGELES, 12 March 1979, *Chaotic Departure* (oil on canvas, 23 3/4 x 30 1/2 ins / 60.3 x 77.5 cm) USD 1,800. MONACO, 3 Dec 1989, *Mameluke and Horse* (oil on canvas, 25 1/2 x 22 ins / 65 x 55 cm) FRF 48,840.

JOSQUIN DES PRÉS. See **DES PRÉS**

JOSS, Peter
Estonian, 20th century.
Born 1915, in Estonia.
Active in the USA.
Painter. Landscapes.
Peter Joss studied in Berlin until Hitler took power in Germany when he emigrated to the USA. There, he worked with Gottlieb, Leon Karp and Martin Jackson.
His delicate 'paysagiste' works are more written than painted, being made up of indistinct lines laid one over the other.
He has held many solo exhibitions in America.

JOSSAND, Henri
French, 19th century.
Born 19th century, in Bourges.
Sculptor.
Henri Jossand studied at the Bourges École des Beaux-Arts and with M. Pètre. He exhibited at the Salon of French Artists and received an honourable mention in 1901.
MUSEUMS AND GALLERIES:
BOURGES: *Wine Grower from the Berry Region* (wooden bust); *M. Daniel, Public Prosecutor* (plaster bust); *Maker of Images* (wooden bust); *M. Brenquier* (plaster medallion).

JOSSAS, Barthélemy
French, 15th century.
Sculptor (wood).
In 1447, Jossas produced the stalls for the chancel of the abbey of St-Vincent de Lucq in Béarn, working in partnership with Nadal Quere.

JOSSE. See also **JOOS**

JOSSE, François Xavier
French, 20th century.
Born 1910, in Nantes; died 20 October 1991.
Painter, sculptor, draughtsman. Nudes.
François Xavier Josse studied at the École des Beaux-Arts in Nantes under the direction of Paul Deltombe. He created the Nantes independent regional group. In 1930, he went to Paris and continued his studies at the Grande Chaumière and Colarossi free academies. He ran the teaching studio of the sculptor Ossip Zadkine. He painted in oils and watercolours, drew female nudes and also worked as a sculptor. Josse took part in group exhibitions in Nantes, and a solo exhibition of his work was held in Paris in 1989.
AUCTION RECORDS:
LA VARENNE-ST-HILAIRE, 13 Dec 1989, *Méral* (watercolour, 22 x 19 ins / 55 x 48 cm) FRF 2,000. VERNON, 18 Feb 1990, *Thérésa Resting* (watercolour, 24 1/2 x 18 1/2 ins / 62 x 47 cm) FRF 2,300. TONNERRE, 15 April 1990, *Nude Study of Véro* (watercolour, 21 1/4 x 15 ins / 54 x 38 cm) FRF 2,200.

JOSSE, Guillaume. See **JASSE**

JOSSE, Jacques
French, 16th century.
Born in Paris.
Active c. 1562.
Painter.
Josse is mentioned by Siret.

JOSSE, Joris
Dutch, 15th century.
Sculptor.
In 1440, Josse produced a statue of *James of Bavaria* for the chapel of the court of The Hague.

JOSSE VAN DER BEKE. See **BEKE**

JOSSELIN DE JONG, Pieter
Dutch, 19th century.
Born 2 August 1861, in St Oedenrode (Brabant); died 2 June 1906, in The Hague.
Painter. History painting, portraits, genre scenes.
Pieter Josselin de Jong was a pupil of P. Slager and also studied under Cabanel in Paris for a time. He settled and worked in The Hague and was awarded medals in Munich in 1897 and at the Paris Exposition Universelle of 1900.
MUSEUMS AND GALLERIES:
AMSTERDAM: a watercolour - AMSTERDAM (Comm.): *Gypsies* - ROTTERDAM: *The Painter Rochussen*; *M. Viruly*; *Mr Sjoerd Vening* - THE HAGUE (Gemeentemus.): *The Painter Stortenbeker*; *Child Sleeping*.
AUCTION RECORDS:
NEW YORK, 15 Oct 1991, *Still-life with Flowers in an Upturned Basket* (oil on canvas, 21 x 25 1/2 ins / 53.4 x 64.8 cm) USD 1,540. AMSTERDAM, 27-28 May 1993, *Foundry* (oil on canvas, 17 3/4 x 27 1/4 ins / 45 x 69 cm) NLG 3,450.

JOSSELIN-DARDE, Marguerite Louise
French, 19th century.
Born in Dangé (Vienne).
Miniaturist.
Marguerite Louise Josselin-Darbe was a pupil of Madame Georges Grimblot,a member of the Société des Artistes Français from 1908. She was represented at the salon as part of this group.

JOSSERANT, François André
French, 19th century.
Born in St-Tropez (Var); died 24 December 1859, in Toulon.
Painter.
François André Josserant was a former officer who went to Holland and produced a number of copies of the great Dutch masters.
MUSEUMS AND GALLERIES:
TOULON: *Portrait of Baron de Beurmann.*

JOSSERME, François. See **L'ANGE**

JOSSET, Guillaume
French, 17th century.
Painter.
Josset became a widower in 1655.

JOSSET, Raoul
French, 20th century.
Born 9 December 1892, in Four (Nièvre).
Active in the USA.
Sculptor. Religious subjects, figure compositions, figures. Monuments.

Raoul Josset studied under Injalbert and became a member of the Salon des Artistes Français in Paris. He was awarded a travel bursary in 1923. Josset produced numerous sculptures in the state of Texas, particularly in Dallas.

JOSSO, Camille
French, 20th century.
Born 6 June 1902, in Nantes.
Engraver, illustrator.

Camille Josso was a member of the Salon of the Société Nationale des Beaux-Arts in Paris. He also exhibited at the Salon d'Automne after World War II and in Rabat and Casablanca during the 1930s. He illustrated some 30 books.

JOSSO, Xavier
French, 20th century.
Born 1894, in Nantes; died 1983.
Painter, watercolourist, engraver, draughtsman, illustrator. Landscapes.

Xavier Josso studied at the École des Arts Décoratifs; he painted landscapes of Brittany of the Guérande peninsula, the Gulf of Morbihan and Cornouaille. The Musée de Pont-Aven held a retrospective of his work (2003).

JOSSOT, Henri Gustave, also known as Abdul Karim
French, 19th - 20th century.
Born 16 April 1866, in Dijon; died 7 April 1951, in Sidi Bou Saïd, Tunisia.
Painter, draughtsman, caricaturist, engraver, illustrator, lithographer, poster artist.
Orientalism.

Henri Gustave Jossot studied under Jean-Paul Laurens and Eugène Carrière. He collaborated on several Paris magazines, in particular special editions of *L'Assiette au Beurre*, *Cocorico*, *L'Épreuve*, *La Plume*, *Le Rire* and *L'Estampe Originale*. He travelled in Brittany, Corsica, Switzerland and Tunisia and, after extended visits in 1896 and 1904, settled in Tunisia in 1910. He converted to Islam in 1913 and took the name Abdul Karim Jossot. His work is a virulent attack on the established powers: the middle classes, priests, judges and the military. He wrote and illustrated various books, including *Artistes et Bourgeois* published by Louis Michaud; *Mince de trognes* published by Hazard in 1896; and *Viande de Bourgeois* published by Michaud in 1906. His drawing style with its sinuous, thick lines and flat, black areas contrasting with the whitness of the paper was no doubt influenced by Félix Valloton. After converting to Islam Jossot drew orientally-inspired subjects in brush and wash. He took part in group exhibitions in Paris, including the Salon of the Société Nationale des Beaux-Arts in 1895, the Salon d'Automne from 1908 to 1911 and the Salon des Indépendants in 1910 and 1911.

BIBLIOGRAPHY:
Bouchard, Marie, '*Henri Gustave Jossot*' in *Bulletin du Club Français de la Médaille* n° 70-71, periodical, Paris, 1st trimester 1981. Osterwalder, Marcus (ed.), *Dictionnaire des illustrateurs 1800-1914*, Ides et Calendes, Neuchâtel, 1989.

MUSEUMS AND GALLERIES:
TUNIS (MAM): *Rue du Persan*.

AUCTION RECORDS:
NEW YORK, 12 June 1980, *Anti Nabis* (1894, oil on canvas, 36 1/4 x 28 3/4 ins / 92 x 73 cm) USD 1,400. PARIS, 18 June 1993, *Wadi in Southern Tunisia* (oil on canvas, 32 x 39 ins / 81 x 99 cm) FRF 6,000. PARIS, 26 March 1996, *The Wave* (1894, lithograph) FRF 18,500. PARIS, 3 Dec 2001, *Morning at the Soup Seller's* (1909, oil on canvas, 28 x 43 ins / 70 x 110 cm) FRF 80,000.

JOST, Josef
German, 20th century.
Born 6 August 1875, in Heckendalheim (Rhineland-Palatinate); died 1948.
Sculptor, painter. Figures, genre scenes, animals. Busts.

Josef Jost worked in Munich, having studied in Strasbourg and Munich. He made his debut in 1903 at the Krystallpalast in Munich with a relief *Evening Prayer*, following this with busts, sculptures of subjects from everyday life, and animals.

MUSEUMS AND GALLERIES:
HAMILTON, NJ (AG): *Awakening* - MUNICH (Stadtmus.): *Europa* (group).

AUCTION RECORDS:
COLOGNE, 14 June 1977, *Standing Nude* (bronze, h. 22 ins / 55 cm) DEM 1,100. LONDON, 14 Feb 1979, *Vase of Flowers* (oil on canvas, 26 1/2 x 21 1/4 ins / 67 x 54 cm) GBP 1,000. ZURICH, 19 July 1984, *Still-life with Apples* (1927, oil on panel, 37 1/2 x 26 ins / 95 x 66 cm) CHF 3,000. ZOFINGEN, 30 Nov 2001, *Flowers in Delft Vase* (oil on canvas, 27 x 23 ins / 68 x 58 cm) CHF 3,100.

JOST, Joseph
Austrian, 20th century.
Born 13 January 1888, in Vienna.
Painter. Portraits, still-lifes.

Joseph Jost started by teaching himself, copying the old masters, and then studied at the Akademie der Bildenden Künste in Vienna. He became a war artist in 1914, and from 1918 devoted himself almost exclusively to still-lifes. He featured in the jubilee exhibition of the Vienna group of artists in 1908 with *The Right to Death*; in 1911 as a member of the same group with *Medusa*; in 1913 at the autumn exhibition with *Still-life with Glass of Water, Rolls and Napkins* and in 1914 *Still-life with Oranges*. He featured in the Grosse Kunstausstellung in Berlin in 1916, in the Vienna group of artists in 1916 and 1917, and in the exhibition of war paintings in 1918 in Vienna. From 1919, he showed still-lifes, flowers, fruit, vegetables and chickens. His portraits include: *Colonel General von Kövess*; *Count Clam-Martinitz*, Governor-General of Montenegro; *General von Hoen* and *Staff Colonel Baron von Waldstätten*.

AUCTION RECORDS:
VIENNA, 14 Sept 1976, *Vase of Flowers* (oil on canvas, 23 1/2 x 19 3/4 ins / 60 x 50 cm) ATS 22,000. VIENNA, 10 June 1980, *Bouquet of Flowers* (oil on panel, 17 3/4 x 13 1/4 ins / 45 x 33.5 cm) ATS 28,000. LONDON, 25 Nov 1992, *Still-life of a Staffordshire Tea Service* (oil on panel, 25 1/4 x 31 1/2 ins / 64 x 80 cm) GBP 9,680. LONDON, 18 March 1999, *Grapes, Apples, Pears, Lemon, Pitcher and Glass on Table* (oil on panel, 22 x 27 ins / 55 x 68 cm) GBP 1,600. VIENNA, 15 June 1999, *Still-life of Mixed Flowers* (oil on canvas, 23 x 27 ins / 58 x 69 cm) ATS 28,000. NEW ORLEANS, 17 March 2000, *Floral Still-life of Fuschias, Marigolds and Other Flowers in a Vase* (oil on panel, 14 x 11 ins / 36 x 28 cm) USD 3,400. LONDON, 22 Feb 2001, *Gladioli, Peonies, Carnations and Fuchsias in Vase on Draped Table* (oil on canvas, 39 x 30 ins / 98 x 77 cm) GBP 1,600. VIENNA, 30 Oct 2001, *Flower Posy* (oil on panel, 10 x 8 ins / 26 x 21 cm) ATS 28,000. VIENNA, 2 April 2002, *Flowers in a Jug* (oil on canvas, 27 x 24 ins / 68 x 60 cm) EUR 3,400. LONDON, 18 Sept 2003, *Tea Table* (oil on panel, 25 x 32 ins / 64 x 81 cm) GBP 7,000.

JOST, Melchior. See **JOBST**

JOST, Ottilie E.
Maiden name: Palm
Canadian, 20th century.

Born 13 February 1878, in Hamilton (Ontario); died 1961, in Oberhausen, Germany.
Active in Germany.
Painter, illustrator. Portraits, genre scenes, landscapes, still-lifes.

Ottilie Jost studied at the School of Fine Arts of Hamilton. She drew illustrations for such papers as the *Hamilton Herald* and the *Toronto Globe*. In 1908, she painted a *Resurrection* for the church of St Paul in Hamilton. She exhibited with the Ontario Society of Artists in Toronto and the Académie des Beaux-Arts in Montreal, showing portraits, genre paintings and landscapes. In 1914 she married the German sculptor Josef Jost and settled in Munich, where she exhibited landscapes.

MUSEUMS AND GALLERIES:
HAMILTON, NJ (AG): *Old Woman; Hartz Peasant Woman.*

JOST VON WORMS. See **DOTZINGER Jost**

JOSUI SOEN. See **SOEN**

JOSZ, Italo
Italian, 20th century.
Born 1878, in Florence.
Painter. Figures.

Josz studied at the Accademia di Belle Arti di Brera, Milan, where he first exhibited on 1 May 1898. He was subsequently represented in many exhibitions, and was awarded the gold medal at the National Exhibition, Ferrara, in 1919 for *Head of a Woman*. He painted mainly female figures.

JOSZA, Karoly. See **JOZSA K.**

JOSZA, Sándor, or Alexandre
Hungarian, 20th century.
Born 1910.
Active in France from c. 1930.
Painter. Scenes with figures.

Sándor Josza lived and worked near Fontainebleau in France. The forest appears frequently in his works. The colours are lively and tender, the compositions consisting of a dreamlike juxtaposition of symbolic images that seem to depict the occupations of daily life through an unreal space in compositions reminiscent of Chagall.

The Budapest Museum held a retrospective exhibition of his work in 1983.

AUCTION RECORDS:
PARIS, 29 June 1990, *Composition with Sailing Boats* (1947, oil on canvas, 28 1/2 x 36 ins / 72.5 x 91.5 cm) FRF 3,000; *Abstract Landscape* (oil on canvas, 24 x 35 3/4 ins / 61 x 91 cm) FRF 3,000.

JOTTHIER, Louis
Belgian, 19th - 20th century.
Born 1866, in Ghent; died 1942, in Heverlee.
Painter, sculptor.

Louis Jotthier was a student at the Académie des Beaux-Arts in Ghent, and a lecturer at the Académie des Beaux-Arts in Louvain.

AUCTION RECORDS:
AMSTERDAM, 3 Nov 1992, *A Dog* (1895, oil on canvas, 38 1/4 x 28 1/4 ins / 97 x 72 cm) NLG 3,220.

JOTTI, Carlo
Italian, 19th - 20th century.
Born 1826, in Milan; died 1905.
Painter. Genre scenes, landscapes.

Jotti exhibited in Milan, Turin and Venice.

AUCTION RECORDS:
MILAN, 28 Oct 1976, *Procession* (oil on card, 7 x 6 ins / 18 x 15.5 cm) ITL 600,000. MILAN, 14 March 1978, *Canobbio* (oil on canvas, 10 1/2 x 20 1/2 ins / 26.5 x 52 cm) ITL 1,300,000. MILAN, 5 April 1979, *Fishermen's Island* (oil on canvas, 13 3/4 x 27 1/2 ins / 35 x 70 cm) ITL 1,100,000. MILAN, 9 June 1987, *Village by a Lake* (oil on canvas, 35 3/4 x 57 3/4 ins / 91 x 147 cm) ITL 8,000,000. MILAN, 1 June 1988, *Peasants in the Simplon Region* (oil on canvas, 15 1/4 x 19 3/4 ins / 39 x 50 cm) ITL 5,000,000. MILAN, 19 March 1992, *Church on Lake Como* (1897, oil on canvas/card, 12 1/2 x 16 1/4 ins / 31.5 x 41 cm) ITL 8,000,000. ROME, 27 April 1993, *Landscape of Lake Como* (watercolour/card, 5 x 7 1/2 ins / 13 x 19 cm) ITL 2,139,500. ROME, 31 May 1994, *Soldiers in Venafro* (1861, oil on canvas, 22 x 30 ins / 55 x 76 cm) ITL 17,678,000. MILAN, 4 Dec 2000, *Marine with Figures* (oil on canvas, 16 x 22 ins / 40 x 56 cm) ITL 7,000,000. MILAN, 23 Oct 2002, *Lugano* (oil on card, 9 x 16 ins / 23 x 40 cm) EUR 10,000. VIENNA, 22 May 2003, *Scipione Castle near to Salsomaggio* (oil on canvas, 17 x 22 ins / 43 x 57 cm) EUR 6,000. MILAN, 8 June 2004, *Scipione Castle* (oil on canvas, 17 x 22 ins / 43 x 57 cm) EUR 8,000.

JOTTRAND, Lucien Gustave
Belgian, 20th century.
Born 12 December 1873, in St Joost-ten-Node; died 1957, in Ixelles (Brussels).
Painter, engraver, writer. Landscapes, seascapes.

Jottrand featured at the Brussels Exhibition of 1900. He was a member of the Société Royale des Beaux-Arts in Brussels and was made a Chevalier of the Ordre de Léopold.

JOU SENABRE, Luis, or Louis, known as Louis Jou
Spanish, 20th century.
Born 29 May 1881, in Barcelona; died 3 January 1968, in Les Baux-de-Provence, France.
Active in France.
Painter, engraver, illustrator.

In the first half of the 20th century, which saw the revival of books in de luxe editions, Luis Jou Senabre, more commonly known as Louis Jou, stands out as one of the master artists and craftsmen of the book. He became famous for his typography and also illustrated and engraved for books. Edmond Joseph mentions that Luis Jou did not hesitate to put on the overalls belonging to the handyman in order to paint a sign for the Champion Bookshop near the Institut.

Luis Jou and his work were the subject of an important study by M.J. Cassou: *Notre Ami Jou* (*Our Friend Jou*). Jou illustrated works in French, including Montaigne's *Essays*, the *Physionomie des Saints* (*Physiognomy of the Saints*) by Ernest Hello, *Le Jaloux Garrizales d'Estremadures* (*The Jealous Man of Extremadura*), a translation of Cervantes' *El Celoso Extremeño*, Machiavelli's *The Prince*, Victor Hugo's *Selected Poems*, Oscar Wilde's *Salome*, Boccaccio's *Decameron*, illustrations for the works of Anatole France, *La Petite Ville* (*The Little Town*) by Rémy de Gourmont, *Alphabet* by Paul Valéry, *The Poems* of Alfred de Vigny and *The Return of the Prodigal* by André Gide.

BIBLIOGRAPHY:
Arnáiz, José Manuel/López Jiménez, Javier/Merchán Díaz, Manuel (ed.), *Cien años de pintura en Espana y Portugal (1830-1930)*, Antiqvaria, Madrid, 1990.

JOU SENABRE, Ramón
Spanish, 20th century.
Born 1893.
Painter, draughtsman, illustrator. Landscapes with figures, still-lifes.

Ramón Jou Senabre was the younger brother of Luis Jou Senabre. He studied at the La Lonja Art School in Barcelona. At the age of eighteen, he left Barcelona for Paris, where he attended art school in the evenings after work for just one month, so he truly studied painting by himself in his spare time. Not until 1928 was he able to devote himself entirely to painting. He then went to live and work in Marseilles and Corsica. He returned to his native Catalonia in around 1935 and then went back to Paris around 1950.

Jou Senabre featured in a number of group exhibitions in Barcelona, Paris and Tangier, and also held solo shows, the first of which, in a small, short-lived gallery in the Montparnasse district, passed unnoticed. Between 1929 and 1932, he featured regularly in exhibitions organised by Parisian galleries. On 15 February 1936, an exhibition of his paintings was organised at the Museo de Arte Moderno in Madrid. It was received enthusiastically by the press and several of his paintings were bought for Catalan and Spanish collections. On returning to Paris in the 1950s, he showed paintings and watercolours there.

In 1925, Jou Senabre was commissioned to design for the Loïe Fuller Ballets, for whom he produced fabric designs, accessories, and compositions consisting of slabs of luminous colours. In his native Catalonia, he painted fishermen, marine landscapes and still-lifes of fish and shells, fruits and flowers. He is well known for his satirical illustrations.

BIBLIOGRAPHY:

Arnáiz, José Manuel/López Jiménez, Javier/Merchán Díaz, Manuel (ed.), *Cien años de pintura en Espana y Portugal (1830-1930)*, Antiqvaria, Madrid, 1990.

JOU WEN-CHOU. See **RU WENSHU**

JOU-T'AI. See **RUTAI**

JOUAFF

French, 16th century.

Sculptor, architect.

Jouaff was of Breton origin, and worked at the church in Trédrez, in the Côtes d'Armor region of France, in 1565. His monogram is engraved on the capitals of the chancel.

JOUAN, Claude

French, 16th - 17th century.

Painter.

Jouan's name was recorded on an official identification document in Paris in 1600. He was a master painter.

JOUAN, Jean Pierre

French, 20th century.

Born 22 January 1943, in Deauville.

Painter. Seascapes, landscapes.

Jean Pierre Jouan was self-taught. He exhibits in Paris, Lyons, Honfleur, Montpellier and Deauville.

AUCTION RECORDS:

DOUAI, 1 April 1990, *Black Cows at Houlgate* (1982, oil on canvas, 18¼ x 25½ ins / 46.6 x 65 cm) FRF 4,500.

JOUAN, Michel

French, 17th century.

Painter.

Jouan became a godfather in 1608.

JOUANDOT, Amédée

French, 19th century.

Born 2 September 1831, in Bordeaux; died 9 March 1884.

Sculptor.

Amédée Jouandot worked with Jouffroy. He was represented at the Paris Salon from 1867. His most important works were: *St Catherine* (stone statue in Nevers Cathedral), *St Baudile* (wooden statue for the pulpit of Nîmes church), *Religion* (wooden statue for the pulpit of the church in Marmande), *Groups of Children and Dauphins*, a decoration of the base of the fountain of the Three Graces in the Place de la Bourse in Bordeaux.

MUSEUMS AND GALLERIES:

BORDEAUX: *Eternal Rest*.

JOUANEAUX, Louis

French, 18th century.

Painter, draughtsman. Maps.

MUSEUMS AND GALLERIES:

NANTES (Mus. des Archives): *Map of the City of Nantes* (wash heightened with watercolour).

JOUANIN, Auguste Adrien

French, 19th century.

Born 5 April 1806, in Cosne (Nièvre); died 1887, in Paris.

Engraver (aquatint/mezzotint).

Auguste Adrien Jouanin entered the École des Beaux-Arts on 13th May 1826 and was a pupil of Sixdeniers. He made his debut at the Paris Salon in 1846 and continued to take part in exhibitions until 1874. He gained third class medals in 1859, and again in 1861 and 1863. He engraved in the style of Guet, Eduard Girardet, Muller, Landelle, Jalabert, Portaels, Brochard, Graeffe, Mm. De Châtillon, Toulmouche, Comte calix, Riedel, Coomans, Schlesinger, Bouguereau, Holfeld, Rubens, Winterhalter and Le Guide. He sometimes signed himself: *graveur de S. M. l'Impératrice* (*engraver to Her Majesty the Empress*).

JOUANNAUD, Yves

French, 20th century.

Born 1924, in La Madeleine.

Painter.

Yves Jouannaud studied first at the École des Beaux-Arts in Lille in 1941 and 1942 and then in Paris from the end of World War II until 1947. He also worked at the Académie Julian and, with Zadkine, at the Académie Colarossi. Originally taking a figurative approach, Jouannaud gradually moved towards abstraction around 1960. His painting then became Abstract Impressionist in style.

JOUANNE, Léon

French, 19th century.

Died 1897.

Active in Paris.

Painter.

Léon Jouanne was a member of the Société des Artistes Français and exhibited at the Salon as part of this group.

JOUANNE-HUGONET, Marthe

French, 20th century.

Born 11 August 1871, in Paris.

Painter, pastellist. Portraits, flowers.

Marthe Jouanne-Hugonet studied under Léandre and from 1894 to 1938 exhibited from time to time at the Salon des Artistes Français, of which she was a member. She was awarded a silver medal and the Marie Bashkirtseff prize in 1920. Her portraits and intimate subjects are bathed in a diffuse, hazy light.

MUSEUMS AND GALLERIES:

CAEN: *Vase of Flowers* - VERNON (Mus. Alphonse-Georges-Poulain): *Rest*.

JOUANNEAU (Abbé)

French, 19th century.

Active in Blois.

Painter. Landscapes.

JOUANT, Jules

French, 19th - 20th century.

Born 19th century, in Paris.

Active in Neuilly-sur-Seine.

Sculptor.

From 1885, Jules Jouant exhibited frequently at the Salon of the Société des Artistes Français and the Salon of the Société Nationale, showing genre statues and busts. In 1913 he received a commendation. Jouant executed the monument to the irregular soldiers in the Place St-Ferdinand, Ternes.

JOUAS, Abel
French, 20th century.
Engraver.
Abel Jouas exhibited at the Brussels Exhibition of 1910.

JOUAS, Charles
French, 19th - 20th century.
Born 5 December 1866, in Paris; died 1942.
Engraver (etching), illustrator.
Charles Jouas was president of the engraving section of the Société Nationale des Beaux-Arts. He was perhaps the last exponent of Romantic inspiration and technique before the advent of Modernism. His finest plates were inspired by the work or Huysmans. Jouas produced engravings of historical sites and was particularly adept at depicting Paris and the city's historic buildings. The books he illustrated include *The Cathedral* by Huysmans, *Reims dévasté* by P. Adam; and *Albert Savarus* by Balzac.

AUCTION RECORDS:
PARIS, 20-22 May 1920, *The Main Door and Left Door of the Royal Porch of Chartres Cathedral in Flames* (red chalk) FRF 380. PARIS, 10 Feb 1932, *The Seine in Paris during the 1910 Flood (the Arcevêché Bridge)* (drawing in colouring pencil heightened with gouache) FRF 430. PARIS, 11 Dec 1935, *Cour de Rohan: the Vine Arbour and Mounting Block* (colouring pencil) FRF 180. NEW YORK, 18 Feb 1993, *Construction of the Métro in Paris* (watercolour/paper, 26 3/4 x 36 1/4 ins / 68 x 92 cm) USD 5,500. PARIS, 5 Nov 1993, *The Seine in Paris during the 1910 Flood* (1910, lead pencil and coloured pencil heightened with white gouache, 10 x 16 1/4 ins / 25.3 x 41 cm) FRF 5,300. PARIS, 9 April 1999, *Notre Dame de Paris* (black crayon and white and red chalk, 19 x 12 ins / 48 x 31 cm) FRF 12,500. PARIS, 22 Nov 2000, *Gargoyle at Notre Dame* (black crayon, 13 x 9 ins / 34 x 24 cm) FRF 17,200. PARIS, 23 March 2001, *Binding Workshop* (black crayon heightened with red chalk, seven, 13 x 9 ins / 32 x 22 cm) FRF 50,000.

JOUAS, Édouard-Étienne
French, 19th century.
Born 19th century, in Brie-Comte-Robert (Seine-et-Marne).
Painter. Landscapes.
Édouard-Étienne Jouas took pleasure in painting Norman sites. He exhibited at the Paris Salon from 1878.
MUSEUMS AND GALLERIES:
LOUVIERS: *Farmyard in La Morenier (Eure); Farm in Montreuil-l'Argellé.*
AUCTION RECORDS:
PARIS, 11 Dec 1946, *River in the Woods,* FRF 520. VIENNA, 17 March 1982, *Landscape with River* (oil on canvas, 18 x 25 1/2 ins / 46 x 65 cm) ATS 25,000. PARIS, 3 June 1994, *Landscape with Mill and Poplars* (oil on canvas, 43 1/4 x 30 ins / 110 x 76 cm) FRF 6,000. NEW ORLEANS, 26 Jan 2002, *Choppy Seas at Sunset* (oil on canvas, 20 x 25 ins / 51 x 64 cm) USD 4,200. PARIS, 17 Nov 2003, *Springtime, Hens* (oil on canvas, 30 x 44 ins / 76 x 112 cm) EUR 2,500.

JOUAS-POUTREL, Louis Marie Ernest
French, 20th century.
Born 17 February 1874, in Rouen.
Engraver (etching).
Louis Marie Ernest Jouas-Poutrel studied under Cormon and Mongin. He became a member of the Société des Artistes Français in Paris in 1905, receiving a commendation the same year.

JOUATTE, Alphonse
French, 19th century.
Born 1827, in Paris; died 1892.
Painter. Genre scenes.
Alphonse Jouatte exhibited at the Salon from 1861 to 1880.
MUSEUMS AND GALLERIES:
LIMOGES: *Wounded Clown.*

JOUATTE-BIVA, Julienne
French, 19th century.
Active in Paris.
Painter.
Julienne Jouatte-Biva was a member of the Société des Artistes Français in Paris from 1893 and exhibited at the Salon as part of this group.

JOUAULT, André Gustave
French, 20th century.
Born 24 July 1904, in Domfront (Orne); died 1987.
Painter. Figures, portraits, rustic scenes, landscapes, waterscapes, harbour scenes, seascapes, architectural views, still-lifes, flowers. Wall decorations.
André Gustave Jouault studied at the Bernard Palissy École des Arts Appliqués in Paris under M. Decamps. He became a member of the Salon des Artistes Français in Paris and was awarded a silver medal and a travel bursary in 1929. He received numerous prizes and medals during the course of his career, including the Grand Prix in 1970 and in 1976 the Salon des Artistes Français medal of honour. Jouault decorated the church of St-Christophe and the Oratoire chapel in the diocese of Sées in Normandy. His landscapes and still-lifes are bathed in a dark and bluish light as if seeking to capture the moment when daylight changes into darkness, concealing objects and places. He also painted many African landscapes, masks and figures in brown and ochre tones, using contrast to enhance the feeling of heat and the richness of the textures of plants, fabrics and bodies. He took part in group exhibitions, including, from 1927: the Salon des Artistes Français, the Salon des Indépendants and the Salon d'Automne; in 1962, Décades de Provence; and in 1977, *Maîtres de l'Art Français* (*Masters of French Art*) in Kuwait. In 2003, Le Toit de la Grande Arche de la Défense held a retrospective of his work.
AUCTION RECORDS:
PARIS, 26 May 1988, *Vase of Roses* (oil on canvas, 24 x 19 3/4 ins / 61 x 50 cm) FRF 8,800.

JOUBEL, Guillaume
French, 17th century.
Active in Nantes c. 1651.
Glass painter.

JOUBERT, Andrée
French, 20th century.
Born 1894, in Paris; died 13 February 1959.
Painter, draughtsman. Portraits, landscapes, urban landscapes, flowers.
In 1910, Andrée Joubert joined the École des Arts Décoratifs in Nice and in 1912 exhibited at the Salon des Beaux-Arts de Nice. Joubert did not make her Paris début at the Salon des Indépendants until 1924, however, as she decided to abandon art in 1917 to care for the war wounded. After this she went to Algiers and to Palestine to 'learn about light'. From 1920 to 1930, she travelled in Syria and North Africa. On her return, she again exhibited at the Paris salons, including the Salon des Artistes Français, the Salon des Tuileries, the Salon des Indépendants, the Salon of the Société Nationale des Beaux-Arts and the Salon d'Automne, of which she was made a member. She also took part in the Venice Biennale of 1930, the International Exhibition in Paris in 1937 (where she decorated the pavilion of the Ville de Paris, the architecture pavilion and the pavilion of the Côte d'Azur). She exhibited regularly with Marcel Blenheim in Paris in 1926, 1933 and 1940 in solo exhibitions. In 1940 Joubert again volunteered

to care for the war wounded. She decorated the offices of the French navy.

Her paintings inspired by Nice include *Woman at a Window; Wild Flowers; Spring Bouquet.*

JOUBERT, Bernard
French, 20th - 21st century.
Born 23 October 1946, in Paris.
Painter.

Bernard Joubert's work was marked from the outset by a certain amount of minimalism. First, starting from glued geometric strips, he obtained chromatic effects from shaded colours. Then his painting became even more pared down, simply delimiting space from slanting, parallel or perpendicular lines generally drawn diagonally on canvases without frames. He also investigated the line itself and the bracketing of two lines, one black, and the other white, overturning the usual perceptions of straight lines. He has taken part in exhibitions such as: *Onze Peintres Actuels* (*Eleven Contemporary Painters*), Dijon; Paris Biennale, 1975; Orleans National Theatre, 2003. Solo exhibitions include: Galerie Yvon Lambert, Paris, 1974; Galerie Françoise Lambert, Milan, 1974; Galerie Delta, Brussels, 1975 and Galerie Regards, Paris, 1991.

JOUBERT, F. E. (father)
French, 19th century.
Engraver (burin).

F. E. Joubert was the author of a *Manual for the Amateur Engraver* (1821).

JOUBERT, Ferdinand Jean
French, 19th century.
Born 15 September 1810, in Paris; died 1884, in Menton (Alpes-Maritimes).
Engraver (burin).

Ferdinand Joubert entered the École des Beaux-Arts on March 31 1829 as part of the studio of Henriquel Dupont. He began engraving for illustration around 1830 and also produced portraits for Thiers' *History of the Revolution.* He made his debut at the Paris Salon in 1840 and his work featured again in the 1878 exhibition. He was awarded a third class medal with a rappel in 1859 and 1863.

Joubert spent some time in London and exhibited at the Royal Academy from 1855 to 1881. His works include portraits and genre subjects in the style of Murillo, Winterhalter, Lejeune and Greuze and also *Parable of Our Lord Illustrated* in the manner of John Franklin.

JOUBERT, Henri
French, 20th century.
Born 14 May 1873, in Paris.
Painter, sculptor.

Henri Joubert exhibited in Paris at the Salon des Indépendants from 1902.

JOUBERT, Jean
French, 17th century.
Draughtsman, miniaturist. Natural history.

Jean Joubert is mentioned about 1688. He executed natural history paintings and was the master of Claude Aubriet.

AUCTION RECORDS:
PARIS, 23 March 1937, *Portrait of a Grenadier* (miniature) FRF 240.

JOUBERT, Laurent
French, 20th - 21st century.
Born 1952, in Narbonne.
Painter.

Laurent Joubert's approach is to enlarge extracts of documents, texts, captions, ex-libris, emblems, coats of arms, imprimaturs and scenes taken from old engravings or drawings from the time of the Conquistadors for example, and incorporate them into his paintings. In the painting *Les Allemands - Wie des Königs* (*The Germans - Wie des Königs*), 1987, a cannibal scene taken from a 16th-century engraving is engraved as if encrusted on or superimposed, with a caption written in gothic letters. The background, in warm colours, is painted with big brushes. Through the dual perspective of a deconstruction company Joubert denounces the hold that the West as inquisitor and colonist has over written and pictorial signs: media that culturally signifies a suggestion, or better still, imposes values. Joubert shows us the ideological working and make-up of images.

Laurent Joubert has appeared in collective exhibitions such as: Musée des Beaux-Arts, Tours, 1984; Salon de Montrouge, 1984, 1985, 1986; Galerie Yvon Lambert, Paris, 1985; Fondation Cartier, Paris, 1986; ARC, Musée d'Art Moderne de la Ville de Paris, 1986; *Les Éléphants Sont Parmi Nous* (*Elephants Are Among Us*), Château-Musée de Dieppe, 1987; Salon des Indépendants, 1988; *La Peinture au Quotidien. France 1984-1988* (*Painting in Everyday Life. France 1984-1988*), a travelling exhibition in Latin America; *Les Années quatre-vingt* (*The Eighties*), Fondation Cartier, Jouy-en-Josas, 1989; First Johannesburg Biennale of Contemporary Art, 1995.

Solo exhibitions of his work include: Galerie Philippe Fregnac, Paris, 1982, 1983; Galerie Beau Lezard, Paris, 1986; *Du Trou du Pot à Ma Chatte* (*From the Hole in the Pot To My Cat*), Galerie Triebold, Basel, 1987; *Les Cannibales n'ont pas de Cimetière* (*Cannibals do not have Cemeteries*), French Cultural Institute, Prague, 1988; *Missio*, Galerie Charles Cartwright, Paris, 1989; *Le Bateau ou la Forêt* (*Boat or Forest*), Le Quartier, Contemporary Art Centre, Quimper, 1992; *Le Maître Court*, Espace des Arts, Coulommiers, 1994; Musée National des Arts d'Afrique et d'Océanie, Paris, 1996.

BIBLIOGRAPHY:
Enrici, M., *Les Peintres et l'Architecture antique*, Musée des Beaux-Arts, Tours, 1984. Gibbal, Jean Marie, *Les Ruines de l'esprit*, Toulouse, 1985. Mercadé, Bernard, *Du trou du pot à ma chatte*, Gal. Triebold, Basel, 1987. Bourriaud, Nicolas, '*La Légende noire*' in *Art Press*, n° 125, periodical, Paris, 1988. Tío Bellido, Ramón, *Fonds National d'Art Contemporain, acquisitions 1989*, Centre National des Arts Plastiques, Paris, 1990. Huitorel, Jean-Marc, '*Laurent Joubert*' in *Art Press*, n° 173, periodical, Paris, 1992.

MUSEUMS AND GALLERIES:
MARSEILLES (FRAC Provence-Alpes-Côte d'Azur): *Eigenstein/Astrolabe* (1994) - PARIS (FNAC): *Germans; Wies Des Königs* (1987); *Réseau signalétique basé sur une iconographie.*

AUCTION RECORDS:
PARIS, 7 Oct 1996, *Adam's Skull* (1990-1991, acrylic and wax/canvas, 18 x 24 ins / 46 x 61 cm) FRF 11,000.

JOUBERT, Léon
French, 19th century.
Born 19th century, in Quimper (Finistère).
Painter. Landscapes.

Léon Joubert was a pupil of Pelouze and Ch. F. Cormon. He was a member of the Société des Artistes Français from 1883 and exhibited his work at the Salon as part of this group. He received an honourable mention in 1884, a third class medal in 1889 and a bronze medal in the Exposition Universelle of 1889 and 1900.

MUSEUMS AND GALLERIES:
MONTPELLIER: *Mouth of the Arguenon* - MONTREAL: *The Area around Rochefort; Tomb of Chateaubriand in St-Malo* - ST-BRIEUC: *Autumn in Clairefontaine.*

AUCTION RECORDS:
PARIS, 27 April 1897, *Landscape of Clourière,* FRF 195. PARIS, 28 Dec 1898, *View of Netheuil (Seine-et-Oise),* FRF 205. PARIS, 18-21 Dec 1918, *Low Tide,* FRF 100. PARIS, 30 Dec 1925, *The Area around St Jean-de-la-Mer,* FRF 280. PARIS, 16 May 1947, *Landscape,* FRF 2,500. VIENNA, 16 March 1976, *Seashore* (oil on panel, 10 1/2 x 13 3/4 ins / 26.5 x 35 cm) ATS 28,000. RHEIMS, 29 Oct 1978, *River Bank* (oil on canvas, 36 1/4 x 25 1/2 ins / 92 x 65 cm) FRF 7,500. NEW YORK, 20 May 1986, *Cape Finistère* (1877, oil on canvas, 35 1/4 x 59 1/2 ins / 89.5 x 151.1 cm) USD 3,000. PARIS, 7 April 2000, *Views of Vetheuil* (oil on canvas, a pair, 35 x 51 ins / 90 x 130 cm) FRF 90,000. PITTSFIELD, 8 Sept 2001, *The Port of Antibes* (oil on canvas, 11 x 16 ins / 28 x 41 cm) USD 3,500. LONDON, 21 March 2002, *The Town on the River* (oil on canvas, 14 x 21 ins / 36 x 53 cm) GBP 2,000. PARIS, 25 June 2003, *Steam Boat on a River* (oil on canvas, 34 x 50 ins / 86 x 127 cm) EUR 6,000. COLOGNE, 13 Dec 2003, *Outside the Town* (oil on canvas, 24 x 30 ins / 61 x 76 cm) EUR 5,000.

JOUBERT, Louis
French, 18th century.
Engraver.
Louis Joubert was living in Lyons in 1758 and 1786. He made dies for medals, and engraved with a burin after Delamonce.

JOUBERT, Louise Adéone. See **DROLLING Louise Adéone**

JOUBERT, Pierre
French, 20th century.
Born 27 June 1910, in Paris; died 14 January 2002, in La Rochelle.
Draughtsman, illustrator. Figures.
Pierre Joubert studied at the École des Arts Appliqués in Paris before working for the magazine *L'Illustration*. During the 1930s he soon became an illustrator on the main French scouting magazines such as *Scout de France* and on adventure magazines for young people produced by several publishing houses such as Toison d'Or, Marabout and Hachette. He worked alongside Henri Vernes on the creation of the celebrated character Bob Moranne, whose stories ran to around 100 issues. His name is particularly associated with publications in the 'Signe de Piste' collection published by Éditions Alsatia of Paris and with the Prince Éric adventure stories which were very popular with several generations of readers. Joubert came under fierce criticism when he went over to the Vichy government and continued to illustrate the magazine *Scout*. Joubert is known principally as an illustrator of adolescence. The adolescence he exalts in his carefully executed realist compositions is one of boys and girls who display courage, brotherly love and a fondness for the outdoor life. It is an idealised world composed of stereotypes.
BIBLIOGRAPHY:
Foncine, Jean-Louis/Dalens, Serge, *Pierre Joubert - Illustrateur de l'adolescence*, Éd. Universitaires, Paris, 1979. Mauriès, Dominique, '*Pierre Joubert - Chefs d'œuvre*' in vol. I, Alain Littaye, Paris, 1981. Rivière, François/Joubert, Pierre, '*Pierre Joubert - Chefs d'œuvre*' in vol. II, Alain Littaye, Paris, 1982. Rivière, François/Foncine, Jean-Louis, '*Pierre Joubert - Chefs d'œuvre*' in vol. III, Alain Littaye, Paris, 1983.

JOUBIN, Diane
French, 20th century.
Born 1906.
Painter.
Diane Joubin worked in the region of Toulon.

JOUBIN, Georges
French, 20th century.
Born 25 January 1888, in Digny (Eure-et-Loir); died 8 February 1983, in Paris.
Painter. Figure compositions, nudes, portraits, urban landscapes, still-lifes, flowers.
School of Montmartre.
In 1906, Georges Joubin joined the Académie Julian, studying at the studio of Jean Pierre Laurens and in 1908 moved to Gabriel Ferrer's studio at the École des Beaux-Arts. In 1929, with Dignimont, Asselin, Pascin and Bonnard, he became one of the founders of the Montmartre School. Although he painted still-lifes, flowers, portraits and nudes, it is for his urban landscapes, views of Paris and of the area in which he lived, with its street vendors, that he is best known. A vigorous realist in the tradition of Marquet, he remained attached to the style of the 1930s in which forms are clearly outlined and colours applied in flat tints. Joubin exhibited at the Salon des Indépendants in Paris from 1920 and at almost all the Paris salons, including the Salon des Tuileries, the Salon d'Automne, the Salon de Luxembourg and the Salon of the Société Nationale des Beaux-Arts, of which he became a committee member in 1935. An exhibition of his work was held at the Musée de Montmartre in Paris in 1988.

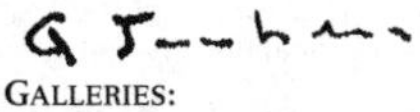

MUSEUMS AND GALLERIES:
PARIS (former Mus. du Luxembourg).
AUCTION RECORDS:
PARIS, 21 Oct 1974, *Kiosks in the Snow,* FRF 10,500. PARIS, 3 Feb 1988, *Banks of the St-Bernard Quay, Paris* (oil on canvas, 21 1/4 x 25 1/2 ins / 54 x 65 cm) FRF 7,000. PARIS, 6 May 1988, *Woman Seated in a Forest* (oil on panel, 32 x 25 1/2 ins / 81 x 65 cm) FRF 7,000. PARIS, 23 June 1988, *Chestnut Grove* (oil on panel, 28 3/4 x 36 1/4 ins / 73 x 92 cm) FRF 16,500. LONDON, 21 Oct 1988, *Fishing Boats at St-Jean-de-Luz* (oil on panel, 25 1/2 x 21 1/4 ins / 65 x 54 cm) GBP 1,430. VERSAILLES, 11 Jan 1989, *Brittany Landscape* (oil on paper, 19 x 24 3/4 ins / 48 x 63 cm) FRF 8,300. PARIS, 10 April 1989, *Market, Rue Lepic* (oil on canvas, 46 x 35 ins / 116 x 89 cm) FRF 86,000. RHEIMS, 23 April 1989, *Conversation* (oil on canvas, 37 x 43 1/4 ins / 94 x 110 cm) FRF 13,500. LA VARENNE-ST-HILAIRE, 21 May 1989, *Andelys Landscape* (oil on panel, 25 1/2 x 32 ins / 65 x 81 cm) FRF 29,000. RHEIMS, 11 June 1989, *Resting in a Clearing* (oil on panel, 32 x 25 1/2 ins / 81 x 65 cm) FRF 20,000. PARIS, 11 July 1989, *Cour de Rome* (oil on canvas, 28 3/4 x 35 3/4 ins / 73 x 91 cm) FRF 92,000. STRASBOURG, 29 Nov 1989, *Andelys Landscape* (oil on panel, 25 1/2 x 32 ins / 65 x 81 cm) FRF 43,000. LA VARENNE-ST-HILAIRE, 3 Dec 1989, *Dance* (oil on panel, 13 3/4 x 11 ins / 35 x 27 cm) FRF 15,200. RHEIMS, 17 Dec 1989, *The Card Game* (oil on panel, 19 x 25 1/4 ins / 48 x 64 cm) FRF 40,000. CALAIS, 4 March 1990, *Rue Lepic* (1950, oil on canvas, 28 3/4 x 23 1/2 ins / 73 x 60 cm) FRF 60,000. PARIS, 26 March 1990, *La loge* (oil on panel) FRF 130,000. PARIS, 10 May 1990, *Figures in a Forest Interior* (oil on panel, 36 1/4 x 28 3/4 ins / 92 x 73 cm) FRF 64,000. PARIS, 30 May 1990, *Rue Lepic* (oil on canvas, 28 3/4 x 23 1/2 ins / 73 x 60 cm) FRF 60,000. PARIS, 17 Oct 1990, *People Walking along the River in Les Andelys* (oil on card, 21 x 25 1/2 ins / 53.5 x 65 cm) FRF 30,000. LOUVIERS, 10 Feb 1991, *Studio in Montmartre* (oil on panel, 51 1/4 x 38 1/4 ins / 130 x 97 cm) FRF 69,000. PARIS, 5 July 1991, *Vue de Robinson* (1923, oil on card, 21 1/4 x 25 1/2 ins / 54 x 65 cm) FRF 7,500. STOCKHOLM, 21 May 1992, *Two Women outside a Sunny Farmhouse* (oil on panel, 19 x 24 1/2 ins / 48 x 62 cm) SEK 7,700. PARIS, 26 Oct 1993, *Rue Lepic* (oil on canvas, 28 3/4 x 23 1/2 ins / 73 x 60 cm) FRF 20,000. NEUILLY, 12 Dec 1993, *Betty* (1932, oil on canvas, 32 x 25 1/2 ins / 81 x 65 cm) FRF 26,000. PARIS, 14 March 1994, *Unloading on the Banks of the Seine* (1923, watercolour and charcoal, 18 x 21 1/4 ins / 45.5 x 54 cm) FRF 4,500. CALAIS, 4 July 1999, *Breton Market* (oil on panel, 20 x 26 ins / 50 x 65 cm) FRF 14,000. PARIS, 13 Oct 2000, *Card Game* (oil on panel, 51 x 38 ins / 129

x 97 cm) FRF 11,500. PARIS, 13 Oct 2000, *Woman Reading* (oil on canvas, 51 x 38 ins / 130 x 97 cm) FRF 13,500.

JOUCLARD, Adrienne
French, 20th century.
Born 4 September 1882, in Onville (Meurthe-et-Moselle); died 1972.
Painter. Portraits, scenes with figures, sporting subjects, animals.

Adrienne Jouclard studied under Maurice Humbert at the École des Beaux-Arts in Paris. Technically accomplished, she also had a breadth of vision, execution and power that give her work an undeniable mastery. She was well-known among the women artists of the period, particularly for her dance scenes. She exhibited in Paris at the Salon des Artistes Français, receiving a commendation in 1908 and a bronze medal in 1911. She also exhibited at the Salon des Femmes Peintres, the Salon des Indépendants, the Salon d'Automne and the Salon des Tuileries. Jouclard took part in the *Le Trait* exhibition held by the Société de Gravure and in the Salon des Animaliers. She was awarded the Rosa Bonheur prize in 1914 and was made a Chevalier of the Légion d'Honneur. One of her pieces is kept at the city hall in Vienna.

MUSEUMS AND GALLERIES:
SAN FRANCISCO.

AUCTION RECORDS:
PARIS, 28 June 1923, *Chinese Figure Playing a Tambourine*, FRF 600. PARIS, 20 June 1944, *The Gardens of Versailles*, FRF 130. PARIS, 19 Dec 1944, *Harvest*, FRF 4,000. VERSAILLES, 25 Oct 1976, *Animals at Saint Julien-sur-Woevre* (oil on canvas, 18 x 24 ins / 46 x 61 cm) FRF 2,500. PARIS, 28 Feb 1985, *Boat* (print, 5 1/2 x 11 1/2 ins / 14 x 29 cm) FRF 10,000. PARIS, 28 Feb 1985, *Celebration under the Chestnut Trees* (oil on canvas, 36 1/2 x 51 1/4 ins / 93 x 130 cm) FRF 27,000. PARIS, 14 March 1988, *La Guinguette* (oil on canvas, 32 x 37 3/4 ins / 81.5 x 96 cm) FRF 6,800. VERSAILLES, 24 Sept 1989, *At the Circus: The Three Rigettis* (oil on card, 16 1/4 x 12 1/2 ins / 41 x 32 cm) FRF 4,200. VERSAILLES, 21 Jan 1990, *Villerey Road* (oil on canvas, 15 x 22 ins / 38 x 55 cm) FRF 5,300. PARIS, 17 June 1990, *Harvest Scene with Huts* (oil on canvas, 12 1/2 x 20 3/4 ins / 32 x 53 cm) FRF 5,000. METZ, 14 Oct 1990, *The Slide at Besançon* (oil on canvas, 13 x 18 ins / 33 x 45.5 cm) FRF 12,000. PARIS, 12 Feb 1991, *Summer* (oil on canvas, 28 3/4 x 39 1/4 ins / 73 x 100 cm) FRF 30,000; *Celebration at Lessy* (oil on canvas, 25 1/2 x 32 ins / 65 x 81 cm) FRF 21,000. PARIS, 27 April 1992, *Celebration at Bayonville* (oil on canvas, 21 1/4 x 25 1/2 ins / 54 x 65 cm) FRF 4,800. PARIS, 18 Nov 1992, *Burial of President Doumer* (oil on canvas, 36 1/4 x 28 3/4 ins / 92 x 73 cm) FRF 8,500; *Haymaking* (oil on canvas, 21 1/4 x 28 3/4 ins / 54 x 73 cm) FRF 7,000. PARIS, 14 March 1994, *Bedouin Women* (oil on canvas, 34 1/2 x 37 3/4 ins / 87.5 x 96 cm) FRF 15,000. PARIS, 2 Dec 1994, *Harvest at Guyancourt* (oil on canvas, 13 x 16 1/4 ins / 33 x 41 cm) FRF 5,000. PARIS, 13 March 1995, *Conversation in the Sunshine* (gouache, 18 x 23 1/2 ins / 46 x 60 cm) FRF 5,000. NANCY, 27 June 1999, *Basket of Cherry Plums* (oil on canvas, 26 x 36 ins / 66 x 91 cm) FRF 11,500. NANCY, 17 Oct 1999, *Harvest* (oil on canvas, 24 x 35 ins / 61 x 90 cm) FRF 22,000. PARIS, 3 April 2000, *Bedouin Women in Tunisia* (1921, distemper, 31 x 24 ins / 80 x 60 cm) FRF 15,000. PARIS, 12 May 2000, *Discussion* (gouache, 19 x 24 ins / 47 x 61 cm) FRF 15,000.

JOUDERVILLE, Isaac de, or Souderville
Flemish School, 17th century.
Born c. 1612, in Leiden; died c. 1645.
Painter. Portraits.

In 1632, Isaac de Jouderville was a student at the academy in Metz. In 1641 he went to Deventer and in 1643 to Amsterdam. He appears to have been a pupil of Rembrandt between 1627 and 1631. According to some biographers, he had two daughters who married Frédérick Moucheron and Julian Teniers.

BIBLIOGRAPHY:
Sumowski, Werner, *Gemälde der Rembrandt-Schuler*, PVA, Landau, 1983.

MUSEUMS AND GALLERIES:
DUBLIN: *Portrait of a Young Man*.

AUCTION RECORDS:
AMSTERDAM, 15 May 1979, *Portrait of a Young Man of Quality* (oil on panel, 14 1/4 x 13 1/2 ins / 36 x 34 cm) NLG 15,000. NEW YORK, 10 Oct 1990, *Portrait of a Bearded Man Wearing a Turban* (oil on panel, 18 3/4 x 14 1/4 ins / 47.7 x 36.2 cm) USD 14,300. PARIS, 12 Dec 1995, *Portrait of a Young Woman in Profile* (oil on panel, 15 3/4 x 12 1/2 ins / 40 x 31.5 cm) FRF 230,000. AMSTERDAM, 10 Nov 1997, *An Officer Standing in a Guardroom by a Staircase, a Helmet on a Barrel, a Shield, a Saddle, a Flag and a Bag on the Floor in the Foreground* (oil on panel, 25 x 18 3/4 ins / 63.5 x 47.7 cm) NLG 14,991. LONDON, 11 April 2002, *Portrait of a Young Man, Traditionally Called Rembrandt* (oil on paper/canvas, 11 x 10 ins / 29 x 25 cm) GBP 13,000. NEW YORK, 2 Oct 2002, *Portrait of a Man with a White Beard and Turban* (oil on panel, 19 x 14 ins / 48 x 36 cm) USD 10,000. VIENNA, 29 Sept 2004, *Portrait of a Young Man* (oil on canvas, 26 x 20 ins / 66 x 52 cm) EUR 560,000.

JOUENNE (Mme)
Maiden name: Bossey
Belgian, 19th century.
Active in Brussels during the first half of the 19th century.
Painter. Flowers.

JOUENNE, Alexandre
French, 20th century.
Born 8 July 1885, in Paris; died 1 June 1977.
Medallist, miniaturist.

Alexandre Jouenne studied under Gaillard. He was president of the Châtillon society of artists.

JOUENNE, Charles
French, 20th century.
Born 8 October 1877, in Paris; died during World War I, on the battlefield.
Engraver (wood).

Charles Jouenne studied under his father Léon Michel Marie Jouenne. He became a member of the Salon des Artistes Français in 1909, having received a commendation at the Salon in 1908.

JOUENNE, Léon
French, 20th century.
Born 2 December 1873, in Paris; died 23 May 1961, in Noyen-sur-Sarthe.
Engraver (wood).

Léon Jouenne studied under his father, Léon Michel Marie Jouenne and under Truphème and Tournay. He became a member of the Salon des Artistes Français in Paris in 1905, receiving a commendation in 1904, a bronze medal in 1908 and a gold medal in 1925. He was made a member of the engraving jury.

JOUENNE, Léon Michel Marie
French, 19th - 20th century.
Born 23 October 1845, in St-Hilaire-du-Harcouët (Manche); died 21 April 1912, in Châtillon.
Engraver (wood).

Léon Michel Marie Jouenne was the father of Alexandre Jouenne, Léon Jouenne and Charles Jouenne. He studied under Hanoteau and exhibited in Paris at the Salon des Artistes Français. He received a commendation in 1902.

JOUENNE, Michel
French, 20th century.
Born 25 January 1933, in Boulogne-Billancourt.
Painter. Landscapes, seascapes.

Michel Jouenne studied modelling at the studio of the sculptor Muguet before becoming a painter. Jouenne worked in the Aix-en-Provence area, following in the footsteps of Cézanne, and also in Corsica. He favours warm colours and thickly applied pigment. He exhibited at exhibitions in Paris, including various salons. He also showed his work in solo exhibitions, particularly at the Galerie Guigné in Paris; in 2003 at the Galerie Alexandre Léadouze in Paris, and in 2003 in the *Décalages Horaires* exhibition at the Galerie St-Hubert, Lyons.

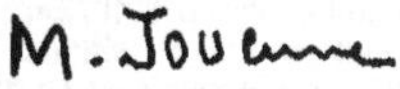

Auction records:
Paris, 21 May 1979, *Landscape* (oil on canvas, 29 1/4 x 39 1/4 ins / 74 x 100 cm) FRF 5,000. Versailles, 17 June 1987, *Road to the Farmhouse* (oil on canvas, 39 1/4 x 39 1/4 ins / 100 x 100 cm) FRF 17,000. Versailles, 15 May 1988, *Sunny Countryside* (oil on canvas, 21 1/4 x 28 1/2 ins / 54 x 72.5 cm) FRF 11,000. Paris, 23 June 1988, *Road with Almond Trees* (oil on canvas, 28 3/4 x 39 1/4 ins / 73 x 100 cm) FRF 16,500. Paris, 18 June 1989, *Red Vines* (oil on canvas, 25 1/2 x 36 1/4 ins / 65 x 92 cm) FRF 25,500. Versailles, 7 June 1990, *Corsican Village* (oil on canvas, 28 3/4 x 39 1/4 ins / 73 x 100 cm) FRF 30,000. Paris, 25 June 1990, *The Pond* (oil on canvas, 38 1/2 x 51 1/4 ins / 98 x 130 cm) FRF 100,000. Calais, 8 July 1990, *Little House with a Pink Roof* (oil on canvas, 43 1/4 x 43 1/4 ins / 110 x 110 cm) FRF 27,000. Paris, 7 Dec 1990, *Sunny Countryside* (oil on canvas, 21 1/4 x 28 1/2 ins / 54 x 72.5 cm) FRF 25,000. Le Touquet, 19 May 1991, *White Village* (oil on canvas, 39 1/4 x 39 1/4 ins / 100 x 100 cm) FRF 38,000. Calais, 7 July 1991, *Vineyards in Corbières* (oil on canvas, 21 1/4 x 28 3/4 ins / 54 x 73 cm) FRF 28,000. Paris, 18 March 1992, *Three Trees* (oil on canvas, 35 1/2 x 35 1/2 ins / 90 x 90 cm) FRF 25,500. Le Touquet, 30 May 1993, *Provence Landscape* (oil on canvas, 18 x 23 1/2 ins / 46 x 60 cm) FRF 22,000. Calais, 25 June 1995, *Village Church* (oil on canvas, 18 x 24 ins / 46 x 61 cm) FRF 8,100. Paris, 4 Nov 1997, *Pond with Flowers* (oil on canvas, 51 1/4 x 51 1/4 ins / 130 x 130 cm) FRF 20,000. Paris, 5 March 1998, *Mountain near Mouries* (oil on canvas, 32 x 39 1/4 ins / 81 x 100 cm) FRF 20,000. Calais, 23 May 1999, *Summer Landscape in Provence* (oil on canvas, 21 x 29 ins / 54 x 73 cm) FRF 16,500. Calais, 12 Dec 1999, *Road in the Guarrigue* (oil on canvas, 29 x 39 ins / 73 x 99 cm) FRF 35,500. Calais, 12 March 2000, *Church and Village of Zahara* (oil on canvas, 35 x 46 ins / 89 x 116 cm) FRF 40,000. Calais, 5 Nov 2000, *Market in Birmanie* (oil on canvas, 29 x 39 ins / 73 x 100 cm) FRF 34,000. Calais, 6 May 2001, *Road to Baux de Provence* (oil on canvas, 29 x 39 ins / 73 x 100 cm) FRF 42,000. Calais, 1 July 2001, *Alpilles Landscape* (oil on canvas, 29 x 39 ins / 73 x 100 cm) FRF 38,000. Calais, 7 July 2002, *Spring in Brittany* (oil on canvas, 29 x 39 ins / 73 x 100 cm) EUR 5,500. Calais, 15 Dec 2002, *Small Farm in Provence* (oil on canvas, 29 x 39 ins / 73 x 100 cm) EUR 5,000. Paris, 9 July 2003, *Lake* (oil on canvas, 39 x 39 ins / 100 x 100 cm) EUR 3,500. Calais, 9 Nov 2003, *Landscape in Provence* (oil on canvas, 35 x 35 ins / 90 x 90 cm) EUR 4,400. Calais, 30 May 2004, *Fishermen's Return* (oil on canvas, 29 x 39 ins / 73 x 100 cm) EUR 4,700. Calais, 4 July 2004, *Forest* (oil on canvas, 39 x 29 ins / 100 x 73 cm) EUR 2,000.

JOUENNE, Sylviane, known as Sylviane
French, 20th century.
Designer, illustrator. Stage sets, stage costumes.

Sylviane Jouenne studied at the École des Beaux-Arts in Paris. She has produced and collaborated on numerous stage sets, maquettes, costumes and masks for the ballets of Maurice Béjart. She also illustrates children's books and has exhibited at salons.

JOUET
French, 18th century.
Active in St-Calais (Sarthe) in 1725.
Sculptor. Statues.

Jouet is known to have sculpted a statue of *St Blaise* in the church at St-Calais (Sarthe).

JOUET, or Jouette
French, 18th century.
Painter. Still-lifes, flowers.

Jouet took part in the *Exposition de l'Académie* in 1719, and the *Exposition du Colisée* in 1797.

JOUET, Lambert, or Jonet
Flemish School, 17th century.
Active in Châtelet-sur-Sambre (Hainaut).
Painter.

Lambert Jouet was the son of Pierre Jouet. Between 1651 and 1665 he painted the high altar of the parish church in Châtelet.

JOUËT, Michel
French, 20th century.
Born 9 November 1943, in Cholet.
Painter, draughtsman, sculptor, engraver, mixed media.

Michel Jouët was attracted to art early on. From the start he applied himself to working on the geometric expression of abstract art which was itself, for some of its advocates, the mathematical representation of the world. His vocabulary is minimal, the line or metaphors of the line, his colours binary, black and white but worked in varied techniques. Michel Jouët creates series of works, on rhythms in 1962, optical games in 1967, superimposition of frameworks in 1969, repetitions of sequences of straight lines in 1969, random distribution of black and white rope segments in 1971, problems of the line from 1973 to 1975, craquelure in 1975, white strips on a black background in 1978 or on volume in 1986, cracks in a beam from 1980 to 1985, string in 1989 and more recently, monochrome marking and masking old figurative paintings. He also makes sculptures. His meticulous research is multiple, classed as conceptual by some people, and while it is not marked with even a toned down mysticism, it is certainly open to more casuistic than normative metaphysics. Principally through the line and repetition of its course, Michel Jouët makes us feel a new relationship with the world, and at the same time, the materiality of the work.

He has participated in group exhibitions such as: Salon des Arts, Cholet, 1971 and 1972; Galerie Argos, Nantes, 1972, with Morellet, Gorin, Seuphor, Del Pezzo and Peire. In 1973 he was selected for the international festival of contemporary art in Royan. After 1973 he refused to exhibit for 15 years in order to dedicate himself to research, projects and sketches. He started exhibiting again in 1987, and took part in many collective and thematic exhibitions on Art Construit and Neo-Constructivism, including: *Hommage à Pythagore* (*Homage to Pythagoras*), Galerie Carré Estampes, Luxembourg, 1989; *Arte Strucktura*, Milan, 1990; *Nouvelles Tendances de l'Art Construit* (*New Trends in Art Construit*), Galerie Denise René, Paris, 1991.

Solo exhibitions of his work include: Cholet, 1987; Galerie La Cour 21, Nantes, 1989; *Du Géométrique et du Conceptuel* (*Geometric and Conceptual*), Musée des Arts, Cholet, 1990; Galerie Quadri, Brussels, 1991; Galerie 42, Oldenburg, 1992; Foire International d'Art Contemporain (International Contemporary Art Fair), Paris, 1996.

Bibliography:
Fauchille, Bernard (preface), *De la nature des choses du géométrique au conceptuel*, exhibition catalogue, Musée des Arts, Cholet, 1990. Molnar, F. (preface), *Volupté ou austérité*, exhibition catalogue, Musée des Arts, Cholet, 1990.

JOUET, Pierre, or Jonet
Flemish School, 16th - 17th century.
Died 1638.
Active in Châtelet-sur-Sambre (Hainaut).
Painter.

Nothing is know of Pierre Jouet's birth place or whom he studied under, however in 1596 he had already acquired the title of 'master' in Châtelet. Jouet was a prolific artist, producing many works for the churches abbeys and castles of the Châtelet-sur-Sambre region. In 1621, he illustrated a manuscript for Dom Henri Velpen, abbot of the monastery at Aulne. This work, entitled *Life of the Blessed Lay Brother S Simon at the Abbey of Aulne*, was decorated with 52 pen and ink drawings. The Soleilmont Abbey at Gilly has a painting of St Lutgarde and Christ on the cross by the artist dated 1617. Which was destroyed in a fire in 1963. The chapel of St Roch in Châtelet has a picture of the death of St Roch dated 1634.

Bibliography:
Nihoul, Marcel, '*Une vie d'artiste au XVIe siècle. Le peintre Pierre Jouet*' in *Le Vieux Châtelet*, periodical, Châtelet, 1980.

JOUETT, Matthew
American, 19th century.
Born 22 April 1788, in Lafayette (North Carolina); died 10 August 1827, in Lexington (Kentucky).
Painter. Portraits.

Matthew Jouett had a reputation as a good painter in the western and southern USA.

Museums and Galleries:
New York: *Portrait of John Grimes*.

Auction records:
New York, 19 April 1968, *Portrait of John Brand*, USD 1,100.
New York, 11 April 1973, *Portrait of John Brand*, USD 1,600.
Raleigh, 5 Nov 1985, *Portrait of Arnold Harbach* (oil on panel, 26 1/2 x 21 1/2 ins / 67.5 x 54.8 cm) USD 5,000. New York, 6 June 1987, *Mr and Mrs Parsons* (oils on panel, a pair, 28 x 22 ins / 71.2 x 56 cm) USD 9,000. New York, 23 May 2000, *Portrait of Dr William Hall Richards* (oil on panel, 28 x 24 ins / 71 x 61 cm) USD 22,000. New York, 16 Jan 2001, *Portrait of Thomas Jefferson* (oil on panel, 29 x 24 ins / 74 x 60 cm) USD 40,000.

JOUETTE
French, 18th century.
Engraver.

Jouette was the wife of the painter and draughtsman Jouette. She engraved in the style of a pencil drawing.

JOUETTE
French, 18th century.
Painter, draughtsman.

Jouette was a member of the General Commission on the Arts in 1793. He may be the same artist as Jouet, who was active in Paris.

JOUETTE. See also **JOUET**

JOUFFROY, or Jauffroy, or Sauffrois
French, 18th century.
Painter. Portraits.

Jouffroy was perhaps the son of Pierre Jouffroy.

Museums and Galleries:
Amsterdam: *Portrait of a Man* (1767, oil) - Semur: *Portrait of the Marquis de Thiard* (1749).

Auction records:
Paris, 17 June 1983, *Portrait of Monsieur Jean-Baptiste Suster* (1762, oil/glass, 16 x 11 3/4in/40.5 x 30cm) FRF 12,000.

JOUFFROY, François
French, 19th century.
Born 1 February 1806, in Dijon; died 25 June 1882, in Laval (Mayenne).
Sculptor.

François Jouffroy was the son of a baker and at the age of 11 entered the École des Beaux-Arts in Dijon. At that time, the school was directed by Anatole Devosges and the teacher of sculpture was Nicolas Bornier. Following his success in obtaining the departmental prize he continued his studies in Paris.

He entered the École des Beaux-Arts on April 10 1824, gaining the second Prix de Rome in 1826 and the first in 1832. After his return to Rome in 1835 he regularly displayed his work in Salon exhibitions up till 1877 and quickly became one of the best sculptors of his generation.

He was awarded a second class medal in 1838, first class in 1839 and second class in 1848. In the same year he became a Chevalier of the Légion d'Honneur, a member of the Institute in 1857, an officer of the Légion d'Honneur in 1861 and a teacher at the École des Beaux-Arts in 1863. Jouffroy was, above all, an official sculptor and received an amazing number of commissions. Among his most important works it is worth including: *St Bernard* (marble statue in the church of Saint Genevieve), *St John* (statue for the St-Gervais church in Paris), *Monument to St Bernard* (Dijon), *Statue of Napoleon I* (Auxonne), *St Bernard* (stone statue on Napoleon III Square), *Punishment and Protection* (Palais de Justice), *Christ and his Twelve Apostles* (bas-reliefs on the façade of the church of St Augustine).

Museums and Galleries:
Dijon: *Disillusion*; *Erigone*; *Reverie*; *Gaspard Monge*; *Bonaparte 1st Consul*; *Death of Orion*; *Prometheus*; *Crowning of the Font at St-Germain l'Auxerrois*; *First Secret Confided to Venus*; *Philomela and Progneus*; *St Benedict*; *St Bruno*; *Louis Dietsch*.

JOUFFROY, Jean Pierre
French, 20th century.
Born 20 April 1933.
Painter, draughtsman, engraver, sculptor. Figures.

Jean Pierre Jouffroy is keen on trying new techniques and has been known to rework various subjects as line engravings, etchings and aquatints and then altuglass in order to assess the different effects. He draws a great deal but also paints and sculpts. His drawing style is lively and his representation allusive. He moves easily from the figurative to the abstract. In the post-war years, he exhibited on two occasions at the annual group exhibition of the École de Paris. He later exhibited at the Salon de Mai and Groupe 109 and at the major Paris galleries in 1954, 1956, 1957, 1958, 1959 and 1960. More recent exhibitions include: in 1972 *La Sphynge*; 1975 *L'Enlèvement des Sabines*; 1978 *L'Inventaire de Vénus*; 1980 *Delacroix, ses Filles et Fils*; 1982 *Figures Humaines* at the Sallaumines town hall (Pas-de-Calais). In 1983, he showed at the Centre Culturel de la Maison des Arts et Loisirs, Sochaux; in 1984 at the Maison de la Culture, Bourges; in 1986 at the Galerie Septentrion, Marcq-en-Barœul; and in 1987 at the Galerie Michèle Brouta, Paris. He was awarded the Pacquement prize in 1957.

Bibliography:
Fernàndez-Recatalà, Denis, *Jean-Pierre Jouffroy: anthropométries*, Le Temps des cerises, Pantin, 2000.

Museums and Galleries:
Paris (MNAM-CCI).

JOUFFROY, Marthe de
French, 19th century.

Born 19th century, in Paris.
Painter.
Marthe de Jouffroy's flower subjects were represented at the Salon de Paris from 1878-1879.

JOUFFROY, Pierre
French, 18th century.
Active from 1742 to 1786.
Painter. Mythological subjects, religious subjects, portraits. Glass painting.
A glass painter of the name of P. Jouffroy exhibited in London from 1765 to 1767 at the Free Society and the Society of Artists, and this may be the same artist as Pierre Jouffroy of Pontarlier. He worked about 1743 in Pontarlier (Doubs), where the church has an *Christ Appears* by him.
MUSEUMS AND GALLERIES:
VALENCIENNES: *Venus and Cupid*.
AUCTION RECORDS:
PARIS, 6 April 1976, *Young Woman Dressed as Diana* (fixed under glass) FRF 8,500. PARIS, 16 Nov 1990, *Rinaldo and Armida* (1750, oil on canvas, 54 x 77in/137 x 195.5cm) FRF 82,000. ROME, 26 Nov 1992, *Portrait of a Gentleman; Portrait of a Lady* (1786, oil on canvas, a pair, 25 1/2 x 21in/64.5 x 52.5cm) ITL 5,000,000. PARIS, 20 Dec 1993, *Portrait of Mademoiselle de Félix* (1774, oil on canvas, 26 x 22in/66 x 55cm) FRF 9,000. PARIS, 24 March 2004, *Portrait of Young Woman Holding Garland of Flowers* (1756, oil on canvas, 32 x 26 ins / 81 x 65 cm) EUR 3,500.

JOUFFROY, Pierre Henri
French, 20th century.
Born 21 September 1912, in Voujeaucourt (Doubs); died 11 October 2000.
Painter. Figures, portraits, landscapes, still-lifes.
Pierre Henri Jouffroy was a self-taught painter who lived and worked in his château at Belvoir. He painted domestic scenes in the manner of Le Nain and Courbet. He is known for his landcapes of the Doubs, Jura and Franche-Comté and also for his still-lifes which are often based on hunting themes. He exhibited from 1931 in Paris at the Salon des Indépendants and in 1935 and 1941 at the Salon d'Automne. He became a member of the Salon in 1938. He exhibited, again in Paris, at the Salon des Artistes Français in 1941, receiving a silver medal in 1942, a first gold medal and, in 1944, the critics' prize and the Prix Chardin in 1953.
AUCTION RECORDS:
PARIS, 25 May 1997, *Still-life with a Bag of Flour* (1951, oil on canvas, 32 x 39 1/4 ins / 81 x 100 cm) FRF 10,000. BESANÇON, 3 April 2004, *Still-life with Jug* (oil on canvas, 29 x 36 ins / 73 x 92 cm) EUR 2,300.

JOUHAN, René
French, 19th century.
Born 25 September 1835, in Angers.
Painter. Portraits, landscapes, still-lifes.
René Jouhan was a pupil of Ingres and was guided by Jules Joseph Dauban and Jean Michel Mercier. He was active at the Salon de Paris from 1870 to 1880. His portraits are elegant and strongly constructed, as are his landscapes, though the latter are more loosely constructed and highlighted with brush strokes of luminous colour.
MUSEUMS AND GALLERIES:
BREST: *Fruits in an Architectural Design* - DIEPPE: *Portrait of M. Durenty*.
AUCTION RECORDS:
PARIS, 29 March 1994, *Still-life with Fruit* (1866, oil on canvas, 38 1/4 x 51 1/4 ins / 97 x 130 cm) FRF 40,000.

JOUHANNEAU, Claude
French, 20th century.
Born 1 January 1931, in Tours.
Painter. Landscapes, still-lifes.
Claude Jouhanneau studied at the École des Beaux-Arts in Tours, the Académie de la Grande-Chaumière and the École des Arts Appliqués in Paris. His painting is characterised by a technique of sensually applied impasto and black and grey harmonies shot through with strident notes of colour. He has taken part in group exhibitions, including the Salon de la Jeune Peinture in Paris in 1959 and 1961, and at the Salon d'Automne in Paris in 1965 and 1967, of which he became a member in 1971. He has also held solo exhibitions at the Galerie Sisley in Brussels in 1967; at the Galerie du Haut Pavé in Paris in 1969; at Lons-le-Saunier in 1980; at Rambouillet in 1990; in Paris at the Galerie Espace 51 in 1992; and at the Musée de la Poste in Paris in 1996.

JOUHASSIN, C.
French, 19th century.
Active in Paris.
Painter.
C. Jouhassin received an honourable mention in Paris in 1887, a second class medal in Barcelona and a bronze medal in the Exposition Universelle of 1900.

JOUHAUD, Léon
French, 20th century.
Born 1874, in Limoges; died 1950.
Painter, pastellist, designer. Genre scenes, landscapes, still-lifes.
In 1910, Léon Jouhaud began exhibiting at the Salon of the Société des Artistes Indépendants and the Salon of the Société des Artistes Français in Limoges and Paris, showing pastel landscapes and paintings on enamel (genre scenes, decorative and still-lifes).
MUSEUMS AND GALLERIES:
PARIS (Mus. des Arts décoratifs).

JOUI
Flemish School, 17th century.
Painter. History painting.
According to Siret, Joui is not mentioned in any biography; his name appears in Spanish catalogues. He may be the same as the artist Gouwi or Gow (Jacob Peter).

JOUILLAT, Jean Michel
French, 20th - 21st century.
Born c. 1959.
Painter.
AUCTION RECORDS:
LA VARENNE-ST-HILAIRE, 6 March 1988, *Forgotten Moment* (oil on canvas, 25 1/2 x 39 1/4 ins / 65 x 100 cm) FRF 6,500.

JOUIN, Jacques
French, 17th century.
Active in Le Mans in 1693.
Painter.

JOUKOVSKI, Pavel Vassiliévitch von
German, 19th - 20th century.
Born 1845, in Frankfurt am Main; died 26 August 1912, in Weimar.
Painter.
Symbolism.
Pavel Vassiliévitch von Joukovski was the son of Vassili Andreevitch Joukovski. He painted portraits of members of the family of Richard Wagner in Bayreuth. He took part in the staging of the first performance of *Parsifal*.
MUSEUMS AND GALLERIES:
ST PETERSBURG (Gosudarstvennyj Russkij Muz.): *Virgin near the Body of Christ; St Cecilia;* other works.

JOULIN, Lucien
French, 19th century.
Born 20 September 1842, in Paris.
Painter.

Lucien Joulin was represented at the Paris Salon with still life and genre subjects from 1865 to 1878.
AUCTION RECORDS:
PARIS, 25 April 1947, *Still-life with Fruit*, FRF 650.

JOULLAIN. See also **JOLLAIN**

JOULLAIN, François
French, 18th century.
Born 1697, in Paris; died 5 October 1778, in Paris.
Engraver (etching, burin), watercolourist (?). Religious subjects, mythological subjects, figures, portraits, nudes, scenes with figures, rustic scenes, costumes.

According to Mariette, François Joullain was a pupil of Gillot, which seems all the more likely since the numerous reproductions he executed after this master marvellously preserve Gillot's style. He may also have received advice from Laurent Cars. Joullain engraved after Watteau: *The Pleasures of Summer*, after Nicolas Lancret: *The Pleasures of the Countryside, The Pastoral Concert* and *Rustic Recreation*, after Gillot, the delightful costumes: *Man of Quality in Evening Dress, Woman of Quality in a Ball Gown, Another Woman of Quality in a Ball Gown, Italian Abbot, Woman of Quality, Man of Quality, Faces of Actors*, 14 pieces, *Series of Costumes*, six pieces in the vertical, *New Costume Designs for Use in Ballets, Operas*, a series of 94 numbered pieces, *Adolescence, Virility, Childhood, Old Age*, four pieces. However, he was above all the engraver of Charles-Antoine Coypel, after whom he executed: *The Annunciation of the Virgin Mary, Ecce Homo, Jesus Placed in the Tomb, History of the Italian Theatre*, 18 plates under the title *Subjects Drawn from the Comedies of Molière*, six plates under the title *The Adventures of Don Quixote*, 25 plates, in collaboration with Cochin, Ravenet, Surugue and Tardieu, *Rinaldo Abandoning Armida, Cyrus Consulting Daniel, Aymon I* and *The Card Houses*. He also engraved after Cabari two plates from the Crozat collection, the *Portrait of François Desportes*, by himself. Three watercolours in the name of Joullain appear in the catalogue of an auction sale in Paris on 3 April 1909: *Young Woman Seated*, FRF 175, *Young woman on a Bed*, FRF 31, and *Female Nude on a Cushion*, FRF 60. These works could perhaps be by François Joullain.
AUCTION RECORDS:
PARIS, 18 March 1998, *Georges Dandin; M de Pourceaugnac; The School for Wives; The Learned Women* (engraving, four works in the same frame after Coypel, 10¼ x 12½in/26 x 32cm) FRF 2,800. NEW YORK, 27 Jan 1999, *Head and Shoulders of Male Nude* (red and black chalk heightened with white chalk, 18 x 14 ins / 46 x 36 cm) USD 2,500. PARIS, 30 March 2004, *Female Nudes* (black crayon/red chalk, a pair, 8 x 11 ins / 21 x 29 cm) EUR 1,800.

JOULLAIN, Jean
French, 17th century.
Active in Angers.
Sculptor.

Jean Joullain was commissioned by the city of Angers to execute statues to be placed on the St-Aubin Gate on the occasion of the solemn entry into the city of Louis XIII and Marie de Médicis in 1614.

JOULLIN, Amedee
American, 19th - 20th century.
Born 13 June 1862, in San Francisco; died 3 February 1917.
Painter. Figures.

Amedee Joullin began his art education at the San Francisco Art Institute, before going to Paris where he studied under Bouguereau and Robert-Fleury. He later attended the École des Beaux-Arts. He painted mostly Native Americans.
AUCTION RECORDS:
SAN FRANCISCO, 21 June 1984, *Squaw Weaving* (oil on canvas, 18 x 24 ins / 46 x 61 cm) USD 4,000. NEW YORK, 12 March 1992, *Mexican Peasant Girl* (1912, oil on canvas, 24 x 30 ins / 61 x 76 cm) USD 4,620.

JOULLIN, Lucile Wilcox, married name Benjamin
American, 20th century.
Born 6 August 1876, in Genesee (Illinois); died 1924, in San Francisco.
Painter. Landscapes, figures.

Lucile Wilcox Joullin attended the Art Institutes in Chicago and San Francisco before studying in Paris, where she took part in the Salon des Artistes Français in 1908. She married her former tutor Amédée Joullin in 1907, and after his death in 1917, she married Edward H. Benjamin. She was known for her paintings of the Native Americans of New Mexico.
MUSEUMS AND GALLERIES:
SAN FRANCISCO (Bohemian Club): *Algerian Slave*.

JOULY, Hugues
French, 14th century.
Born to a family originally from Bourges.
Sculptor.

Jouly was invited to work in Riom by John, Duke of Berry, who commissioned him to sculpt the portal of the château chapel. He was deputy master of works under Guy de Dammartin.

JOUMARD, Germaine
French, 20th century.
Painter.

After a career as a painter of portraits of women and children and a painter of birds, in the 1950s Germaine Joumard became known for a series of paintings she produced from the first negatives obtained using an electron microscope. This made it possible to rise well above a magnification of 2000 to one in the order of 150,000, a new world of microphotography under polarized lights.

JOUMARD, Véronique
French, 20th - 21st century.
Born 1964, in Grenoble.
Installation artist.

Véronique Joumard lives and works in Paris. In her pared-down theatre sets basic physical phenomena survive, mainly linked to light, energy, electricity or sound. Taking into account the visitor's body Véronique Joumard installs a wall covered in heat-sensitive paint like a wall picture that takes on the imprint caused by human body heat. Fascinated by the light, she renders it in a thousand styles as with the glaring 44,000 watt *Ligne de lumières* (*Line of Lights*). A DIY digital clock counts down time at the frenetic rhythm of a thousandth of a second. Through her work Véronique Joumard encourages people to look at things and events and their interconnection with new, misplaced eye. Several ladders fixed to the walls at the exhibition at FRAC Languedoc-Roussillon's La Galerie in 1999 invite the spectator to climb them to select new vantage points. Her installation at the Galerie Cent8 in 2001 deforms reality and the spectators' image by means of convex surveillance mirrors.

She has taken part in collective exhibitions including: *Comme Rien d'Autre que des Rencontres* (*Like Nothing Other than Meetings*), MuHKA, Antwerp, 1994, where she showed a magnetic and gravitational environment; Artissima, Contemporary Art Fair, Turin, 2000; *De Concert, Œuvres d'une Collection Privée* (*In Unison, Works from a Private Collection*), Loire area FRAC, Carquefou, 2002. Solo exhibitions include: Le Consortium, Dijon, 1993; *Le Bel Aujourd'hui* (*The Beautiful Today*), Institut d'Art Contemporain, Villeurbanne, 1997; FRAC Franche-Comté, Musée des

Beaux-Arts, Dole, 1997; FRAC Languedoc-Roussillon at La Galerie de Montpellier, 1999; Galerie Cent8, Paris, 2000; Shizuola Stadium Ecopa, Fukuroi City, Japan, 2001; FRAC Lorraine, Metz, 2001; Le Parvis, Centre d'Art Contemporain, Ibos, 2002; Galerie Cent8-Serge Le Borgne, Paris, 2003.

BIBLIOGRAPHY:

Parsy, Paul-Hervé, *Sylvia Bossu, Yves Brochard, Claude Darras, Véronique Joumard, Marylène Negro, Véronique Verstraete*, exhibition catalogue, Centre national des arts plastiques, Paris, 1988. Douroux, Xavier/Chavanne, Blandine/Dary, Anne/Joumard, Véronique, *Véronique Joumard. Œuvres 1985-1998*, travelling exhibition catalogue, Le Consortium, Dijon, Fonds régional d'Art contemporain du Languedoc-Roussillon, Montpellier, Temps réel, Dijon, 1998.

MUSEUMS AND GALLERIES:

DÔLE (FRAC Franche-Comté): *Suns, Moons* (1993).

JOUNEAU, Prosper

French, 19th century.
Born 19th century, in Parthenay (Deux-Sèvres).
Sculptor.

Prosper Jouneau was a former Resident of the town of Niort and a pupil of A. Dumont. He exhibited at the Salon de Paris with busts and fantasy subjects from 1874 gaining an honourable mention in 1876. He became director of the École des Beaux-Arts in Montpelier.

JOUNI, Hassan

Lebanese, 20th century.
Born 1942, in Roumin.
Painter. Figure compositions, figures.

Hassan Jouni studied painting in the Fuster Academy in Valencia, Spain. In 1970 he taught drawing at the San Fernando Institute in Madrid. In 1971 he joined the staff of the University of Lebanon, where he became head of the department of drawing and painting.

He showed work in group exhibitions: in Damascus in 1971; Mannheim, 1972; Kuwait, 1972-1973; at the Sursock Museum in 1974, 1982 and 1988; at the Alexandria Biennale in 1974; at the São Paulo Biennale where he showed a painting, *Migrants from the South*, in 1975; Baghdad, 1985; and Paris also in 1985. His solo exhibitions included those at: Dar el Fan in 1971, 1972; at the Contact Gallery, 1974, 1975; at the Spanish Cultural Centre in 1973, 1980, and 1981; at the Meridian Hotel in Kuwait in 1982; at the Hilton Hotel in Kuwait in 1982, 1984 and 1988; and at the Al Munda Gallery in 1987.

BIBLIOGRAPHY:

Liban. Le Regard des peintres. 200 ans de peinture libanaise, exhibition catalogue, Institut du Monde Arabe, Paris, 1989.

JOUNIEAU, Alfred Aimé

French, 19th century.
Died 1896.
Active in Paris.
Sculptor.

Alfred Aimé Jounieau was a member of the Société des Artistes Français and was represented at the Salon as part of this group.

JOURDAIN, Al, known as Aljourdain

French, 20th century.
Born 15 March 1920, in Paris.
Painter, illustrator. Figures, portraits.

Aljourdain exhibited in Europe and the USA. She took her inspiration from the Far East, the Primitives and from modern trends. She specialised in portraits of society ladies.

JOURDAIN, Auguste

French, 19th century.
Born 19th century, in Paris.
Engraver.

Auguste Jourdain collaborated on the journal *Illustration*, producing engravings of reproductions of the masters which are worthy of note. He exhibited at the Salon from 1863.

JOURDAIN, Francis

French, 20th century.
Born 2 November 1876, in Paris; died 31 December 1958.
Painter, designer, engraver. Genre scenes, nudes, landscapes, gardens, still-lifes. Designs (wallpapers/fabrics), designs for stained glass, theatre decoration.
Art Deco.

Francis Jourdain was the son of the writer, art critic and architect Franz Jourdain. He studied painting and colour engraving under Henri C. Guérard, and worked in the evenings at the studio of Eugène Carrière. He also studied under Albert Besnard and collaborated with him for three months on the decoration of the chapel of the Berck hospice. He took part in exhibitions of the Société Nationale des Beaux-Arts and was made an associate member of the Society. With his father - for many years the president - he was one of the founder members of the Salon d'Automne. He collaborated on the magazine *Les Cahiers d'Aujourd'hui*. He was interested in both decorative art and pure art and built furniture and designed wallpaper, fabric and stained glass. He was a supporter of rationalism against Modern Style. At the Exposition Universelle of 1900, he decorated the theatre of the dancer Loïe Fuller. Jourdain also produced colour engravings and paintings of gardens. In 2001, the Musée d'Art et d'Industrie in Roubaix held an exhibition of Jourdain's work.

BIBLIOGRAPHY:

Gonzalez, Sylvie, '*Francis Jourdain. Un parcours moderne*' in *Nouvelles de l'Estampe*, periodical, Bibliothèque nationale de France, Paris, 2000.

MUSEUMS AND GALLERIES:

ROUEN (MBA).

AUCTION RECORDS:

PARIS, 23 April 1925, *The Bath*, FRF 475. PARIS, 1 July 1943, *Capuchin Nuns* (1912) FRF 1,200. PARIS, 24 April 1947, *Seashore Landscape*, FRF 2,100. PARIS, 9 Nov 1990, *Still-life with Flowers and Fruit* (1906, oil on canvas, 25 1/2 x 19 3/4 ins / 65 x 50 cm) FRF 17,000. PARIS, 24 June 1991, *Open Window by a Desk* (1905, gouache, 5 x 6 3/4 ins / 13 x 17 cm) FRF 3,590. PARIS, 20 Nov 1994, *Woman against a Multi-coloured Background* (pastel/card, 39 1/4 x 25 1/4 ins / 100 x 64 cm) FRF 11,500. PARIS, 22 Feb 1995, *Back View of Female Nude* (pastel/card, 24 x 20 ins / 61 x 51 cm) FRF 17,000. PARIS, 18 March 1996, *Still-life on a Persian Background* (1910, oil on canvas, 37 1/2 x 31 1/2 ins / 95 x 80 cm) FRF 37,000. PARIS, 15 Aug 2000, *Portrait of a Woman on a Blue Background* (pastel, 26 x 21 ins / 65 x 53 cm) FRF 22,000. PARIS, 15 Aug 2000, *Woman on a Blue Background* (pastel and collage, 36 x 28 ins / 91 x 72 cm) FRF 22,000. PARIS, 22 June 2001, *Vase of Flowers in the Studio* (1905, 7 x 5 ins / 17 x 13 cm) FRF 11,500. PARIS, 25 Oct 2001, *Bay of St-Tropez* (1908, oil on canvas, 21 x 29 ins / 54 x 73 cm) FRF 15,000.

JOURDAIN, François

French, 18th century.
Active in Besançon from 1738 to 1755.
Portrait painter.

François Jourdain was the father of Laurent Bruno François Jourdain.

JOURDAIN, Henri

French, 19th - 20th century.
Born 1864 or 1865, in Paris; died August 1931, in Paris.
Painter, watercolourist, illustrator. Landscapes.

According to the *Annuaire de la Curiosité*, Henri Jourdain exhibited in Paris at the Salon of the Société Nationale des Beaux-Arts and the Salon des Artistes Français. He is known for his watercolours and drawings. Works illustrated by him include Flaubert's *Madame Bovary, Monsieur des Lourdines* by A. de Chateaubriand and Daudet's *Letters from my Windmill.*

AUCTION RECORDS:

PARIS, 20-22 May 1920, *St-Cloud* (watercolour) FRF 280. PARIS, 4 Nov 1924, *Outside the Château* (watercolour) FRF 950. PARIS, 17-18 June 1927, *Mortmoulin* (watercolour) FRF 500. PARIS, 7 May 1943, *Sea Shore* (charcoal, heightened with pastels) FRF 700. PARIS, 4 Dec 1944, *Outer Wall on the Banks of the Loire,* FRF 2,900. VERSAILLES, 26 March 1972, *Windmill in Moonlight* (oil on canvas, 21 1/4 x 28 1/4 ins / 54 x 72 cm) FRF 650. PARIS, 22 Jan 1988, *View of Paris and Notre Dame* (watercolour and gouche, 9 x 12 3/4 ins / 22 x 32.5 cm) FRF 3,100. RHEIMS, 22 Oct 1989, *Winter Landscape* (oil on panel, 19 3/4 x 25 1/2 ins / 50 x 65 cm) FRF 3,000. BERN, 12 May 1990, *Winter Landscape* (watercolour and gouache, tondo, diam. 21 ins / 53.5 cm) CHF 900. NEW YORK, 15 Oct 1991, *Afternoon at a Rustic House in France* (watercolour/canvas, 19 1/4 x 23 1/2 ins / 49 x 59.8 cm) USD 935.

JOURDAIN, Jules
Belgian, 19th - 20th century.
Born 30 December 1873, in Namur.
Active in Brussels.
Sculptor.

Jules Jourdain featured in the Exposition de Bruxelles of 1910.

JOURDAIN, Laurent Bruno François
French, 18th - 19th century.
Born 6 October 1745, in Besançon; died 18 April 1815, in Besançon.
Painter. Religious subjects, portraits.

Laurent Bruno François Jourdain painted canvases for numerous churches in the Besançon region, and also some portraits. He exhibited a *Study of a Head* at the Salon of 1802.

JOURDAIN, Philippon
French, 14th century.
Active in Poitiers.
Sculptor.

Jourdain worked on the decoration of the château belonging to John, Duke de Berry, in Poitiers in 1383.

JOURDAIN, Pierre Gaston
French, 19th century.
Born 19th century, in Villeneuve-l'Archevêque (Yonne).
Active in Paris.
Painter, illustrator.

Pierre Jourdain was a pupil of S. Cornu in Paris and his works appeared at the Salon in 1866, 1870 and 1872. From 1877 to 1881 his genre paintings were seen and in 1875, the painting *Attack on the Redoubt of Montretout on 19th January 1871.*

JOURDAIN, Roger Joseph
French, 19th - 20th century.
Born 11 December 1845, in Louviers; died 19 August 1918, in Paris.
Painter, watercolourist. Genre scenes, landscapes.

Roger Joseph Jourdain studied under Cabanel, Chabanne and Pils and first exhibited at the Salon de Paris in 1869. He became a member of the Société des Artistes Français in 1883 and received a bronze medal in 1879, a silver medal in 1881 and a silver medal at the Exposition Universelle of 1889. He was made a Chevalier of the Légion d'Honneur in 1889 and received a bronze medal at the Exposition Universelle of 1900.

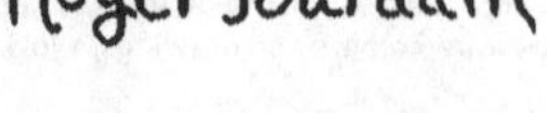

MUSEUMS AND GALLERIES:

CHÂTEAU-THIERRY: *Japanese Fantasy* - LOUVIERS: *Gladiator.*

AUCTION RECORDS:

PARIS, 1880, *The Telegram,* FRF 360. PARIS, 27 Feb 1893, *An Accident* (watercolour) FRF 175. PARIS, 12-15 April 1899, *Group of Trees at St-Cossin near Cannes* (watercolour) FRF 200. PARIS, 27 Feb 1909, *The Footbridge,* FRF 170. PARIS, 7 and 8 March 1911, *The Carpet Bazaar in Cairo,* FRF 550. PARIS, 12 March 1911, *La Herse* FRF 135. PARIS, 4 March 1926, *The Model's Advice,* FRF 200. PARIS, 27 March 1947, *Two Women Towing a Barge,* FRF 1,600. NEW YORK, 15 Dec 1978, *Travellers Under Attack* (oil on canvas, 28 1/2 x 23 1/2 ins / 72.5 x 59.5 cm) USD 3,750. LONDON, 24 March 1982, *The Fortune Teller* (oil on canvas, 19 x 24 ins / 48.5 x 61 cm) GBP 4,500. NEW YORK, 28 Oct 1986, *Woman Dreaming in a Boat* (oil on canvas, 23 3/4 x 28 3/4 ins / 60.3 x 73 cm) USD 12,000. NEW YORK, 22 May 1991, *Sunday at La Grande Jatte* (oil on canvas, 37 x 61 ins / 94 x 154.9 cm) USD 143,000. NEW YORK, 20 Feb 1992, *Towing the Dinghy* (oil on canvas, 36 3/4 x 60 ins / 93.3 x 152.4 cm) USD 35,750. NEW YORK, 16 Feb 1995, *Before Lunch* (oil on canvas, 26 3/4 x 32 ins / 67.9 x 81 cm) USD 20,700. LONDON, 17 March 1995, *The Boat Shed* (oil on canvas, 32 x 43 3/4 ins / 81 x 111 cm) GBP 20,125.

JOURDAIN, Tanguin
French, 17th century.
Born 1626, in Brest (Finistère); died 1651; buried on 23 May in Paris.
Wood carver.

JOURDAIN-LEMOINE, André
French, 20th century.
Born 1879, in Paris; died 1918, in Rheims, reported missing 29 May.
Painter. Landscapes, still-lifes.

André Jourdain-Lemoine exhibited in Paris at the Salon des Indépendants.

AUCTION RECORDS:

PARIS, 25 Oct 1978, *Woman Making Her Toilette* (1910, oil on canvas, 32 1/4 x 24 ins / 82 x 61 cm) FRF 10,000. LONDON, 2 April 1981, *Woman at Her Toilette* (1910, oil on canvas, 31 1/2 x 24 ins / 80 x 61 cm) GBP 2,300.

JOURDAN (Mme)
French, 18th century.
Active in Paris.
Engraver (burin).

Mme Jourdan engraved subjects from everyday life, after Boucher, and plates for an *Illustrated Journey in Switzerland.*

JOURDAN, Adolphe
French, 19th century.
Born 4 August 1825, in Nîmes; died 1889.
Painter. Portraits, genre scenes.

Adolphe Jourdan entered the École des Beaux-Arts on April 3 1844 and worked in the studio of Jalabert. He was awarded medals in 1864 and 1866 and displayed genre subjects and portraits at the Salon de Paris from 1855. He also exhibited in New York in 1876.

MUSEUMS AND GALLERIES:

NÎMES: *Fisherman* - TOLEDO, OH: *The First Step.*

AUCTION RECORDS:

PARIS, 3 April 1879, *Girl Getting out of the Bath,* FRF 980. PARIS, 16 and 17 May 1892, *Love's Secrets,* FRF 125. PARIS, 20 Nov 1900, *Woman Bathing,* FRF 170. NEW YORK, 17 Jan 1902, *Love's Secrets,* USD 470. PARIS, 12 May 1919, *Head of a Young Woman,* FRF 550. LONDON, 20 June 1979, *Nymph* (1870, oil on canvas, 28 3/4 x 45 ins / 73 x 114 cm) GBP 1,300. LONDON, 22 June 1983, *Nymph on the Shore* (1870, oil on canvas, 28 3/4 x 45 ins / 73 x 114 cm) GBP 3,800. TORONTO, 30 Nov 1988, *Innocence* (oil on canvas, 53 1/2 x 34 ins / 136 x 86.5 cm) CAD 30,000. NEW YORK, 24 Oct 1990, *Mother Love* (oil on canvas, 40½ x 32¾ ins / 102.8 x 83.2 cm) USD 35,200. AMSTERDAM, 5-6 Nov 1991, *Flower Seller* (1845, oil on canvas, 22 x 15¾ ins / 56 x 40 cm) NLG 11,500. PARIS, 10 Feb 1993, *Romantic Scene* (oil on canvas) FRF 125,000. PARIS, 31 May 2001, *Nymphs and Satyrs* (oil on canvas, 51 x 26 ins / 130 x 65 cm) FRF 110,000. LILLE, 21 Oct 2001, *Elegant Woman in an Interior* (oil on canvas, 41 x 28 ins / 104 x 70 cm) FRF 17,000. WASHINGTON, 13 Dec 2003, *Mother and Child* (oil on canvas, 47 x 36 ins / 119 x 91 cm) USD 32,000.

JOURDAN, Étienne
French, 17th - 18th century.
Active in Grenoble at the end of the 17th century and at the beginning of the 18th century.
Sculptor.

Étienne Jourdan sculpted a door in the house of the Oratorians and, in 1693, executed a ceiling for the Chambre des Comptes.

JOURDAN, Étienne
French, 18th century.
Active in Paris in 1785.
Engraver (line-engraving).

JOURDAN, Félix
French, 20th century.
Born 1890; died 31 March 1971.
Painter. Landscapes.

Félix Jourdan was a friend of Jules Flandrin and was influenced by him. He took part in the *150 Ans de Peinture Dauphinoise* (*150 Years of Painting from the Dauphiné Region*) exhibition at the Château de la Condamine, Corenc Town Hall in 1980.

JOURDAN, Félix Désiré Joseph
French, 19th century.
Born 17 November 1818, in La Rochelle; died 20 August 1896, in Vivonne (Vienne).
Painter (including gouache).

MUSEUMS AND GALLERIES:
LA ROCHELLE: a gouache.

JOURDAN, Jacques Jean Raoul
French, 20th century.
Born 22 June 1880, in Paris; died 25 March 1916, on the battlefield, near Verdun.
Painter. Portraits.

Jacques Jean Raoul Jourdan studied under Gabriel Ferrier. He became a member of the Salon des Artistes Français in Paris in 1907. He also exhibited at the Salon of the Société Nationale des Beaux-Arts in Paris.

AUCTION RECORDS:
PARIS, 20 Nov 1942, *Two Vases of Flowers*, FRF 1,150. NEW YORK, 26 May 1993, *Afternoon Tea* (oil on canvas, 65 x 73 ins / 165.1 x 185.4 cm) USD 11,500. PARIS, 5 July 2000, *Souk in Tunis* (oil on canvas, 27 x 22 ins / 68 x 57 cm) FRF 14,000.

JOURDAN, Louis
French, 20th century.
Born 7 March 1872, in Bourg-en-Bresse; died 3 May 1948, in Paris.
Painter. Landscapes.

Louis Jourdan signed his work *L. Jourdan*. He studied art by visiting the Musée de Lyon when the need to earn a living made it impossible for him to attend the art academies. He painted nature, basing his approach solely on what he had learned from the masters in the museum, and produced sensitive landscapes of the Bresse and Dombes regions, often choosing to show them at night or in twilight. His paintings include *Twilight and Morning Mists*, Lyons 1898; *Evening*, Lyons 1899; *The Saraband* and *Edge of the Wood*, Lyons 1902, for which he received a medal; *Stormy Evening*, Paris 1907, commended; and *The Road to the Pond at Verfey*, Paris 1910. He exhibited in Lyons from 1891 and in Paris from 1900, notably at the Salon des Artistes Français. He was awarded a gold medal, declared *hors concours* and received the Rosa Bonheur prize in 1914.

BIBLIOGRAPHY:
Deshairs, Léon, *Louis Jourdan*, Chelles, 1951. *Louis Jourdan 1872-1948. Peintre de la Dombes*, Musée de Brou, Bourg-en-Bresse, 1989.

MUSEUMS AND GALLERIES:
BOURG-EN-BRESSE (Mus. de Brou): *Oxen at Verfey Pond*.

AUCTION RECORDS:
PARIS, 19 Nov 1992, *The Great Tree* (1933, oil on card, 25½ x 36¼ ins / 65 x 92 cm) FRF 7,500. PARIS, 30 March 2004, *Brittany* (oil on canvas, 49 x 76 ins / 125 x 192 cm) EUR 4,200.

JOURDAN, Pierre
French, 17th century.
Born in Vaulnaveys (Isère); died 1690, in Grenoble.
Wood carver.

From 1664 to 1683, Pierre Jourdan executed retables and tabernacles for the churches of the Jesuits and Jacobins in Grenoble, and for the Carthusian monastery at Durbon. He also worked for Bishop Étienne le Camus at the bishop's palace.

JOURDAN, Prosper Émile Marie
French, 19th - 20th century.
Born 30 July 1860, in Vannes; died 28 December 1931, in Quimperlé.
Painter, watercolourist. , figures, portraits, landscapes, landscapes with figures, urban landscapes, seascapes, still-lifes.
School of Pont-Aven.

From 1880 to 1886, Prosper Émile Marie Jourdan studied at the École des Beaux-Arts in Paris under William Bouguereau and Tony Robert-Fleury. He also studied at the Académie Julian where he was elected 'student in charge' of his studio. In 1883, he made a trip to Algeria. In 1886 or 1888, he went to Pont-Aven where he became friends with Henry Moret, Ernest de Chamaillard, Charles Laval and Émile Bernard and met Paul Gauguin. In 1891, on a journey to Finland, his boat was shipwrecked off Riga and he remained there for some months. He moved back to Pont-Aven in 1892 with his wife and lived in a house adjoining the Kerluen studio rented by Henry Moret, Émile Bernard and Paul Gauguin. He was visited there by Maurice Denis in 1905. The death of his mother in 1907 was a financial help to Jourdan, but eventually resulted in him leading a poverty-stricken existence. From 1911 to 1920 he led a nomadic life in Brittany, staying with artists such as Maurice Asselin and Jacques Vaillant, and with the writers Roland Dorgelès and Pierre Mac-Orlan. He produced little work. From 1920 to 1930, he led a solitary life and in 1931 succumbed perhaps to alcoholism and certainly to poverty, dying alone at the Quimperlé hospice.

Jourdan's chaotic existence was in many ways typical of the bohemian artist and in his case ended with belated recognition among art lovers and the public, after several decades of neglect. He did little during his lifetime to promote his own success and produced relatively little work, to the despair of his handful of patrons. Stylistically, at Pont-Aven and Le Pouldu he was a faithful follower of Gauguin. Pont-Aven, famous for the school of that name, owed its reputation to the fact that between 1886 and 1896 it became home to some 20 artists, including Émile Bernard, and Gauguin, with whom it is most closely associated. Jourdan mixed with these artists and even worked in Gauguin's studio. However, unlike other artists, and Gauguin in particular, Jourdan remained in Pont-Aven and the surrounding area for 43 years and continued to paint there at his own pace. Originally a traditional figurative artist in a realist and naturalist vein - and an unrivalled draughtsman - he first came under the influence of Impressionism, retaining its touch and its concern with the depiction of light through colour until 1892 (as in *Rue de Concarneau, Pont-Aven*). However, from 1895 new elements began to enter his work.

Biographical information about Jourdan is scarce, and only a handful of paintings from the period between 1888 and 1896 are known to us, as many of his works are undated. Nevertheless, his style developed and changed. Jourdan defines the planes of his compositions clearly, separating them with outlines. He also begins to work with expanses of colour, juxtaposing bright shades (as in *Fishing Boats in the Port of Brigneau*), and in some paintings unlocks perspective by shortening it, if only timidly, as in *Trémalo Chapel*. However, he was far from adopting the 'synthetist' approach, his subjects generally remaining inspired by reality treated in a naturalist and narrative way. It is this duality that characterises Jourdan's endearing style. His fishermen at work, his peasants exposed to the harsh climate of Brittany, his portraits of men and women represented with restraint and simplicity, all display a respect for their subjects. However, works such as *The Red Road, Trémalo Chapel, Threshing* (1915) and *The River Aven at Le Hénant* (1926) seem inspired by more spiritual and poetic considerations rather than strict naturalism. They display a sense of the decorative and an unusual use of colour. Jourdan also tackled less conventional and even amusing subjects in works such as *Loft Scene* and *Still-life with Rats*.

Jourdan had always refused to show his work at salons and exhibitions or at art dealers' galleries, and it did not become known until 1946 when it was shown in retrospective exhibitions devoted to the School of Pont-Aven. These include *Pont-Aven Gauguin et ses Amis* (*Pont-Aven Gauguin and his Friends*), Paris 1951; *Hommage à Sérusier et aux Peintres du Groupe de Pont-Aven* (*Homage to Sérusier and to the Painters of the Pont-Aven Group*), Pont-Aven 1958; *Gauguin and the Pont-Aven School*, London 1966; *Gauguin und sein Kreis in der Bretagne* (*Gaugin and His Circle in Brittany*), Zurich 1966; *Rétrospective de Pont-Aven aux Nabis* (*Retrospective from Pont-Aven to the Nabis*), Paris 1971; and *Autour de Gauguin à Pont-Aven* (*Around Gauguin at Pont-Aven*), Marcq-en-Barœul 1985. In 1987, the Musée de Pont-Aven held a retrospective exhibition of Jourdan's work.

Bibliography:

Dauchot, Fernand, '*Jourdan, peintre de Pont-Aven*' in *Le Panorama des Arts*, periodical, Paris, August 1943. Parceveaux, Henri de, *Rétrospective Henry Moret, Émile Jourdan, Roderic O'Conor, Wladyslaw Slewinski*, exhibition catalogue, Musée de Limur, Vannes, 1966. Jaworska, W., *Gauguin et l'École de Pont-Aven*, Ides et Calendes, Neuchâtel, 1971. *Émile Jourdan 1860-1931*, exhibition catalogue, Musée de Pont-Aven, Pont-Aven, 1987.

Museums and Galleries:

Brest (MBA): *Fishing Boats in the Port of Brigneau; The River Aven Seen from the Bridge* - Paris (Mus. d'Orsay): *Rain at Pont-Aven* - Pont-Aven: *Still-life with Palette; The Trémalo Chapel; The Lanriot Chapel by Moonlight* - Quimper (MBA): *Loft Scene* - Vannes (MBA La Cohue): *Bunch of Wildflowers*.

Auction records:

Brest, 19 Dec 1976, *River Banks* (oil on card, 18 x 13 ins / 46 x 33 cm) FRF 2,800. Enghien-les-Bains, 25 Nov 1984, *View of Pont-Aven* (c. 1895, oil on canvas, 18 1/4 x 22 ins / 46.5 x 55 cm) FRF 370,000. Lorient, 17 May 1986, *The Wave* (1915, oil on canvas, 32 x 46 ins / 81 x 116 cm) FRF 356,000. Enghien-les-Bains, 15 March 1987, *Landscape with Two Breton Women* (charcoal, 12 x 12 1/4 ins / 30.5 x 31 cm) FRF 47,000. Paris, 23 Nov 1989, *Brigneau Port* (oil on canvas, 23 1/2 x 32 ins / 60 x 81 cm) FRF 1,300,000. Lorient, 10 June 1990, *Still-life with Mice* (oil on canvas) FRF 62,000. Paris, 30 Oct 1995, *Breton Woman in a Wood by the River Aven* (pastel, 12 1/2 x 19 3/4 ins / 32 x 50 cm) FRF 90,000. Paris, 17 Oct 1997, *Nude on a Radiant Background* (pastel, 39 1/4 x 25 1/4 ins / 100 x 64 cm) FRF 5,000. London, 8 Dec 1999, *Harbour at Pont Aven* (1891, oil on canvas, 17 x 26 ins / 43 x 65 cm) GBP 37,000. Brest, 19 Dec 1999, *Chapel of Lanriot in the Moonlight* (oil on panel, 32 x 31 ins / 81 x 80 cm) FRF 255,000. Brest, 10 Dec 2000, *Wrack Collecting on the Breton Coast* (1909, oil on canvas, 23 x 29 ins / 59 x 73 cm) FRF 170,000. Calais, 9 Dec 2001, *Boat on the Sea in Severe Weather* (1923, oil on canvas, 26 x 21 ins / 65 x 53 cm) FRF 123,000. Brest, 16 Dec 2001, *Brigneau Harbour* (1914, oil on panel, 43 x 39 ins / 110 x 100 cm) FRF 780,000. Brest, 20 July 2002, *View of Aven* (oil on cardboard, 22 x 18 ins / 55 x 46 cm) EUR 38,700. Brest, 15 Dec 2002, *Shipwreck* (1914, oil on canvas, 32 x 39 ins / 81 x 100 cm) EUR 98,000. Brest, 11 May 2003, *Brigneau, Semaphore and Wrack Collectors* (oil on panel, 35 x 31 ins / 89 x 78 cm) EUR 71,455. London, 3 Feb 2004, *Red Sailing Boats* (1889, oil on canvas, 33 x 45 ins / 84 x 115 cm) GBP 15,000.

JOURDAN, Théodore

French, 19th century.

Born 29 July 1833, in Salon-de-Provence; died 1906.

Painter. Genre scenes, landscapes.

Théodore Jourdan was a pupil of Émile Loubon and began his career at the Salon de Paris in 1865, obtaining an honourable mention in 1888. He took particular pleasure in reproducing scenes of Provençal life.

Museums and Galleries:

Aix-en-Provence: *Flock in Provence* - Cognac: *Return of the Flock* - Digne-les-Bains: *The Flock* - Draguignan: *Corner of the Sheepfold* - Tourcoing: *Sheep at the Drinking Trough*.

Auction records:

Vienna, 5 Dec 1984, *Sheep in the Byre* (oil on canvas, 17 1/4 x 25 1/4 ins / 44 x 64 cm) ATS 70,000. Paris, 21 June 2000, *Shepherdess* (oil on canvas, 19 x 29 ins / 48 x 73 cm) FRF 23,000.

JOURDEUIL

French, 19th century.

Died 1868, in Lyons.

Painter.

Jourdeuil was a teacher of ornamentation at the École St-Pierre in Lyons where he was also museum curator. He lived in St Petersburg from 1845 to 1855. He had a son during this time who became the painter Adrien Jourdeuil.

JOURDEUIL, Adrien Louis Marie

French, 19th - 20th century.

Born 18 September 1849, in St Petersburg; died August 1907, in Chambéry (Savoy).

Painter, architect. Landscapes, still-lifes.

Adrien Louis Marie Jourdeuil was the son of Jourdeuil, the painter and teacher of ornamentation. He studied at the École des Beaux-Arts in Lyons and in Paris and trained as an architect. He first exhibited in Paris in 1877, showing a salon design for Great Duchess Helena of Russia. He went on exhibiting from 1878, receiving a bronze medal in 1888 and a silver medal in 1894. He was also awarded a bronze medal at the Paris Exposition Universelle of 1900. Jourdeuil initially exhibited still-lifes, then oil and pastel landscapes showing views of Normandy, Savoy and Provence, often at sunset or in moonlight.

Museums and Galleries:

Béziers: *Banks of the Seine* - Chambéry: *Meadows by a Lake* - Dieppe: *Landscape* - Louviers (Mus. municipal): *On the Road to Le Var*.

Auction records:

Paris, 19 Nov 1924, *Morning*, FRF 420. Paris, 27 March 1947, *River Banks with Cows*, FRF 400. Bern, 1 May 1980, *Summer Landscape with Cows* (oil on panel, 12 1/4 x 17 3/4 ins / 31 x 45 cm) CHF 3,600. London, 24 June 1987, *Washerwomen by a River* (oil on canvas, 17 1/4 x 29 ins / 43.5 x 73.5 cm) GBP 1,800.

JOURDHEUIL, or Jourdeville, or Jourdheul
French, 18th century.
Born 1759, in Poitiers; died 1781, in Paris.
Engraver (burin).
Jourdheuil was a pupil of J.-F. Beauvarlet. He worked in Paris, engraving subjects from everyday life after J. Raoux, G. Dou and Aubry.

JOURDIER-CHABAS, Marie
French, 19th century.
Born 19th century, in Versailles.
Painter.
Marie Jourdier-Chabas was a pupil of Boulanger and Jules Lefebvre and was a member of the Société des Artistes Français from 1891. She received an honourable mention in 1893.

JOURDOGNE, Gilles de. See **JODOIGNE**

JOURDY, Paul
French, 19th century.
Born 17 December 1805, in Dijon; died 28 October 1856, in Paris.
Painter, watercolourist. Religious subjects, mythological subjects, portraits, genre scenes, landscapes.
Jourdy entered the École des Beaux-Arts on 30th October 1820. He was a pupil of Lethière and Ingres. He obtained the second Prix de Rome in 1828 and the first in 1834. He exhibited portraits and historical subjects from 1831 to 1853. His *Seven Sacraments* can be seen at the church of St-Élisabeth in Paris.
BIBLIOGRAPHY:
Les Années romantiques, la peinture française de 1815 à 1850, exhibition catalogue, Musée des Beaux-Arts, Nantes, Galeries nationales du Grand Palais, Paris, 1996.
MUSEUMS AND GALLERIES:
DIJON: *Achilles and Scamander; Prometheus in Chains; Theseus Recognised by his Father* - ROANNE: *St Louis* - TROYES (Mus. d'Art, d'Archéologie et de Sciences Naturelles): *Portrait of Simart at the Age of Twenty-Five* (1831) - VERSAILLES: *Malebranche*.
AUCTION RECORDS:
PARIS, 1895, *Pompeii* (watercolour) FRF 39; *Pompei: the Forum* (watercolour) FRF 85. BERN, 18 Nov 1966, *Views of Rome* (two pendants) CHF 16,000.

JOURET, Henry
British, 18th century.
Active in London.
Painter. Figures.
Henry Jouret exhibited at the Free Society in London in 1773 and 1774.

JOURET, Walter
Belgian, 20th century.
Born 1937, in Berchem (Antwerp).
Painter, sculptor.

JOURJON, Toussaint François
French, 19th century.
Born 1809, in St-Genest-Lerp (Loire); died 1857, in Rennes.
Painter, sculptor.
Toussaint Jourjon was the son of an armourer and a pupil of Augustin Dumont. He received the second Rome Prize in 1836. He exhibited at the Salon de Paris, notably between 1844 and 1849. He is known for his busts of children and his portraits.
BIBLIOGRAPHY:
Les Années romantiques, la peinture française de 1815 à 1850, exhibition catalogue, Musée des Beaux-Arts, Nantes, Galeries nationales du Grand Palais, Paris, 1996.
MUSEUMS AND GALLERIES:
RENNES (MBA): *Portrait of Charles-Louis Jourjon*.

JOURNAULT, Alexandre Adolphe
French, 19th century.
Born 19th century, in Paris.
Painter.
Alexandre Journault worked with Hersent and Watelet. His landscapes were represented at the Salon from 1824 to 1852.
MUSEUMS AND GALLERIES:
LE HAVRE: *Wadi-Schile*.

JOURNAULT, Ernest
French, 19th century.
Born 19th century, in Paris.
Painter. Landscapes, seascapes.
Ernest Journault began his career at the Salon de Paris in 1864 and continued to take part in its exhibitions. He painted many scenes of Italy, Switzerland and Arabia.
MUSEUMS AND GALLERIES:
BAYONNE (Mus. Bonnat): *Beach at Dinard*.

JOURNAUX
French, 20th century.
Painter. Landscapes.
AUCTION RECORDS:
PARIS, 19 March 1947, *Village Street*, FRF 1,800.

JOURNET, Élise Marie Thomate
French, 19th century.
Died 30 November 1866, in Paris.
Painter. Portraits, genre scenes, still-lifes.
Élise Journet exhibited at the Salon de Paris from 1833 to 1845.
BIBLIOGRAPHY:
Les Années romantiques, la peinture française de 1815 à 1850, exhibition catalogue, Musée des Beaux-Arts, Nantes, Galeries nationales du Grand Palais, Paris, 1996.
MUSEUMS AND GALLERIES:
BREST: *Laboratory Items* - QUIMPER (MBA): *Vase of Flowers; Brauwer and Craesbeke* (1845).

JOURNET, Joseph or Jean Louis
French, 18th century.
Born 18th century, to a family originally from Le Vigan (Gard).
Sculptor.
Journet worked first of all in Paris. About 1755, he moved to Copenhagen, where he collaborated with the sculptor J.F. Saly on the monument to *Frederick V*. He received the title of 'Sculptor to the King of Denmark', and became a professor at the Kunstakademi in Copenhagen. On returning to France in 1769, he set up in Montpellier, where he executed the sculptures of the fountain in the Place de la Préfecture. At the exhibition of the Société des Beaux-Arts of Montpellier in 1779, the following works by him were on show: a marble copy of the relief *Diogenes*, by Saly, terracotta models of two tombs, plaster models of a *Vulcan* and an urn.

JOURNIAC, Michel
French, 20th century.
Born 7 October 1943; died 15 October 1995, in Paris.
Performance artist, sculptor, painter, poet. Multimedia.
Michel Journiac studied philosophy and scholastic theology. He taught aesthetics at the University of Paris I (Panthéon-Sorbonne) and was formerly a teacher in art schools in Versailles, Nancy and Rheims.

He started by painting and making objects appropriate to the body. His first body performances were *Parcours Piège du Sang* (*Course, Blood Trap*), which he showed in Paris in 1968, *Piège Pour un Voyeur* (*Trap for a Voyeur*), 1969 and *Messe Pour un Corps* (*Mass for a Body*), 1969, in which he gave communion with a blood sausage made from his own blood. From the outset Journiac gave his art a factual character. While his investigations on the body, its expressiveness, its social role, likens him to body art artists, Journiac did not practise this art of posing but offered a deliberately troubling, even shocking discourse. 'Social meat', the body is also the site of sociological and psychoanalytical investigations. Above all he placed the emphasis on the inherent trans-sexuality of the body: *Piège pour un Travesti* (*Trap for a Tranvestite*), 1972, *Hommage à Freud* (*Homage to Freud*), 1972 where he dresses simultaneously as his mother and father, *Le Saint Vierge* (*Virgin Mary*), *Vingt-quatre Heures de la Vie d'une Femme Ordinaire* (*Twenty-four Hours in the Life of an Ordinary Woman*), 1974, a photograph album, etc. These often summary 'reflections' were accompanied by a fairly acute sense of the expressiveness of the theatre. He used the written word, film, objects, photographs and video. From the end of the 1980s Journiac kept away from the art scene. In an article paying homage to him in 1995 Geneviève Breerette stressed that his was 'A misunderstood career, often rejected, because it was shocking, blasphemous and scandalous and its impact was symbolic and underrated.'

Michel Journiac appeared regularly in collective exhibitions from the 1971 exhibition *Piège Pour une Exécution Capitale* (*Trap for Capital Punishment*), University of Paris I, Paris, and then among others: *L'Art Corporel* (*Body Art*), 1975, during which he presented a performance: *Célébration de Messe pour un Corps* (*Mass for a Body*), Galerie Stadler, Paris; *Mythologies Quotidiennes* (*Everyday Mythologies*), Musée d'Art Moderne de la Ville de Paris, 1975; *L'Art Corporel* (*Body Art*), 1981, at which he presented a performance: *Corps Interdit I, le 7 Février* (*Banned Body I, 7th February*), Community Arts Centre, Nevers; *Écritures dans la Peinture* (*Writing in Painting*), Villa Arson, Nice, 1984; *Splendeur et Misère du Corps* (*Splendor and Wretchedness of the Body*), Musée d'Art Moderne de la Ville de Paris, 1988; *Fémininmasculin. Le Sexe de l'Art* (*Masculinefeminine. Gender of Art*), Musée National d'Art Moderne, Pompidou Centre, Paris, 1995. Posthumous collective exhibitions include: *L'art au corps. Le Corps Exposé de Man Ray à nos Jours* (*Body Art: The Exposed Body from Man Ray to the Present*), Musée d'Art Moderne, Marseilles, 1996; *L'Empreinte* (*Imprint*), Musée National d'Art Moderne, Pompidou Centre, Paris, 1997; *Les années 70: l'Art en Cause* (*The 1970s: Art in Question*), Capc-Musée d'Art Contemporain, Bordeaux, 2002.

He exhibited mainly in Paris following *Parcours. Piège du Sang* (*Course. Blood Trap*), at the Cloître des Billettes, Paris in 1968. Exhibitions since then include: *Piège pour un Voyeur* (*Trap for a Voyeur*), Galerie Marc Martin-Malburet, Paris, 1969; *Referendum Journiac* (*Journiac Referendum*), Galerie Daniel Templon, Paris, 1970; *Contrat de Prostitution* (*Prostitution Contract*), Galerie Stadler, Paris, 1973; *24 Heures de la Vie d'une Femme Ordinaire* (*24 Hours in the Life of an Ordinary Woman*), Galerie Stadler, Paris, 1974; *Rituel Pour un Mort* (*Ritual for Someone who has Died*), Galerie A. Zerbib, Paris, 1976; *Action de Corps Exclu* (*Excluded Body Performance*), George Pompidou Centre, 1983; *Meurtre et Sacré* (*Murder and Sacred*), Galerie J. & J. Donguy, Paris, 1985; 12 things sent through the post and other initiatives during the year 1993 to 1994, including the action *Icône des Mots et du Sang* (*Icon of Words and Blood*) in the La Différence festivals at the Salon du Livre in Paris. Exhibitions after his death include: *24 Heures de la Vie d'une Femme ordinaire* (*24 Hours in the Life of an Ordinary Woman*), La Galerie, Ville de Noisy-le-Sec, 2001; Musée d'Art Moderne et Contemporain, Strasbourg, 2004. He also published poems such as *Délit du Corps* (*Body Violation*), 1967 and *Le Sang Nu* (*Naked Blood*), 1968.

BIBLIOGRAPHY:

Journiac, Michel, *L'Objet du corps et le corps de l'objet*, Paris, 1970. *Vingt-quatre heures de la vie d'une femme ordinaire*, Arthur Hubschmid, Paris, 1974. Paquet, Marcel/Journiac, Michel, *Ossuaire de l'esprit*, La Différence, Paris, 1977. Daviot, Jean/Marcadé, Bernard, *Contrat pour un corps*, Éd. Daviot, Paris, 1994. Breerette, Geneviève, '*Michel Journiac un plasticien hors limites*' in *Le Monde*, periodical, Paris, 18 October 1995. *L'Art au corps. Le Corps exposé de Man Ray à nos jours*, exhibition catalogue, Musée d'Art contemporain, Marseilles, 1996. Labaume, Vincent, *Tombeau de Michel Journiac*, Éd. Al Dante, Paris, 1998. Goldberg, RoseLee, *Performances, l'art en action*, Thames & Hudson, Paris, 1999. *Vingt-quatre heures de la vie d'une femme ordinaire*, exhibition leaflet, La Galerie, Noisy-le-Sec, 2001 (extensive documentation). Fréruchet, Maurice, et al., *Les Années soixante-dix: l'art en cause*, exhibition catalogue, Capc Musée d'Art Contemporain, Bordeaux, 2002.

MUSEUMS AND GALLERIES:

LIMOGES (FRAC Limousin): *Les Vingt-Quatre Heures de la Vie d'une Femme* (*Twenty-four Hours in the Life of a Woman*) (1974).

AUCTION RECORDS:

RHEIMS, 20 Dec 1987, *Massacre of the Innocents* (celluloid on canvas, 45 1/4 x 29 1/2 ins / 115 x 75 cm) FRF 2,300. PARIS, 25 April 1990, *Homage to Freud* (1972, silk screen print/hardboard, 31 x 22 ins / 79 x 55 cm) FRF 16,000. PARIS, 21 May 1992, *Gilles de Rais' Cupboard* (1966, painting, sheet and plaster on canvas, 51 1/4 x 35 ins / 130 x 89 cm) FRF 3,000. PARIS, 26 Oct 1994, *Gilles de Rais' Cupboard* (1966, linen, plaster and oil on canvas, 35 x 51 1/4 ins / 89 x 130 cm) FRF 4,000. PARIS, 28 Oct 2000, *Untitled* (c. 1970, sponge, painted wood and fabric, 13 x 9 ins / 34 x 23 cm) FRF 13,000. PARIS, 19 June 2002, *Large Wash of Modern Art* (1969, trousers and mixed media on panel, 69 x 31x2 ins / 175 x 80x6 cm) EUR 1,800. PARIS, 24 April 2004, *Self-portrait* (1965, oil on canvas, 51 x 38 ins / 130 x 97 cm) EUR 1,500.

JOURNO, Victor
French, 20th century.
Born 20 October 1917, in Tunis.
Painter.

Victor Journo studied in Tunis before becoming a student of Léger in 1948. He first exhibited in Tunis, and later in Paris at the Salon de la Jeune Peinture until 1955 and then at the Salon des Indépendants. A figurative artist, he borrowed a few elements from late Cubism.

JOURNOD, Monique
French, 20th century.
Born 1935, in Rome.
Painter.

Monique Journod studied at the École Nationale des Beaux-Arts in Paris. She was awarded the Prix de Rome for painting in 1962 and has exhibited at group exhibitions in France, notably in Paris at the Salon des Peintres Témoins de leur Temps, as well as abroad. She received a gold medal at the Salon des Artistes Français in Paris. Journod is president of the painting division of the Salon des Artistes Français. Several of her works, in vitrified steel, decorate public buildings. Some of her canvases have been purchased by the Ville de Paris.

AUCTION RECORDS:

CALAIS, 26 May 1991, *Vase of Flowers* (oil on canvas, 15 3/4 x 15 3/4 ins / 40 x 40 cm) FRF 6,500.

JOURNOT
French, 19th century.
Engraver.

Among his works is: *Rouget de L'isle Singing the Marseillaise* in the manner of Pils.

JOURNOT, Laurent
French, 16th century.
Active in Amiens.
Sculptor.

Journot produced various decorations, including salamanders, lilies and coats of arms of the king and the town, for the Montre-Ecu door in Amiens in 1534.

JOURNOT, Louis Isidore
French, 19th - 20th century.
Born 27 August 1867, in Port-Marly.
Engraver (burin).

Louis Isidore Journot studied at the École Nationale des Arts Décoratifs under Alphonse Lamotte. He became a member of the Salon des Artistes Français in Paris in 1904. Journot received a commendation in 1892, a bronze medal in 1893, a silver medal in 1897 and a travel bursary in 1899. He also exhibited at the Brussels Exhibition of 1910.

JOUSETTE, Guillaume
French, 17th century.
Active in Paris.
Painter.

Jousette became a widower in 1663.

JOUSSAUME, Georges
French, 20th - 21st century.
Born 27 May 1946, in La Rochelle.
Painter.

Georges Joussaume was taught by Brianchon at the École des Beaux-Arts in Paris from 1965 to 1967. He was inspired by Pop Art and some effects in the style of Linder can be seen in his work.

JOUSSAUME, Michel
French, 20th century.
Born 1931, in Bordeaux.
Painter. Interiors with figures, landscapes, still-lifes (shellfish), flowers.

Michel Joussaume lives and works in Bordeaux. His paintings contain few or no figures - a painting entitled *Dressed in Red* in fact shows a cooked lobster. His starting point is landscape and still-life. In his early period Joussaume painted from nature and, although freely interpreted, his subjects were at that time more or less identifiable, as can be seen in works such as *Between Two Waters* and *Flowers and Jug* of 1977. After this he became more interested in translating the flavour, the odour, the 'murmur' of objects through the colour and rhythm of their composition, which varied uniquely with each subject. He began to take only brief notes on site, and in the paintings executed in the studio sought to convey the poetic atmosphere and original emotion of the moment of perception. Examples include *Jeux de soleil* of 1990 and *Interior* of 1993. The period of transition between reality and sensation appears to have taken place in 1986 and reached its culmination in the abstract work of 1988 *Fires on the Hill*. In this the flames licking and scorching the vegetation are already, in their mission to destroy reality, an abstract phenomenon. In *Interior* of 1993 the process of abstraction based on an external reality is found again in an approach similar to that practised by Maurice Estève since the 1940s.

He has taken part in numerous group exhibitions since 1968, mainly in Bordeaux and the surrounding area, receiving prizes and awards, and in Saarbrücken, Fréjus, Bilbao, Frankfurt, Berlin, Nantes, San Francisco and Vannes. He has also exhibited in Paris, notably from 1975 to 1987 at the Salon of the Société Nationale des Beaux-Arts, of which he is a member, from 1987 to 1991 at the Salon d'Automne, of which he is also a member, and in 1993 at the Salon des Réalités Nouvelles. Joussaume has shown his work in solo exhibitions since 1971: regularly in Bordeaux, notably at Atelier 80, in 1973 at the Maison de la Culture in Villeneuve-sur-Lot and in 1991 at the Musée Marzelles in Marmande.

BIBLIOGRAPHY:

Dussol, Dominique, et al., *M. Joussaume*, exhibition catalogue, Gal. A 80, Bordeaux, 1993 (good documentation).

JOUSSAY, Jacques, sometimes called Jules
French, 19th century.
Born 1 October 1821, in Rochetaillée-sur-Saône (Rhône); died 1889.
Painter. Genre scenes, portraits, interiors, landscapes, flowers, fruit, still-lifes.

Jacques Joussay was a pupil of Bonnefond at the École des Beaux-Arts in Lyons where he studied under him from 1837 to 1841 and 1850 to 1852. From 1857 to 1877 he exhibited portraits, still-lifes (especially fruit), interiors and landscapes in Lyons. He is mainly known for: *Childhood Friends Singing a Song by P. Dupont* (1858), *Interior of a Mill, Repiquage de la meule* (1861), *Fishing the Depths, Banks of the Saône* (1867), *Landscape in Optevoz* (1870), *Autumn Grapes* (1877). He signed himself *J. Joussay*

AUCTION RECORDS:

LONDON, 17 June 1994, *Roses in a Vase* (1878, oil on canvas, 23 1/2 x 19 3/4 ins / 59.7 x 50.2 cm) GBP 1,840.

JOUSSE, Mathurin
French, 17th century.
Born 27 August 1607, in La Flèche (Sarthe); died before 1692.
Painter, sculptor, engraver, writer.

Jousse worked on the decoration of the church of the college at La Flèche. He is remembered for *The Faithful Servant*, a series of 52 plates.

JOUSSELIN, Auguste
French, 19th century.
Landscape painter.

Auguste Jousselin exhibited landscapes of Paris and its surroundings and seascapes at the Salon de Paris from 1834 to 1842.

JOUSSELIN, François
French, 20th century.
Born 1926, in Laval (Mayenne).
Painter. Figure compositions, landscapes, urban landscapes, still-lifes.

François Jousselin studied history of art and archaeology at the faculty of letters in Toulouse before going on to study at the École des Beaux-Arts. There he met Marfaing and Igon and went with them to Paris in 1949. In 1953 he was awarded a bursary by the Dutch government which enabled him to paint in The Hague and Amsterdam. He also travelled to London, Montreal and New York. After an early abstract period that coincides with his first submissions to the Salon des Réalités Nouvelles - large pieces showing totemic signs in black, grey and white in the spirit of Soulages - he returned firmly to a figurative language equally well suited to drawing, wash, gouache and oil.

While it is possible to trace the development of his technique from a deliberately heavy and free use of pigment to a smoother and more finely drawn style of painting from 1968 onwards, it is perhaps more interesting to observe the way his choice of subject develops. It often includes the female form, sometimes partially clothed in erotic garments; the female presence in urban folklore; man alone or looking at himself in a mirror. These themes reappear regularly in various forms with different implications in their relationship with existential anguish. Jousselin also painted views of Paris and his own district from various angles and perspectives.

He has taken part in numerous group exhibitions in Paris, including the second Salon des Jeunes Peintures, 1951; the Salon Comparaisons, 1957, 1959, 1968, 1975 and 1976; the Salon des Surindépendants, 1952 and 1953; the École de Paris exhibition, 1962; the Salon des Réalités Nouvelles from 1954 to 1964, then again in 1969; and the Salon de Mai, 1964. In the provinces, he participated in *Climat 66* at the Musée de Grenoble; *Rencontres de Nantes* at the Musée de Nantes, 1966. Abroad, he was included in exhibitions at the Recklinhausen Museum, Germany, 1958; at the Verviers museum in Belgium in 1962; at the first Galeries Pilotes international salon at the Musée de Lausanne in 1963 and at the Musée Royal des Beaux-Arts, Antwerp, in 1969. He has also shown his work in solo exhibitions: at the Galerie Jacques Massol, Paris, in 1962, 1963, 1966, 1968, 1970, 1972, 1975, 1977 and 1981; at the Galerie Simone Boudet, Toulouse, 1968; at the Norland gallery, Östersund, 1968; the Galerie Auvernier-Neauchâtel, 1968; the Galerie Nord, Lille, 1969; and the Galerie Jean Peyrole, Paris, in 1988, 1990 and 1992.

BIBLIOGRAPHY:

François Jousselin, exhibition catalogue, Gal. Jacques Massol, Paris, 1968.

MUSEUMS AND GALLERIES:

BUDVA - LAUSANNE (Cantonal MFA): *War* (1961); *The Accident*; two drawings; *Demonstration* - OSTEND (Municipal Mus.): *The Matches* (1968) - SKOPJE: *Figures* (1961) - TOULOUSE: *The Work* (1953); *Clouds* (1958, gouache).

JOUSSELIN, Paul

French, 19th century.
Active in Paris.
Painter. Landscapes.

Paul Jousselin exhibited views of Switzerland, the Pyrenées, the Dauphiné and the Paris environs.

JOUSSELIN, Renée

French, 20th century.
Born 24 January 1905, in Paris.
Painter.

Renée Jousselin exhibited at the Salon des Artistes Français in Paris from 1926 to 1960.

JOUSSELIN, Stéphane A.

French, 19th century.
Active in Paris.
Sculptor.

Stéphane Jousselin was a member of the Société des Artistes Français from 1888 and exhibited his works in the Salon of the society.

JOUSSERANDOT, Louise. See **GUGNON Louise**

JOUSSERANDOT, Lucien

French, 19th century.
Painter. Religious subjects.

BIBLIOGRAPHY:

Les Années romantiques, la peinture française de 1815 à 1850, exhibition catalogue, Musée des Beaux-Arts, Nantes, Galeries nationales du Grand Palais, Paris, 1996.

MUSEUMS AND GALLERIES:

LONS-LE-SAUNIER: *St Jerome*.

JOUSSET, Charles

French, 19th century.
Born 18 June 1857, in Nantes; died 1907.
Painter.

Charles Jousset was a member of the Société des Artistes Français and exhibited at the Salon as part of this group.

JOUVE, Auguste

French, 19th century.
Born 11 July 1846, in Lyons.
Painter.

Auguste Jouve was a pupil of Reignier and Guichard at the École des Beaux-Arts in Lyons where he studied from 1861 to 1864. He was then a pupil of Comte. He exhibited his work in Lyons from 1866 and in Paris from 1877. He painted flowers, still-lifes, portraits, figures and landscapes (paintings, drawings, enamelled wash drawings, and original lithographs).

MUSEUMS AND GALLERIES:

AMSTERDAM: *Flowers*.

JOUVE, Georges

French, 19th century.
Born 27 August 1867, in Paris.
Painter, art restorer. Interiors.

Georges Jouve was a pupil of Cabanel and of Jules Lefebvre. He was a member of the Société des Artistes Français from 1899 and was represented at the Salon as part of this group.

JOUVE, Georges

French, 20th century.
Born 1910; died 1964.
Ceramicist, designer, decorative artist. Designs for furniture, objets d'art.

Jouve was an important figure in the applied arts during the 1950s.

BIBLIOGRAPHY:

Faré, Michel, *Georges Jouve*, Art et Industrie, Paris, 1965.

JOUVE, Joseph

French, 19th century.
Born 19th century, in Le Pont-de-Beauvoisin (Isère).
Painter.

Joseph Jouve was a pupil of Cabanel, Hébert and Barrias. He was represented at the Salon de Paris in 1876 and 1877.

JOUVE, Louis

French, 19th century.
Born 1829, in Le Puy-en-Velay; died 23 December 1903.
Painter.

Louis Jouve was a pupil at the École des Beaux-Arts.

JOUVE, Paul

French, 20th century.
Born 16 March 1878 or 1880, in Marlotte (now Bourron-Marlotte), near Fontainebleau; died 1973.
Painter (gouache), watercolourist, engraver, draughtsman, illustrator. Animals. Murals.

Paul Jouve was only 15 years old when he showed *The Lions of Ménélick* at the Salon of the Société Nationale des Beaux-Arts. He made studies from life in all the major zoos of Europe and, having mastered the lion, travelled as far afield as Angkor in order to see elephants in the wild. He was therefore the obvious choice to illustrate Kipling's *Jungle Book*. He also illustrated *Un pélerin d'Angkor* (*A Pilgram fom Angkor*) by Pierre Loti and Leconte de Lisle's *Les Poèmes Barbares*. Jouve also produced panels for the Vincennes colonial exhibition of 1931.

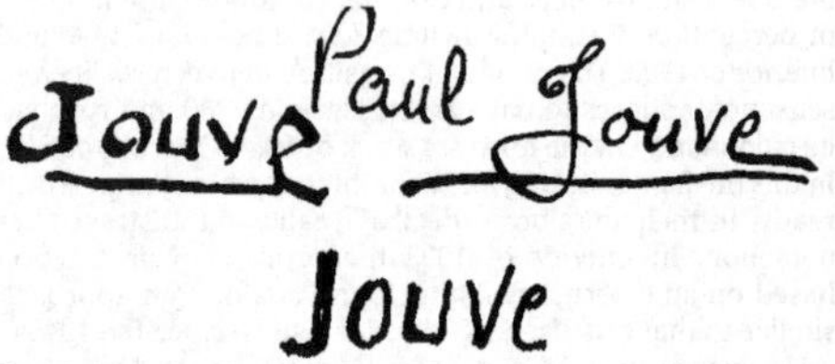

BIBLIOGRAPHY:

Mornand, Pierre/Thomé, Jules-René, *Vingt artistes du livre*, A. Cymboliste, Paris, 1950. Marcilhac, Félix, *Paul Jouve, peintre sculpteur animalier*, Amateur, Paris, 2005.

AUCTION RECORDS:

PARIS, 20-22 May 1920, *Young Eagle Fighting a Snake* (pencil) FRF 5,900. PARIS, 29 April 1921, *Black Cat* (watercolour) FRF 500. PARIS, 10 Feb 1932, *Panthers Reclining* (lead pencil heightened with paint) FRF 1,020. PARIS, 18 May 1942, *Panthers at Rest* (wash heightened with watercolour, gouache and paint) FRF 4,400. PARIS, 22 Feb 1943, *The Snake* (charcoal) FRF 2,500. PARIS, 26 Feb 1945, *Lioness and Lion Cubs*, FRF 32,000. PARIS, Oct 1945-July 1946, *Black Panther* (drawing) FRF 6,000. PARIS, 7 Nov 1946, *Bird of Prey*, FRF 4,800. PARIS, 27 March 1947, *Tiger* (gouache) FRF 3,400. PARIS, 11

March 1949, *Tiger Drinking at a Lake*, FRF 29,000. Paris, 13 March 1972, *Lion Devouring a Wild Boar* (bronze) FRF 4,200. Paris, 29 May 1974, *Ceremonial Elephant outside a Temple* (watercolour, 116 1/4 x 133 3/4 ins / 295 x 340 cm) FRF 27,500. Paris, 14 June 1976, *Python* (gouache and charcoal, 21 1/4 x 30 1/4 ins / 54 x 77 cm) FRF 4,000. Enghien-les-Bains, 29 Oct 1978, *Bengal Tiger* (1905, low relief, patinated bronze, l. 7 3/4 ins / 20 cm, w. 19 3/4 ins/50 cm) FRF 4,500. Paris, 24 Nov 1978, *Panther Attacking a Peacock* (oil on panel, arched at the top, 72 3/4 x 65 ins / 185 x 165 cm) FRF 27,100. Paris, 6 April 1979, *Profile View of a Panther Walking* (charcoal, 19 3/4 x 43 ins / 50 x 109 cm) FRF 6,500. Monte Carlo, 23 June 1979, *Large Panther* (c. 1925, engraving/gilt background, 41 1/4 x 29 3/4 ins / 105 x 75.5 cm) FRF 6,000. Enghien-les-Bains, 28 Oct 1979, *Lionness and Lion Cubs* (oil on panel, 28 1/4 x 43 ins / 72 x 109 cm) FRf 14,000. Paris, 24 June 1980, *Cléo, le chien à la gradée* (patinated bronze, h. 17 3/4 ins / 45 cm) FRF 9,500. Monte Carlo, 7 Dec 1981, *Two Elephants in Profile View* (c. 1925, oil on panel, 36 x 63 1/2 ins / 90.5 x 161 cm) FRF 40,000. Monte Carlo, 25 Oct 1982, *Lion Cub, c. 1925* (green-patinated bronze, h. 16 1/2 ins / 42 cm) FRF 57,000. Enghien-les-Bains, 26 June 1983, *Two Meharists* (graphite and Indian ink heightened with gouache, 13 3/4 x 16 1/2 ins / 35 x 42 cm) FRF 20,500. Enghien-les-Bains, 26 June 1983, *Panther Walking* (oil on panel, 29 1/2 x 51 1/4 ins / 75 x 130 cm) FRF 230,000. Paris, 23 Nov 1983, *Elephants in a Jungle Setting* (natural bronze, a pair of doors, each 107 3/4 x 78 ins / 274 x 198 cm) FRF 320,000. Monte Carlo, 11 March 1984, *Panther Sitting in a Tree* (1930, pastel gouache and oil/gold-leaf background/panel, 30 1/4 x 31 1/2 ins / 77 x 80 cm) FRF 55,000. Enghien-les-Bains, 2 Dec 1984, *Tigers* (dry-point/bistre-coloured paper, 18 x 41 ins / 46 x 104 cm) FRF 12,000. Monte Carlo, 6 Oct 1985, *Lion Cub* (c. 1925, greenish-patinated bronze, h. 16 1/2 ins / 42 cm) FRF 50,000. Paris, 7 May 1986, *Two Panthers Walking* (gouache and charcoal/mounted paper, 43 1/4 x 92 1/2 ins / 110 x 235 cm) FRF 122,000. Paris, 1 July 1987, *Lionness Devouring Her Prey* (Indian ink and stump pencil, 18 1/2 x 25 1/2 ins / 47 x 65 cm) FRF 29,000. Paris, 13 Nov 1987, *The Angkor Temple with Snakes* (oil on panel, 17 x 36 1/4 ins / 43 x 92 cm) FRF 48,000. Paris, 9 Dec 1987, *Sacred Elephants at the Angkor Temple* (oil on canvas remounted/panel, 94 1/2 x 76 3/4 ins / 240 x 195 cm) FRF 132,000. Paris, 26 Feb 1988, *Panther and Cobra* (watercolour and gouache, 20 x 39 1/4 ins / 51 x 100 cm) FRF 20,000. Paris, 7 March 1988, *Lion* (oil on card, 16 1/4 x 20 1/4 ins / 41.5 x 51.5 cm) FRF 5,000. Paris, 24 April 1988, *The Monkey and the Idol* (black-green patinated bronze, l. 6 1/4 ins / 16 cm, h. 6 ins/15 cm) FRF 11,600. Paris, 6 May 1988, *Seated Tiger* (watercolour, 11 1/2 x 9 ins / 29 x 22 cm) FRF 9,000. Paris, 12 June 1988, *Elephants and Their Mahouts* (oil on canvas remounted/panel, 70 3/4 x 132 ins / 180 x 335 cm) FRF 165,000; *Tigers Drinking* (oil on canvas remounted/panel, 69 x 132 ins / 175 x 335 cm) FRF 430,000. Paris, 22 June 1988, *Three Tigers* (gouache and Indian ink on gold background, 11 3/4 x 37 1/2 ins / 30 x 95 cm) FRF 50,000. Paris, 16 Oct 1988, *Panther* (gouache and watercolour, 12 1/2 x 20 1/2 ins / 31.5 x 52 cm) FRF 36,000. Paris, 14 Dec 1988, *Two Panthers* (gouache and charcoal, 18 1/2 x 27 1/2 ins / 47 x 70 cm) FRF 55,000. Paris, 9 April 1989, *Sacred Elephants at Angkor Temple* (two drawings heightened with gouache, 40 1/2 x 28 3/4 ins / 103 x 73 cm and 41 1/4 x 29 1/4 ins/105 x 74 cm) FRF 140,000. Paris, 13 Dec 1989, *Simonos Petra Monastery, Mount Athos* (oil on paper, 55 x 72 3/4 ins / 140 x 185 cm) FRF 175,000. Paris, 20 Feb 1990, *Blue Panther* (watercolour, 12 1/2 x 20 1/2 ins / 32 x 52 cm) FRF 35,000. La Varenne-St-Hilaire, 20 May 1990, *Panther and Prey* (etching, 18 x 26 1/2 ins / 46 x 67 cm) FRF 21,100. Paris, 28 Oct 1990, *Two White Bears* (oil on card, 12 1/2 x 22 ins / 32 x 55 cm) FRF 70,000. Paris, 25 March 1993, *Eagle* (charcoal and chalk, 20 3/4 x 29 ins / 53 x 73.5 cm) FRF 30,000. Paris, 8 April 1993, *Profile View of Black Panther Walking* (oil and charcoal/paper, 19 x 42 1/2 ins / 48.5 x 108 cm) FRF 55,500. Paris, 9 June 1993, *Tiger and Young* (dry-point, 15 3/4 x 20 ins / 40 x 51 cm) FRF 3,200. Paris, 6 Dec 1993, *Pair of Condors* (pencil, 45 x 34 1/4 ins / 114 x 87 cm) FRF 15,000. Paris, 9 March 1994, *Royal Eagle and Pheasant* (oil on panel, 37 1/2 x 26 3/4 ins / 95 x 68 cm) FRF 72,000. Paris, 16 Dec 1994, *Elephants Bathing in the Perfumed River at Hué* (ink heightened with gouache, 10 1/2 x 16 1/4 ins / 26.5 x 41 cm) FRF 4,500. Paris, 19 Dec 1994, *Elephants and Their Mahouts* (oil on canvas/panel, 72 x 135 1/4 ins / 183 x 343.5 cm) FRF 710,000. Nanterre, 26 Oct 1995, *The Meharists' Halt* (oil on card, 21 1/4 x 25 1/4 ins / 54 x 64 cm) FRF 42,000. Paris, 17 April 1996, *Elephant and Mahout* (gouache, 17 3/4 x 13 3/4 ins / 45 x 35 cm) FRF 10,000. Paris, 24 Nov 1996, *Royal Elephants and Their Mahouts* (1923, oil on card, 14 1/2 x 20 1/2 ins / 37 x 52 cm) FRF 10,000. Paris, 14 March 1997, *Black Panther* (lithograph heightened with gouache through a stencil, 21 3/4 x 15 1/2 ins / 55.5 x 39.5 cm) FRF 10,000. Paris, 28 May 1997, *Black Panther* (lithograph, 40 1/2 x 28 3/4 ins / 103 x 73 cm) FRF 10,000. Paris, 17 June 1999, *Leopard on a Rock* (oil on panel, 35 x 35 ins / 90 x 90 cm) FRF 280,000. Paris, 22 Nov 1999, *Crouching Tiger* (charcoal, Indian ink and oil on paper on board, 17 x 24 ins / 43 x 60 cm) FRF 120,000. Paris, 26 June 2000, *Leopards on the Prowl* (mixed media, oil, lacquer and gold leaf ground on panel, 33 x 79 ins / 85 x 200 cm) FRF 260,000. Paris, 20 Nov 2000, *Tuareg on Horseback* (charcoal and pastel, 29 x 38 ins / 74 x 97 cm) FRF 300,000. Paris, 21 May 2001, *Panther's Head and Snake, Hammer* (black and gilt patinated bronze, 18 x 19 ins / 45 x 48 cm) FRF 540,000. Paris, 22 June 2001, *Lioness and Cubs* (oil and Indian ink on cardboard, 29 x 43 ins / 73 x 109 cm) FRF 175,000. Paris, 5 April 2002, *Tigers on a Mountain Background* (oil, charcoal and Indian ink on paper, 19 x 39 ins / 47 x 100 cm) EUR 35,000. Calais, 29 Sept 2002, *Lion on the Prowl* (c. 1920, coloured patinated bronze, h. 16 ins / 41 cm, w. 30 ins/76 cm) EUR 34,000. Paris, 2 Oct 2003, *Lion on the Prowl* (patinated bronze, h. 28 ins / 72 cm) EUR 26,000. Paris, 3 Dec 2003, *Elephants in the Swamp* (oil on paper on panel, 26 x 38 ins / 66 x 96 cm) EUR 16,000. New York, 15 June 2004, *Study of a Tiger* (oil, gouache and charcoal on paper on board, 42 x 28 ins / 107 x 71 cm) USD 30,000. New York, 15 June 2004, *Miroir aure boussois* (oil on glass on panel, nine, 76 x 100 ins / 193 x 254 cm) USD 260,000.

JOUVEAU

French, 19th century.
Active in Avignon c. 1860.
Painter.

JOUVEN, Romain

French, 19th - 20th century.
Born 1874; died 1929.
Painter, watercolourist. Landscapes.

AUCTION RECORDS:

Neuilly, 3 Feb 1991, *Provençal Landscape* (watercolour, 14 1/2 x 21 1/4 ins / 37 x 54 cm) FRF 7,100. Neuilly, 12 Dec 1993, *The Little Landing Stage at Magaud* (watercolour, 13 x 17 3/4 ins / 33 x 45 cm) FRF 3,800.

JOUVENEL, Adolphe

Belgian, 19th century.
Born 1798, in Lille; died 9 September 1867, in Brussels.
Medallist, engraver.

JOUVENEL, H.

French, 19th century.
Active in Lille at the beginning of the 19th century.
Engraver (burin).

H. Jouvenel engraved *Theatre of the Siege of Valenciennes in 1793* in the style of Coste.

JOUVENEL, Nicolas Wulfran

French, 19th century.

Born 1788, in Abbeville; died 11 April 1878, in Amiens.
Landscape painter.

MUSEUMS AND GALLERIES:
AMIENS: *Forest of Compiègne.*

JOUVENET, François, the Younger

French, 17th - 18th century.
Born 19 December 1664, in Rouen; died 8 April 1749, in Paris.
Painter. Portraits.

François Jouvenet the Younger was the son of Laurent the Younger and brother of Jean the Great. He studied in Paris as a portrait painter and was admitted to the Académie on 25 June 1701. He exhibited very frequently at the Salon from 1704 to 1747, and, to judge by his clientele, it would seem that his reputation was considerable.

MUSEUMS AND GALLERIES:
CAEN: *Portrait of François Romain* - ORLÉANS: *Mlle de Scuderi.*

AUCTION RECORDS:
PARIS, 21 June 1897, *Portrait of an Abbot,* FRF 230. PARIS, 27 April 1900, *Portrait of a Magistrate,* FRF 200. PARIS, 12 June 1906, *Portrait of a Man of Letters,* FRF 400. PARIS, 17 April 1920, *Bust Painting of the Virgin Feeding the Infant Jesus,* FRF 130. PARIS, 30 March 1998, *Portrait of a Man with an Embroidered Waistcoat* (oil on canvas, 40 1/4 x 32in/102 x 81cm) FRF 280,000. LONDON, 14 April 1999, *Madonna and Child* (1719, oil on canvas, 83 x 54 ins / 211 x 136 cm) GBP 3,500.

JOUVENET, François Dagobert

French, 18th century.
Born between 1688 and 1694, in Paris; died 24 April 1756, in Paris.
Painter.

François Dagobert Jouvenet was a member of the Académie de St-Luc in Paris.

JOUVENET, Isaac

French, 17th century.
Born c. 1659, in Rouen; died 27 September 1692, in Paris.
Active in Paris.
Sculptor.

Isaac Jouvenet was married to Gabrielle Lamotte, and he is mentioned on 16 December 1691 in connection with the death of a child. He is believed to be the brother of Jean Jouvenet.

JOUVENET, Jacques

French, 17th century.
Born probably on 16 August 1649, in Paris; died 1674; buried on 12 November in Paris.
Painter.

Jacques Jouvenet was the son of Laurent Jouvenet II and younger brother of Jean-Baptiste Jouvenet. He moved to Paris to work at the École de l'Académie and obtained, in 1673, the second prize for painting with *The Crossing of the Rhine.* His premature death, the following year, means that it is impossible to tell how his talent could have developed.

JOUVENET, Jean Baptiste

French, 17th - 18th century.
Born April 1644, in Rouen; died 5 April 1717, in Paris.
Painter, decorative designer. Historical subjects, mythological subjects, religious subjects, portraits.

Jean Baptiste Jouvenet was the son of Jouvenet the Younger and Catherine Leuze. He started out as a pupil of his father who, in view of his aptitude, sent him to pursue his studies at the École de l'Académie Royale in Paris in 1661. On 29 September 1668, he received the second prize for drawing, with the subject: *The First Conquest of the Franche-Comté,* Verdier taking first prize. The Académie further decided, 'that it would be permissible for Jouvenet to execute the painting of his drawing, on which the Académie will judge if he deserves to be sent to Rome'. Jouvenet, either because he did not execute the painting, or because his painting was not good enough, did not go to Rome, but, in 1673, having been commissioned by the corporation of goldsmiths to execute the painting which was to be submitted that year for the decoration of Notre-Dame, painted *Jesus and the Paralysed Man.* The work was very well received, in particular by Le Brun, who employed Jouvenet at the Palais de Versailles, and proposed him for the Académie, where he was admitted on 27 March 1675. He married Marie Baronneau, who was a member of a family of goldsmiths and artists, and there may be a connection between this marriage and the commission for the votive painting of 1673. At all events, he was very well thought of in the corporation. There were two children from the marriage: Jean-Baptiste-Antoine, born on 13 October 1686, for whom Antonin Veaucour, goldsmith, was a godparent with the wife of Philippe Vendicourt, also a goldsmith. This son died at the age of ten months, on 30 July 1687, and Marie-Thérèse, born in 1690, died on 1 December 1698. Jouvenet lost his wife, who was aged 47, on 6 February 1701. At the Académie he held all the posts: assistant professor on 3 July 1676; professor on 29 November 1681; assistant education officer on 24 July 1702; chief education officer on 31 December 1707; director from 30 June 1705 to 7 July 1708. During his last years he suffered cruelly from gout and, in 1713, stricken with hemiplegia, he lost the use of his right hand. He then learnt to work with his left.

At the start of his career, Jouvenet had unreserved admiration for Poussin, and it was in his style that he executed his first painting: *Moses Striking the Rock.* Later, under the influence of Le Brun, he came closer to the purely Italian idea of the 17th century. Apart from his collaboration at Versailles (Salon de Mars), mention should be made of his decoration of the Parlement de Rennes, in 1695 (perhaps destroyed during the fire of 1997); in 1702, the *Apotheosis of the Apostles,* in Les Invalides; at St-Martin-des-Champs, four paintings: *Jesus at the House of the Pharisee, The Traders Driven from the Temple, Lazarus Raised from the Dead* and *The Miraculous Draft of Fishes,* all four now in the Louvre. Louis XIV had them reproduced as tapestries by the Manufacture des Gobelins, and these were later presented to Tsar Peter the Great on his visit to France; at the church of the Fathers of Nazareth in the Rue du Temple: *Jesus at the House of Martha and Mary; Jesus Healing the Sick,* for the church of the Carthusians in Paris; *The Descent from the Cross,* for the altar of the church of the Capuchin Convent at the Rue Neuve-des-Petits-Champs, whose Baroque style was very much inspired by Rubens; *The Ascension of Jesus Christ,* for the chapels in the church of St Paul; *Innocence Pursued by Deceit,* for the ceiling of the Parlement de Rouen.

After Jouvenet lost the use of his right hand, whilst he was giving a painting lesson to his nephew Jean Restout, the son of Jean Restout I and his sister Marie-Madeleine, he used his left hand to make an alteration. The result was so satisfactory that, after a little practice, he was able to carry on his work, executing the *Magnificat* for Notre-Dame, his last work, in 1716. For a long time it adorned the high altar, and is now in one of the chapels.

It is perhaps regrettable that Jouvenet's ability to work fast sometimes led to be him being over-hasty. However, he certainly had remarkable qualities as a decorator, like Le Brun and Mignard. While these two were alive, Jouvenet occupied a place second to them, but on their deaths, he remained the uncontested master of the French Classical School.

Posthumously, Jouvenet has featured in themed exhibitions on the reign of Louis XIV, including: 1968, *Tricentenaire du rattachement de Lille à la France. Au temps du Roi Soleil, les peintres de Louis XIV* (Tercentenary of the Attach-

ment of Lille to France. At the time of the Sun King, the Painters of Louis XIV), Palais des Beaux-Arts, Lille; 2003, *Les Grands décors peints de Louis XIV. Esquisses et dessins* (*The Grand Decorative Schemes of Louis XIV: Sketches and Designs*), Château de Versailles. He was also the subject of a retrospective in 1966, at the Musée des Beaux-Arts, Rouen.

BIBLIOGRAPHY:

Schnapper, Antoine, '*De Nicolas Loir à Jean Jouvenet. Quelques traces de Poussin dans le troisième tiers du XVII siècle*' in *Revue du Louvre et des Musées de France*, no. 3, periodical, 1962. Schnapper, Antoine, *Jean Jouvenet: 1644-1717*, exhibition catalogue, Musée des Beaux-Arts, Rouen, 1966. *Tricentenaire du rattachement de Lille à la France. Au temps du Roi Soleil, les peintres de Louis XIV*, exhibition catalogue, Palais des Beaux-Arts, Lille, 1968. Morel, Guillaume, '*Versailles, l'envers du décor*' in *L'Œil*, no. 544, periodical, Librairie Léonce Laget, Paris, 1974. Bailey, Colin, et al., *Les Amours des Dieux: La Peinture Mythologique de Watteau à David*, exhibition catalogue, RMN, Paris, 1991. Bajou, Thierry, *La Peinture à Versailles, XVIIè siècle*, Buchet/Chastel, Paris, 1998. Milanovanic, Nicolas, '*Les Plafonds des grands appartements de Versailles: un traité du bon gouvernement*' in *Monuments et mémoires de l'Académie des Inscriptions et Belles-Lettres*, vol 78, Institut de France, Paris, 2000. Arrizoli-Clémentel, Pierre (preface)/Milovanovic, Nicolas, *Les Grands décors peints de Louis XIV. Esquisses et dessins*, exhibition catalogue, Actes Sud, Arles, château de Versailles, Versailles, 2003.

MUSEUMS AND GALLERIES:

ALENÇON (Mus. de Peinture): *Marriage of the Virgin* - AMIENS: *The Miraculous Draft of Fishes* - ARRAS (MBA): *The Meal at Simon's; Christ Chasing the Moneylenders out of the Temple* - BROUG-EN-BRESSE (Mus. de L'Ain): *Esther and Ahasuerus* (1675, oil on canvas) - CAEN (MBA): *Portrait of a Clergy Member* - DIJON (MBA): *The Desposition of the Cross* - FLORENCE (Uffizi): *St Anne and the Virgin* - FONTAINEBLEAU (Mus. National du Chateau): *Latona and the Farmers of Lycia* (1700, oil on canvas) - GRENOBLE: *Martyrdom of St Ovidus; Triumph of Justice* - LA FÈRE (Church): *St Peter Healing the Wounded with his Shadow* - LA FLÈCHE: *Annunciation* - LE MANS (Mus. Tessé): *Presentation of Christ in the Temple* - LILLE (MBA): *Jesus Healing the Sick; Lazarus Raised from the Dead* - LYONS: *Jesus Drives the Traders from the Temple* (1706); *The Meal at the House of Simon* (1706); *St Bruno at Prayer; Academy* (red chalk) - METZ (Mus.): *The Ascension of Christ* - MONTREUIL-SUR-MER: *The Ascension of Christ* - MUNICH (Alte Pinakothek): *Portrait of Louis Bourdaloue* (oil on canvas) - ORLÉANS (MBA): *Christ in the Olive Garden* (1707, oil on canvas) - PARIS (Cathedral of Notre-Dame): *The Visitation of the Virgin Mary* (1716, oil on canvas) - PARIS (Chapelle de L'Hopital Laënnec): *St Peter Healing with His Shadow the Sick* - PARIS (Louvre): *Jesus at the House of Martha and Mary; Jesus Healing the Sick* (1689, oil on canvas); *The Miraculous Fish; Lazarus Raised from the Dead; Descent from the Cross; The Extreme Unction; Portrait of Doctor Raymond Finot; The Mass of the Clergy de la Porte* - PARIS (Lycée Louis-le-Grand): *Darius' Family* (c. 1680, oil on canvas) - PONTOISE (Church of St-Maclou): *Deposition of the Cross* - RENNES (MBA): *Christ in the Garden of Gethsemane* (1964); *The Triumph of Justice* - RENNES (Palais de Justice): *Christ on the Cross* - RENNES (Parlement de Bretagne): group of six paintings mounted*Decor for the Grand'chambre* - ROUEN (MBA): *Self Portrait; The Rapture of St Teresa; Presentation of Jesus in the Temple; Isaac Blessing Jacob; Death of St Francis; Departure of Phaeton; The Ascension; The Annunciation; St Philip; St James the Less; St Mathias; St John; St Peter; St Paul; St Simon; St Bartholomew; St James the Great; St Jude Thaddaeus; St Andrew; St Thomas; Apotheosis of St Luke and St John* - ST PETERSBURG (Hermitage): *Portrait of a Man* - ST RIQUIER (Abbey Church): *Louis XIV Touching the Sick* - ST-GERMAIN-EN-LAYE (Musée Municipal): *St Louis Holding the Crown of Thorns* - STOCKHOLM: *St Bruno Praying on his Knees* - TOULOUSE (MBA, Mus. des Augustins): *Descent from the Cross; Founding of a Town in Germania by the Tectosages* - TOURS (MBA): *The Centurion at the Feet of Christ* - TROYES (Mus. des Beaux-Arts et d'Archéologie): *The Sacrifice of Iphigeneia* (1685, oil on canvas) - VERSAILLES (Cathedral of St Louis): *The Ressurection of Widow Naïms' Son* - VERSAILLES (Mus. national des châteaux de Versailles et de Trianon): *Victory by Hercules* (Grand appartement, Salon de Mars) - VERSAILLES (Mus. national des châteaux de Versailles et de Trianon, Chapelle Royale): *Pentecost* (1709); *St Louis Visiting the Wounded after the Battle of Al Mansurah; Zephyr and Flora* (1688, oil on canvas); *Apollo and Tethys* (1700, oil on canvas) - VERVINS (Church): *Christ in the Olive Tree Garden* (1707); *Christ Eating at Simon Pharisee*.

AUCTION RECORDS:

PARIS, 1776, *Sacrifice of Iphigenia*, FRF 3,000. PARIS, 1861, *The Marriage of the Virgin*, FRF 430. PARIS, 2 April 1874, *Portrait of the Painter by Himself*, FRF 1,120. PARIS, 1897, *Portrait of an Abbot*, FRF 230. PARIS, 28 April 1900, *The Education of the Virgin*, FRF 400. PARIS, 14 Dec 1901, *Portrait of the Artist's Mother*, FRF 1,000. NEW YORK, 12-14 March 1906, *Portrait of Madame de Celvoy*, USD 960. LONDON, 14 Dec 1907, *The Adoration of the Magi*, GBP 4. NEW YORK, 9 and 10 April 1908, *Vertumnus and Pomona*, USD 525. PARIS, 25 and 26 March 1924, *Portrait of a Man*, FRF 10,100. PARIS, 6 May 1925, *The Adoration of the Shepherds*, FRF 10,000. BRUSSELS, 6 Dec 1938, *Judgement of Solomon*, FRF 7,000. VERSAILLES, 7 June 1962, *Christ Placed in the Tomb*, FRF 4,000. VERSAILLES, 16 May 1965, *Christ Placed in the Tomb*, FRF 4,200. VERSAILLES, 15 May 1966, *Jesus Healing a Sick Woman*, FRF 7,500. ROUEN, 4 May 1972, *Lazarus Raised from the Dead*, FRF 14,000. PARIS, 2 Feb 1976, *Latona Changing the Peasants into Frogs* (oil on canvas, 51 1/4 x 43 1/4in/130 x 110cm) FRF 3,100. PARIS, 4 March 1977, *Portrait of a Man* (oil on canvas, 22 3/4 x 17in/58 x 43cm) FRF 18,000. LONDON, 12 Dec 1979, *Latona Changing the Peasants into Toads* (oil on canvas, oval, 49 1/4 x 42 1/2in/125 x 108cm) GBP 2,500. LONDON, 5 July 1984, *Christ Placed in the Tomb* (oil on canvas, 51 x 31 1/2in/129.5 x 80cm) USD 16,500. PARIS, 29 Nov 1985, *The Birth of Bacchus* (oil on canvas) FRF 300,000. LONDON, 14 April 1986, *The Virgin and Child Appearing to a Saint* (grey wash heightened with white/outlines in black chalk, rounded at the top, 17 1/2 x 10in/44.5 x 24.5cm) GBP 950. PARIS, 30 March 1987, *St Paul in Meditation* (oil on canvas, 31 x 25 1/4in/78.5 x 64cm) FRF 120,000. MONACO, 17 June 1988, *Portrait of an Officer* (1704, oil on canvas, 35 x 28in/89 x 70.2cm) FRF 24,420. PARIS, 9 April 1990, *The Assumption of the Virgin* (oil on canvas, 92 1/2 x 60 1/2in/235 x 153.5cm) FRF 400, 000. MONACO, 5-6 Dec 1991, *Study of a Man* (red chalk heightened with white chalk, 17 x 11 3/4in/42.3 x 30.1cm) FRF 4,440. NEW YORK, 17 Jan 1992, *St Paul in Meditation* (oil on canvas, 30 3/4 x 25in/78.4 x 63.8cm) USD 33,000. LONDON, 11 Dec 1992, *The Assumption of the Virgin* (oil on canvas, 92 1/2 x 60 1/2in/235 x 153.5cm) GBP 4,620. LONDON, 2 July 1996, *The Assumption of the Virgin* (black chalk and brown wash heightened with white/blue paper, 14 x 8in/35.7 x 20.3cm) GBP 4,140. NEW YORK, Jan 1998, *King St Louis Washing the Feet of a Poor Man* (oil on canvas, 44 1/4 x 57 1/4in/112.1 x 145.1cm) USD 46,000. MONTPELLIER, 16 May 1998, *Study for a Figure in the Miraculous Draft of Fishes* (1712, black chalk heightened with white chalk/paper, 17 x 22in/43 x 56cm) FRF 205,000. PARIS, 24 March 1999, *St Paul in Meditation* (oil on canvas, 29 x 23 ins / 73 x 59 cm) FRF 40,000. LONDON, 6 July 1999, *Nude Seen from Behind, Holding Dagger and*

Kneeling on Rock (chalk, 10 x 6 ins / 26 x 16 cm) GBP 4,500. NEW YORK, 18 Oct 2000, *Venus at the Forge of Vulcan* (oil on canvas, 32 x 26 ins / 81 x 65 cm) USD 37,000. PARIS, 20 Oct 2000, *Study of Figure for the Left Side of 'The Raising of Lazarus'* (black crayon/white chalk, 10 x 17 ins / 25 x 42 cm) FRF 40,000. PARIS, 11 March 2003, *Portrait Presumed to be of Francois d'Aubigne* (oil on canvas, oval, 36 x 29 ins / 92 x 74 cm) EUR 6,500. NEW YORK, 29 Jan 2004, *Deposition* (brush/brown ink/wash, 15 x 10 ins / 37 x 26 cm) USD 2,400.

JOUVENET, Jean I, the Elder
French, 16th - 17th century.
Born in Italy; died before 1615.
Painter, sculptor.
Rouen School.

Jouvenet visited Lyons and then settled in Rouen, where he lived until 1580, becoming a master there. He was the first Jouvenet in a long line of artists of this name.

JOUVENET, Jean II, the Younger
French, 17th century.
Born in Rouen; died 1675, in Rouen.
Painter, sculptor.
Rouen School.

Jean Jouvenet II the Younger was the son of Noël the Elder as well as his pupil, and brother of Laurent the Younger. The glass painter Guillaume the Elder married one of his daughters in 1665.

JOUVENET, Laurent I, the Elder
French, 17th century.
Born in Rouen; died 1616, in Rouen.
Painter, sculptor.
Rouen School.

Laurent Jouvenet I the Elder was the son of Jean Jouvenet the Elder. Nothing is know about him, except that he was a member of the guild of master painters of Rouen.

JOUVENET, Laurent II, the Younger
French, 17th century.
Born 1609, in Rouen; died 1681, in Rouen.
Painter, sculptor.
Rouen School.

Laurent Jouvenet II the Younger was a pupil of his father Noël the Elder. He is mentioned as a master painter-sculptor, and as the first teacher of his son Jean. He had 15 children by his wife Catherine Leuze, including Jean-Baptiste or the Greater, Marie-Madeleine, Jacques, a painter, Isaac, a sculptor, François, Noël III, a sculptor and Noël IV, a painter. The Jouvenet family occupied an important position in the guild of painters and sculptors in the city. After the brilliant success of Jean-Baptiste, his brothers moved to Paris and found advantageous posts thanks to his patronage. The *Presentation of Christ in the Temple* (Orleans Museum) is attributed to Laurent Jouvenet the Younger.

MUSEUMS AND GALLERIES:
ORLÉANS: *Presentation of Christ in the Temple* (attributed).

JOUVENET, Louis
French, 16th century.
Painter, carver.

Louis Jouvenet worked in Lyons in 1548 on preparations for the official visit of Henri II. He may have been the father of Jean Jouvenet the Elder.

JOUVENET, Marie Madeleine
French, 17th - 18th century.
Born c. 1655, in Rouen; died before 1729.
Painter.
Rouen School.

Marie Madeleine Jouvenet was the sister and pupil of Jean Jouvenet the Great. She married in Rouen Jean Restout I, the son of Marc Restout, of Caen. She bore him a son, Jean Restout II, on 26 March 1692. She had died by the time of the latter's marriage on 14 November 1732.

JOUVENET, Noël
French, 17th century.
Born 17th century, in Rouen.
Sculptor.

Noël Jouvenet was the son of Noël II the Younger. He was Sculptor to the King and worked for the royal châteaux, including those at Versailles, Clagny, Marly and St-Germain.

JOUVENET, Noël
French, 17th century.
Born in Rouen; died 1693, in Rouen.
Active in Paris.
Painter, sculptor.
Rouen School.

Noël Jouvenet was the son of Laurent II the Younger, and also his pupil. He is mentioned in Rouen as a master painter and sculptor, but he also worked in Paris, where he is mentioned on 13 February 1682 as Sculptor to the King's Buildings. He was married to Isabelle Guichard.

JOUVENET, Noël
French, 17th century.
Born in Rouen; died 1698.
Painter. Historical subjects, portraits.

Noël Jouvenet was the brother of Jean the Great and fifteenth child of Laurent Jouvenet. He worked at Padua in 1684, where he painted *The Family of Charles Patin*. He was summoned at this period by the Duke of Brunswick, and is mentioned as having painted a *Portrait of Karl Philip of Hanover* (now in the possession of the University of Göttingen). Houel, in his dissertation on Jean Jouvenet, states that Noël Jouvenet was painter to the Duke of Hanover, and Dussieux observes that this portrait seems to justify that assertion.

JOUVENET, Noël I, the Elder
French, 17th century.
Born in Rouen; died 1675, in Rouen.
Painter, sculptor. Historical subjects, portraits.
Rouen School.

Noël Jouvenet I the Elder was the son and pupil of Laurent Jouvenet the Elder, and a master painter-sculptor at Rouen. Bellier de la Chavignerie states this to be in 1658, which is inaccurate as it applies to his son Noël. Noël the Elder is mentioned as one of the masters of Poussin, who left Normandy about 1613. He was the father of Laurent the Younger, Noël II the Younger, and Jean II the Younger.

AUCTION RECORDS:
PARIS, 1865, *Portrait of the Artist by Himself,* FRF 245.

JOUVENET, Noël II, the Younger
French, 17th century.
Born in Rouen; died 17th century, in Rouen.
Painter, sculptor.
Rouen School.

Noël Jouvenet II the Younger was the son of Noël the Elder and a pupil of his father. He was admitted as a master painter-sculptor in 1658 at Rouen.

JOUVENOT, Stanislas Charles
French, 19th century.
Born 7 May 1861, in St-Martin-de-Ré (Charente-Maritime).
Active in Charpont (Eure-et-Loir).
Engraver (etching).

Stanislas Jouvenot was a pupil of Cabanel and of Lancelot. As a member of the Société des Artistes Français, he was represented at the Salon from 1902. He received the Belin-Dollet prize in 1926.

JOUVENSEL
French, 20th century.
Engraver.
Jouvensel became a member of the Société des Artistes Français in Paris in 1908. He exhibited at the Society's salons.

JOUVET-MAGRON, Dominique
French, 20th century.
Born 20th century, in Vire.
Engraver (etching).
Dominique Jouvet-Magron worked in Paris and became a member of the Salon des Artistes Français in Paris in 1908.

JOUVRAY, Madeleine
French, 19th century.
Born 19th century, in Paris.
Sculptor. Figures, landscapes. Busts.
Madeleine Jouvray was an associate of the National École des Beaux-Arts and she exhibited at the Salon in this capacity. She obtained an honourable mention at the Société des Artistes Français in 1889.
MUSEUMS AND GALLERIES:
CHÂTEAU-THIERRY: *Wild Pansy* - COMPIÈGNE: *Bust of Bacchante* - GRAY: *Slave* - TOURCOING: *A Spring*.

JOUX, Claude de. See **DEJOUX Claude**

JOUY, Jehan de. See **JEHAN de Jouy**

JOUY, Joseph Nicolas
French, 19th century.
Born 11 September 1809, in Paris.
Painter, engraver. Military subjects, portraits.
Joseph Jouy entered the École des Beaux-Arts on 10 May 1824 as a pupil of Ingres. He was awarded a second class medal in 1835 and first class in 1839. His work appeared at the Salon de Paris from 1827 to 1880. Among his works is cited a romantic etching: *Urbain Grandier* in the style of his 1839 painting as well as *Torture of Urbain Grandier*.
BIBLIOGRAPHY:
Les Années romantiques, la peinture française de 1815 à 1850, exhibition catalogue, Musée des Beaux-Arts, Nantes, Galeries nationales du Grand Palais, Paris, 1996.
MUSEUMS AND GALLERIES:
BORDEAUX: *Urbain Grandier; The Torture of Urbain Grandier* - MÂCON: *Portrait of Madame Nonjon and her Two Daughters* (1839) - ST-OMER: *Portrait of Madame Nonjon and her Two Daughters* (1839) - VERSAILLES: *Portrait of Aubeterre de Lusson; Battle of Heilsberg 10 January 1807; Batle of Rocroy; Siege of Landau; The Taking of Furnes; Crossing the Mincio and the Battle of Pozzola; The Taking of la Lunette St Laurent 14 December 1832; Battles of Tirlement and Goizenhoven*.
AUCTION RECORDS:
PARIS, 15 Nov 1900, *The two Sisters*, FRF 172. PARIS, 6 March 1979, *Family Meeting in the Park* (1842, oil on canvas, 30¾ x 40½ ins / 78 x 103 cm) FRF 10,000.

JOVAN IZ PECI, also known as John of Pec
Serb, 14th century.
Active during the first half of the 14th century.
Painter.
John of Pec is believed to have been a monk who painted frescoes for the church of St Demetrios from 1316 to 1324. The frescoes depict the ecumenical council and the council of Njemanjic. Although he was required to follow an iconographical protocol for these works, the frescoes show evidence of his spontaneous, rather crude style.

JOVANE, Achille
Italian, 19th century.
Active in Naples at the beginning of the 19th century.
Painter. Mythological subjects, religious subjects, historical subjects.
Jovane was a pupil at the Accademia in Naples and first exhibited at the city's fine art exhibition of 1837 with two paintings, *Mercury and Apollo* and *Dying Gladiator*; in 1839 he showed an *Annunciation* there. Among his historical paintings is a *Departure of Charles III of Bourbon for the Battle of Velletri in 1744*. He also painted religious pictures such as *St Catherine* for the church of S Caterina, Naples, and *Martyrdom of St Crispin* for the church of this name in Naples.

JOVANOVIC, Anastas
Bulgarian, 19th century.
Born 1817, in Vratsa.
Lithographer, painter (?). Portraits.
Anastas Jovanovic worked in Belgrade and Vienna. He engraved lithograph portraits of many well-known personalities from the southern Slav states, including, notably, *The Philosopher D. Obradovic, The Poet L. Musicki, Prince Milos, Patriach Rajacic*, and *Prince Danilo*.

JOVANOVIC, Paja, or Yovanovitch
Serb, 19th - 20th century.
Born 4 June 1859, in Vrsac; died 30 November 1957, in Belgrade.
Sculptor.
Paja Jovanovic studied at the Akademie der Bildenden Künste in Vienna and under Henri M.-A. Chapu and Jean-Antoine Injalbert in Paris. He was elected member of the Royal Serbian Academy of Sciences in 1888. He was Serbia's preeminent historical artist (one of his most famous works is *The Migration of the Serbs*) and also painted religious works and portraits in the traditional academic style. Jovanovic won prizes in Vienna in 1893, Berlin in 1900, a bronze medal at the 1889 Exposition Universelle in Paris and the gold medal at the 1900 Exposition Universelle for *Coronation of Tsar Dushan* (now in the Belgrade Museum). After World War I, Jovanovic divided his time between Belgrade and Vienna.
MUSEUMS AND GALLERIES:
BELGRADE: *Coronation of Tsar Dushan*.

JOVANOVIC, Pajo
Slav, 19th century.
Painter.
He painted a picture entitled *Rescue Party*.

JOVÁNOVICS, György
Hungarian, 20th century.
Born 1939, in Budapest.
Painter (mixed media).
György Jovánovics studied at the schools of fine art in Budapest (1958-1960), Vienna (1964-1965), then Paris (1965-1966). He spent time in Berlin between 1980 and 1983 thanks to a grant. He lives in Budapest.

In 1973, he exhibited wooden objects and plaster motifs called *Ecstatic Sign*, which had nothing to do with any idea of ecstasy in their form, content and crude craftsmanship, except as derision of conventional attitudes. He then practised the Surrealist technique of 'frottage' (rubbing). He took part in many avant-garde events in Hungary and collective exhibitions in Europe, notably in Germany, where he is represented in the Ludwig collections. He appeared at the 8th Biennale in Paris in 1973 and at the Venice Biennale in 1995.
BIBLIOGRAPHY:
Sinkovincs, P., *Jovánovics*, Budapest, 1985. Kovalovszky, Marta K., *György Jovánovics*, exhibition catalogue, Szent István Király Múzeum, Székesfehérvár, 1995.

JOVENAU, Jean, called Jean-Jovenau
French, 20th century.
Born 17 September 1888, in Paris.
Painter. Portraits, landscapes, still-lifes.
Jean Joveneau studied at the École des Beaux-Arts in Paris and under Tony Robert-Fleury at the Académie Julian. The

first pieces he exhibited were views of the Île St-Louis. In 1903, he exhibited *Studio Corner* at the Salon of the Société des Artistes Français in Paris; in 1913, at the first international Sezessionist exhibition in Rome, he showed a still-life entitled *Pot of Gaillardias* and in 1912 at the Cologne Federation exhibition a piece entitled *Delta Square*. After producing landscapes in a tame, Impressionist style, Joveneau came under the spell of Braque's aesthetic approach. One of his still-lifes, *Hare and Statue of Cupid* was purchased by the French State.

AUCTION RECORDS:

PARIS, 4 May 1923, *Seascape*, FRF 380. PARIS, 26 Feb 1927, *Opium Smoke*, FRF 800. PARIS, July 1946, *Violin and Score*, FRF 2,600. LONDON, 10 April 1962, *Still-life with Fruit and Teapot*, GBP 420. PARIS, 4 July 1969, *Still-life*, Gns 650. ZURICH, 6 June 1985, *Still-life with Guitar* (oil on canvas, 35½ x 28¾ ins / 90 x 73 cm) CHF 5,500. PARIS, 8 Nov 1989, *Still-life with Coffee Pot* (oil on card, 18½ x 22 ins / 47 x 56 cm) FRF 8,000. PARIS, 4 March 1991, *Château Carp* (oil on canvas, 39¼ x 32 ins / 100 x 81 cm) FRF 5,800.

JOVER CASANOVA, Francisco

Spanish, 19th century.

Born c. 1830, in Muro (Alicante); died 22 February 1890, in Madrid.

Painter. History painting, portraits.

Francisco Jover Casanova studied at the school of painting in Madrid. He first exhibited at the exhibition of the national fine arts society of Madrid in 1862. In 1864 his painting *The Last Moments of Philip II* was purchased for the national museum. He went to Rome and remained there until 1870. When he returned to Spain, he painted numerous portraits and also frescoes for the church of S Antonio in Cádiz. He was appointed teacher of drawing at the Madrid conservatory.

MUSEUMS AND GALLERIES:

MADRID (Prado): *The Last Moments of Philip II; 16th-Century Soldier* - VALLADOLID: *Christopher Columbus before King Ferdinand and Queen Isabella*.

JOVER CASTELLS, Francisco

Spanish, 20th century.

Born in Barcelona.

Painter. Landscapes.

Francisco Jover Castells studied at the La Lonja art school in Barcelona. He exhibited in both group exhibitions and solo shows.

BIBLIOGRAPHY:

Arnáiz, José Manuel/López Jiménez, Javier/Merchán Díaz, Manuel (ed.), *Cien años de pintura en Espana y Portugal (1830-1930)*, Antiqvaria, Madrid, 1990.

JOVI, Bruno Jean

French, 20th century.

Born 26 August 1939, in Kouba, Algeria.

Active in Canada since 1980.

Painter, draughtsman, illustrator.

Bruno Jean Jovi studied at the École des Beaux-Arts in Algiers. He began exhibiting in Algeria and received the association of French North African artists' prize in 1959. He was also awarded a bronze medal by the circle of artist in Quebec.

JOVIN, Aimée. See **CHÉRON Aimée, Mme**

JOVINO, Félix

Italian, 20th century.

Born 1882, in San Paolo Bel Sito (Caserta).

Active in Paris.

Sculptor.

A pupil at the Accademia di Belle Arti in Naples, Félix Jovino worked in Naples and Paris, where he exhibited in 1910 and from 1920 to 1922 at the Salon des Artistes Français with *Bust of Verlaine*, *Bacchante* and *Dance of Love* (marble relief). For Thiviers, in the Dordogne, he carved a marble monument, and in the cemetery of Pont-Audemer there is a low relief by him in memory of an officer killed in World War I. He was a member of the Société des Artistes Français.

JOVY-NAKATENU, Marianne

German, 20th century.

Born 1906, in Bonn.

Sculptor.

Marianne Jovy-Nakatenu was a student at the school of fine art in Düsseldorf, and in 1932 attended the courses offered by the École des Beaux-Arts in Paris. She exhibited in Germany and elsewhere in Europe, with sculpted figures in marble, porphyritic rock, sandstone and bronze moulds.

JOWETT, Percy Hague

British, 20th century.

Born 1 June 1882, in Halifax (Yorkshire); died 4 March 1955, in London.

Painter, watercolourist. Landscapes, interiors, rural scenes.

Percy Jowett was a British painter whose legacy as an art teacher has superseded the achievements of his artistic career. He studied at Leeds School of Art and the Royal College of Art (1904-1907). After serving during the World War I for the Royal Garrison Artillery, his professional career as an artist began to unfold. He was one of the founding members of the Seven and Five Society (1919), where he met Paul Nash, Ben Nicholson and Henry Moore, amongst others, and his work was exhibited at the Royal Academy from 1907 until the 1920s. Jowett's future as an art teacher and administrator began with his role as Head of the Chelsea School of Art (1927-1929). He became Director of the Central School of Art (1929-1935) and Principal of the Royal College of Art (1935-1947). During his tenure at the Royal College of Art, Jowett was invited to join the War Artists' Advisory Committee in 1939. He was one of the three artists named by the committee to direct a project called 'Recording Britain'. Together with Kenneth Clark, then Director of the National Gallery, and William Russell, Jowett put in place a series of governmental commissions designed to leave a visual record of Britain before the country suffered the effects of the World War II.

The St George's Gallery in London held solo exhibitions of his work in 1923, 1925, 1927 and 1929. Other solo exhibitions in London were also organised by the Perkin Gallery, in 1974 and 1983, and the Clarges Gallery, in 1978.

BIBLIOGRAPHY:

Watercolours by P.H. Jowett: St. George's Gallery, exhibition catalogue, St. George's Gallery, London, 1929. *Percy Hague Jowett 1882-1955: Watercolours*, exhibition catalogue, Clarges Gallery, London, 1978. *Percy Hague Jowett, 1882-1955: An Exhibition of Early Paintings and Watercolours*, exhibition catalogue, Parkin Gallery, London, 1983.

MUSEUMS AND GALLERIES:

MANCHESTER (Whitworth Art Gallery, University of Manchester): *The River Kent at Staveley* (1924) - NEWCASTLE (Laing Art Gallery): *Cider Press Farm, Llantarnam* (1931).

AUCTION RECORDS:

PENZANCE, 27 July 2000, *Cattle Grazing in a Meadow* (1907, oil on board, 19 x 23 ins / 49 x 59 cm) GBP 1,000. SALISBURY, 1 Oct 2003, *Holy Family. Virgin Mary and an Angel* (1915, oil on board, a pair, 16 x 18 ins / 41 x 46 cm) GBP 1,100.

JOY, Albert Bruce. See **BRUCE-JOY Albert**

JOY, Arthur

Irish, 19th century.

Born c. 1808, in Dublin; died 16 November 1838, in London.

Painter. History painting, genre scenes, landscapes.

Arthur Joy exhibited his painting *View of Dublin Bay* in 1830 at the Academy in Dublin. In 1838, he showed a small painting entitled *Young Welsh Girl* at the British Institution in London. In Dublin again in 1836, he showed his *Don Quixote at the Inn* at the Academy exhibition. There is also mention of watercolour paintings including *Views of Rouen*.

JOY, François
French, 18th century.
Active in Nantes c. 1755.
Glass painter.

JOY, George William
British, 19th - 20th century.
Born 1844, in Dublin; died 28 October 1925.
Active in Bristol.
Painter. History painting, genre scenes, figures.

George William Joy was the son of William Joy. He studied initially in Paris and then at the Royal Academy in London, where he exhibited for the first time in 1872 - and subsequently, with some success. His charming work *The Danaides* was shown at the Salon des Artistes Français in 1892, winning a bronze medal. He also obtained a jury commendation at the Exposition Universelle in Paris in 1900, and was awarded a medal in Munich in 1896. His painting *Joan of Arc*, exhibited in 1896, was bought by the French state and is now in the Musée des Beaux-Arts in Rouen.

Museums and Galleries:
Bristol (City Museum and Art Gallery): *Kirkman Daniel Hodgson* (oil on canvas) - Leeds (City AG): *Cordelia Comforting her Father, King Lear, in Prison* (1886, oil on canvas); *General Gordon's Last Stand* (exhibited in 1893, oil on canvas) - Oldham: *A Supper of Grasses* - Rouen: *Joan of Arc*.

Auction records:
London, 24 Oct 1980, *Truth* (oil on canvas, 101 x 37 1/4 ins / 256.5 x 94.5 cm) GBP 7,000. New York, 25 Feb 1983, *Joan of Arc* (oil on canvas, 65 x 45 ins / 165.1 x 114.3 cm) USD 4,500. London, 12 May 1993, *Wood Nymph* (oil on canvas, 15 1/4 x 19 ins / 39 x 48 cm) GBP 1,437.

JOY, Jessey (Miss)
British, 19th century.
Active in Richmond (Yorkshire).
Painter. Figures.

Jessey Joy exhibited in London at the Royal Academy, the British Institution and at the Suffolk Street Gallery from 1843 to 1869.

JOY, John Cantiloe
British, 19th century.
Born 1806, in Yarmouth; died 1857 or 1867, in Chichester.
Painter. Seascapes.

John Cantiloe Joy, like his brother William, was self taught. He worked principally in Yarmouth, and exhibited at Suffolk Street in London in 1826 and 1827.

Auction records:
London, 7 March 1910, *Man of War at Anchor; Stiff Breeze* (two watercolours forming a pendant) GBP 17. London, 6 Nov 1973, *Fishing Boats at Sea* (watercolour) Gns 650. London, 29 Jan 1999, *Scene on Yarmouth Beach from Nature* (watercolour, 6x9 ins / 16x24 cm) GBP 2,600. Aylsham, 23 April 1999, *Boat in Distress by Jetty with Numerous Figures* (watercolour, 6x9 ins / 15x23 cm) GBP 480. Knowle, 26 July 2000, *British Frigate with Other Shipping* (watercolour, scratching out, 8x12 ins / 21x30 cm) GBP 3,300. London, 9 Nov 2000, *Inshore Anchorage* (pencil, pen, brown ink and watercolour, 9x14 ins / 23x35 cm) GBP 600. Knowle, 14 Feb 2001, *Shipping off a Harbour* (watercolour, 5x9 ins / 12x22 cm) GBP 1,750. Norfolk, 14 June 2001, *French Lugger Prize to a British Brig of the War* (watercolour, 8x11 ins / 20x28 cm) GBP 1,400. London, 19 June 2002, *Cutter Running up Southampton Water with Calshot Castle off her Port Bow* (pencil and watercolour, 5x9 ins / 12x22 cm) GBP 2,400. London, 31 Oct 2002, *Inshore Squadron* (watercolour, 7x10 ins / 18x26 cm) GBP 320. London, 22 Jan 2003, *Shipping off the Norfolk Coast* (pencil and watercolour, 6x9 ins / 16x23 cm) GBP 4,000. London, 14 Sept 2004, *Queen Victoria, in the Royal Yacht Victoria and Albert I* (watercolour heightened with white, 8x11 ins / 20x29 cm) GBP 4,000.

JOY, Thomas Musgrave
British, 19th century.
Born 1812, in Boughton Monchelsea (Kent); died 7 April 1866.
Painter. Portraits, genre scenes.

Thomas Musgrave Joy was a pupil of Drummond. He first exhibited in London at the Society of British Artists in 1832; he exhibited at the Royal Academy in 1833. For Queen Victoria, he painted portraits of the Prince and Princess of Wales. There is also mention of several genre scenes inspired by Molière's comedies, as well as Joy's 1864 painting, *Meeting at Tattersall before the Races* which shows all the famous English sportsmen of the time.

Museums and Galleries:
York: *Mother*.

Auction records:
London, 23 Nov 1982, *Hyde Park in the season, entrance of Her Majesty and HRH the Prince Consort* (1860, oil on canvas, 20 x 36 ins / 51 x 91.5 cm) GBP 1,700. London, 13 June 1984, *The Post Office* (1856, oil on canvas, oval, 22 3/4 x 19 ins / 58 x 48 cm) GBP 4,800. London, 12 June 1985, *Entry of the Royal Carriage into Hyde Park* (oil on canvas, 19 3/4 x 28 3/4 ins / 50 x 73 cm) GBP 4,600. New York, 23 Feb 1989, *On the Way to School* (1860, oil on canvas, 36 1/4 x 24 1/2 ins / 92 x 62.2 cm) USD 19,800. New York, 17 Feb 1993, *Barber of Seville* (1861, oil on canvas, 28 1/4 x 36 1/2 ins / 71.8 x 92.7 cm) USD 4,600. New York, 26 May 1993, *Help Getting onto the Autobus* (oil on canvas, 30 x 25 ins / 76.2 x 63.5 cm) USD 17,250. Ludlow, 29 Sept 1994, *The Vicar of Wakefield's Family on their Way to Church* (1857, oil on canvas, 27 1/2 x 35 1/2 ins / 70 x 90 cm) GBP 8,625. London, 29 March 1996, *Test of Love, A German Legend* (1843, oil on canvas, 43 x 31 1/2 ins / 109.2 x 80 cm) GBP 4,370. London, 7 June 1996, *Traveller in 1760: Your Money or Your Life; Traveller Today: Tickets, Please* (1861, oil on canvas, a pair, 11 1/4 x 16 1/2 ins / 28.5 x 42 cm) GBP 5,750. London, 9 June 1999, *Brighton Diamonds* (1856, oil on canvas, 18 x 22 ins / 45 x 56 cm) GBP 8,000. London, 11 June 2002, *Portrait of a Lady. Portrait of a Gentleman* (1864, oil on canvas, a pair, 36 x 28 ins / 91 x 71 cm) GBP 1,800. London, 20 Feb 2003, *Charing Cross to Bank Omnibus* (oil on canvas, 30 x 25 ins / 76 x 63 cm) GBP 29,000.

JOY, William
British, 19th century.
Born 1803, in Great Yarmouth; died 1867, in Chichester.
Painter, watercolourist. History painting, landscapes, seascapes.

William Joy taught himself to paint and, with his brother, John, became known as a painter of seascapes. The two brothers worked mainly in Great Yarmouth where they were known as The Brothers Joy. William exhibited in London from 1823 to 1845, at the Royal Academy, the British Institution and at Suffolk Street.

Museums and Galleries:
London (Victoria and Albert Mus.): *King George IV Passing through Yarmouth on his Return from Edinburgh in 1822* (watercolour) - Norwich (Castle Mus. and AG): *Boat Going to a Vessel in Distress; Saving a Crew, Yarmouth; Lifeboat Going to a Vessel in Distress*.

AUCTION RECORDS:
LONDON, 7 Dec 1807, *Hampstead Heath*, GBP 2. LONDON, 30 July 1928, *Phoenix; Roebuck; The Tarter on the Hudson*, GBP 567. LONDON, 12 Dec 1972, *Seascape* (watercolour) Gns 1,000. LONDON, 4 April 1973, *Fishing Boat at Sea*, GBP 3,600. LONDON, 1 April 1976, *Ma at Sea* (watercolour, 10 1/4 x 14 1/4 ins / 26 x 36 cm) GBP 750. LONDON, 18 June 1976, *Seaside Scene* (oil on canvas, 25 3/4 x 44 ins / 65.5 x 112 cm) GBP 1,800. LONDON, 13 Nov 1979, *Boats off the Coast* (watercolour and pencil, 11 1/2 x 17 1/4 ins / 29.3 x 43.5 cm) GBP 1,000. LONDON, 18 March 1981, *Boats and Sailing Ships in a Landscape* (1832, oil on canvas, 40 3/4 x 64 ins / 103.5 x 162.5 cm) GBP 13,000. LONDON, 2 March 1983, *English Men o' War and other Vessels off the Coast* (oil on canvas, 20 x 29 ins / 51 x 73.5 cm) GBP 8,000. LONDON, 12 July 1984, *Boat off the Coast* (1856, watercolour, 11 x 14 1/4 ins / 28 x 36 cm) GBP 1,300. LONDON, 20 Nov 1986, *Sailing Boats in a Strong Breeze* (1859, watercolour, 12 1/4 x 18 1/2 ins / 31 x 47 cm) GBP 2,100. LONDON, 31 May 1989, *Fishing Boats in the Evening* (watercolour/paper, 9 x 11 1/2 ins / 22 x 29 cm) GBP 1,650. LONDON, 20 July 1990, *Greenwich seen from the Thames with the Lord Mayor Embarking and Fishermen in the Foreground* (oil on canvas, 59 3/4 x 139 ins / 152 x 353 cm) GBP 7,700. LONDON, 22 May 1991, *English Man o'War approaching Portsmouth* (watercolour, 11 x 14 ins / 27 x 35.5 cm) GBP 3,960. LONDON, 8 April 1992, *Panoramic view of Harting Hill in Sussex* (1838, oil on canvas, 24 1/4 x 33 3/4 ins / 61.5 x 86 cm) GBP 3,960. LONDON, 16 July 1993, *English Man o'War off a Port* (watercolour, 9 3/4 x 16 1/2 ins / 25 x 42 cm) GBP 2,530. LONDON, 9 Nov 1994, *The Royal Yacht Reviewing the Fleet* (oil on canvas, 17 1/2 x 26 1/2 ins / 44.5 x 67 cm) GBP 3,220. LONDON, 3 May 1995, *English Man o'War in a Rough Sea* (*English Man o'War in a Rough Sea*) (oil on canvas, 17 x 26 ins / 43 x 66 cm) GBP 2,990. LONDON, 29 May 1997, *Dutch Ships in a Strong Breeze* (*Dutch Ships in a Strong Breeze*) (1859, watercolour heightened with scratches, 12 1/4 x 18 1/4 ins / 31 x 46.5 cm) GBP 3,680. BISHOPS STORTFORD, 9 Feb 1999, *Shipping in Distress off the Coast with Figures in Wreckage* (watercolour heightened with white and scratching out, 8 x 11 ins / 21 x 29 cm) GBP 4,800. LONDON, 25 Nov 1999, *American Man of War and Other Shipping. British Shipping in Rough Seas* (watercolour and pencil heightened with gouache, scratching out and stopping out, a pair, 11 x 16 ins / 27 x 40 cm) GBP 4,200. LONDON, 9 Nov 2000, *British Frigate in Pursuit of the Enemy* (1854, pen, brown ink, watercolour and scratching out, 8 x 11 ins / 20 x 29 cm) GBP 3,000. LONDON, 29 Nov 2000, *English and Dutch Shipping at Anchor* (watercolour over pencil heightened with gouache, gum arabic and stopping out, 6 x 8 ins / 14 x 21 cm) GBP 3,200. GENOA, 6 June 2001, *Portrait of Sailing Ships* (oil on canvas, 17 x 26 ins / 42 x 65 cm) ITL 17,050,000. BURY ST EDMUNDS, 2 Oct 2001, *Off Yarmouth* (watercolour, 9 x 15 ins / 24 x 37 cm) GBP 3,600. LONDON, 31 Oct 2002, *Men-o-War, Art Spithead* (1857, pencil and watercolour heightened with white, 11 x 15 ins / 27 x 39 cm) GBP 3,500. LONDON, 31 Oct 2002, *Frigate Anchored in the Roadstead, Another Following Her In* (oil on canvas, 20 x 28 ins / 51 x 72 cm) GBP 12,000. PENZANCE, 11 Dec 2003, *British War Ships and Other Shipping Under Sail in a Stiff Breeze* (1854, watercolour, 10 x 14 ins / 26 x 36 cm) GBP 5,000. PENZANCE, 11 Dec 2003, *British War Ships at Anchor and Other Shipping in a Calm Anchorage* (1857, watercolour, 11 x 15 ins / 28 x 39 cm) GBP 5,000. PENZANCE, 15 June 2004, *Still Day, Two Warships at Anchor with Much Other Shipping* (1857, watercolour, 11 x 15 ins / 28 x 38 cm) GBP 3,200. PENZANCE, 15 June 2004, *Line of Battleship and Frigate Getting Under Way, Sunrise, Bright Morning* (1854, watercolour, 10 x 14 ins / 25 x 36 cm) GBP 3,500.

JOYAN
French, 19th century.
Died 1874.
Sculptor.

Joyan worked in London in 1855 and remained there for more than 20 years.

JOYANT, Jules Romain, or Joyan
French, 19th century.
Born 16 August 1803, in Paris; died 6 July 1854, in Paris.
Painter, engraver, watercolourist. Landscapes, urban landscapes, architectural views.

Jules Joyant was a pupil of Xavier Bidauld and Guillaume Lethière. Following a meeting with Bonington at the beginning of 1828, he decided to go to Italy. He made three journeys to Italy between 1828 and 1835.

He exhibited his works at the Salon de Paris between 1835 and 1854. He was awarded a second class medal in 1835 as well as first class medals in 1840 and 1848. He was decorated by the Légion d'Honneur in 1852.

He specialised in representing scenes of Venice in the style of the Italian Veduttists of the 18th century: Pannini, Canaletto, and Guardi. He was a brilliant colourist with impeccable design. His works include views of Rome, Florence and Bologna. He engraved several views of Venice.

Among his individual exhibitions can be cited: 1978 museum of Art and History, Louis Senlecq, L'Isle Adam, 2003, *Sur la route de Venice Jules-Roamin Joyant. Les Voyages en Italie du 'Canaletto français'* (*On the Road to Venice. Jules Romain Joyant. Travels of the 'French Canaletto' in Italy.*)

Stamp of sale

BIBLIOGRAPHY:
Les Années romantiques, la peinture française de 1815 à 1850, exhibition catalogue, Musée des Beaux-Arts, Nantes, Galeries nationales du Grand Palais, Paris, 1996. Fossier, François/Julia, Isabelle, et al., *Sur la route de Venise, Jules-Romain Joyant: les voyages en Italie du Canaletto français*, exhibition catalogue, Musée Louis Senlecq, L'Isle-Adam, Somogy, Paris, 2003.

MUSEUMS AND GALLERIES:
ALBI (Mus. Toulouse-Lautrec) - AMIENS: *View from the Rialto Bridge in Venice* (1841) - DIJON (MBA): *View from the Campo Vaccino in Rome* (1843) - DIJON (Mus. Magnin): *View of the Forum from Santa-Francesca-Romana church* - L'ISLE-ADAM (MAH Louis-Senlecq): gift of five hundred drawings - NANTES (MBA): *View of the Santa-Maria della Salute in Venice* (1835); *Oriental Landscape* - POITIERS: *The Rialto; Palace of Manin, the last Doge of the Venetian Republic on the Grand Canal in Venice* (1848) - TOULOUSE (MBA, Mus. des Augustins): *The Ancient Palais des Papes in Avignon* (1845); *View of Venice*.

AUCTION RECORDS:
PARIS, 1886, *View of Venice*, FRF 800. PARIS, 30 Nov-2 Dec 1920, *Venice, Scene near the Rialto* (sepia) FRF 1,200. PARIS, July 1946, *Canal in Venice*, FRF 4,500. LONDON, 14 March 1969, *View of Venice*, Gns 2,000. LONDON, 6 May 1977, *View of Venice* (1834, oil on canvas, 65 x 40 1/2 ins / 165.1 x 102.8 cm) GBP 2,200. LONDON, 28 Nov 1980, *Entrance to the Grand Canal, Venice* (oil on panel, 46 1/2 x 63 1/4 ins / 118.2 x 160.6 cm) GBP 8,000. LONDON, 29 Nov 1982, *Grand Canal at Dusk, Venice* (1839, oil on canvas, 18 x 25 1/2 ins / 46 x 65 cm) GBP 2,800. NEW YORK, 25 Oct 1984, *View of Bologna* (oil on panel, 12 1/2 x 9 1/2 ins / 31.7 x 24.2 cm) USD 1,500. PARIS, 12 Dec 1990, *Stepped Street near the Piazetta* (lead pencil, pen and sepia wash, 16 x 10 3/4 ins / 40.5 x 27.5 cm) FRF 15,000. PARIS, 25 Nov 1993, *View of the Salute in Venice* (pen and bistre wash, 16 1/4 x 22 3/4 ins / 41 x 58 cm) FRF 12,000. NEW YORK, 19 Jan 1994, *Rialto Bridge at Sunset* (1830, oil on canvas,

18¼ x 25¾ ins / 46.4 x 65.7 cm) USD 2,990. LONDON, 28 June 1999, *The Doge's Palace* (1834, oil on canvas, 41 x 65 ins / 104 x 165 cm) GBP 20,000. PARIS, 25 Oct 1999, *Square in Venice* (oil on canvas, 14 x 11 ins / 36 x 28 cm) FRF 48,000. BILLINGSHURST, 1 Feb 2000, *View of the Rialto Bridge, Venice* (1841, oil on panel, 14 x 12 ins / 36 x 30 cm) GBP 5,000. PARIS, 23 March 2001, *View of Venice* (colour ink/colour wash, 16 x 23 ins / 41 x 58 cm) FRF 23,000. PARIS, 28 Nov 2002, *View of the Capitol* (crayon/watercolour, 16 x 20 ins / 40 x 51 cm) EUR 3,500. LYONS-LA-FORÊT, 12 Oct 2003, *View of a Ruelle in Venice* (oil on panel, 9 x 6 ins / 22 x 15 cm) EUR 1,600. MILAN, 18 May 2004, *Venice, Campo SS Giovanni e Paolo* (1838, oil on canvas, 18 x 26 ins / 46 x 65 cm) EUR 10,000.

JOYARD, Angel
French, 19th century.
Born 21 June 1809, in Lyons.
Painter.

Angel Joyard studied at the École des Beaux-Arts in Lyons where he was admitted in 1822. From 1841 to 1847 in Paris he exhibited religious and historical subjects and a portrait. His most significant works are: *Babylon in Captivity, Ruth and Boaz* (1841), *The Druidesses of Armorica* (1842), *The Holy Women* (1845), and *The Holy Rosary* (1846).

JOYAU
French, 18th century.
Painter.

Joyau specialised in painting bunches of flowers at the royal porcelain factory known as the Manufacture de Sèvres from 1766 to 1775. He worked with other artists on the paintings for a table service which Louis XVI gave to the Court of Sweden, and which is kept in the royal castle at Stockholm.

JOYAU, Amédée
French, 19th - 20th century.
Born 1872, probably in Nantes; died 7 August 1913, in Fontainebleau.
Painter, watercolourist, engraver. Landscapes.

Amédée Joyau became an associate of the Salon of the Société Nationale des Beaux-Arts in 1901 and exhibited at the Society's salon in Paris and at the exhibitions of the Salon d'Automne. He left 35 engravings dating from 1895 to 1913, mainly multi-coloured wood engravings.

BIBLIOGRAPHY:
Curtis, A., *Catalogue de l'œuvre gravé de Amédée Joyau*, Prouté, Paris, 1938.

AUCTION RECORDS:
PARIS, 29 May 1929, *Beech Trunks* (watercolour) FRF 150. PARIS, 7 March 1988, *Mosques and Houses in Old Cairo* (watercolour, 10½ x 7¾ ins / 26.5 x 19.5 cm) FRF 3,500.

JOYBERT, de (Mme la Comtesse)
French, 19th century.
Born 31 December 1851, in Cuisy-les-Fiers (Aisne).
Active in Paris.
Painter.

Mme la Comtesse Joybert was a member of the Société des Artistes Français from 1885 and presented her work at the Salon as part of this group.

JOYET, Jean
French, 20th century.
Born 25 May 1919, in St-Victumien (Haute-Savoie).
Painter.

Jean Joyet's paintings sometimes border on abstraction. He exhibits at the Salon Comparaisons in Paris and is a member of the Salon d'Automne and the Salon des Indépendants.

JOYEUX, Pierre
French, 20th century.
Born 11 July 1881, in Angoulême.
Sculptor.

Pierre Joyeux studied under Coutan and became a member of the Salon des Artistes Français in Paris.

JOYEUX, Pierre Samuel Louis
Swiss, 18th - 19th century.
Born 1749, in La Tour-de-Peil; died 1 December 1818, in Vevey.
Engraver.

Pierre Joyeux was a burgher of La-Tour-de-Peilz and Vevey. Six engravings on copper (signed: Joyeux et Wexalberg) were shown at the National Exhibition in Geneva in 1896 (four of them coloured). They are views of Vevey.

JOYSE, Cardin
French, 16th century.
Born in Rouen; died c. 1512.
Painter (glass).
Rouen School.

Joyse produced stained glass windows for the church of St-Ouen in Rouen.

JOZAN, real name: Watanabe Teiko, given name: Shukuho, nickname: Goro, artist name: Jozan
Japanese, 19th century.
Born 1817; died 1837.
Painter. Landscapes.

Jozan was a Nanga (literati) painter and the younger brother of the painter Kazan (179⅔-1841).

AUCTION RECORDS:
PARIS, 5 July 1994, *Boat Trip* (oil on canvas, 17 x 24 ins / 43 x 61 cm) FRF 14,000.

JOZAN, Saintin François
French, 19th century.
Born 28 January 1797, in Paris; died 1867 or 1868.
Painter, draughtsman.

Saintin Jozan was a pupil of Lafon. He entered the École des Beaux-Arts on 6 April 1819 and presented his work at the Salon from 1831 to 1859 with portraits, still-lifes and genre subjects.

AUCTION RECORDS:
PARIS, 20 March 1920, *Virgin and the Child Jesus* (pastel) FRF 160.

JOZANT, E.
French (?).
Painter. Portraits.

AUCTION RECORDS:
PARIS, 18 Feb 1926, *Portrait of a Young Man*, FRF 580.

JOZEN. See **JOKI**

JOZON, Jeanne
French, 19th - 20th century.
Born 15 July 1868, in Paris; died 1946.
Sculptor.

Jeanne Jozone studied at the École des Beaux-Arts in Bourges under M. D. Puech. She became a member of the Salon des Artistes Français in Paris in 1906, receiving a commendation in 1897.

JOZSA, Karoly
Hungarian, 20th century.
Born 16 December 1872, in Budapest.
Engraver, draughtsman, painter, illustrator.

Karoly Jozsa studied in Vienna, Munich and at the Académie Julian in Paris. He worked in Munich and later in Budapest. He engraved figure compositions on wood: *Evening; Victorious; Amazons, Indian Chief*, and portraits. He also produced etchings and paintings and worked as an illustrator and designer of medals.

AUCTION RECORDS:
PARIS, 27 Oct 1988, *Rebellion* (1919, oil on paper, 35½ x 25¼ ins / 90 x 64 cm) FRF 23,000. PARIS, 27 April 1989, *Rebellion* (1919, oil on paper, 35½ x 25¼ ins / 90 x 64 cm) FRF 17,500.

JU JIE, or Chu Chieh, sobriquet: Shanggu, style name: Shizhen
Chinese, 16th century.
Born in Suzhou (Jiangsu).
Painter.

Ju Jie was a disciple of Wen Zhengming (1470-1559) and of Wen Peng (1498-1573). He painted mainly landscapes.

MUSEUMS AND GALLERIES:

NEW YORK (Metropolitan Mus. of Art): *View from a High Mountain: Observing the Stream* (1559, ink on paper, with inscription by the artist) - STOCKHOLM (Nationalmus.): *Mountains in Springtime after the Rain* (signed and dated 1575) - TAIPEI (National Palace Mus.): *Spring in Jiangnan* (signed and dated 1531, colour on silk); *Landscapes* (colour/paper, eight album leaves, poems by the artist, last leaf signed and dated 1523).

JU LIAN, or Chü Lien
Chinese, 19th century.
Born 1828/9; died 1904.
Painter. Birds and flowers, animals, flowers, insects.

The Museum of East Asian Art in Cologne has in its collection a signed album leaf *Lychees and Cicadas* (colour on silk), by Ju Lian.

BIBLIOGRAPHY:

Yang Xin and others, *Three Thousand Years of Chinese Painting*, Yale University Press, 1997 (Mentioned briefly in relation to his pupils Gao Jianfu (1879-1951) and Gao Qifeng (1889-1933)).

MUSEUMS AND GALLERIES:

COLOGNE (Mus. für Ostasiatische Kunst): *Lychees and Cicadas* (colour on silk, album leaf).

AUCTION RECORDS:

HONG KONG, 17 Nov 1988, *Flowers and Insects* (1898, ink and colours on silk, twelve-leaf album, each leaf 8 1/2 x 11 1/4 ins / 21.5 x 28.4 cm) HKD 57,200. HONG KONG, 15 Nov 1989, *Flowers and Insects* (1896, ink and colours on silk, set of four albums) HKD 77,000. NEW YORK, 31 May 1990, *Flowers and Birds; Fish* (ink and colour on paper, a pair of painted fans, 7 1/2 x 21 1/2 ins / 19 x 54.6 cm) USD 3,850. HONG KONG, 30 March 1992, *Chrysanthemums and Insect* (ink and colour on paper, hanging scroll, 24 3/4 x 12 1/2 ins / 63 x 32 cm) HKD 17,600. HONG KONG, 22 March 1993, *Flowers* (ink and colours on silk, Ten-leaf album, each 10 1/4 x 12 1/2 ins / 26 x 31.5 cm) HKD 195,500. HONG KONG, 29 April 1993, *Peonies and Butterflies* (ink and colours on silk, hanging scroll, 35 x 8 1/2 ins / 88 x 21.9 cm) HKD 34,500. HONG KONG, 3 Nov 1994, *Peony; Flowers and Grasshopper* (1898, ink and colours on silk, a pair of circular paintings, diam. 9 3/4 ins / 24.8 cm) HKD 59,800. HONG KONG, 4 May 1995, *Flowers* (ink and colours on gilded paper, Ten leaf album, each 7 1/4 x 8 1/2 ins / 18.1 x 21.9 cm) HKD 276,000. HONG KONG, 29 April 1996, *Fish and Vegetables* (1887, ink and colour on paper, 7 1/4 x 21 ins / 18.6 x 53.5 cm) HKD 115,000. HONG KONG, 6 May 2002, *Ten Kinds of Flowers* (ink colour on silk, album of ten, 12 x 10 ins / 31 x 25 cm) HKD 100,000. HONG KONG, 27 Oct 2003, *Two Fish* (ink and colour, hanging scroll and fan painting, 7 x 21 ins / 18 x 54 cm) HKD 32,000.

JU MING, or Zhu Ming
Chinese, 20th century.
Born 1938, in Miaoli, Taiwan.
Sculptor (including metal).

Ju Ming learned woodcarving from Li Jinchuan, a famous woodcarver in the folk tradition, and Yang Yingfeng, a sculptor with an international reputation. He first exhibited in Taiwan in 1976 and has since had numerous exhibitions there, as well as in Japan, Hong Kong, elsewhere in Asia, and in Europe and the USA. He has been one of the ten young Taiwanese artists honoured each year by the People's Republic of China.

Ju works mainly in wood, creating series of progressively stylised hieratic figures, sometimes coloured and sometimes culminating in unidentifiable shapes. A major exhibition of Ju Ming's work toured Singapore, Beijing, and Shanghai in Spring 2005.

BIBLIOGRAPHY:

Tsong-zung, Chang, '*Ju Ming*' in *Orientations*, vol 15, no. 5 (May 1984). Chang Tsong-zung/Wong, Harold, '*Ju Ming: International Chinese Sculpture*' in *Arts of Asia*, vol 16, no. 6, Nov-Dec 1986. Chalumeau, Jean-Luc, *Ju Ming*, Éd. Cercle d'Art, Paris, 2002.

AUCTION RECORDS:

TAIPEI, 22 March 1992, *Tai Chi* (1990, sculpted wood, h. 30 1/4 ins / 77 cm, w. 49 1/4 ins/125 cm) TWD 1,870,000. NEW YORK, 27 March 2003, *Split Taichi* (bronze, 114 x 87x59 ins / 289 x 220x150 cm) USD 210,000. HONG KONG, 26 Oct 2003, *Taiji Shadow Boxing* (1991, green patinated bronze, a pair, h. 30 ins / 76 cm) HKD 650,000. HONG KONG, 25 April 2004, *Thrust* (1991, camphor wood, h. 39 ins / 99 cm) HKD 1,200,000. HONG KONG, 26 April 2004, *Taichi Arch* (1986, bronze, 28 x 43x14 ins / 71 x 108x35 cm) HKD 500,000.

JU WEN-SHU. See **RU WENSHU**

JU-T'AI. See **RUTAI**

JUAN, or Juan de Ávila
Spanish, 16th century.
Sculptor.

Juan lived in Guadeloupe. He was a monk of the order of St Jerome and in 1520 worked in the monastery of the Hieronymites of Guadeloupe.

JUAN. See also **JAN, JEAN** and **JOHANN**

JUAN, Francisco
Spanish, 15th century.
Active in Médème.
Sculptor.

JUAN, José
Spanish, 16th century.
Active in Seville during the second half of the 16th century.
Painter.

José Juan was also an expert in painting materials.

JUAN, Maxime
Spanish, 20th century.
Born 1900, in Valencia.
Active in France from 1912.
Painter, draughtsman, engraver, watercolourist.
Landscapes, urban landscapes.

In his dry-point engravings in particular, Maxime Juan succeeded in recreating the atmosphere of harbours and of the streets of old Paris. He also produced paintings and Indian ink drawings of views of Breton landscapes and the limestone country of les Causses.

JUAN, Ronaldo de
Argentinian, 20th century.
Born 1930 or 1933, in Córdoba; died 1989.
Painter, pastellist.

Ronaldo de Juan studied at the National University of Córdoba. In 1970 he was awarded a bursary by the Guggenheim Foundation. He held many solo exhibitions in Latin America, the USA and Europe.

AUCTION RECORDS:

NEW YORK, 17 Oct 1979, *Untitled* (1979, acrylic, 72 x 72 ins / 183 x 183 cm) USD 3,250. NEW YORK, 28 May 1985, *Untitled* (1979, acrylic/canvas, 72 x 72 ins / 183 x 183 cm) USD 2,500. NEW YORK, 18 May 1994, *Untitled* (1984, acrylic and pastel/canvas, 72 x 72 ins / 182.6 x 182.9 cm) USD 5,175.

JUAN ALEMÁN, the Elder
Spanish, 15th century.
Active in Toledo.
Sculptor.
He is probably identical with Sanchez Alemán (Juan).

JUAN ALEMÁN, the Younger
Spanish, 16th century.
Active in Seville in 1511.
Sculptor (wood).
Juan Alemán carved the choir stalls for the convent of Valle, directed at that period by an abbess known as Magnificent Lady Doña Leonor de Pontocarreno. This work, consisting of 43 stalls, panels, statues (or statuettes) and columns, appears to have been held in the highest esteem. He also did other work of this kind, in particular a carved retable that included figures.

JUAN D'AVILA. See also **DAVILA**

JUAN DE ALCANTARA. See **ALCANTARA**

JUAN DE ANGES
Spanish, 16th century.
Born 1504, in Palencia.
Active in León.
Sculptor (wood).
Between 1587 and 1590, in collaboration with Diego de Solis, he carved the stalls of the cathedral in Orense to his own designs. He also worked in Valladolid.

JUAN DE ARAGON
Spanish, 16th century.
Active in Granada, in 1580.
Painter.

JUAN DE ASTORGA
Spanish, 16th century.
Active in Medina del Campo, c. 1553.
Sculptor.

JUAN DE AUSTRIA (Don)
Spanish, 17th century.
Born 1629, in Madrid; died 17 September 1679.
Painter, engraver (burin).
Don Juan de Austria was the son of King Philip IV of Spain and Maria Calderón. He was viceroy of Aragon and minister to Charles II. Some experts claim that he studied under Jusepe Martinez, others that he was taught by Eugenio de las Cuevas. The national library in Madrid has an etching by him after Callot.
MUSEUMS AND GALLERIES:
MADRID (Biblioteca Nacional): (etching).

JUAN DE BORGOÑA, or Junze de Borgoña, or Jean de Bourgogne
French, 15th - 16th century.
Born c. 1470, in Burgundy; died c. 1535-1536.
Painter, fresco artist. Religious subjects. Murals, designs for stained glass.
Toledo School.
Juan de Borgoña was the brother, or father, of Felipe Vigarni and may also have been known as Jean Bourguignon. He is thought to have been from the Burgundy region of France, and to have been familiar with Flemish painting. It is also believed that he visited Italy on more than one occasion, and possibly studied in the workshop of Ghirlandaio. What is certain is that he had a good knowledge of fresco techniques, and that his painting shared similarities with the work of Piero della Francesca and Melozzo da Forli, demonstrating an awareness of the Italian Renaissance. Despite this, he also remained a follower of the late Quattrocento, using golden, or Spanish-type backgrounds, and Gothic, or Toledo-style architectural settings.

Juan entered the service of the archbishop of Toledo in 1495, working mostly at Toledo Cathedral, where he produced an altarpiece entitled *The Conception* in about 1502, and another entitled *Epiphany* in approximately 1504. He also produced stained glass windows for the cathedral in Burgos, for the convent in Batalha, and at the theatre of the university of d'Alcala de Henares.

As Juan's fame spread, he became the head of a workshop in Toledo and replaced Berruguete following the latter's death in 1508. This gave him the opportunity to complete the altarpiece *St Thomas of Avila*, producing the panels featuring *Nativity*, *The Purification*, *The Transfiguration*, and *Descent into Limbo*. He also received commissions from the chapter house to paint murals entitled *Life of the Virgin*, *Calvary*, and *The Last Judgement*, dated between 1509 and 1511, as well as the commission for mural decorations in the mozarabic chapel in the cathedral, *The Fall of Oran*, dated 1514.

In 1993, the Louvre acquired his painting *The Virgin, St John, Two Holy Women and St Dominic*. This painting shows the Virgin in mourning after the crucifixion, her earthly grief highlighted by the dark clothing in which she is wrapped from head to foot. The simplicity of the landscape is inspired by Tuscan painting, the sharply defined folds in the clothing are Gothic in inspiration, while St Anne - painted in profile looking at the sky - and the faces of the three women, including the Virgin - serious without betraying emotion, and serene bordering on ethereal - are inspired by Florentine art. St Dominic, identifiable by his black and white robes, is notable, above all, for the finely executed painting of his right hand holding a lily, which, in its delicacy, anticipates the Renaissance.
MUSEUMS AND GALLERIES:
DALLAS (Meadows Mus.): *The Investiture of St Ildefonsus* (1508-1514, tempera and oil on wood) - PARIS (Louvre): *The Virgin, St John, Two Holy Women and St Dominic*.
AUCTION RECORDS:
NEW YORK, 1895, *Legend of St Catherine of Alexandria*, FRF 11,750. PARIS, 22 May 1985, *St Francis and St Dominic at the Foot of the Cross* (oil on panel, 17½ x 11 ins / 44.5 x 28 cm) FRF 50,000. MILAN, 24 Oct 1989, *St John the Baptist* (oil on panel with a gold background, 34¼ x 20 ins / 87 x 51 cm) ITL 28,000,000. PARIS, 15 Dec 1991, *The Virgin, St Anne and the Holy Child* (oil on panel/panel, 38½ x 30¼ ins / 98 x 77 cm) FRF 280,000.

JUAN DE BRUXELAS, or Jean de Bruxelles
Flemish, 14th century.
Born to a family originally from Brussels.
Painter.
Juan de Bruxelas worked for the bishop Lope Fernandez de Heredis from 1379.

JUAN DE BRUXELAS, or Jean de Bruxelles
Flemish, 16th century.
Born to a family originally from Brussels.
Sculptor.
Juan de Bruxelas produced small statues for the altarpiece of St Ildefonsus at the cathedral, working with his brother Bernandino of Brussels. He also sculpted the coats of arms of the archbishop in the chapter hall, and in 1525, statues of the apostles to decorate the main door of the chapter hall.

JUAN DE BURGOS
Spanish, 15th century.
Active c. 1450.
Painter.
MUSEUMS AND GALLERIES:
CAMBRIDGE, MA (Fogg AM, Harvard University): *Annunciation* (c. 1450, part of triptych).

JUAN DE BURGOS
Spanish, 16th century.
Active in Seville.
Sculptor.
Juan de Burgos is listed in the record of privileges no. 125 as resident in Palmas Street in 1534 and as working on public buildings in 1540. He is referred to again in 1565.

JUAN DE CAFRANCA. See **CAFRANCA**

JUAN DE CATRES
Spanish, 16th century.
Active in Seville c. 1508.
Painter.

JUAN DE CORDOBA
Spanish, 15th century.
Active in Cordova.
Painter, sculptor (wood) (?).

JUAN DE CORDOBA
Spanish, 16th century.
Active in Seville at the beginning of the 16th century.
Painter.

JUAN DE FLANDES
Flemish, 15th - 16th century.
Died before 16 December 1519, in Palencia.
Active in Spain.
Painter. Religious subjects, portraits.
Juan de Flandes was a painter at the court of Isabella of Spain from 1496 to 1504. He produced small paintings for the queen's oratory, working with Michel Sittow, of which 15 are still extant in Madrid. He also painted the master altar of the university chapel in Salamanca, as well as the master altar of the cathedral in Palencia, which shows 12 scenes from the *Life of Christ*, and an altarpiece featuring St Michael. His other works include *Young Girl with a Rose in her Buttonhole*, and *Child with a Dead Bird*. He painted only in muted colours - mauves, pinks and blue greys - and his figures give the impression of being weightless. The suave delicacy and fragility of his art recall the work of Hugo van der Goes.

Juan's work has featured in several thematic exhibitions, including: 1994, *Hans Memling*, in the section devoted to copies of lost works; 2002, *The Age of Jan Van Eyck: the Mediterranean world of early Netherlandish painting, 1430-1530* at the Groeningsmuseum in Bruges; and 2003, *Hispano-Flemish Gothic Painting, Bartolomé Bermejo and his time*, at the Museu Nacional d'Art de Catalunya in Barcelona. His work was also shown in an individual exhibition in 1985 at the Memlingmuseum in Bruges.

BIBLIOGRAPHY:
Vandevivere, Ignace, *Juan de Flandes*, exhibition catalogue, Memlingmuseum, Bruges, 1985. *Juan de Flandes*, Sarpe, Madrid, 1990. *The 'Retablo de la Reina Católica'*, dissertation, University Microfilms International, Ann Arbor, 1990. *Juan de Flandes*, Ediciones Rayuela, Valencia, 1992. Borchert, T., *The Age of Jan Van Eyck: the Mediterranean world of early Netherlandish painting, 1430 - 1530*, exhibition catalogue, Groeningemuseum, Bruges, Thames and Hudson, London, 2002. *Hispano-Flemish Gothic Painting. Bartolomé Bermejo and his time*, exhibition catalogue, Museu Nacional d'Art de Catalunya, Barcelona, 2003 (text in Spanish, Catalan and English).

MUSEUMS AND GALLERIES:
BRUSSELS (Mus. royaux des Beaux-Arts de Belgique): *Child with a Dead Bird* - DETROIT (IA) - GENEVA (MAH): *The Beheading of St John the Baptist* - LONDON (Apsley House, Wellington Mus.): *The Last Supper, with the institution of the Eucharist and Christ washing the Disciples' Feet* (before 1504, oil/panel, fragment of a series of 47 wings painted for the Queen of Spain, Isabella, now in numerous collections) - LONDON (NG): *Christ Appearing to the Virgin with the Redeemed of the Old Testament* (before 1505, oil/wood) - MADRID (Prado) - PARIS (Louvre) - VIENNA: *Christ Bearing the Cross; Christ Nailed to the Cross* - WASHINGTON DC (NGA): *The Temptation of Christ* (c. 1500-1504, oil/panel); *The Nativity* (c. 1508-1519, oil/panel); *The Baptism of Christ* (c. 1508-1519, oil/panel); *The Annunciation* (c. 1508-1519, oil/panel); *The Adoration of the Magi* (c. 1508-1519, oil/panel).

AUCTION RECORDS:
LONDON, 23 June 1967, *The Marriage at Cana*, Gns 83,000. LONDON, 21 June 1968, *Annunciation*, Gns 3,200. COLOGNE, 8 May 1969, *Portrait of a Gentleman*, DEM 23,500. LONDON, 10 Dec 1986, *Christ at the Pillar* (oil on panel, 15 x 11 ins / 38 x 27 cm) GBP 15,500.

JUAN DE GANTE, or Jan van Gent
Flemish, 16th century.
Born to a family originally from Ghent.
Sculptor.
Juan de Gante worked in Spain, where he produced decorative sculptures and figures in Salamanca cathedral in 1531, and also in Granada in 1541, where he worked on the decoration of the palace belonging to Charles V. He then settled in Seville, where he produced sculptures for the organ of the cathedral. He also sculpted scenes from the life of *St John the Baptist* in 1541.

JUAN DE HOLLANDE
Dutch, 16th century.
Painter.
Juan de Hollande painted an altarpiece in 1505 for Jerome de Fonseca, who was bishop of Palencia and ambassador to King Ferdinand in Brussels. He also produced an *Our Lady of Compassion* for the cathedral in Palencia. According to C. Justi, Juan de Hollande was the same artist as Jan Mostaert, although evidence appears to contradict this claim. He may, however, have been the same artist as Jean de Holland, who worked in Lyons in 1492 and 1507.

JUAN DE HOROZCO
Spanish, 16th century.
Born 16th century, in Tal Orozco.
Sculptor, architect.
Juan de Horozco did a great deal of work for the cathedral in Salamanca.

JUAN DE LA GUARDIA. See **LA GUARDIA**

JUAN DE LEVI
Spanish, 14th - 15th century.
Painter. Religious subjects.
Between 1392 and 1403, Juan de Levi painted for the cathedral in Tarazona an altar consisting of 32 small paintings and three larger ones that are still preserved, though they have also been restored. In 1403, he painted a retable for the church of Montalbán, and in 1405 a retable for the church of La Hoz de la Vieja; the paintings of the St Catherine altar of the cathedral in Tudela are probably also by him.

AUCTION RECORDS:
LONDON, 23 April 1993, *Crucifixion with Two Prophets* (tempera/panel with gilt ground, 43¾ x 39¼in/111 x 100cm) GBP 11,500.

JUAN DE MALINAS, or Jean de Malines
Flemish, 15th century.
Born to a family originally from Mechelen.
Sculptor (wood).
Juan de Malinas worked in Spain, and began work on the richly decorated stalls in the cathedral of León in 1467. These stalls were completed in 1480 by Teodorico.

JUAN DE OLMEDO
Spanish, 15th century.

Active in Toledo.
Painter.
In 1440, Juan de Olmedo painted the tomb of the archbishop of Rojas in the chapel of St Peter in the cathedral in Toledo.

JUAN DE PARIS. See **PARIS**

JUAN DE PLASENCIA. See **PLASENCIA**

JUAN DE SALES
Spanish, 16th century.
Active in Majorca.
Sculptor (wood).
Between 1526 and 1529, he carved a *St Sebastian* for the St Sebastian chapel of the cathedral in Palma, and reliefs for the porch depicting the *Passion of Christ* and the *Martyrdom of St Sebastian*.

JUAN DE SANTIAGO. See **SANTIAGO**

JUAN DE SEGOVIA. See **SEGOVIA**

JUAN DE SEVILLA, Romero y Escalante
Spanish, 17th century.
Born 1643; died 1695.
Painter. Religious subjects. Murals.
Juan de Sevilla was a pupil of Andrés Alonso Arguells and of Pedro de Moya.

In collaboration with Pedro Atanasio Bocanegra he painted a number of trompe l'œil decorations for the Carmelite and Augustinian churches in Granada. These include: *Triumph of the Eucharist with St Augustine and St Thomas* and *Miracle of St Nicolas of Tolentino*. He is also known for a *Last Supper*, which he painted for the Jesuit refectory and for several paintings at the monastery of St Jerome.

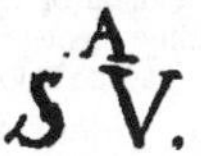

MUSEUMS AND GALLERIES:
BUDAPEST: *Holy Family* - GRANADA: *Communion of St Agatha; Miracle of St Nicolas of Tolentino* - MADRID (Prado): *The Rich Man Epulon and the Poor Man Lazarus* - NEW YORK (Hispanic Society of America): *Virgin and Child with Angels*.
AUCTION RECORDS:
NEW YORK, 7 June 1984, *Return from the Flight into Egypt* (oil on canvas, 65 x 46 1/2 ins / 165 x 118 cm) USD 3,500. NEW YORK, 31 May 1991, *Holy Family* (oil on canvas, 21 x 27 ins / 53.3 x 68.6 cm) USD 2,860.

JUAN DE TOLEDO. See **TOLEDO**

JUAN DE UDINE. See **UDINE**

JUAN DE VALENCINES. See **JEAN de Valenciennes**

JUAN DEL CAMPON. See **CAMPON**

JUAN DEL SANTISSIMO SACRAMENTO. See **GUZMAN Juan de**

JUAN FLAMENCO
Flemish, 15th century.
Active in Spain at the end of the 15th century.
Painter.
The charterhouse of Miraflore owned five paintings by Juan Flamenco of *Scenes from the Life of St John the Baptist*, which were probably destroyed during the sacking of the charterhouse by Armagnac's troops. He has often been wrongly confused with Juan de Flandes.

JUAN GONZALEZ
Spanish, 13th century.
Calligrapher, miniaturist.
The Library of the Escorial has an important manuscript by this artist, *Las cantigas del rey sabio*, that is decorated with rich miniatures, and which was probably written for King Alfonso X (1252-1284).

JUAN JAQUES, or Johannes Jacobus or Johannes filius Jacobi
Dutch, 16th century.
Probably born in Holland.
Painter (glass).
Jaques Juan worked in Spain where he produced paintings on glass in Seville Cathedral.

JUAN PEDRO, or Johan Pere, or Johan de Vallfogona or Wallfogona
Spanish, 15th century.
Born to a family originally from Barcelona; died probably in 1445, in Saragossa.
Sculptor.
The son and pupil of Jordi de Deu, he probably worked with him on the decoration of the home of the municipal council of Barcelona, for the façade of which he carved an *Archangel Raphael*. Also in Barcelona, he sculpted a statue of *St George* above the porch of the *Diputación* (council office). In 1425, the archbishop of Tarragona commissioned him to make a high altar for the city's cathedral and the socle of a large retable, both in alabaster. The Metropolitan Museum of Art, New York, possesses a fragment of an alabaster altar by him that comes from the Archbishop's palace in Saragossa.
MUSEUMS AND GALLERIES:
NEW YORK (Metropolitan Mus. of Art): fragment of an alabaster altar piece.

JUANELO, Francisco
Spanish, 17th century.
Active in Seville in 1614.
Painter.
Francisco Juanelo painted an altarpiece for the chapel prison.

JUANES
Spanish, 16th century.
Active in Seville c. 1539.
Sculptor.

JUANES. See also **JUAN**

JUANES, Juan de. See **MASIP Vicente Juan**

JUARA, Filippo. See **JUVARRA**

JUÁREZ, José, or Xuarez
Mexican, 17th century.
Painter. Religious subjects.
José Juárez studied under Artagea and imitated his style. He painted many religious works.
MUSEUMS AND GALLERIES:
MEXICO CITY (Mus. Nacional de San Carlos): *The Miracle of St Francis; The Martyrdom of St Just and St Pastor; Adoration of the Magi; Communion of St Francis*.

JUÁREZ, José
Mexican, 20th century.
Born 22 March 1939, in Acapulco, Mexico.
Painter.
After studying in Mexico City, José Juárez travelled extensively in Europe, the East and the Far East. He has shown work in Mexico, Europe and the USSR. His painting shows the clear influence of the Latin American tradition.

JUÁREZ, Lorenzo, or Suárez
Spanish, 17th century.
Active in Murcia.
Painter. History painting.
Lorenzo Juárez was at the height of his powers during the first half of the 17th century and was considered at that period to be a great master. He executed decorative paintings

for several convents and monasteries in Murcia, including *Martyrdom of St Angelo* at the Carmelite monastery and *St Ramon* at the Merced convent; both works received high praise from Cean Bermudez. Juárez is known to have worked in collaboration with Avecedo. The collegiate church in Lorca has an *Adoration of the Shepherds* and an *Adoration of the Magi* by Juárez.

JUÁREZ, Luis
Mexican, 17th century.
Born 1585, in Mexico City; died 1637/1638.
Painter. Religious subjects.

Luis Juárez painted religious subjects. His Mannerist style was similar to that of other Mexican painters of the day.

BIBLIOGRAPHY:
Mexico: Splendors of Thirty Centuries, 1990.

MUSEUMS AND GALLERIES:
MEXICO CITY (Mus. Nacional de San Carlos): *Martyrdom of St Laurence; Christ in the Garden of Gethsemane; The Miracle of St Ildephonsus; Holy Family; Ascension; Annunciation.*

JUÁREZ, Manuel
Spanish, 17th century.
Active in Valladolid c. 1671.
Painter. Genre scenes.

Manuel Juárez worked with Diego Valentin Diaz.

JUÁREZ, Nicolás Rodríguez, sometimes Juan, or Xuárez
Spanish, 17th - 18th century.
Born 1667; died 1734.
Active in Mexico.
Painter. Religious subjects, portraits.

Nicolás Rodríguez Juárez painted a *St Christopher* for the college of Nuestra Señora de Guadalupe in Zacatecas and a *Triumph of Mary* for the Mount Carmel church in Celaya.

MUSEUMS AND GALLERIES:
AIX: *Immaculate Conception* - MEXICO CITY (Mus. Nacional): *Adoration of the Magi; Portrait of D Joaquin Munez de Santa Cruz at Four Years Old.*

AUCTION RECORDS:
NEW YORK, 7 May 1981, *Adoration of the Shepherds* (oil on panel, oval, 74 x 43 3/4 ins / 188 x 111 cm) USD 16,000. NEW YORK, 11 June 1982, *Nuestra Senora de los Dolores (Our Lady of Sorrows); Nuestro Senor de los Dolores (Man of Sorrows)* (two oils on canvas, 32 1/4 x 24 1/2 ins / 82 x 62.2 cm) USD 10,000. NEW YORK, 15 Jan 1988, *Scenes from the Life of St Libania* (oil on canvas, 65 1/2 x 46 3/4 ins / 166.4 x 118.7 cm) USD 24,200.

JUBANY Y CARRERAS, Francisco
Spanish, 19th century.
Born 1787, in Barcelona; died 11 June 1852.
Painter. Genre scenes.

Francisco Jubany y Carreras went to France around 1811 as a prisoner, having been captured during the Peninsular War, and was interned in Tournus. In 1827 he worked as a miniaturist in Lyons. A series of lithographs were made in Lyons after drawings by Jubany, including: *31 July 1830; Portraits of J.-M. Mioland, Archbishop of Toulouse*; of *Roux Martin*, the composer; *Entrance of the Madeleine Cemetery; View of the Croix-Rousse Gate; Homme de la Roche (The Man of the Rock)*; and the *Tragic End of Thérèse and Faldoni.* Jubany also made lithographs for a ballad entitled *The Prisoner's Dog*. A painter by the name of Jubany lived in Lyons and exhibited *St Mary Magdalene* (1849-1850) and *The Apparition of the Angels to the Shepherds* at the Lyons exhibition. He trained many students in Lyons.

MUSEUMS AND GALLERIES:
BARCELONA: *Flowers* - TOURNUS: *Basket of Fruit; Young Woman Painting.*

JUBEAU, Henri
French, 19th century.
Born 19th century, in Paris.
Lithographer.

Jubeau exhibited at the Salon of French Artists in Paris receiving an honourable mention in 1908.

JUBERT
French, 15th century.
Active in Troyes.
Sculptor.

The name Jubert is engraved on a stone pendant, which was previously in the convent of Cordeliers in Troyes, but which is now in the town's archaeological museum. The museum of sculpture (now the museum of French monuments) owns a mould of it. A low relief by Jubert of two angels holding a shield bearing the arms of Champagne, also from the convent of Cordeliers, is in the museum of Lyons.

MUSEUMS AND GALLERIES:
LYONS: a low relief, attributed - PARIS (Mus. des Monuments Français): a casting - TROYES (Mus. d'Art, d'Archéologie et de Sciences Naturelles).

JUBERT, Cécile
French, 20th century.
Born 29 December 1885, in Sedan.
Engraver, lithographer.

Cécile Jubert was awarded a silver medal at the Salon des Artistes Français in Paris in 1924.

JUBERT, Guillaume Jules Laurent
French, 19th century.
Born 19th century, in Orléans.
Painter. Seascapes.

Guillaume Jubert was a pupil of Gudin. He displayed his work, made up of maritime scenes of Toulon, Iport, Gibraltar, England and Holland at the Salon de Paris from 1837 to 1852.

JUBERT, Jacques
French, 16th century.
Born to a family originally from Troyes.
Sculptor.

Jacques Jubert may have been the son of the sculptor Jacques Jubert, who lived in Troyes in the 15th century. He produced a *Mater Dolorosa* which is in the church of St-Pantaléon in Troyes. He also produced several figures for the church of St-Ayoul in Provins, and six statues in 1526 for the Maladrerie de Close-Barbe chapel in Provins, which included *Our Lady of Pity.*

JUBIEN, Antoine François Louis
French, 19th century.
Born 30 August 1833, in Trévoux (Ain); died 10 December 1909, in Lyons.
Painter, pastellist, draughtsman. Figures, portraits.

Antoine Jubien studied at the Lyons École des Beaux-Arts from 1847 to 1852 and was a pupil of Guy. He exhibited still-lifes, figures and especially portraits (mainly pencil or pastel from 1869) in Lyons from 1854-55 and in Paris from 1872.

MUSEUMS AND GALLERIES:
GRENOBLE: *Portrait of A. Gerin* - LYONS: *Portrait of J. Soulary.*

AUCTION RECORDS:
LONDON, 17 June 1994, *Portrait of Sarah Bernhardt* (1885, pastel/paper, 26 3/4 x 22 3/4 ins / 67.9 x 57.8 cm) GBP 5,750.

JUBIER, C. L.
French, 18th century.
Active in 1760.
Engraver.

Jubier was the pupil of Bonnet. He engraved in the style of a pencil drawing, and executed *Everyday Subjects* and *Mythological Subjects* after J.-B. Huet, J. Sarrasin and Siccardi. His works are very sought after.

AUCTION RECORDS:
PARIS, 27 Nov 1997, *View of a Classical Fountain; Farm Interior* (coloured engraving, two plates in a set of four, 11 x 14in/28.2 x 35.5cm) FRF 3,000.

JUBIER, Frédéric
French, 20th century.
Born 2 March 1870, in Vannes.
Painter, engraver. Figure compositions, figures, portraits, genre scenes, landscapes.
Frédéric Jubier worked in Paris. He studied under Albert Maignan and exhibited from 1903 at the Salon of the Société des Artistes Français in Paris. He first showed genre scenes and landscapes, and original etchings from 1920, including *Portrait, Stag on the Watch, Flight into Egypt* and *Mary at the Tomb of Jesus*.

JUBIN, Ernestine
Maiden name: Solié
French, 19th century.
Active in Paris.
Painter.
Ernestine Jubin was a member of the Société des Artistes Français in Paris from 1888 and presented her work at the Salon as part of the group.

JUBRÉAUX, Joseph
French, 19th century.
Born 20 May 1834, in Rheims.
Painter. Still-lifes (flowers).
Joseph Jubréaux was a pupil of Lequien. He exhibited flower studies and still-lifes at the Salon de Paris from 1869 to 1880.
AUCTION RECORDS:
PARIS, 29 Sept 1993, *Vase of Flowers and Fruits* (oil on canvas, 39 1/4 x 25 3/4 ins / 100 x 65.5 cm) FRF 51,000.

JUCH, Ernst
Austrian, 19th century.
Born 25 April 1838, in Gotha (Saxony); died 5 October 1909, in Vienna.
Painter, caricaturist, illustrator, sculptor. Portraits, genre scenes, landscapes.
As an illustrator, Ernst Juch worked for the humorous Viennese review *La Râpe* and subsequently *L'Air viennois*, a supplement of *Der Figaro*, then finally *Kikeriki*. As a painter, he made oil sketches of the lives of ordinary people, especially the Viennese, and portraits, including one of his friend *L. Anzengruber* and a *Caricature of Himself*. Landscapes were another genre he painted. As a sculptor, he is noted for humorous renderings of his friends in the form of painted terracotta statuettes, reliefs and small busts.
MUSEUMS AND GALLERIES:
GRAZ (Landesmus. Joanneum, Neue Gal.): *Landscape* - LINZ (Landesgal.): *Relief Portrait of the Painter A. Obermüller* - VIENNA (Kunsthistorisches Mus.): *Anzengruber in front of His Monument* (humorous painting); *Mask of Anzengruber* (polychrome plaster); *Mask of Anzengruber Smiling* (patinated plaster); *Anzengruber Sitting Smoking* (bronze, relief).
AUCTION RECORDS:
LONDON, 16 June 1993, *Street Scene in Vienna* (oil on panel, 15 3/4 x 23 1/2 ins / 40 x 60 cm) GBP 3,220.

JUCHANOWITZ, Albert Wilhelm Adam
German, 19th century.
Born 6 December 1817, in Danzig (now Gdansk, Poland).
Painter, lithographer. Landscapes, architectural views.
Juchanowitz studied in Danzig and Berlin. His first works were mainly views of streets in Danzig and nearby landscapes. He first exhibited in the city in 1838. Noted works of subsequent years include *Danzig Town Hall, St Brigitta's Church*, and *Stations of the Cross* in Magdeburg Cathedral. From 1846, he painted Norwegian landscapes, e.g. *View of Christiania (Oslo)*, and from 1853 Italian landscapes (*Chiavari*, a *Lake Bracciano* and the *Ruins of Lucullus's Villa*).

JUCKER, Hans
Swiss, 15th century.
Active in Bern c. 1499.
Painter (glass).

JUCKOFF-SKOPAU, Paul
German, 19th - 20th century.
Born 2 August 1874, in Merseburg.
Sculptor.
Paul Juckoff-Skopau was a student at the academy in Leipzig, setting up in Skopau, near Merseburg, in 1901. He executed numerous commemorative monuments including those of Gustavus-Adolphus in Weissenfels and in Meuchen near Lützen, those of Luther in Saalfeld and Weissenfels, and of Bismarck in Halle and Scharnhorst on the battlefield at Gross-Görschen.

He also produced fountains in Wiessenfels, Stendal, Schönebeck and Hildesheim, busts, including one of Prince Eitel Frederick of Prussia, and a relief portrait of the Empress of Germany. He featured in the Grosse Kunstausstellung in Berlin in 1904, 1907 and 1910.

JUCLAR. See **JUGLAR**

JUDA, Andreas
Austrian, 16th - 17th century.
Painter.
Juda was a banner painter who worked in Graz. He was commissioned to produce paintings for the tower of the palace of the states-general in 1587, and for the altar of the chapel at Weinburg castle in 1592.

JUDD, Donald
American, 20th century.
Born 3 June 1928, in Excelsior Springs (Missouri); died 12 February 1994, in New York.
Painter, sculptor.
Minimal Art.
Donald Judd served one year in the US army in Korea before attending the Art Students League in New York. At the same time, he studied philosophy at Columbia University where he would return, 10 years into his art career, in the early 1960s to attend Meyer Shapiro's art history course. Judd worked as an art critic from 1959 to 1965. He was an instructor at the Brooklyn Institute of Arts and Sciences from 1962 to 1964, was Visiting Artist at Dartmouth College, Hanover, New Hampshire in 1966, and in 1967 taught sculpture at Yale University in New Haven. He operated from New York, then Marfa (Texas). In 1993, he received the Rembrandt award in Amsterdam.

Donald Judd wanted to break away from the historical past of painting, calling for art's total autonomy from perceptible reality. Unhappy with his own first exhibition, he gave up painting to study and write about art. Between 1959 and 1963, he honed the analysis of outward reality which would release him from the 'illusionism' he deplored in existing art. In one of his articles, *Specific Objects* (1965), considered as the seminal text of minimal art, he insists the canvas is an exclusively two-dimensional plane. His painting shuns all references to an outward reality to allow only for its formal components. This pictorial geometry would, in 1961, be translated into a set of six equidistant black stripes on a white background with a black circle at its exact centre. For Judd, illusionism endures whenever shapes, no matter how abstract-geometric, are projected into space. His first way around this would be to insert objects in his paintings, after the time-honoured technique of assemblage.

His experiments led to what he called 'open structures' or 'specific objects'. His first object took the shape of a cadmium red aluminium incline on which a rectangle of fine black enamelled blades framed in red is set at an angle. In 1963, he showed in New York sculptures consisting in closed boxes set on the floor: primary geometric structures, 'real materials in real space', utterly non-organic, yet not devoid of complexity. He went outside the fully invested surface of paintings to explore space and the use of space with his objects, often evolved from a cuboids. 'Three-dimensional', taking up as well as opening up real space, these objects do not belong in the history of sculpture, with its anthropomorphic references and shapes and values hierarchised by the artist.

Consistent with his plastic analysis, he forewent the use of wood in favour of metal and Plexiglas, insisting on man-made materials. *Untitled* (1965), consists of a box on the ground with two sides made of metal, and the others of Plexiglas. This material, through its transparency, shows both the solidity of the volume and its openness. The viewer is invited to look through the piece as well as at it.

The mid-1960s also saw his first *Progressions*. The first horizontal sets of aluminium boxes connected by a bar were followed by the famous vertical cantilevered progressions counting from 7 to 10 open boxes made of diverse materials. Their geometric arrangements relied on the adoption of mathematical progressions though Judd claimed mathematics meant little to him.

By 1965, he had defined a 'method' so exact that it allowed for little else than repetition. The narrow focus on the object itself would be eased by the deft use of materials - brass, copper, stainless steel, Plexiglas - and colour, while the dialectics between open and filled space played on. Faithful to machined materials, such as plywood, he developed asymmetrical compositions, subdivided his open boxes, modulating the volumes in depth. On smaller objects, he explored the impact of colour on perspective by using aluminium painted in different shades.

From 1970, Judd was preoccupied with the given space, the relationship between the object, the viewer and their environment, the setting of the object within an architecture. In response, he created the *Chinati* Foundation, having bought in Marfa, Texas, buildings in which, along with other artists (Flavin, Chamberlin and others), he could define the setting of the works so that their authors were also in control of the conditions in which they were perceived/received. In this respect, Judd follows in the line of the Bauhaus architects, Mies van der Rohe in particular, for whom the time of the visual encounter with the piece is critical. His objects set no perception criteria: the physical properties of space, scale, and materials are explored as phenomena of interest in their own right.

Judd was one of the most important artists of the post-war period, who changed the face of modern sculpture through his exploration of space, colour, interval and volume. His pared-down forms and use of industrial materials remain highly influential in contemporary art, architecture and design.

He has taken part in numerous collective exhibitions in galleries and museums all over the world, notably in New York: *Primary Structures: Young British and American Sculptors* at the Jewish Museum in 1966 and *Attitudes* at the Brooklyn Museum of Art; *Sculpture from all directions*, and *Plastic and New Art*, at the Philadelphia Institute of Contemporary Art; in Washington: *A New Aesthetic*, 1967; at the 1965 São Paulo Biennale; at Gravenhage (*Minimal Art*) and at Documenta IV in Kassel. He featured in exhibitions dedicated to minimal art: several Whitney Museum biennials; several events in France including *Paintings for Today*, and *What is Modern Art?* in Paris; the 1980 Venice Biennale and Documenta VII in Kassel.

He has shown his works in solo exhibitions in numerous New York venues, including *Shape and Structure* at the Tibor de Nagy Gallery in 1965, and a retrospective at the Whitney Museum of American Art in 1968, and also in Pasadena, Los Angeles, Paris, Amsterdam, London, Bern, Berlin, Eindhoven, Düsseldorf and Barcelona. In 2004, the first travelling exhibition since the artist's death was set up at the Tate Modern in London and the K20 in Düsseldorf and Basel.

BIBLIOGRAPHY:

Don Judd, Art Museum, Pasadena (CA), 1971. Smith, B., *Donald Judd, catalogue raisonné de peintures, objets et planches en bois 1960-1974*, Gal. nationale du Canada, Ottawa, 1975. *Donald Judd, Complete Writings, 1958-1975*, The Press of Nova Scotia College of Art and Design, Halifax, 1975. *Donald Judd - Drawings 1956-1976*, Kunstmuseum, Basel, 1976. Friedrich, Heiner, *Donald Judd, 15 Works*, New York, 1977. *Donald Judd*, Waddington Gall., London, 1986. *Donald Judd, Complete Writings 1975-1986*, Stedelijk Van Abbemuseum, Eindhoven, 1987. *Donald Judd*, exhibition catalogue, Whitney Museum of American Art, New York, 1988. *Donald Judd*, exhibition catalogue, ARC musée d'Art moderne de la Ville de Paris, Paris, 1988. Schellmann, Jörg/Jitta, Mariette Josephus, *Donald Judd: Prints and Works in Editions, a Catalogue Raisonné*, Edition Schellmann, Cologne and New York, 1993 (text in German and English). *Donald Judd: Selected Works*, exhibition catalogue, Museum of Modern Art, Saitama, 1999 (text in Japanese and English). Kellein, Thomas, *Donald Judd: 1955-1968*, exhibition catalogue, Distributed Art Publishers, New York, 2002. Batchelor, David/Fuchs, Rudi, et al., *Donald Judd. Das Werk*, exhibition catalogue, DuMont Literatur und Kunstverlag, Cologne, 2004 (exhibition: Kunstmuseum, Basel). Serota, Nicholas (ed.), *Donald Judd*, exhibition catalogue, Tate Gallery, London, 2004. *Donald Judd: Large-Scale Works*, exhibition catalogue, PaceWildenstein, New York, 2004.

MUSEUMS AND GALLERIES:

BASEL (Kunstmus.): *Untitled* (1962) - COLOGNE (Mus. Ludwig): *Untitled* (1969) - DAYTON (AI): *Untitled* (1982) - DUNKIRK (FRAC Nord-Pas de Calais): *Untitled* (1985) - EINDHOVEN (Van Abbe Mus.): *Untitled* - HOUSTON (MFA): *Untitled* (1975) - MARFA (Chinati Foundation): *Untitled* (1963); *Untitled* (1963); *Untitled* (1979); *Untitled* (1979); *Untitled* (1979) - MILWAUKEE (AM): *Untitled* (1968) - MINNEAPOLIS (Walker Art Center): *Untitled* (1965); *Untitled - 1971* - MONTREAL (MAC): *Untitled* (1974); *Untitled* (1974) - NEW YORK (Whitney Mus. of American Art): *Untitled* (1965); *Untitled* (1966); *Untitled* (1968); *Untitled* (1984) - PARIS (FNAC): *Yellow Wallpiece* (1987) - PARIS (MNAM-CCI): *Untitled* (1965); *Stack* (1973); *Untitled* (1974-1975); *Untitled* (1978) - SOPHIA ANTIPOLIS (Daniel Templon Institute): *Untitled* (1980) - ST LOUIS (AM): *Untitled* (1969) - ST-ÉTIENNE (Mus. d'Art et d'Industrie): *Untitled* (1972) - STOCKHOLM (Moderna Mus.): *Untitled* (1965) - WASHINGTON DC (Hirshhorn Mus. and Sculpture Garden): *Untitled* (1969).

AUCTION RECORDS:

PARIS, 22 March 1977, *Untitled* (box in steel with green paint, 25 1/2 x 5 x 6 1/2 ins / 65 x 12.5 x 16.5 cm) FRF 7,500. NEW YORK, 18 May 1979, *Untitled* (1970, copper and aluminium, 6 1/4 x 110 3/4 x 6 ins / 15.6 x 281.3 x 15.2 cm) USD 12,000. NEW YORK, 13 May 1981, *Untitled* (1970, galvanised iron, 4 3/4 x 25 1/2 x 8 1/2 ins / 12 x 65 x 21.5 cm) USD 4,000. NEW YORK, 10 May 1983, *Untitled* (1972, aluminium, 14 1/2 x 76 1/2 x 25 1/2 ins / 37 x 194.5 x 65 cm) USD 14,000. NEW YORK, 5 Nov 1985, *Untitled* (1976-1977, stainless steel, 21 items, 4 x 236 x 108 ins / 10.3 x 599.4 x 274.4 cm) USD 45,000. NEW YORK, 5 May 1987, *Untitled* (1970, copper, 8 1/2 x 69 1/4 x 5 ins / 21.6 x 175.9 x 12.7 cm) USD 80,000. NEW YORK, 3 May 1988, *Untitled* (1970, galvanised iron, 5 x 25 1/2 x 8 1/2 ins / 12.7 x 64.7 x 21.5 cm) USD 42,900. NEW YORK, 9 Nov 1988, *Untitled* (1972, inox and light cadmium red varnish, group of spaced items, in all 102 x 27 x 24 ins / 259.1 x 68.6 x 61 cm) USD 242,000. NEW YORK, 2 May 1989, *Untitled* (1968, stainless steel and yellow Plexiglas in 10 parts with 23 cm between each part, each élément: 9 x 40 x 31 ins / 23 x 101.7 x 78.8 cm) USD 286,000. PARIS, 9 Oct 1989, *Untitled* (1974, anodised purple aluminium and brass, 5 x 75 x 5 ins / 13 x 190.5 x 12.7 cm) FRF 720,000. PARIS, 15 Feb 1990, *Untitled* (1985, painted aluminium, 11 3/4 x 47 1/4 x 11 3/4 ins / 30 x 120 x 30 cm) FRF 520,000. NEW YORK, 23 Feb 1990, *Untitled* (stainless steel and amber Plexiglas, 6 x 27 1/4 x 24 1/4 ins / 15.5 x 69 x 61.3 cm) USD 57,200. NEW YORK, 27 Feb 1990, *New Progression* (1985, spray paint on aluminium, 11 3/4 x 71 x 11 3/4 ins / 29.8 x 180.3 x 29.8 cm) USD 88,000. PARIS, 9 May 1990, *Untitled* (1972, pencil drawing, 19 3/4 x 23 1/2 ins / 50 x 60 cm) FRF 43,000. PARIS, 18 June 1990, *Galvanised Sheet Metal* (1972, 23 x 26 3/4 ins / 58.5 x 68 cm x 4 1/4 ins/10.5 cm) FRF 150,000. NEW YORK, 7 Nov 1990, *Untitled* (1969, brass and electric blue aluminium, 6 1/4 x 110 3/4 x 6 ins / 15.7 x 281.5 x 15 cm) USD 99,000. PARIS, 20 Jan 1991, *Untitled; Galvanised Metal Sheet* (27 mars 1972, 4 1/4 x 27 x 23 ins / 10.5 x 68.6 x 58.5 cm) FRF 190,000. NEW YORK, 14 Feb 1991, *Progression* (1978, blue and red aluminium, 5 x 75 x 5 ins / 13 x 190.5 x 12.7 cm) USD 44,000. NEW YORK, 1 May 1991, *Progression* (1974, mauve aluminium and brass, 5 x 75 x 5 ins / 13 x 190.5 x 12.7 cm) USD 82,500. NEW YORK, 13 Nov 1991, *Untitled* (1972, copper parallelepiped and light cadmium red varnish on top, 36 x 60 x 60 ins / 91.4 x 152.4 x 152.4 cm) USD 165,000. PARIS, 23 March 1992, *Corner Chair* (1990, sculpture in painted aluminium, 29 1/2 x 19 3/4 x 19 3/4 ins / 75 x 50 x 50 cm) FRF 7,500. NEW YORK, 5 May 1992, *Untittled* (1969, aluminium and brown Plexiglas, 33 x 48 x 68 ins / 83.8 x 121.9 x 173 cm) USD 66,000. LOKEREN, 23 May 1992, *Mural Pannel* (1986, aluminium and Plexiglas, 28 x 28 ins / 71 x 71 cm) BEF 260,000. NEW YORK, 19 Nov 1992, *Untitled* (1982, steel and purple Plexiglas, 19 3/4 x 39 1/4 x 19 1/2 ins / 50.2 x 100 x 49.8 cm) USD 35,200. NEW YORK, 3 May 1993, *Untittled* (stainless steel and green Plexiglas in 10 parts, in all 120 x 27 x 24 ins / 304.8 x 68.6 x 61 cm) USD 233,500. NEW YORK, 10 Nov 1993, *Untittled* (1964, red lacquer on wood, 5 x 25 1/2 x 8 1/2 ins / 12.7 x 64.8 x 21.6 cm) USD 255,500. LONDON, 2 Dec 1993, *Lippencott* (1985, aluminium and Plexiglas, wall sculpture, 10 x 45 x 10 ins / 25.5 x 114.3 x 25.5 cm) GBP 17,250. PARIS, 17 Oct 1994, *Untitled* (1986, painted aluminium, 11 3/4 x 23 1/2 x 11 3/4 ins / 30 x 60 x 30 cm) FRF 59,000. NEW YORK, 2 Nov 1994, *Untitled* (1962, oil/mixture of Liquitex and sand/synthetic resin and yellow Plexiglas, 48 x 96 x 2 3/4 ins / 122 x 244 x 7 cm) USD 288,500. LONDON, 21 March 1996, *Untitled* (1987, spray paint/aluminium, 12 x 23 1/2 x 11 3/4 ins / 30.5 x 60 x 30 cm) GBP 11,500. NEW YORK, 7 May 1996, *Untitled* (1968, eight units in turquoise-lacquered steel, each 48 x 120 1/2 x 8 ins / 121.9 x 305.8 x 20.3 cm) USD 409,500. PARIS, 16 Oct 1996, *Untitled* (1971, stainless steel and Plexiglas, 4 1/4 x 27 1/4 x 23 1/4 ins / 11 x 69 x 59 cm) FRF 15,000. NEW YORK, 6-7 May 1997, *Folded Meters Numbers 13, 16, 19* (1982, stainless steel, in three parts, each 39 1/2 x 39 1/2 x 3/4 ins / 100.3 x 100.3 x 2 cm) USD 39,100. NEW YORK, 7-8 May 1997, *Untitled* (1980; *Untitled* (1987, aluminium and Plexiglas, in six parts, 118 x 19 3/4 x 10 ins / 300 x 50.2 x 25.1 cm) USD 112,500; *Progression* (1970, brass, relief, 5 x 25 1/2 x 8 1/2 ins / 12.8 x 64.8 x 21.6 cm) USD 178,500. NEW YORK, 19 Nov 1997, *Untitled* (1992, coloured Plexiglas and Corten steel, 10 x 19 3/4 x 9 3/4 ins / 25.3 x 50.3 x 24.7 cm) USD 129,000. NEW YORK, 6 and 7 March 1998, *Untitled* (three wooden panels, complete series, each, 14 1/4 x 19 3/4 x 19 3/4 ins / 36.5 x 50 x 50 cm) USD 9,775. NEW YORK, 19 May 1999, *Untitled* (1976, galvanized steel, 10 x 72x26 ins / 25 x 183x66 cm) USD 180,000. NEW YORK, 16 Nov 1999, *Untitled* (galvanized iron, 26 x 9x5 ins / 65 x 22x12 cm) USD 200,000. NEW YORK, 17 May 2000, *Untitled* (1967, lacquer on iron, 5 x 26x9 ins / 13 x 65x23 cm) USD 400,000. NEW YORK, 14 Nov 2000, *Untitled* (steel and red Plexiglas, 180 x 40x31 ins / 457 x 102x79 cm) USD 740,000. NEW YORK, 17 May 2001, *Untitled* (1987, galvanized iron and Plexiglas, ten elements, 120 x 27x24 ins / 305 x 68x61 cm) USD 570,000. NEW YORK, 14 Nov 2001, *Untitled - Stack Sculpture* (stainless steel and green aluminium, ten units, 94 x 27x24 ins / 240 x 69x61 cm) USD 600,000. NEW YORK, 14 May 2002, *Untitled* (1966-1967, stainless steel and Plexiglas, six units, 34 x 34x34 ins / 86 x 86x86 cm) USD 4,200,000. NEW YORK, 13 Nov 2002, *Untitled* (1969, copper, ten units, 120 x 27x24 ins / 305 x 68x61 cm) USD 1,300,000. NEW YORK, 14 May 2003, *Untitled* (1978, anodized aluminium, ten parts, 6 x 27x24 ins / 15 x 69x61 cm) USD 750,000. NEW YORK, 15 May 2003, *Untitled - Progression* (1970, clear anodized and purple anodized aluminum, 8 x 161x8 ins / 21 x 409x20 cm) USD 580,000. NEW YORK, 11 May 2004, *Untitled - DSS 107* (1967, blue lacquer on galvanised iron, 5 x 69x9 ins / 13 x 175x23 cm) USD 700,000. NEW YORK, 12 May 2004, *Untitled* (1980, galvanised iron and blue Plexiglas, ten parts) USD 1,000,000.

JUDD, John
British, 18th century.
Active in Chelmsford.
Painter. Landscapes.

John Judd exhibited in London from 1774 to 1793 at the Society of Artists and at the Royal Academy.

JUDE, Marin
French, 17th century.
Born c. 1595; died 1675; buried on 8 December in Paris.
Painter.

JUDE, Patrick
French, 20th century.
Born 5 September 1944, in Perpignan.
Painter (mixed media).
Citationism.

Patrick Jude studied at the École des Beaux-Arts in Perpignan from 1962 to 1964 and then at the École des Beaux-Arts in Nancy from 1965 to 1967. Since 1968 he has taught at the École Nationale d'Art Décoratif in Limoges, where he made friends with Claude Viallat, Louis Bec and Ramon. He does not restrict himself to traditional painting techniques. His creations are often three dimensional, such as some busts of soldiers or other official figures. He has produced varnished aluminium triptychs, as well as using audiovisual montages, in which each image is the negative of a previously made painting, the whole thing making up an animation. Whatever the support, his intention is to highlight the state of alienation that is automatically conferred by all regulated dress, whether it is of a judge, a soldier, bishop or managing director. Jude always wears a monk's habit. At the beginning of the 1980s he created *Murs de Mémoire* (*Memory Walls*), a series of works combining the techniques of drawing, acrylics and collage. The walls are in two rooms of a house and he scrupulously painted them with wallpaper patterns. Similarly, he re-transcribed popular images from white bathroom tiles. The whole thing works on the principle of visual shock. This same procedure applies to the series *Machinations*, 1982-1983, which more clearly incorporates quotations from old and modern works of art on the theme of female nudity. Later, the quotation became his favoured form of comment. He cuts up and enlarges selected pieces of old works by David, Fouquet or Caravaggio for example, and subjects them to a special pictorial treatment and integrates them in his own figuration. Placing the image in an already known and acknowledged awkward position like this poses the much discussed question of the end of the painting cluttered with its own history.

Since 1970, he has participated in collective exhibitions in Limoges, Toulouse, Aix-en-Provence, Paris, Céret *Impact II* and Perpignan. Other exhibitions include: Salon des Réalités Nouvelles, Paris, 1973; Rencontres Internationales de La Rochelle, 1973; *Marginales 74* (*Fringe 74*), Marseilles, 1974; *Mostra del Larzac*, 1974; *Les Artistes sur le Pavé* (*Artists on the Street*), Angoulême, 1974; Limousin Fonds Regional d'Art Contemporain, 1982; *Vivant/Artificiel* (*Living/Artificial*), Avignon festival, 1984; *Cas de Figure* (*Scenario*), travelling exhibition, Angoulême, Edinburgh, Dôle and other places; Salon de Montrouge, 1986.

Solo exhibitions of his work include: Céret, 1971; Galerie Guénant, Limoges, 1973; Galerie Alternative, Paris, 1975; Montmorillon Community Art Centre, 1975; Brive Cultural Centre, 1976, with Jean-François Demeure, 1976; École Régionale des Beaux-Arts, Clermont-Ferrand, 1984; École Nationale d'Art Décoratif, Limoges, 1985; Musée d'Art Moderne, Céret, 1987.

BIBLIOGRAPHY:

Jude, exhibition catalogue, Maison de la Culture, Montmorillon, 1975. *Jude*, exhibition catalogue, Musée d'Art Moderne de la Ville de Paris, Céret, 1987.

JUDEICH, Theresa
German, 19th - 20th century.
Born c. 1831; died 1914.
Active in Dresden.
Landscape artist.

Theresa Judeich is remembered for *Evening in Venice* and *Party in the Woods*.

JUDERIAS CABALLERO, Maximo.
See **CABALLERO Maximo Juderias**

JUDKIN, Thomas James or T.K. (Revd.)
British, 19th century.
Born c. 1788; died October 1871, in London.
Active in Southgate.
Painter. Landscapes with figures, landscapes.

Thomas James Judkin was a churchman. He exhibited in London from 1822 to 1849, especially at the Royal Academy, the British Institution and at Suffolk Street.

JUDKINS, Elisabeth
British, 18th century.
Active in London.
Engraver (mezzotint).

Elisabeth Judkins is believed to have been a pupil of J. Watson. She exhibited at the Society of Artists in 1773 and 1775. There is mention of three engravings after J. Reynolds: *The Good Shepherdess, Lady Nardale and her Son, Harriet Powell* and *Lady F. Bridges*.

JUDL. See **JODL**

JUDLIN, Alexis
French, 18th century.
Miniaturist.

Judlin featured at the Salon, from 1791 to 1793, with miniature portraits and allegorical compositions such as: *Liberty, Equality* and *The Republic and the Rights of Man*. He also exhibited at the Royal Academy, London, from 1773 to 1776.

MUSEUMS AND GALLERIES:

ROUEN: *Portrait of Descroizilles.*

JUDSON, Alice
American, 20th century.
Born in Beacon (New York); died 1948.
Painter.

Alice Judson studied at the Art Students League in New York. She was a member of the Pen and Brush Club and of the League of American Art Teachers.

AUCTION RECORDS:

NEW YORK, 7 Dec 1984, *Cos Cob Spring* (oil on canvas, 26 x 20 ins / 66 x 50.7 cm) USD 2,600. NEW YORK, 17 March 1988, *Stream near a Farm* (oil on canvas, 19¾ x 23½ ins / 50 x 60 cm) USD 2,750. NEW YORK, 24 Jan 1989, *Harbour* (oil on canvas, 15¾ x 19¾ ins / 40 x 50 cm) USD 880.

JUDSON, Minnie Lee
American, 19th - 20th century.
Born 29 October 1865, in Milford (Connecticut); died 1938.
Painter. Landscapes.

Minnie Lee Judson was a member of the American Federation of Arts.

JUDSON, William Lee
British, 19th - 20th century.
Born 1 April 1842, in Manchester; died 1928.
Active in Los Angeles.
Painter, writer. Landscapes.

William Lee Judson studied in Paris under Boulanger and J. Lefebvre, and with John Beaufain Irving in New York. He is the author of the book *Building of a Picture*.

AUCTION RECORDS:

TORONTO, 26 May 1981, *Landscape with Waterfall* (1880, watercolour, 21½ x 12½ ins / 54.4 x 31.9 cm) CAD 2,200. LOS ANGELES-SAN FRANCISCO, 10 Oct 1990, *Canyon* (oil on canvas, 18 x 15 ins / 46 x 38 cm) USD 4,125. NEW YORK, 12 Sept 1994, *Haymaking* (oil on canvas, 30 x 50 ins / 76.2 x 127 cm) USD 2,300.

JUEGEL, Johann Friedrich
German, 18th - 19th century.
Active in Berlin.
Engraver (burin).

Johann Juegel engraved portraits and history subjects. Among the latter, mention may be made of various pieces associated with the Napoleonic Wars, including *The Allies Entering Berlin, Napoleon I Entering Berlin* (after Wolf), *Napoleon I Inspecting the Imperial Guard in the Pleasure Garden in Berlin* (1807), *The Allied Monarchs Entering Paris, The Apotheosis of Queen Louisa of Prussia*, and *Blücher Arriving in the Champs Elysées* (after Kirchhof, 1824). Also by him are the 36 figures of the *Royal Prussian Infantry*, after F. Lieder.

JUEL, Jens, or Jorgensen
Danish, 18th century.
Born 12 May 1745, in Balslev; died 27 December 1802, in Copenhagen.
Painter. Portraits, genre scenes, landscapes.
Naturalist.

Jens Juel was a pupil of Johann Michael Gehrmann. As a successor to Peder Als, Juel made a substantial contribution to Danish portraiture. Following his studies with Gehrmann in Hamburg, he attended the Kunstakademi in Copenhagen and received a gold medal. The next year he left for Rome, Paris and Geneva. Upon his return in 1780 he was named court painter and became member, professor, and later director at the academy. He taught and exerted considerable influence over Caspar David Friedrich and Philipp Otto Runge.

Juel excelled in his execution of heads and hands, although his treatment of torsos was less accomplished. His bodies often seemed somewhat rigid and lacking in elegance. In his painting of small-format portraits, however, he was an evident master. His works are still greatly esteemed today. Although his landscapes are lesser known, they may be counted with the best of his work.

He was featured in the exhibition *Twee gouden eeuwen: schilderkunst uit Nederland en Denemarken* (*Two Golden Ages: Masterpieces of Dutch and Danish Painting*) at the Rijksmuseum in Amsterdam in 2001.

BIBLIOGRAPHY:

Poulsen, E., *Jens Juel*, Gyldendal, Copenhagen, 1961. Poulsen, E., '*Jens Juel: Master Portrait Painter*' in *Connoisseur, pp. 70-75*, Feb 1962. Monrad, Kasper, *Danish Painting: The Golden Age*, exhibition catalogue, National Gallery, London, 1984. Lerberg, E., et al., *Fire Danske Klassikere: Nicolai Abildgaard, Jens Juel, Christoffer Wilhelm Eckersberg og Bertel Thorvaldsen*, exhibition catalogue, Nasjonalgalleriet, Oslo, 1992.

MUSEUMS AND GALLERIES:
COPENHAGEN (Statens Mus. for Kunst): *Hjelmstjerne; The Copper Engraver Clemens; Harch; A. W. Hauch; Countess A. J. Dameskjold Laurvig; Admiral F. C. Risbrick; J. Juel and his Wife; Mrs Abidgaard, Mother; Paulli; Gerner and his Wife; Four Portraits of Women; A Dwarf, Beggar in Rome; A Farm; Fruit; The Snoghöij* (1787); *Maria Ubrica Schow; Mrs Gojertrud Hage; Landscape; J. S. Conninck; Holstein's Young Daughter; Brother of the Painter Henrick; Julie Holm; The Painter's Children; Landscape in Joegerspris; Two Spouses; Two Dwarves;* two sketches; *Mrs Moltke; The Sculptor Nic. Dajon; Henrik Gernery* - COPENHAGEN (Thorvaldsens Mus.): *The Surroundings of Middelfort* - HAMBURG: *Flowers; View of a City* - HILLERØD: *C. F. Numsen; H. H. Könnemann; N. Dajon; F. V. Schested; C. Rantzau; B. Sporon; Mrs Sporon; A. P. Bernstorff; W. A. Müller; Johan Bülow; P. A. Heiberg; Mme Gyllembourg; P. S. Suhm; M. Rosing; Klopstock; J. F. Clemens; N. Abildgaard* - ODENSE: *Storm* - OSLO: *Bernt Anker* - STOCKHOLM: *The Singer Carolina Müller; The Sculptor Johan Tobias Sergel.*

AUCTION RECORDS:
PARIS, 5 June 1920, *Portrait of a Man,* FRF 2,200. LONDON, 18 May 1938, *Artist in Coat and Cap,* GBP 95. COPENHAGEN, 7 Nov 1960, *Landscape,* DKK 8,900. COPENHAGEN, 28-29 May 1963, *Portrait of Princess Louisa Augusta,* DKK 28,000. COPENHAGEN, 26-27 Oct 1966, *Portrait of Sophie Charlotte Cederfeld,* DKK 25,000. COPENHAGEN, 19 March 1969, *Mother and Child* (pastel) DKK 11,500. COPENHAGEN, 8 May 1969, *Portrait of Christopher Battier,* DKK 20,000. LONDON, 8 Dec 1971, *Little Girl and her Dog,* GBP 2,900. COPENHAGEN, 30 Oct 1973, *Portrait of Christine Frederikke Bruhn,* DKK 38,000. COPENHAGEN, 4 Sept 1974, *Emilie Kilde,* DKK 100,000. COPENHAGEN, 31 Aug 1976, *Portrait of Frederik VI* (oil on panel, 15 x 11 ins / 38 x 28 cm) DKK 25,000. COPENHAGEN, 3 May 1977, *Wooded Landscape with Figures* (oil on canvas, 16 1/2 x 20 1/2 ins / 42 x 52 cm) DKK 35,000. COPENHAGEN, 6 Nov 1979, *View of Helsingør or Kronborg* (c. 1790, oil on canvas, 11 1/2 x 22 1/2 ins / 29.5 x 57 cm) DKK 85,000. COPENHAGEN, 16 March 1982, *View of Marienlyst near Helsingør and Kronborg* (oil on canvas, 117 x 22 1/2 ins / 297 x 57 cm) DKK 107,000. COPENHAGEN, 12 April 1983, *Portrait of a Young Russian Prince (Serge Metchekoff)* (1798, oil on canvas, 26 3/4 x 21 1/4 ins / 68 x 54 cm) DKK 225,000. COPENHAGEN, 16 April 1985, *Portrait of Charlotte Bartholin Eichel* (c. 1800, oil on canvas, 36 1/2 x 28 3/4 ins / 93 x 73 cm) DKK 240,000. COPENHAGEN, 11 June 1986, *Portrait of Queen Marie-Sophie Frederikke* (pastel, 16 1/2 x 11 ins / 42 x 27 cm) DKK 28,000. COPENHAGEN, 23 April 1987, *Portrait of Cecilia Andrea Krabbe* (oil on canvas, oval, 27 1/2 x 21 1/2 ins / 70 x 54.5 cm) DKK 150,000. COPENHAGEN, 5 April 1989, *Portrait of a Man* (1777, oil on canvas, oval, 26 x 21 1/4 ins / 66 x 54 cm) DKK 145,000. COPENHAGEN, 21 Feb 1990, *Portrait of Berte Brockenhuus, Countess Scheel* (oil on canvas, oval, 27 1/2 x 21 1/4 ins / 70 x 54 cm) DKK 171,000. LONDON, 28 Feb 1990, *Portrait of a Lady* (1773, oil on canvas, 37 3/4 x 32 3/4 ins / 96 x 83.5 cm) GBP 12,100. LONDON, 29 March 1990, *Portrait of a Young Woman in White Dress and Black Shawl Holding a Book* (oil on canvas, 13 3/4 x 10 1/2 ins / 35 x 26.5 cm) GBP 12,650. COPENHAGEN, 25-26 April 1990, *Nordic Landscape near Mjosen* (oil on canvas, 15 3/4 x 19 ins / 40 x 48 cm) DKK 305,000. COPENHAGEN, 6 May 1992, *View of Petit Saleve near Mont Blanc* (oil on canvas, 18 x 28 ins / 46 x 71 cm) DKK 240,000. COPENHAGEN, 18 Nov 1992, *Landscape with Mill and Church* (oil on canvas, 20 1/2 x 24 ins / 52 x 61 cm) DKK 180,000. NEW YORK, 14 Jan 1993, *Bust Portrait of Seated Lady in Brown Dress and White Shawl in a Landscape* (1778, oil on canvas, 28 1/2 x 22 1/2 ins / 72.4 x 57.2 cm) USD 16,500. LONDON, 10 Dec 1993, *Three-quarter Length Portrait of a Young Woman in Circassian Costume* (oil on canvas, 38 3/4 x 29 1/4 ins / 98.3 x 74 cm) GBP 17,250. COPENHAGEN, 2 Feb 1994, *Portrait of Amalie Christiane Juel* (oil on canvas, oval, 27 1/2 x 22 ins / 70 x 55 cm) DKK 70,000. LONDON, 26 Oct 1994, *Portrait of a Lady* (oil on canvas, 26 1/4 x 20 3/4 ins / 66.5 x 53 cm) GBP 3,680. COPENHAGEN, 23 May 1996, *Portrait of the Administrator Niels Collin* (1770, oil/copper, 19 1/4 x 15 1/4 ins / 49 x 39 cm) DKK 72,000. NEW YORK, 14 Oct 1999, *Portrait of Madame Senebier* (1778, oil on canvas, 28 x 22 ins / 70 x 57 cm) USD 42,500. COPENHAGEN, 30 Nov 1999, *Portrait of Maria Helena Kortright* (oil on canvas, oval, 28 x 21 ins / 70 x 54 cm) DKK 240,000. COPENHAGEN, 29 Feb 2000, *Portrait of Jacqueline H E Senebier, née Morsier* (1778, oil on canvas, 28 x 22 ins / 70 x 57 cm) DKK 600,000. COPENHAGEN, 22 March 2000, *Portrait of a Young Woman* (pastel, oval, 13 x 10 ins / 32 x 25 cm) DKK 96,000. COPENHAGEN, 27 Nov 2001, *Portraits of Frederikke Christine Hellsen and Rasmus Hanson Lange* (pastel, a pair, 15 x 11 ins / 38 x 27 cm) DKK 55,000. COPENHAGEN, 27 Nov 2001, *Portrait of Countess Juliane Sophie Rosenkrantz-Levetzau* (1783, oil on canvas, 32 x 26 ins / 81 x 67 cm) DKK 580,000. COPENHAGEN, 2 Dec 2002, *Portraits of Henrik Even Moe and his Wife Henriette Frederikke* (oil on canvas, oval, a pair, 27 x 21 ins / 69 x 54 cm) DKK 330,000. COPENHAGEN, 2 Dec 2002, *Johan Carl von Moller as a Three-year-old Holding a Whip* (oil on canvas, 39 x 27 ins / 100 x 68 cm) DKK 460,000. COPENHAGEN, 2 Dec 2003, *Sigismund Ludvig Schulin as a Child* (oil on canvas, oval, 29 x 22 ins / 73 x 57 cm) DKK 260,000. COPENHAGEN, 9 Dec 2003, *Sophie Hedvig Adeler as a Child* (pastel, oval, 12 x 9 ins / 30 x 24 cm) DKK 48,000.

JUELB. See **JÜLB**

JUELL-GLEDITSCH, Ralf
Norwegian, 20th century.
Active c. 1937.
Painter.

JUENGER. See **JÜNGER**

JUENGLING, Friedrich, or Jüngling
German, 19th century.
Born 18 October 1846, in Leipzig; died 31 December 1889, in New York.
Active in New York.
Engraver, painter.

Juengling studied engraving on wood in Leipzig, worked in Berlin and in 1866 settled in New York. Numerous engravings by him were published in *Century Magazine* and other American reviews. He was also a painter.

JUERGENS. See also **JÜRGENS**

JUERGENS, Alfred
American, 19th - 20th century.
Born 5 August 1866, in Chicago; died 18 April 1934, in Oak Park (Illinois).
Painter. Murals.

Alfred Juergens began his art education in Chicago before working in Munich under Robert Kochler, Professor Gysis and Diez. He was awarded medals in Madrid and Munich. He was member of the Munich Artist Association, the Artists Association of Germany and the International Society of Fine Arts.

JUEZ SARMIENTO, Andrés
Spanish, 19th century.
Born 19th century, in Madrid.
Painter. History painting, portraits.

Andrés Juez Sarmiento studied at the Real Academia de San Fernando and exhibited in Madrid.

JUG, Master of the. See **KRUG Ludwig**

JUGAN, Vladimir
Russian, 20th century.
Born 1926, in Dnepropetrovsk.
Painter. Landscapes, flowers.

Vladimir Jugan studied at the school of fine art in Dniepropetrovsk from 1946 to 1951. He became a member of the Union of Ukranian Painters in 1964.

He held regular exhibitions in Dniepropetrovsk.

AUCTION RECORDS:

PARIS, 13 March 1992, *On the Sea of Azov* (oil on canvas, 20 1/2 x 30 1/4 ins / 52 x 77 cm) FRF 5,000. PARIS, 27 March 1994, *Water Moons on the Lake* (oil on canvas, 23 1/2 x 27 1/4 ins / 60 x 69.5 cm) FRF 4,000.

JÛGASEI. See **SHUNSHO**

JUGBLUT. See **JUNGBLUT**

JUGE-LAURENS, Suzanne Nanny Adrienne. See **ADAM-LAURENS Suzanne**

JÜGEL, Johann Friedrich. See **JUEGEL**

JUGELET, Auguste Jean Marie

French, 19th century.

Born 25 August 1805, in Brest (Finistère); died 1875, in Versailles.

Painter. Landscapes, seascapes.

Auguste Jugelet was a pupil of Théodore Gudin. He exhibited his work at the Salon de Paris from 1831 to 1870, gaining a third class medal in 1836. He was decorated by the Légion d'Honneur in 1847.

His scenes of Brittany, Normandy, the Mediterranean coast and Italy are often diffused with a dramatic light. Also accredited to him are seascapes of a historical character such as *Battle Between la Belle-Poule and Arethusa* or *Wreck of the Sloop Le Gool in Dieppe in July 1858*.

BIBLIOGRAPHY:

Les Années romantiques, la peinture française de 1815 à 1850, exhibition catalogue, Musée des Beaux-Arts, Nantes, Gal. nationales du Grand Palais, Paris, 1996.

MUSEUMS AND GALLERIES:

BREST: *Study of a Tree* - DIEPPE: *Louis-Philippe Entering Dieppe* - LE PUY-EN-VELAY: *Seascape* - RHEIMS: *Three Seascapes* - ROCHEFORT: *Watch on the Koat Ven; Battle between Belle-Poule and Arethusa* (1778) - ST-OMER: *Two Landscapes in Brittany* (1833) - TARBES: *Jesus Christ Calming the Storm* (1845).

AUCTION RECORDS:

PARIS, 1890, *Seascape*, FRF 350. PARIS, 28 March 1928, *Sunset Near St-Valéry-sur-Somme*, FRF 500. LONDON, 5 June 1985, *Seashore at Dusk* (oil on canvas, 21 1/2 x 38 1/2 ins / 54.5 x 98 cm) GBP 1,700. PARIS, 20 May 1992, *Ship on a Rough Sea* (oil on panel, 7 1/2 x 11 3/4 ins / 19 x 30 cm) FRF 4,500. LONDON, 28 Oct 1992, *Dusk in Le Havre* (oil on canvas, 12 1/2 x 20 3/4 ins / 32 x 53 cm) GBP 770. ZURICH, 5 Sept 2001, *Coastal Landscape with Ships, Animals and Figures* (1836, oil on canvas, 15 x 24 ins / 38 x 62 cm) CHF 3,000. BRUSSELS, 10 Nov 2003, *Seascapes* (oil on canvas/glass, a pair, 4 x 5 ins / 9 x 13 cm) EUR 1,800.

JUGLAR, Jean

French, 14th century.

Sculptor, architect.

Jean Juglar worked at the palace in Riom in 1383 under his father, Pierre Juglar. He was commissioned to produce two stone statues of *St Lazarus* and *St Louis, Bishop of Toulouse*, in the following year by the town authorities of Marseilles. The statues were for the Lauret door.

JUGLAR, Pierre

French, 14th century.

Sculptor, architect.

Pierre Juglar worked under Guy de Dammartin on the decoration of the chapel of the Duke de Berry at the palace in Riom in 1383. He often acted as Dammartin's replacement.

JUGLAR, Victor Henri

French, 19th century.

Born 25 July 1826, in Châlons-sur-Marne; died in Châlons-sur-Marne.

Active in Paris.

Painter. Portraits, genre scenes, animals.

Victor Juglar was a pupil of Thomas Couture. He was represented at the Salon de Paris from 1857. He donated two of his works to the museum in his hometown.

MUSEUMS AND GALLERIES:

CHÂLONS-EN-CHAMPAGNE: *The Spy* (1880); *Ash Wednesday* (1879).

AUCTION RECORDS:

LONDON, 10 July 1997, *Water Spaniel* (oil on canvas, 13 1/4 x 10 1/2 ins / 33.5 x 26.7 cm) GBP 1,380.

JUGLARIS, Tommaso

Italian, 19th century.

Born 1845, in Moncalieri.

Painter. Genre scenes, portraits.

A pupil at the academy in Turin and of Thomas Couture in Paris, Tommaso Juglaris exhibited in 1879 and 1880 at the Paris Salon, in 1894 at the exhibition of fine art in Milan, in 1898 in Turin, and elsewhere. Among his works are *Sacrifice to the Household Gods*, *The Corso, Venice*, and *Invasion*, a prehistoric scene.

JUGNET, Anne-Marie

French, 20th - 21st century.

Born 1958, in La Clayette (Saône-et-Loire).

Installation artist, painter. Multimedia.

Conceptual Art.

Since 1997, Anne-Marie Jugnet has been producing work in collaboration with Alain Clairet. In her early work, Jugnet often used a photographic process and neon lighting, which constructed and conceptualised around words or phrases which she 'brought into dialogue' with different environments. Working with Alain Clairet, the two artists seek to define the conditions of production of an object, to understand how it exists within reality, what it represents. To do this they deconstruct. Hence the 'American Series' in which elements of town plans, including empty, unbuilt areas that are displayed in guide books, are enlarged to a human scale. These works question the notions of emptiness, of flat geometric areas, of non-perspective, of reference, of a different way of perceiving. Another series of paintings, the *Switch* series (2002), captures the moment when a television is switched off and the image becomes a vanishing dot, as if inhaled by the cathode-ray tube.

She has taken part in group exhibitions, including: in 1991, the *Mouvement 1 et 2* exhibition at the Contemporary Galleries of the Musée Nationale d'Art Moderne, Paris; in 1993, at the International Contemporary Art Exhibition, Paris; in 2001, the *Esprit de Famille* (*Family Spirit*) exhibition at Villa du Parc, Annemasse; and in 2003, the exhibition *Un Tableau dans le Décor: Peintures 1970-2000* (*A Painting in the Décor: Paintings 1970-2000*) celebrating 20 years of the FRAC, held at the Château des Ducs de Bretagne, Nantes. She has also shown her work in solo exhibitions, including: in 1991 and 1993 at the Galerie Froment-Putman, Paris, and in 1994 at the Centre d'Art Contemporain, Vassivière, Limousin, where she executed a government-commissioned sculpture for the gardens. In 1995, she was selected for the 10th monumental art bursary awarded by Ivry-sur-Seine. In 1997, she exhibited at the Villa Arson, Nice. In 2000, she exhibited with Alain Clairet at the Fonds Régional d'Art Contemporain of Haute-Normandie, Sotteville-lès-Rouen; in 2003 with Alain Clairet in the *Alpine + Cádiz, 1997-2003* exhibition at the Fondation Mamco and Musée d'Art Contemporain, Geneva; and again with Alain Clairet in 2003 at the cultural centre in Milan.

Bibliography:
Sans, Jérôme, '*Anne Marie Jugnet: Eclipses*' in *Mouvements: cinq artistes français*, group exhibition catalogue, Éd. du Centre Georges-Pompidou, Paris, BASF Aktiengesellschaft, Ludwigshafen, 1991 (French edition, allemand). Bourel, M./Ditche, Stéphanie, *Anne-Marie Jugnet*, exhibition catalogue, Centre d'Art contemporain de Vassivière en Limousin, Beaumont-du-Lac, 1994. Piguet, Philippe, *L'écrit, le mot, le texte*, group exhibition catalogue, Fondation d'art contemporain Daniel et Florence Guerlain, Les Mesnuls, 1999. Donnadieu, Marc/Negro, Marylène/Scherübel, Klaus, *Anne-Marie Jugnet et Alain Clairet*, exhibition catalogue, Fonds régional d'Art contemporain de Haute-Normandie, Sotteville-lès-Rouen, 2000 (texts in French and English). Boyer, Charles-Arthur, '*Anne-Marie Jugnet & Alain Clairet*' in *Art Press* n° 287 p. 35, periodical, Paris, February 2003.
Museums and Galleries:
Geneva (Mamco) - Sotteville-lès-Rouen (FRAC Haute-Normandie): *Fishing with John No. 6* (2001); *Fishing with John No. 5* (2001); *The Baby of Macon No. 1* (2001).

JUGONI, Giovanni Battista. See **INGONI**

JUGUINE, Leon
Russian, 20th century.
Born 1891, in Moscow.
Painter, illustrator.
Leon Juguine was close to new ideas about painting and founded the group Painting's Route.

JUHASZ, Arpad
Hungarian, 19th - 20th century.
Born 29 June 1863, in Zombor; died 30 May 1914, in Budapest.
Painter.
Arpad Juhasz was a student at the Design School in Budapest. He toured Hungary for several years in order to study popular art there. His drawings and watercolours illustrated an important ethnographic work by Malonyay. In 1912 he exhibited ethnographic pictures at the Nemzeti Salon in Budapest, two of which reached the Ethnographic Museum in Budapest. He executed two frescoes inspired by the same motifs for a school in the same town.

JUHASZ, Gyulia
Hungarian, 19th - 20th century.
Born 1876, in Eger; died 6 January 1912, in Budapest.
Medallist, sculptor.
Gyulia Juhasz studied in Budapest, then at the academy in Vienna and spent time studying in Florence. He worked in Budapest, where he produced medals in particular and appeared at several exhibitions.
Museums and Galleries:
Budapest (Szépmuvészeti Múz.): *Woman* (bronze statue).

JUHEL
French, 19th century.
Painter, watercolourist, lithographer. Historical subjects, genre scenes.
Juhel exhibited his work at the Salon de Paris from 1812 to 1831. After depicting serious subjects such as *Christ in the Tomb* (1812) and *Oedipus and Antigone* (1814) he exhibited *An Old Caretaker Reading his Newspaper and Admiring his Parrot* in 1831.
Also cited is Juhel, a pupil of Charlet, who is accredited with a series of *Fantastic Sketches* and a series of six lithographs with dates of 1806 and 1830. Possibly a relative of the painter.

JUILLART, Dominique
French, 20th - 21st century.
Born 16 February 1961, in Lyons.
Painter, designer. Landscapes, urban landscapes, mountainscapes, seascapes. Murals.
Dominique Juillart studied at the École Nationale des Beaux-Arts in Paris from 1980 to 1987. In 1985 he created a wall painting for the museum of mechanical musical instruments in Paris and for Malakoff parish in 1987. Essentially a landscape and seascape painter, in some *Impressions*, he moves away from strict figuration to strive for poetic abstraction. He has taken part in group exhibitions in Paris, including: Salon des Indépendants, 1985; Salon des Artistes Français, 1986, 1989 and 1990; Salon d'Automne regularly since 1988 and the Salon de Bernay in 1989. Solo exhibitions have been held at the Île d'Yeu Town Hall in 1990; Espace Jean-Charles Ribes, Paris in 1992; Pontault-Combault; Tourist Office, Île d'Yeu, 1995.

JUILLERAT, Clotilde
Maiden name: Gérard
French, 19th century.
Born 14 November 1806, in Lyons; died 1904 or 1905.
Painter, pastellist, draughtswoman. Historical subjects, portraits, genre scenes.
Clotilde Juillerat was a pupil of P. Delaroche and exhibited her portraits (paintings, drawings and especially pastels) and a few historical paintings and genre subjects in Paris from 1833 to 1861 (under her maidene name until 1839). They included *Beggar and his Child Asleep* (1836), *Childhood of St Theresa* (1839), *St Elizabeth, Queen of Hungary, Taking a Small Beggar Child to the Castle*, and portraits in pastel (1841) for which he gained a first class medal, *Anne of Austria* (1845), *The Great Condé Beaten at the Gate of St-Antoine* (1849)
Museums and Galleries:
Versailles: *Portrait of the Duke of Duras; Portrait of Henrietta of England; Portrait of François d'Aubeterre; Portrait of François de Bourbon, prince of Conti; Portrait of the Countess of Fiesque*.
Auction records:
Paris, 22 May 1996, *Anne de Beaujeu Pursued by the English* (1838, oil on canvas, 22¾ x 42¼ ins / 57.7 x 107.2 cm) FRF 41,000.

JUILLERAT, Eugène
French, 19th - 20th century.
Born 17 April 1856, in Paris.
Painter, sculptor, engraver, watercolourist.
Eugène Juillerat studied lithography under Pierre Lehoux; he also studied under Carolus Duran and exhibited at the Salon des Artistes Français, becoming a member of the society in 1888. He received a commendation in 1893, a bronze medal in 1895, a silver medal in 1899 and a silver medal at the Paris Exposition Universelle of 1900. Juillerat was made a Chevalier of the Légion d'Honneur in 1909. Known mainly for his lithographs, he also exhibited generously proportioned sculptures and produced paintings and watercolours which display a facility for combining drawing and volume.

JUILLERAT, Jacques Henri
Swiss, 19th century.
Born 1777, in Moutier (Bern canton); died 1860, in Bern.
Painter, watercolourist. Landscapes.
A pupil of Tavanes, Holzach, Birmann and Wuest, Jacques Juillerat was appointed professor of drawing in the Bern academy in 1823. He spent 1828-1855 in Italy for the sake of his health, notably in Nice, Turin and Rome. He painted landscapes, especially of Switzerland and Italy, with great feeling.
Auction records:
Paris, 18-19 Dec 1940, *Monuments and Figures: The Louvre, Palais de Luxembourg, etc.* (watercolour, series) FRF 650. Paris, 2 Dec 1946, *The Swiss Chalet* (1816, watercolour) FRF 2,400. Bern, 29 Nov 1976, *View of Bern* (1920, watercolour, 7 x 9¼ ins / 18 x 23.5 cm) CHF 6,200. Zurich, 5 June 1996,

View of the Palatine in Rome (1848, watercolour, 9 1/2 x 13 ins / 24 x 33 cm) CHF 4,025. BERN, 13 May 2004, *La Sorne* (watercolour, 16 x 21 ins / 40 x 53 cm) CHF 2,400.

JUILLERAT, Marie
Swiss, 19th century.
Born 1843, in Rolle (Lake Geneva).
Painter, watercolourist. Landscapes, flowers.
A pupil of Mme Hegg de Landerset and B. Menn in Geneva, Marie Juillerat worked and exhibited in the same city.

JUILLET, Jacques
French, 18th century.
Born 1739, in Paris.
Engraver (burin).
Juillet engraved *Ornaments*, after Sallembier.

JUILLIOT, Louis Laurent
French, 19th century.
Born 1827, in Paris.
Sculptor.
Louis Juilliot was a pupil of Langlois and Cézanne. His work appeared at the Salon from 1852 to 1859.

JUIVEN, E.
French, 19th century.
Painter.
MUSEUMS AND GALLERIES:
NIORT: *Peaches and Grapes*.

JUKES, Francis
British, 18th - 19th century.
Born 1747, in Martley; died 1812.
Active in London.
Painter, engraver (aquatint).
Francis Jukes holds an important place among English engravers. He is generally mentioned as having engraved views of Ireland and England after Nicholson; however, he also engraved genre and sports scenes. In connection with the latter, his production met with popular success, in particular with *The Life and Death of a Racehorse*, a series of six pieces after Ansell. Jukes also made many engravings on nautical themes. *The Adventures of the Ship Essex*, consisting of four pieces made in collaboration with Wells; *Admiral Graves's Squadron Beset by a Tempest* (1787) a series of four pieces after Robert Dodd. Quite a number of his works have been printed in colour; his landscapes and seascapes were often coloured, giving them the impression of being drawings. Of interest was the 1786 engraving, *A Doctor Assaulted by a Troop of Skeletons of People Killed by his Ignorance* after Collings; the 1787 *Gallantry*; *Marriage* (1787); views after A. Calanders and Clevely; twelve views of Mysore after Ambéry; views of the docks after R. Thew; Views of Italy and Tunis after C. Tuliv; views of Italy after Freebain. Jukes also made four plates for *Voyage of Captain Cook*.
AUCTION RECORDS:
LONDON, 13 Nov 1997, *Portrait of a six-year-old Horse* (1791, aquatint and etching, eight items) GBP 3,220; *Cape of Good Hope* (1794, aquatint, a pair, oval, 2 x 2 1/2 ins / 5 x 6.1 cm) GBP 4,370.

JUKES, J.
British, 18th - 19th century.
Miniaturist.
J. Jukes worked in London where, between 1775 and 1802, he exhibited at the Society of Artists and, especially, at the Royal Academy.

JUKO. See **SHUKO**

JUKOV, Dimitri Igorovich
Russian, 19th century.
Born 17 July 1820 or 1841; died 1903.
Painter. History painting.
MUSEUMS AND GALLERIES:
MOSCOW (State Tretyakov Gal.): painting.

JUKOV, Innokenti Nikolaevich
Russian, 20th century.
Born 1875; died 5 November 1948.
Sculptor.
Jukov studied at the University of St Petersburg and with the sculptor Bourdelle in Paris from 1911 to 1914.

JUKOV, Vladimir
Russian, 20th century.
Born 1921, in Vladivostok.
Painter. Figure compositions.
Vladimir Jukov studied at the Repin Institute in Leningrad (now St Petersburg) with Bobychev. He was a member of the Union of Painters of the USSR.
MUSEUMS AND GALLERIES:
KRASNODAR (MFA) - MOSCOW (Ministry of Culture) - ST PETERSBURG (Academy).
AUCTION RECORDS:
PARIS, 26 April 1991, *Market Scene* (1947, oil on canvas, 14 1/4 x 23 1/2 ins / 36.5 x 59.5 cm) FRF 4,000.

JUKOVSKI, Rudolph Casimirovich
Russian, 19th century.
Born 1814; died 5 or 17 November 1866, in St Petersburg.
Painter, lithographer.
Among Rudolph Jukovski's lithographs are a series of 35 plates depicting *Scenes from Everyday Russian Life*, and 15 *Views of Chablykino* as well as portraits.
MUSEUMS AND GALLERIES:
ST PETERSBURG (Gosudarstvennyj Russkij Muz.): *Baptism*; *Portrait of N V Kukolnik*; and drawings.

JUKOVSKI, Stanislav Joulianovich
Russian, 20th century.
Born 1873, in Russia; died 1944.
Painter. Genre scenes, landscapes, flowers.
Jukovski's Impressionist-style landscape paintings show a good feeling for variations in climate and season.
MUSEUMS AND GALLERIES:
MOSCOW (State Tretyakov Gal.): *In the Moonlight*; *Autumn Evening*; *Spring Evening*; *Spring Day* - ST PETERSBURG (Gosudarstvennyj Russkij Muz.).

JUKOVSKI, Vassili Andreievich
Russian, 19th century.
Born 9 February or 29 January 1783, in Tula; died 1 April 1852, in Baden-Baden.
Draughtsman, engraver. Landscapes.
Vassili Joukovski was the father of Pavel Jukovski. He was a poet and made drawings and etchings of views of Switzerland, Tsarskoe-Selo, Gatchina and Pavlosk, among others.
MUSEUMS AND GALLERIES:
ST PETERSBURG (Academy) - ST PETERSBURG (Public Library): 14 plates - ST PETERSBURG (Winter Palace Library).

JÜLB, Franz G.
German, 19th century.
Active in Offenbach.
Potter.
MUSEUMS AND GALLERIES:
KASSEL (Hessisches Landesmus.): signed plate (1807).

JULEMONT, Jean Henri
Belgian, 20th century.
Born 1904, in Cornesse-Pepinster; died 1979, in Cornesse-Pepinster.
Painter, fresco artist, watercolourist, draughtsman. Religious subjects, figures, portraits, landscapes. Designs for stained glass.

Jean Henri Julemont was a student at the Académie des Beaux-Arts de St-Luc, later becoming one of its lecturers. He gave expression to rural France and Belgium. He painted the frescoes in the chapel of Mont de la Salle in Ciney and numerous Ways of the Cross, notably in Jemappes, Theux, Franchimont and Charneux en Condroz. Several of his works have been purchased by the Belgian State and the Province of Liège.

AUCTION RECORDS:
LIÈGE, 11 Dec 1991, *In the Woods* (1935, oil on canvas, 14 3/4 x 18 3/4 ins / 37.5 x 47.5 cm) BEF 30,000.

JULES, Mervin
American, 20th century.
Born 1912; died 1994.
Painter.
Jules Mervin featured in the 1946 Carnegie Selection.

JULIA, Ascensio
Spanish, 18th - 19th century.
Born before 1771, in Valencia; died 1816, in Madrid.
Active in Spain.
Painter, engraver. Genre scenes.
Ascensio Julia is mentioned by Florence Levy. He was a pupil of Goya and assisted him with the frescoes for the church of S Antonio de la Florida in 1798. Goya painted Julia's portrait. Julia painted by applying touches of pure colour without any preliminary drawing.

MUSEUMS AND GALLERIES:
VALENCIA: *Shipwreck Victims*; *Smuggler*.

AUCTION RECORDS:
NEW YORK, 23 and 24 Feb 1906, *The Letter*, USD 750.

JULIA, Jean Baptiste
French, 18th century.
Born in Toulouse; died 1803, in Toulouse.
Sculptor. Mythological subjects.
Julia was a member of the Académie des Beaux-Arts de Toulouse, and owed his admission to a relief depicting *Apollo*, with ornamental panels (Toulouse Museum). He executed sculptures for the church of St-Pierre at Toulouse. He is probably identical to the woodcarver Julia who worked with Pajou on the decoration of the auditorium of the Opéra de Versailles.

MUSEUMS AND GALLERIES:
TOULOUSE: *Apollo* (relief).

JULIA, Léon Félix
French, 19th century.
Active in Castres (Tarn) at the end of the 19th century.
Painter. Genre scenes.

AUCTION RECORDS:
NEW YORK, 26 May 1983, *In the Train* (oil on canvas, set of four, each 59 1/4 x 19 1/2 ins / 150.5 x 49.8 cm) USD 8,500.

JULIA, Rafael
Spanish, 19th century.
Born 19th century, in Madrid.
Painter. Genre scenes.
Rafael Julia was a pupil of C. Ribera. He first exhibited around 1873.

JULIÀ VENTURA, Francisco
Spanish, 20th century.
Born 1900, in Sabadell (Catalonia).
Painter. Scenes with figures, landscapes.
Francisco Julià Ventura studied at the Sabadell school of applied arts, then completed his training in Barcelona. From 1944, he took part in various Barcelona exhibitions. He also held solo exhibitions, most notably in 1947 at the Pallarés Gallery in Barcelona. He painted local landscapes and country scenes in Montseny, Sant Cugat and the Aran Valley in a conventional Post-Impressionist manner.

BIBLIOGRAPHY:
Arnáiz, José Manuel/López Jiménez, Javier/Merchán Díaz, Manuel (ed.), *Cien años de pintura en Espana y Portugal (1830-1930)*, Antiqvaria, Madrid, 1990.

JULIA Y CABRERA, Emilio
Spanish, 19th century.
Sculptor.
Emilio Julia y Cabrera studied at the school of fine arts in Valencia. He first exhibited his work in around 1869.

JULIA Y CARRERE, Luis
Spanish, 19th century.
Born 19th century, in Madrid.
Painter. Animals.
Luis Julia y Carrere first exhibited around 1864. He specialised in painting bullfight scenes. He was a remarkable artist and very highly regarded in Spain.

MUSEUMS AND GALLERIES:
MURCIA: *Group of Bulls*.

JULIAN, Rodolphe
French, 19th century.
Born 13 June 1839, in La Palud (Vaucluse); died 12 February 1907, in Paris.
Painter, engraver, illustrator. Portraits, genre scenes.
Rodolphe Julian was a pupil of L. Cogniet and Cabanel. His work appeared at the Salon de Paris from 1865. He was decorated by the Légion d'Honneur in 1881.

Without the foundation of the academy that bears his name, Julian would have remained a minor figure among French painters. By drawing the most well-known teachers into his entourage, he attracted a considerable number of pupils, painters, sculptors and draughtsmen. The Académie Julien became a powerful artistic force with a worldwide reputation. Julian had to give up painting almost entirely to concentrate on his directorial role. He was an excellent administrator and, thanks to his school, he amassed quite a large fortune. He was also a benevolent master and, with his generosity, he enabled many artists to pursue studies they would otherwise have been obliged to interrupt. Julian enjoyed great popularity with his pupils to the end of his life.

Although his paintings are few, his illustrations are more numerous. He illustrated *Ompdrailles, the Tomb of the Fighters*, by Leon Cladel, and collaborated with *Republic of Letters* as its illustrator.

JULIAN-DAMAZY, William
French, 19th - 20th century.
Born 19th century, in Paris.
Engraver (burin).
William Julian-Damazy became a member of the Société des Artistes Français in 1907. He received a commendation in 1891 and a silver medal in 1905. He illustrated *Madame Thérèse* by Erckmann-Chatrian in 1925.

JULIANA Y ALBERT, José
Spanish, 19th century.
Born 19th century, in Sabadell.
Painter, watercolourist. Genre scenes.
José Juliana y Albert was a pupil of José Sevra in Barcelona. He completed his studies in Rome and first exhibited in Barcelona in 1866.

AUCTION RECORDS:
PARIS, 17 May 1897, *Window with Flowers*, FRF 85. PARIS, 26 Jan 1945, *Young Gentleman in a Garden* (watercolour) FRF 150. LONDON, 6 June 1990, *Monks Distributing Food to the Poor* (oil on canvas, 15 1/4 x 20 ins / 39 x 51 cm) GBP 1,980. COLUMBIA, 25 Sept 1999, *Portrait of Lady in Interior* (watercolour, 12 x 8 ins / 30 x 20 cm) USD 2,200. MADRID, 12 March 2002, *Gallant Scene* (oil on board, 7 x 11 ins / 19 x 28 cm) EUR 4,250. MADRID, 20 May 2003, *Figures by the Fountian* (oil on canvas, 19 x 15 ins / 47 x 39 cm) EUR 1,500.

JULIANCE. See **HENRIANCE Pierre**

JULIANI. See **ZULIANI**

JULIANIS, Caterina de

Italian, 17th - 18th century.
Active in Naples c. 1695-1742.
Modeller (wax), painter. Religious subjects, genre scenes.
Neapolitan School.

Caterina de Julianis produced a number of small statues and reliefs in multicoloured painted wax. Naples preserves examples of these, including an *Ecce Homo* and a *Virgin of Sorrow* in the church of Girolamini, and a *St Rose of Lima* and a *St Dominic* in the church of S Severe al Pendino. The Duca di Martina Museum in Naples has her statuettes of an *Apostle* and a *St Agatha*. It also has genre works by her (such as the *Cobbler's Family*, the *Confectioner's Shop*, the *Forge*, and the *Boat Ride*). She also produced oil paintings of landscapes, some of which can be found in the Valetta Museum.

MUSEUMS AND GALLERIES:

NAPLES (Mus. Nazionale di Ceramica Duca di Martina): *Apostle* (statuette); *St Agatha* (statuette); *Cobbler's Family*; *Confectioner's Shop*; *Forge*; *Boat Ride*.

JULIANUS. See **GIULIANO**

JULIARD, Alexandre

French, 19th century.
Born 3 March 1817, in Orléans.
Painter. Portraits, military portraits, genre scenes.

Alexandre Juliard was a pupil of Michel Drolling and François Picot. He presented his work at the Salon de Paris from 1844 to 1874 gaining a third class medal in 1846. He came from a military family which seems to have been the inspiration for numerous portraits of officers. His genre paintings include: *Pifferari Neapolitan Brigands Waiting in Ambush*.

BIBLIOGRAPHY:

Les Années romantiques, la peinture française de 1815 à 1850, exhibition catalogue, Musée des Beaux-Arts, Nantes, Gal. nationales du Grand Palais, Paris, 1996.

MUSEUMS AND GALLERIES:

NANTES (Mus. Dobrée): *Portrait of Madame Th. Dobrée* - RENNES (MBA): *Portrait of General Baron Rapatel* (1846).

JULIARD, Germaine

French, 19th - 20th century.
Active in Paris.
Painter.

Germaine Juliard became a member of the Société des Artistes Français in 1907 and exhibited at the society's salons.

JULIARD, Nicolas Jacques Bernard, or Julliard or Juliart or Julliar

French, 18th century.
Born 1715, in Paris; died 19 April 1790, in Paris.
Painter. Portraits, landscapes with figures, landscapes.

Juliard was the pupil of François Boucher. He was elected to the Académie on 31 August 1754, and was an academician in 1759. He exhibited at the Salon from 1755 to 1785. He signed himself *Jq N. Julliar fecite*. Juliard was probably one of the artists employed by F. Boucher in his studio to help him in the execution of his numerous works. At all events, he worked for the tapestry workshops known as the Manufacture d'Aubusson in 1757. He was also employed by M de la Ferte, Steward of the King's Lesser Pleasures, to whom he supplied two small landscapes in 1765.

Although he specialised in executing landscapes, his work also includes village festivals.

MUSEUMS AND GALLERIES:

LA FÈRE: *Landscape* - MONTPELLIER: *Landscape* - STOCKHOLM: *View of Frascati*; *Area around Tivoli* - TOURS: *Landscape*.

AUCTION RECORDS:

PARIS, 1884, *The Watermill*; *The Stone Bridge* (two pendants) FRF 4,500. PARIS, 1888, *Portrait of a Young Woman*, FRF 620. PARIS, 4 March 1905, *Landscape with Mill*, FRF 3,200; *The Mill*, FRF 3,200. PARIS, 10 April 1919, *The Pleasures of Fishing*; *Pastoral Scene* (pair) FRF 3,640. PARIS, 21 Nov 1919, *The Wooden Bridge*; *Ruins in a Landscape*, FRF 150. PARIS, 3 May 1928, *Flock near a Mountain Stream*, FRF 4,020. PARIS, 26 Feb 1931, *The Stone Bridge*, FRF 4,000. PARIS, 28 May 1931, *The Watermill* (gouache) FRF 2,500. PARIS, 9 March 1954, *The Smallholding*, FRF 300,000. PARIS, 18 June 1965, *The Smallholding by the River*, FRF 8,200. NEW YORK, 14 Nov 1979, *Wooded River Scene* (oil on canvas, 22 x 17in/56 x 43cm) USD 7,500. PARIS, 24 March 1983, *The Smallholding by the Water* (oil on canvas, 15 1/4 x 19 1/4in/38.5 x 49cm) FRF 37,000. PARIS, 17 June 1985, *Landscape with Waterfall* (oil on canvas, 17 3/4 x 29 1/2in/45 x 75cm) FRF 16,000. PARIS, 18 Dec 1987, *Italian Landscape with Figures* (oil on canvas, 38 1/4 x 52in/97 x 132cm) FRF 85,000. NEW YORK, 7 April 1988, *Jupiter and Callistes* (oil on canvas, 21 x 25 1/4in/52.5 x 64cm) USD 9,350. ROME, 7 March 1989, *Portrait of a Noble Lady and a Child* (oil on canvas, 39 1/4 x 31 1/2in/100 x 80cm) ITL 13,500,000. LONDON, 12 Dec 1990, *Wooded Landscape with Figures* (oil on canvas, a pair, each 14 3/4 x 18in/37.5 x 46cm) GBP 8,250. PARIS, 30 Jan 1991, *Rustic Landscapes* (two oils on canvas, 60 3/4 x 38 1/2in/154.2 x 98cm) FRF 110,000. PARIS, 18 April 1991, *Italian Landscape with Figures* (oil on canvas, 38 1/4 x 52in/97 x 132cm) FRF 82,000. PARIS, 17 June 1994, *Pastoral Scene near a River* (oil on canvas, 24 1/2 x 32in/62.5 x 81cm) FRF 30,000. LONDON, 30 Oct 1996, *Fishermen in a Rocky Riverscape* (oil on canvas, 51 1/2 x 38 3/4in/130.5 x 98.6cm) GBP 10,350. LONDON, 16 April 1997, *Fishermen in a Rocky Wooded Riverscape* (oil on canvas, a pair, each 20 x 23in/50.5 x 58.5cm) GBP 6,325. PARIS, 12 July 2000, *Fishing Port with Figures* (oil on canvas, 10 x 15 ins / 26 x 37 cm) FRF 65,000. PARIS, 6 Dec 2000, *Rest of Peasants by the River* (oil on panel, 14 x 10 ins / 35 x 26 cm) FRF 43,000. PARIS, 11 March 2003, *Pairs of Fishermen* (oil on panel, a pair, 6 x 8 ins / 16 x 21 cm) EUR 16,000. NEW YORK, 22 Jan 2004, *Figures Resting on River Banks* (1752, oil on canvas, a pair, 33 x 40 ins / 83 x 102 cm) USD 190,000. LONDON, 22 April 2004, *Pastoral Landscape with Shepherd, Shepherdess and Farmhouse* (1748, oil on panel, 9 x 14 ins / 23 x 35 cm) GBP 8,000.

JULIBERT GUAL, Joaquín

Spanish, 20th century.
Born 1898, in Barcelona.
Painter, engraver, draughtsman, illustrator.

Joaquín Julibert Gual studied at the Gali y Labarta academy and became an etcher. He showed in both group and solo exhibitions in Spain and abroad, winning several awards, including a first prize in a competition in Ripoll in 1933.

BIBLIOGRAPHY:

Arnáiz, José Manuel/López Jiménez, Javier/Merchán Díaz, Manuel (ed.), *Cien años de pintura en Espana y Portugal (1830-1930)*, Antiqvaria, Madrid, 1990.

JULIEN. See also **JULLIEN**

JULIEN, Albert

French, 19th century.
Active in Paris.
Painter, architect.

Albert Julien was a member of the Société des Artistes Français from 1888 and exhibited at the Salon as part of this group.

AUCTION RECORDS:

PARIS, 31 May and 1 June 1929, *Old Bridge at Vittel* (watercolour) FRF 210.

JULIEN, Alfred
French, 19th century.
Active in Paris.
Painter.
Alfred Julien was a member of the Société des Artistes Français from 1893 and exhibited at the Salon as part of this group.

JULIEN, Anne J. F.
French, 19th century.
Born 10 July 1855.
Painter.
Anne Julien was a member of the Société des Artistes Français from 1892 and exhibited at the Salon as part of this group.

JULIEN, Bernard Romain
French, 19th century.
Born 16 September 1802, in Bayonne; died 3 December 1871, in Bayonne.
Painter, draughtsman, engraver.
Bernard Julien was a pupil of Gros and was represented at the Salon de Paris from 1833 to 1850 with paintings, drawings and lithographs.

He was particularly well-known for his models of drawings with: *Studies in Two Crayons in the Manner of the Masters of the Classical School*, then in 1841: *Le Petit Cours, Les Grands Éléments* and *Les Grands Groupes* from 1860 to 1865, *Studies in the Style of Antiquity*.

His output includes around 600 pieces. Julien's portraits demonstrate perfect technical skill but are often kind and flattering.

AUCTION RECORDS:
PARIS, 21 Dec 1928, *Portrait of George Sand* (drawing) FRF 380.

JULIEN, Blaise
French, 18th century.
Born 18th century, in Poissy.
Sculptor.
Blaise Julien exhibited a low relief and a statue at the Salon in 1795.

JULIEN, Edouard
French, 20th century.
Born 1883, in Albi; died 1966, in Vence.
Active in Spain.
Painter, draughtsman.
Edouard Julien studied at the École des Beaux-Arts in Toulouse and then at the Académie Julian in Paris. He was curator of the Musée Toulouse-Lautrec in Albi from 1934 to 1963. He rarely exhibited during his lifetime, the last occasion being in Paris in 1960. Julien's work was featured at the *Vingt-cinq ans d'acquisitions 1959-1984* (*25 Years of Acquisitions 1959-1984*) exhibition at the Musée d'Art et d'Histoire in Narbonne in 1984. A retrospective exhibition of his work was held at the Musée de Sète in 1984.

MUSEUMS AND GALLERIES:
NARBONNE (MAH): *Interior*.

JULIEN, Élisabeth Charlotte
French, 19th century.
Born 2 December 1850, in Le Havre.
Painter.
Élisabeth Julien was represented at the salon in 1866, 1868,1870.

JULIEN, Emile. See **JULIEN Rémy Eugène**

JULIEN, Georges Jules
French, 19th - 20th century.
Born 20 February 1872, in Paris.
Sculptor.
Georges Jules Julien studied under Thomas and Larche. He became a member of the Salon des Artistes Français in Paris in 1902.

JULIEN, Gustave Marius
French, 19th century.
Born 1825, in Lambese (Bouches-du-Rhône); died 1881.
Painter. Seascapes.
Gustave Julien exhibited at the Salon de Paris in 1864, 1865 and 1866.

AUCTION RECORDS:
NEUILLY, 5 Dec 1989, *Entering the gate of Marseilles* (oil on canvas, 14 3/4 x 21 1/2 ins / 37.5 x 54.5 cm) FRF 12,000.

JULIEN, J. Laurent
French, 18th century.
Active in Paris.
Draughtsman, engraver.
Laurent Julien was the nephew and possibly the student of Simon Julien, whose portrait he engraved after Simon Julien's painting at the museum in Toulon. His works, depicting various genre subjects, include *Religious Feeling; Bacchic Reflections; Good-Day, Mother* after Simon Julien; *Rose Defended*, also after Simon Julien; *Study Scattering Flowers Over Time; Poor Ruined Rentier; Whiting For Frying; Rich Man of the Day; Pawnbroker*.

JULIEN, Jacques
French, 20th - 21st century.
Born January 1967.
Painter, sculptor. Sporting subjects.
Jacques Julien lives and works in Paris. He makes fun of the sporting world, by, for example, putting a penguin in a basketball net, or turning a tennis court around so that the net looks like the wings of a geometrical bird. By this ironic subversion of the codes and models of sport, he questions the rules in force, and provokes a debate about the nature and reception of art.

Exhibitions in which his work has featured include: 1995, *Champ Libre* (*Clear Field*), Musée des Beaux-Arts, Dole; and 2000, *La Beauté du geste* (*The Beauty of the Gesture*), Centre d'Art de Vassivière. He has shown his work in solo shows including: 1995, Espace Jules Verne, Bretigny-sur-Orge; 1998, Villa Arson, Nice; and 2003, Triangle, Rennes.

BIBLIOGRAPHY:
Ateliers 94, group exhibition catalogue, Musée d'Art moderne de la Ville de Paris, Paris, 1994. *Champ libre*, group exhibition catalogue, Musée des Beaux-Arts, Dole, 1995. *Jacques Julien*, exhibition catalogue, Espace Jules-Verne, Brétigny-sur-Orge, 1995. *Jacques Julien*, exhibition catalogue, Villa Arson-Centre national des Arts plastiques, Nice, 1998. Huitorel, Jean-Marc, "*Jacques Julien. L'Exercice auquel je m'applique*" in *Art Press*, n° 255 p. 46, periodical, Paris, March 2000.

MUSEUMS AND GALLERIES:
DÔLE (FRAC Franche-Comté): *Four Tables* (1993).

JULIEN, Jean Antoine, called Julien de Parme or Giuliano da Parma
Swiss, 18th century.
Born 23 April 1736, in Cavigliano; died 28 July 1799, in Paris.
Active in France from 1748.
Painter. History painting, portraits.
Despite the similarity of dates, Jean Antoine Julien should not be confused with Simon Julien. Jean Antoine Julien went to Berry in France in 1748. In 1756, he was given advice by Carle van Loo and Slodtz in Paris. He visited Champagne and Burgundy, painting portraits for a living, before moving on to Italy, where he entered the service of the Duke of Parma. He returned to Paris, but contrary to what *Bryan's Dictionary* says, he did not put himself up for the academy. It

was Simon Julien who unsuccessfully sought academy membership on 17 June 1787.

MUSEUMS AND GALLERIES:

AIX: *Caracalla Killing His Brother Geta* - ORLÉANS: drawings - PARIS (Louvre) - VIENNA (Albertina Mus.).

AUCTION RECORDS:

NEUILLY-SUR-SEINE, 13 May 1950, *Bust-length Portrait of a Young Girl*, FRF 28,000. LONDON, 19 April 1991, *Personification of Painting* (oil on panel, 10 1/4 x 13 3/4 ins / 26.2 x 35 cm) GBP 7,150. PARIS, 27 June 1991, *Bust-length, Almost Full-face Portrait of a Man* (1795, oil on canvas, oval, 25 1/2 x 21 ins / 65 x 53.5 cm) FRF 63,000.

JULIEN, Jean Pierre

French, 20th century.

Born 12 May 1888, in Marseilles; died 1974

Painter. Landscapes, seascapes, still-lifes.

Jean Pierre Julien studied under Cormon and became a member of the Salon des Artistes Français in Paris. He exhibited at the Salon from 1910 to 1967 and was awarded a gold medal.

AUCTION RECORDS:

BEAUNE, 10 April 1994, *Lunch at Amalfi* (1923, oil on canvas, 80 3/4 x 94 1/2 ins / 205 x 240 cm) FRF 93,500. LONDON, 22 June 2000, *Rest under a Tree on a Summer's Day* (oil on canvas, 38 x 51 ins / 97 x 130 cm) GBP 2,500.

JULIEN, Joseph

Belgian, 19th century.

Painter. Scenes with figures, landscapes with figures.

Joseph Julien is known primarily for his works sold at public auctions, often in New York. He painted mainly rural subjects.

AUCTION RECORDS:

NEW YORK, 1900-1903, *Haymaking in Belgium*, USD 210; *Haymaking*, USD 200. NEW YORK, 25 March 1904, *Shepherd Returning Home with his Flock*, USD 195. NEW YORK, 3 Feb 1906, *Sheep by a Pond*, USD 300. NEW YORK, 7 Oct 1977, *Harvest Scene* (oil on canvas, 38 1/2 x 52 ins / 98 x 132 cm) USD 9,500. NEW YORK, 29 May 1980, *Harvesters Resting* (oil on canvas, 13 3/4 x 19 3/4 ins / 35 x 50 cm) USD 3,500. NEW YORK, 13 Feb 1981, *Harvesters* (oil on canvas, 31 1/2 x 39 ins / 80 x 99 cm) USD 4,500. BRUSSELS, 20 June 1984, *Country Picnic* (oil on canvas, 18 1/2 x 26 3/4 ins / 47 x 68 cm) BEF 160,000. ZURICH, 21 June 1985, *Harvest Scene* (oil on canvas, 24 1/2 x 33 1/2 ins / 62.5 x 85 cm) CHF 13,000. NEW YORK, 15 June 1999, *Haymakers* (oil on canvas, 12 x 15 ins / 30 x 38 cm) USD 13,000.

JULIEN, Joseph Toussaint, also called Julien de Paris

French, 18th - 19th century.

Born in Paris.

Draughtsman, engraver (etching), miniaturist. Local figures, portraits.

From 1810-1818, Joseph Toussaint Julien was a painter of miniatures and an engraver in Lyons. He engraved etchings from his own drawings, such as the *Portrait of M. A. Petit*; *The Choir of Fourvière*; *Homage to the Sacré-Cœur* (after Revoil); many engravings, including a series portraying various kinds of people in the street, entitled *Cries of Lyons*; *Cinderella's Musician*; *Guard of Honour's Costume*; *Poor Michel*; *J.-B. Julien, Also Known as Mirabeau* (possibly one of his relatives), *Man Selling Ink*; *Woman Selling Needles* and many portraits of people of Lyons, mainly actors and actresses of the town. Many of these works are signed *Julien de Paris*.

JULIEN, L.

French.

Painter. Seascapes.

L. Julien may be identical with Jean.

MUSEUMS AND GALLERIES:

NICE: *Vessel in Sudden Squall*.

JULIEN, Marie Pauline. See LAURENT Marie Pauline

JULIEN, Pierre

French, 18th century.

Born 20 June 1731, in St-Paulien, near Le Puy-en-Velay; died 17 December 1804, in Paris.

Sculptor. Busts, statues, groups, monuments.

In Le Puy, Pierre Julien was the student of G. Samuel; then in Lyons he studied with Antoine Michel Perrache. In 1753, he won the medal for sculpture and in 1758 he went to join Guillaume Coustou in Paris. On 31 December 1760, he won the first medal of the quarter at the Académie Royale and on 31 August 1765 he won the Grand Prix de Rome for a low relief: *Albinus Offering His Chariot to the Vestals*. From 1765 to 1768, he stayed at the school for sponsored students run by Louis-Michel Vanloo, left for Rome on 1 December 1768 and returned to Paris in 1773. He was accepted by the Académie Royale on 25 April 1778. His reception piece was *Dying Gladiator*, which is at the Louvre. In 1790, he was given lodgings at the Louvre; then in 1801 he was lodged at the Palais de l'Institut. The catalogue of the museum in Le Puy states that he was made a Chevalier of the Légion d'Honneur shortly before he died.

Julien is one of the best sculptors of his era. He resists the influence of the more extreme forms of antique style. His principal works are the following: *Bust of Albinus* (museum of Le Puy); part of the *Mausoleum of the Dauphin* (cathedral in Sens), 1777; *Ganymedes* (Rothschild collection at Ferrières), 1776; *Dying Gladiator* (Louvre), 1778-1779; *Nymph Clipping Cupid's Wings* and *Head of a Woman* (Salon of 1779); *Atalanta* (château of St-Bonnet-Les-Oules, Loire), 1781; *Erigone* and *Head of a Vestal* (Salon of 1781); *La Fontaine* (plaster cast, at Château-Thierry); *Shepherd Killing a Snake*; *Young Camilla*; *Nymphs Clipping Cupid's Wings*, Salon of 1783; sketch for a *Monument for the Aerostation*, 1784; *La Fontaine* (marble, at the Palais de l'Institut); *Ganymedes* (marble, at the Louvre); *Silent Love* (terracotta, Salon of 1784). He exhibited at the Salon of 1788: *Cadet*, marble (Palais de l'Institut); *Leda*, marble (Rothschild collection at Ferrières); *Study*, plaster cast, executed in marble in 1789 (Cramail collection at Rueil). In 1791, he carried out the decorative work on the dairy at Rambouillet, of which there remains *Young Girl with a Goat* at the Louvre, and some works at the Pantheon. At the Salon in 1791, he exhibited: *Marble Clock* (probably the subject of Study) and in 1795 he exhibited four sketches: *Maternal Tenderness, Narcissus, Adolescent Love* and *Charity*; in 1796, in Le Puy, he produced: *Hygiea, Nymph, Echo* and *Matronly Woman of Ephesus*. In 1804, he made a bust of Napoleon from life that was sent to Le Puy and disappeared in 1816.

MUSEUMS AND GALLERIES:

ANGERS - LE PUY-EN-VELAY: *Bust of Albinus*; *Self-portrait* (low relief); *Amalthea, the Nymph*; *Albinus Offering His Chariot to the Vestals*; *Hygiea, Goddess of Health*; various maquettes and designs for statues; *Demosthenes* (1802) - PARIS (Louvre): *Bather* (marble); *Dying Gladiator* (1778-1779); *Ganymedes* (marble); *Young Girl with a Goat*.

AUCTION RECORDS:

PARIS, 13 May 1976, *Bust of a Woman* (1763, white marble) FRF 11,000. LONDON, 21 June 1999, *Young Girl with Doves* (1789, sculpture, terracotta) GBP 6,500.

JULIEN, Rémy Eugène, called Émile

French, 19th century.

Born 27 July 1797, in Laon (Aisne); died 17 November 1868, in Caen.

Painter. Military subjects, genre scenes.

Rémy Julien started off in a military career but abandoned it in 1830. He settled in Caen where he devoted himself to painting and the teaching of drawing. His work appeared at the Salon de Paris from 1834 to 1839.

BIBLIOGRAPHY:

Les Années romantiques, la peinture française de 1815 à 1850, exhibition catalogue, Musée des Beaux-Arts, Nantes, Gal. nationales du Grand Palais, Paris, 1996.

MUSEUMS AND GALLERIES:

BAYEUX: *Battle of Formigny* - CAEN: *Children Playing* - LISIEUX: *Two Neapolitan Brigands Fighting* (1831).

JULIEN, René

Belgian, 20th century.
Born 1937, in Hollogne-aux-Pierres.
Painter, sculptor. Designs for tapestries, stage sets.

René Julien was a student of the Académie des Beaux-Arts in Liège, and later director of the Académie des Beaux-Arts in St-Josse-ten-Node.

BIBLIOGRAPHY:

Provoyeur, Pierre, *René Julien: 10 ans de sculpture en Lubéron*, Éd. Château vert, Cavaillon, 1999.

AUCTION RECORDS:

ANTWERP, 20 Oct 1976, *The Colour of the Night* (oil on panel, 28 3/4 x 36 1/4 ins / 73 x 92 cm) BEF 20,000. LOKEREN, 8 Oct 1994, *Girl with a Hat* (silver, h. 13 1/2 ins / 34 cm) BEF 40,000. BRUSSELS, 17 April 2000, *Journeys* (1973, oil on canvas, 50 x 37 ins / 128 x 94 cm) BEF 90,000. BRUSSELS, 15 Oct 2002, *Violonist* (oil on canvas, 60 x 38 ins / 152 x 97 cm) EUR 2,000. ANTWERP, 21 Oct 2003, *Woman Playing Cello* (patinated bronze, h. 10 ins / 26 cm) EUR 1,700.

JULIEN, Simon

French, 18th century.
Born 28 October 1735, in Toulon; died 23 February 1800, in Paris.
Painter, engraver. History painting, allegorical subjects, mythological subjects, portraits.

A student of Dandré Bardon in Marseilles and of Carle van Loo in Paris, Simon Julien was awarded the first Prix de Rome in 1760 for *Sacrifice of Manoah, Father of Samson* (museum of Le Mans). He remained in Italy until 1776. When he arrived in Paris to continue his studies, his father, who had always discouraged his artistic leanings, refused to send him any money. Continuing to paint, Simon had to turn his hand to dealing in engravings in order to survive. He was made an associate of the Académie Royale on 29 March 1783 and exhibited at the Salon in 1783, 1785, 1787 and (posthumous submission) 1800. Prosper de Baudicour describes eight engravings by him. On either 17 June 1787 or 27 June 1789, he presented his picture *Aurora and Tithonus* (museum of Caen) in order to gain acceptance as an academician but he was not elected. The highly remarkable catalogue in Toulon museum states that he was made a professor of the Académie Royale in 1790; there seems to be some doubt about this, given that his name does not appear with this position in the registers of the academy.

MUSEUMS AND GALLERIES:

CAEN: *Aurora and Tithonus* - LE MANS: *Sacrifice of Manoah, Father of Samson* - ORLÉANS: *Daphne Fleeing Apollo* - TOULON: *Triumph of Aurelian; Portrait of His Parents.*

AUCTION RECORDS:

PARIS, 21 June 1920, *Angel*, FRF 2,000. PARIS, 23 Nov 1927, *Return of Ulysses* (black chalk heightened) FRF 820. PARIS, 2-3 Nov 1948, *The Sciences* (four supra portas (overlintels)) FRF 48,000. PARIS, 21 Dec 1977, *Minerva Arranging Her Hat* (1775, oil on canvas, 100 1/2 x 78 ins / 255 x 198 cm) FRF 26,000. PARIS, 30 March 1980, *Jesus Chasing the Merchants from the Temple* (oil on canvas, 23 1/4 x 28 3/4 ins / 59 x 73 cm) FRF 9,500. PARIS, 19 June 1987, *Psyche Clipping Cupid's Wings; Coveted Child* (1780, painting/copper, a pair, each 10 x 12 3/4 ins / 24.5 x 32.5 cm) FRF 50,000. MONACO, 5-6 Dec 1991, *Scene from Ancient History* (oil on canvas, 25 1/4 x 32 1/4 ins / 64.2 x 81.8 cm) FRF 77,700. PARIS, 24 June 1996, *Aeneas; Plague* (pen with brown ink wash, a pair, each 11 x 15 3/4 ins / 28 x 40.3 cm) FRF 6,000.

JULIEN DE HONGRIE. See **HONGRIE**

JULIEN DE PARIS. See **JULIEN Joseph Toussaint**

JULIEN DE PARME. See **JULIEN Jean Antoine**

JULIEN L'ARCHEVESQUE. See **L'ARCHEVESQUE Julien**

JULIENNE, Eugène

French, 19th century.
Active between 1800 and 1874.
Painter (porcelain).

Eugène Julienne painted two vases that were presented to the king of Portugal in 1856 by Napoleon III. His works include lithographs, a romantic cover for the *Treatise on Colour in Lithographs*, an engraving by Meilhac (1836) and various ornamental plates and industrial decoration.

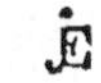

AUCTION RECORDS:

PARIS, 15 Dec 1926, *Roses, Tulips, Bindweed, Peaches and Grapes* (gouache) FRF 1,250.

JULIENNE, Jean de. See **JULLIENNE**

JULIN, Johan Fredrik

Swedish, 19th century.
Born 1798, in Askersund; died 1843, in Stockholm.
Watercolourist.

One of Johan Julin's works is in the museum in Stockholm.

JULIN, Raymond

Belgian, 20th century.
Born 1921, in Liège.
Painter.

Raymond Julin studied at the Académie des Beaux-Arts de St-Luc, where he became a lecturer.

JULIO, pseudonym of Pereira, Julio Dos Reis

Portuguese, 20th century.
Painter, draughtsman.

Julio was also a poet, under the pseudonym of Saul Dia, and introduced Expressionism and Surrealism to Portugal. He collaborated on the review *Presença*. His Expressionism was influenced by Grosz before becoming truly personal, and he painted mainly figures, whose features he deformed. During the 1920s, he became an adherent of Surrealism and subsequently produced a large number of drawings, including the series *Circus, Music* and *The Poet*.

BIBLIOGRAPHY:

Elle Poeta, exhibition catalogue, Gal. Gilde, Lisbon, 1985.

JULIOT. See also **JULYOT**

JULIOT, Antoine

French, 16th century.
Born in Troyes.
Sculptor.
Fontainebleau School.

Antoine Juliot was a member of the Juliot family, and like his parents, worked on the decoration of the Château de Fontainebleau from 1540 to 1550.

JULIOT, François

French, 16th century.
Born in Troyes.
Sculptor.
Fontainebleau School.

François Juliot worked on the decoration of the Château de Fontainebleau from 1537 to 1540.

JULIOT, Hubert or Imbert
French, 16th century.
Born in Troyes.
Painter, sculptor.
Fontainebleau School.
Hubert Juliot worked at the Château de Fontainebleau from 1535, and repaired antique marble statues that had been brought from Rome between 1540 and 1550. He also seems to have worked at the Château de Polizy in the Aube region of France in 1548.

JULIOT, Jacques I, or Julyot
French, 16th century.
Died c. 1552.
Sculptor.
In 1511, Jacques Juliot I produced the altarpiece for the altar of Notre-Dame, featuring the *Last Supper*, in the church of St-Jean in Troyes. The work still exists today. In 1516, he worked on the portal overlooking the cemetery at the church of Ste-Madeleine, and in 1534 produced the tomb for the abbot of the convent of Montier-la-Celle. He was also responsible for the main altarpiece of the Larrivour abbey (1539) - a major work that is now part of the Julien Gréau collection in Troyes - and another marble altarpiece for the church of St-Nizier, showing, like its predecessor, the life of the Virgin. Two damaged fragments of this work are in the museum of Troyes.
MUSEUMS AND GALLERIES:
TROYES: *Altarpiece of the Life of the Virgin* (fragments).

JULIOT, Jacques II, the Younger
French, 16th century.
Died 12 November 1567, in Troyes.
Sculptor.
Fontainebleau School.
Jacques Juliot II may have been the son of Jacques Juliot I. He worked on the decoration of the Château de Fontainebleau from 1540 to 1550. After returning to Troyes, he produced a large altarpiece for the church of St-Urbain.

JULIOT, Jacques III
French, 16th century.
Born 16 September 1544, in Troyes.
Sculptor.
Works produced by Jacques Juliot III are not known.

JULIUS. See **GIULIO**

JULIUS
German, 20th century.
Born 1939, in Wilhelmshaven.
Installation artist. Multimedia.
Julius studied from 1961 to 1969 at the school of fine art in Bremen and then Berlin, and from 1972 to 1977 taught drawing in Brake and Bremen. Since 1974 he has worked with photography, and since 1975 he has included music in his three dimensional work. In 1983 and 1984 he spent time in the USA, thanks to a bursary awarded by the PS1 in New York. He set up in Berlin.

He has featured in exhibitions in Germany: Kunstmuseum in Düsseldorf (1980); Kunstverein Brunswick (1982); Kunstverein Heidelberg (1983); and in France, in Paris in 1984 at the Goetheinstitut, and in 1999 at the Galerie Lara Vincy.

His work consists in associating different colours with music: 'red music', 'yellow music', and so on. He puts tiny loudspeakers into small piles of pigment and plays music 'which causes one to see and hear music that is static or that flows slowly'.

JULIUS, Gyula
Hungarian, 20th - 21st century.
Born 1958, in Budapest.
Screen printer.
Gyula Julius studied in the graphic art section of the academy of fine arts in Budapest. His silk-screen creations take on an unusual perspective through their use of geometric figures. His work has featured in collective exhibitions in Hungary, Germany, Sweden and Poland and he won the Hermann foundation prize in 1983.

JULIUS, Per
Swedish, 20th - 21st century.
Born 1951, in Örnsköldsvik.
Painter. Landscapes.
Per Julius paints traditional Swedish landscapes with birch woods, fjords and snow-covered mountains. Since 1986 he has lived in Annecy in France.
AUCTION RECORDS:
STOCKHOLM, 21 Nov 1988, *Nordic Landscape* (watercolour, 5 3/4 x 9 ins / 14.5 x 23 cm) SEK 3,900. STOCKHOLM, 22 May 1989, *Spring Evening - Nordingra* (oil on canvas, 12 1/2 x 19 1/4 ins / 32 x 49 cm) SEK 8,500. STOCKHOLM, 5-6 Dec 1990, *Nordic Landscapes* (watercolour, a pair, 6 1/2 x 9 1/2 ins / 16.5 x 24 cm and 6 x 9 1/4 ins/15.5 x 23.5 cm) SEK 18,000. STOCKHOLM, 26 May 1999, *Winter Landscape* (watercolour, 30 x 21 ins / 75 x 54 cm) SEK 15,000. STOCKHOLM, 24 Nov 1999, *Northern Winter Landscape* (watercolour, 37 x 61 ins / 93 x 155 cm) SEK 30,000. STOCKHOLM, 28 Nov 2000, *Ice Thawing* (watercolour, 31 x 44 ins / 79 x 111 cm) SEK 17,500. STOCKHOLM, 5 Dec 2000, *River Landscape, Angermanalven* (watercolour, 22 x 29 ins / 55 x 74 cm) SEK 28,000. STOCKHOLM, 22 May 2001, *Northern Landscape* (watercolour, 28 x 42 ins / 72 x 107 cm) SEK 29,000. STOCKHOLM, 4 June 2003, *Northern Landscape in Autumn Colours* (watercolour, 29 x 21 ins / 74 x 54 cm) SEK 26,000. STOCKHOLM, 30 Nov 2004, *Mountain Landscape* (oil on canvas, 13 x 20 ins / 33 x 50 cm) SEK 15,500.

JULIUS, Victor
American, 20th century.
Born 26 July 1882, in Boston (Massachusetts); died 1958.
Painter, watercolourist.
Julius Victor studied at the Art Students League in New York. He was a member of the Salmagundi Club.

JULLIAN, Philippe
French, 20th century.
Born 1919; died 1977.
Painter, watercolourist, draughtsman. Genre scenes.

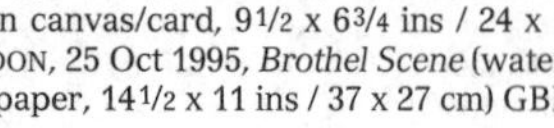

AUCTION RECORDS:
VERSAILLES, 29 Oct 1989, *The Painter's Studio* (oil on card, 14 1/2 x 11 ins / 37 x 28 cm) FRF 4,200. PARIS, 5 April 1991, *Avenue Marigny Gallery, Christmas 1972* (watercolour, 11 1/2 x 8 1/4 ins / 29 x 21 cm) FRF 6,500. PARIS, 24 Nov 1993, *The Antiquarian Mademoiselle Rémy* (watercolour, 10 3/4 x 5 1/2 ins / 27.5 x 14 cm) FRF 8,500. PARIS, 29 March 1995, *Coquette* (1971, oil on canvas/card, 9 1/2 x 6 3/4 ins / 24 x 17 cm) FRF 5,500. LONDON, 25 Oct 1995, *Brothel Scene* (watercolour and Indian ink/paper, 14 1/2 x 11 ins / 37 x 27 cm) GBP 1,840.

JULLIARD
French, 19th century.
Painter. Flowers.
MUSEUMS AND GALLERIES:
BREST: two paintings.

JULLIARD (Mlle)
later Mme George-Julliard
Swiss, 19th century.
Enameller.
Mlle Julliard exhibited in Geneva in 1851 and 1852.

JULLIARD, Nicolas Jacques. See **JULIARD**

JULLIEN. See also **JULIEN**

JULLIEN, Amédée, Marie, Antoine
French, 19th century.
Born 1819, in Clamecy (Nièvre); died 1887, in Clamecy.
Painter, engraver (including etching). Landscapes.
Amédée Jullien was a pupil of Jean Charles Rémond and Harpignies. He was a lawyer as well as a painter until 1860 when he sold his practice. He made his home in Entrains near Clamecy but stayed regularly in Paris. He was the founder and first curator of the museum in Clamecy.

He exhibited at the Salon de Paris from 1841 to 1878 and was a member of the Société des Artistes Français.

He painted mainly landscapes inspired by the Nivernais but also some views of Morvan, the Alps and Normandy. Influenced by the style of Corot he introduced atmospheric effects into his landscapes to convey a poetic impression. He experimented with decoration on earthenware. In 1883 he published: *The Nièvre through the Ages, Historical Topography and Principal Towns* illustrated with 33 engraved plates.

In 2001 he was represented in the exhibition devoted to *Paysages de Bourgogne, de Corot à Laronze* (*Landscapes of Bourgogne from Corot to Laronze*) at the Musée des Beaux-Arts in Dijon.

BIBLIOGRAPHY:
Barthélémy, Sophie/Tran, Catherine, *Paysages de Bourgogne, de Corot à Laronze*, exhibition catalogue, Musée des Beaux-Arts, Dijon, 2001.

MUSEUMS AND GALLERIES:
AUXERRE: *Meadow in a Valley of the Yonne; After the Rain* - CLAMECY: *Return from the Market; Still-life; Three Episodes from the War of 1870; Two Landscapes* - NEVERS (Mus. Frédéric Blandin): *Gust of Wind During a Downpour in Maupertuis (Yonne)* (1870, oil on canvas) - VARZY (Mus. Auguste Grasset): *The Chemin de la Fontaine in Entrains-sur-Nohain* (1864, oil on canvas).

AUCTION RECORDS:
LONDON, 4 Oct 1991, *Pond in the Forest* (1854, oil on canvas, 35 x 46 ins / 89 x 117 cm) GBP 4,400.

JULLIEN, Anthelme Joseph Claude Julien
French, 19th century.
Born 26 December 1840, in Lyons; died 27 January 1867, in Lyons.
Painter, draughtsman. Portraits, landscapes.
Anthelme Jullien was the son of a weaver. While still quite young he went to work for an architect. He followed courses given by Vibert and Danguin at the École des Beaux-Arts in Lyons from 1859-60 while earning his living designing for architects, for a railway company and for the Lyons Museum. He exhibited in Lyons in 1863 and 1867. He died of tuberculosis.

His legacy, along with a few portraits and landscape studies, is a number of pen and pencil drawings that are impressive for their energy, sureness of touch and freedom of expression. These drawings represent mainly Jullien's relations or neighbours going about their daily work. A retrospective exhibition in Lyons in 1904 revealed this, until then, unknown artist.

MUSEUMS AND GALLERIES:
LYONS (MBA): *Portrait of a Woman; Six Drawings, among which: Worker Reading; Old Woman Seated; Old Woman Eating; Old Woman Repairing her Spinning Wheel* (1864) - PONTOISE: *Head of a Woman*.

JULLIEN, Cécile
French, 19th century.
Born 19th century, in Charenton (Hauts-de-Seine).
Engraver, lithographer.
Cécile Jullien was a pupil of M. Guillon. She was a member of the Société des Artistes Français from 1894 and exhibited at the Salon as part of this group.

JULLIEN, Hippolyte André
French, 19th century.
Born 1840, in Gap (Hautes-Alpes).
Sculptor.
Hippolyte Jullien worked with Duret, Guillaume and Lequesne. He exhibited at the Salon de Paris from 1866 to 1876 and executed the marble bust of A. -L. de Jussieu. He taught at Winterthur from 1875 to 1887.

MUSEUMS AND GALLERIES:
ANGERS: *Fawn*.

JULLIEN, Jacques
French, 17th century.
Painter.
On 24 September 1616, Jacques Jullien received a payment for various works carried out at the residence of the Connétable de Lesdiguières in Grenoble. He settled in Grenoble and married there. Certain biographers give Toulon as his birth-place.

JULLIEN, Marcelle, short for Julie Marcelle Madeleine
Maiden name: Tachard
French, 19th - 20th century.
Born 13 April 1867, in Montauban; died 6 April 1947, in Montauban.
Painter. Flowers.
Marcelle Jullien was an amateur painter. She did not exhibit and her works were known only within her family circle. However, they were rediscovered and restored and have become highly regarded for their fineness of observation and precision of execution in keeping with the tradition of flower painting. She signed her work: *Marcelle*.

JULLIEN, Maurice
French, 19th century.
Born 19th century, in Paris.
Engraver (wood).
Maurice Jullien was a pupil of Émile Tilly. He received an honourable mention in 1902.

JULLIEN, Robert, or Jullient
French, 16th - 17th century.
Illuminator.
The name of Robert Jullien appears in the 'List of Domestic Officers of the King' in 1599, and in the list of 'painters and manservants' under the subheading 'other painters and craftspeople', as 'A. Robert Julien, illuminator'. His name appeared again in 1609.

JULLIENNE, Jean de, or Julienne
French, 18th century.
Born 29 November 1686, in Paris; died 20 March 1766, in Paris.
Engraver, reproductions engraver, collector. Genre scenes, figures, nudes.
A good friend of Watteau, Jean de Julienne published four volumes of engravings after the works of this artist following his death. One of these volumes contains a short biography of Watteau that appears as an introduction. He made a gift of these volumes to the Académie Royale in Paris. They are preserved by the library at the École des Beaux-Arts. There are four etchings by him: *Beggar and Cripple*, after Téniers, two portraits of *Warriors with Helmets* after E. van Heemskerk and a *Male Nude* after J. Restout.

JULLIO, César. See **GILIO Cesare**

JULLIOTT, Made
French, 20th century.

Born in Thomery.
Painter.
Made Julliott exhibited interiors and landscapes in Paris at the Salon des Indépendants from 1913.

JULYEN. See **JULIEN**

JULYOT. See also **JULIOT**

JULYOT, Jean, or Juliot
French, 16th century.
Active in Besançon.
Sculptor.
Julyot is thought to have produced the stalls for the church of the abbey of Montbenoît in the Doubs region of France, from 1525 to 1527. The work was commissioned by Abbot Ferry Carondelet, who was the master of commissions at the main council of Mechelen, and procurer at the court of Rome and of Margaret of Austria.

JULYOT, Rémond, or Juliot
French, 16th century.
Sculptor.
Rémond Julyot was the son of Jean Julyot. In 1555, he sculpted a stone altarpiece for one of the chapels in the church of St-Maurice in Besançon.

JUMEL, Anthoine or Antoine
French, 17th century.
Died 1663; buried 3 May.
Painter.
Anthoine Jumel was a burgess of Paris and master painter.

JUMEL, Jean
French, 17th century.
Active in Paris in 1606.
Painter.

JUMEL DE NOIRETERRE, Antoine Valentin
French, 19th century.
Born 26 January 1824, in Paris; died 21 July 1902, in La Landelle-Palleville (Tarn).
Painter.
Antoine Jumel de Noireterre was a pupil of Flers. He was a former pupil of the Polytechnic and an aide-de-camp to Napoleon III. He painted scenes of the Crimean war and of the Italian countryside (Paris, Musée de l'Armée). In 1948, M. G. Poulain, curator of the Castres museum, found, in the attic, a portrait of the imperial prince aged two signed by Jumel de Noireterre.
MUSEUMS AND GALLERIES:
CASTRES: *Batle of Inkermann; Nightmare; The Duel* - PARIS (Mus. de l'Armée): *Battle of Alma; Battle of the Balaklava; Battle of Traktir; Battle of Sebastopol; Battle of Solferino; Battle of Magenta.*

JUMELLE. See also **JUMEL**

JUMELLE, Pierre, or Jumel
French, 17th century.
Painter, sculptor.
Pierre Jumelle was made an associate of the Académie Royale on 11 April 1674. He lived at the Louvre galleries.

JUMIERE-GILGENGRANTZ, Adèle
French, 19th century.
Born 19th century, in Colmar (Upper Rhine).
Painter.
Adèle Jumiere-Gilgengrantz was a pupil of Fontaine and of A. Dubufe. She exhibited at the Salon from 1878.

JUMILHAC, Armand de
French, 19th century.
Born 1849, in Paris.
Painter. Landscapes.
Armand de Jumilhac was a pupil of Collin. He exhibited *Interior of a Monastery* at the Salon in 1869 and in 1870 *Ruins of Charbonnières*

JUMONT, A.
French, 19th - 20th century.
Born in Lyons.
Painter.
A. Jumont studied under Madame D. de Cool. She exhibited in Paris from 1873 to 1887, showing portraits (watercolours, enamels, pastels and miniatures).

JUMP, R.
British, 19th century.
Active in London.
Painter. Seascapes.
R. Jump exhibited at the Royal Academy in 1842.
AUCTION RECORDS:
LONDON, 3 May 1909, *Seascape; River Scene,* GBP 1.

JUNAYD
Persian School, 14th century.
Born probably in Baghdad.
Active at the end of the 14th century.
Painter.
Junayd has been identified as the painter whose signature *Imperial Painter* appears on the miniatures of the *Diwan* of Khwaju Kirmani (1396), in the British Museum. These miniatures are elegantly designed, combining brilliant colours with an idealised landscape and characters which reappear repeatedly over the course of the following centuries.
BIBLIOGRAPHY:
Canby, Sheila R., *Persian Painting,* Geneva, 1961. Gray, Basil, *Persian Painting,* Geneva, 1961. Lentz, Thomas W./Lowry, Glenn D., *Timur and the Princely Vision,* exhibition catalogue, Los Angeles County Museum of Art, Los Angeles, 1989.
MUSEUMS AND GALLERIES:
LONDON (British Mus.): miniatures of the 'Diwan' of Khwaju Kirmani.

JUNCA, Jan
French, 20th century.
Born 20th century.
Sculptor, ceramicist.

JUNCADELLA COLLET, María
Spanish, 20th century.
Born in Barcelona.
Painter. Landscapes.
María Juncadella Collet studied at the school of fine arts in Barcelona. She took part in the portrait and landscape exhibition in Barcelona in 1910.

JUNCEAU, Brandt
American, 20th - 21st century.
Born 1957.
Installation artist.
Brandt Junceau held his first solo exhibition at Galerie Meert-Rihoux in Brussels in 1993. His installations are rooted in his own highly personal and family associations.

JUNCK, Ferdinand
British, 19th century.
Active in London.
Sculptor.
Ferdinand Junck exhibited in London from 1858 onwards, especially at the Royal Academy, the British Institution and at Suffolk Street.

JUNCK, Oscar Alexander
British, 19th century.
Active in London.
Sculptor.

Alexander Oscar Junck began in 1880 to exhibit in London, especially at the Royal Academy.

JUNCKER, Frederick
French, 19th century.
Born in Paris; died 1906.
Painter. Genre scenes, landscapes, still-lifes.
Frederick Juncker was a pupil of L. Cogniet and took part in Salon exhibitions between 1839 and 1882. His life remains something of a mystery. He is best known for his panoramic views of towns. Even when they are executed in the smallest format, they succeed in portraying the essence of his impression.

JUNCKER, Hans, the Elder
German, 17th century.
Born 1582; died after 1621.
Sculptor.
Hans Juncker the Elder's works are found in the region of Würzburg, e.g. a high altar in the village church in Darstadt, and tombs in Fröhstockheim and Würzburg Cathedral. More works by him are found in Aschaffenburg and Mainz Cathedral. He is possibly associated with Zacharias Juncker.

JUNCKER, Isaac
German, 18th century.
Born 1727, in Frankfurt; died 1789, in Frankfurt.
Painter. Genre scenes.
Isaac Juncker was the son and pupil of Justus Juncker, and made himself a name chiefly as an operatic tenor.

JUNCKER, Johann Jakob, or Jungker
German, 18th century.
Born in Düsseldorf; died 1 October 1786, in Mainz.
Sculptor.
Johann Juncker was granted civic rights in Mainz on 29 August 1744. A noted work by him is an *Assumption* (wood carving). A *St Ignatius* on the doorway of the church of St Ignaz and a *St Nicholas* on an altar in the same church are also attributed to him.

JUNCKER, Justus, or Junker
German, 18th century.
Born 24 July 1703, in Mainz; died 1767, in Frankfurt am Main.
Painter, engraver (etching). Portraits, genre scenes, landscapes, still-lifes.
A pupil of Schlegel in Frankfurt, then of Thomas Wyck, Heem and Van Huysum, Justus Juncker painted portraits, landscapes, genre scenes and still-lifes.
MUSEUMS AND GALLERIES:
AIX: *Chemist* - DARMSTADT: *Fruit* - FRANKFURT AM MAIN: *A Scholar in His Study* - KASSEL: *Scholar in his Laboratory; Master at His Easel; Man Reading; Kitchen with Cook and Kitchen Boys; Kitchen with Two Young Girls; Woman with Kitchen Provisions* - MAINZ: *Fruit* - STUTTGART: *Calm Sea.*
AUCTION RECORDS:
PARIS, 28-29 Nov 1923, *Preparations for the Meal,* FRF 1,420; *The Housewife,* FRF 1,420. LONDON, 22 May 1968, *Cabaret Scene,* GBP 350. PARIS, 4 June 1970, *The Painter's Studio; The Sculptor's Studio,* FRF 6,300. VIENNA, 20 March 1973, *The Painter's Studio,* ATS 60,000. VERSAILLES, 20 July 1976, *The Young Mother* (oil on wood, 9 3/4 x 13 3/4 ins / 25 x 35 cm) FRF 9,800. LONDON, 29 Oct 1980, *Preparations for the Meal* (oil on canvas, 36 3/4 x 12 ins / 93.5 x 30.5 cm) GBP 2,900. NEW YORK, 9 Jan 1981, *Huntsmen in a Tavern* (oil on canvas, 9 x 14 1/2 ins / 23 x 37 cm) USD 7,500. MONTE CARLO, 8 Dec 1984, *An Alchemist in His Workshop* (oil on panel, 19 x 14 1/4 ins / 48 x 36 cm) FRF 55,000. ZURICH, 29 Nov 1985, *Still-life with Fruit* (oil/copper, 12 1/2 x 10 ins / 32 x 25.5 cm) CHF 20,000. PARIS, 30 Oct 1986, *Kitchen Interior; The Spinner* (oil on canvas, a pair, 13 x 17 1/4 ins / 33 x 43.5 cm) FRF 60,000. PARIS, 16 March 1988, *Still-life with Fruit beneath a Sculpted Vase in a Landscape* (1761, oil on canvas, 32 1/4 x 26 1/2 ins / 82 x 67 cm) FRF 150,000. LONDON, 19 May 1989, *Inn Interior with a Boy Playing the Violin; Peasants Smoking while a Man Reads to Them* (oil on panel, a pair, each 9 1/4 x 12 1/2 ins / 23.5 x 31.7 cm) GBP 4,620. LONDON, 8 July 1992, *Portrait of a High-Ranking Officer* (1767, oil on canvas, 49 1/2 x 39 1/4 ins / 126 x 100 cm) GBP 4,400. LONDON, 11 Dec 1992, *Portrait of the Artist Sitting at His Easel with a Pupil behind Him* (oil on panel, 16 3/4 x 12 3/4 ins / 42.5 x 32.5 cm) GBP 33,000. PARIS, 28 June 1993, *Woman Scouring; The Countrywoman* (oil on panel, a pair, each 16 1/4 x 13 ins / 41.5 x 33 cm) FRF 60,000. NEW YORK, 19 May 1995, *Bird Taking Off; Mother and Child Talking to the Grandfather* (1765, oil on panel, a pair, each 13 1/4 x 11 ins / 33.7 x 27 cm) USD 14,950. NEW YORK, 27 Jan 1999, *Awaiting the Doctor's Reply* (1765, oil on panel, 13 x 16 ins / 33 x 41 cm) USD 4,500. LONDON, 16 April 1999, *Alchemist in His Study* (1751, oil on panel, 20 x 17 ins / 50 x 42 cm) GBP 55,000. LONDON, 2 Nov 2000, *Interior with Two Young Men Counting Money at a Table. Interior with Turbaned Man Reading* (oil on panel, a pair, 10 x 8 ins / 26 x 20 cm) GBP 3,800. ZURICH, 30 March 2001, *Still-life with Vegetables. Still-life with Cheese* (oil on canvas, a pair, 14 x 19 ins / 35 x 47 cm) CHF 60,000. MUNICH, 26 June 2002, *Old Man at a Table Smoking a Pipe* (1752, oil on canvas, 19 x 16 ins / 48 x 41 cm) EUR 6,500. LONDON, 10 Dec 2002, *Interior with Man Seated before a Table Smoking a Pipe* (1752, oil on canvas, 19 x 16 ins / 47 x 40 cm) GBP 4,000. VIENNA, 27 March 2003, *Scholar in Study Sharpening a Quill* (oil on panel, 17 x 13 ins / 44 x 34 cm) EUR 12,000. AMSTERDAM, 5 Nov 2003, *Kitchen Interior with Maid and Child Conversing. Kitchen Interior with Maid and Man Conversing* (oil on panel, a pair, 13 x 10 ins / 33 x 26 cm) EUR 7,000. STOCKHOLM, 25 May 2004, *Still-life with Flowers in a Vase* (1764, oil on panel, a pair, 11 x 9 ins / 28 x 22 cm) SEK 145,000.

JUNCKER, Käthe. See **JUNCKER-STREIT**

JUNCKER, Michael
German, 16th century.
Sculptor.
Juncker is recorded as having lived in Walldürn, in the German region of Baden from 1588 to 1591, and in Miltenberg from 1598 until his death in 1616 or 1619. The only work that has been attributed to him with complete confidence is a relief in the 'hospital of servants' in Würzburg. Other attributions include commemorative monuments in the church in Messelhausen in the Mosbach region of Germany.

JUNCKER, Wilhelm Karl
German, 19th century.
Born 8 July 1820, in Wenden; died 17 April 1901, in Dresden.
Painter. History painting, portraits, genre scenes.
Wilhelm Juncker trained at the academies of Dresden and Antwerp. A noted work is a *Portrait of the History Painter K. Baehr.*
MUSEUMS AND GALLERIES:
DRESDEN: *Portrait of the Painter Moritz Müller* - RIGA: *Portrait of a Woman.*

JUNCKER, Zacharias, the Elder
German, 17th century.
Born between 1578 and 1580; died c. 1657.
Sculptor.
Zacharias Juncker the Elder was granted civic rights in Würzburg in 1608, and was admitted to the Guild of St Luke in 1611. He worked for Würzburg Cathedral, but his works are also recorded in nearby Walldürn (altar), in Mittenberg (pulpit in the parish church), in Eibelbach (font) and in

Schneeberg near Amorbach (high altar of the pilgrimage church). He was possibly associated with Hans Juncker.

JUNCKER-STREIT, Käthe
German, 19th - 20th century.
Born 1858, in Dresden; died 1919, in Novaggio (Ticino), Switzerland.
Painter. Portraits, genre scenes.

Käthe Juncker-Streit was a pupil of her father, Wilhelm Juncker, and of Gussow in Berlin. She subsequently studied in Munich and paid a visit to Paris in 1892. She exhibited in Munich in 1891, and is remembered for *Little Red Riding Hood* and a portrait of her father.

JUNCKHER. See **JUNCKER** and **JUNKER**

JUNCOSA, Joaquín (Fray)
Spanish, 17th century.
Born 1631, near Tarragona; died 1708, near Rome.
Painter. History painting.

Joaquín Juncosa was a member of the Carthusian order. He was taught by his father, Juan Juncosa, and developed sufficient talent to gain the protection of the Marquis of La Quardia and, through him, to receive a commission for four large paintings for Cagliari town hall in Sardinia. In 1660 Juncosa joined the Scala Dei charterhouse as a lay brother. He executed many works at the monastery including a *Nativity* and a *Coronation of the Virgin* for the monastery church; these works revealed him to have a talent worth nurturing and the prior decided he should be sent to Rome to study the masters. When he returned from Italy, Juncosa painted several decorative works for the monastery, also for the Reus hermitage (1680), the Montealegre charterhouse, and at other religious establishments. According to tradition, his work as an artist was interrupted by a change of prior at the monastery. The problems that ensued led him to flee the monastery and move to Rome where he was closer to the pope. We do know that at the beginning of the 18th century Juncosa was in Rome and was given permission by the pope to live alone in a hermitage on the outskirts of the city; he remained there until his death.

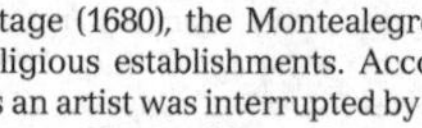

JUNCOSA, Josep
Spanish, 17th century.
Born in Cornudella; died at the beginning of the 18th Century, in Tarragona.
Painter. History painting.

Josep Juncosa was a nephew and pupil of Joaquin Juncosa. After working as a painter he entered holy orders and became a doctor of theology. In this capacity he preached at Tarragona Cathedral. As a painter he collaborated with his uncle and, in 1680, assisted him with the decoration of the Reus hermitage. In 1682 he painted some frescoes for Diego Giron de Rebolledo in the chapel of the Concepción in Tarragona Cathedral as well as the *Martyrdom of St Thecla*. He also executed various paintings for the Merced convent.

JUNCOSA, Juan
Spanish, 17th century.
Painter.

Juan Juncosa was the father and teacher of Joaquin Juncosa. Nothing is known of his work. He appears to have worked between 1630 and 1640 in Tarragona.

JUND, Bernard
French, 20th century.
Born 21 November 1934, in Alfortville.
Sculptor.

Bernard Jund exhibits mainly in the French provinces. He works in metal, fur and various precious stones, producing objects that are fetishistic.

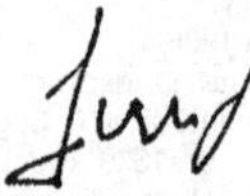

JUNDT, Gustave Adolphe
French, 19th century.
Born 21 June 1830, in Strasbourg; died 15 May 1884, in Paris.
Painter, caricaturist, engraver, illustrator. Genre scenes, landscapes.

Gustave Jundt entered the École des Beaux-Arts in Paris in 1850 and worked in the studios of Drolling and Biennoury. He was active at the Salon de Paris from 1857 to 1882, gaining medals in 1868 and 1873. He was decorated by the Légion d'Honneur in 1880.

His themes from the Alsace region were so individual in their execution that Théophile Gautier remarked that Jundt was one of the few painters who did not need to sign his work for it to be recognised as his. He engraved illustrations for children's books.

MUSEUMS AND GALLERIES:
ABBEVILLE: *Sunday Morning* - BERNAY: *Farewell, Landscape* - CARCASSONNE: *First Light* - DIEPPE: *Return from the Festival* - MULHOUSE: *Grandparents' Celebration; Return of the Storks; Baptism in the Tyrol; The Farm* - STRASBOURG: *Sunday in the Grand Ducal Museum; Woman Making Hay; Peasant Woman sewing; The Eldest.*

AUCTION RECORDS:
PARIS, 1875, *Islands of the Rhine,* FRF 4,500. PARIS, 1884, *Sunday Morning,* FRF 2,200. PARIS, 21 May 1904, *First-Born,* FRF 360. PARIS, 28 Feb 1944, *Lady of Fashion on the Beach,* FRF 5,900. PARIS, 27 June 1949, *Visit to the Museum,* FRF 12,000. PARIS, 31 May 1972, *At the Museum of natural History* (oil on canvas, 28 1/4 x 35 1/2 ins / 72 x 90 cm) FRF 1,400. VERSAILLES, 22 April 1990, *Young Girl at the Lakeside* (oil on canvas, 23 1/2 x 15 3/4 ins / 59.5 x 40 cm) FRF 7,500. AMSTERDAM, 5-6 Nov 1991, *Ladies of Fashion Strolling on the Beach* (oil on canvas, 18 x 25 1/4 ins / 45.5 x 64 cm) NLG 9,430. PARIS, 27 May 1994, *Beach Games* (oil on canvas, 15 x 22 ins / 38 x 55 cm) FRF 9,000. NEW YORK, 28 June 2001, *By the Riverbank* (oil on canvas, 46 x 63 ins / 116 x 160 cm) USD 10,000. PARIS, 1 July 2002, *Young Girl with Distaff and Cat* (oil on canvas, 22 x 18 ins / 55 x 46 cm) EUR 1,600.

JUNE, J.
British, 18th century.
Active c. 1740-1770.
Engraver (burin).

J. June found work mainly with publishers; however, he also made engravings of landscapes after Collet, of genre scenes after Hogarth and portraits and horses after Sertorins. There were also some portraits.

JUNEAU, Denis
Canadian, 20th century.
Born 1925, in Montreal.
Active in France.
Painter, sculptor.

Denis Juneau studied at the École des Beaux-Arts in Montreal from 1943 to 1950 and at the Centro Studi Arte Industria in Novara, Italy from 1954 to 1956. He has benefited from several grants from the Canada Council for the Arts. Around 1958, his compositions leaned more towards Herbin than Mondrian. In the early 1960s, he executed a set of highly dynamic orthogonal compositions before creating kinetic pieces in which he favoured primary colours: *Mobiles in co-*

lour, 1967. The *Spectrograms* he showed at the Montreal Museum of Fine Arts in 1970 is an exploration in depth of colour possibilities. He is also a sculptor, and has created sculptures with a practical use. His more recent paintings use more muted colour ranges in warm tones superimposed with a subtle, dreamlike figuration reminiscent of Klee.

He took part in collective exhibitions in Ottawa, Montreal, Vienna, Spoleto, Basel and Paris. He has shown his works in solo exhibitions in Paris, Montreal in the early 1980s, later in Ottawa, Paris, Toronto and Québec (2001, *Punctuations*). He became a member of the Royal Canadian Academy of Arts in 1973 and, in 1986, was awarded the Gershon Iskowitz prize for his contribution to contemporary art.

MUSEUMS AND GALLERIES:
MONTREAL (MAC): *Mobile in Colour* (1967); *Blue against Red Space* (1965); *Green Tales* (1969); *Rounds in Blue Space* (1975); *Untitled* (1965); *Fourth dimension* (1961); *Untitled* (1977); *Red Background* (1960); *Untitled* (1959); *Untitled* (1962); *Abstraction* (1958) - MONTREAL (MBA) - OTTAWA (NG. of Canada) - QUEBEC (Mus. du Quebec).

JUNEC, Lorris
French (?), 20th century.
Born 1899; died 1993.
Active in France.
Painter. Landscapes.

Lorris Junec lived and worked for many years at Orsay. He modelled, simplified and structured his landscapes using bright, lively colours in a patchwork effect. He may have been the same person as the artist Leo Junek. In 1969 an exhibition of his watercolours was presented by Jean Bazaine. In 2001 a tribute to Junec took place at the auditorium of the Espace Jacques Tati in Orsay, organised by the faculty of science.

BIBLIOGRAPHY:
Le Gouic, Jean-Claude/Junec, Suzanne, *Une vision de la peinture: extraits des carnets de 1950 à 1989,* L'Harmattan, Paris, 2001.

JUNEK, Leo
Croat, 20th century.
Born 1899, in Zagreb.
Painter. Landscapes.

Leo Junek appeared at the exhibition that opened in Paris in 1946, at the Musée d'Art Moderne, sponsored by the United Nations Organisation.

JUNEK-VIDAL, Sebastián
Spanish, 20th century.
Born in Catalonia.
Painter.

According to the critic J. Junoy, the earliest of Sebastián Junek-Vidal's landscapes showed a spirit of 'magical transfiguration'. Later, he gradually returned to a more direct feeling for nature. One of his best-known works is *Calanque de Deya.*

JUNES, David
French, 19th - 20th century.
Born 5 March 1874, in Tunis; died 1938.
Active in France and Tunisia.
Painter. Portraits, genre scenes.

David Junes studied under Benjamin-Constant, Jean-Paul Laurens and Jean-Léon Gérome. He divided his time between Tunis and Paris and made numerous visits to the area around Marseilles and to Brittany. His broad strokes of bright colour make both his souk scenes and his portraits shimmer with light. He exhibited in Paris at the Salon des Artistes Français between 1897 and 1937 and, until his death, at the Salon de la Société Coloniale des Artistes Français.

BIBLIOGRAPHY:
Lumières tunisiennes, exhibition catalogue, Association française d'action artistique, Pavillon des arts, Paris, 1995.

JUNG. See also **JÜNGER** and **JUNGE**

JUNG, Frédéric Charles, or C
French, 19th - 20th century.
Born 12 July 1865, in Lyons; died 1936.
Painter. Still-lifes, flowers.

Frédéric Charles Jung studied under Jean-Marie Reignier and later his successor Adolphe Louis Castex-Dégrange, attending their classes at the École des Beaux-Arts in Lyons from 1882 to 1885. Jung began exhibiting in Lyons in 1886 and in Paris in 1905. He was awarded a gold medal in Lyons in 1908. He signed his work: *Jung* or *C. Jung.*

Jung specialised in painting decorative still-lifes. He painted a still-life for the Préfecture of the Rhone and *Spring Flowers* for the town hall of the 6th district of Lyons. A large-scale still-life by Jung, now in a private collection, decorated an entire wall of a café or restaurant in Lyons. This piece, lit by bright sunlight, leads the eye to the vista of a background landscape; the still-life elements, with their warm, golden tones spread out across the painting's breadth, are bottles of champagne, one in an ice bucket, glasses both empty and full, grapes on a plate, and bunches of flowers, some stems of which overhang as if spilling out of the canvas over a frame painted to look like dark marble that surrounds the composition on all four sides and enhances it.

MUSEUMS AND GALLERIES:
LYONS: *Blackthorns.*

AUCTION RECORDS:
LYONS, 13 May 1982, *Still-life with Flowers* (oil on canvas, 53 1/4 x 76 3/4 ins / 135 x 195 cm) FRF 10,600. NEW YORK, 22 Oct 1997, *Basket of Oranges* (1916, oil on canvas, 38 1/4 x 51 1/2 ins / 97.2 x 130.8 cm) USD 12,650.

JUNG, Jacob
German, 19th century.
Born 12 September 1819, in Frankfurt am Main; died 28 June 1844, in Frankfurt am Main.
Painter. History painting.

Jung was a pupil of P. Veit at the Städelsches Institut from 1832 to 1844.

JUNG, Jakob
German, 19th - 20th century.
Born 25 January 1862, in Darmstadt; died 15 May 1920, in Mainz.
Painter, draughtsman.

Jakob Jung was a lecturer at the professional school of design in Mainz. He executed numerous portraits, landscapes with figures, architecture paintings and still-lifes, in oils, watercolour and pastel.

JUNG, Johann Christian
Bavarian School, 18th century.
Active in Augsburg at the beginning of the 18th century.
Engraver (burin).

JUNG, Julius
German, 19th - 20th century.
Born 24 November 1851, in Kassel.
Painter. Landscapes.

Julius Jung studied in Frankfurt am Main and at the academy in Kassel. He featured in the exhibitions at Berlin (1909), Kassel (1913), Düsseldorf (1911) and Munich (1904).

MUSEUMS AND GALLERIES:
ERIE (AM) - KASSEL (Municipal Gal.) - KASSEL (Town Hall).

JUNG, Karl
German, 19th century.
Born 24 April 1852, in Rathenow (near Berlin).
Painter. Portraits, genre scenes.

Jung trained in the studios of Ernst Hildebrand at the academies of Munich and Berlin, and later settled in Berlin.

JUNG, Kaspar
Swiss, 16th century.
Painter.

Jung was a member of the guild of St Luke in Lucerne in the second half of the 16th century.

JUNG, Michel
French, 20th century.
Born 16 October 1939, in Anneville.
Painter.

Michel Jung spent his childhood in Alsace and studied there. As a university student in 1965 he decided to become a painter and began teaching himself. It was not until 1973 that he held his first exhibition at the Galerie Septentrion in Marcq-en-Barœul. He also exhibited at the Salon d'Automne and in 1974 held a solo exhibition of his work, also in Paris.

JUNG, Moriz
Czech, 20th century.
Born 22 October 1885, in Nikolsburg (now Mikulov, Czech Republic); died 11 March 1915.
Painter, draughtsman, engraver, illustrator, lithographer.

Moriz Jung studied at the school of arts and crafts in Vienna. He devoted himself to wood engraving and lithography. In 1906 he published a series of engravings on coloured wood representing animals. In 1907 he made some humorous engravings for the cabaret *Die Fledermaus* (*The Bat*). In 1913 he decorated Louis Hirschfeld's sketches: *That's a Red Letter Day!*. As an illustrator he collaborated on Viennese sports and comic magazines. A wood engraving of the Emperor *Franz Joseph I* is attributed to him.

JUNG, Otto
German, 20th century.
Painter. Landscapes.

Otto Jung worked in Stuttgart, exhibiting in Berlin in 1909.

JUNG, Simonetta Irène
Italian, 20th century.
Born 1917, in Palermo.
Also active in Belgium.
Painter, lithographer, sculptor.

During her studies in Florence, Simonetta Jung concentrated on music, and it was only after marriage and World War II that she began to paint portraits, landscapes and still-lifes - early works that prepared her technically for the periods that were to follow. She stopped working for a time after the death of her husband, A.E. Vigevani, whose name she used on several paintings. She remarried in 1962, this time to a Belgian diplomat, and she took Belgian nationality. They lived in Naples, Rome and San Francisco, and then settled in Brussels. She has taken part in group exhibitions since 1953, including: 1955, Xth Triennale of Milan; 1962, *Contemporary Italian Work in Colour* at the Mexican National Museum of Modern Art; 1976, *Femmes de Diplomates* (*Diplomats' Wives*) at the Palais d'Egmont, Brussels; 1979, *20 peintres du Réalisme Magique en Belgique* (*20 Magic Realist Painters in Belgium*), an exhibition that travelled in Poland, etc. She has also had many solo shows throughout the world: Milan 1954, 1976; Florence, Venice and Rome 1954; Brussels 1970, 1975, 1979, 1981, 1990; San Francisco 1971; Antwerp 1980; Cologne 1985, etc.

Her work falls into five groups so clearly that she has herself given a collective title to the paintings included in each. Between 1950 and 1955, the *Forme-Luce* (*Form-Light*) series is geometric-abstract in character and consists solely of curves, circles, and spirals, perspective views in indeterminate space. When she began work again after her husband's death, she painted, between 1958 and 1972, the series *Tensioni Formative* (*Formative Tensions*), paintings in the lyrical-abstraction style; in her case highly gestural and always suggesting a subject, sometimes, like De Kooning, the presence of a human body. From 1972 to 1979, she painted the *Homo Novus* (*New Man*) series, in which her style changes radically, depicting, in volumes that seem to have been painted from sculpture, small figures that are half-man, half-machine. The fourth period *Elountha*, named after a place of residence in Greece, began in 1979 and is linked to the previous one. The small figures become progressively less human and more like abstract sculptures, though certainly soothing and decorative as they are depicted in the painting. In 1982, the *Anthroposcopies* period begins, in which the small figures reappear, break apart and decompose physically, sometimes bringing to mind similar processes in Francis Bacon's paintings. René Huyghe writes of them, 'in contrast with the strongly structured background, she suspends a sort of faceless mummy that, peering into its own bowels, collapses and falls to the ground'. In 1986, the decomposition of the bodies of the *Anthroposcopies* seems to be more marked in the *Onto-Rythmes* (*Being-Rhythms*), of which the artist has said that she is aiming to capture the vibrations of the whole of Being.

BIBLIOGRAPHY:

Claessens, Bob, et al., *Simonetta Jung*, exhibition catalogue, Gal. Veranneman, Brussels, 1970. Goyens de Heusch, Serge, et al., *Simonetta Jung*, Fondation pour l'Art belge contemporain, Brussels, 1981. Richter, Horst, et al., *Simonetta Jung*, exhibition catalogue, Das Belgische Haus, Cologne, 1985. *Simonetta Jung*, exhibition catalogue, Gal. BP, Brussels, 1990.

MUSEUMS AND GALLERIES:

GREENWICH, CT (Bruce Mus.) - MINNEAPOLIS (IA): *Abstract* (1960, oil on canvas) - NEW YORK (Pratt Institute) - NORTHAMPTON, MA (Smith College MA) - STANFORD (Iris and B. Gerald Cantor Center For Visual Arts, University) - TEL AVIV (MA).

JUNG, Théodore
French, 19th century.
Born 20 September 1803, in Strasbourg; died 13 January 1865, in Strasbourg.
Watercolourist, painter (gouache). History painting, military subjects, landscapes.

Théodore Jung began his studies with Gabriel Guérin in Strasbourg and Simeon Fort. He made his debut at the Salon de Paris in 1834 and continued to exhibit there until 1864. He was awarded a third class medal in 1841 and decorated by the Légion d'Honneur in 1860.

When he was attached to the War Ministry he executed a considerable number of battle scenes of which a large number belong to the Ministry of War. The Versailles Museum also has 12 watercolours. He is probably the painter cited by Siret around 1840.

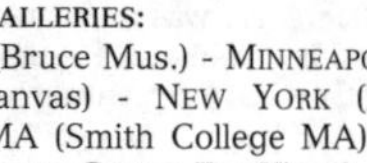

MUSEUMS AND GALLERIES:

VERSAILLES: 12 watercolours.

AUCTION RECORDS:

PARIS, 23 Feb 1925, *Military Convoy in the Snow* (watercolour) FRF 400. PARIS, 7 April 1927, *Bois de Boulogne in 1840* (gouache) FRF 1,200. PARIS, July 1946, *Military Inspection* (watercolour) FRF 7,000. PARIS, 7 Feb 1951, *Military Scenes* (four watercolours) FRF 15,000. VERSAILLES, 16 Nov 1980, *Surrender of the Town of Ulm* (watercolour, 15 1/4 x 23 ins / 38.5 x 57.5 cm) FRF 4,500. PARIS, 22 June 1982, *The Old Town Hall* (1835, watercolour, 10 1/4 x 14 1/2 ins / 26 x 37 cm) FRF 15,000. PARIS, 12 Dec 1983, *Napoleon III in Wimereux* (watercolour, 23 1/2 x 37 3/4 ins / 60 x 96 cm) FRF 20,200. MONACO, 20

June 1994, *Napoleon III Inspecting the Troops on the Military Esplanade, graphite* (watercolour and gouache, 5 1/4 x 9 ins / 13.5 x 22 cm) FRF 16,650. PARIS, 4 June 1997, *Inspection of an Infantry Regiment on the Military Esplanade in front of the Ecole Militaire* (pencil heightened with gouache, 23 1/2 x 35 1/2 ins / 60 x 90 cm) FRF 14,000. PARIS, 1 Dec 1999, *Battlefield at Valmy* (1842, watercolour/gouache, 10 x 18 ins / 26 x 46 cm) FRF 15,000. PARIS, 20 Oct 2000, *Battle of 17 October 1844* (watercolour crayon/heightened white gouache, 13 x 19 ins / 33 x 49 cm) FRF 13,000. PARIS, 23 Nov 2001, *View of Tunis* (watercolour/gouache, 10 x 17 ins / 25 x 42 cm) FRF 12,000. PARIS, 16 Dec 2002, *The Aqueduct of Wad-El-Raml, near Constantine* (1833, watercolour, 8 x 12 ins / 21 x 30 cm) EUR 1,600. ST-GERMAIN-EN-LAYE ENCHERES, 23 March 2003, *Algerian Countryside* (watercolour, 11 x 16 ins / 27 x 41 cm) EUR 1,800. PARIS, 23 June 2003, *The Entrance to the Jardin des Tuileries under the Snow* (watercolour, 8 x 13 ins / 21 x 34 cm) EUR 7,500.

JUNGBLUT, or Jugblut
18th century.
Active at the end of the 18th century.
Draughtsman, engraver.

JUNGBLUT, Emil
German, 20th century.
Born 1 June 1888, in Düsseldorf.
Sculptor. Monuments.

Emil Jungblut studied at the school of art and design and then at the academy in Düsseldorf, and spent some time in Paris. He featured in the Düsseldorf exhibitions of 1913 and 1920 with masks and statues of famous persons. His works include a monument in Oldenburg and a monument to members of the German armed forces who died during World War I in the cemetery at Thiaucourt (Meurthe-et-Moselle).

JUNGBLUT, J.
German, 19th century.
Painter. History painting, portraits.

A pupil of Schadow at the academy in Düsseldorf, J. Jungblut is documented in Aachen c. 1842.

JUNGBLUT, Johann. See **SANDER**

JUNGBLUT, Victor
Luxembourg, 20th century.
Born 1914, in Luxembourg.
Painter. Nudes.

JUNGBLUT, Walter J.
German, 20th century.
Born 9 April 1892, in Düsseldorf.
Painter. Figures.

Walter Jungblut specialised in figure painting. He executed a fresco at the Ministry of Finance building in Düsseldorf, *The Brass Farthing*. In 1920 he featured in the great exhibition of fine art in Düsseldorf with the paintings *Melody of Life*, *Exhausted* and *Portrait of a Woman*.

JUNGBLUTH, Alfred L.
French, 19th - 20th century.
Born 1865, in Trémentines; died May 1914, in Paris.
Sculptor, draughtsman. Figures. Statuettes.

Alfred L. Jungbluth exhibited in Paris from 1898 to 1909 at the Salon de la Société Nationale des Beaux-Arts and in 1907 at the Salon de la Société des Artistes Indépendants, showing genre drawings and statuettes of dancers and women of the Parisian demi-monde.

JUNGBLUTH, Chrysis
French, 20th century.
Born 23 January 1907, in Boulogne-sur-Mer.
Painter. Nudes, portraits, genre scenes.

Chrysis Jungbluth studied under Humbert and exhibited at the Salon des Artistes Français, the Salon de la Société Nationale and the Salon des Indépendants. She also painted dance-hall scenes.

AUCTION RECORDS:
PARIS, 21 April 1943, *Cabaret de Matelots (Seamen's Cabaret)*, FRF 700. PARIS, 21 Nov 1995, *La Boule Blanche at Montparnasse* (gouache, 18 x 14 1/2 ins / 46 x 37 cm) FRF 8,000.

JUNGCLAUSEN, Christian Hermann Diedrich
German, 19th century.
Born 15 January 1798, in Altona (Hamburg); died 19 December 1867, in Hamburg.
Painter.

Jungclausen exhibited a *Holy Family* in Altona in 1821. In 1822, he won the small silver medal in Copenhagen for a drawing after B. Schidone, and exhibited copies and portraits in the same city until 1830. In 1839, he settled in Hamburg as a portrait painter.

JUNGE, Friedrich August, or Jung
German, 19th century.
Born 22 April 1781, in Leipzig; died 21 January 1841, in Leipzig.
Painter, draughtsman. Portraits.

He produced a considerable number of works, mainly miniatures on ivory, and lightly coloured pencil drawings.

MUSEUMS AND GALLERIES:
HANOVER (Kestner-Mus.): a miniature - LEIPZIG (Mus. der Bildenden Künste): two pencil drawings and a watercolour - LEIPZIG (Stadtgeschichtliches Mus.): four miniatures.

JUNGE, Gottlob, or Jung
German, 18th century.
Born in Leipzig; died 1806.
Active in Leipzig.
Draughtsman, painter, engraver, caricaturist.

MUSEUMS AND GALLERIES:
LEIPZIG (Stadtgeschichtliches Mus.): sketch (sepia); *Mill* (1796, small etching).

JUNGE, Margarete
German, 20th century.
Born 1874, in Dresden; died 1966, in Dresden.
Draughtswoman. Designs (objets d'art, furniture, decorative motifs).
Jugendstil.

Margarete Junge was trained in the decorative arts at Dresden, then at the Woman's academy in Munich. From 1907 to 1933, she taught at the Kunstgewerbeschule in Dresden. From 1901 to 1902, she supplied models of furniture and decorative textile motifs to the Dresdener Werkstätten für Handwerkskunst (Dresden Studios), a very important centre for the creation of decorative art, situated in the Dresden region, which became the focus of so much artistic activity at the turn of the century.

BIBLIOGRAPHY:
Kern, Andrea, et al., *Jugendstil in Dresden, Aufbruch in die Moderne*, exhibition catalogue, Staatliche Kunstsammlungen, Dresden, 1999.

MUSEUMS AND GALLERIES:
DRESDEN (Kunstgewerbemus.).

JÜNGER, Christoph von, or Jung
Austrian, 18th century.
Born 1736, in Vienna; died 21 July 1777.
Engraver, metal chaser.

JÜNGER, Johann Christoph
German, 18th century.
Active in Dresden.
Painter. Historical subjects.

Jünger is represented in the Stadtmuseum in Dresden, which has five oil paintings and a wash by him, mostly showing fires that took place in Dresden.

Museums and Galleries:

Dresden (Stadtmus.).

JÜNGER, Johann J., or Jung

Austrian, 18th century.

Enameller, metal chaser.

Jünger worked in Vienna until 1780, and collaborated with his brother Christoph von Jünger. Two Sèvres-style pots preserved in Vienna are signed *J. Jünger 1778.*

Museums and Galleries:

Vienna (Österreichisches Mus. für Angewandte Kunst): two pots.

JUNGESBLUTH, Anton Ernst Wilhem

German, 18th century.

Born c. 1740; died 7 September 1799, in Brunswick.

Painter (porcelain).

Jungesbluth worked at the Fürstenberg pottery, where he was a painter of figures.

JUNGHANNS, Julius Paul

Austrian, 20th century.

Born 1876, in Vienna; died 1953 or 1958, in Düsseldorf.

Painter. Genre scenes, landscapes with figures.

Julius Paul Junghanns was a lecturer in Düsseldorf. He was awarded a gold medal in Berlin in 1907. He specialised in painting peasant subjects and landscapes with figures.

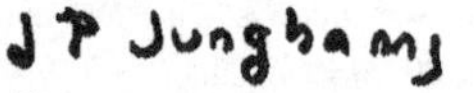

Museums and Galleries:

Bonn (Kunstmus.): *Goats Close Beside Woodland* - Düsseldorf: *Among the Broom Bushes; Goats; Sun* - Mannheim: *Animal Study* - Munich: *Noon* - Pittsburgh (Carnegie MA): *Sun.*

Auction records:

Cologne, 15 March 1968, *Winter Landscape with a Cart,* DEM 4,500. Cologne, 26 March 1971, *Riverbank,* DEM 3,800. Cologne, 12 Nov 1976, *Draught Horse* (oil on canvas, 35 3/4 x 47 1/4 ins / 91 x 120 cm) DEM 9,500. London, 12 Oct 1977, *Shepherd and Flock* (oil on canvas, 16 1/2 x 22 3/4 ins / 42 x 58 cm) GBP 2,100. Cologne, 11 June 1979, *Flock at Pasture* (oil on canvas, 15 3/4 x 23 1/2 ins / 40 x 59.5 cm) DEM 26,000. Cologne, 19 Nov 1981, *Siesta* (oil on panel, 19 3/4 x 23 1/2 ins / 50 x 60 cm) DEM 24,000. Heidelberg, 3 April 1982, *Horses at the Drinking Trough* (watercolour, 7 x 5 1/2 ins / 18 x 14 cm) DEM 3,300. Düsseldorf, 15 June 1983, *Rustic Scene* (oil on canvas, 15 3/4 x 23 1/2 ins / 40 x 60 cm) DEM 22,000. Düsseldorf, 6 June 1984, *Return from the Fields* (oil on canvas, 16 x 19 3/4 ins / 40.5 x 50 cm) DEM 16,000. Cologne, 21 Nov 1985, *The Encounter* (oil on canvas, 17 x 30 1/4 ins / 43 x 77 cm) DEM 11,000. Hamburg, 4 Dec 1987, *Shepherdess and Flock of Goats* (oil on canvas, 15 3/4 x 19 3/4 ins / 40 x 50 cm) DEM 9,000. Cologne, 18 March 1989, *Young Peasant with a Goat and Its Young* (oil on canvas, 15 3/4 x 19 3/4 ins / 40 x 50 cm) DEM 8,000. Cologne, 20 Oct 1989, *Alpine Landscape* (oil on canvas, 15 1/4 x 23 1/2 ins / 39 x 60 cm) DEM 3,000. Cologne, 29 June 1990, *Cattle Drinking from the River* (1918, oil on paper, 9 x 13 ins / 23 x 33 cm) DEM 3,300. Cologne, 28 June 1991, *Young Peasant Girl Watching Her Cow Grazing in a Field* (oil on canvas, 19 3/4 x 23 1/2 ins / 50 x 60 cm) DEM 5,500. Munich, 22 June 1993, *Young Peasant Watering His Horses by a Stream* (1905, oil on panel, 11 x 10 ins / 28 x 25.5 cm) DEM 8,280. Cologne, 25 March 1999, *Forest Worker with Logs on Horse-cart* (oil on canvas, 16 x 24 ins / 41 x 60 cm) DEM 12,000. Cologne, 28 Oct 1999, *Peasant Woman with Cow and Goats in Spring Landscape* (1903, oil on canvas, 41 x 31 ins / 103 x 80 cm) DEM 10,000. Stuttgart, 14 April 2000, *Farmer with Two Goats* (oil on canvas, 24 x 20 ins / 61 x 50 cm) DEM 10,000. Amsterdam, 18 April 2000, *Spring* (oil on canvas, 22 x 26 ins / 55 x 66 cm) NLG 16,000. Lindau, 30 June 2001, *Peasant with Goat and Kid under Tree* (oil on canvas, 24 x 20 ins / 60 x 50 cm) DEM 10,500. Munich, 26 Sept 2001, *Two Peasants with Horses Pulling Logging Wagon* (oil on panel, 12 x 21 ins / 30 x 54 cm) DEM 13,000. Amsterdam, 23 Oct 2002, *Horse-drawn Cart with Figures near a Farmhouse* (oil on panel, 9 x 11 ins / 22 x 28 cm) EUR 3,200. Cologne, 21 Nov 2002, *Peasant with Four Horses Pulling Cart* (oil on canvas, 17 x 30 ins / 43 x 77 cm) EUR 6,000. Cologne, 10 April 2003, *Peasant with Four Horses Pulling Cart* (oil on canvas, 16 x 24 ins / 40 x 60 cm) EUR 4,500. Cologne, 20 Nov 2003, *Four Horses Pulling Cart* (oil on canvas, 21 x 30 ins / 54 x 77 cm) EUR 5,500. Cologne, 1 April 2004, *In the Alps* (oil on panel, 12 x 19 ins / 31 x 48 cm) EUR 2,200. Munich, 24 Sept 2004, *Transporting Wood* (oil on panel, 12 x 21 ins / 30 x 53 cm) EUR 1,800.

JUNGHANNS, Reinhard Paul

German, 20th century.

Painter. Genre scenes, still-lifes.

Reinhard Paul Junghanns exhibited in Berlin in 1909. He worked in Hamburg, and also painted on porcelain.

JUNGHANNS, Reinhold Rudolf

German, 20th century.

Born 29 September 1884, in Zwickau.

Active in Switzerland.

Painter, draughtsman, engraver, lithographer.

Portraits, landscapes, landscapes with figures, urban landscapes, still-lifes.

Reinhold Rudolf Junghanns studied at the academies in Dresden and Munich and set up in Switzerland. He exhibited in Munich, in particular still-lifes, drawings and landscapes with figures. He also painted subjects from the North Sea and the ports of Hamburg and Copenhagen, as well as executing lithographs. He is also remembered for 12 etchings of portraits, landscapes and interiors, as well as nine original etchings: *Variations on a Female Theme.*

JUNGHANNS-GRULICH, Herta

German, 20th century.

Born 1912, in Velbert (Rhineland).

Painter. Designs for tapestries.

Herta Junghanns-Grulich studied at the academy of fine art in Dresden in 1934 and 1935. She set up in Düsseldorf in 1936, exhibiting in Germany and abroad.

JUNGHANS

German, 15th century.

Born 15th century, in Nuremberg.

Engraver (wood).

Junghans produced a series of crude wood engravings in 1472. He is almost certainly the same artist as Hans Sporer.

JUNGHEIM, Julius

German, 20th century.

Born 1878; died 1957, in Düsseldorf.

Active in Düsseldorf.

Painter. Landscapes.

Julius Jungheim exhibited in Berlin in 1909.

Auction records:

Cologne, 18 March 1989, *Winter near Mühlenbach* (oil on canvas, 31 1/2 x 25 1/2 ins / 80 x 65 cm) DEM 3,000.

JUNGHEIM, Karl

German, 19th century.

Born 6 February 1803, in Düsseldorf; died 6 June 1886, in Düsseldorf.

Painter. Landscapes.

Jungheim trained at the academy in Düsseldorf, in the studios of Schadow and Schirmer. He exhibited in Vienna (1869), Basel (1871) and Geneva (1876), and won medals in

Paris, Vienna and Philadelphia. He visited Germany, Tyrol, Switzerland and Italy.
MUSEUMS AND GALLERIES:
BASEL: *Capri.*
AUCTION RECORDS:
VIENNA, 22 March 1966, *Alpine Landscape with Lake,* ATS 30,000. COLOGNE, 24 March 1972, *View of Traunsee Lake,* DEM 2,800. LUCERNE, 11 Nov 1987, *Sorrento Landscape* (oil on canvas, 48 1/2 x 63 1/2 ins / 123 x 161 cm) CHF 9,000. MUNICH, 7 Dec 1993, *View of Berchtesgaden with Mount Watzmann in the Background* (1858, oil on canvas, 30 1/4 x 38 1/2 ins / 77 x 97.5 cm) DEM 7,475. MUNICH, 6 Dec 1994, *Capri Fishermen* (1865, oil on canvas, 42 3/4 x 61 ins / 108.5 x 154 cm) DEM 23,000. MUNICH, 25 June 1996, *Watermills in the Mountains* (1859, oil on canvas, 32 3/4 x 28 ins / 83 x 71 cm) DEM 3,360. BERN, 17 May 1999, *Italian Landscape with Figures* (1878, oil on canvas, 18 x 26 ins / 45 x 65 cm) CHF 8,500. WARSAW, 24 Oct 1999, *Mountain Landscape near Berchtesgaden* (1854, oil on canvas, 37 x 48 ins / 93 x 121 cm) PLN 28,000. VIENNA, 23 May 2000, *Lake Gosau, View to the Dachstein* (oil on canvas, 33 x 49 ins / 83 x 125 cm) ATS 40,000. BREMEN, 30 March 2001, *Swiss Alpine Landscape with Buildings and Cows* (oil on canvas, 34 x 48 ins / 87 x 122 cm) DEM 6,500. BOSTON, 11 May 2001, *Villa Borghese* (oil on canvas, 18 x 14 ins / 46 x 36 cm) USD 6,000. MUNICH, 20 March 2002, *Bernese Oberland* (oil on canvas, 37 x 50 ins / 93 x 126 cm) EUR 4,400. AMSTERDAM, 1 July 2003, *Cowherds by a Lake in an Extensive Mountain Landscape* (1859, oil on canvas, 25 x 37 ins / 63 x 94 cm) EUR 1,800. KEMPTEN, 8 Jan 2004, *Successful Hunt in the Dolomite Mountains* (oil on canvas, 30 x 41 ins / 76 x 104 cm) EUR 1,700. COLOGNE, 22 May 2004, *Fishermen on Capri* (1865, oil on canvas, 43 x 61 ins / 108 x 154 cm) EUR 22,000.

JUNGHOLTZ, Andreas
German, 16th century.
Born 16th century, in Bavaria, or probably in Poland.
Painter.
Jungholtz moved from Bavaria to settle in Cracow in 1536. He signed his pictures *Andris Jungholtz* and *Bavaria de Monte-Sancto, pictor.*

JUNGI, Giovanni. See **PEROXINO**

JUNGK, Elfriede
German, 20th century.
Born 29 May 1889, in Berlin.
Active in Berlin.
Painter, engraver (wood). Landscapes.

JÜNGKER. See **JUNCKER**

JÜNGLING. See **JUENGLING**

JUNGMANN, Maarten Johannes Balthasar
Dutch, 20th century.
Born 7 September 1877, in Rotterdam.
Painter, engraver.
Maarten Johannes Balthasar Jungmann was awarded a prize by the academy in Rotterdam in 1909, and the Vigelius Prize. He executed figure paintings, landscapes, still-lifes and flower paintings. He also produced lithographs.

JUNGMANN, Nico Wilhelm
Dutch, 19th - 20th century.
Born 1872; died 1935.
Painter, pastellist, watercolourist. Figure compositions, local scenes, genre scenes.
Nico Wilhelm Jungmann worked in Holland and Brittany, seeking out typical figures, depicting old sea dogs with weather-beaten faces or girls in traditional costume.

AUCTION RECORDS:
LONDON, 20 Feb 1909, *Wedding Procession,* GBP 42. PARIS, 11 Dec 1926, *The Final Touch,* FRF 180. PARIS, July 1946, *Two Old Women,* FRF 920; *Young Dutch Woman in Local Costume* (watercolour) FRF 4,000. LONDON, 19 May 1976, *Quays, possibly in Amsterdam* (oil on canvas, 30 x 25 1/4 ins / 76 x 64 cm) GBP 250. LONDON, 7 May 1980, *Portrait of a Young Norwegian Woman* (pastel, 22 x 33 ins / 56 x 84 cm) GBP 400. LONDON, 20 June 1985, *Young Couple* (pencil and coloured chalk, 16 1/2 x 13 1/2 ins / 42 x 34.5 cm) GBP 900. LONDON, 3 Dec 1985, *Waiting for Father* (gouache, 14 1/4 x 8 1/4 ins / 36 x 21 cm) GBP 1,500. MELBOURNE, 21 April 1986, *Portrait of a Lady* (mixed media, 48 3/4 x 18 ins / 124 x 46 cm) AUD 4,800. LONDON, 12 Nov 1987, *Love Needs No Words...* (tempera/panel, 11 1/2 x 8 1/4 ins / 29 x 21 cm) GBP 1,100. LONDON, 8 Nov 1990, *Kevelaar Procession* (oil on panel, 29 1/2 x 100 1/2 ins / 75 x 255 cm) GBP 3,300. LONDON, 22 Nov 1990, *Little Dutch Girl in Traditional Costume* (watercolour heightened with white, 7 1/4 x 5 1/2 ins / 18.4 x 14 cm) GBP 506. LONDON, 4 Nov 1994, *Looking for Jaunette; Young Hostess* (oil on panel, a pair, 14 1/2 x 10 ins / 36.8 x 25.4 cm) GBP 4,600. AMSTERDAM, 16 April 1996, *Woman Weaving* (watercolour, 13 x 9 ins / 33 x 23 cm) NLG 1,062.

JUNGNICKEL, Ludwig Heinrich
German, 20th century.
Born 27 July 1881, in Wunsiedel (Upper Franconia); died 1965, in Vienna.
Active then naturalised in 1918 in Austria.
Painter, engraver (wood), draughtsman, illustrator, lithographer, watercolourist, illustrator. Figures, animals. Designs for carpets, designs (wallpapers).
Jugendstil.
Ludwig Heinrich Jungnickel studied at the Kunstgewerbeschule in Munich in 1896, and then, after his family moved to Austria, at the Akademie der Bildenden Künste in Vienna in 1899, under the supervision of Christian Griepenkerl and August Eisenmenger. In Vienna, he worked for various design companies, producing designs for wallpaper and similar work, and starting his collaboration with the Wiener Werkstätte (Vienna Studio) in 1903. Around 1906, he completed his training at the Vienna Akademie der Bildenden Künste in graphic art, where he learned engraving with William Unger. He taught at the Kunstgewerbeschule in Frankfurt from 1911. He was a member of the Deutscher Werkbund. He formed a friendship with Egon Schiele and Kokoschka. He obtained Austrian nationality in 1918 and, between 1921 and 1930, travelled regularly to Italy, visiting Rome, Naples and Sicily. The Nazis banned him from practising his art and subjected him to persecution. He withdrew to Split in 1938. On returning to Austria in 1952, he was rehabilitated and received the title of professor, and his art was acclaimed.

As an artist, he made very beautiful drawings of animals (cats, donkeys, tigers, cocks, parrots, monkeys, and beasts of prey) which he began to draw in 1909 in the royal menagerie of Schoenbrunn in Vienna. He also made colour engravings of them. It has to be admitted that his style, which was at once naturalistic and expressive, sometimes idealised the animals. He also did a remarkable series of engravings on wood of views of Frankfurt-on-Main. On his return from a stay in Italy, his *Livre d'esquisses italiennes* (*Book of Italian Sketches*) was published, along with the oil paintings: *Via Appia; Positano;* and *Castel Gandolfo.* The books that he illustrated included: *Animaux de fables* (*Animals from Fables*); and *Tierfabeln des klassischen Altertums* (*Animal Fables from Classical Antiquity*), by Viktor Fleischer. In 1911, he assisted Klimt in the decoration of the Palais Stoclet in Brussels. He is generally considered to have made a contribution to the formation of Expressionism.

His work was shown in exhibitions in Vienna, Berlin, Munich, Amsterdam, Leipzig and San Francisco. In 1930, he was awarded the national prize of the Austrian State.

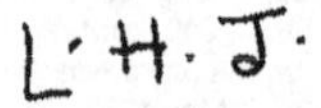

Bibliography:
Oskar Laske, Ludwig Heinrich Jungnickel, Franz von Zülow: 3 österreichische Künstler der Jahrhundertwende und Zwischenkriegszeit, Graphische Sammlung Albertina, Vienna, 1978. Spielvogel-Bodo, Ilse, *Ludwig Heinrich Jungnickel: ein Leben für die Kunst*, J. Heyn, Klagenfurt, 2000 (with a catalogue raisonné of his drawings).
Museums and Galleries:
Lódz (Mus. Sztuki) - Vienna (Albertina Mus.): large format drawings.
Auction records:
Vienna, 17 March 1976, *Two Donkeys* (charcoal, red chalk and watercolour, 12¼ x 16¼ ins / 31 x 41 cm) ATS 11,000. Vienna, 18 March 1977, *Cat and Kittens* (watercolour/charcoal outlines, 20¾ x 17 ins / 53 x 43 cm) ATS 15,000. Vienna, 18 March 1977, *Undergrowth* (c. 1902, oil on canvas, 36½ x 39¼ ins / 93 x 100 cm) ATS 70,000. Vienna, 22 Sept 1978, *Cat* (oil on paper, 16¼ x 18¼ ins / 41.5 x 46.5 cm) ATS 18,000. Vienna, 22 June 1979, *Landscape* (1928, oil on canvas, 28 x 37½ ins / 71 x 95 cm) ATS 60,000. Vienna, 18 March 1981, *Tiger* (1957, watercolour and charcoal, 19¼ x 17¾ ins / 49 x 45 cm) AUD 20,000. Vienna, 16 March 1982, *Tree* (Indian ink and chalk, heightened with white, 19¼ x 15 ins / 49 x 38 cm) ATS 38,000. Vienna, 15 Nov 1983, *Cockfight* (oil on canvas, 36 x 35½ ins / 90.5 x 90 cm) ATS 110,000. Vienna, 13 March 1984, *Little Donkey* (watercolour and charcoal, 13½ x 10 ins / 34.5 x 25.5 cm) AUD 16,000. Vienna, 18 June 1985, *Smoking Goat* (hand-coloured woodcut, 16¼ x 18 ins / 41 x 46 cm) ATS 60,000. Vienna, 18 June 1985, *Nude Dancing* (charcoal, 16½ x 13¼ ins / 42 x 33.5 cm) ATS 20,000. London, 25 Feb 1987, *Two Donkeys* (watercolour, 11¼ x 14 ins / 28.6 x 35.8 cm) GBP 1,400. Vienna, 17 March 1987, *View of Vesuvius* (oil on paper, 14 x 17¾ ins / 35.5 x 45 cm) ATS 40,000. Amsterdam, 12 Dec 1991, *Study of a Horse* (1928, black chalk/paper, 15 x 13 ins / 38 x 33 cm) NLG 1,035. New York, 2 May 1996, *Lady with a Muff* (1912, watercolour/paper, 15¾ x 10 ins / 40 x 25.4 cm) FRF 4,312. Vienna, 12 Oct 1999, *Cock Fight* (oil on canvas, 38 x 42 ins / 97 x 107 cm) ATS 300,000. Vienna, 25 May 2000, *Donkey* (charcoal and watercolour, 10 x 15 ins / 26 x 39 cm) ATS 75,000. Vienna, 29 Nov 2000, *Tigercat Sleeping* (charcoal and watercolour, 8 x 11 ins / 21 x 29 cm) ATS 50,000. Vienna, 30 May 2001, *Relatives* (charcoal, 9 x 13 ins / 24 x 33 cm) ATS 30,000. Vienna, 14 May 2002, *Animals from Fables* (coloured woodcut, 11 x 7 ins / 28 x 17 cm) EUR 20,000. Vienna, 15 Oct 2002, *Chicken and Cockerel* (coloured woodcut, 11 x 11 ins / 29 x 28 cm) EUR 3,400. Vienna, 28 Oct 2003, *Wild Cat* (oil on canvas, 14 x 19 ins / 36 x 47 cm) EUR 7,000. Vienna, 26 Nov 2003, *Landscape near Castelgandolfo* (oil on canvas, 27 x 41 ins / 68 x 105 cm) EUR 34,000. Vienna, 22 June 2004, *Southern Town with Palm Trees* (oil on canvas, 15 x 18 ins / 38 x 46 cm) EUR 9,000. Vienna, 12 Oct 2004, *Two Girls* (1932, oil on canvas and board, 34 x 25 ins / 86 x 64 cm) EUR 11,000.

JUNGSTEDT, Axel Harold
Swedish, 19th century.
Born 1859, in Sweden.
Painter. Rustic scenes, landscapes.
Museums and Galleries:
Copenhagen (Statens Mus. for Kunst): *The Stone Cutters* - Göteborg: *Haul of Herring on the Banks of Stockholm* - Oslo: *The Mines of Dannemore* - Stockholm: *In the Quarry*; *Self-portrait*.

JUNGSTEDT, Kurt
Swedish, 20th century.
Born 21 May 1894, in Stockholm; died 1963.
Painter, draughtsman, decorative designer, illustrator. Genre scenes.
Kurt Jungstedt specialised in interior decoration and scenes from everyday life. He illustrated Voltaire's *Candide* (1925).
Auction records:
Stockholm, 6 June 1988, *Beach in Summer with a Pontoon and Boats* (oil, 17¾ x 21¼ ins / 45 x 54 cm) SEK 6,200. Stockholm, 17 May 1999, *Flamenco* (oil on canvas, 35 x 56 ins / 90 x 141 cm) SEK 28,000. Stockholm, 27 Nov 2000, *Interior Scene with Woman Reading* (1921, oil on canvas, 45 x 29 ins / 115 x 73 cm) SEK 62,000. Stockholm, 2 May 2001, *Umbrellas in Expectation* (oil on canvas, 18 x 26 ins / 46 x 66 cm) SEK 21,000. Stockholm, 6 Nov 2001, *Interior Scene with Woman* (1937, oil on panel, 26 x 21 ins / 65 x 54 cm) SEK 46,000. Stockholm, 5 Nov 2002, *Scherzo* (oil on canvas, 13 x 16 ins / 33 x 41 cm) SEK 15,000. Stockholm, 7 May 2003, *View from Stockholm* (oil on canvas, 32 x 21 ins / 81 x 54 cm) SEK 20,000.

JUNGWIRTH, Franz Xaver, or Jungwierth
German, 18th century.
Born c. 1720, in Munich; died 1790.
Engraver (burin).
Jungwirth, a pupil of Mörl, engraved religious subjects, history subjects and portraits. He left a considerable body of work.

JUNGWIRTH, Joseph
Austrian, 20th century.
Born 1869; died 1950.
Painter.
Joseph Jungwirth worked in Vienna. He was awarded a medal in Munich in 1905, and exhibited in Berlin in 1909.
Auction records:
Vienna, 14 Jan 1976, *Still-life with Flowers* (oil on canvas, 26¾ x 32 ins / 68 x 81 cm) ATS 12,000. Lindau, 5 Oct 1983, *Spring Awakening* (oil on canvas, 48 x 67¼ ins / 121 x 171 cm) DEM 8,500. London, 18 June 1993, *Still-life with a Lobster, Vegetables, Kitchen Utensils and a Fowl on a Table* (1926, oil on canvas, 33¾ x 49¼ ins / 86 x 125 cm) GBP 8,970. New Orleans, 8 April 2000, *The Welcome* (oil on canvas, 36 x 60 ins / 91 x 152 cm) USD 2,500. Vienna, 12 April 2000, *Still-life of Flowers in Vase* (1920, gouache on card, 16 x 20 ins / 41 x 50 cm) ATS 30,000. Lindau, 4 Oct 2001, *Fighting for the Dummy* (1893, oil on panel, 9 x 11 ins / 22 x 29 cm) DEM 4,800. Uppsala, 8 Dec 2002, *Views from Italy* (oil on canvas) SEK 25,000. Stockholm, 3 Dec 2003, *Spring Landscape with Girls Playing* (oil on canvas, 24 x 30 ins / 62 x 76 cm) SEK 20,000. Stockholm, 30 Nov 2004, *Summer Landscape with Girls* (oil on canvas, 24 x 30 ins / 61 x 76 cm) SEK 14,000.

JUNGWIRTH, Martha
Austrian, 20th century.
Born 1940, in Vienna.
Painter, draughtswoman.
Wirklichkeiten (Realities) group.
From 1956 to 1963, Martha Jungwirth studied at the Hochschule für angewandte Kunst in Vienna, under the direction of Carl Unger and Rader Sulek. She was awarded the Joan Miró prize in 1966, as well as a prize in Innsbruck in 1969 and another at the Florence Biennale of Graphic Art in 1974. She was one of the co-founders of the group Wirklichkeiten (Realities) in 1968.

She has taken part in group exhibitions, including *Wirklichkeiten* in 1968, the first exhibition of the group of that name; the Vienna Secession; *In Praise of Painting* in 2002, a retrospective exhibition of the Wirklichkeiten group at the KunstHaus Wien in Vienna, and, in 2003, *Selbst und Andere. Das Bildnis in der Kunst nach 1960* (*Self and Others: Portraiture since 1960*), an exhibition on the theme of portraiture at the Rupertinium in Graz. She also had a solo show in 1999 at the Museum Moderner Kunst in Passau.

With the other members of the Wirklichkeiten group, Martha Jungwirth participated in the resurgence of realist painting in Austria in the 1960s, even before Pop Art arrived in Vienna. It was an informal, unstructured group, which left its mark on the period, and all its members expressed themselves in different styles. Over the years, Jungwirth's own style tended more and more towards the abstract. Her drawings, consisting of many variations on the theme of women in different truncated states, sometimes verging on caricature, are both disturbing and ludicrous.

BIBLIOGRAPHY:
Martha Jungwirth, exhibition catalogue, Landesgalerie im Schloss Esterhazy, Eisenstadt, 1976. Breicha, Otto von (ed.), *Wirklichkeiten: Aspekte einer Gruppierung*, exhibition catalogue, Museum des 20. Jahrhunderts, Vienna, 1988. *Martha Jungwirth - 'Malfluchten'*, exhibition catalogue, Museum Moderner Kunst, Passau, 1999.

MUSEUMS AND GALLERIES:
SALZBURG (Rupertinum).

JUNGWIRTH, Maximilian, or Jungwierth
German, 18th century.
Died 1768; young.
Engraver (burin).

Maximilian Jungwirth was the son and pupil of Franz Xaver Jungwirth.

JUNI, Isaac de
Spanish, 16th century.
Active in Valladolid.
Sculptor.

A natural son of Juan de Juni, he married Juana Martinez de Cuellar, by whom he had several children. Isaac had a genuine artistic gift and worked with his father and with Innocencio Berruguete. He was always rather overshadowed by his famous father, but was nonetheless a painter of the first rank. He collaborated in the retable of the cathedral in Burgo de Osma and in works of art in the chapels in Burgo de Osma, in Aronda, and in Santo Domingo de la Calzada, Valladolid.

JUNI, Juan de
French, 16th century.
Born c. 1507, in Joigny (Yonne); died 19 April 1577, in Joigny.
Active in Spain.
Painter, sculptor.
Valladolid School.

Juni worked mostly in Spain, but was invited to Rome by Pedro Alvarez de Acosta, the bishop of Oporto, to build the episcopal palace there, where he produced an altarpiece in the chapel of Dona Francisca de Villafana. For many years he was also believed to have been the author of an altarpiece in the church of Sta Eulalia, but it is now thought that it was made by the working partnership of Berruguete and Esteban Jordan. However, Juni is undoubtably the author of the *Adoration of the Kings* in the parish church of Santiago in Valladolid, and in 1545 he and Giralte sculpted the chapel of the bishop of Mondonedo and the statues that decorate it. His other works include the *Entombment*, made for the church of Sto Francisco in Valladolid, and *The Body of Christ*, which is now in the museum in Valladolid.

Juni executed works in almost all of the major churches of his time. In the church of Sto Francisco in Medina de Rioseco, he produced a series of clay statues on the themes of *The Martyrdom of St Stephen*, and *The Penitence of St Jerome*. In about 1540, in Salamanca, he sculpted the tomb of the archdeacon Gutierre de Castro and produced a *Virgin* for the monastery of Veruela in Saragossa, a *Entombment*, for the cathedral in Segovia, and many other altarpieces for monasteries and chapels in other towns. In the main, however, he worked in Valladolid, where he sculpted altarpieces for the churches of Antigua, Sto Benito and the convent of Sta Isabel, amongst others.

Despite the fact that he was born in France, Juni received his artistic training in Italy before settling in Valladolid, where he was a friend of Berruguete. His baroque style is somewhat expressionistic, tempered with influences from the classical Renaissance, and he favoured pathetic figures. According to J. J. Martinez Gonzalez: 'From French and Spanish art, Juni drew more on spirit than on form, from Italian art, he drew more on form than on spirit.' His main influences seem to have been Claus Sluter and Jacopo della Quercia, and his art shared similarities with that of Grünewald. His later works are more relaxed, and less centred around horror and terror. He left a son, born out of wedlock, who was his student and artistic equal.

MUSEUMS AND GALLERIES:
VALLADOLID: *The Body of Christ*.

JUNIGE, Ernst
German, 19th century.
Active in Dresden.
Painter. Genre scenes.

Junige is noted for *Small Boy Praying*.

JUNIUS, Franciscus, or François du Jon
German, 17th century.
Born 1589, in Heidelberg; died 1677, in Windsor, England.
Painter.

Junius was a noted writer and philologist as well as a painter, and became famous with his work on the painting of old masters. He lived in England for a long time.

JUNIUS, Isaak
Dutch, 17th century.
Painter. Battles.

Isaak Junius was a master artist in Delft in 1640, who painted in the style of Palamedes. His *Horsemen in Combat* is in the Budapest museum.

JUNIUS, Yves
French, 20th century.
Born 1 August 1937, in Montfermeil.
Painter, draughtsman. Landscapes, landscapes with figures, still-lifes.

Yves Junius studied under Brianchon at the École des Beaux-Arts in Paris in 1961.

JUNK, Rudolf
Austrian, 20th century.
Born 23 February 1880, in Vienna; died 1943, in Rekawinkel.
Painter, engraver, illustrator, pastellist. Landscapes, landscapes with figures. Models (banknotes).

Rudolf Junk studied at the Akademie der Bildenden Künste in Vienna from 1903 to 1908, under the direction of Heinrich Lefler. From 1904, he exhibited landscapes in pastels and oils at the *Hagenbund* and, from 1906, wood engravings in colour. He was a member of the Hagenbund from 1909 to

1922. He was greatly influenced by the *Exhibition of Viennese Impressionists* and applied Seurat's technique of 'divisionism' of colours to some of his paintings.

Between 1907 and 1909 and in 1911, Junk was commissioned to illustrate the Hagenbund catalogues. Among the books he decorated were *Old Vienna* by Stifter, *Aucassin and Nicolette, Waves of Love and the Sea,* and Max Eisler's publications *Historical Atlas of the City of Vienna* and *Baroque Vienna*. His major work, *Sixteen Little Songs by Goethe,* is engraved on wood and decorated with ornate letters and decorative borders. He produced a large number of designs for banknotes for the National Bank of Austria, as well as a series of decorative plates for the Exposition Internationale des Arts Industriels in Paris in 1925. He featured in the exhibition *Art in Vienna around 1900* at Schloss Halbturn.

AUCTION RECORDS:

VIENNA, 9 Dec 1987, *Spring* (oil on canvas, 19 3/4 x 27 1/2 ins / 50 x 70 cm) ATS 100,000. PARIS, 7 March 1989, *Rainstorms over Lake Atter* (oil on canvas, 19 3/4 x 26 ins / 50 x 66 cm) FRF 67,000. LONDON, 5 May 1989, *Twilight* (1904, oil on canvas, 22 1/2 x 27 1/4 ins / 57 x 69.3 cm) GBP 3,300. VIENNA, 6 March 2001, *View over Rooftops* (oil on canvas, 20 x 20 ins / 50 x 50 cm) ATS 28,000. VIENNA, 26 Nov 2003, *Forest Clearing* (oil on canvas, 26 x 20 ins / 66 x 51 cm) EUR 6,000.

JUNKA

French.

Painter. Seascapes.

MUSEUMS AND GALLERIES:

TOURNUS: *Wrecked Vessel* (painting).

JUNKER, C. L.

18th century.

Died 1797.

Draughtsman, engraver.

JUNKER, Hermann

German, 19th - 20th century.

Born 21 March 1867, in Frankfurt am Main.

Painter. Sporting subjects, military subjects, animals.

Hermann Junker was the son of Hermann I. Junker studied at the Städelsches Kunstinstitut in Frankfurt am Main and at the Akademie der Bildenden Künste in Karlsruhe. He became known for his portraits of horsemen and officers from Berlin and for his pictures of horses.

MUSEUMS AND GALLERIES:

DONAUESCHINGEN (Fürstlich Fürstenbergisches Sammlungen): *Mare and Foals* - FREIBURG IM BREISGAU: *Interior of a Stable*.

AUCTION RECORDS:

LINDAU, 8 May 1985, *Young Horseman* (oil on canvas, 69 x 56 ins / 175 x 142 cm) DEM 9,200.

JUNKER, Hermann I

German, 19th century.

Born 18 September 1838, in Frankfurt am Main; died 1899.

Painter. History painting, genre scenes.

Junker was a pupil at the Städelsches Institut in Frankfurt, in the studio of Jacob Becker. He worked in Paris and the Low Countries, but exhibited in Vienna and Munich from 1868 to 1883.

JUNMING, or Chun-ming, sobriquet: Jigu, style name: Zhiqin

Chinese, 19th century.

Born in Dantu (Jiangsu).

Active towards the middle of the 19th century.

Painter.

Junming was a priest, poet, calligrapher and painter, and a friend of the painter Mu Dashou (active around 1850). He is not mentioned in the artists' biographies. His landscapes are in the tradition of Jing Hao (end of the 9th and beginning of the 10th century), Ma Yuan and Xia Gui (active c.1190-1230). He is known for *Temple Garden*, signed and accompanied by a poem.

JUNOT

Swiss, 19th century.

Active in Neuchâtel.

Painter. Topographical views.

JUNQUERA LAVIN, Augusto

Spanish, 20th century.

Born 1 September 1869, in Oviedo (Asturias); died 1942, in Oviedo.

Painter. Religious subjects, figures, portraits, genre scenes.

Augusto Junquera Lavin studied at the Real Academia de Bellas Artes de San Fernando in Madrid, and was a pupil of his compatriot Luis Menéndez Pidal. He became a magistrate, but took up a post as an assistant teacher of drawing in Gijon. He took part in the national exhibitions in 1904 and 1906, where he received awards.

Junquera Lavin painted genre scenes and family scenes, such as *The Soldier's Return* and *In the Asylum*, in an academic style with overtones of realism.

BIBLIOGRAPHY:

Arnáiz, José Manuel/López Jiménez, Javier/Merchán Díaz, Manuel (ed.), *Cien años de pintura en Espana y Portugal (1830-1930)*, Antiqvaria, Madrid, 1990.

JUNYENT SANS, Olegario

Spanish, 20th century.

Born 1876, in Barcelona; died 1956, in Barcelona.

Painter, decorative designer. Landscapes, urban landscapes, still-lifes. Murals.

Olegario Junyent Sans was the brother of the painter Sebastián Junyent Sans. He studied at the La Lonja school of fine arts in Barcelona between 1890 and 1895. He travelled round the world in 1909 and wrote a book about it. He studied and worked on stage sets with Francisco Soler. He also painted murals and cartoons for stained glass windows, and was interested in ceramics.

Junyent Sans exhibited paintings at the St-Luc art group exhibition in 1893 and 1904 and himself organised exhibitions on themes relating to decoration throughout the centuries. His painting technique follows the traditional line, without innovation, yet producing compositions - landscapes, city views and still-lifes - that are well-structured and attractive.

BIBLIOGRAPHY:

Arnáiz, José Manuel/López Jiménez, Javier/Merchán Díaz, Manuel (ed.), *Cien años de pintura en Espana y Portugal (1830-1930)*, Antiqvaria, Madrid, 1990.

AUCTION RECORDS:

MADRID, 24 May 1977, *Palma de Majorca* (oil on panel, 13 1/2 x 18 1/2 ins / 34.5 x 47 cm) ESP 80,000. MADRID, 19 Feb 2001, *Hanging the Linen* (1942, oil on canvas, 20 x 26 ins / 50 x 65 cm) ESP 325,000. MADRID, 9 April 2001, *Market* (1936, oil on canvas, 26 x 20 ins / 65 x 50 cm) ESP 400,000. MADRID, 21 Jan 2003, *Allegory of Bacchus* (oil on canvas, oval 39 x 51 ins / 98 x 130 cm) EUR 2,800. MADRID, 30 June 2003, *Basket with Grapes* (1952, oil on canvas, 21 x 26 ins / 54 x 65 cm) EUR 2,100.

JUNYENT SANS, Sebastián

Spanish, 19th - 20th century.

Born 1865, in Barcelona; died 1915.

Painter, art critic. Religious subjects, genre scenes, landscapes.

Sebastián Junyent Sans studied at the academy of fine arts in Barcelona. As well as a painter, he was art critic of the review *Joventut* (*Youth*). He took part in the Barcelona exhibitions of 1894, 1896 and 1898. His paintings were sober in composition and clearly drawn.

BIBLIOGRAPHY:

Arnáiz, José Manuel/López Jiménez, Javier/Merchán Díaz, Manuel (ed.), *Cien años de pintura en Espana y Portugal (1830-1930)*, Antiqvaria, Madrid, 1990.

JUNYER, Joan, or Junyer y Pascual
Spanish, 20th century.
Born 1904, in Barcelona; died 1994, in Barcelona.
Also active in the USA from 1942.
Painter (including gouache), watercolourist, sculptor, draughtsman. Scenes with figures, figures, portraits. Stage costumes.

Joan Junyer began studying at the academy in Barcelona in 1918. He lived in Paris from 1925 to 1939, and finally settled in Manhattan in 1942. During the 1920s and 1930s, his paintings, on a variety of subjects and using various techniques, fell within the Spanish tradition as a moderate form of Expressionism. From 1944 onwards, without becoming Abstract, he developed a synthetic schematisation of form, with the human presence remaining a constant feature of his work. He also produced ballet costumes and painted sculptures, notably for the auditorium of the New York Ballet. His figures in silhouette are sometimes reminiscent of the work of Oscar Schlemmer.

Junyer took part in many group exhibitions, including the 1926 Salon des Indépendants in Paris and the exhibition of *Modern Catalan Art* at the Madrid Fine Arts Society; the 1934 Paris Salon des Surindépendants; the 1936 exhibition of *Contemporary Spanish Art* in the Musée du Jeu de Paume in Paris; the 1944 *Homage to the Salon d'Automne* at the Pierre Matisse Gallery in New York and the 1980 *121 Catalan Artists* in Madrid. He also held solo exhibitions, in 1925 at the Veda Gallery in Palma de Majorca and the Dalmau Gallery in Barcelona; 1931 at the Galerie Percier in Paris; 1934 at the museum of modern art in Madrid; 1939 at the Leicester Gallery in London; 1946 at the Wyte Gallery in Washington; 1949 at the Delius Gallery in New York and a 1989 retrospective at the Palau Robert in Barcelona. He also exhibited at the Chicago Institute of Art, and the museums of modern art in Toledo, Madrid, Copenhagen, St Louis, New York, Cleveland, Manhattan and San Francisco. He was awarded a prize by the Carnegie Institute in 1929.

AUCTION RECORDS:

BARCELONA, 23 April 1980, *Majorcan Hermit* (oil on card, 41 1/4 x 29 1/2 ins / 105 x 75 cm) ESP 200,000. BARCELONA, 14 May 1981, *Majorcan Hermit* (oil on card, 41 1/4 x 29 1/2 ins / 105 x 75 cm) ESP 235,000. PARIS, 27 Oct 1988, *Portrait of a Woman* (1927, oil on canvas, 16 1/4 x 13 ins / 41 x 33 cm) FRF 20,000. PARIS, 27 April 1989, *Portrait of a Woman* (1927, oil on canvas, 16 1/4 x 13 ins / 41 x 33 cm) FRF 28,000.

JUNYER VIDAL, Sebastián
Spanish, 20th century.
Born 1879, in Castelló d'Empúries (Catalonia).
Painter, draughtsman.

Sebastián Junyer Vidal studied drawing and painting at the Trias school in Barcelona. He was a founder member of the group Art and Artists along with Canals, Nogues and Nonell. He showed his works in group exhibitions, for instance in Barcelona in 1918, and solo shows. He specialised in the landscapes of Catalonia and the Balearic Islands.

BIBLIOGRAPHY:

Arnáiz, José Manuel/López Jiménez, Javier/Merchán Díaz, Manuel (ed.), *Cien años de pintura en Espana y Portugal (1830-1930)*, Antiqvaria, Madrid, 1990.

JUNYER-VIDAL
Spanish, 19th - 20th century.
Active late 19th and early 20th century.
Painter. Landscapes.

Junyer-Vidal was a friend of Picasso, who produced a caricature of him. They went to Paris together in 1901. He painted mainly Majorcan landscapes.

JUNZE DE BORGOÑA. See **JUAN de Borgoña**

JUPÉON. See **XU BEIHONG**

JUPILLE, Raymond
French, 20th century.
Born 28 May 1913, in Bretteville-en-Saire (Manche); died 24 February 1997.
Painter (including gouache), watercolourist, draughtsman, lithographer. Landscapes, seascapes, harbour scenes. Frescoes, designs for tapestries and stained glass windows.

Raymond Jupille studied at the École des Beaux-Arts in Cherbourg and at the equivalent institution in Paris. He taught at the Centre de Formation Professionnelle in Pantin. He was also General Secretary of the Salon du Dessin et de la Peinture à l'Eau, and a member of the Société des Beaux-Arts. He painted mainly landscapes and views of harbours, in geometrical compositions in which the shapes dissolve into a warm colour wash.

In Paris he exhibited at the Salon des Indépendants, the Salon d'Automne, the Salon de la Marine, the Salon du Dessin et de la Peinture à l'Eau, and at the Salon Comparaisons. In 1999, the Fondation Taylor in Paris presented a retrospective of his work.

MUSEUMS AND GALLERIES:

CHERBOURG (musée).

JUPPE, Ludwig, or Jupe
German, 15th century.
Born c. 1465, in Marburg.
Sculptor (including wood).

Juppe produced many works for the church of St Elizabeth in Marburg which have survived, including tombs, statues, coats of arms, and altars, and he left a *Virgin* in sculpted wood in the church of the village of Wehrhausen, near Marburg.

JUPPIN, Jean Baptiste
Flemish School, 18th century.
Born 25 November 1675, in Namur, in 1678 according to Siret; died 5 September 1729, in Namur.
Painter. Landscapes with figures, mountainscapes.

Jean Baptiste Juppin studied in Brussels. Following some study trips to Italy he settled in Liège in 1717. His painting *Mountain Landscape* is in the Liège museum. The figures in his landscapes were painted by Plumier.

AUCTION RECORDS:

BRUSSELS, 28 Oct 1987, *Landscape with Figures* (1717, oil on canvas, 37 1/2 x 54 ins / 95 x 137 cm) BEF 110,000.

JURADO, Luis
Spanish, 17th century.
Born c. 1595, in Saviote.
Active in Seville.
Sculptor.

JURADO Y GARCIA, Manuel
Spanish, 19th century.
Born 19th century, in Cádiz.
Painter. Genre scenes.

Manuel Jurado y Garcia was awarded a bronze medal in Cádiz in 1879.

JURAKOVSKY, Mikhail
Ukrainian, 20th century.
Born in the Ukraine.
Sculptor.

Jurakovsky studied at the Moscow academy of fine art. He exhibited at the Salon de Paris from 1926.

JURAN, or Chu-jan
Chinese, 10th century.
Born in the Nanjing region.
Active c. 960-980.
Painter. Landscapes, landscapes with figures.

In the 10th century, in the region of the Blue River, two great painters, Dong Yuan and Juran, played a very important role in the history of Chinese landscape painting and became patriarchal figures of what is known as the Southern School. The works of Juran, a Buddhist monk, were known throughout China from the days of his youth. Two periods can, be distinguished in his work. First there are landscapes of the Nanjing region where he was born. These are typified by the elongated lines of the mountains and round shapes of the copses. Then his style becomes purer and more spiritual. In 975, the last emperor of the Tang dynasty in the South was taken prisoner and held in Kaifeng, the capital of the Song. Juran followed him and entered the monastery of Kaibao there. He became a disciple of Dong Yuan and painted the same landscapes as he did with the a similar impressionist technique. For Juran, nature is more peaceful, with fewer contrasts, and the ink which he uses is lighter and more fluid. Hills and mountains are a series of pure undulations, finely shaded by the layers of ink, against which trees with luxuriant foliage stand out in thick dark strokes. The eye is led with ease through the delicacy of the forms and the subtlety of the materials: grass grows spontaneously and the road winds without our being aware of it.

The theoretician Guo Ruoxu (around 1070) wrote of him that he was a skilful landscape artist with great richness in his brush and ink technique. He was a master of misty atmosphere and vast mountain and river panoramas. These mountains, structured in round masses one on the other, are interrupted by terraces of vegetation of which the ascent is proportional to the distance. Their uncontoured relief is sometimes underlined by black patches of ink. Among works attributed to him the scroll *Seeking the Dao in Autumn Mountains* is one of the most authentic. At the foot of the rounded mountain which forms the whole landscape, a little pathway runs alongside a river. It leads to isolated cottages in the pine trees. Higher up, wooded copses and bushes conceal the many undulations of the ground which is done in *pima cun*, that is to say furrows in hemp fibre painted with a soft, light brushstroke. An impression of evanescence and unreality emanates from this painting.

BIBLIOGRAPHY:
Cahill, James, *Chinese Painting*, Skira, Geneva, 1960. Ching-lang, Hou, *'Tong Yuan et Kiu-Ran'* in *Encyclopaedia Universalis* vol. XVI, Paris, 1973. Yang Xin and others, *Three Thousand Years of Chinese Painting*, Yale Univ. Press, New Haven and London, 1997. Fahr-Becker, Gabriele (ed.), *The Art of East Asia: Volume 1*, Konemann, Cologne, 1998.

MUSEUMS AND GALLERIES:
BEIJING (Palace Mus.): *Mountain Retreat* (small handscroll, signed); *High Mountains and Twisting Stream*; *Riverscape with Boat Returning* (attributed); *Mountain Valley with Pines and a Boy Following Two Men Crossing a Bridge* (album leaf, attributed) - TAIPEI (National Palace Mus.): *Seeking the Dao in Autumn Mountains* (ink and light colour on silk, hanging scroll); *Xiao Yi Attempting to Rediscover a Masterpiece* (ink on silk, hanging scroll); *Autumn Mountains*; *Distant Mountain Forests* (c. 980, ink on silk, hanging scroll); *Crane and Musical Instrument in an Autumn Landscape of Mountains and Woods* - WASHINGTON DC (Freer Gal. of Art): *Changjiang Wanli Tu* (*View of Yang-zijiang*) (handscroll, colophons by Lu Shen and Dong Qichang, attributed - possibly from the Song period).

JURAND, Jean
French, 17th century.
Active in Besançon in 1628.
Sculptor.

JURAVLEV, Anatoli
Russian, 20th - 21st century.
Born after 1960

JURAVLEV, Firs Sergeevich, or Jouravliov, Jouravlev, Chouravlev
Russian, 19th century.
Born 10 (22) December 1836, in Saratov; died 4 September 1901, in St Petersburg.
Painter. Genre scenes.

Juravlev was a student at the fine art academy in St Petersburg, where he was awarded a fellowship in 1874 for a painting entitled *Before the Wedding*. He exhibited in Philadelphia. Later he showed two works in Paris at the 1878 Exposition Universelle: *Dinner after a Funeral* and *Blessing of the Bride and Groom*. Another of his works is entitled *Unfaithful Peasant*.

MUSEUMS AND GALLERIES:
MOSCOW (State Tretyakov Gal.): *Baggage Porter*; *Dinner after the Funeral of a Merchant*; *Before the Wedding* (variant); *Self-portrait* - ST PETERSBURG (Gosudarstvennyj Russkij Muz.): *Before the Wedding*.

JURAVLIOV, Mikhail Pavlovich
Russian, 20th - 21st century.
Born 1952, in Magnitogorsk.
Painter. Figure compositions, landscapes with figures.

Mikhail Juravliov was a student at the USSR cinematographic institute. His paintings stem from popular imagery. He depicts family and comical scenes, complex compositions that use a highly skilled technique and which are deliberately populist, caricature, almost: *Cinema Studio Arrest*; *Branch Station*. He became a member of the association of Leningrad (St Petersburg) painters and from 1985 has exhibited regularly in Moscow and particularly in St Petersburg. His work was seen in Osaka, Japan, in 1986, and in 1990 he took part in exhibitions in Helsinki and Warsaw. A solo exhibition of his works was held in Helsinki in 1987.

BIBLIOGRAPHY:
L'École de Léningrad, auction catalogue, Drouot, Paris, 19 November 1990.

MUSEUMS AND GALLERIES:
HELSINKI (Gal. of Contemporary Art) - MOSCOW (Ministry of Culture) - ST PETERSBURG (Gosudarstvennyj Muz. Istorii) - ST PETERSBURG (Mus. of Performing Arts).

AUCTION RECORDS:
PARIS, 27 Nov 1989, *Square by the Station* (tempera/hardboard, 19¾ x 27½ ins / 50 x 70 cm) FRF 12,500. PARIS, 11 June 1990, *Cinema Studio* (oil on card, 19¾ x 27½ ins / 50 x 70 cm) FRF 14,000. PARIS, 19 Nov 1990, *Communal Kitchen* (oil/hardboard, 23½ x 31½ ins / 60 x 80 cm) FRF 19,000. PARIS, 15 May 1991, *Bride and Groom Celebrating their Marriage* (oil on canvas, 11 x 16¼ ins / 27 x 41 cm) FRF 4,000. PARIS, 25 Nov 1991, *Christmas Eve* (oil on canvas, 18 x 22 ins / 46 x 55 cm) FRF 16,500. PARIS, 6 Dec 1991, *Meal* (oil on canvas, 17¾ x 21¼ ins / 45 x 54 cm) FRF 4,500. PARIS, 13 April 1992, *Still-life with Fruit* (oil on canvas, 20¾ x 19¾ ins / 53 x 50 cm) FRF 15,000. PARIS, 7 Oct 1992, *Two Sisters* (oil on canvas, 25½ x 21¼ ins / 65 x 54 cm) FRF 15,000. PARIS, 29 Nov 1993, *On the Balcony* (oil on canvas/card, 22 x 18 ins / 55 x 46 cm) FRF 11,000. PARIS, 4 May 1994, *Going For a Walk* (oil on canvas, 15 x 18 ins / 38 x 46 cm) FRF 5,500.

JURDAK, Halim
Lebanese, 20th century.
Born 1927, in El Metn.
Painter, engraver. Figures, scenes with figures.

Halim Jurdak came from El Metn. He began his education in the Lebanon and continued it in Paris in the Brianchon studio at the École des Beaux-Arts. A grant from his home country enabled him also to attend the studios of Goetz, Brayer and André Lhote, as well as the Académie de la Grande Chaumière. He visited Germany, England, Switzerland and other parts of Europe. He returned to the Lebanon in 1966, was appointed to teach painting and engraving at Lebanon University and became a member of the Cultural Council of Northern El Metn. In 1974 he collaborated in the creation of a monumental decorative piece, *The International Wall*, for the Canadian festival of French-speaking countries. He created other such pieces in Saudi Arabia and elsewhere.

His work has been included in numerous collective exhibitions: in Paris at the *Salon Nationale* of the École des Beaux-Arts in 1958; at the Salon of the Sursock Museum in 1967, 1982, 1984, and 1988; at the São Paulo Biennale in 1967; and at the Baghdad *Biennale* in 1970, 1974 and 1981. It has featured also in exhibitions in Beirut, Kuweit, Mannheim, Bradford, London, Paris (*Liban, le regard des peintures, 200 ans de peinture libanaise* (*Lebanon as Seen by Painters - 200 Years of Lebanese Painting*), Institut du Monde Arabe, 1989, and others. He has had solo exhibitions at the Rudolph Steiner Gallery in Stuttgart since 1961, at the Galerie Triades in Paris in 1963, 1964 and 1965, and at Dar El Fan in 1970 and 1980. He also has solo shows in Beirut.

His painting is highly individual, with hints of the surreal but constructed in an almost expressionist manner. He peoples his dream-spaces with often rather haggard figures or nudes.

BIBLIOGRAPHY:

Liban. Le Regard des peintres. 200 ans de peinture libanaise, exhibition catalogue, Institut du Monde Arabe, Paris, 1989.

JURETZEK, Tina

German, 20th - 21st century.
Born 1952, in Leipzig.
Painter, collage artist.

Tina Juretzek lives and works in Düsseldorf, having studied at the Kunstakademie in Düsseldorf from 1971 to 1978. Tina Juretzek's paintings from the 1990s appear to have an enormous desire for a 'fight' with the forms, space and depth of the canvas. She covers it with impassioned dots, dribbles, splashes, scratches and brush strokes, all swirling round in an interplay and atmosphere of cold tones. As Jean-Paul Schneider wrote, this contributes to 'tracing the signs of an imaginary topography of areas of adventure, of dreams, of the exploration of the artist's intimate mythologies'. Her collages on paper, dating from 1992, whether overpainted or not, are more structured. She has taken part in many group exhibitions in Düsseldorf, Kiel, Cologne and Leipzig. She has exhibited in solo shows since 1979 in Cologne, followed by 1981 at the Stadthalle in Marburg; 1983, 1984, 1986 and 1990 at the Galerie Zimmer in Düsseldorf; 1985 at the Kunstverein in Bremerhaven; 1986 at the 6th New Delhi Triennial; 1985, 1987 and 1989 at the Galerie Marghescu in Hanover; 1990 at the Goethe Institute in Brussels and in 1990, 1992 and 1998 at the Galerie de Luxembourg in Luxembourg, and in 1998, 2001 and 2003 at the Gallery Borkowski in Hanover.

BIBLIOGRAPHY:

Schneider, Jean Paul (preface), *Noces vives de formes et de couleurs*, exhibition catalogue, Gal. du Luxembourg, Luxembourg, 1992.

JURGA, Jerzy

Polish, 20th century.
Born 1940, in Srem.
Painter, poet.

Jerzy Jurga studied at the Adam Mickiewicz University in Poznan. He was a professor of fine arts, and exhibited his works at exhibitions in Poland as well as in Sweden and Japan.

JÜRGEN BILDENSCHNEIDER. See GOWER Jürgen

JÜRGEN-FISCHER, Klaus

German, 20th century.
Born 1930, in Krefeld.
Painter, draughtsman.

Klaus Jürgen-Fischer studied at the academies in Düsseldorf and Stuttgart, where he was influenced by Willi Baumeister. An art critic and philosopher, he became the editor of the review *Das Kunstwerk* (*The Work of Art*), and then a member of the Deutscher Künstlerbund (Association of German Artists). He took part in many group exhibitions of young German painters, including the Salon de Charleroi in 1958, the first Biennale des Jeunes in Paris and the first Tokyo Biennale of Graphic Arts. He has also held solo shows in Krefeld, Heidelberg, Wuppertal, Munich, Turin and Venice, and was a winner of the *Kunstpreis der Jugend* for graphic arts. His early work was mainly graphic, and featured accumulations of graffiti on large surfaces, lying somewhere between the abstract and the cartoon.

JÜRGENS, Alfred. See JUERGENS

JÜRGENS, Grethe

German, 20th century.
Born 1899; died 1981.
Painter.
Neue Sachlichkeit (New Objectivity).

Grethe Jürgens was one of the artists of the German New Objectivity movement. She featured in the exhibition *Neue Sachlichkeit, Magische Wirklichkeit* (*New Objectivity, Magical Realism*) in Bielefeld and Kaiserslautern.

MUSEUMS AND GALLERIES:

HANOVER (Sprengel Mus.): *The Fabric Sellers* (1932).

AUCTION RECORDS:

HAMBURG, 7 June 1985, *Gypsy and Child* (1923, watercolour, 12 x 11 ins / 30.5 x 27 cm) DEM 5,000. MUNICH, 25 May 2004, *Portrait of Gustav Schenk* (watercolour, 25 x 19 ins / 64 x 48 cm) EUR 2,200.

JÜRGENS, J. F.

German, 18th - 19th century.
Painter (porcelain).

Jürgens worked at the Brunswick pottery, where he did ornamental and decorative painting. He specialised in silver painting, giving the porcelain a silver look.

MUSEUMS AND GALLERIES:

BRUNSWICK: numerous works.

JÜRGENS, Johann Wilhelm

German, 19th century.
Born 14 April 1845, in Lübeck; died 4 March 1906, in Wiesbaden.
Engraver. Landscapes.

Jürgens was taught by W. Friedrich and T. Hagen at the art academy in Weimar. He exhibited in Berlin (1886) and Munich (1889).

JÜRGENSEN. See JORGENSEN

JURIE, A.

French, 19th century.
Born 19th century, in Lyons.
Draughtsman, engraver.

A. Jurie produced etchings and signed his landscapes with his intitials, notably *The Château of Charly in the region of Lyons* (1835).

JURIMY (Mlle)

French, 19th century.
Painter. Genre scenes, portraits.

Mlle Jurimy exhibited her work at the Salon from 1824: *Baptismal Fonts at the Metropolitan in Aix* and in 1831: *The Mad Woman from the Valley* and two portraits.

JURJANE, Aija

Latvian, 20th century.

Painter. Figure compositions.

Aija Jurjane began studying art at the Rozental School in Riga and continued at the Academy of Fine Art in Latvia. She currently manages the Rozental School and is a Member of the Union of Artists.

Her painting is of the youthful games of childhood, idealised perhaps, but certainly happy and colourful. The representation is simple in its drawing and the colours are controlled as flat tints. She appears at exhibitions in Riga.

MUSEUMS AND GALLERIES:
RIGA (Nat. Institute For the Fine Arts).

AUCTION RECORDS:
PARIS, 11 July 1990, *Schoolboys in the Playground* (1990, oil on canvas, 28 1/4 x 36 1/4 ins / 72 x 92 cm) FRF 6,500.

JURJANS, Juris

Latvian, 20th century.

Born 1944.

Painter. Landscapes, flowers.

Juris Jurjans attended the Rozental school in Riga from 1955 to 1962 before continuing his studies at the Latvian academy of fine arts from 1963 to 1969. He became a member of the artists' union. Jurjans is a decorative painter whose sole aim is to please his viewers. He has exhibited in Riga and Moscow and overseas in the USA, Japan, Belgium, Finland, Germany, France, Bulgaria, Romania and Poland.

MUSEUMS AND GALLERIES:
MOSCOW (Ministry of Culture) - MOSCOW (State Tretyakov Gal.) - RIGA (Valsts makslas muzejs).

AUCTION RECORDS:
PARIS, 11 July 1990, *Le pré debout* (1990, oil on canvas, 35 x 47 1/4 ins / 89 x 120 cm) FRF 3,000.

JURJEWICZ, Franz

Polish, 19th century.

Born 9 August 1849, in Pskov.

Active in Vilna (now Vilnius, Lithuania).

Painter.

Franz Jurjewicz studied for a time in Paris with E. Dardoize. He settled in Vilna and exhibited in Cracow (1894, *Procession*, after Kalwarya), Warsaw (1910, *View of Vilna*) and Lemberg (now Lviv, Ukraine).

JURKIEWICZ, Zdzislaw

Polish, 20th century.

Born 1931, in Wolsztyn.

Photographer, mixed media.

Conceptual Art.

Zdzislaw Jurkiewicz's art concurs completely with conceptual art in its form (the use of photograph negatives) and in its descriptive and external intention. He photographed odd moments of sunshine in his kitchen, the sun being seen as a circle, or instead reconstituted different perceptions one could have of the planet Saturn. He appeared at the Retrospective on Polish conceptual art in 1999: *Conceptual Reflections in Polish Art. Experience of Discourse: 1965-1975*, Ujazdowski Castle, Warsaw.

JURRES, Johannes Hendricus

Dutch, 20th century.

Born 17 January 1875, in Leeuwarden; died 1946.

Painter, draughtsman, illustrator. Religious subjects, figure compositions, genre scenes.

Johannes Jurres studied at the Rijksakademie in Amsterdam, where he became a professor in 1921. He featured in exhibitions in Holland and in Paris, where he won a silver medal for his painting *Richard III's Equerry Finding the Body of the King* at the Salon de la Société des Artistes Français in 1913. In 1914, he showed *The Death of Jezebel*. He also took part in several exhibitions in St Louis, USA as well as the international Panama-Pacific exhibitions, held in San Francisco in 1915 and in Venice in 1920.

Among the books he illustrated were a Dutch edition of Cervantes' *Don Quixote* and some children's books by Stamperius. He worked for the weekly magazine *Graphic*. As a painter, he was influenced by Decamps, Diaz and Delacroix, and studied Rembrandt, Rubens and Velazquez. During a visit to Spain, he produced a number of works, including *Spanish Peasants, the Good Samaritan, the Stoning of Don Quixote, Christ Healing the Lepers, St John and St Peter Healing the Palsied* and a few pictures of Don Quixote, as well as figure compositions on themes drawn from the Old Testament and from Romantic literature. There is an altarpiece by him in St Agnes' Church in Amsterdam.

BIBLIOGRAPHY:
Van Calker, Henri H., *J. H. Jurres*, Hollandsche uitgeversmaatschappij, Amsterdam, 1947.

MUSEUMS AND GALLERIES:
ST LOUIS: *Christ Healing the Lepers*.

AUCTION RECORDS:
AMSTERDAM, 7 Sept 1976, *Judith and Holofernes* (oil on canvas, 21 1/4 x 28 ins / 54 x 71 cm) NLG 2,200. AMSTERDAM, 5 Dec 1978, *Women Prisoners* (oil on canvas, 30 x 35 ins / 76 x 89 cm) NLG 4,200. AMSTERDAM, 15 May 1979, *Reclining Nude* (oil on canvas, 29 1/2 x 57 ins / 75 x 144.5 cm) NLG 3,300. GIEN, 26 June 1988, *Medieval Horsemen* (oil on panel, 22 x 11 1/2 ins / 55 x 29 cm) FRF 9,800. TORONTO, 30 Nov 1988, *St Martin and the Beggars* (oil on canvas, 29 1/2 x 39 ins / 75 x 99 cm) CAD 2,000. AMSTERDAM, 28 Feb 1989, *Roman Soldier Drinking by a Well* (oil on canvas, 28 1/4 x 40 1/4 ins / 72 x 102 cm) NLG 1,725. AMSTERDAM, 5 June 1990, *Don Quixote and his Horse with a Shepherd and his Flock in the Background* (oil on canvas, 16 x 19 3/4 ins / 40.5 x 50 cm) NLG 1,955. AMSTERDAM, 11 Sept 1990, *Rest During the Flight into Egypt* (oil on canvas, 25 3/4 x 21 ins / 65.5 x 52.5 cm) NLG 3,220. AMSTERDAM, 23 April 1991, *The Lion Hunt* (oil on canvas, 35 1/2 x 51 1/4 ins / 90 x 130 cm) NLG 5,750. AMSTERDAM, 14-15 April 1992, *The Good Samaritan* (oil on canvas, 15 x 22 ins / 38 x 55 cm) NLG 4,025. AMSTERDAM, 2-3 Nov 1992, *Warrior on Horseback* (oil on panel, 7 1/2 x 5 1/2 ins / 19 x 14 cm) NLG 2,070. AMSTERDAM, 20 April 1993, *Joel and Barah* (1933, oil on canvas, 39 1/4 x 29 1/2 ins / 100 x 75 cm) NLG 4,830. AMSTERDAM, 19-20 Feb 1997, *View of the Harbour in Nice* (1910, oil on canvas, 30 x 41 ins / 76 x 104 cm) NLG 3,459. AMSTERDAM, 21 Jan 1998, *The Death of Jezebel* (oil on canvas, 51 1/2 x 36 1/4 ins / 131 x 92 cm) NLG 29,983; *Samson and Delilah* (oil on canvas, 30 3/4 x 52 1/4 ins / 78 x 133 cm) NLG 23,064; *The Trumpet Call* (1941, oil on canvas remounted/card, 39 1/2 x 29 3/4 ins / 100.5 x 75.5 cm) NLG 10,955. AMSTERDAM, 19 Jan 1999, *Three Musketeers* (1900, oil on canvas, 29 x 41 ins / 74 x 103 cm) NLG 5,000. AMSTERDAM, 7 July 1999, *Warriors Taking Refreshment* (oil on canvas, 50 x 24 ins / 126 x 60 cm) NLG 7,000. THE HAGUE, 31 Oct 2000, *Jehu and Jezabel* (charcoal and pastel, 30 x 40 ins / 75 x 102 cm) NLG 4,200. THE HAGUE, 31 Oct 2000, *Death of Izebel* (charcoal and pastel, 48 x 27 ins / 121 x 69 cm) NLG 4,400. AMSTERDAM, 25 April 2001, *Entrance of Peace* (pastel on paper on canvas, 32 x 57 ins / 81 x 145 cm) NLG 6,500. AMSTERDAM, 22 Oct 2001, *Battle* (oil on canvas, 15 x 25 ins / 38 x 64 cm) NLG 5,500. AMSTERDAM, 22 April 2002, *Negro* (oil on canvas, 37 x 27 ins / 94 x 69 cm) EUR 3,800. AMSTERDAM, 3 Sept 2002, *Cavalrists Resting* (oil on canvas, 52 x 35 ins / 131 x 88 cm) EUR 3,500. AMSTERDAM, 15 March 2004, *Hannibal Crossing the Alps* (1823, oil on canvas, 34 x 51 ins / 86 x 129 cm) EUR 7,000. NEW YORK, 29 June 2004, *Samson and Delilah* (oil on canvas, 36 x 46 ins / 92 x 118 cm) USD 5,000.

JÜRSS, Julius

German, 19th century.

Active in Munich, then in Berlin.

Painter. Genre scenes.

Jürss exhibited in Munich in 1889.
AUCTION RECORDS:
LONDON, 10 June 1909, *Brigands*, GBP 27.

JURY, Julius
German, 19th century.
Born 30 July 1821, in Konikow (near Köslin/Koszalin), Pomerania.
Painter. Genre scenes.
Jury settled in Munich in 1870.
AUCTION RECORDS:
LONDON, 10 Feb 1978, *Little Rapscallions* (oil on canvas, 21 3/4 x 16 3/4 ins / 55.2 x 42.5 cm) GBP 4,500.

JURY, Wilhelm
German, 18th - 19th century.
Born 13 May 1763, in Berlin; died 21 June 1829, in Berlin.
Active in Berlin.
Painter, engraver (burin).

JUSARTE, Felipe, or Iusarte
Spanish, 16th century.
Active in Valladolid.
Sculptor.
Felipe Jusarte worked on the statue of the empress and, around 1563, lived for some years in Madrid.

JUSEPE DE BURGOS
Spanish, 16th century.
Active in Seville in 1550.
Sculptor.

JUSIDMAN, Yishai
Mexican, 20th - 21st century.
Born 1963, in Mexico City.
Painter. Figures, landscapes.
Yishai Jusidman uses photographs for his oil or tempera paintings and tapestries. The figures he creates seem to dematerialise or conflict with a coded reality. Thus, in the 1996 *Sumo* series, the combatants are shown on an abstract geometric background, the dynamic cinematic qualities of which dominate the fighters' movements. The depiction of isolated standing individuals challenges the illusionism of the image as well as the movement of typologies in the imagination.

Yishai Jusidman took part in the 2001 Venice Biennale. Solo exhibitions of his work include: University Gallery, San Diego, California, an exhibition that toured the USA (1996); *en/treat/ment*, Galería Ramis, Mexico City (1999) and Art Centre, Vassivière, Limousin, France (2000).
BIBLIOGRAPHY:
Gallo, Rubén, '*L'orientalisme dans l'art mexicain*' in *Art Press* n° 243, periodical, Paris, February 1999. Gonzales-Day, Ken, '*Sourires distants: les peintures de Yishai Jusidman*' in *Art Press* n° 260 p. 38, periodical, Paris, September 2000.

JUSSAUD, Émile
French, 19th century.
Born 6 November 1820, in Naples; died May 1874.
Painter.
Émile Jussaud was the son of a Nîmes family. He studied in Zurich and settled in Bergedorf in Germany where he painted a number of portraits.

JUSSERAND, Antoine Louis
French, 19th century.
Born 1838, in Issoudun (Indre).
Active in Paris.
Sculptor.
Antoine Jusserand was a pupil of Dumont and Bonnassieux. He exhibited statues and busts at the Salon from 1848 to 1877.
MUSEUMS AND GALLERIES:
CHÂTEAUROUX: *Amazon*.

JUSTE, André
Italian (then naturalised French), 16th century.
Born c. 1487, in Italy.
Active in France.
Sculptor.
The brother of Antoine and Jean Juste, he settled in Tours, took French nationality in 1513, and was appointed sculptor to the king. It is likely that he collaborated in the works of his brothers and that he worked with Jean Juste on the tomb of Louis XII.

JUSTE, Antoine
Italian (then naturalised French), 16th century.
Born 1479, in Corbignano, near Settignano, according to some sources, in San Martino, near Florence, according to others; died 1519, in Tours.
Active in France.
Sculptor.
Antoine Juste went to France in about 1504 with his brothers Jean and André. In 1507, he sculpted in stone for the cathedral in Dol, Brittany, the tomb of Thomas James, bishop of Dol; this monument is still extant on the wall of the left transept, only the statue of the bishop having disappeared. For the chapel of Cardinal d'Amboise in the château of Gaillon, he carved between 1508 and 1509 12 statues of the Apostles, and for the gallery a large marble low relief (*Battle of Genoa*) and then a bust of Cardinal d'Amboise. In 1514, he settled in Tours, had Carrara marble brought there, and with his brother Jean worked on the tomb of Louis XII and Anne de Bretagne. This was ornamented with magnificent low reliefs and was placed in St-Denis in 1531. The Louvre has a marble head of a young warrior thought to be by him that came from the château of Gaillon.
MUSEUMS AND GALLERIES:
PARIS (Louvre): *Head of Young Warrior* (marble).

JUSTE, Estelle
Belgian, 20th century.
Born 1894; died 1962, in Ukkel (Brabant).
Painter.

JUSTE, Javier
Spanish, 19th century.
Born 19th century, in Valencia.
Painter. Genre scenes.
Javier Juste first exhibited in Valencia in 1875.
AUCTION RECORDS:
NEW YORK, 25 Feb 1983, *Landscape with River* (oil on canvas, 19 x 35 1/2 ins / 48.2 x 90.2 cm) USD 1,500.

JUSTE, Jean I
Italian, 16th century.
Born 1485, in San Martino, near Florence; died 1549, in Tours.
Naturalised in France.
Sculptor. Funerary monuments (recumbent statues).
A brother of Antoine Juste, he finished the tomb of the bishop of Dol and settled in Tours. He took French nationality in 1513 and was appointed sculptor to the king. He went to St-Denis to oversee the installation of the tomb of Louis XII and Queen Anne de Bretagne. He carved the kneeling statues of the king and queen and the two recumbent figures. The statues of the 12 Apostles and the 4 Virtues placed at the corners are by his nephew Juste de Juste, and the low reliefs are the work of Antoine Juste. Between 1532 and 1539, he carried out a commission from Hélène de Hangest, making for the chapel of the château of Oiron (Deux Sèvres) the tomb of her husband Artus Gouffier and that of Philippe de Montmorency.

JUSTE, Jean II
French, 16th century.
Born 1510, in Tours; died c. 1579.
Active in Tours.
Sculptor.

The son of Jean Juste, in 1558 Jean Juste II sculpted the tomb of Claude Gouffier, the principal equerry to the French court, and private tutor to Henri II and his first wife Jacqueline de la Trémoïle. The tomb was destroyed in 1793, and only the statue of Gouffier has survived. He is also thought to have produced, in Oiron, the tomb of Guillaume Gouffier, who was known as admiral Bonnivet and who died near Pavia in 1525, as well as the tomb of Guy d'Espinay in the old collegiate church in Champeaux, near Vitré. In 1561, in the Place de la Foire-le-Roi, he sculpted a marble and hard-stone fountain decorated with bronze low reliefs of nymphs and naiads. He possibly worked in Avignon, as records survive of a man named Jean Juste, from Tours, who produced work there in the 16th century.

JUSTE, Juste de
French, 16th century.
Born 1505, in Tours; died 1559, in Tours.
Sculptor, engraver.
First Fontainebleau School.

The son of Antoine Juste, Juste de Juste studied under Jean Juste, and was involved in producing the monument to Louis XII, sculpting statues of the Apostles and the Virtues. In 1529, he sculpted various marble statues for François I, in particular a Hercules and a Leda. He was appointed as a sculptor to the king in 1533, and worked in the main gallery of the Château de Fontainebleau in 1535 and 1536, under Rosso. On returning to Tours, he produced a statue of the Virgin for the portal of the church of Notre-Dame-de-la-Riche in 1538.

AUCTION RECORDS:
LONDON, 9 Dec 1982, *Back View of a Man Leaning on a Staff* (etching, 6 3/4 x 3 1/2in/17.3 x 9.2cm) GBP 2,500. LONDON, 6 Dec 1983, *Man Standing with One Arm Raised* (etching, 7 1/4 x 3 1/2in/18.5 x 9.1cm) GBP 3,800. LONDON, 29 June 1987, *Back View of a Man Holding a Stick* (etching, 6 3/4 x 4in/17.4 x 9.3cm) GBP 14,500.

JUSTE, René Camille, pseudonym René-Just
French, 19th century.
Born 12 June 1868, in Paris.
Active in Marlotte (now Bourron-Marlotte), near Fontainebleau.
Painter. Landscapes.

René Juste was in the forefront of the Société des Artistes Français from 1902. He was a colourist of great power, profoundly moved in the presence of nature and gifted with the secret of conveying his emotion on canvas. A little of Guillaume's early style can be detected in his work but this similarity of conception causes Juste to lose none of his originality. He liked to translate the poetic quality of old village dwellings, the overwhelming calm of the snow. His works are highly regarded.

MUSEUMS AND GALLERIES:
PARIS (former Mus. du Luxembourg): *Old Corner of Marlotte* - TOURS: *Before the Rain.*

AUCTION RECORDS:
PARIS, 27 Feb 1919, *Footpath Alongside the River,* FRF 175. PARIS, 28 Nov 1924, *Leaving Marlotte in the Snow,* FRF 750; *Steeple of Larchand: around Fontainebleau,* FRF 580.

JUSTE DE GAND, or Giusto da Guanto, real name: Wassenhove Joos van, or Joost, Jodocas or Jodocus
Flemish, 15th century.
Born c. 1435; died c. 1480.
Painter.

Juste de Gand's biographical dates are unrecorded, as is his birthplace and where he died. However, he is known to have been a master in Antwerp in 1460, and to have entered the guild in Ghent in 1464. The archives of the brotherhood of Corpus Christi in Urbino indicate that he received two payments on 11 April 1473 and 15 October 1474, for a painting produced for the brotherhood, and on 7 March 1745, he entered into a second agreement to paint a banner for them. After this date no further references to him are found.

An important exhibition in Ghent in 1957, entitled *Juste de Gand, Berruguete and the Court of Urbino,* shed light on this artist's role in the art of his time. Juste de Gand is thought to have been the same artist as Joos van Wassenhove, and three important facts support this claim: his friendship with Hugo van der Goes, the close similarity of the first names Juste and Joos, a trip to Italy, and the complete lack of references to them (or him) after 1475.

The only authentic work by Juste de Gand is *Communion of the Apostles,* which is now in the ducal palace of Urbino. Among the works attributed to him are an *Adoration of the Kings* in the Metropolitan Museum of New York, a *Crucifixion* in a private collection in Brussels, a *Triptych of the Crucifixion* in the St-Bavon Cathedral in Ghent, and the 28 *Portraits of Famous Men,* of which 14 are in the ducal palace of Urbino, and 14 in the Louvre. *Frederick of Montefeltro, his Son, and Members of his Court* is in Windsor Castle, England. Not all of these portraits, produced for the studio of the duke of Montefeltro, have been attributed to Juste de Gand; Berruguete was almost certainly the author of some of them, although determining which of them were his works is a difficult task.

MUSEUMS AND GALLERIES:
GHENT (St-Baafskathedraal): *Crucifixion* (triptych) - NEW YORK (Metropolitan Mus. of Art): *Adoration of the Kings* - PARIS (Louvre): *Portraits of Famous Men* (14 works) - URBINO (Gal. Nazionale Delle Marche): *Communion of the Apostles; Portraits of Famous Men* (14 works) - WINDSOR (Windsor Castle, Royal Collection): *Frederick of Montefeltro, his Son, and Members of his Court.*

JUSTER, Joseph
Italian, 17th century.
Active in Venice c. 1690.
Engraver (burin).

Juster engraved religious subjects and portraits in the style of Da Vinci, Titian and Noel Jouvenet. His works notably included panels for *Tabulae Selectae, Catharinae Patin.*

JUSTIN
French, 19th century.
Portrait painter.

The Douai museum has a *Full-length Portrait of Louis-Philippe* donated by the government in 1841 which indicates the period during which Justin worked.

MUSEUMS AND GALLERIES:
DOUAI: *Full-length Portrait of Louis-Philippe.*

JUSTIN, Auguste François
French, 19th century.
Born 1847, in Bordeaux.
Painter. Genre scenes, animals, landscapes.

Auguste Justin was a pupil of Yvon. He exhibited a few genre subjects at the Salon from 1869 to 1870.

AUCTION RECORDS:
NEW YORK, 19 July 1990, *Cows in a Landscape* (1881, oil on canvas, 49 1/2 x 61 ins / 125.5 x 155.1 cm) USD 2,310.

JUSTIN, Marie Jules
French, 19th century.
Born in Paris; died 1891.
Painter. Genre scenes, landscapes, still-lifes.

Marie Jules Justin was a pupil of Luminais. He began exhibiting his works at the Salon in 1880 with *Office Corner* and continued to exhibit landscapes, still-lifes and genre subjects in the following years. In 1888 he put *Cheese Symphony in Brie Major* up for exhibition.

Museums and Galleries:

Castres: *The Barn of the Vatinet in Criquebeuf* - Soissons: *Cheese Symphony in Brie Major.*

Auction records:

Lindau, 9 May 1979, *Young Breton Woman Knitting* (oil on canvas, 13 x 9 1/2 ins / 33 x 24 cm) DEM 2,100.

JUSTIN, Pierre
French, 18th century.
Active in Dieppe in 1700.
Ivory worker.

JUSTINART, Berthe A.
French, 19th - 20th century.
Active in Paris.
Painter.

Berthe A. Justinart became a member of the Société des Artistes Français in 1898 and exhibited at the society's Salons.

JUSTINAT, Augustin Oudart, or Justinar
French, 18th century.
Died 12 March 1743.
Active in Paris.
Painter. Portraits.

Augustin Oudart Justinat was a member of the Académie St-Luc and court painter to Louis XV. He painted a portrait of the king, of which he made 11 copies. Engravings have been made after two of his portraits: those of *E. Baugier* and the *Cardinal L. A. de Noailles.*

JUSTITZ, Alfred
Czech, 20th century.
Born 19 July 1879, in Nova Cerekev; died 9 February 1934, in Bratislava.
Painter. Figures, landscapes, still-lifes.

Alfred Justitz studied at the Academy in Prague with Professor Thiele, then in Karlsruhe under Schmid-Reutte and in Berlin. He spent some time in Paris in 1910, where he studied Ingres, Puvis de Chavanne, Courbet and Cézanne. He spent more time there in 1923 when he got to know André Derain, who was to be a dominant influence on his work. His career was interrupted by World War I, in which he was involved as a soldier.

He painted landscapes, still-lifes and figures. The female nudes and still-lifes he painted at the height of his powers are strongly influenced by the Cubist works of Georges Braque, toned down a little as in the works of Jean Souverbie. His major works include: *Gypsies,* which expresses a mixture of the formalism of Cézanne and Czech Expressionism, and *Bathsheba* (1927), a picture painted in a synthetic Cubist style. Alfred Justitz is regarded as a key figure in modern Czech painting. He exhibited several times in Prague, in 1911 in Munich and in 1921 in Berlin.

Bibliography:

Zykmund, Vaclav, *Alfred Justitz,* Nakladatelstui, Prague, 1962. *Fifty years of Czechoslovak Painting from the Collections of the Galleries, 1918-1958,* exhibition catalogue, Slovenska Národna Gál., Bratislava, 1968 (in commemoration of the 50th anniversary of the Republic of Czechoslovakia).

Museums and Galleries:

Prague (Národní Gal.): three works.

Auction records:

London, 13 March 1996, *Washing* (1928, watercolour and coloured chalks/charcoal, 18 x 15 ins / 46 x 38 cm) GBP 1,265. London, 19 March 1997, *Female Bathers* (1919, watercolour/paper, 16 1/2 x 20 1/2 ins / 42 x 52 cm) GBP 8,970. Prague, 18 Nov 2000, *Susanna Bathing* (oil on plywood, 32 x 24 ins / 81 x 61 cm) CZK 400,000. Prague, 18 Nov 2000, *Still-life with Vase and Fruit* (1932, oil on canvas, 22 x 28 ins / 55 x 70 cm) CZK 600,000. Munich, 19 May 2001, *Still-life with Fruit* (1931, oil on canvas, 18 x 22 ins / 46 x 56 cm) DEM 12,000. London, 24 Oct 2001, *Still-life with Bowl of Fruit* (1931, oil on canvas, 19 x 22 ins / 47 x 56 cm) GBP 5,000. Prague, 30 Nov 2002, *Bouquet of Yellow Flowers in a Vase* (oil on plywood, 22 x 17 ins / 57 x 43 cm) CZK 140,000. Boston, 16 May 2003, *Still-life with Chrysanthemums* (oil on canvas, 26 x 21 ins / 65 x 54 cm) USD 3,500.

JUSTO, Johannes de
15th century.
Painter.

In 1469 King Ferdinand of Naples sent Johannes de Justo to Bruges to study painting. On 20 January 1470 Johannes received a payment of 34 ducats.

JUSTO ALEMÁN
Spanish, 16th century.
Active in Seville at the beginning of the 16th century.
Painter.

On 18 September 1519, five Flemish crosses were bought from him.

JUSTUS, Elisabeth
German, 20th century.
Sculptor.

Elisabeth Justus was active in Hamburg.

JUSTUS, Paul
French, 19th century.
Painter. History painting, portraits.

Paul Justus exhibited religious subjects and portraits at the Salon in 1845 and 1846.

JUSTUS D'ALLAMAGNA. See **GIUSTO d'Allamagna**

JUSTUS DA PADUA. See **MENABUOI Giusto di Giovanni de**

JUSTUS VERUS AB EGMONT. See **EGMONT Justus van**

JUSTUS VON RAVENSBURG. See **GIUSTO d'Allamagna**

JUSTYNE, P. William
British, 19th century.
Born 1812, in Rochester (Kent); died 6 June 1883.
Active in London.
Painter, draughtsman. Landscapes.

P. William Justyne worked mainly as an illustrator. Nottingham Museum and Art Gallery houses fourteen of his works in watercolour, India ink, and sepia. He exhibited landscapes in London in 1837 and 1838, at the Royal Academy and at Suffolk Street.

Museums and Galleries:

Nottingham (Castle Mus. & AG): 14 illustrations.

JUSZKÖ, Jeno
Hungarian, 20th century.
Born 1880, in Hungary.
Active in the USA.
Sculptor, medallist.

Jeno Juszkö was a student of E. von Hellmer in Vienna and G.J. Thomas in Paris. He settled in New York in 1906, and was a member of the Salmagundi Club. He taught at the Academy of Fine Art in Philadelphia in 1913-1914 and at the National Academy of Design in New York from 1919 to 1924.

He modelled portrait medals in particular, including a series of portraits of illustrious men. He created a monument to Archbishop J.B. Lamy in Santa Fé (New Mexico). He exhibited in 1904 in Paris and appeared at the International Exhibition in 1903 in Milan.

JUTAND, Pierre
French, 20th century.
Born 27 December 1935, in Paris.
Painter, designer. Landscapes with figures, urban landscapes, landscapes.

After leaving the École Boulle, Pierre Jutand studied under Gromaire, Lurçat and Brianchon. His landscapes and still-lifes are painted in a figurative style. He exhibited in Paris at the Salon des Indépendants and at the Salon de la Société Nationale des Beaux-Arts. He also showed his work in solo exhibitions, including at the Galerie St-Hubert in Lyons in 2003.

JUTEAU, Emma Cécile
French, 19th - 20th century.
Born 1875, in Le Havre.
Painter. Flowers.

MUSEUMS AND GALLERIES:
MULHOUSE: *Flowers*.

JUTOVSKY, Boris
20th century.
Born 1932.
Painter.

JUTREM, Arn Jan
Norwegian, 20th century.
Born 1929, in Oslo.
Painter.

Lyricism and emotion underlies Arn Jan Jutrem's abstract paintings.

JUTSAYTIS, Antoine
Lithuanian, 19th - 20th century.
Born 30 October 1868, in Lithuania.
Active in France.
Sculptor.

Antoine Jutsaytis studied in Odessa, Munich and Paris. He exhibited at the Salon of the Société Nationale des Beaux-Arts in Paris in 1912 and 1922 showing the following works: *Marble Bust of G. Kutschinki*; a decorative piece entitled *Tree*; statuettes entitled *Girl from Alsace*, *Day* and *Small Beauce Shepherd Dog*. He also exhibited a granite *Head of an Eskimo* at the Salon d'Automne, Paris (1921).

JUTSUM, Henry
British, 19th century.
Born 1816, in London; died 3 March 1869, in St John's Wood.
Painter, watercolourist. Genre scenes, landscapes with figures, landscapes.

Henry Jutsum studied art in Devon and Kensington; he was also a student of James Stark. His work was first seen in 1836 at the Royal Academy. In 1843, he became a member of the New Water-Colour Society. He exhibited at the British Institution. After 1847, he worked nearly exclusively in oils.

MUSEUMS AND GALLERIES:
BLACKBURN: a watercolour - LONDON (Victoria and Albert Mus.): a watercolour; *Landscape*.

AUCTION RECORDS:
LONDON, 1863, *Cornfield*, FRF 3,415. LONDON, 30 Nov 1907, *Edge of the Wood*, GBP 1. LONDON, 19 July 1909, *Hunters in a Wood* (1846) GBP 12. LONDON, 24 April 1911, *Thames at Low Tide*, GBP 8. LONDON, 17 Sept 1943, *Near Godalming* (drawing) GBP 99; *Near Sevenoaks* (drawing) GBP 105; *Near Tunbridge Wells* (drawing) GBP 42. LONDON, 9 June 1967, *River Landscape with Figures*, Gns 950. LONDON, 23 June 1971, *Landscape*, GBP 1,300. LONDON, 20 Nov 1973, *Wooded Landscape with Figures*, GBP 1,300. LONDON, 6 Jan 1976, *Landscape* (oil on canvas, 18 x 25 ins / 46 x 63.5 cm) GBP 300. LONDON, 13 May 1977, *Children Beside a Pool* (1845, oil on canvas, 18 1/2 x 33 ins / 47 x 84 cm) GBP 900. LONDON, 19 May 1978, *Landscape by the River, Berwickshire* (oil on canvas re-mounted/panel, 14 1/2 x 20 ins / 37 x 51 cm) GBP 750. LONDON, 20 July 1979, *Hatfield Park, Hertfordshire* (oil on canvas, 15 1/2 x 28 3/4 ins / 39.3 x 73 cm) GBP 1,100. LONDON, 11 March 1980, *Children sitting in a Landscape* (1862, watercolour and gouache, 11 3/4 x 20 ins / 30 x 50.5 cm) GBP 650. LONDON, 6 Feb 1981, *Shepherd and Flock in a Wooded Landscape* (1861, oil on canvas, 13 1/2 x 27 1/2 ins / 34.2 x 70 cm) GBP 1,500. AUCHTERARDER, 28 Aug 1984, *The River Nidd, near Knaresborough, Yorks* (1845, oil on canvas, 30 x 48 ins / 76.2 x 122 cm) GBP 2,500. LONDON, 21 Nov 1984, *A Gentleman with his Water Spaniels out Shooting* (1865, watercolour on pencil outlines heightened with gouache, 6 1/2 x 11 ins / 16.5 x 27 cm) GBP 1,800. LONDON, 16 April 1986, *Valley in Devon* (1861, oil on canvas, 14 1/4 x 28 1/4 ins / 36 x 72 cm) GBP 1,900. LONDON, 9 Feb 1990, *Small Farm near the River with a Servant Feeding Ducks* (oil on canvas, 13 3/4 x 17 3/4 ins / 35 x 45.2 cm) GBP 2,420. LONDON, 25-26 April 1990, *Mother and Child by a Stile* (1869, watercolour, 11 1/2 x 8 1/4 ins / 29 x 21 cm) GBP 715. LONDON, 15 June 1990, *The Remains of Last Winter* (1856, oil on canvas, 27 1/2 x 40 ins / 69.9 x 101.6 cm) GBP 4,950. LONDON, 27 Sept 1994, *The Cavalier's Courtship* (1866, oil on panel, 12 x 9 ins / 30.5 x 22 cm) GBP 1,035. NEW YORK, 12 Dec 1996, *Harvesters in a Landscape* (oil on canvas, 17 x 24 1/2 ins / 43.2 x 62.2 cm) USD 7,475. LONDON, 5 Nov 1997, *Cattle Beside a River* (oil on canvas, 24 x 35 3/4 ins / 61 x 91 cm) GBP 4,140. LONDON, 19 April 1999, *Going to Market. Crossing the Brook* (1850, watercolour, a pair, 11 x 7 ins / 29 x 19 cm) GBP 1,900. LONDON, 9 Sept 1999, *Woodcutters Resting by Stream* (oil on canvas, 15 x 23 ins / 38 x 58 cm) GBP 2,000. LONDON, 9 March 2000, *Cattle Watering in a Wooded River Landscape* (1843, oil on panel, 10 x 13 ins / 25 x 34 cm) GBP 1,300. ILKLEY, 21 June 2000, *Landscape with Figures and Cottage* (1859, watercolour, 16 x 12 ins / 41 x 30 cm) GBP 1,500. BURY ST EDMUNDS, 8 March 2001, *Highland River Landscape with Sheep on the Village Path* (1860, watercolour, 15 x 26 ins / 39 x 66 cm) GBP 3,400. LONDON, 8 March 2001, *Herd of Deer in a Wooded River Landscape, near Kenilworth* (1860, oil on canvas, 24 x 38 ins / 61 x 96 cm) GBP 4,000. LONDON, 7 March 2002, *Family Resting by a Path* (oil on canvas, 14 x 25 ins / 36 x 63 cm) GBP 2,800. LONDON, 28 Aug 2002, *Highland Loch* (1871, oil on canvas, 35 x 59 ins / 88 x 150 cm) GBP 3,200. LEEDS, 4 Feb 2003, *Angler by a River* (1853, pencil and watercolour, 11 x 19 ins / 28 x 47 cm) GBP 2,400. CHESTER, 14 July 2004, *Cows Being Driven Across a Stone Bridge* (1859, oil on canvas, 11 x 15 ins / 27 x 37 cm) GBP 1,800. CHESTER, 3 Nov 2004, *Hunting Party in a Woodland Clearing* (1867, oil on panel, 19 x 12 ins / 47 x 31 cm) GBP 1,950.

JUTTI, Pierre Adolphe
French, 19th century.
Born 16 March 1800, in Paris; died 15 June 1831, in Paris.
Painter, decorative designer.

Pierre Jutti was a pupil of Daguerre and Ciceri. In 1821 he went to Warsaw as the guest of Osinski, director of the National Theatre of Warsaw. During his stay there Jutti produced several decorative works. He was also the director of the little French theatre at the Saxony palace in Warsaw. At the Warsaw exhibition in 1823 he exhibited his *Entrance to a Gothic Church*. In 1824 he left Warsaw for Paris and worked as a director at the Variety theatre.

JUTTNER, Franz
German, 20th century.
Painter, draughtsman, watercolourist.

Franz Juttner was active in Friedenau. He exhibited drawings, watercolours and caricatures in Berlin in 1909.

JÜTTNER, Franz Albert
German, 20th century.
Born 23 April 1865, in Lindenstadt.

Painter, watercolourist, draughtsman, illustrator.
Franz Albert Jüttner lived in Wolfenbüttel. He began his career as a decorative painter, turned next to drawing illustrations for comic magazines, novels and children's books, and then to caricatures of politicians, students and animals. He painted in oils and watercolours and did pen and ink drawings. His works include *The Guitar, Curiosity, Gossip* and *Birch Trees in the Wind.*
Museums and Galleries:
Berlin (Nationalgal.): original designs.

JUTZ, Adolf Gustav
German, 20th century.
Born 20 June 1887, in Freiburg in Breisgau.
Painter, draughtsman. Religious subjects, portraits, landscapes.
Adolf Jutz studied at the Akademie der Bildenden Künste in Karlsruhe and also at the Académie Ranson in Paris. He featured regularly in the New Secession exhibition, mainly with graphic works.

JÜTZ, Julie Dorothea
Maiden name: Schmid
Swiss, 19th century.
Baptised 28 April 1795 in Bern; died 29 September 1852, in Bern.
Painter.
Jütz exhibited in Bern in 1830.

JUTZ, Karl
German, 19th - 20th century.
Born 22 September 1838, in Windschläg; died 1916, in Paffendorf (Koblenz).
Painter. Genre scenes, animals, farmyard scenes, landscapes with figures, still-lifes.
Karl Jutz studied in Munich and Düsseldorf. He won medals in Vienna in 1873, in Sydney in 1879 and in Melbourne in 1881.
Museums and Galleries:
Düsseldorf: *Poultry Yard* - Frankfurt am Main: *Henhouse* - Kaliningrad: *Ducks; Chickens* - Leipzig: *Hen, Ducks and Chickens* - Mulhouse: *Dead Wild Boar.*
Auction records:
New York, 17 Jan 1902, *Chickens,* USD 210. Cologne, 22 Oct 1965, *The Henhouse,* DEM 12,000. Cologne, 26 Nov 1970, *The Poultry Yard,* DEM 10,800. Cologne, 26 March 1971, *The Poultry Yard,* DEM 21,000. Vienna, 10 April 1973, *The Duckpond,* ATS 70,000. Cologne, 12 Nov 1976, *The Poultry Yard* (1896, oil on panel, 5 1/4 x 6 3/4 ins / 13.5 x 17 cm) DEM 30,000. Munich, 9 March 1978, *Wild Ducks Taking Off* (1898, oil on panel, 7 3/4 x 12 ins / 20 x 30.5 cm) DEM 14,000. Cologne, 22 Nov 1979, *Birds by a Pond* (oil on panel, 7 x 9 ins / 17.7 x 23 cm) DEM 50,000. Cologne, 21 May 1981, *The Duckpond* (1892, oil on panel, 5 1/4 x 6 1/2 ins / 13.5 x 16.7 cm) DEM 48,000. London, 22 June 1983, *Poultry Yard* (1870, oil on canvas, 9 x 11 ins / 23 x 28 cm) GBP 8,000. London, 19 March 1986, *Peacock, Turkey and Other Fowls in a Farmyard* (oil on canvas, 14 1/2 x 18 1/2 ins / 37 x 47 cm) GBP 32,000. Cologne, 25 June 1987, *Cockfight* (pen and wash, 14 1/2 x 18 1/2 ins / 37 x 47 cm) DEM 6,000. London, 23 March 1988, *Ducks by a Pond* (oil on canvas, 9 x 12 1/4 ins / 22 x 31 cm) GBP 9,900. Cologne, 15 Oct 1988, *The Poultry Yard* (oil on panel, 5 1/4 x 6 1/2 ins / 13.5 x 16.6 cm) DEM 46,000. New York, 23 Feb 1989, *The Duckpond* (1874, oil on panel, 5 1/4 x 7 1/4 ins / 13.3 x 18.7 cm) USD 18,700. Munich, 10 May 1989, *On the Farm* (1897, oil on canvas, 15 x 19 1/4 ins / 38 x 49 cm) DEM 82,500. Munich, 31 May 1990, *Ducks by a Pond* (oil on panel, 3 3/4 x 5 ins / 9.5 x 13 cm) DEM 30,800. New York, 20 Feb 1992, *The Duckpond* (oil on panel, 5 1/4 x 6 1/2 ins / 13.3 x 16.8 cm) USD 27,500; *Poultry in a Farmyard* (oil on panel, 8 x 10 1/4 ins / 20.3 x 26 cm) USD 13,200. Munich, 10 Dec 1992, *Kid Coming to Play by a Hen and her Chicks* (1868, oil on canvas, 20 x 27 1/2 ins / 50.5 x 70 cm) DEM 53,110. Munich, 7 Dec 1993, *Anglers beside a Mountain Tarn* (oil on canvas, 11 1/2 x 9 ins / 29 x 23 cm) DEM 28,750. New York, 16 Feb 1994, *Poultry in a Farmyard* (oil on canvas, 15 x 19 ins / 38.1 x 48.3 cm) USD 51,750. London, 15 Nov 1995, *Poultry in front of a Barn* (oil on canvas, 8 3/4 x 11 ins / 22.5 x 27 cm) GBP 13,800. Paris, 26 March 1996, *The Poultry Yard* (1862, oil on canvas, 26 1/2 x 32 3/4 ins / 67 x 83 cm) FRF 320,000. Munich, 25 June 1996, *Ducks by the Pond* (oil on panel, 9 x 7 ins / 22 x 18 cm) DEM 55,200. New York, 24 Oct 1996, *Peacock in a Poultry Yard* (1902, oil on canvas, 15 x 19 ins / 38.1 x 48.3 cm) USD 46,000. London, 9 Oct 1997, *Behind the House: Peacock, Hen and Ducks* (oil on canvas, 15 x 19 ins / 38 x 48.4 cm) GBP 36,700.

JÜTZ, Karl (Jr.)
German, 20th century.
Painter.
Karl Jütz was active in Düsseldorf. He exhibited in Berlin in 1909.

JUUEL, Andreas Thomas
Danish, 19th century.
Born 17 October 1817, in Copenhagen; died 21 August 1868, in Copenhagen.
Painter (including porcelain). Portraits, landscapes.
Andreas Juuel studied at the royal Copenhagen porcelain factory and at the Kunstakademi in Copenhagen. He exhibited landscapes from 1836 to 1855. Two of these, *View of Skanderborg* and *Laaland Farm,* are in the royal collection. In 1847 he won a prize for his painting *Storm on an Autumn Day.* He also executed a medallion portrait of the Landgrave family member *G. Hesse* for the Queen of England.
Museums and Galleries:
Bergen: porcelain service of King Frederik VII - Hillerød: *Portrait of the Preacher Jens Hornsyld* (after W. F. Bendz).
Auction records:
London, 4 Nov 1977, *The Broberg Family's Summer Residence in Springforbi, Denmark* (1852, oil on canvas, 22 x 30 ins / 56 x 76 cm) GBP 2,200. London, 5 Feb 1982, *A Country House in Springfors* (1852, oil on canvas, 22 x 29 1/2 ins / 55.7 x 75 cm) GBP 2,600. London, 24 June 1983, *Geels Bakke, near Copenhagen* (1851, oil on canvas, 14 x 19 3/4 ins / 35.5 x 50 cm) GBP 6,200. London, 7 Feb 1986, *Children in a Landscape* (oil on canvas, 24 1/2 x 35 ins / 62 x 89 cm) GBP 3,500. Copenhagen, 28 Oct 1987, *Landscape with Lake* (1845, oil on canvas, 18 1/2 x 26 1/2 ins / 47 x 67 cm) DKK 27,000. Copenhagen, 25-26 April 1990, *Wooded Path Leading to a Thatched Cottage* (1843, oil on canvas, 12 1/4 x 15 ins / 31 x 38 cm) DKK 12,000. Copenhagen, 6 March 1991, *View from Furesøen through Flowered Branches* (1860, oil on canvas, 9 x 11 ins / 22 x 28 cm) DKK 6,400. Copenhagen, 5 Feb 1992, *Partial View of Furesøen Surrounded by a Garland of Flowers* (1860, oil on canvas, 9 x 11 ins / 22 x 28 cm) DKK 5,500. London, 27 Nov 1992, *Geels Bakke near Copenhagen* (1851, oil on canvas, 34 x 20 ins / 86.2 x 50.6 cm) GBP 7,150. Ahlden, 23 April 1999, *Bright Summer's Day in an Upper Bavarian Village* (1854, oil on canvas, 22 x 31 ins / 55 x 78 cm) DEM 16,000. Aarhus, 28 Aug 2000, *Seascape* (oil on canvas, 9 x 13 ins / 22 x 32 cm) DKK 13,000. Copenhagen, 6 Sept 2000, *Beach at Öresund* (oil on canvas, 23 x 33 ins / 59 x 85 cm) DKK 70,000. Copenhagen, 5 March 2001, *Street Scene with Figures, Lumskebugten* (1852, pen and pencil, 8 x 11 ins / 20 x 29 cm) DKK 20,000. Vejle, 14 March 2001, *Coastal Landscape with Figures and Boats* (oil on canvas, 15 x 23 ins / 38 x 58 cm) DKK 18,000.

JUUL, Ole
Norwegian, 19th century.
Born 1852.
Painter. Landscapes.
Ole Juul studied in Bergen and at the academy in Düsseldorf. He was unknown until he showed his landscape studies in

Oslo in December 1922, and in Drontheim and Bergen in 1924. These exhibits resulted in his becoming a sensation. Some of his works are in the Drontheim gallery.

JUVANIS, Francesco. See **GIOVANI**

JUVARA, Aloisio Tommaso
Italian, 19th century.
Born 13 January 1809, in Messina; died 30 May 1875, in Rome.
Draughtsman, engraver.

Aloisio Juvara studied at the Accademia di S Luca, Rome, and in Parma. He was first recognised for engraving two plates for the studio of engraving in Rome, *St John*, after Guercino, and *St Bartholomew*, after Camuccini. He exhibited at the Exposition Universelle in Paris in 1855 and 1857, in London in 1862, and at the academy in Berlin in 1868, where he received the lesser gold medal for his most important work, *Madonna of the Palace of Naples*, after Raphael. Among his other works are *St Charles Borromeo*, after Mancinelli, and *Portrait of the Marquis Niccola Santangelo*, from a drawing of his own. Other plates by him are mainly portraits after Rembrandt, Rubens and other masters.

JUVARRA, Filippo, or Juvara or Juara or Ivara
Italian, 18th century.
Born 1676, in Messina; died 1736, in Madrid.
Active in Italy and Spain.
Architect, engraver (etching).

Juvarra trained under Carlo Fontana in Rome. In 1714, Victor Amadeus II summoned him to the court in Turin, where he remained almost 20 years, with the exception of the quite considerable number of journeys which he made. He built several churches in Turin, including the Basilica de Superga. He also built the Madame Palace and drew plans for the Palace of Stupinigi. He died during a journey to Madrid. He engraved 37 panels for *Raccolta di varie Targhe*. He worked in Italy and Spain. He is particularly known as an architect. Nevertheless, modern critics have been attracted by his architectural designs, which were etched in the style of Piranesi in a surprisingly bold manner.

AUCTION RECORDS:
LONDON, 7 July 1976, *Architectural Fantasy* (pen and wash, 5¼ x 7¾ ins / 13.2 x 19.8 cm) GBP 1,000. LONDON, 25 June 1981, *Façade of an Italian Palace (front); Arches (back)* (pencil, pen and wash, study, 9¼ x 15¼ ins / 23.5 x 38.5 cm) GBP 2,600. LONDON, 13 Dec 1984, *Scenery Plan* (black chalk, pen and wash, 7¾ x 7½ ins / 19.9 x 19.2 cm) GBP 14,000. LONDON, 11 Dec 1985, *Scenery Plan; an Ampitheatre* (black chalk, pen and wash, 7½ x 6¾ ins / 19.3 x 17.1 cm) GBP 7,000. LONDON, 3 July 1995, *Study of Decoration for an Altar Top Dedicated to St Joseph in the Church of St Teresa of Turin* (ink and black chalk, 6½ x 8¾ ins / 16.5 x 22.1 cm) GBP 3,220.

JUVENALIS DE URBE VETERI.
See **GIOVENALE Johanalis**

JUVENEL, Esther, or Juvenell
Bavarian School, 17th century.
Born in Nuremberg; died after 1673, in Pozsony (now Bratislava, Slovakia).
Painter.

Esther Juvenel was the daughter and pupil of Paul Juvenel.

JUVENEL, Friedrich, or Juvenell
Bavarian School, 17th century.
Born 1609, in Nuremberg; died 1642 or 1647.
Painter, decorative designer. Perspectives.

Friedrich Juvenel was the son and pupil of Paul Juvenel.

AUCTION RECORDS:
PARIS, 5 Nov 1941, *The Circumcision*, FRF 2,880. PARIS, 11 April 1945, *The Circumcision*, FRF 4,200.

JUVENEL, Johann, or Juvenell
Bavarian School, 17th century.
Born in Nuremberg; died 1641.
Painter. History painting.

Johann Juvenel was the son and pupil of Paul Juvenel. He lived in Vienna for some years.

JUVENEL, Johann Philipp, or Juvenell
Bavarian School, 17th century.
Born in Nuremberg; died 1650.
Painter, decorative designer. Perspectives.

Johann Philipp Juvenel was the son and pupil of Paul Juvenel; he lived in Vienna.

JUVENEL, Nicolas, or Juvenell, pseudonym: Nicola Nicolai
Bavarian School, 16th century.
Born probably in 1540, in the Netherlands; died 1597, in Nuremberg.
Painter, architect.

Nicolas Juvenel was the son of a painter. On finishing his apprenticeship, he moved to Nuremberg to work as a stained glass artist, and as a painter of portraits, historical scenes, architecture and miniatures. His works have often been confused with those of his son, Paul. They include *Christ and the Woman Taken in Adultery*, in the castle in Nuremberg, the *Annunciation*, in the art gallery in Vienna, and 82 figures, each representing a different nation, in Bamberg.

MUSEUMS AND GALLERIES:
MUNICH: *Duke Louis of Bavaria; A Couple* - NUREMBERG (Germanisches Nationalmus.): *Portrait of a Woman* - VIENNA: *Annunciation*.

JUVENEL, Paul, the Elder, or Juvenell
Bavarian School, 17th century.
Born 1579, in Nuremberg; died 1643, in Pozsony (now Bratislava, Slovakia).
Painter. Religious subjects, landscapes, church interiors.

Paul Juvenel was the son of Nicolas Juvenel. After an initial grounding from his father, he became a pupil of Adam Elsheimer in Frankfurt. He remained there some time, decorating churches and making excellent copies of old Flemish and German masters, particularly Dürer, adopting in turn the styles of Frans Franken, Tintoretto and Callot. Noted works of his at the Rathaus in Nuremberg include *The German Emperor on His Throne*, *Horatius Cocles*, and *Attila Marching on Rome*. Other works include an *Assumption of the Virgin* in Frankfurt and a *View of Rome* at the gallery in Munich. He had three sons and a daughter who were also painters.

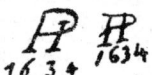

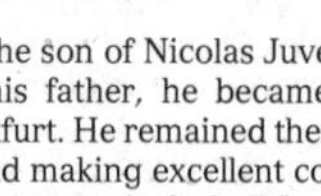

MUSEUMS AND GALLERIES:
VIENNA: *View of Rome*.

AUCTION RECORDS:
PARIS, 5 Nov 1941, *The Adulterous Woman* (1632) FRF 20,000. VIENNA, 15 June 1971, *The Last Supper*, ATS 90,000. LONDON, 5 July 1989, *Church Interiors with Figures* (1629, oil on panel, 18¾ x 15¾ ins / 47.5 x 40 cm) GBP 8,800. LONDON, 27 Oct 1993, *The Baptism of Christ* (1621, oil on panel, 19¼ x 33 ins / 49 x 84 cm) GBP 5,980. LONDON, 10 July 2001, *Interior of the Augustan Church in Nuremberg with Elegant Figures* (1626, oil on copper, 15 x 11 ins / 38 x 29 cm) GBP 5,500. PARIS, 31 March 2003, *Tribute to Caesar* (1630, oil on panel, 38 x 52 ins / 97 x 132 cm) EUR 5,200. MUNICH, 19 Sept 2003, *In the Temple* (1630, oil on panel, 13 x 24 ins / 34 x 62 cm) EUR 9,000.

JUVENELL. See **JUVENEL**

JUVIA, Jean de
French, 16th century.
Painter.
Siret refers to him as a native of the diocese of Laon.

JUVIAC, Jean de
French, 14th century.
Painter.
He is recorded as having worked in Avignon in 1390, and was also active in Laon.

JUVIN, Françoise
French, 20th century.
Born 3 August 1926, in Nancy.
Painter. Landscapes.
Lyons School.
From 1942 to 1947 Françoise Juvin studied at the École des Beaux-Arts in Lyons. From 1947 to 1999 she was an art teacher. Her work is similar to that of Truphémus. A colourist, Juvin paints landscapes of the Nord region of France, of Provence and of Italy. She took part in numerous group exhibitions, including: at the Salon de la Jeune Peinture in Paris (1958); at the Galerie Romanet in Paris (1959, 1960, 1961); and at the *École Lyonnaise* (*Lyons School*) exhibition at the Galerie Berlioz in Sausset-les-Pins (1988).

JUVIN, Juliette
French, 20th century.
Born 26 June 1896, in Paris.
Painter. Figures, interiors with figures, flowers.
Juliette Juvin was a self-taught artist. Originally an amateur, she was encouraged by Pascin, Heuzé and Chas-Laborde. Her work was shown in 2002 as part of the *Elles de Montparnasse* (*Women of Montparnasse*) exhibition at the Musée de Montparnasse which aimed to show the emancipation of female artists between World War I and II.

BIBLIOGRAPHY:
Campagne, Jean-Marc, *Louise Hervieu, Andrée Joubert, Juliette Juvin*, exhibition catalogue, La Palette bleue, Maison nationale des artistes, Paris, 1964.

AUCTION RECORDS:
PARIS, 19 Dec 1944, *Pot of Asters*, FRF 1,000. PARIS, 20 Feb 1990, *Interior* (oil on canvas, 23 1/2 x 32 ins / 60 x 81 cm) FRF 4,000. NEW YORK, 15 Nov 1990, *Women Bathing* (oil on panel, 12 1/2 x 12 1/4 ins / 31.8 x 31.1 cm) USD 16,500.

JUWEEL, Nicolaas
Dutch, 17th century.
Born in Rotterdam.
Still active c. 1690.
Miniaturist, draughtsman.
Nicolaas Juweel also painted in oils and watercolours in the style of Van der Werff. He is known for his town views.

JUYS, Jean de, or Juyf
French, 15th century.
Died between 1477 and 1479.
Painter, glassmaker.
Jean de Juys is recorded as living in Lyons in 1446, where he painted escutcheons, banners, canopies and decorations for the municipality. In 1463, he was commissioned, along with Jean Hortart and Étienne Du Puy, to prepare stage settings for performances that were due to be put on for the official visit to Lyons of Louis XI. Although the visit never took place, he prepared, with Hortart, portraits for the mystery play *Modus and Ratio*, which was due to be performed for the king.

JYNGE, Gert
Norwegian, 20th century.
Born 1904.
Painter.

K

K'I SIU. See **QI XU**

K'I-TSONG. See **QIZONG**

K'IAO TCHONG-TCH'ANG. See **QIAO ZHONG CHANG**

K'IEN-LONG. See **QIANLONG**

K'IEOU CHE. See **QIU SHI**

K'IEOU TI. See **QIU DI**

K'IEOU WEN-PO. See **QIU WENBO**

K'IEOU YING. See **QIU YING**

K'IEOU YU-K'ING. See **QIU YUQING**

K'IU YING-CHAO. See **QU YINGSHAO**

K'O CHE-HOUANG. See **KE SHIHUANG**

K'O CHIU-SSU. See **KE JIUSI**

K'O KIEOU-SSEU. See **KE JIUSI**

K'O SHIH-HUANG. See **KE SHIHUANG**

K'OUEN-TS'AN. See **KUNCAN**

K'UN T'SAN. See **KUNCAN**

K. F.
German, 16th century.
Monogram of a sculptor (ivory).
Ris-Paquot makes a reference to this artist.

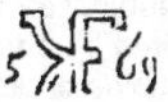

K. I. P.
French, 16th - 17th century.
Mark of an enameller.
This monogram is probably that of an enamel artist who worked in Limoges during the 16th and 17th centuries in Jean Penicaud II's workshop. According to Dr von Wurzbach, he was Jean Poillevé, a Limoges-based artist. His enamels include *Two Nude Children Playing the Lute and the Flute* (Paris, former Beurdeley collection) and *Battle between Cavaliers* (Paris, former collection of Charles Davillier).

AUCTION RECORDS:
PARIS, 1874, *Various Battle Scenes,* FRF 3,400. PARIS, 1884, *Warriors Fighting on Foot and on Horseback* (two plates) FRF 3,500.

KA, Peter van der
Flemish School, 18th century.
Born 21 February 1688, in Antwerp.
Sculptor.
Peter van der Ka was a member of the Jesuit Order and created the white marble communion bench in the church of the Assumption of the Virgin in Cologne.

KA-FO-TO
Chinese, 5th century.
Active in China at the end of the 5th century.
Painter.

KAA, Jan van der
Dutch, 19th century.
Born 1 November 1813, in Dordrecht; died 23 November 1877, in Rotterdam.
Painter. Figures, portraits, interiors, landscapes with figures.
A pupil of P. Hofman and J.-C. Bendorp, he worked in Rotterdam and travelled in Belgium and Germany.

AUCTION RECORDS:
NEW YORK, 30 June 1981, *The Rhine Guard* (1851, oil on canvas, 48 x 66 1/4 ins / 122 x 168 cm) USD 3,250. AMSTERDAM, 25 April 1990, *Figures in a Boat in a Mountain Landscape* (oil on canvas, 22 3/4 x 28 3/4 ins / 58 x 73 cm) NLG 3,450.

KAAN, Arthur
German, 19th - 20th century.
Born 24 February 1867, in Klagenfurt; died 1940.
Sculptor. Mythological figures, historical figures. Busts, statues.
Arthur Kaan studied with Zajouk in Vienna. He is best known for busts of children. His works include a *Statue of the Emperor Franz Joseph.*
AUCTION RECORDS:
VIENNA, 18 June 1985, *Achilles and Penthesilea* (bronze, 20 ins / 50.5 cm) ATS 25,000.

KAAN, I or J. See **KAENEN I.** or **J.,** or **Theodorus**

KAAN-ALBEST, Julius von
German, 19th - 20th century.
Born 8 March 1874, in Munich.
Painter, illustrator.
Julius von Kaan-Albest was active in Austria, especially in Steinach, in the Tyrol. He painted a huge canvas of *The Battle of Wagram* for the Theresienstadt Museum.

KAARBOE, Ragnhild
Norwegian, 20th century.
Painter.
Ragnhild Kaarboe was active around 1937.

KAARSGITER, F. J.
Dutch, 18th century.
Active in Amsterdam c. 1700.
Draughtsman.

KAAS, Jaap
Dutch, 20th century.
Born 1898, in Amsterdam; died 1972, in Amsterdam.
Active in Belgium.
Sculptor. Animals.
Jaap Kaas studied at the Rijksakademie in Antwerp. He became a professor at the Rotterdam academy.
MUSEUMS AND GALLERIES:
ANTWERP (Antwerp Zoo).

KAASKAMER, Claes Jansz.
Dutch, 17th century.
Active in Leiden c. 1653.
Sculptor (wood). Allegorical subjects.
MUSEUMS AND GALLERIES:
LEIDEN: *Allegorical Figure of Justice.*

KAAY, Cornelis
Dutch, 20th century.
Born 1905, in Haarlem.
Painter.
Cornelis Kaay was a street paver, who painted poetic rural landscapes depicting figures, usually lovers.
BIBLIOGRAPHY:
Gans, Louis, *Meesters der Europese naïven*, exhibition catalogue, Centraal Museum, Utrecht, 1970.

KAAZ, Carl Ludwig
German, 18th - 19th century.
Born 22 January 1773, in Karlsruhe; died 14 July 1810, in Dresden.
Engraver. Landscapes.
Kaaz is said by the *Boetticher Artists Dictionary* to have taught himself, drawing inspiration from Claude and Ruysdael. He worked in Italy and Paris from 1804 to 1807. On the other hand, *Bryan's Dictionary* says that his parents sent him to the academy in Stuttgart to study engraving with Johann Gotthard von Müller.
MUSEUMS AND GALLERIES:
KARLSRUHE: *Landscape.*
AUCTION RECORDS:
ZURICH, 9 June 1972, *Lakeside Landscape,* CHF 4,000. ZURICH, 25 Sept 2000, *Huon's Flight from Oberon* (gouache, 21 x 30 ins / 53 x 76 cm) CHF 5,000.

KABAKOV, Ilya Iossifovitch
Ukrainian, 20th century.
Born 30 September 1933, in Dnepropetrovsk.
Active since 1992 in the USA.
Painter (mixed media), watercolourist, collage artist, installation artist, draughtsman, illustrator.
Sots Art, Perestroika Art, Conceptual Art.
Boulevard Stretensky group.
Ilya Kabakov was evacuated in 1941 to Samarkand in Uzbekistan. In 1945 he was transferred to Moscow, where he studied from 1945 to 1951 at a secondary-level art school. From 1951 to 1957 he took courses in design and graphics at the Surikov Institute of Art. He was awarded an illustrator's diploma. He was a member of the Boulevard Stretensky group of conceptual artists. He took his first trip outside the Soviet Union in 1987-1988, taking advantage of a study grant from the city of Graz in Austria. In 1989 he spent some time in Germany with a grant from the city of Berlin. Since 1992 he has lived and worked in New York.

From the end of the 1950s, Kabakov worked as a children's book illustrator. In 20 years or so he illustrated over 100 books. His illustrations were traditional to begin with, although sometimes (even for official commissions), he would introduce irony, stamped with a humour that often borders on the absurd.

He works with coloured crayons, with very pale shades, and this gives his works a strong luminosity. With a simple, bare and carefully drawn stroke he makes the most of the theme of partial vision defined, for example, through a window or a plank with holes in. His subjects show the strength and vitality of his imaginative powers and give dreams an important position (as shown by his portrait of *Olga Markovna Ducouvercle and Matchenka Delacorne*) or, more often, verge on Surrealism, following on from Kafka and Ionesco. Works that he was not able to show at the time in his native country, which integrated the influence of Cézanne's late representation and of Abstract Expressionism, were displayed in Paris in the 1960s at the Galerie Dina Vierny. From 1970 onwards, he produced his series of more than 50 *Albums* presented as shirts filled with leaves, each album consisting of an illustrated account inspired by heroes of classical literature or invented characters. His modernity is in no way spectacular. Conventional practices remain, to the extent that Kabakov does not practise an art de rupture (fractured art). He nevertheless became the leader of the Muscovite avant-garde.

In addition to his illustrations and drawings, he painted the series of *Kitchens* (1981-1988), monochrome pictures in the midst of which hangs the most banal, everyday object possible (a cup or a saucepan) These unusual assemblages are invariably captioned, but with different names, as follows: "Olga Llinichna Suiko: To Whom does this Scraper Belong?, reply by Anna Petrovna Selenchuck: To Olga Markovna". His most spectacular designs since the beginning of the 1980s are his installations, such as that entitled *The Man Who Flew off into Space From His Apartment* (1981-1988), which was shown at the exhibition *Les Magiciens de la Terre* (*Magicians of the Earth*) in 1989 at the Centre Georges-Pompidou in Paris. This installation recreates an interior, the ceiling of which has been ripped off by the flight of this Leonardian dreamer with a rudimentary elastic seat. This work was part of a wider exhibition entitled *Ten Characters,* which had already been the subject of an album in the 1960s in Moscow. This exhibition was organised in 1988 at the Feldman gallery in New York, where Kabakov had changed the exhibition space for this occasion into 10 cramped rooms typical of Soviet communal dwellings in order to recreate their ambience and atmosphere. Each of these rooms was inhabited by a fictitious character. There, in addition to the person who dreamed of travelling through the cosmos, one could meet the man who had never thrown anything away or the collector of the opinions of others. 'The communal apartment is not a real object to me, but a metaphor', he stated. According to Kabakov, the urban environment of the Muscovites was favourable to the wanderings of the imagination: 'Everything, he says, is at a demolition or construction stage... but without always being able to tell them apart'. This unleashed imagination is the nerve centre of *Ten Characters.*

In *Incident in a Museum or Water Music* (1992), he twists head-on the themes of Socialist Realism, painting in this style, but still using the accompanying text. His installations also consist of his installation projects in the form of drawings. They are sometimes made up of hundreds of drawings, as in *River of Gold* (1986), which retrace the ups and downs of everyday life, the state-controlled fear of chaos and invariably the need for a bureaucratic search to measure order.

Text and image go hand in hand in Kabakov's works. He believes that the strength and advantage of the written word is its ability to deal with much wider problems than painting. The origin of this attitude lies in the history of the Russian avant-garde, which is unfamiliar to the Russian people themselves. Since the history of the avant-garde has been deliberately blurred, Russian citizens lack information about their past. In this sense Kabakov tries to include in his works all the reactions that this past has caused and that it continues to cause: interpretation, incomprehension, amazement... Leaving enough space for pluralism, he avoids splits and rifts between the commentators and the work and ironically relocates the latter in Russia's Realist, sentimental tradition. This physical presence of the text is also an indirect reference to the many observations and controls of the rights and responsibilities accompanying Soviet citizens throughout their lives.

Karbakov's art is more a consideration of the mechanisms of Socialist Realism than a head-on battle against it. In the 1960s, with others, he said the opposite of what the Muscovite avant-garde said and had been trying to say for a decade in its stormy relationship with authority, advocating an attitude that would negate Soviet values. Outside this trend, Kabakov became one of the main representatives, with Boulatov, of 'Soc Art' or 'Sots Art' (terms invented in 1972 by Komar and Melamid, by analogy with the terms pop art and Socialist Realism). Artists associated with this trend actually have a particular rapport with the Stalinist myth. They tend not to deny it, but to sublimate its form by including it as an historic period of contemporary thought. This apparent neutrality, for which some would criticise them, is in fact merely their almost scientific contact with ideology as a system of signs. In retrospect some, such as Margarita Tupitsyn, were able to describe this approach as 'an unprecedented case of Post-Modernist practice' and, as a result, include it in the history of the Western avant-garde.

Kabakov exhibited his works at solo exhibitions in Paris at the Galerie Dina Vierny, from the 1960s until the exhibition listed in 1992. A retrospective of his work was displayed at the Vieille Charité centre in Marseilles, at the Kunstverein in Düsseldorf then at the Centre National des Arts Plastiques in Paris in 1986. He also exhibited in 1988 at the Kunstverein in Graz; in 1989, *10 Characters*, Ronald Feldman Gallery in New York; in 1989, *Qui sont ces petits hommes blancs?* (*Who are these little white men?*), Galerie de France in Paris; in 1989, *10 Characters*, Riverside Studios in London; in 1989, Kunsthalle in Zurich; in 1989, *He Lost His Mind, Undressed, Ran Away Naked*, Ronald Feldman Gallery in New York; in 1990, Hirschhorn Museum, Washington; in 1992, Municipal Workshops in Marseilles; in 1993, Stedelijk Museum in Amsterdam; in 1994, Museum of Contemporary Art in Helsinki; in 1994, Centre of Contemporary Art, Le Magasin in Grenoble; in 1995, *C'est ici que nous vivons* (*This is Where We Live*), monumental installation, Musée national de l'art moderne, Centre de Création Industrielle in Paris; in 1998, *16 Installations*, Munkha in Antwerp; in 1999, Sprengel Museum in Hanover; in 2001, Continua Gallery in San Gimignano.

He has taken part in collective exhibitions, notably: in 1989, *Les Magiciens de la Terre* (*Magicians of the Earth*), Centre Georges-Pompidou in Paris; Documenta 9 in Kassel; in 1990, *Contemporary Russian Artists*, Luigi Pecci Museum of Contemporary Art, Prato (Tuscany); in 1992, Universal Exhibition in Seville; in 1993, he represented Russia at the Venice Biennale; in 1997, *Skulptur. Projekte in Münster 1997* (*Sculpture. Projects in Münster 1997*) in Münster; in 2003 *Esprit des Lieux* (*The Spirit of Places*), contemporary work and his display space, exhibition organised as part of the *Trésors publics, 20 ans de création dans les Fonds régionaux d'art contemporain (FRAC)* (*Public Treasury, 20 Years of Creation in the Regional Collection of Contemporary Art (FRAC)*), Palais des Papes in Avignon; in 2003, *Traumfabrik Kommunismus - die Visuelle Kultur der Stalinzeit* (*Dream Factory Communism, the Visual Culture of the Stalin Period*), Schirn Kunsthalle, Frankfurt; in 2003, *Berlin-Moscow/Moscow-Berlin 1950-2000*, a panorama exhibition which, following the exhibition covering 1900-1950, provided discussion material on 50 years of Germano-Russian artistic and cultural relations influenced by the political changes at the Martin-Gropius Bau in Berlin and the Tretyakov Gallery in Moscow.

Bibliography:

L'Avant-garde Russe, Moscou 73, exhibition catalogue, Paris, 1973. *Ilya Kabakov*, exhibition catalogue, Centre National des Arts Plastiques, Paris, 1987. Jolles, Claudia, '*Moscou années 80*' in *Les Cahiers du Musée National d'Art Moderne*, periodical, Paris, winter 1988. Tupitsyn, Margarita, '*Le Pop à la mode soviétique*' in *Les Cahiers du Musée National d'Art Moderne*, periodical, Paris, winter 1988. Martin, Jean-Hubert/Mark, Francis/Magnin, André/Marcadé, Bernard, *Les Magiciens de la terre*, group exhibition catalogue, Éd. du Centre Georges-Pompidou, Paris, 1989. '*Interview avec Kabakov*' in *Art International* n° 8, periodical, Paris, 1989. *Contemporary Russian Artists*, exhibition catalogue, Centro per l'Arte Contemporanea Luigi Pecci, Prato, 1990. Zahm, Olivier (preface), et al., *Trésors publics, 20 ans de création dans les Fonds régionaux d'art contemporain*, Flammarion, Paris, 2003 (text in French and English). Hollein, Max, et al., *Dream Factory Communism, the Visual Culture of the Stalin Period*, exhibition catalogue, Schirn Kunsthalle, Frankfurt, 2003 (text in English and German). '*Berlin-Moskau/Moskau-Berlin 1950-2000*' in *2 vols.*, exhibition catalogue, Martin-Gropius-Bau, Berlin, 2003 (text in German).

Museums and Galleries:

Châteaugiron (FRAC Brittany): *52 entretiens dans la cuisine communautaire* (*52 Interviews in the Communal Kitchen*) (1991) - Marfa, Texas (Chinati Foundation) - Oiron (Château).

Auction records:

Moscow, 7 July 1988, *Responses from the Experimental Group* (1970-1971, oil, Alkit enamel and a manuscript in black ink/card, 57 3/4 x 146 ins / 147 x 370 cm) GBP 22,000. London, 27 Oct 1994, *Victor Popov Says...* (1992, mixed media/paper, 9 x 13 ins / 23 x 33 cm) GBP 2,070. Paris, 29-30 June 1995, *Horse* (1965, colouring pencil/paper, 8 x 11 ins / 20.5 x 27 cm) FRF 31,000. New York, 22 Feb 1996, *Ivan Petrovich, may I install this stool here in this corner and settle down comfortably?* (1991, ink and colouring pencil/paper, 17 1/2 x 14 1/4 ins / 44.2 x 36.2 cm) USD 4,600. Paris, 28 April 1997, *Untitled* (1963, drawing pencil and collage/paper, 12 1/2 x 11 3/4 ins / 31.5 x 30 cm) FRF 16,000; *Komarov's Flight* (1972-1975, watercolour and ink/paper, 7 3/4 x 10 1/2 ins / 20 x 26.5 cm) FRF 31,000. Cologne, 10 Nov 2000, *Untitled* (1972, ink and colour pencil, 9 x 18 ins / 22 x 45 cm) DEM 5,500. Paris, 29 Jan 2001, *Zoia Alexandrovna Lech, Whose Is This Grater, Kitchen Series* (oil and grater on panel, 28 x 48 ins / 70 x 121 cm) FRF 120,000. London, 26 June 2003, *Untitled* (1968, 1970, colour pencil and ink on card, a pair, 8 x 11 ins / 20 x 27 cm) GBP 7,500. New York, 12 Nov 2003, *List of What I Was Supposed To Do before March 1961* (1989, enamel on masonite, pants and shirt, 102 x 75 ins / 260 x 190 cm) USD 120,000. New York, 29 June 2004, *Fly* (1997, watercolour and pencil, 4 x 9 ins / 10 x 24 cm) USD 3,500.

KABANOV, Andrei

Russian, 20th century.

Born 1927.

Painter. Genre scenes, figures.

Andrei Kabanov studied at the School of Art in Leningrad. He adopted the Divisionist and Pointillist technique of the French Neo-Impressionists, which he applied to genre scenes: *Silence*, *Waiting* and *Summer Reading*. He appeared from 1987 onwards at collective exhibitions of Russian art in

Moscow, Leningrad and Tallinn and in Western Europe in Brussels and Berlin.

BIBLIOGRAPHY:

L'École de Léningrad, auction catalogue, Drouot, Paris, 19 November 1990.

AUCTION RECORDS:

PARIS, 11 June 1990, *Silence* (oil on canvas, 19¾ x 15¾ ins / 50 x 40 cm) FRF 5,000. PARIS, 19 Nov 1990, *Inseparable Friends* (oil on canvas, 33½ x 23¼ ins / 85 x 59 cm) FRF 16,000. PARIS, 13 April 1992, *Meeting in the Park* (oil on canvas, 19¾ x 15¾ ins / 50 x 40 cm) FRF 11,500. PARIS, 17 June 1992, *Small Music and Dancing Restaurant* (oil on canvas, 17¾ x 22 ins / 45 x 56 cm) FRF 7,200. PARIS, 16 Nov 1992, *Terrace at the Edge of the Water* (oil on canvas, 23¼ x 19¾ ins / 59 x 50 cm) FRF 5,600.

KABANOV, Ivan Andreevich

Russian, 19th century.

Born 1819; died 12 December 1869.

Painter. Landscapes.

MUSEUMS AND GALLERIES:

MOSCOW (State Tretyakov Gal.): *Terrace near Rome*.

KABATCHEK, Leonid

Russian, 20th century.

Born 1923, in St Petersburg.

Painter. Figure compositions, landscapes.

Leonid Kabatchek studied at the Repin Institute of the Academy of Fine Art in Leningrad (now St Petersburg). He was a member of the Union of Artists of the USSR. From 1950 onwards, he exhibited in his native country and, from 1957, abroad, particularly in Tokyo. He also showed work at *L'Art de Leningrad* (*Art of Leningrad*) in Le Havre in 1983; at *Contemporary Art of the USSR* in Montreal in 1986 and *L'Art Russes, des Scythes à nos jours* (*Russian Art from the Scythians to Today*) at the Musée du Grand Palais de Paris in 1967.

BIBLIOGRAPHY:

L'École de Léningrad, auction catalogue, Drouot, Paris, 19 November 1990.

MUSEUMS AND GALLERIES:

DRESDEN (Gemäldegal.) - KIEV (Mus. of Russian Art) - MOSCOW (State Tretyakov Gal.) - ST PETERSBURG (Gosudarstvennyj Russkij Muz.) - ST PETERSBURG (MFA).

AUCTION RECORDS:

PARIS, 19 Nov 1990, *The Ball* (1951, oil on canvas, 6 x 11¼ ins / 15.5 x 28.5 cm) FRF 20,000. PARIS, 25 March 1991, *Village Fete* (1957, oil on card, 18 x 37¾ ins / 46 x 96 cm) FRF 34,000.

KABEL, Adrian and Adrian van der.

See **CABEL**

KABELL, Ludwig

Danish, 19th century.

Born 21 July 1853, in Veilby; died 1 February 1902, in Fredensborg.

Painter. Landscapes.

MUSEUMS AND GALLERIES:

COPENHAGEN (Statens Mus. for Kunst): *Path through the Village*.

AUCTION RECORDS:

COPENHAGEN, 16 March 1976, *Landscape* (1898, oil on canvas, 35 x 49¼ ins / 88 x 125 cm) DKK 2,700. STOCKHOLM, 19 April 1989, *Summer Afternoon in Kattegatt* (oil on canvas, 15¾ x 24½ ins / 40 x 62 cm) SEK 11,000. COPENHAGEN, 16 May 1994, *Peasant Woman with Little Boy in a Kitchen* (oil on canvas, 18½ x 15¾ ins / 47 x 40 cm) DKK 6,800. COPENHAGEN, 14 Feb 1996, *Summer Idyll in front of Country House with Beehives* (oil on canvas, 13¾ x 16¼ ins / 35 x 41 cm) DKK 5,600. STOCKHOLM, 18 May 1999, *Summer Landscape with Woman and Boy on Road* (oil on canvas, 19 x 29 ins / 48 x 74 cm) SEK 16,000. AHLDEN, 22 Sept 2000, *Summer's Day* (1881, oil on canvas, 28 x 43 ins / 71 x 110 cm) DEM 4,000. AARHUS, 26 Feb 2002, *Coastal Landscape with Rainbow* (oil on canvas, 36 x 58 ins / 91 x 147 cm) DKK 16,000. COPENHAGEN, 2 Dec 2002, *Kalkovn Woods near Holckenhavn, Nyborgfjord* (1899, oil on canvas, 29 x 48 ins / 74 x 123 cm) DKK 12,000. VIENNA, 22 May 2003, *Summer's Day* (1899, oil on canvas, 29 x 48 ins / 74 x 123 cm) EUR 5,000. VEJLE, 12 Jan 2004, *Landscape from Mons Klit with Rainbow, Cow and Milkmaid* (oil on canvas, 36 x 58 ins / 91 x 148 cm) DKK 70,000. COPENHAGEN, 25 Feb 2004, *Road through Hilly Landscape with Sheep Grazing, Lonstrup* (1899-1900, oil on canvas) DKK 14,000.

KABURAGI, Kiyokata, or Kaburaki, given name: Ken'ichi

Japanese, 20th century.

Born 1878, in Tokyo; died 1972.

Painter, draughtsman.

In 1890, in his report to the Japan Art Institute (Nihon bijutsuin), the painter Okakura Tenshin (1862-1913), who was the head of the Institute, defined six principles for the future direction of Japanese art. The first five insisted on the value of personal expression and the artistic spirit, on the dignity and the nobility of themes and on a solid technical basis. The sixth set out the broad lines of Nihon-ga (Japanese painting) of the modern era, emphasising historical painting in particular and *ukiyo-e*. By *ukiyo-e*', he said, 'I don't mean simply the usual wonderful portraits of men, women and children, because the *ukiyo-e*, just like the old scrolls (*emakimono*) should also describe the customs and appearances of the modern age. In fact historical painting may be called the *ukiyo-e* of the past and *ukiyo-e* the historical painting of the present.'

Of all the artists of the Nihon-ga of the end of the 19th century and the beginning of the 20th century none was more responsive to the ideas of Okakura than Kaburagi Kiyokata. He would be styled the creator of the new *ukiyo-e*. From a very early age Kaburagi began his technical education in this tradition in the studio of Mizuno Toshikata, a young disciple of Tsukioka Yoshitoshi, himself a pupil of Kuniyoshi (1797-1861), a late Edo master. It was there that Kaburagi would succeed in mastering the *ukiyo-e* watercolour technique, which would remain the fundamental chracteristic of all his work. But he was also a man of his time and quickly embraced realist and impressionist styles of Western painting. He applied himself to studying not only the *yo-ya* (Western style painting) of his predecessors and contemporaries, such as Kurudoa Seiki (1868-1912), but also the work of Renoir, especially his portraits of women. His first paintings were exhibited in 1897. They sought to establish a synthesis between Western-style realism and traditional *ukiyo-e*, and already contained all the elements that would later be found, albeit in more refined form, in the work of his maturity: emotion, the contemporary historical context, the compromise between realism and abstraction, from which shadow virtually disappears. Although not the most important and indeed not the only artist working in the *ukiyo-e* tradition, he is noteworthy for the way in which he perpetuates the style without losing any of its freshness or purity. He brought a human warmth and an emotional depth to the old *bijin-ga* (portraits of beauties) that it had never had: his bijin-ga portraits rival his Western-style oils in their realism. As a painter of the Meiji period (1868-1912), he was necessarily faced by thematic and stylistic problems connected with the encounter between East and West. That the synthesis he achieved in his work was so successful was largely due to his critical intelligence, which enabled him to draw on he widest range of sources without falling into confusion or the trap of eclecticism. In 1917, he was awarded the grand prize at the *Bunten* exhibition (the annual exhibition organised by the Ministry of Education) for a pair of screens entitled *Black*

Hair. In 1929 he became a member of the Imperial Academy and in 1954 was awarded the Order of Cultural Merit. Thereafter he exhibited annually and major retrospectives of his work were organised by the newspapers Asahi and Mainichi in Tokyo and Yokohama. Kiyokata spent the last four years of his life in quiet retreat at Kamakura, where he devoted himself to his writing. The first part of his autobiography *Koshikata no ki* appeared in 1961, which was followed by a second part *Zoku koshikata no ki* in 1969. Yet they were only part of his literary output.

BIBLIOGRAPHY:

Read, Louisa, '*Kaburagi Kiyokata*' in *Apollo p. 404-406*, periodical, London, March, 1975.

KACELI, Sadih

Albanian, 20th century.
Born 1914.
Painter, engraver. Landscapes.

Sadih Kaceli painted scenes of Albania. He also engraved on linoleum.

MUSEUMS AND GALLERIES:

TIRANA (AG): *Peasant*; *Seaside*; *Kruja Landscape* (engraving on lino).

KACER, Mania

German, 19th - 20th century.
Active in Mannheim.
Sculptor, painter.

Having started as a painter, Mania Kacer studied with Rodin and became a sculptor in the naturalist style.

KACERE, John

American, 20th century.
Born 23 June 1920, in Walker (Iowa); died 1999.
Painter. Nudes.

John Kacere showed artistic aptitude at an early age. He first trained as a commercial artist in Chicago where his exposure to the great masters, from Holbein to Degas, in the city's museums led to a shift in his career. During World War II, his interest turned to the moderns, for example, Picasso and Klee. After graduating from the university of Iowa, he taught first at the University of Manitoba in Winnipeg, Canada, moving on to, among others, the Rhode Island School of Design and the University of New Mexico. He rose to fame around 1970, in the wake of hyperrealism and its photo-realist variety although his technique differs as he works in layers of paints distributed all over the canvas.

The obsessive manner in which he has treated the female body, seeking to capture the sheen of a stocking or the interaction of delicate fabrics with womanly curves did not endear him to feminists and led some critics to dismiss his work as 'improbable eroticism, devoid of naturalism'. However, Kacere claimed that his work is not sexist, but praises the aspect of womanhood which is the 'source of all life, the source of regeneration'.

He took part in numerous group exhibitions from the early 1970s in the USA, all over Europe and in Japan (Tokyo Biennale). He showed his works in solo exhibitions in New York, Tucson, Paris and Hamburg.

BIBLIOGRAPHY:

Brach, Paul, *Kacere*, exhibition catalogue, Gal. Lavignes-Bastille, Éd. Filipacchi, Paris, 1989.

AUCTION RECORDS:

NEW YORK, 13 May 1977, *Blue Panties: Silken Slip (front view)* (1972, oil on canvas, 50 1/2 x 78 ins / 128 x 198 cm) USD 3,750. NEW YORK, 18 May 1979, *Study* (1975, graphite, 20 3/4 x 29 ins / 53 x 73.5 cm) USD 1,800. NEW YORK, 19 Oct 1979, *Marsha D.* (1972, oil on canvas, 55 x 81 ins / 140 x 205.8 cm) USD 8,250. NEW YORK, 13 May 1981, *Beth* (1972, oil on canvas, 57 1/4 x 80 3/4 ins / 145.5 x 205 cm) USD 11,000. NEW YORK, 3 May 1985, *Blue Panties: Silken Slip (front view)* (1972, oil on canvas, 50 x 78 ins / 127 x 197.2 cm) USD 8,000. NEW YORK, 20 Feb 1987, *Kathy M.* (1972, oil on canvas, 55 x 67 ins / 139.7 x 170.2 cm) USD 13,500. PARIS, 18 Feb 1990, *Cynthia* (1987, graphite/paper, 26 3/4 x 32 ins / 68 x 81 cm) FRF 13,500. NEW YORK, 23 Feb 1990, *M. Garibaldi I* (1974, acrylic/canvas, 54 x 80 ins / 137.2 x 203.2 cm) USD 19,800. NEW YORK, 27 Feb 1990, *Jutta* (1973, acrylic/canvas, 53 x 78 1/2 ins / 134.6 x 199.5 cm) USD 33,000. PARIS, 29 Oct 1990, *M. Garibaldi* (1974, 54 x 80 ins / 137 x 203 cm) FRF 100,000. PARIS, 14 Nov 1990, *Peggy* (1977, oil on canvas, 35 3/4 x 56 ins / 91 x 142 cm) FRF 155,000. PARIS, 16 June 1991, *M. Garibaldi I or Marsha I* (1974, oil on canvas, 54 x 80 ins / 137 x 203 cm) FRF 120,000. NEW YORK, 6 Oct 1992, *Allison* (oil on canvas, 38 x 78 ins / 96.5 x 198.1 cm) USD 14,300. PARIS, 11 June 1993, *Lorraine* (1983, graphite, 19 x 25 ins / 48 x 63.5 cm) FRF 10,000. PARIS, 18 Sept 1993, *Sally T.* (1972, acrylic/canvas, 66 1/4 x 72 ins / 168 x 182 cm) FRF 125,000. PARIS, 28 June 1994, *Transition* (1951, oil on harboard panel, 25 1/2 x 48 1/2 ins / 65 x 123 cm) FRF 12,500. PARIS, 11 Dec 1997, *Maija* (1974, watercolour and graphite/paper, 14 1/4 x 20 ins / 36 x 51 cm) FRF 20,500. PARIS, 27 April 2000, *Untitled* (oil on panel, 25 x 47 ins / 64 x 120 cm) FRF 31,000. SAN FRANCISCO, 24 Oct 2000, *Kelly, Red 77* (oil on canvas, 62 x 40 ins / 157 x 102 cm) USD 8,000. PARIS, 27 May 2004, *Dara* (1989, oil on canvas, 40 x 60 ins / 101 x 152 cm) EUR 17,000. PARIS, 27 May 2004, *Lorena* (1991, oil on canvas, 40 x 60 ins / 101 x 152 cm) EUR 40,000.

KACEROWSKY, W.

Russian, 20th century.
Painter. Landscapes with figures.

Kacerowsky's painting in heavy, coloured pastes tends towards abstraction.

AUCTION RECORDS:

PARIS, 14 May 1990, *Village in the Trees* (1989, oil/hardboard, 25 1/2 x 31 1/2 ins / 65 x 80 cm) FRF 5,000.

KACHAMAKOV, Atanas

Bulgarian, 20th century.
Born 18 January 1898, in Leskovetz.
Sculptor. Statues, busts, monuments.

Atanas Kachamakov received his artistic training in Sofia. He exhibited his sculptures in Bulgaria, Germany, Italy and America, and was awarded numerous distinctions, including a $1,500 prize for a representation of a Native American Indian at the American Society of Arts in 1931.

He sculpted a bust of the Bulgarian poet Zany Ginchev and several architectural sculptures, notably for the Deutschebank in Berlin.

KACHAROV, Oscar

Ukrainian, 20th century.
Born 1924, in Kiev.
Painter. Figure compositions, figures.

Oscar Kacharov studied art between 1934 and 1937 in the figurative art studio in Kiev, before attending the Chevchenko school of fine arts in Kiev from 1937 to 1941. He fought in the war and in 1946 enrolled at the institute of applied and decorative arts in Lviv, where he studied mural painting until 1948 and became the student of R. Selski. He completed his studies at the Surikov institute of fine arts in Moscow. From 1953 to 1962 he taught at the Ilya Repin school of fine arts in Moldavia. Using a technique that complied with the precepts of Socialist Realism, he painted scenes of the Revolution and World War II, as well as compositions on sport, work and leisure. His painting was representative of the trends in Soviet art of the 1950s and 1960s.

From 1954 he regularly exhibited both in the USSR and at international exhibitions.

BIBLIOGRAPHY:

Tableaux soviétiques, auction catalogue, Salle Drouot, Paris, 3 October 1990.

MUSEUMS AND GALLERIES:

MOSCOW.

AUCTION RECORDS:
PARIS, 3 Oct 1990, *A Communist Saturday* (1975, oil on canvas, 48 x 59 ins / 122 x 150 cm) FRF 20,000.

KACHE, Serge van
French, 20th - 21st century.
Born 18 November 1946, in Angoulême.
Painter.
Serge van Kache's mother was French and his father Asian. He studied art at the École des Beaux-Arts in Angoulême. He worked as a graphic designer on the magazines *Lui* and *Playboy*. A meticulous painter, Kache is a distant heir of the Flemish masters and in particular works with the light in landscapes that often comprise architectural elements. In 1985 he was a prizewinner at the Salon de la Peinture Fantastique d'Avoriaz (Avoriaz Exhibition of Fantasy Painting) in 1985. His work has been shown at the Salon d'Automne in Paris since 1988 and he became a member there in 1990. He exhibited at the Galerie Vendôme Rive Gauche in 1983 and 1991 and the Galerie Râ in 1987 and 1989. He has also exhibited regularly at the Galerie Michelle Boulet in Paris.

KACHEL, Johann Wilhelm Friedrich
Dutch, 19th century.
Born 11 October 1826, in The Hague; died 1 June 1873, in The Hague.
Draughtsman, painter, lithographer.
A pupil of Van der Berg and Henry Brown, he took his subjects mostly from everyday life. He also reproduced paintings and sculptures by contemporary artists and illustrated Milton's *Paradise Lost.*

KACHEL, Ludwig
German, 19th century.
Born 10 December 1830, in Karlsruhe; died 17 October 1858, in Karlsruhe.
Painter. History painting.
Kachel exhibited in Munich, but worked in Baden.
MUSEUMS AND GALLERIES:
KARLSRUHE: *Minne.*

KACHLER, Johann
Swiss, 16th century.
Active in Uri at the end of the 16th century.
Glass painter.
Most of Kachler's work was undertaken in Altdorf.

KACI CHAOUCH, Farid
Algerian, 20th - 21st century.
Born 5 March 1953.
Sculptor. Figures.
Kaci Chaouch studied design at the school of fine arts in Paris from 1977 to 1979. From 1979 to 1981 he studied history of art at the university of Oslo, returning to France to follow courses in sculpture in the studios of Étienne Martin, Pol Bury and Lebel from 1982 to 1984. He teaches at the school of fine arts in Tours. Chaouch has been commissioned to restore the casts of pieces at the Rodin museum in Paris, and has also created several posters.

Kaci Chaouch's work has been represented in the following group exhibitions: the exhibition at the Algerian cultural centre in Paris in 1985, the biennial of contemporary art in Vichy in 1986 and the exhibition at the Vivenel museum in Compiègne in the same year, the *Festival of Arab Culture* in Orléans and the *Forum for Algerian Creators in France* at the Château des Blondes in Sassenague, both in 1987. He has also exhibited his work in solo shows, such as those at the Studio gallery in Grenoble in 1989 and the Algerian cultural centre in Paris in 1990.

KACIMI, Mohamed
Moroccan, 20th century.
Born 1942, in Meknès.
Painter, draughtsman, installation artist, draughtsman.
Kacimi became interested in painting while following a fine arts course of the ministry for youth in Morocco and was subsequently influenced by the work of the Moroccan painter Gharbaoui. He travels regularly in Europe.

His work has appeared in various group exhibitions, including *Peintres du Maroc* (*Moroccan Painters*) at the Institut du Monde Arabe in Paris in 1991, at the Mukhta museum in Antwerp in 1992 (where his work was shown alongside that of Fouad Bellamine), and *Suites Africaines* (*African Sequels*) at the Cordeliers convent in Paris in 1997. Exhibitions of his work have also been staged in Africa, the Far East, and (several times) in Bourges and Amiens in France and in Madrid.

First and foremost a painter, Kacimi works mainly in large format, executing major installations in towns such as the painted walls of Asilah, the standards of Harhoura and the haiks of Marrakech. He had very close connections with the painter Miloud Labied and also practised abstract painting which, while conveying an impression of vegetation, was completely gestural. However, he introduced the presence of human beings symbolically into his work in order to represent them as being at the heart of the world. In his more recent work, Kacimi has reconciled the abstract image in a symbolic context with elements of written texts. He sometimes introduces a variety of different materials into his work such as string, pieces of wood and other collages. His works include *Seven Figures in Meditation* and *Time of the Storytellers*, which are superimposed with memories, traces and impressions.
BIBLIOGRAPHY:
M' Rabet, Khalil, *Peinture et identité - L'Expérience marocaine*, L'Harmattan, Rabat, apr. 1986.

KACZIANY, Aladar
Hungarian, 20th century.
Born 15 October 1887, in Nograd Surany.
Painter, engraver.
Aladar Kacziany studied at the Royal Academy in London, then in Rome and Florence before settling in Budapest, where he often executed decorative paintings.

KACZIANY, Œdoen
Hungarian, 19th century.
Born 8 January 1852, in Marosvásárhely.
Active in Budapest.
Painter. Landscapes.
Œdoen Kacziany was a pupil of Dietz. He exhibited at the 1900 Exposition Universelle and gained an honourable mention.

KACZOR-BATOWSKI. See **BATOWSKI-KACZOR Stanislas**

KÁDÁR, Bela
Hungarian, 20th century.
Born 1877; died 1956.
Painter (including gouache), draughtsman. Figure compositions, figures. Stage sets.
Bela Kádár began by working in a naturalist style then, in 1921, moved towards an Expressionist manner. His style then became harder, even disjointed. He executed certain paintings in a Cubist spirit. He exhibited in 1921 with Hugo Scheiber in Budapest. From 1922 until 1930, he exhibited paintings at *Der Sturm* (*The Storm*) gallery in Berlin. In 1936 he left Berlin to go back to Budapest. He became the Director of *Der Sturm* (*The Storm*) gallery and newspaper. He also produced stage sets. He exhibited in 1938 in the USA, having appeared at the exhibition of the Anonymous Society in New York, and had a solo exhibition in 1932 in Budapest at the Tamas Gallery. In 1971, a retrospective exhibition of his work was organised in Budapest. He appeared in many exhibitions that historically retraced the pictorial activities of

the Hungarian Avant-Garde of the years between 1900 and 1930.

BIBLIOGRAPHY:

Hevesty, Ivan, *Kádár*, Budapest, 1922. Mezei, Ottó Arpad, *Béla Kádár*, exhibition catalogue, Gal. Nabert, Geneva, 1992.

AUCTION RECORDS:

LOS ANGELES, 10 June 1976, *Traffic Police* (1929, watercolour/mounted paper/card, 19¼ x 14¼ ins / 49 x 36 cm) USD 500. NEW YORK, 3 Nov 1978, *Constructivist Composition* (1920-1925, gouache, 26¾ x 20 ins / 68 x 51 cm) USD 4,250. LOS ANGELES, 6 Nov 1978, *Still-life with Pipes* (oil on canvas, 37½ x 33 ins / 95.3 x 84 cm) USD 1,300. LOS ANGELES, 19 June 1979, *Concert* (gouache, 46¾ x 61¾ ins / 118.7 x 156.9 cm) USD 12,500. LOS ANGELES, 16 Oct 1979, *Accordion Player* (oil on canvas, 41 x 37 ins / 104 x 94 cm) USD 2,400. LOS ANGELES, 17 March 1981, *Mannequin* (1929, gouache, 23½ x 17¼ ins / 59.7 x 43.7 cm) USD 1,700. NEW YORK, 18 March 1982, *Bareback Rider* (oil on card, 37¼ x 40¼ ins / 94.3 x 102.5 cm) USD 4,750. NEW YORK, 18 May 1983, *Abstract Composition* (c. 1925, gouache, 18½ x 13½ ins / 47 x 34.5 cm) USD 6,000. LONDON, 28 June 1983, *Nude Seated* (brown pencil heightened with brown watercolour/pencil outlines/paper, 17½ x 11½ ins / 44.5 x 29 cm) GBP 1,600. MUNICH, 6 June 1984, *Nude Girl and Cat* (1924, oil on canvas, 40¼ x 26¾ ins / 102 x 68 cm) DEM 18,000. ZURICH, 25 Sept 1986, *Nude Seated* (charcoal and coloured chalks, 16½ x 23½ ins / 42 x 59.5 cm) CHF 9,000. ZURICH, 25 Sept 1986, *Cubist Still-life* (gouache/card, 11 x 9 ins / 27 x 22 cm) CHF 17,000. NEW YORK, 18 Feb 1988, *Egyptian Composition* (oil on canvas, 19¾ x 24 ins / 50.1 x 61 cm) USD 1,980. LONDON, 24 Feb 1988, *Portrait of Two Women* (watercolour and gouache, 34 x 23¾ ins / 85.5 x 60.5 cm) GBP 3,300. PARIS, 22 April 1988, *Woman (front); Baby's Lunch (back)* (watercolour, 17¼ x 11 ins / 44 x 28 cm) FRF 9,500. TEL AVIV, 26 May 1988, *Girl Seated* (pastel and gouache, 39¼ x 27½ ins / 100 x 70 cm) USD 16,280. NEW YORK, 6 Oct 1988, *Embrace* (gouache/paper, 35½ x 23½ ins / 90.2 x 60 cm) USD 8,800. NEW YORK, 12 Nov 1988, *Female Nude Standing with Fruit Bowl* (gouache/paper, 40 x 29¼ ins / 101.5 x 74 cm) USD 26,400. ROME, 21 March 1989, *Villlage* (mixed media/card, 18 x 13¾ ins / 45.5 x 34.8 cm) ITL 1,000,000. NEW YORK, 3 May 1989, *Outdoors* (gouache/paper, 23¼ x 32¼ ins / 59.1 x 81.9 cm) USD 17,760. LONDON, 24 May 1989, *Dairymaid* (gouache and watercolour/paper, 29¼ x 22½ ins / 74 x 57 cm) GBP 2,090. TEL AVIV, 30 May 1989, *Composition with Horserider and Birds* (gouache/paper, 22¾ x 33 ins / 58 x 84 cm) USD 3,300. TEL AVIV, 3 Jan 1990, *Women in a Room* (ink, 10¾ x 11¼ ins / 27.5 x 28.5 cm) USD 880. PARIS, 20 Feb 1990, *Girl with Cat* (mixed media, 26¾ x 18½ ins / 68 x 47 cm) FRF 56,000. PARIS, 8 April 1990, *Abstraction, Red Circle* (gouache, 8¾ x 11¼ ins / 22.5 x 28.5 cm) FRF 40,000. TEL AVIV, 19 June 1990, *Landscape with Figures* (gouache, 16¼ x 11½ ins / 41 x 29 cm) USD 3,960. LONDON, 17 Oct 1990, *Small Girl in Her High Chair* (gouache, 34 x 23½ ins / 86.5 x 59.5 cm) GBP 3,300. LUCERNE, 24 Nov 1990, *Composition with Two Female Nudes* (watercolour and ink/paper, 7¾ x 11 ins / 20 x 27 cm) CHF 2,700. PARIS, 9 Dec 1990, *Woman, Cubist Composition* (ink and gouache/bistre-coloured paper, 12¼ x 8¼ ins / 31 x 21 cm) FRF 19,000. TEL AVIV, 1 Jan 1991, *Still-life with Statue and Table* (watercolour, 18 x 11 ins / 45.5 x 27 cm) USD 1,100. NEW YORK, 13 Feb 1991, *Interior* (gouache/card, 23 x 33½ ins / 58.5 x 85 cm) USD 6,050. PARIS, 5 July 1991, *Amazons* (ink and wash, 18 x 11¼ ins / 45.5 x 28.5 cm) FRF 4,500. TEL AVIV, 26 Sept 1991, *Composition* (gouache, 22¾ x 10¼ ins / 58 x 26 cm) USD 3,300. PARIS, 14 April 1992, *Horse Rider* (gouache, 18 x 11¼ ins / 46 x 28.5 cm) FRF 13,500. TEL AVIV, 20 Oct 1992, *Mother and Child* (gouache, 19 x 12¾ ins / 48.5 x 32.7 cm) USD 4,950. LUCERNE, 21 Nov 1992, *Composition with Figures* (ink and tempera/paper, 9 x 11½ ins / 22 x 29 cm) CHF 1,400. AMSTERDAM, 9 Dec 1992, *View of a Village* (oil on paper/canvas, 22 x 27¾ ins / 55 x 70.5 cm) NLG 4,600. LONDON, 7 April 1993, *Leaving the Church* (gouache, 31 x 22¾ ins / 79 x 58 cm) GBP 3,450. PARIS, 12 May 1993, *Self-portrait of the Artist with His Daughters* (1918, oil on canvas/wood, 21 x 13½ ins / 52.5 x 34 cm) FRF 23,000. ZURICH, 24 June 1993, *On a Village Square* (gouache, 18¼ x 11¼ ins / 46.5 x 28.5 cm) CHF 4,600. LOKEREN, 12 March 1994, *Abstract Composition* (watercolour, 3¼ x 5¾ ins / 8 x 14.5 cm) BEF 33,000. PARIS, 14 March 1994, *Composition* (gouache, 15¾ x 11 ins / 40 x 27 cm) FRF 8,000. LONDON, 29 June 1994, *Model with Cat* (oil on canvas, 40 x 27¼ ins / 101.6 x 69.2 cm) GBP 10,925. TEL AVIV, 27 Sept 1994, *Three Figures* (gouache, 31 x 23¼ ins / 78.5 x 59 cm) USD 3,680. NEW YORK, 24 Feb 1995, *Young Girl in Hat Decorated with Flowers* (gouache/paper, 18½ x 11½ ins / 46.7 x 29.5 cm) USD 2,415. LONDON, 20 March 1996, *Young Girl* (gouache, 19 x 13¼ ins / 48 x 33.5 cm) GBP 2,530. TEL AVIV, 7 Oct 1996, *Village* (gouache, 11½ x 18 ins / 29 x 46 cm) USD 3,680. LONDON, 22 Oct 1997, *Interior* (oil on canvas, 23¾ x 31½ ins / 60.5 x 80 cm) GBP 2,300. NEW YORK, 23 Feb 2000, *Portrait of a Woman* (watercolour, 34 x 23 ins / 86 x 58 cm) USD 11,000. BUDAPEST, 1 May 2000, *Woman with a Guitar* (mixed media, 27 x 19 ins / 69 x 48 cm) HUF 3,400,000. BUDAPEST, 27 April 2001, *Mother and Child* (tempera on paper, 28 x 39 ins / 71 x 100 cm) HUF 4,400,000. BUDAPEST, 27 April 2001, *Before Dinner* (pastel, 25 x 19 ins / 64 x 47 cm) HUF 10,000,000. TEL AVIV, 7 April 2002, *Seated Girl* (pastel and gouache, 39 x 28 ins / 100 x 70 cm) USD 28,000. BUDAPEST, 13 Sept 2002, *Still-life with Flowers, Glass and Grapes* (tempera on canvas, 33 x 23 ins / 84 x 59 cm) HUF 8,000,000. BUDAPEST, 11 April 2003, *Girl in a Flowery Hat* (mixed media, 28 x 20 ins / 70 x 50 cm) HUF 5,500,000. BUDAPEST, 4 Oct 2003, *Woman in a Veil with a Fruit Bowl* (tempera on paper, 28 x 20 ins / 70 x 50 cm) HUF 8,000,000. BUDAPEST, 12 Oct 2004, *Lovers* (mixed media, 9 x 14 ins / 24 x 35 cm) HUF 4,200,000. BUDAPEST, 12 Oct 2004, *Nudes with Still-life of Fruit* (tempera on paper, 27 x 19 ins / 68 x 48 cm) HUF 6,500,000.

KADAR, Gyorgy

Hungarian, 20th century.

Born 1912, in Budapest.

Painter, draughtsman, illustrator. Designs for mosaics. Gyorgy Kadar studied art in Budapest and Paris. He won the Kossuth and Munkácsy Prizes, and taught at the Higher School of Fine Art in Budapest. His works are held in national collections.

He was active to begin with as a poster artist and only began painting continuously in 1945, having produced a series of drawings in 1944 that seized on what he had seen when he was deported to Germany. He painted historical pictures around 1950 in the academic style of the 19th century which was advocated at that time in the Eastern Bloc countries. He then painted a few works outdoors, and subsequently worked on a series of monumental paintings in which, circumstances having changed, he introduced a few ideas of the international Neo-Cubist style, while remaining cautiously figurative. He appeared at collective exhibitions (in 1958 at the International Exhibition in Brussels, and at solo exhibitions in 1962 in Budapest and in Rome in 1964).

BIBLIOGRAPHY:

Hongrie 68, Budapest, 1968.

AUCTION RECORDS:
Bern, 20 June 1973, *Profile of Young Girl,* CHF 3,000. London, 6 Dec 1973, *Composition* (gouache) GBP 720.

KADAR, Joseph
20th century.
Painter.
Joseph Kadar's abstract painting alternates strict geometric structures with fluid shadowy forms, using this contrast to achieve a balance. Sometimes elements in relief are attached to the picture. He has had solo exhibitions of his work, such as that in the Galerie Marcel Lenoir Claude Namy in Paris in 1985.
MUSEUMS AND GALLERIES:
Amsterdam (Stedelijk Mus.) - Antwerp (Koninklijk Mus. voor Schone Kunsten) - Avallon (Mus. de L'Avallonais) - Bayonne (Mus. Bonnat) - Beauvais (Mus. départemental de l'Oise) - Budapest (Szépmuvészeti Múz.) - Caracas (MAC Sofía Imber) - Debrecen (Déri Muz.) - Dijon (MBA) - Ghent (Stedelijk Mus. voor Actuele Kunst) - Grenoble (Mus. de Grenoble) - Honfleur (Mus. Eugène Boudin) - Kassak (Emlek Mus.) - Liège (Mus. of Modern and Contemporary Art) - Lille (MBA) - Los Angeles (County MA) - Mâcon (Mus. des Ursulines) - Mexico City (MMA) - New York (MoMA) - Ostend (Mus. voor Schone Kunsten) - Pécs (Janus Pannonius Mus.) - Rome (Gal. Nazionale d'Arte Moderna) - San Francisco (MoMA) - São Paulo (MA) - St-Étienne (Mus. d'Art et d'Industrie) - Strasbourg (Mus. d'Art Moderne et Contemporain) - Villefranche-sur-Mer (Fondation Volti).

KADDI, Kikusui
Japanese, 20th century.
Painter.
Kaddi Kikusui was represented at the exhibition of Japanese art at the Jeu de Paume Museum in Paris in 1929.

KADERSCH, Gustav Adolph
German, 19th century.
Born 30 May 1804, in Bernstadt (Saxony).
Painter, lithographer.
Kadersch was a pupil of portrait painter T.L. Pochmann, and worked in Dresden.

KADID, Djilali
Algerian, 20th - 21st century.
Born 25 January 1956, in Sfizef.
Active in France.
Painter (including gouache/mixed media), watercolourist, engraver. Scenes with figures, portraits, still-lifes, landscapes.
Djilali Kadid studied in Siddi Bel-Abbes and then from 1978 at the Sorbonne in Paris. In 1983 and 1984 he exhibited his work in Paris, in 1985 at the Syrian cultural centre in Paris, in 1987 at the Bernheim gallery in Paris, and in 1993 at the Tammouz gallery in Brussels. He also mounted solo exhibitions at the Bernheim gallery in Paris in 1984, the gallery of the Algerian cultural centre in 1987, the Tammouz gallery in 1993 and also participated in the Salon of sacred art (1984, 1987, 1988) and the Salon des Réalités Nouvelles (1989 and 1990). In 1995 he took part in the tribute to the writer Kateb Yacine at the Palais de Congres in Béziers. Kadid is also a journalist, art critic and author of *Benanteur, Impressions of a Development.*

Kadid is a painter of 'interior realism', who sees himself in a line of development represented by Georges Rouault, Chaim Soutine and Fautrier. His works attempts to convey the spiritual dimension of tangible objects, represented through landscapes, figures, or bunches of flowers.
BIBLIOGRAPHY:
Memmi, Albert, *Djilali Kadid,* Centre culturel syrien, Paris, 1985. '*Tableaux à partir de Kateb Yacine*' in *Algérie-Actualité,* periodical, Paris, 1987 (conversation with B. Souibès). Yacine, Kateb, *Djilali Kadid, peintre tragique,* Bernheim-Jeune, Paris, 1987. Pélégri, Jean, *Pour entrer dans l'univers d'un peintre,* Paris, 1989. Harouak, Djémila, '*Entretien avec le peintre Djilali Kadid*' in *El-Forçane,* periodical, Paris, 1989. *Djilali Kadid,* Monique Boucher, Ivry, 1997. Kadid, Djilali, *Benanteur, empreintes d'un cheminement,* Myriam Solal, Paris, 1998.

KADISHMAN, Menashe
Israeli, 20th century.
Born 1931 or 1932.
Painter, sculptor (including bronze). Figures, interiors with figures, animals.

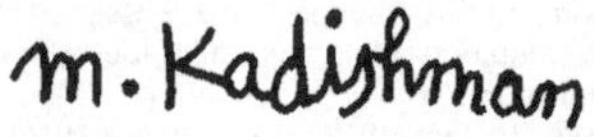

AUCTION RECORDS:
New York, 19 Nov 1981, *In Suspense* (1967, steel, h. 114 ins / 289.5 cm) USD 21,000. New York, 5 May 1982, *Untitled* (aluminium, 6 3/4 x 18 1/2 x 5 1/2 ins / 17.2 x 47 x 14 cm) USD 2,000. New York, 21 May 1983, *Head* (1979-1980, oil on canvas, 82 x 93 ins / 208.3 x 236.2 cm) USD 18,500. New York, 6 May 1987, *Two Heads* (1981, oil on canvas mounted/canvas, 53 3/4 x 89 ins / 136.8 x 226.1 cm) USD 20,000. New York, 4 May 1989, *Sheep's Head* (1984, acrylic and oil on canvas, 51 x 38 ins / 129.5 x 96.5 cm) USD 11,000. Tel Aviv, 3 Jan 1990, *Female Figure in a Bedroom* (1982, oil on canvas, 43 3/4 x 29 1/2 ins / 111 x 75 cm) USD 3,080. Tel Aviv, 19 June 1990, *Head* (acrylic/canvas, 51 1/4 x 38 1/4 ins / 130 x 97 cm) USD 9,900. New York, 10 Oct 1990, *Untitled* (acrylic/printed paper/canvas, 39 x 27 1/2 ins / 99.1 x 70 cm) USD 1,870. Tel Aviv, 1 Jan 1991, *Head* (1989, acrylic/canvas, 39 x 32 ins / 99 x 81 cm) USD 7,700; *Head* (bronze, h. 10 1/4 ins / 26 cm) USD 4,180. Amsterdam, 22 May 1991, *Lamb* (oil on paper/canvas, 39 1/4 x 27 1/2 ins / 100 x 70 cm) NLG 6,325. Tel Aviv, 12 June 1991, *Head of an Animal* (1983, acrylic/paper/canvas, 34 x 23 3/4 ins / 86.5 x 60.5 cm) USD 1,980. Amsterdam, 14 Sept 1993, *Head of a Lamb* (acrylic/canvas, 29 1/2 x 23 1/2 ins / 75 x 60 cm) NLG 2,300. Tel Aviv, 27 Sept 1994, *The Shepherdess (Homage to Van Gogh)* (1987, oil on canvas, 79 1/4 x 60 3/4 ins / 201.5 x 154.3 cm) USD 11,500. Tel Aviv, 12 Oct 1995, *Birth* (sculpture in cut metal, h. 24 1/2 ins / 62.1 cm) USD 6,900. Tel Aviv, 11 April 1996, *Reclining Woman* (iron, 19 3/4 x 38 1/2 ins / 50 x 98 cm) USD 12,650. Tel Aviv, 12 Jan 1997, *Head* (c. 1990, iron, l. 14 1/4 ins / 36 cm) USD 5,060; *Tension* (1963-1966, aluminium, h. 12 1/4 ins / 31 cm) USD 2,070. Tel Aviv, 26 April 1997, *Boy and Donkey* (1991, cut iron, 16 1/2 x 31 1/2 ins / 42 x 80 cm) USD 10,925. Tel Aviv, 10 April 1999, *Birth* (iron, h. 24 ins / 60 cm) USD 5,000. London, 3 Dec 1999, *Megalithic Landscape* (oil on canvas, 22x36 ins / 56x91 cm) GBP 2,800. Tel Aviv, 29 June 2000, *Head* (acrylic, 39x39 ins / 100x100 cm) USD 6,000. Tel Aviv, 15 Jan 2001, *Head* (acrylic, 46x35 ins / 118x89 cm) USD 8,000. Tel Aviv, 16 Jan 2001, *Nami* (bronze, h. 22 ins / 57 cm) USD 18,500. Tel Aviv, 16 April 2001, *Flock of Sheep* (1985, oil on canvas, 69x69 ins / 175x175 cm) USD 18,000. Tel Aviv, 7 April 2002, *Lamentation* (iron, h. 20 ins / 50 cm) USD 2,000. San Francisco, 23 April 2002, *Untitled, Sheep in a Pasture* (acrylic, 37x30 ins / 95x77 cm) USD 1,500. Radford, 8 Feb 2003, *Figure of Abraham and Isaac* (oil on canvas) USD 4,000. Paris, 27 Nov 2003, *Sheep* (oil on canvas, 31x24 ins / 80x60 cm) EUR 4,500. Tel Aviv, 1 May 2004, *Sheep's Head* (acrylic, 43x43 ins / 110x110 cm) USD 4,050. Tel Aviv, 1 Sept 2004, *Shepherdess with Sheep* (acrylic, 43x43 ins / 110x110 cm) USD 3,800.

KADLETZ, Willi
German, 20th century.
Born 25 September 1895.
Painter, engraver.

Willi Kadletz was active in Krieglach. He studied with Rotky and Fessel in Munich. Among his works is a *Portrait of the poet Bruno Ertler*.

KADLIK, Franz, or Tkadlik, Frantisek
Czech, 19th century.
Born 23 November 1786, in Prague; died 16 January 1840, in Prague.
Painter. History painting, genre scenes.
Kadlik was a pupil of Birgler at the school of fine arts in Prague in 1803. In 1817, he went to Vienna as a protégé of Count Czernin, and worked there until 1824, at which date he set off for Rome with a bursary from the emperor in his pocket. In 1835, he was appointed director of the academy of fine arts in Prague.
MUSEUMS AND GALLERIES:
VIENNA (Czernin'sche Gemäldegal.): *Child with an Angel*.

KADO, Eduard
German, 20th century.
Born 15 August 1875, in Memel (now Klaipeda, Lithuania).
Painter, sculptor, decorative designer.
After studying at the Académie Julian in Paris and travelling across Europe, Eduard Kado settled in Königsberg (now Kaliningrad), where he decorated a number of churches.

KADORIZI, Wolfgang Joseph
Austrian, 18th century.
Active in Linz c. 1700.
Painter.
Kadorizi is known for a large miniature of *The Painter in His Studio*.

KADOW, Gerhard
German, 20th century.
Born 1909, in Uelzen (Hanover).
Painter, draughtsman.
Gerhard Kadow was active in Krefeld. From 1929 to 1932, he studied at the Bauhaus, mainly in the weaving workshop, where he created designs on fabrics, but also with Kandinsky and Klee. He later became a teacher of both textiles and painting.
BIBLIOGRAPHY:
Leymarie, Jean/Herzogenrath, Wulf/Grote, Ludwig/Gropius, Walter, *Le Bauhaus*, exhibition catalogue, Württembergischer Kunsteverein, Stuttgart, Musée national d'Art moderne, Paris, 1969.

KAEGI, Gottlieb
Swiss, 19th - 20th century.
Born 20 August 1856, in Riedl.
Painter. Landscapes.
After studying in Nuremberg, Gottlieb Kaegi visited Italy in 1881 and 1884, before returning to settle in Zurich, where he worked for a porcelain factory. He painted mainly landscapes, sometimes in watercolour, and a few portraits by him are also still known. He took part in the Brussels Exhibition in 1910.

KAEHLER, Heinrich
German, 19th century.
Born 22 February 1804, in Rostock; died 5 April 1878, in Güstrow.
Sculptor.
Kaehler was a pupil of J.G. Schadow at the academy in Berlin, and exhibited at the royal academy several times between 1837 and 1844. He left Berlin only infrequently, to go to Italy or, occasionally, England.

KAEHRLING, Suzanne Blanche
French, 20th century.
Born in Paris.
Painter, designer.
Suzanne Blanche Kaehrling exhibited at the Salon d'Automne in Paris.

KAELIN, Charles Salis
American, 19th - 20th century.
Born 19 December 1858, in Cincinnati; died 1929.
Painter, pastellist. Seascapes, landscapes.
Charles Salis Kaelin studied at the Art Students League in New York. He exhibited in Paris in 1900, at the Exposition Universelle.
AUCTION RECORDS:
NEW YORK, 2 Dec 1982, *Harbour* (oil on canvas, 20 1/4 x 24 ins / 51.5 x 61 cm) USD 3,000. NEW YORK, 28 Sept 1983, *Craggy Coastline* (pastel/black paper, 14 1/4 x 16 1/4 ins / 36 x 41.1 cm) USD 3,600. NEW YORK, 21 Oct 1983, *Fishing Harbour, Massachusetts* (oil on canvas, 22 1/4 x 24 ins / 56.5 x 61 cm) USD 6,500. NEW YORK, 25 Oct 1985, *Autumn Landscape* (pastel, 15 1/4 x 13 1/2 ins / 38.6 x 34.5 cm) USD 2,800. NEW YORK, 15 March 1986, *Spring Landscape* (oil on canvas, 20 x 24 ins / 50.8 x 61 cm) USD 2,600. NEW YORK, 24 June 1988, *Boats in the Port* (pastel/paper, 15 x 16 ins / 37.2 x 40.8 cm) USD 5,775. NEW YORK, 24 Jan 1989, *Fishing Boats at Anchor* (pastel/paper, 16 1/4 x 13 1/4 ins / 41.2 x 33.8 cm) USD 1,650. NEW YORK, 24 Jan 1990, *Green Trees* (pastel/paper, 17 x 10 ins / 43 x 25.4 cm) USD 605. NEW YORK, 21 May 1991, *Forest in Winter* (pastel/card, 14 x 16 ins / 35.6 x 40.6 cm) USD 3,850.

KAELIN, Joseph
Swiss, 20th century.
Born 1870, in Einsiedeln (Zug).
Painter, engraver. Landscapes.
Joseph Kaelin was active in Zurich. He painted mainly Swiss landscapes.

KAEMMERER, Ernst
German, 18th - 19th century.
Born in Rudolstadt; died 23 May 1807, in Rudolstadt (near Saalfeld).
Painter, engraver.
Kaemmerer taught drawing in Rudolstadt. Noted works by him include *Views of Schloss Leutenberg* and *Views of Schwarzburg*.

KAEMMERER, Frederik Hendrik, or Kammerer
Dutch, 19th century.
Born 1839, in The Hague; died 4 April 1902, in Paris.
Also active in France.
Painter. Genre scenes, landscapes.
Frederik Kaemmerer studied under Gérôme in Paris and divided his time between Paris and The Hague. At the age of 63 he put an end to his life in a Paris studio.

Kaemmerer exhibited at the Paris Salon from 1870; he was awarded a medal in 1874 and a silver medal at the Exposition Universelle of 1889. He was made a chevalier of the Légion d'Honneur the same year. Kaemmerer achieved great success with his small, highly polished pictures of subjects under the Directoire and the First Empire. He sought to please the public at large and his *Merveilleuses* (*Marvels*) were much sought after by his American clientèle. Towards the end of his life his style became freer and he demonstrated a speed of execution that allies him with the Impressionists.
MUSEUMS AND GALLERIES:
MULHOUSE: *The Clothes Mender*.
AUCTION RECORDS:
PARIS, 14 April 1891, *Baptism*, FRF 13,860. NEW YORK, 13-14 Feb 1900, *Going to Church*, USD 680. NEW YORK, 3 Feb 1905, *Woman Bathing*, USD 1,100. PARIS, 10 May 1926, *Marriage under the Directory* (watercolour and gouache) FRF 1,420. PARIS, 22 June 1942, *Young Woman with a Shawl*, FRF 1,600. NEW YORK, 10 Dec 1958, *The Flower Girl*, USD 550. LONDON, 28 Feb 1973, *The Outing*, GBP 1,700. NEW YORK, 9 Oct 1974, *Love Potions*, USD 4,000. AMSTERDAM, 27 April 1976, *Portrait*

of a Young Girl with a Flowery Hat (oil on canvas, 9¾ x 6¼ ins / 25 x 16 cm) NLG 7,400. NEW YORK, 12 May 1978, *After the Masked Ball* (oil on canvas remounted/panel, 13¾ x 8½ ins / 35 x 21.5 cm) USD 2,600. NEW YORK, 26 Jan 1979, *Skaters* (oil on canvas, 18¼ x 12½ ins / 46.5 x 32 cm) USD 4,000. NEW YORK, 11 Feb 1981, *Young Woman with a Fan by the Sea* (oil on canvas, 15¼ x 8½ ins / 39 x 21.5 cm) USD 8,250. NEW YORK, 27 May 1983, *Young Woman with a Flowery Hat* (oil on canvas, 11¼ x 7¼ ins / 28.5 x 18.5 cm) USD 1,500. NEW YORK, 13 Feb 1985, *In the Nursery* (oil on canvas, 23½ x 16 ins / 60 x 40.5 cm) USD 9,000. NEW YORK, 24 Nov 1987, *Lady Walking* (oil on canvas, 22 x 15 ins / 56 x 38 cm) USD 5,500. NEW YORK, 24 May 1988, *Picking Roses in the Garden* (oil on canvas, 36 x 24 ins / 91.5 x 61 cm) USD 9,625. PARIS, 16 Dec 1988, *Woman with Mandolin* (oil on canvas, 25½ x 19¾ ins / 65 x 50 cm) FRF 15,500. LONDON, 4 Oct 1989, *The Young Harpist* (oil on canvas, 23¾ x 13¾ ins / 60.5 x 35 cm) GBP 7,700. NEW YORK, 28 Feb 1990, *By the Sea* (oil on canvas, 22 x 15 ins / 56 x 38 cm) USD 22,000. NEW YORK, 1 March 1990, *Scheveningen Beach in Holland* (oil on canvas, 9 x 15¾ ins / 23 x 40 cm) USD 82,500. PARIS, 4 April 1990, *Footman Putting on a Glove* (oil on canvas, 17 x 11½ ins / 43 x 29 cm) FRF 10,500. NEW YORK, 24 Oct 1990, *The Pretty Schoolgirls* (oil on canvas, 22 x 13 ins / 55.9 x 33 cm) USD 11,000. STOCKHOLM, 14 Nov 1990, *Interior with a Young Woman Writing a Letter* (oil on canvas, 15¾ x 9¾ ins / 40 x 25 cm) SEK 64,000. CALAIS, 9 Dec 1990, *The Intruder* (oil on panel, 11 x 7½ ins / 27 x 19 cm) FRF 13,000. NEW YORK, 19 Feb 1992, *Women Selling Fish* (oil on canvas, 43½ x 29¾ ins / 110.5 x 75.6 cm) USD 17,600. NEW YORK, 26 May 1992, *Elegant Young Woman Standing* (charcoal and white chalk/beige paper, 20½ x 13 ins / 52 x 33 cm) USD 2,200. AMSTERDAM, 28 Oct 1992, *The Recital* (oil on canvas/paper, 11 x 7 ins / 28 x 18 cm) NLG 2,185. AMSTERDAM, 21 April 1994, *Elegant Young People Fishing* (watercolour/paper, 9½ x 13¾ ins / 24 x 35 cm) NLG 10,350. NEW YORK, 26 May 1994, *Scheveningen Beach in Holland* (oil on canvas, 27½ x 55 ins / 69.9 x 139.7 cm) USD 827,500. PARIS, 13 June 1994, *Elegant Lady* (charcoal heightened with white chalk, 22¾ x 14¾ ins / 58 x 37.5 cm) FRF 4,200. LONDON, 21 March 1997, *An Elegant Woman* (oil on canvas, 43½ x 23¾ ins / 110.5 x 60.4 cm) GBP 11,500. NEW YORK, 22 Oct 1997, *An Elegant Gentleman* (oil on canvas, 16¼ x 10 ins / 41 x 25.7 cm) USD 12,650. NEW YORK, 12 Feb 1998, *Apple Picking* (oil on canvas, 23¾ x 15¾ ins / 60.4 x 40 cm) USD 25,300. ROTTERDAM, 20 April 1999, *Young Woman Walking over a Bridge* (oil on canvas, 18 x 13 ins / 45 x 32 cm) NLG 22,000. GRAVENHAGE, 28 April 1999, *Elegant Lady with Fireplace in Sitting Room* (oil on canvas, 23 x 16 ins / 59 x 40 cm) NLG 36,000. GRAVENHAGE, 31 Oct 2000, *Musical Wedding Procession on a Quay* (watercolour, 12 x 20 ins / 30 x 51 cm) NLG 4,800. PARIS, 19 Dec 2000, *On Scheveningen Beach* (oil on canvas, 9 x 16 ins / 23 x 40 cm) FRF 355,000. GRAVENHAGE, 25 April 2001, *Getting Ready for the Masked Ball* (oil on canvas, 20 x 15 ins / 52 x 39 cm) NLG 68,000. NEW YORK, 1 May 2001, *At the Seashore* (oil on canvas, 11 x 17 ins / 29 x 43 cm) USD 60,000. NEW YORK, 29 Oct 2002, *On the Lookout* (oil on canvas, 16 x 10 ins / 40 x 25 cm) USD 120,000. NEW YORK, 29 Oct 2002, *Beach at Scheveningen, Holland* (oil on canvas, 28 x 56 ins / 70 x 141 cm) USD 425,000. AMSTERDAM, 21 Oct 2003, *Flirtation* (oil on canvas, 15 x 9 ins / 37 x 24 cm) EUR 20,000. LONDON, 3 Dec 2003, *Proud Moment* (oil on canvas, 43 x 30 ins / 110 x 75 cm) GBP 38,000. NEW YORK, 23 April 2004, *Wedding Procession* (oil on canvas/masonite, 39 x 63 ins / 99 x 160 cm) USD 60,000. ROTTERDAM, 11 May 2004, *Worshipper* (watercolour, 13 x 9 ins / 33 x 22 cm) EUR 2,400.

KAEMON. See **GOSHUN**

KAEMPFFER, Eduard, or Kaempfer
German, 19th century.
Born 13 May 1859, in Münster.
Painter, sculptor. Historical subjects, genre scenes.

Kaempffer was a pupil of Peter Janssen in Düsseldorf, where he worked until 1891 before going to Munich. In 1893, he won gold medals in Munich and in Berlin. He lived mainly in Breslau (now Wroclaw, Poland).

KAENDEL, Joerg
German, 16th century.
Active in Biberach.
Painter.

Joerg Kaendel worked in the Biberach region of Germany, and specialised in religious decorations. He produced altarpieces in the churches in Oberliezheim, Tinzen and Seewis. The Kaiser Friedrich museum (now the Bode Museum) in Berlin and the Kunsthaus in Zurich own work by this artist.

KAENEN, I. or J., or Theodorus, or Caenen, Canen, or Kaan
German, 18th century.
Born probably in Germany.
Painter.

Kaenen became a member of the guild in Middelburg (Holland) in 1736 under the name of Canen, but lived for many years in Nijmegen as Theodorus. He returned to Germany to settle after 1744 and became a court painter.

KAEPPEL, Carl
German, 19th century.
Active in Nuremberg.
Painter, engraver. Landscapes.

Kaeppel painted mainly watercolour views of Nuremberg.

KAEPPELIN, Dominique
French, 20th - 21st century.
Born 19 August 1949, in Le Puy-en-Velay.
Sculptor, engraver.

Dominique Kaeppelin was the son of Philippe Kaeppelin. He studied at the École des Beaux-Arts in Paris. He has created altars and constructions with altar tables in many religious buildings, such as: the church of Ste-Bernadette in Lourdes, the chapel of St-Clair in the little village of Aiguilhe in the upper parts of the Puy, the church of Ste-Bernadette d'Albigny in Annecy, the church of Annemasse, the church of Notre-Dame du Mont-Roland in Dôle and the church of St-Paul in Sophia-Antipolis near Nice. He also made wooden sculptures on the theme of the Santiago de Compostella pilgrims in the Baptistery of St-Jean in Pay-en-Velay, which are particularly interesting.

KAEPPELIN, Olivier. See **KAEPPELIN Philippe**

KAEPPELIN, Philippe, pseudonym: Olivier Kaeppelin
French, 20th century.
Born 22 October 1918, in Le Puy-en-Velay.
Sculptor, collage artist, designer, engraver, illustrator. Figures, bestiaries.

Philippe Kaeppelin was the father of Dominique Kaeppelin. He carved figures and produced a bestiary in lead, copper and bronze. He received many commissions for church works, including: the churches of Ponthierry and St-Laurent-au-Puy; the cathedral of Notre-Dame in Puy-en-Velay; the oratory of St-Gabriel and the chapel of St-Clair in the small village of Aiguilhe (near Le Puy); the church of the Holy Sepulchre in Jerusalem; and the parish church of St-Germain-l'Auxerrois. Much of his work consists of decorating altars with gilded lead figures. He also produced decorative work for French high schools (the girls' high school in Le Puy and the Lycée de Meaux, among others), specialising in brass birds. Kaeppelin illustrated the *Œuvres* of Jules Vallès and *Le Train de 8 Heures 47* by Courteline.

MUSEUMS AND GALLERIES:
ÉPINAL (Mus. départemental d'Art ancien et contemporain): *Birds*.

KAEPPLER, Johann
German, 16th - 17th century.
Active in Munich.
Painter.
According to *Bryan's Dictionary*, Johann Kaeppler studied under Donauer and worked at the beginning of the seventeenth century. These two facts, however, are contradictory. Donauer worked at the beginning of the 16th century, and left works, for example, dated 1532. He would therefore have been a very old man if indeed he ever worked with Kaeppler.

KAERFVE, Fritz Eduard
Swedish, 19th - 20th century.
Active in Malmö.
Painter. Figures, landscapes.
Fritz Kaerfve exhibited and worked in Stockholm, Munich, Paris and Copenhagen.

KAERGLING, Franz
Hungarian, 19th century.
Active in Budapest c. 1834.
Painter, musician.
Franz Kaergling produced landscapes as well as historical and religious paintings. He was the son and pupil of Johann Tobias Kaergling.

KAERGLING, Johann Tobias
German, 19th century.
Born 9 February 1780, in Augsburg; died 11 April 1845, in Budapest.
Miniaturist.

KAERGLING-PACHER, Henriette
Austrian, 19th century.
Born 10 May 1821, in Budapest.
Painter. Genre scenes, portraits, flowers, fruit.
Henriette Kaergling-Pacher was the daughter of Johann Tobias Kaergling and wife of Pacher the pianist; she worked in Vienna.

KAERIUS. See **KEERE Pieter Van der**

KAERLE, Antoine, or Caerle
Flemish School, 15th century.
Died 15th century.
Painter, decorative artist.
Bruges School.
Antoine Kaerle was the son of Jean Caerle, and was a master in Bruges in 1483. In 1485, he taught Jean de Wilde. He died in the battle of Bevertoutsveld, fought against the Ghentish army.

KAERLE, Johann
German, 19th - 20th century.
Born 1835, in Hinterhornbach; died 1913.
Painter. History painting.
Johann Kaerle was active in Augsburg and Munich, and was responsible for the decoration of a number of churches, including those at Holzgau, Bach, Elmen and Imsterberg.

KAERLEN, Jean, or Caerlius
Flemish School, 15th century.
Died before 1474.
Active in Bruges.
Painter, decorative artist.
Jean Kaerlen taught Arnould Paesschedach from 1453 to 1456, and Jean de Meessene in 1465.

KAERNER, Theodor
German, 20th century.
Born 10 January 1884, in Holenberg.
Sculptor.
Theodor Kaerner worked in Munich, mainly for porcelain factories.

KAESBACH, Rudolf
German, 20th century.
Born 22 July 1873, in Munich; died 1955.
Sculptor. Mythological subjects.
Rudolf Kaesbach was active in Paris, Düsseldorf and Brussels. Works such as *Woodland Idyll, Nausicaa and Aphrodite* show his predilection for mythological subjects.
AUCTION RECORDS:
LONDON, 16 May 1986, *Greek Warrior* (black-patinated bronze, h. 17 1/4 ins / 43.5 cm) GBP 2,400. STOCKHOLM, 6 June 1988, *Europa and the Bull* (bronze, h. 12 1/4 ins / 31 cm l. 18 ins/46 cm) SEK 12,000. SYDNEY, 10 Aug 1999, *Nausicaa, Female Nude* (1911, gilt patinated bronze, h. 19 ins / 47 cm) AUD 3,400. FRANKFURT, 17 Nov 2001, *Figure* (bronze, h. 13 ins / 33 cm) DEM 3,300. COLOGNE, 21 Nov 2002, *Mountain Goat* (dark brown patinated bronze) EUR 1,600. RUDOLSTADT, 30 May 2003, *Woman* (brown bronze, h. 23 ins / 58 cm) EUR 2,200. LONDON, 30 Sept 2003, *Fighting Athlete* (green-brown patinated bronze, h. 22 ins / 56 cm) GBP 1,800.

KAESBERG
German, 20th - 21st century.
Born 1964, in Leipzig.
Painter.
Kaesberg is a self-taught artist. Since 1987, he has featured in exhibitions in Leipzig, Basel, Bern and in 1993 at the Goethe Institute in Paris.

KAESELAU, Charles
American, 20th century.
Born 1889, in Stockholm, Sweden; died 1972, in Boston (Massachusetts).
Painter.
Charles Kaeselau studied under Hawthorne at the Art Institute of Chicago. He exhibited his works in the USA, at the Corcoran Gallery, the Whitney Museum of American Art, the Pennsylvania Academy of Fine Art, and the Art Institute Chicago, and also in Sweden.

KAESER-RUEFF, Rudolf
Austrian, 19th - 20th century.
Born 6 April 1870, in Vienna.
Painter, engraver, lithographer.
Rudolf Kaeser-Rueff was active in Munich, Strasbourg, Mannheim and Kiel. He exhibited regularly, mainly in Munich, from 1891 on.

KAESSMANN, Franz
Slav, 18th - 19th century.
Born c. 1760, in Windischfeistritz; died 2 May 1833, in Vienna.
Sculptor.
Franz Kaessmann worked for the church of St Michael in Vienna and for the church in Kalksburg. He produced a group of sculptures entitled *Jupiter and Thetis*.

KAETELHOEN, Hermann
German, 20th century.
Born 22 September 1884, in Hofgeismar.
Engraver, potter. Portraits, scenes with figures, industrial landscapes.
After first studying in Karlsruhe, Hermann Kaetelhoen became a pupil of Peter Halm in Munich. He later settled in Essen. He engraved portraits and scenes of contemporary industrial life. He was also a potter.

KAFFSACK, Josef
German, 19th century.
Born 21 October 1850, in Regensburg; died 7 September 1890, in Wannsee, Berlin, by drowning.
Sculptor.

Kaffsack was a pupil of Hanel in Dresden.
MUSEUMS AND GALLERIES:
LEIPZIG (Mus. der Bildenden Künste): *Portrait of Kaiser Wilhelm II.*

KAFKA, Bohumil
Czech, 20th century.
Born 14 February 1878, in Nova Paka.
Sculptor.
Bohumil Kafka exhibited in Paris at the Salon de la Société Nationale des Beaux-Arts and also worked in London, Vienna, Berlin and Rome. He settled in Prague.
MUSEUMS AND GALLERIES:
PRAGUE (Národní Gal.): a bronze.
AUCTION RECORDS:
PARIS, 26 Oct 1988, *Faun's Kiss* (brown-green patinated lost-wax bronze, h. 9 ins / 22 cm, l. 18 1/2 ins/47 cm, w. 12 1/4 ins/31 cm) FRF 30,000. PARIS, 25 March 2002, *Military Leader* (1932, patinated bronze, 38 x 35x9 ins / 96 x 90x23 cm) EUR 3,800.

KAFKA, Cestmir
Czechoslovak, 20th century.
Born 14 November 1922, in Jihlava.
Painter.
Cestmir Kafka studied in Zline from 1940 to 1945, then in Prague from 1945 to 1949. He painted poetic transcriptions of reality reminiscent of Paul Klee's linear arrangements. He took part in group exhibitions in Czechoslovakia and in the São Paulo Biennale in 1963, in Paris, Bochum and Baden-Baden in 1965 and in Munich in 1966.
BIBLIOGRAPHY:
Fifty years of Czechoslovak Painting from the Collections of the Galleries, 1918-1958, exhibition catalogue, Slovenska Narodna Gal., Bratislava, 1968 (in commemoration of the 50th anniversary of the Republic of Czechoslovakia).

KAFKA, Vysheslav Antonovich
Russian, 19th century.
Born in Russia; died 1889.
Sculptor.
Vysheslav Kafka received a commendation in 1888, and a silver medal in 1889 Exposition Universelle in Paris.
AUCTION RECORDS:
PARIS, 14 Oct 1983, *Prometheus* (patinated bronze, h. 24 3/4 ins / 63 cm) FRF 10,000.

KAGAMI, Kozo
Japanese, 20th century.
Born 1896, in Gifu Prefecture; died 1985.
Glass artist.
Kagami Kozo graduated from the Tokyo Higher Industrial School in 1915, where he had studied with Rudolph Ina. In 1927 he went to Germany where he studied under Wilhelm von Eiff at the Stuttgart Polytechnic, graduating in 1929. In 1930, back in Japan, he founded his own crystal technology research institute and in 1934 his own crystal factory, the Kagami Kurisutaru Seisakujo.
Kagami exhibited his art glass from 1932, when he won the distinction Special Selection at the Teiten for a glass vase, and went on to win many Japanese and foreign awards. He was also a member of the jury of the Nitten. Kagami's work, classically proportioned and of great beauty, is highly sought after.

KAGEI, family name: Tatebayashi (later Hirabayashi, Shirai), given name: Rittoku, artist names: Kagei, Tsuruoka Itsumin, Kingyu-sanjin, Kiusai
Japanese, 18th century.
Born in Kaga (now Ishikawa).
Painter.
Kagei was a physician in the service of the Maeda family, the lords of Kaga, but soon gave up this position and moved to Edo (now Tokyo) where he devoted himself to painting and especially to painting flowers. He was a disciple of Ogata Kenzan (1663-1743) and belonged to the Korin School (1658-1716).

KAGEMATSU, nickname: Utagawa, artist names: Ipposai, Goryutei
Japanese, 19th century.
Active c. 1840-1841.
Print artist.
Kagematsu is probably the same artist as Utagawa Kagematsu, who was active in Edo (now Tokyo) around 1830-1840.

KAGEN, real name: Niwa Yoshiro, nicknames: Shoho, Shinji, artist names: Shuchindo, Fukuzensai, Shaan
Japanese, 18th century.
Born 1742, in Nagoya; died 1786.
Painter.
Nanga (literati) school.
Kagen was one of the close friends of Ike no Taiga. He worked in the style of Chinese literati painting of the Ming period (1368-1644).

KAGENOBU, real name: Kano Kagenobu, original name: Fujiwara, nickname: Dewajiro
Japanese, 15th century.
Born in Izu province.
Active at the beginning of the 15th century.
Painter.
Kagenobu was the father of the famous Kano Masanobu (1434-1530), the founder of the Kano School.

KAGER, Erica von
Swiss, 20th century.
Born 28 April 1890, in Zurich.
Painter, illustrator. Portraits, flowers.
Erica von Kager studied in Basel and Munich before taking lessons at the Académie Julian in Paris.

KAGER, Johann Mathias
German, 17th century.
Born 1575, in Munich; died 1634, in Augsburg.
Painter, miniaturist, engraver, draughtsman, architect. Religious subjects, allegorical subjects, portraits. Murals.
Kager was a pupil of Pieter de Witte. He subsequently went to Rome and continued his studies with the best teachers. On his return to Germany, the Elector Maximilian of Bavaria appointed him court painter.
Kager decorated several monuments in Munich, notably the Senate Room, where he painted a *Last Judgment,* and the Frauenkirche, where he did a *Discovery of the Holy Cross.* In 1612, he painted a miniature of the *Baptism of Christ* for the Duke of Stettin's album. Towards the end of his life, he moved to Augsburg, where he painted façades and was elected mayor.
During his lifetime, Kager enjoyed a considerable reputation. The best engravers - Sadeler, Killian and Reichel - reproduced his works (almost 60 of them). As an engraver himself, Kager produced a certain number of prints and etchings on religious subjects, finished with a burin. Some of them are dated (1600 to 1603)..

AUCTION RECORDS:
PARIS, 30 Jan 1933, *Portrait of the Director of the Freiberg Silver Mines in Saxony,* FRF 5,100. AMSTERDAM, 29 Oct 1979, *The Raising of Lazarus* (pen and wash/traces of red chalk, 16 x 41 1/2 ins / 40.5 x 105.5 cm) NLG 6,000. HEIDELBERG, 11 April 1992, *Allegories of Mercy and Truth - Justice and Peace* (ink, 5 1/4 x 6 3/4 ins / 13.5 x 17.2 cm) DEM 2,700. LONDON, 4 July

1994, *Kneeling Man near a Woman* (ink and ochre wash, 9 x 8 ins / 22 x 20.3 cm) GBP 575. MUNICH, 22 March 2000, *Madonna and Child with Infant St John the Baptist* (oil on copper, octagonal, 6 x 4 ins / 15 x 11 cm) DEM 4,000. COLOGNE, 15 Nov 2003, *Madonna with Child and Infant St John* (1606, oil on copper, 6 x 4 ins / 14 x 11 cm) EUR 2,600.

KAGER, Karel von
German, 19th century.
Born 1819; died 1866, in Trento (Italy).
Painter.

Kager exhibited in Bozen (now Bolzano, Italy), Vienna and Munich, especially military paintings.

KAGETANE, given name: Hyobu
Japanese, 16th century.
Active during the Muromachi era (1338-1573).
Painter.
Suiboku School (ink painting).

KAGETOSHI
Japanese.
Active probably in Edo (now Tokyo).
Print artist.

Sources suggest there may have been multiple Kagetoshis. One was a disciple of Utagawa Sadakage. Another, a netsuke carver, was active in the early to mid-19th century; an example of his work, *Hotei and Chinese Boys*, is in the Los Angeles County Museum of Art. Also recorded is a late 19th-century woodcut artist called Kagetoshi Imao.

KAHANA, Aharon
German, 20th century.
Born 1 March 1905, in Stuttgart; died 1967.
Active then naturalised in Israel.
Painter. Religious subjects. Murals.
Symbolism.
New Horizons Group.

Aharon Kahana studied at the Stuttgart and Berlin academies, and then in Paris from 1922 to 1925. He settled in Palestine (later Israel) in 1934. In 1947, he was one of the cofounders of the New Horizons group. He painted a number of murals in various buildings in Israel. His work evolved from archaistic Symbolism to Abstract Expressionism, with its use of rhythmic lines and suggested forms. However, he could also be considered a painter of religious subjects. As with Soutine and Chagall, traces of the mystical can be glimpsed in his use of thick, malleable paint to emphasise outlines in his work. Kahana took part in the Venice Biennale in 1948, 1954 and 1958, and the São Paulo Biennale in 1953 and 1961.

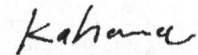

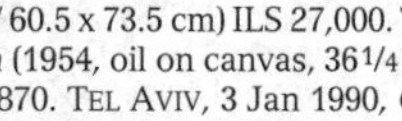

BIBLIOGRAPHY:
Aharon Kahana: The Human Figure in His Work, Museum of Modern Art, Haifa, 1978. Kampf, Avram, *Chagall to Kitaj: Jewish Experience in 20th Century Art*, Barbican Art Gall., London, 1990.

AUCTION RECORDS:
TEL AVIV, 3 May 1980, *Maritime Landscape* (1938, oil on canvas, 23¾ x 29 ins / 60.5 x 73.5 cm) ILS 27,000. TEL AVIV, 2 Jan 1989, *Composition* (1954, oil on canvas, 36¼ x 28½ ins / 92 x 72.5 cm) USD 1,870. TEL AVIV, 3 Jan 1990, *Children* (1949, oil on canvas, 23½ x 31¾ ins / 59.5 x 80.5 cm) USD 5,720. TEL AVIV, 19 June 1990, *Forms* (1955, oil on canvas, 28¼ x 35¾ ins / 71.5 x 91 cm) USD 7,480. TEL AVIV, 1 Jan 1991, *Odalisque on a Grey Background* (1955, oil on canvas, 28 x 36 ins / 71 x 91.5 cm) USD 7,040. TEL AVIV, 6 Jan 1992, *Composition* (1956, oil on paper/card, 18½ x 26 ins / 47 x 66 cm) USD 2,750. TEL AVIV, 30 June 1994, *View of the Street from a Window* (1942, oil on canvas, 29¾ x 39¼ ins / 75.5 x 100 cm) USD 6,900; *Jacob and Esau* (1952, oil on canvas, 32¾ x 24½ ins / 83.5 x 62.5 cm) USD 12,075. TEL AVIV, 11 April 1996, *Still-life with an Open Window* (1945, oil on canvas, 31½ x 23½ ins / 80 x 60 cm) USD 14,375. TEL AVIV, 7 Oct 1996, *Still-life with Fruit* (1947, oil on paper/canvas, 18¼ x 21¼ ins / 46.5 x 54 cm) USD 5,750.

KAHAR, Ibrahim. See **IBRAHIM KAHAR**

KAHILL, Joseph B.
Egyptian, 20th century.
Born 15 May 1882, in Alexandria, Egypt.
Active in France and in the USA.
Painter. Portraits.

This artist was a pupil of Charles Fox, Collin and Prinet in Paris. He was a member of the American Artistic Association in Paris.

KAHL, Karl
Latvian, 19th - 20th century.
Born 1873, in Riga.
Active in Germany.
Painter. Landscapes.

Karl Kahl studied in Düsseldorf, then lived in Munich and Karlsruhe.

MUSEUMS AND GALLERIES:
TOLEDO.

KAHLE, Anna von
German, 19th - 20th century.
Born 17 February 1853; died June 1920, in Berlin.
Sculptor.

Anna von Kahle produced mainly busts and mythological sculptures. Between 1876 and 1880, she studied with Fritz Schaper in Berlin.

KAHLE, August
German, 19th - 20th century.
Born 30 July 1869, in Brandenburg.
Painter. Landscapes.

August Kahle exhibited in Berlin in 1910.

KAHLE, Julie von
German, 19th century.
Born 6 April 1841, in Berlin.
Watercolourist, draughtswoman.

Kahle did illustrations for Goethe's *Italienische Reise*.

KAHLER, Eugen von
Czech, 20th century.
Born 6 January 1882; died 13 December 1911.
Painter, draughtsman.

Eugen von Kahler spent a long time in Paris and was profoundly influenced by French 19th-century painting. He admired Delacroix, and imitated the work of Cézanne, Van Gogh and Gauguin. He brought back from his many travels highly structured landscapes and even took part in the Blaue Reiter (Blue Rider) Foundation in Munich in 1911.

KAHLER, Karl
Austrian, 19th century.
Born 1855, in Linz.
Active in Munich.
Painter, watercolourist. Genre scenes, animals, cats.

Kahler made his Berlin debut c. 1880, but also exhibited in Dresden, Munich and Vienna. He travelled widely, and even visited Australia. His works are prized.

AUCTION RECORDS:
NEW YORK, 22-24 Nov 1899, *Studio Interior*, USD 270; *The Happy Family*, USD 470. NEW YORK, 10-11 Jan 1907, *The Artist's Studio in Melbourne*, USD 525. LONDON, 3 Oct 1979, *Flirtatious Conversation* (oil on canvas, 51¼ x 31 ins / 130 x 78.5 cm) GBP 850. NEW YORK, 18 June 1982, *Portrait of Lilian Russell* (oil on canvas, 30 x 40½ ins / 76 x 103 cm) USD 2,000. MELBOURNE, 7 Nov 1984, *The Arab Slave* (oil on canvas, 68½

x 39 1/4 ins / 174 x 100 cm) AUD 6,500. NEW YORK, 4 June 1987, *The Horse His Highness in a River Landscape* (1899, oil on canvas, 32 1/2 x 48 ins / 82.5 x 121.9 cm) USD 16,000. NEW YORK, 24 Oct 1990, *Teatime in Paris in 1900* (oil on canvas, 32 1/4 x 51 ins / 82 x 129.5 cm) USD 13,200. NEW YORK, 7 June 1991, *The Horse His Highness in a River Landscape* (1899, oil on canvas, 32 1/2 x 48 ins / 82.6 x 121.9 cm) USD 16,500. LONDON, 7 April 1993, *White Cat under Observation* (1877, oil on canvas, 27 1/4 x 22 ins / 69 x 55 cm) GBP 7,475. NEW YORK, 19 Jan 1995, *Cat Looking at Itself in a Mirror* (watercolour/paper/card, 20 x 15 1/4 ins / 50.8 x 38.7 cm) USD 2,300. LONDON, 18 Dec 1997, *A Black Persian Cat on a Partly Covered Table* (oil on canvas, 31 1/2 x 23 1/2 ins / 80 x 59.6 cm) GBP 1,725. VEJLE, 20 May 1999, *Portrait of a Girl with a Cat on a Sofa before Drapery* (oil on canvas, 41 x 30 ins / 103 x 76 cm) DKK 45,000. NEW YORK, 15 June 1999, *Elegant Lady at Flower Stand* (oil on canvas, 51 x 31 ins / 130 x 79 cm) USD 4,000. BILLINGSHURST, 24 July 2000, *Portrait of a Young Girl with a White Cat* (oil on canvas, 39 x 29 ins / 99 x 74 cm) GBP 2,000. VICTORIA, 8 Aug 2000, *Portrait of Baroness Marie Vetsera* (1889, pastel, 37 x 33 ins / 93 x 84 cm) AUD 3,000. MELBOURNE, 27 Nov 2000, *Secret* (1884, oil on canvas, 31 x 52 ins / 79 x 131 cm) AUD 11,500. MILFORD, 24 April 2003, *Interoir with Artist Sketching* (oil on canvas, 38 x 54 ins / 97 x 137 cm) USD 8,500. NEW YORK, 7 Oct 2003, *Lost in Thought* (oil on canvas, 25 x 30 ins / 63 x 76 cm) USD 7,250. SAN FRANCISCO, 18 May 2004, *Proud Mother* (1894, oil on canvas, 34 x 38 ins / 86 x 97 cm) USD 6,500.

KAHLO, Frida

Mexican, 20th century.

Born 6 July 1907, in Coyoacan (Mexico City); died 13 July 1954.

Painter, lithographer. Portraits, figure compositions, allegorical subjects.

Frida Kahlo was Hispano-Indian on her mother's side and German on her father's. She met Diego Rivera while studying medicine when he was painting a mural at the medical school. They married in 1929 and, like Rivera, she became passionately interested in revolutionary politics. She had contracted polio at the age of six and never fully recovered the use of her right leg. In 1925 she also suffered a serious bus accident and became permanently physically handicapped as a result. It was during her convalescence that she began to paint.

The couple spent several years in New York and then returned to San Angel in Mexico where they lived in a double house - each with their own studio - which had been designed by Juan O'Gorman, a pupil of Le Corbusier. In 1937 Trotsky stayed in Kahlo's blue house in Coyoacan. In 1938 she met André Breton in Mexico City. Kahlo and Rivera divorced in 1939 but remarried a year later. Kahlo made a trip to Paris with her husband in 1939 for an exhibition entitled *Mexique* (*Mexico*) organised by Breton, and there she became associated with the Surrealist group. She also met Wolfgang Paalen and his wife Alice Rahon and became friends with Duchamp, Picasso and Kandinsky.

Kahlo painted a series of self-portraits that convey her sufferings in a strange and surreal atmosphere. One of the best known is *Self-portrait with Loose Hair* (1947). Her painting possesses the ingenuousness of naive art while her imagination suggests deeper, disturbing connotations that draw strongly on popular ancestral customs dating back to the Pre-Colombian period: woman as suckling, woman as root, woman as stag. She painted her last self-portrait, entitled *Self-portrait with Diego on my Heart* in 1953-1954. André Breton, who was interested in her work, wrote: 'The art of Frida Kahlo y Rivera is a ribbon tied around a bomb'. She also painted works that recounted different stages in her life such as her miscarriage in 1934. She often showed herself accompanied by small monkeys, a dog, flowers and fruit. Kahlo is one of the major figures of pre-war Mexican art and exerted a noticeable influence on the Surrealist Movement that emerged after the war.

Kahlo took part in collective exhibitions of Surrealist and Mexican art in Mexico and the USA. She held her first solo exhibition in 1938 in the USA at the Julian Levy Gallery in New York and then in Europe. Her first solo exhibition in Mexico City took place in 1953 at the gallery of contemporary art. In Paris there were no solo exhibitions until 1992 when the department store *Printemps* showed some of her paintings as part of the commemoration of the fifth centenary of the discovery of Latin America in 1492. In Switzerland an exhibition entitled *Diego Rivera - Frida Kahlo* was held at the Gianadda Foundation in Martigny in 1998 and then at the Dina Vierny Foundation - Musée Maillol in Paris, also in 1998. In 2001 the National Gallery of Australia in Canberra hosted an exhibition on the theme *Frida Kahlo, Diego Rivera and Mexican Modernism*.

BIBLIOGRAPHY:

Obituary, New York Times Magazine, July 13th 1954. Herrera, Hayden, *Frida: A Biography of Frida Kahlo*, Harper and Row, 1983 and further editions (Also printed by Amazon Books). Jamis, Rauda, *Frida Kahlo, autoportrait d'une femme*, Presses de la Renaissance, Paris, 1985. Prignitz-Poda, Helga/Grimberg, Salomon/Kettenmann, Andrea, *Frida Kahlo, das Gesamtwerk*, Verlag Neue Kritik, Frankfurt am Main, 1988. Zamora, Martha, *Frida Kahlo - La Gerbe d'angoisse*, Chronicle Books, San Francisco, Herscher, Paris, 1990. Herrera, Hayden, *Frida Kahlo: the Paintings*, London, 1991. Lindauer, M.A., *The Art History and popular Celebrity of Frida Kalho*, Middletown (CT), 1998. *Diego Rivera-Frida Kahlo*, exhibition catalogue, Fondation Pierre Gianadda, Martigny, 1998. Noël, Bernard, '*Frida et Diego*' in *Beaux-Arts Magazine* n° 166, periodical, Paris, March 1998. Littman, Robert R./O'Brien, Gregory/White, Anthony/Carr, Barry, *Frida Kahlo, Diego Rivera and Mexican Modernism*, exhibition catalogue, National Gall. of Australia, Canberra, 2001. *Frida Kahlo et Leo Matiz. Un regard sur le Mexique des années 40*, exhibition catalogue, Paris Musées, Paris, 2003.

MUSEUMS AND GALLERIES:

BUFFALO (Albright-Knox AG): *Self-portrait with Monkey* (1938, oil/Masonite) - MEXICO CITY (Mus. Casa de Frida Kahlo): *The Two Fridas* (1939) - OLMEDAO PATINO (Dolores Mus.): *The Broken Column* (1944) - PHOENIX (AM): *El suicidio de Dorothy Hale* (*The Suicide of Dorothy Hale*) (1939, oil/Masonite and painted frame).

AUCTION RECORDS:

NEW YORK, 26 May 1977, *Arbol de la Esperanza Mantente Firme* (*Tree of Hope Stand Firm*) (1946, hardboard, 22 x 16 ins / 56 x 40.6 cm) USD 19,000. NEW YORK, 11 May 1979, *Self-portrait* (1940, hardboard, 22 x 17 1/4 ins / 55 x 43.5 cm) USD 40,000. NEW YORK, 5 May 1981, *Self-portrait* (1932, oil/metal, 12 1/4 x 13 3/4 ins / 31 x 35 cm) USD 35,000. NEW YORK, 29 Nov 1983, *What the Water Gave Me* (1939, oil on canvas, 35 3/4 x 27 3/4 ins / 91 x 70.5 cm) USD 235,000. NEW YORK, 28 May 1985, *Self-portrait* (1929, charcoal, 32 x 25 1/4 ins / 81.3 x 64.2 cm) USD 12,000. NEW YORK, 26 Nov 1985, *Moses* (1945, hardboard, 24 x 29 3/4 ins / 61 x 75.6 cm) USD 210,000. NEW YORK, 19 May 1987, *Portrait of Mrs Jean Wight* (1931, oil on canvas, 25 x 18 ins / 63.5 x 45.6 cm) USD 42,000. NEW YORK, 20 May 1987, *Still-life* (watercolour, 11 x 13 1/2 ins / 28 x 344 cm) USD 16,000. NEW YORK, 17 April 1988, *Barbarous Figures* (1938, 7 3/4 x 9 3/4 ins / 20 x 25 cm) USD 74,250. NEW YORK, 21 Nov 1988, *Self-portrait with Diego on my Heart* (1954, oil/synthetic resin, 23 1/2 x 15 3/4 ins / 59.7 x 40 cm) USD 143,000; *Portrait of Cristina* (1928, oil on panel, 31 x 23 1/2 ins / 79 x 60 cm) USD 198,000; *Frida and the Abortion* (1932, lithograph/Japanese paper, 8 1/4 x 5 3/4 ins / 21 x 14.5 cm) USD 20,900. NEW YORK, 17 May 1989, *Your Mother-in-Law's Canteen* (1927, watercolour/paper, 74 1/2 x 9 3/4 ins / 189.5 x 25 cm) USD 30,800. NEW

YORK, 21 Nov 1989, *Earth Itself or Two Nudes in the Jungle* (1939, oil/tin, 10 x 12 ins / 25.1 x 30.2 cm) USD 506,000. NEW YORK, 2 May 1990, *Diego and I* (1949, oil/synthetic resin, 11 3/4 x 8 3/4 ins / 29.8 x 22.4 cm) USD 1,450,000. NEW YORK, 20-21 Nov 1990, *Sketch for my Ancestors, My Parents and Me* (1943, pencil/paper, 12 x 13 3/4 ins / 30.7 x 35 cm) USD 33,000. NEW YORK, 15-16 May 1991, *Self-portrait with Loose Hair* (1947, oil/synthetic resin, 24 x 17 3/4 ins / 61 x 45 cm) USD 1,650,000. NEW YORK, 18-19 May 1992, *Memory* (1937, oil on canvas, 15 3/4 x 11 1/4 ins / 40 x 28.3 cm) USD 935,000. NEW YORK, 17 May 1995, *Self-portrait with Chango and Loro* (1942, oil/synthetic resin, 21 1/2 x 17 ins / 54.6 x 43.2 cm) USD 3,192,500. NEW YORK, 14-15 May 1996, *Four Inhabitants of Mexico City* (1937, oil/synthetic resin, 12 1/4 x 18 3/4 ins / 31.4 x 47.9 cm) USD 882,500. NEW YORK, 20 Nov 2000, *Lips* (Wood, metal box and objects) USD 47,500. NEW YORK, 20 Nov 2000, *Self-portrait* (oil on panel, miniature, 2 x 2 ins / 5 x 4 cm) USD 200,000. NEW YORK, 30 May 2001, *Karma. Portrait of Nacho Aguirre* (1946 and 1935, sepia ink and pencil, a pair, one double-sided, 9 x 11 ins / 22 x 27 cm) USD 65,000. NEW YORK, 31 May 2001, *Portrait of Cristina, My Sister* (1928, oil on panel, 31 x 24 ins / 79 x 60 cm) USD 1,500,000. MEXICO, 17 Oct 2002, *Handwritten Letter to Frida's Sisters Elenita and Tere* (1952, ink, 11 x 8 ins / 27 x 21 cm) MXP 24,000. NEW YORK, 28 May 2003, *View of Central Park* (1932, watercolour and pencil, 11 x 8 ins / 27 x 20 cm) USD 70,000. NEW YORK, 18 Nov 2003, *Self-portrait with Curly Hair* (1935, oil on tin, 7 x 6 ins / 18 x 14 cm) USD 1,200,000. PARIS, 10 June 2004, *Frida and the Miscarriage* (1932, lithograph, 12 x 9 ins / 31 x 24 cm) EUR 70,000.

KAHN, Annelies
American, 20th century.
Ceramicist.

Annelies Kahn studied at the Rhode Island School of Design and taught ceramics in a number of American universities, including Mountain View College from 1971 to 1974. She has taken part in collective exhibitions in the USA (Corcoran Gallery, Washington, in 1959) and Germany. She has shown her works in solo exhibitions, notably in 1971 at the University of Texas. She has received many awards.

KAHN, Leo
Israeli, 20th century.
Born 1893; died 1983.
Painter. Figures, landscapes, Still-lifes.

In 1981 the Ulmer Museum mounted a retrospective exhibition of the work of Leo Kahn.

AUCTION RECORDS:

TEL AVIV, 2 Jan 1989, *Figure on a Balcony in Safed* (oil on canvas, 32 x 39 1/4 ins / 81.5 x 100 cm) USD 3,740. TEL AVIV, 3 Jan 1990, *Still-life with a Vase and Fruit* (oil on canvas, 19 1/2 x 28 1/2 ins / 49.5 x 72.5 cm) USD 990. TEL AVIV, 19 June 1990, *Landscape* (oil on canvas, 21 1/4 x 29 ins / 54 x 73.5 cm) USD 660. TEL AVIV, 1 Jan 1991, *Still-life with a Vase and Fruit* (oil on canvas, 19 1/2 x 28 1/2 ins / 49.5 x 72.5 cm) USD 1,100. TEL AVIV, 22 April 1995, *View from a Room in La Cadière* (1931, watercolour and pencil, 22 1/2 x 19 1/4 ins / 57.3 x 48.7 cm) USD 5,750. TEL AVIV, 14 April 1996, *Still-life with a Mandolin* (oil on canvas, 23 1/2 x 32 ins / 60 x 81 cm) USD 11,500. STUTTGART, 14 April 2002, *Village Road* (oil on board, 9x14 ins / 24x35 cm) DEM 3,080. TEL AVIV, 1 Dec 2003, *Landscape of the Sharon Valley* (oil on canvas, 19x27 ins / 49x69 cm) USD 1,100.

KAHN, Max
German, 19th century.
Born 22 April 1857, in Mannheim.
Painter. Portraits, genre scenes.

Kahn was a pupil of Tony-Robert Fleury at the Académie Julian in Paris. His works include landscapes of Brittany, particularly views of the Île de Bréhat. In 1899, he gained an honourable mention in Paris.

AUCTION RECORDS:

PARIS, 16 May 1979, *Rembrandt Bugatti* (oil on canvas, 39 1/4 x 28 3/4 ins / 100 x 73 cm) FRF 6,000.

KAHN, Nicole
French, 20th century.
Born 31 March 1914, in Paris.
Painter.

Nicole Kahn studied under André Lhote.

KAHN, Robin
American, 20th - 21st century.
Born 1961, in New York.
Painter (mixed media).

Robin Kahn has exhibited regularly in New York galleries since 1987.

AUCTION RECORDS:

PARIS, 16 Dec 1990, *Women Stay Put II* (1990, embroidery/canvas, 59 3/4 x 36 1/4 ins / 152 x 92 cm) FRF 5,200.

KAHN, Wolf
German, 20th century.
Born 1927, in Stuttgart.
Active from 1941 in the USA.
Painter. Landscapes, urban landscapes, flowers.

Wolf Kahn left Germany in 1939, spent a year in London, then settled in New York. In 1950, he took lessons from Hans Hoffmann at the University of Chicago.

He took part in many group exhibitions, including the Whitney Annual in 1957, 1958 and 1961, *Young America* at the Whitney Museum in 1960, and the Japan Biennale in 1961. He had solo shows in New York in 1954, 1955, 1956, 1958, 1961 and 1962.

MUSEUMS AND GALLERIES:

NEW YORK (MoMA) - NEW YORK (Whitney Mus. of American Art) - VIRGINIA (MFA).

AUCTION RECORDS:

NEW YORK, 2 Oct 1985, pastel, 10 1/4 x 13 1/4 ins / 26 x 33.6 cm) USD 1,300. NEW YORK, 4 Dec 1987, *River* (oil on canvas, 44 x 64 ins / 111.7 x 162.5 cm) USD 14,000. NEW YORK, 26 April 1988, *After Sunset II* (oil on canvas, 42 x 66 ins / 106.7 x 167.6 cm) USD 18,700. NEW YORK, 30 Sept 1988, *A Corner of Blue Sky* (oil on canvas, 32 x 54 1/4 ins / 81 x 137.5 cm) USD 7,700. NEW YORK, 8 Oct 1988, *Landing Ground* (1983, oil on canvas, 36 x 52 ins / 91.5 x 132.2 cm) USD 12,100. NEW YORK, 24 Jan 1989, *Flowers in a Vase* (pastel/paper, 10 3/4 x 8 1/2 ins / 27.5 x 21.3 cm) USD 1,760. NEW YORK, 25 May 1989, *Summer Flowers in a Glass Vase* (oil on canvas, 34 x 25 ins / 86.2 x 63.4 cm) USD 6,050. NEW YORK, 28 Sept 1989, *Crab-apple Trees in Tennessee* (1981, oil on canvas, 36 x 52 ins / 91.5 x 132 cm) USD 11,000. NEW YORK, 24 Jan 1990, *Stuyvesant Square* (pastel/paper, 14 x 17 ins / 35.5 x 43.2 cm) USD 1,320. NEW YORK, 27 Feb 1990, *River Banks near the Sheep Farm* (1987, oil on canvas, 32 1/4 x 52 ins / 82 x 132 cm) USD 13,200. NEW YORK, 26 Sept 1990, *The Big Barn* (1972, oil on canvas, 36 x 52 ins / 91.4 x 132 cm) USD 8,800. NEW YORK, 14 March 1991, *The Connecticut River at Dawn* (1975, oil on canvas, 22 x 36 1/2 ins / 56 x 92.5 cm) USD 8,250. NEW YORK, 22 May 1991, *The Sawmill* (1975, oil on canvas, 42 1/2 x 54 1/4 ins / 108 x 138 cm) USD 11,000. NEW YORK, 26 Sept 1991, *Late Afternoon* (oil on canvas, 50 x 41 1/2 ins / 127 x 105.5 cm) USD 13,200. NEW YORK, 12 March 1992, *Jenk's Farm* (oil on canvas, 22 x 32 ins / 55.9 x 81.3 cm) USD 2,860. NEW YORK, 31 March 1993, *Mr Hamilton's Heifers* (oil on canvas, 24 x 29 3/4 ins / 61 x 75.6 cm) USD 5,175. NEW YORK, 24 Feb 1995, *Railroad beside a River* (1991, oil on canvas, 44 1/4 x 66 ins / 112.4 x 167.6 cm) USD 18,400. NEW YORK, 10 Oct 1996, *The Adams' Farm* (1976, oil on canvas, 14 x 22 ins / 35.6 x 55.9 cm) USD 2,760. NEW YORK, 3 Dec 1996, *Orchards, Green Mountain II* (oil on canvas, 24 x 34 ins / 61 x 86.3 cm) USD 6,325.

KAHN DE CHAUMESNIL, Louise (Mme)
French, 19th - 20th century.
Active in Paris.
Painter.
Louise Kahn de Chaumesnil became a member of the Société des Artistes Français in 1909.

KÄHR, Jakob
Swiss, 19th century.
Born 27 May 1865, in Bern.
Sculptor.
Kähr studied successively with the sculptor Lorenti in Bern, then at the Brera in Milan and finally with Sartorio in Geneva. He worked in Lyons, Bern and Zurich.

KAHRER, Max
Romanian, 20th century.
Born 8 July 1878, in Temesvár (now Timisoara); died 1937.
Painter. Landscapes.
Max Kahrer studied at the Akademie der Bildenden Künste in Vienna, where he regularly exhibited views (mainly of Austria and Bavaria).

AUCTION RECORDS:
PARIS, 22 Feb 1943, *Cathedral* (1902) FRF 500. VIENNA, 22 June 1976, *View of Klosterneuburg* (1917, oil on canvas, 19 x 20¾ ins / 48.5 x 53 cm) ATS 13,000. VIENNA, 18 March 1977, *View of Chiemsee* (oil on canvas, 28 x 32 ins / 71 x 81 cm) ATS 20,000. VIENNA, 13 March 1984, *Danube in Vienna* (oil on card, 12½ x 17¼ ins / 32 x 44 cm) ATS 25,000. VIENNA, 19 May 1987, *Bisamberg at Sunset* (1907, oil on canvas, 20½ x 31 ins / 52 x 79 cm) ATS 35,000. VIENNA, 31 Oct 2000, *Landscape* (1931, oil on wood, 24 x 19 ins / 61 x 47 cm) ATS 55,000. VIENNA, 29 Nov 2000, *At the Danube* (1923, oil on canvas, 21 x 26 ins / 54 x 66 cm) ATS 75,000. VIENNA, 30 May 2001, *Klosterneuberg, Kritzendorf Bathing Beach, Kahlenberg beyond* (1931, oil on panel, 24 x 38 ins / 62 x 96 cm) ATS 65,000. VIENNA, 16 Oct 2001, *By the Danube, Leopoldsberg beyond* (1981, oil on panel, 15 x 24 ins / 38 x 61 cm) ATS 38,000. VIENNA, 12 Nov 2002, *Autumn in Schiessstattgraben* (1934, oil on panel, 20 x 24 ins / 50 x 60 cm) EUR 1,900. VIENNA, 26 Nov 2002, *Danube meadows near Klosterneuburg* (oil on canvas, 36 x 36 ins / 92 x 92 cm) EUR 2,200. AMSTERDAM, 18 Feb 2003, *Alpine Village, South Tyrol. Kitchen Garden* (1914, oil on canvas, a pair, 29 x 31 ins / 74 x 79 cm) EUR 8,000.

KAHRS, Johannes
German, 20th - 21st century.
Born 1965, in Bremen.
Painter, draughtsman, video artist. Figures, self-portraits.
Johannes Kahrs' work questions the presence of images in our society. Faces and bodies, sometimes placed in violent situations, emphasise the transformation in relationships between individuals. He is also interested in the extent to which the real or the virtual disrupts these changes. Since 1994, he has been working on a series of self-portraits.

He has participated in group exhibitions including: 1994, *Postconceptional Painting* at the Kunstwerke in Berlin; 1997, *Korrespondenzen* (*Correspondences*) at the Berlinische Galerie Martin Gropius-Bau in Berlin and at the Scottish National Gallery of Modern Art in Edinburgh; 1997, *Fenêtre sur Cour* (*Window overlooking Courtyard*) at the Galerie Almine Rech in Paris; 1998, Berlin Biennale; 1999, *Rue Louise Weiss*, Centre d'Art Contemporain in Meymac; 2002, *Indoor* at the Stedelijk Museum voor Aktuele Kunst in Ghent; 2002 Taipei Biennale and 2002, *Cardinals* at the MARCO - Museo de Arte Contemporánea in Vigo, Spain. He has also shown his works in solo exhibitions, including 1993 at the Galerie Mutzek in Berlin; 1997, 1999 and 2000 at the Galerie Almine Rech in Paris; 2001, a travelling exhibition at the Stedelijk Museum voor Aktuele Kunst in Ghent, the Fonds Régional des Pays de la Loire in Nantes and the Munich Kunstverein. In 2003, he featured in *Berlin-Moscow/Moscow-Berlin 1950-2000*, a panoramic exhibition at the Martin Gropius-Bau in Berlin and the Tretyakov Gallery in Moscow, that was a follow up to a previous exhibition covering the period 1900-1950, opening up a discussion of 50 years of artistic and cultural relations between Germany and Russia marked by sweeping political changes.

BIBLIOGRAPHY:
Johannes Kahrs, Rencontres 3, Gal. Almine Recherches et Images Modernes, Paris, 2000. *A - h*, exhibition catalogue, Fonds régional d'Art contemporain des Pays de la Loire, Nantes, Stedelijk Museum voor Aktuele Kunst, Gent, Kunstverein, Munich, 2001. '*Berlin-Moskau/Moskau-Berlin 1950-2000*' in *2 vol.*, exhibition catalogue, Martin-Gropius-Bau, Berlin, 2003 (text in German).

KAI, Jakob
German, 16th century.
Born in Lützen.
Painter.
Würzburg School.
Jakob Kai worked in Würzburg between 1566 and 1590.

KAI, Masayuki
Japanese, 20th - 21st century.
Born 1958, in Hiroshima.
Active in France from 1976.
Painter.
Masayuki Kai studied under Claude Viallat at Marseille-Luminy Arts School in 1976, graduating in 1981. He lives and works in Paris and Aix-en-Provence. Influenced by the ideas of the Support-Surface group on the materiality of painting, he shapes the texture of the surface of his 'canvases' by burying them in the ground for a time and then takes them from the ground covered in stains like a shroud, washes them, cuts them into geometric figures which he then reapplies onto a new support by sewing them into place.

Kai has taken part in group exhibitions since 1980, among which were: *Contemporary Presence*, Aix-en-Provence; the Biennale de la jeune peinture méditerranéenne, Nice; Salon Grands et Jeunes d'Aujourd'hui, Paris; the Salon de Mai, Paris; *Contemporary Japanese Artists*, East Forum Junku, Paris. He mounted solo exhibitions in 1980 at the Yokota Gallery, Hiroshima; in 1980 at Studio 37, Marseilles; in 1981 at the Psyche Gallery, Martigues; and in 1982 at the Ginza Gallery, Surugadai, Tokyo. In 1984 he was awarded the grand prize in the 16th Festival international de la peinture at Cagnes-sur-Mer.

KAI CH'I. See **GAI QI**

KAI K'I. See **GAI QI**

KAIGETSUDO, Anchi, or Kwaigetsudo, Yasumoto, artist name: Choyodo
Japanese, 18th century.
Died 1716.
Active in Edo (Tokyo) at the beginning of the 18th century.
Painter, print artist. Screens.
Anchi Kaigetsudo was a pupil of Kaigetsudo Ando and used the first two syllables of his master's first name for his own. He is the only one of Ando's direct disciples to have had the name of a studio as his own and some think that he was granted this privilege because he was actually Ando's son. His known works consist of about seventeen paintings and seven prints as well as one extremely rare work: a small *hina-byobu* (miniature screen), the only one (as far as is known) which ever emerged from the Kaigetsudo studio. The article is in fact a pair of six-leaf screens. Anchi was a painter of courtesans and succeeded in imbuing them with a more openly erotic character than his master did. His tech-

nique is that of an print artist rather than a painter. His prints contain a certain coldness and rigidity.
MUSEUMS AND GALLERIES:
CHICAGO (AI): *Courtesan* (c. 1710).

KAIGETSUDO, Ando, or Yasunobu, popular name: Genshichi Okazaki, artist names: Kan'unshi, Ando, Kaigetsudo Ando
Japanese, 18th century.
Painter.
Ukiyo-e (pictures of the floating world).
Ando Kaigetsudo and the school that he founded, and to which he gave his name, belong to the 'primitive' stage of the ukiyo-e movement. The pictures produced by the school were predominantly of beautiful women about town; they were mass-produced and have a particularly stylised look about them, which adds a boldness to the rhythmic movement of their sumptuous robes. Such pictures would become the stock-in-trade of later ukiyo-e artists. But the reason we know Ando's name is because of his involvement in a scandal between Ejima, a lady-in-waiting at the court of the shogun, and Ikushima Shingoro, a celebrated *kabuki* actor; it caused a great stir in Edo (Tokyo) in 1714 and as a result, Ando was forced to take exile on the island of Oshima. It is not known whether he ever returned to Edo.

His paintings, which are his only known works, perfectly symbolise the early 18th century and the close of the famous Genroku era (1688-1704), which saw the zenith of the wealth of the merchant class and its taste for elegance. Working in his studio in the Asakusa quarter in Edo, not far from the Yoshiwara, the pleasure quarter, Ando continued in the style of the genre painters of the end of the preceding century, specialising in the portrayal of *bijin* or beautiful women, who were in fact the most famous courtesans. He created a type of monumental woman, with clothes sumptuously decorated with thick, flexible lines that contrast with the delicate features of the faces with their slightly plump cheeks. It is not known whether he himself practised the art of printing, but his disciples would leave several of what are now extremely rare examples of sumizuri-e (monochrome woodcut prints). These are large and divided into two horizontally-joined halves. Other than his immediate disciples who bore the name of his studio, he also had many followers up to the middle of the 18th century, such as Tosendo, Rifu, Takizawa, Shigenobu, Baiyuken Katsunobu, Baioken Nagaharu and Takeda Harunobu. It is possible that he is the same person as the artist Kaigetsudo Ankei.
BIBLIOGRAPHY:
Seiichiro, Takashi, *Kaigetsudo Ando*, Charles E. Tuttle Co., Rutland (USA), Tokyo, 1959.

KAIGORODOFF, Anatol
Russian, 20th century.
Born 2 November 1878, in St Petersburg.
Painter.
Anatol Kaigorodoff was a student of Simon Hollosy in Munich and of Colarossi in Paris.
MUSEUMS AND GALLERIES:
ST PETERSBURG (Gosudarstvennyj Russkij Muz.): several landscapes.

KAIHO, Terumichi. See **YUTOKU**

KAIHO, Yusen
Japanese, 18th century.
Active in Kyoto during the first half of the 18th century.
Painter.

KAIHO, Yusho, nickname: Jomon, artist names: Shogen, Yokumon, Yusho
Japanese, 19th century.
Born 1817; died 1868.
Painter.
Kaiho School.

KAIHO DOKI. See **YUSETSU**

KAIKAN. See **FUJIWARA Nagataka**

KAIKEI, religious name: An-amidabutsu, artist name: Kaikei
Japanese, 12th - 13th century.
Active during the Kamakura period (1185-1337).
Monk-sculptor.
A monk in the Shunjobo Chogen (Pure Land) sect of Buddhism, Kaikei was a disciple of Kokei, the father of Unkei (d. 1123), and together the three sculptors defined the new Kamakura style of sculpture, with its revival of the realism of the Nara period (8th century). Yet while the works of Unkei are imbued with strength and power combined with extreme spirituality, those of Kaikei are more reflective of Chinese Song dynasty Buddhist painting, in that they are typified by the gentleness of the faces and the suppleness of delicate bodies, approaching a kind of formal beauty without exaggerated sweetness or prettiness. Kaikei brought touches of grace and calm to his work, thereby creating a new and distinctive style that was his alone. He took the religious name Annamidabutsu, from which the term Annami style was derived to describe his art. In 1203 he was awarded the rank of hokkyo, and in 1210 promoted to hogen.

Many of his works are extant, such as the *Miroku* (Sanskrit: Maitreya) in the Boston Museum, dated 1189, the *Jizo* (Sanskrit: Ksitigarbha) of the Kodai-ji temple in Nara, the *Amida* (Sanskrit: Amitâbha) of the same temple, dated 1208, the *Amida* of the Kodai-in temple in Koya-san, dated 1221 and other works, as well as several copies of old masters.
BIBLIOGRAPHY:
Kuno, Takeshi, *A Guide to Japanese Sculpture*, Mayuyama, Tokyo, 1963. Fahr-Becker, Gabriele (ed.), *The Art of East Asia: Volume 2*, Konemann, Cologne, 1998 (mentioned briefly).
MUSEUMS AND GALLERIES:
BOSTON (MFA): *Miroku, the Bodhisattva of the Future* (1189).

KAIKINGER, Marie
French, 20th century.
Born 8 May 1933.
Painter.
Marie Kaikinger exhibited at the Salon d'Automne, the Salon Comparaisons and the Salon des Indépendants in Paris. She was awarded first prize at the Salon de Luchon.

KAINER, Ludwig
German, 20th century.
Born 28 June 1885, in Munich; died 1967.
Painter, draughtsman, illustrator, poster artist, decorative designer, lithographer. Stage costumes and sets.
Ludwig Kainer started out as a doctor and only later became an artist. From 1904 to 1914, he lived in Paris. In 1910, he married the artist Lene Schneider, known as Schneider-Kainer. They were in Berlin in 1912, but separated in 1926. Kainer spent some time in India in 1924-1925.

He worked on the magazine *Simplicissimus* and also for Diaghilev's Ballets Russes and the Berlin Opera. He produced the illustrations for *Russisches Ballett* (*Russian Ballet*) (1909), an album presenting the dancers Nijinsky and Karsavina. He was interested in fashion and produced illustrations for *Die Dame* (*The Lady*). He achieved success with his posters and book illustrations. His use of colour attracted attention. He owned a painting by Monet, *Au Parc Monceau* (*In the Parc Monceau*), which his descendants were forced to sell in 1935 under pressure from the Nazis and their policy of robbing and marginalising the Jews.

KAIOKU, real name: Nukina Ho, given name: Kane, alternate names: Kummo, Shizen, nicknames: Yasujiro, Seizaburo, artist names: Kaioku, Shuo, Suo, Hochiku Shujin, Kaikyaku, Kaisen, Kaiso, Sankando, Shuseido, Tekishuo
Japanese, 19th century.
Born 1778, in Awa (now Tokushima); died 1863, in Kyoto.
Painter. Landscapes.
Late Edo period.
Nanga (literati) school.

Kaioku was a teacher of Confucian studies, a calligrapher and landscape painter.

KAISEKI, real name: Noro Ryu, alternate names: Ryunen, Shorei, Daigoryu, Kuichiro, artist names: Kaiseki, Waibai, Shiheki-dojin, Daigaku-shosha, Chomei, Juyu, Konsai
Japanese, 18th - 19th century.
Born 1747, in Wakayama; died 1828.
Painter.
Nanga (literati) school.

Kaiseki is said to have studied with Kakutei, the monk-painter of the Nagasaki school, before returning to Kyoto to study with Ike no Taiga. He is known for his copy of Huang Gongwang's Stone Cliffs between Heaven and Earth (in Senju-in, Tonomine) and for his treatise on painting, the *Shihekisai gawa*.

KAISEN, real name: Oda Ei, nicknames: Kyokai, Ryohei, artist names: Hyakukoku, Kaisen
Japanese, 19th century.
Born 1785, in Nagano; died 1862, in Kyoto.
Painter.
Nanga (literati) school.

Kaisen was a disciple of Goshun (1752-1811) and Rai San'yo (1780-1832). He later turned towards towards landscape and figure painting, as well as birds and flowers, becoming a leading figure in the Nanga (Southern school) style.

KAISER, Adolf
German, 19th century.
Born 1804, in Geisa (near Fulda); died 21 April 1861, in Weimar.
Landscape painter.

Kaiser studied at the Munich academy; he later worked in Italy and exhibited in Munich and Weimar. In 1834, he was appointed director of the school of fine arts in Weimar. The museum in Weimar has a *Landscape* by him.

KAISER, Anton
Austrian, 19th - 20th century.
Born 5 November 1863.
Engraver.

Anton Kaiser is best-known for his engravings of old paintings.

KAISER, Edouard
Swiss, 19th - 20th century.
Born 21 September 1865, in La Chaux-de-Fonds.
Painter. Interiors with figures, landscapes.

Edouard Kaiser studied with Hirschy at La Chaux-de-Fonds and then worked in Paris, Milan, Venice, Belgium and Holland. From 1886, he exhibited at the Salons des Amis des Arts in Geneva and at the Société Suisse des Beaux-Arts. In 1887, he was appointed professor at the art school in La Chaux-de-Fonds.

MUSEUMS AND GALLERIES:
LA CHAUX-DE-FONDS: *Interior of an Engraver's Studio; The Box-Makers* - NEUCHÂTEL: *Near Beaufonds* - ST GALL: *The Blümisalp*.

KAISER, Eduard
Austrian, 19th century.
Born 22 February 1820, in Graz; died 30 August 1895, in Vienna.
Watercolourist, lithographer.

Kaiser was a pupil of Danhauser and is noted for a *Portrait of the Emperor Franz Joseph on Horseback and with his Retinue*.

AUCTION RECORDS:
VIENNA, 16 May 1984, *Portrait of a Young Girl* (oil on canvas, 15 3/4 x 12 1/2 ins / 40 x 32 cm) ATS 30,000. LONDON, 19 April 1999, *Portrait of a Young Boy, Seated, with a King Charles Spaniel* (miniature, oval, h. 6ins / 15cm) GBP 2,300.

KAISER, Ernst
Bavarian School, 19th century.
Born 20 July 1803, in Rain-am-Lech (Bavaria); died 23 December 1865, in Munich.
Painter, watercolourist. Historical subjects, landscapes with figures, landscapes, mountainscapes.

Kaiser was trained by his father (still-life painter Georg Kaiser), the academy in Munich and Preller, with whom he went to Rome in September 1828. He remained there for a year, then returned to settle in Munich, where he first exhibited (1836). He later also exhibited in Berlin, Hanover and Cologne.

Kaiser started out with history painting, but turned to landscapes following a trip to the Bavarian Alps and the Tyrol. He was a protégé of Ludwig of Bavaria, who put up the funds for him to visit the Styrian Alps. He had a distinctive style as a painter of mountains.

MUSEUMS AND GALLERIES:
HANOVER: *Lake Gossar* - KALININGRAD: *Hintersee Lake* - MUNICH: *Landscape*.

AUCTION RECORDS:
VIENNA, 29-30 Oct 1996, *Herd of Heifers Drinking beside a Lake* (1857, oil on canvas, 13 1/4 x 20 ins / 33.5 x 50.5 cm) ATS 402,500. LONDON, 29 Jan 2003, *Collecting Hay* (oil on canvas, 25 x 25 ins / 63 x 63 cm) GBP 1,100.

KAISER, Friedrich
German, 19th century.
Born 21 January 1815, in Lörrach (Baden); died 13 October 1889, in Berlin.
Painter, engraver. Historical subjects, battles.

Kaiser went to Paris and studied lithography based on the works of Horace Vernet. He then returned to Munich and took up painting. In the wars of 1864, 1866 and 1870, he endeavoured especially to reproduce battle scenes. He exhibited mainly in Berlin.

AUCTION RECORDS:
LONDON, 23 Feb 1977, *Kaiser Wilhelm I Surrounded by His Generals* (oil on canvas, 9 x 13 ins / 23 x 33 cm) GBP 600. ROME, 6 March 1984, *The Defeat (The Retreat)* (oil on canvas, 11 1/2 x 22 3/4 ins / 29 x 58 cm) ITL 2,200,000. VIENNA, 29-30 Oct 1996, *Cavalry Battle in the Middle Ages* (1849, oil on canvas, 31 x 44 ins / 78.5 x 112 cm) ATS 109,250. HAMBURG, 5 May 1999, *King Wilhelm I Inspecting His Troops* (oil on canvas, 9 x 12 ins / 22 x 30 cm) DEM 8,000. MUNICH, 24 Sept 2003, *Prussian Cavalry near Koniggratz* (oil on canvas, 17 x 24 ins / 43 x 60 cm) EUR 2,300. AMSTERDAM, 28 Oct 2003, *Battle of Balaklawa at the Sapoune Heights on the Crim-25th October 1854* (oil on canvas, 60 x 86 ins / 153 x 218 cm) EUR 95,000. COLOGNE, 1 April 2004, *Prussian Cavalry on the March in the Dunes* (oil on canvas, 11 x 16 ins / 29 x 40 cm) EUR 3,600.

KAISER, Georg
German, 18th - 19th century.
Born 1767; died c. 1835.
Active in Neuburg an der Donau.

Painter. Still-lifes.
The father of Ernst Kaiser, who was his pupil.

KAISER, Johan Wilhelm
Dutch, 19th century.
Born 5 January 1813, in Amsterdam; died 21 November 1900, in Leiden.
Engraver.
Johan Kaiser studied under A.-B. Taurel. From 1833 to 1839 he served in the Dutch artillery. In 1859 he was director of a school of engraving and in 1870 taught at the academy. He became director of the Rijksmuseum in Amsterdam in 1874 and was made a chevalier of the Légion d'Honneur in 1869. His works include *The Trustees; The Night Watch, Portrait of Burgomaster Six* after Rembrandt; *Celebration of the Peace of Münster* after Van de Helst; *Jan Steen as a Child* after Steen; *The Death of Admiral de Ruyter* after N. Pieneman; *The Widow Oldenborneveld before Prince Maurice* after H.-H. Scholten; *The Assassination of Prince William I, 18 March 1582* after M. Pieneman; *Woman Knitting* after J. Israels; *J.-W. Pieneman* after N. Pieneman; *Jan Pietersz. Koen, Governor of the Indies*; and 50 *Engravings after Pictures from the Six Gallery in Amsterdam*.

KAISER, Joseph, or Kayser, or Keiser
Swiss, 18th - 19th century.
Born 1763, in Dagmersellen (Lucerne canton); died c. 1820.
Sculptor.
Kaiser was a pupil of Schäfer in Lucerne from 1775 to 1779 and subsequently worked in Bern, Strasbourg and Mannheim, where he won various medals. In 1798, he settled in Karlsruhe.

KAISER, Karl Georg
Swiss, 19th - 20th century.
Born 20 April 1843, in Stans; died 20 August 1916, in Stans.
Painter.
After studying in Karlsruhe, Karl Kaiser returned to Switzerland, where he painted a few portraits but mainly focused on religious pieces.

KAISER, Ludwig Friedrich
German, 19th century.
Born 28 February 1779, in Ulm; died 3 February 1819, in Vienna.
Painter, engraver (burin). History painting, battles.
Kaiser was a pupil of Christian von Mechel in Basel. Friedrich Bertuch, in Weimar, got him to do several plates for his *Bilderbuch für Kinder* (picture-book for children). In Paris, he engraved some classical heads under the direction of Bervic in 1806, and in Naples in 1809, he did colour engravings representing views and popular scenes after Pinelli. In 1814, he went to Vienna and was appointed court painter.

KAISER, Nicolas
German, 18th - 19th century.
Born 1751, in Bamberg; died 1829, in Warsaw.
Painter.
Kaiser went to Poland during the reign of Stanislaw II Augustus Poniatowski and became a teacher of painting and drawing.

KAISER, Raffi
Israeli, 20th century.
Draughtsman. Landscapes.
Raffi Kaiser studied at the art school in Tel Aviv and then from 1952 to 1954 at the École des Beaux-Arts in Paris, followed by the art college in Florence from 1955 to 1957.

His work was featured in collective exhibitions: 1963, at the Salons d'Automne and de la Jeune Peinture in Paris; 1969, *Five Israeli Painters* at the Saginaw Museum, Michigan; 1970, *International Biennale of Graphic Art* in Bradford; 1975, *International Art Fair* in Basel, and at the Jewish Museum in New York; 1977, *Perspective israélienne* (*Israeli Perspective*) at the Galerie Nationale du Grand Palais in Paris. His solo shows included: 1968, Brussels; 1968, 1972, Tel Aviv; 1977, New York; 1978, Haifa; and 1981, the Galerie Noire in Paris.

He produced strongly drawn pen and ink work in the tradition of Renaissance painters, evoking in careful detail various landscapes, but principally those of Israel, the land of his forebears.

KAISER, Richard
German, 19th - 20th century.
Born 13 August 1868, in Magdeburg; died 1941.
Painter, engraver. Waterscapes, landscapes.
Richard Kaiser was active in Munich, winning a medal there in 1905, as well as at the 1900 Exposition Universelle in Paris.
Museums and Galleries:
Munich (Pinakothek): *Lake Constance*.
Auction records:
Vienna, 18 March 1987, *Stormy Landscape* (1919, oil on canvas, 61 x 74 3/4 ins / 155 x 190 cm) ATS 90,000. Columbia, 25 Sept 1999, *Landscape with Country Road* (oil on canvas, 18 x 23 ins / 46 x 58 cm) USD 2,050. Munich, 5 July 2000, *Lower Alpine Landscape in Summer* (1918, oil on canvas, 18 x 24 ins / 46 x 61 cm) DEM 5,500. Munich, 27 Sept 2000, *Summer River Landscape, possibly in Franken* (1934, oil on canvas, 24 x 31 ins / 61 x 80 cm) DEM 9,000. Munich, 4 June 2002, *Fraueninsel, Chiemsee* (oil on canvas, 28 x 33 ins / 72 x 85 cm) EUR 2,500. Munich, 25 Sept 2002, *Summer Evening near Diessen* (oil on canvas, 40 x 59 ins / 101 x 151 cm) EUR 2,600. Furth, 17 Oct 2003, *Woodland Pond* (1909, oil on canvas, 16 x 20 ins / 41 x 50 cm) EUR 1,600. Munich, 30 June 2004, *Landscape with Trees by a River* (1902, oil on canvas, 67 x 83 ins / 170 x 210 cm) EUR 4,000.

KAISER-HERBST, Carl
Austrian, 19th - 20th century.
Born 8 November 1858, in Vienna; died 1940, in Vienna.
Painter. Landscapes.
Kaiser-Herbst is represented by a substantial number of works in the collection of the Princes of Liechtenstein.
Auction records:
Vienna, 12 Nov 1980, *Banks of the Danube at Klosterneuburg* (1929, oil on canvas, 22 1/2 x 31 1/2 ins / 57 x 80 cm) ATS 22,000. Vienna, 14 Sept 1982, *View of Vienna from the Belvedere* (oil on card remounted/panel, 15 3/4 x 22 3/4 ins / 40 x 58 cm) ATS 35,000. Vienna, 11 June 2002, *Sunny Monastery Garden* (oil on board, 14 x 17 ins / 35 x 43 cm) EUR 2,500. Vienna, 25 May 2004, *Garden* (oil on board, 14 x 17 ins / 35 x 43 cm) EUR 3,000.

KAISERMAN, Franz. See **KAISERMANN**

KAISERMANN, Franz, or Keiserman, Keizerman
Swiss, 18th - 19th century.
Born 27 February 1765, in Yverdon (Lake Geneva); died 3 January 1833, in Rome.
Painter, watercolourist. Landscapes, architectural views.
Kaisermann was the son of a stone mason. In 1783, he set off for Rome, where he was a pupil of Ducros for a while. Noticed by Prince Borghese, he did several paintings for him. After remaining in Naples for six years, he settled in Rome, renouncing his Protestant faith in 1828. He painted landscapes and monuments.
Auction records:
London, 9 April 1910, *The Colosseum and St Peter's in Rome* (watercolour) GBP 4. Paris, 28-31 Dec 1925, *Peasants Resting* (watercolour and gouache) FRF 115. Paris, 2 March 1928, *The*

Colosseum in Rome (watercolour) FRF 130. PARIS, 4 May 1928, *View of the Arch of Constantine* (ink and wash) FRF 400. PARIS, 15 April 1944, *Washerwomen beside a River*, FRF 2,700. LONDON, 4 July 1972, *The Colosseum; the Foro Romano; the Pantheon; the Temple of Paestum* (watercolour) Gns 1,100. LONDON, 15 June 1976, *The Tivoli Falls* (watercolour and pencil, 20 1/2 x 14 1/4 ins / 52 x 36 cm) GBP 240. LONDON, 25 Oct 1977, *View of Rome from Monte Mario* (1816, watercolour and pencil, 21 1/4 x 29 3/4 ins / 54 x 75.5 cm) GBP 750. LONDON, 13 March 1980, *View of Lake Geneva* (1819, watercolour and pencil, 17 1/2 x 23 3/4 ins / 44.2 x 60.6 cm) GBP 1,300. NEW YORK, 8 Aug 1980, *View of Paestum* (1824, watercolour, 26 1/2 x 41 1/4 ins / 67.5 x 104.5 cm) USD 2,000. LONDON, 24 Nov 1983, *View of the Colosseum, Rome* (1818, watercolour and pen, 26 x 40 1/4 ins / 66 x 102.2 cm) GBP 7,000. AMSTERDAM, 26 Nov 1984, *View of Rome* (watercolour and pencil, 41 1/4 x 26 1/2 ins / 104.5 x 67.5 cm) NLG 9,000. LONDON, 19 June 1986, *View of the Terni Falls in Twilight* (1819, watercolour and pencil, 22 x 30 ins / 55 x 76 cm) GBP 4,400. LONDON, 1 April 1987, *View of Tivoli at Sunset; View of the Tivoli Falls at Dawn* (drawing in black chalk and wash, a pair, 16 x 21 1/2 ins / 40.6 x 54.7 cm) GBP 3,200. ROME, 14 Dec 1988, *View of the Colosseum* (watercolour/paper, 21 1/4 x 29 1/4 ins / 54 x 74 cm) ITL 12,000,000. NEW YORK, 11 Jan 1989, *View of Campovacino at Sunrise; View of Campovacino at Sunset with the Capitol* (a pair, 21 x 29 1/2 ins / 53.5 x 75 cm) USD 13,200. ROME, 31 May 1990, *View of the Pantheon* (watercolour/paper, 25 1/2 x 39 1/4 ins / 65 x 100 cm) ITL 49,000,000. MONACO, 8 Dec 1990, *View of the Foro Romano* (watercolour, 25 1/4 x 38 1/4 ins / 64 x 97 cm) FRF 44,400. MONACO, 18-19 June 1992, *View of the Colosseum in Rome* (watercolour and ink, 11 1/2 x 16 1/2 ins / 29.5 x 42 cm) FRF 33,300. PARIS, 23 June 1993, *Pyramid of Caius Cestius and English Cemetery in Rome* (watercolour, 5 1/4 x 8 ins / 13.5 x 20.5 cm) FRF 7,200. LONDON, 5 July 1993, *Temple at Paestum* (1802, ink and watercolour, 26 3/4 x 38 1/2 ins / 68 x 98 cm) GBP 4,830. ROME, 8 March 1994, *View of the Arch of Titus* (watercolour/paper, 40 1/2 x 26 1/2 ins / 103 x 67 cm) ITL 34,500,000. PARIS, 18 Oct 1995, *View behind the Sirens' Grotto in Tivoli* (1811, watercolour, 20 1/4 x 26 ins / 51.5 x 66 cm) FRF 55,000. HEIDELBERG, 11-12 April 1997, *The Falls of Tivoli; The Falls of Tivoli Seen Through an Arch* (1813, watercolour and gouache and pencil outlines, a pair, 17 1/4 x 12 1/4 ins / 43.8 x 31.4 cm and 16 3/4 x 12 ins/42.8 x 30.5 cm) DEM 28,000. ROME, 2 Dec 1997, *Vagrants in a Landscape* (watercolour/paper, 20 1/2 x 29 1/4 ins / 52 x 74 cm) ITL 11,500,000.

KAISH, Morton
American, 20th century.
Born 1927, in Newark (New Jersey).
Painter.

Morton Kaish studied at Syracuse University and then for a time at the Academie de la Grande Chaumiere in Paris, the Istituto d'Arte in Florence and the Accademia delle belle Arti in Rome. He exhibited several times in New York. He lived in Rome from 1971 to 1973, when he produced paintings halfway between figuration and abstraction.

KAISIN, Lucien
Belgian, 20th century.
Born 1901; died 1963, in Ixelles (Brussels).
Painter.

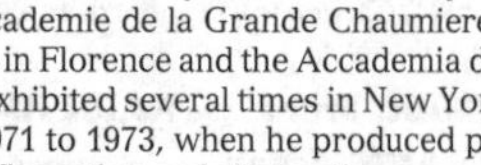

KAIVANTO, Kimmo
Finnish, 20th century.
Born 1932, in Tampere.
Painter.

KAJI, Tameya
Japanese, 19th century.
Born in Wakayama Prefecture; died 1894, in Tokyo.
Painter.

Kaji painted in the Western style. In 1875 he travelled to the USA then to Germany where he studied oil painting.

KAJIWARA, Takuma
Japanese, 20th century.
Born 15 November 1876, in Japan; died 1960, in the USA.
Painter, photographer. Portraits.

Kajiwara Takuma emigrated to the USA in about 1900. He was a member of the American Federation of the Arts and won many awards including a silver medal for portraits in Kansas City in 1926.

KAKABADZE, David
Russian, 20th century.
Born 1889, in Georgia; died 1952.
Painter, watercolourist, sculptor, decorative designer.

David Kakabadze studied from 1910 to 1916 at Dimitriev Kavkazski's workshop. Initially he taught the natural sciences in Moscow. In 1919 the Georgian government offered him a study grant to go and work in Paris. He remained in Paris from 1919 to 1927 where he painted and regularly exhibited at the Salon des Indépendants from 1920 onwards. In 1927 his work was exhibited at the Brooklyn International Exhibition (New York).

Abandoning Post-Cubism, he ventured into a more pronounced abstraction. He published a manifesto around 1926. His presence in the Société Anonyme's Collection seems to indicate the esteem in which he was held at this time of the first steps of abstract art. However, his return to Georgia in 1928 forced him to submit to the Realist representation code of landscapes and city views. He designed stage sets in Kutaissi from 1928 to 1930 and taught in Tbilisi.

MUSEUMS AND GALLERIES:
PHILADELPHIA (La Société Anonyme Coll.) - TBILISI (NM).

AUCTION RECORDS:
NEW YORK, 2 Nov 1993, *Composition* (1925, mirror, metallic plaster, silvering, varnish/panel in a frame by the artist, 14 x 20 ins / 35.3 x 50.8 cm) USD 31,050.

KAKEI. See **KEIBUN**

KAKINOUCHI
Japanese, 20th century.
Painter. Animals.

Kakinouchi lived and worked in Kanazawa, where he painted pictures of birds on silk. His work was exhibited at the 1900 Paris Exposition Universelle.

KAKIUCHI, Seiyo
Japanese, 20th century.
Painter.

Kakiuchi was included in the exhibition of Japanese art held at the Musée du Jeu de Paume in Paris in 1929.

KAKS, Olle
Swedish, 20th century.
Born 1941, in Hedemora.
Painter.

Olle Kaks depicts childhood memories with meticulous accuracy while transforming them into fantasy. He exhibited in Paris in 1971 as one of a group of eight Swedish artists. In 2002 the Konsthall in Malmö in held a major retrospective of his work.

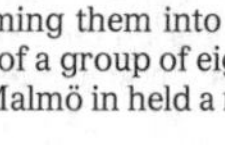

AUCTION RECORDS:
STOCKHOLM, 22 May 1989, *Landscape* (1961, oil on canvas, 19 x 26 3/4 ins / 48 x 68 cm) SEK 16,000. STOCKHOLM, 14 June 1990, *Composition with the Photograph of a Model on the*

Cover of a Pad of Paper (1967, oil and collage, 36 1/2 x 30 ins / 93 x 76 cm) SEK 15,000. STOCKHOLM, 5-6 Dec 1990, *Emblem II* (1974, oil on canvas, 36 1/4 x 28 3/4 ins / 92 x 73 cm) SEK 29,000. STOCKHOLM, 30 May 1991, *Composition* (1975, mixed media, 24 1/2 x 19 3/4 ins / 62 x 50 cm) SEK 7,200. STOCKHOLM, 10-12 May 1993, *The Pomegranate - from the Appolinaire Suite* (oil on canvas, 51 1/4 x 36 1/4 ins / 130 x 92 cm) SEK 24,000. STOCKHOLM, 27 April 1999, *Lou - The Wolf Lady* (1988, oil on canvas, 51 x 36 ins / 130 x 92 cm) SEK 32,000. STOCKHOLM, 13 March 2000, *Composition* (oil on canvas, triptych, 83 x 106 ins / 210 x 270 cm) SEK 17,000. STOCKHOLM, 2 May 2000, *Untitled* (1994, oil on canvas, 77 x 39 ins / 195 x 98 cm) SEK 25,000. STOCKHOLM, 24 April 2002, *Japan* (watercolour, 18 x 46 ins / 46 x 116 cm) SEK 15,000. UPPSALA, 26 May 2002, *Ophelia* (1986, oil on canvas, twenty pieces, 96 x 100 ins / 244 x 255 cm) SEK 36,000. STOCKHOLM, 3 Nov 2004, *Untitled* (1967, oil on canvas, 59 x 55 ins / 150 x 140 cm) SEK 48,000.

KAKUJO
Japanese, 10th - 11th century.
Died 1077.
Sculptor.
Late Heian period.

Kakujo was the son of the famous sculptor Jocho (d. 1057). He was one of the sculptors who worked for the Fujiwara family and was granted the title Hogen (eye of the law, a title of the Buddhist clergy bestowed as an honorific title on certain artists) in 1070 in recognition of his statues in the Hossho-ji, Byodo-in and Kofuku-ji temples in Nara. He founded the Schichijo Bussho studio in Kyoto which would later be developed further by his son Raigo (1054-1119) and Injo (d. 1108) and where the talent of Unkei (d. 1223) would blossom. No work is at present directly attributable to Kakujo.

KAKUMYO, religious name: Kakumyo, Shinga, nickname: Tayubo, artist name: Saibutsu
Japanese, 12th century.
Painter.

Kakumyo was a Buddhist monk-painter.

KAKUSHU, real name: Sumiyoshi Hirotsugu (later Hironatsu), nickname: Kuranosuke, artist name: Kakushu
Japanese, 17th - 18th century.
Born 1650; died 1731.
Painter.
Sumiyoshi School.

Kakushu was the son of Sumiyoshi Hiromichi and the founder of the Shofuku-ji monastery in Takamatsu.

KAKUSHU, real name: Watanabe Shujitsu, nickname: Gensei, artist names: Kakushu, Kyoi Shujin
Japanese, 19th century.
Born 1778; died 1830.
Painter.
Nagasaki School.

Kakushu was a disciple of his father Watanabe Shusen (1736-1834). He specialised in landscapes, figures, flowers and birds.

KAKUTEI, given names: Johaku, Zenno, Joko, religious name: alternate names: Kaigen, Etatsu, artist names: Kakutei, Jubeio, Gojian, Hakuyo Sanjin, Nanso-o, Baiso-o
Japanese, 18th century.
Born 1722, in Nagasaki; died 1785, in Edo, (now Tokyo).
Monk-painter.
Middle Edo period.

Kakutei was a monk painter of the realistic style of painting practised at the school of Nagasaki, which he later introduced into the Osaka-Kyoto region. A friend of Ike no Taiga, he also produced work in the Nanga (literati) style. His work was held in high esteem.

KAKUYU, popular name: Toba Sojo, monk name: Kakuyu
Japanese, 11th - 12th century.
Born 1053; died 1140.
Painter.
Late Heian period.

A monk-painter of the Tendai Buddhist sect, Kakuyu was the son of Minamoto no Takakuni. He was one of the best-known painters of his generation and is traditionally believed to be the author of *Choju Giga* (*Animal Scrolls*) although no positive proof exists. These scrolls, which are currently preserved in the Kozan-ji temple near Kyoto, bear witness to a remarkable technique of monochrome drawing whose origin is to be found in Buddhist art.

KAL, Adam
German, 16th century.
Born 28 June 1539, in Würzburg; died 1594, in Würzburg.
Painter.
Würzburg School.

Adam Kal was also a poet and an architect.

KALAB, Frantisek
Czech, 20th century.
Born 14 November 1908, in Brno; died 1950, in Brno.
Painter, illustrator. Figure compositions.

Frantisek Kalab studied at the school of applied art in Prague from 1925 to 1927, then at the academy of fine art in Prague from 1927 to 1929. He continued his studies at the Académie Moderne in Paris in 1929. He took many trips to France, Italy, the former Yugoslavia and England. He executed figure compositions very much influenced by Georges Braque, whose highly decorative Post-Cubism was appreciated in Czechoslovakia between the two World Wars. He exhibited his works at several exhibitions in Brno, where he taught in 1940.

BIBLIOGRAPHY:
Fifty years of Czechoslovak Painting from the Collections of the Galleries, 1918-1958, exhibition catalogue, Slovenska Narodna Gal., Bratislava, 1968 (in commemoration of the 50th anniversary of the Republic of Czechoslovakia).

KALACHNIKOV, Alexander Nikailovich
Russian, 19th century.
Born 24 November 1776.
Engraver, lithographer.

Kalachnikov produced a *Virgin*, from a work by Annibale Carracci, and a large number of portraits.

KALAEF, Alexis
Russian, 20th century.
Born 16 March 1902.
Active from 1926 in France.
Painter. Portraits, still-lifes.

Alexis Kalaef was a student at the School of Fine Art in Odessa in 1918 and 1919. He left a few years later and took refuge in France where he lived from 1926 onwards. He resumed his studies there and became Othon Friesz' student at the Académie de la Grande Chaumière. A painter of still-lifes and portraits, he remained faithful to the figurative tradition. He exhibited on a regular basis in the Salon des Tuileries, the Salon des Indépendants and the Salon des Artistes Français in Paris.

KALAJIC, Dragos
Yugoslav, 20th century.

Born 1943.
Painter.
Dragos Kalajic is not only a painter but also an art critic and journalist. He came to public prominence in the 1990s, during the Yugoslav conflict, for his nationalist Serb views.

KALAND, Moritz Jan
Norwegian, 19th - 20th century.
Born 30 September 1869, in Bergen.
Painter, sculptor, lithographer.
Moritz Kaland was the curator of the Bergen Museum. His views of the surroundings of this city are particularly notable.

KALAS, Ernest
French, 19th century.
Born 10 February 1861, in Rheims.
Painter, architect.
Ernest Kalas was a pupil at the École des Beaux-Arts, of Guadet and of Galland.
MUSEUMS AND GALLERIES:
RHEIMS: *Choice of a Print*; *Model for the Mumon House*; a watercolour.

KALB, Wilhelm
German, 20th century.
Born 26 April 1870, in Albersweiler.
Painter. Animals, landscapes.
Wilhelm Kalb exhibited in Frankfurt, Düsseldorf and Weimar.

KALBA, Hans von
German, 16th century.
Painter.
Hans von Kalba painted and gilded low reliefs in the church in Annaberg in 1522 and 1524, working in partnership with Balthasar Muller.

KALBERMATTER, J.-Alf
French, 17th century.
Active in Besançon towards the middle of the 17th century.
Draughtsman.

KALBERMATTER, Johannes
Swiss, 16th century.
Died 1551.
Draughtsman.
Johannes Kalbermatter was the nephew of the bishop Adrian de Riedmatten, and was his official painter. He produced drawings for a *Cosmography*.

KALCEVSKI, Risto
Yugoslav, 20th century.
Born 1933, in Prilep (Macedonia).
Painter.
Risto Kalcevski completed his studies in 1957 at the Academy in Ljubljana and took part in many Macedonian art exhibitions from this date in Skopje where he lived in 1961, 1965 and 1968.

His painting is abstract with material effects. He had informal structures changed to end in organic compositions. His paintings are often reduced to monochrome surfaces with nuances due to the relief.
MUSEUMS AND GALLERIES:
SKOPJE: several canvases.

KALCHOVENNE, Pieter van den
Flemish School, 14th - 15th century.
Active in Tournai.
Painter.
The master painter Pieter van den Kalchovenne worked on the canopy of the church of Our Lady in Tournai from 1369 to 1409.

KALCKREUTH, Christine von (Countess)
German, 20th century.
Born 22 March 1898, in Karlsruhe.
Illustrator.
Christine von Kalckreuth was the daughter of Karl Walter Leopold von Kalckreuth. She illustrated *Woman with a Mirror* by Felix Salten.

KALCKREUTH, Karl Walter Leopold von (Count)
German, 19th - 20th century.
Born 15 May 1855 or 1858, in Düsseldorf; died 1928, in Eddelsen, near Hamburg.
Painter, sculptor, lithographer. Portraits, genre scenes.
Karl Walter Leopold von Kalckreuth was the son of the landscape painter Stanislas von Kalckreuth. From 1879 to 1884, he studied at the Akademie der Bildenden Künste in Munich with Benezur and Piloty. He was a professor at the Weimar academy from 1885 to 1905, and returned to live in Munich in 1890. He became a professor at the Akademie der Bildenden Künste in Karlsruhe from 1895 to 1899, then director of the Stuttgart academy from 1900 to 1905. From 1903, he was the president of the Neue Künstlervereinigung (New Artists' Association), which brought together the various Secessions. He was also associated with the artists Paul Lichtwark and Max Liebermann.

Von Kalckreuth later worked in Dachau, then visited Holland. His early work was inspired by Millet, but he then he turned to a rustic symbolism, painting agricultural labourers at work. His portraits are naturalistic, and his landscapes of the Silesian Plain and the port of Hamburg are reminiscent of the flat landscapes of Holland.

Von Kalckreuth exhibited in Munich, Berlin, Dresden and Weimar. He was awarded medals in Munich in 1888 and at the Expositions Universelles in Paris in 1889 and 1900. The Bibliothèque Nationale mounted a retrospective of his works in 1928.
MUSEUMS AND GALLERIES:
BERLIN: *The Castle of Klein-Ols in Silesia* - BREMEN: *Winter Landscape*; *Old Woman*; *Summer* (1890) - COLOGNE (Wallraf-Richartz Mus.) - DRESDEN: *Portrait of the Artist's Wife* (1902) - HAMBURG (Kunsthalle): *Fräulein A. Wohlwill*; *Teaching* (sculpture); *Justus Brinckmann*; *Friedrich Chrysander*; *Herr Behrmann*; *Marie Zacharias* (times three); *The President of the Tribunal of the Hanseatic Provinces*; *Portrait of the Artist*; *Crouching Wolf* (1900); *Returning Travellers on the Elbe* (1894); *Alfred Lichtwark* (1912) - MUNICH: *Rainbow*; *Life* (1898) - STUTTGART (Staatsgal.): *Landscape*; *Woman Gleaning* - WEIMAR: *Skating*; *Funeral at Dachau* - WIESBADEN.
AUCTION RECORDS:
HAMBURG, 24 June 1968, *Evening on the Balcony*, DEM 5,200. HAMBURG, 2 June 1977, *Fisherman on the Beach* (1883, card, 8 3/4 x 14 ins / 22.1 x 35.7 cm) DEM 2,500. AMSTERDAM, 14-15 April 1992, *Portrait of the Painter Gamper Playing the Cello* (1913, oil on canvas, 18 1/2 x 25 1/4 ins / 47 x 64 cm) NLG 7,475.

KALCKREUTH, Maria von (Countess)
German, 19th century.
Born 30 December 1857, in Düsseldorf; died 30 April 1897 or 1898, in Dachau (Bavaria).
Painter, illustrator. Portraits, genre scenes, landscapes.
Von Kalckreuth first exhibited in Berlin in 1889, and later also in Munich.
AUCTION RECORDS:
COLOGNE, 20 Oct 1989, *House beneath the Trees* (1894, oil on canvas, 22 x 16 1/2 ins / 56 x 42 cm) DEM 2,000.

KALCKREUTH, Patrick von
German, 20th century.
Born 1892, in Starnberg; died 1970.
Painter. Seascapes.

Patrick von Kalckreuth painted lakeside scenes, often depicting the shores of Lake Starnberg.

AUCTION RECORDS:

COLOGNE, 15 June 1989, *View of a Lake* (oil on canvas, 19 3/4 x 23 1/2 ins / 50 x 60 cm) DEM 1,500. COLOGNE, 20 Oct 1989, *Lakeside Landscape* (oil on canvas, 23 1/2 x 35 1/2 ins / 60 x 90 cm) DEM 1,500. LONDON, 14 Feb 1990, *A Three-Master out at Sea* (oil on canvas, 27 1/2 x 39 ins / 70 x 99 cm) GBP 4,400. HEIDELBERG, 15 Oct 1994, *Approaching Storm at Sea* (oil on canvas, 27 1/2 x 47 1/4 ins / 70 x 120 cm) DEM 1,300. HAMBURG, 6 Feb 1999, *Zeppelin, Graf Zeppelin over Sea* (oil on canvas, 32 x 47 ins / 81 x 120 cm) DEM 6,000. BERN, 3 Nov 1999, *Fully Rigged Ship on the High Seas* (oil on canvas, 28 x 39 ins / 70 x 100 cm) CHF 2,600. LINDAU, 3 May 2000, *Marina at Sunset* (oil on canvas, 28 x 40 ins / 70 x 101 cm) DEM 4,900. MUNICH, 27 Sept 2000, *Coast of Cornwall* (oil on canvas, 28 x 42 ins / 70 x 106 cm) DEM 4,000. COLOGNE, 5 April 2001, *Marina with Fishing Boat* (oil on canvas, 24 x 35 ins / 60 x 90 cm) DEM 4,000. BERN, 8 Nov 2001, *Waves Breaking on the Beach* (oil on canvas, 28 x 39 ins / 70 x 100 cm) CHF 2,400. WARSAW, 16 June 2002, *Masted Ship in Rough Seas* (oil on canvas, 31 x 28 ins / 80 x 70 cm) PLN 8,500. COLUMBIA, 22 June 2002, *Shoreline and Waves* (oil on canvas, 24 x 36 ins / 61 x 91 cm) USD 2,500. BREMEN, 5 Dec 2003, *Rolling Seas* (oil on canvas, 27 x 47 ins / 69 x 120 cm) EUR 2,200. MUNICH, 17 March 2004, *Stormy Sea* (oil on canvas, 24 x 35 ins / 61 x 90 cm) EUR 1,500. AHLDEN, 26 Nov 2004, *Surf* (oil on canvas, 24 x 36 ins / 60 x 91 cm) EUR 1,500.

KALCKREUTH, Stanislas von (Count)
German, 19th century.
Born 24 December 1821, in Kozmin, Poland; died 25 November 1894, in Munich.
Painter. Landscapes.

Von Kalckreuth was a lieutenant in the guards regiment in Berlin for five years, but then took up painting under the direction of Gustav Wegener. He subsequently worked in the studio of Wilhelm Krause in Berlin and W. Schirmer in Düsseldorf. In 1854, he settled in Weimar and became director of the academy there. He was also a member of the academies in Berlin, Amsterdam and Rotterdam. He exhibited in Paris in the Exposition Universelle of 1878 and won medals in Berlin, Vienna and Bordeaux (1853-1868).

MUSEUMS AND GALLERIES:

BERLIN: *Canigai Valley* - COLOGNE: *Landscape*; *Tyrol* - HANOVER: *Lake Lucerne* - KALININGRAD: *Lake Goube* - SZCZECIN: *The Wetterhorn* - WEIMAR: *Alpine Landscape* - WROCLAW: *Finsteraarhorn*.

AUCTION RECORDS:

COLOGNE, 23 March 1973, *Alpine Landscape*, DEM 3,300. COLOGNE, 25 June 1976, *Mountain Lake* (1852, oil on canvas, 26 1/2 x 36 1/4 ins / 67.5 x 92 cm) DEM 3,000. COLOGNE, 19 Oct 1979, *View of Lake Lucerne* (1870, oil on canvas, 20 x 30 1/4 ins / 51 x 77 cm) DEM 7,000. LONDON, 19 June 1981, *View of Innsbruck* (1857, oil on canvas, 45 1/4 x 63 ins / 115 x 160 cm) GBP 2,600. MUNICH, 29 Nov 1984, *Lake Segl and View of Sils (Segl Maria), near St Moritz* (oil on canvas, 9 x 12 1/2 ins / 22 x 31.5 cm) DEM 4,800. LONDON, 26 Nov 1986, *View of Traunsee, Salzkammergut* (1882, oil on canvas, 12 1/4 x 15 1/4 ins / 31 x 39 cm) GBP 1,800. LONDON, 18 June 1993, *The Jungfrau from the Lauterbrunn Valley* (1867, oil on canvas, 35 3/4 x 50 ins / 90.8 x 127 cm) GBP 6,900. MUNICH, 7 Dec 1993, *Mountain Landscape* (1876, oil on canvas, 33 1/4 x 45 ins / 84.5 x 114.5 cm) DEM 4,600. MUNICH, 23 June 1999, *Schlossel Ort on the Traunsee in Upper Austria* (oil on canvas, 17 x 22 ins / 43 x 57 cm) DEM 3,000. MUNICH, 8 Nov 2000, *Mountain Landscape* (1850, oil on canvas, 30 x 38 ins / 76 x 97 cm) DEM 3,500. MUNICH, 2 July 2003, *Mountain Landscape by Twilight* (1859, oil on canvas, 15 x 25 ins / 38 x 63 cm) EUR 2,400. COLOGNE, 15 Nov 2003, *Konigsee with Watzmann* (oil on canvas, 8 x 11 ins / 20 x 27 cm) EUR 1,500.

KALDENBACH, Hans
German, 15th century.
Died c. 1503.
Painter.

Hans Kaldenbach worked in Frankfurt from 1467.

KALDENBACH, Johan Anthoni
Dutch, 18th - 19th century.
Born 22 January 1760, in Zutphen; died 29 April 1818, in Zutphen.
Portrait painter, draughtsman.

He worked in Zutphen and was rector of the Latin school.

MUSEUMS AND GALLERIES:

AMSTERDAM: *The Directors of the Vrouwen Hospital* - HAARLEM: *Portrait of Fr van der Burck*.

KALDENBACH, Martin, called Hesse
German, 15th - 16th century.
Born c. 1470, in Frankfurt am Main; died 1518, in Frankfurt am Main.
Painter. Religious subjects, portraits.
Frankfurt School.

Martin Kaldenbach was the son of Hans Kaldenbach.

MUSEUMS AND GALLERIES:

FRANKFURT AM MAIN - MUNICH.

AUCTION RECORDS:

COLOGNE, 19 Nov 1981, *Jesus Taking Leave of his Mother* (oil on panel, 25 1/2 x 31in/65 x 79cm) DEM 40,000.

KALDENBACH-SCHROTER, Gustav
German, 19th century.
Born 21 February 1821, in Rheinfelden; died 10 October 1901, in Rheinfelden.
Painter, draughtsman.

Kaldenbach-Schroter is known mainly for painted, watercoloured or drawn landscapes.

KALDORI, André
Hungarian, 20th century.
Born in Hungary.
Active then naturalised in France in 1950.
Painter. Portraits.

André Kaldori studied in Budapest. He exhibited and worked in the South of France and in America in Los Angeles, Miami, New York and Washington.

In addition to his *Portrait of President Eisenhower*, *Portrait of Princess Grace of Monaco* and *Portrait of Princess Caroline*, he painted the *Portrait of Lady Silvia Churchill* and many important people in theatre and film.

MUSEUMS AND GALLERIES:

KANSAS CITY: *Portrait of President Eisenhower*.

KALEDIN, Rurik
Russian, 20th century.
Born 1944, in Leningrad (now St Petersburg).
Painter. Scenes with figures, local scenes.

Rurik Kaledin studied at the Moukhina school of fine arts in Leningrad where he became friends with Shemyakin. He was the pupil of Mushin. His paintings are Figurative, in a style that might almost be described as naive, depicting popular scenes of typical Russian festivities, seen from new angles. His work featured in collective exhibitions from 1986, including the 1990 exhibition *Sept peintres soviétiques contemporains* (*Seven Contemporary Soviet Painters*) organised by UNESCO in Paris. He has also had solo exhibitions, including one in Finland in 1988.

KALENDAROV, Yuri Acherovich
Russian, 20th - 21st century.
Born 1947.
Painter.

KALER, Johann
Dutch, 16th - 17th century.
Born 1564, in Nuremberg; died 1638, in Nuremberg.
Painter, engraver (etching).

Johann Kaler engraved the *Geschelcht-Buch des Heiligen Reichs Stat Nürnberg von 300 Jahren*, which is dated 1610.

KALESHI, Ömer
Turkish, 20th century.
Born c. 1932.
Painter. Figures, still-lifes.

Omer Kaleshi's work has appeared in such group exhibitions as the Salon de Mai in 1973 and 1974, an exhibition at the Régine Lussan gallery, Paris in 1981, and *Contemporary Mediterranean Painters* at the Institut du Monde Arabe, Paris, in 1988. He also mounted solo exhibitions in 1986, 1988, 1990, 1993, 1995 (at Galerie Art 50 in Paris), 1997, 1999 and 2001. His most recent exhibitions have been at UNESCO in Paris and at the Tem Sanat Galerisi in Istanbul in 2003.

KALF, Willem
Dutch, 17th century.
Born 1619, in Rotterdam; died 31 July 1693, in Amsterdam, suddenly.
Painter. Genre scenes, interiors with figures, still-lifes, vegetables.
Amsterdam School.

After studying with Heindrick Pot, a painter of history and portraits, Willem Kalf abandoned these heroic, solemn subjects to concentrate exclusively on painting realistic subjects, particularly still-lifes.

His works are generally of medium size; the majority are painted on wood, although he did also use canvas. He rarely signed his work. Unlike many Dutch painters of the period whose work was perhaps over-polished, Kalf painted with a firm touch, applying the paint with a full brush and defining the character of the objects he painted, demonstrating a similarity to Rembrandt. He sought strong contrasts in his light effects which draw the viewer's eye. His palette, like that of Rembrandt, showed great restraint, with no aggressive reds, yellows or blues. He used pale yellow and warm tones, painting the light rather than colouring his work in some more or less agreeable way.

Kalf produced many paintings of interiors, often kitchens, cellars and storerooms, focusing on the most humble of items, although from time to time he also painted more ostentatious gold or silverware. According to Houbraken he would spend entire days contemplating an object, no matter how humble. He also liked to paint unusual objects or items that were interesting for their form or texture, such as shells. He deliberately shunned the human figure in order to concentrate on the plastic nature of his surroundings, painting everything that related to man but without showing man himself. His *Kitchen Interiors* are typical of this genre; his work is very different from that of 'anecdotal' artists such as Jan Steen or Van Ostade. When he included figures he tucked them away into some obscure corner in the background. Kalf was content to sing the praises of the humble cabbage, the cooking pot, the upturned pail - anything that revealed the picturesque side of domestic life. It was a formula that was to enrich generations of 19th-century painters, including Bonvin, Ribot and many others.

For many years most of Kalf's paintings remained in private houses in Holland and Flanders but gradually they became more widely dispersed. By the 18th century many of his works had been copied, often by very good painters. During the same period, Lebrun (the husband of Mme Vigée-Lebrun), the famous art dealer, said of Kalf, 'He has always been much sought after by art lovers; there are few collections in Paris that do not include his work.' It is said that Boucher, a painter of more elegant and frivolous subjects, held Kalf in great esteem as an artist.

MUSEUMS AND GALLERIES:

AACHEN: *Woman at a Well; Still-life* - ALENÇON: *Laundry; Kitchen* - AMIENS: *Still-life*; two kitchen interiors - AMSTERDAM: *Still-life* - BERLIN: *Kitchen*; three still-lifes - BESANÇON: *Kitchen; Rustic Interior; Saying Grace* - BREST: *Kitchen Utensils* - BUDAPEST: *Rustic Scene* - COPENHAGEN: painting - DARMSTADT: *Still-life* - DIJON: *Kitchen Interior* - DRESDEN: painting - EDINBURGH: *Rustic Scene* - ÉPINAL: *Kitchen Interior* - FRANKFURT AM MAIN: *Still-life* - GENEVA (Mus. Ariana): *Dutch Interior* - GLASGOW: *Rustic Scene* - HANOVER: painting - LA FÈRE: *Still-life* - LE MANS: two still-lifes; *Kitchen Interior* - LE PUY-EN-VELAY: *Still-life* - LYONS: *Kitchen Interior* - METZ: *Kitchen Interior* - MONTPELLIER: *Kitchen Interior* - PARIS (Louvre): *Kitchen Interior* - PÉRIGUEUX: *Still-life* - POTSDAM (Schloss Sanssouci): *Kitchen Interior* - ROTTERDAM: painting - ROUEN: painting - SCHWERIN: painting - ST PETERSBURG (Hermitage): painting - ST-LÔ: *Kitchen Interior* - STRASBOURG: *Still-life* - TOULOUSE: *Kitchen Interior* - VALENCIENNES: *Still-life* - WEIMAR: painting.

AUCTION RECORDS:

PARIS, 1864, *The Blue Vase,* FRF 4,100. PARIS, 27 April 1874, *Still-life,* FRF 3,100. PARIS, 27-28 May 1892, *Still-life,* FRF 10,000. PARIS, 10-15 May 1900, *Silver Objects,* FRF 500. LONDON, 21 Dec 1907, *Kitchen Interior,* GBP 7. LONDON, 3 April 1909, *Still-life,* GBP 8. LONDON, 11-12 March 1911, *Kitchen Interior,* GBP 17. PARIS, 19 March 1919, *Still-life,* FRF 1,500. PARIS, 3 June 1920, *Lemons and Pomegranates,* FRF 1,500. PARIS, 23-24 Nov 1923, *Kitchen,* FRF 1,305. LONDON, 12 Dec 1924, *Still-life,* GBP 141. PARIS, 25 March 1925, *Table Laden with Fruit, Shellfish and Various Objects* (pen and Indian ink wash) FRF 2,500. PARIS, 27-28 May 1926, *Kitchen Interior,* FRF 195,000. PARIS, 20 May 1927, *The Storeroom,* FRF 10,000. LONDON, 10 June 1927, *Still-life,* GBP 231. NEW YORK, 10 May 1930, *Still-life,* USD 3,700. LONDON, 12 April 1935, *Still-life,* GBP 2,100. PARIS, 5 April 1938, *Dish of Fruit,* FRF 80,000. PARIS, 12 May 1938, *Golden Ewer,* FRF 70,000. AMSTERDAM, 15 Nov 1938, *Still-life,* NLG 9,800. LONDON, 2 July 1947, *Still-life,* GBP 260. NEW YORK, 2 March 1950, *Still-life,* USD 1,050. NEW YORK, 8 May 1957, *Still-life,* USD 1,500. PARIS, 9 Dec 1960, *Pieces of Precious Plate,* FRF 25,000. LONDON, 17 May 1961, *Still-life,* GBP 1,900. PARIS, 9 Dec 1961, *Still-life with Delft Vase,* FRF 16,500. LONDON, 27 March 1963, *Kitchen Interior,* GBP 3,100. LONDON, 29 Nov 1968, *Still-life,* Gns 31,000. LONDON, 29 June 1973, *Still-life,* Gns 17,000. VIENNA, 3 Dec 1974, *Farmyard,* ATS 150,000. ZURICH, 12 Nov 1976, *Still-life* (c. 1678, oil on canvas, 23 x 20 1/2 ins / 57.5 x 52 cm) CHF 67,000. AMSTERDAM, 9 June 1977, *Still-life* (oil on canvas, 14 x 11 1/4 ins / 35.5 x 28.5 cm) NLG 21,000. LONDON, 30 March 1979, *Kitchen Interior* (oil on panel, 9 3/4 x 7 3/4 ins / 25 x 20 cm) GBP 4,200. LONDON, 8 July 1983, *Still-life with Oranges and Lemon* (oil on canvas, 30 1/2 x 25 ins / 77.5 x 63.5 cm) GBP 65,000. NEW YORK, 15 Jan 1987, *Peasant Woman Asleep by a Well* (oil on panel, 23 1/4 x 19 1/4 ins / 59 x 49 cm) USD 29,000. LONDON, 8 July 1988, *Vegetables in a Barrow with Pots and Pans in a Storeroom* (oil on panel, 19 x 15 1/4 ins / 48.2 x 38.7 cm) GBP 13,200. MILAN, 12 Dec 1988, *Storeroom Interior with Vegetables and Kitchen Utensils* (oil on panel, 19 x 15 ins / 48 x 38 cm) ITL 44,000,000. AMSTERDAM, 20 June 1989, *Barn Interior with a Barrel, Pitcher, Copper Pan and Other Objects* (oil on panel, diam. 8 3/4 ins / 22.3 cm) NLG 10,925. LONDON, 18 May 1990, *Basket of Vegetables and Var-*

ious Utensils in a Country Kitchen (oil/copper, 6 1/4 x 8 1/4 ins / 16 x 21.2 cm) GBP 5,500. LONDON, 9 Dec 1992, *Landscape with a Peasant by a Well and a Still-life with Vegetables in the Foreground* (oil on copper, 20 x 13 1/2 ins / 51 x 34.5 cm) GBP 19,800. NEW YORK, 16 May 1996, *Large Still-life with Arms and Pieces of Armour, Trumpets, a Sabre and a Nautilus Shell with Various Pieces of Precious Plate on a Table* (oil on canvas, 60 1/4 x 65 1/4 ins / 153 x 165.7 cm) USD 129,000. LONDON, 16 April 1997, *Kitchen Interiors with figures* (1644, oil on canvas, 11 x 15 3/4 ins / 28.2 x 40 cm) GBP 5,520. AMSTERDAM, 6 May 1997, *Still-life with Fruit, a Roemer Glass and a Flute Glass on a Table Covered with an Oriental Rug* (oil on canvas, 14 1/2 x 11 3/4 ins / 37 x 30 cm) NLG 49,560. AMSTERDAM, 10 Nov 1997, *Maid in a Kitchen with a Copper Pan, a Cabbage, Gherkins, a Pumpkin, Utensils in a Basket and Other Objects with a Woman Seated by a Fire in the Background* (oil on panel, 14 1/4 x 10 3/4 ins / 36.2 x 27.3 cm) NLG 20,757. VIENNA, 30 March 2000, *Woman by the Fountain* (oil on panel, 13 x 10 ins / 32 x 25 cm) ATS 130,000. LONDON, 14 Dec 2000, *Still-life of a Peeled Lemon, Roemer, Wine Glass and a Knife on Rug upon a Draped Table* (1660, oil on canvas, 20 x 17 ins / 51 x 44 cm) GBP 320,000. NEW YORK, 26 Jan 2001, *Steeple Cup with Upturned Cover, Glass of Wine, an Orange and a Knife on an Oriental Rug* (oil on panel, 22 x 17 ins / 55 x 43 cm) USD 65,000. LONDON, 1 Nov 2001, *Domestic Interior with a Figure Sweeping, Maid Spinning by a Fire Beyond* (oil on copper, 5 x 7 ins / 13 x 17 cm) GBP 20,000. BREMEN, 18 June 2004, *Still-life with Vase, Fruit and Pocket Watch* (oil on canvas, 37 x 30 ins / 93 x 77 cm) EUR 9,500.

KALFAS, Christos
20th century.
Painter. Architectural views.

In 1996 Christos Kalfas had a solo exhibition in the Jesuit chapel at Chaumont, where he arranged some 15 canvases on a low circular wall built of breeze blocks. Catherine Ulmer, in an article for *Art Press*, described them as 'metaphors which evoke the world - its birth, its meaning - our place in the cosmos, which appear like an Ariadne's thread in an attempt to understand it'.

BIBLIOGRAPHY:
Ulmer, Catherine, '*Christos Kalfas*' in *Art Press* n° 203, periodical, Paris, May 1996.

KALFAYAN, Zareh
Turkish, 20th century.
Born in Constantinople.
Active in France.
Painter. Landscapes.

A painter of Armenian origin, Kalfayan showed views of Dieppe, Tréport and St-Cloud at the Salon des Indépendents in Paris from 1921 onwards. He also exhibited his work at the Salon des Artistes Libres Arméniens in Paris in 1945.

KALI, pseudonym of Michel Kalitowicz
Polish, 20th century.
Born 6 May 1909, in Warsaw.
Active then naturalised in France in 1946.
Painter, illustrator. Portraits, still-lifes. Stage sets, posters.

Kali studied first at the school of fine arts in Warsaw in 1930 and 1931 before going to France, where he worked with Ozenfant and Olga Boznanka, in particular in 1933. In 1937 he won a bronze medal at the Exposition Universelle in Paris. Known particularly as a portrait painter, he was also a painter of still-lifes, as well as producing stage sets, illustrations and advertising posters. He was a member of the Salon des Indépendants in Paris and he also regularly exhibited at the Salon d'Automne.

KALIDE, Theodor Erdmann
German, 19th century.
Born 8 February 1801, in Königshütte (Harz); died 26 August 1863, in Gleiwitz (Gliwice), Silesia.
Sculptor.

Kalide was initially a foundry worker, but then went to Berlin to study with G. Schadow. He subsequently went to Italy to study Italian masters.

MUSEUMS AND GALLERIES:
BERLIN: *Bacchante on a Panther* (marble, group).

KÄLIN, Anton
Swiss, 18th century.
Active in Einsiedeln in 1750.
Painter, engraver. History painting.

Kälin's work includes two altar paintings depicting *St Anthony* and *St Nicholas*.

KALIN, Boris
Slovene, 20th century.
Born 1905.
Sculptor.

Boris Kalin tried to give psychological content to his sculptures in the tradition of Streten Stojanovic.

KALIN, Dominik Franz
Austrian, 17th century.
Born c. 1630; died c. 1680.
Painter.

Kalin lived at the court of Leopold I. He was also a historian.

KÄLIN, J. Benedikt
Swiss, 19th century.
Active in Einsiedeln.
Lithographer.

Kälin was one of the first Swiss lithographers.

KÄLIN, Joseph
Swiss, 17th - 18th century.
Active in Einsiedeln.
Sculptor.

Kälin sculpted two statues, of *St Joseph* and *St Anne*, for a chapel in 1693, and a *Mater Dolorosa* in 1704.

KÄLIN, Joseph Meinrad
Swiss, 19th century.
Born c. 1790, in Einsiedeln (Zug); died 1834, in Einsiedeln.
Painter, draughtsman, engraver, watercolourist.

Kälin trained in Einsiedeln. In his youth, he painted a lot of miniatures, but then took up landscapes. He engraved from Rembrandt.

KALIN, Zdenko
Slovene, 20th century.
Born 1911.
Sculptor. Nudes.

Zdenko Kalin's sculpture retained a Realist style close to that of Streten Stojanovic.

MUSEUMS AND GALLERIES:
LJUBLJANA: *Female Nude Standing.*

KALININE, Viatcheslav Vassilievitch
Russian, 20th century.
Born 1939, in Moscow.
Painter.

Viatcheslav Kalinine studied at the Abramtsevo School of Industrial Art in Khotkovo in the Moscow area in 1963. He took part in collective exhibitions in Russia, Europe and the USA and had solo exhibitions in 1962, 1965 and 1979 in Moscow, in 1989 in New York, in 1992 in Bern and in 1944 at the Central House of Artists in Moscow.

KALINITCHENKO, Jakoff Jakovlevitch
Russian, 19th - 20th century.
Born 1869, near Poltava.
Painter. Genre scenes, animals.

MUSEUMS AND GALLERIES:
MOSCOW (Rumiantsev Mus.): *Before the Search; Hens.*

KALINOVITCH, Jacek
Polish, 18th century.
Active c. 1771.
Painter.
Jacek Kalinovitch painted a portrait of *Count Nicolas Potoki.*

KALINOWSKI, Horst Egon
German, 20th century.
Born 1924, in Düsseldorf.
Assemblage artist, painter (including gouache), engraver, illustrator. Stage costumes and sets.
Group 53.
Horst Egon Kalinowsky studied at the Staatliche Kunstakademie in Düsseldorf from 1945 to 1948. In 1949-1950, he spent some time in Italy, where he stayed in Rome and Venice. From 1950 to 1952, he was a student in the abstract art classes of Jean Dewasne and Edgard Pillet at the Académie de la Grande Chaumière in Paris. In 1964, he spent some time in Greece and in 1965, he visited Spain and America. In 1966, he was awarded the Carl Einstein prize in Essen and made two further trips to America. He was awarded the Prix Burda, the top prize for sculpture, at the Munich Kunsthaus in 1967, and in 1968, he taught at the Akademie der Bildenden Künste in Karlsruhe and was appointed a member of the Preussische Akademie in Berlin.

Kalinowsky acknowledges the influence of Dewasne and Pillet on his work, inasmuch as he learned from them that the expression of emotion was compatible with formal rigour. Until 1956, he produced non-figurative paintings, but he then abandoned painting for collage and for assemblages of various materials, which he preferred to be all brown and to either resemble, or to be meticulously covered in, leather. These included objects such as branches, logs, planks, packing cases and saddles, and Kalinowsky used the technique from 1958, in his *Tableaux-objets* (*Object-Pictures*) and *Tableaux-Châsses* (*Frame-Pictures*), through to the appearance of the *Caissons* (*Boxes*) in 1960. Some of these *Caissons* look a little like doors or pieces of furniture, and the various items piled up in them are reminiscent of Louise Nevelson's 'altars'. In 1980, Kalinowsky began to work directly on leather, instead of simply imitating it. He used it in conjunction with wood and metal structures, creating sculptural objects in relief, instead of attempting to produce one-dimensional equivalents. In 1961, he began to work on etchings, and in 1964 produced etchings to illustrate Japanese poems. In 1965, the *Caissons* began to resemble stelae, and he produced etchings to illustrate St Francis of Assisi's *Canticle of Brother Sun* and, in 1967, for *The Seven Days of the Creation.*

Kalinowski's *Caissons* are austere, even threatening. They are made of leather, wood and iron, and tend to be heavy constructions, which suggest themes of both sexuality and suffering. In a fairly generalised way, commentaries on Kalinowski's work emphasise, not without justification, the sense of aggressiveness and unease aroused by these sculptures, but the objects, with their carefully patinated framework, leather and seams, are more than just metaphors for acts of cruelty. They can also lay claim to the distinguished decay of luxury items, and this deliberate ambiguity is a part of their twofold power to repel and seduce.

Kalinowski began exhibiting at the Salon des Réalités Nouvelles in Paris in 1953, 1954 and 1956. He took part in numerous group exhibitions, including: 1963, *The Art of Assemblage* at the New York Museum of Modern Art and *Mythologies Quotidiennes* (*Everyday Mythologies*) at the Musée d'Art Moderne in Paris; 1965 and 1968 at the Carnegie Institute, Pittsburgh; 1967 at the Prix Marzotto, Milan, and *Second Decade 1955-1965* at the Maeght Foundation in St-Paul-de-Vence; 1968 *Living Art 1965-1968* at the Maeght Foundation; 1984 *IIe Biennale Européenne de Sculpture de Normandie* (*2nd European Sculpture Biennale in Normandy*) at Jouy-sur-Eure, and others. After 1956, he also had many solo exhibitions in various cities in Germany, several countries in Europe, and in New York. The most notable of these were at the Städtische Kunsthalle in Mannheim, the Lehmbruck Museum in Duisburg, the Städtische Kunstsammlung in Bonn in 1967, the Centre National d'Art Contemporain in Paris in 1968 and the Galerie Chave in Vence in 1991. Other solo exhibitions include those in Paris at the Galerie Arnaud in 1953, 1954 and 1955, the Galerie Creuse in 1956, the Galerie Daniel Cordier in 1958 and 1963, and in Frankfurt am Main, Wuppertal and Brussels.

BIBLIOGRAPHY:
First Exhibition of Horst Egon Kalinowski, exhibition catalogue, Lefebre Gallery, New York, 1969. *Horst Egon Kalinowski: Caissons et Steles*, exhibition catalogue, Centre National d'Art Contemporain, Paris, 1969. Bachmann, Vera, *Horst Egon Kalinowski, das plastische Werk. Werkverzeichnis 1960-1997*, catalogue raisonné, Letter Stiftung, Cologne, 1997.

MUSEUMS AND GALLERIES:
LONDON (Tate Collection) - NEW YORK (MoMA) - PARIS (MNAM-CCI).

AUCTION RECORDS:
MUNICH, 25 May 1976, *The Dilemma of Lynceus* (1965, sculpture in leather, 82¾ x 47¼ x 9 ins / 210 x 120 x 22 cm) DEM 5,600. MUNICH, 1 Dec 1980, *The Remains of the Fire* (1960, burnt watercoloured fabric, collage, 11½ x 22¼ ins / 29.5 x 56.5 cm) DEM 2,200. NEW YORK, 13 May 1981, *Silent Carillon* (1968, wall with leather, wood and nails, 41½ x 27 x 6 ins / 105.5 x 68.5 x 15.5 cm) USD 800. MUNICH, 28 May 1984, *Vamp* (1971, leather relief/panel, 68½ x 27 ins / 174 x 68.5 cm) DEM 6,800. LONDON, 27 June 1985, *Iris in her Micro-Salon* (1961, wooden relief, 49 x 38¼ ins / 124.5 x 97 cm) GBP 1,900. PARIS, 28 March 1988, *Charon's Veil* (1956, oil on panel, 52 x 40¼ ins / 132 x 102 cm) FRF 10,000. PARIS, 27 Oct 1988, *Claire* (1957, mixed media/panel, 5 x 15½ ins / 13 x 39.5 cm) FRF 10,500. PARIS, 26 April 1990, *Claire* (1957, mixed media, 5 x 15½ ins / 13 x 39.5 cm) FRF 8,000. COPENHAGEN, 30 May 1991, *Drum* (1961, collage, 13 x 9½ ins / 33 x 24 cm) DKK 5,000. HEIDELBERG, 5-13 April 1994, *Sunrise in Leather* (collage of leather and stuffing/plywood, 23½ x 36 ins / 59.5 x 91.5 cm) DEM 4,200. NEW YORK, 1 Nov 1994, *Lynceus' Lookout* (1964, leather mounted/wood, 34½ x 31 x 10½ ins / 87.6 x 79 x 26.7 cm) USD 2,990. PARIS, 27 March 1995, *For a Greek Tragedy* (gouache, 19 x 25 ins / 48.5 x 63.5 cm) FRF 5,500. LONDON, 23 Oct 1997, *Sarcophagus for Nagaraja* (1961, wooden box, 29¾ x 56¾ ins / 75.5 x 144.3 cm) GBP 3,450. PARIS, 30 Nov 2004, *Vamp* (1971, leather on wood, 68 x 27 ins / 173 x 68 cm) EUR 2,800.

KALINYTCHEVA, Clara
Russian, 20th century.
Born 1933, in Moscow.
Engraver, lithographer.
Clara Kalinytcheva's naive style is narrative-illustrative. She appeared in Paris at the exhibition *L'Art Russe, des Scythes à nos jours* (*Russian Art from the Scythians to Today*) at the Galeries Nationales du Grand Palais in 1967.

KALISH, Max
Polish, 20th century.
Born 1 March 1891; died 1947.
Active in the USA.
Sculptor. Genre scenes. Groups.
Max Kalish was the student of a certain Adams and of Calder. He was a member of the American Arts Federation.

AUCTION RECORDS:
NEW YORK, 18 Dec 1991, *Family* (1906, white marble, h. 12 ins / 30.5 cm) USD 2,860. NEW YORK, 4 Dec 1992, *Farmer Plough-*

ing (bronze, h. 15½ ins / 39.4 cm) USD 7,150. NEW YORK, 21 Sept 1994, *Shock* (1932, bronze, h. 22½ ins / 57.2 cm) USD 9,487. NEW YORK, 13 March 1996, *Steel Worker* (1926, bronze, h. 18 ins / 46 cm) USD 6,900.

KALISTOV, Vassili Jefimovich
Russian, 19th century.
Painter. Genre scenes.
MUSEUMS AND GALLERIES:
MOSCOW (State Tretyakov Gal.): *Scene in an Educational Establishment.*

KALITOWICZ, Michel. See **KALI**

KALITSCH, Werner von
German, 19th century.
Active in Düsseldorf.
Painter. Landscapes, animals.
Kalitsch first exhibited in Berlin in 1879 and later also in Düsseldorf.

KALKAR. See **CALCAR**

KALKREUTH. See **KALCKREUTH von**

KALLE, Albert Christian
German, 17th century.
Born in Berlin.
Active in Strasbourg from 1620 to 1670.
Engraver (burin).
Kalle worked mainly for booksellers, for whom he engraved portraits and frontispieces. A noted work by him is *Bellum Suedo-Germanicum*, with a portrait of Gustavus Adolphus (1648).

KALLENBACH, Georg Josef
German, 18th - 19th century.
Born 16 June 1751, in Würzburg; died 30 June 1814, in Würzburg.
Miniaturist.
Kallenbach was a pupil of Joseph Appiani and lived in Italy (probably Rome) around 1780.

KALLENBERG, Anders Hansson, or Kallersberg
Swedish, 19th century.
Born 23 October 1834, in Malmö; died 1902.
Painter. Landscapes with figures, landscapes, animals.
Anders Kallenberg was a pupil at the academy in Stockholm as well as Düsseldorf, where he lived for an extended period. At the end of his life he returned to Sweden and settled in Stockholm. He painted scenes of goats and horses under grey, rainy skies.

MUSEUMS AND GALLERIES:
SALFORD (Museum and AG): *Torrent Scene in Norway* - STOCKHOLM: *Farm in Skåne; Chorus in the Forest; Bull.*
AUCTION RECORDS:
MALMÖ, 2 May 1977, *Livestock in a Landscape* (1875, oil on canvas, 39¼ x 58¼ ins / 100 x 148 cm) SEK 23,000. STOCKHOLM, 30 Oct 1984, *Farm Courtyard* (1881, oil on canvas, 10¼ x 15 ins / 26 x 38 cm) SEK 11,500. STOCKHOLM, 20 April 1987, *Seashore in the Moonlight* (1869, oil on canvas, 22¾ x 30¼ ins / 58 x 77 cm) SEK 35,000. STOCKHOLM, 15 Nov 1989, *Mountain Landscape in Sweden with Mill amidst the Birches in Summer* (oil on canvas, 16½ x 23¼ ins / 42 x 59 cm) SEK 27,000. STOCKHOLM, 16 May 1990, *Cow in a Field* (oil on canvas, 8¼ x 10¼ ins / 21 x 26 cm) SEK 5,500. STOCKHOLM, 14 Nov 1990, *Wooded Landscape by the Edge of a Pond* (oil on canvas, 13¾ x 19¾ ins / 35 x 50 cm) SEK 3,500. STOCKHOLM, 31 Aug 1999, *Mountain Landscape* (oil on canvas, 26 x 40 ins / 67 x 102 cm) SEK 14,500. STOCKHOLM, 16 May 2000, *Coastal Landscape with Figures* (1869, oil on canvas, 23 x 31 ins / 59 x 79 cm) SEK 24,000. STOCKHOLM, 26 May 2004, *Paddle-steamer on Fire by Rocky Cliffs on a Moonlit Night* (oil on canvas, 18 x 25 ins / 45 x 64 cm) SEK 17,000.

KALLENBERG, Jakob
Swiss, 16th century.
Painter, engraver (wood).
Bern School.
Jakob Kallenberg worked in Bern from 1535 to 1565 and was a member of the council of Bern in 1545. He married on 4 May 1559. He mostly produced wood engravings for book illustrations.

KALLENBERG, Kaspar
Swiss, 16th century.
Painter.
Kaspar Kallenberg is recorded as having received a payment in Bern in 1538.

KALLENBERG, Peter
Swiss, 16th century.
Active in Bern.
Painter.
Peter Kallenberg was made a burgher of Solothurn in 1511.

KALLENBERG, Samuel
Swiss, 16th century.
Active in Bern.
Painter.
Samuel Kallenberg mostly produced portraits, and was married in Bern on 16 April 1551.

KALLIAUER, Anton
Austrian, 18th - 19th century.
Born 1760, in Styria; died 29 March 1827, in Leoben.
Painter, engraver.
Kalliauer taught at the fine arts academy in Vienna.

KALLMEYER, Hans Julius Bernhard
German, 20th century.
Born 1 September 1882, in Erfurt.
Painter. Landscapes, animals.
Hans Kallmeyer studied and exhibited in Dresden.

KALLMORGEN, Friedrich
German, 19th - 20th century.
Born 15 November 1856, in Altona; died 4 June 1924, in Karlsruhe.
Painter, watercolourist, lithographer. Landscapes, urban landscapes, landscapes with figures.
In 1875, Friedrich Kallmorgen was a student at the Staatliche Kunstakademie in Düsseldorf. In 1877, he studied with Hans Gude, Gustav Schönleber and Hermann Baisch at the Akademie der Bildenden Künste in Karlsruhe, where he himself became a professor in 1891. He won medals in Munich in 1888 and 1905 and Berlin in 1887 and 1908, and also exhibited in Vienna and Dresden. At the 1900 Exposition Universelle in Paris he was awarded bronze medals for painting and engraving.
MUSEUMS AND GALLERIES:
BERLIN: *At Work; Rainy Weather* - MUNICH: *October Evening* - SYDNEY: *Spring Day.*
AUCTION RECORDS:
PARIS, 16 Dec 1942, *Canal in Bruges*, FRF 14,000. COLOGNE, 8 May 1969, *Market Scene*, DEM 4,000. HAMBURG, 14 June 1973, *The Port of Hamburg*, DEM 28,000. MUNICH, 29 Nov 1976, *View of Hamburg* (1901, oil on canvas, 14¾ x 20½ ins / 37.5 x 52 cm) DEM 3,350. STUTTGART, 12 April 1978, *The Port of Hamburg* (oil on canvas, 32¼ x 36¼ ins / 82 x 92 cm) DEM 5,100. HAMBURG, 4 June 1980, *View of Hamburg Harbour* (1917, oil on canvas, 35½ x 47½ ins / 90 x 120.5 cm) DEM 13,000. STUTTGART, 6 March 1981, *The Port of Hamburg* (1917, oil on canvas, 35½ x 47¼ ins / 90 x 120 cm) DEM

10,000. HAMBURG, 10 June 1983, *The Port of Hamburg* (1922, oil on canvas, 18 1/4 x 25 1/2 ins / 46.5 x 65 cm) DEM 17,000. COLOGNE, 22 May 1986, *View of Berlin in Winter* (1914, oil on canvas, 26 1/4 x 40 3/4 ins / 66.5 x 103.5 cm) DEM 25,000. MUNICH, 1 June 1987, *The Pensioners' Walk* (oil on canvas, 12 1/4 x 18 1/2 ins / 31.3 x 47.3 cm) DEM 14,000. HEIDELBERG, 11 April 1992, *The Port of Hamburg* (oil on canvas, 15 3/4 x 20 ins / 40 x 51 cm) DEM 13,000. MUNICH, 25 June 1992, *The Level Crossing at the Muhlburger Tor in Karlsruhe* (1899, oil on canvas, 43 x 66 1/4 ins / 109 x 168 cm) DEM 33,900. HEIDELBERG, 8 April 1995, *Mountainous Landscape* (1907, oil on canvas, 16 x 20 1/4 ins / 40.5 x 51.5 cm) DEM 4,000.

KALLOS, Ede
Hungarian, 19th - 20th century.
Born 22 February 1866, in Hódmezovásárhely.
Sculptor.

Ede Kallos studied at the School of Decorative Arts in Budapest and under Henri Chapu in Paris where he took part in the Exposition Universelle in 1900.

KALLOS, Paul
Hungarian, 20th century.
Born 15 November 1928, in Hernadnemeti; died 10 August 2001.
Active from 1950 in France.
Painter (including wash).

Paul Kallos was interned in a concentration camp in Germany in 1944-1945. Having returned to Hungary, he sat his Baccalaureate in Kiskunhalas. From 1946 to 1949 he studied at the school of fine art in Budapest. He settled in Paris in 1950, where he immediately painted his first abstract paintings.

In his preliminary period until the 1960s, his stroke was jerky, the allusive representation of figures in an interior or of landscapes mixed with Expressionism. He was stylistically close to Bernard Dufour and exhibited in the same gallery, Galerie Pierre in Paris. At the end of this period, he painted a *Balcony* in 1968 after Manet's. After this, he moved in the direction of abstract landscapism. His painting, abstract in appearance, is actually still solidly based on the real: landscapes, interiors, architecture and still-lifes, which he transposed into misty forms bathing a dreamy atmosphere with the technique of transparent flowing lines, which he had been practising since his early period in oil and which only became apparent with Indian ink washes and acrylics. Since the 1970s, he has been consolidating these transparent effects by composing paintings of series of rectangles or squares, horizontally or vertically separated by chinks of white of the untouched canvas, or again of series of spaced-out horizontal or intertwined horizontal and vertical strata superimposed. These processes were then developed at the end of the 1980s in *Tributes on a Palladian Theme* or even with discreet citations in 1996 from *History of Solomon and the Queen of Sheba* by Piero della Francesca and in 1998 in the *Variations on the Tuscan Order*. With the exception of the early period, which was still representational, all of Paul Kallos' work is built up as a kind of tribute to the fluidity of the four elements, to light.

He took part in many collective exhibitions, particularly in Paris: from 1956 to 1964 at the Salon des Réalités Nouvelles, the Salon de l'École de Paris and the Salon de Mai, as well as in many foreign countries. He exhibited sets of his paintings at solo exhibitions: in Paris at the Galerie Pierre in 1955, 1957, 1960, 1962, 1963; Galerie Pierre Domec in 1964, 1966, 1967; Galerie Nane Stern from 1971 to 1982 and in 1985 and 1986; Galerie G in 1986 and 1988; Galerie Le Troisième Œil in 1996 and 1998; in London in 1955; New York in 1958 and 1961; Basel in 1960; Stockholm, Madrid and Tokyo.

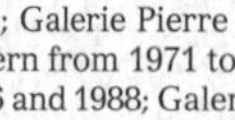

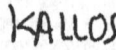

BIBLIOGRAPHY:
Loeb, Pierre, *Kallos*, exhibition catalogue, Gal. Pierre, Paris, 1957 (another catalogue in 1960). *Salon international des Galeries Pilotes*, exhibition catalogue, Musée cantonal, Lausanne, 1963. Marteau, Robert, *Kallos*, exhibition catalogue, Gal. Pierre Domec, Paris, 1966. Zurcher, Bernard, et al., *'Paul Kallos. L'Architecte des Transparences'* in *coll. L'État des Lieux*, La Différence, Paris, 1988.

MUSEUMS AND GALLERIES:
BUDAPEST (Szépmuvészeti Múz.) - DENVER (AM) - DIJON (MBA): *Interior with Figure* (1960) - EINDHOVEN (Van Abbe Mus.) - ÉPINAL (Departmental Museum of Ancient and Contemporary Art): *Painting* (1956) - ÉVREUX (Mus. de l'Ancien Évêché) - METZ (La Cour d'Or) - PARIS (FNAC) - PARIS (MAMVP): *Diptych* (1978) - PARIS (MNAM-CCI) - REHOVOT (Centre for Contemporary Art) - RIO DE JANEIRO (MAM) - ST-ÉTIENNE (MAM) - TEL AVIV (MMA) - TORONTO (AG of Ontario).

AUCTION RECORDS:
NEUILLY, 20 June 1988, *Composition* (1968, oil on canvas, 32 x 39 1/4 ins / 81 x 100 cm) FRF 7,200. PARIS, 10 April 1989, *Horizons* (1984, oil on canvas, 32 x 39 1/4 ins / 81 x 100 cm) FRF 12,000. PARIS, 26 Sept 1989, *Blue Horizon* (acrylic/canvas, 19 3/4 x 19 3/4 ins / 50 x 50 cm) FRF 9,500. PARIS, 17 Dec 1989, *Embrasement* (1983, acrylic/canvas, 45 x 57 1/2 ins / 114 x 146 cm) FRF 40,000. PARIS, 5 April 1990, *Composition* (1954, oil on canvas, 36 1/4 x 23 1/2 ins / 92 x 60 cm) FRF 165,000. NEW YORK, 7 May 1990, *Untitled* (1954, oil on canvas, 23 3/4 x 32 ins / 60.3 x 81.3 cm) USD 18,700. PARIS, 10 May 1990, *Vertical Composition* (acrylic/paper, 26 x 19 3/4 ins / 66 x 50 cm) FRF 12,000. PARIS, 16 May 1990, *Wide Strata* (acrylic/canvas, 59 x 86 1/2 ins / 150 x 220 cm) FRF 140,000. PARIS, 20 June 1990, *Untitled* (1986, acrylic/canvas, 51 1/4 x 32 ins / 130 x 81 cm) FRF 30,000. PARIS, 15 Dec 1990, *Untitled* (1959, oil on canvas, 28 3/4 x 36 1/4 ins / 73 x 92 cm) FRF 71,500. PARIS, 15 April 1991, *Silks* (1983, acrylic/canvas, 45 x 57 1/2 ins / 114 x 146 cm) FRF 40,000. PARIS, 2 Feb 1992, *Composition* (1988, acrylic/canvas, 39 1/4 x 32 ins / 100 x 81 cm) FRF 5,000. LONDON, 26 March 1992, *Untitled* (1957, oil on canvas, 51 3/4 x 38 1/2 ins / 131.5 x 97.5 cm) GBP 3,960. PARIS, 14 April 1992, *Yellow Interior* (1963, oil on canvas, 511 3/4 x 38 1/4 ins / 1300 x 97 cm) FRF 40,000. PARIS, 28 May 1993, *Composition* (1956, oil on canvas, 36 1/4 x 28 3/4 ins / 92 x 73 cm) FRF 9,000. NEW YORK, 30 June 1993, *Untitled* (1955, oil on canvas, 36 x 28 3/4 ins / 91.4 x 73 cm) USD 1,380. PARIS, 28 Sept 1993, *Nude* (1962, oil on canvas, 51 1/4 x 38 1/4 ins / 130 x 97 cm) FRF 23,000. PARIS, 5 July 1994, *Abstraction* (1990, acrylic/canvas, 57 1/2 x 38 1/4 ins / 146 x 97 cm) FRF 8,500. PARIS, 7 Oct 1996, *Menine* (1962, oil on canvas, 57 1/2 x 45 ins / 146 x 114 cm) FRF 12,000; *Composition* (1960, oil on canvas, 36 1/4 x 28 3/4 ins / 92 x 73 cm) FRF 9,000. PARIS, 4 Oct 1997, *Composition* (1957, oil on canvas, 51 1/4 x 31 1/2 ins / 130 x 80 cm) FRF 11,000. PARIS, 19 April 2000, *Composition* (oil on canvas, 29 x 24 ins / 73 x 60 cm) FRF 12,000. PARIS, 26 Nov 2000, *Composition* (acrylic, 57 x 45 ins / 146 x 114 cm) FRF 23,500. PARIS, 21 May 2001, *Composition* (oil on canvas, 36 x 29 ins / 92 x 73 cm) FRF 17,500. PARIS, 16 April 2002, *Composition* (1960, oil on canvas, 46 x 35 ins / 116 x 89 cm) EUR 2,220. PARIS, 28 March 2003, *Composition* (1989, acrylic, 77 x 45 ins / 195 x 114 cm) EUR 2,500. PARIS, 24 April 2004, *Landscape with Tall Trees* (1956, oil on canvas, 39 x 29 ins / 100 x 73 cm) EUR 2,200.

KALLSTENIUS, Evald
Swedish, 20th century.
Born 1898, in Stockholm; died 1957.
Painter. Landscapes.

Évald Kallsteniüs studied at the Konstakademien in Stockholm. He visited France and Italy before settling in Ektorp.

KALLSTENIUS, Gottfrid Samuel Nickolaus
Swedish, 19th - 20th century.

Born 13 July 1861, in Västervik; died 1943.
Painter. Landscapes, seascapes.

Gottfrid Kallstenius lived in Stockholm but travelled and painted throughout Sweden, France, Italy and Germany. He exhibited in Munich, where he won medals in 1890 and 1905. He became a member of the Konstakademien in Stockholm of Fine Arts. The countries Kallstenius visited inspired him to paint numerous landscapes. However, he mostly painted typically Swedish landscapes with pine forests, often paying particular attention to the effects of light, such as the sun, sunsets, twilight and, especially, the light nights.

MUSEUMS AND GALLERIES:

HELSINKI: *Marshland* - MUNICH: *Hill Covered with Pines* - STOCKHOLM: *Untidy Garden; Moonlight, Gottland.*

AUCTION RECORDS:

STOCKHOLM, 24 April 1947, *Park*, SEK 2,875. STOCKHOLM, 26-28 March 1969, *Landscape*, SEK 5,800. GÖTEBORG, 24 March 1976, *Trees by the Waterside* (oil on canvas, 25 1/2 x 32 ins / 65 x 81 cm) SEK 19,000. GÖTEBORG, 9 Nov 1977, *Wooded Landscape with River* (1925, oil on canvas, 25 1/2 x 32 1/4 ins / 65 x 82 cm) SEK 16,500. STOCKHOLM, 30 Oct 1979, *Landscape* (1933, oil on canvas, 34 1/2 x 45 1/4 ins / 87.5 x 115 cm) SEK 16,000. STOCKHOLM, 22 April 1981, *Wooded Landscape* (1924, oil/canvas, 30 3/4 x 35 ins / 78 x 88 cm) SEK 25,200. GÖTEBORG, 9 Nov 1983, *Peasant Women by the Waterside* (1891, oil on canvas, 38 1/2 x 47 1/4 ins / 98 x 120 cm) SEK 33,000. STOCKHOLM, 22 April 1986, *Summer Landscape* (1892, oil on canvas, 47 1/4 x 38 1/4 ins / 120 x 97 cm) SEK 40,000. STOCKHOLM, 20 Oct 1987, *Lone Tree* (1912, oil on canvas, 51 1/4 x 46 ins / 130 x 116 cm) SEK 45,000. LONDON, 23 March 1988, *Sunset Over a Lake* (1927, oil on canvas, 28 3/4 x 59 ins / 73 x 150 cm) GBP 6,600. LONDON, 24 March 1988, *Pine Forest* (oil on canvas, 36 1/4 x 33 ins / 92 x 84 cm) GBP 3,300. STOCKHOLM, 15 Nov 1988, *Trees on the Undulating Slope by a Lake* (1935, oil, 28 1/4 x 39 1/4 ins / 72 x 100 cm) SEK 40,000. LONDON, 16 March 1989, *Sunset over the Archipelago* (1933, oil on canvas, 35 x 46 ins / 88.8 x 116.8 cm) GBP 6,600. STOCKHOLM, 19 April 1989, *Islands Seen from the Wooded Shore on a Summer Afternoon* (oil on canvas, 25 1/4 x 43 3/4 ins / 64 x 111 cm) SEK 50,000. GÖTEBORG, 18 May 1989, *Rocky Coastal Landscape with Trees* (1936, oil on canvas, 27 1/2 x 47 1/4 ins / 70 x 120 cm) SEK 40,000. STOCKHOLM, 15 Nov 1989, *Treelined Shore with a Group of Islands off the East Coast* (1937, oil, 29 1/4 x 55 ins / 74 x 140 cm) SEK 47,000. LONDON, 27-28 March 1990, *Trees by a Lake* (1938, oil on canvas, 36 1/2 x 26 3/4 ins / 93 x 68 cm) GBP 8,800. LONDON, 29 March 1990, *In the Meadow* (1888, oil on canvas, 34 1/2 x 47 ins / 87.5 x 119.5 cm) GBP 57,200. STOCKHOLM, 16 May 1990, *Sunlit Coastal Landscape with Pines* (1917, oil on canvas, 43 1/4 x 59 ins / 110 x 150 cm) SEK 46,000. STOCKHOLM, 14 Nov 1990, *Landscape with Trees beside an Inlet* (1919, oil on canvas, 63 x 78 3/4 ins / 160 x 200 cm) SEK 65,000. STOCKHOLM, 29 May 1991, *Landscape with Pines by the Shore at Dusk* (oil on canvas, 63 x 78 3/4 ins / 160 x 200 cm) SEK 35,000. STOCKHOLM, 28 Oct 1991, *Sunset over a Fjord* (oil on canvas, 30 3/4 x 39 ins / 78 x 99 cm) SEK 20,000. STOCKHOLM, 30 Nov 1993, *Evening beside an Inlet* (oil on canvas, 28 1/4 x 39 1/4 ins / 72 x 100 cm) SEK 21,000. LUND, 23 April 1999, *Winter Road with Mother and Son* (1889, oil on canvas, 27 x 39 ins / 68 x 100 cm) SEK 54,000. STOCKHOLM, 23 Nov 1999, *Sunny Landscape from the Skerries* (1827, oil on canvas, 28 x 39 ins / 72 x 100 cm) SEK 24,000. STOCKHOLM, 16 May 2000, *Glistening: Wooded Landscape* (1921, oil on canvas, 39 x 47 ins / 100 x 120 cm) SEK 28,000. STOCKHOLM, 28 Nov 2000, *Tranquility: Moonlight in the Skerries* (1907, oil on canvas, 40 x 48 ins / 101 x 123 cm) SEK 23,500. COPENHAGEN, 28 May 2001, *Evening by the Fjord* (oil on canvas, 32 x 49 ins / 82 x 125 cm) DKK 32,000. STOCKHOLM, 29 May 2001, *Summer Landscape, Breviksudden* (oil on canvas, 35 x 58 ins / 88 x 147 cm) SEK 380,000. STOCKHOLM, 4 March 2002, *Sunlit Skerries* (1909, oil on canvas, 29 x 59 ins / 73 x 150 cm) SEK 20,000. STOCKHOLM, 4 Dec 2002, *Cupid with Man Resting* (1890, oil on canvas, 20 x 79 ins / 50 x 201 cm) SEK 36,000. STOCKHOLM, 25 Aug 2003, *Coastal Landscape with Vessel* (oil on canvas, 33 x 33 ins / 85 x 83 cm) SEK 15,000. UPPSALA, 7 Dec 2003, *Cliffs in the Skerries at Sunset* (1932, oil on canvas, 25 x 31 ins / 64 x 80 cm) SEK 18,000. STOCKHOLM, 8 March 2004, *Pine Forest in Sunshine* (1923, oil on canvas, 29 x 39 ins / 73 x 99 cm) SEK 15,500.

KÄLLSTRÖM, Arvid

Swedish, 20th century.
Born 17 February 1893, in Påskallavik.
Sculptor.

Arvid Källström trained in Paris, Rome, London and Copenhagen. In Paris, he took part in many exhibitions, including the Salon des Réalités Nouvelles in 1952, 1953, 1955 and 1956. He was awarded a bursary by the Ester Lindahl Foundation. He exhibited abstract sculptures at the Salon des Réalités Nouvelles in Paris and produced many religious and non-religious monuments.

KALMAKOFF, Nikolaï or Nicolas

Russian, 19th - 20th century.
Born 23 January 1873, in Nervi, to Russian parents; died 1955, in the hospice at Chelles, France.
Active from 1924 in France.
Painter (gouache), pastellist. Figure compositions, figures, nudes, self-portraits. Stage sets.
Art Nouveau, Symbolism.

Nikolaï or Nicolas Kalmakoff was of aristocratic origin. Born in Italy, he was trained there in painting. He returned to St Petersburg where he remained until the Revolution. He designed many stage sets, usually for productions by Nicolas Evreinov and Vera Kommissajervski's theatre. His stage sets for Oscar Wilde's *Salome* in 1908 had the play banned on opening night due to its unashamed crudeness, which earned him his notoriety. Based on this same *Salome* and on Flaubert's *Salammbo*, he painted further large decorative compositions. His links with the Russian Symbolist poet and dramatist Sologub, his own satanic concerns and his affiliation to the Skoptsi sect and the Khlistis, to which Rasputin belonged, had Maïakoski describe him in 1913 as a 'Russian Beardsley'. In 1920 he went to Helsinki again and to Tallinn in Estonia. He settled in France around 1924, where he continued to live an increasingly lonely and miserable life. He was taken into a hospice for the destitute in Chelles, where he stopped painting in 1947.

Although he was compared with Beardsley, the technique of Kalmakoff's works is specifically Russian, tortuous admittedly, but with the colour clearly predominant, in flat tints, decorative and sparkling. In his Finnish and Estonian period, he toned down his palette, emphasising the contours. His paintings then resembled one of the trends of the Munich Secession, following on from Franz von Stück. However, while the technique changed, the subjects remained peculiar to him. In France, his development ended in an academic exhibition, tinged with Pre-Raphaelism, in imagery parallel to certain Surrealist works. Female nudes rubbed shoulders with cautious knights in shining armour. His paintings, almost always dated, are often signed with an inscrutable acronym, symbolic of a rootless life and obsessed mind.

He took part in exhibitions by the group Mir Isskoustva (World of Art) led by Sergei Diaghilev, Bakst and Benois among others. In 2003 he was represented at the collective exhibition *Un été russe à Montmartre. Artistes de St-Pétersbourg à Paris au début du XXe siècle* (*A Russian Summer in*

Montmartre. St Petersburg Artists in Paris at the Beginning of the 20th Century) at the Musée de Montmartre in Paris.

BIBLIOGRAPHY:
Gérard, Raphaël/Essaïan, Sergeï, et al., *Un été russe à Montmartre. Artistes de Saint-Pétersbourg à Paris au début du XXe siècle*, exhibition catalogue, Musée de Montmartre, Éditions Fragments, Paris, 2003.
AUCTION RECORDS:
PARIS, 18 June 1971, *Prophet*, FRF 8,000. PARIS, 28 March 1974, *Astarte* (gouache) FRF 47,000. PARIS, 14 June 1976, *The Wife of Satan or Lust* (1919, gouache and Indian ink, 19 1/4 x 10 1/2 ins / 49 x 26.5 cm) FRF 7,000. MUNICH, 28 May 1979, *Asiatic Gods* (1911, pastel, 28 1/4 x 40 ins / 72 x 101.5 cm) DEM 7,000. ENGHIEN-LES-BAINS, 28 Oct 1979, *Underwater Loves* (1914, oil on canvas, with copper disks, 24 x 41 1/4 ins / 61 x 105 cm) FRF 22,000. LONDON, 28 March 1984, *Abduction* (1928, gouache, 19 x 24 3/4 ins / 48 x 63 cm) GBP 11,000. LONDON, 19 March 1986, *Apollo and Daphne* (oil on canvas, 32 1/2 x 22 3/4 ins / 82.5 x 58 cm) GBP 6,000. ENGHIEN-LES-BAINS, 25 Oct 1987, *Rat with Gold Teeth* (1927, oil on panel, 22 x 22 ins / 55 x 55 cm) FRF 35,000. PARIS, 10 Dec 1987, *Snake God* (1911, watercolour and gouache heightened with gold, 13 x 13 ins / 33 x 33 cm) FRF 15,500. LONDON, 18 May 1988, *Crown of Thorns* (1922, oil on panel, 23 1/4 x 18 1/2 ins / 58.8 x 47.2 cm) GBP 1,650. PARIS, 20 May 1988, *St Michael, St Catherine, St Margaret* (1930, watercolour/bistre-coloured paper, 24 3/4 x 20 3/4 ins / 63 x 53 cm) FRF 7,000. PARIS, 16 June 1991, *Medusa* (1924, gouache and pastel, 24 3/4 x 19 ins / 63 x 48 cm) FRF 30,000. PARIS, 7 Dec 1992, *Self-portrait with Black Woman* (1921, oil on panel, 26 x 28 3/4 ins / 66 x 73 cm) FRF 95,000. PARIS, 29 March 1995, *Idol* (1919, gouache/card, 12 1/2 x 6 1/4 ins / 32 x 16 cm) FRF 62,000. PARIS, 20 Feb 1999, *Triumph of Joan of Arc* (1930, oil on canvas, 22 x 31 ins / 56 x 78 cm) FRF 27,000. BILLINGSHURST, 24 July 2000, *Harem Scenes* (watercolour and gouache, a pair, 9 x 24 ins / 22 x 61 cm) GBP 1,400. LONDON, 12 Oct 2000, *Storyteller in the Harem* (oil on canvas, 20 x 47 ins / 50 x 120 cm) GBP 5,000. LONDON, 31 May 2001, *Russian Symbolist Painting with Two Female Figures* (1909, pastel, 28 x 40 ins / 72 x 101 cm) GBP 5,800. PARIS, 25 Nov 2001, *Romantic Scene* (gouache, 23 x 27 ins / 59 x 69 cm) FRF 282,000. LONDON, 20 Nov 2002, *Winged Goddess of Wine* (c. 1930, gouache heightened with gold and silver, 39 x 27 ins / 100 x 69 cm) GBP 35,000. LONDON, 26 Nov 2002, *Astartee* (1926, gouache on paper on panel, 29 x 22 ins / 74 x 55 cm) GBP 20,000. LONDON, 19 Nov 2003, *Salome* (1918, mixed media on card, 41 x 33 ins / 103 x 83 cm) GBP 65,000. BUDAPEST, 12 Dec 2003, *Forerunner of Our Lord, St John, Self-portrait* (1921, oil on cardboard, 27 x 24 ins / 69 x 62 cm) HUF 16,000,000. LONDON, 26 May 2004, *Pharaoh* (1927, tempera on panel, 21 x 21 ins / 54 x 54 cm) GBP 15,000. PARIS, 9 June 2004, *Warrior* (oil on panel, 21 x 53 ins / 54 x 134 cm) EUR 11,400.

KALMAR, Felix
Austrian, 20th century.
Born 31 August 1936, in Vienna.
Painter.
Felix Kalmar studied at the Akademie der Bildenden Künste in Vienna. In his paintings, he always took nature as a starting point, abandoning volume and construction and treating his subjects in terms of light.

KALMBACH, Michael
German, 20th - 21st century.
Born 1962, in Frankfurt am Main.
Active in Frankfurt am Main and Berlin.
Sculptor (plaster), draughtsman, installation artist, watercolourist.
Michael Kalmbach combines drawings and installations. His drawings are based on fairy-tale subjects and show human figures, very often children, in states of depression or sadness. He is known for painting large-format watercolours, which he calls 'human soup'. The lower part of the drawings is spattered with spots of red or pinkish liquid. Isolated figures (of small boys) float in space, regurgitating or absorbing this ambient liquid. He also makes small plaster figures, which he arranges in groups.

Kalmbach's solo exhibitions include *Michael Kalmbach. Menschensuppe, Aquarelle und Skulpturen* (*Michael Kalmbach: Human Soup, Watercolours and Sculptures*) at the Museum für Gegenwartskunst in Basel in 2002.
BIBLIOGRAPHY:
Ammann, Jean-Christophe, *Michael Kalmbach*, exhibition catalogue, Museum für Moderne Kunst, Frankfurt, 2000. *Michael Kalmbach - Aquarelles et sculptures*, exhibition catalogue, Kunstsammlung, Basel, 2002.

KALMIK ERCUMENT. See **ERCUMENT-KALMIK**

KALMSTEINER, Johann
Austrian, 19th century.
Born 23 September 1845, in Sarnthein, South Tyrol.
Sculptor.
Kalmsteiner trained in Dresden and Munich, and subsequently worked much in Vienna, Berlin and Bremen. Various busts by him are documented.

KALMYKOV, Ivan Leonidovitch
Russian, 19th - 20th century.
Born 1866; died 1925.
Painter. Landscapes, seascapes.
Ivan Kalmykov was active in Novotcherkassk. He painted coastal seascapes in particular.
MUSEUMS AND GALLERIES:
MOSCOW (Rumiantsev Mus.): *Seascape* - MOSCOW (State Tretyakov Gal.): *Dusk*; *Coastal Scene* (study).
AUCTION RECORDS:
LONDON, 6 Oct 1988, *Coastal Landscape* (oil on canvas, 39 1/4 x 32 1/2 ins / 99.7 x 82.5 cm) GBP 3,300. PARIS, 27 Nov 2003, *Temple* (1918, watercolour, 20 x 26 ins / 50 x 65 cm) EUR 3,400.

KALNINS, Eduards
Latvian, 20th century.
Born 1904, in Vidzeme.
Active in Sweden.
Painter.
Eduards Kalnins won the Rome Prize of the academy of fine art in Riga in 1935. In 1939, he appeared at the exhibition of Latvian art in Paris.
MUSEUMS AND GALLERIES:
KAUNAS - RIGA.

KALNINS, Rheinhold
Latvian, 20th century.
Born in Pernau.
Painter, pastellist. Nudes, portraits, landscapes.

Rheinhold Kalnins studied at the Académies Libres in Montparnasse, Paris. He spent a fairly long time in Paris, drawing or painting portraits of random clients, in order to pay for his studies, and exhibiting from 1921 at the Salon des Indépendants, Salon d'Automne and Salon des Tuileries. Subsequently, he often travelled to Sweden, Switzerland and Spain. He seems to have made a career in Sweden. He painted in pastel as much as in oil. He preferred drawing and relief, working in a limited range of tones. His simple studies of nudes reveal a particular anxiety.

He took part in collective exhibitions in Riga, Stockholm, Göteborg and Malmö.

MUSEUMS AND GALLERIES:
RIGA (Valsts makslas muz.).

AUCTION RECORDS:
STOCKHOLM, 1947, *Landscape*, SEK 2,500.

KALNROZE, Valdis, or Rozenbergs
Latvian, 20th century.
Born 17 January 1894, in Kuldiga.
Painter. Landscapes.

Valdis Kalnroze studied at the academy of fine art in Riga. He appeared at the exhibition of Latvian art in Paris in 1939.

MUSEUMS AND GALLERIES:
JELGAVA - RIGA.

KALRAET, Abraham Pieterz van, or Kalraat, Calraet
Dutch, 17th - 18th century.
Born 7 October 1642 or 1643, in Dordrecht; died 11 June 1721 or 1722, in Dordrecht.
Painter, sculptor. Religious subjects, genre scenes, landscapes with figures, landscapes, still-lifes (including fruit/shellfish).

Abraham van Kalraet was the son of the sculptor Pieter Jansz. and studied under the sculptors Aemilius and Samuel Huppe. He married on 30 June 1680. Nothing is known of any surviving sculptures by him. His brothers were also wood sculptors (Johan and Hendrick) and painters (Dirk, Barend and Pieter).

MUSEUMS AND GALLERIES:
BIRMINGHAM (Barber Institute of Fine Arts): *Horses and cattle in a landscape* (oil/wood).

AUCTION RECORDS:
LONDON, 13 March 1936, *Landscape with Peasant*, GBP 50. PARIS, 8 Dec 1948, *Still-life: Peaches and Plums*, FRF 50,000. PARIS, 28 May 1954, *The Hunt Halts; Three Huntsmen on Horseback* (pair) FRF 120,000. LONDON, 24 June 1959, *Landscape with Two Draught Horses*, GBP 1,400. LONDON, 20 March 1964, *River Bank with Figures*, Gns 220. AMSTERDAM, 26 April 1976, *Halt at the Inn* (oil on panel, 14 1/4 x 22 1/2 ins / 36 x 57 cm) NLG 34,000. VERSAILLES, 6 March 1977, *Lesson in Dressage* (oil on wood, 15 x 20 3/4 ins / 38 x 53 cm) FRF 15,000. ZURICH, 25 Nov 1977, *Elegant Company on Horseback* (oil on panel, 16 1/4 x 21 1/4 ins / 41 x 54 cm) CHF 13,000. LONDON, 18 May 1979, *Landscape with Huntsmen* (oil on panel, 19 3/4 x 31 1/2 ins / 50 x 80 cm) GBP 4,800. NEW YORK, 8 Jan 1981, *Still-life with Fruit* (oil on canvas, 28 1/4 x 23 1/4 ins / 72 x 59 cm) USD 6,500. NEW YORK, 19 Jan 1984, *Still-life with Fruit, Crawfish and Porcelain Vase* (oil on panel, 24 x 49 ins / 61 x 124.5 cm) USD 32,000. NEW YORK, 31 May 1989, *Still-life with Peaches, Grapes and Butterflies* (oil on panel, 16 3/4 x 14 3/4 ins / 42.5 x 37.5 cm) USD 36,300. AMSTERDAM, 20 June 1989, *Shellfish on a Stone Entablature* (oil on panel, 15 3/4 x 21 1/4 ins / 39.9 x 53.9 cm) NLG 21,850. NEW YORK, 13 Oct 1989, *Still-life with Peaches on a Red Cloth* (oil on canvas, 11 1/4 x 13 3/4 ins / 28.5 x 35 cm) USD 22,000. NEW YORK, 10 Jan 1990, *Christ on the Road to Emmaus* (oil on canvas, 35 1/2 x 57 ins / 90.2 x 144.8 cm) USD 11,000. PARIS, 23 April 1990, *Interior Scene* (oil on panel, 20 x 30 1/4 ins / 50.5 x 77 cm) FRF 95,000. LONDON, 5 July 1991, *River Landscape with Peasants Leading their Animals along a Wooded Road* (oil on panel, 17 x 22 1/4 ins / 43.2 x 56.5 cm) GBP 9,900. NEW YORK, 19 May 1993, *Horsemen Stopping at an Inn* (oil on panel, 19 1/2 x 25 1/2 ins / 49.8 x 64.7 cm) USD 17,250. LONDON, 9 Dec 1994, *Gentlemen with their Horses at the Farrier's Door* (oil on panel, 12 1/2 x 18 1/2 ins / 31.7 x 47 cm) GBP 11,500. AMSTERDAM, 13 Nov 1995, *Landscape with Horseman* (oil on panel, 9 1/4 x 7 3/4 ins / 23.5 x 20 cm) NLG 9,200.

KALRAET, Barend van, or Kalraat
Dutch, 17th - 18th century.
Born 1649, in Dordrecht; died 1737, in Dordrecht.
Painter. Portraits, landscapes.

Barend van Kalraet studied under his brother Abraham Pietersz. from 1662 to 1665 and also under Albert Cuyp. He married on 26 May 1697.

Kalraet painted landscapes, portraits and views of the Rhine in the style of Saftleven, although early in his career he took his inspiration from Cuyp.

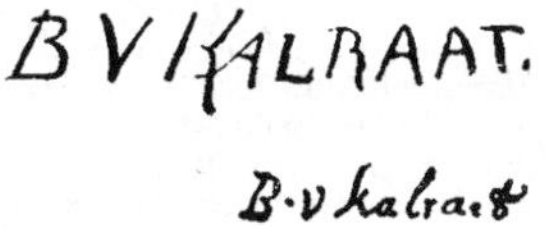

MUSEUMS AND GALLERIES:
LIÈGE: two views of the banks of the Rhine - SCHWERIN: *Cowshed*.

AUCTION RECORDS:
LONDON, 14 Dec 1907, *Cavalry Skirmish*, GBP 5. LONDON, 10 Dec 1910, *Quay with Ships, Figures and Animals*, GBP 42. LONDON, 7 May 1920, *Landscape*, GBP 47. PARIS, 16 April 1951, *River Scenes* (two pendants) FRF 87,000. COPENHAGEN, 22 April 1982, *Banks of the Rhine with Figures* (oil on panel, 6 x 7 1/2 ins / 15.5 x 19 cm) DKK 26,000. PARIS, 15 April 1988, *Timber Being Run Down River in the Rhine Valley* (oil on panel, 15 3/4 x 20 ins / 40 x 51 cm) FRF 42,000. STOCKHOLM, 29 April 1988, *Couple* (oil on canvas, 12 1/2 x 9 1/2 ins / 32 x 24 cm) SEK 44,000.

KALRAET, Pieter Jansz. van
Dutch, 17th century.
Born c. 1615, in Utrecht; died 1680, in Dordrecht.
Sculptor.

Pieter van Kalraet was the father of Abraham and Barend van Kalraet.

KALTEISEN, Heinrich von. See **ACH Heinrich von**

KALTENBACH, Lucile
South African, 20th century.
Born in Durban.
Active in the USA.
Painter, watercolourist.

Lucile Kaltenbach trained at the Art Institute of Chicago and at the studio of André Lhôte in Paris. She was a member of the Art Students League in Chicago. She painted mainly in watercolours.

KALTENHEUZER, Charles
German, 19th century.
Born 19th century, in Barmen.
Sculptor.

Kaltenheuzer exhibited in Paris, and gained an honourable mention in the Salon of 1859.

KALTENMOSER, Kaspar
German, 19th century.
Born 25 December 1806, in Horb am Neckar; died 8 March 1867, in Munich.
Painter, lithographer. Genre scenes.

Kaltenmoser worked as a lithographer in Schweinfurt from 1826 to 1829. From 1830, he worked at the academy in Munich under the direction of Heinrich Hess, travelling in the Black Forest, Switzerland and the Tyrol. Subsequently he settled in Munich, exhibiting there from c. 1831 and also in Karlsruhe and Württemberg.

AUCTION RECORDS:
STUTTGART, 2 Nov 1977, *The Proposal* (oil on canvas, 26 1/2 x 21 1/4 ins / 67 x 54 cm) DEM 8,100. LONDON, 30 Nov 1984, *The Priest's Advice* (1865, oil on canvas, rounded at the top, 35 1/2 x 30 ins / 90 x 76.2 cm) GBP 9,000. CHESTER, 10 July 1986, *Young Couple Seeking Her Father's Consent* (1849, oil on canvas, 33 x 29 1/4 ins / 84 x 74 cm) GBP 8,000. NEW YORK, 19 May 1987, *Peasant Family Playing with a Baby* (1859, oil on canvas, 33 1/2 x 26 3/4 ins / 85 x 68 cm) USD 8,500. MUNICH, 10 Dec 1992, *Italian Family* (1855, oil on canvas, 25 1/2 x 21 1/4 ins / 65 x 54 cm) DEM 22,600. MUNICH, 24 March 1999, *Italian Woman and Her Children Seated outside a House* (oil on canvas, 22 x 19 ins / 55 x 48 cm) DEM 10,000. VIENNA, 20 May 1999, *Interior Scene with Mother Combing Child's Hair* (1848, oil on canvas, 19 x 17 ins / 48 x 42 cm) ATS 90,000. STUTTGART, 30 June 2000, *Young Neapolitan Woman on Terrace* (1854, oil on canvas, 22 x 19 ins / 57 x 48 cm) DEM 23,000. MUNICH, 6 Dec 2000, *Dancing in Upper Bavarian Tavern* (1837, oil on iron, 6 x 7 ins / 15 x 18 cm) DEM 6,000. STUTTGART, 29 March 2001, *Scene with Family* (1854, oil on canvas, 22 x 19 ins / 55 x 48 cm) DEM 10,000. STUTTGART, 6 Dec 2001, *Southern Family* (1849, oil on canvas, 25 x 20 ins / 63 x 52 cm) DEM 24,000. COPENHAGEN, 2 Dec 2002, *Interior Scene with Grandfather Playing Violin and Children Dancing* (1864, oil on canvas, 27 x 38 ins / 68 x 96 cm) DKK 50,000. STUTTGART, 25 Sept 2003, *Southern Mother with Child* (1865, oil on panel, 11 x 9 ins / 29 x 23 cm) EUR 7,000. MUNICH, 3 Dec 2003, *Haircut* (1840, oil on canvas, 13 x 11 ins / 33 x 27 cm) EUR 2,600.

KALTENMOSER, Max
German, 19th century.
Born 1 December 1842, in Munich; died 4 April 1887, in Munich.
Painter. Genre scenes.

Max Kaltenmoser was the son and pupil of Kaspar Kaltenmoser; he was later taught by P. Foltz and A. von Ramberg at the academy in Munich in 1858. He subsequently travelled in the Tyrol, north Germany and the Côte d'Azur. He exhibited in Vienna, Munich, Düsseldorf, Bremen, Dresden and Hanover.

AUCTION RECORDS:
LONDON, 1 Nov 1973, *The Stolen Kiss*, Gns 550. LONDON, 20 July 1977, *The Family Picnic* (oil on canvas, 34 1/4 x 48 1/2 ins / 87 x 123 cm) GBP 6,200. MUNICH, 25 June 1992, *Young Woman Sewing by a Window* (1867, oil on canvas, 23 x 17 3/4 ins / 58.5 x 45 cm) DEM 15,820. LONDON, 17 March 1995, *The Farewell* (1878, oil on canvas, 17 1/2 x 11 ins / 44.5 x 28 cm) GBP 2,300. MUNICH, 20 March 2002, *Midday Meal in Peasant Interior* (oil on canvas, 11 x 17 ins / 29 x 42 cm) EUR 3,500. AMSTERDAM, 18 Feb 2003, *Portrait of Maria Mancini* (oil on canvas, 20 x 16 ins / 50 x 41 cm) EUR 2,800. MUNICH, 28 March 2003, *Mother Cutting Children's Hair* (oil on canvas, 13 x 11 ins / 33 x 27 cm) EUR 3,200.

KALTENOFER, Peter
German, 15th century.
Died c. 1490.
Active in Augsburg.
Painter. Decorative schemes.

The museum in Munich owns some of Kaltenofer's paintings. He also produced large-scale decorations.

MUSEUMS AND GALLERIES:
MUNICH: Portraits.

KALTNER, Josef
German, 18th - 19th century.
Born c. 1758, in Nymphenburg (Munich); died c. 1824.
Painter, engraver. History painting, portraits, genre scenes.

Kaltner worked in Munich, having trained at the academy in Paris. He produced miniature portraits of several members of the Bavarian royal family.

KALTWASSER, Fritz
German, 20th century.
Born 20 November 1889, in Wiesbaden.
Painter. Portraits, landscapes, still-lifes.

Fritz Kaltwasser studied in Munich, then worked mainly in Dresden. His painting was influenced by Hans von Marées.

KALUGUIN, Igor
Ukrainian, 20th - 21st century.
Born 1957, in Kharkov.
Painter.

Igor Kaluguin participated from 1979 in exhibitions held by the union of painters and the Island group.

AUCTION RECORDS:
PARIS, 8 Dec 1990, *Métamorphose* (oil on canvas, 35 1/2 x 43 1/4 ins / 90 x 110 cm) FRF 11,000.

KALVACH, Rudolf
Austrian, 20th century.
Born 1883; died 1932.
Painter.
Wiener Werkstätte group.

Rudolf Kalvach had a brief career because he began to suffer from schizophrenia in 1912. His paintings show affinities with the Viennese Expressionists of the early 20th century. He created a series of postcards for the Wiener Werkstätte (Vienna Workshops).

AUCTION RECORDS:
NEW YORK, 13 March 1982, *Art Exhibition* (1908, gouache, 48 3/4 x 18 1/2 ins / 124 x 47 cm) USD 17,000. LONDON, 23 Sept 1993, *Fantasy* (oil on panel, 23 1/2 x 23 1/4 ins / 60 x 59 cm) GBP 26,450. VIENNA, 14 May 2002, *The Three Kings* (enamel on copper, 4 x 4 ins / 10 x 10 cm) EUR 2,600. VIENNA, 14 May 2002, *Brunhilde, Siegfried and the Dragon* (enamel on copper, 9 x 9 ins / 22 x 22 cm) EUR 6,000.

KALVODA, Alois
Czech, 20th century.
Born 15 May 1875, in Brno; died 1934.
Painter, engraver, illustrator. Landscapes.

Alois Kalvoda spent time in Paris and Munich around 1900, then returned to his native country, where he regularly exhibited in Prague.

AUCTION RECORDS:
BERN, 12 May 1990, *Forest Path* (oil on panel, 10 1/4 x 9 ins / 26 x 22 cm) CHF 1,400. LONDON, 22 Feb 1995, *Winter Landscape* (oil on canvas, 9 3/4 x 14 ins / 25 x 35.5 cm) GBP 690. PRAGUE, 18 March 2000, *Landscape* (oil on canvas, 13 x 19 ins / 33 x 49 cm) CZK 65,000. PRAGUE, 27 May 2000, *Village in Late Afternoon* (oil on canvas, 14 x 14 ins / 36 x 36 cm) CZK 80,000. PRAGUE, 24 March 2001, *Summer Landscape* (oil on canvas, 18 x 22 ins / 45 x 55 cm) CZK 80,000. PRAGUE, 19 May 2001, *Forest Pool in Winter* (oil on canvas on cardboard, 20 x 28 ins / 50 x 70 cm) CZK 90,000. PRAGUE, 4 Oct 2003, *Mountain Landscape with Buildings* (oil on canvas, 22 x 37 ins / 57 x 95 cm) CZK 55,000. PRAGUE, 29 Nov 2003, *Winter in a Forest* (oil on cardboard, 39 x 27 ins / 98 x 68 cm) CZK 180,000. PRAGUE, 2 Oct 2004, *Winter Landscape with Stream* (oil on cardboard, 10 x 14 ins / 25 x 35 cm) CZK 50,000.

KAM, F. van der
Dutch, 18th century.
Active c. 1750.
Engraver.
F. van der Kam produced etchings and line engravings.

KAMADA, Baiseki
Japanese, 19th - 20th century.
Painter (including silk). Landscapes.
Kamada was active in Osaka and exhibited at the 1900 Paris Exposition Universelle.

KAMATANI, Shin'ichi
Japanese, 20th - 21st century.
Born 1948.
Painter.
Kamatani exhibited in Tokyo from 1971. In 1974 he took part in the exhibition *Japanese Art of Today* at the Museum of Contemporary Art in Montreal.

KAMBARA, Tai, real name: Kambara Yasushi, artist name: Tai
Japanese, 20th century.
Born 1898, in Sendai; died 1997.
Painter.
Groups: Action, Plastic.
Kambara was first of all a poet, dramatic author and critic. He became personally linked quite early on with Marinetti and introduced Futurism to Japan. He began exhibiting in 1917 at the fourth Nika Salon. In 1920 he published the *First Manifesto of Kambara Tai*. In 1922 he founded the avant-garde group Action and was responsible for its manifesto at the time of the group's first exhibition. He was also active in the Sanka Association of Fine Arts. After the dissolution of this association he created the group Plastic in 1925, which became the Association of Plasticians, from which he was excluded. Apart from participating in group exhibitions, he also exhibited his paintings in solo exhibitions, the first being in 1920. He eventually gave up painting and devoted himself entirely to his literary career. He could be said to have been the theoretician and one of the actors of the Japanese artistic avant-garde at the beginning of the century. His paintings were abstract with a futuristic inclination towards the expression of movement.

KAMBLI, Heinrich Friedrich
German, 18th century.
Born 1750, in Potsdam; died 1801, in Potsdam.
Sculptor.
Kambli, the son and pupil of Johann Melchior Kambli, was appointed sculptor to the court of Prussia in 1785.

KAMBLI, Johann Melchior
Swiss, 18th century.
Born 1718, in Zurich; died 1783, in Potsdam.
Sculptor.
Kambli entered the service of Frederick the Great, but soon specialised in foundry and bronze work. He was the father of Heinrich Friedrich Kambli.

KAMEI SHIICHI, real name: Kamei Matsunosuke, artist name: Shiichi
Japanese, 19th - 20th century.
Born 1843, in Edo (now Tokyo); died 1915, in Tokyo.
Painter, print artist.

KAMEKE, Egon von
German, 20th century.
Born 13 January 1881, in Luckenwalde.
Painter, lithographer. Seascapes, landscapes.
Before World War I, Egon von Kameke painted mainly seascapes in England and Scandinavia. Later, he became interested in a greater variety of landscapes.

KAMEKE, Otto Werner Henning von, or Kamecke
German, 19th century.
Born 3 February 1826, in Stolp (Slupsk), Pomerania; died 8 June 1899, in Berlin.
Painter. Landscapes, animals.
Kameke worked in Rome c. 1862. Subsequently he attended the school of fine arts in Weimar, where he was taught by Michelès and Böcklin. He travelled around Germany, the Tyrol and Switzerland. In 1886, he became a member of the academy in Berlin, and in 1888 was appointed professor there. He exhibited in Berlin, gaining a gold medal in 1879, and in Vienna, Dresden, Hanover and Munich.
MUSEUMS AND GALLERIES:
BERLIN: *St Gotthard Road* - LEIPZIG: *The Bois Glacier in Chamonix* - WEIMAR: *Königssee Lake (Berchtesgaden).*
AUCTION RECORDS:
BERLIN, 1894, *View of the Ortler*, FRF 625. COLOGNE, 24 March 1972, *Rapallo*, DEM 3,300. COLOGNE, 19 Oct 1979, *Alpine Landscape* (1871, oil on canvas, 37 3/4 x 53 1/4 ins / 96 x 135 cm) DEM 4,000. COLOGNE, 30 March 1984, *Anglers in a River Landscape with Cliffs* (1873, oil on canvas, 37 x 53 1/4 ins / 94 x 135 cm) DEM 6,000. LONDON, 27 Nov 1985, *Young Peasant Woman and Her Goats in a Mountain Landscape* (oil on canvas, 36 x 53 1/4 ins / 91.5 x 135 cm) GBP 4,800. MUNICH, 13 May 1987, *Lake Brienz, Interlaken* (oil on canvas remounted/panel, 19 1/2 x 26 ins / 49.5 x 66 cm) DEM 5,500. AMSTERDAM, 28 Oct 1992, *Mountain Landscape with Waterfall* (oil on canvas, 24 1/4 x 16 3/4 ins / 61.5 x 42.5 cm) NLG 2,760. VIENNA, 20 Nov 2001, *Farmstead in Swiss Alps* (oil on canvas, 36 x 52 ins / 91 x 131 cm) ATS 50,000. BREMEN, 26 March 2004, *High Alpine Valley with Waterfall and Chapel* (oil on canvas, 53 x 37 ins / 135 x 95 cm) EUR 2,400. MUNICH, 26 March 2004, *Garda See Landscape* (oil on panel, 19 x 23 ins / 49 x 58 cm) EUR 5,000.

KAMEL, Brahim
Tunisian, 20th century.
Born in Mahdia.
Painter (mixed media).
Brahim Kamel has taken part in several group exhibitions. These include, among others, exhibitions in Tunisia and Egypt from 1971 onwards, at the International City of Arts in Paris in 1975, at the Salon d'Automne in Paris in 1983, in Basel, Switzerland in 1984, and in Rennes and Paris in 1986. He has also shown his work in solo exhibitions in Tunis since 1974, and at the City of Arts in Paris in 1981.

Brahim Kamel's painting is an accumulation of simple geometric signs and often superimposed surfaces. Taken in its entirety, his work conveys an impression of great turbulence.

KAMEL, Fouad
Egyptian, 20th century.
Born 1919.
Painter.
Fouad Kamel studied at the faculty of fine arts in Cairo. He obtained state funding in 1960. Fouad Kamel produces automatic painting which is extremely gestural, characteristic of the lyrical abstract painting of the 1960s. He taught art in schools in Cairo and his work was presented in collective exhibitions including the 1947 *International Exhibition of Surrealism* in Paris, the 1961 São Paulo Biennale, the 1964 Venice Biennale, and notably *Visages de l'art contemporain égyptien* (*Aspects of Contemporary Egyptian Art*) at the Galliera Museum in Paris in 1971.
BIBLIOGRAPHY:
Badr El-Din Abou Ghazy, *Visages de l'Art contemporain égyptien*, exhibition catalogue, Musée Galliera, Paris, 1971.
MUSEUMS AND GALLERIES:
ALEXANDRIA (MMA) - CAIRO (Egyptian MMA).

KAMEL, Saad
Egyptian, 20th century.
Born 1924, in Cairo.
Painter (textile), engraver.
Saad Kamel studied at the free section of the Cairo school of fine arts and also worked in Rome. He obtained state funding in 1965, and has been the permanent representative of the international trades council in Geneva since 1963. Predominantly a batik painter, Kamel's works are mainly decorative and upbeat in mood, and are characterised by their meticulous execution.

Saad Kamel has exhibited his work in several group exhibitions, including the international craft fair in Florence in 1958, where he was awarded the first prize for engraving, the third Alexandria Biennale in 1968, the international biennial of engraving in Ljubljana in 1967, the Venice Biennale in 1968 and notably *Visages de l'art contemporain égyptien* (*Faces of Contemporary Egyptian Art*) at the Galliera Museum in Paris in 1971.

BIBLIOGRAPHY:
Badr El-Din Abou Ghazy, *Visages de l'Art contemporain égyptien*, exhibition catalogue, Musée Galliera, Paris, 1971.

KAMELOR, J.
German, 18th century.
Painter.

KAMENEV, Igor
Russian, 20th - 21st century.
Born 15 December 1955, in Vladivostok.
Painter.
Igor Kamenev settled in Moscow in 1956. He abandoned his studies at the institute of architecture to join the dissidents' movement in 1974. His protest activities resulted in his spending time in psychiatric clinics on several occasions. Certain of his paintings seem linked to a Surrealist style, while others are directly inspired by religious sentiments of the kind that were prohibited by the Soviet regime. He also produces works that resemble Byzantine-type icons. From 1975, he took part in many exhibitions, both clandestine and public. In 1978, he enrolled with the UNESCO international artists federation and in 1988 he was one of the initiators behind the first exhibition of religious art in the USSR.

KAMENEV, Lieff Livovich
Russian, 19th century.
Born 1834; died 24 January 1886.
Painter. Landscapes.
MUSEUMS AND GALLERIES:
MOSCOW (State Tretyakov Gal.): *Road in Winter; Spring; Red Lake in Moscow, Autumnal Effect.*

KAMENSKY, Fiodor Fidorovitch
Russian, 19th - 20th century.
Born c. 1838, near Leningrad (now St Petersburg); died 1913, in the USA.
Sculptor. Busts.
MUSEUMS AND GALLERIES:
MOSCOW (State Tretyakov Gal.): *P P Vedenetzky Working* - ST PETERSBURG (Gosudarstvennyj Russkij Muz.): *First Step* (marble); *Bust of Th-A Brouny* (bronze).

KAMER, Konrad
German, 17th century.
Born to a family originally from Frankfurt.
Active at the beginning of the 17th century.
Sculptor (wood).
Kamer was an assistant to Jost Stachel and collaborated with him in decorating the sacristy of the church of the Discalced Carmelites in Lucerne.

KAMERLINGH-ONNES, Menso. See **ONNES Menso Kamerlingh**

KAMERMANN
French, 18th century.
Active in Italy and Paris.
Engraver (burin). Portraits.

KAMIEN, Erasmus
Polish, 16th century.
Born in Poznan.
Engraver, goldsmith.
Some engravings of ornaments by Erasmus Kamien are known.

KAMIENSKI, Antoine
Polish, 19th century.
Born during the second half of the 19th century, in Grodus.
Active in Warsaw.
Engraver (etching).
In 1921, Antoine Kamienski showed *Courtyard of the Jagellonian University in Cracow* at the *Exposition des Artistes Polonais* (*exhibition of Polish artists*) organised by the Salon of the Société Nationale des Beaux-Arts.

KAMIGAKI, Horyu
Japanese, 18th century.
Active c. 1700.
Painter.
Edo period.
Kamigaki Horyu was influenced by the early stages of the Torii School. A hanging scroll, Courtesan Seated on a Bench Enjoying the Evening Cool in Summer, in ink and colour on silk, is in the Cleveland Museum.

KAMINAGAI, Tadashi
Japanese, 20th century.
Born 27 September 1899, in Hiroshima; died 14 June 1982, in Paris.
Also active in Brazil.
Painter.
Determined to become a painter, Kaminagai Tadashi went to Paris in 1927 and during the 1930s exhibited at the Salon des Tuileries and the Salon d'Automne as a member of the École de Paris. In 1940 he returned to Japan, leaving the following year for Brazil to escape the conflict, as did many other artists. While in Brazil he won a silver medal at the 1942 Salão Nacional de Belas Artes and exhibited at the São Paulo Biennale in 1951 and 1953. He returned to Japan once more in 1955 but left two years later and returned to Paris, this time for good, exhibiting annually at the Salon d'Automne. In 1987 the Marion Gallery, Tokyo, held a retrospective of his work.

KAMINER, Saul
Mexican, 20th - 21st century.
Born 1952.
Also active in France.
Painter. Scenes with figures.
Saul Kaminer is inspired by observed or imagined reality and produces arabesque drawings in harmonious tones of grey tinged with red, blue and green.

KAMINSKA, Sophie
Polish, 19th - 20th century.
Active in Warsaw.
Painter, sculptor.
Sophie Kaminska's paintings of *Susanna Bathing* and the *Pruszkowski Family Tomb* are cited.

KAMINSKI
Polish, 18th century.
Painter.
The gallery of King Stanislas Augustus contained two *Views of the City of Kasimierz*, two *Views of Solce Mountain* and two *Landscapes* by Kaminski.

KAMINSKI, Aleksander
Polish, 19th century.
Born 3 January 1823, in Warsaw; died 26 February 1886, in Warsaw.
Painter.
Aleksander Kaminski spent ten years in Italy, where he mainly painted scenes from Italian folklore.

KAMINSKI, Aleksandr Stepanovich
Russian, 19th century.
Born 1829; died 1897.
Painter, architect. Architectural views.
MUSEUMS AND GALLERIES:
MOSCOW (State Tretyakov Gal.): *Road in Viterbo; Michaelangelo's House in Rome; Fountain at Viterbo; Interior of St Mark's, Venice; Chapel of the Church of S Maria della Minerva.*

KAMINSKI, Anton
Polish, 19th - 20th century.
Born 1861, in Wilno (now Vilnius, Lithuania).
Engraver (etching).
Anton Kaminski was honoured in 1906. He worked particularly in Warsaw.

KAMINSKI, Sigismond
Polish, 19th century.
Born during the second half of the 19th century, in Poland.
Active in Warsaw.
Draughtsman.
In 1921, Sigismond Kaminski took part in the *Exposition des Artistes Polonais* (*exhibition of Polish artists*) organised by the Salon of the Société des Beaux-Arts.

KAMINSKY, Emmanuil Abramovich
Ukrainian, 20th century.
Born 1927, in Odessa.
Painter. Landscapes, still-lifes.
MUSEUMS AND GALLERIES:
ODESSA (MFA).
AUCTION RECORDS:
PARIS, 19 June 1991, *Haystacks* (1953, oil on canvas, 14 1/4 x 24 ins / 36 x 61 cm) FRF 4,000. PARIS, 16 Nov 1992, *After School* (1972, oil on canvas, 36 1/2 x 29 1/2 ins / 93 x 75 cm) FRF 4,200. PARIS, 1 Dec 1994, *Bouquets of Roses* (1953, oil on canvas, 31 x 23 1/2 ins / 79 x 60 cm) FRF 4,000.

KAMINSKY, Thomas
German, 20th century.
Born 1945, in Dresden.
Painter, draughtsman, mixed media.
Thomas Kaminsky lives and works in Cologne. From the start, his technique has been that of draughtsmanship. He covers huge surfaces with a confusion of lines, using first pencil, then pastels, then mixed media and, most recently, oil paints applied directly with the fingers. Since 1973, he has taken part in group exhibitions and has also had solo shows, notably in 1976 in Munich, 1978 and 1980 in Berlin, 1979 and 1982 at the Galerie Appel und Fertsch in Frankfurt and 1988 at the Galerie Appel und Troschke in Frankfurt.

KAMIR, Leon, also known as Leon Kaufmann
Polish, 19th - 20th century.
Born 8 June 1872, in Pavlovo; died 1933, in Louveciennes.
Painter. Portraits, landscapes, seascapes.
Leon Kamir started his training in Warsaw, then followed courses at the Academy in Munich from 1895 to 1897. He was then a student of Benjamin-Constant in Paris and exhibited there at the Salon de la Société Nationale des Beaux-Arts and the Salon d'Automne. His compositions show views of Normandy and Brittany as well as somewhat stilted portraits of women. He sometimes signed his work as Leon Kaufmann. He also exhibited in Italy, England and Germany.
AUCTION RECORDS:
PARIS, 30 March 1925, *Night*, FRF 345. PARIS, 17 Dec 1943, *Douarnenez Bay*, FRF 180. PARIS, 21 March 1947, *Seascape*, FRF 650. LONDON, 23 Oct 1980, *Tamara Karsavina dressed as Giselle* (1913, pastel, 35 1/2 x 23 ins / 90.2 x 58.5 cm) GBP 2,500. PARIS, 3 March 2003, *Lake Landscape* (oil on panel, 13 x 16 ins / 32 x 41 cm) EUR 1,800. SION, 5 June 2004, *Colombine* (1916, pastel on cardboard, 38 x 28 ins / 96 x 70 cm) CHF 6,000.

KAMIYA, Shin
Japanese, 20th century.
Born 1942, in Tokyo.
Illustrator, print artist.
Kamiya lives and works in Tokyo. He was represented in the 1974-1975 Tokyo International Print Biennale. He also illustrates children's books.

KAMKÉ, Georges Lucien Louis
French, 20th century.
Born 25 May 1889, in Paris.
Painter. Portraits, urban landscapes, landscapes.
Georges Lucien Louis Kamké was the son of a decorative artist and his artistic vocation received his family's support. He studied anatomy, figure drawing and landscape, notably under Pierre Grandsire. He travelled widely and held exhibitions of his work during his travels.

In 1925-1926 the City of Paris commissioned him to paint views of the city, including the gates of Paris, the fortifications and the 'Zone', prior to their demolition. He also painted in various regions of France and in Belgium, The Netherlands, Spain, Brazil, the Canary Islands and the Balearics. He executed numerous portrait commissions, including ambassadors, politicians, the sultan of Morocco, and Spanish ministers, noblemen and noblewomen.
AUCTION RECORDS:
PARIS, 4 Feb 1928, *Boat*, FRF 180; *L'Avenue des Platanes* FRF 120. PARIS, 5 March 1941, *Bust of a Spanish Woman* (1934) FRF 1,350.

KAMKE, Ivar
Swedish, 20th century.
Born 1882; died 1936.
Painter. Landscapes.
Ivar Kamke studied with Gustav Oskar Björck and Axel Kulle at the Konstakademien in Stockholm. His paintings drew inspiration from his teacher Björck and from Anders Zorn.
AUCTION RECORDS:
STOCKHOLM, 30 Oct 1979, 1932, oil on panel, 22 3/4 x 16 1/2 ins / 58 x 42 cm) SEK 9,400. STOCKHOLM, 1 Nov 1983, 1918, oil on canvas, 28 1/4 x 22 3/4 ins / 72 x 58 cm) SEK 23,500. LONDON, 23 March 1988, *Le Pont Quattro Capi à Rome* (1924, oil on canvas, 25 1/2 x 32 3/4 ins / 65 x 83 cm) GBP 4,400. AARHUS, 8 May 2000, *Venetian Canal with Gondolas* (1921, oil on canvas, 21 x 25 ins / 54 x 64 cm) DKK 19,000. STOCKHOLM, 4 Dec 2002, *Models by Water* (oil on canvas, 20 x 24 ins / 50 x 61 cm) SEK 50,000. STOCKHOLM, 29 Sept 2003, *Reclining Female Nude* (1918, oil on canvas, 32 x 39 ins / 81 x 98 cm) SEK 20,000. STOCKHOLM, 30 Nov 2004, *Two Women Doing Needlework* (1920, oil on canvas, 39 x 31 ins / 98 x 80 cm) SEK 19,000.

KAMM, Jean Frédéric
French, 18th century.
Active in Paris in 1759.
Painter.

KAMM, Johann Bernhard
German, 18th - 19th century.
Born 4 February 1736, in Oberluerheim; died 10 March 1816, in Bamberg.
Sculptor.

Kamm worked for several churches in Bamberg, and the nearby churches of Schesslitz, Mainroth and Bischberg.

KAMM, Louis Philippe
French, 20th century.
Born 11 April 1882, in Strasbourg; died 16 June 1959, in Strasbourg.
Painter. Local figures.
Louis Philippe Kamm taught at the École des Arts Décoratifs in Strasbourg. He painted peasants from the north of Alsace. His work is characterised by his monumental style.

KAMM, Marcel
French, 19th - 20th century.
Born 19th century, in Paris.
Engraver (burin).
Marcel Kamm exhibited at the Salon des Artistes Français and received a commendation in 1910.

KAMMERER, Chrétien
French, 19th century.
Born in Mulhouse; died 1903.
Painter. Flowers.
MUSEUMS AND GALLERIES:
MULHOUSE: watercolour.

KAMMERER, Frederik Hendrik.
See **KAEMMERER Frederik Hendrik**

KAMMERER, Marcel
Austrian, 20th century.
Born 4 November 1878, in Vienna; died 1959.
Painter. Flowers.
Marcel Kammerer travelled widely in Europe. He was best known as an architect, a pupil of Otto Wagner and as the designer of the Hotel Maria Schutz in Semmering. However, he also exhibited his paintings in Rome in 1913 and in Vienna in 1923. He was a member of the Künstlerhaus from 1919.
AUCTION RECORDS:
LONDON, 10 Feb 1988, *Chrysanthemums* (1925, oil on canvas, 53 1/4 x 31 1/2 ins / 135 x 80 cm) GBP 5,500. VIENNA, 10 April 2001, *Still-life with Flowers* (oil on canvas) ATS 38,000.

KÄMMERER, Paul
German, 19th century.
Born 5 January 1868, in Stuttgart.
Watercolourist. Landscapes.
Kämmerer trained at the school of fine arts in Stuttgart. He visited Italy, and in 1900 went to join his family in Tägerwilen, just across the Swiss border from Konstanz. One of his noted works is *Sunny Summer*.
AUCTION RECORDS:
MUNICH, 28 Nov 1980, *Isar Landscape in Mist* (1909, watercolour heightened with white, 16 1/2 x 21 1/2 ins / 42 x 54.5 cm) DEM 2,200.

KAMMÜLLER, Paul
German, 20th century.
Born 31 January 1885, in Lahr.
Active in Switzerland.
Painter. Portraits, still-lifes.
Paul Kammüller began his training in Munich and later studied with Jean-Paul Laurens in Paris. He took up residence in Basel.

KAMOCKI, Stanislaus
Polish, 20th century.
Born 18 November 1875, in Warsaw.
Painter. Church interiors, landscapes.
Stanislaus Kamocki spent time in France and Italy before settling in Cracow. He exhibited in Paris at the Salon de la Société Nationale des Beaux-Arts, of which he was a member and where he took part in 1921 in the exhibition of Polish artists organised there with: *Czerna Convent, Spring in Zakopane, Interior of a Country Church.*

KAMOSHITA, Choko
Japanese, 20th century.
Born 1890; died 1967.
Painter, print artist, illustrator.
Kamoshita Choko was represented at the exhibition of Japanese art held at the Musée du Jeu de Paume in Paris in 1929. He illustrated childrens' books and designed new ukiyo-e prints.

KAMOTSAI, Istvan
Hungarian, 20th century.
Born 1923.
Sculptor. Figures. Statues.
From 1942 to 1949 Istvan Kamotsai was a student of Pal Patzay at the Higher College of Fine Art in Budapest. He won the Munkácsy Prize.

His sculptures included: *Athlete* for the stadium of the Vasas club, *Harpist* in Kapuvar, *Statue of the Poet Vörösmarty* in Debrecen and *Statue of Young Girl* at the Institute of Pharmaceutical Research in Budapest.
BIBLIOGRAPHY:
'*Kamotsai*' in *Hongrie 68*, exhibition catalogue (?), Budapest, 1968.

KAMPANYIETS-KYANCHENKO, Nadezha Dimitryieva
Russian, 20th century.
Born 1913.
Painter. Landscapes with figures.
Nadezha Kampanyiets-Kyanchenko lived and worked in Kiev. She painted landscapes with figures in one of the most academic techniques. Initially guided towards agriculture, she became a student at the Institute of Fine Art in Kiev in 1932. She met the painter Kyanchenko there, who became her husband. She often took part with him in collective exhibitions. She became a member of the Union of Artists.

KAMPEN. See also **CAMPEN**

KAMPEN, Cornelis van, or Campen
Dutch, 17th century.
Active in Leiden in 1644.
Draughtsman.

KAMPEN, Jacob van. See **CAMPEN**

KAMPEN, Joos, called Stoffade
Dutch, 16th - 17th century.
Active in Amsterdam.
Painter.
A seascape by Joos Kampen was sold at an auction in Amsterdam on 16 October 1619.

KAMPENER, Peter. See **CAMPANA Pedro**

KAMPER, Godaert
Dutch, 17th century.
Born c. 1614, in Düsseldorf; died 1679, in Leiden.
Painter. Portraits.
In 1648, Godaert Kamper was a member of the Leiden guild and from 1658 to 1674 belonged to the guilds in Amsterdam and Naarden. He returned to Leiden in 1674. He painted portraits and courtly scenes.

MUSEUMS AND GALLERIES:
AMSTERDAM: *Portrait of a Woman; Family Portrait.*
AUCTION RECORDS:
LONDON, 13 Nov 1968, *Landscape with Travellers*, GBP 780. LONDON, 19 April 2000, *Wooded Landscape with Herdsman and Cattle on a Track* (oil on panel, 18 x 26 ins / 46 x 65 cm) GBP 5,500.

KAMPER, Govert
Dutch, 18th century.

Born probably in Leiden.
Active at the beginning of the 18th century.
Painter. Landscapes.

Govert Kamper painted moonlight scenes in the style of Van der Neer.

Auction records:
London, 4 May 1922, *Farm Landscape,* GBP 57. London, 21 Nov 1924, *The Marriage Contract,* GBP 422.

KAMPER, Paul
German, 20th century.
Born 9 July 1926, in Krefeld.
Painter, mosaicist.

Paul Kamper came to France in 1953, where he studied with Roger Chastel and Gustave Singier at the Académie Ranson in Paris. He began exhibiting in Paris in 1954, most notably at the Salon des Réalités Nouvelles in 1957, and has also exhibited in Hamburg, Cologne, Stuttgart, Munich and other cities in Germany. In 1968 he was awarded a UNESCO scholarship for a visit to Japan.

KAMPF, Arthur
German, 19th - 20th century.
Born 28 September 1864, in Aachen; died 1950, in Castrop-Rauxel.
Painter. History painting, figures, portraits.

Arthur Kampf studied with Peter Janssen at the Staatliche Kunstakademie in Düsseldorf. In 1898, he was appointed a professor at the Berlin Academy and in 1907 he became its president. He exhibited in Munich, Dresden and Berlin and was awarded a silver medal at the Exposition Universelle in Paris in 1900. He also won medals in Munich in 1890 and Berlin in 1891 and 1902. He painted simple allegorical subjects in a rather academic manner.

Museums and Galleries:
Berlin: *Professor Steffers Haranguing the People* - Düsseldorf: *L. Knaus; Frederick II* - Leipzig: *Sacrifice* - Munich: *The Night of 13 to 14 March 1888 at Berlin Cathedral.*

Auction records:
Cologne, 12 Nov 1976, *Café Scene with a Standing Violinist* (oil on canvas, 29 1/4 x 25 1/2 ins / 74.5 x 65 cm) DEM 3,000. Cologne, 22 Nov 1979, *Café Scene* (oil on canvas, 30 3/4 x 22 1/4 ins / 78 x 56.5 cm) DEM 10,200. London, 8 Oct 1982, *Spanish Dancer* (oil on canvas, 77 1/4 x 61 1/4 ins / 196.3 x 155.6 cm) GBP 4,100. Cologne, 27 June 1986, *The News of the Death of Kaiser Wilhelm I* (oil on canvas, 31 1/2 x 23 1/2 ins / 80 x 60 cm) DEM 8,500. Lindau, 6 May 1987, *Still-life with Flowers* (oil on canvas, 37 1/2 x 27 1/2 ins / 95 x 70 cm) DEM 5,000. Cologne, 15 Oct 1988, *Old Husband in Regional Costume Sitting in a Flower Garden* (watercolour, 17 3/4 x 24 1/2 ins / 45 x 62 cm) DEM 2,400. Munich, 22 June 1999, *Kiss of Death: Sick Mother, Father Holding Baby* (oil on canvas, 44 x 54 ins / 113 x 138 cm) DEM 10,000. Cologne, 4 Dec 1999, *The Farewell* (oil on canvas, 58 x 68 ins / 147 x 172 cm) DEM 9,500. Düsseldorf, 26 Feb 2000, *Memories* (oil on canvas, 21 x 26 ins / 53 x 67 cm) DEM 5,500. Düsseldorf, 26 Feb 2000, *Torchlight Procession at Brandenburger Tor* (oil on panel, 24 x 20 ins / 62 x 51 cm) DEM 7,000. Cologne, 17 Nov 2001, *Elegant Man in a Nightclub* (oil on canvas, 19 x 14 ins / 48 x 35 cm) DEM 8,500. Cologne, 24 Nov 2001, *Meeting in a Park* (oil on board, 20 x 24 ins / 50 x 60 cm) DEM 7,100.

KAMPF, Eugen
German, 19th - 20th century.
Born 16 March 1861, in Aachen; died 1933, in Düsseldorf.
Painter. Historical subjects, figures, village scenes, landscapes with figures, landscapes, architectural views, seascapes.

Eugen Kampf was the brother of Arthur Kampf. He studied first at the Antwerp academy between 1870 and 1880, then from 1880 to 1883 in Düsseldorf, and finally in 1884-1885 in Brussels. He travelled in Flanders, Holland and the Eifel region of Germany, and during this period, he mainly painted the landscape of Flanders and the Eifel mountains. He received an honourable mention at the 1900 Paris Exposition Universelle and a gold medal in Berlin in 1902.

Museums and Galleries:
Aachen: *The Surrender of Aachen; English Pastor; Seascape; Flanders Landscape; Rough Sea* - Berlin: *Village in the Eifel Mountains* - Cologne: *Mill in Flanders* - Düsseldorf: two landscapes.

Auction records:
Munich, 25 Nov 1976, *Landscape with Mill* (oil on canvas, 23 3/4 x 31 1/2 ins / 60.5 x 80 cm) DEM 5,000. New York, 26 Jan 1979, *The Village Street* (oil on canvas, 19 3/4 x 23 1/2 ins / 50 x 60 cm) USD 2,300. Cologne, 23 Oct 1981, *Peasant Woman in a Summer Landscape* (oil on canvas, 22 x 26 ins / 56 x 66 cm) DEM 8,000. Cologne, 25 Nov 1983, *Village in Flanders* (oil on canvas, 23 1/2 x 31 1/2 ins / 60 x 80 cm) DEM 8,000. Cologne, 25 Oct 1985, *Farmyard* (oil on canvas, 18 1/4 x 24 ins / 46.2 x 61.2 cm) DEM 6,500. Cologne, 30 May 1987, *Flanders Landscape* (oil on canvas, 24 x 31 1/2 ins / 61 x 80 cm) DEM 9,000. Cologne, 20 Oct 1989, *Summer's Day in Flanders* (oil on canvas, 19 3/4 x 23 1/2 ins / 50 x 60 cm) DEM 4,800. Amsterdam, 28 Oct 1992, *Street in a Mountain Village* (oil on canvas, 20 x 23 1/2 ins / 50.5 x 60 cm) NLG 4,600. Ahlden, 17 Sept 1999, *Landscape near Kamen* (pastel on board, 14 x 20 ins / 35 x 51 cm) DEM 3,500. Cologne, 28 Oct 1999, *Figures in a Village Street in Flanders* (oil on canvas, 20 x 24 ins / 50 x 60 cm) DEM 9,500. Cologne, 6 April 2000, *Farmhouse with Trees* (oil on panel, 13 x 17 ins / 33 x 44 cm) DEM 9,500. Cologne, 25 Nov 2000, *Village Street* (oil on canvas, 14 x 20 ins / 35 x 50 cm) DEM 7,700. Bern, 7 Nov 2001, *Summer Village* (1918, oil on canvas, 44 x 65 ins / 111 x 165 cm) CHF 12,000. Munich, 13 Dec 2001, *Farm in North Germany* (oil on canvas, 19 x 24 ins / 47 x 62 cm) DEM 6,500. Cologne, 11 April 2002, *Flanders Farmstead* (oil on canvas, 12 x 16 ins / 30 x 40 cm) EUR 4,000. Hamburg, 8 May 2002, *Lower Rhine Landscape* (oil on canvas, 21 x 26 ins / 53 x 65 cm) EUR 3,000. Cologne, 10 April 2003, *Extensive Landscape on the Lower Rhine with Sheep by a Farmstead* (1892, oil on canvas, 20 x 13 ins / 52 x 34 cm) EUR 2,650. Ahlden, 19 Sept 2003, *Last Rays of the Sun* (oil on board, 12 x 19 ins / 30 x 49 cm) EUR 3,800. Cologne, 1 April 2004, *Flanders Village* (oil on canvas, 24 x 31 ins / 61 x 80 cm) EUR 1,800. Düsseldorf, 25 Sept 2004, *Heathland* (oil on panel, 14 x 18 ins / 35 x 46 cm) EUR 2,800.

KAMPF, Léopold Eugène
French, 19th century.
Born 19th century, in Clairvaux.
Sculptor.

Léopold Kampf executed military subjects. He made his debut at the Salon in 1864. He worked mainly in Dunkirk.

KÄMPF, Max
Swiss, 20th century.
Born 1912, in Basel; died 1982, in Basel.
Painter, draughtsman.

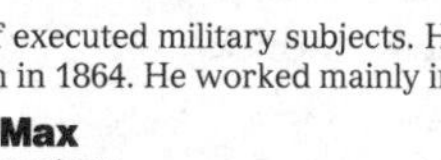

AUCTION RECORDS:
LONDON, 23 May 1985, *The Artist and his Model* (1962, oil on canvas, 25 3/4 x 23 1/4 ins / 65.5 x 59 cm) CHF 8,000. BERN, 26 Oct 1988, *Musician from Basel* (1965, coloured chalk and charcoal, 7 3/4 x 11 ins / 20 x 28 cm) CHF 2,700. ZURICH, 25 Oct 1989, *Portrait of a Woman* (pencil, 22 3/4 x 15 1/4 ins / 58 x 39 cm) CHF 2,000. ZURICH, 18 Oct 1990, *Three Characters* (1963, oil and tempera/paper, 39 x 42 1/2 ins / 99 x 108 cm) CHF 5,000. ZURICH, 17-18 June 1996, *Two Women* (1971, oil on canvas, 23 1/2 x 31 1/2 ins / 60 x 80 cm) CHF 2,000. BERN, 22 June 2000, *Carnival* (1938, oil on canvas, 12 x 39 ins / 30 x 100 cm) CHF 23,000. BERN, 9 May 2003, *Self-portrait* (oil on board, 19 x 17 ins / 49 x 44 cm) CHF 2,500. BERN, 12 Nov 2004, *Portrait of a Standing Boy* (1960, oil on canvas, 33 x 19 ins / 83 x 48 cm) CHF 3,700.

KAMPF, Melissa Q.
American, 19th - 20th century.
Born 1 May 1867, in Philadelphia.
Painter.
Melissa Kampf studied under Chase and Carolus Duran. A member of the Société des Artistes Indépendants, she obtained a gold medal in 1922.

KAMPHUYS, Jan
Dutch, 17th century.
Died 1682.
Active in Amsterdam.
Painter.
There is a signed landscape by Jan Kamphuys.

KAMPHUYSEN. See also **CAMPHUYSEN**

KAMPHUYSEN, Jan, or Camphuysen
Dutch, 18th - 19th century.
Born 1760, in Amsterdam; died after 1840, in Amsterdam.
Painter. Allegorical subjects, portraits, landscapes, urban landscapes. Decorative schemes.
Jan Kamphuysen was a pupil of J. van Dreght and P. Barbiers. He travelled through France in 1781, was in Bordeaux in 1786, and went to Italy in 1792, returning to Amsterdam the following year. In 1816 he executed *Panorama of the Battle of Waterloo.*
MUSEUMS AND GALLERIES:
AMSTERDAM: *Self-portrait.*
AUCTION RECORDS:
PARIS, 10 Dec 1993, *Allegory of William I, King of the Low Countries* (1817, oil on canvas, 33 1/2 x 41 ins / 85 x 104 cm) FRF 33,000. AMSTERDAM, 11 Nov 1997, *Allegory on the Unification of the Schools of Painting of the Low Countries and the Return of Works of Art on the Authority of King William I* (1817, oil on canvas, 33 3/4 x 40 3/4 ins / 85.7 x 103.7 cm) NLG 40,362.

KAMPMANN, Erich
German, 19th - 20th century.
Painter. Landscapes.
Erich Kampmann remains largely unknown, though Hundertwasser was influenced by his instinctive expressionism in his youth. Kampmann painted landscapes with trees, probably using the 'fixed under glass' technique.

KAMPMANN, Gustave
German, 19th - 20th century.
Born 30 September 1859, in Boppard; died 12 August 1917, in Bad Godesberg.
Draughtsman (including charcoal), lithographer. Landscapes.
Gustave Kampmann worked successively in Munich, Lübeck and Schleissheim, and first exhibited around 1886. He exhibited in Berlin, Munich and Vienna, and was awarded an honourable mention at the Paris Exposition Universelle in 1900.
AUCTION RECORDS:
HEIDELBERG, 11 April 1981, *Trees in a Storm* (charcoal, 39 1/4 x 27 1/2 ins / 100 x 70 cm) DEM 2,300.

KAMPMANN, Jack
Danish, 20th century.
Born 1914; died 1989.
Painter. Landscapes, seascapes.
Jack Kampmann was born in London in 1914, of Danish parents, and grew up in England and the USA. He studied under Sigurd Wandel at the Copenhagen Academy from 1933-1934. He lived in Paris from 1938-1939, but was in London when war broke out and decided to join the British army. In 1941, he was sent to Faeroes, where he subsequently married and settled, taking Faeroese citizenship. In 1964, he left the Faeroes and settled in Copenhagen. In addition to painting, he also produced lithographs and engravings, and worked on manuscripts for documentary films about the Faeroes. Kampmann's paintings are mainly of views of towns and villages. He tended to paint seaside and harbour landscapes rather than seascapes.
AUCTION RECORDS:
COPENHAGEN, 29 April 1976, *View of a Harbour* (1961, oil on canvas, 21 1/4 x 25 1/2 ins / 54 x 65 cm) DKK 4,300. COPENHAGEN, 8 March 1979, *Harbour Scene* (oil on canvas, 23 1/2 x 32 1/4 ins / 60 x 82 cm) DKK 6,600. COPENHAGEN, 30 Nov 1988, *Village by the Sea* (oil on canvas, 21 1/4 x 25 1/2 ins / 54 x 65 cm) DKK 6,800. COPENHAGEN, 21-22 March 1990, *Seaside Village* (oil on canvas, 21 1/4 x 25 1/2 ins / 54 x 65 cm) DKK 4,500. COPENHAGEN, 14-15 Nov 1990, *Village* (1968, oil on canvas, 25 1/2 x 32 ins / 65 x 81 cm) DKK 4,000. COPENHAGEN, 1 April 1992, *Town by the Sea* (oil on canvas, 13 3/4 x 16 1/4 ins / 35 x 41 cm) DKK 3,700. COPENHAGEN, 20 Oct 1993, *House by the Sea* (oil on canvas, 21 1/4 x 25 1/2 ins / 54 x 65 cm) DKK 4,500. COPENHAGEN, 26 April 1995, *Houses in the Faeroes* (oil on canvas, 23 1/2 x 32 ins / 60 x 81 cm) DKK 5,500. COPENHAGEN, 1 April 2003, *View of a Village by the Sea, Faroe Islands* (c. 1958, oil on canvas, 26 x 32 ins / 67 x 81 cm) DKK 11,000.

KAMPNER, Peter. See **CAMPANA Pedro de**

KAMPO. See **ARAKI Kampo**

KAMPS, Jean
Dutch, 20th century.
Born 1938, in Wijlre.
Painter. Figure compositions.
Jan Kamps went to Africa as a Catholic priest, but later left the church to become a social worker and start a family. In 1970, he found a new vocation as a painter and spent the rest of his life in Holland. He exhibited in Paris at the Salon International d'Art Naïf. He often chose to illustrate Biblical subjects. The large numbers of people in his compositions have an almost hallucinatory effect.

KAMROWSKI, Gerome
American, 20th century.
Born 1914, in Warren (Minnesota); died 2004.
Painter.
Gerome Kamrowski was already familiar with the novel creation processes with which the French Surrealists were experimenting before World War II, including automatism. In the winter of 1940-1941, he collaborated with William Baziotes and Jackson Pollock on several canvases, some of which prefigured the latter's *Dripping*. He created highly elaborate and imaginative collages using mixed materials. His work is characterised by the unusual juxtaposition of dissimilar colours and the enduring presence of curvilinear biomorphic outlines of mesmerising fluidity.

He featured at the Exposition Internationale du Surréalisme at Galerie Maeght in Paris, in 1947. After 1955, he withdrew from official artistic events and joined in the activities of an American Surrealist group. Kamrowski's exhibitions include *Vital Forms: American Art & Design in the Atomic Age 1940-60,* Brooklyn Museum (2002-2003, touring); *The Worlds of Gerome Kamrowski: Surrealism and Beyond,* University of Michigan Art Gallery, Ann Arbor (2003); *Surrealism in Exile and the Beginning of the New York School,* Musée d'Art Moderne et Contemporain, Strasbourg, and Museo Nacional Centro de Arte Reine Sofia, Madrid (2000); and *The American Century: Art and Culture 1900-1950,* Whitney Museum of American Art (1999). He held a Guggenheim Fellowship from 1937 to 1939, and taught at the University of Michigan School of Art from 1948 to 1982.

BIBLIOGRAPHY:

Gerome Kamrowski: the 1940s, exhibition catalogue, Washburn Gallery, New York, 1989.

MUSEUMS AND GALLERIES:

MINNEAPOLIS (IA) - NEW YORK (Metropolitan Mus. of Art) - NEW YORK (MoMA) - NEW YORK (Whitney Mus. of American Art) - WASHINGTON DC (Smithsonian American AM).

KAMSETZER, Jan Baptist

Polish, 18th century.

Born 1753, in Dresden; died 25 November 1795, in Warsaw.

Architect, draughtsman, engraver.

Jan Baptist Kamsetzer studied with the aid of a bursary from King Stanislas Augustus. The Lazienski palace in Warsaw was built according to his plans. He travelled in Greece, making drawings as he went, the most notable of which is *View of Constantinople from the Japanese Consulate.*

KAN, Mimi, or Mimi Saraga, Mimi Saraga-Maxy, Mimi Maxy-Kan, pseudonym of Saraga Mundeta Nina

Maiden name: Saraga

Romanian, 20th century.

Born 29 December 1923, in Bucharest.

Active in Israel from 1982, in France from 1995.

Painter, draughtswoman, sculptor, collage artist, illustrator. Frescoes.

Mimi Kan studied at the Bucharest Jewish Art School (1941-1944) under the constructivist painter Max Herman Maxy, whom she married in 1947 (he died in 1971). In 1982 she left Romania for Germany, then Israel. In 1995, she married the Frenchman Albert Kan and settled in Brive, France. She became a naturalised French citizen in 1999.

Mimi Kan's work addresses the Shoah and the persecution of peoples under dictatorships. She speaks of suffering and despair in violent images where primary colours are opposed with grey silhouettes outlined in black; or creates jarring Expressionist metal assemblages. She has also illustrated Ion Caraioin's *Les feuilles de Gallad* and Tania Lovinescu's *Ma numesc Alzheimer* (*My Name is Alzheimer*).

Starting in 1948, Mimi Kan took part in various group exhibitions in Romania, including 1965, City of Bucharest, and 1972-1976, Bucharest Painting and Sculpture Biennale. She also took part in the 1965 Venice Biennale. Among her solo exhibitions are 1987, Dannon Shai Gallery, Tel Aviv; 1997, Centre Edmond Michelet, Brive; 2001, Musée du Cloître, Tulle. In 1952 she was awarded the second state prize in Romania.

BIBLIOGRAPHY:

Soutenet, Laurent, *Mimi Kan - Crimes contre l'Humanité,* exhibition catalogue, Centre Edmond Michelet, Brive, 1996. Rooryck, Isabelle, *Mimi Maxy Kan - Une vie de peintre ou La longue clameur de l'humanité,* exhibition catalogue, Musée du Cloître, Tulle, 2001.

MUSEUMS AND GALLERIES:

BRAILA (Museum): *Cry of Revolt; Suffering; Portrait of M.H. Maxy; Self portrait;* important holdings - BUCHAREST (Mus. of the City of Bucharest) - TULLE (Mus. du Cloître).

KAN YOSAI. See **RYOTAI**

KANA AND OLYMPIOS, Katerina and Marina

Cypriot, 20th century.

Active in France.

Installation artists.

Katerina Kana and Marina Olympios exhibited their work in 1996 at the art centre Passages in Troyes, and at the Galerie Renos Xippas in Paris.

They present an accumulation of pieces, from videos to sculpture, from collage to performance, all connected with their own history.

BIBLIOGRAPHY:

Ardenne, Paul, '*Katerina Kana - Marina Olympios*' in *Art Press* n° 211, periodical, Paris, March 1996.

KANAAN, Élie

Lebanese, 20th century.

Born 1926, in Beirut.

Painter. Landscapes.

Georges Cyr, a French painter and critic living in Beirut, encouraged the young Élie Kanaan's interest in art. Kanaan spent time in Italy before 1950, and in 1958 a grant from UNESCO enabled him to train in Paris at the Académie de la Grande Chaumière. He was awarded numerous prizes and distinctions. From 1963 to 1974 he taught drawing and painting at the Jesuit College of Our Lady in Jambur. Later he taught at the University of Lebanon and at the Lebanese academy of fine art.

His pictures, mostly landscapes, tend towards the abstract. They are painted with a vigorous touch and in blazing colours.

His work has been featured in collective exhibitions, including: from 1964, at the Sursock Museum in Beirut, the Paris Biennale, the Alexandria Biennale and so on; in 1989 at *Liban - Le Regard des peintres - 200 ans de peinture libanaise* (*Lebanon as Seen by Painters - 200 Years of Lebanese Painting*) at the Institut du Monde Arabe in Paris. In 1950 he had an exhibition, the first of many, at the Beirut Higher School of Letters, followed by many more in different parts of Beirut and abroad, including: 1967, the Galerie l'Entr'Acte in Lausanne; 1983, the Galerie Castiglione in Paris, and elsewhere.

BIBLIOGRAPHY:

Liban. Le Regard des peintres. 200 ans de peinture libanaise, exhibition catalogue, Institut du Monde Arabe, Paris, 1989. *Élie Kanaan,* exhibition catalogue, Gal. Brigitte Schehadé, Paris, 1990.

KANAMORI, Yoshio

Japanese, 20th century.

Born 1922, in Toyama Prefecture.

Painter, print artist.

Kanamori Yoshio studied at the Imperial School of Art but left with Munakata Shiko when he was evacuated during the war. Kanamori started to exhibit his work while still young at the National Painting Society and the Japan Print Association, and won a prize at the exhibition of Japanese prints at St James' Church, New York.

His figurative style, in which he contrasts black and white with great effectiveness, tends towards naive art.

KANASHIMA, Keika, real name: Kanashima Seita, artist name: Keika

Japanese, 20th century.

Born 1892, in Hiroshima; died 1974.

Painter. Animals.

Kanashima Keika decided to become a painter in 1909 after winning first prize at an exhibition of the Tatsumi Gakai (Southeast Painting Society). He then moved to Kyoto and studied nihonga painting with Takeuchi Seiho. During the 1920s he had considerable success at the Teiten exhibitions, and was included in the exhibition of Japanese art held at the Jeu de Paume Museum in Paris in 1929. Later he moved away from traditional nihonga techniques, tending towards neo-realism. After the war he won a series of awards, being made a member of the academy in 1959.

KANAYAMA, Akira
Japanese, 20th century.
Born 1929, in Osaka.
Painter.
Gutai group.

Kanayama Akira was originally a member of the Zero group, which exhibited at the Shinseisaku Salon. In 1955 these painters were invited by Yoshihara Jiro to join the Gutai group, which had been formed in 1954 with the aim of opening up Japanese art to all possible forms of expression, to all materials, all attitudes, both in open air exhibitions and also in institutions and art galleries. The venue in Tokyo and the influence of the critic Michel Tapié contributed to the group's influence in Europe and the USA. However he curbed the excesses of the group and directed its activity to abstract painting of which he was one of the principal defenders.

Kanayama practised gestural calligraphy with links to the Japanese writing tradition. He took part in very many group exhibitions in the Kansai and in Tokyo. In 1965 the group exhibited at the Stadler Gallery in Paris, under the patronage of the critic Michel Tapié. In 1988 he was included in the exhibition *L'Art moderne à Marseille: La collection du Musée Cantini* (*Modern Art in Marseilles: The Cantini Museum Collection*).

BIBLIOGRAPHY:

Tapié, Michel/Tôre Haga, *Continuité et avant-garde au Japon*, Ed. d'arte Fratelli Pozzo, Turin, 1961 (text in French). *L'Art moderne à Marseille. La Collection du Musée Cantini*, exhibition catalogue, Musée Cantini, Marseilles, 1988. Yamamoto, Atsuo, et al., *Gutai: moments de destruction, moments de beauté*, Blusson, Paris, 2002 (text in French and English).

MUSEUMS AND GALLERIES:

MARSEILLES (Mus. Cantini): *Painting* (1964).

KAND, Helmut
Austrian, 20th - 21st century.
Born 13 December 1946, in Bruck.
Painter.

Helmut Kand studied at the Akademie der Bildenden Künste in Vienna. He now divides his time between Vienna and the Cyclades. His work belongs to the Viennese fantastic movement. At first sight, his very colourful painting may appear primitive, even naive, but closer inspection soon reveals an elaborate design reminiscent of Persian miniatures, with a hint of eroticism. He has had solo shows in Vienna in 1969, Rome in 1970, Düsseldorf in 1971 and Paris in 1973.

KANDEL, David, or Kannel
School of Alsace, 16th century.
Active in Strasbourg.
Painter, engraver (wood). Flowers.

According to Mariette, David Kandel was a highly talented artist. He produced the drawings of all the plants for a book on botany by Tragus, and also the author's portrait. He engraved a *View of Baden in Switzerland*, and a *View of Constantinople*.

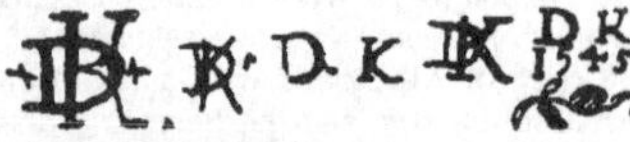

KANDELMAÜLLER, Jörg
Swiss, 16th century.
Active in Biberach.
Painter (?), sculptor (wood) (?).

References to Jörg Kandelmaüller, dating from 1531 to 1535, are to be found in the archives of the town of Tinzen. They state that he produced an altar decoration for the church of St-Blaise in Tinzen, but it is not known if the decoration was a painting or a wooden sculpture.

KANDINSKY, Wassily
Russian, 19th - 20th century.
Born 4 December 1866, in Moscow; died 13 December 1944, in Neuilly-sur-Seine, France.
Active from 1921 and naturalised in Germany in 1928, active from 1934 and naturalised in 1939 in France.
Painter, watercolourist, draughtsman, engraver, illustrator. Stage costumes and sets.
Groups: Phalanx, Der Blaue Reiter, Die Blauen Vier.

Wassily Kandinsky was born in Moscow. His father came from Siberia, near the border with China. After a family trip to Italy, where they stayed in Venice, Rome and Florence, they settled in Odessa in 1871. In 1876, alongside his classical studies, he studied piano and cello. Each summer he spent a few weeks with his father in Moscow, a city that fascinated him all his life. When he was very young, he was already painting interiors of churches in bright colours and was trying his hand at landscape. In 1886, he studied Economics and Roman and Russian Law at the University of Moscow. In 1889, the Society of Natural Science, Ethnography and Anthropology sent him on a study trip to the government of Vologda, to study the legal customs and vestiges of paganism in the local Zyrian peasant communities. It was here that he discovered popular Russian art, having frequently visited peasant houses, the walls, and even ceilings and sometimes furniture of which were covered in brightly coloured paintings. The Science Society published the results of his mission and adopted him as a member. That same year he passed through St Petersburg, where he was impressed by the Rembrandts in the Hermitage Museum. In 1889 he also took a trip to Paris, to the Exposition Universelle. He was awarded his law degree in 1892, married his cousin Anya Chimiakin and took a second trip to Paris. He was appointed assistant in the Faculty of Law of the University of Moscow in 1893, a post he occupied for three years. In 1895, he became Artistic Director of the Kusverev printing works in Moscow. It was in 1896, having seen the exhibitions of French painting in Moscow (which included one of Monet's *Haystacks*), that he refused a chair at the University of Dorpat (now Tartu) in Estonia and decided to spend his time painting, settling in Munich. In 1897 he was a student there at the private workshop of Anton Azbé, where he stayed for two years and where he met Jawlensky and Mariana von Werefkin. In 1899, he worked alone. In 1900 he became Franz von Stuck's student at the Akademie der Bildenden Künste in Munich, where Paul Klee was a fellow student, and made contact with the group Mir Iskusstva (World of Art) in St Petersburg. In 1901 he co-founded the group Phalanx, of which he became chairman in 1902. The group organised 12 exhibitions up to 1904, including one of Monet's works. He set up a school of painting within the group and taught there; Gabriele Münter became his student in 1902. Another student introduced him to Rudolf Steiner's anthropocentrism. This was probably how he got to know the colour symbolism of Goethe's *Farbenlehre* (*Theory of Colour*). However, the Phalanx school closed in 1903 and the group was dissolved in 1904. These years marked the start of his production as a painter with a few small landscapes and his first engravings on wood in 1902.

In 1903 he travelled to Venice, Odessa and Moscow. From 1904 onwards, he lived with Gabriele Münter. He travelled to Holland, Odessa and Tunis, where he stayed until April 1905. His first album of engravings on wood, *Poetry Without Words*, was published in Moscow in 1904. In 1905 he took a trip to Rapallo and, from May 1906 to June 1907, he spent time in Paris, then settled in Sèvres with Gabriele Münter, and met Gertrude Stein, at whose home he saw works by Matisse and Picasso. He spent the summer of 1907 in Switzerland and the end of the year in Berlin (where Matisse had an exhibition). He continued producing small landscapes in oil, wood engravings and tempera paintings on the Russian themes drawn from folklore with which he remained associated throughout his life, as well as with the practices of the Orthodox Church and the icons that accompanied him in all his homes. In 1908 he was in contact with the avant-garde artists in Moscow and returned to Munich, where he met Jawlensky again and renewed his friendship with Klee. With the composer Thomas von Hartmann and the dancer Sacharoff, he worked on his first ballet set designs for *Daphnis* and the *Gelbe Klang* (*Yellow Sound*), a 'stage composition' of which he was the author and the design of which he subsequently continued in Murnau, where he stayed for the first time at the end of 1908. Following a brief contact with the Die Brücke (The Bridge) group in Dresden, he co-founded, with Kubin, the Neue Künstler Vereinigung München (New Association of Munich Artists), NKVM, of which he was elected chairman. The association's first exhibition took place that same year. Tendances Nouvelles published his collection of *Woodcuts*. Gabriele Münter bought a house in Murnau, where they regularly stayed until 1914.

In 1910 he met Franz Marc, travelled to Moscow, St Petersburg and Odessa. In 1911 he made friends with August Macke and, after the committee's refusal to exhibit his *Composition V*, he left the NKVM with Marc, Münter and Kubin. With Franz Marc, Gabriele Münter and Alexei von Jawlensky, among others, he founded the Blaue Reiter (Blue Rider) and the group exhibited at the Thannhauser Gallery in Munich, the exhibition transferring the year after to the *Der Sturm* gallery in Berlin. In 1911 he was also divorced from his first wife, from whom he had lived apart for a long time.

In 1912 he published *Concering the Spiritual in Art* and also, with Franz Marc the *Almanac of the Blaue Reiter*. The group exhibited for the second time, again in Munich, solely graphics, at Hans Goltz's, an exhibition which also toured. The two Blaue Reiter exhibitions were eclectic and international; the work of Braque, Picasso, Delaunay and Le Douanier Rousseau appeared with that of Malevich, Kubin and Klee.

In 1913 *Rückblick* (*Looking Back*) was published in Berlin and *Klänge* (*Sounds*) was published in Munich with 55 black and colour wood engravings. In 1914 he left Munich for Murnau. When war was declared he returned to Moscow and Odessa via Zurich and the Balkans. In 1915-1916, when staying in Stockholm, he separated from Gabriele Münter in 1917 he married Nina de Andreewsky. From 1918 to 1921 he was a member of the *IZO*, Fine Arts Department at the People's Commission for Public Instruction. In 1919 he founded the Museum of Pictorial Culture in Moscow, was involved in setting up 22 provincial museums and taught in the people's workshops of the *Vhutemas*. In 1920 he was appointed professor at the University of Moscow, where a major exhibition of his works was organised. In 1921 he founded the Academy of Art Sciences, of which he was elected Vice-President.

At this time the attitude of the Soviet authorities towards culture was changing. Stalin was growing in importance and became Secretary General of the party in 1922. Innovation in art had been encouraged, but it was now decided that avant-garde art was unnecessary or even harmful and it began to be suppressed.

At the end of 1921, Kandinsky had returned to Germany and in 1922 he executed murals in Berlin in the reception hall of the *Juryfrei* Salon, then settled in Weimar and became a teacher at the Bauhaus, where Paul Klee had preceded him. He became Deputy Director almost immediately and here, once again, the effect of his personal influence was noticed,as well as his aptitude, if not his taste, for positions of responsibility. He followed the Bauhaus (driven out of Weimar in 1925 to Dessau by the future Nazi Party), having taken on a compulsory class there in analytical drawing until 1925, when he became director of the mural workshop and finally manager of the free workshop for painting from 1928 onwards. He also gave many lectures and theory classes at the Bauhaus.

A theoretician by calling, he had already published *Concerning the Spiritual in Art* in 1912; in 1926 *Punkt und Linie zur Fläche* (*From the Point and Line to the Surface*) appeared, in which he set conditions and limits on creative freedom, somewhat contradicting *Concerning the Spiritual in Art* (expression through shape is replaced with expression through colour, austerity has supplanted the unconscious). In 1955 he was to publish *Essays über Kunst und Künstler* (*Essays on Art and Artists*). In 1922 he had published the *Kleine Welt* (*Small World*) collection of wood engravings, etchings and lithographs. In 1924 he had founded Die Blauen Vier (The Blue Four) with Lionel Feininger, Jawlensky and Klee, which exhibited on several occasions. In 1926, for his 60th birthday, the first edition of the magazine *Bauhaus* was dedicated to him at the opening of the new Bauhaus buildings constructed by Gropius in Dessau. In Dessau, where he once again lived near Paul Klee, they renewed their old friendship.

In 1927, he travelled to Austria and Switzerland. In 1928 he painted stage sets and costumes for Mussorgsky's *Pictures for an Exhibition* at the Theatre in Dessau. He travelled to Belgium and the Basque Coast. Marcel Duchamp went to Dessau to meet him. He travelled to Ravenna and discovered the mosaics that reminded him of the style of his youthful paintings. In 1931 he produced mock-ups for the interior design of the concert hall designed by Mies Van der Rohe and presented at the International Exhibition of Architecture in Berlin; later these were executed as ceramics by the Meissen Factory. He travelled to Egypt, Palestine, Syria, Turkey and Greece. He started a collaboration with Christian Zervos' *Art Notebooks*, where he first gave his *Reflections on Abstract Art*.

Following the closure of the Bauhaus in Dessau in 1932 (which he followed to Berlin), and after the Nazis had effectively taken over in Germany, Kandinsky finally emigrated to Paris in 1933, settling in Neuilly-sur-Seine. He was officially banned from Germany as a 'degenerate artist' in 1934; in 1937 57 of his works were withdrawn from German museums. In 1934-1935 he was involved with the Abstraction-Création group in Paris, met Mondrian and Miró and became closer friends with Pevsner, Arp and Magnelli. Two solo exhibitions of his works were organised in Paris in 1934 and 1935 by Christian Zervos in his gallery, *Art Notebooks*, with which he continued his collaboration, publishing his memoirs of Franz Marc there. Jeanne Bucher's gallery took over from Zervos in displaying Kandinsky's works in Paris, although still in a climate of indifference. Leading a humble, secluded life, he only had contacts with Léger, Arp and Delaunay. In 1937 he travelled to Switzerland where he visited Klee and, while his paintings were circulating in Germany with the exhibition of degenerate art, he took part in the major contemporary art exhibition in Paris organised at the Musée du Jeu de Paume during the Exposition Internationale. In 1939 Kandinsky acquired French nationality. At the time of the Nazi occupation of Paris in 1940, he took refuge in Cauterets in the Pyrenées then, after two months, returned to Paris where he resumed painting with surprisingly serene, happy works, inspired by rediscovering the fresh feeling of childhood. In 1944 Kandinsky was working on a stage set project for a ballet with music by Thomas von Hartmann, with whom he had already collaborated in 1908, when he fell ill in March. He died on 13 December, virtually unheard of in France, except by artists who had quite recently become part of the groups Cercle et Carré, Abstraction-Création, Réalites Nouvelles.

From 1900 to 1908, Kandinsky's very mixed production consisted in particular of wood engravings, (usualy black and sometimes black with one colour), 'coloured drawings' (actually tempera paintings), 'studies in oil' and paintings in the strict sense of the word. Until 1900, when he was still an art student, he had produced a few small naturalist landscapes. This was followed from 1900 to 1902 by a second period that can be called Impressionist, then a third period until 1906, a period of Russian Romanticism, in which the influences of Russian popular art penetrated each other, a period of German Expressionism and French Fauvism, when he represented both Neo-Romantic scenes of wandering knights, women in the moonlit forest, and very many landscapes captured during his travels, dream-like landscapes in which the figurative reality could no longer really be captured. From 1904 to 1907 in particular, he painted Russian scenes inspired by popular legends and by operas by Glinka and Rimski-Korsakov. Many of these paintings were executed when he was staying in Sèvres, expressing a nostalgia for his native land which would feel throughout his life in exile. He was painting at the time in clay with a spatula, the strokes building up like mosaics in dazzling colours. It was in 1909 in Murnau that the famous episode took place of the picture hanging upside down: '...picture of extraordinary beauty, shining with an inner radiance... I knew then definitely that *objects* were harmful to my painting.' *Concering the Spiritual in Art* was published in 1912, on which he had been working since 1910. The genesis of his initial approaches to abstract painting corresponds to these years in his work, in line with the ideas expressed in his essay. The fourth period, from 1907 to 1911, referred to as art with no purpose, was the gestation period of abstraction. His dual concern, then and henceforth, consisted of breaking away from folklore, which had long impressed and influenced him, and of not falling into the decorative, to which 'art with no purpose' could drive him. With regard to Kandinsky's culmination in abstraction and the thoughts that materialised in his first book, his wife Nina Kandinsky's recalled:

When he saw the exhibition of Impressionism for the first time, standing in front of Claude Monet's *Haystack*, which impressed him greatly, he asked himself: *Is art not entitled to go further and have complete creative freedom, as composers do in their symphonies?*.... We recognise in this passage thinking that was familiar to the Cubists... And so this question tormented him consciously and unconsciously for several years. He did not come to abstraction by chance, it was something he had been considering and experiencing. I have a poster by Kandinsky from 1909, which is completely abstract. But it was his watercolour in 1910, because of his conclusion, which he regarded as his first abstract work.

On many occasions, Kandinsky explained his thought processes and approaches to art. Thoughts and processes changed and to some extent differentiated themselves according to the various periods of his work that followed one another again: the fifth, the dramatic period from 1911 to 1914, was turbulent and colourful, quiet and dark after 1916; the sixth up to 1925 was a calm period with Constructivist tendencies, the seventh, from 1925 to 1928, was the period of circles. By this time the lyrical, emotional approach of the work before 1916 had been succeeded by something more calculated, as a result of the influence of the Constructivist experiments of Malevich, Pevsner and Gabo. Kandinsky aimed to form a 'science of art' and create a 'lyrical geometry'; nothing was to be left to chance. Nevertheless, these works display elements of fantasy and a dreamy poetry despite their rigorous geometry, possibly thanks to the influence of Paul Klee.

In the eighth period from 1928 to 1934 the Romantic period, he clearly broke free from the Constructivist sectarianism to which he had subscribed under the dual influence of Malevich and Mondrian. The ninth period, form 1934 to 1944 corresponding to his French period, was the period of major synthesis. Abandoning geometrical forms almost entirely, he used irregular figures from a biology of origins in the most exuberant freedom and imaginativeness. While it is generally customary to divide Kandinsky's work into these nine periods, the individual periods are intertwined. Kandinsky himself, around the year 1910, divided his works into three distinct series:

1) Direct impressions of the *external nature* in a drawn and painted form. I called these paintings *Impressions;* 2) Expressions that were unconscious to a large extent and often formed suddenly from events of an internal nature, therefore impressions of the *internal nature.* I call them *Improvisations;* 3) Expressions formed in a similar way but which, having developed slowly, have been adopted, examined and worked on at length from preliminary sketches, almost in a pedantic way. I call them *Compositions*. Intelligence, the conscious, the lucid intention and the precise aim play a crucial role here: simply, it is not the calculation that prevails, it's always intuition.

As an engraver, Kandinsky provided illustrations for the *Tendances Nouvelles* (*New Trends*) publications in 1906, and *Eloquence* in 1937. He illustrated *Poetry Without Words* in 1904; 18 plates, his own treatise *Concering the Spiritual in Art* in 1911; 43 wood engravings and 12 colour illustrations *Klänge* (*Sounds (or Resonances)*) in 1913; the album of the Blaue Reiter with Franz Marc in 1914; *Kleine Welten* (*Small Worlds*) in 1922. His engravings before 1908, generally small in format, were engraved on wood. He printed them by hand with watercolours and sometimes went over them with a brush. These are figurative, inspired by an enchanted imagination, and are influenced by Art Nouveau. In the first few years of the century, when Kandinsky went back to painting, he only produced timid or unsystematic studies. It was not until 1909-1910, at the age of 43, that he was able to extract the logical, ultimate consequences of Germanic Expressionism, Fauvism and Cubism of the Paris School becoming one of the first creators of abstraction and modern art. From the conception of *Concering the Spiritual in Art*, speaking in fact about the three important series of works that he was painting at the same time around 1910, he had planned the three main directions according to which the different periods of his work would differ and, by the same token, the three main directions according to which the various trends of the abstract art of the future would differ: Abstract Expressionism, Constructivist Abstraction, Lyrical Abstraction. In 1909-1910, therefore, he got through and passed the stages of the major artistic revolution of the 20th century and, at the same time as he was becoming more self-aware, he had all the elements that would form the impressive cohesion of his work in the second half of his life, in all its diversity, and which to a large extent would influence the development of art in this century.

Kandinsky took part in many exhibitions throughout his lifetime. From 1902 to 1911 he exhibited annually at the Secession in Berlin, from 1904 to 1910 or 1912 annually at the Salon d'Automne in Paris and in 1905 at the Salon des Indépendants. In 1904 he exhibited with Tendances Nouvelles (New Trends) in Paris, and in 1907 the group invited him to take part in the exhibition organised at the museum of the People of Angers, where he exhibited 109 works. In 1909 he exhibited with Die Brücke (The Bridge) group in Dresden. From 1909 until 1914 he exhibited at the Allied Artists' Association in London.

In October 1912, *Der Sturm* Gallery in Berlin organised his first solo exhibition, which was transferred to Goltz's in Munich. In 1913, he took part in the *First German Autumn Salon* at *Der Sturm* Gallery and at the Armoury Show in New York, then Chicago, an exhibition where his own works were acquired. Four major exhibitions were organised in Germany on his 60th birthday in 1926. In 1928 his first exhibition of watercolours and gouaches took place in Paris at the Galerie Zack. In 1930 a new exhibition took place in Paris at the Galerie de France and he took part in the *Cercle et Carré* (*Circle and Square*) exhibition organised by Michel Seuphor.

Retrospectives of Kandinsky's works multiplied after World War II, including: Stedelijk Museum, Amsterdam in 1947; Kunsthalle, Bern, in 1955; Städtische Galerie, Munich, in 1957; Musée Nationale d'Art Moderne, Paris, in 1957, 1979 and 1984; Musée Nationale d'Art Moderne de Paris, Solomon R Guggenheim Museum in New York, Gemeente Museum in The Hague, Kunsthalle in Basel in 1963; Moderne Museet, Stockholm in 1965; Solomon R Guggenheim Museum, New York, in 1966; Fondation Maeght, St Paul-de-Vence in 1966; Staatliche Kunsthalle, Baden-Baden, in 1970; Kunstmuseum, Bern, in 1971; Scottish National Gallery of Modern Art, Edinburgh, in 1975; National Museum of Modern Art in Tokyo and Kyoto in 1987; Moderna Museet, Stockholm in 1989; Kunstsammlung Nordrhein-Westfalen in Düsseldorf, Staatsgalerie in Stuttgart in 1992; Musée des Beaux-Arts, Nantes, in 1998; *Work on Paper* at the Musée d'Art Moderne et Contemporain, Strasbourg, in 2001.

He is also frequently represented at exhibitions mounted by subject, including: *Le Fauvisme ou 'l'épreuve du feu'. Éruption de la modernité en Europe* (*Fauvism or 'Trial by Fire': The Eruption of Modernity in Europe*), Musée d'Art Moderne de la Ville de Paris, Paris, in 1999; *Musical Analogies: Kandinsky and His Contemporaries*, Thyssen-Bornemisza and Fundación Caja Museum, Madrid, in 2003; *Russian Paris 1910-1960*, exhibition on Russian art and artists in Paris, organised by the Russian Museum of St Petersburg and presented at the Von der Heydt Museum in Wuppertal, then at the Museum of Fine Art in Bordeaux in 2003; *Aux Origines de l'Abstraction (1800-1914)* (*The Origins of Abstraction (1800-1914)*), Musée d'Orsay, Paris, in 2003.

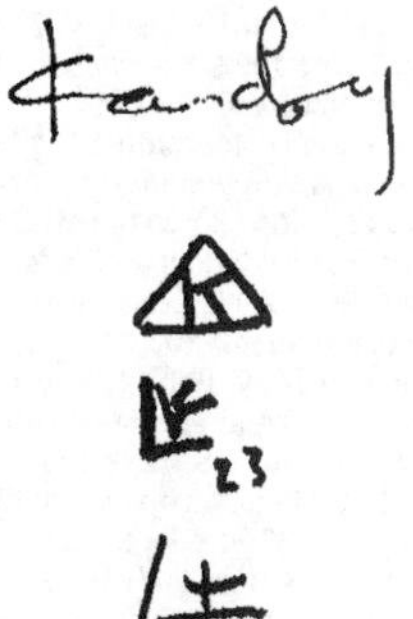

BIBLIOGRAPHY:

Lassaigne, Jacques, *Kandinsky*, periodical, Skira, Geneva, 1964. Grohmann, Will, *Wassily Kandinsky, Life and Work*, Thames & Hudson, London, 1970. Roethel, Hans Konrad, *Kandinsky. Das graphishe Werk*, DuMont Schauberg, Cologne, 1970. *Wassily Kandinsky*, exhibition catalogue, Haus der Kunst, Munich, 1976. Long, Rose-Carol Washton, *Kandinsky: the development of an abstract style*, Clarendon, Oxford, 1980. Lindsay, Kenneth C./Vergo, Peter (ed.), *Kandinsky: Complete Writings on Art*, Faber, London, c. 1982. Roethel, Hans Konrad, *'Kandinsky. Catalogue Raisonné of the Oil Paintings'* in *2 vol.*, Sotheby's Publications, New York, 1982 (Karl Flinker, Paris, 1984). Derouet, Christian/Boissel, Jessica, *Oeuvres de Wassily Kandinsky (1866-1944), collections du Musée National d'Art Moderne*, exhibition catalogue, Musée National d'Art Moderne, Paris, 1984-1985. Tio Bellido, Ramón, *Kandinsky*, Portland House, New York, 1988 (translated by Jane Brenton). *Kandinsky, dessins et aquarelles*, Flammarion, Paris, 1992. Hahl-Koch, Jelena, *Kandinsky*, Rizzoli, New York, 1993. Endicott Barnett, Vivian, *'Kandinsky: aquarelles'* in *2* vol. t. I 1900-1921, t. II 1922-1944, critical catalogue, Philip Wilson Ltd, London, Société Kandinsky, Paris, 1994. Weiss, Peg, *Kandinsky and Old Russia: the artist as ethnographer and shaman*, Yale University Press, New Haven, c. 1995. Endicott Barnett, Vivian/Helfenstein, Josef, *The Blue Four: Feininger, Jawlensky, Kandinsky, and Klee in the New World*, Yale University Press, London, 1998. Rapelli, Paula, *Kandinsky*, DK Pub, New York, 1999 (translated by Fiona Wild). Bowlt, John E. (ed.), *Painting Revolution: Kandinsky, Malevich and the Russian Avant-Garde*, exhibition catalogue, Foundation for International Arts and Education, Bethesda, Maryland, c. 2000. Golding, John, *Paths to the Absolute: Mondrian, Malevich, Kandinsky, Pollock, Newman, Rothko and Still*, Thames & Hudson, London, 2002. *Analogies musicales: Kandinsky et ses contemporains,*, group exhibition catalogue, Museo Thyssen-Bornemisza, Madrid, 2003. Lemoine, Serge/Rousseau, Pascal, et al., *Aux origines de l'abstraction (1800-1914)*, exhibition catalogue, Musée d'Orsay, Paris, 2003. *Kandinsky: the Dissolution of Form, 1900-1920*, Fundacio Caixa Catalunya, Barcelona, c. 2003.

MUSEUMS AND GALLERIES:

AMSTERDAM (Stedelijk Mus.): *Landscapes and Houses* (1909) - BALTIMORE (MA) - BASEL (Beyeler Foundation): *Fugue* (1914, oil on canvas) - BERN (Kunstmus.): *Simplicity* (1943) - COLOGNE (Wallraf-Richartz Mus.): *The Gentle Sharp Rose* (1924) - DÜSSELDORF (Kunstsammlung Nordrhein-Westfalen): *Clarity* (1924, watercolour); *In the Blue* (1925); *Horizontal Blue* (1929, watercolour) - EINDHOVEN (Van Abbe Mus.): *Murnau with Church* (1910) - HAMBURG (Kunsthalle): *Arab Cemetery* (1909) - MARSEILLES (Mus. Cantini): *Development in Brown* (1933) - MONTREAL (MAC): *Oval* (1925) - MONTREAL (MBA): *Highlighted Corners* (1922, watercolour) - MOSCOW (Mus. of Modern Western Art): *Winter No. 1* (1909); *Improvisation No. 20, Horses* (1911) - MOSCOW (State Tretyakov Gal.): *Lake, Boat Ride* (1910); *Composition No. 7* (1913) - MUNICH (Städtische Gal. im Lenbachhaus): *Old Town* (1903); *Beach Huts in Holland* (1904); *Couple on Horseback* (1905-1907); *Street in Murnau* (1908); *Around the Town* (1908); *Through the Griesbrau Window in Murnau* (1908); *Study for Improvisation No. 2, Funeral March* (1909); *Railway near Murnau* (1909); *Lounge on Ainmillerstrasse* (1909-1910); *Church* (1910); *Cow* (1910); *Improvisation XIV* (1910); *Romantic Landscape* (1911); *Impression No. 4, Policeman* (1911); *With Red Stain* (1913) - NEW YORK (MoMA): *Untitled, Known as Spring and Summer* (1914, two of four panels intended for E. R. Campbell's apartment in New York); *Black Report* (1924) - NEW YORK (Solomon R. Guggenheim Mus.): *Blue Mountain* (1908-1909); *Ladies in Crinolines* (1909); *Sketch for Composition II* (1909-1910); *Pastoral* (1911); *Rain* (1911); *Im-*

provisation No. 28 (1912); *Black Features* (1913); *Painting with White Shape* (1913); *Small Joys No. 174* (1913); *Clear Painting* (1913); *Untitled, Known as Autumn and Winter* (1914, two of four panels intended for E. R. Campbell's apartment in New York); *Blue Circle* (1922); *In the Black Square* (1923); *Composition VIII* (1923); *Extension* (1926); *Two Red Sides* (1928); *Stages* (1929); *Defining Rose - 1932; Yellow Canvas* (1933); *Green Emphasis* (1935); *Accompanied Contrast* (1935); *Dominant Curve* (1936); *White Face* (1943); *Ribbon with Squares* (1944) - Paris (MNAM-CCI): *Painting with Red Stain* (1914, oil on canvas); *Landscape with Bell* (1909); *Improvisation III* (1909); *Untitled* (1910, watercolour); *Impression V (Park)* (1911); *With Black Arch* (1912); *Painting with Red Stain* (1914); *In the Grey* (1919); *Yellow-Red-Blue* (1915 or 1925); *Set for the Juryfreie Ausstellung Exhibition recreated in 1977* (1922); *Pink Emphasis* (1926); *Sky BLue* (1940); *Reciprocal Agreement* (1942); *Tempered Impulse* (1944) - Rotterdam (Mus. Boijmans Van Beuningen): *Lyric* (1911) - St Petersburg (Gosudarstvennyj Russkij Muz.): *Black Stain I* (1912) - The Hague (Gemeentemus.): *Promenade* (1905); *View from Apartment Window in Moscow* (1920) - Washington DC (Phillips Collection): *Sketch for Painting with White Border* (1913); *Succession* (1935) - Worcester, MA (AM): *Untitled Painting, No. 629* (1936, oil on canvas) - Wuppertal (Von der Heydt Mus.): *Houses in Munich* (1908); *Landscape with Church* (1908).

Auction records:

Paris, 12 April 1933, *Composition,* FRF 300; *Composition,* FRF 1,200. New York, 14 Feb 1951, *Daydreaming,* USD 350. Bern, 17 May 1958, *Composition with a Wide Triangle* (watercolour) CHF 13,800. Brussels, 25 April 1959, *Solar Composition* (watercolour) BEF 66,000. New York, 27 April 1960, *Blank* (tempera/card) USD 7,200. Stuttgart, 20 May 1960, *Zigzag* (gouache/card) DEM 26,000. London, 13 July 1960, *Mountain Landscape in Winter* (tempera/card) GBP 5,000. Stuttgart, 3-4 May 1962, *Composition with White Shapes* (gouache) DEM 31,000. Milan, 21-23 Nov 1962, *Corner on Circle,* ITL 11,000,000. London, 30 June 1964, *Fan-shaped* (tempera and oil on panel) GBP 6,500; *Improvisation,* GBP 50,000. London, 30 March 1966, *Starnberger See, Tutzing* (1908, oil on card, 12 x 27 1/4 ins / 30.5 x 69 cm) GBP 5,100. Geneva, 28 June 1969, *Three* (watercolour) CHF 67,000. New York, 13 May 1970, *Village Street,* USD 119,000. New York, 20 Oct 1971, *Painting with Three Stains,* USD 300,000. Milan, 2 Dec 1971, *Yellow-Pink* (watercolour) ITL 20,000,000. Geneva, 7 June 1974, *Cold Energy,* CHF 900,000. Bern, 9 June 1976, *Study for a Portrait* (1917, Indian ink, 12 1/4 x 9 ins / 31 x 22 cm) CHF 27,000. London, 29 June 1976, *Tournament* (1902, tempera, 12 x 16 ins / 30.5 x 40.5 cm) GBP 16,000. London, 29 Nov 1976, *Sternberger See, Tutzing* (1908, oil on card, 12 x 27 1/4 ins / 30.5 x 69 cm) GBP 31,500. Munich, 30 Nov 1976, *Orange (Composition in Chequered Pattern)* (1923, lithograph, 16 1/4 x 15 1/4 ins / 41 x 38.5 cm) DEM 26,000. London, 29 March 1977, *Street in Murnau with Woman* (1908, oil on card, 13 x 17 3/4 ins / 33 x 45 cm) GBP 50,000. Bern, 8 June 1977, *Woman with Fan* (1903, woodcut) CHF 25,0000. London, 7 Dec 1977, *Pink-Red* (1927, watercolour remounted on board, 12 1/2 x 19 ins / 32 x 48 cm) GBP 22,000. New York, 17 May 1978, *Improvisation with Horses* (1911, oil on canvas, 28 x 39 ins / 71.2 x 98.8 cm) USD 365,000. Hamburg, 2 June 1978, *Composition.* London, 2 April 1979, *Village Street* (1908, oil on card, 19 x 27 1/2 ins / 48 x 70 cm) GBP 165,000. New York, 16 May 1979, *Composition* (1931, Indian ink, 12 3/4 x 15 ins / 32.5 x 37.2 cm) USD 6,750. New York, 7 Nov 1979, *Early Hour* (c. 1904-1906, tempera/canvas, 38 1/4 x 51 1/4 ins / 97 x 130 cm) USD 240,000. New York, 13 Nov 1979, *Violet* (1923, coloured lithograph, 11 1/2 x 7 1/2 ins / 29.5 x 19 cm) USD 8,000. Milan, 26 Feb 1981, *Gentle Hardness No. 404* (1927, oil/hardboard, 20 x 15 ins / 51 x 38 cm) ITL 142,000,000. Munich, 30 June 1982, *Moonrise* (1904, monotype) DEM 60,000. Bern, 22 June 1983, *The Blue Rider Almanach* (1911, colour woodcut/paper) CHF 62,000. New York, 17 Nov 1983, *Composition* (1924, Indian ink, 12 x 8 3/4 ins / 30.5 x 22.5 cm) USD 18,000. London, 28 March 1984, *Composition* (1917-1918, watercolour and ink, 18 3/4 x 35 ins / 47.5 x 88 cm) GBP 150,000. London, 4 Dec 1984, *Elephant* (1908, card remounted/panel, 18 x 27 ins / 46 x 68.5 cm) GBP 420,000. New York, 13 May 1986, *Accentuated Corners* (1923, oil on canvas, 51 1/4 x 51 1/4 ins / 130 x 130 cm) USD 1,000,000. London, 3 Dec 1986, *Composition* (c. 1915-1917, watercolour and Indian ink, 9 x 13 1/2 ins / 22.8 x 34 cm) GBP 195,000. London, 1 July 1987, *Lyrical Composition* (1922, watercolour and Indian ink, 12 1/2 x 14 3/4 ins / 31.5 x 37.7 cm) GBP 150,000. New York, 10 Nov 1987, *Murnau, Landscape with Church I* (1909, oil on card/remounted/panel, 27 x 37 1/2 ins / 68.3 x 95.2 cm) USD 2,200,000. Paris, 25 Nov 1987, *Blue* (1922, lithograph, 12 3/4 ins / 32.5 cm w. 11 ins/27.8 cm) FRF 46,000. London, 2 Dec 1987, *In Summer* (1904, woodcut in eleven colours, 12 1/4 x 6 1/2 ins / 31.3 x 16.4 cm) GBP 30,000. Paris, 21 March 1988, *Colourful Character* (1927, oil on card, 23 1/2 x 13 1/4 ins / 59.5 x 33.6 cm) FRF 4,000,000. Milan, 24 March 1988, *Flexible* (1931, gouache/light card/ cardboard, 19 x 10 ins / 48 x 25.5 cm) ITL 103,000,000. London, 29 March 1988, *Composition* (1940, gouache/black paper, 13 1/4 x 20 ins / 33.5 x 51 cm) GBP 63,800. London, 30 March 1988, *Composition* (1922, gouache, watercolour, Indian ink, 13 x 19 ins / 33 x 48 cm) GBP 137,500. New York, 11 May 1988, *Landscape with Tree* (1908, oil on card, 13 x 16 1/4 ins / 32.8 x 41 cm) USD 440,000; *Three Columns* (1943, oil on card, 16 1/4 x 22 3/4 ins / 41.5 x 57.8 cm) USD 319,000. New York, 12 Nov 1988, *Composition No. 1* (1915, ink and watercolour/paper, 13 x 8 3/4 ins / 33 x 22.2 cm) USD 156,750. London, 3 April 1989, *Flat-Deep* (1930, oil on card, 19 1/4 x 27 1/2 ins / 49 x 70 cm) GBP 495,000. Paris, 9 April 1989, *Black Two* (1941, mixed media/canvas, 46 x 32 ins / 116 x 81 cm) FRF 10,600,000. New York, 10 May 1989, *Angel of the Last Judgement* (oil on paper/panel, 25 1/2 x 20 ins / 64.7 x 50.5 cm) USD 4,620,000. Paris, 17 June 1989, *4x5=20* (1943, mixed media/card, 23 x 16 1/4 ins / 57.5 x 41.5 cm) FRF 5,300,000. New York, 15 Nov 1989, *Pool in St Cloud Park* (1906, oil on panel, 9 1/4 x 12 3/4 ins / 23.5 x 32.7 cm) USD 176,000. New York, 16 Nov 1989, *Country House with Kochel Church* (1902, oil on card, 9 1/2 x 12 3/4 ins / 24 x 32.7 cm) USD 286,000. Paris, 19 Nov 1989, *Small Values* (1926, oil on card, 17 3/4 x 13 ins / 45 x 33 cm) FRF 4,000,000. Paris, 25 March 1990, *Blue Circle No. 2* (oil on card, 24 x 16 1/4 ins / 61 x 41.5 cm) FRF 11,500,000. London, 3 April 1990, *Murnau - Lower Market* (1908, oil on card, 13 x 17 1/2 ins / 33 x 44.5 cm) GBP 880,000. London, 4 April 1990, *Surrounding Area* (1924, ink, watercolour and gouache, 16 x 12 1/4 ins / 40.7 x 30.8 cm) GBP 418,000. Paris, 17 March 1991, *Clowning* (1932, Indian ink, 7 3/4 x 4 1/4 ins / 19.5 x 11 cm) FRF 75,000. New York, 11 Nov 1992, *Two Movements* (1924, watercolour and coloured inks/paper/card, 13 1/4 x 18 1/2 ins / 33.7 x 47.3 cm) USD 550,000. London, 1 Dec 1992, *Sketches for Composition VII* (1913, oil on canvas, 30 3/4 x 39 1/4 ins / 78 x 100 cm) GBP 5,500,000; *Untitled* (watercolour and ink, 14 1/4 x 11 ins / 36 x 27 cm) GBP 319,000; *Arrow Pointing to the Circle* (1930, oil on canvas, 31 1/2 x 43 1/4 ins / 80 x 110 cm) GBP 506,000. Paris, 3 Feb 1993, *Boatride* (woodcut, 8 3/4 x 22 3/4 ins / 22.5 x 58 cm, 2 3/4 ins/7 cm) FRF 5,200. Paris, 6 April 1993, *Abstract Composition* (1930, Indian ink, 10 x 2 1/4 ins / 24.5 x 6 cm) FRF 84,000. New York, 12 May 1993, *Green in a Cross* (1927, gouache and watercolour/paper mounted/black paper, 19 3/4 x 13 1/2 ins / 50.2 x 34 cm) USD 222,500. London, 21 June 1993, *Constant Greens* (1925, oil on card/panel, 27 1/4 x 20 ins / 69.5 x 49.9 cm) GBP 826,500. Paris, 21 June 1993, *Circuit* (1939, oil on canvas, 36 1/4 x 28 3/4 ins / 92 x 73 cm) FRF 2,910,000. London, 22 June 1993, *Accompanied Centre* (1937, oil on canvas, 45 x 57 1/2 ins / 114 x 146 cm) GBP

3,026,500. NEW YORK, 2 Nov 1993, *Murnau, Landscape with a Church I* (1909, oil on card, 27 x 37 1/2 ins / 68.3 x 95.2 cm) USD 2,752,500. PARIS, 22 Nov 1993, *In the Black Circle* (1923, oil on canvas, 51 1/4 x 51 1/4 ins / 130 x 130 cm) FRF 36,000,000. NEW YORK, 11 May 1994, *Circuit* (1939, oil on canvas, 36 x 28 1/2 ins / 91.4 x 72.4 cm) USD 772,500. PARIS, 13 June 1994, *Submerged or Absorbed* (1929, gouache, watercolour and Indian ink/paper, 19 3/4 x 9 3/4 ins / 50 x 25 cm) FRF 308,000. LONDON, 29 June 1994, *From To* (1930, watercolour, gouache, colouring pencil and ink/paper/card, 7 1/2 x 20 ins / 18.8 x 51.1 cm) GBP 210,500. NEW YORK, 10 Nov 1994, *Untitled* (watercolour and ink/paper, 11 1/2 x 9 ins / 29 x 22.8 cm) USD 354,500. PARIS, 28 Nov 1994, *Red Shape* (1938, oil on canvas, 32 x 23 1/2 ins / 81 x 60 cm) FRF 2,310,000. PARIS, 22 June 1995, *Climbing from the Semi-Circle* (1931, tempera/card, 29 1/2 x 17 3/4 ins / 75 x 45 cm) FRF 1,176,000. LONDON, 11 Oct 1995, *Night* (1903, woodcut in colour/Japanese paper, 11 3/4 x 5 ins / 29.8 x 12.8 cm) GBP 62,000. NEW YORK, 8 Nov 1995, *Sharp Angle* (1926, oil on canvas, 30 3/4 x 48 1/2 ins / 78.1 x 123.2 cm) USD 937,500; *Last Judgement* (1910, oil on canvas, 49 3/4 x 28 3/4 ins / 126.4 x 73 cm) USD 5,227,500. LONDON, 28 Nov 1995, *Arrangement of Signs* (1927, oil on canvas, 32 x 20 1/2 ins / 81 x 52 cm) GBP 441,500. COPENHAGEN, 12 March 1996, *Composition* (lithograph) DKK 32,000. MILAN, 19 March 1996, *Melody* (1924, watercolour and ink/paper/card, 12 1/2 x 9 1/4 ins / 32 x 23.2 cm) ITL 437,000,000. NEW YORK, 1 May 1996, *Sun's Rays* (1929, watercolour, pen and ink/paper/card, 20 3/4 x 13 1/4 ins / 53 x 33.8 cm) USD 107,000. LONDON, 24 June 1996, *Composition VII* (watercolour and Indian ink/paper, sketch, 15 1/2 x 18 ins / 39.2 x 46 cm) GBP 936,500. NEW YORK, 12 Nov 1996, *Watercolour with Red Corners* (1913, watercolour, gouache and Indian ink/paper, 14 1/4 x 15 3/4 ins / 36.2 x 40 cm) USD 1,102,500. NEW YORK, 13 Nov 1996, *Autumnal Landscape with Boats* (1908, oil on panel, 28 x 38 ins / 71 x 96.5 cm) USD 3,852,500. LONDON, 3 Dec 1996, *Divided* (1928, watercolour/mounted paper/card, 18 3/4 x 13 ins / 47.9 x 32.1 cm) GBP 56,500. NEW YORK, 14 May 1997, *4 x 5 = 20* (1943, oil and gouache/panel, 23 x 16 1/4 ins / 57.5 x 41.5 cm) USD 552,500. LONDON, 23 June 1997, *Dunaberg* (1909, oil on panel, 13 x 17 3/4 ins / 33 x 45 cm) GBP 1,651,500. LONDON, 24 June 1997, *Grey-Blue* (1925, watercolour, gouache and brush and Indian ink/paper, 19 x 12 1/2 ins / 48.3 x 31.8 cm) GBP 155,500. LONDON, 25 June 1997, *Solitaire 54* (1934, gouache, watercolour and pen and ink/paper, 23 x 15 1/4 ins / 57.5 x 39 cm) GBP 101,600. NEW YORK, 13 Nov 1997, *Picture Within a Picture* (1929, oil on card, 27 1/2 x 19 1/4 ins / 70 x 49 cm) USD 662,500. NEW YORK, 6 and 7 March 1998, *Small Worlds* (1922, drypoint, 9 1/4 x 7 3/4 ins / 23.8 x 19.7 cm) USD 5,750. NEW YORK, 13 May 1999, *Untitled* (c. 1918, watercolour, pen, brush and ink, 14 x 11 ins / 36 x 27 cm) USD 520,000. LONDON, 28 June 1999, *Untitled* (1923, watercolour, pen and ink, 13 x 19 ins / 33 x 47 cm) GBP 750,000. NEW YORK, 10 May 2000, *From-To* (1930, oil on cardboard, 14 x 19 ins / 35 x 49 cm) USD 520,000. NEW YORK, 11 May 2000, *Kallmunz, Sunset* (oil on canvasboard, 9 x 13 ins / 23 x 33 cm) USD 250,000. NEW YORK, 5 Nov 2001, *Mountain Landscape with Village I* (1908, oil on cardboard, 28 x 38 ins / 70 x 96 cm) USD 4,500,000. NEW YORK, 7 Nov 2001, *Untitled* (1923, watercolour, pen, brush and Indian ink, 19 x 17 ins / 47 x 43 cm) USD 440,000. LONDON, 24 June 2002, *Murnau-Obermarkt* (1908, oil on board, 19 x 28 ins / 49 x 70 cm) GBP 920,000. LONDON, 8 Oct 2002, *Black Triangle* (1923, watercolour, pen and Indian ink, 12 x 16 ins / 30 x 40 cm) EUR 1,000,000. LONDON, 26 June 2003, *Composition with White Shapes* (1940, gouache, 13 x 20 ins / 32 x 50 cm) GBP 100,000. NEW YORK, 4 Nov 2003, *Capricious Stroke* (1924, oil on board, 28 x 19 ins / 70 x 49 cm) USD 1,100,000. LONDON, 3 Feb 2004, *Watercolour for Poul Bjerre* (1916, watercolour, pen, brush and ink, 9 x 13 ins / 23 x 34 cm) GBP 420,000. LONDON, 22 June 2004, *Mountainous Landscape* (1909, oil on board, 13 x 18 ins / 33 x 45 cm) GBP 2,700,000.

KANDL, Lukas
Czechoslovak, 20th century.
Born 29 November 1944, in Prague.
Active in France from 1970, naturalised French.
Painter, draughtsman.

Lukas Kandl studied at the school of applied arts in Prague. In 1967-1968, he studied for a while in France. In 1969, having worked in Alois Fisarek's studio, he won the national diploma from the academy of fine arts in Prague. The Russian occupation of Czechoslovakia in 1968 forced him to emigrate to France. He settled in Saint-Germain-en-Laye in 1985. He has adopted the techniques of the Flemish masters, applying them to a Surrealist-like fantastic inspiration, incorporating overtones of Jerome Hieronymus Bosch, Dali and de Tanguy. His themes are enigmatic and personal to him and he keeps the keys that unlock the meaning of his work to himself. In 1985, he won first prize at the poster competition for the Lancôme Trophy and in 1987 he was awarded a prize at the Prix International in Monaco and was made a member of the Copley Society in Boston. In 1989, he won a painting prize at the *Remontons les Champs-Élysées pour la sauvegarde culturelle de Paris* (*Let's Walk up the Champs-Élysées to Safeguard Parisian Culture*) painting contest. In 1990, he won a top prize at the Osaka art festival. He has taken part in collective exhibitions since 1969 in Prague and Milan and in Paris at the Salon de Paris, the Salon des Indépendants, the Salon des Artistes Français, the Salon des Surindépendants and the Salon d'Automne, of which he is a member, as well as in several group exhibitions in French provincial towns, including Deauville, Château Gontier and Cannes, sometimes being awarded distinctions. He had solo exhibitions in 1973 in Cologne, in 1974 in Saint-Jeannet, in 1975 in Paris, in 1977 in The Hague, in 1978 in Amsterdam, in 1982 in Cologne, in 1986 in Saint-Germain-en-Laye, in 1989 in Douai, in 1990 in Saint-Germain-en-Laye, and in 2002 (*Homage to Audubon*) at the Galerie Ileana Bouboulis in Paris.

AUCTION RECORDS:
PARIS, Oct 1990, *Untitled* (oil on canvas, 18 x 15 ins / 46 x 38 cm) FRF 11,000.

KÄNDLER, Johann Joachim
German, 18th century.
Born 1706, in Fischbach; died 18 May 1775, in Meissen.
Sculptor, faïence painter.

Kändler was a monumental mason and sculptor before becoming famous as a maker and painter of faïence. He worked mainly on tombs in the early part of his career.

KANDLER, Wilhelm
German, 19th century.
Born 28 February 1816, in Kratzau (now Chrastava); died 18 May 1896, in Prague.
Painter. History painting, landscapes.

Kandler enrolled at the academy in Prague in 1830, where he was taught by C. Ruben and Kaldik. From 1842 to 1850 he worked in Italy, notably Venice, Rome, Florence, Bologna and Padua. In 1850, he settled in Vienna and exhibited his works there. He was a literary figure as well as an artist.

KANDLPALTUNG, Hans Ludwig
German, 16th century.
Born in Cologne; died 1592.
Painter, engraver.

Hans Kandlpaltung was a painter who worked mostly in Weiden.

KANE, John
British, 19th - 20th century.

Born 1860, in West Calder, Scotland; died 1934, in Pittsburgh.
Active in the USA from 1879.
Painter. Portraits, interiors, local scenes, urban landscapes, landscapes with figures.

John Kane emigrated to the USA at the age of 19. In Ohio, he worked as a builder, coal miner, steel worker and joiner; he competed in fairground boxing matches, and produced sketches in his spare time. After losing a leg in a railway accident in 1891 he found work as a painter of railway carriages, but became a vagrant and casual worker following the death of his son in 1904. He eventually settled in Pittsburgh, and worked as a house painter. He also produced hand-coloured photographs, and continued to paint childhood memories of Scotland, portraits, street scenes and religious scenes. His earliest surviving paintings - of steel tools, to which he attributed his understanding of the use of colour - date from around 1910. In 1927 Kane's reputation as America's leading Naive artist (the first painter to be officially categorised as such) was established overnight when the jury of the Carnegie International Exhibition in Pittsburgh accepted one of his Highland landscapes. Recognition failed to bring him financial security, however, and he died of tuberculosis in a hospice in 1934.

Kane's early works include naive views of the working-class suburbs of cities in Pennsylvania, especially Pittsburgh. The steel-making capital is seen as a bright, animated city of factories and colonnaded mansions beneath skies filled with dancing smoke-clouds from industrial chimneys, and the tops of the first skyscrapers. In the archetypal Naive manner, his paintings feature highly-detailed renditions of the structural supports of bridges, or the wheels of cars. Another series of landscapes recalls the Scottish mining towns where he spent his early years, characterised by their equally detailed rendering of, for example, the minutiae of a particular tartan. His best-known works include *Touching Up* (a view of the interior of his studio, including a portrait of the artist finishing one of his works amidst numerous other canvases) and a moving *Self-portrait* of 1929, now in the Museum of Modern Art in New York. Here, Kane depicts himself as an emaciated figure in old age, posing in a faded blue worker's overall with muscles flexed pathetically, his gaze fixed and disillusioned. His rigidly symmetrical figure fills the picture, accentuated by a kind of halo.

Kane exhibited frequently during the 1920s, particularly in New York. In 2001, his work featured in the exhibition *Die Naive, Aufbruch ins verlorene Paradies* (*The Naïve Painters, Journey to a Lost Paradise*) at the Kuntshaus in Vienna, which presented almost 200 works by Naive artists from the collection of the Museum Charlotte Zander in Bönnigheim.

Bibliography:

Kane, John, *Shy Hook: the Autobiography of John Kane*, J.B. Lippincott, New York, 1938 (with a foreword by Frank Crowninshield). *Four American Primitives: Edward Hicks, John Kane, Anna Mary Robertson Moses, Horace Pippin*, exhibition catalogue, ACA Galleries, New York, 1972. Kallir, Jane, *John Kane, Modern America's First Folk Painter*, exhibition catalogue, Galerie St Etienne, New York, 1984.

Museums and Galleries:

Bönnigheim (Mus. Charlotte Zander) - Merion (Barnes Foundation): *Along the Susquehanna* (oil on canvas) - New York (MoMA): *Self-portrait* (1929).

Auction records:

New York, 9 Oct 1963, *View of Pittsburgh*, USD 12,500. New York, 14 March 1968, *View of Philadelphia*, USD 12,000. New York, 7 April 1971, *Young Girl with Cat*, USD 2,300. New York, 12 Dec 1974, *Day of Rest*, USD 5,000. New York, 28 Oct 1976, *The Lincoln Highway* (1933, oil on canvas, 21 3/4 x 27 1/2 ins / 55.2 x 70 cm) USD 12,000. New York, 25 April 1980, *Portrait of Maggie* (1929, oil on canvas, 23 x 19 1/4 ins / 58.4 x 48.9 cm) USD 6,250. New York, 29 May 1981, *Scots Day at Kennywood* (oil on canvas, 19 x 27 ins / 48.3 x 68.6 cm) USD 23,000. London, 21 May 1986, *Winter Scene* (oil on canvas, 24 x 26 ins / 61 x 66 cm) GBP 7,000. New York, 24 Jan 1989, *Little Girl with a Collie* (1931, oil on canvas, 11 x 14 ins / 28.2 x 35.4 cm) USD 8,250. New York, 23 May 1991, *St Philomena* (oil on canvas, 20 x 24 ins / 50.8 x 61 cm) USD 19,800.

KANE, Paul

Canadian, 19th century.
Born 3 September 1810, in Mallow (Cork), Ireland; died 2 February 1871, in Toronto.
Painter, watercolourist, engraver, illustrator. Portraits, local scenes, landscapes.

Paul Kane arrived in Toronto with his parents in 1819. After his studies, he started out as a decorative painter in a furniture factory. He was a pupil of Thomas Drury in around 1830, and in 1834he left for Cobourg in Ontario, where he started a career as a portrait painter. In 1836 he left Cobourg for Detroit and then St Louis, and continued to travel around the USA before settling in New Orleans. There he raised sufficient money to travel to Europe in 1841. From 1841 to 1845 he stayed in France and Italy, visiting museums and copying the masters.

He returned by way of Switzerland and London, where he met the painter George Catlin, whose passion for Native American culture pointed Kane's art in a new direction. Kane realised that Native Americans were in danger of extinction and decided to devote his art to them from that point on. When he returned to Toronto he made his first trip by canoe in 1845 to make contact with the Indians around the Great Lakes. He then travelled from eastern to western Canada, painting the Indians, noting their way of life and describing the places. Following this long voyage, he exhibited his work in Toronto in 1848, showing a great panorama of the life of Indians from the Great Lakes to the Pacific.

Between 1848 and 1855 Kane produced 100 canvases depicting the life of Indians. In 1853 he married, settled down and gave up his long journeys. In 1856 he completed the replicas of 12 of his works which had been commissioned by the government. In 1858 he went to London to publish his book *Wanderings of an Artist among the Indians of North America*, which he illustrated with wood engravings. This publication was enormously successful and was translated into French in 1861 and into German and Danish in 1862. He could not complete his other projects, having become blind, and ceased all pictorial activity in the 1860s.

Through his enthusiasm for Indian life, Kane produced work revealing feeling rather than mere documentary fact. His landscapes are grandiose, composed according to the European tradition, and some even evoke Poussin. Sometimes the landscape serves to highlight an Indian and his horse, as in *The Man that Always Rides*, which shows a magnificent rider on a fiery white horse, standing out against a stormy, blazing sky. Kane painted portraits of Indian chiefs in the European Romantic tradition, depicting them before stormy skies, wearing intensely coloured clothes and painting their faces with much emotion. The Indians themselves valued Kane greatly, and one of the chiefs showed his gratitude by offering him a much-prized necklace of grizzly bear teeth.

Bibliography:

Reid, Dennis, *A Concise History of Canadian Painting*, Oxford University Press, Toronto, 1988.

Museums and Galleries:

Montreal (MBA): *Caw-Wacham* (1845-1848); *Mah-min or The Feather* - Ottawa (NG. of Canada): *Chief Black Foot and his Braves; White Mud Portage* - Toronto (AG of Ontario): *Indian Camp on the Banks of Lake Huron* (1845-1846) - Tor-

ONTO (Royal Ontario Mus.): 100 canvases on the life of Indians; *The Man that Always Rides.*

AUCTION RECORDS:

TORONTO, 1 June 1982, *Caw-kee-ka-kesh-a-ko, or The Constant Sky* (oil on canvas, 17 3/4 x 28 1/2 ins / 45 x 72.5 cm) CAD 55,000. TORONTO, 2 June 1999, *Portrait of Maungwudaus* (oil on canvas, 25 x 30 ins / 63 x 76 cm) CAD 475,000. TORONTO, 25 Feb 2002, *Scene in the Northwest: Portrait* (oil on canvas, 20 x 31 ins / 51 x 79 cm) CAD 4,600,000. CALGARY, 1 Dec 2002, *Portrait of Maungwudaus* (1851, oil on canvas, 30 x 25 ins / 76 x 64 cm) CAD 2,200,000.

KANE, Robert or Bob
American, 20th century.
Born 1937, in Cleveland.
Painter. Landscapes, still-lifes.

Robert Kane modelled himself on Matisse. Admiring in particular Matisse's *Goldfish* and *Lilac Branch,* he paints appealing, pieces in clean hues.

KANE KWEI, Samuel
Ghanaian, 20th century.
Born 1924, in Teshie; died 1992.
Sculptor.

Kane Kwei became a sculptor by chance, at the age of 14. His uncle, a fisherman, died at sea and Kane Kwei fashioned a coffin in his honour, in the form of his pirogue (dug-out canoe). The piece was greatly admired during the funeral celebrations, resulting in numerous commissions. Coffins based on the same fundamental concept have since become traditional features at Ghanaian funerals, where they are highly appreciated for their contribution to the dignity and solemnity of the occasion. Kane Kwei is now supported in his work by ten assistants. In 1989 his coffin-sculptures were introduced to a wider, Western public through the film *Les Magiciens de la Terre* (*Magicians of the Earth*), shown at the Centre Pompidou in Paris. The 'pirogue-coffin' has given rise to numerous other polychromed 'coffin-objects', all conceived on a scale dictated by the proportions of the human body: vegetables, a lion and other animals shown flying or swimming, cars, planes, houses and other objects. The coffins are constructed, carved, polished and painted with care and precision, on the basis of models approved by the individual commissioning the work.

KANELBA, Raymond, pseudonym of Kanelbaum Rajmund Mojzesz
Polish, 20th century.
Born 24 February 1897, in Warsaw; died 23 July 1960, in London.
Also active in France from 1915 to 1934, in Britain from 1934 to 1951, and in the USA from 1951.
Painter. Portraits, landscapes.

From 1918-1919 Kanelba studied at the Stuk Pieknych academy in Warsaw and then at the academy of fine arts in Vienna from 1919 to 1922. From 1915 to 1934 he was living and painting in Montparnasse in Paris, where he associated, amongst others, with Kisling, Mané-Katz, Alfred Aberdam, Eugène Zak, Krémègne, Kikoin and Lipschitz.

He was first and foremost a portrait painter, specialising in portraits of women and children. From 1916 he painted portraits of many well-known society figures from Poland (Count Edward Raczynski), France, Germany, England (the daughters of Lord Louis Mountbatten, the parents of the Shakespearean actor John Gielgud, Queen Elizabeth II) and the USA (Margaret Dupont de Nemours, Wendy Vanderbilt). He also painted landscapes of Paris and the banks of the Seine, as well as landscapes of the Polish plains. Before settling in New York in 1951, he had visited the USA on several occasions in 1937, 1938 and 1939 and had received commissions to paint portraits. He died during a visit to London.

Kanelba took part in several collective exhibitions, including the Salon d'Automne, Paris (1925 to 1956); the Salon des Indépendants (1926 to 1928); the Salon des Tuileries (1927 to 1938); England; Belgium; Poland; Germany; Denmark; and the USA.

His solo exhibitions include the Galerie Zborowski, Paris (1928); Berlin (1931); Galerie Berthe Weil, Paris (1932); Galerie Zak, Paris (1933); Galerie Alex Reid et Lefèvre (1936); New York (1937); London and Palm Beach (1938); Edinburgh and Glasgow (1941); and New York (1947, 1952, 1954, 1958, 1959, 1961).

BIBLIOGRAPHY:

Salmon, André, *Kanelba,* Le Triangle, Paris, 1933. Nieszawer, Nadine/Boyé, Marie/Lanzmann, Claude (preface), *Peintres juifs de l'école de Paris 1905-1939,* Denoël, Paris, 2001.

MUSEUMS AND GALLERIES:

ŁÓDZ (Muzeum Sztuki/MFA): *Young Beggar Girl; Portrait of Madame S.* - WARSAW (Muz. Narodowe): *Sleeping Family; Oriental Woman* - WEST PALM BEACH (Norton MA): *Madame Mullard.*

AUCTION RECORDS:

LONDON, 29 July 1988, *Two Children with a Dolls House* (1945, oil on canvas, 23 1/2 x 19 3/4 ins / 60 x 50 cm) GBP 660. PARIS, 4 July 1995, *Portrait of a Woman* (oil on canvas, 24 x 22 ins / 61 x 55 cm) FRF 10,000. WARSAW, 14 March 1999, *Flowers* (c. 1927, oil on canvas, 29 x 24 ins / 73 x 60 cm) PLN 25,000. PARIS, 30 May 2001, *Rue de Tournon* (1930, oil on canvas, 29 x 24 ins / 73 x 60 cm) FRF 20,000. PARIS, 12 Dec 2002, *Still-life with Petrol Lamp* (1929, oil on canvas, 36 x 22 ins / 91 x 57 cm) EUR 3,800. PARIS, 12 Dec 2002, *Little Girl Looking in a Mirror* (1929, oil on canvas, 36 x 26 ins / 92 x 65 cm) EUR 4,200. PARIS, 3 June 2003, *Breton Woman* (oil on canvas, 24 x 15 ins / 61 x 38 cm) EUR 4,000. PARIS, 3 June 2003, *Country Scene* (1958, oil on canvas, 20 x 26 ins / 50 x 65 cm) EUR 6,100. WARSAW, 23 May 2004, *Woman* (oil on canvas, 24 x 18 ins / 61 x 46 cm) PLN 28,000. PRAGUE, 2 Oct 2004, *Port* (oil on canvas) CZK 240,000.

KANEMITSU, Matsumi
American, 20th century.
Born 1922, in Ogden (Utah).
Painter, lithographer.

Matsumi Kanemitsu lived in Japan from 1925 to 1940. Back in the USA, he joined the US army during World War II. Later he studied under Fernand Léger in Paris, and Yasuo Kuniyoshi at the Art Students League in New York. In 1961, he received a grant from the Ford Foundation, thanks to which he studied lithography at the Tamarind Workshop in Los Angeles. Since 1950, he has taken part in collective exhibitions in the USA. He has shown his works in solo exhibitions in New Haven, Seattle, New York and Los Angeles.

KANENARI, family names: Izumiya Yashiro, Izumiya Akihiro, given name: Kimura, artist names: Akatsuki no Kanenari, Keimeisha, Seio
Japanese, 19th century.
Born 1793, in Osaka; died 1860.
Print artist.

Kanenari was an author and illustrator, active sometime between 1810 and 1850.

KANERVA, Aimo
Finnish, 20th century.
Born 1909; died 1991.
Painter, watercolourist. Landscapes.

Aimo Kanerva was one of the founders of the October Group. In 1960, he represented Finland at the Venice Biennale. His work falls into several periods. From 1930 to 1940, his paintings are close to Expressionism, with a tendency towards the mystical, but after World War II, he constructed his landscapes according to Post-Cubist principles while continuing to heighten the depiction of his subjects, strongly emphasising the forms with thick black lines. His watercolours continued in calm and gentle mood.

Auction records:

Stockholm, 10-12 May 1993, *Trees and Blue Sky* (1947, oil on canvas, 32 x 23$^{1/4}$ ins / 81 x 59 cm) SEK 31,000. Helsinki, 25 April 1999, *Marshy Landscape* (1975, watercolour, 20 x 25 ins / 50 x 64 cm) FIM 10,500. Helsinki, 17 Feb 2000, *Self-portrait* (oil on canvas, 21 x 18 ins / 54 x 46 cm) FIM 12,000. Helsinki, 12 May 2001, *View of Utsjoki in Summer* (1964, oil on board, 15 x 16 ins / 39 x 40 cm) FIM 11,500. Helsinki, 28 April 2002, *Vuokatti Mountains* (1949, oil on canvas, 34 x 44 ins / 86 x 112 cm) EUR 4,800. Helsinki, 1 Dec 2002, *Bog-myrtle* (1978, watercolour, 25 x 19 ins / 64 x 48 cm) EUR 2,200. Helsinki, 29 Nov 2003, *Trees on a Sandy Beach, Helsingfors* (1949, watercolour, 8 x 16 ins / 21 x 41 cm) EUR 1,750. Helsinki, 8 May 2004, *Summer Flowers* (1972, watercolour, 20 x 26 ins / 51 x 67 cm) EUR 2,200.

KANERVA, Raimo
Finnish, 20th century.
Born 1941, in Turku; died 1999.
Painter, collage artist, engraver, graphic designer.

Raimo Kanerva began his studies in Turku from 1958 to 1961. In 1963, while studying engraving in Paris, he attended William Stanley Hayter's Studio 17. On his return to Finland, he settled in Tampere. He was both a painter and a graphic artist and is often credited with having revived the graphic arts in Finland, particularly through his borrowings from the world of Surrealism. He drew his inspiration from everyday life, which he combined with purely imaginary scenes, often expressed through the medium of collage. In 1969, he represented Finland at the São Paulo Biennale, where he was awarded an honourable mention.

KANG, Gil-Seong
Korean, 20th - 21st century.
Born 18 March 1962, in Kwang-Joop (South Korea).
Active in France.
Painter.

Kang Gil-Seong studied at the Faculty of Fine Arts in Seoul. He also taught drawing and watercolour in Seoul. In 1989 he went to France to continue his studies. He attended the School of Fine Arts in Angers, where he was the student of Francis Limérat and Pincemein. His work is gestural abstract. He has taken part in various group exhibitions, among them the 1992 and 1993 Salon de la Jeune Peinture, and the Manifestation Internationale d'art contemporain, Le Mans, in 2000. He has also shown his work in solo exhibitions, for example, at the Galerie Le Troisième Œil, Paris, in 1993.

KANG, Jeong-Wan
Korean, 20th century.
Born 1933, in Sancheong, Gyeongnam.
Active in France.
Painter.

In 1975, after years of struggle, Kang Jeong-Wan was awarded the Korean President's Prize, which enabled him to go to Paris the following year to study at the École des Beaux-Arts. He graduated in 1979. Rich in materials and colours, his work is abstract, with figurative echoes from its sources in the landscapes of Korean culture. Kang has taken part in a number of group exhibitions, such as 1977-1978 Salon de Mai, Paris; 1982 *Korean Artists Resident Abroad*, National Museum of Modern Arts in Korea; 1978, 1982, 1984, 1985 and 1987, Salon de la société nationale des beaux-Arts, Paris; 1979, 1981 and 1987, Cité Internationale des Arts, Paris. He has also shown his work in solo exhibitions in 1968 and 1975 in Tokyo, in 1973 and 1976 in Seoul, from 1977 in Paris (notably at the Galerie Marcel Bernheim), and in 1981 and 1988 at the Cité internationale des Arts, Paris.

Museums and Galleries:

Oueno (Mus.) - Seoul (Ho-am Art Mus) - Seoul (NMMA).

KANG HAI, or K'ang Hai, sobriquet: Duishan, style name: Dehan
Chinese, 16th century.
Born 1475, in Nanjing (Shenxi); died 1540/1.
Painter.

Kang Hai was a poet whose devotion to wine, women, and song and his friendship with Wang Rusi (1468-1551) are still legendary. Although he is not mentioned in the biographies of painters, a signed hanging scroll by his hand is known: *Landscape with Pines and Pavilions on the River Bank.*

KANG TAO, or K'ang T'ao, sobriquets: Tiendu Laoren, Maoxin Laoren, etc, style name: Shizhou
Chinese, 18th century.
Born in Qiantang (Zhejiang).
Active c. 1740.
Painter.

Kang Tao specialised in landscapes, flowers and birds. He left a number of signed works.

KANGETSU, real name: Shitomi Tokki, alternate names: Shion, Genji, artist names: Iyosai, Kangetsu, Seigado
Japanese, 18th century.
Born 1747, in Osaka; died 1797.
Painter.

Kangetsu was a pupil of the painter and print artist Tsukioka Settei (1710-1786). Afterward he moved towards the study of old Chinese and Japanese paintings. He is also known for his poems and his calligraphy.

KANGYU, real name: Tokufu Shitomi, given name: Shien, artist names: Teiyoken, Iyosai, Kangyu
Japanese, 19th century.
Died 1843.
Active in Osaka c. 1820.
Print artist.

KANIEWSKI, Xaver Jan
Polish, 19th century.
Born 1809, in Krasilow; died 1867 or 1870, in Warsaw.
Painter, lithographer.

Xaver Kaniewski studied in Warsaw and St Petersburg, where he became a member of the academy. He then moved to Rome for a time. He painted a number of portraits of the Russian imperial family. In 1846, he settled in Warsaw, where he taught at the academy of fine arts and subsequently became its director.

KANIYA, Kuniharu
Japanese, 19th - 20th century.
Sculptor.

Kaniya Kuniharu lived in Tokyo. He exhibited at the 1900 Paris Exposition Universelle.

KANKAI, real name: Araki Shun, nickname: Kyoko, artist names: Kankai, Hosei Gajin, Tatsuan
Japanese, 19th century.
Born 1789, in Edo (now Tokyo); died 1860.
Painter.

KANKAN, real name: Hayashi Hama, artist names: Suiran, Kankan
Japanese, 18th century.
Born 1770, in Edo (now Tokyo); died 1794.
Painter.

Kankan was a famous painter of the Edo period. She was a pupil of her husband the painter Buncho (1763-1840) of the Nanga (literati) School. She painted landscapes as well as flowers and birds.

KANN, Frederick I

Czech, 20th century.

Born 25 May 1884, in Jablonec, in 1886 according to some sources; died 1965.

Naturalised in the USA from 1910.

Painter, sculptor, photographer.

Frederick Kann taught at the École du Louvre and his work was exhibited in Paris along with that of Kandinsky, Calder, Mondrian and Delaunay, as well as at the Salon des Surindépendants and the Salon des Tuileries. A member of the Abstraction-Création group in France and of the Artists Professionnal League in the USA, he had a large following in Europe, his renown being furthered by the support of critics such as Henry Miller, who lived in his studio. He went to the USA in the 1940s and exhibited at the Museum of Modern Art and the Solomon R. Guggenheim Museum in New York, as well as at private galleries. He organised exhibitions for other artists, and introduced Man Ray to the public. A respected teacher in Kansas City and Los Angeles, he established his own school in California, the Kann Institute of Art. His works appear to have been mislaid on his death in 1965, and were only discovered later.

His three-dimensional purist compositions lay particular stress on the dynamic power created by the linking of lines and planes. Miller wrote: 'There is a lot of mystification in Kann's abstract paintings, a curious mix of mathematics and introspection. With no transition, he leaps from the most rigid Academic style to a no man's land which is strange but not yet surreal'.

AUCTION RECORDS:

NEW YORK, 14 March 1991, *Sympatica* (oil/synthetic resin, 18 x 24 ins / 45.9 x 61 cm) USD 9,900.

KANN, Léon

French, 19th - 20th century.

Born 19th century, in Damboch.

Sculptor.

Léon Kann became a member of the Société des Artistes Français in 1904. He received a commendation in 1907 and a bronze medal in 1908.

KANNEGIESSER, Friedrich August

German, 19th century.

Born 16 May 1800, in Dresden.

Draughtsman.

Kannegiesser did views of monuments and landscapes.

KANNEMAES, A. G.

Painter. Seascapes.

A.G. Kannemaes is listed by Florence Levy.

AUCTION RECORDS:

NEW YORK, 12-13 March 1903, *Seascape*, USD 150.

KANNEMANS, Christian Cornelis

Dutch, 19th century.

Born 13 July 1812, in Breda; died 1884.

Painter. Seascapes.

Christian Kannemans was a pupil of J.-B. Frederiks.

AUCTION RECORDS:

PARIS, 16 Feb 1927, *Return to Port before the Storm*, FRF 1,450. DORDRECHT, 25 Nov 1969, *River Landscape*, NLG 4,600. COLOGNE, 22 Oct 1971, *Seascape*, DEM 8,500. PARIS, 29 March 1973, *Boats in Stormy Weather*, FRF 16,000. BRUSSELS, 26 March 1974, *Seascape*, BEF 320,000. NEW YORK, 15 Oct 1976, *Fishing Boats at Sea* (oil on panel, 12 x 17 1/2 ins / 30.5 x 44.5 cm) USD 800. LONDON, 22 July 1977, *Sailing Ships in Stormy Weather at Night* (1854, oil on canvas, 47 x 63 1/2 ins / 119.3 x 161.3 cm) GBP 2,800. COLOGNE, 19 Oct 1979, *Seascape* (1857, oil on panel, 13 x 17 1/2 ins / 33 x 44.5 cm) DEM 28,000. LONDON, 5 June 1985, *Dismasted Boat* (1849, oil on canvas, 35 x 50 3/4 ins / 89 x 129 cm) GBP 1,600. PARIS, 21 April 1988, *Seascape* (1847, oil on panel, 22 3/4 x 32 1/4 ins / 58 x 82 cm) FRF 30,000. AMSTERDAM, 30 Aug 1988, *Commercial Port with a Two-master and Other Vessels* (oil on panel, 20 3/4 x 28 ins / 53 x 71 cm) NLG 13,225. AMSTERDAM, 28 Feb 1989, *Two-master and Other Vessels in an Estuary on Calm Seas* (1852, oil on panel, 16 1/2 x 22 1/2 ins / 42 x 57 cm) NLG 5,750. AMSTERDAM, 2 May 1990, *Fishermen Preparing their Nets near Boats along a Jetty at Low Tide* (1845, oil on panel, 15 1/4 x 16 1/4 ins / 39 x 41 cm) NLG 3,450. AMSTERDAM, 5-6 Nov 1991, *River Landscape with Sailing Boats* (oil on panel, 23 1/2 x 34 1/2 ins / 59.5 x 87.5 cm) NLG 12,650. AMSTERDAM, 14-15 April 1992, *Sailing Vessels in a Sudden Squall* (1850, oil on canvas, 27 1/2 x 38 1/2 ins / 70 x 98 cm) NLG 11,500. AMSTERDAM, 21 April 1994, *Pilot Boat Nearing a Boat in Rough Seas* (oil on panel, 21 1/4 x 29 1/2 ins / 54 x 75 cm) NLG 28,750. AMSTERDAM, 11 April 1995, *Sailing Offshore from a Town* (1848, oil on panel, 23 1/2 x 32 1/4 ins / 59.5 x 82 cm) NLG 14,160. AMSTERDAM, 16 April 1996, *Sailors in Distress* (oil on canvas, 35 1/2 x 51 1/4 ins / 90 x 130 cm) NLG 17,700. AMSTERDAM, 19-20 Feb 1997, *Ship in Distress on a Rocky Coast* (1856, oil on panel, 13 1/4 x 17 1/2 ins / 33.5 x 44.5 cm) NLG 4,612. PARIS, 29 Nov 2000, *Seascape* (1881, oil on panel, 20 x 28 ins / 50 x 70 cm) FRF 36,000. PARIS, 29 Nov 2000, *Boats at Low Tide* (1881, oil on panel, 20 x 28 ins / 50 x 70 cm) FRF 46,000. AMSTERDAM, 23 April 2001, *Sailing Vessels on a Choppy Sea* (1857, oil on canvas, 26 x 35 ins / 66 x 89 cm) NLG 14,000. BISHOPS STORTFORD, 23 Oct 2001, *Sailing Ships off the Dutch Coast* (oil on panel, 8 x 12 ins / 20 x 30 cm) GBP 2,200. AMSTERDAM, 22 Oct 2002, *Shipping off the Coast* (oil on canvas, 22 x 29 ins / 57 x 74 cm) EUR 9,000. LONDON, 16 Dec 2002, *Shipping off the Coast* (1847, oil on canvas, 36 x 49 ins / 92 x 124 cm) GBP 5,000. AMSTERDAM, 29 April 2003, *Tall Ship on Choppy Water by a Lighthouse* (1856, oil on panel, 13 x 17 ins / 33 x 44 cm) EUR 7,000. AMSTERDAM, 20 Oct 2003, *Ships in a Strong Breeze. Ships on a Calm Sea* (oil on panel, a pair, 24 x 33 ins / 60 x 85 cm) EUR 16,000. AMSTERDAM, 21 April 2004, *Two-master Approaching a Harbour on Choppy Waters* (1850, oil on panel, 22 x 30 ins / 55 x 75 cm) EUR 7,000.

KANNENGIESSER, Georg

German, 19th century.

Born 1814, in Neustrelitz; died 27 April 1900, in Neustrelitz.

Painter. History painting, landscapes.

Kannengiesser was a pupil of Ternitre and Blechen at the academy in Berlin, then of Sohn at the academy in Düsseldorf. He set off for Italy in 1842 and worked in Rome, Naples, Sicily and Greece for four years. Subsequently he returned to Germany and settled in Berlin. He exhibited there and in Paris (1855, Exposition Universelle). The church in Friedland has an *Ecce Homo* by him.

KANNING, David Martin

German, 19th century.

Born 31 May 1806, in Hamburg; died 18 October 1884.

Lithographer.

Kanning produced a large number of views of the city of Hamburg.

KANNO, Seiko

Japanese, 20th century.

Born 1933, in Sendai; died 1988.

Painter.

Gutai group.

Seiko Kanno graduated in Fine Arts from Fukushima University. In the 1960s she belonged to the Association of Abstract Arts. She painted geometric abstract works based on patterns of lines. She took her inspiration from poetry, music, philosophy and science.

Seiko Kanno first exhibited with the Gutai group in 1965 and exhibited regularly in group shows in Japan. Her work also appeared in *Japan Contemporary Art Exhibition* (1971) and *Japanese Art Today* at the Museum of Contemporary

Art in Montreal (1975). A retrospective was held of her work at the Nishinomiya City Art Gallery in 1989.

KANO, Eitoku, real name: Kano Tachinobu Kano, popular name: Kumagoro, artist names: Eitoku, Seitsusai
Japanese, 19th century.
Born 1841; died 1891.
Active in Tokyo.
Painter.
Kano School.

Kano Eitoku was the son of Kano Isen (1775-1828). He was a member of the Art Committee of the Imperial Household.

BIBLIOGRAPHY:
Fahr-Becker, Gabriele (ed.), *The Art of East Asia, Volume 2*, Konemann, Cologne, 1998.

KANO, Furunobu, popular name: Shozaburo, artist names: Eisen, Eisen-in
Japanese, 18th century.
Born 1696; died 1731.
Painter.
Kano School.

Kano Eisen was the son of Kano Chikanobu and the fourth generation of the Kobichiko line of the Kano school. He lived and worked in Edo (now Tokyo).

KANÔ, Ichio, real name: Shigenobu Jugo, popular name: Kyuzo, artist name: Ichio
Japanese, 16th - 17th century.
Born 1550; died 1617.
Painter.
Kano School.

Kanô Ichio lived in Odawara and worked in the service of Lord Hojo.

KANO, Isen, real name: Kano Eishin, artist names: Isen, Genshosai
Japanese, 19th century.
Born 1775; died 1828.
Painter.
Kano School.

Kano Isen was the son of Kano Korenobu and the sixth generation of the Kobichiko line of the Kano school. He lived and worked in Edo (now Tokyo).

KANO, Koi, family name Ogawa; given names Sasanobu, Churi; monk's name Shimpo; popular names Saemon, Yahei, Yazaemon
Japanese, 17th century.
Born 1569 or 1564; died 1636.
Painter.
Kano School.

Kano Koi was trained by his father Kano Mitsunobu (1565-1608). He worked in his father's studio, then that of his brother Sadanobu (1597-1623).

AUCTION RECORDS:
NEW YORK, 16 Oct 1990, *Monkeys Trying to Seize the Moon* (a pair of hanging scrolls, each 50 1/2 x 20 3/4 ins / 128.3 x 53 cm) USD 14,300.

KANO, Minoru
Japanese, 20th century.
Born 25 April 1930, in Tokyo.
Active in France since 1957.
Sculptor.

In 1957, after studying classical art under Kikouchi at Tokyo National University of Fine Arts and Music (1949-55), Kano Minoru was awarded a French government scholarship. This enabled him to go to Paris, where he worked at the École des Beaux-Arts and the Académie de la Grande Chaumière. He had already won the Young Sculptor's Prize at the 1954 Shinseisaku exhibition in Tokyo and the 1955 Spring Salon prize (the Spring Salon is an event organised by the French Embassy in Tokyo). Since 1977 he has taught part-time at the Université St-Charles.

At first influenced by the classics and Romanesque sculpture (it is said that he went to Paris to make a copy of Gislebertus d'Autun's *Eve*), in the 1960s he turned towards abstraction. After working in plaster, bronze and stone, he switched to using wood, metals and especially synthetic resins, in which he mixes metal powder, and which lend themselves to flexible, minutely-detailed modelling. He would then compress quantities of the matter to obtain rounded volumes of great density that seemed organic, as if pulsing with some inner force. In the early 1980s his work became more baroque.

Kano has exhibited at the major Paris salons (the Salon de Mai, Salon des Réalités Nouvelles, Salon de la Jeune Sculpture, Salon des Grands et Jeunes d'Aujourd'hui, Salon Comparaisons) since 1962, as well as at the 1965 Paris Biennale and the 1967 Tokyo Biennale. He has also had various solo exhibitions: 1962, Évreux Museum; 1966, galerie Grand-Cerf, Évreux; 1966, Maison des beaux-arts, Paris; 1968, Galerie expérimentale d'art, Paris; 1981, the cultural centres in Noisy-le-Sec and Noisy-le-Grand.

BIBLIOGRAPHY:
Tavernier, Catherine, *20 ans de sculptures Kano*, exhibition catalogue, Noisy-le-Sec, 1983.

MUSEUMS AND GALLERIES:
KAMAKURA (MMA) - PARIS (MNAM-CCI).

AUCTION RECORDS:
PARIS, 1 June 1973, *Sculpture No. 182* (laminated powdered bronze faced with polished brass) FRF 11,500.

KANO, Mitsuo
Japanese, 20th century.
Born 1933, in Tokyo.
Print artist, painter, illustrator.

Kano Mitsuo has no formal artistic training. While still young he developed an interest in poetry, especially French poetry, the work of Lautréamont, Rimbaud and Sade. At the same time, working as an assistant to a botanist, he became fascinated with the study of microbiomorphology and macro-organisms. His talent was discovered by the surrealist poet Shuzo Takiguchi.

Kano has illustrated translations of the works of his favourite French poets, while his study of micro-organisms led him to a style of copper engraving that shows the influence of Max Ernst. Gradually he abandoned drawing his imaginary yet precise forms in favour of applying the acid direct to the copper or zinc, producing biomorphic images that resemble a sort of primordial representation of clouds, fragments of bone, or shapes of flowers. He himself has said that his engravings of this period evoked the poetry of Rimbaud: 'Oh concealed precious stones, flowers intent on gazing.' In his 1960s series entitled *Mirrors*, he demonstrated and exhibited plates eaten away by acid to evoke frozen images of a chaotic planet. With Masuo Ikeda, Kano is one of the most visible print artists of his generation, appreciated for the subtlety of the rhythms which give life to the space of his floating, dreamlike, strangely evocative forms. The image seems to be that of an organic movement which the artist has attempted to capture and which, like every living organism, is constantly moving and evolving, engendering other forms and other images. As Kano has himself said of his art, it is 'engraving in action'.

He has taken part in many international group exhibitions: from 1957, the São Paulo Biennale; from 1959, the Tokyo International Print Biennale, where, in 1962, he won the National Museum of Modern Art Prize; and from 1959, the Ljubljana International Print Biennale. In 1961 and 1965, he won the Award of Excellence at the Japan International Art Exhibition. He had his first solo exhibition in Tokyo in 1956.

KANO, Sansetsu, family name: Chiga, given name: Mitsuie, popular name: Heishiro, court name: Nuido no suke, artist names: Sansetsu, Jasokuken, Shohaku Sanjin, Togenshi
Japanese, 17th century.
Born 1589, in Hizen; died 1651, in Kyoto.
Painter.
Kano School.
Sansetsu was a disciple of his adoptive father Kano Sanraku (1559-1635) and succeeded him as the head of the Kano school in Kyoto. Together they worked on mural paintings for the Tenkyu-in sanctuary of the Myoshin-ji in Kyoto from 1631 to 1635. In 1647 Sansetsu made two panel paintings for the Tofuku-ji in Kyoto, for which he was granted the title hokkyo.

KANO, Tanbi, real name: Tanbi Moritaka, artist name: Tanbi
Japanese, 19th century.
Born 1840; died 1893.
Painter.
Kano Tanbi was the son of Kano Tan'en Morizane and a member of the Kajibashi line of the Kano school. He lived in Tokyo. Tanbi specialised in painting landscapes, flowers and birds in the Japanese style.

KANO, Tanshin Morimichi
Japanese, 18th - 19th century.
Born 1785; died 1835?.
Active at the end of the 18th and beginning of the 19th century.
Painter.
Kano School.
Tanshin Morimichi was the head of the Kajibashi line of the Kano School at the turn of the 19th century. He was the director of the official academy of the shogunate in Edo (now Tokyo).

KANO, Toshun
Japanese, 18th century.
Painter.
Kano School.
The name of several Kano school painters. The first, Kano Toshun Fukunobu (d. 1723), was the grandson of Tan'yu (1602-1674) and the son-in-law of Toun Masunobu (1625-1694). He was the second painter of the Surugadai line of the Kano school in Edo (now Tokyo). The second was Kano Toshun Yoshinobu (1747-1794), who painted screens. The third was Kano Toshun Hidenobu (late 19th century).

KANO, Yoshin, real name: Kano Yoshinobu, popular name: Shozaburo, artist names: Seisen-in, Kaishin-sai, Gyokusen
Japanese, 19th century.
Born 1796; died 1846.
Painter.
Kano School.
Kano Yoshin was the son and disciple of Kano Isen'in (1775-1828). He was the eighth generation of the Kobichiko branch of the Kano school in Edo (now Tokyo). In 1819 he was granted the title hogen and in 1834 that of hoin. On the death of his father he he became painter-in-residence for the shogunate.

KANO, Yoshinobu. See **EINO**

KANO EISHIN. See **KANO Isen**

KANO ENSHIN. See **HOGAI**

KANO GEN'YA. See **GEN'YA**

KANO HARUNOBU. See **TOEKI**

KANO HIDEYORI. See **TOEKI**

KANO HOGAI. See **HOGAI**

KANO ICHIAN. See **ICHIAN**

KANO KAZUNOBU. See **KAZUNOBU**

KANO KOSHIN. See **KANO Isen**

KANO KOYA. See **KOYA**

KANO KUNINOBU. See **EITOKU**

KANO MASANOBU. See **MASANOBU** and **SHOSEN'IN**

KANO MASUNOBU. See **TOUN**

KANO MINENOBU. See **MINENOBU**

KANO MITSUNOBU. See **MITSUNOBU**

KANO MITSUYORI. See **SANRAKU**

KANO MOTONOBU. See **MOTONOBU**

KANO MUNENOBU. See **MUNENOBU**

KANO NAONOBU. See **NAONOBU**

KANO SADANOBU. See **SADANOBU**

KANO SANRAKU. See **SANRAKU**

KANO SHOEI. See **SHOEI**

KANO SHOSEN'IN. See **SHOSEN'IN**

KANO SOSHU. See **SOSHU**

KANO SUENOBU. See **SOSHU**

KANO TAKANOBU. See **TAKANOBU**

KANO TATSUNOBU. See **SOSHU**

KANO TOEKI. See **TOEKI**

KANO TOSHUN. See **TOSHUN**

KANO TOUN. See **TOUN**

KANO YOSHINOBU. See **EINO**

KANO YUKINOBU. See **YUKINOBU**

KANOFF, Alexandre
Painter.
Alexandre Kanoff is listed in the annual price-lists.
AUCTION RECORDS:
PARIS, July 1946, *Hunt in Sologne*, FRF 4,200.

KANOKOGI, Takeshiro
Japanese, 19th - 20th century.
Born 1874, in Okayama Prefecture; died 1941.
Painter.
Kanokogi Takeshiro studied with the Osaka painters Matsubata Sangoro and then Koyama Shotaro. He went to Paris three times, first when he was 26, spending a total of seven years in the city, during which time he studied with Jean-Paul Laurens and Emile René Ménard at the Académie Julian. On his return to Japan, he exhibited his work at the Bunten and Teiten Salons (Imperial Exhibition) and later became a member of the jury. In 1906, he founded his own school in Tokyo, the Kansai Bijutsu-in (Kansai Art School), which helped to introduce Western art into Japan. He belonged to the Taiheiyo Gakai (Pacific Art Society). Kanokogi's works are to be found in museums throughout Japan. His style was influenced by French classicism.
AUCTION RECORDS:
NEW YORK, 29 March 1990, *Boating on a Lake* (watercolour on paper, 18 1/4 x 14 ins / 46.5 x 35.6 cm) USD 12,100. NEW YORK, 16 Oct 1990, *Farmyard with Horse and Cart* (watercolour on paper, 12 1/2 x 19 ins / 31.6 x 48.2 cm) USD 6,600.

KANOLDT, Alexander
German, 20th century.
Born 29 September 1881, in Karlsruhe; died 1939, in Berlin.

Painter (gouache), lithographer. Figure compositions, still-lifes, flowers, landscapes.
Neue Sachlichkeit (New Objectivity).
New Artists' Association of Munich.

Alexander Kanoldt was the son of Edmund Kanoldt. After being taught by his father, a painter in the academic tradition, he entered the Akademie der Bildenden Künste in Karlsruhe in 1899. In around 1906, an exhibition took place in Karlsruhe, which included works by Cézanne and Seurat, artists who were to influence Kanoldt's subsequent artistic development greatly. In 1908, Kanoldt went to Munich to complete his studies, and there he became a member of the Neue Künstlervereinigung (New Artists' Association) in 1909, and later its secretary. He played an active role in the association, alongside Kandinsky and Jawlensky, until its dissolution in 1911. In 1912, he was one of the founders of the New Munich Secession, which he left in 1920.

Until 1914, Kanoldt had travelled widely in Europe, visiting Italy, England, France and Switzerland. He was then mobilised for the duration of the war. After returning to Munich in 1919, he became an active member from 1924 to 1930 of the small Neue Sachlichkeit (New Objectivity) group, which was centred around Otto Dix and George Grosz. He visited Italy in 1924 and in 1925 was appointed professor at the Wroclaw Academy, though he moved from there in 1932 to the Akademie der Künste in Berlin, where he subsequently became director. He had many pupils, some of whom showed signs of his influence in the years following the war.

Like his father, Kanoldt showed a marked predilection for big historical or heroic compositions. His work developed through several periods it was influenced by Post-Impressionism, Cézanne, Neo-Impressionism and Expressionism. His acquaintance with the paintings of Cézanne and Seurat had led him to synthesise detailed forms in favour of structured composition and to adopt a palette of quite bright colours that was sometimes similar to that used by the Fauves. Nevertheless, he was able to reconcile this progressive tendency with the tradition of monumental symbolism inherited from Hans von Marées and Böcklin, to which he remained attached. From 1909 to 1911, he was temporarily susceptible to the innovations of Kandinsky and Jawlensky. In his New Objectivity period, Kanoldt painted a few figures, but mainly focused on still-lifes, often composed of stiff plants, rubber and cactus, inert objects, vases and scarves, which he painted according to the aesthetics of Magic Realism. During his stay in Italy in 1924, he became fascinated by the city of Olevano and painted a series of schematic, almost unreal views of it.

Because of the desire for realistic objectivity which became apparent in his paintings from his New Objectivity period onwards, Kanoldt influenced the Italian painters of the Valori Plastici (Plastic Values) group. After 1930, he painted Mediterranean landscapes with an increased concern towards space and perspective. His paintings from the Nazi period, during which he remained in Germany, express feelings of despair and in 1937, despite his endeavours to maintain discretion, some of his works were declared to be 'degenerate art'.

In 1966, Kanoldt's work featured in the important exhibition *Le Fauvisme français et les débuts de l'Expressionisme allemand* (*French Fauvism and the Beginnings of German Expressionism*) at the Musée National d'Art Moderne in Paris.

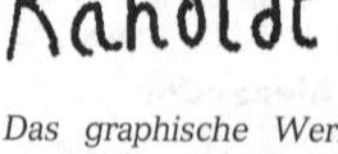

Bibliography:

Ammann, Adith, *Das graphische Werk von Alexander Kanoldt*, exhibition catalogue, Staatliche Kunsthalle, Karlsruhe, 1963. Koch, Michael, *Alexander Kanoldt: 1881-1939, GeMälde, Zeichnungen, Lithographien*, travelling exhibition catalogue, Museum für Neue Kunst, Freiburg im Breisgau, 1987. Jacob-Friesen, Holger, *Alexander Kanoldt: Graphik und Malerei aus dem Besitz der Staatlichen Kunsthalle Karlsruhe*, exhibition catalogue, Staatliche Kunsthalle, Karlsruhe, 2000.

Museums and Galleries:

Berlin (Berlinische Gal.): *Still-life III with Amaryllis* (1926) - Karlsruhe: including all lithographs from 1921 onwards - Stuttgart (Staatsgal.): *Still-life with Guitar* (1926).

Auction records:

Cologne, 4 Dec 1969, *Still-life*, DEM 5,500. Hamburg, 15 June 1973, *Cactus*, DEM 8,600. Heidelberg, 8 Feb 1974, *Still-life*, DEM 8,600. Cologne, 3 Dec 1976, *Still-life* (1922, oil on canvas, 19 3/4 x 15 3/4 ins / 50 x 40 cm) DEM 22,000. Cologne, 3 Dec 1977, *Still-life I* (1924, oil on canvas, 35 3/4 x 28 ins / 91 x 71 cm) DEM 22,000. Munich, 30 Nov 1979, *Bunch of Flowers* (c. 1910, oil on card, 14 1/4 x 10 1/2 ins / 36 x 26.5 cm) DEM 8,000. Munich, 27 Nov 1981, *Daniel I* (oil on paper, 14 1/4 x 19 1/4 ins / 36.5 x 49 cm) DEM 13,500. London, 7 Dec 1983, *Still-life with Cactus* (1920, oil on canvas, 16 1/4 x 13 1/4 ins / 41.3 x 33.5 cm) GBP 5,000. Cologne, 7 Dec 1984, *Still-life* (1922, lithograph/paper, 20 1/2 x 16 1/2 ins / 52.2 x 41.7 cm) DEM 3,200. Amsterdam, 11 Nov 1985, *View of a Town* (1920, oil on canvas, 32 x 25 3/4 ins / 81.5 x 65.5 cm) NLG 14,000. Heidelberg, 14 Oct 1988, *Arums Against a Red Background* (gouache, 27 1/4 x 20 1/4 ins / 69 x 51.7 cm) DEM 7,600. Munich, 31 May 1990, *Still-life* (oil on card, 21 1/2 x 18 ins / 54.5 x 46 cm) DEM 41,800. Munich, 26 May 1992, *Olevano VI* (1925, lithograph, 7 x 9 3/4 ins / 17.5 x 25 cm) DEM 2,415. Berlin, 27 Nov 1992, *Caravans* (1919, oil on canvas, 16 1/4 x 13 ins / 41 x 33 cm) DEM 70,060. Heidelberg, 3 April 1993, *Village in Swabia* (1927, lithograph, 9 1/4 x 12 1/4 ins / 23.8 x 31.3 cm) DEM 1,300. Heidelberg, 8 April 1995, *Still-life with Jugs* (1922, lithograph, 15 3/4 x 12 1/2 ins / 39.9 x 31.6 cm) DEM 4,200. Amsterdam, 18 June 1997, *City by Night* (oil on canvas, 23 1/2 x 31 1/2 ins / 60 x 80 cm) NLG 32,289. New York, 11 May 1999, *Still-life* (1924, oil on canvas, 18 x 29 ins / 45 x 73 cm) USD 18,000. Munich, 20 Nov 1999, *Out of the Tyrol* (1912, oil on board, 20 x 18 ins / 52 x 45 cm) DEM 45,000. Berlin, 26 May 2000, *Still-life with Plants and Apple* (oil on canvas, 21 x 17 ins / 53 x 44 cm) DEM 80,000. Berlin, 24 Nov 2000, *Still-life VIII* (1919, oil on canvas, 22 x 16 ins / 55 x 40 cm) DEM 40,000. Munich, 1 Dec 2001, *Winter Landscape* (watercolour, 19 x 25 ins / 47 x 63 cm) DEM 5,000. Cologne, 4 Dec 2001, *Still-life II* (1922, oil on canvas, 36 x 28 ins / 91 x 70 cm) DEM 260,000. Cologne, 4 June 2002, *Still-life* (1930, oil on canvas, 31 x 24 ins / 80 x 61 cm) EUR 63,000. London, 9 Oct 2002, *Still-life VII* (1926, oil on canvas, 35 x 28 ins / 90 x 70 cm) GBP 26,000. Berlin, 26 April 2003, *Chiemsee Landscape in Winter* (watercolour, 19 x 24 ins / 47 x 62 cm) EUR 1,800. Hamburg, 26 March 2004, *Winter Landscape in Chiemsee* (watercolour, 19 x 24 ins / 47 x 62 cm) EUR 4,500. Berlin, 15 May 2004, *Bridge in Besigheim* (gouache on paper on board, 10 x 17 ins / 26 x 42 cm) EUR 2,800.

KANOLDT, Edmund or Edmund Friedrich

German, 19th century.
Born 13 March 1839, in Grossrudestedt, in 1845 according to some sources; died 27 June 1904, in Bad Nauheim.
Painter. Mythological subjects, genre scenes, landscapes with figures, mountainscapes, landscapes.

Kanoldt was taught by Preller at the school of fine arts in Weimar. From 1869 to 1872, he worked in Italy. In 1876, he took up an appointment in Karlsruhe. He exhibited in Berlin, Weimar, Dresden and Munich.

Bibliography:

Müller-Scherf, Angelika, *Edmund Kanoldt: Leben und Werk*, Centaurus-Verlagsgesellschaft, Pfaffenweiler, 1992.

Museums and Galleries:
Weimar: *Ulysses Hunting.*
Auction records:
Frankfurt am Main, 12 Dec 1892, *Antigone,* FRF 600. Cologne, 6 June 1973, *The Gardens of the Villa d'Este,* DEM 2,600. Lucerne, 30 May 1979, *Mountain Landscape* (oil on canvas, 32 1/4 x 24 1/2 ins / 82 x 62 cm) CHF 2,600. Heidelberg, 11 April 1981, *The Garden of the Villa d'Este* (1891) DEM 3,500. Munich, 2 July 1986, *Iphigenia* (oil on canvas, 35 1/2 x 52 3/4 ins / 90 x 134 cm) DEM 13,000. Amsterdam, 30 Oct 1990, *Oaks during a Storm* (1868, oil on canvas, 45 1/4 x 32 1/4 ins / 115 x 82 cm) NLG 13,225. London, 20 March 1992, *Sappho in the Mountains of Leucas on Lesbos* (1879, oil on canvas, 53 3/4 x 39 3/4 ins / 136.5 x 101 cm) GBP 8,800. Munich, 21 June 1994, *Nightfall (Poem by Schiller)* (oil on canvas, 9 x 22 ins / 23 x 56 cm) DEM 5,750. Vienna, 29-30 Oct 1996, *Monk and Rider on a Mountain Path* (1877, oil on canvas, 53 3/4 x 38 3/4 ins / 136.5 x 98.5 cm) ATS 126,500. Munich, 2 Dec 1997, *Panorama of Olevano* (oil on card, 8 x 12 1/2 ins / 20.5 x 31.5 cm) DEM 3,360. Heidelberg, 14 April 2000, *Lady by Swan Pond* (oil on panel, 18 x 10 ins / 46 x 26 cm) DEM 6,400. Heidelberg, 6 April 2001, *Hero* (oil on canvas, 74 x 87 ins / 188 x 220 cm) DEM 22,000. Heidelberg, 12 Oct 2001, *Psyche Surveying Cupid's Palace* (oil on canvas, 12 x 9 ins / 31 x 23 cm) DEM 5,000. Konigstein, 24 May 2002, *Sea Cliffs, Capri* (oil on canvas/board, 15 x 21 ins / 38 x 53 cm) EUR 6,500. Freiburg, 1 April 2004, *Iphigenia as Priestess of Artemis* (oil on canvas, 51 x 37 ins / 129 x 95 cm) EUR 4,800.

KANOVITZ, Howard
American, 20th century.
Born 1929, in Fall River (Massachusetts).
Painter, draughtsman.

Howard Kanovitz studied until 1949 at Providence College, then at the Rhode Island School of Design, and under Franz Kline in New York. In the late 1950s he travelled around Europe. Teaching at Brooklyn College in the early 1960s, he split his time between New York and Cologne. His early works, inspired by Franz Kline, lean towards Abstract Expressionism. In 1963, his father's death brought Kanovitz face to face with the harsh realities around him, reinforced by the experience of dealing with family photos, now the translation of past events. This had a major impact on his artistic development. From 1965, he worked from photographic documents, first recreating scenes which epitomised the art milieu, such as private views. Then he drew material from the written press to illustrate the American way of life, and finally documented his own very ordinary private life, working from his own snapshots.

Kanovitz' Hyperrealism differs significantly from the traditional urban American pictures it is often associated with. He is much more concerned with mood than with a retraced reality. What he looks for in his starting point image is the moment when objects somehow relate to each other, no matter how absurdly, seeking to account for it 'with logic and common sense'. He does not think that the preliminary photographic data is a given, but responds to elements of the documents which he isolates for further treatment, alongside drawings, other pictures, posters, projection slides, any number of representational techniques which highlight the complexity of pictorial illusion. His work often features architectural elements, doorways and window frames, taken from their context. Likewise, his figures are left to stand against neutral, monochrome backgrounds, exposing their purely representational value whilst the very real banality of their pursuit is plain for all to see.

Since 1969, Kanovitz has taken part in international collective exhibitions concerned with Hyperrealism and Photorealism: in 1969 *Painting from the photo* in New York, *Radical Realism* in Chicago, Documenta V in Kassel, Humlebaek, Denmark, *Fotorealismus* (*Photorealism*) in a number of German cities, and *Kunst aus Fotographie* in Hanover. He has shown his works in solo exhibitions, starting in New York in 1966 at the Jewish Museum.

Bibliography:
Chase, Linda, *Les Hyperréalistes américains,* Éd. Filipacchi, Paris, 1973. Salzmann, Siegfried, *Howard Kanovitz,* exhibition catalogue, Wilhelm-Lehmbruck-Museum, Duisburg, 1974 (text in German and English). *Howard Kanovitz: Works of the 1980s,* exhibition catalogue, Marlborough Gallery, New York, 1988. *Howard Kanovitz: Works of the Sea,* exhibition catalogue, Marlborough Gallery, New York, 1990.
Museums and Galleries:
Aachen (Ludwig Forum für Internationale Kunst): *Lovers* (1965); *Painted Wall* (1968) - Cologne (Wallraf-Richartz Mus.): *Newspaper* (1973) - New York (Whitney Mus. of American Art): *New Yorkers I* (1965).
Auction records:
New York, 3 May 1994, *Elements of Prose* (1972, acrylic and varnish/canvas, 50 x 32 ins / 127 x 81.3 cm) USD 5,750. New York, 14 May 2004, *New Sky with Andre* (1972, liquitex, polymer and acrylic on canvas, 80 x 59 ins / 203 x 151 cm) USD 6,000.

KANT, Marie
German, 20th century.
Born 1942.
Painter (gouache), watercolourist. Stage costumes.

Marie Kant started in haute couture and moved into designing costumes for the theatre. She has worked on many stage and television productions in both France and Germany, most notably Ludwig Thoma's *Moral* at the Kiel theatre in 1969, *La Grande Oreille* (*The Big Ear*) at the Opéra du Rhin in 1972 and Jean Giraudoux's *La Folle de Chaillot* (*The Madwoman of Chaillot*) at the Théâtre de l'Athénée in Paris in 1975.

KANTAN NO KYO. See **FUYO**

KANTCHALOVSKI
Russian, 20th century.
Painter.

Kantchalovski was regarded as a disciple of Cézanne. He remained in Russia after the 1917 Revolution.

KANTEI, or Gantei, popular name: Nara Hogen, monk's name: Kantei
Japanese, 15th - 16th century.
Active during the second half of the 15th century.
Painter.

Kantei was a Zen monk-painter who painted figures and landscapes in different styles that clearly derive from Chinese originals, including those of Shubun and Sesshu.
Bibliography:
Fahr-Becker, Gabriele (ed.), *The Art of East Asia, Volume 2,* Konemann, Cologne, 1998 (mentioned briefly).

KANTER, Michel
French, 20th century.
Born 11 December 1940, in Bordeaux.
Sculptor.

Michel Kanter plasticises pillows, retaining the imprint of the head that has rested on them. He has exhibited mainly in Paris at the Salon de Mai and at group exhibitions held by l'ARC (Art, Recherche, Confrontation) led by Pierre Gaudibert at the Musée d'Art Moderne de la Ville de Paris. He has shown work at exhibitions brought together by Pierre Restany similar in style to those of the New Realists, whose common characteristic was a process of appropriation of reality.

KANTOR, Maxim
Russian, 20th - 21st century.
Born 1957, in Moscow.
Painter, graphic designer. Figures.

Maxim Kantor studied at the polygraphic institute in Moscow. He developed an Expressionist technique, using an exaggerated style of drawing and clashing colours. His prime theme is the sufferings of long-stay patients in psychiatric hospitals, a theme which he sees as a metaphor for the degradation of the human condition in the face of the absurdity of the modern world. He has exhibited frequently in Russia, the USA, Japan and Germany. He exhibited at the Galerie Julia Tocaier in Paris in 1989 and at the Bochum Museum in 1992.

BIBLIOGRAPHY:
Maxim Kantor, exhibition catalogue, Bochum (DEU), 1992.

KANTOR, Morris

Russian, 20th century.
Born 1896; died 1974.
Active in the USA.
Painter. Figures, interiors with figures, landscapes, seascapes. Patterns (fabrics).

A pupil of Homer Boss, Morris Kandor painted fabric designs in his youth to earn a living, and in 1926 he designed a fabric for a famous *Evening Coat* produced by the couturière Valentina, who dressed American high society and the cinema stars of the 1920s. His paintings displayed an awareness of modern European trends.

In 1931 he won first prize and the Logan medal at the Chicago Art Institute. He exhibited at the international salons organised by the Carnegie Foundation in Pittsburgh.

AUCTION RECORDS:
NEW YORK, 9 Sept 1993, *Irridescent Day* (oil on canvas, 28 x 22 ins / 71.1 x 55.9 cm) USD 748. NEW YORK, 28 Sept 1995, *Figure in an Armchair* (1924, oil on canvas, 35 x 27 1/2 ins / 88.9 x 69.9 cm) USD 4,600. NEW YORK, 25 March 1997, *On the Beach* (1938, oil on canvas, 38 3/4 x 31 ins / 98.7 x 78.7 cm) USD 3,565.

KANTOR, Tadeusz

Polish, 20th century.
Born 1915, in Wielopole; died 1990, in Cracow.
Happenings artist, environmental artist, collage artist, painter (gouache), draughtsman.
Conceptual Art.
Cracow Group.

Tadeusz Kantor lived and worked in Cracow. He received his first artistic training at the academy of fine arts in Cracow until 1939. In 1947, in association with artists who had taken part in the underground theatre activities he had organised during the German occupation of Poland, he founded the Modern Artists Club, which lasted until 1949, and the Enthusiasts of Modern Art Association. From 1948 he was one of the organisers of the first modern art exhibition in Cracow. He set up the *Cricot 2* theatre in 1955-1956, a reference to the pre-war *Cricot*. Kantor stated that 'at that time, I was engaged in real painting with canvases, colours, brushes, but I always wanted to quit the space dictated by the canvas - and get involved in life...For me, it's all the same thing: the surface of the picture, theatrical reality, the outside world. I make paintings, I make theatre. I also write too. It's all the same thing, one single whole'. In 1954 he visited Paris, and discovered Abstract trends.

After 1968 his *Cricot 2* theatre took on an international dimension. He almost exclusively put on pieces written by Stanislaw Ignacy Witkiewicz. His stage sets, built from the principle he defined as 'Zero Theatre', clearly showed the anticipatory values of Witkiewicz's plays by integrating situations and 'ready made' objects, by conferring an autonomous function on costume, and by operating a reversal of the rhythmic and modulated values of the text.

In his theatre activities, which he was virtually solely responsible for creating, sometimes even writing the script, in addition to the action, the stage settings, he also designed the props, stage sets and the costumes. As a three-dimensional artist, up until around 1950, and in order to get around the censorship exerted by the Stalinist era and Socialist-Realism, he produced metaphorical paintings which came more and more to resemble Surrealism. In 1957, the artists' colony clustered around Maria Jaréma, Jonasz Stern, revived the association known as the Cracow Group. Between his visit to Paris in 1954 and 1961 he completed strongly gestural, informal abstract paintings. He gave this up in the 1960s, however, and referring back to Gombrowicz and Witkiewicz, Kantor stated that he was engaged in a permanent battle against form (even when informal), authentic creation having 'to directly contain life impulses'. In 1963 he was the first to create an 'environment' at the time of an 'anti-exhibition' or a 'people's exhibition' at the Krysatofory gallery in Cracow. Kantor had assembled 937 objects, all carefully listed, associated with *Cricot 2* and with his other activities, including sketches, texts, and costumes. After this exhibition he devoted most of his time to 'assemblages' which incorporated items of clothing, objects, the 'emballages' of paintings, and people, as he had already done in his earlier theatrical achievements. His '*Emballage*' *Manifesto* was published in Switzerland in 1964. From 1965 he organised 'happenings' in several locations including Warsaw, Cracow, a *Maritime Panoramic Happening* in Osiek, near Koszalin, Basel and Nuremberg. He labelled some of these *Cricotages* so as to stress the presence of certain factors that had previously been seen in his stage sets. In the summer of 1968 he took part in the first Vela Luka symposium in Croatia, devoted to mosaics, and showed a chair that he covered from top to bottom in a mosaic of small stone cubes. A remarkable designer, he later produced a large number of designs and collages, enlivened with gouache, in a spirit approaching automatic Surrealist creation, yet always including a sarcastic dimension, denouncing the absurdity of the human condition with gallows humour.

After a break of several years Kantor began exhibiting his paintings again in 1955 in a number of major international exhibitions, including the Venice Biennale (1960); São Paulo Biennale (1967, winning a prize); and the Marzotto prize (1968, winning an award). Solo exhibitions from 1958 include: Stockholm, Paris, Düsseldorf, Göteborg, New York, Lausanne, Basel and in Baden-Baden with a show put on by the *Zero* theatre. In 1978 he won the Rembrandt prize. He then had two solo exhibitions of paintings, object drawings at the Galerie de France, Paris (1982) *Plus loin, rien* (*Further on, Nothing*) (1989). In 2001 the city hall in Brussels hosted a retrospective designed to present both sides of this artist: theatre, as illustrated by stage props and designs for his first production *Dead Class* (1975), and painting, with works spanning the period 1986 to 1990.

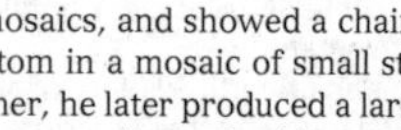

BIBLIOGRAPHY:
Peinture moderne polonaise - Sources et recherches, exhibition catalogue, Musée Galliera, Paris, 1969. Kantor, Tadeusz, *Métamorphoses*, Éd. du Chêne, Hachette, Paris, 1982. *L'Art moderne à Marseille. La collection du musée Cantini*, exhibition catalogue, Musée Cantini, Marseilles, 1988. Kantor, Tadeusz, *'Interview: L'art a remplacé la religion'* in *Le Figaro*, periodical, Paris, 1989. Banu, Georges (ed.), *Kantor, l'artiste à la fin du XXe siècle*, Actes Sud, Arles, 1990. Jedlinski, Jaromir, *Tadeusz Kantor 1915-1990: Leben im Werk*, exhibition catalogue, Kunsthalle, Verlag für moderne Kunst, Nürnberg, 1996.

Museums and Galleries:
Marseilles (Mus. Cantini): *Men* (1953, ink, gouache and collage); *Man Through the Window* (1980, gouache and collage).
Auction records:
Douai, 1 April 1990, *Characters on a Stage with a Geometric Background* (1962, varnished gouache, 8¾ x 11¾ ins / 22.2 x 29.9 cm) FRF 6,100. Paris, 20 May 1992, *Untitled* (1981, felt and pastel/paper, 9¼ x 6¾ ins / 23.5 x 17 cm) FRF 6,000. Paris, 4 Nov 1992, *Judas* (1979, felt pastel and collage/paper, 8¼ x 11 ins / 21 x 27 cm) FRF 5,000. Warsaw, 5 Oct 2000, *Untitled, Project* (mixed media, 16 x 20 ins / 40 x 50 cm) PLN 50,000. Warsaw, 19 Nov 2000, *Metamorphosis* (1949, ink, pencil and pastel, 8 x 12 ins / 21 x 30 cm) PLN 7,000. New York, 6 Feb 2002, *Wrapped Head* (1967, oil on canvas, 39 x 31 ins / 99 x 79 cm) USD 19,000. New York, 6 Feb 2002, *White Umbrella. Black Umbrella* (mixed media on wood on plexiglass, a pair, 53 x 46 ins / 135 x 117 cm) USD 24,000. Copenhagen, 7 Oct 2003, *Composition* (1962, oil on canvas, 28 x 34 ins / 70 x 87 cm) DKK 55,000. Warsaw, 16 Nov 2003, *Composition* (oil and gouache on board, 26 x 38 ins / 67 x 96 cm) EUR 7,500. Copenhagen, 29 March 2004, *Painting* (oil on canvas, 55 x 51 ins / 140 x 130 cm) DKK 90,000. Uppsala, 28 May 2004, *Postac* (1972, oil on canvas, 37 x 27 ins / 93 x 68 cm) SEK 100,000.

KANTOROWICZ, Serge

French, 20th century.
Born 1942, in Paris.
Painter, pastellist, lithographer, draughtsman. Scenes with figures.
Nouvelle Figuration.

Serge Kantorowicz studied at the École Estienne des Arts Graphiques in Paris from 1958 to 1961 and was a private pupil at the École des Beaux-Arts in Brussels in 1967. He portrays the human bestiary in its various forms with a lively and bright technique and with some allusion to Goya or other artists.

He has exhibited in collective and solo exhibitions since 1977, including: Amsterdam, 1977; Galerie Zodiaco, Madrid, 1977 and 1978; Galerie Krikhaar, Amsterdam, 1977 and 1983; Galerie Au Fond de la Cour, Paris, 1979; Galerie Nina Dausset, Paris, 1980 and 1981; Galerie Kutter, Luxembourg, 1981; Galerie Georges Fall, Paris, 1985 and 1988; Luxembourg, London, 1986. In 1990 the Galerie Carmen Cassé in Paris held a solo exhibition of his lithographs and drawings under the title *Chronique d'un Voyeur* (*Chronicle of a Voyeur*), and in 1992 the Centre d'Art et de Plaisanterie in Montbéliard showed a collection of his paintings, pastels and charcoal drawings, under the title *Les Nouveaux Caprices ou La Vie Privée des Animaux* (*New Whims or The Private Lives of Animals*). In 1995 the Galerie Carmen Cassé held another exhibition of his work called *Journal d'un Lithographe. De la Visitation à la Passion* (*Diary of a Lithograph. From the Visitation to the Passion*), and in 2002 the exhibition *Pages Arrachées au Journal de Victor Hugo* (*Pages Torn Out of Victor Hugo's Diary*), at the Hôtel d'Albret, Paris.

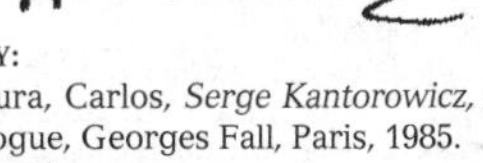

Bibliography:
Semprun-Maura, Carlos, *Serge Kantorowicz, peintures*, exhibition catalogue, Georges Fall, Paris, 1985.
Museums and Galleries:
Brussels (Prints Collection) - Cracow (Prints Coll) - Geneva - Luxembourg (Mus. national d'histoire et d'art) - Luxembourg (Prints Coll) - Paris (FMAC).

Auction records:
Paris, 29 May 1989, *Zig-zag Bar* (1989, 46 x 35 ins / 116 x 89 cm) FRF 24,000. Paris, 30 Oct 1991, *Souvenir* (mixed media/grey paper, 13¾ x 11 ins / 35 x 28 cm) FRF 3,800.

KANZ, C.

French, 19th century.
Born in Paris.
Miniaturist, enameller.

C. Kanz was a pupil of his father Carl Christian Kanz. He exhibited at the Salon betwenn 1835 and 1839 gaining a third class medal in 1839.

KANZ, Carl Christian

German, 18th - 19th century.
Born 1758, in Plauen (Saxony); died probably c. 1818.
Painter (including enamel).

Kanz was a pupil of Hesse and Kemly; he worked in Paris. A number of his paintings are preserved in St Petersburg.
Auction records:
Paris, 1874, *Portrait of a Young Girl* (enamel) FRF 400. Paris, 27-29 May 1929, *Young Woman in a Tall Wig Decorated with Ribbons* (miniature) FRF 5,700; *Young Woman with Her Hair Ringed with Pearls* (miniature) FRF 6,000. Paris, 28 Feb 1939, *Expressive heads* (two miniatures painted on enamel) FRF 1,150. Paris, 1 April 1949, *Portrait Presumed to be of Mme Roland*, FRF 26,000. Paris, 19 Dec 1949, *Young Woman with Blond Hair*, FRF 25,000. London, 22 Nov 1999, *Young Lady in a White Dress and Green Stole* (enamel on copper, miniature) GBP 2,000. London, 6 Nov 2000, *Lady in White Robes with One Breast Exposed* (1787, enamel, miniature, oval, h. 2ins / 6cm) GBP 1,050.

KAO

Japanese, 14th century.
Active 14th century.
Painter.

Kao was a Zen monk and early exponent of monochrome painting in Japan. Little is known about his life, but several important works bearing his stamp have been preserved. They reveal his mastery of brush and wash techniques.

KAO CH'ÊNG-MO. See **GAO CHENGMO**

KAO CH'I-FENG. See **GAO QIFENG**

KAO CH'I-P'EI. See **GAO QIPEI**

KAO CHE-K'I. See **GAO SHIQI**

KAO CHIEN. See **GAO JIAN**

KAO CHIEN-FU. See **GAO JIANFU**

KAO CHOU-TCH'ENG. See **GAO SHUCHENG**

KAO FENG-HAN. See **GAO FENGHAN**

KAO HIANG. See **GAO XIANG**

KAO HSIANG. See **GAO XIANG**

KAO JAN-HOUEI. See **GAO RANHUI**

KAO K'I-FENG. See **GAO QIFENG**

KAO K'I-P'EI. See **GAO QIPEI**

KAO K'O-KUNG. See **GAO KEGONG**

KAO K'O-MING. See **GAO KEMING**

KAO KIEN. See **GAO JIAN**

KAO KIEN-LOU. See **GAO JIANFU**

KAO LOUEN. See **GAO JIANFU**

KAO PIN. See **GAO BIN**

KAO SHIH-CH'I. See **GAO SHIQI**

KAO SHU-CH'ENG. See **GAO SHUCHENG**

KAO T'ING-LI. See **GAO TINGLI**

KAO TCH'ENG-MO. See **GAO CHENGMO**

KAO TS'EN. See **GAO CEN**

KAO TS'ENG-YUN. See **GAO CENGYUN**

KAO YANG. See **GAO YANG**

KAO YEN. See **GAO YAN**

KAO YU. See **GAO YU**

KAO-TSONG SONG. See **QIANLONG**

KAOL, Claude
French, 20th century.
Born 1941.
Sculptor. Figures.

Claude Kaol studied at the École des Beaux-Arts in St-Étienne in 1958 and then in Paris. After a long time working on materials, usually reinforced metal bars and glass fibre but also twisted, bent, kneaded or stroked wood, he creates figures, such as mature women and dancers. His coloured beings shoot off into the air. In 1977 he created stained glass windows and sculptures for the chapel of Pontoise Hospital.

He has exhibited regularly in collective exhibitions at the Salon d'Automne, Salon des Artistes Français and Salon des Indépendants in Paris since 1982. He has also exhibited in Paris galleries such as the Galerie Keramicos since 1982.

AUCTION RECORDS:
PARIS, 17 Nov 1991, *Little Bell* (epoxterre sculpture, h. 13 1/2 ins / 34.5 cm) FRF 3,500; *1st of May Androgyne* (epoxterre mix sculpture, h. 26 3/4 ins / 68 cm) FRF 18,000. PARIS, 4 April 1993, *First Day* (epoxterre sculpture, h. 26 1/2 ins / 67 cm) FRF 8,000. PARIS, 21 Nov 1993, *Stone* (mixed media sculpture, h. 11 ins / 28 cm) FRF 4,000. PARIS, 4 Oct 1994, *Gloomy Dreamer* (epoxterre sculpture, h. 19 3/4 ins / 50 cm) FRF 4,900.

KAPANDJI. See **CHEVALIER Roberte Jeanne Aimée**

KAPELLER
French, 18th century.
Born 18th century, in Marseilles.
Painter. Landscapes, seascapes, flowers.

Kapeller was one of the founders of the academy in Marseilles. He was its director in 1777. He was also a surveyor.

AUCTION RECORDS:
PARIS, 3 March 1926, *Fishing Port* (black chalk) FRF 1,600.

KAPELLER, Josef Anton, the Elder
Austrian, 18th century.
Died 30 July 1763, in Imst.
Active in Imst.
Painter.

KAPELLER, Josef Anton, the Younger, or Kappeller
Austrian, 18th century.
Born 22 February 1761, in Imst (Tyrol); died 1806, near Graz, committed suicide.
Painter, miniaturist, engraver.

Kapeller went to Vienna in 1782 to study at the academy there. In 1787 he went to Warsaw, invited to the court of Prince Jablonowski, for several members of whose family he did portraits. During the revolution in Poland he fought as an ordinary soldier. He was a friend of General Kosciuszko, whose portrait he engraved in colour. In 1794, he left Poland and settled in Innsbruck, then Vienna. Noted engravings include the *Four Defenders of Tyrol*, and a series of 24 *Tyrolean Costumes*.

KAPÉRA, Jean
French, 20th century.
Born 3 October 1920, in Argenteuil; died 29 July 1986, on the Île d'Oléron.
Painter, collage artist, assemblage artist.

After working on the theme of capturing objects using adhesive paint and electric interceptor sculptures, Jean Kapéra's media-related work from 1960 to 1972 was characterised by the use of newspaper and magazine printing plates. In a spirit close to New Realism as defined by Pierre Restany but with a clear concern for the aesthetic, Kapéra assembled printing plates, which retain reliefs of texts and printed reproductions, into collages and structures. From 1974 to 1976 he worked on creating an international language based on drawings using figures and names executed in a variety of media (notably plastic film) and produced on a computer; these take the form of graphic dances of spirals, lacework and asymptotic perspectives. He also worked with photography and tourist events and from 1981 explored the technological imagination.

Kapéra showed work at various exhibitions that took objects or collage as their theme. He also showed collections of his work in solo exhibitions: in Paris (1964, 1969, 1971, 1974); at the Centre d'Action Culturelle in St-Brieuc (1987); at the Musée du Dessin et de l'Estampe Originale in Gravelines (1989); and at the Musée d'Art Moderne et Contemporain in Nice (1993).

BIBLIOGRAPHY:
Kapéra. Hommage à la lettre, exhibition catalogue, Centre d'action culturelle, St-Brieuc, 1987. *Kapéra. L'Imaginaire médiatique*, exhibition catalogue, Musée du dessin et de l'estampe originale, Gravelines, 1989.

KAPFF, Aline von
German, 19th century.
Born 20 July 1842, in Bremen.
Painter. Genre scenes.

Kapff worked in Munich, Bremen and Paris.

KAPITANOVA, Yulia Grigorievna. See **ARAPOVA**

KAPITONOVA, Valentina
Russian, 20th century.
Born 1926.
Painter.

Valentina Kapitonova studied at the school of fine arts in Riga. She was a 'painter emeritus' of the USSR.

AUCTION RECORDS:
PARIS, 9 Dec 1991, *Le Planeur* (1957, oil on canvas, 27 1/2 x 23 1/2 ins / 70 x 60 cm) FRF 4,800.

KAPKOV, Yakov Fedorovich or Iakov Fedorovitch, or Kapkoff
Russian, 19th century.
Born 1816; died 1854.
Painter. History painting.

Works by Yakov Kapkov that were on display in the Tretiakov Gallery in Moscow include *Metropolitan Aleksis Healing a Sick Man, The Virgin and the Baby Jesus, Annunciation* and *The Betrothed*; the Romanianzev Museum housed *Nun at Prayer, Turkish Woman* and *Widow*.

AUCTION RECORDS:
LONDON, 11-12 June 1997, *Widow* (oil on canvas, round, diam. 21 1/4 ins / 54 cm) GBP 4,600.

KAPLAN, Anatole
Russian, 20th century.
Born 1903, in Leningrad (now St Petersburg).
Lithographer, pastellist.

Two of Anatole Kaplan's lithographs, both inspired by popular themes, were shown in the *L'Art Russe des Scythes à nos jours* (*Russian Art from the Scythians to Today*) exhibition, Grand-Palais, Paris (1967).

AUCTION RECORDS:
TEL AVIV, 15 May 1982, *Bewitched Tailor* (1954-1957, portfolio containing 24 lithographs, 24 x 17 3/4 ins / 61 x 45 cm) ILS

21,100. TEL AVIV, 16 May 1983, *Horse-drawn Sleigh by Moonlight* (pastel, 19 x 15 ins / 48.5 x 38 cm) ILS 51,660.

KAPLAN, Jacques
French, 19th - 20th century.
Born 1872, in Sebastopol, to French parents.
Painter, pastellist, miniaturist, draughtsman, illustrator.
Portraits.

Jacques Kaplan went to Paris as a child and joined the École des Arts Décoratifs at the age of 13 and the École des Beaux-Arts at 16, studying there under Bonnat. He worked in a variety of techniques but from 1900 concentrated mainly on portrait painting. He also worked as an illustrator and illustrated works by Guy de Maupassant, among others. In 1890 he exhibited for the first time at the Salon des Artistes Français, continuing to exhibit there and also at the Salon de la Société Nationale des Beaux-Arts. He became well-known following a solo exhibition of his work in 1894.

AUCTION RECORDS:
PARIS, 20 Nov 1994, *Terrace in Aix-en-Provence* (oil on canvas, 29 1/4 x 37 ins / 74 x 94 cm) FRF 8,000.

KAPLAN, Marc
French, 20th - 21st century.
Born 12 November 1950, in Leningrad (now St Petersburg).
Since 1980 active in the Netherlands.
Painter. Landscapes with figures, urban landscapes.

Marc Kaplan was trained at the Leningrad academy of art. He has lived in the Netherlands since 1980. As well as painting he also makes theatre sets. He paints street scenes, markets and beaches connected to reality but seen in the Post-Impressionist style and in paste. He exhibited in Leningrad and Moscow between 1976 and 1979, regularly since 1982 at the Galerie & Faïence in the Netherlands and in 1988 and 1991 at the Galerie Katia Granoff, Paris.

AUCTION RECORDS:
PARIS, 6 Dec 1993, *Figures on a Beach in Biarritz* (oil on canvas, 22 3/4 x 26 3/4 ins / 58 x 68 cm) FRF 9,000. PARIS, 27 March 1994, *Jerusalem* (oil on canvas, 28 x 31 1/2 ins / 71 x 80 cm) FRF 9,000. PARIS, 26 March 1995, *Jerusalem* (oil on canvas, 27 x 35 1/2 ins / 68.5 x 90 cm) FRF 8,000. PARIS, 5 April 1995, *Saturday in Toulon* (oil on canvas, 31 1/2 x 35 1/2 ins / 80 x 90 cm) FRF 7,500. PARIS, 21 June 1996, *Café Terrace* (oil on canvas, 30 1/4 x 22 ins / 77 x 56 cm) FRF 7,500.

KAPLAN, Michel
Ukrainian, 19th century.
Born 19th century, in Odessa.
Sculptor.

Michel Kaplan studied at the fine arts schools in Odessa and Paris. He was taught by Falguière. He received a commendation at the 1900 Exposition Universelle in Paris.

KAPLICKY, Josef
Czech, 20th century.
Born 1899; died 1962.
Sculptor (bronze).

In 1946 work by Kaplicky featured in the exhibition of Czechoslovakian art held at the Musée de l'Orangerie in Paris. His sculptures were influenced by contemporary French art.

MUSEUMS AND GALLERIES:
PRAGUE (Národní Gal.): a bronze.

KAPLINSKY, Léon
Polish, 19th century.
Born 1826, in Lisovo; died 1873, in Miloslaw.
Painter.

Léon Kaplinsky began by studying drawing with Count Severin Mielzynski in Miloslav. He was imprisoned by the Prussians from 1846 to 1848 for his part in the patriotic movement. Later, he went to Paris, where he studied with Scheffer and Robert-Fleury. He was awarded an honourable mention in 1863. The name Kaplinsky appears again in the catalogue of the Salon of 1911, but this must be a mistake.

KAPLUNGER, Rudolph
Bohemian, 18th century.
Born 2 April 1746, in Bechin, Bohemia; died 1795.
Sculptor.

Rudolph Kaplunger worked in Paris, Vienna, Potsdam, Dresden and Prague.

KAPOOR, Anish
British, 20th - 21st century.
Born 1954, in Bombay, to an English father.
Active in London from the beginning of the 1970s.
Sculptor, installation artist, painter (gouache).
New British Sculpture.

Anish Kapoor is half-Indian and spent his early years in India. In 1973, he moved to London and studied at Hornsey College of Art until 1977 and then at Chelsea School of Art in 1977 and 1978. In 1979, he was given a teaching post at Wolverhampton Polytechnic near Birmingham. From 1979, he returned regularly to India, believing that this is where his real roots in art, architecture, philosophy and mythology lie. He was awarded the Premio Duemila at the 44th Venice Biennale in 1990 and the Turner Prize at the Tate in London in 1991. He was made an honorary fellow of the Royal Institute of British Architecture in 2001 and in 2003 received the third Julio Gonzalez international prize awarded by the Valencia institute of modern art in Spain.

Following years of training with Bill Woodrow, Tony Cragg, David Mach, Richard Deacon and Anthony Gormley, Anish Kapoor established himself as part of the Post-Modern British sculpture scene. His early career was marked by the use of a diverse range of materials, free geometric, biomorphic and mixed forms in raw, striking colours reminiscent of Indian ritual. He produced indeterminate, spontaneous objects, 'things' that he used in his installations. They were placed on the floor, on which colour was also used, fixed to walls or suspended from above. He gave them metaphorical meaning, often, and particularly during his early period, with erotic associations. Many of his sculptures are composed of a number of elements with colours in violent, though not unpleasant contrast. From 1986-1987, he abandoned colour, or reduced its function considerably, allowing the material to express itself. In this period, his work shows similarities with Arte Povera - for example, when he arranges a series of rough stone blocks on the ground - though less so than his previous period. Kapoor now began to intervene on the materials chosen - often large, monumental stones, slate, sandstone and travertine - either choosing to retain the primitive roughness of the material or carving it (or having it carved) with the very precise intention to produce regular, rigorous volumes in which he often fashioned apparently random cavities like faults or rifts or, by contrast, geometric, rectangular or vertical shapes, like portals to a dark cavern. For Kapoor, these violations of the wholeness of the stone reveal, through their very form, the opposition between solid and void, interior and exterior or the visible and the hidden, the tensions of which are symbolically transferred to man in the dualisms that form part of Hindu thought: postive-negative, active-passive, beginning-end, life-death, spiritual-material, etc. These contrasts are at the heart of Kapoor's creative impulse.

Kapoor has taken part in international group exhibitions, including in 1985, the Nouvelle Biennale, Paris, in 1990 the London Biennale, where he officially represented Britain, and in 1996 *Un Siècle de Sculpture Anglaise* (*A Century of English Sculpture*) at the Galerie Nationale du Jeu de Paume, Paris. He has also shown his work in solo exhibitions, including in 1980 at the private studio of Patrice Alexandre, Paris; in 1981 in London; in 1982 at the Walker Art Gallery,

Liverpool, and the Lisson Gallery, London. In 1983, he showed at the Lisson Gallery, the Nouveau Musée de Villeurbanne, the Walker Art Gallery, Liverpool, and in Rotterdam; in 1984 in Cologne and New York; in 1987 in Sydney; in 1988 and 1996 at the Lisson Gallery; in 1989 in New York and Nagoya; in 1990 at the Tate Gallery, London, and at the Magasin, Grenoble; in 1991 at the Centro de Arte Reina Sofia, Madrid; in 1996 at the Prada Foundation, Milan; in 1996 at the Galerie Lucien Durand, Paris; in 1998 at Capc-Musée d'Art Contemporain, Bordeaux; and in 2002, in *The Unilever Series: Anish Kapoor* at the Tate Modern, London.

BIBLIOGRAPHY:

Anish Kapoor, exhibition catalogue, Walker Art Gall., Liverpool, Nouveau Musée, Villeurbanne, 1983. Lewison, Jeremy, *Anish Kapoor: Drawings,* exhibition catalogue, Tate Gall., London, 1990. Smulders, Caroline, *'Interview: vers la dématérialisation de l'objet'* in *Art Press* n° 152, periodical, Paris, November 1990. Roberts, James, *Anish Kapoor: White Sand, Red Millet, Many Flowers,* The Arts Council/South Bank Centre, London, 1993. Celant, Germano, *Anish Kapoor,* exhibition catalogue, Fondazione Prada, Ed. Charta, Milan, 1995 (English edition, Ed. Charta, Milano, 1998). Celant, Germano, *Anish Kapoor,* Thames & Hudson, London, 1996. Hilty, Greg, *A Changed World: Sculpture from Britain,* British Council, London, 1997. *Anish Kapoor,* exhibition catalogue, Capc musée d'Art contemporain, Bordeaux, 1998 (text in French and English). McEvilley, Thomas, *Sculpture in the Age Of Doubt,* Allworth Press, New York, 1999. Von Drathen, Doris, *'Anish Kapoor'* in *Kunstforum International* No. 169, March-April 2004.

MUSEUMS AND GALLERIES:

AMSTERDAM (Stedelijk Mus.) - LONDON (Tate Collection): *Three* (1982, pigment, oil and plaster/expanded polystyrene) - MADRID (Mus. Nacional Centro de Arte Reina Sofía) - NEW YORK (MoMA).

AUCTION RECORDS:

NEW YORK, 3 May 1989, *Three* (1982, gesso and pigments/foam) USD 41,250; *Untitled* (1988, gouache/paper, 17 3/4 x 23 1/2 ins / 45.2 x 59.7 cm) USD 1,485. LONDON, 17 Oct 1991, *B10* (1985, pigment, pastel and ink/paper, 23 x 15 1/4 ins / 57.5 x 38.5 cm) GBP 1,760. NEW YORK, 27 Feb 1992, *Untitled* (acrylic and pigment/polystyrene, 39 x 36 1/4 x 11 1/4 ins / 99.1 x 92.1 x 28.6 cm) USD 18,700. NEW YORK, 4 May 1993, *Blue Song* (1984, pigment/polystyrene and cement in three parts, 51 x 107 x 84 ins / 129.5 x 271.8 x 213.4 cm) USD 31,625. LONDON, 3 Dec 1993, *B6* (1985, pigment, pastel and ink/paper, 23 x 15 1/4 ins / 57.5 x 38.5 cm) GBP 1,150. NEW YORK, 3 May 1994, *Untitled (Black Sphere)* (pigment/sea foam, diam. 26 ins / 66 cm) USD 6,900. PARIS, 19 June 1996, *Square* (1985, wood, chalk and blue pigment, 32 1/4 x 31 1/2 x 31 1/2 ins / 82 x 80 x 80 cm) FRF 165,000. NEW YORK, 18 Nov 1999, *Untitled* (polystyrene, plaster, cloth, gesso and raw pigment, 30 x 30x18 ins / 75 x 75x46 cm) USD 20,000. LONDON, 27 June 2000, *Buco* (painted terracotta, h. 67 ins / 170 cm) GBP 18,000. LONDON, 29 June 2000, *Untitled - Vessel* (mixed media and pigment, 24 x 33x24 ins / 61 x 84x61 cm) GBP 50,000. LONDON, 23 Oct 2001, *1000 Names* (1979-1980, wood, gesso and red pigment, 16 x 16x12 ins / 40 x 40x30 cm) GBP 22,000. COLOGNE, 8 Dec 2001, *Untitled* (colour pigment and oil, 15 x 11 ins / 38 x 28 cm) DEM 3,300. LONDON, 8 Feb 2002, *Untitled* (1985, gesso and pigment on wood, 43 x 79x43 ins / 110 x 200x110 cm) GBP 26,000. LONDON, 28 June 2002, *Mountain* (1994, white painted wood, 83 x 46x84 ins / 210 x 116x214 cm) GBP 38,000. LONDON, 7 Feb 2003, *Untitled* (1989, gouache and pencil, 18 x 24 ins / 45 x 60 cm) GBP 3,200. NEW YORK, 14 May 2003, *Pot is Gold* (1985, pigment sculpture, 16 x 20x15 ins / 41 x 51x38 cm) USD 40,000. LONDON, 24 June 2004, *Untitled - from the Volterra Series* (alabaster, 85 x 32x16 ins / 217 x 82x40 cm) GBP 200,000. NEW YORK, 9 Nov 2004, *Mother as a Ship* (1989, pigment on fibreglass, 85 x 46x43 ins / 215 x 116x109 cm) USD 280,000.

KAPP, David

American, 20th - 21st century.
Born 1953, in New York.
Painter.

David Kapp studied at Queens College in New York 1977, and Windham College in Vermont, 1974. His paintings appear crude in style, sharp and contrasted, his oblique figuration is at the confluence of Neo-Expressionism and new figurations, free figuration included. He paints maily urban street scenes. His work has been shown in numerous solo shows including in 2002 at the Tobor de Nagy Gallery, New York. His group exhibitions have been mostly in the USA.

BIBLIOGRAPHY:

Oritz, Lori, *David Kapp at Beitzel Gallery,* periodical, The Brooklyn Rail, Brooklyn, May - June 2001.

AUCTION RECORDS:

PARIS, 13 April 1988, *Van Dam Street* (1985, oil on canvas, 70 x 78 ins / 178 x 198 cm) FRF 10,000. PARIS, 12 Feb 1989, *Long Island* (oil on canvas, 72 1/2 x 66 1/4 ins / 184 x 168 cm) FRF 15,000.

KAPPEL, Philip

American, 20th century.
Born 10 February 1901, in Hartford (Connecticut); died 1966.
Painter, engraver.

Philip Kappel studied at the Pratt Institute. He received many awards, including the Purchase Prize in the First Annual National Art Competition of the Associated American Artists, and the Bijur Prize from the Brooklyn Society of Etchers. He was a noted engraver.

MUSEUMS AND GALLERIES:

PARIS (BNF, Prints Collection).

KAPPELER, Detlef

German, 20th century.
Born 1938, in Stettin (now Szczecin, Poland).
Painter, draughtsman. Allegorical subjects, scenes with figures.

Detlef Kappeler studied at the University of Hanover between 1958 and 1965, and from 1966 to 1968 at the Hochschule für Bildende Künste in Hamburg. After starting out on his career as an artist, he went on study tours to India, Morocco, the USA, Hungary and Poland. In 1972, he was awarded a bursary to study at the Cité Internationale des Arts in Paris, and from 1974, he was professor of drawing and painting in the department of Architecture at the University of Hanover. In his drawings and paintings, he makes use of a hyperrealist technique, which he uses as a vehicle for moral content and protest aimed at the general deterioration of the modern way of life.

Since 1971, Kappeler has taken part in group exhibitions, including *Aktiva* at the Haus der Kunst in Munich in 1971; *German Art of the 1960s,* a travelling exhibition in Germany and abroad in 1972; *The Horrors of War* at the Bielefeld Kunsthalle and an exhibition at the Cité des Arts in Paris, also in 1972; *Aspects of Realist Figuration* in Cologne in 1976, and exhibitions of the Deutscher Künstlerbund (German Artists' Association) in Hanover in 1980 and 1981. He has shown collections of his works in several solo shows, including those in 1969 in Tübingen; 1970 in Dortmund; 1971 at the Hamburg Kunsthalle and the Bielefeld Kunsthalle; 1975 at the Hanover Kunstverein; 1976 at the Bochum Museum; 1983 at the Goethe Institute in Paris, and Transparenzen in 2001 at the Stadtmuseums in Oldenburg, Wroclaw and Szczecin.

KAPPELER, Joseph Damien

Swiss, 19th century.

Born 1792, in Baden (Aargau); died 22 November 1871, in Baden.
Painter, miniaturist, lithographer.
Kappeller lived in Fribourg from 1825 to 1840, doing a large number of religious paintings there, principally for the Bishop of Lausanne and Geneva.

KAPPEN, Francis van der, or Kuppen
Dutch, 17th - 18th century.
Born 1660; died 1723.
Active in Antwerp.
Painter.
Houbraken refers to a history painter known as Studie under the name of Francis van der Kappen, but this name does not appear in the guild registers. Some biographers believe that he worked in Italy.

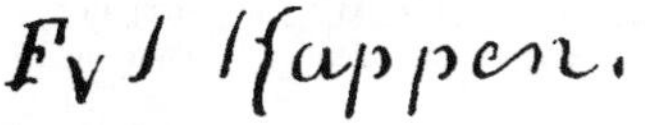

KAPPERS, Anton
Dutch, 18th century.
Born 1 October 1707, in Münster; died 18 July 1762, in Münster.
Painter.
Anton Kappers was a pupil of M. Terwesten. He travelled in France and Brabant and worked for churches. His brother was a copyist in Münster in 1768.

KAPPERS, Gerhard
German, 18th century.
Died 20 August 1750.
Painter.
Kappers decorated the choir of Münster Cathedral.

KAPPES, Alfred
American, 19th century.
Born 1850, in New York; died 1894.
Painter. Genre scenes.
Alfred Kappes was an associate of the National Academy of Design in New York from 1887.
AUCTION RECORDS:
NEW YORK, 9 Jan 1902, *Reading*, USD 80. NEW YORK, 22 May 2001, *Tattered and Torn* (1886, oil on canvas, 40 x 32 ins / 101 x 81 cm) USD 75,000.

KAPPES, Karl
American, 19th century.
Born 28 May 1861, in Zanesville (Ohio); died 16 November 1943.
Painter.
Karl Kappes was a pupil of William M. Chase in New York, Benjamin-Constant in Paris and Carl Marr in Munich. He was a member of the American Federation of Arts.

KAPPES, Karl
German, 19th century.
Born 5 January 1821, in Frankfurt am Main; died 3 January 1857, in Frankfurt am Main.
Engraver.
Kappes was a pupil of Schaeffer in Frankfurt. He did religious paintings inspired by old masters.

KAPPIS, Albert
German, 19th - 20th century.
Born 20 August 1836, in Wildberg; died 18 September 1914, in Stuttgart.
Painter. Genre scenes, landscapes.
Albert Kappis worked successively in Stuttgart, Munich, Düsseldorf and Paris, and travelled in Holland, Belgium and Italy. In 1880, he was appointed professor at the Akademie der Bildenden Künste in Stuttgart.

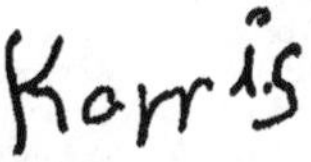

MUSEUMS AND GALLERIES:
BERN: *Fishermen on Lake Constance; Inn in the Tyrol* - COLOGNE: *The Hemp Harvest* - GRAZ: *Landscape* - STUTTGART: *In the Black Forest*.
AUCTION RECORDS:
COLOGNE, 24 Nov 1971, *Fishermen*, DEM 5,000. VIENNA, 4 Dec 1973, *Blessing the Fields*, ATS 110,000. COLOGNE, 20 Oct 1978, *Couple Seated on a River Bank* (1856, oil on canvas, 13 1/4 x 18 1/2 ins / 33.5 x 47 cm) DEM 12,000. LONDON, 30 Jan 1981, *Children beside a Pond* (oil on canvas, 13 1/2 x 18 ins / 34.4 x 45.7 cm) GBP 7,000. MUNICH, 13 Sept 1984, *Farm Scene in Winter* (1877, oil on canvas, 17 3/4 x 31 1/2 ins / 45 x 80 cm) DEM 38,000. MUNICH, 26 Nov 1985, *Fishermen on Lake Constance* (oil on card, 5 x 8 1/4 ins / 12.8 x 20.7 cm) DEM 7,500. HEIDELBERG, 3 April 1993, *Boat Shed and Jetty beside a Lake* (oil on canvas, 13 3/4 x 18 1/2 ins / 35 x 47 cm) DEM 1,900. NEW YORK, 17 Feb 1994, *Bringing in the Nets* (1883, oil on canvas, 20 1/4 x 38 1/2 ins / 51.4 x 97.8 cm) USD 25,300.

KAPPSTEIN, Karl
German, 19th - 20th century.
Born 6 March 1869, in Berlin; died 1933.
Painter. Animals.
Karl Kappstein was a pupil of the animal painter Paul Meyerheim, among others. He first exhibited in Berlin in 1891 and won a medal in 1904.
AUCTION RECORDS:
AMSTERDAM, 21 April 1993, *Flamingoes and Sea Geese* (oil on card, 10 x 12 1/2 ins / 25.5 x 31.5 cm) NLG 3,220.

KAPRASOVA, Ludmila
Czechoslovak, 20th century.
Born 16 May 1941, in Novýbyozov.
Painter. Designs for tapestries.
Ludmila Kaprasova lives in Prague where she began exhibiting in 1964. She has also exhibited in Switzerland, Algeria, Poland and at the universal exhibition in Osaka. She also produces large-scale weavings created from thick plaited wool.

KAPRIELIAN, Yetvart
French, 20th - 21st century.
Born 7 July 1959, in Antony.
Painter. Landscapes, seascapes.
Yetvart Kaprielian exhibits at the regional exhibitions in the Île de France and provincial France. He paints landscapes and seascapes of the Île de France, Normandy, Brittany and Provence. He has shown collections of pictures at solo exhibitions such as Pontoise in 1989, Lyons in 1992 and Paris.

KAPROW, Allan
American, 20th century.
Born 1927, in Atlantic City (New Jersey).
Happenings artist, environmental artist. Multimedia.
Neo-Dadaism.
Allan Kaprow studied under Hans Hofmann in 1947-1948. He wrote his doctoral thesis on Mondrian, under the supervision de Meyer Schapiro. In 1956-1958, he attended John Cage's course at the New College for Social Research in New York. That period was witnessing a resurgence of interest in Dada and the advent of a belated, and quite unexpected wave of successors to Marcel Duchamp. Dada's subversive response to art, its readiness to turn things on their head released Kaprow's energies. He had a chair in art history, was involved in the creation of two galleries in New York, and pursued the activities which befitted a conceptual

artist. He taught Visual Arts at the University of San Diego (California).

His earlier pieces were collages, and more complex assemblages, in which he brought together reclaimed materials, texts and action painting. Like Kurt Schwitters' *Merzbau*, these assemblages could grow in volume. In 1958-1959, Kaprow initiated his 'happenings', a genre he is often credited with although Yves Klein's *The Void* in Paris in 1958 precedes them. These happenings were all-encompassing shows, including a basic script, staging, music, dance. From the very first happenings, the audience was implicated in the action, which led in the following ones, between 1967 and 1971, to a distinctively whimsical orientation, when chance and the participant's improvisation came into their own. Alongside the happenings he developed *environments*, and he took versions of these events, in their varied combinations, around the USA, in Germany, Cologne in particular, in Italy, and in Paris. Kaprow is considered to be one of the founders and leading practitioners of conceptual and performance art.

He has taken part in many collective exhibitions concerned with American avant-garde art, in Amsterdam, Stockholm, Copenhagen; he featured in Daniel Spoerri's 1961 exhibition *Art in motion*, featuring Duchamp, Calder and Tinguely. In 2001, he contributed to *Hypermental: Rampant Reality 1950-2000 From Salvador Dalí to Jeff Koons*, in Hamburg. In 1986, the Museum Am Ostwall in Dortmund dedicated an exhibition to his actions over the past decades.

BIBLIOGRAPHY:

Kaprow, Allan, *Assemblage, environments and happenings*, Abrams, New York, 1966. *Allan Kaprow*, exhibition catalogue, Pasadena Art Museum, Pasadena, 1967. *Allan Kaprow: Collagen, Environments, Videos, Broschüren, Geschichten, Happening und Acti Vity Dokumente 1956-1986*, exhibition catalogue, Museum am Ostwall, Dortmund, 1986. Haywood, Robert E., *Revolution of the ordinary: Allan Kaprow and the invention of happenings*, University of Michigan, Ann Arbor, 1993. *Allan Kaprow*, Fondazione Antonio Ratti, Como, Skira, Milan, 1998. Buchloh, Benjamin H.D./Rodenbeck, Judith R., *Experiments in the everyday: Allan Kaprow and Robert Watts*, exhibition catalogue, Miriam and Ira D. Wallach Art Gall., Colombia University, New York, 1999. Kelley, Jeff, *Childsplay: the Art of Allan Kaprow*, University of California Press, Berkeley, 2004.

MUSEUMS AND GALLERIES:

NÎMES (Carré d'Art, MAC): *Veronica* (1956).

KAPTAN, Arif

Turkish, 20th century.
Born 1906.
Painter. Landscapes.

Arif Kaptan's work was represented in the 1946 exhibition of Turkish art in the Cernuschi Museum in Paris. He painted mainly landscapes, in which one can discern the influence of Utrillo, yet with an oriental flavour. Gradually forsaking realism in favour of abstraction, he drew on the design repertoire of kilims and the carpets of Anatolia.

KAPUP, Christof

German, 17th century.
Active in Nordhausen c. 1600.
Sculptor.

Kapup had several spells working in the cathedral of Magdeburg.

KAPUYNS, N.

Flemish School, 17th century.
Active in Brussels at the end of the 17th century.
Painter. Flowers.

N. Kapuyns is known for *Madonna Surrounded by Flowers* in the church of Notre-Dame in Brussels.

KARAHALIOS, Constantin

Greek, 20th century.
Born 1921, in Tripolis.
Painter, mixed media.

Constantin Karahalios studied at the school of fine arts in Athens between 1947 and 1952, and then went on to train at the École des Beaux-Arts in Paris, where he studied frescoes. He studied engraving at the École Estienne between 1957 and 1960.

Schematised figures of ordinary men in the street aligned into painted spaces populate Karahalios' compositions. Closely approximating hieroglyphic symbols, they feed on both the artist's memory and themes from the distant past. He took part in many collective exhibitions, including the Salon des Réalités Nouvelles, Paris (1961, 1969, 1974); Salon de la Jeune Sculpture, Paris (1965, 1966, 1967, 1968, 1971, and regularly up until 1974); Salon Comparaisons, Paris (1966, 1967, 1968, 1988); Salon de Mai, Paris (1969, 1973, 1975, 1977, 1978); Salon des Grands et Jeunes d'Aujourd'hui, Paris (1983 to 1988).

His solo exhibitions include the Galerie du Haut-Pavé, Paris (1960, 1979); Galerie Stadler, Paris (1965); Apollinaire gallery, Milan (1970); Galerie Raymonde Cazenave, Paris (1971); Musée Cantonal des Beaux-Arts, Paris (1980); Skufa gallery, Athens (1987); and the Galerie 1900-2000, Paris (1988).

MUSEUMS AND GALLERIES:

ATHENS (MMA) - BUFFALO (Albright-Knox AG) - GLYFADA (Pinakothíki Dimitri Pieridi/Pierides Gallery) - MAUBEUGE - PARIS (BNF, Medal Collection) - PARIS (MNAM-CCI) - SÖDERTÄLJE.

KARANDJULOV, Dimitas

Bulgarian, 20th century.
Painter, ceramicist. Scenes with figures. Designs for stained glass, designs for mosaics.

Dimitas Karandjulov looked for ways of simplifying the shapes found in icons and popular frescoes and then applied these in his figurative paintings. This synthesization of shapes informed his decorative works.

KARAS, Vekoslav

Croat, 19th century.
Born 1821, in Karlovac; died 5 July 1858, in Karlovac.
Painter.

Karas spent many years living in Italy before moving to Zagreb and later settling in Karlovac. He painted allegories and religious compositions, and also genre scenes. He was a member of the Illyrian movement and witnessed Croatia's gaining of independence. He was one of Croatia's first national painters.

MUSEUMS AND GALLERIES:

ZAGREB (Mus.): *Roman Girl Playing the Guitar*.

KARAVACK, Louis. See **CARAVAQUE**

KARAVAN, Dani

Israeli, 20th century.
Born 1930, in Tel Aviv.
Active in France.
Sculptor, environmental artist. Monuments.
Land Art.

Dani Karavan began his studies in Tel Aviv and at the Bezalel Academy in Jerusalem, and continued them until 1957, first in Florence, where he learnt techniques of fresco painting with Mordechai Ardon, and then in Paris at the Grande Chaumière. In 1958 he won the competition for the construction of the pavilions celebrating the 10th anniversary of the independence of Israel. In 1995 he was awarded the Great Imperial Prize of Japan.

Until 1973 he created settings for theatre and ballet, including those of the Martha Graham Company, from 1963 onwards also developing his own work of environmental art. In Israel he produced the *Monument of the Negev Desert* and a low relief in the Knesset. He staged a brief *Intervention* in the 1977 Kassel Documenta VI, and since then has set up similar installations in different parts of Europe. He discovers locations where there are vast spaces and then installs major routes to create structures within them, marking nature, dimension, time and reference points, places to pause and reflect, by signs, carvings or simple monuments. On the Paris outer ring road he began in 1980 to create the Cergy-Pontoise *Major Axis*, starting from a square tower set up in the middle of a Ricardo Bofill housing development. The three kilometres are marked out by pyramids, sighting points, gnomons and aeolian harps. His art is classical in form, and humanist in philosophy, as he seeks to bring harmony to the anchoring of human life in its context of a modern city. Karavan's work is usually seen as belonging to Land Art, but most of his creations are not ephemeral and belong rather to the domain of urban architecture.

His solo exhibitions include that of 2002, *Pardes*, IVAM, in Valencia, where he displayed installations specially created for the site.

BIBLIOGRAPHY:

Chaslin, François, '*À Cergy, Karavan passe*' in *Le Nouvel Observateur*, periodical, Paris, February-March 1988. Torres, Anna M./Morgan, Robert, et al., *Dani Karavan: 'Pardes'*, exhibition catalogue, Instituto Valenciano de Arte Moderno (IVAM), Valencia, 2002.

AUCTION RECORDS:

TEL AVIV, 11 Oct 1995, *Project* (assemblage of bronze plates, in all 10 1/4 x 23 1/2 ins / 26 x 59.5 cm) USD 4,600. TEL AVIV, 14 Jan 1996, *Composition* (1976, bronze relief, 9 3/4 x 12 1/2 ins / 25 x 32 cm) USD 2,070. TEL AVIV, 8 April 1999, *Paralleli* (stainless steel, 65x26 ins / 165x67 cm) USD 16,000. TEL AVIV, 4 July 1999, *Jerusalem* (bronze relief, 7x20 ins / 18x51 cm) USD 2,600.

KARAVUSIS, Sarandis

Greek, 20th century.
Born 1938, in Athens.
Active in France from 1967.
Painter, sculptor. Still-lifes, townscapes. Stage sets.

Sarandis Karavusis trained at the school of fine arts in Athens under the direction of Yannis Moralis, and then at the school of fine arts in Paris. From 1964 he designed stage sets for folkloric ballets produced by the northern Greek theatre in Thessalonica.

Using a smooth technique, Karavusis painted still-lifes, ceramic bottles, small jugs, bowls, goblets using matt and dark shades of different greys and ochres. This surrealist or metaphysical tendency is clearly identified in compositions showing the glorious remains of the ancient world: ruins, headless statues, and fallen columns.

Karavusis took part in many collective exhibitions, including the Salon d'Automne, Paris (1970); *Exposition pour Chypre*, Musée Galliéra, Paris (1975); Salon Comparaisons, Paris (1976, 1978, 1980, 1982); *Contemporary Greek Art*, National Gallery, Athens (1976, 1983); São Paulo Biennale (1979); and the Salon Figuration Critique, Paris (1982).

His solo exhibitions include the Ora gallery, Athens (1971, 1976); Galerie Coard, Paris (1974, 1976, 1978, 1981, 1984); and the Zygos gallery, Athens (1978).

MUSEUMS AND GALLERIES:

ATHENS (Gal.) - GLYFADA (Pinakothíki Dimitri Pieridi/Pierides Gallery) - PARIS (BNF) - PARIS (MAMVP) - THESSALONICA (AG).

AUCTION RECORDS:

PARIS, 25 March 1994, *Still-life with Bottles* (oil on canvas, 23 1/2 x 32 ins / 60 x 81 cm) FRF 10,000.

KARAYANNI, Maria

Greek, 20th - 21st century.
Born 25 December 1953.
Painter.

Maria Karayanni began her artistic training in Athens and continued it in Paris where she may have been a student at the École des Beaux-Arts, but in any case lodged at the Cité Internationale des Arts. Her paintings are ambitious, her composition complex and animated. She likes using warm shades with sensual pigmentations in browns, reds, oranges, yellows, earth colours and greens, which breathe life into certain shades of blue. In around 1990, she devoted a cycle of paintings to the book *Journal of an Invisible April* by the Greek poet Odysseus Elytis. She had her first exhibition in Athens in 1983-1984 at the Odeon National and at the Institut Français. This was followed by others, including exhibitions in Paris from 1986 at the Galerie de la Maison des Beaux-Arts and at the gallery of the Cité Internationale des Arts, and in 1988 at the Salon des Réalités Nouvelles.

KARAZIAN, Eduard Arturovich

Armenian, 20th century.
Born 1939, in Yerevan.
Painter. Figure compositions, still-lifes.

A student at the institute of art and theatre in Yerevan, Karazian went on to settle in Moscow.

The structure of his paintings sprang from Post Cubism, although the rich, coloured harmonies which are often shown again dark backgrounds, are from Matisse. His works contain from a juxtaposition of planes enlivened with figures, objects, vases of flowers and purely decorative elements. The final result is always seductive while at the same time preserving a note of modernism. He took part in several national collective exhibitions.

BIBLIOGRAPHY:

Alavarez, José, *Art contemporain soviétique*, exhibition catalogue, Gal. de France, Paris, 1987.

KARAZIN, Nicolai Nikolaevich

Russian, 19th century.
Born 1842; died 19 December 1908, in Gatchina near St Petersburg.
Painter (gouache). Genre scenes.

MUSEUMS AND GALLERIES:

MOSCOW (State Tretyakov Gal.): *Death of a Cavalier.*

AUCTION RECORDS:

LONDON, 16 March 1983, *Nomad* (1901, gouache, 25 1/2 x 19 3/4 ins / 65 x 50 cm) GBP 1,600. LONDON, 28 March 1990, *Nomad* (1881, gouache, 25 1/4 x 19 3/4 ins / 64 x 50 cm) GBP 1,650. LONDON, 19 Dec 1996, *Farmhands at Krasnoe Selo* (1882, gouache/panel, 14 1/4 x 20 1/4 ins / 36.5 x 51.5 cm) GBP 2,185. LONDON, 17 Dec 1999, *Russian Village in the Depths of Winter* (1894, watercolour and bodycolour on paper/card, 9 x 15 ins / 23 x 39 cm) GBP 2,000. LONDON, 26 Nov 2002, *Siam Strand at a Palace Exhibition* (1893, gouache and watercolour on panel/cardboard, 17 x 13 ins / 44 x 32 cm) GBP 1,100. HELSINKI, 1 Dec 2002, *Cossack* (1895, Indian ink, 12 x 16 ins / 30 x 40 cm) EUR 1,600. LONDON, 26 May 2004, *Medieval Russian Scene* (1884, wash and watercolour, 7 x 6 ins / 19 x 16 cm) GBP 6,500. LONDON, 26 May 2004, *Troika by the River* (1900, watercolour over pencil heightened with gouache, 11 x 19 ins / 29 x 48 cm) GBP 8,000.

KARBASIUS, Dirk

Dutch, 17th century.
Died before 1702.
Painter.

In 1646, Dirk Karbasius was a member of the Haarlem guild. He appears to have given up painting by 1650.

KARBOWSKY, Adrien

French, 19th - 20th century.
Born 15 December 1855, in Paris.

Painter, designer, decorative designer. Still-lifes, flowers. Murals, designs for tapestries.

Adrien Karbowsky studied under Alexandre (?) Lequien. He produced decorative murals, notably for the town hall of Nogent-sur-Marne and for the dining room of the prince of Monaco as well as numerous decorative works and fine furniture. He is also known for his fabric designs. He exhibited regularly in Paris at the Salon des Artistes Français, becoming a member in 1883 and receiving a commendation in 1889. He also exhibited at the Exposition Universelle of 1900, at the Salon de la Société Nationale des Beaux-Arts and the Salon des Tuileries and was a committee member of both Salons. Karbowsky took part in the Brussels exhibition of 1910. He was made a Chevalier de la Légion d'Honneur in 1902 and later an Officier de la Légion d'Honneur.

AUCTION RECORDS:

PARIS, 15-16 Dec 1924, *Vase of Roses and Books; Pot of Dahlias on a Faïence Dish Background* (two paintings) FRF 430. PARIS, 10 May 1933, *Tea-time,* FRF 400. MONTE CARLO, 16 June 1982, *Serenade* (1926, oil on canvas, in three parts, 54 x 81 ins / 137 x 206 cm) FRF 11,000.

KARBOWSKY, René

French, 20th century.

Born 18 October 1883, in Paris.

Painter, designer. Still-lifes, flowers.

René Karbowsky was probably the son of Adrien Karbowsky. He exhibited in Paris and at the Salon des Tuileries from 1922.

AUCTION RECORDS:

PARIS, 4 Dec 1944, *Peonies,* FRF 1,200; *Still-life with Young She-goat* (1918) FRF 1,000.

KARCHANSKY, Christine.

See **KOROCHANSKY Christine**

KÄRCHER, Amalie

German, 19th century.

Active in Karlsruhe.

Painter. Still-lifes (flowers/fruit).

Kärcher regularly exhibited flower paintings in Karlsruhe, Kassel and Munich.

AUCTION RECORDS:

LONDON, 1 March 1972, *Still-life with Fruit and Flowers,* GBP 400. ZURICH, 16 May 1980, *Still-life with Flowers and Fruit* (1868, oil on canvas, 39 x 31 1/2 ins / 99 x 80 cm) CHF 30,000. NEW YORK, 26 Feb 1982, *Still-life with Flowers and Fruit* (1867, oil on canvas, 26 3/4 x 21 ins / 68 x 53.3 cm) USD 22,000. LONDON, 20 March 1985, *Still-life with Fruit* (oil on canvas, 20 x 27 1/4 ins / 51 x 69 cm) GBP 12,800. NEW YORK, 1 March 1990, *Still life of a Substantial Composition of Flowers, Fruit and Insects* (1866, oil on canvas, 39 1/4 x 32 1/2 ins / 99.7 x 82.5 cm) USD 66,000. PARIS, 22 June 1990, *Bouquet of Flowers and Fruit on an Entablature* (oil on canvas, 37 1/2 x 30 3/4 ins / 95 x 78 cm) FRF 350,000. NEW YORK, 24 Oct 1990, *Still-life of Grapes, Peach and Butterfly on a Mossy Rock* (oil on canvas, 13 1/4 x 16 ins / 33.6 x 40.7 cm) USD 7,150. VERSAILLES, 17 Nov 1991, *Bouquet of Flowers and Fruit on an Entablature* (oil on canvas, 37 1/2 x 30 3/4 ins / 95 x 78 cm) FRF 580,000. NEW YORK, 26 May 1993, *Still-life of Flowers on an Entablature* (1859, oil on canvas, 16 1/2 x 19 3/4 ins / 41.9 x 50.2 cm) USD 20,700. MUNICH, 23 June 1999, *Still-life with Fruit* (1850, oil on canvas/card, 22 x 18 ins / 56 x 46 cm) DEM 8,200. VIENNA, 19 Feb 2002, *Still-life with Wine Grapes, Peaches, Plums and Raspberries* (1875, oil on canvas, 8 x 10 ins / 21 x 26 cm) EUR 3,000. COLOGNE, 21 Nov 2002, *Still-life with Fruit* (1869, oil on canvas, 11 x 13 ins / 28 x 34 cm) EUR 2,800.

KARCHER, Anton

French, 18th century.

Born c. 1760, in Colmar.

Engraver (burin).

Anton Karcher was a student of Verhelst in Mannheim. He engraved portraits and historical subjects after Raphael, Zampieri, Ribera and others.

KARCHER, Eugène Henri

French, 20th century.

Born 17 November 1881, in Angers.

Sculptor.

Eugène Henri Karcher exhibited in Paris at the Salon des Artistes Français and was a member of the associated society.

KARCHER, Gustave

French, 19th century.

Born 28 May 1831, in Colmar (Upper Rhine); died 23 January 1908, in Lyons.

Painter, watercolourist. Landscapes, still-lifes.

Gustave Karcher was originally a business employee based both in St-Étienne and in Lyons. He took painting lessons from Fonville and exhibited in Lyons from 1858 and in Paris between 1868 and 1880. He was awarded a third medal in Lyons in 1903.

His riverside or poolside paintings, executed in oil, charcoal or watercolour are characterised by the blurring of features by the diffusion of light. He also painted a few still-lifes.

AUCTION RECORDS:

NEW YORK, 17 Jan 1996, *Rose Bush in the Country* (oil on canvas, 36 x 51 1/4 ins / 90.5 x 129.9 cm) USD 5,175. ZURICH, 19 March 1999, *Summer River Landscape with Boat and Figures* (1899, oil on canvas, 51 x 35 ins / 129 x 90 cm) CHF 3,000. NEW YORK, 29 Nov 1999, *Rowboat* (1899, oil on canvas, 50 x 35 ins / 128 x 90 cm) USD 8,500.

KARCHER, Henri

French, 20th century.

Born 25 May 1937, in Strasbourg; died 2 August 1992, in Strasbourg.

Painter, collage artist. Stage costumes and sets.

Henri Karcher trained at the École des Arts Décoratifs in Strasbourg, graduating in 1958. From 1956 he lived and worked in Bischwiller. Karcher produced stage sets and costumes from 1968 to 1976. He also worked at the Malesset studio in Paris which restores historical and national monuments and buildings. Originally a figurative artist, Karcher moved towards Abstraction. He produced very large-format canvases characterised by movement or minute collages with a more structured composition.

He took part in group exhibitions, including: the Pont-Aven festival (1961); the Salon d'Automne and the Salon des Indépendants in Paris; and the Sélest'art exhibition at Sélestat (1989). He showed his work in solo exhibitions in Paris, notably at the Galerie Henri Bénézit, at the Centre Culturel Américain and in Strasbourg.

AUCTION RECORDS:

PARIS, 14 April 1991, *Untitled* (collage and mixed media/paper, 18 1/4 x 22 ins / 46.5 x 56 cm) FRF 4,800.

KARCSAY, Lajos

Hungarian, 19th century.

Born 18 February 1860, in Kis-Kölked.

Painter. Genre scenes.

Lajos Karcsay studied with Gabl and Seitz at the academy in Munich and began his career in 1888. He exhibited in Vienna, Munich and Paris in 1900.

KARCZEWSKI, Julian

Polish, 19th century.

Born 1806, in Ozmiana, Russia; died 1833, in Rome.

Painter.

After first studying in Vilna (now Vilnius), Julian Karczewski studied with Baron Gros and then with Vernet in Paris.

KARCZMAR, Natan

French, 20th century.

Born in Paris.

Active in Canada from 1955.
Painter.
Groupe des Automatistes.

Natan Karczmar was associated with the Canadian Automatists who practised an automatic style of art in the tradition of the Surrealists. He later reduced his artistic vocabulary to simple, irregular bands of colour. His use of highly absorbent linen-finish paper gives his colours the appearance of enamelled varnish.

KARDORFF, Konrad von
German, 20th century.
Born 13 January 1877, in Niederrabnitz.
Painter, engraver.

Konrad von Kardorff studied with the Hungarian artists Simon Hollosy, then at the Académie Julian in Paris. The main influence on his work was Max Liebermann.

KARDOS, Gyula
Hungarian, 19th century.
Born 20 February 1857, in Baya; died 26 January 1908, in Monte Carlo.
Painter. History painting, genre scenes.

Gyula Kardos studied under J. Greguss and C. Lotz and began his career around 1888. He exhibited in Vienna, Munich, Berlin and Paris, winning a bronze medal at the 1900 Exposition Universelle.

AUCTION RECORDS:
LONDON, 4 Oct 1989, *A Gift from the Sea* (1887, oil on canvas, 76 x 20 ins / 193 x 51 cm) GBP 3,850. BUDAPEST, 9 Dec 2003, *Nude* (oil on canvas, 63x37 ins / 160x95 cm) HUF 1,100,000.

KARDOS, Ladislas
Hungarian, 20th century.
Born 1909, in Budapest.
Active in Canada from 1951.
Painter. Townscapes.

Ladislas Kardos arrived in Paris in 1928 and then travelled around the world. In 1951 he settled in Vancouver, where he worked as a forester. From 1957, disabled after a flying accident, he started to produce drawings and wash drawings and then turned to painting. He exhibited from 1963. His paintings are obsessed with the theme of modern cities spreading like tentacles.

KARDOVSKAIA, Olga Ludvigovna
Maiden name: Della Vos
Russian, 19th - 20th century.
Born 14 September 1875, in Chernigov, 2 September 1876 according to some sources, born in Spain.
Painter.
Symbolism.

Olga Kardovskaia studied at the academy of fine arts in St Petersburg. She married Dmitri Kardovsky.

MUSEUMS AND GALLERIES:
ST PETERSBURG (Gosudarstvennyj Russkij Muz.): *Small Woman.*

KARDOVSKI, Dmitri Nicolaevich
Russian, 19th - 20th century.
Born 17 September 1866, near Pereiaslavl-Salessky; died 1943, in Moscow.
Painter, watercolourist. Historical subjects.

Kardovsky studied art in Moscow and St Petersburg, where he went on to teach painting.

In 2003 his work was represented in the collective exhibition *Traumfabrik Kommunismus - die Visuelle Kultur der Stalinzeit* (*Dream Factory Communism, the Visual Culture of the Stalin Period*) at the Schirn Kunsthalle in Frankfurt.

BIBLIOGRAPHY:
Hollein, Max, et al., *Dream Factory Communism, the Visual Culture of the Stalin Period*, exhibition catalogue, Schirn Kunsthalle, Frankfurt, 2003 (text in English and German).

KAREL, or Karel Zlin, real name: Karel Machalek
Czech, 20th century.
Born 1937, in Zlín.
Active and naturalised in France from 1976.
Painter, sculptor.
Symbolism.

Karel trained at the academy of fine arts in Prague from 1957 to 1963, and lived there until 1976, when he left for Paris for political and cultural reasons. In 1992 he was commissioned by the French ministry of culture to create a monumental sculpture, *Solar Boat*, which was erected in the grounds of Rambouillet Château. This was followed in 1995 by another commission from the office of the presidency of the republic.

He painted figures whose bodies were transformed into a staircase, he sculpted heads or hieratical figures to which he attached geometric elements. In parallel with his activities as a painter and sculptor, Karel published collections of poems (*Recherché*, 1969; *La Maison des autres*, 1979). His work was shown in France at the Salon de Montrouge and the Salon de Mai in Paris. From 1989 he went back to exhibiting in his native country. The Czech cultural centre in Paris held a solo exhibition of his works in 2001: *Les Chimères de Nerval par Karel Zlin*.

KAREL D'YPRES. See **FOORT Karel**

KAREL DE NÉRÉE. See **NÉRÉE TOT BARBERICH**

KARES, Johannes
Romanian, 20th - 21st century.
Born 11 February 1953, in Bazna.
Active in Germany from 1980.
Sculptor.
Arte Povera.

Johannes Kares first studied choreography in Cluj before transferring to the theatre institute in Bucharest, from which he graduated in 1978. During the same period he was sculpting life-sized works in the studio of another sculptor, Grigore Minea. Settled in Germany, he continued his training as a sculptor with Baumann at the academy of fine arts in Stuttgart. During his summer holidays, he worked in the marble quarries in Azzano, Italy. He settled in Leonberg in 1981. While at Azzano he executed 50 or so marble sculptures; in Nurtingen in 1982 a *Crucifix* carved in stone 8 1/2 feet (2.6 metres) in height; at Neuhausen in 1983 a *Fountain* in stone; for the Kunstakademie in Stuttgart, also around 1983, a *Sculpture for a Burnt Horse* 26 feet (8 metres) long and 10 feet (3 metres) high. He also executed other monumental sculptures for public squares in Germany. He later devoted himself to carving life-sized works. Starting from planks, beams, carefully squared off pieces of wood, he assembled them in simple, rustic, primarily geometric shapes, comprising angles, triangles, squares, rectangles, polygons, all without curves. They were inspired by popular traditional objects such as troughs, boxes and coffins but they were themselves woodwork with no clear destination. Their three-dimensional function appears to be to circumscribe their interior space. This is evidential sculpture, as much for the material as for the form, fundamentally materialist, linked possibly to Arte Povera rather than to Minimalist Art. Collective exhibitions have included: 1982, Nürtingen sculpture symposium; 1983, first prize in the Neuhausen-Fildern competition; 1985, first prize in the young artists' forum at Bochum Museum and at the Städtische Galerie, Wolfsburg. He had his first solo exhibition in 1981 in Leonberg, following by others in Germany, including one at the Staatliche Kunsthalle in Baden-Baden in 1986.

BIBLIOGRAPHY:
Romanian Artists and the West, American Romanian Academy of Arts and Sciences, Los Angeles, 1986.

KARFATI
Hungarian, 19th - 20th century.
Painter.
AUCTION RECORDS:
PARIS, July 1946, *Head of an Old Man, in profile,* FRF 6,000.

KARFIOL, Bernard
American, 20th century.
Born 1886, near Budapest, to American parents; died 1952.
Painter, watercolourist. Figures, scenes with figures, landscapes, seascapes.
Bernard Karfiol studied under Jean-Paul Laurens in Paris, where he got his first taste of modern art, and, in due course, gained recognition. He contributed to the introduction of Cubism in the USA. He later reverted to a more traditional style and is best remembered for his stylised paintings of classical nudes in interiors or landscapes. In the USA he regularly exhibited at the Carnegie Institute in Pittsburgh.
AUCTION RECORDS:
NEW YORK, 1 May 1946, *Figures Sitting,* USD 1,050. NEW YORK, 19 April 1977, *Bathers* (card, 13½ x 17¼ ins / 34 x 44 cm) USD 1,700. PORTLAND, 12 April 1980, *Beach Scene* (oil on canvas, 30 x 40 ins / 76.2 x 101.5 cm) USD 1,750. PORTLAND, 5 Nov 1983, *Virginie at Perkins Cove* (oil on canvas, 27¼ x 36 ins / 69 x 91.5 cm) USD 3,800. NEW YORK, 31 May 1990, *Three Young Women* (oil on canvas, 12 x 16 ins / 30.5 x 40.7 cm) USD 1,650. NEW YORK, 26 Sept 1990, *Two Sisters* (oil on canvas, 36 x 28 ins / 91.4 x 71.1 cm) USD 5,225. NEW YORK, 10 June 1992, *Mill on a River* (oil on canvas, 30 x 40¼ ins / 76.2 x 102.2 cm) USD 2,420. NEW YORK, 30 June 1993, *Two Women Sitting* (watercolour and ink/paper, 9½ x 12 ins / 24.1 x 30.5 cm) USD 920. NEW YORK, 28 Sept 1995, *In the Boudoir* (oil on canvas, 26 x 20 ins / 66 x 50.8 cm) USD 7,187. MAINE, 11 Sept 1999, *Nude with Book* (1949, oil on canvas, 12 x 16 ins / 30 x 41 cm) USD 1,800. OAK PARK, 5 Dec 1999, *Still-life Composition* (oil on canvas, 36 x 28 ins / 91 x 71 cm) USD 4,500. MAINE, 4 Aug 2001, *Mini and John Laurent* (oil on canvas, 21 x 26 ins / 53 x 66 cm) USD 2,000. FAIRFIELD, 22 Aug 2001, *Landscape with Water* (oil on canvas, 23 x 29 ins / 58 x 74 cm) USD 2,000. NEW YORK, 13 March 2002, *Mirror and model* (oil on canvas, a pair, 16 x 12 ins / 41 x 30 cm) USD 2,500. PORTLAND, 8 Aug 2003, *Young Bathers* (oil on canvas, 14 x 20 ins / 36 x 51 cm) USD 4,800. PORTLAND, 8 Aug 2003, *After a Swim, Ogunquit Beach* (oil on canvas, 39 x 25 ins / 99 x 63 cm) USD 6,000. MAINE, 3 Jan 2004, *Maine Farmhouse* (oil on canvas, 18 x 27 ins / 46 x 69 cm) USD 2,400.

KARG, Georg
German, 17th century.
Active in Augsburg c. 1620.
Painter.

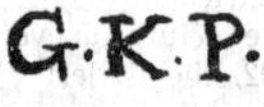

KARG, Joseph Paul
German, 19th century.
Born c. 1791; died 1837, in Mannheim.
Watercolourist.
Karg depicted mainly military scenes.

KARGEN, David
16th century.
Engraver (wood).
David Kargen engraved the plates for Sebastian Münster's *Cosmographia,* published in Basel, 1544.

KARGER, Karl
Austrian, 19th - 20th century.
Born 30 January 1848, in Vienna; died 18 October 1913.
Painter, watercolourist, illustrator. Genre scenes.
Karl Karger began studying at the Akademie der Bildenden Künste in Vienna in 1864, then moved to Munich in 1871. In 1873, he went to work in Italy. On returning to Austria, he was appointed professor at the Hochschule für Angewandte Kunst in Vienna. He was a member of the Belgian Royal Society of Watercolourists, and won medals in Vienna in 1873 and in Berlin in 1886.
MUSEUMS AND GALLERIES:
VIENNA: watercolours.
AUCTION RECORDS:
BERLIN, 1894, *A Staging Post,* FRF 456; *Interior of an Inn,* FRF 455.

KARI, Yrjö
Finnish, 20th century.
Born 1901, in Hollola.
Painter. Local scenes, landscapes with figures.
Yrjö Kari studied at the Helsinki School of Art. He painted arctic landscapes, Eskimos and herds of reindeer in a typical folk-art manner.

KARIMI, Ali
Iranian, 20th century.
Miniaturist.
Ali Karimi was one of the few Iranian miniaturists of the modern age. He was painter to the Shah.

KARINE, Anne
Swiss, 20th century.
Born 1919.
Painter. Figures, portraits, scenes with figures, circus scenes, still-lifes. Stage costumes.
Anne Karine studied at the Hochschule der Künste in Bern and at the École Supérieure des Beaux-Arts in Geneva, and later lived in Paris for several years. In addition to painting, she designed costumes for classical ballets. She began exhibiting in 1949, mainly in Switzerland, but also in Paris in 1960 and in Milan in 1963. Her favourite subjects for painting are those connected with her other vocation: dancers, actors, circus scenes and the world of the theatre.

KARING, Georg Rudolf
Latvian, 19th century.
Born 1807, in Riga; died 9 July 1858, in Riga.
Painter. Genre scenes.
Karing studied under Hansel and worked in Riga and St Petersburg.

KARINGER, Anton
Austrian, 19th century.
Born 29 November 1829, in Laibach (Ljubljana), Slovenia; died 14 March 1870, in Laibach (Ljubljana), Slovenia.
Painter. Landscapes, seascapes.
Karinger was a pupil of Steinfeld in Vienna. He particularly like to paint views of Carinthia and the Adriatic coast.

KARINSKAIA, Anna Nicolaevna
Russian, 19th - 20th century.
Born 1871; died 1931.
Painter. Landscapes.
Anna Karinskaia was active in Vologda.
MUSEUMS AND GALLERIES:
MOSCOW (Rumiantsev Mus.).

KARKOU
Syrian, 20th century.
Born 1 January 1908, in Aleppo.
Active in France.
Painter, draughtsman. Stage sets.
Musicalism (the attempt to interpret music in painting).
Karkou exhibited together with the artists of the musical group of Henri Valensi, who practised an abstraction based

on the correspondences between graphic rhythms, coloured scales and music.

KARL, Georg
German, 16th century.
Born in Nuremberg.
Painter.

Georg Karl worked in Munich, where he settled in about 1490.

KARL, Jean
French, 19th century.
Born in Beaumont-sur-Oise.
Sculptor.

Jean Karl exhibited at the Salon of French Artists from 1908.

KARL, Jo
German, 20th century.
Born 1930, in Merten, near Bonn.
Painter, potter.

Jo Karl studied at the Cologne academy. He has been exhibiting since 1965, mainly in Germany, but also in Rome, Florence and Paris. His tall, coloured ceramics are treated as pictures for decorative purposes. Based on a geometrical construction, but in figurative compositions, his works have a dreamlike, mythical quality.

KARL, Johann
German, 19th century.
Born 1776, in Auerbach.
Active in Munich.
Painter, engraver.

KARL-ROBERT, real name: Georges Meusnier
French, 19th century.
Born 19th century, in Paris.
Painter, watercolourist. Landscapes, waterscapes.

Karl-Robert was a pupil of Allongé and made his debut at the Salon in 1875. He was a member of the Société des Artistes Français from 1883 and an officer of the Académie. He was also involved in buying and selling paintings.

MUSEUMS AND GALLERIES:
PONTOISE: *Sunset on the Banks of the Marne; The River Oise in Stor.*

AUCTION RECORDS:
PARIS, 26 Nov 1920, *Riverside; Farm Beside the Pond* (two charcoals) FRF 260.

KARLEBYE, Jens
Danish, 18th - 19th century.
Born 1730, in Thorsager; died 21 November 1812.
Sculptor.

Jens Karlebye executed several busts of Danish kings, notably *Christian VII* and *Frederik V.*

KARLINGEN, Pierre van
Dutch, 17th century.
Active c. 1610.
Painter.

Pierre van Karlingen is mentioned by Ris Paquot.

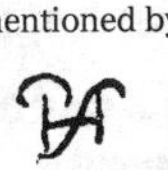

KARLOVSZKY, Bertalan von
Hungarian, 19th - 20th century.
Born 24 October 1858, in Munkács (now Mukachevo in the Ukraine); died 1912 or 1938.
Painter. Portraits, genre scenes, still-lifes.

Karlovszky was the pupil of Mihaly Munkácsy. He won a silver medal at the 1900 Exposition Universelle in Paris.

AUCTION RECORDS:
NEW YORK, 23-24 Jan 1901, *A Bay*, USD 175. LONDON, 18 Feb 1911, *Jealousy* (watercolour) GBP 16. NEW YORK, 26 Jan 1979, *Still-life with Flowers and Fruit* (oil on panel, 39 1/2 x 30 3/4 ins / 100.5 x 78 cm) USD 2,100. NEW YORK, 29 May 1981, *Shepherd* (oil on panel, 8 1/2 x 5 3/4 ins / 21.5 x 14.6 cm) USD 2,400. PARIS, 4 March 1988, *Portrait Study* (oil on panel, 18 x 14 1/2 ins / 46 x 37 cm) FRF 7,000. NEW YORK, 19 July 1990, *Farmer Mowing* (oil on panel, 8 1/4 x 6 1/4 ins / 20.9 x 15.8 cm) USD 1,540. NEW YORK, 27 May 1993, *Young Girl Teaching her Little Dog a New Trick* (oil on canvas, 31 1/2 x 41 3/4 ins / 80 x 106 cm) USD 29,900. LONDON, 26 March 1997, *Admiring the Portrait* (1883, oil on panel, 30 x 40 1/4 ins / 76 x 102 cm) GBP 12,650.

KARLOWSKA, Stanislawa de
Polish, 19th - 20th century.
Born 8 May 1876, in Czeliewy; died 9 December 1952, in London.
Active from c. 1898 then naturalised in England.
Painter. Interiors, landscapes, townscapes, architectural views, still-lifes.

Stanislawa de Karlowska studied art in Warsaw, Cracow and at the Académie Julian in Paris from 1896. Back in Warsaw, she married Robert Bevan, assumed British citizenship and immediately followed her husband to England. There she took part in exhibitions organised by the Women's International Art Club from 1900, and from 1908 her work was shown in exhibitions organised by the Allied Artists Association. She had her first solo exhibition in 1935.

MUSEUMS AND GALLERIES:
LONDON (Tate Collection): *Berkeley Square* (exhibited in 1935, oil on canvas); *Fried Fish Shop* (c. 1907, oil on canvas); *Swiss Cottage* (exhibited in 1914, oil on canvas).

AUCTION RECORDS:
LONDON, 13 June 1986, *The Gate* (1916, oil on canvas, 20 x 16 ins / 50.8 x 40.5 cm) GBP 2,600. LONDON, 3 May 1990, *Morning Sun* (oil on canvas, 18 x 22 ins / 46 x 56 cm) GBP 1,210. LONDON, 13 July 2000, *Wine Shop* (oil on board, 10 x 13 ins / 25 x 33 cm) GBP 2,400. LONDON, 5 Sept 2002, *Devon Landscape* (oil on canvas, 17 x 21 ins / 43 x 53 cm) GBP 1,000. LONDON, 11 March 2004, *Mydlow* (oil on canvas, 17 x 21 ins / 43 x 53 cm) GBP 3,000.

KARLSRUHE PASSION, Master of the.
See **MASTERS**

KARLSSON, C. Göran
Swedish, 20th century.
Born 1944, in Uppsala.
Painter.

C. Göran Karlsson studied at Konsthögskolan in Stockholm from 1967 to 1972. He paints very complex assemblages of boldly coloured geometrical figures that not only completely cover the surface of the picture but even seem to project into space. In March 1992, the Galleri Christina Höglund in Stockholm presented a collection of his silk-screen prints at the SAGA prints exhibition at the Grand Palais in Paris.

AUCTION RECORDS:
STOCKHOLM, 9 Dec 1986, *Semaphore* (1977, tempera, 78 x 29 1/2 ins / 198 x 75 cm) SEK 27,000. STOCKHOLM, 14 June 1990, *Earth - Composition* (1973, acrylic/canvas, 47 1/4 x 80 1/4 ins / 120 x 204 cm) SEK 10,500. STOCKHOLM, 5-6 Dec 1990, *Geometric Composition* (1987, tempera, 30 1/4 x 22 3/4 ins / 77 x 58 cm) SEK 18,000. STOCKHOLM, 30 Nov 1993, *Geometric Composition* (1989, tempera/canvas, 70 3/4 x 59 ins / 180 x 150 cm) SEK 25,000. STOCKHOLM, 26 Oct 1999, *Semaphore* (1978, oil on canvas, 76 x 28 ins / 193 x 72 cm) SEK 34,000. STOCKHOLM, 13 March 2000, *Annunciation* (1993, tempera on pan-

el, 31 x 24 ins / 80 x 60 cm) SEK 20,000. STOCKHOLM, 7 Nov 2000, *Meeting* (1994, oil on panel, 25 x 21 ins / 64 x 53 cm) SEK 15,500. STOCKHOLM, 24 April 2001, *Untitled Composition* (1998, oil on canvas, 59 x 30 ins / 150 x 75 cm) SEK 25,000. STOCKHOLM, 21 May 2001, *Untitled Composition* (1988, oil on canvas, 60 x 83 ins / 152 x 210 cm) SEK 16,000. STOCKHOLM, 28 April 2003, *Untitled* (1999, tempera on canvas, 45 x 33 ins / 114 x 84 cm) SEK 17,500. STOCKHOLM, 7 May 2003, *Semaphore* (oil and tempera on canvas, 78 x 30 ins / 198 x 75 cm) SEK 60,000. STOCKHOLM, 27 April 2004, *Horrods Ballet* (1988, tempera on panel, 31 x 24 ins / 80 x 60 cm) SEK 17,000.

KARLSTEEN, Arfvid
Swedish, 17th - 18th century.
Born 16 March 1647, in Karlskoga; died 8 May 1718, in Stockholm.
Miniaturist, medallist.

Arfvid Karlsteen was a pupil of Jean Varin in Paris and John Roettier in London.

KARMANSKI, Joseph von
Polish, 19th century.
Born 9 January 1865, in Brusztynow; died 3 December 1904, in Brusztynow.
Active in Cracow, Munich and Paris.
Painter.

KARNEC, J. E.
Austrian, 19th - 20th century.
Born 1865; died 1934.
Also active in France.
Painter. Landscapes, seascapes, harbour scenes, waterscapes.
Orientalism.

J.E. Karnec was mainly active in Rouen, but also worked in Paris and Venice. Some of his Orientalist landscapes are painted in a thick paste that tends to blur their outlines.

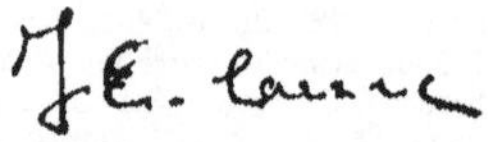

AUCTION RECORDS:
PARIS, 26 Jan 1929, *Narrow Branch of the Seine by the Pont-Neuf*, FRF 350; *View of a Harbour*, FRF 320. PARIS, 10 Jan 1945, *Seascapes* (two paintings together) FRF 3,400. PARIS, 5 March 1945, *The Estuary, Ships at Anchor Within Sight of a Town* (two paintings together) FRF 5,600. PARIS, 7 Feb 1972, *Constantinople* (oil on wood, 9 x 11 ins / 22 x 27 cm) FRF 1,100. PARIS, 14 Nov 1980, *Yachts* (oil on panel, 7 3/4 x 11 1/2 ins / 20 x 29.5 cm) FRF 7,800. PARIS, 13 April 1988, *View of Rouen* (oil on card, 9 1/2 x 7 1/2 ins / 24 x 19 cm) FRF 7,000; *Boats in a Harbour* (oil on card, 6 3/4 x 9 1/2 ins / 17 x 24 cm) FRF 7,500; *Boats at Rouen* (oil on card, 7 1/2 x 9 3/4 ins / 19 x 25 cm) FRF 11,000. VERSAILLES, 6 Nov 1988, *Harbour* (oil on card, 7 3/4 x 10 ins / 20 x 24.5 cm) FRF 6,700. VERSAILLES, 20 June 1989, *Venice* (oil on card, 7 1/2 x 9 1/2 ins / 19 x 24 cm) FRF 11,500. PARIS, 22 March 1990, *Seascape* (oil on panel, 7 3/4 x 12 3/4 ins / 20 x 32.5 cm) FRF 16,000. PARIS, 30 May 1990, *Three-master at the Quayside* (oil on panel, 7 3/4 x 11 1/2 ins / 20 x 29 cm) FRF 21,000. PARIS, 26 April 1991, *Venice, San Giorgio* (oil on panel, 7 1/2 x 9 ins / 19 x 23 cm) FRF 8,500. PARIS, 9 Dec 1991, *Boats* (oil on panel, 9 1/2 x 7 1/2 ins / 24 x 19 cm) FRF 11,000. PARIS, 26 June 1992, *Seascape* (oil on panel, 9 x 12 3/4 ins / 23 x 32.5 cm) FRF 14,000. PARIS, 5 July 1993, *Gondolas in Venice* (oil on card, 7 1/2 x 9 1/2 ins / 19 x 24 cm) FRF 6,500. PARIS, 27 May 1994, *Harbour in Brittany* (oil on panel, 7 1/2 x 9 1/2 ins / 19 x 24 cm) FRF 4,800. PARIS, 19 May 1995, *Yachts and Fishing Boats in a Harbour* (oil on panel, 7 1/2 x 10 ins / 19 x 25.5 cm) FRF 6,500. PARIS, 22 Nov 1996, *Venice* (oil on card, 13 x 7 ins / 33 x 18 cm) FRF 4,600. PARIS, 23 June 1997, *Small Fishing Harbour* (oil on card, 7 1/4 x 9 1/4 ins / 18.5 x 23.5 cm) FRF 5,000. CALAIS, 29 Sept 2002, *Bridge in the Town* (oil on panel, 8 x 11 ins / 20 x 29 cm) EUR 1,750.

KARNEEV, Akim Egorovich, or Carneeff
Russian, 19th century.
Born 5 February 1833, in the Kaluga region; died 1896.
Active in Rome.
Painter. History painting.

MUSEUMS AND GALLERIES:
MOSCOW (State Tretyakov Gal.): *Raising of Lazarus*.

KÄRNER, Theodor
German, 20th century.
Born 1885, in Hohenberg an der Eger; died 1966, in Munich.
Sculptor, modeller, painter (porcelain), draughtsman.
Animals.
Jugendstil.

Theodor Kärner was trained between 1898 and 1903 in C.M. Hutschenreuther's porcelain factory in Hohenberg. He completed his training at the Kunstgewerbeschule at the Munich Academy under the supervision of Heinrich von Zügel. He supplied models of birds to the porcelain factory at Nymphenburg, near Munich, and also to the Rosenthal and Allach porcelain factories in Selb and Munich respectively. He was represented at the exhibition *Traumwelten. Porzellanfiguren zwischen Jugendstil und Art Deco* (*Dream Worlds: German Porcelain Figures from Jugendstil to Art Deco*), at the Museum Huelsmann in Bielefeld in 1999.

BIBLIOGRAPHY:
Franzke, Irmela, *Jugendstil. Glas, Graphik, Keramik, Metall, Möbel, Skulpturen und Textilien von 1880 bis 1915*, exhibition catalogue, Badisches Landesmuseum, Karlsruhe, 1987. Zöller-Stock, Bettina, *Traumwelten: Porzellanfiguren zwischen Jugendstil und Art Deco*, exhibition catalogue, Kunstgewerbemuseum, Berlin, 1998.

MUSEUMS AND GALLERIES:
KARLSRUHE (Badisches Landesmus.): *Seated Dog* (c. 1912, porcelain, model).

KARNOVICH, Stepan Stepanovich
Russian, 18th century.
Born 1746, in St Petersburg.
Engraver.

Karnovich studied at the fine art academy in St Petersburg. His works include a *St Cecilia*, inspired by a work by Raphael.

KARNOVSKY, Mikhail
Russian, 17th century.
Active in Russia.
Engraver (burin).

KAROLIS, Adolfo de. See **CAROLIS**

KAROLUS
Flemish School, 16th century.
Possibly born in Flanders.
Engraver (burin).

According to Le Blanc, prints by Karolus were wrongly attributed to Caraglio.

KAROLUS. See also **CAROLUS**

KAROLYI, Zsigmond
Hungarian, 20th - 21st century.
Born 1952, in Budapest.
Painter.

During his early career, Zsigmond Karolyi painted nudes, landscapes, still-lifes. He then turned to analysing the ingredients of his painting materials in the spirit of Support Surface. At the end of the 1970s, he returned to figuration, but by the 1980s he was producing paintings made up of abstract or symbolic symbols. A retrospective of his work was held in 1992 at the In Situ Gallery, Aalst, Belgium.

KAROW, Hermann Franz Leonhard
German, 19th century.
Born 25 June 1840, in Königsberg (now Kaliningrad, Russia); died 25 June 1899, in Königsberg.
Painter. Portraits, genre scenes.
Karow was a pupil of the academy of fine arts in Königsberg from 1857 to 1861. He exhibited in Berlin and Hanover.
AUCTION RECORDS:
COLOGNE, 26 March 1976, *The Sharpshooter Champion* (1880, oil on canvas, 25 1/4 x 23 1/2 ins / 64 x 60 cm) DEM 6,000.

KAROWSKI, Michael
German, 18th century.
Born c. 1707, in Danzig (now Gdansk, Poland); died 1745, in Göteborg, Sweden.
Painter.
Karowski decorated the great chamber of Gothenburg Town Hall, depicting episodes of Roman history.

KARPATHY, Jeno
Hungarian, 19th - 20th century.
Born 1871.
Painter. Landscapes.
AUCTION RECORDS:
VIENNA, 22 June 1976, *Banks of the Danube in Summer* (oil on canvas, 15 3/4 x 20 ins / 40 x 50.5 cm) ATS 11,000. VIENNA, 19 June 1979, *Summer Landscape* (oil on canvas, 18 1/2 x 28 ins / 47 x 71 cm) ATS 18,000. LOKEREN, 8 Oct 1988, *Flower Meadow* (oil on canvas, 27 1/2 x 39 3/4 ins / 70 x 101 cm) BEF 220,000. LONDON, 22 Feb 1995, *Pond edged by Rhododendron Bushes* (oil on canvas, 30 1/4 x 50 1/4 ins / 77 x 127.5 cm) GBP 1,610. LONDON, 25 May 2000, *Waves Breaking on a Sunlit Shore* (oil on canvas, 26 x 34 ins / 67 x 87 cm) GBP 1,300. BERN, 5 Nov 2003, *Faraglioni Rocks* (oil on canvas, 31 x 52 ins / 80 x 132 cm) CHF 2,400. VIENNA, 24 Feb 2004, *Southern Village Street* (oil on canvas, 39 x 29 ins / 100 x 74 cm) EUR 2,000.

KARPELÈS, Andrée
French, 20th century.
Born 18 May 1885, in Paris.
Painter, illustrator.
Andrée Karpelès studied under René Ménard and Lucien Simon. Her painted work was influenced by the Indian poet Rabindranath Tagore.

KARPELÈS, Jiri. See **KARS Georges**

KARPELLUS, Adolf
Austrian, 19th - 20th century.
Born 8 January 1869, in Neu Sandec; died 18 December 1919, in Vienna.
Painter. Portraits, landscapes, still-lifes.
Adolf Karpellus studied with Christian Griepenkerl at the Akademie der Bildenden Künste in Vienna, then with Jules Lefebvre and Tony Robert-Fleury in Paris.
AUCTION RECORDS:
BERN, 23 Oct 1982, *Little Eve, 1910* (oil on canvas, 32 1/4 x 20 1/2 ins / 82 x 52 cm) CHF 4,000. LONDON, 8 Oct 1986, *The Spirit of Autumn* (1918, oil and gouache/card, 13 3/4 x 18 ins / 35 x 46 cm) GBP 3,200.

KARPF, Anton
German, 18th century.
Born in Lauingen, Bavaria; died 31 August 1770, in Dillingen, Bavaria.
Painter.
Karpf worked mainly for churches such as Steinheim and Gottmannshofen near his home town.

KARPFF, Jean Jacques, or Carp, called Casimir
French, 18th - 19th century.
Born 1770, in Colmar; died 24 March 1829, in Versailles.
Painter, miniaturist, draughtsman, lithographer.
History painting, portraits.
Jean Jacques Karpff was a student of David and lived in Versailles.
MUSEUMS AND GALLERIES:
AVIGNON: *Portrait of Mme Bigand, the Painter's Mother.*
AUCTION RECORDS:
NEW YORK, 30 April 1982, *Portrait of a Young Woman* (pencil and charcoal heightened with white, 14 x 10 1/4 ins / 35.3 x 26.3 cm) USD 2,700. PARIS, 12 Dec 1988, *Full-length Portrait of Marie-Elizabeth Saint Didier, Wife of Andreoli Patochi; Full-length Portrait of M. J. P. Andreoli Patochi* (both in black chalk heightened with white/beige paper, 26 1/2 x 17 3/4 ins / 67 x 45 cm) FRF 125,000.

KARPINSKY, Alfons
Polish, 20th century.
Born 20 February 1875, in Rozvadov; died 1961, in Cracow.
Painter. Portraits, landscapes, still-lifes, flowers.
Alfons Karpinsky trained in Cracow from 1891 to 1899, Munich in 1903, Vienna from 1904 to 1907, and Paris from 1908 to 1912. He visited Venice, Dresden and Budapest. He then returned to Cracow, where he settled after World War I. He was a member of the Vienna Secession and of the Warsaw-based Sztuka artists association.

He first worked as a portrait artist before taking an interest in landscapes and flowers. Sensitive to the elegance of Olga Boznanska's work, he paid great attention to colours. His numerous figures of women show some similarities with those of Degas or Toulouse-Lautrec.

In 2001 his work featured in the *Early Spring. Poland 1880-1920* exhibition at the Palais des Beaux-Arts in Brussels.
BIBLIOGRAPHY:
Morawinska, Agnieszka/Clegg, Elisabeth/Poprzecka, Maria/Crugten, Alain van, *L'Avant-printemps. Pologne 1880-1920*, exhibition catalogue, Palais des Beaux-Arts, Tempera, Brussels, 2001.
MUSEUMS AND GALLERIES:
CRACOW (Muz. Narodowe): *Jane with a Japanese Doll* (1909, oil on canvas).

KARPOV, Boris
Russian, 20th century.
Born 1896, in Kremenchug; died 1968, in Moscow.
Painter.
Socialist Realism.
Boris Karpov studied at the academy of fine arts in Kiev before settling in Moscow. From 1919 he took an active part in collective exhibitions organised by the authorities, and became a member of the Union of Soviet Artists in 1940.

In accordance with official prescriptions, Karpov painted edifying subjects.
BIBLIOGRAPHY:
Tableaux soviétiques, auction catalogue, Salle Drouot, Paris, 3 October 1990.

KARPOV, Ivan
Russian, 20th century.
Born 1898, in Novocherkassk; died 1970, in Milan.
Active in Italy.
Painter. Landscapes with figures, seascapes.
Ivan Karpov's landscapes paid close attention to the influences of the season in which they were painted.
AUCTION RECORDS:
MILAN, 28 Oct 1976, *Beach Scene* (oil on canvas, 17 3/4 x 23 1/2 ins / 45 x 60 cm) ITL 450,000. MILAN, 14 June 1989, *Snowy Landscape* (oil on canvas, 19 1/2 x 27 1/2 ins / 49.5 x 70 cm) ITL 1,500,000. MILAN, 6 Dec 1989, *Autumn Landscape* (oil on canvas, 19 3/4 x 27 1/4 ins / 50 x 69.5 cm) ITL 1,500,000. MILAN, 21 Nov 1990, *Bellagio* (oil on canvas, 27 1/2 x 39 1/4 ins / 70 x 100 cm) ITL 3,000,000. ROME, 16 April 1991, *Landscape with Fig-*

ures (oil on canvas, 27 1/2 x 39 1/4 ins / 70 x 100 cm) ITL 2,990,000. Milan, 6 June 1991, *Shepherd and his Flock* (oil on panel, 15 3/4 x 19 3/4 ins / 40 x 50 cm) ITL 2,000,000. Milan, 12 Dec 1991, *View of a Lake* (oil on canvas, 19 3/4 x 27 1/2 ins / 50 x 70 cm) ITL 4,000,000. Milan, 8 June 1993, *Winter Landscape with Setting Sun* (oil on canvas, 11 1/2 x 15 1/4 ins / 29 x 39 cm) ITL 1,200,000. Milan, 21 Dec 1993, *Haymaking* (oil on canvas, 20 x 28 ins / 51 x 71 cm) ITL 1,495,000. Milan, 20 Dec 1994, *Seascape with Sailboats* (oil on canvas, 15 3/4 x 19 3/4 ins / 40 x 50 cm) ITL 1,610,000. Milan, 14 June 1995, *Bridge over a Canal* (oil on canvas, 15 3/4 x 19 1/2 ins / 40 x 49.5 cm) ITL 2,530,000. Milan, 26 March 1996, *Haywain and Peasant in the Countryside* (oil on canvas, 19 3/4 x 27 1/2 ins / 50 x 70 cm) ITL 3,333,000. Milan, 18 Dec 1996, *Milan Canal* (oil on canvas, 19 3/4 x 27 1/2 ins / 50 x 70 cm) ITL 3,262,000. Milan, 17 Dec 2003, *Snowfall* (oil on board, 28 x 39 ins / 70 x 100 cm) EUR 2,400.

KARPOWICZ, Michel
French, 20th - 21st century.
Born 1955, in Escaudain.
Sculptor. Monuments.

Michel Karpowicz was taught by Henri Derycke in Valenciennes and from 1977 to 1980 at the École des Beaux-Arts in Paris. Several of his works have been made for official commissions in various educational establishments in the Nord region of France. Some of his work has also been bought by the Fonds National d'Art Contemporain.

Auction records:
Paris, 3 June 1991, *Time Love* (1991, granite, metal and wood, 51 1/4 x 15 3/4 x 17 3/4 ins / 130 x 40 x 45 cm) FRF 4,000.

KARS, Georges, pseudonym of Karpeles Jiri
Czech, 20th century.
Born 2 May 1882, in Kralupy nad Vltavou; died 6 February 1945, in Geneva, committed suicide.
Active in France from 1908.
Painter (gouache), pastellist, sculptor, lithographer, draughtsman. Figures, nudes, portraits, still-lifes, landscapes.
Osma Group (The Eight).

Georges Kars studied at the Munich art academy from 1899, where he received guidance from Franz von Stuck and associated with Julius Pascin, Rudolf Lévy and Paul Klee. In Prague he joined the Osma Group (The Eight). He moved to Paris in 1908 and the following year exhibited at various Salons. While travelling in Spain he met Juan Gris in Madrid. On the outbreak of World War I he set up home in Belgium, then in Prague, and returned to France in 1919. He became a friend of Utrillo, of whom he executed several portraits, and of Suzanne Valadon. Fleeing to Geneva during World War II he committed suicide in his hotel in 1945.

As a result of his contacts with Juan Gris and Apollinaire, his painting was strongly, if not markedly, oriented towards the constructive influence of Cubism. His drawings, which use continuous, single, smudged lines, stress their ample volumes.

A number of his works were posthumously featured in the exhibition entitles *Kafka's Metamorphoses* at the Musée du Montparnasse in Paris (2002). Retrospectives include the Galerie des Beaux-Arts, Paris (1945); Galerie Katia Granoff, Paris (1954); Wolfgang Ketterer gallery, Munich (1959); and *Georges Kars, peintures et dessins* at the Musée d'Art Moderne, Troyes (1983).

Bibliography:
Georges Kars, exhibition catalogue, Gal. des Beaux-Arts, Paris, 1945. *Georges Kars, peintures, dessins*, exhibition catalogue, Gal. Katia Granoff, Paris, 1954. Jolinon, Joseph, *Kars, la vie et l'œuvre de Georges Kars*, Imprimerie Générale du Sud-Est, Lyons, 1958. *Osma. Výstava 8, k 70. výroci první výstavy [Le groupe des Huit, soixante dixième anniversaire de leur exposition]*, exhibition catalogue, Gal. Výtvarného Umeni, Roudnice nad Labem, 1978 (text in French). Chabert, Philippe-Gérard, *Georges Kars, peintures et dessins*, exhibition catalogue, Musée d'Art moderne, Troyes, 1983. Siblík, Jirí, *Georges Kars*, Odeon, Prague, 1999. Nieszawer, Nadine/Boyé, Marie/Lanzmann, Claude (preface), *Peintres juifs de l'école de Paris 1905-1939*, Denoël, Paris, 2001. *Métamorphoses de Kafka*, group exhibition catalogue, Musée du Montparnasse, Paris, 2002.

Museums and Galleries:
Cologne - Grenoble - Hamburg - Hanover - Los Angeles - Prague - Troyes (MAM): *Prague* - Vienna.

Auction records:
Paris, 18 Nov 1925, *Artist's Dressing Room*, FRF 350; *Negro*, FRF 750. Paris, 29 Oct 1926, *Road to Rochemaure*, FRF 5,400. Paris, 30 May 1945, *Landscape*, FRF 5,100. Paris, 13 June 1947, *Reclining Nude*, FRF 12,500. Paris, 27 Nov 1950, *Female Bather*, FRF 15,500. Paris, 17 June 1966, *Acrobats*, FRF 12,000. Versailles, 27 June 1976, *The Ballet* (bronze gilded with gold leaf, relief, 9 3/4 x 7 3/4 ins / 25 x 20 cm) FRF 3,000. Versailles, 27 Nov 1977, *The Dance* (bronze gilded with gold leaf, 9 3/4 x 7 3/4 ins / 25 x 20 cm) FRF 4,000. London, 21 Feb 1979, *Still-life with Grapes* (oil on panel, 12 3/4 x 16 ins / 32.5 x 40.5 cm) GBP 680. Zurich, 15 May 1982, *The Ballet* (bronze relief, 4 3/4 x 9 1/2 x 7 ins / 12 x 24 x 18 cm) CHF 2,800. London, 23 Feb 1983, *Seated Nude* (oil on canvas, 24 x 15 ins / 61 x 38 cm) GBP 1,000. Zurich, 6 June 1986, *Reclining Nude* (watercoloured sketch, drawing, 7 x 9 1/2 ins / 18 x 24 cm) CHF 1,700. Paris, 6 April 1987, *Cubist Woman* (1912, oil on canvas, 39 1/4 x 32 ins / 100 x 81 cm) FRF 55,000. Paris, 20 March 1988, *Jewish Wedding* (charcoal drawing, 18 x 20 ins / 46 x 51 cm) FRF 6,000; *Still-life with Mask* (c. 1914, oil on canvas, 35 x 28 1/4 ins / 89 x 72 cm) FRF 32,000; *Portrait of a Woman* (c. 1912-1913, oil on canvas, 39 1/4 x 32 ins / 100 x 81 cm) FRF 68,000. Paris, 16 May 1988, *Woman with Mirror* (gouache, 19 x 12 1/2 ins / 48 x 32 cm) FRF 6,200. Versailles, 25 Sept 1988, *Woman in Pink* (1927, oil on canvas, 25 1/2 x 19 3/4 ins / 65 x 50 cm) FRF 13,000. Paris, 19 Oct 1988, *Acrobats* (1930, oil on canvas, 31 1/2 x 25 1/2 ins / 80 x 65 cm) FRF 110,000. Tel Aviv, 30 May 1989, *Still-life with Teapot and Fruit* (oil on canvas, 25 1/2 x 32 ins / 65 x 81 cm) USD 9,900. Paris, 1 Dec 1989, *Chestnut Trees in Flower* (oil on card, 15 x 18 ins / 38 x 46 cm) FRF 40,000. Tel Aviv, 3 Jan 1990, *Children on a Roundabout* (pencil, 10 1/4 x 11 1/2 ins / 26 x 29 cm) USD 530. Douai, 1 April 1990, *Young Girl Leaning on her Elbows* (1937, oil on canvas, 22 x 18 1/4 ins / 55 x 46.5 cm) FRF 42,000. Paris, 8 April 1990, *Bouquet of Flowers* (c. 1918, oil on canvas, 25 1/2 x 22 ins / 65 x 55 cm) FRF 38,000. Tel Aviv, 31 May 1990, *Resting Place in the Forest* (oil on canvas, 32 x 39 1/4 ins / 81 x 100 cm) USD 17,600. Tel Aviv, 19 June 1990, *Two Little Girls* (1941, charcoal, 23 1/2 x 17 1/4 ins / 60 x 43.5 cm) USD 880. Tel Aviv, 20 June 1990, *Nude on a Bed of Flowers* (1926, pastel, 16 1/2 x 24 1/4 ins / 42 x 61.5 cm) USD 1,540. Paris, 12 Oct 1990, *Still-life with Violins* (pastel, 20 3/4 x 20 ins / 53 x 51 cm) FRF 5,500. Tel Aviv, 1 Jan 1991, *Woman Reading* (oil on canvas, 18 x 14 3/4 ins / 46 x 37.5 cm) USD 4,400; *Two Women* (1928, oil on canvas, 19 3/4 x 13 3/4 ins / 50 x 35 cm) USD 9,350. Paris, 14 April 1991, *Nude with Parrot* (oil on canvas, 25 1/2 x 19 3/4 ins / 65 x 50 cm) FRF 33,000. Paris, 27 May 1991, *Orchestra* (gouache, 19 x 18 ins / 48 x 46 cm) FRF 15,000. Paris, 17 May 1992, *Woman in her Robe* (1922, charcoal drawing, 23 1/2 x 17 3/4 ins / 60 x 45 cm) FRF 7,000. Tel Aviv, 20 Oct 1992, *Landscape* (1928, oil on canvas, 15 x 18 ins / 38 x 46 cm) USD 3,850. Paris, 4 April 1993, *The Dance* (bronze, 9 1/2 x 7 1/4 ins / 24 x 18.5 cm) FRF 8,000. New York, 23 Feb 1994, *Reclining Naked Woman* (1923, oil on canvas, 18 1/4 x 25 3/4 ins / 46.5 x 65.5 cm) USD 4,600. Paris, 15 Nov

1994, *Woman Washing Herself* (oil on panel, 29 1/2 x 17 1/4 ins / 75 x 44 cm) FRF 13,000. PARIS, 26 March 1995, *Woman Washing Herself* (oil on wood, 29 1/4 x 17 1/4 ins / 74.3 x 44 cm) FRF 19,000. TEL AVIV, 11 Oct 1995, *Woman in an Armchair* (1912, oil on canvas, 39 1/4 x 32 ins / 100 x 81 cm) USD 23,000. PARIS, 20 June 1996, *Villefranche, the Main Road* (1948, oil on canvas, 17 1/4 x 28 3/4 ins / 44 x 73 cm) FRF 16,000. PARIS, 16 March 1997, *Rural Landscape* (oil on canvas, 21 1/4 x 25 1/2 ins / 54 x 65 cm) FRF 18,000. NEUILLY, 27 Nov 1997, *Nude* (1937, oil on canvas, 18 x 12 1/2 ins / 46 x 32 cm) FRF 12,800. LYONS, 7 June 1999, *Nude Doing Her Hair* (oil on board, 19 x 15 ins / 47 x 37 cm) FRF 25,000. PARIS, 13 Oct 1999, *Standing Nude* (1926, oil on canvas, 24 x 15 ins / 61 x 38 cm) FRF 27,000. PARIS, 15 March 2000, *Still-life* (oil on canvas, 35 x 29 ins / 89 x 73 cm) FRF 88,000. PRAGUE, 14 Oct 2000, *Parrot* (1897, oil on canvas, 26 x 20 ins / 66 x 52 cm) CZK 600,000. PARIS, 18 Nov 2001, *Nude with Turban* (charcoal and pastel, 19 x 13 ins / 49 x 34 cm) FRF 12,000. PARIS, 18 Nov 2001, *Reclining Female Nude* (oil on canvas, 20 x 26 ins / 50 x 65 cm) FRF 71,000. PARIS, 17 June 2002, *Woman with Basket* (1941, oil on canvas, 26 x 20 ins / 65 x 50 cm) EUR 4,200. PARIS, 18 Dec 2002, *Portrait of a Woman* (oil on canvas, 31 x 24 ins / 80 x 62 cm) EUR 8,000. PARIS, 3 March 2003, *Nude in an Armchair* (charcoal, 19 x 13 ins / 47 x 33 cm) EUR 1,800. LONDON, 20 March 2003, *Still-life* (oil on canvas, 21 x 18 ins / 54 x 46 cm) GBP 7,000.

KARSCH, Eduard Joseph
German, 17th - 18th century.
Born in Münster.
Painter.

Karsch worked initially in Düsseldorf, then spent 1700-1703 in Rome.

MUSEUMS AND GALLERIES:
DÜSSELDORF (Kunstmus.): *Mythological Scene* (oil on canvas, six).

KARSCH, Florian
German, 19th century.
Born 18 February 1831, in Wurzeldorf (Wyrebina), Silesia; died 6 November 1884, in Breslau (now Wroclaw, Poland).
Painter. History painting, portraits.

Karsch was appointed drawing master at the Realgymnasium in Breslau and retained the post until he died.

MUSEUMS AND GALLERIES:
WROCLAW: *St Jerome.*

KARSCH, Joachim
German, 20th century.
Born 20 June 1897, in Breslau (now Wroclaw, Poland).
Sculptor. Groups.

Joachim Karsch settled in Berlin in 1919 and was awarded the National Sculpture prize in 1920. His best-known work is the low relief *The Brothers Karamazov.*

AUCTION RECORDS:
ZURICH, 8 April 1997, *Reclining Girl* (plaster, 4 1/4 x 7 3/4 ins / 11 x 20 cm) CHF 1,300. BERLIN, 5 June 1999, *Boy Praying* (1931, brown patinated bronze, 11 x 7x8 ins / 28 x 18x21 cm) DEM 7,000. BERLIN, 1 Dec 2001, *Drinking Boy* (1937, 12 x 7x7 ins / 30 x 17x17 cm) DEM 6,500.

KARSEN, Eduard
Dutch, 19th - 20th century.
Born 10 March 1860, in Amsterdam; died 1941.
Painter, engraver. Landscapes with figures, urban landscapes.

Eduard Karsen was awarded a medal in Munich in 1905. He took part in the Brussels exhibition of 1910.

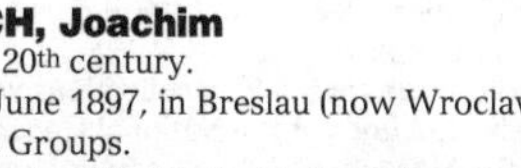

MUSEUMS AND GALLERIES:
AMSTERDAM (Stedelijk Mus.): *The Little Garden.*

AUCTION RECORDS:
AMSTERDAM, 27 April 1976, *Summer Landscape* (oil on canvas, 15 x 20 1/2 ins / 38 x 52 cm) NLG 7,800. AMSTERDAM, 14 April 1986, *Garden in Winter* (oil on canvas, 14 1/4 x 19 1/4 ins / 36 x 49 cm) NLG 5,400. AMSTERDAM, 10 Feb 1988, *Bridge on the Bocht in Amsterdam* (oil on canvas, 31 1/4 x 39 3/4 ins / 79.5 x 101 cm) NLG 1,610. AMSTERDAM, 24 Sept 1992, *Chickens in a Farmyard* (oil on canvas, 14 1/4 x 18 ins / 36.5 x 45.5 cm) NLG 3,680. AMSTERDAM, 27 April 1999, *Boersche buurt* (oil on canvas, 15 x 20 ins / 37 x 50 cm) NLG 18,000. AMSTERDAM, 26 Oct 1999, *Voormalig buitenpad* (oil on panel, 7 x 11 ins / 18 x 28 cm) NLG 4,000. AMSTERDAM, 24 April 2001, *Herengracht, Amsterdam* (chalk, 13 x 17 ins / 34 x 44 cm) NLG 9,000. AMSTERDAM, 4 March 2002, *De cunera-toren van rhenen* (oil on canvas, 17 x 22 ins / 44 x 55 cm) EUR 2,000. AMSTERDAM, 2 Sept 2003, *Achter eene boerderij* (oil on panel, 7 x 11 ins / 17 x 27 cm) EUR 2,000.

KARSEN, Kaspar or Kasparus, or Karssen
Dutch, 19th century.
Born 2 April 1810, in Amsterdam; died 24 July 1896, in Amsterdam.
Painter, lithographer. Urban landscapes, landscapes.

MUSEUMS AND GALLERIES:
AMSTERDAM: *Town on a River; Interior of the Old Stock Exchange* - AMSTERDAM (Stedelijk Mus.): *Dordrecht.*

AUCTION RECORDS:
PARIS, 1844, *View of Haarlem,* FRF 310. ROTTERDAM, 1891, *View of a Village,* FRF 150. LONDON, 29 July 1929, *View of a Dutch Town,* GBP 46. AMSTERDAM, 15-21 April 1947, *Village in Gelderland,* NLG 1,350. AMSTERDAM, 1 May 1951, *Old Houses in Scheveningen,* NLG 1,700. AMSTERDAM, 18 May 1965, *View of Amsterdam,* NLG 11,500. COLOGNE, 16 Nov 1967, *Romantic Landscape,* DEM 10,000. AMSTERDAM, 29-30 Oct 1968, *Street Scene,* NLG 33,000. AMSTERDAM, 20 Nov 1973, *Castle by a River,* NLG 20,000. AMSTERDAM, 26 Nov 1974, *Oud Katwijk* NLG 37,000. AMSTERDAM, 27 April 1976, *View of Amsterdam* (oil on panel, 12 1/2 x 18 1/2 ins / 32 x 47 cm) NLG 22,000. AMSTERDAM, 27 June 1977, *Riverside* (1870, oil on panel, 13 3/4 x 17 ins / 35 x 43 cm) NLG 8,600. AMSTERDAM, 30 Oct 1979, *View of Dresden* (1862, oil on canvas, 21 1/2 x 39 ins / 54.5 x 99 cm) NLG 30,000. LONDON, 24 March 1982, *Dunkirk, a View from the River* (1853, oil on canvas, 15 3/4 x 25 ins / 40 x 63.5 cm) GBP 6,600. LONDON, 23 March 1984, *Town by a River* (oil on panel, 16 1/4 x 23 ins / 41.2 x 58.4 cm) GBP 8,000. AMSTERDAM, 15 April 1985, *View of Koblenz* (oil on canvas, 21 1/4 x 38 1/4 ins / 54 x 97.2 cm) NLG 38,000. LONDON, 6 May 1987, *Figures in a Sunny Street* (oil on canvas, 17 x 21 ins / 43 x 53.5 cm) GBP 3,800. AMSTERDAM, 3 May 1988, *View of a Town on a Summer's Day with Villagers in the Square around the Fountain* (oil on panel, 7 3/4 x 11 ins / 20 x 27 cm) NLG 12,650. LONDON, 6 Oct 1989, *The Ferryman* (1850, oil on panel, 15 3/4 x 20 3/4 ins / 40 x 53 cm) GBP 8,250. AMSTERDAM, 30 Oct 1990, *Dutch Town with Figures in Summer* (oil on canvas, 16 1/4 x 25 1/2 ins / 41 x 65 cm) NLG 103,500. AMSTERDAM, 23 April 1991, *The Weighing House in Amsterdam* (oil on panel, 9 x 11 1/2 ins / 22 x 29 cm) NLG 14,950. AMSTERDAM, 30 Oct 1991, *View of the Von Wied House at Scheveningen with Many Fishermen* (oil on canvas, 22 x 36 1/4 ins / 56 x 92.2 cm) NLG 23,000. AMSTERDAM, 28 Oct 1992, *Fishermen in their Village, Scheveningen* (1874, oil on canvas, 16 3/4 x 25 3/4 ins / 42.5 x 65.5 cm) NLG 9,775. AMSTERDAM, 2 Nov 1992, *Figures on a Quay* (oil on panel, 5 3/4 x 7 3/4 ins / 14.5 x 19.5 cm) NLG 2,530. AMSTERDAM, 20 April 1993, *Village Scene at Scheveningen* (1872, oil on canvas, 16 1/4 x 22 3/4 ins / 41 x 58 cm) NLG 29,900. LONDON, 18 Nov 1994, *Cattle Drinking in a River in a Large Town* (oil on panel, 14 3/4 x 21 1/4 ins / 37.5 x 54 cm) GBP 6,900. AMSTERDAM, 5 Nov 1996, *View of a Town with*

Figures in a Boat (1850, oil on canvas, 24½ x 36¼ ins / 62 x 92 cm) NLG 70,800. AMSTERDAM, 27 Oct 1997, *Village in the Dunes, Probably Scheveningen* (1874, oil on canvas, 17 x 25¾ ins / 43 x 65.5 cm) NLG 21,240. AMSTERDAM, 26 Oct 1999, *Town View with Figures along River* (oil on canvas, 16 x 23 ins / 40 x 59 cm) NLG 35,000. AMSTERDAM, 26 Oct 1999, *Town View along Canal with Figures* (oil on panel, 16 x 20 ins / 40 x 52 cm) NLG 38,000. AMSTERDAM, 18 Jan 2000, *Cappriccio View in City* (oil on panel, 9 x 12 ins / 23 x 31 cm) NLG 7,000. AMSTERDAM, 4 July 2000, *Huis op de Contre Escarpe, Doesburg* (1884, oil on canvas, 15 x 14 ins / 39 x 35 cm) NLG 6,000. GRAVENHAGE, 24 April 2002, *Town View with Many Figures with Market Merchandise* (1883, oil on canvas, 28 x 24 ins / 70 x 60 cm) EUR 12,000. AMSTERDAM, 3 Dec 2002, *Town View with Cows Wading in a River* (oil on canvas, 22 x 39 ins / 56 x 99 cm) EUR 28,000. AMSTERDAM, 29 April 2003, *View of Katwijk Village with a Groot Badhotel in the Background* (oil on canvas, 22 x 36 ins / 57 x 92 cm) EUR 38,000. AMSTERDAM, 21 Oct 2003, *Town on the Waterfront* (oil on panel, 9 x 13 ins / 22 x 32 cm) EUR 12,000. AMSTERDAM, 21 April 2004, *Figures on a Frozen City Canal at Dusk* (1880, oil on panel, 8 x 11 ins / 21 x 27 cm) EUR 8,000.

KARSENTY, Guy

French, 20th century.

Born 16 February 1933, in Bône, now Annaba, Algeria.

Painter (gouache), lithographer. Genre scenes, landscapes.

Guy Karsenty was initially a shop-sign painter and decorator and in 1955 became a student at the École des Beaux-Arts in Tours. He later moved to Paris where he continued to paint signs and posters. He is then believed to have worked as a teacher in Toulon. He took part in numerous regional group exhibitions and received various local awards and honours. He exhibited at the Salon des Surindépendants in Paris in 1976. He also showed collections of his paintings in hotels and galleries in Marseilles, Gap and Lyons. He took part in the 1980 Venice Biennale and in other prestigious exhibitions.

AUCTION RECORDS:

MARSEILLES, 10 May 1980, *Kippur* (oil on canvas, 32 x 25½ ins / 81 x 65 cm) FRF 6,000. MARSEILLES, 21 Jan 1984, *Quays of the Seine* (oil on canvas, 19¾ x 27½ ins / 50 x 70 cm) FRF 10,000. ARLES, 16 Feb 1986, *La Ghriba* (oil on canvas) FRF 25,500.

KARSENTY-SCHILLER, Danièle

French, 20th century.

Born 18 July 1933, in Paris.

Painter. Scenes with figures, landscapes with figures.

Danièle Karsenty-Schiller was the daughter of a family of Hungarian origin who emigrated to North Africa. Her father, a hero of the Resistance during World War II, died in a concentration camp in Poland at the age of 34. Danièle was originally an actor and did not begin painting until 1971. In a style close to Naive she makes the transition from poignant depictions of German concentration camps to more joyful scenes of public celebration, including dances, private viewings, casino interiors and religious processions. Her work is characterised by bright colours and the meticulousness and precision of her draughtsmanship and is inspired by France and Mexico.

Karsenty-Schiller took part in group exhibitions in Paris, including the Salon d'Automne, the Salon des Indépendants and the Salon des Femmes Peintres, of which she was a member. She also exhibited at the Musée de l'Athénée in Geneva and at international painting exhibitions held in Basel, Zurich and Düsseldorf. She showed her work in solo exhibitions, including those at the following: the Galerie Vercamer in Paris (1972); the Galerie Valayer in Valence (1972); the Musée d'Art Naïf in Flayosc (1973); the Musée d'Art Naïf in Carros (1974); the Galerie Antoinette in Paris (1974, 1977, 1985); the Galerie des Peintres Européens in Cannes (1975); the Maison de la Culture in Thonon (1975); the Galerie de l'Angle Aigu (1978); the Pinacothèque du Bilboquet in Paris; the Château-Musée in Vallauris (1985); the Musée du Bastion St-Antoine in Antibes (1986); the Musée de Fréjus (1989); and the Musée St-Paul-de-Vence (1990)

MUSEUMS AND GALLERIES:

FLAYOSC (Mus. of Naive Art) - JERUSALEM (Israel Mus.) - LAVAL (Mus. d'Art naïf) - NICE (Mus. International d'Art Naïf Anatole-Jakovsky) - PARIS (Mus. du Martyr Juif) - TEL AVIV - VICQ (Mus. International d'Art Naïf).

KARSH, Yousuf

Canadian, 20th century.

Born 23 December 1908, in Mardin, Armenia; died 13 July 2002, in Boston.

Active in Canada from 1926.

Photographer. Portraits.

Yousuf Karsh, emigrated to Canada in 1924 with his parents. From 1926 to 1928 he learned photography with his uncle George Nakash at his portrait studio in Sherbrooke. He also studied with John H. Garo in Boston from 1928 to 1931, and had some experience with stage lighting in the Ottawa Little Theatre. He set up his own studio in Ottawa in 1932 and had established a reputation as a portrait photographer of visiting statesman and dignitaries by 1936. He became internationally known when he photographed Winston Churchill at a political meeting in Ottawa in 1941. This photograph was used on the cover of *Life* magazine in December of the same year.

Karsh was famous for his iconic photographs of world figures and celebrities, or 'people of consequence' as he called them. Frequently, a Karsh portrait has become the best known image of the subject, and one of his sitters, Field Marshal Montgomery, coined the phrase 'I've been Karshed'. His work was motivated by a belief in individual excellence and the need for role models in society. He stated that he wished to capture the essential element of greatness in his famous subjects 'as they impressed themselves on their generation', citing three portraits that achieved his objective: Winston Churchill, George Bernard Shaw and Eleanor Roosevelt. Karsh used large format cameras with up to 8 x 10 inch plates, placing the subject against a dark background, and using banks of spotlights to achieve dramatic clarity with remarkable detail and depth. His works are notable for the balance between light and dark, and between form and negative space.

Karsh's photographs are held in collections worldwide, including massive holdings at the National Gallery of Canada, Ottawa, and the Museum of Fine Arts in Boston. In 1973, the National Gallery of Australia purchased the entire collection of 130 prints which had formed his touring exhibition *Men Who Make our World*. The National Archive of Canada in Ottawa holds the bulk of his work, consisting of 250,000 negatives, 12,000 colour transparencies and 50,000 original prints. His works were featured in the Canadian pavilion at the World Expo in Osaka, Japan in 1967. Solo exhibitions include: Corcoran Gallery, Washington DC (1969); National Gallery of Canada (1989, 2003-2004); Museum of Fine Arts, Boston (1996, 2003); and Albany Museum of Art, Georgia (1999). He was an Officer of the Order of Canada, and an Honorary Fellow of the Royal Photographic Society.

BIBLIOGRAPHY:

Portraits by Yousuf Karsh, exhibition catalogue, Corcoran Gallery of Art, Washington DC, 1969. Karsh, Yousuf, *Karsh Canadians*, University of Toronto Press, Toronto, 1978. *Karsh, A Fifty-Year Retrospective*, University of Toronto Press, Toronto, 1983. Borcoman, James, *Karsh: The Art of the Portrait*, exhibition catalogue, National Gallery of Ottawa, Ottawa, 1989. *Karsh: A Sixty-Year Retrospective*, exhibition catalogue, Museum of Fine Arts, Boston, 1996. Vorsteher, Dieter/Yates, Janet (ed.), *Yousuf Karsh: Heroes of Light and Shadow*, Stoddart, Toronto, 2001. *Karsh: A Biography of Images*, exhibition catalogue, Museum of Fine Arts, Boston, 2003.

Museums and Galleries:

Bell Island (Mine Mus.): *Stephen B. Leacock* (c. 1940, gelatin silver photograph); *'Tiny' Stirtzinger of Atlas Steel* (c. 1945, gelatin silver photograph); *Katherine Cornell* (1947, gelatin silver photograph) - Boston (MFA): *Agnes MacPhail* (1934, gelatin silver photograph); *Alexander Fleming* (1954, gelatin silver photograph); *Audrey Hepburn* (1956, gelatin silver photograph); *Man Ray* (1965, gelatin silver photograph); *Norman Rockwell* (1956, gelatin silver photograph); *Sir Edmund Hillary* (1960, gelatin silver photograph); *Georgia O'Keefe* (1956, gelatin silver photograph); *Humphrey Bogart* (1946, gelatin silver photograph) - Canberra (Nat. Gal. of Australia): *Pablo Picasso* (1954, gelatin silver photograph); *Ernest Hemingway* (1957, gelatin silver photograph); *Dr Jonas Edward Salk* (1956, gelatin silver photograph); *Helen Keller with her Companion Polly Thomson* (1948, gelatin silver photograph); *Tennessee Williams* (1956, gelatin silver photograph); *Sir Laurence Olivier* (1954, gelatin silver photograph) - London (UK Government Art Collection): *Sir Winston Churchill* (1941, photograph) - Los Angeles (County MA): *Self-portrait* (1946, gelatin silver photograph); *Winston Churchill* (1941, gelatin silver photograph) - Ottawa (Nat. Gal. of Canada): *Albert Camus* (1954, gelatin silver photograph); *Andy Warhol* (1979, gelatin silver photograph); *Pierre Elliott Trudeau* (1968, gelatin silver photograph); *Grey Owl (Archibald Belaney)* (1936, gelatin silver photograph); *Henry Moore* (1949, gelatin silver photograph); *Kenojuak* (1976, gelatin silver photograph); *Martin Luther King* (1962, gelatin silver photograph); *Charles de Gaulle* (1944, gelatin silver photograph); *Fidel Castro* (1971, gelatin silver photograph) - Toronto (Ryerson University): *Marshall McLuhan at the Royal Ontario Museum, Toronto* (1974, photomechanical reproduction); *Jean Sibelius* (c. 1945, gelatin silver photograph); *Boris Karloff* (1946, gelatin silver photograph); *Men Working in Steel Factory* (c. 1945, gelatin silver photograph); *His Holiness Pope Pius XII* (c. 1945, gelatin silver photograph); *Martha Graham* (1948, gelatin silver photograph); *HRH Faisal Ibn Abdul Aziz* (1945, gelatin silver photograph).

KARSHAN, Linda

American, 20th - 21st century.
Born 1947, in Minneapolis, USA, of Romanian origin.
Active in London from 1969.
Draughtswoman, engraver (including wood).

Linda Karshan studied drawing, painting and colour at Skidmore College in Saratoga Springs from 1965 to 1967 under the direction of the architect Robert Reed. She then studied art history for a year at the Sorbonne in Paris in 1968. Karshan has a Master's degree in psychology.

Remarkably, Karshan works exclusively as a draughtswoman. She started out with still-lifes and went on to draw on Post-Minimalist sources, Eva Hesse in particular, developing architectures and grids through the repetition of short, horizontal and vertical lines and dots that contain great energy.

Karshan has taken part in various group exhibitions, including *The Legacy of Surrealism in Contemporary Art* at the Ben Shahn Galleries of William Paterson College in Wayne in New Jersey in 1988, and *Contemporary British Drawings* at Edward Tyler-Nahem Fine Art in New York in 1997. She has also shown her work in solo exhibitions, including at the following: the ASB Gallery in London (1984, 1985, 1986, 1991); the Bidermann Gallery in London (from 1991); Romania (a touring exhibition, 1998); the Sir John Soane's Museum in London, the Insitituto Valenciano de Arte Moderno in Valencia, and Kettle's Yard in Cambridge in England (a touring exhibition, 2002); and *Linda Karshan: Marks and Moves* at Kettle's Yard in Cambridge (2003).

Bibliography:

Linda Karshan at the Soane: Prints and Drawings 1997-2002, exhibition catalogue, Sir John Soane's Museum, London, 2002. Raeburn, Michael, *Linda Karshan. Marks and Moves*, exhibition catalogue, Kettle's Yard, Cambridge, 2003.

Museums and Galleries:

London (Arts Council Collection, Hayward Gal.) - London (British Mus.) - Munich (Staatliche Graphische Sammlung).

KARSKAYA, Ida

Ukrainian, 20th century.
Born 5 July 1905, in Debdor, near Bender; died 23 March 1990, in Paris.
Active from 1924.
Painter (including gouache/mixed media), collage artist, assemblage artist. Figures, portraits, flowers. Designs for tapestries.

Ida Karskaya studied medicine in Ghent and Paris. She married a painter, Serge Karsky, and his example awakened her own vocation as an artist. The only advice she received was from her husband and their friend, Pascin.

Francis Carco devoted a study to Ida Karaskaya's depictions of flowers, portraits, fields and meats which he likened to the 'scenes from the slaughterhouse' by Soutine, an artist whom she admired. In fact, Carco's study corresponds only to the eary period of Karskaya's work. In her figurative pictures, the figures were only hinted at. She was already particularly drawn to the sensuousness of the pigmented, thick and triturated materials of informal abstraction. From 1949 numerous writers took an interest in her work, including Henri Calet, Francis Ponge and Jean Paulhan. Having evolved towards abstraction, she frequently employed a collage technique, sometimes incorporating scraps of tree bark which particularly suited her gentle, warm and harmonious colours and materials. She often also assembled scrap objects, thus anticipating the practice of appropriating actual things from the real world that was so characteristic of the New Realists. The critic Geneviève Bonnefoi compiled an inventory of the materials that were reutilised: 'thin slats of wood, leather, fraying fabrics, slips of paper, strands of wool and, sometimes, tongue in cheek, the torn blue of a packet of Gauloises'. Extending her researches, she created tapestries and figures in textiles made from animal or vegetable fibres. She referred to a good number of her abstract assemblages as *Unanswered Letters*, conferring nobility and poetry on the most despised materials by assembling their ruined textures and bright colours with humour and a very personal sense of the mystery of creation.

Collective exhibitions include: Salon des Tuileries (from 1938); *Collages*, Galerie Arnaud, Paris (1954); *Collages*, Galerie La Roue, Paris (1957); Salon des Réalités Nouvelles (1956 to 1964); *Fifty Years of Collage*, Musée de St-Étienne (1964); *Rencontres - Cinquante ans de collages* (*Encounters - Fifty Years of Collage*), an exhibition organised by Françoise Monin, Galerie Claudine Lustman, Paris (1991). In 2003 her work was represented in *Russian Paris 1910-1960* an exhibition showcasing Russian art and Russian artists in Paris. Organised by the Russian museum in St Petersburg, the exhibition moved to the von der Heydt museum, Wuppertal, then to the Musée des Beaux-Arts, Bordeaux.

Solo exhibitions include: Montpellier (1943); Galerie Pétridès, Paris (1946); Galerie Colette Allendy, Paris (1949, 1950 and 1954); Galerie Karl Flinker, Paris (1962). Retrospectives include: Beaulieu abbey in Rouergue (1972); Fondation Nationale des Arts Plastiques, Paris (1980); Freiburg, (1981); Paris (1989). In 1995 four simultaneous exhibitions were devoted to her work: *Invités de minuit* (*Midnight Guests*), Galerie Arnoux, Paris; *Les Gris quotidiens* (*Everyday Greys*),

Galerie Pierre Brullé, Paris; *Collages*, Galerie Philip, Paris; and *Paintings*, Limmer gallery, Freiburg. In 1997, the Musée Bibliothèque Pierre André Benoit in Alès organised an exhibition of her work, and in Paris the Galerie Pierre Brullé exhibited works dating from 1947 to 1957.

BIBLIOGRAPHY:

'*Karskaya*' in *XXe Siècle* n° 6, periodical, Paris, 1956. *Ida Karskaya*, exhibition catalogue, Fondation nationale des Arts graphiques et Plastiques, Paris, 1980. Marcadé, Jean-Claude/Pétrova, Evguénia, *Paris russe 1910-1960*, exhibition catalogue, Musée des Beaux-Arts, Bordeaux, 2003.

AUCTION RECORDS:

PARIS, 6 Nov 1983, *Composition in Green and Blue* (1960, oil on canvas, 31 1/2 x 47 1/4 ins / 80 x 120 cm) FRF 10,000. PARIS, 24 Oct 1986, *Untitled, Mauve* (c. 1960, gouache and collage, 25 1/4 x 18 ins / 64 x 46 cm) FRF 9,000. PARIS, 9 April 1987, *Everyday Greys* (mixed media/paper, 9 x 11 1/2 ins / 23 x 29 cm) FRF 17,500. PARIS, 20 March 1988, *Twins* (mixed media, 14 1/4 x 11 ins / 36 x 28 cm) FRF 11,000. PARIS, 21 Nov 1988, *Useless Gestures* (1949, oil on paper, 9 3/4 x 11 3/4 ins / 25 x 30 cm) FRF 10,300. PARIS, 14 Dec 1988, *Composition* (c. 1968, gouache, 25 1/2 x 17 3/4 ins / 65 x 45 cm) FRF 15,000. PARIS, 19 March 1989, *Composition* (oil on paper, 15 3/4 x 11 3/4 ins / 40 x 30 cm) FRF 5,200. PARIS, 26 May 1989, *Composition* (mixed media and chain/paper, 15 x 20 3/4 ins / 38 x 53 cm) FRF 7,000. PARIS, 18 June 1989, *Composition* (mixed media and collage, 11 3/4 x 18 ins / 30 x 46 cm) FRF 10,000. DOUAI, 1 April 1990, *Face* (1962, mixed media and collage/paper, 12 1/2 x 9 1/2 ins / 32 x 24 cm) FRF 29,000. PARIS, 14 May 1990, *Composition in Pink* (mixed media/crumpled paper, 9 3/4 x 7 3/4 ins / 25 x 19.5 cm) FRF 10,000. PARIS, 10 Feb 1991, *Transparent Face* (mixed media collage and canvas, 18 1/4 x 14 ins / 46.5 x 35.5 cm) FRF 7,000. PARIS, 26 Sept 1991, *Everyday Grey* (mixed media/paper, 4 1/4 x 12 1/4 ins / 11 x 31 cm) FRF 5,000. PARIS, 20 April 1994, *Composition* (oil and collage/canvas, 18 x 10 1/4 ins / 46 x 26 cm) FRF 4,600. PARIS, 25 May 1994, *Warrior* (1954, oil on canvas, 31 1/2 x 31 1/2 ins / 80 x 80 cm) FRF 14,000. PARIS, 7 Oct 1995, *Everyday Grey* (oil on canvas, 39 1/4 x 39 1/4 ins / 100 x 100 cm) FRF 20,000.

KARST, Adolf

German, 19th century.

Born 19 November 1815, in Erfurt; died 22 April 1868, in Dresden.

Painter, lithographer. Historical subjects, landscapes.

Karst was a pupil of Kolbe in Berlin in 1836, but subsequently settled in Dresden, where he exhibited from 1845 to 1875.

KARST, Pankratius

Swiss, 17th century.

Active in Lucerne.

Glass painter.

Karst was a member of St Luke's Academy in Lucerne in 1641.

KARSTEN, Elisabet Charlotta, later Mrs Kaschanoff

Swedish, 19th century.

Born 1789, in Stockholm.

Painter. Landscapes.

Elisabet Karsten is known mostly for her works copied from the masters, including Ruysdael.

KÄRSTEN, Johann David

German, 18th - 19th century.

Born 1758, in Hamburg; died 23 August 1839, in Hamburg.

Painter, draughtsman, decorative designer.

Kärsten was a student at the Kunstakademi in Copenhagen.

KARSTEN, Ludvig Peter

Norwegian, 20th century.

Born 8 May 1876, in Christiania (now Oslo); died 1926, in Paris.

Active from 1907 in Denmark.

Painter. Figures, nudes, portraits, interiors with figures, landscapes.

Ludvig Peter Karsten began painting in Munich. He then spent two years in Madrid, before studying in Paris with Eugène Carrière and Henri Matisse. Most importantly, he worked alongside Edvard Munch and became friendly with him.

It is certain that he was consciously influenced by Munch, though by his subject matter - such as figures in interiors, and sick children - much more than by his colours, though Karsten's colours were at least as violent as those used by Munch in his brief early period when he painted *The Scream*. It is hard to tell what he might have taken from Carrière. On the other hand, some of the titles of his paintings, including *The Red Drawing Room, The Blue Kitchen, The Red Kitchen*, show traces of the influence of Matisse, the painter of *The Red Studio*. One of the characteristic features of Karsten's paintings is the contrast between the violence of the colour, an undeniable link with the Expressionist movement or even Fauvism, and the fluid outlines of the shapes and volumes which he seems to have retained from Impressionism. However that may be, after Munch who, with van Gogh and Ensor, was one of the three precursors of modern Expressionism, Karsten no doubt represents an essential link in the history of Scandinavian painting before the rise of the CoBrA painters.

MUSEUMS AND GALLERIES:

OSLO (Nasjonalgal.): *The Red Kitchen*.

AUCTION RECORDS:

PARIS, 29 Oct 1926, *Portrait of my Daughter*, FRF 2,200. COPENHAGEN, 14 March 1972, *Mother and Child*, DKK 9,200. COPENHAGEN, 29 April 1980, *Two Dolls* (1914, oil on canvas, 16 1/4 x 12 1/2 ins / 41 x 32 cm) DKK 8,000. COPENHAGEN, 20 Sept 1989, *Model in an Interior* (1921, oil on canvas, 19 3/4 x 17 3/4 ins / 50 x 45 cm) DKK 160,000. LONDON, 29 March 1990, *Nude in an Interior* (1921, oil on canvas, 19 3/4 x 17 3/4 ins / 50 x 45.2 cm) GBP 99,000. COPENHAGEN, 9 May 1990, *Seated Model* (1925, charcoal, 19 x 15 ins / 48 x 38 cm) DKK 16,000. COPENHAGEN, 31 Oct 1990, *Sick Child* (1916, oil on canvas, 22 x 30 ins / 55 x 76 cm) DKK 210,000. LONDON, 22 May 1992, *Fried Eggs* (1921, oil on canvas, 23 1/4 x 23 1/4 ins / 59 x 59 cm) GBP 28,600. LONDON, 25 Nov 1992, *The Winter Garden at Julebæk* (1918, oil on canvas, 55 1/2 x 57 3/4 ins / 141 x 146.5 cm) GBP 38,500. LONDON, 27 Nov 1992, *Morning Wash* (1921, oil on canvas, 21 1/2 x 26 ins / 54.6 x 66 cm) GBP 33,000. COPENHAGEN, 12-14 Nov 1997, *Portrait of a Girl* (1917, oil on canvas, 21 1/4 x 16 1/2 ins / 54 x 42 cm) DKK 340,000. OSLO, 10 June 1999, *Woman Resting* (1916, oil on canvas, 32 x 41 ins / 82 x 105 cm) NOK 1,200,000. OSLO, 25 Oct 1999, *From my Blue Kitchen* (1913, oil on canvas, 55 x 38 ins / 140 x 96 cm) NOK 2,400,000. OSLO, 8 May 2000, *Street Scene, Tordenskioldsgate* (1891, pastel, 11 x 17 ins / 28 x 42 cm) NOK 28,000. OSLO, 14 Nov 2000, *Woman at her Toilet* (oil on canvas, 22 x 26 ins / 55 x 66 cm) NOK 420,000. OSLO, 7 June 2001, *Still-life with Cups, Jug and Vase* (1923, oil on canvas, 20 x 26 ins / 50 x 66 cm) NOK 570,000. OSLO, 29 Oct 2001, *Red Kitchen* (1913, oil on canvas, 19 x 24 ins / 48 x 60 cm) NOK 1,400,000. OSLO, 18 March 2002, *Portrait of the Actress Betty Kirkeby* (1914, oil on canvas, 56 x 35 ins / 142 x 89 cm) NOK 160,000. OSLO, 21 Nov 2002, *Landscape from Skagen* (1923, oil on canvas, 14 x 17 ins / 36 x 42 cm) NOK 140,000. OSLO, 17 March 2003, *The Art Dealer Mrs Anna Grosell* (1912, oil on canvas, 74 x 35 ins / 189 x 90 cm) NOK 150,000. OSLO, 13 Oct 2003, *Helge Rode* (1919, oil on canvas, 82 x 33 ins / 208 x 85 cm) NOK 680,000. OSLO, 7 June 2004, *Resting in Bed: the Artist's Sister Rikke* (1916, oil on canvas, 32 x 41 ins / 81 x 104 cm) NOK 800,000.

OSLO, 29 Nov 2004, *Portrait of a Man and a Woman* (1915, oil on canvas, 18 x 20 ins / 46 x 51 cm) NOK 195,000.

KARTARO, Christoforo
Italian, 16th century.
Engraver.
Christoforo Kartaro engraved religious subjects and often signed himself: *C. Cart.*

KARTARUS, Marius, or Cartarus, Kartanys, Xtrarus
German (?), 16th century.
Born 1540.
Active in Rome in 1580.
Engraver.
He produced a *Martyrdom of St Catherine* after Salviati, landscapes after Titian, and various compositions after Michelangelo. He also made copies of several prints by Dürer: *Christ in the Garden of Gethsemane*, dated 1567, *St Jerome in his Oratory*, and also *Christ Descending to Hell* after Mantegna. In 1578, he produced a series of engravings of Rome, entitled *Various Perspectives*. The plates are dated from 1567 to 1586. He is also thought to have been a trader in prints, who signed not only his own engravings but also those of other artists who supplied work to him. This would explain the stylistic variations in his work. He was probably also known as Mario Kartovo.

KARTCHEWSKI, Julien
Polish, 19th century.
Born 1802, in Vilna (now Vilnius, Lithuania); died 1832, in Rome.
Painter. Genre scenes, landscapes.
Julien Kartchewski studied with Professor Rustein in Vilna, and later in France and Italy. His painting *Funeral of a Jew* is well known. In 1830, he exhibited with great success in Rome.

KARTH, Jean Nicolas
French, 19th century.
Born 19 July 1795, in Strasbourg; died 21 October 1878, in Strasbourg.
Painter, draughtsman. Landscapes.
Jean Karth began as an amateur artist and carried out many commissions of Alsatian landscapes for the publishers of lithographies.

KARTHAUS, Karl Friedrich
German, 19th century.
Active in Berlin.
Painter. Landscapes, urban landscapes.
Karthaus made his debut in 1886. He exhibited in Berlin, Munich and Magdeburg. His preferred subject was views of Venice.

KARTHAUSER, Margaretha
German, 15th century.
Died 1499, in a Dominican convent.
Miniaturist.

KARUGA, Rosemary, or N'Karuga
Kenyan, 20th century.
Born June 1928, in Meru.
Collage artist.
Rosemary Karuga studied at Makerere University in Uganda. At university she studied mosaic art but later abandoned this technique for practical reasons such as cost and lack of materials, turning instead to mosaic-like collages of paper cut-outs from magazines.

Her work was shown in the collective exhibition *Contemporary African Artists: changing tradition* at the Studio Museum in Harlem in 1990, and by the society 'Cultural Migrations Aquitaine Africa' at the submarine base in Bordeaux in 1998. In 1994 she had a solo show at the Contemporary African Art Gallery in New York.

BIBLIOGRAPHY:
Contemporary African Artists: changing tradition, exhibition catalogue, Studio Museum in Harlem, New York, 1990.

KARUTH, Ethel
British, 19th - 20th century.
Active in London.
Miniaturist.
Ethel Karuth exhibited at the Royal Academy in London from 1901. She is best known for her portrait of *Sarah Bernhardt*.

KARVALY, Mor
Hungarian, 19th century.
Born 1860, in Ungvár (now Uzhgorod, Ukraine); died 9 March 1899, in Meran (now Merano, Italy).
Painter.
Mor Karvaly studied with G. Courtois in Paris. He mainly painted genre scenes.

KASACHINSKY, Andrei Ivanovich
Russian, 18th - 19th century.
Born 17 October 1774; died 16 December 1814.
Engraver.
Kasachinsky produced mainly landscapes and also several historical scenes.

KASAJEZ, Yakov Tichonovich, or Kasanets
Russian, 17th century.
Died c. 1664.
Painter.
Kasajez specialised in icon painting and worked at the court of the Tsars. He is known to have painted a *St Alexis*, a *St Mary of Egypt* and a *Virgin* in 1648. In 1652, he is thought to have overseen the painting of frescoes in the Cathedral of the Archangel in the Kremlin. He was also involved in the decoration of the church of the Trinity of Nikitniki in Moscow. His style contains elements of the baroque that dominated Russian painting of the 17th century.

KASAKOFF, Ivan Semionovich
Russian, 19th - 20th century.
Born 1873.
Painter. Figure compositions, figures.
MUSEUMS AND GALLERIES:
MOSCOW (Rumiantsev Mus.): *Transfiguration; Study of an Old Man.*

KASANZEV, Vladimir Gavrilovich
Ukrainian, 19th century.
Born 1849, in Yekaterinoslav (now Dnepropetrovsk).
Active in St Petersburg.
Landscape painter.
Vladimir Kasanzev exhibited work in Russia and in Germany, in Berlin in 1886 and in Hamburg in 1887.
MUSEUMS AND GALLERIES:
ST PETERSBURG (Gosudarstvennyj Russkij Muz.): *The Kivach Waterfall.*

KASATKIN, Aleksei
Russian, 18th century.
Active in Moscow at the end of the 18th century.
Engraver.
Kasatkin produced portraits of many famous Russians living at the end of the 18th century.

KASATKIN, Nicolai Alekseevich
Russian, 19th century.
Born 1859, in Moscow.

Painter. Genre scenes.
Nikolai Kasatkin exhibited work in Paris in 1900 at the Exposition Universelle where he was awarded a silver medal.
MUSEUMS AND GALLERIES:
MOSCOW (State Tretyakov Gal.): *Miners; Who?; The Rivals; The Joke; Calumny; Young Girl by a Hedge; Arrival of the Tram.*

KASCHANOFF. See **KARSTEN Elisabet Charlotta**

KASCHAUER, Jakob
Austrian, 15th century.
Died before 1463.
Painter, sculptor.
Jakob Kaschauer is known to have been active as early as 1441. In 1449, he produced an altar for the church of St Michael in Vienna. He also worked in Freising and Thalhausen.

KASCHENKOV, Isak Sinoveevich
Russian, 18th century.
Born 14 January 1782; died 5 February 1808.
Sculptor.
Kaschenkov studied at the fine arts academy in St Petersburg from 1788 to 1803.

KASCIUNAITE, Dalia
Lithuanian, 20th - 21st century.
Born 1947, in Vilnius.
Painter.
Dalia Kasciunaite is a skilled technician, whose paintings hover between suggested reality and the temptations of abstraction. She began exhibiting in 1973 in Vilnius. She has taken part in numerous collective exhibitions, notably in 1989 in Moscow at the *USA-USSR: The Way to the Stars* exhibition. Solo exhibitions have included Hungary 1987, Moscow and Helsinki 1988, Austria 1989 and Paris 1990.
AUCTION RECORDS:
PARIS, 1 March 1993, *Three Phrases* (1989, oil on canvas, 51 1/4 x 47 1/4 ins / 130 x 120 cm) FRF 15,000.

KÄSE, Georg Wolrat
German, 18th century.
Active in Schöppenstedt (near Brunswick).
Sculptor.
Käse decorated the churches in Schöppenstedt.

KÄSE, Johann Kaspar
German, 18th century.
Died 1756, in Bad Gandersheim.
Sculptor.
Käse was sculptor to the local ruling family; his work included several tombs.

KASE, Paul George
American, 20th century.
Born 4 November 1893, in Reading (Pennsylvania).
Painter. Landscapes.
Paul Kase studied at the Fine Arts Academy in Philadelphia. He belonged to the American Federation of Arts.
MUSEUMS AND GALLERIES:
READING, PA: *Mountain Landscape.*

KÄSEBERG, Hugo
German, 19th century.
Born 21 November 1847, in Grimma (near Leipzig); died 17 August 1893, in Grimma.
Engraver.
Käseberg was a pupil of Flegel, and with Kaspar Örtel founded a firm of wood engravers.

KASEK, Karel
Czech, 19th - 20th century.
Born 25 May 1861, in Prague; died 20 November 1918, in Prague.
Painter, decorative artist. Figures, landscapes.
Karel Kasek was the pupil of F. Sequens and Maximilian Pirner.
MUSEUMS AND GALLERIES:
PRAGUE (Mus. of the Friends of the Arts): *At the Edge of the Fields* (drawing) - PRAGUE (Národní Gal.): *Story.*

KASELITZ, Albert Friedrich
German, 19th century.
Born 18 February 1821, in Berlin; died 28 May 1884, in Chur, Switzerland.
Painter. Portraits, landscapes.
Kaselitz trained at the academy in Berlin, subsequently travelling to Norway, then Sicily. In 1850 he settled in Chur, where he became a drawing master at the municipal school.
MUSEUMS AND GALLERIES:
CHUR: *Portrait.*

KASELOWSKY, August Theodor
German, 19th century.
Born 26 April 1810, in Potsdam; died 4 January 1891, in Berlin.
Painter. History painting.
Kaselowsky enrolled at the academy in Berlin in 1827 and was taught by Hensel. In 1836, he went to Paris to work in the studio of Léon Cognier. He went to Rome in 1840, then to Venice and Palermo, before returning to Germany in 1850 and settling in Berlin. In 1859, he was appointed professor of the academy of fine arts in Berlin, and gained a medal in Berlin in 1861. In his last years, he travelled to Spain, Greece, Turkey and England.
AUCTION RECORDS:
COPENHAGEN, 9 Nov 1977, *Mother and Child* (1868, oil on canvas, 34 1/4 x 26 1/2 ins / 87 x 67 cm) DKK 8,500.

KASEMANN, Rutger
German, 18th century.
Active in Cologne.
Architect, engraver (etching).
Kasemann engraved plates for *Architectora Lehr Kiolen Bockg, nach reichtiger mas... 1615... giedrock zo Cöllen* (24 pictures).

KÄSEWEISS, Christian
German, 17th century.
Active in Gotha.
Painter.
Käseweiss was a partner of his father Michael, and worked like him for the Dukes of Saxony-Gotha.

KÄSEWEISS, Michael
German, 17th century.
Active in Gotha, towards the middle of the 17th century.
Painter.
Käseweiss worked for Duke Ernst of Saxony-Gotha, notably at Schloss Friedenstein and the church of St Margarete in Gotha.

KASHALOV, Grigori Anikeievich
Russian, 18th century.
Born 1711; died c. 1761.
Engraver.
Kashalov produced portraits as well as views of towns and monuments.

KASHENZOV
Russian, 19th century.
Active at the beginning of the 19th century.
Lithographer.
Between 1835 and 1841, Kashenzov produced portraits of members of the academy of sciences in St Petersburg.

KASHI
Japanese, 19th century.
Active in Osaka c. 1830.
Master engraver.

KASHIHARA, Etsutomu
Japanese, 20th century.
Born 1941, in Kobe.
Painter, draughtsman, mixed media.

Kashihara has lived in Tokyo since 1972, studying at the city's Tama School of Fine Art. He has taken part in collective exhibitions since 1966, most of them in Japan. Outside Japan he has exhibited work at, among others, the San Fedele Gallery in Milan in 1972, the São Paulo Biennale in 1973, the *Japan: Tradition and the Present Moment* exhibition at the Stadtische Kunsthalle in Düsseldorf in 1974 and the 9th Paris Biennale of 1975. He has also had solo exhibitions in Tokyo and Kyoto. Kashihara teaches at the Fujimicho studio in Yokohama. His work is very diverse and strongly influenced by American Pop Art.

BIBLIOGRAPHY:
IXe Biennale de Paris, exhibition catalogue, Idea Books, musée d'Art moderne de la Ville de Paris, Paris, 1975.

KASHO. See also **TAIGA**

KASHO, pseudonym: Nanpitsu
Japanese, 19th century.
Active in Osaka c. 1826.
Master engraver.

KASIMIR, Luigi
Austrian, 20th century.
Born 18 April 1881, in Pettau; died 1962.
Engraver. Urban landscapes, architectural views.

Luigi Kasimir was a pupil of Siegmund L'Allemand at the Akademie der Bildenden Künste in Vienna. He was much influenced by Anders Zorn and Karl von Kalckreuth. His engravings of views of cities and public buildings, which he kept skilfully renewing, made him very famous.

BIBLIOGRAPHY:
Lorenz, Angelika, *Luigi Kasimir*, Wiener Verlag, Vienna, 1944.

AUCTION RECORDS:
VIENNA, 18 Nov 1981, *St Stephen's Church* (1945, graphite and coloured rayon, 11 3/4 x 8 ins / 30 x 20.5 cm) ATS 15,000. VIENNA, 31 March 1984, *View of Salzburg* (1917, colouring pencil and graphite, 12 x 15 1/2 ins / 30.7 x 39.2 cm) ATS 25,000. VIENNA, 15 May 1984, *London, Fleet Street* (mixed media/grey paper, 23 1/4 x 17 1/2 ins / 59 x 44.5 cm) ATS 40,000. VIENNA, 3 Dec 1986, *London, Fleet Street* (mixed media/paper, 23 1/4 x 17 1/2 ins / 59 x 44.5 cm) ATS 55,000. VIENNA, 25 Sept 2001, *Schweizertor, Hofburg Vienna* (pencil and colour pen, 10 x 10 ins / 25 x 25 cm) ATS 28,000. VIENNA, 15 Oct 2002, *Salzburg* (1920, colour pen, 8 x 6 ins / 21 x 15 cm) EUR 2,200.

KASIMIR, Marin
German, 20th - 21st century.
Born 1957, in Munich.
Active in Brussels.
Environmental artist, installation artist, photographer.
Düsseldorf Constructive Sculpture.

Marin Kasimir won the Belgian Prix de la Jeune Peinture in 1985. In 1990, he spent some time working in the studio of Alexander Calder at Saché. In 1996, he was awarded the Belgian Triennial Prize for the integration of monumental sculpture into the urban environment. He lives and works in Brussels.

In October-November 1988, Kasimir created two important 'in situ' environments, one at *La Verrière* in Valenciennes, the other at Charleroi in Belgium. In 1994, he was commissioned to create a *Fountain* for the Place des Droits de l'Homme in Issoudun. These installations offer concrete motifs for reflection in the living space of the city. Since the end of the 1990s, Kasimir's projects for public squares, parks, façades, metro stations and industrial buildings have made him a true creator of urban spaces. He also creates panoramic photographs, both inside and outside buildings, in multiple formats. He prints them on canvas sheets, then scans them, in order to make friezes of gigantic pictures, which he exhibits in underground car parks, shop windows, metro stations and public squares.

Kasimir has taken part in group exhibitions, including: 1980, Dany Keller Gallery, Munich; 1987, *Inside-Outside*, MUHKA, Antwerp; 1989, *Theatergarten Bestiarum*, PS1 Museum, New York; 1992, *Like Nothing Else in Tennessee*, Serpentine Gallery, London; 1994, *La Ville* (*The City*), Centre Georges-Pompidou, Paris; and 2000, *Città: More Ethics, Less Aesthetics*, Venice Biennale of Architecture. He has also had a number of solo shows, including: 1993, Galerie Peyroulet, then Galerie Froment et Putman, Paris; 1998, *Le contexte permanent* (*The Permanent Context*), Galerie Gilles Peyroulet, Paris; 2000, *Projects*, Architekturgalerie, Munich; *Normalemans/exceptionnelemans*, École des Beaux-Arts, Le Mans.

BIBLIOGRAPHY:
Ambo, solo exhibition catalogue, Palais des Beaux-Arts, Charleroi, 1988. *Martin Kazimir*, exhibition catalogue, Gal. "Ils arrivent", St-Étienne, 1989. Brayer, Marie-Ange, '*Marin Kasimir*' in *Art Press* n° 179, periodical, Paris, April 1993. *Zoom in, Turn around*, solo exhibition catalogue, Stroom HCBK, The Hague, 1995.

MUSEUMS AND GALLERIES:
CAEN (FRAC Basse-Normandie): *Düsseldorf Kunstverein* (1991) - DÔLE (FRAC Franche-Comté): *Profile XI Milena-Marin* (1992) - DÜSSELDORF (Kunstverein).

KASIMIR-HOERNES, Tanna
Austrian, 20th century.
Born 31 January 1887, in Vienna.
Engraver. Urban landscapes, architectural views.

Tanna Kasimir-Hoernes was the wife of Luigi Kasimir. Her technique and subjects are similar to those of her husband.

KASINSKI, Jan
Polish, 17th century.
Painter.

Jan Kasinski was court painter to Count Zamoyski and painted a number of portraits of members of the family. His most important works are *Portrait of Prince Ostrogski* and *Portrait of Prince Constantin Basyli*.

KASIULIS, Vytautas
Lithuanian, 20th century.
Born 23 April 1918, in Simnas.
Active in France.
Painter. Scenes with figures.

After working in Lithuania, Vytautas Kasiulis continued his training at Freiburg im Brisgau and then in Paris, where he settled. His compositions express an intimist feeling and display flashes of humour. In 1949 he was awarded a mention in the Hallmark prize. His works were purchased by the authorities in Lithuania, Germany, France, the USA.

KASKAS, J.
Painter. Still-lifes.

MUSEUMS AND GALLERIES:
HELSINKI (Valtion Taidemus.): *Still-life* (two).

KÄSLI, Kaspar
Swiss, 19th century.
Born 11 October 1826, in Altdorf (Uri).
Active in Küssnacht (Lake Lucerne) and Zurich.
Painter. Landscapes.

Käsli was a pupil of Calame in Geneva, and accompanied him to Paris. He specialised in landscape paintings of Italy and the Tyrol.

KASNYA, Bela
Hungarian, 20th century.
Painter. Landscapes.
Bela Kasnya worked in Paris.
AUCTION RECORDS:
PARIS, 29 Oct 1926, *On the Banks of the Seine,* FRF 3,500.

KASPAR, Johann Baptist
German, 18th century.
Died 1774.
Active in Bad Wurzach.
Painter.
Kaspar worked for the church in Ziegelbach, near Bad Wurzach.

KASPAR, Johann Nepomuk
German, 19th century.
Born 22 January 1822, in Obergünzburg (near Kempten); died 23 October 1885, in Obergünzburg.
Painter.
Kaspar, after extensive training at the academy in Munich, devoted himself almost exclusively to religious painting, though he also painted portraits. His works are found in many churches in Swabia; others were executed for German missions in Palestine and Africa.

KASPARIDES, Edouard
Austrian, 19th - 20th century.
Born 18 March 1858, in Markt-Kronau; died 1926, in Bad Gleichenberg.
Painter. Figures, nudes, landscapes.
Edouard Kasparides was a pupil of Frenkwald. He exhibited at the Paris Exposition Universelle in 1900, where he received an honourable mention.
AUCTION RECORDS:
VIENNA, 15 April 1980, *Banks of the Danube* (oil/card, 35 x 44 ins / 89 x 112 cm) ATS 14,000. VIENNA, 15 Nov 1983, *View of the Danube at Dusk* (1922, oil on card, 35 x 43 1/4 ins / 89 x 110 cm) ATS 28,000. LONDON, 12 Feb 1986, *Lovers on the Beach* (1902-1905, oil on canvas, 58 3/4 x 78 ins / 149.5 x 198 cm) GBP 2,200. VIENNA, 9 Dec 1987, *Portrait of a Woman Seated in a Landscape* (oil on card, 13 x 9 1/2 ins / 33 x 24 cm) ATS 50,000. MUNICH, 10 May 1989, *Moonlight on the Sea* (oil on canvas, 38 x 39 1/4 ins / 96.5 x 100 cm) DEM 7,700. LONDON, 20 June 1989, *The Gardens of Greece* (1920, oil on canvas, 45 x 59 ins / 114 x 150 cm) GBP 7,700. LONDON, 18 March 1992, *Reclining Nude* (oil on canvas, 36 1/2 x 62 1/4 ins / 93 x 158 cm) GBP 9,900. LONDON, 25 Nov 1992, *Young Woman by a Lake* (oil on canvas, 36 1/4 x 46 1/4 ins / 92 x 117.5 cm) GBP 4,840.

KASPER, Ludwig
German, 20th century.
Born 1893, in Gurten; died 1945, in Brunswick.
Sculptor.
Ludwig Kasper came from a peasant family. A Viennese patron provided him with the means to go to the Munich academy, where he studied with Hermann Hahn, first from 1912 to 1914 and then, after the war, from 1918 to 1923. In 1928, he stayed for a time in Paris, and settled in Berlin in 1933, visiting Greece in 1937. From 1943 to 1945, he was a professor at the Brunswick school of art. All his works centre around a few themes: young men and girls standing, men walking, and seated women, who are always characterised by the priestly stillness of their poses. He represents the last traces of Adolf Hildebrand's Neo-Classicism. In 1952, the City Gallery in Munich organised a retrospective exhibition of his entire works.

BIBLIOGRAPHY:
Haftmann, Werner, *Der Bildhauer Ludwig Kasper*, catalogue raisonné, Propyläen, Frankfurt am Main, 1978. Ulm, Benno, *Ludwig Kasper: 1893-1945. Ein Innviertler Bildhauer*, exhibition catalogue, Landes-Bildungszentrum, Zelle an der Pram, Oberösterreichischen Landesmuseum, Linz, 1979. Schmidt, Diether, *Ludwig Kasper, Zeichnungen*, Ernst-Rietschel-Kulturring, Pulsnitz, 2000.
AUCTION RECORDS:
COLOGNE, 31 May 1986, *Torso* (1936, patinated bronze, h. 44 3/4 ins / 113.5 cm) DEM 16,000. COLOGNE, 7 June 2000, *Child Head of Beate* (terracotta, h. 10 ins / 26 cm) DEM 4,500. COLOGNE, 7 June 2000, *Portrait of Marianne* (plaster, h. 16 ins / 40 cm) DEM 5,500. HAMBURG, 14 June 2003, *Bust Portrait of Ottilie Kasper* (marble and cement, 26 x 16x9 ins / 65 x 41x23 cm) EUR 3,400.

KASPRZYCKI, Wincenty
Polish, 19th century.
Born 1802, in Warsaw; died 27 May 1849, in Warsaw.
Painter. Landscapes.
Wincenty Kasprzycki studied with Professor Villan in Warsaw, then, with the aid of a bursary from Count Ossolinski, continued his studies at the University of Warsaw. He soon left the house of Ossolinski and in 1821, together with an Italian painter, he went to Vilna (now Vilnius). He worked there until 1828, when he returned to Warsaw. He was often employed by Count Alexandre Potocki.

In 1828, Kasprzycki was commissioned to paint a series of views of Wilanow and its surroundings. Alongside realistic landscapes, he continued the tradition of the 18th-century *vedutà*. A number of his works are preserved in the castle of Potocki at Wilanow, near Warsaw. He exhibited in Warsaw in 1838 and 1895, twice winning a medal. He painted the peaks and slopes of the Carpathian mountains, the romantic sites of Ojcow and the countryside around Cracow.

KASS, Deborah
American, 20th - 21st century.
Born 1952, in San Antonio (Texas).
Painter (oil), printmaker. Portraits.
Pop Art.
Deborah Kass studied at the Art Students' League (1968-1970), the Whitney Museum of American Art Independent Study Program (1972), and Carnegie-Mellon University, obtaining a BFA in painting. She taught at the Rhode Island School of Design, the Art Institute of Chicago, the Boston Museum School of Fine Arts, the State University of New York, and the Skowhegan School of Painting and Sculpture.

Kass's work explores the issues of appropriation and identity, particularly through the imagery of Andy Warhol. Since the early 1990s, she has used Warhol's familiar forms, but substituted Jewish, female and lesbian subjects, for example Barbra Streisand for Jackie Kennedy, Gertrude Stein for Robert Rauschenberg, and the photographer Cindy Sherman for Liza Minnelli. Kass has also produced self-portraits in Warhol's style. She seeks to question stereotypes of beauty and power, as seen in Warhol's work, as well as the fixing of racial, ethnic and gender identities.

Kass has shown work at numerous exhibitions, some of which include: *Too Jewish? Challenging Traditional Identities* at the Jewish Museum in New York (1996); *NowHere: Incandescent* at the Louisiana Museum of Art in Humlebaek in Denmark (1996); *Identity Crisis: Self Portraiture at the End of the Century* at the Milwaukee Art Museum (1997); *The Prophecy of Pop* at the Contemporary Art Center in New Orleans (1997); *Art on Paper* at the Weatherspoon Gallery of Art in Greensboro in North Carolina (1998); *In Your Face* at the Andy Warhol Museum in Pittsburgh (1998);. *The Warhol Project* at the Newcomb Art Gallery at Tulane University in New Orleans (1999); *Queer Visualities* at the Stony Brook

University Art Gallery in New York (2002); *Influence, Anxiety and Gratitude* at the List Visual Arts Center in Cambridge in Massachusetts (2003); *Co-conspirators: Artist and Collector* at the Orlando Museum of Art (2004); *American Art: 1960-Present, Selections from the Permanent Collection* at the Weatherspoon Art Museum in Greensboro (2005); and *Likeness: Portraits of Artists by Other Artists* at the Institute of Contemporary Art in Boston (2005). She received fellowships from Art Matters (1996, 1992) and a fellowship from the New York State Foundation for the Arts (1991).

BIBLIOGRAPHY:
Holmes, A.M., '*Deborah Kass at Fiction/Non-fiction*' in *Arts Magazine*, Journal article, April 1986. *Deborah Kass: Paintings*, exhibition catalogue, Scott Hanson Gallery, New York, 1988. *Deborah Kass: The Warhol Project*, exhibition catalogue, Newcomb Art Gallery, New Orleans, 1999. Goeser, Caroline, '*Deborah Kass: The Warhol Project*' in *ArtLies*, vol 29, journal article, winter 2001.

MUSEUMS AND GALLERIES:
BOSTON (MFA) - CINCINNATI (AM) - GREENSBORO (Weatherspoon AM, University of North Carolina): *Cindy Sherman* (1995, screen print) - LA JOLLA (MCA of San Diego): *Orient Rock* (1983, oil) - NEW YORK (Guggenheim Mus.) - NEW YORK (Jewish Mus.): *Double Red Yentl, Split (My Elvis)* (1993, screen print and synthetic polymer on canvas) - NEW YORK (MoMA) - NEW YORK (Whitney Mus. of American Art).

AUCTION RECORDS:
NEW YORK, 10 Dec 2003, *Six Barbras, the Jewish Jackie Series* (1992, silk screen, 30 x 24 ins / 76 x 61 cm) USD 3,200.

KASS, Janos

Hungarian, 20th century.
Born 1927.
Engraver, illustrator, poster artist.

Janos Kass studied at the school of decorative arts in Budapest from 1945 to 1951, at the school of fine arts in 1961 and 1962, and then at the school of fine arts in Leipzig. He is particularly known for his work as an illustrator and designer of cinema posters. In 1958 he took part in the Exposition Mondiale in Brussels, where he was awarded a silver medal. He showed his work in solo exhibitions in Budapest in 1964 and 1966. He received the Munkácsy prize.

BIBLIOGRAPHY:
Hongrie 68, N.d., Budapest, 1968.

KASSAK, Lajos

Hungarian, 20th century.
Born 21 March 1887, in Érsekujvár; died 1967, in Budapest.
Painter (including gouache), watercolourist, graphic designer, engraver, collage artist, sculptor.
Dadaism, Constructivism.

Lajos Kassák ran away from home aged 13. He started his working life as a blacksmith and locksmith. He came into contact with the workers' movement and contributed to the Social Democrat magazine *Eeszava*. He travelled on foot across Europe, arriving in Paris in 1909, where he met Apollinaire, Cendrars, Picasso, Modigliani. By the time he returned to Budapest shortly after 1910, he was already a writer and poet. In 1912 he met Marinetti. In 1915 he founded the avant-garde political, literary and artistic magazine *A Tett* (*Action*), which was anarchistic and violently hostile to the war. Banned by the government in 1916, it resurfaced in November that same year under the name *Ma* (*Today*). It was this magazine that from 1918 to 1925 brought the Expressionists of the Berlin-based Der Sturm movement and the Dadist movement to Hungary's attention, while at the same time representing the activist movement. Following the fall of the Hungarian Soviet Republic in 1920, which Bela Kun had founded just a year earlier and which had encouraged the circle of intellectuals and artists of the *Today* magazine, Kassák emigrated to Vienna, where he continued to publish the magazine from 1920 to 1926. Arp, Schwitters, Lissitsky, Archipenko had all contributed to it. Up until that time Kassák had primarily been a poet, a novelist, a theoretician, graphic designer, typographer and editor. He became a painter in 1921, and soon had his first exhibition and signed the *Bildarchitektur* manifesto. In 1922, in collaboration with Moholy-Nagy, he published the *Book of New Artists* in Hungarian, German and English, which constituted a detailed list of contemporary artists. In 1925 he had an exhibition with Niklaus Braun at the *Der Sturm* gallery in Berlin. He returned to Hungary in 1926 where he tried to restore his links with the Social Democrats. He gave up painting to set up the New Circle of Advertising Designers with Kurt Schwitters, and then founded two new avant-garde magazines: *Dokumentum* in 1926-1927 and *Munka* (*Work*), which appeared between 1928 and 1938. During the course of his life Lajos Kassák founded several international magazines, and these constituted his literary output which was set on the lines of Surrealism. Following the liberation of Hungary in 1945 he took on an official and active role, contributing to the magazines *Alkotas* (*Creation*) and *Kortars* (*Contemporary*). After 1949, having retired to Bekasmegyer, he kept his silence until the end of the era of intellectual and artistic dogmatism in 1955, two years after Stalin's death. After 1950, then, having resumed his activities as a painter, he sought contact with European artistic life, and several international exhibitions of his work were held, including Galerie Denise René, Paris (1960) and a major retrospective in Budapest in the year of his death (1967). After 1968 exhibitions were organised in many major European cities. He came to be regarded as the father of Hungarian Avant-Garde. His work was extensively represented at the exhibition *L'art en Hongrie 1905-1930. Art et Révolution* (*Art in Hungary 1905-1930. Art and Revolution*) at the Musée d'Art et d'Industrie in St-Étienne and the Musée d'Art Moderne in Paris (1980). In 1987 the Magyar Nemzeti gallery in Budapest organised a new retrospective of his work and in the same year the Hungarian institute in Paris organised an exhibition entitled *Homage to Kassák* to mark the centenary of his birth which ran in parallel with the *Avant-Gardes in Hungary* exhibition. His work was also shown at the Centre Beaubourg, at the Maison des Écrivains and at other Paris venues. During his first Dadaist epoch, from 1921 to 1925, during his time in Vienna, Kassák produced poem-paintings, collages, paintings and sculptures in the spirit of Schwitters' work, in which Moholy-Nagy and the Bauhaus Circle took an interest, thus helping to contribute towards the international genesis of abstract art. After 1924 Kassák also produced architectural models. While his literary output placed him in the Surrealist sphere of influence, his painting was inspired by constructivist tendencies. His first three-dimensional works, created between 1920 and 1922, belong to the last period of Dadaism and comprise montages, dynamic typographic rough drafts. He later rejoined the constructivist camp, where he fell somewhere between the rigorous abstraction of De Stijl and the liberal constructivism of the Bauhaus with his own *Architecture of Images*. After 1926 he probably stopped painting altogether for some 20 years. After World War II, having withdrawn from public life during the repressive Stalinist era, he took up drawing and painting again, producing drawings that take motifs from the landscape and from nature. But in spite of their sensitivity, they represent a regression in his work. From the early 1960s he went back to constructivism, and was regarded by young artists as the master of the geometric abstraction generation. Generally speaking, at least in his constructivist periods, Kassák's art was characterised by a robust strength, fiery dynamism, a saturated chromatism that breathed life into his intellectual compositions and occasionally uneven style.

BIBLIOGRAPHY:
Dorival, Bernard/Hoog, Michel, *Dada*, group exhibition catalogue, Musée national d'Art moderne, Paris, 1966-1967. Laszlo, Carl, *MA-Kassák*, Basel, 1968. Németh, Lajos, *Moderne ungarische Kunst*, Corvina Kiadó, Budapest, 1969. Stravssi, Thomas, *Kassák*, exhibition catalogue, Gal. Gmurzynska, Cologne, 1975. Passuth, Krisztina/Szabó, Júlia, *L'Art en Hongrie 1905-1930. Art et révolution*, exhibition catalogue, Musée d'Art et d'Industrie, Saint-Étienne, musée d'Art moderne de la ville de Paris, Paris, 1980. *Lajos Kassák (1887-1967)*, exhibition catalogue, Gal. nationale hongroise, Budapest, 1987.

MUSEUMS AND GALLERIES:
BUDAPEST (Kassák Múz.): *Sculpture II* (1922-1968, marble); *Collage with Animals* (1923); *Self-portrait Collage* (1923-1964) - BUDAPEST (Magyar Nemzeti Gal.): *Architecture of Image II* (1922); *Painting-Architecture* (1922) - PÉCS (Janus Pannonius Mus.): *Inside Page from the Today magazine* (1923, woodcut) - ST-ÉTIENNE (Mus. d'Art et d'Industrie): *Popular Motifs* (1921, gouache).

AUCTION RECORDS:
BERN, 12 June 1969, *Abstract Composition* (collage and pencil) CHF 7,800. PARIS, 18 Nov 1972, *Architecture* (gouache) FRF 13,000. LONDON, 4 July 1974, *Composition for 'Today'* (watercolour) GBP 1,100; *Forthcomin Gallery*, GBP 1,500. MUNICH, 30 Nov 1979, *Construction* (c. 1925, watercolour and pen, 15 x 12 ins / 38 x 30.5 cm) DEM 5,500. COLOGNE, 17 May 1980, *Composition* (oil on canvas, 39¾ x 35¾ ins / 101 x 91 cm) DEM 4,000. LONDON, 24 Oct 1984, *Composition* (1922-1929, gouache and watercolour, 16¼ x 11½ ins / 41.5 x 29.3 cm) GBP 1,700. LONDON, 4 Dec 1985, *Composition for 'Today'* (1922, watercolour, 15½ x 11½ ins / 39.2 x 29 cm) GBP 6,500. HAMBURG, 9 June 1986, *Composition* (1923, collage and oil on panel, 10¾ x 9 ins / 27.2 x 22.9 cm) DEM 7,000. ZURICH, 26 March 1987, *Suprematist Composition* (1921, gouache/paper, 16 x 11¼ ins / 40.5 x 28.4 cm) CHF 5,000. PARIS, 12 May 1993, *Composition* (1922, gouache/paper, 11½ x 8¾ ins / 29 x 22.5 cm) FRF 63,000. PARIS, 18 March 1995, *Composition* (1922, watercolour) FRF 8,000. AMSTERDAM, 4 June 1996, *Untitled* (1921, ink/paper, 11½ x 9 ins / 29 x 23 cm) NLG 4,956. PRAGUE, 22 May 1999, *Architecture* (watercolour, 10 x 8 ins / 26 x 20 cm) CZK 200,000. MUNICH, 11 Nov 1999, *Abstract Composition* (watercolour and ink on paper on board, 11 x 8 ins / 27 x 21 cm) DEM 11,000. MUNICH, 6 May 2000, *Memento* (1922, collage, sandpaper and felt tip on board, 11 x 8 ins / 27 x 20 cm) DEM 30,000. LYONS, 8 Oct 2000, *Composition* (oil on canvas, 24 x 22 ins / 62 x 56 cm) FRF 66,000. LILLE, 7 April 2001, *Cubist Compostition with Guitar* (1910, crayon and pastel, 13 x 10 ins / 33 x 26 cm) FRF 38,000. LILLE, 7 April 2001, *Cubist Portraits* (crayon and pastel, 17 x 14 ins / 42 x 35 cm) FRF 67,000. COLOGNE, 4 June 2002, *Red Shapes* (pencil, Indian ink and collage on board, 7 x 6 ins / 17 x 15 cm) EUR 2,000. NEW YORK, 18 Sept 2002, *Untitled* (c. 1920, colour paper, newsprint, gouache and crayon, 12 x 9 ins / 30 x 23 cm) USD 3,200. BERLIN, 31 May 2003, *Untitled* (watercolour, 24 x 22 ins / 61 x 55 cm) EUR 9,700. PARIS, 23 Nov 2003, *Composition on an Orange Background* (1922, gouache, 14 x 9 ins / 35 x 23 cm) EUR 9,000.

KASSEBÖHMER, Alex

German, 20th - 21st century.
Born 1952, in Herne.
Painter. Landscapes, still-lifes.

Alex Kasseböhmer studied with Gerhard Richter in Düsseldorf, where he has lived and worked since 1976. He began by reproducing extracts from works of the past, then continued to make use of quotation in his work, by adopting a variety of styles and manners. His work, which is intended to be decorative, has become progressively more denuded. His primitive style with abstract tendencies is reminiscent of children's drawings.

He has taken part in group exhibitions, including 1981, 1982 and 1986 in Munich; 1982, 1985, 1986, 1988 and 1989 in Cologne; 1983 and 1988 at the Düsseldorf Kunsthalle; 1987 at the Royal Scottish Academy in Edinburgh; 1988 at the Boston Institute of Contemporary Art and 1990 at the Museum Haus Esters/Museum Haus Lange in Krefeld. He has also exhibited in solo shows in 1982, 1985 1989 and 1990 in Munich; 1982 in Stuttgart; 1983 in Düsseldorf; 1984, 1985, 1987, 1989 and 1993 in Cologne; 1985 in Rotterdam; 1988 and 1991 in Frankfurt; 1989 at the Westfälischer Kunstverein in Münster; 1990 at the Galerie Nelson in Lyons and 1994 at the Galerie Nelson in Paris 1997 and 1999 at the Galerie Monika Sprüth in Cologne, and 2004 at the Galerie Sprüth/Magers in Munich.

BIBLIOGRAPHY:
Grasskamp, Walter, '*Kasseböhmer Trees*' in *Parkett* n° 39, periodical, Zurich, 1994.

KASSELSTATT, Franz von (Count)

German, 18th - 19th century.
Born 1753, in Trier; died 1841, in Mainz.
Draughtsman.

Kasselstatt, an amateur artist and a canon in the city cathedral, is represented in Mainz museum by a series of 28 drawings. They depict the main sights and monuments of the city, and date from 1810 to 1824. They were watercoloured by J. Caspar Schneider and Johann Jakob Hoch.

MUSEUMS AND GALLERIES:
MAINZ.

KASSIN, Josef

German, 19th - 20th century.
Born 1856, near Klagenfurt, Austria; died 1931.
Sculptor.

Kassin was a pupil of Kundmann. A noted work is a bronze group of *Samson and Delilah*, which won him the Rome prize in 1885.

KASSLER, Charles

American, 20th century.
Born September 1896, in Denver (Colorado); died 1979.
Painter, fresco artist, lithographer.

Charles Kassler Junior studied at Princeton and the Chicago Art Institute. He studied fresco painting in France between 1925 and 1932, when he moved to Los Angeles. He exhibited in the USA and in Paris. One of his extant frescoes decorated the interior of the Beverly Hills Post Office (now the Cultural Centre); another, which was restored in 1997, is in the Plummer Auditorium in Orange County (California).

KASSLER, Marguerite

American.
Born in Tacoma (Washington).
Sculptor.

Marguerite Kassler was married to Charles Kassler; they held joint exhibitions. She practised direct carving.

KÄSSMANN, Josef

Austrian, 19th century.
Born 3 September 1784, in Vienna; died 18 January 1856, in Bad Fischau, near Wiener Neustadt.
Sculptor.

Kässmann was a pupil of his father Franz, then a disciple of Thorvaldsen in Rome. He subsequently became a member of staff at the Akademie der bildenden Künste in Vienna. A noted work is his group of *Jason and Medea*.

Museums and Galleries:
Vienna (Österreichische Gal. Belvedere): several works.

KÄSSMAYER, Karl
Austrian, 19th century.
Born 18 April 1861, in Vienna.
Painter. Portraits, hunting scenes, landscapes.
Kässmayer's work includes large-scale landscapes.
Museums and Galleries:
Linz: several works.

KASTEELE, Abraham Anne van de
Dutch, 19th century.
Born 1 May 1814, in The Hague; died 1893.
Painter. Portraits, genre scenes.
Abraham van de Kasteele was a pupil of Ch. Kruseman.
Auction records:
Antwerp, 1853, *Cavalry Charge*, FRF 215. Amsterdam, 22 April 1992, *Portrait of a Fisherman Bringing in his Nets; Portrait of a Hunter Holding a Pipe* (1838, oil on panel, each 15 3/4 x 12 1/2 ins / 40 x 31.5 cm) NLG 2,070.

KASTEELS, Peter I
Flemish School, 17th century.
Died 1683.
Painter.
Peter Kasteels I was active in Antwerp and became a master artist there in 1629. He does not appear to have been related to the Casteels who were also from Antwerp.

KASTEELS, Peter II
Flemish School, 17th century.
Died c. 1700.
Painter. Battles.
Peter Kasteels II was active in Antwerp and became a master artist there in 1673. He does not appear to be related to the Casteels who were also from Antwerp.

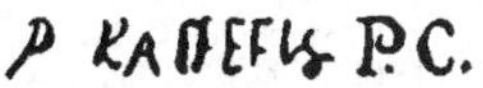

Museums and Galleries:
Oldenburg: *Two Fights between Horsemen.*
Auction records:
Paris, 24 May 1923, *Port with Boats and Numerous Figures* (attributed) FRF 340.

KASTELEYN, Gustave
Belgian, 19th century.
Born 15 July 1848, in Ghent; died 20 April 1900, in Ghent.
Sculptor.
The museum in Ghent has works by Gustave Kasteleyn entitled *The Prisoners* and *Sleeping Child.*

KASTEN, J. E.
German (?), 18th century.
Painter.
Museums and Galleries:
Versailles (Mus.): watercolour.

KASTENS, Erich Walther
German, 20th century.
Born 29 December 1887, in Berlin.
Painter. Stage sets.
Erich Kastens studied with Max Fabian in Berlin.

KASTHOFER, Karl Rudolf
Swiss, 19th century.
Born 1808, in Bern; died 22 March 1874, in Waldau.
Painter, watercolourist.
Kasthofer lived in Genoa for a long time.

KASTMAN, Alexander
Swedish, 18th century.
Painter.
Alexander Kastman executed the *Portrait of Andreas Rydeluis, Bishop of Lund,* which in now in the collection of the university in Lund.

KÄSTNER, Carl August
German, 18th - 19th century.
Born in Raschau (near Chemnitz).
Painter.
Kästner's legacy includes portraits (mainly miniatures), genre scenes and religious paintings. He worked in Dresden and Chemnitz.

KASTNER, Hans. See **CASTNER**

KÄSTNER, Johann Evangelist
Austrian, 19th century.
Born 26 November 1776, in Weiher; died 31 July 1827, in Vienna.
Painter. History painting.
Kästner was a student of the academy in Vienna and exhibited mainly in that city.

KÄSTNER, Josef, the Elder
Austrian, 19th century.
Born in Innsbruck; died 1871, in Vienna.
Painter. History painting.
Kästner did altar paintings for several churches in Vienna.

KÄSTNER, Josef, the Younger
Austrian, 19th century.
Born 1844, in Vienna.
Painter. History painting.
Kästner, after a spell in Italy, returned to Austria and, like his father, worked as a religious painter. He decorated churches in Vienna, Graz and other Austrian towns.

KASTOR, Robert
French, 19th - 20th century.
Engraver.
Robert Kastor exhibited in Paris at the Salon des Artistes Français and became a member of that society in 1894.

KASUKABE, Hiroshi
Japanese, 20th century.
Born 1930, in Tokyo.
Also active in France.
Painter, watercolourist.
Kasukabe graduated from the Graduate School of Arts and Sciences in Tokyo in 1949, before moving to Paris. Since 1963 he has exhibited regularly at the Salon d'Automne, becoming a member in 1971. He also exhibited at the salon of the French Société Nationale des Beaux-Arts in 1963, 1973 and 1975. In the period 1963-1974 he showed work at international exhibitions of figurative art and of contemporary drawings and watercolours at the National Museum of Modern Art in Tokyo. He also exhibited in France in 1971 (Tours) and 1974 (Mérignac). Between 1960 and 1968 he had solo exhibitions every year in Tokyo and Osaka.

KASYN, John
Canadian, 20th century.
Born 1926.
Painter, watercolourist. Urban landscapes.
John Kasyn spent his childhood in Winnipeg. He studied at Ontario College of Art, and is known for his portrayals of the streets and houses of Toronto.
Auction records:
Toronto, 12 June 1989, *Wellesley Street* (watercolour, 9 x 5 1/4 ins / 23 x 13.4 cm) CAD 800. Toronto, 7 Dec 1999, *Richmond Street W, Toronto* (oil on board, 24 x 18 ins / 60 x 45 cm) CAD 13,000. Toronto, 7 Dec 1999, *Early Evening in Cabbagetown* (oil on board, 22 x 30 ins / 56 x 75 cm) CAD 22,000. Vancouver, 9 Nov 2000, *Robert Street Yard* (oil on board, 18 x 24 ins / 46 x 61 cm) CAD 9,000. Toronto, 21 Nov 2000, *On Lowther Near Avenue Road* (oil on board, 26 x 20 ins / 65 x 50

cm) CAD 10,000. Toronto, 29 May 2001, *At Dawn* (oil on board, 30 x 28 ins / 75 x 70 cm) CAD 18,000. Toronto, 4 Dec 2001, *Row of Old Houses on Bleeker St* (c. 1984, oil on board, 24 x 35 ins / 60 x 90 cm) CAD 20,000. Vancouver, 14 Nov 2002, *Along Wellesley Street* (oil on board, 20 x 28 ins / 51 x 71 cm) CAD 19,000. Toronto, 3 Dec 2002, *Shanon St Yard After the Snow* (oil on board, 30 x 28 ins / 75 x 70 cm) CAD 17,000. Vancouver, 15 May 2003, *On McCaul Street Before Demolition* (oil on board, 34 x 30 ins / 86 x 76 cm) CAD 22,500. Toronto, 2 Dec 2003, *Behind Grand Ave - Toronto* (oil on board, 28 x 35 ins / 70 x 90 cm) CAD 23,000. Vancouver, 27 May 2004, *Back Yard on Nepean Street, Ottawa* (1974, oil and lucite on board, 20 x 16 ins / 50 x 40 cm) CAD 7,000. Toronto, 1 June 2004, *Laneway to Bleeker St* (1969, oil on board, 24 x 30 ins / 60 x 75 cm) CAD 11,000.

KAT, Anne-Pierre de

Belgian, 20th century.

Born 1 May 1881, in Delft, to Dutch parents; died July 1968, in La Frette-sur-Seine (Val-d'Oise), France.

Also active in France.

Painter. Figures, nudes, portraits, landscapes, urban landscapes, still-lifes, flowers.

Brabant Fauvism.

Anne-Pierre de Kat studied painting at the Koninklijke Academie in the Hague, and went on to study sculpture at the Academie in Ghent, and also at the Académie in Brussels. He left the Netherlands for good in 1904 and settled in Brussels. He fought in the ranks of the Belgian Army in World War I, which enabled him to become a Belgian citizen in 1919. He was a friend of Wouters, Tytgat and Brusselmans and became a member of the informal group of 'Brabant Fauves'. He won the Prix National des Beaux-Arts in 1939 and was made an Officer of the Ordre de Léopold, then moved to France in 1950.

De Kat's determined style of drawing and his muted harmonies link him with the Flemish Expressionist movement, particularly with Brabant Fauvism, and are also characterised by a moderate Cubist influence. His figures and nudes express contained emotion. He often painted the landscapes of the Brabant countryside and is most appreciated for his rain and snow effects.

Before the war, de Kat exhibited a number of times in Paris at the Salon des Indépendants and in 1914 at La Libre Esthétique in Brussels. After the war, he exhibited in Paris at the Salon des Indépendants and at the Salon d'Automne, where he became an associate. In 1966, he featured in the exhibition *Rick Wouters et quelques artistes Brabançons* (*Rick Wouters and some other Brabant Artists*) at the Musées Royaux des Beaux-Arts in Brussels. His work sometimes appears in thematic exhibitions devoted to Fauvism or Belgian Expressionism.

De Kat also held solo exhibitions, including: 1921, Galerie Le Centaure, Brussels; 1925, Galerie Manteau; 1938, Musée de Tournai; 1941, Galerie de la Toison d'Or, Brussels; 1943, Galrie Brueghel, Brussels; and 1949, retrospective, Forest. Posthumous exhibitions include: 1992, an important retrospective exhibition, organised by the province of Brabant; 2001, homage was paid to him within the framework of the 29th Salon d'Ensemble, devoted to the artists of the Rouge-Cloître in Brussels.

Bibliography:

Muller, Roland/Dhaene, Yvette, *Rétrospective Anne-Pierre de Kat*, exhibition catalogue, Province de Brabant, 1992.

Auction records:

Breda, 26 April 1977, *Girl at the Piano* (1920, oil on canvas, 39 1/4 x 31 1/2 ins / 100 x 80 cm) NLG 2,800. Antwerp, 8 May 1979, *Lady of Fashion* (oil on canvas, 39 1/4 x 31 1/2 ins / 100 x 80 cm) BEF 120,000. Lokeren, 5 March 1988, *View of Tuin* (oil on canvas remounted on board, 16 x 12 ins / 40.5 x 30.5 cm) BEF 33,000. Lokeren, 8 Oct 1988, *Square in the Rain* (oil on canvas, 26 x 21 1/2 ins / 66 x 54.5 cm) BEF 500,000. Amsterdam, 24 May 1989, *View of Liège in Belgium* (1933, oil on canvas, 20 x 24 ins / 51 x 61 cm) NLG 6,900. London, 19 Oct 1989, *Portrait of a Man* (1922, oil on canvas, 28 1/2 x 23 ins / 72.3 x 58.4 cm) GBP 3,300. Amsterdam, 22 May 1990, *Roundabout: Avenue de Tervuren in Brussels* (oil on canvas, 18 x 21 1/4 ins / 45.5 x 54 cm) NLG 32,200. Amsterdam, 12 Dec 1990, *Pensioner* (1919, oil on canvas, 50 1/4 x 30 1/2 ins / 127.5 x 77.5 cm) NLG 9,200. Lokeren, 23 May 1992, *House in the Snow* (1926, oil on canvas, 23 1/2 x 35 3/4 ins / 60 x 91 cm) BEF 240,000. Lokeren, 10 Dec 1994, *Place Ste-Croix in Watermael* (1912, oil on canvas, 29 3/4 x 39 3/4 ins / 75.5 x 101 cm) BEF 750,000. Lokeren, 9 Dec 1995, *Convalescent* (1911, oil on canvas, 39 1/4 x 31 1/2 ins / 100 x 80 cm) BEF 400,000. Lokeren, 18 May 1996, *Dusk over the Pond* (1940, oil on canvas, 35 1/2 x 39 1/4 ins / 90 x 100 cm) BEF 95,000. Amsterdam, 17-18 Dec 1996, *Breakfast* (c. 1912-1913, oil on canvas, 35 x 29 1/4 ins / 89 x 74 cm) NLG 47,200. Antwerp, 28 April 1999, *Pleasure of the Snow* (1928, oil on canvas) BEF 350,000. Amsterdam, 12 Oct 1999, *Still-life with Fruit and Vegetables on a Table* (1933, oil on canvas, 24 x 39 ins / 60 x 100 cm) NLG 13,000. Antwerp, 4 April 2000, *Winter* (c. 1924, oil on canvas, 39 x 47 ins / 100 x 120 cm) BEF 300,000. Antwerp, 24 Oct 2000, *Guitar* (oil on canvas, 33 x 53 ins / 84 x 134 cm) BEF 130,000. Amsterdam, 12 June 2001, *City Life* (oil on canvas, 30 x 25 ins / 76 x 64 cm) NLG 65,000. Amsterdam, 4 Dec 2001, *Landscape* (1932, oil on canvas, 20 x 24 ins / 50 x 61 cm) NLG 8,000. Lokeren, 11 May 2002, *Still-life with Apple* (1929, oil on panel, 6 x 9 ins / 14 x 22 cm) EUR 1,800. Brussels, 13 Oct 2003, *Fauvist Portrait of a Man* (oil on canvas, 24 x 19 ins / 60 x 48 cm) EUR 4,600. Amsterdam, 2 Dec 2003, *Bezon* (oil on canvas, 15 x 19 ins / 39 x 47 cm) EUR 4,300. Lokeren, 13 March 2004, *Descent to the Forest* (1940, oil on canvas, 24 x 20 ins / 60 x 50 cm) EUR 3,000. Brussels, 11 Oct 2004, *Young Sleeping Female Nude* (oil on canvas, 21 x 24 ins / 54 x 60 cm) EUR 9,000.

KAT, Otto B. de

20th century.

Born 1907; died 1995.

Painter (gouache), draughtsman. Interiors with figures, Still-lifes, landscapes.

Auction records:

Amsterdam, 10 April 1989, *Mountainous Landscape in France* (1976, oil on canvas, 13 x 16 1/4 ins / 33 x 41 cm) NLG 1,725. Amsterdam, 12 Dec 1990, *Still-life with Stoneware Pot* (1930, oil on canvas, 21 1/2 x 23 1/2 ins / 54.5 x 60 cm) NLG 1,840. Amsterdam, 17 Sept 1991, *Two Female Nudes on a Bed* (1958, gouache/paper, 13 1/2 x 20 1/2 ins / 34 x 52 cm) NLG 2,070. Amsterdam, 24 Sept 1992, *Street Corner in London* (1968, oil on canvas, 15 1/2 x 25 3/4 ins / 39.5 x 65.5 cm) NLG 4,830. Amsterdam, 10 Dec 1992, *Landscape* (1981, black and coloured chalks/paper, 12 1/2 x 15 3/4 ins / 32 x 40 cm) NLG 1,380. Amsterdam, 31 May 1995, *Still-life* (oil on canvas, 14 1/4 x 20 1/4 ins / 36 x 51.5 cm) NLG 6,136. Amsterdam, 19-20 Feb 1997, *Interior* (oil on canvas, 10 x 13 ins / 24.5 x 33 cm) NLG 3,228. Amsterdam, 16 March 1999, *Tuinparasol* (1969, oil on canvas, 26x18 ins / 65x46 cm) NLG 12,000. Amsterdam, 1 Dec 1999, *Painter's Still-life* (1983, oil on canvas, 12x16 ins / 30x40 cm) NLG 7,500. Amsterdam, 18 Jan 2000, *Still-life with Autumn Leaves* (1983, watercolour, 10x14 ins / 26x35 cm) NLG 2,800. Amsterdam, 28 Nov 2000, *Auverne* (1975, oil on canvas, 11x15 ins / 28x38 cm) NLG 5,500. Amsterdam, 11 June 2001, *De eetkamer te ukkel* (1938, oil on canvas, 26x16 ins / 65x40 cm) NLG 13,000. Amsterdam, 3 Dec 2001, *De gele berg Auvergne* (1966, oil on canvas, 16x20 ins / 40x50 cm) NLG 4,000. Rotterdam, 23 April 2002, *Sands of Olonne* (oil on canvas, 11x15 ins / 28x38 cm) EUR 3,600. AMSTERDAM, 25 Nov 2002, *French Landscape* (1935, oil on canvas, 18x21 ins / 45x53 cm) EUR 4,800. AMSTERDAM, 3 June 2003, *Interior* (1993, oil on canvas, 28x20 ins / 70x50 cm) EUR 3,200. AMSTERDAM, 25 Nov 2003, *Round Table* (1937, oil on canvas, 39x59 ins / 100x150 cm) EUR 6,300. AMSTERDAM, 22 June 2004, *French Landscape* (1975, 20x24 ins / 50x60 cm) EUR 1000. AMSTERDAM, 27 Sept 2004, *View of an Italian Village* (1935, pen, brown ink, watercolour and gouache, 9x11 ins / 23x29 cm) EUR 800.

KATADA, Tokuro

Japanese, 20th century.
Born 1889, in Oita Prefecture (Island of Kyushu); died 1934, in Tokyo.
Painter.

Katada graduated from the oil painting department of the Tokyo School of Fine Art. He was a member of the Imperial Fine Art Committee.

KATANO, Takashi

Japanese, 20th century.
Painter, calligrapher.

In 1989 the Espace Japon in Paris mounted a solo exhibition of Katano's calligraphic paintings on paper after Japanese poets of the past.

KATAOKA, Tamako

Japanese, 20th century.
Born 5 January 1905, in Sapporo (Hokkaido).
Painter. Portraits, landscapes.

In 1923, Kataoka decided to go to Tokyo and enrol in the department of traditional Japanese painting, or *Nihon-ga*, at the School of Fine Art for Women, where she studied under Tadao Yoshimura and took drawing classes with Onichiro Tomita. In 1925 she refused to go back to her family, choosing instead to complete her studies and get married. She decided to become a painter. The following year she graduated from the women's art school and took up a teaching post at Ooka state primary school in Yokohama, where she taught for 30 years. In 1955 she was appointed to teach at the Women's University of Fine Art, a post she held for a further 15 years. In 1962 she visited Europe, travelling to France, the UK and Italy. In 1966 she became head of the *Nihon-ga* department at the Prefectural University of Fine Art in Aichi, where she trained a great many students and sought to modernise the traditional style. She was appointed a member of the Nihongeijutsu-in Academy in 1982 and awarded the Order of Culture in 1989.

Kataoka was trained in the traditional school of Japanese painting known as *Nihon-ga* and used plant pigments rather than the techniques and materials of Western oil painting. In the five years from 1954 she produced her first major series of Kabuki actors, consisting of scenes painted mainly on screens. Next, in 1959, she turned to the sea, then to volcanoes in 1961, before concentrating on Mount Fuji in 1968-1969. In their composition and Fauvist colours, these landscapes reveal her evident familiarity with Western art. In the typically Japanese Bugaku scenes of 1961-1971, she uses bright colours contained within traditional drawing. In 1966 she turned to representing historical figures, including politicians, military leaders and Japanese monks, then, around 1971, to the lithographers of the 19th-century Edo period, such as Hokusai, Sharaku and Hiroshige (1797-1858), who had had such a great influence on Western painting. In 1983 Kataoka started painting female nudes reminiscent of sculptures by Maillol transposed into the world of Japanese painting. This indicates how hard it is to classify her art, which is traditionally Japanese in technique, but whose style sometimes owes much to Western art.

Kataoka showed work at the Inten annual exhibition for the first time in 1930. After 1939 she became a regular participant, winning first prize in 1943 and the Ministry of Education prize in 1961. She was selected to represent Japan at the 9th São Paulo Biennale in 1967 and exhibited at the Salon Comparaisons in Paris in 1976. Her first solo exhibition was held at the Mitsukoshi department store on Nihonbashi in Tokyo in 1959 and she exhibited there again in 1961. The Tamenaga Gallery in Paris mounted an exhibition of her work in 1972 and her first retrospective, in 1979, was held at the Matsuya store in Ginza, the Matsuzakaya store in Nagoya and at the prefectural museums of modern art in Hokkaido and Kamakura. She had a tribute exhibition in 1990 in Tokyo and the Mitsukoshi-Étoile Gallery in Paris mounted an exhibition of her work in 1992.

BIBLIOGRAPHY:

Kataoka, Tamako, *Kanshu Kawakita Michiaki; sekinin henshu Tsuruta Heihachiro, Gakushu Kenkyusha*, Tokyo, 1991. *Kataoka Tamako*, exhibition catalogue, Espace des arts Mitsukoshi-Étoile, Paris, 1992.

MUSEUMS AND GALLERIES:

KAMAKURA (MMA): *Volcano: Mt Asama* (1965); *Swirling Sea* (1962); *Illusion: Bugaku Scene* (1961); *Portrait of Ashikaga Takauji* (1966); *Portrait of Ashikaga Yoshimitsu* (1966); *Portrait of Ashikaga Yoshimasa* (1966); *Portrait of Haku-in* (1968); *Portrait of Nichiren* (1968); *Portraits of Hotaiko and Josui Kuroda* (1970); *Portrait of Toshusai Sharaku* (1971); *Portrait of Katsushika Hokusai* (1971); *Portraits of Kitagawa Utamaro and Kiyonaga Torii* (1972); *Portrait of Hiroshige Ando* (1973); *Portrait of Chobunsai Eishi* (1974); *Portraits of the Monk Benei Yamazaki and of Komano Noritsugu* (1975); *Portrait of Toyokuni III after He Had Taken the Name Kunisada* (1976); *Portrait of Toyokuni I* (1978) - KYOTO (National Mus. of Modern Art): *Portraits of the Zen Monk of the Myoshin-ji temple, Sekko and the Grand Zen Master of the Kobai-in, Tokai Sekimon* (1984) - MITO (Ibaraki Mus. of Modern Art): *Mt Fuji in Spring, Plum Trees* (1988) - OKAYAMA (Prefectural Mus. of Art): *Portraits of the Ukiyo-e Painter Keisai Kuwagata and the Popular Writer Santo Kyoden* (1981) - SAPPORO (Hokkaido Mus. of Modern Art): *Awa Landscape* (1963); *Izu Landscape* (1964); *Extinct Volcano: Mt Myogi* (1966); *Mt Fuji* (1967); *Bugaku: Hassen* (1967); *Gagaku: Goddess and Konju* (1968); *Bugaku: Ni-no-mai, Second Dance, Old Couple* (1969) - TOKYO (Setagaya Art Mus.): *Portrait of the Ukiyo-e Painter Shunsho* (1987).

KATASE, Kazuo

Japanese, 20th - 21st century.
Born 1947, in Shizuoka.
Installation artist, environmental artist.

In 1989, Katase's installations were exhibited at Le Magasin in Grenoble, at the Shedhalle in Zurich and at the International Cultural Centre in Antwerp. In 1995 Katase made a collection of sculptural pieces under the overall title *Temple of the Sea* for Lille-Europe station, including an enormous, hanging, mute bell. His technique involves modifying perceptions of familiar places and spaces by either accentuating or disrupting their structural characteristics.

BIBLIOGRAPHY:

Hutchinson, John, *Kazuo Katase*, exhibition catalogue, Douglas Hyde Gallery, Dublin, 1993. *Umsicht*, exhibition catalogue, Wilhelm-Hack-Museum in Ludwigshafen am Rhein, Cologne, 1999-2000.

KATCHADOURIAN, Sarkis

Iranian, 20th century.
Painter, watercolourist. Local scenes, architectural views.
Orientalism.

This artist signs himself *S. K. Biche*

AUCTION RECORDS:

PARIS, 19 Nov 1942, *Amorous Embrace*, FRF 2,500; *The Frescoes of Ispahan, Techenel-Sutun Palace*, FRF 4,000. PARIS, 28

July 1947, *Young Persian Woman Sleeping* (watercolour) FRF 1,100. PARIS, 11 March 1983, *Young Woman Wearing a White Veil on a Floral Background* (gouache) FRF 6,000. PARIS, 12 Dec 1990, *Young Woman with a Rose* (oil on canvas, 22 x 28 3/4 ins / 55 x 73 cm) FRF 28,000. AMSTERDAM, 21 Jan 1998, *Idle Moments* (oil on canvas, 19 3/4 x 24 ins / 50 x 61 cm) NLG 2,767. BRUSSELS, 12 Oct 1999, *Arab Market Scene* (1922, oil on canvas, 32x26 ins / 82x66 cm) BEF 80,000. NEW ORLEANS, 7 Oct 2000, *Floral Still-life* (oil on canvas, 26x20 ins / 66x51 cm) USD 2,500. BOSTON, 7 Sept 2001, *Draped Figure Study* (crayon and gouache, 17 x 12 ins / 44x30 cm) USD 2,200. PARIS, 26 March 2002, *Couple Embracing* (1930, gouache on cardboard, 21x15 ins / 54x37cm) EUR 1,200. BRUSSELS, 28 May 2002, *Arab Market* (1922, oil on canvas, 32x26 ins / 82x55 cm) EUR 4,800. PARIS, 4 June 2003, *Market at Cairo* (1922, oil on canvas, 32x26 ins / 82x66 cm) EUR 5,800. NEW YORK, 24 Sept 2003, *Ararat* (oil on canvas, 14x18 ins / 36x46 cm) USD 650. NEW YORK, 24 Sept 2003, *Arakatz, Erivan* (1919, watercolour, gouache and pastel on paperboard, 12 x 23 ins / 30x58 cm) USD 750. BRUSSELS, 13 Sept 2004, *Oriental Woman at the Lecture* (gouache, 17x24 ins / 43x60 cm) EUR 650.

KATCHENKO, Mikhail Stepanovich
Ukrainian, 19th century.
Born 1860, in Kharkov.
Painter. Genre scenes, landscapes.

Mikhail Katchenko studied at the imperial academy of fine arts in St Petersburg and with Cormon. His work went on view at several Paris salons. He was made a Chevalier of the Légion d'Honneur in 1889 and received an honourable mention in 1907.

MUSEUMS AND GALLERIES:
ST PETERSBURG (Gosudarstvennyj Russkij Muz.): *In an Artist's Studio* - TOULON: *Arrival in Toulon of the Russian Squadron, 13 October 1893*.

AUCTION RECORDS:
PARIS, 6 March 1920, *Windmills (Sunlight Effect)*, FRF 600; *Calm Sea*, FRF 500. AHLDEN, 17 Sept 1999, *Tirla Kari Mosque in Samarkand* (1893, oil on canvas, 20 x 29 ins / 52 x 74 cm) DEM 4,100.

KATEI, real name: Ken Taki, nickname: Shichoku, pseudonym: Katei
Japanese, 19th century.
Born 1830, in Tokyo; died 1901.
Painter.
Nanga School.

Katei studied under Araki Kankai (1786-1860) and specialised in depicting flowers and birds. He was a member of the Imperial Fine Art Committee.

BIBLIOGRAPHY:
Illing, Richard, *The art of Japanese prints*, Omega Books.

KATEI, real name: Michihiro Kodama, nickname: Shiki, pseudonym: Katei
Japanese, 19th - 20th century.
Born 1841; died 1913.
Painter.
Nanga School.

Katei studied under Chokunyu Tanomura (1814-1907) and painted flowers and birds. He lived in Nagano prefecture.

KATEN, real name: Shiko Mikuma, nickname: Kaido, Shukei, pseudonym: Katen, Kaido
Japanese, 18th century.
Born 1730, in Kyoto; died 1794.
Painter. Landscapes, flowers.

Katen belonged to the realist school of Nagasaki and mainly painted cherry trees in bloom. He seems also to have painted a portrait sold at auction in London.

AUCTION RECORDS:
LONDON, 13 Nov 1989, *Half-length Portrait of a Mother Nursing her Baby* (Aiban Tate-e print, 13 x 8 1/4 ins / 33 x 21.2 cm) GBP 1,155.

KATH, Ludwig
German, 20th century.
Born 2 July 1886, in Kiel.
Painter. Landscapes.

Ludwig Kath lived and worked in Karlsruhe and Charlottenburg. He took part in the Grosse Berliner Kunstausstellung of 1910.

KATHELIN, Ernest
Belgian, 19th century.
Active in Brussels.
Painter. Genre scenes.

Ernest Kathelin exhibited at the Brussels Salon between 1863 and 1866.

KATHELYN, Dina
Belgian, 20th century.
Born 1934, in Ukkel.
Graphic designer, illustrator.

Dina Kathelyn studied with Marcel Hastir and Léon Pringels at the Académie de St-Gilles in Brussels. She began as an advertising artist, and went on to illustrate children's books, which she sometimes wrote herself.

KATICHEV, Aleksei
Russian, 20th century.
Born 1940.
Painter. Genre scenes, sporting subjects.

Aleksei Katichev studied at the school of fine arts in Moscow, at the Surikov institute, and worked in the studio of Evgeniy Adolfovich Kibrik. He was a member of the union of Soviet artists.

AUCTION RECORDS:
PARIS, 18 Oct 1993, *Reapers of Novgorod* (1963, oil on canvas, 39 1/4 x 59 ins / 100 x 150 cm) FRF 8,200. LONDON, 11 April 1997, *Hockey Match* (c. 1970, oil on canvas, 18 x 20 ins / 45.7 x 50.7 cm) GBP 345.

KATMANN, Bernhard
German, 16th century.
Died 1609.
Active in Münster.
Sculptor.

KATO, Akira
Japanese, 20th century.
Born 1937, in Gumma Prefecture.
Painter.

In 1966 Kato showed work at the 7th Exhibition of Contemporary Art in Japan and at the Shell Prize exhibition in Tokyo. In 1969 he exhibited at the 5th International Exhibition of Young Artists and won the Ministry of Trade and Industry prize.

KATO, Hajime
Japanese, 20th century.
Born 7 February 1925, in Tokyo.
Active in France from 1958.
Painter.
Musicalism (the attempt to interpret music in painting).

Kato trained as an economist and was largely self-taught as a painter, though he briefly attended classes at the department of graphic design at the National School of Fine Art. He moved to France in 1958 and exhibited at the Salon d'Automne in Paris.

His abstract painting is in the Far Eastern tradition of calligraphic signs. It is also close to the 'Musicalist' movement and is characterised by a transparency of colour.

MUSEUMS AND GALLERIES:
PARIS (Mus. National du Sport).
AUCTION RECORDS:
PARIS, 25 April 1990, *Composition* (1961, oil on canvas, 28 3/4 x 39 1/4 ins / 73 x 100 cm) FRF 25,000. PARIS, 7 Nov 1990, *Composition* (1962, oil on canvas, 24 x 28 3/4 ins / 61 x 73 cm) FRF 20,000. PARIS, 19 April 1991, *Composition* (1965, oil on canvas, 24 1/2 x 19 ins / 62 x 48 cm) FRF 6,000.

KATO, Kiyomi
Japanese, 20th century.
Born 1931, in Tokyo.
Engraver. Genre scenes.
Kato enrolled in a theatre course at university in Tokyo, but dropped out in 1957 and, in 1959, began to exhibit with the Shunyokai association, immediately winning a prize. He creates familiar scenes in a style with overtones of surrealism, evoking a poetic world that transcends the subject-matter. In Vienna in 1960 he was represented in an exhibition of exchanges between Austria and Japan. In 1960, 1964 and 1966, he exhibited at the Tokyo Print Biennale. In 1962, he received the Newcomer Prize of the Japanese Print Association, of which he became a member.

KATO, Koi-Oun
Japanese, 19th - 20th century.
Sculptor.
Kato lived in Kyoto. He was a sculptor in wood and exhibited at the Exposition Universelle in Paris in 1900.

KATO, Tsuneaki
Japanese, 20th - 21st century.
Born 1948.
Sculptor.
Kato studied at the university of Iwate Prefecture. His works are conceptual in approach, made in stone set with metal. In 1973 he received the prize at the 5th Exhibition of Contemporary Sculpture in Ube. In 1974 he showed work at the *Japanese Art Today* exhibition at the Montreal museum of contemporary art.

KATONA, Nandor
Hungarian, 19th century.
Born 12 September 1864, in Szepes Ofalu.
Painter. Landscapes.
Nandor Katona received an honourable mention at the 1900 Exhibition Universelle in Paris.

KATOW, Paul de
French, 19th century.
Born 17 October 1834, in Strasbourg; died November 1897, in Asnières (Hauts-de-Seine).
Painter. Battles, genre scenes.
Paul de Katow was a pupil of Delacroix. He exhibited at the Salon between 1839 and 1882. He was war correspondent of the *Gaulois* in 1870.

KATSCH, Arnold
German, 19th century.
Born 25 May 1861, in Kassel.
Sculptor.
Katsch spent five years in Rome, and from 1894 exhibited busts in Berlin.

KATSCH, Hermann
German, 19th century.
Born 10 September 1853, in Eisenach.
Painter. History painting, portraits.
Katsch trained at the academy in Munich, subsequently travelling to Italy and Tunisia. He exhibited mainly in Berlin (from 1883).

KATSCHENREITER, G. H.
German, 19th century.
Active in Munich.
Painter. Genre scenes.
Katschenreiter is mentioned in *Art Prices Current*.
AUCTION RECORDS:
LONDON, 10 Jan 1909, *The Latest News*, GBP 6. LONDON, 4 June 1909, *Smoker* (1880) GBP 2.

KATSUDA, Michitaka
Japanese, 20th century.
Born 1944, in Kobe.
Painter.
Katsuda studied at the University of Fine Art in Musashino near Tokyo. He has exhibited regularly in Tokyo since 1966.

KATSUHIRA, Tokushi
Japanese, 20th century.
Born 1904, in Akita Prefecture.
Painter, engraver (wood). Local scenes.
Katsuhira's working life began in his family's paper factory. He started learning the art of wood engraving around 1922. In 1928, he embarked on a more serious study of engraving techniques with Goro Kimura. He made several series of engravings depicting the customs of his native province. These are of particular interest because it was an area where many old traditions were preserved. The backgrounds of his works evoke certain *ukiyo-e* landscapes, giving a special flavour to these scenes of provincial life. In 1929 Katsuhira exhibited at the Japanese Print Association. In 1931 his work was shown in the Imperial Exhibition. From 1931 he took part in exhibitions run by the National Painting Academy. He was awarded a cultural medal by Akita Prefecture.

KATSUKAWA. See **HOKUSAI**

KATSUKAWA SHUNJO. See **SHUNJO**

KATSUKAWA SHUNKO. See **SHUNKO**

KATSUKAWA SHUNSHO. See **SHUNSHO**

KATSUKAWA SHUNZAN. See **SHUNZAN**

KATSULIDIS, Panayiotis
Greek, 20th century.
Born 27 December 1933, in Messini.
Active in France from 1962.
Painter.
Panayiotis Katsulidis took part in several exhibitions in Athens. After moving to France he was invited to exhibit at the São Paulo Biennale (1965) and the Paris Biennale (1967). His painting, abstract, is based on gestural art.

KATSUMATA, Takeo
Japanese, 20th century.
Born in Tokyo.
Painter.
From 1928, Katsumata exhibited in Paris at the Salon des Artistes Français and at the Salon d'Automne.

KATSUMOTO, Fujio
Japanese, 20th century.
Born 1926, in Ishikawa Prefecture.
Painter.
Katsumoto studied at the Kyoto School of Fine Art. He uses touches of abstract colour on slightly geometrical backgrounds, sometimes with a raised, granular surface. His work has been shown in group exhibitions, including the Biennale Internationale des Jeunes Artistes in Paris in 1961, the second exhibition of the JAFA group in 1967 and the 6th Print Biennale in Tokyo in 1968. He has also had a great many solo exhibitions. He is a member of the Japanese Association of Modern Art and the International Art Club.

KATSUNO
Japanese, 19th century.
Active in Osaka c. 1805.
Master engraver.

KATSURA, Yuki
Japanese, 20th century.
Born 1913, in Tokyo.
Painter, collage artist.
Katsura entered art school in 1926 but, as the study of oil painting was not considered suitable for a girl, she had to take private lessons with Shuho Ikegami, Kenichi Nakamura and Sabrosuke Okada. In 1933, she won first prize at the *20th Light and Wind* exhibition in Tokyo. In the 1930s, her work became more contemporary in style and she became a member of the Research Centre for Western Avant-garde Painting. In 1935 she had her first exhibition of collages. In 1936, she founded the Association of Women Painters to publicise the work of women artists. During a stay in France (1956-1961) Katsura met Sam Francis and Kenzo Okada. Her paintings and collages of the 1960s tend towards simplified, slightly humorous forms and brighter colours reminiscent of Miró. In this period she began to include solid materials such as cork and wood in her collages. She had retrospective exhibitions at the prefectural museum in Yamaguchi in 1980 and at the Shimonoseki museum in 1991. In 1966 she won first prize at the 7th Exhibition of Modern Art in Tokyo.
AUCTION RECORDS:
NEW YORK, 27 April 1994, *Owl* (watercolour/paper, kakemono, 24 3/4 x 18 1/4 ins / 62.9 x 46.4 cm) USD 4,830.

KATSUSHIGE, real name: Katsushige Iwasa, nickname: Gembei, pseudonym: Matabei II
Japanese, 17th century.
Died 1673.
Painter.
Katsushige studied under his father Matabei (1578-1650), also known as Katsumochi. He specialised in dancing figures and decorated the doors of Fukui Castle with images of cranes. The doors were restored in 1669.

KATSUSHIKA HOKUSAI. See **HOKUSAI**

KATSUTA, Shokir or Shokin
Japanese, 20th century.
Painter. Still-lifes.
Katsuta's work was shown at the exhibition of Japanese art at the Musée du Jeu de Paume in Paris in 1929.

KATTENHOFFER, Joël Paul
18th century.
Died 1777.
Draughtsman, engraver (burin).

KATTERFELDT, Karl Georg Theodor
German, 19th century.
Died 1881.
Active in Lübeck.
Painter.

KATTIK, Petrus van
Dutch, 17th - 18th century.
Painter. Landscapes.
Two landscapes with ruins by Petrus van Kattik appear in the Hulk sales catalogue in Dordrecht in 1720.

KATY. See **DESLANDES**

KATZ, Alex
American, 20th century.
Born 24 July 1927, in New York.
Painter, collage artist, engraver. Portraits, still-lifes, landscapes. Stage sets, artists' books.
Alex Katz studied at Cooper Union from 1946 to 1949, then at the Skowhegan School of Painting and Sculpture in Maine, where he obtained two studentships. He taught at the Cooper Union. In 1994, Cooper Union Art School created the Alex Katz Visiting Chair in Painting with the endowment provided by the sale of ten paintings donated by the artist.

In the 1960s, he produced small collages of home landscapes, rows of trees and beaches from his native Maine and still-lifes. He showed a short-lived interest in the techniques involved in working from photographs. Since the mid 1950s, he has worked from life, concentrating on portraits and the representation of flowers sometimes presented in *Cut-outs*, painted on both sides and set on a pedestal.

Indifferent to the still powerful hold of Abstract Expressionism and alien to Pop Art, he benefited from the renewed interest in realism at the end of the 1960s, without succumbing to hyperrealism and the need for rivalry with the camera. His painting remained figurative, taken from life, his subjects restricted to a close circle: his wife Ada, their son Vincent, his friends Rauschenberg and Ginsberg, artists, poets and dancers. He captures private moments in the diversely secret smiles, the figures he picks out from the crowd; the soft hues, though contrasted with the deep colours of the backgrounds, confirm the feeling of intimacy. However, the big screen close-up frames contradict it as do the elliptic simplification of the drawing, its economical outline, broad flat tints, and, from 1962, the huge formats, and especially the rejection of any psychological insights into the sitters: he is not interested in psychology, just surfaces. After 1965, he also produced prints. From 1960 to 1977, he designed sets for the Paul Taylor Dance Company.

In 1977, he took on the sheer size of street advertising, by having 23 portraits displayed on Time Square's billboards. By focusing on scale, he was continuing his investigation of formal content and highlighting issues of perception. His portraits have been gradually integrated into backgrounds, he has even dedicated a set to couples (*Pas de Deux*). His brush captures the anecdotal, catches instants in everyday life, casting what he calls his film characters in increasingly vibrant colours. He is interested in what makes appearance: imagery without reality.

He has taken part in numerous collective exhibitions in the USA and in Europe, notably, in New York: *Young America 1960: Thirty American Painters under Thirty-Six, American Drawings 1963-1973*; the 1991 Whitney Biennial and *Two decades of American Painting; Contemporary American Realism since 1960*, set up by the Pennsylvania Academy of Fine Arts in Philadelphia, which travelled to Lisbon, Madrid and Nuremberg; and *Birth of the Cool*, which went from Hamburg to Zurich. In Paris he featured in *By Night* and *Cher Peintre... peintures figuratives depuis l'ultime Picabia* (*Dear Painter, Figurative Paintings since Late Picabia*) at the Pompidou Centre. He has shown his works in solo exhibitions from 1954, first regularly in New York then in Chicago, Los Angeles and Detroit; from the early 1970s in Hanover, Cologne, Helsinki, Montreal, London, Copenhagen, Paris, Valencia and Baden-Baden (*Alex Katz: American Landscape*). In 1986, he had a retrospective at the Whitney Museum and, in 1988, a retrospective of his prints at the Brooklyn Museum of Art; they were followed by many others on diverse aspects of his production.

BIBLIOGRAPHY:
Smith, Roberta, *Alex Katz in the Seventies*, exhibition catalogue, Rose Art Museum, Brandeis University, Waltham, 1978. Kramer, Hilton, '*The Return of the Realists - And a new battle shaping up*' in *The New York Times section C*, periodical, New York, October 25, 1981. Maravell, Nicholas P., *Alex Katz. The Complete Prints 1947-1983*, Alan Wofsy Fine Arts, San Francisco, 1983. *Alex Katz*, exhibition catalogue, Museum of Modern Art, New York, 1986. Beattie, A., *Alex Katz*, New York, 1987. *Alex Katz*, exhibition catalogue, Solomon R. Guggenheim Museum, New York, 1996. *Alex Katz. Twenty-five Years of Painting*, exhibition catalogue, The Saatchi Gall., London, 1997. Schwabsky, Barry, '*A Conversation with Alex Katz*' in *New Art Examiner* vol. 27, n° 6, periodical, New York, March, 2000. *Alex Katz: New Paintings and Drawings*,

exhibition catalogue, Richard Gray Gallery, Chicago, 2003. *Alex Katz: Twelve Paintings*, exhibition catalogue, PaceWildenstein, New York, 2004.

MUSEUMS AND GALLERIES:

NEW YORK (Whitney Mus. of American Art): *The Red Smile* (1963); *Eli* (1963) - PORTLAND, ME (MA): *Black Scarf* (1996) - RICHMOND (Virginia MFA): *Self-portrait with sunglasses* (1969, oil on canvas) - WINSTON-SALEM (Fine Arts Gal., Wake Forest University): *Vincent with Open Mouth* (1971).

AUCTION RECORDS:

NEW YORK, 31 March 1973, *Peony*, USD 1,000. PARIS, 30 Nov 1974, *Iris*, FRF 11,000. NEW YORK, 21 Oct 1976, *Joan* (1971, oil on canvas, 55½ x 68 ins / 141 x 172.5 cm) USD 5,000. NEW YORK, 20 Oct 1978, *Man and Woman* (oil on canvas, 65½ x 50 ins / 166.5 x 127 cm) USD 2,300. NEW YORK, 16 May 1980, *Portrait of Vincent* (1974, pencil, 15¼ x 22¼ ins / 38.6 x 56.5 cm) USD 2,000. NEW YORK, 16 May 1980, *Portrait of Al Held n°2* (oil on canvas, 16¾ x 23¾ ins / 42.5 x 60.3 cm) USD 2,100. NEW YORK, 12 May 1981, *Islebow Ferry* (1976, oil on canvas, 78 x 84 ins / 198 x 213.3 cm) USD 24,000. NEW YORK, 9 Nov 1983, *Ada at her Mirror* (1969, oil on canvas, 32¼ x 48 ins / 82 x 122 cm) USD 8,500. NEW YORK, 7 June 1984, *Ada* (1974, pencil, 15 x 22¼ ins / 38.1 x 56.5 cm) USD 3,250. NEW YORK, 8 Nov 1984, *The Orange Band* (1979, colour silk screen print, 40¼ x 28¼ ins / 102 x 72 cm) USD 2,600. NEW YORK, 10 May 1985, *The Orange Band* (1979, colour silk screen print, 40¼ x 28¼ ins / 102 x 72 cm) USD 2,750. NEW YORK, 5 Nov 1985, *Evening* (1972, oil on canvas, 72 x 96 ins / 182.8 x 243.8 cm) USD 46,000. NEW YORK, 20 Feb 1987, *Vincent facing Right* (1974, pencil, 15 x 22 ins / 38.2 x 55.8 cm) USD 3,000. NEW YORK, 20 Feb 1988, *Untitled* (1965, oil on canvas, 35 x 63 ins / 89 x 160 cm) USD 11,000. NEW YORK, 8 Oct 1988, *Ada in a Red T-shirt* (1980, oil/synthetic resin, 11¾ x 9 ins / 30 x 22.9 cm) USD 9,900. NEW YORK, 10 Nov 1988, *Cityscape* (1963, oil on canvas, 48¼ x 48¾ ins / 122.8 x 124 cm) USD 30,800. NEW YORK, 3 May 1989, *Tiger Lily 1* (1968, oil on canvas, 32 x 48¾ ins / 81 x 124 cm) USD 35,750. NEW YORK, 4 May 1989, *January* (oil on canvas, 48½ x 41½ ins / 123.2 x 105.5 cm) USD 85,800. NEW YORK, 9 Nov 1989, *Interior* (oil/synthetic resin, 18 x 14 ins / 45.6 x 35.5 cm) USD 33,000. NEW YORK, 23 Feb 1990, *Ada* (1976, pencil/paper, 22¼ x 15¼ ins / 56.5 x 38.8 cm) USD 14,300; *Fire III* (oil on canvas, 72 x 120 ins / 182.9 x 304.8 cm) USD 121,000. NEW YORK, 8 May 1990, *Jennifer* (1978, oil on canvas, 48 x 34 ins / 121.9 x 86.3 cm) USD 77,000. NEW YORK, 9 May 1990, *Splendid Lilies 2* (1967, oil on canvas, 72 x 144 ins / 182.8 x 365.5 cm) USD 88,000. NEW YORK, 4 Oct 1990, *Ada at her Mirror* (1969, oil/synthetic resin, 9¾ x 1½ x 14 ins / 25 x 4 x 35.5 cm) USD 11,000. NEW YORK, 5 Oct 1990, *Sketch for a Walk* (oil/synthetic resin, 18 x 20 ins / 45.8 x 50.8 cm) USD 13,200. NEW YORK, 14 Feb 1991, *Dance* (1978, oil on canvas, 78 x 120 ins / 198.1 x 304.7 cm) USD 99,000. NEW YORK, 12 Nov 1991, *Summer Landscape* (oil/synthetic resin, 15 x 20 ins / 38 x 50.8 cm) USD 3,300. NEW YORK, 13 Nov 1991, *Pat 2* (1979, oil on canvas, 48 x 60 ins / 121.9 x 152.4 cm) USD 60,500. NEW YORK, 6 May 1992, *Rex 1* (1975, oil on canvas, 48½ x 48½ ins / 123.2 x 123.2 cm) USD 22,000. NEW YORK, 6 Oct 1992, *Ada in the Wood* (1984, oil/synthetic resin, 20 x 16 ins / 50.8 x 40.6 cm) USD 13,750. NEW YORK, 19 Nov 1992, *Ada with Sunglasses* (1977, oil on canvas, 96 x 72 ins / 243.9 x 182.9 cm) USD 77,000. ZURICH, 21 April 1993, *Alex at Cheat Lake in 1969* (lithograph, 38½ x 24 ins / 98 x 61 cm) CHF 1,800. NEW YORK, 5 May 1993, *The Blue Sweater* (1988, oil on canvas, 70 x 60 ins / 177.8 x 152.4 cm) USD 59,700. NEW YORK, 11 Nov 1993, *Lauren and Peter* (1988, oil on canvas, 90 x 66 ins / 228.6 x 167.6 cm) USD 55,200. NEW YORK, 3 May 1994, *Summer Picnic* (1975, oil on canvas, 78 x 144 ins / 198.2 x 365.8 cm) USD 129,000. ZURICH, 23 June 1995, *Portrait of Ada* (coloured silk screen print, 26 x 26½ ins / 66.2 x 67 cm) CHF 1,300. NEW YORK, 22 Feb 1996, *Ada* (graphite/paper, 15 x 22¼ ins / 38.1 x 56.5 cm) USD 4,025. NEW YORK, 5 May 1996, *Ada Standing* (1987, coloured silk screen print/sheet of double-sided aluminium, 64¾ x 10¼ ins / 164.5 x 25.8 cm) USD 9,775. NEW YORK, 10 Oct 1996, *Swamp Maple* (1981, oil/Masonite, 16 x 12 ins / 40.6 x 30.5 cm) USD 9,200. NEW YORK, 9 Nov 1996, *Ada Standing* (1987, coloured lithograph, 64¾ x 10¼ ins / 164.5 x 25.8 cm) GBP 10,925. NEW YORK, 19 Nov 1996, *Boy with Open Mouth* (1973, graphite/paper, 15 x 22 ins / 37.8 x 55.8 cm) USD 2,990. NEW YORK, 21 Nov 1996, *Folding Chair* (1962, oil on canvas, 48 x 45 ins / 121.8 x 114.4 cm) USD 36,800. BUCKINGHAMSHIRE, 22 Sept 1997, *Portrait of a Woman in a Broad-brimmed Hat* (1973, pencil, 14½ x 22 ins / 36.8 x 55 cm) GBP 1,035. NEW YORK, 19 Nov 1997, *Luisa, Dana, and Joan* (1979, oil on canvas, 72 x 144 ins / 182.8 x 365.7 cm) USD 90,500. NEW YORK, 17 Feb 1999, *Vincent and Ada* (1976, oil on canvas, 72 x 96 ins / 183 x 244 cm) USD 65,000. NEW YORK, 18 Nov 1999, *Dark Glasses* (oil on canvas, 40 x 112 ins / 102 x 284 cm) USD 75,000. NEW YORK, 18 May 2000, *Untitled - Still-life* (oil on masonite, double-sided, 47 x 23 ins / 119 x 58 cm) USD 32,500. NEW YORK, 16 Nov 2000, *Cornice* (1997, oil on canvas, 96 x 126 ins / 244 x 320 cm) USD 30,000. NEW YORK, 14 Nov 2001, *Rowing* (oil on canvas, 49 x 60 ins / 124 x 152 cm) USD 100,000. NEW YORK, 15 Nov 2001, *Blue Umbrella No.2* (1972, oil on canvas, 96 x 144 ins / 244 x 366 cm) USD 600,000. NEW YORK, 14 May 2002, *January IV* (1992, oil on canvas, 91 x 120 ins / 232 x 305 cm) USD 240,000. NEW YORK, 11 Nov 2002, *Ada Ada* (1991, oil on canvas, 60 x 120 ins / 152 x 306 cm) USD 200,000. NEW YORK, 15 May 2003, *Bicycle Rider* (1982, oil on canvas, 72 x 96 ins / 183 x 244 cm) USD 190,000. NEW YORK, 11 Nov 2003, *Nine A.M.* (1999, oil on canvas, 96 x 120 ins / 244 x 305 cm) USD 220,000. NEW YORK, 12 May 2004, *Forsythia* (1997, oil on canvas, 78 x 48 ins / 198 x 122 cm) USD 75,000. LONDON, 24 June 2004, *Ada in Orange Straw Hat* (1990, oil on board, 16 x 11 ins / 41 x 29 cm) GBP 17,000.

KATZ, Franz

Flemish School, 19th century.

Born 1782, in Antwerp; died 28 May 1851, in Cologne.

Draughtsman, miniaturist.

Franz Katz was a pupil of J.P. van Langer at the Düsseldorf academy. He is known for his portraits.

KATZ, Irina

Romanian, 20th - 21st century.

Born 22 March 1952, in Bucharest.

Painter, draughtswoman. Figures, landscapes.

Irina Katz graduated from the institute of art in Bucharest. She has produced stage sets and costumes for several films. She selects a real object for her subjects - a path, a house, a face - then confers on it a mysterious, twilight feeling. Collective exhibitions have included the national graphic art salon, Bucharest, in 1975 and the Salon des Indépendants, Paris, 1982. She has also shown her works in several solo exhibitions, including one at the Centre Rachi in Paris in 1982.

KATZ, Leo

Polish, 20th century.

Born 30 December 1887, in Poznan.

Active in the USA from 1919.

Painter. Portraits.

Leo Katz received his artistic training in Vienna and Munich. After World War I he settled in New York, where he pursued a career as a portrait artist.

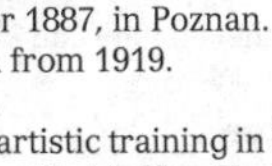

KATZ, Michèle

French, 20th century.

Born 1936, in Paris.

Painter. Artists' books.
Michèle Katz's painting style consists of attractively coloured staining that takes advantage of pleasing random effects. She took part in group exhibitions, beginning with the Salon de la Jeune Peinture in Paris in 1959. She also exhibited at the following: the Salon de Mai (1964-1967); the Salon des Réalités Nouvelles (1964-1967); the Paris Biennale (1969); the Salon de Montrouge (1982); and *Qu'est-ce qu'un Livre d'Artiste?* (*What is an Artist's Book?*) at the Médiathèque in Issy-les-Moulineaux (2001). She showed collections of her work in solo exhibitions at the following: the Musée Rath in Geneva (1967); the Musée d'Art Moderne de la Ville de Paris (ARC section) (1968); the Maison de la Culture in Thonon, Évian and Grenoble (1971); and the Galerie Jean Peyrole in Paris (1986).

KATZ, Moshe
Romanian, 20th century.
Born 2 March 1942, in Bucharest.
Active in Israel and in the USA.
Painter.
Moshe Katz studied at the school of fine arts in Jerusalem in 1962, then at its Chicago counterpart in 1963. He concentrates on breaking down the structure of his canvases, associating geometric shapes and lines with biomorphic figures. He has exhibited solo regularly since 1965 in the USA and in Paris from 1976, notably in 1976 and 1982 at the Galerie Katia Granoff and in 1989 at the Galerie Étienne de Causans. In 1983, he exhibited solo at the Kunsthaus in Bonn and in 1988 and the Haifa cultural centre.

KATZ MANÉ. See **MANÉ-KATZ**

KATZAROFF, Michel
Hungarian, 20th century.
Died c. 1970, in Paris.
Active in France.
Painter, watercolourist, draughtsman. Figures, portraits, landscapes.
In 1946 the Galerie La Boétie in Paris displayed Michel Katzaroff's series of 36 paintings produced from 1931 onwards following a study tour in Vienna. Each one depicted an episode in Beethoven's life. He also completed charcoal drawings depicting other composers and musicians.

KATZENSTEIN, Alois
German, 19th century.
Born 21 June 1859, in Daugendorf (Bavaria); died 30 August 1900, in Munich.
Painter.
Katzenstein trained in Stuttgart and Munich, then specialised in decorating churches.

KATZENSTEIN, Ludwig
German, 19th century.
Born 27 August 1822, in Kassel; died 18 October 1907, in Kassel.
Painter. History painting, portraits, genre scenes.
Katzenstein trained at the academy in Kassel, then studied with Léon Cognier in Paris in 1847. He worked in England, mainly on portraits, then in Italy and Portugal. He finally returned to settle in Kassel.

KATZER, Anton
Austrian, 19th - 20th century.
Born 8 March 1863, in Vienna; died 1938.
Painter. Portraits, genre scenes.
Anton Katzer exhibited in Vienna from 1890.
AUCTION RECORDS:
VIENNA, 16 Sept 1969, *The Horseman and the Woman Gathering Firewood*, ATS 35,000. VIENNA, 15 April 1980, *Picking Flowers* (1894, oil on card, 36 1/2 x 28 1/4 ins / 93 x 71.5 cm) ATS 15,000. LUCERNE, 15 May 1986, *Girl with a Hoop* (1886, oil on canvas, 38 1/2 x 22 1/2 ins / 98 x 57 cm) CHF 12,000. LONDON, 11 April 1995, *The Walk* (1887, oil on canvas, 22 x 48 3/4 ins / 56 x 124 cm) GBP 5,750.

KATZHEIMER, Wolfgang
German, 15th - 16th century.
Active in Bamberg.
Painter, stained glass painter.
Wolfgang Katzheimer produced stained glass windows for churches in Bamberg and Nuremberg, and, in particular, for the church of St Sebald in Nuremberg.

KATZLER
Austrian, 19th century.
Born 1823, in Vienna; died 22 July 1882, in Vienna.
Painter, draughtsman, lithographer.
Katzler established a reputation mainly as a newspaper illustrator. He also did portraits of the *Emperor Franz Joseph* and *Empress Elizabeth*.

KATZNER, Christoph
Austrian, 17th century.
Died 13 December 1661, in Graz.
Painter.
Katzner is known for a *St Veronica with Two Angels*, signed and dated 1658.

KATZOURAKIS, Kyriakos
Greek, 20th century.
Born 1944, in Athens.
Painter.
Nouvelle Figuration.
Kyriakos Katzourakis studied at the school of fine arts in Athens from 1963 to 1968. His paintings are realist in style and use a typeset layout reminiscent of journalistic discourse, juxtaposing images, the aim being to accuse and seek revindication. He has taken part in collective exhibitions and had his first solo exhibition in Athens in 1966.

KAU, Georg
German, 19th - 20th century.
Born 1870, in Neuss.
Painter. Religious subjects.
Georg Kau was a pupil of Martin Feuerstein at the Akademie der Bildenden Künste in Munich. He collaborated with his master on the decoration of St Anne's church in Munich. Later, he decorated many churches in such places as Paxheim, Augsburg, Strasbourg and Padua.

KAU TSE-MING. See **HUXIAN peasant painters of**

KAUB-CASALONGA, Alice
French, 19th - 20th century.
Born 12 March 1875, in Paris.
Painter. Genre scenes, landscapes.
Alice Kaub-Casalonga studied under William Bouguereau and Gabriel Ferrier. She exhibited in Paris at the Salon des Artistes Français, having become a member of that society in 1898.
AUCTION RECORDS:
ENGHIEN-LES-BAINS, 25 April 1976, *Bust of a Seated Female Nude* (oil on canvas, 45 x 34 1/4 ins / 114 x 87 cm) FRF 4,800. NEW YORK, 21 May 1987, *Nude with Roses* (oil on canvas, 41 3/4 x 35 ins / 106 x 89 cm) USD 7,000. NEW YORK, 16 Feb 1993, *An Afternoon Devoted to Sewing* (oil on canvas, 71 x 78 3/4 ins / 180.4 x 200 cm) USD 10,450.

KAUBA, Carl
Austrian, 19th - 20th century.
Born 1865; died 1922.
Active in the USA.
Sculptor. Local scenes.
Carl Kauba devoted himself to typical themes of American folklore, which he treated in small anecdotal pieces, extend-

ing his care for the narrative element to the use of painted bronze.

AUCTION RECORDS:

NEW YORK, 29 April 1976, *Friend in Need* (brown-patinated bronze, H.21 1/2 ins / 54.6 cm) USD 10,000. LONDON, 14 Oct 1977, *The Charge* (patinated bronze, h. 10 ins / 25.4 cm) GBP 6,500. NEW YORK, 23 May 1979, *Indian Chief* (polychrome bronze, h. 16 3/4 ins / 42.4 cm) USD 10,000. NEW YORK, 23 April 1982, *Indian Chief Standing* (brown-patinated bronze, h. 16 1/4 ins / 41.2 cm) USD 10,000. NEW YORK, 5 Dec 1986, *Indian Horse Thief* (polychrome bronze, total height 35 3/4 ins / 90.8 cm) USD 55,000. NEW YORK, 31 May 1990, *Cavalry Soldier* (bronze, h. 21 1/4 ins / 54 cm) USD 5,280. NEW YORK, 10 March 1993, *A Friend in Need of Help* (bronze, h. 20 1/2 ins / 52.1 cm) USD 20,700. NEW YORK, 27 May 1993, *Chief Wolf Robe* (painted bronze, h. 21 3/4 ins / 55.2 cm) USD 18,400. NEW YORK, 31 March 1994, *Indian Smoking the Pipe of Peace* (bronze, h. 16 1/4 ins / 41.3 cm) USD 5,750. NEW YORK, 28 Sept 1995, *Precocious Education* (bronze, h. 16 ins / 40.6 cm) USD 4,025. PERTH, 26 Aug 1996, *Farrier Shoeing a Horse, and its Harness* (bronze, 8 1/4 x 9 3/4 ins / 21 x 25 cm) GBP 1,150. NEW YORK, 25 March 1997, *Cheyenne* (polychrome bronze, l. 12 ins / 30.5 cm) USD 2,300. NORWALK, 3 Jan 1999, *Cowboy with Revolver on Horseback* (green patinated bronze, h. 23 ins / 58 cm) USD 3,300. BOSTON, 9 Jan 1999, *St George and the Dragon* (brown patinated bronze, h. 15 ins / 38 cm) USD 5,000. SANTA FE, 19 May 2001, *Attacking the Fort* (bronze, h. 21 ins / 53 cm) USD 19,000. NEW YORK, 6 June 2001, *How - Kola* (cold painted bronze, h. 24 ins / 61 cm) USD 19,000. BOSTON, 13 July 2002, *Metamorphosis, Art Nouveau Mechanical Figure of a Butterfly Girl* (silvered patina bronze, h. 9 ins / 23 cm, w. 12 ins/30 cm) USD 4,000. PORTSMOUTH, 17 Aug 2002, *Native American Chief* (patinated bronze, h. 11 ins / 28 cm) USD 6,500. PHILADELPHIA, 24 Jan 2003, *Indian on Horseback Roping a Steer* (golden brown patinated bronze, 11 x 6x12 ins / 28 x 15x30 cm) USD 3,750. AMSTERDAM, 11 June 2003, *Horseman Taking Care of his Horse* (brown patinated bronze, h. 10 ins / 25 cm) EUR 5,500. NEW YORK, 7 March 2004, *A Friend in Need* (bronze polychrome, h. 22 ins / 56 cm) USD 19,000. NEW YORK, 2 May 2004, *For Death or for Glory* (bronze, h. 27 ins / 69 cm) USD 18,500.

KAUDERBACH, Sigismund Heinrich

German, 17th century.
Active in Bautzen (Saxony).
Painter.

Kauderbach decorated the town hall and the church of St Michael in Bautzen.

KAUFELER, Bartholomeus

Swiss, 16th century.
Active in Zurich.
Sculptor (wood).

In 1564, Bartholomeus Kaufeler was the leading figure working with wood in Zurich. The museum in the city owns a raised relief by him, depicting two men, one blind, the other lame.

KAUFFER, Edward McKnight

American, 20th century.
Born 14 December 1890, in Great Falls (Montana); died 22 October 1954, in New York.
Active in London from 1914.
Painter, draughtsman.
Vorticism.
The Friday Club, The London Group, Group X.

Edward Kauffer was an American-born artist who became one of Britain's most progressive and influential designers in the 1920s and 1930s. He began his career as an artist, but his fame came from his work as a graphic designer in the advertising industry. He trained as painter at the Mark Hopkins Institute in San Francisco (1910-1912) and studied for six months at the Art Institute of Chicago in 1912. In 1913 Kauffer came into contact with the European avant-garde during his visit to the Armory Show in Chicago. Encouraged by the art movement in Europe, Kauffer left America to study in Paris, where he enrolled at the Académie Moderne (1913-1914). His artistic training was made possible thanks to the financial support of his mentor, Professor Joseph McKnight, from whom he adopted his middle name as a sign of gratitude.

At the outbreak of the World War I in 1914, Kauffer moved to Britain, where he remained until 1940. In England he found a fertile and progressive art scene that allowed his creativity to flourish and mature. He became an active member of avant-garde groups such as the London Group and the Friday Club, joined the Arts League of Service and ran an avant-garde film society that introduced experimental cinema to London. He was also a founding member of Group X, which was formed by leading artists such as Wyndham Lewis who founded the Vorticist Group in 1914. His career as a poster artist began in 1915, when Frank Pick commissioned Kauffer to produce a poster for the London Underground. He designed over 140 posters for London Transport, as well as posters for Shell, British Petroleum and Eastman and Sons. His posters reflect Kauffer's experimentation with modernist styles such as Futurism, Cubism and Surrealism, and he often used abstract or non-figurative elements in his designs. One of Kauffer's best known works is his *Early Bird* (1919) published by the *Daily Herald*. In this composition the act of flying is symbolised by a fusion between nature and machines - very much in line with the manifesto of the Vorticist group.

Apart from his posters, Kauffer also produced illustrations (including for T.S. Eliot's *Ariel Poems*), book covers, set designs and textiles (often in partnership with his wife, the designer Marion Dorn). He was appointed art director of Lund Humphries Publishers in 1930. As well as his experimentation with styles, Kauffer also experimented with techniques such as photomontage and photomurals. He returned to the USA in 1940 and settled in New York, where he continued to work as a graphic designer. The Museum of Modern Art in New York organised a solo exhibition of his work in 1937, and the Victoria and Albert Museum in London held a memorial exhibition in 1955.

BIBLIOGRAPHY:

Kauffer, E. McKnight, *The Art of the Poster: Its Origin, Evolution and Purpose*, Cecil Palmer, London, 1924. *Posters by E. McKnight Kauffer*, exhibition catalogue, Museum of Modern Art, New York, 1937 (preface by Aldous Huxley). *E. McKnight Kauffer: Memorial Exhibition of the Work of E. McKnight Kauffer*, exhibition catalogue, Percy Lund Humphreys & Co., London, 1955. Haworth-Booth, Mark, *E. McKnight Kauffer: A Designer and his Public*, G. Fraser, London, 1979.

KAUFFMAN, Angelica Catharina Maria Anna

Swiss, 18th - 19th century.
Born 30 October 1741, in Chur (Graubünden); died 5 November 1807, in Rome.
Painter (gouache), watercolourist, engraver. Allegorical subjects, mythological subjects, portraits, genre scenes.

Kauffmann's father is supposed to have had boy's clothing made for her so that she could attend courses at the academy more easily. In 1754, she went to Milan with her family and set up as a painter of portraits. She also stood out with her beauty, grace and talent. She spoke German, French, Italian and English, sang, and played several musical instruments. The young English painter Nathaniel Dance, who later figured in the history of English art and politics, fell in love with her. For nine years he followed her from city to city, attempting in vain to persuade her to marry him.

In 1757, after the death of her mother, Angelica and her father set off for Florence. In 1759, they went to Rome, moving thence to Venice in 1764, with Angelica's reputation growing all the time. The wife of the English ambassador, Lady Wentworth, carried her off to London and presented her at court. In 1768, when the Royal Academy was founded, Angelica was put down as one of the founder members. Sir Joshua Reynolds had a great partiality for her, and painted her portrait three times.

A sad episode marred this brilliant career when a young stranger claiming to be Count Frederick Horn of Sweden paid court to her and Angelica agreed to marry him in secret. After the ceremony, she discovered to her mortification that she had fallen victim to a fraudster, and her husband was just a servant of the count. After suffering ill treatment at the hands of the impostor, she managed to get rid of him at the cost of 7,500 francs. In 1781, after the death of this first husband, she contracted a happier marriage with Venetian painter Antonio Zucchi, and shortly after left London for Italy. In 1782 her father died - he had hitherto been constantly with her - and she and Zucchi moved to Rome, where Zucchi died in 1795 and Angelica remained until her death.

The artistic value of Kauffmann's work has been debated because it partakes of the rather prettified, affected, occasionally mannered style of English artists in the 18th century - Reynolds undoubtedly had a considerable influence on her style. Her painted output (portraits, mythological and allegorical subjects) was substantial, and bears witness to considerable facility. She also engraved about 40 prints in a vigorous style. A great many of her works were reproduced as engravings.

An exhibition of her works was organised by the Haus der Kunst in Munich in 1999.

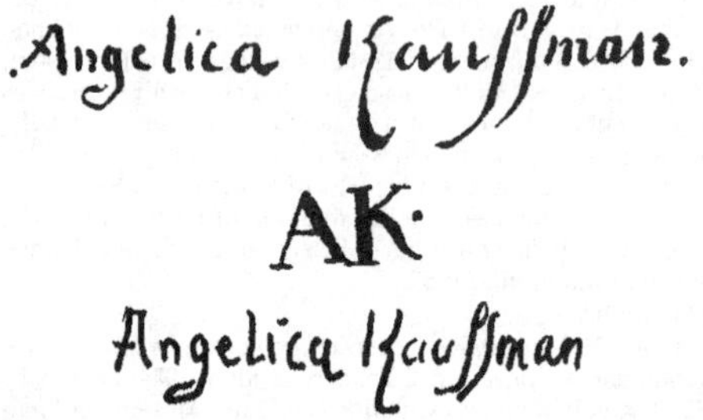

BIBLIOGRAPHY:

De Rossi, G.G., *Vita di Angelica Kauffmann, Pittrice*, Florence, 1811. Gerard, F. A., *Angelica Kauffmann: A Biography*, London, 1892, rev. 1893. Manners, V./Williamson, G.C., *Angelica Kauffmann, RA*, London, 1924. *Exhibition of Paintings by Angelica Kauffmann*, exhibition catalogue, London Kenwood House, 1955 (foreword E. Bayliss). Croft-Murray, E., *Decorative Painting in England, 1537-1837*, London, 1962. Thurnher, E., *Angelika Kauffmann und die deutsche Dichtung*, Bregenz, 1967. Helbok, C., *Miss Angel: Angelika Kauffmann-eine Biographie*, Vienna, 1968. Moulton Mayer, Dorothy, *Angelica Kauffmann, a Biography*, Colin Smythe, Gerrards Cross, 1972. Clark, A.M., *'Roma mi è Sempre in Pensiero'* in *Studies in Roman Eighteenth-century Painting*, E. P. Bowron, Washington DC, 1981 (pp. 125-38). Alexander, David/Roworth, Wendy W., *Angelica Kauffman: a Continental Artist in Georgian England*, Reaktion, London, 1993. Alexander, David/Allen, Brian/Baumgärtel, Brian, et al., *Angelika Kauffmann (1741-1807). Eine Dichterin mit dem Pinsel*, Hatje Cantz, Ostfildern, 1998.

MUSEUMS AND GALLERIES:

BATH (Holburne Mus. of Art): *Henrietta Laura Pulteney* (1777, oil on canvas) - BERLIN: *The Artist* - BERN: *St Cecilia* - BREGENZ: *Bacchus and Ariadne* - BRIGHTON (Hove Mus. and AG): *Penelope at her Loom* (1764, oil on canvas) - BRIGHTON (Mus. and AG): *Mrs Marriott* (oil on canvas, portrait) - BUDAPEST: *Portrait of the Artist; Cyrus and Astyages* - DRESDEN: *Portraits of Women as Sibyls and Vestal Virgins; Ariadne Abandoned* - DUBLIN: *Miss Monroe; Henry Loftus and His Family* - FLORENCE (Uffizi): *Portrait of the Artist* - FRANKFURT AM MAIN: *J. Winckelmann* - INNSBRUCK (Tiroler Landesmus. Ferdinandeum): *J. J. Kauffmann* - LEIPZIG: *Portrait of a Young Man* - LONDON: *John Palmer* - LONDON (National Portrait Gal.): *Angelica Kauffmann* (1770-1775, oil on canvas, other portraits) - LONDON (Royal Academy of Arts): *Invention, Composition, Design, Colour* (c. 1778-1780, oil on canvas, four oval paintings, allegories of painting) - LONDON (Tate Collection): *Portrait of a Lady* (c. 1775, oil on canvas) - LONDON (Victoria and Albert Mus.): *Lady Hamilton; Nymph Asleep and Shepherd; Nymph*; a watercolour - MUNICH: *Portrait of the Artist; Christ and the Samaritan; Ludwig I of Bavaria as the Crown Prince* - PARIS (Louvre): *Baroness von Krudner and Her Daughter* - RICHMOND (Virginia MFA): *Cornelia Pointing to Her Children as Her Treasures* (c. 1785, oil on canvas) - ST PETERSBURG (Hermitage): *The Monk of Calais; Héloise and Abelard; Juliette the Madwoman* - STUTTGART: *Baroness von Bauer* - VALENCIENNES: *Hymen* - VIENNA: *The Return of Arminius after the Battle; Burial of Pallas*.

AUCTION RECORDS:

LONDON, 28 March 1809, *The Duchess of Devonshire*, GBP 73; *The Countess of Bessborough*, GBP 105. PARIS, 1888, *Portrait of a Young Woman*, FRF 2,020. LONDON, 1888, *A Portrait of Miss Harrod*, FRF 9,900. LONDON, 1898, *The Judgment of Paris*, FRF 4,050. NEW YORK, 10-11 April 1902, *Portrait of Miss Craddock*, USD 300. NEW YORK, 26-27 Feb 1903, *Portrait of the Artist*, USD 1,620. NEW YORK, 22-23 Feb 1907, *Portrait of a Woman*, USD 1,000. LONDON, 27 Jan 1908, *Portrait of a Woman*, GBP 6; *Nymph Making a Sacrifice*, GBP 3. LONDON, 29 Feb 1908, *Nymph Scolding Cupid*, GBP 16. LONDON, 10 June 1909, *The Contemplation of Ariadne*, GBP 42. LONDON, 12 March 1910, *Cupid in Chains*, GBP 47. LONDON, 11 Dec 1910, *Portrait of the Earl of Sheffield* (engraved by Smith) GBP 173. LONDON, 11 March 1911, *Miss Dayrell Holding a Guitar*, GBP 52. LONDON, 8 April 1911, *Young Woman in a Pink Dress*, GBP 126. PARIS, 8-9 Dec 1919, *Reading in the Park* (pencil) FRF 1,020. PARIS, 23-25 May 1921, *Portrait of a Woman*, FRF 3,600. LONDON, 4 May 1922, *The Three Daughters of Thomas Coutts*, GBP 273. LONDON, 15 Dec 1922, *Children with a Bird's Nest*, GBP 136. PARIS, 12 May 1925, *The Woman with the Angels*, FRF 1,400. PARIS, 4-5 April 1927, *The Young Mother* (pencil with highlights) FRF 3,500. LONDON, 22 Feb 1928, *Dorothy Holroyd*, GBP 220. PARIS, 23 May 1928, *Venus Lending Her Girdle to Juno* (pen and wash) FRF 420. PARIS, 7-8 June 1928, *Women Bathing* (drawing) FRF 6,200. LONDON, 28 June 1929, *Woman in a Muslin Dress*, GBP 325. LONDON, 10 July 1931, *Discovery of Achilles*, GBP 110. LONDON, 18 April 1932, *Miss Lambton as Psyche*, GBP 60. PARIS, 28 Feb 1938, *Tambourine Player* (red chalk) FRF 200. LONDON, 5 May 1939, *Lady Rushout as a Child*, GBP 840; *Gualtherus and Griselda*, GBP 157. LONDON, 16 Feb 1940, *Mrs Downman*, GBP 157. PARIS, 16 June 1941, *Young Woman beside an Amphora* (gouache) FRF 600. PARIS, 11 Jan 1943, *The Young Tambourine Player* (1757, black chalk, heightened with white) FRF 2,100. PARIS, 31 March 1943, *Tambourin Player* (red chalk) FRF 1,200. NEW YORK, 26 May 1943, *Judgement of Paris*, USD 1,500; *Life of Cupid*, USD 2,300. LONDON, 27 Oct 1943, *Portrait of the Artist*, GBP 230. LONDON, 20 July 1945, *T. Jenkins and His Wife*, GBP 136. PARIS, 6 March 1950, *Young Woman Standing Leaning on a Plinth* (gouache) FRF 11,000. PARIS, 2 July 1951, *Diana and Callisto; Venus and Adonis* (set of two) FRF 17,500. PARIS, 4 March 1955, *Portrait Presumed to be of William Pitt* (pen and wash with gouache highlights)

FRF 6,500. LUCERNE, 1 Dec 1956, *Achilles,* CHF 2,300. LONDON, 6 Nov 1959, *Three Children with Birds and Flowers,* GBP 357. NEW YORK, 6 April 1960, *The Judgement of Paris,* USD 2,000. LONDON, 27 Oct 1961, *Portrait of the British Consul in Naples,* Gns 700. LONDON, 3 April 1968, *Portrait of Lady Anne Maxwell,* GBP 1,600. COPENHAGEN, 13 Feb 1969, *Portrait of King Christian VII,* DKK 20,000. LONDON, 9 Nov 1971, *The Muses of Painting, Architecture and Sculpture* (watercolour and gouache) Gns 1,050. NEW YORK, 3 Nov 1972, *Cupid; Cephisa* (matching pair) USD 7,000. COLOGNE, 27 June 1974, *Madonna and Child,* DEM 12,500. MUNICH, 29 May 1976, *Couple beside a River* (c. 1790, pen, 8 1/4 x 10 3/4 ins / 21 x 27.5 cm) DEM 6,000. LONDON, 19 Nov 1976, *Venus and Adonis* (1786, oil on canvas, 49 3/4 x 35 1/2 ins / 126.5 x 90 cm) GBP 1,700. ZURICH, 20 May 1977, *Lord Windsor and Lady Maria Windsor as Cupid and Amor* (1795, oil on canvas, 55 x 43 1/4 ins / 140 x 110 cm) CHF 11,000. VIENNA, 13 March 1979, *Allegory of Beauty and Wisdom* (oil on canvas, tondo, diam. 25 1/2 ins / 65 cm) ATS 130,000. LONDON, 19 June 1979, *Rebecca and Eliezer at the Well* (pencil and wash heightened with white, 11 x 14 3/4 ins / 27 x 37.5 cm) GBP 750. LUCERNE, 13 Nov 1980, *View of the Campagna Romana* (watercolour, 6 1/4 x 8 ins / 16 x 20.5 cm) CHF 1,600. LONDON, 16 April 1982, *Portrait of Brownlow, 8th Earl of Exeter* (1764, oil on canvas, 40 1/2 x 30 1/2 ins / 102.9 x 77.5 cm) GBP 5,500. LONDON, 16 Nov 1982, *Portrait of an Artist Leaning on an Anchor* (coloured chalks/grey paper, oval, 15 x 11 3/4 ins / 38 x 30 cm) GBP 900. LONDON, 6 July 1983, *Cupid Discovered by Cephisa; The Clipping of Cupid's Wings* (oil on canvas, an oval pair, 23 x 15 3/4 ins / 58.5 x 40 cm) GBP 13,000. LONDON, 11 July 1986, *Portrait of Countess Catherine Skavronska* (1789, oil on canvas, 63 x 47 1/4 ins / 160 x 120 cm) GBP 50,000. HEIDELBERG, 14 Oct 1988, *Cupid Attaches Aglaia to a Laurel and Euphrosyne Disarms Cupid* (two coloured lithographs, each 12 1/2 x 14 1/2 ins / 32 x 36.8 cm) DEM 1,100; *The Three Sisters* (watercolour, 11 1/2 x 10 1/4 ins / 29.2 x 26.2 cm) DEM 3,700. LONDON, 18 Nov 1988, *Marie de Moulins - illustration for Sterne's Sentimental Journey* (oil/metal, 12 3/4 x 10 1/2 ins / 32.5 x 26.5 cm) GBP 3,850; *Portrait of a Lady Sitting on a Sofa Wearing a White Dress with a Blue Sash* (oil on canvas, 28 1/2 x 23 1/4 ins / 72.4 x 59.3 cm) GBP 26,400. LONDON, 15 Nov 1989, *Portrait of Louise-Henrietta Campbell, the Future Lady Abinger* (oil on canvas, 29 1/4 x 24 ins / 74 x 61 cm) GBP 11,550. STOCKHOLM, 16 May 1990, *Mars and Venus* (oil on canvas, 50 x 39 1/4 ins / 127 x 100 cm) SEK 48,000. LONDON, 14 Nov 1990, *Portrait of a Lady Half-Reclining on a Couch in Oriental Dress Looking at a Miniature* (1772, oil on canvas, 24 1/4 x 29 1/4 ins / 61.5 x 74.5 cm) GBP 22,000. ROME, 23 April 1991, *Portrait of a Woman* (oil on canvas, 17 3/4 x 14 1/2 ins / 45 x 37 cm) ITL 9,500,000. PARIS, 6 March 1992, *Study for Dido* (1763, black chalk, 7 x 8 1/4 ins / 17.5 x 21 cm) FRF 6,600. LONDON, 17 July 1992, *Portrait of Lady Rushout in a Yellow Dress, Sitting in a Landscape and Accompanied by Her Daughter* (oil on canvas, 50 1/4 x 40 ins / 127.5 x 101.5 cm) GBP 132,000. LONDON, 10 Nov 1993, *The Resurrected Jesus Appears to Martha and Mary Magdalene; The Madonna with the Child Jesus and St John the Baptist and the Lamb* (oil on canvas, a pair, each 16 1/4 x 18 ins / 41 x 46 cm) GBP 16,675. MONACO, 4 Dec 1993, *Rinaldo and Armida; Tancred and Clorinda* (oil/copper, oval, 7 1/2 x 6 1/4 ins / 19.2 x 15.8 cm) FRF 15,540. LONDON, 13 April 1994, *Portrait of William Henry Lambton, Standing, Dressed in a Red Coat and Blue Cape* (1797, oil on canvas, 86 x 55 1/2 ins / 218.5 x 141 cm) GBP 104,900. PARIS, 13 Oct 1995, *Penelope* (oil/metal, 10 3/4 x 8 1/4 ins / 27.5 x 21 cm) FRF 17,000. NEW YORK, 2 April 1996, *Portrait of Anne Miller, Countess of Albermarle* (oil on canvas, 30 x 25 ins / 76.2 x 63.8 cm) USD 35,650. LONDON, 10 July 1996, *Bust-Length Portrait of the Artist in a Yellow Dress with a Blue Ribbon in Her Hair* (oil on canvas, 27 1/4 x 22 3/4 ins / 69 x 58 cm) GBP 73,000. PARIS, 28 Oct 1996, *Penelope* (oil/metal, 10 3/4 x 8 1/4 ins / 27.5 x 21 cm) FRF 27,000. LONDON, 13 Nov 1996, *Héloise* (oil on canvas, oval, 12 x 10 ins / 30.5 x 25.5 cm) GBP 17,250. NEW YORK, 31 Jan 1997, *Bust Portrait of the Artist in a Pink Dress and Blue Garment Embroidered with Gold* (oil on canvas, 24 x 20 ins / 61.2 x 50.5 cm) USD 123,500. PARIS, 13 June 1997, *Portrait of Henry Kuhff and His Brother, Son of Angelica Kauffman's Lawyer in Basel* (canvas, 49 1/2 x 39 1/4 ins / 126 x 100 cm) FRF 380,000. LONDON, 12 Nov 1997, *Lady Sketching* (oil on canvas, oval, 25 x 20 ins / 63.6 x 51 cm) GBP 42,200. ST GALL, 21 April 1999, *Cupid Tied by Nymphs* (oil on canvas, 25 x 25 ins / 64 x 63 cm) CHF 195,000. LINDAU, 3 Dec 1999, *Fantasy Decorating Shakespeare's Tomb* (1784, pencil and charcoal, 15 x 12 ins / 38 x 30 cm) DEM 10,000. NEW YORK, 23 May 2000, *Portrait of Robert Stearne Tighe and His Wife Catherine in Wooded Landscape* (oil on canvas, 37 x 31 ins / 94 x 80 cm) USD 190,000. LONDON, 28 Nov 2000, *Designs for Illustration to Bell's Poets* (pencil, pen, grey ink and grey and brown wash, feigned circles, three, 4 x 3 ins / 11 x 7 cm) GBP 1,800. NEW YORK, 29 May 2001, *Three Female Allegorical Figures in Front of a Classical Temple* (chalk, pen, and ink wash, 20 x 16 ins / 50 x 41 cm) USD 2,800. LONDON, 14 June 2001, *Self-portrait in a Red Dress, Holding a Porte Crayon* (oil on canvas, 29 x 24 ins / 74 x 61 cm) GBP 380,000. PARIS, 21 March 2002, *Seated Queen* (chalk, pen and ink wash, 6 x 14 ins / 14 x 35 cm) EUR 2,600. LONDON, 28 Nov 2002, *Portrait of Louise Henrietta Campbell, later Lady Scarlett* (oil on canvas, 29 x 24 ins / 74 x 61 cm) GBP 26,000. LONDON, 12 June 2003, *Portrait of Philip Tisdal with His Wife and Family* (oil on canvas, 61 x 75 ins / 154 x 190 cm) GBP 450,000. BERLIN, 27 Nov 2003, *Holy Family* (etching, 10 x 7 ins / 25 x 19 cm) EUR 4,500. NEW YORK, 27 May 2004, *Portrait of Lady Louisa Dorothea Holroyd* (oil on canvas, 31 x 26 ins / 79 x 65 cm) USD 90,000. LONDON, 6 July 2004, *Mirtillo Leaving for the Hunt. Mirtillo and Ergasto Returning from the Hunt* (pen and ink wash, a pair, 88 x 9 ins / 224 x 23 cm) GBP 1,600.

KAUFFMANN, Craig

American, 20th century.

Born 1932.

Painter, sculptor.

Craig Kauffmann freed himself from the picture plane in order to create three-dimensional objects, which he still painted, thereby extending his exploration of painting. Outwardly modernist, his coloured Plexiglas reliefs, shaded in subtle colours, appeal to romantic souls.

AUCTION RECORDS:

NEW YORK, 1 Nov 1994, *Green-orange* (1965, acrylic on moulded plastic, 89 1/2 x 45 1/2 ins / 227.3 x 115.5 cm) USD 3,450.

KAUFFMANN, Hermann, the Elder

German, 19th century.

Born 7 November 1808, in Hamburg; died 24 May 1889, in Hamburg.

Painter, watercolourist, draughtsman. Genre scenes, landscapes, landscapes with figures, seascapes.

Kauffmann merits special mention because of his artistic sincerity - he has often been compared with Millet - and for his lifelong affection for his native city. He studied in Munich (1827-1833), then returned to Hamburg, remaining there for the rest of his life except for a visit to Norway in 1843, whence he brought back a remarkable series of landscapes. He exhibited in Hamburg, Hanover, Munich and Berlin. Kauffmann's output comprises, in the main, views of the Hamburg area, with the city in the background.

MUSEUMS AND GALLERIES:
DARMSTADT: *Seascape* - HAMBURG: *Study; Return of Provost Fischer; Farmworkers at Rest* - LEIPZIG: *Cemetery* - OSLO: *The Diligence.*
AUCTION RECORDS:
BERLIN, 1894, *Forest Interior in Winter, Snow Effect,* FRF 750. PARIS, 28 June 1928, *Eutin from the North West* (watercolour) FRF 300. PARIS, 30 March 1942, *The Farrier, Snow Effect,* FRF 1,550. COLOGNE, 15 March 1968, *The Snow-storm,* DEM 5,000. HAMBURG, 2 June 1976, *The Mill Road* (oil on canvas remounted/panel, 21 3/4 x 31 1/4 ins / 55.2 x 79.5 cm) DEM 8,500. NEW YORK, 13 Oct 1978, *Woodcutters in a Snowy Landscape* (oil on canvas, 26 1/4 x 37 ins / 66.5 x 94 cm) USD 19,000. HAMBURG, 7 June 1979, *Woodcutters in a Winter Landscape* (oil on canvas, 16 x 21 ins / 40.4 x 53.5 cm) DEM 28,000. LONDON, 13 March 1980, *Waiting for the Ferry* (1861, watercolour, 9 1/2 x 14 ins / 24.4 x 35.5 cm) GBP 650. VIENNA, 17 Nov 1981, *Midnight, Hour of the Muses* (1881, oil on panel, 10 1/4 x 8 1/4 ins / 26 x 21 cm) ATS 55,000. COLOGNE, 18 March 1983, *The Woodcutters* (Indian ink, watercoloured, 5 x 8 1/4 ins / 13 x 21 cm) DEM 5,000. HAMBURG, 4 June 1983, *Cab in a Snowstorm* (oil on canvas, 22 x 31 1/2 ins / 55 x 80 cm) DEM 26,000. LONDON, 21 June 1984, *The Return in Snowy Weather* (watercolour and pencil, 8 1/4 x 11 3/4 ins / 21 x 30 cm) GBP 1,300. HAMBURG, 6 June 1985, *The Labourer's Return* (1851, oil on canvas, 25 1/2 x 32 3/4 ins / 64.5 x 83.5 cm) DEM 20,000. HAMBURG, 11 June 1987, *Coaching Inn* (oil on canvas, 17 x 24 1/2 ins / 43.2 x 62.2 cm) DEM 8,000. MUNICH, 18 May 1988, *At the Coaching Inn* (1834, oil on canvas, 27 x 50 3/4 ins / 68.5 x 129 cm) DEM 77,000. COLOGNE, 18 March 1989, *Woodcutters in Winter* (oil on canvas, 22 1/2 x 32 1/2 ins / 57 x 82.5 cm) DEM 17,000. LONDON, 24 Nov 1989, *In Church Lane* (oil on canvas/card, 21 3/4 x 31 ins / 55.1 x 78.7 cm) GBP 7,480. LONDON, 2 Oct 1992, *Riders in a Winter Landscape* (oil on canvas, 20 x 25 1/2 ins / 51 x 65 cm) GBP 4,400. LONDON, 18 March 1994, *The Approaching Storm* (oil on canvas, 12 x 18 3/4 ins / 30.5 x 47.6 cm) GBP 6,325. MUNICH, 6 Dec 1994, *Lunch Break in the Fields* (ink and watercolour/paper, 7 x 9 1/4 ins / 18 x 23.5 cm) DEM 2,070. MUNICH, 3 Dec 1996, *Return with the Hay Crop* (oil on canvas, 11 x 14 1/2 ins / 28 x 37 cm) DEM 19,200. LONDON, 21 Nov 1997, *Peasants Going to Church* (c. 1850, oil on canvas, 22 1/2 x 31 1/2 ins / 57.2 x 80 cm, 2 1/4 ins/6 cm) GBP 14,950. AHLDEN, 23 April 1999, *Horse Race at the Edge of the Village* (1864, watercolour, 7 x 10 ins / 18 x 26 cm) DEM 4,000. HAMBURG, 4 Dec 1999, *Village Winter Scene with Horses Pulling Wood Cart* (oil on canvas, 15 x 20 ins / 37 x 52 cm) DEM 18,000. SAN FRANCISCO, 17 May 2000, *Winter Landscape with Figures Loading Firewood onto a Cart* (oil on canvas, 22 x 31 ins / 56 x 80 cm) USD 8,000. LONDON, 28 Nov 2000, *Logging in a Winter Landscape* (oil on canvas, 28 x 41 ins / 70 x 103 cm) GBP 13,500. HAMBURG, 25 April 2001, *On the Way Home* (oil on canvas, 19 x 26 ins / 47 x 65 cm) DEM 24,000. HAMBURG, 25 April 2001, *Before the Post Office in the Rain* (oil on canvas, 21 x 29 ins / 54 x 73 cm) DEM 24,000. COPENHAGEN, 2 Sept 2003, *Gentleman being Helped onboard a Horse Carriage before a Stable in the Rain* (oil on canvas, 13 x 17 ins / 33 x 44 cm) DKK 45,000. TOESTORF, 6 Dec 2003, *Transporting Hay in the Snowdrifts* (oil on canvas, 16 x 24 ins / 41 x 62 cm) EUR 9,500. LONDON, 21 Jan 2004, *Snowstorm* (oil on canvas, 22 x 31 ins / 56 x 80 cm) GBP 4,200.

KAUFFMANN, Hermann, the Younger

German, 19th - 20th century.
Born 27 February 1873, in Munich.
Painter. Portraits, genre scenes. Miniatures.

Hermann Kauffmann the Younger was the grandson of Hermann Kauffmann the Elder. He studied with Paul Nauen before travelling to Italy and later spending time in Hamburg. He began his career as a painter of miniature portraits.

AUCTION RECORDS:
NEW YORK, 21 Jan 1978, *The Letter* (oil on canvas, 19 1/2 x 14 ins / 49.5 x 35.5 cm) USD 1,700. AHLDEN, 28 Sept 2001, *Italian Landscape* (oil on canvas, 46 x 66 ins / 117 x 168 cm) DEM 9,500. MUNICH, 6 Nov 2002, *Taylor in Workshop* (1896, oil on panel, 11 x 7 ins / 27 x 18 cm) EUR 4,000. COLOGNE, 20 Nov 2003, *Old Traveller on a Country Lane* (oil on panel, 4 x 3 ins / 10 x 7 cm) EUR 3,500.

KAUFFMANN, Hugo Wilhelm

German, 19th - 20th century.
Born 7 August 1844, in Hamburg; died 30 December 1915, in Prien.
Painter. Genre scenes, animals.

Hugo Wilhelm Kauffmann was the son of Hermann Kauffmann the Elder. He studied with Jacob Becker in Frankfurt before moving first to Düsseldorf, then, from 1863 to 1871, in Kronberg. After a brief visit to Paris, he settled in Munich in 1871. From 1870, he exhibited in Munich, Vienna, Berlin, Dresden and Frankfurt.

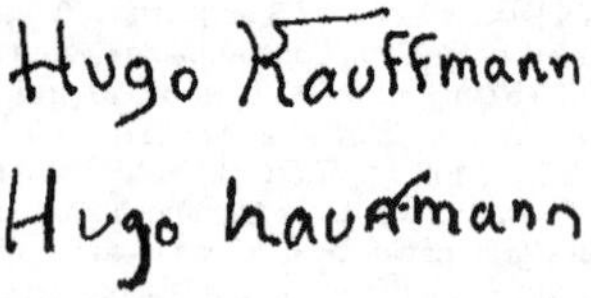

MUSEUMS AND GALLERIES:
BREMEN: *The Meal* - FRANKFURT AM MAIN: *Huntsman and Inn Girls* - GRAZ: *Veterinary Surgeon at the Farm* - KALININGRAD: *Happy Story* - MELBOURNE: *Card-Players* - MUNICH: *Friendly Chat* - STUTTGART: *Huntsman* - TRIESTE: *Gamblers.*
AUCTION RECORDS:
VIENNA, 14 May 1881, *Conversation,* FRF 966. BERLIN, 12 Dec 1899, *A Question,* FRF 1,240. NEW YORK, 1-2 April 1902, *Sale in a Village,* USD 1,425. LONDON, 23 May 1910, *Bavarian Gallantry* (1888) GBP 33. NEW YORK, 12 Jan 1911, *At the Window,* USD 280. LONDON, 20 March 1911, *Pifferari* (1870) GBP 15. PARIS, July 1946, *Tyrolean Scene,* FRF 5,000. COLOGNE, 21 Nov 1957, *Interior,* DEM 4,800. MUNICH, 7 Oct 1959, *Interior of an Inn,* DEM 3,300. COLOGNE, 20 May 1960, *Interior of an Inn,* DEM 1,300. PARIS, 3 Feb 1961, *Drinkers,* FRF 2,250. COLOGNE, 16 Nov 1967, *Hunting Stories,* DEM 13,000. COLOGNE, 8 May 1969, *The Cheat,* DEM 21,000. COLOGNE, 24 Nov 1971, *The Unexpected Visit,* DEM 13,500. VIENNA, 22 May 1973, *Tyrolean Girl,* ATS 50,000. MUNICH, 24 Nov 1973, *The Beer-Drinker,* DEM 15,000. LONDON, 29 Oct 1976, *Confidences* (oil on panel, 4 1/4 x 5 1/2 ins / 11 x 14 cm) GBP 4,800. FRANKFURT AM MAIN, 26 March 1977, *Wounded Soldier* (1872, oil on canvas, 13 1/4 x 16 3/4 ins / 33.5 x 42.5 cm) DEM 15,000. COLOGNE, 11 June 1979, *Girl Playing the Zither* (oil on panel, 14 1/4 x 18 ins / 36.5 x 46 cm) DEM 75,000. LOS ANGELES, 16 March 1981, *Discussing the News* (1877, oil on panel, 6 x 7 1/2 ins / 15 x 19 cm) USD 25,000. MUNICH, 20 Oct 1983, *The Sleeper Disturbed* (1890, oil on panel, 14 1/4 x 17 1/2 ins / 36 x 44.5 cm) DEM 120,000. NEW YORK, 26 Feb 1986, *Peasant Couple in a Kitchen* (1901, oil on panel, 14 1/2 x 18 ins / 36.8 x 45.7 cm) USD 42,000. LONDON, 26 June 1987, *Postillion in an Inn* (1887, oil on panel, 19 1/2 x 24 ins / 49.5 x 61 cm) GBP 40,000. NEW YORK, 25 Feb 1988, *Bavarian Peasant Girl* (oil on panel, 12 1/4 x 9 1/4 ins / 31 x 23.4 cm) USD 17,600. MUNICH, 15 May 1988, *Peasant Girl* (1909, oil on panel, 7 3/4 x 6 ins / 20 x 15 cm) DEM 7,700. MUNICH, 18 May 1988, *Reading the Newspaper* (oil on panel, 4 1/4 x 3 1/4 ins / 11 x 8 cm) DEM 23,100. MUNICH, 29 Nov 1989, *The Payment* (1878, oil on panel, 7 x 6 ins / 18 x 15 cm) DEM 26,400. NEW YORK, 17 Jan 1990, *Flirtatious Conversation* (1899, oil on panel, 3 x 3 ins / 7.9 x 7.6 cm) USD 7,700. NEW YORK, 22 May 1991, *Fiddler in a Tavern* (1878, oil on panel, 10 x 12 ins / 25.4 x 30.5 cm) USD 29,700. MUNICH, 25 June 1992,

The Dead Fox (1877, oil on wood, 6 x 7 ins / 15.5 x 18 cm) DEM 38,420. New York, 18 Feb 1993, *Old Man with a Pipe* (1886, oil on panel, 9 3/4 x 7 3/4 ins / 24.8 x 19.7 cm) USD 8,800. Paris, 23 April 1993, *Russian Girl* (oil on panel, 6 x 4 1/2 ins / 15 x 11.5 cm) FRF 41,000. London, 20 May 1993, *Pretty Reflection in a Mirror* (1901, oil on panel, 6 x 4 ins / 14.3 x 9.3 cm) GBP 9,200. New York, 26 May 1993, *Musical Talent* (1897, oil on panel, 14 1/2 x 18 1/4 ins / 36.8 x 46.4 cm) USD 82,250. Munich, 21 June 1994, *Huntsman Surprising a Young Woman Sleeping at her Spinning-Wheel* (1889, oil on panel, 7 1/4 x 9 1/2 ins / 18.5 x 24 cm) DEM 46,000. London, 13 Oct 1994, *A Good Story* (1877, oil on panel, 7 3/4 x 6 3/4 ins / 19.7 x 17.2 cm) GBP 11,500. London, 10 Feb 1995, *In the Tavern* (1866, oil on canvas, 11 1/2 x 8 3/4 ins / 29.5 x 22.5 cm) GBP 3,910. Munich, 27 June 1995, *Three Peasants in a Tavern* (1878, oil on panel, 7 x 6 ins / 18 x 15.5 cm) DEM 8,280. New York, 20 July 1995, *The Shy Maidservant* (1882, oil on panel, 6 1/4 x 8 1/2 ins / 15.6 x 21.3 cm) USD 29,900. London, 21 Nov 1996, *Foxhunters and Two Girls* (1891, oil on panel, 14 1/2 x 18 1/4 ins / 37 x 46.5 cm) GBP 36,700. Munich, 3 Dec 1996, *Girl and Two Boys in a Tavern* (oil on wood, 14 1/4 x 18 1/4 ins / 36.5 x 46.5 cm) DEM 72,000. New York, 23 Oct 1997, *Gambling Companions* (1890, oil on panel, 6 x 7 1/2 ins / 14.3 x 19.1 cm) USD 14,950.

KAUFFMANN, Ignatius
German, 18th century.
Died 1781.
Active in Teisbach (near Landshut) c. 1755.
Painter.

Kauffmann based himself in the Teisbach area of Bavaria; he painted a number of portraits, but mostly did religious paintings - in Unterneunhausen, Landshut and Diepoltskirchen, among other places.

Auction records:
London, 3 Nov 1978, *The Vision of St Augustine* (oil on canvas, 43 x 25 1/4 ins / 109.2 x 64.1 cm) GBP 2,800.

KAUFFMANN, J. F.
18th century.
Active in Paris c. 1720.
Engraver.

J.F. Kauffmann engraved portraits and subjects from the Bible after Le Brun, Veronese and Conca. His work included *You Old Men who Pass by and See* after Van Schuppen.

KAUFFMANN, Jean
Swiss, 19th - 20th century.
Born 27 November 1866, in Lucerne; died 24 March 1924, in Lucerne.
Medallist, engraver, sculptor, miniaturist.

Jean Kauffmann worked at the École des Beaux-Arts in Lucerne in 1888, and in Geneva in 1888 and 1889. He then travelled and subsequently worked in La Chaux-de-Fonds, Stuttgart, Hamburg and Paris, before returning to settle in Lucerne in 1893. He is best known as a Medallist.

KAUFFMANN, Johann Joseph, or Kaufmann
Swiss, 18th century.
Born 27 February 1707, in Schwarzenberg (Lucerne); died 11 January 1782, in Venice.
Painter. Religious subjects, portraits.

Kauffmann worked in Switzerland and Italy before going to England, where he exhibited paintings with poetical and religious themes at the Royal Academy in London from 1771 to 1779. In 1780, he retired to Rome with his daughter, Angelica Kauffman.

KAUFFMANN, Louis
Swiss, 20th century.
Born 1923.
Painter.

Louis Kauffmann began painting in 1942. He took part in group exhibitions, notably in Paris at the Salon des Réalités Nouvelles in 1949, 1950, 1951 and 1955. He showed a collection of his paintings in a private exhibition in Paris in 1951. He evolved into an abstract painter after 1945. His abstract compositions recall the gaiety of Miro's graphic work.

KAUFFMANN, Paul Adolphe
French, 19th century.
Born 8 July 1849, in Belfort.
Painter, draughtsman, illustrator.

Paul Kauffmann was a significant artist. He specialised in painting a large number of men and women of Alsace (*Our Dear People of Alsace at Home. Notes and Memoirs of the Artist*) but later devoted himself to illustration. His work was suffused with the authority of a serious intellect and great sincerity.

He worked for a large number of publishing houses and his drawings always appealed to the public. Worthy of note is an outstanding illustration for a work on the Chartreux. In 1877 and 1878 as correspondent for the *Monde Illustré* (*Illustrated World*) he followed the Russo-Turkish campaign and created a remarkable series of compositions on the subject. His legacy also includes some charming watercolours. He was a Chevalier of the Légion d'Honneur.

Auction records:
Paris, 26 Feb 1926, *Costumes of Alsace* (six watercolours) FRF 625.

KAUFFMANN, Peter. See **KAUFMANN**

KAUFFMANN-ROY, Marthe
French, 19th century.
Born 15 February 1863, in Asnières.
Painter.

Marthe Kauffmann-Roy artist was a member of the Société des Artistes Français from 1899.

KAUFFUNGEN, Richard
Austrian, 19th century.
Born 24 June 1854, in Unter St Veit, near Vienna.
Sculptor.

Kauffungen exhibited at the Exposition Universelle in Paris in 1900. Noted works include *Phryne before the Areopagus* (Rudolfinum in Prague) and the bronze statue of *Haydn* (municipal museum, Vienna).

KÄUFLER, Rudolf
Swiss, 16th century.
Sculptor (wood).

Rudolf Käufler was a master carpenter and sculptor who worked on the door of the cloister in Einsiedeln in 1577.

KAUFLI, M. L., the Younger
Swiss, 18th century.
Active in Einsiedeln (Schwyz).
Painter.

KAUFMAN, Donald
American, 20th century.
Born 1935, in New Orleans.
Painter.

Donald Kaufman has exhibited at the Whitney Museum in New York since 1968.

He is an exponent of Concrete Art. He proposes to define space by fully occupying it, by running slanting lines across his canvas, which are symmetrical in reference to one given point or axis.

KAUFMAN, John François
Swiss, 19th - 20th century.
Born 31 October 1870, in Uznach.
Active in the USA.
Painter, sculptor.

John François Kaufmann was a pupil of Gérome at the École des Beaux-Arts in Paris. He worked as a portrait painter in the USA, and carved monumental decorations for the church in Richmond, Virginia. He exhibited in Paris, at the Salon des Artistes Français, and was awarded an honourable mention in 1927.

KAUFMANN, Adolf

Austrian, 19th - 20th century.
Born 1848, in Troppau (now Opava, Czech Republic); died 2 December 1916, in Vienna.
Painter. Landscapes.

Adolf Kaufmann exhibited in Paris in 1900 at the Exposition Universelle.

AUCTION RECORDS:

VIENNA, 22 May 1973, *The Amsterdam Quays,* ATS 35,000. VIENNA, 20 Sept 1977, *Summer Landscape* (oil on canvas, 15 1/4 x 22 3/4 ins / 39 x 58 cm) ATS 30,000. COLOGNE, 11 June 1979, *Wooded Landscape* (oil on canvas, 41 1/4 x 26 3/4 ins / 105 x 68 cm) DEM 6,500. VIENNA, 17 Nov 1982, *The Huntsman's Picnic* (oil on canvas, 28 3/4 x 39 1/4 ins / 73 x 100 cm) ATS 55,000. VIENNA, 22 June 1983, *Woodland Stream* (oil on panel, 22 3/4 x 14 1/4 ins / 58 x 36 cm) ATS 40,000. LINDAU, 8 Oct 1986, *Cornfield* (oil on canvas, 21 x 31 ins / 52.5 x 79 cm) DEM 9,000. VIENNA, 18 March 1987, *Spring Landscape* (oil on canvas, 20 3/4 x 31 ins / 53 x 79 cm) ATS 80,000. COLOGNE, 15 Oct 1988, *Storm at Sea with a Sailing Boat in Danger and a Lifeboat* (oil on canvas, 35 1/2 x 49 1/4 ins / 90 x 125 cm) DEM 3,300. GÖTEBORG, 18 May 1989, *The Old Bridge* (oil on canvas, 11 x 15 ins / 28 x 38 cm) SEK 6,300. PARIS, 22 June 1990, *Forest Pool* (oil on canvas, 35 1/2 x 48 3/4 ins / 90 x 124 cm) FRF 82,000. NEW YORK, 24 Oct 1990, *Peasant Girl on a Forest Path* (oil on canvas, 38 1/2 x 56 1/2 ins / 97.8 x 143.5 cm) USD 15,400. MUNICH, 12 June 1991, *Shepherd with his Flock* (oil on canvas, 25 1/2 x 45 ins / 65 x 114.5 cm) DEM 11,000. NEW YORK, 15 Oct 1991, *The Port of Genoa* (oil on canvas, 39 x 43 ins / 99 x 109.3 cm) USD 3,520. AMSTERDAM, 28 Oct 1992, *Peasants with an Ox-Cart on a Forest Road* (oil on canvas, 29 1/4 x 39 1/4 ins / 74 x 100 cm) NLG 8,050. LONDON, 28 Oct 1992, *Ducks and Chickens near a Farm* (oil on panel, 15 x 11 3/4 ins / 38 x 30 cm) GBP 3,300. NEW YORK, 29 Oct 1992, *On a Country Road* (1897, oil on canvas, 24 1/2 x 39 1/4 ins / 62.2 x 99.7 cm) USD 5,500. HEIDELBERG, 5-13 April 1994, *Shepherdess and her Flock under a Birch in Spring* (oil on panel, 21 x 16 1/2 ins / 52.5 x 42 cm) DEM 3,400. MUNICH, 21 June 1994, *Haymaking* (oil on canvas, 25 1/2 x 39 1/4 ins / 65 x 100 cm) DEM 23,000. MUNICH, 27 June 1995, *Peasant Woman with Men Gathering Firewood* (oil on wood, 29 1/4 x 18 1/4 ins / 74 x 46.5 cm) DEM 13,800. MUNICH, 3 Dec 1996, *Peasants Gathering Firewood* (oil on canvas, 12 1/2 x 19 ins / 31.5 x 48 cm) DEM 7,200.

KAUFMANN, Arthur

German, 20th century.
Born 7 July 1888, in Mülheim; died 1971, in Nova Friburgo (Brazil).
Active in the USA and in Brazil.
Painter, engraver. Landscapes.
Group Das Junge Rheinland (Young Rheinland).

Arthur Kaufmann trained in Düsseldorf. He visited England, Italy and France, and studied in Paris with Henri Le Fauconnier. He was a member of the group Das Junge Rheinland (Young Rhineland). He organised a big exhibition of modern art in Düsseldorf in 1922. Forced into exile by the Nazi authorities, he lived in Holland from 1936 to 1939, then in the USA until 1946, after which he lived alternately in the USA and, for different lengths of time, in Brazil. He returned from his travels with many landscapes.

In 2001, Kaufmann featured in the exhibition *Verfemy. Vergessen. Wiederentdeckt. Schicksale expressiver Bildkunst im 20 Jahrhundert* (*Condemned. Forgotten. Rediscovered. The Fate of Expressive Art in the 20th Century*), at the Kulturgeschichtliches Museum in Osnabrück, which was aimed at rediscovering a generation of German and Austrian artists who had appeared in the 1920s and 1930s, but had suffered cultural and political repression at the hands of the Nazis and had fallen into oblivion after the war.

BIBLIOGRAPHY:

Pontual, Roberto, *Dicionário das artes plásticas no Brasil*, Civilização Brasileira, Rio de Janeiro, 1969. *Verfemt. Vergessen. Wiederentdeckt. Schicksale expressiver Bildkunst im 20. Jahrhundert. Sammlung Gerhard Schneider*, exhibition catalogue, Kulturgeschichtiches Museum, Osnabrück, 2001.

MUSEUMS AND GALLERIES:

WASHINGTON DC (National Portrait Gal.): *George Gershwin* (1936).

AUCTION RECORDS:

COLOGNE, 17 May 1980, *Still-life* (oil on canvas, 28 3/4 x 23 1/2 ins / 73 x 60 cm) DEM 3,400. AHLDEN, 22 Sept 2000, *Train Yard* (oil on canvas, 33 x 41 ins / 85 x 105 cm) DEM 10,000.

KAUFMANN, Asmus

German, 19th century.
Born 6 October 1806, in Haderslev (Sønderjylland), Denmark; died 24 June 1890, in Copenhagen.
Painter. Genre scenes, urban landscapes.

Kaufmann was born in Hadersleben (now Haderslev) in what was formerly the Prussian province of Schleswig-Holstein.

MUSEUMS AND GALLERIES:

GRAZ: *A Street in Rome.*

AUCTION RECORDS:

LONDON, 16 March 1989, *View of Salzburg Castle from St Peter's Church* (1878, oil on canvas, 38 1/2 x 49 1/2 ins / 98 x 126 cm) GBP 1,650.

KAUFMANN, Eduard

German, 19th century.
Painter. Portraits.

KAUFMANN, Eugenie

Maiden name: Hiller
Austrian, 19th century.
Born 15 May 1867, in Esseg (Osjek), Croatia; died 1 July 1924, in Vienna.
Sculptor.

Kaufmann, born in what was then the Austrian town of Esseg, studied in Karlsruhe and worked mainly in Germany, including Weimar and Mannheim. She specialised in busts.

KAUFMANN, Ferdinand

German, 19th - 20th century.
Born 17 October 1864, in Oberhausen; died 1942.
Active and naturalised in the USA.
Painter. Landscapes.

Ferdinand Kaufmann trained as a painter in Paris, where he studied with Jean-Paul Laurens, Benjamin-Constant and William Bouguereau at the Académie Julian. He was a member of the American Artists' Association in Paris. After emigrating to the USA, he painted characteristic Californian landscapes.

AUCTION RECORDS:

NEW YORK, 17 March 1988, *Eucalyptus in Spring* (oil on canvas, 29 1/2 x 24 1/2 ins / 75 x 62.5 cm) USD 1,210. LOS ANGELES/SAN FRANCISCO, 7 Feb 1990, *The High Plateaux of California* (oil on canvas, 30 x 30 ins / 76 x 76 cm) USD 8,800. LOS ANGELES/SAN FRANCISCO, 10 Oct 1990, *Seen from My Studio* (oil on canvas, 24 x 20 ins / 61 x 51 cm) USD 4,400. SAN FRANCISCO, 13 June 2001, *Morning at Lumber Wharf, Los Angeles Harbour* (oil on canvas, 20 x 24 ins / 51 x 61 cm) USD 6,000. PASADENA, 23 Oct 2001, *La Loma Street Bridge* (1937, oil on board, 13 x 16 ins / 33 x 41 cm) USD 4,500. PASADENA, 11 June 2002, *Street Scene, Pasadena* (oil on canvasboard, 12 x 16 ins / 30 x 41 cm) USD 8,000. LOS ANGELES, 19 June 2002, *Pacific Coast at Carmel, California* (oil on canvas, 20 x 24 ins / 51 x 61 cm) USD 6,000. PASADENA, 17 June 2003, *Landscape: Where the Wild Flowers are Blooming in the Foothills* (oil on canvas, 25 x 30 ins / 64 x 76 cm) USD 7,500. PASADENA, 18 Nov 2003, *Flint Ridge, West of Rose Bowl, Pasadena* (oil on board, 15 x 16 ins / 38 x 41 cm) USD 4,250.

KAUFMANN, Herbert
German, 20th century.
Born 1924, in Aachen.
Painter.

From 1946 to 1950, Herbert Kaufmann was a student at the Kunstakademie in Düsseldorf, where he lived. He has exhibited in Germany and abroad, and in 1962, he participated in the exhibition *Artists of Düsseldorf* at the Ostend Museum.

KAUFMANN, Hugo
German, 19th - 20th century.
Born 29 June 1868, in Schotten; died 14 May 1919, in Munich.
Sculptor.

Hugo Kaufmann studied art at the Hanau academy, the Städelsches Kunstinstitut in Frankfurt am Main, and with Von Ruemann at the Akademie der Bildenden Künste in Munich. He then settled in Berlin. He exhibited at the Paris Exposition Universelle in 1900 and won a medal in Munich in 1897.

MUSEUMS AND GALLERIES:
BERLIN: *St George* - BREMEN: *Project for a Monument to Moltke; St George; Medallion of Goethe; Satyr; Bearded Man; Johannes Hey; Jacobus Kaufmann.*

AUCTION RECORDS:
NEW YORK, 29 June 1983, *The Zither Player* (1881, oil on panel, 11 1/2 x 9 ins / 29 x 23 cm) USD 5,500.

KAUFMANN, Isidor
Hungarian, 19th - 20th century.
Born 22 March 1853, in Arad; died 1921.
Active in Austria.
Painter, watercolourist, draughtsman. Local figures, local scenes.

Isidor Kaufmann studied at the school of drawing in Budapest and with Josef von Trekwald at the academy of fine arts in Vienna. He travelled around western Europe researching the customs of Jewish communities and making numerous sketches. He was awarded medals in Munich (1897), in Berlin (1899) and in Paris at the 1900 Exposition Universelle.

His paintings of typical scenes from everyday Jewish life are characterised by his close attention to detail.

BIBLIOGRAPHY:
Altshuler, David, *The Precious Legacy: Judaic Treasures from the Czechoslovak State Collections*, exhibition catalogue, Summit Books, New York, Smithsonian Institution Traveling Exhibition Service, Washington DC, 1983.

MUSEUMS AND GALLERIES:
VIENNA (Kunsthistorisches Mus.): *The Rabbi's Visit.*

AUCTION RECORDS:
NEW YORK, March 1950, *The Lesson of the Talmud*, USD 2,800. LUCERNE, 23-26 Nov 1962, *Two Jews in Conversation*, CHF 12,000. LONDON, 10 Nov 1971, *A Chess Problem*, GBP 1,700. VIENNA, 4 Dec 1973, *Young Woman Writing*, ATS 140,000. NEW YORK, 28 April 1977, *Still-life with Red Shawl* (oil on canvas, 18 x 12 1/4 ins / 46 x 31 cm) USD 1,500. LOS ANGELES, 12 March 1979, *Thinker* (oil on panel, 11 1/4 x 13 1/2 ins / 28.7 x 34.2 cm) USD 26,000. NEW YORK, 7 Jan 1981, *Persons in an Interior* (pencil, 7 x 10 1/2 ins / 17.5 x 26.7 cm) USD 1,700. LONDON, 26 March 1982, *Portrait of Hannah, the Artist's Daughter* (oil on panel, 13 1/2 x 10 1/4 ins / 34.3 x 26 cm) GBP 19,000. NEW YORK, 25 Feb 1983, *Jewish Bride* (oil on canvas, 13 1/2 x 11 ins / 34.3 x 28 cm) USD 18,000. LONDON, 29 Nov 1984, *Young Girl with Book* (watercolour and gouache, oval, 19 x 15 1/2 ins / 48.5 x 39.5 cm) GBP 3,000. JERUSALEM, 18 May 1985, *Portrait of a Rabbi* (oil on panel, 15 3/4 x 12 1/2 ins / 40 x 32 cm) USD 75,000. NEW YORK, 21 May 1987, *Garden of the Château* (oil on panel, 13 1/2 x 17 3/4 ins / 34 x 45 cm) USD 7,500. NEW YORK, 24 May 1988, *Young Peasant Boy* (oil on panel, 10 x 6 1/4 ins / 25.4 x 15.9 cm) USD 5,500. NEW YORK, 22 May 1991, *Portrait of a Rabbi* (oil on panel, 12 1/2 x 10 ins / 31.8 x 25.4 cm) USD 45,100. TEL AVIV, 12 June 1991, *In the Apartment of my Maternal Grandmother* (watercolour, 12 x 9 ins / 30.5 x 22 cm) USD 1,980. TEL AVIV, 6 Jan 1992, *Little Girl in a Pinafore* (pencil, 9 1/4 x 6 ins / 23.5 x 15.5 cm) USD 990. NEW YORK, 20 Feb 1992, *Young Rabbi Praying* (oil on card, 18 1/2 x 14 3/4 ins / 47.3 x 37.5 cm) USD 176,000. TEL AVIV, 20 Oct 1992, *Small Boy Studying the Talmud* (oil on panel, 6 1/4 x 4 3/4 ins / 15.6 x 12 cm) USD 44,000. NEW YORK, 29 Oct 1992, *Comments Regarding the Talmud* (oil on panel, 16 1/2 x 20 3/4 ins / 41.9 x 52.7 cm) USD 176,000. NEW YORK, 17 Feb 1993, *Portrait of a Young Hassidic Boy* (oil on panel, 14 x 10 1/2 ins / 35.6 x 26.7 cm) USD 76,750. NEW YORK, 13 Oct 1993, *A Pair of Shoes* (oil on panel, 15 x 12 ins / 38.1 x 30.5 cm) USD 118,000. NEW YORK, 26 May 1994, *Portrait of a Rabbi* (oil on panel, 11 1/4 x 9 1/4 ins / 28.6 x 23.2 cm) USD 55,200. TEL AVIV, 25 Sept 1994, *Young Jewish Boy* (oil on panel, 14 x 11 3/4 ins / 35.5 x 30 cm) USD 140,000. NEW YORK, 16 Feb 1995, *Portrait of a Young Jew* (oil on panel, 9 x 7 ins / 22.9 x 17.5 cm) USD 16,100. NEW YORK, 1 Nov 1995, *Rabbi Before the Wooden Synagogue at Jablonow* (oil on panel, 11 3/4 x 10 1/4 ins / 29.8 x 26 cm) USD 189,500. TEL AVIV, 14 April 1996, *Young Girl at the Synagogue* (oil on panel, 20 1/4 x 15 ins / 51.5 x 37.8 cm) USD 167,500. LONDON, 21 Nov 1996, *Rabbi* (pen, blue ink and oil on panel, 7 3/4 x 6 ins / 19.6 x 15.5 cm) GBP 5,175. TEL AVIV, 23 Oct 1997, *Portrait of a Rabbi Carrying Taleth* (oil on panel, 14 3/4 x 12 ins / 37.5 x 30.3 cm) USD 131,200. NEW YORK, 18 March 1998, *Portrait of a Young Hassidic Jew* (oil on panel, 15 3/4 x 12 1/2 ins / 40 x 31.8 cm) USD 48,875.

KAUFMANN, Jean
Swiss, 19th century.
Born 19th century, in La Chaux-de-Fonds.
Sculptor.

Kaufmann worked in his home town. In 1900, he exhibited in Paris at the Exposition Universelle.

KAUFMANN, Johann Michael
German, 18th century.
Born c. 1713.
Painter.

Kaufmann was portrait painter to the Bavarian court.

KAUFMANN, Joseph
Swiss, 18th century.
Active in Staufen im Breisgau in 1776.
Painter.

KAUFMANN, Joseph Clemens
Swiss, 19th - 20th century.
Born 7 February 1867, in Harw (Lucerne); died 1926, in Zurich.
Painter, pastellist. Military subjects, landscapes, animals.

From 1883 to 1885, Joseph Clemens Kaufmann was a student at the École des Beaux-Arts in Geneva, then studied from 1885 to 1887 with Luc-Olivier Menson and Benjamin-Constant in Paris before settling in Lucerne. He painted mainly dioramas and battle scenes.

MUSEUMS AND GALLERIES:
LUCERNE: *Batteries Firing* (two paintings).

AUCTION RECORDS:
ZURICH, 15 March 1951, *Returning from the Campaign*, CHF 1,500. NEW YORK, 15 Oct 1976, *The Seventh Battalion on Manoeuvres* (1900, oil on canvas, 58 1/2 x 84 1/2 ins / 148.5 x 214.5 cm) USD 1,300. LUCERNE, 17 June 1977, *Ploughing Scene* (1924, oil on canvas, 33 3/4 x 49 1/2 ins / 86 x 126 cm) CHF 6,000. LUCERNE, 30 May 1979, *Flock by an Alpine Lake* (1893, oil on canvas, 33 1/2 x 49 1/2 ins / 85 x 125.5 cm) CHF 10,000. LUCERNE, 8 Nov 1984, *View of Lake Lauerz and the Island of*

Schwanau (1926, oil on canvas, 33½ x 45¼ ins / 85 x 115 cm) CHF 4,200. ZURICH, 29 Nov 1985, *Emperor Wilhelm II Watching the Grand Manoeuvres of 1912* (1912, oil on canvas, 40½ x 57½ ins / 103 x 146 cm) CHF 32,000. STOCKHOLM, 15 Nov 1988, *View of Bari in Italy* (oil, 11¾ x 20 ins / 30 x 51 cm) SEK 14,000. LUCERNE, 3 Dec 1988, *Village near the Julierpass* (1911, pastel, 18½ x 23½ ins / 47 x 60 cm) CHF 950. BERN, 12 May 2000, *Young Swiss Goatherd in Mountain Landscape* (1892, oil on canvas, 43 x 35 ins / 110 x 88 cm) CHF 6,000. LUCERNE, 2 May 2001, *Swiss Militia Resting in Winter Landscape* (oil on canvas, 17 x 13 ins / 44 x 34 cm) CHF 2,700.

KAUFMANN, Julius
French, 20th century.
Born 10 April 1885, in Altkirch.
Painter. Landscapes.

Julius Kaufmann was born in annexed Alsace. He trained in Kassel and Karlsruhe and later in Paris. He often painted landscapes under snow.

KAUFMANN, Karl, pseudonyms: Carnier, Henri, called C. Carlo (?), Marchand, Charles
Austrian, 19th century.
Born 1843, in Neuplachawitz; died 1901, in Vienna.
Painter. Landscapes, waterscapes, urban landscapes, architectural views.
Orientalism.

Kaufmann used pseudonyms, which does not make it easy to identify him, and his identity is still uncertain. It is not impossible that some of his paintings are attributed to otherwise mysterious artists. He specialised mainly in oriental views and prospects of Venice, considered the gateway to the Orient. In some cases, the towns he painted represent an imaginary Orient.

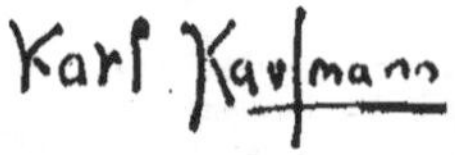

AUCTION RECORDS:
LONDON, 23 July 1976, *Sta Maria della Salute, Venice* (1899, oil on canvas, 17½ x 12¾ ins / 44.5 x 32.5 cm) GBP 420. COPENHAGEN, 7 June 1977, *View of a Venetian Canal* (1891, oil on canvas, 35½ x 49¼ ins / 90 x 125 cm) DKK 10,000. LONDON, 9 May 1979, *View of a Town beside a Canal* (oil on canvas, 26¼ x 41 ins / 66.5 x 104 cm) GBP 600. COLOGNE, 19 Oct 1979, *View of Cordova* (oil on canvas, 20¾ x 37 ins / 53 x 94 cm) DEM 3,000. LONDON, 24 June 1981, *Street Scenes outside a Mosque* (two oil paintings on panel, 12¼ x 7 ins / 31 x 18 cm) GBP 600. VIENNA, 17 Nov 1981, *Zurich* (1892, oil on canvas, 23½ x 41¾ ins / 60 x 106 cm) ATS 150,000. VIENNA, 18 May 1983, *Boats beside the Lake* (1888, oil on canvas, 19¾ x 32 ins / 50 x 81 cm) ATS 28,000. LONDON, 22 June 1983, *View of Venice* (oil on panel, 14¼ x 20¾ ins / 36 x 53 cm) GBP 1,800. VIENNA, 11 Sept 1985, *Street Scene, Istanbul* (oil on panel, 8¾ x 6¾ ins / 22.5 x 17 cm) ATS 45,000. ZURICH, 20 Sept 1985, *View of Rome* (1878, oil on canvas, 20¾ x 37½ ins / 53 x 95 cm) CHF 4,400. LONDON, 7 Feb 1986, *Street Scenes in Baghdad, Alexandria and Tunis* (four oil paintings on panel, each 12 x 6½ ins / 30.5 x 16.5 cm) GBP 1,600. VIENNA, 20 May 1987, *View of Venice* (oil on canvas, 26¾ x 41¾ ins / 68 x 106 cm) ATS 75,000. LONDON, 26 Feb 1988, *Canal in Venice* (1897, oil on canvas, 20 x 32¼ ins / 50.5 x 82 cm) GBP 1,980. NEW YORK, 19 July 1990, *Constantinople and Rome* (1895, oil on canvas, a pair, each 27 x 41 ins / 68.6 x 104.1 cm) USD 7,700. AMSTERDAM, 30 Oct 1990, *The Molo and Doge's Palace, Venice* (oil on panel, 12½ x 20¼ ins / 31.5 x 51.5 cm) NLG 8,050. LONDON, 22 Nov 1990, *Continental Town beside a River* (1884, oil on canvas, 20 x 37 ins / 50.8 x 94 cm) GBP 1,540. CALAIS, 10 March 1991, *Italian Lake* (oil on panel, 16½ x 20¾ ins / 42 x 53 cm) FRF 20,000. AMSTERDAM, 28 Oct 1992, *The Viennese Opera House with Elegant Strollers* (1880, oil on canvas, 27 x 41½ ins / 68.5 x 105.5 cm) NLG 13,800; *View of Naples* (oil on panel, a pair, each 10½ x 8¼ ins / 26.5 x 21 cm) NLG 4,370. LONDON, 28 Oct 1992, *The Grand Canal in Venice* (1893, oil on canvas, 19 x 31 ins / 48 x 79 cm) GBP 2,640. NEW YORK, 20 Jan 1993, *River Landscape in Moonlight* (1891, oil on canvas, 18¼ x 26¾ ins / 46.4 x 67.9 cm) USD 2,875. LONDON, 1 Oct 1993, *On the Bosphorus* (1894, oil on panel, 8 x 12¼ ins / 20.3 x 31.1 cm) GBP 3,450. NEW YORK, 15 Oct 1993, *Arab Village* (oil on canvas, 18½ x 12½ ins / 47 x 31.7 cm) USD 1,150. STOCKHOLM, 30 Nov 1993, *The Grand Canal with the Doge's Palace, Venice* (oil on canvas, 27¼ x 41¾ ins / 69 x 106 cm) SEK 60,000. MUNICH, 7 Dec 1993, *Black Ice on Village Street* (1891, oil on canvas, 23 x 16½ ins / 58.5 x 42 cm) DEM 10,350. NEW YORK, 26 May 1994, *Venice* (1896, oil on canvas, a pair, each 27 x 41½ ins / 68.6 x 105.4 cm) USD 11,500. LONDON, 16 Nov 1994, *View of Constantinople* (1897, oil on canvas, 20 x 30¾ ins / 51 x 78 cm) GBP 4,600. PARIS, 12 June 1995, *Oriental Town* (oil on canvas, 23 x 31¼ ins / 57.5 x 79.5 cm) FRF 43,000. LONDON, 17 Nov 1995, *On the Bosphorus* (1882, oil on canvas, 12½ x 20½ ins / 32 x 52 cm) GBP 9,775. MUNICH, 25 June 1996, *The Grand Canal; The Doge's Palace* (1877, oil on canvas, a pair, each 22¾ x 35½ ins / 58 x 90 cm) DEM 18,000. LONDON, 10 Oct 1996, *The Woodcutter* (oil on canvas, 29 x 45½ ins / 73.6 x 115.5 cm) GBP 2,000.

KAUFMANN, Kaspar
German, 19th century.
Born 15 July 1810, in Rome; died 1855, in Rastatt (near Baden-Baden).
Painter, lithographer.

Kaufmann worked a lot in Weimar, where he did portraits and religiously inspired works.

KAUFMANN, Léon. See **KAMIR Léon**

KAUFMANN, Ludwig
German, 19th century.
Born 5 May 1801, in Rome; died 12 May 1855, in Cracow.
Sculptor.

Kaufmann, a pupil of Thorvaldsen and Canova, established himself in Warsaw, where he did a *Bust of King John III Sobieski*, which gained him fame and numerous commissions. He was the son of Peter Kaufmann.

KAUFMANN, Massimo
Italian, 20th - 21st century.
Born 1961, in Milan.
Painter, installation artist. Multimedia.

In 1990, Kaufmann stayed at the Cartier Foundation for Contemporary Art in Jouy-en-Josas. After discovering Goya's *Caprichos* in the same year, he set up an installation accompanied by typed drawings relating this powerful experience and his encounter with the Spanish painter's demons. He has had solo exhibitions in Geneva (1991) and Nice (Musée d'Art Moderne Contemporain, 1997).

KAUFMANN, Peter, or Kauffmann
German, 18th - 19th century.
Born 16 February 1764; died 2 August 1829, in Weimar.
Sculptor. Busts.

Kaufmann was a pupil of Thorvaldsen and Canova, and lived mainly in Italy. He did numerous busts, including one of *Angelica Kauffman*, his famous cousin.

MUSEUMS AND GALLERIES:
WEIMAR (Schlossmus.): *Grand Duchess Maria Paulowna of Saxony* (bust); *August von Heigendorf in His Youth* (bust).

KAUFMANN, Theodor
German, 19th century.
Born 1814, in Uelzen.
Painter. History painting, portraits.

Kaufmann studied under Hess and Kaulbach in Munich, then subsequently worked in Hamburg and Dresden, exhibiting in Dresden and Vienna. From 1850, he established himself in America, where he mainly did military scenes.
Auction records:
New York, 23 May 1979, *On to Liberty* (1867, oil on canvas, 36 x 56 ins / 91.5 x 142.5 cm) USD 40,000.

KAUFMANN-PFISTER, Elsa
German, 20th century.
Born 3 May 1883, in Strasbourg.
Painter. Religious subjects, portraits, landscapes.
Born in Alsace, when it was part of Germany, Elsa Kaufmann-Pfister studied painting in Berlin and Paris and chose to settle in Darmstadt. She was responsible for the decoration of the church in Balga.

KAUFURAU, A.
Painter. Landscapes with figures.
A. Kaufurau is listed in annual sales records.
Auction records:
Paris, 22 Dec 1943, *Two Horses at the Water Trough; Sheep in the Snow* (both) FRF 3,600.

KAUKE, Johann Friedrich
German, 18th century.
Born in Berlin; died 1777.
Draughtsman, engraver (burin).
Kauke was a pupil of Schleuen; he engraved mythological subjects and portraits after artists such as Fuseli, J. Courtin de la Tour, M.R. Rode, and A. Pesne.

KAUL, August
German, 19th - 20th century.
Born 13 February 1873, in Hamburg.
Painter.
August Kaul settled in Düsseldorf and exhibited in Berlin in 1910.

KAUL, Johann Jakob
German, 18th century.
Active in Mainz.
Painter.
Kaul is represented by a *St Joseph with the Child Jesus* in the archiepiscopal seminary in Mainz.

KAULA, Lee Lufkin
American, 19th - 20th century.
Born 1865, in Erie (Pennsylvania); died 1953.
Painter. Genre scenes.
Lee Lufkin Kaula studied under Charles Melville Dewey in New York, under Aman-Jean and also at the Académie Colarossi in Paris. Married to painter William Jurian Kaula, she settled in Boston.
Auction records:
New York, 24 Oct 1979, *Ann on the Veranda* (1919, oil on canvas, 29 1/4 x 29 1/4 ins / 74 x 74 cm) USD 2,800. Portland, 9 July 1983, *The Letter* (oil on canvas, 29 1/4 x 24 1/4 ins / 74 x 61.5 cm) USD 1,900. Bolton, 19 Nov 1987, *Cornelia* (oil on canvas, 48 x 30 ins / 122 x 76.2 cm) USD 6,500. New York, 30 Sept 1988, *Choosing an Accessory* (oil on canvas, 29 x 24 ins / 73.6 x 61 cm) USD 7,700. New York, 14 Nov 1991, *Eating Porridge* (watercolour/paper, 14 1/2 x 11 3/4 ins / 36.9 x 29.9 cm) USD 1,320. New York, 14 March 1996, *Young Woman in Blue* (oil on canvas, 39 1/4 x 31 3/4 ins / 99.7 x 80.6 cm) USD 18,400. New York, 26 Sept 1996, *The Kimino* (oil on canvas, 39 1/2 x 32 ins / 100.3 x 81.3 cm) USD 8,050. Portland, 4 Aug 1999, *Portrait of Lulu and Florence M Lufkin* (oil on canvas, 40 x 30 ins / 102 x 76 cm) USD 15,000. Milford, 21 Oct 1999, *Washerwomen, France* (watercolour, 12 x 15 ins / 30 x 38 cm) USD 3,250. Milford, 11 May 2000, *Self-portrait in Japanese Kimono* (oil on canvas, 37 x 27 ins / 94 x 69 cm) USD 9,250. Connecticut, 5 Dec 2000, *Table Still-life* (oil on canvas, 23 x 18 ins / 58 x 46 cm) USD 2,400. Boston, 22 Nov 2002, *Portrait of Hathaway Stetson* (oil on canvas, 48 x 30 ins / 122 x 77 cm) USD 9,000. Cincinnati, 7 Dec 2003, *Portrait of a Woman in an Interior* (c. 1920, oil on canvas, 35 x 25 ins / 89 x 64 cm) USD 10,000.

KAULA, William Jurian
American, 19th - 20th century.
Born 1871, in Boston; died 1952.
Painter. Landscapes.
William Jurian Kaula studied art at the Normal Art School in Boston, and under Raphaël Collin in Paris. His landscapes show a great sensitivity to the play of light and shadows and to the mood of the seasons.
Auction records:
Portland, 9 July 1983, *The Brink of Spring* (oil on canvas, 35 x 46 ins / 89 x 117 cm) USD 6,600. East Dennis, 28 March 1986, *Willoughby Hills* (oil on canvas, 25 1/2 x 29 ins / 65 x 73.5 cm) USD 3,500. New York, 20 March 1987, *Mountain Laurel, Ashby, Massachusetts* (watercolour, 22 1/4 x 18 1/4 ins / 56.5 x 46.1 cm) USD 2,200. East Dennis, 31 July 1987, *Landscape* (oil on canvas, 24 x 29 ins / 61 x 73.5 cm) USD 7,000. New York, 17 March 1988, *Winter Landscape* (oil on canvas, 11 1/2 x 14 1/4 ins / 29 x 36 cm) USD 1,980. New York, 26 May 1988, *Millstream, Ipswich, New Hampshire* (oil on canvas, 46 x 35 ins / 116.9 x 89.1 cm) USD 52,800. New York, 14 Feb 1990, *The River Swale* (watercolour/paper, 17 x 21 ins / 43.2 x 53.3 cm) USD 2,750. New York, 14 March 1991, *Shadows and Sun* (oil on card, 17 1/4 x 23 ins / 44 x 58.5 cm) USD 3,300. New York, 21 May 1991, *Track in Winter* (1913, oil on card, 8 1/4 x 10 ins / 21 x 25.4 cm) USD 1,100. New York, 15 Nov 1993, *Landscape with Blue Sky* (gouache/card, 20 x 25 1/2 ins / 50.8 x 64.7 cm) USD 690. New York, 21 Sept 1994, *Near Ipswich in New Hampshire in October* (oil on canvas, 35 x 46 ins / 88.9 x 116.8 cm) USD 10,350. Portland, 4 Aug 1999, *Autumn Landscape with Billowing Clouds* (oil on canvas, 32 x 39 ins / 81 x 99 cm) USD 3,800. Milford, 21 Oct 1999, *Temple Hills in Winter, New Hampshire* (oil on board, 21 x 26 ins / 53 x 66 cm) USD 6,000. Boston, 10 March 2000, *Sunshine and Clouds* (oil on canvas, 24 x 29 ins / 61 x 74 cm) USD 13,000. New York, 28 Nov 2000, *Autumn Effect, North-West Wind* (oil on canvas, 24 x 29 ins / 61 x 74 cm) USD 6,500. Boston, 9 March 2001, *Cheshire Hills* (oil on canvas, 35 x 46 ins / 89 x 116 cm) USD 9,500. Los Angeles, 7 Nov 2001, *Hills of New Ipswich, New Hampshire* (oil on canvas, 32 x 39 ins / 81 x 100 cm) USD 20,000. Boston, 22 Nov 2002, *Upright Landscape* (oil on canvas, 29 x 24 ins / 74 x 61 cm) USD 2,000. Boston, 22 Nov 2002, *Hillside* (oil on board, 10 x 13 ins / 26 x 33 cm) USD 3,500. Boston, 16 May 2003, *Danville Hills, Vermont* (oil on canvasboard, 10 x 13 ins / 26 x 33 cm) USD 5,000. East Dennis, 21 Nov 2003, *Landscape with Trees and Cloud-scattered Sky* (oil on canvas, 18 x 22 ins / 46 x 56 cm) USD 6,750. Milford, 6 May 2004, *September Skies* (oil on canvas, 24 x 29 ins / 61 x 74 cm) USD 7,000.

KAULBACH, Friedrich
German, 19th century.
Born 8 July 1822, in Bad Arolsen (Hesse); died 5 September 1903, in Hanover.
Painter. History painting, portraits, landscapes, flowers.
Kaulbach was a cousin and pupil of Wilhelm Kaulbach, whose studio he worked in until 1845, and the father of Friedrich August Kaulbach. He travelled to Italy, returned to Munich, then set off for Hanover. He won medals in Berlin (1872) and Munich (1883), and was appointed to the staff of the academy of fine arts in Berlin.

He was particularly susceptible to the influence of Karl Theodor von Piloty, whose stagey effects he exaggerated, but he also learnt from the Venetian painters in the richness of his coloration. He did a large number of portraits of the royal House of Hanover.

Museums and Galleries:

Hanover: *Portrait of the Royal Family of Hanover.*

Auction records:

Paris, 12 June 1985, *Portrait of Marie-Marthe de Choiseul-Praslin, Marchioness of Montalembert d'Esse* (1863, oil on canvas, 80 3/4 x 52 ins / 205 x 132 cm) FRF 40,000. Venice, 19 Sept 1999, *Lament for Abel* (oil on canvas, 39 x 46 ins / 100 x 116 cm) ITL 10,000,000. New Orleans, 3 June 2000, *Crown Prince* (oil on canvas, 30 x 25 ins / 76 x 64 cm) USD 1,800. Munich, 8 Nov 2000, *Portrait of a Girl* (oil on canvas, 24 x 20 ins / 62 x 52 cm) DEM 11,000.

KAULBACH, Friedrich August von

German, 19th - 20th century.

Born 2 June 1850, in Munich; died 26 July 1920, in Ohlstadt.

Painter, pastellist. Religious subjects, genre scenes, portraits.

Friedrich August von Kaulbach was the son of Friedrich Kaulbach. He was first taught by his father, then studied with Karl Raupp at the Nuremberg art school and, from 1872, with Wilhelm von Diez at the Akademie der Bildenden Künste in Munich. In 1873 he travelled to Italy, and from 1883 to 1885, he lived in Paris. He was appointed a member of the Akademie der Bildenden Künste of Munich in 1882 and became a member of the Berlin Academy in 1883 and the Akademie der Bildenden Künste of Munich in 1888, succeeding Karl Piloty. He exhibited in Paris in 1878 and 1889 and at the Exposition Universelle in 1900. He won gold medals in Berlin, Munich and Vienna.

Museums and Galleries:

Aachen: *Portrait of Adam Bock* - Cologne: *Wilhelm II* - Frankfurt am Main: *Portrait of the Artist's Wife* - Leipzig: *Max von Pettenkofer* - Munich: *The Entombment of Christ; Portrait of the Artist's Wife; Councillor von Pettenkoffer Luitpold of Bavaria* - San Francisco (FAM): *Self Portrait* (1916, dry-point); *Portrait of a Young Girl* (1916, dry-point); *In the Park (Classic Dance)* (1917, dry-point) - Vienna: *The Luteplayer.*

Auction records:

Zurich, 15 March 1951, *Portrait of a Girl,* CHF 1,200. New York, 10 Oct 1973, *Mother and Child,* USD 1,700. Cologne, 25 June 1976, *Portrait of a Woman* (oil on canvas, 39 1/4 x 29 1/2 ins / 100 x 75 cm) DEM 11,000. Munich, 1 Dec 1976, *Portrait of a Child* (1883, pastel, 15 3/4 x 11 1/2 ins / 40 x 29.5 cm) DEM 3,200. Zurich, 12 May 1977, *Nude at the Well* (1918, oil on card, 16 1/4 x 9 ins / 41 x 22 cm) CHF 2,800. Zurich, 20 May 1977, *Children Dancing to the Sound of a Tambourine* (watercolour, 17 3/4 x 14 ins / 45 x 35.5 cm) CHF 5,000. Cologne, 17 March 1978, *Girls Dancing in a Spring Landscape* (oil on canvas, 13 x 16 1/4 ins / 33 x 41.5 cm) DEM 2,600. New York, 2 May 1979, *The Writing Lesson* (oil on panel, 14 x 10 3/4 ins / 35.6 x 27.3 cm) USD 30,000. Los Angeles, 17 March 1980, *Portrait of a Young Woman* (pastel, 22 x 18 ins / 56 x 45.7 cm) USD 1,700. New York, 28 May 1981, *Portrait of a Young Woman* (oil on paper remounted/canvas, 39 x 24 1/2 ins / 99 x 62 cm) USD 5,500. New York, 27 Feb 1982, *Portrait of a Woman* (c. 1897-1914, pastel, 23 x 18 ins / 58.5 x 45.5 cm) USD 1,500. Cologne, 22 March 1985, *Portrait of a Girl* (oil on panel, 16 1/4 x 12 ins / 41 x 30.5 cm) DEM 10,000. Munich, 21 Oct 1987, *Allegory of Architecture* (pastel/mounted paper/canvas, 30 1/4 x 38 1/2 ins / 77 x 98 cm) DEM 4,800. New York, 23 Feb 1989, *Portrait of Max Beckmann's Mother-in-Law* (1916, oil on canvas, 43 x 35 ins / 108.3 x 88.8 cm) USD 8,800. London, 24 Nov 1989, *Hedda* (oil on panel, 44 x 28 ins / 112 x 71 cm) GBP 18,700. London, 29 Nov 1991, *Portrait of Master Eckstein Standing in a Grey Coat, with his Elbows Leaning on a Brown Drape* (1902, oil on canvas, 64 x 39 1/4 ins / 162.5 x 99.7 cm) GBP 9,900. New York, 20 Jan 1993, *Young Woman Carrying a Tray of Fruit in a Landscape* (oil on canvas, 38 3/4 x 29 ins / 98.4 x 73.7 cm) USD 8,338. London, 12 Feb 1993, *Portrait of a Lady on a Day-Bed with a Little Dog on her Knees* (oil on panel, diam. 23 1/4 ins / 59.1 cm) GBP 3,520. London, 20 May 1993, *Head and Shoulders Portrait of a Young Woman* (1915, oil on card, 24 3/4 x 23 3/4 ins / 62.9 x 60.3 cm) GBP 4,600. New York, 26 May 1993, *Portrait of a Young Woman* (oil on canvas, 23 1/4 x 23 1/4 ins / 59.1 x 59.1 cm) USD 9,775. Munich, 22 June 1993, *Portrait of a Girl* (pastel/card, 23 1/2 x 17 1/4 ins / 59.5 x 43.5 cm) DEM 2,875. New York, 19 Jan 1994, *The Infant Bacchus* (oil on card, 21 1/2 x 15 ins / 54.6 x 38.1 cm) USD 3,738. Paris, 21 June 1996, *Profile Portrait of a Young Boy* (oil on card, 14 1/4 x 12 1/4 ins / 36 x 31 cm) FRF 8,000. Vienna, 29-30 Oct 1996, *Festival in Arcadia* (oil on canvas, 50 1/2 x 90 1/4 ins / 128 x 229 cm) ATS 138,000. Paris, 25 June 1997, *Elegant Lady in a Landscape* (1905, oil on canvas, 53 1/4 x 39 3/4 ins / 135 x 101 cm) FRF 14,000.

KAULBACH, Hermann

German, 19th century.

Born 26 July 1846, in Munich; died 9 December 1909, in Munich.

Painter, draughtsman, illustrator. Religious subjects, portraits, genre scenes.

Kaulbach was the son of Wilhelm von Kaulbach and became a pupil of Karl Theodor von Piloty. Medals came his way in Vienna (1873), Berlin (1886) and Munich (1901). An honorary member of the academy in Munich, he was appointed professor in 1888.

Museums and Galleries:

Munich: *Immortality.*

Auction records:

New York, 3 Feb 1905, *Madonna and Child,* USD 400. Düsseldorf, 20 June 1973, *Outside the Cobbler's Workshop,* DEM 110,000. Zurich, 5 May 1976, *Young Girl* (oil on panel, 8 1/4 x 6 1/4 ins / 21 x 16 cm) CHF 4,800. Zurich, 20 May 1977, *Little Red Riding Hood* (1879, card, 35 x 25 3/4 ins / 88 x 65.5 cm) CHF 4,000. Los Angeles, 17 Nov 1980, *Two Good Friends* (oil on panel, 11 3/4 x 15 1/2 ins / 30 x 39.5 cm) USD 20,000. San Francisco, 18 March 1981, *The Little Storyteller* (oil on panel, 16 1/4 x 12 1/2 ins / 41.5 x 31.5 cm) USD 55,000. Munich, 30 June 1983, *Pierrette* (1891, oil on panel, 9 x 7 ins / 22 x 18 cm) DEM 5,000. New York, 13 Feb 1985, *The Intruders* (oil on panel, 21 1/2 x 15 3/4 ins / 54.5 x 40 cm) USD 37,000. New York, 24 May 1988, *An Odd Thing* (oil on panel, 15 3/4 x 11 1/2 ins / 40 x 29 cm) USD 28,600. New York, 23 May 1990, *Portrait of a Lady with a Mandolin* (oil on canvas, 59 x 28 1/2 ins / 149.9 x 72.7 cm) USD 17,600. New York, 23 Oct 1990, *The Imps* (oil on panel, 17 1/4 x 13 ins / 43.8 x 33 cm) USD 66,000. London, 17 May 1991, *On the Swing* (oil on panel, 10 x 6 1/2 ins / 25.2 x 16.2 cm) GBP 3,300. New York, 29 Oct 1992, *The Clown's Audience* (oil on panel, 24 1/2 x 18 1/2 ins / 62.2 x 47 cm) USD 46,750. Munich, 10 Dec 1992, *King Ludwig II of Bavaria on His Deathbed* (1886, pencil/paper, 7 1/4 x 9 ins / 18.2 x 23.1 cm) DEM 9,492. London, 14 June 1996, *The Drawing Lesson* (oil on panel, 15 x 10 3/4 ins / 38 x 27.4 cm) GBP 36,700. Munich, 25 June 1996, *Young Peasant with a Bowl of Soup* (oil on panel, 13 x 9 ins / 33 x 22 cm) DEM 7,200. London, 10 Oct 1996, *Ulrich with Ruth in the Forest* (oil on canvas, 35 x 25 3/4 ins / 88.9 x 65.5 cm) GBP 3,000. Amsterdam,

18 June 1997, *Bavarian Farmhouse Interior* (oil on canvas, 20 1/4 x 25 ins / 51.5 x 63.5 cm) NLG 10,955. New York, 22 Oct 1997, *Returning Home* (oil on canvas, 38 1/2 x 27 ins / 97.8 x 68.6 cm) USD 10,925. Munich, 27 Feb 1999, *All Beginnings are Difficult: Joker Tries Spinning* (oil on panel, 30 x 23 ins / 76 x 58 cm) DEM 30,000. New York, 3 Nov 1999, *Reading by the Fire* (oil on canvas, 15 x 11 ins / 37 x 29 cm) USD 44,000. New York, 25 Oct 2000, *Sitting for a Meal* (oil on panel, 14 x 10 ins / 35 x 26 cm) USD 19,000. New York, 25 Oct 2000, *Story Time* (oil on panel, 24 x 19 ins / 61 x 49 cm) USD 24,000. Lindau, 7 Dec 2001, *Small Girl Sitting in a Chair Looking at Apples* (oil on panel, 6 x 8 ins / 15 x 21 cm) DEM 5,000. Munich, 4 Dec 2002, *Young Mother Sitting at the Fireside Feeding Her Two Small Girls* (oil on panel, 14 x 10 ins / 35 x 25 cm) EUR 35,000. Munich, 6 Dec 2002, *Bible Study for Small Children* (oil on panel, 24 x 19 ins / 61 x 49 cm) EUR 28,000. Munich, 17 March 2004, *Little Boy Holding Flowers* (oil on panel, 9 x 6 ins / 24 x 15 cm) EUR 4,400. Munich, 17 March 2004, *Dwarf with Toothache* (oil on panel, 18 x 13 ins / 45 x 33 cm) EUR 5,000.

KAULBACH, Karl

German, 19th century.
Born 5 March 1808, in Bad Arolsen.
Sculptor, painter.

Kaulbach was a pupil of Schwanthaler in Munich, then taught drawing in Würzburg.

KAULBACH, Wilhelm von

German, 19th century.
Born 15 October 1805, in Bad Arolsen; died 7 April 1874, in Munich.
Painter, watercolourist, fresco artist, draughtsman, illustrator. History painting, allegorical subjects, mythological subjects, portraits.

Kaulbach was the son of a goldsmith, under whom he started to train. In 1821, he went to the academy in Düsseldorf and was admitted to the studio of Cornelius, whom he followed to Munich in 1825. Despite his youth, Kaulbach showed quite exceptional artistic qualities. The occasion to demonstrate them came in 1826 when he painted the *Apollo among the Muses* at the Odeon in Munich. It was much noticed, and was followed by two important frescoes in the garden palace. Kaulbach also painted various subjects from the works of Goethe, Wieland, Klopstock and Hermann in the palace of Duke Maximilian.

By then, the young Kaulbach had established his reputation. Count Roczynski got him to do a large-scale *Battle of the Huns*, which took him from 1834 to 1837. He also did a *Destruction of Jerusalem* for the Pinakothek in Munich. In 1839, he went to Rome and in 1847 he began work on his great work of decorating the staircase of the new Berlin Museum. In the same year, he was appointed director of the academy of fine arts in Munich.

Though a master of the classical German school, he was not above doing illustrations, and provided interesting compositions to accompany the works of Goethe, Schiller and Shakespeare. Among his numerous allegories, he defined his artistic programme in a painting that became famous - a young woman celebrating ideal beauty is enclosed in a cage guarded by monsters, represented here by the Romantic French barbarians; while brave knights, among whom we can identify the features of Kaulbach himself along with his friends Overbeck, Cornelius and several others, courageously attempt to rescue her.

Museums and Galleries:

Antwerp: *The Scattering of the Nations; The Gods of Greece; The Crusaders; Battle of the Huns; Cartoons for Murals for the Berlin Museum* - Bremen: *Nero* - Munich: *Destruction of Jerusalem by Titus; Heinrich Heinlen at the Masked Ball; Dietrich Monten as a Captain of the Lansequenets*; 20 sketches; *Ludwig I; Max II of Bavaria; Ludwig I of Bavaria* - Stuttgart: *The Huns on the Catalaunian Fields; Battle of Salamis* - Weimar: *Cupid Riding a Lion.*

Auction records:

Paris, 27 April 1929, six sketches for the frescoes on the outside of the Neue Pinakothek in Munich) FRF 3,000. Paris, 17 Oct 1932, *Young Woman*, FRF 440. London, 5 Oct 1979, *The Broken Violin* (oil on canvas, 28 x 34 ins / 71.2 x 86.4 cm) GBP 2,200. Munich, 4 June 1981, *The Water Sprite* (c. 1830-1840, pencil, tondo, diam. 11 1/2 ins / 29 cm) DEM 2,300. London, 15 June 1982, *Lohengrin Taking Leave of Elsa* (1866, pencil, 57 x 45 3/4 ins / 144.5 x 116.5 cm) GBP 5,000. Hamburg, 8 June 1983, *Self-portrait* (c. 1835, pencil, 8 x 4 1/4 ins / 20.6 x 11 cm) DEM 1,900. Hamburg, 7 June 1984, *The Flirtatious Conversation* (1860, watercolour, 15 1/4 x 11 ins / 39 x 28 cm) DEM 4,200. New York, 21 May 1986, *Charity* (oil on canvas, 30 1/2 x 24 1/2 ins / 77.5 x 62.2 cm) USD 5,500. Munich, 10 Dec 1991, *Reform* (1862, pencil and ink, 62 1/4 x 75 1/2 ins / 158 x 192 cm) DEM 6,325. London, 22 May 1992, *Lotte (The Sorrows of Werther)* (oil on canvas, 74 3/4 x 53 ins / 190 x 134.6 cm) GBP 7,700. Munich, 10 Dec 1992, *Mythological Scene* (watercolour, 13 1/2 x 17 3/4 ins / 34 x 45 cm) DEM 3,390. Munich, 7 Dec 1993, *Portrait of a Young Italian Woman* (oil on canvas, 37 3/4 x 28 3/4 ins / 96 x 73 cm) DEM 10,925. Munich, 25 June 1996, *Small Boy Playing; Small Girl at Her Drawing Book* (oil on canvas, a pair, each 12 1/4 x 8 3/4 ins / 31 x 22.5 cm) DEM 18,000. Munich, 22 June 1999, *Still-life with Roses* (oil on panel, 6 x 8 ins / 15 x 20 cm) DEM 4,800. Melbourne, 2 May 2000, *Anacreon* (oil on canvas, 45 x 67 ins / 114 x 171 cm) AUD 5,000. Cologne, 20 Oct 2000, *Judgement of Reineke Fuchs* (pencil and wash on board, 8 x 8 ins / 20 x 20 cm) DEM 13,000. Vienna, 23 Sept 2002, *Girl with Grapes* (oil on canvas, 40 x 33 ins / 102 x 83 cm) EUR 4,000.

KAULE, Otto

German, 19th - 20th century.
Born 5 November 1870, in Thiendorf.
Painter. Landscapes.

Otto Kaule studied in Dresden and settled in Bardowiek.

KAULITZ, Christian Ludwig

German, 18th century.
Born in Berlin; died 1744, in Nuremberg.
Illuminator, draughtsman.

Kaulitz wrote and illustrated *Patricie Reipublicæ Marimbergea.*

KAULUM, Haakon Jensen

Norwegian, 19th century.
Born 12 June 1863, in Bergen; died 1933.
Painter. Landscapes.

Haakon Kaulum's *Landscape with Fjord* is in the museum of Oslo.

KAUPER, Kurt

American, 20th - 21st century.
Born 1966, in Indianapolis.
Painter. Figures.

Kurt Kauper is a graduate in fine arts from Boston University with a further degree from UCLA. He began teaching at Yale University in 2000. He has received many awards, including the Tiffany Foundation Grant in 1999. He paints huge canvases in a Hyperrealist style. He presents real or fictitious divas in blunt colours, exposing the artificiality of their status. In his full-length portraits of actor Cary Grant, a casual pose or a mundane setting contrasts with the nude representation: Kauper makes a point of demystifying the heroic male nude images dear to 19th-century artists. The size of the paintings and the clash in their content between archetypal subjects and a Pop version of classical portraiture explode representational stereotypes and cannot fail to provoke the viewer. He began taking part in collective exhibitions in 1990 and has been included in the Whitney Biennial, New York, and *Cher Peintre... Peintures figuratives depuis l'ultime Picabia* (*Dear Painter, Figurative Paintings since Late Picabia*), Centre Georges Pompidou, Paris. He has shown his works in solo exhibitions notably in 2000 at Deitch Projects, New York.

BIBLIOGRAPHY:
Miles, Christopher, '*Kurt Kauper at ACME*' in *Artweek* vol. 28, periodical, San Jose (CA), July 1997. *Form Follows Fiction*, group exhibition catalogue, Castello di Rivoli, Turin, 2000. Gingeras, Allison M., '*Kurt Kauper, Deitch Projects*' in *Art Press* n° 260, periodical, Paris, September 2000. Weinhart, Martina, '*Kurt Kauper*' in *Cher Peintre... Peintures figuratives depuis l'ultime Picabia*, group exhibition catalogue, Éd. du Centre Georges-Pompidou, Paris, 2002.

KAUPERT, Gustav
German, 19th century.
Born 4 April 1819, in Kassel; died 4 December 1897, in Kassel.
Sculptor, medallist.

Kaupert was a pupil of Wehmuth, and later of Werner Henschel and Ruhl. He travelled widely in Germany and also in Italy. His sculptural works, often mythologically inspired, display a moving naturalism. His works include sculptures for the Capitol in Washington.

KAUPERZ, Jakob Melchior
Austrian, 18th century.
Born 6 July 1744, in Graz; died 20 January 1795, in Graz.
Engraver.

Kauperz was the son of Johann Michael Kauperz, also an engraver. His works are rare.

KAUPERZ, Johann Veit
Austrian, 18th - 19th century.
Born 15 June 1741, in Graz; died 31 December 1816.
Painter, engraver (etching/burin).

Kauperz was a pupil of J.M. Schmutzer, later becoming a member of the academies of Vienna and Florence. He lived mainly in the latter city. He engraved historical, genre and religious subjects after G. Terbusch, Maulpertsch, D. Teniers, Kupetzky, Gerrit Dou and P. de Pomis. He was the brother of Jakob Melchior Kauperz and was represented at the exhibition on the subject of *Still Lesen* (*Silent Reading*) at the Residenzgalerie in Sazburg in 2001.

BIBLIOGRAPHY:
Leitner, Karin, *Johann Veit Kauperz (1741-1815)*, dissertation, University, Graz, 1998.

KAUPISCH, Leonard
German, 20th century.
Born 1 September 1878, in Bitterfeld.
Painter. Portraits, landscapes.

Leonard Kaupisch began painting as an amateur. In his landscapes he often painted winter effects.

KAUS, Max
German, 20th century.
Born 11 March 1891, in Berlin; died 5 August 1977, in Berlin.
Painter, watercolourist. Figures, scenes with figures, landscapes with figures, flowers.

Max Kaus was one of the generation of Expressionists in the 1910s. For this reason his works were banned and withdrawn from museums by the Nazis after 1933. Until then, and again after World War II, he exhibited regularly in Berlin. His preferred medium was watercolour. He often painted figures in landscapes and flowers.

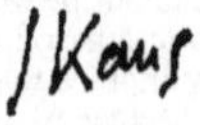

BIBLIOGRAPHY:
Schmitt-Wischmann, Ursula, *Max Kaus Werkverzeichnis der Gemälde*, catalogue raisonné, Nicolai, Berlin, 1990.

AUCTION RECORDS:
MUNICH, 28 May 1974, *Women Bathing on the Beach* (watercolour) DEM 4,800. MUNICH, 29 Nov 1976, *Seaside* (watercolour, 15 1/4 x 22 1/2 ins / 38.5 x 57.3 cm) DEM 1,600. COLOGNE, 21 May 1977, *Man with a Mirror* (1919, lithograph, 15 x 12 3/4 ins / 37.8 x 32.5 cm) DEM 2,200. COLOGNE, 5 Dec 1979, *Nude with Amaryllis* (1975, gouache, 30 x 21 1/4 ins / 76 x 53.7 cm) DEM 6,000. COLOGNE, 30 May 1981, *Town in Italy* (1956, oil on canvas, 35 1/2 x 29 1/4 ins / 90 x 74 cm) DEM 8,500. COLOGNE, 4 June 1983, *Two Women on the Beach* (1938, watercolour/chalk outlines, 21 x 26 3/4 ins / 52.5 x 68 cm) DEM 4,000. MUNICH, 25 Nov 1983, *Portrait of Mrs Valentiner* (1920, pencil, 22 3/4 x 17 ins / 58 x 43 cm) DEM 2,180. HAMBURG, 7 June 1985, *Nude on a Chaise Longue* (1921, watercolour/graphite outlines, 14 1/4 x 17 1/4 ins / 36.3 x 43.8 cm) DEM 17,000. MUNICH, 14 June 1985, *Self-portrait* (1919, woodcut in watercolour, 13 1/2 x 11 3/4 ins / 34 x 30 cm) DEM 3,400. HAMBURG, 9 June 1986, *Town in Italy* (1956, oil on canvas, 35 1/2 x 29 1/4 ins / 90 x 74 cm) DEM 14,500. COLOGNE, 10 Dec 1986, *Woman at her Mirror* (1975, Indian ink, 30 x 25 1/4 ins / 76 x 64 cm) DEM 2,800. MUNICH, 28 Oct 1987, *Head of a Woman* (1921, brush and Indian ink, 22 3/4 x 17 1/2 ins / 58 x 44.5 cm) DEM 5,500. MUNICH, 31 May 1990, *Sleeping Girl* (watercolour and charcoal, 14 1/4 x 17 1/4 ins / 36 x 44 cm) DEM 38,500. LONDON, 13 Oct 1994, *Sleeping Woman* (1932, ink/paper, 19 x 24 3/4 ins / 48 x 63 cm) GBP 4,025. NEW YORK, 24 Feb 1995, *Fishing Nets* (1932, oil on canvas, 28 x 39 1/2 ins / 71.1 x 100.3 cm) USD 16,675. HEIDELBERG, 8 April 1995, *Dune Landscape on Sylt* (1965, brown wash and noir, 25 1/4 x 30 ins / 64.4 x 76.3 cm) DEM 1,200. LONDON, 11 Oct 1995, *Breisach I* (black and brown lithograph/paper canvas, 19 1/4 x 23 1/4 ins / 48.8 x 59 cm) GBP 2,990. AMSTERDAM, 4 June 1996, *Women Bathing* (watercolour and pencil/paper, 20 1/2 x 26 3/4 ins / 52 x 68 cm) NLG 4,720. LONDON, 9 Oct 1996, *Sleeping Girl* (1930, lithograph, 18 1/2 x 22 1/2 ins / 47 x 57 cm) GBP 5,520. LONDON, 9 Oct 1997, *Back View of a Woman in Front of a Mirror* (1922, lithograph, 23 x 16 1/2 ins / 57.5 x 41.6 cm) GBP 1,495. BERLIN, 5 June 1999, *On the Elbe* (1926, watercolour heightened with white pencil, 17 x 25 ins / 44 x 63 cm) DEM 16,000. MUNICH, 30 Nov 1999, *Fish Pots* (1932, oil on canvas, 28 x 39 ins / 70 x 100 cm) DEM 20,000. HAMBURG, 9 June 2000, *Bathers* (c. 1946, tempera on canvas, 21 x 27 ins / 53 x 68 cm) DEM 12,000. LONDON, 17 Oct 2000, *Woman at Table I* (1931, oil on canvas, 35 x 29 ins / 90 x 74 cm) GBP 30,000. BERLIN, 30 Nov 2001, *Seated Figure at the Beach* (1923, watercolour over crayon, 17 x 13 ins / 42 x 32 cm) DEM 35,000. BERLIN, 1 Dec 2001, *Sand Mountains, in Middle Elbe* (1932, oil on canvas, 31 x 39 ins / 80 x 100 cm) DEM 20,000. BERLIN, 7 June 2002, *Coast at Hiddensoi* (1922, oil on canvas, 28 x 39 ins / 70 x 100 cm) EUR 35,000. BERLIN, 7 June 2002, *Walk* (1934, oil on canvas on cardboard, 39 x 31 ins / 100 x 80 cm) EUR 40,000. COLOGNE, 29 May 2003, *Women in Meadow* (oil on canvas, 45 x 35 ins / 115 x 90 cm) EUR 16,000. BERLIN, 29 Nov 2003, *Passau: Inn Shore II* (1928, oil on canvas on paper, 37 x 46 ins / 95 x 118 cm) EUR 15,000. BERLIN, 11 June 2004, *Reclining Lady* (1922, watercolour, ink and chalk, 18 x 25 ins / 46 x 63 cm) EUR 18,000. COLOGNE, 4 Dec 2004, *Tulips and Oranges* (1924, oil on panel, 23 x 20 ins / 58 x 50 cm) EUR 21,000.

KAUTH, Johann
German, 18th century.
Active in Düsseldorf c. 1789.
Miniaturist, draughtsman.

KAUTSCH, Heinrich
Austrian, 19th century.
Born 28 January 1859, in Prague.
Sculptor, medallist.
Kautsch, a pupil of Injalbert and Roubaud, won an honourable mention in 1897 and a silver medal in 1900 (outside the competition).
MUSEUMS AND GALLERIES:
SÈTE: *Bust of Jules Sandeau.*
AUCTION RECORDS:
PARIS, 25 June 1937, *Bust Portrait of the Artist,* FRF 95.

KAUTSKY, Franz
Moravian, 18th century.
Born 1705; died 6 October 1761, in Brno.
Painter.
One portrait by Franz Kautsky is known.

KAUTSKY, Johann
Bohemian School, 19th century.
Born 13 September 1827, in Prague; died 4 September 1896, in Vienna.
Painter. Hunting scenes, landscapes with figures.
Johann Kautsky studied at the academy in Prague, then with Schirmer in Düsseldorf. He was a painter at the royal theatre in Vienna. He exhibited in Vienna and Brussels, where he won a gold medal in 1888.
AUCTION RECORDS:
COLOGNE, 29 June 1984, *Hunters with a Pack of Hounds in a Wooded Landscape* (oil on panel, 14 1/2 x 19 ins / 37 x 48 cm) DEM 4,800.

KAUTZ, Amélie. See **LACÉPÈDE**

KAUTZHAMMER, Johann Philipp
German, 17th century.
Died c. 1647.
Active in Lübeck.
Engraver (wood).
Kautzhammer engraved a *Judgment of Solomon.*

KAUW, Albrecht, the Elder
School of Alsace, 17th century.
Born 1621, in Strasbourg; died 1681, in Bern.
Painter. Genre scenes, still-lifes.
Albrecht Kauw the Elder worked mainly in Bern, where he had already settled by 1640. He carried out a large number of decorations for public buildings in this town and for various châteaux.
MUSEUMS AND GALLERIES:
BERN: *Cavalry Combat in the 17th Century; Shipwreck; Brigands Attacking; Path to Happiness.*
AUCTION RECORDS:
BERN, 18 Nov 1966, *Still-life with Game and Huntsman,* CHF 20,000. ZURICH, 12 Nov 1976, *Still-life* (oil on canvas, 52 x 43 ins / 132 x 109 cm) CHF 19,000. BERN, 25 Oct 1986, *Still-life with Game, Pewter Dishes and Fruit* (1657, oil on canvas, 43 x 61 3/4 ins / 109 x 157 cm) CHF 60,000.

KAUW, Albrecht, the Younger
Swiss, 17th century.
Active in Basel.
Painter.
Kauw was the son of Albrecht Kauw the Elder. No works by him are known.

KAUW, Gabriel
Swiss, 17th century.
Baptised 14 September 1646 in Bern.
Painter.
Kauw was the son and pupil of Albrecht Kauw the Elder. He worked in Bern and painted mainly landscapes.

KAUZLARIC-ATTAC, Zlatko
Yugoslav, 20th century.
Born 30 June 1945, in Koprivnica (now in Croatia).
Painter. Scenes with figures.
School of Hlebine.
Zlatko Kauzlaric-Attac was the pupil of Miljenko Stancic at the academy of fine arts in Zagreb until 1968, but then went to work in the studio of Kristo Hegedusic, who initiated the Naive peasant painters group in Hlebine. He translates the everyday world through the astonished eyes of the child for whom reality can no longer be distinguished from the unreal. It is a deliberate naivety that might well stem from the teachings of Hegedusic. More Expressionist than Naive, however, his technique shows a knowledge of Goya and of Spanish artists in general. He has taken part in collective exhibitions in many towns of the former Yugoslavia, including Zagreb, where his work featured in the 1968 May festival, in 1970 at the third salon of young artists in Rijeka, Belgrade, as well as in Cairo, Florence and Poland. Venus for solo exhibitions include Koprivnica, 1969; Zagreb, 1970; Belgrade, Dubrovnik, Rijeka, Koprivnica, and Paris (where he lived for a while), 1971.
BIBLIOGRAPHY:
Waldberg, Patrick, *Kauzlaric-Attac,* exhibition catalogue, Gal. Lambert, Paris, 1971.

KAVALSKY, Alfred
Polish, 19th century.
Born 1849.
Painter.
Alfred Kavalsky taught at the academy in Munich. He painted snow scenes and picturesque scenes of Polish life.

KAVAN, Franta
Austrian, 20th century.
Active in Vienna in 1900.
Painter. Landscapes.
Franta Kavan received an honourable mention at the Paris Exposition Universelle in 1900.

KAVANAGH, Joseph F.
Irish, 20th century.
Born 24 September 1903, in Birr.
Sculptor, painter. Figures. Busts.
Joseph F. Kavanagh trained initially at Liverpool School of Art, in 1910 and 1921, and later at the Royal College of Art in London in 1925. He was a pupil of Henry Moore from 1925 to 1930, and studied in Italy from 1930 to 1933. Upon returning to England, he taught in Leeds until 1939. He was chiefly active as a sculptor of portraits.
MUSEUMS AND GALLERIES:
LONDON (Tate Collection): *Russian Peasant* (c. 1935-1939, bronze).

KAVANAGH, Joseph Malachy
Irish, 19th - 20th century.
Born 1856; died 1918.
Active in Dublin.
Painter. Religious subjects, landscapes.
Joseph Malachy Kavanagh exhibited at the Royal Academy in London and at the Paris Salon.
AUCTION RECORDS:
LONDON, 5 March 1976, *Landscape with Gypsy Encampment* (oil on canvas, 28 x 36 ins / 71 x 91.5 cm) GBP 850. CELBRIDGE, 29 May 1980, *Windmill beside a River* (oil on canvas, 10 x 13 1/2 ins / 25.6 x 34.2 cm) GBP 620. LONDON, 12 Nov 1987, *Landscape* (1903, oil on panel, 6 1/4 x 10 ins / 16 x 25.5 cm) GBP 1,800. LONDON, 16 May 1996, *Stream on the Outskirts of a Town* (1903, oil on card, 14 1/4 x 10 1/4 ins / 36 x 26 cm) GBP 1,725. NEW YORK, 18-19 July 1996, *Vision of St Dominic* (oil on canvas, 30 x 19 3/4 ins / 76.2 x 50.2 cm) USD 575. BILLINGSHURST, 29 April 1999, *Winding River Landscape with Cattle* (1893, oil on canvas, 13 x 9 ins / 32 x 22 cm) GBP 3,900. BELFAST, 6 Oct 1999, *Looking Out to Sea for the Return* (oil on

canvas, 30 x 20 ins / 76 x 51 cm) GBP 3,600. LEWES, 14 Feb 2000, *Sweet Watercress* (1906, oil on board, 12 x 16 ins / 30 x 41 cm) GBP 6,400. DUBLIN, 31 May 2000, *Carting Seaweed on Sutton Sands* (1895, oil on canvas, 28 x 36 ins / 71 x 91 cm) IEP 30,000. DUBLIN, 12 June 2001, *Gambling for a Goose* (oil on canvas, 20 x 30 ins / 51 x 76 cm) IEP 4,600. DUBLIN, 29 May 2002, *Poachers* (oil on canvas, a pair, 20 x 24 ins / 50 x 60 cm) EUR 20,000. DUBLIN, 24 Sept 2003, *In the Baskin Fields, Fingal* (1903, oil on board, 9 x 13 ins / 24 x 34 cm) EUR 5,200. DUBLIN, 25 Nov 2003, *Stately Elm, Rathfarnham Park* (1903, oil on panel, 14 x 10 ins / 35 x 25 cm) EUR 4,000. DUBLIN, 21 Sept 2004, *Old Dublin: Marrowbone Lane* (oil on canvas, 28 x 37 ins / 70 x 93 cm) EUR 22,000.

KAVANAGH, Marion. See **WACHTEL**

KAVEL, Martin. See **MARTIN-KAVEL François**

KAVLI, Arne Texnes

Norwegian, 20th century.

Born 27 May 1878, in Bergen; died 1970.

Painter, engraver, lithographer. Figures, portraits, scenes with figures, landscapes, still-lifes.

Arne Texnes Kavli studied first at technical college, then in Antwerp, and finally in Copenhagen in 1898, where he was taught by Krøyer and Tuxen. He stayed in Paris from 1900 to 1904, and the influence of the Parisian movements of the time can be seen in his early works. He had his first exhibition in Bergen in 1895. He rarely exhibited outside Norway, but showed in New York in 1912 and 1936, as well as in Paris and Brazil.

During his early youthful period, Kavli's works still had links with the Post-Romantic tradition. In around 1910, he began employing Impressionist and Fauvist techniques, with a more emphatic use of colour. Norwegian artistic circles are rediscovering the boldness of the decorative values of his works and consider him to be the link between French and Norwegian painting. His most striking paintings date from the 1920s, and are reminiscent of Dufy and Bonnard in their subject matter and colour.

MUSEUMS AND GALLERIES:

COPENHAGEN (Statens Mus. for Kunst): *Interior; Autumn Sun*.

AUCTION RECORDS:

LONDON, 25 March 1987, *A Seaside Café* (oil on canvas, 18½ x 24½ ins / 47 x 62 cm) GBP 4,800. LONDON, 23 March 1988, *Morning Conversation* (oil on canvas, 26 x 31¾ ins / 66 x 80.5 cm) GBP 8,800; *Still-life with Fruits on a Kitchen Table* (oil on canvas, 13½ x 17½ ins / 34 x 44.5 cm) GBP 7,700; *Garden Path* (1905, oil on canvas, 39¼ x 42½ ins / 99.5 x 108 cm) GBP 12,100. LONDON, 24 March 1988, *Seated Woman with an Orange Parasol* (1917, oil on canvas, 31½ x 31½ ins / 80 x 80 cm) GBP 13,200. LONDON, 16 March 1989, *Summer Afternoon* (oil on canvas, 36 x 38 ins / 91.5 x 96.5 cm) GBP 30,800. LONDON, 20 June 1989, *Summer Day* (oil on canvas, 48 x 43¼ ins / 121 x 110 cm) GBP 22,000. LONDON, 27-28 March 1990, *Terrace* (oil on canvas, 54¾ x 62½ ins / 139 x 159 cm) GBP 55,000. LONDON, 29 March 1990, *Circus Artist* (1915, oil on canvas, 18½ x 15¼ ins / 47 x 38.5 cm) GBP 33,000. LONDON, 6 June 1990, *Elegant Woman Seated at a Table* (1919, oil on canvas, 25½ x 30¼ ins / 65 x 77 cm) GBP 8,250. LONDON, 17 May 1991, *Fjord in Summer* (oil on canvas, 37 x 51¾ ins / 93.7 x 131.5 cm) GBP 15,400. LONDON, 19 June 1991, *Summer* (oil on canvas, 31 x 34¼ ins / 79 x 87 cm) GBP 38,500. STOCKHOLM, 21 May 1992, *Portrait of Johanne Heiberg* (oil on canvas, 26¾ x 22 ins / 68 x 55 cm) SEK 20,000. STOCKHOLM, 5 Sept 1992, *Still-life with a Salad Bowl, Jugs and Earthenware Cups* (oil on canvas, 21½ x 25½ ins / 54.5 x 65 cm) SEK 24,000. OSLO, 26 April 1999, *Woman on Garden Bench* (oil on canvas, 31 x 24 ins / 78 x 60 cm) NOK 220,000. OSLO, 25 Oct 1999, *Karl Johan's Street seen from Eger Square* (1930, oil on canvas, 44 x 44 ins / 111 x 111 cm) NOK 740,000. LONDON, 7 April 2000, *In the park* (oil on canvas, 34 x 29 ins / 86 x 74 cm) GBP 40,750. OSLO, 8 May 2000, *Apple Tree* (1928, oil on canvas, 46 x 70 ins / 117 x 177 cm) NOK 400,000. STOCKHOLM, 2 May 2001, *Summer in Fiskebackskil* (oil on canvas, 31 x 35 ins / 80 x 90 cm) SEK 420,000. OSLO, 27 Nov 2001, *Woman Seated on Garden Steps* (oil on canvas, 22 x 24 ins / 56 x 61 cm) NOK 215,000. OSLO, 18 March 2002, *Rain* (oil on canvas, 37 x 38 ins / 93 x 96 cm) NOK 130,000. OSLO, 17 June 2002, *Summer's Day in Fiskebackskil* (oil on canvas, 32 x 35 ins / 82 x 90 cm) NOK 450,000. OSLO, 26 May 2003, *On the Steps* (oil on canvas, 52 x 48 ins / 131 x 121 cm) NOK 250,000. OSLO, 26 May 2003, *Open Air Restaurant on the Pier and Sailing Boats* (1928, oil on canvas, 46 x 70 ins / 117 x 178 cm) NOK 300,000. OSLO, 25 May 2004, *Dronningen Restaurant by Oslo Fjord* (oil on canvas, 37 x 30 ins / 95 x 76 cm) NOK 300,000. OSLO, 25 May 2004, *Woman at Table* (1909, oil on canvas on panel, 27 x 26 ins / 68 x 67 cm) NOK 410,000.

KAVOLIN, Valentin

Russian, 20th century.

Born 1930; died 1978.

Painter. Nudes, landscapes with figures.

Valentin Kavolin completed his studies at the Repin institute in Leningrad (now St Petersburg) and worked under the direction of V. Orechnikov. He became a member of the union of Soviet artists and was awarded the title 'painter emeritus'.

MUSEUMS AND GALLERIES:

KIROVSK (MFA) - MOSCOW (Ministry of Culture) - OMSK (Mus. of Contemporary Soviet Art) - YAROSLAVL (Mus. of Russian Art).

AUCTION RECORDS:

PARIS, 25 Nov 1991, *Seated Nude* (1956, oil on canvas, 40¼ x 29½ ins / 102 x 75 cm) FRF 6,600. PARIS, 20 May 1992, *In Leningrad* (1959, oil on card, 27½ x 17 ins / 70 x 43 cm) FRF 6,500.

KAWA, Éliane

French, 20th century.

Born 12 May 1937, in Paris.

Painter.

Éliane Kawa studied at the École des Beaux-Arts in Paris from 1959. In 1968 she moved without transition from figurative to Abstract art, having discovered the evocative power of signs through Christian Byzantine iconography. She was later influenced by Paul Klee, without this leading to problems of incompatibility. She exhibited in Paris at the Salon d'Automne and the Salon des Indépendants from 1970. She also showed her work in solo exhibitions, including in Brussels in 1974 and Amsterdam in 1975.

KAWABATA, Gyokusho, pseudonyms: Keitei, Shoo

Japanese, 19th - 20th century.

Born 1842; died 1913.

Painter, draughtsman. Landscapes, animals, flowers.

Kawabata was a painter of the Shijo School and studied under Raisho Nakajima. He was a member of the Imperial Fine Art Committee and the Society of Japanese Art and taught at the Fine Art University in Tokyo. He won a silver medal at the Exposition Universelle of 1900 in Paris and showed work at the exhibition of Japanese art at the Musée du Jeu de Paume in Paris in 1922. He specialised in landscapes, flowers and birds.

AUCTION RECORDS:

NEW YORK, 17 Oct 1989, *Landscape* (ink/paper, kakemono, 68 x 35¾ ins / 172.5 x 91 cm) USD 1,870.

KAWABATA, Minoru
Japanese, 20th century.
Born 1911, in Tokyo.
Active in the USA from 1964.
Painter.

Kawabata graduated from the School of Fine Art in Tokyo in 1934 and studied in France and Italy from 1937 to 1939. He taught at the Tama School of Fine Art in Tokyo from 1950 to 1955, then at the New School for Social Research in New York from 1958-1961. He then returned to Japan but, in 1964, decided to settle in New York. His work is in the tradition of lyrical abstraction and is reminiscent of the work of Pierre Soulages. He showed work at the São Paulo Biennales of 1951, 1957 and 1959, receiving a prize in 1959. He also exhibited at the Salon de Mai of 1952 in Paris, at the Guggenheim National Exhibition in New York in 1958 and 1961 and at the Venice Biennale of 1962. He has had solo exhibitions in Tokyo, Milan and New York.

BIBLIOGRAPHY:
Beckh, Erika, '*Contemporary art in Japan*' in *College Art Journal,* vol 19, no. 1 (Autumn 1959).

MUSEUMS AND GALLERIES:
SÃO PAULO (MAM) - TOKYO (MMA).

AUCTION RECORDS:
NEW YORK, 27 April 1994, *Dark Oval* (oil on canvas, 63 3/4 x 51 1/2 ins / 162.2 x 130.5 cm) USD 27,600.

KAWABATA, Ryushi, real name: Shotaro Kawabata, pseudonym: Ryushi
Japanese, 20th century.
Born 1885, in Wakayama Prefecture; died 1966.
Painter.

Kawabata began his career by painting in a Western style, having gone to the USA in 1913 to finish his training. Back in Japan, he turned towards traditional Japanese painting. In 1917, he became a member of the Japanese Academy of Fine Art, leaving it in 1928 to found his own group, Seiryusha (the Blue Dragon Association). In 1959 he was awarded the Culture Medal. The decorative aspects of his fluid, dynamic style are reminiscent of the 17th- to 18th-century painter Korin.

BIBLIOGRAPHY:
Yamada, Chisaburo, '*Japanese Modern Art: Part II*' in *Monumenta Nipponica,* vol 5, no. 2 (July 1942). Beckh, Erika, '*Contemporary art in Japan*' in *College Art Journal,* vol 19, no. 1 (Autumn 1959).

KAWABE, Seiran
Japanese, 19th - 20th century.
Painter (including silk). Genre scenes.

Kawabe lived and worked in Osaka. In 1900 she exhibited work at the Univeral Exhibition in Paris.

KAWAFUNE, Misao
Japanese, 20th century.
Painter.

In 1929, Kawafune's work was shown at the exhibition of Japanese art at the Musée du Jeu de Paume in Paris.

KAWAGUCHI, Masahiro
Japanese, 20th century.
Born 1936.
Sculptor.
Op Art.

In 1973 Kawaguchi's work was shown at the 5th Exhibition of Contemporary Japanese Sculpture in Ube and, in 1974, at the *Japanese Art Today* exhibition at the Montreal museum of contemporary art.

KAWAGUCHI, Tatsuo
Japanese, 20th century.
Born 1940, in Kobe.
Painter, sculptor of assemblages. Multimedia.
Conceptual Art.

Kawaguchi studied at the Tama School of Fine Art in Tokyo, graduating in 1962. He teaches at the University of Akashi. Kawaguchi's interest in conceptual art appeared early in his career. Since then, he has used the new media of light, video, photography and film. He creates assemblages of markers arranged in a space, some of which can be electronically stimulated. Interested in making his art available outside normal gallery and museum spaces, he has produced two works for Japanese high schools: *Relation-Circle/Departure* (1987) and *Sun Circle* (1989).

His work was included in the 1965 and 1966 shows by Group I, of which he was a member, the 10th Tokyo Biennale of 1970, the 1st Kyoto Biennale of 1972, the 3rd Paris Biennale of 1973 and the *Japanese Art Today* exhibition at the Montreal museum of contemporary art in 1974. He has also had several solo exhibitions in Japan since his first in Osaka in 1962. In 1968 and 1973 he won the JAFA prize.

BIBLIOGRAPHY:
Kawaguchi, Tatsuo, '*Kawaguchi Tatsuo fuinsareta jikan*' in *Mito-shi: Mito Geijutsukan Gendai Bijutsu Senta,* 1998.

KAWAI, Gyokudo, real name: Yoshisaburo Kawai, pseudonyms: Gyokushu, Gyokudo
Japanese, 19th - 20th century.
Born 1873, in Eichi Prefecture; died 1957.
Painter. Figure compositions, landscapes with figures.

Kawai studied under Gyokusen Mochizuki and Barei Kono. He later went to Tokyo to study under Gaho Hashimoto. He regularly exhibited work at the Bunten exhibition, for which he was a member of the selection committee. In 1929 he showed work at the exhibition of Japanese art at the Musée du Jeu de Paume in Paris. He taught at the Tokyo School of Fine Art, was an attaché of the Imperial Fine Arts Committee and a member of the Imperial Academy of Art. In 1940, he was awarded the Order of Cultural Merit and the *Asahi* Culture Prize.

BIBLIOGRAPHY:
Shin'ichi Nagai, Sentaro Namba, *Kanzan Shimomura, Gyokudo Kawai,* Shueisha, Tokyo, 1976.

AUCTION RECORDS:
NEW YORK, 16 Oct 1990, *Fisherman under a Tree in Summer* (ink and pigments/silk, 50 x 19 3/4 ins / 127 x 50.4 cm) USD 38,500. NEW YORK, 16 Oct 1990, *Woodcutters in an Autumn Landscape* (ink and pigments/paper, 17 1/2 x 21 1/2 ins / 44.3 x 54.6 cm) USD 82,500.

KAWAI, Koji
Japanese, 20th - 21st century.
Born 1947.
Painter.

In 1974 Kawai exhibited at the *Japanese Art Today* exhibition at the Montreal museum of contemporary art. In the same year he had his first solo exhibition in Tokyo. He works in acrylics, creating clearly outlined patches of colour on a plain ground.

KAWAI, Shinzo
Japanese, 19th - 20th century.
Painter. Landscapes.

Kawai exhibited at the Exposition Universelle in Paris in 1900.

AUCTION RECORDS:
LONDON, 29 April 1977, *Tokyo Street; Painting* (oil on canvas, 35 x 63 ins / 89 x 160 cm) GBP 3,000.

KAWAI, Shivsaï
Japanese, 19th - 20th century.
Painter. Animals.

Kawai was an exponent of the traditional technique of painting on silk. He exhibited at the Exposition Universelle in Paris in 1900.

KAWAKAMI, Sumio
Japanese, 20th century.
Born 1895, in Yokohama; died 1972.
Engraver (wood), illustrator, painter, glass painter.
Figures, urban landscapes, still-lifes.
First Thursday Society.

Kawakami had no formal training as an artist and always regarded himself as an amateur. However, he attended the studo of the engraver Kiyoshi Goda (1862-1938). At this time, young Japanese people tended to be drawn to Europe, however in 1917 Kawakami set off for Canada and Alaska, where he worked first as a sign-painter and then in a fish-canning factory. On his return to Japan, he tried to live by his painting in Tokyo, but bowed to his family's insistence that he should get a 'proper' job and became a primary school teacher in the country town of Tsuruda from 1921-1945. After this, he taught English in a school in Tochigi Prefecture. Kawakami had an independent nature and remained outside Tokyo society, having little contact with the post-war avant-garde movements and the world of art. His isolation did not prevent him painting or writing and illustrating his own poems. Throughout this period, and despite his absolute refusal to sell his works, which he preferred to give as presents to friends and students, he illustrated at least 40 collections of his own poems and short stories. He did not become a professional artist until 1958, when he was 63 years old. Nevertheless his early works had already influenced some of his contemporaries, notably Shiko Munakata (born 1903), who became the best-known Japanese engraver of his day.

From 1920 onwards Kawakami's art was characterised by his total devotion to painting subjects and objects that were foreign to the Japanese tradition, such as men with red beards, half-length portraits of women, clocks and watches, lamps, leather-bound books and pipes. All were manifestations of the exoticism that had fascinated the Japanese since the 16th century, when the first Portugese and Dutch traders arrived. Influenced by the Sosaku Hangan movement, he joined the Nihon Sosaku Hanga Kyokai (Creative Japanese Prints Association). After the great earthquake of 1923, Kawakami, Unichi Hiratsuka and Koshiro Onchi (died 1955) published an important series of prints entitled *100 Views of the New Tokyo*. While his contemporaries turned to social and proletarian subjects, Kawakami concentrated on the Meiji period (1868-1912) and *Namban* art (Japanese Christian art). At this time, he was painting glass-pictures. He joined the First Thursday Society, founded by Koshiro Onchi. From 1942 to 1944, Kawakami published 21 collections of prints and texts, whch he engraved himself character by character on separate wood blocks, in order to give a heightened sense of the simultaneity of text and image. The first of these books, *Namban Sen-ki* (*Documents on the Christian Ships*) was published in 1942, followed in 1943 by *Documents on the Arrival of Tobacco* and in 1944 by *Images of the Southern Barbarians, Christian Buddhas* and a series of views for magic lantern. Nothing in any of these works suggests that the country was in the midst of an international war at the time they were made.

However, Kawakami was exhausted by the privations of the time and by this intense creativity. He had to leave Tsuruda on a freight train, moving to a small village on Hokkaido, the northernmost island of the Japanese archipelago, in order to escape the difficulties of defeat. It was there that he and the poet Genzo Sarashina (born 1904) became interested in the *Mingei* (traditional craft) movement, to which Kawakami gave great support. In 1949 he returned to his teaching post and worked with Shiko Munakata and Shoji Hamada (born 1895), the famous ceramicist known as the 'Living National Treasure'. The town of Kanuma in Togichi Prefecture has opened a Sumio Kawakami Museum of Engraving entirely devoted to his work.

When finally recognised as one of the most important and original figures of Japanese art, Kawakami found himself the subject of many exhibitions and was awarded official honours. In 2002 he was represented in the exhibition *Japanese Prints during the Allied Occupation, 1945-1952* at the British Museum in London.

BIBLIOGRAPHY:
Sumio, Kawakami, '*Hanga*' in *Toho Shoin, Showa 34*, 1959. Read, Louisa, '*Kawakami, a Modern Print-Maker*' in *Apollo* n° 157, periodical, London, March, 1975. Merritt, Helen/Yamada, Nanako, *Guide to Modern Japanese Woodblack Prints: 1900-1975*, University of Hawaï Press, Honolulu, 1992. Smith, Lawrence, *Japanese Prints during the Allied Occupation, 1945-1952: Onchi Kôshirô, Ernst Hacker and the First Thursday Society*, The British Museum Press, London, 2002.

MUSEUMS AND GALLERIES:
KANUMA (Kawakami Sumio Mus. of Engravings): important collection of works.

KAWAKITA, Kaho
Japanese, 20th century.
Born 1875; died 1940.
Painter.

Kawakita's work was shown at the exhibition of Japanese art at the Musée du Jeu de Paume in Paris in 1929.

KAWAKITA, Michisuke
Japanese, 19th century.
Born 1850; died 1907.
Painter.

Kawakita was a Western-style painter who studied under Kan Kawakami (1827-1881) and worked in Tokyo. After travelling in Europe, he studied in Paris and, in 1900, was a member of the selection committee for the Exposition Universelle. He later taught at the Japanese Martial Arts Academy.

KAWAKUBO, Masana
Japanese, 20th century.
Active in Tokyo in 1900.
Painter.

Kawakubo exhibited at the Exposition Universelle in Paris in 1900.

KAWALEROWICZ, Marzena
Polish, 20th - 21st century.
Born 1952.
Draughtswoman. Figures.

Marzena Kawalerowicz graduated from the school of fine arts in Warsaw. As if obsessed with the subject, she draws mysterious blind beings who have no mouth, no nose, a single ear. They are extended by columns of smoke, billowing drapes. The faces, their integrity wounded, their eyes bloodred, are timeless. She has taken part in collective exhibitions in Random, Sopot, Copenhagen and Warsaw. Solo exhibitions have been held regularly in Warsaw from 1978; in Lódz, Cracow and Pozna in 1979; at the Galerie Jean-Pierre Lavignes, Paris, in 1980.

BIBLIOGRAPHY:
Kawalerowicz, exhibition catalogue, Gal. Jean-Pierre Lavignes, Paris, 1980.

KAWAMATA, Tadashi
Japanese, 20th - 21st century.
Born 1953, on Hokkaido Island.
Installation artist, environmental artist.

Kawamata graduated from the painting section of the Tokyo University of Fine Art in 1979. In addition to his main activity in Japan, his work is often seen abroad. In 1982 his work was shown at the Venice Biennale, in 1984 at the exhibition *Ex-*

change of Contemporary Art, Tokyo-Paris in Paris and in 1987 at the 8th Documenta in Kassel with *Destroyed Church*. Also in 1987, he was invited to work in France for three months, making installations for the Vieille Charité Centre in Marseilles in the context of the *Japan Living Art* event, and at the École supérieure d'art in Grenoble. He has made numerous pieces in the USA and Europe, notably for the Courtrai Beguinage in 1989-1990 and *Transfert* for the Centre de Création Contemporaine (CCC) in Tours. He made pieces for the CCC and the Calder studio in Saché in 1994, for the St Louis Chapel of the Hôpital La Salpétrière in Paris in 1997 and for *Skulptur. Projekte in Münster 1997* (*Sculpture. Projects in Münster 1997*).

From 1997, he and his assistants created site-specific installations for spaces that he selected or had been offered on demolition and construction sites, surrounding them with tightly spaced, recycled planks and beams, with which he made ephemeral structures. These are like frames open to the air and light and to the external space, part of which they also contain. He also erected huts and alleyways in traditional exhibition spaces or public places. His piece at the St Louis chapel at the Salpétrière in Paris consisted of a tower made from hundreds of church chairs. With these ephemeral constructions that alter the pre-existing space, he invites reflection on the cultural contrast between the style of the setting and his own unstable constructions.

BIBLIOGRAPHY:

L'Art Moderne à Marseille. La Collection du Musée Cantini, exhibition catalogue, Musée Cantini, Marseilles, 1988. Kawamata, Tadashi, *Projects 1982-1990: 3 May-19 May 1990, installation at Annely Juda Fine Art, London*, Annely Juda Fine Art, Kerber Verlag, London, Bielefeld, 1990, 2003. Gould, Claudia/Bois, Yue-Alain/Kawamata, Tadashi, *Kawamata Project on Roosevelt Island*, Princeton Architectural Press, New York, 1993. Kawamata, Tadashi, *Relocation*, Annely Juda Fine Art, London, 1997. Kawamata, Tadashi, *Tadashi Kawamata bridge and archives*, Kerber Verlag, Bielefeld, 2003 (photos by Leo van der Kleij).

MUSEUMS AND GALLERIES:

MARSEILLES (Mus. Cantini): *Untitled* (1987, collage/wood) - ORLÉANS (FRAC Centre).

KAWAMATA, Tsunemasa
Japanese, 18th century.
Born 1720; died 1750.
Active in Kyoto.
Painter.

Kawamata studied under Tsuneyuki Kawamata (b. 1677, d. after 1741) and painted pretty women in genre scenes, often in studied poses, with a perspective reminiscent of the older painted scrolls of *yamato-e*.

KAWAMATA, Tsuneyuki
Japanese, 17th - 18th century.
Born 1677, in Edo, now Tokyo; died after 1741.
Painter.

Kawamata specialised in genre scenes with pretty women. His *1740s Male Prostitute Leaving a Brothel* (Gitter-Yelen Collection) provides an interesting twist on the 'pretty women' theme. The figure is dressed entirely as a woman and identifiable as a man only by the title, adding another layer of ambiguity to the 'floating world'.

KAWAMURA, Chiaki
Japanese, 20th century.
Sculptor.

In 1972 Kawamura showed work at the Second JAFA exhibition and, in 1974, at the *Japanese Art Today* exhibition at the Montreal museum of contemporary art.

KAWAMURA, Kiyo-o
Japanese, 19th - 20th century.
Born 1852, in Tokyo; died 1934, in Tokyo.
Painter.

Kawamura studied under Kan Kawakami. He travelled in Europe and studied at the Venice School of Art. Although he never exhibited his work, he was extremely well known during his own lifetime.

MUSEUMS AND GALLERIES:

KYOTO (Municipal Mus. of Art) - TOKYO (National Mus.) - TOKYO (SFA).

KAWAMURA, Kogai
Japanese, 20th century.
Painter.

Kawamura's work was shown at the exhibition of Japanese art at the Musée du Jeu de Paume in Paris in 1929.

KAWAMURA, Manshu
Japanese, 20th century.
Born 1880; died 1942.
Painter.

Kawamura exhibited at the Exhibition of Japanese Art at the Jeu de Paume Museum in Paris in 1929.

KAWAMURA, Naoko
Japanese, 20th century.
Born 1932, in Tokyo.
Painter.

Kawamura has participated in collective exhibitions, including the Fifth International Exhibition of Young Artists in Tokyo in 1969 and the Ninth Exhibition of Contemporary Japanese Art.

KAWANARI, real name: Kawanari Aguri, original forename: Kudara no Kawanari
Japanese, 9th century.
Born 782; died 853.
Painter.

Kawanari is sometimes said to have been of Korean origin. He was painter to the Imperial court, an officer in the Imperial guard and is one of the great painters of the Heian period (794-1184) in Japan. He is known for the extraordinary realism of his work.

KAWANISHI, Hide
Japanese, 20th century.
Born 1894, in Kobe; died 1965.
Engraver. Landscapes.
First Thursday Society.

Kawanishi was born into a rich family of merchants and shipowners. In 1914 he graduated from the Commercial College in Kobe and devoted himself to wood engraving, whose techniques he had been learning since childhood, taking a correspondence course in art. He took over the management of a private post office owned by his family, becoming an employee of the Japanese post office when it was nationalised. He won the prize at the National Academy of Painting (Kokugakai) in 1929, the Hyogo Prefecture Culture Prize in 1949 and the Kobe Shinbun Peace Prize in 1962.

His favourite subjects were views of gardens and Japanese houses, particularly those of his native city of Kobe. Examples can be seen in his series *Scenes of Kobe Across 12 Months* (1931) and *100 Views of Kobe* (1961). He worked with a round tool and his style is distinguished by a harmonious arrangement of brilliant colours and simple composition skilfully combining decorative and realistic elements, without black outlines. He was a member of the First Thursday Society led by Koshiro Onchi.

In 2002 Kawanishi was included in the *Japanese Prints during the Allied Occupation, 1945-1952* exhibition, presenting the members of the First Thursday Society and the Sosaku Hanga movement at the British Museum in London.

BIBLIOGRAPHY:
Koshiro, Onchi, *Shikashû Anthology of Contemporary Japan: Nohon no Hana Flowers of Japan*, Hongakusha, Tokyo, Shôwa 21 (1946). Merritt, Helen, *Modern Japanese Woodblock Prints: The Early Years*, University of Hawaii Press, Honolulu, 1990. Smith, Lawrence, *Japanese Prints during the Allied Occupation, 1945-1952: Onchi Kôshirô, Ernst Hacker et la Société du Premier Jeudi*, exhibition catalogue, The British Museum Press, London, 2002.

KAWANISHI, Yuzaburo
Japanese, 20th century.
Born 1923, in Kobe.
Engraver. Urban landscapes.

Kawanishi studied political economy in Tokyo before turning to wood engraving. In 1912 his works were selected by the Ministry of Education and the Japanese Print Association, of which he became a member. In 1947 he received the prize of the National Academy of Painting (Kokugakai). His views of the little town of Kurashiki made him well-known. His realism is tempered by a highly decorative approach, which never becomes mannered.

KAWANO, Kaoru
Japanese, 20th century.
Born 1916, on Hokkaido Island; died 1965.
Engraver.

From 1934, Kawano studied at the Kawabata School of Fine Art in Tokyo. In 1944, his works were selected by the Japanese Print Association. From 1944 to 1949 his artistic activity was interrupted when he was deported to Siberia as a prisoner. His style is figurative and his compositions are enhanced by impasto with various substances. From 1952, he exhibited at the National Academy of Painting, winning the Academy's prize in 1954. From 1959 he participated in international collective exhibitions and had several solo exhibitions in the USA.

KAWARA, On
Japanese, 20th century.
Born 1933, in Kariya (Aichi).
Active in the USA from c. 1962.
Painter, collage artist. Multimedia.
Conceptual Art, Mail Art.

Kawara is a self-taught artist. After painting his early works in Japan, he emigrated to the USA in the early 1960s. His first works from the 1950s express a desire to exploit the grotesque, as in the swollen female torsoes surrounded by scattered, apparently floating limbs of the *Bathrooms* and *Storerooms* of 1953-1954. Such works define and describe spaces, places and situations that reflect the existentialist tendencies of the Japanese artistic currents of the day, still affected by the apocalyptic outcome of the war. Kawara was highly sceptical about the social role of art and was interested in using the mass media. After this time his work became more conceptual with *Rulers* of 1964, showing graduated rulers drawn in perspective, the *Location Paintings* of 1965, giving the latitude and longitude of particular places, and the *Codes*, which simulate linguistic characters. On 4 January 1966 he began the *Today* series, consisting of 'date paintings', After his first approach to the media, using directly printed text, Kawama created a series of pictures composed entirely of letters and figures, painted in white on a monochrome ground in the local language, often simply indicating the date and time, confirmed by a fragment from a local newspaper. He painted over 1700 date paintings, which are divided into sub-groups. The sub-group *Read* begins in 1966 and consists of newspaper cuttings. *Met* begins in 1968 and consists of typed notes mentioning people the artist has met. *Went* retraces his movements on maps of the local area. At the time of his series of postcards (*I Got up at...*) and telegrams (*I Am Still Alive*), Kawama was the best-known exponent of Mail Art, in which he expressed himself through messages sent by post to a comparatively restricted audience. However, in the 1970s Mail Art became a real movement, to the point where an entire section was devoted to it at the Paris Biennale of 1971. Kawara was living in New York at the time and had a certain influence over local and western European artistic circles through this speciality. He would manifest his presence in particular places for a given period, often a month, by sending a postcard or a telegramme to his chosen correspondents. All his graphic activity was based around the notion of where and when he was in a particular place, what was happening there - the more insignificant the better - how long he stayed there and so on. All this information was preserved and confirmed in different ways, whose unity arose out of their multiplicity, which could not be synthesised in words. The main aim of the messages was identification: they mentioned what time he got up, what he had had to eat or simply confirmed that he was still alive, but only at the time the message was sent. Of a different order, but still based on an expression of the relativity of time and all other phenomena, particularly art, in 1970-1971 Kawara composed *One Million Years: Past* and, in 1980, *One Million Years: Future*, representing a million years in 10 books of typescript.

The evident derision of all his approaches denotes the malaise expressed by a number of artists from about 1968 onwards. This malaise was inherent to the position of the artist, ill-defined in a society whose values they challenged and which actions of this kind only served to render more confused. What is peculiar to Kawara is perhaps the great care he took over the material and graphic execution of this evidence of his geographical, physical and mental wanderings. It is through this that, as though in parenthesis, these documents acquire their status as works and become transferable. By voluntarily confining his activity to this almost maniacal updating, and in the ostentatious modesty of his expression, which was, however, ratified by the market and artistic circles, Kawara sought to prove the relativity of all positions and thus all artistic discourse, by reducing them to the absurd.

Since 1963, he has shown his work in collective exhibitions of conceptual art throughout the world. These have included *Conceptual Art and Conceptual Aspects* in Seattle in 1969, the *Conception Exhibition* at the Staedtisches Museum in Leverkusen in 1970, the Paris Biennale of 1971, *Painting on the Move*, presenting a century of contemporary painting, staged simultaneously at the Kunstmuseum, the Kunsthalle and the Museum für Gegenwarskunst in Basel in 2002, *Les années 70: l'art en cause* (*The 1970s: Art in Question*) at the CAPC Musée d'Art Contemporain in Bordeaux, 2002 and *Un tableau dans le décor. Peintures 1970-2000* (*A Painting in the Décor: Paintings 1970-2000*) an exhibition marking the 20th anniversary of FRAC at the Château des Ducs de Bretagne in Nantes, France. Solo exhibitions of Kawara's work have been held at the Bern Kunstalle in 1973, the Moderna Museet in Stockholm, the Folkwang Museum in Essen and the Van Abbe Museum in Eindhoven in 1980-1981, the Dijon Consortium in 1985 and 1990, the Nouveau Musée in Villeurbanne in 1996 and the Centre d'Art Contemporain in Geneva in 2003.

BIBLIOGRAPHY:
Denizot, René, *Les Images quotidiennes du pouvoir, On Kawara au jour le jour*, Yvon Lambert, Paris, 1979. *On Kawara: Continuity/Discontinuity, 1963-1979*, exhibition catalogue, Moderna Museet, Stockholm, 1980. *On Kawara*, exhibition catalogue, Le Coin du miroir, Dijon, 1986. Pagé, Suzanne, *L'Art conceptuel, une perspective*, exhibition catalogue, Musée d'Art moderne de la Ville de Paris, Paris, 1989-1990 (extensive documentation). Denizot, René, *On Kawara*, exhibition catalogue, Museum für Moderne Kunst, Frank-

furt am Main, 1991. *On Kawara: Whole and Parts*, Les presses du réel, Paris, 1996. *On Kawara: Horizontality/Verticality*, exhibition catalogue, Städtische Galerie im Lenbachhaus, Munich, 2000. Mendes Bürgi, Bernhard, et al., *Painting on the Move*, exhibition catalogue, Kunstmuseum, Kunsthalle, Museum für Gegenwartskunst, Basel, 2002. Watkins, Jonathan, *On Kawara*, Phaidon, London, 2002. Fréruchet, Maurice, et al., *Les Années soixante-dix: l'art en cause*, exhibition catalogue, Capc musée d'Art contemporain, Bordeaux, 2002. Gilbran, Khalil/Adachi, Ikuro, et al., *On Kawara: Consciousness. Meditation. Watcher on the hills*, catalogue raisonné, Presses du réel, Paris, 2003.

MUSEUMS AND GALLERIES:

BORDEAUX (FRAC Aquitaine): *Feb 6, 1982* (1982) - DUNKIRK (FRAC Nord-Pas de Calais): *Dec 8* (1994); *Dec 9, 1994* - LOS ANGELES (MCA) - STUTTGART (Staatsgal.): *Date Pictures* (1966).

AUCTION RECORDS:

LONDON, 5 Dec 1978, *Apr 5* (1966, Liquitex/canvas, 8 x 10 ins / 20.5 x 25.5 cm) GBP 1,700. PARIS, 20 Jan 1991, *Dec 30 1988* (acrylic/canvas and cardboard box designed to hold daily newspaper cuttings, 8 x 10 1/4 ins / 20.5 x 26 cm) FRF 240,000. NEW YORK, 13 Nov 1991, *I Got up at...* (mounted postcards from Tokyo with text on the back, each card 4 x 5 3/4 ins / 10.3 x 14.5 cm) USD 15,400. NEW YORK, 14 Nov 1991, *June 2, 1971* (Liquitex/canvas, 10 1/4 x 13 ins / 26 x 33 cm) USD 35,750. PARIS, 23 March 1992, *I Got up at...* (12 mounted postcards addressed to Dan Graham in New York between 5 June 1968 and 11 March 1969) FRF 53,000. LONDON, 26 March 1992, *Sept 6, 1978* (Liquitex/canvas, 17 3/4 x 24 1/2 ins / 45 x 62 cm) GBP 22,000. NEW YORK, 7 May 1992, *I Got up at...* (1973, 20 mounted postcards from Nova Scotia with text on the back, each 3 1/2 x 5 1/2 ins / 8.9 x 14 cm) USD 16,500. NEW YORK, 24 Feb 1993, *8 Oct 1976* (acrylic/canvas, 10 1/2 x 13 ins / 26.4 x 33 cm) USD 24,200. NEW YORK, 10 Nov 1993, *13 July 1977* (acrylic/canvas, 10 1/4 x 13 ins / 26 x 33.3 cm) USD 25,300. FRANKFURT AM MAIN, 14 June 1994, *26 Aug 1993 and Box* (acrylic/canvas, 8 x 10 ins / 20.5 x 25.5 cm) DEM 40,000. LONDON, 26 June 1997, *2 Dec 1976* (1976, acrylic/canvas, 10 x 13 ins / 25.3 x 33 cm) GBP 27,600. NEW YORK, 17 Nov 1999, *December 17, 1989 Today Series* (liquitex on canvas/cardboard box with newspaper clipping, 8 x 10 ins / 20 x 25 cm) USD 20,000. NEW YORK, 17 Nov 1999, *Feb 17 1982 Today Series* (liquitex on canvas/cardboard box with newspaper clipping, 13 x 17 ins / 33 x 44 cm) USD 26,000. NEW YORK, 17 May 2000, *Apr.22. 1967 - Today Series* (liquitex on canvas/cardboard box with newspaper collage, 10 x 13 ins / 25 x 33 cm) USD 95,000. NEW YORK, 18 May 2000, *Tuesday Aug 12 1975* (liquitex on canvas with newspaper and cardboard, 10 x 13 ins / 26 x 33 cm) USD 32,000. NEW YORK, 16 May 2001, *Feb. 27, 1987* (liquitex and newspaper on cardboard box, 52 x 76 ins / 133 x 194 cm) USD 140,000. NEW YORK, 16 Nov 2001, *I Got Up* (1969-1977, 72 mailed postcards) USD 38,000. NEW YORK, 15 May 2002, *Wednesday 20 Oct 1974* (liquitex on canvas/cardboard box with newspaper clipping, 8 x 10 ins / 20 x 25 cm) USD 28,000. NEW YORK, 13 Nov 2002, *July 12-18 1998 - Today Series Nos. 18-24* (8 x 10 ins / 20 x 25 cm) USD 260,000. NEW YORK, 14 Nov 2003, *Monday Sept 6 1999 - Today Series No.34* (liquitex on canvas/cardboard box with newspaper clipping, 13 x 17 ins / 34 x 44 cm) USD 38,000. NEW YORK, 14 May 2004, *Thursday November 19, 1981, Today Series no 43* (liquitex on canvas/cardboard box with newspaper clipping, 13 x 17 ins / 33 x 43 cm) USD 56,000.

KAWARABAYASHI, Mutsuo

Japanese, 20th century.
Born 1934, in Fukuoka Prefecture.
Sculptor.

Mutsuo Kawarabayashi's works are abstract, tending towards the geometrical. They have been shown in many international exhibitions, including the 1967 Young Artists' Biennale in Paris, the *Manifestation (Demonstration)* exhibition of 1968 in Fontainebleau, the Paris exhibition of New Realities and the Kyoto exhibition of *Trends in Contemporary Japanese Art* in 1969.

KAWASAKI, Shoko or Shako

Japanese, 20th century.
Born 1886, in Gifu; died 1977, in Tokyo.
Painter. Landscapes with figures.

Kawasaki came from a family of artists and writers. In 1905, he entered the School of Fine Art in Tokyo, where he was in the same year as Fujita. Several of his works were bought by the state, including *Deserted Landscape: A Squirrel in the Autumn Wood*. As their titles suggest, his works express his feeling for nature. He showed work at the official national and Ministry of Education exhibitions, becoming a panel judge for the latter in 1927. In 1929, his work was shown at the exhibition of Japanese art at the Musée du Jeu de Paume in Paris. In 1934 he was appointed professor at the School of Fine Art in Tokyo. In 1940, he sent *Life on the Marshes* to the Universal Exhibition in New York. In 1961, he received the Geijutsuin prize. From 1968 to 1973 he exhibited in Tokyo, Nagoya and Osaka. For his 88th birthday in 1974, a large exhibition of his work was mounted in Tokyo, during which he died of pneumonia. In 1978 a retrospective was held at the Yamatane Museum.

KAWASHIMA, Riichiro

Japanese, 20th century.
Born 1886, in Tochigi Prefecture; died 1971.
Also active in France.
Painter.

Kawashima studied in the USA, where he graduated from the Corcoran School of Art in Washington in 1910. He then moved to Paris until 1919 and exhibited there at the Independents Salon from 1921. In 1919 he had gone back to Japan, where he became one of the founders of Kokugakai and a member of the Nihon Bijutsu-in. He also taught at the Women's School of Fine Art in Tokyo. His painting was strongly influenced by the post-Cézannism widespread in the Paris School in the early 20th century.

AUCTION RECORDS:

NEW YORK, 12 Oct 1989, *Beautiful Philippino Girl* (oil on panel, 11 x 8 1/2 ins / 27 x 21.5 cm) USD 8,800.

KAWASHIMA, Takeshi

Japanese, 20th century.
Born 1930, in Takamatsu (Kagawa).
Active in the USA from 1963.
Painter.

Kawashima graduated from the School of Fine Art in Musashino near Tokyo in 1956. In 1963 he moved to New York. He is an abstract artist who works with the repetition and juxtaposition of well-constructed forms in squares. From 1958, he participated in a number of collective exhibitions and showed collections of his works in solo exhibitions in Tokyo and the USA.

MUSEUMS AND GALLERIES:

NEW YORK (MoMA) - TOKYO (Kyobashi Mus. of Modern Art).

AUCTION RECORDS:

NEW YORK, 24 Feb 1994, *New York - M.33* (1966, oil on canvas, 68 x 68 ins / 172.7 x 172.7 cm) USD 6,038.

KAWAUCHI, Kigai

Japanese, 20th century.
Born in Wakayama-ken.
Painter.

Kigai Kawauchi exhibited in Paris.

KAWECKI, Roman

Polish, 19th - 20th century.
Born 9 August 1870.
Painter.

Roman Kawecki studied art in Cracow and was later a pupil of Henri Morisset in Paris.

KAWENBERG, Aegidius and Christian.
See **COUWENBERG**

KAWERAN, Johanna
German, 19th century.
Active in Berlin.
Portrait artist.

Kaweran exhibited in Berlin and Munich, first exhibiting c. 1878.

KAWIAK, Tomek
Polish, 20th century.
Born 1943.
Active in France from 1971, naturalised French 1976.
Sculptor, painter, draughtsman.

Tomek Kawiak graduated from the Warsaw academy of fine arts in 1968. From 1971 to 1973, he studied sculpture at the École des Beaux-Arts in Paris, graduating in 1983, and then in César's studio. He was granted French nationality in 1976 and since 1977 he has taught at the École des Beaux-Arts in Orléans. His sculptures, generally monumental in size, carefully prepared and complemented with paintings and drawings, are in wood, pottery and, of preference, use both marble and bronze. In around 1984, he completed his bronze *Packs of Strings* then, again in bronze, earthenware, bundles of wood, a number of *Bags of Bricks*. After the bag, his emblematic theme became the pocket - jeans pockets or the pocket in the door of a car (Mercedes) - not an object in itself, but rather a receptacle as much as an empty space. He fills these voids with all kinds of bric-a-brac, reinterpreted on a majestic scale, which can be crammed into pockets. By defining the contents of a pocket, the identity of the person wearing the jeans can also be identified. Kawiak's sculptures also act as a mirror for the everyday things we all share, although his treatment of them imbue them with a mythology all of their own. Collective exhibitions have included *Art Jonction Internationale* in Nice in 1986 Salon de Montrouge, *Art Jonction Internationale* again and Salon Mac 2000 at the Grand-Palais de Paris in 1987; *Line Art*, Ghent, in 1989, and Salon Saga au Grand-Palais, and *9 Sculptors* at Bernay Abbey (Eure) in 1990. Solo exhibitions have included Orléans and Stockholm, 1985; Rome, 1986; Saint Tropez, 1987; 1987 Hôtel du Département à Clermont-Ferrand and Issoire and Ville d'Avray cultural centre, 1988; Madrid and Barcelona, 1989; Galerie Artuel and Galerie 10, Paris, 1991.

BIBLIOGRAPHY:
Tomek Kawiak, exhibition catalogue, Gal. Artuel, Paris, 1991.

AUCTION RECORDS:
PARIS, 25 June 1986, *A Brick in the Pocket* (bronze, 12 1/2 x 11 x 2 1/4 ins / 32 x 27 x 6 cm) FRF 8,000.

KAWSHORE, H. L.
19th century.
Painter. Genre scenes.

H.L. Kawshore is listed in *Art Prices Current*.

AUCTION RECORDS:
LONDON, 7 and 8 Nov 1910, *Sunday Evening*, GBP 4.

KAWUN, Ivan
French, 20th century.
Born 25 November 1925, in Rheims, to Ukrainian parents; died 16 July 2001, in Montchanson.
Painter, lithographer, illustrator, sculptor.

Ivan Kawun was an artist who led a picaresque life. Born in Rheims while his parents were emigrating, he studied at secondary school in Troyes and Rheims and then at the École des Beaux-Arts in Paris. Kawun's atavistic expansiveness made him one of the most colourful existentialist personalities in St-Germain-des-Prés in the years immediately after World War II. He earned a moderate living working as stage manager at one of the theatres in the district where his duties included operating the stage curtain. In 1953 he married Denise Portefaix and after a period of training at the École de Bergerie de Rambouillet, they moved to the Portefaix family home at Montchanson and raised sheep in the depths of the Central Massif.

Immediately after the war, as a member of the Mains Éblouies (*Dazzled Hands*) group formed around the new Galerie Maeght, Kawun was part of the second generation of Abstract painters of the Paris School, displaying gestural spirit and a colourful imagination. He experimented with the bright colours and freshness inspired by Pop Art, which he applied to assemblages of humorous form-signs, but soon returned to the use of impasto in earthy tones extended into reds, inspired by his close contact with the harshness of the Auvergne landscape. During the late 1980s Kawun had the opportunity to spend time in Venice and painted its churches, palaces and museums, blending the driving force of the rhythms and colours of his former Abstraction with the imaginary Venice that filled his mind.

Kawun took part in group exhibitions, including the following: the *Les Mains Éblouies* exhibition at the Galerie Maeght in Paris (1949); the Salon des Moins de Trente Ans (Salon of the Under-30s) in Paris (1950); *Le Mur Vivant* at the Galerie Mai in Paris (1951-1953); the Salon d'Octobre in Paris (1952, 1953); the Salon de Mai in Paris (from 1956); the Salon des Réalités Nouvelles in Paris (from 1957); Stockholm (1950); Lausanne (1951); the Düsseldorf Kunsthaus (1957); the Salon Comparaisons in São Paulo (1964); the Musée de Lille (1968); the French Cultural Centre in Moscow (1991); and St'art, the contemporary art fair in Strasbourg (2002). He also held regular solo exhibitions of collections of his work, mainly in Paris (1956, 1961, 1963, 1968, 1987) but also in the following: Rouen (1973); Nantes (1976); Le Havre (1977); Tours (1978); Aurillac (1982); Grasse (1985); Vichy (1988); St-Flour (1989); Clermont-Ferrand (1989); a double exhibition at Galerie 17 in Clermont-Ferrand and at the Musée d'Art Contemporain in Chamalières (1990); Orléans (1991); Clermont-Ferrand (1992); Galerie Kara in Geneva (1993); Les Écuries in Aurillac (1995); and Galerie Claude Martinon in Clermont-Ferrand (1997).

BIBLIOGRAPHY:
Kawun, exhibition catalogue, Musée d'Art contemporain, Chamalières, 1990. Vercier, Florence, '*Une certaine Venise*' in *Ivan Kawun, peintures 1988-1992*, exhibition catalogue, Gal. Kara, Geneva, 1993 (extensive documentation). Harambourg, Lydia, *L'École de Paris 1945-1965. Dictionnaire des peintres*, Ides et Calendes, Neuchâtel, 1993. Moreau, Marcel/Vercier, Florence, et al., *Kawun*, exhibition catalogue, Espace Les Écuries, Aurillac, 1995 (good documentation).

AUCTION RECORDS:
PARIS, 12 July 1988, *Composition with Circles* (gouache and collage, 19 3/4 x 25 1/2 ins / 50 x 65 cm) FRF 3,200. PARIS, 19 March 1989, *Untitled* (1962, gouache/paper, 10 1/4 x 13 ins / 26 x 33 cm) FRF 5,000. DOUAI, 11 Nov 1990, *Composition* (1963, oil on canvas, 51 1/4 x 38 1/2 ins / 130 x 98 cm) FRF 6,000. PARIS, 4 April 1993, *Le Bois de la Dame* (1958, oil on canvas, 35 x 46 ins / 89 x 116 cm) FRF 5,000.

KAY, Archibald
British, 19th - 20th century.
Born 1860, in Glasgow; died 1935.
Painter. Genre scenes, landscapes with figures, landscapes.

Archibald Kay was a pupil of Benjamin-Constant, Gustave Boulanger and Jules Lefebvre at the École des Beaux-Arts in Paris. In London, he exhibited at the Royal Academy from 1890 to 1921.

AUCTION RECORDS:
PARIS, 3 Feb 1919, *Dordrecht*, FRF 140. PARIS, 4-5 March 1930, *Dordrecht*, FRF 266. EDINBURGH, 30 Aug 1988, *Fruit-*

seller on the Banks of a River (oil on canvas, 12 x 16 1/4 ins / 30.5 x 41 cm) GBP 1,650. GLASGOW, 7 Feb 1989, *Shepherd and his Flock* (oil on canvas/card, 7 x 9 3/4 ins / 17.5 x 25 cm) GBP 1,045. GLASGOW, 6 Feb 1990, *Road through the Trossachs, between Aberfoyle and Loch Achray* (oil on canvas, 23 3/4 x 36 ins / 60.5 x 91.5 cm) GBP 1,870. PERTH, 27 Aug 1990, *Ploughing Beside a Stream in a Forest* (oil on canvas, 30 x 25 ins / 76 x 63.5 cm) GBP 2,640. GLASGOW, 22 Nov 1990, *Children Playing on Swings on Market Day* (oil on card, 10 x 14 ins / 25.4 x 35.6 cm) GBP 1,045. PERTH, 26 Aug 1991, *The River Leny* (oil on canvas, 20 x 30 ins / 51 x 76 cm) GBP 3,300. EDINBURGH, 23 March 1993, *Late Afternoon in Callander* (oil on canvas, 18 x 36 ins / 46 x 91.5 cm) GBP 1,207. PERTH, 30 Aug 1994, *Lobster Fisherman* (1889, oil on canvas, 36 1/4 x 48 1/2 ins / 92 x 123 cm) GBP 2,760. GLASGOW, 16 April 1996, *By a Quiet River* (oil on canvas, 12 1/4 x 16 1/4 ins / 31 x 41 cm) GBP 862. GLASGOW, 21 Aug 1996, *The River Leny* (oil on canvas, 18 x 36 ins / 45.7 x 91.4 cm) GBP 1,092. GLASGOW, 26 Aug 1996, *Woodland River* (oil on canvas, 30 x 40 1/4 ins / 76.5 x 102 cm) GBP 2,300. EDINBURGH, 7 May 1999, *Logging* (oil on canvas, 24 x 35 ins / 60 x 90 cm) GBP 3,200. EDINBURGH, 4 June 1999, *Sheep Grazing by a Celtic Cross* (oil on canvas, 18 x 13 ins / 45 x 33 cm) GBP 1,350. LONDON, 10 April 2000, *River in Torrent* (oil on canvas, 28 x 36 ins / 71 x 92 cm) GBP 4,000. LEYBURN, 13 April 2000, *Harvest Scene* (oil on canvas, 16 x 24 ins / 41 x 61 cm) GBP 3,400. LONDON, 9 April 2001, *Sunlit Slopes of Ben Ledi* (ink over pencil and watercolour, 14 x 21 ins / 35 x 53 cm) GBP 1,100. EDINBURGH, 24 Aug 2001, *Sheep in a Summer Landscape* (oil on canvas, 13 x 17 ins / 32 x 42 cm) GBP 2,200. VANCOUVER, 19 March 2002, *Clock Tower, Aberdeen* (watercolour, 17 x 21 ins / 43 x 53 cm) CAD 4,000. LONDON, 15 April 2002, *Sunshine and Shower* (oil on canvas, 24 x 40 ins / 61 x 102 cm) GBP 3,000. LONDON, 27 Aug 2003, *Coming from Church* (watercolour, 21 x 15 ins / 54 x 39 cm) GBP 2,000. LONDON, 27 Aug 2003, *Autumn Sunset* (oil on canvas, 30 x 40 ins / 76 x 102 cm) GBP 3,800. EDINBURGH, 28 May 2004, *On the Leny* (oil on canvas, 34 x 44 ins / 87 x 112 cm) GBP 3,000. EDINBURGH, 18 Aug 2004, *Figures on a Links Course, possibly Kilchattan Bay, Bute* (oil on canvas, 12 x 18 ins / 30 x 45 cm) GBP 2,200.

KAY, Helena de, later Mrs Gilder
American, 19th - 20th century.
Born c. 1846, in New York; died 28 May 1916, in New York.
Painter.

Helena de Kay exhibited mostly portraits and decorations in New York from 1874.

KAY, Hermann
German, 19th century.
Born 31 August 1839, in Hanover; died December 1902, in Berlin.
Painter. Genre scenes.

Kay, a product of the academies of Königsberg and Munich, lived in Berlin, Dresden, Vienna and Munich.

KAY, James
British, 19th century.
Born 1858, in Lambash, Scotland; died 1942, in Whistlefield (Dumbartonshire).
Active in Glasgow.
Painter (gouache), watercolourist. Genre scenes, landscapes, waterscapes, seascapes.

James Kay held an important place in the Glasgow school. He was a member of the Royal Scottish Watercolour Society. He took part in the Exposition Universelle held in Paris in 1900; at the Salon des Artistes Français in Paris in 1903 where he was awarded a medal for third place; and in the Brussels Fair of 1910. He was a member of the Royal Scottish Watercolour Society and the Royal Scottish Academy.

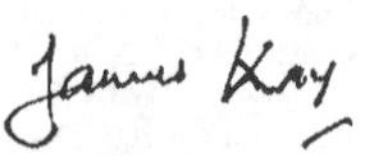

MUSEUMS AND GALLERIES:
BRISTOL: *Launch of the Lusitania* - GLASGOW: *Launch of the Lusitania* - LEEDS (City AG): *Launched* (oil on canvas); *Winter on the River Clyde* (1874, oil on canvas).

AUCTION RECORDS:
GLASGOW, 1 Dec 1943, *Winter in the Valley*, GBP 57. PARIS, 5 Feb 1951, *Harbour*, FRF 9,000. LONDON, 19 May 1972, *Promenade des Anglais, Nice*, Gns 420. SCOTLAND, 24 Aug 1976, *Holidays by the Seaside* (oil on card, 11 1/2 x 17 1/2 ins / 29 x 44.5 cm) GBP 250. AUCHTERARDER, 30 Aug 1977, *Embankment of the Seine in Paris* (oil on card, 22 x 33 1/2 ins / 56 x 85 cm) GBP 1,100. PERTH, 24 April 1979, *Wooded Landscape* (oil on canvas, 14 1/4 x 18 ins / 36 x 46 cm) GBP 600. GLASGOW, 3 July 1980, *Place du Grand Sablon, Brussels* (oil on canvas, 24 1/2 x 20 ins / 62 x 51 cm) GBP 1,100. AUCHTERARDER, 30 Aug 1983, *Beach scene* (coloured chalk, 19 x 23 ins / 48 x 58.5 cm) GBP 1,000. GLASGOW, 19 April 1984, *Mediterranean Port* (oil on panel, 23 x 33 ins / 58.4 x 83.8 cm) GBP 2,600. GLASGOW, 28 Aug 1985, *Fontainebleau* (oil on canvas, 23 x 34 1/2 ins / 58.3 x 87.6 cm) GBP 4,200. GLASGOW, 11 Dec 1986, *Young Girl wearing a White Dress, carrying a Parasol in a street in Paris* (watercolour, 19 x 24 ins / 48.2 x 61 cm) GBP 6,500. AUCHTERARDER, 1 Sept 1987, *Fish Market in Le Havre* (gouache, 9 1/2 x 11 3/4 ins / 24 x 30 cm) GBP 5,800. LONDON, 9 June 1988, *No. 3 Place de Paris* (1931, oil on card, 24 1/2 x 29 1/2 ins / 62.5 x 75 cm) GBP 6,380. EDINBURGH, 30 Aug 1988, *Marketplace in Dieppe* (oil on canvas, 24 3/4 x 30 ins / 63 x 76 cm) GBP 6,600. EDINBURGH, 22 Nov 1988, *Near Gareloch* (oil on card, 9 3/4 x 13 3/4 ins / 24.8 x 35 cm) GBP 1,700. GLASGOW, 7 Feb 1989, *Sailing boats in a Port* (watercolour, 19 1/4 x 23 1/4 ins / 49 x 59 cm) GBP 2,200. PERTH, 29 Aug 1989, *Cattle Grazing near a Farm* (oil on card, 18 x 22 ins / 46 x 56 cm) GBP 1,210. GLASGOW, 6 Feb 1990, *Autumn Festival* (1893, oil on canvas, 30 x 24 3/4 ins / 76 x 63 cm) GBP 1,430. PERTH, 27 Aug 1990, *Rue de Majorque* (oil on panel, 20 x 24 1/2 ins / 51 x 62 cm) GBP 20,350. GLASGOW, 22 Nov 1990, *Fisher Folk on the Beach* (1896, oil on canvas, 24 x 36 ins / 61 x 91.4 cm) GBP 3,080. GLASGOW, 5 Feb 1991, *Promenade* (oil on card, 21 x 30 3/4 ins / 52.5 x 78 cm) GBP 13,200. SOUTH QUEENSFERRY, 23 April 1991, *Children in a Field* (1896, watercolour, 8 1/4 x 11 1/4 ins / 21 x 28.5 cm) GBP 1,320. EDINBURGH, 2 May 1991, *Sweetness of Summer* (oil on canvas, 10 x 14 ins / 25.3 x 35.6 cm) GBP 6,600. PERTH, 26 Aug 1991, *Navigating on the Clyde* (gouache, 18 1/4 x 22 ins / 46.5 x 56 cm) GBP 4,400. EDINBURGH, 28 April 1992, *The Grosse Horloge, Rouen* (oil on card, 30 x 25 ins / 76 x 63.5 cm) GBP 11,000. PERTH, 1 Sept 1992, *On the Beach* (oil on canvas, 23 x 36 ins / 57.5 x 91.5 cm) GBP 6,380. PERTH, 31 Aug 1993, *The John Knox House in Edinburgh* (oil on card, 19 1/4 x 22 3/4 ins / 49 x 58 cm) GBP 6,900. GLASGOW, 14 Feb 1995, *Cottage in the Highlands* (oil on canvas, 24 x 20 ins / 61 x 51 cm) GBP 2,875. PERTH, 29 Aug 1995, *Sunset over the Clyde* (oil on card, 20 x 22 3/4 ins / 51 x 58 cm) GBP 4,255. GLASGOW, 21 Aug 1996, *Boat Drawing near an Island in the Evening* (oil on canvas, 24 3/4 x 30 ins / 62.8 x 76.2 cm) GBP 632; *Parade on the Beach* (pastel, 6 1/2 x 9 3/4 ins / 16.5 x 24.7 cm) GBP 1,840; *Regatta on the Clyde* (oil on card, 7 1/2 x 11 ins / 19 x 28 cm) GBP 632. PERTH, 26 Aug 1996, *On the Beach* (gouache, 13 1/2 x 19 1/4 ins / 34 x 49 cm) GBP 2,415. GLASGOW, 25 Aug 1997, *Le Havre* (gouache, 8 3/4 x 11 3/4 ins / 22.2 x 29.8 cm) GBP 1,610. EDINBURGH, 26 Nov 1997, *Figures with a Carriage on a Parisian Boulevard* (heightened watercolour, 19 x 23 1/2 ins / 48.5 x 59.5 cm) GBP 5,175. GLASGOW, 25 Feb 1999, *Departure from the Clyde - Bound for the Front* (oil on canvas, 30 x 50 ins / 76 x 127 cm) GBP 9,500. LONDON,

28 Oct 1999, *View of the Bay of Naples* (oil on canvas, 30 x 50 ins / 76 x 127 cm) GBP 5,000. LONDON, 30 Aug 2000, *The Strand, London* (oil on board, 24 x 20 ins / 61 x 51 cm) GBP 11,000. LONDON, 30 Aug 2000, *Notre-Dame, Paris* (oil on board, 24 x 20 ins / 61 x 51 cm) GBP 13,500. LONDON, 5 Sept 2001, *Paris Sunshine* (oil on canvas, 25 x 30 ins / 64 x 76 cm) GBP 18,000. AYLSHAM, 14 Dec 2001, *Busy French Street Market* (oil on canvas, 19 x 24 ins / 48 x 61 cm) GBP 7,500. LONDON, 28 Aug 2002, *Paris Street Scene* (oil on canvas, 24 x 20 ins / 62 x 51 cm) GBP 7,500. EDINBURGH, 6 Dec 2002, *Church Square* (oil on canvas, 30 x 25 ins / 76 x 63 cm) GBP 7,800. LONDON, 27 Aug 2003, *The Grosse Horloge, Rouen* (oil on canvas, 30 x 25 ins / 77 x 63 cm) GBP 15,000. LONDON, 27 Aug 2003, *Rue Saint Romain, Rouen* (oil on canvas, 36 x 28 ins / 91 x 71 cm) GBP 22,000. EDINBURGH, 18 Aug 2004, *Shipping on the Clyde* (oil on panel, 10 x 14 ins / 25 x 35 cm) GBP 4,200. LONDON, 28 Oct 2004, *Skating, Early Morning* (oil on canvas, 10 x 13 ins / 26 x 33 cm) GBP 8,200.

KAY, John

British, 18th - 19th century.

Born April 1742, near Dalkeith; died 21 February 1826, in Edinburgh.

Miniaturist, caricaturist.

John Kay's unhappy childhood was the prelude to his becoming a barber, a profession he practiced in Dalkeith and then in Edinburgh. His natural artistic bent soon came to the fore and, working on his own, he became a fine painter of miniatures. In 1782, one of Kay's best patron's died; however, his son guaranteed Kay a pension which enabled him to dedicate himself completely to art. In 1784, Kay etched a caricature of a well known Edinburgh personality. It was the first of many as his ability to make comical, very recognisable caricatures marked the new direction his art would take. Although his success was remarkable, it had its counterpart in the ill-humour it provoked in some of his models. He was sued and a number of his works were bought only so that they could be destroyed. Kay was not less prolific in his production of portraits of which 900 can be counted. His etchings were published under the title *Kay's Edinburgh Portraits*.

KAY, Nancy

American, 20th - 21st century.

Born 1949, in La Jolla (California).

Painter (mixed media).

Nancy Kay trained in a variety of colleges and institutions from 1967-1973. She now lives and works in Santa Monica. Her work is characterised by highly coloured geometric, abstract-decorative compositions on pieces of card featuring low relief surfaces, mounted on monochrome supports.

Kay's work has featured in a number of group exhibitions: since 1982, New York, Los Angeles, and the Suzanne Bollag Gallery in Zurich; 1985, Museum of Contemporary Art, La Jolla; 1987-1988, cities in the USA and Tokyo; 1990, cities in the USA, etc. Her work has also been the subject of a number of solo exhibitions, including: 1983, Zurich, New York, Los Angeles; 1987, Santa Monica Heritage Museum; 1989, Los Angeles; 1991, Venice and Los Angeles; 1992, Suzanne Bollag Gallery, Zurich.

BIBLIOGRAPHY:

Nancy Kay, exhibition catalogue, Gal. Suzanne Bollag, Zurich, 1992.

KAY, Willem. See **KEY**

KAY-SCOTT, Cyril

American, 20th century.

Born 3 January 1879, in Westport (Montana); died 1960.

Painter. Portraits.

Cyril Kay-Scott studied at the Académie Colarossi in Paris, and under Tony Robert-Fleury, Léon Bonnat and Gustave Moreau. He made portraits of famous European and American figures.

KAYAMA, Matazo

Japanese, 20th century.

Born 1927, in Kyoto.

Painter (including mixed media). Flowers, insects.

Kayama graduated from the department of Japanese painting at the University of Fine Art in Tokyo. In 1957, he won the Asahi Young Painters prize. Around 1960, he travelled abroad, exhibiting and giving lectures. In 1973, he won the Japanese Art prize and in 1980 was awarded the Ministry of Culture prize. In 1988, he took up a teaching post at the University of Fine Art in Tokyo.

Kayama's works look like a montage of painting and photographs. In 1950 he began to include discreet elements of Cubism and Italian Futurism applied to series of birds and other animals. In 1964, he designed a ceramic mural for the Taiseki-ji temple in Fujinomiya and, in 1974, designed a stone pagoda for the Jindai-ji temple as a homage to his friend Misao Yokoyama, who had recently died. In the late 1970s, he received several government commissions for murals, including one for the Japanese Embassy in Washington DC. He was awarded the Order of Culture by the Japanese government in 2003.

From 1950, Kayama showed work at the exhibitions of the Association of Young Artists (Shinseisaku gakai). He won first prize of four occasions. He participated in international exhibitions of modern Japanese art from 1958. In 1967, his work was shown in the *Masterpieces of Modern Japanese Painting* exhibition at the Hermitage Museum in St Petersburg and at the Pushkin Museum in Moscow. A collection of his work was also shown at the De Francony Gallery in Paris in 1990.

AUCTION RECORDS:

NEW YORK, 27 April 1994, *Mizube (Waterside)* (oil and gouache/paper, 46 1/4 x 36 1/4 ins / 117.5 x 92.1 cm) USD 145,500. NEW YORK, 31 Oct 1995, *Insects* (mineral pigment/paper/mounted and varnished card, 14 1/4 x 17 1/4 ins / 35.9 x 43.7 cm) USD 57,500. NEW YORK, 24 April 1997, *Flowers* (coloured ink and gold/paper, 17 x 24 1/2 ins / 43.2 x 62.2 cm) USD 134,400. NEW YORK, 10 May 2000, *Solitude* (colour ink, 47 x 35 ins / 120 x 88 cm) USD 450,000. PARIS, 23 Nov 2000, *Le Kaki* (colour lithograph, 13 x 10 ins / 32 x 26 cm) FRF 37,000. NEW YORK, 24 March 2003, *Flock of Birds in a Winter Forest* (ink and colour, 36 x 46 ins / 91 x 117 cm) USD 85,000.

KAYE, Otis

American, 20th century.

Born 1885, in Michigan; died 1974.

Painter. Genre scenes, still-lifes.

Otis Kaye was taken back to Germany by his immigrant mother after his father's death in 1905; he read engineering in Dresden. He moved back to the USA in 1920 and set up an engineering firm with a cousin in Chicago.

In his art, he perpetuated William M. Harnett and John Frederick Peto's tradition, focusing on *trompe l'œil* for which his talent was uncanny. He is famous for his reproductions of American notes and coins and the absolute accuracy of his drawings and reproductions. He cited Rembrandt and Whistler as major inspirations as well as N.A. Brooks, and they all found their way into a highly original and little-known production.

AUCTION RECORDS:

NEW YORK, 4 Dec 1986, *Money to Burn* (oil on canvas remounted/panel, 8 x 9 1/2 ins / 20.3 x 24.1 cm) USD 14,000. NEW YORK, 3 Dec 1987, *Make Sense* (1929, oil on canvas remounted/panel, 8 x 10 ins / 20.4 x 25.4 cm) USD 22,000. NEW YORK, 24 May 1989, *Target Practice* (oil on panel, 14 1/2 x 18 ins / 36.8 x 45.7 cm) USD 45,100. New York, 14 March 1991, *In the Bag* (oil on panel, 6 3/4 x 9 1/2 ins / 17.3 x 24 cm) USD 22,000. New York, 12 April 1991, *One Dollar Bill* (1921, oil on panel, 9 1/4 x 14 3/4 ins / 23.5 x 37.5 cm) USD 13,200. New York, 22 May 1991, *Target Practice* (oil on panel, 14 1/2 x 18 ins / 36.7 x 45.8 cm) USD 38,500. New York, 28 May 1992, *How to Stamp out Poverty* (oil on panel, 5 x 9 1/2 ins / 13 x 24.1 cm) USD 19,800. New York, 24 Sept 1992, *US Musical Notes* (oil on panel, 30 x 24 3/4 ins / 76.2 x 62.9 cm) USD 101,200. New York, 22 Sept 1993, *Easy Come - Easy Go* (oil on panel, 21 x 26 ins / 53.1 x 65.1 cm) USD 107,000. New York, 1 Dec 1994, *What a Hit* (oil on canvas, 30 x 25 ins / 76.2 x 63.5 cm) USD 112,500. New York, 13 Sept 1995, *Five Dollar Bill* (1955, watercolour, ink, oil and pencil/paper, 3 1/4 x 7 1/4 ins / 8 x 18.7 cm) USD 9,200; *Land of the Free, Home of the Brave* (oil on panel, 25 1/2 x 36 1/4 ins / 64.6 x 92 cm) USD 156,500. New York, 26 May 1999, *Key to Success* (oil on canvas laid on panel, 8 x 10 ins / 20 x 25 cm) USD 62,000. New York, 26 May 1999, *Joshua's Horn* (oil on canvas, 24 x 36 ins / 61 x 91 cm) USD 240,000. New York, 24 May 2000, *Octopus Ticker Company* (watercolour, 23 x 30 ins / 58 x 77 cm) USD 5,000. New York, 24 May 2000, *Hidden Assets* (oil on panel, 14 x 20 ins / 36 x 51 cm) USD 80,000. New York, 23 May 2001, *Bid and Ask* (oil on panel, 12 x 15 ins / 31 x 38 cm) USD 65,000. New York, 21 May 2002, *Fool and his Money* (1929, oil on panel, 5 x 7 ins / 13 x 18 cm) USD 26,000. New York, 3 Dec 2003, *Two to Win* (oil on panel, 11 x 13 ins / 27 x 32 cm) USD 45,000. New York, 19 Dec 2003, *Rembrant's Etching of The Goldsmith with 10 Dollar Eagle Note* (etching and oil, 4 x 3 ins / 10 x 8 cm) USD 4,250. New York, 19 May 2004, *Washington and the Half-dollar* (oil on panel, 6 x 8 ins / 15 x 20 cm) USD 19,000. New York, 19 May 2004, *Fool and his Money* (oil on panel, 6 x 9 ins / 15 x 23 cm) USD 20,000.

KAYLER, Richard
French, 20th century.
Born 1927, in Paris; died 31 May 1997.
Painter (including gouache), watercolourist, draughtsman.

Richard Kayler began painting in 1946, moving towards Abstraction in 1952. Difficult living conditions and an unyielding personality did nothing to help his success. His paintings consist of surfaces of contrasting and conflicting values. In his early period these were outlines cut with great geometric purity and in the following period became freer, more lyrical forms and rhythms. He exhibited in Paris at the Salon des Réalités Nouvelles in 1955. In 1998 an exhibition of a collection of his paintings was held at the Centre Culturel in Sucy-en-Brie.

Bibliography:
Kayler, Stéphane (preface), *Richard Kayler*, exhibition catalogue, Centre culturel, Sucy-en-Brie, 1998.

Auction records:
Paris, 16 June 1988, *Abstract Composition* (1987, acrylic/canvas, 32 x 25 1/2 ins / 81 x 65 cm) FRF 2,300; *Abstract Composition* (1986-1987, acrylic/canvas, 35 x 46 ins / 89 x 116 cm) FRF 3,300.

KAYMAX, Eduard
German, 17th century.
Born in Nuremberg; died July 1626.
Painter.

Kaymax worked in Rotterdam.

KAYNOOT, Hans. See **KEYNOOGHE**

KAYO, real name: Kagehiro Shirai, nickname: Shijun, pseudonyms: Kayo, Baisen, Garo
Japanese, 19th century.
Active c. 1840.
Painter.

Kayo studied under Ganku (1756-1838) and painted flowers and birds. He wrote the *Gajo Yoraku* treatise on painting.

KAYSER, Conrad
German, 20th century.
Born 26 August 1880, in Achern; died 1954, in Achern.
Painter, engraver. Portraits, landscapes, still-lifes.

Conrad Kayser spent time in both Karlsruhe and Munich.

Auction records:
Heidelberg, 15-16 Oct 1993, *Summer Landscape* (oil on canvas, 22 1/2 x 19 3/4 ins / 57 x 50 cm) DEM 2,800. Heidelberg, 8 April 1995, *Swiss Landscape with a Stream* (1943, oil on card, 19 1/4 x 15 ins / 49 x 38 cm) DEM 2,800. Staufen, 3 Dec 1999, *Going to Church in Glottertal* (1926, oil on canvas, 20 x 16 ins / 50 x 40 cm) DEM 3,500.

KAYSER, Edmond Charles
French, 20th century.
Born 1882, in Paris; died 1965, in Paris.
Painter. Urban landscapes, seascapes, landscapes.

Edmond Charles Kayser received guidance from Eugène Carrière but studied in museums and was mainly self-taught. At first an artistic affinity led him to associate with Léopold Lévy, Linaret and Vergé-Sarrat, but later he spent time with Despiau, Dunoyer de Segnonzac, André Lhote, Charles Dufresne and Zadkine. Around 1937 Kayser married the painter Mercedes Legrand. In 1938 he was appointed director of the École des Arts Décoratifs and curator of the Musée Adrien-Dubouché in Limoges, a post from which he was dismissed in 1941 because he was Jewish. He then took refuge in Avignon.

A landscape painter, Kayser also painted views of Paris and the Côte-d'Azur, mainly the ports of Cassis, Bandol and Sanary. As his friendships show, he was very much a part of the inter-war Paris School. Alhough a figurative artist, Kayser incorporated elements of Cézanne's constructional approach into his work when observing and describing an emotive reality.

He exhibited in Paris, including at the following: the Salon des Indépendants (from 1907, and notably at the Salon's retrospective exhibition of 1926); the Salon d'Automne; the Salon des Peintres-Graveurs Français; the Salon des Tuileries; and the Salon des Peintres-Graveurs Indépendants. He took part in numerous group exhibitions and was invited to exhibit at the Venice Biennale of 1926. The Salon des Indépendants organised a posthumous exhibition of Kayser's work in 1979.

Museums and Galleries:
Paris (MNAM-CCI): *Landscape*; *Garden Path*.

Auction records:
Paris, 18 April 1929, *Ste-Maxime*, FRF 3,600. Paris, 12 Dec 1946, *Éventaire* FRF 6,000. Paris, 11 July 1989, *Place de la Concorde* (oil on canvas, 16 x 22 ins / 40.5 x 55 cm) FRF 10,200.

KAYSER, Elba
Swedish, 19th century.
Born 15 February 1846, in Stockholm.
Painter. Landscapes, flowers.

Elba Kayser exhibited regularly in Austria and Germany.

KAYSER, Engelbert
German, 19th - 20th century.
Born 1840; died 1911
Designs (pewter).
Jugendstil.

Engelbert Kayser was director of the creative studio in Cologne belonging to the foundry of Johann Peter Kayser, situated in Krefeld-Bochum. Kayser gave this business an aesthetic orientation towards Jugendstil. The firm developed his famous 'Kayser Pewter' (or Kayserzinn) for use in the manufacture of tableware. This was a pewter made with silver, without lead. The company, which employed as many as 800 workers, also had artists on its books, including Hugo Leven (1874-1956), Karl Geyer (1858-1912), Hermann Fauser (1874-1947), Karl Berghof (1881-1967), Johann Christian Kröner (1838-1911), a painter who developed hunting scene motifs, and Jean Garnier, from France.

BIBLIOGRAPHY:

Kayserzinn und andere Zinngeräte des Jugendstils, Die Stiftung Henrich im Kaiser Wilhelm Museum, Krefeld, 1984.

MUSEUMS AND GALLERIES:

HAMBURG (Mus. für Kunst und Gewerbe).

KAYSER, Eska

French, 20th century.

Born 11 September 1936, in Boulogne-Billancourt.

Painter.

Nouvelle Figuration.

Eska Kayser studied at the École des Beaux-Arts in Nancy and later at the École des Beaux-Arts in Paris where she was awarded the Grand Prix de Rome for painting in 1963 and received a post-graduate degree in art (with distinction) in 1965. In 1960 she was awarded a diploma in the history of modern art at the Sorbonne. In 1961 she obtained the Prix Rocheron and the Prix Lefranc, in 1964 the Prix Othon Friesz., and in 1965 a state travel bursary and the second-place Prix du Dôme and Prix de Barbizon. In 1977 Kayser produced a mosaic for a secondary school in Versailles, in 1979 a mural painting for the Banque de France in Versailles, and in 1988 was co-author of the book *Un Tableau, un Enfant, un Peintre, une Histoire* (*A Picture, a Child, a Painter, a Story*), published by Éditions de Fleurus.

Kayser soon developed her own artistic language. During her early period her painting was a savagely deformed expression of reality. She had a period close to Abstract Expressionism when she painted on raw canvas, integrating strange elements such as fragments of wire netting or a piece of gauze. Her exhibition of 1996 marked a return to a more clearly defined figuration, with multiple female faces and scattered eyes which stare or wait. The work is still removed from any realism unless one argues its quality of dream-like realism. Through the course of her artistic development, Kayser's world reveals itself as one of intense, disturbed and silent questioning.

From 1960 she took part in group exhibitions: the Salon de la Jeune Peinture in Paris; an exhibition organised by the Asahi newspaper in Tokyo (1963); the *Le Temps du Regard* exhibition in Paris (1984); the Art Expo in Geneva (1984); a group exhibition in Athens (1984); the Foire Internationale d'Art Contemporain in Ghent (1988, 1991); and with Groupe 109 in Paris (during the 1980s and 1990s). Kayser also showed her work in solo exhibitions: at the Galerie des Beaux-Arts in Paris (1960, 1961); at the Club des Arts in Nancy (1961, 1963); again in Paris (1966, 1968); in Rouen and Avignon (1970); in Paris and Avignon (1974); in Paris (1977); at the Galerie Sculptures in Paris (1986, 1991); at the Galerie Étienne de Causans in Paris (1990); in Lacoste (1991); at the Centre Culturel in Toulouse (1992); at the Galerie Étienne de Causans in Paris (1995); at the Galerie Yves Fay in Paris (1996); in the *Le Temps du Regard* exhibition at the Hôpital Paul Brousse in Villejuif (1997); and at the Orangerie of the Palais du Luxembourg in Paris (1997).

AUCTION RECORDS:

PARIS, 28 Oct 1990, *Mirror of Uncertainty* (oil on canvas, 51 1/4 x 38 1/4 ins / 130 x 97 cm) FRF 15,000. PARIS, 4 May 1994, *White Silence* (1979, oil on canvas, 46 x 35 ins / 116 x 89 cm) FRF 5,000.

KAYSER, Felix

German, 20th century.

Painter. Genre scenes.

Felix Kayser lived and worked in Düsseldorf. He exhibited in Berlin in 1909.

KAYSER, Gabrielle

French, 20th century.

Born 6 February 1902, in Strasbourg.

Painter. Nudes, landscapes.

Gabrielle Kayser exhibited in Paris at the Salon d'Automne. A landscape artist, she mainly painted her native region of Alsace in a restrained traditional style.

KAYSER, Joachim

French, 18th century.

Active in Hanover.

Painter.

Kayser painted portraits of the princes of Hanover and of George I and George II of England.

KAYSER, Joseph. See **KAISER**

KAYSER, Leo

German, 19th - 20th century.

Born 15 November 1868.

Engraver. Landscapes.

Leo Kayser studied art in Stockholm and Munich, then stayed for a time in Florence, before settling in Darmstadt. He engraved views of Alsace and Italy.

KAYSER, Paul or Jean Paul

German, 19th - 20th century.

Born 22 September 1869, in Hamburg; died 1942.

Painter, engraver. Harbour scenes. Wall decorations.

Paul Kayser studied art in Munich and Dresden. He painted mainly large decorative pieces. From 1910, he was considerably influenced by the style of Albert Marquet.

AUCTION RECORDS:

HAMBURG, 11 June 1986, *A Small Harbour on the Elbe* (1916, oil on card, 9 3/4 x 12 3/4 ins / 24.8 x 32.5 cm) DEM 5,200. HAMBURG, 3 Dec 1999, *Still-life with Books and Vase of Flowers* (oil on canvas, 19 x 20 ins / 49 x 51 cm) DEM 4,600. HAMBURG, 8 Dec 2001, *Fisherman and Cargo Boat in a Rural Port* (oil on board, 17 x 23 ins / 43 x 58 cm) DEM 4,200.

KAYSER, Robert

Belgian, 20th century.

Born 1933, in Mons.

Painter, sculptor, lithographer.

Robert Kayser studied with Émile Salkin and Claude Lyr. He became professor of the history of engraving at the academy of art in Watermael-Boitsfort.

KAYSER, Tilman

German, 20th century.

Born 2 October 1941, in Lisbon, to German parents.

Also active in France.

Painter.

Tilman Kayser studied in Berlin from 1963 to 1969. While staying in France in 1970, he decided to take up residence there. Though he had previously exhibited in Germany, his first exhibition in France was in 1971. His painting is a strange mixture of Tachiste and very structured backgrounds. Allowing glimpses of the 'cracks' resulting from this contrast, it tends towards a notion of space, expressed in a varied plastic vocabulary.

KAYSER, Victor

French, 16th century.

Active in Augsburg.

Sculptor. Religious subjects, mythological subjects, figures.

Victor Kayser was certainly an important artist, although only a few works can be confidently attributed to him. Among these are a *Muse* in a private collection in Munich, *Suzanne Bathing* in the museum in Berlin, and a *Holy Family* after Dürer, which is in the Louvre museum in Paris.

MUSEUMS AND GALLERIES:
BERLIN (Bodemus.): *Suzanne Bathing* - PARIS (Louvre): *Holy Family* (after Dürer).

KAYSER-EICHBERG, Carl
German, 19th - 20th century.
Born 5 April 1873, in Eichberg.
Painter, engraver. Landscapes.
Carl Kayser-Eichberg exhibited in Berlin in 1910.
AUCTION RECORDS:
MUNICH, 25 Nov 1976, *Landscape with Lake* (1896, oil on canvas, 31 1/2 x 23 1/2 ins / 80 x 60 cm) DEM 1,800. MUNICH, 25 Sept 2002, *Shepherd Talking to a Man on a White Horse in a Spring Landscape* (1908, oil on canvas, 37 x 46 ins / 95 x 118 cm) EUR 3,500.

KAZAK, Marie. See **ERISTOFF-KAZAK Marie, princesse**

KAZAKOS, Tryphon
Greek, 20th century.
Born in Athens.
Painter.
Tryphon Kazakos travelled around France where he was a pupil of Jean-Paul Laurens and where, from 1928, he exhibited in Paris at both the Salon des Artistes Français and the Salon d'Automne.

KAZAKS, Jekabs
Latvian, 20th century.
Born 1895, in Riga; died 1920, in Riga.
Painter.
Jekabs Kazaks studied art in Riga and Paris.
AUCTION RECORDS:
LONDON, 6 June 1979, *Exotic Dancer* (oil on canvas, 80 3/4 x 48 3/4 ins / 205 x 124 cm) GBP 3,400.

KAZAN, real name: Issho Yokoyama, nickname: Shunro, pseudonym: Kazan
Japanese, 19th century.
Born 1784; died 1837.
Active in Kyoto.
Painter. Figures.
Kazan studied under Ganku (1756-1838) and was then influenced by Goshun (1752-1811), but eventually found his own style in depicting figures.
AUCTION RECORDS:
NEW YORK, 17 Oct 1989, *Swallows* (ink/silver paper, two-panelled folding screen, 61 1/2 x 69 3/4 ins / 156.2 x 177.4 cm) USD 3,850.

KAZAN, Watanabe, real name: Sadayasu Watanabe, nicknames: Shian and Hakuto, nickname: Noboru, pseudonyms: Kazan, Gukaido, Zenrakudo, Sakuhi Koji, Kintonkyo and Zuian Koji
Japanese, 19th century.
Born 1793, in Edo (now Tokyo); died 1841.
Painter. Portraits, genre scenes.
Kazan's tragic life and work are emblematic of the difficult period in Japanese history. He stands out as an innovator who nevertheless remained a traditionalist, straddling the transition from the old regime to the modern era and from a pictorial tradition in decline to its revitalisation with ideas from the West. Kazan was the son of a samurai from the Tawara clan in Mikawa (now Aichi Prefecture) and received a good education, although his family's financial difficulties obliged them to steer him towards painting. So Kazan led a double life as both a painter and man of the sword, devoted to his clan, whose lands he administered as chief among his co-vassals. He frequented progressive intellectual circles (*rangaku-sha*) and formed a group in which possible reforms were discussed in the light of texts from the Netherlands. Though not at all revolutionary, this group was misunderstood and was hated by the Confucian conservatives. In 1839, Kazan and his friends were charged with conspiracy and imprisoned. Kazan risked the death penalty but, thanks to the intervention of high-ranking supporters, was spared and put under house arrest in Tawara. Stripped of his functions, he became extremely poor and had to live by his painting, meanwhile continuing to suffer the ill will and defamatory opinions of his detractors. He committed suicide in 1841 out of loyalty to his lord, for whom he feared he was causing difficulties. He was 48 years old.

Kazan had his first experience of painting in the studio of Buncho (1763-1840), who realised his student was particularly talented. Buncho is known, among other things, for introducing literati painting to Edo, combining it with the traditions of Tosa and Kano to create a style imbued with eclecticism. Kazan had a comparatively realist touch, which grew stronger as the European influence reinforced his desire for objectivity and truth. His own talent can be seen less in his official works than in his many sketchbooks, sketches and studies, which combine freshness, freedom, dynamic yet bare lines, poetry and European principles. His portraits are in the front rank of Japanese painting, maintaining a balance between ancestral tradition and the new realism. His subjects are captured on paper with an extreme economy of means and bold simplification, all their personality contained in the eyes. Kazan's line and colour bring both heightened realism and decorative effect, to which he adds volume, with a particularly successful depiction of three dimensions. His explorations were very fruitful for Japanese painting for, while willing to learn lessons from the West, he was able to remain within Japanese tradition, creating his own original form of realism.
BIBLIOGRAPHY:
Kozyreff, C., '*Kazan Watanabe*' in *Encyclopædia Universalis* vol. IX, Paris, 1971. Abiko, Bonnie, '*Persecuted Patriot: Watanabe Kazan and the Tokugawa Bakufu*' in *Monumenta Nipponica*, 44:2 (Summer 1989).
AUCTION RECORDS:
NEW YORK, 26 March 1991, *Drinking Tea Deep in the Valley* (1838, ink and pigments/silk, kakemono, 49 1/2 x 22 ins / 125.5 x 55 cm) USD 187,000. NEW YORK, 24 March 2003, *Bamboo and Rock* (1832, ink, hanging scroll, 51 x 11 ins / 129 x 28 cm) USD 2,200. NEW YORK, 24 March 2003, *Autumn Grasses* (1846, ink, colour and gold leaf, two-panel screens, a pair, 65 x 63 ins / 164 x 159 cm) USD 16,000. NEW YORK, 23 March 2004, *Fisherman* (1832, colour ink, hanging scroll a pair, 11 x 7 ins / 28 x 18 cm) USD 3,200. NEW YORK, 23 March 2004, *Peach Blossoms* (1836, colour ink, silver and mica, fan, 16 x 6 ins / 41 x 16 cm) USD 3,200.

KAZANOVSKA, Maria
Maiden name: Klass
Polish, 20th century.
Born 1898, in Zhitomir, Ukraine.
Painter. Landscapes.
Maria Kazanovska studied in Warsaw.

KAZANZEV, Vladimir
Russian, 19th century.
Born in Russia.
Painter.
Kazanzev was awarded a bronze medal at the Exposition Universelle in Paris in 1889.

KAZARIN, Viktor
Russian, 20th - 21st century.
Born 1948, in Moscow.
Painter.
Viktor Kazarin studied in Sokolov's studio. He graduated from the faculty of painting and graphic art in Moscow. He was one of the founders of Russian Neo-Expressionism. He uses a Tachiste technique that comes close to 'dripping'. His

apparently abstract paintings often suggest figures drawn from reality, often animals, involving an element of guesswork, detection, deciphering in the style of a Rorshach test.
AUCTION RECORDS:
PARIS, 15 Dec 1989, *Black Cow* (1986, 39 1/4 x 59 ins / 100 x 150 cm) FRF 110,500.

KAZMIERCZAK, Karl
German, 20th century.
Born 1894, in Holbra.
Painter. Genre scenes.
Karl Kazmierczak lived in Hamborn, where he worked until 1958 in the blast furnaces of the Thyssen factories. He painted intimist scenes and scenes of family life.
BIBLIOGRAPHY:
Bihalji-Merin, Oto, *Les Peintres naïfs*, Delpire, Paris, 1960.

KAZUKI, Yasuo
Japanese, 20th century.
Born 1911, in Yamaguchi Prefecture; died 1974.
Painter.
Kazuki graduated from the School of Fine Art in Tokyo in 1936. During World War II, from 1943 to 1945, he served in the Japanese army in Manchuria. He was taken prisoner and spent two years in Siberia, an experience that marked him deeply and provided him with a great many themes for his work. In 1953 he travelled in Europe. From childhood, Kazuki was much influenced by the work of Sesshu (1420-1506) and his successors and sought to translate the effects of ink wash (*sumi*) into oils. He generally starts a painting with a monochrome sketch, which he then paints over several times until a form appears. This creates a tendency towards abstraction arising out of a sense of calligraphy. In 1951 and 1957, he exhibited at the São Paulo Biennale. From 1952, he was a regular exhibitor at the Tokyo Biennale. In 1989-1990, the prefectural museum in Yamaguchi mounted an exhibition of his work, entitled *Yasuo Kazuki, Siberia Series*. He was awarded the Taisho Prize in 1969.

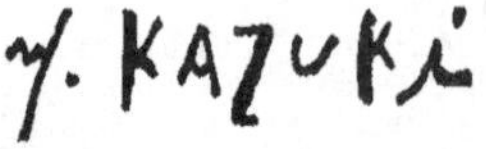

BIBLIOGRAPHY:
Kazuki, Yasuo, *Gashu Kazuki Yasuo [Collected works of Yasuo Kazuki]*, Asahi shimbunsha, 1979. *Kazuki Yasuo-Sono zokei to jojo no kiseki [Yasuo Kazuki-His Formation and the Traces of his Self-Expression]*, exhibition catalogue, Prefectural Museum, Yamaguchi, 1981.
MUSEUMS AND GALLERIES:
TOKYO (MMA) - YAMAGUCHI (Prefectural Mus. of Art).
AUCTION RECORDS:
NEW YORK, 27 April 1994, *Fields in Winter* (oil on canvas, 28 3/4 x 19 3/4 ins / 73.3 x 50.2 cm) USD 101,500.

KAZUMASA, Nakagawa. See **NAKAGAWA Kazumasa**

KAZUNOBU, real name: Shigenojo Kano, original name: Wada, nicknames: Jonosuke, Kumenosuke, pseudonyms: Chinshido, Hakuchiso, Hakusan Yajien, Shounsai Risshi
Japanese, 18th century.
Active c. 1740.
Painter.
Kano School.
Kazunobu studied under his father Shoun and worked in the service of the Lord of Tsukushi.

KCHO, pseudonym of Leyva Machado, Alexis
Cuban, 20th - 21st century.
Born 12 February 1970, in Nueva Gerona (Juventud Island).
Sculptor, installation artist, draughtsman.
Kcho studied at the Nueva Gerona school of art from 1983 to 1986 and at the Escuela Nacional de Artes Plásticas in Havana from 1984 to 1990. He lives and works in Havana. He has taken part in numerous collective exhibitions in Latin America and Europe and since 1991 has shown his work in solo exhibitions, including: in Cuba and Montreal (1996); Los Angeles Museum of Contemporary Art (1997); Jeu de Paume National Gallery, Paris (1998); Galleria d'Arte Moderna e Contemporanea, Turin (2001).

KE JIUSI, or K'o Chiu-ssù or K'o Kieou-sseu, nickname: Jingzhong, pseudonym: Danqiu
Chinese, 14th century.
Born 1312; died 1365.
Active in Daizhou (Zhejiang).
Painter.
Ke Jiusi was an eminent connoisseur of painting, calligrapy and antiques who was appointed to evaluate the Imperial collection during the reign of Tianli (1328-1330). His paintings of bamboo and ancient trees are in the style of the painter Wen Tong Song (died 1079).
MUSEUMS AND GALLERIES:
BEIJING (Palace Mus.): *Bamboo near a Rock Garden* (dated 1338, poem by ther Qing emeror Qianlong (1736-1796)); *Frozen Trees and Rocks* (dated 1342, long painter's colophon); *Two Bamboo Plants*; *Bare Trees and Bamboo near a Rock* - TAIPEI (National Palace Mus.): *River Landscape* (dated 1344, colophon by Yo Yu); *Bare Tree and Bamboo near a Rock*.

KE SHIHUANG, or K'o Che-houang or K'o Shih-huang, nickname: Wuxia
Chinese, 16th century.
Active in Putian (Fujian) c. 1580.
Painter.
Ke painted flowers in colour and has left two dated works: *Flowers*, signed and dated 1577, and *Banana Trees*, signed and dated 1580.

KEAN, Michael
British, 19th century.
Born in Dublin; died 1823, in London.
Miniaturist, draughtsman.
Michael Kean was a student of the sculptor Edward Smith. He also trained at the Academy of Dublin where he was awarded a gold medal in 1779. During a stay in London from 1786 to 1790, he exhibited his drawings at the Royal Academy and at the Free Society. He was also associated with a porcelain factory in Derby.

KEANE, Tina
British, 20th - 21st century.
Born 1948.
Active in London.
Video artist.
Tina Keane studied at the Hammersmith College of Art and the Sir John Cass School of Art (1967-1970). She later did an MA in Independent Film and Video at the London College of Printing (1995-1996). She is a founder member of the group Circles: Women in Distribution, and has been a lecturer in film and video at the Central St Martin's College of Art and Design in London since 1982. In 1985 she co-curated the exhibition *New Pluralism* with Michael O'Pray at the Tate Gallery.

Although interested in women's issues, Keane explores a wide range of themes in her work, including social issues, aesthetics and the possibilities and limits of new technology, the latter being particularly pertinent to her chosen media of film and video. Her films combine and reflect her interest in all these issues. In her well-known film *Shadow of a Journey* (1980), filmed in the Western Isles of Scotland, Keane interviewed a number of women, bringing to light and documenting the stories of their ancestors, particularly their experience of being forcibly removed to make room for sheep-farming. In an effort to not only focus on stories of suffering but also emphasise the positive nature of the strong links between the generations of the crofters, she used the image of the waves in the sea in her film, seeing them as a metaphor for constant energy. There are echoes of this in Keane's reaction to the giant trucks on the streets of New York, filmed on her first trip there, and the energy of the women's performance group 'Disband', which she also experienced during her trip. She describes being impressed by both the trucks and the group, finding both to be 'larger than life and threatening; also intriguing, intelligent and funny'.

Screenings of her work include: *Unbridled Echoes*, commissioned projections in the New Forest in England (2000); *Couch*, a live internet performance and video projection work at the Piano Nobile Gallery in Geneva (2000); *Transposition*, a two-screen video projection and installation also at the Piano Nobile Gallery (2000); *Faded Wallpaper* at the Video Project Space in the Anthony Wilkinson Gallery in London (2001); *Making of Dandy Dust* in the Mix Experimental Film/Video Festival at the Anthology Film Archives in New York (2001); *Ghost Train*, a video installation with neon and sound at Transit Space in London and the Paço das Artes in São Paulo in Brazil (2002); and *Gate*, a live outdoor film event on Dartmoor in Devon (2002).

BIBLIOGRAPHY:

MacRitchie, L., '*Transposition*' in *Mute, Issue 4*, 1996. O'Pray, Michael, *British Avant Garde Film*, 1996. Darke, C., '*Deviant Beauty: Tina Keane*' in *The Raw and the Cooked*, Institute of Contemporary Arts, London, 1997.

KEARNAN, Thomas
British, 19th century.
Active in London.
Watercolourist. Urban landscapes.

Thomas Kearnan was a member of the New Water-Colour Society which exhibited twenty-five of his works. He also showed two of his paintings at the Royal Academy in London between 1821 and 1850.

KEARNE, Andreas
German, 17th century.
Active in England.
Sculptor.

Of German origin, Kearne established himself in London and sculpted busts and decorative sculptures.

KEARNEY, William Henry
British, 19th century.
Born c. 1800; died 25 June 1858, in London.
Watercolourist.

William Henry Kearney was, for the most part, a painter of landscapes and genre scenes. He was one of the founders, later to become vice-president, of the New Water-Colour Society. He exhibited at the Royal Academy and, more frequently at the New Water-Colour Society, from 1823 to 1858.

MUSEUMS AND GALLERIES:

DUBLIN - LONDON (Victoria and Albert Mus.).

KEARNY, Francis
American, 18th - 19th century.
Born c. 1785, in Perth Amboy (New Jersey); died 1837, in Perth Amboy.
Active in New York and Philadelphia.
Engraver.

Francis Kearny specialised in book illustration.

KEARSE, Mary (Mrs)
Maiden name: Lawrence
British, 18th - 19th century.
Active in London.
Painter. Flowers.

Mary Kearse (née Lawrence) exhibited at the Royal Academy in London under her maiden name, from 1794 to 1813 and, as Mrs Kearse, from 1814 to 1830.

AUCTION RECORDS:

LONDON, 10 July 1980, *Still-life with Flowers* (1807, watercolour heightened with gouache, 23 1/2 x 18 1/2 ins / 59.5 x 47 cm) GBP 450. CREWKERNE, 16 Oct 2003, *Glories of the Garden* (1799, gouache, 26 x 21 ins / 65 x 53 cm) GBP 3,500.

KEARSLEY, H. (Miss)
British, 19th century.
Active in London.
Painter. Figures.

Miss Kearsley exhibited very frequently at the Royal Academy, at the British Institution and at Suffolk Street in the period between 1824 and 1858.

KEARSLEY, Thomas
British, 18th - 19th century.
Active in London.
Painter. Portraits.

Thomas Kearsley was known especially for his portraits of actors. He exhibited his paintings at the Royal Academy in London from 1792 to 1802.

KEASBEY, Henry Turner
American, 20th century.
Born 23 September 1882, in Philadelphia.
Painter. Landscapes.

Henry Keasbey exhibited in New York from 1922.

KEAST, Suzette
American, 20th century.
Born 6 August 1892, in Philadelphia; died 1932.
Painter. Landscapes.

Suzette Keast read art in Philadelphia where she also showed her work. She painted numerous views of Japan.

KEATE, George
British, 18th century.
Born 30 September 1729, in Trowbridge; died 28 June 1797, in London.
Painter, watercolourist. Landscapes, landscapes with figures.

George Keate was destined to become a lawyer; however, he became an amateur painter instead. In 1779, he published an album of nature sketches made on a trip to Margate. He showed his work from 1766 to 1789 in the exhibitions of the Society of Artists, of which he was a member, and at the Royal Academy.

MUSEUMS AND GALLERIES:

LONDON (Victoria and Albert Mus.): a watercolour.

AUCTION RECORDS:

LONDON, 16 March 1982, *Margate* (1771, watercolour, 13 x 19 ins / 33 x 48 cm) USD 1,200. LONDON, 15 Nov 1983, *Bathing Machines at Margate* (watercolour and pen with touches of white, 19 1/2 x 30 ins / 49.7 x 76.2 cm) GBP 2,400.

KEATE, Georgiana. See **HENDERSON**

KEATING, George
Irish, 18th - 19th century.
Born 1762, in Ireland; died 3 February 1842, in London.
Engraver (stippling/mezzotint).

George Keating was trained by W. Dickinson. He worked in London between 1784 and 1799, mostly making engravings of portraits and genre subjects after Reynolds, Gainsborough and Morland. His work is considered to be among the best in the English school; his engravings of *A Party Angling* and *The Angler's Repast* are much sought after. A George Keating exhibited paintings of expressive faces at the Free Society in 1775 and 1776; this may have been the same artist, trying his hand at painting before opting for the artform in which he would excel.

Museums and Galleries:

London (National Portrait Gal.): *George Fordyce* (1795, mezzotint, after Thomas Phillips); *Edward Smith Stanley* (1797, mezzotint, after Gainsborough).

Auction records:

London, 13 Nov 1997, *Children and Nanny in the Fields and other Country Scenes* (1791, mezzotints and dry-point engraving, 38 items) GBP 6,900.

KEATING, John

Irish, 20th century.
Painter. Portraits.

John Keating lived and worked in Dublin.

KEATING, R. H. (Mrs)

British, 19th century.
Active in London.
Painter.

Mrs R.H. Keating exhibited at the Royal Academy between 1884 and 1888.

KEATING, Sean

Irish, 20th century.
Born 29 September 1889, in Limerick; died 21 December 1977, in Dublin.
Painter, watercolourist. Rural scenes, historical subjects, portraits.

Sean Keating was one of Ireland's leading painters during the first half of the 20th century. His work has strong nationalist connotations and is generally regarded as representative of Irish nationalist art. His rural views of Ireland recall the writings of Yeats and Synge. Keating's idealised depiction of a heroic Ireland is best represented by his *Men of the West* (1915) and *Men of the South* (1921). In 1961 Keating painted a mural for the main hall of the International Labour Office in Geneva, and was asked to paint a series of works depicting the Shannon hydro-electrical scheme in the 1920s. In terms of style, his compositions and craftsmanship are very traditional as Keating rejected the application of modernist schools; his work remained faithful to the figurative tradition. Keating trained as an artist at the Metropolitan School of Fine Art in Dublin, thanks to a scholarship which he received in 1911, and won the Taylor scholarship whilst studying there. He studied under William Orpen and worked as his assistant in London for one year in 1915. Back in Dublin, Keating began to teach at the Metropolitan School of Art in 1919, and was appointed Professor of the National College of Art in Dublin in 1934. Keating was asked to join the Royal Hibernian Academy in 1923, and acted as its Director from 1948 to 1962. He begun exhibiting at the Academy in 1914 and continued to do so for 61 years. Keating visited New York on several occasions and held a one-man exhibition at the Hackett Gallery in New York in 1930. His work was also exhibited regularly at the Victor Waddington Gallery in Dublin during the 1930s.

Bibliography:

Sean Keating 1889-1977, exhibition catalogue, Royal Hibernian Academy of Arts, Dublin, 1989.

Museums and Galleries:

Cork (Crawford Municipal Art Gallery): *Men of the South* (1921, oil on canvas) - Dublin (Hugh Lane Gallery): *Men of the West* (1915, oil on canvas).

Auction records:

Slane Castle, 25 June 1979, *Portrait of Eamonn de Valera* (1971, oil on canvas, 19 x 14½ ins / 48 x 37 cm) GBP 620. London, 6 Feb 1985, *Irish Peasant* (coloured chalk/grey paper, 19 x 14 ins / 48 x 35.5 cm) GBP 480. London, 8 Nov 1985, *Christy and the Widow Quin in 'Playboy of the Western World'* (oil on canvas, 30 x 25 ins / 76.2 x 63.5 cm) GBP 2,000. Dublin, 24 Oct 1988, *Turf Boats, Aran* (oil on card, 36 x 48 ins / 91.5 x 122 cm) IEP 9,350; *Sunday Evening* (oil on canvas, 25 x 30¼ ins / 63.5 x 76.8 cm) GBP 12,100. Belfast, 28 Oct 1988, *Portrait of a Gypsy Woman* (oil on panel, 20 x 16 ins / 50.8 x 40.7 cm) GBP 2,420. Dublin, 26 May 1993, *Couple of Aran Islanders beside a Boat* (charcoal, 28 x 20 ins / 71 x 50.8 cm) IEP 2,420; *Fishing Boats in the Shelter of a Jetty in the West of Ireland* (oil on card, 34½ x 44½ ins / 87.6 x 113 cm) IEP 26,400. London, 2 June 1995, *Trawler from the Island of Aran* (oil on canvas, 25 x 30 ins / 63.5 x 76 cm) GBP 13,800. London, 9 May 1996, *The Playboy of the Western World, after the stage play of the same name* (oil on card, 48 x 48 ins / 122 x 122 cm) GBP 15,525. London, 20 May 1999, *Launching the Curragh* (pencil, pastel and oil on paper on board, 33 x 42 ins / 85 x 106 cm) GBP 36,000. Dublin, 8 Dec 1999, *West of Ireland Coastal Scene with Fishermen in a Currach* (oil on canvas, 20 x 24 ins / 51 x 61 cm) IEP 56,000. Dublin, 29 March 2000, *Unloading the Turf Boats, Aran* (oil on canvas, 25 x 31 ins / 63 x 79 cm) IEP 52,000. London, 18 May 2000, *Three Fishermen on Aran* (colour chalk, 19 x 28 ins / 48 x 70 cm) GBP 7,500. Dublin, 5 Dec 2001, *Irish Gothic* (oil on board, 20 x 24 ins / 50 x 60 cm) IEP 15,000. Dublin, 5 Dec 2001, *Exposition of Irish History* (watercolour and gouache, 17 x 39 ins / 43 x 99 cm) IEP 16,000. London, 17 May 2002, *Boatmen of Aran* (charcoal, 22 x 31 ins / 56 x 78 cm) GBP 19,000. Dublin, 3 Dec 2002, *Unloading a Turf Boat, Aran* (oil on canvas on board, 24 x 31 ins / 62 x 78 cm) EUR 135,000. London, 15 May 2003, *Feast of St Bridget* (oil on canvas, 38 x 46 ins / 96 x 117 cm) GBP 120,000. Dublin, 16 Sept 2003, *Head of the Turf Gatherer* (pastel, 20 x 16 ins / 50 x 41 cm) EUR 17,000. Dublin, 27 April 2004, *Self-portrait in Bainin Hat* (pastel, 19 x 15 ins / 48 x 38 cm) EUR 13,500. Dublin, 26 May 2004, *Self-portrait: Man of Aran* (oil on canvas, 36 x 28 ins / 91 x 70 cm) EUR 170,000.

KEBOT, I. Gusti Ketut

Balinese, 20th century.
Born 1917.
Painter. Landscapes.

Auction records:

Singapore, 27 Sept 1997, *Balinese Village Scene* (1955, oil on canvas, 59 x 79 ins / 150 x 200.5 cm) SGD 36,800.

KECK, Charles

American, 19th - 20th century.
Born 9 September 1875, in New York; died 1951.
Sculptor. Statues, monuments.

Charles Keck studied at the Art Students League in New York and rounded off his training by visiting Greece, Florence and Paris. He was a member of the American Federation of Arts. In 1926, he was awarded a Gold Medal by the Archaeological Institute of America. His works can be seen in many large American cities, either in museums or as commemorative public monuments such as the *Jackson Monument* in Charlottesville.

Auction records:

New York, 30 Sept 1988, *In Memoriam, Bronze Commemorative plaque for the USS Maine* (1913, bronze, 12¾ x 17½ ins / 32.4 x 44.5 cm) USD 2,200.

KECK, Emil

German, 19th - 20th century.
Born 2 May 1867, in Wildfeldsried.
Painter. Genre scenes.

Emil Keck was active in Munich. He exhibited there and also in Vienna.

KECK, Jean

German, 19th century.
Active in Saarbrücken.
Painter.

KECK, Otto

German, 19th - 20th century.
Born 20 March 1873, in Oberstaufen; died 1948.

Painter. Portraits, genre scenes, landscapes.

AUCTION RECORDS:

BERN, 30 April 1988, *Village Musicians in an Interior* (1921, oil on canvas, 31 1/2 x 40 1/2 ins / 80 x 103 cm) CHF 12,000. KEMPTEN, 8 July 1999, *View on Burgberg with Allgau Alpine Panorama and Figures* (1941, gouache, 11 x 16 ins / 29 x 40 cm) DEM 3,000. KEMPTEN, 5 Nov 1999, *Spring Day on Christlessee with Snowy Mountains of the Allgau* (1942, oil on canvas, 31 x 39 ins / 80 x 100 cm) DEM 8,300. KEMPTEN, 9 Nov 2000, *Still-life with Flowers and Apples* (1947, oil on board, 20 x 28 ins / 50 x 70 cm) DEM 3,500. KEMPTEN, 9 Nov 2000, *Farmers Talking* (1937, oil on canvas, 25 x 30 ins / 64 x 77 cm) DEM 9,000. KEMPTEN, 8 Nov 2001, *Portrait of a Girl with Plaits* (1932, oil on canvas, 16 x 13 ins / 40 x 33 cm) DEM 5,000. KEMPTEN, 4 Nov 2004, *Pond near Lindenberg in Winter* (1917, oil on canvas, 26 x 50 ins / 66 x 126 cm) EUR 2,700. KEMPTEN, 4 Nov 2004, *Three Local Allgau Peasants in Conversation Round a Table* (1923, oil on canvas, 28 x 39 ins / 71 x 98 cm) EUR 5,500.

KECK, Peter

Bohemian, 18th century.
Died 14 August 1730, in Prague.
Painter. Religious subjects.

Peter Keck was court painter in Prague. He also painted for the church of St Augustine in Wittingau (Trebon) and the church of the Friars Minor in Prague.

KEDWEELLI, David de

British, 14th century.
Born probably in Kidwilly, Wales.
Illuminator, copyist.

David Kedweelli illuminated a two-volume work in a style very untypical of clerical works, which was described by Fleury as 'both sublime and ridiculous'. He was a talented artist who succeeded in painting grotesque subjects with finesse. This work, which was previously kept in the cathedral, is now in the public library in Laon.

KEDZIERSKI, Apolonius

Polish, 19th century.
Born 1851, in Suchedniow.
Painter.

Apolonius Kedzierski studied art in Warsaw, and then in Munich. He painted landscapes among other subjects. He exhibited in Poland, Germany, France and the USA. In 1921, he showed two canvases: *The Fisherman* and *Woman Carrying Water* at the *Exposition des Artistes Polonais* (*exhibition of Polish artists*) organised by the Salon of the Société Nationale des Beaux-Arts.

KEEB, Gustav E.

German, 19th century.
Active in Berlin.
Lithographer.

Keeb specialised in religious painting.

KEEBLE, William, or Keable

British, 18th century.
Active in London.
Portrait artist.

William Keeble or Keable was a member of St Martin's Lane Academy in London in 1754. A portrait of him by Sir Crips Gascoyne was made into an engraving by MacArdell.

KEEFE, Daniel, or O'Keefe

British, 18th century.
Active in London.
Miniaturist.

Daniel Keefe or O'Keefe exhibited at the Royal Academy and at the Free Society between 1769 and 1786.

KEEL, Anna

German, 20th century.
Born in Chemnitz.
Active in Switzerland.
Painter, draughtsman, sculptor. Figures, nudes, portraits, still-lifes, flowers.

Anna Keel studied with the painter Albers Pfifer from 1964 to 1966. She lives and works in Zurich. In 1984, she received a bursary from the Berlin academy. She has taken part in group exhibitions: in 1977, *Papier sur nature* (*Paper on Nature*) at the Autumn Festival in Paris, an exhibition conceived by Jean Clair in the midst of the argument about the return to drawing and figurative painting; and in 1979 at the Musée des Arts Décoratifs in Paris. Since 1971, she has also had solo shows in 1971, 1976, 1979, 1983, 1987 and 1991 in Zurich, as well as in 1983, in Munich, and in 1988 in Essen.

KEELER, Charles B.

American, 20th century.
Born 2 April 1882, in Cedar Rapids (Iowa); died 1964, in Los Angeles County.
Painter, engraver.

Charles Keeler studied under John Christen Johansen and John Calvin Stevens in Chicago. In 1915, he was awarded a silver medal in San Francisco.

KEELEY, John

British, 19th century.
Active in Birmingham.
Painter, watercolourist. Landscapes.

John Keeley exhibited at the New Water-Colour Society from 1883 and 1892 and at the Royal Academy in 1897.

KEELEY, Shelagh

Canadian, 20th - 21st century.
Born 1954, in Oakville (Ontario).
Active in the USA.
Painter, draughtswoman, mixed media.

Shelagh Keeley studied at York University, Toronto. In a varied output centred on drawing, she likes to improvise, integrating sculpture, installations and photographs relevant to her theme. She has held solo shows regularly since 1980, and has exhibited in Canada, the USA, Europe, Australia and India.

KEELHOFF, Alice

Belgian, 20th century.
Born 1896, in Ghent; died 1983.
Painter. Nudes, portraits, still-lifes, flowers.

Alice Keelhoff studied with Jacques Ochs at the Académie des Beaux-Arts in Liège and continued her training in Paris.

MUSEUMS AND GALLERIES:

GHENT.

AUCTION RECORDS:

BRUSSELS, 12 June 1990, *Flowers* (1938, oil on canvas, 36 1/4 x 28 3/4 ins / 92 x 73 cm) BEF 48,000.

KEELHOFF, Frans

Belgian, 19th century.
Born 2 May 1820, in Neerharem; died 19 December 1891 or 1893, in Brussels.
Painter. Landscapes, mountainscapes.

Frans Keelhoff studied at the Koninklijke Academie voor Schone Kunsten in Antwerp and was made a Chevalier of the Ordre de Léopold in 1866. He was awarded medals at exhibitions in Brussels, Vienna and Lyons.

Museums and Galleries:
Antwerp: landscapes - Brussels: landscapes.
Auction records:
Paris, 1890, *Landscape* (with figures by Verboechoven) FRF 1,500. Bern, 3 May 1979, *Mountain Landscape with Stream* (oil on canvas, 28 1/4 x 22 1/2 ins / 72 x 57 cm) CHF 4,600. New York, 15 Dec 2000, *At the Farm* (1851, oil on canvas, 30 x 39 ins / 75 x 99 cm) USD 7,000. Lokeren, 8 Dec 2001, *Landscape in Neerhaeren, Limburg* (oil on canvas, 35 x 56 ins / 90 x 142 cm) BEF 120,000. Brussels, 18 March 2002, *Troops Depart in a Clearing* (oil on canvas, 37 x 46 ins / 94 x 117 cm) EUR 12,400. Brussels, 13 May 2002, *Washerwoman and Fisherman on a Boat* (1882, oil on canvas, 24 x 29 ins / 60 x 74 cm) EUR 2,200. Antwerp, 26 April 2004, *Woodview with Pond and Shepherdess* (1858, oil on canvas, 39 x 28 ins / 100 x 70 cm) EUR 3,200.

KEELHOL, A.
19th century.
Painter. Still-lifes.
A. Keelhol is mentioned in *Art Prices Current*.
Auction records:
London, 20 Feb 1911, *Poultry* (1856) GBP 6.

KEELING, Michael
British, 18th - 19th century.
Died 1820, near Stone (Staffordshire).
Painter.
Michael Keeling worked in Staffordshire. Between 1782 and 1809, he exhibited eight portraits at the Royal Academy.
Auction records:
London, 17 July 1908, *Portraits of Mr and Mrs J. Hall* (1819) GBP 9. London, 29 Feb 1984, *Portrait of Thomas Carlton Whitmore* (1811, oil on canvas, 50 3/4 x 40 3/4 ins / 129 x 103.5 cm) GBP 4,800. San Francisco, 26 May 1999, *Portrait of Sir Thomas Sheppard, Bart.* (1817, oil on canvas, 36 x 28 ins / 91 x 71 cm) USD 1,800. Detroit, 14 March 2003, *Thomas Charlton Whitmore* (oil on canvas, 19 x 16 ins / 49 x 40 cm) USD 15,000. London, 12 Oct 2004, *Portrait of a Gentleman in a Blue Coat. Portrait of a Lady in a White Dress* (1818, oil on canvas, a pair, 29 x 24 ins / 73 x 60 cm) GBP 1,000.

KEELING, William Knight
British, 19th century.
Born 1807, in Manchester; died 21 February 1886, in Boston-on-Irwell (Manchester).
Painter, watercolourist.
William Knight Keeling began as an apprentice to a wood engraver in Manchester. Still a young man, he went to London to become an assistant to W. Bradley, the portrait artist. In 1835, he returned to Manchester and established himself as a portrait painter. He spent a period in Spain, which resulted in some interesting watercolours. He was one of the founders of the Manchester Academy of Fine Arts, serving as president from 1864 to 1877.

From 1840 to 1885, Keeling exhibited his work in London at the Royal Academy and, more particularly, at the New Water-Colour Society of which he was named associate in 1840 and became a member in 1841.
Museums and Galleries:
London (Victoria and Albert Mus.): two watercolours - Salford (Museum and AG): *William Bow*.

KEEN, Oscar
Swedish, 19th - 20th century.
Born 1867; died 1949.
Painter. Landscapes with figures, urban landscapes, landscapes.
Auction records:
Stockholm, 20 Oct 1987, *Winter's Day* (1895, oil on canvas, 24 1/2 x 17 ins / 62 x 43 cm) SEK 60,000. Stockholm, 19 April 1989, *Undulating Wooded Meadow in Summer* (1929, oil on panel, 15 3/4 x 12 1/2 ins / 40 x 32 cm) SEK 5,000. Stockholm, 14 Nov 1990, *Town with a Fortified Bridge over the River Pegnitz* (oil on canvas, 55 x 37 1/2 ins / 140 x 95 cm) SEK 21,000. Stockholm, 19 May 1992, *Bell-Tower in a Village in the Auvergne in France* (oil on canvas, 41 x 28 1/4 ins / 104 x 72 cm) SEK 9,200. Stockholm, 30 Nov 1993, *Two Children in a Village Street in Winter* (1888, oil on canvas, 26 1/2 x 40 1/2 ins / 67 x 103 cm) SEK 18,000. Stockholm, 28 May 2002, *He Loves Me, He Loves Me Not* (1896, oil on canvas, 22 x 18 ins / 56 x 46 cm) SEK 30,000.

KEENAN (Mrs)
British, 19th century.
Active in Windsor.
Painter. Landscapes, architectural views.
Mrs Keenan was the wife of John Keenan. She exhibited at the Royal Academy in London between 1807 and 1813.

KEENAN, John
British, 18th - 19th century.
Miniaturist.
John Keenan worked in Bath, Exeter, London and Windsor. He exhibited his work at the Royal Academy from 1791 to 1815 and was nominated court painter to Queen Charlotte in 1809.

KEENAN, L.
British, 19th century.
Active in London.
Painter.
L. Keenan exhibited her work at the Royal Academy from 1834 to 1836.

KEENAN, William
American, 19th century.
Active in Philadelphia c. 1830, and in Charleston.
Engraver.

KEENE, Alfred John, called Jack
British, 19th - 20th century.
Born 1864, in Derby; died 1930, in Derby.
Watercolourist. Landscapes, figures.
Jack Keene was born into a family of Midlands artists. His brother was the illustrator William Caxton Keene and his father was an art dealer and photographer; his wife was also an artist. He is known for his very accurate landscapes, with old Derbyshire buildings in pale colour and in vignette form. His later palette is more colourful and the tone of his work more atmospheric. He was also skilled at figure drawing. He exhibited *After the Winter* and *Morning Breeze, Guernsey* at the Society of British Artists (1892).
Museums and Galleries:
Derby (Art Gallery).

KEENE, Charles Samuel
British, 19th century.
Born 10 August 1823, in Hornsey; died 4 January 1891, in London.
Watercolourist, engraver, draughtsman, caricaturist.
Charles Samuel Keene was one of the important artists of his time, holding a place equal to that held by Daumier in France. After working with a lawyer and an architect, he was placed as a pupil with the well-known Whymper brothers, engravers.

Keene's first illustrations were for *Robinson Crusoe* and *The Adventures of Dick Boldhero in search of his Uncle*. He also collaborated on an amusing work entitled *Book of Beauty*. In 1851, he began working for *Punch* with a satirical drawing of Louis Bonaparte; however, it was not until 1860 that he was assigned a pre-eminent position on the magazine.

Keene's wit and concern with his art led to his producing types which quickly became popular. He gave life to a series of picturesque London figures and placed them in superbly drawn settings around the city. He collaborated on the magazine *Once a Week*. He also illustrated *The Voyage of the Constance* by M. Gillier; *Sea Kings and Naval Heroes* by J.G. Edgar; *The Cambridge Grisette* by Herbert Vaughan; and *Eyebright, The Round about Papers* by Thackeray. He exhibited his work in Paris in 1890 and won a gold medal.

MUSEUMS AND GALLERIES:

LONDON (National Portrait Gal.): *Sir John Everett Millais* (pen and ink); *John Laird* (1872, three pencil sketches); *Charles Samuel Keene* (c. 1885, pen and ink).

AUCTION RECORDS:

LONDON, 24 July 1911, *Irish Court; Dry and Wet* (two ink drawings) GBP 1. PARIS, 27 Feb 1919, *The Androgynœceum Club* (pen) FRF 190. PARIS, 28 Nov 1924, *Illustrations for Punch* (four drawings) FRF 880. PARIS, 31 May 1928, *The Cliff* (watercolour) FRF 300. LONDON, 24 April 1929, *Sitting Lady Reading* (pen) GBP 44. LONDON, 27 May 1935, *Collection of Drawings*, GBP 135. LONDON, 19 June 1979, *Two Artists Painting by Lamplight* (pen, 7 x 5 ins / 18 x 12.5 cm) GBP 2,800. LONDON, 27 April 1982, *Self-portrait in the Studio* (pen, 12 1/2 x 7 1/2 ins / 32 x 19 cm) GBP 850. LONDON, 14 June 1991, *The Assault of Makakoff* (ink and watercolour heightened with white/grey paper, 11 x 16 ins / 27.9 x 40.7 cm) GBP 1,100. LONDON, 23 Nov 2004, *Artist's Repose* (oil on board, 7 x 9 ins / 18 x 23 cm) GBP 4,200.

KEENE, E.
British, 19th - 20th century.
Painter.

E. Keene was awarded a gold medal at the Paris Exposition Universelle of 1889.

KEENE, Peter
British, 20th century.
Born in Birmingham.
Active since 1986 in France.
Assemblage artist.

Peter Keene was represented by Galerie Luc Queyrel at the 1993 Salon Découvertes, held in Paris at the Grand Palais. His 'sculptures' are assemblages of heterogeneous, carefully finished elements, which exploit the comic potential of their highly unexpected combinations. The plastic presence of the works is accentuated by the inclusion of often quite incongruous recorded noises.

KEENE, W. C.
British, 19th century.
Painter, engraver. Landscapes.

W.C. Keene exhibited in London at the Suffolk Street Gallery from 1877 to 1891 and, more particularly, at the Royal Academy from 1880 to 1891.

KEENER, Anna Elizabeth, or married name: Wilton
American, 20th century.
Born 16 October 1895, in Flagler (Colorado); died 1982, in Santa Fe (New Mexico).
Painter.

Anna Keener studied under Sven Birger Sandzen. She was a member of the American Federation of Arts. Her works can be seen in the museums of the American West.

KEENS, H. L.
British, 19th century.
Active in London.
Painter. Fruit.

H.L. Keens exhibited in London at the Royal Academy, the Suffolk Street Gallery, and the British Institution from 1822 to 1860.

KEERBERGER, Johannes de
Dutch, 18th century.
Active in Rotterdam in 1772.
Sculptor.

Johannes de Keerberger created the Delft gate in Rotterdam.

KEERDT
German, 19th century.
Active in Frankfurt c. 1842.
Painter. Landscapes.

KEERE, Pieter van der or van den, or Keerke, called Kaerius
Flemish School, 16th - 17th century.
Born c. 1571, in Ghent; died after 1624.
Engraver, print publisher.

Pieter van der Keere was married on 18 September 1599 to Anna Burth, from Ghent, and was later remarried, on 10 March 1623, to Anneken Wennings. He worked in Amsterdam. The year of his birth, claimed by biographers to be 1571, is probably inaccurate. His magnificent illustrations in a book by Guiccardini, published by Plantin in 1588, seem to be the work of a mature artist, not a boy of 17. His works include *A Description of the Low Countries* by Loys Guiccardini, *A Description of Lower Germany*, by Petri Berti, *A Procession of Monks of All Orders, The Duke of Guise marrying Elizabeth of France on the authorisation of the King of Spain, View of Nuremberg, The Death of Maurice near Wesel*, and a *View of Bigorne in Scherminkel*.

KEERINCX, Alexander, or Keerinck, Keirinck, Kierings, Carings, Cierings
Flemish School, 17th century.
Born 23 January 1600, in Antwerp; died c. 1652, in Amsterdam.
Painter, engraver. Religious and mythological subjects, landscapes with figures, landscapes.

Alexander Keerincx was a member of the Antwerp guild in 1619. He married in the city on 18 June 1622 and remained there until 1626, when he went to England to work for the king. In 1643 he was living in Amsterdam and received citizen's rights in 1652. He is also believed to have lived in Utrecht as many of his landscapes were decorated by C. Poelenbourg and Paul van Hellegaer, who both worked there; other artists he collaborated with include S. Vrancx, Fr Franken, Esaias van de Velde, E.T. van Hagelstein, Jurian Jacobs, David Teniers and Ad Brouwer. In 1624 he had Aertus Verhoeven as his pupil. English historical records show that a J. Keirincx or Carings, born in Utrecht in 1590, worked for Charles I and died in Amsterdam in 1646. We believe this to be the same artist.

Keerincx painted a number of royal castles and palaces in Scotland. He painted in a powerfully realist manner and also produced engravings of landscapes. His lyrical interpretation of nature makes him, to some extent, a link between the painting of Coninxloo and that of Rubens. However, his landscapes gradually became almost monochrome like those of Van Goyen.

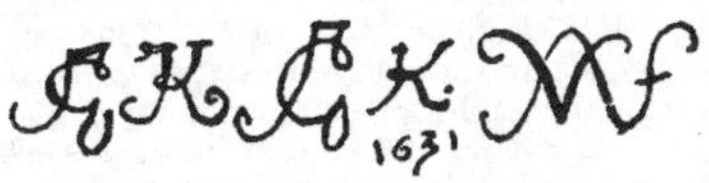

Museums and Galleries:
Aachen: *Road in the Forest* - Antwerp (Koninklijk Mus. voor Schone Kunsten): *Landscape with Stag Hunt* - Basel: *Landscape* - Bremen: *Figures in a Landscape* - Brunswick: *Nymphs in a Forest; Landscape with Peasants; Evening Landscape with Shepherds* - Copenhagen: *Forest* - Darmstadt: *Attack on a Stage Coach* - Dresden: *Forest and River; Fish Pond in the Forest; Path on a Hill; Path beside the Water* - Hamburg: *Landscape* - Hanover: *Landscape* - La Fère: *Landscape* - Leipzig: *Temple Ruins* - Mainz: *Landscape* - Montpellier (Mus. Fabre): *Landscape with Callisto* (oil on wood) - Munich: *Hunt in the Forest* - Oberschleissheim: *Temptation of Christ* - Rennes: *The Creation of Man* - Richmond (Virginia MFA): *Landscape with Cephalus and Procis* (c. 1620, oil/wood) - Rotterdam: *Forest with the Figure of Hillegaert* - Schwerin: *Forest; Forest Landscape* - St Petersburg (Hermitage): *Diana Bathing; Forest with Hunt* - The Hague: *Landscape with Figures*.
Auction records:
London, 11-12 May 1911, *Rest on the Flight into Egypt*, GBP 8. Paris, 21 Feb 1919, *Hunting with Falcons*, FRF 1,550. Paris, 28 Feb 1919, *Winter in Holland*, FRF 1,000. Paris, 5 Dec 1923, *Diana Discovering the Pregnancy of Callisto*, FRF 720. London, 31 July 1925, *Landscape*, GBP 52. Paris, 24 March 1955, *Road on the Plain*, FRF 420,000. Paris, 4 June 1958, *Wooded Landscape*, FRF 1,020,000. Paris, 24 June 1960, *River Banks*, FRF 14,300. London, 10 July 1963, *Wooded Landscape*, GBP 2,400. London, 21 April 1967, *River Landscape with Diana and Actaeon*, Gns 1,700. Paris, 24 Oct 1968, *The Ford*, FRF 14,000. Vienna, 22 Sept 1970, *Shepherds Resting in a Wooded Landscape*, ATS 250,000. London, 24 Nov 1971, *Wooded River Landscape*, GBP 2,000. Zurich, 12 Nov 1976, *Landscape with Argus and Mercury* (oil on panel, 17 3/4 x 29 1/2 ins / 45 x 75 cm) CHF 41,000. Zurich, 25 Nov 1977, *Wooded River Landscape with Figures* (oil on panel, 22 x 33 1/2 ins / 55 x 85 cm) CHF 50,000. New York, 9 Oct 1980, *Travellers in a Wooded Landscape* (oil on panel, 26 x 37 3/4 ins / 66 x 96 cm) USD 95,000. London, 11 Dec 1984, *Peasants on a Path in a Wooded Landscape* (oil on panel, 9 1/2 x 8 ins / 24.1 x 20.3 cm) GBP 7,000. London, 11 April 1986, *View of Pontefract, Yorkshire* (oil on panel, 20 3/4 x 27 ins / 53 x 68.5 cm) GBP 15,000. New York, 21 Oct 1988, *Hunt Scene in an Extensive Wooded Landscape* (oil on canvas, 46 1/2 x 62 3/4 ins / 118 x 159.5 cm) USD 44,000. London, 8 Dec 1989, *Falcon Hunt in a Wooded River Landscape* (oil on panel, 15 1/2 x 11 1/4 ins / 39.2 x 28.5 cm) GBP 34,100. New York, 1 June 1990, *Hunting Party in an Extensive Wooded River Landscape* (oil on canvas, 45 1/2 x 62 1/2 ins / 115.5 x 159 cm) USD 60,500. Amsterdam, 12 June 1990, *Forest Pond* (oil on panel, 19 1/4 x 15 1/4 ins / 49.2 x 38.5 cm) NLG 8,625. Paris, 22 June 1990, *Forest Landscape with River* (oil on oak panel, 18 1/2 x 20 3/4 ins / 47 x 53 cm) FRF 100,000. London, 3 July 1991, *Wooded Landscape with Hunters on a Path Crossing a Pond* (oil on panel, 15 1/4 x 19 1/4 ins / 39 x 48.8 cm) GBP 6,600. Monaco, 5-6 Dec 1991, *Hunters' Call* (oil on panel, 15 3/4 x 23 ins / 40 x 58.2 cm) FRF 532,800. London, 15 April 1992, *Extensive Landscape with an Artist Drawing a Town in the Distance* (oil on panel, 17 3/4 x 27 ins / 45.4 x 68.6 cm) GBP 9,000. Monaco, 2 July 1993, *Return from the Market* (oil on canvas, 26 x 41 ins / 66 x 104 cm) FRF 333,000. Amsterdam, 16 Nov 1993, *Pastoral* (oil on panel, 12 1/2 x 24 1/2 ins / 31.5 x 62 cm) NLG 48,300. New York, 19 May 1994, *Rest on the Flight into Egypt* (oil on panel, 19 1/4 x 14 1/2 ins / 48.9 x 36.8 cm) USD 13,800. New York, 15 May 1996, *Wooded Landscape with the Chariot of Venus Pulled by Swans* (oil on canvas, 41 1/2 x 37 1/2 ins / 105.5 x 95 cm) USD 34,500. London, 11 Dec 1996, *Hunting Party by a Lake* (oil on canvas, 36 1/2 x 44 ins / 93 x 112 cm) GBP 87,300. New York, 31 Jan 1997, *Rest on the Flight into Egypt* (oil on remounted panel, 22 1/2 x 33 1/2 ins / 57.2 x 85 cm) USD 55,200. Paris, 13 June 1997, *Wooded Landscape by a River with Two Figures on a Road* (oak panel, 13 x 18 1/2 ins / 33 x 47 cm) FRF 140,000. Amsterdam, 10 Nov 1997, *Nymphs Hunting Deer by a Pond in a Wooded Landscape* (oil on panel, in collaboration with Cornelis Van Poelenbourg, 30 1/2 x 24 1/2 ins / 77.2 x 62.5 cm) NLG 32,289. London, 3 Dec 1997, *Wooded Landscape with Peasants in a Cart and Travellers on a Road* (oil on panel, 12 x 19 1/4 ins / 30.7 x 49 cm) GBP 36,700. Lyons, 17 Oct 1999, *Horseman on the Edge of a Town* (oil on panel, 22 x 32 ins / 57 x 81 cm) FRF 200,000. Paris, 8 Dec 1999, *Pastoral Scene in a Forest Landscape* (oil on canvas, 75 x 98 ins / 190 x 248 cm) FRF 280,000. Amsterdam, 9 May 2001, *Peasant Women on a Forest Track by a River* (1664, oil on panel, 44 x 31 ins / 112 x 80 cm) NLG 60,000. Lille, 21 Oct 2001, *Apollo and Daphne. Venus and Adonis. Silvio and Dorinda* (wood cabinet) FRF 950,000. London, 12 Dec 2002, *Landscape with Pond by Woods and Figures on a Track* (oil on panel, 15 x 19 ins / 39 x 49 cm) GBP 13,000. New York, 24 Jan 2003, *Wooded Landscape with Stream and Stag* (oil on panel, 7 x 9 ins / 19 x 24 cm) USD 15,000. Stockholm, 26 May 2003, *River Landscape* (oil on panel, 5 x 4 ins / 12 x 10 cm) SEK 29,000. London, 21 April 2004, *Wooded Landscape with the Hunt of Diana* (oil on panel, 31 x 48 ins / 78 x 121 cm) GBP 12,000.

KEERKE, Pieter Van der. See **KEERE**

KEERLE
German, 19th century.
Born 1823; died 1875.
Painter. History painting.
Keerle was a pupil of Cornelius.

KEERLE, Christian
Flemish School, 17th century.
Active in Ypres.
Painter.
Christian Keerle worked in Vienna in 1684.

KEERSTBACH, Claeys Heynderics von, or Keisbac
German, 15th century.
Born in Cologne.
Painter.
Von Keerstbach was a master in Bruges in 1475, and taught Looykin Boch in 1477.

KEERT
German, 19th century.
Active in Frankfurt in the middle of the 19th century.
Painter. Landscapes.
Museums and Galleries:
La Fère: two landscapes.

KEETELHOET, Willem
Dutch, 18th century.
Born 1740, in Amsterdam.
Painter, draughtsman.

Willem Keetelhoet was a pupil of G. van der Myn at The Hague in 1778. He was in Leiden in 1793 and painted portraits, including group portraits.

KEFER, Philipp
German, 16th century.
Active in Amberg in 1594.
Painter.

KEFFER, Frances Alice
American, 20th century.
Born 6 January 1881, in Des Moines (Iowa); died 21 March 1953, in San Diego.
Painter.
Frances Keffer studied at the Pratt Institute and under Alexander Robinson. She was a member of the Pen and Brush Club.

KEGEL
Flemish School, 18th century.
Active in Vienna between 1700 and 1740.
Painter. Landscapes.
Kegel was originally from Antwerp. Nothing is known of any surviving works by him.

KEGEL, Hans
German, 15th century.
Born in Fulda.
Painter.
He worked in Würzburg.

KEGEL, Jules de. See **KEGHEL**

KEGELJAN, Franz or Frans
Belgian, 19th - 20th century.
Born 1847, in Namur; died 1920, in Profonde.
Painter, pastellist, engraver. Historical subjects, landscapes, waterscapes, urban landscapes.
Franz Kegeljan travelled in France, Germany and Italy. He painted mainly landscapes on the banks of the Meuse, the Ourthe and the Semois, as well as in France and Italy. He painted 40 canvases showing the history of the city of Namur, but they were burnt in 1914. He reconstituted them and donated them to the city of his birth.
AUCTION RECORDS:
AMSTERDAM, 2 Nov 1992, *View of Venice* (pastel, 15 1/4 x 23 3/4 ins / 38.5 x 60.5 cm) NLG 6,900. BRUSSELS, 26 Nov 2002, *Young Women in the Dunes* (oil on canvas, 16 x 24 ins / 40 x 60 cm) EUR 2,800.

KEGHEL, Désiré de
Belgian, 19th century.
Born 1839, in Ghent; died 1901, in Ghent.
Painter. Flowers.
There are works by Désiré de Keghel in the museums of Ghent and Courtrai (*Azaleas*).

KEGHEL, Joseph de
Belgian, 19th century.
Glass painter, lithographer.
Among other clients, Joseph de Keghel worked for Tournai Cathedral.

KEGHEL, Jules de, or Kegel
Belgian, 19th century.
Born 1828 or 1835, in Ghent; died 15 March 1879, in Ghent.
Painter, miniaturist. Religious subjects, portraits, genre scenes, still-lifes.
Jules de Keghel is known for his still-lifes, portraits and religious paintings.

KEGLER, August
German, 19th century.
Active in Berlin.
Portrait artist.
Kegler exhibited in Berlin in 1866 and 1878.

KEGYES, Jozsef
Hungarian, 19th - 20th century.
Born 15 June 1834, in Bölcske; died 1914.
Painter.
Jozsef Kegyes lived in Budapest and painted portraits and scenes from peasant life.

KEHR, Albert
French, 20th century.
Born 25 April 1914, in Strasbourg.
Painter. Still-lifes.
Albert Kehr studied under Émile Schneider. He later became a drawing teacher.

KEHR, Johann Philipp
German, 19th century.
Born c. 1800, in Bad Kreuznach.
Lithographer.
Kehr established himself in Cologne and mainly illustrated religious books.

KEHR, Karl
German, 19th - 20th century.
Born 16 March 1866, in Nuremberg; died 9 December 1919, in Neuenstein.
Painter. Landscapes.
Karl Kehr painted landscapes and still-lifes.

KEHREN, Josef
German, 19th century.
Born 30 May 1817, in Hülchrath; died 12 May 1880, in Düsseldorf.
Painter, fresco painter. Religious subjects.
Kehren was a pupil of Schadow at the academy in Düsseldorf. He worked with Rethel in Aachen and completed frescoes begun by his teacher.
AUCTION RECORDS:
MUNICH, 12 June 1991, *The Lorelei* (oil on canvas, 54 3/4 x 43 ins / 139 x 109 cm) DEM 16,500.

KEHRER, Christian Wilhelm Karl
German, 18th - 19th century.
Born 30 May 1770, in Erbach; died 29 February 1869, in Erbach.
Painter. Animals.
Kehrer was the brother of Karl Kehrer and father of Eduard Kehrer. He exhibited for the first time in 1800 at the academy in Berlin. He did a lot of work for Frederick I, king of Württemberg.
AUCTION RECORDS:
COLOGNE, 9 May 1983, *Wild Cats; Foxes; Stag and Other Animals* (1835-1836, oil on canvas, series of six, 20 3/4 x 18 1/2 ins / 53 x 47 cm) DEM 38,000. NEW YORK, 24 Jan 2002, *Rhinoceros* (1821, oil on canvas, 21 x 32 ins / 53 x 82 cm) USD 45,000.

KEHRER, Eduard
German, 19th century.
Born 9 December 1812, in Erbach; died 25 October 1863, in Erbach.
Painter. Horses.
Kehrer was the son of Christian Kehrer; he spent quite a while in Vienna.
MUSEUMS AND GALLERIES:
DARMSTADT: several works.

KEHRER, Karl Christian
German, 18th - 19th century.
Born 14 August 1755, in Dillenburg; died 7 April 1833, in Ballenstedt.

Painter. Portraits, genre scenes.
Kehrer was a pupil of A.W. Tischbein in Hanau, near Frankfurt. In 1782 he was court painter to the Prince of Anhalt-Bernburg. He subsequently worked in Dresden, where he sought advice from Casanova, then settled down in Ballenstedt (Harz). In 1793, he was admitted to the academy in Berlin. He exhibited in Berlin and Dresden.

KEHRLI, Heinrich
Swiss, 19th century.
Born 21 April 1811; died 14 November 1866, in Willigen.
Engraver (wood).

KEHRMANN, Jean Louis
German, 19th century.
Born 8 July 1865, in Koblenz; died 20 March 1891, in Rhens, near Koblenz.
Watercolourist. Landscapes.
Kehrmann trained at the academy in Düsseldorf, then with Schönleber in Karlsruhe. He first exhibited in Berlin in 1887, and won a gold medal there in 1888. He also exhibited in Munich and Bremen.
AUCTION RECORDS:
COLOGNE, 23 May 1985, *View of Niederfell* (watercolour, 15 1/4 ins / 38.50 cm) DEM 2,800.

KEIBUN, real name: Keibun Matsumara, nickname: Shiso, Kamane, pseudonym: Kakei, Keibun
Japanese, 19th century.
Born 1779; died 1843.
Active in Kyoto.
Painter. Landscapes, animals, flowers.
School of Shijo.
Keibun studied under his brother Goshun (1752-1811) and was a member of the Shijo School. His delicate works and refined touch helped to enhance the reputation of his brother's school in the Kyoto-Osaka region. He worked with the Confucian Genzui Koishi and was particularly well-versed in the artistic theories of the Chinese Ming (1368-1644) and Qing (1644-1911) dynasties. He was a painter of flowers and birds.
AUCTION RECORDS:
NEW YORK, 23 Oct 1991, *Winter Landscape*; *Summer Landscape* (ink and diluted pigments/silk, a pair, kakemono, 49 1/2 x 18 1/2 ins / 125.5 x 47 cm) USD 13,200.

KEIBUN, Matsumura. See **KEIBUN**

KEIEN
Japanese, 14th century.
Active during the first half of the 14th century.
Sculptor.
Keien was a *dai busshi* (master sculptor) and *koshi* (lecturer) in Omi province, who made the statue of Buddha Amida (Sanskrit: Amithâba) preserved at the Kongorin-ji temple (Shiga Prefecture), dated the 30th day of the fifth month 1326. This fine, powerful and technically assured work is an excellent representative of the style of the En School created by Myoen (died 1199).

KEIGA, real name: Keiga Kawabara
Japanese, 19th century.
Active c. 1890.
Painter.
School of Nagasaki.

KEIGERLIN, Alois, or Ketterlin
Swiss, 19th century.
Active in Basel.
Miniaturist.

KEIHO
Japanese, 19th century.
Draughtsman.
Keiho was a draughtsman working in the characteristic, lively style which brought 19th-century Japanese artists international success. His *Woman with Cage* was seen in Paris.

KEIJ, Adriaen Thomasz. See **KEY**

KEIKAKU. See **HAKUIN**

KEIKOKU, real name: Masao Gejo, pseudonym: Keikoku
Japanese, 19th - 20th century.
Born 1842; died 1920.
Painter.
Keikoku was a painter of the Nanga School (literati painting). He lived in Tokyo and was a member of the Academy of Fine Art.

KEIKYO DOJIN. See **HOITSU**

KEIL, Alfredo
Portuguese, 19th century.
Born 1851 or 1854, in Lisbon; died 24 October 1907, in Hamburg, Germany.
Also active in Germany.
Painter, musician. Portraits, genre scenes, interiors with figures, landscapes, seascapes, animals.
Alfredo Keil was German by birth. He studied under August van Kreling in Nuremberg and Wilhelm von Kaulbach in Munich. In Portugal he studied under master Miguel Angelo Lupi. He was awarded a bronze medal at the Paris Exposition Universelle of 1900. Keil was also a musician, and composed several operas as well as the Portuguese national anthem.

At the start of his career, under the influence of the German masters, Keil painted anecdotal subjects and interiors, executing these with great precision. Later, in Portugal, he was attracted to the landscape and became skilled at rendering the fine light of the Collares region in a style similar to that of the Barbizon School.
MUSEUMS AND GALLERIES:
LISBON (Mus. do Chiado): *A Flock*; *Study Table* (1868); *The Letter*; *Seascape*.
AUCTION RECORDS:
LISBON, 23-24 Oct 1973, *Sea Shore*, PTE 49,000.

KEIL, Bernhardt or Ebehardt, or Keyl or Keilhau, also known as Monsù Bernardo
Danish, 17th century.
Born 1624, in Helsingborg; died 3 February 1687, in Rome.
Painter. Genre scenes.
Bernhardt Keil was a pupil of Martin van Steenwinkel in Copenhagen. He went to Amsterdam in 1647 and worked in Rembrandt's studio for eight years until the Dutch master's financial ruin. In 1656 he went to Kiel, followed by Rome, where he converted to Catholicism. He worked for various churches but was most known for his treatment of comic subjects. Among his works are *God the Father, The Son* and *The Virgin*, which were donated by Prince Metternich to the church in Mainz. These paintings are now in the church in Loerzweeler.
BIBLIOGRAPHY:
Heimbürger, Minna, '*Bernardo Keilhau a Venezia Minna Heimburger*' in *Arte Veneta a. 39 (1985) p. 65-76*, periodical, 1985. Heimbürger, Minna, *Bernardo Keilhau, detto Monsù Bernardo*, Bozzi, Rome, 1988. Koester, Olaf/Keil, Bernhard, *Bernardo Keilhau i Holland og Italien*, Statens Museum for Kunst, Copenhagen, 1991.
MUSEUMS AND GALLERIES:
CHAMBÉRY (MBA): *The Chestnut Merchant*; *Family Education* - COPENHAGEN: *The Evening Visit*.

AUCTION RECORDS:
LONDON, 26 July 1950, *The Piper*, GBP 220. PARIS, 30 May 1951, *Lady with a Book*, FRF 95,000. PARIS, 13 Dec 1954, *Young Boy with Flowered Hat*, FRF 60,000. MILAN, 16 May 1962, *Genre Scene*, ITL 950,000. MILAN, 19 Nov 1963, *The Market*, ITL 1,100,000. LONDON, 6 Nov 1964, *Two Musicians Tuning their Instruments*, Gns 850. LONDON, 11 July 1973, *Sleeping Girl*, GBP 9,000. NEW YORK, 22 Jan 1976, *Old Man Warming his Hands by a Fire* (oil on canvas, 38 1/4 x 28 1/4 ins / 97 x 72 cm) USD 6,750. MILAN, 29 April 1977, *Market Scene* (oil on canvas, 37 1/2 x 53 1/4 ins / 95.5 x 135.5 cm) ITL 8,500,000. LONDON, 12 Dec 1979, *Sleeping Boy* (oil on canvas, 21 3/4 x 41 3/4 ins / 55.5 x 106 cm) GBP 8,500. NEW YORK, 28 Oct 1981, *The Road of Nations* (oil on canvas, 48 1/2 x 78 1/2 ins / 123.2 x 199.4 cm) USD 4,200. LONDON, 10 Dec 1986, *Little Girl with Cat* (oil on canvas, 19 1/2 x 37 3/4 ins / 49.5 x 96 cm) GBP 9,000. NEW YORK, 7 April 1988, *Young Woman with a Guitar* (oil on panel, diam. 15 ins / 38 cm) USD 15,400. MONACO, 16 June 1989, *Bread Carrier with Woman Nursing her Baby* (oil on canvas, 55 x 69 3/4 ins / 140 x 177 cm) FRF 310,800. LONDON, 11 April 1990, *Man Sealing a Letter and Woman with a Candle Approaching from Behind* (oil on canvas, 38 x 28 1/4 ins / 96.5 x 72 cm) GBP 22,000. PARIS, 30 Jan 1991, *Nativity* (oil on canvas, 28 1/2 x 53 1/4 ins / 72.5 x 135.5 cm) FRF 100,000. MONACO, 5-6 Dec 1991, *Portrait of a Child* (oil on canvas, 16 3/4 x 13 1/4 ins / 42.5 x 33.5 cm) FRF 28,860. LONDON, 13 Dec 1991, *Seated Little Girl Tatting Lace near Little Girl Holding a Letter (Allegory of Sight)* (oil on canvas, 28 1/4 x 39 ins / 72 x 98.2 cm) GBP 27,500. LONDON, 8 July 1992, *Study Room* (oil on canvas, 42 3/4 x 56 1/2 ins / 108.5 x 143.5 cm) GBP 55,000. NEW YORK, 14 Oct 1992, *Two Lacemakers* (oil on canvas, 35 1/4 x 27 ins / 89.5 x 68.6 cm) USD 14,300. LONDON, 22 April 1994, *Pilgrim Offering a Bowl of Food to a Spaniard While Peasants Eat and Drink* (oil on canvas, 43 x 56 1/2 ins / 109 x 143.5 cm) GBP 67,500. LONDON, 5 July 1995, *Personification of the Senses: Sight, Touch, Hearing and Taste* (collection of four oils on panel, each diam. 14 ins / 35.5 cm) GBP 45,500. ROME, 22 Nov 1995, *Head of an Old Man* (oil on canvas, 15 1/4 x 11 1/2 ins / 38.5 x 29 cm) ITL 5,290,000. NEW YORK, 11 Jan 1996, *Four Peasants in a Landscape: Allegory of Hearing and Sight* (oil on canvas, 39 x 54 1/2 ins / 99.1 x 138.4 cm) USD 101,500. LONDON, 5 July 1996, *Young Couple of Musicians* (oil on canvas, 29 x 38 1/4 ins / 73.6 x 97.3 cm) GBP 42,000. NEW YORK, 29 Jan 1999, *Young Man and Girl Tuning Musical Instruments* (oil on canvas, 29 x 38 ins / 74 x 97 cm) USD 54,000. NEW YORK, 28 May 1999, *Old Man and Woman Placing Wax Seal on Letter* (1683, oil on canvas, 23 x 38 ins / 59 x 96 cm) USD 46,000. MADRID, 4 July 2000, *Drunkards* (oil on canvas, 46 x 58 ins / 116 x 148 cm) ESP 900,000. VENICE, 15 Dec 2000, *St James the Apostle* (oil on canvas, 24 x 18 ins / 62 x 46 cm) ITL 19,500,000. LONDON, 25 April 2001, *Allegory of Autumn. Allegory of Winter* (oil on canvas, a pair, 38 x 28 ins / 97 x 72 cm) GBP 30,000. LONDON, 12 Dec 2001, *Recumbent Shepherd Boy with Sleeping Dog by his Side* (oil on canvas, 20 x 50 ins / 52 x 127 cm) GBP 105,000. AMSTERDAM, 14 May 2002, *Old Lady at her Toilette* (oil on panel) EUR 9,500. PARIS, 25 June 2002, *Allegory of Touch* (oil on canvas, 33 x 51 ins / 85 x 130 cm) EUR 7,500. LONDON, 10 Dec 2003, *Seated Boy Holding a Red Pot in his Left Hand* (oil on canvas, 38 x 28 ins / 96 x 72 cm) GBP 32,000. LONDON, 10 Dec 2003, *Young Man with Pot of Roses* (oil on canvas, 38 x 28 ins / 96 x 72 cm) GBP 42,000. STOCKHOLM, 26 May 2004, *Three Children* (oil on canvas, 28 x 37 ins / 70 x 94 cm) SEK 290,000.

KEIL, Carl
German, 20th century.
Died before 1910.
Active in Berlin.
Sculptor.
Carl Keil won a gold medal in Berlin in 1866.

KEIL, Christian
German, 19th century.
Born 4 June 1826, in Siegritz (Thuringia); died 19 June 1890, in Munich.
Sculptor.
Keil completed his studies in Regensburg, then worked mainly for churches, including those in Landshut, Dingelstadt (Thuringia) and above all Munich.

KEIL, Franz Friedrich
German, 19th century.
Born 2 July 1813, in Liebau (Lubawka), Silesia; died 17 January 1875, in Breslau (now Wroclaw, Poland).
Painter. Genre scenes, portraits.
Keil was a pupil of his father Johann Friedrich Keil and of Wach at the academy in Berlin.
MUSEUMS AND GALLERIES:
BERLIN (Nationalgal.): *Portrait of Blaser the Sculptor* (1853).

KEIL, Gerhard
German, 20th century.
Born 1912, in Dresden; died 1992.
Painter. Genre scenes. Murals.
National Socialist Art.
Gerhard Keil studied in Dresden at the Kunsthochschule and then at the Kunstakademie. He won the Prix de Rome in 1938 and remained in Italy until 1940. He celebrated the Nazi regime in his genre paintings and also created fairground decorations.
BIBLIOGRAPHY:
Pagé, Suzanne/Winock, Michel/Michaud, Éric/Vidal, Aline, *Les Années trente en Europe. Le Temps menaçant*, exhibition catalogue, Musée d'Art moderne de la Ville de Paris, Paris musées, Flammarion, Paris, 1997.
MUSEUMS AND GALLERIES:
DRESDEN (Gemäldegal. Neue Meister): *Gymnast* (1939); *Gymnasts* (1939).

KEIL, Hélène
Belgian, 20th - 21st century.
Born 1948, in Tongeren (Limburg).
Painter, sculptor, assemblage artist, screen printer.
Conceptual Art.
Hélène Keil studied at the Hoger Institute for the Fine Arts. She is a member of the Research Group of Hasselt. She exhibits mainly in Belgium and teaches at the Art Academy in Genk. In 1971, she won the painting prize awarded by the Province of Limbourg. She works in the areas of ready-made art and conceptual art. Her assemblage sculptures, placed beneath transparent cubes, give an important place to the vocabulary of geometry, using spirals, spheres etc, while preserving a spirit of play.
MUSEUMS AND GALLERIES:
BRUSSELS (Bibliothèque royale Albert Ier, Prints Collection).

KEIL, Hermann
German, 20th century.
Born 13 January 1889, in Darmstadt.
Painter, engraver.
After beginning his artistic studies in Darmstadt, Hermann Keil went on to study in Munich and Paris. He exhibited in Darmstadt and Frankfurt am Main.

KEIL, Ignaz Franz
Swiss, 18th - 19th century.
Born c. 1734; died 25 January 1814, in Bern.
Active in Umhausen.
Painter.
Keil settled in Bern in 1788 and remained there until his death.

KEIL, J.
Austrian, 19th century.
Active in Vienna at the beginning of the 19th century.

Engraver (burin).
Keil is noted for his plates based on the paintings of Karel Dujardin.

KEIL, Paul
German, 16th - 17th century.
Born 1573, in Neustadt-an-der-Orla; died 28 July 1646, in Schleiz.
Painter.
Paul Keil worked mostly for churches, including those in the towns of Wernburg and Keila.

KEILHAU, Bernhardt. See **KEIL Bernhardt** or **Ebehardt**

KEILWERTH, Johann Joseph
German, 18th century.
Born in Waldsassen (Bavaria).
Sculptor.
Keilwerth did the altar at the church of Amorbach, among other works.

KEIM, Benno
German, 19th century.
Born 1798, in Nymphenburg (Munich); died 1826, in Nymphenburg.
Painter (porcelain).
Keim painted hunting and battle scenes after Snyders and Hess.

KEIMEL, Hermann
German, 20th century.
Born 24 February 1889, in Munich.
Painter, engraver. Portraits, still-lifes.
Hermann Keimel studied with Hugo Diez at the Akademie der Bildenden Künste in Munich.

KEINEN, real name: Imao Eikan, nickname: Shiyu, pseudonyms: Keinen and Yososai
Japanese, 19th - 20th century.
Born 1845; died 1924.
Painter. Flowers, birds.
Keinen studied under Hyakunen Suzuki (1825-1890). He was active in Kyoto and was a member of the Imperial Fine Art Committee and the Imperial Academy of Fine Art. In Paris he received a silver medal at the Exposition Universelle of 1900 and his work was shown in the *Japanese Art* exhibition at the Musée du Jeu de Paume in Paris in 1929.

KEINENEN, Sigfrid August
Finnish, 19th - 20th century.
Born 7 February 1841, in Kuopio; died 26 April 1914, in Lempälä.
Painter. Genre scenes.
Sigfrid August Keinenen received an honourable mention at the 1889 Exposition Universelle in Paris.
MUSEUMS AND GALLERIES:
HELSINKI: *In the Antichamber of the Law Courts; Rest.*
AUCTION RECORDS:
LONDON, 23 March 1988, *The Traveller* (1882, oil on canvas, 18 1/2 x 22 1/2 ins / 47 x 57 cm) GBP 7,700.

KEININ, real name: Keinin Sumiyoshi
Japanese, 13th century.
Painter.
Keinin was a painter of *yamato-e* (national style) and is thought to have painted the *Kako-genzai Inga-kyo* scroll with his son Shojumaru in 1252. His name was long misread as Keion.

KEINKE, Karl
German, 19th century.
Born 10 August 1852, in Hamburg.
Painter. Portraits, genre scenes.
Keinke trained at the school of fine arts in Weimar, with A. Baur and Ferdinand Schauss. He exhibited in Berlin and London, winning a gold medal in London in 1890.

KEINSELEN, Martin van
German, 16th century.
Active in Bruges in 1505.
Painter.
Van Keinselen was a master painter.

KEIO. See **UNCHIKU**

KEIRINCK, Alexandre. See **KEERINCX**

KEIRSBILCK, Jules van
Belgian, 19th century.
Born 12 December 1833, in Ghent; died 10 November 1896, in Schaerbeek (Brussels).
Painter. History painting, portraits, genre scenes.
Jules van Keirsbilck studied under Navez and collaborated with Gallait, for whom he copied a large number of paintings. He exhibited regularly at the Brussels Salon.
AUCTION RECORDS:
NEW YORK, 25 Oct 1984, *The Artist's Studio* (oil on canvas, 27 x 32 3/4 ins / 68.6 x 83.2 cm) USD 8,500. NEW YORK, 16 Feb 1993, *Artist's Studio* (1885, oil on canvas, 36 x 24 ins / 91.4 x 61 cm) USD 4,400. LOKEREN, 18 May 1996, *Working Class District, the St Roch Impasse* (oil on canvas, 32 x 27 1/2 ins / 81 x 70 cm) BEF 90,000.

KEISAI, nickname: Tsukioka
Japanese, 18th century.
Active in Osaka c. 1785.
Master engraver.

KEISAI, real name: Shoshin Kawagata, original name: Tsuguzane Akabane, nickname: Sanjiro, pseudonyms: Shikei, Masayoshi, Kesai, Tsuguzane, Kitao Masayoshi, Shosai, Kitao Masami, religious name: Shoshin Kuwagata
Japanese, 18th - 19th century.
Born 1761 or 1764, in Edo (now Tokyo); died 1824, in Edo.
Master engraver, illustrator, painter.
Ukiyo-e (pictures of the floating world).
Keisai was the son of a maker of *tatami* (straw mats), who studied the style of Korin (1658-1716) and the old Japanese *yamato-e* scrolls. He trained under Shigemasa (1738-1820) and became a genre painter. Several of his views of the city of Edo in the style of Kano have been preserved. Keisai entered the service of Lord Matsudaira and later became a monk, taking the name Shoshin Kuwagata. He began by making single prints of women, landscapes and warriors. Between 1780 and 1796 he specialised in book illustrations. It was then that he entered the service of Lord Tsuyama and studied painting with Kano Yosenin Korenobu. His *Ryakuga Shiki Sketchbooks* of 1795 were known to the Nabi painters. Keisai eventually abandoned prints for painting, producing works in a near-caricatural, cursive style.
AUCTION RECORDS:
NEW YORK, 21 March 1989, *Two Figures on a Beach with Mt Fuji in the Background* (dai-oban yoko-e print, excerpt from the Kanadehon Chushingura series, 11 3/4 x 16 1/4 ins / 30.1 x 41.5 cm) USD 1,320.

KEISAI, real name: In Onishi, nickname: Shukumei, pseudonyms: Yukei, Issa Enkaku and Shochi Dojin
Japanese, 19th century.
Active in Edo (now Tokyo) c. 1820.
Painter.
Nanga School.
Keisai studied under Buncho (1763-1840) and painted flowers and birds.

KEISAI EISEN. See **EISEN**

KEISBAC, Claeys Heynderics von.
See **KEERSTBACH**

KEISEN, real name: Shigegoro Tomita, pseudonyms: Keisen, Kei Sanjin, Kyukoan, Kyuko, Sanjin
Japanese, 20th century.
Born 1879; died 1935.
Painter. Landscapes, flowers, birds.

Keisen studied under Kako Tsuji (1877-1927). He was active in Kyoto and was a member of the National Academy of Fine Art and the Imperial Academy of Fine Art.

KEISER, Johann Albert
Swiss, 19th century.
Born 13 January 1825, in Zug; died 19 July 1905, in Zug.
Sculptor.

Keiser, a pupil of Ludwig Schwanthaler in Munich, executed a large number of monuments for the cemetery in Zug.

KEISER, Johann Ludwig, or Kaiser, Keyser
Swiss, 19th century.
Born 14 December 1816, in Zug; died 8 January 1890, in Zurich.
Sculptor.

Keiser was initially a pupil of the painter Moas in Zug, but once he took up sculpture he went to work in Munich, where Ludwig Schwanthaler was his teacher. He remained in Munich from 1837 to 1853, returned to Zug for a time, then settled in Zurich, where he was appointed professor of sculpture and modelling at the polytechnical college. He worked mainly in Winterthur, Zurich and Zug. Among other works, a *St Agatha* for a chapel in Zug is noted.

KEISER, Josef
Swiss, 19th century.
Born 16 May 1859, in Zug.
Draughtsman, watercolourist.

Keiser worked in Stuttgart and Karlsruhe, and subsequently exhibited regularly in Zug.

KEISER, Joseph. See also **KAISER**

KEISER, Karl Albert
Swiss, 19th century.
Born 28 April 1834, in Zug; died 27 March 1885, in Fribourg.
Painter.

Keiser worked successively in Zug, Einsiedeln, St Gall, Fribourg, Bonn and Strasbourg. In 1858, he travelled to Italy and spent time particularly in Naples. In 1871 to 1883, he settled in Lucerne and became a member of the school of fine arts there. He mainly painted portraits.

KEISER, Karl Josef
Swiss, 18th century.
Born 25 April 1702, in Zug; died 3 October 1765.
Painter.

Keiser was a pupil of Johann Brandenberg and worked in Germany, Austria and Rome. He painted landscapes and portraits.

KEISER, Lorenz
Swiss, 16th century.
Active in Bern.
Glass painter.

Lorenz Keiser worked for the town hall of Huttwil, among other places.

KEISER, Oswald
Swiss, 17th century.
Active in Zug at the end of the 17th century.
Painter.

Keiser was a pupil of Johann Brandenberg.

KEISERMAN, Franz or François.
See **KAISERMANN**

KEISHI, nickname: Hanabusa, pseudonym: Reikinsha
Japanese, 18th century.
Born 1719; died 1786.
Active c. 1760-1780.
Painter, illustrator.

KEISHI, Mori. See **IPPO**

KEISHOKI. See **SHOKEI**

KEISHU, real name: Hiromasa Itaya, original name: Sumiyoshi, nickname: Hiroyoshi
Japanese, 18th century.
Born 1729, in Edo, now Tokyo; died 1797.
Painter.

Keishu was a a traditional painter who studied under Hiromori Sumiyoshi. Keishu specialised in genre painting and worked for the Tokugawa government.

KEISON, pseudonym: Kyugetsusai
Japanese, 15th - 16th century.
Painter.

Keison was a painter of the Muromachi School, active in the 15th-16th century. He painted in ink.

KEISTER, Lorenz de
Dutch, 17th century.
Active in Schleswig-Holstein c. 1610.
Painter.

In 1611, Lorenz de Keister was working in Tönning. He later returned to his native Low Countries.

KEISTER, Roy C.
American, 20th century.
Born 2 January 1886, in Ohio.
Painter, illustrator. Portraits, landscapes.

Roy C. Keister studied at the Art Institute in Chicago. He lived and worked in California. He painted the portraits of many famous people and, at one time, the portraits of Native Americans. He took part in numerous exhibitions in the USA, and was awarded several distinctions.

KEITA, Bouba
Senegalese, 20th century.
Born 1940, in Thiès.
Painter.

Bouba Keita studied in Dakar and then at the École des Beaux-Arts in Montpellier and in Florence. His work is very much influenced by the popular art of his native country of Senegal. He has taken part in group exhibitions in Senegal, France and Italy and showed his paintings in a solo exhibition in Moscow.

KEITA, Souleymane
Senegalese, 20th - 21st century.
Born 1947.
Painter, watercolourist, pastellist, potter. Designs for tapestries, murals.

Souleymane Keïta lived in New York from 1980 to 1985, where he taught pottery and painting. He lives and works in Senegal, on the Island of Gorée (Dakar). There is a strong lyrical (in the sense that the artist mingles various different styles) and poetic aspect to his art, which draws its subjects and motifs from life and the immediate environment: nature, music, and spiritualism. He is regarded as one of the leading exponents of abstract art in Senegal.

His work featured in the exhibition *Contemporary African Artists: Changing Tradition* at the Studio Museum in Harlem, New York, in 1990.

Bibliography:
Contemporary African Artists: changing tradition, exhibition catalogue, Studio Museum in Harlem, New York, 1990. Sankale, Sylvain, *Souleymane Keïta*, Sépia, 1994.

KEITEL, Otto
German, 19th century.
Born 15 September 1862, in Brunswick; died 3 August 1902, in Pasing (Munich).
Painter, engraver. Animals.
Keitel trained at the academy in Düsseldorf, then with A. Bundel at the school of fine arts in Weimar. He exhibited in Munich, Vienna and Weimar.

KEITH, Dora
Maiden name: Wheeler
American, 19th - 20th century.
Born 8 March 1865, possibly in New York; died 1940.
Painter, illustrator.
Dora Keith was designer Candace Wheeler's daughter. She lived and worked in New York, where she had studied under William Merrit Chase. A gifted student, she went on to win several Louis Prang awards for his Christmas card competition and was counted among the best-known commercial artists of her day. She gained an honourable mention in 1901 in Buffalo, and became, in 1906, an associate member of the National Academy of Fine Arts.

KEITH, Elizabeth
British, 20th century.
Born 30 April 1887, in Macduff; died 1956.
Painter, draughtswoman.
Elizabeth Keith exhibited in London in 1925.

KEITH, Martin Morrow
American, 20th century.
Born 1911; died 1983.
Painter.
Martin Keith was an abstract painter who studied at the Art Institute of Chicago. As a member of the US army, he lived in European locations including Iceland, England, France and Germany. He also worked in collage in the 1950s and 1960s. Martin received an honorary doctorate from the Maryland Institute College of Art in 1981. He is remembered for the paintings he made of Iceland during World War II.

KEITH, Walter Castle
American, 19th - 20th century.
Born 1864, in Detroit; died 1927.
Active in the Netherlands.
Painter. Landscapes with figures, interiors with figures. Laren Artists' Colony.
Walter Castle Keith was one of many American artists who went to work in Laren and Leende in the Netherlands.
Auction records:
Amsterdam, 23 April 1991, *Kitchen Interior* (oil on canvas, 19 3/4 x 23 1/2 ins / 50 x 60 cm) NLG 2,070. Amsterdam, 24 Sept 1992, *Riverscape* (oil on canvas on panel, 12 x 16 ins / 30.5 x 40.5 cm) NLG 1,150. Amsterdam, 16 April 1996, *Peasant Woman with Goats in a Stable* (oil on canvas on cardboard, 16 x 13 1/4 ins / 40.5 x 33.5 cm) NLG 2,360.

KEITH, William
British, 19th - 20th century.
Born 21 November 1838, in Old Meldrum (Aberdeenshire), Scotland; died 13 April 1911, in Berkeley (California).
Painter, engraver. Landscapes, animals, portraits.
William Keith emigrated to the USA in 1850. He worked as a wood-engraver for Harper and Brothers publishing in 1857, before moving to San Francisco where he did small jobs in an engraver's shop. By 1859, he was an established engraver, and received commissions for country scenes from rail companies. Keith was a prolific artist, influenced by the work of Andreas Achenbach, the Hudson River School, the Barbizon School and the religious philosophy of Swedenborg. He travelled to Europe from 1869-1872, studying art in Düsseldorf and visiting Paris. He visited to Europe from 1883 to 1885 including informal study in Munich and again from 1893 to 1899. In 1906, 2,000 of his paintings were lost in a studio fire caused by the San Francisco earthquake.

By the 1870s, Keith had gained a reputation for painting large-format panoramic landscapes of the Pacific coast and mountainous areas such as the High Sierras, as in *Mount Lyell, California Sierra* (1874). By the 1890s he preferred to paint scenes of forests in sunsets, such as *Evening Glow* (1891). His early works were characteristically objective and accurate portrayals of specific places, but evolved over time to a more subjective style to express feelings, using broader brushwork, complicated scumbles and glazes, and with scenes of bright sunlight, hazy meadows or twilight. Keith was an influential artist in California in the late 19th-century, and is considered to be one of the leading artists in San Francisco during this period. He received a bronze medal at Buffalo in 1901. Keith's works were featured in exhibitions in San Francisco in 1913 and at Hearst Art Gallery, Saint Mary's College of California, Moraga.

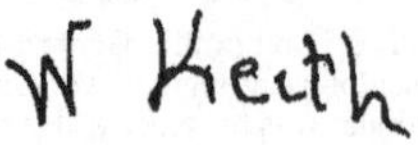

Bibliography:
Harmon, E.N., *The William Keith Collection of Paintings*, exhibition catalogue, San Francisco, 1913. Hay, Emily P.B., *William Keith as Prophet Painter*, exhibition catalogue, Paul Elder, San Francisco, 1916. Cornelius, Brother, *Keith, Old Master of California*, exhibition catalogue, Putnam, New York, 1942-1957 (2 vols). *Introduction to the Art of William Keith*, exhibition catalogue, Oakland Museum, Oakland (CA), 1956. Harris, Alfred C., *William Keith: the Saint Mary's College Collection*, exhibition catalogue, Hearst Art Gallery, Saint Mary's College of California, Moraga (CA), 1988. Harlow, A., '*William Keith, California's Poet-Painter*' in *American Art Review*, vol 6, no. 6, journal article, 1994-1995. *William Keith: the Artist and his Times, Featuring Paintings in the Saint Mary's College Collection*, exhibition catalogue, Hearst Art Gallery, Saint Mary's College of California, Moraga (CA), 1995.
Museums and Galleries:
Boston (MFA): *California Landscape* (1870s, oil); *The Lone Pine* (1881, watercolour); *Wooded Landscape* (1865, pen and ink, wash) - Chicago (AI) - Claremont (Ruth Chandler Williamson Gal., Scripps College): *The Murky Pool* (oil); *Mt Tamalpais* (1893, oil) - Frankfurt am Main: *Oak Forest in America* - Los Angeles (County MA): *Yosemite Valley* (1875, oil); *California Press* (1878, oil) - Moraga, CA (Hearst Art Gallery, Saint Mary's College of California): *Evening Glow* (1891, oil); *Grey Rain Cloud, Cattle in Meadow* (late 1880s, watercolour and gouache); *Polemics (Ideal Head of Junipero Serro)* (c. 1884, oil); *Mount Lyell, California Sierra* (1874, oil); *San Anselmo Valley near San Rafael* (1869, oil) - New York (Metropolitan Mus. of Art): *Approaching Storm* (1880, oil); *Yosemite Falls, from Glacier Point* (1879, oil) - San Francisco (AI) - San Francisco (FAM): *California Ranch* (1908, oil); *Breaking of the Storm* (oil); *California Oaks and Field* (oil); *Evening* (oil); *Hetch Hetchy Side Canyon I* (c. 1908, oil); *The Glory of the Heavens* (1891, oil) - Stanford, CA (Cantor Arts Center, Stanford University): *Upper Kern River* (1876, oil) - Washington DC (Corcoran Gal. of Art).
Auction records:
New York, 10 Feb 1903, *Landscape with Pond and Animals*, USD 85. New York, 9 Feb 1906, *Harvest*, USD 750; *Majesty of the Oaks*, USD 2,300. New York, 9 April 1929, *San Francisco of Old*, USD 425. New York, 14 March 1968, *Landscape with*

Waterfall, USD 2,000. NEW YORK, 28 Oct 1971, *Into the Mystery,* USD 1,300. LOS ANGELES, 22 May 1973, *California Landscape,* USD 4,000. NEW YORK, 29 April 1976, *River Landscape with Figures* (oil on canvas, 18 x 24 ins / 45.7 x 61 cm) USD 1,200. NEW YORK, 28 Jan 1977, *California Landscape* (oil on canvas, 20 x 30 ins / 51 x 76.2 cm) USD 1,100. LOS ANGELES, 18 June 1979, *Mountain Landscape* (oil on canvas, 24 x 18 3/4 ins / 61 x 47.6 cm) USD 4,250. NEW YORK, 21 Oct 1983, *San Anselmo Valley, California* (oil on canvas, 23 x 34 ins / 58.5 x 86.4 cm) USD 7,500. SAN FRANCISCO, 28 Feb 1985, *Yosemite* (oil on canvas, 24 x 36 ins / 61 x 91.5 cm) USD 15,000. NEW YORK, 1 Oct 1987, *Wooded Landscape with Figures* (oil on canvas remounted on hardboard, 20 x 30 ins / 50.8 x 76.5 cm) USD 2,800. NEW YORK, 28 Sept 1989, *Autumn Dusk* (oil on canvas, 20 x 30 ins / 51 x 76.5 cm) USD 3,300. LOS ANGELES-SAN FRANCISCO, 7 Feb 1990, *Glimmers of Dawn* (oil on panel, 24 x 72 ins / 61 x 183 cm) USD 8,250; *Cattle Grazing beneath Mount Tamalpais* (1889, oil on canvas, 30 x 50 ins / 76 x 127 cm) USD 27,500. LOS ANGELES-SAN FRANCISCO, 12 July 1990, *Cows in a Clearing* (oil on canvas, 15 x 18 ins / 38 x 46 cm) USD 4,675. LOS ANGELES-SAN FRANCISCO, 10 Oct 1990, *Pastoral Landscape* (oil on canvas, 22 x 32 ins / 56 x 81 cm) USD 6,600. NEW YORK, 14 March 1991, *Carmel Mission* (1889, oil on canvas, 16 x 30 ins / 40.5 x 76 cm) USD 8,800. NEW YORK, 14 Nov 1991, *Californian Landscape* (oil on canvas, 15 x 11 ins / 38.1 x 27.9 cm) USD 2,420. NEW YORK, 4 May 1993, *Evening* (oil on canvas, 24 x 36 ins / 61 x 91.5 cm) USD 4,025. NEW YORK, 9 March 1996, *El Capitan, Yosemite Valley* (oil on canvas, 21 x 14 ins / 53.5 x 35.5 cm) USD 12,650. NEW YORK, 27 Sept 1996, *Mount Tamalpais from Lagunitas Creek* (1878, oil on canvas, 30 1/4 x 25 1/4 ins / 76.9 x 64.1 cm) USD 17,250. NEW YORK, 30 Oct 1996, *Wooded Landscape* (1898, oil on canvas, 21 x 27 1/4 ins / 53.3 x 68.9 cm) USD 4,600.

KEIZERMAN, François. See **KAISERMANN Franz** or **François**

KEIZO, real name: Morishita
Japanese, 20th century.
Born 1944.
Painter.

In 1963 Keizo received a grant to study at the Accademia di Brera in Milan, where he worked with Marino Marini from 1964 to 1968.

AUCTION RECORDS:

MILAN, 7 Nov 1989, *Archipelago* (1974, acrylic/canvas, 39 1/4 x 31 1/2 ins / 100 x 80 cm) ITL 2,500,000.

KÉLAN
French, 17th century.
Active at Versailles in 1687.
Sculptor.

KELCK, Anthonys Dionys
Dutch, 17th century.
Sculptor.

In 1642, Anthonys Kelck worked on the great organ in Alkmaar.

KELDER, C.
Dutch, 17th century.
Active at the end of the 17th century.
Painter.

C. Kelder is believed to have worked in Deventer.

KELDER, Toon
Dutch, 20th century.
Born 24 November 1894, in Rotterdam; died 1973.
Painter, sculptor. Figures, nudes, portraits, interiors with figures, landscapes, still-lifes, flowers.

Toon Kelder studied at the art academies in Rotterdam and The Hague. Though living in The Hague, he made frequent visits to Paris after 1945. He took part in a large number of group exhibitions in the Netherlands and abroad, including the Venice Biennale and the Pittsburgh International Exhibition at the Carnegie Foundation in 1958 and the Sculpture Biennial in Antwerp-Middelheim in 1961. He has shown collections of his works in solo exhibitions in 1950 in Paris and notably at the City Museum in The Hague in 1963.

Until 1945, Kelder worked only as a painter, at first in a Post-Cubist style, then, after 1953, in a sensual, Expressionist manner, making use of symbols. After World War II, he became unsure that painting could adapt to the expression of modern ideas and, at the age of fifty, he began to produce a kind of drawing in space, using wire to form masks and stylised animals. He then perfected his technique, soldering the wires, enriching the three-dimensional form, then carving three-dimensional shapes in wood and covering them with metal foil. Although he continued to draw inspiration from natural forms, his sculptures, with their precise and complex articulations, sometimes dominated by straight lines and sometimes by curves, have evolved towards abstraction. Using this technique, he created a large sculpture for the entrance hall of the post office laboratories in Leidschendam, near The Hague.

BIBLIOGRAPHY:

Elgar, Frank, '*Kelder*' in *XXe Siècle*, periodical, Paris, June 1957.

MUSEUMS AND GALLERIES:

AMSTERDAM (Stedelijk Mus.) - THE HAGUE (Gemeentemus.).

AUCTION RECORDS:

AMSTERDAM, 19 May 1976, *Portrait of Jan Toorop* (1925, oil on canvas, 39 1/4 x 32 ins / 100 x 81 cm) NLG 1,800. AMSTERDAM, 1 Nov 1977, *Still-life* (oil on canvas, 27 x 22 1/4 ins / 68.5 x 56.5 cm) NLG 2,800. AMSTERDAM, 24 March 1980, *Reclining Nude* (oil on canvas, 22 x 28 1/4 ins / 55 x 72 cm) NLG 11,000. AMSTERDAM, 11 Nov 1985, *Reclining Nude* (oil on canvas, 16 1/2 x 21 ins / 42 x 52.5 cm) NLG 7,000. AMSTERDAM, 24 May 1989, *Interior* (oil on canvas, 18 1/2 x 16 1/2 ins / 47 x 42 cm) NLG 1,495. AMSTERDAM, 13 Dec 1989, *Two Women* (1948, oil on canvas, 38 1/4 x 24 1/2 ins / 97.2 x 62.5 cm) NLG 12,650. AMSTERDAM, 22 May 1990, *Nude seen from Behind* (1945, oil on canvas, 19 3/4 x 31 ins / 50 x 79 cm) NLG 14,950. AMSTERDAM, 5 June 1990, *Still-life with Fish on a Table in front of a Window* (1926, oil on canvas, 62 1/2 x 50 1/2 ins / 159 x 128 cm) NLG 1,092; *Standing Nude from the Back* (oil on canvas, 34 1/4 x 17 1/2 ins / 87 x 44.5 cm) NLG 3,450. AMSTERDAM, 11 Sept 1990, *Tulip Field at Dawn* (oil on canvas, 19 3/4 x 27 1/2 ins / 50 x 70 cm) NLG 3,680. AMSTERDAM, 13 Dec 1990, *Nudes* (oil on canvas, 28 3/4 x 36 1/4 ins / 73 x 92 cm) NLG 12,650. AMSTERDAM, 23 May 1991, *Still-life with Flowers* (oil on canvas, 20 x 16 1/2 ins / 51 x 42 cm) NLG 3,680. AMSTERDAM, 17 Sept 1991, *Circus Horses* (1944, oil on canvas, 15 3/4 x 13 1/2 ins / 40 x 34 cm) NLG 2,300. AMSTERDAM, 11 Dec 1991, *View of a Marble Quarry* (oil on canvas, 36 x 43 1/4 ins / 90.5 x 110 cm) NLG 4,600. AMSTERDAM, 12 Dec 1991, *Don Quixote* (1944, oil on canvas, 17 1/4 x 22 3/4 ins / 44 x 58 cm) NLG 2,300. AMSTERDAM, 21 May 1992, *Reclining Nude* (oil on card, 27 1/4 x 35 ins / 69 x 88 cm) NLG 12,650. AMSTERDAM, 9 Dec 1992, *Still-life with Flowers* (oil on canvas, 21 x 14 1/4 ins / 53.5 x 36 cm) NLG 16,100. AMSTERDAM, 8 Dec 1993, *Standing Nude* (oil on panel, 22 x 10 ins / 56 x 24.5 cm) NLG 8,625. AMSTERDAM, 7 Dec 1994, *White Horse and Silhouette* (oil on canvas, 25 1/2 x 21 1/4 ins / 65 x 54 cm) NLG 3,450. AMSTERDAM, 18 June 1996, *Café at Night* (1924, gouache/paper, 17 1/4 x 13 1/2 ins / 43.5 x 34 cm) NLG 2,070. AMSTERDAM, 2-3 June 1997, *Female Nude* (oil on panel, 22 x 26 1/4 ins / 55 x 66.5 cm) NLG 23,010. AMSTERDAM, 4 June 1997, *Reclining Nude* (oil on canvas, 39 1/4 x 47 1/4 ins / 100 x 120 cm) NLG 74,958. AMSTERDAM, 1 Sept 1999, *Portrait of the Wife of the Artist and their Daughter Renee*

(1941, oil on canvas, 31 x 24 ins / 80 x 60 cm) NLG 28,000. AMSTERDAM, 1 Dec 1999, *Reclining Nude* (1940, oil on canvas, 32 x 50 ins / 82 x 126 cm) NLG 20,000. THE HAGUE, 9 May 2000, *Still-life with Flowers* (oil on canvas, 24 x 19 ins / 60 x 49 cm) NLG 20,000. AMSTERDAM, 7 June 2000, *Circus Scene* (oil and gouache on paper, 18 x 25 ins / 46 x 64 cm) NLG 11,000. AMSTERDAM, 19 June 2001, *Untitled. Male Nude Study* (1952, gouache, a pair, 18 x 11 ins / 45 x 29 cm) NLG 6,000. AMSTERDAM, 3 Dec 2001, *Female Nude* (1933, oil on canvas, 33 x 22 ins / 85 x 57 cm) NLG 30,000. AMSTERDAM, 26 Nov 2002, *Zittend Naakt* (oil on canvas, 43 x 35 ins / 110 x 90 cm) EUR 4,000. AMSTERDAM, 3 Dec 2002, *Spanish Woman* (c. 1925, oil on canvas, 44 x 35 ins / 111 x 90 cm) EUR 16,000. AMSTERDAM, 27 May 2003, *Portrait of Mina* (ink and watercolour, 28 x 22 ins / 71 x 55 cm) EUR 4,000. AMSTERDAM, 2 Dec 2003, *Untitled* (1950, oil on canvas, 42 x 55 ins / 106 x 140 cm) EUR 18,000. AMSTERDAM, 2 Dec 2004, *Circus* (oil on linen, 21 x 26 ins / 53 x 65 cm) EUR 8,000. AMSTERDAM, 2 Dec 2004, *Figure* (wood kernel and copper, h. 40 ins / 102 cm) EUR 9,000.

KELDERMAN, Jan
Dutch, 18th - 19th century.
Born 8 August 1741, in Dordrecht; died 22 June 1820, in Dordrecht.
Painter. Animals, birds, still-lifes (including flowers/fruit).

Jan Kelderman was a pupil of Wouter Dam. He specialised in painting birds.

AUCTION RECORDS:

NEW YORK, 14 Jan 1994, *Still-life with a Floral Composition in an Urn with a Nest on an Entablature; Still-life with Flowers and Fruit around an Urn with a Pheasant Perched on the Lid* (oil on panel, a pair, each 37 1/2 x 28 1/4 ins / 95.3 x 71.8 cm) USD 310,500.

KELDERMANS, Andries, the Elder,
called van Mansdale
Flemish School, 15th century.
Died 1481 or before 1488.
Active in Mechelen.
Sculptor, architect.

In 1446, Andries Keldermans the Elder followed his father, Jan Keldermans II, to become the city architect and engineer of Mechelen. The Keldermans family produced five generations of architects and sculptors and became immensely famous for their works. Andries also completed several of his father's projects, among them the city gates of Hanswyck and Neckerspoel and also the renovation of the city hall. He was also responsible for the Romboutsturme (Towers of Rombout) and the magnificent front of the Scheppenhuis. In 1439, under his father's supervision, he sculpted the décor for the city hall in Louvain, in 1454 he began the towers of the Lievensmonsterkerk (not completed), in 1468 city houses in Middelburg, in 1470 the city hall in Veere, and in 1471 he worked on the church of Bergen-op-Zoom with his son Anthonis Keldermans I. With Anthonis he also undertook projects for the Katarinenkirche (church of St Catherine) in Mechelen and the Peterskirche (church of St Peter) in Louvain.

BIBLIOGRAPHY:

Galland, G., *Geschichte die holländische Baukunst*, Frankfurt am Main, 1890.

KELDERMANS, Andries, the Younger
Dutch, 16th century.
Active in Mechelen c. 1518.
Sculptor.

Andries Keldermans the Younger worked mostly in Mechelen, but also in Wetteren and Werchter.

KELDERMANS, Anthonis, the Elder
Flemish School, 15th - 16th century.
Born c. 1450; died 15 October 1512, in Mechelen.
Sculptor, architect.

Antonis Keldermans the Elder worked with his father, Andries Keldermans the Younger, at the church of St Sulpice in Diest, and at the church of Berg-op-Zoom in 1471, as well as at the church of the Virgin in Veere in 1479. He created the façade of the town hall in Middelburg in flamboyant gothic style, decorating it with colossal statues of the counts of Holland. Like his father, Anthonis I was the city architect and engineer of Mechelen. He took over his father's position about 1480 and continued the work for the towers of the Lievensmonsterkirk in Zieriksee and the city hall in Veere. Between 1483 and 1489 he completed the church of St Sulpice in Diest and managed the construction of the towers of St Rombout in Mechelen. He is also associated with the enlargement of the church of St John and the Notre Dame on the Dyle, the church in Alkmaar in 1502, and the construction of the towers of the church of St Bavo in Harleem in 1505. In 1507 he was contracted to build a palace in Mechelen for Margaret of Parma and in 1509, together with his son Anthonis II, he was commissioned by the Emperor Maximillian to complete the 'Cour de Bailled' at the royal palace in Brussels.

BIBLIOGRAPHY:

Schayes, A.G.B., in *Histoire de l'architecture en Belgique*. Van Even, E., *Biographie Nationale de Belgique, vol X*, 1888/1889. Galland, G., *Geschichte die holländische Baukunst*, Frankfurt am Main, 1890. *Inventaire des objets d'art de la province d'Anvers*, 1902. Druckfehler, *Bulletin van den Nederlanddische Oudheidkund, 2nd series, no. VII*, 1914.

KELDERMANS, Anthonis, the Younger
Flemish School, 16th century.
Died 5 December 1515, in Mechelen.
Sculptor, architect.

Anthonis Keldermans the Younger was active during the reign of Charles V. He worked in Louvain, and was married on 27 April 1502. The son of Anthonis Keldermans the Elder, he worked with his own son, with whom he also shared a name, in Brussels. He was made a burgher of Antwerp in 1543.

KELDERMANS, Frans
Flemish School, 17th century.
Born c. 1660.
Engraver.

There is an engraving by Frans Keldermans of *The Mausoleum of Frédéric de Marselaer*.

KELDERMANS, Hendrik
Flemish School, 16th century.
Active in Louvain.
Glass painter.
Antwerp School.

Hendrik Keldermans was the son of Mathias Keldermans, and was made a master in Antwerp in 1490. He ran an inn in Mechelen called the Golden Head. Albrecht Dürer stayed there during his visit to Mechelen in 1521.

BIBLIOGRAPHY:

Michiels, A., *Histoire de la peinture*, 1866. Van Even, E., *École de peinture de Louvain*, 1870. Rombouts, Ph./Van Lerius, Th., *De Liggeren*, Antwerp, 1872. Siret, A., *Dictionnaire des peintres, Vol I*, 1883. Van Mander, C., *Livre des peintres*, Éditions Huysmans, Paris, 1884. *Biographie nationale de Belgique, no. XIII*, 1895.

KELDERMANS, Jan
Flemish School, 14th century.
Active in Mechelen.
Sculptor, architect.

Jan Keldermans produced the tomb of Frans de Mirabelle in the church of St-Rombout. Known as Jan Keldermans I, he was the first in a long line of artists. A member of the stonecutters' guild in Brussels at the end of the 14th century, he worked at the county magistrates' lodge in Louvain in 1385. His son, Jan Keldermans II, was a master in Brussels in 1399, and directed the works at the collegiate church of St-Gommaire in Lierre for 20 years. He also worked at the church of St Peter in Louvain.

BIBLIOGRAPHY:

Biographie nationale de Belgique, no. XIII, 1894/1895.

KELDERMANS, Laurijs

Flemish School, 16th century.
Died 1534, in Mechelen.
Sculptor.
Antwerp School.

Laurijs Keldermans studied in Antwerp from 1503 to 1532. He was a master sculptor, and worked at the town hall in Ghent after Rombout Keldermans. He produced sculptures for the palace of the parliament in Mechelen in 1527, and for the church in Diest in 1534. He also worked for the cathedral in Antwerp.

BIBLIOGRAPHY:

Busscher, E. de, *Sur les peintres à Gand*, Ghent, 1866. Graul, R., *Beitrage zur Geschichte der Dekor. Skulptur in den Niederlands*, Leipzig, 1889.

KELDERMANS, Mathias, the Elder

French, 15th - 16th century.
Died between 1520 and 1525.
Sculptor, architect. Monuments.

Mathias Keldermans the Elder was of Flemish origin, and took part in work on the cathedral in Antwerp in 1487. He worked with Jean de Bourgogne on the jube of the church in Bourbourg, which Jean de Bourgogne had started in 1485. Keldermans completed this jube alone in 1491, following the death of his colleague in 1490. The jube was destroyed in 1580. In 1491, records place him in Berg-op-Zoom, and, in 1498, he worked on the Brussels gate in Mechelen. He was appointed master of works for the town of Louvain in 1504.

BIBLIOGRAPHY:

Van Even, E., *Biographie nationale de Belgique, vol X*, 1888/1889. Galland, G., *Geschichte die holländische Baukunst*, Frankfurt am Main, 1890.

KELDERMANS, Mathias, the Younger

Flemish School, 16th century.
Died c. 1526.
Sculptor, architect.

He worked with his father, Mathias Keldermans the Elder, on the church in Brecht.

BIBLIOGRAPHY:

Van Even, E., *Biographie nationale de Belgique, vol X*, 1888/1889.

KELDERMANS, Pieter

Flemish School, 16th century.
Active in Brussels c. 1539.
Sculptor.

Possibly the brother of Hendrik Keldermans, Pieter Keldermans completed the altar in the church of St-Gudule in Brussels, as well as a number of statues for the altars of St Stephen and St Catherine.

KELDERMANS, Rombout, known as Rombout I

Flemish School, 15th century.
Died 17 March 1489.
Active in Louvain from 1455 to 1488.
Glass painter.

A student of Niclas Yewen, one of the most-admired masters of his time, Rombout Keldermans worked on the stained glass windows in the town hall in Louvain in 1469, and in the church of St-Gommaire in Lierre in 1475.

BIBLIOGRAPHY:

Van Even, E., *Journal des Beaux-Arts, p 4*, Brussels, 1864. Van Even, E., *École de peinture de Louvain*, 1870. Van Even, E., *Biographie nationale de Belgique, no. X*, 1888/1889.

KELEMEN, Alicia

Venezuelan, 20th - 21st century.
Born 1960, in Caracas.
Also active in France.
Sculptor.

Alicia Kelemen studied architecture in Venezuela in 1984, then at the Pilchuck School of Art in Washington in 1988 and finally at the academy in Stuttgart in 1989-1990. Her glass and metal sculptures are more like abstract two-dimensional pictures than sculptures. She has taken part in several collective exhibitions, including: Valencia (1988, 1991 and 1995); Munich (1989); Caracas (1989, 1990, 1991, 1993 and 1994); Japan (1990); Atlanta and Kansas (1991 and 1992); Romont stained glass museum, Boston (1992 and 1994); Salon des Artistes Plasticiens, Paris (1994). She has also shown her work in solo exhibitions in Caracas and Boston (1993) and in London (1995).

MUSEUMS AND GALLERIES:

EBELTOFT (Glasmus.).

KELEMEN, Laszlo

Hungarian, 20th century.
Born in Budapest.
Painter (mixed media).

Laszlo Kelemen studied at the school of fine arts in Budapest. He was a member of the young artists' studio. He used various materials, including powdered minerals in acrylic colours. His painting used an informal technique, the result approximating to 'cloudism'. He has exhibited in collective shows since 1986 and was awarded the Hermann prize (1989).

KELETI, Gabor

Hungarian, 19th - 20th century.
Born 1870, in Budapest.
Painter.

Gabor Keleti studied in Munich before returning to Budapest, where he made his debut in 1895.

AUCTION RECORDS:

MILAN, 26 March 1996, *Urchins on the Banks of a Torrent in a Wood* (1892, oil on canvas, 38 1/4 x 28 1/4 ins / 97 x 72 cm) ITL 9,775,000.

KELETTI, Gustav

Hungarian, 19th century.
Born 13 December 1834, in Pressburg (now Bratislava); died 2 September 1902, in Budapest.
Painter. Landscapes.

Gustav Keletti studied under I. Fischbach and Fr. Voltz at the academy in Munich. He was a member of the academy in Budapest.

AUCTION RECORDS:

VIENNA, 14 Oct 1980, *Landscape* (1874, oil on panel, 7 x 18 1/4 ins / 18 x 46.5 cm) ATS 25,000.

KELETY, Alexandre

Hungarian, 20th century.
Born in Budapest.
Active in France.
Sculptor. Genre scenes.

Kelety was active from 1918 to 1940, and completed several statuettes.

AUCTION RECORDS:

PARIS, 26 June 1979, *Couple of Ara Parrots* (polychrome patinated bronze, h. 24 3/4 ins / 63 cm) FRF 9,500. NEW YORK, 3 April 1982, *Modern Medusa* (polychrome bronze, h. 15 3/4 ins / 40 cm) USD 5,000. LONDON, 29 June 1983, *Nude Dancer* (brown and silver patinated bronze, h. 15 3/4 ins / 40.2 cm)

GBP 5,000. New York, 15 June 1985, *The Archer* (gilt bronze, h. 44 1/2 ins / 113 cm) USD 9,000. Paris, 4 Dec 1987, *Disobedient* (polychrome brown, silver and gold patinated bronze chryselephantine sculpture, h. 7 1/2 ins / 19 cm) FRF 7,500. Paris, 20 Nov 1991, *Nude Woman with Veil* (bronze, h. 11 1/2 ins / 29 cm) FRF 3,800. Paris, 18 Nov 1993, *Mermoz* (bronze, h. 15 1/4 ins / 38.5 cm) FRF 15,000. Paris, 21 March 1996, *Genie and the Lamp* (bronze, h. 18 1/4 ins / 46.5 cm) FRF 10,200. Paris, 22 March 1996, *Young Man and His Horse* (lost-wax bronze, h. 14 1/4 ins / 36 cm) FRF 8,000. Lyons, 1 June 1996, *Dog Handler* (bronze) FRF 20,000.

KELLAR, James
British, 18th - 19th century.
Born 1750, in London; died 1810, in Riga (Latvia).
Painter.

James Kellar lived for a long time in France and Italy before going to Riga, where he taught and eventually died.

KELLE, Émile
French, 19th century.
Born in Paris.
Painter. Landscapes.

Émile Kelle made his debut at the Salon in 1879.

KELLEN, David van der, the Elder
Dutch, 19th century.
Born 23 September 1804, in Amsterdam; died 30 March 1879, in Utrecht.
Painter, engraver, lithographer. Portraits.

David van der Kellen the Elder is known for his portraits and engravings after works by Braekeleer and classical painters.

KELLEN, David van der, the Younger
Dutch, 19th century.
Born 2 January 1827, in Utrecht; died 9 September 1895, in Amsterdam.
Painter, engraver. Historical subjects, portraits, genre scenes, interiors with figures, architectural views.

David van der Kellen the Younger studied under his father, the medallist, under Bruno van Straeten, W.-P. Hœvenaer and J.-A. Kruseman. He went to Düsseldorf in 1845 and married in Amsterdam in 1850. In 1859 he held the post of librarian of the *Arli et Amicitiae* society. He executed many pieces with archeological subjects.

Museums and Galleries:
Amsterdam (Stedelijk Mus.): *Interior* - Strasbourg: *Interior* - Utrecht: *The Inhabitants of Veendal Take Refuge in the Church of St Gertrude in Utrecht During the Flood of 1855.*

Auction records:
Amsterdam, 5 June 1990, *Portrait of a Gentleman on his Balcony* (oil on panel, 14 1/2 x 11 ins / 37 x 27 cm) NLG 1,150. Amsterdam, 19 Oct 1993, *Happy Family* (oil on panel, 25 1/2 x 20 ins / 64.5 x 50.5 cm) NLG 5,750.

KELLEN, Hendrika Frederika van der, later Mme Landré
Dutch, 19th century.
Born 8 October 1846, in Utrecht; died 4 April 1903.
Painter.

Hendrika van der Kellen was a pupil of Haanen.

KELLEN, Jan van der
Dutch, 19th century.
Born 1843, in Utrecht; died 2 September 1895, in Rotterdam.
Engraver.

Jan van der Kellen is known for the plates he produced after works by Claude Mellan and Robert Nanteuil.

KELLEN, Johan Philip van der
Dutch, 19th century.
Born 9 July 1831, in Utrecht; died 7 June 1906, in Bussum.
Engraver, lithographer.

Johan van der Kellen was director of the Amsterdam engravings collection from 1875 until his death. He copied works by the old masters.

KELLENS, Anne
Belgian, 20th - 21st century.
Born 1954, in Etterbeek (Brussels).
Painter, lithographer, draughtsman.

Anne Kellens studied at the academies in Brussels and Watermael-Boitsfort.

KELLER, A.
Swiss, 19th century.
Active in Bern.
Painter. Landscapes.

KELLER, Achill
German, 19th century.
Born 26 April 1815, in Rome.
Painter.

KELLER, Adam
French, 17th century.
Died c. 1625, in Colmar.
Sculptor.

The only known work by Adam Keller is a wooden *Statue of a Man*.

KELLER, Adam
German, 18th century.
Born 1767, in Bamberg; died 24 July 1791, in Bamberg.
Painter, engraver. Portraits, still-lifes, fruit.

Keller was a pupil of Mattenheimer, and worked for churches in Bamberg.

KELLER, Adolphe
Belgian, 20th century.
Born 21 June 1880, in Brussels; died 10 January 1968.
Painter. Genre scenes, landscapes, flowers.

Adolphe Keller studied in Brussels. He took part in the Brussels exhibition in 1910. From 1934, he lived at the Rouge-Cloître in Auderghem and was an ardent defender of it.

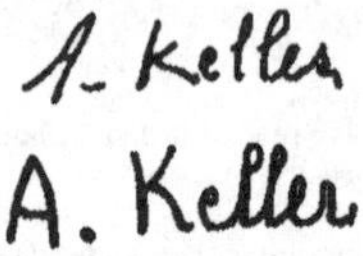

Auction records:
Amsterdam, 8 Dec 1988, *Woman Reading in a Garden Chair* (oil on canvas, 14 x 19 1/2 ins / 35.5 x 49.5 cm) NLG 4,140. Brussels, 27 March 1990, *View of Bruges* (oil on panel, 11 3/4 x 22 ins / 30 x 55 cm) BEF 34,000. Lokeren, 10 Oct 1992, *Orchard in Blossom* (1936, oil on canvas, 28 3/4 x 36 ins / 73 x 91.5 cm) BEF 140,000. Lokeren, 15 May 1993, *The Road from Panpelonne to St Tropez* (1931, oil on canvas, 19 3/4 x 23 1/2 ins / 50 x 60 cm) BEF 80,000. Lokeren, 4 Dec 1993, *Skaters* (1928, oil on canvas, 31 1/2 x 39 1/4 ins / 80 x 100 cm) BEF 140,000. Lokeren, 12 March 1994, *Flemish River* (oil on canvas, 23 1/2 x 39 1/4 ins / 60 x 100 cm) BEF 80,000. Amsterdam, 9 Nov 1994, *Reverie* (oil on canvas, 14 x 19 1/2 ins / 35.5 x 49.5 cm) NLG 2,300. Lokeren, 7 Oct 1995, *Boat near a Lock* (1914, oil on card, 28 x 35 ins / 71 x 89 cm) BEF 36,000. Lokeren, 9 March 1996, *View of a Harbour in Flanders* (oil on canvas, 28 1/4 x 36 ins / 71.5 x 91.5 cm) BEF 130,000. Lokeren, 7 Dec 1996, *Sunny Street in Stockel* (1905, oil on canvas, 20 3/4 x 29 1/4 ins / 53 x 74 cm) BEF 180,000. Brussels, 23 April 2001, *Breakfast on the Terrace* (oil on canvas, 19 x 24 ins / 48 x 60

cm) BEF 85,000. LOKEREN, 11 Oct 2003, *Harbour at Saint Tropez* (1931, oil on canvas, 29 x 36 ins / 73 x 92 cm) EUR 3,300. BRUSSELS, 10 Dec 2003, *Harbour at Cassis* (1938, oil on canvas, 29 x 36 ins / 74 x 92 cm) EUR 2,800. BRUSSELS, 15 June 2004, *Stokel* (oil on canvas, 33 x 47 ins / 85 x 120 cm) EUR 1,700. BRUSSELS, 15 June 2004, *Sunlit Forest Interior* (oil on canvas, 33 x 39 ins / 85 x 100 cm) EUR 11,000.

KELLER, Albert von
Swiss, 19th - 20th century.
Born 27 April 1844, in Gais; died 14 July 1920, in Munich.
Painter. History painting, portraits, genre scenes.

Albert von Keller studied under Franz von Lenbach and Arthur Ramberg at the Akademie der Bildenden Künste in Munich, after which he spent several years in Paris. He settled in Munich, where he was appointed professor at the academy in 1886. He won medals in Munich in 1883 and 1889, in Berlin in 1886 and 1891 and at the Paris Exposition Universelle in 1889 and 1900.

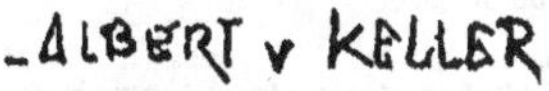

MUSEUMS AND GALLERIES:
MUNICH: *The Raising of Jairus' Daughter*; *Portrait of the Artist's Wife*; *Madeleine G.*; *Cassandra*; *Chopin* - ST PETERSBURG: *Portrait of Mme Jurieva*.

AUCTION RECORDS:
LUCERNE, 26 June 1965, *Portrait of a Young Woman in a White Dress*, CHF 7,500. BERLIN, 4 Nov 1970, *The Big Dinner*, DEM 16,000. ZURICH, 25 Nov 1977, *Woman in a White Dress* (oil on canvas, 35 1/4 x 28 1/4 ins / 89.5 x 71.5 cm) CHF 4,600. VIENNA, 16 March 1979, *Young Woman in her Boudoir* (oil on canvas, 20 3/4 x 16 1/2 ins / 53 x 42 cm) ATS 45,000. ZURICH, 1 June 1983, *Woman with a White Umbrella* (oil on card, 16 1/4 x 12 1/2 ins / 41 x 31.5 cm) CHF 7,000. HAMBURG, 4 Dec 1987, *Portrait of Tsarina Alexandra Feodorovna* (oil on canvas, 23 1/2 x 20 1/2 ins / 60 x 52 cm) DEM 10,500. COLOGNE, 20 Oct 1989, *Female Nude* (oil on canvas, 26 x 17 1/4 ins / 66 x 43.5 cm) DEM 5,000. NEW YORK, 15 Oct 1991, *Female Nude Reclining on a Lion Skin* (oil on panel, 9 x 15 ins / 23 x 38 cm) USD 5,500. ZURICH, 2 June 1994, *Characters from Antiquity* (oil on card, 9 1/4 x 13 1/2 ins / 23.5 x 34 cm) CHF 1,725. NEW YORK, 19 Jan 1995, *The End of the Evening* (oil on canvas, 57 1/2 x 38 ins / 146.1 x 96.5 cm) USD 2,587. NEW YORK, 24 May 1995, *Study in Grey* (1909, oil on panel, 23 1/2 x 12 ins / 59.7 x 30.5 cm) USD 5,750. ZURICH, 12 June 1995, *Nude with Mask* (oil on canvas, 21 1/4 x 9 1/2 ins / 54 x 24 cm) CHF 8,050. VIENNA, 29-30 Oct 1996, *Dance in the Forest at Night* (1876, oil on panel, 30 3/4 x 22 ins / 78 x 56 cm) ATS 80,500. MUNICH, 3 Dec 1996, *Gisela von Wehner in her Finest Clothes* (1906, oil on canvas, 57 1/2 x 38 1/2 ins / 146 x 98 cm) DEM 21,600.

KELLER, Alfred
Austrian, 20th century.
Born 1 February 1877, in Vienna.
Sculptor.

Alfred Keller spent some time in Rome before settling in Munich.

KELLER, Alois
Swiss, 19th century.
Born in Bavaria; died 1866.
Painter. History painting.

Keller was the son and pupil of Swiss painter Josef Keller; he subsequently worked in Vienna. He was a brother of Friedrich and Karl Keller, with whom he worked on the restoration of frescoes at the church in Einsiedeln.

KELLER, Anton
Croat, 19th century.
Active in Zagreb at the beginning of the 19th century.
Painter. Religious subjects.

Religious paintings by Keller are in the towns of Kneginec and Vinice.

KELLER, Antonius, the Elder
Swiss, 16th - 17th century.
Born 22 July 1548; died before 1611.
Active in Schaffhausen.
Painter (glass).

He married in 1576.

KELLER, Antonius, the Younger
Swiss, 17th century.
Born 1578.
Active in Schaffhausen.
Painter (glass).

Keller was the son of Antonius Keller the Elder.

KELLER, Arthur Ignatius
American, 19th - 20th century.
Born 4 July 1866 or 1867, in New York; died 1924, in New York.
Painter, watercolourist, illustrator.

Arthur Keller studied under Edgar Ward and Lemuel E. Wilmarth at the National Academy of Design in New York, then under Ludwig von Loefftz in Munich.

Around the turn of the century, he illustrated Longfellow's *Hanging of the Crane*, F. Hopkinson Smith's *Caleb West, Master Diver*, Wister's *The Virginian*, *Her Letter* by B. Harte, Irving's *Legend of Sleepy Hollow* and *A Christmas Carol* by Charles Dickens.

In 1900 and 1904 he received medals at the Exposition Universelle in Paris, and at the World's Fair, St Louis and one for drawing at Buffalo. In 1903, he was chairman of the Society of Illustrators.

BIBLIOGRAPHY:
Arthur Ignatius Keller, 1866-1924, exhibition catalogue, Brandywine River Museum, Chadds Ford, 1988. Osterwalder, Marcus (ed.), *Dictionnaire des illustrateurs 1800-1914*, Ides et Calendes, Neuchâtel, 1989.

KELLER, Christoph Heinrich Carl
German, 18th century.
Active in Nuremberg.
Engraver.

Keller is noted for a *Portrait of the Last Margrave of Ansbach*.

KELLER, Clyde Leon
American, 19th - 20th century.
Born 2 February 1872, in Salem; died 1962.
Painter. Landscapes. Wall decorations.

Clyde Keller created decorative paintings in Portland (Oregon).

KELLER, David Emil
Swiss, 19th - 20th century.
Born 6 March 1871, in Zurich.
Painter, potter.

David Emil Keller started by working as a potter in Lausanne. He went to Munich in 1893, where he studied with August Spiess. He specialised in heraldic painting.

KELLER, Delphine Gabrielle
French, 19th century.
Born 15 March 1836, in Paris.
Painter, lithographer.

Delphine Keller was a pupil of Rosa Bonheur and Soulange Teissier. She made her debut at the Salon de Paris in 1859.

KELLER, Ella
Swiss, 20th century.
Born 1876, in Aarau.
Draughtswoman, watercolourist.

Ella Keller studied art in Berlin and Bern.

KELLER, Emmanuel
French, 19th century.
Born 1806, in Troyes.
Painter. Genre scenes.

Emmanuel Keller exhibited his work at the Salon de Paris between 1833 and 1848.

BIBLIOGRAPHY:

Les Années romantiques, la peinture française de 1815 à 1850, exhibition catalogue, Musée des Beaux-Arts, Nantes, Gal. nationales du Grand Palais, Paris, 1996.

MUSEUMS AND GALLERIES:

TROYES (Mus. d'Art, d'Archéologie et de Sciences Naturelles): *Farewells.*

KELLER, Evelyn R. (Mrs)
British, 19th century.
Active in Walton-on-Thames.
Miniaturist.

Mrs Evelyn R. Keller exhibited in London at the Royal Academy in 1892.

KELLER, Fanny H. M.
British, 19th century.
Active in London.
Miniaturist.

Fanny H.M. Keller exhibited in London at the Royal Academy from 1883 to 1892.

KELLER, Ferdinand
German, 19th - 20th century.
Born 5 August 1842, in Karlsruhe; died 8 July 1922, in Baden-Baden.
Painter. History painting, portraits, landscapes. Murals. Symbolism.

Ferdinand Keller accompanied his parents to Brazil as a teenager, and lived there for four years. He was delighted by the country and returned home at the age of twenty with masses of studies and sketches, determined to make the splendours of Brazil known through his landscape painting. He studied first with Johann Wilhelm Schirmer at the Akademie der Bildenden Künste in Karlsruhe, then with Hans Gude, and later with the Viennese painter Hans Canon. In 1866, he travelled to Switzerland and France, where he took part in the 1867 Paris Exposition Universelle. He lived in Rome from 1867 to 1869, where he made the acquaintance of Anselm Feuerbach. After returning to Karlsruhe in 1870, he taught portrait and history painting at the academy there, becoming a professor in 1873 and then its director. He visited Spain in 1889 and England in 1892.

At the time when Keller was Schirmer's pupil, he became famous for his picture *Alexander von Humboldt on the Orinoco*, which was immediately bought by a Karlsruhe art-lover in 1862. After Schirmer's death, the influence of Hans Canon led Keller to abandon landscape for figure painting. He returned from Italy with a large number of studies of sites and figures, which he used in his big painting *Nero and the Burning of Rome*. In 1870, his project for the curtain of the royal theatre successfully defeated those of ninety competitors. In 1875, he painted *Margrave Ludwig Defeating the Turks at the Battle of Slankamen*, which he later called his sin of youth. An *Assumption of the Virgin* for the Jesuits' church in Heidelberg marked the start of his career as a painter of frescoes and murals. This was followed by the stairwell of the Karlsruhe Museum, then the great mural for the assembly hall of the University of Heidelberg, and later by two large paintings for the National Museum of Arts and Crafts in Stuttgart, in which he traces the history of Württemberg. *The Apotheosis of Emperor Wilhelm I* dates from 1887 and *Hero Finding the Body of Leander* from 1888.

At the beginning of 1890, Keller completed the *Apotheosis of Emperor Friedrich III*, which was on a smaller scale than the work of 1887. The emperor who defeated MacMahon is shown controlling his rearing horse on the battlefield at Froeschwiller, ready to receive the imperial crown, half shrouded in storm clouds, from the hands of a spirit, while the distant horizon is illuminated by a golden light. Though Keller often refused commissions, he painted some remarkable portraits, such as *the Grand Duke of Baden; Wilhelm I; Wilhelm II; the Grand Duchess of Oldenburg and her Daughters*. Around 1900, he was very much influenced by Arnold Böcklin and painted Symbolist landscapes such as *Arcadia* in 1899 and *The Tomb of Böcklin*, 1901-1902, which is a homage to the master, offering a kind of synthesis of his famous themes. Some elements, such as a young man playing the flute, or swans, juxtaposed with cypresses, misty, morbid colours and masks, endow his landscapes with melancholy, magic and symbolism. He was very comfortable with all techniques, and with fresco, chalks, pastels, oils, and tempera. He had hundreds of pupils and helped to give the Baden school a particular brilliance. German critics have compared him to Menzel, adding that though the latter may have complained that he was not a colourist, this was certainly not true of Keller.

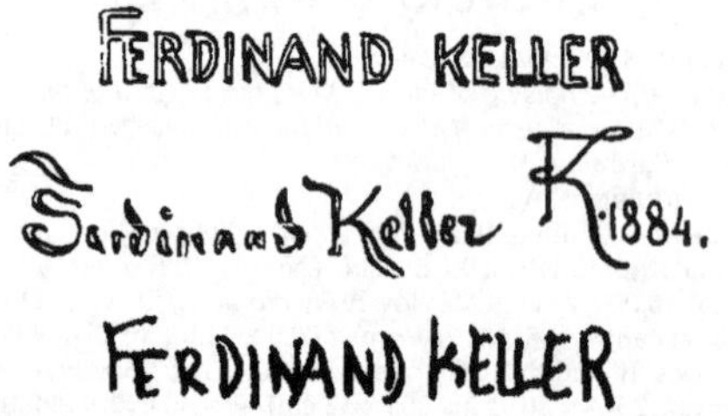

BIBLIOGRAPHY:

Jenderko, Ingrid, *Le Symbolisme en Europe*, exhibition catalogue, Rotterdam, Brussels, Baden-Baden, Gal. nationales du Grand Palais, Paris, 1976. Koch, Michael, *Ferdinand Keller (1842-1922)*, Leben und Werk, Muller, Karlsruhe, 1978.

MUSEUMS AND GALLERIES:

AACHEN: *The Departure* - HAMBURG: *Brazilian Landscape* - KARLSRUHE (Staatliche Kunsthalle): *The Tomb of Böcklin.*

AUCTION RECORDS:

PARIS, 12 Dec 1892, *The Villa d'Este at Tivoli*, FRF 2,875. PARIS, July 1946, *Symbolic Scene* (1899) FRF 28,000. LOS ANGELES, 28 Feb 1972, *Hero Finding the Body of Leander*, USD 4,000. NEW YORK, 12 June 1980, *Woman Playing the Harp* (1910, oil on card, 16½ x 10 ins / 42 x 25.5 cm) USD 1,600. LONDON, 15 March 1983, *Stiftungsfest* (*Foundation Day Celebration*) (1874, oil on canvas, 79¼ x 57 ins / 201 x 145 cm) GBP 3,000. LONDON, 19 June 1985, *Landscape with Pond* (1911, oil on canvas, 42¼ x 49¼ ins / 107 x 125 cm) GBP 3,500. NEW YORK, 17 May 1989, *View of Rio de Janeiro* (1863, oil on canvas, 12½ x 17½ ins / 31.7 x 44.5 cm) USD 7,150. NEW YORK, 25 Oct 1989, *Flora* (1883, oil on canvas, 70 x 38½ ins / 178 x 98 cm) USD 22,000. MILAN, 6 Dec 1989, *Vanity* (1896, oil on canvas, 17 x 20¾ ins / 43 x 53 cm) ITL 2,000,000. MUNICH, 12 June 1991, *Baroque Fountain with Nymph and Triton* (1893, oil and chalk/canvas, 78¾ x 65 ins / 200 x 165 cm) DEM 11,000. MUNICH, 10 Dec 1991, *The Prairie Rose* (1869, oil on canvas, 96 x 59 ins / 244 x 150 cm) DEM 25,300. NEW YORK, 16 July 1992, *Mythological Scene* (oil on canvas, 15½ x 29 ins / 39.4 x 73.7 cm) USD 1,210. MUNICH, 1 July 1998, *Southern Island with Cypress Trees and Castle* (oil on canvas, 37 x 47 ins / 95 x 120 cm) DEM 14,000. AHLDEN, 23 April 1999, *Brazilian Coastal Landscape with Beached Fishing Boat* (1873, oil on canvas, 45 x 61 ins / 114 x 154 cm) DEM 70,000. AMSTERDAM, 4 July 2000, *Toteninsel* (oil on canvas, 37 x 47 ins / 95 x 120 cm) NLG 26,000. COLOGNE, 30 Nov 2000,

David Playing Harp for Bathsheba (oil on canvas, 34 x 63 ins / 86 x 160 cm) DEM 24,000. NEW YORK, 28 June 2001, *Beauty and Butterfly* (1870, oil on canvas, 54 x 40 ins / 138 x 102 cm) USD 18,000. AHLDEN, 28 Sept 2001, *Roman Bridge* (oil on canvas, 39 x 46 ins / 98 x 117 cm) DEM 32,000. LONDON, 9 April 2002, *Give me Your Paw!* (1891, oil on canvas, 48 x 34 ins / 122 x 86 cm) GBP 8,000. MELBOURNE, 25 Nov 2002, *Beauty and Butterfly* (1870, oil on canvas, 54 x 40 ins / 138 x 102 cm) AUD 35,000. LONDON, 3 June 2003, *Frieze with Putti, Music* (1882, oil on canvas, 32 x 73 ins / 82 x 185 cm) GBP 10,000. MUNICH, 28 March 2003, *King Friedrich the Great of Prussia* (1891, pastel/paper/canvas, 32 x 26 ins / 82 x 65 cm) EUR 14,000. SYDNEY, 15 May 2004, *Study of a Woman's Head* (1897, pastel tinted paper, 17 x 17 ins / 43 x 43 cm) AUD 7,000. COLOGNE, 1 July 2004, *The Ceres Festival* (1874, oil on canvas, 80 x 57 ins / 203 x 146 cm) EUR 12,000.

KELLER, Franz
Swiss, 19th century.
Born 15 March 1800, in Gähwil; died 5 September 1883, in Kloster Magdenau, Wolfertswil.
Glass painter.

Keller, who was a monk, did a series of stained glass windows for the monastery in Wettingen.

KELLER, Franz
German, 19th century.
Born 1821, in Linz am Rhein; died 3 November 1896, in Düsseldorf.
Engraver.

Keller illustrated Overbeck's Gospels.

KELLER, Franz Xaver
German, 18th century.
Active in Straubing c. 1780.
Sculptor.

Keller did figures of *St John* and the *Virgin* for the church of St Jacob in Straubing.

KELLER, Friedrich von
German, 19th - 20th century.
Born 18 February 1840, in Neckarweihingen; died 26 August 1914, in Abtgemünd.
Active in Stuttgart and Munich.
Painter. History painting, genre scenes.

Friedrich von Keller was a student of B. Neher at the school of fine arts in Stuttgart.

MUSEUMS AND GALLERIES:
BUCHAREST (Muz. National de Arta al României): *The Forge* - STUTTGART (Staatsgal.): *The Laying in the Tomb*.

AUCTION RECORDS:
NEW YORK, 10 Oct 1973, *Artist Sitting at a Table in a Tavern, Drawing*, USD 6,000. LONDON, 30 Nov 1977, *The Ballad* (oil on canvas, 11 3/4 x 17 3/4 ins / 30 x 45 cm) GBP 3,000. NEW YORK, 24 May 1985, *Grandmother with her Two Grandchildren* (1874, oil on canvas, 23 1/2 x 19 ins / 60 x 48.3 cm) USD 13,000. LONDON, 25 March 1987, *Artist Drawing in a Tavern* (1878, oil on canvas, 20 x 26 3/4 ins / 51 x 68 cm) GBP 8,500.

KELLER, Georg
German, 16th - 17th century.
Born 15 September 1568, in Frankfurt am Main; died c. 1640, in Frankfurt am Main.
Painter, engraver (burin). History painting, landscapes.
Frankfurt School.

Georg Keller studied under Jost Amman and Ph. Uffenbach. His works include *Coronation of Emperor Ferdinand III*, dated 1627, and views of towns and castles. He produced altarpieces for the abbey church and the Franciscan church in Regensburg.

KELLER, Georg or Jorg (father and son)
Swiss, 16th century.
Active in the first half of the 16th century.
Sculptors.
Lucerne School.

The father was made a burgher of Lucerne in 1500. He and his son were both members of the guild of that city.

KELLER, Gottfried
Swiss, 19th century.
Born 19 July 1819, in Zurich; died 15 July 1890, in Zurich.
Painter, watercolourist. Landscapes.

Keller was torn between literary and artistic vocations as a young man; he opted for literature, but nonetheless continued as an amateur painter all his life. His output consists mainly of realistic landscapes including views of Lake Zurich and the Alps, but also symbolical paintings such as an *Ossianic Landscape* and *Ossianic Landscape with a Horse*.

AUCTION RECORDS:
MUNICH, 1 Dec 1976, *The Village Street* (1839, watercolour, 8 3/4 x 14 ins / 22.5 x 35.5 cm) DEM 4,500. ZURICH, 3 Dec 1987, *View of a Church beside a Stream* (1838, watercolour, 12 x 9 1/4 ins / 30.5 x 23.5 cm) CHF 6,500. LUCERNE, 12 April 2000, *Study of Tree with Deer* (1834, wash heightened with white and Indian ink, 11 x 8 ins / 28 x 20 cm) CHF 9,700.

KELLER, Gustav
German, 19th - 20th century.
Born 20 October 1860; died 18 August 1911.
Painter, draughtsman.

After studying at the Munich academy, Gustav Keller worked mainly as an illustrator of works on geology and the natural world.

KELLER, Hans
Swiss, 17th century.
Active in Zurich in the first half of the 17th century.
Painter (glass).

Keller is known to have been a pupil of glass painter Hans Heinrich Bardorf in 1619.

KELLER, Hans
Swiss, 20th century.
Born 1884, in Zurich; died 1983.
Painter. Figures, portraits, landscapes, still-lifes, flowers, animals.

Hans Keller was initially a student of the painter Ernst Würtenberg before studying in Stuttgart from 1906 to 1907, and in Paris at the Académie Julian.

BIBLIOGRAPHY:
Ateliers: Georges Roubaudo, Henri Auchère, Hans Keller, auction catalogue, Maître Gilles Néret-Minet, Paris, 26 February 2001.

KELLER, Hans Balthasar
Swiss, 17th century.
Active in Zurich.
Glass painter.

KELLER, Hans Jakob
Swiss, 17th century.
Active in Zurich c. 1610.
Painter (glass).

KELLER, Heinrich
Swiss, 16th century.
Born 1518; died 1567.
Active in Rapperswil.

Calligrapher, miniaturist.
Heinrich Keller was a prior at the cloister of St Gall.

KELLER, Heinrich
Swiss, 18th - 19th century.
Born 17 February 1771, in Zurich; died 21 December 1832, in Rome.
Sculptor, scholar. Mythological subjects. Busts.
Keller left several busts such as those of *Abbot Koch* and *J.J. Bodmer* and mythological sculptures such as *Electra at the Tomb of Agamemnon* and *Ariadne*.

KELLER, Heinrich
Swiss, 19th century.
Born 11 October 1778, in Zurich; died 18 September 1862, in Zurich.
Draughtsman. Landscapes.
Keller was known chiefly for his panoramas, maps and similar.
AUCTION RECORDS:
NEW YORK, 1 Feb 1958, *Woman with a Mask*, USD 200. BERN, 24 June 1983, *View of Zurich* (c. 1830, watercoloured etching, 20 1/2 x 29 ins / 52.3 x 73.6 cm) CHF 8,200. BERN, 21 June 1985, *View of Baden* (c. 1810, tinted coloured etchings, 9 x 11 1/2 ins / 22 x 29.5 cm) CHF 21,000.

KELLER, Henri
French, 18th century.
Draughtsman. Rustic scenes.
Henri Keller was working in 1743. He is mentioned by Mariette.

KELLER, Henry George
American, 19th - 20th century.
Born 3 April 1870, in Cleveland (Oklahoma); died 1949.
Painter. Landscapes, still-lifes.
Henry George Keller studied under Julius Hugo Bergmann at the Kunstakademie in Düsseldorf, and continued his studies in Karlsruhe and Munich where he won a silver medal and an award worth 1,600 dollars. Keller ran an informal art school in Berlin Heights, Ohio from 1903 to 1914. He was an influential teacher of watercolour and drawing techniques, and his pupils included Charles Burchfield, Paul Travis and Frank Wilcox. He exhibited in the 1913 Armory Show.
MUSEUMS AND GALLERIES:
CLEVELAND: *Several Landscapes* - WASHINGTON DC (Phillips Collection): *In the Sandpit*; *Still-life*.

KELLER, Johan
German, 15th century.
Active in the region of Meran (now Merano, Italy).
Painter.

KELLER, Johan
Dutch, 19th century.
Born 13 November 1863, in The Hague.
Sculptor.
Johan Keller taught at the Glasgow school of fine arts from 1895.
MUSEUMS AND GALLERIES:
ROTTERDAM (Mus. Boijmans Van Beuningen): *Sculpture*.

KELLER, Johann Christoph
German, 18th century.
Born 12 June 1737, in Nuremberg; died 5 March 1795, in Erlangen.
Painter, miniaturist, engraver. Portraits.
Keller was a pupil of J.J. Preisler in Nuremberg and a drawing master at the University of Erlangen. Noted works are subjects taken from Kabener's *Satires* (11 pieces) and engravings from a work called *Plantae Rariores*.

KELLER, Johann Heinrich
Swiss, 18th century.
Born 1692, in Zurich; died 1765, in The Hague.
Painter, draughtsman, decorative designer.
Mythological subjects, figures, scenes with figures, genre scenes, interiors with figures, landscapes with figures, seascapes. Ornaments.
Keller was the son of a Basel sculptor who set up in Zurich, which some biographers also give as his birthplace. He studied painting initially with Andreas Holzmüller, but then went to Munich to continue his studies with Nicolaus Sluber, finally ending up as a student at the Académie Royale in Paris. In 1726, he moved to The Hague as a painter decorator, and did a lot of work for great houses in the area.
Keller is a fascinating subject for study in that his style is a mixture of David Teniers and Watteau.

MUSEUMS AND GALLERIES:
AMSTERDAM: *Five Child Musicians*; *Aeneas and Anchises* - STUTTGART: *Storm at Sea*.
AUCTION RECORDS:
LONDON, 18 April 1947, *Pastoral Figures*, GBP 147. NEW YORK, 9 May 1947, *In the Woods*, USD 480. LONDON, 27 June 1969, *Pastoral Dance*, Gns 1,200. PARIS, 19 Oct 1973, *Interior of an Inn*, FRF 9,500. MARSEILLES, 10 March 1974, *Young Woman Bathing with Cupids*, FRF 10,600. ZURICH, 26 May 1978, *Inn Scene* (1756, oil on canvas, 30 1/2 x 27 1/4 ins / 77.5 x 69.5 cm) CHF 7,000. ZURICH, 30 Nov 1984, *Bacchanal* (oil on canvas, 21 1/2 x 26 1/4 ins / 54.5 x 66.5 cm) CHF 15,000. EDINBURGH, 30 April 1986, *Diana Resting after the Hunt* (1759, oil on canvas, irregular pediment, 42 x 40 ins / 106.7 x 101.6 cm) GBP 12,000. MILAN, 3 March 1987, *The Soap Bubbles* (oil on canvas, 52 1/4 x 46 ins / 133 x 117 cm) ITL 18,500,000. PARIS, 3 July 1996, *Spring Dance* (oil/copper, 16 x 19 1/2 ins / 40.5 x 49.5 cm) FRF 22,000. PARIS, 30 March 1998, *Ornamental study* (grey wash, pen and brown ink, 10 3/4 x 5 1/4 ins / 27.3 x 13.2 cm) FRF 3,400. LUCERNE, 19 May 1999, *Time Helps Truth and Peace to Conquer All* (1746, oil on canvas, 31 x 25 ins / 78 x 63 cm) CHF 4,000. LUCERNE, 13 Oct 1999, *Venus and Adonis* (1751, oil on canvas, 28 x 35 ins / 71 x 90 cm) CHF 10,000. MUNICH, 5 July 2000, *Venus and Adonis in Wooded Landscape* (1759, oil on canvas, 28 x 35 ins / 70 x 89 cm) DEM 13,000. LONDON, 1 Nov 2000, *Allegory of the Arts* (oil on canvas, 22 x 17 ins / 55 x 44 cm) GBP 1,900. NEW YORK, 3 Oct 2001, *Mirtillo Playing Blind Man's Buff with Amarillis. Crowning of Mirtillo* (1751, oil on canvas, a pair, 18 x 21 ins / 46 x 54 cm) USD 15,000. BERN, 9 Nov 2001, *Shepherd with Cows, Goats and Sheep in Front of a Ruin* (oil on canvas, 14 x 17 ins / 35 x 44 cm) CHF 5,800.

KELLER, Johann Jacob
Swiss, 17th - 18th century.
Born 1665, in Basel; died November 1747, in Basel.
Sculptor.
Keller was the father of Johann Heinrich Keller. He trained in his home city, then travelled round Germany, Italy and France, including a spell working at the palace of Versailles. On his return to Basel in 1691, he married Susanna Keller. Among his works are a large number of tomb monuments in Basel and all kinds of statues in the churches of the city.

KELLER, Johann Sigmund
German, 18th century.
Active in Freiburg im Breisgau.
Painter.

Keller trained in Düsseldorf. His works include views of churches.

KELLER, Josef
German, 19th century.
Born 31 March 1849, in Nesselwang (Bavaria).
Sculptor.

Keller worked in Frankfurt, noted works of his being *Neptune*; a *Monument to the Warriors*; and a bust of *J. Mönch-Offenbach*.

KELLER, Josef or Joseph
Swiss, 18th - 19th century.
Born 1740, in Pfronten (Bavaria); died 1823.
Painter.

Keller is noted for a fresco in the church of Menzingen (Zug canton), signed *Joseph Keller invenit et pinxit 1793* (Joseph Keller made and painted this).

KELLER, Joseph von
German, 19th century.
Born 31 March 1811, in Linz am Rhein; died 30 May 1873, in Düsseldorf.
Engraver.

Von Keller initially studied art at the school in his village, then went on at 16 to a major engraving workshop in Bonn. In 1835, he moved on to Düsseldorf, working there under the direction of Hübner. In 1838, he went to Paris to study with Desnoyers and Forster. The following year, he was appointed to the staff of the academy in Düsseldorf to teach engraving. In 1841, he won a grant to go and work in Rome, where he drew Raphael's *Dispute of the Holy Sacrament*. From there he went on to London, where he engraved a *Portrait of Prince Albert*.

In 1846, he resumed his position at the academy in Düsseldorf. Enjoying great fame, he was admitted to membership of the academies of Berlin, Brussels, St Petersburg and Vienna. Von Keller applied himself in particular to engravings from German painters, especially Hübner, Deger, Hermann and Götzenberg.

KELLER, L. G.
French, 20th century.
Sculptor, designer.

L. G. Keller was a sculptor until 1939. He went on to work in lacquer, creating pictures inspired by contemporary poets.

KELLER, Laurent Friedrich
French, 20th century.
Born 3 May 1885, in Monaco.
Active in Switzerland.
Sculptor.

Laurent Friedrich Keller studied in Paris and worked mainly in Zurich.

MUSEUMS AND GALLERIES:
OLTEN - SOLOTHURN.

KELLER, Ludwig
German, 19th - 20th century.
Born 20 June 1865, in Duisburg; died 28 December 1925, in Düsseldorf.
Painter.

Ludwig Keller exhibited in 1910, and on other occasions, in Berlin.

MUSEUMS AND GALLERIES:
DÜSSELDORF: *Portrait of Peter Jansen, Director of the Fine Arts Academy*.

AUCTION RECORDS:
VIENNA, 18 March 1977, *Seated Nude* (card, 22 1/2 x 19 3/4 ins / 57 x 50 cm) ATS 25,000.

KELLER, Maximilien
German, 20th century.
Born 25 August 1880, in Tübingen.
Active in Munich.
Painter.

Maximilien Keller exhibited in Paris in 1911 and 1912.

KELLER, Meinrad
Swiss, 18th century.
Active in Baden c. 1745.
Draughtsman, painter.

KELLER, Nicolas
French, 18th century.
Painter, designer.

Nicolas Keller was resident in Lyons in 1788 and 1790.

KELLER, Pierre
Swiss, 20th century.
Born 9 January 1945, in Gilly.
Sculptor, engraver, draughtsman, photographer.
Conceptual Art.

Pierre Keller studied at the École Cantonale des Beaux-Arts et d'Art Appliqué in Lausanne from 1961 to 1985. He has lived in Grandvaux since 1970.

In 1966, he began creating his first modifiable objects, which led him to produce modifiable structures in the Constructivist manner. His manifestations and realisations are extremely diverse. He attempts a new kind of performance focused on the concept of 'Kilo Art' that he himself created, by having the quantities measured by official organisations and thus causing ideas of value in the world of art to be permanently questioned and changed. At the 1975 Paris Biennale, he presented a different kind of work, emphasising the way the artist behaves, using autobiographical photographs, montages and mascots.

He has taken part in group exhibitions since 1969. These have included 1969, *Jeunes graveurs suisses* (*Young Swiss Engravers*) at the National Museum in Santiago in Chile; 1970 *Jeunes graveurs suisses* (*Young Swiss Engravers*) in a number of Latin American capital cities and at the National Museum in Stockholm; 1971, *Multiples* at the Philadelphia Museum of Art and the International Biennale of Engraving in Ljubljana; the 1972 Venice Biennale; the 1974 Wroclaw Triennial of Drawing and the 1975 Paris Biennale. He has also shown collections of his works in solo exhibitions since 1969 in Switzerland, Italy, Germany and Poland and in 1994 he showed his photographic works *Horses* at the Swiss Cultural Centre in Paris.

BIBLIOGRAPHY:
IXe Biennale de Paris, exhibition catalogue, Idea Books, Musée d'Art moderne de la Ville de Paris, Paris, 1975.

MUSEUMS AND GALLERIES:
LAUSANNE (Cantonal MFA): *Small Modifiable Cubes*.

KELLER, Pyton Stepanovich
Russian, 20th century.
Born 1909, in Rostov-on-Don.
Painter. Landscapes.

Pyton Keller graduated from the Donprofobra school of fine arts in Rostov in 1930. From 1936 he was a member of the union of Soviet artists. He lived in Rostov.

AUCTION RECORDS:
GLASGOW, 4 Dec 1991, *On the Verdant Isle* (1966, oil on card, 19 x 25 1/4 ins / 48 x 64 cm) GBP 440.

KELLER, Richard
Swiss, 20th century.
Born 6 July 1885, in Plauen.
Painter. Landscapes.

KELLER, S.
German, 18th century.
Active in Freiburg c. 1780.
Painter. Architectural views.

MUSEUMS AND GALLERIES:
STUTTGART (Staatsgal.): *Church Interior* (two).

KELLER, Salomon
Swiss, 17th century.
Born 1582; died 1642.
Active in Zurich.
Painter (glass).

KELLER, Stéphane (Mme)
French, 19th century.
Active in Paris.
Painter.
Stéphane Keller was a member of the Société des Artistes Français from 1908.

KELLER, Wolf
German, 16th century.
Active in Kulmbach.
Painter.

KELLER-HERMANN, Marie
Austrian, 19th - 20th century.
Born 26 November 1868, in Vienna.
Painter. Genre scenes, flowers.
Marie Keller-Hermann was a student of Olga Wisinger-Florian and worked in the Dachau region.

KELLER-LEUZINGER, Franz
German, 19th century.
Born 30 August 1835, in Mannheim; died 18 July 1890, in Munich.
Painter, engineer.
Keller-Leuzinger was the brother of the painter Ferdinand Keller. He is noted for landscapes of Brazil, among other things.

KELLER-REUTLINGEN, Paul Wilhelm
German, 19th - 20th century.
Born 2 February 1854, in Reutlingen; died 10 January 1920, in Munich.
Painter. Landscapes with figures.
Paul Keller-Reutlingen was a student at the fine arts academies in Stuttgart and Munich. His landscapes often include figures - farmers at work, people tending animals, children playing and loving couples - and are sensitive to changes of light according to the hours and seasons. He exhibited from 1879 in Vienna, Munich (where he received a medal in 1892), Düsseldorf, Stuttgart and Berlin.

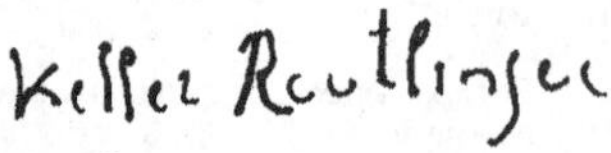

MUSEUMS AND GALLERIES:
FRANKFURT AM MAIN: *Windmill in Bruck* - LEIPZIG: *Dusk* - MUNICH: *Beneath the Moss Roof* - STUTTGART: *Evening Bells.*
AUCTION RECORDS:
MUNICH, 19 June 1974, *The Goose Girl,* DEM 7,000. COLOGNE, 16 June 1977, *Houses by the Water* (oil on canvas, 32 x 48 ins / 81 x 121 cm) DEM 7,500. LONDON, 21 March 1980, *Little Girl Feeding the Chickens* (1882, oil on canvas, 19 x 26 ins / 48 x 66 cm) GBP 10,000. NEW YORK, 28 Oct 1982, *After the Storm* (oil on canvas, 29¾ x 41½ ins / 75.5 x 105.5 cm) USD 17,500. LONDON, 3 June 1983, *The Vegetable Market in Verona* (oil on canvas, 26 x 58 ins / 66 x 147.3 cm) GBP 8,500. LUCERNE, 6 Nov 1986, *The Goose Girl* (oil on canvas, 22 x 33½ ins / 55 x 85 cm) CHF 5,000. VIENNA, 18 March 1987, *View of a Village by the Sea* (1880, oil on panel, 12½ x 19¾ ins / 32 x 50 cm) ATS 50,000. AMSTERDAM, 16 Nov 1988, *The Goose Girl* (oil on canvas, 25¼ x 32 ins / 64 x 81 cm) NLG 41,400. MUNICH, 29 Nov 1989, *Children Playing in a Garden by a River* (oil on canvas, 20¼ x 26¾ ins / 51.5 x 68 cm) DEM 33,000. COLOGNE, 29 June 1990, *Summer Landscape with a Shepherd and his Flock* (oil on canvas, 28 x 43 ins / 71 x 109 cm) DEM 3,800. MUNICH, 12 Dec 1990, *Village at Nightfall* (oil on canvas, 29¾ x 39¼ ins / 75.5 x 100 cm) DEM 22,000. MUNICH, 12 June 1991, *Washing Drying on the Line* (oil on canvas, 30¾ x 46½ ins / 78 x 118 cm) DEM 33,000. MUNICH, 10 Dec 1991, *Swabian Idyll* (oil on canvas, 21 x 27 ins / 53.5 x 68.5 cm) DEM 28,750. LONDON, 19 June 1992, *The View from my Studio Window* (oil on canvas, 19¼ x 26½ ins / 49 x 67.3 cm) GBP 13,200. MUNICH, 10 Dec 1992, *On the Way Home* (oil on canvas, 14½ x 23¼ ins / 37 x 59 cm) DEM 25,990. LONDON, 20 May 1993, *Swabian Idyll* (oil on canvas, 21¾ x 29½ ins / 55.3 x 75 cm) GBP 12,650. MUNICH, 7 Dec 1993, *Nightfall* (1898, oil on canvas, 14¼ x 23 ins / 36 x 58.5 cm) DEM 12,650. MUNICH, 6 Dec 1994, *Portrait of Gräf (verso)* (1914, oil on canvas, 27½ x 20 ins / 70 x 51 cm) GBP 1,981,500.

KELLER-VYLIANDI, J. P.
Russian, 19th century.
Born 1826.
Painter. History painting, portraits, genre scenes.
MUSEUMS AND GALLERIES:
MOSCOW: *An Italian Shepherd; Galileo* - MOSCOW (State Tretyakov Gal.): *Portrait of the Composer A. N. Serov.*

KELLERHOVEN, Franz
German, 19th century.
Born c. 1814, in Cologne; died 23 September 1872, in Cologne.
Lithographer.
Kellerhoven was a pupil of Ödenthal; he subsequently spent a lot of time in Holland and France. Noted works include his *Imitation of Christ* and reproductions of illuminated manuscripts.

KELLERHOVEN, Josef
German, 19th century.
Born 1798, in Mannheim; died 1840, in Speyer.
Painter, lithographer.
Kellerhoven was the son of Moritz Kellerhoven. A noted work is his *Portrait of Princess Charlotte Augusta of Bavaria.*

KELLERHOVEN, Moritz
German, 18th - 19th century.
Born 1758, in Altenrath; died 15 December 1830, in Munich.
Painter, engraver.
Kellerhoven started out as a natural philosopher, but then went over to art. He trained in Düsseldorf, then Antwerp, finally settling in Vienna in 1779. A member of staff at the Munich academy and court painter to Elector Karl Theodor from 1784, he was made principal professor in 1808. He did paintings and engravings of talent on historical subjects and portraits, often from Rembrandt.

MUSEUMS AND GALLERIES:
MUNICH: *Portrait of Michael Gilbert.*

KELLERINI, Alberick
Austrian, 17th century.
Born 1623, in Rouen; died 25 October 1672, in Zwettl Abbey (near Zwettl).
Painter.
Kellerini painted several altar paintings, including some in the Lilienfeld area near St Pölten.

KELLERTHALER, Daniel
German, 17th century.
Active in Dresden in 1613.
Goldsmith, engraver. Mythological subjects.
Kellerthaler is known for his engravings.

KELLERTHALER, Hans
German, 16th century.
Active in Dresden.
Engraver.

Hans Kellerthaler was certainly a gold and silversmith, and could also have been a painter.

KELLERTHALER, Johan, the Elder, or
Kellerdaller
German, 16th century.
Born c. 1530, in Dresden.
Active in Dresden from 1558 to 1575.
Engraver.

His works include engravings produced from drawings of subjects from the Old Testament and secular history by Giovanni Maria Nosseni, an Italian artist living in Dresden.

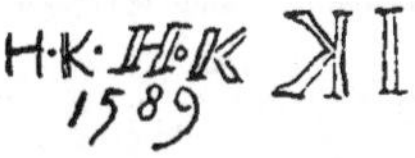

KELLERTHALER, Johann, the Younger
Dutch, 17th century.
Active in Dresden from 1620 to 1625.
Engraver (burin).

Johann Kellerthaler the Younger produced engravings of historical, mythological and religious subjects.

KELLEY, Gary
American, 20th century.
Born 1945.
Painter, illustrator.

Gary Kelley works essentially for the press and publishing industry, executing illustrations and posters. Inspired by the classics of fantastic literature from Edgar A. Poe to Maupassant or Washington Irving, he creates a strange, unsettling universe through a discerning distribution of light and shade. His work has appeared in magazines including *New-Yorker Magazine, Rolling Stone, Playboy, Atlantic Monthly, Time*, and *Newsweek*. He has also painted murals including two for the Barnes and Nobel bookstore in New York City.

He took part in the exhibition: *Fantastic Art: a Spirited View* in Bobigny.

KELLEY, Mike
American, 20th - 21st century.
Born 27 October 1954, in Detroit.
Sculptor of assemblages, installation artist, draughtsman, mixed media, illustrator. Multimedia.
Neo-Conceptual Art.

Mike Kelley received a BFA from University of Michigan, Ann Arbor, in 1976, and an MFA from the California Institute of the Arts, Valencia, in 1978. He lives and works in Los Angeles. His work is critical of psychoanalysis, capitalism and post-industrial American culture, particularly the injustices, crudity and hypocrisy concerning racism, physical taboos, political conscience and machismo.

While a graduate student, Kelley developed a unique performance style in which his sculptures were demonstrational, being used as props during his performances, such as *Monkey Island* (1982-1983) and *Plato's Cave, Rothko's Chapel, Lincoln's Profile* (1985). Kelley gave a series of performances from 1981 to 1986 in Buffalo, Los Angeles, the University of California, San Diego, Venice (California) and New York. His work was influenced by the music and stage manner of a rock band he founded with artist Tony Oursler in 1974, Destroy All Monsters, and by Sun Ra and other jazz performers. In 1986, Kelley changed from performance to the creation of stand-alone sculptures and mixed media installations, the first of which was his series *Half a Man*, which was shown at the Hirshhorn Museum and Sculpture Garden in Washington DC in 1991.

Kelley's work, which uses a variety of media, is often based on troubled periods of childhood or on nostalgia, interlaced with elements of pop psychology. He has sewn old stuffed toys onto knitted afghans, or arranged partially blacked-out photographs in an installation piece to represent repressed memory syndrome, as in *Blackout* (2001). In 1997 he collaborated with Tony Oursler on the project *The Poetics*, shown at *Documenta X* in Kassel, which included video, sound, images and objects drawn from popular culture.

Kelley's exhibitions include: 1996, *Thinking Print: Books to Billboards, 1980-95*, Museum of Modern Art, New York; 2000, *Présumés innocents: l'art contemporain et l'enfance (Presumed Innocent: Contemporary Art and Childhood)*, Capc Musée d'Art Contemporain, Bordeaux; 2000, *Consolation Prize: Mike Kelley and John Miller*, Belkin Art Gallery, Vancouver; 2002, *The Object Sculpture*, Henry Moore Institute, Leeds; 2003, *C'est Arrivé Demain (It Happened Tomorrow)*, Lyons Biennale; 2003, *The Poetics Project 1977-1997*, The Curve, Barbican Center, London, and other venues; 2004, *WOW (The Work of the Work)*, Henry Art Gallery, University of Washington, Seattle; and 2004, *Mike Kelley: The Uncanny*, Tate Liverpool and Museum Ludwig, Vienna.

He has received a Louis Comfort Tiffany Foundation Grant (1984), National Endowment for the Arts Grants (1985, 1990), an Artists Space Interarts Grant (1986), an Awards in the Visual Arts Grant (1987), a Skowhegan Medal in Mixed Media (1997), a University of Michigan School of Art and Design Distinguished Alumnus Award (1998), a California Institute of the Arts Distinguished Alumnus Award (2000) and a Guggenheim Fellowship (2003).

BIBLIOGRAPHY:

Jones, Nancy, '*Anxieux objets made in U. S. A.*' in *Artstudio* n° 19, periodical, Gal. Templon, Paris, winter 1990. Kellein, Thomas, *Mike Kelley*, exhibition catalogue, Edition Cantz, Basel, 1992. Miyoshi Barosh/Bartman, William S., *Mike Kelley*, illustrated book, Artpress, New York, 1992. *Mike Kelley: 1985-1986*, exhibition catalogue, Museu d'Art Contemporani de Barcelona, Barcelona, 1992. Adams, Brooks, '*Mike Kelley ou l'Esthétique de l'échec*' in *Art Press* n° 170, periodical, Paris, June 1992. Sussman, Elisabeth, et al., *Mike Kelley*, Abrams, New York, 1993. Bois, Yve Alain/Krauss, Rosalind, *L'Informe-mode d'emploi*, Éd. du Centre Georges-Pompidou, Paris, 1996. Bernadac, Marie-Laure/Moisdon-Tremblay, et al., *Présumés innocents: l'art contemporain et l'enfance*, exhibition catalogue, Capc musée d'Art contemporain, Bordeaux, 2000. Arden Roy (ed.)/ Watson, Scott, *Consolation Prize: Mike Kelley and John Miller*, exhibition catalogue, Morris and Helen Belkin Art Gallery, Vancouver, 2000. Monk, Philip, *Mike Kelley and Paul McCarthy: Collaborative Works*, exhibition catalogue, Power Plant Contemporary Art Gallery at Harborfront, Toronto, 2000. *Mike Kelley: Extracurricular Activity Projective, Reconstruction #1*, Video, Electronic Arts Intermix, New York, 2000. '*Mike Kelley. Se penser en tant qu'objet. Entretien*' in *Art Press* n° 282 p. 36, periodical, Paris, September 2002. Zahm, Olivier (preface), et al., *Trésors publics, 20 ans de création dans les Fonds régionaux d'art contemporain*, Flammarion, Paris, 2003 (text in French and English). Weibel, Peter (ed.), '*Phantom der Lust. Visionen des Masochismus in der Kunst*', *2 vol.*, exhibition catalogue, Neue Galerie am Landesmuseum, Graz, Belleville Verlag, Munich, 2003. Cooper, Dennis, '*Mike Kelley Talks to Dennis Cooper*' in *Artforum*, journal article, April 2003. Welchman, John C. (ed.), *Mike Kelley: Minor Histories - Statements, Conversations, Proposals*, illustrated book, MIT Press, Cambridge (MA), 2004.

MUSEUMS AND GALLERIES:

BOSTON (MFA): *No Exit* (1987, installation) - DETROIT (Institute of Arts) - EINDHOVEN (Van Abbe Mus.): *Categorical Imperative and Morgue* (1999, installation) - GHENT (Stedelijk Museum voor Actuele Kunst): *Incorrect Sexual Model: Mommy's Penis* (1987, acrylic on wood); *Innards* (1990, multi-media) - HUMLEBÆK (Louisiana Mus) - LOS ANGELES (County MA) - MADRID (Fundación La Caixa) - MONTPELLIER (FRAC Languedoc-Roussillon): *Dialogue #1* (1991) - NEW YORK

(Guggenheim Mus.): *Riddle of the Sphinx* (1991, multi-media) - NEW YORK (Metropolitan Mus. of Art) - NEW YORK (MoMA) - NEW YORK (Whitney Mus. of American Art) - PARIS (FNAC) - PARIS (MNAM-CCI) - PITTSBURGH (Carnegie MA): *Gussied Up* (1992, installation) - WASHINGTON DC (Hirshhorn Mus. and Sculpture Garden): *Untitled #7* (1994, enamel on aluminium).

AUCTION RECORDS:
NEW YORK, 6 May 1992, *Untitled* (1983, ink/panel, 16 1/2 x 13 3/4 ins / 42.2 x 35.2 cm) USD 5,280. NEW YORK, 22 Feb 1993, *Detritus no. 37* (acrylic/paper, 23 1/2 x 31 1/2 ins / 59.8 x 80 cm) USD 3,850. NEW YORK, 4 May 1993, *Two Frogs and Two Cats* (1990, soft toy animals, 20 x 69 x 7 ins / 50.8 x 175.3 x 17.8 cm) USD 13,800. LONDON, 3 Dec 1993, *Rainbow of Death* (1985, acrylic/paper, 60 x 60 ins / 152.5 x 151.5 cm) GBP 9,775. NEW YORK, 23 Feb 1994, *Untitled* (1982, gesso, ink and felt pen/three sheets of paper, 30 x 66 1/2 ins / 76.2 x 169 cm) USD 12,650. NEW YORK, 15 Nov 1995, *Fruit of Thy Loins* (1990, wall assemblage of soft toys, 38 x 20 x 10 ins / 96.4 x 50.8 x 25.4 cm) USD 51,750. NEW YORK, 19 Nov 1996, *Travelogue: From Monkey Island* (1982-1983, acrylic/paper, set of eight works, each 24 1/2 x 19 1/2 ins / 62.2 x 49.5 cm) USD 36,800. NEW YORK, 20 Nov 1996, *Incorrect Sexual Model: Utopia* (1987, synthetic polymer/panel, two pendants, each 72 x 48 ins / 182.9 x 121.9 cm) USD 19,550. NEW YORK, 19 Nov 1997, *Charte de morphologie des métiers* (1991, 60 black and white photographs, each 12 3/4 x 8 ins / 32.3 x 20.4 cm) USD 96,000. NEW YORK, 19 May 1999, *Incorrect Sexual Model Corrected* (1987, acrylic on canvas, diptych, a pair, 72 x 48 ins / 183 x 122 cm) USD 60,000. NEW YORK, 16 Nov 1999, *The Sublime, The Sublime Framed* (1983, synthetic polymer on paper, ten parts, 140 x 41 ins / 356 x 103 cm) USD 150,000. NEW YORK, 16 May 2000, *Estral Star 1* (tied stuffed cloth animals, 31 x 12x6 ins / 80 x 30x16 cm) USD 110,000. NEW YORK, 16 Nov 2000, *Pagan Altar* (synthetic polymer on panel and dried corn, 98 x 100 ins / 249 x 254 cm) USD 60,000. NEW YORK, 15 May 2001, *Untitled* (two rag dolls sewn together, 30 x 13x3 ins / 76 x 33x8 cm) USD 60,000. NEW YORK, 17 May 2001, *Human Geometry* (acrylic on paper, triptych, 93 x 214 ins / 236 x 543 cm) USD 130,000. NEW YORK, 16 May 2002, *Unwilling Splendour* (1984, acrylic on canvas, two parts, 54 x 48 ins / 138 x 122 cm) USD 20,000. NEW YORK, 16 May 2002, *If Orange Is Beautiful/Orange and Purple Flux/If Purple Is Tragic* (1985, acrylic on fabric, three parts, 48 x 146 ins / 122 x 372 cm) USD 32,500. NEW YORK, 12 Nov 2003, *Hierarchical Figure* (1989, acrylic on four panels with ribbon, 94 x 48 ins / 240 x 122 cm) USD 55,000. NEW YORK, 14 Nov 2003, *Memory Ware Flat no.30* (2001, plastic, glass and wooden beads on panel, 70 x 46x4 ins / 178 x 117x10 cm) USD 82,000. NEW YORK, 13 May 2004, *Head's the Same as between the Legs Symmetrical Sets round Eye, Straight Line of Mouth* (acrylic on paper, triptych, 50 x 38 ins / 127 x 96 cm) USD 150,000. NEW YORK, 10 June 2004, *Memory Ware Flat no. 10* (mixed media and synthetic resin on wood panel, 85 x 61x7 ins / 216 x 155x18 cm) USD 180,000.

KELLIN, Nicolas Joseph
French, 19th century.
Born c. 1789; died 18 May 1858, in Samer.
Painter, watercolourist. Landscapes, architectural views.

Nicolas Kellin was a pupil of Roqueplan and Bonington. He exhibited his work at the Salon de Paris between 1833 and 1842.

MUSEUMS AND GALLERIES:
BOULOGNE-SUR-MER - COMPIÈGNE (Mus. national du Château): several works.

AUCTION RECORDS:
PARIS, 27 June 1945, *Road in Normandy* (1836, watercolour) FRF 1,500. PARIS, 15 June 1983, *View of Tréport* (watercolour and gouache) FRF 8,400. PARIS, 16 March 1990, *View of the Pantheon* (1832, watercolour heightened with white, 6 1/2 x 9 3/4 ins / 16.5 x 24.8 cm) FRF 30,000. PARIS, 22 Nov 1991, *Rue de Paris?* (watercolour and gouache, 10 x 7 ins / 25.5 x 18 cm) FRF 12,000. PARIS, 23 Nov 2001, *View of the Pyramids* (1830, watercolour/crayon, 6 x 9 ins / 15 x 23 cm) FRF 25,000. PARIS, 5 July 2002, *Dieppe, Beach and Castle* (1840, watercolour, 14 x 17 ins / 35 x 42 cm) EUR 3,800.

KELLNER, August Friedrich
German, 20th century.
Born 22 January 1885, in Nuremberg.
Glass painter.

August Kellner made the windows for a church in Nuremberg.

KELLNER, Carl
German, 19th century.
Born 1852, in Nuremberg; died in Friedrichshafen.
Painter.

KELLNER, Carl Philipp
German, 20th century.
Born 27 November 1886, in Nuremberg.
Painter, engraver.

Carl Kellner painted a *Christ on the Cross* for the church in Affalterthal.

KELLNER, Charles Harry
American, 20th century.
Born 13 September 1890, in Kasa (Czechoslovakia), to American parents; died 1979, in Chicago.
Painter. Landscapes.

Charles Harry Kellner studied under Wellington Reynolds and Pierre Bonnard. He lived for some time in France in Bellevue near Paris, and obtained local recognition.

He is remembered for *Sunny Morning in St-Cloud*, which was acquired by the US government.

KELLNER, Dorothea
German, 20th century.
Born 11 January 1875, in Gentzrode.
Active in Berlin.
Miniaturist.

KELLNER, Georg, the Elder
German, 19th century.
Born 15 May 1811, in Oberreichenbach; died 22 August 1892, in Nuremberg.
Painter, glass painter. Portraits.

Kellner worked with his father and brothers, making his contribution to the establishment of the great Kellner stained glass window business. He provided works for churches in the Nuremberg area - in Viersen, Rothenburg and elsewhere - but especially for a private clientele in London, Paris, Vienna and St Petersburg.

AUCTION RECORDS:
LONDON, 1894, *Portrait of a Woman Seen in Three Quarters Profile*, FRF 725.

KELLNER, Georg, the Younger
German, 19th - 20th century.
Born 1 May 1874, in Nuremberg; died 30 July 1924, in Nuremberg.
Painter, glass painter, engraver. Landscapes.

Georg Kellner received commissions in the Nuremberg area for the church in Wieseth and the castle in Roth.

KELLNER, Hermann, the Elder
German, 19th century.
Born 9 April 1814, in Bruckberg; died October 1877, in Friedrichshafen.
Glass painter.

Kellner was a pupil of his father Johann Jakob Kellner; he worked in England, then mainly in Nuremberg and Ulm.

KELLNER, Hermann, the Younger
German, 19th - 20th century.
Born 27 September 1849, in Nuremberg; died 14 November 1926, in Munich.
Painter. History painting, genre scenes.
Hermann Kellner was the son of the glass-painter Johann Stephan Kellner and the brother of Samuel Kellner. He was a student of Kreling in Nuremberg and of Diez at the academy in Munich, where he subsequently worked.
MUSEUMS AND GALLERIES:
GLASGOW: *The Ravages of War*.

KELLNER, Johann Friedrich
Russian, 17th century.
Active in Reval (now Tallinn).
Painter. Portraits.

KELLNER, Johann Georg Michael
German, 19th century.
Born 24 April 1825, in Nuremberg; died 13 October 1859, in Nuremberg.
Glass painter.
Kellner worked for Count Raczynski in Berlin.

KELLNER, Johann Jakob
German, 19th century.
Born 1788, in Nuremberg; died 20 December 1873, in Schwabach.
Engraver, glass painter.
Kellner studied under his father and worked for the church in Bremen.

KELLNER, Johann Stephan, the Elder
German, 19th century.
Born 25 October 1812, in Bruckberg; died 26 July 1867, in Nuremberg.
Painter (glass).
Kellner worked in Amberg, Göttingen and elsewhere.

KELLNER, Johann Stephan, the Younger
German, 19th century.
Born 1851, in Nuremberg; died in Friedrichshafen.
Glass painter.

KELLNER, Josef
Austrian, 20th century.
Born 22 March 1876, in Vienna.
Painter. Landscapes.

KELLNER, Joseph
German, 18th - 19th century.
Born 1749, in Nuremberg; died 4 September 1814.
Engraver.
Kellner's work is represented for us by only a single plate. However, he was the founder of the Kellner dynasty of artists.

KELLNER, Samuel Benjamin
German, 19th century.
Born 5 October 1848, in Nuremberg; died in Friedrichshafen.
Painter (glass).
Kellner was the son of Johann Stephan Kellner.

KELLO, Esther, also known as Inglis
French, 16th - 17th century.
Born 1561 or 1571, probably in Dieppe; died 30 August 1624.
Painter, draughtswoman, illuminator, calligrapher.
Esther Kello was the daughter of Nicholas Langlois, a Huguenot who had taken refuge in England. She illuminated, or provided calligraphy for, a large number of books destined for the Scottish kings in Edinburgh. She produced some much-admired manuscripts, in particular the Psalms of David, in French, which she made for James I, and which are in the library of Christ Church College, Oxford.

KELLOGG, Mary Kilbourne
American, 19th century.
Born 1814; died 1889.
Active in Cincinnati.
Painter. Portraits.
Mary Kilbourne Kellogg painted the notable figures in her town, and exhibited at the Royal Academy in London in 1858.

KELLOW, Kate
British, 19th century.
Active in London.
Miniaturist.
Kate Kellow exhibited in London at the Royal Academy in 1893.

KELLY, Bernadette
French, 20th century.
Born 1933, in Bousquet d'Orb.
Painter, engraver, illustrator.
Bernadette Kelly featured in *De Bonnard à Baselitz - Dix Ans d'enrichissements du cabinet des estampes 1978-1988* (*From Bonnard to Baselitz: A Decade of Acquisitions by the Prints Collection 1978-1988*) at the Bibliothèque Nationale in Paris in 1992.
MUSEUMS AND GALLERIES:
PARIS (Prints Collection): *Invitation to Travel* (1979).

KELLY, Elisabeth
Swiss, 19th century.
Born 10 April 1825, in St Gall; died 1 May 1890, in St Gall.
Painter, engraver. Landscapes.
MUSEUMS AND GALLERIES:
ST GALL (Kunstmus.): *Landscape* (three).

KELLY, Ellsworth
American, 20th century.
Born 31 May 1923, in Newburgh (New York).
Active from 1948 to 1954 in France.
Painter, sculptor, engraver.
Post-painterly Abstraction.
Ellsworth Kelly attended the Pratt Institute in Brooklyn in the early 1940s. In 1943, he was called up and sketched views of the French countryside and Paris while taking part in the Liberation. Back in the USA in 1945, he studied under Karl Zerbe at the Boston Museum School. He returned to France and enrolled at the École des Beaux-Arts in Paris under the GI bill. He stayed on for six years, getting to know Jean Arp, Georges Vantongerloo, Michel Seuphor, Brancusi, Picabia, Magnelli, Giacometti, Miró and Calder. In 1954, he returned to New York.

Whilst in France, Kelly studied Byzantine and Roman art whose use of triptychs would have a lasting influence - as did the thriving art scene. By 1949, he had resolutely adopted abstraction. As Jackson Pollock and Franz Kline's Abstract Expressionism reigned supreme in New York, Kelly was learning from the purity of the coloured shapes in Matisse's papiers découpés, the cleanness of Vantongerloo's lines and Jean Arp's aleatoric method. Yet Kelly's lines, forms, and colours are derived from the direct observation of the shapes taken from the world around him, echoing Georgia O'Keefe.

Kelly's Paris sketch books brim over with staircases, plants, a wall structure here, a window there, chimneys and roofs, the mirror reflection of light hitting the Seine through the arch of a bridge. Drawing from this relationship to reality, Kelly's paintings would follow the approach adopted in his 1952-1955 *Relief Blanc* and later described by Jonathan Binstock: 'The original image has been sacrificed, but the object of Kelly's representation has not. The flat, taut sculptural cut-outs separated by a decisive seam cast the work in sharp relief against its surroundings and charge it with its own palpable reality.' At this early stage, Kelly had already made the radical experience of the power of pure colour, with his juxtapositions of panels each of which was entirely covered in one single uninflected colour, each panel underscoring the size and hue of the others, which the 1952 *Painting for a White Wall* illustrates at its best.

On his return in New York in the 1960s he was among the instigators of Hard Edge, forerunner to Minimal Art. Personally averse to any abstract dogmatism, he remained attached to the object as seen, and to the process of an almost instinctive creation which allowed for chance. With the exception of the pure colour experiments, his paintings at the time are made up of a few ultra-simple, straight or curved lines which delimit scarce, rigorously shaped surfaces shaded in flat tint. Kelly deftly played on the harmonies and dissonances between the colours, working towards bold and dynamic compositional balance, setting off optical vibrations at the abutting edges, and creating effects of relative depths between light and warm hues and the deeper and colder ones. Later he would remove the background, simply cutting around the outline in the so-called shaped canvas in which the surrounding space serves as background. He extended his explorations by superimposing several plane shapes into reliefs, then venturing into volumes and thus sculpture which would grow in importance in his production.

Ellsworth Kelly said of his work in 1969: 'The form of my painting is the content. My work is made of single or multiple panels: rectangle, curved or square. I am less interested in marks on the panels than the 'presence' of the panels themselves (...) made to exist forever in the present, (...and which) can be repeated anytime in the future.' While rooted in nature, his work confronts the viewer with purely visual considerations of colour and scale and also shape in an almost exclusively optical experience of the work of art.

He has taken part in numerous collective exhibitions in America and abroad. In his Paris days he featured in *Les Mains Éblouies* (*Dazzled Hands*) (Galerie Maeght 1948), the Salon de la Jeune Peinture, and the Salon des Réalités Nouvelles; in New York he featured in *Sixteen Americans* at the MoMA and *Geometric Abstraction in America* at the Whitney Museum, among others. He has featured at the Venice Biennale and Documenta IV in Kassel.

He had his first solo show in Paris in 1951, and many others followed, (including *Ellsworth Kelly. The French Years 1949-1954* and *Henri Matisse/Ellsworth Kelly*). His works have been exhibited in New York, Washington, San Francisco, Amsterdam, Münster, Lausanne (*Tablet 1948-1973*, a travelling exhibition) and Basel.

The recipient of prestigious art awards, he became a member of the National Institute of Arts and Letters; in France, he was made a Chevalier de l'Ordre des Arts et Lettres.

BIBLIOGRAPHY:

Paintings, Sculpture and Drawings by Ellsworth Kelly, exhibition catalogue, Gall. of Modern Art, Washington DC, 1963-1964 (extensive documentation). Waldman, Diane, *Ellsworth Kelly, Drawings, Collages, Prints*, New York Graphic Society, Greenwich, 1971. Hulten, Pontus, *Ellsworth Kelly, peintures et sculptures, 1968-1979*, exhibition catalogue, Éd. du Centre Georges-Pompidou, Musée national d'Art moderne, Paris, 1980. Axsom, Richard Hayden, *The prints of Ellsworth Kelly: a catalogue raisonné 1949-1985*, travelling exhibition catalogue, Hudson Hills Press, New York, 1987. Kelly, Ellsworth, *Fragmentation and the single form*, 1990. *Ellsworth Kelly, les années françaises 1949-1954*, exhibition catalogue, Gal. nationale du Jeu de Paume, Paris, 1992. Bois, Yve-Alain, *Ellsworth Kelly, the Years in France 1948-1954*, exhibition catalogue, National Gallery of Art, Washington DC, 1992. *Ellsworth Kelly: the Paris Prints*, exhibition catalogue, Susan Sheehan Gallery, New York, 1992. Kelly, Ellsworth, '*Fragmentation et forme unique*' in *Art Press* n° 167, periodical, Paris, March 1992. Waldman, Diane, *Ellsworth Kelly*, exhibition catalogue, Solomon R. Guggenheim Museum, New York, October, 1996. *Kelly*, Hatje Cantz, Ostfildern, 2002. *Henri Matisse et Ellsworth Kelly*, exhibition catalogue, Éd. du Centre Georges-Pompidou, Gallimard, Paris, 2002. Zegher, Catherine/Aupetitallot, Yves/Bois Yve-Alain, *Tablet 1948-1973*, exhibition catalogue, Musée cantonal des Beaux-Arts, Lausanne, 2002. Kelly, Ellsworth, *in Max Beckmann*, exhibition catalogue, essay, Tate Modern, London, 2002. Grynsztejn, Madeleine, *Ellsworth Kelly in San Francisco*, exhibition catalogue, Museum of Modern Art, San Francisco, 2002. Wylie, Charles, *Ellsworth Kelly in Dallas*, exhibition catalogue, Dallas Museum of Art, Dallas, 2004. Axsom, Richard H., *Drawn from Nature: the Plant Lithographs of Ellsworth Kelly*, exhibition catalogue, Grand Rapids Art Museum, Grand Rapids, 2005.

MUSEUMS AND GALLERIES:

AMSTERDAM (Stedelijk Mus.): *Blue Red Rocker* (1963 or 1967, sculpture); *White Curve I* (1972) - BIELEFELD (Kunsthalle): *Dark Gray* (1986) - CHICAGO (AI): *White Disk III* (1961) - CHICAGO (Lincoln Park): *Curve XXII* (1981) - DALLAS (MA): five items*Colored Paper Images* (1976, pressed and coloured paper pulp); *Red Panel* (1980, oil on canvas); *Untitled Stainless* (1983, stainless steel); *White* (1985, oil on canvas) - HOUSTON (MFA) - HOUSTON (Sculpture Garden): *Houston Triptych* (1986, sculpture) - LOS ANGELES (County MA): *White Sculpture II* (1968) - MINNEAPOLIS (Walker Art Center): *Green Rocker* (1968) - NEW YORK (Metropolitan Mus. of Art): *Curve XXXII* (1982) - NEW YORK (MoMA): *Sixty-four Panels: Colors for a Large Wall* (1951); *Sculpture for a Large Wall* (1957); *Running White* (1959); *Curve II* (1973, sculpture) - NEW YORK (Solomon R. Guggenheim Mus.): *One Stroke* (1962); *White Angle* (1966) - NEW YORK (Whitney Mus. of American Art): *Atlantic* (1957) - NÎMES (Carré d'Art, MAC) - PARIS (MNAM-CCI): *Window* (1949, relief); *Kite II* (1952); *Yellow Red* (1972); *Dark Blue Panel* (1985); *Black White* (1988) - ST LOUIS (AM): *Spectrum II* (1966-1967, oil on canvas) - ST-ÉTIENNE (MAM): *Blue Diagonal with Curve* (1988) - ST-PAUL-DE-VENCE (Fondation Maeght): *Red Yellow Blue I* (1963).

AUCTION RECORDS:

NEW YORK, 13 May 1964, *Charter*, USD 3,750. NEW YORK, 15 Feb 1968, *Composition in Red and White*, USD 3,000. NEW YORK, 18 Nov 1970, *Palisade* (acrylic) USD 14,000; *Gate* (painted iron) USD 18,000. NEW YORK, 26 Oct 1972, *Black and White*, USD 18,000. MILAN, 5 Dec 1974, *Yellow-white*, ITL 28,000,000. NEW YORK, 21 Oct 1976, *Blue Curve V* (1973, oil on canvas, 107 3/4 x 93 ins / 274 x 236 cm) USD 32,000. LONDON, 29 June 1977, *Yellow and White* (1962, oil on canvas, 43 x 32 3/4 ins / 109.5 x 83 cm) GBP 9,500. NEW YORK, 23 May 1978, *Two Panels: Yellow Black* (1968, oil on canvas, 94 x 95 ins / 239 x 241.5 cm) USD 46,000. NEW YORK, 18 May 1979, *A Lines* (1958, gouache and graphite, 11 x 13 3/4 ins / 27 x 35 cm) USD 2,200. NEW YORK, 18 May 1979, *Wave Motif* (1959, oil on canvas, 60 x 94 ins / 152.5 x 239 cm) USD 45,000. NEW YORK, 19 Oct 1979, *Portrait of a Chinese Boy* (1948, pen, 17 x 11 1/2 ins / 43 x 29 cm) USD 2,000. LOS ANGELES, 22 Sept 1980, *Large Blank Curve* (1974, silk screen print in black, 12 1/2 x 72 1/4 ins / 32 x 183.5 cm) USD 1,900. NEW YORK, 13 May 1981, *Orange-blue I* (1965, oil on canvas, 60 x 54 ins / 152.5 x 137 cm) USD 80,000. NEW YORK, 4 May 1982, *Black and White Venus* (c. 1958, painted steel relief, 85 x 36 x 2 1/2 ins / 216 x 91.5 x 6.5 cm) USD 37,000. NEW YORK, 11 May 1982, *Spectrum* (1973, silk screen print in colour, 17 1/2 x 67 ins / 44.5 x 170.4 cm) USD 2,500. NEW YORK, 8 Nov 1983, *Red Yellow, Blue* (1968, oil on canvas, 81 x 27 ins / 205.5 x 68.5 cm) USD 80,000. NEW YORK, 9 Nov 1983, *Wild Grape* (1960, graphite, 26 3/4 x 23 ins / 68 x 57.5 cm) USD 7,000. NEW YORK, 16 Nov 1983, *Blue, Green, Yellow, Orange. Red* (1977, laminated papier mâché, 9 x 41¼ ins / 22 x 105 cm) USD 3,000. New York, 10 Nov 1986, *Block Island* (1959, oil on canvas, 88¼ x 68 ins / 224 x 173 cm) USD 220,000. New York, 17 Nov 1987, *Blue, Yellow in Red Squares* (1971, silk screen print in colour, 72 x 23¾ ins / 182 x 60.3 cm) USD 6,000. New York, 4 May 1988, *Tropical Plant, St-Domingue* (1981, black ink in pen/paper, 24 x 18 ins / 61 x 45.7 cm) USD 22,000. New York, 2 May 1989, *White over Black* (1963, painted aluminium, 72 x 76 x 8 ins / 183 x 193 x 20.4 cm) USD 577,500. New York, 3 May 1989, *Black Triangle with White Stripe* (oil on canvas, 107¼ x 113½ ins / 272.5 x 288.3 cm) USD 715,000. New York, 31 Oct 1989, *Lily* (1983, pencil/paper, 14 x 11 ins / 35.6 x 28 cm) USD 12,100. New York, 7 Nov 1989, *Red, Blue, Green, Yellow*, (1965, oil on canvas, two panels: one vertical, the other horizontal, 87½ x 54 x 87½ ins / 222.2 x 137.1 x 222.2 cm) USD 660,000. Rome, 6 Dec 1989, *Abstract Composition* (tempera/paper, 30¼ x 21½ ins / 76.7 x 54.7 cm) ITL 57,500,000. New York, 7 May 1990, *Black and White* (1970, oil on canvas, diptych, in all 27½ x 157½ ins / 70 x 400 cm) USD 385,000. New York, 1 May 1991, *Black Curve IX* (1976, oil on canvas, 90 x 95¼ ins / 228.5 x 242 cm) USD 495,000. New York, 13 Nov 1991, *Blue Panel* (1986, acrylic/canvas, 99½ x 94 ins / 252.7 x 238.8 cm) USD 220,000. New York, 5 May 1992, *Rogue* (1956, oil on panel, 34 x 38 ins / 86.4 x 96.3 cm) USD 110,000. New York, 18 Nov 1992, *Blue White* (1980, oil on canvas, 112¼ x 115 ins / 285.1 x 292.1 cm) USD 209,000. New York, 24 Feb 1993, *Brooklyn Bridge* (1958, oil on canvas, 34 x 13 ins / 86.4 x 33 cm) USD 55,000. New York, 4 May 1993, *Black Venus* (1959, painted aluminium, wall relief, 85 x 36 x 2½ ins / 216 x 91.5 x 6.5 cm) USD 145,500; *Blue-red* (1965, oil on canvas, 65 x 150 ins / 165 x 381 cm) USD 222,500. New York, 9 Nov 1993, *Black and White* (1988, oil on canvas, 103 x 141 ins / 261.6 x 357.3 cm) USD 266,500. Frankfurt am Main, 14 June 1994, *Oak Leaf* (1992, coloured lithograph, 30 x 36 ins / 76.2 x 91.4 cm) DEM 7,800. New York, 3 Nov 1994, *Untitled* (1962, oil on canvas, 22 x 22 ins / 55.8 x 55.8 cm) USD 71,800. New York, 2 May 1995, *Purple-red Curve* (1982, oil on canvas, 72¼ x 135½ ins / 183.2 x 344.2 cm) USD 266,500. Zurich, 23 June 1995, *Orange Green* (two coloured lithographs, 34¾ x 23¼ ins / 88.5 x 59.2 cm) CHF 1,800. New York, 9 Nov 1996, *Nine Squares* (1976-1977, coloured lithograph, 40½ x 40½ ins / 103 x 103 cm) USD 19,550. New York, 7 May 1997, *Red Blue Green Yellow* (1965, oil on canvas and oil on canvas/ Masonite, two panels, 87½ ins / 222 cm, ¾ x 54 x 87½ ins/2 x 137.1 x 222.2 cm) USD 530,000. New York, 7-8 May 1997, *Untitled* (1986, stainless steel, 83¾ x 94 x 49 ins / 212.8 x 238.7 x 124.5 cm) USD 442,500. New York, 6 and 7 March 1998, *Colored Paper Image* (1976, pressed papier mâché, 32¼ x 31 ins / 82 x 79 cm) USD 4,600. New York, 13 May 1999, *Milkweed* (1970, pen and ink, 30 x 22 ins / 75 x 56 cm) USD 48,000. New York, 18 May 1999, *Red White* (1966, acrylic on canvas, 65 x 90 ins / 165 x 229 cm) USD 600,000. New York, 14 Nov 2000, *White, Dark Blue* (1962, oil on canvas, 58 x 33 ins / 147 x 84 cm) USD 500,000. New York, 15 Nov 2000, *Falcon* (1959, oil on canvas, 60 x 49 ins / 152 x 124 cm) USD 975,000. New York, 15 May 2001, *Blue Green I* (1968, oil on panel, two joined panels, 91 x 91 ins / 231 x 231 cm) USD 1,100,000. New York, 14 Nov 2001, *Red White Blue* (1986, oil on canvas, 102 x 30 ins / 259 x 76 cm) USD 1,300,000. New York, 12 Nov 2002, *Diagonal Curve XXI - EK790* (1988, stainless steel, 51 x 93x0 ins / 129 x 236x1 cm) USD 320,000. New York, 13 Nov 2002, *Untitled - Red and Blue Squares* (1976, colour on pressed paper pulp, 22 x 33 ins / 56 x 85 cm) USD 32,500. New York, 13 May 2003, *Curve in Relief III - EK561* (1978, aluminium, 15 x 132x2 ins / 38 x 335x4 cm) USD 380,000. New York, 14 May 2003, *Green White* (1968, oil on canvas laid on panel, 71 x 141 ins / 180 x 358 cm) USD 1,200,000. New York, 11 May 2004, *White Black* (1988, oil on panel, two attached panels, 103 x 141 ins / 262 x 357 cm) USD 800,000. New York, 12 May 2004, *Chatham XIII - Yellow Red* (1971, oil on canvas, overlap two parts, 96 x 81 ins / 244 x 207 cm) USD 2,600,000.

KELLY, Felix

New Zealander, 20th century.
Born 1916, in New Zealand.
In Britain from the late 1930s or early 1940s; also active in the USA.
Painter, illustrator, set designer. Landscapes with figures, seascapes, landscapes, murals.

Felix Kelly was born in New Zealand and came to Britain before World War II. He worked in advertising for a time, then took up painting seriously during the war. He also worked in the USA and became known as a painter of country houses in both countries. He painted in a Neo-Romantic style, depicting imaginary and fantastic landscapes and buildings (*Cities of Enchantment* series). He also painted murals in public places like the ship RMS Windsor Castle. His imaginative buildings have inspired architects, as in the case of the Henbury Rotonda, Macclesfield, Cheshire, which was rebuilt according to his painted caprice.

As a stage set designer, Kelly is remembered for *A Day by Sea* and the *Merchant of Venice* at the Old Vic, London.

Auction records:
London, 12 Nov 1976, *No. 28, Brompton Square* (oil on card, 22 x 16½ ins / 56 x 42 cm) GBP 350. London, 9 June 1978, *Waterloo Steps and Carlton House Terrace* (oil on card, 19 x 23¾ ins / 48 x 60.5 cm) GBP 1,000. Oxfordshire, 20 March 1979, *The Beacon* (oil on card, 16½ x 22 ins / 42 x 55 cm) GBP 600. Norfolk, 22 Oct 1986, *Sheringham Hall* (1977, oil on card, 23 x 33½ ins / 57.5 x 85.2 cm) GBP 4,000. London, 14 Oct 1987, *Buscot House* (1951, oil on card, 19 x 25½ ins / 48 x 65 cm) GBP 2,000. London, 12 May 1989, *Middle Lodge* (1945, oil on card, 9½ x 14¼ ins / 24.3 x 36.2 cm) GBP 770. London, 9 June 1989, *Well Walk in Hampstead* (1943, oil on card, 16½ x 13¼ ins / 42 x 33.7 cm) GBP 3,080. London, 21 Sept 1989, *Boat at Dawn, Eagle at Auckland* (1952, oil on card, 16½ x 21¾ ins / 42 x 55.2 cm) GBP 1,870. London, 8 March 1990, *Young Couple in a Classic Park* (oil on card, 13¾ x 9½ ins / 35 x 24.2 cm) GBP 1,650. Monaco, 16 June 1990, *The House of the Painter* (oil/plywood, 14¼ x 18 ins / 36 x 46 cm) FRF 21,090. London, 25 Jan 1991, *The National Gallery in Trafalgar Square* (1951, oil on card, 20 x 15 ins / 51 x 38 cm) GBP 3,300. London, 6 June 1991, *Steamer on a River in Bangkok* (1977, oil on card, 17 x 22 ins / 43 x 56 cm) GBP 3,850. London, 28 Nov 1991, *Low Tide* (1945, gouache, 11¼ x 15¼ ins / 28.6 x 38.7 cm) GBP 990. London, 6 Nov 1992, *The Awning Above the Alley* (oil on card, 17 x 22 ins / 43 x 56 cm) GBP 1,980. New York, 19 Jan 1995, *Cameron Gallery, the Steps* (1970, oil/synthetic resin, 22 x 28 ins / 55.9 x 71.1 cm) USD 1,380. London, 5 March 1999, *End of the Line* (1951, oil on board, 15 x 20 ins / 38 x 51 cm) GBP 6,500. Bury St Edmunds, 23 June 1999, *At the Fort* (1946, oil and gouache on board, 14 x 18 ins / 35 x 46 cm) GBP 4,600. London, 22 March 2000, *River Steamer on the Bangkok River* (1977, oil on canvas, 17 x 22 ins / 43 x 56 cm) GBP 4,000. London, 6 Dec 2000, *Orchard, Narraganset Avenue, Newport, Rhode Island* (1968, oil on board, 26 x 34 ins / 66 x 86 cm) GBP 5,500. London, 5 April 2001, *Set Design for a Day by the Sea* (oil on board, 10 x 14 ins / 25 x 35 cm) GBP 4,000. London, 5 April 2001, *Day by the Sea* (1950, oil on board, 14 x 20 ins / 36 x 50 cm) GBP 4,200. London, 13 June 2002, *Strange Adventure in the Life of Miss Laura Mildmay* (gouache, with two others, 11 x 7 ins / 28 x 19 cm) GBP 1,500. Exeter, 2 July 2002, *Whiteway House* (1950, oil on board, 15 x 20 ins / 37 x 50 cm) GBP 2,200. London, 24 June 2003, *The Lodge, Marble Arch* (1965, oil on

board, 19 x 28 ins / 49 x 71 cm) GBP 1,800. LONDON, 3 July 2003, *Nuns on the Beach* (1969, tempera on board, 22 x 28 ins / 56 x 71 cm) GBP 16,000. LONDON, 21 Sept 2004, *Lighthouse Winch* (oil on board, 14 x 11 ins / 36 x 28 cm) GBP 1,700. LONDON, 24 Nov 2004, *Mid-winter Meeting* (1945, oil on board, 12 x 16 ins / 30 x 40 cm) GBP 2,400.

KELLY, Gerald Festus (Sir)
British, 19th - 20th century.
Born 9 April 1879, in London; died 5 January 1972, in London.
Painter, printmaker, etcher. Local figures, portraits, landscapes.

Sir Gerald Kelly was educated at Eton. As a young man he travelled to Paris to study, and met Monet, Cézanne and Degas. He also visited Spain, Burma and South Africa. Later he became an established portrait artist, receiving commissions from celebrities and from royalty. He was known as a sound portrait painter of elegant ladies and beautiful children. He also painted *Eton School after Bomb Attack*, 1940. In the early days of television after World War II he made himself a name as a populariser of art. He was a member of the Royal Academy and its president in 1950.

BIBLIOGRAPHY:
Hudson, D, *For the Love of Painting: The Life of Gerald Kelly KVCO PRA*, P. Davies, 1975.

MUSEUMS AND GALLERIES:
LONDON (National Portrait Gal.): *Ralph Vaughan Williams* (1958-1961, oil on canvas); *Marie Charlotte Carmichael Stopes* (1953, oil on canvas); *Ernest Thesiger* (1920, oil on canvas); *Lewis Waller*; *Hug Richard Lawrie (Dick) Sheppard* (1932, oil on canvas); *Montague Rhodes James* (1936, oil on canvas); *King George VI* (c. 1941, oil on canvas); *Queen Elizabeth, the Queen Mother* (c. 1938, oil on canvas); *Dame Caroline Harriet Haslett* (c. 1949, oil on canvas) - LONDON (Tate Collection): *The Jester (W. Somerset Maugham)* (1911, oil on canvas); *Boulevard Montparnasse* (1904); *Alex and Demary Dancing in a Music Hall at Algiers* (1906); *Terrace at Monte Carlo* (1908); *Beach at Etretat* (1908); *Ma Si Gyaw, Pose IV* (1909-1914); *The Vicar in his Study* (1912) - OTTAWA (Nat. Gal. of Canada).

AUCTION RECORDS:
LONDON, 8 March 1937, *Joaquina IV, Seville* (drawing) GBP 44. LONDON, 4 Nov 1966, *Sao Ohn Nyunt*, Gns 720. LONDON, 14 Dec 1973, *Huts on the Beach*, Gns 900. LONDON, 12 Nov 1976, *My Seyn Nu* (1919, oil on canvas, 43¼ x 31 ins / 110 x 78.5 cm) GBP 1,400. LONDON, 4 March 1977, *Ma Seyn Nu (Pose III)* (1908, oil on canvas, 18 x 11 ins / 46 x 27 cm) GBP 950. LONDON, 16 May 1979, *Market at Taungdwingyi* (oil on canvas, 41½ x 50 ins / 105.5 x 127 cm) GBP 1,800. LONDON, 13 March 1981, *Sao Ohn Nyun XIX* (oil on canvas, 42¾ x 35 ins / 108.5 x 88 cm) GBP 1,900. LONDON, 9 March 1984, *Siesta* (1919-1921, oil on canvas, 37 x 61 ins / 94 x 155 cm) GBP 12,000. LONDON, 15 May 1985, *Ma Seyn Me XII, the Spendid* (oil on canvas, 48 x 32 ins / 122 x 81 cm) GBP 13,000. LONDON, 5 March 1987, *Burmese Dancers* (oil on canvas, 48 x 75 ins / 122 x 190.5 cm) GBP 4,000. LONDON, 9 June 1988, *Baraques, the Beach* (1906, oil on panel, 8½ x 10½ ins / 21.3 x 26.4 cm) GBP 3,300. DUBLIN, 24 Oct 1988, *Beautiful Spanish Girl* (oil on canvas, 30¾ x 25½ ins / 78.2 x 64.6 cm) IEP 1,100. LONDON, 8 June 1989, *The Cox in the Hozu Rapids* (1937, oil on canvas, 15¾ x 11¾ ins / 40 x 30 cm) GBP 4,620. LONDON, 21 Sept 1989, *Portrait of Saw Nyun III* (1931, oil on card, 15¼ x 11¼ ins / 38.8 x 28.6 cm) GBP 2,420. LONDON, 2 May 1991, *Twisted Tree* (oil on canvas, 28 x 22½ ins / 71 x 57 cm) GBP 1,430. DUBLIN, 26 May 1993, *Spanish Woman* (oil on canvas, 30 x 24 ins / 76.2 x 61 cm) IEP 495. NEW YORK, 17 Jan 1996, *Seated Nude* (oil on canvas, 20¾ x 16 ins / 52.7 x 40.6 cm) USD 3,450. DUBLIN, 26 May 1999, *Beach Scene* (oil on board, 10 x 8 ins / 25 x 20 cm) IEP 3,400. LONDON, 5 Nov 1999, *La plage des baraques* (1906, oil on panel, 10 x 13 ins / 25 x 34 cm) GBP 3,500. LONDON, 9 June 2000, *Mangosteens and a Casket* (oil on canvas, 25 x 30 ins / 63 x 76 cm) GBP 3,000. LONDON, 24 Nov 2000, *Ma Than E II* (1932, oil on canvas, 24 x 20 ins / 60 x 50 cm) GBP 6,500. DUBLIN, 28 May 2001, *Tuscan Landscape* (oil on panel, 13 x 17 ins / 32 x 42 cm) IEP 5,000. LONDON, 8 June 2001, *Punta del Cuppo, Portofino* (1932, oil on panel, 13 x 17 ins / 33 x 42 cm) GBP 4,000. LONDON, 19 Feb 2002, *Neac Sumuy IV* (oil on canvas, 33 x 27 ins / 84 x 69 cm) GBP 2,800. PARTRIDGE GREEN, 14 March 2002, *Jean Brady I* (oil on canvas, 19 x 39 ins / 49 x 100 cm) GBP 1,900. LONDON, 15 May 2003, *Portrait of Mrs Kelly* (oil on canvas, 34 x 35 ins / 86 x 90 cm) GBP 4,800. BATH, 1 Dec 2003, *On the Beach* (oil on panel, 16 x 13 ins / 40 x 33 cm) GBP 4,900. LONDON, 14 May 2004, *Taungdwingyi, Myanmar* (oil on board, 6 x 7 ins / 15 x 18 cm) GBP 3,500. LONDON, 14 May 2004, *Portrait of Mrs Boardman* (oil on canvas, 80 x 36 ins / 203 x 92 cm) GBP 3,800.

KELLY, J.
British, 19th century.
Sculptor.

J. Kelly exhibited in London at the Royal Academy in 1834.

KELLY, James Edward
American, 19th century.
Born 30 July 1855, in New York; died 1933.
Sculptor, illustrator.

James Edward Kelly worked on various periodicals but is best known for his sculpted portraits of *General P. H. Sheridan*, the inventor *Edison*, and other American personalities.

AUCTION RECORDS:
NEW YORK, 21 June 1978, *Sheridan's Ride* (1879, bronze, h. 18 ins / 46 cm) USD 2,000. NEW YORK, 18 Sept 1980, *Sheridan's Ride* (brown-patinated bronze, h. 20 ins / 50.8 cm) USD 1,200. NEW YORK, 3 Dec 1996, *Sheridan's Ride* (1879, bronze, h. 20½ ins / 52 cm) USD 3,450. NEW YORK, 26 May 1999, *Sheridan's Ride* (1879, bronze, h. 19 ins / 48 cm) USD 5,500. NEW YORK, 10 Dec 2002, *Sheridan's Ride* (1879, green and brown patinated bronze, h. 19 ins / 48 cm) USD 3,500.

KELLY, John
Irish, 18th century.
Active in Dublin.
Sculptor.

John Kelly exhibited low reliefs such as *Fire* and *Hibernia* in Dublin.

KELLY, John
Irish, 19th century.
Active in Belfast at the beginning of the 19th century.
Painter.

John Kelly painted portraits including *John Cunningham* and *Hugh Mc Kibbin*.

KELLY, Leon
American, 20th century.
Born 1901, in Philadelphia; died 1982.
Painter, watercolourist, draughtsman. Figures.

Leon Kelly studied at the Pennsylvania Academy of the Fine Arts before completing his art education in Europe. He exhibited at the Carnegie International in Pittsburgh.

AUCTION RECORDS:
NEW YORK, 27 March 1985, *Abstraction* (pastel, 19¼ x 12¼ ins / 49 x 31 cm) USD 1,000. NEW YORK, 24 Oct 1986, *Facade* (1923, oil on canvas, 26¼ x 21¼ ins / 66.5 x 54 cm) USD 2,500. NEW YORK, 24 Jan 1989, *The Absinthe Drinker* (ink, watercolour and gouache/paper, 21 x 15¾ ins / 52.5 x 40 cm) USD 1,760. NEW YORK, 15 May 1991, *The Bird of Wisdom* (1945, ink/paper, 12 x 8½ ins / 30.5 x 21.6 cm) USD 1,980. NEW YORK, 25 March 1997, *Farm in Pennsylvania* (oil on can-

vas, 43 x 64 ins / 109.2 x 162.6 cm) USD 2,875. NEW YORK, 4 Oct 2000, *Compote with Fruit* (1924, oil on canvasboard, 9 x 12 ins / 22 x 30 cm) USD 4,500. NEW YORK, 4 Oct 2000, *Standing Nude Figure* (1924, pastel, 20 x 13 ins / 51 x 33 cm) USD 5,000. NEW YORK, 13 June 2001, *Insects and Cliffs* (1943, oil on canvas, 28 x 44 ins / 71 x 112 cm) USD 10,000. MILFORD, 23 Oct 2003, *Mountain Village* (1920, pastel, 14 x 20 ins / 36 x 51 cm) USD 6,000. PHILADELPHIA, 7 Dec 2003, *Disenchantment of love* (1959, oil on canvas, 38 x 22 ins / 97 x 56 cm) USD 2,000.

KELLY, Louise Minert
American, 20th century.
Born 14 June 1879, in Waukon (Iowa); died 1945.
Painter.

Louise Kelly studied in Philadelphia, in France and in Italy. She was a member of the American Federation of Arts.

KELLY, Mary
American, 20th century.
Born 7 June 1941, in Albert Lea (Minnesota).
Installation artist, multimedia artist.
Conceptual Art.

Mary Kelly studied fine art and music at the college of St Teresa in Winona in Minnesota, receiving a BA in 1963, and fine art and aesthetics in Italy at the Pius XII Institute in Florence, obtaining an MA in 1965. She also obtained a diploma in 1970 from the St Martin's School of Art in London. She taught at the American University of Beirut and the Whitney Independent Study Program, and was director of studios and artist-in-residence at New Hall, Cambridge in the UK. She was on the editorial board of *Screen* magazine. She married the British artist Ray Barrie, and spent her formative years as an artist in London. She moved to New York in 1989.

Kelly's work is concerned with maternal subjects and the situation of post-maternal women. She also addresses issues of cultural identity, women's power in capitalist society and contemporary feminist thought, by examining the psychology of Sigmund Freud and the cultural theories of Jaques Lacan. In her first solo exhibition *Post-partum Document (1973-1977)* in 1976 at the London Institute of Contemporary Arts, Kelly explored a mother's anxiety about weaning her child by displaying faecal stains on nappy liners in recessed frames, along with a daily diary of the baby's food intake and sound recordings. Later, in *Documentation IV*, she examined fetishism, namely maternal attitudes of keeping souvenirs of children's infancy, such as locks of hair and baby shoes. In this work, Kelly displayed children's undershirts and plaster casts of a child's hands. Her later work addresses the issue of older women and their identity crises, as in *Interim* (1984-1989), a work divided into the parts Corpus (body), Pecunia (money), Historia (history) and Potestas (power), with photographs of garments, pop-up steel cards, narrative scenes of daily life, and texts describing the personal lives of feminists.

She exhibited in *Women and Work* at the South London Art Gallery in 1975. Solo exhibitions include those at the Museum of Modern Art in Oxford (1977); the Institute of Contemporary Arts in London (1976); *Interim* at the New Museum of Contemporary Art in New York (1990-1991); and *Gloria Patri* at the Herbert F. Johnson Museum of Art in Ithaca in New York (1992). She received a Lina Garnade Memorial Foundation Award (1978), an Arts Council of Great Britain Award (1977) and a fellowship from the National Endowment for the Arts (1987).

BIBLIOGRAPHY:

Kelly, Mary/Mulvey, Laura, '*Mary Kelly and Laura Mulvey in Conversation*' in *Afterimage*, vol 13, no. 8, 1986. *Mary Kelly: Interim*, exhibition catalogue, New Museum of Contemporary Art, New York, 1990. Langer, Cassandra, '*Mary Kelly's Interim*' in *Woman's Art Journal*, vol 13, no. 1, Journal article, 1992. *Mary Kelly*, illustrated book, Phaidon Press, London, 1997. Mastai, Judith (ed.), *Social Process - Collaborative Action: Mary Kelly 1970-75*, exhibition catalogue, Charles H. Scott Gallery, Vancouver, 1997. Kelly, Mary, *Imagining Desire*, Book, MIT Press, Cambridge (MA), 1997. Kelly, Mary, *Post-Partum Document*, illustrated book, University of California Press, Berkeley, 1999.

MUSEUMS AND GALLERIES:

CAMBRIDGE (New Hall): *Extase* (1986, screen print and acrylic) - CANBERRA (Nat. Gal. of Australia): *L10: From Documentation V* (1977); *Documentation V: Classified Specimens, Proportional Diagrams* (1977, multimedia) - HELSINKI (City Mus.) - LONDON (Tate Collection): *Post-Partum Document* (1975, multimedia) - NEW YORK (New Mus. of Contemporary Art) - VANCOUVER (AG) - ZURICH (Kunsthaus).

KELLY, Richard Barret Talbot
British, 20th century.
Born 20 August 1896, in Birkenhead; died 1971.
Painter, watercolourist, illustrator. Birds.

AUCTION RECORDS:

LONDON, 25 Feb 1992, *Small Kestrel and Alpine Chough* (ink and watercolour, 11 x 7 1/4 ins / 27.7 x 18.1 cm) GBP 528. LONDON, 16 March 1993, *Wild Ducks* (watercolour/paper, 14 1/2 x 22 1/4 ins / 36.9 x 56.5 cm) GBP 805. LONDON, 28 Nov 2002, *Redshanks* (watercolour, 46 x 51 ins / 117 x 130 cm) GBP 1,000.

KELLY, Robert George
British, 19th - 20th century.
Born 22 January 1822, in Dublin; died 9 May 1910, in Chester.
Painter. Portraits, landscapes with figures, landscapes.

Robert George Kelly exhibited in London, at the Royal Academy, the British Institution and the Suffolk Street Gallery, from 1853 to 1888.

AUCTION RECORDS:

LONDON, 18 May 1990, *Group of Four Children Playing in a Garden* (1846, oil on canvas, 35 3/4 x 28 ins / 90.8 x 71 cm) GBP 9,020.

KELLY, Robert George Talbot
British, 19th - 20th century.
Born 1861; died 1934, in Birkenhead.
Painter, watercolourist. Genre scenes, landscapes.
Orientalism.

Robert George Talbot Kelly was a member of the Royal Institute of Painters in Watercolour and of the Royal British Academy.

MUSEUMS AND GALLERIES:

GLASGOW: *Arid Desert Landscape* - LIVERPOOL (Walker AG): *Flight of the Caliph after his Defeat at the Battle of Omdurman, 2nd September 1898* (1899, oil on canvas).

AUCTION RECORDS:

LONDON, 14 May 1976, *Landscape at Sunset* (1892, oil on panel, 23 1/2 x 35 1/2 ins / 59.7 x 90 cm) GBP 500. LONDON, 1 June 1983, *Mosque in Cairo* (1894, watercolour on pencil outlines heightened with gouache, 17 1/2 x 13 ins / 44.5 x 33 cm) GBP 1,700. LONDON, 26 Jan 1984, *Drifting down the Nile* (1913, oil on card, 25 x 36 3/4 ins / 63.5 x 93.5 cm) GBP 4,000. NEW YORK, 24 May 1985, *Street Scene in Cairo* (watercolour heightened with gouache/pencil outlines, 21 1/2 x 14 ins / 54.6 x 35.4 cm) USD 3,800. PARIS, 2 Dec 1985, *Harbour at Tangier* (1889, watercolour, 21 1/4 x 13 1/2 ins / 54 x 34 cm) FRF 25,000. NEW YORK, 21 May 1991, *Feluccas on the Nile* (oil on panel, 10 x 14 ins / 25.4 x 35.6 cm) USD 2,640. PARIS, 19 Nov 1991, *Pyramids at Giza* (watercolour, 18 1/2 x 28 3/4 ins / 47 x 73 cm) FRF 6,000.

NEW YORK, 16 Feb 1993, *Village on the Banks of the Nile* (1912, watercolour/card, 20 1/2 x 28 1/2 ins / 52 x 72.3 cm) USD 1,980. NEW YORK, 17 Feb 1994, *Charge of Arab Horsemen* (1910, oil on canvas, 12 1/4 x 20 1/4 ins / 31 x 51.4 cm) USD 863. LONDON, 27 Sept 1994, *Outskirts of Cairo* (1900, watercolour, 14 x 22 ins / 35.5 x 56 cm) GBP 517. PARIS, 13 March 1995, *Filling the Storage Jars* (1899, watercolour/card, 11 x 22 3/4 ins / 28 x 58 cm) FRF 15,000. NEW YORK, 20 July 1995, *Afternoon in an Oriental Market* (1889, watercolour/card, 21 1/2 x 15 1/4 ins / 54.6 x 38.7 cm) USD 5,462. LONDON, 29 March 1996, *North Wind on the Upper Nile* (1916, oil on canvas, 22 x 45 ins / 56 x 114.3 cm) GBP 4,600. LONDON, 13 Oct 1999, *Turkish Advance on Egypt in a Sandstorm* (watercolour heightened with white, 18 x 31 ins / 45 x 78 cm) GBP 2,400. LONDON, 13 Oct 1999, *The Hunter* (1895, watercolour, 15 x 22 ins / 39 x 56 cm) GBP 2,800. LONDON, 6 Feb 2001, *On the Banks of the Nile* (1896, watercolour heightened with scratching out, 11 x 17 ins / 27 x 42 cm) GBP 1,200. LONDON, 26 March 2003, *Tombs of the Khalifs* (1888, watercolour, 21 x 37 ins / 54 x 94 cm) GBP 1,900. LONDON, 20 Nov 2003, *View of the Temple of Hatshepsut, Deir El Bahri, Egypt* (pencil and watercolour, 16 x 22 ins / 41 x 57 cm) GBP 2,200. AUCKLAND, 29 July 2004, *Geysers and Steam, Tarawera* (1890, watercolour, 20 x 37 ins / 50 x 93 cm) NZD 7,000.

KELLY, Thomas
American, 19th century.
Died c. 1841, in New York.
Engraver.

Thomas Kelly was of Irish birth and moved to the USA. He specialised in portraits of famous men.

KELPE, Paul
American, 20th century.
Born 1902; died 1985.
Painter, watercolourist, draughtsman.
Constructivism.

Paul Kelpe was an abstract painter. His pieces are strictly geometric, structured around straight lines, squares, rectangles, triangles and circles.

AUCTION RECORDS:

MUNICH, 1 Dec 1980, *Abstraction* (1934, watercolour, 11 3/4 x 7 3/4 ins / 30 x 20 cm) DEM 4,000. NEW YORK, 29 May 1981, *Abstraction* (1927, oil on canvas, 12 x 22 ins / 30.5 x 56 cm) USD 8,250. NEW YORK, 3 Dec 1987, *Man and Machinery* (1934, pencil, 13 1/4 x 9 1/2 ins / 33.5 x 24 cm) GBP 16,500. NEW YORK, 6 Oct 1989, *Composition* (1930, watercolour and pencil/paper, 10 1/4 x 7 1/2 ins / 26 x 19 cm) USD 9,350. NEW YORK, 2 Dec 1993, *Composition #353* (1932, watercolour/paper, 11 1/4 x 7 3/4 ins / 28.3 x 20 cm) USD 17,250. NEW YORK, 25 May 1994, *Composition #499* (1934, oil/synthetic resin, 23 1/2 x 14 ins / 59.7 x 35.6 cm) USD 25,300. NEW YORK, 23 May 1996, *Untitled* (1934, oil on canvas/synthetic resin, 18 3/4 x 16 ins / 47.6 x 39.7 cm) USD 20,700.

KELPIN, Carl Martin Ludwig
German, 19th century.
Born 27 April 1838, in Penzlin.
Painter.

Kelpin painted three portraits of emperors for the town hall in Fraustadt (Wszowa), Silesia.

KELS, Franz
German, 19th century.
Born 1828, in Derendorf (Düsseldorf); died 20 April 1893, in Düsseldorf.
Painter. Genre scenes, landscapes.

Kels studied at the academy in Düsseldorf. He exhibited in Düsseldorf, Dresden and Vienna.

AUCTION RECORDS:

NEW YORK, 13 Oct 1978, *A Young Artist* (1853, oil on canvas, 24 1/2 x 30 ins / 62 x 76 cm) USD 11,500. COLOGNE, 20 Oct 1989, *Family by a Spring* (oil on panel, 9 1/4 x 7 1/4 ins / 23.5 x 18.5 cm) DEM 1,700. STUTTGART, 10 Dec 1999, *Young Peasant Girl Sitting at River's Edge* (1863, oil on canvas, 19 x 15 ins / 48 x 38 cm) DEM 7,200. MUNICH, 6 Dec 2000, *Young Family in a Boat on a Calm River* (1864, oil on canvas, 27 x 38 ins / 69 x 97 cm) DEM 5,000. RADOLFZELL, 31 March 2001, *Young Boy with Grandparents Looking at Fountain* (oil on panel, 9 x 7 ins / 23 x 18 cm) DEM 3,200.

KELSEY, Charles J. Samuel
British, 19th century.
Active in London.
Sculptor.

Charles Kelsey occasionally exhibited in London at the Royal Academy from 1840 to 1877.

KELSEY, Francis
British, 18th century.
Painter.

Francis Kelsey exhibited at the Free Society in 1776.

KELSEY, Frank
British, 19th century.
Painter. Waterscapes, seascapes.

Frank Kelsey exhibited in London at the Royal Academy and the Suffolk Street Gallery between 1887 and 1893.

AUCTION RECORDS:

LONDON, 20 May 1992, *Pilot Boat* (watercolour, a pair, each 13 1/4 x 19 ins / 33.5 x 48.5 cm) GBP 1,650. LONDON, 11 May 1994, *In Southampton Waters* (oil on canvas, 28 x 36 ins / 71 x 91.5 cm) GBP 2,530.

KELSEY, J.
British.
Painter, watercolourist.

J. Kelsey is listed in *Art Prices Current*.

AUCTION RECORDS:

LONDON, 7 Feb 1910, *The Fleet under Lord Hood at Spithead 17 August 1791* (watercolour) GBP 3.

KELTENBORN, Adolf
German, 19th century.
Born in Stettin (now Szczecin, Poland).
Painter. Genre scenes, portraits.

Keltenborn worked in Königsberg (now Kaliningrad) and Berlin.

KELTENHOFER, Christoph
German, 15th - 16th century.
Born in Augsburg.
Painter.

Christoph Keltenhofer worked in Ravensburg from 1480 until 1516 on decorations for the altar of the municipal church.

KELTERBORN, Ludwig Adam
German, 19th century.
Born 1811, in Hanover; died 6 June 1878, in Basel.
Painter, draughtsman, caricaturist. History painting, portraits.

In 1828, Kelterborn was a draughtsman in a factory in Mulhouse. Having moved to Basel, he was appointed drawing master in the municipal schools (1837) and married Augusta Märklin (1839). His political caricatures of about 1830 were inspired by the French masters Daumier, Raffet and Traviès. Noted among his best history canvases are *The Temptation of Christ* (Basel Museum) and *Mephistopheles and the Pupil*.

MUSEUMS AND GALLERIES:

BASEL: *The Temptation of Christ*.

AUCTION RECORDS:

ZURICH, 2 June 1994, *Portrait of Caroline Schmidt-Fäsch* (1841, oil on canvas, 16 1/4 x 13 ins / 41 x 33 cm) CHF 4,025. SWITZERLAND, 1 Dec 2000, *Der Freischutz* (1835, oil on panel, 13 x 1 ins / 33 x 3 cm) CHF 5,500.

KELY, Jean de
Flemish School, 15th century.
Active in Tournai during the second part of the 15th century.
Sculptor.

Jean de Kely created the tomb of Jehan de Melun and his two wives.

KELZ, Franz Xaverius
Austrian, 19th century.
Born 18 December 1826, in Rettenbach (near Kitzbühel); died 24 December 1876, in Graz.
Sculptor.

Kelz decorated churches in Graz, Styria and elsewhere.

KEMAL
Persian School, 16th century.
Active in Tabriz.
Illuminator.

MUSEUMS AND GALLERIES:
VIENNA (Österreichische Nationalbibliothek).

KEMAL, pseudonym of Sirberegovic Kemal
Bosnian, 20th century.
Born 1 January 1939, in Modrica.
Active in France from 1972.
Painter, engraver, watercolourist, illustrator.
Landscapes. Murals, designs for tapestries, designs for mosaics.

Kemal studied at the school of fine arts in Belgrade from 1957 to 1965, then attended a special course in 1965. He worked on the conservation and restoration of frescoes and mosaics from 1958 to 1962, then in Hayter's studio in Paris, where he lived from 1972 onwards.

During the 1970s his painting had yet to benefit from the maturity he was to prove in his engravings. He uses a firm language, devoid of revolutionary excess, marked by the Post-Cubist plenitude of Georges Braque and tending towards abstraction. The subject matter, the differences in quality, the epidermis of his paintings and particularly his engravings, which look like collages, point towards the preponderant role played by his desire to express his feelings. He painted a world that was sometimes nearly abstract, which seized the harmonies of nature with just a few scant means. A few geometric shapes, a few lines are enough to evoke the Seine or a cloud. He perfected a particular technique of lino-engraving which enabled him to highlight areas of shadow and light. He then turned to watercolours, developing a technique by which he created new fluid spaces, less structured, and discovered another, less vague, light. In this work colour is freely deployed, using gradated hues applied in lines or blotches using delicate brush strokes that leave the grain of the paper visible. He also completed several painted murals and mosaics, as well as ceramics, tapestries and illustrations for book collectors.

After 1962 Kemal took part in several collective exhibitions, including the October Salon in Belgrade from 1963; Belgrade triennale and *Exhibition of Contemporary Yugoslav Art* in Iraq, Lebanon, Syria and Libya (1967); Vela Luka (1968); *Exhibition of Young Yugoslav Artists* in Tunisia and Morocco, and the engraving Biennale, Ljubljana (1969); Salon de Mai, Paris (1972 to 1975); FIAC (Foire Internationale d'Art Contemporain), Paris (1974); Cologne art fair (1975); Tokyo Museum (1977); Washington, New York and Pittsburgh (1979); New York International Fair (1981); Sarajevo (1984); and the Musée d'Art, Chamalières (1985). His solo exhibitions include Banja Luka (1957, 1962, 1967, 1968, 1973 and 1978); Modrica (1964); Belgrade (1965, 1975 and 1979); Novi Sad (1967); Paris (1967, 1972, 1975 to 1977, 1980, 1983 and 1986); and Sarajevo (1968 and 1970). He has been awarded numerous prizes and distinctions, including first prize from the school of fine arts in Belgrade (1960 and 1962), first prize from the Banja Luka Salon (1966), a prize from the museum of modern art in Sarajevo (1967), a prize from the museum of modern art in Sarajevo (1967), and first prize from the Subotica engraving Triennale (1975).

BIBLIOGRAPHY:
Begic, Azra, *K. Sirbegovic*, exhibition catalogue, Gal. Mala, Sarajevo, 1968. Boudaille, Georges, *Kemal*, exhibition catalogue, Gal. Camille Renault, Paris, 1972. *Kemal*, exhibition catalogue, Gal. d'Art contemporain, Chamalières, 1986. *Kemal*, exhibition catalogue, Helge Steensen, Oslo, 1987.

MUSEUMS AND GALLERIES:
BELGRADE (Muz. savremene umetnotsi) - KRAGUJEVAC (Narodni Muz.) - KRALJEVO (Narodni Muz.) - LAUSANNE (Bibliothèque cantonale et universitaire) - LES SABLES-D'OLONNE (Mus. de L'Abbaye Ste-Croix) - LJUBLJANA (Dom Jna Coll.) - NIŠ (Narodni Muz.) - PARIS (BNF) - PARIS (MAMVP) - PARIS (MNAM-CCI) - SARAJEVO (Zemalsjski Muz. BiH) - SKOPJE (Muz. na Sovremena Umetnost) - SUBOTICA (Yugoslav Mus. of Contemporary Art).

KEMAL KASHMIRI
Indian, 16th century.
Active on the Indian subcontinent.
Miniaturist.

KEMAN, Georges Antoine
French, 18th - 19th century.
Born 7 August 1765, in Schlettstadt (now Sélestat); died 1830, in Schlettstadt.
Miniaturist.

Georges Antoine Keman exhibited frequently at the Royal Academy in London between 1793 and 1827. After working in Strasbourg, he exhibited in Paris and from there he went to London, where he spent a large part of his life.

AUCTION RECORDS:
PARIS, 15-16 Nov 1920, *Woman Leaning on a Balustrade* (miniature) FRF 645.

KEMBLE, Edward Windsor
American, 19th - 20th century.
Born 18 January 1861, in Sacramento (California); died 19 September 1933.
Draughtsman, newspaper cartoonist, illustrator. Local scenes, figures.

Edward Windsor Kemble was self-taught. He worked on numerous papers, in particular the New York Daily Graphic which printed his first pieces in 1881. He specialised in the depiction of African Americans' everyday lives.

BIBLIOGRAPHY:
Dictionnaire des illustrateurs, 1800-1914, exhibition catalogue, Ides et Calendes, Neuchâtel, 1989.

AUCTION RECORDS:
NEW YORK, 6 Feb 1981, *Boy with the Gun* (pen, 7¾ x 6 ins / 20 x 15 cm) USD 3,800. NEW YORK, 16 Nov 1984, *Illustration for 'Cape Cod Ballads and other Verse' by Joseph C. Lincoln* (pen drawing, series of 23 drawings, 7¼ x 6 ins / 18.7 x 14.4 cm and 9¾ x 7¼ ins/24.6 x 18.6 cm) USD 7,000. NEW YORK, 11 May 2002, *Dour Democratic Donkey with Broadside* (c. 1900, pen and ink, 8 x 6 ins / 20 x 15 cm) USD 2,000.

KEMENEDY, Jeno
Hungarian, 19th - 20th century.
Born 8 April 1860, in Orastie; died 25 June 1925, in Budapest.
Painter. Genre scenes.

A pupil of both Benczur and Seitz at the academy in Munich, Jeno Kemenedy first exhibited around 1883 in Munich and Vienna.

AUCTION RECORDS:
FRANKFURT AM MAIN, 1894, *The Diva Strolls By*, FRF 2,750. CREWKERNE, 21 July 1977, *Bibliophiles* (1886, oil on panel, 7¾ x 9¾ ins / 19.5 x 25 cm) GBP 9,000. LONDON, 4 April

2000, *Talk of the Town* (1891, oil on panel, 10 x 13 ins / 25 x 33 cm) GBP 5,200. BUDAPEST, 7 Dec 2001, *Bunch of Wildflowers* (oil on canvas, 27 x 22 ins / 69 x 56 cm) HUF 800,000.

KEMENY, Nandor

Hungarian, 20th century.
Born 22 January 1885, in Salgótarján.
Painter. Portraits, genre scenes, still-lifes.

Nandor Kemeny spent time in Munich and Paris before settling in Budapest.

AUCTION RECORDS:

VIENNA, 18 May 1976, *Reapers* (oil on canvas, 35 x 44 1/2 ins / 88 x 113 cm) ATS 8,000.

KEMENY, Zoltan

Hungarian, 20th century.
Born 21 March 1907, in Banica, Transylvania; died 14 June 1965, in Zurich.
Active from 1942 and naturalised from 1957 in Switzerland.
Watercolourist, painter, draughtsman, mixed media. Murals.

The son of a station master in Hungary, Zoltan Kemeny was introduced to painting at an early age by a naive painter who made a living painting shop signs. In the meantime Kemeny had started to learn carpentry, a skill that would play a role in his later output, and in 1924 he enrolled in the school of decorative arts in Budapest. While it is true to say that he appears to have taken this step in order to learn the rudiments of interior architecture, which might seem a way of extending his training as a carpenter, in 1927 he enrolled at the school of fine arts. It is unclear what courses he followed, but he did confide that during this period he was initiated into the major contemporary artistic movements - Cubism, Surrealism, Dadaism, Constructivism. What particularly complicates this version of events is that Frank Popper reports that in 1922 Kemeny, along with Moholy-Nagy, signed the *Manifesto on the System of Dynamic-Constructive Form*, regarded as one of the first demonstrations of research into and experimentation with kinetics. While the role of Moholy-Nagy is clearly established, that of Kemeny remains virtually unknown. He arrived in Paris in 1930, where he remained until 1940, working as a skilled craftsman in several media and as a designer in wrought iron, constructing lighting devices. He married in 1933 and turned to fashion design, abandoning any idea of pursuing an artistic career. He did not complete a single painting for the next 13 years, and relied on fashion design to make his living. He fled to Zurich during World War II, and it was during this period that he started painting again.

Having returned to painting, Kemeny attracted the attention of Dubuffet, by whom he was certainly then influenced. Like the latter, Kemeny introduced a range of different materials into his paintings - sand, twine, pebbles, beads. He then found his own means of expression with tableaux-reliefs of the sort that make up the *His Friends' Gardener* series, which draws a psychological portrait of imaginary people using materials appropriate to their supposed professions: collage of rags for a rag-picker, beaten copper for a goldsmith, collection of herbs for a herbalist, buttons for a haberdasher, clay for a potter and so on. He immediately went on to product luminous reliefs, lit either through transparency or by electricity. According to the definition given in the *Manifesto on the System of Dynamic-Constructive Form*, Kemeny and Moholy-Nagy believed that constructivism consisted of an activation of space through the tension of forces in real space, and they set out their programme as follows: 'To replace the static principle of classic art with the dynamic principle of universal life' In this perspective of constructivism, defined by the word 'dynamic' but not yet 'kinetic', the material is no longer a medium for forms, but a medium for forces. However in Kemeny's work, this principle was left to one side because, although the material continued to be a medium for forces, its form was nevertheless far from being neglected. From 1954 onwards, no longer content with finding ingenious ways of using scrap materials chanced upon, he instead put himself in a position where he could meticulously mill his montages, whether melted metallic parts affixed onto a wooden panel using an array of bolts, or melted and welded to each other. He expressed this obsession with machinism most notably in *Fear Grinder* (1958). These milling operations were very time-consuming and during this period of his career he scarcely completed more than 15 to 20 reliefs each year. Even though all of his reliefs, completed from 1954 onwards using a similar process, are connected to sculpture, and even though he knew how to use fire to colour his metals, he nonetheless insisted on describing them as 'paintings'. He did produce paintings, in fact, that started off using paint, but which then took on a greater complexity, collages in different thicknesses, before achieving real relief. Michel Ragon commented that these reliefs 'show an astonishing diversity. One could say that each one raises a different problem, both because of the material used as by the space suggested and the always surprising composition'. Sarane Alexandrian comments that: 'From the formal point of view, each work is in fact constituted on the basis of a formal element from which Kemeny drew hallucinatory, ever-renewable effects through the simple device of repetition, of amassing, through variations in size or colour'. In 1963 he was commissioned to produce a mural relief in brass for the École des Hautes Études Économiques et Sociales in St Gall. He also completed a spatial sculpture suspended from the ceiling, 33 feet high, 380 feet long and some 40 feet wide, for the foyer of the theatre in Frankfurt am Main. In 1964 he executed a triptych in copper for the Swiss national exhibition in Lausanne.

Kemeny took part in numerous collective exhibitions, including at the Kuntshalle, Bern (1945); Stedelijk Museum, Amsterdam (1950); Carnegie Institute, Pittsburgh (1958 and 1961); Documenta II, Kassel (1959); Musée d'Art Moderne de la Ville de Paris (1960); and at the Tate Gallery, London (1964 and 1965). His solo exhibitions included Zurich (1945, 1949, 1959 at the Kuntshaus, 1967 and 1980; Paris (1946, 1950 at his studio, 1955, 1957, 1959, 1960, 1966, at the Musée National d'Art Moderne); Chicago (1954); Berlin (1956); London (1958 and 1967, at the Tate Gallery); the Kunsthaus, Düsseldorf (1959); Musée des Beaux-Arts, La Chaux-de-Fonds (1961); Kröller-Müller museum, Otterlo (1963); Palais des Beaux-Arts, Brussels (1967); and the Fondation Maeght, St Paul de Vence (1974). The Musée National d'Art Moderne in Paris devoted a permanent salon to his work, and in 1966 organised a major retrospective which was shown again in 1967 at the Palais des Beaux-Arts in Brussels, the Tate Gallery in London, and the Wallraf-Richartz museum, Cologne. In 1986 the Kunstmuseum in Bern and the Peccolo Gallery in Livorno put his works on display. In 1964 he was awarded the Grand Prix for sculpture at the Venice Biennale.

BIBLIOGRAPHY:

Kemeny, exhibition catalogue, Musée national d'Art moderne, Paris, 1966. Popper, Frank, *Naissance de l'Art cinétique*, Gauthier-Villars, Paris, 1967. Kemeny, Madeleine/ Picon, Gaëtan/Rathke, Ewald, *Kemeny - Reliefs en métal*, Maeght, Paris, 1973. *La Collection du Musée national d'Art moderne*, Éd. du Centre Georges-Pompidou, Paris, 1986. Heusser, Hans-Jörg, *Zoltan Kemeny. Peintures, sculptures et reliefs-collages: la première période 1943-1953*, catalogue raisonné, Séguier, Paris, 1993.

MUSEUMS AND GALLERIES:

BERLIN (National Gal.) - BUFFALO (Albright-Knox AG) - CHICAGO (AI) - GENEVA (MAH): *Tempérament ligné* (1955); *Rythmes No. 2* (1958) - LA CHAUX-DE-FONDS (MBA) - LONDON

(Tate Collection): *Cat Mask* (1947, mixed media/panel); *Suburb of Angels* (1957, metal, relief) - Otterlo (Kröller-Müller Mus.) - Paris (MNAM-CCI): *Humanity* (1948); *Conception of Time* (1961); *Thought Treated in Form* (1962); *Pacific* (1963) - Skopje (Muzej na Sovremena Umetnost).

Auction records:

Paris, 29 Nov 1962, *Colour without Wright* (copper) FRF 10,800. New York, 19 May 1966, *Nothing* (metal) USD 5,500. New York, 14 May 1970, *Images of the Present* (copper) USD 5,000. Paris, 16 March 1971, *Composition* (iron and cement) FRF 10,000. Milan, 6 Nov 1973, *Division of the Night* (iron) ITL 10,000,000. New York, 1 May 1974, *Seeker of Friendship* (1956, forged metal) USD 18,000. Zurich, 12 May 1977, *Relief* (1958-65, metal, h. 28 3/4 ins / 73 cm, w. 33 1/2 ins/85 cm, depth 6 ins/15 cm) CHF 48,000. Zurich, 24 Oct 1979, *Relief* (1958/65, nails/wood, 28 3/4 x 33 3/4 x 6 ins / 73 x 86 x 15 cm) CHF 42,000. Paris, 27 Oct 1982, *Embroideries of Herculine* (1960, metal accumulation, iron, nuts attached and welded to a pile of bars, 46 1/2 x 35 ins / 118 x 88 cm) FRF 31,000. Zurich, 6 June 1984, *Relief* (1958-1965, metal, 28 3/4 x 33 3/4 x 6 ins / 73 x 86 x 15 cm) CHF 44,000. Zurich, 6 June 1986, *Junction of Thought and the Actual* (1962, bronze, high relief, 37 x 41 3/4 ins / 94 x 106 cm) CHF 95,000. Zurich, 7 Oct 1987, *Young Doctors Strolling By* (1946, oil on canvas, 22 1/2 x 19 ins / 57 x 48 cm) CHF 13,000. London, 23 Feb 1989, *Light Breaker* (1958, white iron welded on plastic panel, 26 1/2 x 34 1/2 ins / 67.5 x 87.5 cm) GBP 13,200. Paris, 23 June 1989, *Study* (1961, pencil/tracing paper, 5 x 10 ins / 13 x 25.5 cm) FRF 6,000. New York, 7 Nov 1990, *Mathematical Chance* (welded copper and bronze, 29 x 34 1/4 ins / 73.7 x 87.3 cm) USD 14,300. London, 21 March 1991, *Interior Geography 2* (copper wall relief, 98 x 1/2 x 28 ins / 248.9 x 1.493.5 x 71.1 cm) GBP 37,400. London, 26 March 1992, *Association of Two Optics* (1962, copper tubes/zinc/card, 26 3/4 x 32 3/4 ins / 68 x 83 cm) GBP 9,350. Amsterdam, 19 May 1992, *Abstract Composition* (1963, watercolour and coloured chalks/paper, 20 1/2 x 15 1/4 ins / 52 x 39 cm) NLG 5,520. London, 23 June 1993, *Bloody Friendship* (1956, relief of copper and painted nails/panel, 21 1/2 x 35 x 5 1/2 ins / 54.6 x 89 x 14 cm) GBP 17,000. New York, 23 Feb 1994, *Last Supper No. 2* (1961, welded copper/wood). Paris, 12 Oct 1994, *Mildewed Flower* (1955, sculpture in cut copper oxide sheeting, 35 x 32 1/4 x 1 1/2 ins / 88 x 82 x 3.5 cm) FRF 67,000. Paris, 29-30 June 1995, *Zephyr* (1964, relief sculpture with welded copper parts and polychrome resin/panel, 52 3/4 x 42 1/4 ins / 134 x 107 cm) FRF 110,000. Zurich, 14 Nov 1995, *Signs-Lines* (1958, copper sculpture/black background, 26 3/4 x 38 1/2 ins / 68 x 98 cm) CHF 22,000. London, 5 Dec 1996, *Three Winds* (1963, painted aluminium, screws and nails, 59 1/4 x 45 1/2 x 7 1/4 ins / 150.5 x 115.6 x 18.4 cm) GBP 13,225. London, 9 Dec 1998, *Broken Wings* (1954, welded sheet metal and wood) GBP 5,000. Stuttgart, 29 Jan 2000, *Light Breakers* (copper plates) DEM 7,000. Paris, 19 Dec 2001, *Composition no 21* (soldered copper on panel, 36 x 46 x 3 ins / 92 x 118 x 7 cm) FRF 115,200. Paris, 1 July 2003, *Nature, K42* (half-tubes on brass plaque, 29 x 31 x 6 ins / 74 x 78 x 15 cm) EUR 8,000. Zurich, 8 June 2004, *Junction between Thought and Reality* (brass relief, 37 x 42 x 126 ins / 94 x 106 x 320 cm) CHF 32,000. Munich, 30 Nov 2004, *Light Breakers* (copper resin) EUR 18,000.

KEMENYFFI, Jeno

Hungarian, 20th century.

Born 19 February 1875, in Budapest; died 6 September 1920, in Budapest.

Painter.

Jeno Kemenyffi exhibited in Berlin, Darmstadt, London, Munich and Venice.

KEMEYS, Edward

American, 19th century.

Born 31 January 1843, in Savannah (Georgia); died 11 May 1907, in Washington (DC).

Sculptor. Animals.

Edward Kemeys studied in New York and Paris. On his return to the USA he quickly became known as a good animal sculptor. He produced, notably, a group of dead game for Central Park in New York, *Wolves* for Fairmount Park in Philadelphia, and *Lions* to decorate the Art Institute of Chicago. He exhibited in Philadelphia in 1876, in London in 1877 and at the Paris Salon in 1878.

Museums and Galleries:

Washington DC (Smithsonian American AM): *American Panther and Her Cubs* (c. 1878, bronzed plaster); *Fox Terrier and Rat* (1871-1885, bronzed plaster/wood base); other sculptures.

Auction records:

New York, 29 April 1976, *Chief Sitting Bull* (c. 1884, bronze, 31 x 22 ins / 79 x 56 cm) USD 2,500. New York, 17 Oct 1980, *Big Snake* (patinated bronze, high relief, 24 x 18 ins / 61 x 45.7 cm) USD 6,000. New York, 28 Sept 1983, *Deer Stalker* (dark brown patinated bronze, h. 7 1/2 ins / 19 cm and l. 16 1/4 ins/41.3 cm) USD 2,600. New York, 30 May 1986, *The Still Hun* (black-brown patinated bronze, h. 11 3/4 ins / 29.9 cm) USD 13,000. New York, 28 Sept 1989, *Two Tigers* (bronze, h. 7 1/2 ins / 19 cm, w. 13 3/4 ins/34.9 cm) USD 1,980. New York, 22 Sept 1993, *Chief Sitting Bull* (bronze, relief, h. 31 3/4 ins / 80.6 cm, w. 23 1/2 ins/59.6 cm) USD 1,150. Pasadena, 15 Feb 2000, *Wolf* (bronze, relief, 20 x 16 ins / 51 x 41 cm) USD 3,750.

KEMINCKX, Philippus

Flemish School, 18th century.

Engraver.

Philippus Keminckx was active during the second half of the 18th century. He worked in Antwerp.

KEMLEIN, William

German, 19th century.

Born 31 March 1818, in Jena; died 11 January 1900, in Weimar.

Painter, art restorer.

Kemlein was a pupil of H.G. Arnold in Dresden. He did a series of major British personalities.

KEMLY

French, 18th century.

Painter.

KEMM, Robert

British, 19th century.

Born 1830; died 1897.

Active in London 1874-1885.

Painter. Figures, genre scenes.

Robert Kemm exhibited at the Suffolk Street Gallery from 1874 onwards. Importantly, he travelled to Seville and painted numerous canvases of what he had seen there. His work is much sought after.

Museums and Galleries:

Sunderland: *Sleeping Priest.*

Auction records:

London, 22 Feb 1908, *Fruit Market in Seville,* GBP 12. London, 8 May 1908, *Going to the Market in Seville,* GBP 5. London, 21 Nov 1908, *Seville, Refreshment Halt,* GBP 8. London, 15 July 1910, *Going to the Bullfight,* GBP 42. London, 24 July 1973, *The Ferry,* GBP 520. London, 9 July 1974, *Andalusian Shepherds,* GBP 700. New York, 2 April 1976, *Leaving for the Fair* (oil on canvas, 40 x 50 ins / 101.5 x 127 cm) USD 1,600. London, 22 July 1977, *Labourage Nivernais* (1860, oil on canvas, after Rosa Bonheur, 51 x 102 ins / 129.5 x 259 cm) GBP 800. London, 18 April 1978, *The Toreador and the Spanish Beauty* (oil on canvas, 36 x 28 ins / 91.5 x 71 cm) GBP 600. London, 20 March 1979, *A Night at 'La Traviata'* (oil on canvas, 20 1/2 x 16 1/4 ins / 52 x 41 cm) GBP 750. London, 31 July

1981, *Market Scene in Spain* (oil on canvas, 38 x 50 1/2 ins / 96.5 x 128.2 cm) GBP 2,500. LONDON, 5 Nov 1982, *The Lady Musician* (oil on canvas, 28 x 36 ins / 71 x 91.4 cm) GBP 2,000. LONDON, 19 Oct 1983, *Fisher Women Beside the Sea* (oil on canvas, 20 x 24 ins / 51 x 61 cm) GBP 980. LONDON, 12 June 1985, *Matador's Wedding* (oil on canvas, 25 1/2 x 41 1/4 ins / 65 x 105 cm) GBP 4,000. LONDON, 23 March 1988, *Muleteers* (oil, 32 x 40 ins / 81.3 x 101.6 cm) GBP 3,520. LONDON, 2 June 1989, *Slave Market* (oil on canvas, 30 x 20 ins / 76 x 50.5 cm) GBP 4,400. LONDON, 13 June 1990, *Card Players in Seville* (oil on canvas, 40 1/4 x 50 ins / 102 x 127 cm) GBP 9,350. EDINBURGH, 2 May 1991, *Cleaning the Nets* (oil on canvas, 44 x 33 ins / 111.8 x 83.7 cm) GBP 4,950. NEW YORK, 19 Feb 1992, *Teller of Good Fortunes* (oil on canvas, 34 1/4 x 44 1/4 ins / 87.3 x 112.4 cm) USD 6,050. LONDON, 12 June 1992, *Matador's Bride* (oil on canvas, 35 1/2 x 27 1/2 ins / 90.2 x 69.8 cm) GBP 2,750. LONDON, 3 March 1993, *Spanish Gypsy* (oil on canvas, 36 x 28 ins / 91.5 x 71 cm) GBP 1,725. NEW YORK, 12 Oct 1994, *In the Market Place* (oil on canvas, 35 x 50 ins / 88.9 x 127 cm) USD 37,375. LONDON, 4 Nov 1994, *Blessing before the Bullfight* (oil on canvas, 28 x 36 ins / 71.1 x 91.4 cm) GBP 4,830. NEW YORK, 20 July 1995, *On the Breton Coast* (oil on canvas, 20 x 24 ins / 50.8 x 61 cm) USD 2,875. LONDON, 7 Nov 1996, *Fisherman's Daughter* (oil on canvas, 34 x 21 ins / 86.3 x 53.2 cm) GBP 2,070. AMSTERDAM, 27 Oct 1997, *Market Scene in Seville* (oil on canvas, 28 x 36 ins / 71 x 91.5 cm) NLG 18,880. LONDON, 5 Nov 1997, *The Halt* (oil on canvas, 50 1/2 x 40 1/4 ins / 128 x 102 cm) GBP 5,175. MADRID, 28 Sept 1999, *Song at the Fountain* (oil on canvas, 36 x 28 ins / 91 x 71 cm) ESP 1,900,000. MADRID, 20 Dec 1999, *Galant at the Fountain* (oil on canvas, 28 x 36 ins / 71 x 92 cm) ESP 2,500,000. LONDON, 22 March 2000, *Spanish Gossip* (oil on canvas, 36 x 28 ins / 91 x 71 cm) GBP 12,000. MADRID, 3 April 2000, *The Christening* (oil on canvas, 37 x 54 ins / 94 x 137 cm) ESP 5,500,000. ANTWERP, 5 Feb 2001, *Gypsies on the Way to Seville Market* (oil on canvas, 42 x 60 ins / 106 x 152 cm) BEF 750,000. LONDON, 11 June 2002, *Spanish Musicians* (oil on canvas, 36 x 28 ins / 91 x 71 cm) GBP 3,600. LONDON, 17 July 2002, *Spanish Guitar* (oil on canvas, 36 x 28 ins / 92 x 71 cm) GBP 2,000. LONDON, 17 June 2003, *Return from Market* (oil on canvas, 40 x 60 ins / 102 x 153 cm) GBP 13,000. LONDON, 2 July 2003, *Blessing Before the Fight* (oil on canvas, 28 x 36 ins / 72 x 91 cm) GBP 4,800.

KEMMEL, Charles van
Belgian, 19th century.
Born 20 September 1834, in Ypres.
Painter. History painting.
Charles van Kemmel studied at the academy and with Alma Tadema. His *Return of Ulysses* is in the Ypres museum.

KEMMER, Johann
German, 16th century.
Born c. 1495, in Lübeck.
Painter.
Lübeck School.
Johann Kemmer studied under Lucas Cranach the Elder, before settling in Lübeck. His masterpiece is an altarpiece produced for the church of Our Lady in Lübeck. He also produced a votive picture for the church of St Catherine.

KEMMER, Otto
German, 19th century.
Born 7 February 1853, in Tauberbischofsheim (near Würzburg).
Painter.
Kemmer established himself in Karlsruhe and did murals for the principal houses there, among them Prince Karl's town house and the grand duke's palace.

KEMMERICH, Joseph Louis Benoît
Belgian, 19th - 20th century.
Born 25 February 1868, in Liège.
Painter, sculptor. Busts, groups.
Joseph Kemmerich was a student at the fine arts academy in Brussels. He exhibited two drawings at the Exposition Universelle in Brussels in 1910.

KEMNER, Helge
Swedish, 20th century.
Born 3 August 1883, in Malmö.
Painter, draughtsman. Landscapes.
Helge Kemner studied in Copenhagen, Munich and Paris.

KEMNITZ
Flemish School, 18th century.
Active at the beginning of the 18th century.
Engraver.
Kemnitz is known for his engravings of *The Brussels Court* and *Delights of the Low Countries*.

KEMNITZ, Ludwig von
German, 19th century.
Born in Berlin.
Active in Frankfurt.
Painter. Landscapes, seascapes.
Kemnitz exhibited in Berlin, Munich, Dresden and Vienna.

KEMP, Edith
British, 19th - 20th century.
Born in Bushey (Hertfordshire).
Painter. Landscapes, flowers.
Edith Kemp exhibited in London at the Royal Academy from 1898 to 1914.

KEMP, J.
British, 19th century.
Painter.
J. Kemp painted two portraits that are now in the Melbourne museum, and which were apparently painted in Australia: *John Pascol Fawkner, one of the Founders of Melbourne* and *Edward Henty, the First Inhabitant of Portland*. He is possibly the same artist as the painter John Kemp, who lived in Gloucester and exhibited landscapes at the Suffolk Street Gallery from 1868 to 1876.
MUSEUMS AND GALLERIES:
MELBOURNE: *Portrait of John Pascol Fawkner, one of the Founders of Melbourne* (1877); *Portrait of Edward Henty, the First Inhabitant of Portland*.

KEMP, Jan, or de Kemp
Dutch, 17th century.
Born c. 1611; died c. 1665.
Active in Haarlem.
Painter.
Jan Kemp was the son of Nicolaes Kemp the Elder.

KEMP, Jeka
British, 19th - 20th century.
Born in Glasgow.
Active in France.
Painter. Portraits, still-lifes, flowers.
Jeka Kemp was active from 1902 to 1921. She settled in Paris, and exhibited at the Société Nationale des Beaux-Arts from 1912.
AUCTION RECORDS:
GLASGOW, 7 July 1983, *Mother and Children on a Doorstep* (watercolour, 12 x 12 ins / 30.5 x 30.5 cm) GBP 460. LONDON, 3 May 1990, *Still-life with Lemons and Vase of Flowers* (oil on canvas, 28 x 28 ins / 71 x 71 cm) GBP 1,320. LONDON, 7 June 1990, *Black Poodle* (watercolour and gouache, 15 x 15 ins / 38 x 38 cm) GBP 2,640. GLASGOW, 14 Feb 1995, *Marseilles* (oil on card, 14 1/2 x 18 ins / 37 x 46 cm) GBP 1,035. GLASGOW, 16 April 1996, *Concarneau* (oil on card, 13 1/2 x 17 ins / 34 x 43 cm) GBP 1,150. EDINBURGH, 12 May 2000, *Harbour, Menton* (oil on board, 14 x 17 ins / 36 x 44 cm) GBP 1,200. LONDON, 9 April 2001, *Menton* (oil on board, 15 x 18 ins / 38 x 45 cm)

GBP 2,000. LONDON, 5 Sept 2001, *Market Scenes in Morocco* (oil on panel, a pair, 13 x 16 ins / 33 x 40 cm) GBP 3,500.

KEMP, John
British, 19th century.
Watercolourist.

John Kemp was a teacher at the School of Arts in Gloucester. He exhibited at the British Institution from 1868 to 1876.

MUSEUMS AND GALLERIES:
LONDON (Victoria and Albert Mus.): a work.

KEMP, Nicolaes de, the Elder
Dutch, 16th - 17th century.
Born c. 1574; died 1646, in Haarlem.
Painter, decorative artist. Seascapes.

Nicolaes de Kemp studied under H.-C. Vroom and Karel van Mander. He is known to have still been alive in 1635, and certain biographers claim that he was active from 1580. His works include *View of Löwenstein*, which is in the museum in Haarlem.

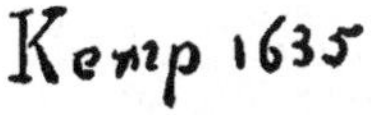

KEMP, Nicolaes or Klaes de, the Younger
Dutch, 17th century.
Born 4 February 1609, in Haarlem; died c. 1674, in Haarlem.
Painter. Seascapes.

Nicolaes Kemp the Younger was the son of Nicolaes Kemp the Elder. He was senior member of the Guild of St Luke in 1655.

KEMP, Oliver
American, 20th century.
Born 13 May 1887, in Trenton; died 1934.
Painter, illustrator.

Oliver Kemp studied under Pyle, Chase and, in Paris, Gérôme. He worked on several New York papers.

AUCTION RECORDS:
NEW YORK, 14 March 1986, *Taken by Surprise* (oil on canvas remounted on board, 17 3/4 x 26 3/4 ins / 45.4 x 67.8 cm) USD 5,500. HAYDEN, 28 July 2001, *Huron Waters* (oil on canvas, 24 x 54 ins / 61 x 137 cm) USD 32,500. MICHIGAN, 6 Nov 2001, *White Water Man* (oil on canvas, 24 x 30 ins / 61 x 76 cm) USD 4,500. WASHINGTON, 14 Sept 2002, *Elk Chase* (oil on canvas, grisaille, 12 x 36 ins / 30 x 91 cm) USD 6,500. HAYDEN, 26 July 2003, *Long Shot* (oil on canvas, grisaille, 36 x 24 ins / 91 x 61 cm) USD 12,000.

KEMP, Robert
French, 19th - 20th century.
Born 21 May 1849, in Cadillac.
Draughtsman, illustrator.

Robert Kemp illustrated a number of books.

KEMP, Robert
Australian, 20th century.
Born 1912.
Painter.

Robert Kemp is the principal Australian exponent of pictorial Abstraction and Expressionism based on a new concept of form, analogous to the work of Klee and Kandinsky.

KEMP, Roger
Australian, 20th century.
Born 1908 or 1912; died 1987.
Painter.

Roger Kemp's gestural paintings are characterised by their use of thickly applied impasto and multiple calligraphic signs.

BIBLIOGRAPHY:
Creating Australia: 200 Years of Art 1788-1988, exhibition catalogue, Art Gall. Board of South Australia, Adelaide, 1988.

MUSEUMS AND GALLERIES:
MELBOURNE (Monash University Gallery): *The Cross* (1967).

AUCTION RECORDS:
MELBOURNE, 26 July 1987, *No. 29, Ascent* (oil on card, 31 x 40 1/4 ins / 78.5 x 102 cm) AUD 6,500. MELBOURNE, 30 April 1997, *Abstract Composition* (c. 1960, oil on panel, 40 1/4 x 32 ins / 102 x 81 cm) AUD 3,220. VICTORIA, 3 Aug 1999, *Rhythm Six* (oil on paper, 55 x 63 ins / 139 x 161 cm) AUD 4,500. MELBOURNE, 3 May 2000, *Sequence Fifteen* (synthetic polymer on paper on canvas, 59 x 102 ins / 149 x 259 cm) AUD 20,000. MELBOURNE, 28 June 2000, *St Francis and Birds* (oil on board, 72 x 48 ins / 183 x 122 cm) AUD 32,000. MELBOURNE, 9 May 2001, *Untitled* (oil on board, 31 x 46 ins / 78 x 117 cm) AUD 8,500. MELBOURNE, 27 Nov 2001, *Geometric Progression* (acrylic on board, 53 x 71 ins / 135 x 181 cm) AUD 36,000. MELBOURNE, 30 April 2002, *Untitled* (oil on board, 36 x 48 ins / 91 x 122 cm) AUD 20,000. MELBOURNE, 27 Nov 2002, *Untitled* (synthetic polymer on paper on canvas, 58 x 69 ins / 147 x 174 cm) AUD 26,000. MELBOURNE, 4 June 2003, *Opus I* (enamel on composition board, 24 x 36 ins / 60 x 91 cm) AUD 5,500. MELBOURNE, 2 Sept 2003, *Untitled* (oil on board, 31 x 46 ins / 78 x 117 cm) AUD 13,200. MELBOURNE, 16 June 2004, *Untitled* (oil on canvas, 59 x 92 ins / 150 x 234 cm) AUD 34,000. MELBOURNE, 8 Sept 2004, *Untitled* (c. 1975, synthetic polymer on paper on linen, 60 x 101 ins / 153 x 256 cm) AUD 40,000.

KEMP, Walter M.
British, 19th century.
Active in London.
Sculptor.

Walter M. Kemp exhibited at the Royal Academy and the Suffolk Street Gallery between 1870 and 1889.

KEMP-WELCH, Lucy Elisabeth
British, 19th - 20th century.
Born 1869, in Bournemouth; died 27 November 1958, in Watford.
Painter, engraver, illustrator, watercolourist. Animals.

Lucy Kemp-Welch trained at Bushey in Hertfordshire, where she subsequently taught painting. She was a member of the Royal Society of British Artists and the Royal Institute of Painters in Watercolours, and a regular exhibitor at the Royal Academy and the Suffolk Street Gallery in London. She also exhibited at the Société Nationale des Beaux-Arts in Paris. Kemp-Welch was a talented artist, whose pictures were noted for their lively, dashing execution. She also produced an interesting body of original etchings.

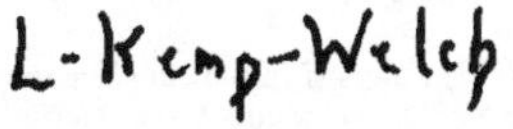

BIBLIOGRAPHY:
Messum, David, *The Life and Work of Lucy Kemp-Welch*, Antique Collectors' Club, Woodbridge, 1976. Osterwalder, Marcus (ed.), *Dictionnaire des illustrateurs 1800-1914*, Ides et Calendes, Neuchâtel, 1989. Wortley, Laura, *Lucy Kemp-Welch, 1869-1958: the Spirit of the Horse*, Antique Collectors' Club, Woodbridge, 1996.

MUSEUMS AND GALLERIES:
BRISTOL (City Mus. & AG): *Timber-hauling in the New Forest* (oil on canvas) - CAPE TOWN: *Calves* - LONDON (Tate Collection): *Colt Hunting in the New Forest* (1897, oil on canvas) - MELBOURNE: *Horses Bathing in the Sea*.

AUCTION RECORDS:
LONDON, 2 May 1924, *Noonday Heat*, GBP 56. LONDON, 13 Oct 1930, *Rocky Coastline*, GBP 48. LONDON, 31 July 1979,

Draught Horse (black chalk, 13¾ x 14¼ ins / 35 x 36 cm) GBP 650. LONDON, 31 July 1979, *Horses in a Field of Wheat* (oil on canvas, 28 x 36¼ ins / 71 x 92 cm) GBP 2,600. LONDON, 25 May 1983, *The Plough Team* (oil on canvas, 16 x 18½ ins / 40.5 x 47 cm) GBP 3,000. LONDON, 1 March 1984, *The Children's Pony* (watercolour heightened with white, 13 x 16¼ ins / 33 x 41 cm) GBP 3,000. CHESTER, 30 March 1984, *The Plough Team* (oil on panel, two panels, 6½ x 8½ ins / 16.5 x 21.5 cm) GBP 950. LONDON, 15 May 1985, *The Starting Gun* (pastel, 9 x 23¼ ins / 23 x 59 cm) GBP 3,800. LONDON, 2 March 1989, *Horses Drinking* (oil on canvas, 19¾ x 26½ ins / 50 x 67.5 cm) GBP 46,200. LONDON, 27 Sept 1991, *Mare and her Foal* (1903, oil on canvas, 16 x 22½ ins / 40.5 x 57 cm) GBP 3,850. LONDON, 7 Nov 1991, *Harvest Home* (1938, oil on card, 22¾ x 17 ins / 58 x 43 cm) GBP 3,850. NEW YORK, 30 June 1993, *Women at Work during the Great War of 1914-1918* (gouache, watercolour and pencil/paper/card, 56 x 37 ins / 142.2 x 94 cm) USD 805. LONDON, 4 June 1997, *Sheep at Rest* (1919, oil on canvas, 33¾ x 44 ins / 86 x 111.5 cm) GBP 4,140. NEWBURY, 14 July 1999, *Study of Shire Horses Galloping through the Landscape* (1913, oil on canvas, 12 x 18 ins / 31 x 46 cm) GBP 3,300. HAVERHILL, 20 Oct 1999, *Morning Ride: Daughter of the Hon Stanhope Tollemache Riding her Pony* (watercolour, 22 x 25 ins / 56 x 63 cm) GBP 7,800. LONDON, 26 May 2000, *Happy Autumn Fields* (oil on canvas on board, 19 x 24 ins / 47 x 62 cm) GBP 11,500. LONDON, 24 Nov 2000, *Midday Heat* (1933, oil on canvas, 18 x 24 ins / 46 x 62 cm) GBP 22,000. LONDON, 22 Nov 2001, *Haywain* (watercolour and gouache, 7 x 10 ins / 19 x 25 cm) GBP 1,900. LONDON, 5 Dec 2001, *Study for The Riders* (1910, oil on canvas, 20 x 24 ins / 51 x 61 cm) GBP 12,000. BRISTOL, 9 April 2002, *Over the Uplands* (pastel, 14 x 18 ins / 35 x 45 cm) GBP 6,600. LONDON, 7 June 2002, *Carthorse on the Downs* (1914-1917, oil on canvas, 18 x 24 ins / 46 x 61 cm) GBP 31,000. LONDON, 2 Dec 2003, *Down!* (1915, watercolour and gouache heightened with white, 12 x 8 ins / 30 x 20 cm) GBP 5,500. LONDON, 2 Dec 2003, *I'll Drive You Straight to the Hospital* (1916, watercolour and gouache heightened with white pencil, 15 x 10 ins / 38 x 26 cm) GBP 6,000. BATH, 21 June 2004, *Horse Carts Beneath the End of the Pier at St Ives, Low Tide* (oil on board, 12 x 18 ins / 30 x 45 cm) GBP 4,000. LONDON, 3 Nov 2004, *Skylark* (oil on canvas, 30 x 40 ins / 76 x 101 cm) GBP 18,000.

KEMP-WELCH, Margaret
British, 19th - 20th century.
Born in Streatham.
Painter, engraver. Genre scenes, landscapes.

Margaret Kemp-Welch is noted for her landscapes, chiefly of Italy, France and Spain.

KEMPA, Ernst
German, 19th century.
Born 1 December 1858, in Kronau.
Painter.

Kempa established himself in Berlin, executing portraits of *Nietzsche, Kaiser Wilhelm II* and *A. van Menzel.*

KEMPE, Charles Emer
British, 19th century.
Born 29 June 1837, in Ovingdean (Sussex); died 29 April 1907, in London.
Glass painter.

Charles Emer Kempe made several stained-glass windows for Winchester Cathedral and the College chapel at Eton.

KEMPE, Francon de. See **FRANCON de Kempe**

KEMPE, Harriet (Miss)
British, 19th century.
Active in London.
Painter. Genre scenes.

Harriet Kempe exhibited frequently at the Royal Academy and at the Suffolk Street Gallery from 1867 to 1892.

KEMPE, Roland
Swedish, 20th century.
Born 13 August 1907, in Borås; died 1991.
Painter, illustrator.

Roland Kempe was a student at the school of fine arts in Stockholm from 1925 to 1930. He visited Paris in 1926, where he frequently returned, and made trips to Spain, England, France, Italy, the East, Greece (including Crete), Turkey, Egypt, Mexico and the USA.

His work has been shown in several group exhibitions, including two at the Carnegie Institute in Pittsburgh in 1950 and 1952. His first solo show was held in Stockholm in 1936, followed by others in Scandinavia.

MUSEUMS AND GALLERIES:
STOCKHOLM (Nationalmus.).

AUCTION RECORDS:
STOCKHOLM, 14 June 1990, *The Golden Fleece* (1959, oil on canvas, 7½ x 13 ins / 19 x 33 cm) SEK 5,200. STOCKHOLM, 21 May 1992, *Guitarist and Model* (1957, oil on canvas, 20½ x 23¼ ins / 52 x 59 cm) SEK 6,500. UPPSALA, 28 May 2004, *Lucretzia Fiorentina* (1965, oil on canvas, 38 x 51 ins / 96 x 130 cm) SEK 18,000.

KEMPEN, B. van
Dutch, 18th century.
Active in Rotterdam.
Engraver.

B. van Kempen is known for a plate after E. van Nimweegen.

KEMPEN, Godofredus van.
See **GODOFREDUS van Kempen**

KEMPEN, Hans P. Melchior
German, 19th - 20th century.
Born 10 April 1874, in Cologne.
Painter.

MUSEUMS AND GALLERIES:
BAUTZEN - CHEMNITZ - DRESDEN - ZWICKAU.

KEMPEN, Renée
Belgian, 20th century.
Born 1914, in Antwerp.
Painter. Figures, interiors, landscapes, seascapes, flowers.

Renée Kempen produces expressive paintings that range from moods of serenity to high drama.

KEMPENER, Jacob
Flemish School, 16th century.
Active in Brussels.
Painter.

Nothing is known of this artist's work.

KEMPENER, Jacob
German, 17th century.
Active probably in Cologne.
Painter. Flowers.

Kempener specialised in still-lifes.

KEMPENER, Jan
Flemish School, 16th century.
Active in Brussels.
Painter.

KEMPENER, Juan Bautista de.
See **CAMPANA**

KEMPENER, Peter. See **CAMPANA Pedro**

KEMPER, Coco
Belgian, 20th century.
Born 1943, in Heemstede.
Sculptor, potter. Figures.

Coco Kemper studied at the Academie voor Kunst in Breda.

KEMPER, Georg
German, 20th century.
Born 20 November 1880, in Oelde (Nordrhein-Westphalia).
Active in Munich.
Sculptor.
Kemper exhibited in Munich and Berlin.

KEMPF, Anna, later Anna Gumlich-Kempf
German, 19th century.
Born 26 November 1860, in Berlin.
Painter. Still-lifes, flowers.
Kempf exhibited in Berlin from 1888.

KEMPF, Carl
German, 19th century.
Active in Nuremberg in 1826.
Draughtsman, engraver.

KEMPF, Hans
Swiss, 16th century.
Active in 1551.
Glass painter.

KEMPF, Heinrich
German, 19th century.
Born 13 July 1814, in Mainz; died 13 July 1852, in Mainz.
Painter. Portraits, landscapes.
Kempf lived in England for a long time.
MUSEUMS AND GALLERIES:
MAINZ: *Two Views of the Old Fischturm; Portrait of the Artist; Joseph Leské and His Wife; The Freiherr of Lichtenberg.*
AUCTION RECORDS:
COLOGNE, 20 March 1981, *Wooded Landscape with Figures* (oil on canvas, 21 1/4 x 27 3/4 ins / 54 x 70.5 cm) DEM 11,000.

KEMPF, Jean Baptiste
French, 20th century.
Born 1941, in Belfort.
Engraver.
Jean Baptiste Kempf works with G.F. Kammerer-Luka and uses a computer to create his works. He took part in the exhibition *De Bonnard à Baselitz - Dix Ans d'enrichissements du cabinet des estampes 1978-1988* (*From Bonnard to Baselitz: A Decade of Acquisitions by the Prints Collection 1978-1988*), at the Bibliothèque Nationale in Paris in 1992.
BIBLIOGRAPHY:
Beaumont-Maillet, Laure/Woimant, Françoise/Pernoud, Emmanuel, *De Bonnard à Baselitz - Dix ans d'enrichissements du Cabinet des estampes 1978-1988*, exhibition catalogue, Bibliothèque nationale de France, Paris, 1992. '*Kammerer-Luka, Jean-Baptiste Kempf: Méta-Écritures, signes + textes*' in *Nouvelles de l'Estampe* n° 167, periodical, Bibliothèque Nationale de France, Paris, 2000.
MUSEUMS AND GALLERIES:
PARIS (Prints Collection).

KEMPF, Jörg
Swiss, 16th century.
Born in Rheineck; died 1564, in Freiburg im Brisgau.
Sculptor, architect.
Jörg Kempf was an architect and a sculptor who worked almost exclusively in Constance, Strasbourg and Fribourg.

KEMPIN, Kurt
German, 19th - 20th century.
Born 7 April 1874, near Halle.
Painter, decorative designer. Stage sets.
Kurt Kempin worked as a set designer at the Darmstadt theatre for much of his adult career. His painting of *Eve* was exhibited in Munich in 1900.

KEMPIN, Richard
German, 20th century.
Born 21 June 1885.
Active in Osterburg.
Painter. Landscapes.
Richard Kempin studied in Weimar.
MUSEUMS AND GALLERIES:
OLDENBURG.

KEMPLEN, Alfred
British, 20th century.
Painter.
Alfred Kemplen lived and worked in London. His work featured at the Brussels Exposition Universelle of 1910.

KEMPS, Niek
Dutch, 20th century.
Born in Nijmegen.
Active in Amsterdam.
Sculptor (mixed media).
Niek Kemps creates huge coloured screens in a wide range of materials (including polyester, glass, steel and concrete), which depict figures and interior landscapes and play on effects of transparency and light.

He has taken part in many group exhibitions, including *Documenta VIII* in Kassel; *Nieuwe aanwinsten*, Stedelijk Van Abbemuseum (with work by Boltanski, Bustamente, Cragg, Munoz, Vercruysse); 1992, *Universal Exhibition*, Seville; 1994, *Art - Pays-Bas - XXe siécle - Du concept à l'image* (*Twentieth Century Dutch Art: From Concept to Image*), Musée d'Art Moderne de la Ville de Paris. Solo shows include: 1979, Arnhem; 1988, Musée d'Art Moderne, St-Étienne; 1988, Boymans van Beuningen Museum, Rotterdam; and 1996, Tramway, Glasgow.
BIBLIOGRAPHY:
Kemps, N./Schampers, K./Wiethoff, C., *Niek Kemps: Twee/Two/Deux*, exhibition catalogue, Museum Boymans van Beuningen/Musée d'Art Moderne, Rotterdam/St-Étienne, 1988. Kemps, Niek, *Niek Kemps*, Stedelijk Van Abbemuseum, Eindhoven, 1992. French, Christopher, *Like a Body without a Shadow: L. C. Armstrong, James Drake, Ilya Kabakov, Niek Kemps, Claudia Matzko, Buzz Spector*, exhibition catalogue, Marsha Mateyka Gallery, Washington DC, 1993. Cueff, Alain/Jansen, Bert, *Art - Pays-Bas - XXe siècle. Du concept à l'image*, exhibition catalogue, Musée d'Art Moderne de la Ville de Paris, Paris, 1994. Koplos, Janet, '*Off Sight: Niek Kemps Installation Art*' in *Art in America*, Corcoran Gallery, Washington DC, May 1996.

KEMPSON, M. Freeman (Miss)
British, 19th century.
Active in Croydon.
Painter. Landscapes.
Miss M. Freeman Kempson exhibited at the Suffolk Street Gallery from 1868 to 1884. She may be the same person as Mary Freeman.

KEMPTER, Caroline or Lina
German, 19th - 20th century.
Born 5 February 1856; died 27 August 1925, in Munich.
Active in Munich.
Landscape artist.
Kempter first came to notice around 1889. She exhibited in Munich and Berlin.

KEMPTER, Ernst
Swiss, 20th century.
Born 6 July 1891, in Olten (Solothurn).
Active in Paris and Berlin.
Painter, engraver.
Ernst Kempter exhibited in Zurich from 1910.

KEMPTER, Hugo
German, 19th century.

Born 23 January 1855, in Neustadt.
Painter. Genre scenes.
Kempter was a pupil of Pauwels in Dresden, and first exhibited around 1880.

KEMPTEUR, Joseph
French, 19th century.
Active c. 1800.
Engraver.

KEN'EN
Japanese, 12th century.
Active during the first half of the 12th century.
Sculptor.
Ken'en was the grandson of the sculptor Chosei (1010-1091) and studied under Jocho (died 1057). He and his brother Choen (died 1150) worked in Jocho's studio at a time of intense creativity in the temples. He is responsible for some well-known stylistic advances.

KENAR, Antoni
Polish, 20th century.
Born 1906, in Iwonicz.
Sculptor.

KENCKEL, Benjamin
German, 18th century.
Active at the beginning of the 18th century.
Engraver.
Kenckel was probably born in Augsburg. He worked in Nuremberg, Frankfurt, Graz and Vienna, mainly doing views of towns and monuments.

KENCKEL, Johann
German, 18th century.
Born 14 February 1688, in Augsburg; died 20 December 1722, in Nuremberg.
Painter, engraver.
Kenckel was a pupil of Isaac Fischer, then Martin Schuster. Subsequently he travelled around Europe - especially Germany, France and Holland - painting portraits of all the personalities of his day. He also engraved historical subjects after Schuster, Brandel and Cranach, working mainly in Nuremberg.

KENCKEL, Kaspar
Swedish, 17th - 18th century.
Born 1650, in Brandenburg; died 1724, in Stockholm.
Painter.
Kaspar Kenckel arrived in Sweden at a very young age and specialised in portraiture. Noteworthy among his works is *Portrait of Count Karl Bonde with his Wife and Son*.

KENCKEL, Matthäus
German, 18th century.
Miniaturist.
Kenckel worked mainly in Vienna.

KENDALL, Beatrice
American, 20th century.
Born 14 January 1902, in New York; died 1968.
Painter. Portraits, landscapes.
Beatrice Kendall studied under William Seargent Kendall. She belonged to the American Federation of Arts.

KENDALL, J. G.
British, 19th century.
Active in London.
Painter, watercolourist. Landscapes, architectural views, architectural interiors.
J.G. Kendall exhibited frequently from 1843 to 1854 at the Royal Academy, and until 1892 at the British Institution and at the Suffolk Street Gallery.

AUCTION RECORDS:
PARIS, 10 Dec 1926 (with no first name), *Cottage in a Park* (watercolour) FRF 185; *Autumn Landscapes* (two watercolours) FRF 480.

KENDALL, John
British, 18th century.
Active during the first half of the 18th century.
Engraver (mezzotint), draughtsman.
John Kendall mostly made engravings of portraits.

KENDALL, Margaret
Maiden name: Stickney
American, 19th - 20th century.
Born 29 November 1871, in Staten Island.
Miniaturist.
Margaret Kendall was married to the painter-sculptor William Sergeant and she studied under him. She also worked with J. Alden Weir and Julius Rolshoven. She lived in New York. She featured in the Exposition Universelle in Paris in 1900 and the St Louis World's Fair in 1904 (bronze medal).

KENDALL, William Sergeant
American, 19th - 20th century.
Born 20 January 1869, in Spuyten Duyvil; died 1938.
Painter, sculptor.
William Sergeant Kendall first studied at the Art Students League in New York, then under Thomas Eakins in Philadelphia and Luc Olivier Merson at the École des Beaux-Arts in Paris. He exhibited at the Salon des Artistes Français in Paris gaining an honourable mention in 1891. Renowned for his portraits and his paintings of children, he obtained numerous distinctions, among which are medals at the Carnegie Institute and at the Paris Exposition universelle of 1900; the Shaw Prize of the Society of American Artists and the Shaw Fund Purchase Prize. In 1901 he was elected an associate and in 1905, an academician of the National Academy of Design. He became head of the department of fine arts at Yale.
AUCTION RECORDS:
NEW YORK, 5 Dec 1985, *The Artist's Wife and Daughter* (1904, pastel/brown paper, 28 1/2 x 19 ins / 72.4 x 48.3 cm) GBP 6,750. NEW YORK, 29 May 1986, *The Sphinx* (oil on canvas, 48 1/4 x 36 ins / 122.6 x 91.4 cm) USD 42,500. NEW YORK, 17 March 1988, *Snow in Connecticut* (pastel/brown paper, 11 3/4 x 19 ins / 30 x 48 cm) USD 4,950. NEW YORK, 31 March 1993, *Autumn Landscape with Meadows and Hills in the Distance* (oil on canvas, 21 x 21 ins / 53.3 x 53.3 cm) USD 4,888. NEW YORK, 22 May 1996, *Little Girl in Blue with her Dog* (1909, oil on canvas, 30 x 25 ins / 76.2 x 63.5 cm) USD 74,000. CINCINNATI, 7 May 2000, *Portrait of a Woman* (c. 1900, pastel, 20 x 12 ins / 51 x 30 cm) USD 6,000. PITTSFIELD, 8 Sept 2001, *Reclining Nude in an Interior* (oil on canvas, 40 x 63 ins / 102 x 160 cm) USD 2,750. DETROIT, 19 July 2002, *Paradise Rocks and Purgatory-New-Port* (oil on board, 13 x 16 ins / 33 x 41 cm) USD 2,500. BETHESDA, 13 Dec 2003, *Two Brittany Girls* (1918, oil on canvas, 30 x 22 ins / 76 x 56 cm) USD 16,000.

KENDE, István
Hungarian, 19th - 20th century.
Born 2 January 1865, in Körtvefája.
Painter, watercolourist. Landscapes.
István Kende was the pupil of Greguss.

KENDE, Jacques Samu
Hungarian, 19th - 20th century.
Born 10 June 1865, in Nagykanizsa.
Painter.
Jacques Kende went to Munich and was a pupil of de Piloty and F.A. Kaulbach. In Paris he was influenced by the painters of the Barbizon School.

KENDLBACHER, Johann
German, 18th century.
Painter. Religious subjects.

Kendlbacher is represented by works in Bavarian churches, such as those in Isen and Raitenhaslach.

KENDRICK, Emma Eleonora
British, 19th century.
Born 1788; died 6 April 1871.
Miniaturist, writer.

Emma Eleonora Kendrick was the daughter of Josephus Kendrick. Her works include *Cupid and Psyche* and *Death of Dido*. In 1830, she published a work on the miniature and was named miniaturist to King William IV the following year. She began exhibiting at the Royal Academy in 1811. She also exhibited at the Water-Colour Society, at the Suffolk Street Gallery and at the Society of British Artists, from 1811 to 1840.

KENDRICK, Josephus
British, 18th - 19th century.
Sculptor.

Josephus Kendrick trained at the schools of the Royal Academy. He worked on public buildings, notably on St Paul's Cathedral, and two projects for a national monument are mentioned as having been exhibited in 1815 and 1819. He began exhibiting his work relatively late, in 1813, when he won a gold medal with *Adam and Eve Lamenting the Death of Abel*. in 1817, he exhibited *Prometheus in Chains*. His name is last mentioned in the catalogues of the London exhibitions in 1829.

Kendrick was the father of the painter Emma Kendrick, who enjoyed far greater success.

KENDRICK, Matthew
Irish, 19th century.
Born c. 1797, in Dublin; died 1 November 1874, in London.
Painter. Seascapes.

Matthew Kendrick painted *The Queen's Departure for Kingstown*, which is in the British Royal Collection. He began exhibiting his work in Dublin in 1827; he went on to exhibit in London at the Royal Academy as well.

AUCTION RECORDS:
LONDON, 6 June 1984, *Sailing-boat at Sea* (oil on canvas, 14 1/2 x 22 3/4 ins / 37 x 58 cm) GBP 1,800.

KENDRICK, Mel
American, 20th - 21st century.
Born 1946 or 1949.
Sculptor, mixed media.

Mel Kendrick attended Phillips Academy, where he studied film and photography, and considered a career in mathematics. After his graduation in 1967, he went to Trinity College, Hartford, obtaining a BA in 1971. At Hunter College, New York, where he received an MA in 1973, Kendrick studied under the sculptors Robert Morris and Tony Smith. He later worked for Dorothea Rockburne as a studio assistant. He has taught in the graduate studio art programme at Hunter College, New York.

An abstract sculptor, he uses a variety of woods as his primary medium. His early work in the 1970s was geometric and based on a grid formula. He soon developed his unique style of using a saw to cut, gouge and pierce the wood, then re-assembling the pieces in new configurations, highlighting the artificiality of his process, as in his work *Reverse Stump* (1995). His sculptures may have appendages on which they are balanced off the ground, such as *Black Trunk* (1997). The wood sculptures are often used as a basis for bronze casting. Since the 1980s, Kendrick has also created (often massive) woodblock prints, which he calls his drawings in wood. Using his saw to create a relief image on plywood with interesting natural patterns, he then inks the surface with rollers and handprints the image onto Japanese paper. Twenty-one of his prints were used to illustrate a book of poems by William Carlos William's *Kora in Hell*. He has used some of his sculptures and their by products as subjects for large photographs made from Polaroid negatives, for example, the 2002 works *Open Core* and *Tubes*.

In 2002 he showed his Core Samples (1995-2001) at the Hood Museum of Art, Hanover (New Hampshire), a series of sculptures which reflect the growth patterns and exterior textures of trees. Other solo exhibitions include those at the Contemporary Art Museum, Houston (1986) and the St Louis Art Museum (1987). His work has also been included in: 1984, *The International Survey of Painting and Sculpture*, the Museum of Modern Art, New York; 1985, Whitney Biennial; 1988, *Art of the 80s*, Metropolitan Museum, New York; 1989, *Four Americans: Aspects of Current Sculpture*, at the Brooklyn Museum, New York; 2000, *Hunter College Art Department Faculty Exhibition*; and 2004, *Drop Out*, at the Julie Saul Gallery, New York.

He has received grants from the Creative Artists Public Service Program (1974, 1978) and from the National Endowment for the Arts (1978, 1981).

BIBLIOGRAPHY:
Siersma, Betty, *Mel Kendrick: Recent Sculpture*, exhibition catalogue, Massachusetts University, Amherst Art Gallery, Amherst, 1986. Boodro, Michael, '*Mel Kendrick's Calculated Risks*' in *Art News*, journal article, May 1991. Princenthal, Nancy, '*Mel Kendrick at John Weber*' in *Art in America*, journal article, March 1994. Williams, William Carlos, *Kora in Hell: Improvisations*, illustrated book, Arion Press, San Francisco, 1998 (woodblock prints by Kendrick). Hart, Katherine W., *Mel Kendrick: Core Samples*, exhibition catalogue, Hood Museum of Art, Hanover (NH), 2002.

MUSEUMS AND GALLERIES:
ANDOVER, MA (Addison Gal. of American Art): *Behind the Cross* (1982, sculpture) - ATLANTA (High Mus. of Art) - BALTIMORE (MA) - HAMILTON, NJ (Grounds for Sculpture): *Black Trunk* (1997, bronze sculpture) - MINNEAPOLIS (Walker Art Center) - MOUNTAINVILLE (Storm King Art Center) - NEW YORK (Metropolitan Mus. of Art) - NEW YORK (Whitney Mus. of American Art) - TAMPA (MA): *Reverse Slices, Two Blues* (1997-1999, woodblock print) - TOLEDO (MA): *Sculpture No. 4* (1994, bronze sculpture) - WASHINGTON DC (NGA): *Giraffe* (1990, relief print); *Little Cock* (1990, relief print); *6 Locks* (1996, woodcut); *7 Locks* (1996, woodcut) - WASHINGTON DC (Smithsonian American AM): *Woodprints* (portfolio of six prints).

AUCTION RECORDS:
NEW YORK, 10 Nov 1988, *Untitled* (1983, painted wood and white chalk, 27 1/2 x 13 1/4 x 9 ins / 70 x 33.6 x 23 cm) USD 17,600. NEW YORK, 4 May 1989, *Small Iron Cast* (1985, cast iron, 59 3/4 x 9 x 9 ins / 151.8 x 22.8 x 22.8 cm) USD 17,600. NEW YORK, 9 Nov 1989, *Permission* (1982, painted wood with tar and graphite, h. 25 ins / 63.5 cm) USD 8,800. NEW YORK, 27 Feb 1990, *Lime Tree* (1984, lime and ink/plaster, 64 x 22 x 7 3/4 ins / 162.5 x 56 x 19.7 cm) USD 23,100. NEW YORK, 17 Nov 1992, *Untitled* (1984, green-patinated bronze, 12 1/2 x 14 x 11 ins / 31.8 x 35.6 x 28 cm) USD 2,750. LONDON, 25 March 1993, *Three Woods* (graphite and adhesive on wood, 54 1/4 x 26 1/2 x 29 ins / 137.9 x 67.3 x 73.7 cm) GBP 5,060. NEW YORK, 4 May 1993, *Untitled* (1987, bronze, 73 x 44 x 33 ins / 185.4 x 111.8 x 83.8 cm) USD 25,300. NEW YORK, 3 May 1994, *Poplos, Black and Green* (1983, glued wood, oil and graphite with a steel base, 62 3/4 x 10 1/2 x 10 ins / 159.4 x 26.6 x 25.4 cm) USD 5,750. NEW YORK, 5 May 1994, *Large Cast Poplar* (bronze, 58 1/2 x 34 x 28 ins / 148.6 x 86.4 x 71.1 cm) USD 24,150. NEW YORK, 17 Feb 1999, *Tall Osage* (1988, oiled wood, 64 x 24x15 ins / 163 x 61x38 cm) USD 4,000. NEW YORK, 7 Nov 2000, *Black Silver* (steel, 74 x 32x41 ins / 188 x 81x104 cm) USD 3,800. NEW YORK, 12 Feb 2004, *No.11181 Untitled* (1982, painted wood, 78 x 4x17 ins / 197 x 10x42 cm) USD 3,250.

KENDZRIERSKI, Apolonius
Polish, 19th century.
Born in Parchow.
Active in Warsaw.
Painter. Genre scenes.

Apolonius Kendzrierski studied in Warsaw and at the academy of fine arts in Munich. He won a bronze medal at the Exposition Universelle in 1900. He was influenced by Brand, and took from nature those elements that suited his sensitivity and inner vision.

AUCTION RECORDS:
NEW YORK, 21 May 1991, *Peasant Woman in a Cart* (oil on canvas, 17 x 25 ins / 43.2 x 63.4 cm) USD 1,100.

KENES, Marcel
Belgian, 20th century.
Born 1898, in Molenbeek-St-Jean; died 1960.
Painter. Landscapes.

Marcel Kenes studied at the fine arts academy in Molenbeek-St-Jean and was influenced by Laermans.

KENGEL
Painter. Landscapes.

MUSEUMS AND GALLERIES:
ÉPINAL (Mus. départemental d'Art ancien et contemporain): *Landscape with Ruins* (two).

KENGEN, Éric
Belgian, 20th - 21st century.
Born 1952.
Painter. Figures.

Éric Kengen has had solo shows in Brussels. He depicts man set against backgrounds of fabulous scenery, which have become less complex over the course of time.

KENHOVE, Marijke van
Belgian, 20th century.
Painter (mixed media). Scenes with figures.

Marijke van Kenhove exhibited in various galleries in Belgium.

KENJI
French, 20th - 21st century.
Born 3 February 1958, in Paris.
Sculptor. Figures.
Banlieue-Banlieue Group.

Kenji lived in Tokyo from 1963 to 1978 and studied at the École des Beaux-Arts in Paris from 1980 to 1985. He was one of the three members of the group *Banlieue-banlieue*, from 1984 to 1988, when the group separated in 1988. Kenji's sculptures are made from cut outs in thin metal sheets and generally portray figures running with waving legs and excessively long arms. He has held solo exhibitions since 1988, including: Tokyo, 1988; Galerie l'Horloge, Paris, 1989, 1990 and 1992 and Toulouse and Ivry-sur-Seine in 1991.

KENKADO, real name: Kokyo Kimura, nickname: Seishuku, nicknames: Ko, Kotaro, pseudonyms: Sonsai, Kenkado
Japanese, 18th century.
Born 1736, in Osaka; died 1802.
Painter. Landscapes.

Kenkado belonged to the Nanga School (literati painting). His works were later much appreciated by Chikuden (1777-1835).

AUCTION RECORDS:
NEW YORK, 17 Oct 1989, *Bamboo* (ink/paper, kakemono, 46¾ x 15¾ ins / 118.7 x 40 cm) USD 11,000.

KENNARD, E. C. (Miss)
British, 19th century.
Active in London.
Sculptor.

Miss E.C. Kennard exhibited at the Royal Academy in 1866 and in 1869.

KENNEDY, Cecil
British, 20th century.
Born 4 February 1905.
Painter. Still-lifes, flowers, portraits.

Cecil Kennedy was the son of the landscape painter and designer Thomas Robert Kennedy, from whom he received some early instruction. He painted portraits in his early career, but became a prominent member of the English Contemporary School for his highly detailed paintings of flowers. After attending art school in London, he studied on the continent with a number of influential artists, including the Dutch artist and illustrator Nico Jungmann.

He began exhibiting at an early age at the Royal Academy, the Royal Hibernian Academy, and the Royal Scottish Academy. He embraced the style and technique of Dutch and Flemish Old Master still-life paintings, for which he became popular while stationed in Antwerp during World War II. The elaborate flower arrangements created by his wife, Winifred Aves, whom he married in the early 1930s, were the foremost source of inspiration for his vibrant oil paintings. He often juxtaposed exotic hybrid blooms with English flowers and grasses and traditional plants. He knew much about flowers and his use of all white flower arrangements reflected his awareness of 20th-century horticultural trends such as Vita Sackville-West's *White Garden* at Sissinghurst.

He was awarded a silver medal at the Paris Salon in 1956 and a gold medal in 1970, and exhibited regularly at the Fine Art Society and MacConnal-Mason Gallery in London until his death.

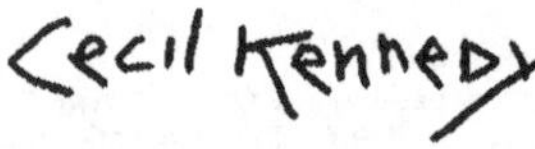

MUSEUMS AND GALLERIES:
MERTHYR TYDFIL (Art Gallery) - ROCHDALE (Art Gallery).

AUCTION RECORDS:
LONDON, 17 March 1976, *Flowers* (oil on canvas, 19½ x 15½ ins / 49.5 x 39.5 cm) GBP 950. LONDON, 16 March 1977, *Roses* (oil on canvas, 19½ x 15½ ins / 49.5 x 39.5 cm) GBP 1,600. LONDON, 19 Sept 1979, *Red Roses* (oil on canvas, 11¾ x 9¾ ins / 30 x 25 cm) GBP 2,700. LONDON, 6 Nov 1981, *Summer Plenty* (oil on canvas, 36 x 28 ins / 91.5 x 71.2 cm) GBP 5,500. LONDON, 4 Nov 1983, *Flowers in a Vase* (oil on canvas, 36 x 28 ins / 91.5 x 71.2 cm) GBP 8,000. LONDON, 7 Nov 1985, *Flowers in a Vase* (oil on canvas, 40 x 30 ins / 101.6 x 76.2 cm) GBP 10,000. LONDON, 13 May 1987, *Mixed Flowers* (oil on canvas, 25 x 30 ins / 63.5 x 76 cm) GBP 16,000. LONDON, 9 June 1988, *Still-life with Roses in a Glass Vase* (1927, oil on canvas, 23½ x 19¾ ins / 60 x 50 cm) GBP 2,860. LONDON, 29 July 1988, *Chrysanthemums in a Vase* (1928, oil on canvas, 23½ x 19¾ ins / 60 x 50 cm) GBP 1,210. LONDON, 2 March 1989, *Flower Composition in a Recess* (oil on canvas, 29½ x 24½ ins / 75 x 62.5 cm) GBP 23,100. EDINBURGH, 22 Nov 1989, *Still-life with Flowers in an Oriental Vase* (1928, oil on canvas, 24 x 20 ins / 61 x 50.8 cm) GBP 3,850. LONDON, 20 Sept 1990, *Still-life with Fruits* (oil on canvas, 19½ x 25¼ ins / 49.5 x 64 cm) GBP 4,400. LONDON, 8 Nov 1990, *Composition with Summer Flowers in a Basket* (oil on canvas, 24½ x 29¾ ins / 62 x 75.5 cm) GBP 6,380. NEW YORK, 12 June 1991, *Flowers in a China Vase* (oil on canvas, 24 x 20 ins / 61 x 50.8 cm) USD 3,300. LONDON, 27 Sept 1991, *Still-life with Flowers* (oil on canvas, 25¼ x 30¼ ins / 64 x 77 cm) GBP 4,180. LONDON, 7 Nov 1991, *Pink Roses* (1954, oil on canvas, 19 x 15¼ ins / 48 x 38.5 cm) GBP 4,180. ST ASAPH, 2 June 1994, *Still-life with Flowers: Irises, Carnations and Gladioli* (oil on canvas, 36 x 28 ins / 91.5 x 71 cm) GBP 43,300. EDINBURGH, 23 May 1996, *Anemone, Forsythia, Hellebore, Narcissi in a Glass Vase* (oil on canvas, 20 x

16 ins / 50.8 x 40.6 cm) GBP 10,350. GLASGOW, 21 Aug 1996, *Summer Flowers* (oil on canvas, 30 x 25 ins / 76.2 x 63.5 cm) GBP 17,825. LONDON, 5 March 1999, *Late Summer* (oil on canvas, 24 x 20 ins / 61 x 51 cm) GBP 18,000. LONDON, 2 Nov 1999, *Madame Butterfly Roses in a Glass Vase* (oil on canvas, 20 x 16 ins / 51 x 41 cm) GBP 13,000. LONDON, 9 June 2000, *Summer* (oil on canvas, 40 x 30 ins / 102 x 76 cm) GBP 70,000. LONDON, 24 Nov 2000, *Summer Flowers* (1968, oil on canvas, 25 x 30 ins / 63 x 76 cm) GBP 29,000. WOODBRIDGE, 26 June 2001, *Still-life with Flowers on a Silver Pedestal Vase* (oil on canvas, 36 x 28 ins / 91 x 71 cm) GBP 68,000. LONDON, 5 Dec 2001, *Still-life with Summer Flowers in a Glass Vase* (oil on canvas, 30 x 25 ins / 76 x 63 cm) GBP 49,000. LONDON, 2 July 2002, *Hibiscus and Mermaid Roses in a George III Silver Wine Cooler* (oil on canvas, 30 x 25 ins / 76 x 63 cm) GBP 82,000. SALISBURY, 9 Oct 2002, *Summer Group: Still-life with Flowers* (oil on canvas, 30 x 25 ins / 76 x 63 cm) GBP 57,000. LONDON, 6 June 2003, *Summer Flowers* (oil on canvas, 30 x 25 ins / 76 x 63 cm) GBP 50,000. LONDON, 2 Dec 2003, *Still-life with Summer Flowers* (oil on canvas) GBP 58,000. AMSTERDAM, 26 Oct 2004, *Summer, Bouquet of Flowers* (1964, oil on canvas, 30 x 25 ins / 77 x 64 cm) EUR 50,000. LONDON, 25 Nov 2004, *Romneya* (oil on canvas, 24 x 20 ins / 62 x 52 cm) GBP 32,000.

KENNEDY, Charles Napier
British, 19th century.
Born 1852, in London; died 17 January 1898, in St Ives.
Painter, watercolourist. Mythological subjects, portraits, genre scenes.

Charles Napier Kennedy was the son of Lieutenant-Colonel John Pitt Kennedy. He trained at the Slade School in London and in Paris. He made his debut at the Royal Academy in 1872 and continued to exhibit at the London exhibitions until his death. He was a member of the Royal Institute of Painters in Watercolours and an associate of the Royal Hibernian Academy.

MUSEUMS AND GALLERIES:
DUBLIN: *Young Boy and Dryad* - MANCHESTER (City AG): *Fair-haired Slave* - SHEFFIELD: *Rest.*

AUCTION RECORDS:
SLANE CASTLE, 13 May 1980, *The legend of the Irish Harp* (1895, oil on canvas, 22 3/4 x 35 ins / 58 x 89 cm) GBP 520. MONTRÉAL, 21 Oct 1986, *Perseus and Andromeda* (1890, oil on canvas, 102 1/4 x 68 ins / 260 x 173 cm) CAD 7,000. LONDON, 13 Nov 1992, *Fountain of Youth* (1892, oil on canvas, 71 x 45 ins / 180.3 x 114.3 cm) GBP 9,350. NEW YORK, 13 Oct 1993, *Perseus and Andromeda* (1890, oil on canvas, 101 3/4 x 68 1/4 ins / 258.4 x 173.4 cm) USD 39,100. LONDON, 4 April 2000, *Cain's First Crime* (oil on canvas, 65 x 57 ins / 166 x 144 cm) GBP 9,500. HASLEMERE, 21 Feb 2001, *Portrait of Mrs Willats Seated in a Cane Chair* (1884, oil on canvas, 54 x 38 ins / 137 x 97 cm) GBP 2,000. STOCKHOLM, 29 May 2001, *The Letter* (oil on canvas, 30 x 18 ins / 76 x 46 cm) SEK 50,000. STOCKHOLM, 2 Dec 2003, *Elegant Visitor at the Artist's Studio* (1879, oil on canvas, 24 x 18 ins / 61 x 46 cm) SEK 25,000. BATH, 26 July 2004, *Portraits of William Boyd, his Wife Charlotte and their Son John Dopping* (1896, oil on canvas, oval, three, 47 x 35 ins / 120 x 90 cm) GBP 1,150.

KENNEDY, Edward Sherard
British, 19th century.
Born c. 1837, in Camberwell (Surrey).
Painter. History painting, genre scenes.

Edward Sherard Kennedy exhibited from 1863 to 1890 in London at the Royal Academy, the Suffolk Street Gallery, and the Water-Colour Society.

AUCTION RECORDS:
LONDON, 2 Dec 1907, *Flight after St Bartholomew's Day*, GBP 4. LONDON, 13 June 1910, *Prayer for Those at Sea* (1874) GBP 4. LONDON, 15 May 1979, *Prayer for Sailors* (1874, oil on canvas, 23 1/2 x 39 ins / 60 x 99 cm) GBP 500. NEW YORK, 20 April 1983, *Summer Afternoon* (oil on canvas, 22 x 16 ins / 56 x 40.5 cm) USD 2,500. LONDON, 27 Sept 1989, *Travelling Comedians on their Way* (oil on canvas, 25 x 39 1/4 ins / 63.5 x 100 cm) GBP 1,980. DETROIT, 14 June 2002, *Sudden Shower* (oil on canvas on masonite, 33 x 27 ins / 84 x 69 cm) USD 1,900.

KENNEDY, J.
British, 19th century.
Active in Oxford.
Painter.

J. Kennedy may have been the artist who exhibited his work at the Royal Academy in 1823.

KENNEDY, Jack
American, 20th century.
Born 1922, in Otterbein (Indiana).
Painter.

Jack Kennedy studied in Chicago. He started painting in 1942. In 1949, he travelled to Paris and took in many other European countries. His paintings favour curvilinear shapes, inspired by Arp's work. In what he called his *Formessences*, he disregarded the orthogonal frame. He has shown his works in solo exhibitions in Chicago in 1949, Paris in 1951 and around Europe.

KENNEDY, James
American, 18th century.
Active in New York.
Engraver.

James Kennedy produced *George Washington* and *Retreat on York.*

KENNEDY, John
British, 19th century.
Painter, watercolourist. Landscapes.

John Kennedy taught at the Dundee School of Art for a period of time.

MUSEUMS AND GALLERIES:
LONDON (Victoria and Albert Mus.): *Rumbling Bridge, near Dunkeld* (watercolour).

KENNEDY, Joseph
British, 19th century.
Active in Kidderminster.
Painter, watercolourist. History painting, genre scenes.

Joseph Kennedy exhibited in London at the Royal Academy and at the Suffolk Street Gallery between 1861 and 1888.

AUCTION RECORDS:
LONDON, 6 Feb 1909, *Ivanhoe, Richard the Lionheart returning from the Crusade* (watercolour) GBP 2. LONDON, 6 Nov 1995, *Visit to the Toyshop* (1870, oil on canvas, 36 x 56 ins / 91.5 x 142 cm) GBP 5,175.

KENNEDY, Reinier Willem
Dutch, 20th century.
Born 16 August 1881, in Dordrecht.
Active in Brussels.
Painter, watercolourist.

Reinier Kennedy exhibited at the Exposition Universelle in Brussels in 1910.

KENNEDY, Samuel James
American, 20th century.
Born 7 June 1877, in Mount Pleasant.
Painter.

Samuel Kennedy studied under Henri Martin in Paris. He settled in Chicago.

KENNEDY, William
British, 19th - 20th century.
Born 1 August 1860, in Glasgow; died 1918.
Painter. Genre scenes, landscapes.

William Kennedy was a pupil of William Bougeureau and Tony Robert-Fleury in Paris. He is best known for his paintings of rural life and his military scenes.

Auction records:
Glasgow, 3 July 1980, *The Kelvingrove Museum and Art Galleries, Glasgow* (1910, oil on canvas, 20 x 30 ins / 51 x 76 cm) GBP 1,300. Perth, 29 Aug 1989, *Children and Rabbits* (oil on canvas, 20 x 24 ins / 51 x 61 cm) GBP 3,080. Glasgow, 6 Feb 1990, *Bringing in the Hay* (oil on canvas, 20 x 24 ins / 51 x 61 cm) GBP 2,640. Glasgow, 22 Nov 1990, *Picking Flowers* (oil on canvas, 10 1/4 x 7 1/4 ins / 26 x 18.4 cm) GBP 1,650. Edinburgh, 2 May 1991, *Moorish Warriors* (oil on canvas/card, 20 x 16 ins / 50.8 x 40.6 cm) GBP 880. Edinburgh, 28 April 1992, *View of Stirling from the River* (oil on canvas, 11 1/4 x 15 1/4 ins / 28.5 x 39 cm) GBP 2,750. New York, 14 Oct 1993, *Tea on a Terrace by Moonlight in Tangier* (oil on card, 11 3/4 x 14 1/2 ins / 29.8 x 36.8 cm) USD 5,175. London, 13 March 1997, *In Camp* (oil on canvas, 11 x 15 ins / 27.9 x 38.2 cm) GBP 3,400. Edinburgh, 7 May 1999, *The Haycart* (oil on canvas, 20 x 24 ins / 51 x 61 cm) GBP 1,500. Dallas, 16 Oct 1999, *Southern Courthouse* (oil on canvas, 38 x 48 ins / 97 x 122 cm) USD 22,500. Edinburgh, 25 Aug 2000, *Hitching up the Haycart* (oil on canvas, 19 x 23 ins / 49 x 59 cm) GBP 2,400. Edinburgh, 8 Dec 2000, *Between Manoeuvres* (oil on canvas, 39 x 35 ins / 100 x 90 cm) GBP 17,000. London, 5 Sept 2001, *Filling the Water Barrel, Thatcham, Berkshire* (oil on canvas, 16 x 24 ins / 40 x 61 cm) GBP 2,000. Edinburgh, 7 Dec 2001, *Loading the Hay Cart* (oil on canvas, 36 x 48 ins / 91 x 122 cm) GBP 2,800. Edinburgh, 24 May 2002, *Arab Camp, Evening* (oil on board, 11 x 14 ins / 29 x 36 cm) GBP 1,100. Edinburgh, 24 May 2002, *Old English Village* (oil on canvas, 16 x 24 ins / 40 x 60 cm) GBP 1,300. London, 27 Aug 2003, *Arab Camp* (oil on panel, 11 x 13 ins / 28 x 34 cm) GBP 1,500. London, 27 Aug 2003, *News from the Front* (oil on panel, 11 x 15 ins / 29 x 38 cm) GBP 4,000. New York, 16 Jan 2004, *Little Girl with Black Cat* (c. 1840, oil on canvas, 32 x 22 ins / 81 x 56 cm) USD 140,000. Portsmouth, 6 Aug 2004, *Clarke and Sarah Gardner Swallow, Portraits* (oil on board, a pair, 16 x 12 ins / 41 x 30 cm) USD 7,000.

KENNEDY, William Deuholm
British, 19th century.
Born 16 June 1813, in Dumfries; died 2 June 1865, in London.
Painter. Portraits, landscapes.

William Deuholm Kennedy was a student at the school of the Royal Academy in 1833. In 1835, he won a gold medal with his two works, *Apollo* and *Hylas*. In 1840, he won a travel scholarship which allowed him to live in Italy. After a brief return to London, he again left for Rome and stayed there for three years. His works were strongly influenced by those of his close friend William Etty, and stand out for their wealth of colours and superb composition. He was also a distinguished critic.

Kennedy exhibited regularly at the Suffolk Street Gallery and at the Royal Academy.

Museums and Galleries:
Dublin: a study.

Auction records:
London, 13 April 1908, *Two Landscapes*, GBP 3. London, 19 March 1910, *Camille and Gil Blas*, GBP 13. London, 1 April 1980, *Playtime* (oil on canvas, 12 x 26 1/2 ins / 30.5 x 67.5 cm) GBP 650.

KENNER, Anton von or Anton Josef Ritter von
Czech, 19th - 20th century.
Born 11 September 1871, in Brno; died 1951.
Active in Austria.
Painter, illustrator.

Anton von Kenner taught at the school of applied arts in Vienna. He worked particularly in Vienna, where he completed several major decorative compositions and book illustrations.

Auction records:
London, 8 Oct 1986, *Taborstrasse in Vienna* (1903, oil on canvas, oval, 21 1/4 x 18 ins / 54 x 46 cm) GBP 2,600. Ahlden, 23 April 1999, *Illustrated Proverbs* (1932, oil on panel, cycle of 12, 39 x 28 ins / 100 x 71 cm) DEM 10,000.

KENNERLEY, Ino
British, 19th century.
Active at the beginning of the 19th century.
Engraver, draughtsman.

Ino Kennerley made a considerable number of portraits.

KENNERLEY, J.
British, 19th century.
Active in London at the beginning of the 19th century.
Painter. Religious subjects, portraits.

J. Kennerley exhibited on occasion between 1803 and 1828 at the Royal Academy and at the Suffolk Street Gallery.

Museums and Galleries:
London (National Portrait Gal.): *John Isaacs as Hawthorne in Bickerstaff's 'Love in a Village'* (1818, stipple engraving, three versions); *Henry Gatti as Monsieur Marbleu in Moncrief's 'Monsieur Tonson'* (1826, stipple engraving); *Princess Charlotte Augusta of Wales* (stipple engraving).

KENNES, Arseen
Belgian, 20th century.
Born 1890, in Herzele.
Painter. Figures, still-lifes, flowers.

Arseen Kennes studied at the fine arts academy in Antwerp under Brunin and H. Luyten.

KENNET, Kathleen (Lady)
Maiden name: Hilton Young
British, 20th century.
Born 27 March 1878, in Carlton in Lindrick (Nottinghamshire); died 24 July 1947, in London.
Sculptor. Figures. Busts.

Kathleen Kennet studied at the Slade School of Fine Art, London, and exhibited at the Royal Academy from 1913 until her death. She joined the Royal Academy of British Sculptors in 1946.

Museums and Galleries:
London (Tate Collection): *The Rt. Hon. H.H. Asquith* (c. 1912-1913, bronze).

KENNINGTON, Eric Henri
British, 20th century.
Born 12 March 1888, in London; died 13 April 1960, in Reading.
Painter, draughtsman, sculptor, illustrator, pastellist.
Military subjects, portraits.

Eric Henri Kennington was the son of the painter Thomas Kennington. He was an Official War Artist for the British government in both World Wars, painting a large number of military scenes and portraits of private soldiers. He exhibited in London from 1908, and held his first solo show in 1916. He became a member of the Royal Academy in 1959. In 1920, he travelled to Arabia to work on illustrations for T.E. Lawrence's autobiographical work *The Seven Pillars of Wisdom*. Kennington painted the portraits of a number of Arab dignitaries during his stay. His non-military portraits (especially of children) were noted for their unusual oil-on-glass technique. He also produced a number of sculptural works, notably the 1924 war memorial to the 24th Division in Battersea Park, London, the memorial to the Allied Forces in Soissons, France (1928), and the tomb effigy of T.E. Lawrence for St Martin's church in Wareham, Dorset (1939).

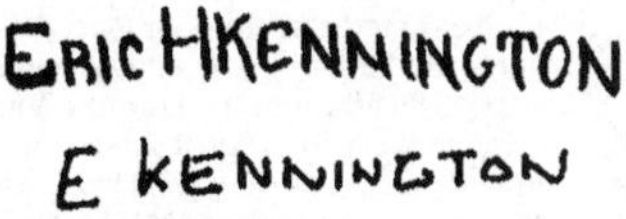

Museums and Galleries:
London (Tate Collection): *Raider with a Cosh* (1917, pastel/paper); *Earth Child* (c. 1936-1937, stone).

Auction records:
London, 24 Nov 1976, *Abdulla El Zaagi* (pastel/grey paper, 29½ x 21 ins / 75 x 53.5 cm) GBP 1,000. London, 8 June 1979, *Wind* (1926, pen and gouache, illustration for 'The Seven Pillars of Wisdom' by Lawrence of Arabia, 10¼ x 14¼ ins / 26 x 36 cm) GBP 580. London, 14 Nov 1979, *Sheriff Ali Ibn el Hussein* (pastel/grey paper, 30 x 20 ins / 76 x 51 cm) GBP 4,300. London, 2 Nov 1983, *The Arras-Bapaume Road* (1918, gouache/pencil outlines, 19 x 13 ins / 48 x 33 cm) GBP 800. London, 2 Nov 1983, *T.E. Lawrence* (1926, bronze, h. 16½ ins / 42 cm) GBP 2,500. London, 21 May 1986, *Wounded Soldier* (black chalk, 18 x 24 ins / 46 x 61 cm) GBP 2,200. London, 22 July 1986, *Hands* (bronze, h. 13 ins / 33 cm) GBP 1,000. London, 6 March 1987, *Sergeant-Major A.F. Sutton DCM, Essex Regiment* (1942, pastel, 30 x 20½ ins / 76.2 x 52 cm) GBP 2,500. London, 10 Nov 1989, *Portrait of a Young Girl* (pastel and white chalk/grey paper, 18 x 15¼ ins / 45.5 x 38.8 cm) GBP 2,420. London, 3 March 1999, *Portrait of Robert Graves* (1921, black and white chalk, 19 x 12 ins / 47 x 30 cm) GBP 30,000. Bury St Edmunds, 23 June 1999, *Portrait of Sir Ronald Storrs* (colour chalk, 18 x 19 ins / 45 x 48 cm) GBP 2,500. London, 2 Nov 2000, *Signaller Off Duty* (colour chalk, 19 x 25 ins / 48 x 63 cm) GBP 5,200. Edinburgh, 8 Dec 2000, *Palm Trees* (oil on board, 26 x 19 ins / 66 x 48 cm) GBP 3,800. London, 21 Nov 2001, *The Eighth* (1943, colour chalk, 29 x 20 ins / 74 x 51 cm) GBP 6,000. London, 21 Nov 2001, *Lance Corporal Smith, 1st Argyll Battalion, Home Guard* (colour chalk, 20 x 28 ins / 51 x 71 cm) GBP 6,500. London, 3 July 2002, *Signaller Off Duty* (c. 1916, colour chalk, 20 x 26 ins / 50 x 65 cm) GBP 9,500. London, 20 Nov 2003, *Alice* (1920, pastel and watercolour on buff paper, 15 x 11 ins / 37 x 29 cm) GBP 2,800.

KENNINGTON, Thomas Benjamin

British, 19th - 20th century.
Born 7 April 1856, in Great Grimsby; died 10 December 1916, in London.
Painter. Portraits, genre scenes.

Thomas Benjamin Kennington trained at the Royal College of Art and the Académie Julian in Paris. He was a founder member of the New English Art Club, and exhibited at the Royal Academy and the Suffolk Street Gallery in London from 1880. He won a bronze medal at the Paris Exposition Universelle of 1900. His paintings are notable for their emphatic handling and pathos. He was the father of the British war artist Eric Henri Kennington.

Museums and Galleries:
Liverpool: *Daily Bread* - London (Tate Collection): *Orphans* (1885, oil on canvas) - Manchester: *Robert Dukinfield Darbishire*.

Auction records:
London, 9 June 1967, *Young Woman Sitting on the Beach, Working at her Embroidery*, Gns 400. London, 10 July 1973, *Three Young Women Gossiping*, GBP 4,200. London, 31 Jan 1979, *Anne Kennington Reading at a Window* (oil on panel, 13¾ x 11 ins / 35 x 27 cm) GBP 850. London, 4 June 1982, *Widow and Orphan* (1888, oil on canvas, 48 x 71½ ins / 121.9 x 181.6 cm) GBP 2,600. London, 21 July 1983, *Portrait of a Young Girl* (1901, oil on canvas, 26 x 20 ins / 66 x 51 cm) GBP 1,600. London, 11 June 1986, *Motherhood* (oil on canvas, 54 x 72 ins / 137 x 183 cm) GBP 19,000. New York, 28 Feb 1990, *No Gossiping!* (1907, oil on canvas, 20 x 30 ins / 50.8 x 76.2 cm) USD 28,600. London, 11 Oct 1991, *The Letter* (1912, oil on canvas, 37¼ x 52 ins / 94.6 x 132.1 cm) GBP 3,520. New York, 16 Feb 1994, *Oriental Beauty* (oil on canvas, 30¼ x 25 ins / 76.8 x 63.5 cm) USD 8,050. London, 29 March 1995, *Shepherdess* (1901, oil on canvas, 39¼ x 78¼ ins / 99.5 x 198.5 cm) GBP 29,900. London, 6 Nov 1996, *Curiosity* (1906, oil on canvas, 78¼ x 39 ins / 198.5 x 99 cm) GBP 25,300. New York, 12 Feb 1998, *Portrait of a Woman in a Pink Dress* (oil on canvas, 21 x 15 ins / 53.3 x 38.1 cm) USD 29,900. London, 3 June 1999, *Idle Hours* (1892, oil on canvas, 15 x 17 ins / 37 x 43 cm) GBP 12,000. London, 3 June 1999, *Autumn* (1900, oil on canvas, 22 x 18 ins / 56 x 46 cm) GBP 31,000. London, 13 June 2000, *Maternal Advice* (oil on canvas, 26 x 39 ins / 65 x 99 cm) GBP 9,000. Wellington, 30 Aug 2000, *Morning Relaxation* (oil on canvas, 13 x 17 ins / 34 x 44 cm) NZD 82,000. London, 8 Nov 2001, *At the Kitchen Table* (1912, oil on board, 14 x 10 ins / 36 x 26 cm) GBP 4,200. London, 11 June 2002, *Picture Book* (oil on board, 16 x 20 ins / 40 x 51 cm) GBP 19,000. Leyburn, 21 April 2004, *Figurative Subject with Two Young Girls Seated on Stone Steps* (1889, oil on canvas, 35 x 24 ins / 88 x 62 cm) GBP 4,800. London, 11 June 2004, *Glory of Womanhood* (oil on canvas, 60 x 39 ins / 153 x 100 cm) GBP 13,000.

KENNION, Charles John

British, 19th century.
Born 1789; died 1853.
Watercolourist.

Charles John Kennion was the son of Edward Kennion. He exhibited at the Royal Academy and the Suffolk Street Gallery from 1804 to 1853.

KENNION, Edward

British, 18th century.
Born 15 January 1744, in Liverpool; died 14 April 1809.
Painter, draughtsman, engraver. Natural history (botanical subjects).

Edward Kennion started out as a trader in the West Indies. He came to London in 1798 and established himself as a drawing teacher. He provided illustrations for the *Journal of a Voyage to New South Wales* (1790) by J. White. He also produced an album containing studies of trees and a series of eight etchings.

KENNIS, Ignace Jacques Lucien

Belgian, 20th century.
Born 26 June 1888, in Mechelen; died 25 January 1973, in Mechelen.
Painter. Religious subjects, portraits, interiors, landscapes.

Ignace Kennis was a student of W. Rosier and A. Geudens at the Kensington Art School, and taught at St-Rombouts College and at the fine arts academy in Mechelen. His works, of which his portraits are best known, belong to the Impressionist tradition.

Kennis exhibited frequently in Belgium. He was an Officier de l'Ordre de la Couronne, Officier de l'Ordre de Léopold II, Commandeur de l'Ordre de St-Grégoire le Grand and Commandeur de l'Ordre de St-Sylvestre.

Museums and Galleries:
Brussels (Mus. de l'Estampe).

Auction records:
Lokeren, 7 Oct 1995, *View of St-Rombouts in Mechelen* (oil on canvas, 27½ x 31½ ins / 70 x 80 cm) BEF 26,000.

KENNY, Michael
British, 20th century.
Born 10 June 1941, in Liverpool; died 28 December 1999.
Sculptor, draughtsman.

Michael Kenny studied at the Liverpool College of Art (1959-1961) under sculptor Philip Hartas and painter Arthur Ballard, at the Slade School of Fine Art, London (1961-1964) under sculptor Reg Butler, and held a University of London Fellowship in Fine Art (1964-1965). He taught as visiting lecturer at the Slade from 1970 to 1982, was Head of Fine Art at Goldsmiths College, London from 1983 to 1988, became Head of the City and Guilds School of Art in 1995, and was elected as Treasurer of the Royal Academy of Art in 1995. Kenny spent the period from 1988 to 1992 in New York City, Paris and Japan.

Kenny worked in stone, aluminium, wood, and plaster. His sculptures in the 1960s were slim, spatially open works. In the late 1960s, Kenny began to experiment with welded or fabricated metal sculptures, but he normally used softer metals. In the 1970s, floorboard bases and steel underpinning were common in his work, as in *Crucifixx* (1976). Kenny's drawings tended to be three-dimensional with architectural-style draughtsmanship. His drawings increased in scale since 1975, and in the 1980s he began to draw nature and landscape. Kenny executed commissions, including sculptures for Nene College, Northampton (1997), Docklands, London (1993), Yokohama Business Park, Japan (1990), and Addenbrookes Hospital, Cambridge (1989).

Kenny had solo exhibitions at Bear Lane Gallery, Oxford (1964); Tokyo Gallery (1983, 1985, 1989); a retrospective at Wilhelm-Lehmbruck Museum, Duisburg (1984); and Royal Academy of Art, London (1986, 1995, 1997). Other exhibitions include Cumberland House Museum, Portsmouth (1967); Whitechapel Art Gallery, London (1968, 1981); Centre of Art and Communication, Buenos Aires (1972); Hayward Gallery, London (1976); *Documenta VI*, Kassel (1977); *The Sculpture Show*, Hayward Gallery, London (1983); *Sculptors' Drawings*, British Council (1984, tour); *A Private View*, École des Beaux-Arts, Nantes (1984); Summer Exhibitions at the Royal Academy (1990-1993, 1995); *Goldsmiths' Centenary Exhibition*, Goldsmiths Gallery (1991); *Academicians*, Royal Academy of Art (1991-1992, tour); and *The Contemporary Print Show*, Barbican Centre, London (1993).

BIBLIOGRAPHY:

Michael Kenny, exhibition catalogue, Hanover Gallery, London, 1969. *Michael Kenny: Sculpture and Drawings*, exhibition catalogue, Serpentine Gallery, London, 1977. *Michael Kenny: Sculpture and Drawings*, exhibition catalogue, Bluecoat Gallery, Liverpool, 1981. *Juda Rowan Gallery at Tokyo Gallery: Michael Kenny*, exhibition catalogue, Tokyo Gallery, Tokyo, 1983 (text in Japanese and English). *Michael Kenny: New Work 1987-1989*, exhibition catalogue, Annely Juda Fine Art, London, 1989. '*Michael Kenny: Profile*' in *Print Quarterly*, periodical, May 1996. Davies, Peter, *Michael Kenny*, illustrated book, Scolar Press, Brookfield (VT), 1997.

MUSEUMS AND GALLERIES:

BELFAST (Ulster Mus.): *Lot's Wife and the Shadow & the First Circle* (1983-1984, 1984, sculptures) - BUCHAREST (Muz. National de Arta al României) - DUBLIN (Irish MMA): *Study for 'Tranquil Night II'* (1980, polished aluminium, bronze and pencil) - DUISBURG (Wilhelm-Lehmbruck Mus.): *Un-Named Person* (wood and metal sculpture) - LEEDS (Henry Moore Institute): *Tranquil Night* (1980, mixed media sculpture) - LIVERPOOL (University of Liverpool AG): *St Katherine's Wheel III & the Magician and the Fool* (1983-1984, 1984, sculptures) - LIVERPOOL (Walker AG): *Bougainville 0.9% & Et in Arcadia Ego...* (1975, 1989, sculptures); *Blood and Pure Wine* (1991-1992, stone sculpture) - LONDON (Arts Council of Great Britain): *Lazarus (In This Awful Place)* (1978-1980, sculpture); *The First Step Toward a Final Gesture* (1975-1976, plaster, wood, metal sculpture) - LONDON (British Council) - LONDON (British Mus.): *Instruments of Passion, V* (1982-1983, pencil, charcoal, pastel, paint on paper) - LONDON (Contemporary Art Society) - LONDON (Royal Academy of Arts): *Arcangel* (1984-1985, wood sculpture) - LONDON (Tate Collection): *The Astronomer* (1984, mixed media sculpture); *Place* (1967, metal sculpture) - LONDON (UK Government Art Collection): *In Solitude (with Clouds)* (1978, lithograph) - LONDON (Victoria and Albert Mus.): *Elementa Curvarum* (1979, mixed media on paper) - MANCHESTER (Whitworth AG): *The Dancer* (sculpture) - STUTTGART (Staatsgal.) - TOKYO (Hara MCA).

AUCTION RECORDS:

LONDON, 26 Oct 1994, *Alone in a Large Room* (pencil, charcoal, gouache and oil on paper, 35 3/4 x 48 1/2 ins / 91 x 123.5 cm) GBP 1,380. LONDON, 5 Oct 1999, *Mixed blessings II, Mixed blessings IV* (1987, charcoal and acrylic, two, 27 x 37 ins / 69 x 93 cm) GBP 1,100.

KENNY, Nicholas
Irish, 19th century.
Born c. 1807, in Kilkenny.
Painter.

Nicholas Kenny worked mostly in Dublin.

KENNY, Thomas Henry
American, 20th century.
Born 12 January 1918, in Bridgeport (Connecticut).
Painter, engraver.

Thomas Henry Kenny's early works show his debt to Pollock and Miró. He has worked all over the world. He was a member of the Institute of Contemporary Art and of the American Federation of Arts in New York.

KENOY, Frans van. See **DUQUESNOY François**

KENRETSU, real name Kenretsu Yamada
Japanese, 20th - 21st century.
Born 1947, in Hyogo Prefecture.
Sculptor.

Kenretsu studied architecture before turning to sculpture. In 1970 he was awarded the President's Prize at the 5th JAFA (Japan Art Festival Association) exhibition.

KENSAI, real name: Shin Hirai, nicknames: Kimpu, Genjiro, Jiroku, pseudonyms: Kensai, Sankoku Sansho
Japanese, 19th century.
Born 1802, in Totomi, now Shizuoka; died 1856.
Painter.
Nanga School.

Kensai studied under Buncho (1763-1840) and Kazan (1793-1841). After Kazan's death he worked with Hanko Fukuda (1804-1864).

KENSETT, John Frederick
American, 19th century.
Born 22 or 23 March 1818, in Cheshire (Connecticut); died 14 or 16 December 1872, in New York.
Painter. Landscapes with figures, landscapes, seascapes.
Hudson River School.

John Frederick Kensett entered Dagget's banknote engraving studio at a very young age, and studied art in his spare time. In 1840 he went to England where he produced landscapes. He sent work to the Royal Academy for the first time in 1845. Kensett stayed in Europe for seven years, living in Rome for two years and visiting Naples, the Italian lakes, Switzerland and the banks of the Rhine. When he returned to the USA in 1847, his reputation as a landscape artist was already firmly established through the many works he had sent there. He became a member of the National Academy of

Design in New York in 1849. In 1850 his *View of Windsor Castle* was warmly welcomed by critics.

He liked to depict the most scenic sites of the USA, and his works quickly became even more popular. Kensett was one of the Second Generation of the Hudson River School, also known as Luminists. Unlike the First Generation, these painters moved away from untouched nature, in favour of the familiar landscape of city surroundings, where people went to relax.

Kensett took part in the major American exhibitions and in the Paris exhibitions of 1867 and 1878. His work featured in the following group exhibitions on landscape: *200 Ans de Peinture Américaine. Collection du Wadsworth Atheneum (200 Years of American Painting. The Wadsworth Atheneum Collection)* at the Galeries Lafayette in Paris (1989); and *American Sublime* at the Tate Britain in London (2002). His work was also the subject of the 1985 travelling exhibition at Worcester Art Museum, Los Angeles County Museum of Art and the Metropolitan Museum of Art in New York.

BIBLIOGRAPHY:

Sullivan, Mark White, *John F. Kensett, American landscape painter*, dissertation, Bryn Mawr College, 1981. Driscoll, John Paul, *John Frederick Kensett, an American master*, travelling exhibition catalogue, The Metropolitan Museum of Art, New York, 1985. Wilton, Andrew/Barringer, Tim, *American sublime in the United States 1820-1880*, exhibition catalogue, Tate Britain, London, 2002.

MUSEUMS AND GALLERIES:

BALTIMORE (Peabody Art Collection): *On the Thames, near Windsor* (1868, oil on canvas) - HARTFORD (Wadsworth Atheneum): *Mount Washington from the Conway Valley* (oil on canvas); *Bergen Park, Idaho Springs, Colorado* (oil on canvas).

AUCTION RECORDS:

NEW YORK, 19 March 1969, *Landscape*, USD 5,250. NEW YORK, 28 Oct 1971, *Landscape with Waterfall*, USD 15,000. NEW YORK, 19 April 1972, *Mount Chocorua, New Hampshire*, USD 11,000. NEW YORK, 29 April 1976, *White Mountains* (oil on canvas, 11 x 16 1/2 ins / 28 x 42 cm) USD 3,250. NEW YORK, 21 April 1977, *Waterfall* (1853, oil on canvas, 35 x 29 1/4 ins / 89 x 74.3 cm) USD 8,500. NEW YORK, 20 April 1979, *Does in a Landscape* (1853, oil on canvas, 48 x 72 1/2 ins / 122 x 184.1 cm) USD 90,000. NEW YORK, 22 Oct 1981, *Hunters by a River* (1850, oil on mounted canvas on board, 30 x 25 ins / 76.2 x 63.5 cm) USD 50,000. LONDON, 25 March 1982, *Lake George* (1868, oil on canvas, 13 x 16 1/4 ins / 33 x 41 cm) GBP 7,000. NEW YORK, 8 Dec 1983, *Eagle Cliff, Coast of Massachusetts* (1859, oil on canvas, 28 1/2 x 45 1/2 ins / 72.4 x 115.6 cm) USD 540,000. NEW YORK, 6 Dec 1985, *Long Island Sound at Darien* (oil on canvas, 15 1/2 x 30 3/4 ins / 39.5 x 78 cm) USD 100,000. NEW YORK, 3 Dec 1987, *Seaside at Newport* (oil on canvas, 20 x 31 ins / 50.8 x 78.8 cm) USD 560,000. NEW YORK, 1 Dec 1988, *Mountain Lake in Summer* (oil on canvas, 10 1/4 x 14 ins / 26 x 35.6 cm) USD 11,550. NEW YORK, 24 Jan 1989, *Middlebury in Vermont* (1851, pencil heightened with white, 9 1/4 x 13 1/4 ins / 23.2 x 33.5 cm) USD 5,775. NEW YORK, 25 May 1989, *Mount Kearsarge* (oil on paper/canvas, 12 x 14 ins / 30.5 x 35.6 cm) USD 19,800. NEW YORK, 1 Dec 1989, *Forty Steps at Newport, Rhode Island* (1871, oil on card/synthetic resin, 10 1/2 x 18 1/2 ins / 26.6 x 47 cm) USD 60,500. NEW YORK, 16 March 1990, *Niagara Falls* (oil on canvas, oval, 25 x 36 1/4 ins / 63.5 x 92 cm) USD 308,000. NEW YORK, 26 Sept 1990, *Morning* (oil on canvas, 34 x 27 ins / 86.4 x 68.6 cm) USD 24,200. NEW YORK, 22 May 1991, *Narragansett Beach* (1865, oil on canvas, 12 1/4 x 20 ins / 30.9 x 51.1 cm) USD 104,500. NEW YORK, 27 May 1992, *Black Mountain, Lake George* (oil on canvas, 14 1/4 x 24 ins / 36.2 x 61 cm) USD 286,000. NEW YORK, 3 Dec 1992, *Beach at Newport* (oil on canvas, 10 x 17 ins / 25.4 x 43.2 cm) USD 104,500. NEW YORK, 26 May 1993, *Passage of the Storm* (1848, oil on canvas, 18 x 24 ins / 46 x 61.2 cm) USD 43,700. NEW YORK, 3 Dec 1993, *Landscape* (oil on canvas, 34 x 26 3/4 ins / 86.5 x 68 cm, 2 ins/5 cm) USD 27,600. NEW YORK, 21 Sept 1994, *Autumn Landscape* (oil on canvas, 14 x 24 ins / 35.6 x 61 cm) USD 17,250. NEW YORK, 29 Nov 1995, *River Landscape in Autumn* (oil on canvas, 18 1/4 x 30 1/4 ins / 46.4 x 76.8 cm) USD 28,750. NEW YORK, 9 March 1996, *Afternoon in Newport* (1871, oil on card, 8 1/2 x 12 ins / 21.7 x 30.7 cm) USD 77,300. NEW YORK, 5 June 1997, *Franconia Mountains* (1854, oil on canvas, 40 x 60 ins / 101.6 x 152.3 cm) USD 332,500. NEW YORK, 5 June 1997, *Newport Hills, Rhode Island* (oil on canvas, 12 x 20 ins / 30.5 x 50.8 cm) USD 23,000. NEW YORK, 6 June 1997, *Narragansett Coast* (oil on canvas, 14 x 24 ins / 35.6 x 61 cm) USD 85,000. NEW YORK, 26 May 1999, *Near Newport, Rhode Island* (oil on canvas, 10 x 24 ins / 25 x 61 cm) USD 420,000. NEW YORK, 30 Nov 1999, *Coastal Scene* (oil on canvas, 9 x 16 ins / 23 x 41 cm) USD 120,000. NEW YORK, 15 March 2000, *Trout Brook* (1871, oil on canvas, 16 x 14 ins / 41 x 36 cm) USD 45,000. NEW YORK, 24 May 2000, *Connecticut Shoreline in Autumn* (oil on canvas, 14 x 24 ins / 36 x 62 cm) USD 110,000. CLEVELAND, 23 April 2001, *Rydau Falls* (c. 1868, pen, ink and watercolour, 11 x 7 ins / 28 x 18 cm) USD 1,900. NEW YORK, 5 Dec 2001, *Lily Pond, Newport, Rhode Island* (oil on canvas, 10 x 18 ins / 25 x 46 cm) USD 230,000. NEW YORK, 21 May 2002, *Catskills* (1859, oil on canvas, 11 x 17 ins / 27 x 42 cm) USD 200,000. NEW YORK, 3 Dec 2002, *Sunset over Lake George* (1867, oil on canvas, 28 x 46 ins / 71 x 117 cm) USD 480,000. NEW YORK, 22 May 2003, *Mountain Lake* (1866, oil on canvas, 24 x 36 ins / 61 x 91 cm) USD 200,000. NEW YORK, 4 Dec 2003, *Waterfall in the Woods with Indians* (1850, oil on canvas, 17 x 24 ins / 43 x 61 cm) USD 400,000. NEW YORK, 18 May 2004, *View of Mount Washington* (1852, oil on canvas, 30 x 45 ins / 76 x 114 cm) USD 750,000. NEW YORK, 19 May 2004, *On the Coast, Beverley Shore, Massachusetts* (1872, oil on canvas, 18 x 30 ins / 46 x 76 cm) USD 875,000.

KENSETT, Thomas

British, 19th century.
Born 1786; died 1829, in Hampton.
Engraver.

Thomas Kensett is known for his *Map of Canada*.

KENT, John

British, 18th century.
Active in London.
Painter, draughtsman. Urban landscapes, landscapes.

John Kent exhibited his views of Italy at the Royal Academy from 1771 to 1773.

KENT, Rockwell

American, 20th century.
Born 21 June 1882, in Tarrytown Heights (New York); died 13 March 1971, in Plattsburgh.
Painter, draughtsman, illustrator, printmaker. Genre scenes, landscapes. Murals.

Rockwell Kent initially studied architecture at Columbia University (1906-1910), but switched to studying art in night and summer classes at the New York schools of William Merritt Chase, Robert Henri, Kenneth Hayes Miller and Abbot Handerson Thayer. He worked as an architect for about 10 years, before moving to Maine to concentrate on painting and printmaking. Kent travelled on sketching trips to Alaska, Greenland, Canada, Latin America, Europe and the Straits of Magellan. In 1967 he received the Lenin Peace Prize in Moscow.

Kent is one of the best known American illustrators of the 20th century, producing works for many journals and books, such as Voltaire's *Candide* (New York, 1928), and Herman Melville's *Moby Dick* (Chicago, 1930). By the 1920s, he had developed a style of bold sculptural patterns of landscape and solitary figures, created by sharp contrasts of light and dark. He was a committed socialist, a situation which caused him to come under investigation in the 1950s, and his social activism was reflected in some of his work, such as the engraving *Workers of the World Unite* (1937). His political views did not prevent him from accepting commissions from large corporations, including a series of nine paintings for the Bituminous Coal Institute and the Benton and Bowles Advertising Agency in New York City. Kent painted murals for the Ministries of Justice and of the Post in Washington DC, and was the author of a number of memoirs.

Kent had his first solo exhibition in 1908, and his work has been shown at the National Academy of Design, New York (1905); Kunstakademie, Berlin (1910); a solo, Everson Museum of Art, Syracuse (1937); Cleveland Museum of Art (1940); Whitney Museum of American Art, New York (1940); *Diversity of Line: Works in Pen and Ink from the Collection*, Brandywine River Museum, Chadds Ford, Pennsylvania (1998); *Art of the Far North*, Anchorage Museum of History and Art (1999); *The View from Asgaard: Rockwell Kent's Adirondack Legacy*, Adirondack Museum, Blue Mountain Lake, New York (1999-2000); and *Distant Shores: The Odyssey of Rockwell Kent*, Norman Rockwell Museum in Stockbridge, Appleton Museum of Art at Florida State University in Ocala, Terra Museum of American Art in Chicago, and Anchorage Museum of History and Art (2000-2001). He was one of the organisers of the *Independent Artists* exhibition in 1910 and a member of the National Institute of Arts and Letters.

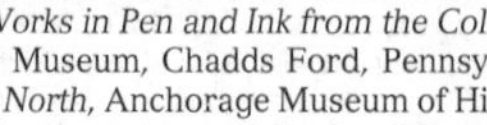

BIBLIOGRAPHY:

Burne Jones, Dan, *The Prints of R. Kent*, The University of Chicago Press, Chicago, 1975. Traxel, David, *An American Saga: the Life and Times of Rockwell Kent*, Harper & Row, New York, 1980. Ferris, Scott R., *Rockwell Kent's Forgotten Landscapes*, Down East Books, Camden (ME), 1998. Welsh, Caroline Mastin, *The View from Asgaard: Rockwell Kent's Adirondack Legacy*, exhibition catalogue, Adirondack Museum, Blue Mountain (NY), 1999. Martin, Constance, *Distant Shores: the Odyssey of Rockwell Kent*, exhibition catalogue, Chameleon Books, Chesterfield (MA), 2000. Roberts, Dan, *Rockwell Kent: the Art of the Bookplate*, Fair Oaks Press, San Francisco, 2003.

MUSEUMS AND GALLERIES:

BALTIMORE (MA) - BOSTON (MFA) - CHICAGO (AI): *Mount Equinox, Winter* (1921) - CHICAGO (Terra Foundation for American Art Collection): *Cranberrying, Monhegan* (c. 1907, oil); *Three Stumps* (1919, oil); *Flame* (1928, wood engraving); *The Lovers* (1928, wood engraving); *Summer, Greenland* (1932-1933, oil) - CLEVELAND (Art Museum): *Beowulf: Beowulf* (1931); *The Cheshire Academy* (1947); *Twilight of Man* (1926); *The Lookout* (1930); *Hero* (1931) - CLEVELAND (MA): *Maine Coast* (1907) - DAYTON (AI): *Endless Energy for Limitless Living* (c. 1945, oil) - DETROIT (IA) - HOUSTON (MFA) - JACKSON HOLE (National Mus. of Wildlife Art): *Mount Equinox, Fall* (1921-1923, oil) - LETHBRIDGE, ALBERTA (University of Lethbridge): *Indian Summer, Alaska* (1919, oil) - LONDON (British Mus.) - LONDON (Victoria and Albert Mus.) - MINNEAPOLIS (IA): *Macy Island, Strait of Magellan* (1922, brush and ink) - MOSCOW (Pushkin MFA): *Eskimo in a Kayak* (1933) - NEW YORK (Metropolitan Mus. of Art) - NEW YORK (Whitney Mus. of American Art) - PORTLAND, ME (MA): *Mt. Monadnock* (1903); *Wreck of the D.T. Sheridan* (c. 1948-1953) - SAN FRANCISCO (FAM): *Revisitation* (lithograph); *Workers of the World Unite* (1937, wood engraving); *Self-portrait, Reading in Winter* (1930-1935, woodcut); *Convalescent* (1920, linoleum cut or woodcut); *And Women Must Weep* (1937, lithograph); *Twilight of Man* (1926, wood engraving) - ST PETERSBURG (Hermitage): *Greenland Tryst* (1929, oil); *Cloudy Day, Fjord in Northern Greenland* (1932/33, oil); *Maine Lobsterman* (1955, oil); *Asgaard* (1950, oil); *Sunglare: Alaska* (1919, oil); *Mount Assiniboine, Canadian Rockies* (1952, oil) - WASHINGTON DC (Hirshhorn Mus. and Sculpture Garden): *The Seiners* (1910-1913, oil); *Landscape with Distant Mountains (Tierra del Fuego)* (1928-1930, oil) - WASHINGTON DC (NGA): *Foreboding* (1926, transfer lithograph on zinc); *Almost* (1929, wood engraving) - WASHINGTON DC (Phillips Collection) - WASHINGTON DC (Smithsonian American AM): *Fair Wind* (1931, wood engraving); *Eternal Vigilance is the Price of Liberty* (1945, lithograph); *Imperishable* (1927, engraving); *Oarsman* (1931, wood engraving); *Prometheus* (1931, engraving); *Snow Fields (Winter in the Berkshires)* (1909, oil).

AUCTION RECORDS:

NEW YORK, 15 April 1970, *Driftwood*, USD 1,600. NEW YORK, 16 May 1973, *Seaside*, USD 3,750. NEW YORK, 29 April 1976, *The City* (1928, pen, 19¼ x 17¼ ins / 49 x 43.5 cm) USD 1,000. NEW YORK, 28 Oct 1976, *Study for a War Poster* (1941, tempera/paper, 14½ x 11½ ins / 37 x 29.2 cm) USD 2,100. NEW YORK, 23 May 1979, *Anni McGinley* (1926, oil on canvas, 38 x 54¼ ins / 96.5 x 137.5 cm) USD 8,500. NEW YORK, 2 Dec 1982, *Cornfield* (1926-1927, oil on canvas, 38 x 54 ins / 96.5 x 137.2 cm) USD 25,00. NEW YORK, 2 June 1983, *Skaters* (oil on canvas, 28 x 42 ins / 71.2 x 106.7 cm) USD 19,000. NEW YORK, 3 June 1983, *My Reminiscences as a Cowboy* (red, black and blue ink, 8½ x 11½ ins / 21.6 x 29.2 cm) USD 1,700. NEW YORK, 22 June 1984, *Greenland* (watercolour, 10 x 14 ins / 25.4 x 35.5 cm) USD 3,250. NEW YORK, 12 Sept 1985, *Nightmare* (1941, lithograph, 11 x 8 ins / 27.7 x 20.3 cm) USD 750. NEW YORK, 29 May 1986, *Haystack Farm, Ausable Fork, New York* (1946, oil on canvas, 27¾ x 44 ins / 70.5 x 111.8 cm) USD 46,000. NEW YORK, 3 Dec 1987, *Birches* (1921, oil on canvas, 34 x 44¼ ins / 86.4 x 112.3 cm) USD 57,500. NEW YORK, 26 May 1988, *Christmas, Adirondacks* (gouache, watercolour and pencil, 11 x 15 ins / 27.9 x 38.1 cm) USD 7,150. LOS ANGELES, 9 June 1988, *Scene from Faust* (ink, 7¼ x 11 ins / 18.5 x 28 cm) USD 1,045. NEW YORK, 1 Dec 1988, *Fresh Snow, Greenland* (oil on canvas, 20 x 24 ins / 50.8 x 61 cm) USD 12,650. NEW YORK, 28 Sept 1989, *Motherhood* (1913, oil on canvas, 32¼ x 42 ins / 82 x 106.8 cm) USD 22,000. NEW YORK, 14 March 1991, *Monhegan Village at Night* (oil on panel, 12 x 16 ins / 30.5 x 40.5 cm) USD 12,100. NEW YORK, 27 May 1992, *Garden of Oak Ridge, Virginia* (1956, oil on canvas, 28 x 38¼ ins / 71.1 x 97.2 cm) USD 17,600. NEW YORK, 23 Sept 1993, *Aasgard Farm* (oil on panel, 20 x 24 ins / 50.8 x 61 cm) USD 18,400. NEW YORK, 1 Dec 1994, *Igdlorssuit in Winter* (oil on canvas, 34 x 44 ins / 86.4 x 111.8 cm) USD 112,500. NEW YORK, 14 March 1996, *Greenland Landscape* (oil on canvas, 26 x 47 ins / 66 x 119.4 cm) USD 156,500. NEW YORK, 26 Sept 1996, *Calm (Tierra del Fuego)* (1922-1925, oil on canvas, 34 x 44 ins / 86.4 x 111.8 cm) USD 26,450. NEW YORK, 7 Oct 1997, *The Yacht Sara at Dawson Island* (oil on canvas, 27¼ x 42¼ ins / 69.2 x 107.4 cm) USD 36,800. NEW YORK, 1 Dec 1999, *Hay Bales, Evening. Below Whiteface* (oil on canvas, 35 x 44 ins / 88 x 112 cm) USD 65,000. NEW YORK, 1 Dec 1999, *Monhegan Harbour* (oil on canvas, 28 x 38 ins / 71 x 96 cm) USD 120,000. NEW YORK, 29 Nov 2000, *Rocky Inlet, Monhegan* (1909, oil on canvas, 38 x 44 ins / 96 x 112 cm) USD 170,000. NEW YORK, 30 Nov 2000, *April Ice* (1935-1937, oil on canvas, 34 x 44 ins / 86 x 113 cm) USD 120,000. NEW YORK, 17 May 2001, *Time Magazine Deluxe* (c. 1938, pen, ink, crayon and wash on board, six, 11 x 15 ins / 29 x 37 cm) USD 40,000. NEW YORK, 29 Nov 2001, *Wilderness* (oil on canvas laid on board, 28 x 34 ins / 71 x 86 cm) USD 120,000. NEW YORK, 2 May 2002, *Sermilik Fjord* (colour lithograph, 13 x 19 ins / 34 x 48 cm) USD 3,200. NEW YORK, 21 May 2002, *Untitled - Greenland Mountains and Sea* (oil on panel, two framed together, 24 x 90 ins / 61 x 229 cm) USD 24,000. NEW YORK, 21 May 2003, *Sermilik Fjord, Greenland* (oil on canvas laid on panel, 20 x 24 ins / 51 x 61 cm) USD 75,000. NEW YORK, 3 Dec

2003, *Blue Day, Greenland* (1935-1937, oil on canvas, 34 x 44 ins / 86 x 113 cm) USD 200,000. NEW YORK, 19 May 2004, *America's Steel Industry* (c. 1945, brush, pen, ink and lithographic crayon on paper, 13 x 18 ins / 33 x 46 cm) USD 18,000. NEW YORK, 19 May 2004, *Ice, Sea and Rock* (c. 1932-1933, oil on canvas, 26 x 47 ins / 66 x 119 cm) USD 100,000.

KENT, William

British, 18th century.

Born 1685, in Yorkshire; died 12 April 1748, in London.

Painter, engraver, draughtsman, architect. History painting, portraits, architectural views, designs for furniture.

William Kent came from a poor family. He was apprenticed to a carriage painter but ran away and set himself up as a portrait painter in London around 1704. He made enough friends to gather sufficient funds for a trip to Rome in 1710. There, he became a pupil of Luti and won a second-class medal at the academy. When his money was about to run out, a compatriot guaranteed him a living of 40 pounds sterling for seven years. After a brief return to England, he came back to Rome again.

In 1719, Kent returned permanently to London, where the patronage of Lord Burlington and later Sir Robert Walpole assured his success. Together with Lord Burlington Kent played an important role in forming contemporary English artistic taste, in line with the tastes he himself had formed during a series of Grand Tours with various patrons. A leading architect in the Palladian style, he was employed by Lord Burlington, for whom he decorated ceilings at Burlington House (which now houses the Royal Academy in London), as well as designed the interiors at Chiswick House. He worked on a number of major private and public buildings including Houghton, Holkham and Stowe; buildings in London for the Horse Guards and the Treasury. He was also a pioneering figure in landscape gardening, creating a style which asserted that 'all gardening is landscape painting'.

Kent produced paintings and engravings, though his abilities in these media did not match his excellence in architecture and garden design. He published architectural plates, including the *Designs of Inigo Jones* (1727) and illustrated works by Pope and Spenser as well as Gay's *Poems* (1720) and Thomson's *Seasons* (1730). He also designed the royal barge now exhibited at the National Maritime Museum in Greenwich.

On questions of taste in English court and aristocratic circles, Kent ruled supreme. He was consulted about the shape of furniture, ornaments and even clothes. He was named architect and first painter to the court and put in charge of conserving the Royal Collection of paintings. In 1730, he travelled to Italy for the third time. He enjoyed the protection of Lord Burlington up to his death, and was buried at his patron's home in Chiswick.

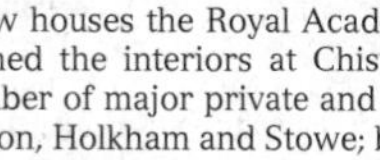

BIBLIOGRAPHY:

Wittkower, Rudolf, '*The Earl of Burlington and William Kent*' in *York Georgian Society, Occasional Papers* n° 5, periodical, York, 1948. Gilbert, Christopher, '*James Moore the Younger and William Kent at Sherborne House*' in *Burlington Magazine* vol. CXI n° 792, periodical, March 1969. Beard, Geoffrey, '*Willilam Kent and the Royal Barge*' in *Burlington Magazine* vol. CXII n° 809, periodical, August 1970. Beard, Geoffrey, '*William Kent and the Cabinet Makers*' in *Burlington Magazine* vol. CXVII n° 873, periodical, December 1975. Hayward, Helena/Kirkham, Pat, et al., *Two Eighteenth Century London Cabinet Makers*, London, 1980. Colvin, Howard, *A Biographical Dictionary of British Architects, 1600-1840*, London, 1995. Beard, Geoffrey, '*Kentian furniture by James Richards and others*' in *Apollo* vol. CLVI n° 491, periodical, January 2003.

MUSEUMS AND GALLERIES:

LONDON (Royal Collection): *The Battle of Agincourt (?)*; *The Marriage between Henry V and the Queen of France*; *The Marriage of Henry V* (1729).

AUCTION RECORDS:

LONDON, 14 Dec 1982, *The Garden of Eden* (pen and wash, 8 x 13 1/2 ins / 20.2 x 34.5 cm) GBP 1,500. LONDON, 7 July 1983, *Project for the Decoration of the Saloon, Houghton Hall, Norfolk* (pen and wash, two drawings, 10 3/4 x 10 ins / 27.5 x 25.7 cm) GBP 14,000. LONDON, 30 April 1987, *Project for a Mantlepiece* (pen and brown wash/pencil outlines, 13 1/4 x 9 1/2 ins / 33.5 x 24 cm) GBP 16,500. PARIS, 13 June 2001, *Study for Royal Coat of Arms* (c. 1725, pen, ink and wash, 12 x 19 ins / 31 x 48 cm) FRF 185,000. PARIS, 13 June 2001, *Study for Fireplace* (pen, ink and wash, 16 x 13 ins / 40 x 32 cm) FRF 225,000. CHICAGO, 1 June 2003, *Alder Ffly* (carved sugar and maple, 16 x 15x55 ins / 41 x 38x140 cm) USD 2,000. LONDON, 18 Nov 2004, *Design for a Chimney-piece for Thomas Coke for Holkham Hall, Norfolk* (black-brown ink and brown wash, 12 x 10 ins / 31 x 26 cm) GBP 5,800.

KENTISH, P.

British, 18th century.

Landscape artist.

P. Kentish exhibited at the Free Society in 1783.

KENTON, Mary Jean

American, 20th century.

Born in Grindstone (Pennsylvania).

Painter, installation artist, mixed media. Stage sets, artists' books.

Mary Jean Kenton has featured in several collective exhibitions, including: 1992, *De Bonnard à Baselitz - Dix ans d'enrichissements du Cabinet des estampes 1978-1988* (*From Bonnard to Baselitz: A Decade of Acquisitions by the Prints Collection 1978-1988*), in Paris and *Botanica: Contemporary Art and the World of Plants*, a travelling exhibition organised by the Tweed Museum of Art, University of Minnesota, Duluth. She was involved in the creation of the set for the ballet *Breakers* (1994) for Merce Cunningham.

BIBLIOGRAPHY:

Beaumont-Maillet, Laure/Woimant, Françoise/Pernoud, Emmanuel, *De Bonnard à Baselitz - Dix ans d'enrichissements du Cabinet des estampes 1978-1988*, exhibition catalogue, Bibliothèque nationale de France, Paris, 1992.

MUSEUMS AND GALLERIES:

PARIS (Prints Collection).

KENTRIDGE, William

South African, 20th - 21st century.

Born 28 April 1955, in Johannesburg.

Draughtsman, engraver, graphic designer, designer, film producer, sculptor. Multimedia, animated films. Land Art.

William Kentridge is the son of a human rights lawyer. He studied at King Edward VII School in Johannesburg and from 1973 to 1976 at the University of Witwatersrand, where he received a degree in political science and African studies. From 1976 to 1978, he studied at the Johannesburg Art Foundation under the direction of the painter Bill Ainslie. From 1978 to 1980, Kentridge taught engraving at the Johannesburg Art Foundation and in 1981-1982 studied mime and drama at the École Jacques Lecocq in Paris. He worked as an artistic director for television and in 1988 became one of the founders of the Free Filmakers Co-operative in Johannesburg. He was a member of the Junction Avenue Theatre Company from 1975 to 1991. It operated in Johannesburg and Soweto. He also worked as a theatre director. Kentridge was awarded the Carnegie Prize in 1999. He lives and works in Johannesburg.

In 1989, Kentridge made his first film in the *Soho Eckstein/Felix Teitlebaum* series, in which two contrasting but physically identical individuals confront their destinies. One is a corrupt capitalist industrialist and the other a poet in love with Mrs Eckstein. In 1992, he created his first theatre play, *Woyzeck on the Highveld*, in association with the Handspring Puppet Company. He also wrote an opera, *Il Ritorno d'Ulisse*. His multimedia oratorio *Zeno at 4 am* is a synthesis of animation, puppet theatre and shadow theatre to a composition by Kevin Volans. Kentridge takes his inspiration from the character of Zeno created by Italo Calvino and addresses the history of apartheid combined with his own personal history. He uses charcoal and pastel drawings as a storyboard when directing theatre and assembles them to create films. His method is not to add drawings but to erase them as the narrative sequences progress. This accentuates the theme of disappearance and personal deprivation, already very present in his work which is a poetic satire on South African society and the world of capitalism. His drawing style is powerful and expressive, his use of colour very restrained with landscape playing the role of 'metaphor of memory and oblivion'.

Kentridge has also produced Land Art, including *Memory and Geography*, 1995, on which he collaborated with Doris Bloom. This project has two parts. The first is an anatomical diagram of an enormous heart, drawn in white chalk in an arid landscape as if projected from the sky onto the earth. The drawing does not invade the landscape but is written on it like a sign. He also makes reference to the cave drawings of South Africa, celebrating the country's earliest artistic creations in a partnership between earth and the human body, which is one of Kentridge's main themes. The second part of the piece is an immense portal in the form of a stylised heart, placed flat in front of the Newton power station in Johannesburg. When night falls, hundreds of light bulbs around the edge of the portal are illuminated, giving the impression of a utopian entrance into the earth itself. The proximity of the power station enhances the quality of energy associated with the symbol of the heart and the way into a better world. In this piece, Kentridge successfully combines the metaphor of the living social body with the theme of liberation in the very land that produced the oppression of apartheid. The land thus becomes a symbol of history (artistic and political history) and of transition to a new and liberated modernity.

More recent work involves large-format etchings - for example, of processions of figures for casting in bronze.

Kentridge has taken part in many group exhibitions, including in 1994, *Un Art contemporain d'Afrique du Sud* (*Contemporary Art of South Africa*) at the Galerie de l'Esplanade, La Défense, Paris. In 1995, he showed his piece *Memory and Geography* at the Johannesburg Biennale. In 1997, he showed at Documenta X, Kassel, and at the Havana Biennale. In 2002, he took part in *Moving Pictures*, an exhibition exploring the use of photography, film and video in art since the late 1960s, shown at the Guggenheim Museum, New York. In 2003, he took part in *Apparition: the Action of Appearing* at Kettle's Yard, Cambridge, and in 2004 he exhibited at the Musée de Valence.

In 1998, the Palais des Beaux-Arts in Brussels presented a collection of Kentridge's work, which also toured the Kunstverein, Munich, the Museu d'Art Contemporani, Barcelona, the Serpentine Gallery, London, the Centre de la Vieille Charité, Marseilles and the Neue Galerie Graz at the Landesmuseum Joanneum in Austria. He also showed his work solo in 1999 at the Galerie Marian Goodman, Paris; in 2000 at the Stephen Friedman Gallery, London; in 2001-2002 at the New Museum, New York, the Museum of Contemporary Art, Chicago, the Hirshorn Museum and Sculpture Garden, Washington DC, the Contemporary Arts Museum, Houston, the Los Angeles County Museum and the South African National Gallery in Cape Town. In 2002, he had a solo exhibition, *William Kentridge: Felix in Exile*, at the Sprengel Museum, Hanover. In 2002, the *William Kentridge Retrospective* was held at the South African National Gallery, Cape Town; in 2004, he showed solo at the Castello di Rivoli, Turin, and in 2004, at K20 Kunstsammlung Nordrhein-Westphalia, Düsseldorf.

Bibliography:

Godby, Michael, '*William Kentridge: Four Animated Films*' in *William Kentridge: Drawings for Projection*, exhibition catalogue, Goodman Gall., Johannesburg, 1992. Kentridge, William, '*Image et Langage, Problèmes, Approches, Méthodes*' in *Cynos*, vol. II n° 1, periodical, Nice, 1994 (conference paper given by William Kentridge). Williamson, Sue/Jamal, Ashraf, '*William Kentridge: Devils and Angel*' in *Art in South Africa: The Future Present*, David Philip, Cape Town, Johannesburg, 1996. *Documenta X*, exhibition catalogue, Documenta, Kassel, 1997. Enwezor, Okwui, '*Reframing the Black Subject*' in *Third Text*, n° 40, periodical, London, Autumn 1997. Christov-Bakargiev, Carolyn, *William Kentridge*, exhibition catalogue, Société des Expositions du Palais des Beaux-Arts, Brussels, 1998. Cameron, Dan/Christov-Bakargiev, Carolyn/Coetzee, J.M., *William Kentridge*, Phaidon, London, 1999. Passera, Jean-Louis, '*William Kentridge*' in *Ohm*, n° 13, periodical, École supérieure d'Art, Caen, November 1999. Lebovici, Elisabeth, '*Kentridge, l'art de la gomme*' in *Libération*, periodical, Paris, 20 July 2000. Boris, Staci/Cameron, Dan/Benezra, Neal, et al., *William Kentridge*, exhibition catalogue, Museum of Contemporary Art, Chicago, 2001. *Moving Pictures*, group exhibition catalogue, Solomon R. Guggenheim Museum, New York, 2002. Kentridge, William, in *Max Beckmann*, exhibition catalogue, Tate Modern, London, 2002 (essay). Champenois, Michèle, '*Éloge de l'insomnie par Kentridge*' in *Le Monde*, periodical, Paris, 20 September 2002. Malbert, Roger, *Apparition: the action of appearing*, group exhibition catalogue, Arnolfini, Bristol, 2003. Bakargiev, Carolyn Christov/Taylor, Jane, *William Kentridge*, Skira, Geneva, 2004.

Museums and Galleries:

Bremen (Kunsthalle): *Eye-to-Eye* (1994, mixed media on paper) - Durban (AG): *Miners in Tunnel* (1991, charcoal on paper) - Johannesburg (AG): *Crowd and Covered Monument 1* (1990, charcoal on paper) - London (Tate Collection): *Arc/Procession: Develop, Catch Up, Even Surpass* (1990, charcoal and pastel/paper) - New York (MoMA): *Soho Leaking* (1999, charcoal and pastel on paper) - New York (Solomon R. Guggenheim Mus.): *History of the Main Complaint* (1996, animation film); *Felix in Exile* (1994, animation film) - San Diego (MCA Downtown): *Industrial Landscape* (1997-1998); *Soho with Head on Rock* (1997-1998); *Soho Holding Cup and Stone to Ear* (1997-1998, charcoal and pastel on paper) - Washington DC (Hirshhorn Mus. and Sculpture Garden): *Blue Head* (1993-1998, aquatint, drypoint and etching/paper); *Drawing from 'Stereoscope'* (1999, charcoal and pastel/paper); *Reeds* (1996, etching, aquatint, drypoint and hand coloring/paper).

KENZAN, real name: Koremasa Ogata, original forename: Iin, nickname: Kenzan, Gompei, Shinsei, pseudonyms: Shisui, Shuseido, Reikai, Toin
Japanese, 17th - 18th century.
Born 1663, in Kyoto Prefecture; died 1743.
Potter, painter.

Kenzan was the brother of Korin Ogata, the great Edo painter (1658-1716), and became known first as a ceramicist. He and Ninsei Nonomura introduced a new form of richly decorated ceramic art, which was very successful in the Genroku period (1668-1703). The son of Soken Ogata, Kenzan received a very good education and revealed clear gifts for calligraphy and poetry. He was also initiated into Zen and took the name Shinsei. In 1697 he opened his own kiln at Narutaki, in the hills to the north of Kyoto, and definitively adopted the name Kenzan. He made square dishes on which he asked his brother Korin to draw light sketches in iron brown, reminiscent of his ink drawings. Kenzan then added Japanese or Chinese poems, in his highly personal calligraphy. In 1713 he closed his kiln and opened a ceramics shop in the city centre. His output was very varied, as were his motifs, from birds or Chinese dragons in panels, to large flowers in bright colours and sketches drawing on ink wash techniques. In 1731 Kenzan moved to Edo (now Tokyo) and set up a kiln in Iriya. At the very end of his life he devoted himself primarily to painting, combining his talent as a decorator with his sense of poetry. His calligraphy, which often figures in his painting, creates a pleasant harmony in, for example, *Hollyhocks, Plant with its Fruit* and *Willows in Spring*, or a square pauwlonia-wood basket, with a decoration in ink enhanced with gold and colours, all of which are preserved at the Yamato Bunkakan museum in Nara. Kenzan left disciples in Edo and Kyoto, so that his style persisted for many years, although with less elegance and without the refined, poetic sensibility that give a particular flavour to the work of this master.

Bibliography:
Paine, Robert Treat/Soper, Alexander, *The Art and Architecture of Japan*, Penguin, London, 1955. Paul-David, Madeleine, '*Kenzan Ogata*' in *Encyclopædia Universalis* vol. IX, Paris, 1971. Kawahara, Masahiko, *The Ceramic Art of Ogata Kenzan (Japanese Arts Library, Vol 13)*, Kodansha America, New York, 1985. Wilson, Richard L., *The Art of Ogata Kenzan: Persona and Production in Japanese Ceramics*, Weatherhill, New York, 1991. Wilson, Richard L., *The Potter's Brush: The Kenzan Style in Japanese Ceramics*, Washington, D.C.: Freer Gallery of Art: Arthur M. Sackler Gallery, Smithsonian Institution, New York, 2002.

KEOU YUE-KI
Chinese, 20th - 21st century.
Born 1955.
Painter.

Keou is a painter in the Huxian region. She was a member of the brigade of Siaowangtchouang, a poor district in Tawang.

KEOU-LONG CHOUANG. See **SHUANG GOULONG**

KEPES, György
Hungarian, 20th century.
Born 1906, in Selyp.
Active in the USA.
Painter. Murals, designs for stained glass, designs for mosaics.

György Kepes studied at the academy of fine arts in Budapest, and at the end of the 1920s took part in the activities of the Munka group. From 1930 to 1932 he worked in Berlin, where he met Moholy-Nagy. He then worked as a teacher in the USA, and collaborated on the publication of scientific works devoted to art.

He exhibited regularly, particularly in Chicago and New York.

He engaged in numerous artistic activities: photogrammes, paintings and mural decorations.

Auction records:
New York, 2 Nov 1984, *Sanctuary 2* (1965, sand and oil on canvas, 14 x 18 ins / 35.5 x 45.7 cm) USD 1,300. New York, 7 May 1986, *Colour Harvest* (1968, sand and oil on canvas, 60 x 60 ins / 152.4 x 152.4 cm) USD 2,200. New York, 10 April 1987, *Moon* (1955, sand and oil on canvas, 36 x 72 ins / 91.5 x 183 cm) USD 2,800. New York, 29 Sept 1993, *Broken Light* (1959, oil on canvas, 25 x 30 ins / 63.5 x 76.2 cm) USD 2,070.

KEPFER, Maximilien Pierre
French, 19th century.
Born 1798.
Active in Paris.
Painter, draughtsman.

Maximilien Kepfer was a pupil of Abel de Pujol.

KEPHISODOROS. See also **CEPHISODOROS**

KEPPEL-HESSELINK, Herman Gysbert
Dutch, 19th century.
Born 21 November 1811, in Zutphen.
Painter.

Herman Keppel-Hesselink was a pupil of W. van der Worp and B.-J. van Hove in The Hague.

KEPPENS, Jules
Belgian, 20th century.
Born 1910, in Lebbeke; died 1992.
Painter. Local scenes, interiors, landscapes, architectural views, seascapes, flowers.

Jules Keppens was a student of F. Willaert and Félix Gogo at the fine arts academy in Termonde.

Auction records:
Lokeren, 11 March 1995, *View of Baasrode* (1943, oil on canvas, 39 1/4 x 47 1/4 ins / 100 x 120 cm) BEF 36,000. Lokeren, 9 March 1996, *View of Baasrode* (1943, oil on canvas, 39 1/4 x 47 1/4 ins / 100 x 120 cm) BEF 36,000. Lokeren, 8 March 1997, *Vissersboten te temse* (oil on canvas, 23 1/2 x 31 1/2 ins / 60 x 80 cm) BEF 20,000.

KEPPLER, Richard Ernst
German, 19th century.
Born 27 March 1851, in Stuttgart.
Painter, illustrator.

Keppler worked mainly in Munich and Vienna, and towards the end of his life concentrated principally on book illustrations.

KERBOUR, Jean, or Kerbourc'h
French, 20th century.
Born 22 April 1930, in Quimper.
Painter. Landscapes.

Jean Kerbour taught himself to paint. He moved to Paris in 1950 and while continuing to paint decided to study philosophy at the Sorbonne. At the same time he pursued a career as a journalist. In his early career he painted landscapes of Brittany but his work gradually became more abstract. Despite the austerity of his approach, dominated by black, his Abstract work retains a lyrical quality. He exhibited at the Salon des Réalités Nouvelles in Paris but exhibited relatively little and showed his work in Paris on just a few occasions (1966, 1971, 1974, 1975, 1986 and 1988).

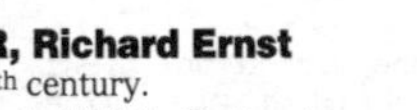

Auction records:
Paris, 8 Oct 1989, *Untitled* (1954, oil and gouache/paper, 25 1/4 x 19 ins / 64 x 48 cm) FRF 4,800.

KERBRAT, Jean
French, 20th century.
Born 28 September 1939, in Mayenne.
Sculptor, installation artist.

Jean Kerbrat studied at the École des Beaux-Arts in Caen, the École des Beaux-Arts in Rouen and the École des Beaux-Arts in Paris from 1959 to 1964. In 1967 he became a teacher at the École d'Architecture of Normandy.

An official sculptor, Kerbrat executed some 50 monumental pieces including fountains and low reliefs for private and public commissions in the following: Creil (1975-1984); Juvisy (1984); Val de Reuil (1986); St-Pierre-du-Vauvray (1988); Évreux (1989); Darnétal (1990); and Rouen, Vésoul, Amiens, Cléon and Nancy. He later abandoned this form of expression to work on engaged art, such as his *Direct Action*, a cart immersed in a galvanizing bath. He also uses photographs and slides which allow him to combine family recollections with historical documents and the collective and individual memories. He was an active and outspoken opponent of the Gulf War. In his installation *Numina Sunt Nomina* of 1993 he assembled blocks composed half of black granite and half of white marble onto which he projected the engraved photographic image of his grandmother institutionalised in a psychiatric hospital in Mayenne. Each block is linked by a glass bar on which are engraved the names of political prisoners and their prison numbers, which appear and disappear.

Kerbrat has taken part in numerous group exhibitions: *Formes Humaines* (*Human Forms*) at the Musée Rodin in Paris (1966-1982); at the École d'Architecture of Normandy (1987); at the Foire Internationale d'Art Contemporain in Paris (1989, 1992); at the Abbaye St-Ouen in Rouen (1991); at the Hôtel des Arts in Paris (1992); and at the Centre d'Art CREDAC in Ivry-sur-Seine (1993). Since 1973 he has shown his work in numerous solo exhibitions, including at the following: the Musée du Havre (1973); the Musée de Bayeux (1975); the École d'Architecture of Normandy (1988); the Galerie du Génie in Paris (1990); the Centre d'Art Contemporain in Jouy-sur-Eure (1991); Barcelona (1992); and the A.B. galleries and contemporary galleries of the Musée National d'Art Moderne in Paris (1993).

BIBLIOGRAPHY:

Smulders, Caroline, '*Jean Kerbrat*' in *Art Press*, no. 155, periodical, Paris, February 1991. Piguet, Philippe, '*Jean Kerbrat*' in *Art Press*, no. 183, periodical, Paris, July-Aug 1993.

KERCKHOFF, Frans

Dutch, 17th century.
Active in Groningen c. 1661.
Painter. Still-lifes.

AUCTION RECORDS:

NEW YORK, 18 May 1994, *Still-life with Partridges, Sparrows, Ducks and Woodcocks Hanging or on a Stone Entablature* (oil on panel, a pair, each 23 x 18 1/2 ins / 57.5 x 46.7 cm) USD 10,120.

KERCKHOVE, Antoine Joseph van den, called Nelson

Belgian, 19th century.
Born 1 May 1849, in Brussels.
Sculptor.

Antoine van den Kerckhove was the son of Augustin van den Kerckhove and lived for many years in London and Paris (1890-1910).

MUSEUMS AND GALLERIES:

BRUSSELS.

AUCTION RECORDS:

LOKEREN, 11 March 1995, *Merveilleuse* (bronze, h. 22 1/4 ins / 56.5 cm, w. 13 1/2 ins/34 cm) BEF 75,000. LOKEREN, 10 March 2001, *Young Woman with a Rose* (dark brown patinated bronze, 27 x 17 ins / 68 x 42 cm) BEF 110,000. AHLDEN, 9 May 2003, *Bust of a Woman* (gold patinated bronze, h. 28ins / 70cm) EUR 1,900.

KERCKHOVE, Antoine van den

Belgian, 19th century.
Sculptor.

Antoine van den Kerckhove worked in Antwerp and exhibited in Brussels at the Salon of 1851.

KERCKHOVE, Antonia van den

Belgian, 19th century.
Active in Brussels.
Sculptor.

Antonia van den Kerckhove exhibited at the Brussels Salon of 1848.

KERCKHOVE, Arthur van den

Belgian, 19th century.
Sculptor.

Arthur van den Kerckhove exhibited in Brussels and Antwerp around 1872 to 1873.

KERCKHOVE, Auguste van den

Belgian, 19th century.
Born 1825, in Antwerp; died 1895, in Brussels.
Sculptor. Still-lifes.

Auguste van den Kerckhove worked mainly in Brussels but exhibited at the Royal Academy in London.

AUCTION RECORDS:

NEW YORK, 25 Feb 1987, *Autumn Bouquet* (oil on canvas, 21 1/2 x 26 ins / 54.6 x 66 cm) USD 5,500.

KERCKHOVE, Ernest van den

Belgian, 19th century.
Born 1840, in Brussels; died 19 March 1879, in Schaerbeek.
Painter. History painting, genre scenes.

Ernest van den Kerckhove won the Grand Prix de Rome. He lived in Rome and Paris for many years.

AUCTION RECORDS:

LONDON, 10 Oct 1969, *The Antique Dealer's*, Gns 650. NEW YORK, 2 April 1976, *Choosing a Fan* (1877, oil on panel, 28 1/4 x 21 ins / 72 x 52.5 cm) USD 1,800. BRUSSELS, 28 Sept 1999, *Betrayal* (1874, oil on panel, 29 x 20 ins / 73 x 52 cm) BEF 120,000. BRUSSELS, 29 Feb 2000, *Betrayal* (1874, oil on panel, 29 x 20 ins / 73 x 52 cm) BEF 140,000.

KERCKHOVE, Godefroid van de

Belgian, 19th - 20th century.
Born 1841, in Antwerp; died 1913, in Brussels, in 1915 in Ukkel, according to some sources.
Sculptor. Allegorical subjects. Busts.

Godefroid van de Kerckhove was the son of Jan van den Kerckhove. He was a student at the academy in Antwerp and later professor at the Schaerbeek academy.

MUSEUMS AND GALLERIES:

BRUSSELS.

KERCKHOVE, J. B. van der

Flemish School, 18th century.
Died 1772.
Painter.

J.B. van der Kerckhove worked for the church of St Peter in St Petersburg.

KERCKHOVE, Jan van de

Belgian, 20th century.
Born 1927, in Courtrai.
Sculptor, potter.

Jan van de Kerckhove was a student at the fine arts academy in Courtrai, where he subsequently taught. His works are figurative verging on the abstract.

KERCKHOVE, Jean Baptiste van den

Belgian, 19th century.
Active in Brussels in 1866.
Sculptor.

Jean Baptiste van den Kerckhove exhibited his sculpture *Eve* at the Brussels Salon.

KERCKHOVE, Jean François van den

Belgian, 19th century.

Born c. 1815, in Antwerp; died 29 November 1885, in St Joost, near Brussels.
Sculptor.
Jean François van den Kerckhove was a pupil of G. Geef and exhibited at the Brussels Salon from 1848 to 1872.

KERCKHOVE, Jean Ives van den
Belgian, 19th century.
Active in Brussels.
Sculptor.
Jean Ives van den Kerckhove exhibited busts at the Salon of 1873.

KERCKHOVE, Joseph van den.
See **KERKHOVE**

KERCKHOVE, Louis van den
Belgian, 19th century.
Born 1814, in Antwerp; died in Brussels.
Sculptor.
The museum in Ypres has a statue entitled *Veiled Cupid* by Louis van den Kerckhove.

KERCKHOVE, Louise van de
Flemish School, 19th - 20th century.
Born 1860.
Active near Bruges.
Painter, engraver. Landscapes, seascapes.
Louise van de Kerckhove was the daughter of Jan van de Kerckhove.

KERCKHOVE, Paul van den
Belgian, 20th century.
Born 23 October 1876, in St Joost.
Sculptor. Busts, monuments.
Paul van den Kerckhove was the son of the sculptor Josef Anton van den Kerckhove, and a student of Léon Mignon in Brussels and of J.L. Gérôme in Paris. He spent many years in England. He produced portrait busts and commemorative monuments.

KERCKHOVEN, Jacob van de.
See **KERKHOVEN**

KERCKX, Jean Baptiste
Belgian, 19th century.
Born 1 May 1853, in Antwerp.
Sculptor.
Jean Baptiste Kerckx studied at the Koninklijke Academie voor Schone Kunsten in Antwerp. In 1833 he was given a temporary teaching post at the academy and a permanent one in 1892.

KERELS, Henri
Belgian, 20th century.
Born 1896, in Molenbeek-St-Jean; died 1956, in Ixelles (Brussels).
Painter, engraver.
Henri Kerels was a student at the fine arts academy in Brussels and later became a teacher at the academy in his native town. His style evolved towards *Art informel.*
AUCTION RECORDS:
LOKEREN, 21 March 1992, *Composition* (1956, oil on canvas, 17¾ x 22 ins / 45 x 55 cm) BEF 26,000. BRUSSELS, 7 Dec 2004, *Congolese Woman* (oil on canvas, 24 x 20 ins / 60 x 50 cm) EUR 1,500.

KERENYI, Jeno
Hungarian, 20th century.
Born 1909; died 1975.
Sculptor. Groups, monuments.
After studying at the college of fine arts, Jeno Kerenyi travelled around Italy. His work ranges from small sculptures to groups to monumental statues. He completed his *Monument to Ostapenko* in Budapest in 1951 and the *Monument to the Workers' Movement* in Nagykanizsa in 1964.

He exhibited from 1938 and took part in the Venice Biennale. He was awarded the Grand Prix in Brussels (1960), the Kossuth prize and the Munkácsy prize.
BIBLIOGRAPHY:
Gabor, Pogany Ö., *Kéréyi Jeno. 1908-1975*, exhibition catalogue, Magyar Nemzeti Galéria, Budapest, 1976.
MUSEUMS AND GALLERIES:
BUDAPEST (Magyar Nemzeti Gal.).

KEREVEL, Tiennick
Belgian, 20th - 21st century.
Born 1956, in Kinshasa.
Active in France.
Engraver, draughtsman.
From 1975 to 1979, Tiennick Kerevel studied engraving at the Académie Royale des Beaux Arts in Brussels. He lives and works in Marseilles. He took part in the exhibition *De Bonnard à Baselitz - Dix ans d'enrichissements du Cabinet des estampes 1978-1988* (*From Bonnard to Baselitz: A Decade of Acquisitions by the Prints Collection 1978-1988*) at the Bibliothèque Nationale in Paris in 1992.
BIBLIOGRAPHY:
Beaumont-Maillet, Laure/Woimant, Françoise/Pernoud, Emmanuel, *De Bonnard à Baselitz - Dix ans d'enrichissements du Cabinet des estampes 1978-1988*, exhibition catalogue, Bibliothèque nationale de France, Paris, 1992.
MUSEUMS AND GALLERIES:
PARIS (Prints Collection) - TOULOUSE (Bibliothèque Municipale).

KERG, Théo
Luxembourg, 20th century.
Born 2 June 1909, in Niedercorn.
Active in France.
Painter, sculptor, draughtsman, illustrator.
Théo Kerg was a student in the design faculty of the École Nationale des Beaux-Arts in Paris, and then at the Institut d'Art et d'Archéologie. He spent time in Munich and Luxembourg, where he became a professor of drawing, and subsequently settled in Paris.

Kerg was associated with the Abstraction-Création group, though he cannot be strictly classified as an abstract artist. Kerg's canvases consist of a network of innumerable interlacing lines and luminous colours - reds and oranges - which create an enamel-like surface of tiny spaces. However, the titles of his works reveal his intentions: *Vaults of the Night, The Street Turns in the Light*, and *The Mathematics of Roofs*, as well as cityscapes, including views of *Basel, Bern, Fribourg*, and *Paris - In the Shadow of Notre-Dame*. Between 1957 and 1959, he developed a technique based on touch, known as *tactilism*, which used materials such as wood, cardboard, sand, pebbles or polyester that respond differently to the play of light. From 1959 to 1970, as these materials began to encroach on the third dimension, he progressed to the construction of reliefs.

Kerg exhibited at the Salon de l'Art Mural, the Salon des Indépendants, at exhibitions of the *Abstraction-Création* group, and under the general title *Lunar and Terrestrial Tactilism* (1959). He illustrated Paul Éluard's *Dignes de vivre* (*Fit to Live*) and Paul Valery's *Cimetière marin* (*Cemetery by the Sea*).

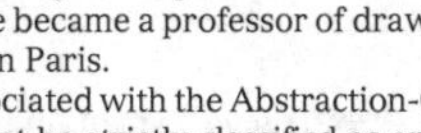

BIBLIOGRAPHY:
Cichy, Bodo, *Moderne Malerei, Beginn und Entwicklung*, E. E. Thoma, Munich, 1965. Kerg, Théo, *Théo Kerg: Naissance et Evolution du Tactilisme, 1956-1974. Tableaux Tactilistes, Graphismes, Vitraux, Environnements*, exhibition catalogue, Musée de Rennes, Rennes, 1974. Kerg, Théo, *Retrospective:*

Théo Kerg, exhibition catalogue, Musée des Beaux-Arts, Moutier, 1981.

MUSEUMS AND GALLERIES:

BASEL (Kunstmus.) - BERN (Kunstmus.) - FRIBOURG (MAH) - GENEVA (Petit Palais) - GRENOBLE (Mus. de Grenoble) - LAUSANNE (Cantonal MFA) - LILLE (MMA) - LUXEMBOURG (Mus. national d'histoire et d'art) - PARIS (MAM) - PARIS (Prints Collection): *Tombstone for the Rights of Man* (1965, lithograph) - TOULOUSE (Musée Municipal D'art Moderne) - ZURICH (MMA).

AUCTION RECORDS:

PARIS, 31 May 1954, *Fishmongers*, FRF 50,000. VERSAILLES, 7 March 1976, *On the Coast* (oil on canvas, 19 3/4 x 27 1/2 ins / 50 x 70 cm) FRF 2,500. NEUILLY, 20 June 1988, *Big Margot* (oil on paper, 11 1/2 x 13 1/2 ins / 29.5 x 34 cm) FRF 5,500. PARIS, 3 March 1989, *Rocky* (oil on canvas, 15 x 24 ins / 38 x 61 cm) FRF 10,500. PARIS, 18 Feb 1990, *Flames* (1961, oil and various materials/canvas, 35 3/4 x 22 1/2 ins / 91 x 57 cm) FRF 15,500. PARIS, 27 Jan 1992, *Les filets verts* (oil on canvas, 9 1/2 x 13 ins / 24 x 33 cm) FRF 5,500. NEUILLY, 17 June 1992, *Derricks* (oil on canvas, 28 3/4 x 21 1/4 ins / 73 x 54 cm) FRF 14,000. PARIS, 27 March 1995, *Untitled* (1960, oil on paper, 5 x 7 ins / 12.8 x 17.5 cm) FRF 7,000.

KERGA
French, 20th century.
Born 1899; died 1956.
Painter. Landscapes, seascapes.

In 1994 the Musée des Jacobins in Morlaix held a retrospective exhibition of Kerga's work entitled *Kerga, le Peintre de la Baie de Morlaix* (*Kerga, the Painter from Morlaix Bay*).

KERGEL, Carl Franz Ludwig
German, 19th century.
Born 23 January 1814, in Strehla (Elbe); died 2 November 1874, in Dresden.
Painter. Genre scenes, architectural views.

Kergel trained at the academy in Dresden, and first exhibited in about 1837. He exhibited in Dresden, Munich and Vienna.

KERHOR, Jean, pseudonym of André Dupuis Kerhor
French, 19th - 20th century.
Born 2 April 1876, in Langres; died 7 January 1974, in Paris.
Illustrator, engraver.

Jean Kerhor was a member of the Société Coloniale des Artistes Français. He worked for the Ministry of Colonies, producing stamps and drawings. Kerhor was made a Chevalier de la Légion d'Honneur.

KERI, Adam
Hungarian, 20th century.
Mixed media. Artists' books.

Adam Keri took part in *De Bonnard à Baselitz - Dix ans d'enrichissements du Cabinet des estampes 1978-1988* (*From Bonnard to Baselitz: A Decade of Acquisitions by the Prints Collection 1978-1988*) at the Bibliothèque Nationale in Paris in 1992. He made a lithograph for the *Homage to Bartok* collective album (1979).

BIBLIOGRAPHY:

Beaumont-Maillet, Laure/Woimant, Françoise/Pernoud, Emmanuel, *De Bonnard à Baselitz - Dix ans d'enrichissements du Cabinet des estampes 1978-1988*, exhibition catalogue, Bibliothèque nationale de France, Paris, 1992.

MUSEUMS AND GALLERIES:

PARIS (Prints Collection).

KERIN, Patrick
Irish, 17th century.
Born c. 1618.
Sculptor.

Patrick Kerin worked in the area of Limerick as well as in Emly and Kilkenny.

KERIN, Walter
Irish, 16th - 17th century.
Sculptor.

Walter Kerin produced sculptures in Callan and Dungarvan.

KERINGER, Albert Joseph
French, 20th century.
Born in Mulhouse.
Painter. Landscapes.

Albert Joseph Keringer exhibited in Paris at the Salon des Indépendants from 1905.

KERIUS, Peter
Dutch, 16th - 17th century.
Active in Amsterdam, between 1590 and 1620.
Engraver.

Peter Kerius produced a *View of Nuremberg* and a work entitled *Procession of Monks*.

KERKEN, Willem
Flemish School, 18th century.
Active in Antwerp.
Sculptor.

Willem Kerken's son was a painter of historical subjects in Antwerp around 1736. Willem Kerken is known for his work in churches, including altars, low reliefs and epitaphs.

KERKHAM, Earl
American, 20th century.
Born 1890, in Virginia; died 1965.
Painter. Portraits.

Earl Kerkham attended the Académie de la Grande Chaumière in Paris, around 1930 and after World War II. He has taken part in collective exhibitions and has had several solo shows in the USA. Jacques Villon had a major influence on his work, which is particularly noted for its long series of self-portraits.

AUCTION RECORDS:

NEW YORK, 11 May 1967, *Self-portrait No. 8*, USD 1,200. NEW YORK, 31 March 1994, *Female Nudes* (watercolour and pencil/paper, three drawings, 18 x 12 ins / 45.7 x 30.5 cm and 15 x 10 3/4 ins/38.1 x 27.3 cm) USD 978. CHICAGO, 9 May 1999, *Self-portrait* (red chalk, 15 x 11 ins / 38 x 28 cm) USD 2,600. CHICAGO, 1 June 2003, *Self-portrait No. 2* (oil on board, 24 x 15 ins / 61 x 38 cm) USD 4,250.

KERKHOFF, Daniel
Dutch, 18th - 19th century.
Born 1766, in Amsterdam; died 1831, in Amsterdam.
Draughtsman, watercolourist.

Daniel Kerkhoff painted mainly military scenes. He studied under P. Pietersz. Barbier and was very highly regarded by his contemporaries.

MUSEUMS AND GALLERIES:

HAARLEM (Teylers Mus.): drawings - ROTTERDAM (Mus. Boijmans Van Beuningen): several works - VIENNA (Albertina Mus.): drawings.

KERKHOVE, Frédéric Jean Louis van de
Flemish School, 19th century.
Born 4 September 1862, in Bruges; died 12 August 1873, in Bruges.
Painter.

Frédéric van de Kerkhove was a child prodigy and by the age of 11 had made over 600 drawings and landscapes, mostly copied from illustrations in *Tour du Monde* and *Magasin Pittoresque*.

AUCTION RECORDS:

PARIS, 19 Sept 1946, *Riverbank* (note indicating that the artist executed this painting at the age of 10 and a half) FRF 3,700. PARIS, 18 March 1955, *Landscape* (1872) FRF 12,500.

KERKHOVE, Jaak van de
Belgian, 20th century.
Painter.

KERKHOVE, Jean van de
Flemish School, 19th century.
Born 1822; died 26 December 1881, in Schaerbeek.
Active in Thielt.
Painter, engraver. History painting, genre scenes.
Jean van de Kerkhove was a pupil of Wappers and Rudder.

KERKHOVE, Johannes van den
Flemish School, 16th century.
Painter.
Antwerp School.
Johannes van den Kerkhove worked in the guild of Antwerp in 1575 and 1580.

KERKHOVE, Joseph van den, or Kerckhove
Flemish School, 17th - 18th century.
Born 4 May 1667, in Bruges; died 8 August 1724, in Bruges.
Painter. Religious subjects, portraits, still-lifes.
In 1682, Joseph van den Kerkhove was a pupil of J. van Meunincxhove and later of E. Quellinus in Antwerp. He became a master artist in 1695 and after a trip to Frankfurt founded the Bruges academy and became its director. He is known to have been in Angers in 1691 and in Nantes in 1693 under the name Joseph van den Kerchove. He painted the ceiling of Ostend town hall and also produced paintings of churches.

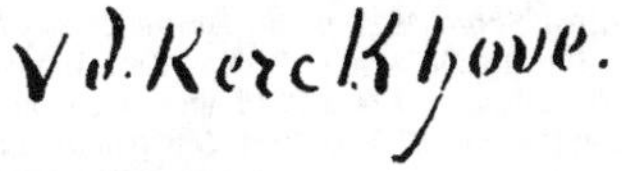

MUSEUMS AND GALLERIES:
BRUGES: *St Catherine of Siena* - CLAMECY: *Flemish Burghers*.
AUCTION RECORDS:
MILAN, 27 Oct 1987, *Still-life with Fruits and Doves* (oil on canvas) ITL 34,000,000. MONACO, 3 July 1993, *Still-life with Fish* (oil on canvas) FRF 144,300. MILAN, 4 Nov 1986, *Still-life with Game and Fruits* (oil on canvas, 53 1/4 x 69 ins / 135 x 175 cm) ITL 34,000,000.

KERKHOVEN, van den
Flemish School, 19th century.
Lithographer.
Van den Kerkhoven worked for the *Portrait Gallery of Flemish and Dutch Painters*, 1826.

KERKHOVEN, Conrad van den
Flemish School, 17th century.
Active in Mechelen c. 1637.
Sculptor.

KERKHOVEN, Jacob van de, called Giacomo da Castello
Flemish School, 17th century.
Born c. 1637, in Antwerp; died c. 1712, in Venice.
Painter. Still-lifes.
This artist is believed to have been born in Antwerp where he studied with Jan Fyt in 1649. He settled in Venice in about 1660 and is last mentioned in 1712. His work was represented in the exhibition *Stille Welt. Italienische Stilleben aus drei Jahrhunderten* (*Still World: Three Centuries of Italian Still-lifes*) held at the Kunsthalle der Hypo-Kulturstiftung in Munich in 2003.
BIBLIOGRAPHY:
Safarik, E./Bottari, F., *La natura morta in Italia*, Electa, Milan, 1989. Gregori, Mina/Prinz, Johann Georg, *Stille Welt. Italienische Stilleben aus drei Jahrhunderten*, exhibition catalogue, Kunsthalle der Hypo-Kulturstiftung, Munich, 2003.
MUSEUMS AND GALLERIES:
STUTTGART (Staatsgal.).
AUCTION RECORDS:
NEW YORK, 15 Jan 1988, *Still-life with Fish, Shells and Vegetables on a Table* (oil on canvas, 18 x 23 ins / 45.7 x 58.5 cm) USD 17,600. LONDON, 12 Dec 1990, *Cock, Hens and Ducks with a Jewel* (oil on canvas, 38 1/2 x 45 ins / 98 x 114 cm) GBP 13,200. LONDON, 10 Dec 1993, *Goose, Ducks, Turkey and Other Fowl with Onions, Oysters and Cabbages on a Entablature* (oil on canvas, 47 1/4 x 61 ins / 119.8 x 154 cm) GBP 23,000. LONDON, 16 April 1997, *Still-life with a Hare, Birds in a Basket and Vegetables* (oil on canvas, oval, 30 x 37 1/2 ins / 75.3 x 95 cm) GBP 3,220.

KERKHOVEN, Léonard van den
Belgian, 19th century.
Born c. 1828; died September 1898, in Geneva.
Painter, engraver.
Léonard van den Kerkhoven was a pupil of Wiertz. He exhibited a painting entitled *River in Flanders* at the Salon of 1848.
AUCTION RECORDS:
NEW YORK, 15 Nov 1946, *Flowers and Fruit*, USD 300.

KERKOVIUS, Ida
Latvian, 20th century.
Born 31 August 1879, in Riga; died 7 July 1970, in Stuttgart.
Active in Germany.
Painter, pastellist, watercolourist, mixed media.
Figures, nudes, landscapes, still-lifes. Designs for tapestries.
In 1903 Ida Kerkovius travelled around Italy and Germany. She studied art in Berlin and was a pupil of A. Hölzel at the academy of fine arts in Stuttgart. From 1920 to 1923 she attended the Bauhaus, notably the weaving studio, where she met Klee, Kandinsky and Itten. In 1933 the Nazi regime banned her from painting, her work being denounced as 'degenerate art'. She then travelled until 1939, when she returned to Stuttgart. In 1944 her studio was destroyed and the vast majority of her works were lost. She obtained a job as a teacher in 1958, and in 1963 she was appointed honorary president of the Deutscher Künstlerbund (German artists' association).

Her works, with their luminous colours, come close to abstraction due to her use of symbols, whose task it is to convey the real world and owes much to Hölder, Klee and Jawlensky.

BIBLIOGRAPHY:
Leonhard, Kurt, *Ida Kerkovius - Leben und Werk*, DuMont Schauberg, Cologne, 1967.
MUSEUMS AND GALLERIES:
AMSTERDAM (Stedelijk Mus.) - DUISBURG - MANNHEIM - STUTTGART (Staatsgal.): *Nudes Standing* (1911); *Abstract Still-life* (1935).
AUCTION RECORDS:
COLOGNE, 30 Nov 1971, *Figure and Angel* (pastel) DEM 4,600. COLOGNE, 30 Nov 1973, *Strolling*, DEM 8,400. HAMBURG, 3 June 1976, *Mountainous Landscape* (c. 1960, coloured chalks, 19 1/2 x 26 1/2 ins / 49.4 x 67.2 cm) DEM 3,600. HAMBURG, 3 June 1977, *Flowers Against Blue* (1968, oil on panel, 17 3/4 x 25 ins / 45.1 x 63.7 cm) DEM 7,000. MUNICH, 28 May 1979, *Animals* (1969, oil on canvas, 15 3/4 x 19 3/4 ins / 40 x 50 cm) DEM 6,800. MUNICH, 27 Nov 1979, *Mountain People* (c. 1925, watercolour/canvas, 15 1/4 x 19 3/4 ins / 38.5 x 50 cm) DEM 29,000. BERN, 24 June 1981, *Garden Shelter* (c. 1930, oil on canvas remounted on board, 9 x 12 ins / 23 x 30.5 cm) CHF 11,000. HAMBURG, 12 June 1982, *Bird* (coloured chalks,

10¼ x 11 ins / 26.2 x 28 cm) DEM 4,200. BERN, 23 June 1982, *Composition* (c. 1950, pastel, 5 x 6¾ ins / 12.6 x 17 cm) CHF 2,900. HAMBURG, 10 June 1983, *Abstract Still-life* (1954, gouache, 7 x 9¼ ins / 17.7 x 23.4 cm) DEM 3,200. HAMBURG, 10 June 1983, *Portrait of Frau F. with Dog* (1951, oil on canvas, 28¾ x 20 ins / 73 x 50.5 cm) DEM 8,200. MUNICH, 30 Nov 1984, *Woman Standing and Woman Seated* (c. 1940, coloured chalks, 19¾ x 31 ins / 50 x 79 cm) DEM 16,000. HAMBURG, 7 June 1985, *Composition in Blue* (1956, watercolour and gouache, 21¼ x 27½ ins / 53.8 x 69.7 cm) DEM 17,000. MUNICH, 2 June 1986, *Winter Landscape* (oil/hardboard, 22 x 17¼ ins / 55.7 x 43.9 cm) DEM 12,000. MUNICH, 24 Nov 1986, *View of Heiligenblut and the Grossglockner* (coloured chalks, 8¼ x 10 ins / 21 x 24.5 cm) DEM 5,800. MUNICH, 26 Oct 1988, *Abstract Composition* (pastel, 8¼ x 10¼ ins / 20.9 x 26.2 cm) DEM 6,160. PARIS, 26 Oct 1988, *Woman* (mixed media, 14½ x 4½ ins / 37 x 11.5 cm) FRF 6,000. BERLIN, 30 May 1991, *Little Composition in Three Sections* (1960, oil on card, 14 x 12 ins / 35.5 x 30.5 cm) DEM 12,210. MUNICH, 1-2 Dec 1992, *Composition with Light Playing on a Landscape* (1959, mixed media, 14 x 18¾ ins / 35.5 x 47.5 cm) DEM 9,200. HEIDELBERG, 8 April 1995, *Adoration* (pastel and pencil, 4½ x 5½ ins / 11.6 x 14.1 cm) DEM 4,700. MUNICH, 3 Dec 1996, *Children's Game; Greetings Cards* (oil on card and watercolour on card on greetings cards, two works, 6 x 8¾ ins / 15.5 x 22.5 cm and 4¼ x 6 ins/11 x 15.5 cm) DEM 6,000.

KERLING, Anna E.
Dutch, 19th - 20th century.
Born 19 March 1862, in The Hague.
Painter. Flowers.

Anna Kerling was a student of Erelman and S. Robertson. Her work featured in the Exposition Universelle in Paris in 1900, receiving an honourable mention.

KERMABON, Adèle Marie
French, 19th century.
Born in St-Malo.
Miniaturist, painter (enamel/porcelain).

Adèle Kermabon was a pupil of Madame de Cool and Beauregard. She began exhibiting her works at the Salon in 1875.

KERMADEC, Eugène Nestor de
French, 20th century.
Born 21 May 1899, in Paris; died 1976.
Painter, sculptor, illustrator. Figures, still-lifes.

After spending his childhood in his father's native Guadeloupe, Eugène Nestor de Kermadec went to Paris to study sculpture at the École des Arts Décoratifs and drawing at the École des Beaux-Arts from 1915 to 1917. Although his work was shown at the Salon des Indépendants in Paris and several collections of his work were also exhibited, De Kermadec appears to have preferred to keep out of the public eye and was relatively unknown. In 1961 he was awarded the European Foundation of Culture Prize in Amsterdam for his painting *Blasonnage Blessant*.

De Kermadec could certainly have aspired to a higher profile among the painters of his generation. Although cold and uncompromising, his intensely rhythmic work was a considerable influence on many younger artists. He painted mainly female figures, standing, reclining or seated, but transposed half way to abstraction, so that only the essential interlinking lines remained, creating the basic forms. The viewer is surprised to find his eye following a path and discovering a link between space and time in the invention of rhythm. In 1949 De Kermadec illustrated *Verre d'Eau* by Francis Ponge.

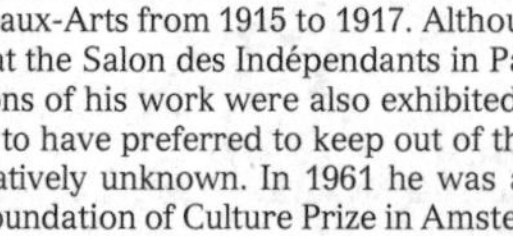

BIBLIOGRAPHY:
Eugène de Kermadec: Opere 1931-1975, exhibition catalogue, Gall. Seno, Milan, 1987.

AUCTION RECORDS:
PARIS, 24 Nov 1928, *Young Woman Viewed from Behind*, FRF 110. PARIS, 4 March 1943, *Landscape; Nude; Still-life* (three canvases) FRF 2,000. PARIS, 18 June 1976, *Man with Pipe* (1945, oil on panel, 13 x 9½ ins / 33 x 24 cm) FRF 2,550. ZURICH, 30 May 1979, *Torso of a Woman Bathing* (1957, oil on canvas, 28¾ x 23½ ins / 73 x 60 cm) CHF 2,000. LONDON, 3 Dec 1985, *Female Nude with Black Stockings* (oil on canvas, 25½ x 21¼ ins / 64.6 x 54 cm) GBP 4,200. PARIS, 24 Nov 1987, *Woman with Cushion* (1939, oil on canvas, 31½ x 51¼ ins / 80 x 130 cm) FRF 53,000. PARIS, 24 Nov 1987, *Woman with Cushion* (1939, oil on canvas, 35 x 51¼ ins / 89 x 130 cm) FRF 53,000. MILAN, 8 June 1988, *House of the Hanged Man* (1944, oil on canvas, 19¾ x 25½ ins / 50 x 65 cm) ITL 6,500,000. VERSAILLES, 15 June 1988, *Second Impression of Algiers* (1948, oil on canvas, 19¾ x 25½ ins / 50 x 65 cm) FRF 59,500. PARIS, 23 June 1988, *Small Incarnation* (1955, oil on canvas, 18 x 13 ins / 46 x 33 cm) FRF 20,000. PARIS, 20 Nov 1988, *Series of Impasses* (1950, oil on canvas, 25½ x 19¾ ins / 65 x 50 cm) FRF 50,000. PARIS, 12 Dec 1988, *Still-life* (oil on canvas, 18 x 25½ ins / 46 x 65 cm) FRF 36,000. PARIS, 8 Nov 1989, *A Certain Order* (1955, oil on canvas, 13 x 18 ins / 33 x 46 cm) FRF 35,000. PARIS, 20 Nov 1989, *Woman with Red Dressing-gown* (1932, oil on canvas, 36¼ x 23½ ins / 92 x 60 cm) FRF 130,000. PARIS, 25 March 1990, *Macroscopic* (1956-1957, oil on canvas, 38¼ x 51¼ ins / 97 x 130 cm) FRF 380,000. PARIS, 29 March 1990, *Shore* (1929, oil on canvas, 21¼ x 25½ ins / 54 x 65 cm) FRF 160,000. PARIS, 26 Nov 1990, *Woman Seated* (1936, oil on canvas, 36¼ x 23½ ins / 92 x 60 cm) FRF 280,000. AMSTERDAM, 23 May 1991, *Navigation of a Site* (oil on canvas, 38¼ x 51¼ ins / 97 x 130 cm) NLG 26,450. PARIS, 27 Jan 1992, *Abstract Composition* (1949, oil on canvas, 25½ x 19¾ ins / 65 x 50 cm) FRF 50,000. LONDON, 15 Oct 1992, *Untitled* (1953, oil on canvas, 28¼ x 39¼ ins / 72 x 99.5 cm) GBP 4,070. PARIS, 19 March 1993, *Composition* (oil on canvas, 18 x 25½ ins / 46 x 65 cm) FRF 28,000. LONDON, 25 March 1993, *Dédale en Expansion* (1965, oil on canvas, 38¼ x 51¼ ins / 97 x 130 cm) GBP 6,325. LONDON, 14 March 1995, *Marine Wildlife* (oil on canvas, 17¾ x 24 ins / 45 x 61 cm) GBP 2,990. PARIS, 21 Nov 1995, *Nude* (1929, oil on canvas, 18 x 25½ ins / 46 x 65 cm. PARIS, 15 April 1996, *Woman with Still-life* (oil on canvas, 39 x 25½ ins / 99 x 65 cm) FRF 55,000. PARIS, 10 June 1996, *Pink Building* (1949, oil on canvas, 23½ x 28¾ ins / 60 x 73 cm) FRF 22,000. PARIS, 20 June 1996, *Essential Landscape* (watercolour and coloured pencil/paper, 9¾ x 12½ ins / 25 x 32 cm) FRF 4,000. COPENHAGEN, 22-24 Oct 1997, *Study for a Series on Algeria* (watercolour, 12½ x 9½ ins / 32 x 24 cm) DKK 7,000. PARIS, 14 Dec 1997, *Nude* (1931, oil on canvas, 36¼ x 23½ ins / 92 x 60 cm) FRF 50,000. PARIS, 15 Dec 1997, *Untitled* (1959, watercolour and pencil/paper, 9½ x 13¾ ins / 24 x 35 cm) FRF 5,800. STOCKHOLM, 2 May 2000, *Intimacy* (oil on canvas, 18 x 15 ins / 46 x 38 cm) SEK 34,000. STOCKHOLM, 7 Nov 2000, *Model* (oil on canvas, 29 x 20 ins / 73 x 50 cm) SEK 52,000. MUNICH, 19 May 2001, *Borborygme plastique* (oil on canvas, 29 x 39 ins / 73 x 100 cm) DEM 8,000. LONDON, 9 April 2002, *Banner Woman* (oil on canvas, 29 x 20 ins / 73 x 50 cm) GBP 6,500. PARIS, 11 Dec 2002, *Woman with Lantern* (oil on canvas, 26 x 20 ins / 65 x 50 cm) EUR 5,000. LONDON, 20 March 2003, *Black Corset* (oil on canvas, 29 x 20 ins / 73 x 51 cm) GBP 5,200. MILAN, 26 March 2003, *My Surroundings* (1959, gouache, 9 x 12 ins / 24 x 31 cm) EUR 1,500. PARIS, 26 May 2004, *Red Pyjamas with Still-life* (oil on canvas, 29 x 20 ins / 73 x 50 cm) EUR 12,000. PARIS, 17 Oct 2004, *Shattering Collision* (oil on canvas, 24 x 32 ins / 60 x 81 cm) EUR 4,500.

KERMARREC, Joël
Belgian, 20th century.
Born 20 January 1939, in Ostend.

Active from 1958 and naturalised in France.
Painter, sculptor, draughtsman, installation artist, collage artist, mixed media.
Surrealism.
Distances.

Kermarrec studied at the École des Beaux-Arts in Paris from 1958 to 1963 and, during the same period, was one of the organizers, with Pierre Gaudibert and Jacques Poli, of the *Distances* group at the Musée d'Art Moderne de la Ville de Paris. The group aimed to bring together young artists who were developing new modes of expression. From 1975 to 1987, Kermarrec was professor at the École des Beaux-Arts in Marseilles and, from 1987, at the École in Paris.

In 1970, Pierre Gaudibert said of Kermarrec: 'Kermarrec is a unique talent at the heart of a trend...around [which] revolve the preoccupations of those artists...seeking a synthesis of surrealism, pop art and op art.' At this point, Kermarrec's work consisted of body parts - like limbs from an écorché that can be taken to pieces - executed in flesh pink celluloid or plastic, presented in an indeterminate space and considered dispassionately, as if disinfected or as symbols of a personal syntax. Kermarrec aims to disassociate his objects from any emotive response, a feature reinforced by his titles, which borrow from the language of contemporary advertising: *Spend your Holidays in the Body's Mazes!*. His works are produced in series - *Slate-greys* (1969-88), *Canvases in the Raw* (1970), *Black Canvases* (1970-71), *Khaki Canvases* (1972), *Trousers* (autumn 1972), *White Canvases* (1973), *Skin, Order and Knowledge* (1973), *Ostend and the Pantograph* - but he avoids the implication of narrative, insisting that one canvas has the same value as another.

In the mid-1970s, Kermarrec abandoned oil painting to explore other artistic processes: drawing, language, collage, assemblage and photography. However, certain forms and themes recur, such as smiling angels, hares, stripes, sticks, laces or feathers, drawn on to a background of flat colour. He also produced complex drawings in black lead and coloured pencil, combined with collaged objects and gold-leaf. Kermarrec describes his work as follows: 'I've spent 25 years breaking down what I was making, as well as the image I had or was beginning to have through my work, and the value of this image. Above all, what I want to find out is how to be whole by making things piece by piece.' In 2002, Kermarrec published an book entitled *Funny Science by Tom Tit in 50 Experiments: Vignettes*.

Since 1960, Kermarrec has taken part in numerous group exhibitions, particularly those dedicated to new trends in painting: 1964, 1965 and 1966, Salon de la Jeune Peinture, Paris; from 1965, Salon de Mai and Salon des Grands et Jeunes d'Aujourd'hui, Paris; 1965, 1967, 1969, Paris Biennale; 1965, 1967, Fine Arts Museum, Ostend; 1968, Salon des Réalités Nouvelles, Paris; 1969, 1973, 1977, 1979 and 1981, Musée d'Art Moderne de la Ville de Paris; 1972, Guggenheim Museum, New York; 1978, Gulbenkian Foundation, Lisbon; 1979, São Paulo Biennale; 1986, New Delhi Triennale; 1990 and 1992, Musée National d'Art Moderne, Paris. Solo exhibitions include: 1968, 1970, Brussels; 1969, 1971, 1973, 1974, 1977, 1985, 1987, Paris; 1975, CAPC, Bordeaux; 1978, Musée de Grenoble; 1989, Musée Picasso, Antibes; Galerie Baudoin-Lebon, Paris. He was awarded the Prix du Dôme in 1964, and, in 1965, a scholarship from the Salon de Mai and the Prix Fénéon from the University of Paris.

Bibliography:

Gaudibert, Pierre, *Joël Kermarrec*, exhibition catalogue, Gal. Withofs, Brussels, 1970. Naggar, Carole/Le Bot, Marc, *Joël Kermarrec*, exhibition catalogue, Musée d'Art Moderne de la Ville de Paris, Paris, 1973. Le Bot, Marc, '*Éloge du formalisme, les peintures de Joël Kermarrec*' in *Figurations 1960-1973 coll. 10/18*, UGE, Paris, 1973. *Joël Kermarrec*, exhibition catalogue, Gal. de France, Paris, 1980. Millet, Catherine, *L'Art contemporain en France*, Flammarion, Paris, 1987. Michaud, Yves, *Pratiques d'envoûtements*, exhibition catalogue, Gal. de France, Paris, 1987. *L'Art moderne à Marseille - La Collection du musée Cantini*, exhibition catalogue, Musée Cantini, Marseilles, 1988.

Museums and Galleries:

Marseilles (Mus. Cantini): *Crystal Hammer* (1974); *Blue Oval* (1979-1980) - Paris (MNAM-CCI): *Blue Background Plus Object* (1970); *Rabbit - Skull* (1972); *ANA with Blue Ruler* (1980-1981).

Auction records:

Paris, 24 June 1977, *Composition* (1969, oil on canvas, 76¾ x 59 ins / 195 x 150 cm) FRF 5,100. Paris, 22 April 1983, *Composition* (1972, oil on canvas, 57½ x 45 ins / 146 x 114 cm) FRF 10,000. Paris, 15 March 1985, *Background Plus Object* (oil and acrylic/canvas, 63¾ x 51¼ ins / 162 x 130 cm) FRF 18,000. Paris, 27 Nov 1987, *Black Square on Red Ground* (1979, oil on canvas, 62¼ x 36¼ ins / 158 x 92 cm) FRF 15,000. Paris, 29 Jan 1988, *The Knot* (acrylic/canvas, 25½ x 21¼ ins / 65 x 54 cm) FRF 2,500. Paris, 20 March 1988, *Composition* (1969-1970, oil on canvas, 63 x 51¼ ins / 160 x 130 cm) FRF 23,000. Paris, 12 June 1989, *Composition* (1970, mixed media and collage, 25½ x 19¾ ins / 65 x 50 cm) FRF 8,000. Paris, 13 Oct 1989, *Composition* (1973, collage and painting, 42½ x 29¼ ins / 108 x 74 cm) FRF 25,000. Paris, 29 Nov 1989, *Ostend and the Pantograph* (1974-1975, oil and collage /canvas, 39¼ x 39¼ ins / 100 x 100 cm) FRF 32,000. Paris, 21 June 1990, *Composition* (1969, acrylic/canvas, 31¼ x 31¼ ins / 79.5 x 79.5 cm) FRF 21,000. Paris, 15 Oct 1990, *Untitled* (1973, colouring pencil, collage, Indian ink and gouache/paper, 41 x 29¼ ins / 104 x 74 cm) FRF 11,000. Paris, 8 Oct 1991, *Mauve* (1970, oil on canvas, 78¾ x 59 ins / 200 x 150 cm) FRF 17,000. Paris, 4 Nov 1992, *Composition* (1973, oil on canvas, 47¼ x 47¼ ins / 120 x 120 cm) FRF 10,000. Paris, 25 May 1994, *Untitled* (1976, oil on canvas, 50¾ x 50¾ ins / 129 x 129 cm) FRF 11,500. Paris, 13 Dec 1996, *Composition* (1972, collage and oil on canvas, 39¼ x 32 ins / 100 x 81 cm) FRF 6,500. Paris, 3 April 1998, *Knot on Pink Ground* (1969, oil on canvas, 39¼ x 32 ins / 100 x 81 cm) FRF 4,000.

KERMOAL, Alexis de

French, 20th century.
Born 1958, in Singapore, to French parents; died 2002.
Painter, engraver.

Alexis de Kermoal lived and worked in Bordeaux. He catalogued the world around him in the minutest detail in his paintings and engravings and transposed them into skilful graphics in muted tones in rare patinas. He took part in the exhibition *De Bonnard à Baselitz - Dix Ans d'enrichissements du cabinet des estampes 1978-1988* (*From Bonnard to Baselitz: A Decade of Acquisitions by the Prints Collection 1978-1988*), at the Bibliothèque Nationale in Paris in 1992. In 1996 the Galerie Thierry Spira organised a solo exhibition of his works.

Bibliography:

Beaumont-Maillet, Laure/Woimant, Françoise/Pernoud, Emmanuel, *De Bonnard à Baselitz - Dix ans d'enrichissements du Cabinet des estampes 1978-1988*, exhibition catalogue, Bibliothèque nationale de France, Paris, 1992. Lascault, Gilbert/Sarre, Michel, *Alexis de Kermoal. Gravures, peintures*, exhibition catalogue, Médiathèque municipale, Lorient, 2004.

Museums and Galleries:

Mulhouse (MBA, Prints Collection) - Paris (BNF, Prints Collection): *Tennis* (1986, etching) - Paris (MAMVP) - Sète (Mus. Paul Valéry) - Strasbourg (Library des Mus.).

KERN, Achilles

German, 17th century.

Born 6 November 1607, in Forchtenberg; died 20 January 1691, in Forchtenberg.
Sculptor.

Kern worked from his youth on decorating a chapel in Dettelbach, then undertook regular work in Schöntal, Waldenburg, Mergentheim and principally Forchtenberg.

KERN, Anton, or Korne
Bohemian School, 18th century.
Born 1709 or 1710, in Tetschen (now Decín); died 8 June 1747, in Dresden.
Painter. Religious subjects, mythological subjects. Bohemian School.

Anton Kern studied with Pittoni in Venice. On his return to Germany, the king of Saxony awarded him a pension to continue his studies in Rome. When Kern returned to Dresden in 1741, having painted *Massacre of the Innocents*, Augustus III appointed him painter to his court. Kern also painted a carriage for the royal wedding. He is best known for *Pretty Flower-girl* and *The Four Seasons*. He died at the height of his powers, leaving some interesting drawings.

He was represented in the exhibition *Lumière et ténèbres, art et civilisation du Baroque en Bohême* (*Light and Darkness. Baroque Art and Civilisation in Bohemia*) at the Palais des Beaux-Arts in Lille in 2002.

BIBLIOGRAPHY:
Preiss, Pavel, *Anton Kern (1709 - 1747): Ölskizzen, Zeichnungen und Druckgraphik*, exhibition catalogue, Verlag des Salzburger Barockmuseums, Salzburg, 1993. Preiss, Pavel, *Anton Kern*, exhibition catalogue, Národní galerie, Prague, 1998. Vlnas, Vit (ed.), *Lumière et ténèbres, art et civilisation du Baroque en Bohême*, exhibition catalogue, Palais des Beaux-Arts, Lille, Réunion des musées nationaux, Paris, 2002.

MUSEUMS AND GALLERIES:
DRESDEN (Gemäldegal.): *Massacre of the Innocents*.

AUCTION RECORDS:
PARIS, 23 Nov 1927, *Offerings*, FRF 3,100. PARIS, 10 Nov 1928, *Young Women Bearing Gifts for the Gods*, FRF 3,400. LONDON, 7 Dec 1988, *Trinity* (oil on canvas, 11 x 4 3/4 ins / 28 x 12 cm) GBP 7,480. VIENNA, 24 March 1999, *Wedding at Cana* (oil on canvas, 19x30 ins / 47x76 cm) ATS 1,000,000. LONDON, 7 July 2000, *Bacchus and Ariadne* (oil on panel, 26x45 ins / 66x114 cm) GBP 32,000. BERLIN, 31 May 2002, *Thymbraus, Son of Laocoon, with Snake* (1726, chalk, 17x11 ins / 42x28 cm) EUR 1,900. PARIS, 23 June 2004, *Visitation* (oil on canvas, 14x12 ins / 36x31 cm) EUR 4,800.

KERN, Endrüs
German, 16th century.
Active in Forchtenberg c. 1596.
Sculptor.

KERN, Éric
French, 20th - 21st century.
Born 1961, in Ingwiller.
Painter.

Éric Kern lives and works in his native town of Ingwiller.

BIBLIOGRAPHY:
Beaumont-Maillet, Laure/Woimant, Françoise/Pernoud, Emmanuel, *De Bonnard à Baselitz - Dix ans d'enrichissements du Cabinet des estampes 1978-1988*, exhibition catalogue, Bibliothèque nationale de France, Paris, 1992.

MUSEUMS AND GALLERIES:
PARIS (Prints Collection): *Violinists* (1984, lithograph).

KERN, Haim
German, 20th century.
Born 1930, in Leipzig.
Active in France.
Engraver.

Haim Kern studied at the École des Beaux-Arts in Paris and at several other academies. He worked in the studio of Georges Visat in Paris, and, in 1971 was awarded a grant to spend a period at the Contemporary Engraving Centre in Geneva. His work was exhibited in Paris, from 1970, at the Salon des Réalités Nouvelles and the Salon d'Automne, as well as in Switzerland, Turkey and Germany.

KERN, Hans Ulrich
Swiss, 19th century.
Born 2 October 1787, in Berlingen; died 17 October 1818, in Zurich.
Painter.

Kern married Elisabeth Kern from Berlingen in 1814.

KERN, Hermann
Hungarian, 19th - 20th century.
Born 1839, in Liptouivar; died January 1912, in Maria-Enzersdorf.
Painter. Portraits, genre scenes.

Hermann Kern settled in Vienna in 1880, exhibiting both in the Austrian capital and in Munich.

AUCTION RECORDS:
LONDON, 4 Dec 1909, *The Antiquary and the Naturalist* (two pendants) GBP 33. VIENNA, 28 Nov 1967, *Game of Cards*, ATS 45,000. BERLIN, 7 July 1971, *Old Gardener*, DEM 8,000. VIENNA, 20 March 1973, *Botanist*, ATS 100,000. NEW YORK, 9 Oct 1974, *Preparations for a Feast*, USD 4,000. NEW YORK, 2 April 1976, *First Grape* (oil on panel, 22 3/4 x 14 1/4 ins / 58 x 36 cm) USD 3,500. VIENNA, 20 Sept 1977, *Two Old Village Musicians* (oil on canvas, 17 3/4 x 26 1/4 ins / 45 x 66.5 cm) ATS 100,000. CANNES, 30 Oct 1979, *Card Players* (1903, oil on panel, 16 1/4 x 20 1/2 ins / 41 x 52 cm) FRF 40,000. ZURICH, 15 May 1981, *Game of Cards* (1880, oil on canvas, 24 x 18 1/2 ins / 61 x 47 cm) CHF 12,000. VIENNA, 16 Nov 1983, *Old Wine Waiter* (oil on panel, 18 x 11 3/4 ins / 46 x 30 cm) ATS 130,000. VIENNA, 4 Dec 1986, *Reading the Newspaper* (1909, oil on canvas, 16 3/4 x 20 3/4 ins / 42.5 x 53 cm) ATS 220,000. VIENNA, 18 March 1987, *A Good Drink* (1904, oil on panel, 16 1/4 x 20 1/2 ins / 41 x 52 cm) ATS 200,000. LONDON, 26 Feb 1988, *Fortune Teller; Itinerant Musician* (oil on canvas, two pendants, each 20 3/4 x 17 ins / 52.7 x 43.2 cm) GBP 4,400. NEW YORK, 24 May 1988, *Ornithologist* (oil on panel, 18 1/4 x 24 ins / 46.4 x 61.1 cm) USD 5,775. PARIS, 7 March 1989, *Young Hawkers* (oil on canvas, 28 1/4 x 22 3/4 ins / 72 x 58 cm) FRF 35,000. LONDON, 4 Oct 1989, *Young Violinist* (oil on canvas, 30 3/4 x 21 1/2 ins / 78 x 54.5 cm) GBP 4,180. NEW YORK, 23 May 1990, *Wrong Note* (oil on canvas, 22 3/4 x 31 1/2 ins / 57.7 x 80 cm) USD 15,400. NEW YORK, 23 Oct 1990, *Violinist* (oil on panel, 18 1/2 x 12 1/2 ins / 47 x 31.8 cm) USD 8,250. LONDON, 22 Nov 1990, *First Drink; Last Drink* (oil on panel, a pair, each 18 1/2 x 12 1/2 ins / 47 x 31.8 cm) GBP 4,620. MUNICH, 10 Dec 1991, *Heaviest Melon* (oil on panel, 18 1/2 x 12 1/4 ins / 47 x 31 cm) DEM 12,650. NEW YORK, 20 Feb 1992, *At the Greengrocer's* (oil on panel, 18 1/2 x 27 ins / 47 x 68.6 cm) USD 8,250. NEW YORK, 26 May 1992, *Bassoon Player Drinking a Tankard of Beer* (oil on panel, 18 1/2 x 12 ins / 47 x 30.5 cm) USD 5,280. LONDON, 25 Nov 1992, *Enjoying a Good Wine* (oil on panel, 26 x 17 3/4 ins / 66 x 45 cm) GBP 3,520. LONDON, 12 Feb 1993, *Musician; Chef* (oil on panel, a pair, 19 x 12 1/2 ins / 48.2 x 31.8 cm) GBP 7,920. NEW YORK, 17 Feb 1993, *Bassoon Tuner* (1900, oil on canvas, 14 1/4 x 20 ins / 36.2 x 50.8 cm) USD 7,475. AMSTERDAM, 21 April 1993, *A Refreshing Drink* (oil on canvas, 18 3/4 x 27 1/4 ins / 47.5 x 69 cm) NLG 12,650. MUNICH, 22 June 1993, *Peasant Lighting his Pipe* (oil on panel, 15 3/4 x 12 1/2 ins / 40 x 31.5 cm) DEM 7,820. LONDON, 17 March 1995, *Horticulturalist; Gardener* (oil on panel, a pair, 18 1/2 x 12 1/4 ins / 47.2 x 31 cm) GBP 8,970. AMSTERDAM, 11 April 1995, *Scattering Grain to the Geese* (1878, oil on canvas, 28 1/4 x 22 3/4 ins / 71.5 x 58 cm) NLG 9,676. LONDON, 22 Nov 1996, *Cithara Player* (oil on canvas, 19 x 12 ins / 48 x 30.5 cm) GBP 1,265. NEW YORK, 15 June

1999, *Drink between Songs* (oil on panel, 12 x 18 ins / 30 x 46 cm) USD 17,000. LONDON, 17 June 1999, *Hunter. Fiddler* (oil on panel, a pair, 19 x 12 ins / 47 x 31 cm) GBP 14,000. VIENNA, 23 May 2000, *In the Vegetable Cellar* (oil on panel, 18 x 27 ins / 46 x 68 cm) ATS 140,000. LONDON, 14 June 2000, *Musician's Workshop* (1906, oil on canvas, 14 x 20 ins / 35 x 50 cm) GBP 6,500. BREMEN, 30 March 2001, *Clarinetist* (1907, oil on canvas, 19 x 13 ins / 48 x 32 cm) DEM 16,500. COLOGNE, 24 Nov 2001, *Old Fiddler Drinking in a Tavern* (oil on canvas, 19 x 13 ins / 48 x 32 cm) DEM 17,000. AMSTERDAM, 23 April 2002, *Game of Cards* (1903, oil on panel, 16 x 20 ins / 41 x 52 cm) EUR 25,000. VIENNA, 13 May 2002, *Instrument Maker* (oil on panel, 18 x 27 ins / 45 x 68 cm) EUR 15,500. BUDAPEST, 12 April 2003, *Mender of Old Instrument* (oil on canvas, 18 x 13 ins / 46 x 32 cm) HUF 1,500,000. VIENNA, 24 Nov 2003, *Thirsty Fiddler* (oil on panel, 18 x 12 ins / 46 x 31 cm) EUR 6,500. VIENNA, 27 May 2004, *Tricky Card Group* (1903, oil on canvas, 23 x 31 ins / 58 x 80 cm) EUR 9,500. LONDON, 23 Sept 2004, *Musical Refreshments* (oil on panel, a pair, 19 x 12 ins / 48 x 31 cm) GBP 6,000.

KERN, Jean
Swiss, 19th - 20th century.
Born 1874, in Bülach (Zurich).
Active in Paris.
Painter, engraver. Landscapes.

Jean Kern exhibited in Paris between 1899 and 1914.

KERN, Johann Adam
German, 18th century.
Born 10 April 1750, in Frankfurt am Main.
Painter, engraver. Portraits, landscapes.

Kern left a number of portraits, including a *Goethe as a Young Man* and an *Emperor Charles V.*

KERN, Joseph
German, 20th century.
Born 17 February 1878, in Aachen.
Painter, engraver. Landscapes.

Joseph Kern was an art historian and museum conservator.

MUSEUMS AND GALLERIES:
AACHEN - DÜSSELDORF - KOTTBUS.

KERN, Léon
French, 20th century.
Draughtsman.

Léon Kern worked for various satirical publications and created a figure made comical because of his perpetual astonishment.

KERN, Leonhard
German, 17th century.
Born 22 November 1588, probably in Forchtenberg; died 4 April 1662, in Schwäbisch Hall.
Sculptor (ivory).

Kern, who is mentioned by the encyclopedist Ris-Paquot, was in Italy from 1609 to 1644, working in Naples and Rome. Subsequently he carried out important commissions in Oberburg and Forchtenberg, Nuremberg, Heidelberg and especially in Schwäbisch Hall, where he settled in 1620 not far from his home town. His powerful naturalism at a time when Baroque Mannerism was triumphant in Germany makes him one of the outstanding sculptors in his country during the Thirty Years' War.

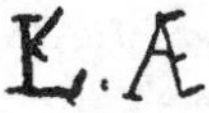

AUCTION RECORDS:
AMSTERDAM, 24 April 1968, *Image of Death* (marble) NLG 23,000. LONDON, 22 April 1982, *Fulvia Holding the Head of Cicero* (c. 1625, ivory, h. 7 1/2 ins / 19 cm) GBP 12,500. LUCERNE, 12 April 2000, *Piggyback Group* (bronze, h. 4ins / 11cm) CHF 6,500. AHLDEN, 20 May 2000, *Caritas, Allegory of Mercy* (ivory, h. 7cm/17ins) DEM 32,000.

KERN, Matthäus
Austrian, 19th century.
Born 5 September 1801, in Riedhausen; died 22 June 1852, in Vienna.
Painter, engraver.

Kern worked in Vienna and did a large number of portraits, some of which were miniatures for the imperial court.

AUCTION RECORDS:
MUNICH, 25 June 1996, *Franz Schubert with Katharina Fröhlich and Her Children* (1841, pencil and watercolour, 9 3/4 x 10 3/4 ins / 25 x 27.5 cm) DEM 5,400.

KERN, Melchior
German, 19th - 20th century.
Born 9 March 1872, in Mainz.
Active in Munich.
Painter. Genre scenes.

Melchior Kern exhibited in Berlin in 1909.

KERN, Michaël, the Elder
German, 16th century.
Active in Pforzheim in 1550.
Painter.

Michaël Kern the Elder also worked in Nuremberg.

KERN, Michaël, the Younger
German, 17th century.
Born 1580, in Forchtenberg am Kocher; died 31 August 1649, in Forchtenberg am Kocher.
Sculptor.

Michaël Kern was the brother of Leonhard and father of Achilles. He was a pupil of Jakob Müller in Heilbronn before working in Würzburg and especially Forchtenberg. Among his works is a *Tomb of Count Ludwig II von Löwenstein* in the church in Wertheim.

KERN, Pascal
French, 20th - 21st century.
Born 1952, in Paris.
Installation artist, painter, sculptor, engraver.

Pascal Kern colours natural components, especially cucurbits and steel objects, cast metal or plaster work, but allows the texture of the material to show through. Then he photographs the 'still-life' that has been meticulously composed, despite its disordered appearance, and presents it in the form of an installation in a heavy steel frame. In the *Factory in Bastos,* at the start of his career, he presented industrial objects retrieved from abandoned factories and found on the land. The series *Fictions Colorées* (*Coloured Fictions*) continued this theme but incorporated painting into the installation. Recently he has been working on engravings.

He has taken part in many collective exhibitions since 1976, such as: Musée d'Art Moderne de la Ville de Paris, 1976; 12th Paris Biennale, 1982; Fontevraud Abbey, 1983; Salon de Montrouge, 1984 and 1985; Musée des Beaux-Arts de Beauvais, 1985; Kunsthalle, Bremen, 1985-1986; New York, 1986; Houston Art Gallery, 1986-1987; Gulbenkian Foundation, Lisbon and the Centre de la veille Charité, Marseilles, 1990; Museo del Arte Moderno, Barcelona, 1992. Solo exhibitions of his work include: Musée National d'Art Moderne, Paris, 1980; Champagne-Ardennes FRAC (Fonds Régional d'Art Contemporain - Regional Contemporary Art Collection) in Chaumont; French Institute in Cologne, 1988; Centre d'Arts Plastiques (Visual Arts Centre) in Villefranch-sur-Saône, 1989; Centre National de la Photographie (National Photographic Centre) in Paris, 1991 and the Centre d'Arts Plastiques (Visual Art Centre) in Royan, 1994. In 1985 the Salon de Montrouge jury awarded him the special prize.

BIBLIOGRAPHY:
Pascal Kern, exhibition catalogue, Gal. Żabriskie, Paris, 1985. Millet, Catherine, *L'Art contemporain en France*, Flammarion, Paris, 1987. *Pascal Kern*, exhibition catalogue, Centre d'Art contemporain Le Parvis, Tarbes, 1992.
MUSEUMS AND GALLERIES:
PARIS (Prints Collection): *Printworks: Factory in Bastos* (1979, book); *Study* (1982-1983, silk screen print).
AUCTION RECORDS:
PARIS, 18 March 1992, *Fiction Colorée* (*Coloured Fiction*) (1983, heightened Cibachrome, 49¼ x 31½ ins / 125 x 80 cm) FRF 7,000.

KERN, Peter, the Elder
German, 17th century.
Born 26 September 1594, in Forchtenberg.
Sculptor.

KERN, Peter, the Younger
German, 17th century.
Died 1635.
Active in Forchtenberg.
Sculptor.

KERN, Stephan
German, 19th - 20th century.
Born 26 December 1860, in Bühlertal; died 4 July 1915, in Bühlertal.
Painter.
Stephan Kern exhibited regularly in Berlin.

KERN, Stephan
German, 20th - 21st century.
Born 1966.
Sculptor, installation artist.
Stephan Kern has exhibited in solo shows, including Portikus in Frankfurt in 2000. He manipulates everyday objects, such as chairs, benches and desks, which he paints in monochrome, generally white, and converts into sculptures.
BIBLIOGRAPHY:
Riese, Ute, *Skulptur 2000*, group exhibition catalogue, Kunsthalle, Wilhelmshaven, 2000.

KERN, Walter
Swiss, 20th century.
Born 26 May 1898, in Küssnacht (Lucerne).
Painter, draughtsman.
Walter Kern worked as a tradesman, travelling to numerous countries between 1919 and 1921 while painting and drawing in his spare time at his home in Uttwil. In Paris he met Paul Éluard and René Crevel and came into contact with Kirchner. His early works were influenced by Surrealism, but, from 1930, he began to produce abstract works with delicate poetic atmospheres. He was also an art critic.
In 1932, Kern exhibited some collages in London beside works by Arp and Ernst.

KERN-LOFFTZ, Marie
German, 20th century.
Sculptor.
Marie Kern-Lofftz exhibited in Berlin in 1909.

KERNE
French, 19th - 20th century.
Portrait artist.
MUSEUMS AND GALLERIES:
ORLÉANS: *Portrait of Madame de St-Amand.*

KERNENDY, Eugen
Hungarian, 19th - 20th century.
Painter, miniaturist.
Eugen Kernendy received an honourable mention at the 1900 Exposition Universelle in Paris.

KERNEUR, Henri
French, 19th - 20th century.
Born 21 December 1866, in Angers; died 24 November 1930, in Paris.
Painter. Landscapes, still-lifes.
Henri Kerneur exhibited at the Salon des Indépendants in Paris.

KERNKAMP, Anny or Anna
Belgian, 19th - 20th century.
Born 19 June 1868, in Antwerp; died 1947, in Brasschaat.
Active 1900-1913.
Painter. Landscapes, urban landscapes, seascapes, still-lifes.
Anny Kernkamp's studied under H. Rul in Antwerp and Blanc-Garin in Brussels.

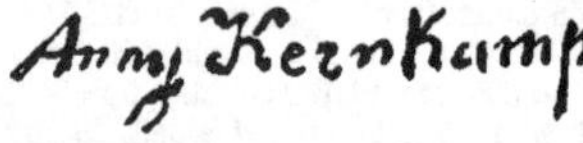

MUSEUMS AND GALLERIES:
ANTWERP: *The Church of St Anthony.*

KERNOFF, Harry
Irish, 20th century.
Born 1900; died 1974.
Painter, watercolourist. Landscapes, still-lifes.
Harry Kernoff is noted for his paintings of typical Irish landscapes.
AUCTION RECORDS:
LONDON, 27 Sept 1991, *Still-life with Fruit and a Beer Mug* (oil on panel, 11½ x 15 ins / 29 x 38 cm) GBP 418. LONDON, 2 June 1995, *The Killarney Mountains* (1943, watercolour, 11 x 14½ ins / 27 x 37 cm) GBP 805. LONDON, 16 May 1996, *Market Lane, Killarney, Wet Day* (1943, pencil and watercolour, 10½ x 14¼ ins / 26.5 x 36.5 cm) GBP 1,495. DUBLIN, 8 Dec 1999, *Back of the Houses* (1936, oil on board, 11 x 15 ins / 28 x 38 cm) IEP 9,000. DUBLIN, 8 Dec 1999, *Dublin Cab* (oil on board, 25 x 38 ins / 64 x 97 cm) IEP 50,000. LONDON, 18 May 2000, *David Byrne's Pub, Duke Street, from the Bailey* (1941, oil on board, 30 x 24 ins / 76 x 61 cm) GBP 70,000. DUBLIN, 27 Sept 2000, *Oysterman or A Bar of a Song* (oil on card, 8 x 6 ins / 20 x 15 cm) IEP 12,000. LONDON, 18 May 2001, *Yonah Shimmel's Knishe Bakery* (gouache, watercolour and black chalk, 12 x 16 ins / 30 x 40 cm) GBP 9,000. LONDON, 18 May 2001, *In Davy's Parlour Snug: Self-portrait with Davy Burne and Martin Murphy* (oil on board, 23 x 28 ins / 58 x 71 cm) GBP 105,000. DUBLIN, 19 Feb 2002, *Bon Viveur* (gouache and charcoal, 22 x 19 ins / 57 x 48 cm) EUR 30,000. DUBLIN, 29 May 2002, *Winetavern Street, Dublin* (watercolour, 18 x 21 ins / 45 x 54 cm) EUR 32,000. LONDON, 16 May 2003, *Winetavern Street, Juky Morning, Dublin* (1940, oil on board, 28 x 32 ins / 71 x 81 cm) GBP 80,000. DUBLIN, 10 Dec 2003, *Currachs in from the Sea, Renvyle, Connemara* (1934, watercolour, 9 x 12 ins / 24 x 30 cm) EUR 12,000. LONDON, 13 May 2004, *Study for 'In Davy's Parlour Snug: Self-portrait with Davy Byrne and Martin Murphy'* (watercolour over pencil, 9 x 13 ins / 23 x 33 cm) GBP 12,000. DUBLIN, 22 June 2004, *Misery Hill, Dublin* (1943, oil on board, 26 x 38 ins / 66 x 97 cm) EUR 52,000.

KERNOTT, James
British, 19th century.
Active in London.
Engraver (burin).
James Kernott made engravings of Murillo's paintings.

KERNSTOK, Karoly
Hungarian, 19th - 20th century.
Born 23 December 1873, in Budapest; died 1940.
Painter. Portraits, interiors with figures. Designs for stained glass, designs for mosaics.
Nyolcak Group (The Eight).

From 1892 Karoly Kernstok studied in Munich, Paris and Budapest. A popular artist in Hungary, he is regarded as one of the creators of modern Hungarian painting. He first joined the community of artists in Szolnok and was a member of the Nyolcak Group (The Eight). He played a role in artistic activities linked to Hungarian political life and also taught, in particular helping to run a free school for young proletarians. From 1919 to 1926 he lived in Berlin. A naturalist painter in his early years, he was later sensitive to the example of Cézanne and subsequently taught that feeling must be subordinated to careful thought. He also had contacts with the German Expressionists. He received a bronze medal at the 1900 Exposition Universelle in Paris.

BIBLIOGRAPHY:
Németh, Lajos, *Moderne ungarische Malerei*, Corvina Kiadó, Budapest, 1969. Passuth, Krisztina/Szabó, Júlia, *L'Art en Hongrie 1905-1930. Art et révolution*, exhibition catalogue, Musée d'Art et d'Industrie, Saint-Étienne, musée d'Art moderne de la ville de Paris, Paris, 1980.

MUSEUMS AND GALLERIES:
BUDAPEST (Magyar Nemzeti Gal.): *Portrait of Bela Czobel* (1907); *Boy Standing* (1909); *Horsemen* (1912); *Rays of Sunlight in the Autumn Forest* (1922).

KERON, Caroline
Flemish School, 19th century.
Active in Brussels c. 1838.
Painter.
Caroline Keron was a pupil of Navez.

KERPEL, Lipot or Leopold
Hungarian, 19th century.
Born 1818, in Kismarton; died 2 April 1880, in Vienna.
Painter, lithographer. Portraits, landscapes.
Lipot Kerpel was a talented portrait and landscape painter. He visited the capitals of Europe from Paris to St Petersburg, but stayed mainly in Vienna, working for the aristocracy.

AUCTION RECORDS:
LONDON, 20 Nov 1996, *Forum in Rome* (1861, oil on canvas, 31 x 40¼ ins / 79 x 102 cm) GBP 8,625. LONDON, 16 Sept 1999, *Panoramic View of Florence* (1847, oil on canvas, 17x23 ins / 43x58 cm) GBP 3,200. MUNICH, 9 July 2003, *Mountain Village with View of Albanian Mountains* (1845, oil on canvas, 12x23 ins / 30x59 cm) EUR 5,000.

KERR, Charles Henry Malcolm
British, 19th century.
Born 22 January 1858; died 27 December 1907.
Active in London.
Painter. Genre scenes.
Charles Henry Malcolm Kerr painted portraits, landscapes and made illustrations. He was a frequent exhibitor at the Royal Academy and at the Suffolk Street Gallery from 1884 to 1893.

MUSEUMS AND GALLERIES:
LONDON (Tate Collection): *Myself* (exhibited in 1899, oil on canvas); *The Visitor* (exhibited in 1905, oil on canvas).

KERR, Edwart
American, 19th century.
Born 1862; died 10 April 1907, in New York, committed suicide.
Painter. Portraits.

KERR, Elizabeth (Mrs)
British, 18th century.
Active in London.
Painter. Flowers.
Mrs Elizabeth Kerr exhibited at the Free Society in 1763.

KERR, George Cochrane
British, 19th century.
Active in London.
Painter, watercolourist. Seascapes.
George Cochrane Kerr was a frequent exhibitor at the Royal Academy, at the Suffolk Street Gallery and at the Water-Colour Society from 1873 to 1893.

AUCTION RECORDS:
LONDON, 9 May 1980, *Naval Battle* (oil on canvas, 33½ x 66 ins / 85 x 167.7 cm) GBP 500. FOLKESTONE, 13 Jan 2001, *Numerous Figures in a Coastal Scene of Kent* (watercolour, 18 x 28 ins / 46 x 71 cm) GBP 1,200.

KERR, Henry Wright
British, 19th century.
Born 1857, in Edinburgh; died 1936, in Edinburgh.
Painter, watercolourist. Figures, genre scenes.
Henry Wright Kerr exhibited at the Royal Academy in Edinburgh, starting in 1890. He was an associate of the Royal Scottish Academy and a member of the Royal Scottish Watercolours Society.

AUCTION RECORDS:
NEW YORK, 27 Jan 1905, *Bailiff of Connemara*, USD 260. LONDON, 13 July 1929, *Waiting* (watercolour) GBP 54. GLASGOW, 14 Feb 1995, *At the Cottage Door* (watercolour, 13¾ x 17¼ ins / 35 x 44 cm) GBP 977. GLASGOW, 21 Aug 1996, *Elderly Woman* (watercolour, 13 x 9 ins / 33 x 22.8 cm) GBP 575. GLASGOW, 25 Feb 1999, *Quiet Smoke* (charcoal and watercolour, 15 x 11 ins / 39 x 29 cm) GBP 1,100. EDINBURGH, 22 Aug 2002, *A Guide Track* (watercolour, 11 x 9 ins / 29 x 24 cm) GBP 2,200. EDINBURGH, 14 Feb 2003, *Study of a Fisherman* (oil on canvas, 15 x 11 ins / 37 x 29 cm) GBP 1,250. BERWICK UPON TWEED, 19 April 2004, *Old Shepherd* (watercolour, 12 x 9 ins / 30 x 23 cm) GBP 2,600. BERWICK UPON TWEED, 28 June 2004, *Cleric* (watercolour, 13 x 9 ins / 33 x 23 cm) GBP 1,200.

KERR, James Wilfried
American, 20th century.
Born 7 August 1897, in New York.
Painter.
James Wilfried Kerr studied under Howard Giles and was a member of the American Federation of Arts and of artists' associations in some Southern and Eastern states.

KERR-LAWSON, James
British, 19th - 20th century.
Born 28 October 1865, in Anstruther; died 1939.
Painter. Landscapes, portraits.
James Lawson-Kerr studied under Lefebvre and Boulanger in Paris, before travelling in Italy. He executed the decorative paintings in the Senate building in Ottawa, Canada. He was also a prolific lithographer.

AUCTION RECORDS:
LONDON, 13 Nov 1985, *Landscape at Dusk, with Ducks* (oil on canvas, 12¾ x 26¾ ins / 32.5 x 68 cm) GBP 3,800. TORONTO, 29 May 1987, *Afternoon in the Garden* (1925, oil on canvas, 20 x 16 ins / 51 x 40.5 cm) CAD 3,200. EDINBURGH, 30 Aug 1988, *Summer's Afternoon in the Shade* (1925, oil on canvas, 20 x 16¼ ins / 51 x 41 cm) GBP 4,810. EDINBURGH, 26 April 1990, *Portait of the Artist's Wife, Reading* (oil on canvas/panel, 9½ x 9 ins / 24.2 x 22.8 cm) GBP 9,900. GLASGOW, 4 Dec 1991, *Tetuan* (1889, oil on panel, 11 x 14 ins / 28 x 35.5 cm) GBP 2,200. LONDON, 9 Sept 1999, *People Bring Much More Than Enough for Service of the Work. And at our Gates..* (oil on canvas, a pair, 20 x 116 ins / 51 x 295 cm) GBP 1,800. TORONTO, 3 June 2002, *Paris Scene* (oil on panel, 5 x 8 ins / 13 x 21 cm) CAD 5,200. BURY ST EDMUNDS, 10 Dec 2003, *Piazzetta with S Giorgio Maggiore, Venice* (oil on canvas, 66 x 46 ins / 168 x 117 cm) GBP 1,600.

KERRE, Joos. See **CARRÉ Joos**

KERREMAN, Balthazar
Flemish School, 16th century.
Active in Antwerp c. 1563.
Painter.

KERRICK, Thomas (Revd.), or Kerrich
British, 18th - 19th century.
Born 1747; died 10 May 1828, in Cambridge.
Painter, engraver.

Thomas Kerrick worked as a librarian at the University of Cambridge, and made pastel portraits of various members of the university. He was awarded a scholarship to travel in Italy.

Kerrick was an outstanding draughtsman, whose drawing style was possibly influenced by Fuseli and his circle. He was an antiquarian who wrote on Gothic architecture as well as providing illustrations for Gough's *Sepulchral Monuments*, and who left a significant collection of early royal portraits to the Society of Antiquaries. Many of his university portraits were made into engravings; he produced architectural etchings and was one of the earliest practitioners of lithography. He was awarded a gold medal in 1776 at the painters' academy in Antwerp.

MUSEUMS AND GALLERIES:
LONDON (National Portrait Gal.): *Portrait (Self-portrait?)* (1774); *Three Portraits* (after Kerrick).

KERRICX, Catherine Claire
Flemish School, 18th century.
Born 1 May 1684, in Antwerp; died 1762.
Painter.

Catherine Kerricx was the daughter of the sculptor Willem Kerricx. She produced mainly copies and watercolours. She died after an illness of 36 years.

KERRICX, Willem
Dutch, 17th - 18th century.
Born 2 July 1657, in Termonde; died 20 June 1719, in Antwerp.
Sculptor.

Willem Kerricx studied under Quellinus the Younger. He was a member of the Antwerp guild in 1674 and married in 1680. His bust of *Maximilian Emmanuel of Bavaria* is in the Antwerp museum.

AUCTION RECORDS:
VIENNA, 24 Sept 1971, *Diana the Huntress*, ATS 70,000.

KERRICX, Willem Ignatius
Flemish School, 18th century.
Baptised 22 April 1682 in Antwerp; died 1745, buried 7 January in Amsterdam.
Painter, sculptor, engineer.

Willem Ignatius Kerricx studied under his father Willem and under Godefries Maes. He was senior member of the guild in 1718 and 1725. Kerricx is known for his low relief *The Bronze Serpent* (on the high altar of the church of Our Lady in Antwerp) and a *St John* (in the church of St James).

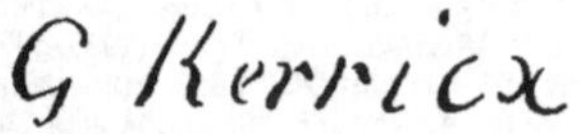

MUSEUMS AND GALLERIES:
ANTWERP: *Mary and St Luke; The Feast of the Passover in Egypt*.

KERROS, Aude de
French, 20th - 21st century.
Born 1947, in Jakarta, Indonesia.
Draughtsman, engraver.

Aude de Kerros lives and works in Paris. She participated in the exhibition *De Bonnard à Baselitz - Dix Ans d'enrichissements du cabinet des estampes 1978-1988* (*From Bonnard to Baselitz: A Decade of Acquisitions by the Prints Collection 1978-1988*) at the Bibliothèque Nationale, Paris, 1992.

BIBLIOGRAPHY:
Beaumont-Maillet, Laure/Woimant, Françoise/Pernoud, Emmanuel, *De Bonnard à Baselitz - Dix ans d'enrichissements du Cabinet des estampes 1978-1988*, exhibition catalogue, Bibliothèque nationale de France, Paris, 1992.

MUSEUMS AND GALLERIES:
PARIS (Prints Collection): *Daytime Frantic Search* (c. 1980, etching).

KERRY, Henry W.
British, 19th century.
Active in Edinburgh.
Painter. Genre scenes, portraits.

Henry W. Kerry exhibited his work regularly in London and in Edinburgh.

KERRY, William L.
British, 19th century.
Active in Liverpool.
Painter. Landscapes.

William L. Kerry exhibited landscapes at the Royal Academy of Arts in London in 1865, 1873 and 1877. In 1909, the Castle Museum in Norwich catalogued three of his works: *Winter's Tale, Mill,* and *Pool at Betws-y-Coed Church*.

KERSBARKE, Romboult van
Flemish School, 16th century.
Painter.

Van Kersbarke worked in London under the name of Rumbolde Casbyck.

KERSCHBAUMER, Anton
German, 20th century.
Born 20 November 1885, in Rosenheim; died 1931.
Painter, engraver. Landscapes.

Anton Kerschbaumer studied in Munich and was inspired by the works of Van Gogh and Matisse.

AUCTION RECORDS:
COLOGNE, 4 Dec 1985, *Still-life* (1921, watercolour heightened with white, 24 3/4 x 22 3/4 ins / 63 x 58.1 cm) DEM 4,800. LONDON, 24 June 1986, *The Landwehrkanal* (1920, oil on canvas, 29 1/2 x 37 ins / 75 x 94 cm) GBP 11,000.

KERSCHENSTEINER, Josef
German, 19th - 20th century.
Born 13 January 1864, in Augsburg.
Active in Augsburg.
Painter. Animals.

Josef Kerschensteiner exhibited in Augsburg, Munich and Berlin.

KERSCHKAMP, Eugen
German, 20th century.
Born 12 April 1880, in Eberfeld.
Painter.

Eugen Kerschkamp studied in Düsseldorf, Paris and Florence before settling in Stettin (now Szczecin, Poland).

KERSEBOOM, Frederic, or Causabon, Korseboom
German, 17th century.
Born 1632, in Solingen; died 1690, in London, buried in St Andrew's church in Holborn.
Active in Britain.
Painter. History painting, portraits.

Frederic Kerseboom worked in Amsterdam, in Paris in 1650 with LeBrun, in Rome where he worked for 14 years with Nicholas Poussin (although Mariette in his *Abecedario* questions whether the Rome stay took place), and in England where he did historical paintings and portraits. His work is often attributed to Poussin.

MUSEUMS AND GALLERIES:
LONDON (National Portrait Gal.): *Portrait of Robert Boyle*.

AUCTION RECORDS:
PARIS, 1892, *The Kiss*, FRF 300. LONDON, 3 Feb 1922, *Robert Boyle* (sketch) GBP 39. LONDON, 17 March 1978, *Portrait of a Lady of the Blunt Family* (oil on canvas, 49 x 39 ins / 124.5 x 99

cm) GBP 650. LONDON, 1 June 1979, *Portrait of a Lady* (oil on canvas, 49 1/2 x 40 ins / 125.6 x 101.5 cm) GBP 1,700. LONDON, 1 June 1979, *Portrait of a Lady* (oil on canvas, 48 1/2 x 40 ins / 123.1 x 101.6 cm) GBP 1,200. NEW YORK, 5 April 1990, *Portrait of a Lady* (oil on canvas, 49 x 39 3/4 ins / 124.5 x 101 cm) USD 2,860.

KERSEBOOM, John or Johann
German, 17th - 18th century.
Active in London 1680-1708.
Painter.

John Kerseboom was the nephew of Frederic Kerseboom. He probably accompanied his uncle to England.

AUCTION RECORDS:
LONDON, 18 Oct 1989, *Portrait of a Naval Officer dressed in Blue with a Red Coat* (oil on canvas, 49 1/4 x 39 1/4 ins / 125 x 100 cm) GBP 6,380. LONDON, 11 July 1990, *Portrait of a Gentleman and his Wife* (oil on canvas, a pair, each 48 3/4 x 39 1/4 ins / 124 x 100 cm) GBP 14,300. LONDON, 8 April 1992, *Three-quarter Portrait of Sir John Harpur dressed in Brown, in a Landscape* (oil on canvas, 48 3/4 x 39 1/4 ins / 124 x 100 cm) GBP 8,800. LONDON, 25 Nov 1998, *Portrait of Admiral Robinson and of his Wife* (oil on canvas, a pair, 49 x 39 ins / 125 x 100 cm) GBP 5,000.

KERSELS, Martin
American, 20th - 21st century.
Born 1960, in Los Angeles.
Sculptor, video artist, photographer, installation artist.

Martin Kersels studied at the University of California in Los Angeles, obtaining a BA in 1984, and later received an MA in 1995. He is co-director of the art programme at the California Institute of the Arts in Valencia. A Los Angeles-based artist, he had his artistic origins in his collaborations with the performance collective SHRIMPS from 1984 to 1993. Since that time, performance has been an integral element of much of his humorous sculpture and photographic work.

His sculptural installations often involve mechanical machines, found objects, moving images and sound. For example, *Piano Drag* (1995) comprises a baby grand piano being pulled across the floor by an electric winch with microphones inside the piano broadcasting the sound, until the performance ends when the moving piano pulls out its own electrical cord. In *Twist* (1993), a prosthetic leg hanging from rubber bands is turned by a motor until the twisted bands cause the leg to fly wildly about and repeatedly hit the wall. Video is used in his installation *Tumble Room* (2001), in which a California girl's bedroom with attached video camera turns 360 degrees, giving the impression that people and a dog are standing on the ceiling. His photographic work also deals with movement, as in his series *Tossing a Friend*, when various people are photographed while being thrown into the air.

Kersels has participated in many exhibitions, including *The Power of Suggestion: Narrative and Notation in Contemporary Drawing* at the Museum of Contemporary Art in Los Angeles (1996); *Commotion: Martin Kersels* at the Madison Art Center (1997); *CA 9001-185* at W-139 in Amsterdam (1997); *COLA: 1996-1997* at the Municipal Art Gallery in Barnsdall Park in Los Angeles (1997); the Whitney Biennial (1997); *Young Americans 2* at the Saatchi Gallery in London (1998); the Melbourne Biennale (1999); the Cahors Festival in France (1999); *Departures: 11 Artists at the Getty* at the Getty Museum in Los Angeles (1999-2000); *Chain Reaction* at the Tang Museum at Skidmore College in Sarasota Springs in New York (2002); *Yankee Remix: Artists Take On New England* at the Massachusetts Museum of Contemporary Art in North Adams (2003-2004); and *Dionysiac* at the Centre Georges-Pompidou in Paris (2005). He received a fellowship from the Foundation for Contemporary Performance Arts in 1999 and a City of Los Angeles Cultural Affairs Department Individual Artist's Grant in 1996.

BIBLIOGRAPHY:
Commotion: Martin Kersels, exhibition catalogue, Madison Art Center, Madison, 1997. Greene, David A., '*Martin Kersels*' in *Art & Text*, vol 56, journal article, 1997. Gerstler, Amy, '*Martin Kersels*' in *Artforum*, journal article, May 1998. Israel, Nico, '*Martin Kersels*' in *Artforum*, journal article, summer 2001.

MUSEUMS AND GALLERIES:
BARCELONA (MAC) - LOS ANGELES (County MA): *Tossing a Friend* (1996, photograph) - LOS ANGELES (MCA): *Swing Film (with Fall)* (1994, installation sculpture); *Piano Drag* (1995, installation sculpture); *Raindrum, Bat Flap, Breather* (1999, sculpture); *Tossing a Friend (Alan)* (1996, photograph) - MADISON (Art Center) - MIAMI (MCA) - PARIS (MNAM-CCI) - SAN DIEGO (MCA).

KERSHAW, Thomas
British, 19th century.
Born 1819, in Standish; died 1898, in London.
Painter, decorative artist.

Thomas Kershaw was responsible for the decoration of the Victoria and Albert Museum in London.

KERSMAKERE, Jean de
Flemish School, 14th century.
Active in Antwerp in 1398.
Painter.

KERSTEL, Theodorus Hendricus
Dutch, 19th century.
Born 15 September 1859.
Engraver.

Theodorus Kerstel worked mainly in Haarlem.

KERSTEN, Wim
Dutch, 20th century.
Born 1908; died 1974.
Painter, draughtsman. Figures, scenes with figures, landscapes.

Wim Kersten was mainly an art critic and historian, as well as a conservator at the Stedelijk Museum in Amsterdam. Through his teaching, he helped stimulate the development of modern art in the Netherlands, bringing it to wider attention. As a painter, he reflected the principal trends of modern art.

AUCTION RECORDS:
AMSTERDAM, 30 May 1995, *The Battle* (1945, black chalk/paper, 25 1/4 x 23 1/2 ins / 64 x 60 cm) NLG 1,125. PARIS, 1 April 1996, *Dutchwoman in a Landscape* (1930, oil on canvas, 32 x 23 1/2 ins / 81 x 60 cm) FRF 50,000.

KERSTING, Georg Friedrich
Danish, 19th century.
Born 31 October 1785, in Güstrow; died 1 July 1847, in Meissen.
Painter, draughtsman. History painting, religious subjects, battles, portraits, genre scenes, landscapes.

Georg Kersting was a pupil at the Kunstakademi in Copenhagen (1805-1808) and Dresden, where he met Caspar David Friedrich, whose influence on Kersting's landscape style is particularly noticeable. In 1811 he exhibited at the Dresden academy. He signed up with the army in Lützow in 1813. Following military service, he lived in Warsaw and executed several historical subjects. Among his finest portraits are those of his two friends, *Caspar David Friedrich in his Studio* and *Gerhard von Kügelgen in his Studio*.

He worked for the Meissen porcelain factory and painted an important set of battle scenes which Duke Frederik-Auguste would in turn offer as a gift to the Duke of Wellington. Goethe appreciated his work, advising Grand Duke Charles

Augustus to buy Kersting's *Embroiderer*. Other works include *Man Reading* and *Man Writing*.

Bibliography:

Gehrig, O., *Georg Friedrich Kersting*, Mecklenburgische Gesellschaft, Mecklenburg, 1932. *Georg Friedrich Kersting, 1785-1847*, exhibition catalogue, Museum der Stadt, Güstrow, 1985. Schnell, W., *Georg Friedrich Kersting*, Deutscher Verlag für Kunstwissenschaft, Berlin, 1994.

Museums and Galleries:

Hamburg (Kunsthalle): *Caspar David Friedrich in his Studio* - Karlsruhe (Staatliche Kunsthalle): *Gerhard von Kügelgen in his Studio* - Weimar (Schlossmus.): *Man Writing; Man Reading; Embroiderer.*

Auction records:

Cologne, 22 Nov 1973, *Woman Viewed from Behind, Descending into a Cellar*, DEM 40,000. Copenhagen, 18 April 1978, *Interior with Young Woman Sewing by Lamplight* (oil on canvas, 15 x 12 ins / 38 x 30.5 cm) DKK 250,000. London, 21 June 1984, *Trompe-l'oeil* (1810, watercolour, $14\frac{1}{4}$ x $20\frac{1}{2}$ ins / 36.5 x 52 cm) GBP 1,000. Heidelberg, 11 April 1992, *Family Scene on a Farm* (pencil, 11 x $8\frac{1}{4}$ ins / 27 x 20.7 cm) DEM 1,550. Munich, 10 Dec 1992, *Couple Seen from Behind* (pencil and grey wash/paper, 5 x $3\frac{3}{4}$ ins / 13 x 9.5 cm) DEM 2,260. Munich, 22 June 1993, *Christ and the Virgin with St John as a Child* (1831, oil on canvas, after Raphael, $17\frac{3}{4}$ x $13\frac{1}{4}$ ins / 45 x 33.5 cm) DEM 28,750.

KERSTING, Hermann Karl

German, 19th century.
Born 19 January 1825, in Meissen (Saxony-Anhalt); died 11 November 1850, in Dresden.
Painter.

Kersting's watercolours, portraits and landscapes in oils established his reputation in Germany.

KERTBENY. See BENKERT

KERVEGUEN, G. de

French, 19th century.
Active in Paris.
Sculptor.

G. de Kerveguen exhibited his work at the Société des Artistes Français from 1887 to 1893.

KERVELLA, Marcel

French, 20th century.
Born 1930, in Loperhet (Finistère).
Active in Paris.
Painter, illustrator.

Marcel Kervella's work featured in the exhibition *De Bonnard à Baselitz - Dix Ans d'enrichissements du cabinet des estampes 1978-1988* (*From Bonnard to Baselitz: A Decade of Acquisitions by the Prints Collection 1978-1988*) at the Bibliothèque Nationale in Paris in 1992.

Bibliography:

Beaumont-Maillet, Laure/Woimant, Françoise/Pernoud, Emmanuel, *De Bonnard à Baselitz - Dix ans d'enrichissements du Cabinet des estampes 1978-1988*, exhibition catalogue, Bibliothèque nationale de France, Paris, 1992.

Museums and Galleries:

Paris (Prints Collection): *Amsterdam* (lithograph).

KERVER, Jacob

German, 16th century.
Born in Germany; died 1583, in Paris.
Draughtsman, engraver (wood), printer.

Jacob Kerver was the son of Thielmann Kerver, and was probably his student. His works include, notably, 128 woodcuts for *Polyphemus's Dream* by Colonna, based on drawings by Mantegna, *The Last Supper*, based on a work by Albrecht Dürer, *A Book of Symbols of the Holy Roman Empire*, and *The Death of Lucretia*. He also produced a series of woodcuts of *Grotesque Figures*, and of *German Door Standards*, which were published in Frankfurt in 1540, and various heads and historical subjects for a work published in Bern that same year. His monogram was often decorated with a pocket knife and a snake.

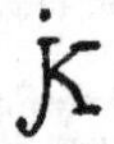

Bibliography:

Füssli, J.R., *Künstlerlexicon*, Zurich, 1779. Bruillot, F., *Dictionnaire des monograms*, 1832/1834. Le Blanc, *Manual de l'amateur d'estampes*, 1854/1890. Marolles, M. de, *Le livre de peintres et graveurs*, 1855 (1677). Christian, M.A., *Origines de l'imprimerie en France*, 1900. Claudin, A., *L'histoire de l'imprimérie en France au 15e et 16e siècles*, 1900/1901. Renouard, Ph., *Documentation sur les imprimeurs à Paris de 1450 à 1600*, 1901.

KERVER, Thielmann

German, 16th century.
Died between 1522 and 1531.
Active in Paris.
Engraver, draughtsman, printer.

Thielmann Kerver is believed to have produced woodcuts for prayer books.

KERVERSEAU, Emmanuel de

French, 19th century.
Born in Rigny (Haute-Saône).
Painter.

Kerverseau exhibited his work in Besançon around 1870.

KERVERSEAU, Gilles de

French, 20th - 21st century.
Born 13 May 1949, in Aix-en-Provence.
Sculptor. Animals.

Gilles de Kerverseau studied at the École des Beaux-Arts and at the École des Arts Décoratifs in Paris. He can be considered a figurative mannerist animal sculptor. He lives in Paris and is active in the provinces where he has his foundry. He makes his sculptures himself. Many contemporary artists also go there to create pieces.

He participates in collective exhibitions such as: *Mac 2000*, at the Grand Palais, Paris, 1987; Galerie de l'Hôtel de Ville, Geneva and the Galerie Verrière, Lyons, 1988 and the Hôtel de la Monnaie, Paris, 1989. He won the Rome Prize in 1973 and also won the Allaud Scholarship.

Auction records:

Paris, 22 Dec 1989, *Canard-Avion* (*Duck-Plane*) (bronze, $18\frac{1}{2}$ x $31\frac{1}{2}$ x $26\frac{1}{2}$ ins / 47 x 80 x 67 cm) FRF 15,000. Paris, 14 May 1990, *L'Éléphant Chasseur d'Ivoire* (*Elephant Ivory Hunter*) (1978, green-patinated bronze, 18 x $6\frac{3}{4}$ x $6\frac{1}{4}$ ins / 46 x 17 x 16 cm) FRF 20,000.

KESAI. See KEISAI

KESEL, Charles Louis de

Belgian, 19th - 20th century.
Born 11 August 1849, in Somergem; died 20 November 1922, in Erlangen.
Sculptor, painter.

Charles Kesel studied in Paris, Rome and Berlin. His work includes the decoration of the Palace of Justice in Ghent.

Museums and Galleries:

Ghent (Mus.): statue; two paintings.

KESELJ, Milan

Yugoslav, 20th - 21st century.
Born 1949, in Savino Selo, Serbia.
Painter.

Milan Keselj trained in the graphic art section of the school of applied arts in Novi Sad. His compositions are inspired by binary computer language. He has been exhibiting since 1973.

KESHAVARZ, Nelly
Iranian, 20th century.
Active in Belgium.
Painter.

Nelly Keshavarz has exhibited her work in solo exhibitions in Belgium. Her brightly coloured paintings recall ancient Persian manuscripts and architectural motifs of the Orient.

KESSEL, Bertel van, called B. de Koster the sacristan
Flemish School, 15th - 16th century.
Painter. History painting.

Bertel van Kessel was the sexton of the church of St Peter in Louvain in 1495. He is known to have still been alive in 1537. He produced heads of Christ for churches.

KESSEL, Ferdinand van
Flemish School, 17th century.
Born 7 April 1648, in Antwerp; died c. 1696, in Breda.
Painter. Allegorical subjects, landscapes, landscapes with figures, animals, flowers. Murals.

Ferdinand van Kessel was the son and pupil of Jan van Kessel. He painted *The Four Elements* (later destroyed) for King Jan Sobieski III and later went to Breda where he became painter to the governor and taught Campo Weyermann. He painted ceilings in the castle of William III and *The Battle of Choszi* (1673) for Sobieski in the church of Zolkiew in Galicia. The figures in his works were painted by Eyckens Maas, Van Opstal and Biset.

MUSEUMS AND GALLERIES:
BESANÇON: *Monkey Barbers Shaving Cats* - BREST: *Ecstasy of St Jerome* - GHENT: *Animal Studies* - RENNES: *Earthly Paradise; Entering the Ark; Landscape with Birds* - VIENNA: *Monkey Seated at a Table; Cats Being Shaved by Monkeys.*

AUCTION RECORDS:
PARIS, 1845, *Landscape,* FRF 305. PARIS, 12 March 1943, *Monkey Eating Grapes by a Basket of Peaches,* FRF 9,500. PARIS, 19 March 1943, *Monkey Barbers,* FRF 16,000. PARIS, 27 Dec 1944, *Choir of Birds,* FRF 122,000. PARIS, 1 June 1949, *Fish and Shellfish,* FRF 43,000. VIENNA, 14 Sept 1965, *Monkey Theatre,* ATS 30,000. VIENNA, 14 March 1967, *Monkeys Playing Cards,* ATS 45,000. COPENHAGEN, 13 Feb 1969, *Allegories* (two pendants) DKK 21,000. LONDON, 7 July 1978, *Insects* (oil/copper, 3½ x 5 ins / 8.6 x 12.7 cm) GBP 30,000. LONDON, 8 July 1981, *Barber Monkeys* (oil/metal, 7½ x 9¼ ins / 19 x 23.5 cm) GBP 2,200. LONDON, 12 Oct 1983, *Musical Birds in a Landscape* (oil/copper, 5¼ x 7 ins / 13.5 x 18 cm) GBP 5,800. LONDON, 18 Oct 1989, *Gathering of Birds in a Landscape* (oil/copper, 5½ x 7¾ ins / 14 x 19.5 cm) GBP 21,450. PARIS, 10 Dec 1993, *Bunches of Flowers in Grisaille in a Niche* (oil/copper, a pair, each 6¾ x 6¼ ins / 17 x 16 cm) FRF 39,000. PARIS, 27 March 1995, *Barber Monkeys* (oil on oak panel, 6½ x 8¾ ins / 16.5 x 22.5 cm) FRF 170,000. NEW YORK, 11 Jan 1996, *Interior with Cats, Monkeys and an Owl Making Music* (oil/copper, 11 x 14¼ ins / 27.9 x 36.2 cm) USD 11,500. PARIS, 1 April 1996, *Two Monkeys in Chains and a Parrot* (oil on canvas, 21 x 26 ins / 53.5 x 66 cm) FRF 75,000. LYONS, 7 Feb 1999, *Birds in a Landscape* (oil on copper, 6 x 8 ins / 15 x 20 cm) FRF 21,000. LONDON, 7 July 1999, *Eagles Attacking Heron and Other Birds* (oil on canvas, 6 x 8 ins / 16 x 20 cm) GBP 2,500. MADRID, 5 June 2000, *Garland of Flowers surrounding St Anthony* (oil on copper, 29 x 22 ins / 73 x 56 cm) ESP 1,300,000. NORTH BETHESDA, 27 Oct 2000, *Boor Smoking a Pipe* (oil on panel, 8 x 7 ins / 20 x 18 cm) USD 1,500. ZURICH, 30 March 2001, *Butterflies* (oil on panel, a pair, 5 x 7 ins / 12 x 17 cm) CHF 140,000. MUNICH, 20 Sept 2002, *Still-life of the Sea* (oil on copper/panel, a pair, 5 x 6 ins / 12 x 16 cm) EUR 15,000. PARIS, 18 Dec 2002, *Monkeys' Meal. Monkeys Playing Cards* (oil on copper, a pair, 6 x 8 ins / 16 x 21 cm) EUR 25,000. PARIS, 18 Dec 2003, *Monkey House, Guardroom Scene* (oil on panel, 8 x 12 ins / 21 x 30 cm) EUR 12,000.

KESSEL, Hieronymus
Flemish School, 16th - 17th century.
Baptised 6 October 1578 in Antwerp; died c. 1636, in Antwerp.
Also active in Germany.
Painter. History painting, portraits, landscapes.

Hieronymus Kessel studied under Cornelis Floris in 1594. In 1606, he visited Frankfurt and Augsburg. In 1609, he went to Strasbourg, where he was a member of the guild in 1615. He worked for the Archduke Maximillian, and returned to Antwerp, where he decorated landscapes by Brueghel, whose daughter he married in 1624. He had two sons, one of whom was a painter. He then left Antwerp, but where he went to is not known.

MUSEUMS AND GALLERIES:
COLOGNE: *Lady in an Armchair* - HANOVER: *Portrait of a Councillor* - NUREMBERG: *A Family* - OBERSCHLEISSHEIM: *Portrait of a Woman.*

AUCTION RECORDS:
LONDON, 7 March 1930, *Portrait of a Woman,* GBP 78. NEW YORK, 4 April 1990, *Portrait of a Young Woman Wearing a Black Dress with a Gold Belt and a White Ruff and Holding a Pair of Gloves* (1617, oil on panel, 40½ x 32½in/102.8 x 82.5cm) USD 3,850.

KESSEL, Jan Baptist van
Flemish School, 18th century.
Born 1693, in Antwerp.
Painter. Historical subjects, animals.

Jan Baptist van Kessel worked for the English court.

AUCTION RECORDS:
PARIS, 6 Nov 1991, *Rabbits and Birds* (oil on canvas, 17 x 24¾ ins / 43 x 63 cm) FRF 26,500.

KESSEL, Jan van I, the Elder
Flemish School, 17th century.
Baptised 5 April 1626 in Antwerp; died 17 April 1679, in Antwerp.
Painter (including gouache), draughtsman. Historical, mythological, religious and allegorical subjects, genre scenes, animals, insects, landscapes, seascapes, interiors, still-lifes (flowers/fruit), insects.

Jan van Kessel the Elder was the son of Hieronymus Kessel and studied under his uncle 'Velvet' Brueghel and Simon de Vos. In 1644 he was a master in the Antwerp guild; he married on 11 June 1647 and had 13 children, two of whom were painters. Van Kessel became captain of the Antwerp civil guard. He painted flowers, fruit, birds and insects in the style of 'Velvet' Brueghel.

MUSEUMS AND GALLERIES:
ABBEVILLE: *Water; Earth* - AIX: *Birds* - AMSTERDAM: *Insects and Fruit* - AUGSBURG: *Crown of Flowers with Butterflies; Rabbits, Vegetables and Kitchen Implements* - BESANÇON: *Two Antique Vases; Flowers* - BORDEAUX: *Flowers* - BRUSSELS (Mus. d'Art ancien): *Cartouche Decorated with Flowers Framing a Temptation of St Anthony* - ÉPINAL: *Forest* - FLORENCE: *Interior with Fish and Fruit; The Virgin Surrounded by Flowers; Virgin and Child; Birds* - HANOVER: *Hen House* - LA FÈRE: *Landscape* - LILLE: *Pan and Syrinx* - MADRID: *Jesus and St John with a Crown of Flowers* (by Th. Van Thulden) - MAINZ: *Flowers; Landscape* - MILAN (Ambrosiana): *Landscape; Flowers* - MILAN (Pinacoteca di Brera): *Musicians* - NAPLES: *Flowers and Fruit* - NUREMBERG: *Madonna Surrounded by Flowers* - OBERSCHLEISSHEIM: *Flowers; The Four Continents* - ORLÉANS: *Landscape; Cat Hallooing and Birds* - PARIS (Louvre): *Grisaille of Franz Francken with Flower* - ST PETERSBURG (Hermitage): *Vegetables and Fruit; Venus and Vulcan; Ornamented Frame* - STOCKHOLM: *Battle between*

Mammals and Owls; Military Emblems - STRASBOURG: *Flowers* - STUTTGART: *Fish and Shellfish; Fish and Shellfish* - THE HAGUE: *Insects; Seascape; Landscape* - VIENNA: *Fight between a Bear and a Snake; Boar Hunts; Landscape and Birds; The Fox and the Stork.*

AUCTION RECORDS:

COLOGNE, 1812, *Stag Hunt,* FRF 656. PARIS, 1871, *Allegory of the Seasons,* FRF 1,150. PARIS, 1885, *The Hunt Sets Out,* FRF 2,050. BERLIN, 1894, *Holy Family,* FRF 2,562. DIJON, 12 Feb 1900, *Venus and Vulcan,* FRF 2,800. LONDON, 28 March 1908, *Flowers in a Vase,* GBP 12. LONDON, 22 July 1910, *Landscape with River and Mill,* GBP 84. PARIS, 22 May 1919, *Bridge,* FRF 2,750. PARIS, 10 Nov 1919, *Discord; Scene in a Church* (both) FRF 1,300. LONDON, 29 June 1923, *Garland of Flowers, Virgin and Child,* GBP 78. PARIS, 17 Feb 1928, *Fruit on a Stone Slab,* FRF 4,600. PARIS, 28 June 1928, *Virgin and Child with Angels* (in collaboration with Van Thulden) FRF 8,000. LONDON, 27 March 1929, *Flowers in a Vase,* GBP 89. LONDON, 14 June 1929, *Hearing* (in collaboration with Jan Brueghel and Van Bâlen) GBP 252. LONDON, 25 Nov 1929, *Artist's Studio,* GBP 47. LONDON, 11 July 1930, *Pier in Amsterdam,* GBP 210. NEW YORK, 15 Jan 1932, *William of Orange's Visit to The Hague,* USD 1,350. PARIS, 30 June 1932, *Flowers and Insects,* FRF 680. PARIS, 31 Jan 1934, *Dance at the Inn; Tavern Interior* (both) FRF 2,200. LONDON, 11 Feb 1938, *Display of Poultry, Fish, Fruit and Vegetables* (four paintings in collaboration with Jan van Brueghel and Van Bâlen) GBP 168. LONDON, 8 April 1938, *Village,* GBP 84. LONDON, 9 June 1939, *Utrecht Gate,* GBP 81. LONDON, 29 Oct 1941, *Choir of Birds,* GBP 462. PARIS, 3 Dec 1941, *The Four Elements,* FRF 52,000. PARIS, 4 June 1943, *Monkeys Eating* (1662) FRF 6,000; *Bird on a Tree,* FRF 5,000. PARIS, 9 June 1943, *Birds in a Landscape; Fish by the Sea* (1675, two pendants) FRF 41,000. LONDON, 9 Dec 1943, *Palace Gardens,* GBP 94. LONDON, 15 Jan 1946, *Birds,* GBP 54. BRUSSELS, 19 April 1951, *Vulcan's Forge,* BEF 6,500. PARIS, 20 June 1951, *Landscape with Fruit, Gourds and Birds; Landscape with a Basket of Fruit and Birds* (two pendants) FRF 42,000. PARIS, 7 June 1955, *Still-life with Monkey and Dog,* FRF 325,000. LONDON, 8 May 1957, *Canal with Village and Windmill,* GBP 480. PARIS, 16 March 1959, *The Four Elements* (on metal) FRF 560,000. PARIS, 16 June 1961, *Butterflies,* FRF 18,000. PARIS, 23 Nov 1962, *The Four Elements,* FRF 25,000. LONDON, 29 Nov 1963, *Still-life with Flowers in front of a Niche,* Gns 2,600. LONDON, 30 Nov 1966, *Still-lifes with Flowers* (two pendants) GBP 2,600. LONDON, 19 April 1967, *The Four Elements: Earth, Air, Fire and Water* (set of four paintings/metal) GBP 6,800. LUCERNE, 22 June 1968, *Bouquet of Flowers* (gouache) CHF 15,000. AMSTERDAM, 25 Nov 1969, *Air,* NLG 30,000. LONDON, 15 July 1970, *Still-lifes with Flowers* (two pendants) GBP 10,500. AMSTERDAM, 23 Nov 1971, *Gods in a Wooded Landscape,* NLG 25,000. PARIS, 23 Nov 1972, *Study of Insects, Flowers and Shells,* FRF 165,000. PARIS, 7 Dec 1973, *Fire; Air* (gouache, a pair) FRF 25,000. LONDON, 28 June 1974, *Still-life with Flowers,* Gns 7,500. AMSTERDAM, 3 May 1976, *Butterflies and Insects* (gouache/parchment, sheet of studies, 4 3/4 x 9 1/4 ins / 11.9 x 23.6 cm) NLG 42,000. PARIS, 9 Dec 1976, *Still-life* (oil/metal, 5 1/2 x 7 3/4 ins / 14 x 20 cm) FRF 22,000. AMSTERDAM, 9 June 1977, *Landscape with Birds (Allegory of Air)* (oil on panel, 20 x 30 1/4 ins / 51 x 77 cm) NLG 46,000. AMSTERDAM, 3 April 1978, *Study of Insects* (watercolour/parchment, 4 1/2 x 6 ins / 11.5 x 15 cm) NLG 7,000. PARIS, 28 March 1979, *Insects and Branches of Flowers* (two gouaches, pendants, each 4 1/2 x 6 ins / 11.5 x 15 cm) FRF 55,000. NEW YORK, 31 May 1979, *Still-life with Flowers* (oil on panel, 21 x 12 1/2 ins / 52.5 x 31.8 cm) USD 75,000. VERSAILLES, 26 Oct 1980, *Vase of Flowers* (oil on wood, 18 1/4 x 13 1/2 ins / 46.3 x 34.2 cm) FRF 115,000. LONDON, 10 April 1981, *Kittens with Fish and Dead Game with Flowers and Fruit* (oil/copper, 13 1/4 x 18 1/4 ins / 33.6 x 46.3 cm) GBP 22,000. LONDON, 15 April 1983, *Flowers in a Glass Vase on an Entablature* (oil on canvas, 23 x 15 3/4 ins / 57.5 x 40 cm) GBP 48,000. LONDON, 12 Dec 1986, *Still-life with Fruit, Oysters and Lemon on a Pewter Dish* (oil on panel, 11 x 15 3/4 ins / 28 x 40 cm) GBP 90,000. LONDON, 11 Dec 1987, *Vase of Flowers and Butterflies on an Entablature* (1676, oil/copper on panel, 8 x 5 1/2 ins / 20.5 x 14 cm) GBP 40,000. NEW YORK, 15 Jan 1988, *Vortumnus and Pomona in a Palace Garden* (oil on panel, 30 1/2 x 37 3/4 ins / 77.5 x 95.8 cm) USD 52,800. LONDON, 22 April 1988, *Still-life with Fruit and Flowers* (oil/copper, 6 1/2 x 8 1/2 ins / 16.3 x 21.8 cm) GBP 35,200. AMSTERDAM, 14 Nov 1988, *Farm Buildings among the Trees with Peasants in the Foreground* (ink and chalk, 7 1/4 x 10 ins / 18.5 x 25.7 cm) NLG 10,580. PARIS, 9 Dec 1988, *Still-lifes* (oil on card, two pendants, 4 1/2 x 7 ins / 11.5 x 18 cm) FRF 90,000. PARIS, 12 Dec 1988, *Bowls of Fruit and a Squirrel on an Entablature; Baskets of Fruit and Figs on an Entablature* (oil/copper, a pair, 6 1/2 x 9 ins / 16.5 x 22 cm) FRF 1,000,000. PARIS, 14 April 1989, *Caterpillars and Spiders; Currants, Butterflies and Insects* (watercolour and gouache/vellum mounted/paper, a pair, 4 1/4 x 5 3/4 ins / 10.5 x 14.5 cm) FRF 440,000. MONACO, 16 June 1989, *Payment of the Tithe, a Monkey Piece* (oil on panel, 14 1/2 x 20 ins / 36.8 x 51 cm) FRF 244,200; *Monkey Overturning a Basket of Fruit with a Cockatoo on Top* (oil/copper, 9 1/4 x 12 1/4 ins / 23.5 x 31 cm) FRF 444,000. PARIS, 27 June 1989, *Allegory of America: Battle between Crocodiles and Hippopotamuses* (copper, 7 x 9 1/2 ins / 17.5 x 24 cm) FRF 38,000. LONDON, 18 Oct 1989, *Gathering of Birds in a Landscape* (1661, oil/copper, 7 3/4 x 11 1/2 ins / 19.5 x 29.5 cm) GBP 90,200. AMSTERDAM, 22 Nov 1989, *Still-life with Fruit* (oil on canvas, 22 x 23 1/2 ins / 55 x 59.5 cm) NLG 103,500. AMSTERDAM, 28 Nov 1989, *Eagle, Peacocks, Doves, a Cockerel and Hens, a Duck and Other Birds* (oil on panel, 10 3/4 x 14 1/2 ins / 27.4 x 36.8 cm) NLG 97,750. PARIS, 11 Dec 1989, *Garland of Flowers, Tulips, Roses, Jonquils, Butterfly* (canvas, 17 1/4 x 28 1/4 ins / 44 x 72 cm) FRF 200,000. LONDON, 23 March 1990, *Monkeys Attacking Penguins on a Beach with a Dutch Man of War Firing a Salvo in the Background* (oil/copper, 7 x 9 1/4 ins / 17.7 x 23.5 cm) GBP 9,900. NEW YORK, 5 April 1990, *God Creating the Birds and Animals of the Earth* (oil on panel, 12 x 30 ins / 30.5 x 76 cm) USD 17,600. PARIS, 9 April 1990, *Roses, Peony, Tulip, Cherry Blossom and Centaurea in a Translucent Vase* (oil on oak panel, 15 1/4 x 10 1/2 ins / 39 x 26.5 cm) FRF 360,000. ROME, 8 May 1990, *Still-life with Fruit and Vegetables with a Monkey* (oil/copper, 6 1/2 x 8 1/2 ins / 16.6 x 21.5 cm) ITL 27,000,000. AMSTERDAM, 22 May 1990, *Travellers on a Road in the Woods* (oil on canvas, 24 1/2 x 30 3/4 ins / 62 x 78 cm) NLG 21,850. AMSTERDAM, 13 Nov 1990, *Still-life with Fruit in a Chinese Porcelain Bowl with a Parrot, Roses, a Water Melon and Dead Birds; Still-life with a Vase of Flowers and Wild Strawberries in Wanli Porcelain with Vegetables and Fish* (oil/copper, a pair, each 5 x 6 ins / 11.8 x 15 cm) NLG 149,500. NEW YORK, 31 May 1991, *Still-life with a Floral Composition in a Vase with a Caterpillar and a Beetle on an Entablature* (1652, oil/copper, 30 1/2 x 23 1/2 ins / 77.5 x 60 cm) USD 495,000. LONDON, 3 July 1991, *Air: Choir of Birds in a River Landscape at Evening* (oil/copper, 9 1/2 x 13 1/2 ins / 24 x 34 cm) GBP 44,000. LONDON, 13 Dec 1991, *Garden of Eden* (25 1/2 x 36 1/2 ins / 64.8 x 92.7 cm) GBP 49,500. PARIS, 3 April 1992, *Study of Arms and Armour* (pen, 5 x 7 1/2 ins / 12.8 x 19 cm) FRF 10,000. AMSTERDAM, 7 May 1992, *Choir of Birds in a Landscape* (oil/copper, 5 1/2 x 7 1/2 ins / 14 x 19 cm) NLG 101,200. NEW YORK, 22 May 1992, *Still-life with Flowers and Insects around the Virgin and Child in a Stone Cartouche* (oil on panel, 21 x 15 ins / 53.3 x 38.4 cm) USD 41,250. LONDON, 8 July 1992, *Still-life with a Bouquet of Roses, Tulips and Other Flowers in a Glass Vase* (oil on panel, 9 x 6 1/4 ins / 23 x 16 cm) GBP 57,200. AMSTERDAM, 18 Nov 1993, *Tulips, Roses, Hyacinths, Cornflowers, Aquilegia and Other Flowers in a Vase with Butterflies and a Beetle on an Entablature* (oil on panel, 15 x 12 ins / 38.2 x 30.2 cm) NLG 149,500. LONDON, 8 Dec

1993, *Still-life with a Stem of Larkspur, Butterflies, Beetles, a Dragonfly and a Snail; Still-life with a Stem of Gooseberries, Butterflies, a Dragonfly, Beetles and Other Insects* (oil/copper, a pair, each 5 x 7 1/2 ins / 11.8 x 19 cm) GBP 80,700. PARIS, 29 March 1994, *Still-life with Fish on a Bank* (oil/copper, 5 1/2 x 7 1/2 ins / 14 x 19 cm) FRF 170,000. PARIS, 28 April 1994, *Still-life* (oil/copper, a pair, each 6 1/4 x 9 ins / 16 x 22 cm) FRF 510,000. AMSTERDAM, 15 Nov 1994, *Still-life with Insects, Fruit and Flowers* (ink, watercolour and gouache, 6 x 7 3/4 ins / 15 x 19.5 cm) NLG 80,500. PARIS, 2 Dec 1994, *Flowers and Insects* (gouache/parchment, a pair, 4 1/2 x 5 3/4 ins / 11.3 x 14.8 cm) FRF 125,000. PARIS, 22 March 1995, *Frugal Still-life; Still-life with Biscuits* (oil/copper, a pair, each 5 3/4 x 8 ins / 14.5 x 20.5 cm) FRF 460,000. LONDON, 5 July 1995, *The Four Elements* (oil/copper, each 5 1/4 x 7 1/2 ins / 13.4 x 19.2 cm) GBP 95,000. AMSTERDAM, 6 May 1996, *Herons and Water Birds by a River with Fish and Reptiles in the Foreground* (oil/copper, 7 3/4 x 11 1/2 ins / 19.5 x 29 cm) NLG 25,960. PARIS, 25 June 1996, *Interior of the Painter's Studio* (oil on panel, 15 1/2 x 23 1/2 ins / 39.5 x 59.5 cm) FRF 320,000. LONDON, 3 July 1996, *Allegory of the Four Elements* (oil/copper, in collaboration with E. Quellinus, 16 x 22 ins / 39.7 x 55.9 cm) GBP 133,500. LONDON, 11 Dec 1996, *Still-life with Flowers in a Basket on a Stone Slab* (oil on wood, 6 1/2 x 9 ins / 16.7 x 22 cm) GBP 63,100. NEW YORK, 30 Jan 1997, *Allegory of Europe* (1670, oil/copper, in collaboration with Erasmus Quellinus the Younger, 19 1/2 x 27 ins / 49.5 x 68.6 cm) USD 354,500. NEW YORK, 31 Jan 1997, *Flowers* (oil on canvas, a pair) USD 178,500. PARIS, 5 March 1997, *Bouquet of Flowers in a Vase on an Entablature* (canvas, 38 1/2 x 28 ins / 98 x 71 cm) FRF 110,000. LONDON, 16 April 1997, *Still-life with Fish with the Sea in the Background* (oil on panel, 6 1/4 x 9 ins / 15.8 x 22 cm) GBP 2,760. LONDON, 18 April 1997, *Butterflies, Insects and Shellfish* (1659, oil/copper, 6 1/4 x 9 1/4 ins / 15.9 x 23.8 cm) GBP 221,500. AMSTERDAM, 6 May 1997, *Still-life with Roses, Tulips and Other Flowers in front of a Painting of Fruit and Flowers on a Stone Entablature* (1653, oil on panel, 17 1/2 x 14 1/2 ins / 44.5 x 37 cm) NLG 31,860. PARIS, 13 June 1997, *Still-life with a Bowl of Grapes, Parrot and Monkey* (copper, 9 1/2 x 12 1/2 ins / 24 x 32 cm) FRF 340,000. LONDON, 3 July 1997, *Study of a Grasshopper, Dragonfly, Caterpillars, Other Insects and a Forget-Me-Not* (1653, oil on panel, 4 1/2 x 5 1/2 ins / 11.5 x 13.8 cm) GBP 238,000. LONDON, 4 July 1997, *Yellow, White and Pink Roses, Tulips, Ranunculus and Other Flowers in a Glass Vase with a Cabbage White Butterfly, a Butterfly, a Dragonfly and a Caterpillar on an Entablature* (oil on panel, 9 1/4 x 7 3/4 ins / 23.8 x 19.7 cm) GBP 67,500. LONDON, 3 Dec 1997, *Pantry Scene with Vegetables, Fruit, Flowers and Fish; Pantry Scene with Vegetables, Fruit, Flowers and Game* (oil/copper, a pair, 9 1/4 x 12 ins / 23.2 x 30.2 cm and 9 x 11 3/4 ins/22.6 x 29.8 cm) GBP 62,000. PARIS, 17 Dec 1997, *Study of Birds against a Cloudy Sky* (copper, 7 1/4 x 9 3/4 ins / 18.5 x 25 cm) FRF 90,000. PARIS, 31 March 1998, *Cat and Dog Fighting in a Pantry* (oil on walnut panel, 13 1/2 x 17 ins / 34 x 43 cm) FRF 560,000. LONDON, 14 Dec 1999, *Still-life with Flowers and Sprig of Cherries in Rummer* (oil on copper, 30 x 23 ins / 77 x 59 cm) GBP 580,000. LONDON, 14 Dec 1999, *Still-life with Flowers in Blue and White Porcelain Vase* (oil on copper, 30 x 23 ins / 77 x 59 cm) GBP 680,000. NEW YORK, 28 Jan 2000, *Sprig of Flowers with Butterflies, Flies, Beetles and a Wasp* (oil on copper, 6 x 7 ins / 14 x 19 cm) USD 675,000. NEW YORK, 25 May 2000, *Study of Butterflies, Spiders, Lizards, a Beetle, an Ant, a Grasshopper and Other Insects* (oil on copper, 16 x 20 ins / 40 x 50 cm) USD 1,500,000. NEW YORK, 26 Jan 2001, *Plaice, Skate and Other Fish Beside a Barrel* (1669, oil on copper, 6 x 8 ins / 14 x 21 cm) USD 70,000. AMSTERDAM, 9 May 2001, *Roses and Other Flowers in Glass Vases with Butterflies and a Caterpillar* (oil on copper, a pair, 5 x 4 ins / 13 x 11 cm) NLG 620,000. LONDON, 12 Dec 2002, *Still-life with Various Fish and Crustaceans on a Beach, with Boats Beyond* (oil on copper, 5 x 7 ins / 12 x 17 cm) GBP 5,200. LILLE, 23 March 2003, *Butterflies and Insects* (1659, oil on copper, 6 x 9 ins / 16 x 23 cm) EUR 630,000. HASLEMERE, 18 June 2003, *Grasshopper, Moths, Butterflies, Insects, Larva* (1664, gouache on vellum, 4 x 9 ins / 10 x 23 cm) GBP 30,000.

KESSEL, Jan van II

Dutch, 17th century.

Born 1641 or 1642, in Amsterdam; died 1680, buried 24 December in Amsterdam.

Painter. Landscapes, landscapes with figures, urban landscapes, still-lifes, animals.

Jan van Kessel II was a friend of Hobbema and probably of Ruisdael. He married on 17 February 1668 in Amsterdam and had two sons, one of whom, Thomas, was the godson of Hobbema. Van Kessel painted landscapes and townscapes and was a talented imitator of Jakob Ruisdael.

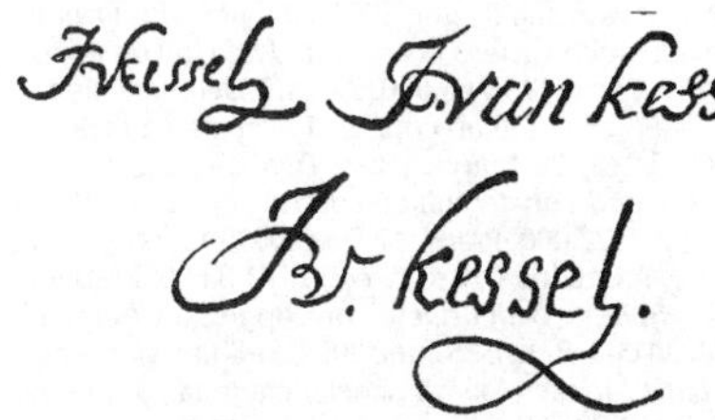

MUSEUMS AND GALLERIES:

AMSTERDAM: *Forest; Waterfall* - ANTWERP: *Landscape* - HAMBURG: *Landscape* - KASSEL: *Landscape* - LA FÈRE: *Landscape* - MILAN (Ambrosiana): *Wood with Game* - MUNICH: *Forest* - ROTTERDAM: *Outskirts of Haarlem; View of Eernhoorsnluis in Amsterdam* - STUTTGART: *The Avenue* - UTRECHT: *Ruin of Utrecht Cathedral after the Storm of 1674* - VIENNA (Liechtenstein Mus.): *Landscape with Valley View.*

AUCTION RECORDS:

AMSTERDAM, 1897, *Forest Edge*, FRF 6,720. PARIS, 1899, *The Old Manor*, FRF 620. PARIS, 19 Dec 1928, *Cottage by the Waterside*, FRF 4,300. PARIS, 15 May 1929, *Flora and Pomona*, FRF 2,800. PARIS, 19 June 1947, *River Shores* (1673) FRF 15,000. PARIS, 28 March 1955, *Hunting*, FRF 190,000. LUCERNE, 26-30 June 1962, *Plain with Horseman and Hunter*, CHF 5,000. PARIS, 10 June 1964, *Landscape with Birds*, FRF 10,200. LONDON, 19 April 1972, *The Collector's Room*, GBP 6,400. COLOGNE, 14 Nov 1974, *Winter Landscape*, DEM 32,000. AMSTERDAM, 28 April 1976, *Wooded Landscape with Hunter* (1666, oil on canvas, 36 1/2 x 46 1/2 ins / 93 x 118 cm) NLG 42,000. ZURICH, 29 Nov 1978, *Still-life with Flowers* (oil on panel, 9 3/4 x 7 3/4 ins / 25 x 19.5 cm) CHF 120,000. BERN, 25 June 1982, *Wooded Landscape with Canal and a Couple in a Boat* (1671, pen and wash, 7 1/4 x 5 3/4 ins / 18.6 x 14.5 cm) CHF 4,000. LONDON, 30 Nov 1983, *View of Heiligewegs Poort, Amsterdam* (oil on canvas, 30 x 42 1/4 ins / 76.5 x 107.5 cm) GBP 20,000. NEW YORK, 6 June 1985, *Allegory of the Four Seasons* (oil on panel, 19 x 29 3/4 ins / 48.5 x 75.5 cm) USD 18,000. LONDON, 9 Dec 1987, *Still-life with Fruit and Vegetables* (oil/copper, 6 1/2 x 8 1/2 ins / 16.5 x 21.5 cm) GBP 15,000. PARIS, 10 April 1991, *Landscape with River* (oil on canvas, 23 1/2 x 19 ins / 60 x 48.5 cm) FRF 17,000. LONDON, 7 Dec 1994, *Wooded Landscape with a Horseman and Huntsman at the Edge of a Pond* (oil on canvas, 40 x 55 1/2 ins / 101.5 x 141 cm) GBP 17,250. LONDON, 9 Dec 1994, *Village in Winter with Peasants and a Man Playing Hockey on a Frozen Canal* (oil on canvas, 19 1/2 x 27 1/4 ins / 49.3 x 69 cm) GBP 36,700. NEW YORK, 19 May 1995, *Still-life with a Monkey Helping Himself from a Basket of Fruit with Wild Strawberries in a Broken Blue and White Bowl on an Entablature* (oil/copper, 6 1/2 x 8 1/2 ins / 16.5 x 21.6 cm) USD 40,250. NEW YORK, 5 Oct 1995, *Fishermen by a River opposite the Ruins of Eyken-*

duynen Chapel near The Hague (oil on canvas, 30 x 26 ins / 76.2 x 66 cm) USD 32,200. NEW YORK, 16 May 1996, *Flowers, Butterflies, Caterpillars, Beetles and Other Insects* (oil/copper, 5 1/2 x 8 ins / 13.7 x 19.4 cm) USD 74,000. LONDON, 1 Nov 1996, *River Landscape with Boats* (oil/copper, 9 3/4 x 13 1/4 ins / 24.8 x 33.7 cm) GBP 21,850. AMSTERDAM, 7 May 1997, *Noah, his Family and the Animals Going on to the Ark* (oil on canvas, 23 1/2 x 33 1/4 ins / 59.6 x 84.4 cm) NLG 98,022. LONDON, 3-4 Dec 1997, *Winter Landscape* (oil on canvas, 45 1/2 x 52 3/4 ins / 115.8 x 134.3 cm) GBP 29,900. NEW YORK, 28 Jan 2000, *Still-life Studies of Fruit and Animals* (oil on copper, four, 6 x 9 ins / 16 x 22 cm) USD 100,000. LONDON, 18 April 2000, *Still-life with Fruit, Monkey and Dog. Still-life with Flowers, Owl and Rabbit* (oil on copper/panel, a pair, 10 x 13 ins / 25 x 33 cm) GBP 115,000. NEUILLY, 12 June 2001, *Allegory of War* (oil on canvas, 19 x 33 ins / 47 x 83 cm) FRF 60,000. PARIS, 19 Dec 2001, *Farmyard Scene* (oil on panel, 9 x 13 ins / 23 x 32 cm) FRF 50,000. NEW YORK, 5 June 2002, *Still-life with Fruit in a Basket. Still-life with Grapes on a White Plate* (oil on copper, 7 x 9 ins / 17 x 22 cm) USD 65,000. PARIS, 5 Dec 2002, *Still-life with Bowl of Flowers* (oil on copper, 7 x 11 ins / 19 x 27 cm) EUR 45,000. LILLE, 23 March 2003, *Two Cats Playing with Fish. Dog, Cat and Lobster* (oil on copper, a pair, 9 x 12 ins / 23 x 31 cm) EUR 32,000. PARIS, 17 Dec 2003, *Allegory of Water* (gouache, 7 x 10 ins / 19 x 25 cm) EUR 8,000. MADRID, 2 March 2004, *Still-life with Fruit* (oil on copper, 5 x 7 ins / 12 x 18 cm) EUR 30,000. PARIS, 25 June 2004, *Still-life with Bowl of Fruit and Little Monkey* (oil on panel, octagonal, 9 x 11 ins / 23 x 28 cm) EUR 20,000.

KESSEL, Jan van III

Flemish School, 17th century.

Born 23 November 1654, in Antwerp; died 1708, in Madrid.

Active in Spain.

Painter. Historical portraits, portraits, animals, insects, still-lifes (including flowers/fruit/vegetables).

Antwerp School.

Jan van Kessel III studied under his father, Jan I. He went to Madrid in 1680 and painted a portrait of Queen Maria Luisa, wife of Charles II and became painter to the court in 1680. He also painted a portrait of Charles II's second wife, Princess Maria-Anna of Palatinate. Van Kessel also worked for Philip V. His Flemish manner was influenced by the Spanish style.

MUSEUMS AND GALLERIES:

ÉPINAL: *Portrait of a Man* - LA FÈRE: *Duck Hunting* - MADRID: *Equestrian Portrait of Philip IV*.

AUCTION RECORDS:

LONDON, 12 Oct 1983, *Landscape with Dogs with a View of Cologne in the Background* (oil/metal, 6 1/4 x 9 ins / 16 x 22 cm) GBP 5,000. AMSTERDAM, 14 Nov 1990, *Gathering of Birds in a Landscape* (oil on canvas, 9 x 11 1/2 ins / 23 x 29.5 cm) NLG 13,225. PARIS, 30 Jan 1991, *Animals in a Landscape* (oil on panel, 10 x 13 3/4 ins / 25.5 x 35 cm) FRF 90,000. LONDON, 17 April 1991, *Still-life with a Dish of Oysters, Almonds, Bread, a Flask of Wine and Glasses and a Fish Grilling on a Brazier; Still-life with a Basket of Grapes, a Bunch of Asparagus and a Cockatoo Pecking at Other Fruit* (oil/copper, a pair, each 6 1/2 x 8 1/2 ins / 16.5 x 21.7 cm) GBP 41,800. LONDON, 5 July 1991, *Still-life with Wild Strawberries in a Chinese Porcelain Dish, Peaches in a Bowl, a Bunch of Asparagus, a Melon etc on a Stone Entablature* (oil/copper, 6 1/2 x 8 1/2 ins / 16.5 x 21.9 cm) GBP 30,800. PARIS, 10 April 1992, *Grasshoppers, Butterflies, Frogs, Currants, a Shrew Mouse, Dragonfly, Caterpillar and Cherry* (copper, a pair, each 6 3/4 x 8 3/4 ins / 17 x 22.5 cm) FRF 250,000. PARIS, 29 March 1994, *Two Cats Playing with Fish; Dog and Cat with a Lobster* (oil/copper, a pair, each 9 1/4 x 12 1/4 ins / 23.5 x 31 cm) FRF 150,000. LONDON, 5 April 1995, *Still-life with a Basket of Flowers, a Blue and White Porcelain Bowl Filled with Wild Strawberries, with a Carnation, a Copper Utensil with a Nightingale on the Handle and a Rabbit* (oil/copper, 9 x 12 ins / 23 x 30.2 cm) GBP 27,600. LONDON, 18 Oct 1995, *Still-life with Game, Hens, Dove, Cat, Dog and a Basket of Fruit on a Step in a Storeroom* (oil/copper, 8 x 11 ins / 20.2 x 28 cm) GBP 8,625. NEW YORK, 12 Jan 1996, *Allegory of Fire: Still-life with a Bellarmine Jug, Silverware and Goldware and a Wanli Porcelain Dish on a Stone Entablature in front of a Burning House* (oil on panel, 11 x 14 3/4 ins / 27.7 x 37.5 cm) USD 52,900. LONDON, 3 Nov 2000, *Wooded River Landscape with Stone Bridge* (oil on canvas, 20 x 27 ins / 51 x 69 cm) GBP 7,500. ZURICH, 28 Nov 2000, *Air* (oil on copper, 8 x 10 ins / 20 x 26 cm) CHF 108,000. LONDON, 9 July 2002, *View of Purmerend Castle, near Monnickendam, Waterland* (oil on canvas, 20 x 27 ins / 51 x 69 cm) GBP 12,500. AMSTERDAM, 3 Dec 2002, *Wooded River Landscape with Fishermen, Hunter and Travellers* (1661, oil on canvas, 37 x 47 ins / 95 x 120 cm) EUR 40,000.

KESSEL, Jean Thomas or Nicolas van

Flemish School, 18th century.

Born 10 September 1677, in Antwerp; died c. 1741, in Antwerp.

Painter. Allegorical subjects, genre scenes, landscapes, landscapes with figures, flowers, animals.

In 1692, Jean Thomas Kessel was a pupil of Peter Eykens and in 1695 studied under his uncle Ferdinand Kessel. He worked in Paris and was a master in Antwerp in 1704. He adopted the style of Teniers and Brauwer and enjoyed considerable success with his village, inn and guardroom scenes and with his flowers and allegorical animal paintings. When Ferdinand Kessel died, the fortune his nephew inherited led him into a life of dissipation which had an adverse effect on his ability and resulted in his ruin. At the end of his life he turned to portraiture but without success. *Bryans' Dictionary* attributes the floral decoration on Teniers' painting *Soap Bubbles* in the Louvre to Kessel. However, it seems more likely that this was the work of Jan van Kessel I.

MUSEUMS AND GALLERIES:

BRUNSWICK - LILLE: *Guardroom Interior; Sense of Smell* - VIENNA (Österreichische Gal. Belvedere).

AUCTION RECORDS:

PARIS, 1853, *Romantic Conversation*, FRF 150. PARIS, 2 Dec 1927, *Monkeys Eating*, FRF 720. PARIS, 12 May 1928, *Assorted Birds on a Branch*, FRF 1,200. NEW YORK, 17 May 1972, *Landscape with Figures*, USD 10,000. ZURICH, 20 May 1977, *Village Celebrations* (oil on canvas, 16 3/4 x 23 1/2 ins / 42.5 x 60 cm) CHF 19,000. LONDON, 28 March 1979, *Still-life with Baskets of Flowers* (two paintings/metal, 7 x 9 ins / 18 x 23 cm) GBP 12,000. PARIS, 16 June 1993, *The Monkey Painter* (oil/copper, 92 x 13 1/2 ins / 233.5 x 34 cm) FRF 120,000. NEW YORK, 16 June 1999, *Elegant Figures Carousing in an Ornamental Garden* (1707, oil on canvas, 24 x 20 ins / 60 x 50 cm) USD 2,200. VIENNA, 6 Oct 1999, *Party Drinking Wine and Merrymaking in the Open Air* (1707, oil on canvas, 24 x 20 ins / 61 x 50 cm) ATS 35,000. MUNICH, 22 March 2000, *Esther before Ahasuerus* (oil on canvas, 17 x 22 ins / 44 x 55 cm) DEM 9,500. PARIS, 8 Dec 2000, *Inn Interiors* (oil on panel, a pair, 11 x 16 ins / 28 x 41 cm) FRF 144,000.

KESSEL, Peter van

Flemish School, 17th century.

Died October 1668, in Ratzeburg (Hamburg).

Active in Antwerp.

Painter. Allegorical subjects, vanitas, flowers.

In 1668, Peter van Kessel went to Lübeck to work with Borchardt Wolff; from there he was summoned to Copenhagen by the king of Denmark. Van Kessel was prosecuted for working as an artist without the council's authority and was released on parole but died in October the same year. He appears to be identical with the Peter van Kessel who was a member of the Delft guild in 1654 and who was known to be in Würzburg in 1658.

Auction records:

New York, 7 April 1989, *Vanitas with Violin, Skull, Flowers and Various Objects* (1664, oil on canvas, 30 x 34¼ ins / 76 x 87 cm) USD 22,000.

KESSEL, Quirin van

Flemish School, 16th century.
Born in Antwerp.
Active in Cologne in 1568.
Painter.

KESSEL, Theodorus van

Dutch, 17th century.
Born c. 1620.
Engraver.

In 1652, Theodorus van Kessel settled in Antwerp. In 1679 an engraver by the name Theodor Andreas van Kessel was a member of the Antwerp guild; he was guild inspector in 1688 and died in 1693.

KESSELER, Will

Luxembourg, 20th century.
Born 1899, in Mersch; died 1983, in Luxembourg.
Active in Luxembourg.
Painter. Still-lifes.

Will Kesseler studied in Paris, from 1919 to 1924, at the École des Beaux-Arts, and then at the Munich Academy. He subsequently spent long periods of time in Africa. He exhibited in several group exhibitions, including that organized by UNESCO at the Musée d'Art Moderne de la Ville de Paris in 1946, where he showed *Still-life with Fish*, and at the São Paulo Biennale. He held solo shows in Luxembourg, Paris, Brussels and New York.

Bibliography:

Cent cinquante ans d'Art luxembourgeois, exhibition catalogue, Musée National d'Histoire et d'Art, Luxembourg, 1989.

Museums and Galleries:

Luxembourg (Mus. national d'histoire et d'art): *Painting* (1954).

KESSELS, A.

Dutch, 18th century.
Active in The Hague in 1719.
Painter.

KESSELS, Matthieu

Dutch, 19th century.
Born 20 May 1784, in Maastricht; died 3 March 1836, in Rome.
Sculptor.

Matthieu Kessels was a pupil of Thorvaldsen. The Brussels academy purchased his sketches after his death.

Bibliography:

Draper, James David/Scherf, Guilhem, et al., *L'esprit créateur de Pigalle à Canova. Terres cuites européennes 1740-1840*, exhibition catalogue, Musée du Louvre, Paris, 2003.

Museums and Galleries:

Brussels (Mus. royaux des Beaux-Arts de Belgique): *Mars at Rest* (c. 1825, terracotta).

KESSELS, Willy

Belgian, 20th century.
Born 1898, in Termonde; died 1974, in Schaerbeek.
Sculptor.

Willy Kessels was self-taught and one of the first Belgian abstract artists.

KESSLER, Adolf

German, 20th century.
Born 16 May 1890, near Landau.
Painter, engraver. Portraits, landscapes, still-lifes.

Adolf Kessler was a student at the fine arts academy in Munich and spent time in Switzerland and Italy.

KESSLER, Adolf Josef

Hungarian, 19th century.
Born 7 April 1859, in Kronstadt (now Brasov, Romania); died 1903, in Budapest.
Sculptor.

Adolf Kessler studied at the Akademie der Bildenden Künste in Vienna, and worked with Huszar and Feszler in Budapest.

KESSLER, Aloys

German, 19th century.
Born 16 October 1777, in Tennenbach; died 1820.
Engraver (burin).

Kessler was a pupil of C. van Meckel and G. von Müller, and is noted for engraving reproductions of classical statues for the French Museum. Among his other works are *Charles II Disembarking in Dover; Battle of Bunker's Hill, near Boston, 17th June 1775*, after J. Trumball; *Funeral of General Graham; Death of General Pierson*, after Singleton (a reduced copy of Heath's engraving); and various portraits.

KESSLER, August or August Friedrich

German, 19th century.
Born 30 December 1826, in Tilsit (now Sovetsk); died April 1906, in Düsseldorf.
Painter. Rustic scenes, landscapes with figures, landscapes, seascapes.

Kessler was a pupil of Schirmer at the academy in Düsseldorf from 1844 to 1851. He subsequently travelled round Germany, Switzerland, the Tyrol and Italy before returning to Düsseldorf to settle. He exhibited in Berlin, Munich, Dresden and Düsseldorf.

Museums and Galleries:

Hanover: *Italian Landscape*.

Auction records:

New York, 14 June 1973, *Wooded Landscape*, USD 1,700. Cologne, 18 March 1977, *Harvest Scene* (1853, oil on canvas, 23½ x 34¼ ins / 60 x 87 cm) DEM 5,000. Cologne, 22 Nov 1979, *The Italian Coast* (1855, oil on canvas, 33 x 51½ ins / 84 x 131 cm) DEM 7,600. New York, 26 Feb 1986, *Bavarian Landscape with Figures* (1858, oil on canvas, 44 x 60½ ins / 112 x 153.7 cm) USD 16,000. Cologne, 6 April 2000, *Shepherds with Cows by Stream* (1857, oil on canvas, 23 x 32 ins / 59 x 81 cm) DEM 14,000. Bremen, 1 July 2000, *Summer Afternoon in the Forest* (1848, oil on canvas, 26 x 35 ins / 66 x 90 cm) DEM 4,600. Stuttgart, 19 Sept 2003, *Romantic Wooded Landscape* (1872, oil on canvas, 13 x 19 ins / 34 x 47 cm) EUR 2,000.

KESSLER, Carl

German, 20th century.
Born 26 October 1876, in Coburg (Bavaria).
Active in Dresden and Munich.
Painter. Landscapes.

KESSLER, Christian Friedrich

German, 19th century.
Born 1799, in Königsberg (now Kaliningrad, Russia); died 26 August 1854, in Tilsit (Sovetsk).
Painter. Portraits, landscapes.

Kessler did a large number of views of cities including Herculaneum, Pompeii, Rome, Berlin, Dresden and St Petersburg.

KESSLER, François Nicolas

French, 19th century.

Born 10 October 1792, in Tavel; died 25 February 1882, in Fribourg.
Sculptor.
Kessler was a pupil of David d'Angers in Paris.

KESSLER, Franz
German, 17th century.
Born c. 1580, in Wetzlar; died c. 1650, in Danzig (now Gdansk, Poland).
Active in Cologne.
Painter.
Kessler was a pupil of Geldorf Gortzius, and was admitted to the guild of painters on 24 October 1615. He travelled from 1620 to 1624, and subsequently returned to Cologne, where he was still living in 1629. There is a *Portrait of a Man* by him in the museum in Budapest and a *Portrait of a Woman* dated 1621 in the museum in Cologne.
AUCTION RECORDS:
COLOGNE, 1862, *Portrait of Mejuffrouw G. Bruyn van Blanckenvoort,* FRF 450; *Portrait of a Man,* FRF 281. PARIS, 1865, *Portraits of Sibert Staden and His Wife,* FRF 250.

KESSLER, Gabriel
Austrian, 17th - 18th century.
Born 1645, in Brixen, South Tyrol (now Bressanone, Italy); died 1719, in Bozen, South Tyrol (now Bolzano, Italy).
Painter.
Kessler was the son of Stephan Kessler and, like his father, painted religious subjects. He worked mostly in the South Tyrolean locations of Chiusa and St Lorenzen near Brunico.

KESSLER, Hans
German, 16th century.
Born in Bremgarten; died before 1525.
Painter.
He lived and worked mostly in Zurich and Lucerne.

KESSLER, Johann Carl
German, 18th century.
Born March 1763, in Frankfurt am Main; died c. 1800, in Frankfurt am Main.
Painter, miniaturist.

KESSLER, Johann Martin Benjamin
German, 18th - 19th century.
Born 17 April 1760, in Frankfurt am Main; died 8 June 1823, in Marburg.
Painter, draughtsman.
Kessler did landscapes and portraits.

KESSLER, Jon
American, 20th - 21st century.
Born 1957, in Yonkers (New York).
Also active in France.
Sculptor, assemblage artist.
Jon Kessler lives and works in New York. His earliest works are relief tableaux featuring kitsch Asian knick-knacks and ornaments (Buddhas, vases, miniature fountains), which form the basis for new, original compositions. Later works use industrial materials (pulleys, cables, cogs) to create monumental mobile sculptures. *Taiwan* (1987) uses lights and motorised parts, sheets of glass and Oriental carpets, porcelain, and small pieces of furniture.

His work has featured in a number of group exhibitions: 1984, Museum of Modern Art, New York and the Whitney Biennial, Whitney Museum of American Art, New York; 1989, New Museum of Contemporary Art, New York; 1991, Martin-Gropius Bau, Berlin; 1992, Hayward Gallery, London. His work has also been the subject of a number of solo exhibitions, including: 1985, International Centre for Contemporary Art, Montreal, and the Institute of Contemporary Art, Boston; 1986, Museum of Contemporary Art, Chicago, and Contemporary Arts Museum, Houston; 1989, Stedelijk Museum, Amsterdam; 1990, Carnegie Museum of Art, Pittsburgh.
BIBLIOGRAPHY:
Kessler, Jon, *Jon Kessler,* Institute of Contemporary Art (University of Pennsylvania), Philadelphia, 1987. Edelman, Robert G., '*Jon Kessler*' in *Art Press 194,* periodical, Paris, September 1994. *In Vivo: Works by Rebecca Horn, Jon Kessler, Dennis Oppenheim, Alan Rath,* University Gallery (University of Massachusetts), Amherst, 1996.
AUCTION RECORDS:
LONDON, 23-24 March 1994, *Battle Crate* (model boat and neon light in a wooden case, 36 1/4 x 61 3/4 x 27 1/2 ins / 92 x 157 x 70 cm) GBP 12,650. NEW YORK, 19 Nov 1996, *The Secret Storm* (1983, acrylic/fibreglass, metal, figurines, electric motor and neon light, 40 x 22 x 8 ins / 101.6 x 55.9 x 20.3 cm) USD 2,530. PARIS, 16 Dec 2000, *Birdrunner III* (1992, neon light, electric motor and bird on colour photo on panel, 39 x 59x12 ins / 98 x 150x30 cm) FRF 27,000. NEW YORK, 16 May 2002, *Days of our Lives* (1983, mixed media construction with lights and motors, 48 x 36 ins / 122 x 91 cm) USD 3,000. NEW YORK, 12 Feb 2004, *X-Ray* (1987, metal and various objects, 20 x 15x13 ins / 51 x 37x32 cm) USD 3,500.

KESSLER, Joseph
Austrian, 19th century.
Born 1826, in Loschitz; died 4 December 1887, in Vienna.
Painter. History painting.
Kessler was a pupil of the academy in Vienna and of Kuppelweiser; he exhibited in Vienna.

KESSLER, Max
Swiss, 20th century.
Born 23 July 1897, in Solothurn.
Painter.
Max Kessler spent time in Paris and was influenced by French Impressionism.

KESSLER, Melchior Kaspar
Swiss, 16th century.
Painter (glass).
Kessler's name appears in accounting records of the Schwyz district in 1573 and 1575. He was married twice.

KESSLER, Michael
Austrian, 17th century.
Born 25 September 1649, in Brixen, South Tyrol (now Bressanone, Italy).
Painter.
Kessler was the son of Stephan Kessler; he worked mainly in Vienna.

KESSLER, Otto
German, 19th century.
Born c. 1830, in Berlin; died c. 1895, in Berlin.
Painter.
Kessler's output mostly consisted of portraits.

KESSLER, Peter
German, 18th - 19th century.
Born 1771, in Frankfurt am Main; died 9 August 1845, in Frankfurt am Main.
Painter. Genre scenes, landscapes.

KESSLER, Raphael
Austrian, 17th century.
Born 1656, in Brixen, South Tyrol (now Bressanone, Italy); died January 1690.
Painter.
Kessler worked in Innsbruck and Brixen.

KESSLER, Stephan
Austrian, 17th century.

Born 1622, in Vienna; died 29 August 1700, in Brixen, South Tyrol (now Bressanone, Italy).
Painter.
Kessler engaged in religious painting and decoration of churches. He worked in numerous Tyrolean and South Tyrolean towns including Bozen (now Bolzano, Italy), Trostberg, Kolmann, Klausen, Feldthurns and Innsbruck, but was active mainly in the vicinity of Brixen.

KESSLER, Ulrich
Swiss, 16th century.
Active in Schwyz.
Painter (glass).
He worked between 1556 and 1572.

KESSNER, August
German, 19th century.
Active in Raschwitz near Leipzig.
Painter. History painting, portraits.
MUSEUMS AND GALLERIES:
RIGA (Mus.): *Portrait of Tsar Alexander I.*

KESTER, Caroline
French, 19th century.
Born 19th century, in Paris.
Painter (including porcelain). Portraits.
Caroline Kester was a pupil of Madame D. de Cool. She began exhibiting her work at the Salon in 1879.

KESTER, Lenard
American, 20th century.
Born 1913.
Painter.

KESTEREN, Chrystian Lodewyk van
Dutch, 19th century.
Born 9 August 1832, in Amsterdam; died 1897, in Amsterdam.
Engraver, lithographer.
Chrystian van Kesteren is known for his portraits and a large number of illustrations he produced for books and almanacs.

KESTING, Edmund
German, 20th century.
Born 1892, in Dresden; died 1970, in Birkenwerder.
Painter. Landscapes.
Edmund Kesting produced figurative work with distorted and stylized forms. His frames, which he considered an intrinsic part of his pictures, were often integrated them with the canvas.
MUSEUMS AND GALLERIES:
BERLIN (Berlinische Gal.): *Village with Spider* (1920).
AUCTION RECORDS:
ZURICH, 23 June 1995, *Untitled* (1925, collage, oil and mixed media, 11¾ x 92 ins / 30 x 233.5 cm) CHF 8,000. BERN, 23 June 2000, *Portrait of Herwarth Walden* (1932, oil on card, 19 x 17 ins / 48 x 43 cm) CHF 44,000. BERN, 23 June 2000, *Picture with Red Zig-zag* (1920, collage, oil, gouache and watercolour on paper, 12 x 12 ins / 30 x 30 cm) CHF 44,000. COLOGNE, 5 May 2001, *Dean Goodelle* (photograph, 11 x 9 ins / 29 x 23 cm) DEM 8,600. COLOGNE, 3 Nov 2001, *Osram* (photograph, 12 x 9 ins / 30 x 24 cm) DEM 56,000. COLOGNE, 4 May 2002, *Dore Hoyer* (photograph, 16 x 12 ins / 40 x 30 cm) EUR 5,200. MUNICH, 4 June 2002, *Scherzando* (mixed media on paper, 12 x 17 ins / 31 x 42 cm) EUR 4,500. COLOGNE, 26 Nov 2003, *Composition in Black* (1922, oil and tempera on hessian, 28 x 28 ins / 72 x 70 cm) EUR 32,000. MUNICH, 14 May 2004, *Houses* (tempera and watercolour over pencil on board, 6 x 6 ins / 16 x 16 cm) EUR 5,000. BERLIN, 25 Nov 2004, *Dore Hoyer* (photograph, 17 x 12 ins / 42 x 30 cm) EUR 3,800.

KESTNER, August
German, 19th century.
Born 28 November 1777, in Hanover; died 5 March 1853, in Rome.
Painter.
Kestner was a diplomat and literary figure as well as an artist. He spent a lot of his life in Rome and painted portraits of a large number of Italian personalities and of Germans passing through the city.

KESTNER, Michael
German, 17th century.
Active in Nuremberg.
Painter, engraver.
Kestner was a pupil of D. Preisler. He painted a number of works on historical themes but mostly concentrated on portraits.

KESU
Indian, 16th century.
Miniaturist.
Kesu worked at the court of the emperor Akbar the Great (1556-1605).

KESU DAS, or the same as/also known as: Kesu; Kesu Kalan; Keshava Kalan
Indian, 16th century.
Miniaturist.
Kesu Das did illuminations at the court of Emperor Akbar the Great (1556-1605).

KESZLER-PUD, Yvonne
French, 19th century.
Painter.
Yvonne Keszler-Pud was a member of the Société des Artistes Français in Paris from 1897.

KESZTHFLYI, Alexander
Hungarian, 19th - 20th century.
Born 31 March 1874.
Active in the USA.
Painter, illustrator.
Alexander Keszthflyi studied in Munich with Herterich and in Vienna with Leffler. In 1903 he won the Harkaniu prize at the Bucharest exhibition and the Rotschild prize in Vienna. He settled in Pittsburgh and was a member of the Carnegie Institute.

KESZY, André Georges
Swiss, 20th century.
Painter.
André Keszy studied at the fine arts school in Zurich. He was awarded a silver medal and the Palme d'Or in Monaco.
MUSEUMS AND GALLERIES:
ZURICH (Prints Collection).

KET, Dick
Dutch, 20th century.
Born 1902, in Den Helder; died 1940, in Bennekom.
Painter, draughtsman. Portraits, landscapes, still-lifes.
Dick Ket studied at the applied arts school in Arnhem. He exhibited little, but took part in the exhibition *Art, Pays-Bas, XXe siècle - La Beauté exacte - De Van Gogh à Mondrian* (*Dutch 20th Century Art: Beauty in Precision, from Van Gogh to Mondrian*) at the Musée d'Art Moderne de la Ville de Paris in 1994. Solo shows include: 1941, Stedelijk Museum, Amsterdam and Gemeentemuseum, The Hague; 1995, Dutch Institute, Paris; 1996, Musée des Beaux-Arts, Valenciennes; and 2004, *Van Dieren, dorpen en landschappen* (*Animals, Villages and Landscapes*), Gemeentemuseum, The Hague.
BIBLIOGRAPHY:
Dick Ket, exhibition catalogue, Gemeentemuseum Arnhem, Nijmegen (NLD), 1988. *Art, Pays-Bas, XXe Siècle - La Beauté exacte, de Van Gogh à Mondrian*, exhibition catalogue, Musée d'Art Moderne de la Ville de Paris, Paris, 1994. *Dick Ket*, exhibition catalogue, Institut Néerlandais, Paris, 1995.

MUSEUMS AND GALLERIES:
AMSTERDAM (Stedelijk Mus.): *Grey Self-portrait* (1931) - ARNHEM (Historisches Mus.): three self-portraits (1930-1939) - ROTTERDAM (Mus. Boijmans Van Beuningen): *Self-portrait with Red Geranium* (1932) - THE HAGUE (Gemeentemus.): *Still-life with Birds' Nests* (1940) - UTRECHT (Centraal Mus.): *Still-life with Several Objects* (1930).
AUCTION RECORDS:
AMSTERDAM, 26 May 1970, *Still-life with Violin,* NLG 7,000. AMSTERDAM, 29 Oct 1980, *Still-life with Violin* (1930, oil on canvas, 31 x 22 3/4 ins / 79 x 58 cm) NLG 46,000. AMSTERDAM, 7 Dec 1981, *Fish* (pen, 35 x 32 3/4 ins / 88 x 83 cm) NLG 5,000. AMSTERDAM, 8 Dec 1988, *Canal in an Ancient City, perhaps Schoonhoven* (1925, ink and pastel/paper, 9 x 6 ins / 22 x 15.5 cm) NLG 1,610. AMSTERDAM, 10 April 1989, *My Grandmother* (oil on panel, 7 x 5 ins / 18 x 13 cm) NLG 2,875. AMSTERDAM, 24 May 1989, *Three Men on a Raft* (1924, charcoal and white paint/cotton, 31 1/2 x 23 3/4 ins / 80 x 60.5 cm) NLG 1,150. AMSTERDAM, 22 May 1990, *Still-life of Bottles near a Flute, with Wrapping Paper and an Enamel Basin on a Draped Entablature* (oil on canvas, 26 x 22 ins / 66 x 56 cm) NLG 109,250. AMSTERDAM, 22 May 1991, *Still-life with Violin* (1932, oil on canvas, 32 x 23 3/4 ins / 81 x 60.5 cm) NLG 40,250. AMSTERDAM, 11 Dec 1991, *Still-life with a Violin, Bread Rolls, and Self-portraits by Schuhmacher and Hynckes* (oil on canvas, 26 x 21 1/4 ins / 66 x 54 cm) NLG 109,250. AMSTERDAM, 19 May 1992, *Still-life of St Nicholas with a White Ewer and Wooden Horses* (1931, oil on canvas, 32 x 23 1/2 ins / 81 x 60 cm) NLG 92,000. AMSTERDAM, 10 Dec 1992, *Self-portrait - the Eater* (oil on canvas, 12 x 10 ins / 30.5 x 25.5 cm) NLG 63,250. AMSTERDAM, 27-28 May 1993, *Portrait of Mej. N. Schilt* (oil on canvas, 39 1/4 x 32 ins / 100 x 81 cm) NLG 69,000. AMSTERDAM, 31 May 1995, *Shoal of All Kinds of Fish* (ink/panel, 35 x 32 3/4 ins / 89 x 83.5 cm) NLG 16,520. AMSTERDAM, 2-3 June 1997, *The Beach at Scheveningen* (1928-1929, oil on canvas, 10 x 12 1/2 ins / 25.5 x 32 cm) NLG 23,600. AMSTERDAM, 16 March 1999, *View of Houses along the Harbour of Hoorn* (oil on canvas, 12 x 16 ins / 30 x 41 cm) NLG 7,000. AMSTERDAM, 7 June 2000, *De Grootmoeder van de Schilder* (black chalk and pencil on card, 10 x 7 ins / 26 x 17 cm) NLG 12,000. AMSTERDAM, 7 June 2000, *Still-life of Flowers* (1925, oil on canvas, 39 x 31 ins / 100 x 80 cm) NLG 50,000. AMSTERDAM, 12 June 2001, *Still-life with Bottles* (c. 1929, oil on canvas, 16 x 11 ins / 40 x 29 cm) NLG 30,000. AMSTERDAM, 12 June 2001, *Self-portrait* (1925, pencil and black chalk, 13 x 10 ins / 33 x 25 cm) NLG 32,000. AMSTERDAM, 16 April 2002, *Self-portrait with a Bread Roll* (c. 1934-1937, oil on canvas, 12 x 10 ins / 31 x 26 cm) EUR 70,000. AMSTERDAM, 3 Dec 2002, *Self-portrait* (1926, pencil and chalk heightened with white, 8 x 6 ins / 21 x 15 cm) EUR 20,000. AMSTERDAM, 30 Nov 2004, *St Nicholas Still-life* (1932, oil on canvas, 32 x 24 ins / 81 x 61 cm) EUR 8,000.

KETEL, Cornelis
Dutch, 16th - 17th century.
Born 18 March 1548, in Gouda; died 1616, buried 8 August in Amsterdam.
Painter, architect, modeller. Allegorical subjects, portraits, group portraits.

Cornelis Ketel was the natural son of G.-J. van Proyen, and was taught in Delft by his uncle, Cornelis Jacobs Ketel, and Anthony Blockland. In 1566, he went to Fontainebleau, and stayed with the painter Jean de la Haine in Paris. Having returned to Gouda in 1568, he then went to London in 1573, where he married a Dutchwoman, and, in 1578, painted the portrait of Queen Elizabeth I. In 1581, he was living in Amsterdam; in 1590, in Gouda. It was rumoured that he stopped painting with a brush altogether, and used his fingertips instead. In 1599, no longer able to work with his hands, he began using his feet. He taught Wouter Crabeth and Pieter Isaaksz. At the time of his death, he was in the service of the king of Denmark.

Ketel painted meetings of arquebusiers, portraits and allegories. He painted group portraits which anticipate the work of Frans Hals. His simple portraits are old-fashioned in their half-length presentation.

BIBLIOGRAPHY:
Bredius, A., *Meisterwerke des Rijksmuseum in Amsterdam.* Walpole, *Anecdotes of Painting in England,* 1762. Van Mander, C., *Het Leven de Nederlandisches Schilders,* H. Huysmans, 1884/1885. Greve, H. E., *De Bronnen van Carel van Mander,* 1903.
MUSEUMS AND GALLERIES:
AMSTERDAM: *Thirteen Arquebusiers; Twenty-two Arquebusiers* - GOUDA: *Arquebusiers* - LONDON (National Maritime Mus.): *Edward Fiennes de Clinton, 1st Earl of Lincoln* (c. 1575, oil/wood, painted after Ketel (?)) - OXFORD: *Martin Frobisher* - UTRECHT: *Family Portrait.*
AUCTION RECORDS:
PARIS, 1900, *Brother and Sister,* FRF 3,675. LONDON, 14 Dec 1907, *Portrait of a Woman,* GBP 3. PARIS, 22 Feb 1936, *Lady Holding Gloves,* FRF 1,250. LONDON, 31 March 1939, *Edward I, the Count of Lincoln,* GBP 48. LONDON, 1 June 1945, *Adriaen Reynertsz Cromhout,* GBP 52. BRUSSELS, 12 March 1951, *Portrait of a Man,* BEF 9,000. LONDON, 26 June 1970, *Study of Bearded Men,* Gns 1,300. PARIS, 26 June 1989, *Portrait of a Young Woman Aged Twenty Seven; Portrait of her Husband Aged Thirty-Three* (1585, two pendants, 4 1/4 x 4 1/2in/11 x 11.5cm) FRF 42,000. PARIS, 12 Dec 1995, *Portrait of Adrien Crombouts, Burgomaster of Amsterdam* (oil on panel, 16 1/4 x 12 1/2in/41 x 32cm) FRF 35,000. LONDON, 12 Nov 1997, *Portrait of Thomas Pead* (1578, oil on panel, 33 3/4 x 27 3/4in/86 x 70.5cm) GBP 34,500. LONDON, 19 April 2000, *Portrait of an Elderly Man* (oil on panel, 13 x 9 ins / 33 x 24 cm) GBP 13,000. LONDON, 4 July 2000, *Portrait of a Bearded Gentleman Wearing a Black Tunic and White Ruff* (oil on panel, 18 x 14 ins / 46 x 35 cm) GBP 2,700.

KETEL, Cornelis Jacobsz.
Dutch, 16th century.
Died c. 1568.
Active in Gouda.
Glass painter.

He was the uncle, and the teacher, of Cornelis Ketel.

KETEL, Jean
Dutch, 19th century.
Painter. Genre scenes.

Jean Ketel was a pupil of J. Ter Beck.

KETELSLEGER
Belgian, 20th century.
Painter.

Ketelsleger's work was influenced by oriental themes and the Middle Ages. He exhibited in Belgium.

KETELTROM. See **BUNNIK Jan van**

KETERLAER, Johannes
Dutch, 17th century.
Engraver.

KETHULLE, Eugène de La. See **LA KETHULLE**

KETOFF, Sacha
20th century.
Active in France.
Assemblage artist.

Sacha Ketoff studied at the Milan art school in 1969 and from 1971 to 1973 he studied architecture in Paris. In 1991 he became interested in numbers, magical signs leading to infinity. In *Hindu Numerals* he placed stick-like symbols made of cord on black phosphorescent rectangles, with the word

SAPTA set in the centre, employing a modern and original language to pay homage to an ancient civilisation. In the 1993 series *Babylon* he united three substances: paper, because it is eternal, gold leaf because it is sacred and unchangeable, and pitch because it is produced by the decomposition of living organisms. He creates an abstract personal space, inspired by architectural forms.

He has shown work in collective exhibitions in Rome, Amsterdam and Paris from 1973 onwards, and has had solo exhibitions in Paris, including that in 1992 at the Salon Découvertes (Discoveries), and others in 1993 at the Bishop's Museum in Limoges, and in Gerona in Spain.

MUSEUMS AND GALLERIES:
HAMBURG (Kunsthalle) - NEW YORK (Cooper-Hewitt Mus.) - PARIS (MNAM-CCI) - PARIS (Mus. des Arts décoratifs).

KETOV, Aleksandr or Alexander
Russian, 20th century.
Born 1914.
Painter. Landscapes.

Aleksandr Ketov painted using thick impasto.

AUCTION RECORDS:
PARIS, 10 Feb 1991, *Gurzuf Landscape* (oil on canvas, 17 1/4 x 20 1/2 ins / 44 x 52 cm) FRF 3,800.

KETT, Willem
Dutch, 18th century.
Painter. Seascapes.

Willem Kett studied in The Hague in 1779; he was an imitator of the seascape painter Vernet.

AUCTION RECORDS:
LONDON, 28 Nov 1958, *River Mouth*, GBP 168.

KETTEN, Maurice
Italian, 20th century.
Born 2 March 1875, in Florence.
Painter, illustrator.

Maurice Ketten was a pupil of Cabanel, Delaunay and Moreau at the École des Beaux-Arts, Paris. His main works are entitled *Such is Life* and *Rest Day*.

KETTENACKER, Anna von. See **JAGEMANN**

KETTENSCHOP, C. V.
17th century.
Draughtsman, engraver (etching).

C.V. Kettenschop was probably a pupil of Rembrandt, whose style he imitated.

KETTERE, Charles Antoine
French, 18th century.
Active in Paris in 1773.
Painter, sculptor.

KETTERLIN, Alois. See **KEIGERLIN**

KETTERLIN, J. J.
Swiss, 18th - 19th century.
Died 1813.
Active in Basel.
Miniaturist.

Ketterlin worked as a drawing teacher.

KETTERLINUS, Christian Wilhelm
German, 18th century.
Born 24 December 1766, in Stuttgart; died 18 May 1803, in St Petersburg.
Engraver.

Ketterlinus studied painting under Guibal and engraving under J. Gotthard Müller, and became court engraver to Duke Karl Eugen in Stuttgart. In 1799 he went to St Petersburg and was accepted into the academy there. A noted work is *The Dutch Drinker* after Mieris. He is probably the same artist as the engraver G. Ketterlinus mentioned by Le Blanc.

KETTLE, Clara E. F.
British, 19th century.
Active in Weymouth.
Miniaturist.

Clara E.F. Kettle exhibited her work at the Royal Academy and the Suffolk Street Gallery from 1845 to 1866.

KETTLE, Henry
British, 18th century.
Active in London.
Painter.

Henry Kettle exhibited at the Society of Artists in 1772.

KETTLE, Rupert A. (Sir)
British, 19th century.
Born 9 January 1817, in Birmingham; died 6 October 1894, in Wolverhampton.
Painter.

Rupert A. Kettle was a lawyer who rose to the position of judge. He was knighted in recognition of the system of arbitration between employers and employees which he established.

MUSEUMS AND GALLERIES:
LONDON (Victoria and Albert Mus.): *The Towyn Coast at Cardigan Bay* (watercolour).

KETTLE, Tilly
British, 18th century.
Born 31 January 1735, in Exeter; died 1786, near Aleppo, Syria.
Painter, pastel artist. History painting, portraits.

Tilly Kettle was the son of a carriage painter. Initially employed in the Duke of Richmond's gallery and later at the Academy of St Martin's Lane, he established himself in London as a portrait painter. He left for India before 1770, staying there for four years and amassing a small fortune. Around 1783, now completely penniless, he left London for Dublin where success eluded him, so he again departed for India but died during the journey. Among the paintings based on his Indian experiences were *The Grand Mogol Reviewing the Troops in the Indian Company* and the historical portrait of the Nawab of Avadh *Choudja-a-ed-Doulah and his son, Myrza-Mani* (Shuja-ud-Daulah) (1770), today at the museum of Versailles.

Kettle showed his work in the exhibitions of the Society of Artists, of which he was a member. He also exhibited at the Royal Academy in London in 1777, 1781, and 1783.

MUSEUMS AND GALLERIES:
LONDON (National Maritime Mus.): *Rear-Admiral Richard Kempenfelt* (1782, oil on canvas, exhibited at the Royal Academy in 1782) - LONDON (National Portrait Gal.): *Anna Seward* (1762, oil on canvas); *Warren Hastings* (c. 1772, oil on canvas) - LONDON (Tate Collection): *Mrs Yates as Mandane in 'The Orphan of China'* (exhibited in 1765, oil on canvas); *Young Man in a Fawn Coat* (c. 1772-1773, oil on canvas) - VERSAILLES: *Shuja-ud-Daulah* (*Choudja-a-ed-Doulah and his son, Myrza-Mani*) (1770).

AUCTION RECORDS:
LONDON, 12 Dec 1908, *Portrait of a Lady; Portrait of a Man* (matching pair) GBP 14. LONDON, 1 Feb 1924, *Anna Seward*, GBP 84; *Sarah Seward*, GBP 84. LONDON, 2 May 1928, *Mr Masson*, GBP 220. LONDON, 2 July 1928, *Warren Hastings*, GBP 94. LONDON, 7 June 1929, *Artist dressed in dark Blue with a Red collar*, GBP 273. LONDON, 26 July 1929, *Man in Buffalo-coloured Jacket*, GBP 157. LONDON, 30 May 1930, *Mrs Drever*, GBP 168. LONDON, 9 April 1937, *John Graham*, GBP 462; *Miss Frances Graham as a Child*, GBP 173; *Mary Helen Graham*, GBP 462. LONDON, 31 March 1943, *Dr Allan D. Graham as a Child*, GBP 220; *Mr John Graham as a Child*, GBP 245. NEW

YORK, 12 Feb 1947, *Children* (pastel) USD 575. NEW YORK, 6 Dec 1958, *The Oldest of the Children*, USD 750. LONDON, 24 July 1959, *Portrait of a young Indian Girl*, GBP 210. LONDON, 12 March 1969, *Portrait of a Woman in a White Dress*, GBP 700. LONDON, 4 April 1973, *Portrait of a Gentleman*, USD 4,500. LONDON, 22 March 1974, *Portrait of Mrs Wayley*, Gns 800. LONDON, 19 Nov 1976, *Portrait of John Hundell* (oil on canvas, 49 1/2 x 39 ins / 125.7 x 99.1 cm) GBP 1,000. LONDON, 25 Nov 1977, *Portrait of Lieutenant James Mayaffre* (1773, oil on canvas, 49 x 39 1/4 ins / 124.4 x 99.6 cm) GBP 2,400. LONDON, 23 March 1979, *Portrait of Sir Richard Sutton* (oil on canvas, 29 1/2 x 24 1/2 ins / 75 x 62.2 cm) GBP 600. LONDON, 26 June 1981, *Group Portrait of Thomas Noel, Viscount of Wentworth, and his Three Sisters* (c. 1766-1768, oil on canvas, 39 x 49 1/4 ins / 99 x 125.2 cm) GBP 14,000. LONDON, 22 April 1983, *Portrait of a Lady* (oil on canvas, 49 x 39 1/4 ins / 124.5 x 99.5 cm) GBP 4,500. LONDON, 20 Nov 1985, *Portrait of Mr Henry Brooke and Mary Aubrey, his Wife* (oil on canvas, a pair, 50 x 40 1/4 ins / 127 x 102 cm) GBP 13,000. NEW YORK, 2 June 1989, *Portrait of Mrs Baldwin*. NEW YORK, 5 April 1990, *Portrait of a Lady (Princess of Orleans?)* (oil on canvas, 48 1/4 x 38 1/4 ins / 122.5 x 97 cm) USD 9,900. LONDON, 15 Nov 1991, *Three-quarter Portrait of John Hundell standing, wearing a white habit over a blue waistcoat with silver frogging, his hand resting on the hilt of his sword.* (oil on canvas, 50 x 40 ins / 127 x 101.6 cm) GBP 8,800. LONDON, 18 Nov 1992, *Three-quarter Portrait of a Gentleman Dreessed in a Blue Habit, in a Landscape* (oil on canvas, 48 x 39 3/4 ins / 122 x 101 cm) GBP 4,180. NEW YORK, 22-23 July 1993, *Portrait of a Young Man* (1769, oil on canvas, 29 x 24 1/4 ins / 73.7 x 61.6 cm) USD 2,990. LONDON, 12 July 1995, *Three-quarter Portrait of a Gentleman Standing Wearing a White Habit and Breeches* (oil on canvas, 49 1/2 x 39 ins / 126 x 99 cm) GBP 11,500. LONDON, 5 Sept 1996, *Portrait of a Gentleman Wearing a Black Habit with Vandyke Collar.*, GBP 2,070. LONDON, 8 June 1999, *Portrait of a Young Indian Boy* (oil on canvas, 35 x 27 ins / 89 x 69 cm) GBP 100,000. LONDON, 24 Nov 1999, *Portrait of a Gentleman, Wearing Red Slashed van Dyck Costume* (oil on canvas, 29 x 24 ins / 74 x 60 cm) GBP 17,000. LONDON, 21 Sept 2000, *Portrait of Umdat-ul-Umara and Amir-ul-Umara, the Two Sons of Nawab Muhammad Ali Khan* (oil on canvas, 50 x 38 ins / 127 x 96 cm) GBP 110,000. LONDON, 30 Nov 2000, *Portrait of Lady Wearing a Lace Bonnet* (oil on canvas, 30 x 25 ins / 75 x 63 cm) GBP 7,000. LONDON, 10 July 2001, *Portrait of George, 3rd Earl of Dartmouth as a Boy* (oil on canvas, 22 x 18 ins / 57 x 45 cm) GBP 9,500. LONDON, 29 Nov 2001, *Portrait of John Graham, Standing in a Landscape* (oil on canvas, 50 x 40 ins / 127 x 101 cm) GBP 9,500. LONDON, 19 March 2003, *Portrait of Lord Charles Spencer-Churchill* (oil on canvas, 30 x 24 ins / 75 x 62 cm) GBP 10,000. LONDON, 21 July 2003, *Portrait of George Rowley of Shropshire and Priory Hill, Cambridgeshire* (oil on canvas, 30 x 24 ins / 75 x 62 cm) GBP 10,000. NEW YORK, 23 Jan 2004, *Portrait of Gentleman in India* (oil on canvas, 51 x 41 ins / 129 x 103 cm) USD 9,500. LONDON, 26 March 2004, *Self-portrait, Wearing Blue Coat with Gold Buttons* (oil on canvas, 29 x 24 ins / 74 x 62 cm) GBP 18,000.

KETTLER, Friedrich

German, 18th century.
Born 1718; died 3 May 1783.
Painter. Flowers.

Kettler was an army general as well as an artist. He concentrated on paintings of flowers.

KETTNER, Ferdinand

Austrian, 19th century.
Born 1779; died 1834, in Vienna.
Miniaturist.

Kettner was noted for portraits on ivory, including one of the painter Steiger (1802).

KETZ, Sigmund von

German, 15th century.
Active in Nuremberg.
Painter.

He worked for the church of Hammersfeld.

KEUDELL, Marie von

German, 19th - 20th century.
Born 16 July 1838, in Launincken; died 7 February 1918, in Berlin.
Landscape artist.

Marie von Keudell was a student of Dressler, E. Pape and O. von Kameke. She worked in Switzerland, Italy and England, and exhibited, from 1866, in Berlin, Dresden, Hanover and Munich.

KEUFFEL, Johann Matthäus

German, 19th century.
Born 5 September 1841, in Frankfurt am Main.
Painter.

Keuffel's work comprises mainly ceilings and decorative frescoes such as those of the Villa Arnoldi in Mainz and the Imperial Palace in Strasbourg.

KEUKEL

German, 18th century.
Miniaturist.

Keukel established himself in Vienna and married the sister of the painter Sedelmeyer, whom he taught.

KEULEMANS, Johannes Gerardus

Dutch, 19th - 20th century.
Born 1842, in Rotterdam; died 1912, in England.
Painter, engraver, illustrator. Natural history (animals/birds).

Johannes Keulemans was an enthusiast for natural history and ornithology, and produced very precise images of many types of birds. He executed the lithographs for Hermann Schlegel and P. L. Pollen's *Research on the Fauna of Madagascar*, published in Leiden in 1868.

MUSEUMS AND GALLERIES:

LONDON (Natural History Mus.): *Cassowary (Casuarius papuanus)* (c. 1900, watercolour, from a series about Cassowaries).

AUCTION RECORDS:

LONDON, 29 Nov 1984, *Australian Kowis* (watercolour gouache and charcoal, 18 x 27 1/4 ins / 45.7 x 69.2 cm) GBP 6,500. LONDON, 20 Nov 1986, *Owl* (watercolour and touches of gouache, 19 1/2 x 14 1/4 ins / 49.5 x 36.5 cm) GBP 4,200. AUCHTERARDER, 1 Sept 1987, *Partridge* (watercolour heightened with gouache, 7 3/4 x 12 ins / 20 x 30.5 cm) GBP 3,200. NEW YORK, 7 June 1991, *Raccoon* (watercolour and pencil/paper, 24 x 32 ins / 61 x 81.3 cm) USD 6,050. LONDON, 25 Feb 1992, *Bird Twittering* (watercolour heightened with white, 7 3/4 x 5 3/4 ins / 19.7 x 14.7 cm) GBP 1,210. LONDON, 16 March 1993, *A Partridge among the Reeds* (watercolour, 13 1/4 x 10 1/2 ins / 33.7 x 26.7 cm) GBP 862. LONDON, 14 May 1996, *Common Fisher Swift* (watercolour and gouache, 10 x 6 1/2 ins / 24.5 x 16.5 cm) GBP 1,035.

KEULEN, Cornelis Janssens, Janson or Jonson van. See **CEULEN**

KEULEN, Johannes van

Dutch, 15th century.
Active in Zwolle c. 1400.
Painter, goldsmith. History painting.

After starting his career as a painter and gold and silversmith, he became a monk.

KEULEN, Simon van

German, 20th century.
Born 1926.
Painter.
Surrealism.

KEULEN, Thomas van
Dutch, 16th century.
Active during the second half of the 16th century.
Painter. History painting.
Thomas van Keulen was taught by Frans Floris. A reference to him is dated 1580.

KEULEYAN, or Keleyan-Lafon, pseudonym of Jean Lafon
French, 20th century.
Born 22 March 1886, in Paris; died 1973.
Painter. Landscapes, seascapes.
Keuleyan specialised in scenes set in moonlight and sunset.
AUCTION RECORDS:
PARIS, 4 July 1945, *Seascape*, FRF 520. ENGHIEN-LES-BAINS, 23 Sept 1984, *Barges at Nightfall* (oil on canvas, 26 x 35 3/4 ins / 66 x 91 cm) FRF 18,500.

KEULLER, Renée
Belgian, 20th century.
Born June 1899, in Antwerp; died 8 March 1981, in Antwerp.
Painter, draughtsman. Nudes, portraits, landscapes, still-lifes.
Renée Keuller was the daughter of the landscape painter Vital Keuller. She mainly painted portraits in different styles, notably *James Ensor*, who gave her artistic guidance, *Queen Astrid, Queen Fabiola*, and *Princess Paola*. She was a Chevalier de l'Ordre de la Couronne.

KEULLER, Vital
French, 19th - 20th century.
Born 1866, in Lille; died 1945, in Mariembourg.
Active in Belgium.
Painter. Portraits, landscapes, seascapes.
Vital Keuller studied under Stallaert and Portaels.
AUCTION RECORDS:
LOKEREN, 21 March 1992, *Dairymaid* (gouache, 28 x 35 3/4 ins / 71 x 91 cm) BEF 38,000. LOKEREN, 15 May 1993, *Forest under Snow* (1941, oil on canvas, 31 1/2 x 39 1/4 ins / 80 x 100 cm) BEF 90,000. LOKEREN, 28 May 1994, *Autumn in the Forest* (oil on canvas, 31 1/2 x 39 1/4 ins / 80 x 100 cm) BEF 50,000. LOKEREN, 11 March 1995, *Jetty and Old Kursaal in Ostend* (oil on card, 13 1/2 x 19 1/4 ins / 34.5 x 49 cm) BEF 60,000. LOKEREN, 9 March 1996, *View of the Beguine Convent of Lier* (1923, oil on panel, 36 x 48 ins / 91.5 x 121 cm) BEF 170,000.

KEULTJES, Gerrit Laurens
Dutch, 19th - 20th century.
Born 10 August 1879, in Utrecht; died c. 1918.
Painter. Portraits, genre scenes, seascapes.
Gerrit Keultjes specialised in seascapes.
MUSEUMS AND GALLERIES:
AMSTERDAM: *Attack of the Dutch Fleet at Algiers* (1816).

KEUN, Catherine
French, 20th - 21st century.
Born 1958, in Courbevoie.
Engraver.
Catherine Keun was selected for the Grav'X prize by the Galerie Michèle Broutta, Paris in 1991. In 2002 she took part in the collective exhibition at the Galerie Madeleine Lacerte, Montreal, as part of an exchange with the Galerie Michèle Broutta.

KEUN, Hendrik, or Keune
Dutch, 18th century.
Born 14 August 1738, in Haarlem; died c. 1788, in Haarlem.
Painter, engraver. Urban landscapes, waterscapes.
Hendrik Keun painted in the style of Berkleyden.
MUSEUMS AND GALLERIES:
AMSTERDAM: *View of Heerengracht.*
AUCTION RECORDS:
LONDON, 14 Dec 1938, *The Niewe Poort, Haarlem* (drawing) GBP 68. NEW YORK, 19 March 1981, *Canal Scene* (oil on canvas, 30 3/4 x 16 1/4 ins / 78 x 41.3 cm) USD 3,250. LONDON, 12 Dec 1985, *The Nieuwe Poort, Haarlem* (1769, watercolour, 10 x 14 ins / 25.4 x 35.6 cm) GBP 1,500. AMSTERDAM, 14 Nov 1995, *Dutch Coastal Landscape with Fishermen Bringing in their Catch and Sailing Ships* (oil on canvas, 12 1/2 x 18 ins / 32 x 46 cm) NLG 8,850. AMSTERDAM, 5 Sept 2000, *Farm by River with Cattle. Peasant Milking Cow near Farm* (oil on canvas, a pair, 9 x 13 ins / 23 x 33 cm) NLG 8,500. AMSTERDAM, 16 April 2002, *Keizersgracht, Amsterdam* (1772, oil on panel, 21 x 30 ins / 53 x 75 cm) EUR 70,000. LONDON, 9 July 2003, *Singel, Amsterdam, with the Munttorren* (oil on panel, 14 x 19 ins / 36 x 48 cm) GBP 11,000. AMSTERDAM, 4 Nov 2003, *View of the Weerdpoort with the Domtorne beyond* (oil on canvas, 19 x 26 ins / 49 x 65 cm) EUR 13,500. AMSTERDAM, 18 May 2004, *Haaelem, View from the South-east* (oil on panel, 13 x 14 ins / 33 x 36 cm) EUR 7,000.

KEUNEN, Alexis
Belgian, 20th century.
Born 1921, in Liège; died 1990.
Painter, engraver.
Surrealism.
Alexis Keunen studied at the St Luke Academy in Liège.
AUCTION RECORDS:
BRUSSELS, 21 Dec 1976, *Resurrection of the Flesh* (1958, oil on canvas, 78 3/4 x 118 ins / 200 x 300 cm) BEF 100,000. LOKEREN, 23 May 1992, *Perpetual Mobile* (1966, oil on canvas, 36 1/4 x 28 3/4 ins / 92 x 73 cm) BEF 26,000. LOKEREN, 20 May 1995, *Violation no. 8* (1973, oil on canvas, 24 3/4 x 31 ins / 63 x 79 cm) BEF 26,000.

KEUNING, Christian. See **KONINCK**

KEUNING, Daan
Dutch, 20th century.
Born 1891, in Hoofdoorp.
Painter. Portraits, local scenes, interiors with figures.
Daan Keuning was a wig-maker who painted scenes from his everyday life - views of his house, family scenes or his wife having a siesta - with minute attention to detail.
BIBLIOGRAPHY:
Gans, Louis, *Meesters der Europese naïven*, exhibition catalogue, Centraal Museum, Utrecht, 1970.

KEUS, A.
Dutch, 20th century.
Born 7 September 1875, in Rotterdam.
Painter, engraver. Landscapes.
A. Keus studied at the fine arts academy in The Hague and exhibited from 1912.

KEUSTERMANS, Jan
Belgian, 20th century.
Born 1940, in Hoboken.
Sculptor.
Jan Keustermans studied at the fine arts institute in Antwerp.

KEUTART, Gérard
Flemish School, 15th century.
Active in Tournai.
Painter.

KEUTH, Hermann
German, 20th century.
Born 6 July 1888, in Ravensburg.
Painter, engraver. Landscapes.
Herman Keuth was a student of P. Halms and painted views of the Sarre valley.

KEUTSCHACH, Johann Ernst van
Austrian, 18th century.

Born 1710, in Salzburg; died 14 July 1773, in Salzburg.
Painter.

Keutschach engaged mainly in decorative work, though he also painted landscapes.

KEUX. See **LE KEUX**

KEVER, Jacob Simon Hendrik

Dutch, 19th - 20th century.
Born 19 June 1854, in Amsterdam; died 1922.
Painter, watercolourist. Figures, portraits, genre scenes, local scenes, interiors with figures, flowers.

Jacob Kever studied with P. F. Greive and at the fine arts academy in Amsterdam. He exhibited in Brussels in 1910, and was awarded medals in Munich in 1901 and 1905 and in Paris at the Exposition Universelle of 1898 and 1900.

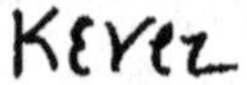

MUSEUMS AND GALLERIES:

AMSTERDAM: *Interior* - THE HAGUE (Gemeentemus.): *Interior; Portrait of the Painter Conrad Metzelaar.*

AUCTION RECORDS:

NEW YORK, 19-20 March 1903, *Keeping Baby Happy,* USD 335. NEW YORK, 27 Jan 1905, *Keeping Baby Happy,* USD 1,330. NEW YORK, 27 April 1906, *The Dress-making School,* USD 1,750. NEW YORK, 10-11 Jan 1907, *The Illustrated Book,* USD 1,300. LONDON, 21 March 1908, *Baby's Soup,* GBP 22. LONDON, 12 June 1908, *Careful Nanny,* GBP 36. NEW YORK, 6 Jan 1911, *The Dress-making School,* USD 2,050. LONDON, 21 June 1929, *New History Book,* GBP 99. LONDON, 11 June 1934, *Sun-lit Period of Life,* GBP 48. NEW YORK, 8 May 1947, *At the Window,* USD 200. AMSTERDAM, 22 Oct 1974, *Young Girl Knitting,* NLG 8,500. AMSTERDAM, 26 May 1976, *Farmers in an Interior* (watercolour, 18 1/2 x 21 3/4 ins / 47 x 55.5 cm) NLG 2,600. AMSTERDAM, 15 Nov 1976, *Farmer's Wife and Child in an Interior* (oil on canvas, 22 1/4 x 30 ins / 56.5 x 76 cm) NLG 14,000. AMSTERDAM, 31 Oct 1977, *Mother and Children in an Interior* (oil on canvas, 37 3/4 x 49 1/2 ins / 96 x 125.5 cm) NLG 17,000. AMSTERDAM, 20 March 1978, *Motherhood* (oil on canvas, 34 3/4 x 31 1/4 ins / 88.5 x 79.5 cm) NLG 14,000. NEW YORK, 26 Jan 1979, *Brother and Sister* (oil on canvas, 18 x 20 3/4 ins / 46 x 53 cm) GBP 5,250. ZURICH, 10 Nov 1982, *Mother and Child* (oil on canvas, 29 3/4 x 36 ins / 75.5 x 91.5 cm) CHF 16,000. AMSTERDAM, 6 June 1983, *Mother and Child* (oil on canvas, 35 1/4 x 27 ins / 89.5 x 68.5 cm) NLG 13,500. NEW YORK, 13 Feb 1985, *The Knitting Lesson* (oil on canvas, 29 x 41 ins / 73.6 x 104.2 cm) USD 20,000. NEW YORK, 28 Oct 1987, *Children Watching Baby Asleep* (oil on canvas remounted on board, 30 x 40 3/4 ins / 76.2 x 103.8 cm) USD 13,000. AMSTERDAM, 30 Aug 1988, *Mother Caressing her Child near a Cradle in an Interior* (oil on canvas, 17 1/4 x 13 1/4 ins / 44 x 33.5 cm) NLG 3,220. AMSTERDAM, 16 Nov 1988, *Farmer's Wife Reading to her Child in an Interior* (oil on canvas, 12 1/2 x 9 1/2 ins / 31.5 x 24 cm) NLG 4,140. AMSTERDAM, 19 Sept 1989, *Child Sat in a Push-chair* (oil on canvas, 11 3/4 x 8 1/2 ins / 29.8 x 21.7 cm) NLG 1,610. NEW YORK, 25 Oct 1989, *Still-life with Peonies* (oil on canvas, 31 1/2 x 35 ins / 80 x 88.8 cm) USD 17,600. NEW YORK, 1 March 1990, *Dressing Baby* (oil on canvas, 29 x 35 1/2 ins / 73.7 x 90.2 cm) USD 15,400. AMSTERDAM, 2 May 1990, *Still-life with Lilacs and Other Flowers in a Crystal Vase* (oil on canvas, 27 3/4 x 24 ins / 70.5 x 61 cm) NLG 14,950. AMSTERDAM, 6 Nov 1990, *Roses in a Bowl* (oil on canvas, 16 1/4 x 14 1/2 ins / 41 x 37 cm) NLG 8,970. AMSTERDAM, 5-6 Feb 1991, *Knitting for Baby* (oil on canvas, 23 1/2 x 30 ins / 60 x 76 cm) NLG 16,100. AMSTERDAM, 24 April 1991, *Mother Cutting Bread for her Children* (oil on canvas, 36 1/4 x 29 1/2 ins / 92 x 75 cm) NLG 9,200. AMSTERDAM, 22 April 1992, *Little Girl Rocking a Baby under the Watchful Gaze of her Mother* (oil on canvas, 16 3/4 x 21 3/4 ins / 42.5 x 55.5 cm) NLG 6,670. AMSTERDAM, 28 Oct 1992, *Spring Idyll* (oil on canvas, 15 3/4 x 16 3/4 ins / 40 x 42.5 cm) NLG 9,775. AMSTERDAM, 2 Nov 1992, *The Reading Lesson* (oil on canvas, 20 3/4 x 25 1/2 ins / 53 x 65 cm) NLG 4,370. NEW YORK, 12 Oct 1993, *Mother's Helper* (oil on canvas, 16 x 20 ins / 40.6 x 51.1 cm) USD 8,625. AMSTERDAM, 9 Nov 1993, *Motherly Tenderness* (oil on canvas, 29 x 34 3/4 ins / 73.5 x 88.5 cm) NLG 17,250. AMSTERDAM, 11 April 1995, *Children Playing with a Goat* (oil on canvas, 15 3/4 x 19 3/4 ins / 40 x 50 cm) NLG 9,440. AMSTERDAM, 5 Nov 1996, *A Happy Family* (oil on canvas, 22 x 32 ins / 56 x 81 cm) NLG 8,850. AMSTERDAM, 19-20 Feb 1997, *Flowers in a Vase* (oil on canvas, 18 1/2 x 16 1/4 ins / 47 x 41 cm) NLG 4,843. AMSTERDAM, 22 April 1997, *Feeding the Goat* (watercolour, 15 x 17 1/4 ins / 38 x 43.5 cm) NLG 23,600.

KEVORKIAN DER. See **DER KEVORKIAN**

KEY, Adriaen Thomas, the Elder

Flemish School, 16th century.
Painter.

Adriaen Thomas Key the Elder is believed to have visited Antwerp, where he gave his sons their artistic training. One of them, Cornelis, is mentioned in a reference dated 1549; the other, Michel, in a document dated 1592. He was probably also the father of Adriaen Thomasz. Key.

KEY, Adriaen Thomasz., the Younger, or Keyen

Flemish School, 16th century.
Born 1544, in Antwerp; died 1589.
Painter. Portraits.
Antwerp School.

He was probably the son of Adriaen Thomas Key the Elder. He was a master in Antwerp in 1568, taught Jean Lossaert in 1582 and Adam van Puttens in 1588, and was still alive in 1589. An artist of the same name worked in Venice between 1558 and 1568.

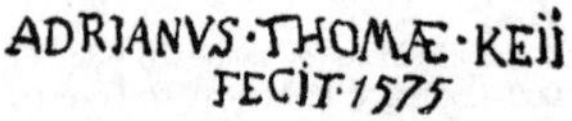

BIBLIOGRAPHY:

Van den Branden, F.J., *Geschichte die Antwerpsche Schilderschool*, 1883. Ring, G.., *Beitrage zu Geschichte die Niederlandische Bildnismalerei im 15. und 16. Jahrhunderte*, 1913. Valentiner, W.R., *Catalogue of a Collection of Paintings*, John G. Johnson, Philadelphia, 1913/1914.

MUSEUMS AND GALLERIES:

AMSTERDAM: *Portrait of a Nobleman* - ANTWERP: *Gilles de Smidt and his Seven Sons; Marie de Deckere, the Wife of the Former, and her Daughters* - BRUSSELS: *Portrait of a Man, and of the Artist* - DUBLIN: *Two Portraits of Men* - HAMBURG: *William of Nassau* - MUNICH: *Portrait of a Man* - SCHWERIN: *Dark-haired Man; Woman Wearing a Pearl Tiara; Portrait of a Man* - THE HAGUE: *William I of Orange-Nassau* - VIENNA: *Gillis Mostraert; Portrait of a Man.*

AUCTION RECORDS:

LONDON, 22 July 1910, *Portrait of a Woman,* GBP 11. LONDON, 8 April 1911, *Lady in a Black Dress,* GBP 16. PARIS, 8 June 1924, *Portrait of Adrien Cromhout, Burgomaster of Amsterdam,* FRF 10,000. LOCHEM, 29 May 1951, *Portrait of a Gentleman,* NLG 3,000. LONDON, 29 Oct 1958, *Portrait of a Gentleman,* GBP 150. LONDON, 3 March 1965, *Portrait of a Gentleman,* GBP 400. NEW YORK, 1 June 1989, *Portrait of a Gentleman* (oil on panel, 17 3/4 x 14 3/4in/45 x 37.5cm) USD 18,700. LONDON, 3 July 1991, *Portrait of Adriaen van Marsellaer of Antwerp* (oil on panel, 19 x 13 3/4in/48 x 35cm) GBP 7,920. LONDON, 13 Dec 1991, *Seated, Three-quarter Portrait of a Gentleman at a Table, his Hand Resting on a Head, and Surrounded by his Three Sons and Three Daughters* (1583, oil on panel, 36 x 45 1/4in/91.5 x 115cm) GBP 374,000. NEW YORK, 14 Jan 1993, *Portrait of a Bearded Gentleman, Standing, Wearing a Black Suit with White Cuffs and Collar* (1564, oil on canvas, 41 1/2 x 30 1/2in/105.7 x 77.5cm) USD 66,000. NEW YORK, 12 Jan 1994, *Bust Portrait of a Bearded Man with a White Ruff* (oil on panel, 20 x 15 1/2in/51 x 39.5cm) USD 19,550. NEW YORK, 31 Jan 1997, *Bust Portrait of a Bearded Man Wearing Gold Chains* (1575, oil on panel, 20 3/4 x 15 1/4in/52.7 x 38.8cm) USD 20,700. PARIS, 22 Oct 1999, *Portrait of William of Orange* (oil on panel, 19 x 14 ins / 48 x 35 cm) FRF 52,000. LONDON, 17 Dec 1999, *Portrait of Lady in Black Brocade Dress with Organza Ruff* (1579, oil on panel, 19 x 14 ins / 48 x 35 cm) GBP 6,500. LONDON, 10 Dec 2002, *Portrait of a Lady aged 31, in a Black Dress* (1573, oil on panel, 19 x 15 ins / 49 x 38 cm) GBP 26,000. VIENNA, 27 March 2003, *Portrait of Gentleman in Ruff* (oil on panel, 19 x 15 ins / 48 x 39 cm) EUR 18,000. LONDON, 30 Oct 2003, *Portrait of a Lady Wearing a Black Coat and White Ruff, Holding a Book* (oil on panel, 41 x 29 ins / 104 x 74 cm) GBP 15,000. ZURICH, 26 March 2004, *Portrait of Man in Black Jacket* (1568, oil on panel, 18 x 13 ins / 46 x 34 cm) CHF 20,000.

KEY, Hendrik
Flemish School, 19th century.
Active in Antwerp c. 1834.
Painter. Genre scenes.

KEY, Henry
British, 18th century.
Died c. 1799, in Hatfield (Yorkshire).
Glass painter.

Henry Key painted pictures of flowers.

KEY, John Ross
American, 19th - 20th century.
Born 1832, in Baltimore; died 1920.
Painter (including gouache). Landscapes, landscapes with figures.

John Ross Key exhibited at the National Academy of Design, the Pennsylvania Academy of the Fine Arts, the Boston Athenaeum, and the Boston Art Club. He won a medal at the Centennial Expo in Philadelphia in 1876. He was a member of the Society of Washington Artists and the Boston Art Club.

AUCTION RECORDS:
NEW YORK, 11 April 1973, *Drewry's Bluff*, USD 9,500. NEW YORK, 23 Jan 1979, *Cattle Grazing* (oil on card, 18 1/2 x 24 1/2 ins / 47 x 62.5 cm) USD 1,100. BOLTON, 21 May 1981, *View of Lake Tahoe* (1871, oil on canvas, 20 x 40 ins / 50.8 x 101.6 cm) USD 11,500. NEW YORK, 21 Sept 1984, *Lake Tahoe* (1879, oil on canvas, 20 1/4 x 37 3/4 ins / 51.4 x 96.2 cm) USD 9,000. SAN FRANCISCO, 27 Feb 1986, *Lone Boat on Lake Tahoe* (1877, oil on canvas, 16 1/4 x 30 1/4 ins / 41 x 77 cm) USD 12,000. NEW YORK, 17 March 1988, *Figures in a Californian Landscape* (oil on canvas, 15 3/4 x 29 1/2 ins / 40 x 75 cm) USD 12,100. NEW YORK, 30 Sept 1988, *Cliffs on the Seafront* (oil on canvas, 14 1/4 x 20 ins / 36 x 50.5 cm) USD 2,860. NEW YORK, 24 May 1989, *Landscape with Lake at Dusk* (1871, oil on canvas, 20 x 40 ins / 50.8 x 101.6 cm) USD 31,900. NEW YORK, 26 Sept 1990, *Californian Coastline* (1872, oil on canvas, 30 1/4 x 50 1/4 ins / 76.8 x 127.6 cm) USD 19,800. NEW YORK, 17 Dec 1990, *Barges along the River* (1877, oil on canvas, 16 1/4 x 26 1/2 ins / 41.3 x 67.4 cm) USD 2,640. NEW YORK, 22 May 1991, *World Trade fair in Chicago in 1892* (gouache/card, 13 1/2 x 21 ins / 34.3 x 53.3 cm) USD 4,400.

KEY, Willem, or Kay
Flemish School, 16th century.
Born c. 1515 or 1520, in Breda; died 5 June 1568, in Antwerp.
Painter. Religious subjects, portraits.
Antwerp School.

Willem Key studied under Peter Cock van Alost and Lambert Lombard in 1529. He was a master of the guild of Antwerp in 1542, became a citizen on 25 April 1550, and a dean of the guild in 1552. While painting the portrait of the Duke of Alba, he overheard the Duke, who did not realise Key could understand Spanish, speaking of the death sentence that had been given to the counts of Egmont and Horn. The distress that either this or the duke's anger caused him made him ill, and he died on the very day of the counts' execution.

Key also painted altarpieces, which have almost all been destroyed. He seems to have renounced Protestantism and to have had sympathies with the followers of Guise.

BIBLIOGRAPHY:
Pacheco, F., *Arte de la pintura*, Cruzada Villaamil, Madrid, 1649. Van den Branden, F.J., *Geschichte die Antwerpsche Schilderschool*, 1883. Van Mander, K., *Het Schilder Boeck*, H. Huysmans, Paris, 1884/1885. Parthey, G., *'Deutscher Bildersaal'* in *Catalogue de la peinture ancienne*, Musée Royale de Belgique, Brussels, 1923. Winkler, F., *Die Altniederlandische Malerei*, Berlin, 1924. Vasari, G., *The Lives of the Artists*, Oxford Paperbacks, 1998.

MUSEUMS AND GALLERIES:
AMSTERDAM: *Lady from the Centen Family* - BUDAPEST: *Portrait of a Man* - HANOVER: *Two Portraits* - POMMERSFELDEN: *Suzanne Bathing* - VIENNA: *Two Portraits*.

AUCTION RECORDS:
PARIS, 24 April 1944, *Portrait of a Man*, FRF 17,000. LUCERNE, 1950, *Virgin with the Holy Child*, CHF 2,800. LUCERNE, 15-16 June 1967, *Portrait of an Old Man*, CHF 12,000. LONDON, 21 June 1968, *Portrait of a Bearded Man*, Gns 700. VIENNA, 6 June 1972, *Suzanne and the Old Men*, ATS 60,000. NEW YORK, 5 June 1979, *Portrait of Marguerite Halscher of Basel* (oil on panel, 13 x 10in/33 x 25.5cm) USD 3,500. LONDON, 21 April 1982, *Portrait of a Gentleman* (oil on panel, 26 1/2 x 20in/67 x 51cm) GBP 3,200. NEW YORK, 15 Jan 1988, *The Four Doctors of the Church* (oil on canvas, 48 1/2 x 41in/123.5 x 104cm) USD 6,600. NEW YORK, 10 Jan 1990, *Portrait of a Gentleman Aged 39, Wearing a Black Habit and a Black Hat and Holding a Pair of Gloves* (1567, oil on panel, 33 x 25in/83.8 x 63.5cm) USD 44,000. NEW YORK, 4 April 1990, *The Four Doctors of the Church* (oil on canvas, 48 1/2 x 41in/123.5 x 104cm) USD 7,700. NEW YORK, 16 Jan 1992, *Portrait of a Man Wearing a Black Habit and a Beret* (oil on panel, 20 x 15 1/4in/50.6 x 38.9cm) USD 19,800. CALAIS, 3 July 1994, *Portrait of Phillip of Montmorency-Nivelle II, the Count of Horn* (oil on canvas, 19 x 15in/48 x 38cm) FRF 31,000. AMSTERDAM, 16 Nov 1994, *Portrait of a Gentleman* (oil on panel, 31 1/4 x 23 1/2in/79.5 x 59.5cm) NLG 41,400. NEW YORK, 30 Jan 1997, *Portrait of a Lady* (oil on panel, 21 1/2 x 17in/54.3 x 43.2cm) USD 90,500. LONDON, 6 July 2000, *Portrait of a Gentleman Standing before a Green Curtain* (oil on panel, 23 x 17 ins / 58 x 44 cm) GBP 55,000. NEW YORK, 22 Jan 2004, *Venus and Cupid* (oil on panel, 37 x 51 ins / 94 x 129 cm) USD 150,000.

KEY, Wouter, or Keyn
Flemish School, 16th century.
Active in Breda.
Painter.
Antwerp School.

Wouter Key was the brother of Willem Key. He studied under Jan de Cock in 1516, and was a master in Antwerp in 1531. He taught Symon van Breda in 1532, and Baptista de Kanksen in 1544. He married in 1540.

KEYER, Ragnihild
Norwegian, 20th century.
Active in the 1930s and 1940s.
Painter.

KEYERT, Ruik
Dutch, 18th century.

Born 1709; died 1775.
Active probably in Friesland in the middle of the 18th century.
Painter, draughtsman. Portraits.

Ruik Keyert worked in The Hague in 1728 and 1731. He drew portraits after old paintings.

MUSEUMS AND GALLERIES:
BERGEN: *Hobbe Baert van Sminia and Brothers.*

AUCTION RECORDS:
AMSTERDAM, 19-20 Feb 1997, *Portrait of a Young Man Standing Holding a Book of Modern History* (1751, oil on canvas, 16 1/4 x 12 3/4 ins / 41.5 x 32.6 cm) NLG 1,153.

KEYL, Bernhardt. See **KEIL Bernhardt** or **Ebehardt**

KEYL, Christian Karl Maximilian
German, 18th - 19th century.
Born 14 January 1766, in Dresden; died 18 November 1818, in Dresden.
Draughtsman, engraver (burin).

Keyl was the son and pupil of Michael Keyl; he drew and engraved topographical maps.

KEYL, Friedrich Wilhelm
German, 19th century.
Born 17 August 1823, in Frankfurt am Main; died 5 December 1871, in London.
Painter, engraver. Animals.

Keyl, a pupil of Verboeckhoeven and then of Landseer in London, exhibited frequently at the Royal Academy and the British Institution between 1847 and 1872.

BIBLIOGRAPHY:
Weber, Horst, *Friedrich Wilhelm Keyl, 1823-1871, a German artist in Victoria's England,* biography, C. Winter, Heidelberg, 1989.

AUCTION RECORDS:
LONDON, 25 June 1908, *Deerhounds,* GBP 27; *Stag at Dawn,* GBP 6; *Sheep on the Hill* (1859) GBP 11. LONDON, 22 Feb 1972, *The Rider, His Horse and His Dogs,* GBP 550. LONDON, 20 March 1979, *Bitch and Her Little Ones* (1870, oil on canvas, 20 x 26 ins / 51 x 66 cm) GBP 600. LONDON, 5 June 1981, *Young Woman Seated, a Horse and a Dog by Her Side* (oil on canvas, 30 1/2 x 28 ins / 77.5 x 71.2 cm) GBP 2,800. LONDON, 1 Oct 1986, *Female Cat and Kittens* (1859, oil on canvas, 26 x 22 3/4 ins / 66 x 58 cm) GBP 2,400. LONDON, 12 March 1997, *In the Highlands* (1851, oil on canvas, 22 x 26 ins / 56 x 66 cm) GBP 10,350. AYLSHAM, 19 Feb 1999, *Figures, Cattle, Sheep Resting in Highland Landscape* (1854, oil on canvas, 12 x 17 ins / 30 x 43 cm) GBP 3,900. LONDON, 29 Nov 1999, *Sheep in the Highlands* (1851, oil on canvas, 26 x 40 ins / 65 x 102 cm) GBP 8,000.

KEYL, Julius
German, 19th century.
Born 25 August 1805, in Dresden; died 3 March 1870, in Dresden.
Engraver.

Keyl is cited for his plates after Georg Wagner.

KEYL, Michael
German, 18th century.
Born 1722, in Nuremberg; died 30 June 1798, in Dresden.
Engraver (burin).

Keyl, a pupil of J. Daniel, J.M. Preissler, Jakob Schubler and Martin Tyroff, set off for Denmark in 1845 and remained there for four years. In 1751, he settled in Dresden. He engraved historical portraits, religious subjects and views, from Ribera, Guerchino and C. Bega.

KEYLL, Johann
German, 17th century.
Active in Germany.
Painter, engraver (wood/mezzotint).

Keyll's works include *St Jerome Reading in a Grotto* and *Luther Reading.*

KEYM
German, 19th century.
Engraver.

KEYM, Alois
German, 18th - 19th century.
Born 1768, in Stuttgart; died 1835, in Nuremberg.
Painter, decorative designer.

Keym initially worked in Schwabach. Between 1805 and 1816, he collaborated with his brother-in-law V.W.P. Keidelhoff on the decoration of the theatre in Stuttgart. In 1828, he went to Coburg. Finally, he became the secretary and bookkeeper of his nephew Karl Heideloff.

KEYMER, M. H.
British, 18th century.
Active in London and in Yarmouth at the end of the 18th century.
Painter.

M.H. Keymer exhibited two portraits and a landscape at the Royal Academy in 1787.

KEYMEULEN, Emile
Belgian, 19th century.
Born 1840, in Antwerp; died 19 September 1882, in Laeken.
Active in Brussels.
Painter. Landscapes.

Emile Keymeulen is known in particular for his paintings of the south of France. He exhibited *Provençal Landscape* and *After the Storm* in Philadelphia in 1876 and was awarded a medal.

MUSEUMS AND GALLERIES:
LIÈGE: *Wooded Site in the Pyrenees* - ROUEN: *Landscape.*

AUCTION RECORDS:
PARIS, 15 Dec 1943, *The Prairies, Landscape,* FRF 2,700. PARIS, 9 Dec 1988, *Landscape with Figures* (oil on canvas, 29 1/2 x 25 1/2 ins / 75 x 65 cm) FRF 4,000. BRUSSELS, 19 Dec 1989, *Landscape with Figures* (oil on canvas, 7 3/4 x 13 3/4 ins / 20 x 35 cm) BEF 28,000. CALAIS, 3 July 1994, *Landscape with Figures* (1880, oil on canvas, 39 3/4 x 61 ins / 101 x 154 cm) FRF 23,500. AMSTERDAM, 21 Jan 1998, *Coastal Landscape at Night* (oil on panel, 6 3/4 x 7 3/4 ins / 17 x 20 cm) NLG 1,845.

KEYMOLEN, Julien, pseudonym of Key Julien
Belgian, 20th century.
Born 1930, in Zaventem.
Draughtsman.

Julien Keymolen specialised in humorous drawings.

KEYNOOGHE, Hans, or Kaynoot, called de Doove (the pigeon)
Flemish School, 16th century.
Died after 1570.
Painter. Landscapes.
Mechelen School.

Hans Keynooghe possibly studied under Mathias Coock in Antwerp. He was certainly a master in Mechelen, painting after Joachim Patinir. His life shows similarities with that of Claes Rogier.

KEYNOOGHE, Jacques
Flemish School, 16th century.
Died after 1597.
Painter.
Mechelen School.

He was a dean of the guild of Mechelen in 1565.

KEYS, Frances M. (Miss)
British, 19th century.
Active in Mitcham.

Painter. Landscapes.
Frances M. Keys exhibited her paintings three times at the Royal Academy and often at the Suffolk Street Gallery between 1856 and 1877.

KEYS, George Scott
British, 19th century.
Active in Hatcham.
Painter. Landscapes.
George Scott Keys exhibited at the Suffolk Street Gallery from 1856 to 1875 and at the Royal Academy in 1861.

KEYSE, Thomas
British, 18th century.
Born 1720 or 1722; died 8 February 1800, in Bermondsey.
Painter. Still-lifes (flowers/fruit), animals, insects.
Thomas Keyse enjoyed a good reputation at his time. As well as being a painter, he had a tea garden in Bermondsey. He was a member of the Free Society and showed his work in its exhibitions.
AUCTION RECORDS:
LONDON, 22 March 1974, *Still-life with Flowers,* Gns 1,500. LONDON, 1 May 1984, *Basket with Grapes and Glass of Wine* (1760, oil on canvas, 27 1/2 x 36 ins / 69.8 x 91.4 cm) GBP 7,500. LONDON, 22 Nov 1985, *Still-life with Fruit* (1767, oil on canvas, 14 x 22 ins / 35.5 x 55.9 cm) GBP 3,500. LONDON, 15 Dec 1987, *Still-life with Fruit in a Basket, an Insect, a Cat and a Squirrel* (1764, oil on canvas, 29 1/2 x 37 1/2 ins / 75 x 95 cm) GBP 8,500. LONDON, 14 March 1990, *Still-life with Fruit on an Entablature* (1767, oil on canvas, 13 1/2 x 21 1/4 ins / 34 x 54 cm) GBP 8,250. NEW YORK, 14 Oct 1992, *Trompe l'Œil with a Page of the London Gazette behind Broken Glass* (1762, oil on canvas, 15 x 11 ins / 38.1 x 27.9 cm) USD 7,700.

KEYSER, Albert de
Belgian, 19th century.
Born 1829; died 1890.
Active in Antwerp.
Painter. Landscapes.

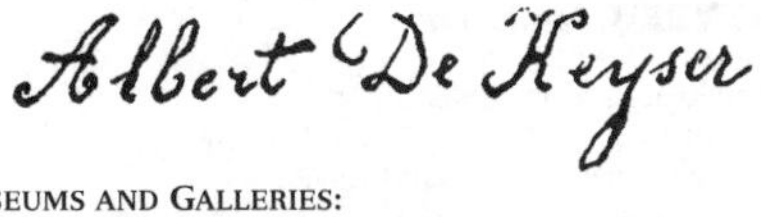

MUSEUMS AND GALLERIES:
ANTWERP: *The Steen, Antwerp, 1875.*
AUCTION RECORDS:
BRUSSELS, 1 Oct 1980, *River Landscape* (oil on canvas, 32 1/4 x 57 3/4 ins / 82 x 147 cm) BEF 40,000. ORLÉANS, 19 May 1984, *Winter Landscape* (1869, oil on canvas, 13 x 16 1/2 ins / 33 x 42 cm) FRF 17,500. LONDON, 22 Feb 1995, *View of the Church of Notre-Dame in Mechelen from the Dyle* (1876, oil on panel, 25 1/4 x 32 ins / 64 x 81 cm) GBP 2,185. ANTWERP, 26 April 1999, *St Pietersvliet* (oil on canvas, 29 x 36 ins / 74 x 92 cm) BEF 280,000. LOKEREN, 15 May 2004, *View of Anvers from the Coast at Escaut* (oil on canvas, 27 x 37 ins / 68 x 93 cm) EUR 3,300.

KEYSER, André de
Belgian, 20th century.
Born 1924, in Schaerbeek.
Draughtsman, sculptor, potter.
André de Keyser studied at the fine arts academy in Brussels.

KEYSER, Auguste Paul de
Belgian, 19th century.
Active in Brussels.
Painter. Genre scenes.
Auguste de Keyser exhibited in Brussels from 1851 to 1869 and later also in Berlin.

KEYSER, Bert de
Belgian, 20th century.
Born 1937, in Berchem-Ste-Agathe (Antwerp).
Painter, draughtsman, engraver, sculptor, potter.
Nudes, landscapes.
Bert de Keyser studied at the St Luke fine arts academy in Brussels, where he subsequently taught.

KEYSER, Cornelis de, or Kayser
Dutch, 17th century.
Painter.
In 1671 and 1682, Cornelis de Keyser was a member of the Middelburg guild. He drew landscapes and book illustrations. In 1696 there was another painter of the same name in Middelburg who was a pupil of Mathaeus Willemse.

KEYSER, Daniel de
Dutch, 18th century.
Born 1739, in Middelburg; died 1806.
Painter.
Daniel de Keyser was a teacher of drawing.

KEYSER, Emiel de
Belgian, 20th century.
Born 1942, in Termonde.
Painter.
Emiel de Keyser studied at the academy of St Luke in Ghent.

KEYSER, Emil
Swiss, 19th - 20th century.
Born 2 June 1846, in Stans; died 20 June 1923, in Munich.
Active in Munich.
Painter. Genre scenes.
Emil Keyser was a student of W. Diez. He exhibited from 1880.
AUCTION RECORDS:
ZURICH, 21 Nov 1986, *Visiting a Sick Child* (oil on canvas, 28 x 39 1/4 ins / 71 x 100 cm) CHF 20,000. BERN, 26 Oct 1988, *Indiscreet Young Woman* (oil on card, 17 1/4 x 9 1/4 ins / 43.5 x 23.5 cm) CHF 1,300.

KEYSER, Ephraim
American, 19th - 20th century.
Born 6 October 1850, in Baltimore; died 1937.
Sculptor. Figures. Busts, monuments.
Ephraim Keyser studied under Widmann at the Munich Art Academy and Albert Wolff in Berlin. In 1872, he was active in Munich. In 1876, he was awarded the Michael Beer prize for his *Psyche*; this enabled him to spend a year in Rome. He taught at the Maryland Institute of Art. He sculpted the busts of Sidney Lanier and John Hopkins, as well as other commemorative monuments.
AUCTION RECORDS:
NEW YORK, 12 March 1992, *Young Girl Feeding a Dove* (1878, white marble, h. 34 ins / 86.3 cm) USD 9,350.

KEYSER, Ernest Wise
American, 20th century.
Born 1875 or 1876, in Baltimore; died 1959.
Sculptor, painter. Monuments.
Ernest Keyser began his art education at the Maryland Institute Art School in Baltimore, moving on to the Académie Julian in Paris, and with Augustus St-Gaudens in New York, where he lived. He was awarded a gold medal in New York in 1923. He created commemorative monuments and fountain subjects.

KEYSER, Franz
Swiss, 19th century.
Born 1804, in Stans (near Lucerne); died 1883, in Stans.
Sculptor.
Keyser completed his studies at the academy in Munich and spent some time there before going on to Rome.

MUSEUMS AND GALLERIES:
GENEVA (MAH): (terracotta).

KEYSER, Heinrich
Swiss, 19th century.
Born 1813, in Stans (near Lucerne); died 28 December 1900, in Munich.
Painter. Religious subjects, portraits.
Keyser worked in Milan in his younger days, then in Rome, where he painted a *Portrait of Pope Gregory*. Subsequently he painted portraits and religious works in Switzerland, Alsace and America.

KEYSER, Hendrik de, the Elder
Dutch, 16th - 17th century.
Born 15 May 1565, in Utrecht; died 15 May 1621, in Amsterdam.
Painter, sculptor, medallist, architect. Religious subjects, portraits. Monuments, funerary monuments, busts.
Amsterdam School.
Hendrik de Keyser the Elder was taught by the sculptor C. Bloemaert in Dordrecht, and the painter Abr. Bloemaert. He was awarded the freedom of the city of Amsterdam on 24 October 1591, and was an architect to the town in 1594. He married on 6 August 1591, and had four sons and two daughters. Three of his sons - Pieter, Thomas and Willem - became artists. He taught Hans Stenwinckel. His architectural masterpiece was the tomb of William of Orange in the church in Delft. His sculptures include *Cup of the Guild of St Martin*, in the church of St Martin in Haarlem, *Relief in the Lucarne of the Portal*, in a spinning works in Amsterdam, and *Portrait of the Antique Dealer Abr. van Gooro* (on a medallion). His paintings include *The Pharisees and the Money Collectors Praying in the Temple*, on a stained glass window in the church of St John in Gouda.

BIBLIOGRAPHY:
Berger, K.J., *Der Holländische Stadttorbau*, university dissertation, Munich, 1908. Weissman, A. E., '*Keyser als baumeister*' in *Bouwkunst*, 1909. Six, J., *Hendrick de Keyser als beeldhouwer*, Amsterdam, 1910. Pit, A., *La sculpture hollandaise au Musée Nationale d'Amsterdam*, exhibition catalogue, 1915. Scholten, Fritz, '*Hendrick de Keyser's Erasmus*' in *Apollo* n° 475 p. 11, periodical, Paris, September 2001.
MUSEUMS AND GALLERIES:
THE HAGUE: *Bust of the Statthalter William I of Orange* (sculpture).

KEYSER, Hendrik de, the Younger
Dutch, 17th century.
Born 1613, in Amsterdam; died 1665, in Amsterdam.
Sculptor.
Hendrik de Keyser the Younger was the son of Hendrik de Keyser the Elder. In 1633 he went to England and worked in the studio of Nicholas Stone.

KEYSER, Hendrik de III
Dutch, 17th century.
Painter. Genre scenes.
In 1613, Hendrik de Keyser III was a pupil of Joachim Uytewall in Utrecht. He is known for his *Lute Player* and *Lacemakers* which appeared at the Neufville sales of 1829.

KEYSER, Hilda Elisabeth
Swedish, 19th century.
Born 1851, in Stockholm; died 1898.
Painter.
Hilda Keyser received a bronze medal at the Exposition Universelle in Paris in 1889. There is a self-portrait by her in the museum in Stockholm.

KEYSER, Huybrecht de
Dutch, 17th century.
Born 1592, in Utrecht; died 1678, in Amsterdam.
Sculptor.
Huybrecht de Keyser worked mainly in Amsterdam, but also in Delft. He was the nephew of Hendrik de Keyser the Elder.

KEYSER, Jacob
Dutch, 18th century.
Engraver.
Jacob Keyser is known for his maps of towns and countries.

KEYSER, Jean Baptiste de
Belgian, 19th century.
Born 22 April 1857, in Curreghem.
Sculptor.
Jean Baptiste de Keyser received a commendation at the Salon of 1882.

KEYSER, Johann Ludwig. See **KEISER**

KEYSER, Marie de
Belgian, 20th century.
Born 1899, in Ghent; died 1971, in Merelbeke.
Painter, sculptor.
Marie de Keyser was a student of Géo Verbanck.

KEYSER, Marie Isabelle de
Maiden name: Telghuys, or Telghuis
Belgian, 19th century.
Born 26 July 1815, in Verviers; died 30 May 1879, in Antwerp.
Painter. History painting, genre scenes.
Marie de Keyser was a pupil of Nicaise de Keyser and married him in 1846.

KEYSER, Martin de
Dutch, 15th century.
Painter.
He was the son of Renier de Keyser. He is recorded as being a master in Antwerp in 1557, and a citizen of the town in 1561. In 1571, he painted an *Ascension*, in grey monochrome for the church of St James.

KEYSER, Michel de
French, 19th century.
Active in Paris in 1880.
Sculptor.
Michel de Keyser made mainly busts.

KEYSER, Monique de
Belgian, 20th century.
Born 1902, in Ghent.
Painter. Children.

KEYSER, Nicaise de
Belgian, 19th century.
Born 26 August 1813, in Santvliet; died 16 July 1887, in Antwerp.
Painter. History painting, portraits. Murals.
Orientalism.
Nicaise de Keyser studied under Joseph Jacobs and Mathieu van Bree in Antwerp. In 1840 he married Isabelle Telghuys, also a painter, after a trip to Italy. He was awarded numerous medals at exhibitions, notably in Paris in 1839 and in Philadelphia in 1876. He was made a Chevalier of the Ordre de Léopold in 1839, an officer in 1855 and commander in 1872. In 1845 Keyser was made a member of the Belgian academy, a member of the teaching body in 1852 and was appointed president in 1856. From 1855 to 1879 he was director of the academy in Antwerp and was accepted as a corresponding member of the Institut de France. He was also made an officer of the Légion d'Honneur and was decorated with the Lion of the Netherlands.

After the 1830 Revolution in Belgium and the proclamation of independence, Keyser composed his passionate *Bat-*

tle of Woeringen, which was instrumental in the Romantic renaissance of Belgian art. He also produced major decorations for the courts of Belgium, Sweden, Bavaria and Wurttemberg as well as decorating the church of the Catholic sisters in Manchester, England.

MUSEUMS AND GALLERIES:
AMSTERDAM (Fodor Mus.): *Francis I at the House of Benvenuto Cellini* - AMSTERDAM (Rijksmus.): *Count Eberhard of Wurtemberg* - AMSTERDAM (Stedelijk Mus.): *Van Dyck Bids Farewell to his Friends; Albanian Woman; Columbus; Italian Woman with Butterfly; The Giaour* (after Byron); *Marino Faliero; Dante; The Final Moments of Charles Marie de Weber; Margaret of Austria and Margaret of Burgundy Visiting Memlinc; William II, King of the Netherlands; The Queen; The Queen Mother; Princess Sophia; The King of Wurtemberg; Great Duchess Olga; Princess Louisa; Weber's Last Thought* - ANTWERP: *Self-portrait; Baron Baut de Rasmon; Fighting Bull; Hendrik Leys at the Age of 19; Good Friday Procession; Charles V Liberates the Christian Slaves after the Capture of Tunis* - BERLIN: *Charles V Liberates the Christian Slaves after the Capture of Tunis; Pierre of Amiens* - BRUSSELS: *The Battle of Woeringen; Justus Lipsius; The Painter Henri de Coene; Portrait of a Woman* - COLOGNE: *After the Battle* - COURTRAI: *The Battle of the Spurs* - DOUAI: *Sir Henry Berthoud* - GHENT: *Massacre of the Holy Innocents* - MUNICH: *Monk* - NICE: *Antiquity* - THE HAGUE: *Portrait of the Painter Wynand Jan Joseph Nuyen.*

AUCTION RECORDS:
PARIS, 1850, *The Battle of New Port*, FRF 11,970; *The Battle of Senef*, FRF 15,769. LONDON, 4 June 1909, *To the Wheel* (1847) GBP 15. PARIS, 9 March 1929, *Diane de Poitiers in the Studio of Jean Goujon in the Presence of Henri II* (watercolour) FRF 1,220. ANTWERP, 14 Feb 1938, *Apotheosis of the Antwerp School*, BEF 11,000. BRUSSELS, 25 March 1938, *Basket of Flowers*, BEF 2,400. LONDON, 6 March 1974, *The Necklace*, GBP 900. LONDON, 23 Feb 1977, *Young Lovers in Ancient Greece* (1869, oil on canvas, 57 x 42 1/4 ins / 145 x 107 cm) GBP 600. PARIS, 23 Feb 1979, *The Painter's Studio* (oil on panel, 33 1/2 x 48 1/2 ins / 85 x 123 cm) FRF 28,000. PARIS, 23 Feb 1979, *The Painter's Studio* (1865, oil on panel, 33 1/2 x 48 1/2 ins / 85 x 123 cm) FRF 28,000. AMSTERDAM, 16 Nov 1988, *Two Elegant Women Looking at a Parrot in an Opulent Drawing Room* (oil on panel, 22 x 16 1/4 ins / 55 x 41 cm) NLG 9,775. PARIS, 16 March 1989, *Scenes of English History* (1840, oil on canvas, 40 1/2 x 49 1/2 ins / 103 x 126 cm) FRF 18,000. PARIS, 17 Oct 1990, *Portrait of Sir John Everett Millais* (1878, oil on canvas, 26 x 22 ins / 66 x 55 cm) FRF 5,300. AMSTERDAM, 6 Nov 1990, *The Battle of the Spurs* (1836, oil on canvas, 22 1/2 x 27 1/2 ins / 57 x 70 cm) NLG 7,475. LONDON, 19 Nov 1993, *Petrarch and Laura* (1842, oil on panel, 41 1/4 x 32 ins / 105 x 81 cm) GBP 10,580. PARIS, 31 March 1998, *Portrait of a Man with a Hat* (1855, oil on canvas, 30 1/4 x 25 1/4 ins / 77 x 64 cm) FRF 11,000. VIENNA, 20 Nov 2001, *Court of Lorenzo dei Medici* (1864, oil on panel, 32 x 43 ins / 82 x 109 cm) ATS 100,000. LONDON, 29 Nov 2001, *Figures in an Interior* (1844, oil on panel, 27 x 22 ins / 68 x 56 cm) GBP 2,200. LONDON, 21 June 2002, *Two Oriental Ladies* (1854, oil on canvas, 68 x 50 ins / 172 x 128 cm) GBP 13,500. PARIS, 16 Dec 2002, *Odalisques with Pearl Necklace* (1854, oil on canvas, 68 x 51 ins / 172 x 130 cm) EUR 145,000. BRUSSELS, 18 Nov 2003, *Sappho and his Model* (oil on canvas, 11 x 9 ins / 28 x 22 cm) EUR 2,000. ANTWERP, 22 March 2004, *Woman with Tambourine* (oil on canvas, 25 x 19 ins / 63 x 48 cm) EUR 4,000.

KEYSER, Nicolaes de
Dutch, 18th century.
Born 1681, in Antwerp.
Painter.

Nicolaes de Keyser was a pupil of Matthys Vermeeren.

KEYSER, Pieter de
Dutch, 17th century.
Born 1595, in Amsterdam; died 1676, in Amsterdam.
Sculptor, architect.

In 1625, Pieter de Keyser married Magd Geens and in 1639 married Catherine Begyn. His most important work was the tomb of Count Willem Lodewyk, now destroyed. He was the eldest son of Hendrik de Keyser.

KEYSER, Raoul de
Belgian, 20th century.
Born 1930, in Deinze (East Flanders).
Painter.

Raoul de Keyser is a hyperrealist painter who studied at the academy in Deinze. His *Loft* series consists of 16 small monochrome panels exploring matter and movement.

He has exhibited in Belgium and Paris, and taken part in group exhibitions, including *Painting on the Move* in 2002, which presented a century of contemporary painting at the Kunstmuseum, Kunstshalle and Museum für Gegenwartskunst in Basel. He held a solo exhibition *Landing* in 1996, and another at the Whitechapel Gallery in London in 2004.

BIBLIOGRAPHY:
Barak, Ami, '*Raoul de Keyser*' in *Art Press* n° 170, periodical, Paris, June 1992. Jacobs, Steven, *Raoul De Keyser: Paintings 1980 - 1999*, Ludion, Ghent, 2000. Bürgi, Bernhard Mendes, et al., *Painting on the Move*, exhibition catalogue, Kunstmuseum, Kunsthalle, Museum für Gegenwartskunst, Basel, 2002 (texts in English and German).

AUCTION RECORDS:
LOKEREN, 21 March 1992, *Composition in Green and White* (1972, gouache, 22 3/4 x 29 3/4 ins / 58 x 75.5 cm) BEF 70,000. LOKEREN, 28 May 1994, *The Hosepipe* (oil on canvas, 47 1/4 x 59 ins / 120 x 150 cm) BEF 330,000. FRANKFURT AM MAIN, 14 June 1994, *Torso* (1988, oil on canvas, 19 3/4 x 15 3/4 ins / 50 x 40 cm) DEM 9,500. LOKEREN, 7 Oct 1995, *Corner* (1969, acrylic/canvas, 59 x 47 1/4 ins / 150 x 120 cm) BEF 440,000. LOKEREN, 9 March 1996, *Corner* (1969, acrylic/canvas, 59 x 47 1/4 ins / 150 x 120 cm) BEF 330,000. ANTWERP, 22 March 1999, *Supervised Freedom* (1972-1973, oil on canvas, 47 x 47 ins / 120 x 119 cm) BEF 160,000. ANTWERP, 19 Oct 1999, *Landscape* (oil on paper, 28 x 18 ins / 70 x 45 cm) BEF 80,000. ANTWERP, 23 Oct 2001, *Composition* (1972, oil on canvas, 16 x 12 ins / 40 x 30 cm) BEF 100,000. ANTWERP, 23 Oct 2001, *De Vlakte Misschien* (acrylic on canvas, 38 x 30 ins / 97 x 76 cm) BEF 320,000. ANTWERP, 23 April 2002, *Composition* (1972, gouache, 30 x 23 ins / 76 x 58 cm) EUR 2,000. NEW YORK, 14 May 2002, *Front* (1992, oil on canvas, 65 x 48 ins / 165 x 123 cm) USD 36,000. LOKEREN, 17 May 2003, *Traces II* (1973-1974, oil on canvas, 59 x 48 ins / 150 x 121 cm) EUR 25,500. LOKEREN, 15 May 2004, *Visp* (1968, oil on canvas, 47 x 35 ins / 120 x 90 cm) EUR 22,000.

KEYSER, René de
Belgian, 20th century.
Born 1883, in Letterhoutem.
Painter, sculptor.

René de Keyser explores contrasts of tone, from the aggressive to the gentle.

KEYSER, Thomas de, sometimes known in error as Theodore or Dirk
Dutch, 17th century.
Born c. 1596, in Amsterdam; died 1667, buried 7 June in Amsterdam.
Painter. Group portraits, portraits.

Thomas de Keyser was the second son of the sculptor and architect Hendrik de Keyser. He was probably a pupil of Cornelis de Voort in Amsterdam and is known to have studied under Aert Pietersz. and Pickenoy. He married twice, first in 1626 to Machteld Andries and then in 1640 to Aaltze Heymerick. He was a great influence on portrait painters of the 17th-century Dutch School and Rembrandt himself was influenced by him early in his career.

De Keyser, it should be noted, had painted *The Anatomy Lesson* in 1619 (in the Amsterdam museum) and several versions of *Militia Companies* (also in the Amsterdam museum). However, too much importance should not be attributed to this coincidence as these were popular subjects at the period. His best-known portraits include *Constantijn Huygens and his Clerk*, 1627 (in the National Gallery in London) and *Dutch Family*, 1640 (in Cologne) in which the red and black elements of the costumes stand out harmoniously against the grey background; *Seated Lady* (in a private collection in New York), a solemn yet lively portrait, is a typical example of Dutch humanism. Keyser was one of the most highly regarded portraitists of his time but modern art critics have quite rightly rediscovered the fineness of his line, the strict sumptuousness of his range of colour and his sense of space and light, all of which make him a distinguished figure in 17th-century Dutch art and not unworthy of comparison with Frans Hals and Rembrandt.

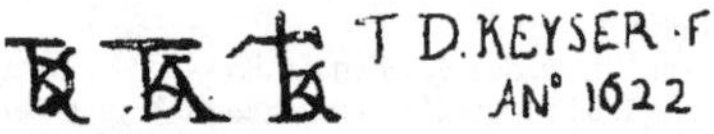

Museums and Galleries:

Aix: two portraits of men - Amsterdam: *The Anatomy Lesson; The Militia Companies of Captains Allard Cloeck and Jacob Symonsz; Portait of Four Men; Portrait of Three Children; Portrait of Two Families; Portrait of Pieter Pietersz. Heyn; Portrait of Pieter Schout* - Berlin: *Old Man and his Son; Old Lady and her Daughter* - Brussels: *Herman Dircksz von de Kolck; Marguerite and Eva Fredericx* - Budapest: *Portrait of a Woman* - Darmstadt: two portraits - Dublin: *Interiors with figures* - Frankfurt am Main: *Horseman* - Haarlem: *Claes Fabricius* - Hamburg: *Portrait of a Lady* - Kassel: *Portrait of a Man; William VI of Hesse at the Age of 18* - London (NG): *Portrait of Constantijn Huygens and his (?) Clerk* (1627, oil/wood) - Mainz: *Dutch Couple* - Munich: *Interior Scene* - Naples: *Magistrate* - Rotterdam: *Portrait of a Man* - Rouen: *The Music Lesson* - St Petersburg (Hermitage): *Portrait of a Man* - St-Omer: *Portrait of Elisabeth van der Aa; Portrait of Hendrick Verburg* - Stockholm: *Dutch Family* - Strasbourg: *Amsterdam Silver Engravers* - The Hague: *Scholar; The Burgomaster of Amsterdam Welcoming Maria de Medici in 1638* - Utrecht: *Group* - Valenciennes: *Family of Ship Owners* - Versailles: *Portrait.*

Auction records:

Paris, 1881, *Portrait of a Young Woman,* FRF 8,100. Paris, 1881, *Interior with Dutch Family,* FRF 19,500; *Astronomer with Sphere,* FRF 44,500. Paris, 1889, *Portrait of a Man of Law,* FRF 22,000. Antwerp, 1898, *Interior with Dutch Family,* FRF 36,500. Paris, 20 April 1898, *Portrait of a Man,* FRF 11,700. Folkestone, 1899, *Portrait of a Gentleman with his Greyhound,* FRF 5,720. New York, 6 and 7 April 1905, *Portrait of a Dutch Gentleman,* USD 3,500. London, 21 Dec 1907, *Portrait of a Man,* GBP 11. London, 15 May 1908, *Portrait of a Man,* GBP 115. London, 3 July 1908, *Portraits of a Man and a Woman* (two pendants) GBP 204. London, 23 July 1909, *Equestrian Portrait of a Gentleman,* GBP 27. London, 11 and 12 May 1911, *Gentleman in Grey,* GBP 31. London, 25 and 26 May 1911, *Lady in Black Holding a Book,* GBP 131. London, 26 May 1922, *Horseman and his Wife,* GBP 189. Paris, 15 Nov 1922, *Portrait of a Man with a Ruff,* FRF 520. London, 4 July 1924, *Two Huntsmen,* GBP 399. Paris, 20 May 1927, *The Philosopher,* FRF 12,500. London, 8 June 1928, *Figures* (1632) GBP 304. New York, 16 April 1930, *Lady with White Ruff,* USD 1,450. New York, 25 and 26 March 1931, *Lady Holding a Box,* USD 600; *Gentleman in Black,* USD 375. Stockholm, 13-15 Dec 1933, *Portrait of a Man,* SEK 925. Geneva, 28 Aug 1934, *Portrait of a Young Girl,* CHF 1,000. London, 28 June 1935, *Musician and his Daughter,* GBP 483. Stockholm, 25-27 Sept 1935, *Portrait of an Old Man,* SEK 2,200. Paris, 8 Dec 1948, *Portrait of a Gentleman,* FRF 100,000. London, 9 Dec 1959, *Portrait of a Man and his Wife with their Four Children,* GBP 420. London, 1 April 1960, *Portrait of a Man,* GBP 472. Cologne, 5 May 1960, *Artist,* DEM 7,500. Lucerne, 26-30 June 1962, *Family Portrait,* CHF 24,000. Amsterdam, 24 May 1966, *Portrait of a Gentleman,* NLG 21,000. London, 12 June 1968, *Portrait of a Gentleman with his Son,* GBP 6,500. London, 5 Dec 1969, *Family Group,* Gns 4,500. London, 29 June 1973, *Portraits of a Gentleman and a Lady of Quality,* Gns 14,000. London, 28 June 1974, *Portrait of a Young Woman,* Gns 2,500. London, 9 July 1976, *Portrait of a Young Woman* (1638, oil on panel, 44½ x 33½ ins / 113 x 85 cm) GBP 3,000. London, 6 April 1977, *Frans van Limborch* (1632, oil on canvas, 46 x 34 ins / 116 x 86.5 cm) GBP 6,000. Paris, 20 May 1980, *Lady of Quality Standing* (oil on wood, 18 x 13 ins / 45.5 x 33 cm) FRF 98,000. Milan, 8 May 1984, *Portrait of a Gentleman* (oil on panel, 43¼ x 29½ ins / 110 x 75 cm) ITL 8,000,000. London, 5 July 1989, *Portraits of a Gentleman and a Lady* (oil on panel, a pair, each 22¼ x 16½ ins / 56.5 x 42 cm) GBP 110,000. London, 10 Dec 1993, *Scholar Holding a Nautilus Shell* (oil on panel, 9¼ x 6¾ ins / 23.5 x 17.3 cm) GBP 20,700. London, 7 Dec 1994, *Young Woman as Flora with a Shepherd Playing the Flute* (1637, oil on panel, 36½ x 28¼ ins / 93 x 72 cm) GBP 98,300. London, 5 July 1995, *Portrait of a Gentleman; Portrait of a Lady* (oil on panel, each 9¼ x 7 ins / 23.5 x 17.5 cm) GBP 24,150. St-Germain-en-Laye, 30 June 1996, *Portrait of a Gentleman and his Son* (oil on canvas, 19¾ x 16½ ins / 50 x 42 cm) FRF 520,000. London, 16 April 1999, *Portrait of a Seated Lady, with her Son and Daughter* (1635, oil on panel, 26 x 20 ins / 67 x 51 cm) GBP 18,000. Copenhagen, 29 Feb 2000, *Portrait of a Gentleman in Black Costume with a White Collar* (1642, oil on panel, 22 x 17 ins / 56 x 44 cm) DKK 80,000. Amsterdam, 9 May 2000, *Portrait of a Gentleman in his Forties in Black Costume* (oil on panel, 20 x 16 ins / 50 x 41 cm) NLG 220,000. London, 13 July 2001, *Portrait of a Gentleman in Black Costume with Gloves in his Hand* (oil on copper, 15 x 11 ins / 38 x 28 cm) GBP 7,500. London, 14 June 2002, *Portrait of a Silversmith, though to be Christian van Vianen* (1630, oil on panel, 26 x 21 ins / 65 x 53 cm) GBP 580,000. London, 11 Dec 2002, *Group Portrait of Three Gentlemen* (1635, oil on canvas, 41 x 39 ins / 104 x 99 cm) GBP 150,000. New York, 23 Jan 2003, *Portrait of a Family Group* (1634, oil on panel, 34 x 24 ins / 86 x 60 cm) USD 40,000. Stuttgart, 24 June 2004, *Portrait of a Man in black costume with a White Collar and Cuffs Holding a Hat* (oil on canvas, 25 x 19 ins / 63 x 47 cm) EUR 22,000.

KEYSER, Willem de I

Dutch, 17th century.

Born 1603, in Amsterdam; died c. 1674.

Sculptor, painter (?), architect.

In 1658, Willem de Keyser I went to London. He was the son of Hendrik de Keyser and worked as a sculptor to the city of Amsterdam and as an architect.

KEYSER, Willem de II

Dutch, 17th century.

Born c. 1647, in Antwerp; died 1692, in London.

Painter, miniaturist, goldsmith. Religious subjects, portraits.

Willem de Keyser II painted enamels, miniatures and pictures for the churches of Antwerp and later those of Dunkirk. He went to England where he became a favourite of James II. His daughter was also a miniaturist. Willem de Keyser lived a very unsettled existence; as a result of his success at the English court he decided to abandon his work as a goldsmith in Antwerp and to bring his family to England; however, the fall of James II deprived him of the majority of his patrons. He began to research into the transmutation of metals and lost everything he owned. It is thought that this calamity played a part in his early demise.

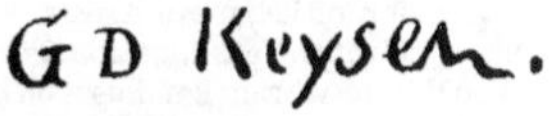

KEYSERE, Clara de

Flemish School, 15th - 16th century.
Born c. 1470; died 1545, in Ghent.
Painter, illuminator.

Clara de Keysere travelled in Germany, Italy, France and Spain. Sanderus identifies her father as a painter in Ghent.

KEYSSERSWERDE, Lewe von

German, 15th - 16th century.
Died c. 1544.
Glass painter.

He worked for the cathedral in Cologne between 1499 and 1509.

KEYWORTH, William Day, the Elder

British, 19th century.
Active in Hull.
Sculptor.

William Day Keyworth the Elder exhibited his sculpture at the Royal Academy from 1837 to 1844.

KEYWORTH, William Day, the Younger

British, 19th century.
Active in London.
Sculptor.

William Day Keyworth the Younger exhibited his sculpture at the Royal Academy from 1863 to 1893.

KEZDI-KOVACS, Laszlo

Hungarian, 19th - 20th century.
Born 11 January 1864, in Puszta Alsócikola.
Painter. Landscapes.

Laszlo Kezdi-Kovacs was the pupil of Liget in Budapest. He is also notable for his contributions to literature.

KHADDA, Mohamed

Algerian, 20th century.
Born 14 March 1930, in Mostghanem; died 1991.
Painter, watercolourist, illustrator, engraver. Stage sets.

Mohamed Khadda, a self-taught painter, was a communist who wrote the theoretical treatise *Élément pour un art nouveau* (*Component of a New Art*) on Algerian painting. Although Kadda's art has its basis in the abstract, he by no means renounces all contact with nature, which underpins all his landscape paintings. Unexpected signs, inspired by Arab-Berber symbols, invest his canvases with violence and emotion. By trade a typographer, Khadda took great pleasure in devising a form of abstract calligraphy that he constantly renewed. This technique is at its most unashamedly exuberant in his painting *Seaweed Calligraphy*.

Khadda participated in the Salon des Nouvelles Realities from 1955 to 1958 and the Salon of the national society of fine arts in 1962, and also exhibited his works in solo exhibitions in Paris in 1961, in Algiers in 1963, 1968, 1971 and 1974, and in Lyons in 1964. In 1996, and again in 2001, the Algerian cultural centre in Paris staged retrospectives devoted to his work.

Bibliography:

Tio Bellido, Ramon (ed.), *Le XXe siècle dans l'Art Algérien*, exhibition catalogue, AICA Press / AFAA, Paris, 2003.

Museums and Galleries:

Algiers (Mus. National des Beaux-Arts): *Dahra* (1959, oil on canvas); *Totem* (1957, oil on canvas); *Free Alphabet* (1954, oil on canvas) - Paris (Mus. de l'Institut du Monde Arabe): *Kabylia* (1960, oil on canvas).

KHAKHAR, Bhupen

Indian, 20th century.
Born 1934, in Bombay (now Mumbai).
Painter. Scenes with figures, local scenes, landscapes.

Bhupen Khakhar studied economics and accountancy, a profession he pursued throughout his working life, as he felt he was carrying out, as he put it, 'the work of the social individual'. From 1963 to 1965 he studied art history in the faculty at Baroda, where he lives and works, but he received no practical instruction. He began painting in 1963 and travelled to the USSR, Yugoslavia and England (in 1976). He taught painting at the Bath School of Art and Design in 1979 and visited Italy the same year.

Khakhar started with collages, using images from calendars as his base and reworking them with varnish. His composition evolved and while he was heavily influenced by the Indian miniature tradition, he still drew his subjects from daily life. In 1972, at a time when his painting style, with its almost kitsch colours (Windsor green, Prussian blue, indigo) was becoming disturbing, he set about depicting as accurately as possible the humble workers in street bazaars such as watch repairers, tailors and barbers. These figures became the actors in his work and increased in number. His travels in the West enriched his thematic repertoire, as in *The Man in the Pub* and *The Meteorologist*, and he ceased to be an 'Indian, exotic' painter. His more recent work is characterized by the same naivety and the same simplicity of depiction, which some called clumsy. Khakhar acknowledged the influence first of the Le Douanier Rousseau and then of Bruegel who became essential to his work 'because he is concerned with the same human qualities'. Khakhar is not afraid of vulgarity and feels close to calendar and postcard painters, for whom nothing is sacred. His chief desire is that 'painting should be part of our lives and a daily necessity'.

Khakhar's work was first exhibited in India, in 1965, and has participated in numerous collective exhibitions including: São Paulo Biennale, New Delhi Triennale, Menton Biennale and at the *Contemporary Indian Art* exhibition, Royal Academy London (1982). He has had regular solo shows in London and has exhibited in 1986 in the galleries for contemporary art of the Musée National d'Art Moderne in Paris.

Bibliography:

Bhupen Khakhar, exhibition catalogue, Musée national d'Art moderne, Paris, 1986.

Museums and Galleries:

New Delhi (NGMA): *Man with Bouquet of Plastic Flowers* (1975).

KHAL, Helen

American, 20th century.
Born 1923, in Pennsylvania, to Lebanese parents.
Also active in Lebanon.
Painter.

Helen Khal began painting at age 21. In 1946, she settled in Beirut, where she studied at Lebanon's Academy of Fine Arts until 1948. Back in the USA in 1949, she attended the Art Students League in New York. In 1963, she settled in Beirut, where she took charge of the first permanent art gallery. She taught at the American University of Beirut from 1967 to 1976. She reviewed art in two Lebanese papers. Later living in Washington, she has taken part in collective exhibitions, notably the Alexandria and São Paulo Biennials and, in 1989, the event *Liban - Le Regard des peintres - 200 ans de peinture libanaise* (*Lebanon Seen by its Painters - 200 Years of Lebanese Painting*), at the Institut du Monde Arabe in Paris. She had her first solo exhibition in Beirut, in 1960, followed by others in the USA and Jamaica.

BIBLIOGRAPHY:

Liban. Le Regard des peintres. 200 ans de peinture libanaise, exhibition catalogue, Institut du Monde Arabe, Paris, 1989.

KHALACHEV, Simeon

Bulgarian, 20th century.
Painter.
Socialist Realism.

Simeon Khalachev was one of the leaders of the young Bulgarian School, and spent much of his career exalting collective labour.

KHALED, Ali

Syrian, 20th century.
Born 1942.
Painter.

Ali Khaled attended the lithography workshop at the school of fine arts in Paris. His work appeared in the exhibition *De Bonnard à Baselitz - Dix ans d'enrichissements du Cabinet des estampes 1978-1988* (*From Bonnard to Baselitz: A Decade of Acquisitions by the Prints Collection 1978-1988*) at the Bibliothèque Nationale in Paris in 1992.

BIBLIOGRAPHY:

Beaumont-Maillet, Laure/Woimant, Françoise/Pernoud, Emmanuel, *De Bonnard à Baselitz - Dix ans d'enrichissements du Cabinet des estampes 1978-1988*, exhibition catalogue, Bibliothèque nationale de France, Paris, 1992.

MUSEUMS AND GALLERIES:

PARIS (Prints Collection).

KHALIDY, Wifac

Lebanese, 20th century.
Born 1907, in Beirut.
Painter, watercolourist. Landscapes.

Wifac Khalidy studied at the American University of Beirut, where she was taught by Frick, H. Khal and John Carswell. Her work featured in collective exhibitions in the 1970s in Beirut and in the 1989 exhibition *Liban - Le Regard des peintres. 200 ans de peinture libanaise* (*Lebanon as Seen by Painters - 200 Years of Lebanese Painting*) at the Institut du Monde Arabe in Paris. She had solo exhibitions from 1980 onwards in São Paulo and Rio de Janeiro.

She made watercolour paintings of the Lebanese countryside.

BIBLIOGRAPHY:

Liban. Le Regard des peintres. 200 ans de peinture libanaise, exhibition catalogue, Institut du Monde Arabe, Paris, 1989.

KHALIFA, Sayed

Egyptian, 20th century.
Born 1933, in Cairo.
Engraver. Scenes with figures.

Sayed Khalifa gained a diploma from the institute of applied arts in 1957, and in 1964 the diploma of the institute for the arts in Florence, where he studied from 1962 to 1965. His engravings often touch on the limits of figural representation. He evokes elusive visual impressions of the Islamic world, which he blends with more typically decorative elements.

Khalifa has been represented in several international group exhibitions in Florence, Spain, Venice and other venues, as well as in applied arts exhibitions in Russia, Germany, the Czech Republic and elsewhere. He also occasionally shows his work in solo shows. He received the first prize for engraving in the Alexandria Biennale in 1968.

BIBLIOGRAPHY:

Badr El-Din Abou Ghazy, *Visages de l'Art contemporain égyptien*, exhibition catalogue, Musée Galliera, Paris, 1971.

KHALIFÉ, Jean

Lebanese, 20th century.
Born 1923, in Hadtoun; died 1978.
Painter.

Jean Khalifé trained first at the Lebanese art college and then with the help of a bursary at the Beaux-Arts in Paris and at the Grande Chaumière. He then spent time in Rome, London and again in Paris. From 1967 to 1969, he was President of the Association of Lebanese Artists, Painters and Sculptors. In his *Composition in Orange and Blue* of 1972 the colours are laid on thickly, vibrant flat tints which connect in a dancing movement.

He has shown work in a number of collective exhibitions: the 1960 and 1966 Biennales in Alexandria; the 1966 and 1971 Biennales in São Paulo; in 1971 at the Tate Gallery in London; in 1973 at the Nika Museum in Tokyo; in 1989 at the exhibition in honour of those artists who have disappeared since 1975 at the Sursock Museum in Beirut; in 1989 at *Liban - Le Regard des peintres - 200 ans de peinture libanaise* (*Lebanon as Seen by Painters - 200 Years of Lebanese Painting*) at the Institut du Monde Arabe in Paris. He has had solo shows in Beirut, Paris, Damascus and elsewhere. In 1979 he received the Lebanese Order of Merit.

BIBLIOGRAPHY:

Liban. Le Regard des peintres. 200 ans de peinture libanaise, exhibition catalogue, Institut du Monde Arabe, Paris, 1989.

KHALIL, Mohamed Omar

Sudanese, 20th century.
Born 1936, in Burni.
Active in the USA.
Engraver. Local scenes.

Mohamed Khalil studied initially at the academy of fine arts in Florence, and thereafter settled in New York. He took part in the exhibition *Graphic Arab Arts* in Le Havre. His subjects are drawn from everyday life.

KHALIL GIBRAN. See **GIBRAN Khalil**

KHALZOV, Nikolai

Russian, 20th century.
Born 1923, in Samara.
Painter. Landscapes.

Nikolai Khalzov enrolled at the school of fine arts in Penza in 1951. He became a member of the Union of Soviet Artists in 1962. He took part in numerous regional and national collective exhibitions and had four solo exhibitions in Samara.

AUCTION RECORDS:

PARIS, 27 Jan 1992, *Autumn in Gurzuf* (oil on canvas, 34 3/4 x 47 ins / 88.5 x 119.5 cm) FRF 15,000. PARIS, 13 March 1992, *Gurzuf* (oil on canvas, 27 1/4 x 31 1/2 ins / 69 x 80 cm) FRF 6,500. PARIS, 3 June 1992, *Coast at Gurzuf* (oil on canvas, 31 1/2 x 23 1/2 ins / 80 x 59.5 cm) FRF 5,500.

KHAN, M., pseudonym of Khan de Hanssens Monawar-Ul-Nussa

Belgian, 20th century.
Born in Dar-es-Salaam, to Belgian parents.
Active in Spain.
Painter.

M. Khan studied painting in her native city, then undertook further training in Pakistan, the USA and Paris, before settling in Barcelona.

She produces gestural painting that mixes different cultures and explosions of violent colour (red, turquoise, yellow), which is designed to have an emotive effect and to conjure up fantastical landscapes.

Her work has featured in group exhibitions in Barcelona, Madrid, Valencia, Bilbao and Lérida. She has also had solo shows in Barcelona and Gerona.

KHAN ILTJI, Ibrahim. See **IBRAHIM KHAN ILTJI**

KHANIN, Aleksandr

Russian, 20th - 21st century.

Born 1955.

Painter. Figure compositions, nudes, portraits.

Aleksandr Khanin graduated from the Orenbourg school of art in 1980. He lives and works in Orenbourg and became a member of the Union of Soviet Artists in 1989. He tackles a wide range of subjects: *Nude on the Mountain*; *My Friend*; *Early Morning Reverie*; *Pastorale*. He is fond of depicting the effects of light.

AUCTION RECORDS:

PARIS, 25 Nov 1991, *Pastorale* (oil on canvas, 57 x 52 ins / 145 x 132 cm) FRF 10,000. PARIS, 11 Dec 1991, *Soldier's Wedding Feast* (oil on canvas, 82 3/4 x 118 ins / 210 x 300 cm) FRF 7,500. PARIS, 16 Feb 1992, *Cubist Pastorale* (oil on canvas, 59 x 47 1/4 ins / 150 x 120 cm) FRF 11,000. PARIS, 2 Feb 1998, *Symphony* (oil on canvas, 42 1/2 x 42 1/2 ins / 108 x 108 cm) FRF 4,500.

KHANNA, Balraj

Indian, 20th century.

Born 1943.

Painter.

Balraj Khanna exhibited in Paris in 1966 and 1968. From the solid composition of his painting he creates an uneasy, somewhat romantic atmosphere.

KHANNA, Krishen

Indian, 20th century.

Born 1925, in Lahore.

Painter.

Krishen Khanna worked initially in a bank and only began painting in 1950 after coming into contact with the Progressive Artists' Group set up in Bombay (now Mumbai) by Raza, Husain and Souza, among others. The first phase of Khanna's artistic development is notable for its figurative works depicting the life and inhabitants of southern India. Khanna's style subsequently evolved into one of poetic abstraction, close to Rothko's expressionism. He then returned to figurative painting, in socially committed works derived from photographs.

His work has been shown in important exhibitions of modern Indian art in India and abroad. He has also exhibited in England and the USA.

MUSEUMS AND GALLERIES:

NEW DELHI (NGMA).

KHARCHENKO, Boris

Russian, 20th century.

Born 1927; died 1985.

Painter. Figure compositions, landscapes.

Boris Kharchenko studied under Boris Ioganson at the Repin Institute in Leningrad (now St Petersburg). He was a member of the Artists Union and People's Artist. He took part in all-Union and international exhibitions from 1949.

MUSEUMS AND GALLERIES:

MOSCOW (Mus. of the Ministry of Culture) - MOSCOW (Pushkin MFA) - MOSCOW (State Tretyakov Gal.) - ST PETERSBURG (Academy) - ST PETERSBURG (Gosudarstvennyj Russkij Muz.).

AUCTION RECORDS:

PARIS, 11 June 1990, *Self Portrait with Model* (1959, oil on canvas, 53 1/4 x 28 3/4 ins / 135 x 73 cm) FRF 23,000.

KHARITONOV, Aleksandr V.

Russian, 20th century.

Born 1931, in Moscow; died 1993.

Painter.

Aleksandr Kharitonov studied with the painters Dubinina and Krassilnikov. He was deeply interested in the challenges posed by light, both from the theoretical and scientific points of view and the question of how to express it. He used a pointillist technique to translate a poetic vision of an imaginary world: 'In my paintings I do my best to depict an invisible world that has an undoubted existence.'

He showed his works in regular solo exhibitions in Moscow: Lomonossov University (1958); Karpov institute of chemistry and physics (1965); united trade union committee of artists and designers (1985); central house of artists (1991); headquarters of the newspaper *Argumenty i fakty*;(1993); and the Tretyakov gallery (1994). He also exhibited at the city museum in Dmitrov (1973).

KHASTAGIR, Sudhir, or Khastgir or Khastagira

Indian, 20th century.

Born 1907, in Chittagong (now in Bangladesh).

Painter. Religious subjects, genre scenes, local scenes.

Sudhir Khastagir studied under Nandalal Bose at Shantiniketan in 1929. He explored national and religious subjects. One of the well-known artists of the Bengal School, his *Charkha, Symbol of Prosperity* was shown at the international exhibition organized by UNESCO at the Musée d'Art Moderne, Paris in 1946. He was awarded the Padma Shri award (1957).

BIBLIOGRAPHY:

Sudhir Ranjan Khastgir, State Lalit Kala Akademi, Uttar Pradesh, 1978.

KHASTGIR, Sudhir. See **KHASTAGIR**

KHÄTSCHER, M.

German, 18th century.

Active in Düsseldorf.

Miniaturist.

Khätscher did portraits and illustrated numerous mythological subjects. The museum in Munich possesses several of his works.

MUSEUMS AND GALLERIES:

MUNICH.

KHAYACHI, Hédi

Tunisian, 20th century.

Born 1882; died 1948.

Painter. Portraits, genre scenes, landscapes.

After working under the guidance of Émile Pinchart in Tunis, Khayachi continued his studies in Paris at the free academies of Montparnasse. He then spent some time in Italy, where he specialised in portraiture. Khayachi painted mainly portraits of princes and other public figures, but also genre scenes and landscapes.

BIBLIOGRAPHY:

Lumières tunisiennes, exhibition catalogue, Association française d'action artistique, Pavillon des arts, Paris, 1995.

MUSEUMS AND GALLERIES:

TUNIS (MAM): *Sidi Bou Said*.

KHAYATT, Dora, Mrs John Plant

Egyptian, 20th century.

Born 18 January 1912, in Cairo.

Watercolourist, painter (gouache). Portraits, Still-lifes, flowers, landscapes, seascapes.

Dora Khayatt painted landscapes in Egypt, France, Italy and Scotland, using a knife to lay on her pigments with a lyric touch. Her work was included in a collective exhibition at the British Institute in Cairo in 1950, and in 1956 at the Salon d'Automne in Paris. She had solo exhibitions in London from 1950; at the New York Wildenstein Galleries in 1961; at the Birmingham Museum of Art in 1973; and at the Union League in Philadelphia in 1976.

BIBLIOGRAPHY:

Dora Khayatt - Oscar Dalvit, exhibition catalogue, Redfern Gall., London, 1950. *Dora Khayatt*, exhibition catalogue, Gal.

Durand-Ruel, Paris, 1956. *Dora Khayatt*, exhibition catalogue, Wildenstein Gall., New York, 1961.
MUSEUMS AND GALLERIES:
BIRMINGHAM (Mus. and AG).

KHAYNACH, Friedrich von
German, 19th - 20th century.
Born 10 December 1867; died November 1920, in Berlin.
Painter. Portraits, still-lifes.
Friederich von Khaynach studied in Düsseldorf and Berlin and was also an author. His works include his *Portrait of Otto Erich Hartleben*. He exhibited in Düsseldorf, Berlin and Munich from 1909.
AUCTION RECORDS:
AMSTERDAM, 2 May 1990, *Still-life with Cabbages, Tomatoes and Other Vegetables* (oil on canvas, 25 1/2 x 31 1/2 ins / 65 x 80 cm) NLG 3,220.

KHEIDT, Thomas
Austrian, 17th century.
Active in Salzburg.
Painter.
Kheidt worked for churches in Salzburg and the surrounding region.

KHEIMON, Mathias
Flemish School, 17th century.
Active in Antwerp c. 1614.
Painter.

KHEMAKER
French, 18th century.
Died c. 1748.
Sculptor.
Khemaker was a member of the Académie St-Luc in Paris.

KHERN, Mathias
Austrian, 17th century.
Active in Styria.
Sculptor.
Khern worked mainly in Graz.

KHIEN, Jacobus
Hungarian, 16th - 17th century.
Active in Besztercebánya.
Painter.
Jacobus Khien painted portraits and worked for the church in Berzevice, among others.

KHIMOUNE, Rachid
Algerian, 20th - 21st century.
Born 1953, in Decazeville.
Active from 1958 in France.
Intervention artist, assemblage artist.
Khimoune settled in Paris in 1958, where he studied at the school of fine arts. A militant figure of the new generation, he was involved with the radical Radio-Beur. A solo exhibition of his work was staged at the K. foundry in Aubervilliers in 1995.

Khimoune was involved in street art, creating an assemblage of mundane, everyday objects such as taps, electric plugs, and manhole covers. He also executed sculptures and casts, most notably for the series *Tortoises*, in which the shell suggests the appearance of a military helmet.
BIBLIOGRAPHY:
Rachid Khimoune: regards, les enfants du monde, exhibition catalogue, Paris musées, Somogy, Paris, 2001.

KHITH, Robert
Norwegian, 19th century.
Painter. Landscapes.
Robert Khith is mentioned by Florence Levy.
AUCTION RECORDS:
NEW YORK, 28-30 Jan 1903, *Norwegian Fjord*, USD 130.

KHLOCKHENDON. See **GLOCKENDON**

KHMELKO
Russian, 20th century.
Born 1903.
Painter.
Khmelko was a painter of Soviet inspiration; the *Breaching of Kiev* is attributed to him.

KHMELUK, Vassyl, or Chmeljuk
Russian, 20th century.
Born 1903.
Active in France.
Painter. Figures, portraits, landscapes, still-lifes.
Vassyl Khmeluk trained in Prague before settling in Paris. He figured amongst the painters of his generation who became known as the Paris School, although he also retained some links with Expressionism, a fact that occasionally resulted in similarities between his work and the later works of Vlaminck.
MUSEUMS AND GALLERIES:
LUCERNE - LVIV - PARIS (MAM): *Still-life* - STOCKHOLM: *Figure*.
AUCTION RECORDS:
PARIS, 15 Jan 1943, *Crayfish*, FRF 3,500. PARIS, July 1946, *Bust of a Woman* (pastel) FRF 3,100. PARIS, 24 Feb 1947, *Bust of a Gypsy*, FRF 14,100. PARIS, 23 May 1949, *Houses in Montmartre*, FRF 29,000. PARIS, 28 Jan 1955, *Rue Belliard*, FRF 26,100. PARIS, 25 June 1959, *Peach Trees in Blossom*, FRF 260,000. PARIS, 5 March 1972, *Landscape of the Loire*, FRF 8,300. VERSAILLES, 12 May 1976, *Banks of the Loir in Autumn* (oil/hardboard, 24 x 19 3/4 ins / 61 x 50 cm) FRF 3,300. PARIS, 10 Dec 1979, *Vase of Roses* (1969, hardboard, 22 x 17 3/4 ins / 55 x 45 cm) FRF 4,500. PARIS, 5 March 1984, *Outskirts of Brantôme* (watercolour, 16 1/2 x 11 1/2 ins / 42 x 29 cm) FRF 8,300. PARIS, 17 Feb 1988, *Countryside in Bloom* (1903, gouache, 13 1/2 x 19 1/4 ins / 34 x 49 cm) FRF 3,500. VERSAILLES, 17 April 1988, *River Banks* (oil on paper, 25 1/2 x 19 3/4 ins / 65 x 50 cm) FRF 5,000. PARIS, 16 April 1989, *Bouquet* (1959, oil on panel, 32 x 21 1/4 ins / 81 x 54 cm) FRF 16,000. PARIS, 1 Dec 1989, *House on the Sea Shore* (oil on card, 7 x 15 ins / 18 x 38 cm) FRF 4,000. PARIS, 7 Nov 1990, *Vase of Flowers* (oil/hardboard, 20 3/4 x 28 3/4 ins / 53 x 73 cm) FRF 10,000. PARIS, 9 Nov 1990, *Small Girl Resting on her Elbows* (1948, oil on canvas, 16 1/4 x 13 1/4 ins / 41.5 x 33.5 cm) FRF 6,200. AMSTERDAM, 22 May 1991, *Girl in Green* (1938, oil on canvas, 31 1/2 x 20 3/4 ins / 80 x 53 cm) NLG 1,150. AMSTERDAM, 7 Dec 1994, *Still-life with Fruit* (oil on card, 9 1/2 x 12 ins / 24 x 30.5 cm) NLG 1,495. ZURICH, 23 June 1995, *Still-life with Apples* (oil/plywood, 15 x 18 ins / 38 x 46 cm) CHF 1,800. PARIS, 28 May 1997, *Portrait of a Woman* (oil on canvas, 22 x 18 ins / 56 x 46 cm) FRF 5,000.

KHNOPFF, Fernand, or Knopff
Belgian, 19th - 20th century.
Born 12 September 1858, in Grembergen-lez-Termonde; died 12 November 1921, in Brussels.
Painter, decorative designer, pastellist, watercolourist, sculptor, draughtsman, illustrator. Nudes, figures, landscapes.
Symbolism.
Les Vingt, Libre Esthètique.
Fernand Khnopff initially studied law, which he abandoned to concentrate on painting. He was a student of Mellery at the fine arts academy in Brussels, and of Jules Lefebvre in Paris, where he studied painting in the manner of Gustave Moreau and Delacroix. In 1891, he visited England for the first time, returning there regularly for exhibitions. In England, he met the Maquet family, whose three daughters,

Elsie, Lily and Nancy, were often the inspiration for Khnopff's female figures. He was also a friend and admirer of the poet Verhaeren, whose work he helped to make known in France, and was a member of the Essor group, Les Vingt (The Twenty), of which he was a founder, and Libre Esthètique (Free Aesthetic). From 1894, he contributed to the journal *Le Studio* (*The Studio*) and, after 1900, retired to lead a solitary life in Bruges.

Khnopff was a man of letters as well as an artist. He admired the Pre-Raphaelite painters Rossetti and Burne-Jones, as well as the Belgian Symbolists, later becoming one of their most important members. Some of his best-known works (*The Sphinx*) clearly belong to their time, but others, such as *Medusa* or the *Temptation of St Anthony*, which combine the influence of Moreau and the Pre-Raphaelites, can seem somewhat contrived. His younger sister Marguerite was Khnopff's main inspiration during his life - alternately sphinx and angel - and posed for *Souvenirs* (*Memories*) in 1889, *From Silence* in 1890, and *Le Secret* (*The Secret*) in 1902. In an enigmatic portrait of her in a white dress leaning against a door of 1887, she evokes the 15th-century madonnas that Khnopff so admired during his childhood in Bruges. The themes of Khnopff's paintings are echoed in his sculptures, which mix bronze, enamel and ivory. Khnopff also illustrated several literary works, notably Maeterlinck's *Pelléas et Mélisande*, Péladan's *Le Vice suprême*, and Verhaeren's *Poems*, and was responsible for the decorative scheme at the Théâtre de la Monnaie in Brussels, as well as designs for his own house.

Khnopff exhibited in London with the Essor group, and in Paris, in 1892 and 1893, at the Salon de la Rose-Croix. He was awarded a silver medal at the Exposition Universelle in Paris in 1892 and 1893, and a further medal in Munich in 1905. In 2001, Khnopff's paintings appeared in the exhibition *Painters of Silence* organized by the Hôtel de Ville in Brussels and the Centre Wallonie-Bruxelles in Paris. In 2003, his work was shown in *Phantom der Lust. Visionen des Machochismus in der Kunst* (*Phantom of Desire. Visions of Masochism in Art*), an exhibition dedicated to Sacher-Masoch (after whom sadomasochism is named) at the Neue Galerie in the Landesmuseum in Graz. In 2004, a retrospective was held at the Royal Fine Arts Museums of Belgium in Brussels and at the Fine Arts Museum in Montreal.

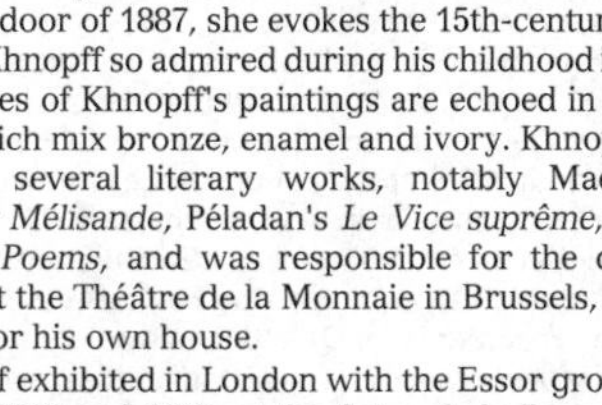

BIBLIOGRAPHY:

Delevoy, Robert L./Croës, Catherine de/Ollinger-Zingue, Gisèle, *Fernand Khnopff - catalogue raisonné de l'œuvre*, La Bibliothèque des Arts, Paris, Lausanne, 1979. Juin, Hubert, *Fernand Khnopff et la littérature de son temps*, Lebeer Hossmann, Brussels, 1980. Howe, Jeffrey, W., *The Symbolist Art of Fernand Khnopff*, UMI Research Press, Ann Arbor, 1982. Kempler, Cheryl, *Fernand Khnopff and the Belgian Avant-Garde*, Friedman, New York, 1983. Kelder, D., *L'Héritage de l'impressionnisme*, La Bibliothèque des Arts, Paris, 1986. Croës, Catherine De/Ollinger-Zinque, Gisèle, *Fernand Khnopff et ses rapports avec la sécession viennoise*, exhibition catalogue, Musées royaux des Beaux-Arts de Belgique, Centre international pour l'étude du XIXe siècle, Brussels, 1987. *Fuerunan Kunopufu ten Fernand Khnopff*, exhibition catalogue, Tokyo Shimbun, Tokyo, 1990. Draguet, Michel, '*Khnopff ou l'ambigu poétique*' in *coll. Monographies de l'art moderne*, Snoeck-Ducaju & Zoon, Ghent, 1995. Carrette, Francis/Croes, Catherine de, *Les Peintres du silence*, exhibition catalogue, Hôtel de Ville, Bruxelles, Centre Wallonie-Bruxelles, Paris, 2001. Draguet, Michel, *Fernand Khnopff: Portrait of Jeanne Kéfer*, Getty Publications, Los Angeles, 2004. *Fernand Khnopff*, exhibition catalogue, Musées royaux des Beaux-Arts de Belgique, Brussels, 2004. Leen, Frederick, Marechal, Dominique, van Vliet, Sophie, *Fernand Khnopff: 1858-1921*, Musées Royaux des Beaux-Arts de Belgique, Brussels, 2004.

MUSEUMS AND GALLERIES:

BRUSSELS (MAM): *Portrait of Germaine Wiener* - BRUSSELS (Mus. royaux des Beaux-Arts de Belgique): *Solitude* (1891, photograph enhanced with pastel, reproduced from the central panel of the 'Isolation' tryptic); *Art, or Caresses* (1896); *The Abandoned Town* (1904); *Beneath the Pines at Fosset*; *Posthumous Portrait of Marguerite Landuyt* (1896, oil on canvas) - MUNICH (Pinakothek): *I Lock my Door upon Myself* (1891) - OSTEND (Mus. voor Schone Kunsten) - PARIS (Mus. d'Orsay): *Marie Mommon* - TOURNAI (Musées des Beaux-Arts): *Roses* (1912, oil on canvas).

AUCTION RECORDS:

LONDON, 14 March 1908, *St Anthony and the Queen of Sheba*, GBP 54. ANTWERP, 14 Oct 1969, *Woman in an Interior*, BEF 11,000. LONDON, 2 July 1974, *In the Forest*, Gns 2,300. LONDON, 29 March 1977, *The Silver Tiara* (pastel) GBP 6,500. LONDON, 6 Dec 1977, *Danaïdes* (pen and wash, 11 1/2 x 7 ins / 29 x 18 cm) GBP 1,600. LONDON, 27 June 1978, *Naked Woman* (coloured chalks, 9 1/4 x 6 3/4 ins / 23.3 x 17.2 cm) GBP 6,200. LONDON, 29 Nov 1979, *Young Woman Wearing a Bonnet in Profile, Facing Right* (lead pencil, 5 x 6 3/4 ins / 12.5 x 17 cm) GBP 1,000. ANTWERP, 22 April 1980, *Garden at Famellettes* (oil on canvas, 9 x 11 3/4 ins / 22 x 30 cm) BEF 120,000. LONDON, 26 Nov 1980, *Sire Halewyn* (1903, coloured drypoint/Japanese Imperial paper, 6 3/4 x 9 1/2 ins / 17 x 24.2 cm) GBP 600. LONDON, 26 Nov 1980, *Sleeping Medusa* (c. 1896, pastel, 11 x 5 ins / 28 x 12.4 cm) GBP 27,000. LONDON, 26 Nov 1980, *A Mask* (1897, polychrome plaster, 7 1/4 x 11 x 2 1/2 ins / 18.6 x 28 x 6.5 cm) GBP 10,000. LONDON, 29 June 1981, *Bruges, the Church of Our Lady* (c. 1904, oil on canvas, 17 1/4 x 34 1/4 ins / 44 x 87 cm) GBP 26,000. LONDON, 23 June 1983, *Profile of a Woman* (charcoal and pencil, 9 x 4 1/4 ins / 22 x 11 cm) GBP 8,800. LONDON, 22 Nov 1983, *Portrait of Jules Philippson* (1890, oil on canvas remounted/panel, 25 1/4 x 14 1/2 ins / 64 x 37 cm) GBP 21,000. LONDON, 21 June 1984, *Bruges, the Hospital of St John* (1904, pastel and pencil, 11 x 19 1/4 ins / 28 x 49 cm) GBP 17,000. HAMBURG, 7 June 1985, *Study for a Woman's Head* (c. 1912, pastel and coloured chalk, 10 x 8 1/2 ins / 25.2 x 21.4 cm) DEM 37,000. LONDON, 19 June 1986, *Listening to the Flowers* (c. 1892, pencil, 13 1/4 x 4 1/4 ins / 33.5 x 10.5 cm) GBP 35,000. BRUSSELS, 29 Oct 1986, *Fosset: the Village* (oil on panel, 12 1/4 x 9 ins / 31 x 22 cm) BEF 360,000. ENGHIEN-LES-BAINS, 25 Oct 1987, *Study of a Woman* (1887, red chalk/bistre-coloured paper, 5 x 3 1/4 ins / 13 x 8.5 cm) FRF 320,000. NEW YORK, 24 May 1988, *The Three Muses: Painting, Music and Poetry* (oil on canvas, 126 x 94 1/2 ins / 320 x 240 cm) USD 132,000. LOKEREN, 28 May 1988, *Portrait of Rubens* (1915, pencil, 9 x 5 1/2 ins / 22 x 14 cm) BEF 95,000. LONDON, 27 June 1988, *The Silver Tiara* (1909, pastel/paper, diam. 10 ins / 24.5 cm) GBP 187,000; *Portrait of a Young Woman* (oil on canvas, 5 1/2 x 4 1/4 ins / 14 x 11 cm) GBP 17,600. LONDON, 19 Oct 1989, *Mist at Fosset* (oil on canvas, 12 3/4 x 15 3/4 ins / 32.4 x 40 cm) GBP 52,800. LONDON, 1 Dec 1989, *A Musician* (watercolour and colouring pencil, 4 3/4 x 3 1/4 ins / 12 x 8 cm) GBP 181,500; *Souvenir of Flanders: a Canal* (1904, pencil and pastel, 10 x 16 1/2 ins / 25.4 x 41.9 cm) GBP 121,000. LONDON, 3 April 1990, *Portrait of Henri de Woelmont* (1885, oil on canvas, 10 1/2 x 11 1/2 ins / 26.4 x 29 cm) GBP 93,500. LONDON, 19 June 1990, *Portrait of a Woman* (oil on canvas/card, 5 1/2 x 4 1/2 ins / 14 x 11.5 cm) GBP 27,500. LONDON, 28 Nov 1990,

Portrait of a Young Girl, perhaps Elsie Maquet (red chalk and blue pencil, 7 1/4 x 5 ins / 18.5 x 12.5 cm) GBP 33,000. NEW YORK, 28 Feb 1991, *Portrait of Marguerite, the Painter's Sister* (oil on canvas/panel, 38 1/4 x 29 3/4 ins / 97.2 x 75.5 cm) USD 880,000. LONDON, 19 March 1991, *The Virgin, after Botticelli* (1909, red chalk/card, 15 3/4 x 12 1/2 ins / 40 x 31.5 cm) GBP 17,600. LONDON, 29 Nov 1991, *Portrait of Jeanne de Bauer* (1890, oil on panel, 20 3/4 x 13 3/4 ins / 53 x 35 cm) GBP 231,000. LONDON, 3 Dec 1991, *His Royal Highness Prince Leopold of Belgium, Duke of Brabant* (pencil, charcoal and red chalk/paper, 25 1/4 x 15 3/4 ins / 64.2 x 40 cm) GBP 12,100. LONDON, 20 March 1992, *The Mask with the Black Curtain* (coloured chalks heightened with white/paper, 11 x 6 3/4 ins / 27 x 17 cm) GBP 39,600. PARIS, 10 June 1992, *View of the Beguin Bridge in Bruges* (lead pencil and stump, 10 1/2 x 65 ins / 26.5 x 165 cm) FRF 195,000. LONDON, 17 Nov 1993, *The Minnewater in Bruges* (pencil and pastel, 18 1/2 x 39 3/4 ins / 47 x 101 cm) GBP 210,500. LONDON, 19 Nov 1993, *Requiem* (1907, pencil, charcoal and watercolour/paper, 31 1/2 x 31 1/2 ins / 80.3 x 80.3 cm) GBP 144,500. LOKEREN, 28 May 1994, *Study for a Nude* (red chalk, 10 1/4 x 7 1/2 ins / 26 x 19 cm) BEF 220,000. PARIS, 24 June 1994, *Woman Leaning* (graphite, 6 x 3 3/4 ins / 15 x 9.5 cm) FRF 8,000. LONDON, 17 Nov 1995, *Dawn Breaking over Fosset* (oil on canvas, 12 1/2 x 15 3/4 ins / 32 x 40 cm) GBP 45,500. NEW YORK, 23-24 May 1996, *Victoria, her Long Red Hair like Flames* (pastel/paper, 27 3/4 x 11 1/2 ins / 70.5 x 29.2 cm) USD 79,500. LONDON, 12 June 1996, *The Flood at Fosset* (1881, oil on panel, 4 1/4 x 8 1/4 ins / 11 x 21 cm) GBP 13,800. NEW YORK, 12 Feb 1997, *Drawing* (c. 1898, pencil and black chalk/paper, 7 x 3 1/2 ins / 17.8 x 8.9 cm) USD 112,500. LOKEREN, 6 Dec 1997, *Past; Future* (c. 1908, engraved marble, a pair, each 37 1/2 x 25 ins / 95 x 63.5 cm) BEF 900,000. NEW YORK, 18 March 1998, *Head of a Woman* (pencil and charcoal/paper, diam. 6 1/4 ins / 16 cm) USD 11,500. AMSTERDAM, 15 Oct 1998, *The Blood of Medusa* (coloured chalk and watercolour/lithograph, 9 x 6 ins / 22 x 14 cm) NLG 32,000. BRUSSELS, 12 May 1998, *Landscape at Fosset* (oil on canvas, 7 x 9 ins / 18 x 23 cm) BEF 700,000. AMSTERDAM, 25 Oct 1999, *A Bruges, l'Hopital St-Jean* (coloured chalk, pencil/paper/panel, 11 x 20 ins / 27 x 50 cm) NLG 200,000. LONDON, 22 June 2000, *M. Neve's Children* (oil on panel, 19 x 16 ins / 49 x 40 cm) GBP 280,000. LONDON, 23 Nov 2000, *Caresses* (pencil black, brown crayon and tracing paper/paper) GBP 80,000. LONDON, 28 June 2001, *Air, Water, Fire and Earth* (pastel and charcoal, set of four, 23 x 22 ins / 58 x 56 cm) GBP 21,000. AMSTERDAM, 4 Dec 2001, *Study of a Woman* (c. 1891, coloured chalk, 8 x 6 ins / 20 x 14 cm) NLG 240,000. LONDON, 13 June 2002, *Portrait of Marguerite Landuyt* (oil on canvas, 28 x 29 ins / 72 x 74 cm) GBP 350,000. BRUSSELS, 11 Nov 2002, *Study of a Woman* (pencil, 7 x 5 ins / 18 x 12 cm) EUR 10,000. LONDON, 6 Feb 2003, *Insense* (1917, charcoal and coloured pencil, 11 x 7 ins / 27 x 19 cm) GBP 90,000. LONDON, 17 June 2004, *Hypnosis* (dark brown-patinated bronze on a marble plinth) GBP 32,000. LONDON, 22 June 2004, *Portrait of a Woman* (coloured crayon and chalk/card, 5 x 3 ins / 12 x 7 cm) GBP 67,000.

KHODASEVICH, Valentina Mikhailovna

Russian, 20th century.
Born 1894, in Moscow; died 1968, in Moscow.
Painter, watercolourist, decorative artist. Stage sets.

After studying in Moscow and Munich, Valentina Khodasevich studied at the Académie Witte with van Dongen in Paris from 1911 to 1912. She completed numerous stage sets and from 1920 to 1930 helped decorate the assembly rooms in Leningrad (now St Petersburg). She also worked as a propaganda artist. Valentina Khodasevich started exhibiting in 1912.

BIBLIOGRAPHY:
Halturin, Aleksandr/Hulten, Pontus/Gunar, Karl (ed.), *Paris-Moscou*, group exhibition catalogue, Éd. du Centre Georges-Pompidou, Paris, 1979.

AUCTION RECORDS:
LONDON, 6 Oct 1988, *Draft of decorations for Commemorative Celebrations held 7 November 1932 in Petrograd* (1932, watercolour and gouache/paper, 7 x 12 1/4 ins / 17.8 x 31.1 cm) GBP 1,320. LONDON, 21 Nov 2001, *Costume Designs for a Peasant and Liusetta in Moliere's Monsieur de Pourceugnac* (1921, watercolour over pencil and mixed media, a pair, 15 x 9 ins / 37 x 23 cm) GBP 1,500. PARIS, 21 Oct 2003, *Study for Harlequin's Costume in Arlequin Squelette* (1921, watercolour and pencil, 13 x 9 ins / 33 x 23 cm) EUR 3,000.

KHODJA, Amine Saddek

Algerian, 20th - 21st century.
Born 15 August 1949, in Constantine.
Painter (mixed media).

Khodja studied art, archaeology and aesthetics at the school of fine arts in Paris. He is director of the subsidiary of the Constantine school of fine arts.

His work has been shown in several solo exhibitions since 1972: in 1973 at the Constantine cultural centre, in 1976 and 1977 at the gallery of the school of fine arts in Paris, in 1978 in Stockholm, in 1979 at the cultural centre in Grenoble, in 1986 at the Cirta museum in Constantine, in 1987 at the Mohammed El Khalifa cultural centre in Constantine, in 1988 in Libya, in 1992 the Algerian cultural centre in Paris, and in 1994 in the French town of Quimper.

Khodja's works, which have evocative titles, are strongly influenced by abstract expressionism.

KHOL, Robert

Austrian, 20th century.
Born 6 February 1891.
Painter, engraver, illustrator.

Robert Khol's work includes illustrations for the works of Shakespeare (1921-1922).

KHOLODOVSKY, Mikhail

Russian, 19th - 20th century.
Painter. Genre scenes.

Kholodovsky received a bronze medal at the 1889 Exposition Universelle in Paris and his work also featured in the 1900 exhibition.

KHONGKHAKUL, Itthi

Thai, 20th century.
Born 1942, in Bangkok.
Engraver.

Work by Itthi Khongkhakul was shown at the international print biennale in Tokyo in 1974.

KHONRAAD, M. C.

Flemish School, 19th century.
Active at the beginning of the 19th century.
Engraver.

Khonraad was a pupil of Goubaud in Brussels. He produced engravings after various artists including Raphael.

KHROMIN, Viktor

Russian, 20th - 21st century.
Born 1948.
Painter. Scenes with figures.

Viktor Khromin studied at the Serov school of art in Leningrad (St Petersburg). He became a member of the Leningrad painters' association. His paintings are evocative of Chagall, his compositions slightly naive and executed in dark colours. His works have been seen in national and international exhibitions in Germany, Scandinavia and the USA.

MUSEUMS AND GALLERIES:
MOSCOW (Ministry of Culture) - RIGA (Valsts makslas muzejs/National Gallery of Art) - TATLIN (Museum of Fine Arts).

AUCTION RECORDS:
PARIS, 10 Feb 1991, *Igra (The Games)* (oil on canvas, 25 1/2 x 35 ins / 65 x 88 cm) FRF 9,000.

KHUEN, Theodor Franz Maria
Austrian, 19th century.
Born 13 July 1860, in Vienna.
Sculptor.
Khuen was a pupil of Hugo Härdtl, Tilgner and Hans Gasser. He left a large number of busts, tombs and monuments, most notably an *Equestrian Statue of the Prince of Liechtenstein.*

KHVOSTENKO, Aleksei, or Khovostenko
Russian, 20th century.
Born 1940, in Leningrad (now St Petersburg).
Painter, collage artist.
Khvostenko studied at the school of fine arts in Leningrad (now St Petersburg). Also a poet and singer, he expressed himself particularly through the technique of collage, which he occasionally complemented with painting.
AUCTION RECORDS:
PARIS, 7 Nov 1988, *Composition* (1988, collage/black background, 20 x 16 ins / 50.5 x 40.5 cm) FRF 3,500. PARIS, 14 May 1990, *Cathedral of Love* (1989, oil and collage/paper, 18 x 13 ins / 46 x 33 cm) FRF 5,000.

KI K'NAG. See **JI KANG**

KI KONG. See **QI GONG**

KI NO BAITEI, real name: Ki Tokitoshi, original name: Ki no Tokitoshi, given name: Shikei, popularly known as: Ki no Bin, artist names: Baika, Baitei, Gan'iku, Kyuro (Sanjin)
Japanese, 18th - 19th century.
Born 1734, in Kyoto; died 1810.
Painter. Flowers, birds.
Nanga School.
Ki no Baitei is thought to have been a pupil of Buson and as he lived in the town of Omi he was known as Omi Buson.

KI TCHAI-KIA. See **QI ZHAIJIA**

KI TCHEN. See **JI ZHEN**

KIA CHE-KOU. See **JIA SHIGU**

KIA TS'IUAN. See **JIA QUAN**

KIA YU-K'IEN. See **XIE YUQIAN**

KIAER, Ian
British, 20th - 21st century.
Born 1971.
Installation artist, painter, draughtsman.
Ian Kiaer trained from 1991 to 1995 at the Slade School of Art and from 1998 to 2000 at the Royal College of Art in London. In 2001, he was artist in residence at Seoul National University in Korea. In 1998, he received a prize and bursary from the Basil H. Alkazzi Foundation. Kiaer's art focuses on private architecture which may be imagined and utopian. He often refers to historical figures whose artistic concerns were at odds with the spirit of their time - for example, the Russian poet Irina Ratushinskaya and her relationship with Constructivism, the writer Curzio Malaparte and the scholar Yan Paeng Son. He is especially interested in their views on architecture. In reference to them, Kiaer uses maquettes of buildings, small-scale models of housing, paintings, drawings and everyday objects in his installations. These are carefully arranged to generate associations and specific feelings. Kiaer has taken part in group exhibitions, including in 1999 *New Contemporaries 99* at Sir John Moore's, Liverpool; in 2000 *UBS Painting Prize: A Tribute to the Painting of Tomorrow* at the Whitechapel Art Gallery, London; in 2002 *Artists Imagine Architecture* at the Institute of Contemporary Arts, Boston, an exhibition exploring the relationship between sculpture and architectural models. He held his first solo exhibition in 2001 at the Asprey Jacques Gallery, London.

KIAER, Soren
Danish, 17th century.
Active at the beginning of the 17th century.
Painter.
Soren Kiaer executed mythological paintings and portraits for the Danish court.

KIAERSKOU, Frederik Christian, or Kiaerschou, Kiaerskov
Danish, 19th century.
Born 26 March 1805, in Copenhagen; died 6 June 1891, in Copenhagen.
Painter. Landscapes with figures, landscapes.
Frederik Kiaerskou was a pupil of J.P. Møller. He worked mostly in Munich, exhibiting there as well as in Vienna. He often painted large decorative panels.
AUCTION RECORDS:
LONDON, 26 Nov 1980, *On the Beach in Øresund, near Elsinore* (1833, oil on panel, 11 1/4 x 15 1/2 ins / 28.5 x 39.5 cm) GBP 3,000. LONDON, 26 Nov 1982, *Wooded Landscape with River* (1848, oil on canvas, 19 3/4 x 27 1/2 ins / 50 x 70 cm) GBP 2,200. LONDON, 5 Oct 1983, *Summer Landscape* (1858, oil on canvas, 17 x 25 1/2 ins / 43 x 64.5 cm) GBP 1,600. COPENHAGEN, 27 Feb 1985, *View of Stockholm* (1849, oil on canvas, 29 1/2 x 43 1/4 ins / 75 x 110 cm) DKK 65,000. LONDON, 25 March 1987, *View of a Lake in Summer* (1860, oil on canvas, 26 1/2 x 42 1/2 ins / 67.5 x 108 cm) GBP 11,000. LONDON, 24 March 1988, *The Academy of Sorø* (1875, 32 x 44 ins / 81.2 x 112 cm) GBP 11,000. STOCKHOLM, 19 April 1989, *Landscape with Constructions near a Road* (oil on panel, 15 3/4 x 22 ins / 40 x 55 cm) SEK 12,000. LONDON, 5 May 1989, *View of Helsingborg* (1854, oil on canvas, 14 1/4 x 19 3/4 ins / 36 x 50 cm) GBP 2,200. LONDON, 16 Feb 1990, *Wooded Landscape with Dog* (1883, oil on canvas, 25 x 20 1/2 ins / 63.5 x 52 cm) GBP 2,200. COPENHAGEN, 21 Feb 1990, *Rowboat in a Fjord* (oil on canvas, 13 1/2 x 17 3/4 ins / 34 x 45 cm) DKK 7,500. COPENHAGEN, 25-26 April 1990, *Manor in Krogerup Park* (oil on canvas, 20 x 27 1/4 ins / 51 x 69 cm) DKK 20,000. STOCKHOLM, 14 Nov 1990, *Wooded Landscape with Road Leading to a House on a Hill* (1876, oil on panel, 15 3/4 x 22 ins / 40 x 55 cm) SEK 10,500. STOCKHOLM, 29 May 1991, *Landscape with Houses by the Edge of a Road* (oil on panel, 15 3/4 x 22 ins / 40 x 55 cm) SEK 5,000. LONDON, 4 Oct 1991, *Figures in a Park Looking at the Statue of Adam Molthe* (1862, oil on canvas, 37 1/2 x 56 ins / 95.2 x 142.3 cm) GBP 2,200. COPENHAGEN, 18 Nov 1992, *Soldiers of the Danish Regiment on Manoeuvres* (1848, oil on wood, 7 3/4 x 11 ins / 20 x 28 cm) DKK 4,000. NEW YORK, 15 Oct 1993, *Landscape with Basnaes Manor* (1849, oil on card, 10 1/4 x 14 1/4 ins / 26 x 36.2 cm) USD 690. LONDON, 11 Feb 1994, *Wooded Landscape with Castle* (1852, oil on canvas, 34 x 47 1/2 ins / 86.3 x 120.6 cm) GBP 6,900. COPENHAGEN, 16 May 1994, *Summer Day by a Fjord* (1869, oil on canvas, 19 1/4 x 28 ins / 49 x 71 cm) DKK 21,000. MUNICH, 24 March 1999, *Farmhouse in a Mountain Valley* (1856, oil on panel, 12 x 18 ins / 31 x 45 cm) DEM 3,800. COPENHAGEN, 22 June 1999, *Southern Landscape with Cliffs* (1865, oil on canvas, 36 x 51 ins / 91 x 130 cm) DKK 18,200. COPENHAGEN, 6 Sept 2000, *Winter Landscape with Children Sledging and Skating* (1872, oil on canvas, 28 x 38 ins / 70 x 96 cm) DKK 28,000. ZURICH, 25 Sept 2000, *Mountain Landscape* (1841, oil on canvas, 14 x 19 ins / 35 x 49 cm) CHF 4,000. COPENHAGEN, 29 Aug 2001, *View towards Koldinghus in Summer* (1837, oil on canvas, 13 x 18 ins / 34 x 45 cm) DKK 26,000. STOCKHOLM, 28 Nov 2001, *Mountain Landscape with Figures on Road* (1861, oil on canvas, 37 x 52 ins / 93 x 133 cm) SEK 36,000. PARIS, 27 Sept 2002, *View of Copenhagen* (oil on canvas, 15 x 20 ins / 38 x 51 cm) EUR 3,300. COPENHAGEN, 2 Dec 2002, *Ruins at Kolding-*

hus (1837, oil on canvas, 14 x 17 ins / 35 x 44 cm) DKK 21,000. HAVNEN, 24 May 2003, *Landscape from Dronningeborg near Randers* (1863, oil on canvas, 33 x 51 ins / 83 x 130 cm) DKK 34,000. COPENHAGEN, 2 Sept 2003, *Hilly Landscape with Lake in Foreground, Jylland* (1868, oil on canvas, 55 x 78 ins / 140 x 198 cm) DKK 42,000. COLOGNE, 1 April 2004, *Burg Stolzenfels* (1852, oil on canvas, 13 x 18 ins / 33 x 45 cm) EUR 1,600.

KIANCHENKO, Georgy Vasilievich
Russian, 20th century.
Born 1911, near Kiev; died 1989.
Painter. Portraits, genre scenes.

Georgy Kianchenko graduated from the institute of fine arts in Kiev in 1932 and painted traditional landscapes in soft, almost pastel shades. He became a member of the Union of Russian Artists in the same year. His work featured in a large number of exhibitions.

MUSEUMS AND GALLERIES:
KIEV (MFA).

AUCTION RECORDS:
PARIS, 18 March 1991, *In the Village* (1976, oil on canvas, 18 x 39 1/4 ins / 46 x 100 cm) FRF 4,500; *Springtime in Sednev* (1971, oil on canvas, 15 3/4 x 27 1/2 ins / 40 x 70 cm) FRF 4,600.

KIANG, Jacqueline
American, 20th century.
Born 1930, in New York.
Active since 1976 in France.
Painter, watercolourist, draughtswoman, engraver.

Jacqueline Kiang has shown her works in Paris, where she is based. Her piece *Poets' Pages* presents watercolours and tiny texts on hallmarked papers. Her work exudes lightness.

BIBLIOGRAPHY:
Beaumont-Maillet, Laure/Woimant, Françoise/Pernoud, Emmanuel, *De Bonnard à Baselitz - Dix ans d'enrichissements du Cabinet des estampes 1978-1988*, exhibition catalogue, Bibliothèque nationale de France, Paris, 1992.

MUSEUMS AND GALLERIES:
PARIS (Prints Collection): *Shadows of Desnos* (1980, wood).

KIANG CHE-TSIE. See **JIANG SHIJIE**

KIANG CHEN. See **JIANG SHEN**

KIANG EUL-CHE. See **JIANG ERSHI**

KIANG FENG. See **JIANG FENG**

KIANG HENG. See **JIANG HENG**

KIANG KIAI. See **JIANG JIE**

KIANG LI-KANG. See **JIANG LIGANG**

KIANG LING-KIEN. See **JIANG LINGJIAN**

KIANG SIAO-KIEN. See **JIANG XIAOJIAN**

KIANG SIUN. See **JIANG XUN**

KIANG SSEU-TCHEOU. See **JIANG SIZHOU**

KIANG TA-LAI. See **JIANG DALAI**

KIANG TCH'ENG-TSONG. See **JIANG CHENGZONG**

KIANG TCHOU. See **JIANG ZHU**

KIANG TS'AN. See **JIANG CAN**

KIANG YIN. See **JIANG YIN**

KIANG YU. See **JIANG YU**

KIAR, Mesko
Slovene, 20th century.
Born 1936, in Murska Sobota.
Painter, engraver, mixed media.

Mesko Kiar studied at the academy of fine arts in Ljubljana, where he lived and worked.

His work is difficult to classify. There is some collage, particularly of known or unknown faces, and a few borrowings from Pop Art. He traces networks of lines scratched out against a uniformly black background, creates stars and constellations, suggests infinite or alternatively delimitated areas. His work focuses on nocturnal spaces from which the figures in his collages emerge, still rubbing the sleep from their eyes, and this places him firmly apart from tried and tested trends.

Mesko Kiar took part in collective exhibitions designed to introduce Yugoslavian painting both in his own country and abroad, including the Mediterranean Biennale in Alexandria (winning the first prize for engraving in 1965); the 33rd Venice Biennale; and *Expo 67* in Montreal. His solo exhibitions include Yugoslavia, Düsseldorf, Verona, Macerati and Klagenfurt.

BIBLIOGRAPHY:
'*Mesko Kiar*' in *Salon des Galeries Pilotes*, exhibition catalogue, Musée cantonal, Lausanne, 1970.

KIBARDIN, Georg
Russian, 20th century.
Born 1899; died 1989.
Painter. Landscapes.

Kibardin taught at the Surikov academy of fine arts.

MUSEUMS AND GALLERIES:
MOSCOW - ST PETERSBURG.

AUCTION RECORDS:
PARIS, 16 June 1991, *Flower-filled Garden* (1940, oil on canvas, 31 1/2 x 27 1/2 ins / 80 x 70 cm) FRF 6,500.

KIBEL, Wolf
Polish, 20th century.
Born 16 December 1903, in Grodzisk, near Warsaw; died 1938, in Cape Town.
Active in South Africa, then naturalised.
Painter, watercolourist, pastellist, draughtsman, engraver, monotype artist. Portraits, landscapes, figures, nudes, still-lifes, genre scenes, religious subjects, street scenes, interiors with figures.

Wolf Kibel fled Poland in 1923, moving first to Czechoslovakia, then Austria, where he studied privately under Pick-Moroni in Vienna (1923-1925). He then left for Tel Aviv, where he established himself as a painter before moving on to Cape Town in 1929. Kibel's Jewish heritage can be seen in his work, which treats both scenes from the Bible and of Jewish life. His impulsive, nervous brushwork and confused outlines create painful, deformed images reminiscent of those of Soutine, whose work, along with that of Chagall, he helped introduce into South Africa.

Kibel exhibited in Cape Town in 1931, 1933, 1935 and 1937. Retrospective exhibitions were held in 1947 and 1950 in Johannesburg and in 1976 in Cape Town's National Art Gallery. Subsequently, a number of exhibitions of his work were held in Cape Town, Johannesburg and Pretoria.

AUCTION RECORDS:
JOHANNESBURG, 17 March 1976, *Landscape* (watercolour and gouache, 9 x 10 1/4 ins / 23 x 26 cm) ZAR 750. JOHANNESBURG, 17 May 1999, *Two Men in Conversation* (watercolour, 12 x 15 ins / 30 x 39 cm) ZAR 35,000. JOHANNESBURG, 8 May 2000, *Vase of Flowers* (pastel, 22 x 16 ins / 55 x 41 cm) ZAR 24,000. JOHANNESBURG, 13 May 2002, *Three Figures* (oil on board, 8 x 7 ins / 21 x 19 cm) ZAR 16,000. JOHANNESBURG, 4 Nov 2003, *Flowers in a Vase* (pastel on paper laid on board, 24 x 19 ins / 60 x 47 cm) ZAR 14,000. JOHANNESBURG, 31 May 2004, *Flowers in a Vase* (pastel on paper laid on board, 24 x 19 ins / 60 x 47 cm) ZAR 35,000.

KIBLER, Friedrich
Austrian, 18th - 19th century.
Born 1747; died 15 February 1816, in Vienna.
Draughtsman.

Kibler is best known for his illustrations for J.H. Eckhel's work *Selection of the Engraved Stones in the Imperial Cabinet in Vienna*.

KIBRIK, Evgeniy Adolfovich or Yevgeny
Russian, 20th century.
Born 1906.
Painter. Portraits.
Socialist Realism.
Kibrik worked in Moscow. He also taught painting.
MUSEUMS AND GALLERIES:
MOSCOW (Central Lenin Mus.): *Lenin at the Soviet* - ST PETERSBURG (Mus. of the History of the Revolutionary Movement in 1880-1890): *Lenin and Stalin in Smoly*.

KICHI
Japanese, 15th century.
Painter.
Kichi was an artist of the Muromachi period and was active in the 15th century. He painted with ink. Nothing is known of his life, except that he is thought to have studied under Sesshu (1420-1506).

KICHIBEI. See **MORONOBU**

KICHLER, Augusta
German, 19th - 20th century.
Born 22 May 1870, in Darmstadt (Hesse).
Active in Darmstadt.
Painter. Still-lifes, flowers.
Augusta Kichler studied under W. Bader, C. von Marr, and H. Heim.

KICK, Cornelis, or Kik
Dutch, 17th century.
Born 1635; died 18 June 1681, in Amsterdam.
Active in Amsterdam.
Painter. Figures, portraits, still-lifes (flowers/fruit).
Cornelis Kick studied under his father Simon Kick. He married in 1661, was widowed, and remarried in 1674. His pupils included Jakob van Walskappel in 1667.

Early in his career, Cornelis Kick followed in the tradition of his father. Later, much impressed by the works of Jan David de Heem, he specialised in painting flowers and fruit and was particularly successful with his pictures of hyacinths and tulips. However, his meticulous approach to his work, together with a certain tendency towards indolence, resulted in a limited output and his paintings are therefore rare. His works include *Bouquet of Flowers* which appeared in the Fechenbach sale in Cologne in 1889, *Flowers* (Leipzig exhibition of 1890) and *Flowers* (in the Fesch catalogue).
AUCTION RECORDS:
PARIS, 25 May 1949, *Still-life,* FRF 350,000. LONDON, 8 Feb 1961, *Summer Flowers,* GBP 240. LONDON, 24 Nov 1967, *Still-life with Flowers,* Gns 1,400. LONDON, 21 March 1973, *Still-life,* GBP 7,500. COLOGNE, 18 Nov 1982, *Still-life with Flowers* (oil on canvas, 17 3/4 x 13 3/4 ins / 45 x 35 cm) DEM 18,000. COLOGNE, 9 May 1983, *Still-life with Flowers* (oil on panel, 16 3/4 x 12 1/2 ins / 42.5 x 32 cm) DEM 13,000. PARIS, 25 Nov 1985, *Bouquet of Flowers in a Basin on an Entablature* (oil on canvas, 30 x 25 ins / 76 x 63.5 cm) FRF 100,000. PARIS, 22 June 1990, *Vase of Flowers on an Entablature with Four Butterflies* (oil on oak panel, 23 1/2 x 18 1/4 ins / 60 x 46.5 cm) FRF 1,400,000. AMSTERDAM, 10 Nov 1992, *Composition with Grapes, Apricots, Plums, Peaches, Cherries and Currants on a Stone Entablature* (oil on canvas, 22 x 18 1/2 ins / 55.8 x 47 cm) NLG 27,600. NEW YORK, 19 May 1993, *Still-life with Tulips, Guelder Roses, Roses, Carnations and Other Flowers in a Glass Vase on the Corner of a Table* (oil on canvas, 24 1/2 x 19 ins / 62 x 48 cm) USD 23,000. AMSTERDAM, 10 May 1994, *Still-life with Flowers in a Vase* (oil on panel, 22 1/4 x 17 3/4 ins / 56.5 x 45 cm) NLG 59,800. LONDON, 3 July 1996, *Still-life with Roses, Poppies, Ranunculus, Irises and Other Flowers in a Glass Vase on an Entablature* (oil on panel, 19 1/4 x 16 1/4 ins / 49 x 41 cm) GBP 67,500. LONDON, 3 Dec 1997, *Silver Brandy Glass, Silver Spoon and an Orange on a Pewter Plate with a Venetian Style Wine Glass and a Lemon on a Table* (oil on panel, 17 1/4 x 13 1/4 ins / 43.8 x 33.6 cm) GBP 33,350. ZURICH, 30 March 2001, *Still-life with Flowers in a Glass Vase, Plums and a Snail* (oil on canvas, 11 x 16 ins / 28 x 40 cm) CHF 13,000. NEW YORK, 24 Jan 2002, *Still-life with Silver Brandy Cup, Silver Spoon and an Orange on a Pewter Plate* (oil on panel, 17 x 13 ins / 43 x 34 cm) USD 80,000.

KICK, Symon
Dutch, 17th century.
Born 1603; died 1652, in Amsterdam.
Painter.
Symon Kick was the son of Willem Kick. On 5 September 1631 he married the sister of the painter W. Duyster. Kick painted soldiers and small portraits. His work was featured in the exhibition *Twee gouden eeuwen: schilderkunst uit Nederland en Denemarken* (*Two Golden Ages: Masterpieces of Dutch and Danish Painting*) at the Rijksmuseum in Amsterdam in 2001.
MUSEUMS AND GALLERIES:
BASEL: *Soldiers Playing Cards* - BERLIN: *Soldiers Resting in a Stable* - COPENHAGEN (Statens Mus. for Kunst): *The Homecoming of a Fowling Party*.
AUCTION RECORDS:
LONDON, 7 May 1909, *Three Gentlemen Playing Musical Instruments,* GBP 110. LONDON, 1 June 1911, *Officers and Soldiers in a Guardroom,* GBP 78. PARIS, 26 Feb 1923, *The Guitar Player,* FRF 520. LONDON, 13 Dec 1935, *Sentry,* GBP 52. LONDON, 12 July 1946, *Interior,* GBP 147. PARIS, 5 Dec 1951, *The Guardroom,* FRF 260,000. NEW YORK, 17 May 1972, *Soldier,* USD 1,600. LONDON, 10 April 1981, *Guardroom* (oil on panel, 48 x 48 ins / 122 x 122 cm) GBP 20,000. MONTE CARLO, 20 June 1987, *Portrait of a Man with a Beard* (oil on panel, 25 1/2 x 21 1/2 ins / 65 x 54.5 cm) FRF 80,000. LONDON, 3 July 1997, *Officer Putting on his Boot while a Servant Removes his Slippers* (oil on panel, 14 3/4 x 12 1/2 ins / 37.3 x 31.5 cm) GBP 23,000. NEW YORK, 29 Jan 1999, *Company of Soldiers in Guardroom Preparing for Battle* (oil on panel, 48 x 48 ins / 122 x 122 cm) USD 400,000. NEW YORK, 24 Jan 2003, *Rabbi Reading* (1637, oil on panel, 26 x 20 ins / 67 x 51 cm) USD 13,000. AMSTERDAM, 4 Nov 2003, *Soldiers in a Barn Playing Cards* (oil on panel, 30 x 41 ins / 75 x 105 cm) EUR 18,000. ZURICH, 26 March 2004, *Gendarme and Party* (oil on panel, 36 x 30 ins / 91 x 75 cm) CHF 65,000.

KICKEL
German.
Painter.
Kickel is mentioned by Ris-Paquot.

KICKERT, Conrad Jean Théodore, called Conrad-Kickert
Dutch, 20th century.
Born 1882, in The Hague; died 26 June 1965, in Paris.
Active from 1906 in France.
Painter, engraver (etching). Figures, nudes, interiors with figures, landscapes, seascapes, still-lifes (fish/seashells), flowers, animals. Theatre decoration.
Conrad Kickert was a professor at a free academy in Montparnasse and played an important role in establishing the Paris school. After World War I, he came under the influence of Dunoyer de Segonzac, especially the latter's preoccupations with returning to reality. Kickert's works are brightly coloured and highly detailed, often meticulously depicting the artist's studio or a landscape. He also executed a

decorative scheme for the Belfort theatre. Kickert gifted some 50 French works to the municipal museum in The Hague: *Abundance, The Hunter,* and *Woman with a Fan* by Le Fauconnier, other works by the same artist, and canvases by Goerg, Formaire, Mondrian, Osterlind; and organized exhibitions of French art in Amsterdam between 1910 and 1916, introducing a number of major artists to the Netherlands: Braque, Derain, Dufy, Herbin, Gleizes, Gromaire, Le Fauconnier, Léger, Metzinger and Picasso.

He exhibited in Paris at the Salon d'Automne, of which he was a member, the Salon des Indépendants and the Salon des Tuileries. A solo exhibition of his work took place in Amsterdam in 1931, and he was awarded the gold medal at the Exposition Universelle in Paris in 1937. He was a Chevalier de la Légion d'Honneur and a Chevalier de l'Ordre Orange-Nassau.

MUSEUMS AND GALLERIES:

ALGIERS: *Still-life of the Four Arts* - AURILLAC: *Portrait of an Architect* - BELFORT: *Woman Sleeping; Flowers; Landscape* - COLLIOURE: *Snow in Upper Savoy* - GRENOBLE: *Landscape* - LE HAVRE: *Woman with Dragon; Still-life* - ORAN: *Still-life* - PARIS (former Mus. du Jeu de Paume): *The Pretty Farmer's Wife* - PARIS (Mus. du Petit Palais): *Getting Up; Shells* - ST-QUENTIN: *Seascape of the Island of Yeu* - THE HAGUE: *The Ploumanach Album* (1913, six etchings); *Kiss by the Sea; Portrait of the Artist; The Painter and his Model; Rabbits and Pheasants; Seascape of the Island of Yeu; Cap d'Ail.*

AUCTION RECORDS:

PARIS, 22 March 1926, *Vases, Tankard and Fruit,* FRF 920. PARIS, 11 April 1927, *Entrance to the Talou Enclosure,* FRF 360. PARIS, 20 Feb 1928, *Nude Lying on a Red Sofa,* FRF 300. PARIS, 11 Oct 1928, *Fish and Scallop Shells,* FRF 1,050. PARIS, 14 June 1929, *Tree above the Yvette,* FRF 810. PARIS, 27 March 1930, *Seascape,* FRF 200. PARIS, 23 April 1937, *Nasturtiums in a Green Vase,* FRF 60. PARIS, 23 March 1938, *Flowers in Jars with Frog,* FRF 700. PARIS, 1 April 1942, *Our Lady of Grace, Honfleur* (1925) FRF 400. PARIS, 3 Nov 1944, *Gorges,* FRF 500. AMSTERDAM, 20 March 1978, *Flowers* (1935, oil on canvas, 28 3/4 x 23 1/2 ins / 73 x 60 cm) NLG 8,800. AMSTERDAM, 24 March 1980, *Vase of Flowers* (1934, canvas) NLG 4,800. AMSTERDAM, 10 April 1990, *The Branse Valley* (1937, oil on panel/canvas, 28 1/4 x 36 ins / 72 x 90.5 cm) NLG 4,830. PARIS, 19 June 1990, *Trees at Bréhat* (oil on panel, 19 x 22 ins / 48 x 55 cm) FRF 18,000. PARIS, 6 Feb 1991, *Waves at Sea* (1920, oil on canvas, 19 3/4 x 25 1/2 ins / 50 x 65 cm) FRF 18,000. AMSTERDAM, 12 Dec 1991, *Still-life* (oil on canvas, 23 1/2 x 29 ins / 60 x 73.5 cm) NLG 2,875. PARIS, 18 May 1992, *The Farm in the Rain, as if in Autumn* (1944, oil on panel, 39 1/4 x 32 ins / 100 x 81 cm) FRF 6,000. AMSTERDAM, 27-28 May 1993, *Landscape* (1930, oil on panel, 19 1/2 x 28 1/2 ins / 49.7 x 72.5 cm) NLG 1,380. PARIS, 3 Dec 1993, *Inlet* (1950, oil on hardboard, 15 x 18 ins / 38 x 46 cm) FRF 10,300. PARIS, 12 July 1994, *Flowers* (1951, oil on panel, 28 3/4 x 24 ins / 73 x 61 cm) FRF 4,500. AMSTERDAM, 8 Dec 1994, *Landscape on the Coast* (1956, oil on card, 25 1/2 x 32 ins / 64.5 x 81 cm) NLG 2,415. AMSTERDAM, 31 May 1995, *Morbihan* (1928, watercolour and black chalk/paper, a pair, each 14 3/4 x 17 1/2 ins / 37.5 x 44.7 cm) NLG 1,062. AMSTERDAM, 5 June 1996, *Road to the Talou Enclosure* (1920, oil on canvas, 39 1/4 x 31 3/4 ins / 100 x 80.5 cm) NLG 2,185.

KIDD, Joseph Bartholomew

British, 19th century.

Born c. 1808, in Edinburgh; died May 1889, in Greenwich.

Painter, engraver. Portraits, landscapes, animals.

Joseph Bartholomew Kidd was a pupil of Thomson and Duddington, and is known for some etchings. In 1829, he was one of the founders of the Royal Scottish Academy. In 1836, he established himself in Greenwich. He resigned from the Academy in 1858.

AUCTION RECORDS:

LONDON, 31 March 1978, *Jamaica Landscape* (1835, oil on canvas, 15 1/2 x 23 1/2 ins / 39.4 x 59.7 cm) GBP 3,000. LONDON, 26 Jan 1984, *Fort Georges from Hyde Park, Grenada* (oil on panel, 9 1/4 x 12 1/4 ins / 23.5 x 31 cm) GBP 3,000. NEW YORK, 25 May 1994, *Peregrine Falcons* (oil on canvas, after Audubon, 26 1/4 x 20 3/4 ins / 66.7 x 52.7 cm) USD 46,000. NEW YORK, 3 Dec 2003, *Baltimore Oriole* (c. 1831-1833, oil on canvas, 26 x 20 ins / 66 x 52 cm) USD 25,000.

KIDD, Peter

Irish, 19th century.

Active in Limerick c. 1825.

Painter.

KIDD, William

British, 19th century.

Born c. 1790; died 24 December 1863.

Painter. History painting, genre scenes, portraits.

William Kidd was a young boy when he began working with the animal painter James Howe. At 13, he began exhibiting his work. Little is known of his life apart from the fact that his very real talent never drew much public success. He got by with the generosity of his friends and an allowance from the Royal Academy, but died poor. He exhibited his work from 1817 to 1853, mostly at the Royal Academy and at the Suffolk Street Gallery. He was elected an honorary member of the Royal Scottish Academy in 1849.

MUSEUMS AND GALLERIES:

CAPE TOWN: *Reading the Ballad of Jim Crow* - EDINBURGH (Nat. Gal. of Scotland): *Indulging* (1832, oil/panel); *Fisher Folk* (oil on canvas) - GLASGOW: *Art Lover.*

AUCTION RECORDS:

LONDON, 30 Nov 1907, *Beggar,* GBP 5. NEW YORK, 20 Jan 1911, *Portrait of the Artist,* USD 60. LONDON, 6 March 1970, *Street Battle,* Gns 320. GLASGOW, 2 Oct 1980, *Dancer and Bagpiper* (oil on canvas, 17 1/4 x 13 ins / 44 x 33 cm) GBP 580. EDINBURGH, 2 July 1981, *Return of the Fishermen* (oil on canvas, 11 3/4 x 15 3/4 ins / 30 x 40 cm) GBP 1,600. LONDON, 3 April 1987, *My Mother Dozed before the Fire* (oil on canvas, 22 x 26 3/4 ins / 55.9 x 68.2 cm) GBP 1,800. MONTRÉAL, 19 Nov 1991, *Victory* (oil on canvas, 12 x 10 ins / 30.5 x 25.4 cm) CAD 1,200. LONDON, 22 June 1999, *Good Move. News from Afar* (oil on panel, a pair, 8 x 7 ins / 21 x 19 cm) GBP 1,450. LONDON, 4 April 2000, *Fair Exchange* (oil on panel, 11 x 13 ins / 28 x 33 cm) GBP 2,000. LONDON, 8 March 2001, *Pensive Cobbler* (oil on panel, 12 x 15 ins / 30 x 38 cm) GBP 1,100. LONDON, 5 Sept 2001, *Naughty Boys* (1833, oil on panel, 16 x 13 ins / 41 x 32 cm) GBP 2,000. LONDON, 28 Aug 2002, *Fair Exchange* (oil on panel, 12 x 14 ins / 30 x 36 cm) GBP 3,000. LONDON, 20 Feb 2003, *By the Campfire* (oil on canvas, 20 x 25 ins / 52 x 64 cm) GBP 13,000.

KIDDER, James

American, 19th century.

Active in Boston (Massachusetts).

Engraver.

James Kidder produced *Views of Boston.*

KIDOKORO, Sho

Japanese, 20th century.

Born 1934, in Tokyo.

Engraver.

Kidokoro began exhibiting work in 1958. His style is at once figurative and highly stylised, on carefully worked grounds. He was represented at the 1964 and 1966 International Print Biennales in Tokyo, the Biennale Internationale des Jeunes Artistes in Paris in 1967 and the São Paulo Biennale of 1967.

KIDSON, H. E.

British, 19th - 20th century.

Painter. Portraits.

H.E. Kidson settled in Liverpool, where he exhibited at the Liverpool Academy of Arts.
MUSEUMS AND GALLERIES:
LIVERPOOL: *Portrait of W. G. Herdman.*

KIDWELL, William
Irish, 19th century.
Died 1836, in Dublin.
Sculptor.

KIE ZIWEN
Chinese, 20th century.
Born in Sichuan.
Engraver.
He studied at the Shanghai Academy.

KIEBOOM, Barend van den
Dutch, 20th century.
Born 28 July 1875, in Dordrecht.
Draughtsman.

KIEBOOM, Guillaume van den
Flemish School, 18th century.
Born in Antwerp; died 26 July 1778, in Antwerp.
Sculptor.
Guillaume van den Kieboom was director of the Koninklijke Academie voor Schone Kunsten in Antwerp in 1774.

KIECHL, Josef
Austrian, 19th century.
Born 1808, in Sarntal, South Tyrol; died 1838.
Painter.
MUSEUMS AND GALLERIES:
INNSBRUCK: *Landscape near Brixen (South Tyrol).*

KIECOL, Hubert
German, 20th - 21st century.
Born 1950.
Sculptor, draughtsman. Architectural views.
Hubert Kiecol produces highly sculptural designs for buildings - small houses, towers, staircases, stations, and so on - in unadorned concrete in the tradition of pre-war German vernacular architecture. He also creates simplified drawings and wrote and illustrated *Là où je vais je suis déjà* (*I'm Already in the Place I'm Going To*) published by the Villa Arson.

Kiecol's work has been shown in group exhibitions, including *10 ans - 10 œuvres 1983-1992* (*Ten Years, Ten Works 1983-1992*) at the Fonds Régional d'Art Contemporain in 1993. He has also exhibited at Villa Arson, Nice, and regularly at the Max Hetzler Gallery in Cologne.
AUCTION RECORDS:
NEW YORK, 23 Feb 1994, *Schrank* (*Cupboard*) (1989, varnished metal plaque, 74 x 32 3/4 x 18 3/4 ins / 188 x 83.2 x 47.6 cm) USD 1,380. COLOGNE, 12 Nov 1999, *Stairs* (concrete, two, h. 6 ins / 16 cm) DEM 12,000. COLOGNE, 12 Nov 1999, *Six Houses* (concrete, six, 10 x 4x5 ins / 26 x 9x13 cm) DEM 19,000. MUNICH, 26 Nov 2000, *White-on-black-print* (woodcut, 68 x 52 ins / 173 x 133 cm) DEM 13,000.

KIEDERICH, Franz, or Kiedrich
German, 19th - 20th century.
Born 25 July 1873, in Düsseldorf; died 1950, in Düsseldorf.
Active in Düsseldorf.
Painter. Genre scenes, figures, landscapes.
Franz Kiederich won a gold medal in Berlin in 1907.
MUSEUMS AND GALLERIES:
DÜSSELDORF: *Late Departure.*
AUCTION RECORDS:
COLOGNE, 12 June 1980, *Resting in the Fields* (oil on canvas, 23 3/4 x 31 1/2 ins / 60.5 x 80 cm) DEM 3,400. COLOGNE, 30 March 1984, *The Potato Harvest* (oil on canvas, 31 1/2 x 47 1/4 ins / 80 x 120 cm) DEM 3,800. COLOGNE, 20 Oct 1989, *In the Fields* (oil on canvas, 23 1/2 x 31 1/2 ins / 60 x 80 cm) DEM 1,600. AMSTERDAM, 25 April 1990, *Young Woman with a Glass of Champagne, Sitting on a Bearskin* (oil on card, 36 1/2 x 30 ins / 93 x 76 cm) NLG 5,750. AMSTERDAM, 19 April 1994, *In the Fields* (oil on canvas, 19 3/4 x 23 1/2 ins / 50 x 60 cm) NLG 1,495.

KIEDERICH, Paul Joseph
German, 19th century.
Born 15 September 1809, in Cologne; died 4 April 1850, in Düsseldorf.
Painter. History painting, portraits.
Kiederich was a pupil of Kuntze in Cologne and Theodor Hildebrandt at the acdemy of fine arts in Düsseldorf.
MUSEUMS AND GALLERIES:
COLOGNE: *Portrait of Peter Fererius Cremer.*
AUCTION RECORDS:
COLOGNE, 16 June 1978, *The Reading Lesson* (1835, oil on canvas, 39 x 28 3/4 ins / 99 x 73 cm) DEM 7,000. NEW YORK, 19 July 1990, *The Bivouac* (oil on canvas, 48 x 61 1/4 ins / 122 x 155.7 cm) USD 6,600.

KIEF, Jan, or Kieft
Dutch, 17th century.
Born in Haarlem.
Painter.
Jan Kief was senior member of the Guild of St Luke in 1683.

KIEF, Jan. See also **KIEFT**

KIEFER, Anselm
German, 20th century.
Born 1945, in Donaueschingen.
Active in France.
Painter, sculptor, mixed media. History painting, interiors with figures, architectural views, landscapes, animals, flowers.
New Fauves.
Anselm Kiefer began studying literature, law and art at the University of Freiburg in Germany, then travelled in Italy, Switzerland and France. He was a pupil of Joseph Beuys at the Staatliche Kunstakademie in Düsseldorf at the beginning of the 1970s. He lived and worked at Hornbach/Odenwald, then in the 1980s he settled in France at Barjac in the Ardèche. Kiefer made his debut with conceptual performances, then created environments characterised by a taste for the splendours of antiquity, casting a slightly disillusioned glance in the direction of western culture as, for instance, when he fills a container with peas and slabs of lead to suggest a population census. What is memorable about these installations is the spectacular element: lead books weighing 675 lbs (300 kilos) collected together in a library of a hundred or so books, a cataclysmic atmosphere, which cannot leave the spectator unmoved; a rocket pointing skywards, broken glass and lumps of earth containing teeth brought together in *Das Grab in den Lüften* (*The Tomb in the Breezes*) of 1991, or lead beds, devoid of all human presence, with a puddle of water in the hollow where a person would have slept, in *Women of the Revolution* of 1992.

At the same time, he employs the more traditional technique of painting, creating sombre images in black, brown and grey. He paints in large formats with violent brush strokes, spreading the material thickly. Kiefer mixes his paint with straw, tar, gold leaf, ashes, sand, earth, hair, snakeskin or lead; he superimposes layers on top of one another, inserts words - influencing the meaning, changing its direction, adding a note of humour or gravity; he exposes the canvas to the weather in order to evoke a mysterious world, apparently hostile to man, dedicated to metamorphosis. He develops only a few themes: architectural subjects copied from the Hitler era, as in the series *To the Unknown Painter*, interiors such as the artist's studio, bare, deprived landscapes crossed by paths that plunge into the very heart of the canvas, in which there is sometimes a man getting lost as he meditates on death, or cows with the eyes of saints, with holes full of stars in their bellies, because for Kiefer their digestive system evokes the idea of transformation, which for him is 'linked to the stars'.

On the occasions when Kiefer makes references to history, borrowing from and freely interpreting the iconography of the Nazi period, Nordic mythology and Wagnerian myths, he is putting forward a way of exorcising that part of the past that has been concealed and suppressed, the Nazi ideology of his native country for which deep down every German feels partly responsible. Especially in *Interior* of 1991, where he copied the monumental public buildings of Albert Speer from contemporary photographs (sometimes even integrating the photographs into the paintings), Kiefer shows his desire to restore the history of his homeland, which is an essential element in the development of his own creative activity. To do this, he rejects the bright colours, the smooth textures and the prettiness that were dear to the National Socialists in favour of gritty, bitter, tumultuous surfaces. In other series, he goes further back in time, drawing on the universal heritage of the Bible, the Kabbalah and French history, particularly in the series inspired by the names of Merovingian and Carolingian rulers. Since 1969 he has been working on the *Books*, more personal works created from a wide variety of materials stuck on to paper, showing a decaying world. He also experiments with photographic works to accompany his paintings, as in the series devoted to sunflowers, where - in book form - he shows the flower photographed in ever greater close-up until what he called the 'firmament and the stars' appear, echoing the surface of the canvases with their patterns of sunflowers seeds that have been coated in glue and incorporated into the thick texture of the painting.

Drawing inspiration from history - at the risk of appearing to wallow in unhealthy nostalgia - and from nature and its metamorphoses, Kiefer experiments with original kinds of sculpture that often show him as a modern rather than a backward-looking artist, who is misunderstood for his references to the holocaust and his spiritual landscapes evoking death. By exploring materials and natural, biological elements, Kiefer poses questions about the course of life and - not without a certain humour - meditates on transfiguration in works with tortured surfaces and austere tones.

He has been taking part in group exhibitions since 1968. The list includes: 1969 at the Hanover Kunstverein; 1970, an exhibition of the most recent trends in art in the streets of Montpellier; 1973 at the Staatliche Kunsthalle in Baden-Baden; 1977 at the Louisiana Museum of Modern Art in Humlebæk, Denmark; 1978 at the Museum of Contemporary Art in Teheran; 1980 *Après le Classicisme* (*After Classicism*) at the Musée d'Art et d'Industrie in St-Étienne; 1981 at the Royal Academy of Art in London and the Musée d'Art Moderne de la Ville de Paris; 1982 and 1987, Documenta in Kassel; 1984 and 1990 at the Stedelijk Museum in Amsterdam; 1984 at the Palais des Beaux-Arts in Charleroi; the 1985 Paris Biennale; the 1987 São Paulo Biennale; 1988 at the Carnegie Institute in Chicago; 1989 at the National Museum of Art in Osaka and 1990 at Museet for Samtidskunst in Oslo.

He has been showing in solo exhibitions since 1969, when he exhibited at the Galerie im Kaiserplatz in Karlsruhe. Since then he has exhibited in Cologne from 1973 to 1978 at the Galerie Michael Werner and 1981, 1982, 1984 1986 and 1989 at the Galerie Paul Maenz; 1977 at the Bonn Kunstverein; 1978 at the Kunsthalle in Bern; 1979 at the Stedelijk van Abbemuseum in Eindhoven; the 1980 Venice Biennale, the Mannheim Kunstverein and the Stuttgart Kunstverein; 1981 at the Whitechapel Art Gallery in London and the Folkwang Museum in Essen; 1984 at the Musée d'Art Moderne de la Ville de Paris and the Israel Museum in Jerusalem. He has shown regularly at the Marian Goodman Gallery in New York since 1985. In 1986, he exhibited at the Stedelijk Museum in Amsterdam; 1987 at the Art Institute of Chicago, the Los Angeles Museum of Contemporary Art, the Museum of Modern Art in New York and the Philadelphia Museum of Art; 1990 at the Städelsches Kunstinstitut in Frankfurt and the Kunsthalle in Tübingen; 1991 at the National Gallery in Berlin; 1993 at the Sezon Museum of Art in Tokyo, the National Museum of Art in Kyoto and the Museum of Contemporary Art in Hiroshima; 1996 at the Centro Cultural Arte Contemporáneo de Mexico and the Galerie Yvon Lambert in Paris, and in 2001 *Les Sept Palais du Ciel* (*The Seven Palaces of Heaven*) at the Fondation Beyeler in Basel.

BIBLIOGRAPHY:

Anselm Kiefer, exhibition catalogue, Whitechapel Art Gall., London, 1981. *Anselm Kiefer*, exhibition catalogue, Musée national d'Art moderne, Paris, 1984. *Anselm Kiefer*, exhibition catalogue, Museum of Art, Philadelphia, 1987. Gilmour, John, *Fire on the Earth: Anselm Kiefer and the Postmodern World*, Philadelphia, 1990. Arasse, Daniel, *Anselm Kiefer, cette obscure clarté qui tombe des étoiles*, exhibition catalogue, periodical, Gal. Yvon Lambert, Paris, 1996. Comment, Bernard, '*Interview: Anselm Kiefer, cette obscure clarté qui tombe des étoiles*' in *Art Press* n° 216, exhibition catalogue, periodical, Paris, September 1996. Kiefer, Anselm, *20 ans de solitude*, exhibition catalogue, periodical, Éd. du Regard, Paris, 1998. Schütz, S., *Anselm Kiefer: Geschichte als Material: Arbeiten 1969-1983*, exhibition catalogue, periodical, Cologne, 1999. Saltzman, Lisa, *Anselm Kiefer and Art after Auschwitz*, exhibition catalogue, periodical, Cambridge University Press, Cambridge (NY), 1999. Arasse, Daniel, *Anselm Kiefer*, exhibition catalogue, periodical, Éd. du Regard, Paris, 2001. Arasse, Daniel, *Anselm Kiefer*, Thames & Hudson, London, 2001 (Trans. Mary Whittall). Kiefer, Anselm, *The Seven Heavenly Palaces, 1973-2001, with an essay by Christoph Ransmayr and contributions by Markus Brüderlin, Mark Rosenthal, Katharina Schmidt*, New York, 2001.

MUSEUMS AND GALLERIES:

AACHEN (Ludwig Forum für Internationale Kunst) - AMSTERDAM (Stedelijk Mus.): *March Sand* (1980-1982); *Interior* (1981) - BUFFALO (Albright-Knox AG): *Die Milchstrasse* (*The Milky Way*) (1985-1987) - COLOGNE (Mus. Ludwig): *Tree and Wing* (1979) - EINDHOVEN (Van Abbe Mus.): *Varus* (1976) - FRANKFURT AM MAIN (Städel): several paintings, a sculpture - LONDON (Tate Collection): *Parsifal* (1973, oil (and blood)/paper/canvas, series of three paintings); *Ways of Wordly Wisdom - Arminius' Battle* (1978, acrylic, shellac and woodcut/paper); *The Rhine* (1981, book of woodcuts/paper); *Lilith* (1987-1989, oil, ash and copper wire/canvas); *Let a Thousand Flowers Bloom* (2000, oil, shellac, dried brambles, thorns, roses and wire/canvas) - PARIS (MNAM-CCI): *To the Supreme Being* (1983); *The Secret Life of Plants* (2001, set of ten panels) - RICHMOND (Virginia MFA): *Landscape with Wing* (1981, oil, straw, lead/canvas) - ST LOUIS (AM): *Breaking of the Vessels*.

AUCTION RECORDS:

NEW YORK, 18 Nov 1992, *Birch* (oil on sacking) USD 209,000. COLOGNE, 7 Dec 1984, *Head of a Woman* (1961, oil on card, 36 1/4 x 27 1/4 ins / 92 x 69 cm) DEM 20,000. NEW YORK, 3 May 1985, *Your Golden Hair, Margarete* (1981, gouache and straw/photograph, 23 1/4 x 33 ins / 59 x 83.8 cm) USD 10,500. NEW YORK, 6 May 1986, *How to Paint* (1976, oil on sacking, 37 1/2 x 49 1/2 ins / 95 x 126 cm) USD 75,000. LONDON, 3 Dec 1987, *Untitled* (1968, tempera, collage and pencil/paper, 16 3/4 x 22 3/4 ins / 42.5 x 58 cm) GBP 6,000. NEW YORK, 3 May 1988, *Studio of Fruits* (painting/photograph, 21 1/2 x 25 1/2 ins / 54.7 x 65 cm) USD 20,900. NEW YORK, 4 May 1988, *Midsummer Night* (oil, straw and acrylic/photographic paper, 23 x 32 1/2 ins / 58.6 x 82.4 cm) USD 90,200. LONDON, 6 April 1989,

The Banks of the Danube (book cover in oil paint, 12 x 8 1/2 ins / 30.5 x 21.3 cm) GBP 33,000. PARIS, 16 April 1989, *Father, Son and Holy Ghost* (1976, oil on canvas, 57 x 45 1/4 ins / 145 x 115 cm) FRF 1,270,000. LONDON, 25 May 1989, *Untitled* (1961, oil on paper, 36 1/4 x 27 1/4 ins / 92 x 69 cm) GBP 16,500. NEW YORK, 8 Nov 1989, *Your Blonde Hair, Margarete* (1981, oil and straw/canvas, 46 1/2 x 57 ins / 118 x 145 cm) USD 220,000. NEW YORK, 27 Feb 1990, *How to Paint* (1975, oil on canvas, 19 3/4 x 23 1/4 ins / 50 x 59 cm) USD 68,750. NEW YORK, 9 May 1990, *To the Unknown Painter* (1983, watercolour/paper, 22 1/2 x 30 ins / 57.2 x 76.5 cm) USD 77,000. NEW YORK, 4 Oct 1990, *The Mastersingers* (watercolour and straw/photograph, 23 x 32 3/4 ins / 58.5 x 83 cm) USD 44,000. NEW YORK, 1 May 1991, *Manne* (lead, acrylic, rubber lacquer and straw on a photograph mounted on card, 26 3/4 x 33 3/4 ins / 68 x 85.7 cm) USD 88,000. NEW YORK, 27 Feb 1992, *The Artist's Studio* (1981, acrylic and charcoal on a black and white photograph, 23 x 31 ins / 58.4 x 78.7 cm) USD 49,500. NEW YORK, 5 May 1992, *Capital* (1983, oil, Shellac and straw/canvas, 110 1/4 x 110 1/4 ins / 280 x 280 cm) USD 638,000. NEW YORK, 7 May 1992, *The Ride to the Vistula* (oil/material, 52 x 69 ins / 132.1 x 175.3 cm) USD 154,000. LONDON, 2 July 1992, *The Tomb of the Unknown Painters* (1982, oil and shellac/canvas, 51 1/4 x 66 3/4 ins / 130 x 169.8 cm) GBP 88,000. NEW YORK, 18 Nov 1992, *Birch* (1974, oil on sacking). LONDON, 3 Dec 1992, *Noch ist Polen nicht verloren IV* (*Poland is Not Yet Lost IV*) (1987, oil and collage of paper/sacking, 74 3/4 x 112 1/4 ins / 190 x 285 cm) GBP 176,000. NEW YORK, 3 May 1993, *The Broken Vase* (1986, emulsion and photograph/card, acrylic lacquer, twigs and lead under glass in a steel frame, 33 3/4 x 46 ins / 86 x 115.9 cm) USD 200,500. LONDON, 29 June 1994, *Midsummer Night* (oil gouache and straw/print, 23 1/4 x 32 ins / 59 x 81 cm) GBP 29,900. NEW YORK, 2 Nov 1994, *Untitled* (emulsion, oil, Shellac acrylic, charcoal and straw on a photograph mounted on canvas with pebbles covered with lead and suspended by metal wire, triptych, 122 3/4 x 215 3/4 ins / 312 x 548 cm) USD 596,500. LONDON, 26 Oct 1995, *Palette and Snake* (photograph on a treated lead background in a frame by the artist, 51 1/4 x 67 ins / 130 x 170 cm) GBP 31,050. NEW YORK, 14 Nov 1995, *The Sephiroth* (emulsion, acrylic, shellac, lead, straw and copper wire/canvas, 74 3/4 x 103 ins / 189.9 x 260.7 cm) USD 299,500. LONDON, 29 Nov 1995, *The Ridgeway* (1983, oil, emulsion, Shellac and straw/sacking, 52 3/4 x 90 ins / 134 x 228.5 cm) GBP 320,500. NEW YORK, 21 Nov 1996, *Untitled* (1982, woodcut and oil on paper/canvas, 79 1/4 x 64 1/2 ins / 201.3 x 163.8 cm) USD 90,500. LONDON, 23 Oct 1997, *Shebirath ha Kelim* (1986-1988, lead treated with acid, glass, metal, wire, graphite and paper, 95 1/4 x 39 3/4 ins / 242 x 101 cm) GBP 41,100. NEW YORK, 19 Nov 1997, *Midsummer Night* (1982, oil and fern/canvas, 51 x 67 ins / 129.5 x 170.2 cm) USD 541,500. NEW YORK, 16 Nov 1999, *Tomb of the Unknown Artist* (oil and shellac on canvas, 51 x 67 ins / 130 x 170 cm) USD 320,000. NEW YORK, 16 Nov 1999, *Your Golden Hair, Margarethe (Midsummer Night)* (oil, acrylic, emulsion and straw on canvas, 51 x 63 ins / 130 x 161 cm) USD 400,000. LONDON, 27 June 2000, *Rhine* (acrylic, shellac and woodcut on paper, 146 x 115 ins / 372 x 291 cm) GBP 130,000. NEW YORK, 17 Nov 2000, *Tree of Jesse* (palm roots, gelatin silver print, resin and oil on canvas, 95 x 52 ins / 241 x 131 cm) USD 110,000. LONDON, 8 Feb 2001, *Untitled* (emulsion, acrylic, shell, sunflower, chalk and charcoal on canvas, 75 x 110 ins / 190 x 280 cm) GBP 330,000. NEW YORK, 14 Nov 2001, *Athanor* (oil, sand, ash, gold leaf and lead foil on canvas, 111 x 150 ins / 282 x 382 cm) USD 1,050,000. NEW YORK, 15 May 2002, *Naglfar* (1988, mixed media and soldered lead on wood, 75 x 118 ins / 190 x 300 cm) USD 500,000. NEW YORK, 12 Nov 2002, *Five Foolish Virgins* (oil, acrylic, emulsion, shellac and straw on mirror, 94 x 134 ins / 240 x 340 cm) USD 600,000. LONDON, 26 June 2003, *The Ridge Way* (1983, oil, emulsion, shellac and straw on burlap, 53 x 90 ins / 134 x 228 cm) GBP 420,000. LONDON, 22 Oct 2003, *Yggdrasil* (black and white photo, branch, charcoal and lead on board, 83 x 40 ins / 211 x 102 cm) GBP 85,000. NEW YORK, 14 May 2004, *Weichsel, Weichsel, weisse Weichsel ach was trauerst du so sehr* (*Vistula, Vistula, White Vistula, How Sad you are*) (oil, sand, wood shavings and charcoal on canvas, 51 x 63 ins / 130 x 160 cm) USD 145,000. LONDON, 24 June 2004, *Der Eingergorene* (1991, dried foliage, roses and photo lead, 40 x 28 ins / 101 x 72 cm) GBP 72,000.

KIEFER, Karl

German, 19th century.

Born 9 February 1871, in Jettenbach.

Sculptor.

Kiefer was a pupil of W. van Rümann. He won a medal in Munich in 1897.

KIEFER, Oscar Alexander

German, 19th - 20th century.

Born 26 February 1874, in Offenburg.

Sculptor.

Oscar Kiefer worked mainly in Karlsruhe, where he decorated the façades of several buildings. He also created monuments to Bismark, Goethe and Liszt.

KIEFFER, Clément

French, 20th century.

Born 1881, in Variez; died 1964, in Metz.

Painter, engraver. Landscapes.

Clément Kieffer attended the École des Arts Décoratifs in Strasbourg in 1900 and the academy of Düsseldorf in 1904. He also mixed with Courbet's students and studied at the Académie Delécleuze in Paris from 1910. He remained in Paris until 1914 before returning to the Moselle region where he produced most of his work. Kieffer taught drawing at the Metz vocational college and was appointed director of the École des Arts Appliqués in 1950, the year it was created. He played an important role in the arts and popular traditions of Moselle, of which Metz was the main beneficiary. In 1934 he produced wood engravings for the *Dictionnaire des Traditions Populaires Messines* (*Dictionary of the Popular Traditions of Metz*) by R. de Westphalen.

Kieffer produced paintings but also engravings, using a wide variety of techniques including wood, etching, drypoint, burin and aquatint. His draughtsmanship is classical and traditional in style and reveals a meticulous attention to detail. His paintings, however, show a discreet influence of Manet. Gradually the two disciplines of drawing and engraving became harmonised in a complementary figurative style characterised by small-format works in shimmering blacks and whites.

The Musée d'Art et d'Histoire of Metz held an exhibition of Kieffer's work in 1967.

BIBLIOGRAPHY:

Collot, Gérard, *Clément Kieffer*, exhibition catalogue, Musée de Metz, Metz, 1967.

MUSEUMS AND GALLERIES:

METZ (La Cour d'Or).

KIEFFER, Hans

Swiss, 16th century.

Active probably in Lucerne in 1568.

Glass painter.

Dr Brun makes a reference to this artist.

KIEFFER, Johann Jakob

German, 19th century.

Born 14 September 1814, in Trier; died 28 January 1891, in Trier.

Painter. History painting.

Kieffer completed his studies with Schadow in Düsseldorf, then travelled around Europe for ten years before returning to his home town. His subsequent output consisted almost entirely of religiously inspired works.

KIEFFER, Philipp
German, 19th century.
Died 18 December 1833, in Mainz.
Painter.
Kieffer lived and worked in Mainz in the early 19th century, painting portraits of notable citizens of the city in oils or as miniatures.

KIEFT, Jan, or Kief
Dutch, 19th century.
Born 17 July 1798, in Ryp; died 20 December 1870, in Amsterdam.
Painter. Portraits.
Jan Kieft studied under Bianchi. In 1828 he visited Belgium and Germany.

MUSEUMS AND GALLERIES:
AMSTERDAM: *Portrait of Gijsbertus Martinus Cort-Heijilgers* - HAARLEM: *Portrait of Doctor Abr de Vries.*

KIEFT, Pieter
Dutch, 17th century.
Painter.
In 1683, Pieter Kieft was a member of the Haarlem guild. His painting *River with Boat Passing under a Bridge* appeared in the Bosch sale in Amsterdam in 1785.

KIEHLMANN, Carl Heinrich
German, 19th century.
Born 22 March 1801, in Dresden.
Painter. History painting, portraits.
Kiehlmann is noted for an *Assumption of the Virgin, Oedipus and Antigone* and above all for oil portraits of people in Dresden.

KIEHTREIBER, Albert Konrad.
See **GÜTERSLOH Paris von**

KIEKEBUSCH, Albert Gustav Adolf
German, 19th - 20th century.
Born 23 March 1861, in Zechin.
Painter, draughtsman. Genre scenes, landscapes.
Kiekebusch studied in Berlin.

KIEL, Lev Ivanovich
Russian, 19th century.
Died 1851, in Paris.
Watercolourist, engraver.
Kiel was a military officer and amateur artist who produced many portraits and landscapes, notably, *Views of St Petersburg.*

KIELBERG, Ole
Danish, 20th century.
Born 1911; died 1985.
Painter. Scenes with figures, landscapes.
AUCTION RECORDS:
COPENHAGEN, 30 Nov 1988, *The Corn Market* (oil on canvas, 25½ x 39¼ ins / 65 x 100 cm) DKK 14,000. COPENHAGEN, 20 Sept 1989, *Summer Landscape at Langstrup* (1954, oil on canvas, 30 x 41¼ ins / 76 x 105 cm) DKK 7,500. COPENHAGEN, 21-22 March 1990, *Rural Landscape* (1945, oil on canvas, 25½ x 39¼ ins / 65 x 100 cm) DKK 4,000. COPENHAGEN, 9 May 1990, *Summer Landscape* (1957, oil on canvas, 29¼ x 39¼ ins / 74 x 100 cm) DKK 11,000. COPENHAGEN, 14-15 Nov 1990, *Two Calves* (oil on canvas, 18 x 25½ ins / 46 x 65 cm) DKK 5,500. COPENHAGEN, 1 April 1992, *Sun on the Snow* (oil on canvas, 22¾ x 25½ ins / 58 x 65 cm) DKK 12,000. COPENHAGEN, 21 Oct 1992, *Rocks at Foraar* (1966, oil on canvas, 15 x 24 ins / 38 x 61 cm) DKK 4,500. COPENHAGEN, 13 April 1994, *Summer Landscape* (1958, oil on canvas, 23½ x 37¾ ins / 60 x 96 cm) DKK 5,000. COPENHAGEN, 17 April 1996, *Spring Landscape* (oil on canvas, 29¼ x 38½ ins / 74 x 98 cm) DKK 4,000. COPENHAGEN, 23 March 1999, *View from Stenhojen, Spring* (1970, oil on canvas, 35 x 51 ins / 89 x 130 cm) DKK 12,500. COPENHAGEN, 25 April 2001, *View across the Tile Works in Nivaa, Summer* (oil on canvas, 30 x 39 ins / 75 x 100 cm) DKK 13,000. COPENHAGEN, 19 June 2001, *Espergaerde Harbour* (oil on canvas, 15 x 24 ins / 38 x 61 cm) DKK 14,500.

KIELDRUP, Anton Edvard
Danish, 19th century.
Born 16 February 1826, in Haderslev; died 22 May 1869.
Painter. Landscapes, animals.
Anton Kieldrup travelled in Norway, Germany and Switzerland, but he executed mostly Danish landscapes.
MUSEUMS AND GALLERIES:
COPENHAGEN.
AUCTION RECORDS:
LONDON, 26 Nov 1980, *Wooded Landscape* (oil on canvas, 45¾ x 14¾ ins / 116.5 x 37.5 cm) GBP 220. COPENHAGEN, 22 Aug 1984, *Wooded Landscape* (oil on canvas, 24 x 30¾ ins / 61 x 78 cm) DKK 15,000. COLOGNE, 27 June 1986, *Landscape with Fjord* (1852, oil on canvas, 24¾ x 33¼ ins / 63 x 84.5 cm) DEM 20,000. LONDON, 26 Feb 1988, *Salzburg* (1858, oil on canvas, 11½ x 16¼ ins / 29.5 x 41 cm) GBP 3,080. COPENHAGEN, 1 May 1991, *Cows at the Entrance of a Forest* (oil on canvas, 19 x 23½ ins / 48 x 60 cm) DKK 4,500. COPENHAGEN, 10 Feb 1993, *The Entrance of a Forest* (1863, oil on canvas, 20¾ x 28¼ ins / 53 x 72 cm) DKK 7,200. COPENHAGEN, 16 Nov 1994, *Water Mill near Silkeborg* (1849, oil on canvas, 19 x 24¾ ins / 48 x 63 cm) DKK 9,500. NEW YORK, 20 July 1995, *Gathering Wild Berries* (oil on canvas/card, 18¼ x 23¼ ins / 46.4 x 59.1 cm) USD 1,150. COPENHAGEN, 1 Dec 1998, *Landscape from Moens Klint* (oil on canvas, 24 x 31 ins / 60 x 78 cm) DKK 48,000. COPENHAGEN, 5 March 2001, *Landscape from Taarbaek* (1848, oil on canvas, 11 x 15 ins / 29 x 38 cm) DKK 13,000. VEJLE, 9 May 2001, *Summer Monument at Mons Klint with Figures Walking* (1847, oil on canvas, 15 x 20 ins / 37 x 52 cm) DKK 14,500. COPENHAGEN, 27 Feb 2002, *Edge of Forest with Brook* (1862, oil on canvas, 42 x 55 ins / 106 x 140 cm) DKK 15,000. VEJLE, 13 Jan 2003, *Wooded Landscape with Footbridge across River* (1862, oil on canvas, 41 x 55 ins / 105 x 140 cm) DKK 24,000. COPENHAGEN, 5 March 2003, *View from Ermelunden towards Charlottenlund* (oil on canvas, 20 x 27 ins / 50 x 68 cm) DKK 21,000. COPENHAGEN, 2 March 2004, *Marienborg at Sunset* (1862, oil on canvas, 20 x 31 ins / 52 x 78 cm) DKK 14,000.

KIELHOLZ, Heiner
Swiss, 20th century.
Born 1942, in Rheinfelden.
Painter, draughtsman, watercolourist. Figures, landscapes, still-lifes.
Heiner Kielholz studied at the Kunstgewerbeschule in Zurich. He lives and works in Aarau. He paints in watercolours, tempera and oils in a Neo-Impressionist style. He also works in Indian ink, in small dots, with simple subjects such as figures. He took part in the São Paulo Biennale in 1971 and the 1972 exhibition *28 Swiss Artists* in Lucerne.
AUCTION RECORDS:
LUCERNE, 23 May 1992, *The Elder Tree* (1988, oil on canvas, 15¾ x 11¾ ins / 40 x 30 cm) CHF 2,800. LUCERNE, 15 May 1993, *Innocenti* (1986, tempera/plywood, 14 x 14 ins / 35.7 x 35.7 cm) CHF 3,400. LUCERNE, 20 May 1995, *Woman Reading*

(mixed media/packaging paper, 38¼ x 28 ins / 97 x 71 cm) CHF 3,400. LUCERNE, 25 Nov 2000, *Black - White* (acrylic on canvas, 35 x 46 ins / 89 x 116 cm) CHF 4,600. LUCERNE, 1 June 2002, *Untitled* (oil on canvas, 24 x 20 ins / 61 x 50 cm) CHF 2,400.

KIELISINSKI, Kajetan Wincenzy
Polish, 19th century.
Born 1808, near Cracow; died 1849, near Posen (now Poznan).
Painter, draughtsman, engraver, caricaturist. Genre scenes.

Kajetan Kielisinski studied in Warsaw with Jan Pivarski, and also in Paris. He travelled in Poland and Russia, and in 1832 was in Cracow. In 1834 and 1839, he is known to have been working for Polish noblemen. He engraved landscapes, views, coats of arms, animals, portraits, costumes, and above all, the Russo-Byzantine churches of the Polish region of Galicia.

KIELLAND, Else Christie
Norwegian, 20th century.
Born 1903, in Bergen.
Painter. Landscapes.

Else Kielland was a student of Krogh, Ström and Revold at the fine arts academy in Oslo, from 1923 to 1927, and travelled to Italy and France, Greece, Egypt and London (1947).

Her work was influenced by Harriet Backer. The majority of her works are landscapes imbued with an expressive quality, while other paintings are more composed, tending towards abstraction. She was also an author.

KIELLAND, Gabriel
Norwegian, 19th - 20th century.
Born 7 July 1871, in Drontheim.
Painter. Religious subjects, portraits, landscapes.

Gabriel Kielland was a pupil of Alfred Roll in Paris and worked largely in his native Drontheim. He was also an architect.

KIELLAND, Ketty or Kitty Lange
Norwegian, 19th - 20th century.
Born 8 October 1843, in Stavanger; died 1 October 1914, in Christiania (now Oslo).
Painter. Figures, portraits, landscapes.
Realism.

Ketty Kielland was born into a wealthy family that did not approve of her artistic vocation. In 1873, she left for Karlsruhe, where she studied under H.F. Gude at the fine arts school, then went to Munich, where she remained until 1878. In 1879 she moved to Paris, returning periodically to Norway before settling in Oslo in 1889. During the summers of 1886 and 1887, she worked at Fleskum with Skredswig and Peterssen and, in the late 1880s, was part of the new Romantic movement in Norway with Eilif Peterssen. She was a friend of Harriet Backer.

Kielland painted the landscapes south of Stavanger and in south-west Norway in a style clearly inspired by the French school. Under the influence of Impressionism, she began to paint in the open air, often bringing a poetic atmosphere to her scenes. She won a silver medal in Paris in 1889 at the Exposition Universelle, where she also exhibited in 1900. In 2001, her work was included in *Da Dahl a Munch. Romanticismo, realismo e simbolismo nella pittura di paesaggio norvegese* (*From Dahl to Munch: Romanticism, Realism and Symbolism in Norwegian Landscape Painting*) held at the Palazzo dei Diamanti in Ferrara.

BIBLIOGRAPHY:

Lange, Marit, *Harriet Backer (1845-1932), Kitty L. Kielland (1843-1914: Stiftelsen Modums Blaafarvevaerk*, Stiftelsen, Amot, 1983. Fogelström, Lollo/Robbert, Louise/Aaserud, Anne, *'Harriet Backer och Kitty Kielland i Paris pa 1880-talet'* in *De drogo till Paris*, Liljevalchs Konsthall, Stockholm, 1988. Terjesen, Marianne, *Kitty Kielland: et portrett*, Glydendal, Oslo, 1999. Lange, Marit (ed.), *Da Dahl a Munch. Romanticismo, realismo e simbolismo nella pittura di paesaggio norvegese*, exhibition catalogue, Palazzo dei Diamanti, Ferrara Arte editore, Ferrara, 2001.

MUSEUMS AND GALLERIES:

OSLO (Nasjonalgal.): *Study of Kvianes at Ogna, near Jæren* (1878, oil on canvas mounted on card); *Study of the Beach at Ogna, near Jæren* (1878, oil on paper mounted on card); *Summer Night* (1886, oil on paper mounted on canvas).

AUCTION RECORDS:

LONDON, 25 March 1987, *By the Sea* (1879, oil on canvas remounted on board, 13 x 23 ins / 33 x 57.5 cm) GBP 6,000. LONDON, 24 March 1988, *Sandvikens* (1891, oil on canvas, 17¾ x 33½ ins / 45 x 85 cm) GBP 22,000. LONDON, 27-28 March 1990, *Autumn Morning* (oil on canvas, 14¾ x 21¾ ins / 37.5 x 55.5 cm) GBP 4,400.

KIELLAND, Kirstine, known as Manna
Norwegian, 20th century.
Born 1882, in Christiania (now Oslo); died 1979, in Oslo.
Painter. Landscapes.

AUCTION RECORDS:

COPENHAGEN, 21 Feb 1990, *Northern Landscape* (1922, oil on canvas, 27¼ x 26 ins / 69 x 66 cm) DKK 10,600.

KIELLAND, Per Axel Smith
Norwegian, 20th century.
Born 19 September 1891, near Christiania (now Oslo); died 24 September 1921, near Hamar.
Painter. Landscapes, portraits.

Per Kielland was a career diplomat and travelled to Germany, Belgium and Italy.

KIELLAND, Valentin Axel
Norwegian, 19th - 20th century.
Born 21 July 1866, in Stavanger.
Sculptor. Religious subjects.

Valentin Kielland was a student of Léon Bonnat in Paris and was deeply influenced by Rodin. His works are largely religious in theme executed in a realist style.

KIELLBERG, Agnes
Swedish, 19th century.
Painter.

Agnes Kiellberg received an honourable mention in 1893. She is probably the same person as Agnes de Frumerie.

KIELLBERG, Johannes Frithiof
Swedish, 19th century.
Born 5 February 1836, in Jönköping; died 16 February 1885, in Stockholm.
Sculptor.

Johannes Kiellberg exhibited sculptures and busts, mostly of mythological subjects, in Stockholm, Copenhagen, Berlin, Paris and Rome. Twenty-one of his works are in the museum in Stockholm, including the busts *Linné, L. J. Hierta, Nils Ericson, Aug. Blanche, Per Wieselgren, B. E. Malmstrom* and *El. Schlestedt The Singer H. Salomon*. Among his other works at the museum are *The God Tyr, The Goddess Freya* and *Jesus Christ*.

KIELLBERG-JUEL, Astrid
Swedish, 20th century.
Born 1877, in Oskarshamm.
Painter. Portraits, genre scenes.

Astrid Kiellberg-Juel is known mainly for her portraits of children.

KIELLERUP, Theodor Julius
Danish, 19th century.
Born 7 March 1818, in Copenhagen; died 14 May 1850, in Munich.

Active in Germany.
Painter. Landscapes, animals.
Theodor Kiellerup settled in Munich and worked there from 1841 onwards.

KIELMANN, Andreas
German, 19th century.
Born 1825, in Weimar; died c. 1880, in Schwerin.
Painter. Genre scenes.
Kielmann began his studies in Berlin (1845-1847), and continued them in Paris, Brussels and Antwerp.

KIELWEIN, Ernst
German, 19th century.
Born 25 April 1864, in Ludwigsburg; died 6 October 1902, in Stuttgart.
Painter. Landscapes, seascapes.
Kielwein studied with Grünewald, Kappis and F. Keller at the Stuttgart art school from 1881 to 1893. In 1888 he made a journey to Venice; later, he went to Paris (1895 to 1897), spending most of his time there in the Louvre copying Dutch old masters. In 1899, he returned to Frankfurt and settled there.
MUSEUMS AND GALLERIES:
STUTTGART (Staatsgal.): *A Farm* (1899); *Seaport* (1901).

KIEMENEIJ, Jan
Belgian, 20th century.
Born 1889, in Antwerp.
Painter.
Jan Kiemeneij's early works were abstract in nature. He later turned to painting in a more traditional manner.

KIEMLEN, Emil
German, 19th - 20th century.
Born 15 January 1865, in Cannstatt.
Sculptor.
Emil Kiemlen's works include the statue of Bismarck at Heilbronn and monuments of Charles and William II in Stuttgart.
AUCTION RECORDS:
MONTE CARLO, 15 April 1978, *Dancer with her Skirt Hitched Up* (bronze and ivory) FRF 9,000.

KIEN, real name: Rikyo Yanagisawa, original forename: Ryu, nicknames: Kobi, Gondayu, pseudonyms: Kien, Chikukei and Gyokkei
Japanese, 18th century.
Born 1706; died 1758.
Active in the Yamato region.
Painter.
In the early-18th century, *bunjin-ga* or *Nanga* was introduced to Japan from China, at a time of great curiosity about the outside world. The arrival of Chinese painters in Nagasaki helped to spread the new techniques of painting with ink. These were first adopted by the literate intellectuals, somewhat uncertainly and with a degree of stylistic confusion. Kien was one of these early innovators and his works (landscapes, figures, flowers and birds) had not yet broken free of the Chinese models. It was from him that Taiga (1723-1776) first learned the skills which, in the second half of the century, enabled him to assimilate the new techniques properly, opening the way to a new vision of landscape.

KIEN, real name: Gen Minagawa, nicknames: Hakkyo, Bunzo, pseudonyms: Kien, Yuhisai, Kyosai, Donkaishi
Japanese, 18th century.
Born 1734; died 1807.
Active in Kyoto.
Painter.
Kien studied under Gyokusen (1692-1755) and then Oko (1733-1795). He was a Confucian literati painter, specialising in landscapes, orchids and bamboo.

KIEN, Emmanuel Marcel
French, 20th century.
Born 1907, in Pondicherry, India; died 1985, in Royan.
Sculptor. Religious subjects. Busts.
Emmanuel Marcel Kien moved to Indochina in 1929, where he met a former student of Rodin who encouraged him to paint and sculpt. Back in France he began studying at the École des Beaux-Arts in Paris in 1945 and met Despiau, Belmondo and Landowski. He returned to his teaching post in Indochina but asked, successfully, to be posted to Africa. In 1962 he returned permanently to France and concentrated on sculpture. During the periods he spent abroad, Kien produced many statues of different Asian and African ethnic groups.

Kien exhibited at the Salon des Artistes Français in Paris, of which he became a member, the Salon d'Automne and the Salon de la Société des Beaux-Arts de la France d'Outremer (French Overseas Fine Arts Salon). He exhibited in Saigon and went on to hold numerous further exhibitions of his work. In Paris he was awarded a bronze medal at the Salon des Artistes Français in 1955, a gold medal in 1959 and the Prix de l'Institut at the Salon of 1969.
MUSEUMS AND GALLERIES:
MONT-DE-MARSAN (Mus. Despiau-Wlérick): *Bust of a Young Vietnamese Boy* - ROYAN.

KIEN, Ferdinand
Austrian, 18th century.
Active in Vienna.
Painter. Battles.
Ferdinand Kien should perhaps be identified with Johann Kien.

KIEN, Johann
German, 18th century.
Active c. 1770.
Painter. Military subjects, battles.
MUSEUMS AND GALLERIES:
VIENNA (Kunsthistorisches Mus.): *Sunset; Mounted Combat.*

KIENAST, pseudonym of Baumann Kienast, Anna
Swiss, 20th century.
Born 18 November 1880, in Horgen (Zurich).
Sculptor.
Kienast exhibited regularly in Switzerland. One of her bronzes was sited on San Michele hill in Lugano.

KIENBUSCH, William Austin
American, 20th century.
Born 1914, in New York; died 1979.
Painter, draughtsman, watercolourist. Landscapes.
William Kienbusch graduated from Princeton in 1936 before attending the Art Students League in New York and the Académie Colarossi in Paris. He studied under Rattner and was also advised by Anton Refregier and Stuart Davis in New York. He painted at Monhegan Island in Maine.

He took part in collective exhibitions in the USA and received a number of awards: for drawing from the Metropolitan Museum in New York; for watercolour at the Boston Arts Festival in 1961; a Guggenheim fellowship and a Ford Foundation prize. He had solo shows in New York.
MUSEUMS AND GALLERIES:
BUFFALO (Albright-Knox AG) - NEW YORK (MoMA) - NEW YORK (Whitney Mus. of American Art).
AUCTION RECORDS:
NEW YORK, 17 Dec 1990, *Black Pines at Camp Island* (1952, gouache/paper, 22 1/4 x 26 ins / 56.5 x 66.1 cm) USD 990. CHICAGO, 15 Dec 2003, *Fog, Oceanville Quarry* (1955, casein on paper laid on board, 27 x 35 ins / 69 x 89 cm) USD 3,000.

KIENER, Henry
French, 20th century.
Born 13 June 1943, in St-Nabord.

Sculptor. Figures. Statuettes, groups.

Henry Kiener lives and works in Cannes. Completely self-taught, he began to tackle sculpture in 1985. In 1989 he undertook a period of work experience to learn bronze moulding and casting bronze techniques.

He sculpts recumbent or seated bodies and groups of women and children. His first statuettes sometimes comprised a mobile head whose position could be changed. These figures are more recalled than described and progressively lean towards relative abstraction. Their smooth and supple forms suggest the influence of Arp and Henri Laurens.

His work was first shown in galleries in Mougins and Paris. In 1992 he held his first solo exhibition of 13 bronzes in Cannes.

KIENER, Joseph

German, 19th - 20th century.

Born 21 July 1856, in Schwarzenfeld; died 2 February 1918, in Eichstätt.

Painter, engraver, illustrator. Portraits, landscapes, genre scenes, altarpieces.

Joseph Kiener studied in Munich.

KIENER, Robert

Swiss, 19th - 20th century.

Born 14 February 1866, in Bollingen (Bern); died 1945, in Bern.

Painter. Genre scenes, landscapes.

Robert Kiener studied at the fine arts school in Bern, from 1883 to 1887, and, from 1887 to 1889, at the École des Arts Decoratifs in Paris, where he was awarded first prize in 1888. After returning to Bern, he illustrated works of literature and became professor of drawing.

Museums and Galleries:

Bern: *Winter Day in the Jura* - Coire: *Meadow in Flower* - Le Locle: *House in the Jura.*

Auction records:

Lucerne, 30 Sept 1988, *Jura Landscape in Winter* (1903, oil on card, 10¾ x 14¾ ins / 27.5 x 37.5 cm) CHF 650. Bern, 12 May 1990, *Löwenzahn in Spring* (oil on treated card, 12½ x 16 ins / 32 x 40.5 cm) CHF 800.

KIENERK, Giorgio

Italian, 19th - 20th century.

Born 5 May 1869, in Florence; died 1948, in Poggio Fornia.

Painter, sculptor. Genre scenes, animals, farmyard scenes, landscapes with figures.

Giorgio Kienerk was a pupil of Signorini and painted landscapes influenced by Impressionist technique. His work as a sculptor was profoundly affected by the art of his teacher, Cecioni.

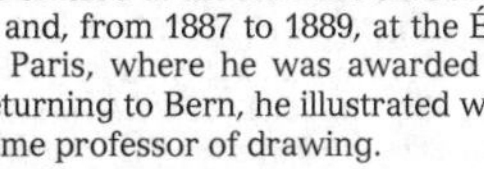

Auction records:

Milan, 28 Oct 1976, *Cocks and Hens* (oil on panel, 11 x 19¾in/27 x 50cm) ITL 500,000. Milan, 26 May 1977, *September in Fauglia* (1941, oil on panel, 9¾ x 19¾in/25 x 50cm) ITL 2,400,000. Milan, 5 April 1979, *Farmyard* (oil on panel, 10½ x 8½in/26.5 x 21.5cm) ITL 1,900,000. Milan, 17 June 1982, *Child in a Wooded Landscape* (1882, oil on canvas, 29½ x 43¼in/75 x 110cm) ITL 12,000,000. Milan, 13 Oct 1987, *Farmyard* (oil on panel, 10¼ x 19¼in/26 x 49cm) ITL 6,000,000. Milan, 6 Dec 1989, *Carding Wool* (oil on card, 8¾ x 11in/22.5 x 27cm) ITL 5,000,000. Milan, 18 Oct 1990, *Sunset over the Tuscan Countryside* (1922, oil on panel, 19¾ x 24in/50 x 61cm) ITL 15,000,000. Rome, 11 Dec 1990, *Light through Branches* (oil on panel, 11¾ x 14¼in/30 x 36cm) ITL 16,100,000. Rome, 5 Dec 1995, *Light through the Trees* (oil on panel, 7 x 4in/18 x 10cm) ITL 3,771,000. Milan, 19 Dec 1995, *Narrow Street in Bagni di Vasciana* (oil on panel, 18 x 27½in/45.5 x 70cm) ITL 19,550,000. Milan, 18 Dec 1996, *Monk and Hayricks, Fauglia* (1925, oil on panel, 7½ x 12½in/19 x 32cm) ITL 8,155,000. Milan, 16 June 1999, *Haystack at Fauglia* (1920, oil on board, 20 x 26 ins / 50 x 66 cm) ITL 15,020,000. Milan, 16 June 1999, *June Flowers* (oil on board, 29 x 24 ins / 74 x 62 cm) ITL 30,000,000. Milan, 7 Nov 2000, *Trees in Bloom at Fauglia* (oil on canvas, 15 x 28 ins / 37 x 70 cm) ITL 20,000,000. Rome, 27 May 2002, *Swing* (oil on panel, 16 x 25 ins / 41 x 63 cm) EUR 9,000. Florence, 9 Dec 2003, *Filicchi Garden, Fauglia* (oil on board, 7 x 10 ins / 18 x 26 cm) EUR 3,200. Florence, 21 June 2004, *Portrait of Pio Gatteschi* (1901, pastel, 18 x 11 ins / 46 x 27 cm) EUR 3,000.

KIENHOLZ, Edward

American, 20th century.

Born 1927, in Fairfield (Washington); died 10 June 1994.

Environmental artist, assemblage artist.

Funk Art.

Edward Kienholz was self-taught and pursued a number of activities before creating his own works. Attracted by the arts, he ran two avant-garde art galleries. Since 1981, his wife Nancy has been closely associated with the realisation and execution of his environments. Edward Kienholz was able to live in Berlin on an academic exchange in 1973. He and his wife shared their time equally between Berlin and Hope (Idaho).

The Kienholz' assemblages are usually three-dimensional scenes, often in real volume and dimension, and are fully focused on the seamier side of life. Reconstructions of brothels (*Roxy's*) and uncompromising treatment of sexual intercourse (*While Visions of Sugar Plums Danced in their Heads, The Back Seat Dodge '38*) caused a stir at Kassel and nearly had their retrospective exhibition closed in Los Angeles. The realistic, coarse confrontation of unpalatable realities, often using mannequins for dramatic effect, is subverted by the replacement, addition or subtraction of body parts which provide a running commentary on the flaws of consumer society. *State Hospital*, showing a madman whose head is a bowl with two black fish swimming in it, tied to his bed speaks transparently of alienation. For many these tasteless images were a gratuitous insult to America. Kienholz' 1969 *Portable War Memorial* struck even closer to home: its faceless soldier figures busy planting the flag, Iwo Jima/Arlington-like, in the sunshade hole of a garden table proclaim the ugliness of war and the vanity of glorious myths.

His works can be seen as an assault on cherished and comfortable conventions, but also as a confrontation with deeper truths. For the treatment is not restricted to the shortcomings of the American Dream. *The Wait* shows an almost decaying woman in rags awaiting death in a clutter of dusty, disintegrating objects below a yellowing photograph of her departed husband, a portent of the emptiness of all things. Their reflection on the human condition finds echoes in pieces like *The Birthday*, a visual testimony to the pain but also the hope of birth. To see any kinship between the Kienholz' works and Madame Tussaud's chamber of horrors would be entirely to miss both the symbolic language and the multilayered manipulation of the image which continues Dada both aesthetically and politically. The Kienholz' work is not to be reduced to sex, alcohol, loneliness and war, which are only symptoms displayed by the diseased society which is their real target. There is more to their graphic account than an indictment, there is anger and sorrow, a deep awareness of modern tragedy. They may 'overdo the sordid' but their concern is genuine.

From the 1960s onwards, they took part in numerous collective exhibitions in Pasadena, New York, Chicago, Los Angeles, Helsinki, several Documentas in Kassel; the 1977 Venice Biennale; *La Sculpture contemporaine après 1970*

(*Contemporary Sculpture after 1970*) in Fréjus; *Les années 70: l'art en cause* (*The 1970s: Art in Question*), in Bordeaux, and *Berlin-Moscow/Moscow-Berlin 1950-2000*, surveying 50 troubled years in the artistic and cultural relationship between Russia and Germany through the Martin-Gropius-Bau in Berlin and the Tretyakov Gallery in Moscow. They have also shown their works in solo exhibitions frequently in Los Angeles, Pasadena, Boston, Washington, San Francisco, Spokane (Washington), *Kienholz in Context*, 1984; and in Stockholm, Berlin, Paris, Düsseldorf, Munich, Humlebaek and Bremen. In 1986, *The Oxymandias Parade* travelled from the Portland Center to Düsseldorf and Vienna.

BIBLIOGRAPHY:

Tuchman, M., *Edward Kienholz*, exhibition catalogue, Contemporary Museum of Art, Los Angeles, 1966. *Kienholz*, exhibition catalogue, Centre national d'Art contemporain, Paris, 1970. *Edward Kienholz: 11+11 Tableaux*, exhibition catalogue, Mod. Mus., Stockholm, 1970. Scott, D., *Edward Kienholz: Tableaux, 1961-1979*, exhibition catalogue, Trinity College, Hyde Gallery, Dublin, 1981. Forrester, Viviane, '*Kienholz*' in *coll. Repères. Cahiers d'art contemporain* n° 3, Gal. Lelong, Paris, 1983. Harten, J., *Kienholz*, exhibition catalogue, Städt. Ksthalle, Düsseldorf, 1989.

MUSEUMS AND GALLERIES:

AMSTERDAM (Stedelijk Mus.) - BERLIN (Berlinische Gal.): *The Art Show* (1963-1977, realised with Nancy Reddin Kienholz) - BERLIN (Nationalgal.) - HUMLEBÆK (Louisiana Mus. for Moderne Kunst) - LOS ANGELES (County MA) - MINNEAPOLIS (Walker Art Center) - NEW YORK (Whitney Mus. of American Art): *The Wait* (1964-1965) - PARIS (CNAC) - PARIS (MNAM-CCI): *While Visions of Sugar Plums Danced in their Heads* (1964) - STOCKHOLM (Moderna Mus.): *State Hospital, 1964-1966* - STUTTGART (Staatsgal.) - TOKYO (MMA) - WASHINGTON DC (NGA): *Sawdy* (published in 1971, various materials including car door, mirrored window, automotive lacquer, polyester resin, silkprint, fluorescent light, and galvanized sheet metal, sculpture).

AUCTION RECORDS:

PARIS, 12 March 1972, *The Meat Eater* (wood, cotton, fur and plastic) FRF 35,600. LOS ANGELES, 22 Jan 1973, *Hope for 36* (wood, canvas, oil and tar) USD 3,500. LONDON, 5 July 1973, *Dumb Pudding* (assemblage and mixed media) GBP 3,500. PARIS, 29 Oct 1974, *Besforum* (1960) FRF 10,000. PARIS, 17 Nov 1977, *Feet on Foot* (metal, bone, glass, 50 x 33 1/2 x 11 ins / 127 x 85 x 28 cm) FRF 9,100. MUNICH, 12 Dec 1978, *Broom Painting* (1955, oil on panel, 29 1/2 x 34 ins / 75 x 86.5 cm) DEM 3,500. LOS ANGELES, 19 June 1979, *Untitled* (painted wood, 88 x 48 ins / 223.5 x 121.9 cm) USD 2,300. PARIS, 23 Oct 1981, *Stretcher* (mixed media, 13 1/4 x 22 x 59 3/4 ins / 33.5 x 56 x 152 cm) FRF 17,000. NEW YORK, 6 May 1982, *They Tar and Feather the Angel of Peace* (oil on wooden relief, 35 x 48 ins / 89 x 122 cm) USD 6,000. LONDON, 23 March 1983, *Queen for the Day* (1961, mixed media, 17 3/4 x 19 3/4 x 5 ins / 45 x 50 x 13 cm) GBP 2,800. VERSAILLES, 16 Nov 1986, *The Casualty* (1960, objects/support with electric lighting, assemblage, h. 61 ins / 154 cm and l. 27 1/2 ins/70 cm) FRF 126,000. NEW YORK, 2 May 1989, *Walter Hopps, Hopps, Hopps* (1959, construction in mixed media, 78 x 34 x 12 ins / 198 x 86.3 x 30.5 cm) USD 176,000. LONDON, 29 June 1989, *Mural Object* (collage with packing board, resin, plastic wood and tar/card, 24 1/4 x 24 1/4 ins / 61.5 x 61.5 cm) GBP 18,700. COPENHAGEN, 20 Sept 1989, *Suitcase* (1973, object and mixed media, 48 1/2 x 118 ins / 123 x 300 cm) DKK 17,000. PARIS, 18 Feb 1990, *Deluxe Billionaire* (1977, portable television monitor lit by a barrel of oil, 10 3/4 x 14 3/4 x 13 3/4 ins / 27.5 x 37.5 x 35 cm) FRF 33,000. NEW YORK, 7 May 1991, *Untitled* (1974, watercolour and ink/paper, 11 3/4 x 15 3/4 ins / 29.8 x 40 cm) USD 2,200. PARIS, 5 Dec 1991, *Deluxe Billionaire* (1977, portable television monitor lit by a barrel of oil, 10 3/4 x 14 3/4 x 13 3/4 ins / 27.5 x 37.5 x 35 cm) FRF 8,500. NEW YORK, 17 Nov 1992, *The Little Eagle Rock Incident* (1958, oil and deer trophy/wood, 61 3/4 x 49 x 20 ins / 156.8 x 124.5 x 50.8 cm) USD 44,000. NEW YORK, 3 May 1993, *House in Semi-darkness* (1983, wood, plastic and metal, 85 x 23 x 52 ins / 215.9 x 58.4 x 132.1 cm) USD 40,250. LONDON, 3 Dec 1993, *Double Cross* (steel, copper, brass and oil/plastic, 16 1/4 x 13 x 13 ins / 41 x 33 x 33 cm) GBP 2,300. PARIS, 17 Oct 1994, *The Block Head* (1979, mixed media, radio, 120 volts light source, 13 x 9 x 12 1/4 ins / 33 x 23 x 31 cm) FRF 6,000. NEW YORK, 3 Nov 1994, *The Last Worley Buffalo* (1986, lead, varnished wooden chair, electric lightbulbs, bull horns and vinyl shoe, 40 x 22 1/2 x 60 ins / 101.6 x 57.2 x 152.4 cm) USD 17,250. NEW YORK, 20 Nov 1996, *Girl Running through Goat* (1981, mixed media, in collaboration with Nancy Kienholz, 16 x 25 1/2 x 6 ins / 40.6 x 64.8 x 15.2 cm) USD 9,775. PARIS, 16 March 1997, *For 209 $* (watercolour, ink and print/paper, 12 1/4 x 16 1/4 ins / 31 x 41 cm) FRF 10,000. STOCKHOLM, 27 April 1999, *Untitled - Assemblage* (1969-1970, wall relief, 24 x 24x? ins / 60 x 60x? cm) SEK 37,000. LOS ANGELES, 9 June 1999, *Sawdy* (1971, galvanized sheet metal screenprint, 39 x 36x6 ins / 100 x 92x15 cm) USD 5,000. ZURICH, 21 March 2000, *The Opti-Can-Royal, Volks-TV-Emfanger* (sculpture, 11 x 9x6 ins / 28 x 23x14 cm) CHF 7,000. LOS ANGELES, 5 Dec 2000, *Black Bird* (taxidermed bird, mallet, shell casings, porcelain and oil on wood, 71 x 23x10 ins / 181 x 59x26 cm) USD 15,000. COLOGNE, 5 Dec 2001, *The Block Head* (transistor radio in wood, 13 x 8x12 ins / 32 x 21x31 cm) DEM 4,400. STOCKHOLM, 24 April 2002, *AM-FM York* (1967, mixed media object, 7 x 11x3 ins / 19 x 29x8 cm) SEK 27,000. NEW YORK, 14 May 2003, *Future as Afterthought* (1962, dolls, wood and sheet metal, 52 x 21x19 ins / 132 x 53x48 cm) USD 120,000. NEW YORK, 13 Nov 2003, *Spit in the Ocean* (1984, mixed media assemblage, 38 x 72x17 ins / 97 x 184x43 cm) USD 45,000. LONDON, 4 Feb 2004, *Reliefs* (1969-1973, mixed media on melamine, in three parts, 24 x 24x? ins / 60 x 60x? cm) GBP 4,500. PARIS, 9 June 2004, *Econo-can* (radio and jerrican, 12 x 9x9 ins / 30 x 22x24 cm) EUR 1,800.

KIENHOLZ, Hans

Swiss, 19th century.
Born 1856, in Brienz.
Sculptor, metal chaser.

Kienholz worked in his home town, then in Paris at the École des Arts Décoratifs. In poor health, he returned to Brienz and joined the staff at the school of fine arts.

KIENING, Isaac

German, 16th century.
Active in Isny.
Painter.

Isaac Kiening worked in several towns and castles in Württemberg, mostly in Isny, but also in Heiligen and Achstetten, among others. He also worked in Ravensburg and Wangen.

KIENLEN, Maximilian Ludwig

German, 17th century.
Born 1634, in Ulm; died 1704, in Ulm.
Painter, engraver.

Kienlen is known for his plates after the Flemish painter Franz Floris.

KIENLIN, Jules Georges

French, 19th century.
Born c. 1830, in Bitche.
Painter. Genre scenes, portraits.

Jules Kienlin was a pupil of Picot and Antigna. He began exhibiting at the Salon in 1863.

AUCTION RECORDS:

PARIS, 3 Dec 1941, *Two Women Holding Stoneware Pitchers from the Rhine*, FRF 650.

KIENZER, Michael

Austrian, 20th - 21st century.
Born 21 June 1962, in Steyr.

Installation artist, sculptor, draughtsman, illustrator. From 1977 to 1979, Michael Kienzer studied at the Kunstgewerbeschule in Graz. He lived in Berlin from 1979 to 1982. He makes sculptures from ropes, fabric, iron and glass, creating balls, pipes and rolled up carpets. He also creates geometric shapes, whose transparent glass surfaces are covered with traces of paint reminiscent of the paintings of Franz Kline. He uses charcoal for his abstract drawings. He says his work is characterised by 'the brutal nature of the material and its natural integration into the surrounding space'. He has been showing in group exhibitions since 1984; in Graz in 1984, 1985, 1987, 1988 and 1990; Vienna in 1984, 1985, 1986, 1989, 1990 and 1991; in 1985 at the Bochum Museum; 1986 and 1987 in Budapest; 1990 at the Toulon museum and 1992 at the Salon des Découvertes in Paris. Since 1985, he has also held solo shows in Vienna, Linz, Graz and Ostend.

KIEPERT, Hermann August Moritz
German, 19th century.
Born 1828, in Königsberg (now Kaliningrad, Russia); died 21 December 1887, in Mitau (now Jelgava, Latvia).
Painter. History painting, portraits.

Kiepert lived for a while in Riga, then in St Petersburg.

KIER, Christopher
Canadian, 20th - 21st century.
Born 1959, in Canada.
Painter.

Christopher Kier trained at the Ontario College of Art. He lives and works in Toronto and Vancouver. Since 1984 his work has featured in a number of group exhibitions, and in solo exhibitions in Toronto, Ottawa and Vancouver.

AUCTION RECORDS:
Paris, 24 May 1992, *Réunion* (1992, encaustic/canvas, 59 3/4 x 35 ins / 152 x 89 cm) FRF 8,000.

KIERDORF, Céline
French, 19th century.
Born 19th century, in Paris.
Painter, watercolourist. Flowers.

Céline Kierdorf was a pupil of Adèle Richet. She exhibited her work at the Salon between 1850 and 1855.

KIERDORFF, Franciscus
Dutch, 19th century.
Born 1777, in Trier; died 1855, in The Hague.
Lithographer.

Franciscus Kierdorff was a pupil and friend of Senefelder. He founded two lithographical institutes, one in Ghent, the other in The Hague. He worked in The Hague with his two sons.

KIERS, Elisabeth Alida. See **HAANEN**

KIERS, Georg Laurens
Dutch, 19th - 20th century.
Born 26 January 1838, in Amsterdam; died 1916.
Painter, draughtsman. Landscapes, seascapes.

Georg Kiers was the son of Petrus Kiers and a student of Louis Leyer.

AUCTION RECORDS:
London, 21 March 1972, *View of Amsterdam*, GBP 760. Amsterdam, 15 April 1985, *View of the River Ij near Amsterdam* (1871, oil on canvas, 18 1/2 x 31 ins / 47.2 x 78.5 cm) NLG 15,000. Amsterdam, 10 April 1990, *Fisherman in a Sailing Boat at Sea* (pencil and watercolour heightened with white/paper, 4 x 5 1/2 ins / 10 x 14 cm) NLG 1,495. Amsterdam, 24 Sept 1992, *River by Moonlight, with Moored Boats and People on a Jetty* (oil on canvas/panel, 16 1/4 x 25 1/4 ins / 41.5 x 64 cm) NLG 1,035. Amsterdam, 7 Nov 1995, *Jetty South of Ijmuiden* (oil on canvas, 25 1/2 x 37 3/4 ins / 65 x 96 cm) NLG 2,360. Amsterdam, 19-20 Feb 1997, *Fisherman Bringing a Boat In* (oil on canvas, 25 1/4 x 37 1/2 ins / 64 x 95.5 cm) NLG 10,955.

KIERS, Petrus
Dutch, 19th century.
Born 5 January 1807, in Gröneveld; died 17 November 1875, in Amsterdam.
Painter, engraver. Genre scenes.

Petrus Kiers was a pupil of Douwe de Hoop in Amsterdam and later became a member of the Amsterdam academy. He married the painter Elisabeth Alida Haanen. Kiers excelled at painting night scenes and light effects.

MUSEUMS AND GALLERIES:
Montpellier: *Dutch Woman Reading the Bible.*

AUCTION RECORDS:
Amsterdam, 1881, *Lady Going out into her Garden by Lamp Light*, FRF 200. Paris, 18 June 1930, *Children Eating*, FRF 1,000. Amsterdam, 1-4 July 1947, *Fruit Seller*, NLG 1,400. Vienna, 15 March 1951, *Family Scene*, ATS 3,000. Cologne, 19 Oct 1979, *The Letter* (1853, oil on panel, 30 1/2 x 25 1/4 ins / 77.5 x 64 cm) DEM 46,000. Gargrave (North Yorkshire), England, 26 Oct 1982, *Young Couple in Conversation at a Window* (oil on card, 17 x 13 1/2 ins / 43 x 34 cm) GBP 3,400. Amsterdam, 15 May 1984, *Interior with Mother and Children in Candle Light* (1850, oil on canvas, 28 1/4 x 22 3/4 ins / 71.5 x 58 cm) NLG 9,000. Amsterdam, 14 April 1986, *The Mussel Seller, Night Scene* (1851, oil on panel, 21 3/4 x 16 1/2 ins / 55.2 x 42 cm) NLG 17,000. Amsterdam, 10 Feb 1988, *Young Woman Spinning by Candle Light* (1874, oil on panel, 35 1/2 ins / 90 cm x 30 ins/76 cm) NLG 2,760. London, 16 Feb 1990, *At the Dressing Table* (1846, oil on panel, 19 1/4 x 15 1/4 ins / 49.2 x 38.8 cm) GBP 2,750. Amsterdam, 16 April 1996, *Evening at Home* (oil on panel, 20 1/2 x 15 1/4 ins / 52 x 39 cm) NLG 5,310. Amsterdam, 16 March 1999, *Two Ladies by Candlelight* (oil on panel, 4 x 4 ins / 10 x 10 cm) NLG 5,000. Amsterdam, 24 April 2001, *Goodbye* (1852, oil on panel, 29 x 24 ins / 74 x 60 cm) NLG 32,000.

KIES, Symon Jansz., called Simon van Amsterdam
Dutch, 17th century.
Born in Amsterdam; died 1620.
Painter. History painting, allegorical subjects.

Symon Kies may have been a pupil of Fr Floris. He made pen drawings of works by Floris executed for Klass Jongeling in Antwerp and produced 17 engravings, including 10 showing the *Labours of Hercules* and seven allegories depicting the seven liberal arts. According to *Bryan's Dictionary* he was a pupil of Heemskerk.

KIES, Wolfgang von. See the entry **PRACHNER Wolfgang**

KIESEL, Carl Maria
French, 20th century.
Born 1903; died 13 July 1971.
Painter.

Carl Maria Kiesel studied at the fine arts academy in Karlsruhe under Ernst Würtenberger in 1922 and 1923 and at the academy in Düsseldorf under Ernst Aufseeser in 1923 and 1924. He also studied in Munich. Kiesel left Germany in 1935 and went first to Belgium, then to Paris and Montauban in France. He returned to Germany after World War II and lived at Kaiserlautern until 1956.

KIESEL, Conrad
German, 19th - 20th century.

Born 29 November 1846, in Düsseldorf; died 28 May 1921, in Berlin.
Active in Berlin and Munich.
Painter, sculptor. Portraits, genre scenes.

Conrad Kiesel initially studied under the sculptor F. Schaper, then with the painter F. Paulsen in Berlin and, finally, with W. Sohn in Düsseldorf. He was a member of the fine arts academy in Munich and exhibited in Berlin, receiving gold medals in 1889 and 1890, and in Paris at the Exposition Universelle, where he received an honourable mention.

AUCTION RECORDS:

LONDON, 1896, *The Harem,* FRF 4,200. NEW YORK, 26 Jan 1906, *The Duo,* USD 825. LONDON, 22 Feb 1908, *Head of a Young Girl,* GBP 52. LONDON, 29 June 1908, *Favourites* (1885) GBP 126; *The Model,* GBP 115; *Spanish Woman,* GBP 44; *Italy, Land of Song,* GBP 84. LONDON, 10 Jan 1909, *The Model,* GBP 33. LONDON, 11 June 1909, *Head of a Woman,* GBP 42. NEW YORK, 27 Jan 1911, *The Duo,* USD 385. LONDON, 17 Feb 1928, *In the Studio,* GBP 105. LONDON, 2 Nov 1973, *The Gold Necklace,* Gns 350. LONDON, 20 Feb 1976, *The Bath* (1888, oil on canvas, 62 1/2 x 42 1/4 ins / 159 x 107 cm) GBP 1,100. NEW YORK, 13 May 1978, *Dreaming* (oil on panel, 12 1/4 x 9 1/2 ins / 31 x 24 cm) USD 2,000. COLOGNE, 30 March 1979, *Young Woman in a Kimono* (oil on panel, 15 1/4 x 10 ins / 39 x 24.5 cm) DEM 3,300. NEW YORK, 19 Oct 1984, *Women Playing Music in the Harem* (1904, oil on canvas, 69 x 47 1/2 ins / 175.5 x 120.6 cm) USD 30,000. LONDON, 18 June 1986, *Portrait of the Artist's Wife* (1881, oil on canvas, 50 1/2 x 29 1/4 ins / 128.5 x 74 cm) GBP 7,500. LONDON, 26 Feb 1988, *Spanish Woman* (oil on panel, 17 1/2 x 13 1/4 ins / 44.5 x 33.6 cm) GBP 1,100. NEW YORK, 28 Feb 1990, *At the Window* (oil on canvas, 36 3/4 x 22 1/2 ins / 93.4 x 57.2 cm) USD 52,250. NEW YORK, 1 March 1990, *The Lesson* (1877, oil on canvas, 42 x 33 1/2 ins / 106.7 x 85.1 cm) USD 60,500. LONDON, 19 June 1991, *Elegant Young Women after the Ball* (oil on canvas, 28 3/4 x 36 1/2 ins / 73 x 93 cm) GBP 69,300. NEW YORK, 22-23 July 1993, *Young Woman Lost in Thought* (oil on canvas, 21 1/2 x 17 ins / 54.6 x 43.2 cm) USD 3,450. NEW YORK, 1 Nov 1995, *Young Spanish Woman with a Fan* (1885, oil on canvas, 29 1/2 x 21 3/4 ins / 74.9 x 55.2 cm) USD 23,000. LONDON, 12 June 1996, *Hesitation* (oil on canvas, 33 x 20 ins / 84 x 51 cm) GBP 12,075. LONDON, 10 Oct 1996, *Beautiful Young Woman* (oil on panel, 12 3/4 x 9 1/2 ins / 32.4 x 24.2 cm) GBP 3,200. NEW YORK, 26 Feb 1997, *Elegant Lady in a Feathered Hat* (oil on panel, 10 3/4 x 8 1/2 ins / 27.4 x 21.5 cm) USD 4,025.

KIESER, Eberhard
German, 17th century.
Active in Frankfurt am Main from 1612 to 1630.
Engraver (burin).

Kieser engraved portraits of famous people, notably *Gonzalvo de Córdoba,* and views of cities in Germany, Spain and Italy.

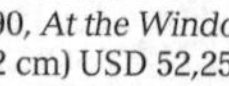

KIESER, Richard
German, 19th - 20th century.
Born 15 March 1870, in Coburg (Bavaria).
Active in Krefeld and Dessau.
Sculptor.

KIESER, Walter
German, 20th century.
Born 27 August 1894, in Krefeld.
Active in Dresden and Dessau.
Sculptor.

KIESEWALTER, Heinrich
German, 19th century.
Born 14 November 1854, in Breslau (now Wroclaw, Poland).
Sculptor.

Kiesewalter was a pupil of Wolff in Berlin. He left a number of equestrian statues.

KIESEWETTER, Wilhelm
German, 19th century.
Born 1811; died 30 August 1865, in Gotha.
Painter.

Kiesewetter made a trip round Sweden, Finland, Russia, Tartary, Central Asia and Caucasia, publishing sketches depicting things he saw during his journey in 1854.

KIESLER, Frederick J.
Austrian, 20th century.
Born 1880 or 1896, in Vienna; died 1965, in New York.
Active and naturalised in the USA.
Sculptor.
Surrealism.

Frederick Kiesler was an architect who became involved with the Surrealists in 1937. He constructed the *Art of this Century* gallery in 1942 and designed the *Hall of Superstitions* for the international Surrealist exhibition in Paris in 1947. He also produced sculptures consisting of forms that initially seem incompatible, which are indebted to Duchamp.

Kiesler's work was exhibited posthumously in group shows, including *Vision Machine* (artists' and architects' 'seeing machines') at the Musée des Beaux-Arts in Nantes. Solo exhibitions include: 1989, the Whitney Museum of American Art, New York; 1996, Centre Georges-Pompidou, Paris; 2000, Center for Art and Architecture, Los Angeles, and 2003, Museum für Moderne Kunst, Frankfurt am Main.

BIBLIOGRAPHY:

Kiesler, Frederick, *Frederick Kiesler: Environmental Sculpture,* exhibition catalogue, Solomon R. Guggenheim Museum, New York, 1964. Phillips, Lisa, *Frederick Kiesler,* exhibition catalogue, Whitney Museum of American Art, New York, 1989. *Frederick Kiesler artiste-architecte,* exhibition catalogue, Éd. du Centre Georges-Pompidou, Paris, 1996. Safran, Yehuda, *Frederick Kiesler (1890-1965),* Architectural Association, London, 1996. Gohr, Siegfried, Luyken, Gunda, *Frederick J. Kiesler: Selected Writings,* Verlag Gerd Hatje, Ostfieldern bei Stuttgart, 1996. Bogner, Dieter (ed.), *Frederick J. Kiesler: Endless space,* exhibition catalogue, Center for Art and Architecture, Los Angeles, Hatje Cantz, Ostfildern-Ruit, 2000. Davidson, Susan/Rylands, Philip, *Peggy Guggenheim and Frederick Kiesler: The Story of Art This Century,* Guggenheim Foundation, New York, 2004.

AUCTION RECORDS:

NEW YORK, 10 Nov 1982, *Sheep's Head* (1963-1964, bronze, 7 x 15 ins / 17.7 x 38 cm) USD 2,200.

KIESLING, Eduard Franz
German, 19th century.
Born 1820, in Hildburghausen; died 1858.
Portrait painter.

MUSEUMS AND GALLERIES:

MUNICH: *Portrait of Prince Eduard of Saxony-Altenburg.*

KIESLING, Ernst
German, 19th century.
Born 21 October 1851, in Berlin.
Landscape painter.

Kiesling first exhibited in Berlin about 1874.

KIESLING, Ferdinand
German, 19th century.

Born 8 August 1810, in Brandenburg; died 5 October 1882, in Siethen, near Berlin.
Landscape painter.
Kiesling exhibited in Leipzig and Berlin.

KIESLING, Louis
German, 19th century.
Born 11 March 1811, in Berlin; died 10 July 1875, in Leicester.
Painter.
Kiesling lived in Berlin until 1853, then settled in North America and finally in England.

KIESNINGER, Vincenz George.
See **KININGER**

KIESSLING, Franz Julius
German, 19th century.
Born 22 June 1811, in Altenburg; died 12 August 1858, in Altenburg.
Painter.
Kiessling, in his youth, worked in Munich, where he did portraits of princesses at the Bavarian court.

KIESSLING, Johann Paul Adolf
German, 19th - 20th century.
Born 8 January 1836, in Breslau (now Wroclaw, Poland); died 10 January 1919, in Dresden.
Painter. Mythological subjects, portraits.
Johann Kiessling was a student of Schnorr at the fine arts academy in Dresden, where he later became a teacher. He visited Italy, Antwerp, Paris and Rome. He exhibited in Berlin in 1891, where he was awarded a gold medal, and in Paris, in 1900, at the Exposition Universelle.
MUSEUMS AND GALLERIES:
WROCLAW: *The Moon and Endymion*.
AUCTION RECORDS:
NEW YORK, 4 May 1979, *Diana and Endymion* (1860, oil on canvas, 24 3/4 x 30 1/4 ins / 63 x 77 cm) USD 2,100. COPENHAGEN, 8 Nov 1983, *The Artist and his Wife, Surrounded by a Muse, Cupid and Bacchus* (1865, oil on canvas, 72 1/2 x 55 ins / 184 x 140 cm) DKK 20,000. NEW YORK, 27 May 1993, *Europa* (oil on canvas, 47 1/4 x 70 3/4 ins / 120 x 180 cm) USD 36,800.

KIEST, Jan
Flemish School, 18th century.
Painter.
In 1794, Jan Kiest was a member of the Haarlem guild. The Albertina gallery in Vienna has a wash tint landscape by a painter of the same name.

KIETZ, Gustav Adolph
German, 19th century.
Born 26 March 1824, in Leipzig; died 24 June 1908, near Dresden.
Sculptor.
Kietz became a fashionable sculptor while still very young. He did works inspired by mythological themes but principally executed an impressive number of monuments for various German cities, notably Dresden, Kassel, Leipzig and Berlin.

KIETZ, Julius Ernst Benedikt
German, 19th century.
Born 9 March 1815, in Leipzig; died 31 May 1892, in Dresden.
Painter, pastellist.
Kietz was the elder brother of Dresden sculptor Gustav Kietz and trained in France at the École des Beaux-Arts and with Paul Delaroche. He exhibited at the Salon from 1841 to 1857. When war broke out in 1870, he returned to Germany, where he did several portraits of the princesses of Schleswig-Holstein.

KIETZ, Theodor Benedikt
German, 19th century.
Born 27 September 1829, in Leipzig; died 26 July 1898, near Dresden.
Sculptor.
Kietz did busts of *Kaiser Wilhelm I* and pianist *Friedrich Wieck*.

KIFF, Ken
British, 20th century.
Born 1935, in Dagenham; died 15 February 2001, in London.
Painter (including gouache/mixed media), watercolourist, pastellist, draughtsman, engraver (etching). Scenes with figures, landscapes.
One of the most distinctive British artists of the late 20th century, Ken Kiff studied at Hornsey from 1955 to 1961. In 1981 he travelled to India, staying at The artists' camp in Kasauli. His paintings and drawings, frequently the result of a long period of gestation and meticulous reworking, display a mastery of colours in vibrant tones, and are often characterised by fantastic flights of imagination, inspired by artists such as Klee and Miró. His lush, radiant paintings and prints spring directly from his imagination; glowing colours are used to create exotic landscapes and fantastic creatures. His pictures are colourful and joyous, occasionally menacing and sinister, and driven by his fascination with colour. He is best known for his sequences of over 200 images charting a process of integration through fantasy. He has taught at various art colleges including the Chelsea School of Art and the Royal College of Art. He has also worked as an illustrator (*Folk Tales of The British Isles*, 1977) and as an engraver (woodcuts and etchings).

Kiff became a member of the Royal Academy in 1989 and was appointed Artist in Residence at the National Gallery in 1991. His solo exhibitions include *Ken Kiff 1965-1985*, Arts Council; *New Work*, Fischer Fine Arts Gallery, London (1988); and *Ken Kiff: Encaustic Paintings*, Marlborough Gallery, London (2000). He also participated in *The Subjective Eye: New Tendencies in British Figurative Art*, Northumbria University Art Gallery, Newcastle (1982).
BIBLIOGRAPHY:
Lambirth, Andrew, *Ken Kiff*, Thames and Hudson, London, 2001.
MUSEUMS AND GALLERIES:
CLEVELAND (MA) - LONDON (Tate Collection): *Triptych: Shadows* (1983-1986, oil on canvas); *Person Cutting an Image* (1965-1971, oil on canvas) - NEW YORK (Metropolitan Mus. of Art) - NEW YORK (MoMA).
AUCTION RECORDS:
LONDON, 13 June 1986, *Walking House* (watercolour and gouache, 7 1/2 x 9 ins / 19 x 22.8 cm) GBP 900. LONDON, 22 Oct 1987, *Seated Figure in a Landscape* (1972, tempera/plaster/panel, 7 x 7 3/4 ins / 18 x 20 cm) GBP 2,000. LONDON, 20 Oct 1988, *Woman in a Landscape no. 38* (acrylic/paper, 10 x 12 1/2 ins / 25.4 x 31.8 cm) GBP 2,750. LONDON, 23 Feb 1989, *Man Looking in two Directions* (gouache/card, 7 1/2 x 12 ins / 19 x 30.5 cm) GBP 2,200. LONDON, 10 Nov 1989, *Primitive Man at Colour Emerging from a Somber World* (1983, pastel, coloured chalk and charcoal, 52 1/2 x 37 ins / 133.4 x 94.1 cm) GBP 4,400. LONDON, 26 March 1993, *Sun Above Houses and a Dog in the Shade* (1986, charcoal and pastel, 53 x 31 ins / 134.7 x 78.9 cm) GBP 2,530. NEW YORK, 24 Feb 1994, *At the Table: Sequence 151* (acrylic/paper, 29 1/2 x 22 1/2 ins / 74.9 x 57.2 cm) USD 920. LONDON, 3 July 2003, *Man Climbing a Ladder* (1979, oil on board, 24 x 20 ins / 61 x 50 cm) GBP 4,200. LONDON, 16 March 2004, *Two People Walking Separately* (watercolour and gouache, 12 x 10 ins / 31 x 26 cm) GBP 3,600.

KIFFER, Charles
French, 20th century.
Born 8 June 1902, in Paris; died 1992.
Painter, engraver, sculptor. Portraits.

Charles Kiffer studied under Cormon and exhibited at the Salon des Indépendants, the Salon d'Automne and the Salon des Tuileries in Paris. He was a painter and engraver known for the emotive quality of his work. His figures, paintings, engravings and posters were mainly devoted to the theatre, music hall and circus. He produced an album of no fewer than 10 drypoint engravings of the singer Maurice Chevalier and is also known for an excellent portrait of the actress Valentine Tessier and portraits of Marcel Marceau, Edwige Feuillère, Brigitte Bardot, Edith Piaf, Carmen Amaya, and other performers. Kiffer also engraved medals for the Paris Mint and designed theatrical sets.

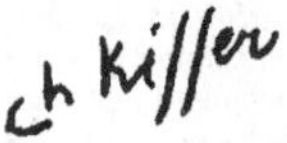

AUCTION RECORDS:
PARIS, 30 April 1945, *Dancers in the Foyer,* FRF 2,450. PARIS, 20 June 1947, *Portrait of a Star,* FRF 4,000. VERSAILLES, 26 Nov 1989, *Dancer in a Black Dress* (gouache/card, 29 1/2 x 20 3/4 ins / 75 x 53 cm) FRF 13,500.

KIGYOKU, real name: Yasusada Kurokawa, nicknames: Shiho, Mangoro, pseudonyms: Shorakan, Shozan Shoshi
Japanese, 18th century.
Born in Edo (now Tokyo); died 1756.
Painter.

Kigyoku studied under Kyushin Kano before working in the style of Okamoto Zen-etsu.

KIHARA, Moshu
Japanese, 20th century.
Sculptor.

Kihara worked in Tokyo in the early 20th century. He received a bronze medal at the Exposition Universelle of 1900 in Paris.

KIHARA, Yasuyuri
Japanese, 20th century.
Born 1932, in Nayoro (Hokkaido).
Active in France from 1970.
Painter, engraver.

Kihara lives and works in Paris. His engravings show a complex design of meticulously precise abstract motifs and are above all concerned with technique, decoration and repetition. The same concern for technical perfection can be seen in his paintings, consisting of mysterious diagrams drawn in black lines and dominated by the colours yellow, green, red, blue and violet. These works combine geometrical rigour with serpentine forms, which can be seen as representing objects, for example traditional Japanese garments in works from 1997. As well as showing work in collective exhibitions, he has had solo shows in many Japanese cities, including Tokyo in 1980, 1984, 1988 and 1990, Osaka in 1980, 1984 and 1988, Nagoya in 1980, 1984 and 1988, and also in Paris, at the Médicis Gallery in 1978 and the Jean-Claude Riedel Gallery in 1986, 1991, 1993, 1995 and 1997.

BIBLIOGRAPHY:
Beaumont-Maillet, Laure/Woimant, Françoise/Pernoud, Emmanuel, *De Bonnard à Baselitz - Dix ans d'enrichissements du Cabinet des estampes 1978-1988,* exhibition catalogue, Bibliothèque nationale de France, Paris, 1992. Lannes-Lacroutz, Maïté, *Kihara,* exhibition catalogue, Gal. Jean-Claude Riedel, Paris, 1993.

MUSEUMS AND GALLERIES:
PARIS (Prints Collection): *Metamorphosis 4* (1977, illustrations for La Mort and la Métamorphose).

KIHLE, Harald Joachin
Norwegian, 20th century.
Painter. Portraits, landscapes.

KIHN, William Langdon
American, 20th century.
Born 5 September 1898, in Brooklyn; died 1957.
Painter. Portraits.

William Langdon Kihn studied under Homer Boss and at the Art Students League in New York. He was a member of the Salmagundi Club. He is remembered for his portraits of Native Americans.

AUCTION RECORDS:
NEW YORK, 26 Oct 1984, *A Town in the West, Montana* (oil on panel, 36 x 44 ins / 91.2 x 111.8 cm) USD 8,250. SANTA FE, 20 Nov 1999, *Mt Fusilade, Glacier Park, Montana* (oil on board, 36 x 44 ins / 91 x 112 cm) USD 4,000.

KIICHI, Suzuki, or Suzuki Kiitsu, real name: Motonaga Suzuki, nickname: Shi-en, nickname: Tamesaburo, pseudonyms: Kiitsu, Kaikai, Seisei, Niwabyoshi, Shukurinsai, Isando, Hitsuan
Japanese, 19th century.
Born 1796; died 1858.
Active in Edo (now Tokyo).
Painter. Portraits, animals, flowers.

Kiitsu was the adopted son of Reitan Suzuki and studied under Hoitsu (1761-1828) and at the school of Korin (1658-1716). He developed a particular technique known as *murasaki zome* (purple dye).

BIBLIOGRAPHY:
Kiichi Suzuki: Edo Rinpa no kisai Suzuki Kiitsu ten, Itabashi Kuritsu Bijutsukan, Tokyo, Heisei 5 (1993).

AUCTION RECORDS:
NEW YORK, 16 April 1988, *Cranes and Autumn Flowers* (ink and colour/silk, 43 1/4 x 17 ins / 110 x 43 cm) USD 14,300. NEW YORK, 21 March 1989, *Portrait of a Messenger of the Heian Period Squatting by his Horse* (Kakubuan print, 8 3/4 x 7 1/2 ins / 22.2 x 18.9 cm) USD 3,300.

KIJNO, Ladislas or Pierre Ladislas
Polish, 20th century.
Born 27 June 1921, in Warsaw.
Active in France from 1925.
Painter (gouache/mixed media), sculptor, engraver, illustrator, decorative artist. Designs for tapestries, designs for mosaics.

Ladislas Kijno made his first pictorial experiments while studying philosophy at the University of Lille between 1941 and 1945. In 1950 he founded the *Cadran* group with Paul Gay.

In the same year he painted a *Last Supper* for the crypt of the church in Assy. From 1954 he devoted himself to painting full-time. After his early works, in which he tirelessly returned to motifs of the violin and of figures in gouache or pencil, he evolved towards abstraction. He worked in series, seeking new means of expression, as witnessed in the *Pebbles* series (1957 to 1959). After 1948 he perfected a personal technique of using crumpled paper, then crumpled fabrics, thus giving relief to the surface of his works. He also achieved a synthesis between traditional painting techniques and industrial discoveries, particularly in the fields of spray painting and colorants, and especially in his use of glycerophtalic paints. Challenging the differentiation between abstraction and figuration, Kijno elaborated a sort of modern mythology that relied on emblems and curved symbols, what is described as a 'violent graphism, lofty, of a magnificent and hieratical development'. He also devoted himself to mural art and the place of art in society. Kijno completed numerous mosaics, notably at the sports hall in Juvisy-sur-Orge. He also illustrated various works, in particularly Jean Grenier's *The Islands* and Aragon's *Brocéliande*.

A member of the management committee of the Salon de Mai in Paris, he took part in numerous exhibitions, including the Venice Biennale (1980); FIAC (Foire Internationale d'Art Contemporain), Paris (1990); and *De Bonnard à Baselitz - Dix ans d'enrichissements du Cabinet des estampes, 1978-1988* (*From Bonnard to Baselitz: A Decade of Acquisitions by the Prints Collection 1978-1988*) at the Bibliothèque Nationale, Paris (1992). His solo exhibitions include Paris (1954, 1956, 1958, 1963, 1972, 1975); Musée d'Antibes (1957); *L'Art au village* in St-Jeoire-en-Francigny (1958); Cercle Noroit-Arras (1965); Geneva (1965 and 1973); Maison de La Culture, Rennes and the museum of fine arts, The Hague (1971); Manège Royal, St-Germain-en-Laye (1985); Musée de Toulon (1986); Galerie Patrick Trigano, Paris, Lille, Toulouse, Marseilles (1991).

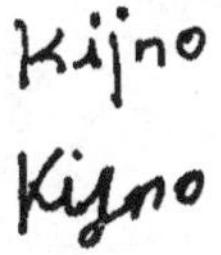

Bibliography:

Damase, Jacques, *Les Dessins de Kijno*, Éd. Pierre Tisné, Paris, 1961. Kréa, Henri, *Introduction à la méthode de Kijno*, 1965. Solier, René de, '*Kijno*' in *coll. Musée de poche*, Georges Fall, Paris, 1972.

Museums and Galleries:

Antibes (Mus. Picasso) - Créteil (FDAC Val-de-Marne): *Homage to Victor Hugo - 1985* - Dresden (Prints Collection) - Dunkirk (MMA) - Marseilles (Mus. Cantini) - Paris (MNAM-CCI) - Paris (Prints Collection): *Friend, Can you Hear?* (1985, lithograph) - St-Paul-de-Vence (Fondation Maeght).

Auction records:

Paris, 18 June 1971, *Composition on White Background*, FRF 5,000. Paris, 26 Feb 1973, *Lerin Islands*, FRF 6,000. Paris, 9 April 1974, *Composition* (gouache) FRF 8,200. Paris, 12 March 1976, *Composition* (gouache/crumpled paper, 27½ x 22 ins / 70 x 55 cm) FRF 4,200. Paris, 14 March 1976, *Composition on Red Background C 269* (oil on canvas, 38½ x 51½ ins / 97.5 x 130.5 cm) FRF 6,200. Paris, 14 Dec 1977, *Initial Study for La Grande Forme or Homage to Elsa* (1966-1970, oil on canvas, 42½ x 59¾ ins / 108 x 152 cm) FRF 7,500. Paris, 27 Oct 1980, *Composition* (1960, oil on canvas, 76½ x 60¼ ins / 194 x 153 cm) FRF 6,000. Versailles, 13 May 1981, *Composition* (oil on canvas, 51¼ x 38¼ ins / 130 x 97 cm) FRF 10,000. Paris, 6 Nov 1983, *Composition in Violet, White, Black and Green* (1960, oil on panel, 46 x 29½ ins / 117 x 75 cm) FRF 11,500. Douai, 24 March 1985, *Composition in Diptych* (wash, two drawings, 15¼ x 13 ins / 39 x 33 cm) FRF 8,000. Paris, 4 Dec 1986, *Composition* (oil on canvas, 46½ x 35½ ins / 118 x 90 cm) FRF 20,000. Paris, 11 Feb 1987, *Composition* (watercolour, 50 x 32¾ ins / 127 x 83 cm) FRF 12,500. Paris, 5 April 1987, *Icon in Homage to Gustav Mahler* (1986-1987, painting and crumpled paper/canvas, 51¼ x 38¼ ins / 130 x 97 cm) FRF 29,000. Paris, 20 March 1988, *Composition* (mixed media/crumpled paper, 24 x 19¾ ins / 61 x 50 cm) FRF 6,500. Paris, 22 April 1988, *Composition* (acrylic/crumpled paper, 30¼ x 29¼ ins / 77 x 74 cm) FRF 8,000. Paris, 24 April 1988, *Hierogrlyph of the Future* (1977-1979, acrylic/creased canvas, 82¾ x 67 ins / 210 x 170 cm) FRF 42,000. Paris, 29 April 1988, *Composition* (oil on canvas, 24 x 18½ ins / 61 x 47 cm) FRF 15,000. Paris, 18 May 1988, *Abstract Composition* (crumpled paper, 12½ x 5 ins / 32 x 13 cm) FRF 3,200. Paris, 27 June 1988, *Composition* (oil on crumpled paper, 32¾ x 24¾ ins / 83 x 63 cm) FRF 7,500. Douai, 23 Oct 1988, *Composition* (crumpled paper, 33½ x 23½ ins / 85 x 60 cm) FRF 11,600. Paris, 26 Oct 1988, *Composition* (1973, oil on canvas, 51½ x 38¼ ins / 131 x 97 cm) FRF 10,500. Paris, 28 Oct 1988, *Image for A. Roublev* (1972, acrylic/canvas, 51¼ x 38¼ ins / 130 x 97 cm) FRF 28,000. Paris, 16 Nov 1988, *Composition* (tapestry, 78 x 67¾ ins / 198 x 172 cm) FRF 30,000. Versailles, 18 Dec 1988, *Composition* (oil on canvas, 24 x 19¾ ins / 61 x 50 cm) FRF 9,000. Paris, 3 March 1989, *Les Sept Chemins du couchant* (1974, oil on canvas, 51½ x 38¼ ins / 131 x 97 cm) FRF 23,000. Paris, 12 June 1989, *Série des mécaniques mentales A* (1977, oil on canvas, 46 x 34¾ ins / 116 x 88.5 cm) FRF 48,000. Paris, 6 Nov 1989, *Composition* (watercolour, 11¾ x 15¼ ins / 30 x 39 cm) FRF 11,500. Le Touquet, 12 Nov 1989, *Neruda Composition* (1973-1983, oil, acrylic and crumpled paper/canvas, 50¾ x 38½ ins / 129 x 98 cm) FRF 92,000. Paris, 20 Nov 1989, *Composition* (crumpled paper, 32¾ x 25¼ ins / 83 x 64 cm) FRF 24,000. Douai, 3 Dec 1989, *Composition* (acrylic/crumpled paper, 25½ x 19 ins / 65 x 48 cm) FRF 20,000. Paris, 26 Jan 1990, *Composition* (25¼ x 17¼ ins / 64 x 44 cm) FRF 23,000. Paris, 31 Jan 1990, *Composition* (oil on paper, 19¾ x 25½ ins / 50 x 65 cm) FRF 45,000. Paris, 8 March 1990, *Composition* (mixed media/crumpled paper, 46 x 33½ ins / 116 x 85 cm) FRF 100,000. Paris, 31 March 1990, *Untitled* (gouache, Indian ink and projection/crumpled paper, 32¼ x 23¼ ins / 82 x 59 cm) FRF 120,000. Paris, 10 May 1990, *Abstract Composition* (crumpled paper, 24¾ x 25¼ ins / 63 x 64 cm) FRF 82,000. Paris, 20 June 1990, *Abstract Composition from the Maia Kovski Series* (1976, crumpled paper, 40½ x 32¾ ins / 103 x 83.5 cm) FRF 120,000. Paris, 1 Oct 1990, *Composition* (1974, oil on canvas, 24 x 19¾ ins / 61 x 50 cm) FRF 25,000. Douai, 11 Nov 1990, *Composition* (1968, acrylic/card, 41 x 29½ ins / 104 x 75 cm) FRF 51,500. Le Touquet, 11 Nov 1990, *Composition* (mixed media/crumpled paper remounted/canvas, 22 x 18 ins / 56 x 46 cm) FRF 28,000. Calais, 9 Dec 1990, *Composition* (mixed media/crumpled paper, 25½ x 19¾ ins / 65 x 50 cm) FRF 36,000. Paris, 14 Feb 1991, *Composition* (1959, oil on canvas, 32 x 39¼ ins / 81 x 100 cm) FRF 70,000. Paris, 15 April 1991, *Composition* (gouache, 23½ x 20 ins / 60 x 51 cm) FRF 25,000. Neuilly, 1 Dec 1991, *Composition* (acrylic/crumpled paper, 32¾ x 25½ ins / 83 x 65 cm) FRF 29,900. Paris, 18 Dec 1991, *Composition on Red Background* (gouache/crumpled paper, 32¾ x 23½ ins / 83 x 60 cm) FRF 14, 500. Paris, 2 Feb 1992, *Buddha* (mixed media/canvas, 76¾ x 51¼ ins / 195 x 130 cm) FRF 80,000. Lucerne, 21 Nov 1992, *Composition* (gouache/paper, 16½ x 11¾ ins / 42 x 30 cm) CHF 1,100. Paris, 1 Oct 1993, *Buddha of Da Tong (Return from China)* (acrylic/crumpled paper/canvas, 32 x 25½ ins / 81 x 65 cm) FRF 10,000. Lokeren, 12 March 1994, *Composition* (gouache/paper, 23½ x 17¾ ins / 60 x 45 cm) BEF 44,000. Rome, 8 Nov 1994, *Untitled* (crumpled paper, 31½ x 22¾ ins / 80 x 58 cm) ITL 3,680,000. Paris, 15 Dec 1994, *Dancer from Hong Kong* (1983, oil on canvas, 51¼ x 38¼ ins / 130 x 97 cm) FRF 22,000. Paris, 22 Nov 1995, *Composition* (oil on crumpled paper/canvas, 36¼ x 28¾ ins / 92 x 73 cm) FRF 14,000. Paris, 20 June 1996, *Hommage aux fruits détruits* (oil on canvas, 36½ x 48 ins / 93 x 122 cm) FRF 13,500. Paris, 11 July 1996, *Abstract Composition* (1974, mixed media/canvas, 36¼ x 28¾ ins / 92 x 73 cm) FRF 10,000. Paris, 24 Nov 1996, *Return from Tahiti* (1989-1990, acrylic/crumpled paper/canvas, 49½ x 37½ ins / 126 x 95 cm) FRF 9,000. Paris, 20 Jan 1997, *Composition* (crumpled paper, 28 x 20½ ins / 71 x 52 cm) FRF 5,500. Paris, 28 April 1997, *Composition* (acrylic/crumpled paper/panel, 42¼ x 35¾ ins / 107 x 91 cm) FRF

8,000. PARIS, 5 Dec 1997, *Port of Antibes - night* (pastel, 14 1/2 x 22 ins / 37 x 55 cm) FRF 2,700. PARIS, 15 Dec 1997, *Untitled* (acrylic/crumpled paper, 33 3/4 x 22 ins / 86 x 56 cm) FRF 4,000. PARIS, 23 March 1998, *Stele to Berthold Brecht* (1972, acrylic and oil on canvas, 46 x 35 ins / 116 x 89 cm) FRF 11,100. LILLE, 25 Oct 1998, *The Cosmonaut or the Elastic Monster* (c. 1965-1967, oil on canvas, 76 x 59 ins / 194 x 151 cm) FRF 39,000. PARIS, 5 Aug 1999, *The Eye of Count K* (1993, oil on crumpled paper, 57 x 57 ins / 146 x 146 cm) FRF 20,000. PARIS, 28 June 2000, *Mirror for Andrei Roublev I* (1973, oil on canvas, 16 x 13 ins / 41 x 33 cm) FRF 110,000. PARIS, 5 Oct 2001, *Composition* (mixed media/crumpled paper, 35 x 24 ins / 88 x 62 cm) FRF 25,000. LILLE, 27 Oct 2001, *Pebbles from Antibes* (1958, oil on paper on canvas, 38 x 57 ins / 97 x 146 cm) FRF 46,000. VERSAILLES, 30 June 2002, *Icons for a Solar Night* (1991, mixed media/paper/canvas, 64 x 50 ins / 162 x 128 cm) EUR 3,800. PARIS, 27 Nov 2002, *Tiki* (1990, oil on canvas, 52 x 41 ins / 132 x 104 cm) EUR 4,000. LILLE, 23 March 2003, *Hommage to Roublev* (1973, oil on canvas, 32 x 25 ins / 81 x 64 cm) EUR 14,000. PARIS, 25 Nov 2003, *Mechanical Elements After Leger* (1969, oil on canvas, 77 x 61 ins / 196 x 154 cm) EUR 7,000. PARIS, 9 June 2004, *Composition* (1962, mixed media/canvas, 51 x 64 ins / 130 x 162 cm) EUR 9,000. PARIS, 24 March 2004, *Variations on Jazz* (1960, oil on canvas, 46 x 35 ins / 116 x 89 cm) EUR 3,600.

KIK, Cornelis. See **KICK Cornelis**

KIKEI, nickname: Takahashi
Japanese, 18th century.
Active in Kyoto, c. 1770.
Painter.

Kikei is known as a designer of theatre programmes in Kyoto. He is thought to have drawn the portraits of young actors in the Kyoto edition of the *Ehon Butai Ogi* fan collection of 1778.

KIKI DE MONTPARNASSE
French, 20th century.
Born 1901, in Châtillon-sur-Seine; died 1953, in Paris.
Painter.

During the years between World War I and II, Kiki de Montparnasse was the model and also the companion of many celebrated Montparnasse painters. Like Suzanne Valadon she also tried her hand at art and exhibited for the first time in 1927.

BIBLIOGRAPHY:
Klüver, Billy/Martin, Julie, *Kiki et Montparnasse*, Flammarion, Paris, 1998.

AUCTION RECORDS:
PARIS, 3 March 1989, *Tightrope Artist* (1927, oil on canvas, 22 x 18 ins / 55 x 46 cm) FRF 6,200.

KIKKAWA, Reika
Japanese, 20th century.
Born in Tokyo.
Painter. Figures, scenes with figures.

After painting in the styles of Tosa and Kano, Kikkawa turned to less decorative subjects, including Buddhas, fairies and ancient Chinese legends.

KIKKERT, Jean Conrad Théodore.
See **KICKERT**

KIKKERT, Pieter, or Kikkart
Dutch, 18th century.
Active in Leiden in 1798.
Draughtsman, engraver.

Pieter Kikkert is known for his *Proeve van Estkundige Uitspanningens* after C. Chalon, B.-H. Their, J.-H. Prins and J.-C. Janson.

KIKOINE, Michel
Russian, 20th century.
Born 31 May 1892, in Homel; died 4 November 1968, in Paris.
Active and from 1922 naturalised in France.
Painter (including gouache/mixed media), watercolourist, pastellist. Figures, nudes, portraits, genre scenes, still-lifes, flowers, landscapes.

Michel Kikoine's grandparents were rabbis, and his father was a bank manager in Minsk. When he was 16, Kikoine enrolled at the school of fine arts in Vilnius and then in Minsk, where he met Soutine and Kremegne. He went to Paris in 1912, where he worked for a short time in Cormon's studio at the École des Beaux-Arts, although he was particularly sensitive to the work of Pissaro and Cézanne. During this time he also discovered Rembrandt, Zurbaran, El Greco and Courbet at the Louvre. He lived at 'La Ruche', a rickety building in the Vaugirard area. He fought in World War I and in 1926 bought a farm at Annay-sur-Serein in the Yonne region. Numerous companions joined him, including Soutine, Kremegne, Pailes, Russel, Rittmann, Brenner and Chermiansky. During the German occupation of France he fled to the area around Toulouse. At the end of the war he returned to Paris. He made a couple of trips to Israel, and during the last ten years of his life he often withdrew to La Garoupe on the shores of the Mediterranean.

In 1920 he visited the Midi region of France, and painted a number of landscapes around Cagnes-sur-Mer in a very typical Expressionist manner. From 1926, while in Annay-sur-Serein, he engaged in an uninterrupted series of landscapes of the region, portraits and nudes, subjects taken from nature, flowers and compositions, animals, the flavour of the countryside being so uppermost in his mind that everything he subsequently painted seemed to have been painted in Annay. During a one-year trip to Israel in 1954, he was led to make a significant revision of the spirit and the manner of his painting, breaking the bounds of Expressionism and returning to his former themes with a more supple style. A series of self-portraits, including nudes, and of compositions depicting hunting and fishing scenes, date from this time. At La Garoupe he painted numerous seascapes. Kikoine contributed to the essentially figurative style with Expressionist undertones that was characteristic of the inter-war Paris School.

BIBLIOGRAPHY:
Pillement, Georges, et al., *Kikoine*, Éd. Pierre Cailler, Geneva, 1957. Cassou, Jean/Parinaud, André, '*Kikoine*' in *Galerie des Arts*, periodical, Paris, September 1969. Roditi, E./Mann, M./Hankel, J., *Kikoine - catalogue raisonné de l'œuvre*, Piazza Éd., Paris, 1973. Cassou, Jean/Parinaud, André, *Kikoine*, Gal. Kriegel, Paris, December 1974.

MUSEUMS AND GALLERIES:
EIN HAROD MEUCHAD: *Composition* (1950); *Portrait of Madame Kikoine*; *Yonne Landscape*; *Flowers* - GRENOBLE (Mus. de Grenoble): *Flowers* (1938) - JERUSALEM: *Landscape* (1950) - MENTON: *Landscape of Nice* (1951) - MONTPELLIER: *Self-portrait* (1946); *Snowy Landscape* - MOSCOW: *Portrait on a Red Background* (1930) - PARIS (MNAM-CCI): *Flowers* - PHILADELPHIA: *Landscape* (1930); *Still-life* - SAFED: *Young Girl Reading* (1954) - SYDNEY: *Children at the Piano* (1954) - TEL

AVIV: *Burgundy Landscape* (1950) - TOKYO: *Landscape of the Yonne Region* (1933) - TOULOUSE: *Paysage de l'Union* (1945).
AUCTION RECORDS:
PARIS, 30 April 1921, *Landscape*, FRF 100. PARIS, 4 Dec 1925, *St-Denis* (1918) FRF 400. PARIS, 22 March 1926, *Burgundy Landscape*, FRF 500. PARIS, 28 Feb 1930, *The Road*, FRF 600. PARIS, 13 July 1942, *Landscape*, FRF 1,300. PARIS, 14 Oct 1942, *Music Lesson*, FRF 3,800. PARIS, 12 May 1944, *Vase of Flowers*, FRF 1,000. PARIS, 5 March 1945, *Flowers*, FRF 7,000. PARIS, 27 Feb 1946, *Landscape*, FRF 3,300. PARIS, 24 March 1947, *Seated Nude*, FRF 1,750. PARIS, 24 Nov 1950, *Road out of the Village*, FRF 10,000. PARIS, 6 Dec 1954, *Still-life with Violin*, FRF 45,000. PARIS, 26 June 1957, *Arab Souk*, FRF 160,000. PARIS, 17 June 1960, *Vase of Roses*, FRF 1,000. PARIS, 26 Feb 1962, *Cottages and Cypress Tree*, FRF 8,000. MILAN, 9 April 1968, *Landscape with Cottage and Two Figures*, ITL 1,500,000. VERSAILLES, 30 Nov 1969, *Still-life with Flowers and Fruit*, FRF 13,600. PARIS, 8 June 1970, *Houses with Red Roofs*, FRF 12,500. PARIS, Dec 1973, *Landscape* (gouache and pastel) FRF 5,600. PARIS, 5 June 1974, *Winter in the Forest*, FRF 20,500. VERSAILLES, 12 May 1976, *Vase of Flowers* (1938, gouache, 19 x 15 1/4 ins / 48 x 39 cm) FRF 4,200. VERSAILLES, 5 Dec 1976, *Village Windmill* (oil on panel, 18 1/2 x 26 1/2 ins / 47 x 67 cm) FRF 15,100. VERSAILLES, 20 Feb 1977, *Vase of Peonies* (c. 1920, oil on canvas, 24 x 19 3/4 ins / 61 x 50 cm) FRF 22,000. VERSAILLES, 10 June 1979, *Fruit and Flowers* (1918/1920, oil on canvas, 32 x 25 1/2 ins / 81 x 65 cm) FRF 15,000. VERSAILLES, 28 Oct 1979, *Little Girls Under the Trees in the Forest* (watercolour, 18 3/4 x 12 1/2 ins / 47.5 x 32 cm) FRF 7,900. ZURICH, 24 Nov 1982, *Houses in the Suburbs* (oil on canvas, 25 1/2 x 21 1/4 ins / 65 x 54 cm) CHF 14,000. LONDON, 24 March 1983, *Young Girl with Mandolin* (c. 1950-1952, oil on panel, 25 x 20 1/2 ins / 63.5 x 52 cm) GBP 8,000. TEL AVIV, 4 June 1984, *Landscape with Figures* (gouache and watercolour, 12 1/2 x 18 ins / 31.5 x 45.5 cm) USD 800. VERSAILLES, 12 June 1985, *Still-life with Lemons* (1936-1938, oil on canvas, 24 x 19 3/4 ins / 61 x 50 cm) FRF 37,000. VERSAILLES, 23 Nov 1986, *Homage to Soutine* (pastel, watercolour, gouache and diluted oil paint, 11 1/2 x 14 3/4 ins / 29 x 37.5 cm) FRF 17,000. PARIS, 20 March 1988, *Village* (oil on canvas, 21 1/4 x 25 1/2 ins / 54 x 65 cm) FRF 46,000; *Fishing Port* (oil on canvas, 23 1/2 x 28 3/4 ins / 60 x 73 cm) FRF 105,000. PARIS, 21 April 1988, *Bouquet of Roses* (oil on canvas, 14 x 10 3/4 ins / 35.5 x 27.5 cm) FRF 16,000. VERSAILLES, 15 May 1988, *Fisherman at Low Tide* (watercolour, 9 1/2 x 12 1/2 ins / 24 x 31.5 cm) FRF 4,800. TEL AVIV, 26 May 1988, *Village Through the Trees* (oil on canvas, 21 1/4 x 25 1/2 ins / 54 x 65 cm) USD 9,020. VERSAILLES, 15 June 1988, *Corner of the Studio* (oil on canvas, 32 x 39 1/4 ins / 81 x 100 cm) FRF 95,000. PARIS, 23 June 1988, *Vase of Roses* (oil on canvas, 13 3/4 x 11 ins / 35 x 27 cm) FRF 37,000. LONDON, 19 Oct 1988, *View of Rooftops* (oil on card, 21 1/4 x 25 1/2 ins / 54 x 65 cm) GBP 4,620. VERSAILLES, 23 Oct 1988, *Woman in the Turban* (watercolour, gouache and pastel, 11 3/4 x 9 ins / 30 x 22 cm) FRF 13,500. PARIS, 20 Nov 1988, *Landscape of the Yonne Region* (c. 1930-40, oil on canvas, 19 3/4 x 25 1/2 ins / 50 x 65 cm) FRF 60,000. PARIS, 14 Dec 1988, *Landscape of the Yonne Region* (c. 1950, oil on panel, 14 1/4 x 18 ins / 36 x 46 cm) FRF 28,500. VERSAILLES, 18 Dec 1988, *Still-life and Bouquets of Flowers* (oil on canvas, 18 x 22 ins / 46 x 55 cm) FRF 54,000. TEL AVIV, 2 Jan 1989, *People in a Meadow Landscape* (pastel, 15 1/4 x 12 1/4 ins / 39 x 31 cm) USD 1,540. LA VARENNE-ST-HILAIRE, 12 March 1989, *Path through the Undergrowth* (oil on canvas, 28 3/4 x 21 1/4 ins / 73 x 54 cm) FRF 49,500. NEW YORK, 3 May 1989, *Bouquet of Flowers* (oil on panel, 16 1/4 x 13 1/4 ins / 41 x 33.5 cm) USD 44,400. TEL AVIV, 30 May 1989, *Card Players* (oil/synthetic resin, 21 1/4 x 25 1/2 ins / 54 x 65 cm) USD 9,350. PARIS, 26 April 1990, *Girl Looking After a Cow* (1935-1940, oil on canvas, 19 3/4 x 25 1/2 ins / 50 x 65 cm) FRF 140,000. TEL AVIV, 31 May 1990, *Still-life with Flowers and Mandolin* (oil on canvas, 32 1/4 x 25 3/4 ins / 82 x 65.5 cm) USD 41,800. PARIS, 13 June 1990, *Young Girl Reading* (oil on panel, 22 x 18 ins / 55 x 45.5 cm) FRF 80,000. TEL AVIV, 20 June 1990, *Landscape at Safed* (1952, oil on card, 24 x 15 ins / 61 x 38 cm) USD 13,750. PARIS, 7 Dec 1990, *At the Forest Edge* (1913-1914, oil on canvas, 21 1/4 x 25 1/2 ins / 54 x 65 cm) FRF 50,000. TEL AVIV, 1 Jan 1991, *Landscape* (oil on canvas, 33 1/2 x 22 1/2 ins / 85 x 57 cm) USD 19,800. PARIS, 17 June 1991, *Landscape* (watercolour/paper, 11 1/2 x 16 3/4 ins / 29.5 x 42.5 cm) FRF 8,500. PARIS, 18 Dec 1991, *Child in Red Hat* (oil on card, 11 x 11 ins / 28 x 28 cm) FRF 10,000. TEL AVIV, 6 Jan 1992, *Rural Landscape* (oil and mixed media/paper/card, 10 1/2 x 14 ins / 26.5 x 35.5 cm) USD 3,630. NEW YORK, 12 June 1992, *Landscape with Houses* (oil on canvas, 25 1/2 x 21 ins / 64.8 x 53.3 cm) USD 8,800. PARIS, 12 June 1992, *Young Girl Reading* (oil on canvas, 32 x 25 1/2 ins / 81 x 65 cm) FRF 61,000. CALAIS, 14 March 1993, *Vase of Flowers and Basket of Fruit* (oil on canvas, 22 x 28 ins / 56 x 71 cm) FRF 60,000. TEL AVIV, 14 April 1993, *Nude* (oil on canvas, 28 3/4 x 23 1/2 ins / 73 x 60 cm) USD 34,500. NEW YORK, 2 Nov 1993, *Bathers* (1926, oil on canvas, 35 1/2 x 46 ins / 90.2 x 116.8 cm) USD 23,000. AMSTERDAM, 8 Dec 1993, *Suburban Landscape* (oil on canvas, 32 x 39 1/4 ins / 81 x 100 cm) NLG 18,400. PARIS, 27 March 1994, *Landscape of Annay-sur-Serein* (1928, oil on canvas, 23 3/4 x 28 3/4 ins / 60.5 x 73.2 cm) FRF 63,000. DEAUVILLE, 19 Aug 1994, *Musicians* (mixed media/paper/canvas, 12 1/2 x 16 1/2 ins / 32 x 42 cm) FRF 30,000. TEL AVIV, 22 April 1995, *Landscape* (oil on canvas, 24 x 29 ins / 61 x 73.5 cm) USD 21,850. NEW YORK, 14 June 1995, *Landscape* (oil on canvas/panel, 21 1/4 x 25 1/2 ins / 54 x 64.8 cm) USD 7,475. PARIS, 28 March 1996, *Christmas Day* (oil on paper/canvas, 31 x 15 ins / 79 x 38 cm) FRF 55,000. NEW YORK, 10 Oct 1996, *Still-life with Fruit and Coffee Pot* (oil/Masonite, 19 3/4 x 25 1/2 ins / 50.2 x 64.8 cm) USD 4,312. PARIS, 13 Nov 1996, *Portrait of a Young Woman* (c. 1935, oil on canvas, 22 x 18 ins / 55 x 46 cm) FRF 80,000. CALAIS, 15 Dec 1996, *Still-life with Fruit* (oil on panel, 19 3/4 x 25 1/2 ins / 50 x 65 cm) FRF 26,000. TEL AVIV, 12 Jan 1997, *On the Beach* (oil on canvas, 10 1/4 x 11 ins / 26 x 27 cm) USD 1,840. PARIS, 16 March 1997, *Portrait of a Woman or Woman Sitting under the Trees* (oil on canvas, 32 x 23 1/2 ins / 81 x 60 cm) FRF 47,000. PARIS, 16 March 1997, *Landscape* (oil on canvas, 18 x 25 1/2 ins / 45.5 x 65 cm) FRF 35,000. TEL AVIV, 26 April 1997, *Coast at Molay-sur-Serein* (oil on canvas, 15 x 18 ins / 38 x 46 cm) USD 16,100. PARIS, 5 June 1997, *Still-life with Figures* (oil on canvas, 18 x 20 1/2 ins / 46 x 52 cm) FRF 31,000. PARIS, 6 June 1997, *Vase Filled with Flowers* (gouache, 14 1/4 x 11 1/2 ins / 36 x 29 cm) FRF 10,000. PARIS, 19 Oct 1997, *Landscape* (c. 1920, oil on canvas, 23 1/2 x 28 1/2 ins / 60 x 72.5 cm) FRF 41,000. PARIS, 22 March 1998, *Man in a Landscape* (gouache and pastel/paper, 11 x 13 3/4 ins / 28 x 35 cm) FRF 4,200. PARIS, 24 March 1998, *Landscape* (1918, oil on canvas, 19 3/4 x 25 1/2 ins / 50 x 65 cm) FRF 28,000. LONDON, 24 March 1999, *Still-life* (c. 1915-1920, oil on canvas, 24 x 29 ins / 60 x 73 cm) GBP 13,000. MELBOURNE, 26 April 1999, *Landscape* (oil on canvas, 28 x 35 ins / 71 x 90 cm) AUD 18,000. PARIS, 15 March 2000, *Two Friends* (oil on canvas, 26 x 32 ins / 65 x 81 cm) FRF 90,000. PARIS, 15 March 2000, *Joan of Arc - Israel* (oil on canvas, 24 x 29 ins / 60 x 73 cm) FRF 105,000. CALAIS, 9 Dec 2001, *Village of Annoy-sur-Serein* (1950-1955, oil on canvas, 21 x 29 ins / 53 x 73 cm) FRF 50,000. PARIS, 11 May 2002, *Landscape in Bourgogne, France* (oil on canvas, 29 x 36 ins / 73 x 92 cm) EUR 15,000. PARIS, 12 Dec 2002, *Cap d'Antibes* (oil on canvas, 32 x 26 ins / 81 x 65 cm) EUR 7,800. PARIS, 12 March 2003, *Still-life with Basket of Fruit* (oil on canvas, 18 x 22 ins / 46 x 55 cm) EUR 9,000. PARIS, 15 Dec 2003, *Three Bathers* (oil on canvas, 32 x 26 ins / 81 x 65 cm) EUR 13,800. PARIS, 25 Jan 2004, *Bouquet of Flowers in an Interior* (oil on canvas, 32 x 26 ins / 81 x 65 cm) EUR 8,000. LONDON, 20 Oct 2004, *Still-life* (oil on canvas, 24 x 18 ins / 60 x 46 cm) GBP 7,500.

KIKUCHI, Keigetsu, real name: Kanji Kikuchi, pseudonym: Keigetsu
Japanese, 19th - 20th century.
Born 1879, in Nagano Prefecture; died 1955.
Painter.

Kikuchi studied first under Kodama Katei, who taught him the Nanga style (literati painting). Then, at the age of 18, he went to study at the Shijo School in Kiyoto under Hobun Kikuchi, who adopted him. In 1907, Keigetsu Kikuchi opened a school in Kyoto, the Kyoto Shiritsu Kaiga Seimon Gako. In 1922, he travelled in Europe. He was a member of the Imperial Academy of Fine Art. Kikuchi was drawn to Japanese classicism and developed a neo-classical style while working for the Imperial family.

KIKUHATA, Mokuma
Japanese, 20th century.
Born 1935, in Nagasaki (Fukuoka Prefecture).
Painter, engraver, decorative artist.

Kikuhata studied at the Fukuoka Prefectural Graduate School from 1950 to 1953. From an early, highly decorative, geometric abstraction, he moved to hyperrealism. In 1964 he decorated the interior of Kanagawa Prefecture's power station. In 1964 he received the Stralem Prize at the International Exhibition of Young Artists in Tokyo. In 1965 he received the prize at the 2nd Exhibition of Contemporary Art at the Nagaoka Museum.

He showed work in many group exhibitions, including *Adventure of Japanese Art* at the Museum of Modern Art in Tokyo in 1961 and *Contemporary Japanese Painting and Sculpture* at the Museum of Modern Art in New York in 1965. He exhibited at the Fukuoka Cultural Centre in 1967, at the Kitakyushu Municipal Museum of Art in 1976, at the National Museum of Modern Art in Tokyo (1981-1982), at the Gumma Prefectoral Museum of Fine Art in 1984, at the Museum of Modern Art in New Delhi, at the Metropolitan Art Museum in Tokyo and the Museum of Modern Art in Oxford, England, in 1985. He was represented in the exhibition *Le Japon des avant-gardes 1910-1970* (*Avant-Garde Japan 1910-1970*) at the Centre Georges Pompidou in Paris in 1986 and at the Metropolitan Art Museum in Tokyo in 1989-1990. He had his first solo exhibitions in Tokyo in 1962. After that he had a number of solo exhibitions in Japanese cities.

MUSEUMS AND GALLERIES:
NEW YORK (MoMA).

AUCTION RECORDS:
NEW YORK, 27 April 1994, *Roulette: old design* (1964, varnish and wood assemblage, 38 1/2 x 31 1/4 x 4 3/4 ins / 97.5 x 79.1 x 12.1 cm) USD 90,500.

KIKUMARO. See **TSUKIMARO**

KIKUTI, Hobun
Japanese, 20th century.
Painter (including silk). Landscapes.

Kikuti exhibited at the Exposition Universelle of 1900 in Paris. He painted on silk.

KILB, Gustav Adolf
German, 19th - 20th century.
Born 13 July 1870, in Frankfurt am Main; died 24 April 1908, in Frankfurt am Main.
Painter. Interiors, landscapes, urban landscapes.

KILBERT, Robert P.
German, 20th century.
Born 14 September 1880.
Painter.

Robert Kilbert was a student of Francis Smith at the Art Institute in Chicago, and of Laurens in Paris. He was a member of the American Art Federation.

MUSEUMS AND GALLERIES:
CHICAGO.

KILBURN
British, 18th century.
Active in London.
Painter. Flowers.

Kilburn exhibited at the Society of Artists and at the Free Society from 1770 to 1775.

KILBURN, Lawrence
American, 18th century.
Died c. 1775, in New York.
Painter. Portraits.

Lawrence Kilburn produced a *Portrait of Dr William Beekmann and his Wife*.

KILBURN, William
Irish, 18th - 19th century.
Born 1745, in Dublin; died 23 December 1818, in Wellington.
Draughtsman, engraver.

William Kilburn was a pupil of John Lisson in Dublin. He later set himself up in London.

KILBURNE, George Goodwin, the Elder
British, 19th - 20th century.
Born 24 July 1839, in Norfolk; died September 1924, in London.
Painter, watercolourist, engraver, draughtsman. Genre scenes, sporting subjects.

George Kilburne trained in London with the Dalziel Brothers, a firm of engravers and illustrators. He is known for his popular paintings and prints of genre scenes and interiors with fashionable well-to-do figures, and also provided illustrations for magazines such as *The Graphic*, *The Illustrated London News* and *Cassell's Magazine*.

He exhibited at the Royal Academy from 1862 to 1918, the Royal Society of British Artists, the Royal Institute of Painters in Watercolours (of which he was a member from 1868), the Royal Miniature Society, the Royal Society of Arts in Birmingham, the Glasgow Institute of Fine Arts, the Walker Art Gallery in Liverpool, and Manchester City Art Gallery.

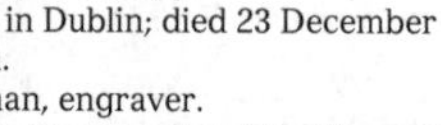

MUSEUMS AND GALLERIES:
LIVERPOOL (Walker AG): *Poor Relations* (1875, oil on canvas) - SHEFFIELD (Sheffield Art Gallery) - SYDNEY: *Visit to the Artist's Studio*.

AUCTION RECORDS:
LONDON, 7 Dec 1907, *Dance Lesson* (watercolour) GBP 22. LONDON, 4 April 1908, *Ray of Sunlight* (1876, watercolour) GBP 12. LONDON, 21 Nov 1908, *Dispute* (watercolour) GBP 35. LONDON, 21 May 1909, *Eavesdropping* (watercolour) GBP 32. LONDON, 9 June 1911, *Sword of the Ancestors* (watercolour) GBP 19. LONDON, 3 April 1922, *Morning in Class; Good News* (two drawings) GBP 38. LONDON, 27 Feb 1925, *Pack Barks*, GBP 37. LONDON, 4 Oct 1973, *London-Liverpool Stagecoach*, Gns 440. LONDON, 21 Oct 1977, *Witness* (1901, oil on panel, 12 3/4 x 7 3/4 ins / 32.3 x 20 cm) GBP 600. LONDON, 22 May 1979, *Singer* (watercolour heightened with white, 39 1/4 x 29 1/4 ins / 100 x 74 cm) GBP 900. TOKYO, 15 Feb 1980, *Slave Capturing a Lion* (oil on canvas, 40 1/4 x 50 ins / 102 x 127 cm) JPY 1,800,000. LONDON, 22 Nov 1982, *Wedding Dress* (oil on canvas, 18 x 24 ins / 46 x 61 cm) GBP 1,300. LONDON, 18 March 1983, *Hearts are Trumps* (oil on canvas, 40 1/4 x 30 1/4 ins / 102.2 x 76.8 cm) GBP 3,800. LONDON, 16 Feb 1984, *Garden Spoil* (1878, watercolour and pencil, 34 x 24 ins / 86.5 x 61 cm) GBP 5,800. LONDON, 12 June 1985, *Hunting Scenes* (oil on canvas, four items, 24 1/2 x 41 1/4 ins / 62 x 105 cm) GBP 38,000. LONDON, 21 Jan 1986, *Looking through the Portfolio* (1877, heightened watercolour, 13 1/2 x 17 1/2 ins / 34 x 44.5 cm) GBP 3,400. CHESTER, 8 Oct 1987, *The Bill* (watercolour, 14 1/4 x 20 1/2 ins / 36 x 52 cm) GBP 2,800. LONDON, 25 Jan

1988, *Repetition of the Lesson at Home* (watercolour, 5 1/2 x 7 3/4 ins / 14 x 20 cm) GBP 1,650. NEW YORK, 25 May 1988, *To the King!* (watercolour and gouache, 11 x 14 1/2 ins / 27 x 37 cm) USD 3,850. LONDON, 3 June 1988, *Departure* (1905, oil on canvas, 12 x 18 ins / 30.5 x 45.7 cm) GBP 3,300. LONDON, 23 Sept 1988, *Suitors at the Stable Door* (oil on card, 6 1/4 x 9 ins / 16 x 23 cm) GBP 1,430. LONDON, 25 Jan 1989, *Aunt's Visit* (watercolour, 10 x 14 ins / 25.5 x 35.5 cm) GBP 6,600. PARIS, 15 March 1989, *Race at the Arch* (1887, oil on paper, 5 x 8 1/2 ins / 12.5 x 21.5 cm) FRF 3,000. CHESTER, 20 July 1989, *Absence Makes the Heart Heavy* (oil on canvas, 27 1/2 x 35 1/2 ins / 70 x 90 cm) GBP 7,700. NEW YORK, 25 Oct 1989, *Admiring the Baby* (oil on canvas, 50 x 36 ins / 127 x 91.5 cm) USD 12,100. LONDON, 3 Nov 1989, *Mother and Her Young Maid* (1874, oil on canvas, 21 x 17 ins / 53.5 x 43.3 cm) GBP 10,120. LONDON, 9 Feb 1990, *No Fireplace* (1874, oil on canvas, 29 3/4 x 36 1/4 ins / 75.6 x 92.1 cm) GBP 10,450. LONDON, 26 Sept 1990, *Gondola* (1877, watercolour, 22 1/2 x 37 1/2 ins / 57 x 95 cm) GBP 4,950. LONDON, 30 Jan 1991, *At the Piano* (1880, watercolour and gouache, 9 x 6 1/4 ins / 23 x 16 cm) GBP 4,180. LONDON, 14 June 1991, *Family History* (pencil and watercolour, 14 1/2 x 20 ins / 36.8 x 51 cm) GBP 4,180. LONDON, 29 Oct 1991, *Pigeons in St Mark's Square, Venice* (1876, pencil and watercolour, 14 1/2 x 25 ins / 37 x 63.5 cm) GBP 3,850. LONDON, 19 Dec 1991, *Woman and Child by the Statue of Demeter in the British Museum* (watercolour, 6 x 11 1/2 ins / 15.2 x 29 cm) GBP 3,080; *Music Room* (oil on panel, 12 x 16 ins / 30.4 x 40.6 cm) GBP 7,480. LONDON, 13 Nov 1992, *Fatherly Advice* (watercolour, 10 1/4 x 14 ins / 26 x 35.5 cm) GBP 1,650. NEW YORK, 17 Feb 1993, *In the Garden* (watercolour and pencil/paper, 8 1/2 x 11 1/2 ins / 21.6 x 29.2 cm) USD 7,188. LONDON, 3 Nov 1993, *Miss Pinkerton's Academy* (watercolour and gouache, 27 1/4 x 38 1/2 ins / 69 x 98 cm) GBP 18,400. NEW YORK, 20 July 1994, *Breakfast at the Old Manor* (watercolour heightened with white/paper/card, 19 x 27 ins / 48.3 x 68.6 cm) USD 2,070. LONDON, 17 Nov 1994, *View of the Death Chamber of Napoleon II at Camden Place in Chislehurst, Kent* (1873, pencil and watercolour, 9 x 13 1/4 ins / 22.7 x 33.7 cm) GBP 16,100. LONDON, 6 Nov 1995, *Nubia, Last Days of Pompeii* (oil on canvas, 84 x 48 1/4 ins / 213.5 x 122.5 cm) GBP 19,550. LONDON, 5 June 1996, *Rose for Mummy* (watercolour, 6 3/4 x 9 ins / 17 x 23 cm) GBP 1,150. LONDON, 5 Sept 1996, *Secret Meeting* (oil on card, 8 x 13 ins / 20.1 x 33 cm) GBP 920. LONDON, 6 Nov 1996, *Presentation* (oil on canvas, 22 1/4 x 29 ins / 56.5 x 73.5 cm) GBP 7,475; *Charming Music* (watercolour, 6 3/4 x 10 ins / 17 x 24.5 cm) GBP 2,300. NEW YORK, 26 Feb 1997, *Her First Dance* (oil on canvas, 36 x 48 ins / 91.5 x 122 cm) USD 5,175. LONDON, 12 March 1997, *Seven Hours of Morning; Seventh Hour of Evening* (1873, watercolour heightened with gouache, a pair, each 23 1/4 x 17 1/2 ins / 59 x 44.5 cm) GBP 15,525. LONDON, 13 March 1997, *First Meeting* (1898, oil on panel, 10 x 14 ins / 25.5 x 35.5 cm) GBP 2,800. LONDON, 6 June 1997, *Three Generations* (1879, oil on canvas, 29 1/2 x 40 1/2 ins / 75 x 103 cm) GBP 8,280. LONDON, 5 Nov 1997, *Basket; Midnight Feast; Cutting the Cake* (watercolour, three items, each 4 x 4 ins / 10 x 10 cm) GBP 3,335; *Feeding the Parrot* (oil on canvas, 18 x 12 ins / 46 x 30.5 cm) GBP 3,220. ISLE OF MAN, 7 May 1999, *Story of the Hunt. Only the Dressmaker* (watercolour, a pair, 14 x 20 ins / 36 x 51 cm) GBP 7,000. LICHFIELD, 26 May 1999, *Traveller on Horseback Appreciating a Glass of Wine* (1896, oil on canvas, 26 x 20 ins / 67 x 50 cm) GBP 7,500. LONDON, 8 June 2000, *Miss Pinkerton's Academy, Chiswick Mall* (pencil and watercolour heightened with white, 27 x 39 ins / 68 x 98 cm) GBP 28,000. LONDON, 15 June 2000, *Watching the Cheshire Hunt* (oil on canvas, 25 x 42 ins / 64 x 107 cm) GBP 14,000. LONDON, 7 June 2001, *May I Have the Pleasure* (pencil, watercolour and gum arabic heightened with gouache and scratching out, 14 x 17 ins / 35 x 43 cm) GBP 3,800. LONDON, 6 Sept 2001, *At the Breakfast Table* (oil on canvas, 20 x 30 ins / 51 x 76 cm) GBP 5,800. LONDON, 11 June 2002, *Lullaby* (oil on canvas, 20 x 16 ins / 51 x 41 cm) GBP 12,000. LONDON, 21 Nov 2002, *Afternoon Rest* (1876, pencil and watercolour heightened with gouache, 7 x 9 ins / 18 x 23 cm) GBP 4,500. LEYBURN, 19 Nov 2003, *Affectionate Pets* (pencil and watercolour, 15 x 11 ins / 38 x 27 cm) GBP 5,600. EDINBURGH, 4 Dec 2003, *Recital. Welcome Advances* (oil on panel, a pair, 9 x 6 ins / 24 x 16 cm) GBP 6,000. LONDON, 4 March 2004, *Her First Appearance* (oil on canvas, 32 x 44 ins / 81 x 112 cm) GBP 14,000. LONDON, 11 June 2004, *Hopeless Case* (oil on canvas, 30 x 46 ins / 77 x 117 cm) GBP 18,000.

KILENYI, Julio

Hungarian, 20th century.
Born 1885.
Active in the USA.
Sculptor, medallist.

Julio Kilenyi was a member of the American Arts Federation. He sculpted medallions of Benjamin Franklin, Edison Pershing and Lindbergh, as well as many commemorative medals.

KILGALLEN, Margaret

American, 20th - 21st century.
Born 1967, in Washington DC; died 26 June 2001 of breast cancer.
Painter, printmaker. Murals, hand-painted photographs, etchings.

Margaret Kilgallen studied at Colorado College, obtaining a BA in printmaking in 1989. She received an MFA at Stanford University in 2001, where she held a fellowship in studio art during her studies. She was married to the artist Barry McGee. She was employed as a librarian and book conservator at the San Francisco Public Library until 1997, which resulted in her considerable knowledge and interest in 15th and 16th-century typography, illustrations in manuscripts, letterpress, printmaking and signs drawn from American folk tradition.

Kilgallen cited images of plants and animals in books as being influential in the flat and graphic nature of her own painting. She painted on discarded endsheets from books, on primed wood and on metal trays for storing letterpress type. She also painted shapes and letters directly onto walls, frequently incorporating found objects such as cakes of soap or organic material such as seeds or insects placed in matchboxes. Kilgallen typically painted female figures with full, dark lips surfing, weeping or fighting, or simply standing or smoking. Text figures prominently in her paintings, as seen in the mural *To Friend and Foe* (1999), which was painted in a 'Wild West' style and contains words such as 'Cheat Steel Lie'.

In addition to her paintings, she hand-painted documentary-style photographs, such as her series *Hand-painted Trainyard Photos* (2000). Most of her murals were designed to be painted over and are, therefore, no longer extant. She created public murals in San Francisco, São Paulo, Boston, Minneapolis and New York.

Kilgallen showed work in *East Meets West* at the Institute of Contemporary Art in Philadelphia (2001). Her prints were exhibited posthumously in the Whitney Biennial (2002); *Art/Women/California, 1950-2000* at the San Jose Museum of Contemporary Art (2002); *Surf Culture: The Art History of Surfing* at the San Jose Museum of Art (2003); *For the Record: Drawing Contemporary Life* at the Vancouver Art Gallery (2003); and *Beautiful Losers: Contemporary Art and Street Culture* at the Orange Museum of Art in Newport Beach in California (2005). Solo exhibitions of her work include those at the Drawing Center in New York (1997) and at the Armand Hammer Museum at the University of California in Los Angeles (2000). She was awarded a Eureka Fellowship from the Fleishhaker Foundation in 1995.

BIBLIOGRAPHY:
Margaret Kilgallen, exhibition catalogue, UCLA Hammer Museum, Los Angeles, 2000.
MUSEUMS AND GALLERIES:
SAN JOSE (MA): *Sloe* (1998, colour aquatint).

KILIAN, family of artists
16th - 17th - 18th century.
Engravers.

The Kilian family has an important place in the history of engraving. From the 16th century to the 18th their name occurs on almost 700 catalogued items, chiefly portraits and also subjects from mythology, topography and religion.

KILIAN, Bartholomäus, the Elder
German, 16th century.
Born 1548, in Silesia; died 1588, in Augsburg.
Goldsmith, engraver.

Bartholomäus Kilian was the first in a long line of artists in the Kilian family. He came from Silesia and settled in Augsburg. Three of his sons - Lukas, Wolfgang and Magnus - were engravers. Nothing is known of his works, and he died while his children were still young. He was almost certainly a trader in prints, as were most gold and silversmiths at that time. His widow married the Antwerp painter and print-trader Dominicus Balten, otherwise known as Custos or Custodis, shortly after Kilian's death.

KILIAN, Bartholomäus, the Younger
German, 17th century.
Born 6 May 1630, in Augsburg; died 15 January 1696, in Augsburg.
Draughtsman, engraver (etching/burin).
Bohemian School.

Kilian was the younger son of Wolfgang Kilian and grandson of the elder Bartholomäus Kilian. He was initially taught by his father, but then went to Frankfurt to train with Mathäus Merian for two and a half years. From there he moved on to Paris, getting advice from F. de Poilly, doing a *Crucifix* there after Testelin and engravings after P. de Champaigne. On his return to Germany, he settled in Augsburg and established a reputation as an excellent engraver. He is known for more than 60 portraits of sovereigns and leading figures of his day, notably the lifesize *Emperor Joseph on Horseback*, one of the largest engravings known. He also did engravings for theses.

Kilian's engraving style was alert and spiritual. His work was represented at the *Lumière et ténèbres, art et civilisation du Baroque en Bohême* (*Light and Darkness. Baroque Art and Civilisation in Bohemia*) at the Palais des Beaux-Arts in Lille in 2002 by an engraving celebrating the accession of Emperor Leopold I to the throne of Bohemia.

BIBLIOGRAPHY:
Appuhn-Radtke, Sibylle, *Das Thesenblatt im Hochbarock: Studien zu einer graphischen Gattung am Beispiel der Werke Bartholomäus Kilians*, Anton H. Konrad, Weissenhorn, 1988.
Vlnas, Vit (ed.), *Lumière et ténèbres, art et civilisation du Baroque en Bohême*, exhibition catalogue, Palais des Beaux-Arts, Lille, Réunion des musées nationaux, Paris, 2002.

KILIAN, Christoph Gustav
German, 18th century.
Born 14 March 1724, in Augsburg.
Engraver (mezzotint).

Kilian was the third son of Georg Christoph Kilian and is noted for a fine portrait of *Maria Theresia of Austria*.

KILIAN, Georg
German, 18th century.
Born 30 December 1683, in Augsburg; died 18 July 1745, in Augsburg.
Painter, pastellist, engraver (burin).

Georg Kilian was the son of Wolfgang Philipp Kilian. He studied painting with Isaak Fischer and engraving with his father. After visiting Berlin, Dresden and Vienna, he devoted himself to engraving and worked for Christoph Weigel in Nuremberg. He engraved religious subjects, portraits and landscapes.

KILIAN, Georg Christoph
German, 18th century.
Born 4 January 1709, in Augsburg; died 15 June 1781, in Augsburg.
Engraver (etching/burin/mezzotint).

Georg Christoph Kilian was the elder son and pupil of Georg Kilian. He visited Austria and Hungary, but spent most of his life in Augsburg. He engraved some historical subjects, but concentrated mainly on portraits. He is known to have produced over a hundred, most notably those of famous painters.

KILIAN, Georg Martin
German, 18th century.
Born 1739, in Augsburg; died 1760, in Augsburg.
Engraver.

Georg Martin Kilian was the son and pupil of Philipp Andreas Kilian. He is known for one engraving after Boucher.

KILIAN, Jakob
Dutch, 18th century.
Painter. Portraits.

In 1762, Jakob Kilian was a student in The Hague. He was born in Germany and is believed to have belonged to a celebrated family of engravers. He is known to have worked in Voorburg and, in 1776, in Schoonhoven.

KILIAN, Jeremias, the Elder
German, 17th - 18th century.
Born 22 July 1665, in Augsburg; died 23 August 1730, in Augsburg.
Engraver.

Jeremias Kilian the Elder was the younger son and pupil of Philipp Kilian. He engraved mainly portraits.

KILIAN, Jeremias, the Younger
German, 18th century.
Born c. 1693; died 8 April 1712.
Active in Augsburg.
Engraver.

Jeremias the Younger was the son of Jeremias Kilian the Elder. No works by him are known.

KILIAN, Johann Jakob
German, 18th century.
Born 5 June 1678, in Augsburg.
Engraver.

Johann Jakob Kilian was the eldest son of Wolfgang Philipp Kilian. He painted portraits and views.

KILIAN, Johannes
German, 18th century.
Born 22 April 1716, in Augsburg; died 4 October 1744, in Augsburg.
Painter, engraver.

KILIAN, Lukas
German, 17th century.
Born 1579, in Augsburg; died 27 March 1637, in Augsburg.
Painter, draughtsman, engraver (burin).

Lukas Kilian was the elder son of the goldsmith and seller of engravings, Bartholomäus Kilian, who died when the boy was barely eight years old. His widowed mother then married the painter Dominique Custos of Antwerp, and it was he who took charge of his stepson's artistic education. After studying painting, Lukas went to Italy, where he stayed mostly in Venice. During his travels he appears to have worked mainly as an engraver, as he made a number of plates after Tintoretto, Paolo Veronese, Jacopo Palma and other Venetian masters. He established himself as an excellent burin engraver, with a style reminiscent of Goltzius. He showed the same skill in religious subjects as in his many portraits.

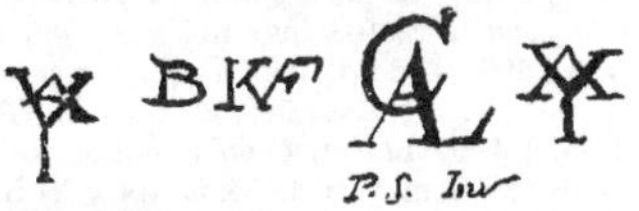

KILIAN, Magnus
German, 17th century.
Active in Munich.
Painter.
Magnus Kilian worked mainly for the Margrave Joachim Ernst of Ansbach.

KILIAN, Max Philipp
German, 18th century.
Born 29 July 1679, in Augsburg; died 1716, in Nuremberg.
Engraver.
Max Philipp Kilian is known for his portraits and views.

KILIAN, Paul
German, 18th century.
Born 20 July 1687, in Nuremberg; died 1718, in Breslau (now Wroclaw, Poland).
Engraver.
Paul Kilian was the youngest son of Wolfgang Philipp Kilian. He worked in Augsburg, Nuremberg, Vienna and Breslau.

KILIAN, Philipp
German, 17th century.
Born 8 July 1628, in Augsburg; died 14 October 1693, in Augsburg.
Draughtsman, engraver (burin).
Bohemian School.
Philipp Kilian was the second son of Wolfgang Kilian. He was first taught by his father, then completed his studies by travelling in Germany and Italy. After returning to Germany, he engraved theses and portraits, collaborated on the engraving of the works of Sandrart, engraved animals after J. H. Roos and, above all, produced portraits.

He was represented in the exhibition: *Lumière et ténèbres, art et civilisation du Baroque en Bohême* (*Light and Darkness. Baroque Art and Civilisation in Bohemia*) at the Palais des Beaux-Arts in Lille in 2002.

Bibliography:
Vlnas, Vit (ed.), *Lumière et ténèbres, art et civilisation du Baroque en Bohême*, exhibition catalogue, Palais des Beaux-Arts, Lille, Réunion des musées nationaux, Paris, 2002.

KILIAN, Philipp Andreas
German, 18th century.
Born 20 October 1714, in Augsburg; died 18 January 1759, in Augsburg.
Draughtsman, engraver (etching/burin).
Philipp Andreas Kilian was the younger son of Georg Kilian. He studied with Andreas Friedrich in Augsburg and Georg Martin Preissler in Nuremberg. He travelled in Germany and Holland and produced a large body of work. He is known for having reproduced a number of paintings in the Dresden Gallery. He also engraved for publishers, notably biblical illustrations and the plates for Schneudzer's *Physica sacra*. He had the patronage of King Augustus III.

KILIAN, Wolfgang
German, 17th century.
Born 10 May 1581, in Augsburg; died 1662, in Augsburg.
Painter, engraver (etching/burin).
Wolfgang Kilian was the younger brother of Lukas Kilian and studied first with his stepfather Dominicus Custos. He continued his studies in Venice, where he made engravings after the Venetian masters in a similar style to that of his elder brother. On returning to Augsburg, he painted a number of portraits, and this was the genre in which he became most famous, both as a painter and as an engraver.

KILIAN, Wolfgang Philipp
German, 17th - 18th century.
Born 1 May 1654, in Augsburg; died 3 April 1732, in Königsberg (now Kaliningrad, Russia).
Engraver.
Wolfgang Philipp Kilian was the son of Philipp Kilian, and probably also his pupil. He worked mainly for publishers. He is best known for a number of plates for *Vitae et Effigies Procancellariorum Academiae Altorfinae*, published in Nuremberg in 1721, and for *Icones Consiliariorum de Illustri Republica Noribergensis*, published in the same city in 1733. He produced accomplished portraits, including one of the Margrave Christian Ernst of Brandenburg.

KILIMNIK, Karen
American, 20th - 21st century.
Born 1955, in Philadelphia.
Installation artist, environmental artist.
Karen Kilimnik studied at the Temple University, Philadelphia, from 1974-1976. Like Process Art of the late 1970s, Kilimnik's 'scatter pieces' of the 1980s explore themes of dispersal, using everyday found objects and materials. Toys, cosmetics, pillows, photographs and found objects are strewn across the floor in apparent chaos; collectively, however, they form a specific narrative. The installation *Mrs Peel... We're needed* (1992), based on the popular cult television series *The Avengers*, mixed fact and fiction with a scattering of clues, Polaroid photographs, newspaper cuttings, phials containing drugs and poisoned chocolates. Kilimnik's sculptures feature similarly assorted materials, assembled into dolls (bits of cotton, thread, plastic toy horses). Her works convey an atmosphere of violence and anxiety, born of her sense of helplessness in the face of the seemingly unstoppable forces of disintegration and obsessive manipulation at the heart of modern life, where anything is possible. Kilimnik's later work concentrates on fairy tales and landmarks - most especially those in New York City.

Her work has featured in a number of group exhibitions: 1987, 1989, 1990, 1991, New York; 1991, Cologne, Los Angeles and Villa Arson, Nice; 1992, Salon Découvertes, Paris; 1992, Institute of Contemporary Art, London; 1992, Centre for Contemporary Art, Warsaw; 1992, Museum of Contemporary Art, Prato; 2001, *The Way I See It*, Galerie Jennifer Flay, Paris. Her work has also been the subject of a number of solo exhibitions, including: 1991, 303 Gallery, New York; 1992, 1995, Galerie Jennifer Flay, Paris; 1994, White Cube, London; 1996, Transmission Gallery, Glasgow; 1998, Galerie Ghislaine Hussenot, Paris; 2000, South London Gallery, London; 2001, Gallery Side 2, Tokyo.

Bibliography:
Bankowski, Jack, '*Slackers*' in *Artforum*, periodical, New York, November, 1991. Feldman, Melissa, *Karen Kilimnik: Escape in Time*, exhibition catalogue, ICA Philadelphia, Philadelphia, 1992. *True Stories: Mark Dion, Renée Green, Larry Johnson, Karen Kilimnik, Raymond Pettibon, Jack Pierson, Jim Shaw*, Institute for Contemporary Arts, London, 1992. Nobbe, Nora, *Karen Kilimnik*, Patrick Frey, New York, 2001. Melandri, Lisa, *Painted Faces: Mary Cassatt, Alice Neel, Karen Kilimnik*, exhibition catalogue, Moore College of Art and Design, Philadelphia, 2002.

Museums and Galleries:
Geneva (Mamco).

KILLAM, Walter Milton
American, 20th century.
Born 1907; died 1979.
Painter.

KILLER, Karl
German, 19th - 20th century.
Born 30 August 1873, in Munich.
Sculptor.

Karl Killer was a student of F. von Miller. His works include a *Tomb of the Industrialist Heinrich Kumm* and an *Equestrian Statue of the Prince Regent Leopold of Bavaria*.

KILLIGREW, Anne
British, 17th century.
Born c. 1660, in London; died c. 1685.
Painter.

Anne Killigrew was a celebrity in her own time for her beauty, her wit and her talent for painting and poetry. Both Dryden and Antony Wood sang her praises. The daughter of Dr Henry Killigrew, the Canon of Westminster, she was Maid of Honour to the Duchess of York. She painted landscapes and portraits in the style of Peter Lely, including portraits of the Duchess of York, James II and Mary of Modena, his second wife. She also painted historical subjects and still-lifes. Her poems were published after her death with an engraving by Beckel after her own self-portrait. She died of smallpox.

MUSEUMS AND GALLERIES:
LONDON (National Portrait Gal.): several portraits by Isaac Beckett after Killigrew's self-portrait.

KILLINGBECK, Benjamin
British, 18th century.
Painter, engraver. Portraits, hunting scenes, sporting subjects.

Benjamin Killingbeck exhibited his work at the Society of Artists, the Free Society and at the Royal Academy in London from 1769 to 1789.

MUSEUMS AND GALLERIES:
LONDON (National Portrait Gal.): *Portrait* (after B. Killingbeck).

AUCTION RECORDS:
LONDON, 29 June 1966, *Hunting Dog*, GBP 300. LONDON, 21 July 1967, *Horse Rider on a Bay in a Landscape*, Gns 300. LONDON, 25 Nov 1977, *Thoroughbred in a Landscape* (1774, oil on canvas, 40 x 51 ins / 101.3 x 129.3 cm) GBP 3,500. LONDON, 24 Nov 1978, *Thoroughbred in a Landscape* (oil on canvas, 40 x 51 ins / 101.3 x 129.3 cm) GBP 1,500. LONDON, 22 June 1979, *Racehorse with Jockey* (1781, oil on canvas, 23 1/2 x 29 ins / 59.6 x 73.6 cm) GBP 2,500. LONDON, 6 July 1983, *Alabucalla, the Winner of the First St Leger, 1776, with his Owner* (oil on canvas, 23 x 28 ins / 58.5 x 71 cm) GBP 13,000. LONDON, 18 April 1986, *Black and White Greyhound in a Landscape* (painting, 45 x 63 ins / 114.2 x 160 cm) GBP 38,000. LONDON, 24 April 1987, *Pointers in a Landscape* (1777, oil on canvas, 41 1/2 x 60 ins / 105.4 x 152.4 cm) GBP 40,000. LONDON, 14 July 1989, *A Brown Thoroughbred Bay held by a Groom in front of Rubbing Down House at Newmarket* (oil on canvas, 41 x 51 ins / 104 x 129.5 cm) GBP 7,150. NEW YORK, 9 April 1999, *Edward Parker with his Son John and his Horse Button* (oil on canvas, 41 x 52 ins / 104 x 133 cm) USD 36,000.

KILLMANN, F. von
German, 19th century.
Active in Düsseldorf at the beginning of the 19th century.
Draughtsman, engraver.

KILPACK, Sarah Louise
British, 19th - 20th century.
Painter. Seascapes.

Sarah Louise Kilpack was active from 1880 to 1909. She was a painter of decorative seascapes, harbour views and fishing scenes, often in pendant pairs.

AUCTION RECORDS:
LONDON, 22 Nov 1991, *Harbour at Twilight; Fishermen in Boats at Anchor at Dawn* (oil on card, a pair, 12 1/2 x 10 ins / 31.7 x 25.4 cm) GBP 1,210. LONDON, 13 Nov 1992, *Fresh Breeze* (oil on card, 6 1/2 x 9 1/2 ins / 16.5 x 24.2 cm) GBP 682. LONDON, 3 Feb 1993, *Landing the Catch; Stormy Sea* (oil on card, a pair, each 11 1/2 x 23 1/4 ins / 29 x 59 cm) GBP 2,070. LONDON, 11 May 1994, *Stormy Evening* (oil on card, a pair, diam. 12 3/4 ins / 32.5 cm) GBP 1,035. LONDON, 27 Sept 1994, *Return of the Fishing Fleet; Unloading the Catch* (oil on card, a pair, each 5 3/4 x 9 ins / 14.5 x 22 cm) GBP 1,840. JERSEY, 17 March 1999, *Unloading Lobster Pots on the Beach* (oil on board, 9 x 13 ins / 24 x 34 cm) GBP 2,600. LONDON, 28 April 1999, *St Michael's Mount, Cornwall* (oil on canvas, 22 x 32 ins / 56 x 81 cm) GBP 3,400. LONDON, 11 May 2000, *On the Causeway at Sark with Storm Brewing* (oil on board, 5 x 7 ins / 13 x 19 cm) GBP 1,100. JERSEY, 29 Nov 2000, *Rocks at Etretat* (1864, oil on card, 11 x 18 ins / 27 x 46 cm) GBP 1,200. PENZANCE, 24 April 2001, *Plymouth Hoe with Smeaton's Tower. Drakes Island and Fishing Boats* (oil on board, a pair, 9 x 12 ins / 23 x 30 cm) GBP 3,600. HONITON, 14 Dec 2001, *Winter Snow-covered Cottage on the Coast. Windmill near Boulogne* (watercolour, a pair) GBP 1,150. LEEDS, 12 March 2002, *Martello Tower, St Leonards. St Michael's Mount, Cornwall* (oil on board, a pair, 4 x 7 ins / 9 x 18 cm) GBP 2,500. JERSEY, 27 Nov 2002, *Just Come Ashore at Portel* (oil on board, 8 x 11 ins / 21 x 29 cm) GBP 2,700. BATH, 14 March 2003, *Figure Retrieving Wreckage under a Storm-swept Cliff* (oil on canvas, 24 x 20 ins / 61 x 51 cm) GBP 2,100. LONDON, 21 May 2003, *Seaweed Gathering, Guernsey. West Pier, Boulogne* (oil on board, a pair, 9 x 12 ins / 23 x 31 cm) GBP 2,800. GUERNSEY, 1 April 2004, *Approaching Storm* (oil on canvas, 9 x 7 ins / 23 x 18 cm) GBP 1,250. GUERNSEY, 1 April 2004, *Salvaging the Wreck. The Peastacks, Guernsey* (oil on board, a pair, 8 x 12 ins / 21 x 30 cm) GBP 1,400.

KILPATRICK, Dereid Gallatin
American, 20th century.
Born 21 September 1884, in Uniontown (Pennsylvania).
Painter, sculptor. Portraits. Statues.

Dereid Gallatin Kilpatrick studied in Paris, under Lucien Simon, Antoine Bourdelle and Collin. He sculpted statues of Georges Washington, Lincoln, and Colonel William Crawford.

KILSDONCK, Adriaen van
Dutch, 18th century.
Born in Leiden.
Painter. Religious subjects.

Adriaen van Kilsdonck also worked in Rome.

AUCTION RECORDS:
VERSAILLES, 5 March 1978, *The Stage* (wood, 16 x 12 ins / 40.5 x 30.5 cm) FRF 9,800.

KILTENHOF, Hans
German, 16th century.
Painter, glass painter.

In 1527, he produced the stained glass windows of the town hall in Lüneburg.

KILVINGTON, Patrick
Australian, 20th century.
Painter. Genre scenes.

Patrick Kilvington painted ensemble views and compositions with figures depicting a variety of subjects, notably racing scenes.

AUCTION RECORDS:
SYDNEY, 17 April 1988, *Night Run to Oxenford* (oil on canvas) AUD 1,300. SYDNEY, 4 July 1988, *From Lower Paddock* (oil on

canvas, 15 3/4 x 20 ins / 40 x 51 cm) AUD 950. SYDNEY, 21 Nov 1988, *Gentle on the Heffers* (oil on canvas, 16 1/4 x 19 3/4 ins / 41 x 50 cm) AUD 1,100. SYDNEY, 20 March 1989, *Lap of Honour* (oil on canvas, 15 3/4 x 19 3/4 ins / 40 x 50 cm) AUD 1,200. SYDNEY, 3 July 1989, *The Ringer from Jubilee Station* (oil on canvas, 24 x 30 ins / 61 x 76 cm) AUD 3,200. SYDNEY, 26 March 1990, *A Right Bloody Caper* (oil on canvas, 16 1/4 x 20 ins / 41 x 51 cm) AUD 1,200. SYDNEY, 2 July 1990, *The Sewage Works from Lower Paddock* (oil on canvas, 15 3/4 x 19 3/4 ins / 40 x 50 cm) AUD 1,000.

KIM, Byron
American, 20th century.
Painter, sculptor.

Byron Kim is based in New York, where he shows his works. His paintings are rooted in minimal abstraction. His previous work has included colour field portraits representing the skin pigmentation of his friends and family; site-specific wall paintings made with the grime collected from the building's vacuum cleaners, and 'action' paintings achieved by splashing latex wall paint onto an earlier painting while it hangs installed in an exhibition. Kim is influenced by monochrome painters such as Ad Reinhardt and Brice Marden, as well as by Mark Rothko and other New York School painters. Kim's paintings merge aspects of Minimalist abstraction with evocative representation, while confronting issues of race, community, and cultural biases.

In *Permanent*, an exhibition held at the Hosfelt Gallery in San Francisco in 2004, Kim created three bodies of work. The first, *Sunday Paintings*, which acted as diary entries made every Sunday for the last three years, was inspired by Kim's chance encounter with the writing of Chuang Tze, an early Taoist, who wrote eloquently about the relationship of the infinite to the infinitesimal. The second work was an ephemeral sculpture, *A Theory of Everything*, which involved a loaf of brown bread going steadily mouldy. The third body of work was the *Permanent Paintings* that Kim created using a mixture of pigment, wax, and mineral oil. These works are closely related to the *Belly Paintings*, shown in his mid-career survey exhibition at the Berkeley Art Museum, *Threshold: Byron Kim 1990-2004*, which also travelled to the Museum of Contemporary Art in San Diego in 2005.

BIBLIOGRAPHY:

Damianovic, Maia, *'La Peinture au risque du dilemme'* in *Art Press* n° 211, periodical, Paris, March 1996.

KIM, Byung Jong
Korean, 20th - 21st century.
Born 1953.
Painter.

Kim studied at the Art College of the University of Seoul until 1983. He uses the materials, concentration and tension of traditional calligraphy on prepared grounds, drawing large, abstract signs that symbolically refer to the great, universal mystery. He showed work at the University of Art exhibition at the National Museum of Contemporary Art in Seoul in 1979, where he won first prize. He exhibited in Osaka in 1983, in Berlin in 1989, at the Fukuoka Museum in Japan in 1991, in Beijing in 1992 and at the National City Museum in Seoul in 1994. He was included in the exhibition of *Contemporary Korean Art* at UNESCO House in Paris in 1995, and was represented in the selection from Korean galleries invited to the FIAC (Foire Internationale d'Art Contemporain) in 1996 in Paris. Kim had solo exhibitions in Seoul in 1988, 1990, 1992, 1994 and 1995, in Berlin in 1989 and 1993, in Gyor, Hungary, and Wroclaw, Poland, in 1989.

KIM, Chang Hee
Korean, 20th century.
Born 1938, in Jang Jung-li.
Sculptor.

Kim began studying sculpture at Hongik University in 1960 and graduated in 1967. In 1975 he took a teaching post in the sculpture department of the University of Seoul. Kim's art is a search for the essential. His sculptures link the human body to architectural forms and the result is a kind of co-existence of realism and fantastical elements, as the art relates simultaneously to two structural orders - human beings and the city - that have been thought of as inter-dependent since the Ancient Greeks and throughout humanist thought.

In 1980, he curated an exhibition of Korean sculpture in Rome. In addition to participating in collective exhibitions, Kim has had a number of solo shows, including at the Hankook Gallery in New York in 1981, at the Kukche Gallery in Barcelona in 1983, at the Pyo Gallery in Seoul and at the Korean Cultural Centre in Tokyo in 1986. A retrospective of his work was held at the Museum of Eastern Art in Moscow in 1991. He had solo exhibitions at the Juliana Gallery in Seoul in 1994, at the Guiter Gallery in Paris and at the Fair mounted by the Akié Aricchi Gallery in Cologne in 1996.

BIBLIOGRAPHY:

Restany, Pierre/Xuriguera, Gérard, *Kim Chang-Hee*, Éd. Garnier Nocera, Paris, 1996.

KIM, Hong-do
Korean, 18th - 19th century.
Born 1745; died 1814(?).
Painter. Genre scenes, landscapes, birds, flowers.
Screens.

Kim Hong-Do was the father of Kim Yang-Ki.

BIBLIOGRAPHY:

Cambon, Pierre, *'Un paravent de Kim Hong-Do récemment restauré'* in *Revue du Louvre* n° 1 p. 51, periodical, Paris, 2001.

MUSEUMS AND GALLERIES:

PARIS (Musée Guimet): screen.

KIM, Hui Kyong
Korean, 20th - 21st century.
Born 1948, in Seoul.
Active in France.
Painter, screen printer.

Kim trained at the Seoul University School of Fine Art, then at the École des Beaux-Arts in Paris. He lives and works in Paris. In his works, abstract, sharply outlined forms (lines, strips of colour) are apparently superimposed. He has shown work in collective exhibitions, among others at the Kieffer Gallery in Paris in 1993 and in the exhibition *Estampes contemporaines. 18 ans d'édition 1982-2001* (*Contemporary Prints: 18 Years of Production 1982-2001*) mounted by the Contemporary Print Connoisseur association at the Villa Tamaris in La Seyne-sur-Mer, France.

MUSEUMS AND GALLERIES:

PARIS (BNF, Prints Collection) - SEOUL (MCA).

KIM, Ku Lim
Korean, 20th century.
Born 1936, in Seoul.
Engraver.

Kim participated in the 9th International Print Biennale in Tokyo.

KIM, Po
Korean, 20th century.
Active in the USA from 1967.
Painter, draughtsman. Still-lifes.

Kim lives in New York. He specialises in vividly coloured figurative paitings, sometimes with a faux-naive air to them.

AUCTION RECORDS:

NEW YORK, 16 Oct 1981, *At the Drawing Table* (1981, pencil, 21 1/2 x 30 1/2 ins / 54.5 x 77.5 cm) USD 1,200. MUNICH, 1-2 Dec 1992, *Three Walnuts* (graphite and pencil, 8 1/2 x 4 3/4 ins / 21.5 x 12 cm) DEM 2,070.

KIM, Soo-ja
Korean, 20th - 21st century.
Born 1957, in Taegu.
Active in the USA.
Installation artist, sculptor, performance artist, video artist.

Kim Soo-ja settled in New York. She uses Korean cloth in her work, which she folds, crumples or hangs; for her the fabric has symbolic weight, one tied to the culture of her country. The cloth becomes a metaphorical relation with her body. Rolled in a bundle to form a *bottari* (bundle), cloth becomes a symbol of nomadic life and migration: her performance *Bottari Truck* involved driving a truck loaded with *bottari* for several days. In her performance *Needle Woman* (1999-2001), which was filmed and then shown as an installation, she had herself filmed from the back on a street in large cities, such as London, Cairo, Lagos, Mexico City - static, unmoving, facing the world around her and the passers-by, who look at her or ignore her. She was featured at the 2000 Whitney Biennial in New York and had solo exhibitions at PS1 in New York in 2001, the Peter Blum Gallery in New York in 2002 and the Musée d'Art Contemporain in Lyons, France, in 2003.

BIBLIOGRAPHY:

'*Kim Sooja*' in *Flah Art*, periodical, New York, January-February 1997 (interview with Hans-Ulrich Obrist). *Kim Sooja: conditions d'humanité*, 5 continents, Milan, 2003 (Trilingual text (English, French and German)). Ardenne, Paul, '*Kim Sooja. Coudre des corps dans le tissu du monde*' in *Art Press* n° 286, periodical, Paris, January 2003.

KIM, Tschang Yeul
Korean, 20th century.
Born 1929, in Seoul.
Active in France.
Painter.

Kim studied at the Seoul School of Fine Art and at the Art Students League in New York before settling in Paris. During the 1970s, his painting was confined to a very skilful trompe l'oeil effect of drops of water running down the untreated canvas. During the 1990s, he abandoned his water drops and used his techniques of illusion to create rough or smooth granite surfaces, on which he draws Chinese ideograms. Kim's works radiate an almost metaphysical serenity and calm. They have been shown in many collective exhibitions, including the Paris Biennale of 1961, the São Paulo Biennale of 1965 and the Salon des Réalités Nouvelles and the Salon de Mai in Paris in 1972-1976. He participated in exhibitions in Seoul in 1987, at the Tate Gallery in Liverpool in 1992 and at the International Contemporary Art Fair in Paris in 1995. He has had solo exhibitions in Seoul in 1963, in Paris in 1973, in Berlin and Hamburg in 1975, in Tokyo in 1976, in Milan in 1978, in New York in 1978 and 1979. He showed at the Paris International Contemporary Art Fair exhibition presented by the Moos Gallery in Toronto in 1979, at the Basel Fair in 1984, at the Chicago International Art Fair in 1989, at the National Museum of Contemporary Art in Seoul in 1993, at the Enrico Navarra Gallery in Paris in 1996 and, with Nam June Paik, at the Jeu de Paume in Paris in 2003.

BIBLIOGRAPHY:

Tschang-yeul Kim: Recent Paintings. Nov. 20-Dec. 22, 1979, exhibition catalogue, Staempfli Gallery, New York, 1979. Cohen, Ronny, *Tschang Yeul Kim*, Hudson Hills Press, New York, 1993. Ch'ang-nyol, Kim, *Kim tschang-yeul*, exhibition catalogue, Museum of Contemporary Art, Korea, 1993. *Kim Tschang-Yeul*, exhibition catalogue, Galerie National du Jeu de Paume, Paris, 2004.

AUCTION RECORDS:

PARIS, 3 Oct 1997, *Water Drops* (1973, acrylic/canvas, 19 3/4 x 19 3/4 ins / 50 x 50 cm) FRF 38,000.

KIM, Yang-ki
Korean, 19th century.
Born 1770; died 1842.
Painter. Genre scenes, landscapes, flowers, birds. Screens.

Kim Yang-ki was the son of the painter Kim Hong-Do. He painted in the style of his father. Kim is regarded as the bridge between traditional 18th century Korean painting and the new, realistic painting of the 19th century.

BIBLIOGRAPHY:

Cambon, Pierre, '*Un paravent coréen au musée Guimet sur le thème des jeux et des saisons, attribué au peintre Kim Yang-Ki*' in *Revue du Louvre* n° 2 p. 56, periodical, Paris, April 2003.

MUSEUMS AND GALLERIES:

PARIS (Musée Guimet): eightfold screen on the theme of games and the seasons, attributed.

KIM EN JOONG
Korean, 20th century.
Born 10 September 1940, in Booyo.
Active in France from 1975.
Painter. Designs for stained glass.

A calligrapher's son, Kim studied at the Seoul School of Fine Art from1959 to 1967 in the department of Western painting, and worked there as an assistant from 1967 to 1968. After his military service on the border between North and South Korea, he studied theology at the University of Freiburg in Switzerland and at the Catholic Institute in Paris (1970-1976). He was ordained a priest in the Dominican order in 1974 and lived in Paris from 1975.

Kim was first influenced by the French Impressionist painters, who had a profound effect on the contemporary Japanese School. In Switzerland, he turned to action painting. After working in black and white, he went back to painting in colour, using first acrylics, then oils. His painting is abstract and lively. Its lines form transparent, superimposed spaces. Discreet, yet strong, it has been described by Claude Bouyeure as 'the explosion of sublimated violence'. His works look like washes and owe the fundamentals of their technique and poetics to traditional Far Eastern calligraphy. Their abstract signs seem to invoke the climate of marine horizons or nocturnal mysteries. Kim adopted a round format in some of his works, to create 'the illusion of conquering a larger space'. He created the stained glass for the Dominican Chapel in Dax.

Kim participated in the 1975, 1976 and 1978 Salon of New Realities in Paris. His many solo shows include three in Seoul, of which the first, at the Sin Moon Haekwan Gallery in 1965, won him the National Exhibition First Prize. In 1973, 1977 and 1978, he exhibited at the Jacques Massol Gallery in Paris, in 1977 at the Benador Gallery in Switzerland, in 1978 at the École Régionale des Beaux Arts in Besançon, France, and in 1994 with Jean Messagier at the Korean Cultural Centre in Paris. He had a double exhibition at the Fanny Guillon-Laffaille and Larock-Granoff galleries in Paris in 1996 and, in 2003, showed recent works at the Musée de Borda in Dax, France.

BIBLIOGRAPHY:

Kim en Joong, exhibition catalogue, Gal. Massol, Paris, 1973 (other catalogue in 1975). Bouyeure, Claude, '*Kim en Joong*' in *Opus international* n° 95, periodical, Paris, autumn 1984. Kim en Joong, *Fragments d'un monde inconnu*, Éditions du Cerf, Paris, 1996. Dunoyer, Jean-Marie, *Kim en Joong*, Éd. du Cerf, Paris, 1997. Kim en Joong, *Expositions du Jubilé de l'an 2000*, Éditions du Cerf, Paris, 2000. *Kim En Joong, les retrouvailles*, Cerf, Paris, 2002 (text in French and English). Danneels, Godfried/Kim En Joong, *Ave Maria: En hommage à Jean-Paul II*, Éditions du Cerf, Paris, 2004.

AUCTION RECORDS:
PARIS, 21 Jan 1998, *Composition* (1980, collage, 15 3/4 x 15 3/4 ins / 40 x 40 cm) FRF 3,500.

KIM HAI LIM
Malayan, 20th century.
Active in France.
Painter. Scenes with figures, still-lifes.

Kim Hai Lim began his studies at the school of fine arts in Singapore and continued them from 1975 to 1982 at the École des Beaux-Arts in Paris.

He puts side by side, or else superimposes, hyperrealist depictions of objects like apples with images of an abstract nature worked with an equal amount of care.

A member of the Salon d'Automne in Paris from 1980, Kim Hai Lim's work was shown at other collective exhibitions including: Salon des Artistes Français, Paris (1981, 1982 when he won a gold medal, 1983 and 1986). Solo exhibitions include: Galerie Valmey, Paris and Singapore Museum (1988). He was awarded the Henri Lehman prize (1986).

KIM PRISU. See **PRISU Kim**

KIMBALL, Alonzo Myron
American, 19th - 20th century.
Born 14 August 1874, in Wentworth (Iowa); died 27 August 1923, in Evanston.
Sculptor.

Alonzo Myron Kimball studied at the Art Students League in New York, and, in Paris, under Jules Lefebvre, Whistler and Courtois.

AUCTION RECORDS:
NEW YORK, 21 May 1991, *Camilla and Alice* (oil on card, 26 x 31 1/2 ins / 66.1 x 80 cm) USD 1,980.

KIMBALL, Charles F.
American, 19th century.
Born 1835, in Monmouth (Oregon).
Painter, engraver. Landscapes.

Charles F. Kimball worked mainly in Portland, Oregon, having previously been a pupil of the portrait painter Charles Octarius Cole.

AUCTION RECORDS:
NEW YORK, 16 March 1990, *Landscape 4* (oil on canvas, 22 x 16 1/4 ins / 56 x 41 cm) USD 2,200.

KIMBALL, Isabel Moore
American, 20th century.
Born in Wentworth (Iowa).
Sculptor.

Isabel Moore Kimball studied under Herbert Adams. She is member of the American Federation of Arts. She sculpted subjects to adorn the fountains in some American parks and some memorials for World War I.

KIMBALL, Katharine
American, 19th - 20th century.
Born 1866, in New Hampshire; died 1949.
Active in England.
Draughtswoman, illustrator, engraver. Landscapes, urban landscapes.

Katharine Kimball lived in London. She visited France and painted views of Paris, Rouen, Les Andelys and Moret. She is remembered for her book illustrations.

KIMBEL, Richard M.
American, 19th - 20th century.
Born 1865, in New York; died 1942.
Painter. Local scenes, interiors with figures.

Richard Kimbel was a member of the Salmagundi Club, who awarded him the Vezin Prize in 1930.

MUSEUMS AND GALLERIES:
PHILADELPHIA (Pennsylvania Academy of the Fine Arts Gal.): *The Old Antique Shop*.

KIMBEL, Wilhelm
German, 20th century.
Painter.

Wilhelm Kimbel is probably the eponymous architect born in Breslau (now Wroclaw, Poland) in 1868. He was awarded a gold medal in Berlin in 1908.

KIMBERLEY, Edward I
Irish, 18th century.
Died 1783, in Dublin.
Sculptor.

KIMBERLEY, Edward II
Irish, 18th century.
Active in Dublin.
Sculptor.

KIMBERLEY, Edward III
Irish, 19th century.
Active in Dublin at the beginning of the 19th century.
Sculptor.

KIMBERLEY, John
Irish, 18th century.
Active in Dublin.
Sculptor.

KIMBERLY, Denison
American, 19th century.
Born 1814, in Guilford (Connecticut); died 1863.
Active in Boston.
Painter, engraver. Portraits.

Denison Kimberly engraved illustrations and portraits.

KIMBROUGH, Frank Richmond
American, 19th century.
Born in Tennessee; died 1902, in England.
Active in England.
Draughtsman, illustrator.

Frank Richmond Kimbrough produced book illustrations in England.

KIMFFY
Hungarian, 20th century.
Painter.

Kimffy received an honourable mention at the 1900 Exposition Universelle in Paris.

KIMIKO, real name: Oka
Japanese, 20th century.
Born 1943, in Hyogo Prefecture.
Painter.

Kimiko works in liquitex and acrylics on canvas. In 1969, he showed work in the *Contemporary Japanese Art* exhibition at the Metropolitan Museum in Tokyo and the following year in the 5th JAFA (Japan Art Festival Association) exhibition in New York.

KIMITADA, real name: Kose
Japanese, 10th century.
Painter.

Kimitada was a court painter in the Heian period, active around 950.

KIMMEL, Cornelis
Dutch, 19th century.
Born 23 March 1804, in Middelburg; died 3 January 1877, in Middelburg.
Painter, miniaturist, lithographer. Portraits, landscapes, animals.

Cornelis Kimmel was a pupil of J.-H. Koekkoek and P. van Hanselaere in Ghent.

AUCTION RECORDS:
COLOGNE, 22 June 1979, *Mountain Landscape* (oil on canvas, 24 3/4 x 30 1/4 ins / 63 x 77 cm) DEM 5,000. AMSTERDAM, 11 May 1982, *Winter Scene* (oil on canvas, 21 1/2 x 27 1/2 ins / 54.5

x 70 cm) NLG 8,000. AMSTERDAM, 15 April 1985, *Skaters in a Winter Landscape* (1855, oil on panel, 18 1/4 x 24 1/4 ins / 46.5 x 61.5 cm) NLG 20,000. COLOGNE, 19 Nov 1987, *Landscape with Church and Figures* (oil on canvas, 24 3/4 x 30 ins / 63 x 76.5 cm) DEM 5,500. AMSTERDAM, 17 Sept 1991, *Landscape with Cows and Sheep by a Pond and Ruins in the Distance* (1866, oil on panel, 14 1/2 x 19 3/4 ins / 37 x 50 cm) NLG 4,370. AMSTERDAM, 27 Oct 1997, *Skaters by a Horse-Drawn Carriage, a Koek en Zopie [refreshment stand] in the Distance* (oil on canvas, 14 1/2 x 17 ins / 37 x 43 cm) NLG 10,030.

KIMMICH, Karl
German, 19th century.
Born 23 March 1850, in Blaubeuren; died 2 May 1905, in Ulm.
Painter, draughtsman.

Kimmich studied in Vienna and Berlin, then settled in Ulm, where he taught drawing and became an art historian.

KIMNACH, Ladislaus
Hungarian, 19th century.
Born 1 July 1857, in Budapest; died 9 November 1906, in Budapest.
Painter. Genre scenes.

Ladislaus Kimnach studied at the academy in Munich and also with Benczur at the academy of fine arts in Budapest. He was one of the representatives of an anecdotal, more modernist style that succeeded the history painting favoured in Hungary until the end of the 19th century. He was also a teacher, and Gustave Mikos was one of his pupils.

KIMPE, Raimond
Belgian, 20th century.
Born 1885, in Ghent; died 1970, in Goes, the Netherlands.
Painter.

Raimond Kimpe was a self-taught painter. His style evolved from symbolism to expressionism, and then towards abstraction.

AUCTION RECORDS:

AMSTERDAM, 29 Oct 1980, *Two Farmers* (1938, oil on canvas, 37 x 42 3/4 ins / 94 x 108.5 cm) NLG 6,500. LOKEREN, 28 May 1988, *Woman* (1961, oil on canvas, 22 x 17 3/4 ins / 55 x 45 cm) BEF 36,000. AMSTERDAM, 10 April 1989, *On the Beach* (oil on canvas, 51 1/4 x 39 1/4 ins / 130 x 100 cm) NLG 9,200. AMSTERDAM, 19 Sept 1989, *Woman with a Vase of Flowers* (oil on canvas, 29 1/2 x 25 1/2 ins / 75 x 65 cm) NLG 4,830. AMSTERDAM, 13 Dec 1989, *Abstract Composition* (1961, oil on canvas, 15 3/4 x 11 3/4 ins / 40 x 30 cm) NLG 2,300. AMSTERDAM, 10 April 1990, *Portrait of a Woman* (1943, oil on canvas, 24 3/4 x 17 ins / 63 x 43 cm) NLG 6,900. AMSTERDAM, 22 May 1990, *Man and Woman* (1932, oil on canvas, 27 3/4 x 23 3/4 ins / 70.5 x 60.5 cm) NLG 10,925. AMSTERDAM, 12 Dec 1990, *The Lamp* (1932, oil on canvas, 26 3/4 x 33 3/4 ins / 68 x 86 cm) NLG 8,280. AMSTERDAM, 22 May 1991, *Moored Boats in Zeeland* (oil on canvas, 7 3/4 x 11 3/4 ins / 20 x 30 cm) NLG 3,220. AMSTERDAM, 11 Dec 1991, *Composition with the Faces of Four Young Women* (oil on canvas, 29 1/2 x 19 3/4 ins / 75 x 50 cm) NLG 7,475. AMSTERDAM, 19 May 1992, *Farmer's Wife in Zeeland Province Dress* (1943, oil on canvas, 27 x 19 3/4 ins / 68.5 x 50 cm) NLG 10,350. AMSTERDAM, 8 Dec 1994, *Priest* (oil on sacking, 22 x 20 ins / 55.7 x 51 cm) NLG 6,440. AMSTERDAM, 7 Dec 1995, *View of the Port at Veere* (1937, oil on canvas, 34 1/4 x 36 1/2 ins / 87 x 93 cm) NLG 12,390. AMSTERDAM, 5 June 1996, *The Port at Monnickendam* (oil on canvas, 23 1/2 x 27 1/2 ins / 60 x 70 cm) NLG 6,900. AMSTERDAM, 10 Dec 1996, *Mother and Child* (1961, oil on canvas, 20 1/2 x 19 3/4 ins / 52 x 50 cm) NLG 3,690. AMSTERDAM, 17-18 Dec 1996, 1931, oil on canvas, 26 3/4 x 25 3/4 ins / 68 x 65.5 cm) NLG 9,676. AMSTERDAM, 2-3 June 1997, *Mother and Child* (1963, oil on canvas, 41 1/2 x 33 3/4 ins / 105.5 x 86 cm) NLG 16,520. LOKEREN, 11 Oct 1997, *Young Girl by a Window* (1943, oil on canvas, 29 1/2 x 25 1/2 ins / 75 x 65 cm) BEF 300,000. AMSTERDAM, 21 Jan 1998, *The Stompetoren and Town Hall in Veere* (oil on panel, 11 3/4 x 12 1/4 ins / 30 x 31 cm) NLG 4,036. AMSTERDAM, 1 Dec 1999, *In the Theatre* (1959, oil on canvas, 37 x 26 ins / 95 x 65 cm) NLG 16,000. AMSTERDAM, 1 Dec 1999, *Young Girl* (oil on canvas, 14 x 12 ins / 35 x 30 cm) NLG 20,000. AMSTERDAM, 18 Jan 2000, *Boerenerfje* (1931, oil on canvas, 31 x 33 ins / 80 x 85 cm) NLG 30,000. AMSTERDAM, 30 Nov 2000, *Two Girls* (1962, oil on canvas, 40 x 28 ins / 101 x 70 cm) NLG 22,000. AMSTERDAM, 12 June 2001, *The Street Organ* (c. 1950, oil on canvas, 41 x 33 ins / 104 x 84 cm) NLG 28,000. AMSTERDAM, 26 Nov 2001, *Portrait of Zeeuwse Woman* (1958, oil on canvas, 17 x 11 ins / 44 x 29 cm) NLG 19,000. LOKEREN, 11 May 2002, *Mills in Middelburg* (1931, oil on canvas, 32 x 35 ins / 81 x 90 cm) EUR 18,000. AMSTERDAM, 28 May 2002, *At the Shooting Gallery* (1959, oil on canvas, 39 x 28 ins / 100 x 70 cm) EUR 10,000. AMSTERDAM, 3 June 2003, *Mannequins* (1958, oil on canvas, 37 x 24 ins / 95 x 60 cm) EUR 7,500. AMSTERDAM, 2 Dec 2003, *Boerinnetje* (1936, oil on panel, 15 x 13 ins / 38 x 33 cm) EUR 6,500. AMSTERDAM, 7 June 2004, *Farm in the Snow* (1931, oil on canvas, 31 x 35 ins / 80 x 90 cm) EUR 6,500. LONDON, 20 Oct 2004, *Woman with Cactus* (1950-1955, oil on canvas, 22 x 20 ins / 55 x 50 cm) GBP 6,000.

KIMPFEL, Johann Christoph
German, 18th century.
Born 15 October 1750, in Breslau (now Wroclaw, Poland); died 21 June 1805, in Berlin.
Painter, caricaturist. Historical subjects, portraits, genre scenes. Frescoes.

Kimpfel is known for a *History of Wine*, a series of grisailles, and for a large number of frescoes for castles in the area around Berlin.

KIMURA, Hideki
Japanese, 20th - 21st century.
Born 1948, in Kyoto.
Engraver.

In 1974, Kimura participated in the 9th International Print Biennale in Tokyo.

KIMURA, Kentaro
Japanese, 20th century.
Born 1928, in Tokyo.
Sculptor.

Kimura studied in the department of sculpture, especially working with metal, at the Fine Art University in Tokyo. In his youth, he was fascinated by gadgets and machines, so that sculpting with metal seemed an obvious choice. However, he also took to sculpting in stone, which he felt to be more alive. To avoid objects being in any way predetermined, his works start as uncut stone, generally a block from the quarry, as a kind of nothingness from which the shape emerges. His only rules are concepts of morphology, stability and colour. All traces of the chisel disappear from his polished surfaces. Kimura greatly admired Brancusi for his economy of means. He won a prize at the *New Face of Today* exhibition at the Museum of Modern Art in Kamakura in 1955. In 1957, he showed work at the São Paulo Biennale and in 1965 was awarded the Grand Prize in the 8th International Biennale in Tokyo. From 1967, he exhibited at the JAFA (Japan Art Festival Association).

BIBLIOGRAPHY:

Kentarô, Kimura, *Kimura Kentarô chôkoku sakuhinishû: 1953-1980*, Kimura, Kashiwa, 1982.

AUCTION RECORDS:

LONDON, 11 Dec 1997, *Abstract I and II* (1961, granite, h. 11 ins / 28 cm and 5 ins/13 cm) GBP 1,495.

KIMURA, Kosuke
Japanese, 20th century.
Born 1936.
Engraver.
Kimura's figurative style tends towards symbolism. In 1971, he won the International Grand Prize at the 9th International Print Biennale in Ljubljana and in 1972 at the 1st Print Biennale in Norway. In 1973, he won first prize in the worldwide print competition in San Francisco. In 1974, he participated in the *Japanese Art Today* exhibition at the museum of contemporary art in Montreal.

KIMURA, Reiji
Japanese, 20th century.
Born 1926, in Tokyo.
Active from 1956 in the USA.
Painter, engraver, mixed media.
After graduating from Chiba University in Tokyo in 1948, Reiji Kimura taught drawing in secondary school. His style tends towards the abstract, with oil and metallic paint often combined on canvas, paper or wood. He has lived in New York since 1956. In 1953 and 1954, his work was shown at the Nika exhibition of painting and sculpture. He has had several solo shows in the USA and in Honolulu.

KIMURA, Risaburo
Japanese, 20th century.
Born 1924, in Yokosuka (Kanagawa Prefecture).
Engraver.
After studying philosophy, Kimura turned to engraving. In 1968 he participated in the 8th Exhibition of Contemporary Japanese Art and the International Print Biennale in Tokyo, where he received a prize. He has had several solo exhibitions.
BIBLIOGRAPHY:
Risaburo, Kimura, *Abstract*, Printed by the author, 1975.

KIMURA, Shintaro
Japanese, 20th century.
Active in Tokyo in 1900.
Painter (silk).
Kimura's work was shown at the Exposition Universelle of 1900 in Paris.

KIMURA, Tchuta
Japanese, 20th century.
Born 25 February 1917, in Takamatsu; died 1987.
Active in France from 1953.
Painter, pastellist. Landscapes.
Kimura attended the Academy of Fine Art in Tokyo in 1937 and began exhibiting in 1938 at the Dokuritu exhibition. He remained in his native city until the age of 36, when he moved to Paris. In 1962 he met and became friends with Jean Grenier. Kimura's particular admiration for Bonnard emerged after a period of almost naive paintings, recalling the imagery of Bombois and using a pointillist technique. Almost all his paintings are landscapes in which silhouetted figures sometimes appear. He gives back to Western landscapes what the Nabis and Bonnard had borrowed from Japanese art, seeing Paris in a light of soft greys with hints of gold, heightened with pink. The landscape of the Île de France is bathed in yellow and orange sunlight. His main biographer Jean Grenier explains, 'His ambition is to express the magnificence of things through their tumult.' Kimura himself said of his work, 'What I want most is to paint the world of inner light, to generate forms other than the forms of objects. It's a kind of Impressionism of the soul.' To achieve this, Kimura skilfully used a modern language, combining impasto, drips, scratching, graffiti and flat colour, and giving colour its full force. He participated in many group exhibitions, both in France and abroad. He also showed his work in solo exhibitions, including 1955, 1961, 1964, 1965, 1967, 1969, 1971, 1973, 1975, 1976, 1977, 1980, 1982 in Paris, 1958 in New York, 1959, 1960 in Lyons, 1966, 1968, 1971, 1976, 1978, 1981 and 1983 in Tokyo, 1969 in Antibes, 1974 and 1976 in Brussels and 1982 in Geneva.
BIBLIOGRAPHY:
Grenier, Jean, *Kimura*, exhibition catalogue, Gal. Kriegel, Paris, 1967. Rey, Jean Dominique, *Kimura*, Gal. Takarashi, Tokyo, 1983. *Kimura: Paintings and Works on Paper*, exhibition catalogue, Phillips Collection, Washington DC, 1985. Chuta, Kimura, *Kimura Chuta ten*, National Museum of Modern Art, Tokyo, 1994.
MUSEUMS AND GALLERIES:
PARIS (FNAC): *House in Clos St-Pierre* - PARIS (MAM): *Chatenay Garden* - TOKYO (National MMA): *Valley*.
AUCTION RECORDS:
PARIS, 22 April 1982, *Apple-trees in the Field* (oil on canvas, 35 x 46 ins / 88 x 116 cm) FRF 13,500. NANTERRE, 24 April 1990, *Bunch of Flowers* (oil on canvas, 8 3/4 x 6 1/4 ins / 22.5 x 16 cm) FRF 12,500. PARIS, 17 Oct 1990, *River Marne* (oil on canvas, 9 1/2 x 6 1/4 ins / 24 x 16 cm) FRF 35,000. PARIS, 24 March 1996, *Composition* (oil on canvas, 48 x 47 1/4 ins / 121 x 120 cm) FRF 58,000. PARIS, 20 June 1997, *Versailles* (c. 1963, oil on canvas, 39 1/4 x 39 1/4 ins / 100 x 100 cm) FRF 87,000. PARIS, 22 March 1998, *Still-life* (oil on canvas, 11 x 18 ins / 27 x 46 cm) FRF 10,500.

KIN CHE. See **JIN SHI**

KIN CHENG. See **JIN SHENG**

KIN K'AN. See **JIN KAN**

KIN K'OUEN. See **JIN KUN**

KIN LI-YING. See **JIN LIYING**

KIN NONG. See **JIN NONG**

KIN T'ING-PIAO. See **JIN TINGBIAO**

KIN TA-CHEOU. See **JIN DASHOU**

KIN TSIUN-MING. See **JIN JUNMING**

KIN TSOUEN-NIEN. See **JIN ZUNNIAN**

KIN WEN-TSIN. See **JIN WENJIN**

KIN YUE. See **JIN YUE**

KINAI
Japanese, 17th century.
Print artist.
Kinai appears to have been born in Kyoto. His prints are highly appreciated in Japan.

KINARD, Patricia
Belgian, 20th century.
Painter. Architectural views, landscapes.
Patricia Kinard's works combine elements from architecture (doors, arches, porches) with motifs of whirlwinds, wave forms and clouds, and occasionally uses gold. She travelled to Italy and the USA. In 1992, she took part in *Journey of Artists* organized by the Commune de St-Gilles, and has also held solo exhibitions, particularly in Brussels.

KINCH, Hayter
British, 19th century.
Active in Fareham.
Painter. Sporting subjects, animals.
Hayter Kinch exhibited his work at the Royal Academy in London from 1811 to 1824.
AUCTION RECORDS:
LONDON, 16 May 1990, *Doxy, the Dapple-Grey Mare owned by John Bourke, Earl of Mayo* (1835, oil on canvas, 19 1/2 x 25 1/2 ins / 49.5 x 64.5 cm) GBP 880. LONDON, 20 Nov 1992, *Cyrus, the Bay Horse Owned by Mrs Whitby, in a Coastal Landscape* (1816, oil on canvas, 27 1/2 x 36 ins / 69.8 x 91.4 cm) GBP 4,180. LONDON, 15 June 2000, *Mr Whitby's Hunter Cyrus*

near Newlands Manor (oil on canvas, 26 x 35 ins / 67 x 89 cm) GBP 5,500.

KINCH, Helvig Agnete
Danish, 19th - 20th century.
Born 10 December 1872, in Copenhagen.
Painter. Animals.

Helvig Kinch is known for her pictures of horses and birds.

KIND, Auguste
French, 19th - 20th century.
Born 1 April 1863, in Forbach.
Painter. Flowers.

Auguste Kind studied under P. Thomas, Pierre Bourgogne and Jules Lefebvre. He became a member of the Société des Artistes Français in 1901 and received a commendation in 1903.

MUSEUMS AND GALLERIES:
NANCY (MBA): painting.

AUCTION RECORDS:
PARIS, 26 Jan 1945, *Cypress,* FRF 1,500. PARIS, 28 Feb 1997, *Still-life with Poppies* (oil on card, 18 x 15 ins / 46 x 38 cm) FRF 3,800.

KIND, Georg
German, 20th century.
Born 24 January 1897, in Dresden.
Sculptor, engraver. Animals. Busts, statues.

Georg Kind became a regular artist after World War I, producing busts and groups of dancers and animals.

KINDBERG, Johan Ludwig, or Kindborg
Swedish, 19th century.
Born 30 January 1861, in Stockholm; died 4 January 1907, in Stockholm.
Painter. Figures, landscapes, architectural views.

Johan Kindberg's *View of Stockholm* is in the museum in Stockholm.

AUCTION RECORDS:
STOCKHOLM, 30 Oct 1979, *Landscape* (1890, oil on canvas, 30 x 46 ins / 76 x 117 cm) SEK 14,200. STOCKHOLM, 26 April 1982, *Wooded Landscape* (1889, oil on canvas, 29 1/4 x 49 1/4 ins / 74 x 125 cm) SEK 15,500. STOCKHOLM, 26 April 1983, *Seashore* (1892, oil on canvas, 56 x 32 ins / 142 x 81 cm) SEK 20,500. STOCKHOLM, 8 Dec 1987, *Young Woman with her Dog in Undergrowth* (1882, oil on canvas, 35 3/4 x 28 1/4 ins / 91 x 72 cm) SEK 25,000. STOCKHOLM, 27 May 1999, *Lake Landscape with Flowering Water Lilies* (1886, oil on canvas, 43 x 33 ins / 110 x 84 cm) SEK 32,000. STOCKHOLM, 23 Nov 1999, *Landscape with Man and Cows* (1888, oil on canvas, 26 x 18 ins / 65 x 45 cm) SEK 15,000. STOCKHOLM, 29 May 2000, *Woman in Summer Wood* (1887, watercolour, 12 x 17 ins / 31 x 42 cm) SEK 17,500. STOCKHOLM, 3 Dec 2003, *Girl on Country Road* (1885, oil on canvas, 9 x 7 ins / 23 x 18 cm) SEK 25,000.

KINDBORD, Y.
Swedish, 19th century.
Painter.

Y. Kindbord was a painter in and around Stockholm.

KINDER, Jean de
Flemish School, 18th century.
Born 1675, in Brussels; died 7 December 1739, in Brussels.
Sculptor.

Jean de Kinder travelled in Italy and then spent time in Copenhagen before returning to settle in Brussels. He executed a bust for the tomb of the Alvaredos family in the Dominican church in Brussels.

KINDERDIJK, Bert
Dutch, 20th - 21st century.
Born 1952, in Baarn.
Painter. Still-lifes.

Bert Kinderlijk imitates the 17th-century masters of the trompe l'oeil genre.

BIBLIOGRAPHY:
Nieuwendijk, Koen, *Met engelengeduld (The Patience of a Saint)*, exhibition catalogue, Gal. Lieve Hemel, Amsterdam, 1995.

KINDEREN, Antonius Johannes der.
See **DERKINDEREN**

KINDERMAN, called Tulipano
Dutch, 18th century.
Painter. Flowers.

In Rome Kinderman took the name of Tulipano. In 1722 he was a member of the Pictura group in The Hague. A painter by the name of Kracht Kinderman was in The Hague in 1690.

KINDERMANN, Adolph
German, 19th century.
Born 23 April 1823, in Lübeck; died 16 September 1892, in Hamburg.
Painter. Portraits, genre scenes.

Adolph Kindermann exhibited in Munich, Hanover and Hamburg.

AUCTION RECORDS:
LONDON, 16 June 1982, *Dog Sitting Up and Begging* (1857, oil on canvas, 24 3/4 x 31 1/2 ins / 63 x 80 cm) GBP 4,200. BREMEN, 7 Nov 1987, *The Reunion* (1858, oil on canvas, 37 1/2 x 47 1/4 ins / 95 x 120 cm) DEM 10,000. STOCKHOLM, 19 May 1992, *Man and Woman in an Interior* (oil on canvas, 23 1/2 x 35 3/4 ins / 60 x 91 cm) SEK 13,500. LONDON, 17 March 1995, *Forest in Spring* (1872, oil on canvas, 31 x 25 1/2 ins / 78.8 x 64.7 cm) GBP 7,130. PARIS, 24 March 2002, *Portrait of Antoine Edouard Thouvenel* (1854, oil on canvas, 39 x 32 ins / 100 x 81 cm) EUR 20,000. CRANBROOK, 17 Nov 2002, *Mother and Her Three Children in an Elegant Interior* (oil on canvas, 22 x 18 ins / 56 x 46 cm) GBP 1,350.

KINDERMANN, Anton
German, 18th century.
Born 1725, in Dresden; died 19 April 1793, in Dresden.
Painter.

Anton Kindermann was sent to Italy by King Augustus III. He remained there for 16 years and bought several paintings for the Dresden Gallery.

KINDERMANN, Dominik
Bohemian, 18th - 19th century.
Born 8 November 1739, in Schluckenau (Sluknov); died 9 June 1817, in Vienna.
Painter. History painting.

Dominik Kindermann was a pupil of his uncle, the sculptor Klein, in Prague. He also studied with the painter Rab and with Franz Palko at the Akademie der Bildenden Künste in Vienna. In 1769, a protector enabled him to work in Rome under the direction of R. Mengs, where Raphael and Annibal Carracci were the masters he preferred to study. He remained in Rome for six years, and his most important painting from this period was an altarpiece of *St Pius*.

Kindermann then went to Naples, where he studied the ruins of Pompeii. His most notable paintings are *Death of Joseph* and the *Birth of Christ* (in the cathedral at Ehrenberg) and *Martyrdom of St Sebastian and St Jude* (in the cathedral at Schawink). Among his many portraits, that of the count of Harrach is worthy of mention.

KINDERMANS, Jan Baptist
Belgian, 19th century.
Born 1821 or 1822, in Antwerp; died 11 August 1876, in Antwerp.
Painter. Landscapes.

Jan Kindermans lived in Switzerland; he travelled in England and Italy and exhibited from time to time in Paris. He was made a member of the Order of Leopold in 1863 and was an active Belgian member of the teaching body in 1866. His paintings from nature of the Ardennes region are reminiscent of Courbet.

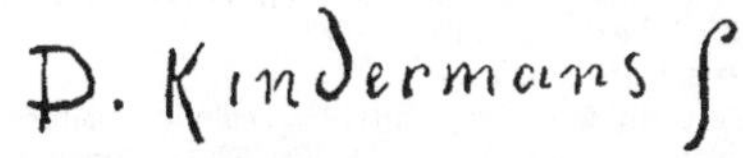

Museums and Galleries:
Antwerp: views and landscapes - Brussels: landscapes - Rheims: *Animals.*
Auction records:
Paris, 1866, *The Storm,* FRF 380. Paris, 25 June 1943, *The Little Shepherd Boy,* FRF 12,600. Paris, 14 March 1955, *Landscape,* FRF 90,000. Brussels, 29 Oct 1980, *Landscape* (oil on canvas, 23½ x 35½ ins / 60 x 90 cm) BEF 280,000. Vienna, 14 March 1984, *Young Fishermen by a River* (oil on canvas, 22¾ x 33¾ ins / 58 x 86 cm) ATS 45,000. New York, 23 May 1985, *Summer Landscape* (oil on canvas, 20 x 23½ ins / 50.7 x 59.6 cm) USD 3,750. Lokeren, 11 March 1995, *The Nature Lover* (1849, oil on panel, 21¼ x 15¾ ins / 54 x 40 cm) BEF 180,000. New Orleans, 8 Dec 2001, *Landscape with Church* (oil on canvas, 17 x 23 ins / 43 x 58 cm) USD 2,400. Lokeren, 11 May 2002, *View of the Ourthe* (oil on canvas, 35 x 51 ins / 90 x 129 cm) EUR 8,000. Lokeren, 7 Dec 2002, *The Banks of the Semois* (1868, oil on canvas, 37 x 55 ins / 94 x 139 cm) EUR 5,000.

KINDLER, Albert
German, 19th century.
Born 1833, in Allenbach; died 14 April 1876, in Meran (now Merano, Italy).
Painter. Genre scenes.

Kindler studied at the academy of fine arts in Munich, then with R. Jordan in Düsseldorf before travelling in Spain and settling in Düsseldorf. He exhibited in Düsseldorf, Vienna, Hanover and Berlin, where he won a gold medal in 1868.
Auction records:
Rotterdam, 1891, *Disappointment in Love,* FRF 220. Munich, 19-20 March 1969, *The Wedding,* DEM 9,000. Lucerne, 30 June 1973, *The Proposal,* CHF 13,000. New York, 14 May 1976, *Reading to Grandmother* (oil on panel, 16¼ x 12½ ins / 41 x 32 cm) USD 1,500. Cologne, 12 June 1980, *Visiting Grandfather* (oil on canvas, 20 x 26½ ins / 51 x 67 cm) DEM 5,000. Cologne, 26 June 1981, *Wedding on the Banks of the Rhine* (oil on canvas, 42¼ x 56¾ ins / 107.5 x 144 cm) DEM 40,000. Cologne, 19 May 2001, *Reading Session* (oil on panel, 6 x 5 ins / 16 x 13 cm) DEM 4,500. Berlin, 30 Nov 2001, *Girl with Doll's Pram* (oil on canvas, 26 x 21 ins / 67 x 54 cm) DEM 3,700. London, 7 Oct 2004, *Enchanting Entertainment* (oil on canvas, 25 x 31 ins / 64 x 79 cm) GBP 1,500.

KINDLER, Ludwig
French, 19th - 20th century.
Born 16 March 1875, in Strasbourg.
Active in Munich.
Sculptor. Busts.

Ludwig Kindler executed busts of King Ludwig III of Bavaria and his wife.

KINDLUND, Anna Belle Wing
American, 19th - 20th century.
Born 18 February 1876, in Buffalo; died 1922.
Miniaturist. Portraits.

Anna Belle Wing Kindlund worked in New York.

KINDON, Mary Evelina
British, 19th - 20th century.
Born 1849; died 1919, in Watford.
Active in Croydon.
Painter, watercolourist. Genre scenes, urban landscapes.

Mary Kindon was a frequent exhibitor at the Royal Academy and the Suffolk Street Gallery in London. She also exhibited at the Institute of Painters in Watercolours from 1874.
Auction records:
London, 12 June 1987, *Street Scene with Figures* (oil on canvas, 21¼ x 17¼ ins / 54.1 x 43.5 cm) GBP 3,000. London, 3 June 1999, *Poem* (oil on canvas, 30 x 40 ins / 76 x 101 cm) GBP 7,000.

KINDT, David, or Kind
Flemish School, 17th century.
Born 1580, in Hamburg; died 26 February 1652, in Hamburg.
Painter.

David Kindt, son of Johann Kind, was a portrait painter.
Museums and Galleries:
Hamburg: *Portraits of the Artist, his Mother, Ditmar Koel, Gertrud Moller and a Couple.*
Auction records:
Paris, 22 May 1951, *Portrait of an Elderly Lady,* FRF 17,000.

KINDT, Isabelle
Maiden name: Van Asche
Belgian, 19th century.
Active in Brussels c. 1830.
Watercolourist.

KINDT, Johann
Flemish School, 16th century.
Born in Courtrai; died 20 June 1608, probably in Hamburg.
Also active in Germany.
Painter.
Hamburg School.

Johann Kindt fled from religious persecution in Courtrai to Hamburg, where he became a master on 10 February 1587.

KINDT, Laurence
Belgian, 19th century.
Born 1805, in Brussels; died 25 March 1863, in Charleroi.
Painter. Landscapes.

Laurence Kindt was a pupil of Edouard Delvaux and painted many views of Brussels and Liège.

KINDT, Marie Adélaïde, called Adèle
Belgian, 19th century.
Born 16 December 1804, in Brussels; died 1884, in Brussels.
Painter. History painting, genre scenes, portraits.

Marie Kindt was the sister of Laurence. For a time she was a pupil of Louis David and also worked with Sophie Fremiet and Navez. In 2002 the Koninklijk Museum voor Schone Kunsten (Royal Museum for Fine Art) in Antwerp held a major exhibition of her work.
Museums and Galleries:
Brussels: *Philip II and Elizabeth of France* - Courtrai: *Van Dyck Allows Peasants to Admire his St Martin; The Vine Grower.*
Auction records:
Brussels, 20 Feb 1980, *Melanchton Presiding over the Future of the Young Prince of Orange, the Future William I* (1828, oil on canvas, 45 x 51¼ ins / 114 x 130 cm) BEF 110,000. London, 25 March 1987, *Portrait of a Woman Sitting in a Landscape* (1829, oil on canvas, 69¼ x 52 ins / 176 x 132 cm) GBP 12,000. London, 16 Nov 1994, *Portrait of a Lady Dressed in Black in a Landscape* (1829, oil on canvas, 69¼ x 52 ins / 176 x 132 cm) GBP 4,025.

KINDYNIS, Anna
Greek, 20th century.
Born 19 March 1914.
Active in France from 1945.
Painter.

Anna Kindynis lived in Paris from 1945 and started to exhibit there in 1947. Her painting style is realist with overtones of pathos.

KINEL, T.
Painter. Portraits.
MUSEUMS AND GALLERIES:
MOSCOW (State Tretyakov Gal.): *Self-portrait*.

KING, Agnes Gardner
British, 19th century.
Active in London.
Miniaturist.
Agnes Gardner King exhibited at the Royal Academy, at the Suffolk Street Gallery and, especially, at the New Water-Colour Society, beginning in 1882.
MUSEUMS AND GALLERIES:
LONDON (National Portrait Gal.): *James Thomson* (1838, pencil, after Elizabeth King, née Thomson); *Baron Kelvin with his Brother and Sister* (charcoal).

KING, Albert Francis
American, 19th - 20th century.
Born 1854; died 1934.
Painter. Still-lifes (flowers/fruit).
AUCTION RECORDS:
NEW YORK, 19 June 1981, *Still-life with Watermelon* (oil on canvas, 22 x 27 ins / 55.9 x 68.6 cm) USD 19,000. NEW YORK, 2 June 1983, *Still-life with Watermelon and Knife* (oil on canvas, 18 x 24 1/4 ins / 45.8 x 61.5 cm) USD 8,500. NEW YORK, 30 May 1985, *Still-life with Watermelon* (oil on canvas, 20 x 27 ins / 50.8 x 68.5 cm) USD 9,000. NEW YORK, 1 Oct 1987, *Pears, Grapes, Apples and Cantaloupe Melon* (1894, oil on canvas remounted on board, 18 x 27 1/4 ins / 45.7 x 69.2 cm) USD 4,500. NEW YORK, 24 June 1988, *Basket of Cherries* (oil on canvas, 9 3/4 x 13 3/4 ins / 25 x 35 cm) USD 3,410. NEW YORK, 30 May 1990, *Pears and Apples in a Plate* (1901, oil on canvas, 14 x 18 ins / 35.6 x 45.5 cm) USD 2,420. NEW YORK, 14 March 1991, *Peaches and Melon* (oil on canvas, 12 x 18 ins / 30.5 x 46 cm) USD 4,400. NEW YORK, 26 Sept 1991, *Copper Pan Full of Apples* (oil on canvas, 12 x 18 ins / 30.5 x 45.5 cm) USD 3,850. NEW YORK, 18 Dec 1991, *Still-life with a Watermelon and Other Fruit* (1884, oil on canvas/card, 4 x 5 3/4 ins / 10.2 x 14.9 cm) USD 2,750. NEW YORK, 15 April 1992, *Still-life with a Pipe, Pretzels and Cheese* (oil on canvas, 14 x 20 ins / 35.6 x 50.8 cm) USD 1,760. NEW YORK, 31 March 1994, *Geranium and Cherries* (oil on canvas, 20 x 13 ins / 50.8 x 33 cm) USD 8,913. NEW YORK, 27 Sept 1996, *Apples in a Basket* (oil on canvas/panel, 18 x 24 ins / 46 x 61 cm) USD 5,175. NEW YORK, 23 April 1997, *Still-life with a Melon and Peaches* (oil on canvas, 14 x 18 ins / 35.5 x 45.7 cm) USD 3,450.

KING, Berkeley
British, 19th century.
Active in London at the beginning of the 19th century.
Painter, engraver, lithographer. Landscapes.
Berkeley King mostly painted moonlit scenes. He occasionally exhibited his work at the Royal Academy, the British Institution and at the Suffolk Street Gallery between 1814 and 1835.

KING, Brian
Irish, 20th century.
Born 1942, in Dublin.
Sculptor, painter.
Minimal Art.
Brian King studied in Dublin at the National College of Art. In 1969, he took part in the Paris Biennale, where he was awarded a bursary, and in 1973, again in Paris, in the *Art Irlandais Actuel* (*Contemporary Irish Art*) exhibition at the Musée d'Art Moderne de la Ville. He held his first solo exhibition in Dublin in 1968. In 1965, he received the Carroll Prize at the *Irish Living Art* exhibition. King's work can be described as minimal abstract.
BIBLIOGRAPHY:
Art irlandais actuel, exhibition catalogue, Musée d'Art Moderne de la Ville de Paris, Paris, 1973.
MUSEUMS AND GALLERIES:
BELFAST (Ulster Mus.): *Zig* (*Zig*) (1969, sculpture, painted plywood, plexiglas); *Red Shift* (*Red Shift*) (1969, sculpture, painted wood, plastic) - DUBLIN (Hugh Lane Gal.).

KING, Carl Friedrich
German, 18th century.
Born c. 1708; died 1738, in Halle.
Painter, engraver (etching).
King studied with Pesne.

KING, Cecil George Charles
British, 20th century.
Born 6 August 1881, in Gunnersburg.
Painter, illustrator. Seascapes, landscapes.
Cecil George Charles King trained in Paris under Jean-Paul Laurens and De Steinlen. He exhibited in London from 1906, and in Paris from 1907. He was a regular contributor to the *Illustrated London News*.

KING, Charles
British, 18th century.
Born in England; died 1756, in Berlin.
Active in Germany.
Sculptor.
Charles King established himself in Berlin where he was the official court sculptor for King Frederick I of Prussia.

KING, Charles Bird
American, 19th century.
Born 1785 or 1786, in Newport (Rhode Island); died 1862, in Washington DC.
Painter, illustrator. Portraits, local figures, still-lifes, vanitas.
Charles Bird King was a pupil of the portrait artist and engraver Edward Savage between 1800 and 1805. He worked in London between 1805 and 1812 under Benjamin West, Charles Leslie and Washington Allston. He spent 40 years in Washington DC, where he painted many eminent people. As well as his portraits, he painted *Vanitas* and still-lifes in *trompe l'œil*, exceptional in the USA.

King is particularly famous for producing the portraits of Native American chiefs who visited Washington DC in 1821. He worked on the highly valued *History of the Indian Tribes of North America, with Biographical Sketches and Anecdotes of the Principal Chiefs* (1836-1844) by Thomas L. McKenney, former director of the Office of Indian Affairs, and James Hall. This work is an essential witness to the history of the Native Americans of the USA. In 1865 a fire at the Smithsonian in Washington DC destroyed most of the original works which were used for the lithographs for the book.

King's work was the subject of an exhibition at the Smithsonian Institute in Washington DC in 1977.
BIBLIOGRAPHY:
Cosentino, Andrew J., *The paintings of Charles Bird King*, Smithsonian Institution Press, Washington DC, 1977.
Moore, Robert John, *Native Americans: a portrait. The art and travels of Charles Bird King, George Catlin, and Karl Bodmer*, Stewart, Tabori and Chang, New York, 1997.
MUSEUMS AND GALLERIES:
CAMBRIDGE, MA (Fogg AM, Harvard University): *The Vanity of the Artist's Dream* - CORAL GABLES (Lowe AM, University of Miami): *Portrait of Julcee Mathla (Tukose Emathla), a Seminole Chief* (1826, oil/panel) - WASHINGTON DC (Smithsonian American AM): *Portrait of Four Indians* (1821, oil on canvas).

Auction records:
New York, 21 May 1970, *Red Jacket, a Senaca Chief,* USD 27,000. New York, 11 April 1973, *A Potawatomi Chief,* USD 26,000. New York, 10 June 1976, *Portrait of Miss M. M. Calhoun* (1858/1859, oil on canvas, 30 x 25 ins / 76.2 x 63.5 cm) USD 700. New York, 29 April 1977, *Portrait of Keesheswa* (charcoal, 9 x 6 1/4 ins / 23 x 15.8 cm) USD 2,900. New York, 2 June 1983, *Rantchewaime* (charcoal/grey paper, 9 1/2 x 6 1/2 ins / 24.1 x 16.5 cm) USD 4,000. New York, 3 June 1983, *Unhappy Love* (oil on panel, 30 1/4 x 25 ins / 77 x 62.6 cm) USD 3,200. New York, 31 May 1985, *Red Ribbon* (oil on panel, 24 x 19 ins / 61 x 48.2 cm) USD 2,600. New York, 25 May 1989, *Still-life with Apples, Pears, Plums and Grapes* (oil on canvas, 25 x 30 ins / 63.4 x 76.4 cm) USD 55,000. New York, 24 May 1990, *'Nesouaquoit', Bear in a Fork in the Branches, an Indian Chief* (oil on canvas, 35 1/2 x 29 1/2 ins / 90.2 x 74.9 cm) USD 385,000. New York, 17 March 1994, *'No-Tin' (The Wind), Chippewa Indian* (charcoal and white chalk/paper, 10 1/4 x 6 1/4 ins / 26 x 15.9 cm) USD 5,463. New York, 25 May 1995, *Still-life with Game* (1806, oil on canvas, 14 x 11 ins / 35.6 x 27.9 cm) USD 14,950. New York, 27 Sept 1996, *Portrait of Mrs William Creighton* (oil on canvas, 36 x 28 ins / 91.5 x 71.1 cm) USD 2,530. New York, 12 Jan 1999, *Pomegranetes, Grapes and Pineapples* (oil on canvas, 25 x 30 ins / 63 x 76 cm) USD 14,000. Pittsfield, 12 May 2001, *Portrait of Samuel L. Southard. Portrait of William Wirt* (oil on canvas, a pair, 24 x 20 ins / 61 x 51 cm) USD 9,000.

KING, Charles Brady
American, 19th - 20th century.
Born 2 February 1869, on Angel Island (California); died 1957, in Rye (New York).
Painter, engraver.
Charles B. King studied under Jean-Paul Laurens in Paris.

KING, Daniel
British, 17th century.
Died c. 1664, in London.
Engraver (burin).
Daniel King was probably a pupil of Hollar, with whom he worked and whose style he imitated. He engraved the plates for Dugdale's *Monasticon* which, however, did not please the author. In 1656, he published *The Cathedral and Conventual Churches of England and Wales,* a series of 50 engravings after his own drawings; Hollat also supplied some engravings for the publication. The same year, King published *The Vale Royal of Cheshire,* which he illustrated with engravings based on his drawings. He is also mentioned as having produced views of castles, churches and ancient monuments.

KING, Edith Lawrence
American, 19th - 20th century.
Born in Chelsea (Massachusetts).
Painter.

KING, Edward
British, 19th - 20th century.
Born 1863, in London.
Painter. Genre scenes, landscapes.
Edward King was a student of Bouguereau and Robert Fleury in Paris. In 1913 and 1914, he exhibited at the Salon des Artistes Français.
Auction records:
London, 3 Feb 1993, *Tower Bridge* (1912, oil on canvas, 24 x 30 ins / 61 x 76 cm) GBP 747. New York, 18-19 July 1996, *A Considerate Suitor* (oil on canvas, 20 x 30 ins / 50.8 x 76.2 cm) USD 8,050. Penzance, 12 July 2001, *Tug of War, St Ives Harbour* (1894, oil on canvas, 24 x 30 ins / 60 x 75 cm) GBP 6,600.

KING, Edward R.
British, 19th century.
Active in Petersfield (Hampshire).
Painter. Genre scenes.
Edward R. King was a frequent exhibitor at the Royal Academy in London beginning in 1889. He does not appear to be the same person as the Edward King born in 1863.

KING, Eleonore
American, 20th century.
Born 5 April 1909, in Manlow (Oklahoma).
Painter, watercolourist, decorative designer. Battles, figures, nudes, landscapes, seascapes, still-lifes, flowers.
Eleonore King has exhibited in the USA since 1937, and, since 1964, she has shown her works regularly in Paris, notably in 1982 and 1983. She was awarded the Médaille d'Argent de la Ville de Paris in 1968. She paints seascapes with energy, and a streak of Expressionism.
Museums and Galleries:
Denver (History Mus.) - Wheaton (Cantigny Mus.).

KING, Emma B.
American, 20th century.
Born in Indianapolis.
Painter. Figures.
Emma King studied under William M. Chase in New York and, in Paris, under Boulanger, Jules Lefebvre, Carolus Duran, and Frank. E. Scott. She lived and worked in Indianapolis.
Auction records:
New York, 10 June 1976, *Young Woman Carrying her Child on her Back* (oil on canvas, 54 x 44 ins / 137 x 112 cm) USD 1,300.

KING, Emma Brownlow (Mrs)
British, 19th century.
Painter. Genre scenes.
Mrs Emma Brownlow King was active in London, where she was a frequent exhibitor at the Royal Academy, the British Institution and at the Suffolk Street Gallery from 1852 to 1873.
Museums and Galleries:
London (Foundling Mus.): *Foundling Girl at Christmas Dinner* (1877, oil on canvas); *The Foundling restored to its Mother* (1858, oil on canvas).
Auction records:
London, 7 Nov 1997, *Foundling Returned to its Mother* (1863, oil on canvas, 25 1/4 x 30 1/4 ins / 63.9 x 76.9 cm) GBP 8,280.

KING, Eric
British, 20th century.
Born 1904.
Engraver.
Eric King was a print-maker and book illustrator specialising in woodcuts.

KING, Ethel Slade
British, 19th century.
Active in London.
Painter, draughtswoman.
Ethel Slade King was a frequent exhibitor at the Royal Academy after 1884.

KING, Francis Scott
American, 19th century.
Born 24 March 1850, in Auburn (New York State); died 1913, in Newark (New Jersey).
Active in Ledgewood (New Jersey).
Painter, illustrator, engraver (wood).
Francis Scott King was a pupil of John W. Orr and August Will in New York. He won medals at the Exposition Universelle in Paris in 1889, in Chicago in 1893 and in Buffalo in

1901. His work also featured in the Exposition de Paris in 1900. He founded the Society of American Wood Engravers.

KING, Frederic Leonard
American, 19th - 20th century.
Born 31 August 1879, in New York; died 1947, in Rockport.
Painter.

Frederic Leonard King studied under Bridgman, Chase and Arthur W. Dow. He was a member of the Salmagundi Club.

KING, G.
British, 18th century.
Active in London.
Sculptor.

G. King was an occasional exhibitor at the Society of Artists and at the Free Society between 1771 and 1778.

KING, George
British, 18th century.
Active c. 1740.
Engraver.

George King worked mostly for publishers although he also produced some portraits. Of these, the most noteworthy are *Richard Gwinnel, Poet; Lady Falconberg;* and *Mrs Elizabeth Thomas.*

KING, Giles
British, 18th century.
Born in London.
Active in the middle of the 18th century.
Engraver.

Giles King lived in London and made engravings of the works of Arnout van Aken.

KING, Gillis
American, 20th century.
Born 8 February 1904, in Dewville (Texas).
Painter. Landscapes.

Gillis King studied under Michel Jacobs and George Bridgman. He was a member of the American Federation of Arts.

KING, Gunning. See **KING William Gunning**

KING, H.
British, 19th century.
Active in London.
Sculptor.

H. King exhibited at the Royal Academy and at the Suffolk Street Gallery between 1828 and 1845.

KING, Hamilton
American, 19th - 20th century.
Born 21 December 1871, in Lewiston (Maine); died 1952.
Painter.

Hamilton King studied at the Académie Julian in Paris. He was a member of the American Federation of Arts.

AUCTION RECORDS:
NEW YORK, 5 Feb 1902, *American Beauty,* USD 110.

KING, Haynes
British, 19th century.
Born 1831, in Barbados; died 17 May 1904, in London, as the result of an accident.
Painter, watercolourist. Genre scenes, rustic scenes, interiors with figures, flowers, fruit.

Haynes King came to England from Barbados in 1854 and worked in London at Leigh's Academy. He died an accidental death, crushed by a train.

He began to exhibit in 1855 and thereafter his work was seen very frequently in the exhibitions at the Royal Academy, at the British Institution and, in particular, at the Suffolk Street Gallery. He was named a member of the Society of British Artists in 1864. His work is sought after.

MUSEUMS AND GALLERIES:
LEEDS (City AG): *An Interesting Paragraph* (oil on canvas) - LONDON (Victoria and Albert Mus.): *Jealousy and Flirtatiousness.*

AUCTION RECORDS:
LONDON, 24 June 1909, *In the Springtime* (1863) GBP 5. LONDON, 4 Dec 1909, *The Tender Mother* (1879) GBP 32. LONDON, 28 Jan 1972, *Country Woman Sitting on the Doorstep,* Gns 320. LONDON, 9 April 1974, *An Incident at the Farm,* GBP 850. VIENNA, 13 Jan 1976, *Rest Under the Trees* (1874, oil on canvas, 20 x 24 ins / 51 x 61 cm) ATS 18,000. LONDON, 14 June 1977, *The New Dress* (oil on canvas, 13½ x 17½ ins / 34 x 44.5 cm) GBP 750. LONDON, 6 June 1980, *An amusing incident* (oil on canvas, 17¾ x 23¾ ins / 45 x 60.2 cm) GBP 1,000. LONDON, 12 Feb 1982, *Taking it easy* (oil on panel, 12 x 10 ins / 30.5 x 25.4 cm) GBP 1,200. LONDON, 2 March 1984, *Repairing the Nets* (oil on canvas, 18 x 14 ins / 46 x 35.6 cm) GBP 1,500. LONDON, 18 Dec 1985, *Family in an Interior* (1872, oil on canvas, 28 x 37 ins / 71 x 94 cm) GBP 7,500. LONDON, 15 June 1988, *Anxious Look* (1866, oil on canvas, 12 x 10 ins / 30.5 x 25.5 cm) GBP 2,640. LONDON, 13 Feb 1991, *Waiting for the Fishermen to Return* (oil on canvas, 12 x 8¼ ins / 30.5 x 21 cm) GBP 1,430. AMSTERDAM, 19 April 1994, *Young Goose-girls in a Farmyard* (oil on canvas, 23½ x 35¾ ins / 60 x 91 cm) NLG 3,220. LONDON, 7 June 1995, *Fruit and Flowers* (1863, oil on canvas, 30½ x 25¼ ins / 77.5 x 64 cm) GBP 4,830. DONCASTER, 18 July 1999, *Lesson in Lacemaking* (oil on canvas, 8 x 6 ins / 20 x 15 cm) GBP 1,050. LONDON, 6 June 2001, *Letter* (1872, oil on canvas, 20 x 16 ins / 51 x 41 cm) GBP 10,000. LONDON, 26 Sept 2001, *Little Sunshine* (1868, oil on canvas, 14 x 18 ins / 35 x 46 cm) GBP 7,500. LONDON, 1 May 2002, *Interesting News* (oil on canvas, 14 x 18 ins / 36 x 46 cm) GBP 7,500. LONDON, 2 Dec 2002, *Homeless* (1872, oil on canvas, 36 x 28 ins / 91 x 71 cm) GBP 13,000. LONDON, 23 March 2004, *Reading the News* (oil on canvas, 14 x 12 ins / 36 x 31 cm) GBP 4,000. KNOWLE, 29 June 2004, *Taking it Easy* (oil on panel, 12 x 10 ins / 30 x 25 cm) GBP 2,900.

KING, Henrietta
American, 20th century.
Painter.

KING, Henry John Yeend
British, 19th - 20th century.
Born 21 August 1855, in London; died 10 June 1924.
Painter, watercolourist. Genre scenes, landscapes with figures.

Henry John Yeend King trained in Paris under Léon Bonnat and Fernand Cormon. He exhibited regularly in London at the Royal Academy from 1879, and at the Suffolk Street Gallery from 1874. He was a member of the Royal Society of British Artists, and vice-president of the Royal Institute of Painters in Watercolours. He exhibited in Berlin and Munich, and won a bronze medal at the Paris Exposition Universelle of 1889. The Tate Gallery in London acquired his painting *Milking Time* in 1898. His paintings of farm-girls in rustic landscapes are popular and highly sought after.

BIBLIOGRAPHY:
'*Henry King*' in *Pall Mall Pictures of 1911,* periodical, Pall Mall, London, 1911.

MUSEUMS AND GALLERIES:
LIVERPOOL: *From Green to Gold* - READING: *Old Newbury; Meditation; Aldermaston; Poet and Countryman* - ROCHDALE (Art Gallery): *River Banks and Blossoms* - SHEFFIELD: *Garden by a River; Farm on the Kentish Coast* - SYDNEY: *Garden by a River.*

AUCTION RECORDS:
LONDON, 30 Nov 1907, *Old Cottages near Blandford* (watercolour) GBP 6. LONDON, 9 Dec 1907, *The Fisherman's Corner,* GBP 36. LONDON, 25 April 1908, *Summer,* GBP 31. LONDON, 23 April 1910, *In the Garden,* GBP 40. LONDON, 14 April 1924,

Milkmaid, GBP 36. LONDON, 24 April 1925, *Field Path,* GBP 39. LONDON, 4 June 1926, *Path in Buckinghamshire,* GBP 34. LONDON, 5 Dec 1927, *Ducks,* GBP 22. LONDON, 20 Feb 1970, *Inn by a River,* GBP 200. LONDON, 2 Nov 1971, *Picking Flowers,* GBP 180. LONDON, 20 Nov 1973, *Summer Landscape,* GBP 1,300. LONDON, 8 June 1976, *Girls Fishing at Low Tide* (oil on canvas, 22½ x 35½ ins / 57 x 90 cm) GBP 320. NEW YORK, 7 Oct 1977, *Spring Landscape* (oil on canvas, 34¼ x 44 ins / 87 x 112 cm) USD 1,100. LONDON, 12 Dec 1978, *The Miller's Daughter* (oil on panel, 17½ x 13½ ins / 44.5 x 34.5 cm) GBP 1,500. LONDON, 15 May 1979, *Fetching Water* (oil on canvas, 29¼ x 44 ins / 74 x 112 cm) GBP 1,900. LONDON, 6 Oct 1983, *At the Garden Gate* (oil on canvas, 24 x 36 ins / 61 x 91.5 cm) GBP 4,300. NEW YORK, 1 March 1984, *Boat Trip* (oil on canvas, 20 x 29¾ ins / 50.8 x 75.5 cm) USD 3,200. LONDON, 1 Oct 1986, *Farm by a Duck Pond* (oil on canvas, 23½ x 35¾ ins / 60 x 91 cm) GBP 6,200. LONDON, 15 Dec 1987, *End of the Village* (watercolour and pencil heightened with gouache, 20 x 30 ins / 50.8 x 76.2 cm) GBP 1,000. LONDON, 15 June 1988, *May Day* (oil on canvas, 24 x 36 ins / 61 x 91.5 cm) GBP 3,850. LONDON, 23 Sept 1988, *Young Boys Crabbing on the Quay* (oil on canvas, 26¼ x 37 ins / 66.5 x 94 cm) GBP 9,350. LONDON, 27 Sept 1989, *Day Dreams* (oil on canvas, 18 x 24 ins / 46 x 61 cm) GBP 9,350. NEW YORK, 25 Oct 1989, *Picking Apple Blossoms* (oil on canvas, 36 x 28¼ ins / 91.4 x 72 cm) USD 12,100. LONDON, 13 Dec 1989, *Flower Garden in May* (oil on card, 24 x 18 ins / 61 x 46 cm) GBP 5,500. LONDON, 21 March 1990, *Children Feeding the Ducks* (oil on reinforced canvas, 14¼ x 9¾ ins / 36 x 25 cm) GBP 2,090. STOCKHOLM, 16 May 1990, *Homewards - Summer Landscape with Buildings* (oil on canvas, 16¼ x 24 ins / 41 x 61 cm) SEK 18,500. LONDON, 15 June 1990, *Lyndale, Devon* (oil on canvas, 62 x 87¾ ins / 157.5 x 223 cm) GBP 7,700. LONDON, 26 Sept 1990, *Country Lane* (watercolour heightened with gouache, 14 x 10 ins / 35.5 x 25.5 cm) GBP 1,210. NEW YORK, 24 Oct 1990, *Two Peasant Girls Picking Faggots on Path* (oil on canvas, 24 x 36 ins / 61 x 91.5 cm) USD 8,800. MONTREAL, 5 Nov 1990, *Young Boy Fishing* (oil on canvas, 18 x 24 ins / 46 x 61 cm) CAD 1,320. LONDON, 5 June 1991, *Driving Geese* (oil on canvas, 14½ x 20¾ ins / 37 x 53 cm) GBP 1,815. LONDON, 11 Oct 1991, *Crossing the Lake* (oil on canvas, 36¼ x 60 ins / 92 x 152.5 cm) GBP 4,400. LONDON, 12 June 1992, *The Last Assignation* (oil on canvas, 40¼ x 31¼ ins / 102.2 x 79.5 cm) GBP 3,080. LONDON, 13 Nov 1992, *Elegant Conversation* (oil on canvas, 18 x 26 ins / 45.9 x 66 cm) GBP 3,850. NEW YORK, 17 Feb 1993, *Expected Arrival* (oil on canvas, 50½ x 49 ins / 128.3 x 124.5 cm) USD 8,050. NEW YORK, 28 May 1993, *Off to School* (oil on canvas, 36 x 28¼ ins / 91.6 x 71.7 cm) USD 6,900. LONDON, 5 Nov 1993, *Duck Pond* (oil on canvas, 41 x 59¼ ins / 104.2 x 150.5 cm) GBP 17,250. NEW YORK, 20 July 1995, *My Pet Rabbit* (oil on canvas, 18 x 14 ins / 45.7 x 35.6 cm) USD 5,462. LONDON, 27 March 1996, *Waiting for the Ferry* (oil on canvas, 37 x 28¾ ins / 94 x 73 cm) GBP 6,440. LONDON, 5 June 1996, *Road to the Mill* (oil on canvas, 48 x 72 ins / 122 x 183 cm) GBP 84,000. LONDON, 6 Nov 1996, *At the Garden Gate* (oil on panel, 15¾ x 12 ins / 40 x 30.5 cm) GBP 3,450; *Peaceful Village* (oil on canvas, 54¼ x 40¼ ins / 137.5 x 102 cm) GBP 20,700. LONDON, 8 Nov 1996, *Picking Poppies* (oil on canvas, 29¾ x 40 ins / 75.7 x 101.4 cm) GBP 19,000. LONDON, 12 March 1997, *Feeding the Geese* (oil on canvas, 52½ x 39 ins / 133.5 x 99 cm) GBP 18,400. NEW YORK, 6 May 1999, *Rest on the Way* (oil on canvas, 40 x 30 ins / 102 x 76 cm) USD 26,000. LONDON, 4 Nov 1999, *Gossips* (oil on canvas, 20 x 30 ins / 51 x 76 cm) GBP 13,000. LONDON, 13 June 2000, *Haymaking* (oil on canvas, 60 x 40 ins / 153 x 102 cm) GBP 40,000. PORTLAND, 2 Aug 2000, *At the Duck Pond* (oil on canvas, 40 x 30 ins / 102 x 76 cm) USD 40,000. PORTLAND, 8 Aug 2001, *In the Garden* (oil on canvas, 40 x 30 ins / 102 x 76 cm) USD 16,000. TORONTO, 26 Nov 2001, *Feeding the Swans* (oil on canvas, 36 x 28 ins / 91 x 71 cm) CAD 26,000. TORONTO, 3 June 2002, *Rush Gatherers* (oil on canvas, 20 x 30 ins / 51 x 76 cm) CAD 15,000. LONDON, 19 Nov 2002, *Tranquil Moment* (oil on canvas, 54 x 41 ins / 137 x 103 cm) GBP 11,000. UPPSALA, 25 May 2003, *Summer Landscape with Women at a Well* (oil on canvas, 36 x 28 ins / 92 x 71 cm) SEK 135,000. LONDON, 27 Nov 2003, *Days at the Well* (oil on canvas, 36 x 28 ins / 92 x 72 cm) GBP 18,000. EXETER, 2 March 2004, *Gathering Water from a Summer Stream* (oil on canvas, 23 x 35 ins / 59 x 89 cm) GBP 4,800. BUENOS AIRES, 11 Aug 2004, *Watching the Bees* (oil on canvas, 40 x 30 ins / 102 x 76 cm) USD 17,900.

KING, J. Arthur

British, 19th century.

Active in London.

Painter. Landscapes.

KING, J. B.

British, 19th century.

Painter. Seascapes.

MUSEUMS AND GALLERIES:

BRISTOL: *South-easterly Wind and Rain on the Cornish Coasts.*

KING, J. W.

British, 19th century.

Active in London c. 1850.

Painter. Genre scenes.

J.W. King exhibited at the Royal Academy, the British Institution and at the Suffolk Street Gallery from 1838 to 1853.

KING, James S.

American, 19th - 20th century.

Born 26 December 1852, in New York; died 1925, in New York.

Painter, watercolourist, engraver. Portraits, landscapes.

James S. King studied under Gérôme at the Paris École des Beaux-Arts. He lived in Upper Montclair.

AUCTION RECORDS:

NEW YORK, 6-7 April 1904, *Montclair, Evening,* USD 140. NEW YORK, 23 Sept 1993, *Summer Afternoon* (oil on canvas, 25 x 30 ins / 63.5 x 76.2 cm) USD 17,250. NEW YORK, 21 May 1996, *The River Cove at East Gloucester in Massachusetts* (oil on canvas, 20 x 30 ins / 51 x 76 cm) USD 3,220.

KING, Jessie Marion

British, 20th century.

Born 1875; died 1949.

Draughtswoman, illustrator.

Jessie M. King trained at Glasgow School of Art. She taught book decoration at the same school from 1899 to 1908, the year in which she married the painter Ernest Archibald Taylor. She won a bursary enabling her to travel in France and Italy, and lived in Paris from 1911 to 1913 before settling in Kirkcudbright in Scotland.

Her earliest works are strongly influenced by Art Nouveau. In 1912 she met the American Frank Zimmerer, from whom she learnt the technique of batik. Zimmerer and King began using chemical dyes similar to those used for the costumes and decor of Diaghilev's Ballets Russes. King began using silk instead of cotton. The resulting prints - sold through Liberty's department store in London - were hugely successful. King's new, brilliant colour palette subsequently lent itself to more strident Art Deco designs. Her illustrations, for works by Kipling and Milton among others, show the influence of the Pre-Raphaelites. Her work was also published in *The Studio*. King is regarded as one of the most successful exponents of the Glasgow style.

BIBLIOGRAPHY:

Oliver, C., *Jessie M. King,* Scottish Arts Council, Edinburgh, 1971. White, Colin, *The Enchanted World of Jessie M. King,* Canongate, Edinburgh, 1989.

AUCTION RECORDS:
AUCHTERARDER, 30 Aug 1977, *The Wish* (watercolour and pen, 9 x 6 ins / 23 x 15 cm) GBP 1,000. AUCHTERARDER, 28 Aug 1979, *The Fairy Glade* (pen and colour wash heightened with white/parchment, 13 x 17 ins / 33 x 43 cm) GBP 1,200. NEW YORK, 13 June 1980, *Design for a Book Cover: Summer and Winter* (watercolour and pen on paper mounted on card, 11 1/2 x 9 1/4 ins / 29 x 23.5 cm) USD 3,750. NEW YORK, 2 April 1981, *Wynken, Blynken and Nod* (watercolour and pen on paper mounted on card, 13 3/4 x 12 ins / 35 x 30.7 cm) USD 4,500. NEW YORK, 27 Feb 1982, *Parisian Life* (pen and watercolour, 12 3/4 x 10 ins / 32.4 x 24.5 cm) USD 850. AUCHTERARDER, 30 Aug 1983, *In that Green Wene Kilmeny Lay her Bosom Happed wi' the Flowerets Gay* (1907, pen heightened with silver and gold, 9 1/2 x 13 ins / 24 x 33 cm) GBP 850. EDINBURGH, 27 March 1984, *The Frog Prince* (tempera, 12 1/2 x 25 ins / 31.5 x 63.5 cm) GBP 700. GLASGOW, 30 Jan 1985, *Beauty in the Beast's Garden* (watercolour heightened with gold and silver, 10 1/2 x 9 1/4 ins / 26.5 x 23.5 cm) GBP 2,600. NEW YORK, 24 May 1985, *The Song of the Fearless* (pen and black ink/parchment, 9 x 6 ins / 22.8 x 15 cm) USD 1,400. EDINBURGH, 22 Nov 1988, *Washday* (ink and watercolour, 11 3/4 x 14 3/4 ins / 29.8 x 37.5 cm) GBP 1,700. PERTH, 28 Aug 1989, *Youth* (1915, watercolour and ink, 9 1/2 x 4 1/4 ins / 24 x 11 cm) GBP 1,100. EDINBURGH, 26 April 1990, *The Blessed Damozel* (ink and watercolour/vellum, 14 1/4 x 19 1/2 ins / 36.2 x 49.5 cm) GBP 2,090. PERTH, 27 Aug 1990, *Ali Baba-style Storage Jar* (hand-painted varnished pot, h. 15 1/2 ins / 39.5 cm) GBP 11,000. GLASGOW, 5 Feb 1991, *Yon Far Isle Beyond the Enchanted Sea* (batik/silk, 31 x 31 ins / 79 x 79 cm) GBP 4,950. EDINBURGH, 13 May 1993, *Halloween* (ink heightened with gold/vellum, 10 x 13 3/4 ins / 25.5 x 35 cm) GBP 2,860. PERTH, 31 Aug 1993, *The Wish* (black ink and blue wash heightened with gold and silver, 11 x 9 ins / 28 x 23 cm) GBP 8,050. GLASGOW, 16 April 1996, *The Enchanted Clearing* (watercolour and ink heightened with gouache, 12 3/4 x 17 ins / 32.5 x 43 cm) GBP 2,875. EDINBURGH, 15 May 1997, *Blue Butterflies* (pen, black ink and watercolour/vellum, 12 x 10 1/2 ins / 30.5 x 26.6 cm) GBP 10,350. LONDON, 29 Nov 1999, *Washing Time* (pen, ink and watercolour, 12 x 15 ins / 30 x 37 cm) GBP 3,000. LONDON, 29 Nov 1999, *There Was a Joyous Hostler who Knelt on Christmas beside a Radiant Manger where his Lord was Born* (1932, watercolour, pen and ink on vellum, 15 x 19 ins / 37 x 49 cm) GBP 7,000. LONDON, 1 Nov 2001, *Joy of Wilding Things* (pencil, pen, ink and watercolour on vellum, 8 x 7 ins / 21 x 19 cm) GBP 5,500. CAMBRIDGE, 1 Nov 2001, *Idleness, from The Romaunt of the Rose by Chaucer* (pen and ink on vellum, 11 x 6 ins / 27 x 14 cm) GBP 6,400. LONDON, 24 Sept 2002, *Queen of the Garden. Rembrance* (pen, ink and watercolour, a pair, 12 x 10 ins / 31 x 26 cm) GBP 4,000. EDINBURGH, 2 Nov 2002, *Sleeping Angel* (pen, ink and watercolour, 16 x 5 ins / 40 x 12 cm) GBP 2,600. LONDON, 27 Aug 2003, *Pont Neuf, Paris* (pen and ink on vellum, 7 x 6 ins / 18 x 16 cm) GBP 2,200. LONDON, 27 Aug 2003, *March* (pen, ink and watercolour on vellum, 11 x 8 ins / 28 x 20 cm) GBP 4,400. EDINBURGH, 21 April 2004, *Flying a Kite* (ink and watercolour, 13 x 17 ins / 34 x 43 cm) GBP 3,800. EDINBURGH, 21 April 2004, *Town by the River* (ink on vellum, 7 x 8 ins / 18 x 20 cm) GBP 5,400.

KING, John
British, 17th century.
Engraver (burin).
John King is noted as having been active in the 17th century; however, it seems more likely that he worked at the beginning of the 18th century. The following works by him are cited: *Chastity of Joseph*; *Christ Tempted in the Desert*; *Herodias Holding the Head of St John the Baptist*; *The Three Theological Virtues*; *Charity*; *Venus and Cupid*; and *Rinaldo and Armida*.

KING, John
British, 19th century.
Born 1788, in Dartmouth; died 12 July 1847, in Dartmouth.
Painter. History painting, portraits.
John King began exhibiting his paintings featuring historical and religious themes in 1817. Seeking to improve his lot, he went to London around 1820 where he enrolled at the Royal Academy. Success continued to elude him, so he turned to portraiture, a genre at which he probably would have made a better living, but which he disliked. He courageously returned to his larger-scale works which guaranteed him only extreme poverty. After his death, his paintings, most of them still unsold, were disposed of for a pittance.
MUSEUMS AND GALLERIES:
LONDON (National Portrait Gal.): *Sir John Bowring* (1826, oil on canvas).

KING, John Baragwanath
British, 19th - 20th century.
Born 1864, in Cornwall.
Painter, watercolourist.
John Baragwanath King exhibited in Paris at the Salon des Artistes Français, as well as in London, Manchester, Vienna and the USA.

KING, John Crookshanks
British, 19th century.
Born 1806, in Scotland; died 1882, in Boston (USA).
Sculptor.
John Crookshanks King left for America around 1829, where he travelled to New Orleans before settling permanently in Boston.

KING, John Duncan
British, 19th century.
Born 1789; died 21 August 1863, in Windsor.
Painter. Landscapes.
John Duncan King was a distinguished and talented amateur artist, who painted the landscapes of the Spanish and Portuguese coasts before turning to the coasts of Ireland. At the end of his life, he was attached to the military household of Queen Victoria. He exhibited at the Royal Academy and at the British Institution from 1824 to 1858.

KING, John M.
American, 20th century.
Born 1 July 1897, in Richmond (Indiana).
Painter. Portraits.
John M. King studied under H.H. Wessel. He was a member of the Salmagundi Club. He painted portraits and many of his sitters were women.

KING, John or Yeend. See **KING Henry John Yeend**

KING, Lilian Yeend. See **YEEND-KING Lilian**

KING, Margaret
British, 18th century.
Draughtswoman.
Margaret King exhibited pencil portraits at the Royal Academy in 1779. She exhibited again in 1786.

KING, Michel
French, 20th century.
Born 2 July 1930, in Normandy.
Active in Dieppe and Paris.
Painter, engraver, lithographer, illustrator. Seascapes.
Michel King studied under François Dunoyer and also studied sculpture and decorative art. In 1959 he was made an associate naval painter and later given full official status. King illustrated *La Phœbé* by Jean de la Varence, *Parallèlement* by

Paul Verlaine (18 etchings) and *Les Contes de La Fontaine*. He is known principally as a seascape painter.

From 1959 he took part in numerous group exhibitions in Paris, the Salon d'Automne and the Salon Comparaisons and was a member of the Société des Artistes Indépendants and the Société Nationale des Beaux-Arts. He held around a dozen solo exhibitions of his work in France, including five in Paris.

MUSEUMS AND GALLERIES:

PARIS (FNAC) - PARIS (Mus. de la Marine).

KING, Paul

American, 19th - 20th century.

Born 9 February 1867, in Buffalo (New York State); died 1940 or 1947.

Painter. Landscapes, seascapes.

Paul King studied under Mowbray at the Art Students League in New York. He was a member of the Salmagundi Club, who awarded him many distinctions, and of the American Federation of Arts. He won a silver medal at the 1915 San Francisco Exhibition.

AUCTION RECORDS:

NEW YORK, 12 Oct 1978, *Wiscasset Harbour under Snow* (oil on canvas, 32 x 40 ins / 81.3 x 101.5 cm) USD 3,000. NEW YORK, 8 Aug 1980, *After the Storm* (oil on canvas, 32 x 40 1/4 ins / 81.5 x 102 cm) USD 2,200. LOS ANGELES, 3 May 1982, *The Passing of Winter* (oil on canvas, 50 x 60 ins / 127 x 152.5 cm) USD 5,000. NEW YORK, 28 Sept 1983, *Riverscape with Birch* (oil on canvas, 16 1/4 x 20 1/4 ins / 41 x 51.2 cm) USD 5,000. NEW YORK, 30 May 1985, *Birch Trees along a Brook* (oil on canvas, 30 1/4 x 25 1/4 ins / 77 x 64 cm) USD 8,500. NEW YORK, 1 Oct 1987, *Silver Sails* (oil/hardboard, 25 1/4 x 30 ins / 64 x 76.5 cm) USD 5,500. NEW YORK, 17 March 1988, *Fishing Boats* (oil on canvas, 15 3/4 x 11 3/4 ins / 40 x 30 cm) USD 2,200. NEW YORK, 25 May 1989, *Winter in the Adirondacks* (oil on canvas, 68 1/2 x 100 1/2 ins / 174 x 255.3 cm) USD 13,200. NEW YORK, 28 Sept 1989, *The Return of the Fishermen* (1929, oil on canvas, 25 1/4 x 30 ins / 64 x 76.5 cm) USD 8,800. NEW YORK, 14 Feb 1990, *Trawlers and Fishermen* (oil/synthetic resin, 24 1/4 x 30 1/4 ins / 61.5 x 77 cm) USD 6,600. NEW YORK, 21 May 1991, *Craggy Coast* (oil on canvas, 12 1/4 x 16 1/4 ins / 31.1 x 41.3 cm) USD 1,540. NEW YORK, 14 Nov 1991, *Harbour Scene* (oil on canvas, 40 x 50 ins / 101.6 x 127 cm) USD 10,450. NEW YORK, 14 Nov 1991, *Wooded Landscape in the Winter* (oil on canvas, 50 x 60 ins / 127 x 152.5 cm) USD 4,620. MILFORD, 22 April 1999, *Chester Harbour* (oil on canvas, 40 x 32 ins / 102 x 81 cm) USD 3,500. NEW YORK, 12 Aug 1999, *The Red Maple* (oil on canvas, double-sided, 40 x 32 ins / 102 x 81 cm) USD 3,250. MILFORD, 11 May 2000, *Camden Harbour, Maine* (oil on canvas on board, 12 x 16 ins / 30 x 41 cm) USD 4,500. MILFORD, 26 Oct 2000, *Winter in Lansdowne* (1919, oil on board, 8 x 10 ins / 20 x 25 cm) USD 2,750. PHILADELPHIA, 24 June 2001, *Autumn* (oil on canvas) USD 3,000. FAIRFIELD, 22 Aug 2001, *Stone Brook Gold Autumn Adirondacks* (oil on canvas, 29 x 24 ins / 74 x 61 cm) USD 6,500. WASHINGTON, 14 Dec 2002, *Golden Autumn* (oil on masonite, 20 x 24 ins / 52 x 62 cm) USD 2,800. MILFORD, 24 April 2003, *Harbour Scene* (oil on canvas, 20 x 16 ins / 51 x 41 cm) USD 3,750. PHILADELPHIA, 7 Dec 2003, *Hunting Season* (1917, oil on canvas, 22 x 28 ins / 56 x 71 cm) USD 6,000. MILFORD, 6 May 2004, *Ships in a Harbour* (oil on canvas, 30 x 24 ins / 76 x 61 cm) USD 3,000.

KING, Philipp

German, 18th century.

Died c. 1750, in Berlin.

Painter.

Philipp King was the son of Carl Friedrich King. He worked for King Frederick William I of Prussia.

KING, Phillip

British, 20th century.

Born 1934, in Tunisia.

Active from 1945 in England.

Sculptor, environmental artist.

Phillip King went to England at the age of 11, where, after completing his preparatory arts studies, he attended St Martin's School of Art from 1957 to 1958. Here he studied under Anthony Caro, and then became Henry Moore's assistant from 1958 to 1960. He subsequently taught at St Martin's from 1959 to 1978, at the Slade School of Fine Arts in London from 1967 to 1968, at the Berlin college of art from 1979 to 1980, and at the Royal College of Art in London from 1980 to 1990. From 1999 to 2005 he was President of the Royal Academy.

King's formal vocabulary is limited to a few primary elements, planes assembled in empty spaces, occasionally incorporating cones made in fibreglass, plastic and sometimes metal. Colour plays a predominant role in his sculptures, either increasing the significance of spaces, or, conversely, diminishing them through the effects of contrast or fusion. King sometimes juxtaposes opaque and transparent materials, and is more concerned with the surfaces delimiting the sections of spaces than with the actual spaces themselves. Space circulates between the various elements that make up the assemblage, the principle of circulation being particularly dominant in his large-scale works, creating what may be termed 'environments'. He also uses recycled and industrial materials in his work. The most cited of his works is his *Genghis Khan* of 1963, a sort of cone in blue turned deep purple fitted with bat-like wings.

King's work has been represented in a great many group exhibitions, in particular those devoted to contemporary English sculpture: in 1961 and 1966 he exhibited at the Jewish Museum in New York, in 1963 at the biennial of young artists in Paris, in 1964 and 1968 at Documenta in Kassel, in 1966 at the Stedelijk Museum in Amsterdam, in 1968 and 1988 at the Venice Biennale, in 1969 at *Arts 69* at the Athenaum Museum in Helsinki, in 1969 and 1970 at the museum of modern art in Tokyo, in 1970 at the Institute of Contemporary Art (ICA) in London, in 1972, 1987, 1990 and 1992 at the Royal Academy in London, in 1973 at the palace of fine arts in Brussels, in 1977 at the Paris Biennale and the Tate Gallery in London, in 1982 in a touring exhibition of Japan, in 1985 at the Cartier foundation in Jouy-en-Josas, in 1989 at Le Havre Museum, and in 1996 in the exhibition *A Century of English Sculpture* at the Jeu de Paume gallery in Paris. From 1957 onwards, he has also mounted solo exhibitions: in 1964, 1970, 1972, 1973, 1975, 1977, 1979, 1983 and 1990 at the Rowan Gallery in London, in 1968 at the Whitechapel Art Gallery in London and the Boymans van Beuningen Museum in Rotterdam, in 1974-1975 a touring exhibition in Otterlo, Düsseldorf, Bern, Paris and Belfast, in 1975-1976 a touring exhibition in Great Britain, in 1981 at the Hayward Gallery in London, in 1987 in Tokyo, in 1992 at the municipal art centre in Mannheim, and in 1993 at the La Filature cultural centre in Mulhouse. He was awarded first prize at the international exhibition of sculpture in Bratislava.

BIBLIOGRAPHY:

Harrison, C., '*Phillip King: Sculpture 1960-1968*' in *Artforum vii, 4*, periodical, 1968. King, P., *Phillip King: Sculptures 1970-1975*, exhibition catalogue, Pal., Paris, 1975. Cooke, L., '*Phillip King's Recent Sculpture*' in *Artscribe* no. 18, periodical, Paris, 1979. Kudielka, R. (ed.), *Phillip King*, exhibition catalogue, Hayward Gallery, London, 1981. Rossignol, Claude, '*Phillip King*' in *Art Press* n° 185, periodical, Paris, November 1993.

MUSEUMS AND GALLERIES:

BELFAST (Ulster Mus.): *Through* (1965, painted fibre glass, sculpture); *Ascona* (1972, painted steel, sculpture) - BRUSSELS (Mus. royaux des Beaux-Arts de Belgique) - HUMLEBÆK (Louisiana Mus. for Moderne Kunst) - LEEDS (City AG): *Through* (1965, mixed media, sculpture) - LISBON (Centro de

Arte Moderna José de Azeredo Perdigão, Fundação Calouste Gulbenkian) - LONDON (Tate Collection): *And the Birds Began to Sing* (1964, acrylic and metal, sculpture); *Within* (1978-1979, metal, stone and wood, sculpture) - LOS ANGELES (County MA) - MELBOURNE (Nat. Gal. of Victoria) - NEW YORK (MoMA) - OSAKA (NMA) - OTTERLO (Kröller-Müller Mus.): *Open bound* (1973) - PARIS (MNAM-CCI) - TURIN (Gal. Civica d'Arte Moderna e Contemporanea).
AUCTION RECORDS:
LONDON, 5 July 1973, *Trough* (1965, painted fibreglass) GBP 5,000. LONDON, 3 April 1974, *Stant* (1965, armorite) GBP 4,000. LONDON, 7 June 1991, *Au travers* (construction of green and red fibreglass, 84 1/4 x 132 1/4 x 107 3/4 ins / 214 x 336 x 274 cm) GBP 9,020. LONDON, 22 Oct 1997, *Model for Cross-Bend* (1980, metal, 42 1/2 x 46 1/2 x 24 3/4 ins / 108 x 118 x 63 cm) GBP 3,220. LONDON, 4 July 2001, *Maquette for Hanover* (1974, painted slate) GBP 2,800.

KING, Thomas
British, 18th century.
Died c. 1769.
Active in London.
Painter.
Thomas King was a student of Knapton. Although he had considerable artistic talent, his laziness and love of pleasure prevented him from receiving his due. He appears to have been connected to the world of the theatre; there is mention of a portrait of the actor Maddox, which was later engraved by Houston.

KING, Thomas
British, 18th century.
Born in Bath.
Sculptor.
Thomas King the sculptor worked mostly for churches, notably in Bath, Salisbury and Gloucester.

KING, Thomas
British, 19th century.
Died 9 August 1845.
Draughtsman, engraver.
Thomas King was an antique dealer. He published a series of engravings of Chichester Cathedral and of other old buildings in the city.

KING, Thomas R.
British, 19th century.
Active in London.
Landscape artist.
Thomas R. King was a frequent exhibitor at the Suffolk Street Gallery from 1839 to 1846.

KING, Wilhelmina (Miss)
British, 18th century.
Painter. Still-lifes.
Miss Wilhelmina King exhibited one of her paintings at the Royal Academy and seven at the Society of Artists between 1770 and 1775.

KING, William
British, 18th century.
Active in Totteridge.
Painter. Flowers.
William King exhibited his paintings at the Free Society and at the Society of Artists from 1761 to 1767.

KING, William
British, 18th century.
Active in London.
Sculptor.
William King exhibited at the Free Society between 1769 and 1782.

KING, William Charles Holland
British, 20th century.
Born 1884.
Sculptor. Busts.
William King trained at the Royal Academy in London and exhibited in Edinburgh, Liverpool and Bristol. He is best known for his portrait busts of the *Duke and Duchess of Beaufort*.

KING, William Dickey
American, 20th century.
Born February 1925, in Jacksonville (Florida).
Sculptor.
William Dickey King studied at the Cooper Union Art School in New York; the Skowhegan School of Painting and Sculpture in Maine; the Brooklyn School in New York; the Academy of Fine Arts in Rome, and the Central School of Arts and Crafts in London. He travelled around Italy and Greece. In 1968-1969, he taught sculpture at the Art Students League in New York. He has taken part in collective exhibitions since 1949 in prestigious venues in New York and Pittsburgh. He has shown his works in solo exhibitions in New York, Detroit, Los Angeles and Miami.
MUSEUMS AND GALLERIES:
ANDOVER, MA (Addison Gal. of American Art).
AUCTION RECORDS:
NEW YORK, 7 May 1990, *Heat* (vinyl on aluminium and wood, h. 70 1/2 ins / 179 cm) USD 6,600. NEW YORK, 9 May 1992, *Afterwards* (1982, dacron and aluminium, 88 1/2 x 32 x 21 ins / 224.7 x 81.3 x 53.3 cm) USD 4,400. NEW YORK, 29 June 2004, *Evening* (black patinated bronze, h. 51 ins / 129 cm) USD 6,500.

KING, William Gunning
British, 19th - 20th century.
Born 1859; died 1940.
Painter, draughtsman, illustrator. Portraits.
William Gunning King trained at South Kensington School of Art and later at the Royal Academy in London. He was a regular contributor to *Punch* and exhibited at the Sketching Society. From 1878 he exhibited at the Royal Academy, the Grosvenor Gallery and the Royal Institute of Oil Painters.
BIBLIOGRAPHY:
MUSEUMS AND GALLERIES:
BRADFORD (Cartwright Hall AG): *Saturday Afternoon* (1893, oil on canvas).
AUCTION RECORDS:
LONDON, 26 Sept 1984, *He Loves Me, He Loves Me Not...* (1883, oil on canvas, 19 x 13 1/2 ins / 48.2 x 34.3 cm) GBP 1,200. LONDON, 1 Oct 1986, *Little Shepherd Boy* (oil on card, 13 3/4 x 17 3/4 ins / 35 x 45 cm) GBP 7,800. LONDON, 8 June 1989, *Assignation* (1893, oil on canvas, 41 1/4 x 25 1/2 ins / 105 x 65 cm) GBP 9,350. LONDON, 13 Dec 1989, *Landscape with Herders and Cattle* (oil on canvas, 16 1/4 x 26 ins / 41 x 66 cm) GBP 1,210. LIVERPOOL, 24 Nov 1999, *Don't be a Donkey* (1903, oil on canvas, 16 x 11 ins / 41 x 29 cm) GBP 1,500. EDINBURGH, 8 Dec 2000, *Feeding Birds* (1890, oil on canvas, 20 x 11 ins / 50 x 27 cm) GBP 7,500. EDINBURGH, 8 Dec 2000, *Scrumping Apples* (1890, oil on canvas, 20 x 11 ins / 50 x 27 cm) GBP 8,500. CAMBRIDGE, 27 June 2001, *Feeding Time, Farmer and Cattle* (1934, oil on canvas, a pair, 17 x 21 ins / 43 x 53 cm) GBP 1,900. LONDON, 23 May 2002, *Milking Time* (1914, oil on canvas, 17 x 18 ins / 43 x 46 cm) GBP 1,800. NANTWICH, 28 April 2004, *Milking Time, Shorthorn Dairy Cow* (1918, oil on canvas, 17 x 19 ins / 43 x 47 cm) GBP 1,500.

KING, Wyncie
American, 20th century.
Born 21 September 1884, in Covington; died 1961.
Painter, illustrator.
Wyncie King exhibited in Chicago.

KING HAO. See **JING HAO**

KINGELEZ, Bodys Isek
Congolese, 20th - 21st century.
Born 27 August 1948, in Kimbembele Ihunga (now in Democratic Republic of Congo).
Sculptor. Architectural views.

Bodys Isek Kingelez is self-taught. He lives and works in Kinshasa. After working on the restoration of traditional masks, Kingelez launched out into making maquettes in paper, cardboard, plastic or adhesive, inspired by the colonial architecture of the 1930s and 1950s. He makes meticulous, perfectly designed maquettes of imaginary furniture from pieces of recycled paper and cardboard. Each of his extraordinary creations, decorated with symbols, flags or signs, is accompanied by a text with a long descriptive commentary.

He has taken part in group exhibitions including 1988 *Les Magiciens de la Terre* (*Magicians of the Earth*), organised by the Musée National d'Art Moderne at the Grande Halle de la Villette in Paris; 1996, *7 artistes zaïrois* (*7 Zairean Artists*) at the Palais des Beaux-Arts in Charleroi; 2002, *Artists Imagine Architecture* at the Boston Institute of Contemporary Arts, an exhibition showing the relationships between sculpture and the architectural model, and in 2003, *The American Effect, A Look at How America is Seen by Artists Around the World*, an exhibition inquiring into the way some 30 foreign artists perceived the USA as a superpower at the Whitney Museum of American Art in New York.

BIBLIOGRAPHY:
Serageldin, Ismail/Olalquiaga, Celeste/Pinte, Jean-Louis/Patras, Jean-Marc, *Home and the world, Architectural sculpture by two contemporary African artists: Aboudramane and Bodys Isek Kingelez*, exhibition catalogue, Museum for African Art, New York, 1993. *Bodys Isek Kingelez*, exhibition catalogue, Fondation Cartier pour l'art contemporain, Paris, 1995. Magnin, André, et al., *Bodys Isek Kingelez*, Kunstverein, Hamburg, 2001 (text in French and German). Rinder, Lawrence, et al., *The American Effect, A Look at How America is Seen by Artists Around the World*, exhibition catalogue, Whitney Museum of American Art, New York, 2003. *Bodys Isek Kingelez*, Snoeck-Ducaju & Zoon, 2003.

MUSEUMS AND GALLERIES:
PARIS (FNAC): *Germany in the Year 2000*; *Italy*; *New Paris* (three maquettes).

KINGENHEIMER, Wilhelm
German, 19th century.
Born 30 September 1830, in Frankfurt am Main; died 3 March 1857, in Kettenheim.
Painter. History painting.

Kingenheimer was a pupil of J. Becker and Passavant. He exhibited in Berlin, Frankfurt and Stettin (now Szczecin).

KINGMAN, Dong, real name Zeng Jingwen
American, 20th century.
Born 31 March 1911, in Oakland (California); died May 2000.
Painter (mixed media), watercolourist, lithographer. Landscapes, urban scenes.

Dong Kingman was born in California, and moved with his family to Hong Kong at the age of five. He learned calligraphy and watercolour at Chan Sun Wen School, and studied at the Lingnan Academy under Szeto Wai. In 1929, Kingman returned to California, studying at the Fox Morgan Art School. He was a participating artist from 1936 in the Works Progress Administration created by the US government to support the arts, painting about 500 works in this programme. He served as a cartographer with the Office of Strategic Service during World War II, and taught at Columbia University (1946-1958); at Hunter College (1948-1953); at Hewitt Painting Workshops; and at the Academy of Art College, San Francisco. Kingman was a founding member of the Famous Artists Painting School, Westport, Connecticut. In 1954, he served as a cultural ambassador for the America on an international lecturing tour for the Department of State.

Kingman did illustrations for magazine covers, such as *Time*, *Life*, *Fortune*, and *Saturday Review*. He was commissioned to paint murals for the Bank of California in San Francisco, the Washington Mutual Bank in New York, the Ambassador Hotel in Hong Kong, and the Boca Raton Hotel in Florida. His watercolours were used for title sequences in films such as *Flower Drum Song* (1961) and *55 Days at Peking* (1963). Kingman was awarded a First Purchase Prize, San Francisco Art Association (1936); an International Watercolor Exhibition Award, Art Institute, Chicago (1941); Guggenheim Fellowships in 1941 and 1942; the Gold Medal of Honour, Audubon Artists (1946); the 150th Anniversary Gold Medal Award, National Academy of Design, New York (1975); and an honorary doctorate, Academy of Art College, San Francisco (1987). In 2002, the School of Visual Arts at Columbia University established the Dong Kingman Fellowship. He was a member of the National Academy of Design and the American Watercolor Society.

Kingman's solo exhibitions include: San Francisco Art Association (1936); *Second Annual Exhibition of Watercolors, Pastels and Tempera on Paper*, San Francisco Art Association (1937); Ministry of Culture, China (1981); Taipei Modern Art Museum, Taiwan (1995); Taichung Provincial Museum, Taiwan (1999); *Dong Kingman: An American Master in Hollywood*, Academy of Motion Picture Arts and Sciences (2000, tour); *Dong Kingman in San Francisco*, Chinese Historical Society of America and Museum, San Francisco (2001-2002); and Beijing National Museum, China (2002-2003, tour).

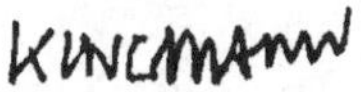

BIBLIOGRAPHY:
Gruskin, Alan D., *The Water Colors of Dong Kingman, and How the Artist Works*, Studio Publications, New York, 1958. *Watercolors around the World by Dong Kingman*, exhibition catalogue, Dalzell Hatfield Galleries, Los Angeles, 1973. Kingman, Dong/Kingman, Helena Kuo, *Dong Kingman's Watercolours*, exhibition catalogue, Watson-Guptill Publications, New York, 1980. Kingman, Dong, *Paint the Yellow Tiger*, exhibition catalogue, Sterling Publishing Co, New York, 1991.

MUSEUMS AND GALLERIES:
ANDOVER, MA (Addison Gal. of American Art) - BOSTON (MFA): *Blue Moon* - CHICAGO (AI): *Passing Locomotive* - COLUMBUS, GA (Museum of Arts and Crafts) - FORT WAYNE (Fort Wayne Art Institute) - HARTFORD (Wadsworth Atheneum) - HONOLULU (Academy of Arts) - LINCOLN (Sheldon Memorial AG, University of Nebraska): *New York after the Storm* (1942, watercolour) - LOS ANGELES (County MA) - NEW YORK (Brooklyn Mus.) - NEW YORK (Metropolitan Mus. of Art): *South Street Bridge* - NEW YORK (MoMA) - NORMAN (Fred Jones Jr MA, University of Oklahoma): *Piqua, Ohio* (1948, oil) - PHILADELPHIA (Pennsylvania Academy of the Fine Arts) - SAN FRANCISCO (California Palace of the Legion of Honor): *The Raised Bridge* (c. 1935, watercolour/graphite/paper); *Bay at Sunrise* (mid 20th century, lithograph) - SAN FRANCISCO (Chinese Cultural Center) - SAN FRANCISCO (MoMA): *A Hill* (1935) - SEATTLE (Frye AM) - TAIPEI (Taipei Fine Arts Museum) - TOLEDO (MA) - WASHINGTON DC (Hirshhorn Mus. and Sculpture Garden): *Station Platform* (1946, watercolour) - YOUNGSTOWN (Butler Institute of American Art): *Lighthouse*.

AUCTION RECORDS:
NEW YORK, 28 Oct 1976, *The Green House* (1944, watercolour, 15 1/4 x 22 1/4 ins / 38.5 x 56.5 cm) USD 1,600. NEW YORK,

21 April 1977, *San Francisco* (1944, watercolour, 20 x 27 1/4 ins / 51 x 69 cm) USD 1,700. LOS ANGELES, 18 June 1979, *The Brooklyn Bridge* (watercolour, 21 x 29 ins / 53.3 x 73.6 cm) USD 2,800. NEW YORK, 19 June 1981, *Moon and Locomotive* (1952, watercolour, 20 1/2 x 29 ins / 52 x 73.6 cm) USD 5,250. NEW YORK, 21 Oct 1983, *Acapulco* (watercolour, 21 3/4 x 29 1/2 ins / 55.2 x 74.9 cm) USD 2,000. NEW YORK, 5 Dec 1985, *House with Eyes* (1959, watercolour, 21 3/4 x 29 3/4 ins / 55.3 x 75.7 cm) USD 10,000. NEW YORK, 22 Sept 1987, *Boat* (watercolour, 19 x 25 1/2 ins / 48.3 x 65 cm) USD 1,700. NEW YORK, 30 Sept 1988, *Blast Furnace* (watercolour and gouache/paper, 18 1/4 x 15 1/4 ins / 46.5 x 38.5 cm) USD 3,300. NEW YORK, 1 Dec 1988, *Place de l'Ange* (1951, watercolour/paper, 30 x 44 ins / 76.2 x 111.8 cm) USD 26,400. NEW YORK, 24 Jan 1990, *San Francisco* (1944, watercolour/paper, 20 x 27 ins / 50.8 x 68.6 cm) USD 8,250. NEW YORK, 31 May 1990, *Harbour Scene* (watercolour/paper, 19 1/4 x 15 1/4 ins / 48.8 x 38.7 cm) USD 4,400. NEW YORK, 26 Sept 1990, *The Blue Bay, Hong Kong* (watercolour/paper, 26 x 40 1/2 ins / 66 x 102.8 cm) USD 14,300. NEW YORK, 15 May 1991, *Square in Buenos Aires* (1968, watercolour and pencil/paper, 15 x 22 ins / 38.1 x 55.9 cm) USD 3,330. NEW YORK, 18 Dec 1991, *San Francisco* (1972, mixed media and collage/paper/card, 16 1/4 x 11 1/2 ins / 41.3 x 29.2 cm) USD 3,850. NEW YORK, 10 March 1993, *A Hundred Fishermen* (watercolour/paper, 30 1/2 x 22 1/4 ins / 77.5 x 56.5 cm) USD 6,900. TAIPEI, 18 April 1993, *Marymount College Bell Tower* (1944, watercolour/paper, 22 x 15 ins / 56 x 38 cm) TWD 345,000. NEW YORK, 9 Sept 1993, *New York Harbour* (watercolour/paper, 22 x 30 ins / 55.9 x 76.2 cm) USD 2,875. NEW YORK, 31 March 1994, *View of a Chinese Village* (watercolour/paper, 22 1/2 x 30 ins / 57.2 x 76.2 cm) USD 4,600. NEW YORK, 14 Sept 1995, *Georgetown, Washington State* (watercolour/paper, 15 1/4 x 22 3/4 ins / 38.7 x 57.8 cm) USD 6,037. NEW YORK, 21 May 1996, *Statue and Butterfly* (watercolour/paper, 20 1/2 x 27 1/2 ins / 52.3 x 70 cm) USD 4,625. NEW YORK, 25 March 1997, *The Depot* (watercolour and gouache/paper, 15 x 22 1/4 ins / 37.8 x 56.5 cm) USD 3,450; *Antigua, Guatemala* (watercolour/paper, 15 x 22 1/2 ins / 38.4 x 57.2 cm) USD 2,587. SAN FRANCISCO, 17 June 1999, *Candlestick Park* (watercolour, 15 x 22 ins / 38 x 55 cm) USD 5,500. LOS ANGELES, 9 Dec 1999, *Botanical Garden, Golden Gate Park* (watercolour, 14 x 21 ins / 36 x 53 cm) USD 4,500. NEW YORK, 22 May 2001, *Columbus Circle* (oil on canvas) USD 4,000. SAN FRANCISCO, 12 Dec 2001, *Down Hyde Street to Fisherman's Wharf* (pencil and watercolour, 22 x 30 ins / 56 x 76 cm) USD 4,750. SAN FRANCISCO, 9 June 2002, *Road to the Capital* (1942, watercolour, 22 x 29 ins / 55 x 74 cm) USD 3,750. SAN FRANCISCO, 9 June 2002, *Street in Chinatown* (watercolour, 22 x 15 ins / 56 x 38 cm) USD 4,750. SAN FRANCISCO, 11 June 2003, *From the Opening Credits of the Film 'Flower Drum Song'* (pencil and watercolour, eight, 11 x 23 ins / 28 x 59 cm) USD 13,000. NEW YORK, 3 Dec 2003, *Junks Under the Brooklyn Bridge* (watercolour heightened with white board, 19 x 28 ins / 47 x 72 cm) USD 9,000. ALAMEDA, 11 Sept 2004, *South Bay Panorama* (watercolour, 14 x 21 ins / 36 x 53 cm) USD 4,000. NEW YORK, 5 Oct 2004, *Washington Square* (1946, watercolour, 22 x 30 ins / 56 x 76 cm) USD 6,000.

KINGMAN, Edouardo

Ecuadorean, 20th century.

Born 1911 or 1913.

Painter. Figures, genre scenes. Murals.

Eduardo Kingman collaborated with Camilo Egas on the decoration of the Ecuadorean pavillion at the International Exhibition in New York in 1939.

He often painted figures typical of the Ecuadorean lower classes. He is best known for his painting *The Visit*.

AUCTION RECORDS:

NEW YORK, 8 May 1981, *Washerwoman* (1940, oil on canvas, 27 1/4 x 33 1/4 ins / 69.2 x 84.5 cm) USD 5,250. NEW YORK, 30 May 1984, *Untitled* (1973, oil on canvas, 35 x 25 1/4 ins / 89 x 64.2 cm) USD 1,300. NEW YORK, 19 Nov 1987, *Flute Player* (1963, oil on canvas, 39 x 31 1/4 ins / 99 x 79.4 cm) USD 3,000. NEW YORK, 21 Nov 1988, *Clown* (1940, oil on canvas, 52 1/4 x 29 1/2 ins / 133 x 75 cm) USD 6,050; *Untitled - Interior with Two Indian Women* (1941, oil on canvas, 23 3/4 x 39 ins / 60.5 x 99 cm) USD 7,700. NEW YORK, 17 May 1989, *Untitled* (1941, oil on canvas, 22 3/4 x 20 3/4 ins / 58 x 53 cm) USD 7,150. NEW YORK, 20 Nov 1989, *Woman Working* (1964, ink/paper, 39 x 27 1/4 ins / 99.1 x 69.2 cm) USD 1,760. NEW YORK, 21 Nov 1989, *Beggars* (1974, oil on canvas, 40 1/4 x 51 3/4 ins / 102 x 131.5 cm) USD 7,700. NEW YORK, 2 May 1990, *Woman in Red and Black* (1985, oil on canvas, 31 1/2 x 25 1/2 ins / 80 x 65 cm) USD 4,675. NEW YORK, 19 May 1992, *Young Native Girl* (1945, oil on canvas, 23 1/4 x 19 ins / 58.8 x 48.4 cm) USD 7,480. NEW YORK, 22-23 Nov 1993, *Guitar Player* (1963, oil on canvas, 31 1/4 x 39 ins / 79.1 x 99.1 cm) USD 3,450. NEW YORK, 23-24 Nov 1993, *Fireworks* (1947, oil on canvas, 41 1/4 x 31 1/2 ins / 104.7 x 80 cm) USD 11,500. NEW YORK, 16 May 1996, *And then Fatigue...* (1982, oil on canvas, 28 3/4 x 35 1/2 ins / 73.3 x 90.2 cm) USD 4,830. NEW YORK, 25-26 Nov 1996, *Woman* (1966, oil on canvas, 39 1/4 x 31 1/4 ins / 99.4 x 79.1 cm) USD 12,650. NEW YORK, 28 May 1997, *Woman Filled with Anxiety* (1964, oil on canvas, 47 x 63 ins / 119.3 x 160 cm) USD 14,950. NEW YORK, 24-25 Nov 1997, *Figures in the High Plateaus* (1939, oil on canvas, 30 1/4 x 28 3/4 ins / 76.7 x 73 cm) USD 36,800. MIAMI, 10 Jan 1999, *Patio* (1965, oil on canvas, 39 x 31 ins / 99 x 79 cm) USD 12,000. NEW YORK, 23 Nov 1999, *Child* (1965, oil on canvas, 27 x 31 ins / 69 x 79 cm) USD 5,500. NEW YORK, 21 Nov 2000, *The Wait* (1948, oil on canvas, 31 x 32 ins / 80 x 82 cm) USD 30,000. NEW YORK, 30 May 2001, *Victory* (1939, oil on canvas, 30 x 36 ins / 75 x 91 cm) USD 20,000. NEW YORK, 31 May 2001, *Maternity* (1970, oil on canvas, 46 x 23 ins / 117 x 58 cm) USD 12,000. FLORIDA, 14 May 2002, *Beggar* (1962, oil on sand, 31 x 47 ins / 79 x 119 cm) USD 3,500. FLORIDA, 14 May 2002, *Mother and Child* (1963, oil on canvas, 47 x 31 ins / 119 x 79 cm) USD 7,000. NEW YORK, 29 May 2002, *Workmen* (1941, oil on canvas, 29 x 30 ins / 74 x 77 cm) USD 15,000. MONTEVIDEO, 24 Nov 2003, *Unity* (1989, oil on canvas, 55 x 28 ins / 140 x 70 cm) USD 8,000.

KINGSBURY, Edward Reynolds

American, 20th century.

Born in Boston; died 1940.

Painter. Murals.

Edward Reynolds Kingsbury studied in Paris. He was a member of the Salmagundi Club and of the American Federation of Arts. One of his works, the mural *Time and the World*, can be seen at Charlestown High School.

KINGSBURY, Henry

British, 18th century.

Active in London 1750-1780.

Draughtsman, painter, engraver (stippling/mezzotint). Portraits, landscapes.

Henry Kingsbury made engravings of portraits and religious subjects. He may have been the same person as the painter Henry Kingsbury who exhibited landscapes at the Society of Artists and at the Royal Academy from 1776 to 1791.

KINGSLEY, Elbridge

American, 19th - 20th century.

Born 17 September 1841, in Carthage; died 1915, in Brooklyn.

Engraver.

Elbridge Kingsley studied at the Cooper Union. He engraved after D.W. Tryon and Francis Murphy. He featured in World's Fair in Chicago and the Exposition universelle in Paris, winning Gold medals in 1893 and 1900.

KININGER, Vincenz Georg
Austrian, 18th - 19th century.
Born 24 April 1767, in Regensburg; died 18 May 1851, in Vienna.
Painter, watercolourist, engraver, draughtsman.
Portraits, genre scenes.

Kininger studied with Schmutzer and Jacobé at the academy of fine arts in Vienna. He was a brilliant student, winning a prize in 1784. In 1786 he studied mezzotint engraving. He also did aquatints. He was an excellent draughtsman and his many engravings of portraits, historical subjects and genre scenes show remarkable qualities.

AUCTION RECORDS:
VIENNA, 1823, *Peasant Woman and Little Girl Looking at a Holy Image* (watercolour) FRF 32; *Scene from the Play 'Weiberehre' (Women's Honour)* (watercolour) FRF 55. MUNICH, 24 May 1976, *The Archbishop's Palace at Sankt Veit, near Vienna* (watercolour, 11¼ x 15 ins / 28.5 x 38.2 cm) DEM 750. LONDON, 26 March 1981, *Hunting Scenes, Genre Scenes and Military Subjects* (pen and wash, book of 70 sketches, 7 x 9 ins / 18 x 23 cm) GBP 3,300. MUNICH, 10 Dec 1992, *Girl Wearing a Golden Helmet and Carrying a Shepherd's Crook, with Two Suitors, in Front of a Wedding Chapel* (watercolour heightened with white/paper, 9¼ x 12¼ ins / 23.6 x 31.4 cm) DEM 2,825.

KINKEAD, Alice S.
Irish, 19th - 20th century.
Born in Tuam.
Painter.

Alice Kinkead exhibited in Paris at the Société Nationale des Beaux-Arts from 1897 to 1922.

KINKELIN, Eduard
Swiss, 19th century.
Born 25 September 1797, in Bern; died 2 November 1879, in Geneva.
Painter, draughtsman. Still-lifes (flowers/fruit).

Eduard Kinkelin's *Portion of Fruit* was shown at the Bern Art Exhibition in 1857.

KINKELIN, Karl
German, 19th - 20th century.
Born 13 August 1842, in Munich; died 3 October 1920, in Munich.
Painter, decorative designer. Stage sets.

Karl Kinkelin executed the decorative scheme of the Bavarian Court Theatre in Munich.

KINKOKU, real name Yokoi Myodo, artist names Kinkoku, Komori, Dojin
Japanese, 18th - 19th century.
Born 1761; died 1832.
Painter, draughtsman. Landscapes.
Nanga (literati) school.

AUCTION RECORDS:
NEW YORK, 16 April 1988, *Travellers on the Shu Highway* (ink and light colours on silk, 12 x 16¾ ins / 30.5 x 42.5 cm) USD 1,870. NEW YORK, 17 Oct 1989, *Spring and Autumn Landscapes* (ink and light colours on paper, a pair of hanging scrolls, each 52¾ x 24¾ ins / 134 x 63 cm) USD 16,500.

KINKOKU, real name Ken Yamamoto; given name Shijo; childhood name Satsuemon; artist names Chichisai, Kando, Kinkoku, Shokuro
Japanese, 19th century.
Born 1811; died 1873.
Painter. Landscapes.
Nanga (literati) school.

Yamamoto Ken (Kinkoku) was a samurai in the service of Lord Kamei in Iwami (Shimane Prefecture). He moved to Edo (now Tokyo) to study painting under Watanabe Kazan (1793-1841.

KINLEN
Dutch, 18th century.
Active at the beginning of the 18th century.
Engraver.

Kinlen is known for his plate engraving *Drunken Silenus, Beast and Bacchante* which is signed *Pater Kinten Fecit.*

KINLEY, Peter
Austrian, 20th century.
Born 16 July 1926, in Vienna; died 1988.
Active in England.
Painter. Figures, interiors with figures, gardens, plants, flowers, animals.

Peter Kinley came to England as a child. After service in the British army, he studied at St Martin's School in London, where he subsequently taught, and was influenced by the work of Nicolas de Staël. He had solo exhibitions in London in 1954, and in New York in 1961.

MUSEUMS AND GALLERIES:
LONDON (Tate Collection): *Yellow Flower* (1966-1967, oil on canvas); *Walking Figure* (1957, oil on canvas); *Flowers on a Table* (1966-1967, oil on canvas); *Figure in a Doorway* (1967, oil on canvas); *Four Sheep* (1970, oil on canvas); *Large House with Two Gables* (1980, oil on canvas); *Fire* (1982, oil on canvas); *Two Cows* (1983-1985, oil on canvas).

AUCTION RECORDS:
LONDON, 12 May 1989, *Study for The Black Monkey* (1977, oil on canvas, 21 x 25 ins / 52.5 x 63.8 cm) GBP 2,640. LONDON, 21 Sept 1989, *Study for 'Tortoise 1975'* (diluted oil and gouache/paper, 10 x 10 ins / 25.4 x 25.4 cm) GBP 880. LONDON, 3 May 1990, *Interior of a Studio with a Figure* (1961, oil on card, 12 x 6 ins / 30.5 x 15.5 cm) GBP 825. NEW YORK, 15 Nov 1990, *Study of Plants; Study of Flowers* (1960, oil on card, a pair, 11 x 8 ins / 28 x 20.3 cm) USD 8,800. LONDON, 2 May 1991, *Study of Flowers* (1960, oil on card, 10 x 7 ins / 25.5 x 18 cm) GBP 825. LONDON, 7 June 1991, *Garden* (1975, oil on canvas, 54¼ x 83½ ins / 138 x 212 cm) GBP 3,300. LONDON, 26 March 1993, *Painting - Blue and Black* (1955, oil on canvas, 50 x 25 ins / 127 x 63.5 cm) GBP 4,140. LONDON, 26 Oct 1994, *Interior of a Studio* (oil on canvas, 48 x 36 ins / 122 x 91.5 cm) GBP 3,220. LONDON, 25 Oct 1995, *Grey Interior with Picture* (1967, oil on canvas, 16 x 20 ins / 40.6 x 50.8 cm) GBP 1,035. NEW YORK, 12 Nov 1996, *Interior with Standing Figure* (1960, pencil outlines and oil on paper/panel, 11 x 8 ins / 28 x 20.4 cm) USD 1,093.

KINLOCH, George W.
British, 19th century.
Active in Edinburgh.
Sculptor.

George W. Kinloch exhibited three of his sculptures at the Royal Academy in 1884.

KINNAIRD, Henry John or Henry James John
British, 19th - 20th century.
Died after 1920.
Painter (gouache), watercolourist. Landscapes.

Henry Kinnaird exhibited in London at the Royal Academy and the Suffolk Street gallery from 1880 to 1891.

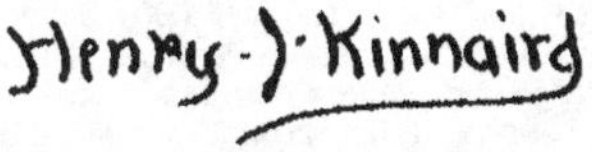

AUCTION RECORDS:
NEW YORK, 1-2 April 1902, *Summer* (watercolour) USD 35. LONDON, 7 June 1973, *Banks of the Thames at Bray, Berkshire*, Gns 350. LONDON, 18 May 1976, *Sussex Landscape* (oil on canvas, 17½ x 31¼ ins / 44.5 x 79.5 cm) GBP 580. LONDON, 2 Oct 1979, *Wheatfield in Sussex; The Thames near Abingdon* (oil on canvas, a pair, 19 x 29½ ins / 48 x 75 cm) GBP

4,800. LONDON, 21 Feb 1980, *Sussex Landscape* (watercolour heightened with white, 10 x 21 1/4 ins / 25.5 x 54 cm) GBP 600. CHESTER, 29 Oct 1981, *Sussex Landscape* (watercolour heightened with gouache, 19 3/4 x 14 1/4 ins / 50 x 36 cm) GBP 1,300. NEW YORK, 27 May 1983, *Harvest Time in Sussex* (watercolour, 13 1/2 x 20 1/4 ins / 34.3 x 51.4 cm) USD 1,000. LONDON, 14 July 1983, *Cornfield near Pangbourne, Bucks; On the River Lea, near Hertford* (oil on canvas, a pair, each 18 x 32 ins / 46 x 81 cm) GBP 3,200. LONDON, 28 Oct 1986, *Harvest Scene near Salisbury* (watercolour heightened with white, 20 x 14 3/4 ins / 50.8 x 37.5 cm) GBP 2,000. LONDON, 21 July 1987, *Shepherd and Flock in a Sussex Landscape* (watercolour and pencil heightened with white, 20 x 14 3/4 ins / 51.1 x 37.7 cm) GBP 2,400. LONDON, 25 Jan 1988, *Meadow in Sussex; The Thames near Goring* (watercolour, two pendants, each 7 3/4 x 15 ins / 20 x 38 cm) GBP 3,740. LONDON, 25 Jan 1989, *Meadow in Sussex* (watercolour, 11 x 7 1/2 ins / 28 x 19 cm) GBP 2,420. NEW YORK, 24 May 1989, *Wheatfield in Sussex* (watercolour and gouache, 10 x 18 ins / 24.5 x 44.8 cm) USD 2,310. CHESTER, 20 July 1989, *Wheatfield near Arundel; Country Track in Sussex* (watercolour, a pair, 10 x 14 3/4 ins / 25.5 x 37.5 cm) GBP 4,180. LONDON, 27 Sept 1989, *View of Windsor Castle from the Thames* (oil on canvas, 30 x 50 ins / 76 x 127 cm) GBP 3,850. LONDON, 25-26 April 1990, *The River Arun, Sussex* (watercolour and gouache, 7 x 11 ins / 18 x 27 cm) GBP 1,430. LONDON, 1 Nov 1990, *Countryside around Lewes, Sussex* (watercolour, 13 1/4 x 20 1/4 ins / 33.4 x 51.7 cm) GBP 3,950. SOUTH QUEENSFERRY, 23 April 1991, *Countryside around Dalmally, Argyll* (watercolour and gouache, 7 x 10 1/2 ins / 18 x 26.5 cm) GBP 770. LONDON, 5 June 1991, *The Thames near Pangbourne* (watercolour, 11 x 16 1/2 ins / 28 x 42 cm) GBP 1,210. LONDON, 7 Oct 1992, *On the River Kennet near Reading* (watercolour heightened with white, 9 3/4 x 14 3/4 ins / 25 x 37.5 cm) GBP 935. LONDON, 5 March 1993, *Farm at Burpham* (watercolour heightened with white, 20 1/4 x 14 3/4 ins / 51.4 x 37.5 cm) GBP 1,610. LONDON, 12 May 1993, *Wheatfield in Sussex* (watercolour and gouache, 13 3/4 x 20 1/2 ins / 35 x 52 cm) GBP 2,070. NEW YORK, 22-23 July 1993, *View of Wensleydale in North Yorkshire* (oil on canvas, 30 x 50 ins / 76.2 x 127 cm) USD 4,600. LONDON, 2 Nov 1994, *The Thames near Wallingford* (watercolour heightened with white, 13 3/4 x 19 3/4 ins / 35 x 50 cm) GBP 2,990. LONDON, 9 May 1996, *View of the Countryside around Steyning in Sussex* (watercolour heightened with white, 13 1/2 x 20 1/4 ins / 34.5 x 51.5 cm) GBP 1,322. BILLINGSHURST, 26 Jan 1999, *Arundel Castle, Sussex. Wargrave Church, Thames.* (watercolour heightened with white, a pair, 13 x 9 ins / 34 x 24 cm) GBP 2,600. BILLINGSHURST, 18 May 1999, *Sussex Hayfield. On the Arun, Sussex* (watercolour heightened with white, a pair, 19 x 14 ins / 48 x 35 cm) GBP 3,600. BILLINGSHURST, 1 Feb 2000, *View near Pulborough, Sussex* (watercolour heightened with gouache, 13 x 20 ins / 34 x 51 cm) GBP 2,300. LEEDS, 14 Nov 2000, *Thames near Wallingford* (watercolour over pencil heightened with white, 9 x 22 ins / 24 x 55 cm) GBP 3,600. LONDON, 9 Jan 2001, *Country River Landscape. Harvest Scene* (oil on board, a pair, 15 x 23 ins / 38 x 59 cm) GBP 4,400. BILLINGSHURST, 23 May 2001, *Near Streatley. Near Cooksbridge* (oil on canvas on board, a pair, 15 x 23 ins / 39 x 59 cm) GBP 7,000. AYLSHAM, 12 April 2002, *Thames near Sonning* (watercolour, 13 x 19 ins / 33 x 48 cm) GBP 1,600. LONDON, 19 Sept 2002, *Sussex Lane. Country Lane, Perth* (pencil and watercolour heightened with white, a pair, 14 x 11 ins / 35 x 27 cm) GBP 1,800. LONDON, 12 June 2003, *View near Arundel. View near Salisbury* (watercolour and gouache, a pair, 7 x 11 ins / 18 x 27 cm) GBP 3,400. CREWKERNE, 16 Oct 2003, *Haymaking Scene* (oil on canvas, 15 x 24 ins / 39 x 60 cm) GBP 1,900. LEWES, 27 Jan 2004, *Cornstalks in a Field, Extensive Landscape beyond* (oil on canvas, 18 x 32 ins / 46 x 81 cm) GBP 1,400. BIRMINGHAM, 18 May 2004, *Near Pulborough, Sussex* (watercolour, 20 x 13 ins / 52 x 34 cm) GBP 2,100.

KINNEAR, James
British, 19th century.
Active in Edinburgh c. 1880.
Painter, watercolourist. Landscapes.

AUCTION RECORDS:
LONDON, 27 Sept 1989, *Gathering Buttercups and other Wildflowers* (oil on canvas, 26 x 40 1/4 ins / 66 x 102 cm) GBP 2,860. GLASGOW, 6 Feb 1990, *The River Tay near Stanley* (oil on canvas, 24 x 35 3/4 ins / 61 x 91 cm) GBP 2,420. MONTRÉAL, 30 April 1990, *Coastal Scenes with Children and Boats* (oil on canvas, a pair, each 16 1/4 x 24 ins / 41 x 61 cm) CAD 2,640. EDINBURGH, 23 March 1993, *Edinburgh from Braid Hills* (watercolour heightened with white, 19 1/4 x 29 1/4 ins / 49 x 74 cm) GBP 920. DETROIT, 16 July 1999, *Shepherd with Sheep by Lake* (oil on canvas, 36 x 46 ins / 91 x 117 cm) USD 1,900. EDINBURGH, 12 May 2000, *Fisherman on the Tummel Looking to Ben Venue* (watercolour, sold with a companion, 13 x 20 ins / 34 x 51 cm) GBP 1,150. LONDON, 8 March 2001, *Shepherd with his Flock on the Scottish Coast* (oil on canvas, 30 x 46 ins / 76 x 117 cm) GBP 1,300. LONDON, 8 March 2001, *Figure in a Rowing Boat in a Tranquil River Landscape, Castle Beyond* (1877, oil on canvas, 24 x 42 ins / 61 x 107 cm) GBP 1,600. LONDON, 27 Aug 2003, *Links at St Andrews* (oil on board, 12 x 17 ins / 30 x 42 cm) GBP 12,000.

KINNEBROOK, W. A.
British, 19th century.
Active in London.
Painter.

W.A. Kinnebrook exhibited at the Royal Academy and at the Suffolk Street Gallery from 1843 to 1863.

KINNEY, Troy
American, 19th - 20th century.
Born 1 December 1871, in Kansas City; died 1938, in Falls Village.
Painter, engraver, decorative designer.

Troy Kinney studied at Yale University and the Art Institute of Chicago. He was a both a figure painter and illustrator, but was most famous as an etcher and drypoint artist. He became a member of the Chicago Society of Etchers, the Brooklyn Society of Etchers, the Philadelphia Paint Club and the New York Architectural League. He depicted nudes and dance scenes, particularly of the ballet, and he portrayed leading ballerinas such as Vera Fokina, Totola Valencia and the Russian dancer, Pavlova.

BIBLIOGRAPHY:
West Kinney, Margaret, *The Etchings of Troy Kinney*, Doubleday, New York, 1929.

MUSEUMS AND GALLERIES:
CHICAGO (AI) - CLEVELAND (MA) - HONOLULU (Bishop Mus.) - NEW YORK (Public Library) - WASHINGTON DC (Library of Congress).

KINOSHITA, Suchan
Japanese, 20th - 21st century.
Born 1960, in Tokyo.
Active in the Netherlands.
Installation artist. Animated films, multimedia.

Kinoshita studied music at the Musikhochschule in Cologne, Germany, from 1981 to 1984, and experimental theatre at the Jan van Eyck Akademie in Maastricht, The Netherlands, from 1988 to 1990. She lives and works in Maastricht.

She interprets everyday objects in new ways: in Ghent, she exhibited vacuum-cleaner bags filled with dirt from the museum in which they were exhibited. Her work also tries to involve the viewer, stressing the relativity of art in space and time. At the MUHKA (Museum van Hedendaagse Kunst) in Antwerp, she exhibited a number of hut-shaped wooden structures in which the viewer could experience a variety of sensory stimuli (auditory, tactile, visual and so on). She creates highly detailed scenographic works using music, text, theatre techniques, photography, video and sculpture to disrupt perception.

Among the group exhibitions in which Kinoshita has taken part are: 1995, Venice and Istanbul Biennales; and 1997, Johannesburg Biennale, *Connexions implicites (Implicit Connections)* at the École des Beaux-Arts and *Delta* at the Musée d'Art Moderne in Paris. She has also had a number of solo shows, including: 1991, De Fabrick, Eindhoven; 1996, White Cube, London; 2002, *Premier Mariage (First Marriage)*, MUHKA, Antwerp.

BIBLIOGRAPHY:

Berndes, Christiane, *Contemporary Art from the Netherlands*, group exhibition catalogue, Stedelijk Van Abbemuseum, Eindhoven, 1998. *Suchan Kinoshita: Meaning is Moist*, exhibition catalogue, S.M.A.K. Stedelijk Museum voor Actuele Kunst, Ghent (BEL), Chisendale Gall., London, 1998. Bonami, Francesco, *Suchan Kinoshita*, Phaidon, London, 1998. Lambrecht, Luk, '*Suchan Kinoshita S.M.A.K*' in *Flash Art* n° 204, periodical, January-February 1999. Ramade, Bénédicte, '*Noces de coton*' in *L'Oil* n° 544, periodical, Paris, February 2003.

MUSEUMS AND GALLERIES:

LYONS (MAC).

KINOSHITA, Tomio
Japanese, 20th century.
Born 1923, in Mie (Kyoto Prefecture).
Print artist.
Sosaku hanga.

Kinoshita Tomio graduated from Nagoya Applied Art School in 1941. He makes woodblock prints in the tradition of the Modernist *sosaku hanga* (creative print) movement founded by Yamamoto Kanae. His prints are of repetitive forms using lines carved deep into the block. He is a member of the Japanese Print Association and an associate member of the National Art Academy. Since 1957, he has exhibited with these bodies and won prizes several times. He has also exhibited outside Japan on a number of occasions.

KINOT, Joseph
Belgian, 20th century.
Born 1903; died 1968.
Painter. Landscapes.

KINRYO, real name Kaneko Inkei; given name Kunsho; artist names Kinryo, Jitsuutei
Japanese, 19th century.
Died 1817.
Active in Edo (now Tokyo).
Painter.

Kinryo was a pupil of Buncho (1763-1840). He was a bird and flower painter.

KINSARVIK, Lars
Norwegian, 19th - 20th century.
Born 8 September 1846, in Hardanger; died 23 June 1925, in Hardanger.
Sculptor (wood).

Lars Kinsarvik was a student of Askevold in Bergen. He aimed to create an original approach for ornamental sculpture and decorated several churches in western Norway.

KINSBOURG, L. (Mme)
French, 20th century.
Active in Paris.
Sculptor.

KINSBURGER, Sylvain
French, 19th century.
Born 21 January 1855, in Paris.
Sculptor, medallist, draughtsman.

Sylvain Kinsburger was a pupil of A. Dumont and Thomas. He began exhibiting his work at the Salon de Paris in 1878, then became a member of the Société des Artistes Français. He obtained honourable mentions in 1884 and 1886; a third class medal in 1888; bronze medals in 1889 and 1900 at the Exposition Universelle and a second class medal in 1899.

AUCTION RECORDS:

WASHINGTON DC, 24 Feb 1980, *Tennis Players* (bronze and ivory, a pair, h. 16 1/2 ins / 42 cm) USD 1,100. PARIS, 29 April 1988, *Woman Playing Tennis* (brown-patinated bronze and ivory, h. 13 ins / 33 cm) FRF 17,000. PARIS, 15 Dec 1995, *Amphitrite* (terracotta, h. 6 3/4 ins / 17 cm, w. 4 3/4 ins/12 cm) FRF 4,200. BRUSSELS, 17 May 1999, *The Course of the Stream* (sculpture, bronze, h. 24 ins / 62 cm) BEF 85,000. BILLINGSHURST, 11 April 2000, *The Gallant* (sculpture, variegated patinated bronze and ivory, h. 24 ins / 60 cm) GBP 2,500. DETROIT, 14 April 2000, *Fillette à la rose* (sculpture, brown patinated bronze, h. 23 ins / 58 cm) USD 3,500. BRUSSELS, 12 Feb 2001, *Rural Love* (sculpture, brown patinated bronze, h. 28 ins / 70 cm) BEF 95,000. PARIS, 28 June 2001, *Bird-charmer* (c. 1880, sculpture, Florentine patinated bronze, 24 x 10x10 ins / 60 x 25x25 cm) FRF 11,500.

KINSCHOT, Gaspard Louis François van
Dutch, 19th century.
Born 31 May 1811, in Amsterdam; died 24 December 1861, in Maastricht.
Painter, engraver, writer.

Gaspard van Kinschot is known for his drawings of tombs in churches in Amsterdam, Arnhem, Gouda, Maastricht and others.

KINSELLA, James
American, 19th - 20th century.
Born 14 December 1857, in New York; died 5 January 1923, in New York.
Painter. Landscapes.

James Kinsella rounded off his art education at the École des Beaux-Arts in Paris.

KINSEY, Helen Fairchild
American, 19th - 20th century.
Born 12 August 1877, in Philadelphia; died 4 Dec 1959.
Painter.

Helen Kinsey studied under Thouron, Chase, Dow and Anschutz. She was a member of the American Federation of Arts.

KINSLER, Anna
French, 20th century.
Born 11 November 1892, in Paris.
Painter.

Anna Kinsler exhibited at the Salon d'Automne in Paris.

KINSLEY, Albert
British, 19th - 20th century.
Born 26 June 1852, in Hull; died 1945.
Painter, watercolourist. Landscapes.

Albert Kinsley came to the city of Leeds as a child and lived there until 1879, when he settled in London. He was a member of the Royal Society of British Artists and the Royal Institute of Painters in Watercolours, and an associate of the Royal Cambrian Academy. He exhibited in London at the Royal Academy and the Suffolk Street Gallery, and at the Royal Society of Painters in Watercolours from 1881. A watercolour by Kinsley featured at the Paris Exposition Universelle of 1900.

MUSEUMS AND GALLERIES:

LEEDS (City AG): *Burnham Beeches* (1882, oil on canvas).

AUCTION RECORDS:

LONDON, 29 Jan 1910, *In Bolton Wood*, GBP 4. LONDON, 30 June 1999, *Where the Burn Winds its Moorland Course* (watercolour, 24 x 39 ins / 60 x 98 cm) GBP 1,100.

KINSLEY, Nelson Gray
American, 19th century.

Born 14 July 1863, in Canton (Massachusetts); died 2 May 1945, in Kronburg, Germany.
Painter. Landscapes, animals.

Nelson Gray Kinsley went to Europe at an early age and studied art in Düsseldorf and Karlsruhe. He exhibited in Berlin, Bremen, Vienna and Munich.

AUCTION RECORDS:

MUNICH, 27 May 1978, *Stag on the Edge of a Wood* (oil on mounted canvas/panel, 7¾ x 11¼ ins / 20 x 28.5 cm) DEM 2,700. CALAIS, 3 July 1988, *Return to the Village in Snow* (1879, oil on canvas, 22½ x 38¼ ins / 57 x 97 cm) FRF 52,000.

KINSMAN-WATERS, Ray
American, 20th century.
Born 21 July 1887, in Columbus (Ohio); died 1962.
Painter.

Ray Kinsman-Waters studied at the Columbus Art School. He was a member of the Société des Artistes Independants.

KINSON, François Joseph, or Kinsoen
Flemish School, 18th - 19th century.
Born 28 February 1771, in Bruges; died 18 October 1839, in Bruges.
Active and naturalised in France.
Painter. History painting, portraits.

François Kinson studied at the Bruges academy. In 1801 he married the daughter of the architect Leprince and became court painter to Jerome of Westphalia. He went to Paris to work as a portrait painter and took French citizenship. He returned to Paris after the fall of the empire and was appointed painter to the Duke of Angoulême.

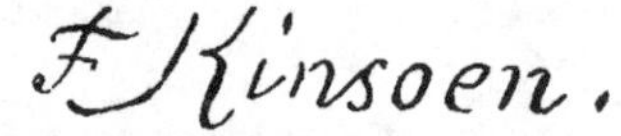

BIBLIOGRAPHY:

Guédron, Martial, '*Suvée, Odevaere, Kinsoen et Ducq: quatre peintres brugeois à Paris au temps du néo-classicisme*' in *Jaarboek*, Stedelijke Musea, Bruges, 1995-1996. *Les Années romantiques, la peinture française de 1815 à 1850*, exhibition catalogue, Musée des Beaux-Arts, Nantes, Gal. nationales du Grand Palais, Paris, 1996.

MUSEUMS AND GALLERIES:

ARRAS: *Young Girl* - BORDEAUX: *Duke of Angouleme* - BRUGES: *Death of Antonina, Wife of Belisarius; Portraits of the Préfet of Very and a Lady* - MOULINS: *Portrait of Mme Thuret* (1824) - THE HAGUE (Gemeentemus.): *Portraits of William II of Orange and his Wife Anna Polowna* - VERSAILLES: *Charles Leclerc; Bernadotte; Jérôme Bonaparte; Louis-Antoine d'Artois.*

AUCTION RECORDS:

PARIS, 1879, *Portrait of a Man Plucking the Strings of a Guitar,* FRF 3,000. PARIS, 7 Dec 1922, *Portrait Presumed to be of Prince Borghese,* FRF 300. PARIS, 8 Feb 1935, *Portrait of General Leclerc,* FRF 3,100. MONTE CARLO, 8 Dec 1984, *Portrait of the Duchess of Berry* (oil on canvas, 24¾ x 20¾ ins / 63 x 53 cm) FRF 75,000. MONTE CARLO, 22 Feb 1986, *Portrait of Jérôme of Westphalia in Regal Attire* (oil on canvas, 104¾ x 68½ ins / 266 x 174 cm) FRF 150,000. PARIS, 15 June 1988, *Portrait of the Duke of Angouleme in the Costume of Grand Admiral* (oil on canvas, 46 x 35½ ins / 117 x 90 cm) FRF 102,000. MONACO, 2 Dec 1989, *Portrait of the Duchess of Mac-Mahon Standing with her Son* (1827, oil on canvas, 95½ x 65¼ ins / 242.5 x 166 cm) FRF 532,800. PARIS, 11 Dec 1989, *Portrait of a Young Woman in a Blue Dress* (oil on canvas) FRF 100,000. PARIS, 22 June 1990, *Portrait of a Young Woman in a Park* (oil on canvas, 27½ x 21¼ ins / 70 x 54 cm) FRF 200,000. PARIS, 16 Dec 1996, *Portrait of the Duchess of Berry* (1823, oil on canvas, 26 x 21¼ ins / 66 x 54 cm) FRF 30,000. NEW YORK, 23 May 1997, *Bust Portrait of a Lady with her Left Hand Holding a Muslin Shawl Draped around her Chest* (1820, oil on canvas, 25½ x 21½ ins / 64.8 x 54.5 cm) USD 23,000. PARIS, 19 March 1999, *Elegant Portrait* (c. 1830, oil on canvas, 45 x 35 ins / 115 x 90 cm) FRF 52,000. PARIS, 12 June 2001, *Portrait of the Duchess of Berry in Mourning* (oil on canvas, 24 x 16 ins / 60 x 40 cm) FRF 148,000. PARIS, 19 June 2001, *Portrait of the Duchess of Angouleme* (oil on canvas, oval, 26 x 21 ins / 65 x 53 cm) FRF 80,000. PARIS, 10 April 2002, *Young Mother and her Three Children in a Castle* (oil on canvas, 25 x 21 ins / 63 x 53 cm) EUR 9,500. SAN FRANCISCO, 14 May 2003, *Portrait of a Lady in a Blue Dress Resting against a Parapet* (oil on canvas, 75 x 50 ins / 190 x 126 cm) USD 12,000. PARIS, 2 Dec 2003, *Portrait of a Woman in a Blue Dress* (oil on canvas, 75 x 50 ins / 190 x 126 cm) EUR 18,000.

KINT, Dirk, or Kindt
Dutch, 18th century.
Born 6 December 1676, in The Hague; died 27 May 1762, in The Hague.
Painter. History painting, portraits.

Dirk Kint was a pupil of Daniel Haaring and Const Netscher. In 1706 he was a member of the Pictura group in The Hague. Unable to earn a living from painting, he became a bookseller. He was senior member of the guild and director of the academy.

KINT, Magda
Belgian, 20th century.
Born 1936, in Ninove.
Painter, watercolourist.

Magda Kint was self-taught.

KINTS, Pieter
Flemish School, 17th century.
Engraver.

Pieter Kints worked in Brussels between 1610 and 1620, though some biographers also say 1635. He made wood engravings after drawings by Anthonie Sallaert; he signed himself *P K.*

KINUTANI, Koji
Japanese, 20th century.
Born 24 January 1943, in Nara.
Painter. Murals.

Kinutani Koji graduated from the Tokyo National University of Fine Arts and Music in 1966 before going to Venice, where he studied at the Academy. He later became a Professor at the Tokyo College of Art. He has lived outside Japan, more than once staying in China. He paints sculptural heads with decorative motifs on them, such as flowers and graphic signs. In 1987, he painted a monumental work for the Ichinomiya Municipal Museum. Kinutani has exhibited his work in group shows, and since 1959 has exhibited regularly in Japan, especially at the Nichido Gallery, Tokyo. He has been awarded Japan's Fine Arts Grand Prize.

KINZEL, Josef
Austrian, 19th - 20th century.
Born 4 May 1852, in Lobenstein; died 4 August 1925, in Spitz am Donau.
Painter. Genre scenes.

Josef Kinzel was a student at the fine arts academies in Vienna and Munich. He exhibited in both cities from 1882.

AUCTION RECORDS:

VIENNA, 29 Nov 1966, *The Village Politician,* ATS 30,000. VIENNA, 14 March 1967, *Reading the Newspaper,* ATS 35,000. VIENNA, 17 Oct 1972, *The Wine-tasting Cup,* ATS 30,000. COLOGNE, 29 March 1974, *A Good Drink,* DEM 4,400. VIENNA, 13 April 1976, *A Good Drink* (oil on panel, 10¼ x 8 ins / 26 x 20.5 cm) ATS 18,000. VIENNA, 11 April 1978, *Cabaret Scene* (oil on canvas, 27¼ x 22 ins / 69 x 56 cm) ATS 30,000. NEW YORK, 2 May 1979, *Serving Woman in the Kitchen* (1900, oil on panel, 20 x 13¼ ins / 50.8 x 33.7 cm) USD 4,200. NEW YORK, 28 May 1981, *A Wrong Note* (1892, oil on canvas, 25 x

35 1/2 ins / 63.5 x 90 cm) USD 16,000. VIENNA, 5 Dec 1984, *Grandfather's Favourites* (1893, oil on canvas, 20 3/4 x 16 3/4 ins / 53 x 42.5 cm) ATS 50,000. VIENNA, 20 March 1985, *Is Your Lover There?* (oil on panel, 20 3/4 x 16 1/4 ins / 53 x 41 cm) ATS 80,000. VIENNA, 10 Dec 1987, *Inn Scene* (1887, oil on panel, 15 3/4 x 12 1/2 ins / 40 x 32 cm) ATS 100,000. MUNICH, 21 June 1994, *Visitor Receiving a Warm Welcome* (1884, oil on canvas, 23 3/4 x 32 1/4 ins / 60.5 x 82 cm) DEM 18,400. MUNICH, 2 Dec 1997, *Headstrong (Cabaret Scene)* (1900, oil on canvas, 28 3/4 x 25 1/4 ins / 73 x 64 cm) DEM 34,500.

KINZEL, Liesl or Élise
Austrian, 20th century.
Born 18 May 1886, in Vienna; died 1961.
Painter. Landscapes.

Élise Kinzel exhibited in Vienna from 1913.

AUCTION RECORDS:
LONDON, 5 Feb 1982, *Reading the Letter* (oil on canvas, 26 1/2 x 20 ins / 67.4 x 50.9 cm) GBP 1,400. VIENNA, 20 May 1999, *Flowers on Window Sill, View of River Danube through Window* (oil on board, 24 x 32 ins / 60 x 81 cm) ATS 100,000. ZOFINGEN, 8 June 2001, *Summer River Landscape with Village* (oil on board, 16 x 18 ins / 40 x 46 cm) CHF 2,800. LINDAU, 4 Oct 2001, *Flowering Geraniums* (oil on board on panel, 23 x 31 ins / 59 x 79 cm) DEM 3,500.

KIOELER, Pehr. See **KÖHLER Per**

KIOELSTROEM, J.
German, 18th century.
Active at the end of the 18th century.
Engraver.

There is a plate, *Portrait of Princess Sophie Wilhelmine as a Child*, signed by Kioelstroem, in the library in Karlsruhe.

KIOERBOE, Carl Fredrik
Swedish, 19th century.
Born 1 June 1799, in Christiansfeld, to Swedish parents; died 1876, in Dijon.
Painter. Portraits, hunting scenes, animals.

Carl Kioerboe was a pupil of Henning. He worked in Berlin, Paris and Stockholm. He was a painter at the Swedish court and a member of the fine arts academy in Stockholm. He was awarded a third-class medal in 1844, a second-class medal in 1846, and became a Chevalier of the Légion d'Honneur in 1860.

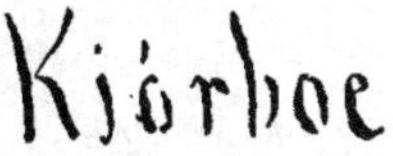

MUSEUMS AND GALLERIES:
AMIENS: *Dog with her Young* - OSLO: *The Fox Hunt* - STOCKHOLM: *The Fox Hunt*; *Portrait of Charles XV*.

AUCTION RECORDS:
PARIS, 1861, *Fox Eying Rabbits*, FRF 335. PARIS, 14-15 Dec 1925, *The Breeder with her Young*; *Dogs and Fox* (pair) FRF 800. PARIS, 1 March 1942, *The Escaped Horse*, FRF 1,200. PARIS, 7 Feb 1951, *Foxes Devouring a Dead Duck*, FRF 36,000. STOCKHOLM, 23 April 1980, *Summer Landscape* (oil on canvas, 21 1/4 x 25 1/2 ins / 54 x 65 cm) SEK 12,500. STOCKHOLM, 29 Oct 1985, *Foxes Chasing Hare* (oil on canvas, 42 1/4 x 35 ins / 107 x 88 cm) SEK 38,000. STOCKHOLM, 13 Nov 1987, *Foxes Chasing Horses* (oil on canvas, 17 3/4 x 20 3/4 ins / 45 x 53 cm) SEK 21,000. MILAN, 14 June 1989, *The Taking of the Fox* (1843, oil on canvas, 35 1/2 x 46 1/4 ins / 90 x 117.5 cm) ITL 4,500,000. STOCKHOLM, 14 Nov 1990, *Wooded Landscape with Fox* (oil on canvas, 29 1/2 x 41 1/4 ins / 75 x 105 cm) SEK 20,000. PARIS, 13 Nov 1991, *Child with Pony* (oil on canvas, 28 3/4 x 36 1/4 ins / 73 x 92 cm) FRF 56,500. STOCKHOLM, 10-12 May 1993, *Wolves Attacking a Reindeer in a Forest in Winter* (oil on canvas, 36 1/4 x 28 1/4 ins / 92 x 72 cm) SEK 24,000. LONDON, 11 Feb 1994, *Newfoundland Dog* (oil on canvas, 51 1/4 x 64 1/4 ins / 130.2 x 163.2 cm) GBP 10,580. STOCKHOLM, 26 May 1999, *Portrait of a Horse* (oil on canvas, 24 x 29 ins / 60 x 73 cm) SEK 38,000. STOCKHOLM, 9 Oct 1999, *Karl XV on Horseback in Uniform Inspecting French Troops* (oil on canvas, 57 x 44 ins / 145 x 112 cm) SEK 74,000. AHLDEN, 24 Nov 2000, *Habdanis Blanc* (oil on canvas, 29 x 36 ins / 74 x 92 cm) DEM 9,000. COPENHAGEN, 4 Dec 2000, *Dogs in Landscape* (oil on canvas, 23 x 29 ins / 59 x 73 cm) DKK 38,000. STOCKHOLM, 22 May 2001, *Hunting Wild Boar with Dogs* (oil on canvas, 19 x 22 ins / 47 x 56 cm) SEK 17,000. STOCKHOLM, 3 Dec 2002, *King Karl XV on Horseback* (oil on canvas, 34 x 30 ins / 86 x 75 cm) SEK 24,000. STOCKHOLM, 26 May 2003, *Fox Hunting* (oil on canvas, 22 x 18 ins / 55 x 46 cm) SEK 15,000. STOCKHOLM, 26 May 2003, *Two Dogs* (oil on canvas, 23 x 29 ins / 59 x 73 cm) SEK 25,000. NEW YORK, 10 Feb 2004, *Head of Bassett Hound* (oil on canvas, 25 x 21 ins / 64 x 53 cm) USD 2,600.

KIOPINI, Christian
Canadian, 20th - 21st century.
Born 1949, in Sorel (Quebec).
Painter, sculptor.

Christian Kiopini began his artistic career working in sculpture, but has subsequently focused increasingly on painting and drawing. His earlier works (until the late 1970s) combine geometric rigour and an expressionistic use of gesture. Since the early 1980s he has explored the expressive potential of the support - cut out, superposed and fragmented, or extended and reinforced, creating veritable Minimalist structures heightened by the application of pure colour.

MUSEUMS AND GALLERIES:
MONTREAL (MAC): *Shadow* (1983).

KIP, Jan
Dutch, 17th - 18th century.
Born c. 1653, in Amsterdam; died 1722, in Westminster, London.
Engraver.

Jan Kip married Elisabeth Breda on 5 April 1680 in Amsterdam. He went to England in 1697. His daughter was also a painter. Kip is known for his *Views of English Castles* after Leonard Knyff; *View of the Dutch Church in London*; *View of Amsterdam*; *Groningen* and numerous *Portraits*.

KIP, Willem or William
Dutch, 17th century.
Active in London c. 1600.
Engraver.

Willem Kip engraved views of a *Triumphal Arch* and a *Monumental Gate*. He is mentioned by Walpole and biographers generally consider him to be English.

KIPKE, Zeljko
Yugoslav, 20th - 21st century.
Born 1953.
Painter.

Zeljko Kipke lives and works in Zagreb. An art critic and theoretician he has been influenced by Malevich, Dada, Magritte, medieval frescoes and Byzantine art. He reproduces geometric shapes, fragments of machines, cylinders, pistons, wheels, freely interpreting them in order to come up with motifs detached from their context which appear to float across the canvas. He has shown his works at several solo exhibitions, notably at the Castres contemporary art centre in France in 1990.

KIPLIK, Dmitri Jossifovich
Russian, 19th century.
Born 1865.
Active in St Petersburg.
Painter.

Kiplik worked in Nizny-Novgorod and exhibited work in Berlin.

KIPLING, John Lockwood
British, 19th - 20th century.
Born 1837; died 1911.
Active in India.
Illustrator, sculptor, designer.

John Lockwood Kipling was a British artist and a scholar. He moved to India with his wife Alice in 1865, where his first son Rudyard Kipling was born. In India Kipling taught architectural sculpture at the Jejeebhoy School of Art and Industry, and was curator of the Lahore Museum. Aspects of his character are known through the work of his son Rudyard, the famous writer, who won the Nobel Prize for Literature in 1907. John Lockwood Kipling illustrated several of Rudyard's works and appears as one of his characters in the first chapter of his novel Kim. Kipling designed the Dunbar Room at Osborne House and was involved in the decoration of the Victoria and Albert Museum. He is also the author of *Beast and Man in India* (1891).

BIBLIOGRAPHY:
Kipling, John Lockwood, *Beast and Man in India: A Popular Sketch of Indian Animals in their Relations with People*, Macmillan and Co., London and New York, 1891 (with contributions by Rudyard Kipling).

KIPLING, Mary
British, 19th century.
Active in London.
Miniaturist.

Mary Kipling exhibited at the Royal Academy from 1843 to 1848.

KIPLING, Rudyard
British, 19th - 20th century.
Born 30 December 1865, in Bombay; died January 1936, in London.
Draughtsman, illustrator.

Rudyard Kipling, the celebrated novelist, short story writer and poet, also produced illustrations for his *Just So Stories*.

KIPMAN, Ladislas
Polish, 19th century.
Painter.

Ladislas Kipman was a realist painter, with a tendency towards anecdotalism.

KIPP, Lyman
American, 20th century.
Born 24 December 1929, in Dobbs Ferry (New York).
Sculptor.
Minimal Art.

Lyman Kipp studied in the early 1950s at the Pratt Institute in New York and then the Cranbrook Academy at Bloomfield Hills. In large sculptures made up with ultra-simple volumes evolved from Minimal Art aesthetics, he has focused on the complexities of colour in sculpture. His deliberately austere works achieve great poise.

He has taken part in collective exhibitions in Baltimore, Providence, New York (frequently at the Whitney Annual), Los Angeles, San Diego, the 1963 São Paulo Biennale, *L'Art du réel, U.S.A. 1948-1968* (*The Art of the Real, USA, 1948-1968*), Paris, and Zurich. He has shown his works in solo exhibitions since 1954 in New York, Buffalo, Boston, Dallas and Chicago.

BIBLIOGRAPHY:
Friedman, Martin, *Ten Sculptors*, Biennale de São Paulo, São Paulo, 1963. Pincus-Witten, Robert, '*Lyman Kipp*' in *Artforum*, periodical, New York, February, 1966. *L'Art du réel, U.S.A., 1948-1968*, exhibition catalogue, Gal. nationales du Grand Palais, Paris, 1968.

MUSEUMS AND GALLERIES:
ATLANTA (High Mus. of Art) - BUFFALO (Albright-Knox AG) - FORT WORTH (MMA): *Untitled* (1973) - NEW YORK (Whitney Mus. of American Art).

KIPPENBERGER, Martin
German, 20th century.
Born 1953, in Dortmund; died 7 March 1997, in Vienna.
Painter, collage artist, sculptor, installation artist, draughtsman.
Neo-Conceptual Art.

Martin Kippenberger studied at the academy in Hamburg from 1972 to 1976. After a stay in Florence, he had his first exhibition in Hamburg in 1977. The following year, he moved to Berlin, where he was responsible for the programme scheduling for S.O. 36, a concert and cinema complex and, together with Gisela Capitain, founded Kippenbergers Büro, where he organised exhibitions. He also started a punk rock group, 'Die Grugas'. In the late 1960s, he worked with the artist Albert Oehlen, reacting against the art of the period. In 1979, he travelled to the USA, where he acted in a number of films. From 1980 to 1983, he divided his time between Paris, Siena and Germany, moving to Cologne in 1983. In 1986, he moved to Mexico, 1988 to Spain, 1989 to Los Angeles, and in 1992 to the Black Forest. At this time he taught in Kassel then in Syros in Greece, where he founded a museum of modern art in 1993. In 1984, he produced sculptures and photographs and also made records with the painters Jörg Immendorf and A.R. Penck.

In 1976, he began work on the series *Uno di voi, un tedesco in Firenze* (*One of You, a German in Florence*), made up of 70 black and white pictures, measuring approximately 20 x 24 in (50 x 60 cm), inspired by postcards and by his own photographs. He did not manage to achieve his objective, which was that, when placed one on top of the other, these works would reach a height of 6 feet 2½ in (189 cm), the artist's own height. He continued to work, branching out into many different activities and not hesitating to get other artists to work in his place. Expressionist paintings, very often deliberately botched, drawings, sculptures, ready-made art, collages, photographs, posters, not to mention performances, articles, catalogues and novels, all are represented in the work of this prolific and insatiable artist, who adopts every style, appropriates and recycles the works of other artists - a chair by Aldo Rosso or a painting by Richter - drawing inspiration from the everyday and parodying the art world. As an artist, he is impossible to classify. He offers organised chaos, insolent and provocative, in an age where anything can become the subject of an exhibition.

He was the curator of a number of exhibitions, notably *Eurostroll I-III* in Cologne and Graz. In 1993, he founded the *Kippenberger Kunstverein* at the Fridericianum Museum in Kassel. He was awarded the Käthe Kollwitz Prize in 1996.

From 1979 on, he took part in many group exhibitions including 1987 at the Museumsverein in Wuppertal and the Museum of Modern Art, San Francisco; 1988 at the Cologne Kunstverein and the St Louis Art museum; 1989 at the Hamburg Kunstmuseum and the Solomon R. Guggenheim museum, New York; 1999 at the Centre for Contemporary Art in Barcelona and Villa Arson in Nice; 1992 at the Musée d'Art Moderne de la Ville de Paris; 1997, *Skulptur. Projekte in Münster 1997* (*Sculpture. Projects in Münster 1997*) in Münster. His work was shown posthumously in 2001, *L'Esprit de Famille* (*Family Spirit*) at the Villa du Parc in Annemasse; 2002, *Cher Peintre... peintures figuratives depuis l'ultime Picabia* (*Dear Painter, Figurative Paintings since Late Picabia*) at the Centre Georges Pompidou in Paris and also in 2002, *Painting on the Move*, presenting a century of contemporary painting simultaneously at the Kunstmuseum, Kunsthalle and Museum für Gegenwartskunst in Basel. In 2003, he was chosen to represent Germany at the Venice Biennale and also featured in *Berlin-Moscow/Moscow-Berlin 1950-2000*, a panoramic exhibition at the Martin-Gropius-Bau in Berlin and the Tretyakov Gallery in Moscow, a follow-up to the one on the period 1900-1950, presenting 50 years of Germano-Russian artistic and cultural relations that were marked by political changes.

He has also exhibited in the following solo shows: 1977 at the Galerie Petersen, Hamburg; 1979 and 1981 in Berlin; 1981 and 1983 in Stuttgart; 1983 in Munich; 1985 at the CDD Gallery, Düsseldorf; 1987, 1989 and 1990 at the Galerie Gisela Capitain, Cologne; 1985, 1987, 1989, 1991 and 1992 in New York; 1986 at the Kunstverein in Oldenburg; 1987 at the Villa Arson, Nice; 1988 at the Kunsthalle in Winterthur; 1988, *Aperto*, Venice Biennale; 1989 at the Museum of Contemporary Art in Seville; 1991, Museum of Modern Art, San Francisco; 1992, Munich Kunstverein; 1993, Musée National d'Art Moderne de Paris, Centre Georges Pompidou, Paris; 1994, Boymans van Beuningen Museum, Rotterdam; 1995, Hirchshorn Museum and Sculpture Garden, Washington DC and 1997, Musée d'Art Moderne et Contemporain in Geneva, where 800 works were on show. There have been posthumous exhibitions in 2001 at the Österreichische Galerie Belvedere in Vienna; 2002, Frac Poitou-Charentes, Château d'Oiron (Deux-Sèvres) and an exhibition of 74 subverted posters at the Château d'Oiron and in 2003, a retrospective at the Van Abbenmuseum in Eindhoven.

BIBLIOGRAPHY:
Martin Kippenberger: Petra, exhibition catalogue, Gal. Gisela Capitain, Cologne, 1987. Hermes, Manfred, *'Repetition, disguises, documents'* in *Flash Art (International Edition)* n° 148, periodical, October, 1989. *Martin Kippenberger: I Had a Vision*, exhibition catalogue, San Francisco Museum of Modern Art, San Francisco, 1991. Kippenberger, Martin, *Martin Kippenberger*, San Francisco Museum of Modern Art, San Francisco, 1991 (produced in conjunction with the exhibition Martin Kippenberger: New York organised by the San Francisco Museum of Modern Art, June 13 - August 25 1991). Kippenberger, Martin (ed.)/Noever, Peter, *Martin Kippenberger: The Last Stop West*, MAK Centre for Art and Architecture, New York, 1991. Muthesius, Angelike, *Kippenberger*, Taschen, Cologne, 1991. Diederchsen, Diedrich/Ohrt, Roberto, *Mehr rauchen! Der Zigarettentester im Test*, Cologne, 1994. *Martin Kippenberger: Kippenberger sans peine avec des clichés de reconnaissance*, exhibition catalogue, Musée d'Art moderne et contemporain, Geneva, 1997. Orht, Roberto, *Kippenberger*, Tashen, Cologne, 1997. Breerette, Geneviève, *'Martin Kippenberger - L'Enfant terrible de la scène allemande'* in *Le Monde*, periodical, Paris, 15 March 1997. Wahler, Marc Olivier, *'Martin Kippenberger'* in *Art Press* n° 223, periodical, Paris, April 1997. *Martin Kippenberger*, exhibition catalogue, Kunsthalle, Basel, 1998. *Martin Kippenberger: The Happy End of Franz Kafka's 'Amerika'*, exhibition catalogue, Deichtorhallen, Hamburg, 1999. Kippenberger, Martin, *'Art's Filthy Lesson'* in *Dickhoff, Wilfried, After Nihilism: Essays on Contemporary Art*, Cambridge University Press, 2000. Folie, Sabine, et al., *Cher Peintre... peintures figuratives depuis l'ultime Picabia*, exhibition catalogue, Éd. du Centre Georges-Pompidou, Paris, 2002. Bürgi, Bernhard Mendes, et al., *Painting on the Move*, exhibition catalogue, Kunstmuseum, Kunsthalle, Museum für Gegenwartskunst, Basel, 2002. *'Berlin-Moskau/Moskau-Berlin 1950-2000', 2 vol.*, exhibition catalogue, Martin-Gropius-Bau, Berlin, 2003 (text in German).

MUSEUMS AND GALLERIES:
GENEVA (Mamco): *Untitled* (T-shirt) - NEW YORK (MoMA).

AUCTION RECORDS:
NEW YORK, 3 Oct 1991, *She Seeks Colour, He Seeks Forms, They Meet* (1984, oil and rubber/canvas, 59 x 71 ins / 150 x 180.5 cm) USD 7,150. LONDON, 25 March 1993, *Lantern* (1990, steel, glass and a red lightbulb, h. 109½ ins / 278.2 cm) GBP 8,625. LONDON, 26 May 1994, *Untitled* (1990, acrylic and rubber/canvas, 35½ x 29 ins / 90.2 x 73.5 cm) USD 2,300. PARIS, 17 Oct 1994, *Untitled* (1988, pencil and letraset/writing paper from the Alfa Theater Hotel in Antwerp, 11½ x 8¼ ins / 29 x 21 cm) FRF 4,500. NEW YORK, 15 Nov 1995, *Lantern* (1990, steel, glass and red light bulb, h. 109½ ins / 278.2 cm) USD 4,830. LONDON, 24 Oct 1996, *Das war Brehmes Goldener Elfer (That was Brehme's Golden Penalty)* (1991, acrylic and silk/canvas, 24 x 36 ins / 61 x 91.5 cm) GBP 1,035. VIENNA, 13 Oct 1999, *Cancer or Caries* (1984, mixed media, 63 x 53 ins / 160 x 135 cm) ATS 360,000. NEW YORK, 16 Nov 1999, *Untitled* (oil on canvas, 79 x 94 ins / 200 x 240 cm) USD 650,000. NEW YORK, 17 May 2000, *Under Eiffel Tower in Tokyo Lauworm* (steel, wood, styrofoam, glass and photographs, 45 x 54x44 ins / 115 x 136x112 cm) USD 55,000. NEW YORK, 16 Nov 2000, *Portrait of Paul Schreber, Designed by Himself* (1994, oil, lacquer and silicon on canvas, 94 x 79 ins / 240 x 200 cm) USD 150,000. LONDON, 7 Feb 2001, *Woman is the Most Dangerous Weapon of the Apartment* (1984, oil, paper collage and staples on canvas, six, 89 x 71 ins / 227 x 181 cm) GBP 160,000. LONDON, 28 June 2001, *Untitled, Hotel Series* (1995, crayon, ink, marker pen, watercolour and colour pencil, three, 11 x 8 ins / 29 x 21 cm) GBP 26,000. NEW YORK, 15 May 2002, *Theoretical Picture: My Toothpick* (1983, oil on canvas, 47 x 38 ins / 120 x 97 cm) USD 90,000. COLOGNE, 3 Dec 2002, *Proceeds Mountain* (oil and silicon on canvas, 35 x 30 ins / 90 x 75 cm) EUR 46,000. LONDON, 26 June 2003, *We Don't Have Problems with Disco Door-waiters* (1986, oil, silkscreen, plexiglas and silicon, 59 x 71 ins / 150 x 180 cm) GBP 105,000. LONDON, 21 Oct 2003, *Waiter Des* (wall-lights, oil on canvas on panel, 79 x 94x7 ins / 200 x 240x19 cm) GBP 170,000. NEW YORK, 14 May 2004, *Wie komme ich in Kriegszeiten mit Knochenbruch und Futurismus klar* (1984, oil and metallic paint on panel, six, 87 x 70 ins / 222 x 178 cm) USD 620,000. NEW YORK, 11 Nov 2004, *Untitled, Lamp* (electric lamp, glass, silicone and welded steel, 39 x 46x12 ins / 98 x 118x31 cm) USD 220,000.

KIPPER, Nicolaus. See **KNUPFER**

KIPRENSKY, Orest Adamovich, or Kiprenski, called sometimes Schwalb
Russian, 19th century.
Born 24 March 1778, in Koporie; died 24 October 1836, in Rome.
Painter, draughtsman. Portraits, genre scenes, landscapes.

Kiprensky was the liberated son of a serf, whose master was the property owner Diakonov. He studied under G. Ugryumov and H. Doyen at the fine arts academy in St Petersburg from 1788 to 1803. He was awarded his first gold medal in 1805. He lived in Italy, travelled in Switzerland and Prussia, and spent a period living in Paris where he exhibited work in 1822. After a brief stay in St Petersburg, he returned to Italy. A Romantic painter, he had a special talent for capturing the warmth and expressiveness in his subjects' eyes. In 1809, while living in Moscow, he moved in the capital's intellectual circles, and his portrait of Davidov is considered to be the best example of his work of that period.

His talent for portraiture earned him the nickname 'the Russian Van Dyck'. His early portraits, particularly those painted in St Petersburg, show some similarities to the work of Gros or Géricault. His later work, painted in Italy, was influenced by Canova and the Danish artist Thorvaldsen, which resulted in a noticeable toning down of his style.

By 1816 he was an advisor at the fine arts academy and received a grant to prolong his stay in Italy, remaining there until 1823. He painted a portrait of Aleksandr Pushkin in Russia in 1829.

At the end of the 1820s he returned to Italy, and remained there until his death in 1836.

MUSEUMS AND GALLERIES:

MOSCOW (State Tretyakov Gal.): *Portrait of Cluchmarev; Portrait of a Woman; Portrait of Catherine Aleksandrowno Telechova; Madonna; Sketch; Portrait of the Countess Rostopchin; Portrait of V. S. Chvostov; Self-portrait; Portrait of the Poet Poreshkir; Portrait of Mme D. W. Chvoslava; Portrait of Cluchmarev; Portrait of an Italian Doctor in St Petersburg* - ST PETERSBURG (Gosudarstvennyj Russkij Muz.): *Portrait of General Albrecht; Portrait of Thorvaldsen; Self-portrait; Portrait of the Father of the Artist Adam Schwalb; Young Gardener; Young Spaniard in 17th-century Costume.*

AUCTION RECORDS:

PARIS, 13 March 1985, *Study of a Man* (charcoal heightened with white/blue paper, 18 x 12¼ ins / 46 x 30.8 cm) FRF 33,000. LONDON, 10 Oct 1990, *Portrait of Prince Eugene Grigorevich Gagarin as a Child* (1812, oil on canvas, 22 x 19¼ ins / 55.8 x 49.2 cm) GBP 22,000. LONDON, 14 Dec 1995, *Portrait of the Abbot Sartory* (charcoal, 9 x 7 ins / 22 x 18 cm) GBP 2,300. VIENNA, 29-30 Oct 1996, *Portrait of Petr Vassilievich Basin* (1829, oil on canvas, 18¾ x 14¾ ins / 47.5 x 37.5 cm) ATS 1,785,000. WARSAW, 4 June 2000, *Portrait of a Gentleman* (1813, oil on canvas, 5 x 4 ins / 13 x 10 cm) PLN 52,000.

KIPRIYANOV, Vassili
Russian, 18th century.
Active c. 1700.
Engraver.

Kipriyanov engraved views of towns. He was the director of the Peter the Great Library.

KIPS, Alexander
German, 19th - 20th century.
Born 22 July 1858, in Berlin; died 6 May 1910, in Berlin.
Painter. Landscapes, architectural views.

Alexander Kips was director of the Berlin porcelain factory.

KIPS, Erich
German, 19th - 20th century.
Born 17 January 1869, in Berlin; died 1945.
Painter. Genre scenes, landscapes.

Kips took part in the Berlin Exhibition in 1909.

AUCTION RECORDS:

LONDON, 23 March 1988, *Japanese Village* (oil on canvas, 31½ x 43 ins / 80 x 109 cm) GBP 3,850. LONDON, 25 March 1988, *Piazza Santa Maria Maggiore, Rome* (oil on canvas, 23 x 27½ ins / 58.5 x 70 cm) GBP 4,400. NEW YORK, 1 Nov 1995, *Open-air Café in Grunewald, Berlin 1911* (oil on paper/canvas/card, 40½ x 60¼ ins / 102.9 x 153 cm) USD 167,500. AHLDEN, 23 April 1999, *Panoramic View of Riva on Lake Garda* (oil on canvas, 28 x 39 ins / 71 x 100 cm) DEM 11,000. HAMBURG, 5 May 1999, *Sailing Boat and Steam Tugs Entering Hamburg Harbour* (oil on canvas, 37 x 51 ins / 94 x 130 cm) DEM 28,000. AMSTERDAM, 7 March 2000, *Hong Kong, Street Scene at Victoria Hill* (oil on board, 19 x 13 ins / 49 x 34 cm) NLG 6,000. HAMBURG, 2 Sept 2000, *Steamer in the Shipyard* (oil on canvas, 37 x 51 ins / 93 x 130 cm) DEM 11,000. AHLDEN, 5 May 2001, *Mountain Landscape* (oil on canvas, 38 x 58 ins / 97 x 148 cm) DEM 8,500. MUNICH, 4 July 2001, *Town Wall* (oil on board, 13 x 20 ins / 34 x 50 cm) DEM 3,500. BERN, 6 Nov 2002, *Asiatic River Scene* (oil on panel, 14 x 20 ins / 35 x 50 cm) CHF 3,600. BREMEN, 5 Dec 2003, *View of Malcesine at Gardasee* (oil on canvas, 40 x 60 ins / 101 x 152 cm) EUR 2,400.

KIPSHAVEN, Isaack van
Dutch, 17th century.
Active in Amsterdam.
Painter. Portraits, still-lifes.

Isaack van Kipshaven worked in the style of W. van der Aelst.

MUSEUMS AND GALLERIES:

VERSAILLES: *Portrait of Louisa Henrietta of Nassau* (1663).

AUCTION RECORDS:

LONDON, 22 Feb 1935, *Still-life*, GBP 152. LONDON, 16 July 1980, *Portrait of a Huntsman* (oil on canvas, 48 x 39 ins / 121 x 99 cm) GBP 11,000. LILLE, 12 Dec 1982, *Still-life* (oil on canvas, 30¾ x 38½ ins / 78 x 98 cm) FRF 82,000. LONDON, 26 Oct 1994, *Still-life with Game* (oil on canvas, 24 x 21 ins / 61 x 53.5 cm) GBP 2,300.

KIRALYFALVI-KRAFT, Karoly
Hungarian, 20th century.
Born 29 May 1879, in Zlaté Moravce.
Painter.

Karoly Kiralyfalvi-Kraft studied at the academy of fine arts in Budapest and worked in Florence for a while. On his return to Hungary he made a particular name for himself as a portrait artist.

KIRBERG, Otto
German, 19th - 20th century.
Born 16 May 1850, in Elberfeld; died 16 May 1926, in Düsseldorf.
Painter. Genre scenes.

Otto Kirberg began studying at the fine arts academy in Düsseldorf in 1869, and then became a student of Sohn. In 1870, he went to live in Düsseldorf, and some years later to Munich. He exhibited in Düsseldorf, Dresden, Vienna and Berlin, where he was awarded a gold medal in 1879, and in Antwerp, where he won a medal in 1888.

AUCTION RECORDS:

VIENNA, 20 March 1973, *Motherhood*, ATS 25,000. ZURICH, 20 May 1977, *The Happy Family* (oil on canvas, 39¼ x 30¾ ins / 100 x 78 cm) CHF 3,800. ZURICH, 26 May 1978, *The Happy Family* (oil on canvas, 39¼ x 30¾ ins / 100 x 78 cm) CHF 3,200. COLOGNE, 30 March 1979, *Young Dutchwoman in an Interior* (oil on canvas, 29¼ x 21¼ ins / 74 x 54 cm) DEM 5,000. LONDON, 26 Nov 1982, *Woman in an Interior, Cleaning the Pewterware* (oil on canvas, 26½ x 21½ ins / 67 x 54.5 cm) GBP 2,200. COLOGNE, 24 June 1983, *Maternal Joy* (1876, oil on canvas, 26¾ x 33¾ ins / 68 x 86 cm) DEM 17,000. COLOGNE, 15 Oct 1988, *The Suitor* (oil on canvas, 26½ x 18¼ ins / 67 x 46.5 cm) DEM 4,500. NEW YORK, 28 Feb 1991, *Two Women in a Garden* (oil on canvas, 24½ x 31¾ ins / 62 x 80.6 cm) USD 24,200. NEW YORK, 16 Feb 1995, *The New-born* (1882, oil on canvas, 35 x 28 ins / 88.9 x 71.1 cm) USD 14,950. AMSTERDAM, 5 Nov 1996, *The New-born* (oil on canvas, 20¾ x 24½ ins / 53 x 62.5 cm) NLG 9,440.

KIRBERGER, Nikolaus
German, 16th century.
Born probably in Passau.
Painter.

The Albertina in Vienna owns a monogrammed drawing that has been attributed to Kirberger.

KIRBY, John Joshua
British, 18th century.
Born 1716, in Parnham (Suffolk); died 20 June 1774, in Kew (Surrey).

Painter, draughtsman, engraver, watercolourist.
John Joshua Kirby was the son of John Kirby, the antique dealer and former schoolmaster and miller who settled in Ipswich where, in 1735, he published *The Suffolk Traveller*, an informative guide to interesting old sites in the county.

Kirby certainly inherited his father's taste for artistic things. He was initially employed by a painter of carriages and buildings in Ipswich. In all likelihood, he had already practised as an artist before a meeting with Gainsborough which resulted in his artistic talent coming to the fore. Probably encouraged by the great artist, he began to paint landscapes. In 1748, he published a series of his etchings illustrating views of the region. As he had studied perspective at St Martin's Lane Academy, he was named teacher of architectural drawing to the Prince of Wales, later George III, who would subsequently employ him at Kew Palace. In 1761, he published a treatise on architectural perspective. Woollett made an engraving of his *View of Kew Gardens*.

A member of the Free Society and the Society of Artists, Kirby took part in their exhibitions from 1761 to 1771.

AUCTION RECORDS:
LONDON, 23 Oct 1996, *Heatwave* (oil on card, 17 x 14 3/4 ins / 43.2 x 37.5 cm) GBP 3,220.

KIRBY, V. (Miss)
British, 19th century.
Active in London c. 1850.
Miniaturist.
Miss V. Kirby exhibited at the Royal Academy from 1855 to 1857.

KIRCH, Willy
German, 20th century.
Born 24 March 1892, in Erfurt (Thuringia).
Painter, watercolourist. Landscapes, flowers.
Willy Kirch began exhibiting after World War I.

KIRCHBACH, Ernst Sigismund
German, 19th century.
Born 23 April 1830, in Meissen (Saxony-Anhalt); died 16 August 1876, near Dresden.
Painter. History painting.
E. S. Kirchbach studied with Z. Schnor and also at the Dresden academy. In 1856 he went to work in England, returning to Germany in 1860. He went to Chile in 1869 and worked in Santiago until 1876. He then returned to Dresden, where he soon died.

KIRCHBACH, Franck
German, 19th century.
Born 2 June 1859, in London, of German parents.
Painter, sculptor. History painting.
Franck Kirchbach was the son of Ernst Kirchbach. He studied with L. Pohle at the Dresden academy and then worked with A. Wagner in Munich. In 1884, he went to Paris, where he studied with Munkácsy. In 1889, he succeeded M. Ritter as professor at the Frankfurt Institute of Art. He exhibited for the first time in 1881 in Munich, Berlin, Vienna and Dresden. He received an honourable mention in Paris in 1895.

KIRCHBERGER
French, 18th century.
Active in Strasbourg.
Painter. Landscapes.

KIRCHBICHLER. See **SOLL Ignaz II**

KIRCHEBERGER, Günther C.
German, 20th century.
Born 1928, in Kornwestheim (Baden-Württemberg).
Painter.
Gunther Kircheberger was a student at the fine arts academy in Stuttgart and studied philosophy in Tübingen and London, which enabled him to become a professor. His early works were influenced by Tachism. Until 1960, he tended towards white monochrome painting, but then turned towards a form of abstraction involving wide dark bars (or beams) reminiscent of Soulages. Together with Pfahler and others, he founded the XI group, which exhibited in various cities in Germany and abroad. Solo exhibitions include: 1959, Frankfurt am Main; 1961, Stuttgart; 1962, Darmstadt, Mainz, Berlin and London. He was selected for the young artists' prize in 1954, 1955, 1958 and 1962.

KIRCHEBNER, Alois
Austrian, 19th century.
Born 1823, in Götzens; died 1868, in Bozen, South Tyrol (now Bolzano, Italy).
Painter, engraver.
Alois Kirchebner is known for church paintings and also for portraits, several of which can now be found in the Innsbruck Museum.

KIRCHEBNER, Anton
Austrian, 18th century.
Born 1702, in Axams; died 17 August 1779, near Innsbruck.
Painter.
Anton Kirchebner decorated a large number of churches in southern Bavaria and North Tyrol, for instance in Inzing, Ischgl and Wertach.

KIRCHEBNER, Franz Xaver
Austrian, 18th - 19th century.
Born 6 December 1736, in Götzens; died 15 November 1815, in Götzens.
Painter.
Franz Kirchebner was the son of Anton. Like his father, he painted altarpieces and decorated churches, including those in Umhausen, Gröden, Sistrans, Vill and Inzing.

KIRCHEBNER, Josef
Austrian, 18th - 19th century.
Born 1 March 1756, in Götzens; died 1814, in Birgitz.
Painter.
After studying with his father Anton, Josef Kirchebner spent some time in Vienna, but returned to work with his father on the decoration of the church in Inzing.

KIRCHEBNER, Peter Paul
Austrian, 19th century.
Died 1842, in Innsbruck.
Painter.
MUSEUMS AND GALLERIES:
INNSBRUCK: *Virgin and Child*; *Landscape*; several portraits.

KIRCHEISEN, Eugen Victor
German, 19th - 20th century.
Born 21 August 1855, in Johanngeorgenstadt; died 13 December 1913, in Brunswick.
Sculptor.
Eugen Kircheisen was a student of Schilling. He produced several busts, including his *Monument to Bismarck* in Holzminden, and was commissioned to produce the *Monument to the Memory of Ludwig Richter* in Dresden.

KIRCHENBAUM, J. D.. See **KIRSCHENBAUM Jules D.**

KIRCHER, Alexander
German, 19th century.
Born 26 February 1867.
Painter, illustrator. Seascapes, landscapes.
Before settling in the Dresden area, Alexander Kircher travelled across Europe and as far afield as America.
MUSEUMS AND GALLERIES:
BERLIN - VIENNA.

KIRCHER, Athanasius
German, 17th century.

Born 2 May 1602, in Geisa; died 28 November 1680, in Rome.
Draughtsman, engraver.
Athanasius Kircher was a Jesuit who travelled widely in Europe, especially in Germany. Everywhere he went, he returned with landscapes and views of public buildings.

KIRCHER, William
British, 19th - 20th century.
Born 1835, in England; died April 1911.
Painter.

KIRCHGESSNER, Ferdinand
German, 19th century.
Born in Nuremberg.
Painter.
Kirchgessner studied in Antwerp and later worked mainly in Munich.

KIRCHHOFF, Hans Wilhelm
German, 17th century.
Born 1584; died 15 December 1636, in Kassel.
Active in Kassel.
Painter.
H. W. Kirchhoff is best known for the decorative paintings he did for the castle of Ziegenheim, near Kassel.

KIRCHHOFF, Johann Jakob
German, 19th century.
Born 13 July 1796, in Berlin; died 30 December 1848, in Leipzig.
Painter, illustrator, lithographer. Historical subjects.
J. J. Kirchhoff exhibited in Berlin from 1828 to 1841. He worked for a number of different periodicals.
BIBLIOGRAPHY:
Osterwalder, Marcus (ed.), *Dictionnaire des illustrateurs 1800-1914*, Ides et Calendes, Neuchâtel, 1989.
AUCTION RECORDS:
ROME, 10 April 1990, *Koilon* (1989, oil on canvas, 59 x 39 1/4 ins / 150 x 100 cm) ITL 7,000,000.

KIRCHHOFFER, Henry, or Kirchoffer
Irish, 19th century.
Born c. 1781, in Dublin; died 20 March 1860, in London.
Painter. Genre scenes, portraits.
Henry Kirchhoffer was one of the founders of the Royal Hibernian Academy which, however, he left when he went to settle in London, where he exhibited his paintings from 1837 to 1843.
MUSEUMS AND GALLERIES:
DUBLIN (NG of Ireland): *Portrait of Miniature Painter Charles Robertson* (watercolour).
AUCTION RECORDS:
LONDON, 13 Nov 1973, *View of Edinburgh* (1851) GBP 200.
LONDON, 18 Nov 2003, *Thomas Henry Gray* (1804, miniature, oval) GBP 1,300.

KIRCHMAIER, Franz
German, 16th century.
Died 1589.
Painter, draughtsman. History painting.
Franz Kirchmaier worked in Regensburg and produced, among other works, a heightened drawing of the *Coronation Procession of Emperor Rudolf of Habsburg*.

KIRCHMAIER, Sebastian
German, 17th century.
Active in Regensburg c. 1600.
Painter.
Kirchmaier is known exclusively for paintings inspired by the Christian religion.

KIRCHMAIR, Joseph
German, 19th century.
Born 1806, in Munich; died 1846, in Munich.
Painter (glass/porcelain).
Kirchmair studied at the Munich academy.
AUCTION RECORDS:
LONDON, 20 June 1979, *Setting off for the Hunt* (oil on canvas, 13 1/2 x 18 ins / 34 x 45.5 cm) GBP 1,800.

KIRCHMAYER, Friedrich
German, 19th century.
Born 1813, in Munich; died 1871, in Munich.
Sculptor.
Friedrich Kirchmayer is known for his statues of *Prince Puprecht I* and *King Ruprecht*, which decorate the façade of the Bavarian National Museum in Munich.

KIRCHMAYER, Michael
German, 19th century.
Active c. 1837.
Painter. Landscapes.

KIRCHMAYR, Anton
Austrian, 20th century.
Born 4 June 1887, in Schwaz.
Active in Innsbruck.
Painter.

KIRCHMAYR, Cherubino
Italian, 19th century.
Born 1848, in Venice.
Painter. Portraits, genre scenes.
Cherubino Kirchmayr was a pupil at the academy of fine arts in Venice, and painted portraits of many aristocratic Venetians.
AUCTION RECORDS:
PARIS, 12 May 1923, *Small Schoolboy*, FRF 300.

KIRCHMAYR, Johann
Austrian, 19th century.
Born in Oberperfuss (Tyrol); died 1846, in Oberperfuss (Tyrol).
Sculptor.

KIRCHMAYR, Joseph
German, 19th century.
Born 8 March 1775, in Rockersing; died 1845, in Munich.
Sculptor.
MUSEUMS AND GALLERIES:
HAMBURG: *Bust of Abbé Vogler*.

KIRCHNER, Albert Emil
German, 19th century.
Born 12 May 1813, in Leipzig; died 4 June 1885, in Munich.
Painter, watercolourist, engraver, draughtsman. Landscapes, architectural views.
Albert Kirchner studied at the academy of fine arts in Munich, and later with Dahl in Dresden. In 1832, he settled in Munich and became a member of the academy. He exhibited in Dresden, Breslau (now Wroclaw, Poland), Munich and Berlin. He was a talented watercolourist.
MUSEUMS AND GALLERIES:
LEIPZIG: *South Tyrol* - MUNICH: *Four Views of Castles; Verona; Tomb of Castelbarco in Verona; Rothenburg* - STUTTGART: *View of Genoa* - WROCLAW: *In the Etschthal; Basilica in Verona.*
AUCTION RECORDS:
PARIS, 21 Feb 1919, *Square in Trento* (pencil and sepia) FRF 18. VIENNA, 14 March 1978, *View of the Castle of Taufers* (1870, oil on canvas, 38 1/4 x 31 1/2 ins / 97 x 80 cm) ATS 120,000. MUNICH, 18 Sept 1985, *Venice* (1867, oil on panel, 16 1/4 x 22 3/4 ins / 41.5 x 58 cm) DEM 14,000. MUNICH, 12 Dec 1990, *View of the Prater with the River Isar* (ink/brown paper, 11 1/2 x 16 3/4 ins / 29 x 42.5 cm) DEM 3,300. COPENHAGEN, 1 May 1991, *Mountain Landscape with a Woman and Child*

Walking to the Chapel (1852, oil on canvas, 32 1/4 x 24 3/4 ins / 82 x 63 cm) DKK 41,000. MUNICH, 27 Feb 1999, *Castle Rendelstein in South Tyrol next to River Talfer* (1860, oil on panel, 11 x 9 ins / 27 x 23 cm) DEM 20,000. MUNICH, 29 Sept 1999, *View over Fontana di Ferro in Verona* (1863, oil on panel, 15 x 21 ins / 39 x 53 cm) DEM 26,000. STUTTGART, 8 Dec 2000, *Watermill* (1861, oil on canvas, 47 x 39 ins / 120 x 100 cm) DEM 8,000. MUNICH, 26 Sept 2001, *Venice* (1859, oil on canvas, 23 x 17 ins / 59 x 44 cm) DEM 22,000. MUNICH, 21 June 2002, *Renaissance Castle* (oil on canvas) EUR 3,200. MUNICH, 26 March 2003, *Sonnenburg near St Lorenzen in Pustertal in Tyrol* (1872, oil on canvas, 28 x 39 ins / 70 x 100 cm) EUR 11,500.

KIRCHNER, Carl Anton
German, 19th century.
Born 7 January 1822, in Bremen; died 1 September 1869, in Bremen.
Painter.

Carl Anton Kirchner was professor of drawing in Bremen and worked in all genres.

KIRCHNER, Carl Friedrich
German, 18th century.
Died 1755, in Dresden.
Sculptor.

Carl Friedrich Kirchner may have worked on the Japanese Palace in Vienna-Neustadt.

KIRCHNER, Christian
German, 18th century.
Born in Merseburg; died 28 December 1732, in Dresden.
Sculptor.

Christian Kirchner is best known for the monumental statues of mythological characters that he created for the great garden in Dresden.

KIRCHNER, Ernst Ludwig
German, 20th century.
Born 6 May 1880, in Aschaffenburg (Bavaria); died 15 June 1938, in Frauenkirch, near Davos (Grisons).
From 1917 active in Switzerland.
Painter, draughtsman, engraver, sculptor, illustrator.
Nudes, portraits, local scenes, landscapes.
Die Brücke group.

Ernst Ludwig Kirchner began studying architecture in Dresden in 1901, and went on to qualify as an architect, while at the same time becoming active as an artist. He initially worked with the painter Hermann Obrist, who was painting in a manner close to *Jugendstil*. In 1904, he became friends with Erich Heckel (also an architecture student), and Bleyl, with whom he studied the colour theories of Goethe, Helmholtz, Newton and Rood. In 1905, Heckel introduced Kirchner to Karl Schmidt-Rottluff (another architecture student), and the four founded Die Brücke (The Bridge). In 1911, Kirchner settled in Berlin, where the journal *Der Sturm* (*The Storm*) published some of his engravings and, with Pechstein, founded a school of modern painting, though it attracted few pupils. In 1913, Kirchner's friends were beginning to disapprove of the way he had dealt with the Brücke *Chronik* (*Chronicle*), alleging, it seemed to him, that he was responsible for too many of its initiatives, and the group disbanded.

Kirchner was horrified by the declaration of World War I and refused to enlist. Declared unfit for service, he was sent to a sanatorium in Königstein im Taunus, where he painted frescoes on the sanatorium staircase, but developed an obsessive fear of being called up and became addicted to drugs. In 1917, he was able to move to Davos in Switzerland, where he decided to settle after the war on account of the grandeur and serenity of its surroundings, which soothed his anxiety. From 1922 to 1938, he collaborated with Lise Gujer on the weaving of tapestries. In December 1925, he returned to Germany for the first time, encountering in Dresden the Marej Wigman dance troupe, which inspired a series of sketches and watercolours. In 1925-1926, he became friendly with a group of young painters in Basel - Camenisch, Albert Müller and Hermann Scherer - with whom he set up the *Rot-Blau* (Red-Blue) group. By now, he was beginning to establish a reputation in Germany, but, in 1933, while he was working on a commission for a decorative scheme for the Folkwang Museum in Essen, the Nazis cancelled the commission, removed him from his position at the Berlin academy and declared his work 'entartete Kunst' (degenerate art). Over 600 of his works were seized. Despite the important exhibitions dedicated to his work in the USA, Kirchner could not bear to see the political and spiritual developments occurring in his country, and, with his health under attack from an infectious disease, he committed suicide.

Kirchner's early paintings reveal a variety of influences, including the Neo-Impressionists (seen at an exhibition organized by the Phalanx group in Munich in 1904), Japanese prints and African art (seen at the ethnographic museum). In 1905, Kirchner made his first woodcut prints, a medium that had a long history in Germany dating to the Middle Ages. Its rudimentary and uneven style was a particularly suitable mode of expression for the anxiety and spiritual confusion that characterised Germany at the beginning of the century. From 1907 to 1909, Kirchner's works were similar to those of the other Brücke members. These strove to provide immediate artistic responses to aspects of city life - narrow streets, semi-nude women, circus athletes - expressed in patches of pure colour and broken line. Kirchner's Berlin-period works - portraits, street scenes - are sharper and more acid and, in their approach to space, are influenced to a certain extent by the pre-Cubist manner of Picasso's *Les Demoiselles d'Avignon*. In 1912, Kirchner and Heckel painted the murals for the chapel at the *Sonderbund* exhibition in Cologne and, in 1917-1918, Kirchner completed a set of engravings for Petrarch's *Triumph of Love*. In 1924, *The Shadow of Life* (*Umbra vitæ*) by Georg Heym appeared, illustrated with engravings by Kirchner.

Kirchner's output consists of more than 2,000 items. Graphic work, which is the largest category, includes countless drawings, etchings, lithographs, watercolours and woodcut prints, which are regarded by critics as among his most spontaneous and poignant expressions. Kirchner drew all the time, striving to understand the essence of things, for which he created a kind of short-hand method for capturing reality in perpetual motion, a 'personal approach to movement, opposite to that of the academic model'. Kirchner also made sculptures - roughly 100 between 1910 and 1925 - inspired by African art, carved directly into wood and painted. In 1913, he wrote: 'Sculpting figures...makes drawing more concise and gives sensual pleasure as the figure emerges from the block, stroke by stroke'.

The first and second exhibitions of the Brücke took place in 1906, in Löbtau, a district of Dresden, and also included works by Cuna Amiet, Axel Gallein, Nolde, and Pechstein. Kirchner was invited to exhibit at the first and second *Blaue Reiter* (Blue Rider) exhibitions in Munich and Berlin, and 32 of Kirchner's works were included in the notorious *Entartete Kunst* (*Degenerate Art*), which toured several cities in Germany. Kirchner works have featured in all the major exhibitions dedicated to Expressionism, including: 1992, *Figures du moderne - L'Expressionnisme en Allemagne 1905-1914* (*Figures of the Modern - Expressionism in Germany 1905-1914*), Musée d'Art Moderne de la Ville de Paris; 1999, *Le Fauvisme ou 'l'épreuve du feu'. Éruption de la modernité en Europe* (*Fauvism or 'Trial by Fire': The Eruption of Modernity in Europe*), Musée d'Art Moderne de la Ville de Paris; 2001,

Die Brücke in Dresden. 1905-1911 (*The Brücke in Dresden. 1905-1911*), Staatliche Kunstsammlungen, Dresden; and *Le Fauvisme en noir et blanc. De Gauguin à Vlaminck, l'estampe des fauves et son environnement* (*Fauvism in Black and White. From Gauguin to Vlaminck, Fauvist Engraving and its Setting*), Musée d'Art Moderne, Villeneuve d'Ascq.

Solo exhibitions of Kirchner's work were held, from 1913, at the Folkwang Museum in Hagen; 1914 and 1917, Kunstverein, Iena; 1918, Kunsthaus, Zurich; 1933, Kunstmuseum, Bern; 1937, Kunsthalle, Basel and the Art Institute, Detroit. Retrospective exhibitions, held posthumously, include: 1952, Kunsthaus, Zurich; 1954 and 1973, Kunsthalle, Bremen; 1960, Kunsthalle, Düsseldorf; 1968, Deutsche Akademie der Kunst, East Berlin; 1968-69, Seattle Museum, Pasadena Art Museum and Museum of Fine Arts, Boston; 1976, Kestner-Museum, Hanover; 1979-80, Nationalgalerie, Berlin, Haus der Kunst, Munich, and Ludwig Museum, Cologne; 1986, Dortmund am Ostwall; 1990, Brücke Museum, Berlin; 1999, Kunsthalle der Hypo-Kulturstiftung, Munich; 2001, *Kirchner. Engravings*, Musée Jenisch, Vevey; 2001, Kunsthalle, Hamburg and Saarland Museum, Saarbrücken; 2002, a retrospective that brought together 150 paintings, drawings, watercolours and woodcut prints, Fondazione Mazzota, Milan; 2003, *Ernst Ludwig Kirchner - Mountain Life*, Öffentlich Kunstsammlung, Basel, which covered Kirchner's early period in Davos; 2002, *Œuvres sur papier* (*Works on Paper*), Musée d'Art Moderne et Contemporain, Strasbourg, and Kunstmuseum, Winterthur; 2003, *Ernst Ludwig Kirchner: Der Maler Als Bildhauer* (*Ernst Ludwig Kirchner: The Painter as Sculptor*), Staatsgalerie, Stuttgart.

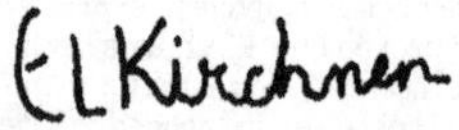

BIBLIOGRAPHY:

Gordon, Donald, E., *Ernst Ludwig Kirchner*, Harvard University Press, Cambridge (MA), 1968. Kirchner, Ernst Ludwig, *Ernst Ludwig Kirchner: A Tribute of the Artist's Centennial Year*, Worthington Gallery Inc, Chicago, 1980. Ketterer, Roman Norbert, *Ernst Ludwig Kirchner: Drawings and Pastels*, Alpine Fine Arts, 1982. Brandt, F./Hight, E./Kistler, A./Schultz, S., *German Expressionist Art: the Ludwig and Rosy Fischer Collection*, exhibition catalogue, Virginia Museum of Fine Arts, Richmond (USA, VA), University of Washington Press, Seattle, 1987. Grisebach, Lucius, *Ernst Ludwig Kirchner 1880-1938*, Taschen, New York, 1996. Wolf, Norbert, *Kirchner*, Tashen, Berlin, 2003. Lloyd, Jill/Moeller, Magdalena M., *Ernst Ludwig Kirchner: The Dresden and Berlin Years*, Royal Academy of Arts, London, 2003. Gee, Malcom, '*Ernst Ludwig Kirchner*' in *The Burlington Magazine* vol. CXLV n° 1206, periodical, London, September 2003.

MUSEUMS AND GALLERIES:

AMSTERDAM (Stedelijk Mus.): *Young Girl Nude Behind a Curtain* (1909); *Woman Dancing* (1911) - BALTIMORE (MA): *Portrait of Hugo* - BASEL (Kunsthalle): *The Mouth of the Amsel River* (1923) - BERLIN (Brücke Mus.): *Nude Attending to her Hair* (1913) - BERLIN (Nationalgal.): *Nude in the Studio* (1910-1911) - BERLIN (Neue Nationalgal.): *Der Belle-Alliance-Platz in Berlin* (*The Belle-Alliance-Platz in Berlin*) (1914); *Potsdamer Platz* (1914) - CAMBRIDGE, MA (Busch-Reisinger Mus., Harvard University): *Self-portrait with Cat* (1918) - COLOGNE (Mus. Ludwig) - COLOGNE (Wallraf-Richartz Mus.): *Female Bust with Hat* (1911); *Woman Wearing a Hat, her Breasts Bare* (1911); *Five Women in the Street* (1913) - DÜSSELDORF (Kunstmus.): *Moonrise at Fehmarn* (1914) - EDINBURGH (Scottish Nat. Gal. of Modern Art): *The Japanese Theatre* (1909) - ESSEN (Folkwang Mus.): *Leipziger Strasse with Tramway* (1914) - FRANKFURT AM MAIN (Städel): *Two Women at the Basin* (1913) - HAGEN (Karl Ernst osthaus-Mus.): *Portrait of Heckel* (1908) - HAMBURG (Kunsthalle): *Selbstbildnis mit Modell* (*Self-portrait with Model*) (1907) - KIEL (Kunsthalle): *Mountain Life* (1924-1925) - LONDON (Tate Collection): *Bathers at Moritzburg* (1909-1926, oil on canvas) - MINNEAPOLIS (IA): *Woman on a Blue Divan* (1907); *Young Girl Seated: Fränzi* (1910-1920, oil on canvas) - MUNICH (Bayerische Staatsgemaldesammlungen): *Boys Playing Cards* (1914); *Interior* (1914) - MUNICH (Staatsgal. Moderne Kunst): *Nudes Playing Beneath a Tree* (1910) - NEW YORK (MoMA): *The Road to Dresden* (1908); *Die Strasse* (*The Street*) (1913); *The Gunner* (1915) - NUREMBERG (Germanisches Nationalmus.): *Selbstbildnis als Trinker* (*Self-portrait as a Drunkard*) (1914) - OBERLIN (Allen Memorial AM): *Self-portrait in Uniform* (1915) - PARIS (MNAM-CCI): *Bathers* (1911); *Getting Ready* (1912-1913) - RICHMOND (Virginia MFA): *Seated Woman with Wood Sculpture* (1912, oil on canvas) - SAARBRUCKEN (Saarland Mus.): *Women Bathers in a Room* (1908) - SEATTLE (AM): *Frau und Mädchen* (*Woman and Girl*) (c. 1922-1923, oil on canvas) - STOCKHOLM (Moderna Mus.): *Marzella* (1909-1910) - STUTTGART (Staatsgal.): *Street Scenes* (1914); *Redheaded Woman* (1914) - THE HAGUE (Gemeentemus.): *Czardas* (1907) - TORONTO (AG of Ontario): *Young Girls Nude Standing near the Stove* (1908) - VIENNA (Mus. Moderner Kunst Stiftung Ludwig): *The Green House* (1907) - WUPPERTAL (Von der Heydt Mus.): *Woman in the Street* (1914) - ZURICH (Kunsthaus): *The Sertig Valley* (1920).

AUCTION RECORDS:

STUTTGART, 26 Oct 1949, *Sailing Boats*, DEM 3,500. STUTTGART, 26 April 1951, *Head of a Young Girl*, DEM 1,200. STUTTGART, 26 Nov 1957, *View of the Village of Davos* (pen and Indian ink) DEM 3,400. NEW YORK, 15 Jan 1958, *Mountain Slope with Yellow Trees*, USD 2,800. LONDON, 6 May 1959, *Mountain Landscape at Davos*, GBP 2,400. NEW YORK, 16 March 1960, *Nude Lying Down* (watercolour) USD 1,500. HAMBURG, 25 Nov 1961, *Female Nude on a Violet Background* (watercolour) DEM 6,000. MILAN, 21-23 Nov 1962, *Japanese Theatre*, ITL 7,500,000. NEW YORK, 30 Oct 1963, *Negro Dancers*, USD 26,000. BERN, 28 May 1964, *Seated Woman* (watercolour) CHF 9,500. COLOGNE, 21 May 1965, *Women Bathing (recto); Two Nudes (verso)*, DEM 98,560. HAMBURG, 19 Nov 1966, *In the Café* (watercolour) DEM 9,500. COLOGNE, 1 June 1967, *Couple Sitting at a Table beneath a Japanese Umbrella*, DEM 92,000. BERN, 15 June 1968, *Alpine Way; Women Dancing* (low relief/wood, double doors) CHF 108,000. NEW YORK, 9 April 1969, *Nude Lying Down with Cat* (watercolour) USD 8,000. BERN, 18 June 1970, *Two Nudes* (pastel) CHF 55,000. MILAN, 2 Dec 1971, *Carpet of Flowers* (1906) ITL 20,000,000. HAMBURG, 9 June 1972, *The Acrobats* (1911) DEM 215,000. HAMBURG, 15 June 1973, *Standing Nude* (sculpture) DEM 82,000. LONDON, 4 April 1974, *Reimann the Pantomime*, GBP 4,000. MUNICH, 28 May 1976, *Still-life with Roses* (woodcut in colour, 17 x 8 1/4 ins / 43 x 21 cm) DEM 11,000. BERN, 9 June 1976, *Vase of Flowers* (c. 1935, watercolour on pencil outlines, 20 x 14 ins / 51 x 35.7 cm) CHF 16,500. ZURICH, 12 Nov 1976, *Dunes by the Sea* (1913, oil on canvas, 35 3/4 x 48 ins / 91 x 121 cm) CHF 90,000. ZURICH, 20 May 1977, *The Forest* (1920-1921, oil on canvas, 80 x 58 1/4 ins / 203 x 148 cm) CHF 68,000. BERN, 8 June 1977, *Nude Wearing a Japanese Hat and Sitting in Front of a Mirror* (1909, pastel, 35 1/2 x 24 3/4 ins / 90 x 62.8 cm) CHF 50,000. LONDON, 30 June 1977, *Head of Ludwig Schames* (1918, woodcut, 22 1/4 x 10 ins / 56.5 x 25.5 cm) GBP 5,500. HAMBURG, 8 June 1979, *Nude Lying Down* (c. 1908, Indian ink, 13 1/4 x 17 ins / 33.9 x 43.1 cm) DEM 12,000. ZURICH, 1 Nov 1979, *Forest Path in Königstein* (1916, watercolour/pencil outlines, 21 1/2 x 13 3/4 ins / 54.7 x 35.1 cm) CHF 13,500. MUNICH, 27 Nov 1979, *Mountainous Landscape by Moonlight* (1918, woodcut in colour, one of two copies/Japanese paper, 12 1/4 x 11 1/2 ins / 31 x 29.5 cm) DEM 150,000. MUNICH, 30 Nov 1979, *Tango Tea* (1919-1921, oil on canvas, 28 x 31 1/2 ins / 71 x 80 cm) DEM 160,000. BERN, 19 June 1980, *How Women Dance; Alpine Cable-car to the*

Stafelalp (bronze, relief, a pair copied from the wooden reliefs of 1919, h. 69 ins / 175 cm) CHF 44,000. Bern, 26 June 1981, *Man Walking Towards the Sea* (lithograph) CHF 240,000. Bern, 26 June 1981, *Kaspar Cadiepolt* (1919, woodcut, 22¾ x 13¾ ins / 57.7 x 34.8 cm) CHF 55,000. New York, 5 Nov 1981, *Self-portrait with Pipe* (1907, oil on canvas, 20½ x 17 ins / 52 x 43 cm) USD 185,000. London, 23 March 1983, *The Wardrobe* (c. 1912, watercolour and gouache on pencil outlines, 20¾ x 15¼ ins / 53 x 39 cm) GBP 27,000. New York, 17 May 1983, *Semi-naked Figure with Raised Arms (recto)* (1910; *Sunflowers (verso)* (1913, oil on canvas, 30 x 26 ins / 76 x 66 cm) USD 160,000. Bern, 22 June 1983, *Mother Nini Müller at the Spinning Wheel, with a Neighbour Knitting* (1918, pencil and black and purple chalk, 23¼ x 16½ ins / 59 x 42 cm) CHF 70,000. Hamburg, 9 June 1984, *Nude Wearing a Black Hat* (1912, woodcut/Japanese Imperial paper) DEM 145,000. Bern, 20 June 1984, *David Ambühl Carrying a Cane and Wearing a Bowler Hat* (1918, bronze, h. 13½ ins / 34 cm) CHF 12,500. Bern, 21 June 1985, *Portrait of Self, Drawing* (etching) CHF 295,000. Bern, 21 June 1985, *Albertplatz in Dresden* (1910-1911, coloured chalks/pencil outlines, 10½ x 13½ ins / 26.5 x 34.5 cm) CHF 88,000. New York, 13 Nov 1985, *Monocyclist* (1911, oil on canvas, 33½ x 37½ ins / 85 x 95.5 cm) USD 590,000. Bern, 20 June 1986, *The Pipe Smoker* (1924-1925, larch wood with red and blue polychromy, h. 39¾ ins / 101 cm) CHF 60,000. New York, 19 Nov 1986, *Portrait of Two Girls* (c. 1907-1908, watercolour/pencil outlines/paper, 18 x 23½ ins / 45.8 x 60 cm) USD 70,000. London, 1 Dec 1987, *Two Women, One Dressed One Nude, Sitting on a Divan* (1914, charcoal and lead pencil, 19½ x 26 ins / 49.5 x 66 cm) GBP 28,000. New York, 18 Feb 1988, *Group of Four People* (pencil, 14½ x 19¼ ins / 37 x 49 cm) USD 5,500. New York, 12 May 1988, *Seated Female Nude* (coloured chalk and pastel/paper, 17½ x 13½ ins / 44.5 x 34 cm) USD 26,400. Munich, 8 June 1988, *Two Women Chatting* (ink/pencil, 5¾ x 7½ ins / 14.5 x 19 cm) DEM 11,000; *Court Scene from the Inquisition* (woodcut, 7 x 7¾ ins / 18 x 19.5 cm) DEM 23,100. Los Angeles, 9 June 1988, *Artist in his Studio with Two Models* (pencil/paper, 16½ x 12½ ins / 42 x 32 cm) USD 11,000. London, 28 June 1988, *Houses in Davos in Winter* (1927, oil on canvas, 47¼ x 35½ ins / 120 x 90 cm) GBP 126,500. New York, 6 Oct 1988, *The Baptism: Group of Countryfolk* (1920, charcoal/paper, 15½ x 19¾ ins / 39.5 x 50 cm) USD 7,700. Heidelberg, 14 Oct 1988, *View of Frankfurt am Main* (1916, pencil sketch, 9 x 6¾ ins / 22 x 17.3 cm) DEM 2,000. Munich, 26 Oct 1988, *Seated Nude* (Indian ink, 19½ x 14¾ ins / 49.5 x 37.5 cm) DEM 23,100. New York, 16 Feb 1989, *Nude Woman Wrapping Herself in a Bathrobe* (1912, pencil/paper/card, 22½ x 17½ ins / 57.1 x 44.5 cm) USD 7,700. London, 3 April 1989, *Sunflowers* (oil on canvas, 26¾ x 22¾ ins / 68 x 58 cm) GBP 198,000. Paris, 21 Sept 1989, *Females Nudes* (drawing, 7½ x 6 ins / 19 x 15 cm) FRF 12,000. New York, 13 Nov 1989, *Two Nudes on a Blue Divan* (oil on canvas, 19¾ x 27¾ ins / 50.2 x 70.5 cm) USD 1,540,000. Munich, 13 Dec 1989, *Couple in an Interior* (watercolour, ink and pencil, 16¼ x 12½ ins / 41.3 x 31.8 cm) DEM 49,500. Tel Aviv, 3 Jan 1990, *Sketch of Trapeze Artists* (1910, pencil, 8¼ x 6¾ ins / 21 x 17.2 cm) USD 1,980. New York, 17 May 1990, *The Tightrope Walkers* (1908, oil on canvas, 47¼ x 59 ins / 120 x 149.9 cm) USD 1,650,000. New York, 18 May 1990, *Portrait of Carl Sternheim* (oil on canvas, 24 x 17¾ ins / 61 x 45 cm) USD 275,000. New York, 14 Nov 1990, *Couple Beneath Japanese Umbrellas (recto)*; *Two Figures in a Landscape (verso)* (1912, oil on canvas, 39¼ x 29½ ins / 100 x 75 cm) USD 1,540,000. London, 4 Dec 1990, *Seated Nude* (pastel and charcoal/paper, 35½ x 27¼ ins / 90.2 x 69.2 cm) GBP 176,000; *The Cathedral in Frankfurt* (1916, oil on canvas, 27¾ x 23½ ins / 70.5 x 60 cm) GBP 440,000. Zurich, 7-8 Dec 1990, *Erna Kirchner and Anni Müller with their Children* (1925, pastel, 15¾ x 19¾ ins / 40 x 50 cm) CHF 60,000. New York, 15 Feb 1991, *Farmer with a Calf* (1917, watercolour and pencil/paper, 8¾ x 9½ ins / 22.2 x 24 cm) USD 6,600. New York, 8 May 1991, *Quarry in Wildenboden (Switzerland)* (1923, oil on canvas, 47 x 35½ ins / 119.5 x 90.2 cm) USD 330,000. Amsterdam, 22 May 1991, *Nudes in a Forest* (blue pencil and watercolour/paper, 8¼ x 11¾ ins / 21 x 29.7 cm) NLG 16,100. Zurich, 29 April 1992, *Man with Cat* (pencil, 10 x 6 ins / 25.5 x 15 cm) CHF 4,600. Munich, 26 May 1992, *Landscape with a Windmill* (1908, ink, 3½ x 5½ ins / 9 x 14 cm) DEM 14,950. New York, 12 Nov 1992, *Couple in a Landscape (recto); Horse and Cart (verso)* (1919, gouache and watercolour/paper, 13¾ x 18¾ ins / 35 x 47.5 cm) USD 63,800. London, 20 May 1993, *Demi-mondaines on the Friedrichstrasse, Berlin* (pastel and charcoal/paper, 15¾ x 11¾ ins / 40 x 30 cm) GBP 309,500. Zurich, 24 June 1993, *Three Deer and a Cow in a Meadow* (watercolour, 10¾ x 13½ ins / 27.2 x 34 cm) CHF 24,000. Heidelberg, 5-13 April 1994, *Trapeze Artists* (ink, 7¼ x 6½ ins / 18.5 x 16.7 cm) DEM 3,500. London, 13 Oct 1994, *Woman Lying Down* (hand-painted woodcut, long. 27 ins / 68.5 cm) GBP 276,500; *Königstein and the Red Church* (1916, oil on canvas, 31¾ x 25¼ ins / 80.6 x 64.2 cm) GBP 496,500. New York, 9 Nov 1994, *Spring Landscape in Sertig* (1925, oil on canvas, 39¼ x 47½ ins / 100 x 120.5 cm) USD 596,500. London, 11 Oct 1995, *Pair of Russian Dancers* (1909, coloured lithograph/paper canvas, 12¾ x 15¼ ins / 32.7 x 38.5 cm) GBP 177,500. Zurich, 26 March 1996, *Old Countrywoman* (1917, watercolour, gouache and ink, 19 x 13¾ ins / 48 x 35 cm) CHF 30,000. New York, 1 May 1996, *Mother and Child* (Indian ink/paper, 19¾ x 15 ins / 50 x 38 cm) USD 9,200; *Young Dorli* (1917, woodcut, 18½ x 14¾ ins / 47 x 37.5 cm) USD 59,700. London, 9 Oct 1996, *Landscape with Chesnut Trees* (oil on canvas, 37¾ x 34 ins / 96 x 85.5 cm) GBP 441,500; *Man Walking Towards the Sea* (1913, coloured lithograph, 28¼ x 20 ins / 71.6 x 51 cm) GBP 194,000. London, 4 Dec 1996, *Two Nudes* (c. 1906-1908, chalk and pencil/paper, 16¾ x 13½ ins / 42.5 x 34 cm) GBP 20,700. Heidelberg, 11-12 April 1997, *Man's Head and Female Nude* (1908, lithograph, 15¼ x 13 ins / 39 x 32.8 cm) DEM 30,000. Amsterdam, 18 June 1997, *Dancers* (c. 1926, pencil and watercolour/paper, 14¼ x 20¼ ins / 36 x 51.5 cm) NLG 32,289. London, 24 June 1997, *Street Scene (recto)* (1913; *Portrait of Gräf (verso)* (1914, oil on canvas, 27½ x 20 ins / 70 x 51 cm) GBP 1,981,500. London, 9 Dec 1997, *Sertigweg in Summer (recto); Fehmarn Coast with Green Sky (verso)* (1923 and 1913, two oils on canvas, 47¼ x 35½ ins / 120 x 90 cm) GBP 397,500. London, 10 Dec 1997, *The Valley at Taunus: Landscape with Small Wooden Bridge* (1916, oil on canvas, 31¾ x 27¾ ins / 80.6 x 70.5 cm) GBP 221,500. London, 7 Oct 1999, *Female Nude with Bathtub. Female Nude Reading* (1912, oil on canvas, double-sided, 38 x 25 ins / 96 x 64 cm) GBP 950,000. London, 7 Oct 1999, *Two Nude Women in Wood* (1909, oil on canvas, 34 x 47 ins / 87 x 120 cm) GBP 1,250,000. London, 17 Oct 2000, *Alpleben* (oil on canvas, triptych, 28 x 24 ins / 70 x 60 cm) GBP 850,000. London, 17 Oct 2000, *Two Nudes on a Blue Sofa* (1910, oil on canvas, 20 x 28 ins / 50 x 70 cm) GBP 1,550,000. London, 11 Oct 2001, *Hafen Burgstaaken, Fehmarn* (1913, oil on canvas, 38 x 33 ins / 96 x 85 cm) GBP 850,000. New York, 5 Nov 2001, *Fehmarntee* (oil on canvas, 47 x 35 ins / 120 x 90 cm) USD 2,300,000. London, 24 June 2002, *Nudes in the Sun, Moritzburg* (c. 1910, oil on canvas, 39 x 47 ins / 100 x 120 cm) GBP 3,200,000. London, 9 Oct 2002, *Red Nudes* (1912, oil on canvas, 47 x 35 ins / 120 x 90 cm) GBP 2,000,000. Stuttgart, 2 April 2003, *Cowshed: Alpine Peasant Milking* (oil on canvas, 24 x 28 ins / 61 x 70 cm) EUR 170,000. Bern, 20 June 2003, *Two Women in Variety in Dresden* (1905, coloured chalk over pencil, 26 x 35 ins / 65 x 88 cm) CHF 880,000. London, 3 Feb 2004, *Ice Hockey Players* (1934, oil on canvas, 31 x 28 ins / 80 x 70 cm) GBP 180,000. London, 1 July 2004, *Wettertannen* (colour woodcut from three blocks, 26 x 158 ins / 67 x 402 cm) GBP 200,000.

KIRCHNER, Eugen
German, 19th - 20th century.
Born 20 February 1865, in Halle; died 1938, in Munich.
Painter, draughtsman, engraver, illustrator, caricaturist. Waterscapes.
Jugendstil.

Eugen Kirchner was trained at the academy in Berlin, then in Dachau. He belonged to the Munich Secession, of which he had become a founder member in 1892. He was awarded a medal in Munich in 1897. His cartoons for the periodical *Fliegende Blätter* were held in high esteem. He worked for the Dresdener Werkstätten für Handwerkskunst (Dresden Studios), designing mainly toys.

BIBLIOGRAPHY:
Lehrs, Max, *Eugen Kirchner*, Dresden, 1911. Kern, Andrea, et al., *Jugendstil in Dresden, Aufbruch in die Moderne*, exhibition catalogue, Staatliche Kunstsammlungen, Dresden, 1999.

MUSEUMS AND GALLERIES:
SCHWEINFURT (Mus. Georg Schäfer).

AUCTION RECORDS:
LONDON, 16 Feb 1979, *Lake in Bavaria* (oil on canvas, 21 3/4 x 18 1/2 ins / 55.2 x 47 cm) GBP 1,600.

KIRCHNER, Gottlob
German, 18th century.
Born c. 1706, in Merseburg.
Sculptor, painter.

Gottlob Kirchner worked for many years for a porcelain factory in Meissen, but also created a number of sculptures for the decoration of Belvedere Castle near Weimar.

KIRCHNER, Heinrich
German, 20th century.
Born 1902, in Erlangen (Bavaria).
Sculptor.

Heinrich Kirchner studied in Munich, from 1924 to 1932, with H. Hahn, and in Paris at the Académie Julian. He taught bronze-casting in Munich from 1932, and was made professor in 1953. His *Good Shepherd* was exhibited at the international exhibition of contemporary sculpture in Paris in 1956.

AUCTION RECORDS:
MUNICH, 25 Nov 1983, *Madonna* (1953, patinated bronze, h. 13 1/2 ins / 34.5 cm) DEM 4,500. SAARBRUCKEN, 9 July 2004, *Motorbike and Sidecar* (brown patinated bronze, 17 x 15x13 ins / 44 x 37x32 cm) EUR 3,300. SAARBRUCKEN, 9 July 2004, *The Walker* (gold brown patinated bronze, h. 19 ins / 48 cm) EUR 4,200.

KIRCHNER, Johann Jakob
German, 19th century.
Born 1796, in Nuremberg; died May 1837, in Nuremberg.
Painter, watercolourist, engraver. Landscapes with figures, landscapes.

Johann Kirchner studied with Kock in Vienna, and later travelled to Munich and Italy.

AUCTION RECORDS:
BERLIN, 5 Dec 1986, *The Prodigal Son Guarding Swine in a Landscape* (pencil, 4 1/4 x 6 ins / 10.5 x 15.3 cm) DEM 9,000.

KIRCHNER, Matthias
Austrian, 18th century.
Born 1735, in Kitzbühl; died 1805.
Painter.

Matthias Kirchner was mainly a painter of frescoes.

KIRCHNER, Otto
German, 20th century.
Born 15 March 1887, in Eckartshausen; died 1960.
Painter. Portraits, genre scenes.

Otto Kirchner studied in Düsseldorf and Munich. He produced religious paintings in the early part of his career.

AUCTION RECORDS:
VIENNA, 6 June 1972, *The Village Notary*, ATS 25,000. COLOGNE, 1 June 1978, *Reading the Newspaper* (oil on panel, 10 x 7 ins / 24.5 x 18 cm) DEM 3,200. NEW YORK, 4 May 1979, *Monks in a Library* (oil on panel, 19 3/4 x 23 1/2 ins / 50 x 60 cm) USD 2,000. LOS ANGELES, 28 June 1982, *Portrait of a Man* (oil on panel); *Portrait of a Woman* (oil/hardboard, 9 3/4 x 7 3/4 ins / 25 x 19.8 cm) USD 2,200. MUNICH, 30 June 1983, *Reading a Letter* (oil on panel, 9 1/2 x 7 ins / 24 x 18 cm) DEM 3,700. BERN, 26 Oct 1988, *Portrait of an Old Man Reading a Letter in his Library* (oil on panel, 12 1/2 x 9 1/2 ins / 32 x 24 cm) CHF 2,600. GÖTEBORG, 18 May 1989, *Portrait of a Man Smoking his Pipe* (oil on panel, 7 x 5 1/2 ins / 18 x 14 cm) SEK 7,500. COLOGNE, 15 June 1989, *The Professor* (oil on card, 9 1/4 x 7 ins / 23.5 x 17.5 cm) DEM 1,300. AMSTERDAM, 6 Nov 1990, *Cheers!* (oil on panel, 7 1/4 x 5 1/2 ins / 18.5 x 14 cm) NLG 2,530. MUNICH, 7 Dec 2000, *Men Playing Cards* (oil on panel, 22 x 26 ins / 55 x 65 cm) DEM 3,500. LONDON, 18 Jan 2001, *Good Vintage. Reading News* (oil on board, a pair, 9 x 7 ins / 23 x 17 cm) GBP 4,200. DORCHESTER, 31 Oct 2002, *Old Man Reading a Letter* (oil on panel, 7 x 5 ins / 18 x 13 cm) GBP 1,200. MUNICH, 3 Dec 2003, *Four Art Lovers from the Rococo Period Poring over Pictures Together* (oil on panel, 24 x 20 ins / 60 x 50 cm) EUR 1,800.

KIRCHNER, Raphaël
Austrian, 20th century.
Born 1876, in Vienna; died 2 August 1917, in New York.
Painter, draughtsman, illustrator, watercolourist.
Portraits.

Raphaël Kirchner worked on Parisian newspapers, notably *Vie Parisienne* (*Paris Life*). He exhibited in Paris at the Salon des Artistes Français.

BIBLIOGRAPHY:
Osterwalder, Marcus (ed.), *Dictionnaire des illustrateurs 1800-1914*, Ides et Calendes, Neuchâtel, 1989. Beaumont-Maillet, Laure/Woimant, Françoise/Pernoud, Emmanuel, *De Bonnard à Baselitz - Dix ans d'enrichissements du Cabinet des estampes 1978-1988*, exhibition catalogue, Bibliothèque Nationale de France, Paris, 1992.

MUSEUMS AND GALLERIES:
PARIS (BNF, Prints Collection): *The Puppets* (c. 1900, three postcards).

AUCTION RECORDS:
PARIS, 15-16 June 1923, *The Swing* (fan-shaped watercolour) FRF 80; *Elegance* (watercolour heightened with gouache) FRF 155. LONDON, 10 May 1979, *The Friends* (pastel, 25 x 21 ins / 63.5 x 53.5 cm) GBP 1,400. VERSAILLES, 11 Dec 1983, *The Dream* (gouache and pastel, 27 1/4 x 19 1/4 ins / 69.5 x 49 cm) FRF 20,500. PARIS, 20 Nov 1985, *Woman in Blue* (gouache, 15 1/4 x 8 ins / 39 x 20.5 cm) FRF 14,000. PARIS, 11 Dec 1987, *Child with a Rose* (colouring pencil heightened with gouache, 9 x 6 3/4 ins / 23 x 17 cm) FRF 9,000. PARIS, 23 Dec 1987, *Child with a Rose* (colouring pencil heightened with gouache, 9 x 6 3/4 ins / 23 x 17 cm) FRF 9,000. PARIS, 14 March 1990, *Rocking-chair* (pencil, gouache and ink/bistre-coloured paper, 18 1/2 x 9 ins / 47 x 23 cm) FRF 5,500. PARIS, 22 March 1991, *The Rustling* (watercolour and pencil, 13 x 9 3/4 ins / 33 x 25 cm) FRF 4,800. LONDON, 13 Oct 1994, *Altar to Bacchus* (oil on canvas, 33 x 23 1/4 ins / 83.8 x 59.2 cm) GBP 5,980. LONDON, 10 Feb 1995, *Temptation* (1915, pencil, watercolour, gouache and coloured chalk/paper, 26 1/2 x 11 ins / 67.2 x 28 cm) GBP 2,530.

KIRCHNER, Zdenek or Zilenek
Czechoslovak, 20th century.
Born May 1934, in Jablonec; died September 1987.
Active in France from 1970.
Painter, engraver.
Visual Poetry.

Zdenek Kirchner studied at the school of decorative arts in Prague from 1955 to 1961 under Adolf Hoffmeister. Writing forms an integral part of his works. His canvases are dotted with unknown symbols inspired by Oriental calligraphies which the viewer is then invited to decipher but which do not give up their secret. A gestural artist, his painting is rhythmic. His work with words and symbols has something in common with the so-called visual or concrete poetry movements and with certain aspects of French lettrism.

From 1958 to 1968 Zdenek Kirchner took part in many exhibitions in his country. He first exhibited outside his homeland in 1965 in Vienna followed by Italy, Japan and Germany. He took part in various Paris salons: Salon Comparaisons (1974); Salon des Réalités Nouvelles (1975 to 1978); Salon des Grands et Jeunes d'Aujourd'hui (1977); exhibitions organised by the Signes Espaces - Ensemble de signes group in Paris (from 1977). He has shown his works in several solo exhibitions in Paris.

MUSEUMS AND GALLERIES:

PARIS (BNF, Prints Collection): *Message A* (1979, engraving) - PARIS (MAMVP) - SÉLESTAT (FRAC Alsace).

KIRCHNER-MOLDENHAUER, Dorothea

German, 20th century.

Born 19 September 1884, in the Posen (now Poznan) region, Poland.

Sculptor, engraver. Animals.

Dorothea Kirchner-Moldenhauer was a student of Heinrich Johann Zügel and worked in porcelain manufacture.

KIRCHOFFER, Henry. See **KIRCHHOFFER**

KIRCHOV, Theodor Johann Friedrich

Russian, 19th century.

Born 8 March 1837, in Moscow.

Sculptor.

Kirchov settled in Dresden, where he trained as an artist. His works include a bust of the editor *J.J. Weber*, and another of *Princess Georg of Saxony*.

KIRCHSBERG, Ernestine von

Austrian, 19th century.

Born 12 August 1857, in Verona.

Illustrator, possibly a painter. Landscapes.

Ernestine von Kirchsberg studied with A. Schaeffer and Hugo Darnaut in Vienna. She worked in Vienna and Graz.

KIREEVSKY, Étienne

Russian, 20th century.

Born in Moscow.

Active in France.

Painter.

Étienne Kireevsky was the pupil of Bonnat and Callias. In 1900 he exhibited at the Exposition Universelle in Paris, where he lived.

AUCTION RECORDS:

PARIS, 7 July 1943, *Nude on a Divan*, FRF 200.

KIREI, real name Kameoka Mitsushige, given name Shikyo, childhood name Kijuro, artist name Kirei

Japanese, 18th - 19th century.

Born 1770; died 1835.

Active in Kyoto.

Painter.

Kirei was a pupil of Maruyama Okyo (1733-1795). He painted flower-and-bird subjects and landscapes.

KIRILI, Alain

French, 20th - 21st century.

Born 1946, in Paris.

Since 1979 also active in the USA.

Sculptor, environmental artist. Statues, multimedia.

Alain Kirili followed courses in Chinese art in Paris during the 1960s, and then travelled in the USA, India, Japan and Indonesia. In 1979 he set up his studio in New York. At the time he associated with Sollers and the group from the review Tel Quel. He lives and works in Paris and New York.

Kirili was very quickly considered as a promising figure in the avant-garde in France, even before his style was fully defined. Starting with strokes and markings, his painting is now directed towards a more pictorial definition in space.

From 1972 he devoted himself to sculpture, which is minimalist in appearance, even though he claims for it the status of statuary. In the *India Curves* he plants an iron stem in a base of baked earth, emphasising the curve, the verticality and the linearity, wanting his work to be seen as calligraphic. These first sculptural works are influenced by David Smith (the base) and Barnett Newman (the erect part), but also by the work of Giacometti. The series of *Commandments*, begun in 1979, rejoins works in forged iron, or later, cut with a blowlamp. As well as forged metal, which he approaches with rigour, he explores such materials as earth and plaster in a freer manner, revealing the handworking, the bumpy surface still carrying traces of the fingers. For several years he has been developing work in stone and marble, which permits him to endow his sculptures with a monumental character. Often his abstract works are placed on pedestals and evoke primitive stele, thus making the exhibition a place of ceremony.

He takes part in public exhibitions: 1975, New York; 1976, Akademie des Künste de Berlin-Ouest; 1977, Documenta in Kassel; 1978, museum of the Abbaye-Ste-Croix at Sables-d'Olonne; 1979, Museum of Modern Art in New York; 1980, Kulturhistorische Museum in Bielefeld; 1981, Hirshhorn Museum in Washington; 1990, FIAC (Foire Internationale d'Art Contemporain) in Paris; 1991, *La Sculpture contemporaine apres 1970* (*Contemporary Sculpture after 1970*) at the Daniel Templon Foundation in Fréjus; 1992, From Bonnard to Baselitz - Ten Years of Additions to the Engravings Exhibition 1978-1988 at the Bibliothèque Nationale in Paris; 1998-1999, *Stages of Sculpture* at the Centre Régional d'Art Contemporain in Montbéliard.

He has shown his work in numerous solo exhibitions since 1969: 1970, 1989, 1992, 1993, 1996 in the Galerie Daniel Templon, Paris; 1981, Museum of Fine Arts, Dallas; 1983, a travelling exhibition in Germany; 1984, museum of St-Pierre de Lyons and museum of Besançon; 1985, Musée Rodin and Galerie Maeght in Paris; 1986, Jardin des Tuileries in Paris; 1991, Brooklyn Museum, New York; 1992, Villa Arson at Nice and Musée d'Art Moderne of St-Étienne; 1998, Musée de Grenoble; 2002, *Kirili talks to Carpeaux*, Musée des Beaux-Arts, Valenciennes; 2003, Instituto Valenciano de Arte Moderno, Valencia.

BIBLIOGRAPHY:

Dagen, Philippe, '*Alain Kirili*' in *Artstudio* n° 3, periodical, Gal. Templon, Paris, winter 1986-1987. Millet, Catherine, '*Interview: Alain Kirili - une abstraction autobiographique*' in *Art Press* n° 170, periodical, Paris, June 1992. Fargier, J.-P./Thuot, S./Kirili, A., *Alain Kirili*, Centre d'Art contemporain de Vassivière en Limousin, Beaumont-du-Lac, 1993. Kirili, Alain, *Sculpture et Jazz*, Stock, Paris, 1996. Dagen, Philippe, '*Interview d'Alain Kirili: la transversalité dans l'art répond à un besoin vital*' in *Le Monde*, periodical, Paris, 25 June 1996. Marmande, Francis, *Kirili à Montmajour*, Éd. du Patrimoine, Paris, 2002. Morgan, Robert C., *Alain Kirili*, Flammarion, Paris, 2002. *Alain Kirili. Homage to Julio González*, exhibition catalogue, Instituto Valenciano de Arte Moderno, Valencia, 2003.

MUSEUMS AND GALLERIES:

NEW YORK (MoMA) - PARIS (BNF, Prints Collection): *Untitled* (1984, lithograph).

AUCTION RECORDS:

NEW YORK, 13 Nov 1986, *Trembling VII* (1980, wrought iron, 26 1/4 x 8 3/4 x 8 3/4 ins / 66.7 x 22.2 x 22.2 cm) USD 5,200. NEW

YORK, 21 Feb 1990, *Untitled (Number 10107)* (rolled and cast steel, 55½ x 12 x 12 ins / 141 x 30.5 x 30.5 cm) USD 7,150. NEW YORK, 4 Oct 1990, *Untitled (Alliance III)* (1982, wrought iron, 62 x 48 x 38 ins / 157.5 x 122 x 96.5 cm) USD 24,200. PARIS, 14 March 1993, *Red Sequence 4* (1971, acrylic/card, 51 x 39¼ ins / 129.5 x 100 cm) FRF 9,600. PARIS, 4 Oct 1997, *Triptich 11 - Sequence in Red Tones* (1971, painting/panel, triptych, 25½ x 59 ins / 65 x 150 cm) FRF 5,000. WASHINGTON DC, 18 Sept 1999, *A.U.M.* (1980, forged iron, 28 x 8x8 ins / 71 x 20x20 cm) USD 2,000. NEW YORK, 12 Feb 2004, *Laocoön II* (1978, forged iron, 98 x 7x6 ins / 249 x 18x15 cm) USD 3,750.

KIRILIUK, Michel
French, 20th - 21st century.
Born 4 November 1952, in Casablanca.
Sculptor (including bronze), assemblage artist, designer. Furniture.

Using a variety of objects and materials, Michel Kiriliuk creates what he calls furniture - tables, consoles and standard lamps - the extremely Baroque nature of which renders their use problematic. He has exhibited at various Salons in Paris, including the Salon des Artistes Décorateurs and the Salon d'Automne.

KIRILLOV, Ivan
Russian, 17th century.
Born in Kostroma.
Icon painter.

It is possible that Kirillov worked in Moscow.

KIRILLOV, Mirón
Russian, 17th century.
Born 17th century, in Tobolsk.
Painter. Icons.

Mirón Kirillov worked for various churches between 1674 and 1691. In 1691, he began working for the Tsars.

KIRK, Douglas
American, 20th century.
Painter.

Douglas Kirk's Abstract Geometric paintings are dominated by the geometry of the square challenged by the presence on the canvas edge of Barnett Newman-inspired zips. He has shown his works in solo exhibitions in Paris.

BIBLIOGRAPHY:
Boulbès, Carole, '*Douglas Kirk*' in *Art Press* n° 204, periodical, Paris, July-August 1995.

KIRK, Eliza
Irish, 19th century.
Active in Dublin.
Sculptor.

Eliza Kirk exhibited at the Academy in Dublin from 1838 to 1859.

KIRK, Eve
British, 20th century.
Born 22 July 1900, in London; died 1969.
Painter. Landscapes.

Eve Kirk trained at the Slade School of Fine Art, London, from 1919 to 1922, and subsequently travelled in Italy, France and Greece. Her first exhibition was held in 1930, in London, followed by others in 1932, 1935, 1943 and 1949.

MUSEUMS AND GALLERIES:
LONDON (Tate Collection): *Avignon* (1939, oil on canvas).

KIRK, Frank C.
Russian, 20th century.
Born 11 May 1889; died 1963.
Active in the USA.
Painter. Interiors, still-lifes.

Frank C. Kirk studied at the Academy of Fine Arts in Philadelphia. He was a member of the Society of Independent Artists.

AUCTION RECORDS:
NEW YORK, 4 May 1993, *A Corner of the Studio* (oil on canvas, 30¼ x 30 ins / 77 x 76.2 cm) USD 1,380.

KIRK, J.
British, 19th century.
Active in Birmingham.
Sculptor.

J. Kirk exhibited at the Royal Academy and at the British Institution from 1847 to 1854.

KIRK, John
American, 19th century.
Born in Great Britain; died c. 1862, in the USA.
Engraver.

John Kirk worked for various New York publishers.

KIRK, Joseph Robinson
Irish, 19th century.
Born 1821; died 30 August 1894, in Bray.
Active in Dublin.
Sculptor.

Joseph Robinson Kirk was a member of the Royal Hibernian Academy. He occasionally exhibited at the Royal Academy in London between 1845 and 1862.

KIRK, Thomas
British, 18th century.
Born c. 1765; died 18 November 1797.
Painter, engraver, illustrator. Historical subjects, portraits, genre scenes.

Thomas Kirk was a student of Cosway. His drawing skills, choice of subjects and the quality of his colours enabled him to hold his own among other painters of historical subjects and genre scenes. He was equally successful with illustration and miniatures, and is also noted for his engravings. He exhibited at the Royal Academy from 1785 to 1796.

KIRK, Thomas
Irish, 19th century.
Born 1781, in Cork; died 10 April 1845, in Dublin.
Active in Dublin.
Sculptor.

Thomas Kirk worked mostly in Dublin and, in 1832, was one of the founding members of the Royal Hibernian Academy. He is known for statues in Dublin (*George IV*, the *Duke of Wellington*, and several busts in the library of Trinity College); in Londonderry (*Clemency* and *Justice*, at the courthouse); and in Limerick (*Lord Monteagle*). He is also mentioned as executing a colossal statue of *Nelson*. He occasionally exhibited at the Royal Academy between 1825 and 1845.

MUSEUMS AND GALLERIES:
DUBLIN: *Portrait of Dr Bartholomew Lloyd*.

KIRK, William Boyton
Irish, 19th century.
Born 24 May 1824; died 5 July 1900, in Ashton-under-Lyne (Lancashire).
Sculptor, writer.

William Boyton Kirk was the son of Thomas Kirk. He did his art training in Dublin, going on to exhibit his work there.

KIRKALL, Elisha
British, 18th century.
Born c. 1682 or 1692, in Sheffield; died December 1742 or 1750.
Engraver, illustrator.

Elisha Kirkall was the son of a locksmith. After working on his drawing skills in his home town of Sheffield, he went to London where he made engravings of coats of arms and book decorations. It is believed that he made excellent wood engravings for an edition of Terence published in 1713. In 1732, he subscribed to the publication of 12 mezzotints using a technique he had invented himself. It involved a combination of etching and engraving wood which itself supplied the half-tones, as in chiaroscuro engraving. Kirkall did not exploit his technique particularly well and, in any case, it seems not to have been overly successful. Nonetheless, he went on to publish 17 engravings after Van de Velde. Most of his work was as an illustrator; he also made engravings of animals after J.E. Ridinger.

MUSEUMS AND GALLERIES:

LONDON (National Portrait Gal.): *Sir Christopher Wren (after Henry Cooke)* (1720-1742, chiaroscuro).

AUCTION RECORDS:

LONDON, 5 Dec 1985, *Maritime Pieces* (c. 1720, green mezzotint, series of 15 works, 17 1/4 x 12 1/4 ins / 44 x 31.2 cm) GBP 11,000. PARIS, 7 July 1992, *Seascapes: Fort William, Saint Helena, Bombay, Telllichery* (four plates in blue, for the East India Company) FRF 16,000.

KIRKBY, Thomas

British, 18th - 19th century.
Active in London.
Painter.

Thomas Kirkby was a frequent exhibitor at the Royal Academy and the British Institution from 1796 to 1847.

AUCTION RECORDS:

LONDON, 7 Nov 1980, *Portrait of Pierre Wynne Yorke* (oil on canvas, 51 1/4 x 39 1/2 ins / 130.2 x 100.2 cm) GBP 750. CHESTER, 6 July 1984, *Portrait of Sir Watkin Williams Wynn of Wynnstay* (1834, oil on canvas, 49 1/2 x 39 ins / 126 x 99 cm) GBP 1,700.

KIRKE-BROWN. See BROWN Henry Kirke

KIRKEBY, Per

Danish, 20th century.
Born 1 September 1938, in Copenhagen.
Also active in Germany.
Painter, sculptor, draughtsman, watercolourist, engraver, performance artist, environmental artist.
Landscapes.
Neo-Impressionism.
Fluxus, Nouveaux Fauves.

Per Kirkeby took a doctorate in geology and has participated in several scientific expeditions to Greenland, central America, central Asia and Ireland. In the 1960s, he was a member of the experimental art school in Copenhagen, which was close to the Fluxus group, and, in 1978, was made professor at the fine arts academy in Karlsruhe. He has lived and worked in Copenhagen, on Læsø island (north Jutland) and in Karlsruhe.

Kirkeby's modes of expression are eclectic: he is a painter, sculptor and draughtsman, but also a poet and maker of prints, environments, models, films and documentaries. At the beginning of his career, he was inspired by Surrealism and Pop Art, calling himself a 'superrealist'. He subsequently produced collages based on a spontaneous form of associationism, which incorporated dried vegetable elements and were sometimes arranged in letter shapes. Later, he became involved in the Fluxus group and took part in performances with Joseph Beuys in Copenhagen, with Immendorf in Aachen and with Nam June Paik in New York. He also mounted exhibitions that brought together various objects he had gathered during his travels. Nothing remains of his work from this period.

From performances, Kirkeby turned to painting and sculpture. His paintings fall within the Western tradition that stretches from Delacroix to Monet and from Turner to Jorn. Interior landscapes, nature in tumult, the universe in flux and undergrowth and caves are all starting points for abstract works that appear to be in the process of coming into being. The artist says: 'You can make images, but you cannot reproduce things. From this we can say that art consists in reproducing images of images.' Kirkeby's earthy colours (browns, ochres, greens) and his matter and forms (fissures, holes, waves) all quiver when the light falls on them and the image itself becomes faint. With layer piled on layer and stratum on stratum, Kirkeby sets up a topographical summary of a world in metamorphosis, both opaque and transparent. More recently, Kirkeby has begun working in bronze, introducing into his work the human figure.

Kirkeby has taken part in group exhibitions since 1962, including: 1970, Kunstverein, Cologne; 1973, *L'Art danois 1945-1973* (*Danish Art 1945-1973*), Galeries Nationales du Grand Palais, Paris; 1976, Venice biennale; 1981, *A New Spirit in Painting*, Royal Academy, London; 1982, *Documenta VII*, Kassel; 1982, *Zeitgeist*, Berlin; Sydney biennale; 1984, *An International Survey of Recent Painting and Sculpture*, New York; 1985, Paris biennale; 1989, *Les Magiciens de la Terre* (*Magicians of the Earth*), Musée Nationale d'Art Moderne, Paris; 1997, *Skulptur. Projekte in Münster 1997* (*Sculpture. Projects in Münster 1997*), Münster; 2001, *Von Rodin bis Baselitz. Der Torso in der Skulptur der Moderne* (*From Rodin to Baselitz: The Torso in Modern Sculpture*), Staatsgalerie, Stuttgart; *Paysages* (*Landscapes*), Fonds régionaux d'art contemporain [FRAC], Centre Européen d'Actions Artistiques Contemporaines, Strasbourg.

Solo exhibitions of Kirkeby's work include: 1968, Fyns Stifsmuseum, Odense; 1975, Statens Museum for Kuns, Copenhagen; 1979, Kunsthalle, Bern; 1982 and 1984, Stedelijk Van Abbemuseum, Eindhoven; 1984, Musée d'Art Moderne, Strasbourg; 1987, Ludwigmuseum, Cologne; 1992, Le Magasin - Centre National d'Art Contemporain, Grenoble; 1995, Musée des Beaux-Arts, Nantes; 1998, Tate Gallery, London; 2002, Louisiana Museum für Moderne Kunst, Humlebæk, Denmark; and 2003, Galerie Vidal-St-Phalle, Paris.

BIBLIOGRAPHY:

Posner, Helaine, *Per Kirkeby: Paintings and Drawings*, MIT Visual Arts Center, Cambridge (MA), 1991. Kirkeby, Per, *Per Kirkeby*, Michael Werner, New York, 1992. Morell, Lars, *Per Kirkeby: The Art of Building*, Aristo, Denmark, 1996. Lloyd, Jill, *Per Kirkeby*, exhibition catalogue, Tate Gallery Publications, London, 1998. Tœjner, Poul Erik, *Per Kirkeby: 122 x 122, Paintings on Masonite*, Humlebaek, Denmark, 2002.

MUSEUMS AND GALLERIES:

AARHUS (Kunstforening) - BUFFALO (Albright-Knox AG): *Holz IV* (*Wood IV*) (1994, oil on canvas) - COPENHAGEN (Statens Mus. for Kunst) - DUNKIRK (FRAC Nord-Pas de Calais): *Pride of Science* (1982) - HUMLEBÆK (Louisiana Mus. for Moderne Kunst): *Six Animals* (1965) - NEW YORK (MoMA) - ODENSE (Fyns Kunstmus.): *Women's Hats* (1964) - PARIS (BNF, Prints Collection) - PARIS (FNAC): *Wood no. II* (1994) - PARIS (MNAM-CCI) - RANDERS (Kunstmus.) - SILKEBORG (Kunstmus.).

AUCTION RECORDS:

COPENHAGEN, 26 Nov 1986, *Sea* (1965, oil on canvas, double-sided, 48 x 48 ins / 122 x 122 cm) DKK 160,000. COPENHAGEN, 26 Nov 1987, *Composition* (1980, watercolour, gouache and Indian ink, 22 x 16 1/2 ins / 56 x 42 cm) DKK 8,500. COPENHAGEN, 30 Nov 1988, *Black Picture* (1977, oil on canvas, 48 x 48 ins / 122 x 122 cm) DKK 45,000. COPENHAGEN, 10 May 1989, *Composition* (1971, oil on canvas, 48 x 48 ins / 122 x 122 cm) DKK 80,000. COPENHAGEN, 22 Nov 1989, *Two Compositions* (mixed media/synthetic resin, each 48 x 48 ins / 122 x 122 cm) DKK 200,000. COPENHAGEN, 21-22 March 1990, *Composition* (1974, paint/synthetic resin, 48 x 48 ins / 122 x 122 cm) DKK 200,000. LONDON, 5 April 1990, *Messen* (1982, oil on canvas, 51 1/4 x 39 1/4 ins / 130 x 100 cm) GBP 9,900. COPENHAGEN, 14-15 Nov 1990, *Composition* (1978, oil on canvas, 82 x 65 ins / 208 x 165 cm) DKK 310,000. STOCKHOLM, 5-6 Dec 1990, *IV* (1981, oil on canvas, 78 3/4 x 51 1/4 ins / 200 x 130 cm) SEK 300,000. COPENHAGEN, 30 May 1991, *Composition* (1972, oil on paper/panel, 24 3/4 x 19 3/4 ins / 63 x 50 cm)

DKK 62,000. NEW YORK, 13 Nov 1991, *Untitled* (1988, charcoal, gouache, soft chalk and black ink/paper, 29 1/2 x 21 1/4 ins / 75 x 54 cm) USD 5,500. COPENHAGEN, 20 May 1992, *Composition* (1968, oil/synthetic resin, 48 x 48 ins / 122 x 122 cm) DKK 90,000. NEW YORK, 18 Nov 1992, *Picture II* (1988, oil on canvas, 59 x 39 1/4 ins / 149.9 x 99.7 cm) USD 16,500. COPENHAGEN, 10 March 1993, *Composition* (1981, oil on canvas, 46 x 37 1/2 ins / 116 x 95 cm) DKK 100,000. NEW YORK, 5 May 1993, *Green Summer* (1988, oil/material, 78 3/4 x 67 ins / 200 x 170.2 cm) USD 34,500. AMSTERDAM, 26 May 1993, *Antinous* (1982, oil on canvas, 35 1/2 x 45 1/4 ins / 90 x 115 cm) NLG 18,400. LONDON, 24 June 1993, *Smoky Quay* (1982, oil on canvas, 78 3/4 x 51 1/4 ins / 200 x 130 cm) GBP 26,450. COPENHAGEN, 3 Nov 1993, *Composition* (oil on canvas, 78 3/4 x 59 ins / 200 x 150 cm) DKK 230,000. AMSTERDAM, 8 Dec 1993, *Silver Birches* (1985, oil on canvas, 78 3/4 x 51 1/4 ins / 200 x 130 cm) NLG 43,700. FRANKFURT AM MAIN, 14 June 1994, *Untitled* (1990, drawing in colour/paper, 38 1/2 x 25 1/4 ins / 98 x 64 cm) DEM 14,000. COPENHAGEN, 14 June 1994, *Composition* (1983, oil on canvas, 78 3/4 x 51 1/4 ins / 200 x 130 cm) DKK 185,000. COPENHAGEN, 21 Sept 1994, *Arms and Head* (bronze, h. 11 3/4 ins / 30 cm) DKK 30,000. COPENHAGEN, 8-9 March 1995, *Composition* (1970, oil/synthetic resin, 48 x 48 ins / 122 x 122 cm) DKK 81,000. LONDON, 26 Oct 1995, *No 1* (1981, oil on canvas, 94 1/2 x 79 1/4 ins / 240 x 201 cm) GBP 13,800. PARIS, 15 Dec 1995, *Untitled* (1981, oil on canvas, 37 1/2 x 46 ins / 95 x 116 cm) FRF 45,000. COPENHAGEN, 12 March 1996, *Salzburg 7* (1982, oil on panel, 39 1/4 x 47 1/4 ins / 100 x 120 cm) DKK 105,000. COPENHAGEN, 15 March 1997, *Hejsa* (1963, etching) DKK 1,900. AMSTERDAM, 2-3 June 1997, *Messen* (1982, oil on canvas, 51 1/4 x 39 1/4 ins / 130 x 100 cm) NLG 29,500. LONDON, 27 June 1997, *Marts* (1984, oil on canvas, 59 1/4 x 78 3/4 ins / 150.5 x 200 cm) GBP 23,000. COPENHAGEN, 22-24 Oct 1997, *The Maya Mountains I* (1976, oil/Masonite, 48 x 48 ins / 122 x 122 cm) DKK 65,000. STOCKHOLM, 26 Oct 1999, *Trust in Wood II* (1986, oil on canvas, 46 x 37 ins / 117 x 95 cm) SEK 215,000. STOCKHOLM, 26 Oct 1999, *Untitled* (1981, oil on canvas, 80 x 51 ins / 203 x 130 cm) SEK 295,000. COPENHAGEN, 28 March 2000, *Car Series I-IV* (mixed media on masonite, four, 48 x 33 ins / 122 x 83 cm) DKK 530,000. LONDON, 28 June 2000, *Untitled* (oil on canvas, 46 x 37 ins / 116 x 95 cm) GBP 13,000. LONDON, 28 June 2001, *Inferno I* (1992, oil on canvas, 79 x 51 ins / 200 x 130 cm) GBP 38,000. LONDON, 28 June 2001, *Untitled* (1985, oil on canvas, 91 x 157 ins / 230 x 400 cm) GBP 45,000. LONDON, 27 June 2002, *Silber* (1982, oil on canvas, 52 x 79 ins / 131 x 201 cm) GBP 24,000. COPENHAGEN, 1 Oct 2002, *Laeso - Composition* (1997, oil on canvas, 63 x 63 ins / 160 x 160 cm) DKK 340,000. COLOGNE, 28 May 2003, *Changes of the Surface* (1990, oil on canvas) EUR 60,000. COPENHAGEN, 26 Nov 2003, *Salzburg 7* (1984, oil on canvas, 39 x 47 ins / 100 x 120 cm) DKK 250,000. LONDON, 5 Feb 2004, *Smaland* (1984, oil on canvas, 59 x 79 ins / 150 x 200 cm) GBP 40,000. COLOGNE, 4 June 2004, *With Absalon* (1988, oil on canvas, 79 x 51 ins / 200 x 130 cm) EUR 52,000.

KIRKEGAARD, Anders

Danish, 20th - 21st century.
Born 1946, in Holstebro.
Painter. Figures.

Anders Kirkegaard studied at the Kongelige Danske Kunstakademi in Copenhagen, but was mainly self-taught. He took part in his first group exhibition in 1963 at the Copenhagen autumn exhibition, followed by several others, notably at the Grand Palais in Paris in 1973. Since 1963, he has also exhibited in solo shows in Scandinavia.

He depicts human nature in torment, the martyred spirit. His painting is violent, the opposite of fine painting, and makes the viewer think about human degradation.

BIBLIOGRAPHY:

Galy-Carles, Henry, *Art danois, 1945-1973*, exhibition catalogue, Gal. nationales du Grand Palais, Paris, 1973.

MUSEUMS AND GALLERIES:

AALBORG (Nordjyllands Kunstmus.): *Portrait of Degradation in Three Phases* (1968-1970) - ODENSE (Fyns Kunstmus.): *Presentation of Masochistic Fetishes* (1966-1967) - RANDERS (Kunstmus.): *While We Await a New Saint John* (1971-1972).

AUCTION RECORDS:

COPENHAGEN, 2 March 1988, *Moderne Times, Reincarnation of Archibold* (58 1/4 x 48 ins / 148 x 122 cm) DKK 10,000. COPENHAGEN, 20 Sept 1989, *Hunting Scene* (acrylic and oil, 39 1/4 x 37 ins / 100 x 94 cm) DKK 27,000. COPENHAGEN, 22 Nov 1989, *Frembæring af spørgsmål og sønnen i 3 stadier* (*Offering of Questions and the Son in 3 Stages*) (1967, oil on canvas, 51 1/4 x 63 3/4 ins / 130 x 162 cm) DKK 16,000. COPENHAGEN, 28 Feb 2001, *Composition* (1965, oil on canvas, 41 x 51 ins / 105 x 130 cm) DKK 12,000. COPENHAGEN, 17 Sept 2003, *Portrait of a Wise Man Holding Back His Wisdom* (1971, oil on panel, 37 x 45 ins / 94 x 114 cm) DKK 11,000.

KIRKLEY, Caroline

British, 18th century.
Active in London at the end of the 18th century.
Miniaturist, engraver.

Caroline Kirkley exhibited her miniatures at the Royal Academy in 1796 and 1797. She also made engravings.

KIRKMAN, Augusta Josepha

British, 19th century.
Active in London at the beginning of the 19th century.
Painter. Landscapes, architectural views.

Augusta Josepha Kirkman exhibited at the Royal Academy from 1815 to 1825.

KIRKOV, Ivan

Bulgarian, 20th century.
Born 1 January 1932, in Assenovgrad.
Painter, sculptor, mosaicist, illustrator. Decorative panels, frescoes, stage sets, patterns (fabrics).

Ivan Kirkov studied at the national academy of fine arts in Sofia where he attended painting classes with Ilia Petrov and Kirk Tsonev, completing his training there in 1955.

Ivan Kirkov's artistic output covers a wide range of themes and a wide register of genres. He worked simultaneously on illustrations, monumental three-dimensional creations, murals, mosaics and decorative fabrics. As his painting style evolved, there were times when the realist approach predominated, and others when problems were dealt with in a formal order. Kirkov belonged to that circle of Bulgarian painters who knew how to safeguard their artistic freedom within the context of the normative, crushing aesthetic of the totalitarian regime in power in Bulgaria between 1945 and 1989. In 1974 he completed the metal panel that stands in the central train station in Sofia. In 1976 he worked on murals and on a curtain for the Ivan Vazov national theatre in Sofia. In 1984(1985 he created mosaics, murals and a curtain for the Yordan Yovkov theatre in Dobrich.

Ivan Kirkov has taken part in many collective exhibitions including salons organised by the union of Bulgarian painters (regularly from 1957); Autumn exhibitions in Plovdiv (1972, 1973, 1981 and 1995). Solo exhibitions include: gallery of the union of Bulgarian painters, Sofia (1969 and 1978); Budapest (1971, 1973); Plovdiv (1972); Rakovski 125 gallery, Sofia (1987); Art 36 gallery, Sofia (1995).

BIBLIOGRAPHY:

Ivan Kirkov, exhibition catalogue, Balgarski Houdojnik, Sofia, 1978.

MUSEUMS AND GALLERIES:

SOFIA (Nat. Gal. of Fine Arts) - SOFIA (Other Bulgarian Regional Galleries).

KIRKPATRICK, Ethel
British, 19th century.
Active in Harrow.
Painter. Seascapes, flowers, landscapes.
Ethel Kirkpatrick exhibited at the Royal Academy starting in 1891.

KIRKPATRICK, Ida
British, 19th century.
Active in London.
Painter. Seascapes.
Ida Kirkpatrick frequently exhibited at the Suffolk Street Gallery after 1888.

KIRKPATRICK, Joseph
British, 19th - 20th century.
Born 1872, in Liverpool; died c. 1936.
Painter, watercolourist. Landscapes, animals.
Joseph Kirkpatrick lived and worked in Curdridge (Hampshire). He painted mainly rustic scenes, and exhibited regularly at the Royal Cambrian Academy.
MUSEUMS AND GALLERIES:
LIVERPOOL: *Flaming June*.
AUCTION RECORDS:
LONDON, 27 April 1908, *Geese* (watercolour) GBP 3. LONDON, 23 April 1910, *Troublemaker* (watercolour) GBP 7. LONDON, 28 Nov 1984, *The Gentle Art* (1898, watercolour and gouache, 19 3/4 x 31 ins / 50 x 78.5 cm) GBP 3,600. MANCHESTER, 24 July 1986, *The Lost Lamb* (watercolour, 35 x 25 ins / 88 x 63.5 cm) GBP 2,600. LONDON, 8 Feb 1991, *Young Woman in a Cottage Garden in Cheriton, Hampshire* (watercolour, 14 1/2 x 10 1/2 ins / 37 x 26.7 cm) GBP 935. LONDON, 3 March 1993, *Three Calves who have Broken through a Fence and Brought Down a Line of Laundry in a Field* (watercolour, 25 1/2 x 37 1/2 ins / 65 x 95 cm) GBP 4,025. NEW YORK, 14 Oct 1993, *El Baia Souk, Tangier* (1902, watercolour/paper, 15 1/2 x 23 3/4 ins / 39.4 x 60.4 cm) USD 1,150. LONDON, 29 March 1996, *Blackberry Pickers* (watercolour, 6 1/2 x 19 1/2 ins / 16.2 x 49.8 cm) GBP 1,035. LONDON, 30 June 1999, *At the Cottage Door* (watercolour, 10 x 14 ins / 25 x 35 cm) GBP 1,800. LONDON, 2 Sept 1999, *Feeding the Calf. Gathering Blossom* (pencil and watercolour, a pair, 13 x 9 ins / 34 x 24 cm) GBP 3,200. LONDON, 3 Feb 2000, *Feeding the Ducks* (pencil and watercolour, 13 x 9 ins / 34 x 23 cm) GBP 1,400. LONDON, 5 March 2002, *Amongst the Summer's Blooms* (watercolour heightened with gouache, 13 x 9 ins / 34 x 24 cm) GBP 1,300. NOTTINGHAM, 29 May 2003, *Gloucestershire Lane, a Young Girl Carrying a Basket of Flowers* (watercolour and gouache heightened with white, 13 x 9 ins / 33 x 23 cm) GBP 1,800. TORONTO, 17 Nov 2003, *In the Orchard* (watercolour, 14 x 10 ins / 35 x 25 cm) CAD 2,900.

KIRKPATRICK, Marion Powers
American, 19th - 20th century.
Born in London, to American parents.
Painter, illustrator.
Marion Powers Kirkpatrick was married to W.A.B. Kirkpatrick. She studied under Garrido in Paris. Her painting *Treasures* was bought by the French government at the Salon des Artistes Français in 1904. She won the Lippincott prize in 1907.
AUCTION RECORDS:
NEW YORK, 2 Feb 1979, *The Toast* (oil on canvas, 51 x 35 ins / 129.5 x 89 cm) USD 2,250.

KIRKPATRICK, Richard
British, 19th century.
Active in London at the beginning of the 19th century.
Painter.
Richard Kirkpatrick exhibited at the Royal Academy from 1812 to 1817.

KIRKPATRICK, W.
British, 19th century.
Active in London in 1841.
Painter. Landscapes.

KIRKPATRICK, William Arber Brown
British, 20th century.
Born 7 November 1880.
Active in the USA.
Painter.
William Arber Brown Kirkpatrick studied under Jean-Paul Laurens in Paris, and exhibited at the Salon des Artistes Français in 1903, before settling in Boston in the USA.

KIRKUP, Seymour Stockes
British, 19th century.
Born 1788, in London; died 3 January 1880, in Livorno (Tuscany), Italy.
Painter, engraver.
Seymour Stockes Kirkup was enrolled at the Royal Academy in 1809, when he was very young; there, he became friends with William Blake and Haydon. Due to his poor health, he went to Italy where he settled in Rome. He made etchings as well as some portraits of his friends. He was a great lover of art and beautiful things; this led him to the lucky discovery, on 21 July 1840 and in the company of his friends, Bezzi and Wilde, of the portrait of Dante in the Palazzo della Podestà in Florence. Long attributed to Giotto, the painting had been considered lost for many years. When the kingdom of Italy was restored, he was made a Cavaliere di Gran Croce dell'Ordine dei SS Maurizio e Lazzaro by King Victor Emmanuel II. In 1872, he settled in Livorno.
MUSEUMS AND GALLERIES:
EDINBURGH (Scottish National Portrait Gallery): *John Scott* (1819, pencil) - LONDON (National Portrait Gal.): *Edward John Trelawny* (lithograph).

KIRKWOOD, George
Irish, 19th century.
Active in Dublin.
Engraver.
George Kirkwood was the son of John Kirkwood. At the beginning, he worked with his father.

KIRKWOOD, Henry
British, 19th - 20th century.
Engraver.
Henry Kirkwood followed his father, George Kirkwood, into a career as a print-maker.

KIRKWOOD, James
Irish, 19th century.
Active in Dublin.
Engraver.

KIRKWOOD, John
Irish, 19th century.
Active in Dublin.
Engraver.
John Kirkwood made engravings of portraits and, especially, illustrations for magazines with his father, James Kirkwood.

KIRMER, Michael, or Kirchmaier, Kirchmeyer
German, 16th century.
Died 1589.
Active in Regensburg from 1550 to 1560.
Draughtsman, engraver (wood).

KIRNER, Johann Baptist
German, 19th century.
Born 24 June 1806, in Furtwangen; died 19 November 1866, in Augsburg.
Painter, illustrator, caricaturist. Genre scenes.

Johann Baptist Kirner was the son of a shoemaker, who encouraged him to take up art. He was a pupil of C. Zimmermann at the school of fine arts in Augsburg from 1822 to 1824 and then went to work in the studio of Cornelius in Munich. After several study tours to Switzerland and Italy and a year spent in Vienna, he settled in Munich in 1838. In 1840, he was appointed court painter and he became a member of the Munich academy in 1856.

MUSEUMS AND GALLERIES:

KARLSRUHE: *Harvest* (1841) - LEIPZIG: *Swabian National Guard* - MUNICH: *Woman Shuffling Cards; Three Men from Baden.*

AUCTION RECORDS:

COLOGNE, 25 Oct 1985, *After the Celebration* (1860, oil on canvas, 27 1/2 x 33 ins / 70 x 84 cm) DEM 6,000. LONDON, 16 Feb 1990, *Attacked by Highwaymen* (1836, oil on canvas, 19 x 22 ins / 48.3 x 55.9 cm) GBP 3,300. STOCKHOLM, 24 Nov 1999, *My Favourite Pony: Young Italian Couple Playing with Their Child* (1838, oil on canvas, 24 x 18 ins / 60 x 46 cm) SEK 50,000.

KIRNER, Lukas

German, 19th century.

Born 18 October 1794, in Furtwangen; died 7 July 1851, in Furtwangen.

Painter.

Several of his portraits of members of his family have survived.

KIRNIG, Alois

Czechoslovak, 19th - 20th century.

Born 10 June 1840, in Prague; died 25 January 1911, in Prague.

Painter. Landscapes.

Alois Kirnig exhibited in Vienna and Dresden.

AUCTION RECORDS:

LONDON, 13 March 1996, *Pilgrimage to the Church of Maris Pocs in the East of Hungary* (1865, oil on canvas, 20 3/4 x 28 ins / 53 x 71 cm) GBP 1,840. BERN, 9 May 2001, *Contexta Factory in Schlimmdorf am Schlacker* (1891, oil on canvas, 31 x 63 ins / 80 x 160 cm) CHF 3,000. VIENNA, 30 Oct 2001, *Bordighera with View of Mentone* (1880, oil on panel, 9 x 21 ins / 22 x 54 cm) ATS 25,000. BRATISLAVA, 26 March 2002, *Inside the Forest* (c. 1875, oil on canvas, 28 x 40 ins / 70 x 101 cm) SL.K 115,000. PRAGUE, 8 March 2003, *Landscape* (1910, oil on canvas on board, 11 x 21 ins / 29 x 53 cm) CZK 65,000. PRAGUE, 8 March 2003, *Alpine Landscape* (oil on canvas, 21 x 26 ins / 53 x 65 cm) CZK 80,000.

KIROV, Dimitri

20th century.

Painter.

Dimitri Kirov had a solo exhibition in Paris in 1990.

KIRSCH, August Christoph

German, 18th century.

Born 22 May 1763, in Dresden; died 8 October 1787, near Tivoli.

Painter. History painting.

Kirsch studied first at the Dresden academy then in the studio of Casanova. In 1786, he was commissioned to paint an altarpiece for the church of the Holy Cross for the Elector of Saxony. He then went to Rome. A painting by him of the *Holy Family* is known.

KIRSCH, Hugo Franz

German, 19th - 20th century.

Born 15 July 1873, in Haindorf (now Hejnice, Czech Republic).

Sculptor, potter.

Hugo Franz Kirsch sculpted models for ceramics.

KIRSCH, Jean

French, 20th century.

Born 1921, in Bagnolet.

Painter. Nudes, landscapes, still-lifes.

Jean Kirsch studied at La Ruche in Montparnasse and then at the École des Beaux-Arts in Paris under Florot and Nouillac. He did not devote himself entirely to painting until 1956. He became director of the Académie Libre in Antibes and was made an Officier des Arts Sciences et Lettres. He produced a painting of Christ for the altar of the chapel of St-Jacques in Bagnolet. His work is often executed in thickly applied paint with yellow dominating and enhancing the quality of the light.

KIRSCH, Johanna

German, 19th century.

Born 1856, in Chemnitz.

Painter. Portraits, genre scenes.

Johanna Kirsch showed her first painting in 1884, and subsequently exhibited in Dresden, Berlin and Munich.

KIRSCH, Vincent

German, 19th - 20th century.

Born 25 January 1872, in Heimbach.

Painter. Cartoons for stained glass.

Vincent Kirsch worked for the church of St-Gervais in Geneva.

KIRSCHBERGER, Christian Wilhelm

German, 19th century.

Born 1779, in Königsberg (now Kaliningrad, Russia).

Painter.

Kirschberger is known for portraits and history paintings. He spent his entire life in the town where he was born.

KIRSCHENBAUM, J. D. for Jecheskiel Dawid, or Chaskiel David, pseudonym: Duvtivani or Duwdivani

Polish, 20th century.

Born 15 August 1900, in Strashov; died 1954, in Paris. Active in Germany between 1920 and 1933, and in France from 1933.

Painter (including gouache). Religious subjects, figures, portraits, landscapes with figures.

The son of a Jewish theologian, J.D. Kirschenbaum from the age of 12 put his artistic gifts to practical use by painting shop signs. He left Poland in 1920. Drawn by the fame of Klee and Kandinsky, he attended their courses at the academy of fine arts in Weimar. He was forced to leave for Berlin, however, and made his living as a newspaper designer and caricaturist under the pseudonym Duvtivani. When the Nazis swept into power he fled to France, where he discovered the work of Soutine and Chagall. His paintings, made up entirely of strokes and lines and Expressionist in form, are witness to the painter's whimsical spirit and the influences of Jewish folklore. He also painted abstract works.

In Paris he exhibited in the major official salons. Solo exhibitions include: Weimar (1923); Berlin (1927); Paris (1935); Lyons (1946); Galerie Quatre Chemins, Paris (1947); Rio de Janeiro (1948); Galerie André Weil (1951); Galerie du Pont des Arts, Paris (1953).

BIBLIOGRAPHY:

Nieszawer, Nadine/Boyé, Marie/Lanzmann, Claude (preface), *Peintres juifs de l'École de Paris 1905-1939*, Denoël, Paris, 2001.

MUSEUMS AND GALLERIES:

JERUSALEM (Israel Mus.): *Head of a Girl; Walking Musician; Head of an Old Jew* (1937); *Old Jew in Snowy Landscape; Woman's Portrait* (watercolour); *Wandering Jews* (1938); *Forest Interior* (1935); *Jewish Villagers Greeting the Messiah* (1937).

AUCTION RECORDS:
NEW YORK, 23 Sept 1993, *Double Portrait* (1959, tempera/synthetic resin, 27 1/4 x 29 1/2 ins / 69.2 x 74.9 cm) USD 6,900.

KIRSCHFINK-HEINEN, Léonie
Belgian, 20th century.
Sculptor, assemblage artist.
Léonie Kirschfink-Heinen showed her works in solo exhibitions held in Belgium. After having used salvaged material, she combined Plexiglass with stone in sculptures which are reminiscent of totem poles or stela.

KIRSCHNER, Friedrich
German, 18th century.
Born 1748, in Bayreuth; died 1789, in Augsburg.
Painter, miniaturist, engraver (etching).
Friedrich Kirschner was a pupil of Gottlieb F. Riedl in Ludwigsburg, and then went into porcelain manufacturing. After that, he went to Nuremberg, then Altdorf, where he painted for the botanical gardens. He also worked in Augsburg. He painted and engraved mainly flowers, fruit and insects, with great delicacy and talent. He is also known for landscapes and for 28 plates for *Sammlung von Blumen zum zeichnen und stichen (Collection of flowers for drawing and embroidering).*

KIRSCHNER, J. J.
German.
Active in Nuremberg.
Engraver (etching).

KIRSCHNER, Ludwig
German, 19th - 20th century.
Born 7 June 1872, in Tettenweis (Bavaria).
Painter. Portraits, landscapes.
Ludwig Kirschner lived and worked notably in Munich.

KIRSCHNER, Marie Louise
Austrian, 19th century.
Born 7 January 1852, in Prague.
Painter. Landscapes, still-lifes.
Marie Louise Kirschner studied with Lier in Munich, then with Jules Dupré and Alfred Stevens in Paris. She worked in Prague, Berlin and Rome. She exhibited for the first time in 1873 at the Vienna Salons and took part in the Paris Exposition Universelle in 1900.

KIRSCHNER, Wolfgang
German, 16th century.
Died 1548, in Schneeberg.
Painter.
It seems possible that Kirschner worked for the church of Our Lady in Zwickau.

KIRSCHT, Émile
Luxembourg, 20th century.
Born 1913, in Rumelange.
Painter (gouache). Landscapes.
Émile Kirscht was one of the founders of the Salon des Iconomaques in Luxembourg in 1954.
BIBLIOGRAPHY:
Cent cinquante ans d'Art luxembourgeois, exhibition catalogue, Musée national d'Histoire et d'Art, Luxembourg, 1989.
MUSEUMS AND GALLERIES:
LUXEMBOURG (Mus. national d'histoire et d'art): *Oasis* (1971, gouache); *Indian Summer* (1978, gouache).

KIRSSANOV, Nicolai
Russian, 18th century.
Engraver.
Works by Kirssanov include, notably, a *Portrait of Catherine the Great*. He specialised in book illustration.

KIRSTEIN, Adolf
French, 19th century.
Born 1814, in Strasbourg; died September 1873, in Königsfeld.
Painter, lithographer. Landscapes.
Adolf Kirstein was a pupil of Bertin in Paris. He exhibited in Dresden from 1860.
AUCTION RECORDS:
COLOGNE, 21 Oct 1977, *Winter Landscape* (oil on canvas, 24 x 29 1/2 ins / 61 x 75 cm) DEM 8,000. LONDON, 6 Oct 1989, *Winter Landscape with Skaters at the Foot of a Castle near Strasbourg* (oil on canvas, 26 3/4 x 34 1/4 ins / 68 x 87 cm) GBP 4,620.

KIRSTEIN, Alfred
German, 19th - 20th century.
Born 25 June 1863, in Berlin; died 2 December 1922, in Berlin.
Painter. Landscapes.
Alfred Kirstein exhibited regularly at the Salon des Artistes Français in Paris between 1909 and 1914.

KIRSTEIN, Edith
German, 20th century.
Born 24 August 1881, in Sagnitz; died 2 December 1922, in Berlin.
Sculptor.
Edith Kirstein trained under Fr. Moritz.

KIRSTEIN, Gabriel
German, 16th century.
Born in Fulda.
Painter.
Kirstein worked mostly in Frankfurt am Main.

KIRSTEIN, Jakob Friedrich
French, 18th - 19th century.
Born 25 May 1765, in Strasbourg; died 4 June 1838, in Strasbourg.
Sculptor, goldsmith.
Jakob Friedrich Kirstein exhibited at the Salon between 1810 and 1834.

KIRSTEIN, Joachim Friedrich
French, 19th century.
Born 1805, in Strasbourg; died 22 January 1860, in Strasbourg.
Sculptor, goldsmith.
Joachim Kirstein was a pupil of his father Jakob Friedrich. He exhibited his work at the Salon between 1838 and 1842.

KIRSTEIN, Max
German, 19th century.
Died 1871, in Munich.
Painter. Still-lifes.
Max Kirstein was the brother of Adolf Kirstein.

KIRTLAND, G.
British, 18th century.
Active in Woodstock at the end of the 18th century.
Painter.
G. Kirtland is known for his *Portrait of Admiral Howe*.

KIRTSOVA, Alyona
Russian, 20th - 21st century.
Born 24 January 1954, in Barentsburg, Spitsbergen.
Painter.
From 1959 to 1963, Alyona Kirtsova lived in Canada. She now lives and works in Moscow. She was initially a pupil at the private school of Vassily Sitnikov, himself a painter of typical landscapes, whose style she emulated for a while. This brought her some success, which she regarded as having been won too easily. In 1978, she enrolled in the painting section of the Gorkon Institute for Graphic Arts. In 1986, she was one of the organisers of the Hermitage, an arts and culture association. Having turned her back on the landscapes

of her early years, after some long and painful soul-searching about the raison d'être for her art, she started painting again, following in the footsteps of Constructivism. She often based her geometric compositions on her observation of architectural details - for example, the angles formed where corridors turned. More recently, a number of more radically abstract compositions compensated for the austerity of an orthogonal geometry through her use of pigmented materials applied with a sensual touch. Her 1990 composition, Stair Treads, comprises alternate bands suggesting the treads of a staircase, the widths gradually narrowing thanks to the effects of perspective. Since 1977, she has taken part in collective exhibitions, including those organised by the Gorkon Institute in private apartments and clubs, and by the hermitage. She had her first solo exhibition in 1990 at Moscow University.

Museums and Galleries:

Avignon (Musée d'Art Contemporain) - Moscow (State Tretyakov Gal.): *Inkombank* - New Brunswick (Zimmerly Art Museum) - New York (Solomon R. Guggenheim Mus.) - St Petersburg (Gosudarstvennyj Russkij Muz.).

KIRVES, Dietmar

German, 20th century.

Born 1941, in Fürstenwalde an der Spree.

Assemblage artist, environmental artist, sculptor, photographer, mixed media. Artists' books.

During the 1960s, Dietmar Kirves worked with artists such as Joseph Beuys, Jochen Gerz and Terry Fox. He has lived in Berlin and Antwerp. He featured in the exhibition *De Bonnard à Baselitz - Dix ans d'enrichissements du Cabinet des Estampes* (*From Bonnard to Baselitz: A Decade of Acquisitions by the Prints Collection 1978-1988*) at the Bibliothèque Nationale in Paris in 1992.

Bibliography:

Beaumont-Maillet, Laure/Woimant, Françoise/Pernoud, Emmanuel, *De Bonnard à Baselitz - Dix ans d'enrichissements du Cabinet des estampes 1978-1988*, exhibition catalogue, Bibliothèque nationale de France, Paris, 1992.

Museums and Galleries:

Paris (BNF, Prints Collection).

KIRWAN, William Burke

Irish, 19th century.

Born c. 1814, in Dublin.

Miniaturist.

William Burke Kirwan exhibited his work at the Royal Academy in Dublin between 1836 and 1846.

KIRZBAUM, Alexandre, or Kirszbaum

French, 20th century.

Painter (mixed media). Figures, landscapes.

Figuration Libre.

Alexandre Kirzbaum exhibited his work in Paris galleries, notably in 1987 and 1988 at the Galerie du Jour. His work is Figurative and Primitive.

Auction records:

Paris, 12 Feb 1989, *Building* (1988, mixed media/paper, 39 1/4 x 27 1/4 ins / 100 x 69 cm) FRF 8,000.

KISCHKA, Isis

French, 20th century.

Born 1908, in Paris; died December 1973, in Montmorency.

Painter, illustrator, ceramicist. Landscapes, still-lifes, flowers. Designs for tapestries.

Isis Kischka's parents were Russian. He taught himself to paint while working in another profession. In 1941 he was arrested by the Gestapo and imprisoned until 1944. He took part in artistic propaganda activities at St-Denis, where he lived. In 1946 he began to paint again. Kischka created the Salon des Peintres Témoins de leur Temps (Salon of Painters Witnesses of their Time) in 1951.

He exhibited at various Paris Salons including the Salon des Indépendants of 1938. He also showed his work in solo exhibitions in Paris, the French provinces and abroad.

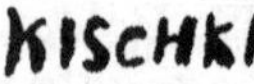

Bibliography:

Dornand, Guy, *Kischka, avec une biographie, une bibliographie et une documentation complète sur le peintre et son oeuvre*, Cailler, Geneva, 1962. Nieszawer, Nadine/Boyé, Marie/Lanzmann, Claude (preface), *Peintres juifs de l'école de Paris 1905-1939*, Denoël, Paris, 2001.

Auction records:

Paris, 29 June 1955, *Honfleur* (gouache) FRF 22,000. Versailles, 8 June 1972, *Sailing Boats on a Lake*, FRF 7,800. Zurich, 30 Oct 1982, *Blue Vase with Irises* (oil on canvas, 23 1/2 x 29 1/4 ins / 60 x 74 cm) CHF 3,400. Versailles, 13 Dec 1987, *Morens Tower at Annecy* (oil on canvas, 18 x 15 ins / 46 x 38 cm) FRF 10,200. Versailles, 20 March 1988, *Bunch of Flowers* (1957, oil on canvas, 15 x 18 ins / 38 x 46 cm) FRF 14,000. Versailles, 25 March 1990, *Vase of Flowers* (oil on canvas, 21 1/4 x 25 1/2 ins / 54 x 65 cm) FRF 15,000. Paris, 4 May 1990, *Quay at Honfleur* (oil on canvas, 23 3/4 x 11 1/2 ins / 60.5 x 29.5 cm) FRF 19,000. Paris, 25 June 1990, *Grand Canal, Venice* (oil on canvas, 51 1/4 x 19 3/4 ins / 130 x 50 cm) FRF 5,200. Paris, 17 Nov 1992, *Flower Seller* (oil on canvas, 11 x 9 ins / 27 x 22 cm) FRF 4,500. New York, 26 Feb 1993, *Training Ship* (1956, oil on canvas, 19 1/2 x 8 ins / 49.5 x 20.3 cm) USD 978. Paris, 27 Oct 1993, *Bouquet in Ochre Pink* (oil on canvas, 19 3/4 x 7 3/4 ins / 50 x 20 cm) FRF 3,000. Paris, 20 March 2001, *Still-life* (oil on canvas, 20 x 24 ins / 52 x 61 cm) FRF 18,000.

KISCHKO

20th century.

Painter.

Pop Art.

In the 1960s Kischko exhibited light and cheerful paintings clearly derived from American Pop Art.

KISEL

Polish, 18th century.

Painter.

Kisel was active during the reign of Stanislas Augustus. He painted landscapes in watercolour and gouache, and scenery for the Warsaw theatre.

KISEL, Conrad. See **KIESEL**

KISELEFF, Margareta

Finnish, 19th - 20th century.

Born 26 June 1862, in Helsinki; died 15 August 1924, in Helsinki.

Painter.

Margareta Kiseleff trained in Switzerland under Rosalie Gay.

KISELEV, Victor Petrovich

Russian, 20th century.

Born 1895, in Moscow; died 1984.

Painter. Stage sets.

Victor Kiselev studied at the Stroganov institute in Moscow from 1906 to 1912, then at the institute of painting, sculpture and architecture from 1912 to 1918. He became a member of the Society of Russian Artists in Moscow in 1926. His art was designed for propaganda purposes.

Bibliography:

Paris - Moscou, exhibition catalogue, Éd. du Centre Georges-Pompidou, Paris, 1979.

KISELEVA, Elena Andreevna

Russian, 20th century.

Born 1878; died 1974.

Painter. Rustic scenes.
Elena Kiseleva is known for a picture entitled *Russian Peasant Girls* which won a State prize in 1908.

KISELIOV, Aleksandr Aleksandrovich, or Kisseljoff
Russian, 19th - 20th century.
Born 6 June 1838, in Sveaborg; died 1911, in Moscow.
Painter. Genre scenes, landscapes.
Aleksandr Kiseliov studied in St Petersburg before settling in Moscow, where he taught landscape painting.
MUSEUMS AND GALLERIES:
MOSCOW - RIGA - ST PETERSBURG.
AUCTION RECORDS:
STOCKHOLM, 27 April 1983, *Summer Landscape* (1890, oil on canvas, 8 1/4 x 10 1/4 ins / 21 x 26 cm) SEK 10,200. LONDON, 1 May 1987, *Water Mill* (1890, oil on canvas, 29 x 48 1/2 ins / 73.5 x 123.5 cm) GBP 14,000. AMSTERDAM, 24 April 1991, *Peasant Girl Doing her Washing on the Banks of a River in Summer* (1879, oil on canvas, 20 1/4 x 26 1/4 ins / 51.5 x 66.7 cm) NLG 9,200. AMSTERDAM, 21 April 1993, *Harvest Scene* (1877, oil on canvas, 11 x 17 3/4 ins / 27 x 45 cm) NLG 1,725.

KISFALUDI-STROBL, Zsigmond
Hungarian, 20th century.
Born 1 July 1884, in Also Rajk; died 1975.
Sculptor.
From 1900 to 1903 Zsigmond Kisfaludi-Strobl studied at the school of decorative arts, followed by tuition from 1904 to 1905 from Alajos Strobl, and finally a year in Vienna. An eminent artist, he taught at a college for further education. Between the two wars he lived in England for a fairly long time.

He painted portraits of G. B. Shaw, Istvan Csok, Béla and Ivanyi Grünwald, as well as sculpting statues for public places (*Archer*, Budapest, in a park) and monuments including the main figure for the Kossuth monument (Freedom).

He featured in many retrospective exhibitions in Hungary and abroad including Artists' House, Müvészhaz (1909); Venice Biennale (1913); Paris (1932 and 1935); London (1935); and Moscow (1955). He won the Kossuth Prize.
BIBLIOGRAPHY:
Pogány, Gábor Ö., *Kisfaludi Strobl Zsigmond*, exhibition catalogue, Magyar Nemzeti Galéria, Budapest, 1974.
MUSEUMS AND GALLERIES:
BUDAPEST (Magyar Nemzeti Gal.).

KISFALUDY, Karoly
Hungarian, 19th century.
Born 5 February 1788, in Tet; died 21 November 1830, in Pest.
Painter. Landscapes.
Karoly Kisfaludy is mainly known for his landscapes, which are often romantically inspired.

KISHI, Ku. See **GANKU**

KISHI, Shoroku. See **CHIKUDO**

KISHIDA, Ryusei
Japanese, 20th century.
Born 1891, in Tokyo; died 1929.
Painter.
Groups: Sodo-sha, Shun'yo-kai.
Kishida Ryusei studied at the Hakuba-kai Art Institute, going on to exhibit at the Bunten (Ministry of Education) exhibitions and to work in a charcoal drawing society. In 1916, he founded the Sodo-sha artists' society, which would have a marked influence on western-style Japanese painting during the years 1910-1920. Later, together with a number of humanist friends, he would found the Shun'yo-kai society. After an initial interest in the work of Dürer and Van Eyck, he turned towards the study of Chinese painting of the Song and Yuan dynasties (960-1279 and 1279-1368), and to literati painting.

KISHIKUNI, artist name Hogado
Japanese, 19th century.
Active in Osaka c. 1820.
Print artist.

KISHINEVSKY, Solomon Yakovlevich, or Kichnewsky or Kinschinevskii
Ukrainian, 19th - 20th century.
Born 1863, in Odessa; died 1941.
Painter. Genre scenes.
From 1897 Solomon Kishinevsky lived in Paris, where he exhibited at the Salon des Artistes Français.
MUSEUMS AND GALLERIES:
MOSCOW (State Tretyakov Gal.): *A Request*.

KISHIO, Suga. See **SUGA Kishio**

KISLAKOV, Serge
Russian, 20th century.
Born 1897, in Yalta; died 1980.
Active in France.
Painter, decorative artist. Figures, local scenes, landscapes.
Serge Kislakov received a good and full artistic education but had to leave Russia in 1920. After spending a time in England he set off for Latin America, but on his way he fell in love with Corsica, where he settled. Before devoting himself full-time to painting, he worked as a designer for the Gaumont company. He restored many Corsican churches. Thanks to his numerous trips abroad, he left views of Stockholm harbour and other Swedish landscapes, as well as scenes of the carnival in Nice. Seduced by Montmartre, he knew how to convey the atmosphere of this lively and highly picturesque district.

He took part in numerous exhibitions including: Nice (1931, 1946); Paris (1946, 1949, 1950, 1952, 1954 and 1959); Sweden (1950); Manchester (1951); Brussels (1958).
MUSEUMS AND GALLERIES:
NICE (MBA Jules-Chéret): *The Market in Nice, in summer*.
AUCTION RECORDS:
RHEIMS, 1 Dec 1985, *Masked Ball* (1950, oil on canvas, 32 x 25 1/2 ins / 81 x 65 cm) FRF 17,000. RHEIMS, 25 Oct 1987, *Venice Carnival* (1950, oil on canvas, 28 3/4 x 35 3/4 ins / 73 x 91 cm) FRF 8,500. RHEIMS, 17 Dec 1989, *Nice Carnival, night-time illuminations* (oil on canvas, 23 1/2 x 28 3/4 ins / 60 x 73 cm) FRF 6,000.

KISLING, Franz Joseph
German, 18th century.
Painter, miniaturist.
Franz Joseph Kisling was the official portrait painter to the Mannheim court.

KISLING, Gabriel
Swiss, 20th century.
Born 6 May 1915, in Geneva.
Watercolourist. Landscapes.
Gabriel Kisling was an electrical engineer by profession, but took art courses by correspondence. He paints in the Alps, in Provence and in Brittany. He lived for two years in Morocco and Tunisia. His landscapes in watercolours have been reproduced as picture postcards. He has taken part in a great many collective regional exhibitions in France and Switzerland. Since 1982, he has participated in the Salon d'Automne, the Salon des Artistes Français and Salon de la Société Nationale des Beaux-Arts in Paris, and has been awarded various honours. He has held solo exhibitions in several Swiss towns and cities.

KISLING, Moïse
Polish, 20th century.
Born 22 January 1891, in Cracow; died 29 April 1953, in Sanary-sur-Mer, France.
Active from 1910 and from 1924 naturalised in France.

Painter, watercolourist, draughtsman, illustrator.
Figures, nudes, portraits, animals, landscapes, still-lifes, flowers.

Moïse Kisling attended the school of fine arts in Cracow whilst still very young. Here he was the pupil of the painter Pankiewicz, who was an excellent teacher and who himself subsequently went to live in Paris and become a representative of Impressionism. Pankiewicz's particular gift was his clarity of vision, since he very soon suspected that his pupil was going to have a brilliant future. He immediately suggested that Kisling move to Paris, a city in which many of the artists today regarded as masters of modern French art lived since 1910. This was an era marked by grand discussions, by violent battles, when everything was challenged. Life was not easy. Though Kisling at that time produced works marked with uneasiness, they nonetheless all showed signs of having been most intelligently researched. Then came the war. Having joined the Foreign Legion on the very first day, he was wounded in 1915 and invalided out. In the immediate aftermath of World War I, Kisling's studio in Paris became the venue for extraordinary meetings where artists like Derain or Modigliani or writers like Max Jacob, Jean Cocteau and Raymond Radiguet met. In 1940, Kisling fought for France and then went to the USA, in New York (1942 to 1946), and also spent several weeks in Beverly Hills, California. In 1946 he was back in France.

Kisling painted several portraits, a number of figures, still-lifes (particularly of fish and flowers) and landscapes. In his early years he was apparently drawn to unhappy figures such as children doomed to misfortune and poor people unable to escape their lives of poverty. Slowly though, and while never turning his back on humanity, he became a painter celebrating the joys of life. He achieved this through the exaltation of a beautiful nude, or the shimmering ingredients of a good bouillabaisse, and even by transposing those southern landscapes in a way that only a few artists after Renoir knew how to. In 1916 he illustrated *La Guerre du Luxembourg* by Blaise Cendrars.

Kisling exhibited in Paris at the Salon des Indépendants, the Salon d'Automne (from 1912), the Salon des Tuileries, and also abroad. His first solo exhibition was in 1919 at the Galerie Druet, Paris. During his time in the USA he exhibited at the Whitney Museum in New York, where he showed his portrait of the lady ambassador of Brazil, in Hollywood where he showed various portraits, including one of the pianist Rubinstein, and again at the Barnes Foundation in Philadelphia. A retrospective exhibition was organised in 1984 at the Grand Palais, Paris and his work was included in *Paris-Barcelone de Gaudí à Miró* (*Paris-Barcelona - from Gaudi to Miró*), also held at the Grand Palais (2001).

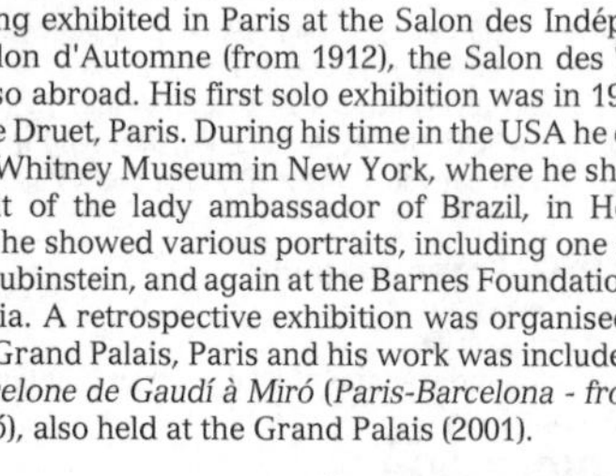

BIBLIOGRAPHY:

Kessel, Joseph, *Kisling, 1891-1953*, Jean Kisling, 1971. '*Kisling*' in *3 vol, 1971, 1982, 1995*, catalogue raisonné, Jean Kisling, Paris, 1982 (texts by J. Kessel/H. Troyat/Jean Dutourd). *L'Art moderne à Marseille - La Collection du Musée Cantini*, exhibition catalogue, Musée Cantini, Marseilles, 1988. De Voort, Claude, *Kisling, 1891-1953. Biographie*, Jean Kisling, 1996. Léal, Brigitte (ed.), *Paris-Barcelone de Gaudí à Miró*, exhibition catalogue, Grand Palais, Réunion des Musées nationaux, Paris, 2001.

MUSEUMS AND GALLERIES:

BELGRADE: *Bust of a Young Girl* - BROOKLYN, NY: *Portrait* - COLOGNE (Wallraf-Richartz Mus.) - GENEVA (Petit Palais): *Still-life with Fruit* (1913); *Young Boy in the Striped Pullover* (1937) - LISBON: *Young Fisherman* - LOS ANGELES: *Seated Nude* - MARSEILLES (MBA): *Belgazou (Portrait of Colette's Daughter)* - MOSCOW: *Head of a Woman* - PARIS (MAMVP): *Head of a Young Girl* - PARIS (MNAM-CCI): *Woman in Shawl* (1928) - STOCKHOLM (Nationalmus.): *Figure* - TEL AVIV: *Nude Lying on a Bed* - VENICE: *Young Dutch Girl*.

AUCTION RECORDS:

PARIS, 19 May 1920, *Golden Nude*, FRF 920. PARIS, 22 Nov 1922, *Hills and Orchards*, FRF 500. PARIS, 3 July 1924, *Woman with Shawl*, FRF 600. PARIS, 21 Dec 1925, *La Charrette* FRF 1,400. PARIS, 19 May 1926, *Nude Lying on a Bed*, FRF 2,600. PARIS, 21 Nov 1928, *Still-life with Gold Fish*, FRF 2,000. PARIS, 2 March 1929, *Portrait of a Young Boy*, FRF 10,800. PARIS, 14 June 1930, *Nude Model*, FRF 10,500. PARIS, 24 Feb 1936, *Fishing Net*, FRF 6,000. PARIS, 23 March 1938, *Young Girl with Plaits*, FRF 3,000. PARIS, 5 Dec 1940, *Reclining Nude against a Landscaped Background*, FRF 3,100. PARIS, 24 April 1942, *Blond Nude*, FRF 11,200. PARIS, 7 April 1943, *Landscape of the Midi* (1916) FRF 6,000. PARIS, 31 Jan 1944, *Roses*, FRF 27,000. PARIS, 8 Dec 1944, *Male Nude in the Bath*, FRF 33,000. PARIS, 30 Nov 1945, *Still-life with Lemons*, FRF 28,000. PARIS, 24 Jan 1947, *Bust of a Little Girl* (1919, watercolour) FRF 11,200. PARIS, 23 June 1950, *Roses in a Vase*, FRF 52,000. COLOGNE, 28 Oct 1958, *Female Nude*, DEM 3,800. PARIS, 20 March 1959, *Woman in the Red Dress*, FRF 400,000. NEW YORK, 16 March 1960, *Male Nude in the Garden*, USD 3,500. NEW YORK, 26 April 1961, *Harbour Scene*, USD 2,700. NEW YORK, 21 March 1962, *Kiki de Montparnasse*, USD 3,600. VERSAILLES, 2 June 1965, *Large male nude on a Couch*, FRF 76,000. LONDON, 3 May 1967, *Portrait of Edith Mera*, GBP 4,500. PARIS, 17 March 1969, *Red-headed Male Nude*, FRF 150,000. PARIS, 3 Dec 1971, *Large Nude Stretched out on a Sofa*, FRF 190,000. NEW YORK, 5 May 1973, *Sailboats in the Harbour* (watercolour) USD 2,100. PARIS, 11 June 1974, *Tulips*, FRF 248,000. VERSAILLES, 12 May 1976, *Bandstand in Montsouris Park* (graphite, 12 1/2 x 9 1/2 ins / 32 x 24 cm) FRF 3,500. NEW YORK, 28 May 1976, *Path Bordered with Trees* (1944, oil on canvas, 28 1/2 x 21 ins / 72.5 x 53.5 cm) USD 14,000. LONDON, 27 June 1977, *Kiki de Montparnasse* (1924, oil on canvas, 45 x 31 ins / 114 x 79 cm) GBP 13,000. ZURICH, 30 May 1979, *Nude Woman in a Garden* (1918, watercolour, 20 x 14 1/4 ins / 51 x 36 cm) CHF 6,000. NEW YORK, 7 Nov 1979, *Seated Nude* (1920, oil on canvas, 28 1/4 x 35 3/4 ins / 72 x 91 cm) USD 87,500. LONDON, 26 March 1980, *Bouquet of Flowers* (1916, pencil, 16 3/4 x 10 1/2 ins / 42.5 x 26.5 cm) GBP 850. NEW YORK, 20 May 1981, *Dutch Girl* (1922, oil on canvas, 39 3/4 x 29 1/4 ins / 101 x 74 cm) USD 70,000. LONDON, 23 March 1983, *Vase of Flowers* (watercolour, 22 x 13 1/2 ins / 55 x 34.5 cm) GBP 4,000. PARIS, 14 Dec 1983, *Large Bouquet Seen Against a Window* (oil on canvas, 39 1/4 x 28 3/4 ins / 100 x 73 cm) FRF 400,000. LONDON, 2 Dec 1986, *Portrait of a Young Brunette* (1947, oil on canvas, 36 1/2 x 27 1/2 ins / 93 x 70 cm) GBP 70,000. PARIS, 6 April 1987, *Harbour of St Tropez* (1925, graphite, 12 1/2 x 10 1/4 ins / 32 x 26 cm) FRF 28,000. PARIS, 24 Nov 1987, *Orchid in a Vase* (oil on canvas, 21 x 14 1/4 ins / 53.5 x 36 cm) FRF 220,000. NEW YORK, 18 Feb 1988, *Young Swedish Girl* (oil on canvas, 11 x 9 1/4 ins / 28 x 23.5 cm) USD 44,000. PARIS, 20 March 1988, *Vase of Red Flowers* (oil on canvas, 28 3/4 x 23 1/2 ins / 73 x 60 cm) FRF 590,000. PARIS, 21 March 1988, *Yellow Tulips* (oil on canvas, 25 1/2 x

21¼ ins / 65 x 54 cm) FRF 800,000. Tel Aviv, 26 May 1988, *Vase of Flowers* (oil on canvas, 22 x 18 ins / 55 x 46 cm) USD 115,500. Paris, 2 June 1988, *Still-life with Radish* (1949, oil on canvas, 18¼ x 21¾ ins / 46.5 x 55.5 cm) FRF 255,000. Paris, 12 June 1988, *Church at the Foot of the Mountain* (watercolour, 20 x 16½ ins / 51 x 42 cm) FRF 28,000. Paris, 22 June 1988, *Young Girl with Blue Corsage* (oil on canvas, 16¼ x 13 ins / 41 x 33 cm) FRF 390,000. Paris, 24 June 1988, *Bouquet of Anemones* (1937, oil on canvas, 16¼ x 11 ins / 41 x 27 cm) FRF 495,000. London, 28 June 1988, *Flowers in a Green Vase* (1938, oil on canvas, 24¾ x 21¼ ins / 63 x 54 cm) GBP 104,500. New York, 6 Oct 1988, *Kiki in a Low Cut Dress* (1918, oil on canvas, 21¾ x 15 ins / 55.2 x 38.4 cm) USD 88,000. Paris, 20 Nov 1988, *Red Roofs in Spain* (1919, oil on canvas, 19¾ x 24 ins / 50.2 x 61 cm) FRF 360,000. Paris, 24 Nov 1988, *Bouquet of Dahlias* (1948, oil on canvas, 28¾ x 21¼ ins / 73 x 54 cm) FRF 1,500,000. Paris, 23 Jan 1989, *Bouquet of Flowers* (oil/canvas, 16¼ x 13 ins / 41 x 33 cm) FRF 445,000. London, 4 April 1989, *The Spaniard* (1925, oil on canvas, 39¼ x 28¾ ins / 100 x 73 cm) GBP 220,000. New York, 10 May 1989, *Nude Female Lying on a Bed* (1923, oil on canvas, 28¼ x 38¾ ins / 71.5 x 98.5 cm) USD 275,000. Le Touquet, 14 May 1989, *Portrait of Madame Ella Brailowska* (1930, oil on canvas, 18 x 14¼ ins / 46 x 36 cm) FRF 440,000. Amsterdam, 24 May 1989, *Still-life with a Rose, an Arum Lily, Tulips and Irises in a Vase* (oil on canvas, 25½ x 19¾ ins / 65 x 50 cm) NLG 201,250. Tel Aviv, 30 May 1989, *Flowers in a White Terracotta Vase* (oil on canvas, 21½ x 15 ins / 54.5 x 38 cm) USD 187,000. Paris, 17 June 1989, *Vase of Lilies* (oil on canvas, 21¼ x 28¾ ins / 54 x 73 cm) FRF 1,170,000. New York, 5 Oct 1989, *Portrait of Madame Brailowsky* (oil on canvas, 25¾ x 19¾ ins / 65.4 x 50.2 cm) USD 242,000. Paris, 11 Oct 1989, *Two Cockerels* (1948, oil on canvas, 21½ x 29 ins / 54.5 x 73.5 cm) FRF 330,000. New York, 15 Nov 1989, *The Park at Gressy Château* (1949, oil on canvas, 33¾ x 45¾ ins / 85.7 x 116.2 cm) USD 352,000. Paris, 19 Nov 1989, *Portrait of a Woman* (oil on canvas, 21¾ x 15¼ ins / 55.5 x 38.5 cm) FRF 1,100,000. London, 28 Nov 1989, *Madeleine Sologne* (1949, oil on canvas, 46 x 35 ins / 116 x 89 cm) GBP 275,000. Paris, 30 March 1990, *Seated Female Nude* (1938, 21½ x 16½ ins / 54.5 x 41.9 cm) FRF 750,000. Paris, 31 March 1990, *Bouquet of Tulips* (oil on canvas, 22 x 15¼ ins / 55 x 39 cm) FRF 1,150,000. Vernon, 27 April 1990, *Bouquet of Yellow Flowers* (oil on canvas, 22 x 15 ins / 55 x 38 cm) FRF 780,000. Paris, 10 May 1990, *Vase of Flowers* (oil on canvas, 22 x 15 ins / 55 x 38 cm) FRF 800,000. New York, 16 May 1990, *Vase of Lilies* (oil on canvas, 25¾ x 21¼ ins / 65.3 x 54 cm) USD 242,000. Tel Aviv, 31 May 1990, *Vase of Tulips* (oil on canvas, 22 x 18 ins / 55 x 46 cm) USD 220,000. Versailles, 6 June 1990, *Madame Esders* (1948, oil on canvas, 28¾ x 21¼ ins / 73 x 54 cm) FRF 850,000. London, 26 June 1990, *Vase of Narcissus* (1931, oil on canvas, 16¼ x 13 ins / 41 x 33 cm) GBP 88,000. Paris, 27 June 1990, *Landscape* (1938, oil on canvas, 18 x 22 ins / 46 x 55 cm) FRF 430,000. New York, 14 Nov 1990, *Mimosa Blossoms* (oil on canvas, 25¾ x 39½ ins / 65.4 x 100.4 cm) USD 319,000. Paris, 26 Nov 1990, *Vase of Lilies* (1937, oil on canvas, 22 x 18 ins / 56 x 46 cm) FRF 900,000. London, 4 Dec 1990, *La Garçonne (Tomboy)* (1928, oil on canvas, 14 x 10¾ ins / 35.5 x 27.5 cm) GBP 55,000. Tel Aviv, 1 Jan 1991, *Landscape with a Little Girl under a Tall Tree* (1916, pencil, 12½ x 10 ins / 32 x 24.5 cm) USD 4,400. New York, 15 Feb 1991, *Tulips* (1942, oil on canvas, 22 x 15 ins / 55 x 38 cm) USD 132,000. London, 19 March 1991, *Portrait of a Young Girl* (1930, oil on canvas, 17¾ x 11 ins / 45 x 27 cm) GBP 49,500. New York, 8 May 1991, *Tulips* (1928, oil on canvas, 28¼ x 21¼ ins / 71.5 x 54 cm) USD 154,000. New York, 9 May 1991, *Young Girl Seated* (1923, oil on canvas, 25¾ x 19¾ ins / 65.4 x 50.2 cm) USD 159,500. Amsterdam, 22 May 1991, *Sketch of Volendam* (oil on canvas, 21¾ x 15¼ ins / 55.5 x 38.5 cm) NLG 69,000. Tel Aviv, 26 Sept 1991, *Portrait of a Young Girl* (1926, oil on canvas, 28¾ x 21½ ins / 73 x 54.3 cm) USD 165,000. Paris, 28 Nov 1991, *Bouquet of Flowers* (1938, oil on canvas, 25½ x 21¼ ins / 65 x 54 cm) FRF 580,000. London, 3 Dec 1991, *Bouquet of Flowers: Dahlias, Lys and Liliums* (1945, oil on canvas, 32 x 21½ ins / 81 x 54.5 cm) GBP 79,200. Auxerre, 5 April 1992, *Woman in Blue* (oil on canvas, 28¾ x 21¼ ins / 73 x 54 cm) FRF 720,000. New York, 11 Nov 1992, *Seated Male Nude* (1928, oil on canvas, 28¾ x 21¼ ins / 73 x 54 cm) USD 60,500. Amsterdam, 10 Dec 1992, *Portrait of a Young Girl* (oil on canvas, 16¼ x 13 ins / 41 x 33 cm) NLG 74,750. Paris, 15 March 1993, *Nude with His Back to the Artist* (oil on canvas, 39¼ x 29¼ ins / 100 x 74 cm) FRF 440,000. New York, 13 May 1993, *Vase of Mimosa Blossoms* (1950, oil on canvas, 29¼ x 24¼ ins / 74.6 x 61.9 cm) USD 189,500. Paris, 8 June 1993, *Young Girl* (1930, oil on canvas, 39¾ x 29¼ ins / 101 x 74 cm) FRF 540,000. Tel Aviv, 4 Oct 1993, *Bouquet of Mimosa Blossoms* (1939, oil on canvas, 27½ x 36¼ ins / 70 x 92 cm) USD 288,500. Paris, 27 March 1994, *Nude in Pink Drape* (lithograph, 24½ x 16½ ins / 62 x 42 cm) FRF 15,000. Toulouse, 3 May 1994, *Poppies in a Vase* (oil on canvas, 28¾ x 23½ ins / 73 x 60 cm) FRF 460,000. Paris, 6 May 1994, *Nude with Scarf* (graphite, 13 x 9 ins / 33 x 23 cm) FRF 31,500. New York, 12 May 1994, *Bouquet of Mixed Flowers and Mimosa Blossom* (1929, oil on canvas, 31¾ x 25¾ ins / 80.6 x 65.4 cm) USD 200,500. Paris, 1 June 1994, *Les Sablettes, Côte d'Azur* (1935, oil on canvas, 63 x 47¼ ins / 160 x 120 cm) FRF 910,000. Paris, 27 June 1994, *Two Female Bathers* (1917, oil on canvas, 32¼ x 59½ ins / 82 x 151 cm) FRF 900,000. London, 28 June 1994, *Kiki de Montparnasse* (1924, oil on canvas, 45 x 31 ins / 114 x 79 cm) GBP 144,500. St-Germain-en-Laye, 11 Dec 1994, *Festival of Flowers, St Tropez* (1917, oil on canvas, 28¾ x 21¼ ins / 73 x 54 cm) FRF 511,000. Tel Aviv, 12 Oct 1995, *Mimosa Blossoms* (1943, oil on canvas, 40 x 30 ins / 101.6 x 76.2 cm) USD 156,500. London, 29 Nov 1995, *Nude* (1938, oil on canvas, 28¾ x 21¼ ins / 73 x 54 cm) GBP 105,000. Paris, 7 Dec 1995, *Large Bouquet in Front of a Window* (1928, oil on canvas, 39¼ x 28¾ ins / 100 x 73 cm) FRF 710,000. Tel Aviv, 11 April 1996, *Brother and Sister* (1952, oil on canvas, 46 x 35 ins / 116 x 89 cm) USD 162,000. Paris, 13 June 1996, *Girl from Marseilles* (1950, oil on canvas, 39¾ x 28¾ ins / 101 x 73 cm) FRF 900,000. Paris, 13 Nov 1996, *Portrait of a Young Woman* (c. 1910-1913, pastel, 11¼ x 9 ins / 28.5 x 22 cm) FRF 15,000. New York, 13 Nov 1996, *Still-life with Fruit* (1925, oil on canvas, 21 x 28½ ins / 53.3 x 72.4 cm) USD 104,250. London, 3 Dec 1996, *Vase of Flowers* (1947, oil on canvas, 22 x 18 ins / 55 x 46 cm) GBP 45,500. London, 19 March 1997, *St Mandrier* (1935, oil on canvas, 9½ x 13¾ ins / 24 x 35 cm) GBP 13,800. Calais, 23 March 1997, *Young Girl with the Red Veil* (1941, oil on canvas, 22 x 18 ins / 56 x 46 cm) FRF 260,000. Paris, 4 April 1997, *Seated Nude* (1927, engraving/Arche vellum, 26½ x 19¾ ins / 67 x 50 cm) FRF 8,500. Tel Aviv, 26 April 1997, *Large Bouquet* (1927, oil on canvas, 38½ x 28¾ ins / 98 x 73 cm) USD 156,000. Paris, 11 June 1997, *Young Girl in the Red Dress* (1936, oil on canvas, 28¾ x 21¼ ins / 73 x 54 cm) FRF 650,000. Paris, 16 June 1997, *Mixed Flowers* (1946, oil on canvas, 23½ x 28¾ ins / 60 x 73 cm) FRF 450,000. London, 25 June 1997, *Provence Landscape* (1933, oil on canvas, 9½ x 13 ins / 24 x 33 cm) GBP 17,825. Tel Aviv, 23 Oct 1997, *Motherhood* (1952, oil on canvas, 46 x 32 ins / 116 x 81 cm) USD 129,000. Tel Aviv, 25 Oct 1997, *Bouquet of Flowers in a Vase* (oil on canvas, 17¾ x 11¼ ins / 45 x 28.5 cm) USD 70,700. Paris, 31 March 1998, *Provence Landscape* (1952, oil on canvas, 36½ x 46 ins / 93 x 116 cm) FRF 410,000. Biarritz, 12 April 1998, *Young Boy with his Arms Crossed* (oil on canvas) FRF 452,000. Paris, 2 Dec 1998, *Large Varied Bouquet* (1947, oil on canvas, 32 x 39 ins / 81 x 100 cm) FRF 940,000. Tel Aviv, 10 April 1999, *Bouquet of Flowers* (1951, oil on canvas, 29 x 24 ins / 73 x 60 cm) USD 200,000. New York, 9 Nov 1999, *Large Bouquet of Tulips* (1952, oil on canvas, 34 x 39 ins / 86 x 100 cm) USD 200,000. TEL AVIV, 29 April 2000, *Bouquet of Mimosas in a Red Pot* (1941, oil on canvas, 35 x 43 ins / 89 x 110 cm) USD 170,000. TEL AVIV, 26 Oct 2000, *Vase of Mimosas* (1952, oil on canvas, 24 x 29 ins / 60 x 73 cm) USD 140,000. TEL AVIV, 16 April 2001, *Large Varied Bouquet* (1947, oil on canvas, 32 x 39 ins / 81 x 100 cm) USD 300,000. NEW YORK, 9 May 2002, *Large Bouquet of Tulips* (1952, oil on canvas, 34 x 39 ins / 86 x 100 cm) USD 290,000. PARIS, 3 July 2002, *Mimosas* (1942, oil on canvas, 36 x 25 ins / 92 x 63 cm) EUR 133,000. NEW YORK, 8 May 2003, *Large Bouquet of Mimosas* (1942, oil on canvas, 37 x 51 ins / 95 x 130 cm) USD 425,000. LONDON, 22 June 2004, *Poppies* (1950, oil on canvas, 29 x 21 ins / 73 x 54 cm) GBP 70,000.

KISLING, Philip Heinrich
German, 18th century.
Born 24 November 1713, in Eggenstein.
Painter.

Philip Heinrich Kisling worked in Durlach as official painter to the court of the Margarve Karl Friedrich of Baden-Durlach.

KISLING-PELATI, Violette
Swiss, 20th century.
Pastellist, draughtswoman. Animals.

Violette Kisling-Pelati is the wife of Gabriel Kisling. She takes part in collective exhibitions, notably in Paris at the Salon des Artistes Français, and has been awarded various regional honours. She also has solo exhibitions in Switzerland.

KISPERT, Gustav
Swiss, 19th century.
Born 13 August 1856, in Rorschach; died 6 March 1887, in Munich.
Painter.

Gustav Kispert studied in Stuttgart and Munich. He is known for a number of canvases of rustic idylls.

AUCTION RECORDS:
LONDON, 18 March 1983, *Duty Calls* (1883, oil on panel, 11 1/2 x 8 1/4 ins / 29 x 21 cm) GBP 1,600.

KISS, August Karl Eduard
German, 19th century.
Born 11 October 1802, in Paprotzah; died 24 March 1865, in Berlin.
Sculptor.

Kiss studied at the Berlin academy with Rauch, Tieck and Schinkel.

MUSEUMS AND GALLERIES:
ANTWERP: *Amazon Defending Herself against a Tiger; Bust of the Artist* - BERLIN: *Faith, Hope and Charity; Fox-hunting; End of the Chase; Returning from the Hunt; Portrait of the Artist.*

KISS, Balint
Hungarian, 19th century.
Born 21 December 1802, in Szentes; died 19 January 1868, in Pest.
Painter.

Balint Kiss studied in Vienna before settling in Pest. He was curator of the museum there. He worked in many different genres, painting altarpieces, portraits, large historical pictures, and even a few landscapes.

KISS, György
Hungarian, 19th - 20th century.
Born 17 August 1852, in Szászvár; died 24 September 1919, in Budapest.
Sculptor.

A silver medallist in Paris at the 1900 Exposition Universelle, György Kiss sculpted his allegorical work *Religion* and a *St Stephen* for Esztergom cathedral.

KISS, Ilona
Hungarian, 20th century.
Born in Budapest.
Painter (mixed media), collage artist.

Ilona Kiss studied graphic art and went on to work professionally in that medium. A member of the young artists' workshop group, her paintings were influenced by graphic techniques in terms of their lay out, shifts in what they signified, and by the vogue for Surrealism.

KISS, István
Hungarian, 20th century.
Born 1927.
Sculptor.

István Kiss studied at the school of fine arts in Budapest from 1948 to 1953 with Kisfaludi, Strobl, Mikus and Patzay. He sculpted monumental statues: *Peace* (1955); *Lenin* in Diosgyor (1959); monument to the workers' movement in Debrecen (1961); and Dozsa monument in Budapest (1956-1960).

Kiss exhibited from 1949 and was awarded the Munkácsy Prize.

BIBLIOGRAPHY:
Bereczky, Lóránd, *Kiss Istvan*, exhibition catalogue, Mücsarnok, Budapest, 1977.

MUSEUMS AND GALLERIES:
BUDAPEST (Magyar Nemzeti Gal.).

KISS, Jozsef
Hungarian, 19th century.
Born 10 January 1833, in Eisenstadt; died November 1900, in Vienna.
Painter. History painting, genre scenes, portraits.

Jozsef Kiss studied at the academy of fine arts in Vienna. He showed his first painting in Vienna in 1873.

KISS, Jozsef
Hungarian, 20th century.
Born 6 March 1875, in Budapest.
Sculptor.

Jozsef Kiss studied at the Académie Julian in Paris.

KISS, Kalman
Hungarian, 20th century.
Born 17 July 1878, in Kalocsa.
Painter.

After studying in Munich and Rome, Kalman Kiss exhibited for the first time in Budapest in 1902.

KISS, Rezso
Hungarian, 20th century.
Born 26 December 1889, in Budapest.
Painter, engraver.

Rezso Kiss was the pupil of L. Simon, Jean-Paul Laurens and G. Courtois in Paris.

KISS, Sarolta, married name Komaromi-Kacz
Hungarian, 20th century.
Born 24 March 1883.
Painter, watercolourist.

MUSEUMS AND GALLERIES:
BUDAPEST (Municipal Mus.).

KISS KOVACS, Gyula
Hungarian, 20th century.
Born 1925.
Sculptor, medallist.

Gyula Kiss Kovacs was a pupil of Ferenc Sidlo and Pal Patzay from 1942 to 1949. He was interested in all types of sculpture but showed a marked preference for small works and medals. He took part in many exhibitions.

KISS NAGY, Andras
Hungarian, 20th century.
Born 1930.

Sculptor, medallist.

Andras Kiss Nagy studied at the academies of fine arts in Budapest and Leningrad (now St Petersburg) from 1949 to 1957 under the direction of Pal Patzay and Sandor Mikus. He primarily sculpted medals and statues which showed a very individual interpretation of the archaism of Tanagra figurines and the monumental three-dimensional works of a Henry Moore.

A member of the young artists' studio, where he regularly exhibited from 1957, he also showed his works in Moscow, Prague, Berlin, The Hague and Vienna. In 1963 a comprehensive exhibition was held in Budapest. He was awarded many prizes in Hungary including the Munkácsy Prize (1965) and the first prize at the first Pécs Biennale.

BIBLIOGRAPHY:

Csorba, Géza, *L'Art hongrois contemporain*, exhibition catalogue, Musée Galliera, Paris, 1970.

KISSEL, Gernot

German, 20th century.

Born 1939, in Worms-am-Rhein.

Painter. Figures.

Gernot Kissel started painting at the age of 18, while studying architecture. He lives and works in the Palatinate. He exhibits in Vienna, Switzerland, Germany, Antwerp, The Hague, Luxembourg and London. Since 1993 he has exhibited in France, notably at the Galerie AkkA in Paris in 1998.

KISSEL, Monique

French, 20th century.

Painter.

Monique Kissel has exhibited her work at various exhibitions, including: in Auch (1992); at the Marset plant nurseries in Le Seilhan; and in Paris (1993). She works in series, producing *Icons* (1985-1986) and *Fluids* (1990). In *My Zen Gardens* (1991) she creates poetic landscapes in which faint signs, branches and leaves stand out against an exceptionally white background.

BIBLIOGRAPHY:

Dagbert, Anne, '*Monique Kissel*' in *Art Press*, no. 176, periodical, Paris, January 1993.

KISSELEVA, Olga

Russian, 20th century.

Born in Leningrad (now St Petersburg).

Installation artist, photographer.

Olga Kisseleva belongs to a new generation of Russian artists who have found their place on the international scene. She usually works abroad, but also exhibits in Russia. She exhibited her installations at the Russian Museum (*Where Are You?* in 2001), and at the Arctic and Antarctic Museum (*Hybrid Space* in 2002). Her works explore the double meanings of people and places.

KISSELIOV, Aleksandr Alekseevich, or Kisselioff

Russian, 19th century.

Born 2 August 1855; died 1927.

Painter, draughtsman. History painting, genre scenes, landscapes.

Kisseliov studied at the imperial academy of arts and sciences in St Petersburg under Beklemichev. He showed work in an exhibition in Moscow in 1894, and showed five paintings at his former academy in St Petersburg in 1904.

His early work was in a rather overdone academic style, which evolved into a mildly impressionistic style by 1900.

MUSEUMS AND GALLERIES:

ST PETERSBURG (Gosudarstvennyj Russkij Muz.): several landscapes and studies.

AUCTION RECORDS:

PARIS, 23 April 1989, *Celebration at Denfert-Rochereau* (oil on canvas, 34 3/4 x 30 1/2 ins / 88.5 x 77.5 cm) FRF 28,000.

KISSELIOV, Ossip

Russian, 19th century.

Active during the first half of the 19th century.

Engraver.

Works by Kisseliov include the *Portraits of the Tsar Nicholas I and his Wife*, and a *Portrait of the Tsar Alexander II.*

KISSLING, Ernest

Swiss, 20th century.

Born 12 August 1890, in Zurich; died 1973.

Sculptor. Nudes, portraits.

MUSEUMS AND GALLERIES:

WINTERTHUR: *Head of Woman.*

AUCTION RECORDS:

ZURICH, 27 May 1982, *Nude Walking* (lost-wax bronze, h. 35 ins / 88 cm) CHF 6,000.

KISSLING, Eugène

French, 19th - 20th century.

Born in Châtenois.

Painter.

Eugène Kissling exhibited at the Salon des Indépendants in Paris from 1901 onward.

KISSLING, Gottlieb

Lithuanian, 19th century.

Active in Vilnius.

Engraver.

Gottlieb Kissling travelled widely in Europe, particularly in Italy. He made a large number of copies of paintings from the Italian Renaissance.

KISSLING, Leopold

Austrian, 18th - 19th century.

Born 8 October 1770, in Schönleben; died 26 November 1827, in Vienna.

Sculptor.

One of Kissling's marbles, *Mars, Venus and Love*, symbolising Napoleon's marriage to the empress Marie-Louise, can be seen in the Austrian Belvedere Gallery in Vienna.

MUSEUMS AND GALLERIES:

VIENNA (Österreichische Gal. Belvedere).

KISSLING, Richard

Swiss, 19th - 20th century.

Born 15 April 1848, in Wolfwil (Solothurn); died 19 July 1919, in Zurich.

Sculptor.

Richard Kissling trained under Ferdinand Schloth in Rome and at the Academy of St Luke from 1870 to 1883. He settled in Zurich. His works include the *Alfred, Esther Monument* in Zurich, the *William Tell Monument* in Altdorf, several fountain sculptures in Coize, and the *Statue of Switzerland* in St Gall. He exhibited at the Royal Academy in London in 1887 and at the Exposition Universelle in Paris in 1889, receiving an honourable mention.

MUSEUMS AND GALLERIES:

BASEL: marble statue.

KISSNER, Erwin

German, 20th century.

Born 13 December 1885, in Berlin.

Sculptor. Animals.

KISTE, Adolph

German, 20th century.

Born 2 August 1912, in Hamburg; died in London.

Painter, engraver. Landscapes.

Adolph Kiste travelled a great deal in Scandinavia, Great Britain and Germany and brought back paintings from all his trips.

KISTENFEGER, Jakob

German, 15th - 16th century.

Active in Munich.

Glass painter.
Kistenfeger worked in Munich, Holzkirchen and Gauting.

KISTLER, Bartholomäus
French, 15th century.
Active in Strasbourg at the end of the 15th century.
Painter.

KISTLER, Samuel Sigmund
Swiss, 19th century.
Born 1814; died 9 December 1865, in Bern.
Watercolourist.

KISTNER, Thomas
German, 16th century.
Died August 1569, in Würzburg.
Active in Würzburg.
Sculptor.
Kistner studied under Peter Dell the Elder, and sculpted funerary monuments in the cathedral in Würzburg.

KITA, Genki
Japanese, 17th century.
Painter.
Kita Genki was active at Nagasaki in about 1671. This port at the westernmost extremity of the Japanese archipelago was the point where, in the 17th century, elements of foreign art and culture (Chinese as well as Western) entered Japan. Among the former were portraits of Zen monks in a heightened realist style. Local painters, Kita Genki among them, adopted these models, adding touches reminiscent of western painting to the style of the Chinese portrait painters.

KITA, Renzo
Japanese, 20th century.
Born 1876; died 1949.
Painter (oil painting). Genre scenes.
Kita Renzo is known to have worked in Tokyo in 1900. He took part in the Paris Exposition Universelle in that year.

KITAGAWA, Kenji
Japanese, 20th - 21st century.
Born 1952, in Fukui Prefecture.
Print artist, copperplate prints.
Kenji Kitagawa graduated from Tama Art University in 1976. He had started to exhibit at the International Young Artists Exhibition in Tokyo in 1973, and in the Japanese Print Association in 1974. He also showed his work at the *Japanese Art Today* exhibition held at the Musée d'Art Contemporain, Montréal.

KITAGAWA, Tamiji
Japanese, 20th century.
Born 1894, in Shizuoka Prefecture; died 1989.
Painter, print artist.
Kitagawa Tamiji went to the USA in 1914 to continue his studies at the Art Students League in New York. He then moved to Mexico, where he attended the Accademia de San Carlos in Mexico City, staying for ten years. He returned to Japan in 1937 and became a member of the Nika (two disciplines - painting and sculpture) Society. In 1955-1956 he travelled once more to Mexico and also visited Europe. His work, especially his copper and wood engravings, but also his painting, has a Mexican feel. He wrote extensively on his travels and published an album of prints.
AUCTION RECORDS:
NEW YORK, 31 Oct 1995, *Mother and Child with Dog* (lithograph, 20 x 14 1/2 ins / 51.1 x 36.8 cm) USD 3,450.

KITAGAWA UTAMARO. See **UTAMARO**

KITAIKIN, Anatoli
Russian, 20th - 21st century.
Born 1948, in Nogimsk.
Painter. Portraits.
Anatoli Kitaikin is a member of the Malaia Gruzhinski association of painters and designers. He studied at the school of fine arts in Moscow where he lives and works. He has taken part in several collective exhibitions, notably in Hamburg and Frankfurt and in 1990 at the Galerie A.L. Expo in Paris with A. Djavid, A. Fonin and B. Otarov. He also took part in an exhibition in Berlin in 1990.
AUCTION RECORDS:
PARIS, 17 Nov 1990, *Beethoven* (1989, oil and acrylic/canvas, 78 3/4 x 67 ins / 200 x 170 cm) FRF 3,000.

KITAJ, Ronald B., or Kitay
American, 20th century.
Born 1932, in Cleveland (Ohio).
From 1958 active in England.
Painter, draughtsman, pastellist. Figures, nudes, scenes with figures.
Pop Art, Nouvelle Figuration.
School of London.
Ron Kitaj, a merchant seaman in the early 1950s, first went to sea on a Norwegian freighter which called at Havana and Mexico. His brief spell at the Cooper Union, New York, was followed by studies at the Vienna Academy of fine arts. From 1955 to 1957, he served in the US army in Europe, and went on to study on a GI scholarship at the Ruskin Academy of Drawing in Oxford, then at the Royal College of Art in London where he became friends with David Hockney. He also toured South America, North Africa and Spain. He took on teaching positions at the Camberwell School of Arts and Craft then at the Slade School in London, making numerous connections with young English artists including Francis Bacon. He has been credited with the idea of the School of London. In 1967, he was a guest professor at the University of California, Berkeley and he also taught at UCLA. He is the third US artist to be elected to the British Royal Academy.

Although Kitaj was loosely associated with the British Pop Art movement of the 1960s, his works differ in their complexity and use of figurative imagery. In Kitaj's work, the elements others found in cartoons and magazines were more likely to draw on literature, history and art history, with a strong biographical element where nostalgia, loss, and the question of Jewish identity loomed large. These collages illustrated the impact Walter Benjamin's *The Work of Art in the Age of Mechanical Reproduction* had on Kitaj. When he returned to painting, he produced vibrant figurative pieces. His subjects, who can be down-and-out types, prostitutes or crooks, are caught in the act, as it were, vivid and allusive at the same time. Alive to art present and past, upon discovering Degas' work he mastered the use of pastel and executed numerous nudes and portraits.

Since 1955, he has taken part in numerous collective exhibitions in London(*Pop' art* and *Young Contemporaries*); Eindhoven, Kassel (1964 and 1968 Documenta); the Venice Biennale; Paris (*La Figuration narrative* (*Narrative Figuration*)); Brussels (*Nouvelle Subjectivité* (*New Subjectivity*), 1979); Basel, Cincinnati, Berlin, Milan and Tokyo. He has shown his works in solo exhibitions in London, New York, Los Angeles, Amsterdam, Cleveland, Rotterdam and Washington.

BIBLIOGRAPHY:
Ashbery, John/Shannon, Joe/Livingston, Jane, *Kitaj. Paintings, drawings, pastels,* Thames & Hudson, London, 1983. Kitaj, Ronald Brooks, *Ronald B. Kitaj,* exhibition catalogue, Marlborough Fine Art, London, 1985. Ashbery, John/Hyman, T./Livingston, J./Shannon, J., *Kitaj. Paintings, Drawings, Pastels,* Thames & Hudson, New York, 1986.

Livingstone, Marco, *Kitaj*, Phaidon, London, 1992 (with preface by Kitaj). Morphet, Richard/Wollheim, Richard, *R. B. Kitaj, a retrospective*, travelling exhibition catalogue, County Museum of Art, Los Angeles, Metropolitan Museum of Art, New York, Tate Gall., London, 1994. Kinsman, Jane, *The Prints of R.B. Kitaj*, Scolar Press, Aldershot, 1994. Calvocoressi, Richard/Cohen, David/Bruce, Bernard, *From London. Bacon, Freud, Kossof, Andrews, Auerbach, Kitaj*, travelling exhibition catalogue, British Council, London, Scottish National Gall. of Modern Art, Edinburgh, 1995. Livingstone, Marco/San Martín, Francisco Javier/Hanak, Werner, *R.B. Kitaj, an American in Europe*, exhibition catalogue, Astrup Fearnley Museet for Moderne Kunst, Oslo, 1998 (text in German and English). Aulich, James/Lynch, John, *'Critical Kitaj. Essays on the work of R. B. Kitaj'* in coll. *The Barber's Institute critical perspectives in art history series*, Manchester University Press, Manchester, 2000. Rudolf, Anthony, *Kitaj: In the Aura of Cézanne and Other Masters*, exhibition catalogue, National Gall., London, 2001 (including a conversation with the artist).

MUSEUMS AND GALLERIES:

ADELAIDE (AG of South Australia) - AMSTERDAM (Stedelijk Mus.) - BALTIMORE (MA) - BASEL (Kunsthalle) - BERLIN (Nationalgal.) - BUFFALO (Albright-Knox AG) - CHICAGO (AI) - CINCINNATI (AM): *Apotheosis of Groundlessness* (painting); *Go and Get Killed Comrade, We Need a Bryon in the Movement* (engraving) - CLEVELAND (MA): *The Garden* (1981) - COLOGNE (Wallraf-Richartz Mus.): *Austro-Hungarian Infantryman* (1961) - GÖTEBORG (Konstmus.) - HAMBURG (Kunsthalle) - LONDON (Tate Collection): *The Murder of Rosa Luxembourg* (1960); *London WC2* (1983-1984); *Cecil Court*; *The Refugees*; *Lord Sieff of Brimpton* (1985) - LONDON (Victoria and Albert Mus.) - NEW YORK (Metropolitan Mus. of Art): *John Ford on his Death Bed* - NEW YORK (MoMA) - OSLO (Nasjonalgal.): *The Sensualist* (1973-1984) - OXFORD (MA) - PARIS (MNAM-CCI) - ROTTERDAM (Mus. Boijmans Van Beuningen) - SÃO PAULO (MAM) - THE HAGUE (Gemeentemus.).

AUCTION RECORDS:

NEW YORK, 12 April 1967, *Yamhill County Court House and Jail*, USD 1,750. LONDON, 19 July 1968, *Welcome Every Dread Delight*, Gns 800. LONDON, 20 March 1970, *Books*, Gns 380. LONDON, 3 Dec 1974, *Synchromy with F.B. - General of Hot Desire* (diptych) Gns 27,000. LONDON, 29 June 1977, *Te Deum* (1963, oil on canvas, 48 1/4 x 72 1/2 ins / 122.5 x 184 cm) GBP 18,000. NEW YORK, 8 Nov 1979, *Warburgh as Maenad* (1962, oil and collage/canvas, 76 x 36 ins / 193 x 91.5 cm) USD 34,000. LONDON, 4 Dec 1980, *Two Nudes Sitting* (1974, pastel and charcoal, 22 x 15 1/4 ins / 56 x 39 cm) GBP 4,800. NEW YORK, 12 Nov 1982, *Primo de Rivera* (1969, oil on canvas, 18 x 15 1/4 ins / 46 x 38.5 cm) USD 9,500. LONDON, 25 June 1985, *The Ohio and Indiana of Anderson and Dreiser* (1965, oil on canvas, 30 x 19 3/4 ins / 76 x 50 cm) GBP 2,800. NEW YORK, 5 May 1987, *Juan de la Cruz* (1967, oil on canvas, 72 1/4 x 60 ins / 183.5 x 152.7 cm) USD 350,000. LONDON, 20 Oct 1988, *The Agony of the Model* (pastel/paper, 22 1/2 x 30 1/4 ins / 57 x 77 cm) GBP 15,400. MILAN, 14 Dec 1988, *French Subjects* (1956, mixed media/paper, 38 1/2 x 25 1/4 ins / 98 x 64 cm) ITL 4,200,000. LONDON, 29 June 1989, *Germania (The Engine Room)* (oil on canvas, 48 x 48 ins / 122 x 122 cm) GBP 121,000. LONDON, 24 May 1990, *Richard Wollheim: Study for Three Philosophers* (1976, charcoal/paper, 22 1/4 x 30 1/4 ins / 56.5 x 77 cm) GBP 17,050. LONDON, 28 June 1990, *Viennese Student* (oil and collage/canvas, 36 1/4 x 36 1/4 ins / 92 x 92 cm) GBP 82,500. NEW YORK, 13 Nov 1991, *To Live in Peace (Singers)* (1974, oil on canvas, 30 1/2 x 84 1/2 ins / 77.5 x 214.5 cm) USD 330,000. LONDON, 26 March 1992, *The 'Londonist'* (1987, oil on canvas, 120 x 36 ins / 305 x 91.5 cm) GBP 55,000. NEW YORK, 6 May 1992, *Rockery (the Nation)* (oil on canvas, 48 x 48 ins / 121.9 x 121.9 cm) USD 154,000. LONDON, 2 July 1992, *First Elements of Motifs I* (1965, oil on canvas, 60 x 60 ins / 151.5 x 151.5 cm) GBP 154,000. NEW YORK, 4 May 1993, *Small View of a Hovel* (1968, oil on canvas, 30 x 24 ins / 76.2 x 61 cm) USD 51,750. LONDON, 30 Nov 1994, *Value, Price, Profit* (oil on canvas, 60 1/4 x 60 1/4 ins / 153 x 153 cm) GBP 243,500. LONDON, 30 Nov 1995, *Golem* (oil on canvas/card, 59 1/4 x 20 3/4 ins / 150.5 x 53 cm) GBP 56,500. LONDON, 26 June 1997, *The Cézanist* (1980-1985, oil on canvas, 60 x 24 ins / 152.2 x 61 cm) GBP 34,500. LONDON, 21 Oct 1999, *Yamhill* (1961, oil on canvas, 40 x 50 ins / 101 x 126 cm) GBP 28,000. LONDON, 9 Dec 1999, *The Drivist* (1985-1987, oil on canvas, 72 x 37 ins / 183 x 93 cm) GBP 40,000. LONDON, 29 June 2000, *Messianist* (1985, oil on canvas, 72 x 24 ins / 183 x 61 cm) GBP 30,000. LONDON, 29 June 2000, *The Red and the Black* (pastel and charcoal, 31 x 23 ins / 78 x 58 cm) GBP 60,000. LONDON, 8 Feb 2001, *New York Madman* (1979, charcoal, 22 x 15 ins / 56 x 38 cm) GBP 20,000. NEW YORK, 23 May 2001, *Manchu Decadence* (charcoal, 45 x 22 ins / 115 x 56 cm) USD 37,500. LONDON, 7 Feb 2002, *Germania - Engine Room* (1983-1986, oil on canvas, overlap, 48 x 48 ins / 122 x 122 cm) GBP 35,000. LONDON, 6 Feb 2003, *Piccadilly* (1992, oil on canvas, 48 x 48 ins / 123 x 123 cm) GBP 18,000. LONDON, 6 June 2003, *After Soutine's Only Nude* (1997-2000, charcoal and pastel, 30 x 22 ins / 77 x 57 cm) GBP 7,500. LONDON, 5 Feb 2004, *Value, Price and Profit* (1963, oil on canvas, 60 x 60 ins / 153 x 153 cm) GBP 220,000. LONDON, 1 April 2004, *Louis Jouvet as Anne* (oil on canvas, 12 x 10 ins / 30 x 25 cm) GBP 5,500.

KITAKATSU, Tokuhiro

Japanese, 20th century.
Born 28 May 1926, in Kobe.
Painter.

Kitakatsu studied at Kobe Art Academy. In 1963-1964 he went to Europe, stopping in Paris and returning there in 1970. His painting is refined in tonality and subject matter, and reminiscent of the poetic climate that Paul Klee brought to abstract art. He has exhibited since 1955, winning various local prizes. He has also held a number of one-man shows of his painting in Paris.

BIBLIOGRAPHY:

Kitakatsu, exhibition catalogue, Gal. Roque, Paris, 1975.

KITAMURA, Kazuo

Japanese, 20th - 21st century.
Born 1951.
Painter.

Kitamura exhibited at the 9th Kanagawa Prefecture exhibition held in Kamakura in 1974 and in the *Japanese Art Today* exhibition held at the Musée d'Art Contemporain, Montréal.

KITAO, Masanobu, real name Haida Sei or Iwase Sei; given name Samuru; popular names Denzo, Hakkei, later Yusei, Yusai; author's pseudonym Santo Kyoden; artist names Rissai, Santokyo, Santokutsu, Santoan, Seisai

Japanese, 18th - 19th century.
Born 1761; died 1816.
Active in Edo (now Tokyo).
Print artist.

Masanobu studied under Kitao Shigemasa (1739-1820). Between 1778 and 1791 he was influential as both artist and writer (as poet, he went by the name Migaru Orisuke). Thereafter he devoted himself to writing fiction. He produced woodblock prints of beautiful women and illustrated many books. His most characteristic work was *Yoshiwara Keisei Shin Bijin Awase Jihitsu Kagami* (Yoshiwara Courtesans: A New Collection of Beauties. An autobiographical mirror). He was famous as the author of works of light fiction, the *Ukiyo-e Ruiko Tsuiko* (Biographies of Ukiyo-e Artists, 1802), and the *Kinsei Kisekiko* (Notes on Unusual Present-day Events, 1815). One of the driving forces behind late 18th-century Japanese middle-class culture, he forged a link between art and literature.

KITAO SHIGEMASA. See **SHIGEMASA**

KITAOJI, Rosanjin, real name Kitaoji Fusajiro, artist name Rosanjin
Japanese, 20th century.
Born 1883, in Kyoto; died 1959.
Painter, calligrapher, potter.

Rosanjin grew up in an adoptive family after being abandoned by his mother. When he was only ten, he discovered the art of calligraphy and was deeply impressed. On being turned down by the Kyoto Municipal Art School he taught himself virtually on his own, mastering the arts of calligraphy and engraving by the age of 20. In 1915, after completing various calligraphic works in Tokyo, he travelled abroad, going to China and Korea. He returned to Kanazawa to study ceramics under Suda Seika for two years. In 1917 he settled in Kita-Kamakura as a ceramic artist. He only travelled to the West once, in 1954, for the exhibition of his work in Europe and the USA. For eleven years, Rosanjin worked in close collaboration with the owners of Tokyo's most renowned restaurant, making all the ceramic wares used in the establishment. His work defies categorisation; he touched on many disciplines in many styles.

AUCTION RECORDS:
NEW YORK, 29 March 1990, *Sparrows among Pines* (ink on paper, two-panelled folding screen, 58¼ x 54½ ins / 148 x 138.4 cm) USD 88,000. NEW YORK, 27 April 1994, *Bizen-Style Brazier* (stone, ash, burnt patches, 8¼ x 16½ x 16½ ins / 21 x 41.9 x 41.9 cm) USD 21,850. NEW YORK, 31 Oct 1995, *Dragonfly and Flower Vase* (ink and diluted colours on paper, hanging scroll, 10¼ x 9¼ ins / 26 x 23.5 cm) USD 4,025; *Rectangular Hollow Dish in Oribe Style* (glazed with wooden casket, 9¼ x 15 ins / 23.5 x 38 cm) USD 13,800.

KITAOKA, Fumio
Japanese, 20th century.
Born 1918, in Tokyo.
Print artist (traditional Japanese woodcut and western-style engraving).
First Thursday Society.

Kitaoka Fumio graduated from the oil painting and print department of Tokyo School of Fine Arts in 1941 and in 1942 became a member of the Japan Print Association. From 1955 to 1956, he studied wood engraving techniques at the École Nationale des Beaux-Arts in Paris. He went to the USA where he taught at the Minneapolis Museum School of Art in 1964-1965 and at the Pratt Graphic Arts Center, New York. After working at first in a realist style, Kitaoka gradually moved towards a more abstract style; yet the meticulous quality of his work has remained unchanged. He has used both traditional Japanese wood engraving techniques and Western engraving processes.

Kitaoka has exhibited at the Tokyo International Print Biennale and the São Paulo Biennale since 1957. He has also had many one-man shows, in Japan, Switzerland, Yugoslavia and the USA, where he often goes to lecture on printing and engraving. In 2002, he was included in the exhibition *Japanese Prints during the Allied Occupation, 1945-1952* held in the British Museum, London.

BIBLIOGRAPHY:
Merritt, Helen/Yamada, Nanako, *Guide to Modern Japanese Woodblock Prints: 1900- 1975*, University of Hawaii Press, Honolulu, 1992. Smith, Lawrence, *Japanese Prints during the Allied Occupation, 1945-1952: Onchi Kôshirô, Ernst Hacker and the First Thursday Society*, British Museum, London, 2002.

MUSEUMS AND GALLERIES:
BOSTON (MFA) - CHICAGO (AI) - NEW YORK (MoMA).

KITARO
Japanese, 19th century.
Active in Kyoto, c. 1810.
Print artist.

KITATSUJI, Yoshihisa
Japanese, 20th - 21st century.
Born 24 April 1948, in Osaka.
Painter, draughtsman, sculptor.
Conceptual Art.

Kitatsuji Yoshihisa studied at the Tama Art School, Tokyo, from 1968 to 1972. The next year he travelled to the West, visiting France, Germany, Italy and The Netherlands. He lives and works in Osaka. His work is first and foremost a reflection on painting itself, how the image fades and wastes away; at the same time, his work is concerned with the artist's eye, which gives the image its quality. He uses photocopying techniques to produce modified repetitions of an original drawing.

Kitatsuji has taken part in a number of group shows, including: 1969, Metropolitan Art Gallery, Tokyo; 1970 and 1976, National Museum of Modern Art, Tokyo; 1972, Kyoto Biennale; 1973, 8th Paris Biennale; 1974, Düsseldorf Kunsthalle and Louisiana Museum, Humlebaek, Denmark; 1982, Nürnberg Kunsthalle; and has had one-man shows at Osaka, Tokyo and Kyoto.

KITAWAKI, Noboru
Japanese, 20th century.
Born 4 June 1901, in Nagoya (Aichi Prefecture); died 1951.
Painter.

Kitawaki studied under Kanokoji Takeshiro. He started exhibiting with the Nika (two disciplines - painting and sculpture) and the Dokuritsuten (Independent Art Association) in 1932. In 1939, together with a number of friends, he founded the Bijutsu Bunka Kyokai (Art Culture Association). He played a highly original role in the Japanese surrealist group; his paintings were influenced by Max Ernst and Salvador Dalí.

BIBLIOGRAPHY:
Noboru Kitawaki: A Retrospective, exhibition catalogue, National Museum of Modern Art, Tokyo, 1997 (text in Japanese and English).

KITAYAMA, Kangan, real name: Ba (Ma) Moki, alternate name: Bunkei, popular name: Gonnosuke, artist names: Kangan, Kangen
Japanese, 18th century.
Born 1767, in Edo (now Tokyo); died 1801, in Edo.
Painter. Landscapes, figures, birds and flowers.

Kangan lived and worked in Edo (now Tokyo). He modelled his style on the Ming artists Wu Wei, Lin Liang and Zhu Duan and was also strongly influenced by Western painting. He was the mentor of the painter Buncho (1763-1840).

KITAYAMA, Taito
Japanese, 20th century.
Born 1931, in Kagawa Prefecture.
Painter.

Kitayama Taito graduated from Musashino Art School, Tokyo, in 1954. Between 1966 and 1969 he took part in the Contemporary Japanese Art exhibition held in Tokyo and the JAFA (Japan Art Festival Association) exhibition.

KITCHEN, George
British, 18th century.
Active in the middle of the 18th century.
Engraver.

George Kitchen made illustrations for books, including very witty vignettes. He also made maps. There is mention of a Thomas Kitchen in the same period who was probably a relative of his but who was mostly involved in map-making.

KITCHEN, H.
British, 19th century.

Active in London at the beginning of the 19th century.
Miniaturist.
H. Kitchen exhibited his work at the Royal Academy in 1802.

KITCHEN, T. S.
British, 19th century.
Active in London.
Painter. Landscapes.
T.S. Kitchen was a frequent exhibitor at the Royal Academy, the British Institution and at the Suffolk Street Gallery from 1833 to 1852.

KITCHIN, Thomas, or Kitchen
British, 18th century.
Active c. 1750.
Engraver.
Thomas Kitchin made engravings of portraits.
MUSEUMS AND GALLERIES:
LONDON (National Portrait Gal.): *Starkey Middleton after M. Jenkin* (18th century, line engraving); *Nathaniel Lardner after unknown artist; John Cennick after M. Jenkin* (1800-1826).

KITCHINGMAN, John
British, 18th century.
Born c. 1740; died 28 December 1781, in London.
Miniaturist.
John Kitchingman worked with William Shipley before going on to be a brilliant student at the Royal Academy. He was interested mainly in painting miniatures but also painted fine landscapes and seascapes. An unhappy marriage damaged his artistic career irreparably; became dissipated and died after the amputation of a leg. He exhibited at the Free Society and at the Royal Academy.

KITE, Jim, pseudonym of Erlikiliakirra
Australian, 19th - 20th century.
Born 1873.
Sculptor. Animals.
BIBLIOGRAPHY:
Creating Australia: 200 Years of Art 1788-1988, exhibition catalogue, Art Gall. Board of South Australia, Adelaide, 1988.
MUSEUMS AND GALLERIES:
ADELAIDE (South Australian Mus.): *Frog* (1902).

KITE, Joseph Milner, or Milner-Kite
British, 19th - 20th century.
Born 11 October 1862, in Taunton; died 1946.
Active in France.
Painter. Figures, scenes with figures, genre scenes, interiors, landscapes.
Joseph Milner Kite settled in Paris and trained under Bouguereau and Jean-Paul Laurens at the Académie Julian. In 1907 he travelled to Pont-Aven in Brittany, where he met Gauguin and Emile Bernard. He exhibited at the Royal Academy in London, the Carnegie Institute in Pittsburgh and the Salon des Artistes Français in Paris, as well as in Liverpool, Manchester and Birmingham, and in Germany. His carefully organised canvases are characterised by their use of rich impasto, but eschew the Cloissonism practised by Gauguin and Bernard in the late 1880s.
AUCTION RECORDS:
LONDON, 11 March 1981, *Young French Peasant* (oil on canvas, 20 3/4 x 14 1/4 ins / 53 x 36.5 cm) GBP 2,400. LONDON, 14 Oct 1987, *Inspecting the Nets* (oil on canvas, 18 x 22 ins / 46 x 56 cm) GBP 3,000. GÖTEBORG, 18 May 1989, *Winter Landscape near Arles* (oil on canvas, 19 3/4 x 25 1/2 ins / 50 x 65 cm) SEK 7,500. LONDON, 7 March 1991, *Sunlight and Shadows* (oil on canvas, 14 1/2 x 17 3/4 ins / 37 x 45 cm) GBP 3,850. GLASGOW, 21 Aug 1996, *Crowded Street Market* (oil on canvas, 27 x 40 ins / 68.5 x 101.6 cm) GBP 1,897. LONDON, 4 June 1999, *Young Girls in a Hammock on a Summer's Day* (oil on canvas, 22 x 29 ins / 55 x 73 cm) GBP 3,000. SYDNEY, 10 Aug 1999, *Still-life, Vittel Water* (oil on canvas, 23 x 28 ins / 59 x 72 cm) AUD 7,600. LONDON, 6 Sept 2000, *Brittany Square* (oil on canvas, 20 x 26 ins / 51 x 65 cm) GBP 1,500. LONDON, 2 Nov 2000, *Girl in a Cabbage Field* (1914, oil on canvas, 20 x 14 ins / 51 x 35 cm) GBP 1,800. NEUILLY, 5 April 2001, *Young Model Undressing* (oil on canvas, 46 x 29 ins / 116 x 73 cm) FRF 55,000. LONDON, 28 June 2001, *Market Day in Concarneau* (oil on canvas, 20 x 25 ins / 51 x 63 cm) GBP 4,500. NEUILLY, 14 March 2002, *Coastal Landscape* (oil on canvas, 26 x 21 ins / 65 x 54 cm) EUR 2,700. NEUILLY, 14 March 2002, *Bedecked Boat* (oil on canvas, 22 x 18 ins / 55 x 46 cm) EUR 4,000. NEUILLY, 16 Dec 2003, *Girl Reclining* (oil on canvas, 22 x 5 ins / 55 x 13 cm) EUR 2,800.

KITO, Akira
Japanese, 20th century.
Born 1925, in Tokyo.
Active in France 1953-1970.
Painter.
Kito Akira studied at Tokyo Fine Art University from 1943 to 1948 and at the École des Beaux-Arts, Paris, from 1953 to 1957. During his first period, the heads of demons are found alongside automobiles and helicopters, in pictures where the artist's intention vacillates between fear and humour. In his second period, Kito made a radical shift to informal, darkly sumptuous painting with sensual subject matter. After 1961, he returned to evocative representational work, this time with a more openly sarcastic tone.

Kito has exhibited in group shows since 1955, including: 1957, Paris, Galerie Ventadour, *Christ*; 1958, Paris, Musée Galliéra, *Artistes japonais à Paris* (*Japanese Artists in Paris*) and Galerie Iris Clert, *Micro Salon 58*; 1960-1963, Paris, Salon Comparaisons; 1961-1962, Paris, Galerie Charpentier, *École de Paris* (*Paris School*); 1961, 1966, 1967, Paris, Salon d'Automne; 1962, Vienna, Künstlerhaus *Fantastic Art*; 1963, Vienna, MUMOK (Museum Moderner Kunst), *Idols and Demons*; 1963, Paris, Salon Grands et Jeunes d'Aujourd'hui (The Great and the Young Today); and 1964-1966, Nantes, Galerie Argos, *Japanese Painters*. He has also had a number of one-man shows: between 1956 and 1962, in Paris, Galerie Lara Vincy; and in 1986, Paris, Galerie Cical-Lefèbvre, *Akira Kito 1958-1964*.
BIBLIOGRAPHY:
Harambourg, Lydia, *L'École de Paris, 1945-1965. Dictionnaire des Peintres*, Ides et Calendes, Neuchâtel, 1993.
MUSEUMS AND GALLERIES:
GRENOBLE (Mus. de Grenoble) - PARIS (MAMVP) - SAN FRANCISCO (California Palace of the Legion of Honor): *Enfant (Child)* (1964, colour lithograph on Arches paper, from the book Prints from the Mourlot Press, two works) - VIENNA (Mus. Moderner Kunst Stiftung Ludwig).
AUCTION RECORDS:
VERSAILLES, 15 June 1986, *Zoo* (oil on canvas, 35 x 51 1/4 ins / 89 x 130 cm) FRF 23,000. PARIS, 27 June 1988, *Prière de Lutin* (*Imp's Prayer*) (1958, oil on canvas, 28 3/4 x 19 3/4 ins / 73 x 50 cm) FRF 9,000. PARIS, 7 Oct 1989, *Dame Crépusculaire* (*Twilight Lady*) (1960, oil on canvas, 51 1/4 x 35 ins / 130 x 89 cm) FRF 47,000. NEUILLY-SUR-SEINE, 7 Feb 1990, *Vent Disparu* (*Vanished Wind*) (1960-1961, oil on canvas, 25 1/2 x 18 ins / 65 x 45.5 cm) FRF 13,000. DOUAI, 1 April 1990, *Ombre de la Lune* (*Shadow of the Moon*) (1959, oil on canvas, 28 3/4 x 21 1/2 ins / 73 x 54.5 cm) FRF 20,100. PARIS, 1 Oct 1990, *Pays Natal* (*Native Land*) (1959, oil on canvas, 39 1/4 x 28 3/4 ins / 100 x 73 cm) FRF 20,000. NEUILLY, 1 Dec 1991, *Alcestis* (1960, oil on canvas, 57 x 38 1/4 ins / 145 x 97 cm) FRF 24,500. PARIS, 28 Jan 1994, *Fantastique* (*Fantastical*) (1961, oil on canvas, 36 1/4 x 25 1/2 ins / 92 x 65 cm) FRF 10,000. PARIS, 8 June 1994, *Rêve* (*Dream*) (1974, oil on canvas, 14 1/2 x 17 1/2 ins / 37 x 44.5 cm) FRF 4,500. PARIS, 28 April 1997, *Aubade* (1975, oil on canvas, 38 1/4 x 51 1/4 ins / 97 x 130 cm) FRF 9,000. PARIS, 19 Nov 1999, *Transplanted Soul* (1959, oil on canvas, 39 x 5 ins / 100 x 13

cm) FRF 16,000. AMSTERDAM, 9 June 2004, *Stroll at Sunset* (1965, oil on canvas, 24 x 23 ins / 61 x 59 cm) EUR 2,200.

KITSCHENREITER, P.
German, 19th century.
Active in Germany.
Painter.
P. Kitschenreiter is mentioned in *Art Prices Current*.
AUCTION RECORDS:
LONDON, 9 Dec 1907, *In Spring*, GBP 7.

KITSEN, G.
Dutch, 19th century.
Active in Rotterdam c. 1800.
Engraver, illustrator.
Kitsen was a pupil of Dirk Langendyck and M. de Sallieth. His works include *Landscape, River at Night* after E. Hoogerheyden; *General Toussaint Louverture* after Barneville; and *The Theologian G. Bonnet*.

KITSLAAR, Hans
Dutch, 20th century.
Born 1944, in Roermond.
Active in Belgium.
Painter. Nudes, portraits, interiors with figures, animals, flowers.
Hans Kitslaar studied at the Academie Beeldende Kunsten in Maastricht and the Nationaal Hoger Instituut voor Schone Kunsten in Antwerp.
AUCTION RECORDS:
LOKEREN, 20 May 1995, *Children's Games* (oil on canvas, 23 1/2 x 19 3/4 ins / 60 x 50 cm) BEF 33,000.

KITSON, Henry Hudson
British, 19th - 20th century.
Born 9 April 1865, in Huddersfield; died 1947.
Active in the USA.
Sculptor. Busts, monuments.
Henry Hudson Kitson trained under Bonnaissieux at the École des Beaux-Arts in Paris. He won a bronze medal at the Paris Exposition Universelle of 1889; he also won numerous prizes at American exhibitions, notably in Chicago in 1893. Kitson produced a number of commemorative monuments. At his suggestion, a series of portraits of reigning monarchs was commissioned for the inauguration of the National Gallery of Art in Washington. Kitson painted the portrait of Victor Emmanuel III of Italy, which remained on show until 1976.
AUCTION RECORDS:
NEW YORK, 30 Sept 1985, *St George and the Dragon* (dark green patinated bronze, door latch, h. 8 1/2 ins / 21.3 cm) USD 1,400. NEW YORK, 30 Sept 1988, *Bust of Victor Emmanuel III of Italy* (bronze, h. 38 ins / 96.5 cm) USD 2,200. NEW YORK, 26 Sept 1996, *Ganymede* (1892, brown-patinated bronze, h. 46 3/4 ins / 118.7 cm) USD 5,750.

KITSON, Samuel James
British, 19th century.
Born 1 January 1848, in Huddersfield; died 9 November 1906, in New York.
Sculptor.
Samuel James Kitson trained under the direction of Todesti and Jacometi at the Accademia di San Luca in Rome. In 1878, he went to the USA, where he settled. He was the most important sculptor employed by William K. Vanderbilt in decorating his hotel in New York. Kitson also sculpted the *Sheridan Monument* in Arlington, the north frieze honouring soldiers and sailors on the triumphal arch in Hartford, and the *Bust of Governor Greenhalge* at the State building in Boston. He worked in Boston and New York at the same time. He exhibited at the Royal Academy after 1880.
AUCTION RECORDS:
NEW YORK, 17 March 1994, *Buffalo Hunt* (1887, bronze, h. 14 ins / 35.6 cm) USD 11,500. LONDON, 11 July 2001, *Abel* (1877, white marble, h. 56 ins / 142 cm) GBP 20,000.

KITSON, Theo Alice
Maiden name: Ruggles
American, 19th - 20th century.
Born 1876, in Brooklyn; died 1932.
Sculptor. Groups, statues.
Theo Alice Kitson was married to Henry Hudson Kitson and studied under him; she also worked in Paris with Dagnan Bouveret. She was awarded an honourable mention at the Paris Salon in 1890 and a bronze medal in St Louis in 1904. She executed groups to decorate memorials and some equestrian statues.

KITSUZAN MINCHO. See **MINCHO**

KITTELSEN, Theodor Severin
Norwegian, 19th - 20th century.
Born 27 April 1857, in Kragerø; died 21 January 1914, in Jeloy.
Painter, watercolourist, draughtsman, illustrator. Landscapes.
Theodor Severin Kittelsen started his artistic training in Kragerø, then from 1874 to 1876, he trained at the Royal Art School in Christiania (Oslo), under the supervision of Julius Middelthun. From 1876 to 1879 he lived in Munich, where he attended the Academy along with other Norwegian artists, such as Erik Werenskiold, Eilif Peterssen and Gerhard Münthe. His works are inspired by legends and are developed with a great knowledge of landscape. He showed a preference for drawing, and from 1882, he began to illustrate popular tales and folklore in this technique.
In 2001, his work appeared in the exhibition *Da Dahl a Munch. Romanticismo, realismo e simbolismo nella pittura di paesaggio norvegese* (*From Dahl to Munch: Romanticism, Realism and Symbolism in Norwegian Landscape Painting*) held at the Palazzo dei Diamanti in Ferrara.
BIBLIOGRAPHY:
Holaas, Odd, '*Theodor Kittelsen: den norske faun*' in *coll. Kunst og kultur*, Glydendal norsk forlag, Oslo, 1942. Ostby, Leif, *Theordor Kittelsen*, Dreyer, Oslo, 1975. *Sommeren med Theodor Kittelsen*, exhibition catalogue, Stiftelsen Modums, Blaafarveværk, 1995. Koefoed, Holger/Okland, Einar/Sundseth, Arnt Bryde, *Theodor Kittelsen: kjente og ukjente sider ved kunstneren*, exhibition catalogue, Stenersens forlag, Oslo, 1999. Lange, Marit (ed.), *Da Dahl a Munch. Romanticismo, realismo e simbolismo nella pittura di paesaggio norvegese*, exhibition catalogue, Palazzo dei Diamanti, Ferrara Arte editore, Ferrara, 2001.
MUSEUMS AND GALLERIES:
OSLO: eight drawings for a publication on witchcraft.
AUCTION RECORDS:
LONDON, 27-28 March 1990, *Havsulua* (1893, oil on canvas, 23 1/4 x 39 ins / 59 x 99 cm) GBP 12,100. LONDON, 17 May 1991, *Alfeland* (watercolour and coloured chalks/paper, 24 x 18 3/4 ins / 61 x 47.7 cm) GBP 11,000. LONDON, 22 May 1992, *Krogskogen* (1921, watercolour and blue chalk on paper, 32 1/2 x 24 ins / 82.5 x 61 cm) GBP 7,700. NEW YORK, 29 Oct 1992, *Farm at the Edge of a Wooded Path* (watercolour on paper, 12 1/2 x 12 1/2 ins / 31.7 x 31.7 cm) USD 2,860.

KITTENDORFF, Johann Adolf
Danish, 19th century.
Born 5 April 1820, in Copenhagen; died 20 April 1902, in Copenhagen.
Draughtsman, engraver (wood), watercolourist.
Mention has been made of Johann Kittendorff's *Christian IV of Denmark*, copied from a bust in the museum in Copenhagen.

KITTENSTEYN, Cornélis van
Dutch, 17th century.
Born c. 1600, in Delft.
Painter, draughtsman, engraver.
Cornelis van Kittensteyn was married on 30 July 1624 in Haarlem. He was senior member of the guild in 1631 and director fht the St Barbe hospital in 1635. His works include *Admiral Pieter Hein; Doctor Augustinus Tylingius; Hendrik Cornelisz. Loncq; Men's and Women's Costumes,* six pages; *The Senses,* five pages; *Beached Whale* after P. Molyn; *Seven Women around a Man's Trousers; Vrouwe and Weduwe (Wife and Widow); Woman Knocked Down by a Man; Men and Women Seated around a Table; The Entry of William of Orange* after Buytenwegh; *The Siege of Haarlem* after Saenredam; *Title Page; The Silver Fleet Enter the Gulf of Matanca; Dutch Victories,* two title pages; *De Hollandsche Lys,* 17 pages; and *Pages* for another publication.

KITTER-FERRUS, Irène, real name Irina Wladimirovna Kitter
Georgian, 20th century.
Born 1904, in Tiflis (now Tbilisi); died 1991, in Bordeaux.
Active and naturalised in France.
Painter. Portraits, landscapes, seascapes, still-lifes, flowers, horse racing scenes.
Kitter-Ferrus was the youngest child of an officer in the army of Tsar Nicholas II. She left Russia with her family in 1920. In 1928, she settled in south western France in Hasparren with her husband. A self-taught painter, she depicted a variety of subjects in a vigorous pictorial manner. She is known for *Eyhartzia: House of Francis Jammes* painted in Hasparren in 1954. She signed her first works in Cyrillic.

She exhibited regularly at the Union Basquaise des Arts from 1952, and, in the same year, at the Salon d'Hiver in Paris. She had a solo exhibition of her work at the Musée Basque in 1957, and in London in 1953 and 1956. In 1952, she received the Grand Prix in painting in Dauville. She stopped working in 1961, due to partial blindness. In 2002, the Association Les Amis d'Irène Kitter-Ferrus was established. In 1979, the city hall of Hasparren organised a retrospective of her work. Another exhibition was held in 2002 at the St Andrew Carthusian monastery in Bordeaux.

BIBLIOGRAPHY:
Suffran, Michel, *Les Pyrénées de Francis Jammes,* Edisud, Aix-en-Provence, 1985. *Femmes artistes d'hier à aujourd'hui,* Éd. Regards, Pau, 1986.

KITTLER, Hermann
German, 19th century.
Born 20 February 1866, in Leipzig.
Sculptor, painter.
Hermann Kittler was active in Berlin from 1887. He is known for landscapes and a large number of portraits that are sometimes paintings but more often sculptures.

KITTLER, Philipp
German, 19th century.
Born 18 June 1861, in Schwabach, near Nuremberg.
Sculptor.
Philipp Kittler was a famous sculptor in Nuremberg and received a great many commissions for funerary monuments. He is also known for his statues for the parks and public buildings of Nuremberg, such as his *Entrance to the Zoological Gardens.*

KITTNER, Gallus, the Elder
German, 17th century.
Active in Potsdam in 1603.
Painter.
Gallus Kittner the Elder also worked in Berlin, Caputh and Saarmund, usually for the princes of Brandenburg.

KITTNER, Gallus, the Younger
German, 17th - 18th century.
Born c. 1655, in Königsberg (now Kaliningrad, Russia); died 25 April 1715.
Painter.
Gallus Kittner the Younger worked in Amsterdam and Danzig (now Gdansk, Poland).

KITTNER, Patrizius
Moravian, 19th century.
Born 16 March 1809, in Brno; died 18 June 1900, in Hirtenberg.
Miniaturist, lithographer.
At the end of his life, Patrizius Kittner worked mainly in Vienna. A number of his works are in the museum in Brno.

KITTON, Frederick George
British, 19th century.
Born 5 May 1856, in Norwich; died 10 September 1904, in St Albans.
Engraver, illustrator, writer.
Frederick George Kitton made illustrations for books by Charles Dickens.

KITZEL, Herbert
German, 20th century.
Born 5 May 1928, in Halle; died 25 August 1978, committed suicide.
Painter, draughtsman, sculptor (bronze, ceramics).
New Figuration.
Herbert Kitzel studied from 1945 to 1950 at the Burg Art College in Halle. He would go on to teach at the Fine Arts Academy in Karlsruhe.

Kitzel was born in East Germany. Following his emigration to West Germany, he became involved in the New Figuration movement, a group which comprised other teachers at the fine arts academy in Karlsruhe, including Hap Grieshaber and Wilhelm Loth. The group as a whole advocated a return to figurative art as opposed to abstraction. This was reflected in Kitzel's work from the 1950s, when he started to draw inspiration from figurative models found in primitive and Expressionist art. By the 1960s, Kitzel was producing spectral figures that he incorporated into his compositions in the manner of Informal or Abstract Expressionism. He produced a series of head profiles in the 1970s. A general sense of existential angst, pain and morbidity pervades Kitzel's body of work, which is nonetheless both imaginative and demanding.

His solo exhibitions and retrospectives include his first showing at the Henning Gallery in Halle in 1950, followed by other exhibitions at the fine arts academy in Karlsruhe in 1958, and at the Fine Arts Museum in Baden-Baden in 1974. His work has also featured at group exhibitions, including in 2002 at the Schlichtenmaier Gallery in Grafenau *Neue Figurationen Karlsruhe* (*Karlsruhe New Figuration*) and the Alfred Knecht Gallery in Karlsruhe in 2003.

BIBLIOGRAPHY:
Herbert Kitzel: Arbeiten 1951-1978, exhibition catalogue, Kunstverein, Karlsruhe, 1981. *Herbert Kitzel: Keramik,* catalogue raisonné, Brinkschulte, Berlin, 1988. *Herbert Kitzel: Die Zeit in Halle. Malerei 1948-1978,* exhibition catalogue, Städtische Galerie, Karlsruhe, 1994. Forstbauer, Nikolai B., *Neue Figurationen Karlsruhe,* exhibition catalogue, Gal. Schlichtenmaier, Schloss Dätzingen, Grafenau, 2002.

KITZEROW, Carl Heinrich
German, 19th century.
Born 13 February 1799, in Hamburg; died 11 February 1874, in Milan.
Painter, lithographer.
Kitzerow is known for lithographs of landscapes and portraits.

KITZINGER, Abraham Felix, the Elder
Bohemian, 17th - 18th century.
Born in Tetschen (now Decín, Czech Republic).
Sculptor.
Abraham Kitzinger worked for the church in Ossek, among others.

KITZINGER, Felix, the Younger
Bohemian, 18th century.
Born 21 April 1697, in Ossek.
Sculptor.
Felix Kitzinger is known to have been in Prague in 1724.

KIU TCHE-P'OU. See **QU ZHIPU**

KIU TSIE. See **JU JIE**

KIU-JAN. See **JURAN**

KIU-LIEN. See **JU LIAN**

KIUSAI. See **KAGEI**

KIVERLEY
Irish, 18th century.
Died 1789, in Dublin.
Painter. Landscapes.

KIVSHENKO, Aleksei Danilovich
Russian, 19th century.
Born 22 March 1851; died 1 October 1895, in Heidelberg.
Painter, watercolourist. Historical subjects, military subjects, figures, hunting scenes, rustic scenes, genre scenes, animals.
Aleksei Kivshenko studied under J. Brandt and F. Adam in Munich, and became a member of the academy of St Petersburg. He began his artistic career in around 1875.
MUSEUMS AND GALLERIES:
MOSCOW (State Tretyakov Gal.): *St-Valéry-en-Caux; The Military Council in 1812; Studies* - ST PETERSBURG: *Watercolour.*
AUCTION RECORDS:
LONDON, 11 Feb 1976, *Peasants on their Way to the Fields* (oil on canvas, 9 3/4 x 29 1/4 ins / 25 x 74 cm) GBP 500.

KIYOCHIKA, commonly known as Kiyochika Kobayashi
Japanese, 19th - 20th century.
Born 1847; died 1915.
Painter, print artist. Historical subjects, figures, genre scenes, still-lifes.
Kiyochika was the son of a low-ranking samurai who lost his inheritance after the Meiji Restoration in 1868. Largely self-taught, he especially admired the prints of Hiroshige (1797-1858) and Kuniyoshi. He studied photography, an art-form then new in Japan, and Western painting through the work of Charles Wirgman, a British journalist who was also his teacher. Kiyochika had always been drawn to *ukiyo-e* ('pictures of the floating world'), but had to adapt it to his time and more particularly to the Western style that was invading Japan. The result was a body of rather exotic work, in which the artist sought to depict his country's native customs but was unable to ignore its modernisation. His pictures are often bizarre, especially for Western collectors: one finds Japanese men wearing bowler hats and carrying black umbrellas. Kiyochika may be said to straddle two worlds, one facing forwards, the other backwards: he can be regarded as the last *ukiyo-e* master or as the first master of the modern Japanese print. In addition to the usual *ukiyo-e* scenes, he also produced still-lifes and war scenes (from the Russo-Japanese and Sino-Japanese Wars); these are not considered to be the best of his work.
BIBLIOGRAPHY:
Lane, R., *L'Estampe japonaise*, Somogy, Paris, 1962. Lane, Richard, *Images from the Floating World*, Konecky and Konecky, New York, 1978. Merritt, Helen/Yamada, Nanako, *Guide to Modern Japanese Woodblock Prints: 1900-1975*, University of Hawii Press, Honolulu, 1992.
AUCTION RECORDS:
NEW YORK, 27 March 1991, *Three Geishas: Kayo of Kyoto, Hitotsuru of Osaka and Kokichi of Tokyo* (oban tate-e print, 14 x 9 1/2 ins / 35.7 x 24.3 cm) USD 1,430.

KIYOHARA, Tama, artist name Eleonora Ragusa
Japanese, 19th - 20th century.
Born 1861, in Tokyo; died 1939.
Painter, watercolourist, lacquerer.
Tama Kiyohara started by studying Japanese painting but switched to Western painting, studying with Vincenzo Ragusa, whom she later married. She left for Italy, where she worked with Lo Forte. She settled in Palermo and only returned to Japan in later years. She exhibited in both Rome and Palermo, won the Grand Prize at the New York International Exhibition and exhibited at the Venice Biennale. She mainly painted flowers and fruit.

KIYOHARU, real name Kondo Kiyoharu, childhood name Sukegoro, also known as Torii Kiyoharu
Japanese, 18th century.
Active in Edo (now Tokyo).
Print artist.
Kiyoharu was a disciple of Kiyonobu I (1664-1729). A book illustrator, he also wrote humorous works and produced plates of beautiful women.

KIYOHARU, nicknames Fujiwara, Hishikawa V; personal names Kichizaemon, Noritaka (or Hirotaka) Ono; artist names Shun'yosai (or Seiyosai), Keisensai, Settei, Yosai
Japanese, 19th century.
Active in Osaka c. 1820-1830.
Print artist.

KIYOHIDE. See **SHUNSENSAI**

KIYOHIRO, real name: Torii Kiyohiro, popular name: Shichinosuke
Japanese, 18th century.
Active in Edo (now Tokyo) c. 1737-1776.
Print artist.
Kiyohiro was a pupil of Kiyomitsu I. He made large format *benizuri-e* prints, two or three colour prints in which pink *(beni)* dominates, to rival Ishikawa Toyonobu's masterpieces. He was also one of the first *ukiyo-e* artists to depict female nudes (a genre that starts at this time).

KIYOKATA. See **KABURAGI KIYOKATA**

KIYOKUNI, nickname Toyokawa; artist names Jushodo, Kiyokuni
Japanese, 19th century.
Active in Osaka c. 1827.
Print artist.

KIYOMASU I, real name Torii Kiyomasu, popular name Shojiro
Japanese, 18th century.
Born 1697; died c. 1722.
Active in Edo (now Tokyo).
Print artist, painter. Posters.
The details of Kiyomasu I's life remain unclear, especially his relationship with Kiyonobu: he may have been his son, perhaps his elder son, or simply a very close disciple. He was part of the first flowering of the Japanese print during the first three quarters of the 18th century, following in the footsteps of Moronobu (late 17th century) and developing his style and accentuating its lines and stylisation, especially in his portraits of *kabuki* actors. He is known for many fine works, both *sumizuru-e* (works in Indian ink) and *tan-e* (works in Indian ink, hand coloured with cinnabar), most of

which are large, vertical portraits of actors and courtesans, published between 1713 and 1716 and signed *Kiyomasu*. These prints have an elegant charm that distinguishes them from the work of Kiyonobu.

BIBLIOGRAPHY:

Fahe-Becker, Gabriele, *Japanese Prints*, Taschen, Cologne, 1999.

AUCTION RECORDS:

NEW YORK, 21 March 1989, *Poster for Ichimura-za Theatre* (oban tate-e print, 18$1/2$ x 12$1/4$ ins / 46.8 x 31 cm) USD 13,200.

KIYOMASU II, real name Torii Kiyomasu, popular name Hanzaburo
Japanese, 18th century.
Born 1706; died 1763.
Active c. 1720-1750.
Print artist, painter.

The details of Kiyomasu II's life are uncertain. He produced actor portraits of the types known as *urushi-e* (hand-coloured prints with glue added to the colours) and *benizuri-e* (two- or three-colour prints with *beni* (pinkish red) as the dominant colour).

AUCTION RECORDS:

NEW YORK, 21 March 1989, *Portrait of the Actor Sagawa Kikunojo in the role of Matsukaze* (colour print, hoso-ban, 13 x 5$3/4$ ins / 32.1 x 14.8 cm) USD 4,400.

KIYOMINE, real name: Torii, Kiyomine
Japanese, 19th century.
Born 1787, in Edo (now Tokyo).
Print artist.

Kiyomine was the grandson of Kiyomitsu (1735-1785) and the disciple of Kiyonaga (1752-1815), whom he succeeded as the fifth head in succession of the Torii studio in Edo, remaining there until 1868. Also known under the name Kiyomitsu II, he produced prints and paintings as well as book illustrations.

KIYOMITSU, real name Torii Kiyomitsu, popular name Kamejiro
Japanese, 18th century.
Born 1735; died 1785.
Active in Edo (now Tokyo).
Print artist, painter, illustrator.

Kiyomitsu, the son and disciple of Kiyomasu II, was the third head of the Torii school. A highly prolific artist, he illustrated theatre posters, books, and programmes. He produced a large number of actor portraits, both *beni-e* (hand-coloured Indian ink prints using the pinkish red *beni*, saffron yellow and other colours, and sometimes pieces of copper foil) and *nishiki-e* (full polychrome prints, register-printed using from five to ten colours). The earliest work known from his hand is a 1747 book illustration entitled *Furisode Seminaru Taimen no Biwa*. His graceful, delicate women point the way stylistically to Harunobu's masterpieces some years later.

BIBLIOGRAPHY:

Fahr-Becker, Gabriele, *Japanese Prints*, Taschen, Cologne, 1999.

AUCTION RECORDS:

NEW YORK, 1989, *Portrait of Ichikawa Danjuro II in the role of Siga no Goro, with a Long Arrow* (dai-oban tate-e print, 16$1/2$ x 11$1/2$ ins / 42.1 x 29.5 cm) USD 7,700.

KIYONAGA, real name Torii Shinsuke; family name Sekiguchi; popular name Ichibei; artist name Kiyonaga
Japanese, 18th - 19th century.
Born 1752, in Edo (now Tokyo); died 1815.
Print artist, painter, draughtsman. Figures, portraits, genre scenes, interiors with figures, landscapes.

Kiyonaga - painter, draughtsman and master of the woodblock print - was one of the most accomplished *ukiyo-e* artists and a central figure in the movement. In just eight years, he succeeded in establishing a new ideal of beauty and developing a style, both of which would dominate the art of the late 18th century and leave their mark on that of the 19th. The son of Shirokaya Ichibei, an Edo book dealer, he was born in one of the city's theatre districts. The story that he was born in Uraga, in Sagami Province, moved to Edo when he was still young, was placed with a tobacco merchant and opened a bookstore, seems rather to apply to his father.

From the book trade, Kiyonaga soon became familiar with the *kibyoshi*, the small, yellow-covered, illustrated books of fiction popular at the time, and the bright, colourful posters embellishing the theatres in the district. While still quite young, he entered the studio of Kiyomitsu (1735-1785), the head of the Torii family of artists who specialised in producing pictures of the world of the stage - posters, programmes, portraits of actors on stage and about town. This was the Anei Period (1772-1780), when a growing taste for realism was leading the print down new paths, when portraits of actors started to be published as they really looked, in settings from everyday life. Although Kiyonaga worked as an artist for over forty years, his talent blossomed fully only from 1780 to 1790. His first known work dates from 1770, when he was eighteen. Until about 1780 he mostly drew actors and scenes from the theatre, mainly for *ehon banzuke* (programmes) and, after 1775, *kibyoshi*. During this period, his work was still influenced by artists such as Harunobu, Koryusai, and Shigemasa (1739-1820); he would sign himself Torii Kiyonaga, joining his own name to that of his master.

Towards about 1780, however, Kiyonaga finally perfected his own style, achieving mastery over his expression, and creating a new form of beauty. The years that followed (1781-1786) were the period of his *bijin-ga* (pictures of beautiful women), which he usually signed with his real name, Seki Kiyonaga, or simply Kiyonaga, as if to distance himself from the Torii school. In these few years he brought the woodblock print to a new height of perfection. His fashionable beauties, tall, slender and noble, dainty and airy of gait, with full, youthful faces, and dressed in flowing kimonos with floating sleeves, seem to fit harmoniously into the background against which they move. Be this a beautiful landscape, a famous spot in Edo, or an elegant interior, it is always imbued with poetry and poised happily between realism and idealism, without ever blurring the line between the lyrical atmosphere of the print and its overall plastic effect. In these young women, beyond their physical beauty, there is something spiritual that is missing in Utamaro, something that conveys a fresh, luminous vision of the world while showing us a thoroughly lifelike view of the Yoshiwara, the pleasure-quarter of Edo.

Because of the technical progress that the printers had made, Kiyonaga's works have clear, subtly diffused colouring rendered livelier by a judicious use of black. The layout of his compositions on the page, always perfect regardless of whichever format he used, conveys a special sense of balance and spaciousness. His planes link up effortlessly, his groups are ingenious, their attitudes natural. He was also one of the first artists to produce diptychs and triptychs, both horizontal and vertical, whose every sheet can stand alone as a work of art in its own right *(tsuzuki-mono)*.

Kiyonaga was at the height of his powers throughout the Temmei Period (1781-1788), dominating his contemporaries; and then his inspiration ran dry. After the death of Kiyomitsu, his former master, the Torii school directors brought him back into the fold, where once more he took to designing actor prints, again signing them Torii Kiyonaga. In 1795, out of fidelity to his master, he blocked his own son Kiyomasa from continuing in the world of *ukiyo-e*, despite his talent, and devoted himself to the artistic education of Kiyomitsu's grandson, the thirteen-year-old Shonosuke, who until 1868 would be the fifth head of the Torii school, under the name Kiyomine.

Kiyonaga's style is as far removed from the ethereal dreams of Harunobu (1725-1770) as it is from the sensuality of Utamaro (1754-1806). In the serenity, grandeur, and perfect balance of its classicism, Kiyonaga's work cannot be confused with that of any other *ukiyo-e* artist.

BIBLIOGRAPHY:

Akiyama, Terukazu, *La Peinture japonaise*, Skira, Geneva, 1961. Kozyreff, C., '*Kiyonaga (Torii)*' in *Encyclopædia Universalis* vol. IX, Paris, 1971. *Six maîtres de l'estampe japonaise au XVIIe siècle*, exhibition catalogue, Musée de l'Orangerie, Paris, 1971. Forrei, Matthi, *The Baur Collection: Japanese Prints*, Geneva, 1995. Fahr-Becker, Gabriele, *Japanese Prints*, Taschen, Cologne, 1999.

AUCTION RECORDS:

NEW YORK, 16 Oct 1989, *Actors Ichikawa Yaozo, Mimasu Tokujiro and Nakamura Sukegoro Playing a Scene* (oban tate-e print, 15 1/4 x 10 1/4 ins / 38.7 x 26 cm) USD 3,520. LONDON, 13 Nov 1989, *Ushiwakamura Serenading Princess Joruri with a Flute* (oban tate-e print, 15 1/4 x 10 ins / 38.8 x 25.3 cm) GBP 2,200. LONDON, 22 March 1990, *Portrait of a Young Woman* (hashira-e print, 26 1/2 x 5 ins / 67.2 x 12.8 cm) GBP 990. NEW YORK, 27 March 1991, *Three women and Two Children Walking* (oban tate-e print, 14 3/4 x 9 1/4 ins / 37.3 x 23.4 cm) USD 6,600. PARIS, 3 June 1992, *The Courtesan Takigawa from the Ogiya House* (1783, print, 15 1/4 x 10 1/2 ins / 38.8 x 26.5 cm) FRF 40,000. PARIS, 25 Nov 2003, *Untitled* (ink, a pair, 15 x 11 ins / 38 x 27 cm) EUR 1,500. PARIS, 25 Nov 2003, *Leisure* (colour print, 14 x 9 ins / 36 x 24 cm) EUR 10,000. NEW YORK, 23 March 2004, *Young Woman Seated on a Bamboo Bench* (print, 15 x 11 ins / 39 x 27 cm) USD 16,000.

KIYONOBU I, real name Torii Kiyonobu, popular name Shobei
Japanese, 17th - 18th century.
Born 1664, in Osaka; died 1729.
Print artist, poster artist.

Torii Kiyonobu was the son of the poster designer Kiyomoto, who had moved with his family to Edo in 1687. He was the real founder of the Torii school after succeeding his father in 1702 as the head of the studio he had founded. The line, which is still active today, would go on to produce a succession of eminent print artists. Kiyonobu studied the Kano and Tosa styles and seems to have fallen under the influence of Moronobu (d. 1694) and perhaps Ando (fl. c. 1700-1715), unless it was he who influenced them, as several authorities maintain. He specialised in *kabuki* posters and programme illustrations, portraits of actors on stage, and occasionally women. He excelled in depicting actors in *aragoto* roles (warriors in battle), whom he drew with bold strokes, thick outlines and accentuated gestures and attitudes. He also illustrated books, the earliest in 1692, entitled *Kokon Shibai Hyakunin Isshu*, and the last in 1728, and produced a number of *shunga* (spring pictures, or erotic prints). He produced *sumizuri-e* (works in ink), *tan-e* (works in ink, hand-coloured with cinnabar red) and *urushi-e* (hand-coloured works with colours containing glue).

BIBLIOGRAPHY:

Fahr-Becker, Gabriele, *Japanese Prints*, Taschen, Cologne, 1999.

KIYONOBU II, real name Torii Kiyonobu, popular name Shubei
Japanese, 18th century.
Born 1706; died 1763.
Active in Edo (now Tokyo) c. 1720-1750.
Painter, print artist. Portraits, genre scenes.

Kiyonobu's exact identity and dates are disputed: he may have been either the son or the son-in-law of Kiyonobu I, while the historian Inoue Kazuo has his dates as 1702-1752. Be that as it may, he produced a large number of small-format portraits of actors on stage in both *urushi-e* (hand-coloured works with colours containing glue) and *benizuri-e* (prints with the pinkish-red *beni* as the dominant colour).

He had a capable technique but one inclined to stiffness; nonetheless his work is imbued with the charm of the so-called primitive prints from the first flowering of *ukiyo-e*.

BIBLIOGRAPHY:

Fahr-Becker, Gabriele, *Japanese Prints*, Taschen, Cologne, 1999.

AUCTION RECORDS:

NEW YORK, 21 March 1989, *The Actor Sanjo Kantaro in the Role of a Courtesan* (coloured print, hosoban-e, 12 1/4 x 5 3/4 ins / 31 x 14.6 cm) USD 7,150. NEW YORK, 16 Oct 1989, *The Actor Ichikawa Ebizo in the Role of Rokuemon* (coloured print, hosoban-e, 12 1/2 x 6 ins / 31.7 x 15.3 cm) USD 5,500. NEW YORK, 15 June 1990, *Portrait of the Actor Tomizawa Montaro in the Role of Osawa before a Teahouse* (urushi-e print, 12 x 6 ins / 30.7 x 15.4 cm) USD 4,400.

KIYOSADA, or Torii Kiyosada
Japanese, 19th century.
Born 1844; died 1901.
Active in Osaka.
Print artist. Actor prints.

Kiyosada was a disciple of Hirosada (d. 1865). He deliberately signed in the same manner as his master.

KIYOSAI. See **SHIGEHARU**

KIYOSHIGE, real name Torii Kiyoshige, artist name Seichoken
Japanese, 18th century.
Born 1720; died c. 1760.
Active in Edo (now Tokyo).
Print artist.

Kiyoshige may have been a pupil of Kiyomitsu (1735-1785) and was a late pupil of Kiyonobu; he was active up to about 1760. He produced *hoso-e* (long, narrow-format) and Torii-style portraits of actors using both *urushi-e* and *benizuri-e* techniques. His large prints, executed in the style of Masonobu, are held to be some of the finest products of the Torii school.

BIBLIOGRAPHY:

Fahr-Becker, Gabriele, *Japanese Prints*, Taschen, Cologne, 1999.

KIYOTADA, real name Torii Kiyotada
Japanese, 18th century.
Active in Edo (now Tokyo) c. 1723-1750.
Print artist.

Kiyotada, a disciple of Kiyonobu I (1664-1729), seems to have also been influenced by Okumura Masanobu (1686-1764). He produced a number of very beautiful *urushi-e* prints (hand-coloured prints using colours containing glue) and several large *uki-e* perspective prints, all of which were published during the 1740s.

AUCTION RECORDS:

NEW YORK, 21 March 1989, *Portrait of Nakamura Kichibei* (coloured print, hosoban-e, 12 1/2 x 6 1/4 ins / 32 x 15.9 cm) USD 3,520.

KIYOTOMO, real name Torii Kiyotomo
Japanese, 18th century.
Active in Edo (now Tokyo) c. 1720-1740.
Print artist.

Kiyotomo was a disciple of Kiyonobu I (1664-1729) and produced *urushi-e* actor prints. His style is close to that of Kiyonobu II (fl. 1720-1750).

KIYOTSUNE, real name Torii Kiyotsune; popular names Nakajimaya, Daijiro
Japanese, 18th century.

Active in Edo (now Tokyo) 1760-1780.
Print artist.

Kiyotsune, a disciple of Kiyomitsu (1735-1785), produced actor prints in both *benizuri-e* (prints whose dominant colour is the pinkish-red *beni*) and nishiki-e *nishiki-e* (register-printed pictures with five to ten colours, also known as a 'bracade picture'). He also produced book illustrations and a number of pictures of beautiful women in a style similar to that of Haronobu.

BIBLIOGRAPHY:

Fahr-Becker, Gabriele, *Japanese Prints*, Taschen, Cologne, 1999.

AUCTION RECORDS:

NEW YORK, 15 June 1990, *Portrait of the Actor Otani Hiroji in the Role of Nasu no Yoichi Munetaka* (hosoban-e print, 11 1/4 x 5 1/2 ins / 28.7 x 13.8 cm) USD 880.

KIYOYASU

Japanese, 19th century.
Active in Kyoto, probably c. 1826.
Print artist.

KJARVAL, Johannes S.

Icelandic, 20th century.
Born 1885, in Efriey; died 1972.
Painter.

Johannes S. Kjarval trained in London, and then at the Kunstakademi in Copenhagen from 1915 to 1917. He made several journeys, notably to Italy. Together with Jon Stefansson, he is regarded as the most important modern Icelandic artist. He painted a great many portraits and landscapes of Iceland in a figurative technique with a trace of mystery. His painting is characterised by an expressive, powerful and colourful technique. He had his first exhibition in Reykjavik in 1908. He also appeared in a great many exhibitions in Copenhagen at the Salon in Charlottenborg and at the Icelandic Art Exhibition in 1927, as well as showing at the Carnegie Institute International Exhibition in Pittsburgh in 1937. The Pavillon des Arts in Paris dedicated an exhibition to him in September 1993. The Kjarvalsstadir, the Art Centre in Reykjavik, which was inaugurated in 1973, is dedicated to him, and his works are exhibited in a permanent gallery there.

BIBLIOGRAPHY:

Ingólfsson, Adalsteinn/ Johannessen, Matthias, *'Kjarval: Painter of Iceland'* in *Iceland Review*, periodical, Reykjavik, 1981.

MUSEUMS AND GALLERIES:

COPENHAGEN (Statens Mus. for Kunst): *Glacier* (c. 1930); *Impression of Evening in the Rocks* (1931) - REYKJAVIK (Listasafn Islands): *Dream and Desire of Taking Flight* (1935-1955).

AUCTION RECORDS:

COPENHAGEN, 6 April 1976, *Rocky Landscape* (1931, oil on canvas, 18 x 39 1/4 ins / 46 x 100 cm) DKK 15,000. COPENHAGEN, 5 Oct 1977, *Icelandic Landscape* (1948, oil on canvas, 47 1/4 x 71 1/4 ins / 120 x 181 cm) DKK 31,000. COPENHAGEN, 23 Jan 1979, *Icelandic Landscape* (1949, oil on canvas, 35 3/4 x 52 ins / 91 x 132 cm) DKK 33,000. COPENHAGEN, 13 Oct 1981, *Landscape* (oil on canvas, 25 1/2 x 46 1/2 ins / 65 x 118 cm) DKK 18,000. COPENHAGEN, 1 June 1983, *Icelandic Landscape* (oil on canvas, 31 1/2 x 38 1/2 ins / 80 x 98 cm) DKK 52,000. COPENHAGEN, 13 Feb 1985, *Landscape at Thingvallasletten* (oil on canvas, 27 1/2 x 59 ins / 70 x 150 cm) DKK 182,000. COPENHAGEN, 4 May 1988, *Landscape at Alfaborg* (gouache, 15 x 27 1/4 ins / 38 x 69 cm) DKK 20,000. LONDON, 27-28 March 1990, *Panorama from Thinvellir in Iceland* (1939, oil on canvas, 17 3/4 x 22 ins / 45 x 55 cm) GBP 7,700. COPENHAGEN, 9 May 1990, *Rocky Landscape on the Island of Thingvalla in Iceland* (oil on canvas, 20 3/4 x 28 3/4 ins / 53 x 73 cm) DKK 65,000. COPENHAGEN, 31 Oct 1990, *Rocky Coast in Iceland* (oil on canvas, 20 3/4 x 28 3/4 ins / 53 x 73 cm) DKK 78,000. LONDON, 16 June 1993, *Summer* (oil on canvas, 41 1/4 x 63 ins / 105 x 160 cm) GBP 5,750. COPENHAGEN, 26 April 1995, *Coastal Landscape at Thingvalla in Iceland* (oil on canvas, 32 3/4 x 53 1/4 ins / 83 x 135 cm) DKK 56,000. COPENHAGEN, 23 March 1999, *Mountain Landscape, Iceland* (1957, oil on canvas, 40 x 60 ins / 102 x 152 cm) DKK 50,000. COPENHAGEN, 20 Oct 1999, *Mountain Landscape, Iceland* (oil on canvas, 39 x 53 ins / 100 x 135 cm) DKK 90,000. COPENHAGEN, 3 Oct 2000, *Mountain Landscape, Iceland* (oil on canvas, 10 x 15 ins / 25 x 37 cm) DKK 22,000. COPENHAGEN, 3 Oct 2000, *Village in the Mountains, Iceland* (oil on canvas, 14 x 26 ins / 36 x 65 cm) DKK 30,000. COPENHAGEN, 2 April 2001, *Symbolic Portrait Composition* (1933, oil on canvas, 28 x 39 ins / 70 x 100 cm) DKK 75,000. COPENHAGEN, 18 June 2002, *Icelandic Landscape with Waterfall* (c. 1935, oil on canvas, 14 x 20 ins / 36 x 52 cm) DKK 31,000. COPENHAGEN, 7 Oct 2003, *Composition with Female Head* (oil on canvas, 22 x 26 ins / 56 x 66 cm) DKK 30,000. COPENHAGEN, 29 March 2004, *Landscape, Thinkvellir* (1946, Indian ink, 34 x 44 ins / 86 x 112 cm) DKK 15,000. COPENHAGEN, 5 Oct 2004, *Coastal Landscape with Stones* (oil on canvas, 32 x 61 ins / 82 x 155 cm) DKK 95,000.

KJELLBERG. See KIELLBERG

KJERNER, Esther

Swedish, 19th - 20th century.
Born 1873; died 1952.
Painter. Landscapes, still-lifes, flowers.

AUCTION RECORDS:

STOCKHOLM, 30 Oct 1979, *Summer Landscape* (1906, oil on canvas, 23 1/4 x 28 1/2 ins / 59 x 72.5 cm) SEK 9,500. STOCKHOLM, 8 April 1981, *Still-life with Flowers* (oil on panel, 21 1/4 x 24 3/4 ins / 54 x 63 cm) SEK 18,100. STOCKHOLM, 26 April 1983, *Still-life with Flowers* (1941, oil on panel, 19 3/4 x 23 1/2 ins / 50 x 60 cm) SEK 24,500. STOCKHOLM, 29 Oct 1985, *Still-life with Fruit* (1936, oil on canvas, 19 1/4 x 25 1/2 ins / 49 x 65 cm) SEK 20,000. STOCKHOLM, 20 Oct 1987, *Still-life with Flowers* (1945, oil on canvas, 17 3/4 x 14 1/2 ins / 45 x 37 cm) SEK 75,000. STOCKHOLM, 6 June 1988, *Still-life with Grapes and Peaches in a Dish* (oil, 13 x 16 1/4 ins / 33 x 41 cm) SEK 27,000. STOCKHOLM, 15 Nov 1989, *Summer Landscape with a House among the Trees and Ferns* (oil, 17 x 22 ins / 43 x 55 cm) SEK 33,000. STOCKHOLM, 6 Dec 1989, *Still-life with a Saucepan and Globe Artichokes* (1945, oil on panel, 14 1/4 x 15 3/4 ins / 36 x 40 cm) SEK 48,000. STOCKHOLM, 16 May 1990, *Houses Behind the Trees* (tempera on canvas, 9 x 11 1/2 ins / 22 x 29 cm) SEK 7,000. STOCKHOLM, 14 Nov 1990, *Fritillaria in a Terracotta Pot* (oil on panel, 15 3/4 x 12 1/2 ins / 40 x 32 cm) SEK 45,000. STOCKHOLM, 13 April 1992, *Still-life of a Bouquet of Flowers in a Vase* (1947, oil on panel, 18 x 13 3/4 ins / 46 x 35 cm) SEK 8,000. STOCKHOLM, 19 May 1992, *Still-life with a Salad Bowl, Small Jug, Glasses and Fruit* (oil on panel, 19 3/4 x 23 1/2 ins / 50 x 60 cm) SEK 20,000. STOCKHOLM, 18 May 1999, *Girl from Brittany* (1897, oil on canvas, 22 x 18 ins / 55 x 46 cm) SEK 47,000. STOCKHOLM, 26 May 1999, *Still-life with Flowers in a Glass Vase* (1945, oil on panel, 16 x 15 ins / 41 x 37 cm) SEK 52,000. STOCKHOLM, 29 May 2000, *Wood Anemones in a Glass Vase* (oil on panel, 9 x 7 ins / 24 x 18 cm) SEK 41,000. STOCKHOLM, 29 May 2000, *Still-life with White Roses* (oil on canvas, 18 x 15 ins / 45 x 38 cm) SEK 46,000. STOCKHOLM, 22 May 2001, *Flowers in a Vase* (1944, oil on canvas, 24 x 20 ins / 61 x 50 cm) SEK 45,000. STOCKHOLM, 28 Nov 2001, *Still-life with Flowers* (1950, oil on canvas, 28 x 24 ins / 70 x 61 cm) SEK 100,000. STOCKHOLM, 29 May 2002, *Still-life with Wine Jug and Fruit* (1935, oil on canvas, 15 x 18 ins / 38 x 46 cm) SEK 34,000. STOCKHOLM, 29 May 2002, *Still-life with Yel-*

low Roses (1949, oil on panel, 16 x 13 ins / 40 x 33 cm) SEK 40,000. STOCKHOLM, 26 May 2003, *Still-life with Grapes and Lemon* (oil on canvas on panel, 14 x 17 ins / 35 x 42 cm) SEK 31,000. STOCKHOLM, 2 Dec 2003, *Peonies and Honeysuckle in a Blue-White Bowl* (1925, oil on canvas, 25 x 20 ins / 63 x 51 cm) SEK 62,000. STOCKHOLM, 25 May 2004, *Still-life with White Roses* (1932, oil on panel, 14 x 15 ins / 35 x 37 cm) SEK 39,000. STOCKHOLM, 26 May 2004, *Still-life with Fruit* (1930, oil on panel, 18 x 21 ins / 46 x 54 cm) SEK 30,000.

KLAAS. See also **CLAES**

KLAAS, Uschi
German, 20th - 21st century.
Born 1949, in Recklinghausen, near Dortmund.
Painter.

Uschi Klaas studied at the art school and the Folkewangschule in Essen. In 1982, she began working with the sculptor Heinrich Brockmeier, whom she married in 1988. Grey predominates in her work, with its superimposed layers, in which chalky, granular material expresses the weight of time. These flat surfaces have words - usually illegible - and shapes engraved on them. Her paintings match the sculptures of Heinrich Brockmeier. She has exhibited in solo shows in Munich, Hanover, Recklinghausen, Hamburg, Nice and Paris.

BIBLIOGRAPHY:
Planche, Jean, '*Pourquoi la peinture doit-elle ainsi pétrifier? Uschi Klaas et Heinrich Brockmeier*' in *Artension* n° 30, periodical, Rouen, December 1991-January 1992.

KLAASENS. See **CLAESSENS**

KLABER, Gijula
Hungarian, 19th - 20th century.
Born 1 December 1872, in Sopron.
Painter.

Gijula Klaber started training in Vienna and exhibited in Budapest from 1898.

KLAEN, Josua
Swiss, 17th century.
Died 1659, in Altdorf.
Glass painter.

Klaen worked in various monasteries in the canton of Uri.

KLAESENER, Alexander
Dutch, 19th - 20th century.
Born 3 March 1826, in Vallender; died 11 November 1912, in Alkmaar.
Painter. History painting.

Alexander Klaesener trained at Düsseldorf Academy, finished his training in Antwerp, then worked for various different churches in, for example, Gouda, Alkmaar and The Hague.

KLAESTRUP, Peter Christian
Danish, 19th century.
Born 29 May 1820, in Copenhagen; died 9 March 1882.
Draughtsman.

Several of Peter Klaestrup's watercolours and caricatures are in the museum of Frederiksborg.

KLAETTE, Paul. See **KLETTE**

KLAEUI, Heinrich
Swiss, 19th - 20th century.
Born in Zurich.
Painter.

Heinrich Klaeui travelled to Italy and lived in Tessin, exhibiting in Zurich, Munich and Rome.

KLAGMANN, Henri
French, 19th century.
Born 22 May 1842, in Paris; died 1871.
Painter. History painting.

Henri Klagmann was the son of the sculptor J. B. Klagmann. He was a pupil of Picot and Cabanel.

MUSEUMS AND GALLERIES:
CHÂTEAU-THIERRY: *Metamorphosis of Byblis* - NANCY: *Medea*.

KLAGMANN, Jean Baptiste Jules
French, 19th century.
Born 14 April 1810, in Paris; died 18 January 1867, in Paris.
Sculptor, decorative designer. Theatre decoration.

MUSEUMS AND GALLERIES:
AVIGNON: *Bust of Queen René* - COMPIÈGNE (Mus. Antoine Vivenel): *The Holy Man Job* (statue) - TOULON: maquettes.

KLAGSTAD, August
Norwegian, 20th century.
Born 14 August 1886, in Modum.
Active in the USA.
Painter. Religious subjects, portraits.

August Klagstad was trained by Feudell, W.J. Reynolds and at the Art Institute of Chicago. He was a member of the American Federation of the Arts.

KLAGUESS, Th. A.
Russian, 19th century.
Born 1814.
Painter. Genre scenes, landscapes.

MUSEUMS AND GALLERIES:
MOSCOW (State Tretyakov Gal.): *A Poestum*.

KLAHR, Emil
Swedish, 19th - 20th century.
Painter. Animals.

KLAIN, Jacques
French, 18th century.
Active in Paris in 1760.
Painter.

KLAMMER, Mariska
Hungarian, 19th - 20th century.
Born 1873, in Budapest.
Painter. Flowers.

Mariska Klammer was the pupil of Jacques Émile Blanche and L. Simon in Paris.

AUCTION RECORDS:
LONDON, 9 Oct 1997, *Peonies and Summer Flowers on a Window Sill* (oil on canvas, 26½ x 31½ ins / 67.2 x 80 cm) GBP 862.

KLAMROTH, Anton
Russian, 19th - 20th century.
Born 29 April 1860, in Moscow.
Painter. Portraits, genre scenes.

Anton Klamroth first exhibited in Berlin in about 1890. He was an associate member of the national society of fine arts from 1897.

KLAMRY, L. de
French, 20th century.
Painter. Figures, portraits.

L. de Klamry painted in Montmartre from 1930 to 1945. His paintings are mainly of picturesque scenes, particularly night clubs, and are executed in an energetic and deliberately satirical style.

KLAPERER, Anton
Austrian, 19th century.
Died 1824, in Prutz.
Painter.

Klaperer worked in Untermais and Meran (now Merano, Italy).

KLAPHAUER, Johann Georg
German, 17th century.

Active in Cologne c. 1651.

Painter.

Klaphauer was the Noble Master of the guild of painters in Cologne. His portraits are reminiscent of those of Gortzius Geldorp.

Museums and Galleries:
Cologne: *Portrait of a Man.*

KLAPHECK, Konrad

German, 20th century.

Born 10 February 1935, in Düsseldorf.

Painter, engraver.

Phases group.

Konrad Klapheck trained at the Academy of Fine Art in Düsseldorf under Bruno Goller from 1954 to 1958. In 1951 he lived in England, and from 1952 he went regularly to Italy. In 1960 and 1968 he visited Spain, in 1969 the USA and in 1973 Israel and the former East Germany. He lives and works in Düsseldorf. Since 1959 he has participated in the Surrealist-inspired group Phases.

His early works reveal the influence of some of the Surrealists, such as Tanguy, Magritte and Max Ernst, as evidenced in the collection entitled *Die Kleinen*, published in 1957. '...in 1955, I set myself the task of painting a composition that was as strictly opposed as possible to Tachism, which was fashionable at the time. I wished to replace this wave with precision - replace lyrical Expressionism with exalted prosaic reality'. In that period he painted his first *Typewriter*, having at that time discovered the language which then characterised his entire work. He painted series of objects with the objectivity of a draughtsman, notably common machines, such as typewriters, sewing machines, telephones, sirens, taps, showers, shoe trees and bicycle bells. They represented obvious or symbolic links with 'the most hidden wishes and desires'. Thus the carefully depicted equipment fitted with connecting demijohns is entitled *Family Life* and a work depicting two streamlined tap systems is entitled *Slender Women*. José Pierre wrote: 'He ardently strove to retain objectivity of representation, but this did not prevent the machine being depicted from taking on a subjective meaning'. His work was very different in terms of its meaning, form and impersonal grasp of elements of urban folklore; it anticipated certain aspects of Pop Art.

Klapheck's work has shown remarkable continuity throughout the years, both in terms of his mental ability and his technical capacity. His hyperrealistic technique, often encountered in Surrealist painters, is used to depict accurately what were, not long ago, called 'Surrealist objects'. He apparently copied these objects faithfully and realistically, even though upon examination they were totally improbable. On the other hand, their titles are examples of Surrealist humour, tipping the objects over into the realms of the poetic unreal. An example is a huge machine tool entitled: *Super-Mother*; another is a kind of impassable motorcycle entitled: *Fortune Hunting*.

He has participated in group exhibitions, notably in 1960 in New York; 1961 *Phases* in Milan; 1962 *Giving People Something to See* in Paris, London, New York and in Germany, notably at the Art Fair in Cologne; 1964, 1968, 1977 Documenta in Kassel; 1968-1969 *Distances* at the Musée d'Art Moderne in Paris; 1970 Moderna Museet in Stockholm; 1971 National Museum of Modern Art in Tokyo; 1974 Kunstverein in Hanover; 1975 Kunsthalle in Bern; 1976 Kunsthalle in Nuremberg; 2000 *Le Mouvement Phases de 1952 à l'Horizon 2001* (*The Phases Movement from 1952 to the 2001 Horizon*) at the Kiosque cultural centre in Mayenne, and at the Noroit Centre in Arras.

He showed his works in the following solo exhibitions: 1959 in Düsseldorf; 1960, 1963 and 1972 in Milan; 1962 in Essen; 1964 in Berlin and London; 1965 in Paris and at the Palais des Beaux-Arts in Brussels; 1969 in New York; 1972 in Rome; 1974 at the Museum Boijmans-van Beuningen in Rotterdam; 1977 in Cologne; 1980 and 1982 at the Galerie Maeght in Paris; 1985 at the Kunsthalle in Düsseldorf; and 1990, 1997 at the Galerie Lelong in Paris.

Bibliography:
Pierre, José, *Konrad Klapheck - Verzeichnis der Gemälde*, Institut für moderne Kunst, Cologne, 1970. Hofmann, Werner/Klapheck, Konrad, *'Klapheck'* in *coll. Repères. Cahiers d'art contemporain* n° 20, Gal. Lelong, Paris, 1985. Frémon, Jean/Klapheck, Konrad, *'Klapheck'* in *coll. Repères. Cahiers d'art contemporain* n° 62, periodical, Gal. Lelong, Paris, 1990. Jouffroy, Alain, *'Entretien avec Konrad Klapheck sur le "sens caché" de ses tableaux de la fin des années 80'* in *Opus international* n° 118, periodical, Paris, March-April 1990.

Museums and Galleries:
Aachen (Ludwig Forum für Internationale Kunst): *Athletic Self-portrait* (1958) - Antwerp (Koninklijk Mus. voor Schone Kunsten) - Cologne (Wallraf-Richartz Mus.) - Düsseldorf (Kunstmus.) - Hamburg (Kunsthalle) - Humlebæk (Louisiana Mus. for Moderne Kunst): *Logic of Woman* (1965) - Krefeld (Kaiser Wilhelm Mus.): *Censors* (1963) - Paris (BNF, Prints Collection): *Master Thinker* (1980, etching) - Paris (CNAC) - Wuppertal (Von der Heydt Mus.).

Auction records:
Hamburg, 3 June 1977, *Rocking Chair* (1971, oil on canvas, 43 1/4 x 39 1/4 ins / 110 x 100 cm) DEM 28,000. New York, 19 Oct 1979, *Maternal Friend* (1966, oil on canvas, 28 1/4 x 35 ins / 71.7 x 89 cm) USD 6,500. London, 3 Dec 1981, *Legal Expert* (1969, oil on canvas, 90 1/2 x 78 3/4 ins / 230 x 200 cm) GBP 10,500. London, 28 June 1983, *Egocentric Person* (1964, oil on canvas, 43 1/4 x 33 1/2 ins / 110 x 85 cm) GBP 8,000. London, 25 June 1985, *Harem* (1968, oil on canvas, 45 x 39 ins / 114.2 x 99 cm) GBP 12,000. Hamburg, 12 June 1987, *Fanatic Female* (1979, charcoal, 39 1/4 x 33 1/2 ins / 100 x 85 cm) DEM 6,000. London, 23 Feb 1989, *Quibbling Female* (1967, oil on canvas, 43 1/4 x 47 1/4 ins / 110 x 120 cm) GBP 46,200. London, 25 May 1989, *Scene of Married Couple* (1968, oil on canvas, 29 1/2 x 37 1/2 ins / 75 x 95.3 cm) GBP 17,600. London, 30 Nov 1989, *Clairvoyant* (1963, oil on canvas, 32 x 39 1/2 ins / 81 x 100.5 cm) GBP 35,200. Paris, 29 Oct 1990, *Family Life* (1961, oil on canvas, 36 x 39 1/4 ins / 90.5 x 100 cm) FRF 300,000. London, 5 Dec 1991, *Four Lifestyles* (1962, oil on canvas, 31 1/2 x 27 1/2 ins / 80 x 70 cm) GBP 27,500. London, 29 June 1994, *Ambassador* (oil on canvas, 43 1/4 x 31 1/2 ins / 110 x 80 cm) GBP 28,750. Paris, 12 Oct 1994, *Self-Assured* (oil on canvas, 15 3/4 x 27 1/2 ins / 40 x 70 cm) FRF 72,000. Paris, 29-30 June 1995, *Schemer* (1964, oil on canvas, 39 1/4 x 39 1/4 ins / 100 x 100 cm) FRF 270,000. Berlin, 1 Oct 1999, *The Vow* (1961, oil on canvas, 37 x 35 ins / 95 x 90 cm) DEM 38,000. London, 10 Oct 2001, *Emperor* (1966, oil on canvas, 67 x 59 ins / 170 x 150 cm) GBP 36,000. Cologne, 5 June 2002, *Fertility* (acrylic on canvas, 39 x 37 ins / 100 x 95 cm) EUR 29,000. Berlin, 29 Nov 2002, *Chief Ideologist* (1965, oil on canvas, 35 x 39 ins / 90 x 99 cm) EUR 40,000. London, 3 Feb 2003, *Demi-Vierge* (1972, oil on canvas, 63 x 51 ins / 161 x 130 cm) GBP 32,000. Cologne, 27 Nov 2003, *Strong Mother* (oil on canvas, 16 x 35 ins / 40 x 89 cm) EUR 41,000. Paris, 5 Oct 2004, *Winter of Feelings* (oil on canvas, 23 x 20 ins / 58 x 51 cm) EUR 19,000. Paris, 5 Oct 2004, *Real* (1964, oil on canvas, 26 x 30 ins / 65 x 77 cm) EUR 37,000.

KLAPISH, Liliane

French, 20th century.

Born 1933, in Cachan.

Active in Israel from 1969.

Painter, draughtswoman, collage artist. Interiors with figures, landscapes.

Liliane Klapish studied at the Académie Ranson from 1951 to 1954 and under Léon Zack. She lived in Morocco from 1958 to 1959 and moved to Jerusalem in 1969. Her canvases are elegantly composed and painted with a delicate sense of colour and sensitivity towards the impact of the subject matter. The psychological atmosphere of her compositions derives from the intimism of her approach and her fondness for depicting atmospheric interiors. She took part in group exhibitions from 1958, showing work in Germany, Paris, notably at the Salon des Réalités Nouvelles, and Israel. She also showed her work in solo exhibitions: in Paris (1966, 1970, 1975, 1976); in Tel Aviv (1970, 1972, 1988); at the Museum of Israel in Jerusalem (1972); and in Geneva and at the Jewish Museum in Jerusalem (1975).

AUCTION RECORDS:
TEL AVIV, 2 Jan 1989, *View of a Courtyard* (oil on canvas, 21 1/2 x 14 3/4 ins / 54.5 x 37.5 cm) USD 1,760. TEL AVIV, 1 Jan 1991, *Through the Window* (1988, charcoal, ink and gouache, 25 1/2 x 19 3/4 ins / 65 x 50 cm) USD 880. TEL AVIV, 14 April 1993, *Under a Bridge* (oil on canvas, 45 x 57 1/2 ins / 114 x 146 cm) USD 10,350. TEL AVIV, 22 April 1995, *House* (1978, oil on canvas, 25 1/2 x 36 ins / 65 x 90.5 cm) USD 9,200. TEL AVIV, 30 Sept 1996, *Book and Notepad on the Corner of a Table* (1978, collage and oil on canvas, 9 1/2 x 21 1/4 ins / 24 x 54 cm) USD 5,060. TEL AVIV, 24 April 1997, *Backlit Figure* (1988, oil on canvas, 31 1/2 x 15 3/4 ins / 80 x 39.9 cm) USD 6,800.

KLAPMUTS, S.

Dutch, 18th century.
Probably active c. 1768-1774.
Painter, engraver.

S. Klapmuts is known for his paintings of landscapes, studies of heads and a painting entitled *Young Boy and Girl*.

KLAPPER, Karl

German, 20th century.
Born 26 August 1879, in Berlin.
Painter, engraver.

Karl Klapper trained in Paris at the Académie Julian.

KLASEN, Peter

German, 20th century.
Born 18 August 1935, in Lübeck.
From 1959 active in France.
Painter (mixed media), collage artist.

After training at Berlin Art College (1956-1959), where his teacher was Hann Trier, Klasen went to Paris and settled there in 1959. He lives in Vincennes. He is Commandeur de l'Ordre des Arts et des Lettres.

In the 1960s, Peter Klasen clearly belonged to European Pop Art, which incorporated everyday objects into the work. He created his first semi-abstract assemblages, covered in grey, white or black, in which he planted a few identifiable objects. The following year he developed this idea further by integrating current objects of consumption into his works, and photographs from popular magazines. He then underlined the ambiguity between reality and his representation, juxtaposing aggressive utensils (scalpel, forceps and syringe) and particularly vulnerable details of the female figure, such as the mouth and breasts. He retained the airbrushing and stencilling techniques, which enabled him to achieve perfectly smooth surfaces, similar to a photographic rendering. From 1966 he focused on the object itself, or a detail of it, in simpler compositions. He rejected any narration. Pipes, pressure gauges, dials, grating, steel security doors, metal shutters, bath tubs and washbasins are the only subjects in his acrylic paintings, which were generally limited to three colours: yellow, blue and black. He also worked from photographs taken during his trips to disused zones, waste ground, hangars and marshalling yards, reinventing the images of these subjects. Since 1975, he has introduced seams, water leaks or various different dirty marks into this sterile environment, which point to the destruction of the objects being represented. From 1985 to 1988, he worked on the subject of the Berlin Wall, which was comprised of photo-collage paintings, in which he integrated life-sized objects.

He has participated in a great many collective exhibitions since the early 1960s in France, Italy, Germany, the Netherlands, Canada and the USA including, in 2003, *L'État des Choses* (*The State of Things*), a look at the status of daily objects in contemporary art, an exhibition held on the occasion of *Trésors publics, 20 ans de création dans les Fonds régionaux d'art contemporain (FRAC)* (*Public Treasury, 20 Years of Creation in the Regional Collection of Contemporary Art (FRAC)*), Musée des Beaux-Arts, Nantes.

Since 1964, he has exhibited his works in solo exhibitions in a great many galleries, in Munich, Paris, Milan, Brussels, Cologne, Berlin, Duisburg, Los Angeles, Tokyo and several provincial towns in France.

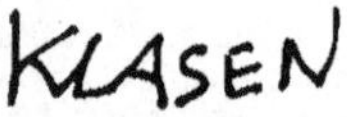

BIBLIOGRAPHY:
Gassiot-Talabot, Gérald, *'Klasen'* in *Chroniques de l'Art vivant*, periodical, Maeght, Paris, April 1971. Tilman, Peter, *Peter Klasen, Pierre Tilman*, periodical, Galilée, Paris, 1979. Lascault, Gilbert (preface), *Peter Klasen, peintures 1977-82*, exhibition catalogue, periodical, Galeria Maeght, Barcelona, 1983. Jouffroy, Alain, *Peter Klasen: The Berlin Wall Cycle (1985-1988). Recent Paintings*, Mayer Schwarz Gallery, Beverly Hills, 1990. Avila, Alin-Alexis, *Peter Klasen, oeuvres 1961-1993*, exhibition catalogue, Centre d'art contemporain, Istres, 1993.

MUSEUMS AND GALLERIES:
BRUSSELS (MAM) - CRÉTEIL (FDAC Val-de-Marne): *Reminder 60* (1980) - LYONS (FRAC Rhône-Alpes): *Bidet* (1968) - MARSEILLES (Mus. Cantini): *Bath Tub and Ventilator* (1970); *Caution, Slow Down* (1980) - NUREMBERG (Kunsthalle) - OSTEND (Mus. voor Moderne Kunst) - PARIS (BNF, Prints Collection): *FIAC Poster* (1983, lithograph) - PARIS (CNAC) - PARIS (MNAM-CCI): *Grey Dumper Trucks* (1974); *Face to Face*; *Forbidden Zone* - ROTTERDAM (Mus. Boijmans Van Beuningen).

AUCTION RECORDS:
PARIS, 27 Nov 1973, *Small Dialogue*, FRF 4,900. ROME, 4 April 1974, *Scissors*, ITL 1,600,000. MILAN, 26 April 1979, *Truck Detail IV* (1974, acrylic on canvas, 45 x 57 1/2 ins / 114 x 146 cm) ITL 900,000. PARIS, 23 Oct 1981, *Keep Out* (1974, acrylic on canvas, 46 x 35 ins / 116 x 89 cm) FRF 16,500. PARIS, 22 April 1983, *Refrigerated Van* (1977, acrylic on canvas, 37 3/4 x 51 ins / 96 x 129.5 cm) FRF 19,000. PARIS, 6 Dec 1985, *Belt No. 2* (1971, acrylic and mixed media, 76 3/4 x 51 1/4 ins / 195 x 130 cm) FRF 42,000. PARIS, 3 Dec 1987, *Tank MK 28* (acrylic on card, 11 1/2 x 16 1/4 ins / 29 x 41.5 cm) FRF 11,000. PARIS, 20 March 1988, *Feeding Bottle + Face* (1969, acrylic on canvas, 32 x 25 1/2 ins / 81 x 65 cm) FRF 17,000. PARIS, 24 March 1988, *Composition* (1935, gouache, 15 1/4 x 12 1/2 ins / 39 x 32 cm) FRF 9,100. PARIS, 5 May 1988, *MT 5* (1978, gouache on card, 19 3/4 x 25 1/2 ins / 50 x 65 cm) FRF 12,000. PARIS, 27 June 1988, *Metal Shutter with Tank* (1980, oil on canvas, 35 x 46 ins / 89 x 116 cm) FRF 31,000. DOUAI, 23 Oct 1988, *S.I.T.A. Truck* (1976, acrylic on canvas, 39 1/4 x 32 ins / 100 x 81 cm) FRF 25,000. PARIS, 23 Jan 1989, *JK3* (collage and gouache on paper, 25 1/4 x 18 ins / 64 x 46 cm) FRF 15,000. PARIS, 12 Feb 1989, *A/V Lock* (1983, acrylic on card, 29 1/2 x 9 1/2 ins / 75 x 24 cm) FRF 38,000. PARIS, 23 March 1989, *Female 2+English*

Key (1972, acrylic on canvas, 32 x 39 1/4 ins / 81 x 100 cm) FRF 105,000. PARIS, 6 April 1989, *Truck Detail II* (1973, acrylic on canvas, 38 1/4 x 51 1/4 ins / 97 x 130 cm) FRF 125,000. PARIS, 16 April 1989, *Good Day Mr S* (1983, acrylic on canvas, 63 x 51 1/4 ins / 160 x 130 cm) FRF 116,000. PARIS, 12 June 1989, *Lock I* (1974, acrylic on canvas, 38 1/4 x 51 1/4 ins / 97 x 130 cm) FRF 125,000. PARIS, 8 Oct 1989, *N for Nîmes* (acrylic and collage on canvas, 36 1/4 x 28 3/4 ins / 92 x 73 cm) FRF 60,000. PARIS, 26 Nov 1989, *Blue/Red Tank Truck G 38* (1986, 39 1/4 x 32 ins / 100 x 81 cm) FRF 145,000. PARIS, 13 Dec 1989, *Shirt* (1971, acrylic on card, 40 1/2 x 28 3/4 ins / 103 x 73 cm) FRF 50,000. PARIS, 17 Dec 1989, *Stethoscope and Switch* (1969, acrylic and object on canvas, 46 x 35 ins / 116 x 89 cm) FRF 55,000. PARIS, 18 Feb 1990, *Untitled* (1964-1965, acrylic on canvas, 28 3/4 x 23 1/2 ins / 73 x 60 cm) FRF 380,000. PARIS, 28 March 1990, *Handle V8/Ochre* (1987, mixed media and collages on card, 25 1/4 x 19 1/4 ins / 64 x 49 cm) FRF 82,000. PARIS, 3 May 1990, *No More Need of a Test* (1967, acrylic on canvas, 7 x 5 1/2 ins / 18 x 14 cm) FRF 30,500. PARIS, 8 May 1990, *Female Object* (1967, acrylic on canvas, 59 x 63 ins / 150 x 160 cm) FRF 460,000. PARIS, 30 May 1990, *Arrow P X 343 Blue* (1987, acrylic on canvas, 39 1/4 x 32 ins / 100 x 81 cm) FRF 180,000. PARIS, 18 June 1990, *Tilt* (1967, acrylic on canvas, 63 3/4 x 45 ins / 162 x 114 cm) FRF 200,000. PARIS, 24 June 1990, *Isotherm* (1973, acrylic on canvas, 63 3/4 x 51 1/4 ins / 162 x 130 cm) FRF 200,000. PARIS, 29 Oct 1990, *Midnight Bathe* (1967, acrylic on canvas, 31 1/2 x 31 1/2 ins / 80 x 80 cm) FRF 150,000. PARIS, 5 Dec 1990, *Covered Truck NM* (gouache, 24 1/2 x 19 ins / 62 x 48.5 cm) FRF 52,000. PARIS, 5 Dec 1991, *Dress No. 3* (1972, acrylic on hardboard, 41 1/4 x 29 1/4 ins / 105 x 74.5 cm) FRF 22,000. PARIS, 2 Feb 1992, *Stethoscope and Switch* (1969, acrylic and stethoscope on canvas, 46 x 35 ins / 117 x 89 cm) FRF 50,000. PARIS, 8 July 1993, *Good Day Mr S* (1983, acrylic collage of wood, card, rope and paper, 64 1/4 x 51 1/4 ins / 163 x 130 cm) FRF 78,000. LOKEREN, 4 Dec 1993, *Composition* (mixed media, 25 1/4 x 19 1/4 ins / 64 x 49 cm) BEF 95,000. PARIS, 10 Feb 1994, *Yellow Tank Truck* (1982, acrylic on canvas, 78 3/4 x 110 1/4 ins / 200 x 280 cm) FRF 95,000. PARIS, 22 April 1994, *Torso, Handle, Screwdriver* (1969, acrylic and airbrush on canvas, 32 x 45 1/2 ins / 81 x 115.5 cm) FRF 66,000. LOKEREN, 11 March 1995, *Insulated Brake* (collage and gouache, 24 3/4 x 19 1/4 ins / 63 x 49 cm) BEF 60,000. PARIS, 8 March 1996, *Shirt + 3 Syringes* (1970, acrylic on canvas, 51 1/4 x 38 1/4 ins / 130 x 97 cm) FRF 40,000. LONDON, 23 May 1996, *Lever + Corrosive Black Background 534* (1989, acrylic on canvas, 39 1/2 x 32 ins / 100.3 x 81.2 cm) GBP 2,300. PARIS, 16 Oct 1996, *Insulated Brake 108* (1988, acrylic on canvas, 36 1/4 x 28 3/4 ins / 92 x 73 cm) FRF 28,000. PARIS, 29 Nov 1996, *Nude Against a Grey Background* (c. 1972, acrylic on canvas, 29 1/2 x 37 1/2 ins / 75 x 95 cm) FRF 51,000; *Circuit Breaker VI* (1972, acrylic and collage on panel, 34 1/4 x 24 1/2 ins / 87 x 62.5 cm) FRF 30,500. PARIS, 4 Oct 1997, *Torso and Light Bulb No. 1* (1968, acrylic on canvas, 39 1/4 x 32 ins / 100 x 81 cm) FRF 32,000. PARIS, 23 Nov 1997, *Lever + 2 Arrows 706* (1995, acrylic on canvas with collage, 31 1/2 x 31 1/2 ins / 80 x 80 cm) FRF 24,500. PARIS, 15 Dec 1997, *Large Nude, Ventilation + Switches* (1969, acrylic on canvas, 51 1/4 x 38 1/4 ins / 130 x 97 cm) FRF 62,000. PARIS, 23 Nov 1999, *Vanne II* (mixed media, 34 x 25 ins / 87 x 63 cm) FRF 50,000. LONDON, 10 Dec 1999, *Tiroir II* (1968, acrylic on canvas, 37 x 29 ins / 94 x 74 cm) GBP 4,500. PARIS, 13 March 2000, *Sourire, Tiroir* (1967, oil on canvas, 39 x 32 ins / 100 x 81 cm) FRF 65,000. PARIS, 15 March 2000, *Poignee and Face no. 2* (1971, oil on canvas, 32 x 46 ins / 81 x 116 cm) FRF 45,000. PARIS, 29 Jan 2001, *Garden by Night* (1966, acrylic on canvas, 11 x 9 ins / 27 x 22 cm) FRF 57,000. PARIS, 20 March 2001, *Nude on a Grey Background* (1973, acrylic on canvas, 29 x 39 ins / 73 x 100 cm) FRF 66,000. PARIS, 4 Feb 2002, *100W Bulb with Portrait* (1968, acrylic on canvas, 36 x 26 ins / 92 x 65 cm) EUR 10,000. PARIS, 4 Feb 2002, *Untitled* (1965, oil on canvas, 5 x 6 ins / 12 x 16 cm) EUR 18,000. PARIS, 29 April 2003, *Paranoiac Lady Version no. 2* (1968, acrylic on canvas, 59 x 24 ins / 150 x 60 cm) EUR 20,000. PARIS, 9 Dec 2003, *Dentist's Chair* (acrylic on canvas, 79 x 75 ins / 200 x 190 cm) EUR 19,000. PARIS, 23 Oct 2004, *Good Magic* (1965, oil on canvas, 63 x 51 ins / 161 x 130 cm) EUR 64,000. VERSAILLES, 12 Dec 2004, *Various Objects* (1963, acrylic and objects, 46 x 35 ins / 116 x 89 cm) EUR 50,000.

KLASENS, Pieter. See **CLAESSENS**

KLASS, Carl Christian

German, 18th century.
Born 1747, in Dresden; died 1793, in Dresden.
Painter. History painting.

Carl Christian Klass was the brother of Friedrich Christian Klass. He studied with Mietsch, Hutin and Casanova, and accompanied the latter to Italy in 1772. He was curator of the print room and a member of the Dresden academy from 1780. One of his best canvases is *The Death of Emilia Galotti*.

KLASS, Friedrich Christian

German, 18th - 19th century.
Born 1752, in Dresden; died 11 April 1827, in Dresden.
Painter, engraver (etching). Landscapes.

Friedrich Christian Klass studied with Casanova and was a member of the electoral academy. He painted in the style of Salvator Rosa and Dietrich. He engraved landscapes and genre scenes.

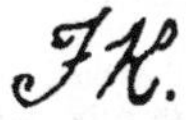

KLASS, Johann Kilian. See **GLAS**

KLASS, Ludwig Friedrich

German, 19th century.
Born 11 October 1784, in Dresden; died February 1830, in Dresden.
Painter.

Ludwig Friedrich Klass studied with J. D. Schubert at the Dresden academy.

KLASSNIK, Robin

South African, 20th - 21st century.
Born 28 January 1947, in Johannesburg.
Active in England from 1960, naturalised British in 1963.
Installation artist.
Mail Art.

Robin Klassnik comes from a Jewish Lithuanian family that was forced to go into exile from South Africa in 1960 and moved to London. He studied at Hornsey Art College from 1963 to 1965 and at Leicester Art College from 1965 to 1968. He teaches painting and sculpture in London. Klassnik paints landscapes and scenes from his life. In 1958, keen to be part a more 'social' art, he created environments in public places. In 1971, disappointed by the response of the public, he turned to Mail Art, sending out documents, plans, instructions and collages which required responses. He used those that arrived (between 8% and 12%) to create a sculpture. Klassnik took part in numerous group exhibitions from 1969, including exhibitions in 1971 at the Kunsthalle, Berlin, and in 1972 and 1973 at the Institute of Contemporary Art in London. He has also shown his work in solo exhibitions in London, Oporto and Poznan.

BIBLIOGRAPHY:

Ball, Keith, *'Yello: Everything Talks with Robin Klassnik'* in *Everything*, No. 14, June-July 1994.

KLATT, Hans

German, 20th century.
Born 13 February 1876, in Hamburg; died 1936.
Painter. Landscapes.

Hans Klatt took part in the Grosse Berliner Kunstausstellung in 1909.

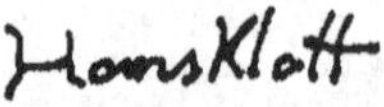

AUCTION RECORDS:
MUNICH, 5 Dec 1979, *Winter Landscape* (1909, oil on canvas, 23 1/2 x 31 1/2 ins / 60 x 80 cm) DEM 2,800.

KLAU, Jacques Grief. See **CLAEUW**

KLAUBER, Catharina
German, 18th century.
Active in Augsburg.
Engraver.

According to some authors, Catharina Klauber may be a misreading of the forename of other engravers of the same family.

KLAUBER, Hans Hug. See **KLUBER**

KLAUBER, Ignaz Sebastian
German, 18th - 19th century.
Born 2 January 1753, in Augsburg; died May 1817, in St Petersburg.
Engraver.

Ignaz Sebastian Klauber was the son and pupil of Johann Baptist Klauber. He pursued his studies further in Rome and, from 1781, in Paris, where he was a pupil of Wille. In 1787, he became a member of the Académie Royale in Paris and engraver to the king. When the Revolution began, he went back to Augsburg, then on to Nuremberg. After that he worked in Denmark and then for the Elector of Trier. Finally, in 1796, he was summoned to St Petersburg by Catherine the Great of Russia and appointed director of the academy there. He engraved portraits and historical subjects.

KLAUBER, Johann Baptist
German, 18th century.
Born 1712, in Augsburg; died c. 1787.
Engraver.

Johann Baptist Klauber worked with his brother, Joseph Sebastian Klauber, on the *Bavarian Calendar of St George* and a *Portrait of Frederick the Great.*

KLAUBER, Joseph Anton
German, 19th century.
Born c. 1779, in Augsburg; died 7 June 1837.
Engraver (burin).

Joseph Anton Klauber was the nephew and pupil of Ignaz Sebastian Klauber.

KLAUBER, Joseph Sebastian
German, 18th century.
Born c. 1700, in Augsburg; died 18 September 1768.
Engraver (burin), miniaturist.

Joseph Sebastian Klauber studied with Antoine Birckhaert in Prague. He engraved religious subjects.

KLAUBER, Joseph Wolfgang Xavier
German, 18th - 19th century.
Born c. 1740, in Augsburg; died 13 April 1813, in Augsburg.
Engraver (burin).

Johann Wolfgang Xavier Klauber was the son of Joseph Sebastian Klauber. He studied in Italy. He engraved portraits and historical subjects.

KLAUBERT, Ignace
French.
Engraver. Portraits.

MUSEUMS AND GALLERIES:
NARBONNE: *Portrait of C. van Loo* (engraving, after the painting by Pierre Lesueur).

KLAUER, Ludwig
German, 19th century.
Born 9 January 1782, in Weimar.
Sculptor.

Ludwig Klauer is known for his busts of Herder, Schiller and Goethe.

KLAUER, Martin Gottlieb
German, 18th century.
Born 29 August 1742, in Rudolstadt; died 4 April 1801, in Weimar.
Sculptor. Mythological subjects, figures, historical figures. Busts.

Martin Gottlieb Klauer is considered a name worthy of note in German sculpture. He appears to have worked mainly for his native city.

MUSEUMS AND GALLERIES:
WEIMAR: *Two wall figures*; *Apollo*; *Eros with a Cornucopia*; *Mercury*; *Herder* (bust); *Wieland* (bust); *Schiller* (bust); *Bertuch* (bust); *Frederick II* (bust); *Charles Augustus of Saxony* (bust); *Duchess Anna Amalia of Saxony* (bust); *Knebel* (bust).

KLAUFLUEGEL, Johann Martin
German, 18th century.
Born 1708, in Biberach; died 1784.
Painter.

Klaufluegel worked for the churches in Biberach and Rottenacker. He is also known for his *Portrait of the Preacher J. J. Doll.*

KLAUGT, Jakob
German, 17th century.
Active in Cologne in 1610.
Sculptor.

Klaugt is known for the *Tomb of Archbishop Sasbout of Utrecht.*

KLAUKE, Jürgen
German, 20th century.
Born 1943, in Kliding, near Cochem.
Painter, draughtsman, performance artist.

Jürgen Klauke studied at the academy of art in Cologne. From 1970 to 1975, he was a contributor to courses at the academy in Cologne and in 1980-1981, he taught at the Hamburg academy. He lives and works in Düsseldorf.

Having started by using the traditional techniques of painting and drawing and the modern techniques of video and photography, since 1975, he has also engaged in performance art. He wants to 'treat the self-portrait as a portrait of society', presenting the individual and his relationships with his body, particularly through erotic expressionist drawings. His work claims to be provocative and engaged, casting an acute gaze on relationships between people and the uncommunicable environment. He has also produced artists' books.

He has taken part in the following group exhibitions: 1977 and 1987 Documenta in Kassel; 1978 Basel Art Fair; 1996, *L'Art au Corps - Le Corps exposé de Man Ray à nos Jours* (*Body Art: The Exposed Body from Man Ray to the Present*) at the Musée d'Art Contemporain in Marseilles; 2002, *Les Années 70: l'art en cause* (*The 1970s: Art in Question*) at the Capc-Musée d'Art Contemporain, Bordeaux; and 2003, *Phantom der Lust. Visionen des Masochismus in der Kunst* (*Phantom of Desire. Visions of Masochism in Art*), an exhibition devoted to Sacher-Masoch, the inventor of masochism, at the Neue Galerie am Landesmuseum in Graz.

He has also exhibited in solo shows: 1973 and 1981 at the Rheinisches Landesmuseum in Bonn; 1976, Artothek, Cologne; 1977 and 1988 in Paris; 1980 Städtisches Kunstmuseum in Düsseldorf; 1981, Kunstmuseum, Lucerne; 1982 Modern Art Galerie in Vienna and Neue Galerie am Landesmuseum Joanneum in Graz; 1986, Karlsruhe Kunstverein,

Hamburg Kunsthalle and Museum Boymans van Beuningen in Rotterdam; 1987, Ludwigsmuseum in Cologne; 1991, Kunsthalle in Baden-Baden; 1996, la Filature in Mulhouse and La Chaufferie - the gallery of the Strasbourg School of Decorative Arts and 2002, *Jürgen Klauke. The Photographic Works* at the Hamburg Kunsthalle.

BIBLIOGRAPHY:
Beaumont-Maillet, Laure/Woimant, Françoise/Pernoud, Emmanuel, *De Bonnard à Baselitz - Dix ans d'enrichissements du Cabinet des estampes 1978-1988*, exhibition catalogue, Bibliothèque nationale de France, Paris, 1992. Brignone, Patricia, '*Jürgen Klauke*' in *Art Press* n° 215, periodical, Paris, July-August 1996. Bronfen, Elisabeth/Diederichsen, Diedrich, et al., *Jürgen Klauke. Das Photographische Werk*, exhibition catalogue, Kunsthalle, Hamburg, 2002. Weibel, Peter (ed.), '*Phantom der Lust. Visionen des Masochismus in der Kunst*', *2 vol.*, exhibition catalogue, Neue Galerie am Landesmuseum, Graz, Belleville Verlag, Munich, 2003.

MUSEUMS AND GALLERIES:
BORDEAUX (FRAC Aquitaine): *Dr Müller's Sex Shop (that's how I imagine love)* (1977) - GENEVA (MAH): *Diptych no. 1* (1988) - PARIS (BNF, Prints Collection).

AUCTION RECORDS:
LONDON, 24 Oct 1996, *The Big Easy* (1989, mixed media/paper, 16 1/4 x 22 ins / 41.5 x 56 cm) GBP 1,265. ZURICH, 18 Nov 1997, *Untitled* (1994, watercolour, 16 1/4 x 21 3/4 ins / 41 x 55.5 cm) CHF 1,500. MUNICH, 8 May 1999, *Two Figures* (1989, watercolour, 16 x 22 ins / 41 x 56 cm) DEM 4,300. LUCERNE, 5 June 1999, *Representative* (1994, watercolour, 17 x 22 ins / 42 x 55 cm) CHF 3,300. COLOGNE, 4 Nov 2000, *So-called Friendships between Men* (black and white, seven, 24 x 20 ins / 60 x 50 cm) DEM 38,000. COLOGNE, 10 Nov 2000, *Dialogue* (1988, gouache on board, 59 x 83 ins / 149 x 212 cm) DEM 18,000. LONDON, 9 Feb 2001, *Hashish Smoker* (1974, colour photo, 16 x 12 ins / 40 x 30 cm) GBP 3,000. COLOGNE, 5 May 2001, *Self-portraits* (1973, photos, a pair, 13 x 19 ins / 33 x 49 cm) DEM 17,000. COLOGNE, 12 April 2003, *Composition: Man with Pile of Hats on His Head* (gelatin silver photo, 85 x 49 ins / 215 x 125 cm) EUR 21,000. COLOGNE, 31 Oct 2003, *Home Game* (gelatin silver photo, 71 x 49 ins / 180 x 125 cm) EUR 13,000. STOCKHOLM, 17 Feb 2004, *From Griffes ins Leere* (1987, watercolour, 16 x 13 ins / 40 x 32 cm) SEK 21,000. LONDON, 24 June 2004, *Artists' Pitch* (1980, gelatin silver print, 24 x 20 ins / 60 x 50 cm) GBP 2,600.

KLAUS, Anton
German, 19th century.
Born 23 October 1810, in Magdeburg; died 1 April 1857, in Berlin.
Painter, lithographer.

Anton Klaus is known for a lithograph of Erfurt Cathedral.

KLAUS, Christian
German, 19th century.
Born 6 July 1843, in Nuremberg; died 15 January 1893, in Munich.
Painter. History painting, genre scenes.

Christian Klaus was a student at the Nuremberg school of fine arts, then completed his studies in Munich from 1872 to 1878 in the studio of W. Lindenschmit. He showed for the first time in 1868 and exhibited in Vienna, Berlin, Munich, Düsseldorf and Dresden. He won a medal in Munich in 1869.

AUCTION RECORDS:
MUNICH, 27 June 1995, *Woman Storyteller* (oil on panel, 16 x 12 1/4 ins / 40.5 x 31 cm) DEM 8,625. KEMPTEN, 19 April 2001, *Interior Scene with Farmwoman Sitting* (oil on panel, 11 x 7 ins / 28 x 19 cm) DEM 4,000. MUNICH, 25 June 2004, *Woman and Child Rubbing Potatoes* (oil on panel, 13 x 10 ins / 34 x 26 cm) EUR 2,000.

KLAUS, Johann
Austrian, 19th century.
Born 19 May 1847, in Vienna; died 20 August 1893, near Linz.
Painter, draughtsman, engraver.

Johann Klaus studied first at the Akademie der bildenden Künste in Vienna, then with Karl Mayer and Wurzinger. He also trained with Jacoby. He won medals in Vienna in 1873, Munich in 1876, and at the Exposition Universelle in Paris in 1878.

KLAUS, Samuel
German, 17th century.
Active in Thuringia.
Painter.

In 1622, Samuel Klaus was painting for the church in Eisenberg. He is also known to have worked in Gera.

KLAUSSNER, Jakob Joseph.
See **CLAUSNER**

KLAUSZ, Ernest
Hungarian, 20th century.
Born 1896, in Eger; died 1970, in Paris.
Active in France from 1931.
Painter, draughtsman, decorative artist. Stage sets, stage costumes.
Musicalism (the attempt to interpret music in painting).
Association of Musicalist Artists.

Ernest Klausz initially studied engineering at the polytechnic in Budapest, but was forced to abandon his studies when World War I broke out. He was taken prisoner and deported to Siberia where he was held until 1922, when he returned to Budapest. He did not stay in Hungary for long, however, but moved to Berlin, where he followed courses at the conservatoire. He worked in the theatre, painting many portraits of actors and designing scenery for shows. With Nazism on the rise, Klausz left Germany in 1931 and went to Paris where he started working for the Opéra designing stage sets. In 1953 he left the Paris Opéra and worked for major lyric theatres across the world while at the same time continuing to paint. He met Henry Valensi and directly joined the Musicaliste group, exhibiting in each of their shows, including the group's very first salon in 1932. He also took part in the Salon des Indépendants in Paris, of which he became a member in 1932, and at the Salon des Réalités Nouvelles.

From 1917 he made several experiments with non-figurative works executed in pastels, but produced his greatest works, the *Symphonies* in the early 1930s. Of all the musical painters, it was Klausz whose output was most oriented towards the fantastic, with fire, the generator of energy and purifying force, the key element. His works are generally speaking strictly abstract, but he also used graphic symbols as well as a geometric construction. In 1949 he designed the scenery, stage sets and costumes for *Birth of Colours*, the first Abstract ballet to be staged by the Paris Opéra, with music by Honegger. As with other musicalist painters, he sought to establish a correspondence between painting and music, and attempted to introduce a time dimension and rhythm into his paintings. Klausz was also particularly interested in the various forms of theatrical shows.

AUCTION RECORDS:
PARIS, 28 March 1988, *Sketch for a Symphonic Portrait* (1941, pastel, 16 1/4 x 20 ins / 41.5 x 50.5 cm) FRF 4,500. PARIS, 22 Nov 1989, *Symphony: The Seasons* (1942-1956, oil on canvas, 37 3/4 x 51 1/4 ins / 96 x 130 cm) FRF 110,000; *Composition* (1949, pastel, 24 1/2 x 18 1/2 ins / 62 x 47 cm) FRF 20,000.

KLAW, Alonzo
American, 20th century.
Born 15 April 1885, in Louisville.
Painter.

Alonzo Klaw studied Art in New York and was a member of the Salmagundi Club.

KLEBAHS, Henrijs
Latvian, 20th century.
Born 1928.
Painter. Landscapes, seascapes.

Henrijs Klebahs attended the Rozental school in Riga and then the Latvian academy of fine arts. His canvases evoke painting from the Far East. The shapes are simplified and the reduced colours highlight the contrasts and harmonies capturing the mood of a particular place. He took part in several exhibitions after 1956.

MUSEUMS AND GALLERIES:
RIGA (Nat. Institute of Fine Arts).

KLECHAR-SAMOKHVALOVA, Maria
Russian, 20th century.
Born 1915.
Painter. Still-lifes.

Maria Klechar-Samokhvalova was the pupil of Aleksandr Nikolaevich Samokhvalov at the school of fine arts in Leningrad (now St Petersburg).

AUCTION RECORDS:
PARIS, 23 March 1992, *Still-life in Blue* (oil on canvas, 26 1/2 x 20 ins / 67 x 51 cm) FRF 8,500.

KLECZYNSKI, Bodhan von
Polish, 19th century.
Born c. 1852; died c. 1920, in Vienna.
Active in Munich and Vienna.
Painter. Hunting scenes, genre scenes, winter landscapes.

AUCTION RECORDS:
NEW YORK, 9 Oct 1974, *Hunting Scene,* USD 4,250. NEW YORK, 30 Oct 1980, *The Master's Sledge* (1889, oil on canvas, 31 3/4 x 52 ins / 80.5 x 132 cm) USD 85,000. NEW YORK, 22 May 1986, *Sleigh Ride* (1888, oil on canvas, 47 x 29 ins / 119.5 x 73.7 cm) USD 8,000. NEW YORK, 25 Oct 1989, *Troika in the Snow* (1887, oil on canvas, 32 x 52 1/4 ins / 81.3 x 132.8 cm) USD 18,700. NEW YORK, 12 Oct 1993, *Two Troikas on the Snow-covered Steppes* (1887, oil on canvas, 30 1/4 x 47 1/2 ins / 76.9 x 120.6 cm) USD 17,250. NEW YORK, 12 Feb 1997, *Return from the Hunt* (1887, oil on canvas, 20 x 37 ins / 50.8 x 94 cm) USD 27,800. BURY ST EDMUNDS, 8 March 2001, *Horse-drawn Troikas in a Snow-covered Landscape* (1888, oil on canvas, 24x39 ins / 60x100 cm) GBP 15,000. ZURICH, 5 Sept 2001, *Landscape with Rider and Dogs* (1883, oil on panel, 10x8 ins / 25x20 cm) CHF 7,500. AMSTERDAM, 24 April 2002, *Hidden Prey* (1883, oil on panel, 10x8 ins / 25x20 cm) EUR 6,000. NEW YORK, 30 Oct 2002, *Waiting to Depart* (1883, oil on panel, 21x35 ins / 54x90 cm) USD 12,000. LONDON, 3 June 2003, *Rescue* (1886, oil on canvas, 29x47 ins / 74x120 cm) GBP 17,000. LONDON, 16 Nov 2004, *Sledge Attacked by Wolves* (1885, oil on canvas, 30x48 ins / 75x121 cm) GBP 8,000.

KLEE, Hermann
Austrian, 19th century.
Born 21 February 1820, in Vienna; died 15 November 1894, in Vienna.
Landscape painter.

Klee first exhibited in Vienna around 1853.

AUCTION RECORDS:
PARIS, 22 Feb 1919, *Ford by Moonlight,* FRF 300.

KLEE, Marguerite
French, 19th - 20th century.
Painter. Genre scenes.

Marguerite Klee exhibited in Paris at the Salon des Artistes Français in 1904 and at the Salon of the Société Nationale des Beaux-Arts between 1907 and 1912.

AUCTION RECORDS:
PARIS, 24 May 1945, *Washing,* FRF 800.

KLEE, Paul
Swiss, 20th century.
Born 18 December 1879, in Münchenbuchsee; died 29 June 1940, in Muralto near Locarno.
Active in Germany.
Painter, draughtsman, engraver, watercolourist.
Groups: Die Blauen Vier, Der Blaue Reiter.

Paul Klee's German father was a singing teacher and his half-French, half-Swiss mother was very musical. Klee himself played the violin and toyed with the idea of a career in music. In 1898, having hesitated between music and painting, he opted for painting. He went to Munich, where he enrolled at Heinrich Knirr's free academy. He then went to Stuck's studio at the Art School. In 1901, he travelled to Italy for the first time. There he admired the work of Michelangelo at the Sistine Chapel and Raphael at the Stanze della Segnatura, although he preferred Da Vinci over both. In 1902 he settled in Bern, before moving to Munich in 1906, the year he married his wife Lily Stumpf, a pianist. She earned their livelihood giving piano lessons, and the two gave small concerts for their own pleasure and that of their close friends, as well as attending many classical concerts at the city's concert halls. He was only ever attracted to traditional classical music and did not like the music of the composers of the Vienna School, such as Arnold Schönberg or Alban Berg, despite the fact that he knew them personally. During this period he became an admirer of Aubrey Beardsley and James Ensor.

In about 1911 he made the acquaintance of August Macke, Franz Marc and Wassily Kandinsky in Munich. Following the outbreak of World War I, he served in various German army corps between 1916 and 1918. In 1920 he was appointed to the staff of the Bauhaus, which was then in Weimar. When the Bauhaus was dissolved in Weimar due to political reasons, it was transferred to Dessau, where Klee and Kandinsky shared a flat in 1925. Klee left the Bauhaus in 1930, as the teaching work monopolised too much of his time and its existence was being threatened by political events. He went to Düsseldorf and was appointed an art teacher at the art school there. Then, in 1933, the Nazis came to power in Germany, and soon declared that modern art in all its forms was 'Degenerate Art'. One hundred and nineteen works by Klee were confiscated by the Nazi authorities, 17 of which featured in the infamous *Entartete Kunst* (*Degenerate Art*) exhibition in 1937. Klee, like all the artists concerned, was forbidden from hunting down his work.

He returned to Switzerland in 1933, where he was able to continue to work. In 1935 he became ill with scleroderma. In 1937 Braque and Picasso went to visit him, aware he was unwell. They did not know one another personally, as Klee had never dared to seek them out when he was passing through Paris. He died in 1940 at the age of 61, the same year his father also died. He wrote his own epitaph: 'I cannot be grasped in the here and now for my dwelling place is as much among the dead as well as the yet unborn; slightly closer to the heart of creation than is usual, but still not close enough.'

At the beginning of his career he applied himself notably to engravings which were grotesque both in their manner and in their content. He was already demonstrating his propensity to fantasy art and a certain kind of humour between derision and poetic nostalgia. He became an admirer of William Blake around 1903-1904, and also of the *Horrors of War* by Goya. When he engraved the *Virgin in a Tree* in 1903, he wrote: 'What does it represent? The truth, I hope. How the restraints and sanctity of virginity serve no purpose. It is thus a criticism of middle-class society.' *Two Men Meet, Each Believing the Other to be of Higher Rank* is also from 1903 and is in the same vein, as the title suggests. Between

1902 and 1905 he only produced 15 etchings. It is possible to deduce from this that the etching preparation is slow, and also that Klee lacked confidence in his ability. Echoes of this can be found in other periods. Between 1905 and 1908 he developed a series of glass-pane drawings, in which he attempted to unite etching and drawing. This popular technique remained in use in Germany. *The Virgin with the Daisy, The Lady Full of Good Intentions* and *The Street with Cart* also date from these years.

In 1908 Klee discovered Van Gogh, saying that Van Gogh had 'opened his eyes'. It was at this point that he effectively opened his mind to modern painting for the first time, somewhat late in life, since he was already 30. Cézanne seemed to him like the 'teacher par excellence; calculated to teach him more than Van Gogh'. Drawing and engraving had been almost exclusively his means of expression until then, although in 1910 he did produce a painting entitled *Young Girl with Pitchers*, which he called his 'first offensive against painting', and which denotes Cézanne's influence linked with that of Matisse, of whose works Klee had just seen an exhibition. Until 1911, Klee's time was monopolised by his illustrations for *Candide* by Voltaire. The engravings which made up this illustration were freer than the preceding ones; the drawing was synthetic, and expressed poetry and imagination. Stylistically speaking, the engravings harmonised with Klee's own judgement on Candide: 'There is a superior element in *Candide* which appeals to me. It is an accurate expression of the precious economy which characterises Voltaire's language.'

The basic principles of Der Blaue Reiter (Blue Rider), 'Do not be inspired either by the past, nor by nature, but by your own inner, spiritual side', which he discovered around 1911, were a spiritual stimulus in his quest for the hypothetical based on real sensations. He also discovered the abstraction of Robert Delaunay, which was slowly evolving, starting from the existence of colours per se and the dynamics between them by the use of alternating contrasting colours. He wrote on Delaunay (for whom he subsequently translated several texts himself for the Bauhaus publications): 'One of the best minds of our time, who, without borrowing anything from nature, makes a motif of it [because he] sees forms on a flat level which have a purely abstract, but genuinely three-dimensional life.'

Klee only exhibited drawings and engravings up to 1910. From 1910 onwards, he exhibited a few watercolours. He wrote: 'I have arrived at painting through drawing'. The opportunity for this lengthily prepared breakthrough occurred on a journey he went on across Tunisia in 1914 in the company of August Macke and the Swiss painter Louis Moillet. He visited notably Kairouan and Hammamet, where he discovered colour. This colour corresponded to what was inside him and needed expressing. He then noted in his diary:

'I am giving up work now. The surroundings penetrate me with such gentleness that without exerting any more ardour, it fills me with increasing confidence. The colour possesses me, I know it. This is the meaning of the happy moment; the colour and I together make up a whole. I am a painter'.

In Tunisia he still expressed himself through watercolours, but from the age of about 35 the greater part of his formal repertoire had been found; the decomposition of space; the combination of planes; and transparency of layers of superimposed colours. They produced a different vision to that of the Cubists and tended towards an abstraction quite similar to that of Delaunay in *Windows*. What radically distinguished Klee from all his contemporaries was the permanent intervention in his painting; poetic, symbolic and humorous inventions, which would make his entire work so emphatically special. His poetics and pictorial technique would concentrate on producing the mobility and constant mutation in nature; the instability of physical appearances. He was the painter of metamorphoses.

In 1915 he perfected a small device, a 'reflecting window' streaked with contradictory lines. The effect was to confuse the unity of vision. Within this same aim of dissociating the world from appearances, he often used the resources of axonometric perspective, which permitted the simultaneous reading of the recessed and bled-off contrast. For him, 'a good form is like movement, an action, doing something. A bad form is like closed inertia, like a terminal halt', and 'the creation of a work originates in the movement, is a fixed movement itself, and is ultimately recorded by movement (the eye muscles)'.

During World War I he was able to continue painting, still favouring the use of watercolours. A watercolour from this era such as *Green Bell in the Centre* showed that he was still under the influence of Delaunay. His reading of Hoffmann, Novalis and Gogol nurtured the ironic and mysterious vigour of his painting. Listening to primitive sources of poetic imagination, he pierced the banality of appearances; he knew how to give his imagination free rein: 'the strokes come from some source or other, like children's words, which stagger or disconcert'. His sense of the magnificent and fantastic was inseparable from his sense of humour. With regard to the laugh in *Dead Souls* by Gogol, he said that 'the most noble lyrical movements of the soul are valuable' on condition that it 'is located a thousand leagues from the contortions of the vulgar entertainer'. His work contained elements of the cartoonist, as was often evidenced in the titles or headings of his paintings, for example: 'The moon was on the wane; she showed me the grimace of an Englishman, a disreputable lord', from 1918. He went as far as to indulge in candid caricature, such as in *Emperor William in a Temper*.

In 1919, at the age of 40, he started to use oil paints, restricting himself to small formats, except towards the end of his life. The simplest techniques and modest formats suited his intimist poetics. In his first oil paintings, such as *Villa R, Composition with B* and *Arctic Thaw*, colour played an important structural role. There was also notably the frequent presence of letters, perhaps following the example of the Cubists, although the letters in Klee's paintings assumed more of a symbolic role, leading to significance, rather than a purely three-dimensional role. Teaching at the Bauhaus led him to question the creative processes and develop them. It is surprising that Klee, who at first sight seemed to be the one painter who gave his imagination and his freed subconscious fantasy the fullest free rein, and was ultimately the most poetic, was able to put into practice the systematic teaching of handling of line and colour for the Bauhaus from 1920 to 1933. By mastering a variety of techniques, Klee was able to set free his creative faculties from the problems he faced in terms of their practical implementation. Right from the time of his early engravings in 1903 in Bern, he noted in his *Diary* that 'Three-dimensional arts never start with poetic sentiment or an idea, but with the construction of one or more figures, and with the action of matching some colours and values'. This was reminiscent of the remark Mallarmé made to Degas: 'Poems are not formed with ideas but with words'. Klee was a poet and subconscious poet, yet was the opposite of a disorganised bohemian, as is evidenced by the way he always wrote the titles at the bottom of his paintings and underlined them with a ruler. For more than 10 years he experimented with the specific properties of dots, lines, surfaces, forms, light, colour, and their reciprocal relationships, together with his pupils.

He identified outstanding teaching methods, which he recorded in a great many written documents, and notably in his *Pedagogical Sketchbook*, which was published in Munich in 1925. He extracted the creative steps from these teaching processes for his own use, and they formed the diversity in his work: *Perspectives* (1921), *Fugues* (1921-1922), the Symbolist inventions: *Under the Sign of the Snail* (1921) or humorous inventions: *The Ex-Kaiser*; variations on dots or crosshatching: *Cosmic Flora* (1923). He combined strictness of construction with deliberate naivety in *Seneccio* (1922) and *Mural* (1926), and trifled with feigned Primitivism in *Puppet Theatre*. He gave his almost theoretic research a supporting role. Thus *Perspectives* could not help being conclusive, and bordered on disturbing.

He knew man's limits: 'Man's intellectual faculties for weighing up terrestrial and superterrestrial things constitute the origin of human nature, while opposing the limits of physical incapacity'. Yet he wanted to place himself at the origin of things and beings, facing the infinitely great and the infinitesimal at the same time. This 'mixture of freshest savage and subtlest intellectual', as F. Cachin-Nora called him, explained in his *Credo of the Creator*: 'I place myself at the point of creation, which is a very long way from the origin of things. This is where I can find a formula both for man, beast, plant, mineral, the elements and for all whirling forms.' This wish to return to the sources of all things, this kind of Primitivism, nevertheless did not lead him to question black art or any other form of ethnological art, but led him more simply to the world of children. He was familiar with Pre-Columbian Art, the Persians, the Byzantine mosaics, and was familiar with the painters who were his contemporaries. Conscious of the link between time and space, he found the duration of space in investigating architecture, and the distance of time in music. These in turn engendered the rhythmic orchestration of lines and mosaics in his personal works. Being an educated man, he increased these numerical connections, similar to those in the universe, until he had created a different world. He wanted to question everything, and particularly the three-dimensional values inherited from the past. In 1902 he wrote: 'I want to be like a newborn baby, knowing absolutely nothing about Europe, unaware of facts and fashions, a virtual primitive tribesman. Then I want to do something very humble, which is to build up quite a small formal motif that my pencil will be capable of mastering without any technique.' Later on, in his lecture entitled: *On Modern Art*, comparing the artist with a tree, he developed reflections on the necessity for the artist to detach himself from all cultural heritage, so that his creative production can flourish in the greatest of freedom, like the branches of a tree: 'No one would advise insisting that a tree should make an exact double of its root system for its branches... but when it's a matter of the artist, people readily forbid him from deviating from the role model.' He contrasted his own freedom to the process used by Kandinsky, who, according to him: 'having been led to abstraction by necessity and discipline, has achieved the same result - pure air - driven by passion and astonishing instinctive freedom'.

Although teaching began to become a burden to him, Klee pursued his educational research, which had beneficial repercussions on his own work. The research on the rhythm and effects of repetition of identical elements produced: *Ancient Air* (1925) or the famous series of *Magic Squares*. Journeys also provided him with formal themes; he was drawn for preference to sun, light and colour in such places as Sicily, mainland Italy and Egypt, where he stayed in 1928-1929. These themes would sustain his work right to the end and after his return: *Main Road and Side Road, Atmospheric Group on the Move, Monument in a Fertile Country, Lagoon Town* and, also from 1929, the *Madman in a Trance*, which Klee gave as 'an example of superimposed movements captured instantaneously'. But it was the original training methods, using the combinative assemblages of dots, lines and modular surfaces, which turned out to be the most fruitful, for example, with the *Old Man Counting* (1929), *Who Floats before the Ascension* (1930) or *Plant Tendril* (1932). There was a certain poetry in the lines in Paul Klee's work, and Henri Michaux expressed this in a poem in prose: 'One line meets another line. One line avoids a line. Adventures with lines. One line for the pleasure of being a line or beginning a new line. Dots. Dot dust. A line dreams. A line had never been allowed to dream until then. A line waits. A line hopes. A line rethinks a face.'

Klee was much less preoccupied with colour than with line, except during a lecture in 1924, when he listed the possibilities offered by combinations of colours. More often than not he used to declare that colour was an 'irrational element', or an 'imaginary phenomenon' which is impossible to explain'. He did not concern himself much with the theoretic point of view, but instead channelled his analytical efforts into dots and lines. However, after being dazzled by Kairouan, he used colour with total confidence, both in the case of harmonious concordance, clashing contrasts and 'chiaroscuro'. During the final phase of his life, around 1931-1932, he used a division of shades in a series of medium-sized compositions. This was known as Divisionism and was effectively inspired by Neo-Impressionism. He doubtless also used this procedure to attempt to recreate light by the addition of the colours of the prism.

He produced several satirical drawings during World War II, including: *He too is a Dictator*. Satire soothed his bitterness. He defined it as: 'Satire should not emanate from an excessively bad mood, but from irritation at the sight of what is superior. Man is ridiculous if God is divine. Or else [satire] should express hatred of the mediocrity of the murky human dregs of society, when you consider the heights man can reach.' In *He Who Must Come*, he multiplied the effects, imitating fish scales or down, on coarse jute canvas or gauze, which were coated in white.

When attempting to place Paul Klee into the history of art, he appears increasingly like the creator of an absolutely new three-dimensional language, or else, as one of his biographers, Werner Haftmann, wrote: 'the Primitive of new sensitivity'. Within the Dada context, Marcel Duchamp also displayed radically different routes. But you can readily see what still links Kandinsky to the French Fauves and the German Expressionists; how Mondrian evolved directly from Cézanne, and that Picasso often summed up the entire history of forms. Confronted by the absolute novelty of Paul Klee's language, it has for a long time been customary to regard him as one of the creators of Abstraction. Although a certain number of his works effectively tend towards Abstraction, the majority remain firmly rooted in reality, but an invented reality corresponding to the definition he gave in his diary concerning his own concept of Abstraction: 'Abstraction with memories'.

He held an exhibition of his engravings in Munich in 1906, but it was not a success. He began to exhibit modestly in Bern, Basel, Zurich and Winterthur, according to what he had produced at the time. He took part in the second *Blaue Reiter* (*Blue Rider*) exhibition in 1912, and in the Moderner Bund exhibition in Zurich. He held a general exhibition and retrospective in Munich in 1920, where he exhibited drawings, engravings, watercolours, paintings and also sculptures. He exhibited his works in New York for the first time in 1924, and in Paris in 1925. In 1935 he had his first solo exhibition in London, followed by a great retrospective exhibition held in Bern, Basel and Lucerne.

Klee is regularly represented in themed exhibitions, including *Primary Vision*, an exhibition on the influential vision of children on 20th-century artists, held at the Tate Gallery, Liverpool, in 2001 and *Aux origines de l'abstraction (1800-1914)* (*The Origins of Abstraction (1800-1914)*), held at the Musée d'Orsay, Paris, in 2003. Likewise, a very great many retrospectives have also been organised: 1945, National Gallery, London; 1948, Kunsthaus, Munich; 1967, Solomon R. Guggenheim Museum, New York; 1969, Musée National d'Art Moderne, Paris; 1970, Gallery of Modern Art, Rome; 1981, Museum of Contemporary Art, Caracas; 1987, Museum of Modern Art in New York, The Cleveland Museum of Art, and Kunstmuseum in Bern; 1995, Kunstsammlung Nordrhein-Westfalen, Düsseldorf; 1998, Thyssen-Bornemisza, Madrid; 2002, *Works on Paper*, Kunstmuseum und Museum für Gegenwartskunst in Basel; 2003, triple exhibition *Klee in the North*: the 1920s at the Kunsthalle in Bremen, the 1930s at the Kunsthalle in Hamburg, and the last years, 1933-1940, at the Sprengel Museum in Hanover.

BIBLIOGRAPHY:

Paul Klee, exhibition catalogue, Solomon R. Guggenheim Museum, New York, 1957. Spiller, Jurg, *Paul Klee: the Thinking Eye. The Notebooks of Paul Klee*, Lund Humphries, London, 1961. *Paul Klee*, exhibition catalogue, Kunstverein, Basel, 1967. *Paul Klee*, exhibition catalogue, Musée national d'Art moderne, Paris, 1970. Short, Robert, *Paul Klee*, Thames & Hudson, London, 1979. Raboff, Ernest, *Paul Klee*, Ernest Benn, London, 1980. Kagan, Andrew, *Paul Klee: Art and Music*, Cornell University Press, Ithaca, 1983. Jordan, Jim M., *Paul Klee and Cubism*, Princeton University Press, Princeton, 1984. Lanchner, Caroline, *Paul Klee*, New York Graphic Society Books, Boston, 1987. Crone, Rainer, *Paul Klee: Legends of the Sign*, Columbia University Press, New York, 1991. Franciscono, Marcel, *Paul Klee: His Work and Thought*, University of Chicago, Chicago, 1991. Endicott Barnett, Vivian/Helfenstein, Josef, *The Blue Four: Feininger, Jawlensky, Kandinsky, and Klee in the New World*, Yale University Press, London, 1998. Connolly, Sean, *The Life and Work of Paul Klee*, Heinemann, Oxford, 2002. Kort, Pamela, et al., *Paul Klee 1933*, exhibition catalogue, Musée des Beaux-Arts, Bern, 2003.

MUSEUMS AND GALLERIES:

AMSTERDAM (Stedelijk Mus.): *Composition with Urns* (1921) - BALTIMORE (MA) - BASEL (Kunsthalle): *Beneath the Black Star* (1918); *Castle Garden* (1919); *Ad Marginem* (1930) - BASEL (Kunstmus.): *Miniature of That which has Faded* (1918); *Villa R* (1919); *Composition with the Letter B* (1919); *Greek and Barbarians* (1920); *Graduation of Crystal* (1921); *Bedroom Occupied, Perspective View* (1921); *Landscape near E. in Bavaria* (1921); *Seneccio* (1922); *Old Air* (1925); *Colonies of Huts* (1932); *Prosperous Port* (1938) - BERLIN (Nationalgal.): *Architecture* (1923) - BERLIN (Sammlung Berggruen): *The Sealed Lady* (1930) - BERN (Kunstmus., Paul Klee-Stiftung): *Sister* (1903); *Two Men Meet, Each Believing the Other to be of Higher Rank* (1903); *Pots of Flowers* (1906); *Drinker* (1907); *Motorboat* (1910); *Reading in Bed* (1910); *Nude* (1910); *Munich, Main Station* (1911); *He is Not a Jesuit* (1911); *Chased Candide Away, Kicking Her in the Behind* (1911); *I have Many Paintings, but I Do Not Look at Them* (1911); *O che sciagura, d'essere senza coglioni* (1912); *They Both Let Themselves Fall Over Backwards* (1912); *And Flung Their Arms Round Her Neck. Candide Stepped Back Frightened* (1912); *Abstraction I* (1913); *Composition* (1913); *Ab ovo* (1917); *Journey of Unklaich to China* (1920); *Study for Bedroom Occupied, Perspective View* (1921); *Rushing Figure* (1923); *Puppet Theatre* (1923); *Mural* (1924); *Model of Female Costume* (1924); *Sketch for a Portrait* (1925); *Sweet (Face KI)* (1925); *Slight Danger at Sea* (1928); *Dispute* (1929); *Colourful Table* (1930); *Who Glides (Before the Ascension)* (1930); *Arab Still-life* (1930); *Small Town in the Rocks* (1932); *J. Still a Child* (1933); *He Who Must Come* (1933); *Triangle on the Scene* (1933); *Sphinx Resting* (1934); *Detachment from the Soul* (1934); *Creator* (1934); *She-Devil* (1935); *St Georges* (1936); *Sky-Blue Fruit* (1938); *Shifting Game* (1938); *Group of Five* (1939); *Torso and Followers under a Full Moon* (1939); *Touching Germination* (1939); *Love Song under a New Moon* (1939); *Destroyed Maze* (1939); *Fama* (1939); *Grave Expression* (1939); *High Care* (1940) - BUFFALO (Albright-Knox AG) - COLOGNE (Mus. Ludwig): *High Roads and By-Roads* (1929) - COLOGNE (Wallraf-Richartz Mus.): *Madman in a Trance* (1929) - DÜSSELDORF (Kunstsammlung Nordrhein-Westfalen): *Red and White Domes* (1914) - HAMBURG (Kunsthalle): *Goldfish* (1925); *Revolution of the Viaduct* (1937) - LONDON (Tate Collection): *The Castle Mountain of S* (1930, gouache on paper); *Comedy* (1921, oil and watercolour on paper); *They're Biting* (1920, pencil and oil on paper); *A Young Lady's Adventure* (1922, watercolour on paper); *Walpurgis Night* (1935, gouache on cloth laid on wood); *The Protector* (1926, pen and ink on paper on board); *Seaside Resort in the South of France* (1927, pencil, crayon and watercolour); *Burdened Children* (1930, pencil, crayon, pen and ink on paper, on board) - MONTREAL (MAC): *Untere und Obere Tiere; Animals of the Lower and Higher Orders* - NEW YORK (MoMA): *Devil on Top of the Ships* (1916); *Around the Fishes* (1926); *Twittering Machine* (1922); *Pastorale* (1927) - NEW YORK (Solomon R. Guggenheim Mus.): *Don Juan of Bade* (1919); *Red Balloon* (1922); *Open Book* (1930); *Rolling Landscape* (1938); *Severing of the Snake* (1938) - PARIS (MNAM-CCI): *St Germain near Tunis* (1914); *Florentine Villas* (1926); *Arrow in the Garden* (1929); *Port and Yachts* (1937); *Aridity Pending* (1940) - PHILADELPHIA (MA): *Jörg* (1924); *Enchanting Display of Fishes* (1925) - SARREBRÜCKEN (Saarland Mus.): *Indian Garden of Flowers* (1922) - STRASBOURG (MBA): *Miniature with the Letter E* (1916); *Night Port* (1917); *Man is the Mouth of the Lord* (1918); *Fitzlibutzli* (1918) - THE HAGUE (Gemeentemus.): *On the Peaks* (1917); *In the Style of Bach* (1919) - ULM (Ulmer Mus.): *Kairouan (Departure)* (1914) - ZURICH (Kunsthaus): *Big Failure* (1937); *At the Hunter's Tree* (1939).

AUCTION RECORDS:

PARIS, 12 April 1933, *Drawing*, FRF 300. NEW YORK, 6 Feb 1947, *Aphrodite's Anatomy*, USD 225. STUTTGART, 10 May 1950, *Branches of Flowers*, DEM 3,850. STUTTGART, 26 April 1951, *World* (watercolour) DEM 1,500. HAMBURG, 26 Nov 1957, *Line Animal* (watercolour) DEM 6,100. BERN, 17 May 1958, *Psychogram with Foot* (pen and Indian ink) CHF 3,850. NEW YORK, 15 April 1959, *House by the Sea* (tempera) USD 6,250. NEW YORK, 27 April 1960, *Seven Flowering Times* (watercolour, pen and ink) USD 6,000. LONDON, 23 March 1961, *Fall* (watercolour) GBP 1,750. BERN, 25 May 1962, *New in October* (tempera on canvas) CHF 102,000. NEW YORK, 30 Oct 1963, *Staircase*, USD 15,000. BERN, 28 May 1964, *Friendly Game* (tempera/plaster background) CHF 132,000. LONDON, 23 June 1965, *Departure of the Boats*, GBP 22,000. NEW YORK, 23-24 March 1966, *Boat and Yacht* (watercolour and gouache) USD 80,000. LONDON, 23 April 1968, *Sextet of Genies* (pastel) GBP 16,000. GENEVA, 28 June 1969, *Gelst im Baum* USD 42,000. BERN, 18 June 1970, *Hat, Table and Woman* (gouache and watercolour/plaster-coated canvas) CHF 206,000. NEW YORK, 10 March 1971, *New Harmony* (1889) USD 110,000. LONDON, 12 April 1972, *Siren Eggs* (1939) GBP 39,000. LONDON, 4 July 1973, *Ostlich-süss* GBP 128,000. LONDON, 4 April 1974, *Polstersitz* GBP 13,000. HAMBURG, 3 June 1976, *Landscape with Canal* (1924, pen, 9 x 11 1/4 ins / 22.8 x 28.4 cm) DEM 16,000. BERN, 9 June 1976, *Tightrope Walker* (1923, coloured lithograph) CHF 50,000. BERN, 9 June 1977, *Red Landscape* (1930, watercolour, 9 3/4 x 13 ins / 24.7 x 33.3

cm) CHF 100,000. NEW YORK, 20 Oct 1977, *Coastal Fruit* (1933, oil on paper, 9 1/4 x 11 3/4 ins / 23.5 x 30 cm) USD 24,000. NEW YORK, 17 May 1979, *Clarification* (1932, oil on canvas, 27 1/2 x 37 3/4 ins / 69.8 x 96.2 cm) USD 435,000. HAMBURG, 8 June 1979, *Tightrope Walker* (1923, lithograph in old rose) DEM 22,000. LONDON, 5 July 1979, *Ausritt auf dem Oger* (1925, pen, 13 1/4 x 19 1/4 ins / 33.5 x 49 cm) GBP 15,800. LONDON, 5 Dec 1979, *Gestime über dem Tempel* (1922-1958, watercolour and Indian ink, 6 1/4 x 11 1/2 ins / 16 x 29.5 cm) GBP 31,000. LONDON, 30 Nov 1981, *Artische Tau* (oil on card, 20 1/2 x 20 ins / 52 x 51 cm) GBP 110,000. LONDON, 21 March 1983, *Keramisch-mystisch (in der Art eines Stillebens)* (1925, oil on card, 13 x 18 3/4 ins / 33 x 47.5 cm) GBP 360,000. NEW YORK, 16 May 1984, *Mehr dort als hier* (*More There than Here*) (1922, pencil/mounted paper/card, 9 x 11 1/4 ins / 22 x 28.4 cm) USD 23,000. HAMBURG, 9 June 1984, *Ein Genius serviert ein kleines Frühstück* (*A Genius Serves a Small Breakfast (An Angel Brings What is Desired)*) (1920, lithograph with watercolour) DEM 125,000. BERN, 22 June 1984, *Higgledy-Piggledy Restless Person* (watercolour and Indian ink drawing, 7 3/4 x 6 1/2 ins / 20 x 16.4 cm) CHF 142,000. LONDON, 3 Dec 1984, *Citronen Ernte* (1937, tempera/sacking mounted/sacking, 27 1/2 x 18 1/4 ins / 70 x 46.4 cm) GBP 225,000. BERN, 20 June 1985, *Aged Phoenix* (etching) CHF 9,000. NEW YORK, 13 Nov 1985, *Mystisches Stadtbild* (1920, tempera/mounted paper/card, 8 1/4 x 7 1/2 ins / 21 x 19.2 cm) USD 200,000. BERN, 20 June 1986, *Fiendish Puppets* (oil and watercolour/black background, 18 1/4 x 14 3/4 ins / 46.5 x 37.7 cm) CHF 410,000. LONDON, 2 Dec 1986, *Ankunft der Luftdrache* (1917, oil on canvas, 14 1/4 x 16 3/4 ins / 36.5 x 42.5 cm) GBP 220,000. NEW YORK, 12 May 1987, *Pleasant Place* (1919, gouache and watercolour/paper/card, 8 x 10 ins / 20.4 x 25.1 cm) USD 300,000. BERN, 17 June 1987, *Metaphor for Flowering Time* (painting in glue and watercolour/brown vellum, 25 3/4 x 13 ins / 65.5 x 33 cm) CHF 320,000. LONDON, 24 Feb 1988, *Landscape with Horses* (1924, pencil and ink, 9 x 13 1/2 ins / 22 x 34 cm) GBP 11,000. PARIS, 22 June 1988, *Music Composition* (1919, graphite, 11 x 8 1/2 ins / 28 x 21.5 cm) FRF 110,000. NEW YORK, 12 Nov 1988, *Barbarian Composition* (1918, watercolour and collage/card, 7 1/4 x 5 ins / 18.5 x 11.8 cm) USD 253,000. ROME, 15 Nov 1988, *Miniature Flower* (1937, distemper/paper/card, 8 1/4 x 13 ins / 21 x 33 cm) ITL 140,000,000. LONDON, 3 April 1989, *Gliding* (1932, oil on canvas, 35 1/2 x 35 3/4 ins / 90 x 91 cm) GBP 3,080,000. NEW YORK, 11 May 1989, *Betrothed Couple in the Autumn of Their Lives* (1930, oil on paper, 8 1/4 x 13 ins / 21 x 33 cm) USD 330,000. LONDON, 26 June 1989, *Chinese Porcelain* (1923, mixed media/plaster and paper, 11 1/4 x 14 1/2 ins / 28.5 x 36.9 cm) GBP 638,000. NEW YORK, 13 Nov 1989, *Rock Chamber* (1929, watercolour and pencil/paper, 10 x 12 1/2 ins / 25.4 x 31.7 cm) USD 418,000. NEW YORK, 15 Nov 1989, *Flower* (1922, watercolour/two sheets of paper mounted on card, 14 x 9 ins / 35.5 x 22 cm) USD 1,320,000. NEW YORK, 16 Nov 1989, *Counterpoint* (1933, oil, watercolour and plaster/fabric mounted on canvas, 9 3/4 x 30 ins / 24.8 x 76.2 cm) USD 1,017,500. LONDON, 28 Nov 1989, *Singer L. in the Role of Fiordiligi* (oil and watercolour/plaster-coated background, 20 x 13 1/4 ins / 51 x 33.5 cm) GBP 2,640,000. LONDON, 2 April 1990, *Junger Mann am Vorabend* (1933, oil and wax crayon/material/card, 22 x 15 3/4 ins / 55.6 x 40.3 cm) GBP 440,000. LONDON, 3 April 1990, *Arrival of the Betrothed* (1933, oil on canvas, 25 1/2 x 20 ins / 65 x 51 cm) GBP 2,200,000. LONDON, 4 April 1990, *Town at Twilight* (1915, watercolour, 7 3/4 x 10 1/4 ins / 19.8 x 26.2 cm) GBP 462,000. NEW YORK, 16 May 1990, *Torwächterstolz* (1929, watercolour/paper/card, en tout 22 1/2 x 16 ins / 57.1 x 40.9 cm) USD 308,000. NEW YORK, 17 May 1990, *Schauplatz eines Dramas* (watercolour/gesso-treated fabric with a grey and purple wash border/card, en tout 18 1/4 x 24 1/2 ins / 46.2 x 62.2 cm) USD 1,320,000. NEW YORK, 2 Oct 1990, *Ageing Venus* (pencil/paper/card, en tout 16 1/2 x 22 ins / 42.2 x 55.6 cm) USD 56,100. NEW YORK, 13 Nov 1990, *Solitary Fir Tree* (1932, oil and sand/card, 21 x 20 ins / 52.5 x 50.8 cm) USD 1,980,000. LONDON, 3 Dec 1990, *Fruit* (1932, oil on sacking, 21 1/2 x 28 ins / 54.6 x 71.1 cm) GBP 726,000. ZURICH, 7-8 Dec 1990, *Reefs in the Shape of Snails* (watercolour heightened with white/paper, 8 x 12 3/4 ins / 20.5 x 32.5 cm) CHF 95,000. NEW YORK, 8 May 1991, *Chinoiseries* (1923, oil and watercolour/card/wood, 12 1/4 x 6 3/4 ins / 31 x 17 cm) USD 209,000; *True Love* (1924, watercolour, gouache and ink/paper/card, en tout 13 1/2 x 18 1/2 ins / 34.6 x 47.3 cm) USD 715,000. LONDON, 26 June 1991, *Small Black Door* (1915, watercolour and gouache, 5 3/4 x 4 1/2 ins / 14.8 x 11.2 cm) GBP 165,000. NEW YORK, 6 Nov 1991, *Small Portraits (with Four Black Quadrilaterals)* (watercolour and ink/Ingres paper/card, en tout 10 x 7 ins / 25.5 x 17.8 cm) USD 264,000. LONDON, 2 Dec 1991, *Moonrise-Sunset* (1919, oil on card, 16 x 13 1/2 ins / 40.5 x 34.5 cm) GBP 814,000. LUGANO, 28 March 1992, *Strange Garlands* (1933, gouache/paper, 11 1/4 x 15 1/4 ins / 28.5 x 39 cm) CHF 190,000; *Balloon Through the Window* (1929, watercolour/paper, 12 1/2 x 9 1/2 ins / 32 x 24 cm) CHF 560,000. NEW YORK, 12 May 1992, *Group of Eyes Wide Open* (1938, oil and gouache/paper, 15 3/4 x 21 3/4 ins / 40 x 55.3 cm) USD 374,000. NEW YORK, 13 May 1992, *Untitled* (watercolour and gouache/paper/card, en tout 9 1/4 x 12 1/2 ins / 23.5 x 31.8 cm) USD 385,000. MUNICH, 26 May 1992, *Tightrope Walker* (1923, lithograph, 17 1/4 x 10 1/2 ins / 44 x 26.5 cm) DEM 69,000. LONDON, 30 June 1992, *House by the Water* (1930, watercolour and ink/paper in a frame by the artist, en tout 17 1/4 x 25 ins / 43.5 x 63.5 cm) GBP 132,000. NEW YORK, 10 Nov 1992, *Concealed Abstractions* (1924, watercolour, gouache and ink/paper/card, en tout 23 x 16 3/4 ins / 57.5 x 42.5 cm) USD 495,000. NEW YORK, 11 Nov 1992, *Sliding* (1930, oil/silk, 13 1/2 x 17 ins / 34 x 43 cm) USD 550,000. NEW YORK, 12 Nov 1992, *Nacelles* (1918, watercolour and ink/paper/paper, en tout 12 1/4 x 8 3/4 ins / 31.1 x 22.2 cm) USD 187,000. LONDON, 30 Nov 1992, *Town Decked with Bunting* (1927, pencil, gouache and mixed media/paper, 11 1/2 x 9 ins / 29 x 22 cm) GBP 616,000. LONDON, 20 May 1993, *Composition with Triangles* (1918, watercolour/paper in a frame by the artist, 12 x 8 1/2 ins / 30.5 x 21.8 cm) GBP 133,500. PARIS, 10 March 1994, *Street in Tunis* (1914, graphite, 7 1/4 x 11 1/4 ins / 18.5 x 28.5 cm) FRF 104,000. NEW YORK, 8 Nov 1994, *Mrs R. Travelling in the South of France* (1924, watercolour and ink/paper/card, 15 x 10 1/2 ins / 38.1 x 26.7 cm) USD 420,500. NEW YORK, 9 Nov 1994, *Diana* (1931, oil on canvas, 31 1/2 x 23 1/2 ins / 80 x 60 cm) USD 1,542,500. PARIS, 19 Dec 1994, *Heavenly Flowers above a Yellow House* (1917, watercolour and gouache/card, 9 x 6 ins / 23 x 15 cm) FRF 780,000. LONDON, 28 June 1995, *Small Still-life of Christmas* (1914, oil on card, 17 x 15 ins / 43.2 x 38 cm) GBP 375,500. NEW YORK, 8 Nov 1995, *Fair* (1940, pastel and charcoal/material/paper/synthetic resin, 16 1/4 x 12 1/4 ins / 41 x 31 cm) USD 112,500. LONDON, 28 Nov 1995, *Scene between Women* (1923, oil and watercolour/thick paper, 15 1/4 x 9 1/4 ins / 39 x 23.7 cm) GBP 287,500. COPENHAGEN, 12 March 1996, *Why is He Running?* (1932, etching) DKK 39,000. MILAN, 19 March 1996, *Something New on an Old Base* (1931, mixed media/paper/card, 9 x 12 1/2 ins / 23 x 32 cm) ITL 483,000,000. ZURICH, 26 March 1996, *Twins* (1933, watercolour, 12 3/4 x 19 1/4 ins / 32.5 x 49 cm) CHF 60,000. NEW YORK, 1 May 1996, *Stage Rehearal* (1925, watercolour and black ink/paper/card, 18 1/4 x 11 1/4 ins / 46.4 x 28.6 cm) USD 332,500. LONDON, 24-25 June 1996, *Brother and Sister* (1930, oil on canvas, 27 3/4 x 17 3/4 ins / 70.7 x 45.2 cm) GBP 2,861,500; *Park in the Freshness of the First Quarter of the Moon* (1926, tempera and oil/plaster glaze/panel, 14 1/4 x 19 1/4 ins / 36 x 49 cm) GBP 551,500. LONDON, 3 Dec 1996, *Mary Magdalene Shortly Before the Resurrection* (1938, gouache, pencil/paper, 11 1/2 x 13 1/2 ins / 29.2 x 34.5 cm) GBP 89,500; *Composition in Red, Orange and Blue (no Green)* (1918, watercolour, gouache and pastel/paper, 6 x 4 3/4 ins /

15.3 x 12.1 cm) GBP 122,500. London, 23 June 1997, *Feier und Untergang* (*Celebration and Downfall*) (1920, oil on paper/panel, 15 1/2 x 11 ins / 39.4 x 27 cm) GBP 364,500. London, 25 June 1997, *Küste bei Gl* (*Coast near Gl*) (1937, white gouache/black-painted paper, 8 x 8 1/4 ins / 20.3 x 20.9 cm) GBP 32,200. London, 9 Oct 1997, *Der Wald der aus dem Samenkorn entstand* (*Wood which was Created from Seed*) (1915, watercolour on paper, 8 3/4 x 8 1/2 ins / 22.2 x 21.5 cm) GBP 243,500. New York, 13 May 1999, *Die Sangerin* (mixed media on paper on board, 20 x 13 ins / 50 x 33 cm) USD 2,400,000. London, 8 Dec 1999, *Coloured Landscape* (1928, tempera and incised plaster on board, 8 x 14 ins / 21 x 36 cm) GBP 900,000. New York, 9 May 2000, *With the Fisherman. Drawing* (1918, watercolour, pencil and chalk, double-sided, 9 x 6 ins / 24 x 16 cm) USD 600,000. New York, 10 May 2000, *Toy* (1931, watercolour, 19 x 27 ins / 48 x 68 cm) USD 600,000. New York, 7 May 2001, *Remote Landscape* (oil on canvas, 16 x 18 ins / 40 x 45 cm) USD 1,400,000. New York, 9 May 2001, *Twins* (1930, oil on canvas, 24 x 20 ins / 61 x 50 cm) USD 1,400,000. New York, 7 May 2002, *Humble Abode* (1928, gessoed gauze over plaster, 15 x 14 ins / 39 x 35 cm) USD 2,000,000. New York, 5 Nov 2002, *Snake Killer* (1923, oil, watercolour, pen and pencil on paper on mount, 16 x 9 ins / 41 x 24 cm) USD 800,000. London, 3 Feb 2003, *Wasservogelenten* (1919, charcoal, watercolour, pen and ink on paper on mount, 9 x 7 ins / 23 x 19 cm) GBP 220,000. Bern, 20 June 2003, *Landscape in Orange with Brown Colour Rhythm* (watercolour, 7 x 10 ins / 18 x 25 cm) CHF 780,000. London, 24 June 2004, *Night in a Southern Town* (1925, pen, ink and wash, 12 x 9 ins / 30 x 23 cm) GBP 280,000. New York, 4 Nov 2004, *Scenery near Pasch* (1936, pastel, 14 x 20 ins / 36 x 50 cm) USD 650,000.

KLEEBERGER, Johann G.
Swiss, 19th century.
Active in Schillingsfürst, in the first part of the 19th century.
Painter, lithographer.

KLEEFT, Henry William Brouwer van der
Dutch, 19th century.
Born 1778, in Dordrecht; died 26 July 1862, in Hamburg.
Painter, sculptor.

Henry van der Kleeft worked for many years in Russia and later in Hamburg and London.

KLEEHAAS, Theodor
German, 19th - 20th century.
Born 9 November 1854, in Germersheim; died after 1914.
Painter. Genre scenes, flowers.

Theodor Kleehaas trained at the Fine Art Academy in Munich. He exhibited in Munich.

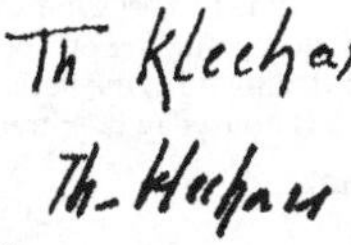

Auction records:
London, 14 April 1967, *Bouquet of Flowers*, Gns 650. London, 19 May 1971, *Children's Games* (1883) GBP 1,250. Cologne, 15 June 1973, *Puppet Theatre*, DEM 2,000. Vienna, 18 Sept 1979, *Romantic Conversation* (oil on canvas, 29 1/4 x 22 ins / 74 x 56 cm) ATS 180,000. Vienna, 5 Dec 1984, *Pinch of Tobacco* (1887, oil on canvas, 30 x 50 ins / 76 x 127 cm) ATS 400,000. Detroit, 26 Oct 1986, *Inn Scene* (1890, oil on canvas, 28 x 43 ins / 71.2 x 109 cm) USD 15,000. New York, 28 Oct 1987, *Child's Game* (oil on canvas, 40 x 30 ins / 101.6 x 76.2 cm) USD 35,000. Munich, 7 Dec 1993, *Children Playing in the Snow* (oil on canvas, 35 x 27 1/4 ins / 89 x 69.5 cm) DEM 10,350. New York, 17 Jan 1996, *Snowball Fight* (oil on canvas, 36 1/2 x 28 1/2 ins / 92.7 x 72.4 cm) USD 5,175. London, 26 March 1999, *Blind Man's Buff* (oil on canvas, 30 x 40 ins / 75 x 101 cm) GBP 9,000. Cologne, 28 Oct 1999, *Boy with Dog in Kitchen Interior* (1886, oil on canvas, 30 x 23 ins / 75 x 58 cm) DEM 26,000. London, 5 April 2001, *Children's Playtime* (oil on canvas, 22 x 28 ins / 56 x 71 cm) GBP 2,800. London, 28 Nov 2001, *Young Girl* (oil on canvas, 39 x 30 ins / 100 x 75 cm) GBP 1,500. Stuttgart, 5 Dec 2002, *Small Girl Sitting with Dog by Mountain Path* (oil on canvas, 39 x 29 ins / 100 x 74 cm) EUR 2,200.

KLEEMAN, Ron
American, 20th century.
Born 24 July 1937, in Bay City (Michigan).
Painter.

Ron Kleeman's work revolves around pictures of lorries, fire-engines, motorbikes and racing cars. He brings the greatest care to the reproduction of reflections from the windows, gleaming chromium plates and bodywork of his vehicles. His painting, photorealist both in its themes and treatment, follows in the footsteps of Bechtle, Goings or Don Eddy, with the success this style has met since the 1970s. He featured in the exhibition *Radical Realism* at the Museum of Contemporary Art in Chicago in 1971 and has since exhibited in New York, Miami, Indianapolis, Paris and Brussels.

Auction records:
London, 3 Dec 1974, *The Way its Spozed to Be 11.30 a.m.*, Gns 3,000. New York, 8 Nov 1979, *Monaco March in May* (1972, oil on canvas, 68 x 89 ins / 172.7 x 226 cm) USD 9,000. New York, 10 Nov 1982, *Sir Cale* (1971, acrylic/canvas, 48 x 48 ins / 122 x 122 cm) USD 4,000. New York, 20 Feb 1987, *Harry Loves Maxine the American Way* (1973, acrylic/canvas, 60 x 60 ins / 152.4 x 152.4 cm) USD 10,000. New York, 8 Oct 1988, *Monaco, Practice in May* (1972, acrylic/canvas, 68 x 90 ins / 172.7 x 228.6 cm) USD 22,000. New York, 27 Feb 1992, *Sear's Point Vettes* (1985, acrylic/canvas, 22 1/4 x 37 3/4 ins / 56.2 x 95.9 cm) USD 8,800. New York, 22 Feb 1993, *Building Site* (1971, acrylic/canvas, 90 x 70 ins / 228.6 x 177.8 cm) USD 1,100. New York, 20 Nov 1996, *Erection Site* (1971, oil on canvas, 70 x 90 ins / 177.8 x 228.6 cm) USD 4,600. New York, 15 May 2002, *Mongoose* (1972, overlap acrylic on canvas, 36 x 48 ins / 91 x 122 cm) USD 48,000. New York, 14 Nov 2002, *Soho Saint 33 and 4 Score* (1974, oil on canvas, 57 x 63 ins / 146 x 159 cm) USD 70,000. New York, 15 May 2003, *Perfect Vision* (1989, oil on canvas, 40 x 66 ins / 102 x 168 cm) USD 68,000.

KLEEMANN, Christian Friedrich Carl
German, 18th century.
Born 10 August 1735, in Altdorf; died 2 June 1789, in Nuremberg.
Painter. Portraits, animals.

Christain Friedrich Carl Kleemann was the son of Nikolaus Moritz Kleemannn. He also trained with J. J. Preisler at the Nuremberg academy. He married the daughter of Rosel Rosenhof. He was famous as a painter and a naturalist and published a work entitled *Contribution to the History of Insects*. He also painted portraits.

KLEEMANN, Christoph Nikolaus
German, 18th century.
Born 24 August 1737, in Altdorf; died 13 September 1797, in Ulm.
Painter.

Christoph Nikolaus Kleemann was the son of Nikolaus Moritz Kleemann.

KLEEMANN, Georg
German, 19th - 20th century.
Born 1863, in Oberwurmbach/Mittelfranken; died 1932, in Eutingen.

Worker in precious metals, painter. Jewels.
Eutingen Artists' Colony.

Georg Kleemann studied at the Kunstgewerbeschule in Munich. In 1887, he became a teacher at the state technical school for precious metals (Staatliche Fachschule für Edelmetal) in Pforzheim, and was appointed head teacher of the Kunstgewerbeschule in the town. He supplied models for the jeweller Theodor Fahrner among others. His style was primarily based on floral and insect motifs, but also on shapes, such as the circle, square or triangle. He was also a painter.

BIBLIOGRAPHY:

Hase, Ulrike von, *Schmuck in Deutschland und Österreich. Symbolismus, Jugendstil, Neohistorismus*, Prestel, Munich, 1977.

MUSEUMS AND GALLERIES:

DARMSTADT (Landesmuseum): *Brooch* (c. 1900-1902) - PFORZHEIM (Schmuckmuseum): several items, including a brooch, c. 1900; *Ornamental Comb*.

KLEEMANN, Johann Conrad
German, 18th century.
Born 1741, in Nuremberg; died 1788, in Nuremberg.
Painter. Landscapes.

Johann Conrad Kleemann was the son of Nikolaus Moritz Kleemann.

KLEEMANN, Johann Jakob
German, 18th century.
Born 4 January 1739, in Altdorf; died 1790, in Nuremberg.
Painter, engraver.

Johann Jakob Kleemann was the son of Nikolaus Moritz Kleemann.

AUCTION RECORDS:

LONDON, 21 March 1973, *Hunting Scene* (gouache) GBP 750. LONDON, 7 July 1987, *Art Gallery, with a Nobleman admiring a Picture and a Lady of Quality, seated* (1762, gouache, 6 1/2 x 9 1/2 ins / 16.8 x 24 cm) GBP 12,000. PARIS, 26 June 2002, *Family Dining* (gouache, 7 x 9 ins / 17 x 24 cm) EUR 6,000. NEW YORK, 23 Jan 2003, *Interior of Gallery* (gouache, 5 x 9 ins / 12 x 22 cm) USD 8,500.

KLEEMANN, Johann Wolfgang
German, 18th century.
Born 24 March 1731, in Altdorf; died 3 March 1782, in Bern.
Painter. Portraits, landscapes, mountainscapes.

Johann Wolfgang Kleemann was the son of Nikolaus Moritz Kleemann. He spent some time in Frankfurt and in Swabia. In 1836, he painted a series of views of the Swiss Alps and glaciers for a work by Wolf.

AUCTION RECORDS:

LONDON, 24 Nov 1983, *General View of the Alps and Glaciers from the Castle of Worb* (gouache, 11 1/4 x 19 1/4 ins / 28.5 x 49 cm) GBP 4,000.

KLEEMANN, Nikolaus Moritz
German, 18th century.
Died 7 February 1756, in Nuremberg.
Painter.

For a long time, Nikolaus Moritz Kleemann was official painter at the University of Altdorf. He settled in Nuremberg in 1740.

KLEEN, Anna Beata
Maiden name: Ehenberg
Swedish, 19th century.
Born 6 September 1813, in Stockholm; died 4 February 1894, in Stockholm.
Miniaturist.

Anna Kleen's *Portraits of Charles XV and his Wife* are in the museum in Stockholm.

KLEEN, Thyra af
Swedish, 19th - 20th century.
Active in Stockholm.
Painter, engraver. Portraits.

Thyra af Kleen worked in Munich and Dresden before settling in Rome.

KLEENE, David. See **KLEINE**

KLEENKNECHT, Barent Cornelisz.
Dutch, 17th century.
Born c. 1610; died 1674, in Amsterdam.
Painter. Landscapes, seascapes.

Although Barent Kleenknecht is mentioned by Bredius, it has never been possible to identify a painting by him.

KLEIBER, Anton
Swiss, 16th century.
Painter, draughtsman. History painting.
Lucerne School.

Anton Kleiber worked in Lucerne between 1550 and 1580.

KLEIBER, Anton
French, 17th century.
Active in Strasbourg at the beginning of the 17th century.
Glass painter.

KLEIJN, Lodewijk Johannes. See **KLEYN Lodewyk Johannes**

KLEIMER, Axel Bernhard
Swedish, 20th century.
Born 13 January 1881, in Christianstad; died 1945.
Painter. Portraits, landscapes.

Axel Bernard Kleimer lived in Malmö.

AUCTION RECORDS:

MALMÖ, 2 May 1977, *Summer Landscape* (1920, oil on canvas, 23 1/4 x 32 ins / 59 x 81 cm) SEK 7,300.

KLEIMINGER, Adolph Frederick
American, 19th - 20th century.
Born 4 December 1865, in Chicago; died 1945, in Tucson (Arizona).
Painter.

A.F. Kleiminger studied under Henri Martin. He was a member of the Société des Artistes Indépendants.

KLEIN, Anna
German, 20th century.
Born 16 February 1883, in Nuremberg.
Painter, engraver. Genre scenes, landscapes, animals.

KLEIN, August, or Augusta
German, 19th century.
Born c. 1777, in Berlin.
Painter.

August Klein studied with Overbeck in Rome in 1821. In the same year she exhibited paintings on religious subjects in Dresden. In 1831 she exhibited at the Paris Salon. Her painting *The Entombment* is housed in the Strasbourg Museum.

KLEIN, Bernat
Serb, 20th century.
Born 1922, in Senta.
Active in Great Britain.
Painter.

Bernat Klein was born in Serbia in an area close to the Romanian and Hungarian borders, but was educated in Czechoslovakia and then at the Bezalel school of art in Jerusalem. His artistic sensitivities were very strongly marked by the light and colours of Central Europe. He went to live in Scotland on the outbreak of World War II. His career really took off in 1945 when he graduated from the Textile Technology Department at Leeds University, Yorkshire, and shortly thereafter was appointed chief designer for Munrospun in Edinburgh. He started painting during this time.

In some of his paintings inspired by flowers, there are affinities with the Vienna Secession. He was fascinated by the way colours continually change in different lights, a phenomenon he attempted to analyse and simplify. In parallel with this, he put his experiments into industrial practice. He designed haute couture fabrics for fashion houses in Paris, winning international acclaim for his work with Chanel in 1962. Perfectly at ease in the use of oils, he gradually introduced the knife, the spatula and the brush. Some of his works tend towards lyrical Abstraction, while others are reminiscent of low reliefs.

Solo exhibitions include London (1966, 1969, 1972); Newcastle (1970); Johannesburg (1971 and 1972); Cape Town (1972); Kirkcaldy (1976); and Edinburgh (1993).

Bibliography:

L'Atelier de Bernat Klein, auction catalogue, Glasgow, November 24, 1994.

KLEIN, Bernhard
German, 20th century.
Born 1888, in Hamburg; died 1968, in Berlin.
Painter. Figures.
Neue Sachlichkeit (New Objectivity).

Auction records:

Copenhagen, 30 May 1990, *Stage Set (Königsberg)* (1951, oil on canvas, 27½ x 24½ ins / 70 x 62 cm) DKK 20,000. Munich, 1-2 Dec 1992, *Occupant of the Attic* (1956, gouache and watercolour, 11¾ x 15¼ ins / 30 x 38.5 cm) DEM 1,955. Hamburg, 9 June 2000, *House with Horse Carriage* (1948, oil on canvas laid on board, 22 x 27 ins / 55 x 69 cm) DEM 4,500. Hamburg, 9 June 2001, *Night Time Street* (1949, watercolour, 11 x 15 ins / 29 x 39 cm) DEM 4,200. Detroit, 12 Dec 2003, *Dutch Genre Scene* (c. 1925, oil on canvas, 35 x 47 ins / 89 x 119 cm) USD 2,500.

KLEIN, Bettina
French, 20th century.
Born 1898, in Niederroedern; died 1986.
Painter (gouache), watercolourist, draughtswoman.
Religious subjects, figures, portraits, flowers.

Bettina Klein exhibited in Paris at the Salon d'Automne and the Salon des Indépendants from 1922.

KLEIN, Catharina, also known as Prussian Eylau
German, 19th century.
Born 4 November 1861, in Preussisch Eylau.
Painter, watercolourist. Flowers.

Catharina Klein exhibited in Berlin from 1890.

KLEIN, Cesar
German, 20th century.
Born 14 September 1876, in Hamburg; died 1954, in Pensdorf, near Lübeck.
Active in Steglitz.
Painter, watercolourist. Landscapes.

Cesar Klein took part in the Grosse Berliner Kunstausstellung in 1909.

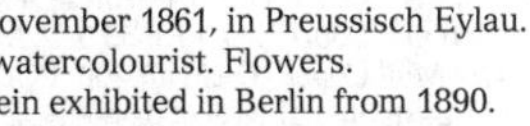

Auction records:

Cologne, 28 Nov 1987, *Harlequin* (tempera, 10¾ x 7½ ins / 27.4 x 19 cm) DEM 4,600. Heidelberg, 5-13 April 1994, *Monte Pincio in Rome* (1914, watercolour, 16½ x 13½ ins / 41.6 x 34.3 cm) DEM 1,350. London, 25 June 1996, *In the Cafe* (1920, oil on canvas, 19¾ x 25½ ins / 50 x 65 cm) GBP 29,900. Berlin, 5 June 1999, *Musicians* (1929, oil on canvas, 39 x 34 ins / 99 x 86 cm) DEM 25,000. Berlin, 26 Nov 1999, *Madonna* (c. 1917, oil on canvas, 67 x 59 ins / 170 x 150 cm) DEM 80,000. Boston, 9 March 2001, *Harbour View* (1912, oil on canvas, 27 x 31 ins / 68 x 78 cm) USD 15,000. Berlin, 30 June 2001, *Harbour* (1917, oil on canvas, 28 x 31 ins / 70 x 80 cm) DEM 52,000. Cologne, 4 Dec 2002, *Seated Female Nude* (gouache, 14 x 17 ins / 35 x 43 cm) EUR 2,000. Hamburg, 2 Dec 2003, *Song of the Sibyls* (1946, 27 x 31 ins / 69 x 79 cm) EUR 6,500. Munich, 24 March 2004, *Fishing Boats on the Southern Coast* (oil on canvas, 28 x 31 ins / 70 x 80 cm) EUR 14,000. Berlin, 12 June 2004, *Still-life with Flower Pots and Jug. Portrait of a Woman in a Hat* (1911, oil on canvas, double-sided, 20 x 24 ins / 50 x 62 cm) EUR 15,000.

KLEIN, Daniel, the Elder
German, 17th - 18th century.
Born 1672, in Danzig (now Gdansk, Poland); died 1744, in Danzig.
Painter.

Auction records:

Paris, 16 Dec 1997, *Portrait of George Clifford holding a Hyacinth* (1736, oil on canvas, 28¼ x 24¼ ins / 72 x 61.5 cm) FRF 15,000.

KLEIN, Daniel, the Younger
German, 18th century.
Active in Paris.
Painter.

Daniel Klein the Younger was the son of Daniel Klein the Elder. He is known for his portraits, said to be a very good likeness, of the Dauphin and Dauphine.

KLEIN, Dominik
German, 18th century.
Active in Troppau (now Opava, Czech Republic) in 1744.
Painter, fresco artist, miniaturist.

A number of altarpieces by Dominik Klein have survived.

KLEIN, Franz
Austrian, 19th century.
Born 27 April 1779, in Vienna.
Sculptor.

Franz Klein studied with Martin Fischer in Vienna, but soon left for Rome. He returned in 1820, after which he carved busts and tombs.

KLEIN, Friedrich Emil
German, 19th - 20th century.
Born 3 March 1845, in Elberfeld; died 1 December 1912, in Düsseldorf.
Painter. History painting, portraits.

Friedrich Emil Klein trained under J. Schrader and at the Art Schools in Düsseldorf, Antwerp and Berlin.

KLEIN, Frits, Frédéric or Fred
Dutch, 20th century.
Born 8 April 1898, in Bandoeng, Java; died 1990.
From c. 1920 active in France.
Painter (including gouache), engraver, decorative designer. Scenes with figures, figures, nudes, animals. Stage sets.

Frits Klein was the father of Yves Klein and the husband of Marie Raymond. He executed stage sets and costumes for the Amsterdam Opera House's performances of: *Cosi Fan Tutte* by Mozart, and *Die Fledermaus* (*The Bat*) by J. Strauss. He worked on the decoration of the Côte d'Azur Pavilion at the World Fair in 1937.

His subject matter, including beaches, circuses, flowers and especially horses in a natural setting, were developed in an unreal light, reminiscent at times of Odilon Redon. He exhibited in Paris at the Salon d'Automne, Salon des Tuileries, Salon des Indépendents and Salon des Surindépendents.

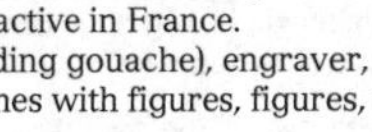

Auction records:
Amsterdam, 7 Nov 1978, *Figures and Horses* (oil on canvas, 19 x 23½ ins / 48 x 60 cm) NLG 7,500. Paris, 16 Oct 1988, *Parasols on the Beach* (oil on canvas, 23½ x 28¾ ins / 60 x 73 cm) FRF 13,000. Amsterdam, 22 May 1991, *Gathering on a Terrace* (oil on card, 7½ x 12¾ ins / 19 x 32.5 cm) NLG 6,325. Amsterdam, 23 May 1991, *Horses* (gouache on paper, 8¼ x 10¼ ins / 20.7 x 26 cm) NLG 2,070. Amsterdam, 12 Dec 1991, *Nude Seated* (1926, oil on canvas, 25½ x 19¾ ins / 65 x 50 cm) NLG 1,725. Amsterdam, 19 May 1992, *Women on a Terrace* (oil on canvas, 18 x 22 ins / 46 x 55 cm) NLG 3,450. Amsterdam, 31 May 1995, *Horses* (oil on card, 15 x 18 ins / 38 x 46 cm) NLG 3,068. Amsterdam, 5 June 1996, *Horseman* (oil on canvas, 24 x 22 ins / 61 x 56 cm) NLG 2,875. Amsterdam, 18 Jan 2000, *Summer Day on the Beach* (oil on paper on canvas, 15 x 18 ins / 38 x 46 cm) NLG 9,500. Amsterdam, 18 Jan 2000, *Beach* (oil on canvas, 21 x 26 ins / 54 x 65 cm) NLG 15,000. Amsterdam, 19 June 2001, *Horses* (oil on canvas, 20 x 24 ins / 50 x 60 cm) NLG 7,000. Amsterdam, 19 June 2001, *Beach* (1927, oil on canvas, 13 x 18 ins / 33 x 46 cm) NLG 8,500. The Hague, 6 Nov 2002, *Horses in Pasture* (oil on canvas, 18 x 22 ins / 46 x 55 cm) EUR 2,400. Amsterdam, 2 Dec 2003, *Garden Scene* (oil on canvas on board, 7 x 15 ins / 17 x 38 cm) EUR 2,400. Amsterdam, 8 June 2004, *Three Horses between Trees with a Setting Sun* (oil on canvas, 26 x 32 ins / 65 x 81 cm) EUR 4,200. Paris, 16 June 2004, *Self-portrait* (1923, oil on canvas, 24 x 20 ins / 60 x 50 cm) EUR 3,800.

KLEIN, Georg Gottfried Christian

German, 19th century.
Born 7 September 1805, in Nuremberg; died 7 June 1826, in Nuremberg.
Draughtsman, engraver (etching).

G. G. C. Klein was the brother of Johann Adam Klein, and a pupil of Ambrosius Gabler and Reindel. He painted landscapes from nature. As an engraver, he reproduced works by his brother and other masters, notably Karel du Jardin and Berchem.

KLEIN, Georges André

French, 20th century.
Born 28 December 1901; died 1992.
Painter. Nudes, still-lifes.

Georges André Klein studied at the Académie Julian. He worked with Bourdelle, patinating plasters and drawing maquettes. He was a friend of Loutreuil and was influenced by his work. Klein lived in Spain, Morocco, Madagascar and the Sahara and made trips to Portugal and Mali in 1968.

He exhibited in Paris at the Salon d'Automne, of which he became a member, and at the Salon des Indépendants and the Salon des Tuileries. He was a member of the Société Nationale des Beaux-Arts. He was awarded the Madagascar Prize in 1957 and the Prix de la Coopération in 1967. Klein was made a Chevalier de la Légion d'Honneur and in 1973 the French State purchased his *Woman at her Toilette*

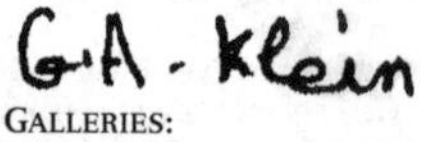

Museums and Galleries:
Paris (MAMVP): *Nude Madagascan Girl* (1937).

Auction records:
Paris, 7 March 1949, *By a Canal*, FRF 11,600. Paris, 15 March 1979, *Public Garden* (oil on canvas, 28¾ x 36¼ ins / 73 x 92 cm) FRF 6,200. Paris, 11 Dec 1991, *Courtyard of the Bahia Palace in Marrakesh* (oil on canvas, 36¼ x 19¾ ins / 92 x 50 cm) FRF 22,500. Paris, 29 Nov 1993, *Painters of Poetic Reality* (1947, oil on canvas, 47¼ x 76½ ins / 120 x 194 cm) FRF 13,000; *Moroccan Woman with an Orange-coloured Dress* (oil on canvas, 39¼ x 25½ ins / 100 x 65 cm) FRF 23,000. Paris, 16 Nov 1999, *Young Girl in Purple. Moroccan Woman in Pink Scarf* (oil on canvas, a pair, 39 x 20 ins / 100 x 50 cm) FRF 30,000. Paris, 16 Nov 1999, *Young Man in Blue. Young Girl in Red* (oil on canvas, a pair, 45 x 23 ins / 115 x 58 cm) FRF 50,000. Paris, 18 June 2001, *Aida in Yellow* (oil on canvas, 31 x 26 ins / 80 x 65 cm) FRF 36,000. Paris, 17 Dec 2001, *Young Girl in Pink* (oil on canvas, 36 x 26 ins / 92 x 65 cm) FRF 45,000.

KLEIN, Johann

Austrian, 19th century.
Born 7 March 1823, in Altlerchenfeld; died 8 May 1883, in Venice.
Painter.

Johann Klein studied with Fuhrich at the Akademie der bildenden Künste in Vienna. He worked mainly in this city. He is known for his designs for the stained glass windows in the churches in Kempen and Bocholt and the frescoes he painted in Vienna, Cracow and Cologne. He was a member of the Akademie in Vienna.

KLEIN, Johann Adam

German, 19th century.
Born 24 November 1792, in Nuremberg; died 21 May 1875, in Munich.
Painter, watercolourist, engraver, draughtsman.
Battles, animals, landscapes.

Johann Adam Klein studied with Zwingen at the school of fine arts in Nuremberg, and from 1805 he studied engraving with W. Gahler. From 1811 to 1815, he attended the Akademie der bildenden Künste in Vienna and travelled through Austria-Hungary. In 1815, he returned to Nuremberg, then went to work in Frankfurt and Lachlens. He returned to Vienna in the company of Chr. Ehrard, and in 1819 he visited Rome and Naples. In 1821, he settled in Nuremberg again and worked there until 1839, when he left for Munich. As an engraver, he reproduced portraits, views, genre scenes and animals.

Bibliography:
Schwemmer, W., *Johan Adam Klein: ein Nürnberger Meister des 19 Jahrh.*, Nürnberg, 1966.

Museums and Galleries:
Berlin: *Hungarian Carters; Walachian Wagons; Animal Trainers* - Bremen: *Landscape* - Kaliningrad: *Coaches and Horses near the Danube* - Mainz: *Coachman Resting* - Munich: *The Tiber near Rome; Horses.*

Auction records:
Vienna, 1823, *Man Riding a Horse Used to Pull Boats* (drawing) FRF 36; *Haywain* (watercolour) FRF 36. Paris, 27 April 1950, *Cavalrymen in a Courtyard*, FRF 53,000. Munich, 15-17 March 1967, *The Mail Coach*, DEM 10,200. Cologne, 17 Oct 1969, *Interior of a Stable*, DEM 9,000. Vienna, 9 June 1970, *The Coaching Inn*, ATS 38,000. Munich, 29 May 1976, *Soldiers and Horses at the Smithy* (1825, watercolour/pencil outlines, 11½ x 15¼ ins / 29 x 39 cm) DEM 2,700. New York, 13 Oct 1978, *Peasant and Horses in the Stable* (1857, oil on canvas, 13¾ x 19 ins / 35 x 48 cm) USD 15,000. Munich, 28 Nov 1979, *The Castle of Durrenstein* (1913, pencil and wash, 9½ x 13¼ ins / 24 x 33.7 cm) DEM 9,000. New York, 30 Oct 1980, *People and Horses outside the Inn* (1846, oil on canvas, 18½ x 23¾ ins / 47 x 60.5 cm) USD 29,000. Munich, 26 Nov 1981, *View of Koblenz* (1815, pen and pencil, 9 x 12¾ ins / 23 x 32.5 cm) DEM 5,500. Cologne, 18 Nov 1982, *At the Smithy* (oil on canvas, 22 x 30¼ ins / 56 x 77 cm) DEM 5,200. London, 29 Nov 1984, *Market Scene in Vienna* (1812, pen and pencil, 6 x 7½ ins / 15.5 x 19 cm) GBP 1,000. Hamburg, 5 June 1985, *The Painter on his Travels* (1819, etching, 8 x 10½ ins / 20.5 x 26.6 cm) DEM 2,500. Munich, 23 Oct 1985, *View of Nuremberg Mögeldorf* (1839, oil on canvas, 16¼ x 22 ins / 41.5 x 56 cm) DEM 22,000. Munich, 5 June 1986, *Slovakian Carters* (pen and watercolour/pencil outlines, 8¼ x 12½ ins / 21 x 32 cm) DEM 2,800. Munich, 13 May 1987, *The Horse Fair* (1841, oil on canvas, 11½ x 14 ins / 29 x 35.7 cm) DEM

20,000. AMSTERDAM, 2 May 1990, *Gypsy Women Resting in a Cowshed with Horses and a Donkey* (1852, oil on canvas, 16 x 21 1/2 ins / 40.6 x 54.7 cm) NLG 32,200. MUNICH, 10 Dec 1992, *Bagpiper with Two Children* (pencil/paper, 5 3/4 x 6 1/4 ins / 14.5 x 16 cm) DEM 3,164. MUNICH, 21 June 1994, *Soldiers* (pencil/paper/paper, 5 1/4 x 7 ins / 13.5 x 18 cm) DEM 2,070. HEIDELBERG, 8 April 1995, *Mounted Cossack* (1815, watercolour, 5 x 4 ins / 12.4 x 10 cm) DEM 3,800. LONDON, 15 March 1996, *Italian Peasant Resting on the Way to Market* (1868, oil on canvas, 11 3/4 x 15 3/4 ins / 30 x 40 cm) GBP 10,120. MUNICH, 2 Dec 1997, *Peasant Resting, with a Loaded Mule* (1822, watercolour/paper, 6 3/4 x 9 3/4 ins / 17 x 25 cm) DEM 10,200. NURNBERG, 22 April 1999, *Cart with Horses by Blacksmith's in Knoblauchsland* (1831, oil on canvas, 12 x 15 ins / 30 x 38 cm) DEM 39,000. MUNICH, 30 Nov 1999, *Polish Soldier from Lancier Garde* (1815, pencil and watercolour, 6 x 9 ins / 14 x 22 cm) DEM 3,800. MUNICH, 8 Nov 2000, *Hungarian Farmer* (1858, watercolour, 10 x 13 ins / 25 x 33 cm) DEM 6,500. MUNICH, 8 Nov 2000, *Horses before Inn* (1864, oil on canvas, 13 x 17 ins / 32 x 43 cm) DEM 12,500. VIENNA, 14 May 2001, *Scene with Hussars on Horses* (watercolour, pen and wash heightened with white, 15 x 19 ins / 37 x 47 cm) ATS 260,000. BERLIN, 31 May 2002, *Self-portrait with Woman* (1817, watercolour, 4 x 6 ins / 9 x 14 cm) EUR 5,200. NURNBERG, 20 June 2002, *Resting by Mountain Lake* (1843, oil on board, 16 x 22 ins / 40 x 55 cm) EUR 21,000. NURNBERG, 26 June 2003, *Resting outside Village in Frank Area* (1842, oil on panel) EUR 8,500. ERLANGEN, 12 July 2003, *Resting outside the City* (1834, oil on canvas, 29 x 37 ins / 74 x 94 cm) EUR 9,000. MUNICH, 16 June 2004, *Ponte Agiore in Tivoli* (1821, oil on cardboard, 7 x 9 ins / 17 x 23 cm) EUR 4,800. LUCERNE, 16 June 2004, *Crashed Beer Transport Coach* (1864, oil on canvas, 13 x 17 ins / 32 x 42 cm) CHF 32,000.

KLEIN, Johann Evangelist
German, 18th - 19th century.
Born c. 1750, in Wiesensteig; died 1815, in Munich.
Painter.

Johann Evangelist Klein worked for the porcelain factory at Nymphenburg. He then went to Munich, where he set up as an artist.

KLEIN, Johann Josef Friedrich
French, 19th century.
Born 31 December 1803, in Strasbourg; died 23 January 1855, in Strasbourg.
Painter, illustrator. History painting, portraits.

Johann Klein was a pupil of Gabriel Guérin and Picot in Paris. He later spent time in Rome, Florence and Pisa. He returned to Strasbourg in 1839.

KLEIN, Jules Auguste (Abbé)
French, 20th century.
Painter.

Jules Auguste Klein took part in various exhibitions in Paris and the French provinces.

KLEIN, Jürgen
German, 20th century.
Born 1924, in Berlin.
Painter and sculptor.

Jürgen Klein studied physics and mathematics before deciding to opt for painting. He has been exhibiting in Berlin and Germany since 1968.

AUCTION RECORDS:
COLOGNE, 3 Dec 1976, *Cordula* (bronze, h. 24 1/2 ins / 62 cm) DEM 2,300. ZURICH, 29 Aug 1984, *Young Boy* (bronze, 19 1/4 x 6 x 4 ins / 49 x 15 x 10 cm) CHF 4,250.

KLEIN, Karl
Czech, 20th century.
Born 25 May 1898, in Nymburk; deported in 1943.
Active in France.
Painter, sculptor. Portraits, genre scenes, landscapes.

After working in Prague and Berlin, Karl Klein settled in Paris. He worked primarily on landscapes depicting various Paris suburbs.

BIBLIOGRAPHY:
Nieszawer, Nadine/Boyé, Marie/Lanzmann, Claude (preface), *Peintres juifs de l'école de Paris 1905-1939*, Denoël, Paris, 2001.

KLEIN, Martina
German, 20th - 21st century.
Born 1962, in Trier.
Painter, draughtsman.

Martina Klein lives and works in Düsseldorf. She has been showing in group exhibitions since 1992, including 1995, at the Düsseldorf Kunstverein, the Fridericianum in Kassel and the Cabinet des Estampes in Geneva and 1977, *Abstract: Torie Begg, Martina Klein, Bernard Rousselot, Juan Usle* at the Quartier Contemporary Arts Centre in Quimper. She has had solo exhibitions in 1992 in Düsseldorf, 1993 in Antwerp and 1997 in Glarus, and has exhibited regularly at the Galerie Arnaud Lefebvre in Paris since 1993.

MUSEUMS AND GALLERIES:
DIJON (FRAC Bourgogne): *Untitled* (1994, oil on canvas).

KLEIN, Max
Hungarian, 19th century.
Born 27 January 1847, in Gönc; died 6 September 1908, in Berlin.
Active in Berlin.
Sculptor.

Max Klein received an honourable mention in Paris in 1883, and was awarded medals in Munich in 1883 and Berlin in 1890.

KLEIN, Paul
French, 20th century.
Born 20 September 1909, in Longwy-le-Haut (Meurthe-et-Moselle).
Painter, engraver, illustrator, sculptor.

Paul Klein studied under François Desnoyer at evening classes in drawing and under Robert Wlerick in the sculpture studio at the École des Arts Décoratifs in Paris. He worked in a style that is a distant extension of Impressionism. He illustrated numerous books, including some by François Villon, La Fontaine's *Fables*, several novels by Balzac, the *Chanson de Roland* (650 illustrations), and *Til Eulenspiegel*. He exhibited at numerous exhibitions in Paris and in French provincial towns and abroad. He was awarded the Hallmarck Prize and the Prix de la Peinture Contemporaine in 1949. He also received the Sole d'Oro Prize in Italy in 1966.

AUCTION RECORDS:
ANTWERP, 23 Oct 1973, *Landscape*, BEF 42,000. ANTWERP, 25 Oct 1977, *Little Kid* (1966, oil on panel, 29 1/4 x 19 1/4 ins / 74 x 49 cm) BEF 32,000. BRUSSELS, 21 May 1980, *Flat Country* (oil on canvas, 39 1/4 x 47 1/4 ins / 100 x 120 cm) BEF 65,000. DOUAI, 24 March 1985, *Fish Merchants* (1968, oil on canvas, 78 3/4 x 78 3/4 ins / 200 x 200 cm) FRF 30,000. BRUSSELS, 25 Nov 1987, *Bulls, Albi* (oil on canvas, 64 1/4 x 51 1/4 ins / 163 x 130 cm) BEF 200,000. BRUSSELS, 12 June 1990, *Winter* (oil on canvas, 31 1/2 x 39 1/4 ins / 80 x 100 cm) BEF 90,000. ANTWERP, 30 Nov 1999, *Hunting Trophy* (oil on canvas, 51 x 64 ins / 130 x 162 cm) BEF 70,000. BRUSSELS, 6 Dec 1999, *Hut* (oil on canvas, 46 x 53 ins / 118 x 134 cm) BEF 90,000. BRUSSELS, 12 Dec 2000, *Kitchen in Inn* (oil on canvas, 74 x 74 ins / 188 x 188 cm) BEF 80,000. BRUSSELS, 18 March 2002, *Nude Young Woman in Stockings* (oil on canvas, 44 x 31 ins / 113 x 80 cm) EUR 2,200. BRUSSELS, 19 Nov 2002, *Circus* (1969, oil on canvas, 79 x 118 ins / 200 x 300 cm) EUR 2,600. ANTWERP, 5 May 2003, *Untitled* (oil on canvas, 45 x 96 ins / 114 x 243 cm) EUR 12,000.

KLEIN, Philipp
German, 19th - 20th century.
Born 16 February 1871, in Mannheim; died 10 May 1907, in Hornegg.
Painter. Genre scenes.

Philipp Klein was awarded a medal in Munich in 1905.

AUCTION RECORDS:

VIENNA, 14 Sept 1982, *New Dress* (1906, oil on canvas, 31 1/2 x 25 1/2 ins / 80 x 65 cm) ATS 45,000. LONDON, 11 Feb 1987, *Market Day* (oil on card, 27 1/4 x 19 1/4 ins / 69 x 49 cm) GBP 2,200. NEW YORK, 3 May 1989, *Boudoir* (oil on canvas, 20 1/4 x 16 1/4 ins / 51.4 x 41.2 cm) USD 9,990. LONDON, 28 Nov 1990, *Women in an Interior* (oil on canvas, 11 x 15 ins / 28 x 38 cm) GBP 3,300. MUNICH, 23 June 1997, *Horseman in a Summer Landscape* (1905, oil on canvas, 26 x 33 3/4 ins / 66 x 80.5 cm) DEM 12,305. MUNICH, 20 May 1999, *Woman Playing Piano* (1902, oil on canvas, 47 x 37 ins / 120 x 95 cm) DEM 7,000. MUNICH, 26 March 2004, *Girls Playing* (1898, oil on canvas, 12 x 19 ins / 31 x 48 cm) EUR 1,600. STUTTGART, 24 June 2004, *Two Girls Playing in a Summer Landscape* (1898, oil on canvas, 12 x 18 ins / 31 x 46 cm) EUR 1,600.

KLEIN, Pierre
Belgian, 20th century.
Born 1909, in Bund.
Painter, glass painter, watercolourist. Religious subjects, landscapes.

Pierre Klein was trained at the Kunstnijverheidsschool in Maastricht and by Opsomer at the Nationaal Hoger Instituut voor Schone Kunsten in Antwerp.

KLEIN, Raoul
French, 20th - 21st century.
Born 1951, in Thionville (Moselle).
Painter, engraver.

BIBLIOGRAPHY:

Beaumont-Maillet, Laure/Woimant, Françoise/Pernoud, Emmanuel, *De Bonnard à Baselitz - Dix ans d'enrichissements du Cabinet des estampes 1978-1988*, exhibition catalogue, Bibliothèque nationale de France, Paris, 1992.

KLEIN, Richard
German, 20th century.
Born 7 January 1890, in Munich.
Painter, sculptor, engraver. Figure compositions, portraits.

Richard Klein trained at the Fine Art School in Munich. He had the opportunity to paint the portraits of *Field-Marshal Hindenburg* and King *Ludwig III of Bavaria*. He was selected for the ideological propaganda exhibition in Munich in 1937, which was opposed to the exhibition of the avant-garde art of the moment, entitled *Degenerate Art*.

KLEIN, Roelof
Dutch, 20th century.
Born 1915.
Painter.

Roelof Klein's career is poorly documented. It is known only that he taught painting and that comic strip author and illustrator Joos Swarte appears to have studied under him.

KLEIN, Simone Marie
French, 19th - 20th century.
Born 24 October 1878, in Neuilly.
Painter. Landscapes, interiors, still-lifes.

Simone Marie Klein exhibited landscapes and still-lifes at the Salon des Indépendants and the Salon d'Automne in Paris. She also painted interiors of houses in Normandy.

KLEIN, Wilhelm
German, 19th century.
Born 18 September 1821, in Düsseldorf; died 10 July 1897, in Remagen.
Painter. Portraits, landscapes.

From 1831 to 1840, Wilhelm Klein studied with Schirmer. He then travelled in Germany, Italy, Switzerland, the Tyrol, Belgium and Holland. From 1840, he exhibited in Berlin, Munich, Cologne and Dresden.

AUCTION RECORDS:

VICHY, 19 May 1984, *Steamer Going Up-river* (oil on canvas, 31 1/2 x 43 1/4 ins / 80 x 110 cm) FRF 21,000. LONDON, 17 May 1985, *Landscape with Hills* (1874, oil on canvas, 35 x 31 ins / 89 x 79 cm) GBP 1,500. NEW YORK, 21 May 1991, *Old Peasant-woman, Head and Shoulders* (oil on panel, 7 x 6 ins / 17.9 x 15.3 cm) USD 1,760. MUNICH, 22 June 1993, *Evening near Weiher* (1864, oil on canvas, 34 x 42 1/4 ins / 85.5 x 107.5 cm) GBP 11,500. MUNICH, 7 Dec 1993, *View of Spielberg Castle, with Emperor Ferdinand's North Road* (oil on canvas, 15 1/2 x 21 1/2 ins / 39.5 x 54.5 cm) DEM 6,900. COLOGNE, 25 March 1999, *Rhenish Landscape with Small Church on Summer's Evening* (oil on canvas, 11 x 16 ins / 29 x 41 cm) DEM 3,300. COLOGNE, 10 April 2003, *Summer Landscape* (1871, oil on canvas, 31 x 44 ins / 78 x 111 cm) EUR 2,000.

KLEIN, Yves
French, 20th century.
Born 28 April 1928, in Nice; died 6 June 1962, in Paris.
Painter, performance artist, sculptor, mixed media.
Conceptual Art, Body Art.
Nouveaux Réalistes group.

Yves Klein was the son of the Dutch Figurative painter Frederick Klein and the Abstract painter Marie Raymond. He was a self-taught artist. In Nice in 1947 he took his first judo classes, discovered Max Heindel's *Rosicrucian Cosmogony* and met Claude Pascal and Armand Fernandez (later known as Arman). In 1948 he became a member of the Californian branch of the Rosicrucian Society of Oceanside. In 1948 he began to write a personal diary, continuing until 1957. In 1949-1950 he spent time in London, where he worked with a picture framer. During the autumn of 1951 Klein moved to Paris and attended classes in Japanese at the École des Langues Orientales. In 1952 he left for Japan where he became a 4th Dan Black Belt. The martial art of judo was ritualistic, as was his art, which was constantly surrounded by ritual. Klein's book *Les Fondements du Judo* (*The Fundamentals of Judo*) was published by Éditions Grasset. His 'spiritual space' thus gradually developed. In 1954 he published a collection of 10 monochrome plates, prefaced by Claude Pascal, of which two variations exist: *Yves Peinture* and *Haguenault Peintures*. In 1956 he exhibited his 'unicolour' paintings. 1958 saw the start of his 'blue period' in Milan. 1958 was marked by the *Exposition du Vide* (*Exhibition of the Void*) and the *Vitesse Pure et Stabilité Monochrome* (*Pure Speed and Monochrome Stability*) exhibition with Jean Tinguely at the Galerie Iris Clert. The same year, Klein won the competition for the decoration of the opera house of Gelsenkirchen, where he executed his first *Sponge Reliefs*. The architect was Werner Ruhnau, with whom Klein also developed the theory of 'air architecture'. In 1959 he gave two lectures at the Sorbonne on *L'Évolution de l'Art vers l'Immatériel* (*The Evolution of Art towards the Immaterial*) and *L'Architecture de l'Air* (*Air Architecture*). He published his pamphlet *Dépassement de la Problématique de l'Art* (*Beyond the Problematic of Art*) in Belgium in 1959. In 1960 Klein produced his first *Cosmogonies*, paintings executed, for example, by the action of rain on prepared paper. On 27 October 1960 he signed the declaration on Nouveau Réalisme drawn up by Pierre Restany. In January 1961 a retrospective of Klein's work was held in Krefeld. He then left for the USA where his first solo exhibition was held at the Leo Castelli Gallery in New York. In 1962 he married Rotraut Uecker but died a few months later. Their son Yves was born after Klein's death.

At least at first, Klein was seeking to achieve a visual and poetic application of Rosicrucianism, in which myth and prophecy are combined towards some anticipated absolute. Klein initially looked beyond line, beyond form and the organisation of space, concentrating solely on pure colour. He began to produce monochrome pieces, from 1955 onwards painting them in different colours. He became truly monochrome, not only producing each of his works with a single colour but painting the majority of them with the same dark, ultramarine blue that he would later patent (19 May 1960 in Paris) under the name 'International Klein Blue' or IKB. In Rosicrucian terms, blue is symbolic of purity of spirit and Klein's blue possesses an incomparable evocative power, an almost innate strength. Klein created monochrome blue objects such as natural sponges impregnated with pigment, believing that sponges were ideally suited to express the maximum capacity of matter to be impregnated. From 1961 onwards he also produced *Planetary Reliefs*.

Blue - this symbol of his pursuit of the immaterial - became an intuitive force that led to his *Exposition du Vide* (*Exhibition of the Void*) of 1958 at the Galerie Iris Clert in Paris, where visitors were invited into a gallery, the walls of which were absolutely bare but which Klein had repainted white. Here, only the artist's sensibility remained. In fact, for Klein, true pictures create rather than represent. In 1959 he developed his famous *Zones de Sensibilité Picturale Immatérielle* (*Zones of Immaterial Pictorial Sensibility*), created in accordance with 'ritual rules'. For example, fine gold was released (in return for payment) in a place where, unrecoverable, it would return to nature - for example in a river - the purchaser being left with nothing to show for this but his receipt. His desire to articulate the elements of this new and highly symbolic syntax led Klein to produce the gold monochrome paintings known as *Monogolds* which symbolise 'the currency of the absolute, this other part of gold required for transfers of the immaterial'. The golden surface of these works is enhanced by numerous fragments of gold leaf in relief. In the triptych *Monoblue, Monopink, Monogold* of 1960, Klein combined blue, pink and gold to illustrate the 'trilogy of colours of flame according to the cosmogony of the Rosicrucians'. His work *Here Lies Space (RP 3)* of 1960 appears to combine the main alchemist components of his declension of the immaterial.

One of the possible characteristics of this enterprise is the involvement of unharnessed forces which the artist must select and capture. Klein invented living brushes in the form of nude women covered in blue paint who made imprints of their bodies on large, white surfaces producing what are known as *Anthropometries*. Between 1960 and 1962 Klein produced some 149 of these *Anthropometries* in a wide range of sizes, some of which were executed as public performances. Some are static, others dynamic. This was not a 'return to the figure' but a continuation of Klein's visual world as a receptacle of forms of life: 'The picture is simply the witness, the sensitive plate which has seen what has happened.' In the same way, in his *Cosmogonies*, Klein introduced other elements of nature whose action is recorded as part of his creative act. He painted with rain, using colour applied in powder form onto paper which was then exposed to the rain, or he used wind, collecting on panels the marks left by its undirected movement. In 1961 he executed his first main series of fire paintings at the Gaz de France test centre at Plaine-St-Denis. In 1962 he exhibited his air architecture ideas at the Pavillon de Marsan as part of the *L'Objet* (*Object*) exhibition. His ideas included plans for the air conditioning of spaces and experimental models (compressed air roofs providing air conditioning of large natural spaces, air beds, walls of fire and light, etcetera). His death meant that he was unable to complete the series of life-size *Relief Portraits* moulded in plaster. Only those of Martial Raysse, Claude Pascal and the painter Arman were finished.

Klein's approach to art was deliberately outside traditional art which, according to the artist, depended on known and accepted means and methods. Neither a Realist nor an Abstract artist, Klein appears to have acted as the catalyst for a form of lyrical art which, on occasions produced in a theatrical manner, became a sensitive space in which art and life were confused, superimposed and enriched; an attempt by Klein to appropriate reality. This new understanding of a work of art and its space resulted in numerous developments, notably with regard to the exhibition space itself. The retrospective exhibition at the museum of Krefeld in 1961, located in the Haus Lange - a house constructed by Mies van der Rohe in the 1920s - deserves particular mention and is considered by some to be at the origin of modern *in situ* exhibitions. Anecdotally Klein is remembered as a likeable illusionist and exhibitionist but there is no doubt that he left his mark on contemporary art. In contrast to the formalism of art in the USA, Klein's work represents more than a simple experiment in post-war European art. His denouncement of the materialist frameworks of art was taken up and extended and his work underlies many trends in contemporary art, the main theme of which can be tangibly appreciated in 'an art that shies away from any material medium', conceptual art, land art and body art being obvious examples.

In 1955, Klein tried to exhibit a monochrome at the Salon des Réalités Nouvelles but the piece was rejected as he refused to add anything that would make it an Abstract work. He subsequently took part in numerous group exhibitions: *Premier Festival d'Art d'Avant-Garde* (*First Festival of Avant-Garde Art*) organised by Michel Ragon and Jacques Polieri at Le Corbusier's Cité Radieuse in Marseilles (1956); the first Paris Biennale (1959); *Works in Three Dimensions* at the Leo Castelli Gallery in New York (1959); *Antagonismes* at the Musée des Arts Décoratifs in Paris (1960) where Klein showed his first gold monochrome *Monogold Frémissant* (*Shivering Monogold*); *New Realists* at the Galleria Apollinaire in Milan (1960); and *Le Nouveau Réalisme à Paris et à New York* (*New Realism in Paris and New York*) at the Galerie Rive Droite in Paris (1961).

Klein also showed his work in solo exhibitions during his lifetime, including: *Yves, Peintures* (*Yves, Paintings*) at the Club des Solitaires in Paris (1955); *Yves, Propositions Monochromes* at the Galerie Colette Alendy (with a catalogue preface by Pierre Restany) in Paris (1956); *Yves Klein, Proposte Monocrome, Epoca Blu* at the Galleria Apollinaire in Milan (1957); a double exhibition, *Yves le Monochrome* at the Galerie Iris Clert in Paris and *Pigment Pur* at the Galerie Colette Allendy in Paris (1957); at the inauguration of the Schmela Gallery in Düsseldorf and at Gallery One in London (1957); *La Spécialisation de la Sensibilité à l'État Matière Première en Sensibilité Picturale Stabilisée*, known by the title *Exposition du Vide* (*Exhibition of the Void*), at the Galerie Iris Clert in Paris (1958); *Bas-reliefs dans une Forêt d'Éponges* (*Low Reliefs in a Forest of Sponges*) at the Galerie Iris Clert in Paris (1959); Klein's first public *Anthropometries* event, featuring three nude models, at the Galerie Internationale d'Art Contemporain in Paris, accompanied by his *Symphonie Monoton* composed in 1949 and performed by 20 musicians (1960); *Monochromes et Feux* (*Monochromes and Fire Pieces*), a retrospective exhibition at the Haus Lange Museum in Krefeld (1961); and *Yves Klein le Monochrome* at the Leo Castelli Gallery in New York (1961).

Following Klein's death, major group exhibitions featuring his work include *Hypermental*, an exhibition on the unreal, the transreal and the reconstruction of reality at the Kunsthalle in Hamburg (2001). Solo posthumous exhibitions include: at the Alexandre Iolas Gallery in New York (1962); *Yves Klein and the Language of Fire* at the Kaiser Wilhelm Museum in Krefeld (1963); *Yves Klein le Monochrome* at the Galerie Tarica in Paris (1963); *Yves Klein le Monochrome* at the Galerie Bonnier in Lausanne (1964); at the Schmela Gallery in Düsseldorf (1964); *Anthologie Rétrospective* (*Retrospective Anthology*) at the Galerie Alexandre Iolas in Paris (1965); at the Stedelijk Museum in Amsterdam (1965); at the Palais des Beaux-Arts in Brussels (1966); at the Jewish Museum in New York (1967); and a touring exhibition that visited the Louisiana Museum in Humlebæk in Denmark, the Institute of Modern Art in Nuremberg in Germany, and the National Gallery in Prague in the former Czechoslovakia (1968). During his life and after his death, cautious French museums paid little attention to Klein, at least until the retrospective exhibition at the Musée des Arts Décoratifs in 1969. Later retrospectives include: a touring exhibition which began in Turin and visited the Museum of Modern Art in Belgrade, the Kunstverein in Hanover, and the Kunsthalle in Bern (1971-1972); at the Château-Musée in Cagnes-sur-Mer (1972); *Anthological Exhibition* at the Stadt Museum in Ludwigshafen (1974); at the Tate Gallery in London (1974); at the Nationalgalerie in Berlin and the Kunsthalle in Düsseldorf (1976); at the Rice University Museum in Houston (1982); a touring retrospective that visited the Contemporary Art Museum in Chicago and the Solomon Guggenheim Museum in New York (1982); at the Pompidou Centre in Paris (1983); a touring exhibition in Japan (1985-1986); and an exhibition at the Hayward Gallery in London (1995).

BIBLIOGRAPHY:

Klein, Yves, *L'Aventure monochrome* (145-page collection of writings, some published). Klein, Yves, *L'Évolution de l'art vers l'immatériel*, RPM, Paris (conference given at the Sorbonne, Paris, 3 June 1959, recorded and copied on disk after Klein's death). Klein, Yves, *Le Dépassement de la problématique de l'art*, Éd. de Montbliard, La Louvière, 1959. Klein, Yves, '*Le Vrai devient réalité*' in *Zero*, no. 3, periodical, Düsseldorf, July 1961. '*Attendu que*' in *Yves Klein*, exhibition catalogue, Alexandre Lolas Gall., New York, 1962. *Yves Klein*, exhibition catalogue, Palais des Beaux-Arts, Brussels, 1966. *Yves Klein*, exhibition catalogue, Jewish Museum, New York, 1967. Restany, Pierre, *Les Nouveaux Réalistes*, Éd. Planète, Paris, 1968. *Yves Klein*, exhibition catalogue, Musée des Arts décoratifs, Paris, 1969. Wember, Paul, *Yves Klein*, DuMont Schauberg, Cologne, 1969. Duparc, Christiane, '*Huit ans de tumulte*' in *Le Nouvel Observateur*, periodical, Paris, February 1969. '*Le Dossier Klein*' in *Chroniques de l'Art Vivant*, periodical, Maeght, Paris, March-April 1969. *Yves Klein*, exhibition catalogue, Gall. Blu, Milan, November 1969. *Yves Klein*, exhibition catalogue, Tate Gall., London, 1974. Restany, Pierre, *Yves Klein*, Éd. du Chêne, Paris, 1974. Stachelhaus, Heiner, *Yves Klein*, Aurel bongers, Recklinghausen, 1976. Rosenthal, Nan, *The Blue World of Yves Klein*, Harvard University, Cambridge (MA), 1976. Restany, Pierre, *Yves Klein*, Éd. du Chêne, Paris, 1982. Millet, Catherine, *Yves Klein*, Flammarion, Paris, 1983. *Yves Klein*, exhibition catalogue, Musée national d'Art moderne, Paris, 1983. *L'Art Moderne à Marseille - La Collection du Musée Cantini*, exhibition catalogue, Musée Cantini, Marseilles, 1988. Stich, S., *Yves Klein*, London, 1995. Restany, Pierre, et al., *Yves Klein - Catalogue raisonné des éditions et sculptures*, Éd. J.- P. Ledeur, Paris, 1999. Descargues, Pierre, *Yves Klein*, monograph, Ides et Calendes, Neuchâtel, 2003.

MUSEUMS AND GALLERIES:

AMSTERDAM (Stedelijk Mus.): *Resonance (MG 16)* (1960); *Blue Harmony (RE 10)* (1960) - COLOGNE (Mus. Ludwig): *Anthropometry* (1960) - EINDHOVEN (Van Abbe Mus.): *Blue Monochrome, Untitled (IKB 63)* (1959) - HOUSTON (The Menil Collection): *Blue Monochrome, Untitled*; *Blue Monochrome, Untitled (IKB)* (1959); *Blue Monochrome, Untitled (IKB 42)* (1960); *Blue Rain (S 36)* (1961) - HUMLEBÆK (Louisiana Mus. for Moderne Kunst): *Large Monopink (MP 16)* (1960); *Blue Sponge, Untitled (SE 100)* (undated) - KREFELD (Kaiser Wilhelm Mus.): *Wall of Fire* (1961) - LONDON (Tate Collection): *IKB 79* (1959, paint on canvas/wood, relief) - MARSEILLES (Mus. Cantini): *Anthropometry, Untitled (ANT 123)* (1961) - NEW YORK (MoMA): *Blue Monochrome, Untitled (IKB)* (1961) - NEW YORK (Solomon R. Guggenheim Mus.): *Blue Sponge, Untitled (SE 160)* (1959) - PARIS (MNAM-CCI): *Green Monochrome (M 77)* (1957); *Maquette de Chèque pour Cession de Zones de Sensibilité Picturale Immatérielle* (c. 1959); *Blue Monochrome, Untitled (IKB 3)* (1960); *Anthropometry from the Bue Period (ANT 82)* (1960); *Ci-Gît l'Espace (RP 3)* (*Here Lies Space (RP 3)*) (1960); *Tree, Large Blue Sponge (SE 71)* (1962); *Fire Colour FC 1* (1962); *Relief Portrait of Arman* (1962) - STOCKHOLM (Moderna Mus.): *Blue Monochrome, Untitled (IKB)* (1958); *Shroud, Untitled (ANT SU 2)* (1961).

AUCTION RECORDS:

PARIS, 14 June 1963, *Handsome Teuton*, FRF 12,000. MILAN, 26 May 1970, *Monocolour* (tempera/canvas mounted on hardboard) ITL 4,500,000. LONDON, 3 April 1974, *Arman, PRI Relief Portrait* (1962, bronze painted blue on gilded background) GBP 15,500. MILAN, 14 June 1976, *Yellow Monochrome* (1957, tempera/card, 6½ x 4¾ ins / 16.5 x 12 cm) ITL 2,200,000. ZURICH, 18 Nov 1976, *Blue Monochrome* (1956, oil on mounted canvas/panel, 31 x 22¼ ins / 78.5 x 56.5 cm) CHF 50,000. NEW YORK, 14 Dec 1976, *Victory of Samothrace* (1962-1973, painted plaster, h. 19 ins / 48 cm) USD 800. NEW YORK, 24 March 1977, *Victory of Samothrace* (1962, painted plaster, h. 19 ins / 48 cm) USD 600. LONDON, 7 Dec 1977, *Blue Monochrome* (1961, mixed media/mounted canvas/panel, 28¾ x 21¼ ins / 73 x 54 cm) GBP 11,000. LONDON, 5 April 1979, *Sponge Relief, RE 11 Blue* (1960, sponges and blue pigment/panel, 78¾ x 65 ins / 200 x 165 cm) GBP 43,000. LONDON, 5 April 1979, *Blue Venus* (blue pigment/bronze, h. 21¼ ins / 54 cm) GBP 2,800. NEW YORK, 19 Oct 1979, *Monochrome Proposition* (1959, gouache, 8½ x 7 ins / 21.6 x 17.8 cm) USD 2,400. LONDON, 30 Nov 1982, *Blue Monochrome, IKB 91* (1959, oil/muslin/panel, 36¼ x 28¼ ins / 92 x 72 cm) GBP 32,000. NEW YORK, 9 May 1984, *Cosmogony of Rain* (1961, ink/mounted paper/canvas, 25½ x 19½ ins / 64.9 x 49.5 cm) USD 22,500. LONDON, 26 June 1984, *Anthropometry* (1960, oil on canvas, 38¼ x 30 ins / 97 x 76.5 cm) GBP 20,000. LONDON, 6 Dec 1984, *Fire Colour* (1959, mixed media/mounted paper/canvas, 32¾ x 26 ins / 83 x 66 cm) GBP 35,000. NEW YORK, 14 May 1985, *Arman* (blue synthetic resin/bronze mounted on card with gold leaf, 69 x 37 x 10¼ ins / 175.5 x 94 x 26 cm) USD 92,500. LONDON, 5 Dec 1985, *IKB 91* (1959, oil on mounted canvas/panel, 36¼ x 28¼ ins / 92 x 72 cm) GBP 130,000. PARIS, 4 Dec 1987, *Blue Monochrome* (pure pigment and synthetic resin, 8½ x 6¼ ins / 21.6 x 16 cm) FRF 200,000. MILAN, 8 June 1988, *F 110* (1961, mixed media, 10¼ x 16¼ ins / 26 x 41 cm) ITL 28,000,000. LONDON, 30 June 1988, *ANT 170* (1960, mixed media, 65¾ x 48½ ins / 167 x 123 cm) GBP 203,500. PARIS, 23 March 1989, *Monochrome* (1957, blue pigment and synthetic resin/wood, 3¼ x 3 ins / 8.5 x 7.5 cm) FRF 230,000. COPENHAGEN, 10 May 1989, *Red Monochrome* (1957, oil on canvas, 7 x 5½ ins / 18 x 14 cm) DKK 105,000. PARIS, 4 June 1989, *Monochrome* (1960, blue pigment and synthetic resin/wood, 7¼ x 5½ ins / 18.4 x 14.2 cm) FRF 300,000. LONDON, 29 June 1989, *AT SU 19* (1960, pigment, synthetic resin and gold paint/linen canvas, 43 x 27½ ins / 109 x 70 cm) GBP 319,000. PARIS, 9 Oct 1989, *IKB 40* (1956, model for the Gelsenkirchen mural, oil on panel, 25 x 19½ ins / 63.5 x 49.5 cm) FRF 1,700,000. PARIS, 13 Dec 1989, *Blue Monochrome* (1959, 8½ x 7 ins / 21.5 x 18 cm) FRF 310,000. PARIS, 18 Feb 1990, *Relief Portrait of Arman, PRI* (April 1962, IKB pigment/panel/gilded bronze, 70 x 37 x 13 ins / 178 x 94 x 33 cm) FRF 2,800,000. MILAN, 27 March 1990, *Anthropometry 145* (blue pigments on mounted paper, 30¼ x 17¼ ins / 77 x 44 cm) ITL 350,000,000. LONDON, 5 April 1990, *IKB 232* (1960, pigment and synthetic resin/fabric/card, 36¼ x 28¾ ins / 92 x 73 cm) GBP 924,000. PARIS, 18 June 1990, *Blue Venus* (1962-1982, polychrome sculpture, h.

27 1/2 ins / 70 cm) FRF 300,000. LONDON, 6 Dec 1990, *RE 36* (1961, pigment and synthetic resin/card, 15 3/4 x 13 3/4 ins / 40 x 35 cm) GBP 132,000. STOCKHOLM, 30 May 1991, *Blue Venus* (blue paint on plaster, h. 26 3/4 ins / 68 cm) SEK 120,000. LONDON, 27 June 1991, *SE 251* (1961, blue pigment/natural sponge/metal stem/stone plinth, h. 29 1/2 ins / 75 cm) GBP 118,800. LONDON, 26 March 1992, *IKB 112* (1961, pigment and synthetic resin/sacking/card, 23 1/2 x 19 ins / 59.5 x 48 cm) GBP 121,000. LONDON, 2 July 1992, *Fire F 2* (burnt card/panel, 57 1/2 x 38 1/4 ins / 146 x 97 cm) GBP 82,500. LONDON, 15 Oct 1992, *Fire FC 5* (1961, pigments and carbonised card/card, 46 x 35 ins / 116 x 89 cm) GBP 83,600. PARIS, 26 Nov 1992, *Blue Venus* (polychrome sculpture, h. 27 1/2 ins / 70 cm) FRF 95,000. LONDON, 3 Dec 1992, *RE 26 Pink, Sponges, Pebbles* (pigment and synthetic resin/card). LONDON, 25 March 1993, *F 89* (1961, burnt card mounted on card, 50 1/2 x 41 1/4 ins / 128.3 x 104.8 cm) GBP 84,000. PARIS, 24 Nov 1993, *Solar Calendar* (1957, yellow monochrome, 3 3/4 x 2 3/4 x 1/2 ins / 9.5 x 7 x 1.5 cm) FRF 60,500. NEW YORK, 4 May 1994, *RE 40* (sponges and pigments in synthetic resin/panel, 78 3/4 x 59 1/4 ins / 200 x 150.2 cm) USD 662,500. PARIS, 17 Oct 1994, *Fire, Anthropometry* (1961, fire paint with anthropometry/card/wood, 35 1/2 x 20 ins / 90 x 51 cm) FRF 230,000. LONDON, 28 June 1995, *IKB 103* (pigment and synthetic resin/fabric/card, 30 3/4 x 22 ins / 78 x 56 cm) GBP 232,500. LONDON, 27 June 1996, *IKB 272* (1957, pigment and synthetic resin/canvas/panel, 30 1/2 x 22 ins / 77.5 x 56 cm) GBP 254,600. LONDON, 5 Dec 1996, *IKB 43* (1958, pigment and synthetic resin/canvas/panel, 30 3/4 x 22 ins / 78 x 56 cm) GBP 287,500. LONDON, 5 Dec 1996, *ANT 154* (1961, pigment and synthetic resin/paper/canvas, 102 x 70 ins / 259 x 178 cm) GBP 441,500; *IKB 160* (1957, pigment and synthetic resin/plaster/panel, 30 3/4 x 22 ins / 78 x 56 cm) GBP 199,500. NEW YORK, 6 May 1997, *IKB 241* (1960, pigment and synthetic resin/fabric/panel, 24 x 19 1/4 ins / 61 x 48.9 cm) USD 266,500. LONDON, 26 June 1997, *IKB 86* (1959, pigment and synthetic resin/card, 36 1/4 x 28 3/4 ins / 92 x 73 cm) GBP 309,500. PARIS, 23 Nov 1997, *SE 78* (pigment/sponge, without casing 7 1/2 x 2 x 1 1/4 ins / 19 x 5 x 3 cm, with casing 12 1/4 x 7 x 7 ins/31 x 18 x 18 cm) FRF 90,000. LONDON, 30 June 1999, *IKB 81* (1957, pigment/synthetic resin on canvas/panel, 39 x 79 ins / 100 x 200 cm) GBP 720,000. LONDON, 9 Dec 1999, *RE 43* (pigment/sponge/synthetic resin on panel, 33 x 15 ins / 85 x 38 cm) GBP 300,000. NEW YORK, 17 May 2000, *RE 40* (c. 1960, sponge/pigment/synthetic resin on panel, 79 x 59 ins / 200 x 150 cm) USD 1,900,000. NEW YORK, 15 Nov 2000, *RE I* (pigment/synthetic resin/sponge, 79 x 65 ins / 200 x 165 cm) USD 6,100,000. NEW YORK, 14 May 2001, *IKB 77* (1955, pigment/synthetic resin on linen, 84 x 34 ins / 213 x 86 cm) USD 2,400,000. NEW YORK, 13 Nov 2001, *Ant 156* (c. 1961-62, blue pigment on paper/canvas, 81 x 32 ins / 205 x 81 cm) USD 1,050,000. LONDON, 6 Feb 2002, *IKB 86* (1959, pigment/synthetic resin on linen/panel, 36 x 29 ins / 92 x 73 cm) GBP 500,000. LONDON, 27 June 2002, *IKB 162* (1958, pigment/synthetic resin on linen/panel, 31 x 22 ins / 78 x 55 cm) GBP 340,000. NEW YORK, 14 May 2003, *Re 2* (1958, sponge/pigment/synthetic resin on board, 53 x 48 ins / 135 x 121 cm) USD 4,700,000. PARIS, 4 Dec 2003, *Fire Painting F 125* (1961, asbestos/cardboard, diptych, 22 x 79 ins / 57 x 200 cm) EUR 290,000. LONDON, 23 June 2004, *Rp. 2 Grenoble* (1961, pigment/synthetic resin on card, 16 x 26 ins / 41 x 65 cm) GBP 180,000. LONDON, 24 June 2004, *Re 29 Blue Sponge Relief* (1957, pigment/synthetic resin/sponge on canvas, 39 x 39 ins / 100 x 100 cm) GBP 950,000.

KLEIN ASTRACHAN, Olga
French, 20th century.
Painter, draughtswoman, designer, ceramicist.

Olga Klein Astrachan was made a Chevalier de l'Ordre National du Mérite.

KLEIN OR, Victor Charles Albert
French, 19th - 20th century.
Born 29 March 1871, in Paris.
Painter, fresco artist.

Victor Charles Albert Klein Or's art is monumental and figurative and executed in a Modernist style. He is known for the triptych entitled *Les Bonnes Heures* (*The Good Hours*). He exhibited at the Salon des Indépendants in Paris and became a member of the Salon committee. He also exhibited at the Salon d'Automne.

KLEIN VON DIEPOLD, Julian
German, 19th - 20th century.
Born 25 January 1868, in Dortmund.
Painter.

Julian Klein von Diepold trained in Düsseldorf. He exhibited in Ghent and Liege in 1892 and 1895.

KLEIN VON DIEPOLD, Leo
German, 19th - 20th century.
Born 27 August 1865, in Dortmund.
Active in the Netherlands.
Painter, engraver.

Leo Klein von Diepold was the brother of Julian and Maximilian Klein von Diepold. He worked initially in Düsseldorf. He then lived in Antwerp and in Noordwijk-aan-See in Holland between 1907 and 1920. After that he returned to Germany and settled in Berlin.

KLEIN VON DIEPOLD, Maximilian
German, 20th century.
Born 1873 or 1878, in Wilhelmshöhe.
Painter, engraver. Hunting scenes, landscapes.

Maximilian Klein von Diepold worked in Düsseldorf. He took part in the Grosse Berliner Kunstausstellung in 1909.

AUCTION RECORDS:

COLOGNE, 24 June 1983, *Landscape* (oil on canvas, 23 1/2 x 31 1/2 ins / 60 x 80 cm) DEM 5,000. COLOGNE, 15 June 1989, *Shooting Party* (oil on panel, 11 x 16 1/2 ins / 28 x 42 cm) DEM 1,400.

KLEIN-CHEVALIER, Friedrich
German, 19th - 20th century.
Born 18 June 1862.
Painter. Portraits, seascapes.

The teacher Friedrich Klein-Chevalier trained in Düsseldorf under Rhenan. He exhibited at the Salon de Paris. He became an associate member of the Salon of the Société Nationale des Beaux-Arts from 1906 onwards, and took part in the Grosse Berliner Kunstausstellung in 1909.

KLEINE, David, or Kleene
Dutch, 18th century.
Born 1753, in Bergen op Zoom; died 1805, in Middelburg.
Draughtsman.

David Kleine was a master artist in Middelburg in 1777 and is known for his drawings of boats.

MUSEUMS AND GALLERIES:

COLOGNE: *Calm Sea* - GOTHA: *Seascape*.

AUCTION RECORDS:

LONDON, 15 April 1983, *Fishing Boats and Other Vessels in an Estuary* (oil on canvas, 20 x 26 1/2 ins / 50.8 x 67.2 cm) GBP 12,000. NEW YORK, 15 Oct 1987, *Dutch Sailing Ships off a Port* (1787, oil on panel, 17 3/4 x 24 3/4 ins / 45 x 63 cm) USD 10,000.

KLEINE, Isidore Carl Heinrich
German, 19th century.
Born 7 August 1810, in Lauchstadt; died 25 October 1844, in Lauchstadt.
Painter. History painting, genre scenes.

Kleine studied with Begas and Johann H. Kretzschmar. He worked in Italy in 1841. He exhibited in Berlin from 1834.

KLEINEH, Oskar Conrad
Finnish, 19th - 20th century.
Born 18 September 1846, in Helsinki; died 16 November 1919, in Helsinki.
Painter. Landscapes, harbour scenes, seascapes.
Oskar Conrad Kleineh worked and exhibited in France. He was awarded a bronze medal in Paris at the Exposition Universelle of 1889, and is probably one and the same as the artist mentioned by the name of Kleinez in the catalogues of the Salon des Artistes Français de Paris.
MUSEUMS AND GALLERIES:
HELSINKI: *Street in Quimper, Port of Douarnenez; Night in Quimper.*
AUCTION RECORDS:
LONDON, 16 March 1989, *View from the Market Place of the South Section of the Port of Helsinki with the Islands of Valkosaari and Suomenlinna in the Distance* (oil on canvas, 27 3/4 x 39 1/4 ins / 70.5 x 99.5 cm) GBP 88,000. STOCKHOLM, 30 Nov 1993, *Seascape with a Hay Transporter Bridge* (oil on canvas, 18 x 15 ins / 46 x 38 cm) SEK 90,000.

KLEINENBROICH, Wilhelm
German, 19th century.
Born 1814, in Cologne; died 22 June 1895, in Cologne-Lindenthal.
Painter. Portraits, genre scenes.
Kleinenbroich studied with Simon Meister and at the academy of fine arts in Düsseldorf.
MUSEUMS AND GALLERIES:
COLOGNE: *Portraits of Thomas Schmitz and his Wife.*
AUCTION RECORDS:
COLOGNE, 11 May 1977, *Students Drinking outside a Tavern* (1843, oil on canvas, 30 3/4 x 38 1/4 ins / 78 x 97 cm) DEM 23,000. NEW YORK, 22-23 July 1993, *Bavarian Bride* (1849, oil on canvas, 28 x 22 ins / 71.1 x 55.9 cm) USD 2,875.

KLEINER, Salomon
German, 18th century.
Born 12 April 1703 or 1700, in Augsburg; died 15 March 1761, in Vienna.
Engraver, draughtsman.
Kleiner was an architect. He engraved plans and views in Augsburg and Frankfurt. He also engraved views of the Belvedere and Viennese churches.
AUCTION RECORDS:
PARIS, 5 April 1990, *View of the Gallery at Pommersfelden* (pen and grey wash, 7 x 16 1/4 ins / 17.5 x 41.2 cm) FRF 75,000. PARIS, 16 June 1993, *Interior View of the Cabinet of Mirrors and Porcelain at Pommersfelden* (pen, Indian ink wash and watercolour, 9 3/4 x 15 3/4 ins / 25 x 40 cm) FRF 50,000.

KLEINERT, Josef Edgar
Austrian, 19th century.
Born 14 April 1859, in Vienna.
Painter.
Josef Kleinert studied with Eisenmenger at the Akademie der bildenden Künste in Vienna. He devoted himself to religious decorative painting.

KLEINERT, Markus Friedrich
German, 18th century.
Born 5 March 1694, in Nuremberg; died 14 May 1742, in Nuremberg.
Painter.
Markus Kleinert was the painter in fashion with the ecclesiastical and lay nobility in southern Germany at the beginning of the 18th century. A large number of his portraits have been engraved.

KLEINERTZ, Alexius
German, 19th century.
Born 16 September 1831, in Cologne; died 9 January 1903, in Cologne.
Painter. History painting.
Kleinertz was a pupil of Michael Weller and collaborated with him on the decoration of the church of St Cunibert. His altarpiece for St Mary's Church in Hanover won him a first prize. Emperor Wilhelm I, the Empress and Pope Leo XIII awarded him decorations.

KLEINEZ, O.. See **KLEINEH**

KLEINHAMMES
German, 20th century.
Painter, draughtsman.
Kleinhammes' works are shown in Germany, and notably in a gallery in Munich. They are little known outside his native country. They belong to 'coldest' Abstraction; a few big forms, executed with a compass and drawing pen, and painted in solid blocks.

KLEINHARD, Johann
Bohemian, 18th century.
Active in Prague.
Painter, engraver.
Johann Kleinhard was a pupil of J.F. Schor. He painted flowers and animals, and landscapes.

KLEINHEMPEL, Erich
German, 20th century.
Born 1874, in Neustadt bei Leipzig; died 1947, in Erbach/Westerwald.
Painter, draughtsman, interior designer, graphic designer. Designs (furniture, fabrics, porcelain, precious metals, jewels).
Jugendstil.
Erich Kleinhempel first trained with Oskar Haebler in his graphics studio in Dresden, then entered the Kunstgewerbeschule in Dresden, where he studied from 1890 to 1893. He then worked in Darmstadt and Einbeck. In 1897, he taught at the Haebler Institute in Dresden. In 1900, with his brother Fritz, and his sister Gertrud, he founded a private art school. He became a teacher at the Kunstgewerbeschule in Dresden in 1910, teaching the painting and drawing of decorative art to the girls at the school. He took over the headship of this school in 1912.

He played an important part in the development of Jugendstil decorative arts in Dresden. He was active in many different areas. He worked for the Dresdener Werkstätten für Handwerkskunst (Dresden Studios). Together with his sister Gertrud he did a great deal of home interior decoration.
BIBLIOGRAPHY:
Kern, Andrea, et al., *Jugendstil in Dresden, Aufbruch in die Moderne*, exhibition catalogue, Staatliche Kunstsammlungen, Dresden, 1999. Ziffer, Alfred, '*Die Geschwister Kleinhempel: Vielfalt im Dresdener Kunstgewerbe*' in *Weltkunst p. 2435-2438*, Munich, 1999.
MUSEUMS AND GALLERIES:
DRESDEN (Kunstgewerbemus.): sample of fabric, before 1914 - MEISSEN (Staatliche Porzellan-Manufaktur) - MUNICH (Die Neue Sammlung, Staatliches Mus. für angewandte Kunst): *Two Glasses* (1905) - PFORZHEIM (Schmuckmuseum): *Necklace* (1908, silver).

KLEINHEMPEL, Gertrud
German, 20th century.
Born 1875, in Leipzig; died 1948, in Althagen near Wustrow.
Illustrator, draughtswoman, decorative designer.
Designs for fabrics, furniture and jewels.
Jugendstil.
Gertrud Kleinhempel studied drawing in Dresden, then in Munich, and made her debut in 1899 as an illustrator in Dresden. From 1900 to 1907, she was head of a private art school that she founded with her two brothers Erich and

Fritz, who were jewellers. She taught fabric creation from 1907 to 1938 at the Kunstgewerbeschule in Bielefeld. She was only the second woman, after Käthe Kollwitz, to achieve the official title of professor. Her work was selected for the principal group exhibitions of decorative art during the first decade of the 20th century: 1899, Dresden; 1902, Turin; 1910, Brussels. She supplied decorative models for the Dresdener Werkstätten für die Handwerkskunst (Dresden Studios). Her work, like that of other artists, was rediscovered thanks to the important exhibition of Jugendstil art in Dresden in 1999: *Jugendstil in Dresden, Aufbruch in die Moderne* (*Jugendstil in Dresden. Beginning of the Modern Age*).

BIBLIOGRAPHY:
Renda, Gerhard, *Gertrud Kleinhempel, Künstlerin zwischen Jugenstil und Moderne*, Historisches Museum, Bielefeld, 1998. Kern, Andrea, et al., *Jugendstil in Dresden, Aufbruch in die Moderne*, exhibition catalogue, Staatliche Kunstsammlungen, Dresden, 1999.

MUSEUMS AND GALLERIES:
BIELEFELD (Historisches Mus.): *Chair* (1905) - DRESDEN (Kunstgewerbemus.): *Glass-Fronted Cabinet* (1906); *Bedroom Furniture* (1901).

KLEINIG, August
German, 19th century.
Born 14 April 1822, in Dresden; died 31 December 1869, in Dresden.
Painter, draughtsman. Landscapes.

August Kleinig was profoundly influenced by Ludwig Richter and often provided his genre scenes with background landscapes.

KLEINIG, Christian
German, 19th century.
Born 19 December 1779, in Dresden; died 26 June 1848, in Dresden.
Draughtsman, engraver. Landscapes.

Christian Kleinig studied with Toscani and Zingg. He is best known for *Bellevue, near Berlin, by Moonlight*.

KLEINJES, J. L.
Belgian, 20th century.
Painter. Portraits.

J.L. Kleinjes took part in the Brussels Exhibition in 1910.

KLEINKNECHT, Friedrich Ernst Wilhelm Georg
German, 18th - 19th century.
Born 25 December 1768, in Bayreuth; died c. 1812, in Ansbach.
Painter, draughtsman.

A *Sicilian Landscape* by Kleinknecht is known, and also that he was interested in large-scale historical painting.

KLEINKNECHT, Hermann
German, 20th century.
Born 1943, in Bad Berneck.
Painter, sculptor.

BIBLIOGRAPHY:
Beaumont-Maillet, Laure/Woimant, Françoise/Pernoud, Emmanuel, *De Bonnard à Baselitz - Dix ans d'enrichissements du Cabinet des estampes 1978-1988*, exhibition catalogue, Bibliothèque nationale de France, Paris, 1992.

KLEINMANN, Alain
French, 20th - 21st century.
Born 1953, in Paris.
Painter, sculptor, lithographer.

Alain Kleinmann is the son of Israeli parents who survived the *Shoah* (Holocaust), of which his paintings all carry reminders. He is currently the only French artist to have had work exhibited at the Beijing fine art museum.

BIBLIOGRAPHY:
Beaumont-Maillet, Laure/Woimant, Françoise/Pernoud, Emmanuel, *De Bonnard à Baselitz - Dix ans d'enrichissements du Cabinet des estampes 1978-1988*, exhibition catalogue, Bibliothèque nationale de France, Paris, 1992.

MUSEUMS AND GALLERIES:
PARIS (BNF, Prints Collection).

AUCTION RECORDS:
PARIS, 8 Oct 1989, *Family Portrait* (oil on canvas, 39 1/4 x 32 ins / 100 x 81 cm) FRF 16,500. PARIS, 26 April 1990, *Reminiscence* (mixed media/canvas, 51 1/4 x 38 1/4 ins / 130 x 97 cm) FRF 38,000. PARIS, 7 Feb 1991, *Memorial* (oil on card and mixed media, 37 1/2 x 24 3/4 ins / 95 x 63 cm) FRF 9,000. PARIS, 14 April 1991, *Theodor Herzl* (oil on canvas, 51 1/4 x 76 3/4 ins / 130 x 195 cm) FRF 21,500. PARIS, 17 June 1991, *Fragment of Memory* (mixed media/canvas, 28 3/4 x 23 1/2 ins / 73 x 60 cm) FRF 18,000. PARIS, 17 May 1992, *Head of Hassidic Jew* (mixed media/card, 33 1/2 x 25 1/2 ins / 85 x 65 cm) FRF 11,000; *Family* (mixed media/card remounted/canvas, 39 1/4 x 31 1/2 ins / 100 x 80 cm) FRF 13,000. PARIS, 6 July 1992, *Fragments of Memory* (lithograph, 31 1/2 x 23 1/2 ins / 80 x 60 cm) FRF 3,500. PARIS, 3 Dec 1993, *Family Photo Composition* (mixed media/canvas, 51 1/4 x 76 3/4 ins / 130 x 195 cm) FRF 30,000. PARIS, 16 Dec 1994, *Water Carrier* (mixed media, 32 x 23 1/2 ins / 81 x 60 cm) FRF 20,000. DOULLENS, 17 Jan 1999, *Temple Entrance* (mixed media, 24 x 29 ins / 60 x 73 cm) FRF 12,000. PARIS, 27 Nov 2000, *Double Portrait* (oil on canvas, 39 x 32 ins / 100 x 81 cm) FRF 13,000. PARIS, 3 Dec 2001, *Souvenirs* (mixed media, 22 x 18 ins / 55 x 46 cm) FRF 19,000. PARIS, 27 Nov 2003, *Childhood Memory* (mixed media, 24 x 29 ins / 60 x 73 cm) EUR 2,400.

KLEINMANN, Alice Adèle
French, 19th - 20th century.
Born 19th century, in Paris.
Painter. Landscapes.

Alice Adèle Kleinmann exhibited in Paris at the Salon d'Automne and from 1904 at the Salon des Indépendants.

KLEINMANN, Joseph
German, 19th century.
Born 1811.
Active in Munich.
Painter (porcelain).

Several paintings on porcelain by Kleinmann after Van Dyck, F. Bol, Dürer, Furini and Guercino are preserved in the Munich Museum.

MUSEUMS AND GALLERIES:
MUNICH.

KLEINMANN, Peter, also known as Peter von Biel
Swiss, 16th century.
Born in Biel; died 1546, in Bern.
Sculptor.

He married Marg. Linserin, who bore him a son, Daniel.

KLEINMICHEL, Ferdinand Julius Theodor
German, 19th century.
Born 5 March 1846, in Rodzonne; died 12 August 1892, in Munich.
Painter. Genre scenes.

Kleinmichel studied at the academy in Königsberg, now Kaliningrad. He then worked in Düsseldorf, Berlin, Leipzig and Munich.

AUCTION RECORDS:
NEW YORK, 9 Oct 1974, *The Pearl Necklace*, USD 3,100.

KLEINSCHMIDT, Johann Jakob
German, 18th century.
Died 30 September 1772, in Augsburg.
Active in Augsburg.
Engraver (burin).

Johann Jakob Kleinschmidt studied with Heckenauer. He engraved religious and historical subjects, portraits and frontispieces.

KLEINSCHMIDT, Johannes
German, 19th century.
Born 22 March 1859, in Niederappenfeld; died 23 December 1905, in Reinhausen.
Painter. Portraits, genre scenes.
Johannes Kleinschmidt studied with Kalitz and Scheusenberg at the Kassel academy, and with O. Seitz in Munich. He exhibited in Berlin and Düsseldorf.

KLEINSCHMIDT, Paul
German, 20th century.
Born 31 July 1883, in Bublitz; died 1949.
Painter, engraver, illustrator. Figures, still-lifes, flowers.
Paul Kleinschmidt trained in Munich in 1904-1905 with Heinrich von Zügel and Peter Hahn. He trained under Anton von Werner at the Fine Art School in Berlin, then settled there. While working independently in Berlin around 1906, he participated in the Secession Exhibitions in several German cities. Despite favourable criticism and offers from Galerie Gurlitt in Berlin, he preferred to retain his independence. In 1927 Erich Cohn, the American collector, organised an exhibition for him in the USA at the Art Institute of Chicago and at Philadelphia Museum of Art. In 1937 his works were included in the exhibition of 'degenerate art' in Munich.

He lived in France during a large part of World War II and many of his works were destroyed by the war or confiscated by the Nazis.

His style was Realist and he was interested in an extremely wide variety of subjects, including nudes, still-lifes and portraits. He was also an illustrator. He was influenced by Adolf von Menzel, Lovis Corinth and also his former teachers Heinrich von Zügel and Peter Halm.

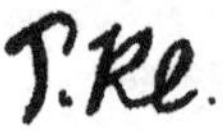

BIBLIOGRAPHY:
Paul Kleinschmidt 1883-1949: Gemälde, Aquarelle, Zeichnungen und Druckgraphik, Galerie der Stadt, Stuttgart, 1983.
Hüneke, Andreas/Lipps-Kant, Barbara/Meier-Graefe, Julius, *Paul Kleinschmidt*, Hatje Cantz, Ostfildern, 1997.

AUCTION RECORDS:
NEW YORK, 19 Nov 1969, *Carnival II*, USD 6,000. MUNICH, 26 Nov 1976, *Ballerina Getting Ready* (1937, oil on canvas, 46 3/4 x 31 1/4 ins / 119 x 79.5 cm) DEM 7,000. MUNICH, 28 Nov 1977, *Equestrian* (1937, oil on canvas, 35 1/2 x 27 1/2 ins / 90 x 70 cm) DEM 6,250. MUNICH, 27 Nov 1979, *Behind the Scenes in a Circus* (1944, watercolour, 25 1/2 x 19 3/4 ins / 64.5 x 50 cm) DEM 3,000. MUNICH, 30 Nov 1979, *Ballerina Getting Ready* (1937, oil on canvas, 46 3/4 x 31 1/4 ins / 119 x 79.5 cm) DEM 10,000. MUNICH, 1 June 1981, *Wasserburg-on-Inn* (1919, watercolour, 13 1/4 x 16 ins / 33.4 x 40.4 cm) DEM 3,200. MUNICH, 7 June 1982, *Ballerina Throwing Her Boots* (1939, oil on canvas, 55 x 39 1/4 ins / 140 x 100 cm) DEM 38,500. MUNICH, 30 May 1983, *Bar Scene* (1938, oil on canvas, 50 3/4 x 25 1/4 ins / 129 x 64 cm) DEM 15,000. COLOGNE, 4 June 1983, *Two Women at the Bar* (1943, watercolour, 27 1/4 x 22 ins / 69 x 55 cm) DEM 6,500. MUNICH, 14 June 1985, *New York, View of Manhattan* (1934, oil on canvas, 39 1/4 x 29 1/2 ins / 100 x 75 cm) DEM 27,000. MUNICH, 6 June 1986, *Carnival in Ulm* (1929, watercolour/pencil outlines, 24 x 23 1/4 ins / 61 x 59 cm) DEM 6,400. MUNICH, 1 June 1987, *Women Undressing* (1947, watercolour and gouache/pencil outlines, 30 3/4 x 22 1/2 ins / 78 x 57 cm) DEM 11,000. MUNICH, 26 Oct 1988, *Still-life of Flowers* (1939, oil on canvas, 24 x 19 3/4 ins / 61 x 50 cm) DEM 29,700. ROME, 21 March 1989, *Two Sisters in a Café* (oil on canvas, 36 1/2 x 30 1/4 ins / 93 x 77 cm) ITL 34,000,000. LONDON, 4 April 1989, *Dancer* (1938, 47 x 35 ins / 119.5 x 89.2 cm) GBP 24,200. MUNICH, 7 June 1989, *Still-life with White Lilac, Daffodils and Fruit* (1926, oil on canvas, 22 1/2 x 16 1/4 ins / 57 x 41 cm) DEM 22,000. LONDON, 27 June 1989, *Young Girl Dressing* (1938, oil on canvas, 49 1/4 x 35 1/2 ins / 125 x 90 cm) GBP 30,800. LONDON, 20 Oct 1989, *Woman Seated* (1937, oil on canvas, 41 1/4 x 28 ins / 105 x 71 cm) GBP 20,900. BERLIN, 30 May 1991, *Still-life with Opera Glasses* (1931, oil on canvas, 24 1/4 x 20 3/4 ins / 61.3 x 52.7 cm) DEM 21,090. MUNICH, 26 May 1992, *Coastal Landscape in the South of France* (1929, watercolour and ink, 14 1/4 x 19 3/4 ins / 36.5 x 50 cm) DEM 9,200. NEW YORK, 24 Feb 1994, *Small Bathroom* (1939, oil on canvas, 49 x 27 1/4 ins / 124.5 x 68.9 cm) USD 90,500. HEIDELBERG, 5-13 April 1994, *Portrait of Woman in Profile from the Left Side* (1939, pencil, 16 1/4 x 12 ins / 41.4 x 30.5 cm) DEM 2,800. NEW YORK, 10 May 1995, *Tease* (1938, oil on canvas, 45 3/4 x 30 ins / 116.2 x 76.2 cm) USD 118,000. NEW YORK, 19 Feb 1997, *Vase of Flowers* (oil on canvas, 23 x 20 ins / 58.4 x 50.8 cm) USD 25,300. LONDON, 9 Oct 1997, *Restaurant* (1938, mixed media/paper, 26 3/4 x 40 1/2 ins / 68 x 103 cm) GBP 28,750. LONDON, 6 Oct 1999, *New York, Manhattan* (1934, oil on canvas, 35 x 28 ins / 90 x 70 cm) GBP 25,000. LONDON, 6 Oct 1999, *Pierrot and Columbine* (1933, oil on canvas, 47 x 33 ins / 120 x 85 cm) GBP 40,000. COLOGNE, 7 June 2000, *Woman with Liqueur Glass* (1935, watercolour and tempera over pencil, 24 x 19 ins / 61 x 47 cm) DEM 26,000. MUNICH, 2 Dec 2000, *Portrait of Margarete K* (1924, oil on canvas, 41 x 30 ins / 105 x 75 cm) DEM 75,000. BERLIN, 30 June 2001, *Concrete Factories* (1931, oil on canvas, 26 x 31 ins / 65 x 80 cm) DEM 40,000. COLOGNE, 4 Dec 2001, *Still-life with Flowers and Cake Dish* (oil on canvas, 28 x 20 ins / 72 x 51 cm) DEM 60,000. MUNICH, 17 May 2002, *Marseilles Landscape* (oil on canvas, 26 x 31 ins / 65 x 80 cm) EUR 14,000. BERLIN, 7 June 2002, *Woman in front of a Mirror* (1922, 13 x 10 ins / 33 x 25 cm) EUR 4,000. HAMBURG, 14 June 2003, *Bar, Blonde Woman* (1938, oil on canvas, 59 x 24 ins / 150 x 61 cm) EUR 30,000. BERLIN, 11 June 2004, *Woman Applying Make-up* (1933, oil on canvas, 35 x 28 ins / 90 x 72 cm) EUR 34,000. BERLIN, 11 June 2004, *Barmaid* (1940, oil on canvas, 61 x 33 ins / 154 x 84 cm) EUR 36,000.

KLEINT, Boris
German, 20th century.
Born 1903.
Painter.
Boris Kleint worked in Saarbrücken. Between 1949 and 1963 he appeared several times in the Salon des Réalités Nouvelles in Paris with abstract paintings, some which showed the influence of Kandinsky, and others that of Léger.

AUCTION RECORDS:
MUNICH, 29 June 1983, *Plastische Windung* (1942, oil on canvas, 50 1/2 x 42 1/2 ins / 128 x 108 cm) DEM 11,000. LUCERNE, 23 Nov 1996, *Unfinished Forms* (1939, oil on canvas, 30 x 30 ins / 76 x 76 cm) GBP 9,000. HAMBURG, 4 Dec 1999, *Composition* (c. 1945, oil on canvas, 9 x 11 ins / 22 x 27 cm) DEM 5,000. LONDON, 25 June 2002, *Play on White* (1940, acrylic on linen, 24 x 36 ins / 60 x 91 cm) GBP 9,000.

KLEINTJES, Jan or Johannes Leonardus, or Kleyntjes
Belgian, 20th century.
Born 24 May 1872, in Rotterdam; died 1955, in Heerde.
Portrait artist.
Kleintjes studied at the academy in Amsterdam from 1891 to 1894. He settled in Nunspeet and then in Heerde. He exhibited in Belgium, Berlin and Liège and took part in the Exposition de Bruxelles in 1910. He was known for his portraits.

BIBLIOGRAPHY:
Kapelle, Jeroen, *Tuin, thee en atelier. Schildersechtpaar Jan Kleintjes en Hedwid Kleintjes-van Osselen*, Walburg Pers, Zutphen, 1999.

Museums and Galleries:
Goningen (Universiteitsmus.).

KLEIST, Emma von
Latvian, 19th century.
Born 29 May 1840, in Lemsern (Kurland); died 17 July 1892, in Riga.
Painter. Landscapes.
After a period spent living in Italy, Emma von Kleist returned to her native Russia. She worked in Riga and Kerklingen.

KLEITSCH, Joseph
American, 20th century.
Born 1885, in Banad; died 1931.
Painter. Portraits, landscapes.
Joseph Kleitsh studied in Chicago, Budapest, Munich and Paris. He won the Gold Medal at the Art Institute of Chicago in 1914 and the Silver Medal at the Painters' and Sculptors' Club.
Auction records:
Los Angeles-San Francisco, 10 Oct 1990, *Indian Women at San Juan Capistrano* (oil on canvas, 20 x 18 ins / 51 x 46 cm) USD 8,800. New York, 18 Dec 1991, *Coastal Landscape* (oil on canvas, 12 x 16 ins / 30.5 x 40.6 cm) USD 3,850. San Francisco, 17 June 1999, *Lakeside Wildflowers, Saugatuck Michigan* (1919, oil on canvas, 30 x 40 ins / 76 x 102 cm) USD 20,000. Los Angeles, 9 Dec 1999, *Angora Cats* (oil on canvas, 21 x 27 ins / 53 x 69 cm) USD 8,500. Los Angeles, 24 Oct 2000, *Rainy Day, Laguna* (oil on masonite, 15 x 20 ins / 38 x 51 cm) USD 10,000. Los Angeles, 24 Oct 2000, *Diver's Cove, Laguna* (oil on canvasboard, 9 x 11 ins / 23 x 27 cm) USD 28,000. Pasadena, 19 June 2001, *Capistrano Mission, Mission Poinsettias* (oil on canvas, 9 x 11 ins / 24 x 29 cm) USD 60,000. Los Angeles, 7 Nov 2001, *Park Avenue, Old Laguna* (oil on canvas, 36 x 40 ins / 91 x 102 cm) USD 300,000. San Francisco, 9 June 2002, *San Juan Capistrano* (oil on canvas, 16 x 20 ins / 41 x 51 cm) USD 60,000. Los Angeles, 20 Nov 2002, *Old Laguna, Foot of Anita Street* (oil on board, 13 x 18 ins / 34 x 45 cm) USD 48,000. Los Angeles, 18 June 2003, *Interrupted Hand* (1911, oil on canvas, 24 x 31 ins / 61 x 80 cm) USD 110,000. San Francisco, 10 Dec 2003, *Park Road* (oil on canvas, 21 x 18 ins / 53 x 46 cm) USD 30,000. Detroit, 12 March 2004, *Still-life of Fruit* (oil on canvas, 22 x 14 ins / 56 x 36 cm) USD 18,000. San Francisco, 8 June 2004, *Le Pont Napoléon* (oil on canvas, 18 x 21 ins / 45 x 53 cm) USD 25,000.

KLEKLER, Hans Ulrich. See **GLÖCKLER**

KLEM, Alfred
French, 20th century.
Born 8 February 1872, in Colmar.
Sculptor.
Alfred Klem studied in Munich under Von Rümann and Eberle. He produced several retables and various other works for churches in Alsace.
Museums and Galleries:
Strasbourg.

KLEM, Théophil
French, 19th - 20th century.
Born 1849, in Colmar; died 20 November 1923, in Colmar.
Sculptor.
After studying in Vienna, Théophil Klem executed various works for churches in Alsace, Lorraine and Switzerland.

KLEMCZYNSKI, Pierre, called Klem
French, 20th century.
Born 31 March 1910, in St-Claude; died 1991.
Active in Bousselange.
Painter, designer. Figures, interiors with figures, landscapes, still-lifes. Stage sets.
Pierre Klemczynski was of distant Polish extraction. He was a set designer for the Théâtre Français before becoming a full-time painter. His work shows reality in an intimist setting. He exhibited at the Salon d'Automne, the Salon des Indépendants and the Salon des Terres Latines in Paris. In 1972 he was awarded the Prix de la Critique and in 1973 the Leonardo da Vinci Prize.

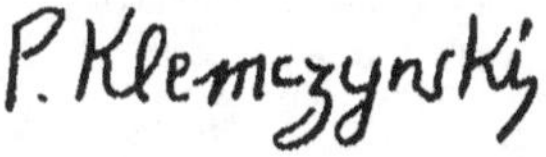

Auction records:
Versailles, 10 Dec 1989, *Bird with Cup* (1968, oil on canvas, 9 1/2 x 13 3/4 ins / 24 x 35 cm) FRF 6,500. Paris, 27 May 1994, *Virgin and Child* (1972, oil on canvas, 36 1/4 x 23 1/2 ins / 92 x 60 cm) FRF 11,000. Paris, 20 March 1998, *Landscape* (1955, oil on canvas, 10 1/2 x 16 1/4 ins / 26.5 x 41 cm) FRF 5,700.

KLEMENS
German, 15th century.
Born in Posen (now Poznan, Poland); died c. 1502.
Painter.
Klemens decorated the Benedictine convent in Lubin and the Dominican church in Koscian.

KLEMENS, Emil
German, 19th century.
Born 5 October 1866, in Berlin.
Sculptor.
Klemens carved a number of monuments in honour of Wilhelm I, emperor of Germany.

KLEMENSIEWICZ, Piotr
French, 20th - 21st century.
Born 1956, in Marseilles.
Painter, sculptor, engraver, screen printer.
Piotr Klemensiewicz is of Polish descent. He studies and teaches at the École d'Art of Luminy in Marseilles. His painting serves as a pretext, not to narrate a history or an event, but to play with colour and representational shapes with vivacity and humour, drawn in a simple, sober style in a checkerboard pattern, bringing out all the richness of pictorial matter.

He has appeared at exhibitions of the Avignon group and in the Paris Galerie Gutharc-Ballin from 1986. He has shown his works in solo exhibitions, mainly in 1986; in 1988 and 1989, a double exhibition at the Musée des Beaux-Arts, Carcassone and the Musée at Toulon; Galerie Gill Favre, Lyons; in 1991, Galerie Gutharc-Ballin, Paris; in 1991, Galerie de Marseille; in 1993, Musée and Centre d'Art Contemporain, château des Ducs de Wurtemberg at Montbéliard; in 1996, Espace 13, Art Contemporain, Aix-en-Provence.
Bibliography:
Pailhas, R./Vedrenne, E., *Klemensiewicz*, Arca, Marseilles, 1986. *L'Art Moderne à Marseille - La Collection du Musée Cantini*, exhibition catalogue, Musée Cantini, Marseilles, 1988. *Piotr Klemensiewicz: travaux récents*, Musée des Beaux-Arts, Carcassonne, musée de Toulon, Toulon, 1989. Beaumont-Maillet, Laure/Woimant, Françoise/Pernoud, Emmanuel, *De Bonnard à Baselitz - Dix ans d'enrichissements du Cabinet des estampes 1978-1988*, exhibition catalogue, Bibliothèque nationale de France, Paris, 1992.
Museums and Galleries:
Marseilles: *Youth of Naples* - Paris (FNAC) - Paris (MAM-VP) - Tournus (Mus. Greuze).

KLEMENTEV, Eugen
Russian, 20th century.
Born 1901, in Rybinsk.
Active in France.
Painter. Figures, still-lifes.

Eugen Klementev exhibited at the Salon des Artistes Indépendants and the Salon d'Automne in Paris from 1926. His paintings mix Cubist representations with Surrealist elements.

AUCTION RECORDS:

CLERMONT-FERRAND, 14 May 1987, *Still-life with Bottle* (1927, oil on canvas) FRF 45,000. PARIS, 16 Oct 1988, *Still-life* (oil on canvas, 24 x 18 ins / 61 x 46 cm) FRF 13,000.

KLEMENTIEV, Boris

Russian, 20th - 21st century.
Born 1972 (?).
Painter. Genre scenes, interiors, landscapes, seascapes.

AUCTION RECORDS:

PARIS, 18 Oct 1993, *In Summer* (oil on canvas, 9 x 11 ins / 22 x 27 cm) FRF 3,800. PARIS, 29 Nov 1993, *Walk Around the Pond* (oil on canvas, 11 x 16 1/4 ins / 27 x 41 cm) FRF 7,600. PARIS, 4 May 1994, *Old Interior* (oil on canvas, 16 1/4 x 11 ins / 41 x 27 cm) FRF 4,000; *Kite* (oil on canvas, 15 3/4 x 31 1/2 ins / 40 x 80 cm) FRF 7,000. PARIS, 1 Dec 1994, *Field of Lavender* (oil on canvas, 23 1/2 x 32 ins / 60 x 81 cm) FRF 19,100. PARIS, 7 June 1995, *Butterfly Chase* (oil on canvas, 24 1/2 x 19 3/4 ins / 62 x 50 cm) FRF 5,200.

KLEMER, Mark

American, 20th - 21st century.
Born 1958, in Gloucester (Massachusetts).
Painter.

Mark Klemer's work featured in a number of shows in Wisconsin, in 1986: *Survival Graphics*, Madison (Wisconsin); *One Person Show* and *Group Show* University of Wisconsin. He also created the *Abandoned House* installation in Madison, and a performance (*Ambient Ruptures*) at the University of Wisconsin.

AUCTION RECORDS:

PARIS, 16 Dec 1990, *Wave of Women* (1989, oil on canvas, 48 x 48 ins / 121 x 121 cm) FRF 5,500.

KLEMM, Franz Joseph

German, 20th century.
Born 1 March 1883, in Cologne.
Painter. Portraits.

Franz Joseph Klemm painted portraits of tycoons from Germany's heavy industry such as *Hugo Stinnes* and *August Thyssen*.

KLEMM, Gottlog Gottfried

German, 20th century.
Born 20 July 1872, in Stuttgart.
Painter, fresco artist, decorative designer.

Gottlog Gottfried Klemm trained under Gussmann and Stuck. He settled in Munich. He received a great many commissions covering a wide variety of genres, decorating churches, restaurants and hospitals.

KLEMM, Joseph Ferdinand

Austrian, 19th - 20th century.
Born 25 December 1868, in Vienna; died 12 February 1916, in Leipzig, Germany.
Painter, lithographer, watercolourist.

Joseph Ferdinand Klemm trained under Brioschi.

MUSEUMS AND GALLERIES:

LEIPZIG: two watercolours.

KLEMM, Walther

German, 20th century.
Born 18 June 1883, in Karlsbad (now Karlovy Vary); died 1957, in Weimar.
Painter, engraver, draughtsman.

Walther Klemm voluntarily extended his training for a thorough study of a very wide variety of techniques and to learn about the history of art.

Although initially enchanted by Japanese art, he ultimately developed a preference for wood engraving. From 1910 onwards he returned to a more personal and more western manner.

AUCTION RECORDS:

MUNICH, 6 June 1986, *Puppet Theatre* (1911, gouache, 9 1/4 x 11 1/2 ins / 23.5 x 29 cm) DEM 2,500. HEIDELBERG, 14 Oct 1988, *Cattle Fair in Dachau* (1910, ink, 5 x 7 ins / 12.4 x 17.6 cm) DEM 1,250. BREMEN, 11 Dec 1999, *Valley in Winter Evening* (oil on canvas, 24 x 31 ins / 60 x 80 cm) DEM 3,500. AHLDEN, 12 May 2001, *Frozen Winter Landscape with Fishermen* (oil on canvas, 9 x 11 ins / 22 x 29 cm) DEM 3,600. AHLDEN, 17 Sept 2004, *Beach* (oil on canvas, 19 x 22 ins / 48 x 57 cm) EUR 4,000.

KLEMME, August

German, 19th century.
Born 30 August 1838, in Hanover; died 30 November 1878, in Hanover.
Painter. History painting, portraits, genre scenes.

Klemme studied with Hildebrandt. He lived most of his life in Munich.

KLEMMER, Frans

German, 20th century.
Born 24 November 1879, in Fischenich; died 1964.
Painter. Religious subjects, military subjects.

Frans Klemmer lived in Munich, where he was a teacher at the School of Fine Art. Work by him appeared in 2003 in the exhibition *1914-1918. Mathurin Méheut un Artiste Combattant* (*1914-1918: Mathurin Méheut, a Fighting Artist*), held at the Musée d'Arras, which showed work which had been executed by both sides at the front.

BIBLIOGRAPHY:

Brodhage, Ursula, *Franz Klemmer: Frontzeichungen*, Brodhage, Nuremberg, 1992. Lankes, Christian, *Franz Klemmer, Künstler im Krieg*, Brodhage, Nuremberg, 1993. *Professor Franz Klemmer (1879 - 1964) und 15 seiner Schüler*, exhibition catalogue, Schloß Wertingen, Wertingen, 1998.

KLEMPNER, Ernest

Austrian, 19th - 20th century.
Born 26 July 1867, in Vienna.
Painter. Portraits.

Ernest Klempner was a pupil of Conrad L'Allemand. He was a member of the American Federation of Arts. He painted the portraits of a great many key figures.

AUCTION RECORDS:

LONDON, 22 Nov 1978, *Conversation* (1896, oil on canvas, 12 3/4 x 10 ins / 32.5 x 24.5 cm) GBP 1,200.

KLEMT, Agathon

Bohemian, 19th century.
Born 1830, in Prague; died 5 July 1889, in Prague.
Painter. History painting, portraits.

KLENAU, Ignaz von (Count)

German, 19th century.
Died 1829, in Regensburg.
Painter, engraver.

One of his best-known works is the altarpiece in the chapel of the castle of Taxis, near Trugenhofen, Wurtemberg.

KLENCK, Paul

Swiss, 19th century.
Born 1844, in Basel.
Also active in France.
Caricaturist.

Klenck lived for some time in Paris, where he worked on *Cri-cri* and *La Caricature pour tous*. Some of his caricatures were shown at the exhibition marking the centenary of the Commune at the Musée St-Denis in 1971. He sometimes signed his work: Filozel.

KLÈNE, Bernardus Henricus. See **BERN-KLÈNE**

KLENGEL, Johann Christian

German, 18th - 19th century.

Born 5 April 1751, in Kesselsdorf, near Dresden; died 9 December 1824, in Dresden.

Painter, engraver, draughtsman. Mythological subjects, genre scenes, landscapes, landscapes with figures.

Klengel was the son of a peasant family and started out as an apprentice bookbinder. He attracted the patronage of Hagedorn, enabling him to enter the academy of fine arts in Dresden, where he became one of Dietrich's favourite students. His work was represented in the exhibition *Expedition Kunst. Die Entdeckung der Natur von C.D. Friedrich bis Humboldt* (*Expedition Art. The Discovery of Nature from C.D. Friedrich to Humboldt*) at the Hamburg Kunsthalle in 2002, an exhibition showing the links between the natural sciences and the painted landscape.

Klengel produced numerous paintings in the style of his master, generally landscapes with figures. In 1790, he travelled to Italy. Later he became a teacher at the academy, and towards the end of his career he painted genre scenes and mythological subjects. As an engraver, he is known for views of Saxony (1771-1773), after his own drawings or those of his master, a landscape after Ruysdael (1787), and two views from the area around Rome (1791).

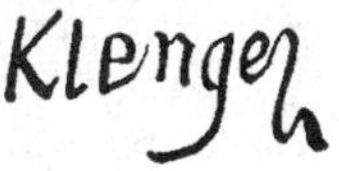

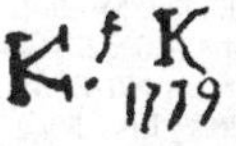

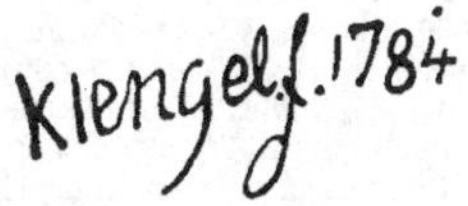

BIBLIOGRAPHY:

Johann Christian Klengel 1751-1824. Gemälde und Zeichnungen, exhibition catalogue, Stadt-und Bergbaumuseum, Freiberg, 1950. Steuer, Egbert, *Johann Christian Klengel 1751-1824*, Heimatkreis Kesselsdorf, Kesselsdorf, 2001. *Expedition Kunst. Die Entdeckung der Natur von C.D. Friedrich bis Humboldt*, exhibition catalogue, Hamburger Kunsthalle, Hamburg, 2002.

AUCTION RECORDS:

VIENNA, 1823, *Mountainous Landscape* (two drawings in pen and black chalk) FRF 40; *Livestock on the Banks of a River* (bistre drawing) FRF 52. PARIS, 2 Dec 1946, *Bringing the Animals Home* (1773, pen and sepia wash) FRF 2,600. PARIS, 6 Dec 1954, *Italian Landscape with Livestock*, FRF 25,000. LONDON, 1 March 1972, *Women Bathing by a River*, GBP 240. NEW YORK, 25 March 1982, *Young Man Reading* (1787, oil on canvas, 9 x 3/4 ins / 23 x 20 cm) USD 1,500. COPENHAGEN, 12 April 1983, *Ruined Aqueduct in the Roman Campagna* (1791, oil on canvas, 12 1/2 x 16 1/4 ins / 32 x 41 cm) DKK 39,000. HAMBURG, 7 June 1984, *View of a Ruin on the Bank of the Elbe* (oil on panel, 9 3/4 x 13 1/2 ins / 25 x 34.2 cm) DEM 4,200. COPENHAGEN, 21 Jan 1987, *Shepherd and Flock* (oil on canvas, 12 1/2 x 18 1/2 ins / 32 x 47 cm) DKK 8,200. NEW YORK, 11 Jan 1989, *Cowherds by a Lake, with a Ruined Castle on a Hill in the Distance* (1779, chalk and ink, 11 1/2 x 17 ins / 29.2 x 43.2 cm) USD 1,650. AMSTERDAM, 30 Oct 1990, *Threatening Weather in an Alpine Valley* (oil on canvas, 25 1/2 x 31 1/2 ins / 65 x 80 cm) NLG 4,025. MUNICH, 26-27 Nov 1991, *Mountainous Landscape with Bathers by a Pond* (ink and wash heightened with white, 10 1/4 x 14 1/4 ins / 26 x 36 cm) DEM 1,552. MUNICH, 10 Dec 1992, *Shepherds and Peasants near Ruins in a Rustic Landscape* (black ink/paper, 7 x 11 3/4 ins / 18 x 29.9 cm) DEM 3,164. LONDON, 22 Sept 1999, *Italianate Landscape with Peasant Ploughing, Hilltop Village beyond* (1793, black pencil and brown wash, 17 x 26 ins / 42 x 65 cm) GBP 2,800. VIENNA, 6 Oct 1999, *Penitent Mary Magdalene in Mountain Landscape* (oil on canvas, 14 x 19 ins / 36 x 47 cm) ATS 70,000. DÜSSELDORF, 31 Jan 2000, *Landscape with Waterfall* (1806, oil on canvas, 27 x 36 ins / 69 x 92 cm) DEM 16,000. DÜSSELDORF, 31 Jan 2000, *Ruins in Extensive Landscape* (oil on canvas, 26 x 39 ins / 67 x 98 cm) DEM 20,000. SAN FRANCISCO, 16 May 2001, *Shepherdess and Flock in an Extensive Landscape* (oil on panel, 10 x 14 ins / 25 x 35 cm) USD 2,500. BERLIN, 18 May 2001, *Hilly Wooded Landscape with Old Oak Tree* (brush over pencil, 15 x 9 ins / 39 x 24 cm) DEM 5,000. MUNICH, 4 Dec 2002, *Wooded Landscape with Young Herdsman and Cattle the on Edge of a Path* (oil on canvas, 22 x 30 ins / 55 x 75 cm) EUR 1,700. MUNICH, 6 Dec 2002, *Romantic Wooded Landscape with Herder and Cattle* (oil on panel, 19 x 29 ins / 48 x 74 cm) EUR 2,500. COLOGNE, 22 May 2004, *Mountain Landscape with Hunter* (oil on canvas, 14 x 18 ins / 36 x 46 cm) EUR 6,500. MUNICH, 25 May 2004, *Landscape with Figures and Ruins* (1770, pen and wash, 8 x 12 ins / 21 x 30 cm) EUR 1,700.

KLENGT, J. C.

18th century.

Draughtsman. Landscapes.

MUSEUMS AND GALLERIES:

AVIGNON: *Landscape with Animals* (drawing).

KLENKE, H.

German, 19th century.

Active in Düsseldorf and in Cologne.

Painter. History painting, portraits.

Klenke is known for his portraits of the Van Baerle family of Worms.

KLENZE, Hippolyte von

German, 19th century.

Born 12 August 1849, in Munich; died 30 April 1892, in Mittelberg.

Painter. Hunting scenes, landscapes.

Hippolyte von Klenze was the son of the painter Leo von Klenze. He studied with Roth and Schmitzberger and exhibited in Munich and Vienna.

KLENZE, Leo von

German, 19th century.

Born 29 February 1784, in Hildesheim; died 27 January 1864, in Munich.

Painter, draughtsman. Landscapes, architectural views.

Leo von Klenze only painted in the rare free moments allowed by his career as an architect, which brought him great fame. He worked in Berlin, Munich, Pau, England, Greece, Italy and Russia. He was the architect of the Hermitage in St Petersburg. In 2001, he was represented in the exhibition *Un Paese incantato. Italia dipinta da Thomas Jones a Corot* (*An Enchanted Landscape. Italy in Paint, from Thomas Jones to Corot*) at the Centro Internazionale d'Arte e di Cultura di Palazzo Tè in Mantua.

BIBLIOGRAPHY:

Leo von Klenze als Maler und zeichner: 1784-1864, exhibition catalogue, Bayerische Akademie der Schönen Künste, Munich, 1977. Lieb, Norbert/Hufnagl, Florian, *Leo von Klenze: Gemälde und Zeichn.*, Callwey, Munich, 1979. Schaefer, Veronika, *Leo von Klenze: Möbel und Innenräume*, Wölfle, Munich, 1980. Hederer, Oswald, '*Leo von Klenze: Persönlichkeit und Werk*' in *2 vol.*, Callwey, Munich, 1981. Haltrich,

Günther-Alexander, *Leo von Klenze, die Allerheiligenhofkirche in München,* dissertation, Stadtarchiv, Munich, 1983 (University, Munich, 1982). Buttlar, Adrian von, *Leo von Klenze: Leben, Werk, Vision,* Beck, Munich, 1999. Nerdinger, Winfried/Hildebrand, Sonja, *Leo von Klenze: Architekt zwischen Kunst und Hof, 1784-1864,* exhibition catalogue, Architekturmuseum, Münchner Stadtmuseum, Munich, 2000.

MUSEUMS AND GALLERIES:

MUNICH: *The Acropolis in Athens; Italian Cloister.*

AUCTION RECORDS:

COLOGNE, 3 Nov 1950, *Fortified Castle in the Apennines,* DEM 2,500. MUNICH, 25 Nov 1976, *Mountain Landscape* (watercolour and pen, 30¾ x 41 ins / 78 x 104 cm) DEM 6,600. MUNICH, 30 Nov 1978, *Amalfi* (1832, oil/copper, 9 x 11 ins / 22 x 27 cm) DEM 23,000. LONDON, 11 Dec 1979, *View of Amalfi* (1824, watercolour, 19 x 26 ins / 48.5 x 66 cm) GBP 800. COLOGNE, 21 May 1981, *A Temple at Paestum* (1859, oil on canvas, 26½ x 33½ ins / 67 x 85 cm) DEM 80,000. MUNICH, 24 Nov 1983, *A Temple at Paestum* (1859, oil on canvas, 26½ x 33½ ins / 67 x 85 cm) DEM 102,000. COLOGNE, 21 Nov 1985, *View of the Castle of Massa di Carrara* (oil on canvas, 30¼ x 39¼ ins / 77 x 100 cm) DEM 360,000. MUNICH, 29 Nov 1989, *Stock Exchange Square in Trieste, Evening* (oil on canvas, 25¾ x 39¼ ins / 65.5 x 100 cm) DEM 143,000. MUNICH, 26 June 2002, *Roman Forum* (1840, oil on canvas, 29 x 39 ins / 73 x 99 cm) EUR 530,000.

KLEPINSKI, Joahan

Polish, 20th century.

Born 29 December 1872, in Lódz.

Painter. Seascapes, landscapes.

Joahan Klepinski was the pupil of Hollósy and Azbe in Munich.

KLEPPER, Jeanne

French, 20th century.

Born in Troyes.

Painter.

Jeanne Klepper exhibited in Paris at the Salon des Indépendants and the Salon d'Automne.

KLEPPER, Max Francis

German, 19th century.

Born 1 March 1861, in Zeitz (Germany); died 5 May 1907, in Brooklyn.

Painter, illustrator. Animals.

In 1876, Klepper went to America with his parents, who later sent him to study in Munich for four years. On his return, he became a distinguished magazine illustrator. However, he was also a painter of animals.

AUCTION RECORDS:

NEW YORK, 28 Sept 1973, *The Attack on Fort Pillow* (watercolour and gouache) USD 5,750. PARIS, 6 Dec 1979, *Trotting Race* (1902, oil on canvas, 15¾ x 22 ins / 40 x 56 cm) FRF 23,000.

KLEPPER-PAAR, Hildegard

Romanian, 20th century.

Born 20 August 1932, in Orsova.

Active in Germany from 1977.

Painter, engraver (etching/aquatint/burin/wood). Interiors with figures, landscapes.

Hildegard Klepper-Paar graduated from the N. Grigorescu institute of fine arts in Bucharest in 1959. In 1977 she left Romania for good and settled in Munich. She joined the union of artists.

Her engravings are complemented with etchings and aquatints; they are chiselled with a burin and take advantage of the natural grain of the wood. Her move to the West freed her from having to rely on socialist-realist themes for inspiration. She turned to depicting landscapes in an Expressionist style, and interiors which at the same time acted as metaphors for her private life and the traits of her personality. She worked in series or cycles.

Hildegard Klepper-Paar took part in numerous collective exhibitions has held solo exhibitions Resita (1971), in other Romanian towns and in Germany.

BIBLIOGRAPHY:

Jianou, Ionel, *Romanian Artists and the West,* American Romanian Academy of Arts and Sciences, Paris, 1988.

KLERK, Willem de

Dutch, 19th century.

Born 28 November 1800, in Dordrecht; died 1874 or 1876, in Dordrecht.

Painter, watercolourist. Landscapes.

Willem de Klerk was a pupil of P. Hofmann and A. van der Koogh. Between 1827 and 1828 he lived in the Ardennes region of Luxembourg; he visited the Rhine in 1835 and Bohemia and Saxony in 1838. In 1840 he married Ida van Bezsekoom.

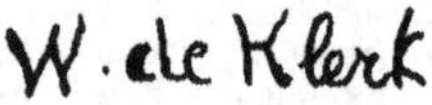

MUSEUMS AND GALLERIES:

NIMEGEN - ROUEN.

AUCTION RECORDS:

LONDON, 31 May 1940, *Frozen River,* GBP 11. LONDON, 22 March 1963, *Frozen River with Skaters,* Gns 510. DORDRECHT, 26-29 May 1970, *Summer Landscape,* NLG 3,400. AMSTERDAM, 22 May 1973, *Banks of the Rhine,* NLG 1,800. LONDON, 14 June 1974, *Wooded Landscapes* (two panels) Gns 2,400. LONDON, 30 Nov 1977, *Wooded Landscape* (oil on canvas, 22½ x 33¼ ins / 57 x 84.5 cm) GBP 1,300. LONDON, 20 June 1979, *Landscape with Mill* (oil on panel, 18½ x 25¼ ins / 47 x 64 cm) GBP 3,900. COLOGNE, 19 Nov 1981, *Imaginary Landscape* (oil on panel, 13½ x 20 ins / 34.5 x 51 cm) DEM 18,000. LONDON, 6 Oct 1982, *Travellers on a Country Road* (1843, oil on panel, 25¾ x 35 ins / 65.5 x 89 cm) GBP 4,800. VIENNA, 14 Sept 1983, *People Gathering Firewood* (oil on canvas, 41 x 35 ins / 104 x 89 cm) ATS 90,000. MUNICH, 8 May 1985, *Undulating Landscape* (oil on panel, 18 x 23¼ ins / 46 x 59 cm) DEM 13,000. COLOGNE, 23 March 1990, *Romantic River Landscape* (oil on panel, 23¼ x 28¾ ins / 59 x 73 cm) DEM 40,000. AMSTERDAM, 25 April 1990, *Cattle in a Mountain Landscape* (watercolour, 11½ x 16¼ ins / 29 x 41 cm) NLG 4,140. AMSTERDAM, 2 May 1990, *Wooded Mountain Landscape with River* (oil on panel, 13½ x 10 ins / 34 x 25.2 cm) NLG 5,750. LONDON, 17 March 1993, *Cart on a Road among the Trees* (oil on panel, 13¾ x 22 ins / 35 x 55 cm) GBP 4,600. AMSTERDAM, 20 April 1993, *Extensive Landscape with Figures on a Road* (oil on canvas, 23¼ x 34¼ ins / 59 x 87 cm) NLG 23,000. AMSTERDAM, 19 April 1994, *Winter Landscape with Figures on a Frozen River* (oil on panel, 15¾ x 21¼ ins / 40 x 54 cm) NLG 57,500. AMSTERDAM, 7 Nov 1995, *River Landscape in Moonlight* (oil on panel, 25¼ x 34 ins / 64 x 85.5 cm) NLG 11,800. AMSTERDAM, 16 April 1996, *Woman on a Forest Road* (oil on panel, 11¾ x 8¾ ins / 30 x 22.5 cm) NLG 2,596. AMSTERDAM, 27 Oct 1997, *Figures on a Frozen River* (oil on panel, 18¾ x 26½ ins / 47.5 x 67 cm) NLG 37,760. AMSTERDAM, 27 April 1999, *Wooded Hilly Landscape with Travellers near Lake* (oil on canvas, 23 x 34 ins / 59 x 86 cm) NLG 12,000. AMSTERDAM, 27 April 1999, *Rhenish Summer Landscape* (oil on panel, 18 x 25 ins / 45 x 63 cm) NLG 28,000. MILFORD, 11 May 2000, *Mountain Waterfall* (oil on panel, 25 x 19 ins / 64 x 48 cm) USD 6,250. AMSTERDAM, 8 Nov 2000, *Winter Landscape with an Ox Cart on a Wooded Road near a Village* (pencil, pen, brown ink and watercolour, 13 x 17 ins / 33 x 43 cm) NLG 7,000. AMSTERDAM, 24 April 2001, *Winter Landscape with Peasant on a Frozen Waterway, with Farmhouses and Windmill beyond* (oil on panel, 16 x 21 ins /

40 x 54 cm) NLG 85,000. COLOGNE, 19 May 2001, *Rhine Landscape* (oil on panel, 13 x 20 ins / 34 x 50 cm) DEM 24,000. AMSTERDAM, 24 April 2002, *Peasant Woman and Child on a Wooded Path by a Forest* (oil on panel, 16 x 21 ins / 41 x 53 cm) EUR 22,000. AMSTERDAM, 29 Sept 2003, *Mountain in Landscape in Evening Sunshine with a Waterfall in the Background* (oil on panel) EUR 3,800. LONDON, 21 Jan 2004, *Cows Watering* (oil on panel, 25 x 35 ins / 64 x 89 cm) GBP 7,800. AMSTERDAM, 21 April 2004, *Sunlit Clearing in a Forest* (oil on canvas, 28 x 39 ins / 70 x 99 cm) EUR 7,000.

KLETT, Hans
German, 20th century.
Born 30 May 1876, in Saafeld (Thuringia).
Sculptor.

Hans Klett took part in the Grosse Berliner Kunstausstellung of 1909. He lived for many years in Italy and travelled to Egypt.

KLETTE, Paul, or Klaette
German, 19th century.
Born 3 September 1854, in Jauer (now Jawor, Poland); died 28 September 1895, in Falkenstein.
Painter. Genre scenes.

Klette lived in Berlin, and exhibited there from 1877.

MUSEUMS AND GALLERIES:
BERLIN (Nationalgal.): *Smoking Den*; *Young Peasants*.

KLETTE VON KLETTENHOF, Karl
German, 19th century.
Born 18 October 1793, in Dresden; died 26 June 1874, in Budapest.
Painter, lithographer. Portraits, genre scenes, landscapes.

Karl Klette von Klettenhof studied in Dresden, Prague and Vienna. He is known for landscapes, portraits and scenes of Hungarian life. In his youth he also produced a few lithographs.

KLETZEL, Martin
German, 17th century.
Died 1699, in Dresden.
Painter, decorative designer, architect. Stage sets.

Kletzel was an architect as well as a painter of stage sets, which he designed and executed, aided only by apprentices.

KLETZINSKY, François
19th century.
Active c. 1837.
Painter. Landscapes.

KLEUDGEN, Fritz von
German, 19th century.
Born 23 February 1846, in Würzburg.
Painter. Landscapes.

Kleudgen studied at the Dresden academy and the school of fine arts in Weimar. In 1878, he settled at Bordighera on the Riviera. He exhibited in Berlin, Munich and Dresden.

AUCTION RECORDS:
MILAN, 28 Oct 1976, *Fishmarket on the Beach at Bordighera* (oil on canvas, 29¼ x 79¼ ins / 74 x 201 cm) ITL 5,000,000. MUNICH, 30 May 1979, *Fishermen Leaving Harbour, Bordighera* (1880, oil on canvas, 11¾ x 21¼ ins / 30 x 54 cm) DEM 3,000. BREMEN, 26 Sept 2003, *Ligurian Coast* (oil on canvas, 21 x 31 ins / 53 x 80 cm) EUR 5,500.

KLEUKENS, Christian Heinrich
German, 20th century.
Born 7 June 1880, in Achim near Bremen; died April 1954, in Darmstadt.
Printer, typographer, draughtsman, graphic designer. Decorative motifs.

Christian Heinrich Kleukens was the brother of Friedrich Wilhelm Kleukens, and was taught by him. He worked with him from 1907 as printer and artistic adviser to the publishing house of Grand Duke Ernst Ludwig of Hesse: the Ernst-Ludwig-Presse, which specialised in art books. After World War I, he founded the Kleukens Presse in Frankfurt, and then the Mainzer Presse. He was senior lecturer at the Staatsschule für Kunst und Handwerk. He published works on the art of printing and the development of typography, notably *Die Kunst der Letter* (*The Art of the Character*) (Leipzig, Insel-Verlag, 1940).

BIBLIOGRAPHY:
Gruschwitz-Kleukens, Ulrike, *Christian Heinrich Kleukens: 1880-1954*, Verein fuer Heimatgeschichte, Ober-Ramstadt, 1980. *Umelecka Kolonie Darmstadt, 1899-1914*, exhibition catalogue, Narodni Galerie, Prague, 1989. Martin, Gerald, *Ein großes Werk blieb unvollendet: Christian Heinrich Kleukens (1880-1954) und die 'Mainzer Presse'*, Mainz, 1990.

KLEUKENS, Friedrich Wilhelm
German, 20th century.
Born 7 May 1878, in Achim, near Bremen; died 22 August 1956, in Nürtingen.
Painter, draughtsman, engraver, illustrator, graphic designer. Portraits, mythological subjects. Decorative motifs, designs (typefaces).
Jugendstil.
Darmstadt Artists' Colony.

Friedrich Wilhelm Kleukens was the brother of Christian Heinrich Kleukens. He first learnt drawing in a silverware factory, then completed his training at the Kunstgewerbeschule in Berlin, under the supervision of Emil Doepler. He was a weaver before becoming a painter, and had to take many different jobs before he was able to take up painting seriously. With Fritz Hellmuth Ehmcke and G. Belwe, he founded a studio in Steglitz. He taught graphic arts from 1903 to 1906 at the Leipzig Akademie für Graphische Künste und Buchgewerbe (Academy of Graphic Arts and the Book Trade). In 1906, he joined the Mathildenhöhe Artists' Colony in Darmstadt, to which he had been introduced by Grand Duke Ernst Ludwig of Hesse, for whom he designed mosaics for the 1914 exhibition. He became the director of the Ernst Ludwig Presse (the publishing house of the Grand Duke of Hesse) from 1907 to 1914. In 1919, he founded the Ratio Presse and the Mainzer Presse. From 1931, he spent time regularly in Majorca, then in Darmstadt, Frankfurt and Nürtingen.

He did illustrations for collector's editions, notably from Martin Luther's Bible, such as *Das Buch Esther* (*The Book of Esther*), 1908) and the *Book of Judith* in 1923. He designed fonts and towards the end of his life devoted himself to painting.

BIBLIOGRAPHY:
Osterwalder, Marcus (ed.), *Dictionnaire des illustrateurs 1800-1914*, Ides et Calendes, Neuchâtel, 1989. *Umelecka Kolonie Darmstadt, 1899-1914*, exhibition catalogue, Narodni Galerie, Prague, 1989. Ernstberger, Harald, *Friedrich Wilhelm Kleukens: Graphik, Illustration, Schrift*, exhibition catalogue, Hessische Landes-und Hochschulbibliothek, Darmstadt, 2000.

MUSEUMS AND GALLERIES:
OFFENBACH (Klingspor-Museum für Internationale Buch und Schriftkunst).

KLEVE, Terkel
Danish, 18th century.
Born 1743, in Aarhus; died 5 December 1797, in Birkerød.
Engraver.

Terkel Kleve imitated the style of Demarteau.

KLEVER, Julius Sergius von or Yuliy Yulevich
Estonian, 19th - 20th century.

Born 31 January 1850, in Tartu; died 1924, in St Petersburg.
Painter. Landscapes.

Julius Klever studied at the academy of fine arts in St Petersburg in 1867 in Vorobev's studio. He exhibited in Russia, Germany, Austria and France, notably in Paris (1878). He won a gold medal in Berlin (1888) and an honourable mention in Paris at the 1889 Exposition Universelle.

Museums and Galleries:

Moscow (Rumiantsev Mus.): *Autumn* - Moscow (State Tretyakov Gal.): *Small River* - St Petersburg (Gosudarstvennyj Russkij Muz.): *Winter; A Forest.*

Auction records:

Paris, Oct 1945-July 1946, *Landscape with Windmill,* FRF 7,600. Paris, 4 Dec 1950, *Twilight,* FRF 10,000. Copenhagen, 14 June 1973, *Winter Landscape with Windmill,* DKK 5,800. New York, 12 May 1978, *Peasant in a Snowy Landscape* (oil on canvas, 13¾ x 21 ins / 35 x 53.5 cm) USD 1,800. New York, 25 Jan 1980, *River Landscape in Spring* (1894, oil on canvas, 42¼ x 33½ ins / 107 x 85 cm) USD 3,750. New York, 25 Feb 1982, *Frozen River* (1894, oil on canvas, 42½ x 34 ins / 108 x 86.5 cm) USD 5,750. Cologne, 18 March 1983, *Seascape under a Stormy Sky* (1907, oil on canvas, 24½ x 39¼ ins / 62 x 100 cm) DEM 6,500. London, 13 Feb 1986, *Cottage on the Edge of a Lake in Winter* (oil on canvas, 22½ x 35 ins / 57 x 88 cm) GBP 7,000. New York, 24 Nov 1987, *Stream Through the Woods* (1899, oil on canvas, 56 x 40¼ ins / 142 x 102 cm) USD 7,500. London, 26 Feb 1988, *Landscape of a River Bordered by Trees at Twilight* (oil on canvas, 23 x 35 ins / 58.4 x 89 cm) GBP 2,640. Paris, 29 June 1988, *Snow-covered Landscape* (oil on canvas, 22¾ x 16¼ ins / 58 x 41 cm) FRF 8,500. New York, 23 Feb 1989, *Snow-covered Forest by Moonlight* (1880, oil on canvas, 59¼ x 41¼ ins / 150.5 x 104.8 cm) USD 22,000. Paris, 17 March 1989, *Woodland and Marsh* (1897, oil on canvas, 23¾ x 17¾ ins / 60.5 x 45 cm) FRF 20,000. London, 17 March 1989, *Winter Landscape with a Village* (1893, oil on canvas, 71 x 85 ins / 180.5 x 216 cm) GBP 8,800. London, 5 May 1989, *Coastal Landscape at Sunrise* (1908, oil on canvas, 23¾ x 32¼ ins / 60.5 x 82 cm) GBP 3,410. Copenhagen, 21 Feb 1990, *Forest Lodge Amongst Fir Trees* (1914, oil on canvas, 31½ x 38¼ ins / 80 x 97 cm) DKK 44,000. Stockholm, 14 Nov 1990, *Winter Landscape with House and Wanderer* (oil on canvas, 27½ x 34¼ ins / 70 x 87 cm) SEK 52,000. New York, 23 May 1991, *Winter Landscape of Trees with a River by Moonlight* (1880, oil on canvas, 58¼ x 41¼ ins / 148 x 105 cm) USD 13,200. Amsterdam, 30 Oct 1991, *Cottages in the Forest in Winter* (oil on canvas, 26½ x 12¼ ins / 67 x 31 cm) NLG 3,220. Stockholm, 10-12 May 1993, *Winter Landscape with House and Figure on Road, Evening* (oil on canvas, 41¾ x 56 ins / 106 x 142 cm) SEK 80, 000. New York, 22-23 July 1993, *Forest* (1916, oil on canvas, 19 x 23 ins / 48.3 x 58.4 cm) USD 2,530. New York, 9 Jan 1997, *Birchwood Forest* (1912, oil on canvas, 45½ x 35¼ ins / 115.6 x 89.5 cm) USD 8,050. London, 11-12 June 1997, *Sunset in the Forest* (oil on canvas, 40½ x 28¼ ins / 103 x 71.5 cm) GBP 4,600.

KLEWER, Maximilian

German, 20th century.
Born 7 December 1891, in Barmen (Wuppertal).
Painter.

Maximilian Klewer trained at Berlin Academy. He brought back landscapes and still-lifes from his trips to Italy.

KLEY, Gils van der

Dutch, 20th - 21st century.
Born 1952, in The Hague.
Painter.

Gils van der Kley studied at the Academie Beeldende Kunsten in Maastricht, where he exhibits most of his work.

KLEY, Heinrich

German, 19th - 20th century.
Born 15 April 1863, in Karlsruhe; died 2 August 1945, in Munich.
Painter, draughtsman, watercolourist, illustrator.
Portraits, genre scenes, interiors with figures, landscapes, still-lifes, animals. Murals.
Jugendstil.

Heinrich Kley was a student of Ferdinand Keller at the Karlsruhe Academy and of C. Fr. Smith in Munich from 1880 to 1885. In 1908, he took up residence in Munich. He began by painting traditional subjects (landscapes, portraits or still-lifes), then became interested in more contemporary themes, such as buildings, factory interiors or commercial ports, and painted several murals. Once he had settled in Munich, he began to draw cartoons for the Munich satirical weekly *Simplicissimus,* and the Munich periodical *Die Jugend,* which from 1896 onwards was promoting the Jugendstil. After his death, Kley was largely forgotten as a painter, but recently there has been a revival of interest in his satirical illustrations. His graphic production indicates an energetic style of drawing, swift but sure, a kind of Expressionism that focused on denouncing bureaucracy, militarism and religion, but which seemed to come fully into its own in a world of fantasy, with animals, mainly elephants.

Publications for which he provided illustrations include Alciphron's *Hetärenbriefe* (*Letters from Courtesans*) (1921); *Die letzte Macht* (*The Last Power*) by P.G. Ehrhardt; *Reineke der Fuchs* (*Reineke the Fox*) (1930) and *Die Reiseschatten* (*Travelling Companions*) by Justinus Andreas Christian Kerner. His work was shown in exhibitions in Munich, Bremen and Berlin.

Bibliography:

Grosz, George (preface), *The drawings of Heinrich Kley,* Borden publishing company, Los Angeles, 1947. *The drawings of Heinrich Kley,* Dover Publications, New York, 1961, reedition 2000. Weeks, Donald, *The drawings of Kley,* exhibition catalogue, Borden Publishing Company, Alhambra (CA), 1968. Franzke, Irmela, *Jugendstil. Glas, Graphik, Keramik, Metall, Möbel, Skulpturen und Textilien von 1880 bis 1915,* exhibition catalogue, Badisches Landesmuseum, Karlsruhe, 1987.

Museums and Galleries:

Karlsruhe (Badisches Landesmus.): oil/card.

Auction records:

New York, 29 Nov 1984, '*Die Schleppe*' (watercolour on Indian ink and colouring pencil outline, 14½ x 12¾ ins / 37 x 32.5 cm) USD 900. New York, 8 May 1999, *Seated Hippo Attended by Monkeys* (c. 1920, pen and watercolour, 14 x 11 ins / 36 x 28 cm) USD 5,000. Munich, 30 Nov 1999, *Sea Monsters* (oil on canvas, 24 x 19 ins / 61 x 47 cm) DEM 10,000. New York, 4 Nov 2000, *Scenes with Devils Attacking Men and Each Other* (pen and ink, sketchbook page, 14 x 10 ins / 36 x 25 cm) USD 2,600. New York, 4 Nov 2000, *Centaurs and Children Frolicking in a Clearing* (pen and ink, 9 x 11 ins / 23 x 28 cm) USD 7,500. New York, 5 May 2001, *Bacchanalian Procession* (pen, ink and watercolour, 5 x 12 ins / 13 x 30 cm) USD 6,500. Hamburg, 15 June 2002, *Spanish Landscape* (1907, watercolour, 9 x 13 ins / 22 x 32 cm) EUR 1,700. Amsterdam, 7 Sept 2004, *Der Karren mit den resten der Deutschen Monarchien* (ink and pencil, 11 x 14 ins / 27 x 36 cm) EUR 4,200. New York, 20 Nov 2004, *Cloudburst* (pen, ink and watercolour, 8 x 10 ins / 20 x 25 cm) USD 4,000.

KLEY, Louis

French, 19th - 20th century.

Born 17 March 1833, in Sens; died 8 March 1911, in Sens.
Sculptor. Animals. Busts, groups.

Louis Kley studied under Lequien père. He exhibited at the Salon de Paris from 1853 and then at the Salon des Artistes Français. He received a silver medal in the Barbedienne competition and a silver medal at the Exposition Universelle of 1889, as well as other awards in Paris and Auxerre.

MUSEUMS AND GALLERIES:

CASTRES: *Bust of Cardinal Bernardon* - SENS: *Allegory; Vestals; Brennus.*

AUCTION RECORDS:

PARIS, 9 May 1940, *Female Faun Seated Holding a Bowl with a Small Bacchante* (terracotta) FRF 520. PARIS, 8 Nov 1995, *Draught Horse in Harness* (bronze, h. 5 ins / 13 cm) FRF 4,000.

KLEYN, Johann Pieter Vaupel
Dutch, 19th century.
Born 20 July 1813, in The Hague.
Painter. Portraits, interiors.

Johann Kleyn was a pupil of W.-G.-F. Heymans and C. Kruseman. He lived in Zalt-Bommel, where he worked as a wine dealer.

KLEYN, Laurenz Ludwig
Dutch, 19th century.
Born 1826, in Demerara, Dutch New Guinea.
Painter. History painting, portraits.

In 1846, Laurenz Kleyn was living in Antwerp and in 1853 in Italy.

AUCTION RECORDS:

RHEIMS, 2 June 1985, *Young Woman on a Swing* (1861, oil on canvas, 86½ x 63 ins / 220 x 160 cm) FRF 19,600.

KLEYN, Lodewyk Johannes, or Kleijn
Dutch, 19th century.
Born 14 January 1852, in The Hague.
Painter.

Lodewyk Johannes Kleyn was a pupil of Christoffel Bischop.

KLEYN, Lodewyk or Lodewijk Johannes, or Kleijn
Dutch, 19th century.
Born 14 August 1817, in Loosduinen; died 11 March 1897, in The Hague.
Painter, watercolourist. Landscapes with figures, waterscapes, landscapes.

Lodewyk Kleyn was a pupil of Andreas Schelfout.

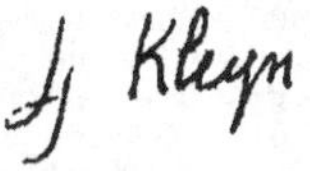

MUSEUMS AND GALLERIES:

CAPE TOWN: *View of Schwenningen* - THE HAGUE (Gemeentemus.): three landscapes.

AUCTION RECORDS:

LONDON, 15 Oct 1969, *View of a Town by a River,* GBP 1,300. LONDON, 1 Nov 1973, *Estuary at Twilight,* Gns 500. LONDON, 29 Sept 1976, *Boats* (oil on panel, 15¼ x 20¾ ins / 38.5 x 53 cm) GBP 2,300. LONDON, 12 Oct 1977, *River Landscape with Mills in the Twilight* (oil on panel, 7¼ x 9¾ ins / 18.5 x 25 cm) GBP 2,000. LONDON, 14 Feb 1979, *River Bank with Figures* (oil on panel, 13¼ x 20½ ins / 33.5 x 52 cm) GBP 4,000. COLOGNE, 19 Nov 1981, *Haarlem Landscape* (oil on panel, 13½ x 20¾ ins / 34 x 53 cm) DEM 20,000. LONDON, 11 July 1983, *Winter Landscape with Skaters* (oil on canvas, 17¼ x 22¾ ins / 44 x 58 cm) GBP 7,000. AMSTERDAM, 15 April 1985, *River Landscape in Summer* (oil on panel, 17 x 21¼ ins / 43 x 54 cm) NLG 38,000. AMSTERDAM, 10 Feb 1988, *Summer: Tranquil River with Villagers in a Ferryboat by a Mill* (oil on panel, 13½ x 20½ ins / 34 x 52 cm) NLG 6,900. AMSTERDAM, 30 Aug 1988, *Winter Landscape with Peasants on a Snowy Road and Skaters on the Canal* (oil on canvas, 22 x 26½ ins / 56 x 67 cm) NLG 2,070. AMSTERDAM, 16 Nov 1988, *Rescuers in a Rowing Boat Coming to the Aid of a Two-Master with Many Villagers by the Lighthouse* (oil on panel, 13 x 17¼ ins / 33 x 44 cm) NLG 8,625. NEW YORK, 24 Oct 1989, *On the Frozen Lake* (oil on panel, 15¼ x 21½ ins / 38.8 x 54.3 cm) USD 25,300. AMSTERDAM, 25 April 1990, *Winter Landscape with Villagers and a Large Town in the Distance* (oil on canvas, 19¼ x 31 ins / 49 x 79 cm) NLG 25,300. COLOGNE, 29 June 1990, *Dutch Landscape in Summer at Sunset* (oil on wood, 16½ x 20¾ ins / 42 x 53 cm) DEM 20,000. AMSTERDAM, 6 Nov 1990, *Winter Landscape with Mills and Skaters* (watercolour, 10¼ x 16¼ ins / 26 x 41 cm) NLG 2,185. AMSTERDAM, 30 Oct 1991, *Winter Landscape with Skaters on a Frozen Canal and Travellers on a Snowy Road* (oil on panel, 13¾ x 20½ ins / 35 x 52 cm) NLG 17,250. AMSTERDAM, 22 April 1992, *Winter Landscape with Skaters on a Frozen Canal near a Mill* (oil on panel, 25½ x 37½ ins / 64.5 x 95 cm) NLG 55,200. AMSTERDAM, 28 Oct 1992, *Dutch Country Landscape with a Boat on a Canal and a Windmill on the Bank Opposite* (oil on canvas, 24½ x 34¼ ins / 62.5 x 87 cm) NLG 57,500. AMSTERDAM, 2-3 Nov 1992, *Winter Landscape with Figures and Sledges on a Frozen Canal* (oil on panel, 13½ x 20¾ ins / 34 x 53 cm) NLG 10,350. AMSTERDAM, 19 Oct 1993, *Extensive Wooded Landscape with The Hague in the Distance and Figures in the Foreground* (oil on panel, 13¼ x 17¾ ins / 33.5 x 45 cm) NLG 27,600. AMSTERDAM, 21 April 1994, *Winter Landscape with Skaters on a Frozen Canal* (oil on panel, 17 x 21¼ ins / 43 x 54 cm) NLG 78,200. NEW YORK, 12 Oct 1994, *Skaters on a Frozen Canal* (oil on canvas, 19½ x 30 ins / 49.5 x 76.2 cm) USD 16,675. AMSTERDAM, 8 Nov 1994, *Figures on a Frozen River* (oil on panel, 13½ x 16¾ ins / 34 x 42.5 cm) NLG 50,600. AMSTERDAM, 7 Nov 1995, *Extensive Summer Landscape with Figures and Cattle among the Dunes* (oil on panel, 15¼ x 20¾ ins / 39 x 53 cm) NLG 33,040. AMSTERDAM, 19-20 Feb 1997, *Winter Landscape with Skaters on a Frozen Lake* (watercolour/paper, 8¼ x 12½ ins / 21 x 31.5 cm) NLG 1,153. AMSTERDAM, 22 April 1997, *The Flower Market at Breda* (oil on canvas, 30¾ x 23½ ins / 78 x 60 cm) NLG 40,120. LONDON, 21 Oct 1999, *Winter Landscape with Figures on Frozen River by a Windmill* (oil on canvas, 28 x 35 ins / 70 x 90 cm) GBP 30,000. AMSTERDAM, 26 Oct 1999, *Peasants Conversing on Sandy Trail along Waterway* (oil on canvas, 21 x 28 ins / 54 x 71 cm) NLG 40,000. AMSTERDAM, 18 Jan 2000, *River Landscape in Autumn* (oil on panel, 17 x 23 ins / 43 x 59 cm) NLG 45,000. AMSTERDAM, 18 April 2000, *Peasants Conversing on a Frozen River, Koek en Zopie beyond* (oil on panel, 15 x 21 ins / 38 x 54 cm) NLG 90,000. AMSTERDAM, 23 April 2001, *Winter Landscape with Figures on a Frozen River* (oil on panel, 19 x 29 ins / 49 x 73 cm) NLG 105,000. AMSTERDAM, 24 April 2001, *Skaters on a Frozen Waterway, a Mansion beyond* (oil on panel, 15 x 20 ins / 37 x 52 cm) NLG 130,000. AMSTERDAM, 21 Oct 2002, *Extensive Landscape with Skaters and Figures* (oil on canvas, 35 x 47 ins / 90 x 120 cm) EUR 28,000. AMSTERDAM, 22 Oct 2002, *Skaters on a Frozen River near Koek en Zopie* (oil on canvas, 19 x 28 ins / 49 x 72 cm) EUR 20,000. AMSTERDAM, 15 April 2003, *Skaters on a Frozen River near Koek en Zopie* (oil on canvas, 19 x 28 ins / 49 x 72 cm) EUR 20,000. AMSTERDAM, 28 Oct 2003, *Figures on a Frozen Waterway with Windmills on the Riverbank* (oil on panel, 10 x 14 ins / 26 x 35 cm) EUR 12,000. AMSTERDAM, 20 April 2004, *Summer Landscape with Figures along a Waterway* (oil on panel, 15 x 20 ins / 37 x 50 cm) EUR 30,000. AMSTERDAM, 20 April 2004, *Summer Landscape with Figure on a Riverbank. Winter Landscape with Skaters on a Frozen Waterway* (oil on panel, a pair, 14 x 19 ins / 36 x 47 cm) EUR 42,000.

KLEYN, Pieter Rudolph
Dutch, 19th century.

Born 17 May 1785, in Hooghe Zwaluwe; died 15 February 1816, in Les Quatre-Bras.
Painter.

Pieter Kleyn was a pupil of Jacob and Abraham van Stry in Dordrecht and also studied under David in Paris in 1808. He achieved the rank of lieutenant and died on the field of battle.

MUSEUMS AND GALLERIES:

AMSTERDAM: *Landscape*; several paintings - HAARLEM (Teylers Mus.): drawings.

KLEYNHENS, Isaak

Dutch, 17th century.
Born 1634, in Haarlem; died 1701, in Haarlem.
Painter. Flowers, fruit.

In 1693, Isaak Kleynhens was a member of the Haarlem guild. He painted a self-portrait at the age of 35.

KLEYNTJES, Jan or Jan Leonard or Johannes Leonardus. See **KLEINTJES**

KLIAVING, Serge

French, 20th - 21st century.
Born 1960.
Performance artist.

Serge Kliaving shows his works in solo exhibitions including at the Galerie Nathalie Obadia, Paris, 1996. His is an art of engagement, close to the work of Hans Haacke. With the aid of flags, images from advertising and oblique logos, he denounces our consumer society.

AUCTION RECORDS:

PARIS, 18 Feb 1990, *Nothing!* (acrylic/canvas, 19 3/4 x 28 3/4 ins / 50 x 73 cm) FRF 6,000.

KLIC, Karl

Austrian, 19th - 20th century.
Born 31 May 1841; died 16 November 1926, in Vienna.
Painter, caricaturist. Genre scenes.

KLICKERMANN, Wilhelm

German, 19th - 20th century.
Born 9 January 1842, in Schleiz; died 3 January 1919, in Stuttgart.
Painter. Landscapes.

AUCTION RECORDS:

COLOGNE, 19 Oct 1979, *Alpine Landscape* (oil on canvas, 27 1/2 x 35 3/4 ins / 70 x 91 cm) DEM 2,700.

KLIEBER, Eduard

Austrian, 19th century.
Born 1 April 1803, in Vienna; died 3 December 1879, in Vienna.
Painter, lithographer.

Eduard Klieber studied at the Akademie der bildenden Künste in Vienna. He painted mainly genre scenes and portraits.

AUCTION RECORDS:

VIENNA, 14 June 1977, *Little Girl Reading* (1853, oil on oval panel, 11 1/2 x 9 1/4 ins / 29.4 x 23.5 cm) ATS 45,000. LONDON, 26 March 1982, *Portrait of the Emperor Franz Josef I* (1851, oil on canvas, 31 x 24 3/4 ins / 78.8 x 62.8 cm) GBP 2,000. VIENNA, 8 April 1999, *Empress Elizabeth of Austria* (1862, oil on canvas, 31 x 24 ins / 78 x 62 cm) ATS 140,000. VIENNA, 2 Dec 1999, *Girl with Basket of Fruit Holding Up a Bunch of Grapes* (1859, oil on canvas, 32 x 26 ins / 82 x 67 cm) ATS 65,000.

KLIEBER, Josef

Austrian, 18th - 19th century.
Born 1 November 1773, in Innsbruck; died 11 January 1850, in Vienna.
Painter, sculptor.

Josef Klieber was the father of Eduard, and had studied with Straub and Fischer. He is known mainly for sculpture and monumental painting.

KLIEBER, Urban

Austrian, 18th century.
Born c. 1740; died 25 March 1803, in Innsbruck.
Sculptor.

Urban Klieber made a large number of statues for public buildings in Innsbruck, both civil and religious.

KLIEMANN, Carl Heinz

German, 20th century.
Born 1942, in Berlin.
Painter, engraver.

BIBLIOGRAPHY:

Kliemann, Helga, *Eberhard Roters. Die Graphik von Carl-Heinz Kliemann 1946-1975*, catalogue raisonné, Städtische Gal., Wolfsburg, 1978. Beaumont-Maillet, Laure/Woimant, Françoise/Pernoud, Emmanuel, *De Bonnard à Baselitz - Dix ans d'enrichissements du Cabinet des estampes 1978-1988*, exhibition catalogue, Bibliothèque nationale de France, Paris, 1992.

KLIEN, Erika Giovanna

Austrian, 20th century.
Born 1900, in Borgo (South Tyrol); died 1957, in New York.
Active from 1929 in the USA.
Painter. Figures, still-lifes. Stage sets, theatre decoration.
Constructivism.

Erika Giovanna Klien trained at the school of applied arts (1918-1922) under Franz Cisek, and then became a teacher in Salzburg from 1926 to 1928. Her work has kinetic leanings and can be compared with the dominant movements of the time, such as Purism, Suprematism and Constructivism. During the 1920s she created a puppet theatre. Her work was also influenced by Mexican mural painters. She took part in collective exhibitions, notably one organised by the Brooklyn Museum, New York, in 1926-1927. She then emigrated to New York in 1929. The Rupertinum in Salzburg held an exhibition of her work entitled *Wien - New York 1900-1957* (*Vienna - New York 1900-1957*) in 2001.

BIBLIOGRAPHY:

Erika Giovanna Klien, Gal. Pabst, Vienna, 1975. *Erika Giovanna Klien: A Retrospective through Drawing*, Rachel Adler Gallery, New York, 1989. Bogner, Dieter/Hapkemeyer, Andreas/Rochowanski, L.W., *Erika Giovanna Klien. Wien New York 1900-1957*, Hatje Cantz, Ostfildern, 2001.

MUSEUMS AND GALLERIES:

SALZBURG (Rupertinum).

AUCTION RECORDS:

HAMBURG, 2 June 1978, *Houses* (1924, oil on canvas remounted on board, 14 3/4 x 19 3/4 ins / 37.5 x 50 cm) DEM 6,400. VIENNA, 19 March 1985, *Head of Dancer* (c. 1923, oil and gold/card, 12 x 10 ins / 30.5 x 25.2 cm) ATS 90,000. LONDON, 26 Feb 1986, *Still-life* (c. 1923-1925, charcoal, 6 x 9 1/2 ins / 15 x 24 cm) GBP 650. LONDON, 7 Oct 1999, *Meeting* (1927, tempera on canvas, 30 x 30 ins / 77 x 77 cm) GBP 35,000. MUNICH, 20 Nov 1999, *Houses* (1924, oil on board, 15 x 20 ins / 38 x 51 cm) DEM 56,000. VIENNA, 15 May 2001, *Woman Walking* (1926, watercolour, 9 x 4 ins / 24 x 11 cm) ATS 190,000. VIENNA, 25 Sept 2001, *Tap Mechanisms* (watercolour on pencil, 11 x 8 ins / 28 x 20 cm) ATS 80,000. VIENNA, 11 June 2002, *Primitive Study: Worship* (watercolour, 5 x 6 ins / 12 x 14 cm) EUR 3,500. VIENNA, 28 Oct 2003, *Flight Rhythm* (1951, oil on canvas, 20 x 16 ins / 51 x 40 cm) EUR 26,000. VIENNA, 28 Nov 2003, *Female Dancer* (black chalk, 20 x 13 ins / 50 x 34 cm) EUR 11,000. VIENNA, 12 Oct 2004, *The Driller* (tempera and watercolour on board, 21 x 21 ins / 54 x 54 cm) EUR 19,000. VIENNA, 12 Oct 2004, *Iron Cutter* (1933, tempera and watercolour on board) EUR 19,000.

KLIM, Hans

German, 16th century.

Born in Nuremberg; died 1550.
Goldsmith, engraver (wood).
His works include woodcuts which were signed with a monogram made up of the letters H and X side by side. Prints of these engravings were published in Wittenberg between 1590 and 1603.

KLIM, Lee
Russian, 20th - 21st century.
Born 1946.
Draughtsman. Nudes.
Lee Klim studied at the Repin institute in Leningrad (St Petersburg), and became a member of the Leningrad painters' association. He works in ink or red chalk, depicting the female body in lascivious poses. He has taken part in many exhibitions since 1975, including *Young Painters*, 1976, Moscow; *Les Jeunes Peintres de l'URSS* (*Young USSR Painters*), 1979, Paris; *Contemporary Soviet Art*, 1988 Tokyo; *Contemporary Soviet Art*, 1990, Helsinki.
MUSEUMS AND GALLERIES:
OMSK (MFA) - ST PETERSBURG (Academy of Fine Art).

KLIMCHENKO, Konstantin Michailovich
Russian, 19th century.
Born 1817; died 29 August 1849, in St Petersburg.
Painter. Genre scenes.
One of Klimchenko's works, *Young Girl with a Mirror*, is in the Russian Museum in St Petersburg.

KLIMCZAK, Adam
Polish, 20th century.
Installation artist.
Conceptual Art.
Adam Klimczak studied at the art academy in Lódz, where he continues to live. He uses his personal experience, well documented in pictures which he shows, to create installations relevant to the social and political history of the community. His work was regularly shown in collective exhibitions in Poland, especially at the museum of international artists in Lódz; he has also exhibited in 1996 at the Lombard/Freid Fine Arts Gallery in New York, in 2001 at the Venice Biennale, and in 2004 at the Centre for Contemporary Art in Haifa.
BIBLIOGRAPHY:
Morgan, Robert C., '*Latitudes éclatées*' in *Art Press* no. 212, periodical, Paris, April 1996.

KLIMEK, Ludwig or Ludwik or Ludovic
Polish, 20th century.
Born 1912, in Cracow; died 1993.
Active in France from 1939.
Painter. Figures, nudes, scenes with figures, landscapes with figures, still-lifes, flowers.
Ludwig Klimek studied at the academy of fine arts in Cracow before settling in the South of France in 1939. He painted solidly structured landscapes of Provence and pictures of female bathers in a lyrical style. Collective exhibitions include: Menton Biennale (1951 to 1972, winning a silver medal in 1953); *Paintings from the Paris School*, Malmö (1948); oceanographic museum, Monaco (1959). He also showed his works in solo exhibitions in France from 1941, particularly in Paris and Menton.

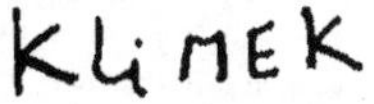

AUCTION RECORDS:
VERSAILLES, 17 April 1988, *Three Women Bathing* (oil on card, 18 x 22 ins / 46 x 55 cm) FRF 2,550. PARIS, 1 July 1988, *Bouquet and Basket of Fruit* (oil on canvas, 25½ x 21¼ ins / 65 x 54 cm) FRF 4,500. PARIS, 16 March 1989, *Sailboats* (oil on canvas, 11 x 13¾ ins / 27 x 35 cm) FRF 3,600. VERSAILLES, 24 Sept 1989, *Bathers on the Sea Shore* (oil on canvas, 19¾ x 25½ ins / 50 x 65 cm) FRF 4,000. VERSAILLES, 26 Nov 1989, *Three Graces* (oil on canvas, 19¾ x 25½ ins / 50 x 65 cm) FRF 5,500. PARIS, 9 Dec 1989, *Bathing Party* (oil on canvas, 35 x 46 ins / 89 x 116 cm) FRF 40,000. VERSAILLES, 10 Dec 1989, *Two Girls Seated* (oil on canvas, 28¾ x 23½ ins / 73 x 60 cm) FRF 7,600. VERSAILLES, 22 April 1990, *Female Bather Sunbathing on the Beach at Juan-les-Pins* (oil on panel, 13 x 16¼ ins / 33 x 41 cm) FRF 9,100. NOYON, 16 Dec 1990, *Broadway* (1960, oil on canvas) FRF 23,000. MONTAUBAN, 24 Feb 1991, *Nude with Cat* (oil on canvas, 32 x 23½ ins / 81 x 60 cm) FRF 26,500. PARIS, 2 Dec 1991, *Nude Model in an Interior* (oil on canvas, 25½ x 19¾ ins / 65 x 50 cm) FRF 7,000. LE TOUQUET, 8 June 1992, *Female Bathers* (1977, oil on canvas, 22 x 27½ ins / 56 x 70 cm) FRF 9,500. PARIS, 6 Dec 1992, *Female Bathers* (oil on canvas, 32 x 25¾ ins / 81 x 65.5 cm) FRF 13,000. LOKEREN, 15 May 1993, *Orange Tree* (1951, oil on canvas, 25½ x 21¼ ins / 65 x 54 cm) BEF 38,000. MONTAUBAN, 20 March 1994, *Beauty and Her Challengers* (1970, oil on canvas and collage) FRF 62,000. MADRID, 18 May 1999, *Nude* (oil on canvas, 13 x 9 ins / 33 x 24 cm) ESP 300,000. CALAIS, 7 Nov 1999, *Nude at Mirror* (oil on canvas, 26 x 20 ins / 65 x 50 cm) FRF 12,000. CANNES, 15 Aug 2000, *Naiads* (oil on canvas, 26 x 36 ins / 65 x 92 cm) FRF 13,000. CANNES, 15 Aug 2001, *Bathing* (oil on canvas, 29 x 37 ins / 74 x 93 cm) FRF 14,000. LYONS, 8 Feb 2004, *Actaeon* (gouache/varnish on paper/canvas, 26 x 36 ins / 65 x 92 cm) EUR 2,700.

KLIMES, F. K.
Polish.
in Lemberg (now Lviv, Ukraine).
Painter, draughtsman.
F.K. Klimes chiefly produced portraits.

KLIMES, Joseph
Bohemian, 19th century.
Born 1775, probably in Bohemia; died c. 1830, in Lemberg (now Lviv, Ukraine).
Painter.
Joseph Klimes settled in Poland, where he painted portraits in oils and miniatures.

KLIMO, Alojz
Slovak, 20th century.
Born 8 March 1922, in Piestany.
Painter.
Alojz Klimo studied in Bratislava from 1941 to 1945 and then at the schools of decorative arts in Prague and Bratislava. His works tend towards Abstraction, though they are based on actual impressions, recomposed either through a geometric organisation or by allowing his instinctive sensitivities free reign.
BIBLIOGRAPHY:
Fifty years of Czechoslovakian Painting from the Collections of the Galleries, 1918-1968, exhibition catalogue, Slovenska Narodna Gal., Bratislava, 1968 (in commemoration of the 50th anniversary of the Republic of Czechoslovakia).

KLIMO, István
Hungarian, 20th century.
Born 8 October 1883, in Debrecen.
Painter. Genre scenes, portraits.
István Klimo worked in Budapest.

KLIMOV, Valentine
Russian, 20th century.
Born 1912, in the Caucasus.
Active in Belgium.
Painter.
Valentine Klimov was the pupil of Jacques Ochs at the Académie des Beaux Arts in Liège.

KLIMOWSKY, Stanislas
Polish, 19th - 20th century.
Active in Cracow.
Painter.

Stanislas Klimowsky painted genre scenes, military scenes, landscapes, as well as portraits.

KLIMSCH, Eugen Johann Georg

German, 19th century.
Born 29 November 1839, in Frankfurt am Main; died 9 July 1896, in Frankfurt am Main.
Painter, watercolourist, engraver. Portraits, genre scenes.

E. J. G. Klimsch was the son of the painter F. K. Klimsch. From 1859 to 1865, he worked in Munich as a pupil of A. Muller, then returned to settle in Frankfurt. He exhibited in Frankfurt and Berlin from 1868, and taught at the Stadel Institute in Frankfurt.

MUSEUMS AND GALLERIES:

FRANKFURT AM MAIN: two paintings.

AUCTION RECORDS:

NEW YORK, 10 Feb 1902, *Horseman* (watercolour) USD 110. NEW YORK, 15-16 April 1909, *The Broken Vase,* USD 150. NEW YORK, 21 Jan 1978, *Pipe-Smoker* (1878, oil on card, 8 3/4 x 6 3/4 ins / 22.5 x 17 cm) USD 1,800. LONDON, 11 Oct 1985, *Reclining Venus with Cherubs* (oil on canvas remounted/panel, 55 x 78 ins / 139.7 x 198.1 cm) GBP 1,600. MUNICH, 23 Sept 1987, *I Am Yours, You Are Mine* (oil on canvas, 31 3/4 x 17 1/2 ins / 80.5 x 44.5 cm) DEM 5,000. LONDON, 31 Oct 1996, *Relaxation* (1894, oil on card, 6 1/4 x 5 ins / 16 x 13 cm) GBP 3,450. FRANKFURT, 20 Nov 1999, *Riders Taking a Drink outside a Tavern* (1879, oil on canvas, 9 x 7 ins / 24 x 18 cm) DEM 7,500. LONDON, 24 Nov 1999, *Portrait of a Minstrel and a Young Lady Riding a White Horse through an Autumnal Forest by Moonlight* (miniature, h. 6ins / 14cm) GBP 1,700. LONDON, 29 March 2001, *Music Lesson* (1888, oil on canvas, 22 x 16 ins / 57 x 40 cm) GBP 6,000. COLOGNE, 24 Nov 2001, *Group Making Music in a Park* (1891, oil on canvas, 17 x 57 ins / 42 x 145 cm) DEM 5,500. HAMBURG, 8 May 2002, *Before the First Ball* (1888, oil on canvas, 35 x 20 ins / 88 x 51 cm) EUR 2,200.

KLIMSCH, Ferdinand Karl

German, 19th century.
Born 12 December 1812, in Bohemia; died 14 September 1890, in Frankfurt am Main.
Painter, engraver. Genre scenes.

F. K. Klimsch studied at the Prague academy. In 1839, he settled in Frankfurt, where he made a reputation as an engraver and lithographer.

KLIMSCH, Fritz

German, 20th century.
Born 10 February 1870, in Frankfurt am Main; died 30 March 1960, in Freiburg im Breisgau.
Sculptor (stone/bronze), draughtsman. Allegorical subjects, mythological figures, figures. Busts, monuments, funerary monuments.
Jugendstil.

Fritz Klimsch was the son of the painter Eugen Johann Georg Klimsch. He began by studying painting, but in 1886 started an apprenticeship in sculpture under the supervision of Fritz Schaper at the Akademie der Künste in Berlin. This continued until 1894, the year in which he received a national prize that gave him the opportunity to visit Vienna, Paris and Italy (1895). He went back to Italy in 1901. He also spent some time in Greece. Living in Berlin, he was a co-founder of the Berlin Secession in 1898. In 1912, he became a member of the Prussian Akademie der Künste in Berlin, then professor at the Akademische Hochschule für bildende Künste in 1916.

Although some of his works were in the style of Jugendstil, especially the statue of the 'femme fatale' *Salome* (1898) (or *Dancer*), essentially his work has more affinity with the classicism that triumphed in Europe in parallel with the coming to power of the National Socialists in Germany in 1933. The Nazis supported his classical aesthetic, which had a great influence on the generation of Arno Breker. After the war, Klimsch was expelled from the Austrian city of Salzburg and went to live in Baden-Baden. From the late 1950s, there was a revival of interest in his work in Germany. He created numerous monuments, including one to Rudolf Virchow in Berlin, a monument to the dead and the *Temple of Flora* in the Carl Duisberg Park in Leverkusen, and the woman symbolising *Wind and Sun* at the Gruga Park in Essen. By far the most popular of his works were the slender female figures with their sleek eroticism, which contrasted with the grandiloquent classical posturing of the men. After the war, he began to roughen the surfaces of his sculptures in order to suggest the inner torments of mankind, without losing sight of his classical aesthetic.

He exhibited at the 1900 Paris Exposition Universelle. He was awarded a gold medal in Berlin in 1907.

BIBLIOGRAPHY:

Braun, Hermann, *Fritz Klimsch: Werke,* exhibition catalogue, Gal. Koch, Hanover, 1980. Braun, Hermann, *Fritz Klimsch: eine Dokumentation,* exhibition catalogue, Kunsthaus am Museum Carola van Ham, Cologne, 1991.

MUSEUMS AND GALLERIES:

BERLIN: *Dancer* - HAMBURG (Mus. für Kunst und Gewerbe) - LEIPZIG (Mus. der bildenden Künste).

AUCTION RECORDS:

COLOGNE, 21 May 1965, *Nude Seated* (patinated bronze) DEM 10,350. COLOGNE, 4 Dec 1974, *Nude with Mirror* (1902, bronze) DEM 7,000. HAMBURG, 3 June 1976, *Portrait of Marianne Hoppe* (bronze, 17 3/4 ins / 45.2 cm) DEM 4,000. COLOGNE, 6 May 1978, *Nude Crouching* (porcelain, h. 16 1/4 ins / 41 cm) DEM 3,400. NEW YORK, 23 Oct 1980, *Nude Crouching* (dark-brown patinated bronze, h. 15 3/4 ins / 40 cm) USD 6,750. HAMBURG, 13 June 1981, *Grosse Jugend* (1940-1941, bronze, h. 62 1/4 ins / 158 cm) DEM 28,000. MUNICH, 28 May 1984, *In the Sun* (1911-1912, marble, 46 1/2 x 26 1/4 x 70 3/4 ins / 118 x 66.6 x 180 cm) DEM 43,000. MUNICH, 24 Nov 1986, *Nude Standing* (brown-patinated bronze, h. 26 ins / 66 cm) DEM 23,100. MUNICH, 26 Oct 1988, *Woman Kneeling with a Towel* (bronze, h. 20 1/2 ins / 52 cm) DEM 27,500. BERLIN, 30 May 1991, *Man Resting* (1925, bronze, h. 29 1/2 ins / 75 cm) DEM 37,740. LONDON, 3 Dec 1991, *Evening* (1919, bronze, h. 19 1/2 ins / 49.5 cm) GBP 13,200. BERLIN, 29 May 1992, *Young Girl with Scarf* (1913, black-patinated bronze, h. 32 1/2 ins / 82.5 cm) USD 54,240. PARIS, 24 Nov 1992, *Female Nude Standing* (bronze, h. 19 3/4 ins / 50 cm) FRF 30,000. LONDON, 20 May 1993, *Nude Seated* (bronze, h. 15 3/4 ins / 40 cm) GBP 10,925. HEIDELBERG, 15-16 Oct 1993, *Female Nude Reclining with a Leg Tucked Up* (earthenware, h. 8 1/4 ins / 21 cm, L.15 1/4 ins/39 cm) DEM 1,400. PARIS, 16 Dec 1994, *Young Woman Seated* (bronze, h. 10 1/2 ins / 26.5 cm) FRF 32,000. AMSTERDAM, 6 Dec 1995, *Dancer* (bronze, h. 31 1/2 ins / 80 cm) NLG 11,500. LONDON, 9 Oct 1997, *Woman Kneeling with a Bath Towel* (brown-patinated bronze, h. 20 3/4 ins / 53 cm) GBP 12,650. BERLIN, 4 June 1999, *Nereid on Seashell* (c. 1936, black patinated bronze, 70 x 23x26 ins / 179 x 58x65 cm) DEM 110,000. BERLIN, 26 Nov 1999, *Spring* (1926, brown patinated bronze, 70 x 16x14 ins / 179 x 41x36 cm) DEM 120,000. COLOGNE, 2 June 2000, *Youth* (zinc, h. 63 ins / 160 cm) DEM 35,000. BERLIN, 24 Nov 2000, *Youth* (black-green patinated bronze, 63 x 24x12 ins / 159 x 61x31 cm) DEM 90,000. COLOGNE, 4 Dec 2001, *Kneeling Bather with Cloth* (black-green patinated bronze, h. 21 ins / 54 cm) DEM 32,000. COLOGNE, 4 Dec 2001, *Evening* (dark brown patinated bronze, h. 18 ins / 46 cm) DEM 32,000. BERLIN, 7 June 2002, *Summer Day* (1937, brown patinated bronze, 18 x 43x18 ins / 45 x 110x45 cm) EUR 45,000. BERLIN, 30 Nov 2002, *Spring* (brown patinated bronze, h. 71 ins / 180 cm) EUR 35,000. COLOGNE, 20 Nov 2003, *Meditation* (marble, 72 x 31x19 ins / 183 x 78x47 cm) EUR 38,000. BERLIN, 29 Nov 2003, *In wind and Sun* (dark brown patinated bronze, h. 58 ins / 147 cm) EUR 32,000. COLOGNE, 2 Dec 2004, *Hallelujah* (1940, marble, h. 90 ins / 228 cm) EUR 36,000. COLOGNE, 4 Dec 2004, *Youth* (bronze, h. 62 ins / 158 cm) EUR 37,000.

KLIMSCH, Hans Paul

German, 19th - 20th century.
Born 15 June 1868, in Frankfurt am Main; died 4 June 1917, in Frankfurt am Main.
Painter, illustrator. Landscapes, animals.

Hans Paul Klimsch specialised in painting mountainscapes.

KLIMSCH, Hermann Anton

German, 19th - 20th century.
Born 18 July 1867, in Frankfurt am Main.
Painter, engraver. Portraits, genre scenes, interiors, landscapes.

Hermann Anton Klimsch was trained by Leopold von Kalckreuth in Weimar.

AUCTION RECORDS:
ROME, 7 June 1995, *Grape-Harvesting Season* (oil on canvas, 39 1/4 x 51 1/4 ins / 100 x 130 cm) ITL 11,500,000.

KLIMT, Ernst, the Elder

Austrian, 19th century.
Engraver.

Ernst Klimt the Elder was active in Vienna. He was the father of the painters Gustav and Ernst Klimt.

KLIMT, Ernst, the Younger

Austrian, 19th century.
Born 3 January 1864, in Vienna; died 9 December 1892, in Vienna.
Painter, draughtsman. Stage sets.

Ernst Klimt the Younger was the son of the engraver Ernst Klimt and younger brother of Gustav Klimt. He studied with Laufberger and J. Berger in Vienna. He had a very promising talent, but died at the age of 28. He painted mainly stage sets in collaboration with his brother Gustav.

AUCTION RECORDS:
VIENNA, 28 Nov 1972, *Portrait of a Woman*, ATS 40,000. LONDON, 10 Feb 1988, *Salome* (brown and black ink and watercolour, 7 x 5 1/2 ins / 17.5 x 14 cm) GBP 22,000. STUTTGART, 2 Dec 1999, *Bathers* (oil on canvas, 30 x 31 ins / 76 x 80 cm) DEM 3,800.

KLIMT, Gustav

Austrian, 19th - 20th century.
Born 14 July 1862, in Baumgarten, near Vienna; died 6 February 1918, in Vienna.
Painter, draughtsman, decorative designer, ceramicist, lithographer. Figure compositions, allegorical subjects, figures, nudes, portraits, landscapes. Wall decorations, designs for tapestries, designs for mosaics.
Symbolism, Art Nouveau.
Vienna Secession group, Wiener Werkstätte group.

Gustav Klimt was the son of a goldsmith and he thus had no difficulty persuading his family to allow him to enrol at the School of Decorative Arts in Vienna in 1876. He trained under Laufberger. In 1879 he worked with Hans Makart, the famous painter of Viennese history, on various decorative compositions, including *The Triumphant Entry of the Emperor* (1879). From 1880 or 1883 he opened a studio for theatre decoration and wall decoration together with his brother Ernst and one of their study companions, Franz Matsch. They received a great many commissions, such as decorations for the National Theatre in Bucharest (1885), Karlsbad theatre (now known as Karlovy Vary, 1884-1886), and Vienna Burgtheater (1886-1888). The most important wall decoration was the one destined for the Kunsthistorisches Museum in Vienna (1890-1892), for which Klimt and his associates had to retrace the history of art from Ancient Egypt to the 16th century in 40 small panels for the pendentives of the staircase of the building. Klimt signed 11 of them. His style at this time was largely academic, in the tradition of the painter Mackart, but with no particular originality, except perhaps for a liking for embellishment and a certain stylisation of the silhouettes. When his brother died in 1892 he practically ceased painting, but he soon opened his own studio, painting a huge amount of portraits. He also painted a few paintings inspired by Impressionism during a very brief period around 1895, having acquainted himself with the style of French Impressionist painting at the beginning of the 1890s, and ideas and the Symbolist movement through his writer friends.

In 1897 Klimt left the Corporation of Austrian Artists (Künstlerhaus) of which he had been a member since 1891 (or 1893?), along with 40 of the painters, sculptors, architects and decorators who were his colleagues. They had decided to break free from the eclecticism in force in the art bodies of the moment by creating the Vereinigung Bildener Künstler (Association of Creative Artists), better known as the 'Vienna Secession'. They founded the journal *Ver Sacrum* (Sacred Spring), which 'spoke' on behalf of their movement. It claimed that its first aim was to destroy the outmoded idealism of the middle-class art of the second half of the 19th century. They also decided to create a new exhibition place, and Klimt entrusted the plans to Joseph-Maria Olbrich. It was inaugurated in 1908. The Vienna Secession thus continued the contemporary revolution in European art which had already found its foundation in the German 'Jugendstil' (Art Nouveau) and was being fast expressed through the French and English 'Modern' style.

Klimt was president of the Vienna Secession until 1903. He appeared at the Exposition Universelle of 1900 held in Paris and was awarded a gold medal. In 1905 he left the Vienna Secession and became a founder member of the Association of Austrian Artists the following year, becoming its president in 1912. The *Kunstschau* in 1908 was the last collective exhibition in which Klimt and his friends (who had left the Secession) participated. In 1909 he spent some time in Paris, becoming acquainted with the paintings of Bonnard, Vuillard and Vallotton. In 1910 and 1911 he was awarded first prize at the International Exhibition of Art in Rome. He became an honorary member of the International Society of Sculptors, Painters and Gravers in London. One year before his death, when the government refused him a post as a teacher, he was elected an honorary member of the Academies of Fine Art in both Vienna and Munich.

His astonishing and escalating monumental paintings entitled: *Philosophy, Medicine and Jurisprudence*, executed from 1900 to 1903 for the ceiling of the Aula Magna of the University of Vienna, encountered incomprehension and hostility when the studies were exhibited at the Secession in 1900, 1901 and 1902. Klimt was accused by the press and university institutions of perverting young people. These paintings were never put up in their intended location, and the Secretary of State for Education, who was his patron, had to resign. They were destroyed by the Nazis in 1945 in Castle Immendorf, but the studies for them have remained in the Albertina Museum in Vienna.

In 1902 the Vienna Secession decided to pay tribute to Beethoven. In the middle of the exhibition hall, around the sculpture - a polychromatic statue featuring the composer executed by Max Klinger - Klimt had designed an interpretation of the *Ninth Symphony* in decorative panels, which he entitled *Beethoven Frieze*. It won the admiration of young artists and established his reputation. It is possible that the relative failure of his ceilings for the University of Vienna made him inclined to abandon the painting of composition, and instead devote himself more to decorative painting. This is what some people have assumed. Yet it seems quite plausible that he did not make any distinction between the two, or even that he was convinced that the supreme aim of painting was precisely to ultimately integrate it perfectly into an architectural framework. His paintings were already very concerned with the harmonious and dense occupation of space, yet still concerned with ambitious meanings. However, the fact remains that from that moment onwards, his paintings developed a complex mass of shapes in their arabesques and volutes, mosaics with abstract ornamental motifs and applications of gold and silver leaf - the pinnacle in terms of range of colours - all resolutely aimed at achieving a jewelled effect. His subject matter of morals, and his symbolic representation of them, resulted in a strange, exclusive cult of women. They were depicted partly as sex objects, and partly as supreme beings. It was a cult which others, such as Werner Hofmann, had no difficulty in likening to Freud's analysis and the myths of Weininger. The faces of these muses or inspiration always appear as patches in the manner of 'collages' within an abundance of the 'peacock's tail' method of decorative flora. They are placed at strange angles and are evocative of past, present or future ecstasy. Examples are *The Kiss* (1902); *Judith II-Salomé* (1903); portrait of *Adele Bloch-Bauer* (1907); *Hope* (1907-1909), which is a representation of his nude pregnant wife; and particularly *Danaë* (1907-1908), where, unlike previous illustrators of this theme, Klimt depicts the act of love as a veritable hymn to female flesh, with shimmering effects like the inside of a shell, set in a symbolically charged oval which occupies the entire space of the composition. Another composition which was characteristic of Klimt's style is *The Three Ages of Life* (1908) and notably *The Kiss* from 1908, a work which was acquired that same year by the Österreichisches Galerie in Vienna. This latter painting formed the subject matter of a great many studies. It was initially called *The Couple*, a motif which Klimt had already handled in an allegorical style. In this instance, the body language of the man and woman and the intensity in their faces express a symbolic state of the imagination. The image of the woman, submissive and yet secretly asserting her identity and individuality, has an ambiguous link to modernity.

Opinions differ as to whether Klimt can be classed as painting in the decorative style or whether he had brilliant intuition. What is conspicuous in all these paintings is the systematic rejection of the third dimension. This had already been tackled by Gauguin and the Nabis, but Klimt applied it with an intransigence which would not surpass the strictest Neo-Plasticists. Thus, having more or less abandoned painting using an easel, he contributed to works of applied art (which would ultimately take him back to the work he produced in his youth when he was working with his brother) for the *Wiene Werkstätten* (*Viennese Studios*), which were founded in 1903 by the architect Josef Hoffmann. Klimt executed, for example, the famous decoration in mosaic, metal, enamel, earthenware, stone and painting, a frieze depicting the theme of love - *Expectation* and *Accomplishment* - for Hotel Stoclet in Brussels, Josef Hoffmann's major work c. 1909.

Following a trip to France at this time, Klimt's manner of painting changed. The gold and wealth of decoration declined. From 1909 onwards, he painted landscapes, and drew a few nudes in interior domestic scenes. The 2003 exhibition held in Vienna showed the decorative and frontal manner with which Klimt handled landscapes, influenced by pointillism, but without ever submitting to it. These works show evidence of lyricism, and give a symbolist vision of nature. However, it was in his parallel career as a fashionable portrait artist that he again found the opportunity to clarify his concept of the 'woman-flower', on backgrounds treated like mosaics with generously coloured floral elements. José Pierre saw this as a transition from obvious Symbolism to a less doctrinaire latent Symbolism, which was more internalised and allocated to both landscapes and portraits. Klimt nevertheless continued to paint allegorical paintings, such as *Young Girl* (1913); *Life and Death* (1911-1916); *Adam and Eve* (1917-1918) and *Bride* (1917-1918). As an illustrator, as well as his work on the *Ver Sacrum* review, he illustrated works, including *Allegories and Emblem*, published in 1883; *Die Hetärengespräche des Lukian* in 1907 and *Women* by Paul Verlaine.

Although Egon Schiele and Oskar Kokoschka were his direct disciples, the entire Blaue Reiter (Blue Rider) movement - referring to Klimt's prodigious ornamental invention - regarded him as one of the precursors of Abstraction. Kurt Schwitters later referred to him as the inventor of the principle of collage, and when he created his *Merzbau*, he was aware that he was both extending the parameters of environmental painting, and opening up the artistic possibilities available to painters and decorative artists of the fin de siècle. Despite his strict will in terms of functionality, which obviously distinguished him from the exuberance of Jugendstil (the German and Austrian form of Art Nouveau), Bauhaus also, in its way, extended the quest for a unity of style, which would coordinate the work of all those participating into one and the same construction, ranging from architecture right to the smallest hand-made objects. It would obviously also affect painters and decorative artists.

Ultimately, after a long eclipse, Jugendstil, and notably Klimt, became influential once again during several art movements in the 1960s. It was not until after 1950 that people abandoned the attitude of derision it had been convenient to adopt until then to treat all art and decorative production which had defined the fin de siècle period and the 1900s. They finally became aware of a pan-European unity of style in terms of this production, its very great degree of originality, and the huge influence it had exercised and continued to exercise in many fields. During this period, works of art - according to the strictest definition of the term - and applied works could no longer be clearly distinguished from one another. They had a reciprocal influence in terms of the deliberate wish to create unity of style, including everything from the concept of the architectural building to the most minor detail on equipment. The house of the Bavarian painter Franz von Stuck and the *Casa Mila* by Gaudí in Barcelona were typical examples of this. However different the concerns of Edward Munch, Ferdinand Hodler or Klimt may have been, however much their creations were at the more gratuitous origin of Symbolism, Expressionism or ornamentalism, and however difficult this huge diversified movement found unity of definition, it can at any rate be defined very precisely in terms of what it set itself up against - Neo-Romanticism - inasmuch as it was radically anti-Realist.

Klimt participated in a number of collective exhibitions, including: 1900, Exposition Universelle, Paris; 1908, *Kunstschau* (Art Show), Vienna; 1910, Biennale in Venice; and 1911, International Exhibition of Art, Rome. In 1960 his work was re-discovered in France, thanks to the exhibition entitled *Twentieth-Century Sources* held at the Musée National d'Art Moderne in Paris. His work has appeared in several solo exhibitions and retrospectives, including: 1967, Gallery Welz, Salzburg; 1969, Galerie Trois plus Deux, Paris; 2001, *Klimt und die Frauen* (*Klimt and Women*), Österreichische Galerie Belvedere, Vienna; and 2003, *Gustave Klimt: Landschaften* (*Gustave Klimt: Landscapes*), Österreichische Galerie Belvedere, Vienna.

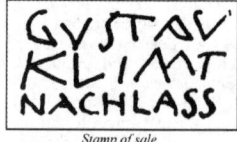

Stamp of sale

BIBLIOGRAPHY:

Comini, Alessandra, *Gustav Klimt: Drawings*, Thames & Hudson, London, 1975. Strobl, Alice, '*Gustav Klimt - Die Zeichnungen*', *4 vol., vol.I 1878-1903, vol.II 1904-1912*, vol. III 1912-1918, vol. IV 1878-1918, Nachtrag, catalogue raisonné, Verlag Gal. Welz, Salzburg, 1980-1989. Sebarsky, Serge, *Gustav Klimt: Drawings*, Fraser, London, 1984. Whitford, Frank, *Gustav Klimt*, Collins and Brown, London, 1993. Fliedl, Gottfried, *Gustav Klimt*, Taschen, Cologne, 1997. Bailey, Colin B., *Gustav Klimt: Modernism in the Making*, exhibition catalogue, National Gallery of Canada, Ottawa, Abrams, New York, 2001. Koja, Stephan/Huemer, Christian, *Gustave Klimt. Landschaften*, exhibition catalogue, Österreichische Galerie Belvedere, Vienna, 2003 (English and German edition).

MUSEUMS AND GALLERIES:

BASEL (Kunstmus.): *Elisabeth Bachofen Echt* - CAMBRIDGE, MA (Fogg AM, Harvard University): *Pear Tree* (1903) - MUNICH (Neue Pinakothek): *Music; Margaret Stonborough-Wittgenstein* (1905) - NEW YORK (MoMA): *Hope II* (1907-1908); *Park* (1909); *Mäda Primavesi* (1912) - NEW YORK (New Gal.): *Dancer* (1916-1918) - OTTAWA (NG. of Canada): *Expectation* (1900-1910); *Hope I* (1903) - PARIS (Mus. d'Orsay): *Rose Bushes beneath the Trees* (1905, oil on canvas) - PRAGUE (Národní Gal.): large decorative composition; *Young Girl* (1912-1913); *The Virgin* (1913) - ROME (Gal. Nazionale d'Arte Moderna): *The Three Ages of Woman* (1905); *Watersnakes (Girlfriends)* (1904-1907) - STRASBOURG (MBA): *The Kiss* (card of the mosaic for the Hôtel Stoclet in Bruxelles); *Plenitude* - VENICE (Gal. d'Arte Moderna): *Judith II* (1909) - VIENNA (Albertina Mus.): *Young Girl Reclining with Arm Folded* - VIENNA (Kunsthistorisches Mus.): *Love* (1895); *Idyll; Pallas Athena* (1898); *Poster for the First Exhibition of the Vienna Secession* (1898); *Philosophy* (preliminary sketch dating from 1899); *Emilie Flöge* (1902) - VIENNA (Leopold Mus.): *Attersee I* (1900, oil on canvas) - VIENNA (Mus. Moderner Kunst Stiftung Ludwig): *Adele Bloch-Bauer II* (1912); *Apple Tree I* (1912) - VIENNA (Österreichische Gal. Belvedere): *Organ Grinder* (1885); *Portrait of Sonja Knips* (1898); *Farm with Silver Birches* (1900); *Judith* (1901); *The Beethoven Frieze; the Longing for Happiness Finds Its Relief in Poetry* (1902); *Judith II - Salomé* (1903); *Farmer's Garden with Sunflowers* (c. 1905-1908); *Portrait of Fritza Riedler* (1906); *Poppy Meadow* (1907); *The Kiss* (1907-1908); *Judith and Holofernes* (1909); *Castle Kammer Park Avenue* (1912); *Apple Tree II* - VIENNA (Österreichisches Mus. für Angewandte Kunst): *Expectation* (1905-1909, preparatory drawing pour la frise du palais Stoclet); *Fulfilment* (1905-1909, preparatory drawing for the Stoclet Palace frieze) - VIENNA (Österreichisches Theatermus.): *Nuda Veritas* (1899).

AUCTION RECORDS:

NEW YORK, 30 Nov 1960, *Nude* (pencil) USD 275. NEW YORK, 26 Oct 1967, *Homage to Poetry* (study for the curtain at the Karlsbad Theatre; *Gustav Klimt and Franz von Matsch*, USD 5,500. VIENNA, 17 March 1970, *Evening Prayer*, ATS 20,000. LONDON, 30 Nov 1971, *Portrait of Hermine Gallia* (1904) Gns 20,000. VIENNA, 28 Nov 1972, *Female Portrait*, ATS 40,000. LONDON, 4 April 1974, *Drawing of a Nude Standing*, GBP 1,400. LONDON, 7 April 1976, *Nude Standing* (drawing, 22 1/4 x 14 ins / 56.5 x 35.5 cm) GBP 2,600. MUNICH, 30 April 1976, *Kunstausstellung Vereinigung bildender Künstler Osterreichs* (*Art Exhibition of the Association of Sculptural Artists of Austria*) (coloured lithograph, poster, 24 1/4 x 17 3/4 ins / 61.5 x 45 cm) DEM 1,700. MUNICH, 23 May 1977, *Portrait of Baron Traun* (c 1896, oil on card, 17 3/4 x 13 1/4 ins / 45 x 33.5 cm) DEM 13,300. NEW YORK, 8 Nov 1979, *Schubert at the Piano* (c. 1900, pencil, study, 17 3/4 x 12 1/2 ins / 45.1 x 31.5 cm) USD 14,000. NEW YORK, 19 May 1981, *Portrait of a Blind Person* (oil on canvas, 26 1/2 x 20 3/4 ins / 67 x 53 cm) USD 50,000. LONDON, 6 Dec 1983, *Life, a Combat (Chevalier d'Or)* (1903, oil on canvas, 39 1/4 x 39 1/4 ins / 100 x 100 cm) GBP 620,000. BERN, 21 June 1984, *Young Girl Reclining, Dress Lifted* (c. 1914) CHF 32,000. LONDON, 5 Dec 1984, *Dear Heart, Where is the Moon?* (1899, gouache and gold/wooden fan, 21 x 11 1/2 ins / 52.5 x 29.5 cm) GBP 60,000. LONDON, 2 Dec 1986, *Nude Reclining* (c. 1913, pencil, 14 1/2 x 22 ins / 37 x 56 cm) GBP 25,000. LONDON, 30 June 1987, *Castle Kammer at Attersee II* (c. 1909, oil on canvas, 43 1/4 x 43 1/4 ins / 110 x 110 cm) GBP 3,000,000. LONDON, 1 July 1987, *Couple of Lovers* (c. 1915, pencil, 14 3/4 x 19 ins / 37.3 x 48.5 cm) GBP 21,000. LONDON, 10 Feb 1988, *Decoration Project for a Proscenium* (oil on canvas, 6 1/4 x 27 1/2 ins / 16 x 70 cm) GBP 35,200; *Nude of Old Woman in Profile* (pencil, 17 1/4 x 12 ins / 44 x 30.5 cm) GBP 6,600; *Portrait of Adele Bloch-Bauer* (1903, soft black chalk, 17 3/4 x 12 ins / 45 x 30.5 cm) GBP 16,500. NEW YORK, 6 Oct 1988, *Female Nude* (pencil on paper, 22 1/2 x 14 3/4 ins / 57 x 37.5 cm) USD 5,280. LONDON, 21 Oct 1988, *Female Portrait*. ROME, 15 Nov 1988, *Maternity* (pencil on paper, 17 1/4 x 11 ins / 43.5 x 27 cm) ITL 8,000,000. LONDON, 22 Feb 1989, *Pregnant Woman with a Man* (pencil, 17 1/2 x 12 ins / 44.5 x 30.4 cm) GBP 3,300. PARIS, 7 March 1989, *Frontal View of Woman Standing* (1916, pencil drawing, 22 1/2 x 14 3/4 ins / 56.9 x 37.5 cm) FRF 85,000. LONDON, 27 June 1989, *Orchard* (oil on paper, 15 1/4 x 11 ins / 39 x 28 cm) GBP 374,000. NEW YORK, 18 Oct 1989, *Portrait of Young Girl with Dangling Hair* (pencil on natural paper, 22 1/2 x 14 3/4 ins / 57 x 37.5 cm) USD 23,100. NEW YORK, 13 Nov 1989, *Bust Portrait of a Lady in Profile from the Left Side* (pencil and red chalk on paper, 23 1/2 x 14 1/2 ins / 60 x 36.8 cm) USD 41,800. LONDON, 28 Nov 1989, *Orchard at the Edge of the Attersee* (1901, oil on canvas, 35 1/2 x 35 1/2 ins / 90 x 90 cm) GBP 2,970,000. LONDON, 3 April 1990, *Figure Slightly Turned Towards the Left* (red, black and blue pencil, 21 1/4 x 14 ins / 54 x 35.5 cm) GBP 28,600. NEW YORK, 16 May 1990, *Three-Quarter's Portrait of the Torso of Young Woman Turned towards the Right* (pencil on paper, 22 1/4 x 14 1/2 ins / 56.5 x 36.8 cm) USD 28,600. PARIS, 20 Nov 1990, *Elegant Woman in a Hat* (1907, lead pencil heightened with red and blue, 21 1/4 x 14 ins / 54 x 35.5 cm) FRF 220,000. LONDON, 4 Dec 1990, *Mother and Daughter* (pencil on paper, 22 1/4 x 15 ins / 56.5 x 37.2 cm) GBP 17,600. LONDON, 20 March 1991, *Figure Seated Turned towards the Left with Hands Placed One over the Other on the Knees* (black chalk, 17 3/4 x 12 ins / 45 x 30.5 cm) GBP 30,800. NEW YORK, 8 May 1991, *Reclining Couple Entwined and Turned towards the Right* (1914, pencil on paper, 14 x 20 3/4 ins / 35.5 x 53 cm) USD 38,500. MUNICH, 26-27 Nov 1991, *Baby Lying Down and Looking to the Right* (pencil and coloured chalk, 14 1/2 x 21 3/4 ins / 37 x 55.5 cm) DEM 74,750. PARIS, 2 Feb 1992, *Man and Pregnant Woman* (lead pencil on paper, 17 1/4 x 11 3/4 ins / 44 x 30 cm) FRF 76,000. LUGANO, 28 March 1992, *Woman Sleeping* (pencil on paper, 14 1/2 x 20 1/2 ins / 37 x 52 cm) CHF 50,000. MILAN, 21 May 1992, *Reclining Nude* (pencil, 14 1/2 x 22 1/4 ins / 37 x 56.5 cm) ITL 34,000,000. LONDON, 30 June 1992, *Nude Standing and Turned towards the Left* (pencil on paper, 17 1/2 x 12 1/4 ins / 44.5 x 30.8 cm) GBP 13,200. HEIDELBERG, 3 April 1993, *Dancer* (22 x 13 3/4 ins / 55 x 34.8 cm) DEM 58,000. NEW YORK, 12 May 1993, *Female Portrait* (pencil on paper, 22 1/2 x 15 ins / 57.2 x 38.1 cm) USD 40,250. NEW YORK, 11 May 1994, *Lady with a Fan* (oil on canvas, 39 1/4 x 39 1/2 ins / 100 x 100.3 cm) USD 11,662,500. LONDON, 28 Nov 1994, *Flower Bed* (oil on canvas, 43 1/4 x 43 1/4 ins / 110 x 110 cm) GBP 3,741,500. LONDON, 14 March 1995, *Nude Lying on Back with Arms Raised* (pencil, 22 x 14 1/4 ins / 56 x 36.5 cm) GBP 12,650. NEW YORK, 2 May 1996, *Female Intimacy* (pencil on paper, 14 1/2 x 22 1/4 ins / 37.1 x 56.5 cm) USD 68,500. LONDON, 23 Oct 1996, *Fe-*

male Portrait (chalk on paper, 20 x 13 ins / 51 x 33 cm) GBP 6,670. LONDON, 3 Dec 1996, *Nude Standing* (c. 1917, pencil on paper, 22 x 14 1/4 ins / 55 x 36 cm) GBP 10,350. LONDON, 4 Dec 1996, *Female Nude Seated, Her Face Hidden by Her Hair* (1907, pencil on paper, 22 x 14 1/2 ins / 56 x 37 cm) GBP 11,500; *Nude Seated with Thighs Spread Out* (c. 1909-1910, pencil on paper, 22 x 14 1/2 ins / 55.8 x 37 cm) GBP 5,750. LONDON, 19 March 1997, *Semi-Nude Model Seated with Right Arm Extended* (1902, pencil on paper, 17 3/4 x 12 1/2 ins / 45 x 31.5 cm) GBP 31,050. NEW YORK, 13 May 1997, *Litzbergerkeller am Attersee* (1915-1916, oil on canvas, 43 1/2 x 43 1/2 ins / 110.5 x 110.5 cm) USD 14,742,500. NEW YORK, 15 May 1997, *Nude Kneeling and Leaning over to the Left* (1904, pencil on paper, 13 3/4 x 21 1/2 ins / 34.9 x 54.9 cm) USD 25,300. LONDON, 9 Oct 1997, *Castle Kammer at Attersee II* (1909, oil on canvas, 43 1/4 x 43 1/4 ins / 110 x 110 cm) GBP 14,521,500. LONDON, 6 Oct 1999, *Die grosse Pappel I* (1900, oil on canvas, 31 x 31 ins / 80 x 80 cm) GBP 1,900,000. VIENNA, 12 Oct 1999, *Helene Klimt* (oil on card, 24 x 16 ins / 60 x 40 cm) ATS 11,000,000. NEW YORK, 11 May 2000, *Kneeling Half Nude* (pencil, 29 x 21 ins / 74 x 54 cm) USD 80,000. NEW YORK, 10 Nov 2000, *Portrait of a Woman* (pencil, 22 x 15 ins / 57 x 37 cm) USD 250,000. LONDON, 10 Oct 2001, *Woman in an Armchair* (oil on board, 20 x 20 ins / 52 x 52 cm) GBP 2,500,000. LONDON, 11 Oct 2001, *Reclining Female Nude* (c. 1913, pencil crayon, 15 x 22 ins / 37 x 56 cm) GBP 210,000. NEW YORK, 4 Nov 2002, *Crouching Nude from the Left* (pencil, 15 x 22 ins / 37 x 56 cm) USD 105,000. NEW YORK, 4 Nov 2002, *Nude with Spread Legs* (oil on panel, 22 x 15 ins / 57 x 37 cm) USD 120,000. LONDON, 26 June 2003, *Two Reclining Female Nudes* (c. 1913, pen, ink and red crayon, 15 x 22 ins / 37 x 57 cm) GBP 50,000. NEW YORK, 5 Nov 2003, *Landhaus am Attersee* (c. 1914, oil on canvas, 43 x 43 ins / 110 x 110 cm) USD 26,000,000. LONDON, 3 Feb 2004, *Girl with Long Hair in Profile* (c. 1899, pastel, 22 x 15 ins / 55 x 37 cm) GBP 160,000. LONDON, 21 June 2004, *Farmhouse with Birch Trees* (1900, oil on canvas, 31 x 31 ins / 80 x 80 cm) GBP 1,800,000.

KLINCKENBERG, Eugen, or Klinkenberg
Dutch, 19th - 20th century.
Born 2 February 1858, in Haus Lemiers; died 1942.
Painter. History painting, genre scenes.

Eugen Klinckenberg studied at the Brussels academy. He later worked in Paris, Rome and Munich and also exhibited in Berlin and Munich.

MUSEUMS AND GALLERIES:
AACHEN: *Trouville.*

AUCTION RECORDS:
COLOGNE, 11 May 1977, *Hunting Scene* (1885, oil on canvas, 22 x 14 1/2 ins / 56 x 37 cm) DEM 2,700. COLOGNE, 11 June 1979, *Elderly Horseman and Young Girl* (1885, oil on canvas, 27 3/4 x 17 3/4 ins / 70.5 x 45 cm) DEM 7,000.

KLINCKERFLUSS, Bernhard
German, 20th century.
Born 23 May 1881, in Stuttgart.
Painter, sculptor. Landscapes.

Bernhard Klinckerfluss was taught by Landenberger and brought back landscapes from his travels in France, England and Italy.

KLINE, Franz
American, 20th century.
Born 1910, in Wilkes-Barre (Pennsylvania); died 1962, in New York.
Painter (including gouache), draughtsman (including ink), collage artist. Figures, portraits, interiors with figures, landscapes, urban landscapes. Murals.
Action Painting.
School of New York.

Franz Kline studied at Girard College, Philadelphia, at Boston University in the early 1930s and then at Heatherly's School of Art in London. Back in New York in 1939, his sound grounding enabled him to teach, notably at the Pratt Institute and the Cooper Union, meeting on the way such artists as De Kooning, Motherwell and John Cage. Between 1940 and 1950, Franz Kline painted in the realist style the landscapes of Pennsylvania, portraits, townscapes, and took an interest in Daumier, Blake and Fuseli's work. He derived an income from the portraits he did in pencil in Greenwich Village and the murals he painted for local taverns, memorably in Bleecker Street, but remained obscure until 1945. From that date his figuration became more allusive, his vision more sweeping, his lines more forceful and his subject matter exploded into dark or paler masses balancing each other out.

In 1949, experimenting with De Kooning, Kline enlarged some ink drawings through a projector, and the expressive power of the magnified shapes and brushstrokes freed from the image confirmed his intent to follow a purely abstract style. Pushing further his experimentation, often by means of collage of papiers froissés, he arrived at an action painting technique he applied to large canvases, thus officially joining Jackson Pollock and Willem de Kooning in the foundation of the School of New York. The ostensibly abstract pieces in his first solo exhibition had not been so in their conception: portraits such as *Nijinsky* (1948) focused on their sitter's psychology whilst the large black lashes at white backgrounds on other paintings evoked the dynamic dash of a train engine or the steel girders of a bridge. His 1950s paintings should not, for all their black and white, be reduced to variations on oriental calligraphies. For Kline, the linear trajectories, stretching beyond the canvas, reflected the cosmic tensions at work around him, and sought to shape the energy, to account for opposing forces (*Requiem*, 1958), to be at one with the mechanics of the industrial world. In 1958, he reintroduced colour in his paintings, gradually coaxing them into the bold and impulsive manner which characterised him (*Orange and black Wall*, 1959). Franz Kline's work belongs with International lyrical abstraction, along with Pollock's; together with him, he is one of the leading figures in the advent of an original American school of painting.

Kline exhibited successfully at the National Academy of Design, winning a major prize in 1943. He featured in the *New Decade* exhibition at the Whitney Museum in New York. Other collective exhibitions took place at Pittsburgh, Biennials in Venice (1956 and 1960 when he took an award); São Paulo, the Documenta in Kassel and all the significant shows of the young American School. His first solo exhibition in New York in 1950 was well received and by the second he was a feature on the American art scene. He had shows in Boston and Chicago. Many retrospective exhibitions were dedicated to him around the world after his untimely death in 1962, notably at Cincinnati and the Whitney Museum, whose *Franz Kline: Black & White 1950-1961* travelled from New York to the Museum of Contemporary Art in Chicago in 1995.

BIBLIOGRAPHY:
Franz Kline (1910-1962), exhibition catalogue, Whitney Museum of American Art, New York, 1968. Sandler, I., *Abstract Expressionism: The Triumph of American Painting*, London, 1970. Gaugh, Harry F., *Franz Kline's Romantic Abstraction*, periodical, Artforum, London, xiii/10 1975. Boime A./Mitchell F. (ed.), *Franz Kline: The Early Works as Signals*, exhibition catalogue, Binghamton, SUNY College, Purchase (NY), 1977. Gaugh, Harry F., *Franz Kline: The Color Abstractions*, exhibition catalogue, Phillips Col., Washington DC, 1979. Caugh, Harry F., *Franz Kline: The Vital Gesture: Cincinnati Art Museum*, Abbeville Press, New York, 1985. Anfam, D., *Franz Kline: Black and White 1950-1961*, exhibition catalogue, The Menil Collection, Houston, 1994. Anfam, D.,

Franz Kline: Black & White, 1950-1961, exhibition catalogue, Menil Col., Houston, 1994.

Museums and Galleries:

Baltimore (MA): *Yellow, Red, Green, Blue* (1956) - Basel: *Andes* (1957) - Düsseldorf (Kunstsammlung Nordrhein-Westfalen): *Untitled* (1957) - Hartford (Wadsworth Atheneum): *Painting* (1952, oil on canvas) - Houston (MFA): *Wotan* (1950) - New York (MoMA): *Chief* (1950); *Painting Number Two* (1954); *Le Gros* (1961) - New York (Solomon R. Guggenheim Mus.): *Painting* (1952) - Pittsburgh (Carnegie MA): *Grey Antique* (1958, casein/paper); *Siegfried* (1958, oil on canvas) - Raleigh (North Carolina MA).

Auction records:

New York, 13 Dec 1961, *Bar Room Painting*, USD 4,500. New York, 13 Oct 1965, *Initial*, USD 18,000. New York, 3 April 1968, *Black Sienne*, USD 28,000. New York, 18 Nov 1970, *Andrus*, USD 52,500. New York, 24 Oct 1974, *Diamond*, USD 95,000. London, 18 March 1976, *Composition 1950 and 1948* (oil on double-sided paper, 29 1/2 x 22 1/2 ins / 75 x 57 cm) USD 4,500. London, 7 Dec 1977, *Untitled* (1955, oil on canvas, 50 3/4 x 86 1/2 ins / 129 x 220 cm) GBP 35,000. New York, 18 May 1979, *Painting No3* (1952, oil on canvas, 60 x 72 ins / 152.5 x 183 cm) USD 240,000. New York, 13 Feb 1980, *The Artist's Studio* (1940, etching/Japanese paper, 5 1/4 x 5 ins / 13.3 x 12.4 cm) USD 1,100. New York, 16 May 1980, *Self-portrait* (c. 1944-1945, ink and pen/mounted paper/card, 10 x 8 ins / 25.5 x 20.5 cm) USD 3,600. New York, 16 May 1980, *Abstraction* (c. 1953-1954, oil on canvas, 35 x 28 3/4 ins / 88 x 73 cm) USD 110,000. New York, 12 Nov 1980, *Untitled* (1957, gouache, 19 3/4 x 14 3/4 ins / 50 x 37.5 cm) USD 25,000. New York, 12 May 1981, *West Brand* (1960, oil on canvas, 93 1/4 x 79 1/2 ins / 237 x 202 cm) USD 350,000. New York, 11 May 1983, *Shenandoah Wall* (1960, brush and black ink/paper and card, study, 11 x 25 ins / 27 x 63.5 cm) USD 29,000. New York, 8 Nov 1983, *Harleman* (1960, oil on canvas, 53 x 102 1/4 ins / 134.5 x 259.5 cm) USD 460,000. New York, 2 Nov 1984, *Untitled* (1952, collage, oil gouache/a page from a phone directory, 10 3/4 x 13 1/2 ins / 27.3 x 34.2 cm) USD 36,000. New York, 1 May 1985, *Untitled* (1960, oil on canvas, 116 1/4 x 79 ins / 295.2 x 200.5 cm) USD 800,000. New York, 11 Nov 1986, *Study for Initial* (c. 1959, ink/mounted paper/card, 12 1/4 x 9 1/2 ins / 31 x 24 cm) USD 35,000. New York, 6 May 1987, *Untitled* (1959, brush and black ink/paper, 15 x 11 ins / 37.8 x 27.7 cm) USD 42,000. New York, 3 May 1988, *Blue Horizontal Lines* (oil on paper, 8 1/2 x 10 1/4 ins / 21.8 x 26 cm) USD 22,000. Paris, 23 March 1989, *Zinc Yellows and Grey* (1958, oil on paper, 22 x 16 3/4 ins / 56 x 42.5 cm) FRF 605,000. New York, 2 May 1989, *Red Painting* (1961, oil on canvas, 110 x 78 1/4 ins / 279.5 x 198.7 cm) USD 1,760, 000. New York, 3 May 1989, *Scudera* (1961, oil on canvas, 111 x 78 1/2 ins / 282 x 199.3 cm) USD 2,860,000. New York, 5 Oct 1989, *Self-portrait* (oil on canvas/card, 10 x 8 ins / 25.5 x 20.3 cm) USD 17,600. New York, 8 Nov 1989, *Third Avenue* (1954, oil on canvas, 37 3/4 x 24 3/4 ins / 96 x 62.8 cm) USD 1,210,000. Paris, 18 Feb 1990, *Figure Woman and Figure Advert* (six drawings, 16 3/4 x 13 3/4 ins / 42.5 x 35 cm) FRF 32,000. New York, 27 Feb 1990, *Untitled* (oil on paper, 11 x 8 1/2 ins / 28 x 21.5 cm) USD 44,000. New York, 7 May 1990, *Abstraction* (1951, oil on canvas, 74 1/2 x 57 1/4 ins / 189.2 x 145.5 cm) USD 1,760,000. New York, 8 May 1990, *Untitled* (oil on paper, 30 x 36 ins / 76 x 91.5 cm) USD 110,000. New York, 6 Nov 1990, *Untitled* (ink/paper, 7 1/2 x 15 ins / 19 x 38.1 cm) USD 3,850. New York, 7 Nov 1990, *Untitled* (1957, oil on canvas, 78 3/4 x 103 1/4 ins / 200.3 x 262 cm) USD 2,640,000. New York, 1 May 1991, *West Brand* (1960, oil on canvas, 93 1/2 x 79 1/2 ins / 237.5 x 201.9 cm) USD 1,870,000. New York, 3 Oct 1991, *Study for Mahoning* (ink/paper, 14 3/4 x 17 ins / 37.5 x 43.2 cm) USD 49,500. New York, 12 Nov 1991, *Henry H II* (oil on canvas, 79 1/2 x 60 ins / 201.9 x 152.4 cm) USD 1,650,000. New York, 5 May 1992, *Black and White* (1954, oil on paper/paper, 9 1/2 x 12 ins / 24.1 x 30.2 cm) USD 104,500. New York, 19 Nov 1992, *Untitled* (1949, ink/paper, 18 x 20 3/4 ins / 45.7 x 52.8 cm) USD 24,200. New York, 23-25 Feb 1993, *Untitled* (ink/paper, 8 1/2 x 11 ins / 21.6 x 27.9 cm) USD 34,500. New York, 3 May 1993, *Untitled (Study for Leda)* (1950, ink/paper, 9 1/2 x 7 ins / 24.1 x 17.8 cm) USD 46,000. New York, 4 May 1993, *Black Triangle* (1961, oil on reinforced canvas, 12 3/4 x 10 ins / 32.7 x 25.2 cm) USD 63,000. New York, 11 Nov 1993, *Untitled* (ink/paper, 11 x 12 1/4 ins / 27 x 30.8 cm) USD 85,000. Rome, 8 Nov 1994, *Untitled* (1958, ink and watercolour/paper/canvas, 10 3/4 x 8 1/2 ins / 27.5 x 21.5 cm) ITL 21,850,000. New York, 2 May 1995, *Figure* (oil on canvas, 71 x 44 1/2 ins / 180.3 x 113 cm) USD 1,047,500. London, 21 March 1996, *Untitled* (tempera/card, 8 x 5 1/2 x 1 1/2 ins / 19.4 x 14 x 4 cm) GBP 9,775. New York, 7 May 1996, *Swanee* (1960, oil on canvas, 35 x 47 ins / 89 x 119.3 cm) USD 965, 000. New York, 8 May 1996, *Accent aigu* (1957, oil on canvas, 78 x 49 ins / 198.1 x 124.5 cm) USD 717,500. New York, 19 Nov 1996, *Untitled* (brush and black ink and coloured chalk/paper/paper, 11 1/4 x 9 1/4 ins / 28.6 x 23.5 cm) USD 6,325. New York, 19 Nov 1996, *Untitled* (c. 1961, oil on paper, 11 x 8 1/2 ins / 27.9 x 21.6 cm) USD 79,500. New York, 20 Nov 1996, *Bruho* (1961, oil on canvas, 37 1/2 x 51 1/2 ins / 95.3 x 130.8 cm) USD 420,500. New York, 6 May 1997, *Crosstown* (1955, oil on canvas, 48 x 65 ins / 121.9 x 165.1 cm) USD 2,202,500. New York, 7 May 1997, *Abstraction* (c. 1950-1951, oil on canvas, 74 1/2 x 57 1/4 ins / 189.2 x 145.5 cm) USD 794,500. New York, 8 May 1997, *Untitled* (brush and black ink and collage/paper, 11 1/2 x 12 ins / 29.3 x 30.6 cm) USD 48,300. New York, 18 May 1999, *Shaft* (1955, oil on canvas, 24 x 29 ins / 61 x 74 cm) USD 380,000. New York, 17 Nov 1999, *Abstraction No.1* (1951, oil on paperboard, 37 x 25 ins / 95 x 63 cm) USD 280,000. New York, 17 May 2000, *Mycenae* (1958, oil on canvas, 101 x 76 ins / 256 x 194 cm) USD 600,000. New York, 15 Nov 2000, *Black Sienna* (1960, oil on canvas, 92 x 68 ins / 234 x 172 cm) USD 2,300,000. New York, 15 May 2001, *Untitled* (1953, oil on canvas, 54 x 28 ins / 137 x 71 cm) USD 700,000. New York, 16 May 2001, *Untitled* (oil on panel, 21 x 16 ins / 53 x 40 cm) USD 240,000. New York, 15 May 2002, *Pennsylvania* (1954, oil on canvas, 49 x 63 ins / 124 x 160 cm) USD 1,100,000. New York, 12 Nov 2002, *Ninth Street* (1951, oil on canvas, 60 x 78 ins / 152 x 198 cm) USD 4,100,000. New York, 11 Nov 2003, *Four Square* (1953, oil on canvas, 78 x 48 ins / 198 x 122 cm) USD 1,700,000. New York, 11 Nov 2003, *Rue* (1959, oil on canvas, 102 x 79 ins / 259 x 201 cm) USD 2,000,000. New York, 12 May 2004, *Untitled* (1954, ink, 12 x 10 ins / 30 x 26 cm) USD 98,000. New York, 13 May 2004, *Untitled* (ink, 6 x 5 ins / 15 x 13 cm) USD 55,000.

KLINE, Hibberd van Buren

American, 20th century.

Born 8 November 1885, in Curiesville (New York).

Painter.

Hibberd Kline attended the art college in Syracuse and the Art Students League (ASL). He was a member of the American Art Union.

KLINE, William Fair

American, 20th century.

Born 3 May 1870, in Columbia (South Carolina); died 1931.

Painter.

William Fair Kline studied at the National Academy of Design in New York and under Bouguereau and Benjamin Constant in Paris. Based in New York, he was rewarded with numerous distinctions: for example, a silver medal in Buffalo in 1901 and a bronze medal in St Louis in 1904. He was an associate member of the National Academy from 1901.

KLING, Anto

Austrian, 20th century.

Born 26 November 1881, in Vienna.

Painter. Cartoons for tapestries, stained glass windows.
Anto Kling worked in the decorative arts, carrying out mostly patterns for material and cartoons for tapestries and stained glass.

KLINGELHÖFER, Fritz
German, 19th century.
Born 4 May 1832, in Marburg; died 9 November 1903, in Marburg.
Active in the USA.
Painter. Landscapes.
Klingelhöfer studied with Achenbach. After spending 19 years in the USA as a press artist, he returned to settle in Germany.
AUCTION RECORDS:
COLOGNE, 28 June 1991, *Coastal Landscape in Southern Italy with a Castle on an Island* (oil on paper, 9 1/2 x 13 3/4 ins / 24 x 35 cm) DEM 2,200. HEIDELBERG, 14 April 2000, *African River Landscape with Natives* (1889, 22 x 17 ins / 57 x 42 cm) DEM 6,200. HEIDELBERG, 13 Oct 2000, *Romantic Tyrolean Landscape* (oil on canvas, 24 x 37 ins / 62 x 93 cm) DEM 4,900.

KLINGELHÖLLER, Harald
German, 20th - 21st century.
Born 1954, in Düsseldorf.
Sculptor, installation artist.
Düsseldorf Constructive Sculpture.
Harald Klingelhöller studied at the Staatliche Kunstakademie in Düsseldorf. He lives and works in Düsseldorf. His work has its origins in 'Düsseldorf constructive sculpture', a rather vague name from the 1980s for German artists of the post-war generation, who were pupils of Joseph Beuys or Klaus Rinke at the Kunstakademie in Düsseldorf. A 'constructive' sculpture is one that can question the different 'natural' and cultural states of artistic creation in contemporary Germany. Klingelhöller himself works with a variety of materials that are *a priori* difficult to reconcile: steel, glass, mirrors and card.

He has taken part in a great many group exhibitions, including: 1980, *Perspektiven 2* at the Düsseldorf Kunsthalle; 1981, *Alles Gute* (*All the Best*) at PS1, New York; 1985, *Les Seconds Ateliers de Fontevraud* at the Abbaye Royale in Fontevraud; 1986, *Europa/America* at the Ludwigsmuseum in Cologne; 1988, Institute of Contemporary Art, Boston; 1990, *Weitersehen* (*Look Further*) at the Krefeld Kunstmuseum; 1991, *Bild und Wort in der Kunst Heute* (*Image and Word in Art Today*) at the Heydt-Muesum in Wuppertal; and the 1992 Documenta in Kassel.

Solo shows have included: 1981 and 1985, Galerie Rüdiger-Schöttle, Munich; 1982, Galerie Schmela, Düsseldorf; 1984, Galerie Fischer, Düsseldorf; 1986, Galerie Philippe Nelson, Lyons; 1988 Museum Haus Esters, Krefeld; 1989, Galerie Ghislaine Hussenot, Paris; 1990, Galerie Philippe Nelson, Lyons, Stedelijk Van Abbemuseum, Eindhoven and the Whitechapel Art Gallery, London; 1991, Galerie Konrad Fischer, Düsseldorf; 1992, Portikus, Frankfurt am Main; 1993, Mukha, Antwerp; 1994, Galerie Ghislaine Hussenot, Paris; and 1997 and 2002, Galerie Nelson, Paris.
BIBLIOGRAPHY:
Harald Klingelhöller, exhibition catalogue, ARC musée d'Art moderne de la Ville de Paris, Paris, 1985. Heyme, J./Deutsch, *Harald Klingelhöller*, Kunstmuseum, Krefeld, 1988. Cassiman, Bart/Zacharopoulos, O.T. Denys, '*I am here, you are here*' in *Harald Klingelhöller*, exhibition catalogue, Stedelijk Van Abbemuseum, Eindhoven (NLD), Whitechapel Art Gall., London, 1990. Cueff, Alain, '*Le Langage à l'œuvre*' in *Art Press* n° 158, periodical, Paris, May 1991.
MUSEUMS AND GALLERIES:
CHÂTEAUGIRON (FRAC Bretagne) - DUNKIRK (FRAC Nord-Pas de Calais) - PARIS (FNAC): *Alle Metaphern werden wahr* (*All Metaphors become True*) (1992).

KLINGEN, Richard
German, 20th century.
Born 9 March 1873; died 8 April 1924.
Painter. Portraits, landscapes.
Richard Klingen attended the art academy in Düsseldorf.

KLINGENDER, Louis Henry Weston
German, 19th century.
Born 22 April 1861, in Liverpool, England; died 1950.
Painter. Hunting scenes, animals.
Klingender exhibited in Berlin, Dresden and Düsseldorf from 1888.
AUCTION RECORDS:
LONDON, 20 June 1986, *Wolves Attacking a Stag* (oil on canvas, 88 x 126 ins / 223.5 x 320 cm) GBP 7,500.

KLINGER, Johan Georg
German, 18th century.
Born 1764, in Nuremberg.
Draughtsman, engraver.
Klinger engraved a large number of portraits.

KLINGER, Julius
Austrian, 20th century.
Born 22 May 1876, in Vienna.
Painter.
Julius Klinger was known above all for his posters.

KLINGER, Klaus
German, 20th century.
Born 1943, in Znaim (now Znojmo, Czech Republic).
Draughtsman, pastellist.
Klaus Klinger has taken part in many group exhibitions, notably in Munich in 1979. He also shows in solo exhibitions, including Regensburg in 1985.

KLINGER, Max
German, 19th - 20th century.
Born 12 February 1857, in Plagwitz, near Leipzig; died 5 July 1920, in Grossjena, near Nuremberg.
Painter, sculptor, engraver. Religious subjects, allegorical subjects, mythological subjects. Statues.
Symbolism.
Max Klinger entered the art school in Karlsruhe at the age of 16, where he studied under Karl Gussov. When Gussov accepted a professorship at the Akademie der Künste in Berlin, Klinger accompanied him to that city from 1875 to 1878. He also worked in the studio of Arnold Böcklin, who was also an influence. He began to exhibit in public in 1878 with a painting, *Walkers*, and eight drawings relating to the life of Christ. The boldness of his expression, with its pronounced realistic tendencies, gave rise to much controversy and he was the object of violent attacks. The acquisition of his drawings by the Neue Nationalgalerie in Berlin inflated the resentment of his enemies. Emboldened by his initial success, Klinger did not modify his artistic style. In the meantime he had taught himself engraving, beginning in this new discipline in 1879 by publishing numerous engravings and aquatints in which the same concern with realism was revealed. As a result of the substantial hostility against him, he decided to travel. He initially went to Brussels in 1879 where he studied the Old Flemish Masters. From there he went on to Austria, spent some time in Munich in 1880, then moved to Berlin from 1881 to 1883 and Paris from 1883 to 1887, settling finally in Rome from 1888 until 1892 or 1893. He decided to return to Germany, but rejected Berlin in preference for Plagwitz, near Leipzig, in his native area.

In 1891 he edited an essay entitled *Malerei und Zeichnung* (*Painting and Drawing*). In 1895 he took up a professorship at the academy in Vienna, but his independent and reflective nature made him somewhat unsuited for the teaching of theory, so he resigned. In 1897 he was appointed a professor at the Leipzig drawing school, while continuing to be a correspondent member of the Vienna Secession, where he exhibited in 1901. In 1912 he was a founder member of the *Leipziger Jahresaustellung* (*Leipzig Annual Exhibition*), of which he was the president. The Museum der Bildenden Künste in Leipzig built a special hall to house his most important works.

Klinger felt equally at home in painting and engraving. Among his most remarkable paintings are *Attack by the Wall*, 1877, then: *The Blue Hour*, 1890, *Nymph at the Seaside; Deputation* and the famous *Crucifixion*, a source of passionate controversy, in which Klinger introduced figures in modern dress, transforming the sacred scene into a naturalist 'slice of life'; just as in his *Christ on Olympus*, he attempted to reconcile paganism and Christianity, inspired by Wagner's work; he also dedicated compositions to the symphonies of Brahms. In his capacity as an engraver he was also very prolific, and in this area, albums such as the *Brahms Fantasy* and, particularly, *A Glove* mean he can be counted as one of the precursors of Surrealism, such works belonging at all events to fantastic art, influenced by Goya. Among his finest series of prints were: *On Death* (25 plates), *Amor and Psyche* (46 plates, published in 1880), *A Life* (20 plates), *Brahms Fantasies* (48 plates) and *Epithalamia* by Asenijeff, his first wife.

He also ventured into sculptural art. In this field too he was innovative, concentrating on statuary in polychrome marble, and infusing it with a boldness and vitality hitherto unknown in the modern German school. His originality was initially baffling but then struck home. His statues include *The Dance*, *Cassandra* and *Beethoven Seated* (1902), which was the central theme of the 1902 Vienna Secession, with friezes surrounding it which were decorated by Klimt.

His one-man shows and retrospectives include: 1977, *Max Klinger l'oeuvre gravé* (*Max Klinger: Engravings*), Goethe Institut, Paris; 1982, *Max Klinger: Gravures* (*Max Klinger: Engravings*), Musée d'Art et d'Histoire, Cabinet des Estampes (Prints Collection), Geneva; 1984, Roemer-und-Pelizaeus-Museum, Hildesheim; 1990, *Max Klinger, Druckgraphiken* (*Max Klinger: Engravings*), Landesmuseum Mainz; 1992, 1995, *Max Klinger*, Museum der Bildenden Künste, Leipzig; 2001, presentation of the spectacular score of the *Brahms Fantasy*, published in 1894, Musée d'Orsay, Paris; 2002, *Max Klinger - Incisioni da una Collezione Privata Bolognese* (*Max Klinger - Engravings in a Private Bolognese Collection*), Museo Morandi, Bologna; 2003, *Max Klinger. Engravings* (*Max Klinger. Engravings*), Musée d'Art Moderne et Contemporain, Strasbourg; 2003, *Éros et Thanatos. Eaux-fortes de Max Klinger sur le Thème de l'Amour et de la Mort* (*Eros and Thanatos: Etchings by Max Klinger on the Themes of Love and Death*), Musée des Beaux-Arts, Bern.

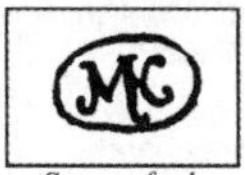

Stamp of sale

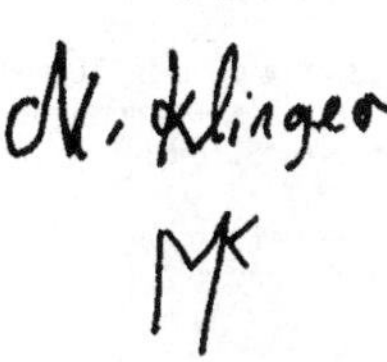

BIBLIOGRAPHY:

Singer, Hans Wolgang, *Max Klinger Radierungen, Stiche und Steindrucke*, Amsler und Ruthardt, Berlin, 1909 (Martin Gordon, New York, 1978, Alan Wolfsy Fine Arts, San Francisco, 1990). *A Glove and Other Images of Reverie and Apprehension: The Graphic Suites of Max Klinger*, Wichita Art Museum, Wichita (KS), 1971. Varnedoe, J. Kirk. T., *Graphic Works of Max Klinger*, Dover Publications, New York, 1977. Holloway, Memory Jockisch, *Max Klinger: Love, Death and the Beyond*, National Gallery of Victoria, 1981. Mason, Rainer Michael, *Max Klinger: gravures*, exhibition catalogue, Musée d'Art et d'Histoire, Geneva, 1982. Gleisberg, Dieter, *Max Klinger*, exhibition catalogue, Museum der bildenden Künste, Leipzig, 1992. Guratzsch, Herwig, *Max Klinger. Bestandskatalog der Bildwerke, Gemälde, und Zeichnungen im Museum der bildenden Künste Leipzig*, exhibition catalogue, catalogue raisonné, Museum der bildenden Künste, Leipzig, 1995. Birnie Danzker, Jo-Anne, al., *Max Klinger: Zeichnungen, Zustandsdrucke, Zyklen*, exhibition catalogue, Stuck-Jugendstil-Museum, Munich, 1996. Klessinger, Angelika, *Max Klinger: eine Liebe (graphischer Zyklus)*, dissertation, Universität, Mainz, 1997. Beyer, Carl, *Max Klinger: das graphische Werk 1909-1909*, exhibition catalogue, Alan Wofsy Fine Arts, San Francisco, 1997 (reprint of the 1930 edition). Priever, Andreas (introduction), *Max Klinger Plastische Meisterwerke*, Seemann, Berlin, 1998. *opus fabulosum, sogno, mito e realtà. Opere grafiche della Fondazione Antonio Mazzotta*, exhibition catalogue, Museo d'Arte Contemporanea, San Donato, 2000.

MUSEUMS AND GALLERIES:

BERLIN (Nationalgal.): *Centaurs and Sea-horses; In the Shells; Water-nymph on a Wave; Triton and Water-nymph* (1883-1884); *Game of Centaurs; Landscape with Marsh; Landscape with Centaur; Amphitrite* (sculpture) - CONSTANZ: *Views of Siena* (watercolour) - DARMSTADT (Hessisches Landesmus.): *Evening* (1882) - DRESDEN: *Pietà* - HAMBURG: *Seven Frescoes from Villa Albert in Steglitz* - KALININGRAD: six etchings - LEIPZIG (Mus. der Bildenden Künste): *The Blue Hour; New Salome* (marble 1902); *Cassandra* (marble); *Girl at her Toilette* (marble); *Beethoven Seated* (1889-1902); *Athlete* (bronze); *Brahmsphantasie, Opus XII* (1894) - MELBOURNE: 12 engravings - VIENNA (Kunsthistorisches Mus.): *Christ on Olympus; Judgement of Paris* (1886-1887).

AUCTION RECORDS:

COLOGNE, 30 Oct 1937, *Landscape with Woman*, DEM 4,700. HAMBURG, 3 June 1971, *Death at the Seaside* (1880) DEM 8,500. BERN, 9 June 1976, *The Embrace* (1879, pen, 15 1/4 x 7 1/4 ins / 39 x 18.6 cm) CHF 13,200. MUNICH, 29 Nov 1976, *Cassandra* (c. 1895, patinated bronze, h. 19 ins / 48 cm) DEM 4,300. HAMBURG, 3 June 1977, *Longing* (1914, aquatint/Japanese Imperial paper) DEM 8,000. HAMBURG, 3 June 1977, *Recumbent Nude* (1910, coloured chalks, 13 x 25 1/4 ins / 33 x 64.1 cm) DEM 4,000. COLOGNE, 16 June 1978, *Bather* (patinated bronze, h. 24 1/2 ins / 62 cm) DEM 2,600. NEW YORK, 9 May 1979, *Brahms Fantasy: Celebration (Roundel)* (etching and dry-point, 10 x 13 3/4 ins / 25.2 x 35 cm) USD 3,800. MUNICH, 30 May 1979, *Self-portrait* (c. 1885?, oil on card, 23 x 19 ins / 57.5 x 48 cm) DEM 12,500. COLOGNE, 19 Oct 1979, *Bather* (c. 1896-1897, bronze, h. 15 3/4 ins / 40 cm) DEM 4,500. MUNICH, 27 Nov 1980, *Promethius* (1879, wash, 9 x 15 3/4 ins / 22 x 40 cm) DEM 5,200. COLOGNE, 5 Dec 1981, *Bather* (1896-1897, bronze, h. 9 3/4 ins / 25 cm) DEM 5,800. HAMBURG, 10 June 1983, *Portrait of a Woman* (1915, pastel, 21 3/4 x 19 1/2 ins / 55.5 x 49.5 cm) DEM 3,000. LONDON, 30 June 1983, *Salome* (c. 1900-1902, bronze, h. 27 1/4 ins / 69 cm) GBP 2,000. LONDON, 4 Dec 1984, *Young Man Seated on Garden Wall* (pen, 5 x 3 1/2 ins / 13 x 9.2 cm) GBP 1,400. MUNICH, 14 May 1986, *Cassandra* (bronze, h. 23 1/4 ins / 59 cm) DEM 17,000. LONDON, 19 June 1986, *Disgrace* (1899, pen, 20 3/4 x 13 1/4 ins / 53 x 33.5 cm) GBP 5,500. MUNICH, 11 Nov 1987, *Homage to Friedrich von Schiller* (1905, pen and Indian ink, 12 1/2 x 11 3/4 ins / 32 x 30 cm) DEM 7,500. LONDON, 24 Feb 1988, *Ride along Sea-front* (1912, oil on panel, 12 1/2 x 10 ins / 32 x 25.5 cm) GBP 2,860. LONDON, 20 June 1989, *Salome* (bronze, h. 23 1/4 ins / 59 cm) GBP 3,080; *Beethoven* (bronze, h. 26 ins / 66 cm) GBP 9,900. LONDON, 1

Dec 1989, *Walk lined with Cherry Trees* (1907, oil on canvas, 20½ x 73 ins / 52 x 185.5 cm) GBP 26,400. MUNICH, 26 May 1992, *Night* (1894, aquatint, 10¾ x 15¼ ins / 27.5 x 39 cm) DEM 1,725. HEIDELBERG, 9 Oct 1992, *Portrait of G. Bock* (1910, charcoal heightened with colour, 25½ x 13½ ins / 64.6 x 34.3 cm) DEM 5,200. NEW YORK, 26 May 1994, *Bather* (bronze, h. 39½ ins / 100.3 cm) USD 16,100. COPENHAGEN, 7 Sept 1994, *Man in Beret* (ink and wash, 5½ x 5 ins / 14 x 12.5 cm) DKK 16,000. LONDON, 11 Oct 1995, *Female Nude on Deserted Coast* (etching, 11½ x 6½ ins / 29 x 16.7 cm) GBP 690. NEW YORK, 6 and 7 March 1998, *Of Death, Part One, Opus XI* (10 engravings and aquatints, complete portfolio, 12¼ x 12½ ins / 31.4 x 31.6 cm) USD 2,070.

KLINGHOFFER, Clara
Austrian, 20th century.
Born 18 May 1900, in Vienna, to Polish parents; died 1970.
Active in the USA from 1939.
Painter.

Clara Klinghoffer studied at the Slade School in London from 1919 to 1921. A member of the New English Art Club from 1933, she also lived in Holland and in France and from 1939 in the USA. A portraitist, she specialised in children's portraits.

MUSEUMS AND GALLERIES:
LONDON (Tate Collection): *The Old Troubadour* (1926, oil on canvas).

AUCTION RECORDS:
LONDON, 13 Nov 1985, *Portrait of Orovida Pissarro* (1962, oil on canvas, 40 x 34¼ ins / 101.5 x 87 cm) GBP 1,500. LONDON, 14 Oct 1987, *Table* (1968, oil on canvas, 28 x 32 ins / 71 x 81 cm) GBP 1,500. LONDON, 29 July 1988, *Portrait of a Woman Near a Grand Piano* (oil on canvas, 27½ x 23½ ins / 70 x 60 cm) GBP 1,078. LONDON, 21 Sept 1989, *Head of a Little Girl* (1928, oil on canvas, 14 x 10 ins / 35.6 x 25.4 cm) GBP 605.

KLINGNER, Albert
German, 20th century.
Born 25 May 1869, in Hamburg; died 5 June 1912, in Berlin.
Painter, decorative designer.

Albert Klingner was the pupil of Götz and produced decorative paintings, frescoes, stained glass and posters.

KLINGNER, Johann Gottlob
German, 18th - 19th century.
Born 1756, in Dresden; died 1815, in Dresden.
Painter, decorative designer, engraver. Landscapes.

Klingner studied with Schenau at the Dresden academy.

KLINGSOR, Tristan, pseudonym of Léon Leclère
French, 19th - 20th century.
Born 8 August 1874, in Lachapelle-aux-Pots; died August 1966, in Le Mans.
Painter, poet, musician.

Tristan Klingsor became known in 1895 for his poetry tinged with Symbolism and a certain humour. Previously he had tried his hand at musical composition. Despite his close friendship with Maurice Ravel, Klingsor began to move in the direction of the visual arts but without abandoning his poetry. He studied at the École du Louvre in Paris. He was in turn a landscape painter, a portraitist, and a painter of still-lifes, and proved to be a moving painter of reality. He also wrote some critical studies, notably on Chardin, Hubert-Robert and Cézanne.

In 1905 he exhibited for the first time at the Salon d'Automne. In 2001 his work was shown as part of *Les Peintres et la Sarthe* (*Painters and the Sarthe Region*) at the Musée de la Reine Bérengère (19th-century artworks) and Épau Abbey (20th-century artworks) in Le Mans.

BIBLIOGRAPHY:
Leclère, Léon, *Tristan Klingsor*, Flammes vives, Paris, 1955. Arpentinier, Jean, *Sarthe, terre d'artistes*, Éd. de la Reinette, Le Mans, 2001.

MUSEUMS AND GALLERIES:
LE MANS: *House on a Hill* - PARIS (Mus. du Petit Palais).

AUCTION RECORDS:
PARIS, 9 Dec 1924, *Still-life*, FRF 103. PARIS, 12 April 1930, *Church Bell Tower*, FRF 1,200. PARIS, 28 Jan 1949, *Taillecourt Mill*, FRF 7,000. PARIS, 25 Nov 1987, *Landscape* (1961, oil on canvas, 19¾ x 23½ ins / 50 x 60 cm) FRF 3,100. PARIS, 30 May 2001, *Still-life with Palette and vase of Daisies* (1912, oil on canvas, 21 x 25 ins / 54 x 64 cm) FRF 11,500. PARIS, 30 May 2001, *Pointe de la Cite, Paris* (oil on canvas, 18 x 23 ins / 46 x 59 cm) FRF 13,000.

KLINGSPOR, Fredrik Filip
Swedish, 18th - 19th century.
Born 5 April 1761, in Jönköping; died 1832, in Stockholm.
Miniaturist.

Fredrik Klingspor's *Portrait of Rubens* is in the museum in Stockholm.

KLINGSTEDT, Karl Gustav, or Klingstel or Clinchetet
Swedish, 17th - 18th century.
Born 1657, in Riga; died 27 February 1734, in Paris.
Miniaturist.

Karl Klingstedt was a career soldier until 1690. From that time on he devoted himself to painting and executed a number of provocative subjects. He was named the 'Raphael of the Snuff-boxes'. He worked mostly in France, and Bernard Picard engraved several of his works.

MUSEUMS AND GALLERIES:
AIX: *Portrait of the Painter's Mother* - LONDON (Wallace Collection): *Venus; Mars and Cupid Surprised by the Sun Chariot; Susanna and the Elders* - ROUEN: *Group of Two Figures*.

AUCTION RECORDS:
PARIS, 1782, *Hot Cockles* (miniature) FRF 292; *Satyrs, Women and Children* (miniature) FRF 600. PARIS, 1898, *Twelve Small Busts of Women* (Indian ink and watercolour) FRF 630. PARIS, 13 Nov 1923, *The Gallant Hunter* (miniature) FRF 780. PARIS, 6-7 April 1925, *Portrait of a Young Woman* (miniature) FRF 750. PARIS, 12 Nov 1938, *The Sleep of Iris* (miniature) FRF 1,150. PARIS, Oct 1945-July 1946, *Romantic Scene with Two Figures* (attributed miniature) FRF 24,000. PARIS, 6 Dec 1991, *The Paternal Lesson* (1720, ink and watercolour, 8¼ x 11¾ ins / 21 x 30 cm) FRF 31,000. LONDON, 28 April 1999, *Masked Ball* (c. 1730, grisaille, miniature, h. 2ins / 5cm) GBP 2,200. LONDON, 12 Sept 2000, *Leda and the Swan* (miniature, oval, h. 3ins / 8cm) GBP 2,200.

KLINK, Age
Dutch, 20th century.
Born 1940, in Vlaardingen.
Painter.

Age Klink exhibited from 1965. In his absurd portrayal of human beings, often in groups, wandering in undefined spaces, his painting verges on Surrealism.

AUCTION RECORDS:
AMSTERDAM, 1 June 1994, *Returning to the Past in the Parental Home* (1970, acrylic/canvas, 39¼ x 78¾ ins / 100 x 200 cm) NLG 1,495.

KLINK, Wilhelm
German, 19th - 20th century.
Born 19 January 1874, in Unterthatheim; died 2 April 1952.
Painter, sculptor, illustrator.

Wilhelm Klink was taught by Vollmer in Regensburg. He is known to have executed the altar of the church at Horb and decorative paintings in the castle of Roseck near Tübingen.

KLINKENBERG, Eugen.
See **KLINCKENBERG**

KLINKENBERG, Johannes Christiaan Karel
Dutch, 19th - 20th century.
Born 14 January 1852, in The Hague; died 1924.
Painter, watercolourist. Landscapes.

A pupil of Christopher Bisschop, Johannes Klinkenberg successfully rendered various picturesque aspects of Dutch towns. His watercolours are much in demand. He took an active part in important worldwide exhibitions. His work featured in the 1900 Exposition Universelle in Paris and in Brussels in 1910. He received medals, notably in Munich in 1888 and in Paris at the Exposition Universelle in 1889.

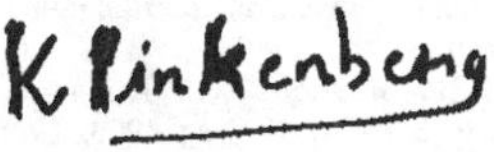

MUSEUMS AND GALLERIES:
AMSTERDAM: *Market Square in Nijmegen* - AMSTERDAM (Stedelijk Mus.): *Episode from the Siege of Leyden; The Hague Town Hall* - FRANKFURT AM MAIN: *Amsterdam in the Snow* - ROTTERDAM: *View of the Hague* - THE HAGUE (Gemeentemus.): *Two Views* - THE HAGUE (Mus. Mesdag): *Two Views* - WEIMAR: *View of Amsterdam.*

AUCTION RECORDS:
LONDON, 14 May 1909, *At The Hague* (watercolour) GBP 46. LONDON, 13 April 1934, *View of Amsterdam,* GBP 78. AMSTERDAM, 21 March 1950, *Oude Gracht in Utrecht,* NLG 1,000. AMSTERDAM, 24 May 1966, *Flower Market at The Hague,* NLG 14,500. AMSTERDAM, 20 March 1974, *View of Rotterdam,* NLG 40,000. AMSTERDAM, 27 April 1976, *View of Haarlem* (oil on panel, 14¾ x 22¾ ins / 37.5 x 58 cm) NLG 20,500. AMSTERDAM, 27 June 1977, *View of Dordrecht* (oil on canvas, 32¾ x 56¾ ins / 83 x 144 cm) NLG 34,000. AMSTERDAM, 31 Oct 1979, *View of Utrecht* (oil on canvas, 27 x 23¼ ins / 68.5 x 59 cm) NLG 25,000. AMSTERDAM, 1 Oct 1981, *View of Amsterdam* (oil on canvas, 15½ x 20¾ ins / 39.5 x 53 cm) NLG 24,000. COLOGNE, 28 Oct 1983, *Sunset over Amsterdam* (oil on canvas, 15¼ x 20¾ ins / 39 x 53 cm) DEM 26,000. AMSTERDAM, 15 April 1985, *View of The Hague* (oil on canvas, 33½ x 46½ ins / 85 x 118 cm) NLG 38,000. AMSTERDAM, 3 May 1988, *Amsterdam with Dome of the Church of St Nicholas in Background* (oil on canvas, 27½ x 39¼ ins / 70 x 100 cm) NLG 166,750. AMSTERDAM, 19 Sept 1989, *View of Amsterdam with the Lutheran Church in Distance* (watercolour/paper, 13¼ x 17½ ins / 33.5 x 44.5 cm) NLG 1,380. AMSTERDAM, 10 April 1990, *View of Dordrecht* (pencil and watercolour heightened with white/paper, 12 x 19¾ ins / 30.5 x 50 cm) NLG 8,050. AMSTERDAM, 2 May 1990, *The Groenburgwal in Amsterdam with the Church of the South in Distance* (oil on canvas, 15¼ x 21 ins / 39 x 53.5 cm) NLG 161,000. NEW YORK, 23 May 1990, *Canal in Winter* (watercolour/paper, 9¾ x 14¼ ins / 24.9 x 36.2 cm) USD 11,000. AMSTERDAM, 30 Oct 1990, *View of Gelderse Kade towards the Schierstoren* (oil on canvas, 15¼ x 18¾ ins / 39 x 47.5 cm) NLG 80,500. AMSTERDAM, 24 April 1991, *View of Pierkade at Alkmaar with the Toll House Tower and Barges Berthed near Pier* (oil on canvas, 15 x 21½ ins / 38 x 54.5 cm) NLG 55,200. AMSTERDAM, 22 April 1992, *Dutch Town with Figures and Horse-drawn Carriage* (1902, oil on canvas, 23½ x 31½ ins / 60 x 80 cm) NLG 86,250. LONDON, 17 June 1992, *View of Amsterdam* (oil on canvas, 15 x 18 ins / 38 x 46 cm) GBP 15,950. AMSTERDAM, 28 Oct 1992, *The Singel in Amsterdam with the Lutheran Church* (watercolour and gouache heightened with white/paper, 13 x 19¾ ins / 33 x 50 cm) NLG 8,625. NEW YORK, 30 Oct 1992, *Canal Scene in Holland* (oil on panel, 23 x 16¼ ins / 57.5 x 41.2 cm) USD 13,200. AMSTERDAM, 2-3 Nov 1992, *Dutch Town* (oil on panel, 6¾ x 9½ ins / 17 x 24 cm) NLG 16,100. AMSTERDAM, 21 April 1993, *View of Prinsengracht in Amsterdam* (oil on canvas, 15¼ x 20¾ ins / 38.5 x 53 cm) NLG 97,750. LONDON, 16 Nov 1994, *Dortrecht* (oil on canvas, 15 x 18 ins / 38 x 46 cm) GBP 12,075. LONDON, 15 Nov 1995, *Dutch Port* (oil on panel, 17 x 12½ ins / 43 x 31.5 cm) GBP 5,175. EDINBURGH, 23 May 1996, *Barges on Canal near The Hague* (oil on canvas, 20¼ x 26¼ ins / 51.4 x 66.5 cm) GBP 32,200. AMSTERDAM, 19-20 Feb 1997, *Zuydthavenpoort, Zierikzee* (oil on panel, 8½ x 10¾ ins / 21.5 x 27.5 cm) NLG 12,685. AMSTERDAM, 22 April 1997, *St Mark's Square, Venice* (watercolour, 9½ x 13½ ins / 24 x 34 cm) NLG 11,800. ROTTERDAM, 20 April 1999, *Inner Harbour* (oil on canvas, 12 x 20 ins / 31 x 51 cm) NLG 6,800.

KLINKERT, Walter
German, 20th century.
Born 1901, in Berlin; died 1959.
Painter, engraver.

Walter Klinkert showed views of the Spree at the exhibition of the German painter-engravers organised in 1929 by the Bibliothèque Nationale in Paris.

KLINKHAMER, Hendrick Abraham
Dutch, 19th century.
Born 9 January 1810, in Amsterdam; died 1 November 1872, in Amsterdam.
Painter, draughtsman, engraver. Landscapes.

Hendrick Klinkhamer was a tobacco broker but took up art and made watercolour copies of works by the Flemish masters.

KLINKHAMMER, Han
Dutch, 20th century.
Painter, collage artist.

KLINKOWSTRÖM, Friedrich August von
German, 19th century.
Born 31 August 1778, in Steinhagen, near Stralsund; died 4 April 1835, in Vienna.
Painter, lithographer. History painting, portraits, genre scenes.

Klinkowström studied with David in Paris, then completed his studies in Dresden. He worked in Hamburg, Dresden and Paris, and finally settled in Vienna.

KLINL, Wilhelm
German, 20th century.
Born 19 January 1874, in Unterhalheim.
Painter, sculptor, illustrator, decorative designer.

Wilhelm Klinl was a pupil of Vollmer in Regensburg. His works include the altar of the church in Horb and decorative pictures in the castle of Roseck near Tübingen.

KLINT, Gustaf Adolf
Swedish, 19th century.
Born 1775, in Stockholm; died 1822.
Sculptor.

Gustaf Klint was a pupil of Sergel. Two plaster medallions by him are in the museum of Stockholm.

KLINT, Hilma af
Swedish, 19th - 20th century.
Born 1862; died 1944.
Painter.

Hilma af Klint's output consisted mainly of representations of constructions and nestling boxes of geometric forms based on the square and circle, which she painted in warm colours on black or grey backgrounds. There is a Hilma af Klint foundation in Stockholm.

AUCTION RECORDS:
STOCKHOLM, 19 May 1992, *Bridge over Canal in Bruges* (1903, watercolour, 93/4 x 133/4 ins / 25 x 35 cm) SEK 31,000. AMSTERDAM, 21 May 1992, *Composition Series III n° 6* (1920, oil on canvas, 193/4 x 113/4 ins / 50 x 30 cm) NLG 11,500. STOCKHOLM, 10-12 May 1993, *Cosmic Birth* (watercolour, 181/2 x 121/2 ins / 47 x 32 cm) SEK 6,200. STOCKHOLM, 29 May 2002, *Andromena by the Sea* (oil on canvas, 52 x 31 ins / 133 x 80 cm) SEK 33,000. STOCKHOLM, 4 Dec 2002, *Park Scene with Buildings and Children Playing, Stockholm* (1889, oil on canvas, 17 x 22 ins / 44 x 56 cm) SEK 180,000. STOCKHOLM, 4 June 2003, *Winter Landscape with Farm* (1891, oil on canvas, 8 x 12 ins / 21 x 30 cm) SEK 20,000.

KLINT, Kaare
Danish, 20th century.
Born 15 December 1888, in Copenhagen; died 1954.
Painter, architect. Landscapes, still-lifes.

Kaare Klint brought back a large number of landscapes from a stay in Indonesia.

AUCTION RECORDS:
COPENHAGEN, 19 Oct 1994, *Six Chairs in Mahogany Covered in Brown Leather* (each h. 35 ins / 89 cm) DKK 17,000.

KLINVÈQUE, J. F.
French, 17th century.
Active in Paris.
Draughtsman.

J. F. Klinvèque worked in the studio of Van der Meulen.

KLIONOV, Vladimir Mikhailovich
Russian, 20th century.
Born 1932, in Rostov-on-Don.
Painter. Landscapes.

Vladimir Klionov was the pupil of D.K. Mochalsky at the V.I. Surikov institute of art in Moscow. He became a member of the Union of Soviet Artists in 1963. He lived and worked in Rostov.

AUCTION RECORDS:
GLASGOW, 4 Dec 1991, *Winter* (1961, oil on card, 193/4 x 271/2 ins / 50 x 70 cm) GBP 462.

KLIOUKINE, Oleg
Russian, 20th century.
Born 1929.
Painter. Scenes with figures.

In 1951 Oleg Klioukine won first prize at the art school. He joined the Union of Artists in 1960. He showed work in Moscow in 1951 and 1954, at the Moscow Youth Festival in 1957, and in the *Soviet Russia* exhibition in 1960. His work has been exhibited regularly since then.

AUCTION RECORDS:
PARIS, 11 April 1992, *Boy Studying* (oil on panel, 24 x 193/4 ins / 61 x 50 cm) FRF 4,800; *Child in a Meadow* (1958, oil on canvas, 491/4 x 44 ins / 125 x 112 cm) FRF 6,500. PARIS, 25 Jan 1993, *Schoolchildren* (oil on canvas, 471/4 x 63 ins / 120 x 160 cm) FRF 4,500. PARIS, 19 April 1993, *Children* (oil on canvas, 283/4 x 361/4 ins / 73 x 92 cm) FRF 5,600.

KLIPPEL, Robert Edward
Australian, 20th century.
Born 1920, in Sydney.
Active in the USA.
Sculptor, draughtsman.

The son of a Polish-born father, Robert Klippel served in the navy during World War II. He subsequently trained at the Slade School of Fine Art, London, from 1944 to 1946. He settled for a time in Paris, where he met André Breton, who organised an exhibition of his work at the Galerie Nina Daussett in 1949. In 1956 his work featured alongside that of the Australian Abstract Expressionists Pasmore, Olsen, R. Smith and Rose in the exhibition *Direction 1* at the Macquarie Galleries in Sydney. He also exhibited in London and New York, where he taught sculpture. He studied the formal language of sculptors such as Picasso, Gaudier-Brzeska and Henry Moore.

His work is informed by motifs and elements from the world of industry. His friend and biographer James Gleson has described his quest to achieve an aesthetic unity between mechanical and organic forms, based on their invisible 'internal logic'. His metal sculptures feature constructions of junk elements and found objects.

BIBLIOGRAPHY:
MacAulay, Bettina/MacAulay, Desmond, *'Forms and Languages'* in *Creating Australia: 200 years of art 1788-1988*, exhibition catalogue, Art Gall. Board of South Australia, Adelaide, 1988. Edwards, Deborah, et al., *Robert Klippel*, exhibition catalogue, catalogue raisonné, Art Gall. of New South Wales, Sydney, 2002.

MUSEUMS AND GALLERIES:
BRISBANE: *Opus 247: Metal Construction* (1965-1968).

AUCTION RECORDS:
SYDNEY, 4 Oct 1977, *Six-foot-six* (1974, metal, h. 78 ins / 198.2 cm) AUD 3,800. SYDNEY, 17 Aug 1999, *Untitled* (ink and gouache, 14 x 9 ins / 35 x 24 cm) AUD 6,000. SYDNEY, 17 Aug 1999, *Opus 209* (1967, bronze, h. 21 ins / 53 cm) AUD 11,000. MELBOURNE, 1 May 2000, *Opus* (1982, bronze, h. 28 ins / 71 cm) AUD 11,000. MELBOURNE, 9 May 2001, *Opus 328: Metal Construction* (brazed and welded steel and found objects, h. 49 ins / 124 cm) AUD 70,000. MELBOURNE, 20 Aug 2001, *Opus 704* (1987, wood assemblage, 56 x 27x12 ins / 141 x 69x30 cm) AUD 34,000. MELBOURNE, 5 March 2002, *LS 26* (1965-1969, lithograph, gouache and collage, 24 x 32 ins / 61 x 81 cm) AUD 5,000. PADDINGTON, 26 Aug 2002, *Sentinel* (grey patinated bronze, h. 67 ins / 120 cm) AUD 78,000. MELBOURNE, 5 May 2003, *Opus: Metal Construction* (c. 1959, welded metal) AUD 64,000. SYDNEY, 30 July 2003, *LS102* (pencil, gouache and collage, 11 x 15 ins / 28 x 39 cm) AUD 4,800. SYDNEY, 26 Aug 2003, *Untitled* (1949, ink and gouache, 13 x 9 ins / 34 x 24 cm) AUD 3,800. MELBOURNE, 4 May 2004, *No. 454* (1982, bronze, h. 44 ins / 113 cm) AUD 26,000. MELBOURNE, 16 June 2004, *LS102* (1978, gouache, pencil and collage, 11 x 15 ins / 28 x 39 cm) AUD 6,000.

KLIPPHAN, Johann
Swiss, 19th century.
Born 13 October 1815, in Damm, near Schaffhausen; died 25 May 1892, in Nuremberg.
Engraver.

Klipphan worked in Schaffhausen until 1871, then settled in Nuremberg.

KLITGAARD, Georgina
American, 20th century.
Born 3 July 1893, in Spuyten Duyvil (New York); died 1976.
Painter.

Georgina Klitgaard gained an honourable mention at the Carnegie international in 1928.

MUSEUMS AND GALLERIES:
BROOKLYN, NY - CHICAGO - NEW YORK (Whitney Mus. of American Art).

AUCTION RECORDS:
NEW YORK, 25 March 1997, *Girl and Child under a Pine-tree* (c. 1938, oil on canvas, 34 x 28 ins / 86.4 x 71.4 cm) USD 2,587. MILFORD, 22 April 1999, *The Colt* (oil on canvas, 24 x 36 ins / 61 x 91 cm) USD 2,750.

KLIVET, Johannes, or Clivet
French, 16th century.

Born c. 1545, in Châlons-sur-Marne; died c. 1600, in Danzig (now Gdansk, Poland).
Painter.
Johannes Klivet settled in Danzig at a very young age, and learnt to paint there.

KLOCK, Hendrick
Flemish School, 16th century.
Glass painter.
He taught van Goyen in Leiden.

KLOCKE, Franziska von
German, 20th century.
Born 6 June 1873, in Hattingen.
Painter. Portraits.
Franziska von Klocke was taught by Starcke in Weimar and subsequently worked largely in Berlin.

KLOCKENDON. See **GLOCKENDON**

KLÖCKER VON EHRENSTRAHL, Anna Maria and David. See **EHRENSTRAHL**

KLOCKOW, Johann Heinrich
Latvian, 18th - 19th century.
Born 29 October 1774, in Riga; died 19 December 1823, in Riga.
Engraver, lithographer.
His works include; *Ruins of the Summer Garden in Riga*.

KLOCZKOVSKI, Walenty
Polish, 17th century.
Active in Cracow.
Painter.
The Annunciation, bearing the signature *Walenti Kloczkovski*, 1675, is in the church in Lorosina.

KLODT VON JURGENSBURG, Mikhail Konstantinovich (Baron), or Clodt von Jurgensburg
Russian, 19th century.
Born 1832, in St Petersburg; died 1902.
Painter. Landscapes.
Mikhail Klodt studied at the academy in St Petersburg from 1851 to 1858. In 1858, he was awarded the first prize for landscapes at the academy, and in 1864 he became a teacher there. He was a founder member of the artistic group Peredvizhniki (the Travellers). He played a key role in the development of naturalist landscape painting in 19th-century Russia.
MUSEUMS AND GALLERIES:
MOSCOW (State Tretyakov Gal.): *Ploughed Field; Midday Landscape; Forested Horizon; Evening Scene in the Countryside; In the Forest; Road in Autumn; Sunset* - ST PETERSBURG (Gosudarstvennyj Russkij Muz.): *Landscape by Night; View in Normandy; Valley of the Aa River in Livonia.*
AUCTION RECORDS:
LONDON, 20 Feb 1985, *Woman on the Banks of a River* (oil on canvas, 41 3/4 x 61 ins / 106 x 154 cm) GBP 16,000. LONDON, 14 Nov 1988, *Landscape* (oil on canvas, 31 x 63 3/4 ins / 79 x 162 cm) GBP 8,250. LONDON, 5 Oct 1989, *Landscape* (1881, oil on canvas, 31 x 63 ins / 79 x 160 cm) GBP 11,000. HELSINKI, 9 Dec 2000, *Calm Day on the Lake* (1882, oil on canvas, 19 x 41 ins / 47 x 104 cm) FIM 125,000. HELSINKI, 10 May 2003, *Moment of Silence* (1891, oil on panel, 14 x 10 ins / 35 x 26 cm) EUR 12,000. STOCKHOLM, 26 May 2003, *Orthodox Nun* (1892, watercolour, 19 x 10 ins / 48 x 25 cm) SEK 88,000.

KLODT VON JURGENSBURG, Mikhail Petrovich (Baron), or Clodt von Jurgensburg
Russian, 19th century.
Born 1835, in St Petersburg; died 1914.
Painter, engraver. Genre scenes.
Mikhail Klodt was the son of Petr Klodt. He spent a long period travelling in France and Germany before returning to live in St Petersburg.
MUSEUMS AND GALLERIES:
MOSCOW (State Tretyakov Gal.): *The Ailing Musician; The Last Spring; Before Leaving; Tatiana.*

KLODT VON JURGENSBURG, Petr Yakov, sometimes P. K. (Baron), or Clodt von Jurgensburg
Russian, 19th century.
Born 1805, in St Petersburg; died 1867, in Finland.
Sculptor. Animals. Monuments, groups.
Petr Yakov Klodt was the son of a general who served under the Tsar Nicholas I. As a young artist his talent was noticed by the Tsar, who helped to launch his remarkable career. He became a member of the fine art academy of St Petersburg in 1838, and later a member of the art academies in Berlin, Paris and Rome. He sculpted many public monuments for the main towns in Russia.
MUSEUMS AND GALLERIES:
MOSCOW (State Tretyakov Gal.): *Mare and Foal* - ST PETERSBURG (Gosudarstvennyj Russkij Muz.): *Study of a Horse for the Group of Statues of the Anitchkov Bridge; Horseman Attacked by a Panther; Horse; Sketch for a Group of Statues for the Anitchkov Bridge; Tsar Nicholas I; Tsar Mikhail Fedorovich; Study of a Horse; Horse at a Watering Place; Mare and Foal; Horseman Resting; Sketch for a Monument of Tsar Nicolas I.*

KLOEBER, August Karl Friedrich von
German, 19th century.
Born 21 August 1793, in Breslau (now Wroclaw, Poland); died 31 December 1864, in Berlin.
Painter. History painting, portraits.
Kloeber studied at the Berlin academy, where later he became a teacher and a member. After fighting in the war of 1813, he worked first in Vienna, then in Breslau. He produced decorative paintings for the theatre in Vienna. He also decorated a number of palaces and public buildings in Berlin, notably the ceiling of the stock exchange. He drew much of his inspiration from Rubens and Correggio. He won a gold medal in Berlin in 1855. His *Jubal as the Inventor of the flute* can be seen in the Berlin Museum and his *Portrait of a child* in the museum in Wroclaw.

KLOETING, Symon
Dutch, 17th century.
Active in Delft.
Engraver, art dealer.
On 13 October 1645, Symon Kloeting was admitted to the Delft guild. A work entitled *Two Children with a Bunch of Grapes* is attributed to him.

KLOHSS, Hans
Austrian, 20th century.
Born 10 June 1879, in Döbling.
Painter. Landscapes.
Hans Klohss took part in the 1909 exhibition in Berlin.
AUCTION RECORDS:
PARIS, 23 June 1969, *Dutch Village*, FRF 200.

KLOKER
Flemish School, 17th century.
Painter.
Kloker worked at the court of Charles I in England.

KLOKUNOV, Ossip
Russian, 17th century.
Icon painter.
Klokunov studied under Ivan Saltanov and worked in Moscow.

KLOMBECK, Johann Bernard, or Klombbek, Clombeck
Dutch, 19th century.
Born 1815; died 1893.
Painter. Landscapes with figures, winter landscapes.

Johann Klombeck appears to have been a pupil of B.-C. Koekkoek. He sometimes collaborated with the painter Eugen Verboeckhoven. Klombeck's principal subject was the Dutch landscape in winter with skaters on frozen canals.

MUSEUMS AND GALLERIES:

THE HAGUE (Gemeentemus.): *A Wood.*

AUCTION RECORDS:

AMSTERDAM, 26 Nov 1946, *Roadway,* NLG 2,700. LONDON, 15 Feb 1967, *Winter Landscape with Figures* (in collaboration with E. Verboeckhoven) GBP 1,300. LONDON, 15 Oct 1969, *Winter Landscape,* GBP 3,300. LONDON, 1 March 1972, *Winter Landscape with Figures* (in collaboration with E. Verboeckhoven) GBP 9,500. LONDON, 6 March 1974, *Wooded Landscape,* GBP 2,600. AMSTERDAM, 25 April 1978, *Snowy Landscape with Skaters* (1846, oil on panel, 12 x 16¼ ins / 30.3 x 41 cm) NLG 60,000. AMSTERDAM, 22 April 1980, *Winter Landscape with Skaters* (oil on panel, 11½ x 16¼ ins / 29.5 x 41 cm) NLG 46,000. SAN FRANCISCO, 3 Oct 1981, *Skaters in a Landscape* (1849, oil on panel, 11 x 14½ ins / 28 x 37 cm) USD 25,000. COLOGNE, 22 Nov 1984, *Wooded Landscape with Chapel* (1852, oil on canvas, 29¼ x 37 ins / 74 x 94 cm) DEM 95,000. COLOGNE, 20 May 1985, *Winter Landscape* (1870, oil on panel, 23¼ x 27½ ins / 59 x 70 cm) DEM 75,000. AMSTERDAM, 10 Feb 1988, *Winter Landscape with a Couple Walking along a Frozen Canal and a Peasant Woman on a Path by a Cottage* (1868, oil on canvas, 24¾ x 32¼ ins / 63 x 82 cm) NLG 32,200. TORONTO, 30 Nov 1988, *Hovel near Gnadenthal* (1861, oil on card, 5¾ x 7¼ ins / 14.8 x 18.7 cm) CAD 3,400. LONDON, 7 June 1989, *Figures on a Path beside a Stream* (1850, oil on panel, 12 x 10 ins / 30.5 x 25.5 cm) USD 8,800. AMSTERDAM, 6 Nov 1990, *Wooded Landscape in Summer with Figures on a Path* (oil on panel, 11¾ x 15¾ ins / 30 x 40 cm) NLG 34,500. AMSTERDAM, 30 Oct 1991, *Extensive Undulating Landscape in Summer with Peasants and Cattle* (1845, oil on panel, 15 x 20½ ins / 38 x 52 cm) NLG 105,800. AMSTERDAM, 2-3 Nov 1992, *Rhineland Landscape with Figures near a Castle* (1845, oil on panel, 6 x 8 ins / 15.5 x 20.5 cm) NLG 51,750. LONDON, 19 Nov 1993, *Wooded River Landscape with Figures on a Path* (1860, oil on canvas, 33 x 45½ ins / 83.8 x 115.5 cm) GBP 56,500. LONDON, 18 March 1994, *Winter Landscape with Villagers on a Footbridge and Skaters* (1865, oil on canvas, 25¾ x 35 ins / 65.4 x 88.9 cm) GBP 45,500. AMSTERDAM, 21 April 1994, *Wooded Valley with Travellers on a Path and a Village and Castle in the Background* (1839, oil on canvas, 21¼ x 27¼ ins / 54 x 69 cm) NLG 46,000. NEW YORK, 23 Oct 1997, *Winter; Summer* (1859, oil on canvas, a pair, each 38 x 46 ins / 96.5 x 116.8 cm) USD 332,500. AMSTERDAM, 27 April 1999, *Wooded River Valley with Peasants on Path, Cattle beyond* (oil on canvas, 39 x 50 ins / 99 x 126 cm) NLG 25,000. COLOGNE, 4 Dec 1999, *Wooded Winter Landscape* (oil on panel, 12 x 16 ins / 31 x 40 cm) DEM 18,000. LONDON, 6 April 2000, *Figures on a Country Road* (1844, oil on panel, 19 x 25 ins / 48 x 63 cm) GBP 30,000. NEW YORK, 18 Oct 2000, *Figures on a Frozen River in Winter* (1844, oil on canvas, 17 x 20 ins / 42 x 52 cm) USD 88,000. PARIS, 31 Jan 2001, *Skaters and Peasants in the Wood* (oil on panel, 12 x 16 ins / 31 x 40 cm) FRF 35,000. GRAVENHAGE, 7 Nov 2001, *Travellers in a Hilly Landscape* (gouache, 8 x 10 ins / 21 x 26 cm) NLG 4,000. AMSTERDAM, 22 April 2002, *Wading Cattle* (1844, oil on panel, 15 x 17 ins / 38 x 44 cm) EUR 78,000. GRAVENHAGE, 24 April 2002, *Landscape with Shepherd and Flock on Wood Path* (oil on canvas, 39 x 49 ins / 98 x 124 cm) EUR 16,000. AMSTERDAM, 15 April 2003, *Figures on a Path in a Snow-covered Landscape* (1843, oil on canvas, 16 x 21 ins / 41 x 54 cm) EUR 32,000. AMSTERDAM, 29 April 2003, *Travellers Resting on a Forest Path in a Wooded Valley* (1849, oil on panel, 25 x 33 ins / 63 x 83 cm) EUR 68,000. NEW YORK, 23 April 2004, *Forest and River Landscape in Winter with Skaters and Villagers on a Path* (1864, oil on canvas, 41 x 48 ins / 103 x 121 cm) USD 42,500.

KLOMP, Albert Jansz., or Clomp

Dutch, 17th century.

Born c. 1618, in Amsterdam; died 20 December 1688, probably in Amsterdam.

Painter, draughtsman. Landscapes, animals.

Apart from the fact that he married Maria du Gardyn, almost nothing is known about Albert Klomp. As an artist he stands alongside Paulus Potter and Albert Cuyp and shared the same magnificent vision of nature which distinguishes the great Dutch landscape artists.

MUSEUMS AND GALLERIES:

AMSTERDAM: *Animals* - BRUSSELS: *Peasants and Animals* - BUDAPEST: *Animals* - CAMBRIDGE (Fitzwilliam Mus.): *Cattle in a Landscape* (oil/panel); *Cattle-Piece* (oil/panel) - COPENHAGEN (Statens Mus. for Kunst): *Bull, Sheep and Goats* - DRESDEN: *Cattle by the Waterside* - FRANKFURT AM MAIN (Städel): *Animals in a Landscape* - GOTHA: *Animals* - LA FÈRE: *Animals* - LIÈGE: *Animals* - MAINZ: *Animals* - OLDENBURG: *Landscape at Evening with Cattle* - SCHWERIN: *Animals Grazing* - STOCKHOLM: *Animals outside a Hut* - TOUL: *Animals.*

AUCTION RECORDS:

COLOGNE, 1862, *Pasture with Cows,* FRF 100. PARIS, 1875, *Landscape with Figures and Animals,* FRF 475; *The Old Sorceress,* FRF 630. PARIS, 1877, *Watering Place,* FRF 1,520. PARIS, 7 July 1926, *Cattle,* FRF 1,650. PARIS, 21 March 1929, *Landscape with a Cow and a Horseman on the Right,* FRF 450. PARIS, 22 Dec 1930, *Pasture,* FRF 950. LONDON, 8 July 1938, *Cattle and Sheep,* GBP 44. LONDON, 30 Oct 1946, *Landscape,* GBP 55. PARIS, 27 June 1951, *Farm Animals Returning,* FRF 15,000. PARIS, 21 June 1955, *Cattle near a Farm,* FRF 30,000. NEW YORK, 9 Feb 1973, *Shepherd and Flock outside an Inn,* Gns 1,300. AMSTERDAM, 30 Oct 1979, *Milking Time* (oil on canvas, 13½ x 12½ ins / 34 x 31.5 cm) NLG 6,500. NEW YORK, 8 Jan 1981, *Animals in a Landscape* (oil on canvas, 22 x 20 ins / 56 x 50.5 cm) USD 12,000. AMSTERDAM, 20 June 1989, *Landscape with Cattle, Goats and Sheep in a Meadow by a Farm* (1666, oil on canvas, 11 x 13¼ ins / 27 x 33.5 cm) NLG 8,050. LONDON, 5 July 1991, *Cattle in a Meadow* (1662, oil on panel, 16¾ x 13½ ins / 42.5 x 34.6 cm) GBP 2,420. AMSTERDAM, 14 Nov 1991, *Shepherds Resting in a Meadow with a Farm in the Background* (1665, oil on panel, 16¾ x 13¼ ins / 42.8 x 33.8 cm) NLG 9,200. AMSTERDAM, 7 May 1992, *Cattle in a Meadow by a Hedge* (oil on canvas, 12¾ x 15¾ ins / 32.5 x 40 cm) NLG 8,625. AMSTERDAM, 15 Nov 1995, *Landscapes with Cows and Sheep in a Meadow near a Farm* (black chalk and watercolour, 10 x 15 ins / 25.3 x 38.2 cm) NLG 10,620. LONDON, 16 Dec 1999, *Cattle and Sheep in an Open Landscape with Figures Resting before a Barn* (1632, oil on canvas, 35 x 48 ins / 89 x 121 cm) GBP 4,000. GRAVENHAGE, 9 May 2000, *Herders and Cattle Resting by the Water* (1662, oil on panel, 16 x 13 ins / 41 x 33 cm) NLG 11,000. GRAVENHAGE, 9 May 2000, *Landscape with Bull and Goats* (1662, oil on panel, 16 x 13 ins / 41 x 34 cm) NLG 16,000. PARIS, 19 Dec 2001, *Animals in a Landscape* (oil on panel, 17 x 13 ins / 42 x 34 cm) FRF 18,000. LONDON, 20 April 2004, *River Landscape with Cattle and Sheep before Farm Buildings* (oil on canvas, 32 x 40 ins / 81 x 102 cm) GBP 2,400. COPENHAGEN, 2 Sept 2004, *Horse, Cattle and Sheep in a Landscape* (oil on canvas, 16 x 19 ins / 40 x 48 cm) DKK 26,000.

KLOMP, C.. See **CLOMP**

KLÖNNE, Hugo

German, 19th century.

Active in Düsseldorf.

Painter. Still-lifes.

Klönne exhibited in Berlin, Hamburg, Düsseldorf and Bremen from 1886.

KLOOT, Jan van der
Dutch, 17th century.
Painter.
Jan van der Kloot was a member of the Delft guild in 1670.

KLOPFER, Karl
Polish, 19th - 20th century.
Born 9 December 1859, in Warsaw.
Painter. Landscapes, waterscapes.
The pupil of Guerson in Warsaw, from 1900 Karl Klopfer worked as a State theatre designer in the Polish capital. His work also featured in the Exposition Universelle in 1900.
MUSEUMS AND GALLERIES:
CRACOW (Mus.): *Forest.*
AUCTION RECORDS:
NEW YORK, 10 Feb 1998, *Ducks on a Lake* (1897, oil on canvas, 36 x 68 1/2 ins / 91.5 x 174 cm) USD 8,625.

KLOPP, Nico
Luxembourg, 20th century.
Born 1894, in Kleinmacher; died 1930, in Luxembourg.
Painter. Landscapes, still-lifes, flowers.
Nico Klopp attended the art academies in Düsseldorf from 1915 to 1918 and Weimar from 1918 to 1920. He regularly visited Germany, Belgium and Paris, living and working in Remich. In 1927 he participated in the first Secession exhibition, of which he was one of the founders.
BIBLIOGRAPHY:
Cent cinquante ans d'Art luxembourgeois, exhibition catalogue, Musée National d'Histoire et d'Art, Luxembourg, 1989.
MUSEUMS AND GALLERIES:
LUXEMBOURG (Mus. national d'histoire et d'art): *The Moselle, near Schengen am Dreiländereck* (1924); *Remich Bridge* (1925); *Still-life with Fruit* (1928); *Martigues, Brescou Point* (1928); *Sunflowers* (1929); *The Moselle* (1930); *Autumn* (1930).

KLOPPENBURG, Lucas, or Cloppenburg
Dutch, 17th - 18th century.
Engraver.
Lucas Kloppenburg is known for his *Leven van den Grooten Apostel Paulus* of 1712.

KLOPPER, Johan
Swedish, 17th - 18th century.
Born 1670; died 1734.
Painter.
Probably of Dutch origin, Johan Klopper lived in Stockholm and taught drawing at the University of Uppsala.
AUCTION RECORDS:
STOCKHOLM, 26 April 1983, *Trompe-l'oeil with Papers, Penholders and Paintings* (oil on canvas, 35 x 30 3/4 ins / 88 x 78 cm) SEK 205,000.

KLOPPER, Johannes
Dutch, 17th century.
Born c. 1666, in Amsterdam.
Engraver (line-engraving).

KLOSE, Johann Bartel
Bohemian, 17th century.
Died 7 September 1679, in Prague.
Painter.
Johann Bartel Klose was a pupil of Skreta. He lived in Würzburg for many years.

KLOSE, Karl Friedrich Wilhelm
German, 19th century.
Born 1804, in Berlin; died c. 1863.
Painter. Architectural views.
In 1824, Klose was a pupil of R. Gropius at the Berlin academy. He exhibited in Berlin from 1824 to 1838.

KLOSE, Paul
Danish, 20th century.
Born c. 1920, in Kolding (Jutland).
From c. 1950 active in Venezuela.
Painter.
Paul Klose attended the academy of Bonen in Copenhagen, the Académie Ranson in Paris and the École des Beaux-Arts in the same city. He lived in Caracas. His work was shown at exhibitions in Paris in 1949, Caracas in 1952, Santiago, Chile, in 1953, the art museum in Caracas in 1958, Bogotá in 1960, Macarïbo in 1961 and the exhibition of Latin-American painting in Bonn in 1963.

KLOSE, Wilhelm
German, 19th - 20th century.
Born 18 November 1830, in Karlsruhe; died 31 August 1914, in Karlsruhe.
Painter. Landscapes.
Wilhelm Klose worked at the academy in Munich from 1846 to 1851 and then continued his studies in Rome, Sicily, Greece and Egypt. He later returned to Karlsruhe, where he exhibited, as well as showing work in Munich and at the Exposition Universelle in Paris in 1867.
AUCTION RECORDS:
ZURICH, 12 Nov 1996, *Landscapes* (oil, 13 studies) CHF 2,400.

KLOSS, Friedrich
German, 18th century.
Active in Königsberg (now Kaliningrad, Russia) c. 1790.
Painter.

KLOSS, Friedrich Theodor
German, 19th century.
Born 19 September 1802, in Brunswick; died 9 June 1876, in Copenhagen.
Painter, lithographer. Historical subjects, battles, seascapes, boats.
F.T. Kloss was a pupil of Schumann in Berlin in 1819. In 1828, he settled in Copenhagen, where he made a name as a painter of seascapes. In 1844, he travelled to Italy. He was a member of the Kunstakademi in Copenhagen and drawing master at the Cadet School. From 1834, he also produced lithographs. He is best known for *The Battle of Lyngør* and *The Prince Christian Frederik after the Battle of Sjællands Odde.*
AUCTION RECORDS:
COPENHAGEN, 16 March 1982, *The Frigate Thetis and the Corvette Flora off the Fortress of Belem* (1843, oil on canvas, 43 1/4 ins / 110 cm 62 1/2 ins/159 cm) DKK 19,000. COPENHAGEN, 12 Aug 1985, *Russian Ships at Anchor in the Sound* (oil on canvas, 23 x 36 1/2 ins / 58.5 x 92.5 cm) DKK 82,000. HAVNEN, 7 Feb 2004, *Seascape with Vessels off Gibraltar* (1843, oil on panel, 12 x 16 ins / 31 x 41 cm) DKK 11,500.

KLOSS, Karl
Polish, 19th century.
Born 19 February 1849, in Warsaw; died 29 May 1881, in Warsaw.
Sculptor.
Karl Kloss studied under Marconi. His known works include a *Tarpeia,* busts and memorial stones.

KLOSS, Robert
Austrian, 20th century.
Born 21 July 1889, in Olmütz (now Olomouc, Czech Republic).
Painter.
Robert Kloss settled in Vienna and was also active in Prague, Leipzig and Paris.

KLOSSOWSKI, Erich
German, 20th century.
Born 21 December 1875, in Ragnit.
Painter, engraver, writer.

Erich Klossowski is primarily known as an art critic. A talented painter, he was influenced by the masters including Daumier, Delacroix, Rembrandt and Klossowski, often drawing on their style or subjects in his large decorative works.

AUCTION RECORDS:

PARIS, 30 May 1921, *Carnival*, FRF 30. MUNICH, 4 June 2002, *Provençal Landscape with Donkey Cart* (oil on canvas, 24 x 30 ins / 60 x 75 cm) EUR 1,800.

KLOSSOWSKI, Pierre

French, 20th century.

Born 9 August 1905, in Paris; died 12 August 2001, in Paris.

Draughtsman, illustrator, sculptor, writer. Figure compositions, figures, nudes.

Pierre Klossowski was the brother of the painter Balthus and came from a background where he mixed with artists and writers on a daily basis. After living in Germany and then Switzerland with his family, Klossowski completed his secondary education in Paris. He met Gide and became his secretary. He then started to move in the world of psychoanalysis and became friends with Georges Bataille. He met André Breton and through Breton met André Masson. Klossowski was part of the creative force behind the Contre-Attaque movement, the Collège de Sociologie and the magazine *Acéphale*. During the German occupation of France he began to study religion and theology and embarked on a novitiate, which he later abandoned. In 1946 he married Denise Marie Roberte Morin-Sinclair. After the war Klossowski published an essay entitled *Sade, Mon Prochain*. His writings are generally a blend of eroticism and theology, and include *La Révocation de l'Édit de Nantes*; *Le Baphomet*; *La Vocation Suspendue*; and *Roberte Ce Soir*. In 1968 he wrote an essay on art entitled *La Décadence du Nu*. Klossowski also translated works by well-known writers, including Virgil, Suetonius, St Augustine, Nietzsche, Kafka, Wittgenstein, Klee and Walter Benjamin. It was not until the 1950s that he began to draw figures, almost certainly as illustrations for his novels.

Klossowski's drawings have an ambiguous attraction and are marked by eroticism and voyeurism. There is a restrained lust that sometimes disturbs the figures and actions and hijacks situations, giving the work as a whole an almost Surrealist quality. Klossowski depicted novelised figures such as *Roberte*, mythological heroes such as *Lucretia* and *Tarquin*, and illustrations of Christian legends such as *St Nicholas*. He sought out the 'underside' of nudity, the erotic unveiling that is part of sexuality, and the transformation of the unthinkable into the 'sayable'. Klossowski drew in lead pencil and coloured pencil. His drawing style is sometimes hieratic, accentuating the drama of the scene and expressing a fascination with the lines of the naked body, while his lucid and almost subdued compositions bring to the narrative a furtive and secret feel. With Henri Michaux, Klossowski was one of the most significant artist-writers of the period.

Klossowski took part in *Alibis* at the Musée National d'Art Moderne in Paris. In 2003 his work was shown as part of *Phantom der Lust: Visionen des Masochismus in der Kunst* (*Phantom of Desire. Visions of Masochism in Art*), a group exhibition devoted to Sacher-Masoch, the creator of masochism, and held at the Neue Galerie am Landesmuseum in Graz. Klossowski's drawings were shown for the first time in a private exhibition at the instigation of Giacometti and Masson in 1956. Other solo exhibitions include those at the Galerie Cadran Solaire in Paris (1967); a retrospective at the Kunsthalle in Bern (1981); at the Musée Chéret in Nice (1982); at the Galerie Beaubourg in Paris (drawings, 1986, 1987); at the Galerie Lelong in Zurich (1988); a retrospective exhibition covering the years 1950 to 1990 at the Musée Cantini in Marseilles and later at the Museo Nacional Centro de Arte Reina Sofia in Madrid, the Casa Parpalo in Valencia and the Arnolfini Gallery in Bristol (1990-1991); at the Galerie Beaubourg for the FIAC (Foire Internationale d'Art Contemporain) in Paris (drawings and sculptures, 1993); and at the Galerie Rachlin-Lemarié-Beaubourg in Paris (1997).

BIBLIOGRAPHY:

'*Pierre Klossowski*' in *coll. Repères. Cahiers d'Art Contemporain*, no. 14, Gal. Lelong, Paris, 1984. Foss, Paul/Taylor, Paul/Weiss, Allen S. (ed.), *Phantasm and Simulacra: The Drawings of Pierre Klossowski*, Art and Text, Melbourne, 1985. Butor, Michel, *Une visite chez Pierre Klossowski le samedi 25 avril 1987*, La Différence, Paris, 1990. *Pierre Klossowski, rétrospective 1950-1990*, exhibition catalogue, Musées de Marseille, Centre national des Arts plastiques, La Différence, Paris, 1990. James, Ian, *Pierre Klossowski: The Persistence of a Name*, Legenda, Oxford, 2000. Hill, Leslie, *Bataille, Klossowski, Blanchot: Writing at the Limit*, Oxford University Press, Oxford, 2001. Weibel, Peter (ed.), '*Phantom der Lust. Visionen des Masochismus in der Kunst*' in *2 vol*, exhibition catalogue, Neue Galerie am Landesmuseum, Graz, Belleville Verlag, Munich, 2003.

MUSEUMS AND GALLERIES:

PARIS (FRAC Île-de-France): *Roberte Giflant l'Aide du Maniaque* (*Roberte Slapping the Maniac's Assistant*) (1982) - PARIS (MNAM-CCI): *Descente au Sous-sol* (1978) - ROCHECHOUART (Mus. Départemental d'Art Contemporain): *Roberte's Siesta in Verona* (1983); *Pan and his Pupil* (1984).

AUCTION RECORDS:

PARIS, 5 April 1987, *Charmide* (1984, coloured pencil/mounted paper/canvas, 59 x 45 1/4 ins / 150 x 115 cm) FRF 90,000. PARIS, 24 March 1988, *Gladiatrix* (pencil, 57 x 39 1/4 ins / 145 x 100 cm) FRF 139,000. MILAN, 6 June 1989, *Roberte Interceptée chez les Routiers* (1973, pencil, 59 x 70 3/4 ins / 150 x 180 cm) ITL 46,000,000. PARIS, 19 March 1992, *Roberte this Evening, First Version* (1984, coloured pencil/paper, 78 3/4 x 37 1/2 ins / 200 x 95 cm) FRF 140,000. PARIS, 1 Oct 1992, *Large Sketch for the Son of William Tell* (1984, coloured pencil, 63 x 59 ins / 160 x 150 cm) FRF 100,000. VERSAILLES, 13 June 1993, *Allo, J'Écoute* (*Hallo, I'm Listening*) (coloured pencil and pastel/paper, 54 x 54 1/2 ins / 137 x 138.5 cm) FRF 70,000. ZURICH, 3 Dec 1993, *Standing Nude* (oil/plywood, 39 1/4 x 27 1/4 ins / 100 x 69.5 cm) CHF 4,400. PARIS, 5 Oct 1996, *Roberte Sleeping with Gulliver* (1980-1982, coloured pencil and collage/paper, 39 x 59 ins / 99 x 149 cm) FRF 50,000. PARIS, 15 Dec 1997, *Le Jeune Ogier chez les Frères Chevaliers du Temple* (1971, graphite/paper, 29 1/2 x 42 1/4 ins / 75 x 107 cm) FRF 80,000. NEW YORK, 10 Nov 1999, *Powerlessness and Seduction* (1982, colour pencil, 65 x 43 ins / 164 x 110 cm) USD 19,000. PARIS, 8 Dec 1999, *Diana and Acteon* (1953, crayon on canvas, 90 x 41 ins / 228 x 105 cm) FRF 340,000. PARIS, 25 March 2001, *Le jeune ogier et le frere chevalier Damiens* (1985, colour crayon on paper/canvas, 46 x 58 ins / 116 x 148 cm) FRF 125,000. PARIS, 21 Nov 2001, *David and Goliath* (1984, pastel on canvas, 71 x 59 ins / 180 x 150 cm) FRF 70,000. PARIS, 9 Dec 2003, *Portrait of Balthus* (crayon, 8 x 6 ins / 21 x 16 cm) EUR 3,300. PARIS, 29 June 2004, *Beautiful Versailles Girl* (1981, colour crayon, 87 x 58 ins / 221 x 147 cm) EUR 28,000. PARIS, 18 July 2004, *Mr de Max and Mlle Glissant in the Roles of Diana and Actaeon* (1991-1992, patinated bronze, 96 x 67x47 ins / 245 x 170x120 cm) EUR 40,000.

KLOSTER, Charles

French, 20th century.

Born 10 January 1884, in Paris; died 27 April 1917, near Avocourt.

Painter.

Charles Kloster was a pupil of Bonnat and Merson. He exhibited in Paris at the Salon des Artistes Français.

KLOSTERMAN. See **CLOSTERMAN Johann Baptist**

KLOTS, Alfred Partridge
American, 19th - 20th century.
Born in St-Germain-en-Laye (Yvelines), France, to American parents.
Painter.
Alfred Partridge Klots received an honourable mention at the Paris Salon of 1907.

KLOTZ, August
German, 19th century.
Born 1808, in Augsburg; died 15 March 1853, in Munich.
Painter. History painting.
August Klotz was the son of Kaspar Klotz. He studied with Cornelius and R. von Langer at the Munich academy and became curator of the city's art collection.

KLOTZ, Carl
German, 19th century.
Born 1810, in Augsburg; died 1834, in Greece.
Painter.
Carl Klotz was the son of August Klotz.

KLOTZ, Edmund
Austrian, 19th century.
Born 25 December 1855, in Inzing; died 1929.
Sculptor.
After spending some time in Italy, Edmund Klotz returned to Austria. He produced mainly large religious sculptures, such as the *Pietà* and the *Four Evangelists* for the church in Breitenfeld.

KLOTZ, Gottlieb
Austrian, 19th century.
Born 3 March 1780, in Imst; died 13 February 1834, in Imst.
Sculptor.
MUSEUMS AND GALLERIES:
INNSBRUCK: *Orestes and Pylades in the Presence of Iphigenia*.

KLOTZ, Hermann
Austrian, 19th century.
Born 11 June 1850, in Imst.
Sculptor.
Hermann Klotz was the nephew of Gottlieb Klotz. He studied with Karl Kaiser in Vienna. He is best known for his polychrome sculptures.

KLOTZ, Joseph
German, 19th century.
Born 1785, in Munich; died 1830, in Munich.
Painter. Urban landscapes.
Joseph Klotz travelled in France and northern Germany. He was appointed painter to the court and theatre in Munich. His painting *The Burning of Moscow in 1814* was a great success.
MUSEUMS AND GALLERIES:
MUNICH: *The Schwabinger Tor before its Demolition* (1817)); *View of Munich* (1817).

KLOTZ, Kaspar Gerhard
German, 19th century.
Born 1775, in Mannheim; died 12 May 1847, in Munich.
Miniaturist.
Kaspar Klotz was the son Matthias Klotz. He studied with his father and with Dorner. In 1794, he became painter to the Elector Charles Theodore, on the death of Emperor Maximilian I. He visited Vienna and Paris and finally settled in Munich.

KLOTZ, Lenz
Swiss, 20th century.
Born 1925, in Coire (Grisons).
Painter.
Lenz Klotz attended the arts and crafts school in Basel from 1945 to 1950 where he taught from 1951 onwards. He contributed to various exhibitions of Swiss abstract art, initially in the major towns of Switzerland, in Berlin in 1957-1958, Charleroi and at the 5th Biennale of São Paulo among others. He was awarded the La Sarraz prize in 1960. His work is abstract and his style of drawing gives the impression of movement.
AUCTION RECORDS:
LUCERNE, 24 Nov 1990, *Frieze in Three Parts* (1980, charcoal and mixed technique/Tibetan paper/canvas, 24 1/2 x 65 ins / 62 x 165 cm) CHF 8,000. ZURICH, 8 Dec 1994, *Grey Space* (1957, oil on canvas, 18 x 23 1/2 ins / 46 x 60 cm) CHF 5,175. ZURICH, 23 March 1999, *Half Slanting* (1960, oil on canvas, 41 x 49 ins / 105 x 125 cm) CHF 19,000. BERN, 9 May 2003, *Picture-sheet* (1965, pencil, 20 x 26 ins / 51 x 66 cm) CHF 2,800. BERN, 9 May 2003, *Graded Lines* (1987, oil on canvas, 24 x 28 ins / 60 x 70 cm) CHF 4,400. ZURICH, 8 June 2004, *I Saw what was Missing* (1990, acrylic and Indian ink, 49 x 57 ins / 125 x 145 cm) CHF 9,500.

KLOTZ, Matthias
French, 18th - 19th century.
Born 1748, in Strasbourg; died 21 March 1821, in Munich.
Painter, designer. Portraits.
Matthias Klotz was a student of Haldenwanger in Strasbourg, then moved to Stuttgart, where he worked with Scotti and Guibal. In 1775, he became a set painter for the theatre in Mannheim, having visited the main towns of Germany. In 1778 he went to Munich, where he seems to have lived until his death, while continuing to provide stage sets for the major German theatres.

KLOTZ, Simon Petrus
German, 19th century.
Born 1776, in Mannheim; died 26 September 1824, in Munich.
Painter, miniaturist, watercolourist, lithographer.
History painting.
Simon Klotz was taught by his father Matthias Klotz and by J. Dorner. He visited Vienna, Dresden, Berlin and Copenhagen. He was appointed professor at Landshut in 1805, then travelled to France and Italy. He produced large numbers of watercolours and sepia drawings.

KLOTZ, Valentyn. See **CLOTS**

KLOUCEK, Celda
Bohemian, 19th century.
Born 6 December 1855, in Senomaty.
Sculptor.
After studying in Vienna and Frankfurt, Celda Kloucek settled in Prague, where he decorated a number of public buildings.

KLOUMAIN, Thoralf
Norwegian, 20th century.
Born 26 April 1890, in Faleide.
Draughtsman, caricaturist.
Thoralf Kloumain worked in Oslo where he contributed to several newspapers.

KLOZE, Jean Hugues
Swiss, 16th century.
Born 1528, in Basel.
Painter. History painting.

KLUBER, Hans Hug.
Swiss, 16th century.

Born 1535 or 1536, in Basel; died 7 February 1578, in Basel, of plague.
Painter. History painting, portraits.
Basel School.

Hans Kluber worked in Basel, where he restored and produced three new paintings for the *Dance of Death*. His painting was influenced by Holbein. He taught Hans Bock the Elder, who later replaced him in his duties.

MUSEUMS AND GALLERIES:
BASEL (Kunstmus.): two portraits.

AUCTION RECORDS:
PARIS, 23 May 1927, *Feast* (watercolour) FRF 1,500.

KLUCIS, Gustav Gustavovich, or Klutsis or Kluzis
Latvian, 20th century.
Born 1895, in Valmiera; died in a labour camp c. 1944.
Painter, collage artist, photomontage artist, poster artist, lithographer, sculptor.
Constructivism.
Groups: Unovis, October.

Gustav Klucis studied at the institute of art in Riga (1913-1915) then at the school of design under the aegis of the society for the promotion of the arts (1915-1917) in Petrograd (now St Petersburg). He completed his training at the V. Meshkov school of design and painting, then in Ilya Mashkov's studio, in the State free art workshop in Moscow (Svomas), then in the high arts and technical workshops (Vhutemas) under the direction of Kasimir Malevich and Pevsner. An associate member of the Inkhuk productivist group (institute of artistic culture) in Moscow from 1921 to 1925, he taught courses at the high arts and technical workshops (Vhutemas) from 1924 to 1930. He was a founder member of the October group in 1928.

Klucis started his career by producing posters in 1919 and from 1920 to 1922 he was particularly influenced by El Lissitsky. These posters often used a photomontage technique but in a new, avant-garde way in relation to perspective, and subject matter. Like Aleksandr Rodchenko, he also produced photo-collages and was a representative of Russian Productivism, a kind of Constructivism, grouped around Tatlin, that banished the conceptual autonomy of art to make way for unity between technique and art designed for the masses. Apart from his political posters, especially those publicising the first annual economic plan (1928-1933) and magazine covers, mention should be made of his propaganda projects. He also wrote books and produced architectural constructions. We know that he produced a lithograph entitled *Dynamic City*, a plan for a Suprematist city (1919-1921).

Collective exhibitions include: *Unovis Exhibition* with the Suprematist group set up in 1919-1920 by Malevich, Moscow (1921); Exposition internationale des arts décoratifs et de l'industrie, Paris (1925); international exhibition, Cologne (1928); Brussels (1929); photomontage exhibition, representing the USSR, Berlin (1931); *Traumfabrik Kommunismus - die Visuelle Kultur der Stalinzeit* (*Dream Factory Communism, the Visual Culture of the Stalin Period*), Schirn Kunsthalle, Frankfurt (2003). Two retrospectives were held in Riga (1959 and 1970).

Klucis published an article entitled *Photomontage as a Means of Agitation and Propaganda* in the anthology *Izo-Fron* (Moscow, 1931).

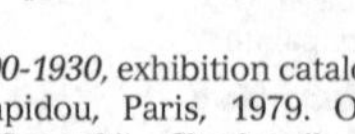

BIBLIOGRAPHY:
Paris Moscou, 1900-1930, exhibition catalogue, Éd. du Centre Georges-Pompidou, Paris, 1979. Oginskaja, Larisa, *Gustav Klucis*, Sovetskij Chudoznik, Moscow, 1981. Gassner, Hubertus/Nachtigäller, Roloand, *Gustav Klucis*, exhibition catalogue, Museum Fridericianum, Kassel, 1991. Buzinska, Irena, *Theoretical Writings and Manifestos by Latvian Artists*, Neputns, Riga, 2002 (Text in Latin and English). Hollein, Max, et al., *Dream Factory Communism, the Visual Culture of the Stalin Period*, exhibition catalogue, Schirn Kunsthalle, Frankfurt, 2003 (text in English and German).

MUSEUMS AND GALLERIES:
MONTREAL (MAC): *Ecrian* (1922) - MOSCOW (State Tretyakov Gal.): *Axonometric Painting* (1920).

KLUG, A. H.
Swiss, 18th century.
Active in Lenzburg.
Possibly a potter, possibly a painter.

KLUG, H. C.
Swiss, 18th century.
Possibly a potter, possibly a painter.

H. C. Klug was related to A. H. Klug.

KLUGE, Constantin
Latvian, 20th century.
Born 1912, in Riga; died 2003.
Active in China and in France.
Painter. Figure compositions, urban landscapes.

Constantin Kluge emigrated to Manchuria and studied in Shanghai before going to Paris where he graduated in architecture. In 1938 he returned to China where he enjoyed the friendship of the philosopher Teilhard de Chardin. He later moved to Hong Kong and finally to Paris. He painted views of Paris, mainly of the Latin Quarter. His works were shown at Wally Findlay Galleries, Paris (1972).

MUSEUMS AND GALLERIES:
WASHINGTON DC (Georgetown University): *View of Notre Dame* (c. 1955, oil on canvas).

AUCTION RECORDS:
NEW YORK, 14 April 1983, *Fisherman in a Landscape* (oil on canvas, 32 x 51 1/4 ins / 81 x 130 cm) USD 1,500. NEW YORK, 13 May 1988, *Harbour Scene* (oil on canvas, 30 3/4 x 30 3/4 ins / 78 x 78 cm) USD 3,740. TORONTO, 30 Nov 1988, *Pont-Neuf After the Storm* (oil on canvas, 28 1/2 x 35 3/4 ins / 72.5 x 91 cm) CAD 4,500. TROYES, 23 March 1989, *Flower Market, Place de la Madeleine* (oil on canvas, 21 1/4 x 25 1/2 ins / 54 x 65 cm) FRF 14,500. NEW YORK, 21 Feb 1990, *Pont-Neuf in Spring* (oil on canvas, 25 1/2 x 32 ins / 64.8 x 81.4 cm) USD 7,700. NEW YORK, 10 Oct 1990, *Flower Market in the Place de la Madeleine* (oil on canvas, 45 x 64 ins / 114.3 x 162.8 cm) USD 8,250. NEW YORK, 13 Feb 1991, *Plailly in Winter* (oil on canvas, 26 x 36 ins / 66 x 91.4 cm) USD 1,870. NEW YORK, 7 May 1991, *Gondoliers in Venice* (oil on canvas, 21 1/4 x 28 3/4 ins / 54 x 73 cm) USD 2,200. LONDON, 15 Oct 1992, *Pont-Neuf* (oil on canvas, 21 1/4 x 25 1/2 ins / 54 x 65 cm) GBP 2,200. NEW YORK, 26 Feb 1993, *Pont des Arts* (oil on canvas, 32 x 51 ins / 81.3 x 129.5 cm) USD 7,188. NEW YORK, 7 Nov 1995, *Quai Conti in Autumn* (oil on canvas, 32 x 32 ins / 81 x 81 cm) USD 4,370. NEW YORK, 10 Oct 1996, *Paris Street Scene* (oil on canvas, 32 x 32 ins / 81.3 x 81.3 cm) USD 3,162.

KLUGE, Harry Axel Edouard Leonardt
Danish, 20th century.
Born 19 November 1879, in Copenhagen; died 1949.
Painter. Landscapes, seascapes.

Harry Kluge's repertoire consisted mainly of seascapes.

AUCTION RECORDS:
LONDON, 2 Oct 1992, *View out of the Window towards Copenhagen* (1905, oil on canvas, 20 1/2 x 16 1/4 ins / 52 x 41.3

cm) GBP 1,980. COPENHAGEN, 5 March 2001, *Entrance to the Surgical Academy in Bredgate 62* (1919, oil on canvas, 39 x 26 ins / 98 x 67 cm) DKK 16,000. COPENHAGEN, 9 June 2004, *Danish Men-o-War Disappearing in the Haze* (1924, oil on canvas, 29 x 38 ins / 73 x 97 cm) DKK 20,000.

KLUGE, Kurt
German, 20th century.
Born 29 April 1886, in Leipzig.
Sculptor.
Kurt Kluge was taught by Sterl and Dorsch in Dresden. Thereafter he settled in Berlin and taught sculpture at the academy there. He sculpted busts and subjects of religious inspiration.

KLUGE, Moriz Ewin
German, 19th century.
Born 1802, in Neustadt Dresden.
Engraver (burin).
Kluge was a pupil of Toschi. He engraved religious subjects after Correggio, Guercino and Carracci.

KLUGT, Hugo
German, 20th century.
Born 14 December 1879, in Hamburg.
Sculptor, engraver.
Hugo Klugt studied in Berlin and Munich. His output includes the war memorial in the town of Volksdorf.

KLUIBENSCHEDL, Heinrich
Austrian, 19th century.
Born 3 March 1849, in Reitz.
Active in Reitz.
Painter. History painting.
Kluibenschedl painted frescoes for churches in the Tyrol.

KLUMB, André
French, 20th century.
Born 28 March 1925, in Paris.
Watercolourist, painter (gouache), designer, engraver, draughtsman. Scenes with figures, still-lifes, flowers, landscapes. Murals, designs for tapestries.
André Klumb worked with André Fraye from 1950, and a few years later met André Derain. A colourist, Klumb began by painting still-lifes, flowers and landscapes and went on to experiment with Abstraction, seeking to evoke his subject rather than simply represent it. He described himself as an aesthetician of surfaces, concerned with movement and the whirlwind of existence. He also produced mural compositions, notably those in the Jansen studio (1967-1973), several decorative works for companies and private individuals as well as reproductions of old paintings.

He exhibited at several of the Paris Salons, including the Salon d'Automne, the Salon des Indépendants and the Salon Comparaisons. He also showed his work in solo exhibitions: at the Galerie de l'Art Moderne in Paris (1961, 1964, 1966, 1967); at the Galerie N. D. in Nantes (1978, 1979); at the Galerie Gorosane in Paris (1982, 1984); at the Musée Francisque Mandet in Riom (1986); and at the Musée Vivenel in Compiègne (1987).

BIBLIOGRAPHY:
André Klumb, exhibition catalogue, Musée Francisque-Mandet, Riom, 1986. *André Klumb, rétrospective 1957-1987*, exhibition catalogue, Musée Vivenel, Compiègne, 1987. *André Klumb*, exhibition catalogue, Bred, Paris, 1990.

MUSEUMS AND GALLERIES:
PARIS (MAMVP) - PARIS (Mus. du Petit Palais) - PARIS (Mus. Galliera) - RIOM (Mus. Francisque-Mandet) - ROCQUEFORT-LES-PINS.

AUCTION RECORDS:
PARIS, 12 Nov 1990, *Green Landscape* (1988, oil on canvas, 32 x 25 1/2 ins / 81 x 65 cm) FRF 12,000.

KLUMPKE, Anna Elizabeth
American, 19th - 20th century.
Born 1856, in San Francisco; died 1942, in Thomery (Seine-et-Marne), France.
Active in France.
Painter. Portraits, genre scenes, animals, still-lifes.
Anna Elizabeth Klumpke studied under Tony Robert-Fleury and Jules Lefebvre at the Académie Julian in Paris. More significantly she became the friend and partner of French artist and women's rights pioneer Rosa Bonheur whose biography (*Rosa Bonheur, Her Life and Work*) she wrote. She created a Prix Rosa-Bonheur at the Paris Salon. Her most famous painting is *The Laundry*. She exhibited at the Paris Salon from 1882 and often won prizes and medals on both sides of the Atlantic (Versailles in 1886, Saint Louis in 1904). She featured in arts events in Pittsburgh, Berlin, Munich and Vienna. She was awarded the Legion d'Honneur in 1924.

MUSEUMS AND GALLERIES:
PHILADELPHIA (Pennsylvania Academy of the Fine Arts Gal.): *The Laundry*.

AUCTION RECORDS:
NEW YORK, 5 Dec 1985, *Girl Sitting in a Field* (1893, pastel, 18 x 21 3/4 ins / 45.7 x 55.3 cm) USD 4,000. PARIS, 10 Dec 1997, *View of the Bay of San Francisco* (1937, oil on canvas, 44 x 32 ins / 112 x 81 cm) FRF 6,800.

KLÜNDER, Alexander Julius
Estonian, 19th century.
Born 20 February 1802; died 8 January 1875, in Reval (now Tallinn).
Painter. Portraits.
Alexander Julius Klünder studied under Senff in Dorpat (now Tartu) and later painted the portraits of the teachers at the university in Dorpat.

KLUNDERT, Phil van der
Dutch, 20th century.
Born 1942.
Sculptor.
Phil van der Klundert exhibits in Holland and Belgium. In 1969, he won the Jacob Maris Prize for young artists. He creates objects in rubber.

KLÜPFEL, Johann Conrad
German, 17th century.
Active c. 1620.
Engraver.
Klüpfel is known for his small plates of the *Cries of Rome*, after Villamena.

KLÜPPEL, Caspar
German, 17th century.
Born 1596, in Pirna; died 1639, in Pirna.
Sculptor.
Klüppel worked for churches in Pirna, Maxen and Wilsdruff.

KLUSEMANN, Georg
German, 20th century.
Born 13 May 1942, in Essen; died 1981.
Since 1969 active in Venezuela then in Italy.
Painter, engraver, draughtsman, illustrator.
From 1961 to 1967, Georg Klusemann studied at the Staatliche Kunstakademie in Düsseldorf under Theo Otto in his stage design and painting workshop. He practised engraving between 1967 and 1968. From 1969 to 1970 he taught engraving at the University of the Andes in Mérida, Venezuela. Since 1970 he has been painting in oils on canvas and wood and producing large numbers of coloured pencil drawings. Since 1971 he has lived and worked in Lucca, Italy.

His painting consists of a series of collections of disparate objects, using a very precise trompe l'œil technique of which he is an undisputed master. These collections of objects, which seem to be suspended in a state of weightlessness within the space of the canvas, generate surrealistic associations. On returning from a trip to the Middle East at the end of the 1960s he published a book of children's stories with his own illustrations, *Die Wundersame Reise nach Esmi* (*The Wondrous Journey to Esmi*). He published another in the Anthology of Children's Literature: *Geh und spiel mit dem Reisen* (*Go and play with travelling*).

In 1969 and 1970, he exhibited at the Art Museum and the Gallery Mendoza in Caracas, at the Centre for Experimental Art in Mérida and then in Maracaibo, and in 1972, at the Galerie du Dragon in Paris.

AUCTION RECORDS:

ZURICH, 20 Nov 1987, *Still-life* (c. 1963-1964, oil on card, 15 1/4 x 11 ins / 39 x 27 cm) CHF 9,500. ZURICH, 31 May 2001, *Still-life* (c. 1963, oil on board, 15 x 11 ins / 39 x 27 cm) CHF 7,000.

KLUTH, Karl

German, 20th century.

Born 1898, in Halle; died 1972, in Hamburg.

Painter.

Hamburg Secession Group.

Karl Kluth studied at the academy in Karlsruhe from 1919 to 1922 before moving to Hamburg. He met Edvard Munch in the course of a visit to Scandinavia. He joined the Hamburg Secession, which advocated breaking free of the constraints of formal academism, and remained a member until the group voluntarily disbanded in 1933 in the wake of demands by the Nazi authorities that it exclude its Jewish members. The advent of the Nazis prevented Kluth from taking up a post as a teacher at the fine arts academy in Hamburg. He returned to Hamburg in 1950, however, and went on to teach at the fine arts academy. He was awarded the Edwin-Scharff Prize in Hamburg in 1957.

Examples of Kluth's work have featured at various exhibitions designed to highlight the importance and influence of the Hamburg Secession in the days of the Weimar Republic, among them *Malerei der Hamburgischen Sezession 1919-1933 aus der Sammlung Hermann-Josef Bunte* (*Paintings of the Hamburg Sezession 1919-1933 from the Hermann-Josef Bunte Collection*), an itinerant exhibition in 2000 which visited various venues in Germany, including the fine arts museum in Hamburg. His work also featured at *Hamburgische Sezession 1919-1933* (*Hamburg Secession 1919-1933*), held in 2003 at the Hamburg arts and crafts museum. Solo exhibitions by Kluth include those at the Oldenburg arts circle in 1970 and the fine arts museum in Hamburg in 1998.

BIBLIOGRAPHY:

Meyer-Tönnesmann, Carsten, *Die Maler Arthur Illies, Friedrich Ahlers-Hestermann, Karl Kluth*, Verein für Hamburg. Geschichte, Hamburg, 1989. Leppien, Helmut R., *Karl Kluth zum 100. Geburtstag: Gemälde*, exhibition catalogue, Hamburger Kunsthalle, Hamburg, 1998.

MUSEUMS AND GALLERIES:

SCHLOSS GOTTORF (Schleswig-Holsteinische Landesmuseen).

AUCTION RECORDS:

MUNICH, 26-27 Nov 1991, *Town House* (oil/synthetic resin, 31 1/2 x 39 1/4 ins / 80 x 100 cm) DEM 5,750.

KLUTH, Robert

German, 19th - 20th century.

Born 1854, in Mecklenberg; died 23 September 1921, in Brooklyn (New York City), USA.

Active in the USA.

Painter. Interiors with figures, landscapes, seascapes.

Robert Kluth's parents emigrated to the USA in 1861. In his youth he worked in Philadelphia and New York. Later he settled in Brooklyn where he was one of the founders of the artists' society.

AUCTION RECORDS:

NEW YORK, 22 Sept 1993, *The First Steps* (oil on canvas, 30 x 48 ins / 76 x 122 cm) USD 10,350.

KLÜVER, Bernt

Norwegian, 20th century.

Painter.

Bernt Klüver was active around 1920.

KLUYT, Adriaen Pietersz. See **CLUYT**

KLUYVER, Pieter Lodewyk Francisco

Dutch, 19th century.

Born 22 March 1816, in Amsterdam; died 4 January 1900, in Amsterdam.

Painter. Landscapes with figures, landscapes.

Pieter Kluyver was a pupil of Root.

MUSEUMS AND GALLERIES:

THE HAGUE (Gemeentemus.): two landscapes.

AUCTION RECORDS:

AMSTERDAM, 1881, *Forest in Winter*, FRF 420. ROTTERDAM, 1891, *Winter Landscape in Twilight*, FRF 200; *Summer Landscape in Twilight*, FRF 180. AMSTERDAM, 26 May 1970, *Landscape*, NLG 13,000. LONDON, 22 Oct 1971, *Wooded Landscape with Figures*, Gns 1,000. LONDON, 6 March 1974, *Landscape*, GBP 3,800. AMSTERDAM, 7 Sept 1976, *River Landscape* (oil on panel, 12 x 15 ins / 30.5 x 38 cm) NLG 6,400. LONDON, 6 May 1977, *View of Haarlem* (oil on panel, 17 1/2 x 25 ins / 44.4 x 63.5 cm) GBP 6,500. AMSTERDAM, 25 April 1978, *Winter Landscape* (oil on panel, 8 x 11 1/4 ins / 20.5 x 28.5 cm) NLG 5,800. AMSTERDAM, 14 June 1979, *Winter Landscape* (oil on canvas, 16 1/4 x 20 1/4 ins / 41 x 51.5 cm) NLG 9,800. NEW YORK, 28 May 1981, *Landscape* (oil on panel, 12 x 16 1/4 ins / 30.5 x 41 cm) USD 5,000. LONDON, 21 Oct 1983, *Wooded Landscape with Figures* (1841, oil on canvas, 40 1/4 x 50 1/4 ins / 102.2 x 127.6 cm) GBP 4,500. LONDON, 26 Feb 1988, *Landscape with a Tree-Lined River and Travellers* (oil on panel, 20 1/2 x 26 ins / 52.1 x 66 cm) GBP 3,300. PARIS, 24 June 1988, *Landscape in Holland* (oil on panel, 14 1/4 x 20 3/4 ins / 36 x 53 cm) FRF 30,000. AMSTERDAM, 25 April 1990, *Forest in Winter with Figures on a Frozen Pond* (oil on panel, 15 x 20 ins / 38 x 51 cm) NLG 12,650. COLOGNE, 29 June 1990, *Outskirts of Haarlem* (oil on canvas, 17 3/4 x 24 1/4 ins / 45 x 61.5 cm) DEM 5,500. AMSTERDAM, 6 Nov 1990, *Houses along a Frozen Canal* (oil on panel, 11 x 17 1/2 ins / 28 x 44.5 cm) NLG 8,970. AMSTERDAM, 24 April 1991, *Winter Landscape with a Man Gathering Firewood on a Snowy Bridge* (oil on panel, 7 3/4 x 11 1/4 ins / 19.5 x 28.5 cm) NLG 10,925. AMSTERDAM, 30 Oct 1991, *Extensive River Landscape with a Peasant in a Boat and Haarlem in the Distance* (oil on panel, 10 3/4 x 16 1/4 ins / 27.5 x 41 cm) NLG 27,600. AMSTERDAM, 14-15 April 1992, *Wooded Landscape with People Gathering Firewood on a Path* (oil on panel, 18 x 21 ins / 45.5 x 52.5 cm) NLG 13,800. AMSTERDAM, 28 Oct 1992, *Harvesters in an Undulating Wooded Landscape* (oil on panel, 14 3/4 x 19 ins / 37.5 x 48 cm) NLG 6,900. AMSTERDAM, 21 April 1993, *Winter: Wooded Landscape in Snow with Figures; Wooded Landscape in Summer with a Church in the Distance* (oil on panel, a pair, each 8 3/4 x 6 1/2 ins / 22.5 x 16.5 cm) NLG 11,500. AMSTERDAM, 8 Nov 1994, *Wooded Landscape with Figures Walking in the Snow* (oil on panel, 16 x 12 1/4 ins / 40.5 x 31 cm) NLG 7,130. AMSTERDAM, 16 April 1996, *Figures on a Road in an Extensive Landscape* (oil on panel, 20 1/2 x 17 ins / 52 x 43 cm) NLG 14,750. AMSTERDAM, 3 Sept 1996, *Peasant on a Path in a Winter Landscape with Windmill* (oil on panel, 7 1/2 x 10 3/4 ins / 19 x 27.5 cm) NLG 3,920. AMSTERDAM, 30 Oct 1996, *Winter: a Frozen Canal with Sailing Boats Covered in Ice and Figures on a Quay by a Mill* (oil on canvas, 13 1/2 x 19 3/4 ins / 34 x 50 cm) NLG 12,685. AMSTERDAM, 5 Nov 1996, *Figures on a Snowy Road* (oil on panel, 10 1/4 x 14 1/4 ins / 26 x 36 cm) NLG 11,800. AMSTERDAM, 27 Oct 1997, *Peasants on a Country Road in Winter* (oil on panel, 15 3/4 x 22 ins / 40 x 55 cm) NLG 28,320. LONDON, 21 Nov 1997, *River Landscape with Windmill* (oil on canvas, 15 1/4 x 22 1/4 ins / 39 x 56.5 cm) GBP 8,970. AMSTERDAM, 19 Jan 1999, *Wooded River Landscape with Eelfisher* (1863, oil on panel, 14 x 21 ins / 35 x 53 cm) NLG 7,500. AMSTERDAM, 26 Oct 1999, *Panoramic Landscape* (oil on panel, 13 x 17 ins / 32 x 44 cm) NLG 32,000. AMSTERDAM, 18 April 2000, *Panoramic Landscape with Haarlem in the Distance* (1868, oil on panel, 15 x 21 ins / 38 x 54 cm) NLG 90,000. BERN, 11 May 2000, *Extensive Plateau with Faraway Town and River* (oil on panel, 11 x 18 ins / 29 x 46 cm) CHF 18,000. AMSTERDAM, 19 June 2001, *Summer Landscape at Dusk with Farm beyond* (oil on panel, 7 x 11 ins / 18 x 27 cm) NLG 11,000. GRAVENHAGE, 7 Nov 2001, *Winter View with Woodgatherers in Forest* (oil on canvas, 30 x 24 ins / 75 x 61 cm) NLG 23,000. AMSTERDAM, 12 March 2002, *Summer Landscapes with Cows, and with a Farm by a Stream* (oil on canvas, a pair, 19 x 26 ins / 47 x 65 cm) EUR 4,800. AMSTERDAM, 24 April 2002, *Panoramic Winter Landscape with Skaters on the Ice* (oil on panel, 12 x 16 ins / 30 x 41 cm) EUR 13,000. AMSTERDAM, 1 July 2003, *Woodgatherers on a Frozen River* (oil on canvas, 30 x 25 ins / 75 x 64 cm) EUR 3,500. STUTTGART, 25 Sept 2003, *Landscape with Sheep and Water* (oil on panel, 19 x 23 ins / 47 x 59 cm) EUR 4,500. STAUFEN, 25 March 2004, *Frozen Dutch River with Horse-drawn Cart and Windmill* (oil on panel, 6 x 9 ins / 16 x 24 cm) EUR 1,800. AMSTERDAM, 19 April 2004, *Woodgatherers on the Ice, with a Mill in the Distance* (oil on canvas, 30 x 29 ins / 76 x 73 cm) EUR 8,000.

KLUZIS, Gustav. See **KLUCIS Gustav Gustavovitch**

KLYUKVIN

Russian, 19th century.

Lithographer.

Klyukvin engraved portraits.

KLYUN, Ivan, or Kliun, Klioun, Klioune, real name: Kliunkov Vasilievich Ivan

Ukrainian, 20th century.

Born 1870 or 1873, in Bolchie or Bolchye Gorki; died 1942, in Moscow.

Painter (including gouache), watercolourist, sculptor. Suprematism.

Brought up in Warsaw, where he studied at the school of design for the promotion of the arts, Ivan Klyun left Poland and moved to Moscow in 1910 where he attended the studio of Ilya Mashkov, V. Fisher and F. Rerberg. In 1913, by now in St Petersburg, he joined a futurist group, the Union of Youth, of which Malevich was also a member, an artist whom Klyun had met some years previously in 1907. He published various articles and essays on the role of art either alone or in collaboration with Malevich. Sympathetic to the Russian Revolution, he went on to run the central exhibitions bureau at the department of fine arts. In 1918 he began teaching at the Free Art Studios in Moscow (Svomas) and at the Higher Artistic-Technical Studios (Vkhutemas) until 1921. In 1922 he was elected to the Institute for Artistic Culture (Inkhuk). In 1927 he joined the society of sculptors.

His very early work, like that of Kasimir Malevich, was marked by the influence of Russian symbolism. In his *Portrait of the Artist's Wife (tuberculosis)* (1910) an unreal and morbid atmosphere hovers over the work. He moved away from this style around 1915 in order to follow Malevich along the Cubo-Futurism route (*Ozonatov*, 1914) and later became an adherent of Suprematism. He was part of the Supremus artistic circle and editor of a periodical to which Rosanova, Udaltsova, Exter and Malevich also contributed. By 1917 his Suprematist style had reached maturity and Klyun sought instead to pursue his research into more individualist channels drawn from other Constructivist experiences, especially within the domain of colour. He researched the *sfumato* technique, and became familiar with the effects of transparencies. His aim is clear in his pictorial order, an approach which differentiated him from rigid Constructivism and Suprematism. In 1919, he used his writings, particularly *The Art of Colour*, to criticise harshly the shapes of Malevich's Suprematism, which according to him were dead and frozen, yet nevertheless continued to refer to his own paintings as 'Suprematist compositions'. His research later concentrated on the movement of light.

Collective exhibitions include *Tramway V*, Moscow and St Petersburg (1915); with Malevich *0.10*, collective Futurist exhibition organised in 1915 by Jean Pougny (I.A. Puni) in Petrograd (now St Petersburg); Bubnovy Valet (Jack of Diamonds) (1916-1917); Russian exhibition, Berlin (1922); *Aspects Historiques du Constructivisme et de l'Art Concret (Historical Aspects of Constructivism and Concrete Art)*, Musée d'Art Moderne de la Ville, Paris (1977); *Traumfabrik Kommunismus - die Visuelle Kultur der Stalinzeit (Dream Factory Communism, the Visual Culture of the Stalin Period)*, Schirn Kunsthalle, Frankfurt (2003). A retrospective was held at the Matignon Gallery, New York (1983).

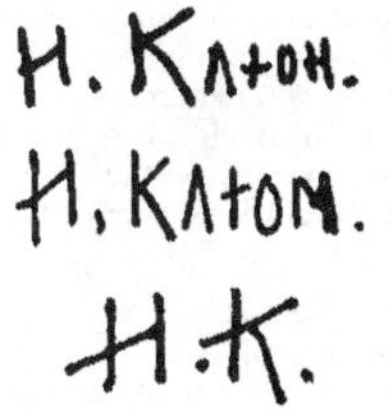

BIBLIOGRAPHY:

La Sculpture et le Dessin des sculpteurs de la fin du XIXe et début du XXe siècle, exhibition catalogue, Gal. Tretiakov, Moscow, 1977. *Paris Moscou, 1900-1930*, group exhibition catalogue, Éd. du Centre Georges-Pompidou, Paris, 1979. Hollein, Max, et al., *Dream Factory Communism, the Visual Culture of the Stalin Period*, exhibition catalogue, Schirn Kunsthalle, Frankfurt, 2003 (text in English and German).

MUSEUMS AND GALLERIES:

MOSCOW (State Tretyakov Gal.): *Suprematism* (1915) - ST PETERSBURG (Gosudarstvennyj Russkij Muz.): *Ozonatov*.

AUCTION RECORDS:

LONDON, 1 Dec 1976, *Harmony of Colours* (c. 1928, watercolour, 11 3/4 x 8 1/4 ins / 30 x 21 cm) GBP 300. NEW YORK, 3 Nov 1978, *Architectonic Construction* (c. 1923, gouache and watercolour/grey paper, 5 3/4 x 5 ins / 14.5 x 12.7 cm) USD 4,000. NEW YORK, 6 Nov 1979, *Purist Composition (Still-life)* (watercolour, 9 1/2 x 7 3/4 ins / 24 x 19.5 cm) USD 16,000. LONDON, 1 Dec 1982, *Suprematist Composition* (1920-25, watercolour, 2 x 2 ins / 5 x 5 cm) GBP 1,000. LONDON, 6 Dec 1983, *Spherical Suprematism* (c. 1923-1925, oil on canvas, 40 1/4 x 27 1/2 ins / 102 x 70 cm) GBP 200,000. NEW YORK, 15 Nov 1984, *Abstraction* (1922, watercolour/green paper, 10 1/2 x 7 3/4 ins / 26.4 x 20 cm) USD 5,000. LONDON, 5 Dec 1984, *Cubist Composition* (1918, pen, 7 x 3 1/4 ins / 17.7 x 8.4 cm) GBP 1,700. NEW YORK, 14 Nov 1985, *Still-life* (1920, watercolour/pencil outlines, 9 1/4 x 8 ins / 23.8 x 19.4 cm) USD 23,000. LONDON, 2 April 1987, *Composition* (c. 1921, pencil, 4 1/2 x 4 3/4 ins / 11.5 x 12 cm) GBP 4,00. LA VARENNE-ST-HILAIRE, 6 Dec 1987, *Composition with Three Centres* (watercolour and gouache, 16 3/4 x 11 3/4 ins / 42.5 x 30 cm) FRF 75,000. LONDON, 6 Oct 1988, *Man Walking* (watercolour/paper, 8 x 6 1/4 ins / 19.4 x 16 cm) GBP 3,300. LONDON, 4 April 1989, *Cubo-Futurist Figure* (oil on canvas, 23 3/4 x 19 1/4 ins / 60.5 x 49 cm) GBP 56,100. LONDON, 6 April 1989, *Architectural Composition* (1921, oil on card, 22 x 16½ ins / 55 x 42 cm) GBP 170,500. LONDON, 4 April 1990, *Suprematism* (oil on panel, 14 x 14 ins / 35.3 x 35.8 cm) GBP 154,000; *Untitled* (charcoal and gouache/paper, 10 x 11 ins / 25.4 x 27 cm) GBP 60,500. PARIS, 28 Nov 1990, *Composition* (gouache/paper, 10¾ x 7½ ins / 27.5 x 19 cm) FRF 40,000. MUNICH, 1-2 Dec 1992, *Composition with Green Rectangle* (1920, oil on paper, 17 x 13 ins / 43 x 33 cm) DEM 131,000.

KMENTOVA, Eva
Czechoslovak, 20th century.
Born 1928, in Prague.
Sculptor. Figures.

Eva Kmentova studied at the school of decorative arts in Prague. She joined the Journey group and started to exhibit with groups in both Czechoslovakia and abroad, particularly in Paris at the 1969 Salon de Mai.

After an initial series of works influenced by Post-Cubism, in 1960 she started producing panels in the form of murals made up of an extremely wide range of objects, some hollow cast, some cast in relief, in which she adopted symbolic colours: blue and green to evoke nature, red for the human form. Then from 1965 she added casts of hands and mouths to her creations, and from 1967 moulds of arms and legs, quickly followed by an entire body, sometimes an amalgam of the body of a man and the body of a woman, often used, in a horizontal position, to evoke landscapist reliefs. By around 1968 she was still producing human silhouettes, cut down into plaster plaques, and dehumanised in *Man-Target* and *Woman-Target*, in which she casts, instead of a heart, the readily understood graphism of an archery target figuratively peppered with bullet holes. She worked primarily in plaster and concrete.

KMETTY, János
Hungarian, 20th century.
Born 23 December 1889, in Miskolc; died 1976.
Painter, draughtsman. Figure compositions, still-lifes.
Szentendre Artists' Colony, Kecskemét Artists' Colony.

From 1909 to 1912 János Kmetty studied at Ferenc Szablya Frischaut's private school. He made a study trip to Paris where he attended the free Russian school. Then from 1911 to 1912 he was the pupil of Karoly Ferenczy. He spent many summers in the artists' colony in Kecskemét. In 1918 he joined the artists' circle known as MA (Today) and worked as the editor of a magazine founded by Kassak. He visited Paris again (1927), then Munich (1932) and the Soviet Union (1955). In 1917 he took part in the Budapest national salon. He taught at the school of fine arts in Budapest.

A painter of compositions with figures and still-lifes, all of his work is strongly influenced by the style of Cézanne, with the occasional Cubist accent. When the Hungarian republic was proclaimed in 1919, he collaborated with Némès Lamperth on designs for political posters.

From 1924 to 1944 his work was included in the exhibitions organised by KUT (new society of artists). In 1936 and 1962 he took part in the Venice Biennale. In 1981 his work featured in the exhibition *Art in Hungary 1905-1930. Art and Revolution L'art en Hongrie 1905-1930. Art et Révolution*, Musée d'Art et d'Industrie, St Étienne and in *Beöthy et l'avant-garde hongroise* (*Beöthy and the Hungarian Avant-Garde*), Galerie Franka Berndt, Paris (1986). He held several solo exhibitions including in Prague (1914 1928, 1937 1960). He was awarded the Kossuth Prize.

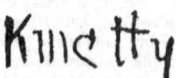

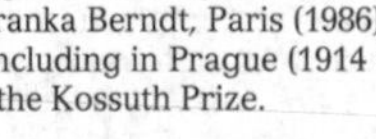

BIBLIOGRAPHY:
Németh, Lajos, *Moderne ungarische Kunst*, Corvina Kiadó, Budapest, 1969. Nemeth, Lajos/Frank, János, *János Kmety*, Mücsarnok, Budapest, 1977. Passuth, Krisztina/Szabó, Júlia, *L'Art en Hongrie 1905-1930. Art et révolution*, exhibition catalogue, Musée d'Art et d'Industrie, Saint-Étienne, Musée d'Art moderne de la ville de Paris, Paris, 1980.

MUSEUMS AND GALLERIES:
BUDAPEST (Magyar Nemzeti Gal.): several works.

AUCTION RECORDS:
PARIS, 15 Dec 1991, *Cubist Still-life* (watercolour/paper, 17 x 11½ ins / 43 x 29 cm) FRF 40,000. PARIS, 19 March 1992, *Cubist Still-life* (watercolour/paper, 12 x 8¼ ins / 30.7 x 20.7 cm) FRF 24,000. PARIS, 3 June 1992, *Still-life with Candlestick* (watercolour/paper, 19 x 14 ins / 48 x 35.5 cm) FRF 32,000. PARIS, 12 May 1993, *Self-portrait* (1917, oil on canvas, 18½ x 12½ ins / 47 x 31.5 cm) FRF 7,000. BUDAPEST, 1 Nov 2000, *A Room, Around 1910* (oil on canvas, 14 x 19 ins / 35 x 49 cm) HUF 2,600,000. BUDAPEST, 1 Dec 2000, *Still-life with Can and Fruits by a Green Curtain* (watercolour, 27 x 23 ins / 69 x 59 cm) HUF 3,000,000. BUDAPEST, 27 April 2001, *Girl with Guitar* (oil on canvas, 39 x 28 ins / 100 x 70 cm) HUF 6,500,000. BUDAPEST, 7 Dec 2001, *Golden Age* (oil on cardboard, 21 x 24 ins / 54 x 62 cm) HUF 9,500,000. BUDAPEST, 6 Dec 2002, *Summer Afternoon in Szentendre* (oil on cardboard, 20 x 28 ins / 50 x 70 cm) HUF 1,800,000. BUDAPEST, 6 Dec 2002, *Plan of the Fresco* (oil on cardboard, 24 x 34 ins / 60 x 87 cm) HUF 3,800,000. BUDAPEST, 16 May 2003, *Hilly Landscape with Rays of Light and Houses* (oil on canvas, 26 x 30 ins / 67 x 77 cm) HUF 7,500,000. BUDAPEST, 12 Dec 2003, *Blue Still-life* (1924, oil on cardboard, 23 x 21 ins / 59 x 54 cm) HUF 3,600,000. BUDAPEST, 16 April 2004, *Still-life with the Kut Magazine* (oil on canvas, 30 x 19 ins / 75 x 47 cm) HUF 27,000,000. BUDAPEST, 28 April 2004, *Still-life with Fruit* (c. 1930, oil on canvas, 24 x 31 ins / 60 x 80 cm) HUF 9,500,000.

KMIELIAUSKAS, Antanas
Lithuanian, 20th century.
Born 1932, in Olenderme, near Butrimonys.
Painter, draughtsman, engraver, sculptor. Religious subjects, figures. Statues, funerary monuments, frescoes.

Antanas Kmieriauskas was born into a peasant family. He graduated at the top of his class from the Lithuanian Art Institute in 1957. At that time artistic creativity was severely controlled by the Soviet regime. Kmieriauskas was banned from the Lithuanian Artists Union for having accepted a commission for a statue of St Christopher from the church authorities (the statue now stands in front of the Church of St Nicholas in Vilnius). Although marginalised, he managed to exhibit a number of bookplates in Poland and Budapest while teaching at Vilnius Art School for Children. Not until 1977 was he reaccepted back into the Lithuanian Art Institute, where he has taught ever since. In 1979 the authorities commissioned frescoes from him for the Quadricentennial of the University of Vilnius. During the 1980s, he took part in a number of alternative exhibitions in Moscow.

Now recognised as an artist and a celebrated figure in his country, Kmieriauskas sculpts and paints themes drawing their inspiration from Lithuanian national tradition in a formal language with Cubist and Futurist undertones.

BIBLIOGRAPHY:
Rimantas Dichavicius, Sudaré, *Antanas Kmieliauskas: Skulptura, freska, tapyba, grafika*, Vilnius, 2001. Vernet, Daniel, '*Antanas Kmieliauskas, tête de l'art à Vilnius*' in *Le Monde*, periodical, Paris, 1 January 2003.

KMITT, Michael, or Kmit
Polish, 20th century.
Born 1910, in Poland; died 1981.
Active in Australia.
Painter.

In 1953 Michael Kmitt won the national prize for sacred art. His style is reminiscent of Chagall's.

Auction records:
Melbourne, 11 March 1971, *Two Figures* (1956) AUD 2,000. Rosebery (Australia), 7 Sept 1976, *Little Girl with Doll* (1948, oil on canvas, 15 1/4 x 13 1/2 ins / 39 x 34 cm) AUD 400. Sydney, 20 Oct 1980, *Little Girl with Cat* (1954, oil on canvas, 16 1/4 x 13 3/4 ins / 41 x 35 cm) AUD 1,000. Melbourne, 26 July 1987, *Man and Woman* (1969, oil on card, 28 3/4 x 26 1/2 ins / 73 x 67.5 cm) AUD 4,000. Sydney, 17 April 1988, *Pianist* (oil on canvas, 39 1/4 x 31 1/2 ins / 100 x 80 cm) AUD 3,400. Sydney, 26 March 1990, *Tree* (pastel, 22 3/4 x 18 ins / 58 x 46 cm) AUD 1,000. Melbourne, 29 April 1997, *Sydney Harbour* (1955, oil on canvas/panel, 35 1/2 x 50 3/4 ins / 90 x 129 cm) AUD 13,800. Sydney, 20 April 1999, *Mardi Gras* (1961, oil on board, 15 x 12 ins / 37 x 30 cm) AUD 2,600. Sydney, 3 Aug 1999, *Candida* (oil on masonite, 22 x 19 ins / 57 x 47 cm) AUD 5,000. Melbourne, 28 June 2000, *Rhythm Fragments* (oil on board, 32 x 48 ins / 81 x 121 cm) AUD 10,000. Melbourne, 29 Nov 2000, *Proprietress* (1962, oil on board, 25 x 21 ins / 63 x 53 cm) AUD 8,000. Melbourne, 9 May 2001, *Stripper* (oil on board, 30 x 26 ins / 75 x 67 cm) AUD 7,000. Paddington, 27 Aug 2001, *Untitled* (1960, oil on board, 29 x 21 ins / 74 x 53 cm) AUD 3,400. Melbourne, 30 April 2002, *Girlhood* (1954, oil on canvas, 25 x 19 ins / 64 x 48 cm) AUD 8,000. Melbourne, 4 June 2003, *Mardi Gras at Luna Park* (oil on board, 23 x 35 ins / 59 x 89 cm) AUD 4,800. Paddington, 25 Aug 2003, *Proprietress* (1963, oil on board, 25 x 21 ins / 64 x 54 cm) AUD 9,000. Melbourne, 10 March 2004, *Girl with a Flower* (oil on board, 48 x 32 ins / 122 x 81 cm) AUD 8,500.

KNAB, Albert
German, 20th century.
Born 26 April 1870, in Oberlaurigen.
Painter, engraver, illustrator. Figures, landscapes.
Albert Knab painted figures and landscapes, though he is better known as an illustrator and drawing professor.

KNAB, Ferdinand
German, 19th century.
Born 12 June 1834, in Würzburg; died 3 November 1902, in Munich.
Painter, decorative designer. Landscapes.
Knab studied with Ramberg, Kirchner and Piloty. He went to Italy, and was then appointed painter to the court of Ludwig II of Bavaria. He decorated the Linderhof and the royal palace and wintergarden in Munich.

Auction records:
Lindau, 10 May 1978, *Italian Landscape* (oil on canvas, 28 1/4 x 22 ins / 72 x 56 cm) DEM 7,500. New York, 30 June 1981, *View of the Roman Campagna* (1891, oil on panel, 14 1/4 x 17 3/4 ins / 36 x 45 cm) USD 2,500. Munich, 17 May 1984, *Roman Ruins at Dusk* (1890, oil on panel, 12 3/4 x 9 1/4 ins / 32.5 x 23.5 cm) DEM 3,500. Cologne, 18 March 1989, *Moonlight on a Watercourse* (oil on canvas, 10 3/4 x 14 1/4 ins / 27.5 x 36 cm) DEM 2,600. London, 1 Dec 1989, *Ancient Roman Baths* (oil on canvas, 46 x 57 1/2 ins / 117 x 146 cm) GBP 14,300. Munich, 3 Dec 1996, *Separation in the Early Morning* (1895, oil on wood, 20 x 15 3/4 ins / 50.5 x 40 cm) DEM 5,400. Ahlden, 26 Nov 1999, *Roman Villa by Still Waters* (1893, oil on canvas, 20 x 16 ins / 50 x 40 cm) DEM 9,000. Zurich, 22 Sept 2000, *Park Landscape with Obelisk* (1882, oil on canvas) CHF 15,000. Munich, 27 Sept 2000, *Classical Ruins at Sunset* (1897, oil on canvas, 33 x 25 ins / 85 x 64 cm) DEM 3,800. Stuttgart, 29 March 2001, *Roman Ruin in the Evening* (1894, oil on canvas, 39 x 51 ins / 99 x 130 cm) DEM 15,000. Zurich, 24 Sept 2002, *Landscape in the Evening* (1884, oil on canvas, 32 x 26 ins / 81 x 67 cm) CHF 4,000. Munich, 25 Sept 2002, *Landscape with Water near Rome at Sunset* (oil on canvas, 33 x 26 ins / 85 x 65 cm) EUR 1,600. Ahlden, 28 Nov 2003, *Coastal Landscape with Temple Ruins* (1892, oil on canvas, 18 x 14 ins / 45 x 35 cm) EUR 2,200. Ahlden, 28 Nov 2003, *Fountain in a Park Landscape* (1900, oil on canvas, 20 x 16 ins / 50 x 40 cm) EUR 2,400. Munich, 26 March 2004, *Byzantine Castle above Mountain Lake* (1884, oil on canvas, 33 x 42 ins / 85 x 107 cm) EUR 2,850. Freiburg, 17 June 2004, *Southern Landscape with Lake, Ruins and a Deer* (1896, oil on canvas, 33 x 26 ins / 85 x 65 cm) EUR 1,600.

KNAB, Sebastian
Swiss, 16th century.
Born 16th century, in Lucerne.
Painter. History painting.
Sebastian Knab produced several paintings on religious themes, which can still be seen in Lucerne. Towards the end of his life he worked with Nicolas Meierhaus.

KNABÉ, Adolf I.
Russian, 19th - 20th century.
Active between 1876 and 1910.
Painter.
Adolphe Knabé was one of the principal representatives of the Russian Symbolist School.

KNABE, Hans
German, 15th - 16th century.
Painter.
Breslau School.
Knabe worked in Breslau (now Wroclaw, Poland) between 1480 and 1520.

KNÄBIG, Maximilian
German, 19th century.
Born 20 August 1804, in Meissen (Saxony-Anhalt); died c. 1876.
Draughtsman, lithographer.
Maximilian Knäbig produced a large number of portraits, though his main profession was newspaper illustration.

KNÄBIG, Otto
German, 19th century.
Born 1 July 1810, in Meissen (Saxony-Anhalt).
Draughtsman, lithographer.
Otto Knäbig was the brother of Maximilian Knäbig. He was mainly interested in landscapes.

KNABL, Josef
German, 19th century.
Born 17 July 1819, in Fliess; died 3 November 1881, in Munich.
Sculptor.
Josef Knabl was a pupil of Franz Renn. He settled in Munich around 1840 and quickly became successful as a sculptor of religious pieces, receiving commissions from many cities, such as Augsburg, Passau, Eichstatt and Marienberg.

KNABL, Karl
German, 19th century.
Born 26 January 1850, in Munich; died 15 June 1904, in Munich.
Painter. Genre scenes, landscapes.
Karl Knabl exhibited in Munich from 1879.

KNACKFUSS, Eduard Heinrich
German, 19th century.
Born 19 October 1855, in Wissen.
Painter. History painting, genre scenes.
E. H. Knackfuss was the brother of Hermann Knackfuss. He studied with Sohn at the Düsseldorf academy. He is known for one major composition, the *Life of St Elizabeth*, painted for the Dominicans. He lived in the monastery of the Preaching Friars in Düsseldorf.

KNACKFUSS, Hermann Josef Wilhelm
German, 19th - 20th century.
Born 11 August 1848, in Wissen; died 17 May 1915, in Kassel.
Painter, draughtsman. Historical subjects, battles, genre scenes, landscapes with figures.

Hermann Knackfuss was taught by Bendemann and Gebbhardt and attended the art academy in Düsseldorf. A travelling scholarship enabled him to continue his studies in Rome. He taught at the art academy in Kassel.
MUSEUMS AND GALLERIES:
KASSEL: *Sun-bath; Battle Scene* (sketch).
AUCTION RECORDS:
LONDON, 19 June 1981, *The Wave* (oil on canvas, 55 x 86 1/2 ins / 140 x 220 cm) GBP 1,700. AMSTERDAM, 19 Oct 1993, *Offering of Early Fruits* (1877, oil on canvas, 27 1/4 x 18 ins / 69.5 x 45.5 cm) NLG 8,625.

KNAEPEN, Armand
Belgian, 20th century.
Born 1887, in Houtain-l'Évêque; died 1982.
Painter, pastellist, engraver. Interiors, landscapes.
Armand Knaepen was taught by J. Marin at the art academy in Tirlemont.

KNAEPEN, Jos
Belgian, 20th century.
Born 1939, in St-Trond.
Painter, glass painter. Cartoons for stained glass.
Jos Knaepen attended the institute of architecture in Hasselt.

KNAGGS, Nancy
British, 19th century.
Active in London.
Painter. Seascapes.
Nancy Knaggs exhibited her seascapes at the Suffolk Street Gallery after 1887.

KNAP, Gerrit Willem or Gereit
Dutch, 19th - 20th century.
Born 2 May 1873, in Amsterdam; died 1931.
Painter. Landscapes, architectural views, still-lifes.
Gerrit Willem Knap took part in the 1910 exhibition in Brussels.
AUCTION RECORDS:
AMSTERDAM, 3 Nov 1992, *Hackney Carriages in the Piazza del Popolo, Rome* (oil on canvas, 15 3/4 x 19 3/4 ins / 40 x 50 cm) NLG 1,725. AMSTERDAM, 20 April 1993, *Embankment in Amsterdam* (oil on canvas, 11 1/2 x 15 3/4 ins / 29 x 40 cm) NLG 1,150. AMSTERDAM, 2 Sept 1997, *Houses along Canal* (oil on canvas, 27 3/4 x 20 ins / 70.5 x 50.5 cm) NLG 1,383.

KNAP, Kassia
Polish, 20th - 21st century.
Born 23 January 1961, in Cracow.
Active in France.
Painter.
Kassia Knap trained at the Cracow academy of fine arts between 1982 and 1987, and was then invited to continue her studies at the École des Beaux-Arts in France. She paints large formal canvases which she calls *Landscapes*. She works directly onto the mounted surface by folding, crumpling then stapling. The folds sometimes in relief, sometimes hollowed, she then paints with clay, ashes, powdered marble or powdered glass. She illustrated Joan Punyet Miró's *Spare Wheel* (2000). She won first prize at the 'jeunes et toiles' (young people and canvases) competition in Paris in 1991. Venues for solo exhibitions have included the Gologorski-Rostworowki Gallery, Cracow, 1988; the Galerie du Haut Pavé, Paris, 1993; the Galerie Larock-Granoff, Paris, 2003.

KNAPEN, Cesar
Romanian, 20th century.
Born 16 December 1879, in Bucharest.
Painter, engraver.
Cesar Knapen studied in Zurich and Munich then went to Paris where he exhibited at the 1913 Salon d'Automne.

KNAPEN, Hélène
Belgian, 20th century.
Born 1944, in Bruges.
Painter.
Hélène Knapen studied at the academy of St Luke in Ghent.

KNAPP, Anton
German, 19th century.
Born 1798, in Mainz; died 15 January 1839, in Mainz.
Painter.
MUSEUMS AND GALLERIES:
MAINZ: two landscapes.
AUCTION RECORDS:
LONDON, 19 March 1980, *Shepherds with their Flock in a Mountain Landscape* (oil on panel, 16 x 21 ins / 40.5 x 53.5 cm) GBP 2,000.

KNAPP, Charles W.
American, 19th century.
Born 1822 or 1823, in Philadelphia; died 15 May 1900, in Philadelphia.
Painter. Landscapes, waterscapes.
AUCTION RECORDS:
LOS ANGELES, 17 March 1980, *Autumn Landscape* (oil on canvas, 20 x 36 1/4 ins / 50.8 x 92 cm) USD 2,250. BOSTON, 12 May 1983, *Landscape and Pool* (oil on canvas, 18 x 32 ins / 45.7 x 81.3 cm) USD 2,000. NEW YORK, 7 Oct 1987, *Figure Seated on a Riverbank* (oil on canvas, 20 x 36 ins / 50.8 x 91.5 cm) USD 5,500. NEW YORK, 24 June 1988, *Landscape* (1876, oil on canvas, 17 3/4 x 31 1/2 ins / 45 x 80 cm) USD 2,090. NEW YORK, 24 Jan 1989, *Mountain Lake at Dusk* (1863, oil on canvas, 29 1/2 x 47 1/2 ins / 75 x 120.7 cm) USD 11,000. NEW YORK, 25 May 1989, *Golden Morning* (oil on canvas, 28 x 50 ins / 71 x 127 cm) USD 26,400. NEW YORK, 6 Dec 1991, *The Valley in Autumn* (oil on canvas, 20 x 36 ins / 50.5 x 91.5 cm) USD 13,200. NEW YORK, 23 Sept 1992, *Rocky Coast* (oil on canvas, 14 x 22 1/4 ins / 35.7 x 56.2 cm) USD 3,300. NEW YORK, 4 Dec 1992, *Early Autumn* (oil on canvas, 28 x 63 1/4 ins / 71.2 x 160.7 cm) USD 11,000. NEW YORK, 9 Sept 1993, *Figures on a Rocky Coast* (oil on canvas, 20 x 36 ins / 50.8 x 91.4 cm) USD 6,038. NEW YORK, 22 Sept 1993, *French Creek* (oil on canvas, 20 x 36 ins / 50.8 x 91.5 cm) USD 3,450. NEW YORK, 15 Nov 1993, *New England Landscape* (oil on canvas, 20 x 36 ins / 50.8 x 91.4 cm) USD 2,530. NEW YORK, 31 March 1994, *Cattle Feeding by a Brook, with Hills in the Background* (oil on canvas/synthetic resin, 20 1/4 x 36 ins / 51.4 x 91.4 cm) USD 4,025. NEW YORK, 28 Nov 1995, *Steam-Boat Crossing a Lake* (oil on canvas, 22 x 36 ins / 56 x 91.5 cm) USD 3,795. NEW YORK, 26 Sept 1996, *View of the River* (oil on canvas, 20 1/4 x 36 ins / 51.4 x 91.4 cm) USD 8,050. NEW YORK, 30 Oct 1996, *Summer in the Adirondacks* (oil on canvas, 28 x 50 ins / 71.1 x 127 cm) USD 6,900. MILFORD, 22 April 1999, *Distant View of the Lake* (oil on canvas, 20 x 36 ins / 51 x 91 cm) USD 4,000. BOSTON, 5 Dec 1999, *Homestead at Sunset* (oil on canvas, 20 x 36 ins / 51 x 91 cm) USD 3,500. NORTH BETHESDA, 3 June 2000, *Mount Washington from North Conway* (1881, oil on canvas, 20 x 36 ins / 51 x 91 cm) USD 8,500. MILFORD, 26 Oct 2000, *Delaware Watergap* (1869, oil on canvas, 20 x 36 ins / 51 x 91 cm) USD 7,000. NORTH BETHESDA, 14 Feb 2001, *Fishing in the Catskills* (1868, oil on canvas, 14 x 22 ins / 36 x 56 cm) USD 3,750. NORTH BETHESDA, 29 Nov 2001, *View of Bear Mountain* (oil on canvas, 18 x 32 ins / 46 x 81 cm) USD 2,600. MILFORD, 25 April 2002, *River Landscape* (oil on canvas, 15 x 28 ins / 38 x 71 cm) USD 5,000. MILFORD, 25 April 2002, *Cows Watering* (oil on canvas, 20 x 36 ins / 51 x 91 cm) USD 8,000. PORTLAND, 8 Aug 2003, *Autumn River Landscape* (oil on canvas, 30 x 46 ins / 76 x 117 cm) USD 11,000. COPAKE, 30 Aug 2003, *Pastoral Landscape, Possibly Delaware Water Gap, Scene with Mountains* (oil on canvas, 20 x 36 ins / 51 x 91 cm) USD 9,500. BANTAM, 14 July 2004, *Pastoral Landscape with*

Farmhouse and Cattle (oil on canvas, 27 x 44 ins / 69 x 112 cm) USD 2,300. PORTLAND, 6 Aug 2004, *New England Pastorale* (oil on canvas, 9 x 17 ins / 24 x 42 cm) USD 5,500.

KNAPP, Johann
Austrian, 19th century.
Born 5 September 1778, in Vienna; died 18 February 1833, in Schönnbrunn.
Painter. Still-lifes, natural history (animals/botanical subjects).
Johann Knapp studied with Drechsler at the Akademie der bildenden Künste in Vienna. He joined his master in 1797. When he returned home, he took up the study of natural history. He published a work entitled *Flora Alpina*. He became court painter to Archduke Anton.
MUSEUMS AND GALLERIES:
VIENNA: a painting.
AUCTION RECORDS:
LONDON, 12 March 1947, *Glass Vase,* GBP 92. VIENNA, 28 May 1963, *Still-life with Flowers,* ATS 80,000.

KNAPP, Joseph
German, 19th century.
Born in Schönbrunn; died 1867.
Painter. Flowers.
Joseph Knapp studied at the Akademie der bildenden Künste in Vienna and also with his father Johann.

KNAPP, Peter
Swiss, 20th century.
Born 5 June 1931, in Baeretschwill.
Active from 1952 in France.
Painter, photographer, film maker. Stage sets.
After attending the Kunstgewerbeschule in Zurich, Peter Knapp went to Paris where he attended the École des Beaux-Arts. Resident in Paris from 1952 onwards, he became, in 1959, artistic director of *Elle* an important Parisian women's weekly. His works were shown in a number of group and one-man exhibitions from 1957: in Zurich, Bern (Kunsthalle), Paris (Salon des Réalités Nouvelles et various galleries), Ascona, Stockholm (Museum of Modern Art), Tokyo (Third Europe-Japan International), Linz, New Delhi, Lausanne (Exposition Nationale), Cologne, Basel, Arles and Geneva. In 1967 he worked with Slavik on a pavilion for the Exhibition Internationale in Brussels. He executed theatrical sets, notably for Eugène Ionesco's *Amédée* (Théâtre de France). He also made documentary films for French television and audiovisual installations 'multivisions'.

KNAPP, Peter
German, 20th century.
Born 21 January 1939, in Frankfurt am Main; died 1978, in Limbourg.
Sculptor.
In 1959 Peter Knapp was in the south of France. From 1960 to 1965 he attended the art academy in Stuttgart with Otto Baum and R. Hoflehner. In 1962 he travelled, staying in Paris and in 1963 in Greece. He contributed to group exhibitions, notably in 1964 the Symposium de Sculpteurs Européens, at the exhibition *Contemporary Sculpture*. His one-man show was held at the Galerie Appel und Fertsch in Frankfurt. He worked almost exclusively in stone, though he did execute a few bronzes. His sculptural output is very severe, consisting of masses made up of trunks of cylinders soldered closely together, forming a block, of which the rounded-off edges could conjure up the human form brought back to its most simple evocation.
BIBLIOGRAPHY:
Peter Knapp, exhibition catalogue, Gal. Appel und Fertsch, Frankfurt am Main, 1968.

KNAPP, Reine
Flemish School, 18th - 19th century.
Born 1761, in Mons; died 1823, in Mons.
Painter.
In 1777, Reine Knapp worked in for the St Wandru cathedral in Mons.

KNAPP, Stefan
Polish, 20th century.
Born 1921, in Belgoraj.
Active in England.
Sculptor, painter (including enamel), decorative artist. Murals.
After he was imprisoned in Siberia, Stefan Knapp served with the Royal Air Force in Britain during World War II. He studied at the Slade School in London. Although he began his career as a sculptor, he also produced highly-coloured abstract paintings. He also painted on enamel and produced mural decorations for the Seagram Building in New York (1959) and for London Airport (1962). His work featured in collective exhibitions in France, Italy, Germany, Poland and Venezuela. He also showed his work in solo exhibitions in London from 1954 and in New York in 1957.
MUSEUMS AND GALLERIES:
CARACAS - DALLAS - HELSINKI - LONDON - NEW YORK (MoMA).
AUCTION RECORDS:
LONDON, 9 March 1990, *Sloping Shape and Red Vertical* (1963, oil on canvas, 46 x 31 1/2 ins / 116.8 x 80.1 cm) GBP 2,640.

KNAPPE, Karl
Russian, 18th century.
Born 1745, in St Petersburg; died 1808.
Painter, engraver. Landscapes, animals, flowers.
Karl Knappe was of German origin and produced paintings of animals and flowers, as well as engravings of views of St Petersburg.

KNAPPE, Karl
German, 20th century.
Born 11 November 1884; died 1970, in Munich.
Sculptor. Religious subjects.
Karl Knappe's career was spent in Munich. In his sculptural works, mostly religious in inspiration, he can be considered to be an exponent of the Expressionist school. He was also interested in different arts and crafts.

KNAPPICH, Johann Georg
German, 17th century.
Born 1637, in Lechbruck (Swabia); died 1704, in Augsburg.
Painter. History painting.
Knappich studied with Johann Heiss. He is best known for a *Nativity,* in Augsburg cathedral, and the *Death of Joseph,* St George's church in Augsburg.

KNAPPING, M. Helen
British, 19th century.
Painter. Flowers.
M. Helen Knapping exhibited her paintings at the Suffolk Street Gallery after 1876.

KNAPTON, Charles
British, 18th century.
Born 1700; died 1760.
Painter, engraver.
Charles Knapton was the brother of George Knapton. Between 1734 and 1735, he published aquatints which imitated drawings. He made engravings of landscapes with figures after Guercino.

KNAPTON, George
British, 18th century.
Born 1698, in London; died 1778, in Kensington (London).

Painter, engraver. Portraits, landscapes.
George Knapton was a student of Jonathan Richardson. In 1740, he went to Italy and published an illustrated description of the excavations at Herculaneum. He was a member of the Dilettanti Society of London and became Keeper of paintings for the King's Pictures in 1765. With Arthur Pond, he made a series of engravings of the most famous paintings. The most notable of these are his landscapes after Guercino.

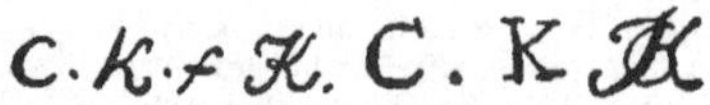

MUSEUMS AND GALLERIES:
LONDON (National Maritime Mus.): *Admiral Sir John Norris* (c. 1735, oil on canvas) - LONDON (Royal Collection): *The Children of Frederick, Prince of Wales; Princess Elizabeth with Prince William Henry and Prince Henry Frederick* (1748); *The Family of Frederick, Prince of Wales* (1751); *Prince Henry Frederick; Princess Louisa Ann (?).*
AUCTION RECORDS:
NEW YORK, 14-15 April 1904, *Portrait of a Woman,* USD 425. LONDON, 1 June 1911, *Portrait of Mrs Whitclocke,* GBP 37. LONDON, 12 Dec 1930, *Three Children,* GBP 63. LONDON, 24 Nov 1965, *Portrait of Windham Quinn of Adare,* GBP 1,900. LONDON, 23 Nov 1973, *Portrait of a Young Man with his Dog,* Gns 4,000. LONDON, 26 March 1976, *Portrait of a Young Man* (oil on canvas, 16 1/2 x 14 ins / 42 x 35.5 cm) GBP 700. LONDON, 27 June 1980, *Portrait of Miss Elizabeth Hatch* (oil on canvas, 49 x 39 ins / 124.5 x 99 cm) GBP 2,400. LONDON, 11 July 1984, *Portrait of Miss Elizabeth Hatch* (oil on canvas, 49 1/4 x 39 1/4 ins / 125 x 99.5 cm) GBP 3,200. LONDON, 18 April 1986, *Portrait presumed to be of Lady Mortley Montagu with a Serving Woman* (oil on canvas, 49 1/4 x 39 1/2 ins / 125.1 x 100.3 cm) GBP 24,000. LONDON, 18 Nov 1987, *Portrait of John, First Earl of Moira and his Wife, Elizabeth* (oil on canvas, 87 1/2 x 59 1/2 ins / 222 x 151 cm) GBP 6,000. LONDON, 15 April 1988, *Portrait of Master Francis Barrell* (oil on canvas, oval, 30 x 25 ins / 75.9 x 63.8 cm) GBP 5,280. LONDON, 12 July 1989, *Portrait of Murrough O'Brien, 5th Earl of Inchiquin, wearing a white tunic with gold frogs and an ermine collar* (oil on canvas, 29 1/2 x 24 1/2 ins / 75 x 62 cm) GBP 8,800. LONDON, 17 Nov 1989, *Portrait of a Seated Gentleman wearing a red habit and surrendering to an experience* (oil on canvas, 49 x 39 ins / 124.5 x 99 cm) GBP 12,100. LONDON, 8 April 1992, *Portrait of John Ross Mackye, Standing, dressed like a Turk and holding a Letter out to a Young Black Servant* (oil on canvas, 93 3/4 x 57 ins / 238 x 145 cm) GBP 20,900. LONDON, 10 Nov 1993, *Portrait of John, First Earl of Moira, wearing a Red Habit, and his Wife, Elizabeth, wearing a White Dress and a Black Shawl* (oil on canvas, 87 1/2 x 59 1/2 ins / 222 x 151 cm) GBP 16,100. LONDON, 11 June 2002, *Group Portrait of Three Children, in a Wooded Landscape, the Eldest Holding a Peach* (1754, oil on canvas, 30 x 36 ins / 77 x 91 cm) GBP 18,000. LONDON, 25 Nov 2003, *Portrait of Mrs Neate, of Donnington, Hampshire, Seated at a Table with her Spaniel* (oil on canvas, 40 x 50 ins / 102 x 127 cm) GBP 26,000. LONDON, 27 Nov 2003, *Portrait of a Lady Wearing a Blue Dress* (oil on canvas, oval, 30 x 24 ins / 75 x 62 cm) GBP 4,500. BURY ST EDMUNDS, 23 June 2004, *Portrait of a Gentleman of the Broughton Adderley Family* (1731, oil on canvas, 36 x 28 ins / 91 x 71 cm) GBP 2,000.

KNARREN, Petrus Renier Hubertus
Belgian, 19th century.
Born 1826; died 1869, in Brussels.
Painter. Genre scenes.
MUSEUMS AND GALLERIES:
HAMBURG: *Jealousy.*
AUCTION RECORDS:
NEW YORK, 27 May 1982, *The Newborn Child* (oil on panel, 23 1/2 x 19 1/2 ins / 60 x 49.5 cm) USD 6,750. VERSAILLES, 19 Nov 1989, *Mother and Child in Interior* (oil on panel, 30 x 23 1/2 ins / 76 x 60 cm) FRF 28,000. LONDON, 10 Feb 1995, *The New Toy* (oil on panel, 27 1/4 x 21 1/4 ins / 69.2 x 54 cm) GBP 12,075.

KNATHS, Otto Karl
American, 20th century.
Born 1891, in Eau-Claire (Wisconsin); died 1971.
Painter.
American Abstract Artists (AAA).
Karl Knaths studied at the Art Institute of Chicago. After a highly formal art education, he became aware of Cézanne and Matisse's work - which he was able to see for himself at the1913 Armory Show in New York. This prompted some further study into Severini, Klee, Mondrian and Kandinsky's theories and the evolution towards a more abstract approach. His Post-Cubist research into the correspondence between sound in music and colour and space in painting shows him to be at the forefront of American modernist art. He was awarded a silver medal in Chicago in 1928, and the first Carnegie Prize in 1946. He exhibited with the American Abstract Artists.
MUSEUMS AND GALLERIES:
LINCOLN (Sheldon Memorial AG, University of Nebraska): *Indian Cover* - WASHINGTON DC (Phillips Collection): *Seascape* (1931).
AUCTION RECORDS:
NEW YORK, 11 Nov 1959, *Elling,* USD 2,000. NEW YORK, 24 March 1974, *House Painters,* USD 6,000. NEW YORK, 29 April 1976, *Fishermen on the Seafront* (gouache, 14 3/4 x 19 3/4 ins / 37.5 x 50.3 cm) USD 2,000. NEW YORK, 28 Oct 1976, *Tide wash* (1947, oil on canvas, 36 x 48 ins / 91.5 x 122 cm) USD 2,500. NEW YORK, 21 April 1978, *Candles* (oil on canvas, 30 x 50 ins / 76.2 x 127 cm) USD 3,000. NEW YORK, 25 Oct 1979, *Drapes and Platens* (1958, oil on canvas, 30 x 42 1/4 ins / 76.2 x 107 cm) USD 9,000. NEW YORK, 19 June 1981, *Provincial Town and Farmyard Scene* (1922, oil on canvas, double-sided, 19 1/2 x 21 1/2 ins / 49.5 x 54.6 cm) USD 5,250. NEW YORK, 4 June 1982, *Beach Scene* (1946, oil on canvas, 36 x 42 ins / 91.5 x 106.6 cm) USD 7,500. NEW YORK, 18 March 1983, *Bananas* (1964, oil on canvas, 30 1/4 x 36 ins / 76.6 x 91.5 cm) USD 5,500. NEW YORK, 31 May 1985, *Johnny Appleseed* (oil on canvas, 50 x 36 ins / 127 x 91.5 cm) USD 5,000. NEW YORK, 28 May 1987, *Fish and Fiddle* (1969, oil on canvas, 30 x 50 ins / 76.2 x 127 cm) USD 7,500. NEW YORK, 1 Dec 1988, *Dusk* (1959, oil on canvas, 27 x 36 ins / 68.5 x 91.5 cm) USD 8,800. NEW YORK, 24 Jan 1990, *Abstraction* (oil on card, 10 1/2 x 13 1/2 ins / 26.7 x 34.1 cm) USD 1,320. NEW YORK, 16 March 1990, *Black Bottle* (1968, oil on canvas, 30 1/4 x 42 1/4 ins / 76.8 x 107 cm) USD 13,200. NEW YORK, 30 May 1990, *Duck and Paper* (1960, oil on canvas, 30 x 42 ins / 76.3 x 106.7 cm) USD 8,800. NEW YORK, 11 March 1993, *Aboriginal Figure* (oil on canvas, 30 x 45 1/2 ins / 75.9 x 115.3 cm) USD 4,600. NEW YORK, 28 Sept 1995, *Black Lines* (oil on canvas, 30 1/4 x 40 1/4 ins / 76.8 x 102.2 cm) USD 2,645. NEW YORK, 3 Dec 1996, *Duck and Paper* (oil on canvas, 30 x 42 ins / 76.2 x 106.7 cm) USD 5,520. NEW YORK, 25 March 1997, *Lilacs* (oil on canvas, 30 x 20 ins / 76.2 x 50.8 cm) USD 3,335. NEW YORK, 3 Feb 1999, *Purple Drape* (1958, oil on canvas, 30 x 42 ins / 76 x 107 cm) USD 3,800. NEW YORK, 3 Feb 1999, *Doorway* (1958, oil on canvas, 40 x 50 ins / 102 x 127 cm) USD 4,000. NEW YORK, 15 June 2000, *Boatman* (1960, oil on canvas, 36 x 42 ins / 91 x 107 cm) USD 6,500. NEW YORK, 15 June 2000, *Blue Bottle* (1969, oil on canvas, 36 x 38 ins / 91 x 97 cm) USD 6,500. WATERTOWN, 29 April 2001, *Portraits of Duncan and Marjorie Philips* (oil on canvas, a pair, 40 x 30 ins / 102 x 76 cm) USD 1,600. PHILADELPHIA, 24 June 2001, *Barker* (oil on canvas) USD 7,000. PORTLAND, 31 July 2002, *Provincetown* (1963, oil

on canvas, 30 x 36 ins / 76 x 91 cm) USD 15,000. PROVINCETOWN, 19 July 2003, *Portrait of Agnes Weinrich* (oil on canvas, 40 x 30 ins / 102 x 76 cm) USD 23,000. NEW YORK, 7 Oct 2003, *Clock* (1951, oil on canvas, 27 x 36 ins / 69 x 91 cm) USD 17,000. NEW YORK, 6 May 2004, *Red Clock* (oil on canvas, 40 x 30 ins / 102 x 76 cm) USD 19,000. NEW YORK, 27 Sept 2004, *Pine Bough* (1952, oil on canvas, 36 x 42 ins / 91 x 107 cm) USD 12,000.

KNAUER-HASE, Paul Emil Hugo
German, 20th century.
Born 9 June 1878, in Bremen.
Painter.

Paul Knauer-Hase was taught by Othon Friesz and Charles Guérin and exhibited at the Salon des Indepéndants. Thereafter he settled in Munich.

AUCTION RECORDS:
NEW YORK, 12 June 1981, *Décor for The Magic Flute* (watercolour and pencil, $13\frac{1}{2}$ x $19\frac{1}{2}$ ins / 34.3 x 49.5 cm) USD 1,400.

KNAUF, Hans Georg
German, 16th century.
Active in Landshut.
Painter.

He produced frescoes for Othon I and Maximillian I, the princes of Bavaria.

KNAUR, Emmanuel August Hermann
German, 19th century.
Born 3 April 1811, in Leipzig; died 1 April 1872, in Leipzig.
Sculptor.

Knaur was the sculptor of the memorial to Gellert.

MUSEUMS AND GALLERIES:
LEIPZIG (Mus. der Bildenden Künste): *Leibnitz* (statuette); *Gellert* (statuette); *Lotter* (statuette); *The Painter Karl Sprosse* (statuette).

KNAUS, Cassian
Swiss, 19th - 20th century.
Born 9 October 1831, in Sevelen (St Gall); died 19 January 1916, in Basel.
Engraver (wood), lithographer.

Cassian Knaus engraved mainly reproductions after drawings of book and magazine illustrations.

KNAUS, Emilie
Polish, 20th century.
Born 1883; died 23 January 1924, in Cracow.
Painter. Portraits, landscapes, flowers.

KNAUS, F.
British, 19th century.
Painter, copyist, art restorer.

F. Knaus appears to have restored and copied works of art. For his decorative panels, he took his inspiration from old masters.

AUCTION RECORDS:
LONDON, 24 Nov 1926, *Fêtes Champêtres* (three paintings, after Watteau) GBP 189; *Mezzetin Playing the Guitar*; *Pastoral Pleasure* (collection) GBP 105.

KNAUS, Ludwig
German, 19th - 20th century.
Born 5 October 1829, in Wiesbaden; died 7 December 1910, in Berlin.
Also active in France.
Painter, engraver, illustrator. Portraits, genre scenes, animals.
School of Düsseldorf.

From 1845 to 1852 he worked in Wilhelm Schadow's studio before living in Paris between 1852 and 1860, except for a one-year Italian sojourn in 1857. On his return to Germany he settled in Berlin and then Düsseldorf. In 1865 he took up a professorship at the academy in Berlin, becoming subsequently a member of the academies in Vienna, Munich, Antwerp, Amsterdam, Oslo and an honorary member of the Royal Academy, London. He participated in several exhibitions in Munich, Berlin and Paris, receiving a first class medal in 1853 and further honours in 1857 and 1859. In 1867 he was elected chevalier de la Légion d'Honneur. He was awarded a medal at the Exposition Universelle in Paris in 1889. His anecdotal scenes which unfurl in a landscape are suffused with a soft light.

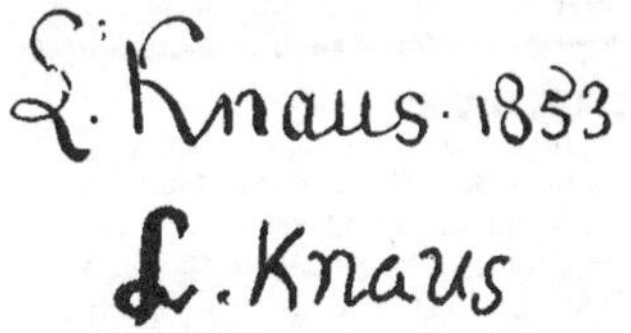

MUSEUMS AND GALLERIES:
AACHEN: *Portrait at the Knees of Barthold Suermondt* - BERLIN: *Children's Party*; *Portraits of Professors Theodor Mommsen and Von Helmholtz*; *The Wisdom of Solomon*; *Tricksters*; *Portrait of Lady* - COLOGNE: *The Empty Bowl* - DÜSSELDORF: *Card Players*; *Modest Pleasures* - HAMBURG: *Drunkard*; *Der Starost* - KALININGRAD: *Bohemians Resting* - LEIPZIG: *Tricksters*; study - LIÈGE: *Old Horse* - MAINZ: *Shoemakers Playing Cards*; *Harlequin* - MONTPELLIER: *Drunken Peasants* - MOSCOW (Rumiantsev Mus.): *Roman Monk* - MOSCOW (State Tretyakov Gal.): *With Congratulations* - PARIS (Louvre): *Promenade* - PARIS (Mus. des Arts décoratifs) - STUTTGART: *Peasant Woman from Hessen*.

AUCTION RECORDS:
NEW YORK, 1 and 2 April 1902, *Old Bohemian Woman*, USD 7,200. NEW YORK, 15-16 April 1909, *The Christening*, USD 8,900. PARIS, 18 June 1930, *Village Cock*, FRF 26,500. LONDON, 11 Jan 1946, *Young Embroideress*, GBP 105. COLOGNE, 17 Nov 1966, *Country Party*, DEM 24,000. COLOGNE, 6 June 1973, *Children Dancing*, DEM 15,000. NEW YORK, 9 Oct 1974, *Camp of Bohemians*, USD 5,000. NEW YORK, 14 May 1976, *Portrait of Girl* (1877, oil on panel, $10\frac{1}{4}$ x $7\frac{3}{4}$ ins / 26 x 20 cm) USD 4,000. LONDON, 6 May 1977, *After the Hunt* (1888, oil on panel, 12 x 9 ins / 30.5 x 23 cm) GBP 1,500. HANOVER, 11 March 1978, *Children's Party* (oil on canvas, $23\frac{1}{2}$ x $35\frac{1}{2}$ ins / 60 x 90 cm) DEM 13,000. LONDON, 3 Oct 1979, *Portrait of Otto von Bismarck* (oil on canvas, 22 x $15\frac{1}{4}$ ins / 56 x 39 cm) GBP 1,900. MUNICH, 1 Dec 1982, *Congratulations* (oil on canvas) DEM 43,000. NEW YORK, 19 Oct 1984, *Potato Harvest* (1889, oil on panel, $33\frac{1}{4}$ x 47 ins / 84.3 x 119.5 cm) USD 55,000. NEW YORK, 24 May 1985, *Spring* (oil on panel, $19\frac{1}{2}$ x 28 ins / 49.5 x 71.1 cm) USD 16,000. VIENNA, 24 Sept 1987, *Bavarian Woodcutter* (1888, oil on panel, $16\frac{3}{4}$ x $10\frac{1}{4}$ ins / 42.5 x 26 cm) ATS 100,000. LONDON, 25 March 1988, *Children Bringing back Vegetables for Evening Soup* (1870, oil on canvas, $31\frac{1}{2}$ x $21\frac{1}{2}$ ins / 80 x 54.3 cm) GBP 9,900. AMSTERDAM, 28 Feb 1989, *Half-length Portrait of a Beautiful Young Italian* (charcoal/paper, 22 x $16\frac{1}{4}$ ins / 55 x 41 cm) NLG 1,265. COLOGNE, 18 March 1989, *Half-length Portrait of a Little Girl* (oil on canvas, 9 x 7 ins / 23 x 18 cm) DEM 9,000. NEW YORK, 24 May 1989, *Birthday* (oil on panel, $23\frac{1}{4}$ x $35\frac{3}{4}$ ins / 59 x 91 cm) USD 49,500. NEW YORK, 24 Oct 1989, *Bohemians in Wood with County Policeman Checking their Documents* (1855, oil on canvas, $43\frac{1}{2}$ x $59\frac{1}{2}$ ins / 110.5 x 151 cm) USD 41,250. AMSTERDAM, 2 May 1990, *Model* (oil on canvas, $16\frac{3}{4}$ x $13\frac{3}{4}$ ins / 42.5 x 35 cm) NLG 16,100. AMSTERDAM, 24 April 1991, *Portrait of a Little Girl* (1879, oil on panel, $10\frac{3}{4}$ x 8 ins / 27.5 x 20.5 cm) NLG 15,525. NEW YORK, 20 Feb 1992, *Armfuls of Kittens* (1865, oil on canvas, 26 x $19\frac{3}{4}$ ins / 66 x 50.2 cm) USD 41,250. MUNICH, 25 June 1992, *Portrait of a Little Girl* (1888, oil on wood, $11\frac{1}{2}$ x $8\frac{1}{2}$ ins / 29.5 x 21.5 cm) DEM 6,215.

MUNICH, 10 Dec 1992, *Little Girl and her Doll* (oil on canvas, 12 1/4 x 9 3/4 ins / 31 x 25 cm) DEM 10,735. NEW YORK, 26 May 1994, *Gipsy and Child* (1886, oil on panel, 23 3/4 x 31 ins / 60.3 x 78.7 cm) USD 20,700. MUNICH, 6 Dec 1994, *Girl Knitting* (pencil/beige paper, 17 1/4 x 11 ins / 43.5 x 27 cm) DEM 1,610. NEW YORK, 16 Feb 1995, *Young Girl* (oil on panel, 7 x 5 1/2 ins / 17.8 x 14 cm) USD 9,200. VIENNA, 29 Oct 1996, *In the Schtetl* (1894, oil on canvas, 42 1/2 x 58 ins / 108 x 147.4 cm) ATS 3,655,000.

KNAUTH, Heinrich

German, 19th century.

Born 1804, in Dresden; died c. 1845, in Dresden.

Painter. History painting, genre scenes.

Knebel is best known for *St George and the Dragon*.

KNEALE, Bryan

British, 20th century.

Born 19 June 1930, on the Isle of Man.

Sculptor (including wood, steel).

Bryan Kneale initially trained as a painter at the Douglas School of Art in 1947, and then at the Royal Academy Schools from 1948 to 1952 under Philip Connard and Henry Rushbury. He went to Italy with the Rome Scholarship, where he studied painting between 1949 and 1951. After his return, Kneale began to move from painting to sculpture, and eventually developed an important career as a sculptor. Apart from his work, Kneale dedicated a considerable amount of his time to teaching. His teaching career was mainly developed at the Royal College of Art, where he was tutor (1963-1980), Senior Tutor (1980-1985), Head of Sculpture (1985-1990) and Professor of Drawing (1990-1995). He was also Head of Sculpture at Hornsey College of Art and Design (1968) and Professor of Sculpture at the Royal Academy Schools (1980-1987).

Kneale's work has been displayed in many group exhibitions in Britain and Europe, including *British Sculpture in the 60s* at the Tate Gallery (1966) and *New Art* at the Hayward Gallery (1975). He also curated the Jubilee Exhibition of British sculpture at Battersea Park in 1977. Retrospectives of his work have been held at the Whitechapel Art Gallery (1966), the Serpentine Gallery (1978), the Royal College of Art (1986) and the Royal West of England Academy (1995). The Natural History Museum held a retrospective of his drawings in 1991. He was commissioned to work for Westminster Cathedral in 1998 and 1999. Kneale was elected Royal Academician in 1974, and is a trustee of the Royal Academy of Arts and a senior fellow of the Royal College of Art.

BIBLIOGRAPHY:

Bryan Kneale: Sculpture 1959-1966, with Paintings and Drawings, exhibition catalogue, Whitechapel Art Gallery, London, 1966. *Bryan Kneale, Sculpture: Work in Progress: Serpentine Gallery*, exhibition catalogue, Arts Council of Great Britain, London, 1978. *Opposing Forces: Bryan Kneale RA*, exhibition catalogue, Hart Gallery, London, 2002.

MUSEUMS AND GALLERIES:

LONDON (British Mus.) - LONDON (Natural History Mus.): *Giant Tortoise* (1986, chalk) - LONDON (Tate Collection): *Knuckle* (1964, metal); *Horse* (1985, drawing on paper); *Marina* (1967, metal); *Journal* (2000, painted aluminium) - MELBOURNE (National Galleries of Victoria) - NEW YORK (MoMA).

KNEASS, William

American, 19th century.

Born 1781, in Lancaster (Pennsylvania); died 27 August 1840, in Philadelphia.

Engraver.

William Kneass produced mainly portraits of famous men and views of cities.

KNEBEL, Franz, the Elder

Swiss, 19th century.

Born 1789, in La Sarraz; died 16 January 1822, in Rome.

Painter, watercolourist. Landscapes.

Franz Knebel the Elder studied with Kaesermann in Rome in 1803. He equalled and even outdid his master, who was not above selling Knebel's paintings as his own.

KNEBEL, Franz, the Younger

Swiss, 19th century.

Born 1809, in La Sarraz; died 1877, in Rome.

Painter, watercolourist, draughtsman. Landscapes, architectural views.

Franz Knebel the Younger lived in Rome and painted Italian landscapes and ruins.

MUSEUMS AND GALLERIES:

NARBONNE: *Lake Nemi and its Surroundings.*

AUCTION RECORDS:

LONDON, 17 Jan 1969, *View of Rome*, Gns 700. LONDON, 7 May 1971, *The Butcher's Boy* (1879) Gns 1,200. LOS ANGELES, 8 April 1973, *The Canary* (1876) USD 4,000. LONDON, 2 Nov 1973, *Ancient Roman Temple*, Gns 2,000. NEW YORK, 26 May 1977, *Ponte Molle* (1875, oil on canvas, 27 3/4 x 41 3/4 ins / 70.5 x 106 cm) USD 1,500. LONDON, 14 Feb 1979, *The Roman Forum* (1850, oil on canvas, 26 1/2 x 40 1/4 ins / 67.5 x 102 cm) GBP 1,400. LONDON, 17 July 1979, *The Arch of Constantine, Rome* (1839, watercolour, 8 1/2 x 12 ins / 21.3 x 30.3 cm) GBP 700. LONDON, 24 June 1981, *Peasants beside an Italian Lake* (1864, oil on canvas, 39 x 54 ins / 99 x 137 cm) GBP 3,200. LONDON, 11 May 1984, *The Temple of Vesta, Rome* (1862, oil on canvas, 27 1/2 x 41 1/4 ins / 70 x 105 cm) GBP 4,000. LONDON, 20 Nov 1984, *Landscape with Figures* (tempera/paper, 20 3/4 x 28 3/4 ins / 53 x 73 cm) ITL 5,200,000. NEW YORK, 27 Feb 1986, *View of the Aqueducts in the Roman Campagna* (1870, oil on canvas, 24 x 39 1/2 ins / 61 x 100.4 cm) USD 4,500. LONDON, 24 Nov 1989, *Tivoli* (1858, oil on canvas, 27 3/4 x 41 ins / 70.5 x 104 cm) GBP 11,000. PARIS, 20 June 1991, *Cicero's House at Tusculum, near Frascati* (1832, watercolour, 7 1/4 x 10 3/4 ins / 18.6 x 27.2 cm) FRF 8,000. PARIS, 28 May 1993, *View of a Village by the Sea* (brown wash and lead pencil/ivory paper, 7 1/2 x 10 ins / 19.3 x 25.4 cm) FRF 7,000. LONDON, 19 Nov 1993, *The Forum in Rome* (oil on canvas, 27 3/4 x 41 1/2 ins / 70.5 x 105.5 cm) GBP 11,500. ROME, 31 May 1994, *Rome, the Temple of Vesta* (1855, oil on panel, 15 x 22 ins / 38 x 56 cm) ITL 23,570,000. ROME, 6 Dec 1994, *Rocca di Ostia* (1840, watercolour/paper, 7 1/2 x 11 1/2 ins / 19 x 29.5 cm) ITL 7,660,000. LONDON, 17 March 1995, *The Temple of Vesta in the Piazza della Verità in Rome* (1860, oil on panel, 14 3/4 x 21 3/4 ins / 37.5 x 55.5 cm) GBP 7,820. MILAN, 14 June 1995, *Tivoli* (watercolour/paper, 13 x 17 3/4 ins / 33 x 45 cm) ITL 4,830,000. LONDON, 13 March 1996, *Shepherds in the Roman Countryside* (oil on canvas, 25 1/2 x 40 1/2 ins / 64.5 x 103 cm) GBP 6,900. BILLINGSHURST, 26 Jan 1999, *Bridge near Rome* (1856, oil on canvas, 26 x 40 ins / 67 x 102 cm) GBP 4,800. LONDON, 17 Feb 1999, *Mountain Scene. Ruins with Coast in Background* (oil on canvas, a pair, 16 x 23 ins / 41 x 58 cm) GBP 3,500. DÜSSELDORF, 31 Jan 2000, *Waterfalls, Tivoli* (1847, oil on canvas, 39 x 53 ins / 99 x 135 cm) DEM 40,000. LONDON, 7 April 2000, *View of Lake Nemi* (1847, oil on canvas, 39 x 54 ins / 99 x 137 cm) GBP 9,600. LEWES, 29 Jan 2002, *Traveller and Cattle beside a Stone Bridge and Castle* (1868, oil on panel, 10 x 15 ins / 25 x 38 cm) GBP 2,700. PLAINVILLE, 18 Nov 2002, *Roman Square with Figures by a Fountain* (1864, oil on canvas, 10 x 15 ins / 25 x 38 cm) USD 4,250. NEUILLY, 27 June 2003, *View of Rome* (oil on canvas, 43 x 71 ins / 110 x 180 cm) EUR 58,000. SION, 12 Dec 2003, *View of the Temple of the Sybil at Tivoli* (1855, watercolour, 13 x 17 ins / 32 x 43 cm) CHF 7,500. NEUILLY, 11 June 2004, *View of Florence* (oil on canvas, 20 x 37 ins / 52 x 94 cm) EUR 12,000.

KNEBEL, Leopold

German, 19th century.

Born 1810, probably in Köpenick.

Painter. Seascapes.

Museums and Galleries:
Hanover: one painting.

KNEBUSCH, Karl von
Latvian, 19th century.
Born 1775, in Holmhof (Kurland); died 1821, in Litau (now Jelgava).
Painter.
Museums and Galleries:
Jelgava: painting.

KNECHT, Frédéric Émile
French, 19th century.
Born 23 July 1808, in Strasbourg; died 1889, in Paris.
Sculptor (wood).
Frédéric Knecht was a pupil of Guérin. He took part in Salon exhibitions between 1849 and 1855.

KNECHT, Gaston
French, 19th - 20th century.
Born 19 May 1875, in Asnières-sur-Oise.
Painter.
Gaston Knecht exhibited in Paris at the Salon des Peintres de Montagne and the Salon des Indépendants.

KNECHT, Jakob
Swiss, 19th century.
Born 1824, in Ennenda; died 1894, in Glarus.
Active in Hinwil.
Engraver.
Jakob Knecht made remarkable miniature reproductions of the Alhambra in Granada and the Crystal Palace in London, engraved on wood and measuring no more than a few centimetres.

KNECHT, Johann Friedrich
German, 19th century.
Born 3 June 1786, in Potsdam; died 18 December 1849, in Hamburg.
Painter.
Johann Knecht painted landscapes and stage sets.

KNECHT, Richard
German, 20th century.
Born 25 January 1887, in Tübingen (Baden-Württemberg).
Painter, sculptor.
Richard Knecht was the pupil of Erwin Kurz at the art academy in Munich. His early output was somewhat derivative of Rodin's works.

KNECHTEL, Johann Jeremias
German, 18th century.
Born 1680, in Chemnitz (Bohemia).
Painter.
Knechtel worked in Bunzlau (now Boleslawiec, Poland) and Liebenthal.

KNECHTELMAN, Lucas
German, 16th century.
Active in Ulm c. 1500.
Painter. History painting.

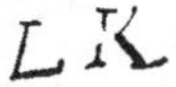

KNECHTELMAN, Marx, called Bayer
German, 15th century.
Born in Ulm.
Painter. History painting, portraits.
Marx Knechtelman, the father of Lucas Knechtelman, settled in Nordlingen and became a burgher of the town in 1440. Prints of his work appeared in the *Wappen des heiligen roemischen Reichs teutscher Nation*, published in Frankfurt in 1540.

KNECHTENHOFER, Adam
Swiss, 16th century.
Baptised 29 December 1542.
Active in Bern.
Glass painter.

KNEELAND, Horace
American, 19th century.
Active in New York c. 1860.
Sculptor.
Museums and Galleries:
Stockholm (Nationalmus.): *Bust of the Inventor John Ericsson*.

KNEEN, William
British, 19th - 20th century.
Born 1 December 1862, on the Isle of Man; died probably in October 1921, in London.
Painter. Genre scenes.
Auction records:
London, 7 Nov 1997, *Portrait of a Moroccan Dignitary* (1900, oil on canvas, 36 1/4 x 28 ins / 92.1 x 71.1 cm) GBP 17,825.

KNEFFEL, Karin
German, 20th - 21st century.
Born 1957, in Marl.
Painter, watercolourist. Landscapes, still-lifes, fruit, animals.
Karin Kneffel studied with Richter in Germany. She exhibits at the Galerie Sophia Ungers in Cologne. When she exhibited at the Galerie Rüdiger Schöttle in Paris in 1992, she showed animal portraits in a conventional figurative style and paintings on the theme of fire.
Bibliography:
Damianovic, Maia, *'La Peinture au risque du dilemme'* in *Art Press* n° 211, periodical, Paris, March 1996.

KNEHCS, Peter
Dutch, 18th century.
Active in Amsterdam c. 1704.
Engraver.
The name Peter Knehcs is an anagram of Peter Schenck. He published his *Christianus Godefridus Carisius* under this pseudonym.

KNEIPP, Georg
German, 19th century.
Born 1793, in Mainz; died 25 August 1862, in Cologne.
Painter.
Georg Kneipp is known for portraits of prelates and views of Mainz.

KNEIPP, Johann
German, 19th century.
Born 1818, in Mainz; died 17 March 1868, in Cologne.
Painter.
Johann Kneipp exhibited in Mainz from 1835. He was the son of Georg Kneipp.
Auction records:
London, 21 March 1980, *River Landscape with Woods* (1864, oil on canvas, 23 3/4 x 28 ins / 60.3 x 71.1 cm) GBP 750.

KNELL, William Adolphus
British, 19th century.
Born 1805; died 10 July 1875.
Active in London.
Painter, watercolourist. Waterscapes, seascapes.

William Adolphus Knell exhibited at the Royal Academy from 1835 to 1866 and at the British Institution and the Suffolk Street Gallery until 1874. Some of his paintings are in the Royal Collection and at the Bridgewater Gallery.

Museums and Galleries:

Edinburgh (Nat. Gal. of Scotland, Print Room): *Vernon Frigate, Malta* (watercolour).

Auction records:

London, 6 Dec 1909, *Seascape*, GBP 2. Paris, 15 and 16 June 1923, *Shipwreck*, FRF 170. London, 12 May 1967, *Boats in Portsmouth Harbour*, Gns 1,400. London, 14 July 1972, *Boats Offshore*, Gns 1,500. Scotland, 30 Aug 1974, *Boats at Sea off Edinburgh*, GBP 1,500. London, 13 Feb 1976, *Men o'War and Sailing Ships* (two oils on canvas, 11 1/2 x 18 ins / 29.5 x 45.7 cm) GBP 1,400. London, 14 Dec 1976, *Boats at Sea off Portsmouth* (watercolour, 9 3/4 x 19 ins / 25 x 48.5 cm) GBP 420. London, 29 July 1977, *Sailing Boats off the Coast* (oil on panel, 15 x 23 ins / 38 x 58.5 cm) GBP 900. London, 12 Dec 1978, *Three-mast Ships in Open Sea off St Thomas* (oil on canvas, 25 x 39 1/2 ins / 63.5 x 100.5 cm) GBP 2,400. London, 25 May 1979, *Sailing Ships in a Breeze* (1825, oil on canvas, 17 x 24 ins / 43.2 x 61 cm) GBP 4,200. Copenhagen, 22 April 1982, *Cape Vincent Naval Battle* (oil on canvas, 70 3/4 x 100 1/2 ins / 180 x 255 cm) DKK 80,000. New York, 20 April 1983, *Battle of Cape Vincent* (1797, oil on canvas, 70 3/4 x 100 1/2 ins / 180 x 255 cm) USD 35,000. London, 19 July 1985, *Opening of the Coal Exchange, 30th October 1849* (oil on panel, 14 x 35 3/4 ins / 35.5 x 90.8 cm) GBP 22,000. London, 5 Oct 1989, *French Fishing Boats* (oil on canvas, 48 1/2 x 62 ins / 123 x 157.5 cm) GBP 10,450. London, 13 June 1990, *Hay Barge; Channel Ferry* (1877, oil on panel, a pair, each 3 3/4 x 5 ins / 9.5 x 12.5 cm) GBP 1,760. Paris, 6 Dec 1990, *Frigate in Trouble, Lower Sails Furled, Moving to Recover a Small Craft.* (watercolour, 9 3/4 x 19 ins / 25 x 48 cm) FRF 15,000. London, 22 Nov 1991, *Small Craft, Fishing Boats and Other Vessels Entering the Mouth of a River* (oil on canvas, 25 x 36 ins / 63.5 x 91.5 cm) GBP 7,700. New York, 28 May 1993, *French Smugglers* (oil on canvas, 18 1/2 x 25 ins / 47 x 63.5 cm) USD 3,220. Montreal, 23-24 Nov 1993, *Approach of a Storm* (watercolour, 13 3/4 x 20 1/2 ins / 35 x 52 cm) CAD 1,000. London, 15 Dec 1993, *Battle of Trafalgar* (oil on canvas, 34 1/4 x 51 1/4 ins / 87 x 130.1 cm) GBP 19,550. London, 3 April 1996, *Two Yachts Racing off The Needles* (oil on panel, 7 1/2 x 12 1/2 ins / 19 x 32 cm) GBP 3,450. New York, 17 Feb 1999, *Sea Rescue* (oil on canvas, 48 x 78 ins / 122 x 198 cm) USD 6,000. San Rafael, 11 Dec 1999, *The Ship Waterloo East Indiaman* (oil on canvas, 27 x 44 ins / 69 x 112 cm) USD 28,000. London, 11 May 2000, *Departure of Fishing Fleet. Returning Fishing Fleet* (pencil and watercolour, a pair, 8 x 19 ins / 21 x 48 cm) GBP 2,000. London, 10 Aug 2000, *Disembarking at Portsmouth* (1825, oil on panel, 6 x 9 ins / 16 x 22 cm) GBP 3,200. London, 23 Jan 2001, *Becalmed. Evening in Downs* (watercolour, a pair, 12 x 22 ins / 30 x 55 cm) GBP 1,050. London, 1 Nov 2001, *Bay of Ostende - Break in the Clouds* (oil on canvas, 24 x 36 ins / 61 x 91 cm) GBP 1,700. London, 16 Jan 2002, *Brig, Dutch Fishing Boat and Steam Ship Off the Harbour Entrance* (oil on canvas, 18 x 24 ins / 45 x 60 cm) GBP 1,450. London, 16 Dec 2002, *Hay Barge. Shipping by Moonlight* (oil on panel, a pair, 5 x 12 ins / 12 x 30 cm) GBP 2,400. London, 18 June 2003, *Leaving Port* (oil on canvas, 22 x 28 ins / 55 x 72 cm) GBP 2,700. London, 1 Oct 2003, *Shipping at Dawn. Returning Home at Dusk* (oil on board, a pair, 7 x 12 ins / 18 x 30 cm) GBP 2,600. London, 26 May 2004, *East Indiaman Reefed Down and Riding Out a Gale* (oil on canvas, 30 x 41 ins / 75 x 104 cm) GBP 4,800. Newbury, 15 Sept 2004, *Three-masted Sailing Ship Upon a Calm Sea at Sunrise. Ship Upon Rough Sea* (oil on panel, 4 x 14 ins / 11 x 35 cm) GBP 3,400.

KNELL, William Calcott

British, 19th century.
Born c. 1830; died c. 1879.

Painter, watercolourist. Waterscapes, seascapes.

William Calcott Knell exhibited at the Royal Academy, the British Institution and at the Suffolk Street Gallery between 1848 and 1871. He continued to produce pictures until 1879.

Auction records:

London, 5 April 1909, *Boats at Anchor* (1863; *View of a Bridge*, GBP 2. Paris, 12 Feb 1945, *Sailing Ships on a Swelling Sea* (watercolour) FRF 400. London, 22 Feb 1972, *View of a Port*, GBP 750. London, 27 March 1973, *Boats in Open Sea* (1864) GBP 1,600. London, 20 March 1979, *View of Dover; View of Folkstone* (1878, two oils on canvas, 7 1/2 x 15 1/2 ins / 19 x 39.5 cm) GBP 1,400. London, 6 Feb 1981, *Men o' War and other Vessels off the Coast* (1864, oil on canvas, 23 1/4 x 35 ins / 59 x 89 cm) GBP 950. London, 21 June 1983, *Boats in a High Sea off the Coast* (oil on canvas, 30 x 50 ins / 76 x 127 cm) GBP 1,050. London, 1 Oct 1986, *Boat and Sailing Ships in a High Sea* (1859, oil on canvas, 28 x 44 ins / 71 x 112 cm) GBP 4,000. London, 18 March 1987, *Summer's Evening off Portsmouth* (1861, oil on canvas, 20 x 36 ins / 51 x 91.5 cm) GBP 2,400. Stockholm, 15 Nov 1988, *Sailing Ships and Boats on the Thames* (oil/canvas, 7 x 11 3/4 ins / 18 x 30 cm) SEK 16,000. Montreal, 1 May 1989, *Shipwreck* (1877, oil on canvas, 12 1/4 x 24 ins / 31 x 61 cm) CAD 1,900. London, 31 May 1989, *Early Morning Calm on the Thames* (oil on canvas, 14 x 23 ins / 35.5 x 58.5 cm) GBP 1,980. Montréal, 19 Nov 1991, *Dover Seen from Admiralty Vessels* (1876, oil on canvas, 18 x 32 1/2 ins / 45.8 x 82.5 cm) CAD 4,000. London, 22 Nov 1991, *All in the Downs the Fleet was Moored* (1876, oil on canvas, 12 x 24 ins / 30.4 x 60.9 cm) GBP 3,080. London, 13 Nov 1992, *Dover Seen from the Admiralty Jetty* (1876, oil on canvas, 18 x 32 ins / 45.7 x 81.2 cm) GBP 2,200. London, 20 Jan 1993, *Merchant Shipping Route* (1872, oil on canvas/card, 12 x 23 3/4 ins / 30.5 x 60.5 cm) GBP 1,092. London, 3 May 1995, *Spanker Preparing to Sail at Sheerness on a Summer's Morning* (1864, oil on canvas, 19 1/2 x 31 ins / 49.5 x 79 cm) GBP 5,175. London, 30 May 1996, *Off Portsmouth* (1855, oil on canvas, 5 1/2 x 9 3/4 ins / 14 x 25 cm) GBP 1,840. Glasgow, 21 Aug 1996, *Fishing Boats Setting Sail from Portsmouth* (oil on card, 9 x 12 ins / 22.8 x 30.4 cm) GBP 690. Glasgow, 31 Oct 1996, *Bad Weather North of the Thames; Dunstanburgh Castle, Northumberland* (1871, oil on canvas, a pair, each 8 x 16 ins / 20.3 x 40.6 cm) GBP 1,725. Edinburgh, 25 Nov 1997, *Armed Barque in a Squall* (1860, watercolour heightened with gouache, 11 1/4 x 19 ins / 28.6 x 48.2 cm) GBP 977. New York, 17 Feb 1999, *Evening off Portsmouth. A Summers Morning in the Channel* (oil on canvas, a pair, 8 x 15 ins / 20 x 38 cm) USD 4,500. London, 17 Aug 1999, *Summer's Afternoon, Mouth of Thames. Dutch Boat Making for Wreck* (oil on canvas, a pair, 8 x 16 ins / 20 x 41 cm) GBP 2,500. Driffield, 4 Aug 2000, *Seascapes, Fishing Vessels on a Stormy Sea* (oil on canvas, a pair, 11 x 21 ins / 28 x 53 cm) GBP 3,300. London, 11 Jan 2001, *Dutch Barges Preparing to Sail. Running Out to Meet the New Arrival* (oil on canvas, a pair, 8 x 15 ins / 20 x 39 cm) GBP 5,500. London, 17 Jan 2001, *Dutch Shipping on the Scheldt* (1860, oil on panel, 30 x 48 ins / 75 x 121 cm) GBP 6,000. Bury St Edmunds, 4 March 2002, *Fishing Boats in Swell* (oil on canvas, 8 x 15 ins / 20 x 39 cm) GBP 1,650. London, 31 Oct 2002, *Fishing Boats in Close Quarters Off the Coast* (1858, oil on canvas, 24 x 36 ins / 61 x 91 cm) GBP 3,000. London, 21 May 2003, *Salvaging the Wreck* (1876, oil on canvas, 18 x 32 ins / 46 x 81 cm) GBP 1,500. Newbury, 24 Sept 2003, *Seascape at Sunset, a Windmill Upon the Shoreline* (1865, oil on canvas, 26 x 42 ins / 66 x 106 cm) GBP 3,000. London, 14 Sept 2004, *Summer Morning at Sheerness Looking from Queensborough* (1864, oil on canvas, 8 x 14 ins / 20 x 36 cm) GBP 2,000. London, 14 Sept 2004, *Experimental Squadron Leaving Spithead. A Breezy Morning in the Downs* (1864, oil on canvas, a pair, 12 x 22 ins / 30 x 56 cm) GBP 5,000.

KNELLER, Gottfried, later Godfrey

German, 17th - 18th century.

Born 8 August 1646, in Lübeck; died 19 or 27 October 1723, in London.

Painter.

A strange sequence of events led to Kneller coming to London during the reign of Charles II to pursue, alongside Peter Lely, the role of great official portrait painter, which had been so brilliantly filled by Anthony Van Dyck during the reign of Charles I. Gottfried Kneller was the son of an inspector of mines in the service of Count Ernst of Monsfeld. He was originally destined for a military career and with this in mind, he was sent to study in Leiden. However, the young student was influenced most of all by the artistic environment, and he showed such ability that his father accepted the idea of making a painter of him and sent him to Amsterdam.

Tradition has it that he studied with Rembrandt, but this is open to doubt, as after his bankruptcy and the dispersal of his property in September 1658, Rembrandt appears to have kept himself apart. Be that as it may, Kneller studied with Ferdinand Bol and thus assimilated Rembrandt's technique.

In 1672, he left Amsterdam for Rome, where he studied with Carlo Maratti and Bernini. He then went to Venice, where he achieved success as a portrait painter. Among his most notable subjects was Cardinal Bassadonna. After spending two years in Italy, he returned to Germany. In Hamburg, a merchant engaged him to go to London, where he achieved considerable success.

Despite the fact that Lely already occupied the post at the court of Charles II, Kneller was made welcome there and placed on an equal footing with his rival. Walpole mentioned that in order to keep the two artists happy, the king had them both paint his portrait at the same time. Kneller painted a considerable number of portraits. All the great names in England had themselves painted by him. On the orders of Charles II, he went to Paris to paint Louis XIV. Other notable subjects were James II, William III, Queen Anne, Peter the Great, Charles VI of Spain and George I. He was made a knight in 1695 and created a baronet in 1715.

Given the brilliant and varied technique of his portraits from around 1685, it is thought that he left England for the continent. However, his series of *Hampton Court Beauties* is rather uninteresting. Other important works are his portraits of the 44 members of the Kit-Kat Club, painted in 1703 and 1713.

His rapid, lively naturalism heralds the art of Hogarth and Richardson. Kneller worked very fast and it is unfortunate that the sheer number of commissions he received sometimes led him to paint rather carelessly. Moreover, he usually painted only the heads, entrusting his pupils with the rest of the portraits. On his death, he left a considerable fortune, and a memorial to him was erected in Westminster Abbey, with an epitaph written by Alexander Pope. Among his pupils were Robert Byng, Van der Roer, Bakker, Baptiste Vergazon and J. Wyck.

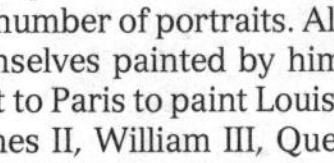

BIBLIOGRAPHY:

Killanin, Michael Morris, *Sir Godfrey Kneller and his Times, 1646-1723, being a review of English portraiture of the period*, Batsford, New York, London, 1948. Stewart, J. Douglas, '*Sir Godfrey Kneller and the English Baroque Portrait*' in coll. *Oxford studies in the history of art and architecture*, Clarendon Press, New York, Oxford University Press, Oxford, 1983.

MUSEUMS AND GALLERIES:

AMSTERDAM: *The Painter Cornelis de Bruyn* - ANTWERP: *Head and Shoulders Portrait in a Wig and Cloak; Portrait of the Canon and Painter François de Cock* - BUDAPEST: *Sir Robert Cecil; Portrait of a Man* - CHAMBÉRY (MBA): *Portrait of a Man* - DRESDEN: *Lord Custon as a Young Man* - DUBLIN: *Richard Steele; King William III at Margate; James, duc d'Ormonde; Godard de Ginkell, Earl of Athlone* - FLORENCE (Uffizi): *Self-portrait* - GLASGOW: *William III* - HANOVER: *Admiral the Duke of Berkeley in a Landscape; Lord Herold; Lord James Tyrawley-Pultney; General Carpenter; The Engraver Smith, Holding a Portrait of the Painter* - LIVERPOOL: *Lady with a Child* - LIVERPOOL (Walker AG): *King Charles II* (1685, oil on canvas) - LONDON (Courtauld Institute of Art): works/paper - LONDON (National Maritime Mus.): *Admiral Edward Russell, 1653-17, 1st Earl of Orford* (c. 1693, oil on canvas); *George, Prince of Denmark, Duke of Cumberland and Lord High Admiral* (1702-1708, oil on canvas, three other portraits) - LONDON (National Portrait Gal.): *King James II* (1684, oil on canvas); *Laurence Hyde, 1st Earl of Rochester* (1685, oil on canvas); *Sir Godfrey Kneller, Bt* (1685 et c. 1706-1711, oil on canvas, two versions); *Anthony Leigh* (1689, oil on canvas); *Charles Montagu, 1st Earl of Halifax* (c. 1690-1695 et c. 1703-1710, oil on canvas, two versions); *William Russell, 1st Duke of Bedford* (c. 1692, oil on canvas); *John Dryden* (1693, oil on canvas); *Charles Sackville, 6th Earl of Dorset* (c. 1697, oil on canvas); *John Somers, Baron Somers* (1700-1709 et c. 1715-1716, oil on canvas, two versions); *Sir Isaac Newton* (1702, oil on canvas); *Charles Townshend, 2nd Viscount Townshend* (1704?, oil on canvas); *James Stanhope, 1st Earl Stanhope* (1705-1710, oil on canvas); *John Churchill, 1st Duke of Marlborough* (c. 1706, oil on canvas); *William Congreve* (1709, oil on canvas); *Anne Churchill, Countess of Sunderland* (c. 1710, oil on canvas); *Charles Montagu, 1st Duke of Manchester* (c. 1710-1712, oil on canvas); *Sir Christopher Wren* (1711, oil on canvas); *William Cowper, 1st Earl Cowper* (1722, oil on canvas) - LONDON (Royal Collection): 25 portraits - LONDON (Tate Collection): *Elijah and the Angel* (1672, oil on canvas); *The Harvey Family* (1721, oil on canvas, group portrait); portraits - LONDON (Victoria and Albert Mus.): *Thomas Betterton* (c. 1690, oil on canvas); *Self-portrait* (c. 1690, oil on canvas) - LÜBECK (Library): *Portrait of an Old Man* - MUNICH: *Henrietta Maria of France* (after Van Dyck) - SCHWERIN: *Man Wearing a Breastplate* (after Rembrandt) - ST PETERSBURG (Hermitage): *John Locke; Grinling Gibbons* - VIENNA: *Johann Philipp of Schönborn, Archbishop of Mainz*.

AUCTION RECORDS:

PARIS, 1846, *Full-length Portrait of an English Lady*, FRF 1,815. PARIS, 1898, *Portrait of the Chancellor Adison*, FRF 1,030. PARIS, 15 March 1899, *Portrait of Chancellor Adison*, FRF 600. NEW YORK, 10-11 April 1902, *Portrait of the Earl of Macclesfield*, USD 500. NEW YORK, 19 Dec 1902, *Portrait of a Nobleman*, USD 1,450. NEW YORK, 26-27 Feb 1903, *Lady Wyndham*, USD 750. NEW YORK, 24 March 1905, *Admiral Edward Russell*, USD 850. NEW YORK, 31 March 1905, *The Duchess of Rutland*, USD 3,050. LONDON, 21 Dec 1907, *The Old Pretender*, GBP 6. LONDON, 27 Jan 1908, *Portrait of Sir William Morice*, GBP 5. LONDON, 8 Feb 1908, *Portrait of Queen Anne*, GBP 54. LONDON, 29 Feb 1908, *Portraits of the Duke and Duchess of Marlborough* (two pendants) GBP 71. LONDON, 17 July 1908, *Portrait of a Young Girl*, GBP 102; *Portrait of Mrs Edward Nicolas*, GBP 79. LONDON, 12 Dec 1908, *Portrait of Prince Maurice of Bohemia*, GBP 32. LONDON, 7 May 1909, *Madonna*, GBP 110. LONDON, 2 July 1909, *The Duke of Marlborough*, GBP 840. LONDON, 19 Nov 1910, *Portrait of the Countess of Pembroke*, GBP 73; *Portrait of the Duchess of Portsmouth*, GBP 44; *Portrait of a Nobleman Holding a Book*, GBP 44. NEW YORK, 25-26 Jan 1911, *George II Wearing the Order of the Garter*, USD 1,900. LONDON, 28 Jan 1911, *Prince Rupert*, GBP 6. LONDON, 1 May 1911, *The Earl of Granville and His Family*, GBP 73; *Lady Carteret*, GBP 57. LONDON, 1 June 1911, *Queen Anne Aged 34*, GBP 71. LONDON, 19 June 1911, *Colonel Keppel*, GBP 60. PARIS, 15 Feb 1923, *Portrait of a Girl Dressed as a Huntress*, FRF 530. LON-

DON, 4 June 1923, *Admiral Henshaw and his Wife*, GBP 110. LONDON, 20 March 1925, *Lady Fairbairn*, GBP 60. PARIS, 22 May 1925, *Portrait of a Nobleman*, FRF 1,650. LONDON, 4 Dec 1925, *Judge Jeffreys*, GBP 75. LONDON, 4 March 1927, *Sarah, Duchess of Marlborough*, GBP 84. LONDON, 10 Feb 1928, *Lady Griffin*, GBP 168. LONDON, 15 June 1928, *John Churchill, Duke of Marlborough*, GBP 241; *Portrait of a Woman*, GBP 168. LONDON, 9 Oct 1928, *Edward Roper*, GBP 483. LONDON, 10 June 1931, *The Duchess of Dorset*, GBP 351. LONDON, 3 July 1932, *John Dryden*, GBP 294. LONDON, 26 June 1936, *Charles II*, GBP 367. LONDON, 8 April 1938, *Baron Jeffreys of Wem*, GBP 152. LONDON, 1 July 1938, *Sir John Cotton*, GBP 152. LONDON, 25 Sept 1942, *The Earl of Oxford*, GBP 147. LONDON, 16 July 1943, *Sir John Sheffield*, GBP 210; *Full-length Portrait of Lady C. S. Sheffield*, GBP 252. LONDON, 1 July 1945, *John Dryden*, GBP 252. PARIS, July 1946, *Portrait of a Woman Holding Flowers* (1696) FRF 8,100. PARIS, 21 Oct 1946, *Young Woman Sitting in a Park, Holding Flowers in Her Hand*, FRF 9,200. DONCASTER, 18 March 1947, *Portrait of a Woman*, GBP 105. MARSEILLES, 23 April 1949, *Portrait of Lady Harry Trelawnay*, FRF 150,000. LONDON, 19 Jan 1951, *Portrait of Admiral George Byng*, GBP 210. LONDON, 3 July 1964, *Portrait of Henry Portman Seymour; Portrait of Milicent Fitch, His Second Wife* (two canvases) Gns 2,000. LONDON, 18 Nov 1966, *Small White Dog on an Entablature between Two Busts of Negroes*, Gns 1,600. LONDON, 13 March 1970, *Portrait of Jemima Crewe*, Gns 380. LONDON, 23 Nov 1973, *Portrait of a Nobleman*, Gns 7,500. LONDON, 23 June 1978, *A Family Group on a Terrace* (1721, oil on canvas). LONDON, 23 March 1979, *Portrait of Sarah Churchill, Duchess of Marlborough* (oil on canvas, 48 3/4 ins / 124 cm, 2 x 39 1/2 ins/5 x 100.3 cm) GBP 2,800. LONDON, 17 Nov 1981, *Portrait of Anthony Henley* (black chalk heightened with white/paper, study, 13 1/4 x 9 1/2 ins / 33.6 x 24 cm) GBP 1,900. NEW YORK, 20 April 1983, *Portrait of John Churchill, 1st Duke of Marlborough* (oil on canvas, 47 x 39 ins / 119.5 x 99 cm) USD 6,750. LONDON, 19 Nov 1986, *Portrait of the Artist* (oil on canvas, 41 1/4 x 44 3/4 ins / 105 x 113.5 cm) GBP 48,000. YEALMPTON (DEVON), 19 Oct 1987, *Portrait of John Banckes* (1676, oil on canvas, 54 x 40 ins / 137.2 x 101.6 cm) GBP 19,000. NEW YORK, 3 June 1988, *Portrait of Henry Jermyn, First Earl of St Albans* (oil on canvas, 29 1/2 x 24 1/2 ins / 75 x 62 cm) USD 20,900. LONDON, 15 July 1988, *Portrait of Whitelock Bulstrode in a Brown Coat and a White Shirt-front* (oil on canvas, 29 3/4 x 24 1/2 ins / 75.5 x 62.5 cm) GBP 6,050. STOCKHOLM, 19 April 1989, *Portrait of a Young Girl* (oil on canvas, 30 1/4 x 24 1/2 ins / 77 x 62 cm) SEK 6,700. LONDON, 18 Oct 1989, *Portrait of Margaret Fitzherbert Wearing a Green Dress* (oil on canvas, 29 1/4 x 24 ins / 74 x 61 cm) GBP 3,740. LONDON, 15 Nov 1989, *Portrait of Charles Fitzroy, 2nd Duke of Grafton, as a Child* (1685, oil on canvas, 48 x 39 1/4 ins / 121 x 99.5 cm) GBP 9,350. LONDON, 28 Feb 1990, *Portrait of Anne Yelverton, Countess of Manchester and Later Countess of Halifax, Dressed in Her Peeress's Robes, with Her Coronet beside Her* (oil on canvas, 50 x 39 1/4 ins / 127 x 100 cm) GBP 4,180. NEW YORK, 4 April 1990, *Portrait of a Nobleman Dressed in a Red Velvet Suit and a Brown Cape in a Park* (oil on canvas, 43 3/4 x 37 ins / 111.1 x 94 cm) USD 6,050. LONDON, 20 April 1990, *Portrait of Algernon Capel, Earl of Essex, in Armour, Standing beside a Table on Which Are His Helmet and a Red Cape* (oil on canvas, 84 1/2 x 50 1/2 ins / 214.5 x 128.2 cm) GBP 9,350. LONDON, 14 Nov 1990, *Portait of Colonel Daniel Parke, Standing, Wearing Armour and Holding His Baton of Office in His Right Hand* (oil on canvas, 49 x 39 1/4 ins / 124.5 x 100 cm) GBP 14,300. LONDON, 12 April 1991, *Portrait of Elizabeth, Vicountess Townshend, Wearing a Blue Dress, Standing by a Balustrade* (oil on canvas, 95 x 58 1/4 ins / 241 x 148 cm) GBP 13,200. LONDON, 8 April 1992, *Three-quarter Portrait of Henrietta, Wife of Thomas Langley of Brossley, Wearing a Red Dress* (oil on canvas, 48 1/2 x 39 3/4 ins / 123 x 101 cm) GBP 7,150. STOCKHOLM, 19 May 1992, *Portrait of a Lady and Her Dog* (oil on canvas, 50 x 39 1/4 ins / 127 x 100 cm) SEK 23,000. LONDON, 18 Nov 1992, *Three-quarter Portrait of Lady Margaret Cavendish, Wearing a Brown Dress* (1683, oil on canvas, 48 1/2 x 39 ins / 123.5 x 99 cm) GBP 8,800. LONDON, 6 April 1993, *Portrait of Don José Carreras y Coligo Seated at a Desk in Clerical Dress* (oil on canvas, 29 x 24 1/4 ins / 73.5 x 61.5 cm) GBP 8,625. PARIS, 23 June 1993, *Portrait Presumed to be of the Duke of Northumberland* (oil on canvas, 49 x 39 3/4 ins / 124.5 x 101 cm) FRF 32,000. LONDON, 10 Nov 1993, *Portrait of Nathaniel Crewe, Bishop of Durham, Wearing Peer's Robes and with His Mitre beside Him* (1698, oil on canvas, 49 1/4 x 40 ins / 125 x 101.5 cm) GBP 10,350. NEW YORK, 11 Jan 1995, *Head and Shoulders Portrait of a Nobleman, Presumed to be Francis, 2nd Lord Godolphin* (oil on canvas, 30 x 25 1/4 ins / 76.2 x 64.2 cm) USD 10,925. LONDON, 3 April 1996, *Portrait of William Western of Rivenhall, Standing, in a Red Suit, with His Greyhound* (oil on canvas, 81 x 55 3/4 ins / 206 x 141.5 cm) USD 20,700. ICKWORTH, 12 June 1996, *Portrait of Elizabeth Hervey, Countess of Bristol* (oil on canvas, 49 x 38 1/2 ins / 124.5 x 98 cm) GBP 38,900. LONDON, 13 Nov 1996, *Portrait of William, Earl Cowper* (1710, oil on canvas, 50 x 40 ins / 127 x 101.5 cm) GBP 8,625. NEW YORK, 26 Feb 1997, *Head and Shoulders Portrait of a Lady, Wearing an Orange Dress and a Mauve Shawl* (oil on canvas, 30 x 25 ins / 76.2 x 63.5 cm) USD 6,900. LONDON, 9 April 1997, *Portrait of John, 3rd Baron Poulett* (oil on canvas, 48 3/4 x 39 3/4 ins / 124 x 101 cm) GBP 10,350. RUMBEKE, 20-23 May 1997, *Full-length portrait of King George I of England* (1721, oil on canvas, 87 1/2 x 57 3/4 ins / 222 x 146.5 cm) BEF 582,650. LONDON, 9 July 1997, *Portrait of Dorothy, Countess Tylney* (oil on canvas, oval, 29 1/4 x 24 ins / 74 x 61 cm) GBP 6,325. VIENNA, 24 March 1999, *Astronomer Studying at his Table* (oil on canvas, 43 x 48 ins / 110 x 122 cm) ATS 1,100,000. BILLINGSHURST, 14 Sept 1999, *Portrait of Charles Howard, 3rd Earl of Carlisle* (1719, oil on canvas, 49 x 39 ins / 125 x 100 cm) GBP 18,000. LONDON, 22 March 2000, *Portrait of Sir William Acton, Seated with Landscape Beyond* (oil on canvas, 49 x 39 ins / 125 x 100 cm) GBP 17,000. LONDON, 1 Dec 2000, *Portrait of Elizabeth, Lady Felton, Seated, in a Blue Dress with Red Wrap, Holding a Monkey* (oil on canvas, 50 x 40 ins / 126 x 102 cm) GBP 14,000. COLOGNE, 24 Nov 2001, *Scholar in Study* (oil on canvas, 49 x 39 ins / 124 x 98 cm) DEM 55,000. LONDON, 28 Nov 2001, *Study of the Head of a Young Girl* (black and white chalk, 6 x 6 ins / 15 x 14 cm) GBP 15,000. LONDON, 21 March 2002, *Portrait of John Dryden Wearing Light Purple Robes* (oil on canvas, 30 x 24 ins / 75 x 62 cm) GBP 52,000. LONDON, 11 June 2002, *Portrait of Charles Fitzroy, Afterwards 2nd Duke of Grafton* (oil on canvas, 47 x 35 ins / 120 x 89 cm) GBP 8,000. LONDON, 19 March 2003, *Portrait of a Lady, Wearing Satin Gown and a Green Cloak, with a Dog at her Feet* (oil on canvas, 69 x 43 ins / 175 x 109 cm) GBP 13,000. CLEVELAND, 28 March 2003, *Sir Charles Sedley* (oil on canvas, 50 x 40 ins / 127 x 102 cm) USD 20,500. NEW YORK, 27 May 2004, *Portrait of Meliora Fitch* (oil on canvas, 50 x 40 ins / 127 x 102 cm) USD 42,500. LONDON, 26 March 2004, *Portrait of Admiral James Berkeley, 3rd Earl of Berkeley* (oil on canvas, 50 x 40 ins / 127 x 102 cm) GBP 16,000.

KNELLER, Johann Zacharias

German, 17th century.

Born 6 October 1644, in Lübeck, in 1635 according to Bryan's Dictionary and Redgrave; died 1702, in London.

Painter (gouache), fresco artist. Portraits, still-lifes, architectural views.

Johann Zacharias Kneller was the brother of Gottfried. He lived with his brother in Rome and after 1674 in England, and made small copies of his paintings. He also painted architectural subjects, as well as interior decorations and frescoes.

Museums and Galleries:
Schwerin: *King William III* (gouache/parchment).
Auction records:
New York, 17 Jan 1992, *Still-life of a Game-bird Hanging by One Leg, with a Game-bag on an Entablature* (oil on panel, 24 1/4 x 18 1/2 ins / 61.6 x 47 cm) USD 10,450.

KNELLER, Zacharias
German, 17th century.
Born 16 November 1611, in Eisleben; died 4 April 1675, in Lübeck.
Painter. History painting, portraits.
Zacharias Kneller was the father of Gottfried and Johann Zacharias. His *Portrait of Caspar von Kobrinck* is owned by Lübeck cathedral.

KNESING, Theodor
German, 19th century.
Born 24 July 1840, in Leipzig.
Painter.
Knesing spent time in Rome and Paris around 1867.

KNESL, Hans
Austrian, 20th century.
Born 1905, in Pyrawarth.
Sculptor.
Knesl was a professor at the academy of applied arts in Vienna.

KNEWSTUB, Walter J.
British, 19th century.
Born 1831; died 1906.
Active in London.
Painter. Genre scenes.
Walter J. Knewstub exhibited at the Royal Academy and at the Suffolk Street Gallery between 1865 and 1881.
Auction records:
London, 23 March 1908, *Oh! If I were Grandmother* (watercolour) GBP 17. London, 12 Nov 1992, *Farm Buildings* (oil on canvas, 7 x 10 ins / 18 x 25.5 cm) GBP 1,100.

KNEZ, pseudonym of Knezevic Radivoye
Serb, 20th century.
Born 1923, in Belgrade; died 8 March 1992, in Paris.
Active in France from 1953.
Sculptor, painter.
While still very young, Knez was already following courses in Mathematics and Physics as well as painting. Since the German occupation force had closed all of the schools in Yugoslavia during World War II with the exception of the schools of fine arts, Knez enrolled at the school in Belgrade, from which he graduated in 1948. He began exhibiting in 1951 in Belgrade and Novi Sad. After a study tour of Italy in 1952 he moved to France in 1953, where he studied monumental painting in the studio of Ducos de La Haille at the École des Beaux-Arts in Paris. During the early 1960s he gave up painting for sculpture. Apart from trips to Yugoslavia, in particular to attend the Vela Luka symposium in 1970 and 1971, he continued to live in France. In 1971 he was the joint winner of a competition in which the prize was a commission to design a monumental fountain. Other commissions followed. He took part in international and French collective exhibitions, particularly in Paris at the Salon des Réalités Nouvelles of which he became a committee member in 1973.

During the course of frequent trips to Corsica, where he loved to paint landscapes sweeping down to the sea, he abandoned strict figuration for more abstract landscapes into which he gradually introduced natural or commonly-found materials which were then assembled onto wooden panels such as sand, copper, tin, lead and nails. As these materials overloaded the surface areas of the panels, Knez inevitably switched to sculpture. From 1964 to 1967 he produced a series of bronze sculptures using the lost polyethylene technique which was then new, and also incorporating rough crystals, ammonites and other precious stones into bronze. From 1968, having finally and fully committed himself to Abstraction, he expanded his techniques and his range of materials to include bronze, tropical hardwoods, stainless steel, in forms that were organic while his style remained abstract. In Port Bacarès in 1970 Knez's work blossomed into monumental sculpture with an iroko wood totem some 26 feet (8 metres) high.
Museums and Galleries:
Paris (MAMVP) - Vela Luka (People's Museum).
Auction records:
Paris, 22 May 1989, *Untitled* (ebony from Gabon and Azobé, 7 3/4 x 5 1/4 x 5 3/4 ins / 19.6 x 13.5 x 14.8 cm) FRF 8,000. Paris, 21 May 1990, *Nicolas Tolentino* (1989, ebony from Gabon and rosewood from Rio, 14 1/4 x 6 1/4 x 7 ins / 36 x 16 x 18 cm) FRF 8,000.

KNEZEVIC, Uros
Croat, 19th century.
Born c. 1818, in Karlovac.
Painter.
Knezevic worked mostly in Belgrade, where he painted portraits.

KNIATOWSKI, Théophile
Polish, 19th century.
Active probably in Paris in 1852.
Painter.
The poet Théophile Gautier mentions Théophile Kniatowski by name in one of the poems from Émaux et Camées (Enamels and Cameos): 'J'ai dans ma chambre une aquarelle/Bizarre et d'un peintre avec qui/Mètre et rime sont en querelle/Théophile Kniatowski' (I have in my room a strange watercolour by a painter with whom metre and rhyme are in dispute, Théophile Kniatowski). The title of the poem, Les Néréides (The Nereids), corresponds to the subject of the watercolour: three nymphs struggling with a triton, and on the horizon, a steamer flying the French tricolore.

KNIAZIEVITCH, Carol
Polish, 18th - 19th century.
Born 4 May 1762, in Courlande; died 10 May 1843, in Paris.
Painter. Portraits, military portraits, landscapes.
Carol Kniazievitch reached the rank of general in the army. He painted portraits and landscapes, and is known for his *Portrait of General Xavier Kossecki* and some paintings that belonged to Princess Alexandra Radziwill.

KNIBBERGEN, Catharina van
Dutch, 17th century.
Active in The Hague in 1656.
Painter. Landscapes.
Catharina van Knibbergen may have been the daughter of the landscape artist François Knibbergen.
Auction records:
London, 30 June 1971, *Wooded Landscape*, GBP 1,600. Vienna, 15 Sept 1981, *Imaginary Landscape* (oil on panel, 7 3/4 x 10 1/2 ins / 19.8 x 26.8 cm) ATS 55,000.

KNIBBERGEN, François, or Knibberch, Knypbergen
Dutch, 17th century.

Born 1597, in The Hague; died 1665.
Probably active in The Hague and in Amsterdam.
Painter. Landscapes with figures, landscapes.

François Knibbergen was a pupil of Van den Zande of Utrecht and travelled with him to Italy in 1614. He joined the guild of The Hague in 1629 and held a sale of his work in the city in 1635. He was a contemporary and imitator of Van Goyen.

MUSEUMS AND GALLERIES:

BASEL: *Path in a Wood; Landscape with Waterfall* - LEIPZIG: *Landscape.*

AUCTION RECORDS:

MUNICH, 1899, *View of a Town on a Hill,* FRF 1,562. COLOGNE, 11 Nov 1964, *Landscape with Castle,* DEM 8,000. AMSTERDAM, 25 Nov 1971, *Summer Landscape,* NLG 6,600. AMSTERDAM, 24 May 1977, *Ruin by a River* (oil on panel, 16 x 14 ins / 40.5 x 35.5 cm) NLG 15,000. AMSTERDAM, 30 Oct 1979, *Landscape with Shepherd and Shepherdess* (oil on panel, 20 1/4 x 26 1/2 ins / 51.5 x 67 cm) NLG 10,500. AMSTERDAM, 18 Nov 1986, *Animals at the Foot of a Fortified Tower* (oil on panel, 16 x 13 ins / 40.5 x 33 cm) NLG 13,000. AMSTERDAM, 6 May 1996, *Figures in a Boat Moored by Ruins with Animals Drinking* (oil on panel, 16 x 13 ins / 40.5 x 33 cm) NLG 11,800.

KNIBILY, Antoine

French, 20th century.
Born 14 June 1920, in Colmar.
Active in Chile and the USA from 1945.
Painter. Landscapes, still-lifes.

Antoine Knibily was ordained as a priest in Strasbourg in 1945 and sent by his Order to teach in Santiago in Chile, where he spent most of his life. He produced his first painting just before Christmas 1958 in order to decorate the nativity scene. This event was a revelation to him and he went on to paint ceaselessly. Untrained and unassociated with any school, Knibily gave free rein to his inspiration and created his own style. His landscapes, like some of his Abstract compositions (*Cosmos* of 1989 and *Under the Microscope* of 1989), are thickly painted in bright colours, characteristics of his work that led to him being dubbed 'the Chilean Van Gogh' by the local press. The sacred, almost mystic quality of his painting also reveals great sensitivity and is an expression of a hymn to life and to faith.

Knibily's first exhibition took place in 1961 at the Galerie Cambacérès in Paris. He then moved to New York where his work was exhibited in numerous galleries as well as in Chile. In 1983 the Musée du Petit Palais in Geneva showed a collection of his paintings and in 1990 he was given a triumphant reception in Chile with a retrospective exhibition of his work.

KNIEB, Johannes

German, 18th century.
Born 1735, in Frankfurt am Main; died 9 March 1796, in Frankfurt am Main.
Painter. Flowers. Decorative schemes.

Knieb studied with Nothnagel.

KNIEBEBE, Walter

German, 20th century.
Born 22 June 1884, in Dortmund.
Sculptor. Figures.

Kniebebe was mainly active in Düsseldorf.

MUSEUMS AND GALLERIES:

ELBERFELD: *Torso.*

KNIEKE, Heinrich

German, 19th century.
Born 5 March 1855, in Macktsum.
Painter, sculptor.

Knieke worked in Hildesheim and Berlin, at first under the direction of Schaper, with whom he collaborated on a *Memorial to Goethe.*

KNIEP, Christoph or Christian Heinrich

German, 18th - 19th century.
Born 1755, in Hildesheim; died 10 July 1825, in Naples.
Painter, watercolourist, draughtsman. Portraits, landscapes.

Kniep studied in Hanover, then lived for a time in Hamburg, Kassel, Berlin and Hanover, visiting Vienna, Warsaw and the Tyrol, before settling in Naples. He produced very few oil paintings, as he devoted himself mainly to watercolours. The famous Goethe Collection in Weimar contains a few of his works.

BIBLIOGRAPHY:

Striehl, Georg, *Der Zeichner Christoph Heinrich Kniep - Landschaftsauffassung und Antikenrezeption,* Georg Olms Verlag, Hildesheim, 1998.

AUCTION RECORDS:

PARIS, 24 June 1929, *Classical Landscapes* (four drawings) FRF 420. MUNICH, 18 May 1988, *Classical Landscape* (brown wash and ink, 20 1/4 x 28 1/4 ins / 51.5 x 72 cm) DEM 4,620. ROME, 21 Nov 1995, *Wooded Landscape with a Washerwoman by a Spring and a Fortified Castle in the Background* (1781, oil on canvas, 17 x 13 1/2 ins / 43 x 34 cm) ITL 7,660,000. LONDON, 16 April 1999, *Extensive River Landscape with Shepherdess and Temples* (chalk, pen and ink wash, 15 x 22 ins / 38 x 57 cm) GBP 3,800. LONDON, 16 April 1999, *River Landscape with Doric Temple, Minerva in Foreground* (chalk, pen and ink wash, 15 x 22 ins / 39 x 57 cm) GBP 6,000. HAMBURG, 7 June 2001, *Idyllic River Landscape with Shepherdess* (chalk, 8 x 10 ins / 20 x 26 cm) DEM 4,600. COPENHAGEN, 27 Nov 2001, *Italian Landscape with Ruins, Shepherd and Women* (1823, watercolour and pencil, 12 x 15 ins / 30 x 39 cm) DKK 55,000. LONDON, 9 April 2003, *Arcadian Landscape with Tomb, Women in Classical Dress and Sheep in the Foreground* (pen and ink, 24 x 32 ins / 61 x 81 cm) GBP 2,000. MILAN, 22 June 2004, *Homage to Karl Theodor Korner* (pencil, 19 x 13 ins / 48 x 33 cm) EUR 3,500.

KNIEP, Frieda

German, 20th century.
Born 9 July 1884, in Lübeck.
Painter.

Kniep worked in Stettin (now Szczecin, Poland) with Gustave Wimmer, then in Frederdorf, near Berlin.

AUCTION RECORDS:

LONDON, 27 July 1973, *Vase of Flowers,* Gns 350.

KNIEPER, Hans

Flemish School, 16th century.
Born to a family originally from Antwerp; died 22 November 1587.
Painter. Historical subjects, landscapes, portraits. Designs for tapestries.

He worked for King Frederick III in Copenhagen in 1578, producing sketches for tapestries showing the Danish kings. In 1586, he painted landscapes for Tycho Brahe. He also produced portraits and sketches for tapestries for the Frederiksborg castle, which were destroyed in a fire at the castle in 1859.

MUSEUMS AND GALLERIES:

COPENHAGEN (Rosenborg Slot): *Portrait of Christian IV as a Child* - HILLERØD (Frederiksborg): *Portrait of Frederick II; Portrait of the Daughter of Frederick II.*

KNIFER, Julije

Croat, 20th century.
Born 1924, in Osijek.
Painter, draughtswoman, screen printer.
Neo-Dadaism, Conceptual Art, Neo-Constructivism.

Gorgona Group.
Julije Knifer was a student at the academy of fine arts in Zagreb. A member of the Dadaist Gorgona group in Yugoslavia at the end of the 1950s, she was also involved with the Neo-Constructivist New Trends group. From 1959 she used the figure of the geometrically-stylised meander and a reduced colour range of black, grey and white. Her work is similar to Morellet's, an artist whom she admired.

She took part in collective exhibitions, including *Un Tableau dans le Décor: Peintures 1970-2000* (*A Painting in the Décor: Paintings 1970-2000*), an exhibition organised to celebrate 20 years of the FRAC, Château des Ducs de Bretagne, Nantes (2003). Solo exhibitions include Galerie Frank, Paris (1999 and 2002).

BIBLIOGRAPHY:
Pierre, Arnauld, *Julije Knifer: méandres*, Adam Biro, Paris, 2001.

MUSEUMS AND GALLERIES:
CHÂTEAUGIRON (FRAC Bretagne) - DIJON (FRAC Bourgogne): *Untitled* (1991-1992) - GRENOBLE (Mus. de Grenoble): *Untitled* - MONTREAL (MAC): *XII, 71-2cs* (silk screen print) - PARIS (FNAC): five drawings in graphite/paper; *1966 K9* (1966, oil on canvas).

KNIGGE, Otto
German, 19th century.
Born 14 December 1835, in Berlin; died 5 March 1883, in Berlin.
Painter. History painting, portraits.

Knigge studied with J. Lüdentz at the Berlin academy, then at the school of fine arts in Weimar and also with Couture in Paris. He made copies of works in the Louvre. He went to Italy in 1869.

KNIGHT, A. Roland
British, 19th - 20th century.
Active from 1810 to 1840.
Painter. Genre scenes.

A. Roland Knight specialised in fishing scenes.

AUCTION RECORDS:
LONDON, 26 July 1985, *'Four-to-one on Jack'* (oil on canvas, 20 x 30 ins / 50.8 x 76.2 cm) GBP 1,400. SOUTH QUEENSFERRY, 1 May 1990, *The Angler's Delight* (oil on canvas, 20 x 30 ins / 51 x 76 cm) GBP 1,045. PERTH, 1 Sept 1992, *Salmon Taking a Fly* (oil on canvas, 14 1/4 x 20 3/4 ins / 36 x 53 cm) GBP 1,980. GLASGOW, 14 Feb 1995, *Hooked Salmon* (oil on canvas, 18 x 24 ins / 45.5 x 61 cm) GBP 920. LONDON, 17 April 1996, *Winter Tragedy* (oil on canvas, 16 x 24 ins / 40.8 x 61 cm) GBP 747. LONDON, 5 Sept 1996, *Trout Fishing* (oil on canvas, 6 1/4 x 9 1/2 ins / 15.9 x 24.2 cm) GBP 690. LONDON, 17 Oct 1996, *Fish Eagles Fighting over their Prey* (oil on canvas, 19 1/2 x 26 1/2 ins / 49.5 x 67.2 cm) GBP 2,185. GLASGOW, 11 Dec 1996, *Warfare in the Highlands* (oil on canvas, 20 x 30 1/4 ins / 51 x 77 cm) GBP 747. LONDON, 18 Dec 1997, *A Regular Fix* (oil on canvas, 18 x 24 ins / 45.7 x 61 cm) GBP 690. LONDON, 2 Nov 1999, *Just Caught* (oil on canvas, a pair, 15 x 20 ins / 37 x 50 cm) GBP 1,700. CRANBROOK, 15 Nov 1999, *Got Away, Study of Leaping Salmon* (oil on canvas, 16 x 24 ins / 41 x 61 cm) GBP 1,450. LONDON, 15 June 2000, *Trout Rising* (oil on canvas, 16 x 24 ins / 41 x 61 cm) GBP 1,800. LONDON, 30 Nov 2000, *Tench, Perch and Roach. Jack in the Roach Swim* (1902, oil on canvas, a pair, 12 x 16 ins / 30 x 41 cm) GBP 1,900. LONDON, 14 June 2001, *Trout in a Net. Salmon on a Line* (oil on card, a pair, 6 x 7 ins / 15 x 18 cm) GBP 4,500. LONDON, 14 June 2001, *Trout on a Line. Trout Leaping* (oil on canvas, a pair, 6 x 8 ins / 16 x 20 cm) GBP 4,900. LONDON, 13 June 2002, *Pike on a Line* (oil on canvas, 20 x 30 ins / 51 x 76 cm) GBP 1,800. LONDON, 13 June 2002, *Grayling. Chub. Lea Trout from the Pied Bull Stream, St Nudent, Hertfordshire* (oil on canvas, 9 x 12 ins / 23 x 30 cm) GBP 3,500. LONDON, 9 Sept 2003, *Jack's Breakfast. Twixt Life and Death. Nemesis or Bitter End* (oil on canvas, 16 x 24 ins / 41 x 61 cm) GBP 1,900. LEYBURN, 19 Nov 2003, *Still-life with Salmon, Pike, other Fish and Fishing Tackle* (oil on canvas, 30 x 50 ins / 76 x 127 cm) GBP 1,800. LONDON, 10 June 2004, *Perch. Salmon and Trout. Roach. Pike. Barbel and Chubb. Trout the First Leap* (oil on board, six, 5 x 9 ins / 13 x 22 cm) GBP 8,000. LONDON, 1 Sept 2004, *On the Banks of the Tweed, Salmon, Salmon Trout, Lake Trout* (oil on canvas, 18 x 32 ins / 46 x 81 cm) GBP 2,800.

KNIGHT, Adah
British, 19th - 20th century.
Active in Gloucester.
Painter, watercolourist.

Adah Knight exhibited at the Royal Academy in London from 1893 to 1926.

KNIGHT, Aston. See **KNIGHT Louis Aston**

KNIGHT, C.
British, 18th - 19th century.
Active in London.
Miniaturist.

C. Knight exhibited on rare occasions at the Royal Academy between 1793 and 1826.

KNIGHT, C. J.
British, 19th century.
Active in London.
Sculptor.

C.J. Knight exhibited his work at the Royal Academy in 1844.

KNIGHT, C. Neil
British, 19th - 20th century.
Active in London.
Painter. Genre scenes, portraits.

C. Neil Knight exhibited at the Royal Academy from 1897.

KNIGHT, Charles
British, 18th - 19th century.
Born 1743; died c. 1826.
Active in London.
Draughtsman, engraver (burin).

Charles Knight made brilliant use of mezzotint and stippling techniques in his engravings, reproducing genre scenes and portraits after the works of J. Reynolds, Romney, Hoppner and Wheatly. He was very prolific and some of his prints today command a very high price.

KNIGHT, Charles Parsons
British, 19th century.
Born 15 February 1829, in Bristol; died 22 January 1897, in Twerton (Somerset).
Painter, watercolourist. Landscapes, seascapes.

Charles Parsons Knight lived in Clifton until 1880, when he moved to Twerton and settled there. His paintings were very popular because of the beautifully rendered skies and the vast horizons in his seascapes. He also painted very beautiful harvesting scenes. His work was exhibited at the Royal Academy, the British Institution and at the Suffolk Street Gallery after 1855.

MUSEUMS AND GALLERIES:
BRISTOL: *Stone Wall; Mardyke Ferry* - BRISTOL (City Mus. & AG): *A Highland Oatfield; Falmouth Harbour* (oil on canvas); *Cawsand Bay* (oil on canvas); *Ramsey Island, off Pembrokeshire* (oil on canvas) - HAMBURG: *Seascape*.

AUCTION RECORDS:
LONDON, 7 July 1929, *Boarding at Gravesend*, GBP 40; *Unloading at Kingston Bridge*, GBP 60. LONDON, 18 Feb 1970, *View from the Window*, GBP 650. STOCKHOLM, 16 May 1990, *Sailing Ships Following the Coast* (oil on canvas, 20 1/2 x 33 ins / 52 x 84 cm) SEK 12,000. LONDON, 4 Nov 1994, *Wheatfield near Runswick* (1858, oil on canvas, 10 x 15 ins / 25.5 x 38 cm) GBP 2,530. LONDON, 24 May 2001, *Fisherfolk on the Jetty* (oil on canvas, 22 x 36 ins / 56 x 91 cm) GBP 1,000. EXETER, 28

June 2001, *West Cornwall Moor* (1873, oil on canvas, 17 x 30 ins / 43 x 77 cm) GBP 1,050. LINDAU, 7 May 2003, *Stormy Seascape with Boat* (oil on board, 11 x 14 ins / 27 x 35 cm) EUR 1,900. BURY ST EDMUNDS, 22 Sept 2004, *Scottish Loch* (1884, oil on canvas, 21 x 45 ins / 54 x 115 cm) GBP 1,500.

KNIGHT, Charles Robert
American, 20th century.
Born 21 October 1874, in Brooklyn; died 15 April 1953, in Middletown.
Painter, draughtsman, illustrator, sculptor. Animals.

Charles Robert Knight studied under Fremiet and Gérôme in Paris, after attending the Art Students League and the Brooklyn Polytechnic. His interest in animals and especially in wildlife was truly scientific: he visited zoological gardens all over the world in order to study his subjects. He also published illustrated books on prehistoric animals, working among others for the American Museum of Natural History as a painter and writer. He is the author and illustrator of: *Animal Anatomy and Psychology for Arts Students; Before the Dawn of History; The Great Adventurer; Life through the Ages* (1946); *Prehistoric Man* (1949).

BIBLIOGRAPHY:
Osterwalder, Marcus (ed.), *Dictionnaire des illustrateurs 1800-1914*, Ides et Calendes, Neuchâtel, 1989.

AUCTION RECORDS:
NEW YORK, 28 Sept 1983, *Dog Gnawing a Bone* (dark red and brown-patinated bronze, h. 6 3/4 ins / 17.2 cm) USD 800. NEW YORK, 8 June 1984, *A Grizzly with his Catch* (1900, watercolour, gouache and pastel, 18 x 30 ins / 45.7 x 76.2 cm) USD 4,800. NEW YORK, 30 May 1990, *Golden Pheasant* (1917, oil on canvas, 32 3/4 x 37 1/2 ins / 83.3 x 95.4 cm) USD 3,300. NEW YORK, 31 May 1990, *Central Park* (1948, oil on canvas, 18 x 24 ins / 45.7 x 60.9 cm) USD 1,210. NEW YORK, 24 Sept 1992, *The Science of the Origins of Stars: Three Studies for a Wall Painting for the Hayden Planetarium* (oil on canvas, in all 24 x 65 ins / 61 x 165.1 cm) USD 5,500. NEW YORK, 12 April 1996, *Bengal Tiger Roaring* (1914, bronze, h. 25 1/2 ins / 64.8 cm) USD 21,850. NEW YORK, 4 Sept 2002, *Seated Puma* (green patinated bronze, h. 7 ins / 17 cm) USD 2,800.

KNIGHT, Daniel Ridgway
American, 19th - 20th century.
Born 13 March 1839, in Philadelphia; died March 1924, in Paris.
From 1861 active in France.
Painter (gouache), watercolourist. Figures, genre scenes, landscapes.

Daniel Ridgway Knight first studied at the Pennsylvania Academy of the Fine Arts. In 1861, he furthered his artistic education in Paris studying under Charles Gleyre and Cabanel at the École des Beaux-Arts. There he made the acquaintance of young Impressionist painters. During the American Civil War, he fought in the Union Army. In 1872, he returned to France, settled in Poissy, and turned to Ernest Meissonier for advice. Knight's gentle account of French peasants' life is more concerned with beautifully rendered landscapes and detailed representation of their clothing than with the reality of their situation. His close friend Meissonier's influence is perceptible in the technical precision of his approach. He was highly rated on both sides of the Atlantic for his female figures and his landscapes including: *Mending, Hailing the Ferry, After the Battle of the Marne.*

He exhibited at the Paris Salon where he received several awards as well as other medals in Munich, Chicago, Antwerp. He was made a Chevalier de la Légion d'Honneur in 1889 and an Officier in 1909.

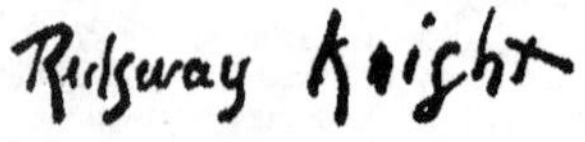

BIBLIOGRAPHY:
Hélène Ahrweiler, Roger Mandle, D. Scott Atkinson, William H. Gerdts, Carole L. Shelby, Jochen Wierich, *Lasting Impressions: American Painters in France 1865-1915*, exhibition catalogue, Musée d'Art américain, Giverny, Terra Foundation for the Arts, Evanston (IL), 1992.

MUSEUMS AND GALLERIES:
CHICAGO (Terra Foundation for American Art Collection).

AUCTION RECORDS:
NEW YORK, 1897, *The Mussel Picker*, FRF 2,000. NEW YORK, 1 Feb 1901, *The Little Shepherdess*, USD 1,700. NEW YORK, 26 to 28 Feb 1902, *Moonlight*, USD 825; *The Spring*, USD 910; *At the Foot of the Steps*, USD 1,250. NEW YORK, 1-2 April 1902, *Laundresses*, USD 1,700. NEW YORK, 23-24 April 1903, *View of the Seine at Poissy*, USD 825. NEW YORK, 12-13 Jan 1905, *In a Garden in Bloom*, USD 1,450. NEW YORK, 19 Jan 1906, *Haymaking near Poissy*, USD 2,000. NEW YORK, 10-11 Jan 1907, *Hailing the Ferry*, USD 2,500. LONDON, 25 Jan 1908, *Forêt de Fontainebleau*, GBP 23. NEW YORK, 6 Jan 1911, *Waiting for the Boat*, USD 2,550. NEW YORK, 4 Feb 1932, *Tall Rosebush*, USD 1,000. PARIS, 16 May 1939, *Country-woman with the Blue Umbrella* (watercolour) FRF 250. NEW YORK, 18 Oct 1944, *Harvest Field*, USD 1,800. NEW YORK, 15 May 1946, *Norman Scene*, USD 2,500. PARIS, 31 March 1950, *Gossiping*, FRF 200,000. PARIS, 30 June 1950, *Returning from the Fields*, FRF 10,000; *The Laundress* (watercolour) FRF 2,800. NEW YORK, 23 Oct 1951, *The Love Letter*, USD 700. NEW YORK, 21 Oct 1959, *The Shepherdess*, USD 900. NEW YORK, 6 Nov 1963, *Country Girl in a Vegetable Garden*, USD 1,500. NEW YORK, 29 April 1965, *Shepherdess*, USD 2,000. NEW YORK, 6 Oct 1966, *Country Woman in a Field*, USD 3,250. NEW YORK, 14 May 1969, *Market Day*, USD 4,400. NEW YORK, 23 Sept 1970, *Shepherdess*, USD 3,000. NEW YORK, 3 June 1971, *Country Girl in a Landscape*, USD 2,200. NEW YORK, 10 Oct 1973, *Two Country Girls and a Shepherd in a Brittany Landscape*, USD 10,000. NEW YORK, 9 Oct 1974, *Grape Harvest*, USD 17,000. LOS ANGELES, 8 March 1976, *Grape Harvest* (oil on canvas, 58 1/2 x 47 3/4 ins / 148.5 x 121.5 cm) USD 5,500. NEW YORK, 14 May 1976, *Portrait of Young Breton Girl* (watercolour, 14 1/2 x 11 ins / 37 x 27 cm) USD 950. NEW YORK, 18 May 1977, *The Luncheon Table* (oil on canvas, 51 x 61 ins / 129.5 x 155 cm) USD 3,750. NEW YORK, 4 May 1979, *After the Storm* (oil on canvas, 46 x 35 1/4 ins / 116 x 89.5 cm) USD 25,000. NEW YORK, 23 May 1979, *Shepherdess* (watercolour, 20 1/2 x 16 3/4 ins / 52 x 42.5 cm) USD 2,000. LOS ANGELES, 8 Feb 1982, *A Rose Garden* (oil on canvas, 23 1/2 x 35 1/2 ins / 60 x 90 cm) USD 14,000. NEW YORK, 27 May 1983, *Girl Picking Flowers* (oil on canvas, 46 1/2 x 35 1/2 ins / 118.1 x 90.2 cm) USD 30,000. NEW YORK, 25 May 1984, *Country Girl Carrying a Bundle* (1883, watercolour and gouache) USD 700. NEW YORK, 6 Dec 1985, *The Gardener's Daughter* (oil on canvas, 32 1/4 x 25 3/4 ins / 81.8 x 65.4 cm) USD 65,000. NEW YORK, 28 Oct 1987, *Peeling an Apple* (1884, watercolour and gouache, 15 x 11 ins / 38 x 27 cm) USD 3,500. NEW YORK, 25 Feb 1988, *Apple-trees in Bloom* (oil on canvas, 31 x 25 1/2 ins / 78.8 x 64.8 cm) USD 28,600. NEW YORK, 26 April 1988, *Apple Blossoms* (oil on canvas, 45 3/4 x 35 ins / 116.5 x 88.8 cm) USD 71,500. NEW YORK, 24 Jan 1989, *The Old Suitor* (1872, oil on panel, 23 1/2 x 18 3/4 ins / 59.5 x 47.5 cm) USD 3,575. NEW YORK, 24 May 1989, *The Golden Sunset* (oil on canvas, 22 x 18 ins / 55.9 x 45.7 cm) USD 15,400. NEW YORK, 1 Dec 1989, *Morning Chill* (oil on canvas, 34 x 26 ins / 86.4 x 66 cm) USD 38,500. NEW YORK, 24 May 1990, *Baiting the Hook* (oil on canvas, 21 1/2 x 18 1/4 ins / 54.6 x 46.3 cm) USD 24,200. NEW YORK, 12 April 1991, *Wash Day* (oil on canvas, 21 x 26 ins / 53.3 x 66 cm) USD 30,800. NEW YORK, 18 Dec 1991, *Potato Harvester*

(watercolour and gouache/paper/card, 14½ x 10½ ins / 36.8 x 26.7 cm) USD 2,640. Stockholm, 19 May 1992, *Girl Fetching Water with Two Clay Ewers* (watercolour, 14½ x 10¼ ins / 37 x 26 cm) SEK 21,000. New York, 27 May 1992, *Waiting* (oil on canvas, 23¼ x 18¾ ins / 59.1 x 47.6 cm) USD 23,100. New York, 28 May 1992, *Summer's Folly* (oil on canvas, 71½ x 43¼ ins / 181.7 x 109.8 cm) USD 52,800. New York, 24 Sept 1992, *Apple Blossoms in Normandy* (oil on canvas, 32½ x 25½ ins / 82.6 x 64.8 cm) USD 16,500. New York, 29 Oct 1992, *Country Woman Standing Carrying Vegetables* (ink/paper, 12½ x 6½ ins / 31.7 x 16.2 cm) USD 990. New York, 4 Dec 1992, *A Lovely Thought* (oil on canvas, 22¼ x 18¼ ins / 56.2 x 46.4 cm) USD 33,000. New York, 9 Sept 1993, *Woman with a Basket* (1885, watercolour/paper/paper, 14¾ x 10¼ ins / 37.5 x 26 cm) USD 1,610. New York, 15 Feb 1994, *Lunch in the Field* (oil on canvas, 33 x 41½ ins / 83.8 x 105.4 cm) USD 96,000. Paris, 20 Nov 1994, *The Washerwomen* (oil on panel, 5½ x 9 ins / 14 x 23 cm) FRF 10,500. New York, 25 May 1995, *Mending* (oil on canvas, 46 x 35 ins / 116.8 x 88.9 cm) USD 87,750. Paris, 27 Oct 1995, *Poissy, the End of School* (oil on canvas, 19 x 22 ins / 48 x 55 cm) FRF 42,000. Paris, 19 April 1996, *Rolleboise, Countryman at his Window (Julia Massé and Old Mr Haranger)* (oil on canvas, 32¼ x 25½ ins / 82 x 65 cm) FRF 30,000. New York, 22 May 1996, *Waiting for the Ferry* (c. 1915, oil on canvas, 26¼ x 32¼ ins / 66.7 x 81.9 cm) USD 41,400. New York, 4 Dec 1996, *The Harvesters* (oil on canvas, 33½ x 46¾ ins / 85.1 x 118.7 cm) USD 36,800. New York, 12 Feb 1997, *Sharing Secrets* (oil on canvas, 26 x 32½ ins / 66 x 82.6 cm) USD 151,000. New York, 25 March 1997, *Breton Country Woman* (oil on panel, 14¾ x 10¾ ins / 37.5 x 27.3 cm) USD 12,650. New York, 6 June 1997, *Woman in a Garden* (oil on canvas, 26 x 21 ins / 66 x 53.3 cm) USD 101,500. New York, 3 Dec 1997, *A Pensive Moment* (oil on canvas, 46 x 35 ins / 116.8 x 88.9 cm) USD 90,500. New York, 12 Feb 1998, *Young Woman Picking Flowers* (oil on canvas, 33 x 26 ins / 83.8 x 66 cm) USD 68,500.

KNIGHT, Harold

British, 19th - 20th century.

Born 27 October 1874, in Nottingham; died 3 October 1961, in Colwall, near Malvern.

Painter. Portraits, interiors with figures, landscapes, animals.

Harold Knight trained under William Foster at Nottingham Art School, where he met his future wife Laura Johnson. In 1894, after receiving the Prince of Wales silver medal, he was awarded a scholarship and went with Laura to Paris, where he attended the Académie Julian, training under Jean-Paul Laurens and Benjamin-Constant.

In 1896 they visited the Staithes Artist Colony on the Yorkshire coast and were both attracted by its ethos of a free brushwork and an Impressionist, bright palette in the Bastien-Lepage tradition. They stayed there until 1910, marrying in 1903. There Harold Knight painted scenes of the hard lives of the fishing community. They then moved to Cornwall, first to Newlyn and later to Lamorna, becoming part of the Lamorna Group with such artists as Lamorna Birch and Alfred Munnings. After World War I they settled in London, though they maintained a studio in Cornwall for a time and frequently paid visits there. Knight was made a member of the Royal Academy in 1937. His work was included in *Painting in Newlyn 1880-1930*, Barbican Art Gallery, London (1985).

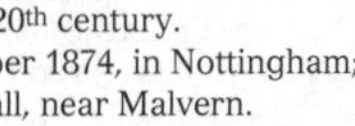

Bibliography:

Greenacre, Francis/Fox, Caroline, *Painting at Newlyn 1880-1930*, exhibition catalogue, Barbican Art Gallery, London, 1985.

Museums and Galleries:

Brighton (Brighton and Hove Museums): *The Reader* (c. 1910, oil on canvas); *A Student* (exhibited 1938) - Cape Town: *Grace* - Cardiff (National Museum and Galleries of Wales): *The Green Book* - Cardiff (National Museums and Galleries) - Cardiff (The National Museum and Galleries of Wales): *W.H. Renwick* - Leeds (City AG): *The Letter* (oil on canvas); *Milking the Goat* (oil on canvas) - London (Burlington House) - London (National Portrait Gal.): *Arthur Balfour, 1st Baron Riverdale* (1936); *Self-portrait* (c. 1923); *George Horation Nelson, 1st Baron Nelson* - London (Tate Collection): *A Student* (exhibited in 1938, oil on canvas) - Nottingham (Castle Mus. & AG): *The Last Fishing Boat* - Perth (Municipal Gallery).

Auction records:

London, 23 May 1910, *Scarborough Harbour* (watercolour and a marine) GBP 10. London, 29 Jan 1947, *The Impression,* GBP 68. London, 16 June 1976, *A Fishergirl* (watercolour, 11½ x 17¾ ins / 29.5 x 45 cm) GBP 120. London, 5 March 1980, *Village Wedding* (oil on canvas, 63½ x 75¼ ins / 161 x 191 cm) GBP 9,800. London, 9 March 1984, *In the Studio* (oil on canvas, 24 x 20 ins / 61 x 50.8 cm) GBP 2,200. London, 15 May 1985, *Reading in a Hammock* (oil on canvas, 14 x 18 ins / 35.5 x 46 cm) GBP 15,000. London, 2 March 1989, *Return of Fishermen at Staithes* (watercolour and gouache, 9¼ x 13¼ ins / 23.7 x 33.7 cm) GBP 6,050. London, 8 June 1989, *Woman with Tikki, the Talisman* (oil on canvas, 29½ x 24½ ins / 75 x 62.5 cm) GBP 2,640. London, 8 Nov 1990, *Tea Time* (oil on canvas, 76 x 59¾ ins / 193 x 152 cm) GBP 79,200. London, 23 June 1999, *Mornie and Her Doll* (oil on canvas, 12 x 14 ins / 30 x 35 cm) GBP 35,000. Birmingham, 1 Oct 1999, *Busy Town Scene with Marketplace* (watercolour, 13 x 24 ins / 33 x 61 cm) GBP 2,500. London, 6 June 2000, *Bric-a-brac* (oil on canvas, 36 x 30 ins / 92 x 77 cm) GBP 30,000. London, 21 Nov 2000, *Morning Sun* (oil on canvas, 30 x 25 ins / 77 x 64 cm) GBP 105,000. London, 26 June 2001, *Letter* (oil on canvas, 18 x 18 ins / 45 x 45 cm) GBP 38,000. Penzance, 25 Oct 2001, *Seamstress* (watercolour, 12 x 15 ins / 30 x 38 cm) GBP 5,000. London, 7 June 2002, *Reading at the Window* (oil on canvas, 24 x 20 ins / 61 x 51 cm) GBP 19,000. London, 3 Dec 2002, *By the Hearth* (oil on canvas, 16 x 12 ins / 40 x 30 cm) GBP 1,800. London, 6 June 2003, *Portrait of Dame Laura Knight Sketching* (oil on canvas, 18 x 18 ins / 46 x 46 cm) GBP 9,000. London, 21 Nov 2003, *Morning Sun* (oil on canvas, 30 x 25 ins / 77 x 64 cm) GBP 95,000. Leyburn, 21 April 2004, *Study of a Young Dutch Girl Seated beside a Window* (oil on canvasboard, 14 x 10 ins / 35 x 25 cm) GBP 8,000.

KNIGHT, John Baverstock

British, 19th century.

Born 3 May 1785, in Langton; died 14 May 1859, near Broadwey (Dorset).

Painter.

Museums and Galleries:

Leicester: *Flora Mae Yvor.*

KNIGHT, John Prescott

British, 19th century.

Born 1803, in Stafford; died 26 March 1881, in London.

Painter, watercolourist, draughtsman. Portraits, genre scenes.

John Prescott Knight was the son of the performer Edward Knight. Initially planning a career in trade, he began with a trader in colonial products. With time on his hands after his employer went bankrupt, he started to copy drawings by West to busy himself. He was so successful at this that he decided to pursue a career in art. At first, he worked with Sass and George Clint and then enrolled at the Royal Academy. After showing his work for the first time in 1824, he set himself up as a portrait painter. His most notable portraits were those of his father, Sir Walter Scott, Miss Chester and Mrs Terry.

In 1828, Knight exhibited a genre scene at the British Institution. He became an associate of the Royal Academy in 1836, a full member in 1844, and was secretary from 1848 to 1878.

MUSEUMS AND GALLERIES:

LEICESTER: *Happy Beggar* - LONDON (National Portrait Gal.): *Sir Charles Barry* (c. 1851, oil on canvas) - LONDON (Tate Collection): *Sacking a Church at the Time of John Knox* (1843, oil on canvas) - LONDON (Victoria and Albert Mus.): watercolours - NOTTINGHAM: *J.D. Handing* - SALFORD (Museum and AG): *Thomas Agnew*.

AUCTION RECORDS:

LONDON, 9 April 1910, *Portrait of David Deans*, GBP 10. NEW YORK, 22-24 March 1911, *Portrait of the Artist's Father*, USD 60. LONDON, 20 July 1979, *The Burning Glass* (oil on panel, 11 3/4 x 9 3/4 ins / 29.8 x 24.7 cm) GBP 1,500. LONDON, 18 May 1990, *Tam O'Shanter* (1833, oil on canvas, 44 x 55 ins / 111.8 x 139.7 cm) USD 3,520. LONDON, 21 July 2003, *Portrait of the Rev. George Lock* (oil on canvas, 35 x 27 ins / 89 x 68 cm) GBP 1,700.

KNIGHT, John William Buxton

British, 19th century.

Born 1843, in Sevenoaks; died 3 January 1908, in Dover.

Painter, watercolourist, engraver (etching/mezzotint).

Landscapes, seascapes, rustic scenes.

John William Buxton Knight was a student at the Royal Academy. He is considered to be the best English landscape artists. He painted in watercolours and in oil, made etchings and mezzotint engravings and, in his large number of works, amply demonstrated his sensitive touch. He belonged to the Constable school, continuing in that painter's grand tradition. He met with rapid success, and his work is much sought after.

Knight began showing his work in the London exhibitions in 1863 at the Royal Academy, at the Suffolk Street Gallery, and the Grosvenor Gallery. He was a member of the Society of British Artists and the Royal Cambrian Academy. He exhibited in Paris, where he won a bronze medal in 1889 at the Exposition Universelle.

MUSEUMS AND GALLERIES:

BRADFORD (Cartwright Hall AG): *Harvest Time on the Conway River* (1890, oil on canvas); *Portsmouth Harbour* (1907, oil on canvas); *Poole Harbour* (oil on canvas); *Hereford Cathedral* (oil on canvas) - MELBOURNE: *Winter Sun* - SYDNEY: *Halcyon near a Stream; Deserted*.

AUCTION RECORDS:

LONDON, 21 Nov 1908, *Breeze*, GBP 12. LONDON, 6 Feb 1909, *Old Dick Shred*, GBP 23. LONDON, 30 April 1910, *Yalding Bridge*, GBP 162; *Poole Harbour* (1889) GBP 168; *Woman by a River Bank* (1881) GBP 89. LONDON, 17 Feb 1922, *The Buck's Head, Godden Green*, GBP 73. LONDON, 2 May 1924, *View of Oxford*, GBP 47. LONDON, 3 April 1925, *On the River*, GBP 89. LONDON, 10 Dec 1926, *When Summer Winds Blow Cold*, GBP 92. LONDON, 6 July 1928, *Near Chertsey* (drawing) GBP 42. LONDON, 17 June 1983, *Seaside Scene* (oil on canvas, 24 x 36 1/4 ins / 61 x 92 cm) GBP 1,800. LONDON, 25 May 1999, *Jetty Scenes* (oil on canvas, a pair, sold with a painting by David Wilson, 20 x 30 ins / 51 x 76 cm) GBP 2,400. LONDON, 28 Oct 1999, *The Tweed at Kelso* (oil on canvas, 18 x 36 ins / 46 x 91 cm) GBP 2,400. LONDON, 9 March 2000, *Church at Sunset* (oil on canvas, 60 x 41 ins / 152 x 103 cm) GBP 7,000.

KNIGHT, Joseph

British, 19th century.

Born 27 January 1837, in Manchester; died 2 January 1909, near Conway.

Active in Sevenoaks.

Painter, watercolourist, engraver. Genre scenes, landscapes.

Joseph Knight may have been related to William Buxton Knight. He began exhibiting his work in London after 1861, in particular, at the Royal Academy. He was a member of the Royal Institute of Painters in Watercolours, of the Royal Cambrian Academy and was an associate of the Royal Society of Painter-Etchers.

MUSEUMS AND GALLERIES:

BLACKBURN: *Landscape* - LIVERPOOL: *Rainy Weather* - LONDON (Tate Collection): *A Tidal River* (1877, oil on canvas) - SALFORD (Museum and AG): *Conway Marsh; A Welsh Grandmother*.

AUCTION RECORDS:

LONDON, 13 Feb 1991, *October Day* (1885, oil on canvas, 33 x 40 1/2 ins / 84 x 103 cm) GBP 2,750.

KNIGHT, Laura (Dame), also known as Orovida

Maiden name: Johnson

British, 19th - 20th century.

Born 4 August 1877, in Long Eaton; died 7 July 1970, in London.

Painter, watercolourist, engraver. Figure compositions, portraits, cartoon for stained glass windows, landscapes.

Laura Johnson was born in Derbyshire and brought up in Nottingham. She received informal instruction from her mother, an art teacher. She attended the Nottingham School of Art, where she met her future husband Harold Knight, and the Royal Academy, winning several awards. She travelled with Knight to Paris. They went together to the Staithes Artists Colony on the Yorkshire coast until 1910, also spending time in another community in Laren, in The Netherlands. They then moved to Cornwall, first to Newlyn and later to Lamorna. Her work at Staithes was influenced by the Hague School but after moving to Cornwall, where she created a scandal by painting scantily dressed models, she embraced Impressionism (*Daughters of the Sun*, 1910; *Flying a Kite*, 1910).

Although Laura Knight painted various subjects, her reputation was founded on paintings of the ballet and the circus, which became predominant after she moved to London after 1918. Technically of a high standard, her narrative realist works, painted in bright colours, occasionally lack depth of expression (*Ballet*, 1936; *Port Sunlight*). She painted backstage during the Diaghilev Ballet's seasons in London and took lessons at Tillers Dancing Academy in St Martin's Lane in order to draw there; she also travelled with the Mills and Carmos Circus. In the 1930s she started painting horses and gypsies at the races, as in *Gypsy* (1938-1939). An accomplished portrait painter, she painted wartime commissions and was the official artist at the Nuremberg war crime trials. Later in life she concentrated on landscapes.

She was also a talented engraver, etching in a mixed technique using aquatint, softground and line engraving as well as pure etching at dry point. Her earliest works in this field date from 1923. She engraved the Bohemian world, circus scenes, ballet and gypsies (*Some Clowns*, 1931; *Merry-Go-*

Round; At the Footlights). She also engraved the female figure (*Make up, Girl Bathing, Putting on Tights*), and landscapes (*Cornish Harbour*, 1927).

She wrote about art and published *Oil Paint and Grease Paint* (1936), *A Proper Circus Omie* (1962) and *The Magic of a Line* (1963). She was a member of the Royal Academy from 1936 and of the Royal Watercolour Society from 1928.

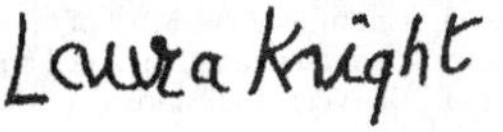

BIBLIOGRAPHY:

Phillips, D., *Dame Laura Knight*, exhibition catalogue, Castle Museum, Nottingham, 1970. Dunbar, J, *Laura Knight*, London, 1975. Fox, C., *Dame Laura Knight*, essay, Oxford, 1988. Bolling, F./Withington, V.E., *The Graphic Work of Laura Knight*, essay, Scholar Press, 1993 (includes catalogue raisonné of her drawings).

MUSEUMS AND GALLERIES:

BRIGHTON (Mus. & AG): study *The Ballet Shoe* (c. 1932, oil/panel) - CARDIFF (National Museum and Galleries of Wales): *The Cornish Coast; Motley* - LIVERPOOL (Walker AG): *Spring in St John's Wood* (1933, oil on canvas) - LONDON (Imperial War Mus.) - LONDON (National Portrait Gal.): *Ella Louise Napier* (1913, oil on canvas); *John Freeman* (1928, charcoal drawing) - LONDON (Tate Collection): *Spring* (1916-1920, oil on canvas); *The Gypsy* (exhibited in 1939, oil on canvas) - LONDON (Victoria and Albert Mus.).

AUCTION RECORDS:

PARIS, 7 April 1943, *The Dancer*, FRF 1,250. LONDON, 12 March 1947, *Letter*, GBP 80. LONDON, 12 July 1961, *Head of Hair*, GBP 320. LONDON, 15 July 1966, *Caravans*, Gns 520. LONDON, 29 Oct 1971, *Dancers*, Gns 1,000. LONDON, 5 March 1976, *Mother and Child by a Riverbank (recto); Young Woman, Head (verso)* (oil on canvas, 30 x 30 ins / 76.5 x 76.5 cm) GBP 700. LONDON, 12 Nov 1976, *Olympia Dwarfs* (1930, watercolour and black chalks, 13 1/2 x 11 ins / 34.5 x 27 cm) GBP 200. LONDON, 14 March 1979, *Under the Big Top* (oil on canvas, 34 1/4 x 42 3/4 ins / 87 x 108.5 cm) GBP 2,300. LONDON, 13 March 1981, *Circus Scene* (watercolour, pen and black chalk, 11 x 14 1/4 ins / 27 x 36 cm) GBP 850. LONDON, 12 March 1982, *Circus Scene* (1930, oil on canvas, 18 x 23 ins / 45.7 x 58.5 cm) GBP 5,000. LONDON, 25 May 1983, *The Fairground, Penzance* (oil on canvas, 54 x 73 3/4 ins / 137 x 187.5 cm) GBP 11,000. LONDON, 9 Nov 1984, *Untrodden Sand* (c. 1912, gouache and tempera, 22 x 23 3/4 ins / 56 x 60.3 cm) GBP 7,000. LONDON, 6 Feb 1985, *The Opera, Amsterdam* (1925, black chalk, pastel and wash, 13 1/2 x 10 ins / 34 x 25.5 cm) GBP 2,300. LONDON, 15 May 1985, *Wind and Sun* (1911, watercolour and gouache/pencil outlines/canvas, 38 x 44 ins / 96.5 x 112 cm) GBP 60,000. LONDON, 12 June 1986, *A Grey Day at Epsom* (oil on canvas, 24 1/2 x 30 ins / 62.5 x 76.2 cm) GBP 22,000. LONDON, 5 March 1987, *Sleeping Nude* (lead pencil, 23 x 15 1/4 ins / 57.5 x 38.6 cm) GBP 3,800. LONDON, 9 June 1988, *Looking at the Waves* (oil on canvas, 15 3/4 x 19 3/4 ins / 40 x 50 cm) GBP 11,000. EDINBURGH, 22 Nov 1988, *Gypsy Camp* (oil on panel, 20 x 14 ins / 50.8 x 35.5 cm) GBP 9,000. LONDON, 8 June 1989, *Malvern Hills* (oil on canvas, 24 1/4 x 35 1/2 ins / 61.6 x 90 cm) GBP 5,280; *Actors before the Curtain Raiser* (1924, watercolour and gouache, 13 3/4 x 11 ins / 35 x 27 cm) GBP 9,900. LONDON, 8 March 1990, *Portrait of Helen Ealand* (oil on canvas, 21 3/4 x 19 ins / 55.2 x 48.1 cm) GBP 10,120. LONDON, 7 June 1990, *The Nursery* (oil on canvas, 11 1/2 x 13 1/2 ins / 29 x 34 cm) GBP 12,100. LONDON, 20 Sept 1990, *Orchestra* (lead pencil, 14 3/4 x 11 ins / 37.5 x 27 cm) GBP 990. LONDON, 8 Nov 1990, *The Curtain Call* (1922, oil on canvas, 23 1/2 x 20 ins / 60 x 51 cm) GBP 7,920. LONDON, 25 Jan 1991, *Circus Scene* (charcoal/paper, 13 1/2 x 9 ins / 34.5 x 22 cm) GBP 825. LONDON, 6 June 1991, *Interior* (oil on canvas, 11 1/2 x 13 1/2 ins / 29 x 345 cm) GBP 14,850. LONDON, 6 March 1992, *May Pole* (oil on canvas, 30 x 40 1/4 ins / 76 x 102 cm) GBP 40,700. LONDON, 12 March 1992, *Bulldog* (pencil, ink and watercolour, 18 3/4 x 23 1/4 ins / 47.5 x 59 cm) GBP 4,025. GLASGOW, 23 Sept 1997, *Circus People* (charcoal, 10 1/2 x 13 3/4 ins / 26.4 x 34.9 cm) GBP 368. LONDON, 26 Nov 1999, *Studio Window* (c. 1935, oil on canvas, 40 x 50 ins / 101 x 127 cm) GBP 70,000. LONDON, 1 Dec 1999, *Marshmallows* (oil on canvas, 30 x 25 ins / 76 x 64 cm) GBP 300,000. LONDON, 14 June 2000, *Boys Bathing, Newlyn Quay* (1910, oil on canvas, 28 x 37 ins / 70 x 93 cm) GBP 75,000. LONDON, 21 June 2000, *Sennen Cove, Cornwall* (oil on canvas, 24 x 30 ins / 61 x 76 cm) GBP 46,000. CREWKERNE, 18 Oct 2001, *Industry* (oil on canvas, 24 x 20 ins / 60 x 50 cm) GBP 17,000. LONDON, 23 Nov 2001, *An O'gust and Two Lions* (oil on canvas, 20 x 18 ins / 51 x 46 cm) GBP 25,000. LONDON, 3 Dec 2002, *Looking in the Mirror* (watercolour over gouache and pencil, 22 x 15 ins / 56 x 38 cm) GBP 8,500. LONDON, 3 Dec 2002, *Before the Performance* (1960, charcoal and colour wash, 22 x 15 ins / 56 x 38 cm) GBP 8,800. LONDON, 4 June 2003, *On the Cliffs* (watercolour and gouache, 29 x 21 ins / 74 x 53 cm) GBP 80,000. LONDON, 21 July 2003, *Fantail Pigeons, Bees, Goat with Kids and Lifeguards* (pencil and charcoal, six, 10 x 14 ins / 25 x 35 cm) GBP 8,500. LONDON, 2 June 2004, *Sennen Cove* (oil on canvas, 20 x 24 ins / 51 x 61 cm) GBP 80,000. LONDON, 19 Nov 2004, *Ballerinas in the Dressing Room* (1957, oil on canvas, 24 x 20 ins / 61 x 50 cm) GBP 20,000.

KNIGHT, Louis Aston

American, 19th - 20th century.
Born 1873, in Paris; died 1948.
Active in France.
Painter. Landscapes.

Louis Aston Knight was the son of Daniel Ridgway Knight, under whom he studied. He also worked under Jules Lefebvre and Tony Robert-Fleury. He was a deft painter of landscapes, particularly adept at drawing the best effects from water which frequently featured in his paintings. He exhibited at the Paris Salons and also featured in the provinces. He obtained many awards including several gold medals in Paris, notably in 1900, at the Exposition universelle. He was made an Officier of the Légion d'Honneur in 1927. He also exhibited in the USA.

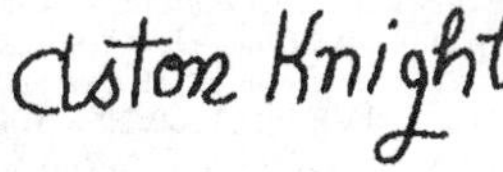

AUCTION RECORDS:

NEW YORK, 8 Feb 1907, *The Stream near the Old Church*, USD 200. PARIS, 15 May 1933, *The River*, FRF 1,020. PARIS, 28 March 1949, *The Riverside*, FRF 15,200. NEW YORK, 14 March 1968, *Young Woman in a Boat Fishing* (watercolour and gouache) USD 1,600. NEW YORK, 14 May 1969, *The End of Summer*, USD 1,700. NEW YORK, 10 June 1976, *Indian Neck, Connecticut* (oil on canvas, 32 x 46 ins / 81.5 x 117 cm) USD 1,200. NEW YORK, 14 Oct 1976, *Young Woman Angler in a Boat* (watercolour and gouache, 36 x 46 ins / 91.5 x 117 cm) USD 1,700. NEW YORK, 13 Oct 1978, *A Cottage in Hattonville* (oil on canvas, 25 3/4 x 33 ins / 65.5 x 84 cm) USD 2,700. LOS ANGELES, 15 Oct 1979, *The Blue Cottage* (oil on canvas, 25 1/2 x 32 ins / 64.7 x 81.3 cm) USD 2,200. NEW YORK, 19 June 1981, *The Poet's Hour* (oil on canvas, 25 3/4 x 32 ins / 65.4 x 81.3 cm) USD 5,750. NEW YORK, 23 June 1983, *Cottage on the Riverside* (oil on canvas, 25 3/4 x 32 ins / 65.4 x 81.3 cm) USD 7,500. NEW YORK, 21 May 1986, *Riversides in Blooms* (oil on canvas, 25 3/4 x 32 ins / 65.5 x 81 cm) USD 19,000. PARIS, 30 Oct 1987, *Cock Pheasant* (1908, watercolour and gouache, 25 1/2 x 32 ins / 65 x 81 cm) FRF 11,000. FONTAINEBLEAU, 28 Feb 1988, *Landscape near Barbizon* (1908, oil on canvas, 26 x 32 3/4 ins / 66 x 83 cm) FRF 20,000. LOS ANGELES, 9 June 1988, *Flowers on the Riverbank* (oil on canvas, 18 x 22 ins / 46 x 55 cm) USD

4,400; *Norman House* (oil on canvas, 18 x 21 1/2 ins / 45.7 x 54.5 cm) USD 7,150. PARIS, 23 June 1988, *Riverside in the Autumn* (oil on canvas, 39 1/4 x 65 3/4 ins / 100 x 167 cm) FRF 60,000. NEUILLY, 22 Nov 1988, *Meadow on the Riverside* (oil on canvas, 39 1/4 x 59 ins / 100 x 150 cm) FRF 25,000. NEW YORK, 24 May 1989, *Dog-rose by a Brook with a Country Church in the Background* (oil on canvas, 45 1/4 x 33 ins / 115 x 84 cm) USD 28,600. VERSAILLES, 24 Sept 1989, *The Cliff at Étretat* (1930, oil on canvas, 22 x 18 ins / 55 x 46 cm) FRF 9,500. NEW YORK, 25 Oct 1989, *Pink Hawthorn by a Norman River* (oil on canvas, 63 1/4 x 35 ins / 160.8 x 88.9 cm) USD 30,800. PARIS, 19 Jan 1990, *Garden in Paris*. NEW YORK, 1 March 1990, *River in France* (oil on canvas, 32 1/2 x 45 ins / 82.5 x 114.3 cm) USD 24,200. NEW YORK, 16 March 1990, *Trees in Flowers in Spring* (oil on canvas, 18 x 22 ins / 46 x 56 cm) USD 6,050. NEW YORK, 22 May 1990, *French River at Dusk* (oil on canvas, 26 x 32 ins / 66 x 81.3 cm) USD 9,350. NEW YORK, 23 May 1990, *Light Effects on the Rio Sant'Aponal in Venice* (oil on canvas, 32 x 25 3/4 ins / 81 x 65.5 cm) USD 20,900. NEW YORK, 14 March 1991, *In the Valley* (oil on canvas, 25 1/2 x 31 3/4 ins / 65 x 80.5 cm) USD 9,350. NEW YORK, 15 May 1991, *On the Riverside* (oil on canvas, 25 3/4 x 32 ins / 65.4 x 81.3 cm) USD 12,100. NEW YORK, 21 May 1991, *Dusk on the River at Thibouville* (oil on canvas, 22 x 18 1/4 ins / 55.9 x 46.4 cm) USD 8,800. NEW YORK, 23 May 1991, *House on the Riverside in France* (oil on canvas, 32 x 26 ins / 81.3 x 66 cm) USD 14,300. NEW YORK, 25 Sept 1992, *Tree in Blooms on a River Bank* (oil on canvas, 21 1/2 x 18 1/4 ins / 54.6 x 46.4 cm) USD 4,125. NEW YORK, 29 Oct 1992, *Meandering Stream at Sunset* (oil on canvas, 32 x 25 1/2 ins / 81.3 x 64.7 cm) USD 9,350. NEW YORK, 27 May 1993, *The Seine near Paris* (oil on canvas, 32 3/4 x 45 3/4 ins / 83.2 x 116.2 cm) USD 9,200. PARIS, 5 Nov 1993, *Diane Cottage: Beaumont-le-Roger (Eure)* (oil on canvas, 18 x 22 ins / 46 x 55 cm) FRF 25,500. NEW YORK, 15 Feb 1994, *Flower-hemmed Path alongside a River* (oil on canvas, 35 1/4 x 45 3/4 ins / 89.5 x 116.2 cm) USD 18,400. PARIS, 23 March 1994, *The Old Mill* (pastel, 22 x 18 ins / 56 x 46 cm) FRF 5,000. PARIS, 5 Nov 1994, *Sailing Boats at Sea* (oil on canvas, 31 1/2 x 23 1/2 ins / 80 x 60 cm) FRF 10,000. LONDON, 11 Oct 1995, *Water Lilies on a Pond* (oil on canvas, 25 1/4 x 31 1/2 ins / 64 x 80 cm) GBP 1,955. NEW YORK, 14 March 1996, *Blue Cottage* (oil on canvas, 25 3/4 x 32 ins / 65.4 x 81.3 cm) USD 35,650. PARIS, 29 Nov 1996, *River Bank* (oil on canvas, 23 1/2 x 31 1/2 ins / 60 x 80 cm) FRF 30,000. NEW YORK, 26 Feb 1997, *Cottage by a Steady River* (oil on panel, a pair, 13 3/4 x 10 1/2 ins / 35 x 26.6 cm and plus) USD 3,680. NEW YORK, 23 April 1997, *East Canaan, Connecticut* (oil on canvas, 21 3/4 x 18 1/4 ins / 55.3 x 46.3 cm) USD 10,350. NEW YORK, 6 May 1999, *The Water Gatherer* (oil on canvas, 48 x 37 ins / 121 x 93 cm) USD 90,000. NEW YORK, 1 Dec 1999, *Sunny Morning at Beaumont-Le-Roger* (oil on canvas, 26 x 32 ins / 65 x 81 cm) USD 47,500. NEW YORK, 18 Oct 2000, *Cottage in Spring, Normandy* (oil on canvas, 26 x 32 ins / 66 x 81 cm) USD 45,000. NEW YORK, 30 Nov 2000, *Flower Garden* (c. 1901, oil on canvas, 26 x 32 ins / 65 x 81 cm) USD 47,500. NEW YORK, 22 May 2001, *Cottage and Garden* (oil on canvas, 18 x 22 ins / 46 x 55 cm) USD 18,000. NEW YORK, 3 Oct 2001, *Skyscraper, New York* (oil on canvas, 32 x 26 ins / 81 x 65 cm) USD 22,000. NEW YORK, 13 Feb 2002, *Path Along the River* (oil on canvas, 26 x 61 ins / 66 x 154 cm) USD 22,000. NEW YORK, 29 Oct 2002, *View of a Château* (oil on canvas, 26 x 33 ins / 67 x 83 cm) USD 29,000. NEW YORK, 21 May 2003, *Summer Garden* (oil on canvas, 35 x 46 ins / 89 x 117 cm) USD 20,000. NEW YORK, 3 Dec 2003, *Above the Mill* (oil on canvas, 26 x 32 ins / 65 x 81 cm) USD 30,000. NEW YORK, 11 March 2004, *On the River* (c. 1920-1930, oil on canvas, 26 x 32 ins / 65 x 81 cm) USD 15,000. NEW YORK, 11 March 2004, *View of Rouen* (c. 1920-1930, oil on canvas, 26 x 32 ins / 65 x 81 cm) USD 19,000.

KNIGHT, Mary Ann
British, 19th century.
Born 7 September 1776, in London; died 1851, in St John's Wood (London).
Miniaturist, draughtswoman.

Mary Ann Knight enjoyed a considerable reputation in her own time as a painter of children. When she was 26 years old, her parents suffered financial problems and she turned to art so as to be able to help them. A pupil of Andrew Plimer, who would later become her brother-in-law, she lost no time in receiving commissions. Most of her work consisted of small portraits which she did in pencil and highlighted with water colour. Between 1807 and 1836, she often exhibited at the Royal Academy.

AUCTION RECORDS:
LONDON, 3 July 1946, *Volume of Portraits* (watercolour) GBP 42.

KNIGHT, Robbert
Dutch, 17th century.
Active in Dordrecht.
Painter.

Robbert Knight may originally have come from England.

KNIGHT, T.
British, 19th century.
Engraver.

T. Knight is mentioned for his portraits. He may be the same person as T.W. Knight.

KNIGHT, T. W.
British, 19th century.
Engraver.

T.W. Knight reproduced drawings for various magazines.

KNIGHT, W.G.
British, 20th century.
Painter.

W.G. Knight was a member of the Royal Institute of Oil Painters.

KNIGHT, Warren
American, 20th century.
Born 23 February 1941, in Minneapolis (Minnesota).
Painter, sculptor, engraver.

Warren Knight has exhibited in the USA, Australia, Canada and Italy. His work is characterised by its use of written script, sometimes modified or 'deformed'.

AUCTION RECORDS:
MILAN, 5 Dec 1974, *From a Secretary...*, ITL 3,000,000.

KNIGHT, William George
British, 19th century.
Active in Chelmsford.
Painter. Portraits, landscapes.

William George Knight exhibited at the Suffolk Street Gallery from 1829 to 1846. Some portraits are also known to have been painted by him.

KNIGHT, William Henry
British, 19th century.
Born 26 September 1823, in Newburg; died 31 July 1863, in London.
Painter. Portraits, genre scenes.

William Henry Knight had planned on following a career in law while painting as an amateur. However, after two of his paintings had been accepted for an exhibition held by the Society of British Artists in the Suffolk Street Gallery, he turned wholeheartedly to a life in art, initially as a portrait painter. He went to London in 1845 to train. His genre scenes are very amusing and often include depictions of children. His work was exhibited at the Royal Academy, the British Institution and at the Suffolk Street Gallery from 1844 to 1864.

Auction records:
London, 30 Nov 1907, *Child Playing,* GBP 10; *District Visitor,* GBP 11. London, 5 March 1910, *Village School,* GBP 21. London, 24 Sept 1943, *Village School,* GBP 68. London, 10 July 1970, *Charge of the Cavalry,* Gns 260. London, 21 Nov 1972, *Children in an Interior,* GBP 740. London, 27 March 1973, *Musical Part,* GBP 2,500. London, 21 July 1978, *Weighted Scales* (1858, oil on panel, 8 x 16 ins / 20.2 x 40.6 cm) GBP 2,400. London, 25 May 1979, *Counterfeit Coin* (1862, oil on panel, 11 3/4 x 15 3/4 ins / 29.8 x 40 cm) GBP 4,800. London, 5 June 1981, *Game of Draughts* (1846, oil on panel, 16 1/2 x 21 1/2 ins / 42 x 54.6 cm) GBP 5,500. London, 21 June 1983, *Snowball Fight* (1853, oil on panel, 20 x 24 ins / 51 x 61 cm) GBP 9,500. London, 9 July 1985, *Who Threw the Stone?* (1855, oil on canvas, 18 1/2 x 13 ins / 47 x 33 cm) GBP 4,000. London, 25 March 1988, *Evening Game of Draughts* (1846, oil on canvas, 17 x 22 ins / 43.2 x 55.9 cm) GBP 7,700. London, 23 Sept 1988, *Playmates* (1862, oil on panel, 11 3/4 x 14 ins / 30 x 35.5 cm) GBP 6,380. New York, 23 Feb 1989, *Hunter on Horseback Surrounded by his Hounds* (1850, oil on canvas, 30 x 25 ins / 76.2 x 63.2 cm) USD 13,200. London, 3 June 1994, *Letter* (1854, oil on panel, 8 3/4 x 6 1/4 ins / 22.3 x 15.8 cm) GBP 2,530. Paris, 30 May 1999, *Young Mother and her Children on the Seashore* (oil on canvas, 31 x 43 ins / 79 x 109 cm) FRF 49,000. London, 30 Nov 1999, *On the Thames, Staines* (oil on panel, 8 x 20 ins / 20 x 51 cm) GBP 8,500. London, 6 June 2001, *Last Change* (oil on panel, 21 x 30 ins / 54 x 76 cm) GBP 50,000. London, 18 Sept 2001, *Maiden* (1851, oil on panel, 22 x 18 ins / 57 x 45 cm) GBP 3,000. San Francisco, 15 May 2002, *Huntsman with his Greyhounds* (1850, oil on canvas, 30 x 25 ins / 76 x 63 cm) USD 6,500. London, 2 Dec 2002, *Peace Versus War, a Troublesome Neighbour* (1862, oil on panel, 10 x 12 ins / 25 x 30 cm) GBP 7,000. Salisbury, 26 March 2003, *Stacking the Bricks* (1860, oil on panel, 8 x 14 ins / 21 x 36 cm) GBP 1,500. London, 23 Nov 2004, *Rivals to Blondin* (1862, oil on board, 19 x 24 ins / 47 x 61 cm) GBP 17,000.

KNIGHT-LAWRENCE, Gwendolyn
Maiden name: Knight
Barbadian, 20th century.
Born 20 April 1913, in Barbados.
Active in the USA.
Painter, engraver, sculptor. Figures, nudes, portraits, animals, still-lifes.

Gwendolyn Knight-Lawrence's family lived in St Louis, then in New York in the 1920s. She studied at Howard University, Washington DC, at the New College of Social Research, and at Skowhegan School of Painting and Sculpture, Skowhegan (Maine). In the 1930s, she worked at the studio led by Augusta Savage as part of the Work Progress Administration, the government programme put in place at the time of the New Deal. She married the painter Jacob Lawrence in 1941. She settled in Seattle. She received honorary doctorates from the Universities of Seattle (Washington State) and Minnesota, at the Twin Cities. She is essentially interested in movement and dance, and her style of painting is clean and uncluttered with strong and contrasting colours.

Her work has been shown at group exhibitions, including in 2003, *Legends,* Center for the Arts of the African Diaspora, Los Angeles. She has also had solo exhibitions, including in 2001, retrospective 1941-1999, Black Mountain College & Arts Center, Ashville (North Carolina) and 2003, Tacoma Art Museum, Tacoma (Washington State).

Bibliography:
Lewis, Samella/Waddy, Ruth G., *Black Artists on Art vol. II,* Contemporary Crafts, Los Angeles, 1969. *Gwendolyn Knight paintings,* exhibition catalogue, Virginia Lacy Jones Gall., Robert W. Woodruff Library, Atlanta University Center, Atlanta, 1988. Conkelton, Sheryl/Earl Thomas, Barbara, *Never late for heaven: the art of Gwen Knight,* exhibition catalogue, University of Washington Press, Seattle, Tacoma Art Museum, Tacoma (WA), 2003.

Museums and Galleries:
Hampton (Hampton University Mus.) - New York (MoMA) - St Louis (AM).

KNIGHTON, Dorothea
Maiden name: Hawker
British, 19th century.
Born 1781, in Plymouth.
Painter. Portraits, genre scenes, landscapes.

KNIGHTS, Winifred Margaret
British, 20th century.
Born 5 June 1899, in London; died 7 February 1947, in London.
Painter, designer. Religious subjects, historical figures, landscapes.

Winifred Margaret Knights worked chiefly as a decorative painter. She became a member of the New English Art Club in 1933. Her works include *The Wedding Feast at Cana* and *St Martin Dividing his Cloak,* painted around 1930 for a chapel in Canterbury Cathedral.

Museums and Galleries:
London (Tate Collection): *Italian Landscape* (1921, oil/wood) - Wellington (Mus. of New Zealand Te Papa Tongarewa): *Wedding Feast at Cana.*

Auction records:
London, 14 Oct 1987, *Cartoon for 'The Deluge'* (pencil on paper mounted on canvas, 59 3/4 x 70 3/4 ins / 152 x 180 cm) GBP 2,400. London, 9 June 1988, *The Deluge* (oil on canvas, 59 x 70 3/4 ins / 150 x 180 cm) GBP 13,200.

KNIJF, Wouter. See **KNYFF Wouter**

KNIKKER, Aris
Dutch, 20th century.
Born 1887, in Haarlem; died 1962, in The Hague.
Painter. Scenes with figures, local scenes, landscapes, animals.

Aris Knikker studied at the Koninklijke Academie van Beeldende Kunsten in The Hague.

Auction records:
Amsterdam, 10 Feb 1988, *Milking Time* (oil on canvas, 26 1/2 x 39 3/4 ins / 67 x 101 cm) NLG 2,760. Paris, 7 March 1988, *Draught-horses* (oil on canvas, 16 1/4 x 11 3/4 ins / 41 x 30 cm) FRF 5,500. Amsterdam, 28 Feb 1989, *Polder Landscape at Dawn with Moored Boat* (oil on canvas, 12 x 15 3/4 ins / 30.5 x 40 cm) NLG 1,092. Amsterdam, 23 April 1991, *Farmer's Wife in Boat* (oil on canvas, 23 x 38 3/4 ins / 58.5 x 98.5 cm) NLG 2,070. Amsterdam, 17 Sept 1991, *Town on River's Edge with Belfry in Distance* (oil on canvas, 24 x 35 1/2 ins / 61 x 90 cm) NLG 4,370. Amsterdam, 18 Feb 1992, *Peasant in Boat near Windmill with Belfry in Background* (oil on canvas, 11 3/4 x 15 3/4 ins / 30 x 40 cm) NLG 1,265. Amsterdam, 11 Feb 1993, *Cattle Drinking in Sunny Meadow* (oil on canvas, 16 1/4 x 24 1/4 ins / 41.5 x 61.5 cm) NLG 2,530. Amsterdam, 2 Sept 1997, *Polder Landscape* (oil on canvas, 9 x 14 1/4 ins / 23 x 36.5 cm) NLG 922. Amsterdam, 1 Sept 1999, *Still-life with Roses* (oil on canvas, 16 x 31 ins / 40 x 80 cm) NLG 4,000. Penzance, 16 Dec 1999, *Barges on Estuary* (oil on canvas, 9 x 14 ins / 22 x 35 cm) GBP 1,050. Amsterdam, 19 April 2000, *Bullfield* (oil on panel, 9 x 14 ins / 23 x 35 cm) NLG 5,000. Amsterdam, 19 April 2000, *Moorland with Cottage* (oil on canvas, 11 x 19 ins / 29 x 49 cm) NLG 9,000. The Hague, 25 April 2001, *Angler by a Pond* (oil on canvas, 9 x 17 ins / 24 x 44 cm) NLG 3,600. Amsterdam, 19 June 2001, *Drawbridge on a Village Canal* (oil on canvas, 16 x 24 ins / 40 x 60 cm) NLG 3,800. Amsterdam, 4 March 2002, *Busy Street Scene, Rotterdam* (oil on canvas, 12 x 20 ins / 30 x 50 cm) EUR 1,900. The Hague, 5 Nov 2003, *Farmer in Rowing Boat* (oil on canvas, 31 x 23 ins / 78 x 58 cm) EUR 1,500.

KNIKKER, Jan, or Jan Knikker Senior
Dutch, 20th century.
Born 1889; died 1957.
Painter. Landscapes, waterscapes, urban landscapes, landscapes with figures.

AUCTION RECORDS:

AMSTERDAM, 15 May 1984, *Paris in Winter* (oil on canvas, 23 1/4 x 31 ins / 59.2 x 79 cm) NLG 6,200. AMSTERDAM, 10 Feb 1988, *Boats on River near Village* (oil on canvas, 22 x 35 1/4 ins / 55 x 89.5 cm) NLG 1,380. LONDON, 21 Oct 1988, *Street Scene, Paris* (oil on panel, 9 1/4 x 14 1/4 ins / 23.4 x 36.2 cm) GBP 605. AMSTERDAM, 16 Nov 1988, *View of Dordrecht with the Cathedral near the Merwede* (oil on canvas, 19 3/4 x 27 1/2 ins / 50 x 70 cm) NLG 1,495. AMSTERDAM, 23 April 1991, *Ducks at Water's Edge* (oil on canvas, 31 x 23 1/4 ins / 79 x 59 cm) NLG 1,265. LOKEREN, 10 Oct 1992, *Dutch River Landscape with Boats* (oil on canvas, 12 x 15 3/4 ins / 30.5 x 40 cm) BEF 55,000. LOKEREN, 15 May 1993, *Mill on Heath* (oil on canvas, 18 1/2 x 30 ins / 47 x 76 cm) BEF 26,000. LOKEREN, 9 Oct 1993, *Village under Snow* (oil on canvas, 15 3/4 x 31 1/2 ins / 40 x 80 cm) BEF 33,000. AMSTERDAM, 9 Nov 1993, *View of Kortenhoef* (oil on canvas, 11 1/2 x 16 1/4 ins / 29.5 x 41.5 cm) NLG 1,495. NEW YORK, 17 Feb 1994, *Windmills at edge of Canal* (oil on canvas, 19 3/4 x 31 1/2 ins / 50 x 80 cm) USD 920. LOKEREN, 12 March 1994, *Village under Snow* (oil on canvas, 15 3/4 x 31 1/2 ins / 40 x 80 cm) BEF 36,000. AMSTERDAM, 19 April 2000, *Fisherman in a Boat on a River* (oil on canvas, 31 x 40 ins / 80 x 101 cm) NLG 11,000. AMSTERDAM, 19 June 2000, *Musicians on a Terrace in Southern Europe* (oil on canvas, 11 x 9 ins / 29 x 24 cm) NLG 3,600. AMSTERDAM, 3 Feb 2004, *Panoramic Landscape with Cows along a River* (oil on canvas, 24 x 39 ins / 60 x 100 cm) EUR 2,200. THE HAGUE, 3 Nov 2004, *Farm by the Water at Giethoorn* (oil on canvas, 31 x 46 ins / 80 x 118 cm) EUR 1,700.

KNIKKER, Jan, or usually referred to as Jan Knikker Junior
Dutch, 20th century.
Born 1911; died 1989 or 1990.
Painter. Landscapes, waterscapes, urban landscapes, landscapes with figures, flowers.

Jan Knikker Jnr was undoubtedly related to the Jan Knikker Snr.

AUCTION RECORDS:

AMSTERDAM, 11 Sept 1990, *Spring Landscape with Farm and Blossoming Trees along River* (oil on canvas, 9 1/2 x 11 3/4 ins / 24 x 30 cm) NLG 1,150. AMSTERDAM, 24 April 1991, *Bunch of Dahlias in Terracotta Vase* (oil on canvas, 35 1/2 x 27 1/2 ins / 90 x 70 cm) NLG 2,530. AMSTERDAM, 5-6 Nov 1991, *The Montelbaanstoren in Amsterdam* (oil on canvas, 19 x 27 1/4 ins / 48.5 x 69 cm) NLG 1,955. AMSTERDAM, 18 Feb 1992, *Town on the Edge of a Canal with Moored Sailing Boats* (oil on canvas, 19 3/4 x 27 1/2 ins / 50 x 70 cm) NLG 1,610. AMSTERDAM, 22 April 1992, *View of the Singel in Amsterdam with the Flower Market and Munttower* (oil on canvas, 20 x 16 ins / 50.5 x 40.5 cm) NLG 1,840. AMSTERDAM, 14 Sept 1993, *Reed-cutters at Sunset* (oil on canvas, 10 x 18 ins / 25.5 x 45.5 cm) NLG 1,725. AMSTERDAM, 19-20 Feb 1997, *Flower Market along the Singel, Amsterdam* (oil on canvas, 15 3/4 x 23 1/2 ins / 40 x 60 cm) NLG 2,537. THE HAGUE, 2 Nov 1999, *Small Bridge over Water, Giethoorn* (oil on canvas, 19 x 27 ins / 48 x 68 cm) NLG 4,000. AMSTERDAM, 19 April 2000, *View of Amsterdam with St Nicolaas Church* (oil on canvas, 20 x 28 ins / 50 x 70 cm) NLG 4,000. ROTTERDAM, 5 May 2001, *View of the Small Port of Leerdam* (oil on canvas, 15 x 31 ins / 39 x 79 cm) NLG 3,800. THE HAGUE, 7 Nov 2001, *Village near Ditch, in Winter* (oil on canvas, 15 x 19 ins / 39 x 49 cm) NLG 6,000. AMSTERDAM, 25 June 2002, *By the Waterside* (oil on canvas, 16 x 24 ins / 40 x 60 cm) EUR 1,600. ROTTERDAM, 6 May 2003, *River Scene near a Town with Many Ships and Figures* (oil on canvas, 23 x 31 ins / 59 x 79 cm) EUR 1,700. AMSTERDAM, 1 July 2003, *River Landscape in Summer* (oil on canvas, 20 x 28 ins / 50 x 71 cm) EUR 1,600. AMSTERDAM, 17 March 2004, *Flower Market in Amsterdam* (oil on canvas, 20 x 28 ins / 51 x 70 cm) EUR 2,000.

KNILLE, Otto
German, 19th century.
Born 10 September 1832, in Osnabrück; died 8 April 1898, in Untermais.
Painter. History painting, genre scenes.

Knille studied with K. Sohn, Th Hildebrandt and W. von Schadow in Düsseldorf and with Couture in Paris. He worked in Munich and Italy, then in 1865 he settled in Berlin, where he painted a large number of decorative works, notably for the University Library. He exhibited in Paris at the 1878 Exposition Universelle. He won medals in Berlin in 1876 and 1881, and the gold medal at the 1881 Berlin academy Exhibition.

MUSEUMS AND GALLERIES:

HANOVER: *The Death of El Cid; Fra Angelico.*

AUCTION RECORDS:

LONDON, 15 Feb 1978, *The Captive Duke* (1852, oil on canvas, 48 x 61 ins / 121 x 154 cm) GBP 1,450. HELSINKI, 11 Dec 1999, *Aristocrats Captured in the German Peasant War* (1853, oil on canvas, 13 x 19 ins / 32 x 47 cm) FIM 29,000.

KNILLER. See **KNELLER**

KNILLING, Joseph
German, 19th century.
Born 1 February 1851, in Munich.
Painter. Genre scenes.

MUSEUMS AND GALLERIES:

GÖTEBORG (Konstmus.): *Card Players.*

KNILLING, Nikolaus
German, 19th century.
Born 28 March 1825, in Mittenwald.
Draughtsman, engraver.

Nikolaus Knilling was the father of Joseph. In 1840, he settled in Munich, where he became an engraver.

KNIP, August
Dutch, 19th century.
Born 11 February 1819, in Amsterdam; died 1852.
Painter. Landscapes, animals.

August Knip was a pupil of August Joseph Knip.

AUCTION RECORDS:

PARIS, 1 June 1931, *The Two Dogs*, FRF 1,360. AMSTERDAM, 28 Oct 1980, *Mountain Landscape* (1843, oil on canvas, 30 1/4 x 41 ins / 77 x 104.3 cm) NLG 21,000. COLOGNE, 25 June 1987, *The Duck Pond* (oil on canvas, 20 x 26 1/2 ins / 51 x 67 cm) DEM 9,500. PARIS, 13 April 1988, *The Two Dogs* (oil on canvas, 14 1/2 x 12 1/4 ins / 37 x 31 cm) FRF 8,000. AMSTERDAM, 16 Nov 1988, *Stag, Doe and Buck on a Promontory above a Valley* (1857, oil on canvas, 19 3/4 x 15 3/4 ins / 50 x 40 cm) NLG 4,025. AMSTERDAM, 25 April 1990, *Landscape with Shepherd and Flock* (1834, oil on canvas, 21 1/4 x 28 1/4 ins / 54 x 72 cm) NLG 5,750. NEW YORK, 7 June 1991, *The Day's Hunt* (oil on canvas, 29 1/2 x 22 3/4 ins / 74.9 x 57.8 cm) USD 1,375. MUNICH, 10 March 1999, *Shepherd with Flock Returning Home* (oil on canvas, 30 x 41 ins / 76 x 105 cm) DEM 7,500. LONDON, 14 Oct 1999, *Deer in a Woodland Clearing* (oil on board, oval, a pair, 21 x 18 ins / 53 x 46 cm) GBP 2,200. COLOGNE, 6 April 2000, *Three Dogs on a Pillow* (1838, oil on canvas, 30 x 23 ins / 77 x 59 cm) DEM 10,000. AMSTERDAM, 4 July 2000, *Summer Landscape with Livestock in a Meadow* (1856, oil on canvas, 24 x 31 ins / 60 x 78 cm) NLG 6,000. AMSTERDAM, 23 April 2001, *Mountainous Landscape with Shepherd and Flock* (1840, oil on canvas, 31 x 45 ins / 80 x 114 cm) NLG 28,000. MUNICH, 26 Sept 2001, *Heron and Ducks in Water* (oil on canvas, 8 x 6 ins

/ 21 x 16 cm) DEM 5,500. LINDAU, 9 Oct 2003, *Poultry Yard* (oil on canvas, oval, 20 x 17 ins / 50 x 42 cm) EUR 1,800.

KNIP, August Joseph

Dutch, 18th - 19th century.

Born 3 August 1777, in Tilburg; died 1 October 1847, in Berlicum, near 's Hertogenbosch.

Painter (gouache), watercolourist, draughtsman. Landscapes.

August Joseph Knip studied under his father, Nicolaas Frederik Knip the Elder. He exhibited at the Paris Salon from 1808 and lived in Paris from 1819 to 1826. Knip returned to Holland in 1827 after visiting Italy, a trip that was to have a decisive influence on his art. He lost his sight in 1832. An exhibition of Knip's works at 's Hertogenbosch in 1978 provided an opportunity to rediscover the artist. His landscapes display simplicity of form, precision in the style of drawing and delicacy in the use of colour.

In 2001 his work was featured in the exhibition *Un Paese Incantato. Italia Dipinta da Thomas Jones a Corot* (*An Enchanted Country. Italy Depicted by Artists from Thomas Jones to Corot*) held at the Centro Internazionale d'Arte e di Cultura di Palazzo del Tè in Mantua.

BIBLIOGRAPHY:

Bergvelt, Ellinoor/Van Boven, Margriet, *Joseph Augustus Knip, 1777-1847*, exhibition catalogue, Noorbrabants museum, 's-Hertogenbosch, Staatsuitgeverij, 's Gravenhage, 1977. Kuyvenhoven, Fransje, *De familie Knip: 3 generaties kunstenaars uit Noord-Brabant*, Waanders, Zwolle, 1988. Ottani Cavina, Anna (ed.), *Un Paese incantato. Italia dipinta da Thomas Jones a Corot*, exhibition catalogue, Electa, Milan, 2001.

MUSEUMS AND GALLERIES:

AMSTERDAM (Historisch Mus.): *View of Tivoli* (pencil, watercolour); *View of Terni* (pencil, watercolour) - AMSTERDAM (Rijksmus.): *View of the Coliseum* (pencil, watercolour/paper); *Landscape near Subiaco* (pencil, watercolour) - DOUAI: *Grotto at Caesar's Palace* - HAMBURG (Kunsthalle): *Lake Albano with the Palazzolo* (oil on paper/card) - ROTTERDAM: *Italian Landscape*.

AUCTION RECORDS:

VIENNA, 14 June 1977, *Landscape with Shepherd Resting* (oil on canvas, 17 3/4 x 21 1/4 ins / 45 x 54 cm) ATS 28,000. BERN, 3 May 1979, *View of Mont Blanc* (1833, gouache, 20 x 29 1/4 ins / 51 x 74 cm) CHF 5,000. COLOGNE, 11 June 1979, *Hunting Dog* (oil on panel, 11 1/2 x 14 1/2 ins / 29.5 x 37 cm) DEM 2,300. AMSTERDAM, 29 Oct 1979, *River Landscape* (colour wash/black chalk, 14 x 19 1/2 ins / 35.7 x 49.5 cm) NLG 4,000. AMSTERDAM, 19 May 1981, *View of the Ruins of Paestum* (1832, oil on canvas, 30 3/4 x 44 1/2 ins / 78 x 113 cm) NLG 16,500. LONDON, 21 June 1984, *Sailors Drinking by the Waterside* (gouache, 24 x 18 ins / 61 x 45.5 cm) GBP 2,000. LONDON, 22 March 1985, *Village of Fluelen, Uri Canton* (gouache, 11 1/4 x 17 ins / 28.5 x 43.2 cm) GBP 1900. LONDON, 17 March 1989, *View of Lake Geneva with the City in the Background* (watercolour and gouache, 19 x 28 3/4 ins / 48.5 x 73 cm) GBP 3,520. AMSTERDAM, 10 April 1990, *Ruins of a Roman Mausoleum near Paestum with the Gulf of Salerno in the Background* (gouache/paper, 19 3/4 x 29 1/4 ins / 50 x 74 cm) NLG 8,625. NEW YORK, 13 Jan 1993, *Landscape in North Italy with an Arched Bridge and Mountains in the Background* (gouache, 9 3/4 x 14 1/4 ins / 25 x 36.5 cm) USD 1,380. AMSTERDAM, 21 April 1993, *Undulating Landscape with a Village by a River and Peasants on a Road* (1822, oil on canvas, 29 1/4 x 37 1/2 ins / 74 x 95 cm) NLG 10,925. PARIS, 30 June 1993, *Italian Landscape with Ruins and a Shepherd Guarding his Flock* (gouache, 18 x 26 1/2 ins / 46 x 67 cm) FRF 20,000. AMSTERDAM, 17 Nov 1994, *View of Lake Albano with Castel Gandolfo in the Distance and a Fountain in the Foreground; View of the Sabine Mountains near Terni* (1816, oil on panel, a pair, each 23 1/2 x 19 ins / 59.8 x 48.1 cm) NLG 103,500. AMSTERDAM, 15 Nov 1995, *Travellers Praying by a Chapel Overlooking the Meuse near Namen* (ink and watercolour, 19 3/4 x 30 1/4 ins / 50.2 x 76.9 cm) NLG 9,440. AMSTERDAM, 7 May 1996, *Italian Landscape with Peasants Stopping on a Hillock Overlooking a River with a Muleteer Crossing a Ford* (1819, oil on canvas, 23 1/2 x 29 ins / 59.6 x 73.6 cm) NLG 12,650. AMSTERDAM, 12 Nov 1996, *Undulating Landscape with Waterfall*. VIENNA, 29-30 Oct 1997, *Summer Landscape with Cows* (1827, oil on canvas, 30 1/2 x 42 1/4 ins / 77.5 x 107 cm) ATS 109,250. AMSTERDAM, 11 Nov 1997, *Port Scene* (gouache, 12 1/2 x 29 1/2 ins / 31.5 x 75 cm) NLG 10,856. GRAVENHAGE, 2 Nov 1999, *Woman Resting in an Italianate Landscape* (oil on canvas, 23 x 30 ins / 58 x 75 cm) NLG 5,600. AMSTERDAM, 9 Nov 1999, *Landscape with Cottage by Pond* (gouache, 15 x 23 ins / 38 x 58 cm) NLG 7,000. NEW YORK, 24 Jan 2001, *Extensive Mountain Landscape with Town atop a Hill* (watercolour and bodycolour, oval, 15 x 19 ins / 38 x 48 cm) USD 16,000. BRUSSELS, 13 March 2001, *Busy Landscape* (1800, gouache, 19 x 25 ins / 48 x 63 cm) BEF 115,000. NEW YORK, 25 Jan 2002, *Temple of Minerva Medica, Rome* (watercolour over black chalk, pen and ink, 14 x 19 ins / 35 x 49 cm) USD 10,000. AMSTERDAM, 23 Oct 2002, *Flock of Sheep in a Stable* (1827, oil on canvas, 22 x 29 ins / 55 x 73 cm) EUR 7,000. AMSTERDAM, 2 Sept 2003, *Oxen Resting by the Lakeside, Italy* (1815, oil on canvas, 22 x 25 ins / 57 x 63 cm) EUR 3,800. AMSTERDAM, 5 Nov 2003, *Ruined Chapel with a Pigsty, Poultry and Peacock* (black chalk and bodycolour, 20 x 25 ins / 52 x 63 cm) EUR 7,000. AMSTERDAM, 19 May 2004, *Basilica of Constantine and Maxentius, Rome* (pen, grey ink, watercolour and black chalk, 14 x 20 ins / 35 x 51 cm) EUR 55,000. AMSTERDAM, 19 May 2004, *Temple of Minerva Medica, Rome* (watercolour, black pencil and black chalk, 17 x 23 ins / 44 x 59 cm) EUR 110,000.

KNIP, Henri or Hendrick Johannes

Dutch, 19th century.

Born 20 April 1819, in 's Hertogenbosch; died after 1897.

Painter (gouache). Still-lifes, landscapes, landscapes with figures, mountainscapes.

Hendrik Knip studied under his father, Marten Derk Knip. He worked in Brussels in 1858.

AUCTION RECORDS:

HAMBURG, 7 June 1984, *Landscape near Interlaken* (watercolour and gouache, 12 x 17 ins / 30.5 x 42.9 cm) DEM 3,400. LUCERNE, 7 Nov 1985, *Carriage in Undergrowth* (oil on canvas, 22 x 29 1/2 ins / 55 x 75 cm) CHF 5,000. AMSTERDAM, 30 Oct 1990, *Gemert Castle, East and West Façades* (1872, watercolour and gouache/paper, a pair, 28 1/4 x 37 ins / 72 x 94 cm) NLG 7,475. NEW YORK, 13 Jan 1993, *Swiss Landscape with a Chalet and a Bridge and Snow-Covered Mountains in the Background* (gouache, 19 1/2 x 28 1/2 ins / 49.5 x 72.5 cm) USD 2,588. AMSTERDAM, 21 April 1993, *Children Playing outside a Chalet by a Pond near Lucerne* (gouache/paper); *Steamer on the Vierwalstädtersee with the Castle of the Habsburgs*, NLG 4,025. AMSTERDAM, 19 April 1994, *View of a Lake with Elegant Figures on a Jetty* (gouache, 19 3/4 x 28 1/4 ins / 50 x 72 cm) NLG 5,750. LONDON, 4 July 1994, *View of an Italian Lake* (ink, watercolour and gouache, 13 1/2 x 19 3/4 ins / 34 x 50 cm) GBP 3,105. LONDON, 17 April 1996, *Still-life with Flowers* (1902, watercolour, 11 3/4 x 10 ins / 30 x 24.5 cm) GBP 1,380. BERLIN, 26 May 2000, *Rhine Landscape near Kaub with Pfalzgrafenstein with Gutenfels Schloss* (watercolour and bodycolour, 14 x 20 ins / 35 x 51 cm) DEM 4,500. NEW YORK, 25 Jan 2002, *View of Pont de Saint Maurice, Canton Vaud, Switzerland* (gouache, 12 x 17 ins / 31 x 44 cm) USD 7,000. COLOGNE, 16 Nov 2002, *Landscape with Small Chapel and Ruins, Moselle* (gouache, 20 x 28 ins / 50 x 70 cm) EUR 1,600. LONDON, 9 July 2003, *Rhine View with Church and Ruined Castle on a Hill, possibly Oberwesel* (gouache, 27 x 28 ins / 69 x 70 cm) GBP 2,000. AMSTERDAM, 29 March 2004, *View of Helmond Castle. View of Hedel Church* (gouache, a pair, 19 x

28 ins / 48 x 71 cm) EUR 4,600. AMSTERDAM, 20 April 2004, *Mountainous Landscape* (watercolour and gouache, 19 x 22 ins / 49 x 57 cm) EUR 2,000.

KNIP, Henriette. See **RONNER-KNIP**

KNIP, Henriette Gertrude or Geertruida
Dutch, 19th century.
Born 19 July 1783, in Tilburg; died 29 May 1842, in Haarlem.
Painter, watercolourist. Still-lifes (including flowers).
Henriette Knip was the sister of Auguste Joseph Knip and studied with G. van Spaendonck in Paris and Van Daël. Her work was exhibited in France, Germany, Flanders, Amsterdam and The Hague.
AUCTION RECORDS:
COLOGNE, 16 June 1977, *Still-life* (oil on canvas, 21 1/4 x 17 1/4 ins / 54 x 44 cm) DEM 7,000. AMSTERDAM, 2 May 1990, *Still-life with Roses, Lily of the Valley and Other Flowers with Peaches and Grapes on a Bed of Moss under an Oak Branch* (1834, oil on panel, 23 x 16 3/4 ins / 57.5 x 42.5 cm) NLG 105,800. LONDON, 16 July 1991, *The Poacher - Still-life of a Store Room with Game and a Tortoiseshell Cat Stealing a Blackbird* (oil on canvas, 28 x 35 3/4 ins / 71.1 x 90.8 cm) GBP 8,250. AMSTERDAM, 21 April 1993, *Still-life with Roses, Tulips and Other Flowers* (watercolour/paper, 21 x 14 ins / 52.5 x 35.5 cm) NLG 2,300. LONDON, 21 Nov 1996, *Summer Flowers and Birds' Nest in a Wood* (1840, oil on panel, 19 3/4 x 15 ins / 50 x 38 cm) GBP 23,000. ANTWERP, 19 Feb 2001, *Still-life with Vase of Flowers on a Table* (oil on panel, a pair, 13 x 7 ins / 34 x 18 cm) BEF 130,000. ZURICH, 3 Oct 2002, *Flowers in Ceramic Vase* (oil on canvas, 14 x 11 ins / 36 x 27 cm) CHF 15,730.

KNIP, Marten Derk
Dutch, 19th century.
Born 30 December 1785, in Tilburg; died 1845, in Vucht, near 's Hertogenbosch.
Painter (gouache). Landscapes.
Marten Derk Knip worked in Paris for many years. He was the brother of Auguste Joseph Knip.
AUCTION RECORDS:
PARIS, 1865, *Landscape with River,* FRF 400. NEW YORK, 28 Jan 1999, *Landscape with Horsemen and Man in Carriage* (pencil, watercolour and bodycolour, 9 x 9 ins / 22 x 22 cm) USD 12,000. LONDON, 17 Nov 1999, *Harengpakkeers-toren on Martelaars Canal, Amsterdam* (gouache, 20 x 29 ins / 50 x 74 cm) GBP 1,500. AMSTERDAM, 20 March 2001, *Extensive Wooded River Landscape with Shepherds and their Animals* (1836, pencil, bodycolour and watercolour, 18 x 22 ins / 45 x 57 cm) NLG 18,000. AMSTERDAM, 4 Sept 2001, *Travellers with Donkey near the Pansilippe* (pencil, watercolour and bodycolour, 10 x 15 ins / 26 x 37 cm) EUR 2,800. PARIS, 18 Dec 2003, *View of Coblenz* (gouache, 20 x 28 ins / 50 x 71 cm) EUR 3,000. PARIS, 18 March 2004, *Park with Fountain Surrounded by Figures and Animals* (pen, brown ink, watercolour and gouache, 11 x 14 ins / 29 x 36 cm) EUR 2,600. LONDON, 6 July 2004, *Mountainous River Landscape with Sailing Boats. Ships on Choppy Sea by a Lighthouse* (watercolour and bodycolour, a pair, 20 x 28 ins / 51 x 72 cm) GBP 4,500.

KNIP, Nicolas Frederik, the Elder
Dutch, 18th century.
Born 12 February 1742, in Nijmegen; died c. 1809, in 's Hertogenbosch.
Painter (including gouache). Landscapes, still-lifes (flowers/fruit).
Up to the age of 31, Nicolas Knip the Elder led the nomadic existence of a travellling painter, going from palace to palace in search of work. He married in Tilburg c. 1752. He appears to have enjoyed success with small-scale paintings of landscapes, animals, flowers and fruit. He went blind around 1795.
AUCTION RECORDS:
PARIS, 21 Feb 1924, *Fruit on a Stone Ledge,* FRF 300. PARIS, 30 April 1924, *Dwelling on the Edge of a Forest with Figures* (gouache) FRF 580. LONDON, 13 June 1973, *Vase of Flowers,* GBP 1,000. LONDON, 31 March 1989, *Floral Composition in a Vase with a Peach and Black Grapes on an Entablature* (oil on canvas, 23 3/4 x 18 3/4 ins / 60.6 x 47.6 cm) GBP 9,680. NEW YORK, 14 Oct 1992, *Still-life with Tulips, Roses and Other Flowers in a Vase with a Butterfly, a Violin, Books and other items on a Stone Entablature* (1789, oil on canvas, 21 3/4 x 29 1/2 ins / 55.2 x 75.2 cm) USD 8,250. LONDON, 3-4 Dec 1997, *Still-life with Flowers in a Vase with a Bunch of Grapes and a Bird's Nest Containing Eggs; Still-life with Flowers in a Vase and Peaches on a Marble Table Top* (oil on panel, each 10 x 11 3/4 ins / 24.5 x 30 cm) GBP 12,650. GRAVENHAGE, 7 May 2003, *Pastoral Landscape* (oil on canvas, 21 x 28 ins / 54 x 71 cm) EUR 15,000.

KNIP, Nicolas Frederik, the Younger
Dutch, 19th century.
Died 1821.
Painter. Landscapes.
Nicolas Frederik Knip the Younger was the son of Nicolas Frederik Knip the Elder.

KNIP, Pauline (Mme)
Maiden name: Rifer de Courcelles
French, 19th century.
Born 26 July 1781, in Paris; died 18 April 1851, in Paris.
Painter. Birds.
Pauline Knip was a pupil of Baraband. She exhibited her work at the Salon between 1808 and 1814 and gained a medal in 1810. She married August Joseph Knip.
AUCTION RECORDS:
LONDON, 26 June 1957, *The Magnificent Crimson Manoura, Bird of Paradise* (gouache) GBP 900.

KNIP, Willem Alexander
Dutch, 20th century.
Born 1883 or 1885, in Amsterdam; died 1967, in Blaricum.
Painter. Landscapes, landscapes with figures, urban landscapes, waterscapes, architectural views, seascapes.
Willem Knip was active throughout Holland and several regions in France and Italy, notably Venice and Florence where he sought typical views.
AUCTION RECORDS:
AMSTERDAM, 10 Feb 1988, *Village in Winter* (oil on canvas, 15 3/4 x 19 3/4 ins / 40 x 50 cm) NLG 1,092. AMSTERDAM, 30 Aug 1988, *Thun Castle* (oil on canvas, 27 1/2 x 39 1/4 ins / 70 x 100 cm) NLG 2,070; *The Grand Canal in Venice and Santa Maria della Salute* (oil on canvas, 23 1/2 x 39 1/4 ins / 60 x 100 cm) NLG 13,800. AMSTERDAM, 3 Sept 1988, *The Pont Marie in Paris, seen from below* (oil on canvas, 16 1/4 x 19 3/4 ins / 41 x 50 cm) NLG 1,725. AMSTERDAM, 16 Nov 1988, *Harbour with Cargo-ships and Boats at Anchor* (oil on canvas, 19 3/4 x 23 1/2 ins / 50 x 60 cm) NLG 2,760. TORONTO, 30 Nov 1988, *Sheep Returning to Pen* (oil on canvas, 19 1/4 x 15 1/2 ins / 49 x 39.5 cm) CAD 1,600. AMSTERDAM, 19 Sept 1989, *Boats near Canal Lock* (oil on canvas, 15 3/4 x 12 ins / 40 x 30.5 cm) NLG 1,150. AMSTERDAM, 11 Sept 1990, *Orange Sail* (oil on panel, 11 1/2 x 15 1/2 ins / 29.3 x 39.5 cm) NLG 1,725. AMSTERDAM, 30 Oct 1990, *Country Road to Vierhouten* (oil on canvas, 10 1/2 x 19 ins / 26.5 x 48 cm) NLG 2,530. AMSTERDAM, 5-6 Feb 1991, *View of Volendam with Bridge over Canal* (oil on canvas, 16 x 20 ins / 40.5 x 50.5 cm) NLG 1,840. AMSTERDAM, 24 April 1991, *View of the Harbour of Concarneau in Brittany* (oil on canvas, 19 3/4 x 23 1/2 ins / 50 x 60 cm) NLG 6,670. AMSTERDAM, 17 Sept 1991, *Shepherd and his Flock on a Path near a Farm* (oil on canvas, 23 1/2 x 32 ins / 60 x 81 cm) NLG 6,325. AMSTERDAM, 5-6 Nov 1991, *Boat in Polder Landscape* (oil on

panel, 9 1/2 x 13 1/2 ins / 24 x 34 cm) NLG 2,243. AMSTERDAM, 14-15 April 1992, *Port in the South of France* (oil on canvas, 11 1/4 x 19 ins / 28.5 x 48 cm) NLG 3,680. AMSTERDAM, 11 Feb 1993, *Boats in a Shipyard* (oil on canvas, 18 1/4 x 21 3/4 ins / 46.5 x 55.5 cm) NLG 2,185. AMSTERDAM, 8 Nov 1994, *The Ponte Vecchio, Florence* (oil on canvas, 31 1/2 x 24 ins / 80 x 61 cm) NLG 2,070. AMSTERDAM, 11 April 1995, *View of Collioure in France* (oil on canvas, 15 3/4 x 31 ins / 40 x 79 cm) NLG 1,416. AMSTERDAM, 16 April 1996, *View of a Harbour in Italy* (oil on canvas, 31 1/2 x 23 1/2 ins / 80 x 60 cm) NLG 3,776. AMSTERDAM, 21 Jan 1998, *Spring* (oil on canvas, 32 x 27 3/4 ins / 81 x 70.5 cm) NLG 4,612. AMSTERDAM, 28 April 1999, *Figures by Farmhouse* (oil on canvas, 12 x 16 ins / 30 x 40 cm) NLG 3,400. AMSTERDAM, 28 April 1999, *Fishing Boats in the Harbour of Concarneau* (oil on canvas, 20 x 16 ins / 50 x 40 cm) NLG 4,000. THE HAGUE, 31 Oct 2000, *O Z Kolkje, Amsterdam* (oil on canvas, 31 x 23 ins / 78 x 58 cm) NLG 7,500. ANTWERP, 12 Dec 2000, *View of Dutch Village* (oil on canvas, 26 x 24 ins / 67 x 60 cm) BEF 400,000. AMSTERDAM, 20 March 2001, *Harbour of St Tropez* (oil on canvas, 24 x 31 ins / 60 x 80 cm) NLG 9,000. AMSTERDAM, 25 April 2001, *Winter Day in a French Village* (1950, oil on canvas, 19 x 23 ins / 48 x 58 cm) NLG 4,200. AMSTERDAM, 4 March 2002, *View of a Bridge, Paris* (oil on canvas, 20 x 16 ins / 51 x 41 cm) EUR 2,000. AMSTERDAM, 25 June 2002, *Grand Canal, Venice* (oil on canvas, 28 x 45 ins / 70 x 114 cm) EUR 2,500. THE HAGUE, 5 Nov 2003, *Prince Henry Quay, Amsterdam* (oil on canvas, 15 x 19 ins / 39 x 49 cm) EUR 1,700. AMSTERDAM, 22 June 2004, *Shipping on the Ij, Amsterdam* (oil on canvas, 15 x 31 ins / 38 x 80 cm) EUR 2,800. AMSTERDAM, 28 June 2004, *View of San Marco, Venice* (oil on canvas, 20 x 16 ins / 52 x 41 cm) EUR 2,000.

KNIPFER, Nic.
German, 17th century.
Active in Germany in 1677.
Engraver (etching).

Knipfer is known to have engraved two plates: *The Game of Boules* and *The Archery Contest*.

KNIPP
19th century.
Painter. Animals.

This Knipp probably belonged to the Knips of Tilburg.

MUSEUMS AND GALLERIES:

NARBONNE: *Stable Interior, Goats, Sheep and Horses at the Manger*.

KNIPPER, Nicolaus. See **KNUPFER**

KNIPSCHILD, Axel
German, 20th century.
Born 1946, in Erfurt; died 1983.
Painter, sculptor.

Axel Knipschild studied at the Staatliche Kunstakademie in Düsseldorf. He exhibited in Germany and Sweden. His drawings, paintings and sculptures play on the possibilities of superimposed forms and lines.

AUCTION RECORDS:

STOCKHOLM, 6 Dec 1989, *Triangular Object* (black plaster with orange diagonal, 39 1/4 x 34 1/4 x 2 1/4 ins / 100 x 87 x 6 cm) SEK 15,500. STOCKHOLM, 14 June 1990, *Space Activator* (grey papier maché with red and blue gouache, 79 1/2 x 6 1/4 ins / 202 x 16 cm) SEK 4,500. STOCKHOLM, 5-6 Dec 1990, *Blue and Yellow Lines on a Black Background* (1975, gouache and ink, 6 1/4 x 6 1/4 ins / 16 x 16 cm) SEK 4,000. STOCKHOLM, 19 May 1992, *Triangular Object* (black plaster with an orange line, 39 1/4 x 34 1/4 x 2 1/4 ins / 100 x 87 x 6 cm) SEK 6,700.

KNIRR, Erwin
German, 19th century.
Active at the end of the 19th century in Munich.
Painter.

Knirr ran a school of painting in Munich, and had the sculptor Burckhardt as his pupil in 1898. Paul Klee began his artistic studies there, before joining Kandinsky in Franz Stuck's class at the academy, also in about 1898.

KNIRR, Heinrich
German, 20th century.
Born 2 September 1862, in Pancsova; died 1944.
Painter. Portraits.

As an exponent of Nazi art, Knirr glorified the Nazi regime in his work. He received a medal in Munich in 1905. In 1937 he painted a *Portrait of the Führer*.

KNITEL, Robert
French, 19th century.
Born 19th century, in Paris.
Painter, pastellist. Fruit.

Robert Knitel took part in Salon exhibitions in 1874 and 1875.

KNITTEL, Adolf
German, 19th century.
Born 10 March 1852, in Freiburg; died 17 May 1909, in Waldkirch.
Sculptor.

Knittel studied in Karsruhe, then worked in Munich and Lorraine.

KNITTEL, Anna
Austrian, 19th - 20th century.
Born 28 July 1841, in Untergibeln; died 28 February 1915, in Wattens.
Painter. Portraits, local scenes, landscapes, flowers.

Anna Knittel produced landscapes, flowers and picturesque scenes of the Austrian Tyrol where she spent most of her life.

KNIZAK, Milan
Czechoslovak, 20th century.
Born 1940, in Plzen.
Painter, draughtsman, performance artist, video artist. Multimedia.
Neo-Dadaism, Fluxus.

Between 1948 and 1956, Milan Knizak studied at the Mariánské Lázne school of music, at the academy of fine arts, and at the faculty of mathematics and physics in Prague. He taught at several American universities and art colleges in Germany and Austria. He was appointed rector of the academy of fine arts in Prague in 1989.

He was one of the first artists in 1962 to initiate happenings and body art in Czechoslovakia as a symbolic gesture for artistic freedom. In 1968 he joined the international Fluxus movement. In parallel with his installation work, the human body became the vehicle for his artistic preoccupations. In the 1970s several happenings and performances were produced to stage gestural and bodily rituals. In the 1980s he turned to clothing as a symbol for his conceptual catechisms on the subject of art. He created moving objects in avant-garde styles such as Cubism and made several films. He also wrote fairly widely on aesthetics and social matters, particularly under the banner of the Aktual group, which he helped to found in 1964.

His work has been shown in collective exhibitions including: *Happening & Fluxus*, Cologne Kunstverein (1970); Stuttgart Kunstverein (1972); 8th Paris Biennale (international young artists exhibition-1973); *L'art au corps. Le corps exposé de Man Ray à nos jours* (*Body Art: The Exposed Body from Man Ray to the Present*), Musée d'Art Contemporain, Marseilles (1996). Solo exhibitions from 1958 include: Germany (1970 and 1972) and Brno.

BIBLIOGRAPHY:

Knizak, Milan, in *V TRE Flux-Newspaper* no. 8, periodical, Fluxus, New York, 1967. *VIIIe Biennale de Paris*, exhibition catalogue, Musée d'Art moderne de la Ville de Paris, Paris, 1973.

KNJAZOVIC, Jano
Serb, 20th century.
Born 1925, in Kovacica near Pancevo.
Painter.

Born of peasant stock, Jano Knjazovic started painting in 1944 and first exhibited his work with a group of other peasant-painters from the same village.

He painted lively scenes of village life. One school for peasant-painters had been set up in Kovacica, and another in Hlebnine, home of Ivan Generalic, both promoting the popular local tradition of glass painting. Knjazovic depicted scenes from everyday peasant life in a style reminiscent of Brueghel He developed a carefully smooth distinctive technique with clearly delineated shades of colour.

BIBLIOGRAPHY:

Bihalji-Merin, Oto, *Les Peintres naïfs,* Delpire, Paris, 1960. Gans, Louis, *Meesters der Europese naïven,* exhibition catalogue, Centraal Museum, Utrecht, 1970.

KNOBELSDORFF, Georg Wenceslaus von (Baron)
German, 18th century.
Born 17 February 1699; died 16 September 1753, in Berlin.
Painter, engraver, architect.

Knobelsdorff was the architect of the Berlin Opera House and the Castle of Sans-Souci. A former captain in the Prussian army, he turned to art in 1730. His portraits and landscapes are highly rated.

KNOBLAUCH, Michelle
Belgian, 20th century.
Born 1943, in Valence.
Active in France.
Painter (mixed media), screen printer, collage artist.

Michelle Knoblauch makes careful use of the substance and textures of paper. Her form of abstraction is very sensitive, introducing elegant poetry coupled with subtle play of colours into the deep spaces of black or blue backgrounds. Since 1977, she has taken part in group exhibitions including: 1979 at the Musée du Luxembourg and the Salon des Femmes Peintres in Paris; 1982 at the Galerie Denise Rene and the Galerie des Femmes, Apt; 1984 at the Municipal Library in Boulogne; 1986 at the Galerie Franka Berndt, Paris and 1989 at the Maison de la Culture, Tournai. She has also had solo shows in 1979 at the Galerie l'Angle Aigu, Brussels; 1981 at the Galerie des Femmes, Paris; 1981 and 1984 at the Galerie Van Hoofdt, Antwerp; 1982 at the Galerie Sastello, Liers; 1986 at the Galerie Art'Mania, Annemasse; 1987 at the Galerie Blum, Paris; 1987, 1990 and 1991 at the Galerie Franka Berndt, Paris and 1995 at the Galerie Natkin-Berta, Paris.

AUCTION RECORDS:

PARIS, 10 June 1993, *Composition* (1991, collage and mixed media/paper, 23½ x 17¼ ins / 60 x 44 cm) FRF 6,000.

KNOBLOCH, Gertrud
German, 19th century.
Born 1 July 1867, in Breslau (now Wroclaw, Poland).
Painter. Genre scenes.

Gertrud Knobloch worked in Breslau and Berlin. She was a pupil of Skarbine.

KNOBLOCH, Josef Rolf, or Knoblauch
Czech, 20th century.
Born 23 August 1891, in Chemnitz.
Painter. Landscapes, mountainscapes, waterscapes.

Josef Knoblock exhibited landscapes in Munich.

AUCTION RECORDS:

VIENNA, 13 Feb 1979, *Autumn Landscape* (1915, oil on canvas, 19¾ x 29½ ins / 50 x 75 cm) ATS 15,000. MUNICH, 21 Oct 1987, *Landscape with Rainbow* (oil on card, 20 x 23½ ins / 51 x 60 cm) DEM 4,800. COLOGNE, 18 March 1989, *Boats on an Alpine Lake* (oil on canvas, 28 x 39¼ ins / 71 x 100 cm) DEM 3,000. MUNICH, 3 Dec 1996, *Foothills of the Alps* (oil on canvas, 27½ x 41¼ ins / 70 x 105 cm) DEM 2,160. MUNICH, 17 March 2004, *Storm Gathering over Kloster Reutberg* (oil on panel, 20 x 31 ins / 50 x 80 cm) EUR 2,000. MUNICH, 20 Oct 2004, *View over the Riegsee with Blossoming Trees in the Foreground* (oil on canvas, 28 x 39 ins / 70 x 100 cm) EUR 2,500.

KNODDE, Nicolas
Flemish School, 15th century.
Illuminator.

His name appears in the records of the brotherhood of booksellers in Bruges between 1457 and 1479.

KNODDER, Ch. de. See **CNODDER Ch. de**

KNODERER, Hans, or Knoder
German, 16th century.
Painter.

Hans Knoderer was a painter at the court of Maximillian I in Augsburg in about 1508. In 1522, he carried out various tasks in Innsbruck, Augsburg and Ulm, amongst other places. The museum in Vienna owns a *View of the Tomb of Rudolf of Habsburg,* a watercolour produced by him which had been commissioned by Maximillian.

KNOEBEL, Imi
German, 20th century.
Born 1940, in Dessau.
Painter (mixed technique), installation artist.

Imi Knoebel was a former pupil of Joseph Beuys at the Kunstakademie in Düsseldorf from 1964 to 1971 where he met Imi Giese and Blinky Palermo, another pupil of Beuys. He had previously begun his studies at the Werkkunstschule in Darmstadt, from which he was excluded as a result of various events. Since 1964 he has lived and worked in Düsseldorf.

From the mid-1960s he was inspired by the abstract painters of the beginning of the century and in particular Kasimir Malevich, to whom he paid homage with his work *Mamatu,* a monument surmounted by a black icon (Malevich's black square). Thereafter he began his investigations into the material nature of painting as a flat surface, elementary colours and forms. He produced sequences, conceiving in 1964 *Line Paintings,* assemblages of straight vertical and horizontal lines painted in black and white, bordering on optical art. These were followed by the series of *Scenes of Dragoons* (1969), then pictures entitled *Projections* (1970-1972) in which a projection of luminous elements on a specially designated wall were arranged and, in 1975, the series of *Constellations of Images.* Using wood henceforth in his compositions, which resembled low reliefs, he reconsidered the idea of painting in its abstract-analytic system - an open system in which several parts come into equilibrium while maintaining their respective independence. Some of these reliefs became increasingly rich in colours and complex in their form. Others evolved as sequences in a minimalist way using virtually 'kitsch' colours (the sequel *Grace Kelly*). He also conceived and carried out 'pieces' or 'objects' in the general sense of the word. Neither sculptures nor paintings, these objects which defy aesthetic categorisation took the form of piles of planks, panels built up in layers or packing cases either placed against a wall or arranged as installations: *Room 19* recreates the old study of the academy of Düsseldorf and *Heerstraße,* his flat. He refused the traditional 'plastic' categorisation and his artistic practice re-echoes the conception of art as a total activity of the subject in its relation to the object which was strongly recommended by Joseph Beuys.

Since 1968 his work has been shown at group exhibitions in Amsterdam, Düsseldorf, Kassel, Winterthur, Mönchengladbach, Frankfurt, Paris, Nice, Bordeaux, Nantes, Lyons and Vienna, including, in 2002, *Les Années 70: l'Art en Cause* (*The 1970s: Art in Question*), CAPC-Musée d'Art Contemporain, Bordeaux; in 2003, *Un tableau dans le décor. Peintures 1970-2000* (*A Painting in the Décor: Paintings 1970-2000*), an exhibition organised on the occasion of 20 years of FRAC, Château des Ducs de Bretagne, Nantes and 2003, *Berlin-Moskau/Moskau-Berlin 1950-2000* (*Berlin-Moskow/Moskow-Berlin 1950-2000*), a panorama-exhibition which, following that relating to the 1900-1950 period, offered debate on this 50-year period of German-Russian artistic and cultural relations marked by political transformations at the Martin-Gropius-Bau of Berlin and the Tretyakov gallery in Moscow.

His solo exhibitions have included: 1968, first exhibition, the palace of Charlottenborg (art academy), Copenhagen; 1969, *Art & Project*, Amsterdam; 1972, Stedelijk Museum, Amsterdam; 1975, Städtiche Kunsthalle, Düsseldorf; 1982 Stedelijk Van Abbemuseum, Eindhoven; 1983, Kunstmuseum, Winterthur; 1983, Städisches Kunstmuseum, Bonn; 1985, Rijksmuseum Kröller-Müller, Otterlo; 1986, Staatliche Kunsthalle, Baden-Baden; 1989, Bonnefentenmuseum, Maastricht; 1989 Barbara Gladstone Gallery, New York; 1989, Vera Muro, Hamburg; 1900 Galerie Hans Strelow, Düsseldorf; 1991, Le Consortium, Dijon; 1992, 1996 Galerie Gilbert Brownstone & Cie, Paris; 1993, Vienna; 1997 Stedelijk Museum d'Amsterdam and the museum in Grenoble (his first retrospective in France).

BIBLIOGRAPHY:

Imi Knoebel - Eingentum Himmelreich, exhibition catalogue, Musée de La Roche-sur-Yon, Le Coin du miroir, Dijon, 1985. *Imi Knoebel*, Dia Art Foundation, New York, 1989. *Imi Knoebel*, exhibition catalogue, Gal. Philippe Casini, Paris, 1990. Grout, Catherine, '*Imi Knoebel, la peinture en devenir*' in *Art Press*, periodical, Paris, 1993. Lemoine, Serge/Fuchs, Rudi/Wechsler, Max/Stüttgen, Johannes/Gassner, Hubertus, *Imi Knoebel*, Musée de Grenoble, Grenoble, 1997. Fréruchet, Maurice, et al., *Les Années soixante-dix: l'art en cause*, exhibition catalogue, Capc Musée d'Art Contemporain, Bordeaux, 2002. '*Berlin-Moskau/Moskau-Berlin 1950-2000*' in *2 vol.*, exhibition catalogue, Martin-Gropius-Bau, Berlin, 2003 (text in German).

MUSEUMS AND GALLERIES:

CHÂTEAUGIRON (FRAC Bretagne): *Zoe* (1992) - DIJON (FRAC Bourgogne): *Hartfaserbild* (1968-1983) - DUNKIRK (FRAC Nord-Pas de Calais) - GRENOBLE (Mus. de Grenoble): *Mamatu* (1986) - NÎMES (Carré d'Art, MAC) - PARIS (FNAC): *Piano Piece* (1984).

AUCTION RECORDS:

NEW YORK, 4 May 1989, *Untitled* (1977, collage of paper and acrylic/paper, 39 x 27 1/2 ins / 99 x 69.8 cm) USD 3,850. NEW YORK, 13 Feb 1991, *Untitled* (1987, acrylic/cut-out panel, irregular 22 1/4 x 20 3/4 x 2 3/4 ins / 56.5 x 52.7 x 7 cm) USD 6,600. NEW YORK, 2 May 1991, *Untitled* (1988, acrylic/wood, 98 x 66 3/4 ins / 249.2 x 169.4 cm) USD 38,500. NEW YORK, 13 Nov 1991, *Painted Geometric Figures* (1987, acrylic/wood, 98 1/2 x 66 3/4 ins / 250.2 x 169.8 cm) USD 33,000. NEW YORK, 14 Nov 1991, *Untitled* (1968, ink and pencil/graph paper) USD 1,870. NEW YORK, 6 May 1992, *Projection* (1968, montage of 20 photographs, in all 60 x 38 ins / 151.5 x 96.8 cm) USD 13,200. NEW YORK, 18 Nov 1992, *White Constellation* (oil/wood in five parts, 101 x 157 ins / 256.5 x 398.8 cm) USD 22,000. NEW YORK, 5 May 1993, *Still-life* (1983, in two parts, wood and acrylic/aluminium, background 97 1/4 x 77 1/2 x 2 ins / 247 x 196.8 x 5.1 cm relief 99 1/2 x 12 1/4 x 11 ins/252.7 x 31.1 x 27.9 cm) USD 17,250. LONDON, 2 Dec 1993, *White Constellation, 4 Elements* (acrylic/plywood, in all 119 x 145 ins / 302.3 x 368.3 cm) GBP 21,850. LUCERNE, 26 Nov 1994, *Untitled* (1972, charcoal/paper, a pair, each 11 1/2 x 16 1/2 ins / 29.5 x 42 cm) CHF 2,000. NEW YORK, 3 May 1995, *DDR* (wood and synthetic resin, 108 x 100 1/2 x 27 ins / 274.3 x 255.3 x 68.6 cm) USD 12,650. LONDON, 12 Dec 1997, *Untitled* (1984, acrylic and varnish/card, 71 1/4 x 65 1/4 ins / 181 x 166 cm) GBP 10,925. LONDON, 2 July 1998, *Figure Painting* (acrylic/panel, 98 x 67 ins / 250 x 170 cm) GBP 55,000. LONDON, 8 Oct 1998, *Untitled* (1970-1971, oil on canvas/panel, 81 x 51 ins / 205 x 130 cm) GBP 27,000. COLOGNE, 28 May 1999, *Untitled - E 3* (1979, collage and acrylic on paper, 39 x 27 ins / 98 x 68 cm) DEM 30,000. BERLIN, 26 May 2000, *Saxony I and II* (1981, corrugated tin, fibreboard and steel, 43 x 52 ins / 109 x 131 cm) DEM 100,000. MUNICH, 26 Nov 2000, *Pure Happiness 1* (acrylic/aluminium, 63 x 45 ins / 160 x 114 cm) DEM 60,000. LONDON, 8 Feb 2001, *Untitled* (1971, black and white photo in 21 parts, 9 x 12 ins / 23 x 30 cm) GBP 16,000. NEW YORK, 13 Nov 2002, *Grace Kelly* (1989, acrylic/wood, 98 x 66 ins / 248 x 168 cm) USD 29,000. MUNICH, 6 Dec 2002, *Grace Kelly* (1990, acrylic/wood, 98 x 67 ins / 250 x 170 cm) EUR 45,000. LONDON, 22 Oct 2003, *39A, 39B, 39C, 39D* (acrylic/four attached wood panels, 67 x 98 ins / 170 x 249 cm) GBP 14,000. NEW YORK, 13 Nov 2003, *Constellation B* (1987, oil on panel, four parts, 130 x 129 ins / 331 x 327 cm) USD 22,500. MUNICH, 14 May 2004, *Untitled* (oil on canvas, 79 x 59 ins / 200 x 150 cm) EUR 26,000. NEW YORK, 11 Nov 2004, *Figure Painting* (1987, acrylic/panel, 98 x 67 ins / 250 x 170 cm) USD 40,000.

KNOEBEL, Robert

German, 20th century.

Born 13 April 1874, in Reichenberg; died 14 July 1924, in Munich.

Painter. Landscapes, portraits.

Robert Knoebel attended the academy of fine arts in Munich where he was the pupil of Ludwig Löfftz and later exhibited landscapes and portraits in the same city.

KNOECHL, Hans

Bohemian, 19th century.

Born 26 July 1850, in Prague.

Painter. Portraits, genre scenes.

Hans Knoechl studied under Trenkwald at the academy in Prague and A. Wagner at the academy in Munich. He also studied with Lindenschmidt and Piloty. He went to Italy, but then settled in Munich.

AUCTION RECORDS:

LONDON, 18 Jan 1980, *Reverie* (oil on panel, 12 1/2 x 10 1/2 ins / 31.7 x 26.6 cm) GBP 800.

KNOELL, Emil

Swiss, 20th century.

Born 24 December 1889, in Basel.

Sculptor.

After attending the academy in Munich, Emil Knoell returned to Switzerland. He also spent time in Paris, where, amongst other places, he exhibited.

KNÖFLER, Gottfried

German, 18th century.

Born 21 March 1715, near Leipzig; died 11 September 1779, in Dresden.

Sculptor.

Knöfler worked at the court of King Augustus III of Saxony and taught sculpture at the Dresden academy from its foundation in 1764.

KNOLL, François Cornelis

Dutch, 18th - 19th century.

Born 1771 or 1772, in Rotterdam; died 23 March 1827, in Utrecht.

Painter, art dealer. Still-lifes.

MUSEUMS AND GALLERIES:

AMSTERDAM: *Stable*.

KNOLL, Konrad von
German, 19th century.
Born 9 September 1829, in Bergzabem; died 14 June 1899, in Munich.
Sculptor.

Konrad von Knoll worked in Karlsruhe, Stuttgart and Munich, before finally settling in Munich, where he taught sculpture. The Hamburg Kunsthalle owns a *Bust of Hans von Marées* by him.

KNOLL, Waldemar
German, 19th century.
Born 19 April 1839, in Berlin; died 26 November 1909, in Coburg.
Painter, watercolourist, draughtsman. Landscapes.

Waldemar Knoll studied at the academy of fine arts in Berlin. He made a study trip to the Caucasus.

AUCTION RECORDS:
NEW YORK, April 1902, *River and Mountains,* USD 150. LONDON, 6 Oct 1988, *The Worontsov Bridge in the Caucasus* (pencil and watercolour/paper, 9 1/4 x 12 3/4 ins / 23.2 x 32.5 cm) GBP 770. MUNICH, 3 Dec 1996, *Morning in Kasbeck in the Caucasus* (watercolour/paper, 19 3/4 x 13 ins / 50 x 33 cm) DEM 1,440. MUNICH, 1 Dec 1999, *Hunters Resting by a Stream in the Caucasus* (oil on canvas, 30 x 44 ins / 76 x 111 cm) DEM 5,500. LINDAU, 9 Oct 2003, *Roaring River in the Caucasus* (oil on canvas, 30 x 44 ins / 76 x 111 cm) EUR 4,800.

KNOLLE, Johann Heinrich Friedrich Ludwig
German, 19th century.
Born 4 May 1807, in Brunswick; died 6 July 1877, in Brunswick.
Engraver.

Knolle studied with Anderloni in Milan. He visited Dresden, London and Paris and became curator of the Brunswick Museum. He engraved historical subjects after Correggio, Titian, Maratta, Murillo and Hildebrandt.

KNOLLER, Martin
Austrian, 18th century.
Born 8 November 1725, in Steinach (Tyrol); died 24 July 1804, in Milan.
Painter, fresco artist. Religious subjects, landscapes.
Neo-Classical.

Considered to be one of the most important painters from the Tyrol, Knoller learned the rudiments from his father, though we do not even know his forename. In 1745, the painter Paul Trogel, having seen the young Martin's first attempts and been struck by his natural ability, took the boy with him to Vienna and got him admitted to the academy. While there, Knoller won the major prize for history painting in 1753 with *Tobias Restoring His Father's Sight.* The following year, he went to Rome and worked in the studio of Raffael Mengs. He was appointed painter to the court of Milan in 1756 and two years later he was summoned to Naples by the Austrian ambassador, Count Firmian, who commissioned major works from him. He returned to Milan in 1760 to take up the post of professor at the academy, a position he held until his death.

Knoller is most appreciated as a painter of frescoes, notable examples of which can be seen in the churches of Ettal, Neresheim, Steinach and various places in the Tyrol. He is also known for the *Ascension of the Virgin* in the town hall in Munich. He was a skilful draughtsman, aided by a powerful imagination. Like Franz Sigrist, Knoller may have followed too closely the lessons of Winckelmann and Anton Raphael Mengs, and definitely paid too much heed to the decree of 1777, in which the Elector Karl Theodor of Bavaria called for 'greater simplicity in the arts'. These artists represent the drying up of the great stream of the Baroque as it gave way to dull academic orthodoxy.

MUSEUMS AND GALLERIES:
MILAN - MUNICH - VIENNA.
AUCTION RECORDS:
LONDON, 25 March 1982, *Elegant Company at Table* (pen and grey wash heightened with white/black chalk outline, 10 1/2 x 12 1/2 ins / 26.7 x 31.7 cm) GBP 580. MILAN, 16 April 1985, *Perseus and Andromeda* (oil on canvas, 28 1/2 x 19 1/4 ins / 72.5 x 49 cm) ITL 13,000,000. MILAN, 11 June 1986, *Sacrifice to Diana; Historical Scenes* (oil on canvas, a pair, 25 1/2 x 32 1/4 ins / 65 x 82 cm) ITL 8,000,000. ROME, 13 April 1989, *View of the Villa Monza from the Garden; A Pavillion in the Garden of the Villa Monza* (oil on canvas, a pair, each 23 1/4 x 29 1/4 ins / 59 x 74.5 cm) ITL 45,000,000. LONDON, 3 July 2000, *St Peter Repentant* (1775, oil on panel, 12 x 10 ins / 31 x 26 cm) GBP 1,100. COLOGNE, 15 Nov 2003, *Childhood of Mary* (oil on canvas, 32 x 24 ins / 81 x 61 cm) EUR 10,000.

KNOOP, August or August Friedrich
German, 19th century.
Born 6 June 1856, in Düsseldorf; died 1900, in Munich.
Painter. Genre scenes.

Knoop is mentioned by Florence Lévy. He studied with Cormon in Paris.

AUCTION RECORDS:
FRANKFURT AM MAIN, 1894, *The Minuet,* FRF 1,262. NEW YORK, 19-20 March 1903, *The Assignation,* USD 115. NEW YORK, 18-19 Feb 1904, *The Charlatan,* USD 120. ANTWERP, 5 Dec 1972, *At the Lawyer's Office,* BEF 75,000. PARIS, 16 March 1976, *Soldiers at the Tavern* (1890, oil on panel, 11 x 15 1/4 ins / 27 x 39 cm) FRF 4,300. LONDON, 12 Oct 1977, *Reading the Newspaper* (1891, oil on panel, 5 3/4 x 7 ins / 14.5 x 18 cm) GBP 1,150. NEW YORK, 27 June 1979, *The Assignation* (1892, oil on panel, 12 1/2 x 17 ins / 32 x 43 cm) USD 1,700. HANOVER, 7 May 1983, *Inn Scene* (oil on panel, 9 x 6 1/4 ins / 22 x 16 cm) DEM 4,500. MUNICH, 5 Nov 1986, *Banquet at Nymphenburg* (1901, oil on canvas, 23 1/4 x 27 1/2 ins / 59 x 70 cm) DEM 16,000. COLOGNE, 20 Oct 1989, *The Antique Dealer's Shop* (oil on canvas, 23 1/2 x 33 3/4 ins / 60 x 86 cm) DEM 3,000. STOCKHOLM, 16 May 1990, *Two Noblemen Conversing after their Meal in a Rich Interior* (oil on panel, 11 1/2 x 15 1/4 ins / 29 x 39 cm) SEK 15,500. COLOGNE, 29 June 1990, *The Chess-Players* (oil on card, 9 3/4 x 12 3/4 ins / 25 x 32.5 cm) DEM 1,500. NEW YORK, 23 May 1996, *Reverie* (1886) USD 14,950. MUNICH, 25 June 1996, *The Inopportune Suitor* (1902, oil on panel, 8 1/2 x 11 ins / 21.5 x 27 cm) DEM 3,600. ANTWERP, 5 Dec 2000, *Music Lesson* (1895, oil on panel, 13 x 10 ins / 32 x 25 cm) BEF 230,000. VLAAMSE KAAI, 12 June 2001, *At the Accountant's* (oil on wood, 13 x 9 ins / 32 x 24 cm) BEF 140,000. VIENNA, 23 Sept 2002, *Entertaining the Clergyman* (oil on canvas, 23 x 31 ins / 59 x 80 cm) EUR 2,500. MICHIGAN, 3 April 2003, *Interiors with figures* (1904, oil on canvas, 17 x 22 ins / 43 x 56 cm) USD 5,500. WARSAW, 15 June 2003, *Game of Chess* (c. 1900, oil on canvas, 11 x 14 ins / 27 x 35 cm) PLN 16,000. LINDAU, 6 May 2004, *Men in 18th C Costume Reading a Contract* (oil on panel, 13 x 17 ins / 32 x 44 cm) EUR 1,900.

KNOOP, Guitou
Dutch, 20th century.
Born 1909, in Moscow, of parents born in Holland; died 1985.
Active from 1927 and from 1933 naturalised in France.
Sculptor.

Guitou Knoop was taken on as a pupil by Émile-Antoine Bourdelle on her arrival in Paris. She received the guidance of Despiau who encouraged her to concentrate on sculpting busts, working in clay and casting in bronze. After World War II she turned her attention to abstract art, notably following a journey to Mexico in 1945 which introduced a Pre-Colombian influence of statuary and Mexican vegetation into her work. In 1949 Jean Arp wrote a preface for one of her exhibitions in New York. Her early abstract output, influenced by her Mexican trip, resembled plant forms and was often worked in brass and lead. From 1949 she preferred stone, producing more monolithic works with taut surfaces, then marble became her favourite medium when she went to work in Carrara, executing works in a Post-Brancusian style.

She participated in a number of group exhibitions in the USA, London and the Salon des Réalités Nouvelles in Paris. Her major one-woman exhibitions were as follows: 1930, 1932 (foreword by Marie Cuttoli), 1949, 1958, 1966, Paris; 1935, Chicago; 1936, 1939, 1942, 1959, 1962, 1964, New York; 1945, Museum of Fine Arts, Houston; 1962, Toronto; 1966, London.

MUSEUMS AND GALLERIES:
BOSTON (MFA) - BUFFALO (Albright-Knox AG) - CHICAGO (AI) - CINCINNATI (AM): *Double Image* (limestone) - DALLAS (MA): *Ion II* (1961, stone) - HOUSTON (MFA) - MINNEAPOLIS (IA): *Two Superimposed Forms* (1957, limestone) - NEW YORK (Metropolitan Mus. of Art) - PROVIDENCE (Rhode Island School of Design) - ROCHESTER (Mus. and Science Center) - SAN FRANCISCO (MoMA): *Méditerranée* (no date, marble) - SANTA BARBARA (MA): *Mediterranee* (c. 1950, marble) - SOUTHAMPTON, USA, NY (Parrish Art Mus.) - ST LOUIS (AM) - ST-ÉTIENNE (Mus. d'Art et d'Industrie) - WASHINGTON DC (Phillips Collection).

AUCTION RECORDS:
NEW YORK, 14 Dec 1976, *Personnage nocturne II* (1963, patinated bronze, h. 17 ins / 43 cm) USD 550.

KNOOP, J. H.
Dutch, 18th - 19th century.
Born 4 August 1769, in Amsterdam; died before February 1834.
Painter, draughtsman. Urban landscapes.

Knoop was a pupil of Barthol and Pieter Barbies Jr. He is known for his views of Amsterdam.

KNOPF, Daniel
Swiss, 17th century.
Active in Solothurn c. 1600.
Painter.

KNOPF, Franz
Swiss, 17th century.
Died 19 December 1615.
Active in Solothurn.
Painter.

KNOPF, Hermann
Austrian, 19th - 20th century.
Born 7 November 1870, in Vienna.
Painter. Genre scenes.

Hermann Knopf received a medal in Munich in 1901 and 1903 and was awarded a distinction in 1903.

MUSEUMS AND GALLERIES:
MUNICH: *Party Evening.*

AUCTION RECORDS:
NEW YORK, 10 and 11 Jan 1907, *Dancing Lesson,* USD 125. LONDON, 3 Feb 1984, *Baby's Meal* (oil on canvas, 31 x 36 ins / 79 x 91.5 cm) GBP 2,600. AHLDEN, 23 April 1999, *Portrait of a Little Dutch Girl* (oil on canvas, 17 x 17 ins / 44 x 43 cm) DEM 3,000. AHLDEN, 20 May 2000, *Dutch Kitchen Maid* (oil on canvas, 35 x 28 ins / 90 x 70 cm) DEM 9,000. MUNICH, 6 Dec 2000, *Child Sleeping in Crib* (oil on canvas, 32 x 36 ins / 81 x 91 cm) DEM 3,600. VIENNA, 30 Oct 2001, *Child Sleeping in Cradle* (oil on canvas, 32 x 36 ins / 81 x 91 cm) ATS 75,000. PHILADELPHIA, 9 Dec 2001, *Young Girl Doing Needlework* (oil on canvas, 36 x 28 ins / 91 x 71 cm) USD 10,000. AHLDEN, 29 Nov 2002, *In a Dream while Reading* (oil on canvas, 36 x 30 ins / 91 x 75 cm) EUR 4,500. SAN FRANCISCO, 16 Nov 2004, *Sleeping Baby in a Cradle* (oil on canvas, 32 x 36 ins / 81 x 91 cm) USD 3,500.

KNOPF, Jakob
Swiss, 16th century.
Active in Solothurn.
Painter.

Knopf worked mostly in Solothurn, but was also active in Bern.

KNOPF, Niklaus
Swiss, 16th century.
Active in Solothurn at the end of the 16th century.
Painter.

Niklaus Knopf produced a decorative fresco at the monastery of St Ursus.

KNOPFF, Adolph
German, 19th - 20th century.
Born 24 November 1851, in Kulpin; died 3 March 1917, in Munich.
Painter. Genre scenes, portraits.

Adolph Knopff lived in Florence for a year and exhibited in Berlin, Bremen and Munich from 1879.

KNOPP, Emerick or Imre
Hungarian, 19th - 20th century.
Born 29 December 1867, in Budapest.
Painter. Genre scenes.

Emerick Knopp was the pupil of Thedy at the Weimar school of fine arts. He exhibited in Paris at the 1900 Exposition Universelle and was awarded a medal in Munich (1905).

KNOPP, Jozsef
Hungarian, 19th century.
Born 1825, in Budapest; died 13 July 1899, in Budapest.
Painter.

Jozsef Knopp studied in Munich, and regularly exhibited portraits in Vienna and Budapest.

KNORR, Charles Émile
French, 20th century.
Born 15 February 1890, in Soultzeren (Haut-Rhin).
Active in Luxembourg.
Illustrator.

Charles Émile Knorr studied under Bernard Naudin. He wrote and illustrated *La Petite Suisse Luxembourgeoise* as well as illustrating other works.

KNORR, Georg David Salomon
German, 19th - 20th century.
Born 24 February 1844, in Löbau; died 10 June 1916, in Königsberg (now Kaliningrad, Russia).
Painter. Genre scenes.

Georg Knorr studied in Berlin and Königsberg and became a professor at the art academy in Königsberg.

AUCTION RECORDS:
COLOGNE, 7 June 1972, *The Invitation,* DEM 3,500. AMSTERDAM, 22 April 1992, *At the Station* (oil on canvas, 32 1/4 x 26 3/4 ins / 82 x 68 cm) NLG 9,200.

KNORR, Georg Wolfgang
German, 18th century.
Born 30 December 1705; died 17 September 1761, in Nuremberg.
Active in Nuremberg.
Engraver (burin), reproductions engraver, painter, art dealer.

Georg Wolfgang Knorr engraved portraits, views and animals after Dürer, Kilian, etc. He published scientific works.

KNORR, Hugo
German, 19th century.
Born 17 November 1834, in Königsberg (now Kaliningrad, Russia); died 29 September 1904, in Karlsruhe.
Painter. Landscapes.

Hugo Knorr worked at the Königsberg academy and devoted himself to landscape painting. He visited Norway, and on his return became professor at the College in Karlsruhe. His *Landscape from the Harz Mountains* can be seen in the Hanover Museum and *Road in the Black Forest* in the Kaliningrad Museum.

KNORR, Theodor Albert Ferdinand
German, 20th century.
Born 30 January 1873, in Kandel.
Painter, art critic. Landscapes.

Theodor Knorr studied in Munich, then worked mostly in Alsace and the occupied region of Lorraine. Following World War I he was in Paris. He was also a prolific art critic.

KNORRE, Johann Friedrich Andreas
German, 18th - 19th century.
Born 1763, in Berlin; died 1841, in Königsberg (now Kaliningrad, Russia).
Painter. Religious subjects.

Johann Knorre was the first professor of drawing at the Provinziale Kunstschule in Königsberg, now Kaliningrad.

MUSEUMS AND GALLERIES:
KALININGRAD: *The Holy Family*.

KNORRE, Julius
German, 19th century.
Born 1807, in Königsberg (now Kaliningrad, Russia); died 22 October 1884, in Königsberg.
Painter. History painting, genre scenes.

Julius Knorre was the son of Johann Friedrich Andreas Knorrre and a pupil of Wach at the Berlin academy. He was professor of art at either the school of fine arts in Düsseldorf or in Königsberg.

KNORST, Leonard
Flemish School, 16th century.
Born in Brussels.
Painter.

Leonard Knorst was made a burgher of Antwerp in 1544.

KNOTEK
Czechoslovak, 20th century.
Born 1945.
Painter, engraver.

KNÖTEL, Richard
German, 19th - 20th century.
Born 12 January 1857, in Glogau (now Glogów Malopolski); died 27 April 1914, in Berlin.
Painter, illustrator, lithographer. Historical subjects, military subjects.

Richard Knötel's repertoire consisted mainly of military subjects and war scenes for Berlin newspapers.

KNOTTER, Jan Adriaensz.
Dutch, 16th century.
Active in Leiden or in Utrecht.
Painter, collector.

KNOWLES, Alison
American, 20th century.
Born 1933, in New York.
Performance artist, environmental artist.
Neo-Dadaism, Fluxus.

BIBLIOGRAPHY:
Beaumont-Maillet, Laure/Woimant, Françoise/Pernoud, Emmanuel, *De Bonnard à Baselitz - Dix ans d'enrichissements du Cabinet des estampes 1978-1988*, exhibition catalogue, Bibliothèque nationale de France, Paris, 1992.

MUSEUMS AND GALLERIES:
PARIS (FNAC): *Wild Goose Moon; Jibway* (1991) - PARIS (Prints Collection).

KNOWLES, Davidson
British, 19th century.
Active in London.
Painter. Portraits, landscapes with figures, landscapes, animals.

Davidson Knowles was a member of the Royal Society of British Artists. He began to exhibit at the Royal Academy and at the Suffolk Street Gallery in 1879. His paintings often include animals.

AUCTION RECORDS:
LONDON, 22 March 1909, *Ducks*, GBP 4. LONDON, 18 July 1984, *Young Girl with a Bunch of Lilac* (1895, oil on canvas, 16 1/4 x 12 ins / 41 x 30.5 cm) GBP 1,600. LONDON, 12 April 1985, *Consolation* (oil on canvas, 28 x 19 3/4 ins / 71 x 50 cm) GBP 2,300. NEW YORK, 14 Oct 1993, *Arab Warrior with a Pistol* (oil on canvas, 20 x 12 1/4 ins / 51 x 31.4 cm) USD 1,265. NEW YORK, 15 Feb 1994, *Drama under the Full Moon* (oil on canvas/panel, 27 x 20 ins / 68.6 x 51.1 cm) USD 5,750. LONDON, 29 Jan 2003, *Sheikh of the Sudan* (oil on board, 9 x 6 ins / 23 x 16 cm) GBP 1,600. LONDON, 4 March 2004, *Sonnet* (oil on canvas, 36 x 28 ins / 91 x 71 cm) GBP 1,300.

KNOWLES, Farquar McGillvray
American, 19th century.
Born 22 May 1860, in Syracuse (New York); died 1932, in Toronto.
Painter, illustrator, miniaturist. Genre scenes, seascapes.

Farquar McGillvray Knowles lived in New York but also spent time in France and England.

KNOWLES, George Sheridan
British, 19th - 20th century.
Born 1863, in Manchester; died 1931.
Painter, watercolourist. Portraits, genre scenes.

George Sheridan Knowles was a member of the Royal Institute of Oil Painters and the Royal Institute of Painters in Watercolours, and an associate of the Royal Cambrian Academy. He exhibited at the Royal Academy, the Suffolk Street Gallery and the Royal Institute of Painters in Watercolours from 1885, and was awarded a jury commendation at the Paris Exposition Universelle of 1900.

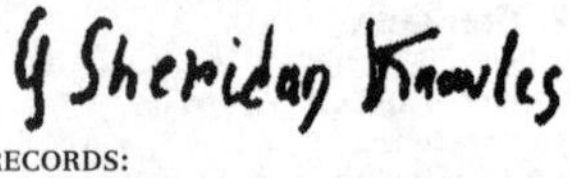

AUCTION RECORDS:
LONDON, 7 Dec 1907, *When Duty Calls* (1901) GBP 24. LONDON, 24 May 1910, *Fairy Tales*, GBP 13. LONDON, 4 March 1911, *Caught Napping*, GBP 26. LONDON, 3 Nov 1944, *General's Council*, GBP 54; *Our Worthy Host*, GBP 57. LONDON, 13 Feb 1976, *Charity* (1906, oil on canvas, 19 1/2 x 29 1/2 ins / 49.5 x 75 cm) GBP 450. NEW YORK, 25 Oct 1977, *Tobogganning* (oil on canvas remounted on board, 35 3/4 x 24 ins / 91 x 61 cm) USD 8,200. LONDON, 26 Oct 1979, *Soldier's Return* (1900, oil on canvas, 23 3/4 x 35 3/4 ins / 60.4 x 90.9 cm) GBP 1,200. LONDON, 20 Oct 1981, *Orphans* (oil on canvas, 48 x 37 1/2 ins / 122 x 95 cm) GBP 4,500. LONDON, 19 Oct 1983, *Companions* (oil

on canvas, 36 x 28 ins / 91.5 x 71 cm) GBP 2,000. NEW YORK, 31 Oct 1985, *Young Woman and Children in a Park* (1901, oil on canvas, 36 x 20 ins / 91.5 x 50.8 cm) USD 8,250. LONDON, 17 Dec 1986, *At the Ball* (1897, oil on panel, 14 1/4 x 10 ins / 36 x 25.5 cm) GBP 3,000. NEW YORK, 29 Oct 1987, *Young Woman and Children Feeding Pigeons* (1903, oil on canvas, 30 x 20 ins / 76.2 x 50.8 cm) USD 13,000. LONDON, 3 June 1988, *Fisherman's Tale* (oil on canvas, 18 x 24 1/4 ins / 45.7 x 61.3 cm) GBP 935. MONTREAL, 1 May 1989, *Woman and Young Girl Sitting on a Bench* (oil on panel, 23 1/2 x 19 ins / 60 x 48 cm) CAD 10,200. NEW YORK, 23 May 1989, *Feeding Pigeons in the Park* (1903, oil on canvas, 30 x 20 ins / 76.2 x 50.8 cm) USD 16,500. STOCKHOLM, 15 Nov 1989, *Interior with Four Men in Conversation* (oil on canvas, 17 1/4 x 23 1/2 ins / 44 x 60 cm) SEK 14,000. LONDON, 13 Dec 1989, *Minstrel's Lay* (oil on canvas, 24 x 16 ins / 61 x 40.5 cm) GBP 3,080. STOCKHOLM, 16 May 1990, *Interior with a Courtly Supper* (oil on canvas, 18 x 24 ins / 46 x 61 cm) SEK 21,000. LONDON, 15 June 1990, *Many Hands Make Light Work* (oil on panel, 18 x 11 3/4 ins / 45.7 x 29.8 cm) GBP 2,200. LONDON, 14 June 1991, *Bust Portrait of Miss Agnes A. Marshall* (1891, oil on canvas, 24 x 20 1/4 ins / 61 x 51.5 cm) GBP 1,430. LONDON, 11 Oct 1991, *Saga of King Olaf* (1892, oil on canvas, 36 x 28 1/4 ins / 91.5 x 71.5 cm) GBP 2,420. NEW YORK, 29 Oct 1992, *Ready for a Walk* (1908, oil on canvas, 21 3/4 x 15 1/2 ins / 55.2 x 39.4 cm) USD 10,450. LONDON, 29 March 1995, *Picking Flowers* (oil on canvas, 24 x 18 ins / 61 x 46 cm) GBP 2,875. NEW YORK, 1 Nov 1995, *Sleigh Ride* (oil on canvas/card, 36 1/2 x 24 ins / 92.7 x 61 cm) USD 48,875. NEW YORK, 23 May 1996, *Happy Hours* (oil on canvas, 35 x 22 1/4 ins / 89 x 56.5 cm) USD 23,000. LONDON, 7 Nov 1996, *Journey's End* (1911, oil on canvas, 30 x 23 ins / 76.2 x 58.4 cm) GBP 2,760. LONDON, 5 Nov 1997, *Imprudence* (1908, oil on canvas, 20 x 30 ins / 51 x 76 cm) GBP 11,500. NEW YORK, 18 March 1998, *Young Beauty* (1900, oil on canvas) USD 13,800. LONDON, 17 March 1999, *Piggybank. Repairing the Broken Doll* (1900, oil on canvas, a pair, 31 x 22 ins / 80 x 57 cm) GBP 16,500. LONDON, 9 June 1999, *Day of Adventure* (1916, oil on canvas, 35 x 46 ins / 90 x 118 cm) GBP 16,000. PORTLAND, 2 Aug 2000, *Woman and Child in a Garden* (oil on canvas, 36 x 24 ins / 91 x 61 cm) USD 12,000. LONDON, 30 Nov 2000, *Nocturne* (1914, watercolour heightened with gouache, 15 x 21 ins / 37 x 53 cm) GBP 5,500. LONDON, 6 Sept 2001, *Adventurer* (oil on canvas, 18 x 24 ins / 46 x 61 cm) GBP 1,200. LONDON, 7 March 2002, *Toast* (oil on canvas, 18 x 24 ins / 46 x 61 cm) GBP 3,400. LONDON, 13 June 2002, *Lunch after the Hunt* (oil on canvas, 18 x 24 ins / 46 x 61 cm) GBP 4,200. SYDNEY, 27 Oct 2003, *Bedtime Stories* (1907, watercolour, 29 x 19 ins / 74 x 49 cm) AUD 3,000. TORONTO, 17 Nov 2003, *Eventide* (oil on canvas, 36 x 24 ins / 91 x 61 cm) CAD 40,000. LONDON, 9 March 2004, *Bedtime Story* (1907, watercolour, 28 x 19 ins / 71 x 47 cm) GBP 2,700. LONDON, 25 Nov 2004, *Gifts of Love* (oil on canvas, 54 x 53 ins / 136 x 135 cm) GBP 16,000.

KNOWLES, Reginald Lionel
British, 20th century.
Died 1925.
Draughtsman, illustrator.

Reginald Knowles worked as a book illustrator with his brother Horace. He was a contributor to *Dent's Everyman's Library* from 1905. Other works illustrated by Knowles include *Legends from Fairyland* by P.C. Asbjørnsen and J. Moe (1908), and *Marie de France* (1913). His style is reminiscent of the work of Arthur Rackham.

KNOWLTON, Helen Mary
American, 19th - 20th century.
Born 16 August 1832, in Littleton (Massachusetts); died 1918.
Painter. Portraits, landscapes.

Helen Mary Knowlton studied under William M. Hunt. She worked in Boston and exhibited at the Boston Art Club and the National Academy. She also wrote books and art reviews.

KNOWLTON, Maud
Maiden name: Briggs
American, 20th century.
Born in Pennacook.
Painter. Landscapes, flowers.

Maud Knowlton studied under Rhoda Holmes Nicholls in New York. She also worked in Holland and in Paris.

KNOX, G. J.
British, 19th century.
Active in London.
Painter, watercolourist. Landscapes, waterscapes, seascapes, architectural views, ruins.

G.J. Knox exhibited at the Royal Academy and at the Suffolk Street Gallery from 1839 to 1859.

MUSEUMS AND GALLERIES:

CAPE TOWN (musée): *Knowle Park (Kent)* (watercolour).

AUCTION RECORDS:

LONDON, 24 July 1911, *Scenes with River and Cottage by a Stream* (three watercolours) GBP 1; *Mill on a River; Fishing Village* (two matching watercolours) GBP 1. GUERNSEY, 20 March 2003, *Prince Albert's Statue and St Peter Port, Guernsey* (watercolour, 7 x 15 ins / 17 x 38 cm) GBP 2,050.

KNOX, James
British, 19th - 20th century.
Born April 1866, in Glasgow.
Active in the USA.
Painter.

James Knox was a member of the American Arts Federation and the Salmagundi Club.

MUSEUMS AND GALLERIES:

WASHINGTON DC: *First Tank Attack.*

AUCTION RECORDS:

NEW YORK, 24 June 1988, *Wooded Landscape with Felled Tree Trunks* (1922, oil on card, 11 3/4 x 13 3/4 ins / 30 x 35 cm) USD 4,400. NEW YORK, 17 Dec 1990, *Summer Landscape* (oil/synthetic resin, 12 x 14 ins / 30.5 x 35.6 cm) USD 1,320.

KNOX, John
British, 19th century.
Born 1778, in Paisley; died 15 January 1845, in Keswick.
Painter. Landscapes.

John Knox was a student of Alexander Nasmyth. His landscapes, mostly showing views of Ben Lomond, Edinburgh, Glasgow and Dublin, were very popular. Two of his students, Horatio MacCulloch and Sir Daniel Macnee, became quite well known. He exhibited at the Royal Academy, the British Institution and at the Suffolk Street Gallery from 1829 to 1849.

MUSEUMS AND GALLERIES:

GLASGOW: four landscapes.

AUCTION RECORDS:

LONDON, 24 Nov 1965, *View of Loch Lomond,* GBP 1,300. SCOTLAND, 31 Aug 1973, *Govan Ferry,* GBP 7,600. LONDON, 25 Nov 1977, *The Nelson Monument on Glasgow Green* (oil on canvas, 26 1/2 x 35 1/2 ins / 67.3 x 90.2 cm) GBP 2,600. LONDON, 24 Nov 1978, *Banks of the Clyde* (oil on canvas, 21 x 29 1/2 ins / 53.3 x 75 cm) GBP 4,800. PERTH, 15 April 1980, *Cottage on the Banks of a River* (oil on canvas, 20 3/4 x 26 1/2 ins / 53 x 67 cm) GBP 800. EDINBURGH, 17 Nov 1981, *View of the Clyde* (oil on canvas, 42 1/4 x 60 ins / 107 x 152.5 cm) GBP 16,000. LONDON, 13 July 1984, *View of Edinburgh from the Village of Canonmills* (oil on canvas, 36 x 50 1/2 ins / 90.5 x 128 cm) GBP 13,000. LONDON, 9 July 1986, *Landscapes around Ben Lomond* (oil on canvas, a pair, 24 1/2 x 61 1/2 ins / 62 x 156 cm) GBP 60,000. LONDON, 12 July 1989, *Loch Coruisk on the*

Isle of Skye (oil on canvas, 20 x 28 ins / 50.5 x 71 cm) GBP 6,600. LONDON, 14 March 1990, *View of Loch Lomond with the Castle of Tulliechewan* (oil on canvas, 24 1/4 x 34 1/4 ins / 61.5 x 87 cm) GBP 15,400. LONDON, 11 July 1990, *View of Regent's Park from Primrose HIll* (oil on canvas, 9 1/2 x 13 1/2 ins / 24 x 34 cm) GBP 18,700. GLASGOW, 5 Feb 1991, *On the Banks of the Clyde* (oil on canvas, 22 x 27 1/4 ins / 55 x 69 cm) GBP 4,950. PERTH, 26 Aug 1991, *Cathcart Castle near Glasgow* (oil on canvas, 26 x 35 1/2 ins / 66 x 90 cm) GBP 7,920. NEW YORK, 21 May 1992, *View of Dunbarton Rock and the Clyde fron Langbank in Scotland* (oil on canvas, 25 1/4 x 35 1/4 ins / 64.1 x 89.5 cm) USD 28,600. PERTH, 1 Sept 1992, *Lismore Castle in Ireland* (oil on canvas, 25 x 35 ins / 63.5 x 89 cm) GBP 5,940. LONDON, 14 July 1993, *View from Ben Lomond Looking South West; View from Ben Lomond Looking North West* (oil on canvas, a pair, each 24 1/2 x 61 1/2 ins / 62 x 156 cm) GBP 67,500. GLASGOW, 1 Feb 1994, *Views of a Loch* (oil on canvas, a pair, each 7 1/2 x 11 ins / 19 x 27 cm) GBP 2,530. EDINBURGH, 23 May 1996, *Panoramic Landscape with Loch Lomond and Ben Lomond in the Background and Figures in the Foreground* (oil on canvas, 24 1/2 x 34 1/4 ins / 62.3 x 87 cm) GBP 20,700. LONDON, 16 Sept 1999, *Approaching Storm* (oil on canvas on board, 19 x 26 ins / 48 x 67 cm) GBP 1,600. LONDON, 26 Oct 2000, *In the Highlands* (oil on canvas, 36 x 50 ins / 91 x 127 cm) GBP 25,000. LONDON, 1 Nov 2001, *On the Banks of the River Clyde, Dumbarton* (oil on canvas, 25 x 35 ins / 63 x 89 cm) GBP 17,000. LONDON, 30 Oct 2003, *The Clyde at Govan, with Figures and a Boat in the Foreground* (oil on canvas, 22 x 30 ins / 56 x 76 cm) GBP 17,000.

KNOX, Susan Ricker
American, 20th century.
Born 1875, in Portsmouth (New Hampshire); died 1959.
Painter. Portraits.

Susan Ricker Knox studied in Philadelphia, New York and in Europe. She was member of the Pen and Brush Club and League of American Art Teachers. She mostly painted portraits.

AUCTION RECORDS:
NEW YORK, 23 June 1983, *Young Woman in Pink* (1902, oil on canvas, 11 x 8 ins / 28 x 20.3 cm) USD 2,100. CHICAGO, 19 June 1999, *Mother and Child, One Sock Missing* (oil on canvas, 40 x 30 ins / 102 x 76 cm) USD 1,800. OAK PARK, 5 Dec 1999, *Untitled, Woman with a Small Girl Sitting on her Lap* (oil on canvas, 40 x 30 ins / 102 x 76 cm) USD 2,300. WASHINGTON, 9 Dec 2000, *Mountainous Desert Landscape* (oil on canvas, 30 x 38 ins / 76 x 96 cm) USD 1,500. PITTSFIELD, 8 Sept 2001, *Adoring Woman in a Lace Shawl Holding a Young Girl* (oil on canvas, 40 x 30 ins / 102 x 76 cm) USD 3,000. MILFORD, 24 April 2003, *Young Girl is the Artist's Favourite Model, Hazel Moulton of Kittery, Maine* (c. 1916, oil on canvas) USD 9,000. BOSTON, 21 Nov 2003, *In the Garden* (oil on canvas, 14 x 16 ins / 35 x 41 cm) USD 3,100.

KNUBEL, Franz Rudolf
German, 20th century.
Sculptor.

Franz Knubel exhibited in Cologne and mainly carried out austere sculptures in aluminium. His works, abstract in conception, show his preoccupation with geometric volumes.

KNUDDEN, E.
Belgian, 19th century.
Active in Antwerp c. 1841.
Painter. Landscapes, urban landscapes, interiors.

Knudden was a pupil of Fr de Braekelaer.

KNUDSEN, Christian
Danish, 20th century.
Born 1945, in Vorup.
Active in Canada.
Painter (mixed media).

Since the early 1960s, Christian Knudsen has taken it upon himself to break down works of art according to their tonal organisation (white, black, yellow) and the composition of their surfaces: canvas stuck on to hardboard panels, acrylic paint, photographic emulsion, adhesive tape and pencil outlines. At first, the composition of his works followed a geometric layout juxtaposed with a photographic image, then from 1976 to 1977, he abandoned the photographic parts and created diptychs and triptychs. He tries to achieve a contrast of textures between geometric shapes and coloured surfaces that are expressionist and gestural, while nevertheless continuing to work in a pronounced minimalist-materialist manner, sometimes reminiscent of the work of the group Support-Surface.

MUSEUMS AND GALLERIES:
MONTREAL (MAC): *Emerging Yellow Rectangle* (1976); *Kite* (1977); *Archer* (1980).

KNUDSEN, Gerda
Norwegian, 20th century.
Active c. 1937.
Painter.

KNUDSEN, Hans
Danish, 19th - 20th century.
Born 16 August 1865, in Roskilde.
Painter. Landscapes.

MUSEUMS AND GALLERIES:
COPENHAGEN (Statens Mus. for Kunst): *Sommerdag. Motiv fra Tange (Summer's Day)* (1898).

KNUDSEN, Henry Jacob
Danish, 19th - 20th century.
Born 10 May 1868, in Copenhagen.
Painter. Landscapes.

Henry Knudsen attended courses at the Académie Julian in Paris, later settling in Egypt after sojourns in Italy and Syria.

KNUDSEN, Leif
Swedish, 20th century.
Born 1928, in Stockholm.
Painter. Murals, cartoons for tapestries, stage sets.

Leif Knudsen studied philosophy at the University in Göteborg in 1947-1948, then went to work in 1948 in the Académie d'André Lhote in Paris and was subsequently taught by André Nemes at the art school in Göteborg. In 1949 he received his diploma and in 1953 he won a scholarship from the French government, which enabled him to stay in Paris again. He executed a tapestry in Aubusson. In 1954 he returned to Sweden while continuing to visit Paris. In 1959 he was awarded the cultural prize of the City of Göteborg. He executed enamels, tapestries and paintings for the VARA company, from 1953 to 1966, an important ceiling for the school of Fässberg in Mölndal, in 1963-1964; from 1955 to 1960, stage sets for plays by Molière, Shakespeare, Holberg and Ibsen. His work is linked to Lyrical Abstraction, through which he expresses his emotions and convictions pertaining to the prevailing social norms.

He participated in numerous group exhibitions including the annual Salons in Stockholm and Göteborg from 1949, the manifestations of the group Nya Valand, in Sweden, Germany, England and Holland from 1953 to 1958; he exhibited with the Kring spontanismen group in several Swedish towns in 1959. His work was shown at *Poetic Abstraction* in Sweden from 1963 to 1965, at *Aspect of Young Swedish Painting* in 1962 in Paris; at the Brooklyn Museum, New York, 1963; the Antibes festival in 1965; the Musée Galliera, Paris, 1964 and the Folkwang Museum in Essen in 1966. He had solo exhibitions in Göteborg in 1954, 1956, 1959, 1961 and 1964; Borås Kunstmuseum, Essen, 1957; Stockholm, 1960; Norrköprings Museum, 1960; Lund, 1962; Malmö, 1966 and Paris, 1966.

Bibliography:
Hellman, Gunnar, *Leif Knudsen*, exhibition catalogue, Gal. Massol, Paris, 1966.
Museums and Galleries:
Halmstad (Länsmuseet) - Karlstad (Värmlands Mus.) - Malmö (Konstmus.) - Paris (Institut Tessin) - Stockholm (Moderna Mus.) - Stockholm (Nationalmus.).

KNUDSEN, Peder
Danish, 19th - 20th century.
Born 1868; died 1944.
Painter. Landscapes.
Auction records:
Copenhagen, 25 Oct 1989, *Park with White Bench in front of Portal* (1931, oil on canvas, 30 x 38 1/2 ins / 76 x 98 cm) DKK 14,000. London, 29 March 1990, *In the Shade* (1919, oil on canvas, 30 x 38 3/4 ins / 76.2 x 98.4 cm) GBP 5,500. London, 11 Oct 1995, *Winter Landscape* (oil on canvas, 33 3/4 x 29 1/4 ins / 86 x 74 cm) GBP 2,300. Vejle, 15 March 2000, *Mountain Landscape, Trolltinder, Romsdalen, Norway* (1932, oil on canvas, 39 x 47 ins / 100 x 120 cm) DKK 13,000. Copenhagen, 2 March 2004, *Waves Breaking on the Rocky Coast at Bornholm* (oil on canvas, 39 x 54 ins / 100 x 136 cm) DKK 12,000. Vejle, 10 May 2004, *Coastal Landscape with Cliffs* (oil on canvas, 29 x 38 ins / 74 x 96 cm) DKK 12,000.

KNUP, Ernst Rudolf
Swiss, 20th century.
Born 30 April 1881, in Zurich.
Painter, engraver.
After studying in Munich, Ernst Knup copied a number of paintings by Spanish, Flemish and Italian masters. He taught drawing in Zoug.

KNUPFER, Benes
Czech, 19th - 20th century.
Born 21 March 1848, near Sychrov; died 20 November 1910, in Ancona, Italy.
Active in Friedstein.
Painter. Allegorical subjects, landscapes.
Benes Knupfer studied at the academy of fine arts in Prague and with Piloty in Munich. He worked in Rome. He was awarded a medal in Munich (1889) and a bronze medal in Paris in 1900 at the Exposition Universelle.
Museums and Galleries:
Düsseldorf: *Scene from 'Goetz von Berlichingen'* - Vienna: *Battle of the Tritons.*
Auction records:
New York, 1st and 2 April 1902, *Sea Nymph,* USD 50. New York, 24 May 1988, *Battle of the Tritons* (oil on canvas, 43 x 88 ins / 109.2 x 223.5 cm) USD 10,450. London, 4 Oct 1989, *Pan Pipes Player* (oil on canvas, 27 1/2 x 55 ins / 70 x 140 cm) GBP 6,380. New York, 12 Feb 1997, *Battle of the Tritons* (oil on canvas, 43 x 88 ins / 109.2 x 223.5 cm) USD 31,050. London, 11 June 1997, *Battle of the Tritons* (oil on canvas, 44 1/2 x 88 1/2 ins / 113 x 225 cm) GBP 17,250. Prague, 20 Nov 1999, *Fishermen's Houses* (oil on canvas, 24 x 13 ins / 62 x 33 cm) CZK 65,000. London, 6 April 2000, *Greeting of Wind and Waves* (oil on canvas, 50 x 40 ins / 128 x 102 cm) GBP 12,000. Prague, 27 May 2000, *Nude Girl* (1870, oil on canvas, 24 x 16 ins / 60 x 40 cm) CZK 100,000. Amsterdam, 24 April 2002, *Siren's Song* (oil on canvas, 20 x 39 ins / 50 x 100 cm) EUR 3,500. Montreal, 10 Dec 2002, *Two Nymphs in a Sunlit Glade* (1884, oil on canvas, 38 x 24 ins / 96 x 62 cm) CAD 11,000. London, 29 Jan 2003, *Embrace* (oil on canvas, 65 x 59 ins / 164 x 150 cm) GBP 5,200. London, 12 Nov 2003, *Dolphins* (oil on canvas, 32 x 57 ins / 82 x 144 cm) GBP 2,000. Vienna, 27 May 2004, *Dolphins* (oil on canvas, 32 x 57 ins / 82 x 144 cm) EUR 8,500.

KNUPFER, Nicolaus
German, 17th century.
Born c. 1603, in Leipzig; died c. 1655-1660, in Utrecht.
Painter. Religious subjects, mythological subjects, battles, portraits, genre scenes.
Knupfer studied with Emmanuel Nyssen in Leipzig. He then worked in Magdeburg, and later with Abraham Bloemaert in Utrecht, where he finally settled. He taught Ary de Vois and possibly Jan Steen in the Hague.

He painted three battles for the king of Denmark, which were lost in the fire at Christiansborg Castle in 1794.

Museums and Galleries:
Amsterdam: *Cincinnatus* - Copenhagen: *Paul before Festus Agrippa and Berenice; Mercury Flying off with Psyche* - Dresden: *The Artist and His Family Making Music* - Kassel: *The Seven Works of Mercy* - Milan (Pinacoteca di Brera): *Lazarus at the Rich Man's Gate* - Oldenburg: *Cupid Opening the Curtains of a Bed on Which Venus is Lying.* - Prague: *Diana Bathing* - Schwerin: *The 'Contento', a Marriage in the Clouds; Joseph in Prison; Christ Washing the Apostles' Feet; Lazarus at the Rich Man's Gate* - St Petersburg (Hermitage): *The Queen of Sheba before Solomon* - Stockholm (Universitet konstsamling): *Fishermen Surprised by Savages* - Turin (Pinacoteca dell'Accademia Albertina di Belle Arti): *Woman Dressed in Yellow Standing on Ruins* - Utrecht: *The Young Tobias and His Wife.*
Auction records:
Paris, 1763, *Mars and Venus,* FRF 478. Paris, 1765, *Christ before Pilate,* FRF 340. Paris, 20 June 1939, *Biblical Scene,* FRF 390. Paris, 25 May 1949, *The Prodigal Son with the Courtesans,* FRF 480,000. London, 10 Dec 1980, *The Prodigal Son Feasting* (oil on panel, 22 3/4 x 28 3/4 ins / 58 x 73 cm) GBP 18,000. London, 22 Oct 1982, *Theagenes and Knemon with the Body of Thisbe* (oil on panel, 14 1/2 x 12 1/2 ins / 37 x 31.6 cm) GBP 3,000. New York, 18 Jan 1984, *The Meeting of Abraham and Melchisedech* (oil on panel, 26 x 32 ins / 66 x 81.2 cm) USD 15,000. Paris, 14 April 1989, *the Death of Orpheus* (oil on oak panel, 28 3/4 x 28 3/4 ins / 73 x 73 cm) FRF 250,000. London, 3 July 1991, *The Banquet of the Gods* (1644, oil on panel, 14 1/4 x 17 3/4 ins / 36 x 45 cm) GBP 16,500. Paris, 24 March 1997, *The Judgement of Solomon* (oil on walnut panel, fragment, 14 1/4 x 11 3/4 ins / 36.5 x 30 cm) FRF 15,000. Stockholm, 3 Dec 2003, *Figures outside a Building* (oil on panel, 14 x 17 ins / 35 x 42 cm) SEK 25,000.

KNUPFER, R.
Painter. Genre scenes.
Museums and Galleries:
Salford (Museum and AG): *Columbus and the Egg.*

KNUS, Jacob
Swiss, 16th century.
Born in Constance.
Active at the end of the 16th century.
Painter.
Jacob Knus worked for, among others, the church of St Peter in Will, in the canton of St Gall.

KNUT, Martin
Czechoslovak, 20th - 21st century.
Born 1964, in Vranov.
Painter.
Martin Knut lives and works in Bratislava. His paintings focus on small imagined anecdotes: here a small figure, man or woman on a see-saw, there another figure sitting and eating an ice cream. Largely devoid of any philosophical implications or social manifesto, the poetic simplicity of his work raises its stature. His works adopt a deliberately naive, clumsy, design, made up of lines and splashes of paint applied onto brightly coloured but otherwise empty backgrounds.

He took part in several collective exhibitions in Czechoslovakia, notably at the national gallery in Bratislava. His work was included in the *Prague-Bratislava: D'une génération à l'autre* (*Prague-Bratislava: From One Generation to Another*) exhibition held in 1992 at the Musée d'Art Moderne de la Ville de Paris.

KNUTSON, Greta

Swedish, 20th century.
Born 10 November 1899, in Stockholm; died 6 March 1983, in Paris.
Active in France.
Painter. Portraits, scenes with figures.

Greta Knutson attended the art school in Stockholm at a very young age. She went to Paris in 1921, where she entered André Lhote's studio. She was introduced into the Dadaïst and Surrealist milieux. In 1924 she married the poet Tristan Tzara by whom she had two children, but separated from him in 1938. During the occupation of France she was involved in René Char's resistance network. She was also an art critic and writer.

Her friendships with Surrealists did not influence her painting. She painted numerous portraits including those of René Char and Alberto Giacometti. For some time her painting was influenced by André Lhote. Her later work in the south of France prompted her to a more faithful representation and generous flamboyancy.

She participated in group exhibitions in Sweden and France and showed regularly at the Salon des Surindépendants in Paris. In 1980 the Centre Culturel Suédois dedicated an important exhibition to her.

BIBLIOGRAPHY:

Bergquist, Lars/Classen, Brigitte, *Greta Knutson*, exhibition catalogue, Centre Culturel Suédois, Paris, 1980. Rosemont, Penelope, *Surrealist Women. An International Anthology*, exhibition catalogue, University of Texas Press, Austin (TX), 1998.

AUCTION RECORDS:

PARIS, 10 Feb 1993, *Composition* (oil on canvas, 13 x 16 1/4 ins / 33 x 41 cm) FRF 4,000. STOCKHOLM, 15 May 2000, *Composition with Woman and Objects on Table* (oil on canvas, 31 x 51 ins / 80 x 130 cm) SEK 48,000. STOCKHOLM, 27 Nov 2000, *Still-life of Objects on Table* (oil on canvas, 30 x 51 ins / 76 x 130 cm) SEK 40,000. STOCKHOLM, 2 May 2001, *Still-life of Fruit* (oil on canvas, 31 x 51 ins / 78 x 130 cm) SEK 35,000.

KNUTSON, Johan

Finnish, 19th century.
Born 28 September 1816; died 13 September 1899, in Helsinki.
Painter, illustrator, lithographer. Landscapes, seascapes.

Johan Knutson was probably a pupil of Gudin in Paris.

MUSEUMS AND GALLERIES:

HELSINKI: *Rokolankoski in the Jamso Parish*; *View of the Southern Port of Helsingfors (Helsinki)*; *Moonlight* (after Gudin).

AUCTION RECORDS:

LONDON, 25 March 1987, *Seashore with Figures* (oil on canvas, 20 3/4 x 26 1/2 ins / 53 x 67 cm) GBP 1,500. STOCKHOLM, 15 Nov 1988, *View from the Borga Archipelago with Small Boats out at Sea* (oil, 7 x 11 3/4 ins / 18 x 30 cm) SEK 56,000. HELSINKI, 25 April 1999, *Fisherman* (oil on canvas, 21 x 31 ins / 53 x 79 cm) FIM 48,000. HELSINKI, 28 Nov 1999, *Ship's portrait - Torsten* (oil on canvas, 20 x 29 ins / 51 x 73 cm) FIM 56,000. HELSINKI, 6 May 2000, *Boats by Jetty* (oil on canvas, 13 x 24 ins / 33 x 61 cm) FIM 29,000. HELSINKI, 13 May 2000, *Coastal Landscape* (oil on cardboard, 9 x 16 ins / 22 x 41 cm) FIM 32,000. HELSINKI, 10 May 2001, *Archipelago* (1866, oil on canvas, 26 x 38 ins / 67 x 96 cm) FIM 85,000. HELSINKI, 1 Dec 2001, *Idyllic Coastal Landscape with Cattle and Figures* (1861, oil on canvas, 31 x 45 ins / 78 x 115 cm) EUR 11,100. HELSINKI, 27 April 2002, *Coastal Landscape* (oil on canvas, 17 x 25 ins / 42 x 64 cm) EUR 4,600. HELSINKI, 1 Dec 2002, *View from Southern Harbour towards Brunnsparken* (oil on canvas, 14 x 22 ins / 36 x 56 cm) EUR 33,000. HELSINKI, 10 May 2003, *Imatra - Landscape with Rapids* (oil on canvas, 12 x 21 ins / 30 x 54 cm) EUR 2,700. HELSINKI, 18 Sept 2003, *Coastal Landscape with Fishermen* (oil on canvas, 9 x 14 ins / 24 x 36 cm) EUR 2,500. HELSINKI, 15 May 2004, *Archipelago* (oil on canvas/board, 9 x 13 ins / 23 x 32 cm) EUR 3,800.

KNYFF, Alfred de (Chevalier)

Belgian, 19th century.
Born 20 March 1819, in Brussels; died 22 March 1885, in Paris.
Painter. Landscapes, seascapes.
Barbizon School.

Alfred de Knyff studied at the fine arts academy in Brussels and in Calame. He was awarded medals in Paris in 1857, 1859 and 1861 and was made a Chevalier of the Légion d'Honneur and of the Order of Leopold in the same year. He spent time at Barbizon and was inspired by Rousseau, Dupré and Daubigny; he also met Corot in France. Knyff enjoyed a certain, possibly exaggerated, amount of success with his gentle, melancholy portrayals of the plains of the River Meuse. He also painted many seascapes and shore scenes.

MUSEUMS AND GALLERIES:

AMIENS: *Marshland in the Campine Region* - ANTWERP: two landscapes and a seascape - BRUSSELS: two landscapes - LIÈGE: four landscapes with animals.

AUCTION RECORDS:

PARIS, 1876, *Sunset in the Campine*, FRF 4,000; *Moonlight on the Banks of the Meuse*, FRF 2,650; *Suresnes Bridge*, FRF 1,700. PARIS, 1882, *Heather in Bloom*, FRF 2,400; *Farm Enclosure*, FRF 1,350. PARIS, 1894, *River*, FRF 500. PARIS, 16 June 1925, *Sheep Pen*, FRF 800. VERSAILLES, 27 Jan 1980, *Shepherdess and Flock in a Meadow* (1881, oil on panel, 16 1/4 x 12 1/2 ins / 41 x 31.5 cm) FRF 7,000. VIENNA, 17 March 1982, *Pastures* (oil on panel, 12 1/2 x 15 3/4 ins / 32 x 40 cm) ATS 30,000. BRUSSELS, 30 Oct 1985, *Seashore with Cattle and a Young Cowherd* (1857, oil on canvas, 43 x 32 3/4 ins / 109 x 83 cm) BEF 115,000. VERSAILLES, 25 Nov 1990, *Farm Animals Returning* (oil on panel, 5 3/4 x 4 1/4 ins / 14.5 x 10.5 cm) FRF 3,500. PARIS, 4 March 1992, *Pasture* (oil on panel, 7 1/2 x 11 1/2 ins / 19 x 29.5 cm) FRF 10,000. MELUN, 10 Dec 2000, *Garden with Trees in Blossom* (oil on panel, 16 x 29 ins / 40 x 73 cm) FRF 25,000. BRUSSELS, 5 Nov 2001, *Cliff View at Sunset* (oil on canvas, 43 x 59 ins / 108 x 151 cm) BEF 220,000. BRUSSELS, 10 Dec 2001, *Sawyers in a Landscape* (oil on panel, 23 x 29 ins / 58 x 73 cm) BEF 145,000. VERSAILLES, 7 April 2002, *Farmyard* (oil on canvas, 16 x 24 ins / 41 x 60 cm) EUR 2,800. LOKEREN, 13 Dec 2003, *River View* (oil on canvas, 28 x 49 ins / 70 x 124 cm) EUR 4,800. PARIS, 30 March 2004, *Ten Horsemen in a Storm* (1846, oil on cardboard, 6 x 8 ins / 15 x 20 cm) EUR 1,800.

KNYFF, Felix
Dutch, 17th century.
Active in Utrecht c. 1630.
Painter.

KNYFF, Jacob, or Knyf
Dutch, 17th century.
Born December 1638; died 1681, in London.
Active in Haarlem.
Painter. Landscapes, seascapes.

Jacob Knyff was the son of Wouter Knyff. After working in Haarlem he went to Paris and studied there under Glauber.

AUCTION RECORDS:
LONDON, 29 Nov 1978, *The English Fleet off Sheerness* (oil on canvas, 42 1/2 x 69 ins / 108 x 175 cm) GBP 9,000. LONDON, 12 March 1980, *Boats off Dover* (oil on canvas, 19 1/4 x 48 ins / 49 x 122 cm) GBP 5,200. LONDON, 23 April 1982, *Dutch Men-o'-war and Turkish Galleys off Constantinople* (oil on canvas, 36 x 76 3/4 ins / 91.5 x 195 cm) GBP 11,000. LONDON, 26 April 1985, *Charles II on board a Man of War off Dover* (c. 1674, oil on canvas, 47 1/4 x 68 ins / 120 x 172.7 cm) GBP 75,000. LONDON, 9 July 1986, *The English Fleet off Sheerness* (oil on canvas, 42 1/2 x 69 ins / 108 x 175 cm) GBP 24,000. PARIS, 12 June 1987, *'Zeven Provincien' - the Ship of Admiral van Ruyter* (1675, oil on canvas, 40 x 55 1/2 ins / 101.5 x 141 cm) FRF 68,000. LONDON, 30 May 1990, *Royal Inspection of the Fleet in the Thames Estuary in 1672* (oil on canvas, 51 1/4 x 61 1/4 ins / 130 x 155.5 cm) GBP 19,800.

KNYFF, Leender or Leonard
Dutch, 17th - 18th century.
Born 10 August 1650, in Haarlem; died 1721, in London.
Painter, draughtsman. Landscapes, architectural views, animals.

Leender Knyff was the son of Wouter Knyff. He lived in London and drew views of English castles and country houses for the *Britannia Illustrata* in 1708.

AUCTION RECORDS:
LONDON, 20 June 1969, *Landscape with Birds and Game*, Gns 1,000. LONDON, 1 June 1977, *Still-life with Game* (oil on canvas, 56 1/4 x 65 ins / 143 x 165 cm) GBP 3,600. LONDON, 10 April 1992, *Perspective of Staunton Harold in Leicestershire* (oil on canvas, 23 1/2 x 50 1/2 ins / 59.7 x 128.2 cm) GBP 17,600. LONDON, 26 Nov 1999, *View from the Side of Richmond Hill towards the Earl of Rochester's New Park* (oil on canvas, 30 x 72 ins / 77 x 183 cm) GBP 180,000.

KNYFF, Willem
Dutch, 17th century.
Born 1646, in Haarlem.
Painter.

Willem Knyff was the son of Wouter Knyff. Another Willem Woutersz. Knyff, who from his name would also seem to have been the son of Wouter Knyff, was buried on 1 March 1665 in St Anne's churchyard in Haarlem.

KNYFF, Wouter, or Knijf
Dutch, 17th century.
Born c. 1607, in Wezel; died c. 1693, in Bergen op Zoom.
Painter. Landscapes, waterscapes.

Wouter Knyff was active in Haarlem after 1640 and in Middelburg in 1652. He was 'foreman' of the Haarlem guild in 1675 and had Pieter Joosten as his pupil. Wouter Knyff had various sons who also became painters: Jacob, Willem and Leender.

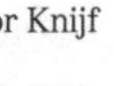

MUSEUMS AND GALLERIES:
AACHEN: *Landscape* - DARMSTADT: *Landscape* - DUBLIN: *Landscape* - GHENT: *Landscape* - HAARLEM: *Landscape* - LEIPZIG: *Landscapes* - ST PETERSBURG (Academy): two paintings - STOCKHOLM: *Landscape*.

AUCTION RECORDS:
LONDON, 23 July 1909, *River Scene*, GBP 22. LONDON, 9 May 1927, *Two Views of Nijmegen*, GBP 63. LONDON, 1 Aug 1929, *Town on a River*, GBP 241. LONDON, 16 Feb 1940, *River Scene*, GBP 78. PARIS, 28 May 1951, *Fishing Port*, FRF 36,000. PARIS, 1 Dec 1951, *Town by a River*, FRF 400,000. LONDON, 30 June 1964, *River Landscape*, Gns 550. PARIS, 5 April 1965, *View of a Castle on a River*, FRF 8,000. AMSTERDAM, 5 Nov 1968, *River Landscape*, NLG 16,000. COLOGNE, 16 June 1973, *River Landscape*, DEM 15,000. AMSTERDAM, 26 Nov 1974, *Town by a River*, NLG 20,000. LONDON, 8 Dec 1976, *River Landscape* (oil on panel, 16 1/4 x 21 1/4 ins / 41 x 54 cm) GBP 7,000. AMSTERDAM, 7 June 1977, *Animals by a River* (oil on panel, 15 1/4 x 22 1/2 ins / 39 x 57 cm) NLG 16,000. NEW YORK, 12 Jan 1979, *Peasants on the Outskirts of a Town* (oil on panel, 17 1/2 x 25 1/2 ins / 44.5 x 65 cm) USD 15,000. NEW YORK, 8 Jan 1981, *River Landscape with Cottages* (1641, oil on panel, 15 1/2 x 23 3/4 ins / 39.5 x 60.5 cm) USD 24,000. NEW YORK, 9 June 1983, *Town by a River* (oil on panel, 18 1/2 x 28 1/2 ins / 47 x 72.5 cm) USD 12,000. NEW YORK, 17 Jan 1985, *River Landscape with Boats and Nets* (oil on panel, 10 3/4 x 13 1/2 ins / 27.5 x 34 cm) USD 4,500. NEW YORK, 5 Nov 1986, *Riverside Scene* (oil on panel, 10 3/4 x 13 1/2 ins / 27.5 x 34 cm) USD 5,250. NEW YORK, 21 Oct 1988, *Landscape with a Castle by a Canal* (1647, oil on panel, 19 1/4 x 25 1/4 ins / 49 x 64 cm) USD 23,100. AMSTERDAM, 29 Nov 1988, *Fortified House by a River with Fishermen Working in their Boat* (oil on panel, 15 3/4 x 23 1/2 ins / 40.2 x 60 cm) NLG 36,800. AMSTERDAM, 22 Nov 1989, *Ruins by a Pool* (oil on canvas, 11 3/4 x 15 1/4 ins / 30 x 38.5 cm) NLG 13,225. AMSTERDAM, 12 June 1990, *View of Overschie with Fishermen in their Boats* (oil on panel, 16 x 32 3/4 ins / 40.5 x 83.2 cm) NLG 21,850. AMSTERDAM, 14 Nov 1990, *River Landscape with Small Boats* (1641, oil on panel, 16 1/4 x 21 1/4 ins / 41 x 54 cm) NLG 50,600. AMSTERDAM, 7 May 1992, *Fortified Village by a River with Fishermen in a Boat* (oil on panel, 18 3/4 x 25 ins / 47.5 x 63.8 cm) NLG 46,000. AMSTERDAM, 10 Nov 1992, *River Landscape with a Fortified Village and a Shepherdess and her Animals in the Foreground* (oil on canvas, 31 x 37 3/4 ins / 79 x 96.2 cm) NLG 9,200. LONDON, 21 April 1993, *River Landscape with Boats below the Town Walls* (oil on canvas, 40 1/4 x 59 3/4 ins / 102.5 x 152 cm) GBP 11,500. PARIS, 29 March 1994, *View of Nijmegen* (oil on oak panel, 15 1/2 x 23 3/4 ins / 39.5 x 60.5 cm) FRF 130,000. LONDON, 16 April 1999, *River Landscape with Fishermen at Landing Stage by Tower* (oil on panel, 15 x 24 ins / 39 x 61 cm) GBP 4,000. AMSTERDAM, 8 Nov 1999, *View of Delft with River Schie* (1632, oil on panel, 24 x 33 ins / 61 x 84 cm) NLG 17,000. NEW YORK, 27 Jan 2000, *River Landscape with Windmill by a Town* (oil on panel, 14 x 20 ins / 35 x 51 cm) USD 12,000. LONDON, 2 Nov 2000, *River Landscape with Castle and Fishermen* (oil on panel, 15 x 21 ins / 38 x 54 cm) GBP 15,000. AMSTERDAM, 6 Nov 2000, *Fortified Town on a River, with Sailing Boat in the Distance, at Sunset* (oil on panel, 10 x 11 ins / 25 x 28 cm) NLG 13,000. STOCKHOLM, 2 Dec 2003, *Coastal Landscape with Castle and Boats* (oil on panel, 19 x 27 ins / 47 x 69 cm) SEK 62,000.

KNYPBERGEN, François. See **KNIBBERGEN François**

KO CHENG-CH'I. See **GE ZHENGQI**

KO I-LUNG. See **GE YILONG**

KO TCHENG-K'I. See **GE ZHENGQI**

KO-JIN
Japanese, 20th - 21st century.
Born 1947, in Tokyo.
Painter.

Ko-Jin studied photography and exhibited at the Ninth Japanese Contemporary Art Exhibition held in Tokyo in 1969.

KOAT PEN. See **PEN-KOAT Pierre**

KOB, Anton
German, 19th century.
Born 7 September 1822, near Meran (now Merano, Italy); died 29 December 1895, in Bozen, South Tyrol (now Bolzano, Italy).
Sculptor.
Kob worked mainly for churches, including the church in Kastebrut and St Nicolas Church in Bozen.

KOBASHI, Yasuhide
Japanese, 20th century.
Born 1931, in Okayama Prefecture.
Active in the USA since 1965.
Print artist, sculptor.
Yasuhide Kobashi graduated from the ceramics department of Kyoto Art School in 1955, but had already started to paint and make woodcuts. He won the 1954 Newcomer's Prize at the National Painting Academy's exhibition and would win it again in 1958. In 1955 he joined the Japanese Print Association. From 1959 to 1962 he lived in New York, settling there permanently in 1965. His woodcut style is deliberately naive.

KOBATAKE, Hiroshi
Japanese, 20th century.
Born 1935, in Tokyo.
Sculptor, print artist.
BIBLIOGRAPHY:
Beaumont-Maillet, Laure/Woimant, Françoise/Pernoud, Emmanuel, *De Bonnard à Baselitz - Dix ans d'enrichissements du Cabinet des estampes 1978-1988*, exhibition catalogue, Bibliothèque nationale de France, Paris, 1992.

KOBAYAKAWA, Kiyoshi
Japanese, 20th century.
Born 1897, in Hakata (Fukuoka Prefecture); died 1948, at Ikegami, Tokyo.
Painter.
Kobayakawa Kiyoshi was a pupil of Kaburagi Kiyokata. He is best known for his woodblock prints of contemporary Japanese women. He began to design a series of six prints, *Kindai jisei sho* (*Modern Fashionable Styles*), in 1930. The prints, carved by Tadano Shichinosuke, were *Tipsy, Powdering the Face, Pedicure, Expression of Eyes, Black Hair,* and *Rouge*. Among these, *Tipsy* was considered daring for its portrayal of a Japanese woman, dressed in the height of western fashion, smoking and drinking.

Kiyoshi was awarded the special rank of *Tokusen* (excellent) for *The Geisha Ichimaru,* executed in 1933. During the 1920s and 1930s, he exhibited *nihonga* (Japanese-style) paintings at several exhibitions including the Kyodokai and the Imperial Academy Exhibition. In 1923, he contributed a print design to the series *Complete Collection of Chikamatsu*. He took part in the 1929 exhibition of Japanese art in the Jeu de Paume, Paris. Twelve of his total output of thirteen prints were exhibited at the 1936 Toledo Exhibition.

KOBAYAKAWA, Shusei
Japanese, 20th century.
Born 1889; died 1973 or 1974.
Painter.
Shusei Kobayakawa took part in the 1929 exhibition of Japanese art in the Jeu de Paume, Paris.

KOBAYASHI, Donge
Japanese, 20th century.
Born 1927, in Tokyo.
Print artist, illustrator.
Kobayashi Donge has exhibited regularly since 1954 with the Japanese Print Association and at the Shunyokai Salon. She won the Onchi Prize in 1956 and helped found the Association of Women Print Artists. The following year she exhibited at the Tokyo International Print Biennale. Her illustrations for *Evening Rainbow,* a collection of poetry by Daigaku Horiguchi, are in a realistic style with surrealist overtones.

KOBAYASHI, Gokiv (?)
Japanese, 20th century.
Painter. Animals.
Kobayashi worked in Tokyo and showed his work at the 1900 Paris Exposition Universelle.

KOBAYASHI, Hisako
Japanese, 20th century.
Painter (mixed media).
Hisako Kobayashi trained at the Pratt Institute in the USA. She paints in a mixture of oils, oil pastels, wax and glazes. Her work is abstract, with definite forms and sculptural plastic qualities. She has exhibited in group shows from 1979 in the USA, Japan and Korea. In 1994, she had solo shows in Paris and New York.

KOBAYASHI, Kanji
Japanese, 20th century.
Painter.
Kobayashi Kanji took part in the 1929 exhibition of Japanese art in the Jeu de Paume, Paris.

KOBAYASHI, Kokei, real name Kobayashi Shigeru, artist name Kokei
Japanese, 20th century.
Born 1883, in Niigata Prefecture; died 1957.
Painter.
Kobayashi Kokei went to Tokyo when he was sixteen, entering the studio of the painter Kajita Hanko. He was first accepted by the Bunken (the Ministry of Education Exhibition) in 1912. In 1922, he went to Europe. The Western painting he saw during his trip there had a lasting influence on his style. He tended towards neo-classicism, mixing Western techniques and Eastern decorative motifs. He became a member of the Imperial Art Academy, and later the Academy of Fine Arts, and was later appointed professor at the Tokyo School of Fine Arts. He was awarded the Order of Cultural Merit.
AUCTION RECORDS:
NEW YORK, 27 April 1994, *Kaki (Persimmons)* (ink and colours on prepared paper, hanging scroll, 53 x 12½ ins / 134.6 x 31.8 cm) USD 27,600.

KOBAYASHI, Mango
Japanese, 20th century.
Born 1870; died 1947.
Painter. Landscapes.
Kobayashi Mango showed his work at the 1900 Paris Exposition Universelle. He was a member of the teaching staff in the Western Art Department at Tokyo School of Fine Arts during the late 1920s.
MUSEUMS AND GALLERIES:
MIE (Prefectural Art Museum) - TOKYO (University Art Museum).

KOBAYASHI, Motoki
Japanese, 20th century.
Born 1945, in Northern Japan.
Painter.
Motoki Kobayashi has exhibited in Tokyo since 1965. He had his first one-man show there in 1969.

KOBAYASHI, Nobuo
Japanese, 20th - 21st century.
Born 1950.
Painter.
Kobayashi Nobuo exhibited in 1972 at the 16th Kyoto Exhibition of Independent Artists and in 1974 at the *Japanese Art*

Today exhibition held at the Musée d'Art Contemporain, Montréal.

KOBAYASHI, Yoshihiro
Japanese, 20th century.
Born in Japan.
Active in France.
Painter. Portraits, landscapes.

KOBBE, Georges G.
German, 20th century.
Born 5 April 1902, in Berlin; died 1934.
Painter, watercolourist, engraver, draughtsman, illustrator.

Georges Kobbe was primarily a book illustrator.

AUCTION RECORDS:
MUNICH, 27 Nov 1981, *The King of the Golden Town* (1920, watercolour/pen outlines, 10 1/2 x 7 3/4 ins / 26.5 x 20 cm) DEM 2,800.

KOBE, Jules Benno
Austrian, 20th century.
Born 4 April 1882, in Klagenfurt.
Painter. Figures, animals.

Jules Benno Kobe exhibited in Vienna, Munich and Holland and in Paris at the Salon des Artistes Français.

KOBEL, Jacob, or Koebel
German, 16th century.
Active in Germany c. 1520.
Engraver (wood) (?).

Certain biographers claim that Kobel was the author of the woodcuts that were published in Frankfurt am Main in 1540 in a book entitled *Wappen des heiligen roemischen Reichs teutscher Nation*. These prints, however, have also been attributed to Jacob Kerver. He is thought to have produced them for the work by Kobel, who was perhaps the author of the text or the drawings.

KOBELL, Anna
Dutch, 19th century.
Born c. 1795, in Gouda; died 7 September 1847, in Rotterdam.
Painter, engraver.

Anna Kobell was the daughter of Jan Kobell.

KOBELL, Ferdinand
German, 18th century.
Born 7 June 1740, in Mannheim; died 1 February 1799, in Munich.
Painter, engraver, draughtsman. Genre scenes, landscapes with figures, landscapes.

Ferdinand Kobell's father was a counsellor at the court of the Elector Charles Theodore of Bavaria. Ferdinand, who was called to occupy the same post, painted for his own amusement. When the Elector saw one of his paintings, he awarded the young man a pension to enable him to study art. Kobell went first to Mannheim, then to Paris in December 1768. There he met the famous engraver Wille who praised his talent very highly in his memoirs. Kobell was already painter to the Elector Palatine at the time he made this journey. On his return, he became a teacher at the academy and in 1793, he became director of the Munich Gallery.

He painted in the style of Berghem. His etchings, in particular, are charming. He also did burin engravings of genre scenes, views and landscapes.

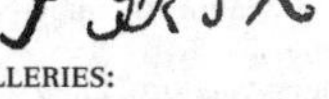

MUSEUMS AND GALLERIES:
BUCHAREST: *Landscape* - DARMSTADT: *Landscape* - MAINZ: *Landscape* - ORLÉANS: *Landscape* - STUTTGART: *Landscape*.

AUCTION RECORDS:
PARIS, 8-10 June 1920, *Wooded Landscape* (pencil) FRF 750. PARIS, 30 June 1925, *Grazing Flock*, FRF 500. MUNICH, 22-24 June 1966, *Mountainous Landscape*, DEM 5,200. ZURICH, 3 Nov 1972, *Beach Scene with Figures*, CHF 4,000. LONDON, 19 May 1976, *Flock beside a River* (oil on panel, 11 x 14 1/4 ins / 27 x 36 cm) GBP 3,300. MUNICH, 1 Dec 1976, *View of the Valley of Tripstatt* (1784, drawing, 17 x 13 1/2 ins / 43 x 34.5 cm) DEM 3,100. MUNICH, 28 Nov 1979, *Pair of Lovers in the Moonlight* (watercolour and gouache, 10 1/4 x 14 3/4 ins / 26 x 37.5 cm) DEM 4,600. MUNICH, 29 Nov 1979, *Two Fishermen in a Landscape* (oil on canvas, 21 1/4 x 29 1/4 ins / 54 x 74.5 cm) DEM 17,500. MUNICH, 29 June 1982, *Young Man at the Edge of a Wood* (1783, pen drawing, watercoloured) DEM 3,000. MUNICH, 28 June 1983, *Wooded River Bank* (pen and sepia wash, 6 3/4 x 8 1/2 ins / 17 x 21.5 cm) DEM 3,000. MUNICH, 28 June 1983, *Shepherd and Flock in a Steep Mountain Landscape* (oil on panel, 13 1/2 x 19 ins / 34 x 48.5 cm) DEM 6,500. HEIDELBERG, 14 Oct 1988, *Stag at Rest in a Vast Landscape* (pencil and ink, 6 x 9 ins / 15.4 x 23 cm) DEM 1,000. LONDON, 28 Feb 1990, *Wooded Landscape with Anglers on the Bank of a Mountain Stream* (oil on panel, a pair, each 30 x 24 1/2 ins / 76 x 62.5 cm) GBP 8,800. MUNICH, 26-27 Nov 1991, *Hunter Resting in a Wooded River Landscape* (ink and wash, 8 1/4 x 7 ins / 21 x 17.5 cm) DEM 2,415. HEIDELBERG, 9 Oct 1992, *Town on a Rocky Summit* (red chalk, 11 1/2 x 9 ins / 29 x 22.7 cm) DEM 1,290. LONDON, 10 Dec 1993, *Moonlit Landscape with Peasants Guarding Horses in a Meadow* (1774, oil on canvas, 26 1/2 x 34 1/4 ins / 67 x 86.7 cm) USD 4,830. MUNICH, 27 Feb 1999, *Rocky Landscape with Waterfall, Horseman and Farmers* (oil on canvas, 10 x 14 ins / 26 x 36 cm) DEM 20,000. LUCERNE, 13 Oct 1999, *Southern Landscapes with Cattle and Herdsmen* (oil on panel, a pair, 17 x 14 ins / 42 x 35 cm) CHF 12,000. COLOGNE, 19 May 2001, *Resting Shepherd* (oil on canvas, 41 x 37 ins / 103 x 94 cm) DEM 11,000. COLOGNE, 13 Dec 2003, *Waterfall in Rocky Landscape* (oil on canvas, 9 x 20 ins / 24 x 51 cm) EUR 4,000.

KOBELL, Franz Innocenz Josef
German, 18th - 19th century.
Born 23 November 1749, in Mannheim; died 14 January 1822, in Munich.
Painter, watercolourist, draughtsman. Landscapes, architectural views, animals.

Franz Kobell was the younger brother of Ferdinand. He was destined for a career in trade, but his brother's example and his own talents led him to follow a career in art. The patronage of the Elector Charles Theodore enabled him to spend nine years working in Italy. While there, he made a particular study of architectural subjects and Roman remains. According to Goethe, he was the greatest landscape artist of his time. On his return to Germany, he almost completely abandoned his brushes, devoting himself to sketches and drawings in pen and pencil. It has been estimated that there are more than 20,000 of these, whereas paintings by him are rare.

MUSEUMS AND GALLERIES:
STUTTGART: two landscapes - WEIMAR: *Stable*; two animal paintings; three landscapes.

AUCTION RECORDS:
PARIS, 10 Nov 1928, *A Shepherd and a Shepherdess Bringing Home Their Flock, in a Landscape* (in collaboration with Wilhelm) FRF 4,100. MUNICH, 25 Nov 1976, *River Bank* (c. 1815, watercolour/pen outlines, 3 1/4 x 4 ins / 8.5 x 10 cm) DEM 1,800. PARIS, 26 March 1979, *Mountain Landscape with Figures* (oil on panel, 13 1/2 x 19 1/4 ins / 34 x 49 cm) FRF 10,100. MUNICH, 28 Nov 1979, *River Landscape with Figures* (1819, pen and wash, 8 1/4 x 13 1/2 ins / 21 x 34.2 cm) DEM 5,600). MUNICH, 28 Nov 1979, *Mountain Landscape with a Flock* (watercolour/pen outlines, 9 x 13 ins / 22 x 33 cm) DEM 12,500. MUNICH, 29 June 1982, *River Landscape with Figures* (1819,

pen wash/pencil outlines, 8 1/4 x 13 1/2 ins / 21 x 34.2 cm) DEM 6,000. MUNICH, 29 June 1982, *Two Women beside a River* (watercolour, 9 x 13 ins / 22 x 33 cm) DEM 15,200. MUNICH, 29 Nov 1984, *Landscape with Two Women by the Water* (watercolour and pen, 9 x 13 ins / 22 x 33 cm) DEM 10,500. MUNICH, 29 Nov 1984, *Italian Landscape with a Castle by the Sea* (c. 1797, pen and wash, 6 1/4 x 8 ins / 16 x 20.5 cm) DEM 4,200. MUNICH, 29 Oct 1985, *Steep Cliff by the Sea* (c. 1800, brown wash/pencil outlines, 8 1/4 x 10 1/4 ins / 21 x 26 cm) DEM 3,400. MUNICH, 26-27 Nov 1991, *Classical Landscape by Moonlight* (1798, ink and watercolour in grisaille, 9 1/4 x 14 3/4 ins / 23.5 x 37.5 cm) DEM 6,440. HEIDELBERG, 11 April 1992, *Mountain Pass* (pencil and grey and brown wash, 12 1/4 x 16 1/2 ins / 30.9 x 42.1 cm) DEM 5,400. MUNICH, 26 May 1992, *Landscape from the Isar Valley* (ink, 6 3/4 x 8 1/4 ins / 17 x 21 cm) DEM 1,840. HEIDELBERG, 9 Oct 1992, *Wooded Landscape* (ink, 7 1/2 x 9 1/2 ins / 19 x 24 cm) DEM 1,500. MUNICH, 10 Dec 1992, *River Landscape with Shepherds* (1814, ink and watercolour, 7 3/4 x 11 ins / 19.9 x 27.7 cm) DEM 10,170. MUNICH, 2 Dec 1997, *Sunlit Landscape; Moonlit Landscape* (two oils on paper, a pair, 9 3/4 x 13 ins / 25 x 33 cm) DEM 12,000. PARIS, 30 March 1998, *Album of 115 Italian Landscapes* (pen and brown ink, occasional grey wash and lead pencil) FRF 50,000. MUNICH, 27 Feb 1999, *Highland Landscape with Castle and Mountain Top* (oil on canvas, 27 x 36 ins / 69 x 91 cm) DEM 28,000. BERLIN, 4 June 1999, *Italian Village in a Forest* (brown, black ink and pen, 11 x 15 ins / 27 x 38 cm) DEM 4,400. MUNICH, 29 May 2001, *Hilly Landscape* (watercolour and pen, 11 x 13 ins / 27 x 33 cm) DEM 4,800. MUNICH, 29 May 2001, *Kochelsee* (watercolour over pencil, 10 x 15 ins / 26 x 37 cm) DEM 31,000. MUNICH, 4 June 2002, *Landscape with Classical Ruins and Female Figures by Water* (1817, pen and wash, 6 x 8 ins / 15 x 21 cm) EUR 2,600. HAMBURG, 7 Dec 2002, *Landscape Studies and Sketches* (Indian ink, 188 in album, 7 x 9 ins / 19 x 23 cm) EUR 19,000. HEIDELBERG, 11 April 2003, *Farmstead in Trees* (sepia brush, 6 x 8 ins / 16 x 20 cm) EUR 1,500. AMSTERDAM, 19 May 2004, *Wooded Landscapes* (brush and brown ink wash, six, 7 x 8 ins / 17 x 21 cm) EUR 8,500. AMSTERDAM, 19 May 2004, *Landscapes* (brush and brown ink wash, six, 7 x 8 ins / 17 x 21 cm) EUR 11,000.

KOBELL, Georg

German, 19th century.
Born 1807, in Worms; died 1894, in Fürstenfeldbruck.
Painter. Landscapes.

Georg Kobell studied at the Munich academy. He spent long periods working in Italy under the direction of Karl Harko.

MUSEUMS AND GALLERIES:

BASEL (Kunstmus.): *Italian Landscape.*

AUCTION RECORDS:

COLOGNE, 19 Oct 1979, *View of the Königssee* (oil on canvas, 35 1/2 x 49 1/4 ins / 90 x 125 cm) DEM 3,800.

KOBELL, Hendrik

Dutch, 18th century.
Born 13 September 1751, in Rotterdam; died 3 August 1779, in Rotterdam.
Painter, engraver, draughtsman. Harbour scenes, seascapes.

Hendrik Kobell's father was a merchant and wanted his son to follow him into commerce. However, Hendrik began painting seascapes and scenes of boats in port for his own pleasure and his aptitude decided him to change career. After trading in Holland and England he studied at the drawing academy in Amsterdam and made such progress that he was admitted as a member of the academy. He received the patronage of Jac de Vos and Ploos van Amstel and went to France. After returning to Holland he married in Delftshaven on 30 October 1774. Kobell exhibited at the Free Society in London in 1770.

He was a frequent visitor to the Rhine and the Meuse and drew and painted some of the most picturesque spots on these rivers. However, he was primarily a painter of seascapes. His works include; *The Boat Yard; River and Boats; Fishermen on the Shore; Seascape with Two-master; Shore* (with Langendyk); *River with Hay Boat; River, Boats and Windmill; Seascape with Boats Pulled Ashore; Oude Hooft in Rotterdam; Houses by the Waterside; Peasant; General Pascal Paoli; Head of a Man Wearing a Fur Cap*; and *Kobell's Wife on her Death Bed.*

MUSEUMS AND GALLERIES:

AMSTERDAM (Academie voor Beeldende Vorming): drawing - CHANTILLY (Mus. Condé): *Ships off the Coast* (drawing); *Ships at Sea* (drawing) - VIENNA (Albertina Mus.).

AUCTION RECORDS:

LONDON, 19 April 1909, *Seascape* (drawing, two drawings by other artists) GBP 3. PARIS, 8-10 June 1920, *Landscape under Trees* (pencil) FRF 750. PARIS, 4 and 5 Feb 1954, *Fleet at Anchor in a Bay* (Indian ink wash) FRF 5,000. AMSTERDAM, 14 Nov 1983, *The Dutch Fleet* (gouache, 12 x 16 ins / 30.5 x 39.8 cm) NLG 4,200. NEW YORK, 19 Jan 1994, *Sailing in Stormy Seas* (1776, ink/paper, 14 x 20 ins / 35.6 x 50.8 cm) USD 1,955. PARIS, 3 April 1998, *Animals Drinking at a Lake* (pen and brown ink, grey wash, attributed, 5 x 7 ins / 13 x 18 cm) FRF 2,700. MUNICH, 23 June 1999, *Ships at Sea* (ink, 14 x 20 ins / 36 x 51 cm) DEM 3,000. PARIS, 16 Dec 2001, *Seascape* (1779, sepia Indian ink, 7 x 11 ins / 19 x 27 cm) FRF 35,000. VEJLE, 10 March 2003, *Seascape - Harbour Scene with Many Sailing Vessels* (1778, oil on canvas, 15 x 20 ins / 37 x 52 cm) DKK 30,000. BERLIN, 13 May 2004, *Sailing Ship off the Dutch Coast* (1777, pen and wash, 4 x 6 ins / 11 x 16 cm) EUR 2,200.

KOBELL, Jan I

Dutch, 18th - 19th century.
Born 1756, in Rotterdam; died 16 July 1833, in Rotterdam.
Painter, engraver. Portraits, seascapes, landscapes.

Jan Kobell I was the younger brother of Hendrik Kobell; he had twelve children. Jan Kobell engraved anatomical subjects and seascapes and in 1787 published a series of historical portraits.

AUCTION RECORDS:

PARIS, Oct 1945-July 1946, *Landscape with Sheep and Shepherds,* FRF 6,200. LONDON, 24 March 1982, *Milkmaid and her Animals* (1803, oil on panel, 18 1/4 x 23 1/2 ins / 46.5 x 60 cm) GBP 5,500. BATH, 16 March 1999, *Landscape with Cattle* (oil on canvas, 13 x 11 ins / 33 x 28 cm) GBP 3,000. HAMBURG, 19 Feb 2000, *Landscape with Herders, Cows and Sheep* (oil on canvas/panel, 9 x 10 ins / 22 x 25 cm) DEM 14,000. LONDON, 22 June 2000, *Pony, Goat and Resting Cattle in a Landscape* (oil on panel, 7 x 10 ins / 19 x 25 cm) GBP 6,500. AMSTERDAM, 23 April 2001, *Cows by a Stream* (oil on panel, 11 x 15 ins / 27 x 38 cm) NLG 6,000. LONDON, 19 April 2002, *Pastoral Landscape with Cow and Sheep by a Tree* (oil on panel, 8 x 9 ins / 21 x 22 cm) GBP 2,500. DORCHESTER, 13 March 2003, *Cattle and Sheep in a Landscape* (oil on panel, 10 x 13 ins / 25 x 33 cm) GBP 1,000. HAMBURG, 24 Oct 2003, *Cows by Lake* (oil on panel, 19 x 25 ins / 49 x 63 cm) EUR 1,500.

KOBELL, Jan II or Jean Baptiste, the Elder

Dutch, 19th century.
Born 8 November 1778, in Delfshaven; died 23 September 1814, in Amsterdam.
Painter, engraver, draughtsman. Religious subjects, landscapes, animals.

Jan Kobell II the Elder was orphaned at an early age and brought up at the orphanage in Rotterdam, though some biographers say that it was the Jansenist orphanage in Utrecht. Later he was placed as a pupil with the landscape and animal painter W.-R. van der Wall, who had no doubt taken an interest in Kobell. He joined the Utrecht guild in 1806. In 1810 he sent a painting to the Paris Salon and was awarded a gold medal. In 1813 he married Maria Stoste. Kobell was extremely successful as an artist and his works were much sought after by art enthusiasts. However, towards the end of his life he began to lead a dissolute existence and his conduct may well have cut short his career. While working from nature, Kobell began a meticulous study of the work of Paulus Potter and assimilated his remarkable vision. He painted scenes from the Old and New Testaments in the Regents room at the hospice in Utrecht.

AUCTION RECORDS:

PARIS, 1866, *Autumn Landscape with Figures and Animals,* FRF 4,860. PARIS, 1869, *Inn,* FRF 2,570. AMSTERDAM, 1881, *Cows in the Meadow,* FRF 1,785. PARIS, 19 Dec 1923, *Animals Grazing,* FRF 150. PARIS, 18 and 19 March 1927, *Grazing by the River,* FRF 1,050. PARIS, 25 Jan 1929, *Landscape with Horse and Goat,* FRF 2,950. PARIS, 9 March 1950, *Grazing Land,* FRF 18,000. PARIS, 5 March 1951, *Cows and Farmer's Wife in a Farmyard,* FRF 33,000. VIENNA, 2 Dec 1958, *Mountain Road in the South,* ATS 18,000. LONDON, 26 April 1968, *Landscape,* Gns 550. LONDON, 18 Oct 1978, *Landscape with Peasant Woman and her Animals* (oil on canvas, 20 x 28 ins / 51 x 71 cm) GBP 2,400. BRUSSELS, 12 June 1990, *Landscape with Animals* (oil on canvas, 25 1/2 x 32 1/4 ins / 65 x 82 cm) BEF 180,000. AMSTERDAM, 11 Sept 1990, *Cows in a Meadow on the Edge of a Forest in a Hilly Landscape* (1804, oil on panel, 18 3/4 x 25 ins / 47.5 x 63.5 cm) NLG 9,200. AMSTERDAM, 5-6 Nov 1991, *Cattle and Figures in a Meadow* (1813, oil on panel, 27 1/2 x 38 1/2 ins / 70 x 98 cm) NLG 6,670. AMSTERDAM, 9 Nov 1993, *Milking Time* (1813, oil on panel, 11 3/4 x 15 1/2 ins / 30 x 39.5 cm) NLG 5,520. PARIS, 31 March 1994, *Landscape with Horse and Goat* (oil on panel, 11 1/2 x 8 3/4 ins / 29.5 x 22.2 cm) FRF 38,000. AMSTERDAM, 14 June 1994, *Milking Time* (oil on panel, 18 x 14 3/4 ins / 46 x 37.5 cm) NLG 2,875. NEW YORK, 12 Jan 1995, *Cow and Sheep in a Meadow near a Farm with the Farmer Sitting by a Fence* (oil on panel, 14 1/2 x 18 1/2 ins / 36.8 x 47 cm) USD 9,200. BRUSSELS, 14 Feb 2000, *Shepherd and his Flock in a Landscape* (oil on canvas, 17 x 24 ins / 44 x 60 cm) BEF 130,000. LONDON, 12 Dec 2000, *Extensive Italianate Landscape with Travellers* (oil on canvas, 19 x 24 ins / 49 x 61 cm) GBP 2,000. MUNICH, 21 March 2001, *Cows and Goat in Meadow* (1809, oil on panel, 15 x 19 ins / 37 x 49 cm) DEM 8,000. MUNICH, 5 Dec 2001, *Peasant Couple with Cows and Goats* (oil on canvas, 24 x 22 ins / 60 x 57 cm) DEM 9,500. COPENHAGEN, 4 March 2002, *Landscape with Cattle Grazing* (1801, oil on panel, 13 x 16 ins / 34 x 40 cm) DKK 15,000. PARIS, 6 Dec 2002, *Shepherd and Flock* (oil on canvas, 10 x 14 ins / 25 x 35 cm) EUR 5,500. AHLDEN, 19 Sept 2003, *Coastal Landscape with Cows and Goat* (oil on panel, 13 x 11 ins / 34 x 29 cm) EUR 2,700. MUNICH, 19 Sept 2003, *Landscape with Cattle* (oil on canvas) EUR 10,000.

KOBELL, Jan III, the Younger

Dutch, 19th century.

Born 13 April 1800, in Rotterdam; died 8 November 1838, in Rotterdam.

Painter. Landscapes, animals.

Jan Kobell III (the Younger) was the son of Jan Kobell I, nephew of Hendrick Kobell and cousin of Jan Kobell II (the Elder). He studied under his cousin Jan Kobell and showed great talent as a painter of animals and enjoyed a notable reputation.

MUSEUMS AND GALLERIES:

AMSTERDAM: *Milking Time.*

AUCTION RECORDS:

LONDON, 19 April 1909, *Ox* (drawing and two additional drawings by others) GBP 4. LONDON, 23 April 1910, *The Dairy,* GBP 54. AMSTERDAM, 27 April 1976, *Landscape with Animals* (oil on panel, 9 x 11 ins / 22.8 x 28 cm) NLG 8,600. VIENNA, 12 Dec 1978, *Dutch Landscape* (oil on panel, 9 x 11 ins / 22.8 x 28 cm) ATS 80,000. COLOGNE, 11 June 1979, *Animals Grazing* (1834, oil on panel, 16 1/4 x 14 1/4 ins / 41 x 36 cm) DEM 6,000. LONDON, 15 Feb 1980, *Farm Animals* (oil on canvas, 17 x 23 1/2 ins / 43.2 x 59.7 cm) GBP 3,800. AMSTERDAM, 14 Sept 1993, *A Brown and White Bull by a Gate in a Meadow with Ducks in the Foreground* (1834, oil on canvas, 20 3/4 x 16 1/2 ins / 53 x 42 cm) NLG 2,185. AMSTERDAM, 12 March 2002, *Cows in a Meadow* (oil on canvas, 24 x 31 ins / 61 x 80 cm) EUR 2,200. AMSTERDAM, 22 June 2004, *Cows by a Pond in Summer* (oil on panel, 11 x 13 ins / 29 x 34 cm) EUR 2,800.

KOBELL, Wilhelm Alexander Wolfgang von

German, 18th - 19th century.

Born 6 April 1766, in Mannheim; died 15 July 1855, in Munich.

Painter, watercolourist, engraver. Battles, rustic scenes, landscapes, landscapes with figures.

Wilhelm Kobell was taught by his father Ferdinand and also studied in Mannheim and Düsseldorf. He became a professor at the Munich academy in 1808. In 1816, he was made a Knight of the Order of Merit by the King of Bavaria. He had been summoned to court by the Elector Charles Theodore. In 1808, he produced a series of paintings relating the noble deeds of the Bavarian army during the Napoleonic Wars under the command of Crown Prince Ludwig, in which he made a particular feature of the landscapes.

MUSEUMS AND GALLERIES:

BERLIN: *The Artist as a Young Man* - DARMSTADT: *The Two Donkeys; Horses and Rider* - FRANKFURT AM MAIN: *Shepherd and Flock* - HAMBURG: *Soldiers on the Parapet; Road through the Forest; Autumn in Bavaria* - KASSEL: *Shepherdess and Flock* - MUNICH: *Battle Scene at Hanau* - NARBONNE: a watercolour - WEIMAR: *Three Huntsmen on Horseback.*

AUCTION RECORDS:

PARIS, 1850, *Meadow with Animals,* FRF 10,200. PARIS, 1868, *Cavalry Halt,* FRF 630. LONDON, 31 July 1929, *Winter Scenes* (watercolour, two) GBP 70. LONDON, 19 April 1937, *Rustic Scene,* GBP 60. PARIS, 11 July 1945, *Military Scene* (watercolour) FRF 14,800; *Soldiers and Peasants* (watercolour) FRF 11,000; *Military Halt* (watercolour) FRF 14,800. STUTTGART, 2 Oct 1949, *Rider and Two Horses* (watercolour) DEM 2,600. STUTTGART, 18 Oct 1950, *The Hunting Party* (watercolour) DEM 4,000. STUTTGART, 29 Nov 1957, *Annual Fair in a Small Town* (watercolour) DEM 5,400. MUNICH, 16 Nov 1959, *Hilly Landscape* (watercolour) DEM 15,000. COLOGNE, 5 May 1960, *Cows in a Landscape,* DEM 9,000. MUNICH, 6-8 Nov 1963, *Shepherdess and her Flock in a Meadow,* DEM 25,000. MUNICH, 14-16 Oct 1964, *The Goatherd* (watercolour) DEM 15,000. COLOGNE, 11 Nov 1964, *Landscape with Flock,* DEM 22,000. MUNICH, 17 May 1966, *Herding Girl with Cows* (watercolour) DEM 17,000. MUNICH, 11 Dec 1968, *The Hunt* (watercolour) DEM 20,000. MUNICH, 30 Nov 1972, *Flock in an Alpine Landscape* (watercolour) DEM 15,000. NEW YORK, 14 June 1973, *Two Horsemen in a Landscape: the Ride,* USD 75,000. MUNICH, 27 Nov 1974, *Peasant Girl and Shepherd Boy in a Landscape* (watercolour) DEM 32,000. MUNICH, 25 Nov 1976, *Young Girl Standing* (drawing, 11 x 9 1/2 ins / 28 x 24 cm) DEM 1,600. MUNICH, 28 Nov 1979, *Portrait of Franz Kobell* (c. 1794, pencil, 9 x 7 1/2 ins / 23 x 19 cm) DEM 2,600. MUNICH, 28 Nov 1979, *View of Lake Ammer* (1844, watercolour, 8 1/4 x 10 1/2 ins / 20.8 x 26.7 cm) DEM 48,000. LONDON, 26 Nov 1980, *Crossing the River* (1804, oil on canvas, 36 1/2 x 45 1/4 ins / 92.5 x 115 cm) GBP 42,000. LONDON, 19 March 1981, *Hunting Scene* (1839, watercolour and pencil, 7 1/2 x 9 3/4 ins / 19 x 24.9 cm) GBP 9,500. MUNICH, 4 June 1981, *Herd amidst Ruins in a Mountain Landscape* (c. 1791, pen and wash, 9 1/4 x 7 ins / 23.5 x 18 cm) DEM 2,800. MUNICH, 29 Nov 1984, *Peasant Girl and Cows beside Lake Ammer* (1803, watercolour and pen, 3 3/4 x 6 ins / 9.5 x 15 cm) DEM 17,000. MUNICH, 29 Nov

1984, *Peasants and Children on a Country Road, with the Castle of Emmingen in the Background* (c. 1800, oil on canvas, 14 1/4 x 19 ins / 36.5 x 48.5 cm) DEM 44,000. MUNICH, 28 Nov 1985, *Horses Grazing* (1793, watercolour, 13 1/2 x 17 1/4 ins / 34.5 x 44 cm) DEM 56,000. MUNICH, 4 June 1987, *Postilion on a Cab in the Fog* (c. 1798, watercolour, 14 1/2 x 19 3/4 ins / 37 x 50 cm) DEM 54,000. LONDON, 25 March 1988, *The Judgement of Paris* (oil on canvas, 35 1/2 x 53 1/4 ins / 90 x 135 cm) GBP 9,350. LONDON, 17 March 1989, *Morning Ride* (1823, oil on panel, 9 3/4 x 7 3/4 ins / 25 x 19.7 cm) GBP 22,000. NEW YORK, 20 Feb 1992, *Peasants from Lake Tegern Encountering an Infantry Company from the Hohenhausen Regiment* (1799, watercolour/paper, 15 x 20 1/2 ins / 38.1 x 52.1 cm) USD 49,500. MUNICH, 26 May 1992, *Alpine Landscape with Huntsmen* (ink, 5 1/2 x 7 3/4 ins / 14 x 19.5 cm) DEM 1,035. MUNICH, 10 Dec 1992, *Alpine Landscape* (ink and watercolour/paper, 5 3/4 x 8 ins / 14.9 x 20.1 cm) DEM 3,390. LONDON, 20 May 1993, *Horsemen near Lake Tegern* (1838, oil on panel, 11 1/2 x 9 3/4 ins / 28.9 x 25 cm) GBP 287,500. MUNICH, 7 Dec 1993, *Group of Horsemen during a Storm near Lake Tegern* (1808, oil on panel, 15 3/4 x 19 1/2 ins / 40 x 49.5 cm) DEM 92,000. LONDON, 13 Oct 1994, *Herding Girl with her Cattle and the Monastery of Lake Tegern in the Distance* (1838, pencil and watercolour/paper, 6 1/4 x 8 1/4 ins / 15.8 x 20.8 cm) GBP 43,300. HEIDELBERG, 8 April 1995, *Munich Seen from the North* (etching, 4 3/4 x 7 1/2 ins / 12.1 x 18.9 cm) DEM 1,600. VIENNA, 29-30 Oct 1996, *Family Encountering Horsemen outside Munich* (pencil, pen, grey ink and watercolour/paper, 11 1/4 x 14 3/4 ins / 28.5 x 37.5 cm) ATS 597,000. MUNICH, 23 June 1997, *Team of Horses* (1794, pencil, Indian ink and watercolour, heightened with white/paper/card, 15 x 18 1/2 ins / 38 x 47 cm) DEM 28,000. VIENNA, 6 Oct 1999, *Courtly Hunting Party beside a Lake* (oil on canvas, 25 x 38 ins / 63 x 96 cm) ATS 1,400,000. MUNICH, 30 Nov 1999, *Two Riders and Hunter before Lake Landscape* (1826, oil on panel, 12 x 17 ins / 31 x 43 cm) DEM 95,000. ZURICH, 29 March 2000, *Resting Peasants in Prayer with Cattle by Tegernsee* (1794, Indian ink and watercolour, 14 x 19 ins / 35 x 47 cm) CHF 32,000. HAMBURG, 7 June 2000, *Dead Boar* (oil on paper, 8 x 12 ins / 21 x 30 cm) DEM 34,000. MUNICH, 5 Dec 2001, *Resting Horses by Menterschweige* (1852, watercolour over pencil, 5 x 5 ins / 13 x 13 cm) DEM 14,000. COPENHAGEN, 6 Feb 2002, *Landscape from Achensee in Bavaria - Loosing the Bull* (1840, watercolour, 6 x 8 ins / 16 x 20 cm) DKK 50,000. MUNICH, 28 March 2003, *Cattle on Isar Shore* (1809, 8 x 11 ins / 20 x 27 cm) EUR 11,000. COLOGNE, 17 May 2003, *Meeting* (watercolour, 15 x 20 ins / 38 x 50 cm) EUR 5,400. MUNICH, 30 June 2004, *Herdsman with Cows in Lower Mountain Landscape* (oil on canvas, 15 x 18 ins / 37 x 46 cm) EUR 16,000.

KOBELT, Johann

Swiss, 19th century.

Born 10 March 1861, in Marbach; died 1903, in St Fidien.

Sculptor.

From 1878 to 1881, Kobelt worked with Widmann in Munich, then from 1881 to 1885 with Lax in Vienna. Notable among his works are four eight-foot-high figures for the Parliament Building in Vienna. In 1886 he is known to have been in Berlin, where he produced a number of busts. On his return to St Gall in Switzerland, he devoted himself to carving funeral monuments and produced interesting sculptures in this genre.

KOBEN

Japanese, 13th century.

Active in Nara during the first half of the 13th century.

Sculptor.

Koben was probably the third son of the great sculptor Unkei (d. 1223). His surviving works are the *Tento-ki* and *Ryuto-ki* statues in the Kofuku-ji temple in Nara, dated 1215. (Ryuto-ki are the imps that support lanterns offered to the Buddha.) These sculptures are masterpieces, full of humour and wholly in the style of Unkei, especially in the treatment of the limbs. They may have been copies after other works from the Nara Period (645-793).

KÖBER, Hélène. See **FRANKEN Hélène von**

KOBER, Martin

German, 16th century.

Born in Breslau (now Wroclaw, Poland).

Active in the second half of the 16th century.

Painter.

Cracow School.

After living in Cracow at the court of the Polish king Stephen Bathory and producing a famous portrait of him, Kober returned to Breslau, his home town.

KOBERSTEIN, Hans

German, 19th - 20th century.

Born 3 June 1864, in Schulpforta.

Painter. Genre scenes, architectural views.

Hans Koberstein particated in the exhibition in Berlin in 1909.

KOBERWEIN, Georg

Austrian, 19th century.

Born 9 February 1820, in Vienna; died 1876, in London.

Painter.

Koberwein exhibited at the Royal Academy in London from 1862 to 1876.

MUSEUMS AND GALLERIES:

LONDON (Corporation of Trinity House): portrait*HRH Alfred, Duke of Edinburgh*.

AUCTION RECORDS:

COLOGNE, 24 June 1983, *Portrait of a Woman in a Straw Hat* (oil on canvas, 24 x 20 ins / 61 x 51 cm) DEM 3,500.

KOBERWEIN, Rosa

British, 19th century.

Active in London.

Painter. Genre scenes.

Rosa Koberwein was the daughter of Georg Koberwein. She exhibited at the Royal Academy from 1876 to 1885.

AUCTION RECORDS:

LONDON, 14 March 1997, *This Maiden Sweetly Fair and Pale...* (1879, oil on canvas, 26 x 20 ins / 66 x 50.8 cm) GBP 9,200.

KOBÈS, Franciska

German, 19th century.

Born 1803, in Berlin.

Painter. Genre scenes.

Franciska Kobès was a pupil of Kretschmar.

KOBIERSKI, Carl von

Austrian, 19th century.

Born 5 November 1848, in Kimpolung; died 29 January 1907, in Vienna.

Painter.

Kobierski started life as an officer. He painted several portraits of Emperor Francis Joseph.

KOBILICA, Ivana

Slovene, 19th - 20th century.

Born 20 December 1861.

Painter.

Ivana Kobilica was a member of the salon of the Société Nationale des Beaux-Arts in Paris from 1891.

KØBKE, Christen Schjellerup

Danish, 19th century.

Born 26 May 1810, in Copenhagen; died 7 February 1848, in Copenhagen.

Painter, engraver, draughtsman. Portraits, genre scenes, landscapes, architectural views, seascapes.

Købke was one of the foremost artists of the Danish Golden Age, praised in particular for his treatment of light and nature. He studied at the academy of Copenhagen (1822-1832), and with Lorentzen and the painter C.W. Eckersberg. He visited Rome and Naples. In 1845 he painted fresco decorations at the Thorvaldsen Museum in Copenhagen.

Købke was one of the great Danish painters. He clearly mastered colour, composition and the rendering of light. His works often took their inspiration from nature, and were at once sombre with a certain element of grandeur. He was also a talented portraitist. *The Mother of the Art Historian N. L. Høyen, Inger Margrethe Høyen, née Schrøder* (Statens Museum for Kunst 1832) demonstrates the subtleties of his technique and his ability to capture the intimate psychology of the sitter, as well as to imbue his subject with a sense of gravity.

In 1838 Købke travelled abroad for the first time, to Dresden and Italy, and on his return from Italy in 1840 his Italian works were not especially popular; in 1846 the work he submitted to the academy as his entry piece was rejected. He died two years later and it is only in retrospect that his importance was recognised.

He has been included in several exhibitions, notably *Twee gouden eeuwen: schilderkunst uit Nederland en Denemarken Two Golden Ages: Masterpieces of Dutch and Danish Painting* at the Rijksmuseum in Amsterdam in 2001 and *Un Paese incantato. Italia dipinta da Thomas Jones a Corot* (*An Enchanted Country. Italy Depicted by Artists from Thomas Jones to Corot*) at the Centro Internazionale d'Arte e di Cultura di Palazzo Te in Mantua in 2001. A notable retrospective exhibition, *Christen Købke: 1810-1848*, was mounted at the Statens Museum for Kunst in Copenhagen in 1996.

BIBLIOGRAPHY:

Nørregård-Nielsen, H. E., '*The Lyricism of Christen Købke*' in *Apollo, cxiii, pp. 372-373*, 1981. Jönsson, H. (ed.), *C. W. Eckersberg og hans Elever (C. W. Eckersberg and his Pupils)*, exhibition catalogue, Statens Museum for Kunst, Copenhagen, 1983. Monrad, Kasper, *Danish Painting: The Golden Age*, exhibition catalogue, National Galllery, London, 1984. Kent, N., *The Triumph of Light and Nature: Nordic Art, 1740-1940*, Thames & Hudson, London, 1987. Schwartz, S., *Christen Købke*, Timken Publishers, New York, 1992. Wivel, Mikael, *Christen Købke*, Blondal, Hellerup, 1993 (text in English). Nørregård-Nielsen, Hans Edvard, *Christen Købke: 1810 - 1848*, exhibition catalogue, Statens Museum for Kunst, Copenhagen, 1996. Ottani Cavina, Anna (ed.), *Un Paese incantato. Italia dipinta da Thomas Jones a Corot*, exhibition catalogue, Electa, Milan, 2001.

MUSEUMS AND GALLERIES:

COPENHAGEN (Den Hirschsprungske Samling): *Portrait of the Landscape Painter Frederik Sodring* (1832) - COPENHAGEN (Ny Carlsberg Glyptotek): *A Natural Arch in Capri* (oil on paper mounted/canvas) - COPENHAGEN (Statens Mus. for Kunst): *Portrait of W. Marstrand; Portrait of Mrs Höyen, Mother; Portrait of Julius Eckersberg; Portrait of Mrs Ployen; Views and Landscapes; View of Copenhagen from Dosseringen* (1837); *Castel dell'Ovo in Naples* (oil on paper mounted on canvas) - NIVÅ (Nivågårds Malerisamling): *View from Limekiln with Copenhagen in the Background* (1836); *The Transept of Arhus Cathedral* - ODENSE (Fyns Kunstmus.): *The Forum of Pompeii* (oil on paper mounted on canvas (?)) - PARIS (Louvre): *Portrait of Adolphina Peterzen* (1832); *Cigar Merchant at the Citadel Gate of Copenhagen.*

AUCTION RECORDS:

COPENHAGEN, 7 Nov 1960, *View of Dosseringen, in the Østerbro Region,* DKK 44,000. COPENHAGEN, 28-29 May 1963, *Portrait of Miss Købke,* DKK 28,000. COPENHAGEN, 26 March 1968, *The Arbour,* DKK 16,000. COPENHAGEN, 19 March 1969, *The Garden,* DKK 100,000. COPENHAGEN, 17 Feb 1970, *Landscape,* DKK 85,000. COPENHAGEN, 11 April 1972, *Portrait of F. C. Krohn* (1839) DKK 15,000. COPENHAGEN, 4 Sept 1974, *The Entry into the Castle,* DKK 130,000. COPENHAGEN, 4 May 1976, *Seashore* (1834, drawing, 7 1/4 x 10 3/4 ins / 18.5 x 27.2 cm) DKK 9,000. COPENHAGEN, 27 Sept 1977, *Seashore, Capri* (1839-1840, oil on canvas, 11 x 15 ins / 27 x 38 cm) DKK 63,500. LONDON, 25 Nov 1981, *Portrait of Conradine, the Artist's Sister* (c. 1838-1839, oil on card, 9 x 7 1/2 ins / 23 x 19 cm) GBP 6,000. COPENHAGEN, 17 March 1982, *The Entry into the Castle* (pencil, 3 1/2 x 4 1/4 ins / 9 x 10.5 cm) DKK 6,500. COPENHAGEN, 2 Oct 1984, *View of Pompeii with Vesuvius in the Background* (1841, oil on canvas, 28 x 35 ins / 71 x 88 cm) DKK 520,000. COPENHAGEN, 1 March 1985, *Portrait of a Man* (1841, pencil, 7 x 4 3/4 ins / 17.5 x 12 cm) DKK 78,000. LONDON, 17 June 1986, *Figures on the Nordre Kastelbro at Sunset* (end of 1837, oil on canvas, 17 1/4 x 25 ins / 43.5 x 63.5 cm) GBP 260,000. COPENHAGEN, 23 April 1987, *View of Pompeii* (1846, oil on canvas, 15 x 20 1/2 ins / 38 x 52 cm) DKK 1,000,000. LONDON, 20 June 1989, *Frederiksborg Castle from Jaegerbakken* (oil on canvas, 29 3/4 x 39 3/4 ins / 75.5 x 101 cm) GBP 37,400. LONDON, 27-28 March 1990, *Family on a Terrace in Capri* (oil on canvas, 27 x 22 1/2 ins / 68.5 x 57 cm) GBP 19,800. COPENHAGEN, 25-26 April 1990, *Portrait of Commander Købke in Uniform* (oil on canvas, 20 3/4 x 17 3/4 ins / 53 x 45 cm) DKK 330,000. COPENHAGEN, 7 Sept 1994, *Standing Woman seen from Behind* (pencil, 7 3/4 x 6 ins / 20 x 15 cm) DKK 18,000. COPENHAGEN, 8 Feb 1995, *In the Garden of a Cloister* (1838, pencil, 7 x 5 1/2 ins / 18 x 14 cm) DKK 12,000. COPENHAGEN, 31 Aug 1999, *Night* (oil on canvas, oval, 35 x 35 ins / 89 x 89 cm) DKK 40,000. COPENHAGEN, 31 Aug 1999, *View of the Marina Grande at Capri with Fishing Boat in Foreground* (1839, oil on canvas, 11 x 15 ins / 27 x 38 cm) DKK 880,000. COPENHAGEN, 29 Feb 2000, *View from a Window in Eckersberg's Studio, Charlottenborg* (oil on canvas, 13 x 10 ins / 32 x 25 cm) DKK 2,500,000. COPENHAGEN, 25 April 2001, *Boats at the Bay of Naples* (1843, 11 x 15 ins / 27 x 39 cm) DKK 95,000. COPENHAGEN, 3 June 2002, *The Sculptor Georg Christian Freund* (oil on canvas, 44 x 34 ins / 111 x 87 cm) DKK 400,000. VEJLE, 5 Aug 2002, *Portrait of Thorvaldsen* (1831, pencil, 11 x 9 ins / 27 x 22 cm) DKK 40,500. COPENHAGEN, 9 Dec 2003, *Sophie Krohn, the Artist's Sister Standing by a Window in the Family Home, Kastellet* (c. 1830, oil on canvas, 12 x 8 ins / 31 x 21 cm) DKK 500,000. COPENHAGEN, 9 Dec 2003, *Coastal Landscape from Southern Capri, Clear Day, Large Waves* (1841, oil on canvas, 48 x 68 ins / 122 x 173 cm) DKK 3,900,000. COPENHAGEN, 25 Feb 2004, *Mr Krohn in High Hat and Coat* (pencil, 8 x 4 ins / 20 x 11 cm) DKK 15,000.

KOBLANSKI

Polish, 18th century.

Born in Warsaw.

Portrait artist.

In 1774, Koblanski painted the portrait of the member of parliament *Jacob Hadzievisck.*

KOBLASA, Jan

Czechoslovak, 20th century.

Born 5 October 1932, in Tábor.

Sculptor, painter, engraver, decorative artist. Murals.

Jan Koblasa studied at the academy of fine arts in Prague from 1952 to 1958.

He was a member of the Smidrové group from 1954, and had works included in the *Exhibition D* in Prague.

One of the leading artists of his generation in Czechoslovakia, he used in his sculptures a range of materials: striated plaster (around 1960); concrete (1966), and always wood which he often exposed to the action of fire. His figures were almost always inspired by the human form: fantastic pieces as if for a gigantic game of chess such as *Kings and Queens* (1962); *Madonnas, Princesses* (1964); and *Dwarfs.* These were followed by the series *Prophets,* improvised masks hoisted on the end of pikes (1966); and *Homages to Kafka, to*

Lautréamont, Arc de Triomphe (1968). Jan Koblasa also produced a fresco for the CSA Agency in Warsaw (1963) and a relief for Prague airport (1967).

Jan Koblasa took part in several collective exhibitions including: festival of young artists, Vienna (1959); *Art Since 1950*, Warsaw and Washington (1962); *Phases*, Ixelles-Brussels (1964); Liège, Rotterdam, Bochum, Baden-Baden, Munich, Heidelberg, Stuttgart, Karlsruhe, Mannheim, Fribourg and Berlin (1965); Syracuse University (New York), Brussels (1966). Solo exhibitions include: Teplice (1958 and 1963 with the painter Medek); Litomerice (1964); Liberec and Berlin (with Kolar and Kotik) (1965); Prague and Bochum municipal gallery (1966).

KOBLER, Peter
Austrian, 18th century.
Active in Vienna.
Painter.

Kobler is known for a large number of portraits of dignitaries of the Imperial Court.

KOBLIHA, Frantisek
Czech, 20th century.
Born 17 November 1877, in Prague; died 12 December 1962, in Prague.
Engraver.

Frantisek Kobliha visited Paris in 1925 and 1926.

KOBOLD, Gottlieb
German, 18th century.
Born 1769, in Kassel; died 1809, in Poland.
Painter, draughtsman. Portraits, landscapes.

Gottlieb Kobold taught at the electoral academy. He was the son of Werner Kobold.

KOBOLD, Werner
German, 18th century.
Born possibly in Eschwege; died 30 April 1803, in Kassel.
Painter, miniaturist, draughtsman, engraver.

Werner Kobold was a draughtsman at the court of Landgrave Frederick II of Hesse-Kassel. He was given the task or reorganising the Kassel academy.

KOBORI, Masamichi
Japanese, 20th - 21st century.
Born 1947, in Saitama.
Print artist, painter.

BIBLIOGRAPHY:

Beaumont-Maillet, Laure/Woimant, Françoise/Pernoud, Emmanuel, *De Bonnard à Baselitz - Dix ans d'enrichissements du Cabinet des estampes 1978-1988*, exhibition catalogue, Bibliothèque nationale de France, Paris, 1992.

KOBORI, Tomone, real name Kobori Keizaburo; original name Sudo; artist names Tomone, Tsurunoya
Japanese, 20th century.
Born 1864, in Tochigi Prefecture; died 1931.
Painter.

Kobori Tomone studied Western painting in Tokyo. He became a member of the Imperial Fine Arts Academy in the early part of the 20th century and took part in the 1929 exhibition of Japanese art in the Jeu de Paume, Paris. In 1897, he was appointed professor at the Tokyo School of Fine Arts.

KOBRO, Katarzyna
Latvian, 20th century.
Born 1898, in Riga; died 1951, in Lódz.
Active in Poland.
Sculptor.
Constructivism, Suprematism.
Groups: Unovis, Blok, Praesens, R.A. (Revolutionary Artists), Abstraction-Création.

Katarzyna Kobro studied sculpture in Moscow between 1917 and 1920, first at the school of painting, sculpture and design in Moscow then at the state free art workshop (Svomas). She met the painter Strzeminsky in Moscow and married him in 1920. As a member of the modern art in the Soviet Union movement she met Medunetsky, Miturich, Rodchenko and Tatlin. In 1920 she moved to Smolensk where she taught at the school of fine arts, came into contact with Malevich and Lissitzky, and thus joined the Unovis group. She ran the *Izo* studio together with her husband until 1922 and in that year they went to live in Poland. Katarzyna Kobro was an active member of several avant-garde art groups in Poland including Bloc (1924) and Praesens (1928). She also founded her own group R.A. (Revolutionary Artists) in 1930. In 1931 she and her husband moved to Lódz where they first established and then provided the driving force for an international centre for avant-garde artists. In 1933 she joined the Paris-based Abstraction-Création group.

Influenced initially by Tatlin, she pursued her researches into Suprematist three-dimensional compositions. These took the form of studies of shapes with geometric surfaces, designed and executed in accordance with the laws of action, energy and polar tensions, in a particular system which could be suspended in space. She also produced Cubist and Figurative sculptures. By the end of the 1920s, she was creating her most famous works: her spatial geometric compositions or *Spatial Sculptures*. These were small constructions made out of sheets of curved, almost folded metal, assembled at right angles and using a reduced palette of black, white and grey. This was the result of a series of accurate calculations founded on the principle of multiplying one modular unit by the Fibonacci series (1, 2, 3, 5, 8). From 1928 her *Spatial Compositions*, to which she added primary colours, used a system of proportionality in their dimensions and planes (in accordance with a ratio of 8:5). She then published her first manifesto *Sculpture and the Solid* in the second issue of *Europa* (1929). With Strzeminski, Katarzyna Kobro formulated theoretical bases for her compositions which were set out in a remarkable work entitled *The Composition of Space and the Calculation of Spatio-Temporal Rhythm*, (Lódz, 1931). The two of them regarded space as a scientifically-articulated phenomenon that might be considered 'Unist', universally applicable. After 1935 she created many 'biological' compositions, the starting point for a new approach to her research but it was cut short by the war. A major part of her work, which the Nazis regarded as 'degenerate art', was destroyed during World War II. A number of pieces were, however, reconstructed.

Katarzyna Kobro participated in all of the Polish Constructivist exhibitions including: *Précurseurs de l'art abstrait en Pologne*, Paris (1957); *Mondrian, De Stijl and their Impact*, New York (1964); *Constructivism in Poland, 1923-1936*, Folkwang museum, Essen (1973); *The Twenties in Eastern Europe*, Gmurzynska gallery, Cologne (1975). Kobro only ever had one solo exhibition during her own lifetime (Cracow, 1935), but her works were exhibited alongside those of her husband, Strzemsinki, posthumously in Lódz and Warsaw (1956 and 1957).

BIBLIOGRAPHY:

Stanislawski, Ryszard/Porebski, Mieczslaw, *Peinture moderne polonaise, source et recherche*, exhibition catalogue, Musée Galliera, Paris, 1969. Fabre, Gladys C., *Abstraction-Création 1931-1936*, exhibition catalogue, Westfälisches Landesmuseum für Kunst und Kulturgeschichte, Münster, Musée d'Art moderne de la Ville de Paris, Paris, 1978. *La Collection du Musée d'Art moderne*, Éd. du Centre Georges-Pompidou, Paris, 1986. *Katarzyna Kobro, 1898 - 1951*, exhibition catalogue, Henry Moore Institute, Leeds, 1999.

MUSEUMS AND GALLERIES:
LÓDZ (Muzeum Sztuki/MBA): *Suspended Composition 2* (1921-1922); *Spatial Sculpture 1* (1925); most of her work - PARIS (MNAM-CCI): *Spatial Sculpture* (1928) - WARSAW (Muz. Narodowe).

KOBZDEJ, Aleksander
Polish, 20th century.
Born 1920, in Olesko; died 1972.
Painter, draughtsman, assemblage artist.
Aleksander Kobzdej lived in Warsaw. Having started by studying engineering in Lviv and Danzig (now Gdansk), he then switched to the academies of fine arts in Cracow and Warsaw, which he attended until 1951. He taught at the academy of fine arts in Warsaw. He 1953 he visited China and Vietnam where he produced realist drawings that were exhibited in Beijing and Warsaw (1954). He also travelled around Europe, Asia and America.

Aleksander Kobzdej started with Realism from 1955 later turning towards Expressionist Abstraction, in which morbid ideas and material effects both figure. He later incorporated elements executed in relief and made out of wood, cardboard and metal into his canvases, at the same time brightening his palette by the addition of almost violent shades of colour. Collective exhibitions include: March Salon; Zakopane Salon; Venice Biennale and Graphic Art Exhibition, Lugano (1954); São Paulo Biennale (where he was awarded a prize, 1959); exhibition of Polish art, Washington (1961). Solo exhibitions include: Paris and New York (1960); Warsaw (1961); Cracow 1962).
MUSEUMS AND GALLERIES:
WARSAW (Muz. Narodowe): *Wide crevice amongst the violets* (1968).

KOCACEMI, Zeki
Turkish, 20th century.
Born 1902, in Istanbul.
Painter. Landscapes.
This artist was represented at the exhibition of modern art organised by the United Nations in Paris in 1946.

KOCH, pseudonym of Kochmeister Samuel
Polish, 20th century.
Born 1887, in Warsaw.
Active in the USA from 1910.
Painter. Figure compositions, flowers.
When Koch first arrived in the USA he turned his hand to any work he could find before he was able to open a sweet shop in New York in 1913 which enabled him to fulfil his vocation as a painter. In 1938 he started to exhibit his work, and Sidney Janis, the renowned collector, took an interest in him. He painted bouquets of flowers in sharp, bright, almost artificial-looking colours set out on a table often covered with a red cloth, groups of people in conversation around a table, stiff and solemn in the Hebrew way, fragile silhouettes lost in the colossal streets of American cities.
BIBLIOGRAPHY:
Bihalji-Merin, Oto, *Les Peintres naïfs*, Delpire, Paris, 1960.

KOCH, Arthur
Polish, 20th century.
Born 16 August 1862, in Rawicz.
Painter. Landscapes. Monuments.
Arthur Koch studied in Dresden and Karlsruhe. He painted the landscapes and monuments he had seen during visits to England, France and Holland.

KOCH, Arthur
American, 20th century.
Born 1934, in Meriden (Connecticut).
Painter, engraver.
Arthur Koch lives and works in Dallas, Texas and has taught at the Southern Methodist University. His works focus on wood and on materials or conditions that influence or affect the wood. He has taken part in collective exhibitions in Dartmouth, the University of Connecticut, Seattle, Washington, Dallas (Texas Painting and Sculpture Exhibition), Museum of Fine Arts and the National Drawing Show, Oklahoma Art Center, Oklahoma City. He has shown his works in solo exhibitions, notably, in 1969, a retrospective at the University of Dallas. He belongs to a number of associations.

KOCH, Carl
German, 19th century.
Born 5 May 1827, in Berlin; died 1 January 1905, in Berlin.
Painter, lithographer.
Carl Koch studied with Thomas Couture in Paris.

KOCH, Carl Friedrich
German, 19th century.
Born 19 February 1856, in Berlin.
Painter. Portraits, genre scenes.
Carl Friedrich Koch studied with Gussow at the Berlin academy. He exhibited in Berlin, notably in 1909.

KOCH, Élisa, or Kock
French, 19th - 20th century.
Born in Livorno (Tuscany), Italy.
Painter, pastellist. Figures, portraits, genre scenes.
Élisa Koch studied under Janmot and Charles Comte. She exhibited in Lyons from 1854 to 1855 and in Paris from 1863 showing numerous oil and pastel portraits and some genre scenes, notably *Dangerous Encounter* (Paris, 1868); *You'll Have None of It* (Paris, 1874); *Misfortune* (Paris, 1881); *Portrait of Mademoiselle J. Dodu* (at the Musée de Lyons in Paris, 1882); *Little Sister* (Paris, 1889); and *Little Savage* (Lyons, 1898). She was awarded a gold medal for her portraits in Lyons in 1889.
MUSEUMS AND GALLERIES:
LYONS: *Portrait of Mademoiselle J. Dodu.*
AUCTION RECORDS:
NEW YORK, 3 Feb 1904, *Not Only For You,* USD 145. LONDON, 7 May 1976, *Temptation* (oil on canvas, 24 1/2 x 16 1/4 ins / 62 x 41 cm) GBP 1,800.

KOCH, Franz
Austrian, 19th - 20th century.
Born 12 September 1832, in Tarrenz (Tyrol); died 12 May 1922, in Vienna.
Sculptor.
Franz Koch's vast output of monumental sculpture included statues for the façade of the Kunsthistorisches Museum in Vienna and for the Treasury and Parliament in that city.

KOCH, Frederic
Belgian, 20th century.
Painter. Still-lifes.
Active in Antwerp, Frederic Koch took part in the exhibition in Brussels of 1910.

KOCH, Friedrich
German, 18th - 19th century.
Born 26 August 1771, in Buchsweiler (Alsace); died 8 January 1832, in Mannheim.
Engraver, miniaturist, draughtsman.
At the start of the French Revolution, Friedrich Koch accompanied his family to Mannheim and set up as a merchant, but continued to study the works of the masters, particularly Rembrandt and Dietrich. He engraved portraits, genre scenes and historical subjects.

KOCH, Friedrich
German, 19th century.
Born 25 December 1859, in Kappeln.
Painter, engraver.

Friedrich Koch studied with Kaulbach in Hanover. He specialised in religious painting. He is known for his work in the churches of Ronnenberg and Mandelsohn.

KOCH, Friedrich Ferdinand
German, 19th - 20th century.
Born 18 February 1863, in Landau; died 24 February 1923, in Landau.
Painter. Landscapes.

Friedrich Ferdinand Koch participated in the Grosse Berliner Kunstausstellung of 1909 and lived for nearly 15 years in Zwyndrecht in Belgium.

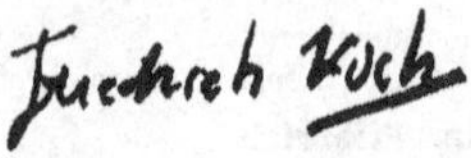

AUCTION RECORDS:
LOS ANGELES, 6 June 1978, *The Newborn Child* (oil on canvas, 29 1/4 x 33 1/2 ins / 74.3 x 85 cm) USD 4,300.

KOCH, Georg
German, 19th century.
Born 19 December 1819, in Kassel; died 10 March 1899, in Kassel.
Painter, draughtsman, lithographer. Landscapes, animals.

Georg Koch studied at the academy of fine arts in Kassel and later visited France and Italy. He exhibited frequently in Saxony and Berlin, winning medals there.

AUCTION RECORDS:
LONDON, 22 Nov 1990, *The Horses of the Keller Stud Farm in a Meadow by the Elbe at Hitzacker* (oil on canvas, 55 x 31 1/2 ins / 140 x 80 cm) GBP 4,950.

KOCH, Georg
German, 19th - 20th century.
Born 1857, in Berlin; died 1926.
Painter. Landscapes with figures.

AUCTION RECORDS:
COLOGNE, 26 March 1976, *Flock at Drinking Place* (oil on canvas, 32 x 39 ins / 81 x 99 cm) DEM 3,300. LONDON, 18 June 1980, *The Hunting Rendezvous* (oil on canvas, 30 3/4 x 46 1/2 ins / 78 x 118 cm) GBP 4,000. VIENNA, 16 March 1982, *Hunting* (oil on canvas, 39 1/4 x 59 ins / 100 x 150 cm) ATS 50,000. COLOGNE, 15 Oct 1988, *Haymaking* (1916, oil on canvas, 25 1/2 x 39 1/4 ins / 65 x 100 cm) DEM 4,500. MUNICH, 25 June 1992, *Horses in Meadow* (oil on canvas, 31 x 54 3/4 ins / 79 x 139 cm) DEM 16,950. HAMBURG, 8 May 1999, *Parforcejagd, Autumn Hunting Scene in Wooded Meadow Landscape* (oil on canvas, 26 x 19 ins / 66 x 49 cm) DEM 6,600. AHLDEN, 22 Sept 2000, *Fox Hunting* (oil on canvas, 32 x 48 ins / 82 x 121 cm) DEM 16,000. NEW YORK, 6 Dec 2000, *Full Cry. Kill* (1896, watercolour and gouache, a pair, 21 x 33 ins / 54 x 83 cm) USD 8,000. STUTTGART, 19 Sept 2002, *Horse Dealer* (oil on canvas, 28 x 42 ins / 71 x 107 cm) EUR 2,800. COLOGNE, 16 Nov 2002, *Fox Hunt* (1891, oil on canvas, 23 x 28 ins / 58 x 70 cm) EUR 3,000. HAMBURG, 14 Feb 2004, *Horses in Meadow* (oil on canvas, 26 x 39 ins / 66 x 100 cm) EUR 4,000. WARSAW, 26 Sept 2004, *Roe Deer in a River Landscape* (1893, oil on canvas, 47 x 63 ins / 120 x 160 cm) PLZ 11,000.

KOCH, Georg Moritz
German, 20th century.
Born 21 December 1885, in Berlin.
Sculptor. Portraits.

Taught by Bruno Wiese, Georg Moritz Koch was pre-eminently a portraitist and an exponent of German Expressionism.

KOCH, Gérard
French, 20th century.
Born 10 March 1926, in Kaiserslautern (Rhineland-Palatinate), Germany.
Sculptor, collage artist.

Gérard Koch became an apprentice to a carpenter in Revel in 1942. From 1950 to 1958 he was mace-bearer at the studios of Auriscote and Zadkine at the Académie de la Grande-Chaumière in Paris. In 1956 he was awarded a Rothschild bursary and in 1965 a bursary by the Ford Foundation in Berlin. From 1968 to 1969 he taught sculpture at the Interlochen Art Academy in Michigan. From 1973 to 1979 he was a part-time lecturer at the École des Beaux-Arts in Paris.

Working in series, Koch produced sculptures cast in bronze between 1950 and 1968, including *Acrobats, Dancers* and *Rondes*. From 1968 to 1974 he produced the series entitled *Cris* (*Cries*), black and white paper collages with sand and drawn in Indian ink. He also produced sculptures in polyester resin, cardboard and wood, covered in fabric. Between 1974 and 1976 he executed the series of pages known as the *Journal à Claire-Voie* (*Openwork Journal*), which are words arranged in a wooden frame with compartments. From 1976 to 1984 Koch worked on linking music with form and in *Fugues, Counterpoints* and *Harmonics* constructed pieces of wood covered in black, blue or white paper in wooden frames and sculptures that were sometimes painted. 1985 to 1989 was marked by the series of tall, slender forms known as *Coloratura*, which consists of collections of small, square or rectangular fragments of painted wood and pieces of glass embedded horizontally, vertically or diagonally into open frameworks. Koch also showed an interest in producing furniture, including chairs and tables. He produced many decorative pieces and sculptures, notably a statue of Pierre Coubertin for the Winter Olympics in Grenoble in 1968, and in 1989 a decorative work for the A41 motorway at Nantua.

Koch exhibited at numerous group exhibitions, notably from 1956 to 1983 in Paris at the Salon de Mai, the Salon des Grands et Jeunes and the Salon de la Jeune Sculpture. Other group exhibitions include *Artists in Residence* at the Ford Foundation in Berlin (1965); *Boîtes* (*Boxes*) at the ARC Musée d'Art Moderne de la Ville de Paris (1976); and *Animation des Autoroutes* at the Centre Georges Pompidou in Paris (1976). His work has also been regularly exhibited by the Galerie Nane Stern at the FIAC (Foire Internationale d'Art Contemporain) in Paris and by the Leif Stahle gallery at the contemporary art fair in Stockholm. Koch showed his work in solo exhibitions, the first in 1956 at the Galerie Spirale in Paris. Others include Basel (1965); in Cleveland (1969); at the Centre Culturel in Villeparisis (1970); at the Galerie Charley Chevalier (1973, 1974); at the Galerie Nane Stern in Paris (1978, 1980, 1983, 1986); at the Galerie Clara Scremini in Paris (1987, 1988, 1989); and at the Abbaye des Cordeliers in Châteauroux (1987).

AUCTION RECORDS:
MANALAPAN (FLORIDA), 20 March 1979, *Acrobats* (c. 1971, black-patinated bronze, h. with base 75 ins / 190.5 cm) USD 1,600.

KOCH, Gottlieb von
German, 19th - 20th century.
Born 15 October 1849, in Hirschberg (now Jelena Gora, Poland); died 21 November 1914, in Alsbach.
Painter, sculptor.

Gottlieb von Koch worked in Jena and Darmstadt, among other towns, and was primarily interested in representing animals.

AUCTION RECORDS:

ZURICH, 29 Oct 1983, *Horse Market* (tempera, 25 1/2 x 16 1/4 ins / 65 x 41 cm) CHF 1,900.

KOCH, Hans, or Kochli, Kôchli
Swiss, 15th - 16th century.
Active in Lucerne.
Glass painter.

This artist is probably the Hans Koch whose name appears in records from 1496. He was also known as Hans Köchli.

KOCH, Hans Heinrich
Swiss, 16th century.
Active in Stein-am-Rhein.
Painter (glass).

KOCH, Heinrich
German, 19th century.
Born 5 September 1806, in Krefeld; died 25 October 1893, in Krefeld.
Painter. Landscapes.

Heinrich Koch studied at the Düsseldorf academy. He imitated the style of Lessing and attempted to become his equal.

AUCTION RECORDS:

COLOGNE, 21 Oct 1977, *The Monastery of Maria Laach* (1849, oil on canvas, 16 1/4 x 23 1/2 ins / 41 x 60 cm) DEM 3,400.

KOCH, Henri
German, 19th century.
Born c. 1804, in Hamburg.
Painter. History painting.

KOCH, Hermann
German, 19th - 20th century.
Born 1856, in Dömitz; died 1939, in Munich.
Painter. Genre scenes.

AUCTION RECORDS:

LONDON, 20 April 1979, *Young Lovers* (oil on canvas, 36 1/4 x 63 ins / 92 x 160 cm) GBP 3,200. MUNICH, 21 June 1994, *The Departure of the Bride and Bridegroom* (oil on canvas, 33 1/2 x 50 ins / 85 x 127 cm) DEM 10,350. LONDON, 11 April 1995, *Tea in the Garden* (oil on canvas, 35 3/4 x 53 1/2 ins / 91 x 136 cm) GBP 20,125. WARSAW, 3 June 2001, *Still-life of Grapes, Peach and a Glass of Wine* (oil on canvas, 15 x 19 ins / 38 x 48 cm) PLZ 6,500. WARSAW, 15 June 2003, *Still-life with Fruit and Goblet* (c. 1900, oil on card, 14 x 20 ins / 36 x 50 cm) PLZ 16,000. AHLDEN, 17 Sept 2004, *Still-life of Fruit* (oil on panel, 11 x 9 ins / 28 x 23 cm) EUR 3,200. WARSAW, 5 Dec 2004, *Still-life of Flowers and Fruit* (oil on canvas, 14 x 10 ins / 35 x 25 cm) PLZ 8,000.

KOCH, Hieronymus. See **COCK Hieronymus** or **Jeronimus**

KOCH, I. H.
Swiss, 18th century.
Draughtsman.

I. H. Koch illustrated Grunes' work: *Les Montagnes de neige de la Suisse* (*The Snow-covered Mountains of Switzerland*).

KOCH, J.
German, 18th century.
Born in Vallendar.
Painter, engraver. Landscapes.

KOCH, Johann
German, 19th century.
Born 1846, in Weilen; died 28 September 1907, in Weilen.
Sculptor (wood).

Johann Koch decorated a large number of churches in Baden and Wurtemberg and taught sculpture in Furtwangen.

KOCH, Johann Carl
German, 19th century.
Born 31 May 1806, in Hamburg; died 11 May 1900, in Speyer.
Painter, lithographer. History painting.

Johann Carl Koch studied with Heinrich Hess in Munich. He contributed to the decoration of St Boniface Church in Munich. In 1836, he was with Overbeck in Rome.

KOCH, Johann Georg
Swiss, 18th century.
Born 1702, in Thoune (Bern); died 1762, in Thoune (Bern).
Painter, copyist. Landscapes.

Johann Georg Koch made copies after Italian painters.

KOCH, Johann Konrad
German, 17th - 18th century.
Active in Berlin.
Sculptor.

King Frederick William I of Prussia commissioned a large number of sculptures from Koch, for Potsdam in particular.

KOCH, John
American, 20th century.
Born 1909 or 1910, in Toledo (Ohio); died 1978, in New York.
Painter. Portraits, genre scenes, still-lifes.

John Koch received minimal formal training other than two summers at the artists' colony at Provincetown, Massachusetts, where he was influenced by Charles Hawthorne. After leaving school he spent four years in Paris, where he studied pictures at the Louvre and won an award at the 1929 Salon de Printemps. On his return to New York, Koch became famous for his portraits of fashionable Manhattan and New England mansion-dwellers. He often used his own apartment as a setting, and many of his pictures feature his wife, the pianist Dora Zaslevsky, and her students, for example, *Music*, which won the Benjamin Altman Figure Prize at the 1959 National Academy of Design exhibition.

A retrospective of Koch's work, *John Koch: Painting a New York Life*, was held at the New York Historical Society in 2002.

BIBLIOGRAPHY:

John Koch: a Memorial Exhibition, exhibition catalogue, Kraushaar Galleries, New York, 1980. Lopate, Philip, et al., *John Koch: Painting a New York Life*, exhibition catalogue, New York Historical Society, New York, 2001.

MUSEUMS AND GALLERIES:

BOSTON (MFA): *At the Museum* (1941, oil on canvas) - ILLINOIS (Rochford Art Museum): *End of the Day* (1970, oil on canvas) - NEW YORK (Memorial AG of the University of Rochester): *Interlude* (1963, oil on canvas) - SAN FRANCISCO (FAM): *The Bridge* (c. 1950, oil on canvas) - WASHINGTON DC (Smithsonian American AM): *My Studio* (c. 1952, oil on canvas) - YOUNGSTOWN (Butler Institute of American Art): *Music* (1956-1957, oil on canvas).

AUCTION RECORDS:

NEW YORK, 21 June 1979, *Little Girl Reading; Little Girl Arranging Flowers* (oil on panel, double-sided, 22 x 24 ins / 56 x 61 cm) USD 2,100. NEW YORK, 4 Dec 1980, *Art Fanatics* (oil on canvas, 25 x 29 3/4 ins / 63.5 x 75.6 cm) USD 34,000. LOS ANGELES, 9 Feb 1982, *Man Putting on a Shirt* (oil on canvas, 30 x 25 ins / 76 x 63.5 cm) USD 4,750. NEW YORK, 3 June 1983, *Excavation* (oil on canvas, 24 x 20 ins / 60.8 x 50.6 cm) USD 8,000. NEW YORK, 26 Oct 1984, *Portrait of Noel Straus* (lead pencil heightened with white, 14 3/4 x 19 ins / 37.5 x 48.2 cm) USD 1,000. NEW YORK, 30 May 1985, *Still-life with laurel*

(1973, oil on canvas, 48 x 36 ins / 122 x 91.5 cm) USD 47,000. NEW YORK, 29 May 1986, *The Plumber* (1966, oil on canvas, 30 x 25 ins / 76.2 x 63.5 cm) USD 30,000. LOS ANGELES, 9 June 1988, *Summer* (oil on canvas, 36 x 40 1/4 ins / 91.5 x 102 cm) USD 8,800. NEW YORK, 30 Sept 1988, *Mary and Michael* (oil on canvas, 16 1/4 x 20 ins / 41 x 51 cm) USD 7,700. NEW YORK, 25 May 1989, *Dora under the Lamp* (oil/synthetic resin, 8 x 10 ins / 20.1 x 25.5 cm) USD 16,500; *The Cocktail* (oil on canvas, 40 x 50 ins / 101.6 x 127.1 cm) USD 363,000. NEW YORK, 28 Sept 1989, *The Window* (oil on canvas, 20 1/4 x 16 1/4 ins / 51.4 x 41 cm) USD 16,500. NEW YORK, 1 Dec 1989, *Putting Clothes Back On* (oil on canvas, 50 x 40 ins / 126.9 x 101.6 cm) USD 52,800. NEW YORK, 16 March 1990, *Monument* (oil on canvas, 49 x 61 ins / 124.3 x 154.9 cm) USD 38,500. NEW YORK, 23 May 1990, *Children's Games* (oil on canvas, 18 x 18 ins / 46 x 45.9 cm) USD 24,200. NEW YORK, 14 March 1991, *The book of drawings* (oil on canvas, 20 x 24 ins / 51 x 61 cm) USD 11,000. NEW YORK, 21 May 1991, *Male nude seated* (pencil and white chalk/paper, 15 1/4 x 12 ins / 38.7 x 30.5 cm) USD 2,420. NEW YORK, 23 May 1991, *Mother and Her Children* (oil on canvas, 40 x 29 ins / 101.6 x 73.7 cm) USD 22,000. NEW YORK, 3 Dec 1992, *Still-life at Dawn* (oil on canvas, 40 x 50 ins / 101.6 x 127 cm) USD 308,000. NEW YORK, 26 May 1993, *The accident n° 2* (1968, oil on canvas, 25 x 30 ins / 63.5 x 76.2 cm) USD 129,000. NEW YORK, 17 March 1994, *The atelier* (oil on canvas, 36 x 30 ins / 91.4 x 76.2 cm) USD 17,250. NEW YORK, 21 May 1996, *Portrait of Mrs Robert Ehrman (Isabel Pickering Beckurts)* (oil on canvas). NEW YORK, 27 Sept 1996, *Playing with Baby* (c. 1947, oil on canvas, 36 x 36 ins / 91.5 x 91.5 cm) USD 26,450. PHILADELPHIA, 12 Dec 1999, *Interior* (oil on canvas, 20 x 24 ins / 51 x 60 cm) USD 6,800. NEW YORK, 29 Nov 2000, *Manuscript II* (1875, oil on canvas, 25 x 30 ins / 63 x 76 cm) USD 28,000. NEW YORK, 29 Nov 2000, *Studio Interior* (oil on canvas, 25 x 30 ins / 63 x 76 cm) USD 70,000. NEW YORK, 29 Nov 2001, *Couple* (oil on canvas, 50 x 40 ins / 127 x 102 cm) USD 13,000. NEW YORK, 23 May 2002, *Chinese Girl, Shu Ching Yang* (c. 1925, colour pastel and watercolour, 34 x 22 ins / 87 x 56 cm) USD 1,700. NEW YORK, 4 March 2003, *Double Portrait* (c. 1955, oil on canvas, 40 x 30 ins / 102 x 76 cm) USD 10,000. NEW YORK, 3 Dec 2003, *Sleeping Boy* (oil on canvas, 20 x 16 ins / 51 x 41 cm) USD 14,000. NEW YORK, 26 May 2004, *Study of a Standing Young Man* (pencil, 18 x 11 ins / 46 x 28 cm) USD 3,000. NEW YORK, 29 June 2004, *Afternoon Labors* (1936, oil on canvas, 50 x 60 ins / 127 x 152 cm) USD 15,000.

KOCH, Josef

Bohemian, 18th century.
Active in Prague at the end of the 18th century.
Engraver.

Josef Koch is known for his portraits and landscapes.

KOCH, Joseph

German, 19th century.
Born 1819, in Munich; died 17 February 1871, in Munich.
Painter, engraver. Landscapes, animals.

Joseph Koch studied with Adam, Voltz and Bernhardt. He went on a study tour to Belgium and spent some time in Antwerp. He also visited Paris and Venice, returning to Munich in 1846.

AUCTION RECORDS:

LONDON, 19 April 1978, *Stag and Hinds in a Landscape* (1849, oil on canvas, 28 x 51 1/4 ins / 71 x 130 cm) GBP 1,500.

KOCH, Joseph Anton

German, 18th - 19th century.
Born 27 July 1768, in Obergibeln (Elbigenalp); died 12 January 1839, in Rome.
Painter, watercolourist, engraver, draughtsman.
Religious subjects, mythological subjects, genre scenes, landscapes, mountainscapes.
Connections to Nazarenes.

Joseph Anton Koch studied in Stuttgart, Strasbourg and Basel. For several years he devoted himself to landscape painting, crossing Switzerland and travelling as far as Naples. He was a corresponding member of the Munich academy. He led a romantic life. He was a pupil at the Karlsschule in Stuttgart and was intended for a career in government, but ran away in 1791, first to France, then to Switzerland, finally reaching Italy, where he arrived on foot. There he met up with Carstens and Thorvaldsen. Several of his works were shown in the exhibition: *Chefs-d'œuvre du Belvédère de Vienne* (*Masterpieces from the Belvedere in Vienna*) at the Musée Marmottan in Paris in 1994. Others appeared in the exhibition *Expedition Kunst. Die Entdeckung der Natur von C.D. Friedrich bis Humboldt* (*Expedition Art. The Discovery of Nature from C.D. Friedrich to Humboldt*) in the Hamburg Kunsthalle in 2003, an exhibition examining the interaction between the art of landscape painting and the natural sciences.

As he had had no artistic training, his technique never lost its naiveté. He remained a Tyrolean peasant, compensating for his lack of culture - which did not prevent him from being in communication with Humboldt, Schlegel and Kotzebue - by the liveliness of his peronality. After some attempts at compositions after Dante, from 1805 onwards he devoted himself to 'Romanised' classically inspired landscapes, apart from a few religious compositions, in which the landscape counts for more than the subject. Like many painters at the time, including even the Italians, he drew his inspiration chiefly from Poussin, but also from Claude Lorraine. He painted the mountainous landscapes of the Sabine, proving to be one of the rare masters of mountain painting. Then, after a stay in Vienna from 1812 to 1815, he returned to Rome, where he became friendly with Overbeck's Nazarenes group and worked with them on the decoration of the Villa Massimi. His closest friends were Reinhart and von Rohden, who were also good representatives of German classical landscape painting. Within this classical movement, Koch himself may be considered as the creator of the romantic landscape. This is mainly due to his feeling for wild nature and mountain scenery, which at the time were considered unaesthetic and barbarous.

BIBLIOGRAPHY:

Expedition Kunst. Die Entdeckung der Natur von C. D. Friedrich bis Humboldt, exhibition catalogue, Hamburger Kunsthalle, Hamburg, 2002.

MUSEUMS AND GALLERIES:

BASEL: *Macbeth and the Witches; Three Italian Landscapes* - BERLIN: *Monastery of San Francesco di Civitella; Landscape; Noah's Sacrifice of Thanksgiving* - DARMSTADT: *Waterfall at Tivoli* - FRANKFURT AM MAIN: *Noah's Sacrifice; The Flight of Hylas; Story of the She-ass of Bethlehem* - HAMBURG: three landscapes - HANOVER: *Italian Landscape* - INNSBRUCK: *Bernese Landscape* (1817) - LEIPZIG: five landscapes; a watercolour - MUNICH: *Italian Wine-growers Festival*; two landscapes - STUTTGART: two landscapes - VIENNA (Österreichische Gal. Belvedere): *Waterfalls at Tivoli, near Rome.*

AUCTION RECORDS:

STUTTGART, 29 Nov 1957, *Heroic Landscape with a Rainbow* (pen) DEM 4,600. MUNICH, 25 Nov 1976, *Meal in the Capuchin Friary* (1793, pen and wash, 9 3/4 x 14 1/4 ins / 25 x 36 cm) DEM 6,500. LONDON, 29 Nov 1977, *St Martin and the Beggar in a Landscape* (pen and wash, 13 x 18 ins / 33.2 x 45.6 cm) GBP 1,900. LONDON, 20 April 1978, *Rebecca and Eliezer at the Well* (1800, watercolour, gouache and pen, 20 3/4 x 29 ins / 53 x 73.5 cm) GBP 4,400. MUNICH, 28 Nov 1979, *View of Ancient Rome* (c. 1803, pencil and pen, 6 x 8 1/2 ins / 15.5 x 21.5 cm) DEM 9,000. COLOGNE, 21 May 1981, *The Holy Family in a Landscape* (pen/two pages joined together, 15 1/2 x 8 1/4 ins / 39.5 x 21 cm) DEM 6,500. LONDON, 23 June 1981, *Ruth and Boaz in a Landscape* (c. 1818/1822, oil on canvas, 33 1/4 x 43 1/4 ins / 84.5 x 110 cm) GBP 60,000. LONDON, 18 March 1983, *Heroic Landscape with a Rainbow* (oil on canvas, 28 3/4 x 23 1/2 ins / 73 x 60 cm) GBP 29,000. NEW YORK, 15 Feb 1985, *Undulating Landscape with Figures* (watercolour/pencil outlines, 9 1/4 x 11 ins / 23.2 x 27 cm) USD 1,600. LONDON, 27 Nov 1986, *Alms to the Cripple* (pencil, 6 x 8 1/4 ins / 15 x 21 cm) GBP 2,800. MUNICH, 18 May 1988, *Italian Landscape* (pencil, 19 1/4 x 32 ins / 49 x 81.5 cm) DEM 3,300. HEIDELBERG, 14 Oct 1988, *Scene of Ancient Sacrifice* (pencil and ink, 6 3/4 x 10 1/4 ins / 17.4 x 26.2 cm) DEM 1,400. LONDON, 19 June 1991, *Imaginary Landscape with Philemon and Baucis Appearing before Zeus and Hermes* (1814, watercolour, 16 3/4 x 23 3/4 ins / 42.5 x 60.5 cm) GBP 7,700. LONDON, 21 June 1991, *Heroic Landscape with a Rainbow* (1824, oil on canvas, 42 1/2 x 37 3/4 ins / 108 x 96 cm) GBP 836,000. LONDON, 13 Oct 1994, *Dante and Beatrice in Paradise; Dante and Vergil at the Gates of Hell* (pencil and ink/paper, 11 1/2 x 14 1/4 ins / 29.5 x 36.2 cm) GBP 4,600. STUTTGART, 19 March 1999, *Scene of Hermann's Battle at Klopstock* (gouache, 11 x 9 ins / 27 x 22 cm) DEM 6,000. LUCERNE, 19 May 1999, *Mountain Landscape* (pen and wash, 17 x 23 ins / 44 x 59 cm) CHF 90,000. DÜSSELDORF, 31 Jan 2000, *Apollo with Shepherds* (oil on canvas, 37 x 59 ins / 95 x 149 cm) DEM 10,000. COLOGNE, 20 Oct 2000, *Italian Landscapes with Figures* (pencil, a pair, 9 x 14 ins / 24 x 35 cm) DEM 18,000. LONDON, 30 March 2001, *Tiber Landscape with Merry Peasant Folk* (1817, oil on canvas, 20 x 29 ins / 52 x 74 cm) GBP 200,000. LONDON, 20 June 2002, *Figures in the Roman Campagna* (c. 1797, watercolour, 27 x 39 ins / 68 x 99 cm) GBP 28,000. NEUILLY, 27 June 2003, *Italian Landscape* (oil on canvas, 24 x 33 ins / 62 x 83 cm) EUR 25,000.

KOCH, Julius
German, 20th century.
Born 1882, in Aachen; died 1952, in Stuttgart.
Painter. Landscapes.

AUCTION RECORDS:
BERN, 26 Oct 1988, *Southern German Landscape* (1921, oil on canvas, 17 x 21 1/4 ins / 43 x 54 cm) CHF 950.

KOCH, Karl Georg
German, 19th century.
Born 27 February 1857, in Berlin.
Painter. History painting.

Karl Koch was a pupil of Steffeck and Gussort, but mainly studied nature. His *Battle of Villiers* aroused great interest. He won a gold medal in Berlin in 1888.

MUSEUMS AND GALLERIES:
LEIPZIG: *French Cuirassiers at Sedan* (1888).

AUCTION RECORDS:
LONDON, 16 March 1983, *Artillery Convoy* (gouache, 19 1/4 x 27 1/4 ins / 49 x 69 cm) GBP 600.

KOCH, Kaspar
Swiss, 15th - 16th century.
Died probably in 1525.
Active in Basel.
Painter, draughtsman.

Kaspar Koch decorated the gallery of the Augustinian convent in Basel. He was appointed to a wide variety of roles in public life in Basel.

KOCH, Leopold
German, 19th century.
Born 28 June 1857, in Klein Mangelsdorf.
Sculptor.

Leopold Koch exhibited for the first time in 1881 at the Berlin academy. He is best known for his *Memorial to King Frederick William I of Prussia*, in Nauen.

KOCH, Lorika
German, 20th century.
Active in France.
Sculptor.

The Musée Bourdelle in Paris organised a one-woman exhibition of Lorika Koch's works in 1988 as a reward for the Bourdelle prize that she received in 1987.

KOCH, Ludwig
Swiss, 16th century.
Probably baptised 31 July 1577 in Bern.
Painter (glass).

KOCH, Ludwig
Austrian, 19th - 20th century.
Born 13 December 1866, in Vienna; died 1934.
Painter. Military subjects.

Ludwig Koch was primarily a painter of war scenes and cavalry charges.

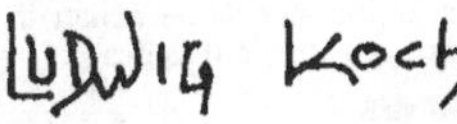

AUCTION RECORDS:
PARIS, 15 Jan 1943, *Fantastic Cavalcade*, FRF 2,100. VIENNA, 3 Dec 1976, *Elegant Horseman* (1905, oil on canvas, 23 1/2 x 30 ins / 60 x 76 cm) ATS 25,000. NEW YORK, 28 April 1977, *Soldiers and Officers of the Great War* (oil on panel, 24 x 37 ins / 61 x 94 cm) USD 1,300. LONDON, 9 May 1979, *The Royal Promenade* (1920, oil on canvas, 27 1/2 x 39 1/4 ins / 70 x 100 cm) GBP 1,300. VIENNA, 12 Nov 1980, *Promenade in the Prater* (watercolour, 23 1/2 x 16 1/4 ins / 60 x 41 cm) ATS 16,000. VIENNA, 18 Nov 1981, *Horse Market* (watercolour, 9 x 13 1/2 ins / 22 x 34 cm) ATS 20,000. VIENNA, 13 March 1984, *Polo Players* (1907, oil on canvas, 28 1/4 x 35 3/4 ins / 72 x 91 cm) ATS 65,000. VIENNA, 19 March 1985, *Studies of Horses Jumping the Fences* (pen and Indian ink, 14 x 10 1/4 ins / 35.5 x 26 cm) ATS 12,000. LONDON, 20 June 1985, *Polo Match* (1911, watercolour and gouache/pencil outline/mounted paper/canvas, 34 3/4 x 59 ins / 88.5 x 149 cm) GBP 26,000. VIENNA, 9 Dec 1987, *Porthos*, (1913, watercolour and pencil heightened with white, 31 x 59 ins / 78.5 x 149 cm) ATS 30,000. NEW YORK, 23 Feb 1989, *Polo Match* (1922, oil on canvas, 36 1/4 x 28 1/4 ins / 92 x 71.7 cm) USD 15,400. LONDON, 11 May 1990, *Stage Coach in the Storm* (1923, oil on canvas, 24 1/2 x 42 1/4 ins / 62 x 107 cm) GBP 2,200. NEW YORK, 15 Oct 1993, *Polo Game* (watercolour and gouache/card, 11 1/2 x 11 3/4 ins / 29.2 x 29.8 cm) USD 4,025. LONDON, 16 Nov 1994, *Hunting Scene* (oil on canvas, 78 x 59 ins / 198 x 150 cm) GBP 12,075. ZURICH, 25 Sept 2000, *Peasants on Horses in Bosnia* (oil on canvas, 65 x 118 ins / 165 x 300 cm) CHF 10,000. LONDON, 22 Nov 2000, *Going for Goal* (gouache, 12 x 12 ins / 30 x 30 cm) GBP 1,000. VIENNA, 30 May 2001, *Wedding Ride* (1934, oil on canvas, 20 x 24 ins / 51 x 61 cm) ATS 35,000. LONDON, 28 June 2001, *Karl I Leading his Troops* (1917, oil on canvas, 52 x 80 ins / 132 x 202 cm) GBP 2,600. LONDON, 25 April 2002, *Off to Battle* (1915, oil on canvas, 52 x 80 ins / 132 x 202 cm) GBP 3,800. PRAGUE, 30 Nov 2002, *Horse Race* (1920, oil on canvas, 43 x 47 ins / 110 x 120 cm) CZK 200,000. SALZBURG, 20 Nov 2003, *Horse-drawn Coach in the Rain* (1923, oil on canvas, 24 x 42 ins / 62 x 106 cm) EUR 6,500. VIENNA, 26 Nov 2003, *Procession of Mounted Soldiers in Vienna* (1929, oil on canvas, 24 x 34 ins / 60 x 86 cm) EUR 6,500. SALZBURG, 9 June 2004, *Horses Drinking* (1928, oil on canvas, 26 x 36 ins / 66 x 91 cm) EUR 1,500.

KOCH, M.
Dutch, 17th century.
Born in the Netherlands.
Active c. 1695.
Engraver.

M. Koch is remembered for his *Procession of William III (5 February 1691)*.

KOCH, Max Friedrich
German, 19th century.

Born 24 November 1859, in Berlin.
Painter. History painting.
Max Koch studied in Berlin, Rome and Paris. He worked on the decoration of the Museum of Fine Arts in Berlin. He won a gold medal in Berlin in 1892.

KOCH, Michael
German, 19th century.
Active in Munich c. 1890.
Painter. Portraits, genre scenes.

KOCH, Michel
German, 19th century.
Born 6 November 1853, in Edingen.
Painter.
Michel Koch studied with Pœckh and Hoff, and for a time followed courses at the Académie Julian in Paris. He is known for genre scenes and landscapes.

KOCH, Niklaus
Swiss, 17th - 18th century.
Active in Bern.
Painter (glass).
Niklaus Koch painted two stained glass windows for the church in Bern in 1609.

KOCH, Ödön
Swiss, 20th century.
Born 1906, in Zurich.
Sculptor.
Ödön Koch produced tapestries before turning his attention to sculpture, which he taught himself in 1938. He worked in fine materials, mostly semi-precious stone. An abstract sculptor, his compositions consisted of monolithic blocks with smoothed-off surfaces, a few simple forms overlapping each other, the softened edges becoming curves. Such arrangements are reminiscent of the works of Lipsi, and ultimately Arp.

He participated in the following group exhibitions: the Expositions Nationales in 1936, 1951, 1966; the plein-air sculpture exhibition in Biel, in 1962 and 1966; in the Kunsthaus in Zurich and in 1960 with Aeschbacher and F. Fisher; at the Exposition Internationale de Sculpture at the Musée Rodin in Paris in 1961 and at the 3rd Salon Internationale des Galeries Pilotes in the Musée Cantonal in Lausanne, in 1970. He showed his work in one-man exhibitions, notably in 1962 and 1967 in Zurich.

KOCH, Paul
French, 20th century.
Born 1927, in Troyes.
Engraver.

BIBLIOGRAPHY:

Beaumont-Maillet, Laure/Woimant, Françoise/Pernoud, Emmanuel, *De Bonnard à Baselitz - Dix ans d'enrichissements du Cabinet des estampes 1978-1988*, exhibition catalogue, Bibliothèque nationale de France, Paris, 1992.

KOCH, Paul Francesco
German, 19th century.
Born 31 March 1845, in Hamburg; died 19 August 1886, in Augsburg.
Sculptor.
Paul Koch studied at the Berlin academy.

KOCH, Peter
German, 20th century.
Born 8 October 1874, near Deidesheim.
Painter. Landscapes.
Peter Koch painted landscapes of different regions in Germany.

AUCTION RECORDS:

LONDON, 24 March 1988, *Dandelions, Poppies and Wild Flowers in a Vase* (gouache, 27 x 14 3/4 ins / 68.5 x 37.5 cm) GBP 1,430. HEIDELBERG, 15 Oct 1999, *Wiesbachtal in Appenzell* (oil on canvas, 35 x 31 ins / 88 x 78 cm) DEM 3,300.

KOCH, Philipp
German, 16th century.
Active in Freiburg, Saxony, c. 1500.
Painter, sculptor (wood).
He worked, notably, for the cathedral in Freiburg.

KOCH, Pieter Frans Christian, called Koch, Pyke, also called Huebner
Dutch, 20th century.
Born 1901, in Beek near Nijmegen; died 1991, in Amsterdam.
Painter. Allegorical subjects, figure compositions. Symbolism, Magical Realism.
Pieter Koch (known as Pyke Koch) began his studies at the University of Utrecht where he met T.J. Botke, a dentist in Maastricht, who became his patron and collected his most important works. During their studies they also met the poet Martinus Nijhoff, the writer Cola Debrot and the painters Erich Wichmann and Charley Toorop, who deeply impressed Koch. In 1927 he abandoned his studies in law for painting. Although he appears to have been self-taught, his early works still show a certain traditional technical perfection while being highly individual. Shortly thereafter he participated in the definition of what was entitled 'Magic Realism' with painters such as Carel Willink, who was to influence him in his turn, and Raoul Hynckes. Koch himself differentiated between Magic Realism and Surrealism as follows: 'Magic Realism is based on possible but improbable situations, whereas Surrealism is based on non-existent and impossible situations. Between the worlds of the impossible and improbable resides the difference between the two.' From 1927 to 1935 he worked on a series *The Café*, a sequence of monumental portraits of imaginary women often dressed as poor street girls, while frequently inspired by the German actress Asta Nielsen whose portrait he painted. Among these popular female figures or *kermesse* figures, *Bertha of Antwerp* is one of the most characteristic of the period. Characteristic also of his crude realism, one of these paintings, *Shooting Gallery*, in its harsh accentuation of the traits and the body of the booth keeper, rather than echoing Surrealism or a single Magic Realism, exemplifies German Expressionism of the beginning of the century and, more especially, the crueller aspects of the Neue Sachlichkeit (New Objectivity) of Otto Dix and Georges Grosz. During this period, Koch also painted after experimental photographs and German Expressionist cinema of the post-war period, especially for *Midnight Poetry* where the nocturnal obscurity seen from an elevated viewpoint, imbues an otherwise fairly common shot with an uncanny atmosphere.

More in keeping with the principles of Magic Realism he introduced unusual elements into certain compositions, such as *Lion in an Interior*. The illusionist interpretation of the subjects - particularly the skin of the figures and the deliberate full-face portraits rigorously framed by the décor - intensify their presence before the viewer. From 1932 he moved on to different subjects. His *Self-portraits*, painted in 1936-1937 following an illness, are indicative of a new emotional potential. Between 1938 and 1940 a trip to Italy enabled him to become familiar with the frescoes of Piero della Francesco in Arezzo, thereby confirming his attachment to the style of the Italian Renaissance, although it should not be forgotten that this influence first reached him through the German Nazarenes of the mid-19th century. On his return, he painted between 1943 and 1944 the *Chimney Sweepers* cycle, some of which bring to mind the attitude and composition of Mantegna's *Saint Sebastian*. Between 1945 and 1953 he worked on *The Four Seasons* series, the characters of which symbolised each season. In 1953 he painted *Harvest*, his largest work, in which traces of the Quattrocento are discernible, perhaps an echo of Paolo Uccello's *Battles* in the rhythmic organisation of elements and frontally placed figures and the receding planes of landscaped décor. In the following period, notably with the *Contortionists*, he was once more preoccupied with the spirit and psychological climate of his characters as in his early paintings. Deliberately less precise in the rendering of detail, his paintings were again evocations rather than descriptions: *Sleepwalker's Rest* 1965, *Memory of a Dream*, 1966.

In an effort to summarise a multifaceted work, Koch wished to express - without abandoning what the Germans called 'gallows humour' - the social realities of his time and the characteristic concerns or sentiments of his generation: sense of fate, morbid anguish, sexual obsessions in paintings which, while related to the Italian Renaissance in their technique, still maintained links with the Surrealist trend.

Koch's group exhibitions included: *Trends in the 1920s* in Berlin in 1977, and *Realisms* in Paris and Berlin 1980-1981. His work was shown at *De blijvende verlokking: Nederlandse kunstenaars in Italië, 1806-1940* (*Lasting Attraction: Dutch Artists in Italy, 1806-1940*), an exhibition which showed the effects of their travels in Italy on Dutch artists (Kunsthal, Rotterdam, 2003). Pyke Koch also showed his paintings in numerous one-man exhibitions from 1930, mostly in the Netherlands, but also abroad, notably in New York. A retrospective of his work was held in 1982-1983 at the Institut Néerlandais, at the Gemeentemuseum in Arnhem and at the museum of modern art in Liège.

Bibliography:

Blotkamp, Carel, *Pyke Koch*, Uitgeverij De Arbeiderspers, Amsterdam, 1972. Blotkamp, Carel, *Pyke Koch*, exhibition catalogue, Institut néerlandais, Paris, 1982. *Art, Pays-Bas, XXe Siècle - La Beauté exacte, de Van Gogh à Mondrian*, exhibition catalogue, Musée d'Art Moderne de la Ville de Paris, Paris, 1994. Zutter, Jörg F./Steen, John/Vovelle, José/Kemper, Bram, *Pyke Koch, réalisme magique aux Pays-Bas*, exhibition catalogue, Musée Cantonal des Beaux-Arts, Lausanne, 1995. *Pyke Koch, Paintings and Drawings*, exhibition catalogue, Museum Boijmans Van Beuningen, Rotterdam, 1995 (text in Dutch and English). *De blijvende verlokking: Nederlandse kunstenaars in Italië, 1806-1940*, exhibition catalogue, Kunsthal, Rotterdam, 2003.

Museums and Galleries:

Amsterdam (Stedelijk Mus.): *Rhapsody of the Slums* (1929); *The Great Contortionist* (1957) - Arnhem: *Mercedes of Barcelona* (1930) - Arnhem (Historisches Mus.): *Nocturne* (1930) - Rotterdam (Mus. Boijmans Van Beuningen): *Shooting Gallery* (1931) - The Hague (Gemeentemus.): *Mercedes of Barcelona* (1930); *The Chimney Sweeper Standing, II* (1944); *Shooting Gallery* (1931); *Bertha of Antwerp* (1931).

Auction records:

Amsterdam, 25 April 1978, *Blind Man's Buff* (oil on canvas, 24 1/2 x 30 ins / 62.5 x 76.5 cm) NLG 42,000. Amsterdam, 9 Dec 1988, *Anna* (1933, oil on canvas, 67 x 51 1/4 ins / 170 x 130 cm) NLG 299,000; *Midnight Poetry* (1931, oil on canvas, 39 1/2 x 39 1/4 ins / 100.5 x 100 cm) NLG 41,400; *The Four Seasons* (oil on canvas, four panels, each 49 1/4 x 33 1/2 ins / 125 x 85 cm) NLG 172,500; *The Harvest* (1953, tempera and oil on canvas, 78 3/4 x 102 1/4 ins / 200 x 259.5 cm) NLG 460,000. Amsterdam, 24 May 1989, *The Young Dead Man - Nephew of the Artist* (1936, tempera/canvas/panel, 14 x 15 ins / 35.5 x 38 cm) NLG 43,700. Amsterdam, 13 Dec 1989, *Memory of a Dream* (oil on canvas, 23 1/2 x 29 1/2 ins / 60 x 75 cm) NLG 207,000. Amsterdam, 22 May 1990, *Daphne* (oil and tempera/canvas, 20 3/4 x 12 ins / 53 x 30.5 cm) NLG 149,500; *Racing Boy* (oil on canvas/panel, 11 3/4 x 10 ins / 30 x 24.5 cm) NLG 57,500. Amsterdam, 13 Dec 1990, *Kermesse in Utrecht* (oil on canvas, 39 1/4 x 43 1/4 ins / 100 x 110 cm) NLG 63,250. Amsterdam, 10 Dec 1992, *The Sign* (1975, oil on canvas, 18 1/4 x 14 3/4 ins / 46.5 x 37.5 cm) NLG 166,750; *Mêlée III* (1969, tempera/canvas, 44 1/4 x 67 1/4 ins / 112.5 x 170.5 cm) NLG 281,750. Amsterdam, 8 Dec 1993, *Daphne* (oil and tempera/canvas, 20 3/4 x 12 ins / 53 x 30.5 cm) NLG 276,000. Amsterdam, 7 Dec 1994, *Portrait of Mrs J. C. Van Boetzelaer in profile* (1948, oil on canvas, 10 x 9 3/4 ins / 25.5 x 25 cm) NLG 184,000. Amsterdam, 6 Dec 1995, *Still-life with Lemons* (oil on canvas, 9 x 16 1/4 ins / 23 x 41 cm) NLG 195,500. Amsterdam, 5 June 1996, *Lion in Interior II* (1972, oil on panel, 23 3/4 x 17 3/4 ins / 60.5 x 45 cm) NLG 138,000. Amsterdam, 2 Dec 1997, *The Sleepwalker's Repose IV* (1971, oil on canvas, 17 3/4 x 29 1/2 ins / 45 x 75 cm) NLG 576,600. Amsterdam, 30 Nov 2000, *Cypress* (1969, oil on canvas, 22 x 12 ins / 55 x 30 cm) NLG 110,000. Amsterdam, 30 Nov 2000, *Daphne* (oil tempera on panel, 11 x 11 ins / 28 x 28 cm) NLG 740,000. Amsterdam, 16 April 2002, *Dead Boy* (tempera on canvas laid on panel, 14 x 15 ins / 35 x 38 cm) EUR 110,000. Amsterdam, 28 May 2002, *Woman with Gramophone* (c. 1928, oil on canvas, 31 x 28 ins / 80 x 70 cm) EUR 140,000. Amsterdam, 2 Dec 2003, *Rustende Slaapwandelaarster I* (1959, oil on canvas, 7 x 14 ins / 18 x 35 cm) EUR 105,000.

KOCH, Renate

German, 20th century.

Sculptor of assemblages, installation artist.

In 1993 Renate Koch exhibited with Claudia Schmacke at the Galerie Patricia Dorfmann, Paris. They met during a stay in Bratislava in 1992. An ecological concern is evident in the celebration of the elements in their arrangements and installations.

KOCH, Rudolf Wilhelm

German, 19th century.

Born 11 January 1834, in Hamburg; died 8 January 1885, in Ottensen.

Painter. Landscapes, architectural views.

Rudolf Koch studied with Martin Gensler in Hamburg and J. W. Schirmer at the Düsseldorf academy. He settled in Hamburg in 1855.

KOCH, Theodor Friedrich

German, 20th century.

Born 24 May 1875, in Wilferdingen.

Painter, engraver. Portraits, landscapes, urban landscapes.

In 1912 Theodor Friedrich Koch settled in Osnabrück, where he painted portraits, landscapes and a number of views of the old town.

KOCH, Udo

German, 20th - 21st century.

Born 1958, in Offenbach.

Sculptor, draughtsman.

Udo Koch lives and works in Frankfurt am Main. He makes sculptures, such as his *Teapots* series, in which some of the facets of each teapot are covered in plaster which perfectly follows the contour of the object. Convex and concave meet, the shapes interact and the contour lines of are strengthened. The same approach can be seen in his drawings, where the object vanishes and is seen in the negative.

Collective exhibitions include: *Kunst in Frankfurt 1986* (*Art in Frankfurt 1986*), Kunstverein, Frankfurt am Main (1986); 8th Ateliers, Fonds Régional d'Art Contemporain des Pays de la Loire (1992); 5th Fellbach Triennale (1992); *Qui, quoi, où? Un regard sur l'art en Allemagne en 1992* (*Who, What, Where? A Look at Art in Germany in 1992*), Musée d' Art Moderne de la Ville de Paris (1992). Solo exhibitions include:

Cologne (1987); Ak gallery, Frankfurt am Main (1988, 1991); Stampa gallery, Base (1980); *Neue Räume*, Museum für Moderne Kunst, Frankfurt am Main (1992); Galerie & Édition Atelier, Graz (1992); Galerie Gilles Peyroulet, Paris (1993).
Auction records:
Zurich, 30 Nov 1995, *Winter* (porcelain and plaster, 10¼ x 7 x 9½ ins / 26 x 17.5 x 24 cm) CHF 3,450.

KOCH, W., or Kock, Kok
Dutch, 18th century.
Born 1761, in Oosterhout; died March 1806, in Amsterdam.
Draughtsman, engraver. Genre scenes.
W. Koch was the pupil of Ch. Philipps in Amsterdam. He worked for some time in Paris, and is especially remembered for his interiors.
Museums and Galleries:
Valenciennes (MBA): *Bad News* (wash drawing).

KOCH, Walter
German, 20th century.
Born 14 April 1875, near Altona; died 30 January 1915, in Zurich.
Painter, engraver, architect. Landscapes.
Walter Koch was taught by Böse at the academy in Berlin. He lived in Davos, Switzerland and produced primarily views of the Alps in this region.
Auction records:
Lucerne, 4 April 1987, *The Lake of Davos* (1911, oil on card, 20¾ x 23½ ins / 53 x 60 cm) CHF 4,200. Zofingen, 4 June 2004, *Spring Landscape with Clouds* (1912, oil on canvas laid on board, 22 x 20 ins / 56 x 52 cm) CHF 6,000.

KOCH, Werner
Swiss, 20th century.
Born 16 July 1884, in Aesch.
Painter, glass painter.
After studying in Munich, Werner Koch returned to work in Switzerland, where he exhibited, most often in Basel and Zurich. In 1925 he was awarded a gold medal at the Exposition des Arts Décoratifs in Paris.

KOCH VON LANGENTREU, Friederike
Italian, 19th - 20th century.
Born 1 January 1866, in Conegliano; died 1941.
Painter. Genre scenes.
She was active in Munich.
Museums and Galleries:
Bucharest (Muz. National de Arta al României): *Peasant Woman Knitting.*

KOCH-GOTHA, Fritz
German, 20th century.
Born 5 January 1877, in Elberstädt.
Painter, illustrator.
Fritz Koch-Gotha attended the art academies in Leipzig and Karlsruhe. From 1902 he lived in Berlin, where he worked as a cartoonist.

KOCH-HANAU, Ludwig
German, 20th century.
Born 1 February 1882, in Hanau (Hesse).
Painter, illustrator. Landscapes.
Ludwig Koch-Hanau was best known for his landscapes.

KOCH-ZEUTHEN, Reinhold
German, 20th century.
Painter.
Reinhold Koch-Zeuthen worked in Berlin and participated in the 1909 Universal Exhibition in Berlin.

KOCHANOWSKY, Roman
Polish, 19th - 20th century.
Born 1857, in Cracow; died 1945, in Freising, Germany.
Painter. Landscapes, portraits.
Roman Kochanowsky studied with Lonkkasievich at the school of fine arts in Cracow, then with Lichtenfelse at the academy of fine arts in Vienna, where he won a gold medal. He took part in the 1909 Berlin exhibition.
Museums and Galleries:
Cracow: *Landscape on the outskirts of Cracow; Winter Landscape.*
Auction records:
Cologne, 17 Oct 1969, *Snowy Landscape*, DEM 4,800. Cologne, 24 Oct 1986, *A Winter's Night* (oil on canvas, 15 x 21¾ ins / 37.2 x 55.5 cm) DEM 5,000. Cologne, 15 Oct 1988, *Autumn Landscape with a Pool and Houses* (oil on panel, 5¾ x 9¼ ins / 14.8 x 23.3 cm) DEM 3,000. Munich, 2 Dec 1997, *Peasants in a Marshy Landscape* (oil on canvas, 14½ x 21¼ ins / 37 x 54 cm) DEM 9,228. Warsaw, 14 March 1999, *Early Spring* (1888, oil on canvas, 17 x 25 ins / 42 x 63 cm) PLZ 44,000. Lyons, 17 Oct 1999, *Landscape with Four Seasons* (1880, oil on canvas, four, 15 x 9 ins / 39 x 24 cm) FRF 75,000. Warsaw, 19 March 2000, *Landscape with Farmstead* (oil on panel, 5 x 8 ins / 12 x 20 cm) PLZ 15,000. Warsaw, 19 March 2000, *Woman by Farmstead, Cow at Pasture* (oil on panel, 10 x 7 ins / 25 x 17 cm) PLZ 18,000. Vienna, 20 Nov 2001, *Farmstead. Winter Landscape* (oil on panel, a pair, 5 x 8 ins / 12 x 20 cm) ATS 50,000. Munich, 2 July 2003, *Woman Gathering Sticks in Moorland* (1892, gouache, 18 x 10 ins / 45 x 26 cm) EUR 2,200. Warsaw, 19 Oct 2003, *Collecting Kindling Wood* (1872, oil on canvas, 18 x 10 ins / 45 x 26 cm) PLZ 15,000. Warsaw, 14 March 2004, *Landscape with a Figure* (oil on canvas, 15 x 21 ins / 37 x 54 cm) PLZ 32,000. Vienna, 22 June 2004, *At the Farm. Winter Landscape* (oil on panel, two, 5 x 8 ins / 12 x 20 cm) EUR 3,600.

KOCHEGURA, Vladimir
Ukrainian, 20th century.
Born 1904, in Yekaterinoslav (now Dnepropetrovsk); died 1970.
Painter. Portraits, landscapes.
Vladimir Kochegura studied at the institute of sculptural arts in Leningrad (now St Petersburg) and was a member of the Union of Soviet Artists.
Museums and Galleries:
Moscow (Central Lenin Mus.) - St Petersburg (Academy) - Sverdlovsk (MFA) - Ulyanovsk (City Museum).
Auction records:
Paris, 24 Sept 1991, *View of Minvodi* (oil on canvas, 19 x 13¾ ins / 48 x 35 cm) FRF 4,500. Paris, 9 Oct 1995, *Children at the Window* (watercolour, 15¾ x 11 ins / 40 x 28 cm) FRF 6,200.

KOCHELEVA, Olga
Russian, 20th - 21st century.
Born 18 December 1956, in Orenburg.
Painter. Figure compositions.
Olga Kocheleva studied at the Kalinin school of fine arts in Moscow and worked under the direction of S. Rakoutine. She executes Expressionist-type figurative paintings in dark colours, the style determined, the perspectives staggered by means of diagonals.

KOCHERSCHEIDT, Kurt, called Kappa
Austrian, 20th century.
Born 1943, in Klagenfurt; died 13 November 1992, in Wels.
Painter, engraver, photographer.
Wirklichkeiten (Realities) group.
From 1961 Kurt Kocherscheidt followed courses at the Academie der Bildenden Künste in Vienna and spent a year in Zagreb. From 1969 to 1971 he lived and worked in London, travelling in South America in 1972-1973. He was a cofounder of the Wircklichkeiten group in 1968. In 1989 he received the painting prize for the City of Vienna. He signed

his works Kappa or K. He married the photographer Elfie Semotan.

As a founder member of the Wirklichkeiten group, Kocherscheidt contributed to the revival of realist painting at the end of the 1960s in Austria before Pop Art reached Vienna. His realism was highly individualistic. He was an exponent of a tendency in Austria to paint or interpret objects or landscapes as pretexts for reflection on experiences and memories. From 1986 Kocherscheidt abandoned the traditional frame, preferring to present his paintings on wooden props placed against the wall.

He exhibited in group shows including: 1968 *Wirklichkeiten* the opening exhibition of the eponymous group; Vienna Secession; 1992 Documenta IX, Kassel: 2002 *In Praise of Painting*, a retrospective presenting the group Wirklichkeiten, Kunst aus Wien, Vienna. His one-man shows are as follows: 1970, 1972, Galerie Würthle, Vienna; 1981 Galerie Heike Curtze, Vienna; 1987, Rupertinum, Salzburg; 1987-1988, Stedelijk Museum, Amsterdam; 1992 Vienna Secession, 1994, Westfälischer Kunstverein, Münster; 2002, *The Continuing Image*, Österreiches Museum für Angewandte Kunst (MAK), Vienna.

BIBLIOGRAPHY:

Breicha, Otto von (ed.), *Wirklichkeiten: Aspekte einer Gruppierung*, exhibition catalogue, Museum des 20. Jahrhunderts, Vienna, 1988. *Kurt Kocherscheidt: Bilder 1976-1986*, travelling exhibition catalogue, Morat-Institut für Kunst und Kunstwissenschaft, Freiburg, Breisgau, Museum des Zwanzigsten Jehrhunderts, Vienna, Waldkircher Verlaggesellschaft, Waldkirch, 1989. Liesbrock, Heinz/Blumberger, Susanne, *Kurt Kocherscheidt: Bilder 1987-1992 und Fotografien aus Südamerika*, exhibition catalogue, Westfälischer Kunstverein, Münster, 1994. Kaiser, Heinz, *Kurt Kocherscheidt (1943-1992)*, dissertation, Salzburg, 2000 (University, Salzburg). Liesbrock, Heinz, *Brustrauschen: Zum Werkdialog von Kurt Kocherscheidt und Wolfgang Rihm*, exhibition catalogue, Hatje Cantz, Ostfildern-Ruit, 2001. Noever, Peter (edition)/Reder, Christian, *Kurt Kocherscheidt. Das fortlaufende Bild. The Continuing Image*, exhibition catalogue, MAK, Vienna, 2003 (bilingual English-German edition).

AUCTION RECORDS:

MUNICH, 26-27 Nov 1991, *Messalina* (1967, mixed media, 19 1/2 x 21 1/2 ins / 49.5 x 54.5 cm) DEM 3,450. VIENNA, 13 Oct 1999, *Memorial to the Resistance in Wood* (1971, mixed media on squared paper, 30 x 22 ins / 76 x 56 cm) ATS 60,000. VIENNA, 13 Oct 1999, *The Melody* (1986, oil on canvas, triptych, 71 x 134 ins / 180 x 340 cm) ATS 600,000. VIENNA, 25 May 2000, *Untitled* (1967, mixed media on card, 14 x 10 ins / 36 x 25 cm) ATS 26,000. VIENNA, 24 Sept 2002, *Teilchengleich* (1982, oil on paper, 24 x 32 ins / 62 x 81 cm) EUR 3,700. VIENNA, 28 Oct 2003, *Untitled* (1979, oil on canvas, 26 x 31 ins / 65 x 80 cm) EUR 10,500. VIENNA, 28 Oct 2003, *Untitled* (1989, oil on canvas, in two parts, 18 x 13 ins / 45 x 34 cm) EUR 13,000. VIENNA, 28 April 2004, *The Song* (oil on canvas, triptych, 71 x 134 ins / 180 x 340 cm) EUR 50,000. VIENNA, 12 Oct 2004, *Untitled* (1983, oil on canvas, 39 x 35 ins / 100 x 90 cm) EUR 7,000.

KOCHESVILI, Boris Petrovich

Russian, 20th century.
Born 1940, in Elektrostal.
Painter.

Boris Kochesvili graduated in 1962. His works are allusions to a fantastic urban universe in a phantasmagorical, almost abstract, projection. He showed his work in Europe and the USA during the 1980s.

BIBLIOGRAPHY:

Alavarez, José, *Art contemporain soviétique*, exhibition catalogue, Gal. de France, Paris, 1987.

KOCHI, Manabu

Japanese, 20th - 21st century.
Born 1954, in Okinawa.
Active in France since 1981.
Painter, pastellist, sculptor, lithographer.

Manabu Kochi acquired his artistic education on his travels across cultures and civilisations, from Tokyo to Florence, from London to Paris, where he eventually settled. He works in acrylics and oil pastels. He is also a lithographer, which allows him to increase the volume of his graphic work, and a sculptor: some of his sculpture is in cast bronze. His artistic identity is a synthesis of different influences - children's drawings, Miró, Brauner, and pop art are dominant in his painting; and primitive art, Miró, Arp, and Max Ernst in his sculpture. His paintings and pastels are a maze of simplified images and juxtaposed graphic signs. Françoise Monnin has described his bestiary sculpture as '... anatomic fragments: a head on a foot, three fingers on a belly... a man with a leaf for a head beside a feather with a mouth....' He exhibited at the Galerie Claude Lemand in Paris in 1989, 1991, and 1994.

BIBLIOGRAPHY:

Monnin, Françoise, *Kochi, peintures, pastels, sculptures, lithographies*, exhibition catalogue, Gal. Cl. Lemand, Paris, 1991.

AUCTION RECORDS:

PARIS, 29 Nov 1991, *Saisir l'Instant* (*Seize the Moment*) (1991, acrylics on canvas, 46 x 35 ins / 116 x 89 cm) FRF 21,500. BOULOGNE-SUR-SEINE, 27 Nov 1994, *Capricorne* (*Capricorn*) (1987, resin on metal frame, unique piece) FRF 20,000.

KOCHLI, Hans. See **KOCH**

KOCHLIN, Regina Emilie

Swiss, 19th century.
Born 15 February 1822, in Zurich.
Painter. Genre scenes.

Regina Kochlin exhibited several canvases between 1854 and 1858. She married the painter Hubert Correns of Cologne, and settled in Munich. She is also known for her portraits.

KOCHORO. See **KUNISADA Kachoro**

KOCIAN, Quido

Czech, 20th century.
Born 1874, in Usti nad Orlicí.
Sculptor. Religious subjects. Statues.

Quido Kocian taught sculpting in the town of Horice. He was drawn to producing statues inspired by the Bible including *Abel* and *Judas*.

KOCINSKI

Polish, 18th century.
Painter.

Kocinski was a painter at the court of Stanislas Leczinski in the 18th century.

KOCK, Albert. See **COECK Albert**

KOCK, Cordt

German, 17th century.
Active in Bremen c. 1600.
Glass painter.

KOCK, David

Swedish, 18th century.
Painter.

A ceiling executed by David Kock was still in the castle in Stockholm in 1816.

KOCK, Elisa. See **KOCH**

KÖCK, Franz
Austrian, 20th century.
Born 4 July 1886.
Painter. Religious subjects.
Franz Köck carried out a number of religious paintings for churches and monasteries in the region of Graz.

KÖCK, Georg
Austrian, 19th century.
Born 1828, in Innichen.
Portrait artist.
Köck settled in Vienna in 1878.

KOCK, Hinrich
German, 17th century.
Active in Bremen at the end of the 17th century.
Glass painter.

KOCK, Jeremias. See **COCK Jeremias**

KOCK, Louis Evrard Conrad de
French, 19th century.
Born c. 1815, in Saumur (Maine-et-Loire).
Painter. Landscapes.
Louis Kock was a pupil of Constant Troyon. He spent his life between Versailles and Saumur. He exhibited at the Salon de Paris between 1839 and 1848, then again in 1859.
AUCTION RECORDS:
LILLE, 30 Nov 1980, *Farmyard* (oil on canvas, 25¼ x 13 ins / 64 x 33 cm) FRF 15,000. PARIS, 29 June 1988, *Seashore* (oil on canvas, 12¼ x 17 ins / 31 x 43 cm) FRF 5,000. PARIS, 16 March 1998, *View on the Marne* (oil on canvas, oval, 18 x 22 ins / 46 x 55 cm) FRF 8,500.

KOCK, Luykas. See **COCK Luykas**

KOCK, Servaes
Dutch, 17th century.
Active in Leiden.
Engraver.
Servaes Kock was an engraver at the University of Copenhagen in 1622.

KOCK, Vilhelm
Danish, 19th century.
Born 1810, in Aalborg.
Painter, lithographer.
Vilhelm Kock exhibited between 1844 and 1846.

KOCK, W.. See **KOCH W.**

KOCK, Yvonne de
French, 19th century.
Born 1843, in Versailles; died November 1869, in Les Vaux-de-Cernay.
Painter. Landscapes, animals.
Yvonne de Kock was a pupil of her father and Lambinet. She took part in Salon exhibitions between 1865 and 1868.
MUSEUMS AND GALLERIES:
ST-BRIEUC: *Study of A Dog*.

KOCKAERT, Ernest
Belgian, 20th century.
Born 24 July 1908, in Vilvoorde (Brabant); died 4 August 1973, in Grimbergen.
Painter. Portraits, genre scenes, landscapes, seascapes, still-lifes.
Although Ernest Kockaert was a precocious pianist, he decided at the age of 16 to become a painter. In his Flemish hometown of Vilvorde he came under the influence of Jules Brouwers. In 1942 and 1944 he exhibited in the Galerie de l'Art Belge in Brussels, subsequently travelling in Brittany and Spain. In 1952 and 1959 he received the 'Art, Sciences and Letters' medals, and another medal in 1965. He participated in several regional competitions. His paintings are solidly constructed with a liberal application of paint in muted tones. After his journey to Spain his painting evinced light and colour.
In 1965 he exhibited at the Galerie Cambacérès in Paris. In 1994 the Galerie Cloots in Brussels dedicated a retrospective to him.
BIBLIOGRAPHY:
Le Peintre Ernest Kockaert, Brussels, 1958.

KÖCKE, Hugo
German, 20th century.
Born 16 April 1874, in Friedenau.
Painter. Landscapes.
Hugo Köcke took part in the Grosse Berliner Kunstausstellung of 1909.
AUCTION RECORDS:
NEW YORK, 19 Jan 1994, *Concert in a Park* (1915, oil on canvas, 27½ x 40 ins / 69.9 x 101.6 cm) USD 10,925. MALMÖ, 24 Nov 2001, *Sunny Rural Landscape with Children in Ditch by Farm* (1939, oil on canvas, 24 x 33 ins / 60 x 84 cm) SEK 17,000. HAMBURG, 11 Sept 2004, *Sheep in the Dunes at Sylt* (oil on canvas laid on card, 14 x 19 ins / 35 x 49 cm) EUR 1,600.

KÖCKERS, George
Dutch, 18th century.
Active in Middelburg at the end of the 18th century.
Engraver, jeweller.

KÖCKERT, Julius
German, 19th - 20th century.
Born 5 June 1827, in Leipzig; died 21 November 1918, in Munich.
Painter, fresco artist. History painting, battles, genre scenes.
From 1850 onwards Julius Köckert worked in Munich. His key work is the *Battle of Salamine*.
MUSEUMS AND GALLERIES:
NUREMBERG: *Otho III in the Tomb of Charlemagne* (fresco).
AUCTION RECORDS:
PARIS, 18 Dec 1950, *Greeting the Mountains*, FRF 21,500. NEW YORK, 26 Jan 1979, *The Signal* (oil on canvas, 38 x 30 ins / 96.5 x 76 cm) USD 1,600. MUNICH, 23 Sept 1987, *Two Children under a Parasol* (oil on panel, 9 x 11½ ins / 22.8 x 29.2 cm) DEM 11,000. NEW YORK, 29 Oct 1992, *Johannes Feuer* (oil on canvas, 38½ x 30½ ins / 97.8 x 77.5 cm) USD 5,225. HEIDELBERG, 15 Oct 1994, *Meditation in a Wood* (1852, oil on canvas, 23½ x 19¼ ins / 60 x 49 cm) DEM 11,500.

KÖCKRITZ, Diepold von
German, 19th century.
Born 16 March 1813, in Breslau (now Wroclaw, Poland); died 8 September 1879, in Gross Sürchen.
Painter. Animals.
Köckritz studied with August von Kloeber and Karl Schultz in Berlin.
MUSEUMS AND GALLERIES:
WROCLAW: *Still-life*.

KOCKS, Jacques de. See **COCK Jacques de**

KOCKX, Peeter and Sebastiaen. See **COCKX Peeter** and **Sebastiaen**

KOCMAN, J. H.
Czechoslovak, 20th - 21st century.
Born 6 August 1947, in Nové Mesto na Morave.
Mixed media.
Conceptual Art, Mail Art, Visual Poetry.
J.H. Kocman is a self-taught artist, and originally trained as a veterinary surgeon. He lives and works in Brno. He is recognised for conceptual art, especially in his own country, particularly in the fields of 'stamp art' and 'mail art', which he associates with body art. In 1996, his work featured in the

exhibition *L'art au corps: Le corps exposé de Man Ray à nos jours* (*Body Art: The Body Exhibited, from Man Ray to Today*) held at the Musée d'Art Contemporain in Marseilles. In 1998, at the Internet launch of a dossier from the Leonardo society, an international society for the arts, sciences and technology devoted to the problems of art and biology, he exhibited a dossier compiled from the exhibition *Art + Bio* held at Central Michigan University in Mount Pleasant in 1998.

KOCSIS, Andras
Hungarian, 20th century.
Born 1905.
Sculptor.
Andras Kocsis studied at the school of fine arts in Budapest from 1928-1931 where he was the pupil of Janos Pasztor and Zsimond Kisfaludi Strobl.
He created a number of public monuments including an aluminium relief for the sports palace, Budapest (1941); *Statue of Petofi*, Miskolc (1951); figures for the *Kossuth Monument*, Budapest (1952); the *Lenin Monument*, Veszprém (1959).
He began exhibiting in 1926 and was awarded the Kossuth and the Munkácsy Prizes.
BIBLIOGRAPHY:
Hongrie 68, Pannonia, Budapest, 1968.
MUSEUMS AND GALLERIES:
BUDAPEST (Magyar Nemzeti Gal.): several works.

KOCSIS, Imre
Hungarian, 20th century.
Born in Hungary.
Painter, screen printer.
BIBLIOGRAPHY:
Beaumont-Maillet, Laure/Woimant, Françoise/Pernoud, Emmanuel, *De Bonnard à Baselitz - Dix ans d'enrichissements du Cabinet des estampes 1978-1988*, exhibition catalogue, Bibliothèque nationale de France, Paris, 1992.

KODA, Katsuta
Japanese, 20th century.
Born in Tokyo.
Painter.
Koda Katsuta exhibited at the Paris Salon d'Automne during the 20th century.

KODA, Saika
Japanese, 20th century.
Painter.
Koda Saika took part in the 1929 exhibition of Japanese art in the Jeu de Paume, Paris.

KODDE, Karel
Dutch, 17th century.
Born c. 1640, in The Hague; died 1698, in The Hague.
Painter. Landscapes.
Kodde is thougt to have been the son of Pieter Codde and the pupil of his cousin Alexander the Younger. He was active about 1657, and in 1662 was a member of the guild. He imitated Nicolaes Berchem. Terwesten mentions a family picture in the Bleiswyk family.
AUCTION RECORDS:
AMSTERDAM, 12 June 1990, *Shepherdess and Cowherd in a Mountain Pass* (1664, oil on canvas, 29 3/4 x 34 1/4 ins / 75.8 x 87 cm) NLG 4,830.

KODDE, Pieter. See **CODDE Pieter Jacobs**

KODET, Jan
Czech, 20th century.
Born 1910.
Sculptor.
MUSEUMS AND GALLERIES:
PRAGUE (Národní Gal.): a bronze.

KODJOMAN, Milos
Yugoslav, 20th - 21st century.
Born 1952, in Skopje, Macedonia.
Painter. Figure compositions.
Milos Kodjoman was the pupil of Korubin and Kondovski and graduated from the school of applied arts and the teacher training academy in Skopje. In 1973, he joined the society of Macedonian painters. In 1976, he visited France, Italy, Germany and Holland. Throughout the 1970s he painted monstrous robots which were not always far from caricature. From 1980, he returned to Expressionist Figuration.
AUCTION RECORDS:
PARIS, 9 Nov 1992, *Public Auditorium* (1978, oil on canvas, 65 x 49 1/4 ins / 165 x 125 cm) FRF 4,500.

KODYM, Ottokar
Swiss, 19th century.
Born 8 November 1864, in Arenenberg.
Painter, draughtsman, decorative designer.
Kodym studied at the school of drawing in St Gall, then with Benjamin-Constant and Laurens at the Académie Julian in Paris. He taught at a school in Barmen in Prussia.

KOE, Laurence
British, 19th - 20th century.
Born in London; died 8 January 1913.
Painter.
Laurence Koe exhibited at the Salon des Artistes Français in Paris, winning a jury commendation in 1904, and a third-class medal in 1905. He exhibited at the Royal Academy, the Suffolk Street Gallery and the Royal Society of Painters in Watercolours in London from 1888.
MUSEUMS AND GALLERIES:
BRIGHTON (Mus. & AG): *Venus and Tannhauser* (oil on canvas); *Idyll* (c. 1908-1911, oil on canvas) - LIVERPOOL: *My Fanny*.

KOEBEL, Franz Georg
German, 19th century.
Born 1807, in Worms; died 10 December 1894, in Fürstenfeldbruck.
Painter.
Koebel spent a long time in Italy, where he painted landscapes and views of ruins.

KOEBEL, Jacob. See **KOBEL Jacob**

KOEBERGER, Wenzel. See **COEBERGHER**

KOECHLIN, Albert
French, 19th century.
Born in Mulhouse.
Painter. Landscapes.
MUSEUMS AND GALLERIES:
MULHOUSE: *Landscape*.

KOECHLIN, Alfred Eugène
French, 19th century.
Born 23 June 1845, in Mulhouse; died 15 January 1878, in Paris.
Painter, draughtsman. Landscapes, seascapes.
Alfred Koechlin was a pupil of Louis Français. He began exhibiting at the Salon in 1869.
MUSEUMS AND GALLERIES:
AUXERRE: *View of the Environs around Cernay-la-Ville* - MULHOUSE: *Woodland path*; *Maritime Pines in the Bay of Beauport*; *Area around Mulhouse*; numerous drawings.

KOECHLIN, Daniel Jules Camille
French, 19th - 20th century.
Born 4 December 1845, in Mulhouse; died 1914, in Kingersheim.
Painter. Landscapes.
Daniel Jules Camille Koechlin came from a family of industrialists and collectors - his father ran the Dolfus-Mieg com-

pany - and was introduced to art at an early age. It was not until the end of the 1870 war, during which he acquitted himself brilliantly, that he was able to become a painter. In 1871 he received guidance from Louis Français before becoming a follower and friend of Jean Jacques Henner.

The art of blending taught by Henner was a considerable influence on Koechlin, who used it to translate the beauty of evening, the mysterious melancholy of twilight, the intense poetry of moonlight on the canals of the sleeping city of Venice, and the penetrating impression of autumn evenings in Alsace.

MUSEUMS AND GALLERIES:
PARIS (Mus. du Petit Palais): *Moonlight in Amsterdam Harbour.*

AUCTION RECORDS:
PARIS, 6 July 1990, *Landscape with Sheep* (oil on canvas, 6 x 11 ins / 15.5 x 27 cm) FRF 3,500.

KOECHLIN, Élisabeth
French, 19th century.
Born 17 December 1853, in Mulhouse; died 27 January 1896, in Paris.
Painter.

Élisabeth Koechlin was a pupil of Mezzara. She made her debut at the Salon in 1876.

KOECHLIN, Émile
French, 19th century.
Born 28 May 1808, in Mulhouse; died 3 May 1883, in Mulhouse.
Draughtsman (charcoal).

MUSEUMS AND GALLERIES:
MULHOUSE: two charcoals.

KŒCHLIN, Florence, later Mme Mezzara
French, 19th century.
Born 20 January 1857, in Mulhouse; died 13 January 1896, in Paris.
Painter. Genre scenes.

Florence Koechlin was a pupil of Madame Ballotée and Mezzara. She began exhibiting at the Salon in 1878.

KOECHLIN, Jean
French, 18th - 19th century.
Born 28 June 1773, in Mulhouse; died 19 November 1861, in Belfort.
Draughtsman.

Following his studies in Paris, Jean Koechlin produced portraits and landscapes.

KOECHLIN, Nicolas
French, 19th century.
Born 31 July 1838, in Mulhouse; died 4 April 1892, in Paris.
Painter, draughtsman. Landscapes.

Nicolas Koechlin began exhibiting at the Salon in 1868.

KOECHLIN, Rodolphe
French, 19th century.
Born 27 August 1778, in Mulhouse; died 11 February 1855, in Mulhouse.
Painter (gouache), watercolourist. Flowers.

Rodolphe Koechlin was a pupil of Regnault.

AUCTION RECORDS:
PARIS, 8 March 1993, *Lilium Tigrinum* (watercolour and gouache, 17 3/4 x 13 1/2 ins / 45 x 34 cm) FRF 9,500; *Roses* (watercolour and gouache, 16 3/4 x 10 3/4 ins / 42.5 x 27.5 cm) FRF 8,800.

KOECHLIN-DOLLFUS, Jean
French, 19th century.
Born in Mulhouse.
Active in the middle of the 19th century.
Draughtsman.

Jean Koechlin-Dollfus was undoubtedly related to Johann Heinrich Dollfus.

MUSEUMS AND GALLERIES:
MULHOUSE: drawings.

KOECHLIN-SCHWARTZ, Alfred
French, 19th century.
Born 15 September 1829, in Mulhouse; died 5 February 1895, in Grasse.
Painter, draughtsman. Landscapes.

Alfred Koechlin-Schwartz exhibited at the Salon de Paris from 1864.

MUSEUMS AND GALLERIES:
MULHOUSE: numerous drawings.

AUCTION RECORDS:
PARIS, 8 March 1993, *Island of Philae in Egypt* (1854, pencil, watercolour and gouache, 12 x 18 ins / 30.5 x 46 cm) FRF 5,100; *Busy Street in Chateldan* (1864, pencil, graphite and colour heightened with white, 12 1/4 x 18 1/2 ins / 31 x 47 cm) FRF 6,800.

KOECHLIN-SCHWARTZ, Jean Leonard
French, 19th - 20th century.
Born in Mulhouse.
Painter, watercolourist. Landscapes.

Jean Leonard Koechlin-Schwartz studied under Édouard Doigneau. He exhibited mainly landscapes at the Salon des Artistes Français in Paris.

AUCTION RECORDS:
PARIS, 8 March 1993, *Law Courts, Bruges* (1851, graphite and white gouache, 11 1/2 x 18 ins / 29.5 x 45.5 cm) FRF 4,200.

KOECK. See also **COECK, COCK**

KOECK, Christian
German, 18th - 19th century.
Born c. 1759, in Mainz; died c. 1825, in Munich.
Sculptor, engraver, lithographer.

Christian Koeck studied with Houdon in Paris. After that, he worked mainly as an illustrator. During a trip to Russia, he received commissions for two busts of Tsar Alexander I.

KOECK, Michael
Austrian, 18th - 19th century.
Born 29 August 1760, in Innsbruck; died 21 November 1825, in Rome.
Painter. History painting.

Michael Koeck studied with Peter Denifle in Innsbruck. His patron, the Count of Engenberg, sent him to Milan, where he studied with Kroller. He remained there for nine years, then went to Rome as a pensioner of the emperor. He became a member of the guild of painters in Rome in 1814. He later became a member of the Academy of St Luke and Curator of Mosaics for the Vatican. The Innsbruck Museum owns a *Story of Achilles* by him, consisting of 14 items forming the designs for a mosaic table to be presented to the king of France by the Pope.

MUSEUMS AND GALLERIES:
INNSBRUCK: *The Story of Achilles* (fourteen items for a mosaic table).

KOECKS, Jacob. See **COCK Jacob**

KOEDYCK, A.
Flemish School, 17th century.
Active c. 1660.
Painter. Genre scenes.

A. Koedyck is remembered for a painting, *Kitchen Interior*, signed and dated 1602, which featured in the Fechenbach sale in 1889.

KOEDYCK, Dirk
Flemish School, 18th century.
Born 1681, in Zaandam.

Active c. 1730.
Painter, engraver.

Dirk Koedyck is confused by certain writers with the painter Nicolaas Koedyk. He is known to have executed: *Landscape with a Woman Lying under a Tree*, after Ph. Wouwermann, *Two Horses*, after Ph. Wouwermann, *Young Violinist Singing, A Man Kissing a Woman*, after J.M. Molenaer, and *The Woman Selling Herrings*, after Metzu.

KOEDYCK, Isaac, or Koedijck
Dutch, 17th century.
Born 1616 or 1617, in Leiden; died 1668, probably in Amsterdam.
Painter. Figures, genre scenes, interiors with figures.

Isaac Koedyck was a merchant in Amsterdam from 1642 onwards, where he had married on 18 March 1641. In 1659 he was the commander of a fleet belonging to the East India Company. The painting catalogued at the museum at Lille, *Interior*, under the name of *J Kocdyk*, must be attributed to this artist. According to Von Wurzbach, the painting *Interior*, of a young man at table, held at the Louvre and traditionally ascribed to Pieter de Hooch, should be attributed to Isaac Koedyck. See also Koedyck (Nicolas).

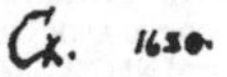

MUSEUMS AND GALLERIES:
ANTWERP: *The Little Nurse* - DARMSTADT: *The Horseman Robbed* - LEIDEN: *The Dead Fledgling* - LILLE: *Interior* - ST PETERSBURG (Hermitage): *Dutch Interior*.

AUCTION RECORDS:
PARIS, 23 June 1941, *A Drinker*, FRF 30,000. PARIS, 25 April 1951, *The Meal*, FRF 500,000. PARIS, 1 Dec 1951, *The Surgeon*, FRF 900,000. LONDON, 24 July 1959, *Interior with a Lawyer*, GBP 630. BRUSSELS, 18-19 and 20 April 1967, *Little Girl in an Interior*, BEF 210,000. LONDON, 11 July 1979, *A Lawyer with his Family* (oil on canvas, 32 1/2 x 27 1/4 ins / 82.5 x 69 cm) GBP 11,500. LONDON, 10 Dec 1993, *Barber-surgeon Tending the Foot of a Peasant* (oil on panel, 35 3/4 x 28 1/4 ins / 91 x 72 cm) GBP 287,500. LONDON, 6 July 1994, *A Man in an Interior Holding a Glass and Two Servants Kissing in a Corner by a Door* (1648, oil on panel, 26 x 22 ins / 66 x 55 cm) GBP 95,000. LONDON, 22 April 2004, *Interior of a Dutch House with a Seated Cavalier Holding an Upturned Glass* (1648, oil on panel, 26 x 22 ins / 66 x 55 cm) GBP 70,000.

KOEDYCK, Nicolas
Dutch, 17th century.
Painter, engraver. Figures, portraits, genre scenes, interiors with figures.

Nicolas Koedyck is mentioned by Van Gool as the pupil and imitator of Pieter de Hooch, but nothing is known about his life and his existence is sometimes even disputed. A painter of the name of Peter Gerritz Koedyk was in the guild at Amersfoort in 1632. On the other hand, certain biographers state that he was protected by Tsar Peter the Great. Siret says that his date of birth was prior to 1681. He is also mentioned as an engraver of scenes from everyday life. He is probably to be identified with Isaac Koedyck.

AUCTION RECORDS:
AMSTERDAM, 1771, *Interior*, FRF 9,030. PARIS, 1892, *Portrait Presumed to be of Van der Meer*, FRF 5,500. ANTWERP, 1898, *The Little Nurse*, FRF 13,000. PARIS, 15 May 1931, *Interiors with figures*, FRF 6,000. LONDON, 8 April 1938, *Disappointed Hunter*, GBP 96.

KOEFOED, Hans Christian
Danish, 19th - 20th century.
Born 16 July 1849; died 5 November 1921, in Nivå.
Painter. Genre scenes.

In Paris Hans Christian Koefoed was taught by Léon Bonnat.

KOEGEL, Linda
Dutch, 19th century.
Born 11 October 1861, in The Hague.
Painter, engraver.

Linda Koegel exhibited for the first time in Munich in 1891. She is remembered for her fresco decorations in several churches in the Munich area.

KOEHLER, Bernhard
German, 19th century.
Born 10 August 1845, in Leipzig.
Painter. Landscapes.

Bernhard Koehler studied with Carl Raupp in Munich. He brought back a large number of landscapes from a trip to Egypt.

KOEHLER, Johann Gustaf
Swedish, 19th century.
Born 3 April 1803, in Södertälje; died 8 June 1881, in Stockholm.
Painter. Portraits, interiors.

After studying in Stockholm, Johann Koehler travelled and worked in Germany.

KOEHLER, Johannes
Hungarian, 16th century.
Active in Bartfa in 1527.
Painter.

A painting by Johannes Koehler is in the cathedral of Košice.

KOEHLER, Karl Christian
German, 19th century.
Born 3 February 1827, in Darmstadt; died 1 March 1890, in Darmstadt.
Painter, watercolourist, draughtsman. Landscapes with figures.

Karl Koehler spent some time in London, where he started to paint watercolours. He was also a writer.

MUSEUMS AND GALLERIES:
DARMSTADT.

AUCTION RECORDS:
LONDON, 10 Feb 1995, *Houses and People on the Shore of Lake Lucerne in Switzerland* (1854, pencil, watercolour heightened with white/paper, 12 1/4 x 19 1/2 ins / 31.3 x 49.6 cm) GBP 1,150.

KOEHLER, Mela
Austrian, 20th century.
Born 1885, in Vienna; died 1960, in Stockholm.
Active from 1934 in Sweden.
Painter (mixed technique), draughtswoman, illustrator. Figures.

From 1905 to 1910 Koehler attended the Kolo Moser school of applied art in Vienna. She became a member of the Wiener Werkstätten (Vienna Studios). She produced paintings in which elegantly attired bourgeois ladies are represented in a somewhat decorative style. Her work was shown in London at an exhibition in 1908 held by the school of applied art in Vienna. She participated in the *Werkbund* exhibition.

KOEHLER, Paul R.
American, 19th century.
Born 1866, in New York; died 1909, in Colorado Springs.
Painter, pastellist. Landscapes.

Paul R. Koehler was self-taught. While working in business, he produced landscapes, notably in pastels, valued by art lovers.

KOEHLER, Robert
German, 19th - 20th century.
Born 27 November 1850, in Hamburg; died 24 April 1917, in Milwaukee, USA.
Painter, engraver.

Robert Koehler came to the USA at the age of three and began his artistic studies in New York. He later worked in Munich with Loefftz and Defregger. In 1889 he exhibited in Paris where he was awarded a distinction. A knight of the order of St Michael of Bavaria, he belonged to a number of Bavarian and American associations. He was also Director of the Minneapolis Institute of Arts.

AUCTION RECORDS:

NEW YORK, 25 Oct 1979, *First Snow* (oil on canvas, 20 x 14 ins / 50.8 x 35.5 cm) USD 4,250. NEW YORK, 28 May 1987, *First Snow* (oil on canvas, 20 x 14 ins / 50.8 x 35.5 cm) USD 10,000.

KOEHLER-EXTER, Judith Anna

German, 19th century.
Born 28 July 1868, in Niederramstadt.
Painter.

Judith Koehler-Exter studied with Paul Weber. After a stay in London, she returned to work in Germany, particularly at the court of Hesse-Darmstadt.

KOEKKOEK, Barend Cornelis

Dutch, 19th century.
Born 11 October 1803, in Middelburg; died 5 April 1862, in Cleves (North Rhine-Westphalia, Germany).
Painter, watercolourist. Landscapes with figures, landscapes.

Barend Cornelis Koekkoek was the pupil of his father Johannes Hermanus Koekkoek and of Schelfhout van Os (?) at the academy in Amsterdam. He married the daughter of the painter J.-A. Daiwaille. In 1845 the King of Holland commissioned several paintings from him. He travelled to Belgium, and frequently visited the banks of the Rhine and the Moselle. In 1841 he founded an art school in Cleves which, on his death, seems to have ceased to function. He took part in the Paris exhibitions, and received a medal in 1840 and 1845. Koekkoek was a member of the academies at St Petersburg and Rotterdam.

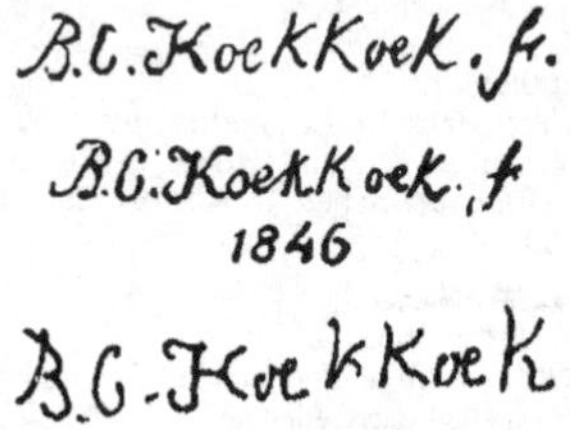

BIBLIOGRAPHY:

Nollert, Angelika/Werd, Guido de, *Barend Cornelis Koekkoek (1803-1862)*, exhibition catalogue, Dordrechts Museum, Dordrecht, 1997.

MUSEUMS AND GALLERIES:

CHELTENHAM (AG and Mus.): *The Coming Storm* (1841); *Trees, Castle and skating figures* - DIJON: *Winter Effect*.

AUCTION RECORDS:

PARIS, 1850, *Landscape*, FRF 7,200. PARIS, 1861, *Landscape*, FRF 8,300. THE HAGUE, 1871, *Ruins of a Castle in Luxembourg*, FRF 10,815. PARIS, 1874, *Landscape*, FRF 27,100. THE HAGUE, 1889, *Forest Exit*, FRF 12,300. NEW YORK, 23-24 Jan 1901, *Dutch Landscape*, USD 175. NEW YORK, 30 Jan 1902, *Area around Cleves*, USD 500. NEW YORK, 15-16 Feb 1906, *Skating Scene*, USD 320. LONDON, 19 June 1908, *Landscape*, GBP 10. LONDON, 30 March 1909, *Farm in the Forest*, GBP 52. LONDON, 19 March 1910, *Forest Scene* (1863) GBP 1. LONDON, 9 April 1910, *Wooded River Banks* (1838) GBP 60. NEW YORK, 7 March 1911, *Landscape*, USD 145. LONDON, 12 April 1911, *Road with Cottages and Figures*, GBP 15. LONDON, 19 May 1922, *Wooded Landscape*, GBP 81. PARIS, 4 July 1927, *The Flock Grazing*, FRF 980. LONDON, 22 July 1927, *Road through a Wood*, GBP 63. PARIS, 26 June 1929, *Dutch Landscape* (watercolour) FRF 2,650. PARIS, 22 Jan 1934, *The Return to the Farm*, FRF 1,300. PARIS, 13 July 1942, *Herd of Cows on the Road* (1848) FRF 1,600. PARIS, 7 Dec 1942, *Forest Landscapes*, FRF 5,000. LONDON, 18 June 1943, *Wooded Pastures*, GBP 44. LONDON, 26 April 1946, *Winter Landscape*, GBP 78. PARIS, July 1946, *Seascape*, FRF 12,500. LONDON, 22 Nov 1946, *Winter*, GBP 63. MILAN, 10-15 Feb 1947, *Pastoral Scene*, ITL 140,000. AMSTERDAM, 21 March 1950, *Panoramic Landscape*, NLG 2,300. PARIS, 12 June 1950, *Peasant, Peasant Woman and Mules Stationary in front of a Fountain*, FRF 25,000. PARIS, 9 March 1951, *The Market Town*, FRF 180,000. AMSTERDAM, 1 May 1951, *Flock on a Road*, NLG 4,500. LONDON, 24 Feb 1960, *Winter in Holland*, GBP 1,500. LONDON, 15 Feb 1961, *Wooded Landscape in Snow*, GBP 980. PARIS, 4 Dec 1963, *The Track in the Valley*, FRF 10,500. AMSTERDAM, 29-30 Sept 1965, *Wooded River Landscape*, NLG 36,500. AMSTERDAM, 19 April 1966, *Summer Landscape*, NLG 35,000. LONDON, 13 Dec 1967, *Village on the Edge of the Wood, in Winter*, GBP 3,000. AMSTERDAM, 25 Feb 1969, *Peasants Going to Market*, NLG 40,000. LUCERNE, 13 June 1970, *Steep Landscape*, CHF 60,000. AMSTERDAM, 23 Nov 1971, *Wooded Landscape*, NLG 16,400. LONDON, 4 Feb 1972, *Wooded Landscape with Figures* (1857) Gns 2,400. LONDON, 19 Jan 1973, *Winter Landscape*, Gns 32,000. AMSTERDAM, 18 Feb 1974, *Landscape with River*, NLG 135,000. AMSTERDAM, 27 April 1976, *Flock in a Wooded Landscape* (1850, oil on panel, 26 x 32 3/4 ins / 66 x 83.5 cm) NLG 235,000. AMSTERDAM, 3 May 1976, *Travellers Resting on a Road in the Mountains* (1853, pen and wash, 8 x 10 3/4 ins / 20.3 x 27.3 cm) NLG 3,600. AMSTERDAM, 26 April 1977, *Shepherdess and Flock in a Wooded Landscape* (1850, oil on canvas, 16 1/4 x 22 ins / 41 x 55 cm) NLG 74,000. LONDON, 22 Nov 1978, *Landscape at Dusk* (1845, oil on panel, 17 x 22 1/2 ins / 43 x 57 cm) GBP 26,000. NEW YORK, 26 Jan 1979, *Before the Storm* (pencil, pen and wash, 7 3/4 x 8 ins / 20 x 20.5 cm) USD 2,750. LUCERNE, 30 May 1979, *Wooded Landscape with Figures* (oil on panel, 12 3/4 x 17 3/4 ins / 32.5 x 45 cm) CHF 68,000. LONDON, 26 March 1981, *Shepherds and Flock in a Wooded Landscape* (1847, pen and grey wash, 8 x 11 1/2 ins / 20.5 x 29 cm) GBP 1,800. COLOGNE, 18 Nov 1982, *Winter Landscape with Castle and Figures* (1846, oil on panel, 15 3/4 x 20 3/4 ins / 40 x 53 cm) DEM 90,000. NEW YORK, 27 May 1983, *Travellers in a Rhenish Landscape* (1856, oil on panel, 23 1/4 x 30 ins / 59 x 76.2 cm) USD 100,000. LONDON, 29 Nov 1985, *Wooded Landscape with Figures* (1854, oil on panel, 24 1/4 x 31 ins / 61.7 x 78.5 cm) GBP 45,000. LONDON, 18 June 1986, *Figures and Sleigh on a Country Track in Winter* (1833, oil on canvas, 22 x 27 3/4 ins / 55 x 70.5 cm) GBP 30,000. NEW YORK, 29 Oct 1987, *Flock on a Country Track* (1849, oil on panel, 18 1/2 x 26 ins / 47 x 66 cm) USD 150,000. AMSTERDAM, 3 Sept 1988, *Peasants Chatting on a Sandy Track with Cows and Sheep in a Meadow and a Church Tower in the Distance* (1822, watercolour and ink/paper, 11 3/4 x 16 1/2 ins / 30 x 42 cm) NLG 4,025. COLOGNE, 15 Oct 1988, *Undulating Landscape with Travellers on a Path and a Ruined Castle in the Background* (1847, watercolour, 7 3/4 x 11 1/4 ins / 19.7 x 28.5 cm) DEM 9,000. AMSTERDAM, 16 Nov 1988, *Wooded Landscape with Figures on a Track Beside a Stream and a Castle on a Cliff in the Background* (1854, oil on panel, 7 x 9 1/2 ins / 18 x 24 cm) NLG 46,000. COLOGNE, 20 Oct 1989, *Peasants Leading their Cattle on a Steep Wooded Track* (1848, watercolour, 13 x 16 1/4 ins / 33 x 41 cm) DEM 8,000. STOCKHOLM, 15 Nov 1989, *Landscape with a Man and Cattle on a Track* (oil on panel, 13 3/4 x 11 1/2 ins / 35 x 29 cm) SEK 28,000. VERSAILLES, 19 Nov 1989, *Landscape with Figures* (oil on panel, 13 3/4 x 20 1/2 ins / 35 x 51.8 cm) FRF 79,000. LONDON, 22 Nov 1989, *Woodmen Working on a Frozen Stream* (1851, oil on canvas, 28 3/4 x 36 1/4 ins / 73 x 92 cm) GBP 79,200. NEW YORK, 28 Feb 1990, *Landscape with Figures in a Squall* (oil on panel, 10 1/4 x 13 1/4 ins / 26 x 33.6 cm) USD 18,700. STOCKHOLM, 16 May 1990, *Mountainous Landscape with Figures* (oil on canvas, 27 1/2 x 33 3/4 ins / 70 x 86 cm) SEK 60,000. AMSTERDAM, 6 Nov 1990, *Winter Landscape with Peas-*

ants Collecting Wood (1856, oil on canvas, 32 x 43 ins / 81.5 x 109.5 cm) NLG 345,000. AMSTERDAM, 23 April 1991, *Wooded Landscape with Herdsmen and their Cattle near a Stream* (1853, oil on canvas, 10 x 11 3/4 ins / 24.5 x 30 cm) NLG 126,500. NEW YORK, 16 Oct 1991, *Village by a River* (oil on panel, 7 x 9 1/4 ins / 17.5 x 23.3 cm) USD 28,600. BORDEAUX, 23 Oct 1991, *Two Fishermen in a Forest Landscape* (1846, oil on canvas, 32 1/4 x 40 1/2 ins / 82 x 103 cm) FRF 490,000. LONDON, 29 Nov 1991, *Winter Landscape with a Skater on a Pond and Men Collecting Bundles of Wood and a Traveller on a Snow Covered Track* (1842, oil on canvas, 23 1/4 x 28 ins / 59 x 71.2 cm) GBP 48,400. HEIDELBERG, 11 April 1992, *Undulating Landscape with Peasants* (watercolour, 5 1/2 x 7 1/4 ins / 14.2 x 18.3 cm) DEM 3,300. AMSTERDAM, 14-15 April 1992, *Summer Landscape with Peasants and Cattle near a Forest Stream* (1856, oil on panel, 24 1/4 x 20 ins / 61.5 x 50.5 cm) NLG 287,500. LONDON, 19 June 1992, *Winter Landscape with Skaters on a Frozen River* (1839, oil on canvas, 26 3/4 x 33 ins / 68 x 83.8 cm) GBP 121,000. AMSTERDAM, 9 Nov 1993, *Winter Landscape with Figures and a Horse and Cart on a Frozen River with a Town in the Background* (1847, oil on panel, 11 1/2 x 16 1/4 ins / 29.5 x 41 cm) NLG 316,250. NEW YORK, 26 May 1994, *Winter Landscape with Peasants Collecting Wood* (1856, oil on canvas, 32 1/4 x 43 ins / 81.6 x 109.5 cm) USD 261,000. LONDON, 17 March 1995, *Herd of Cows with a Steep-sided and Wooded Track in a Mountainous Landscape with a Castle and a Village in the Background* (1848, oil on panel, 8 x 10 1/4 ins / 20.6 x 26 cm) GBP 65,300. AMSTERDAM, 11 April 1995, *Beside the Moselle* (1855, oil on panel, 14 1/4 x 18 1/2 ins / 36 x 47 cm) NLG 47,200. LONDON, 15 Nov 1995, *Landscape in the Rhineland* (1840, oil on canvas, 35 x 44 ins / 88 x 112 cm) GBP 183,000. LONDON, 12 June 1996, *Shepherds Resting* (1835, pencil, sepia and wax, 9 x 12 1/2 ins / 23 x 32 cm) GBP 4,600. LONDON, 14 June 1996, *Wooded Path with Cattle and a Village in the Background* (1848, oil on panel, 8 x 10 1/4 ins / 20.6 x 26 cm) GBP 54,300. LONDON, 21 Nov 1997, *Wooded Landscape with Figures and Cattle on a Path* (1853, oil on panel, 27 1/4 x 36 ins / 69.5 x 90.5 cm) GBP 298,500. NEW YORK, 9 Feb 1999, *Travellers on Wooded Path* (1839, sepia wash, 8 x 10 ins / 20 x 25 cm) USD 10,000. AMSTERDAM, 27 April 1999, *Panoramic Rhine Landscape with Peasants Conversing on a Path* (1855, oil on panel, 21 x 30 ins / 53 x 77 cm) NLG 480,000. AMSTERDAM, 18 April 2000, *View of Cleves with Farmers Reaping Corn in the Foreground* (1838, pencil, brush ink and grey wash, 6 x 8 ins / 15 x 20 cm) NLG 18,000. LONDON, 22 June 2000, *Der Waldweg (Path through the Woods)* (1850, oil on panel, 24 x 32 ins / 61 x 81 cm) GBP 150,000. AMSTERDAM, 24 April 2001, *River View with Town, in the Midday Sun* (1852, oil on panel, 16 x 22 ins / 41 x 55 cm) NLG 420,000. AMSTERDAM, 23 Oct 2001, *Snow Covered Forest with Skaters on a Frozen Waterway* (1838, oil on panel, 14 x 19 ins / 36 x 48 cm) EUR 250,000. AMSTERDAM, 24 April 2002, *Gelders landschap bij afdrijvende donderbuij en brand in de verte* (1849, oil on canvas, 26 x 36 ins / 67 x 92 cm) EUR 330,000. AMSTERDAM, 22 Oct 2002, *Travellers on a Country Road in a Wooded River Landscape* (1852, oil on panel, 28 x 39 ins / 72 x 100 cm) EUR 330,000. NEW YORK, 23 April 2003, *Figure Walking a Dog on a Path in Winter Landscape* (1836, oil on panel, 15 x 20 ins / 37 x 51 cm) USD 95,000. LONDON, 18 Nov 2003, *Cattle Drivers in Landscape* (1839, oil on panel, 44 x 56 ins / 111 x 141 cm) GBP 230,000. AMSTERDAM, 20 April 2004, *Summer Landscape with Travellers on a Path* (1826, oil on canvas, 24 x 29 ins / 61 x 73 cm) EUR 100,000. AMSTERDAM, 20 April 2004, *Wooded Landscape with Figures along a Stream* (1846, oil on canvas, 32 x 42 ins / 82 x 106 cm) EUR 330,000.

KOEKKOEK, Gerard
Dutch, 19th - 20th century.
Born 27 May 1871, in Hilversum.
Painter. Landscapes, seascapes.

Gerard Koekkoek may be related to Hermanus Willem and Marinus Adrianus Koekkoek. His repertoire consisted mainly of views of the northern Dutch coast.

AUCTION RECORDS:
NEW YORK, 30 May 1980, *Fishing Boats in the Harbour* (1892, oil on canvas, 15 x 17 1/4 ins / 38.1 x 43.8 cm) USD 2,600. AMSTERDAM, 9 Nov 1993, *Three-masted Ship off a Harbour* (1891, oil on canvas, 24 1/4 x 32 3/4 ins / 61.5 x 83 cm) NLG 13,800. AMSTERDAM, 25 Oct 1999, *Beached Fishing Boats* (oil on canvas, 25 x 32 ins / 64 x 81 cm) NLG 5,800. AMSTERDAM, 22 Jan 2002, *Horse and Carriage in the Street of Katwijk aan Zee* (oil on canvas, 26 x 39 ins / 65 x 100 cm) EUR 8,500. AMSTERDAM, 23 Oct 2002, *Katwijker Bomschuiten in Open Water* (1897, oil on canvas, 32 x 23 ins / 81 x 58 cm) EUR 9,000. AMSTERDAM, 21 Jan 2003, *Haybarge in a Stiff Breeze* (1893, oil on panel, 7 x 9 ins / 19 x 24 cm) EUR 4,200.

KOEKKOEK, Hendrik Barend
Dutch, 19th - 20th century.
Born 1849; died before 1909.
Painter. Landscapes with figures, landscapes, seascapes.

Hendrik Barend Koekkoek may be a direct descendant of several generations of painters specialising in typical Dutch landscapes, including Johannes and Hermanus Koekkoek the Elder.

AUCTION RECORDS:
LONDON, 20 July 1977, *Firewood Collectors* (oil on canvas, 17 1/4 x 24 1/2 ins / 44 x 62 cm) GBP 1,200. LONDON, 9 May 1979, *Fishing Boats on the Beach* (oil on canvas, 18 x 30 ins / 45.5 x 76 cm) GBP 1,500. NEW YORK, 1 April 1981, *Hunter and Firewood Collectors in a Winter Landscape* (oil on canvas, 30 x 25 ins / 76.5 x 63.5 cm) USD 4,500. LONDON, 29 May 1987, *Hunter, Woman and Child in a Winter Landscape* (oil on canvas, 30 x 25 ins / 76.3 x 63.5 cm) GBP 3,000. STOCKHOLM, 16 May 1990, *Sailing Boats Sheltering near Coast in Rough Sea* (oil on canvas, 17 3/4 x 24 ins / 45 x 61 cm) SEK 12,500. AMSTERDAM, 24 April 1991, *Peasant Walking on a Snowy Path towards a Farm with a Village on Top of a Neighbouring Hill* (oil on canvas, 30 1/4 x 25 1/4 ins / 77 x 64 cm) NLG 18,400. AMSTERDAM, 30 Oct 1991, *Family of Peasants Resting on the Edge of a Path in a Wooded Landscape with a Castle in the Background* (oil on canvas, 19 x 25 3/4 ins / 48.5 x 65.5 cm) NLG 6,900. CALAIS, 4 July 1993, *Path with Figures Leading to River* (1870, oil on panel, 7 x 10 1/4 ins / 18 x 26 cm) FRF 18,000. AMSTERDAM, 16 April 1996, *Peasant on a Forest Path* (oil on canvas, 18 x 12 1/2 ins / 46 x 32 cm) NLG 1,180.

KOEKKOEK, Hendrik Pieter, or sometimes Hermann Pieter
Dutch, 19th century.
Born 1843, in Hilversum; died c. 1890, in Great Britain.
Painter. Scenes with figures, landscapes.

Hendrik Pieter Koekkoek may possibly be a direct descendant of the generation of Johannes and Hermanus Koekkoek the Elder. He established himself in England.

AUCTION RECORDS:
LONDON, 19 May 1976, *Wooded Landscape* (oil on canvas, 24 x 33 1/2 ins / 61 x 85 cm) GBP 1,100. LONDON, 23 Feb 1977, *Landscape in Surrey* (oil on canvas, 13 1/2 x 23 1/2 ins / 34.5 x 59.5 cm) GBP 1,000. LONDON, 3 Oct 1979, *Landscape with Cottages* (oil on panel, 6 x 8 ins / 15.5 x 20.5 cm) GBP 1,000. LONDON, 25 March 1981, *Figures in a Wooded Landscape* (oil on canvas, 35 1/2 x 45 1/2 ins / 90 x 115.5 cm) GBP 4,200. NEW YORK, 27 Oct 1983, *Travellers in a Wooded Landscape* (oil on canvas, 25 1/2 x 38 1/2 ins / 64.8 x 97.8 cm) USD 6,000. NEW YORK, 13 Feb 1985, *Country Track* (oil on canvas, 36 1/2 x 46 1/4

ins / 92.6 x 117.5 cm) USD 15,000. NEW YORK, 28 Oct 1986, *Washerwomen by a River* (1869, oil on canvas, 26 1/2 x 39 1/2 ins / 67.5 x 100.5 cm) USD 15,000. NEW YORK, 24 Feb 1987, *Wooded Landscape with Figures and an Artist at his Easel* (oil on canvas, 24 x 36 ins / 61 x 91.4 cm) USD 9,000. LONDON, 26 Feb 1988, *River through Woodland with Foresters near a Fire* (oil on canvas, 40 x 36 ins / 101.7 x 91.5 cm) GBP 2,420. COLOGNE, 15 Oct 1988, *Landscape with Figures, Large Trees and a Cottage* (oil on panel, 10 1/4 x 13 ins / 26 x 33 cm) DEM 7,500. LONDON, 6 Oct 1989, *Wooded Landscape with a Woman on a Path* (oil on canvas, 14 x 12 ins / 35.5 x 30.5 cm) GBP 1,540. NEW YORK, 23 May 1990, *Landscape with Travellers* (oil on canvas, 24 x 36 ins / 61 x 91.4 cm) USD 9,350. AMSTERDAM, 30 Oct 1990, *Wooded Landscape with Two Elegant Ladies Walking in an Avenue* (oil on canvas, 26 1/2 x 39 1/4 ins / 67 x 100 cm) NLG 14,950. AMSTERDAM, 17 Sept 1991, *A Farm on a Heath* (oil on canvas, 18 x 26 1/4 ins / 46 x 66.5 cm) NLG 2,530. LONDON, 27 Oct 1993, *Figure in a Wooded Landscape* (oil on canvas, 15 3/4 x 23 1/2 ins / 40 x 60 cm) GBP 1,840. PARIS, 5 Nov 1993, *Peasant on a Track* (oil on canvas, 16 1/4 x 24 1/2 ins / 41 x 62 cm) FRF 27,000. AMSTERDAM, 9 Nov 1993, *Wooded Landscape with Figures on a Track* (oil on panel, 11 x 14 3/4 ins / 28 x 37.5 cm) NLG 4,600. AMSTERDAM, 21 April 1994, *Hunting* (oil on canvas, 16 1/4 x 24 1/4 ins / 41 x 61.5 cm) NLG 2,070. LONDON, 11 April 1995, *Anglers in a Summer Landscape* (oil on canvas, 15 3/4 x 23 1/2 ins / 40 x 60 cm) GBP 4,370. LONDON, 31 Oct 1996, *Farmers and Sheep in a Forest* (1864, oil on canvas, 17 3/4 x 23 1/2 ins / 45 x 60 cm) GBP 7,475. NEW YORK, 15 June 1999, *Pulling the Wagon* (oil on canvas, 24 x 36 ins / 61 x 91 cm) USD 4,500. HEIDELBERG, 3 Dec 1999, *Fishermen near a Farmstead* (oil on canvas, 8 x 16 ins / 20 x 40 cm) DEM 8,000. ROTTERDAM, 9 May 2000, *River Landscape with Figures* (oil on canvas, 12 x 16 ins / 31 x 41 cm) NLG 11,500. NEW YORK, 28 June 2000, *Children Fishing on a Riverbank* (oil on canvas, 24 x 16 ins / 61 x 40 cm) USD 4,750. COLOGNE, 19 May 2001, *Wooded Landscape with Travellers* (oil on canvas, 16 x 24 ins / 40 x 61 cm) DEM 23,000. NEW YORK, 22 May 2001, *Wooded Landscape with Figures along a Path* (oil on canvas) USD 6,000. AMSTERDAM, 22 Jan 2002, *Peasants Resting by a Stream at the Edge of a Forest* (oil on canvas, 27 x 39 ins / 68 x 100 cm) EUR 8,500. LONDON, 19 Nov 2002, *Summer Landscape with Figures Netting at a Stream* (oil on canvas, 36 x 46 ins / 91 x 117 cm) GBP 11,000. LONDON, 20 March 2003, *Woodgatherers* (oil on canvas, 12 x 18 ins / 30 x 45 cm) GBP 3,500. BOSTON, 16 May 2003, *Travellers on a Country Lane* (1869, oil on panel, 11 x 16 ins / 29 x 41 cm) USD 4,000. NEW ORLEANS, 5 June 2004, *Forest Landscape with Travellers* (oil on canvas, 40 x 50 ins / 102 x 127 cm) USD 8,500. HARROGATE, 9 Sept 2004, *Meadows in Holland* (oil on canvas, 7 x 9 ins / 18 x 23 cm) GBP 2,000.

KOEKKOEK, Hermanus, the Elder

Dutch, 19th century.

Born 13 March 1815, in Middelburg; died 5 November 1882, in Haarlem.

Painter. Waterscapes, seascapes.

Hermanus Koekkoek the Elder was the son and pupil of Johannes Hermanus Koekkoek, as well as being the father of Willem. He painted with his left hand, and worked in Amsterdam from 1832. There were reputed to have been important collectors of his works in England.

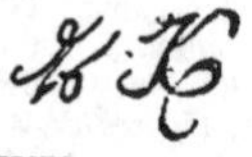

MUSEUMS AND GALLERIES:

COURTRAI: *Seascape* - GLASGOW: *Seascape* - LE HAVRE: *Seascape* - MELBOURNE: *End of the Earth* - SHEFFIELD: *Boats at Sea* (1858); *Seascape*.

AUCTION RECORDS:

LONDON, 18 Jan 1908, *Saved from the Wreck*, GBP 12. LONDON, 27 Feb 1909, *River Scene* (1864) GBP 7. LONDON, 17 June 1910, *Mouth of a River* (1836) GBP 23. PARIS, 28-29 Nov 1923, *Boats at Anchor*, FRF 500. LONDON, 10 Feb 1961, *Scene on the Seashore*, GBP 273. LONDON, 13 July 1966, *The Coast of Holland*, GBP 1,450. LONDON, 12 May 1967, *Sailing Ships in a Calm Sea*, Gns 1,250. SCOTLAND, 30 Aug 1968, *Fishing Port*, GBP 2,500. SCOTLAND, 20 May 1970, *Estuary Scene*, GBP 2,600. SCOTLAND, 8 Nov 1972, *Landscapes in Holland* (two canvases) GBP 14,000. LONDON, 6 March 1974, *Fishing Boats off the Coast*, GBP 3,500. AMSTERDAM, 15 Nov 1976, *River Landscape with Boats* (1862, oil on canvas, 14 3/4 x 22 1/4 ins / 37.5 x 56.5 cm) NLG 42,000. LONDON, 22 July 1977, *Sailing Ships and Boats at Sea* (1857, oil on canvas, 21 1/2 x 29 ins / 54.7 x 73.7 cm) GBP 6,000. AMSTERDAM, 30 Oct 1979, *Scene by the Sea* (1862, oil on canvas, 12 3/4 x 18 3/4 ins / 32.5 x 47.5 cm) NLG 54,000. LONDON, 26 Nov 1982, *Sailing Boats off the Coast in a Calm Sea* (1862, oil on canvas, 21 x 30 1/4 ins / 53.2 x 77 cm) GBP 10,500. NEW YORK, 24 Feb 1983, *The Banks of the Scheldt* (oil on canvas, 13 3/4 x 22 ins / 35 x 55 cm) USD 16,000. AMSTERDAM, 19 Nov 1985, *Sailing Ship and Frigate off the Coast* (1861, oil on canvas, 33 1/2 x 48 ins / 85 x 122 cm) NLG 48,000. LONDON, 26 Nov 1986, *Sailing Ships and Boat in a Calm Sea* (oil on canvas, 14 1/4 x 23 ins / 36 x 57.5 cm) GBP 21,500. NEW YORK, 21 May 1987, *Boats off the Coast of Holland* (1864, oil on canvas, 19 1/4 x 28 1/2 ins / 49 x 72.5 cm) USD 45,000. AMSTERDAM, 28 Feb 1989, *The Port of Edam with a Sailing Ship in a Stormy Sea and a Three-master Moored at a Quay in the Background* (1854, oil on canvas, 15 1/4 x 22 3/4 ins / 39 x 58 cm) NLG 21,275. LONDON, 21 June 1989, *Off the Coast* (1861, oil on canvas, 9 3/4 x 13 1/2 ins / 25 x 34.5 cm) GBP 8,250. LONDON, 16 Feb 1990, *Fishing Boat Towing a Sailing Ship in an Estuary* (1860, oil on canvas, 15 3/4 x 22 1/4 ins / 40 x 56.5 cm) GBP 33,000. AMSTERDAM, 2 May 1990, *Summer River Landscape with Peasants Unloading Goods from Boats and Sailing Boats under way on the River* (oil on canvas, 14 1/2 x 22 1/2 ins / 37 x 57 cm) NLG 92,000. NEW YORK, 23 May 1990, *Boats on the IJ* (oil on canvas, 21 3/4 x 29 1/2 ins / 55.2 x 74.9 cm) USD 52,250. AMSTERDAM, 30 Oct 1990, *Sailors in a Dinghy at Dusk* (1877, oil on panel, 4 3/4 x 7 ins / 12 x 17.5 cm) NLG 11,500. AMSTERDAM, 6 Nov 1990, *Street in a Dutch Town with Figures in Summer* (1867, oil on canvas, 32 3/4 x 47 3/4 ins / 83 x 121.5 cm) NLG 299,000. AMSTERDAM, 23 April 1991, *Boats in a Port* (oil on canvas, 13 3/4 x 22 1/2 ins / 35 x 57 cm) NLG 82,800; *Sailing Ships and Rowing Boats off the Coast* (1853, oil on canvas, 20 3/4 x 28 3/4 ins / 53 x 73 cm) NLG 97,750. LONDON, 19 June 1991, *Boats at Sea* (1863, oil on canvas, 14 1/4 x 22 ins / 36 x 56 cm) GBP 11,000. LONDON, 29 Nov 1991, *Boats off the Coast in a Light Breeze* (1863, oil on canvas, 15 x 23 ins / 38 x 58.5 cm) GBP 26,400. NEW YORK, 20 Feb 1992, *Boating Scenes off the Dutch Coast* (oil on canvas, a pair, each 14 1/2 x 23 ins / 36.8 x 58.4 cm) USD 66,000. AMSTERDAM, 22 April 1992, *A Rowing Boat Approaching a Two-master Anchored in the Open Sea with Sailors on the Shore* (1858, oil on canvas, 22 x 29 3/4 ins / 56 x 75.5 cm) NLG 253,000. AMSTERDAM, 2-3 Nov 1992, *Sailing Ships in an Estuary* (1850, oil on panel, 7 x 10 ins / 18 x 25.5 cm) NLG 23,000. LONDON, 27 Nov 1992, *Sailing Ships off the Cliffs of Folkestone with a Steamer in the Distance* (oil on canvas, 27 x 40 ins / 68.6 x 101.6 cm) GBP 24,200. LONDON, 20 Jan 1993, *Sailors Joining Their Ships in Dinghies on the Zuider Zee* (oil on canvas, 14 1/4 x 22 3/4 ins / 36 x 58 cm) GBP 29,900. LONDON, 19 March 1993, *Estuary with Figures* (1834, oil on canvas, 20 x 25 ins / 50.9 x 63.6 cm) GBP 17,250. AMSTERDAM, 21 April 1993, *Transport Anchored in an Estuary with other Shipping in a Calm Sea* (1848, oil on canvas, 20 1/2 x 28 ins / 52 x 71 cm) NLG 32,200. NEW YORK, 16 Feb 1994, *Fishermen Departing* (oil on canvas, 15 x 22 3/4 ins / 37.8 x 57.8 cm) USD 65,750. AMSTERDAM, 21 April 1994, *Port in the Area around Gronin-*

gen (1865, oil on canvas, 15 x 23 ins / 38 x 58.5 cm) NLG 78,200. LONDON, 14 June 1995, *Unloading the Ferry* (1859, oil on canvas, 22 x 29 1/4 ins / 55 x 74.5 cm) GBP 89,500. LONDON, 12 June 1996, *Large Boat in an Estuary* (oil on canvas, 13 3/4 x 22 ins / 35 x 56 cm) GBP 32,200. VIENNA, 29-30 Oct 1996, *Shipwreck in front of the Lighthouse* (oil on canvas, 15 x 22 3/4 ins / 38 x 58 cm) ATS 299,000. AMSTERDAM, 5 Nov 1996, *Sailing Ship at Sea* (1845, oil on panel, 8 1/4 x 11 1/2 ins / 21 x 29 cm) NLG 11,800. LONDON, 21 March 1997, *Vessels in an Estuary with Fishermen on the Seawall* (1853, oil on canvas, 15 1/2 x 21 3/4 ins / 39.5 x 55.2 cm) GBP 45,500. LONDON, 26 March 1997, *At Sea* (1837, oil on canvas, 15 3/4 x 20 1/2 ins / 40 x 52 cm) GBP 16,675. AMSTERDAM, 22 April 1997, *Beach Scene with Fishermen* (oil on panel, 12 1/2 x 17 ins / 32 x 43 cm) NLG 64,900. LONDON, 21 Nov 1997, *Figures on a River Bank with a Fishing Boat Hoisting its Sail* (oil on canvas, 12 1/2 x 18 1/2 ins / 31.8 x 46.7 cm) GBP 37,800. AMSTERDAM, 21 Jan 1998, *Landscape in Calm Weather with Sailors Unloading a Ship in the Foreground* (oil on panel, 20 x 27 1/4 ins / 50.5 x 69.5 cm) NLG 32,289. LONDON, 21 Oct 1999, *Shipping on the Scheldt with Antwerp in the Background* (1851, oil on canvas, 15 x 22 ins / 39 x 55 cm) GBP 47,000. AMSTERDAM, 26 Oct 1999, *Shipping in a Stiff Breeze* (1855, oil on canvas, 22 x 30 ins / 56 x 76 cm) NLG 160,000. LONDON, 6 April 2000, *In a Calm Estuary* (oil on canvas, 13 x 22 ins / 34 x 56 cm) GBP 40,000. AMSTERDAM, 18 April 2000, *Zeeuws Beurtschip in a Stiff Breeze with Frigate in the Distance* (1836, oil on panel, 16 x 21 ins / 40 x 54 cm) NLG 55,000. AMSTERDAM, 25 April 2001, *Shipping in a Calm* (1855, oil on canvas, 21 x 30 ins / 54 x 75 cm) NLG 630,000. LONDON, 19 June 2001, *Vessels at Anchor in an Estuary with Fishermen Hauling up their Rowing Boats in the Foreground* (1857, oil on canvas, 33 x 45 ins / 83 x 114 cm) GBP 210,000. LONDON, 19 Nov 2002, *On the Scheldt* (1864, oil on canvas, 15 x 23 ins / 38 x 58 cm) GBP 30,000. LONDON, 4 Dec 2002, *Shipping in a Calm* (1852, oil on canvas, 15 x 22 ins / 39 x 55 cm) GBP 35,000. LONDON, 3 June 2003, *Bringing in the Catch* (oil on canvas, 14 x 23 ins / 36 x 58 cm) GBP 37,000. LONDON, 3 June 2003, *Provisioning a Tall Ship at Anchor* (oil on canvas, 15 x 23 ins / 38 x 58 cm) GBP 45,000. LONDON, 23 March 2004, *On the Scheldt* (1853, oil on canvas, 14 x 22 ins / 36 x 55 cm) GBP 26,000. LONDON, 17 June 2004, *Gathering in the Nets in Stormy Seas* (oil on canvas, 26 x 39 ins / 67 x 100 cm) GBP 26,000.

KOEKKOEK, Hermanus, the Younger,

also known as Jan van Couver

Dutch, 19th - 20th century.

Born 1836; died 1909.

Painter. Landscapes with figures, seascapes.

Hermanus Koekkoek the Younger is possibly the son of Hermanus Koekkoek the Elder, part of a family of several generations of painters whose repertoire consisted of typical Dutch landscapes.

AUCTION RECORDS:

LONDON, 7 May 1976, *Harbour Scene* (oil on canvas, 47 x 35 ins / 119.5 x 89 cm) GBP 950. NEW YORK, 15 Oct 1976, *Boats in an Estuary* (oil on panel, 7 3/4 x 10 ins / 20 x 25.5 cm) USD 1,500. LONDON, 11 Feb 1977, *Seaside Scene* (oil on canvas, 32 3/4 x 51 ins / 83 x 129.5 cm) GBP 7,500. LONDON, 22 July 1977, *Estuary Scene* (oil on canvas, 23 1/2 x 35 1/2 ins / 59.6 x 90 cm) GBP 880. LONDON, 10 Feb 1978, *Towns on River Banks* (two canvases, 17 1/2 x 23 1/2 ins / 44.4 x 59.6 cm) GBP 2,200. LONDON, 14 Feb 1979, *Banks of the Scheldt* (oil on canvas, 14 x 22 1/2 ins / 35.5 x 57 cm) GBP 3,600. LONDON, 10 May 1979, *Winter Landscape with Figures* (watercolour and pen, 12 x 17 1/4 ins / 30.5 x 44 cm) GBP 600. LONDON, 2 June 1982, *Harbour Entrance* (1869, oil on canvas, 21 1/4 x 33 ins / 54 x 84 cm) GBP 3,400. LONDON, 3 June 1983, *Sailing Boats off the Coast in the Breeze* (oil on panel, 11 x 15 1/2 ins / 28 x 39.4 cm) GBP 4,800. NEW YORK, 23 May 1985, *View of a Dutch Harbour* (oil on canvas, 24 x 30 ins / 61 x 76.2 cm) USD 4,000. NEW YORK, 24 Feb 1987, *Landscape with Mill and Canal Lock* (oil on canvas, 34 1/4 x 44 ins / 86.7 x 111.7 cm) USD 5,000. PARIS, 29 April 1988, *Marine* (oil on canvas, 25 1/2 x 39 1/4 ins / 65 x 100 cm) FRF 16,000. STOCKHOLM, 15 Nov 1988, *Marine with Sailing Boats and Figures* (oil, 7 x 9 ins / 18 x 23 cm) SEK 17,500. AMSTERDAM, 16 Nov 1988, *Sailing Boat Approaching a Pier and Navigation in an Estuary in a Light Breeze* (oil on panel, 10 1/4 x 13 1/2 ins / 25.8 x 34.3 cm) NLG 5,750; *Boat Full Sail Overtaking a Rowing Boat at the Harbour Entrance* (oil on canvas) NLG 41,400. AMSTERDAM, 28 Feb 1989, *Sailing Boat Driven by Wind on a Rough Sea* (oil on panel, 6 1/2 x 8 ins / 16.5 x 20.5 cm) NLG 4,600. AMSTERDAM, 24 April 1991, *River Landscape with Peasants near a Windmill with a Bell-tower and a Bridge* (oil on canvas, 28 x 36 ins / 71 x 91.5 cm) NLG 4,370. NEW YORK, 15 Oct 1991, *On a Southern Coast* (oil on panel, 6 3/4 x 8 3/4 ins / 17.2 x 22.2 cm) USD 9,350. AMSTERDAM, 30 Oct 1991, *Fishing Boat off Coasts in a Strong Breeze* (oil on canvas, 15 1/2 x 22 ins / 39.5 x 56 cm) NLG 17,250. AMSTERDAM, 5-6 Nov 1991, *Town Around a Bay* (oil on canvas, 19 3/4 x 27 1/2 ins / 50 x 70 cm) NLG 2,415. LONDON, 29 Nov 1991, *Coast Landscape with Transporter Ferry* (1868, oil on panel, 31 x 47 1/4 ins / 78.7 x 120 cm) GBP 14,300. LONDON, 17 June 1992, *Landcape with Figures* (oil on canvas, 26 x 39 ins / 66 x 99 cm) GBP 7,700. NEW YORK, 29 Oct 1992, *Village of Fishermen* (oil on canvas, 23 1/4 x 35 1/4 ins / 59 x 89.5 cm) USD 2,640. AMSTERDAM, 21 April 1993, *Polder Landscape with Sailing Boat on River near Mill* (oil on canvas, 10 x 20 ins / 25.5 x 50.5 cm) NLG 2,530. LONDON, 16 March 1994, *Off the Dutch Coasts* (oil on canvas, 14 1/4 x 22 ins / 36 x 56 cm) GBP 19,550. AMSTERDAM, 19 April 1994, *Sailing Boats on a River* (1855, oil on panel, 24 1/2 x 36 ins / 62.5 x 91.5 cm) NLG 25,300. AMSTERDAM, 9 Nov 1994, *Figure in a Landscape with Ruins* (oil on canvas, 20 1/4 x 30 ins / 51.5 x 76 cm) NLG 2,300. AMSTERDAM, 11 April 1995, *Navigation in an Estuary* (oil on panel, 17 x 26 1/4 ins / 43 x 66.5 cm) NLG 7,670. AMSTERDAM, 16 April 1996, *Sailing Boats in a Port near a Town* (oil on canvas, 10 x 19 3/4 ins / 25.5 x 50 cm) NLG 4,956. AMSTERDAM, 5 Nov 1996, *Boat Drawing Alongside* (oil on panel, 7 1/2 x 11 1/4 ins / 19 x 28.5 cm) NLG 14,160; *River Scene* (oil on canvas, 22 x 35 ins / 56 x 89 cm) NLG 3,540. AMSTERDAM, 27 Oct 1997, *Dutch Sailing Boat on a Choppy Sea* (oil on canvas, 15 x 21 1/2 ins / 38 x 54.5 cm) NLG 7,080; *Harbour View* (oil on canvas, 18 x 24 ins / 46 x 61 cm) NLG 7,670. AMSTERDAM, 21 Jan 1998, *The Needles of the Isle of White* (oil on canvas, 32 1/4 x 40 1/4 ins / 82 x 102 cm) NLG 8,649.

KOEKKOEK, Hermanus Willem

Dutch, 20th century.

Born 1867; died 1925 or 1929.

Painter. Military subjects, battles.

Hermanus Willem Koekkoek is possibly the son of Johannes Hermann Barend, one of several generations of painters of typically Dutch landscapes.

AUCTION RECORDS:

AMSTERDAM, 15 Nov 1976, *Cavalry* (oil on canvas, 15 1/2 x 19 1/2 ins / 39.5 x 49.5 cm) NLG 17,500. AMSTERDAM, 9 Nov 1982, *French Soldiers and Horsemen in a Street in Paris* (oil on canvas, 22 x 25 1/2 ins / 55 x 65 cm) NLG 13,500. LONDON, 3 June 1983, *Horse Trumpet* (oil on canvas, 24 x 17 1/2 ins / 61 x 44.5 cm) GBP 1,500. AMSTERDAM, 5-6 Feb 1991, *Foot-soldier Playing Trumpet* (oil on panel, 8 1/2 x 6 1/4 ins / 21.5 x 16 cm) NLG 4,830. NEW YORK, 17 Oct 1991, *The Charge of the French Cuirassiers* (oil on canvas, 34 3/4 x 50 1/2 ins / 88.3 x 128.3 cm) USD 12,100. AMSTERDAM, 30 Oct 1991, *The Coldstream Regiment on Manoeuvres* (oil on panel, 11 x 8 1/2 ins / 27 x 21.5 cm) NLG 5,750. AMSTERDAM, 18 Feb 1992, *The Charge of the Cuirassiers* (oil on panel, 16 1/4 x 11 1/4 ins / 41 x 28.5 cm) NLG 6,325. LONDON, 18 March 1992, *Cavalry Officers with their Horses* (oil on canvas, 16 3/4 x 23 ins / 42.5 x 58.5 cm) GBP 4,950. AMSTERDAM, 28 Oct 1992, *Sailing Boat on the*

Ij (oil on canvas, 21 1/4 x 29 1/4 ins / 54 x 74.5 cm) NLG 4,830. LONDON, 28 Oct 1992, *The Charge of the Prussians* (oil on canvas, 22 x 25 1/2 ins / 55 x 65 cm) GBP 5,060. AMSTERDAM, 2 Nov 1992, *Soldier in the Mountains* (oil on panel, 7 1/4 x 4 3/4 ins / 18.5 x 12 cm) NLG 1,265. NEW YORK, 19 Jan 1995, *The Charge of the French Cuirassiers* (oil on canvas, 40 1/4 x 54 1/4 ins / 102.2 x 137.8 cm) USD 9,200. AMSTERDAM, 11 April 1995, *Mounted Cuirassiers* (oil on panel, 28 x 14 1/2 ins / 71 x 37 cm) NLG 14,160. LONDON, 17 Nov 1995, *Foot-soldiers of the Second Imperial Prussian Regiment Entering Paris* (oil on canvas, 34 x 49 1/2 ins / 86.3 x 125.7 cm) GBP 3,680. LONDON, 9 Oct 1997, *Scottish Soldier of the Sutherland* (oil on canvas, 20 3/4 x 16 3/4 ins / 53 x 42.7 cm) GBP 3,220. LONDON, 12 May 1999, *Soldiers at Rest* (oil on canvas, 17 x 21 ins / 43 x 53 cm) GBP 4,500. LONDON, 30 Nov 1999, *Sergeant on Horseback* (oil on canvas, 18 x 13 ins / 46 x 32 cm) GBP 7,000. AMSTERDAM, 18 April 2000, *Scout of the Scots Greys Reporting* (oil on canvas, 24 x 20 ins / 62 x 51 cm) NLG 45,000. MONTREAL, 12 Dec 2000, *Troops Returning Home* (oil on canvas, 17 x 21 ins / 43 x 53 cm) CAD 7,250. LONDON, 19 April 2001, *Grenadier Guards* (oil on panel, 11 x 8 ins / 27 x 21 cm) GBP 3,800. LONDON, 5 July 2001, *Cavalry Charge* (oil on canvas, 22 x 26 ins / 56 x 66 cm) GBP 10,000. AMSTERDAM, 29 April 2003, *Troop of Horse Artillery, Gele Rijders* (oil on panel, 11 x 8 ins / 27 x 21 cm) EUR 11,000. AMSTERDAM, 21 Oct 2003, *Battle Scene from the Franco-Prussian War* (oil on canvas, 22 x 26 ins / 56 x 66 cm) EUR 10,000. AMSTERDAM, 21 April 2004, *Trumpeteer of the Third Regiment Hussars* (oil on canvas, 18 x 24 ins / 45 x 60 cm) EUR 32,000. AMSTERDAM, 26 Oct 2004, *Courageous Incursion, French Cuirassiers Charging* (oil on canvas, 34 x 49 ins / 87 x 124 cm) EUR 22,000.

KOEKKOEK, Johannes

Dutch, 19th century.

Born 8 December 1811, in Middelburg; died 28 April 1831, in Breda.

Painter. Seascapes.

Johannes Koekkoek was the son and pupil of Johannes Hermanus Koekkoek. Although he died at a young age, he executed a number of seascapes.

AUCTION RECORDS:

ROTTERDAM, 1883, *Two Seascapes* (forming a pair) FRF 1,200; *Two Seascapes,* FRF 295. ZURICH, 2 Nov 1979, *Seascape* (1830, oil on canvas, 22 1/4 x 27 3/4 ins / 56.5 x 70.5 cm) CHF 8,500. AMSTERDAM, 21 April 2004, *Shipping in a Stiff Breeze off the Dutch Coast* (oil on panel, 8 x 11 ins / 21 x 27 cm) EUR 15,000.

KOEKKOEK, Johannes Hermann Barend

Dutch, 19th - 20th century.

Born 6 July 1840, in Amsterdam; died 24 January 1912, in Hilversum.

Painter. Landscapes with figures, seascapes.

Johannes Hermann Barend Koekkoek was the son and pupil of Hermanus Koekkoek the Elder and was active in Hilversum.

AUCTION RECORDS:

NEW YORK, 1 and 2 April 1902, *Marine,* USD 300. NEW YORK, 1 and 2 Dec 1904, *Landscape,* USD 155. LONDON, 22 Feb 1908, *Ships in Middleburg,* GBP 6. COLOGNE, 22 May 1951, *View of a Port,* DEM 600. COLOGNE, 30 April 1965, *Wooded Landscape with Figures,* Gns 500. DORDRECHT, 10 June 1969, *Fishermen on the Beach,* NLG 11,000. LONDON, 5 June 1970, *Canal Scenes, Holland* (two pendants) Gns 750. LONDON, 2 Nov 1973, *Sailing Boats in an Estuary,* Gns 7,500. LONDON, 1 Nov 1974, *Fishing Boats at Sea,* Gns 3,800. LONDON, 19 May 1976, *Boats off Hilversum* (oil on canvas, 14 x 19 ins / 35.5 x 48.5 cm) GBP 1,800. LONDON, 4 Nov 1977, *Estuary Scene* (oil on canvas, 13 x 19 3/4 ins / 33 x 50.2 cm) GBP 2,000. AMSTERDAM, 15 May 1979, *View of Dordrecht* (1888, oil on canvas, 25 1/2 x 41 3/4 ins / 65 x 106 cm) NLG 24,000. AMSTERDAM, 17 Nov 1981, *Sailing Boats at Sea* (1861, oil on canvas, 25 1/4 x 39 1/4 ins / 64 x 100 cm) NLG 21,000. NEW YORK, 27 May 1983, *Fishing Boats in Surging Sea* (oil on canvas, 14 1/2 x 22 3/4 ins / 36.8 x 57.7 cm) USD 4,000. LONDON, 29 Nov 1985, *Zuyder Zee* (1864, oil on canvas, 38 x 61 ins / 96.5 x 155 cm) GBP 12,000. LONDON, 12 Feb 1986, *Sailing Boats off the Dutch Coast* (oil on panel, 16 3/4 x 26 1/2 ins / 42.5 x 67 cm) GBP 5,200. LONDON, 25 March 1987, *Boats at a Port Entrance* (1883, oil on canvas, 15 x 22 ins / 38 x 56 cm) GBP 11,000. AMSTERDAM, 3 Sept 1988, *Figures Strolling in a Village Street with a Church in the Background* (oil on canvas, 19 x 12 1/2 ins / 48 x 32 cm) NLG 5,175. AMSTERDAM, 16 Nov 1988, *Coastal Landscape with Villagers Collecting Algae on the Shore and Sailing Boats on a Raging Sea* (1881, oil on canvas, 17 x 26 1/2 ins / 43 x 67 cm) NLG 33,350; *Two Fishermen Manoeuvring their Boat under a Bridge with Sailing Boats off the Coast* (oil on panel, 9 1/4 x 12 1/4 ins / 23.5 x 31 cm) NLG 12,650. AMSTERDAM, 28 Feb 1989, *Collectors of Sea Shells with their Carriole on Dunes near Shore* (oil on panel, 15 3/4 x 12 1/2 ins / 40 x 32 cm) NLG 6,900. COLOGNE, 20 Oct 1989, *Marine* (1874, oil on canvas, 16 1/4 x 24 ins / 41 x 61 cm) DEM 4,000. LONDON, 14 Feb 1990, *Rustic Scene* (oil on canvas, 25 1/2 x 38 1/2 ins / 65 x 98 cm) GBP 6,600. NEW YORK, 28 Feb 1990, *The Port of Amsterdam* (1863, oil on canvas, 23 x 32 1/2 ins / 58.4 x 82.5 cm) USD 41,800. AMSTERDAM, 25 April 1990, *Figures in a Sailing Boat in a Turbulent Sea* (oil on canvas, 22 1/2 x 33 ins / 57 x 84 cm) NLG 25,300. AMSTERDAM, 2 May 1990, *Round Boats Stranded on the Beach in Scheveningen at Dusk* (1892, oil on canvas, 49 1/4 x 34 1/4 ins / 125 x 87 cm) NLG 46,000. LONDON, 6 June 1990, *Sailing Boats Leaving Harbour* (oil on canvas, 17 x 24 ins / 43 x 61 cm) GBP 4,950. COLOGNE, 29 June 1990, *In the Dunes with a Stranded Boat in the Background* (1889, oil on wood, 5 x 7 1/2 ins / 12.5 x 19 cm) DEM 11,000. AMSTERDAM, 11 Sept 1990, *Fisherman's Wife and her Child on Path in Dunes near Lighthouse* (oil on canvas, 23 1/4 x 32 ins / 59 x 81 cm) NLG 5,750. AMSTERDAM, 30 Oct 1990, *Fisherman in Horse-drawn Cart Passing by a Fishing Boat Stranded on the Shore* (1892, oil on canvas, 49 1/4 x 34 1/2 ins / 125 x 87.5 cm) NLG 36,800. AMSTERDAM, 23 April 1991, *Boats in Fisheries in Calm Weather* (1888, oil on canvas, 14 x 20 3/4 ins / 35.5 x 53 cm) NLG 34,500. AMSTERDAM, 24 April 1991, *Coastal Landscape with a Woman and her Child in Dunes and Boats Berthed in the Distance* (oil on canvas, 12 1/2 x 19 ins / 32 x 48 cm) NLG 17,250; *Fishermen Busy Around their Trawler Stranded on the Shore of Schevenigen at Sunset* (1892, oil on canvas, 49 1/4 x 34 1/4 ins / 125 x 87 cm) NLG 28,750. LONDON, 21 June 1991, *Arrival of a Strong Gale* (1865, oil on canvas, 22 x 34 1/2 ins / 56 x 87.5 cm) GBP 15,400. LONDON, 20 March 1992, *Navigation of Dutch Vessels in the Open Sea in a Strong Gale* (oil on canvas/card, 15 x 22 ins / 37.2 x 55 cm) GBP 5,720. AMSTERDAM, 9 Nov 1993, *Fishermens' Activities on Katewijk Beach* (1888, oil on canvas, 25 1/4 x 40 3/4 ins / 64 x 103.5 cm) NLG 92,000. AMSTERDAM, 11 April 1995, *Sailing Boats on a River* (oil on panel, 9 3/4 x 14 3/4 ins / 25 x 37.5 cm) NLG 59,000. AMSTERDAM, 16 April 1996, *Navigation in a Calm Sea* (1888, oil on canvas, 15 x 21 1/4 ins / 38 x 54 cm) NLG 31,860. AMSTERDAM, 30 Oct 1996, *Children on the Beach at Sunset* (oil on canvas, 12 3/4 x 19 ins / 32.5 x 48.5 cm) NLG 20,757. AMSTERDAM, 5 Nov 1996, *Fisherman's Family with Horses on the Beach* (oil on panel, 10 1/2 x 14 1/4 ins / 26.5 x 36.5 cm) NLG 11,564. AMSTERDAM, 22 April 1997, *View of the Old Castle of Abcoude* (oil on panel, 10 1/2 x 14 1/4 ins / 26.5 x 36 cm) NLG 15,930.

KOEKKOEK, Johannes Hermanus

Dutch, 19th century.

Born 17 August 1778, in Véré; died 12 January 1851, in Amsterdam.

Painter, watercolourist. Landscapes, seascapes.

Johannes Hermanus Koekkoek married Anna Koolwyk in 1803. He became a member of the academy in Amsterdam, having trained himself to paint from nature during his leisure time from his work in a tapestry factory. He was the father of Barend Cornelis, Marinus Adrianus, Johannes and Hermanus Koekkoek, and the long line of painters of the Koekkoek family, most of whom remained faithful to the tradition of painting typical Dutch subjects.

Museums and Galleries:

Norwich (Castle Mus. and AG): *View on the Scheldt.*

Auction records:

Paris, 1861, *View of the Interior Waterways of Holland,* FRF 1,200. Amsterdam, 1881, *Seascape,* FRF 1,070. Rotterdam, 1891, *Shipwreck on the Coast of England,* FRF 3,000; *Fishing Beach,* FRF 600. New York, 26 Jan 1906, *On the Zuider Zee,* USD 250. London, 6 May 1910, *Dutch Fishing Boats* (1846) GBP 22. London, 4 Feb 1911, *Boats off the Coast of Holland* (1827) GBP 16. London, 25-26 May 1911, *View of Musselburg,* GBP 81. London, 7 May 1926, *Fishing Boats,* GBP 92. Paris, 23 May 1929, *Seascape* (watercolour) FRF 730. London, 9 Nov 1934, *Storm on the Coast,* GBP 56. London, 4 June 1947, *A Courtyard,* GBP 62. Paris, 2 May 1950, *Sailing Ship Approaching Port, in a Storm,* FRF 44,000. Amsterdam, 20 June 1951, *Dutch Frigate and Foreign Boats near the Coast,* NLG 1,900. London, 13 July 1966, *Fishing Boats near the Coast,* GBP 620. Amsterdam, 3 Feb 1967, *The Storm,* Gns 750. Amsterdam, 19 Jan 1968, *Fishing Boats Leaving the Coast,* Gns 1,000. Amsterdam, 25 Feb 1969, *Fishing Boats,* NLG 13,000. London, 14 Nov 1973, *Boats in an Estuary,* GBP 19,000. London, 14 June 1974, *Estuary Scene,* Gns 6,500. London, 24 Nov 1976, *Shipwreck* (1813, oil on panel, 22 x 29 1/4 ins / 56 x 74 cm) GBP 2,900. London, 11 Feb 1977, *Estuary Scene* (1838, oil on panel, 15 1/2 x 21 ins / 39.5 x 53.5 cm) GBP 3,600. Cologne, 1 June 1978, *Boats in a Heavy Sea* (oil on canvas, 33 x 44 1/2 ins / 84 x 113 cm) DEM 32,000. London, 3 Oct 1979, *Boats at Sea* (1809, two oils on panel, 8 1/2 x 10 1/2 ins / 21.5 x 26.5 cm) GBP 2,600. London, 29 Nov 1979, *Sailing Ships* (1804, pen and wash, 10 x 14 1/2 ins / 25.5 x 37 cm) GBP 1,050. London, 24 June 1981, *Fishing Boats in a Rough Sea* (1846, oil on canvas, 27 1/4 x 37 1/2 ins / 69 x 95 cm) GBP 7,000. London, 5 Oct 1983, *Fishermen in a Small Craft Rejoining their Boat.* London, 21 March 1986, *Boats in a Landscape with a Frozen River* (oil on panel, 20 x 27 1/2 ins / 51 x 70 cm) GBP 13,000. Lokeren, 10 Oct 1987, *The Frigate 'Minerva' at her Moorings* (1813, oil on panel, 17 3/4 x 24 ins / 45 x 61 cm) BEF 1,300,000. Amsterdam, 2 May 1990, *Sailing Ships in a River Estuary in Calm Weather* (oil on panel, 9 1/2 x 13 ins / 24.3 x 32.8 cm) NLG 4,370. London, 11 May 1990, *Tarring the Keel of a Boat* (oil on panel, 11 x 14 ins / 28 x 35.5 cm) GBP 6,600. London, 30 Nov 1990, *Coastal Landscape with Figures Repairing a Boat beside the Zuider Zee and Sailing Ships on the Open Sea* (oil on canvas, 14 1/2 x 23 1/4 ins / 37 x 59 cm) GBP 26,400. Amsterdam, 24 April 1991, *River Landscape with Fishermen in their Boat near a Port* (oil on panel, 9 1/4 x 12 1/4 ins / 23.5 x 31 cm) NLG 9,200. London, 22 May 1991, *Dutch Sailing Ship* (oil on panel, 7 3/4 x 10 3/4 ins / 19.5 x 27.5 cm) GBP 3,520. New York, 20 Feb 1992, *Travellers in a Rowing Boat Rejoining their Vessel* (oil on canvas, 15 1/2 x 21 1/2 ins / 39.4 x 54.6 cm) USD 25,300. Amsterdam, 2 Nov 1992, *Fishermen on a Quay opposite a Two-master at Anchor* (oil on panel, 7 1/2 x 11 1/2 ins / 19 x 29 cm) NLG 34,500. London, 25 Nov 1992, *Fishing Boats off a Jetty* (oil on panel, 12 x 17 1/4 ins / 30.5 x 44 cm) GBP 4,950. London, 19 Nov 1993, *Rocky Coast with Sailing Ships Caught in a Storm* (1844, oil on panel, 10 3/4 x 15 ins / 27.2 x 37.2 cm) GBP 6,325. London, 10 Feb 1995, *Dutch Sailing Ship Caught in the Storm* (1842, oil on panel, 8 3/4 x 12 ins / 22.5 x 30.5 cm) GBP 2,300. Amsterdam, 7 Nov 1995, *Boats off a Jetty* (oil on panel, 8 1/2 x 11 ins / 21.5 x 27 cm) NLG 8,024. Paris, 21 Nov 1995, *Ships and Fishing Boats on a Calm Morning* (1833, oil on canvas, 21 1/4 x 29 1/2 ins / 54 x 75 cm) FRF 170,000. London, 21 Oct 1999, *On the Beach* (1823, oil on panel, 12 x 16 ins / 31 x 40 cm) GBP 11,000. London, 21 Oct 1999, *Shipping in Choppy Estuary* (1826, oil on panel, 12 x 17 ins / 30 x 42 cm) GBP 13,000. New York, 18 Oct 2000, *Ships in a Squall with Figures on the Shore* (1831, oil on canvas, 18 x 23 ins / 45 x 59 cm) USD 72,000. Amsterdam, 24 Oct 2000, *De gestrande boot (Beached Three-master with Beachcombers along a Shore)* (1813, oil on panel, 18 x 26 ins / 46 x 65 cm) NLG 220,000. Bremen, 29 June 2001, *Shipwrecked Three-master after Storm* (oil on panel, 18 x 25 ins / 46 x 64 cm) DEM 65,000. Bury St Edmunds, 17 Dec 2001, *Dutch Pinck and Other Vessels Heading for Shore* (1850, oil on canvas, 16 x 22 ins / 40 x 56 cm) GBP 46,000. Bristol, 29 Jan 2002, *Dutch Canal Scene* (1848, oil on canvas, 17 x 23 ins / 44 x 58 cm) GBP 7,400. Amsterdam, 12 March 2002, *Calm* (1857, oil on panel, 8 x 10 ins / 20 x 25 cm) EUR 16,000. London, 2 Dec 2003, *Rescue* (oil on canvas, 30 x 41 ins / 77 x 103 cm) GBP 4,500. London, 4 Dec 2003, *Meeting on the Beach* (1882, oil on panel, 6 x 8 ins / 14 x 20 cm) GBP 5,500. Detroit, 13 Feb 2004, *Landscape with Waterfalls* (oil on canvas/board, 23 x 28 ins / 58 x 71 cm) USD 5,000. Amsterdam, 21 April 2004, *Shipping by a Coast in a Brisk Wind* (oil on panel, 8 x 11 ins / 21 x 27 cm) EUR 9,000.

KOEKKOEK, Marinus Adrianus

Dutch, 19th century.

Born 25 September 1807, in Middelburg; died 1868 or 1870, in Hilversum.

Painter. Landscapes with figures, landscapes, waterscapes.

Marinus Adrianus Koekkoek was the son and pupil of Johannes Hermanus Koekkoek. He lived in Hilversum.

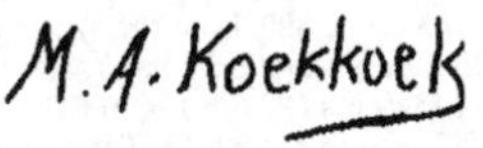

Museums and Galleries:

Courtrai: *A Wood.*

Auction records:

London, 7 Dec 1908, *Wooded Landscape* (1840) GBP 14. London, 18 April 1910, *River Scene* (1844) GBP 15. Paris, 30 April 1919, *In the Forest, Figures Stationary beside a Path,* FRF 175. Paris, 21 March 1938, *Wooded Landscape with Figures and Sheep,* FRF 360. London, 15 June 1945, *Woodland Path* (in collaboration with Verboeckhoven) GBP 89. London, 20 Feb 1946, *Landscape,* GBP 115. New York, 26 Feb 1947, *Landscape with Figures,* USD 525. London, 26 Oct 1960, *Extended Landscape,* GBP 420. London, 26 July 1961, *Extended Landscape,* GBP 270. London, 10 June 1966, *Wooded Landscape with Figures,* Gns 1,700. London, 20 Feb 1970, *The Clearing,* GBP 1,500. London, 12 May 1972, *Wooded Landscape,* Gns 5,500. London, 6 March 1974, *Wooded Landscape with Figures by a River,* GBP 5,200. Amsterdam, 27 April 1976, *Summer Landscape* (1852, oil on panel, 13 x 17 ins / 33 x 43 cm) NLG 30,500. Cologne, 23 Nov 1977, *Wooded Landscape* (oil on canvas, 17 x 24 1/2 ins / 43 x 62.5 cm) DEM 36,000. Amsterdam, 24 April 1979, *Summer Landscape* (1857, oil on canvas, 30 1/4 x 41 ins / 77 x 104 cm) NLG 62,000. New York, 28 May 1981, *Shepherd and Flock in a Sunny Landscape* (1845, oil on canvas, 19 x 25 3/4 ins / 48 x 65.5 cm) USD 20,000. Cologne, 25 Nov 1983, *Wooded Landscape* (1863, oil on canvas, 18 1/2 x 24 1/2 ins / 47 x 62 cm) DEM 56,000. Cologne, 21 Nov 1985, *View of a Town* (1847, oil on canvas, 25 1/4 x 30 3/4 ins / 64 x 78 cm) DEM 30,000. Zurich, 13 June 1986, *Landscape with a Wooden Bridge and a Watermill* (1839, oil on canvas, 35 1/2 x 32 1/2 ins / 90 x 82.5 cm) CHF 40,000. Brussels, 9 Nov 1987, *Landscape with Figures* (oil on canvas, 28 x 37 1/2 ins / 71 x 95 cm) BEF 950,000. London, 25 March 1988, *Cattle and their Herdsman near a Ford in a Shady Meadow* (17 3/4 x 22 3/4 ins / 45 x 58 cm) GBP 9,900. Amsterdam, 16 Nov 1988, *Extensive Landscape with a Figure on a Track with a Windmill and a Church Tower in the*

Distance (oil on panel, 12 3/4 x 15 3/4 ins / 32.5 x 40 cm) NLG 17,250. LONDON, 16 Feb 1990, *Extensive River Landscape with Figures and Animals, and a Town in the Distance* (1845, oil on canvas, 26 1/2 x 37 ins / 67.4 x 94 cm) GBP 14,300. AMSTERDAM, 30 Oct 1990, *River Landscape with Fishermen in a Boat and a Woman and Child Walking along a Track in Summer* (oil on canvas, 19 1/2 x 25 ins / 49.5 x 63.5 cm) NLG 23,000. AMSTERDAM, 6 Nov 1990, *Mountainous Landscape with Figures and Animals* (1851, oil on canvas, 19 1/4 x 25 1/4 ins / 49 x 64 cm) NLG 34,500. LONDON, 28 Nov 1990, *Wooded Landscape with Figures and Animals* (1849, oil on canvas, 24 3/4 x 34 ins / 63 x 85.5 cm) GBP 18,700. AMSTERDAM, 14-15 April 1992, *Figures in a Wooded Landscape* (1854, oil on panel, 11 x 15 1/4 ins / 28 x 39 cm) NLG 8,050. LONDON, 19 June 1992, *Wooded River Landscape with Peasants in a Boat* (1852, oil on canvas, 16 1/2 x 21 1/2 ins / 42 x 54.6 cm) GBP 12,100. AMSTERDAM, 3 Nov 1992, *Figures on a Path in a Wooded Landscape* (1854, oil on panel, 9 1/4 x 12 3/4 ins / 23.5 x 32.5 cm) NLG 6,900. LONDON, 27 Nov 1992, *Goatherd and Shepherd on a Track in a Wooded Landscape* (1859, oil on canvas, 17 1/2 x 23 3/4 ins / 44.4 x 60.4 cm) GBP 13,200. AMSTERDAM, 20 April 1993, *Winter Landscape with Skaters* (1845, oil on canvas, 10 x 13 1/4 ins / 25.5 x 33.5 cm) NLG 26,450. AMSTERDAM, 19 Oct 1993, *Wooded River Landscape with a Fisherman in a Boat and a Herdsman on the Bank* (1853, oil on panel, 16 3/4 x 23 1/2 ins / 42.5 x 59.5 cm) NLG 103,500. AMSTERDAM, 5 Nov 1996, *Traveller near a Cart on a Path in a Wooded Landscape* (oil on panel, 13 1/2 x 17 1/4 ins / 34 x 44 cm) NLG 37,760. AMSTERDAM, 22 April 1997, *Traveller with a Donkey on a Track* (1849, oil on canvas, 11 3/4 x 16 1/4 ins / 30 x 41 cm) NLG 12,390. LONDON, 12 June 1997, *Winter Landscape with Figures Skating on a Frozen River* (1859, oil on panel, 9 1/4 x 13 3/4 ins / 23.5 x 35 cm) GBP 6,325. AMSTERDAM, 27 Oct 1997, *Figures in a River Landscape* (1850, oil on panel, 8 1/4 x 11 1/4 ins / 21 x 28.5 cm) NLG 23,600. SAN FRANCISCO, 26 May 1999, *Extensive Wooded Landscape with Travellers Resting* (oil on canvas, 19 x 24 ins / 48 x 61 cm) USD 8,000. COLOGNE, 26 June 1999, *Extensive Landscape* (1860, oil on panel, 8 x 12 ins / 21 x 30 cm) DEM 30,000. AMSTERDAM, 18 Jan 2000, *Wooded Landscape with Cattle* (1860, oil on canvas, 34 x 39 ins / 86 x 100 cm) NLG 20,000. LONDON, 12 Oct 2000, *Travellers Resting by Side of Path* (oil on canvas, 17 x 16 ins / 44 x 41 cm) GBP 16,000. ROTTERDAM, 5 May 2001, *Wooded Landscape with Herders and Cattle* (oil on canvas, 19 x 24 ins / 47 x 62 cm) NLG 25,000. DETROIT, 14 Dec 2001, *Landscape with Inn* (oil on panel, 7 x 10 ins / 18 x 25 cm) USD 300,000. BRUSSELS, 15 Jan 2002, *Landscape with Figures* (1862, oil on canvas, 18 x 24 ins / 46 x 62 cm) EUR 13,000. AMSTERDAM, 23 April 2002, *Country Scene with Cattle* (1854, oil on panel, 18 x 25 ins / 45 x 64 cm) EUR 17,000. AMSTERDAM, 29 April 2003, *Extensive River Landscape with Figure Unloading a Stone Transport* (1854, oil on canvas, 19 x 26 ins / 49 x 66 cm) EUR 60,000. STOCKHOLM, 26 May 2003, *Pastoral Landscape with Figures and Cattle* (oil on canvas, 35 x 45 ins / 90 x 114 cm) SEK 450,000. COLOGNE, 22 May 2004, *Mountain Landscape with Horse-drawn Cart* (1862, oil on canvas, 24 x 31 ins / 61 x 80 cm) EUR 29,000. BERLIN, 12 June 2004, *Dutch Landscape* (1845, oil on canvas, 29 x 39 ins / 74 x 100 cm) EUR 38,000.

KOEKKOEK, Marinus Adrianus

Dutch, 20th century.

Born 1873; died 1944.

Active in Amsterdam.

Painter (mixed media), watercolourist, pastellist.

Landscapes, animals.

Marinus Adrianus Koekkoek was active in Amsterdam. He may have been a direct descendant of Hermanus Koekkoek the Younger, Willem Koekkoek or Johannes Hermann Barend Koekkoek.

AUCTION RECORDS:

AMSTERDAM, 10 Feb 1988, *A Buffalo* (pastel and watercolour/paper, 17 x 21 ins / 43 x 53.5 cm) NLG 1,725. TEL AVIV, 26 May 1988, *On the Road to Jerusalem* (oil on card, 19 x 27 ins / 48.5 x 68.5 cm) USD 18,150. AMSTERDAM, 11 Sept 1990, *Hens near an Enclosure* (oil on canvas, 10 3/4 x 14 ins / 27.5 x 35.5 cm) NLG 4,600. AMSTERDAM, 5-6 Nov 1991, *Parrot* (oil on paper/panel, 5 1/2 x 7 ins / 14 x 17.5 cm) NLG 2,300. AMSTERDAM, 14 June 1994, *Wooded River Landscape with a Farm and a Figure in a Boat* (oil on panel, 7 3/4 x 11 3/4 ins / 20 x 30 cm) NLG 1,495. AMSTERDAM, 7 Nov 1995, *Goat behind a Door* (oil on card, 7 1/2 x 12 ins / 19 x 30.5 cm) NLG 1,534. NEW YORK, 18 March 1998, *A Popular Place to Rest* (1862, oil on canvas, 23 1/2 x 31 1/4 ins / 59.7 x 79.4 cm) USD 32,200. ROTTERDAM, 20 April 1999, *Flamingos* (1909, oil on canvas, 20 x 25 ins / 50 x 63 cm) NLG 4,000. LONDON, 23 March 2000, *Extensive Wooded Landscape with Travellers* (oil on canvas, 19 x 24 ins / 47 x 62 cm) GBP 1,500. THE HAGUE, 25 April 2001, *Chikens in Farmyard* (1907, oil on panel, 8 x 12 ins / 21 x 30 cm) NLG 3,800. BRUSSELS, 18 Nov 2003, *Skaters in Holland* (oil on panel, 15 x 24 ins / 37 x 60 cm) EUR 3,800.

KOEKKOEK, Willem

Dutch, 19th century.

Born 1839, in Amsterdam; died 1895.

Painter. Landscapes with figures, landscapes.

Willem Koekkoek was the son and pupil of Hermanus Koekkoek the Elder. He established himself in his native city of Amsterdam.

Willem Koekkoek specialised in views of Amsterdam. He displays a very modern sensibility in the way he depicted the regular arrangement of streets, marketplaces and canals for which this appealing city is known.

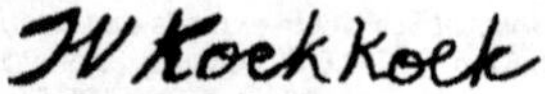

MUSEUMS AND GALLERIES:

MONTREAL: *The Old Town of Hoorn.*

AUCTION RECORDS:

AMSTERDAM, 1886, *View of a Village,* FRF 630. ROTTERDAM, 1891, *Street Covered in Snow,* FRF 700. LONDON, 27 April 1908, *A Highlander,* GBP 2. LONDON, 30 March 1909, *A Street,* GBP 11. LONDON, 26 Nov 1910, *View of Haarlem,* GBP 4. LONDON, 21 Feb 1947, *A Dutch Town,* GBP 178. LONDON, 2 July 1947, *Street Scene in Holland,* GBP 62. LONDON, 11 May 1961, *Continental Street Scene with Figures,* GBP 399. LONDON, 2 May 1962, *A View of Naarden in Winter,* GBP 1,100. LONDON, 9 Oct 1964, *Street Scene in Holland,* Gns 1,400. AMSTERDAM, 5 and 18 Oct 1965, *View of a Dutch Town,* NLG 10,000. LONDON, 21 Jan 1966, *Street Scene in a Small Dutch Town,* Gns 1,550. LONDON, 14 April 1967, *Street Scenes* (forming a pair) Gns 2,400. LONDON, 15 May 1968, *The Auction in an Amsterdam Street,* GBP 4,600. LONDON, 10 Oct 1969, *View of a Small Town in Holland,* Gns 4,800. LONDON, 18 Feb 1970, *View of a Small Town in Flanders,* GBP 4,600. LONDON, 28 Feb 1973, *Street Scene,* GBP 30,000. LONDON, 6 March 1974, *Street Scene,* GBP 23,000. AMSTERDAM, 30 Nov 1976, *Street Scene* (oil on canvas, 17 1/4 x 23 1/2 ins / 44 x 60 cm) NLG 27,000. LONDON, 30 Nov 1977, *Street Scene, Rotterdam* (oil on canvas, 33 x 48 ins / 84 x 122 cm) GBP 20,000. LONDON, 28 Nov 1979, *Street Scene* (oil on canvas, 33 x 48 ins / 84 x 122 cm) GBP 18,000. NEW YORK, 13 Feb 1981, *Street Scene in Delft* (oil on canvas, 21 1/4 x 27 1/4 ins / 54 x 69.3 cm) USD 28,000. LONDON, 22 June 1983, *Street Scene in Winter, Amsterdam* (oil on canvas, 33 x 48 ins / 84 x 122 cm) GBP 15,000. LONDON, 19 June 1985, *Figures near a Canal in a Town in Holland* (oil on canvas, 25 3/4 x 34 1/2 ins / 65.5 x 87.5 cm) GBP 21,000. AMSTERDAM, 14 April 1986, *View of a Town in Holland in Winter* (oil on canvas, 33 x 48 ins / 84 x 122 cm) NLG 86,000. LONDON, 26 June 1987, *View of a Square with Figures* (oil on canvas, 17 x 26 1/2 ins / 43 x 67 cm) GBP 18,000.

LONDON, 4 Oct 1989, *Street in a Quiet Dutch Village* (oil on panel, 18½ x 14¼ ins / 47 x 36 cm) GBP 9,680. LONDON, 30 March 1990, *Street Scene in Holland* (1877, oil on canvas, 21 x 27 ins / 53.5 x 68.5 cm) GBP 37,400. AMSTERDAM, 25 April 1990, *Figures on a Bridge in a Dutch Town in Winter* (oil on canvas, 23¼ x 17¼ ins / 59 x 43.5 cm) NLG 50,600. NEW YORK, 22 May 1990, *Dutch Village in Winter* (oil on canvas, 34 x 49 ins / 86.3 x 124.5 cm) USD 68,200. LONDON, 5 Oct 1990, *Street Scene in a Dutch Village* (oil on canvas, 20 x 15 ins / 50.8 x 38.1 cm) GBP 6,600. AMSTERDAM, 30 Oct 1990, *Village Street with Figures and a Peasant Pushing a Sledge along a Frozen Canal* (oil on canvas, 17¼ x 23½ ins / 44 x 60 cm) NLG 166,750. AMSTERDAM, 6 Nov 1990, *Street with Figures in a Dutch Town in Summer* (1867, oil on canvas, 32¾ x 47¾ ins / 83 x 121.5 cm) NLG 299,000. LONDON, 28 Nov 1990, *Figures in a Snow Covered Street Moving behind a Church* (oil on panel, 13½ x 11 ins / 34 x 28 cm) GBP 6,820. LONDON, 30 Nov 1990, *Dutch Village Street* (1870, oil on canvas, 23¼ x 27½ ins / 59 x 69.8 cm) GBP 19,800. AMSTERDAM, 23 April 1991, *Shopping Street in a Dutch Town* (oil on canvas, 32 x 47½ ins / 81.5 x 120.5 cm) NLG 172,500. LONDON, 21 June 1991, *A Street in Amsterdam* (oil on canvas, 27½ x 35½ ins / 70 x 90 cm) GBP 46,200. AMSTERDAM, 5-6 Nov 1991, *Figures near Flushing Cathedral* (oil on canvas, 33¼ x 48 ins / 84.5 x 122 cm) NLG 97,750. LONDON, 29 Nov 1991, *A Street in Woudrichem* (1883, oil on canvas, 33¾ x 49 ins / 85.7 x 124.5 cm) GBP 19,800. LONDON, 20 March 1992, *A Street in Rotterdam with the Church of St Laurens* (oil on canvas, 21 x 27 ins / 53.5 x 68.6 cm) GBP 18,150. LONDON, 17 June 1992, *Snow Covered Street in a Dutch Town* (oil on canvas, 21¾ x 32¾ ins / 55.5 x 83.5 cm) GBP 28,600. AMSTERDAM, 28 Oct 1992, *Street Scene in a Dutch City in Winter* (oil on canvas, 17½ x 24 ins / 44.5 x 61 cm) NLG 101,200. AMSTERDAM, 21 April 1993, *Winter Landscape with Peasants round a Horse-drawn Sleigh and Road Menders in the Foreground and a Town in the Distance* (oil on canvas, 22¾ x 34 ins / 58 x 85.5 cm) NLG 63,250. NEW YORK, 26 May 1993, *Village Street* (oil on panel, 16¼ x 13 ins / 41.3 x 33 cm) USD 12,650. LUDLOW (SHROPSHIRE), 29 Sept 1994, *Street in a Dutch Town with Passers-by round the Church* (1866, oil on canvas, 33 x 26 ins / 84 x 66 cm) GBP 74,100. AMSTERDAM, 8 Nov 1994, *Figures in the Streets of a Town in Winter* (oil on panel, 12½ x 9 ins / 32 x 23 cm) NLG 43,700. LONDON, 16 Nov 1994, *Street Scene in a Dutch Town with Many Figures* (oil on canvas, 30¾ x 48¼ ins / 78 x 122.5 cm) GBP 118,100. NEW YORK, 24 May 1995, *Street with Figures in Delft* (oil on canvas, 21¼ x 27¼ ins / 54 x 69.2 cm) USD 76,750. LONDON, 17 Nov 1995, *Dutch Town with Figures near a Canal* (oil on canvas, 21½ x 27½ ins / 54.5 x 70 cm) GBP 40,000. AMSTERDAM, 30 Oct 1996, *Townscape with Houses beside a Frozen Canal and Townsfolk near a Drawbridge* (oil on panel, 7¼ x 9¼ ins / 18.5 x 23.5 cm) NLG 39,208. LONDON, 20 Nov 1996, *Street Scene in Holland* (oil on canvas, 17¼ x 24¾ ins / 44 x 63 cm) GBP 19,550. LONDON, 21 Nov 1997, *Street Scene with Figures* (oil on canvas, 33½ x 49 ins / 85 x 124.5 cm) GBP 135,700. NEW YORK, 12 Feb 1998, *Street Scene, Amsterdam* (oil on canvas, 30½ x 44½ ins / 77.5 x 113 cm) USD 222,500. NEW YORK, 18 March 1998, *View of a Dutch Market Town in Summer* (oil on canvas, 15 x 22 ins / 37.2 x 55.9 cm) USD 31,050. LONDON, 26 March 1999, *De Lutherse Kerk, Amsterdam* (oil on canvas, 22 x 28 ins / 55 x 70 cm) GBP 48,000. LONDON, 1 Dec 1999, *Town View with Church* (oil on canvas, 21 x 27 ins / 54 x 69 cm) GBP 75,000. LONDON, 6 April 2000, *Street Scene in a Dutch Town* (oil on canvas, 13 x 19 ins / 34 x 49 cm) GBP 25,000. NORTH BETHESDA, 27 Oct 2000, *Winter in Amersfoort* (oil on panel, 13 x 19 ins / 34 x 48 cm) USD 18,000. LONDON, 30 March 2001, *Street Scene in a Dutch Town* (oil on canvas, 19 x 22 ins / 47 x 57 cm) GBP 58,000. AMSTERDAM, 23 April 2001, *View of a Dutch Town in Winter* (oil on canvas, 22 x 28 ins / 55 x 70 cm) NLG 150,000. LONDON, 4 Dec 2002, *Town in Summer* (oil on canvas, 33 x 49 ins / 84 x 124 cm) GBP 115,000. LONDON, 4 Dec 2002, *Dutch Town in Summer* (oil on canvas, 34 x 49 ins / 86 x 124 cm) GBP 120,000. LONDON, 18 March 2003, *Figures Conversing in a Dutch Town* (oil on canvas, 21 x 28 ins / 54 x 70 cm) GBP 48,000. AMSTERDAM, 29 April 2003, *Winter, Daily Activities on a Sunny Day in Oudewater* (oil on canvas, 24 x 30 ins / 62 x 75 cm) EUR 115,000. EDINBURGH, 28 May 2004, *Figures in a Busy Street* (oil on canvas, 15 x 20 ins / 38 x 51 cm) GBP 15,000.

KOELBEL, Johannes
Norwegian, 20th century.
Engraver.

Koelbel was active around 1937.

KOELER, Johann
Russian, 19th century.
Born 7 March 1826; died 22 April 1899, in St Petersburg.
Painter. Religious subjects, portraits.

MUSEUMS AND GALLERIES:
ST PETERSBURG (Swedish church) - TALLINN (church of St Charles) - WENDEN (church of St John).

KOELLA, Charles Adolphe
Swiss, 19th century.
Born 9 February 1855, in Lausanne.
Painter, watercolourist, architect.

Charles Koella at first studied architecture, then from 1886, he devoted himelf to watercolours. Notable among his works are *Sunrise over the Lac d'Aï*, in the Lausanne Museum, and *Chapel in Valais*, in the Basel Museum.

KOELLA, Heinrich
Swiss, 18th century.
Born 1757, in Stäfa; died 1789, in Stäfa.
Painter.

Heinrich Koella spent a long time in Rome, returning with a large number of drawings, especially views of ruins and portraits. When he returned to Stäfa in 1787, he painted portraits in oils and watercolours. An interesting *Study of a Head* by him can be seen in the ducal castle in Gotha.

KOELLA, Johann
Swiss, 18th century.
Born 22 March 1740, in Stäfa; died 18 January 1778, in Stäfa.
Painter. Portraits, genre scenes.

Johann Koella studied with Füssli. He spent much of the time working alone, conscientiously studying nature in his spare moments. He is known for his *Views of Lake Zurich*, particularly the area around Stäfa. Two of his *Self-portraits*, an *Interior*, 5 genre scenes and some 30 drawings can be seen in Zurich.

KOELLE, Fritz
German, 20th century.
Born 10 March 1895, in Augsburg.
Sculptor.

Koelle travelled extensively in France and Italy and was active mainly in Munich, Berlin, Münster and Baden-Baden.

KOELLIKER, Oscar
Swiss, 19th - 20th century.
Born in Neuchâtel.
Painter. Genre scenes.

Koelliker exhibited at the Salon des Indépendants from 1907.

AUCTION RECORDS:
LONDON, 21 Oct 1988, *Woman Collecting Seaweed* (oil on panel, 10¾ x 18 ins / 27.5 x 46 cm) GBP 715. PARIS, 31 Oct 1997, *Fisherman at Water's Edge* (oil on panel, 14¾ x 18 ins / 37.5 x 45.5 cm) FRF 4,000.

KŒLMAN, Jean
Flemish School, 16th century.

Born 1532, in Ghent; died 1592.
Painter.

KŒLMAN, Johan Daniel
Dutch, 19th century.
Born 30 December 1831, in The Hague; died 16 March 1857, in The Hague.
Painter, watercolourist, draughtsman. Landscapes, animals.
Johan Daniel Kœlman, brother of Johan Hendrik and Johan Philip Kœlman, studied under J.B. Tom and travelled to Germany, France and Italy.

MUSEUMS AND GALLERIES:
THE HAGUE (Gemeentemus.): *Bull in Meadow*; *White Cow*; fourteen studies and sketches on canvas and paper.
AUCTION RECORDS:
PARIS, 27 April 1927, *Landscape with Mill* (watercolour) FRF 105. PARIS, Oct 1945-July 1946, *Flock by the Pond*, FRF 10,100. AMSTERDAM, 10 April 1990, *Cows in a Polder Landscape* (pencil, ink and wash/paper, 6 x 8 1/2 ins / 15 x 21.7 cm) NLG 1,092. AMSTERDAM, 30 Oct 1990, *Shepherd with his Sheep and a Few Cows near a Pond in a Meadow* (1853, oil on canvas, 37 3/4 x 57 1/2 ins / 96 x 146 cm) NLG 12,650. AMSTERDAM, 21 April 1994, *Undulating Landscape with a Shepherd and his Animals* (1850, ink and watercolour/paper, 7 x 9 1/4 ins / 18 x 23.5 cm) NLG 2,300. AMSTERDAM, 23 April 2001, *Landscape with Farmhouse* (oil on panel, 7 x 14 ins / 17 x 36 cm) NLG 5,500. LONDON, 20 March 2003, *Summer Landscape with Cattle Grazing* (1853, oil on canvas, 38 x 58 ins / 97 x 147 cm) GBP 8,500. AMSTERDAM, 29 April 2003, *Peasant Girl and Cattle Resting in a Landscape* (1851, oil on panel, 13 x 18 ins / 32 x 46 cm) EUR 3,000.

KŒLMAN, Johan Hendrik
Dutch, 19th century.
Born 22 January 1820, in The Hague; died 1 February 1887, in Rome.
Painter. History painting, genre scenes.
Johan Hendrik Kœlman was the son of a master joiner and the brother of Johan Daniel and Johan Philip Kœlman. A pupil of C. Kruseman, he gave evidence of remarkable artistic aptitude at a very young age.
AUCTION RECORDS:
MONTE CARLO, 22 June 1986, *Young Woman Writing a Letter* (1847, oil on canvas, oval, 16 1/4 x 13 ins / 41.5 x 33 cm) FRF 58,000.

KŒLMAN, Johan Philip
Dutch, 19th century.
Born 11 March 1818, in The Hague; died 16 January 1893, in The Hague.
Painter, sculptor, draughtsman. Genre scenes, architectural views.
Johan Philip Kœlman worked as a joiner with his father until he was 20 years old, at the same time executing architectural drawings and writing. Encouraged by the example of his younger brother Johann Hendrik, he applied himself to drawing and became the pupil of his brother's teacher, the history painter C. Kruseman. At the exhibition in The Hague in 1866, he exhibited a plaster bust of Duke Bernard-Charles of Saxony-Weimar, and in 1869 models of the statues that decorate the façade of the Netherlands Bank in Amsterdam.
MUSEUMS AND GALLERIES:
THE HAGUE (Gemeentemus.): *Italian Woman near a Well*; *Peace, an Allegory* (watercolour).
AUCTION RECORDS:
LONDON, 23 Feb 1983, *A Family from Italy at the Seaside*; *An Artist Painting Italian Peasants* (oil on card, a pair, 10 x 14 ins / 25.5 x 35.5 cm) GBP 1,250. LONDON, 18 March 1994, *Late Return* (1854, oil on canvas, 25 x 19 1/4 ins / 63.5 x 49 cm) GBP 8,280. PARIS, 5 April 2001, *Children Astride a Statue in Italy* (1859, oil on panel, 17 x 21 ins / 42 x 54 cm) FRF 57,000.

KOEN
Japanese, 13th century.
Born 1207; died 1285(?).
Active in Nara.
Sculptor.
Koen was probably the son of Koun, the second son of the great sculptor Unkei (d. 1223). As the faithful disciple of Unkei, he is representative of the Kei school, whose head he became on the death of Tankei (1178-1256). Koen's work is noteworthy for its powerful expressiveness. Several of his sculptures survive: the central statue for the Rengeo-in, in the Myoho-in temple in Kyoto, which he completed in 1254 as Tankei's assistant; the *Emma Ju O* (Ten Judges of Hell) of 1259 in the Byakugo-ji in Nara; the *Fudo Myoo* (Acala) and *Eight Messengers* of Kannon-ji in Tokyo, dated 1272; *Aizen Myoo* (Ragaraja) in Jingo-ji, Kyoto, dated 1275; and *Manju* (Mañjusri) and *Four Followers* of Daijo-ji in Kofuku-ji temple, Nara, dated 1285.

KOEN, artist name Ichirosai
Japanese, 19th century.
Active in Osaka c. 1810.
Print artist.

KŒNBERGK, Lienhart
German, 15th - 16th century.
Active in Erfurt.
Painter.
Lienhart Kœnbergk is known to have produced an altarpiece for the church in Neustadt-an-der-Orla.

KOENE, Isaac. See **COENE**

KŒNE, Jean
Flemish School, 16th century.
Born c. 1532, in Ghent; died c. 1592.
Painter. History painting, genre scenes.

KŒNEMANN, Hermann
German, 19th - 20th century.
Born 21 April 1871, in Bonn.
Active in Schwerin.
Painter, lithographer. Landscapes, seascapes.
Hermann Kœnemann took part in the Grosse Berliner Kunstausstellung of 1909.

KŒNIG
French, 19th century.
Engraver (burin).
Koenig was active in Paris around 1840. He seems to have produced mainly vignettes. His works include: *Erigone* and *Ariane* in the style of Girodet, *Arrest of the Marquis de Crépière* in the style of Alfred Johannot and others.

KOENIG. See also **KÖNIG**

KŒNIG, Friedrich, or König
Austrian, 19th - 20th century.
Born 1857, in Vienna; died 1941.
Painter. Landscapes.
AUCTION RECORDS:
VIENNA, 17 March 1976, *Night* (oil on canvas, 22 x 33 1/2 ins / 55 x 85 cm) ATS 28,000. VIENNA, 22 Sept 1978, *Fields* (oil on canvas, 26 3/4 x 39 1/4 ins / 68 x 100 cm) ATS 30,000. VIENNA, 14 March 1980, *Cherry Trees in Flower* (oil on canvas, 20 x 15 1/4 ins / 51 x 39 cm) ATS 40,000. MUNICH, 29 June 1983, *Girl with Bouquet of Flowers* (oil on canvas, 27 1/2 x 24 3/4 ins / 70 x 63 cm) DEM 6,200. VIENNA, 15 Nov 1983, *Fresco Study* (c. 1900, pencil, drawing in four parts, each 46 x 20 3/4 ins / 117

x 53 cm) ATS 40,000. VIENNA, 18 June 1985, *Mountain Peaks* (oil on canvas, 26 1/2 x 28 1/4 ins / 67 x 72 cm) ATS 55,000. LONDON, 8 Oct 1986, *The Muses of Music* (c. 1900, watercolour, gouache and gold/panel, a pair, 51 x 20 1/2 ins / 129.5 x 52 cm and 50 1/4 x 20 1/2 ins/127.5 x 52 cm) GBP 22,000. LONDON, 5 Nov 1987, *Secession, Mid-September Opening* (1917, watercolour and pencil, 19 1/2 x 25 1/2 ins / 49.5 x 65 cm) GBP 1,100. PARIS, 7 March 1989, *Pond* (1913, 15 1/4 x 14 1/2 ins / 38.5 x 37 cm) FRF 35,000. LONDON, 17 June 1992, *Girl and Death* (1912, oil on canvas, 81 x 62 3/4 ins / 206 x 159.5 cm) GBP 825.

KŒNIG, Fritz, or König
German, 20th century.
Born 1924, in Würzburg.
Sculptor.

Fritz Kœnig studied under Anton Hiller at the Akademie der Künste in Munich, where he stayed from 1946 to 1952. From 1951 he travelled in the south of France, Italy, Greece and Egypt. Several of his works were devoted to unifying one multiplied element: herds of bulls, or two complementary elements: a man-woman couple, or several disparate elements, for example horses, chariot and driver in *Quadriga* of 1957. From this date onwards he was drawn to abstraction with a geometric tendency.

He participated in the major exhibitions of Die Junge Deutsche Plastik as well as in international exhibitions. In 1949 a retrospective exhibition was held in Munich. He was awarded the Böttcherstrasse prize in Bremen in 1957.

AUCTION RECORDS:
LOS ANGELES, 9 Nov 1977, *Maria Regina Martyrum* (bronze, h. 44 ins / 112 cm) USD 800. MUNICH, 30 May 1980, *Quadriga* (1960, patinated bronze, h. 10 ins / 25.5 cm) DEM 11,000. NEW YORK, 5 May 1982, *Target Figure II* (bronze, h. 21 ins / 53.5 cm) USD 1,500. MUNICH, 29 June 1983, *Target Figure II* (1971, bronze, h. 21 ins / 53.5 cm) DEM 6,200. HAMBURG, 9 June 1986, *Target Figure II* (1971, bronze, h. 21 1/4 ins / 54.2 cm) DEM 5,200. MUNICH, 26 May 1992, *Composition with Calligraphy* (1962, ink, 10 x 14 3/4 ins / 25.5 x 37.5 cm) DEM 3,105. NEW YORK, 14 June 1995, *Derby* (bronze, h. 13 ins / 33 cm, w. 27 ins/68.6 cm) USD 8,050. HEIDELBERG, 11-12 April 1997, *Group of Horsemen* (1959, bronze, 9 x 14 x 2 1/4 ins / 23 x 35.5 x 5.5 cm) DEM 7,200. BERLIN, 1 Oct 1999, *Herd* (c. 1958, black patinated bronze, 2 x 17x13 ins / 6 x 43x34 cm) DEM 33,000. BERLIN, 27 Nov 1999, *Two VIII* (1975, bronze, 66 x 37x10 ins / 168 x 95x26 cm) DEM 50,000. MUNICH, 6 May 2000, *Flora III* (1971, patinated bronze, 23 x 7x7 ins / 58 x 17x17 cm) DEM 23,000. MUNICH, 5 Dec 2000, *Dancing Centaur* (bronze, 14 x 4x4 ins / 35 x 10x10 cm) DEM 22,000. BERLIN, 8 Oct 2001, *Gondolas* (1928, green-brown patinated bronze, 7 x 23x13 ins / 19 x 58x32 cm) DEM 26,000. COLOGNE, 5 Dec 2001, *Untitled - Finish* (bronze, h. 9 ins / 23 cm) DEM 6,500. BERLIN, 30 Nov 2002, *Group* (black-brown patinated bronze, h. 6 ins / 15 cm) EUR 4,000. BERLIN, 30 May 2003, *Call-sign IV* (bronze, h. 94 ins / 238 cm) EUR 68,000. MUNICH, 5 Dec 2003, *Small Quadriga* (gold-brown patinated bronze, 10 x 15x2 ins / 25 x 39x6 cm) EUR 20,000. LONDON, 6 Feb 2004, *Herd* (bronze, 3 x 20x12 ins / 7 x 50x31 cm) GBP 10,000. MUNICH, 14 May 2004, *Derby I* (blackish-brown patinated bronze, 12 x 22x26 ins / 31 x 57x65 cm) EUR 21,000.

KŒNIG, Gustav
German, 20th century.
Born 17 November 1880, in Rudolstadt.
Sculptor.

In 1898 Gustav Kœnig lived in Paris and in 1921 he was awarded the Prix de Rome in Berlin. Thereafter he settled in Berlin-Wilmersdorf.

KŒNIG, Jeanne
French, 19th century.
Born in Thann.
Painter, watercolourist. Flowers.

Jeanne Koenig was a pupil of Madame Regnard. She began exhibiting her works at the salon in 1877.

KOENIG, Johann. See **KÖNIG**

KOENIG, John Franklin
American, 20th century.
Born 24 October 1924, in Seattle (Washington).
From c. 1950 also active in France.
Painter, collage artist, draughtsman, engraver, photographer.

John Franklin Koenig grew up in Seattle, where he made his first acquaintance with far-Eastern art in the local museum. He was drafted in the army in 1943, and saw action in Europe in 1944 and 1945. He bided his time before repatriation by studying at the University for American Soldiers in Biarritz. In 1946, back in Seattle, Koenig studied Romance languages at the University of Washington where he also read art and architecture, having travelled extensively around Mexico. In 1948, he was able to return to France under the G.I. bill and deepen his study of French literature at the Sorbonne. In Paris, he was soon in touch with the artistic and literary vanguard and became a particular friend of Jean-Robert Arnaud with whom he later opened the Galerie Arnaud in St-Germain-des-Près, then a bohemian stamping ground in Paris. He was also, in 1952, co-founder of the art revue *Cimaise* and its dance correspondent. He served as its editorial committee's executive secretary for two terms. After 1980, he returned to Seattle where he curated, in 1984, the exhibition: *Northwest Art in Corporate Collections, 1954-1982*, then, in 1986, the travelling exhibition *Seattle Style* in several provincial museums in France. Since 1988, he has split his time between Paris, Seattle and Central France. In the multi-disciplinary spirit of Bauhaus, he has worked in many media, having at various points in his career practised photography, ceramics, printmaking and textiles.

Whilst attending the University of Washington (Seattle) in the late 1940s, Koenig attended classes in composition, architecture and design, read Moholy-Nagy's *Vision in Motion* and had contacts with the Seattle art scene of Toby, Graves, and Anderson. In 1947, he got to know works by Picasso, Klee, Jean Arp and, a little later, Schwitters and Braque. Miró was also an inspiration. Perhaps better known in France and in Europe than on his native continent, Koenig's vision is no less bathed in the lights of the North-West. His first pieces were figurative as were his gouaches, in the muted colours, the 'calligraphy and mist' of his youth. He also, around 1948, experimented with photography, which he pursued as an art in its own right, and turned his hand to abstract collages, which he saw as a way to 'learn about composition, and to train the eye'. It seems that Paris afforded John Franklin Koenig the possibility of developing an artistic expression where a broad range of influences could be integrated at the confluence of profitable contact with the likes of Ellsworth Kelly, Jack Youngerman, Cesar Domela. His encounter with the Danish lithographer Christian Sorensen in 1954 resulted in 'informal' prints and, in his painting, in the use of superimposed washes which gave free rein to his Abstract Lyricism. In the 1960s, his canvases were taken up with monochrome spaces in ochre, ochre brown or grey-white suggesting movement and spatial intensity, where ridged edges of paint slathered on with a palette knife echoed the edges of torn shapes in earlier collages. From 1965, a 'geometric cosmos' shaped the space of his paintings, triangles and thick impastos being a constitutive part of their composition. Koenig's work and its development can only be understood in the context of what he has seen and heard: his criss-crossing of North America; his visits to Japan, the first one in 1960 being a revelation; the gentle lights of central France; jazz; and dance. Koenig speaks of painting as 'an act of love,' saying, 'The artist must be on the search for beauty and perfection in his own life through the work'.

He has taken part in numerous collective exhibitions: more recently, *Abstractions Lyriques - Paris 1945-1955* (*Lyrical Abstractions - Paris 1945-1955*) and *Aspects de l'art abstrait des années cinquante* (*Aspects of 50s Abstraction*). He regularly exhibits in Paris at the Salon Grands et Jeunes d'Aujourd'hui.

He has shown his works in solo exhibitions since 1948, many of them at Galerie Arnaud in Paris and in numerous venues in North America, specially in Seattle, in Europe, and around the world, in Istanbul, Calcutta, Rangoon, Bamako. He had retrospectives: in 1980, Tacoma; 1983, Montreal; 1985, Reykjavik (prints); 1986, Seattle; 1988, *40 Years of Works*, Bellevue (Washington); 1989, Paris Art Centre; 1990, *Rétrospective de l'Œuvre gravé* (*Retrospective of Engravings*) in the French provinces; 1990-1992, *Œuvres des années 1980* (*Works of the 1980s*), a travelling exhibition in 21 French cities. He was awarded the Prix de la Critique at the Biennale de Paris; Commandeur of the Ordre des Arts et Lettres and the prestigious Médaille de Vermeil de la Ville de Paris.

Bibliography:

Wescher, Herta, '*J.F. Koenig*' in *Cimaise série III* n° 3, periodical, Paris, January-February1956. Ragon, Michel, *L'Aventure de l'Art abstrait*, Laffont, Paris, 1956. Restany, Pierre, *J.- F. Koenig et le Lyrisme de l'étendue*, Éd. Arnaud, Paris, 1960. Deroudille, René, *J.- F. Koenig*, Audin, Paris, 1961. *J.F. Koenig*, exhibition catalogue, Paris, New York, Seattle, 1964 (lettres avec Marc-Albert Levin). Koenig, J.F., '*Ikebana de l'Esprit*' in *Cimaise* n° 78, periodical, Paris, 1966. *J.- F. Koenig*, exhibition catalogue, Paris, New York, Seattle, 1969 (lettres avec Michel Ragon). Arnaud, J.R./Koenig, John-Franklin, *Dialogue. Quelques œuvres de 1969-1971*, Gal. Arnaud, Paris, 1971. Cabanne, Pierre, *Focus, dictionnaire des Arts*, Bordas, Paris, 1971. Ragon, Michel/Seuphor, Michel, '*Art abstrait*' in vol. III et IV, Maeght, Paris, 1973-1974. *Fuji Television*, film, Tokyo, 1977. Koenig, J.F., *La Danse contemporaine*, Fayard, Paris, 1980. Thorn-Petit, Liliane, *Portraits d'artistes*, film, RTL, Luxembourg, 1982. Xuriguera, Gérard, *Regards sur la peinture contemporaine*, Arted, Paris, 1983. '*J.F. Koenig*' in *Cimaise* n° 171-172, periodical, Paris, 1984. Pleynet, Marcelin/Ragon, Michel, '*L'Art abstrait, 1970-1987*' in vol. V, Maeght, Paris, 1988. Persin, Patrick-Gilles, *John-Franklin Koenig - œuvres des années 1980*, exhibition catalogue, Présence de l'Art contemporain, Angers, 1990. Cabanne, Pierre, *John-Franklin Koenig - Rétrospective 1947-1992*, exhibition catalogue, Musées de Metz, Metz, musée Toulouse-Lautrec, Albi, Centre régional d'Art contemporain Le 19, Montbéliard, 1993. Harambourg, Lydia, *L'École de Paris 1945- 1965. Dictionnaire des peintres*, Ides et Calendes, Neuchâtel, 1993. Persin, Patrick-Gilles, *J.-F. Koenig "Les Collages"*, Fragments, Paris, 1994. Koenig, John-Franklin/Harambourg, Lydia (preface), *Voyons voir*, Éd. Main d'œuvre, Nice, 1999.

Museums and Galleries:

Albi (Mus. Toulouse-Lautrec) - Basel (Kunstmus.) - Grenoble (Mus. de Grenoble) - Houston (MFA) - Luxembourg (Mus. national d'histoire et d'art) - Lyons (MBA) - Montreal (MAC) - Montreal (MBA) - Nantes (MBA) - Osaka (National MA) - Ottawa (NG. of Canada) - Paris (BNF) - Paris (MAMVP) - Paris (MNAM-CCI) - San Antonio (Marion Koogler McNay AM) - Seattle (AM) - Seattle (Henry AG, University of Washington) - Tacoma (AM) - Tokyo (National MMA) - Tokyo (National Mus. of Western Art) - Venice (MCA).

Auction records:

Paris, 22 June 1984, *Cleft* (1980, collage, 20 x 14 1/4 ins / 51 x 36 cm) FRF 35,000. Paris, 24 June 1987, *Attendant Oki II* (1961, oil on canvas, 31 1/2 x 31 1/2 ins / 80 x 80 cm) FRF 16,000. Paris, 20 March 1988, *Untitled* (1957, gouache and collage, 18 x 18 ins / 46 x 46 cm) FRF 10,500. Paris, 8 Nov 1989, *Bag's Blues* (1966, oil on canvas, 31 1/2 x 31 1/2 ins / 80 x 80 cm) FRF 42,000. Paris, 7 Oct 1991, *Barytesche* (1974, oil on canvas, 47 1/4 x 23 1/2 ins / 120 x 60 cm) FRF 10,000. Paris, 27 Oct 1994, *Head of a Man* (acrylic/paper, 16 1/4 x 12 1/4 ins / 41 x 31 cm) FRF 15,600. Paris, 19 Oct 1997, *Zones: 121, May 1969, n° 21* (1969, oil on canvas, 69 1/4 x 35 ins / 176 x 89 cm) FRF 11,000. Paris, 19 Oct 2003, *Carvoys* (1972, oil on canvas, 72 x 37 ins / 182 x 94 cm) EUR 1,800.

KŒNIG, Joseph

Belgian, 20th century.
Born 1878; died 1961.
Painter, draughtsman. Figure compositions, portraits.

Joseph Kœnig was from 1925 a member of the Groupe Moderne d'Art and the L'Envol circle.

Museums and Galleries:

Liège - Rheims - Verviers.

KŒNIG, Jules Raymond

French, 19th - 20th century.
Born 2 August 1872, in Ste-Marie-aux-Mines (Haut-Rhin).
Painter, watercolourist. Landscapes.

Jules Raymond Kœnig studied under Luc-Olivier Merson, Jean-Paul Laurens and Gustave Moreau. He made numerous trips to Italy and Belgium, returning with a number of studies. His landscapes in oil or pastel are executed in large areas of bright tones which reveal the influence of Gauguin. Kœnig exhibited at the Salon d'Automne, the Salon de la Société Nationale des Beaux-Arts and the Salon des Tuileries. He received a commendation at the Exposition Universelle in Paris in 1900.

Museums and Galleries:

Chalon-sur-Saône: *River at Pont-Aven* (1902) - Mulhouse: *St Francis*.

KŒNIG, Julius Theodor, or König

German, 19th century.
Born 7 December 1818, in Dresden; died 16 June 1845, in Starnberg.
Painter. History painting.

Kœnig was a pupil of Bendemann.

KŒNIG, Karl

Polish, 19th - 20th century.
Born 1857, in Stryy; died 1917, in Cracow.
Painter.

Karl Koenig studied in Munich. Many of his paintings depict views of the Cracow area.

KŒNIG, Wilhelm

Dutch, 17th century.
Died c. 1640.
Active in Nijmegen.
Sculptor.

Wilhelm Kœnig was the pupil of J.R. Hofman, of Trier. He completed his diploma work in Munich in 1602, where he was a member of the guild.

KŒNIGER, Walter

German, 20th century.
Born 6 May 1881, in Germany; died 1943.
Active in USA.
Painter. Landscapes.

Walter Kœniger was taught by Duecker and Von Gebhard and was a member of the Salmagundi Club in New York. He lived for much of his life in the Catskill Mountains in New York State. He is best known for his winter landcapes.

Auction records:

Los Angeles, 24 June 1980, *Winter Afternoon* (1929, oil on canvas, 38 x 45 ins / 96.5 x 114.3 cm) USD 4,250. New York,

29 May 1981, *After the First Snowfall* (1928, oil on canvas, 38 x 45 1/4 ins / 96.5 x 115 cm) USD 5,750. NEW YORK, 21 Oct 1983, *Streams in a Snowy Forest* (oil on canvas, 38 x 45 ins / 96.5 x 114.3 cm) USD 3,750. NEW YORK, 31 Jan 1985, *A Stream in Winter* (oil on canvas, 25 x 30 ins / 63.5 x 76.2 cm) USD 1,700. NEW YORK, 26 June 1986, *Winter Landscape* (1927, oil on canvas, 32 x 32 ins / 81.5 x 81.5 cm) USD 3,400. NEW YORK, 20 March 1987, *Mountain Waterfalls* (oil on canvas, 32 x 45 ins / 81.5 x 114.5 cm) USD 3,000. NEW YORK, 24 Jan 1989, *Summer Landscape with Birches* (oil on canvas, 31 1/2 x 31 1/2 ins / 80 x 80 cm) USD 3,850. NEW YORK, 16 March 1990, *Mountain Stream in Winter* (oil on canvas, 34 x 36 3/4 ins / 86.3 x 93.6 cm) USD 9,900. NEW YORK, 23 May 1990, *Vermont Landscape in Winter* (oil on canvas, 35 x 37 ins / 89.2 x 94 cm) USD 10,450. NEW YORK, 30 Nov 1990, *The Isolated Hole* (oil on canvas, 25 x 30 1/4 ins / 63.5 x 76.8 cm) USD 7,700. NEW YORK, 4 Dec 1992, *Winter Landscape* (oil on canvas, 32 x 32 ins / 81.1 x 81.2 cm) USD 12,100. NEW YORK, 22 Sept 1993, *Distant Hills in a Winter Landscape* (1928, oil on canvas, 35 x 37 ins / 89 x 94 cm) USD 5,175. NEW YORK, 28 Sept 1995, *Winter Solitude* (oil on canvas, 20 x 24 ins / 50.8 x 61 cm) USD 1,725.

KOENIGSWIESER. See **KÖNIGSWIESER**

KOENRAAD. See **CONRADUS Abraham**

KŒPKE, Carl Friedrich

German, 19th century.
Active in Berlin.
Painter, miniaturist. History painting, portraits.

Kœpke exhibited at the Berlin academy in 1834.

KŒPKE, Robert

German, 20th century.
Born 1893, in Bremen.
Painter, engraver.

BIBLIOGRAPHY:

Beaumont-Maillet, Laure/Woimant, Françoise/Pernoud, Emmanuel, *De Bonnard à Baselitz - Dix ans d'enrichissements du Cabinet des estampes 1978-1988*, exhibition catalogue, Bibliothèque Nationale de France, Paris, 1992.

KOEPP, Wolfgang. See **KÖPP**

KŒPPEL, Reinhold

German, 20th century.
Born 21 April 1887, in Oschersleben.
Painter, illustrator. Landscapes.

Reinhold Kœppel executed views of the Bavarian forest, where he lived, as well as book illustrations.

KŒPPELIN, Georges

French, 19th century.
Born in Colmar.
Painter, watercolourist. Landscapes.

Georges Koeppelin was a pupil of Calame. He began exhibiting at the salon in 1870.

KŒPPING, Karl

German, 19th - 20th century.
Born 24 June 1848, in Dresden; died 15 July 1914, in Berlin.
Painter, engraver. Designs (glassware).
Jugendstil.

After studying chemistry, Karl Koepping studied painting at the Akademie der Bildenden Künste in Munich and engraving with Charles Albert Waltner in Paris. He started out as a painter and engraver in Munich. In 1891 he was made a professor at the Akademie der Künste, Berlin, where he taught both design and engraving. He began to work on glass around 1895. From 1896 he was one of the co-editors (another was Julius Meier-Graefe) of *Pan*, the magazine of the Berlin Symbolists. He became a member of the academy in Berlin in 1889.

Karl Koepping achieved a considerable reputation as an engraver, first for reproduction then for his original prints, but was one of the most famous Jugendstil artists in the area of glass. He produced tall, tapering pieces full of virtuosity but characterised by their simplicity. He was particularly noted for his flower glass goblets (he used the technique of glass-blowing). With Friedrich Zitzmann, a glass-blowing technician, he created glassware with colours of subtle beauty. He ended this co-operation in 1896 when Zitzmann broke his agreement not to use the glassware models for his own profit. Koepping then worked on glass items for studios in Ilmenau (Thuringia). His pieces were sold in Siegfried Bing's 'L'Art Nouveau' shop in Paris.

He exhibited in Paris, where he was highly commended for an engraving in 1879, received a third place medal in 1882, a second place medal in 1887, and the *Grand Prix* in 1889 (with the title of Chevalier de la Légion d'Honneur) and again in 1900, at the Paris Exposition Universelle.

BIBLIOGRAPHY:

Umelecka Kolonie Darmstadt, 1899-1914, exhibition catalogue, Narodni Galerie, Prague, 1989.

MUSEUMS AND GALLERIES:

COPENHAGEN (Danish Mus. of Decorative Art): *Three Stem Glasses* - KARLSRUHE (Badisches Landesmus.): *Stem Glass* (1899).

KŒRBECKE, Johann

German, 15th century.
Painter.
Münster School.

Johann Kœrbecke was the leading painter of the Münster School, whose influence, in the second half of the fifteenth century, overtook that of the Westphalian School. This earlier movement, inspired by its leading painter, Konrad Soest, had put down roots as far afield as Thuringia and Brandenburg.

Kœrbecke was the artist who introduced the Flemish style of painting to Germany. His most characteristic work is the *Crucifixion*, produced in Amelsbüren, which dates from around 1450 and is now in Münster. Although he was the leading painter in Münster for a long time, he also taught students who themselves gained a reputation on a par with his. These artists, such as Derik Baegert, the Heinrich brothers and Victor Dünwege, established the importance of Münster as an artistic centre. In 1457, Kœrbecke painted a major altarpiece for the Cistercian monastery in Marienfeld, Westphalia, various parts of which are now in museums and collections in Münster, Chicago, Avignon (*Resurrection of Christ* in the Calvet Museum) and Berlin. Influences on his work include Stefan Lochner, and the realism of Maître de Flémalle.

MUSEUMS AND GALLERIES:

AVIGNON (Mus. Calvet): *Resurrection of Christ* (1457) - BERLIN: fragment of an altarpiece from Marienfeld (1457) - CHICAGO: fragment of an altarpiece from Marienfeld (1457) - MÜNSTER: *Crucifixion* (c. 1450); fragment of an altarpiece from Marienfeld (1457).

AUCTION RECORDS:

LONDON, 24 June 1938, *Presentation in the Temple*, GBP 3,570. LONDON, 5 July 1984, *St Peter; St Michael* (oil on canvas, two panels, 79 1/2 x 25in/202 x 63.5cm and 81 x 26in/206 x 66cm) GBP 9,000.

KŒRLE, Pancraz

German, 19th century.
Born 21 October 1823, in Munich; died 23 April 1875, in Munich.
Painter. Genre scenes, portraits.

Kœrle studied at the Munich academy and with the porrait painter Bernhard. He spent some time in Vienna. On returning to Munich in 1848, he adopted the Rococo style.

Museums and Galleries:
Cologne: *Horseman* - Leipzig (Mus. der Bildenden Künste): *The Broken Pitcher*.
Auction records:
Munich, 30 Nov 1978, *The Servant Girl and the Rose* (1868, oil on canvas, 32 3/4 x 26 1/2 ins / 83 x 67.5 cm) DEM 4,500. Lucerne, 20 May 1980, *Young Man in an Interior* (oil on wood, 12 x 9 1/2 ins / 30.5 x 24 cm) CHF 6,500. Munich, 27 Sept 2000, *Bird Lover* (1859, oil on canvas, 20 x 17 ins / 52 x 43 cm) DEM 4,000. London, 18 June 2003, *Serving the Refreshments* (1866, oil on canvas, 21 x 17 ins / 53 x 43 cm) GBP 1,500. Cologne, 3 July 2003, *Love Token* (1867, oil on canvas, 22 x 19 ins / 56 x 47 cm) EUR 2,300.

KŒRNER, Edmund
German, 20th century.
Born 23 August 1873, in Dresden.
Painter. Portraits, genre scenes, landscapes, urban landscapes.
Edmund Kœrner was the pupil of Gotthard Kuehl. He worked mostly in Dresden, painting the local beauty spots. He participated in the Grosse Berliner Kunstausstellung of 1909.
Auction records:
Amsterdam, 19 Sept 1989, *View of the Castle of Dresden with a Fountain in the Foreground* (oil on canvas/panel, 24 1/2 x 20 ins / 62 x 51 cm) NLG 1,035.

KŒRNER, Ernest Karl Eugen
German, 19th - 20th century.
Born 3 November 1846, in Stibbe (Prussia); died 30 July 1927, in Berlin.
Painter, pastellist. Seascapes, landscapes.
Orientalism.
Ernest Kœrner was a pupil of Eschke and Biermann. He travelled extensively, visiting North France, Italy and England, and in 1873 and 1874 his travels took him through Egypt, Syria, Palestine and Turkey. He received a medal in Vienna in 1873, Philadelphia in 1876, Berlin in 1887, the Melbourne medal in 1888 and the gold medal in Berlin in 1891.
Museums and Galleries:
Birmingham: *Temple of Edfon* - Hamburg: *Sunset; Beirut* - Kaliningrad: *Landscape; Cleopatra's Needle*.
Auction records:
New York, 15 Dec 1978, *Banks of the Nile* (1873, oil on canvas, 26 x 41 ins / 66 x 104 cm) USD 2,200. New York, 28 Oct 1986, *Mosques at Sunset* (1879, oil on canvas, 33 x 49 1/2 ins / 83.8 x 125.8 cm) USD 9,500. London, 19 Nov 1993, *Palm Grove at Luxor* (1879, oil on canvas, 32 3/4 x 49 1/2 ins / 83 x 126 cm) GBP 25,300. London, 18 March 1994, *Excavation of the Sphinx* (1887, oil on canvas, 39 3/4 x 59 1/2 ins / 101 x 151.1 cm) GBP 43,300. Paris, 7 Nov 1994, *Constantinople* (1910, pastel heightened with gouache, 15 x 23 1/4 ins / 38 x 59 cm) FRF 30,000. New York, 1 Nov 1995, *The Temple of Karnak, the Large Pillared Hall* (1890, oil on canvas, 31 1/4 x 18 1/4 ins / 79.4 x 46.4 cm) USD 26,450. London, 17 Nov 1995, *On the Banks of the Nile* (1889, oil on canvas, 26 x 40 1/2 ins / 66 x 103 cm) GBP 10,580. Vienna, 29-30 Oct 1996, *The Acropolis, Athens* (1911, oil on canvas, 20 1/4 x 39 1/2 ins / 51.5 x 100.5 cm) ATS 138,000. London, 21 Nov 1996, *The Pyramids of Gizeh* (1927, oil on canvas, 33 1/4 x 49 3/4 ins / 84.5 x 126.5 cm) GBP 11,270. London, 21 March 1997, *The Palace of Dolmabahçe on the Bosphorus, Istanbul* (1923, oil on canvas, 32 x 47 1/2 ins / 81 x 120.5 cm) GBP 9,200. London, 11 June 1997, *Coastal Scene in North Africa* (1877, oil on canvas, 31 1/2 x 49 1/4 ins / 80 x 125 cm) GBP 21,850.

KŒRNER, Friedrich Alexander
French, 19th century.
Born 1815, in Brunswick; died c. 1850, in Brunswick.
Painter. Genre scenes.
Friedrich Koerner exhibited at the Salon in 1845 and in 1848. he died young.

KŒRNER, Henry
Austrian, 20th century.
Born 1915.
Active in the USA.
Painter. Figure compositions.
Henry Kœrner left Vienna in 1938, fleeing the Nazi regime and settling in New York in 1939, where he was active as a graphic artist. He began to paint in 1943. The bold realism of his paintings of the 1940s was emphasised by the oblique range of colours of his perspectives. The subject and style of his paintings are to some extent comparable to the work of Paul Cadmus and Philip Evergood whose pictures were also shown in the Midtown Gallery where Kœrner exhibited every year between 1947 and 1952. He had made his debut in Berlin in 1947 in a show which met with success from both the public and critics. The Westmoreland County Museum of Art of Greensburg in Pennsylvania held a retrospective of his work in 1971 and the Carnegie Institute, Pittsburgh organised the exhibition entitled *From Vienna to Pittsburgh - The Art of Henry Kœrner* in 1983.
Auction records:
Los Angeles, 24 June 1980, *Fire on the Beach* (oil on card remounted on hardboard, 16 1/4 x 21 1/2 ins / 41.2 x 54.3 cm) USD 2,100. New York, 12 April 1991, *Pond* (oil/synthetic resin, 30 x 38 ins / 76.2 x 96.5 cm) USD 52,250.

KOERNER, William Henry David
American, 20th century.
Born 1878; died 1938.
Painter, draughtsman, illustrator. Genre scenes.
William Henry David Koerner worked for the Saturday Evening Post, illustrating short stories in the 1920s.
Auction records:
New York, 18 Nov 1977, *Old Pioneer* (oil on canvas, 18 x 30 ins / 45.7 x 76.2 cm) USD 3,600. Los Angeles, 6 June 1978, *Mounted Range Rider* (1931, watercolour and gouache/mounted paper/card, 13 1/2 x 12 1/4 ins / 34.3 x 31.4 cm) USD 1,400. Los Angeles, 15 Oct 1979, *Incantation* (1922, oil on canvas, 36 x 34 ins / 91.5 x 86.5 cm) USD 6,250. New York, 23 April 1981, *When Worries May Occur* (1929, oil on canvas, 22 x 42 1/4 ins / 55.9 x 107 cm) USD 9,000. New York, 6 Dec 1984, *Feathers, Buckskin and Beads* (1931, oil on card, 36 x 60 ins / 91.4 x 152.4 cm) USD 24,000. New York, 24 April 1985, *In Pursuit of Hicks* (1915, oil on canvas, 24 1/4 x 30 ins / 61.6 x 76.2 cm) USD 3,700. New York, 5 Dec 1986, *Illustration for the Trusty Knaves* (1931, oil on canvas, 36 1/4 x 30 ins / 91.8 x 76.2 cm) USD 12,000. New York, 4 Dec 1987, *Herd Crossing a River* (1923, oil on canvas, 24 x 36 ins / 61 x 91.5 cm) USD 10,000. New York, 24 Jan 1989, *Illustration for the Novel 'White Men'* (1918, oil on canvas, 27 1/2 x 35 1/2 ins / 70 x 90 cm) USD 7,425. New York, 24 Jan 1990, *Playground* (ink/paper/card, 15 x 16 1/4 ins / 38 x 41.1 cm) USD 1,100. New York, 26 Sept 1991, *Well Seated* (oil on canvas, 22 x 40 1/4 ins / 56 x 102.3 cm) USD 10,450. New York, 18 Dec 1991, *Distribution* (1917, oil on card in grisaille, 35 1/2 x 25 1/2 ins / 90.2 x 64.8 cm) USD 2,640. New York, 31 March 1993, *Figures in Costumes* (1930, oil on canvas, 27 3/4 x 39 1/2 ins / 70.5 x 100.3 cm) USD 2,070. New York, 14 Sept 1995, *Hunters with a Mule Train* (1922, oil on canvas, 22 x 36 ins / 55.9 x 91.4 cm) USD 11,500. Hayden, 31 July 1999, *Calling Doves* (oil on paper, 9 x 4 ins / 24 x 10 cm) USD 2,500. Hayden, 31 July 1999, *Cattle Stampede* (oil on canvas, 28 x 40 ins / 71 x 102 cm) USD 25,000. New York, 25 May 2000, *Indian Mother* (1934, oil on canvas, 36 x 24 ins / 91 x 61 cm) USD 45,000. New York, 4 Nov 2000, *Cowboy and Burros Crossing Desolate Landscape* (oil on canvas, 26 x 36 ins / 66 x 91 cm) USD 18,000. New York, 28 Nov 2001, *Hunters* (oil on canvas, 26 x 36 ins / 66 x 91 cm) USD 130,000. St Louis, 1 Dec 2001, *Bucking Bronco* (oil on

canvas, 36 x 30 ins / 91 x 76 cm) USD 28,000. BOSTON, 22 March 2002, *Boston Dock Scene* (oil on canvas) USD 5,000. LOS ANGELES, 20 Nov 2002, *I Apologize, Sure* (1918, oil on canvas, 24 x 36 ins / 61 x 91 cm) USD 30,000. DOWNINGTON, 21 May 2004, *Western Scene* (oil on canvas, 36 x 16 ins / 91 x 41 cm) USD 4,800.

KŒRTEN, Johanna, or Koorten
later Mme Adriaan Blok
Dutch, 17th - 18th century.
Born 17 November 1650, in Amsterdam; died 28 December 1715, in Amsterdam.
Draughtswoman.

KŒRTTGÉ, Albert
French, 19th century.
Born 21 January 1861, in Strasbourg.
Engraver (etching).

Albert Koerttgé was a pupil of Meyer Basel. He received an honourable mention in 1908.

KOESTER, Alexander Max. See **KÖSTER**

KŒTS, Andries
Dutch, 17th century.
Born 1622, in Haarlem.
Active in Haarlem.
Painter. Religious subjects, still-lifes.

Andries Kœts was the son of Roelof Kœts the Elder, and was active around 1633. He entered the guild at Haarlem on 2 November 1655, and was in Amsterdam in 1664.

AUCTION RECORDS:
AMSTERDAM, 17 Nov 1993, *Christ Driving the Traders out of the Temple* (oil on panel, 29 1/2 x 41 1/2 ins / 75 x 105.5 cm) NLG 6,670.

KŒTS, Hermanus, or Coets
Dutch, 17th - 18th century.
Born 1663, in Middelburg; died soon after 1711, probably in Amsterdam.
Painter, engraver. Portraits, seascapes.

Hermanus Kœts was the pupil of Blychood and of the English artist Thuardt in Nijmegen. He moved about 1719 to Amsterdam. He also copied the old masters, and made wooden models of boats. He is particularly remembered for: *Title Page for the Work by A. Aleroyns 'Naughty Actions and Harp Songs'*, 1711.

AUCTION RECORDS:
PARIS, 21 Feb 1925, *Seascape in Stormy Weather*, FRF 1,100. PARIS, 27 April 1988, *Boats and a Vessel in a Rough Sea* (oil on panel, 14 1/4 x 18 1/4 ins / 36.5 x 46.5 cm) FRF 8,100.

KŒTS, P.
Dutch, 18th century.
Painter. Portraits.

KŒTS, Roelof, the Elder
Dutch, 17th century.
Born c. 1592
in Haarlem, 1 January 1655 according to Bredius.
Active in Haarlem.
Painter. Still-lifes.

Roelof Kœts the Elder was enrolled in the guild at Haarlem in 1642. He is also reputed to have been a musician.

AUCTION RECORDS:
PARIS, 25 April 1951, *Still-life with Fruit*, FRF 85,000. PARIS, 28 May 1954, *Still-life with Parrot*, FRF 405,000. LONDON, 16 Nov 1960, *Still-life*, GBP 380. MILAN, 29 Oct 1964, *Still-life*, ITL 2,000,000. LUCERNE, 26 June 1965, *Still-life with Glass of Wine*, CHF 12,000. LONDON, 27 March 1968, *Still-life*, GBP 1,700. LONDON, 26 March 1969, *Still-life with Fruit*, GBP 1,400. LONDON, 12 July 1972, *Still-life*, GBP 2,600. LONDON, 11 July 1973, *Still-life*, GBP 6,500. ZURICH, 2 Nov 1979, *Still-life* (oil on canvas, 21 1/4 x 30 ins / 54 x 76 cm) CHF 30,000. NEW YORK, 4 Nov 1982, *Still-life* (oil on canvas, 29 x 42 ins / 73.5 x 106.5 cm) USD 13,000. LONDON, 12 Oct 1983, *Still-life* (oil on panel, 26 1/2 x 32 1/4 ins / 67.5 x 82 cm) GBP 8,000. AMSTERDAM, 29 May 1986, *Still-life with Fruit, Glass, Knife* (oil on panel, 29 x 41 1/2 ins / 73.5 x 105.5 cm) NLG 29,000. NEW YORK, 12 Jan 1989, *Still-life with a Fish, Bread and a Peeled Lemon in Dishes, a Basket of Grapes and a Glass on an Entablature Covered with a Cloth* (oil on panel, 29 1/2 x 43 ins / 75 x 109 cm) USD 99,000. MILAN, 4 April 1989, *Still-life with Grapes and Pears* (oil on panel, 20 x 26 ins / 51 x 66 cm) ITL 34,000,000. NEW YORK, 31 May 1989, *Still-life with a Silver Mould Upside-down in a Dish, a Glass on a Pedestal, Bread, Ham and Fruit on an Entablature Covered with a Cloth* (oil on panel, 25 x 35 ins / 63.5 x 88 cm) USD 33,000. LONDON, 9 July 1993, *Basket of Black and White Grapes on an Entablature* (oil on panel, 18 x 25 ins / 46 x 63.5 cm) GBP 4,830. ZURICH, 8 Sept 1999, *Still-life with Fruit in a Delft Bowl, Blackberry Pie and Pewter Tableware* (oil on canvas, 29 x 42 ins / 74 x 107 cm) CHF 45,000. COLOGNE, 6 April 2000, *Still-life with Little Feast* (1652, oil on canvas, 29 x 38 ins / 74 x 96 cm) DEM 11,000. VIENNA, 22 March 2001, *Still-life with Grapes and Basket of Pomegranates* (oil on panel, 17 x 26 ins / 44 x 65 cm) ATS 130,000. ANTWERP, 4 Dec 2001, *Still-life with Fruit* (1636, oil on wood, 26 x 34 ins / 65 x 87 cm) BEF 260,000. NEW YORK, 24 Jan 2002, *Still-life with Fish, Bread, Peeled Lemon, Grapes in a Basket, Salt and Rummer on a Draped Table* (oil on panel, 30 x 43 ins / 75 x 109 cm) USD 200,000. LONDON, 9 July 2002, *Basket of Fruit with Rummer of White Wine and Sliced Lemon on a Pewter Plate on a Draped Table* (oil on panel, 20 x 26 ins / 51 x 67 cm) GBP 3,000. VIENNA, 27 March 2003, *Still-life with Wine Glasses and Nuts in Ming Dish* (oil on panel, 22 x 27 ins / 56 x 68 cm) EUR 18,000.

KŒTS, Roelof, the Younger
Dutch, 17th - 18th century.
Born probably on 16 January 1655, in Zwolle; died in Zwolle, where he was buried on 28 June 1725 according to von Wurzbach, on 4 July according to the catalogue of Amsterdam Museum.
Painter. Portraits.

Roelof Kœts the Younger, the pupil of Gerard Terborch, is thought to have painted a large number of portraits. He worked in Zwolle, Middelburg and The Hague.

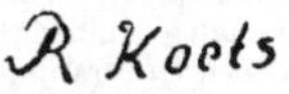

MUSEUMS AND GALLERIES:
AMSTERDAM: *Portrait of a Pastor* (1665); *Lucien Trip van Warfumborg, his Wife and their Children in a Landscape* (1689) - LILLE: *Portrait of a Woman*.

AUCTION RECORDS:
PARIS, 1881, *Portrait*, FRF 900. PARIS, 20 May 1925, *Portrait of a Prelate*, FRF 380. AMSTERDAM, 10 Nov 1992, *Portrait of a Gentleman Wearing a Suit of Armour, with his Right Hand on his Helmet* (oil on canvas, 16 3/4 x 13 3/4 ins / 42.8 x 35.2 cm) NLG 1,725. NEW YORK, 27 Jan 2000, *Grapes on a Stone Ledge* (oil on panel, 17 x 25 ins / 42 x 64 cm) USD 13,000. GRAVENHAGE, 24 April 2002, *Portrait of a Standing Gentleman* (oil on canvas, 17 x 13 ins / 42 x 34 cm) EUR 1,800. CHICAGO, 19 Oct 2003, *Portrait* (oil on canvas, 17 x 14 ins / 43 x 36 cm) USD 1,800.

KŒTSIER, Hans
Dutch, 20th century.
Born 1930, in Amsterdam or in Utrecht.
Painter, draughtsman, lithographer, photomontage artist. Murals.

Hans Kœtsier was invited to the Paris Biennale in 1965 and exhibited in Amsterdam, notably at the Stedelijk Museum in 1966. While he is thought to be in the line of descent from Pop Art - although others counted him as an inheritor of Minimal Art - he limited his universe to painting monograms (comparable to the way Robert Indiana emblazoned pictures with lettering) or fragments of figures which he exploded. His later works involved the use of photomontages. He also carried out large decorative murals for the airport at Amsterdam-Schiphol and for the University at Delft.

KOETSU, real name Honami Koetsu; nickname Jirosaburo; artist names Taikyan, Jitokusai, Kuchuan, Tokuyusai, Ohosha, Taikyoan
Japanese, 16th - 17th century.
Born 1558; died 1637.
Active in Kyoto.
Painter, potter, draughtsman, calligrapher, decorative artist. Portraits, flowers.

Koetsu, a great calligrapher, painter, potter, decorator and patron of the arts, played a major role in the cultured world of Kyoto in the early 17th century. At this period, the city's great merchants, grown wealthy from trade with China, were active in the cultural life of the city, giving themselves over to the tea ceremony, flower arranging, poetry and calligraphy. Koetsu was born into this potent environment to a celebrated family of sword polishers and appraisers who enjoyed the trust of the Ashikaga governors. He received a scrupulous education and followed in his father's footsteps, while cultivating the art of calligraphy. With Konoe Nobutada and Shokado Shojo, he is reckoned as one of the Three Brushes of the early century. His art signals a return to the elegant calligraphy of the Heian period (794-1184), renowned for the beauty of its *kana* (Japanese characters).

In 1614 the shogun, Tokugawa Ieyasu (1542-1616), granted Koetsu permission and assistance to set up in the village of Takagamine, in the hills north of Kyoto, with a few literati (scholar-artist) friends. He surrounded himself with the finest craftsmen of the day: potters, lacquerers, papermakers, brushmakers. It may have been then that he started working together with the painter Tawaraya Sotatsu (fl. c. 1630), his brother-in-law. Sotatsu, who is counted as one of the greatest artists in the history of Japanese art, owned a *machi-e* (painting studio) specialising in the manufacture of fans and decorated paper. The two men worked together on scrolls, Sotatsu creating sumptuous decorations in gold and silver ink, Koetsu writing calligraphic versions of poems from the Heian period. In the minutely-studied rhythms of their writing and decoration we can see how intimate an understanding existed between the two men, and how profound was their understanding of ancient literature.

Several of these scrolls and albums survive (the oldest dating back to 1606). The best, *Flowers of the Four Seasons*, *Lotus Blossoms* and *Deer*, attain a new sythesis of form recalling works of the Heian period, where the movement and the accents of the brushes brilliantly echo Koetsu's slightly mannered and resolutely decorative calligraphic style. This influence is likely to have remained central in his artistic development. Koetsu's name is also linked to pottery for the tea ceremony, for which he produced a number of highly individual pieces, and to several famous pieces of lacquer-ware for which he supplied the decorative motifs and calligraphy. Although they had no direct disciples of any great talent, Koetsu and Sotatsu were to be the key influences on Korin (1658-1716), whose grandfather was among those lucky enough to have worked in the refined circles of Takagamine.

BIBLIOGRAPHY:

Akiyama, Terukazu, *La Peinture japonaise*, Skira, Geneva, 1961. Paul-David, Madeleine, *'Kôetsu Hon Ami'* in *Encyclopædia Universalis* vol. IX, Paris, 1971. Guth, Christine, *Japanese Art of the Edo Period*, Calmann and King, London, 1996. Yamane, Yuzo/Naito, Masato/Clark, Timothy, *Rimpa Art from the Idemitsu Collection, Tokyo*, London, 1998. Fischer, Felice (ed.), *The Arts of Hon'Ami Koetsu: Japanese Renaissance Master*, exhibition catalogue, Museum of Art, Philadelphia, 2000. Little, Stephen, *The Alsdorf Collection of Japanese Paintings*, Honolulu, 2003.

AUCTION RECORDS:

NEW YORK, 16 April 1988, *The Poet Minamoto no Kimitada* (ink and colour on paper, $12\frac{3}{4}$ x $9\frac{1}{4}$ ins / 32.5 x 23.3 cm) USD 7,700.

KOFFERMANS, Isabelle or Marcellus.
See **COFFERMANS**

KOGA, Harue
Japanese, 20th century.
Born 1895, in Kyushu; died 1933.
Painter, poet.

Koga Harue trained as a Buddhist monk, subsequently becoming a poet and then a painter. Influenced by Paul Klee and Giorgio de Chirico, he played an important role in the development of early 20th-century Japanese painting, introducing echoes of the modernist movements in Europe, such as cubism, futurism, constructivism and especially surrealism, which he can be said to represent. His pictures from the late 1920s are full of unusual and bizarre figuration. He exhibited regularly at the Nika (two disciplines - sculpture and painting) Salon and was selected for the 4th Nikakai Exhibition in 1917.

KOGA, Kikuo
Japanese, 20th century.
Born 1934, on Hokkaido.
Painter.

Koga has exhibited regularly at the Nika (two disciplines - sculpture and painting) Salon since 1965.

KOGAN, Anna
Russian, 20th century.
Born 1902; died 1974.
Painter.
Suprematism.
Unovis group.

Born Hannah A. Nathanson, she was the pupil of Malevich at the school of art in Vitbsk from 1919 and 1922 and a member of the Unovis group from 1918 to 1923 in Petrograd (now St Petersburg), participating in many of their exhibitions, including *Artists of All Persuasions and Styles*. In 1924-25, together with the sculptor Pavlov, she worked as Malevich's assistant at the state institute of artistic culture in Leningrad (now St Petersburg) on the construction of his three-dimensional series, *Architectons*.

In the 1920s she was still working on Abstract art projects but then transformed her initial Suprematist-type abstractions into a less formalised style.

BIBLIOGRAPHY:

Nakov, Andréi, *Les Écrits de Malévitch*, G. Lebovici, Paris, 1986.

AUCTION RECORDS:

LONDON, 18 May 1988, *Composition* (oil on canvas, 22 x $27\frac{1}{4}$ ins / 55 x 69 cm) GBP 12,100. LONDON, 6 Oct 1988, *White Suprematism with Circle* (oil on canvas, $21\frac{3}{4}$ x $25\frac{1}{4}$ ins / 55.4 x 64.4 cm) GBP 15,400. LONDON, 6 April 1989, *Composition* (1932, oil on canvas, $25\frac{1}{2}$ x $31\frac{1}{4}$ ins / 65 x 79.5 cm) GBP 35,200. LONDON, 23 May 1990, *Composition* (oil on canvas, $38\frac{1}{2}$ x $28\frac{3}{4}$ ins / 98 x 73 cm) GBP 30,800. LONDON, 20 March 1991, *Composition* (oil on canvas, $28\frac{1}{4}$ x $38\frac{1}{2}$ ins / 72 x 97.5 cm) GBP 15,400. COLOGNE, 29 May 2003, *Suprematist Architectural Composition* (oil on canvas, 30 x 40 ins / 75 x 102 cm) EUR 52,000.

KOGAN, Moisey or Moise or Moisse or Moshé
Moldovan, 20th century.
Born 1879 or 1898, in Orgjejeff; died 1930 or 1942.
Sculptor, ceramicist, draughtsman, engraver.
Moisey Kogan worked in Germany and Paris, where he was strongly influenced by the work of Rodin and Maillol. For a short time he was a member of the artists' association in Munich. He died in a concentration camp.
BIBLIOGRAPHY:
Söhn, Gerhard, *Mossey Kogan: Bausteine zu einer Monographie*, GS-Verlag, Düsseldorf, 1980.
MUSEUMS AND GALLERIES:
PARIS (MAMVP): *Crouching Woman; Female Torso.*
AUCTION RECORDS:
MUNICH, 28 March 1974, *Torso* (before 1927, terracotta) DEM 3,800. HAMBURG, 3 June 1976, *Two Nudes* (bronze in relief, 6 x 2 1/2 ins / 15.3 x 6.4 cm) DEM 2,100. MUNICH, 27 Nov 1979, *Nude Standing* (patinated bronze, 7 1/2 x 1 1/2 x 2 ins / 19.3 x 4 x 4.2 cm) DEM 2,600. COLOGNE, 1 Dec 1982, *Torso* (dark-brown-patinated bronze, h. 11 ins / 27 cm) DEM 3,600. HAMBURG, 10 June 1983, *Three-Quarter Nude* (bronze, h. 33 ins / 84 cm) DEM 8,000. LONDON, 3 Dec 1985, *Torso* (bronze, h. 13 1/2 ins / 34 cm) GBP 1,200. PARIS, 30 Jan 1989, *Venus* (patinated bronze, 33 1/2 x 12 1/2 x 7 ins / 85 x 32 x 18 cm) FRF 13,000. AMSTERDAM, 24 May 1989, *Kneeling Nude* (bronze, h. 7 ins / 18 cm) NLG 3,450. AMSTERDAM, 13 Dec 1989, *Woman Standing* (bronze, h. 9 ins / 23 cm) NLG 3,910. AMSTERDAM, 22 May 1990, *Torso* (bronze, h. 141 3/4 ins / 360 cm) NLG 3,680. TEL AVIV, 1 Jan 1991, *Portrait* (charcoal and sepia, 19 x 15 1/4 ins / 48 x 38.5 cm) USD 770. AMSTERDAM, 22 May 1991, *Nude Seated on a Stool* (bronze relief, 14 1/2 x 11 ins / 37 x 28 cm) NLG 3,680. HEIDELBERG, 12 Oct 1991, *Two Female Nudes Crouching* (linocut, 9 3/4 x 7 1/2 ins / 25 x 19 cm) DEM 1,500. NEW YORK, 22 Feb 1993, *Village Fete* (oil on canvas, 35 1/4 x 48 ins / 89.5 x 122 cm) USD 2,090. AMSTERDAM, 26 May 1993, *Woman Standing with Her Arms Crossed* (bronze, h. 9 1/4 ins / 23.5 cm) NLG 4,025. PARIS, 6 June 1997, *Venus* (patinated gilt bronze, h. 33 1/2 ins / 85 cm) FRF 13,500. AMSTERDAM, 10 June 1999, *Seated Nude* (terracotta, h. 10 ins / 26 cm) NLG 7,000. AMSTERDAM, 1 Dec 1999, *Seated Nude* (bronze, low relief, 15 x 11 ins / 37 x 27 cm) NLG 6,000. HEIDELBERG, 14 April 2000, *Girl's Face* (brown-patinated bronze, 6 x 3x2 ins / 15 x 8x6 cm) DEM 3,900. HAMBURG, 2 Dec 2000, *Three Female Nudes* (terracotta, relief, 15 x 8 ins / 37 x 20 cm) DEM 17,000. AMSTERDAM, 28 May 2002, *Young Woman* (terracotta, h. 10 ins / 25 cm) EUR 1,600. HAMBURG, 4 June 2003, *Bather* (terracotta, 11 x 15x1 ins / 29 x 38x3 cm) EUR 5,300. HAMBURG, 14 June 2003, *Two Nude Women* (bronze, relief, 5 x 3x0 ins / 13 x 7x1 cm) EUR 1,800. HAMBURG, 10 June 2004, *Seated Female Nude by Plant* (bronze, relief, 15 x 11x1 ins / 37 x 27x3 cm) EUR 4,000.

KOGAN, Nina Osipovna
Russian, 20th century.
Born 1887, in Vitebsk; died 1942.
Painter.
Suprematism.
BIBLIOGRAPHY:
Geometrische Abstraktion 1910-1990, exhibition catalogue, Gal. Eremitage, Berlin, 1991.
AUCTION RECORDS:
LONDON, 30 June 1987, *Suprematist Composition* (c. 1922-1923, pencil, 12 1/2 x 8 1/2 ins / 32 x 21.5 cm) GBP 2,200. LONDON, 29 March 1988, *Composition* (watercolour/paper, 20 x 13 ins / 50.5 x 33 cm) GBP 10,450. LONDON, 19 Oct 1988, *Composition* (watercolour, 9 x 3 3/4 ins / 23.1 x 9.5 cm) GBP 2,750. LONDON, 6 April 1989, *Composition* (watercolour, 12 1/4 x 9 1/4 ins / 31.4 x 23.5 cm) GBP 14,300. NEW YORK, 6 Oct 1989, *Composition* (gouache and pencil/paper, 12 x 9 ins / 30.5 x 23 cm) USD 16,500. AMSTERDAM, 5 June 1996, *Balancing Act* (1929, black ink/paper, 7 3/4 x 6 ins / 20 x 15 cm) NLG 2,300. SAN FRANCISCO, 22 April 1999, *Suprematist Composition* (c. 1922, pencil/watercolour, 7 x 6 ins / 18 x 14 cm) USD 3,000. MILAN, 17 Nov 1999, *Untitled* (c. 1910, mixed media on card, 14 x 9 ins / 35 x 23 cm) ITL 7,000,000. LUCERNE, 25 Nov 2000, *Composition* (c. 1921, ink/watercolour over pencil, 7 x 4 ins / 19 x 9 cm) CHF 5,200. MUNICH, 2 Dec 2000, *Suprematist Composition* (gouache/watercolour over pencil on board, 10 x 8 ins / 26 x 21 cm) DEM 5,000. MILAN, 29 May 2001, *Supreme Composition* (tempera on cardboard, 6 x 9 ins / 16 x 24 cm) ITL 5,500,000. MILAN, 29 May 2001, *Super Composition* (tempera on cardboard, 8 x 6 ins / 21 x 15 cm) ITL 9,000,000. TEL AVIV, 7 April 2002, *Suprematist Composition* (collage/gouache/watercolour/ink on card, 12 x 8 ins / 31 x 20 cm) USD 7,000. PARIS, 12 Dec 2002, *Composition* (watercolour/crayon, 16 x 12 ins / 41 x 31 cm) EUR 5,000. VEJLE, 10 March 2003, *Geometric Composition* (mixed media, 10 x 8 ins / 26 x 20 cm) DKK 22,000. COPENHAGEN, 29 March 2004, *Surrealistic Composition* (gouache/Indian ink/pencil, 12 x 9 ins / 30 x 23 cm) DKK 44,000. COLOGNE, 5 June 2004, *Suprematist Composition* (oil on canvas, 22 x 20 ins / 56 x 50 cm) EUR 52,000.

KÖGEL, Henri
Swiss, 19th century.
Born 1816; died 16 March 1867, in Bern.
Engraver (line-engraving). Topographical views.

KÖGEL, Linda. See **KOEGEL**

KOGEVINAS, Lykourgos, called Lyc
Greek, 20th century.
Born 1 July 1887, on Corfu; died 1940.
Painter, engraver. Landscapes.
Lykourgos Kogevinas painted Ancient Greek landscapes and worked in Paris where he exhibited at the Société Nationale des Beaux-Arts and at the Salon d'Automne. He won a gold medal at the 1925 Salon des Arts Décoratifs in Paris and was made Chevalier de la Légion d'Honneur.
AUCTION RECORDS:
LONDON, 16 Nov 1994, *View of Athens; House under the Snow* (oil on card, a pair, 6 1/4 x 9 1/2 ins / 16 x 24 cm and 7 1/2 x 9 1/2 ins/19 x 24 cm) GBP 1,725.

KÖGL, Clement
German, 19th century.
Born 3 April 1808, in Markt Oberdorf; died 3 April 1845, in Leipzig.
Painter. History painting, genre scenes.
Kögl was assistant to the painter Neher, who illustrated the works of Schiller. He was responsible for paintings of scenes from *The Bride of Messina, William Tell* and *Mary Stuart.*
AUCTION RECORDS:
AMSTERDAM, 23 April 1991, *Grandfather's Money* (oil on canvas, 9 1/4 x 7 ins / 23.75 x 18 cm) NLG 3,450.

KOGLER, Gregor
Swiss, 18th century.
Painter.
Kogler withdrew to the monastery in Hergiswil, where he devoted himself to painting. His only known works are church paintings.

KÖGLER, Karl
German, 19th - 20th century.
Born 12 February 1838, in Molsberg; died 1 April 1923, in Wiesbaden.
Painter, illustrator, writer. Genre scenes.

KOGLER, Peter
Austrian, 20th - 21st century.
Born 1959.
Active in the USA.
Painter, collage artist, screen printer, installation artist.

Peter Kogler subjects images to a computer process, converting them into abstract themes for screen prints or for elements of his installations. He lives in Los Angeles. In 1995 he took part in the Venice Biennale and in FIAC (Foire Internationale d'Art Contemporain) in Paris organised by the Krinzinger Galerie, Vienna. Solo exhibitions include: Krinzinger Galerie, Vienna and Maison de la Culture, Le Cargo, Grenoble (1990) and Galerie de l'École Régionale des Beaux-Arts, Nantes (2003).
BIBLIOGRAPHY:
Fleck, Robert, '*Peter Kogler*' in *Art Press* n° 157, periodical, Paris, April 1991.
MUSEUMS AND GALLERIES:
DUNKIRK (FRAC Nord-Pas de Calais): *Untitled* (1997, wall installation).

KOH BYONG JIN
Vietnamese, 20th century.
Painter (mixed media).
Koh Byong Jin's work falls between the abstract and the figurative; it relays a world in its infant state, with mysterious, unidentifiable forms that nevertheless speak of nature.
BIBLIOGRAPHY:
Chalumeau, Jean-Luc, '*Les Territoires de Koh*' in *Opus international* n° 131, periodical, Paris, Spring-Summer 1993.

KOHEN, Leon
Serb, 19th century.
Born 19th century, in Belgrade.
Painter. History painting, genre scenes.
Leon Kohen studied at the royal school in Munich. His work featured in the Exposition Universelle in Paris in 1900. He worked in Munich.

KOHEN-RAZ, Zipporet
Israeli, 20th century.
Painter.
Zipporet Kohen-Raz studied at the Jerusalem art school and in Paris. He showed work at the Paris Salon d'Automne.

KOHL, Andreas
German, 17th century.
Born 31 December 1624, in Nuremberg; died 5 January 1657, in Nuremberg.
Engraver.
Kohl may be the same artist as the engraver from Nuremberg, A Klaol. An example of Kohl's work is a frontispiece for an architectural work executed on copper. It is in imitation of wood engravings resembling ink drawings.

KOHL, Armand Émile Jean Baptiste, or Koel
French, 19th century.
Born 1845, in Paris.
Engraver (wood).
Armand Kohl was a pupil of Fagnière and Laplaute. He exhibited his work at the Salon de Paris from 1869 and received an honourable mention in 1888.

KOHL, Clemens
Austrian, 18th century.
Born 1754, in Prague; died March 1807, in Vienna.
Engraver, draughtsman.
Kohl studied under his brother Ludwig, at the academy in Vienna and under J. Schmutzer. He produced burin engravings of history portraits. He was court engraver and art teacher to Maria Theresa.
AUCTION RECORDS:
NEW YORK, 11 Jan 1989, *Young Man Sleeping on a Rock* (red chalk, 18 x 23 1/2 ins / 45.8 x 59.4 cm) USD 1,650.

KOHL, Franz
Bohemian, 18th century.
Born 1 March 1711, in Kukus.
Sculptor.
Franz Kohl worked in Vienna, where he studied with R. Donner and later collaborated with him.

KOHL, Jeronym or Hieronymus
Bohemian, 17th century.
Born 1631, in Schlaggenwald; died 1709, in Prague.
Sculptor. Religious subjects.
Bohemian School.
Jeronym Kohl is known for his work in the church of St Nicholas in Laun. He was represented in the exhibition *Lumière et ténèbres, art et civilisation du Baroque en Bohême Light and Darkness. Baroque Art and Civilisation in Bohemia* at the Palais des Beaux-Arts in Lille in 2002.
BIBLIOGRAPHY:
Vlnas, Vit (ed.), *Lumière et ténèbres, art et civilisation du Baroque en Bohême*, exhibition catalogue, Palais des Beaux-Arts, Lille, Réunion des musées nationaux, Paris, 2002.

KOHL, Johann Friedrich
Bohemian, 18th century.
Born 10 March 1681, in Prague; died 1763, in Prague.
Sculptor.
Johann Friedrich Kohl was official sculptor to the Prague court from 1709.

KOHL, Ludwig
Austrian, 18th - 19th century.
Born 14 April 1746, in Prague; died 18 June 1821, in Prague.
Painter, draughtsman, sculptor, engraver (etching).
Kohl studied painting under Norbert Grund and engraving under Schmutzer. He was an art teacher at the teacher training college in Prague. He engraved scenes from Bohemian history and views of the city of Prague.
AUCTION RECORDS:
VIENNA, 15 June 1971, *Women Bathing,* ATS 20,000. STUTTGART, 29 March 2001, *Church Interior* (oil on panel, 11 x 13 ins / 27 x 34 cm) DEM 3,200. PRAGUE, 22 May 2004, *Church Interior* (oil on panel, 26 x 34 ins / 65 x 87 cm) CZK 400,000.

KOHL, Pierre Ernest
Monegasque, 20th century.
Born 1897, in Monaco.
Painter, lithographer. Figures, nudes.
Pierre Ernest Kohl exhibited at the Salon des Indépendants, the Salon d'Automne and the Salon des Tuileries in Paris. He also produced lithographs. His nudes are solidly constructed.

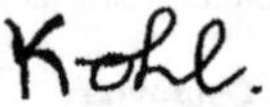

AUCTION RECORDS:
PARIS, 27 Dec 1920, *Portrait of a Woman,* FRF 1,800. PARIS, 10 May 1943, *Young Girl with Couch* (1930) FRF 1,100. PARIS, 16 Dec 1946, *Nude Lying Down,* FRF 2,000. PARIS, 22 Nov 1976, *Woman with Turban* (1928, oil on canvas, 25 1/2 x 19 3/4 ins / 65 x 50 cm) FRF 2,500. BERN, 26 Oct 1988, *Woman Bathing* (1948, oil on panel, 21 1/4 x 17 ins / 54 x 43 cm) CHF 1,100. LA VARENNE-ST-HILAIRE, 3 Dec 1989, *Italian Landscape* (oil on canvas, 24 x 18 1/2 ins / 61 x 47 cm) FRF 9,000. PARIS, 6 Feb 1991, *Portrait of a Woman* (1933, oil on canvas, 17 3/4 x 13 ins / 45 x 33 cm) FRF 4,500. AMSTERDAM, 12 Dec 1991, *Reclining Nude* (1933, oil on canvas, 22 x 15 ins / 55 x 38 cm) NLG 1,725. PARIS, 20 Nov 1994, *Model* (oil on canvas, 29 1/4 x 21 1/2 ins / 74 x 54.5 cm) FRF 50,000. RENNES, 7 Oct 2003, *Woman in Veil* (1930, oil on canvas, 46 x 32 ins / 116 x 81 cm) EUR 5,500. RENNES, 7 Oct 2003, *Salome* (1925, oil on canvas, 46 x 32 ins / 116 x 81 cm) EUR 13,800.

KÖHL, Rudolf
Austrian, 20th century.
Born 26 November 1896, in Vienna.
Engraver.
Rudolf Köhl was an officer during Worl War I. While in a concentration camp he became interested in engraving and begun studies which he was to conclude in Vienna.

KOHL VON KOHLENEGG, Lorenz
Austrian, 19th century.
Born 1783, in Vienna; died 22 January 1851, in Vienna.
Painter, lithographer.
Kohl von Kohlenegg is known mainly as a portrait artist, but he also produced pictures of flowers and genre subjects.

KOHLBRENNER, Martin
German, 18th century.
Born 1682, in Siegsdorf; died 17 July 1740.
Fresco artist, decorative designer.
Kohlbrenner worked mainly in the area around Munich, where he decorated religious buildings.

KÖHLER. See also **KOEHLER**

KÖHLER, Albert
German, 19th century.
Born 1811, in Baden; died 6 July 1849, in Berlin.
Painter. Genre scenes, portraits.
AUCTION RECORDS:
NEW YORK, 11-12 April 1907, *Nymphs and Satyr*, USD 170.

KOHLER, Alfred
German, 20th century.
Born 1916, in Schwabach; died 28 December 1983.
Painter, watercolourist. Figures, portraits, landscapes, still-lifes, flowers.
Alfred Kohler studied under Wertner and Gradle at the art academy in Nuremberg from 1935 to 1937 and worked with Kaspar in Munich. From 1938 he exhibited regularly at the Günter Franke Galerie in Munich with Klee, Nolde, Kokoschka and Heckel. After 1945 he settled in Nuremberg and was one of the promoters of the art society Der Kreis (The Circle) and of the Society to Protect Graphic Artists and Sculptors. He was friendly with Erich Heckel with whom he often went to paint on the Island of Rügen. He is principally appreciated for his watercolours. From 1982 he executed a few erotic figures.
From 1939 to 1970 he exhibited at the Günter Franke Galerie in Munich. A collection of his work was shown in 1985 in Nuremberg by D.M. Klinger.
MUSEUMS AND GALLERIES:
MUNICH (Neue Pinakothek) - NEW YORK (MoMA) - PARIS (Louvre).
AUCTION RECORDS:
AMSTERDAM, 22 May 1990, *Still-life with Bottles* (1956, watercolour/paper, 18 x 23 1/2 ins / 46 x 60 cm) NLG 2,530. STUTTGART, 18 Oct 2002, *Forest Interior* (1963, watercolour, 20 x 31 ins / 51 x 78 cm) EUR 1,800.

KÖHLER, Andreas
Polish, 19th century.
Born 1811, in Szamocin; died 1840, in Berlin.
Painter.
Andreas Köhler studied under Herbig at the academy in Berlin. He is known for war scenes.

KÖHLER, August
German, 20th century.
Born 25 August 1881, in Stuttgart.
Painter, engraver. Portraits, genre scenes.
August Köhler was primarily a portraitist.

KÖHLER, Charles Antoine Népomucène Adrien (Abbé)
Swiss, 19th century.
Born 16 March 1811, in Porrentruy (Bernese Jura); died 10 April 1864, in Porrentruy.
Painter. History painting.
Köhler's teacher was an old sign painter called Father Simon. Köhler visited Paris and Rome, in 1859 and 1862. He produced many copies of great masters. His portraits are notable for their similarity to the originals and a remarkable freshness of colour.

KÖHLER, Christian
French, 19th century.
Born 13 October 1809, in Werben; died 30 January 1861, in Montpellier.
Painter. History painting, religious subjects, portraits.
Christian Köhler pursued his studies at the Berlin and Düsseldorf Academies where he later became a teacher. In 1860, for health reasons, he had to find a more favourable climate and went to Montpellier. He spent the summer on the shores of Lake Geneva and returned to Montpellier to die.
MUSEUMS AND GALLERIES:
COLOGNE: *Mary's Hymn* - DÜSSELDORF: *Agar and Ishmael* - HANOVER: *Jacob Seeking Rachel; Moses; Semiramis* - KALININGRAD: *Discovery of Moses* - LIÈGE: *Semiramis*.
AUCTION RECORDS:
NEW YORK, 22-23 July 1993, *Young David* (1858, oil on canvas, 64 x 47 1/2 ins / 162.6 x 120.7 cm) USD 5,750.

KÖHLER, Emil
German, 19th century.
Born 1815; died 31 August 1876, in Blasewitz.
Painter. Genre scenes.

KÖHLER, Florian
German, 20th century.
Born 1935, in Frankfurt am Main.
Painter.
Geflecht Group.
Florian Köhler participated in the foundation of the Geflecht Network group in 1966, which brought together all young German artists involved in recent trends of world painting and sculpture, namely at that time Pop Art, the New Realists and the Cobra group. He contributed to group exhibitions: 1966, Munich; 1967, Kunsthalle in Kiel; 1967 Kunstverein in Fribourg; 1968, Munich. The group also took part in numerous group exhibitions: 1966, Salon d'Automne in Munich; the association of artists in Essen; 1967, Munich; Berlin; Baden-Baden and Nuremberg. The Geflecht group, which was the result of the conflation in 1965 of the groups Spur Track and *Wir* (*We*), abandoned the principle of the anonymous collective, the works of its members being exhibited individually. The group dissolved in 1967 and was succeeded by the 'Kollektiv Herzogstrasse' which was active until 1981.
AUCTION RECORDS:
MUNICH, 26-27 Nov 1991, *Waiting* (1980, oil on canvas, 27 1/2 x 35 3/4 ins / 70 x 91 cm) DEM 5,175. MUNICH, 26 May 1992, *Oysters 1* (1990, gouache, 11 3/4 x 16 1/2 ins / 30 x 42 cm) DEM 1,035.

KÖHLER, Friedrich Wilhelm
German, 19th century.
Active during the first half of the 19th century in Berlin.
Painter, decorative designer. Landscapes.

KOHLER, Fritz
German, 20th century.
Born 1887, in Moritzberg, near Hildesheim; died 1972, in Düsseldorf.
Painter. Interiors with figures, landscapes, waterscapes, winter landscapes.
After spending his youth in Hamburg, Fritz Kohler was taught by Thedt and Hagen in Weimar. He painted primarily landscapes of northern Germany but also a few interiors.

AUCTION RECORDS:
BREMEN, 21 March 1977, *Banks of the Rhine at Kaiserwerth* (oil on canvas, 19¾ x 29½ ins / 50 x 75 cm) DEM 3,000. COLOGNE, 21 March 1980, *Summer Day* (oil on card, 20 x 28¼ ins / 51 x 72 cm) DEM 2,400. COLOGNE, 23 Oct 1981, *Canal in Winter* (oil on canvas, 23½ x 31½ ins / 60 x 80 cm) DEM 4,000. COLOGNE, 18 March 1983, *Village under Snow* (oil on canvas, 20 x 25 ins / 50.5 x 63.5 cm) DEM 4,400. COLOGNE, 20 Oct 1989, *Forest in Autumn* (oil on canvas, 29½ x 43¼ ins / 75 x 110 cm) DEM 2,000. LONDON, 22 Nov 1990, *The Rhine at Düsseldorf* (oil on canvas, 29 x 39½ ins / 73.6 x 100.3 cm) GBP 1,540. COLOGNE, 26 June 1999, *View of Haarscheidt in Eifel* (oil on canvas, 20 x 30 ins / 50 x 75 cm) DEM 3,400. COLOGNE, 1 April 2004, *Baltic Coast near Arenshoop* (oil on canvas, 102 x 75 ins / 260 x 190 cm) EUR 2,200.

KÖHLER, Georg Johann
German, 20th century.
Born 1 December 1890, in Langenberg.
Painter, engraver.
Georg Köhler worked chiefly in Darmstadt.

KÖHLER, Gustav
German, 19th century.
Born 20 July 1859, in Dortmund.
Painter, illustrator. History painting, genre scenes.
One of Köhler's known works is *Emperor William II Entering Dortmund on 11 August 1899.*
AUCTION RECORDS:
VIENNA, 14 Sept 1965, *Trio*, ATS 30,000. LONDON, 6 May 1977, *Pipe Smoker* (oil on panel, 7 x 5½ ins / 17.8 x 14 cm) GBP 1,350. NEW YORK, 2 May 1979, *Pipe Smoker* (oil on panel, 7 x 5½ ins / 17.8 x 14 cm) USD 3,000. NEW YORK, 25 May 1983, *Portrait of a Hunter* (oil on panel, 7 x 5½ ins / 17.8 x 14 cm) USD 1,700. NEW YORK, 15 Oct 1993, *Lute Player* (oil on panel, 11½ x 9 ins / 29.3 x 22.8 cm) USD 2,760. MUNICH, 29 Sept 1999, *Poacher Holding Gun* (oil on panel, 9 x 7 ins / 23 x 18 cm) DEM 5,000. MUNICH, 9 Dec 2000, *Man Smoking Pipe* (oil on panel, 7 x 6 ins / 18 x 14 cm) DEM 4,800. BOLTON, 1 Feb 2001, *Kitten* (oil on canvas, 25 x 20 ins / 64 x 51 cm) USD 2,900. LUCERNE, 25 May 2002, *Two men in Historical Costume in the Public House* (1894, oil on board, 3 x 4 ins / 7 x 11 cm) CHF 2,800. BETHESDA, 7 May 2004, *Portraits of a Man and a Woman* (oil on paper, a pair, 7 x 5 ins / 18 x 13 cm) USD 3,500.

KÖHLER, Hannelore
German, 20th century.
Born 1929, in Heilbronn.
Painter. Figure compositions, figures.
Hannelore Köhler took part in the exhibition *Artists of Düsseldorf* in the Museum at Ostend in 1962.

KÖHLER, Hans
German, 17th century.
Died 12 September 1616, in Meissen.
Sculptor.
Köhler carved tombs and worked for different churches in Meissen, Bensen and other towns, particularly in northern Bohemia.

KOHLER, Heinrich
German, 19th century.
Born 24 March 1808, in Stuttgart; died 20 March 1885, in Munich.
Lithographer.
Kohler studied under Clemens Zimmermann. His work mainly consisted of reproductions of contemporary works.

KÖHLER, Johann Heinrich Robert
German, 19th century.
Born 14 February 1807, in Leipzig; died 7 December 1872, in New York.
Painter, draughtsman. Figures, portraits, anatomical subjects.
Köhler studied under Johann van Schnorr in Leipzig and Pochmann in Dresden. He left for America in 1848. He is known for his figures and anatomical plates.

KÖHLER, Karl Gottlob
German, 19th century.
Born in Miltiz; died 22 March 1860, in Meissen.
Painter, decorative designer. Landscapes.

KOHLER, Mathieu
French, 19th century.
Born in Niederbronn.
Painter.
Mathieu Kohler studied at the École des Beaux-Arts in Lyons. He began his career at the salon in 1877.
MUSEUMS AND GALLERIES:
MULHOUSE: *Cat and Dog.*

KOHLER, Max
Swiss, 20th century.
Born 1919, in Hubersdorf (Solothurn).
Painter, engraver.
BIBLIOGRAPHY:
Beaumont-Maillet, Laure/Woimant, Françoise/Pernoud, Emmanuel, *De Bonnard à Baselitz - Dix ans d'enrichissements du Cabinet des estampes 1978-1988*, exhibition catalogue, Bibliothèque Nationale de France, Paris, 1992.

KÖHLER, Per
Swedish, 19th century.
Born 1784, in Östergötland; died 30 November 1810, in Stockholm.
Miniaturist. Portraits, genre scenes.
Per Köhler executed copies in miniature, especially of portraits, after the masters.
MUSEUMS AND GALLERIES:
STOCKHOLM: *Genre Scene.*

KOHLER, Rose
American, 20th century.
Born in Chicago.
Painter, sculptor.
Rose Kohler studied under Duveneck at the Art Academy of Cincinnati and was a member of the League of American Art Teachers.

KOHLER-CHEVALIER, Walter
Swiss, 20th century.
Born 1941, in Zofingen.
Draughtsman.
Walter Kohler-Chevalier's drawings have a very distinctive atmosphere that is both oppressive, in that death always seems to be present, and quaint, due to his romanticism. He makes use of the scumbling technique. He has exhibited mainly in Germany, including in Berlin (1969) and Cologne (1970), and in Switzerland, including in Geneva (1971).

KOHLHOFF, Wilhelm
German, 20th century.
Born 6 May 1893, in Berlin; died 1971.
Painter, watercolourist, draughtsman, engraver, lithographer. Portraits, landscapes.
At the beginning of his career, Wilhelm Kohlhoff was a porcelain painter. He exhibited his first works in oil in 1914. His repertoire extended to portraits and landscapes of Prussia. His work was shown in various group exhibitions, including in 2000 *Malerei der Hamburgischen Sezession 1919-1933 aus der Sammlung Hermann-Josef Bunte* (*Painters of the Hamburg Secession 1919-1933 from the Hermann-Josef Bunte Collection*), an exhibition on the artistic importance of the Hamburg Secession during the Weimar Republic. It went to

a number of German cities, most notably the Hamburger Kunsthalle in Hamburg.

Bibliography:

Pfefferkorn, Rudolf, *Wilhelm Kohlhoff*, Stapp, Berlin, 1975. *Wilhelm Kohlhoff: Gemälde, Aquarelle, Zeichnungen*, exhibition catalogue, Altes Rathaus, Schweinfurt, 1981. Schneider, Erich/Choi, Hyeryung, *Wilhelm Kohlhoff. Aquarelle, Gouachen und Zeichnungen aus den zwanziger Jahren*, exhibition catalogue, Schweinfurt, 1989. Kessling, Susanne, *Wilhelm Kohlhoff*, exhibition catalogue, Galerie Pro Art, Verden, 1993.

Museums and Galleries:

Scheinfurt (Mus. Georg Schäfer).

Auction records:

Munich, 31 May 1979, *Reclining Nude* (c. 1925, oil on panel, 18 3/4 x 25 1/2 ins / 47.5 x 65 cm) DEM 3,200. Copenhagen, 16 Sept 1987, *Face and Houses* (c. 1917, oil on canvas, 32 1/4 x 28 3/4 ins / 82 x 73 cm) DKK 60,000. Heidelberg, 11 April 1992, *Interior with Guests at Table* (red chalk, 16 1/2 x 13 3/4 ins / 42 x 35 cm) DEM 1,100. Heidelberg, 3 April 1993, *Still-life of Lilies* (chalk, 16 x 13 1/4 ins / 40.5 x 33.5 cm) DEM 1,200. Heidelberg, 5-13 April 1994, *The Procession* (watercolour, 10 1/2 x 8 1/4 ins / 26.6 x 20.9 cm) DEM 3,200. Heidelberg, 15 Oct 1994, *Seated Figure in Theatrical Costume* (watercolour, 5 1/2 x 3 ins / 14 x 7.5 cm) DEM 1,600. Ahlden, 23 April 1999, *Hour of Reflection* (watercolour, 10 x 14 ins / 26 x 35 cm) DEM 12,800. Bremen, 11 Dec 1999, *Seaside Villa by Moonlight* (oil on canvas, 33 x 26 ins / 85 x 65 cm) DEM 10,000. Berlin, 27 May 2000, *Beach Scene, Promenade in Background* (1930, watercolour and brush, 16 x 20 ins / 40 x 51 cm) DEM 4,800. Berlin, 25 Nov 2000, *Horsewoman in the Circus* (oil on panel, 49 x 41 ins / 124 x 103 cm) DEM 7,500. Ahlden, 5 May 2001, *Mother and Children* (watercolour, 17 x 21 ins / 44 x 53 cm) DEM 16,500. Ahlden, 5 May 2001, *Still-life of Flowers* (oil on canvas, 31 x 39 ins / 80 x 100 cm) DEM 48,000. Bremen, 21 Sept 2002, *Three Workshop Students* (oil on board on panel, 24 x 19 ins / 60 x 49 cm) EUR 2,600. Berlin, 31 May 2003, *Street, Paris* (1930, oil on panel, 31 x 39 ins / 79 x 100 cm) EUR 9,000. Berlin, 29 Nov 2003, *Light Night Sky over Mountain Village* (oil on canvas, 25 x 20 ins / 63 x 51 cm) EUR 15,000. Munich, 14 May 2004, *Nude Girl* (1927, pencil, oil and chalk on paper, 17 x 9 ins / 43 x 22 cm) EUR 1,500. Cologne, 2 Dec 2004, *Still-life of Flowers* (oil on board, 38 x 51 ins / 96 x 130 cm) EUR 6,000.

KOHLMANN, Ejnar

Finnish, 20th century.
Born 1888; died 1968.
Painter. Landscapes with figures, winter landscapes, animals.

Ejnar Kohlmann produced typical landscapes of Scandinavia with wild animals.

Auction records:

Stockholm, 15 Nov 1988, *Winter Landscape with a Fox near a Lake* (oil, 29 1/4 x 21 1/4 ins / 74 x 54 cm) SEK 24,000. Stockholm, 15 Nov 1989, *Coast Line* (oil on canvas, 23 1/2 x 32 ins / 60 x 81 cm) SEK 10,000. Stockholm, 16 May 1990, *Winter Landscape with Ducks Taking Flight in the Marsh* (oil on canvas, 22 x 36 1/4 ins / 55 x 92 cm) SEK 17,500. Stockholm, 14 Nov 1990, *Moorhens in Lake Landscape* (oil on canvas, 28 1/4 x 36 1/2 ins / 72 x 93 cm) SEK 27,000. Stockholm, 29 May 1991, *Edge of Forest with Pheasants near Enclosure* (oil on canvas, 16 1/2 x 22 ins / 42 x 55 cm) SEK 10,000. Helsinki, 14 Sept 2000, *Two White-tailed Eagles* (oil on canvas, 35 x 47 ins / 90 x 120 cm) FIM 12,500. Helsinki, 24 Sept 2000, *Grouse in Coastal Forest* (oil on canvas, 35 x 48 ins / 90 x 121 cm) FIM 15,000. Helsinki, 23 Sept 2001, *Capercaillies Displaying* (1958, oil on canvas, 39 x 52 ins / 98 x 133 cm) FIM 13,000. Stockholm, 10 Dec 2001, *Capercaillies Displaying* (1958, oil on canvas, 39 x 55 ins / 100 x 140 cm) SEK 28,000. Stockholm, 4 March 2002, *Geese by Frozen Lake* (1953, oil on canvas, 37 x 52 ins / 95 x 133 cm) SEK 21,000. Helsinki, 28 April 2002, *Capercaillie* (1949, oil on canvas, 31 x 22 ins / 78 x 57 cm) EUR 2,400. Helsinki, 7 March 2004, *Winter Landscape with Capercaillies* (1954, oil on canvas, 39 x 53 ins / 100 x 134 cm) EUR 2,600. Helsinki, 8 May 2004, *Geese in Early Spring Landscape* (1948, oil on canvas, 33 x 44 ins / 84 x 113 cm) EUR 4,400.

KOHLSCHEIN, Hans

German, 20th century.
Born 5 May 1879, in Düsseldorf.
Painter. Military subjects.

Hans Kohlschein took part in the Grosse Berliner Kunstausstellung of 1909 and favoured subjects of the Napoleonic period.

KOHLSCHEIN, Joseph, the Elder

German, 19th - 20th century.
Born 21 July 1841, in Warburg; died 29 March 1915, in Düsseldorf.
Engraver.

Joseph Kohlschein the Elder mostly copied masters of the Italian Renaissance.

KOHLSCHEIN, Joseph, the Younger

German, 20th century.
Born 1884, in Düsseldorf; died 1958, in Neuss (Rhineland-Westphalia).
Painter, engraver. Portraits, landscapes.

Joseph Kohlschein the Younger cultivated an Impressionist style by imitating French painters.

Auction records:

Cologne, 20 Oct 1989, *The Port of Neuss in Winter* (oil on canvas, 19 x 20 1/2 ins / 48.5 x 52 cm) DEM 4,500.

KOHLSCHÜTTER, Paula

German, 19th century.
Born 10 June 1851.
Active in Dresden.
Painter. Portraits, genre scenes.

Kohlschütter studied under G. Courtois in Paris.

KOHN, Bernard

American, 20th century.
Born 1905, in Philadelphia; died 1989.
Painter, engraver.

Bibliography:

Beaumont-Maillet, Laure/Woimant, Françoise/Pernoud, Emmanuel, *De Bonnard à Baselitz - Dix ans d'enrichissements du Cabinet des estampes 1978-1988*, exhibition catalogue, Bibliothèque nationale de France, Paris, 1992.

KOHN, David

Austrian, 19th - 20th century.
Born 1861, in Vienna; died 1922.
Painter, draughtsman. Portraits.

KOHN, Gabriel

American, 20th century.
Born 1910, in Philadelphia; died 1975.
Painter, sculptor, decorative designer. Stage sets.

Gabriel Kohn's father was an engraver, and he studied under him before being admitted at the Cooper Union in 1929 to study sculpture with Gaetano Cecere. He went on to learn modelling at the Institute of Design, while working for New York sculptors in the early 1930s. From 1934 to 1947, he was a theatre and cinema set designer with contracts in Hollywood. In 1947, he was in Paris and attended Zadkine's studio, moving on to Nice where he learnt to work in clay. He was in Rome in the late 1940s and in France until 1954, before settling back in New York. He has sculpted in stone and clay. As his work became more plainly abstract he turned to plywood for the construction of spatial structures made with geometrically carved, uniformly smooth elements, whose manifold and pliant shapes readily fall in loose, sloping formations.

He has featured in exhibitions at the Whitney Museum of New York, at the São Paulo Biennale in 1959, and in *Recent Sculpture, USA*, at the MoMA of New York. In 1960, he was awarded a Ford Foundation Prize.

KOHN, Georges
French, 19th - 20th century.
Born 14 September 1874, in Paris.
Painter, engraver, medallist.

Georges Kohn is known for his scenes of Jewish folklore in Alsace. He also painted fine Jewish figures and exhibited regularly at the Salon des Indépendants.

KOHN DE BARREIRO, Tanya
Ecuadorean, 20th century.
Born in Prague.
Painter, screen printer.

KOHNERT, Heinrich
German, 19th century.
Born 3 May 1850, in Tilsit (now Sovetsk); died 23 March 1905, in Berlin.
Engraver. Landscapes.

Kohnert was awarded a commendation in Berlin in 1892.

KÖHNHOLZ, Johann Wilhelm Julius
German, 19th - 20th century.
Born 7 March 1839, in Bremen; died 15 January 1925, in Bremen.
Painter. Landscapes.

Johann Köhnholz settled in Bari, Italy, where he was a businessman. It was only in 1869 that he began to paint, working for the most part alone. He was awarded a medal in London in 1874. He is most appreciated for the sincerity in his emotionally charged works.

MUSEUMS AND GALLERIES:
BREMEN: *The Valley of Loisach in the Bavarian Alps*.

AUCTION RECORDS:
VIENNA, 15 April 1980, *Seaside* (oil on canvas, 12 1/4 x 18 3/4 ins / 31 x 47.5 cm) ATS 18,000. COLOGNE, 23 March 1990, *Mountain Lake in Summer* (oil on canvas, 41 1/4 x 37 1/2 ins / 105 x 95 cm) DEM 2,800. LONDON, 21 Nov 1997, *Sunset near Bari* (48 1/2 x 35 1/2 ins / 123.2 x 90.2 cm) GBP 7,475.

KOHO
Cuban, 20th century.
Installation artist.

In 1994, Koho took part in the contemporary art Biennale in Havana. He made an installation consisting of small boats made from a variety of materials - including egg boxes, biscuit packets and beer bottles - all heading in the same direction.

KOHRL, Ludwig
German, 19th century.
Born 4 August 1858, in Graz; died 1927.
Painter. Genre scenes, portraits.

Kohrl studied at the art college in Graz. He worked in Munich.

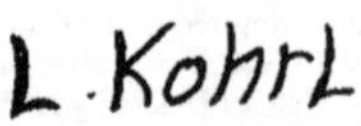

AUCTION RECORDS:
NEW YORK, 29 May 1980, *The Postman Calls* (1886, oil on canvas, 20 1/4 x 27 1/4 ins / 51.5 x 69 cm) USD 3,000. NEW YORK, 24 May 1985, *Young Country Girl Holding a Small Cat* (oil on canvas, 30 x 23 3/4 ins / 76.2 x 60.3 cm) USD 3,000. FRANKFURT, 2 March 2002, *Little Doll's Mother* (oil on canvas, 16 x 12 ins / 41 x 31 cm) EUR 1,700.

KOHTZ, Rudolf
German, 20th century.
Born 3 July 1874, in Magdeburg.
Painter. Genre scenes, still-lifes.

Rudolf Kohtz participated in the Grosse Berliner Kunstausstellung in 1909.

AUCTION RECORDS:
COLOGNE, 23 March 1990, *Brother and Sister in a Forest* (oil on card, 20 x 16 ins / 51 x 40.5 cm) DEM 1,100.

KOIDE, Narashige
Japanese, 20th century.
Born 1887, in Osaka; died 1931.
Painter. Figures, portraits, nudes.

Koide Narashige graduated from the Tokyo School of Fine Arts in 1914 and then returned to Osaka. In 1921 he went to Europe, where he completed his training in oil painting. In 1924 he opened the Shinanobashi Western Art Institute with Nabei Katsuyuki and others. He played an important role in the development of painting in Kansei region (Kyoto-Osaka), and is well known for his female nudes. He won several prizes at the exhibitions of the Nika-kai (two disciplines - painting and sculpture), starting in 1919 and 1920, was made a member in 1923 following his return from France.

KÖIE, Ernst Valdemar
Danish, 19th - 20th century.
Born 19 October 1872, in Bornholm.
Painter, engraver.

KOIN, real name Nagayama Koin; given name Shiryo; artist names Koen, Gorei, Bokusai
Japanese, 18th - 19th century.
Born 1765, in Akita; died 1849.
Painter.

Koin, a disciple of Goshun (1752-1811) from the Shijo school, lived in Osaka, where he specialised in *tanka* (comic poetry) and painted.

KOISTER, Georges
Belgian, 20th century.
Born 1879 or 1880, in Liège; died 1956, in Brussels.
Painter, draughtsman, watercolourist, decorative designer, poster artist. Portraits. Stage costumes.

Georges Koister designed stage costumes and contributed to a number of papers in France and Belgium.

MUSEUMS AND GALLERIES:
LIÈGE: *Portrait of Mme F. W.*

KOISTINEN, Unto
Finnish, 20th century.
Born 1917.
Painter. Portraits, landscapes.

Unto Koistinen began to exhibit in 1940 and soon joined the Expressionist group Octobre. He painted portraits and landscapes in bluish grey tones accentuated by the strong contrast of black. In keeping with the Expressionist trend which was so prevalent in the art of the northern countries, he went in for distortions to express the personality of his figures or the soul of his landscapes.

KOJAN, Jan
Czech, 20th century.
Born 1886; died 1951.
Painter.

The national gallery of modern art in Prague has two oil paintings by Jan Kojan.

KOJEVNIKOV, Vladimir
Russian, 20th - 21st century.
Born 1950.
Painter. Landscapes.

Vladimir Kojevnikov was the pupil of Utkine. He became a member of the union of Leningrad (St Petersburg) painters.
AUCTION RECORDS:
PARIS, 10 June 1991, *Island of Belov* (oil on canvas, 19 3/4 x 27 1/2 ins / 50 x 70 cm) FRF 4,800.

KOJIMA, Kagenobu
Japanese, 20th century.
Active in Tokyo in 1900.
Painter (silk). Still-lifes.
Kojima Kagenobu received an honourable mention at the Paris Exposition Universelle of 1900.

KOJIMA, Nobuaki
Japanese, 20th century.
Born 1935, in Ono (Fukui Prefecture).
Active since 1971 in the USA.
Painter.
Kojima Nobuaki graduated from Osaka Municipal Art School in 1955 and burst into public attention in 1962 when he exhibited himself in a metal drum. It was the first happening to hit Japan. In 1970-1971, he travelled abroad on a scholarship, which took him to Mexico and then New York, where he settled. After a dalliance with Pop Art, he moved towards hyperrealism.

Kojima took part in several exhibitions organised by the journal *Yomiuri*. His work was included in the *New Japanese Painting and Sculpture* exhibition at the Museum of Modern Art, New York, and the *New Trends in Contemporary Art* exhibition held at the Kyoto National Museum of Modern Art. In 1968 he won the prize at the Japanese Contemporary Art Exhibition, and in 1969 that of the Tokyo Biennale.

KOJIMA, Torajiro
Japanese, 20th century.
Born 1881, in Okayama Prefecture; died 1929.
Painter.
Kojima Torajiro graduated from the oil painting department of Tokyo Fine Arts University and went to France to study under Edmond Aman-Jean. He was later appointed to the Imperial Arts Council.

KOJIMA, Zenzaburo
Japanese, 20th century.
Born 1893, in Fukuoka; died 1962, in Chiba.
Painter.
Kojima Zenzaburo worked at Fukuoka. After studying at the Hongo Centre in Tokyo he went to Europe twice, in 1924 and in 1928. On his return to Japan, he was made a member of the Nika-kai but would soon resign, and with a number of friends formed the Independent Art Association. His style is a mixture of Western traits and Japanese traditions from the Momoyama, Rimpa and Nanga schools.

KOJO
Japanese.
Draughtsman, watercolourist. Scenes with figures.
Kojo is probably the same artist as Kojo Kokuwan.
AUCTION RECORDS:
PARIS, 20 Feb 1945, *Cart*; *City View* (two drawings with watercolour) FRF 320.

KOJO, Kokuwan
Japanese, 20th century.
Born in Kagoshima.
Painter.
Kojo exhibited at the Salon des Artistes Français and the Salon d'Automne in Paris.

KOJOVIC, Slobodan
Yugoslav, 20th century.
Born 1942, in Belgrade (now in Serbia).
Active in France from 1969.
Engraver.
BIBLIOGRAPHY:
Beaumont-Maillet, Laure/Woimant, Françoise/Pernoud, Emmanuel, *De Bonnard à Baselitz - Dix ans d'enrichissements du Cabinet des estampes 1978-1988*, exhibition catalogue, Bibliothèque nationale de France, Paris, 1992.

KOK, Jan. See **COK Jan Mathias**

KOK, W.. See **KOCH W.**

KOK, Yew Puah
Malayan, 20th - 21st century.
Born 1947, in Malaya.
Engraver.
Yew Puah Kok lives in Singapore. Works by him in a geometrical abstract style were shown at the international print biennale in Tokyo in 1974.

KOKA, Ferenc
Hungarian, 20th century.
Born 1934.
Painter.
Young Artists' Studio. Szentendre Artists' Colony.
Ferenc Koka lived in the Szentendre Artists' Colony. From 1954 to 1960 he studied in the studio of Aurel Bernath at the academy of fine arts in Budapest and was awarded the Derkovits scholarship from 1963 to 1965. A member of the Young Artists' Studio, he exhibited with them. Other collective exhibitions include: Hungary; Warsaw, Bucharest, Belgrade and São Paulo Biennale. He had his first solo exhibition in Budapest in 1969.
BIBLIOGRAPHY:
Art hongrois contemporain, exhibition catalogue, Musée Galliera, Paris, 1970.

KOKAN, monk's name Myoyo; artist names Koshu, Kokan
Japanese, 17th - 18th century.
Born 1653; died 1717.
Painter.
Kokan, who became the superior at the Hoon-ji temple in Kyoto, studied painting with Eino (1631-1697). He specialised in Buddhist themes as well as humorous subjects verging on caricature.

KOKAN, real name Shiba Shun; alternate name Kungaku; popular names Ando Kichijiro, Katsusaburo; artist names Kokan, Fugendojin, Shumparo, Rantei, Furai Sanjin, Suzuki Harushige
Japanese, 18th - 19th century.
Born 1747, in Edo (now Tokyo); died 1818, in Edo.
Painter, engraver.
Kokan, a pupil of Harunobu (1725?-1770), one of the great *ukiyo-e* masters, is infamous as one of the most brilliant forgers of his master's work, openly admitting his wrongdoing in his autobiography *Shumparo Hikki*. That was the time, he wrote, when 'Master Suzuki Harunobu was known for his talent in depicting the manners and customs of the women of the time. On reaching the age of forty, he suddenly fell ill and died. I then made imitations of these (works) and when they were engraved and printed, nobody recognised them as imitations and everyone took me for Harunobu. But as I was not Harunobu, I did not copy him in a servile manner and, taking the name Harushige, I drew the beauties of our country with the colouring techniques used by Chinese masters such as Qiu Ying and Zhou Chen.' (D. Waterhouse, *Suzuki Harunobu: Some Reflections on the Bicentenary of his Death* in Oriental Art, vol. XVII no. 4, Winter 1971).

The character of Harushige would be the subject of long discussion in both Japan and the West, and no-one wanted to confuse him with Kokan. But the text is unambiguous on this point, and, besides, a work by Harunobu published in 1769 has a preface by Kokan under the signature of his artist name, Furai Sanjin. Kokan was then very young, but he would later become famous for his knowledge of Dutch representational techniques, which he went to study in Nagasaki. He was one of the figures who did much to introduce Western science and techniques into his country. In 1763, after having been a pupil of the Kano school, he started to study with Hiraga Gennai (1723-1779), who taught him the principles of oil painting. He soon abandoned wood engraving for etching, being the first Japanese to experiment with this art form, even attempting Western perspective in some of his landscapes.

BIBLIOGRAPHY:

Guth, Christine, *Japanese Art of the Edo Period*, Calmann and King, London, 1996.

KOKARSKI. See **KUCHARSKI Alexander**

KOKAS, Ignac
Hungarian, 20th century.
Born 1926.
Painter. Murals, designs for mosaics.

Ignac Kokas studied with János Kmetty and Aurel Bernath at the academy of fine arts in Budapest and was awarded a Derkovits scholarship in 1958. He produced abstract landscapes with supple rhythmic surfaces and is known for his generous use of materials and colours. Collective exhibitions include the Hungary and Venice Biennale (1969). His first solo exhibition was held in Budapest in 1969. He won the Munkácsy Prize on several occasions.

BIBLIOGRAPHY:

Art hongrois contemporain, exhibition catalogue, Musée Galliera, Paris, 1970.

KOKEI
Japanese, 12th century.
Active in Nara at the end of the 12th century.
Sculptor.

Kokei was the father of the famous sculptor Unkei (d. 1223). For a while, he was eclipsed by the In school of Inson and the En school of Myoen in Kyoto, but would later distinguish himself by his remarkable work. This includes the *Fukukenjaku Kannon* (the thousand-armed bodhisattva who catches beings in her nets to lead them to the land of the Buddha) and *Hosso Rokuso* (Six Patriarchs of the Hosso Sect) in the Nan'en-do of Kofuku-ji temple, Nara, which he made with his younger brother Jitsugen in 1188.

Kokei opens the way to the development of the Kei school which, with Unkei, Kaikei, Jokei and Tankei, would become the main school of sculpture in the Kamakura period (1185-1337).

KOKEI, real name Yoshimura Kokei; given name Mui; childhood name Yozo; artist names Ranryo, Ryusen
Japanese, 18th - 19th century.
Born 1769; died 1836.
Active in Kyoto.
Painter.

Kokei, a disciple of Maruyama Okyo (1733-1795), is known for his bird and flower paintings.

KOKEN, Anne
German, 20th century.
Born 28 May 1885, in Hanover; died 19 April 1919, in Hanover.
Painter, engraver.

Anne Koken painted landscapes and still-lifes.

KOKEN, Edmund
German, 19th century.
Born 14 June 1814, in Hanover; died 30 October 1872, in Hanover.
Painter. Landscapes.

Koken studied at the college in his home town of Hanover, then in 1836 in Munich. He then visited Italy and Bavaria. He settled in Hanover again and lived there for the rest of his life.

MUSEUMS AND GALLERIES:

HANOVER: *Cemetery; In the Cloister; Two Landscapes; Winter.*

KOKEN, Gustav
German, 19th - 20th century.
Born 8 August 1850, in Hanover; died 6 July 1910, in Hanover.
Painter. Landscapes.

Gustav Koken was the son or nephew of Edmund Koken as well as his pupil. He also worked with Hagen in Weimar. In 1878 he returned to his native Hanover.

MUSEUMS AND GALLERIES:

SYDNEY: *Winter Landscape* - WEIMAR: *Boggenerte near Hanover.*

AUCTION RECORDS:

NEW YORK, 15 and 16 April 1909, *Road through a Wood*, USD 490. COLOGNE, 26 March 1976, *Banks of the Rhine* (oil on canvas, 25 1/2 x 4 1/4 ins / 65 x 11 cm) DEM 2,000. NEW YORK, 26 May 1992, *Returning from School* (1874, oil on canvas, 42 1/4 x 62 1/2 ins / 107.3 x 158.7 cm) USD 9,350. MUNICH, 21 June 1994, *Rest in an Autumn Landscape* (1879, oil on canvas, 27 3/4 x 49 1/4 ins / 70.5 x 125 cm) DEM 7,475.

KOKEN, Paul
German, 19th century.
Born 2 January 1853, in Hanover; died 1910.
Painter. Landscapes, winter landscapes, animals.

Koken was the son and student of Edmund Koken. After his father's death he studied under Lier in Munich and Hagen in Weimar. He settled in Hanover in 1882.

AUCTION RECORDS:

LONDON, 27 July 1973, *Town in Winter*, GNS 1,100. DÜSSELDORF, 8 Dec 1982, *Four Kittens in a Basket* (oil on panel, 6 3/4 x 9 1/2 ins / 17 x 24 cm) DEM 6,000. NEW YORK, 24 May 1985, *Winter Landscape* (1880, oil on canvas, 41 1/2 x 30 ins / 105.4 x 76.2 cm) USD 2,000. ROTTERDAM, 9 May 2000, *Winter Wooded Landscape with Faggot Gatherers at Sunset* (oil on canvas, 47 x 67 ins / 119 x 171 cm) NLG 7,200. AHLDEN, 5 May 2001, *Summer Evening* (oil on canvas, 25 x 38 ins / 64 x 96 cm) DEM 4,000. AHLDEN, 20 Sept 2002, *Church in Winter Landscape* (oil on canvas, 25 x 38 ins / 64 x 96 cm) EUR 2,400. AHLDEN, 29 Nov 2002, *Summer's Day in Ottersdorf Harbour* (oil on canvas/board, 18 x 12 ins / 45 x 31 cm) EUR 1,600. BERLIN, 22 Aug 2003, *Old Town in Summer with River and Stone Bridge* (oil on canvas, 42 x 31 ins / 107 x 78 cm) EUR 1,900. COLOGNE, 1 April 2004, *Northern German City* (oil on canvas, 42 x 31 ins / 106 x 79 cm) EUR 3,300.

KOKER, Anna Maria de
Dutch, 17th century.
Died 17 May 1698, in Amsterdam.
Draughtswoman, engraver. Landscapes.

Anna Maria de Koker was the widow of Jan Camersfelt. She is known for two drawings that formed part of the Geldemcester sale, and landscapes engraved after Hobbema, Van Goyen and Peter de Molyn.

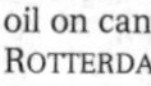

KOKINE, Mikhail, or Kokin
Ukrainian, 20th century.
Born 1921, in Yekaterinoslav (now Dnepropetrovsk).
Painter. Landscapes, seascapes.

Mikhail Kokine studied under the direction of Sergei Grigoriev at the institute of fine arts in Kiev from 1948 to 1954. He joined the union of Ukrainian painters in 1957.

Auction records:
Paris, 13 March 1992, *Reading a Book* (1956, oil on card, 19 3/4 x 13 1/2 ins / 50 x 34.2 cm) FRF 5,500. Paris, 12 Oct 1992, *In the Spring* (1971, oil on canvas, 39 x 42 1/2 ins / 99 x 108 cm) FRF 8,200. Paris, 25 Jan 1993, *Cornflowers* (oil on canvas, 27 1/2 x 27 1/2 ins / 69.7 x 69.7 cm) FRF 4,800. Paris, 20 March 1993, *Red Sailboat* (oil on canvas, 28 3/4 x 43 ins / 73 x 109 cm) FRF 6,500. Paris, 7 June 1995, *Anemones in a Chinese Vase* (oil on canvas, 19 3/4 x 19 3/4 ins / 50 x 50 cm) FRF 8,800. London, 11 April 1997, *On the Beach* (1965, oil on canvas, 22 3/4 x 39 ins / 57.9 x 99 cm) GBP 368.

KOKKADO
Japanese, 18th century.
Active in the Kyoto-Osaka region c. 1770.
Print artist.

KOKKEN, Henry
Belgian, 19th - 20th century.
Born 1860, in Antwerp; died 1941.
Painter. Genre scenes, still-lifes, flowers.

An expert draughtsman, Henry Kokken travelled in Holland, France, Italy and England.

Auction records:
London, 17 Nov 1993, *Still-life with Bunch of Roses and Tray of Peaches* (oil on canvas, 25 1/2 x 32 ins / 65 x 81 cm) GBP 3,680. Lokeren, 9 March 1996, *Guitarist in a Tavern* (oil on canvas, 31 1/2 x 39 1/4 ins / 80 x 100 cm) BEF 500,000. London, 10 Oct 1996, *Roses in a Japanese Vase on a Table* (oil on canvas, 28 x 18 ins / 71.2 x 45.7 cm) NLG 2,200. New York, 26 Feb 1997, *Still-life with Roses and Peaches* (oil on canvas, 25 3/4 x 32 1/4 ins / 65.4 x 81.9 cm) USD 8,625. Lokeren, 9 Oct 1999, *In the Dunes* (oil on panel, 9 x 13 ins / 24 x 32 cm) BEF 110,000. Rome, 4 June 2001, *Family Concert* (oil on canvas, 35 x 47 ins / 90 x 120 cm) ITL 18,000,000. Antwerp, 30 Oct 2001, *Still-life with Bouquet of Flowers* (oil on canvas, 13 x 19 ins / 32 x 48 cm) BEF 70,000. Antwerp, 6 Oct 2003, *Still-life with Roses* (oil on canvas, 29 x 19 ins / 74 x 49 cm) EUR 1,800.

KOKKINAKI, Arta
French, 20th century.
Born 1923, in Marseilles.
Painter, screen printer.

Bibliography:
Beaumont-Maillet, Laure/Woimant, Françoise/Pernoud, Emmanuel, *De Bonnard à Baselitz - Dix ans d'enrichissements du Cabinet des estampes 1978-1988*, exhibition catalogue, Bibliothèque nationale de France, Paris, 1992.

KOKO, nickname Namioka; seal names Hoshi, Yoshiko
Japanese, 18th century.
Active in Osaka c. 1770.
Print artist.

KOKO, Demeter
Austrian, 20th century.
Born 13 June 1891, in Linz; died 29 October 1929.
Painter.

Demeter Koko was a student in Munich from 1910 to 1915 and received the Austrian State prize in 1921.

Museums and Galleries:
Graz - Luz - Vienna.

Auction records:
Munich, 30 Nov 1979, *Woman Walking in Forest* (c. 1915, oil on card, 19 1/4 x 27 3/4 ins / 49 x 70.5 cm) DEM 8,000. Vienna, 14 Oct 1987, *The Farmyard* (oil on card, 13 1/2 x 19 ins / 34 x 48 cm) ATS 35,000. Vienna, 30 May 2001, *Dahlias* (oil on board, 24 x 19 ins / 62 x 49 cm) ATS 65,000. Vienna, 21 Nov 2001, *Spring Morning* (1924, oil on canvas, 31 x 23 ins / 78 x 58 cm) ATS 45,000. Linz, 27 Nov 2003, *Steinerne Mill* (oil on board, 26 x 37 ins / 67 x 94 cm) EUR 5,500. Vienna, 12 Oct 2004, *Hay Card* (oil on board, 14 x 19 ins / 35 x 49 cm) EUR 4,000. Linz, 29 Nov 2004, *Autumn Time on the Heath* (oil on board, 19 x 27 ins / 48 x 69 cm) EUR 8,000.

KOKOLSKY, Hermann
German, 19th century.
Born 12 April 1853, in Berlin.
Sculptor.

Kokolsky carved statues of several German emperors, some of which are in Osnabrück. He decorated churches in Berlin, Dessau and Leipzig.

KOKOREKIN, A.
Russian, 20th century.
Born in Russia.
Painter.

Kokorekin was inspired by Soviet culture. On the occasion of the 30th anniversary of the October Revolution he was awarded first prize by the USSR arts committee for his poster *See our Victorious Working Classes.*

KOKORIN, Anatoli
Russian, 20th century.
Born 1908; died 1989.
Painter. Landscapes.

Anatoli Kokorin attended the academy of fine arts where he was the pupil of Sergei Gerasimov. He was appointed a People's Painter in 1979 and painted in the Academic style. From 1930 he exhibited in both Russia and abroad including: Czechoslovakia, Germany, Holland, Italy, India, Japan, England, France, Finland and Denmark.

Museums and Galleries:
Copenhagen (Andersen Mus.) - Moscow (Pushkin MFA) - Moscow (State Tretyakov Gal.) - St Petersburg (Gosudarstvennyj Russkij Muz.).

Auction records:
Paris, 16 June 1991, *Deep Sea Fishermen* (1953, oil on canvas/card, 13 3/4 x 19 3/4 ins / 35 x 50 cm) FRF 6,500.

KOKOSCHKA, Oskar
Austrian, 20th century.
Born 1 March 1886, in Poechlam; died 22 February 1980, in Montreux (Switzerland).
Active from 1947 and naturalised in England and from 1953 active in Switzerland.
Painter (including gouache), watercolourist, engraver, draughtsman (including ink), illustrator, decorative designer, lithographer. Mythological subjects, allegorical subjects, figure compositions, figures, portraits, self-portraits, landscapes, urban landscapes, still-lifes, flowers. Stage sets, designs for mosaics, wall decorations, posters.

Oskar Kokoschka attended the Kunstgewerbeschule in Vienna from 1904 to 1909, where he was initially taught by Carl Otto Czeschka. Like his contemporary Egon Schiele, was profoundly affected by Gustav Klimt. While still young he was a member of the *Wiener Werkstätte*, founded in 1903 by the architect Josef Hoffman. He initially painted sorrowful emaciated figures, not unrelated to those of Picasso's Blue Period.

Kokoschka was obliged to leave Vienna following a public outcry caused by an exhibition of his work in 1908 at the *Erste Wiener Kunstschau* (*First Viennese Kunstschau*) where he showed his first important illustrations, the coloured lithographs for *Die Träumenden Knaben* (*The Dreaming Boys*) and life-size drawings: *Die Träumtragenden* (*The Dream Carriers*). In this same year, 1908, Kokoschka met the architect Alfred Loos who introduced him to the editors of the publication *Die Fackel* (The Torch) which was to take up his cause. In 1909 he went to Switzerland with Loos, who also introduced him to Herwarth Walden, the editor of the journal *Der Sturm* in Berlin, where he accepted a commission and met the artists of the Neue Sezession (New Secession): Nolde, Pechstein, Kirchner, Heckel and Schmidt-Rottluff.

He had already began his literary work by 1907 when he produced his first book of illustrated poems, *Les Enfants Rêveurs*. His literary output also included several plays, notably *Sphinx and Strawman* and *Mörder Hoffnung der Frauen* (*Murder Hope of Women*), a satirical comedy in which the influence of Klimt is evident and which was to inspire his poster *Pietà*. These plays had a considerable influence on the Expressionist movement after they were performed in the open-air theatre of the second Viennese *Kunstschau* of 1909, where Kokoschka also exhibited paintings. *Mörder Hoffnung der Frauen* (*Murder Hope of Women*) was published in *Der Sturm* in 1916.

Until World War I he painted mainly portraits of his artist and writer friends: *Adolf Loos* (1909), the scientist *August Forel* and *Herwarth Walden* and a few landscapes.

On his return to Vienna in 1911 his play *Der Brennende Dornbusch* (*The Burning of the Thornbush*) was performed, but was much criticised. He frequented Eugène Schwarzwald's circle. In 1912 he met Alma Mahler, the composer's widow, with whom he had a love affair that lasted unteil 1915. In 1913 he was in Italy where he discovered the works of Tintoretto. He volunteered for military service in World War I and was severely wounded on the Eastern Front on 29 August 1915, at Luck. He was looked after in Wladimir Wohlhynsk, convalescing thereafter in Vienna, where, as soon as he had recovered, he had to lead a group of war artists and journalists on the Isonzo front (1916-1917). After various medical examinations in Vienna and then in Stockholm, he settled in Dresden from 1917 to 1924.

His post-war output was greatly shaped by his awareness of a disturbed moral order. In Dresden, working in a milieu of young poets and actors, his humanitarian and mystical preoccupations, exacerbated by the absurdity of the war, inspired him to paint large compositions often of Biblical inspiration, *The Emigrants*, *The Friends*, *The Whirlwind* and *The Knight Errant*. He was in contact with Max Beckmann, Otto Mueller, Käthe Kollwitz and Heinrich Campendonk. He continued to work for the theatre and opera, with *Hiob* (*Job*) and the *The Burning Thornbush* in 1919 at the Max-Reinhart Theatre. When the war had receded into the background, he abandoned his symbolist and mystical inspiration to launch himself again into landscapes and portraits, which he handled with an increased quasi-psychoanalytic acuteness. In 1918 he wrote the play *Orpheus und Eurydike*. The same year saw the appearance of the first monograph on Kokoshcka, written by Paul Westheim. In 1919 the Max-Reinhardt Theatre of Berlin showed *Hiob* and *Der Brennende Dornbusch The Burning of the Thornbush* in stage sets designed by Kokoschka, and he was appointed a professor at the Kunstakademie, Dresden, a post he held until 1924. He published *Vier Dramen* in Berlin in 1919.

In 1924 he executed landscapes during his stay in Blonay, a small village on the Vevey heights, Switzerland, and in Vienna, where he returned on the death of his father, executing the *Portrait of the Composer Arnold Schönberg*. From 1924 to 1933 he travelled widely: from Paris he went to Bordeaux, Biarritz, Avignon, Aigues-Mortes, Marseilles, Toledo, Madrid, Lisbon, Amsterdam and in 1926 he discovered London; from 1928 to 1930 he was in Tunisia, twice in Italy, Istanbul, Jerusalem, Ireland, Egypt and Algeria. In 1931 he returned to Vienna until 1934 from where, after the assassination of Chancellor Dollfuss, he moved to Prague.

In Germany his work was denounced by the Nazis who seized 417 of his works, 16 of which were shown initially at the *Entartete Kunst* (*Degenerate Art*) exhibition in Munich and then in various German. In Prague between 1934 and 1938, he painted the greatest number of views he had ever carried out in one place. On Hitler's invasion of Czechoslovakia he left Prague for London on 19 October 1938, settling in England, where he became a British citizen in 1947. During World War II he once again executed massive allegorical and mythological paintings: *Loreley - Anschluss* and *Anschluss Wonderland*. In 1948 he travelled to Venice and Florence, and in 1949 to Minneapolis, teaching in Tanglewood near Boston.

Apart from his isolated compositions, after World War II, he resumed the double series of portraits and above all landscapes in the Valais and throughout Italy, making colour drip in disorderly striations, conflating natural elements and buildings by applying colours, a technique which invokes Giovanni Boldini's society portraits, even if the result was hardly a synthesis of Impressionism and Expressionism. Kokoschka continued to work as a designer, creating décor and costumes for Mozart's *Die Zauberflöte* (*Magic Flute*) (1953) and also for Verdi's *The Masked Ball* Maskenball (1953); he also carried out cycles of lithographs including *The Odyssey* (1963). From 1953 to 1963 he ran a summer school *Schule des Sehens* (*School of Seeing*) in the Salzburger Akademie and settled in Villeneuve, Switzerland, on Lake Geneva. In 1961 he set out on further journeys to Greece and in 1966 he was in the USA for the fifth time, followed by a stay in Israel and then Sicily in 1973. He painted the cartoons of a mosaic *Ecce Homines* for St Nicholas' Church in Hamburg, finished in 1973. He resumed his Austrian nationality in 1975. During his lifetime he received several distinctions including the Stephan Lochner medal in Cologne in 1951, the Lichtwark prize of the City of Hamburg in 1952, the Erasmus prize in 1960, Honorary Citizen of the City of Vienna, prize of the Town of Salzburg in 1971.

As claimed by his biographers, Kokoschka was clearly one of the greatest portraitists of the 20th century. He went beyond simple psychology, revealing the psychic disequilibrium of his sitters through, for example, his rendering of their expressions and hands. He was clearly in touch with Viennese intellectual circles. The intensity of his psychological portraits informed, as it were, his views of the towns where he stayed. Like El Greco, he painted from an elevated viewpoint looking into the far distance. In his harmonic handling of space and the lyrical expression of the essence of the town, such townscapes were an Expressionist continuation of Francesco Guardi and the view painters of the 18th century, Johannes Vermeer with his 'View of Delft', De Carpaccio and Gentile Bellini. The tense truth of his work, its penetrating psychology, technical virtuosity and dramatic colour contrasts unify his different periods; the two Symbolist periods correspond to the two world wars. In the 1918-1925 period he opted for the rough application of expanses of paint with a spatula in the vein of the Expressionism of Die Brücke; his output after World War II comprised brighter, clearer works. For a long time a profound pessimism which kept him out of society (unlike, for example, Picasso) prevented his work from being placed in the Expressionist current of the 20th century to which it undoubtedly belongs.

Kokoschka is not only one of the most quintessentially Austrian artists but one of the most enthralling painters. His entire output is in line with that of Soutine or Chagall, in that he also translates into painting the Jewish mystique of Central Europe. A similar unfinished, almost frustrated appearance, with the concomitant abundant enthusiasm and above all the hidden meaning and internal reason of things and people, rooted out and exposed, was the hallmark of 20th-century Expressionism and typifies the work of Kokoschka.

He was a contributor to the following group exhibitions: 1908, 1909, Vienna; 1911, 25 of his paintings and a few drawings at the *Hagenbund*, Vienna; 1922 and 1948 Venice Biennale; 1950 Haus der Kunst, Munich; 1955, Vienna Secession. His key one-man exhibitions were as follows: 1910 at Paul Cassirer's gallery, Berlin; between 1912 and 1914 *Der Sturm* showed his works; in 1917 the Galerie Dada, Zurich, showed a production of his play *Sphinx und Strawman* (*Spinx and Strawman*), a satirical comedy, with an exhibition of his paintings; in 1927 a double exhibition in Berlin and Zurich; 1928 in London; 1931 at Galerie Georges Petit, Paris; 1931 in Mannheim; 1938 in Vienna, 1940 in New York; 1947 at the Kunsthalle, Basel; 1948-1949, a travelling exhibition in Boston, Saint Louis and San Francisco; 1954 in Santa Barbara and San Francisco; 1958 at Haus der Kunst, Vienna, Munich and Haus der Künstler, Vienna; 1966 in Karlsruhe, Stuttgart and the Kunsthaus in Zurich; 1971 at Österreische Galerie and the publication of an autobiography under his own auspices *Mein Leben* (*My Life*); 1976, numerous exhibitions to celebrate his 90th birthday; 1978, Japan. His posthumous exhibitions include: 1981, Brussels; 1983, Musée des Beaux-Arts, Bordeaux, then Hotel de Ville, Paris; 2002 *Oskar Kokoschka. Die Kunst des Bildnisses* (*Oskar Kokoscha. The Art of Portraiture*), Kunsthalle, Hamburg; 2002, *Kokoschka: Max Schmidt, Adolf Loos y sus Amigos* (*Kokoschka: Max Schmidt, Adolf Loos and their Contemporaries*), Museo Thyssen-Bornemisza, Madrid; 2002, *Kokoschka Nomade. Dessins et Croquis* (*The Nomadic Kokoschka, Drawings and Sketches*), Musée Jenish, Vevey; 2002, *Oskar Kokoshka. The Modern Portrait*, New Gallery in New York and Kunsthalle, Hamburg. In 2003 his work featured in the group exhibition *Phantom der Lust. Visionen des Masochismus in der Kunst Phantom of Desire. Visions of Masochism in Art*, dedicated to the late-19th-century German novelist Leopold von Sacher-Masoch, the inventor of masochism, at the Neue Galerie am Landesmuseum in Graz.

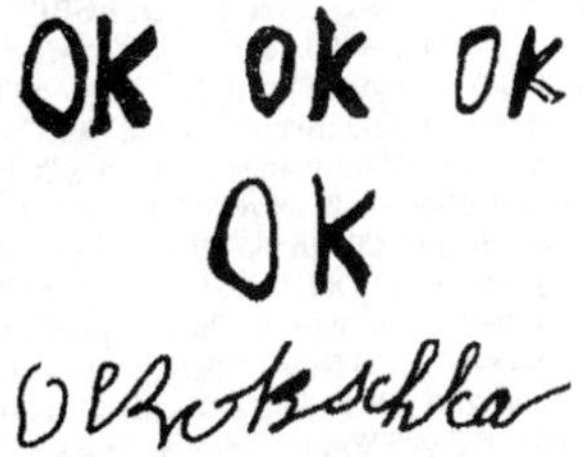

BIBLIOGRAPHY:

Westheim, Paul, *Oskar Kokoschka*, P. Cassirer, Berlin, 1925. Hoffmann, Edith, *Oskar Kokoschka, Life and Works*, Faber and Faber, London, 1947. Kokoschka, Oskar, *Kokoschka: Life and Work*, Faber and Faber, London, 1947. Wingler, Hans Maria, '*Oskar Kokoschka. Das Werk des Malers. Oeuvre-Verzeichnis*' in vol. I: Gemälde, catalogue raisonné, Gal. Welz, Salzburg, 1956. *Kokoschka: A Retrospective Exhibition of Paintings, Drawings, Lithographs, Stage Designs and Books*, Arts Council of Great Britain, London, 1962. Rathenau, Ernest, *Oskar Kokoschka: Handzeichnungen*, Ernest Rathenau, New York, 1973. Wingler, Hans Maria/Welz, Friedrich, '*Oskar Kokoschka, das druckgraphische Werk*' in *2 vols*, catalogue raisonné, Gal. Welz, Salzburg, 1975. Rathenau, Ernest, '*Oskar Kokoschka, Hanszeichnungen*' in *5 vols*, Euphorion, New York Berlin, 1977. Vergo, Peter, *Art in Vienna 1898-1918: Klimt, Kokoschka, Schiele and their Contemporaries*, Cornell University Press, Ithaca (NY), 1981. Sebarsky, Serge, *Kokoschka: Early Drawings and Watercolours 1906-1924*, Thames and Hudson, London, 1985. Kokoschka, Oskar, *Oskar Kokoschka 1886-1980*, Tate Gallery Publications, London, 1986. Kokoschka, Oskar, *Oskar Kokoschka 1886-1980: A Selection of Important Works on Paper*, Marlborough Fine Art, London, 1986. Whitford, F.rank, *Oskar Kokoschka: A Life*, Atheneum, New York, 1986. Calvocoressi, Richard, *Kokoschka: Paintings*, Academy Editions, London, 1992. Keegan, Susanne, *The Eye of God: A Life of Oskar Kokoschka*, Bloomsbury, London, 1999. Winkler, Johann/Gombrich, E. H./Alarcó, Paloma/Llorens, Tomás, *Kokoschka: Max Schmidt, Adolf Loos y sus Amigos*, exhibition catalogue, Museo Thyssen-Bornemisza, Madrid, 2002. *Oskar Kokoshka. Das Moderne Bildnis 1909-1914*, exhibition catalogue, Hamburger Kunsthalle, Hamburg, 2002. Weibel, Peter (ed.), '*Phantom der Lust. Visionen des Masochismus in der Kunst*' in *2 vols*, exhibition catalogue, Neue Galerie am Landesmuseum, Graz, Belleville Verlag, Munich, 2003.

MUSEUMS AND GALLERIES:

AMSTERDAM (Stedelijk Mus.): *Portrait of William Wauer* (1910) - BASEL (Kunsthalle): *Die Windsbraut* (*The Bride of the Wind*) (1914); *The Coast near Dover* (1926) - BASEL (Kunstmus.): *The Tempest or The Bride of the Wind* (1910); *The Tempest* (1914) - BERLIN (Nationalgal.): *Adolf Loos* (1909) - BERLIN (Staatliche Mus.): *Still-life with Pineapple* (1907) - BUFFALO (Albright-Knox AG): *London, Thames Landscape* (1926) - EINDHOVEN (Van Abbe Mus.): *The Power of Music* (1918); *Dresden Bridge* (1923); *Auguste Bridge with Steamer* (1923) - ESSEN (Folkwang Mus.): *Bridges over the Elbe at Dresden* (1923); *Dresden* (1923) - HAMBURG (Philosophy Faculty): *Thermopylae* (1954) - HANOVER (Niedersächsisches Landesmus.): *Delphi* (1956) - LIÈGE (Mus. of Modern and Contemporary Art): *Monte Carlo* (1925) - LINZ (Neue Gal. der Stadt): *Landscape of Linz* (1955); *The Friends* (1917-1918); *Marcel von Nemes* (1929) - LONDON (Tate Collection): *Dr Fannina W. Halle* (1910-1912, drawing on paper); *Polperro II* (1939, oil on canvas); *The Crab* (1939-1940, oil on canvas); *Loreley* (1941-1942, oil on canvas); *Study for Ambassador Ivan Maisky* (1942, drawing on paper); *Marianne-Maquis* (1942, oil on canvas); *View of the Thames* (1959, oil on canvas); *Time, Gentlemen Please* (1971-1972, oil on canvas) - MANNHEIM (Städtische Kunsthalle): *August Forel* (1910); *Portrait of a Little Girl* (1913); *Kloveniersburgwal in Amsterdam* (1925); *Amsterdam* - MUNICH (Bayerische Staatsgemaldesammlungen): *Venice* (1924) - NEW YORK (MoMA): *Portrait of Doctor Tietez and his Wife* (1909) - NEW YORK (Solomon R. Guggenheim Mus.): *Knight Errant* (1915) - PITTSBURGH (Carnegie MA): *Portrait of Tomas Garrigue Masaryk* (1935-1936, oil on canvas); prints - PRAGUE (Národní Gal.): *Charles Bridge in Prague* (1934); *The Wild Egg* (1940-1941); *Charles IV Bridge in Prague* (c. 1940) - ROTTERDAM (Mus. Boijmans Van Beuningen): *Double Portrait* (1919-1921); *The Mandrill* (1926) - STOCKHOLM (Moderna Mus.): *Marquis de Montesquieu* (1910) - STUTTGART (Staatsgal.): *Frau in Blau* (1919); *Herwath Walden* - THE HAGUE (Gemeentemus.): *Giant Tortoises* (1927) - VIENNA (Kunsthistorisches Mus.): *Still-life with Mutton and Hyacinth* (1909); *Pietà* (1908) - VIENNA (Österreichische Gal. Belvedere): *Portrait of Carl Moll* (1913) - WASHINGTON DC (Phillips Collection): *Lyons* (1927) - WINTERTHUR (Kunstmus.): *Hugo Caro* (1910) - ZURICH (Kunsthaus): *Lovers with Cat* (1917); *Else Kupfer* (c. 1911).

AUCTION RECORDS:

NEW YORK, 22 Nov 1949, *Tower Bridge*, USD 5,500. NEW YORK, 14 Jan 1959, *Street Scene in Baka* (watercolour and gouache) USD 1,500. NEW YORK, 23 March 1961, *Alpine Countryside* (1916, colouring pencil) USD 525. STUTTGART, 3 May 1961, *Woman in Red*, DEM 60,000. BERN, 18 June 1965, *Girl at Table* (watercolour) CHF 20,000. NEW YORK, 20 Nov 1968, *Portrait of Italian Peasant Woman*, USD 42,500. LONDON, 1 July 1970, *Still-life with Flowers*, GBP 22,000. LONDON, 29 Nov 1972, *Lake Geneva: Lake Geneva II*, GBP 54,000. DÜSSELDORF, 20 June 1973, *Mother and the Thenody Child* (1946) DEM 100,000. LONDON, 2 and 3 July 1974, *Autumn Flowers* (watercolour) GBP 2,200. NEW YORK, 18 March 1976, *Pilot Kobe and Käthe Richter* (1919, Indian ink, 14 x 18 1/4 ins / 35.5 x 46.5 cm) USD 4,250. HAMBURG, 3 June 1976, *Die Träumenden Knaben* (*The Dreaming Boys*) (1908, complete series of eight coloured lithographs) DEM 5,000. MUNICH, 29 Nov 1976, *Capriccio* (1943, oil on canvas, 24 3/4 x 30 ins / 63 x 76 cm) DEM 100,000. NEW YORK, 16 May 1977, *Florence, View* of the Mannelli Tower (1948, oil on canvas, 33 1/2 x 43 1/4 ins / 85 x 110 cm) USD 110,000. COLOGNE, 19 May 1979, *Portrait of Walter Hasenclever* (1918, lithograph, 24 1/4 x 16 1/4 ins / 61.5 x 41.5 cm) DEM 3,600. HAMBURG, 9 June 1979, *Portrait of Gino Schmidt* (1914, oil on canvas, 35 1/2 x 23 ins / 90 x 57.5 cm) DEM 255,000. MUNICH, 30 Nov 1979, *Portrait of Alma Mahler* (c. 1912-1913, charcoal, 9 3/4 x 8 1/4 ins / 25 x 21 cm) DEM 25,000. MUNICH, 30 Nov 1979, *The Two Friends* (c. 1922, watercolour, 20 x 26 3/4 ins / 50.5 x 68 cm) DEM 37,000. NEW YORK, 7 May 1981, *1908 Exhibition* (coloured lithograph, poster, 37 x 15 ins / 93.7 x 38 cm) USD 19,000. MUNICH, 27 Nov 1981, *Bouquet of Flowers* (1967, watercolour, 19 1/4 x 19 ins / 49 x 48 cm) DEM 36,000. LONDON, 29 Nov 1982, *The Thames from Chelsea Reach* (1957, oil on canvas, 30 x 40 ins / 76 x 101.5 cm) GBP 100,000. BERN, 22 June 1983, *Standing Nude* (1908, charcoal and watercolour, 17 1/4 x 9 3/4 ins / 43.5 x 25 cm) CHF 33,000. LONDON, 28 March 1984, *Venice: Santa Maria della Salute* (1948, oil on canvas, 33 1/2 x 43 1/4 ins / 85 x 110 cm) GBP 162,000. BERN, 21 June 1984, *Corona I* (1918, lithograph in red chalk/Japanese paper) CHF 6,200. LONDON, 27 June 1984, *Roses* (1969, watercolour, 25 x 19 1/2 ins / 63.5 x 49.5 cm) GBP 13,000. LONDON, 26 March 1985, *View of Hamburg with the Binnenalster and Jungfernsteig* (1926, oil on canvas, 27 1/2 x 37 1/2 ins / 70 x 95 cm) GBP 100,000. BERN, 18 June 1986, *Girl in Beret* (c. 1920-1922, black chalk, 24 x 18 ins / 61 x 45.5 cm) CHF 38,000. NEW YORK, 19 Nov 1986, *Seated Girl Smiling with Long Dark Hair* (c. 1921, watercolour/pencil outlines/paper, 27 1/4 x 19 3/4 ins / 69 x 50 cm) USD 115,000. COLOGNE, 10 Dec 1986, *Evelyn (Threnody)* (c. 1942-1945, oil on canvas, 36 x 28 ins / 91.5 x 71 cm) DEM 320,000. HAMBURG, 12 June 1987, *Self-portrait, Hand on Chest* (1911, coloured lithograph) DEM 35,000. MUNICH, 28 Oct 1987, *Portrait of Levin Ludwig Schückling* (1911, pencil, 6 3/4 x 5 1/2 ins / 17 x 14 cm) DEM 75,000. LONDON, 24 Feb 1988, *Portrait of Baron de La Grange* (1964, charcoal, 24 1/4 x 19 1/4 ins / 61.5 x 49 cm) GBP 3,300. MUNICH, 8 June 1988, *Girl with Small Dog* (Indian ink, 27 1/4 x 19 1/2 ins / 69 x 49.6 cm) DEM 10,450. LONDON, 19 Oct 1988, *Portrait of Henry-Louis de La Grange* (1964, charcoal, 23 x 18 ins / 58.4 x 45.8 cm) GBP 3,300. NEW YORK, 16 Feb 1989, *Meeting - Study for a Bach Cantata* (black chalk/paper, 12 1/4 x 16 3/4 ins / 31.1 x 42.5 cm) USD 8,250. ROME, 21 March 1989, *The Fall of Penthesilea* (1970, dry-point, 7 3/4 x 11 1/2 ins / 20 x 29.2 cm) ITL 1,900,000. NEW YORK, 9 May 1989, *Dresden - New City I* (1919, oil on canvas, 32 x 44 1/4 ins / 81.4 x 112.2 cm) USD 2,970,000. NEW YORK, 10 May 1989, *Still-life of a Bouquet by a Window* (1926, oil on canvas, 28 3/4 x 39 1/4 ins / 73 x 100 cm) USD 374,000. NEW YORK, 15 Nov 1989, *Toledo* (1925, oil on canvas, 26 1/2 x 39 1/2 ins / 67.3 x 100.3 cm) USD 418,000; *Prague seen from the Duke of Moldavia* (oil on canvas, 33 1/4 x 45 1/4 ins / 84.4 x 115.2 cm) USD 990,000. MUNICH, 13 Dec 1989, *Olive Branches and Figs* (1949, watercolour, 19 x 25 ins / 48.2 x 63.5 cm) DEM 27,500. PARIS, 23 April 1990, *Self-portrait* (1918, pencil, 11 3/4 x 8 1/2 ins / 30 x 21.5 cm) FRF 40,000. NEW YORK, 16 May 1990, *Reclining Nude* (1953, coloured wax crayon/paper, 18 x 23 3/4 ins / 45.7 x 60.6 cm) USD 33,000; *Prague - View from Strahow* (1934, oil on canvas, 31 x 554 3/4 ins / 79 x 1409.2 cm) USD 770,000. LONDON, 23 May 1990, *Still-life of Flowers* (1955, watercolour, 20 1/4 x 16 ins / 51.5 x 39.7 cm) GBP 20,900. LONDON, 3 Dec 1990, *Portrait of Dr Rudolf Blümmer* (1910, oil on canvas, 31 1/2 x 22 1/2 ins / 80 x 57.1 cm) GBP 990,000. LONDON, 19 March 1991, *Vine Branch* (1953, watercolour/paper, 18 3/4 x 25 ins / 47.7 x 63.3 cm) GBP 12,100. NEW YORK, 9 May 1991, *A Tidy Woman* (1933, oil on canvas, 26 x 33 3/4 ins / 65.1 x 85.6 cm) USD 68,200. BERLIN, 30 May 1991, *Female Nude* (ink, 26 3/4 x 20 ins / 68 x 50.5 cm) DEM 26,640. LONDON, 24 June 1991, *Richmond Terrace* (1926, oil on canvas, 35 x 49 ins / 89 x 124.5 cm) GBP 660,000. MUNICH, 26-27 Nov 1991, *Summer Bouquet* (watercolour, 18 x 20 1/2 ins / 46 x 52 cm) DEM 82,800. PARIS, 24 Feb 1992, *The Three Graces* (1958, watercolour, 25 x 19 ins / 63.3 x 48.5 cm) FRF 132,000. NEW YORK, 25-26 Feb 1992, *Young Gypsy* (gouache/paper, 26 1/2 x 19 ins / 67.3 x 48.3 cm) USD 39,600. ZURICH, 29 April 1992, *Self-portrait with Statuette* (1966, lithograph, 25 1/4 x 19 1/4 ins / 64.2 x 49 cm) CHF 2,600. BERLIN, 29 May 1992, *Annecy Lake* (oil on canvas, 27 1/2 x 35 3/4 ins / 70 x 91 cm) DEM 700,600. ROME, 14 Dec 1992, *Female Nude* (1953, colouring pencil/paper, 15 1/4 x 11 1/2 ins / 39 x 29 cm) ITL 23,000,000. LONDON, 23 June 1993, *Head of a Young Woman* (watercolour/paper/card, 26 1/4 x 19 ins / 66.8 x 48.3 cm) GBP 25,000. HEIDELBERG, 5-13 April 1994, *Christ on the Mount of Olives* (1916, lithograph, 11 x 12 1/2 ins / 28 x 31.5 cm) DEM 2,300. NEW YORK, 9 May 1994, *Portrait of Alice* (black chalk/paper, 22 3/4 x 18 ins / 58.1 x 45.7 cm) USD 13,800. LOKEREN, 8 Oct 1994, *Self-portrait with Tortoise* (1969, lithograph, 26 x 20 1/2 ins / 66 x 52 cm) BEF 33,000. LONDON, 28 June 1995, *Vision of a Dream* (gouache, watercolour and ink on pencil and colouring pencil, 8 x 6 ins / 20.5 x 15.5 cm) GBP 67,500. NEW YORK, 1 May 1996, *Portrait of Dr Robert Freund II* (oil on canvas, 29 1/2 x 20 1/2 ins / 74.9 x 52.1 cm) USD 200,500. ZURICH, 17-18 June 1996, *Grasshoppers* (coloured chalks, 6 x 7 3/4 ins / 14.3 x 20 cm) CHF 1,500. LONDON, 25 June 1996, *Still-life of Flowers* (watercolour, 17 3/4 x 23 ins / 45 x 57.5 cm) GBP 25,300. NEW YORK, 9 Oct 1996, *On the Beach* (1948, watercolour/paper, 19 1/4 x 27 1/2 ins / 48.9 x 69.8 cm) USD 14,950. LONDON, 3 Dec 1996, *Capriccio, Clearing in the Forest* (1943, oil on canvas, 24 1/2 x 29 1/4 ins / 62 x 74.5 cm) GBP 199,500. LONDON, 4 Dec 1996, *Still-life* (c. 1941-1942, watercolour/paper, 18 3/4 x 23 1/2 ins / 47.5 x 60 cm) GBP 18,400. LONDON, 22 Oct 1997, *Seated Woman* (1922, pencil/paper, 9 x 11 1/4 ins / 23 x 28.8 cm) GBP 4,140. NEW YORK, 6 and 7 March 1998, *Un Ballo in Maschera (The Masked Ball)* (1967, complete portfolio of seven lithographs and text by Marcel Jouhandeau) USD 2,300. COLOGNE, 13 Nov 1999, *Sunflowers* (1969, watercolour, 26 x 20 ins / 65 x 50 cm) DEM 86,000. BERLIN, 26 Nov 1999, *Portrait of Brother Bohuslav Kokoschka* (1920, chalk, 28 x 20 ins / 70 x 50 cm) DEM 80,000. LONDON, 17 Oct 2000, *London with the Houses of Parliament* (1967, oil on canvas, 36 x 54 ins / 92 x 137 cm) GBP 280,000. NEW YORK, 9 Nov 2000, *Blumen* (1958, gouache and watercolour, 25 x 19 ins / 63 x 48 cm) USD 20,000. LONDON, 6 Feb 2001, *View of London, with St Paul's Cathedral* (oil on canvas, 40 x 54 ins / 101 x 136 cm) GBP 180,000. LONDON, 26 June 2001, *Amsterdam Kloveniersburgwall* (1925, oil on canvas, 25 x 29 ins / 64 x 74 cm) GBP 130,000. MUNICH, 14 Nov 2002, *Flowers* (1971, watercolour, 26 x 19 ins / 66 x 48 cm) EUR 32,500. AMSTERDAM, 26 Nov 2002, *Standing Woman. Figure* (pencil, double-sided, 16 x 10 ins / 41 x 26 cm) EUR 140,000. NEW YORK, 5 Nov 2003, *London, Richmond Terrace* (1926, oil on canvas, 35 x 51 ins / 89 x 130 cm) USD 850,000. NEW YORK, 6 Nov 2003, *Still-life with Fruit and Jug* (1931, oil on canvas, 24 x 37 ins / 60 x 93 cm) USD 70,000. VIENNA, 27 May 2004, *Girl in Exotic Landscape* (pen, brush and ink over pencil, 13 x 8 ins / 33 x 20 cm) EUR 180,000. VIENNA, 27 May 2004, *Runner* (pen, brush, ink, watercolour and tempera heightened with white over pencil, 9 x 7 ins / 24 x 17 cm) EUR 330,000.

KOKULAR, Alexandre

Polish, 19th century.

Born 9 August 1793, in Warsaw; died 6 April 1846, in Warsaw.

Painter. History painting, portraits.

Alexandre Kokular studied with Vogel in Warsaw. In 1814, he went to Vienna, where he worked with Lampi at the academy of fine arts. Continuing his studies, he spent time in Rome and Paris, returning to Poland in 1818. In 1824, he went to Rome on a state bursary and stayed there for two years. It was there that he painted *Oedipus*. He was elected a member of the Accademia di S Luca in Rome.

KOLAM, Cornelis
Dutch, 17th century.
Born 1656.
Painter.
Kolam was married in Amsterdam on 20 October 1679.

KOLAR, Jiri
Czech, 20th century.
Born 24 September 1914, in Protivín; died 11 August 2002, in Prague.
Active in France from 1981, and since 1999 in the Czech Republic.
Painter (mixed media), collage artist, lithographer, poet. Visual Poetry.
Group 42.
Jiri Kolar was the son of a baker and a seamstress. He lived in the mining town of Kladno for many years earning money wherever he could: as a bricklayer's mate, as a navvy building metalled roads, as a waiter and so on. He received no training and as a painter and a poet was entirely self-taught. He lived in Paris.

At the age of 16, Kolar chanced on a Czech translation of Marinetti's *Parole in Libertà* (*Words in Liberty*). It was a decisive experience and from then on he devoted himself to anything that involved contemporary artistic or poetic creation. But he also retained the freedom of expression found in Surrealism and in around 1934 he began to produce the sort of collages that became a characteristic of his work. After 1938 he produced eight collages that were hung in an avant-garde theatre in Prague. This early experiment with three-dimensional art was not followed up, even though Kolar later composed poems and produced collages. On the occasion of the publication of *Extract from the Birth Certificate* at the end of the war, he met other young painters and became a member of the 42 Group. It was only several years later, however, around 1960, that he repeated his truly three-dimensional experiments. Kolar's poetry was already very close to graphic manipulation but his first visual poems had been completed in 1959: *Poems of Silence*; *Empty Poems* and *Obvious Poetry*. Then in 1961 he wrote his *Analphabetogrammes* and *Dongogrammes*, again poems without words but now hand-written. These were followed by poems made out of knots, string, or razor blades. The relationship between this creative genre and Surrealism seems clear. Eventually Kolar returned to collage, a process that he manipulated and by means of which he obtained results that were as surprising as they were varied. He used a variety of techniques for which it is not possible to draw a chronology, but it seems that after producing his *Pressed Collages* in 1962 he abandoned the written form for the true image. He took old engravings and by crumpling them he managed to animate the scene they were depicting in a spirit reminiscent of Pol Burry's *Kinetisations*. With his *Chiasmages* or *Khiasmage* (around 1965), Kolar returned to letterpress printing, cutting printed texts into a thousand pieces before reassembling them in a random order, either on flat surfaces or on some sort of backing material which could be as varied as a chair or his famous apples. He used the printed image and of typeset texts in alternation throughout his work, and occasionally both are used in a single composition, as in *Weekly Publications*, a sort of journal made up of collages inspired by real events (1967). After 1968 Kolar seems to have become more and more interested in copying paintings. Several different techniques appear simultaneously in his work. In his *Rollages* or *Spreads*, Kolar attempts to add dynamism to his work. Breaking down a reproduction into vertical bands he then puts it back together again in a different order. These *Rollages* lead quite naturally to the *Prollages* where, again using the same découpage technique, works by two different artists are copied, cut into bands and then mixed and reassembled on a single surface - Mondrian with Frans Hals, Guardi with Petrus Christus. In his *Butterflies* series, butterflies are arranged and pinned out as if on an entomologist's board, and fragments of reproductions of famous paintings can be glimpsed through their wings. This series may have a more direct charm but still questions the image and the written word. The creator of a world in which words no longer serve any purpose, Kolar targeted the hiatus between dream and reality.

Jiri Kolar exhibited regularly in Czechoslovakia from 1962 and played an important role in the country's artistic life. He also regularly exhibited abroad, particularly in London, and his work featured in many collective shows, sometimes of Czech art and sometimes in *Visual Poetry* exhibitions. He was also invited to attend major international meetings, notably in 1958 when his work featured at the Venice Biennale, and again at Documenta, Kassel. Other exhibitions include: Galerie Maeght, Paris (1981, 1983 and 1984); Galerie Lelong, Paris (his last poems and first collages, 1988); *Cent méthodes pour sortir du discours* (*One Hundred Ways of Getting Out of an Argument*), Les Cordeliers, Châteauroux (1996); *L'Œil éphémère. Œuvres sur papier de Jiri Kolar et Adriena Simotova* (*Ephemeral Eye. Works on Paper by Jiri Kolar and Adriena Simotova.*), Musée des Beaux-Arts, Dijon (as part of 'Bohemia Magica, a Czech Season in France', 2002).

His work was also shown in the exhibition *Rencontres - Cinquante ans de collages* (*Encounters - Fifty Years of Collage*) organised by Françoise Monin, Galerie Claudine Lustman, Paris (1991). Solo exhibitions include: Miami (1963), Ulm, Munich (1969), Paris (1971), Solomon R. Guggenheim Museum, New York (1975, 1978). He was a prizewinner at the São Paulo Biennale in 1969.

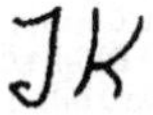

BIBLIOGRAPHY:
'Kolar Jiri' in *coll. BENCHMARKS. CONTEMPORARY SKETCH PADS NO. 8 Repères. Cahiers d'art contemporain* no. 8, Gal. Lelong, Paris. *Jiri Kolar*, exhibition catalogue, Gal. Maeght, Paris, 1981. *Jiri Kolar, artiste tchèque*, exhibition catalogue, Musée des Beaux-Arts, Dijon, 2002.

MUSEUMS AND GALLERIES:
LONDON (Grosvenor Gallery) - MONTREAL (NMMA): *Untitled* (1969) - PARIS (MNAM-CCI) - VIENNA (Mus. Moderner Kunst Stiftung Ludwig).

AUCTION RECORDS:
LONDON, 5 July 1973, *Black and White Collage*, USD 650. LONDON, 2 Dec 1976, *The Bride* (collage/card, 35 x 23 1/4 ins / 89 x 59 cm) GBP 600. ZURICH, 25 May 1978, *King Kong* (1962, collage, 10 1/4 x 8 3/4 ins / 25.9 x 22.5 cm) CHF 1,400. COLOGNE, 19 May 1979, *American Landscape* (1970, collage, 15 3/4 x 13 3/4 x 7 1/4 ins / 40 x 35 x 18.5 cm) DEM 2,200. NEW YORK, 5 May 1982, *Cello* (1973, object chiasmage, 29 3/4 x 17 ins / 75.5 x 43 cm) USD 2,300. NEW YORK, 6 May 1982, *Apple* (1965, object, h. 9 ins / 23 cm) USD 1,600. MILAN, 8 Nov 1984, *Apple* (1966, papier mâché and pieces of newspaper, h. 14 1/4 ins / 36 cm) ITL 1,700,000. MILAN, 10 April 1986, *The Stork Who Brought Modern Art* (1967-1972, wood and collage, 57 3/4 x 30 3/4 ins / 147 x 78 cm) ITL 24,000,000. PARIS, 14 Dec 1987, *Tri Vdalosti* (1963, collage, 15 1/4 x 10 ins / 38.5 x 25.6 cm) FRF 5,500. LONDON, 25 Feb 1988, *Self-portrait* (1979, mixed media, 11 3/4 x 9 ins / 30 x 23 cm) GBP 770. LONDON, 20 Oct 1988, *Untitled* (1972, collage/paper, 10 1/4 x 17 1/4 ins / 26 x 43.5 cm) GBP 935. PARIS, 29 Sept 1989, *Untitled* (1970, collage/card, 10 1/4 x 18 ins / 26 x 46 cm) FRF 13,000. MILAN, 27 March 1990, *Bathroom* (1966, collage, 12 x 9 1/4 ins / 30.5 x 23.5 cm) ITL 5,000,000. NEW YORK, 7 May 1990, *Untitled No. 2* (1968, collage/card, 9 3/4 x 17 1/2 ins / 24.6 x 44.5 cm) USD 4,950. PARIS, 16 May 1990, *Portrait of Joannes Bellinus* (1967, collage, 19 x 15 1/4 ins / 48 x 38.5 cm) FRF 19,000. AMSTERDAM, 22 May

1990, *An Interior: Cycle and Fables* (1987, collage of objects in a box, 15 3/4 x 15 3/4 x 15 3/4 ins / 40 x 40 x 40 cm) NLG 9,775. NEW YORK, 10 Oct 1990, *M. E. V. Kopane* (1976, spots and collage of adhesive stickers/panel, 27 1/2 x 39 1/4 ins / 70 x 99.7 cm) USD 8,800. ROME, 9 Dec 1991, *'Nikdo-Nikde'* (1982, collage and vinyl records/plywood, 15 3/4 x 11 3/4 ins / 40 x 30 cm) ITL 4,025,000. PARIS, 19 March 1992, *Albatross I* (1972, collage on wood, 39 x 27 1/2 ins / 99 x 70 cm) FRF 13,000. NEW YORK, 9 May 1992, *'Autovenuse'* (collage of printed paper/panel, 39 x 27 ins / 99 x 68.6 cm) USD 3,740. ROME, 12 May 1992, *Untitled* (1988, collage/panel, 19 3/4 x 25 1/2 ins / 50 x 65 cm) ITL 8,000,000. STOCKHOLM, 21 May 1992, *Composition: Portrait of a Woman* (collage, 9 x 6 ins / 22 x 15 cm) SEK 3,200. NEW YORK, 12 June 1992, *Untitled (violin)* (collage of objets on a mirror, 34 1/4 x 20 1/2 x 2 1/4 ins / 87 x 52.1 x 6 cm) USD 5,225. NEW YORK, 17 Nov 1992, *Volkswagen* (1969, collage of paper/card, 13 x 9 1/4 ins / 33 x 23.5 cm) USD 880. LONDON, 24-25 March 1993, *Untitled* (1970, collage/paper, 10 3/4 x 18 ins / 27.3 x 46 cm) GBP 1,495. MILAN, 6 April 1993, *'Srepn'* (1985, collage and mixed media/panel, 39 1/4 x 27 1/2 ins / 100 x 70 cm) ITL 8,900,000. PARIS, 5 July 1993, *Portrait* (1969, collage, 9 1/4 x 6 ins / 23.5 x 15.5 cm) FRF 5,000. NEW YORK, 29 Sept 1993, *Babylonian Smile* (1966, mixed media, 39 1/4 x 28 ins / 99.7 x 71.1 cm) USD 2,875. LUCERNE, 4 June 1994, *Collage* (collage and tearing, 9 1/2 x 7 3/4 ins / 24 x 19.5 cm) CHF 1,200. COPENHAGEN, 8-9 March 1995, *Composition* (collage, 39 1/4 x 27 1/2 ins / 100 x 70 cm) DKK 22,000. PARIS, 16 Dec 1996, *Baudelaire* (1973, collage/paper, 10 x 14 1/4 ins / 25.5 x 36 cm) FRF 3,500. PARIS, 23 Nov 1997, *Adoration of the Magi in My Childhood* (1982, collage, 15 3/4 x 11 3/4 ins / 40 x 30 cm) FRF 3,500. PARIS, 15 Dec 1997, *Globe* (1972, collage of paper/globe, h. 11 1/2 ins / 29 cm) FRF 13,500. HAMBURG, 3 Dec 1999, *Tray* (tray with printed wrapped household objects, 12 x 18x2 ins / 31 x 46x5 cm) DEM 4,000. PARIS, 19 April 2000, *Untitled* (collage, pair of skis) FRF 12,000. NEW YORK, 13 Nov 2001, *Chair* (c. 1975, printed paper collage on wood chair, 35 x 17x16 ins / 89 x 44x41 cm) USD 5,500. PRATO, 30 Nov 2001, *M.E.V. Kopane* (collage on board, 28 x 39 ins / 70 x 100 cm) ITL 11,000,000. MILAN, 14 May 2002, *Composition* (mixed media, 10 x 17 ins / 25 x 42 cm) EUR 1,800. HAMBURG, 14 June 2002, *Eye* (mixed media/collage on panel, 39 x 28 ins / 100 x 70 cm) EUR 5,200. MILAN, 13 March 2003, *Composition* (1965, mixed media, 18 x 13 ins / 45 x 33 cm) EUR 3,300. MILAN, 13 Nov 2003, *May Love* (1961, collage on cardboard, 11 x 8 ins / 29 x 21 cm) EUR 2,000. PARIS, 21 March 2004, *Nez prisel lev* (1989, collage on panel, 12 x 16 ins / 30 x 40 cm) EUR 1,800. DÜSSELDORF, 15 May 2004, *Sample book III/Temptation of St Anthony* (collage, 39 x 28 ins / 99 x 70 cm) EUR 3,800.

KOLASINSKI, Jean-Pierre
French, 20th century.
Born 1941.
Painter. Figures, nudes, landscapes, still-lifes.

Jean-Pierre Kolasinski was born in Provence to a Polish mother and a Marseillaise father. He is almost self-taught in painting. He often paints female figures in interiors and nudes, while still covering other traditional themes. His style of working relates to Post-Impressionism; he is able to evoke Renoir in his portraits of young women but with more hazy effects. Landscapes and still-lifes receive a graphic treatment, more precise and with livelier colours.

He takes part in many regional public exhibitions and also shows collections of paintings in solo exhibitions in several cities in the Midi. He exhibited at Bordeaux and at Caracas in 1969, Galerie Marcel Benheim in Paris in 1971, at Antwerp in 1975, Quebec in 1981, New York in 1982, Rome and Dallas in 1983, Paris and Revin (Ardennes) in 1989, Monaco and Chicago in 1992 and has won various prizes, medals and mentions.

KOLASINSKI, Wawrzyniec
Polish, 19th century.
Born 1777, in Pradl, near Cracow; died 1846, in Pilica.
Painter.

Wawrzyniec Kolasinski painted murals for the churches in Pilica.

KOLAWOLE, Lawrence Compton
American, 20th century.
Born 20 August 1931, in Beaumont (Texas).
Painter, sculptor, draughtsman.

Lawrence Compton Kolawole studied at the California School of Fine Arts. During the 1960s and 1970s he lived in Paris and Munich. His work, characterised by simple drawing, lively colours and iconography, belongs to the 1960s African movement in the USA.

He took part in group exhibitions, for example, in 1970, National Center of Afro-American Artists, Boston and in 2005 at the Heckscher Museum of Art, Huntington, New York. His solo exhibitions include in 1955, Lucien Labaudt Gallery, San Francisco; 1967, 1968, Galerie Shrag, Nuremberg; 1967, Goethe House, Lagos; 1969, Galerie Soulange, Paris and in 1971, Museum der Stadt, Witten, Germany.

BIBLIOGRAPHY:
Lewis, Samella/Waddy, Ruth G., *Black Artists on Art vol. I*, Contemporary Crafts, Los Angeles, 1969. *Kolawole, L. C. - Motion Art*, exhibition catalogue, Galerie L 55, Paris, 1973.

KOLB, Alfred
German, 20th century.
Born 1878, in Hörhausen.
Painter.

Alfred Kolb attended the École des Beaux-Arts in Paris in 1898. He came under the influence of Cézanne and Derain.

KOLB, Alois
German, 19th - 20th century.
Born 12 February 1875, in Vienna or Ebersberg; died 1942, in Leipzig.
Painter, engraver, illustrator, lithographer. Figures.

Alois Kolb is best known for his numerous book illustrations, which he carried out mostly from 1971 onwards.

AUCTION RECORDS:
MUNICH, 1 June 1987, *Woman in Fur Coat before Mirror* (1926, oil on panel, 46 3/4 x 33 1/2 ins / 119 x 85 cm) DEM 6,200.

KOLB, Anna. See **JAGEMANN**

KOLB, Augustin
German, 19th century.
Born July 1869, in Guntersleben.
Painter, engraver.

Kolb produced painted and engraved illustrations of biblical and Christian scenes.

KOLB, Franz
Austrian, 19th century.
Born 22 September 1789, in Vienna; died 1865, in Vienna.
Engraver (mezzotint).

Kolb studied under Kininger. He engraved history subjects and portraits.

KOLB, Franz Xaver
German, 19th century.
Born 27 November 1827, in Ehingen; died 30 June 1889, in Ellwangen.
Painter.

Kolb's work mainly involved decorating churches.

KOLB, Jean Louis
French, 20th - 21st century.
Born 1956, in Niort.
Painter.

Jean Louis Kolb studied at the École Nationale d'Art Décoratif of Limoges and obtained a masters degree in fine arts in 1985 at the University of Paris. He lives and works in Nice. His paintings seem to be looking far back to a thought, a figure, a state that shows through the matter, or, according to Giovanni Jappolo, through the 'narrow doorway' which the painting has become, to 'an overflowing of the awareness of the world'.

He shows his work in solo exhibitions: 1985, Centre d'Art Contemporain, Abbaye de Maymac; 1987, *Paintings*, Galerie Krief-Raymond, Paris; 1987, Institut Culturel, Naples; 1989, Institut Français, Naples; 1989, Galerie Le Troisième Œil, Bordeaux; 1989, Centre d'Art Contemporain, Castres; 1990, Galerie Krief, Paris; 1990, Musée des Beaux-Arts de Beaune; 1991, Galerie Artset, Limoges; 1992, Galerie Le Troisième Œil, Paris; 1995, Galerie Krief, Paris.

BIBLIOGRAPHY:

Jappolo, Giovanni, *'Jean Louis Kolb'* in *Opus international*, periodical, Paris, March-April 1990.

KOLB, Johann Christoph

German, 18th century.
Born 1680, in Augsburg; died 1743.
Active in Augsburg.
Engraver.

Kolb's known works include a *Collection of Portraits of Cardinals* and *Landscapes with Cottages*.

KOLB, Joseph Maximilian

German, 19th century.
Active in Munich.
Engraver.

Kolb specialised in views of towns and monuments.

KOLB, Paulus, the Elder

German, 17th century.
Died 5 October 1650.
Active in Nuremberg.
Painter, engraver (etching).

Kolb studied under C. Weyer. He engraved portraits.

AUCTION RECORDS:

COLOGNE, 21 May 1970, *Fantasy Landscape*, DEM 18,000.

KOLB, Paulus, the Younger

German, 17th century.
Died 11 October 1656.
Active in Nuremberg.
Painter.

Kolb was a master painter from 1645.

KOLBE, Carl Wilhelm, the Elder

German, 18th - 19th century.
Born 20 November 1757, in Berlin; died 13 February 1835, in Dessau.
Draughtsman, engraver.

Kolbe was a French teacher and an artist in his spare time. He was almost 30 when his relative Chodowiecki persuaded him to pursue a career in art. He entered the academy in Berlin in 1793, where he studied under Miel. After two years of study, having been accepted by the academy in his home town, he returned to Dessau, where he became an art teacher at the college of higher education. In the meantime he engraved prints after Waterloo and Gessner. He produced mainly landscapes and idyllic compositions. He is noted for his engravings, especially 25 prints, after watercolours by Gessner, produced in Zurich between 1806 and 1811.

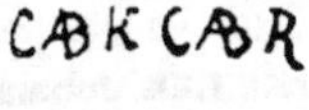

AUCTION RECORDS:

HAMBURG, 7 June 1979, *Hut in the Forest* (pencil and pen, $15\frac{1}{4}$ x 18 ins / 38.6 x 44.8 cm) DEM 3,400. MUNICH, 25 Nov 1982, *Back View of Woman with Parasol* (black chalk, $18\frac{1}{4}$ x $11\frac{3}{4}$ ins / 46.5 x 30 cm) DEM 6,200. HEIDELBERG, 9 Oct 1992, *Oak Trees near a Pond* (black chalk, $12\frac{3}{4}$ x $16\frac{1}{2}$ ins / 32.5 x 41.7 cm) DEM 8,000. HEIDELBERG, 3 April 1993, *Young Shepherds* (etching, $17\frac{1}{4}$ x $14\frac{3}{4}$ ins / 43.6 x 37.5 cm) DEM 1,150. HAMBURG, 8 May 2002, *Tree Study* (1800, pencil, 17 x 22 ins / 42 x 55 cm) EUR 2,700.

KOLBE, Carl Wilhelm, the Younger

German, 19th century.
Born 7 March 1781, in Berlin; died 8 April 1853, in Berlin.
Painter, fresco artist. Religious subjects, genre scenes.
Designs for stained glass.

Kolbe was the son of a gold embroiderer and a relation of his namesake Carl Wilhelm the Elder. As with the latter, it was on the advice of Chodowiecki that he pursued an artistic career and became one of his students at the academy. In 1796 he was awarded first prize for a drawing representing *The Death of Froben in the Battle of Fehrbellin*. He rapidly achieved success. He became a member of the academy in Berlin in 1815, and became a professor and member of the academic council in 1830. He was awarded gold medals in Berlin in 1849 and 1853.

He adopted the style of the old Dutch painters, giving his compositions a rather dramatic appearance, as was the fashion of the time, which only increased their popularity with the public. The cartoons for the stained glass windows in the castle at Marienburg (now Malbork, Poland), in which German chivalric orders triumph, are attributed to Kolbe. His most important works include *The Ascension of Christ*, in the chapel in Potsdam, and the frescoes of the songs of the Niebelungen in the marble Palace in Potsdam.

MUSEUMS AND GALLERIES:

GRAZ: *Othon the Great Fighting the Hungarians* (sketch).

KOLBE, Ernst

German, 20th century.
Born 9 January 1876, in Marienwerder (now Kwidzyn, Poland); died 1945.
Painter, lithographer. Genre scenes, landscapes.

Kolbe took part in the 1909 exhibition in Berlin.

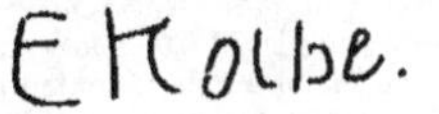

AUCTION RECORDS:

VIENNA, 17 March 1976, *Fields and Houses* (oil on card, $19\frac{3}{4}$ x $23\frac{1}{2}$ ins / 50 x 60 cm) ATS 28,000. AHLDEN, 3 May 2002, *Berlin Cathedral* (oil on canvas, 35 x 30 ins / 90 x 75 cm) EUR 2,700. WARSAW, 16 June 2002, *Interior with Woman Standing by a Window* (oil on canvas, 24 x 20 ins / 60 x 51 cm) PLN 12,000.

KOLBE, Etienne Maria

German, 19th century.
Born 1 January 1809, in Paris; died 1835, in Düsseldorf.
Painter.

Two portraits by Kolbe, entitled: *Herr and Frau Schreiner* can be seen at the museum in Düsseldorf.

KOLBE, Georg

German, 20th century.
Born 15 April 1877, in Waldheim; died 1947, in Berlin.
Sculptor, lithographer. Figures, nudes.

Georg Kolbe began as a painter, but devoted himself to sculpture after meeting Rodin in Paris and Tuaillon in Rome in 1898. After returning to Germany, he met Max Klinger in Leipzig, who became his friend and mentor. Kolbe settled in Berlin in 1903, where he became a member of the Secession. He travelled to Florence in 1905, Egypt in 1913 and Greece in 1931. After volunteering for the army in 1915, Kolbe was commissioned to design war memorials, including one in Eppegem (1916), one in Belgium and another in Therapia, near Istanbul. In 1936, he received the Goethe prize from the City of Frankfurt. His last years were overshadowed by illness and the gradual loss of his sight. Following his death, a Georg Kolbe Museum was set up at Berlin-Charlottenburg.

The influence of Rodin and Maillol is conspicuous in his gracious figures, like the *Dancer* (1912), the *Slave* (1917) and the *Crouching Woman* (1928), and also in his more serious works, such as the *Annunciation* (1924) and *Pietà* (1929). His preoccupation with the aesthetic of the stereotyped male athlete, which found favour with the Nazis, was later eclipsed by his sensibility towards figures, as witnessed in the *Young Girl Standing*, sculpted in 1937 for the Goethehaus in Frankfurt, and restrained male forms, as in *Resting Athlete* (1935).

BIBLIOGRAPHY:

Cassirer, P., *Georg Kolbe Bildwerke*, Berlin, 1973. Berger, Ursel, *Georg Kolbe - Leben un Werk mit dem Katalog der Kolbe-Plastiken im Georg-Kolbe-Mueum*, exhibition catalogue, Mann, Berlin, 1990.

AUCTION RECORDS:

NEW YORK, 26 Oct 1960, *Nude* (bistre wash) USD 500. NEW YORK, 26 Oct 1967, *Allegro*, USD 7,000. NEW YORK, 9 April 1969, *Fourth Model for the Monument to Beethoven*, USD 14,500. NEW YORK, 3 March 1974, *Standing Nude* (black and green-patinated bronze) USD 11,000. NEW YORK, 28 May 1976, *Kneeling Nude* (1944, dark-gold patinated bronze, h. 17 ins / 43 cm) USD 6,500. NEW YORK, 13 May 1977, *Lamentation (Crouching Nude)* (1921, red and brown patinated bronze, h. 16 1/2 ins / 42 cm) USD 7,000. MUNICH, 31 May 1979, *Seated Nude* (Indian ink, 17 3/4 x 9 1/2 ins / 45 x 24 cm) DEM 6,400. MUNICH, 27 Nov 1979, *Kneeling Nude* (1926, patinated bronze, h. 21 1/4 ins / 54 cm) DEM 32,000. MUNICH, 25 Nov 1981, *Kneeling Nude, Arms Stretched Out* (pen and wash, 17 x 13 3/4 ins / 43 x 35 cm) DEM 8,000. LOS ANGELES, 21 June 1982, *Seated Nude Singing* (gilt-patinated bronze, h. 25 1/2 ins / 65 cm) USD 10,000. LONDON, 7 Dec 1983, *Kneeling Nude* (1926, bronze, h. 21 1/4 ins / 54 cm) GBP 17,000. MUNICH, 6 June 1984, *Seated Nude* (pencil and wash, 15 x 9 ins / 38 x 22 cm) DEM 6,100. LUCERNE, 12 Nov 1986, *Two Seated Nudes* (black chalk and charcoal, 14 1/2 x 19 3/4 ins / 37 x 50 cm) CHF 6,500. LONDON, 2 Dec 1986, *Cathedral* (1922, dark-brown patinated bronze, H.22 1/2 ins / 57 cm) GBP 16,000. BERLIN, 23 May 1987, *Kneeling Nude* (brown wash, 17 3/4 x 13 1/2 ins / 45 x 34.4 cm) DEM 10,500. PARIS, 21 March 1988, *Kneeling Woman* (h. 9 1/2 ins / 24 cm) FRF 72,000. LONDON, 28 June 1988, *Woman Bathing* (bronze, h. 28 ins / 71 cm) GBP 44,000. NEW YORK, 6 Oct 1988, *The Grandson* (1930, bronze, h. 9 ins / 23 cm) USD 2,200. LONDON, 21 Feb 1989, *Kneeling Man* (charcoal/paper, 16 3/4 x 13 ins / 42.5 x 32.8 cm) GBP 605. MUNICH, 7 June 1989, *Resurrection* (bronze, h. 30 ins / 76 cm) DEM 77,000. NEW YORK, 5 Oct 1989, *Statuette* (1925, bronze, h. 15 3/4 ins / 40 cm) USD 17,600. NEW YORK, 6 Oct 1989, *Kneeling Woman* (1926, bronze, h. 21 1/4 ins / 54 cm) USD 26,400. NEW YORK, 26 Feb 1990, *Lamentation* (1921, brown-patinated bronze, h. 15 3/4 ins / 40 cm) USD 23, 100. NEW YORK, 10 Oct 1990, *Supplication* (dark-green patinated bronze, h. 17 1/2 ins / 44.6 cm) USD 13,200. NEW YORK, 14 Nov 1990, *Supplication* (1921, bronze, h. 15 1/2 ins / 39.4 cm) USD 29,700. NEW YORK, 14 Feb 1991, *Grovelling Woman* (dark-patinated bronze, l. 9 1/2 ins / 24.1 cm) USD 8,800. LONDON, 25 June 1991, *Couple of Young Women* (brown-patinated bronze, h. 27 1/4 ins / 69.5 cm) GBP 22,000. LONDON, 16 Oct 1991, *Javanese Dancer* (bronze, h. 28 3/4 ins / 73 cm) GBP 28,600. BERLIN, 27 Nov 1992, *Assunta* (black-patinated bronze, h. 77 1/4 ins / 196 cm) DEM 135,600. NEW YORK, 29 Sept 1993, *Running Man* (ink and wash/paper, 18 x 13 1/2 ins / 45.7 x 34 cm) USD 1,610. NEW YORK, 4 Nov 1993, *Resurrection* (bronze, h. 30 ins / 75.9 cm) USD 40,250. LONDON, 1 Dec 1993, *Standing Woman* (1929, bronze, h. 30 ins / 76.5 cm) GBP 17,250. LONDON, 11 Oct 1995, *Peasant Woman with Basket and Dog* (1930, oil on canvas, 35 1/2 x 27 1/2 ins / 90 x 70 cm) GBP 56,500. NEW YORK, 9 Nov 1995, *Benediction* (1940, bronze, h. 30 3/4 ins / 78.1 cm) USD 16,100. NEW YORK, 10 Oct 1996, *Portrait of Young Man* (oil on canvas, 37 1/4 x 23 1/4 ins / 94.6 x 59.1 cm) USD 5,462. NEW YORK, 13 Nov 1996, *Allegro* (1929, dark-brown patinated bronze, h. 28 1/4 ins / 71.8 cm) USD 37,950. NEW YORK, 14 Nov 1996, *Kneeling* (1926, brown-patinated bronze, h. 20 ins / 51 cm) USD 18,400. LONDON, 4 Dec 1996, *Dancer* (1914, bronze, h. 25 1/2 ins / 64.5 cm) GBP 17,250. LONDON, 24 June 1997, *The Bather* (1921, bronze, h. 28 ins / 71 cm) GBP 89,500. BERLIN, 4 June 1999, *Assumption* (1920, black patinated bronze, 31 x 7x7 ins / 78 x 17x19 cm) DEM 115,000. BERLIN, 26 Nov 1999, *Small Dancer* (1917, wood, h. 20 ins / 50 cm, w. 15 ins/39 cm) DEM 250,000. BERLIN, 26 May 2000, *Seated Figure* (yellowish patinated bronze, 11 x 10x7 ins / 28 x 26x18 cm) DEM 95,000. BERLIN, 24 Nov 2000, *Javanese Dancer* (brown-black patinated bronze, 29 x 13x15 ins / 73 x 33x37 cm) DEM 140,000. NEW YORK, 10 May 2001, *The Dancer Nijinsky* (dark brown patinated bronze, h. 25 ins / 64 cm) USD 55,000. BERLIN, 30 Nov 2001, *Kneeling Figure* (yellow-brownish patinated bronze, 22 x 10x9 ins / 55 x 25x22 cm) DEM 68,000. LONDON, 9 Oct 2002, *Woman Bathing* (bronze, h. 28 ins / 71 cm) GBP 70,000. NEW YORK, 5 Nov 2002, *Faller* (brown patinated bronze, 15 x 18x13 ins / 38 x 46x34 cm) USD 80,000. BERLIN, 30 May 2003, *Allegro* (brown patinated bronze, h. 28 ins / 72 cm) EUR 50,000. NEW YORK, 5 Nov 2003, *Female Dancer* (1922, brown patinated bronze, h. 27 ins / 69 cm) USD 55,000. LONDON, 20 Oct 2004, *Statuette* (1925, bronze, h. 16 ins / 41 cm) GBP 16,000. BERLIN, 26 Nov 2004, *Japanese Woman* (1911, black patinated bronze, h. 18 ins / 46 cm) EUR 40,000.

KOLBE, Heinrich Christoph

German, 18th - 19th century.

Born 2 April 1771, in Düsseldorf; died 16 January 1836, in Düsseldorf.

Painter. History painting, portraits.

Kolbe studied at the art college in Düsseldorf. He also worked for some time in Paris. He won a prize at an exhibition in Weimar and was appointed professor at the academy in his home town.

MUSEUMS AND GALLERIES:

COLOGNE: *Portrait of Goethe* - DÜSSELDORF: *Portrait of Goethe.*

AUCTION RECORDS:

LONDON, 14 Feb 1990, *Portrait of Alwine and Robert Uellenberg* (1825, oil on canvas, 27 1/4 x 23 ins / 69 x 58.5 cm) GBP 6,600. NEW YORK, 24 Oct 1996, *Helen and Paris* (1819, oil on canvas, 51 1/2 x 64 1/2 ins / 130.8 x 163.8 cm) USD 68,500. PARIS, 28 June 2000, *Portrait of Three Young Men, Bust of a Woman behind* (1820, oil on canvas, 41 x 50 ins / 105 x 128 cm) FRF 300,000.

KOLBECH, J.

Austrian, 19th century.

Painter.

AUCTION RECORDS:

PARIS, 12 April 1943, *Portrait of Man*, FRF 1,500.

KÖLBEL, Johannes

Norwegian, 20th century.

Born 19 April 1883, in Malmö.

Painter, engraver.

Johannes Kölbel worked in Oslo, Copenhagen, Berlin and Dresden.

KÖLBEL, Rudolf
German, 19th - 20th century.
Born 1826, in Berlin; died 7 January 1910, in Oldenburg.
Sculptor, medallist.
Rudolf Kölbel worked for the grand-ducal court of Oldenburg.

KÖLBER, Dezso
Hungarian, 20th century.
Born 1874, in Budapest.
Painter, decorative artist.
Dezso Kölber is known for his decorations for the Count of Palffy and for Prince Esterhazy's castle in Eisenstadt.

KOLBERG, Andreas Johnsen
Danish, 19th century.
Born 25 November 1817, in Copenhagen; died 10 August 1869, in Copenhagen.
Sculptor.
Andreas Kolberg is noted for *Ruth and Boaz* dated 1843.

KOLBERG, Anton
Polish, 19th century.
Born 1816, in Machory; died 1882, in Warsaw.
Painter.
Anton Kolberg painted mainly historical and religious subjects, also a *Portrait of Chopin*.

KOLBERG, Peter
German, 18th century.
Born c. 1700, in Mehlsack (Pieniezno), Poland.
Painter.
The cathedral in Frombork owns a painting by Kolberg entitled *Nativity*.

KÖLBL, Anton
Austrian, 18th - 19th century.
Born 24 February 1771, in Vienna; died 1832 or 1843, in Vienna.
Engraver.
Kölbl was active between 1799 and 1806, producing mostly history subjects.

KOLDE, Alexander
German, 20th century.
Born 2 March 1886, in Neuhaldensleben.
Painter, engraver.
Kolde lived mainly in Königsberg (now Kaliningrad, Russia) and spent time in New York after World War I. He had a predilection for large coloured and stylised compositions.

KÖLDERER, Yorg
Austrian, 16th century.
Died 1540, in Innsbruck.
Painter, architect.
Kölderer is recorded as working for the court of Emperor Maximillian I in 1497. Later, he would produce a painting that was one of Charles V's, and subsequently Ferdinand I's, favourites, and he continued to receive important commissions until the time of his death. He produced both frescoes and miniatures.

KOLDEWEY, Bernard Marie
Dutch, 19th century.
Born 23 November 1859, in Dordrecht; died 17 December 1898, in Dordrecht.
Painter. Genre scenes, landscapes.
Koldewey was the pupil of C.-J. de Vogel and Roland Lary, and a student at the Koninklijke Academie voor Schone Kunsten in Antwerp. He visited Southern Italy and Corsica. He was awarded a medal in Munich in 1897.

MUSEUMS AND GALLERIES:
STUTTGART: *Unloading Mussels in Philipperno.*
AUCTION RECORDS:
AMSTERDAM, 5-6 Nov 1991, *Farmyard* (oil on canvas, 14 1/4 x 20 ins / 36 x 50.5 cm) NLG 1,380. AMSTERDAM, 24 Sept 1992, *Houses beside a Canal* (1889, oil on canvas, 22 x 17 1/4 ins / 56 x 43.5 cm) NLG 1,092. AMSTERDAM, 14 Sept 1993, *Woman Knitting* (oil on canvas, 17 3/4 x 11 ins / 45 x 28 cm) NLG 1,265. AMSTERDAM, 7 Nov 1995, *On the Track near Blaricum Houses in Holland* (oil on canvas, 42 1/2 x 64 1/4 ins / 108 x 163 cm) NLG 8,260. AMSTERDAM, 18 Jan 2000, *Shepherdess and Flock* (1889, oil on canvas, 17 x 34 ins / 43 x 86 cm) NLG 4,500. GRAVENHAGE, 24 April 2002, *My Dog* (oil on canvas, 10 x 14 ins / 25 x 35 cm) EUR 2,200. GRAVENHAGE, 6 Nov 2002, *Shell Fisherman on the Beach* (oil on canvas, 33 x 42 ins / 83 x 106 cm) EUR 4,000. AMSTERDAM, 1 Sept 2004, *View of Dordrecht on the Meuse* (oil on canvas, 32 x 41 ins / 82 x 103 cm) EUR 1,800.

KOLDING, Peder Jensen. See **JENSEN Peder**

KOLEMANS, Peter
Flemish School, 16th century.
Active in Mechelen.
Painter.
He married Marthe Legwarole in Vienna on 28 April 1590.

KOLESAR, Marijan
Croat, 20th century.
Born 1936, in Zagreb.
Active in Belgium from 1966.
Painter, watercolourist. Figures, nudes, landscapes, seascapes.
Marijan Kolesar studied science at Zagreb university. He painted mainly sensual nudes and seascapes, both influenced by Impressionism.

He has taken part in several collective exhibitions since 1967 including: Centre Culturel, Antwerp (1968); festival of graphic art, Osaka (1980). Solo exhibitions include: cultural centre, Krizevci (1959); Zagreb city museum (1973); cultural centre, Belgrade (1978); Galerie Marcel Bernheim, Paris (1978); retrospective, Krizevci city museum (1979); Galerie Katia Granoff, Paris (1980); Yugoslav cultural centre, Paris (1981).

MUSEUMS AND GALLERIES:
ANTWERP (Jesode Hatora Beth Jacob Mus.) - LAETHEM-ST-MARTIN (MCA) - NEW YORK (Rockefeller Art Institute) - OSTEND (Fine Arts Museum) - OVAR (Ovar Museum) - VICTORIA (AG of Greater Victoria).

KOLESNIK, Boris
Russian, 20th century.
Born 1927, in Kharkov.
Painter.
Boris Kolesnik attended the institute of fine arts in Kharkov between 1949 and 1955.
AUCTION RECORDS:
PARIS, 13 March 1992, *Apple Picking* (oil on canvas, 20 1/2 x 25 ins / 52 x 63.5 cm) FRF 5,500.

KOLESNIKOV, Sergei, or Kolesnikoff
Russian, 20th century.
Born 25 January 1889, in Kalgon; died 1947.
Active in Germany from 1918.
Painter, engraver. Local scenes, genre scenes, still-lifes.
Sergei Kolesnikov lived in St. Petersburg until the outbreak of the Russian Revolution in 1917 and later went to live in Germany.

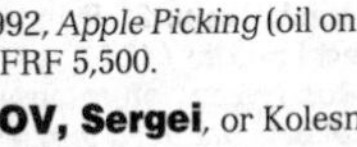

Auction records:
New York, 25 Jan 1980, *Peasants in a Landscape* (1955, oil on canvas remounted on board, 14 1/2 x 19 ins / 37 x 48.5 cm) USD 1,600. London, 5 March 1981, *Mountainous Landscape Enlivened with Figures* (1930, oil on canvas, 34 1/4 x 44 1/2 ins / 87 x 113 cm) GBP 4,500. Cologne, 30 March 1984, *Winter Landscape* (tempera, 19 3/4 x 24 3/4 ins / 50 x 63 cm) DEM 7,500. London, 20 Feb 1985, *Villagers on Their Way to Church* (gouache, 14 1/4 x 18 1/2 ins / 36 x 47 cm) GBP 1,700. London, 1 May 1987, *Two Washerwomen* (oil on panel, oval, 17 1/4 x 20 3/4 ins / 43.5 x 53 cm) GBP 1,800. Paris, 7 Nov 1988, *Evening in front of a Farm* (19 3/4 x 25 1/2 ins / 50 x 65 cm) FRF 13,500; *Woman on the Sea Shore* (oil on canvas, 19 3/4 x 25 1/2 ins / 50 x 65 cm) FRF 9,000. London, 14 Nov 1988, *Encampment of Bohemians* (1913, oil on canvas, 20 3/4 x 30 1/2 ins / 53 x 77.5 cm) GBP 1,210. Stockholm, 14 Nov 1990, *Still-life with Melons* (oil on canvas, 48 x 65 1/4 ins / 121 x 166 cm) SEK 77,000. London, 18 Nov 1999, *Hunter and his Dog* (oil on card, 9 x 11 ins / 24 x 28 cm) GBP 1,700. London, 18 Nov 1999, *After the Service* (oil on canvas, 28 x 39 ins / 72 x 100 cm) GBP 4,500. Zurich, 11 Dec 2001, *Landscape with Washerwoman* (gouache, 19 x 25 ins / 48 x 63 cm) CHF 4,000. Calais, 14 April 2002, *Cart and Peasant Woman in the Mountains* (oil on canvas, 34 x 46 ins / 86 x 117 cm) EUR 7,000. Lindau, 9 Oct 2002, *Bare Trees in Sunny Winter Landscape* (oil on canvas, 19 x 23 ins / 49 x 59 cm) EUR 3,800. Vienna, 24 April 2003, *Winter Landscape* (gouache, 20 x 26 ins / 50 x 66 cm) EUR 3,200.

KOLESOV, A. M.

Russian, 19th century.
Died 1901.
Painter. Portraits.

Museums and Galleries:
Moscow: *Portrait of the Painter S K Zarianko; Portrait of the Painter I I Shishkin; Portrait of the Painter A K Savrasov; Portrait of the Journalist P Guiharov Platanov.*

KOLHOWSTZ

19th century.
Painter. Genre scenes.

Kolhowstz is listed by Florence Levy.

Auction records:
New York, 21 Dec 1910, *Trial of Skill,* USD 107.

KOLIBAL, Stanislav

Czechoslovak, 20th century.
Born 11 December 1925, in Orlová.
Draughtsman, sculptor, installation artist, illustrator, painter. Stage sets.

Stanislav Kolibal lived and worked in Prague. From 1945 to 1950 he studied at the school of decorative arts in Prague and at the academy of dramatic art from 1951 to 1954. He also taught there from 1954 to 1962 while at the same time producing stage designs. He was a member of UB 12. A teacher at the school of fine arts in Prague from 1990, he won a scholarship that enabled him to work in Berlin. In 1992 the Calder Foundation provided him with a studio for six months in Saché, France.

In spite of the long years of cultural authoritarism in Czechoslovakia, Kolibal continued to produce works of art. After one particular period that lasted until 1962, during which his sculptures were inspired by the shape of torsos, he turned more towards abstract forms and began to work in plaster, polyester, sometimes in bronze. In 1965 he gave his creations the appearance of tropical creepers, of blossoms, twisting and writhing, supple and soaring skywards into space: *Monument for the Paper* (1967); *Disappearing Shape* (1968). From 1989 he showed compositions that had large but fine shapes, plates made out of plywood, with flat surfaces, sometimes with the arc of a circle, laid out at a right angle in relation to the ground. These huge, upwardly-soaring ensembles, places of calm yet also of underlying tension, are like the units of some ideal volume to be constructed 'to give' in his words 'an impression of order, of harmony and of silence to the visitors'. He took sculptural compositions originating from drawings done in Berlin in 1988 and then added aluminium and transparent materials. He regarded himself as a conceptual artist in tune with the analytical preoccupations of artists such as Buren or Morellet.

Collective exhibitions include *Czechoslovakian Sculpture from 1900 to the Present Day*, Folkwang museum, Essen (1966); Salon de Mai, Paris (1969); *Dessins tchèques contemporains* (*Contemporary Czech Drawing*) Centre Georges Pompidou, Paris (1983); *Les Praguois, les années de silence People of Prague: the Silent Years* Galerie Lamaignere-St-Germain, Paris (1990); *Prague-Brastilava - D'une génération à l'autre* (*Prague-Brastilava - From One Generation to Another*), Musée d'Art Moderne de la Ville de Paris (1992). He also exhibited in Czechoslovakia, but sometimes this was only under difficult conditions in the wake of the 1968 'Prague Spring', although since the democratisation of the country he has shown his work more frequently.

Solo exhibitions include Prague (1961, 1967, 1970); Turin, New York (1975); Rome (1976, 1977); Walter Storms gallery Munich (1979); Washington (1980); pavilion of contemporary art, Milan (1983); Letohradek gallery, Kolovy Vary-Ostrov nad Ohri (1985); House of the Lords of Kunstat, Prague (1988); Daad gallery, Berlin (1989); Knoll gallery, Budapest (1989); Knoll gallery, Vienna (1990).

Bibliography:
Stanislav Kolibal, exhibition catalogue, Daadgalerie, Berlin, 1989. Nuridsany, Michel, '*Stanislav Kolibal: une fragile stabilité*' in *Art Press* no. 169, periodical, Paris, May 1992.

KÖLIG, Anton

Austrian, 20th century.
Born 1 July 1886, in Neutitschein, Moravia; died 1950, in Nötsch (Carinthia).
Active in France.
Painter, decorative designer. Religious subjects, allegorical subjects, figures, nudes. Murals, designs for tapestries.
Symbolism.
Neukunstgruppe.

Anton Kölig studied at the Vienna School of Arts and Crafts from 1904 to 1906 and at the Kunstakademie from 1906 to 1912. His participation in one of the group exhibitions of modern Austrian art, *Neukunstgruppe* in 1911, drew the attention of Gustav Klimt. He thereby procured a travelling scholarship for Paris between 1912 and 1914 and went to Cassis near Marseilles. After World War I, he returned to Nötsch in Austria. From 1928 to 1943, he taught at the academy in Stuttgart. A retrospective of his work was held in 1981 at the Kunstlerhaüs in Graz. The Albertina in Vienna also organised an exhibition of his work in 1985.

Kölig was initially concerned with renewing religious art, an undertaking in which he was followed by Herbert Boeckl. While aspiring to conflate Impressionism and Expressionism, he is not to be ranked with Oskar Kokoscha in terms of power of expression. From 1922, he launched himself into monumental art, renewing his palette. He carried out decorative frescoes at the crematorium in Vienna (1925) and the Rathaus in Klagenfurt (1930), as well as the tapestries at the Festspielhaus in Salzburg (1926). From 1944, his style was characterised by the attention he accorded to the contrast of colours; his brush stroke became nervous as it evoked his figures, which were principally male nudes.

AK

Museums and Galleries:
Salzburg (Residenzgal.): *Self-portrait* - Vienna (Österreichische Gal. Belvedere): *Wife of the Artist with Flowers* (1913); *General Seibt* (1918); *Family Portrait* (1928).
Auction records:
Vienna, 18 March 1977, *Two Male Nudes* (1925, oil on canvas, 30 1/4 x 22 ins / 77 x 55 cm) ATS 100,000. Vienna, 13 June 1980, *Recumbent Male Nude* (pencil, 23 1/4 x 18 1/4 ins / 59 x 46.5 cm) ATS 15,000. Vienna, 25 May 1982, *Still-life* (1912) ATS 200,000. Vienna, 19 May 1999, *Two Reclining Male Nudes* (c. 1919, pencil, 14 x 19 ins / 35 x 49 cm) ATS 40,000. Vienna, 29 Nov 2000, *Male Nude* (pencil, 14 x 10 ins / 36 x 25 cm) ATS 55,000. Vienna, 27 Nov 2001, *Reclining Male Nude* (pencil, 19 x 13 ins / 48 x 34 cm) ATS 28,000. Vienna, 27 Nov 2001, *Reclining Male Nude* (1920, pencil, 30 x 20 ins / 76 x 51 cm) ATS 60,000. Vienna, 14 May 2002, *Male Nude* (1936, pencil, 15 x 13 ins / 38 x 32 cm) EUR 2,600. Klagenfurt, 15 May 2002, *Reclining Male Nude with Hands behind Head* (1936, graphite, 24 x 18 ins / 62 x 45 cm) EUR 2,600. Cologne, 29 May 2003, *Reclining Nude* (watercolour, tempera and oil on board, 20 x 29 ins / 51 x 73 cm) EUR 13,000. Vienna, 25 Nov 2003, *Male Nude* (1941, charcoal, 18 x 14 ins / 45 x 35 cm) EUR 3,200. Vienna, 27 May 2004, *Standing Male Nude* (1925, charcoal, 24 x 18 ins / 60 x 45 cm) EUR 4,500. Vienna, 27 May 2004, *Woman* (black charcoal, 85 x 69 ins / 215 x 175 cm) EUR 23,000.

KOLIN, Jakob
Swiss, 17th century.
Born 28 September 1634, in Zug; died c. 1692.
Painter.
Kolin became a member of the Guild of St Luke in 1659. He carried out work for the churches in Zug in 1664, 1669 and 1692.

KOLIN, Karl Franz
Swiss, 17th century.
Born 1 January 1629, in Zug.
Glass painter.
Kolin became a member of the guild in 1659.

KOLIN, Lazarus
Swiss, 17th century.
Born 19 January 1632, in Zug; died 16 April 1705, in Zug.
Draughtsman.

KOLITZ, Louis
German, 19th - 20th century.
Born 5 April 1845, in Tilsit (now Sovetsk); died 24 July 1914, in Kassel.
Painter, draughtsman. Historical subjects, battles, portraits, landscapes.
Louis Kolitz attended the academy in Berlin and was taught by Achenbach in Düsseldorf. In 1870, he returned to Germany with a number of sketches of the Franco-Prussian War. He later abandoned himself to history painting and landscapes. From 1880, he was professor and director of the academy of painting in Kassel.
Museums and Galleries:
Berlin: *Two Battle Scenes*; *General von Werder* - Kassel: *Transport of Prisoners*; *Portrait of Hofrats Ruhl*.
Auction records:
London, 14 March 1908, *The Glass of Wine*; *Bacchante* (two pendants) GBP 19. Vienna, 29-30 Oct 1996, *Bay of Albano* (1893, oil on canvas, 37 3/4 x 44 3/4 ins / 96 x 113.5 cm) ATS 299,000.

KOLL, Dieter
German, 20th century.
Born 1940.
Sculptor.
Koll was a member of the Plex group. He participated in the Young Sculpture competition in Mannheim in 1968, the association of German artists in Hanover in 1969 and the association of artists of Baden-Wurtemberg in Karlsruhe in 1969. Koll was also connected with the American New Reality group. He limited his use of space to his primary structures.

KOLL, Heinrich Cristoph
German, 18th (?) century.
Painter.
Museums and Galleries:
Weimar (Goethe-Nationalmus.): *Portrait of Goethe*.

KOLL, Laurent van
Dutch, 16th century.
Born probably in Delft.
Active c. 1530.
Painter (glass). Historical subjects, portraits. Stained glass windows.
Van Koll painted portraits of the lords of Delft on the stained glass windows of their chapel.

KOLLAR, Josef
Slovak, 20th century.
Born 8 March 1899, in Banská Štiavnica.
Painter.
Josef Kollar lived in Slovakia and studied at the academy of fine arts in Munich. He travelled in the picturesque regions of his own country, and then in Italy. In 1932(1933 he was in Poland, Germany and Paris. In 1937 he settled at Banská Štiavnica. At the end of the 1950s and the beginning of the 1960s, he often painted in the Liptov region. His painting stresses the social aspect of art in eastern Slovakia.
Josef Kollar exhibited in Prague (1939, 1942, 1944) and Bratislava (1956). He featured in the *Exposition d'art slovaque* at the Musée d'Art Moderne in Paris (1974). Named as artist emeritus in 1959, he was promoted to national artist in 1972.

KOLLARZ, Franz
Austrian, 19th century.
Born 1829, in Josefstadt; died 1894, in Vienna.
Draughtsman, lithographer.
Kollarz illustrated books and worked in particular for Viennese publications.

KÖLLE, Claus Anton
Danish, 19th century.
Born 25 November 1827, in Sandby; died 2 September 1872, in Copenhagen.
Painter. Landscapes.
Several works by Claus Kölle are in the museum in Copenhagen: *The Edge of a Lake*; *Panorama of the Forest near Himmelbjergel*; *View of the Beach in Moen*; and *Spring in a Crevass*.
Auction records:
London, 7 April 1971, *View of Stockholm* (1872) Gns 450. London, 28 Nov 1979, *Wooded Landscape with River* (1871, oil on canvas, 26 1/2 x 37 3/4 ins / 67 x 96 cm) GBP 1,500. Copenhagen, 27 Sept 1983, *Landscape with Lake in Sollerod* (oil on canvas, 20 1/2 x 26 3/4 ins / 52 x 68 cm) DKK 14,000. London, 7 Feb 1986, *Fasoebing* (1856, oil on canvas, 20 x 26 1/4 ins / 50.8 x 66.6 cm) GBP 2,800. Copenhagen, 4 Sept 2002, *Landscape with Steep Cliff by the Coast* (oil on canvas, 12 x 14 ins / 30 x 35 cm) DKK 15,000.

KÖLLE, Gustav
German, 19th century.
Active in Berlin c. 1890.
Landscape artist.

KOLLE, Helmut. See **HELMUT-KOLLE**

KOLLER, Ben-Ami
French, 20th - 21st century.

Born 14 May 1948, in Oradea, Romania.
Draughtsman. Figures, portraits, self-portraits. Stage costumes and sets.

Ben-Ami Koller studied at the Nicolae Gregorescu school of fine arts in Bucharest from 1967 to 1973, particularly scene painting. He draws with pencil or silver crayons, sometimes in the form of washes. His broad, nervous stroke places and replaces figures, alone or in couples, in different postures, on a neutral background. Elsewhere his stroke is gentler, particularly in his portraits and self-portraits in silver.

Between 1972 and 1974 he created sets and costumes for the theatre in Bucharest.

He takes part in public exhibitions, particularly in the Parisian Salons: Salon de la Figuration Critique, Mac 2000, Salon de Mai, Salon de Montrouge, Salon Comparaisons, in 1990, but also: 1979, Biennale des Jeunes Artistes, Haïfa; 1987, Fonds Départemental d'Art Contemporain, Seine-St-Denis; 1993, Galerie Sanguine, Paris.

He shows his works in private exhibitions, among which are: 1973, Petöfi Sandor House of Culture, Bucharest; 1975, Tzavta Gallery, Tel-Aviv; 1980 Bruno Gallery, Tel-Aviv; 1981, Museum of Petach-Tikva (Israel); 1985, Galerie Bernard Jagot, St Nazaire; 1987, Galerie Nicole Buck, Strasbourg; 1988, 1990, Galerie AA, Paris; 1992, Galerie 27, Toulouse; 1993, Galerie Daniel Duchoze, Rouen.

Bibliography:

Xuriguera, Gérard, *Les Figurations de 1960 à nos jours*, Mayer, Paris, 1985.

Museums and Galleries:

Montluçon (Fonds D'art Contemp.) - Paris (FNAC) - Seine-St-Denis (Fonds D'art Contemp.).

Auction records:

Neuilly, 5 Dec 1990, *Drawing* (graphite/pap, 39¼ x 39¼ ins / 100 x 100 cm) FRF 5,000. Paris, 21 Nov 1993, *Music in Movement* (mixed media/canvas, 52¾ x 39¼ ins / 134 x 100 cm) FRF 10,000.

KOLLER, Broucia

Maiden name: Pinell
Austrian, 19th century.
Born 2 March 1867, in Sanok, Poland.
Painter.

Koller worked in Vienna, where she painted mainly genre scenes and interiors, such as *Adagio* or *Sunday at Grandmother's*, which were exhibited in 1893 and 1890.

KOLLER, E. Leonard

American, 20th century.
Born 8 December 1877, in Hanover (Pennsylvania).
Sculptor. Monuments.

Leonard Koller studied under Pyle and Morse. He was a member of the American Federation of Arts. He sculpted memorial monuments.

KOLLER, Gustav

German, 20th century.
Born 14 February 1870, in Breslau (now Wroclaw, Poland).
Painter, engraver. Genre scenes.

Koller participated in the Berlin exhibition of 1909.

Auction records:

London, 22 Feb 1946, *Faust and Marguerite*, GBP 105. London, 1 Oct 1980, *The Messenger* (oil on panel, 24 x 16½ ins / 61 x 42 cm) GBP 1,150. Brussels, 17 Oct 1983, *Fonts* (oil on canvas, 45¼ x 52 ins / 115 x 132 cm) BEF 110,000. Brussels, 30 April 1986, *Castle Life* (oil on panel, 26 x 43 ins / 66 x 109 cm) BEF 160,000.

KÖLLER, Johann Caspar

Swiss, 19th century.
Born 31 December 1808, in Zurich; died 9 February 1887, in Zurich.
Painter (including gouache), watercolourist.
Landscapes with figures.

Auction records:

London, 16 March 1983, *Local People in an Alpine Landscape* (1841, watercolour heightened with gouache, 13 x 17½ ins / 33 x 44.5 cm) GBP 550. London, 17 April 2002, *Sportsmen Shooting Duck from a Boat* (oil on panel, 11 x 15 ins / 27 x 37 cm) GBP 2,000.

KOLLER, Johann Jakob

Swiss, 18th century.
Born 1746, in Zurich; died c. 1805, in Amsterdam.
Painter, watercolourist, engraver, draughtsman.
Portraits, landscapes, urban landscapes.

Koller's teachers are not known. In order to improve his skills he went to Amsterdam in 1777, where he married and settled. He lived in Frankfurt am Main for several years. A sale of his work took place in Amsterdam on 19 December 1898.

His first works, *Swiss Landscape*, and two *Views of Neidelbald*, are dated 1775. His other known works include his *Self-portrait*; *Peter Florus Cerning, Merchant*; *J. S. Moors*, and six *Views of Frankfurt am Main*.

Auction records:

Paris, Oct 1945-July 1946, *Country People on a Road* (1784) FRF 15,000; *Riders at the Edge of a Forest* (1790) FRF 40,000. Bern, 7 May 1976, *Alpine Landscape* (1776, watercolour/line drawing, 6½ x 9 ins / 16.5 x 22 cm) CHF 1,500. Bern, 23 Oct 1980, *Alpine Landscape*; *River Landscape* (1776, watercolour/line drawing, each 6½ x 9 ins / 16.5 x 22 cm) CHF 6,000. Paris, 11 April 1992, *Landscape with Waterfalls near Zurich* (oil on panel, 15¼ x 21 ins / 39 x 52.5 cm) FRF 38,000. Amsterdam, 4 Nov 2003, *View of the Spui, Amsterdam* (1778, oil on canvas, 17 x 22 ins / 42 x 56 cm) EUR 22,000.

KOLLER, Johann Ulrich

Swiss, 18th century.
Born 3 August 1753, in Winterthur; died 19 July 1789.
Painter, draughtsman.

The Kunsthaus gallery in Zurich owns several landscapes by Koller.

KOLLER, Matthias

German, 17th century.
Born in Augsburg.
Painter.

Koller worked in Brig as well as other places.

KOLLER, Oskar

German, 20th century.
Born 1925, in Erlangen (Bavaria).
Painter, draughtsman.

Oskar Koller showed his works in a number of exhibitions, including: in 1977, at the Galerie Lochte in Hamburg; in 1978, at the Stadt Museum in Minden; in 1979, at the Galerie Gunzenhauser in Munich; in 1980 and 1983, at the Galerie Welz in Salzburg; in 1981, at the Kunstverein in Ulm; in 1981, at the Kunstkabinett in Regensburg; in 1984, at the Offenbacher Kunstkabinett in Offenbach; in 1985, at the Neue Pinakothek in Munich; in 1986, at the Galerie Vita in Bern; and, in 1987, at the Stadtlishes Galerie in Lindau and the Galerie Étienne de Causans in Paris.

KOLLER, Rudolf Johann or Rodolphe

Swiss, 19th century.
Born 21 May 1828, in Zurich; died 5 January 1905, in Zurich.
Painter, draughtsman. Nudes, portraits, animals, landscapes.

Koller studied under Rudolf Obrist, Jacob Ulrich, and then, from 1846 under Carl Ferdinand Sohn at the academy in Düsseldorf. He became friends with Arnold Böklin, with whom he visited the museums of Antwerp and Brussels and the Louvre in Paris in 1847. During the revolution of 1848 he returned home to his parents and he then left on a long journey to Germany. He later travelled to Italy, bringing back several studies from Florence, Rome and Naples. He lost the sight in his right eye in 1870, and then his left eye in 1875. His exhibition in 1898 was a great success. He was awarded gold medals in Bern in 1869, Vienna in 1873 and Munich in 1876, and a silver medal in Paris in 1879.

In 2002 the Kunsthaus gallery in Zurich staged a retrospective of his work. He was essentially an animal painter and had a great admiration for Troyon, whose freedom of colour he adopted in his robustly drawn compositions with their generously applied paint.

BIBLIOGRAPHY:
Becker, Christoph/Pfister, Paul/Waldkirch, Bernhard von, *Rudolf Koller*, exhibition catalogue, Kunsthaus Zürich, Zurich, 2002.

MUSEUMS AND GALLERIES:
BASEL: *Horses in Harness; Sheep; Cattle at the Watering Place; Landscape by the Sea with Cattle* - BERN: *Cow and Calves Straying; Transporting Oxen in Italy* - GENEVA (MAH): *Flock on the Mountain* - NEUCHÂTEL: *Landscape* - ZURICH (Kunsthaus): important collection of works.

AUCTION RECORDS:
LUCERNE, 21-27 Nov 1961, *Watering Place*, CHF 24,000. BERN, 27 Nov 1963, *Bedouins and Thoroughbred*, CHF 31,000. LUCERNE, 3 Dec 1966, *Before the Storm*, CHF 34,000. LUCERNE, 29 June 1973, *Alpine Landscape*, CHF 16,500. LUCERNE, 21 June 1974, *Young Man Sleeping Beside a River*, CHF 15,500. ZURICH, 18 Nov 1976, *Forest at Engelberg* (oil on canvas, 33½ x 26¾ ins / 85 x 68 cm) CHF 24,000. ZURICH, 25 Nov 1977, *Anzio Bay* (1869, oil on canvas, 23½ x 35½ ins / 59.5 x 90 cm) CHF 16,000. ZURICH, 26 May 1978, *Flock Beside a Lake* (c. 1865, oil on canvas, 38¼ x 51¼ ins / 97 x 130 cm) CHF 40,000. ZURICH, 19 May 1979, *Brown Horse in a Landscape* (1854, oil on canvas, 32¼ x 41¾ ins / 82 x 106 cm) CHF 28,000. ZURICH, 11 Nov 1981, *Lost in the Snow* (c. 1853, oil on canvas, 17½ x 24½ ins / 44.5 x 62 cm) CHF 17,000. BERN, 24 June 1983, *Children Sitting in a Landscape* (1855, oil on canvas, 20¾ x 25 ins / 53 x 63.5 cm) CHF 20,000. ZURICH, 9 Nov 1984, *Dog Jumping* (black and white chalk, 36¼ x 37¾ ins / 92 x 96 cm) CHF 3,800. PARIS, 13 June 1990, *Cattle in the Valley* (oil on card, 10 x 8¼ ins / 25.5 x 21 cm) FRF 7,000. ZURICH, 4 June 1992, *Clouds over the Mountains* (oil on canvas, 11½ x 15¾ ins / 29 x 40 cm) CHF 5,650. ZURICH, 9 June 1993, *Young Girl with a Dog Looking After Cattle Beside a Lake* (1863, oil on canvas, 18 x 25 ins / 45.5 x 63.5 cm) CHF 51,750. ZURICH, 13 Oct 1994, *Lion in the Desert* (1864, oil on canvas, 16 x 23½ ins / 40.5 x 59.5 cm) CHF 12,000. ZURICH, 12 June 1995, *Nude Kneeling* (pencil/paper, 21¼ x 13½ ins / 54 x 34 cm) CHF 1,265. BERN, 21 June 1996, *Excursion in the Alps* (1881, oil on canvas, 38½ x 62¾ ins / 97.8 x 159.7 cm) CHF 115,000. ZURICH, 12 Nov 1996, *Cattle Near a Stream* (1900, oil on canvas, 55 x 46½ ins / 140 x 118 cm) CHF 12,000. ZURICH, 10 Dec 1996, *Boy on a Horse and Young Country Girl* (oil on canvas, 39¼ x 46 ins / 100 x 117 cm) CHF 23,000. ZURICH, 4 June 1997, *Young Man on a Horse* (1874, oil on canvas, 24¾ x 30¾ ins / 63 x 78 cm) CHF 36,800. ZURICH, 18 March 1999, *Cowherd on a White Horse with Herd of Horses and Cows* (1877, oil on canvas, 54 x 93 ins / 137 x 236 cm) CHF 33,000. ZURICH, 9 June 1999, *Herdsman with Cattle* (1858, oil on canvas, 29 x 37 ins / 73 x 93 cm) CHF 80,000. BERN, 12 May 2000, *Farmgirl Milking a Cow* (1870, oil on canvas, 36 x 35 ins / 91 x 90 cm) CHF 38,000. ZURICH, 5 Dec 2000, *Cattle and Washerwoman at a Stream* (1865, oil on canvas, 56 x 45 ins / 142 x 114 cm) CHF 30,000. ZURICH, 3 Dec 2001, *Zurichhorn* (1885, oil on canvas, 56 x 44 ins / 141 x 113 cm) CHF 40,000. ZURICH, 10 Dec 2001, *Cattle Descending from the Alps* (1856, oil on canvas, 44 x 52 ins / 112 x 132 cm) CHF 23,000. ZURICH, 25 March 2002, *Girl with Cow on Path* (oil on canvas, 20 x 20 ins / 50 x 50 cm) CHF 3,500. ZURICH, 3 June 2002, *White Horses near Approaching Thunderstorm* (1877, oil on canvas, 40 x 52 ins / 102 x 132 cm) CHF 40,000. ZURICH, 28 March 2003, *Cows by the Zurichhorn* (1882, oil on canvas, 45 x 68 ins / 114 x 173 cm) CHF 50,000. BERN, 20 June 2003, *Cowherd with Cow and Women Cutting Flax in Meiringen* (1867, oil on canvas, 18 x 24 ins / 45 x 61 cm) CHF 86,000. ZURICH, 17 May 2004, *Little Shepherdess Knitting* (1859, oil on canvas, 22 x 22 ins / 57 x 57 cm) CHF 78,000. ZURICH, 26 May 2004, *Sowing* (1882, oil on canvas, 28 x 41 ins / 72 x 104 cm) CHF 55,000.

KOLLER, Wilhelm

Austrian, 19th century.

Born 1829, in Vienna; died 1884 or 1885, near Nancy.

Painter, watercolourist. History painting, genre scenes.

Koller studied at the art academy in Vienna and in Düsseldorf. During a stay in Antwerp he exhibited *Secret Marriage of Philippine Welser and Archduke Ferdinand at Meran Castle*. Most of his subjects are taken from sixth-century German history.

MUSEUMS AND GALLERIES:
HAMBURG: *Farewell; Emperor Maximilian and Albrecht Dürer* - MELBOURNE: *Fiancé's Departure* - VIENNA: a watercolour.

AUCTION RECORDS:
LONDON, 1873, *Seduction*, FRF 5,625. AMSTERDAM, 1881, *Faust and Marguerite*, FRF 6,510; *Marguerite and Martha*, FRF 5,565. LONDON, 1881, *Charles Quint at the Home of Fugger*, FRF 7,100. LONDON, 1898, *Philippine Welter Appealing for Mercy*, FRF 2,875. VIENNA, 4 June 1957, *Drinking Song*, ATS 28,000. NEW YORK, 14 May 1976, *Young Beggar* (1883, oil on canvas, 26 x 20 ins / 66 x 51 cm) USD 800. LONDON, 4 Nov 1977, *Scene from the Life of Durer* (1866, oil on panel, 12 x 17 ins / 30.5 x 43 cm) GBP 1,500. LONDON, 24 June 1988, *Faust and Mephistopheles Watching Women at the Cathedral Door* (1870, oil on panel, 29¼ x 39¼ ins / 74 x 100 cm) GBP 5,500. NEW YORK, 29 Oct 1992, *Faust and Mephistopheles Waiting for Women at the Cathedral Door* (1870, oil on panel, 30½ x 40½ ins / 77.5 x 102.9 cm) USD 27,500. SWITZERLAND, 28 May 1999, *New Jewellery* (oil on panel, 31 x 24 ins / 80 x 62 cm) CHF 12,500. LUCERNE, 13 Oct 1999, *Lady Giving Money to Begging Boy* (1873, oil on panel, 9 x 6 ins / 24 x 15 cm) CHF 4,000.

KOLLER-PINELL, Broncia

Austrian, 19th - 20th century.

Born 1863, in Vienna; died 1934, in Vienna.

Painter. Figures, nudes.

Broncia Koller-Pinell was the wife of the patron Hugo Koller, and she knew the musician Gustav Mahler and the Austrian painter and draughtsman Egon Schiele. She belonged to the Vienna Secession and exhibited at the Kunstschau in 1908. Her works were exhibited at *Chefs-d'oeuvre du Belvédère de Vienna* (*Masterpieces from the Belvedere in Vienna*) at the Musée Marmottan in Paris.

MUSEUMS AND GALLERIES:
VIENNA (Österreichische Gal. Belvedere).

AUCTION RECORDS:
VIENNA, 25 June 1976, *Portrait of Edith Schiele* (oil on canvas, 23½ x 19¾ ins / 60 x 50 cm) ATS 10,000. VIENNA, 12 Nov 1980, *Rest on the Flight into Egypt* (oil on canvas, 33 x 34¾ ins / 84 x 88.5 cm) ATS 70,000. VIENNA, 16 Sept 1981, *Roses in Glass* (oil on canvas, 16¼ x 13 ins / 41 x 33 cm) ATS 38,000. VIENNA, 22 March 1983, *Edith and Egon Schiele* (oil on canvas, 27½ x 27½ ins / 70 x 70 cm) ATS 55,000. LONDON, 8 Oct 1986, *View of Hellbrunn from Salzburg* (oil on card, 22 x 17¼ ins / 56 x 44 cm) GBP 3,800. VIENNA, 9 Dec 1987, *Half-length*

Portrait of Nude (oil on canvas, 29 1/2 x 19 3/4 ins / 75 x 50 cm) ATS 50,000. LONDON, 10 Feb 1988, *Male Nude* (oil on card, 35 x 22 3/4 ins / 89 x 58 cm) GBP 5,280. VIENNA, 15 June 1999, *Portrait of Prof Dr Hans Wilbrandt as a Boy* (oil on canvas, 31 x 24 ins / 80 x 62 cm) ATS 80,000. VIENNA, 12 Oct 1999, *Still-life with Tulips* (card, 33 x 29 ins / 84 x 73 cm) ATS 190,000. VIENNA, 25 Jan 2000, *Still-life with Pineapple* (oil on canvas, 18 x 20 ins / 45 x 50 cm) ATS 45,000. VIENNA, 29 Nov 2000, *Portrait of Daughter Silvia* (c. 1914, oil on canvas, 26 x 36 ins / 66 x 91 cm) ATS 90,000. VIENNA, 11 March 2003, *Grace* (oil on board, 10 x 16 ins / 26 x 40 cm) EUR 2,600. VIENNA, 20 May 2003, *Still-life with Parrot in a Cage* (1927, oil on canvas, 40 x 33 ins / 102 x 83 cm) EUR 10,000. VIENNA, 9 March 2004, *Etka* (oil on canvas, 11 x 11 ins / 29 x 29 cm) EUR 3,400.

KÖLLIKER, David
Swiss, 19th century.
Born 13 November 1807, in Zurich; died 25 May 1875.
Painter, watercolourist. Landscapes, flowers, animals.
Kölliker studied under the landscape artist Johann Wirz. He concentrated on watercolours and gouache at first, painting his landscapes in a pointillist style. After 1845 he studied oil painting and specialised in pictures of animals.

KÖLLIKER, Martin
Swiss, 18th century.
Born 1741, in Zurich; died June 1801.
Sculptor (wood).

KOLLMANN, Carl Ivanovich
Russian, 19th century.
Born 1788; died 25 November 1846.
Painter, watercolourist, engraver, draughtsman, lithographer. Figures, genre scenes, interiors with figures, landscapes with figures.
Carl Kollmann lived mostly in St Petersburg. He produced two well-known series of works entitled *The Stroganov Gallery* and *Memories of St Petersburg*.
AUCTION RECORDS:
LONDON, 14 May 1980, *Peasants in a Sleigh* (1842, watercolour and pencil, 7 x 10 1/2 ins / 18 x 26.4 cm) GBP 560. LONDON, 25 June 1981, *A Drawing Room in the Palace of the Gagarin Princes in St Petersburg* (watercolour, 8 3/4 x 12 ins / 22.5 x 30.5 cm) GBP 2,600. PARIS, 18 April 1983, *Russian Interior; Market* (1845, watercolour, two pendants, 6 x 9 ins / 15 x 22 cm) FRF 9,000. LONDON, 6 Oct 1988, *Peasant Family inside a Hut* (watercolour and pencil, 9 1/4 x 11 3/4 ins / 23.5 x 30 cm) GBP 2,310. LONDON, 5 Oct 1989, *Ice Seller's Sleigh* (1839, watercolour and pencil, 6 1/2 x 9 3/4 ins / 16.2 x 24.8 cm) GBP 1,210. NEW YORK, 12 Jan 1994, *The Pavlino Garden with Peasants Gathering Hay in the Foreground* (1838, watercolour/black chalk, 9 1/2 x 14 1/4 ins / 24.3 x 36.4 cm) USD 1,725. LONDON, 17 July 1996, *Interior of a Tavern in St Petersburg* (watercolour heightened with white, 6 1/2 x 9 ins / 16.5 x 23 cm) GBP 1,035. AMSTERDAM, 21 Jan 1998, *Peasant Man; Peasant Woman* (1837, pencil and watercolour/paper, a pair, 9 1/2 x 7 3/4 ins / 24 x 20 cm) NLG 2,883. LONDON, 31 May 2001, *Russian Genre Scenes* (1842, watercolour over pencil heightened with white, eight, 2 x 3 ins / 6 x 8 cm) GBP 3,500. LONDON, 31 May 2001, *Russian Types* (watercolour and ink, miniatures, eighteen, 15 x 23 ins / 38 x 58 cm) GBP 6,500. LONDON, 20 Nov 2002, *St Petersburg Itinerants* (1846, pencil and watercolour, 6 x 9 ins / 16 x 23 cm) GBP 1,000. LONDON, 21 May 2003, *Roadside Scenes* (1812, watercolour and ink, a pair, 8 x 11 ins / 20 x 28 cm) GBP 1,700. LONDON, 19 Nov 2003, *Coachmen outside the Cathedral of the Mother of God of Kazan, St Petersburg* (1820, watercolour over pencil, 6 x 8 ins / 15 x 21 cm) GBP 2,000.

KOLLMANN, Ignaz
Austrian, 19th century.
Born 16 January 1775, in Graz; died 16 March 1837, in Graz.
Painter.
Kollmann studied in his home town of Graz and accompanied Princess Seraphine Porcia to Italy as her secretary. He painted altarpieces for the churches in Graz.

KOLLMANN, Julius
Austrian, 19th - 20th century.
Born c. 1870, in Vienna; died in Paris.
Painter. Scenes with figures, portraits.
Kollmann participated in the Salon de Paris from 1895 to 1909 and the Salon des Indépendants in 1913. His compositions are suffused with a soft melancholic light.

KOLLMAR, Wilhelm
German, 20th century.
Born 15 March 1872, in Zweibrücken.
Sculptor.
Kollmar attended the academy of Karlsruhe between 1896 and 1903, where he exhibited from 1906.

KÖLLO, Miklos
Hungarian, 19th century.
Born 1861, in Gyergyo-Csomafalva; died 17 September 1900, in Budapest.
Sculptor.
Miklos Köllo studied with Hess and Knabl at the academy in Munich. He is best known for his *Statue of Kossuth* in Maros Vasarhely.

KOLLOCK, Mary
American, 19th - 20th century.
Born 1832, in Norfolk; died 12 January 1911, in New York.
Painter. Landscapes.
Mary Kollock studied under Robert Wylie in Philadelphia and A.H. Wyant in New York. She regularly exhibited at the National Academy of Design in New York, where her work was highly praised. She mostly painted the banks of Lake George and the Adirondacks.

KOLLOFF, Fritz
German, 19th century.
Died 1884, in Karlsruhe.
Landscape artist.
Kolloff studied under Gude. He painted views of Venice.

KOLLONITSCH, Christian (Count)
German, 18th century.
Born 20 November 1730; died 1802.
Portrait artist.
Kollonitsch was an officer in the dragoons in 1784.

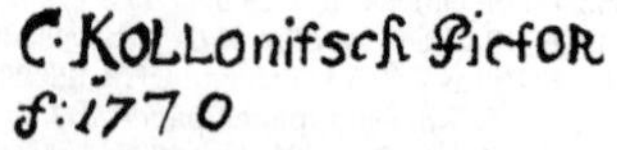

KOLLWITZ, Käthe Schmidt
German, 19th - 20th century.
Born 8 July 1867, in Königsberg (now Kaliningrad, Russia); died 22 April 1945, in Moritzburg Castle, near Dresden.
Engraver, sculptor, illustrator, draughtswoman.
Käthe Schmidt Kollwitz initially learned engraving with Rudolf Mauer and she went on to study painting and drawing in Berlin (in 1855) under Karl Stauffer-Bern and then in Munich (in 1888) under Ludwig Herterich. She received her training in sculpture at the Académie Julian during a stay in Paris in 1904, during which time she met Rodin and Steinlein. In 1907, she went to Italy. During her Italian sojourn, she was awarded the Villa Romana prize. In 1916 she exhibited her first sculpture, *Two Lovers*.

Sympathetic to the proletarian plight, she was active in student organisations and read authors like Ibsen, Tolstoy, Dostoevsky and Zola who, by the standards of the time, were considered to be revolutionary. She was the first woman to enter the Preussische Akademie der Künste (Prussian Academy of Arts), where she held masterclasses in graphic art between 1928 and 1933. Having witnessed the injustices of the war, she opposed the politics of aggression of Nazi Germany, which resulted in her exclusion from the academy in Berlin; she was persecuted and threatened with arrest, and her works were withdrawn from galleries and museums. However, she remained in Berlin: 'I wish to and must stay with the outcasts'. She was eventually evacuated to Moritzburg and was welcomed by Prince Ernst of Saxony, an admirer of her work. In 1937, on the occasion of her 70th birthday, an oppressed and silent Germany paid tribute to this inflexible woman: she received thousands of letters and telegrams. However, she was still banished from public artistic life.

Kollwitz engraved numerous plates, including: *The Rebellion of the Weavers*, a series of six prints begun in 1893, which was inspired by Gerhart Hauptmann's drama and was shown for the first time at the Grosse Berliner Kunstausstellung in 1898; *The Peasants' War*, a series begun in 1902 and finished in 1908; and then *War* and *Proletariat*.

She began to carry out her first sculptures in bronze in 1910. When her son fell in Flanders in 1914, she did the sketches and plans for a *War Memorial*, which was to consist of a couple of parents in the simple eloquence of their mourning; begun in 1914 and not finished until 1932, it was titled *Mourning Parents*, a monument in granite erected in Essen cemetery, near Dixmude in Belgium. She also executed, in poster-form, engravings on the theme of war-induced devastation: *Our Children are Hungry* (1918) and *Help the Russians* (1921). She worked from 1934 to 1936 on a final series of engravings entitled *Death*. A similar inspiration - or, rather, rebellion - animates her *Tower of Mothers* of 1937, in which a group of robust women in a rage squeeze their children in a gesture of refusal to allow them to enlist in the war. The same theme pervades her later works, such as her *Pietà* of 1938. She contributed to the political-satirical magazine *Simplicissimus* and illustrated Gerhart Hauptmann's *The Weaver* in 1897.

In 1947 the Musée Boymans in Rotterdam organised a retrospective of her work including both reproductions of her sculptures and numerous prints. Other retrospective exhibitions included: in 1967, at Bethnal Green Museum in London; in 1975, in Florence; in 1981, in Hamburg; in 1988, in Milan; in 1992, at Kettle's Yard in Cambridge, at the Scottish National Gallery of Modern Art in Edinburgh, at the Institute of Contemporary Arts in London and at the National Gallery of Art in Washington, DC; in 1995, *Käthe Kollwitz, Schmerz und Schuld* (*Käthe Kollwitz, Pain and Guilt*), at the Käthe Kollwitz Museum in Berlin; in 1997, *Käthe Kollwitz: Radierungen, Lithographien, und Holzschnitte* (*Käthe Kollwitz: Etchings, Lithographs and Wood Engravings*), at the Das Museum in Schwerin (Germany); in 2003, *Käthe Kollwitz: The Art of Compassion*, at the Art Gallery of Ontario in Toronto, and *Käthe Kollwitz: "Je veux œuvrer en ces temps..."* (*Käthe Kollwitz: "I wish to work at this time..."*), at the Kunstmuseum in Bern.

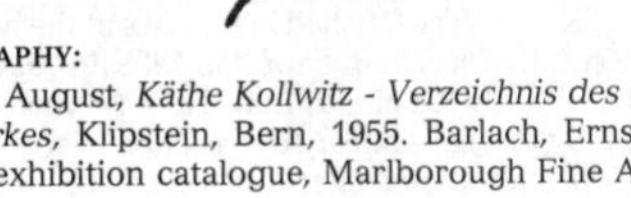

BIBLIOGRAPHY:

Klipstein, August, *Käthe Kollwitz - Verzeichnis des graphischen Werkes*, Klipstein, Bern, 1955. Barlach, Ernst, *Käthe Kollwitz*, exhibition catalogue, Marlborough Fine Art, London, 1967. Kollwitz, Hans, *Käthe Kollwitz - Das plastische Werk*, Wagner, Hamburg, 1967. *Prints and drawings of Käthe Kollwitz*, Dover Publications, New York, Constable, London, 1969. Zigrosser, Carl, *Prints and Drawings of Käthe Kollwitz*, Dover Publications, New York, 1969. Nagel, Otto/Werner, Timm, *Käthe Kollwitz - Die Handzeichnungen*, Henschelverlag Kunst und Gesellschaft, Berlin, 1972. Timm, Werner, *Käthe Kollwitz*, Henschelverlag, Berlin, 1974. Klein, Mina C./Klein, H. Arthur, *Käthe Kollwitz, life in art*, Schocken Books, New York, 1975. Hinz, R., *Käthe Kollwitz - Druckgraphik, Plakate, Zeichnungen*, Elephant Press, Berlin, 1980. *Käthe Kollwitz. Die Zeichnerin*, Kunstverein, Hamburg, 1980. Hinz, Renate (ed.)/Lippard, Lucy (introduction), *Käthe Kollwitz: graphics, posters, drawings*, Writers and Readers, London, 1981 (texts in English and German). Lauter, Estella, *Women as Mythmakers: poetry and visual art by twentieth-century women*, Indiana University Press, Bloomington, 1984. Whitford, Frank/Hartley, Keith, *Käthe Kollwitz 1867-1945: the graphic works*, exhibition catalogue, Kettle's Yard, Cambridge, 1992. Prelinger, Elizabeth/Comini, Alessandra/Bachert, Hildegard, *Käthe Kollwitz*, exhibition catalogue, National Gallery of Art, Washington DC, Yale University Press, New Haven, 1992. *Käthe Kollwitz, Schmerz und Schuld*, exhibition catalogue, Käthe Kollwitz Museum, Berlin, 1995. Kollwitz, Hans (ed.), *The diary and letters of Kaethe Kollwitz*, Northwestern University Press, Evanston (IL), 1995. Achenbach, Sigrid, *Käthe Kollwitz*, exhibition catalogue, Staatliche Museen, Berliner Kupferstichkabinetts, Berlin, 1995. *Käthe Kollwitz: Radierungen, Lithographien, und Holzschnitte*, exhibition catalogue, Das Museum, Schwerin, 1997. Knesebeck, Alexandra von dem, *Käthe Kollwitz. Catalogue raisonné des gravures*, Gal. Kornfeld, Bern, 2002. Thiem, Gunther/Rix, Brenda/Clarke, Jay, *Käthe Kollwitz: The Art of Compassion*, exhibition catalogue, Art Gall. of Ontario, Toronto, 2003.

MUSEUMS AND GALLERIES:

BERLIN (Käthe Kollwitz Mus.) - COLOGNE (Wallraf-Richartz Mus.): *Workman's Wife* (1903) - TORONTO (AG of Ontario): *Lamentation: In Memory of Ernst Barlach* (bronze).

AUCTION RECORDS:

NEW YORK, 30 Nov 1960, *Two Women* (lead pencil) USD 250. HAMBURG, 30 Nov 1963, *Woman and Child* (bronze) DEM 14,000. HAMBURG, 9 June 1972, *Seated Woman, Crossed Arms* (pastel) DEM 26,000. HAMBURG, 7 June 1974, *The Mothers* (1937, patinated bronze) DEM 11,000. HAMBURG, 3 June 1976, *Despair* (1940, bronze relief, $10\frac{1}{2}$ x 10 ins / 26.5 x 25.3 cm) DEM 8,500. BERN, 10 June 1976, *Self-portrait at the Table, Second Version* (etching) CHF 5,000. HAMBURG, 3 June 1977, *Half-length Portrait of Working Woman in Blue* (1903, coloured lithograph) DEM 7,400. NEW YORK, 16 March 1978, *Despair* (1938, reddish-brown patinated bronze relief, 11 x 10 ins / 27 x 25.5 cm) USD 3,600. NEW YORK, 16 May 1979, *Pietà* (1937-1938, brown-patinated bronze, h. 15 ins / 38 cm) USD 9,000. MUNICH, 31 May 1979, *The Happy Mother* (1931, lithograph/yellow-tinted Japanese paper) DEM 8,500. MUNICH, 27 Nov 1979, *Mother and Child Lying Down* (c. 1927, black chalk, $16\frac{1}{2}$ x $23\frac{1}{2}$ ins / 42 x 60 cm) DEM 23,000. COLOGNE, 5 Dec 1979, *Burial Vault of the Innocents* (1904, pastel) DEM 2,800. BERN, 24 June 1981, *Battlefield* (1907, etching) CHF 5,000. NEW YORK, 4 Nov 1982, *Farewell* (brown-patinated gilt bronze, h. 7 ins / 17.5 cm) USD 6,200. MUNICH, 29 June 1983, *Saatfrüchte sollen nicht vermahlen* (1942, lithograph) DEM 95,000. MUNICH, 28 Nov 1983, *Two Women* (1943, bronze, $8\frac{3}{4}$ x 10 x $7\frac{3}{4}$ ins / 22.5 x 24.5 x 20 cm) DEM 36,000. BERN, 21 June 1984, *Self-portrait at the Window* (1900, watercolour/outlines in pen and ink heightened with Indian ink, $22\frac{1}{4}$ x $17\frac{1}{4}$ ins / 56.5 x 43.5 cm) CHF 76,000. COLOGNE, 7 Dec 1984, *Inn in Hamburg* (1901, charcoal heightened with white, 14 x 16 ins / 35.5 x 40.5 cm) DEM 54,000. NEW YORK, 15 May 1985, *Dead Woman and*

Child (c. 1910, charcoal, 26 x 18 1/4 ins / 65.1 x 46.4 cm) USD 31,000. BERN, 19 June 1985, *Plowman with Woman Standing in Foreground* (1905, etching) CHF 30,000. BERN, 19 June 1985, *Seated Nude* (c. 1900, pastel, 29 1/2 x 21 1/4 ins / 74.8 x 54 cm) CHF 43,000. COLOGNE, 31 May 1986, *Tower of Mothers* (1937-1938, dark-brown patinated bronze, h. 11 ins / 28 cm) DEM 39,000. HAMBURG, 12 June 1987, *The Street* (1908, charcoal and Indian ink, 13 1/2 x 12 1/2 ins / 34.5 x 31.5 cm) DEM 30,000. NEW YORK, 12 May 1988, *Affliction* (bronze, h. 10 1/4 ins / 26 cm) USD 13,200. MUNICH, 7 June 1989, *Tower of Mothers* (1938, bronze, h. 11 1/4 ins / 28.5 cm) DEM 66,000. NEW YORK, 5 Oct 1989, *Pietà* (bronze, h. 15 ins / 37.8 cm) USD 37,400. AMSTERDAM, 13 Dec 1989, *Pietà* (brown-patinated bronze, h. 15 ins / 37.8 cm) NLG 25,300. NEW YORK, 3 Oct 1990, *Mother with Two Children* (charcoal/paper, 19 x 12 1/2 ins / 48.2 x 32 cm) USD 24,200. HEIDELBERG, 12 Oct 1991, *Death Reaches into a Group of Children* (1934, lithograph, 19 3/4 x 16 1/2 ins / 50 x 42 cm) DEM 5,000. ZURICH, 16 Oct 1991, *Mother with her Dead Child* (etching, 21 3/4 x 28 3/4 ins / 55.5 x 73 cm) CHF 4,800. MUNICH, 26-27 Nov 1991, *Grief* (bronze, 10 x 9 3/4 ins / 25.5 x 25 cm) DEM 28,750. NEW YORK, 12 May 1992, *Pietà* (brown-patinated bronze, h. 15 ins / 38.1 cm) USD 39,600. MUNICH, 26 May 1992, *Portrait of Servant with Blue Cloth* (1903, coloured lithograph, 13 3/4 x 9 1/2 ins / 35 x 24 cm) DEM 2,300. HEIDELBERG, 9 Oct 1992, *Mother with Child in her Arms* (1916, lithograph, 11 1/2 x 7 1/2 ins / 29 x 19.3 cm) DEM 1,250. BERLIN, 27 Nov 1992, *In the Dining Hall* (sepia and charcoal heightened with white/brown paper, 16 1/2 x 15 1/4 ins / 42 x 38.5 cm) DEM 62,150. NEW YORK, 12 May 1993, *The Sculptor Opanos* (1928, charcoal/paper, 18 1/2 x 26 ins / 47 x 66 cm) USD 17,250. AMSTERDAM, 27-28 May 1993, *The People* (pencil/paper, 13 3/4 x 13 3/4 ins / 35.2 x 34.9 cm) NLG 33,350. PARIS, 11 June 1993, *Self-portrait* (1919, lithograph, 13 1/2 x 11 1/2 ins / 34 x 29 cm) FRF 13,000. ZURICH, 13 Oct 1993, *A Pensive Woman* (1920, lithograph, 15 3/4 x 12 3/4 ins / 40 x 32.5 cm) CHF 2,400. LONDON, 13 Oct 1994, *Mother Carrying her Child on her Shoulder* (bronze, h. 18 ins / 46 cm) GBP 20,700. HEIDELBERG, 15 Oct 1994, *Woman by Cradle* (1897, etching, 10 3/4 x 5 3/4 ins / 27.6 x 14.5 cm) DEM 1,500. NEW YORK, 9 Nov 1994, *The Parents* (black ink wash heightened with white gouache, 16 1/2 x 19 1/4 ins / 41.9 x 48.9 cm) USD 33,350. LONDON, 11 Oct 1995, *Anxious Woman* (1920, lithograph, 21 x 14 1/2 ins / 53.5 x 37 cm) GBP 2,300. BERN, 21 June 1996, *Woman with Child in her Arms* (1926, woodcut heightened with white, 7 3/4 x 5 1/4 ins / 19.6 x 13.2 cm) CHF 66,000. LONDON, 9 Oct 1996, *Pensive Woman* (1920, lithograph, 23 1/2 x 17 1/2 ins / 59.7 x 44.2 cm) GBP 4,370. NEW YORK, 12 Nov 1996, *Embrace* (brown-patinated bronze, h. 6 3/4 ins / 17 cm) USD 8,050. ZURICH, 12 Nov 1996, *The Survivors* (1922-1923, Indian ink and black chalk, 20 x 19 3/4 ins / 51 x 50 cm) CHF 56,000. PARIS, 10 Dec 1996, *Tempest* (1897, etching, 9 1/4 x 11 1/2 ins / 23.4 x 29 cm) FRF 4,000. HEIDELBERG, 11-12 April 1997, *Mother with Child in Arms* (1916, lithograph, 13 x 7 3/4 ins / 33.3 x 19.5 cm) DEM 5,100. NEW YORK, 14 May 1997, *Working Woman* (charcoal/paper/card, 24 1/4 x 18 1/2 ins / 61.9 x 47 cm) USD 85,000. LONDON, 9 Oct 1997, *The Happy Mother* (1931, lithograph, 9 x 12 1/2 ins / 23 x 31.8 cm) GBP 4,025. PARIS, 19 Oct 1997, *Hungry Children* (1924, charcoal, 15 x 11 ins / 38 x 27.8 cm) FRF 46,000. HAMBURG, 12 June 1999, *Portrait of a Working Woman* (c. 1902, lithograph, 11 x 9 ins / 27 x 24 cm) DEM 56,000. NEW YORK, 10 Nov 1999, *Pietà* (1938, brown patinated bronze, 15 x 11x16 ins / 38 x 27x40 cm) USD 40,000. NEW YORK, 11 May 2000, *Arming under an Arch* (charcoal, 18 x 12 ins / 46 x 31 cm) USD 35,000. BERN, 22 June 2001, *Mary and Elizabeth* (c. 1924, chalk, 13 x 15 ins / 34 x 37 cm) CHF 75,000. NEW YORK, 8 Nov 2001, *Pietà* (brown patinated bronze, h. 15 ins / 38 cm) USD 32,500. NEW YORK, 9 May 2002, *Large Lovers II* (brown patinated bronze, h. 28 ins / 71 cm) USD 55,000. SAN FRANCISCO, 14 Oct 2002, *Self-portrait* (colour lithograph, 19 x 13 ins / 49 x 33 cm) USD 110,000. MUNICH, 5 May 2003, *Gretchen* (pencil over chalk, 9 x 7 ins / 24 x 18 cm) EUR 52,000. MUNICH, 5 May 2003, *Self-portrait* (colour lithograph on board, 18 x 13 ins / 45 x 33 cm) EUR 135,000. NEW YORK, 5 May 2004, *Pietà* (1937, brown patinated bronze, h. 15 ins / 38 cm) USD 35,000. BERLIN, 26 Nov 2004, *Two Chatting Women with Children* (1928, etching, India ink and gouache, 9 x 8 ins / 22 x 20 cm) EUR 27,000.

KOLLY
Swiss, 16th century.
Active in Fribourg.
Glass painter.

His name was mentioned in the accounting records of the treasurer of Fribourg.

KOLMAN, Hans Friedrich
Swiss, 16th - 17th century.
Died 1615.
Active in Schaffhausen.
Glass painter.

He studied under Mara Grimm from 1585 to 1588.

KOLMAN, K. K.
Russian, 19th century.
Born 1831; died 1889.
Painter.

MUSEUMS AND GALLERIES:
MOSCOW (State Tretyakov Gal.): a painting.

KOLMAR, Elisabetha
Swiss, 18th century.
Active in Schaffhausen c. 1750.
Painter, draughtswoman.

One of Kolmar's known works is the *Portrait of Eberhard Köchlin*. She produced mostly drawings.

KOLMSPERGER, Waldemar, the Elder
German, 19th century.
Born 5 October 1858, in Berchtesgaden.
Painter. Religious subjects.

Kolmsperger is primarily known for decorative paintings in churches, for example, his great ceilings in the convent and church in Roggenburg, and his paintings in the town hall in Landshut.

KOLMSPERGER, Waldemar, the Younger
German, 20th century.
Born 15 September 1881, in Munich.
Painter, fresco artist. Religious subjects.

Waldemar Kolmsperger the Younger was a pupil of his father, Waldemar the Elder, and, like him, he decorated a number of churches.

KOLOMBI, Zef
Albanian, 20th century.
Born 1907; died 1949.
Painter. Landscapes with figures, landscapes, still-lifes.

Zef Kolombi painted melancholy and magnificent landscapes and still-lifes.

MUSEUMS AND GALLERIES:
TIRANA (AG): *Three Slices of Water Melon; Still-life; Harvest; Painter's Son in the Garden.*

KOLOS-VARY, Sigismond, or Kolos-Vari
Hungarian, 20th century.
Born 19 May 1899, in Banffyhunyad; died 26 June 1983, in La Chaux-de-Fonds, Switzerland.
Active in France from 1926, naturalised in 1955.
Painter, engraver, illustrator.

Sigismond Kolos-Vary finished his studies at the high school for the decorative arts in Budapest in 1925. In 1926, a period of travel and study led him to Italy. Here he was very much influenced by Uccello's linear construction of space. He then went to Switzerland, and later to Paris where he settled. He also visited Spain. In 1941 he was interned in a concentration camp, but escaped to Switzerland in 1943, where he remained until 1946 before returning to France.

It is useful to divide the work of Kolos-Vary into three main periods: from 1921 to 1949, an imaginative, figurative period moving from Impressionism to a kind of Surrealism in which memories of the Transylvanian landscape of his childhood shone through, from 1950 to 1954, a transitory period leading to abstract work; and, from 1954, his abstract period, of which Kolos-Vary writes, 'The earth has become too small. Humanity dreams by ploughing through space, of conquering other stars. The rocket has opened new horizons to us. Art could offer its services to cosmonauts.... My paintings are composed of parallel lines and circles. The succession of parallel lines suggests horizons seen from different distances, and the circles (or solids) give a resting point for the eyes to measure space in depth'.

Solo exhibitions include: Paris (1928, 1935, 1948, 1958, 1963, 1965); Basel (1955);, La Chaux-de-Fonds (1959, 1962, 1966); Rotterdam (1962); municipal gallery of Rosenheim, Germany (1968). Collective exhibitions, mainly in Paris, include: Salon d'Automne and Salon des Indépendants (from 1928); exhibition of Hungarian painters, organised by Jean Cassou, Musée National d'Art Moderne de Paris (1946); Salon de Mai (after World War II for over 10 years); Salon des Réalités Nouvelles (1956 to 1961); exhibition of the school of Paris in Japan (1961).

Bibliography:

'*Sigismond Kolos-Vary*' in *Documents* n° 14, periodical, Geneva, 1955. Van Gindertael, Roger, *Propos sur la peinture actuelle*, Skira, Paris, 1955. *Kolos-Vary*, exhibition catalogue, Gal. Katia Granoff, Paris, 1965. Galy-Carles, Henry, *Kolos-Vary*, Coloquio, c. 1969 (published in Portugal).

Museums and Galleries:

Algiers (Mus. National des Beaux-Arts) - Budapest (Szépmuvészeti Múz.) - Jerusalem - Lille (MBA) - Milwaukee - Paris (MAMVP) - Paris (MNAM-CCI) - Pécs (Janus Pannonius Mus.).

Auction records:

Carcassonne, 27 Oct 1984, *Despair* (1925, oil on canvas, $27\frac{1}{2}$ x 22 ins / 70 x 56 cm) CHF 3,800. Paris, 26 Oct 1988, *Composition* (1957, oil on canvas, 9 x $6\frac{1}{4}$ ins / 22 x 16 cm) FRF 4,000. Paris, 29 Nov 1989, *Composition* (1960, oil on canvas, $4\frac{3}{4}$ x $9\frac{1}{2}$ ins / 12 x 24 cm) FRF 4,500. Paris, 1 July 1991, *Figure* (watercolour and gouache/paper, $38\frac{1}{4}$ x $27\frac{1}{2}$ ins / 97 x 70 cm) FRF 6,800. Lucerne, 26 Nov 1994, *Hitting the Target* (1953, oil on canvas, 19 x $20\frac{1}{2}$ ins / 48 x 52 cm) CHF 2,400. Paris, 7 March 1999, *Composition* (1958, oil on canvas, 44 x 57 ins / 113 x 145 cm) FRF 19,000. Paris, 7 March 1999, *The Infinite* (oil on panel, four, 66 x 65 ins / 167 x 165 cm) FRF 28,500. Paris, 22 Oct 2000, *Woman with Candle* (oil on canvas, 35 x 51 ins / 90 x 130 cm) FRF 22,000. Paris, 22 Oct 2000, *Woman with Tulip* (oil on canvas, 32 x 26 ins / 81 x 65 cm) FRF 22,000. Paris, 25 June 2001, *Instrumental Landscape* (1955, oil on canvas, 29 x 40 ins / 73 x 102 cm) FRF 12,000. Budapest, 12 Oct 2001, *Composition in Blue* (oil on canvas, 39 x 32 ins / 100 x 81 cm) HUF 800,000. Budapest, 11 Sept 2002, *Opening Forms, 1976* (1976, oil on canvas, 32 x 40 ins / 82 x 101 cm) HUF 650,000. Budapest, 11 April 2003, *Landscape* (1964-65, oil on canvas, 38 x 51 ins / 97 x 129 cm) HUF 650,000. Budapest, 28 April 2004, *Tornado* (1957, oil on canvas, 46 x 23 ins / 118 x 59 cm) HUF 650,000.

KOLP, Engelbert
Austrian, 19th century.
Born 28 October 1840, in Flirsch; died 21 August 1877, in Innsbruck.
Sculptor.

Kolp mainly worked for the churches of Upper Bavaria.

KOLPACHNIKOV, Aleksei Yakovleevich
Russian, 18th - 19th century.
Born 28 March 1744; died 17 December 1814.
Engraver.

Aleksei Kolpachnikov engraved mostly historical subjects and works produced to mark special occasions. He worked in St Petersburg.

KOLPAKOV, Ivan Ivanovich
Russian, 18th - 19th century.
Born 17 January 1771; died c. 1840.
Engraver.

Kolpakov engraved a small number of portraits but most of his works are maps and views of monuments.

KOLPAKOV, Nikolai Yakovleevich
Russian, 18th century.
Born 1740; died 17 September 1771, in St Petersburg.
Engraver.

Works by Kolpakov include reproductions of paintings by Guercino, Rigaud and J Stenglin.

KÖLSTO, Fredrik
Norwegian, 19th - 20th century.
Born 5 March 1860, in Haugesund; died 1940.
Painter.

Kölsto was awarded a bronze medal at the Exposition Universelle in Paris in 1889.

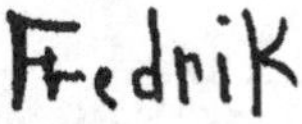

Museums and Galleries:

Oslo (Nasjonalgal.): *Seascape* (two pieces).

Auction records:

Copenhagen, 12 Nov 1986, *Young Street Musician with his Monkey* (1881, oil on canvas, 65 x $39\frac{1}{4}$ ins / 165 x 100 cm) DKK 130,000. Oslo, 22 Nov 1999, *Girl with Headscarf* (1903, oil on canvas on board, 17 x 14 ins / 42 x 36 cm) NOK 66,000. Oslo, 4 Dec 2000, *Landscape from Karmoy* (oil on canvas, 31 x 55 ins / 79 x 139 cm) NOK 78,000. Oslo, 4 Dec 2000, *Winter Fishing from the Shore* (oil on canvas, 27 x 49 ins / 68 x 125 cm) NOK 80,000. Oslo, 7 May 2001, *Red Interior* (oil on canvas, 20 x 24 ins / 52 x 60 cm) NOK 105,000. Oslo, 21 Nov 2002, *Rowing Boats in a Bay* (1886, oil on canvas, 21 x 26 ins / 53 x 65 cm) NOK 58,000. Oslo, 2 Dec 2002, *Farm under the Mountains* (1897, oil on canvas, 17 x 26 ins / 44 x 67 cm) NOK 27,000. Oslo, 28 April 2003, *Afternoon - Interior with Woman Reading* (1886, oil on canvas, 24 x 21 ins / 60 x 53 cm) NOK 88,000. Oslo, 2 June 2003, *Visiting Grandfather* (1885, oil on canvas, 24 x 20 ins / 60 x 52 cm) NOK 135,000. Copenhagen, 9 June 2004, *Hazy Winter's Day* (oil on canvas, 22 x 26 ins / 57 x 67 cm) DKK 14,000. Oslo, 6 Dec 2004, *Two Women Writing Letters* (1892, oil on canvas, 15 x 20 ins / 39 x 52 cm) NOK 82,000.

KOLTONOVSKI, Johann
Polish, 18th century.
Portrait artist.

Johann Koltonovski is known for his portrait of the mother of the famous Polish general Thaddeus Kosciuszko.

KOLTZOV, Sergei
Russian, 20th century.
Born 17 September 1892, in Moscow.
Sculptor.

Sergei Koltzov was a pupil of the school of fine arts in Moscow, where he obtained a gold medal. His realist style has a constructionist aspect.

KOLYN. See **COLYN** and **COLYNS**

KOMAGATA, Katsumi
Japanese, 20th - 21st century.
Born 1953, in Shizuoka.

Also active in the USA.
Graphic designer, illustrator.

Katsumi Komagata eventually settled in Tokyo, where in 1986 he opened his own publishing house, One Stroke. Earlier, from 1977 to 1983, he lived in the USA. From 1990, Komagata produced children's books for the *Little Eyes* series published by Kaisei-sha, Tokyo. He works series by series, experimenting with form and playing on the interactive relations between adults and children. His work is constantly innovative his books are works of art, in which the artist's ingenious cut-outs bring form and colour lyrically to life. In 2003 he created a tactile book for the visually impaired, *Plis et plans* (*Folds and Flat Surfaces*) (Édition Les Trois Ourses/ Les Doigts qui rêvent, Paris, 2003).

He exhibited his work in solo exhibitions in Japan and abroad from 1977. In 1994, his show *1,2,3 Komagata* was seen in Villeurbanne, France; in 1998, *Le monde de Komagata* (*The World of Komagata*) in New Caledonia. In 2003 he had a show at the Bibliothèque Municipale in Aubenas, France. He has been awarded various prizes, including a special mention in 2000 at the Bologna Fiera del Libro per Ragazzi (youth book fair), in the introduction to art category, and the 2002 FEE prize in Switzerland.

KOMAI, Tetsuro

Japanese, 20th century.
Born 1920, in Tokyo.
Engraver, illustrator.

Komai Tetsuro graduated from the oil painting department of Tokyo School of Fine Arts in 1943, where he was appointed assistant. In 1954 he travelled to Europe and studied woodcut and etching techniques at the École des Beaux-Arts, Paris. His style is figurative, tending towards schematic form, with subtle interaction between light and shade playing a major role. He has made many illustrations for poetry anthologies.

In 1948, he started to exhibit at the Japan Print Association and Shonyokai exhibitions. He has exhibited at the Tokyo International Print Biennale since 1957. He was awarded prizes in 1951 at the Lugano International Biennale and São Paulo Biennale, and in 1954 at the Tokyo International Art Exhibition.

KOMAN, Ilhan

Turkish, 20th century.
Born 1921, in Edime.
Active in Sweden.
Sculptor.

Koman studied first at the school of fine arts in Istanbul from 1941 to 1946. He then travelled in Europe until 1950, exhibiting his works in the countries he visited, in particular in France, at the Salon des Nouvelles Realities. Koman has also taken part in various international meetings and was invited to the Venice Biennale in 1956, the São Paulo Biennale in 1957 and the World Fair in Brussels in 1958. Koman's sculptures reveal a sensitivity refined into the starkest abstraction.

MUSEUMS AND GALLERIES:
NEW YORK (MoMA).

KOMANO-KASEICHI

Japanese, 7th century.
Of Korean origin.
Active in Nara in the early 7th century.
Painter.

Komano-Kaseichi is listed as one of the artists on the inscription on the *Tenjukoku Mandara*, a pair of large embroideries in the Horyu-ji Monastery, Nara, dedicated to Prince Shotoku (592-622). It represents the paradise (Tenjukoku) to which the dead prince's soul was supposed to have migrated.

KOMAR AND MELAMID, Vitaly and Aleksandr

Russian, 20th century.
Born in Moscow, Komar born 11 September 1943, Melamid born 14 July 1945.
Active in the USA from 1976.
Painters (mixed media). Figure compositions, figures.
Sots Art, Perestroika Art, Conceptual Art, Neo-Conceptual Art.

Komar and Melamid are the inventors of the name 'art of fools' or 'sots-art', by analogy with the terms 'pop art' and 'socialist realist art'. They borrow themes and very structured stylised productions from socialist realism and twist them with a subversive irony. They began working at the beginning of the 1970s, but they are best known for their work from the 1980s. They produced compositions in a classic, even academic style, in which characters from an idealised history of Soviet socialism are associated with figures from historical paintings or from modern images. In their painting *The Origin of Socialist Realism* (1982-1983), they denounced the Soviet artistic propaganda according to which Russian national culture is expressed only by socialist realism. They showed Stalin sanctified by the Muse and posing for one of his first paintings that created his myth. Komar and Melamid started with large classical formats but later changed to a series of small canvases which, in quick succession, look like quotations from a variety of power symbols. The iconography of thier paintings is far from simplistic. As Boris Groys explains, Komar amd Melamid denounced the monistic conception of art by treating it like a collection of conventions forming one style among others. On the other hand, their art, says Boris Groys, 'relates not only to rationalist academicism, but to magic realism and an academic Surrealism'. For example, the painters dismantle the politico-sexual significance of power in art. By banishing eroticism to sublimate the libido, socialist realist art succeeds in making itself the unconscious mirror of the citizens' fantasies. Acting like a double-faced mirror, reflecting the infernal and fascinating imagery of the West, which socialist realist art had left to the imagination.

Vitaly Komar and Aleksandr Melamid lived and worked in New York since 1976. Collective exhibitions include: *Traumfabrik Kommunismus - die Visuelle Kultur der Stalinzeit Dream Factory Communism, the Visual Culture of the Stalin Period* Schim Kunsthalle, Frankfurt (2003); *Berlin-Moscow/Moscow-Berlin 1950-2000*, a panoramic exhibition following that concerning the period 1900-1950, offering a debate on 50 years of artistic and cultural relations between Germany and Russia marked by political transformations, in the Martin-Gropius building, Berlin and the Tretyakov gallery in Moscow (2003). Solo exhibitions include Moscow (1966, 1973, 1974); Kafe Siniaya Ptitsa, Moscow (1967); Ron Feldman Fine Arts, New York (1976, 1977); Ohio University Gallery of Fine Arts, Columbus (1977); Wadsworth Atheneum, Hartford (1978); Israel Museum, Jerusalem (1978); Hirshhorn Museum and Sculpture Garden, Washington D.C. (1979); Edwin A. Ulrich Museum of Art, Wichita State University, Kansas (1980); Museum of Contemporary Art, Chicago (1981); Portland Center of Visual Arts, Oregon (1983); University of Iowa Museum of Art, Iowa City (1984); The Kitchen, New York (1984); The Fruitmarket Gallery and the Museum of Modern Art, Edinburgh and Oxford (1985); Galérie d'Actualité, Musée des Arts Décoratifs, Paris (1985); Kröller-Müller Rijksmuseum, Otterlo (1985); Arts Council Gallery, Belfast; Haags Gemeentemuseum, The Hague (1986); Institute of Modern Art, Brisbane; The Australian Centre of Contemporary Art, Melbourne; Whitney Museum of American Art, New York; and Artspace, Sydney (1987).

BIBLIOGRAPHY:
Groys, Borys, '*À la recherche du pouvoir artistique perdu*' in *Les Cahiers du Musée national d'Art moderne* no. 26, periodical, Paris, winter 1988. Tupitsyn, Margarita, '*Le Pop à la mode soviétique*' in *Les Cahiers du Musée national d'Art moderne* no. 26, periodical, Paris, winter 1988. Ratcliff, Carter, *Komar and Melamid*, Abbeville Press, New York, 1988. Rapaport, Brooke Kamin, *Komar and Melamid, Yalta in 1945 and Winter in Moscow 1977*, exhibition catalogue, Brooklyn Museum of Art, New York, 1990. Hollein, Max, et al., *Dream Factory Communism: the Visual Culture of the Stalin Period*, exhibition catalogue, Schirn Kunsthalle, Frankfurt, 2003 (text in English and German). '*Berlin-Moskau/Moskau-Berlin 1950-2000*' in *2 vol*, exhibition catalogue, Martin-Gropius-Bau, Berlin, 2003 (text in German).

MUSEUMS AND GALLERIES:
AMSTERDAM (Stedelijk Mus.).

AUCTION RECORDS:
NEW YORK, 8 Nov 1989, *Nike over the Moon* (1985, composition in 8 panels with photographs, oil on canvas, acrylic and coloured chalks/paper, wood, feathers and mirror on panel, 66 x 40¾ ins / 167.6 x 103.5 cm) USD 48,400. NEW YORK, 8 Oct 1992, *Stalin with Hitler's Remains* (1985, oil on canvas, 84¼ x 60¼ ins / 214 x 153 cm) USD 19,800. NEW YORK, 7 May 1993, *Natasha with the Bust of Stalin* (oil on canvas, 72¼ x 47¼ ins / 183.5 x 120 cm) USD 16,100. NEW YORK, 1 Nov 1994, *Bronze Leaves* (1988, oil and copper leaf/canvas, paper and gold leaf/synthetic resin in a Plexiglas frame, oil and gold leaf/panel, 25 x 91 ins / 63.5 x 231.1 cm) USD 4,600.

KOMAROMI-KACZ. See **KISS Sarolta**

KOMÁROMI-KACZ, Endre
Hungarian, 20th century.
Born 9 June 1880, in Komárom.
Painter. Genre scenes.

Endre Komáromi-Kacz was a pupil of Ballo at the academy of fine arts in Budapest, and then of Hollósy in Munich.

AUCTION RECORDS:
VIENNA, 19 March 1986, *The Dance* (oil on canvas, 22¾ x 39¼ ins / 58 x 100 cm) ATS 38,000. VERSAILLES, 24 Sept 1989, *La petite fille assoupie* (oil on canvas, 31½ x 23½ ins / 80 x 60 cm) FRF 5,000. NEW YORK, 19 July 1990, *Tea and Conversation* (oil on canvas, 30¾ x 23½ ins / 78.2 x 59.7 cm) USD 2,200. LONDON, 22 Nov 1996, *The Recital* (oil on canvas, 47 x 34½ ins / 119.4 x 87.8 cm) GBP 1,840.

KOMAROV, Aleksandr or Alexander
Russian, 20th century.
Born 1918; died 1987.
Painter. Scenes with figures.
Collective of Masters of Analytical Art (MAI).

Aleksandr Komarov attended the Repin institute in Leningrad (now St Petersburg), where he was taught by Viktor Orechnikov and Pavel Filonov. A member of the association of painters in Leningrad, he also belonged to the Analytical art group set up by Pavel Filonov.

His painting style is strongly influenced by that of Filonov, a formidably charismatic master. It apparently applies analytical principles of the origin of the universe as an organic whole with drawn and coloured shapes.

Aleksandr Komarov featured in exhibitions in Russia and abroad from 1950.

BIBLIOGRAPHY:
L'École de Léningrad, auction catalogue, Drouot, Paris, 19 November 1990.

MUSEUMS AND GALLERIES:
MOSCOW (Ministry of Culture) - MOSCOW (State Tretyakov Gal.) - NOVGOROD (MFA) - PSKOV (MFA) - ST PETERSBURG (Academy) - ST PETERSBURG (Gosudarstvennyj Muz. Istorii) - ST PETERSBURG (Gosudarstvennyj Russkij Muz.) - YAROSLAVL (Gal. of Russian Art).

AUCTION RECORDS:
PARIS, 11 June 1990, *A Man and a Woman* (oil on canvas, 21¼ x 29½ ins / 54 x 75 cm) FRF 32,000. PARIS, 19 Nov 1990, *Conversation* (oil on canvas, 28¼ x 24¾ ins / 72 x 63 cm) FRF 22,000. PARIS, 23 March 1992, *Game of Billiards* (oil on canvas, 22¾ x 32 ins / 58 x 81 cm) FRF 20,500. PARIS, 20 May 1992, *On the River* (1957, oil on card, 23½ x 32¼ ins / 60 x 82 cm) FRF 18,000. PARIS, 5 Nov 1992, *Road* (1956, oil on canvas, 27¼ x 38¼ ins / 69 x 97 cm) FRF 4,000.

KOMATIS, Henri. See **MATHIS Henri**

KOMATSU, Yuataka
Japanese, 20th century.
Born 1940, in Fukuoka Prefecture.
Painter.

Komatsu Yuataka's canvases, which are made up of spirals and circles, one swallowing the next, have a certain fantastic quality. He was awarded the Shell Prize and second prize in the 1964 *Asahi* oil painting competition. In 1966, he exhibited at the first JAFA Exhibition and other international exhibitions, including the Biennale Internationale des Jeunes Artistes in Paris.

KOMET
Turkish, 20th century.
Painter. Figure compositions.

Komet exhibited at the Briance gallery in the course of the contemporary art fair in Paris in 1992. His painting is narrative, small-format and draws the eye in, depicting a world where people meet.

AUCTION RECORDS:
PARIS, 2 June 1991, *The Kiss* (1982, oil on canvas, 9½ x 12½ ins / 24 x 32 cm) FRF 12,000. PARIS, 3 Feb 2003, *Paysage pour oublier* (1983, oil on canvas, 39x39 ins / 100x100 cm) EUR 680.

KOMIERSKI. See **KANIEWSKI**

KOMLÖSY, Ede
Hungarian, 19th century.
Born 1862, in Turkisch-Kanizsa.
Active in Budapest.
Painter.

Ede Komlösy exhibited in Paris in 1900.

KOMLÖSY, Ferenc
Austrian, 19th century.
Born 17 December 1817, in Temesvár (now Timisoara, Romania); died 14 July 1892, in Vienna.
Painter.

Komlösy exhibited landscapes and flower paintings in Pest, Prague and Vienna. He was the father of Ede and Irma.

KOMLÖSY, Irma
Hungarian, 19th century.
Born 30 August 1850, in Prague.
Active in Vienna.
Painter, watercolourist. Flowers.

Irma Komlösy, the daughter of Ferenc Komlösy, studied with Sturm at the academy of fine arts.

KOMORN, Brigitte
French, 20th century.
Painter.

Brigitte Komorn exhibited at the FIAC (Foire Internationale d'Art Contemporain) in Paris in 1993.

KOMORO, Itaru
Japanese, 20th century.

Born 1941.
Sculptor.
Komoro Itaru won a prize at the Tenth Contemporary Japanese Art Exhibition in Tokyo in 1971. In 1973, he took part in the eighth JAFA show, and the following year in the *Japanese Art Today* exhibition at the Musée d'Art Contemporain, Montréal.

KOMOROWSKA, Wanda
Polish, 20th century.
Born 1883, in Cracow.
Painter, engraver. Portraits, landscapes.
Wanda Komorowska studied at Cracow, Munich and Paris.

KOMPATSCHER, Andreas
Austrian, 19th century.
Born 1864, in Bozen, South Tyrol (now Bolzano, Italy).
Sculptor.
Kompatscher collaborated with Arthur Winder on a polychrome marble entitled *Virgin and Jesus as a Child*, which is kept in the Simu Museum in Bucharest.

KONASHEVICH, Vladimir
Russian, 20th century.
Born 1888; died 1963.
Painter, engraver.
Vladimir Konashevich decorated the palace of the Iusupov princes at St Petersburg.

KONATÉ, Abdoulaye
Malian, 20th - 21st century.
Born 1953, in Diré.
Painter (mixed media), draughtsman, installation artist.
Abdoulaye Konaté studied at the national institute of arts at Bamako until 1976, then between 1978 and 1985 at the school of fine arts in Havana, Cuba. On his return he became a graphic designer, later becoming responsible for the artistic displays at the national museum of Mali. He lives and works in Bamako.

In his often monumental structures, he mingles objects from modern life (scrolls, cartridges), with traditional things (cloth, paintings), in which are inscribed memories of Africa and its links with the West. If it can be said that he uses various pictorial and technical supports, it is painting that he draws on the most.

He has taken part in various public exhibitions, among them: 1984, Centre Culturel Français, Bamako; 1992, Musée National, Mali; 1992, Musée de l'IFAN, Dakar; 1994, Institut du Monde Arabe, Paris; 1995, Biennale *Africus*, Johannesburg; 1996, Biennale, Dakar; 1996, Centre d'Art Moderne de Las Palmas; 1997, *Suites Africaines* (*African Series*) at the Couvent des Cordeliers, Paris; 2002, *Quatre Artistes Maliens Contemporains* (*Four Contemporary Artists from Mali*), Musée de Picardie, Amiens.

KONCHALOVSKY, Piotr Petrovich, or Kontchalovski
Russian, 20th century.
Born 1876, in Slavyansk; died 1956, in Moscow.
Painter. Scenes with figures, portraits.
Groups: Bubnovy Valet (Jack of Diamonds), Association of Artists of Revolutionary Russia (AKhRR).
Piotr Konchalovsky was a pupil at the M.D. Raevskaya-Ivanova drawing school at Kharkov and of V. Sukhanov at the evening classes at the Stroganov Institute in Moscow. From 1892 to 1897 he was in Paris, and took instruction from Jean-Paul Laurens and J.-J. Benjamin-Constant at the Académie Julian. From 1898 to 1905 he was a pupil of Pavel Kovalevski at the Higher Institute of Art in St Petersburg. In 1897 to 1898 he was in Paris for a period, and returned several more times between 1904 and 1925. In 1910 he became a founder-member and president of the Bubnovy Valet (Jack of Diamonds) group.

It is likely that Konchalovsky adopted a Post-Impressionist technique soon after he arrived in Paris. Later, in spite of his title of president, he played a more unassuming role in Bubnovy Valet (Jack of Diamonds) group than Larionov, Goncharova and Malevich, but shared with them their admiration for Cézanne, which they transposed into a more Fauvist, more Russian scale, with discreet borrowings from Cubism or from Matisse. Later still, Konchalovsky later became the painter of the tranquil joys of everyday life, reverting to a softened post-Matisse tradition, having escaped the realist-socialist straitjacket. He painted among others portraits of *Prokofiev* (1934) and *Meyerhold* (1937).

Collective exhibitions include Moscow (1922); Paris (1925); Moscow (1927, 1928, 1929, 1930). He was awarded a Stalin prize (1943). After 1956, the importance of the totality of his work was fully recognised. He was a member and a teacher at the Academy of Arts of the USSR in Moscow.

BIBLIOGRAPHY:
Halturin, Aleksandr/Hulten, Pontus/Gunar, Karl (ed.), *Paris-Moscou*, group exhibition catalogue, Éd. du Centre Georges-Pompidou, Paris, 1979. Pospelov, Gleb G., *Bubnovyj valet, primitiv i gorodskoj folklor v moskovskoj zivopisi 1910*, Sovetskij Chudoznik, Moscow, 1990.

MUSEUMS AND GALLERIES:
MOSCOW (State Tretyakov Gal.): *Portrait of V. Meyerhold* (1937) - ST PETERSBURG (Gosudarstvennyj Russkij Muz.): *People of Novgorod* (1925); *Novgorodians* (1925).

AUCTION RECORDS:
ENGHIEN-LES-BAINS, 7 Dec 1980, *Vase of Flowers* (1918, oil on canvas, 35 x 42 3/4 ins / 88.8 x 108.8 cm) FRF 7,000. ENGHIEN-LES-BAINS, 29 March 1981, *Crystal II* (1917, oil on canvas, 32 x 26 1/2 ins / 81 x 67 cm) FRF 45,000. LONDON, 14 Nov 1988, *Fruits on the Tree* (oil on canvas, 23 1/2 x 28 3/4 ins / 60 x 73 cm) GBP 1,650. LONDON, 10 Oct 1990, *Still-life with Teapot and Lemon* (1929, oil on canvas, 6 3/4 x 9 ins / 17 x 23.1 cm) GBP 3,300. MILAN, 10 Nov 1992, *Townscape* (1926, tempera/paper, cover design for Neva Rouge, 14 1/4 x 11 ins / 36.3 x 27.8 cm) ITL 1,500,000.

KONCZEWSKA
Polish, 19th century.
Sculptor.
Mme Konczewska adapted her talents to suit the new French fashions.

KONDO, Koichiro, real name Kindo Hiroshi, original given name Ko
Japanese, 20th century.
Born 1884, in Yamanashi Prefecture; died 1962.
Active in the early 20th century.
Painter.
Kondo Koichiro started to exhibit at the Teiten (Imperial Salon) after studying in the oil painting department of the Tokyo Fine Arts School. Around 1917, he turned to ink painting (*suiboku-ga*) and was made a member of the Japanese Fine Art Academy, which he would remain until 1936.

KONDO, Komei
Japanese, 20th century.
Born 1924, in Tokyo.
Painter.
Kondo Komei graduated from the oil painting department of Tokyo Fine Arts University. His style is figurative, with surrealist overtones. He was accepted as a member of the Shinseisaku (Young Artists Association) where he exhibited regularly. In 1967 he exhibited at the second JAFA exhibition.

KONDOPOULOS, Alekos
Greek, 20th century.
Born 1905, in Lamia; died 1975.
Painter.

After studying at the school of fine arts in Athens, Alekos Kondopoulos obtained a grant to go to Paris where he attended the free academies between 1931 and 1933. Returning to Greece, in 1941 he became an administrative assistant to the National Museum of Archaeology in Athens. In 1949 he founded the group Extremists whose manifesto he drew up. He is also the author of a book *Painting Today*. From 1964 until his death he lived and worked in Aghia Paraskevi, where his home has become a cultural centre. Alekos Kondopoulos is considered to have introduced abstract art to Greece.

He took part in collective exhibitions, including the Venice Biennale (1960). Solo exhibitions include Athens; Paris (1963); New York (1965, 1967, 1968).

KONDOR, Bela

Hungarian, 20th century.
Born 1931.
Painter, draughtsman, illustrator. Historical subjects. Murals, designs for stained glass.

Bela Kondor was a pupil at the school of fine arts in Budapest from 1951 to 1956, and made a study visit to Paris in 1957.

He first became known with for his illustrations of the modern world and of historic events as well as of literary works. His very varied technique and use of interesting materials combines a variety of influences and expresses an extensive range of feelings.

Collective exhibitions include: Budapest (1960); Miami (1961); Székesfehérvar (1964); Musée Ernst de Budapest (1965). He showed his works in a large solo exhibition in Budapest (1970). In 1964 he won the prize for graphic art in the Venice Biennale. He was also awarded the Munkácsy prize.

BIBLIOGRAPHY:
Hongrie 68, Pannonia, Budapest, 1968. Csorba, Géza, *L'Art hongrois contemporain*, exhibition catalogue, Musée Galliera, Paris, 1970.

KONDOVSKY, Dimitar

Macedonian, 20th century.
Born 1927, in Prilep.
Painter. Murals.

Dimitar Kondovsky completed his studies at the academy of fine arts in Belgrade in 1952. His painting is a good example of the synthesis between traditional medieval and non-figurative, associative art.

Collective exhibitions after 1952 include Yugoslavia; Canada (1959); Britain; Italy; Germany; and the São Paulo Biennale (1967). Kondovsky also held several solo exhibitions in Yugoslavia, and in Rome in 1962 when he was living in that city studying techniques of wall-painting. He produced a large mural in Skopje.

KONDRAT, Dimitri

Russian, 20th century.
Painter.

Dimitri Kondrat worked at Pskov.

AUCTION RECORDS:
PARIS, 7 Nov 1988, *Couple* (1970, 29¼ x 20¾ ins / 74 x 53 cm) FRF 3,600.

KONDRATENKO, Gavriil Pavlovich

Russian, 19th - 20th century.
Born 1854; died 1924.
Painter. Landscapes.

Gavriil Kondratenko lived in St Petersburg and showed at the Exposition Universelle of 1900 in Paris.

MUSEUMS AND GALLERIES:
ST PETERSBURG (Gosudarstvennyj Russkij Muz.): *Ananour (Georgia)*; *Night in the Crimea*.

AUCTION RECORDS:
LONDON, 27 March 1984, *Boats on a Crimean Lake* (1884, oil on canvas, 31 x 62¾ ins / 79 x 159.5 cm) GBP 2,800. LONDON, 14 Nov 1988, *Garden in the Crimea* (oil on canvas, 18¼ x 13¾ ins / 46.5 x 35 cm) GBP 880. NEW YORK, 16 July 1992, *View of Gurzuf on the Black Sea* (oil on panel, 13¾ x 18¼ ins / 34.9 x 46.4 cm) USD 1,320.

KONDRATOVITCH, Daniel

Polish, 18th - 19th century.
Born 1771; died 1844, in Warsaw.
Painter. History painting.

Daniel Kondratovitch studied in Warsaw under Franciszek Smuglewicz (1745-1807), and was director of the art gallery of Count Józef Ossolinski (1748-1826). Among his major works are *Prince Józef Poniatowski Visiting the Tombs of the Kings of Kraków*, *Death of Virginia* and *Old Man* (exhibited in Warsaw in 1819).

KONDRUP, Catinka

Danish, 19th century.
Born 11 December 1851, near Aalborg.
Sculptor.

Catinka Kondrup exhibited at the royal academy in 1880 and 1886.

KONEBERG, Michael

German, 18th century.
Active in Kempten in 1765.
Painter.

Koneberg decorated many churches in Germany and his work includes, in particular, an impressive number of ceilings in Schiff, Kempten, Langenegg, Martinszell and other places.

KONECSNI, Gyögy

Hungarian, 20th century.
Born 1903, in Devecser.
Painter, graphic designer. Murals, designs for mosaics.

Gyögy Konecsni was a pupil of Gyula Rudnay at the school of fine arts in Budapest from 1927 to 1931 and later taught there. He began by producing artistic posters and graphic publicity designs, an area that brought him great success, notably abroad. From 1949 he devoted more time to painting and began with historic compositions in an academic style advocated by the doctrine of socialist realism. Some liberalisation of the system encouraged him to undertake mosaics and murals (in some of which he used purely graphic techniques), in an expressionist style, following the rules of post-Cubism. The influence of Surrealism, even of Abstraction can be seen in his easel paintings. He was awarded the Kossuth prize.

BIBLIOGRAPHY:
Hongrie 68, Pannonia, Budapest, 1968.

KONEK, Ida

Hungarian, 19th century.
Born 13 June 1856, in Pressburg (now Bratislava).
Painter.

Ida Konek was a pupil of Telepy in Budapest. She is known for still-lifes, landscapes and genre scenes.

AUCTION RECORDS:
VIENNA, 20 March 1973, *Old Couple*, ATS 20,000. PARIS, 23 Nov 2001, *Young Artist in Studio* (1896, oil on canvas, 20x15 ins / 50x37 cm) FFR 12,000. LONDON, 21 March 2002, *Artist's Studio* (1886, oil on canvas, 20x15 ins 52x38 cm) GBP 2,300. VIENNA, 10 April 2003, *Girl with Blossom on Twigs* (oil on canvas, 21x17 ins / 54x42 cm) EUR 800.

KONEMANN, C. W.

German, 19th century.
Born in Barmen.
Painter.

KONENKOV, Serguei Timofeievitch, or Konyonkov
Russian, 20th century.
Born 1874, in Karakovichi; died 1971, in Moscow.
Active in the USA from 1922 to 1945.
Sculptor. Allegorical subjects, portraits.
Symbolism.

Serguei Konenkov studied at the Institute of Painting, Sculpture and Architecture in Moscow from 1899 to 1902, in the studio of Pavel Trubetskoy, and at the Institute of Higher Art near the Art Academy in St Petersburg with Vladimir Beklemishev. In 1897 he visited France. From 1918 to 1922 he taught in the Studios of Free Art, at the Vhutemas in Moscow. In 1908 he became a member of the New Association of Artists, in 1917 of the Mir Iskousstva (World of Art), in 1919 of the Union of Russian Artists, and in 1919 of the Academy. On his return to the USSR because his sources of inspiration and his style of expression was being less compatible with the official doctrine of Socialist Realism, he fell from grace between 1947 and 1954; however, he was awarded the Stalin prize in 1951, was made a member of the new Academy of Arts in 1954, he was awarded the Lenin prize in 1957.

Nicknamed the 'Russian Rodin', Serguei Konenkov was also a portrait sculptor and is known for his effigies in wood, most often representing old men, characters from tales of old Russia and gods of ancient Slav civilisations.

His work featured in collective exhibitions including: 14th International Exhibition, Venice (1924); Exhibition of Russian art, New York; Grand Palais, Paris with his 1910 monolithic wooden sculpture of *Stribog*, ancient Slav god of the winds (1967-1968); *Traumfabrik Kommunismus - die Visuelle Kultur der Stalinzeit* (*Dream Factory Communism, the Visual Culture of the Stalin Period*), Schim Kunsthalle, Frankfurt (2003). Solo exhibitions include Moscow (1916, 1917); and New York (1925).

BIBLIOGRAPHY:
Konënkov, S., '*Mastera nachego veka*' in *coll. Les maîtres de notre siècle*, Moscow, 1978. Savelona, E., *Sergueï Timofeevitch Konenkov*, Moscow, 1978. Halturin, Aleksandr/Hulten, Pontus/Gunar, Karl (ed.), *Paris-Moscou*, exhibition catalogue, Éd. du Centre Georges-Pompidou, Paris, 1979. Mamontova, O.V., *S. Konënkov*, Sovetskij Chudoznik, Moscow, 1983. Hollein, Max, et al., *Dream Factory Communism: the Visual Culture of the Stalin Period*, exhibition catalogue, Schirn Kunsthalle, Frankfurt, 2003 (text in English and German).

MUSEUMS AND GALLERIES:
MOSCOW (State Tretyakov Gal.) - STRIBORG (Mus. Konenkov): *Forest Warden*.

KONER, Max
German, 19th century.
Born 17 July 1854, in Berlin; died 7 July 1900, in Berlin.
Painter.

Koner studied at the academy in Berlin. He was a professor and member of the academy from 1893. He was awarded gold medals in Berlin in 1890 and 1894 and in Paris in 1900. His works entitled *Portrait of William II* and *Portrait of Doctor Curtuis* are on display in the Berlin museum.

KONER, Sophie
Maiden name: Schäffer
German, 19th century.
Born 13 July 1855, in London; died 1929.
Painter.

Sophie Koner was the wife of Max Koner. She won a gold medal in Berlin in 1896.

AUCTION RECORDS:
LONDON, 9 Oct 1997, *Head and Shoulders Portrait of Child Wearing a Ribbon in Her Hair and a White Dress* (oil on canvas, 23 3/4 x 19 1/2 ins / 60.5 x 49.5 cm) GBP 5,175.

KONETZKE, August
German, 19th century.
Born 22 May 1858, in Dammerau.
Painter.

Konetzke is known for his decorations and landscapes. He also illustrated a Shakespeare text with silhouettes.

KONEWKA, Paul
German, 19th century.
Born 5 April 1841, in Greifswald; died 10 May 1871, in Berlin.
Draughtsman.

Konewka studied under the sculptor Drake and the painter Adolf Menzel. He is famous for his silhouettes.

KONFAR, Gyula or Giula
Hungarian, 20th century.
Born 1933.
Painter.

Gyula Konfar was a pupil of Endre Domanovsky, Janos Kmetty and Géza Fonyi at the academy of fine arts in Budapest from 1950 to 1957. He won the Munkácsy prize, received the Derkovits grant from 1960 to 1963, and was one of the founders of the Kilencek (The Nine) group. He mainly painted figures and figure compositions that bordered on the abstract in an extremely thick and lumpy texture.

He began exhibiting from 1958 and showed at the Venice Biennale (1960). Solo exhibitions include: London (1964, 1965); and Gyor (1969).

BIBLIOGRAPHY:
Art hongrois contemporain, exhibition catalogue, Musée Galliera, Paris, 1970.

KONG, Yanshi, or K'ung Yan-shih
Chinese, 19th century.
Active c. 1820.
Painter.

Kong Yanshi is known for several works, including the *Shicun Huajue*, a short book of ten chapters dealing with aesthetic and technical matters, from a practical point of view. Except for a detailed acount of a wash technique, the work as a whole lacks originality.

KONG HIEN. See **GONG XIAN**

KONG K'AI. See **GONG KAI**

KONG PO. See **GONG BO**

KONG SOU-JAN. See **GONG SURAN**

KONGSBAK, Albert Georg
Danish, 20th century.
Born 20 February 1877, in Copenhagen.
Painter. Religious subjects, genre scenes.

Kongbak executed an altarpiece for the church of Kleistrup.

AUCTION RECORDS:
LONDON, 17 May 1991, *Children Playing in Courtyard* (1904, oil on canvas, 28 1/4 x 32 3/4 ins / 71.5 x 83.2 cm) GBP 9,020.

KONGSVALD, Rolf
Norwegian, 20th century.
Painter.

Kongsvald was active in 1937.

KONICHEVA, Natalia
Russian, 20th century.
Born 1935, in Moscow.
Painter. Nudes, portraits, scenes with figures.

Natalia Konicheva graduated from the faculty of fine arts of the polygraphic institute in Moscow and was a member of the Union of Soviet artists from 1973.

She produced paintings strongly resonant of a strange dream world, peopled with quantities of miniature figures, angels, clowns, gnomes, more suggested than drawn in lively compositions.

KONIECZNY, Wladimir
Polish, 20th century.
Born 1886, in Jaroslaw; died 5 July 1916.
Sculptor, engraver.
Wladimir Konieczny worked in Cracow, then Paris and Italy.

KÖNIG
German, 19th century.
Born in Coburg.
Active c. 1853.
Painter. History painting.

KÖNIG. See also **KOENIG**

KÖNIG, Albert
German, 20th century.
Born 22 March 1881, in Eschede.
Painter, engraver. Landscapes.
Primarily a landscapist, König attended the academy in Düsseldorf from 1901.

KÖNIG, Alfred
German, 20th century.
Born 1871, in Rodolstadt; died 1940, in Meissen.
Draughtsman. Figures. Designs (porcelain).
Jugendstil.
Alfred König trained at the Kunstgewerbeschule in Dresden, then worked as modeller for a porcelain factory, before becoming a regular supplier for the Meissen porcelain factory.
BIBLIOGRAPHY:
Kern, Andrea, et al., *Jugendstil in Dresden, Aufbruch in die Moderne*, exhibition catalogue, Staatliche Kunstsammlungen, Dresden, 1999.

KÖNIG, Anton Balthazar
German, 18th century.
Born c. 1693, in Berlin; died 1773, in Berlin.
Draughtsman, engraver.
König studied under Blesendoff and Gorbel. He worked in St Petersburg and Dresden. He engraved portraits mainly, notably that of Frederick the Great.

KÖNIG, Anton Friedrich, the Elder
German, 18th century.
Born 1722, in Berlin; died 1787.
Miniaturist, draughtsman, engraver.
König was the son of Anton Balthazar König. He studied under Blesendoff and A. Pesne. He was miniaturist to the Prussian court in 1767. One of his portraits was of *Frederick the Great*.

KÖNIG, Anton Friedrich, the Younger
German, 18th - 19th century.
Born 13 June 1756, in Berlin; died 2 January 1838, in Berlin.
Sculptor, medallist, engraver.
König was the son of Anton Friedrich König the Elder. He studied under Loos. He was in Breslau (now Wroclaw, Poland) in 1776. He engraved portraits.

KONIG, Arthur
Swiss, 20th century.
Born 19 January 1882, in Bern.
Painter.
After receiving an initial artistic training in his native town, Arthur Konig studied further in Basel and, from 1904, he attended the art academy in Munich.

KÖNIG, Benedikt
German, 19th century.
Born 11 April 1842, in Gruberberg (Baden-Württemberg); died 9 July 1906, in Munich.
Sculptor.
König carved a *Statue of Leibniz* for the Polytechnikum in Stuttgart.

KÖNIG, Caroline
Swiss, 19th century.
Born 1793; died 8 April 1823, in Bern.
Painter, watercolourist.
König studied under her father Franz Niklaus König. She exhibited her work in Bern in 1818.

KÖNIG, Catherine Elisabeth. See **KÖNIG Lily**

KÖNIG, E.
French, 19th century.
Painter. Seascapes.
E. König exhibited at the Salon in 1837 and 1838.

KÖNIG, Ferdinand
German, 19th century.
Born 17 June 1827, in Magdeburg; died 5 February 1894, in Munich.
Landscape artist.
König studied in Munich, Norway and Italy. He settled in Munich.

KÖNIG, Franz Niklaus
Swiss, 18th - 19th century.
Born 6 April 1765, in Bern; died 27 March 1832, in Bern.
Painter, engraver. Genre scenes, landscapes.
König was the second son of a draughtsman who had five children. He studied with the painters Wocher and Freudenberger, then became an officer. He married Marie Madeleine Wyss in 1786 and took up painting again. He gained recognition through small works such as *Evening*, *Baptism* and *Wedding*. The war of 1798 interrupted his work, which he took up again enthusiastically on his return to his family. As his talent became recognised his reputation spread through Germany and France. However, his family misfortunes ruined his health, 15 of his 19 children dying before he did.
The majority of his engravings are views of Switzerland.

MUSEUMS AND GALLERIES:
BERN: *Waterfall; Peasants' Houses in Leissingen and the Bernese Oberland; The Hoheweg in Interlaken; Eagle Swooping Down on its Prey; View of Wetterhaw; Workers on a Bernese Farm; Spa at Sigriswyl; Beasts at the Watering Place* - NEUCHÂTEL: a gouache.
AUCTION RECORDS:
PARIS, 30 Nov 1897, *Portrait of Man* (miniature) FRF 150. PARIS, 6 Dec 1923, *Bernese Chalet* (pencil and wash) FRF 1,050. ZURICH, 31 May 1976, *Staubbach Falls in the Lauterbrunnen Valley* (coloured etching, 19 3/4 x 16 ins / 50 x 40.7 cm) CHF 2,900. BERN, 21 Nov 1978, *View of Unterseen* (oil on panel, 10 x 13 3/4 ins / 25.5 x 35 cm) CHF 2,100. LONDON, 15 July 1980, *Child Playing with a Cat* (1827, gouache/grey paper, 4 x 5 3/4 ins / 10 x 14.5 cm) GBP 450. LONDON, 17 July 1980, *Farmyard Scene* (coloured etching, 9 3/4 x 13 1/4 ins / 24.9 x 33.8 cm) GBP 600. BERN, 25 June 1982, *Return from the Alps; Family at Work* (two etchings in colour, 10 1/2 x 13 3/4 ins / 26.5 x 34.8 cm) CHF 12,500. BERN, 25 June 1982, *Wedding in the Church at Unterseen near Interlaken* (pen/pencil outlines) CHF 3,400. HAMBURG, 8 June 1983, *Mountain Landscape* (1805, gouache, 13 1/4 x 18 1/2 ins / 33.8 x 47.3 cm) DEM 4,000. BERN, 24 June 1983, *Staubbach Falls in the Lauterbrunnen Valley* (1804, coloured etching, 23 3/4 x 17 1/4 ins / 60.3 x 43.8 cm) CHF 4,200. LUCERNE, 11 Nov 1983, *Market Scene* (pen and watercolour, 4 x 3 1/4 ins / 10.3 x 8.4 cm) CHF 3,000. BERN, 22 June 1984, *Bern, Drawn from the Enge Road* (coloured etching, 7 3/4 x 12 3/4 ins / 19.7 x 32.3 cm) CHF 2,700. ZURICH, 12 June 1995, *View of the City of Bern at Full Moon* (gouache/paper, 6 x 8 ins / 15.5 x 20.5 cm) CHF 3,450. ZUR-

ICH, 5 June 1996, *View of Geneva* (pencil and ink/paper, 29 1/2 x 41 1/4 ins / 75 x 105 cm) CHF 17,250.

KÖNIG, Franz Xaver
Austrian, 18th century.
Born c. 1711, in Salzburg; died 24 December 1782.
Painter.
König's most important work is the decoration of St Peter's Abbey in Salzburg, in which he painted pictures of the saints.

KÖNIG, Fritz. See **KOENIG**

KÖNIG, Georg Rudolf
Swiss, 19th century.
Born 1 March 1790, in Bern; died 12 June 1815, in Bern.
Painter, draughtsman. Portraits, landscapes.
König studied under his father Franz Niklaus König and Jacques-Louis David in Paris. Towards the end of 1813 he returned to his family and concentrated on producing portraits. He was a political prisoner for several months, and his fragile health deteriorated suddenly. He died prematurely at the age of 25. His final works were drawings of his fellow prisoners.
AUCTION RECORDS:
LUCERNE, 30 May 1979, *Landscape at Lauterbrunnen* (oil on canvas, 23 1/4 x 31 3/4 ins / 59 x 80.5 cm) CHF 6,000.

KÖNIG, Gustav Ferdinand Leopold
German, 19th century.
Born 2 April 1808, in Coburg; died 30 April 1869, in Erlangen.
Painter. History painting.
Konig started out as a porcelain painter. Between 1828 and 1833 he studied successively in Heidelberg, Stuttgart, Strasbourg, Fribourg, Munich and Nuremberg. He devoted himself to religious subjects and history painting.
MUSEUMS AND GALLERIES:
MUNICH: *Nathan Warning David to Repent.*
AUCTION RECORDS:
LONDON, 25 Nov 1982, *Three Children Playing with a Bird* (pen and brown ink, heightened with white, 12 3/4 x 21 3/4 ins / 32.7 x 55.5 cm) GBP 1,500.

KÖNIG, Heinrich Justus
German, 19th century.
Born 22 April 1862, in Elberfeld.
Active in Düsseldorf.
Painter. History painting, portraits.
One of König's known works is entitled *Tigers Fighting in an Arena.*
MUSEUMS AND GALLERIES:
WROCLAW: *Portrait of the Artist's Father.*

KONIG, Henri
Swiss, 20th century.
Born 13 January 1896, in Romanshorn (Thurgau); died 24 June 1983.
Sculptor. Figures. Busts.
In 1917 Henri Konig attended the École des Beaux-Arts in Geneva, and from 1921 to 1924 he was James Vibert's assistant. He was in Rome in 1924 and 1925, and again in 1935 and 1936, when he studied at the Villa Massimo, the German Academy in that city. In 1943 he took up a teaching post at the École des Beaux-Arts in Geneva and was attached to the École d'Architecture (Université) - positions from which he resigned in 1963 and 1969 respectively. Konig's works were bought by the Swiss authorities and he carried out several works for private or public institutions, notably in Geneva for the Quai Gustave-Adar and Mont-Blanc.
BIBLIOGRAPHY:
Ammann, Heinrich, *Thurgauer Jahrbuch*, Verlag Huber, Frauenfeld.
MUSEUMS AND GALLERIES:
GENEVA: *Domenico*; *Angel* (stone).

KÖNIG, Herbert
German, 19th century.
Born 1820, in Dresden; died 13 June 1876, in Niederlössnitz.
Painter, watercolourist, caricaturist. Genre scenes.
König began his studies in Dresden and continued them in different towns in Germany. From 1848 he worked in Munich and for the publications *Fliegende Blätter* and *Hanschronik*. In 1852 he worked in Leipzig, contributing to the publications *Gardenlaube* and *Illustrierte Zeitung (Illustrated News)*. He later went to Berlin and produced illustrations for *Kladderadatsch (Scandal)*. During the wars of 1866 and 1870 he produced studies of battles and a collection of watercolours entitled *Classic Examples of the War Years*, which were bought by Queen Olga of Württemberg.

KÖNIG, Hugo
German, 19th century.
Born 21 May 1856, in Dresden; died 27 July 1899, in Dresden.
Painter. History painting, genre scenes, landscapes.
König studied under Oehme in Blasewitz, and Seitz, Löfftz and Lindenschmit in Munich. He was awarded a medal in Munich in 1892 and diplomas in Dresden and Berlin in the same year, and a silver medal in Vienna in 1893.
MUSEUMS AND GALLERIES:
BUCHAREST: a watercolour - MUNICH: *St Peter's Denials* - STUTTGART: *Evening by the Pond.*
AUCTION RECORDS:
MUNICH, 29 Nov 1979, *Portrait of Young Girl in a Tyrolean Hat* (1885, oil on canvas, 17 x 13 3/4 ins / 43 x 35 cm) DEM 3,000. VIENNA, 15 Sept 1982, *Rural Idyll* (oil on panel, 13 1/2 x 9 1/2 ins / 34 x 24 cm) ATS 28,000. NORTH BETHESDA, 5 March 1999, *Family in Interior* (1896, oil on canvas, 19 x 16 ins / 48 x 41 cm) USD 2,000. NEW YORK, 5 Oct 1999, *Picking Wildflowers* (1885, oil on panel, 17 x 12 ins / 43 x 30 cm) USD 3,500.

KÖNIG, Johann Christoph
German, 18th century.
Active in Kirchheim in 1703.
Painter.
König's best-known work is his decoration of the church in Wilheim with the portrait of Duke Frederick Charles.

KÖNIG, Johann Henrich Christoph
German, 19th century.
Born 11 November 1777, in Brunswick; died 27 October 1867, in Breslau (now Wroclaw, Poland).
Painter. Mythological subjects, portraits, landscapes.
König studied in his home town of Brunswick and then in Berlin, returning at the beginning of the 19th century.
MUSEUMS AND GALLERIES:
WROCLAW: *Death of Cleopatra*; *The Nicolai Gate in Breslau in 1807*; *Portrait of Field Marshall Von Gneisenau.*

KÖNIG, Johann or Hans
German, 17th century.
Born c. 1586, in Nuremberg; died c. 1642.
Painter, miniaturist. Religious subjects, genre scenes.
König seems to have received his early education from Johan Rottenhammer in Augsburg. He was influenced by Tintoretto and Veronese during a stay in Venice in 1609. Between about 1610 and 1615 he stayed in Rome, where he most probably met Adam Elsheimer. He finally returned to Nuremberg in 1630.

He painted works entitled *Last Judgement* and *Story of Ananias and Sapphira* for the town hall in Augsburg. The university of Upsal owns an agate by König, on which he painted *Crossing the Red Sea* on one side and *Last Judgement* on the other. He painted several versions of *Ecce*

Homo on different materials, such as copper, vellum and canvas, for example, in 1615 (part of a private collection in Darmstadt), in 1616 (kept at the Schlossmuseum in Weimar), and in 1622 (part of the Staatliche Graphische Sammlung in Munich). His use of colour and his baroque style, similar to that of Caravaggio, have been likened to the technique of Johann Lyss, and through him to that of Elsheimer.

Museums and Galleries:

Berlin (National Mus.): *Christ and the Samaritan* - Munich (Staatliche Graphische Sammlung): *Ecce Homo* (1622) - Vienna: *Winter, Summer, Spring, Autumn* (painting/copper) - Weimar (Schlossmus.): *Ecce Homo* (1616).

Auction records:

Paris, 1838, *Adam and Eve in the Garden of Eden,* FRF 150. Paris, 4 April 1925, *Danae,* FRF 280. Paris, 9 March 1951, *Jacob's Dream,* FRF 280,000. London, 26 Feb 1958, *Landscape with Abraham and the Angels,* GBP 360. London, 6 Dec 1972, *Leto and the Peasants,* GBP 9,000. London, 13 July 1977, *Women Bathing in a Wooded Landscape* (oil/copper, 12 x 16 1/4 ins / 30.5 x 41 cm) GBP 10,500. London, 7 July 1978, *Diana the Huntress and a Nymph in a Wooded Landscape* (oil/copper, 11 x 8 1/4 ins / 27 x 21 cm) GBP 1,600. London, 4 May 1979, *Stoning of St Stephen* (oil on canvas, 30 1/4 x 19 3/4 ins / 76.7 x 50.2 cm) GBP 4,200. London, 8 July 1981, *St John the Baptist in a Wooded River Landscape* (oil/metal, 3 1/4 x 4 3/4 ins / 8.5 x 12.3 cm) GBP 14,500. New York, 10 June 1983, *Bathsheba* (oil/copper, 13 x 9 ins / 33 x 22.7 cm) USD 35,000. London, 12 Dec 1984, *Flight to Egypt against a Wooded Landscape* (oil/copper, 13 x 19 1/2 ins / 33 x 49.5 cm) GBP 45,000. Amsterdam, 18 Nov 1985, *The Good Samaritan* (gouache heightened with gold/parchment, 3 1/2 x 4 3/4 ins / 8.9 x 11.9 cm) NLG 4,400. Amsterdam, 25 Nov 1991, *Ecce Homo* (ink and wash heightened with white, 10 1/4 x 8 1/4 ins / 25.8 x 21.2 cm) NLG 17,250. Monaco, 2 July 1993, *Ecce Homo* (1618, oil/vellum, 10 1/2 x 8 1/4 ins / 26.5 x 21 cm) FRF 499,500. London, 13 Dec 2001, *Landscape with Rest on the Flight into Egypt* (oil on copper, 11 x 15 ins / 28 x 38 cm) GBP 390,000. Vienna, 5 June 2002, *Flight to Egypt* (oil on copper, 5 x 7 ins / 13 x 19 cm) EUR 7,000. Amsterdam, 17 May 2004, *Susanna in a Landscape with Peacock, Pheasant and Dog* (oil on panel, 10 x 13 ins / 25 x 34 cm) EUR 5,500.

KÖNIG, Julie

Swiss, 19th century.

Born c. 1791; died 17 July 1821.

Active in Bern.

Painter.

König was the daughter of Franz Niklaus König. She exhibited her work in Bern in 1818.

KÖNIG, Julie

Swiss, 19th century.

Born 26 October 1839, in Bern; died 6 January 1881, in Paris.

Painter.

König studied drawing and painting with her father. She specialised in gilding on glass and settled in Paris.

KÖNIG, Leo von (Freiherr)

German, 19th - 20th century.

Born 28 February 1871, in Brunswick; died 20 April 1944, in Tutzing.

Painter. Figures, portraits, landscapes.

In 1887, Leo von König attended the academy in Berlin with Franz Lippisch; then, between 1894 and 1897, he studied under Lefebvre and Tony Robert-Fleury at the Académie Julian in Paris. He travelled to St Petersburg, Moscow, London, Concarneau and Munich. A member of the Berlin Secession, he settled in Berlin in 1899. He imitated the Old Masters with a certain eclecticism, drawing inspiration from Manet, Cézanne, Rembrandt and El Greco.

König's works were exhibited at the Galerie Schulte in Berlin in 1916 and 1917; at the 41st exhibition of the Berlin Secession in 1921; and at the Galerie Günter Franke in Munich in 1941. After his death, other exhibitions were dedicated to him, including in 1950, at the Museum am Ostwall in Dortmund and, in 2001-2002, *Leo von König (1971-1944): Maler der Berliner Sezession* (*Leo von König (1971-1944): Painter of the Berlin Sezession*), at the Landesmuseum für Kunst und Kulturgeschichte in Oldenburg and the Niedersächsisches Landesmuseum in Hanover.

Bibliography:

Schneider, Reinhold, *Gestalt und Seele: das Werke des Malers Leo von König,* Insel-Verlag, Leipzig, 1936. *Leo von König: Gedächtnisausstellung,* exhibition catalogue, Pfalzgalerie, Kaiserslautern, 1974. Bechter, Alexandra, *Leo von König, 1871-1944: Leben und Werk,* dissertation, WP Druck & Verlag, Darmstadt, 2001 (University of Mainz, 1988).

Museums and Galleries:

Berlin (Nationalgal.): *Anna von König im gelben Pelz* (1925, oil on canvas); *Countesse of Vaux St Cyr* (1932, oil on canvas) - Bremen (Kunsthalle): *Damenbildnis (Fräulein Hardy)* (1906, oil on canvas); *Grüner Papagei vor Azaleenblüten* (1908, oil on canvas); *Weg zum Friedhof in Rapallo* (1927, oil on canvas) - Dresden (Staatliche Kunstsammlungen): *Käthe Kollwitz (IV)* (1941, oil on canvas) - Hanover (Niedersächsisches Landesmus.): *Dr. Fritz Nemitz* (1925, oil on canvas); *Aufziehzndes Gewitter in La Ciotat* (1928, oil on canvas).

Auction records:

Cologne, 27 April 1972, *Saint Martin* (1914) DEM 1,600. Bern, 3 March 1974, *Nude Bust of Young Woman,* CHF 7,000. Munich, 25 Nov 1981, *Summer Landscape* (oil on canvas, 18 1/4 x 22 3/4 ins / 46.2 x 58 cm) DEM 14,500. Cologne, 24 June 1983, *Young Woman Holding a Baby on Lap* (oil on canvas, 30 3/4 x 19 3/4 ins / 78 x 50 cm) DEM 3,800. Cologne, 15 Oct 1988, *Young Woman with Cat* (oil on canvas, 37 x 28 ins / 94 x 71 cm) DEM 5,000. Cologne, 15 June 1989, *Portrait of a Lady* (oil on canvas, 41 1/4 x 29 1/2 ins / 105 x 75 cm) DEM 2,600. London, 9 Oct 1997, *Portrait of Emil Nolde* (1937, oil on canvas, 37 x 30 ins / 94 x 76.5 cm) GBP 21,850. Düsseldorf, 31 Jan 2000, *Preparing for a Night Out* (1908, oil on canvas, 62 x 36 ins / 158 x 92 cm) DEM 24,000. Berlin, 27 May 2000, *Sleeping Figure* (1921, oil on canvas, 29 x 22 ins / 74 x 57 cm) DEM 40,000. Vienna, 27 Nov 2001, *Young Woman and Children in Theatre Box* (1940, oil on canvas, 51 x 65 ins / 130 x 164 cm) ATS 140,000. Königstein, 24 May 2002, *Mathilde and Yvonne Reading the Newspaper* (1909, oil on canvas, 30 x 38 ins / 75 x 96 cm) EUR 18,000. Berlin, 8 June 2002, *Young Anna von Konig with Cat* (1926, oil on canvas, 37 x 28 ins / 94 x 71 cm) EUR 80,000. Berlin, 28 Nov 2003, *Ernst Barlach II* (1937, oil on canvas, 36 x 31 ins / 92 x 78 cm) EUR 110,000. Munich, 26 March 2004, *Scholar* (1898, oil on canvas, 47 x 37 ins / 119 x 93 cm) EUR 4,000. Berlin, 27 Nov 2004, *Three Marabou and Pelican* (oil on canvas, 18 x 13 ins / 46 x 33 cm) EUR 2,200.

KÖNIG, Lily

Swiss, 19th century.

Painter, watercolourist.

This artist appears to be Catherine Elisabeth König, who was baptised on 11 August 1799 and married Louis Emmanuel Savary of Payerne in 1823.

KÖNIG, Marie Albert, later Mme Winternitz

British, 19th - 20th century.

Born 14 August 1866, in Bowdon; died 12 February 1927, in Munich.

Painter. Landscapes.

Marie König was chiefly active in Munich. She was the wife of the painter Richard Winternitz.

Museums and Galleries:

Munich (Municipal Mus.): two paintings.

KÖNIG, Mathilde
Swiss, 19th - 20th century.
Born 27 December 1863, in Bern.
Painter, watercolourist. Landscapes.

KÖNIG, Nicolas or Niclas
German, 17th century.
Active in Nuremberg c. 1600.
Painter. Seascapes.
König was the son of Johann König. *Bryan's Dictionary* refers to a painting by him kept at the museum in Dresden, entitled *Stormy Sea*, which is not mentioned in the current catalogue.

KÖNIG, Otto
Austrian, 19th - 20th century.
Born 28 January 1838, in Meissen; died 30 December 1920, in Vienna.
Sculptor.
Otto König was awarded a distinction in Munich 1869.

KÖNIG, Richard
German, 19th - 20th century.
Born 7 February 1863, in Leobschütz; died 1938, in Munich.
Sculptor. Religious subjects, figures. Groups.
Jugendstil.
Richard König was a student at the academy in Berlin (1882-1885) under the supervision of Calandrelli, then at the academy in Dresden (1885-1887), where he was taught by Ernst Julius Hähnel. He made a study visit to Italy in 1888-1889 with the support of a grant. He then worked in Radebeul, near Dresden, and finally in Chemnitz, where he created religious sculpture for the Kreuzkirche in Dresden, and monumental work, principally a group in relief for the Albertinum symbolising glory, and a relief for the Kunstakademie.
BIBLIOGRAPHY:
Kern, Andrea, et al., *Jugendstil in Dresden, Aufbruch in die Moderne*, exhibition catalogue, Staatliche Kunstsammlungen, Dresden, 1999.
MUSEUMS AND GALLERIES:
DRESDEN (Skulpturensammlung): *Büste einer Muse* (*Bust of a Muse*) (1901).

KÖNIG-LORINSER, Minna
Austrian, 19th century.
Born 2 July 1849, in Vienna; died 1 May 1893, in Vienna.
Painter. Still-lifes, flowers.
König-Lorinser studied under J. Sturn.

KÖNIGER, Veit
Austrian, 18th century.
Born 1 July 1729, in Sexten; died 2 December 1792, in Graz.
Sculptor.
Königer worked mostly for the churches in Graz, including the cathedral, the church of St Peter and the church of St Andrew.

KÖNIGSBRUNN, Hermann von (Reichsfreiherr)
Austrian, 19th - 20th century.
Born 1 March 1823, in Radkersburg; died 16 February 1907, in Graz.
Painter, draughtsman. Landscapes.
In 1848, Hermann von Königsbrunn was taught by Carl or Leopold Rottman in Munich. He travelled in Greece, Egypt and Ceylon. On his return to Germany, he lived for three years in Düsseldorf. In 1858, he settled in Graz, and he is documented to have been in Rome from 1963 to 1964. In 1868, he took up a teaching post at the art academy in Graz.
MUSEUMS AND GALLERIES:
GRAZ: *Ceylonese Landscape.*

KÖNIGSWIESER, Heinrich
German, 16th century.
Died c. 1583, in Königsberg (now Kaliningrad, Russia).
Painter.
Königswieser studied under Lucas Cranach the Younger in Wittenberg. He subsequently worked at the court of Duke Albert of Prussia, decorating the castle at Königsberg and producing portraits of those frequenting the court.
AUCTION RECORDS:
LONDON, 7 Dec 1960, *The Madonna and Child with St John*, GBP 1,400. COLOGNE, 6 June 1973, *The Virgin and Child*, DEM 100,000.

KONIJNENBURG, Willem Adriaan van, or Konynenburg
Dutch, 19th - 20th century.
Born 11 February 1868, in The Hague; died 1943, in The Hague.
Painter, watercolourist, pastellist, poster artist.
Religious subjects, figure compositions, landscapes, seascapes.
Symbolism.
After studying under Arnaud Gerkins and then Hendrik Willem Mesdag, Willem van Konijnenburg entered the art academy in The Hague. From 1900, he became a follower of Haagsche Kunstking (Art Circle of The Hague), which had been directed since 1892 by 'Sar' Péladin, and which Verlaine belonged to. It represented the Symbolist movement in opposition to the Realist trend of the Hague School (which was represented by, among others, his old master Mesdag). In this context, Konijnenburg was also a theoretician with philosophical texts to his name, including his 1908 *Nature du Beau, Idee du Beau*.

In his early period, he was influenced by Impressionism, being primarily a painter of landscapes and seascapes. Once won over to Symbolism, however, he handled religious themes, often borrowed from fantastic episodes of the Golden Legend, as illustrated by his 1916 *Legend of St George*. He worked in the English Pre-Raphaelite style and was accordingly influenced by Italian primitive artists, allowing the decorative elements of 1900 to prevail in his works.
MUSEUMS AND GALLERIES:
THE HAGUE (Mus. Mesdag): *View of Maastricht* (1892) - ZWOLLE (Dominican Monastery): *The Triumph of St Thomas Acquinus* (1928).
AUCTION RECORDS:
AMSTERDAM, 8 Dec 1988, *Farmers Preparing a Pair of Oxen in front of the Farm* (1915, pastel and watercolour/paper, 50 x 29 1/4 ins / 127 x 74 cm) NLG 3,910. AMSTERDAM, 24 May 1989, *Couple in a Horse-drawn Sleigh* (chalks and pastel/paper, 35 3/4 x 35 3/4 ins / 91 x 91 cm) NLG 3,220. AMSTERDAM, 13 Dec 1989, *St Joris* (1916, oil on canvas, 32 x 54 1/4 ins / 81 x 138 cm) NLG 57,500. AMSTERDAM, 12 Dec 1991, *Consolation* (1925, oil on panel, 15 3/4 x 12 1/2 ins / 40 x 32 cm) NLG 8,050. AMSTERDAM, 7 Dec 1994, *War Dance* (1919, lead pencil and colour, 48 x 34 1/4 ins / 122 x 87 cm) NLG 63,250. AMSTERDAM, 18 June 1996, *Good Pedagogue* (charcoal and pastel/paper, 39 3/4 x 28 1/4 ins / 101 x 71.5 cm) GBP 1,035. AMSTERDAM, 18 April 2000, *Bridge over the Thames, London* (oil on canvas, 24 x 35 ins / 60 x 90 cm) NLG 10,000. AMSTERDAM, 11 June 2001, *St Joris* (1916, oil on canvas, 32 x 54 ins / 81 x 138 cm) NLG 60,000. GRAVENHAGE, 5 Nov 2003, *Boy with Cow* (charcoal and brown chalk, 42 x 35 ins / 106 x 90 cm) EUR 1,600.

KONINCK. See also **CONINCK**

KONINCK, Andries de
Dutch, 17th century.
Painter. Genre scenes, landscapes, still-lifes.
Andries de Koninck is thought to have been active in Rotterdam.

KONINCK, Christian, or Kerstiaen de, the Elder, or Keunninck, Keuning, Kanninck, Coninck
Flemish School, 16th - 17th century.
Born in Courtrai; died 1635, in Antwerp, c. 1642 according to some sources.
Painter. Religious subjects, mythological subjects, landscapes, landscapes with figures, mountainscapes, urban landscapes.
Antwerp School.

He was the brother of Martin of Coninck, and studied under Hans Bol. He was a master of the Guild of St Luke in Antwerp in 1580, 1585 to 1586, 1589, 1599, and from 1629 to 1639. He taught Engel Ergo in 1629, and Francis Antonisse in 1636.

MUSEUMS AND GALLERIES:
ANTWERP: *Diana and Actaeon* - COLOGNE: *Forest* - COURTRAI: *The Burning of Troy* - FREIBERG: *Tobias and the Angel* - GHENT: *St Agnes* - VIENNA: *Landscape with Mountains.*

AUCTION RECORDS:
COLOGNE, 14 June 1976, *Landscape with a Bridge* (oil on panel, 17 3/4 x 27 1/4in/45 x 69cm) DEM 15,000. LONDON, 27 May 1977, *Wooded Landscape with a River and Figures* (oil on panel, 14 1/2 x 22 1/2in/37 x 57.3cm) GBP 4,200. LONDON, 15 July 1977, *Wooden Landscape with a Village* (oil on panel, 16 x 27 1/2in/40.6 x 70cm) GBP 2,200. LONDON, 30 March 1979, *Wooded Landscape with a River and Figures* (oil/copper, 15 1/4 x 21 3/4in/38.7 x 55.2cm) GBP 7,500. LONDON, 8 July 1994, *Wooded Landscape with Latona Turning the Peasant Lycien into a Frog* (oil on panel, 18 3/4 x 27 3/4in/47.7 x 70.5cm) GBP 17,250.

KONINCK, Christian, or Kerstiaen de, the Younger, or Keunninck, Keuning, Kanninck, Coninck
Flemish School, 17th century.
Born 1587, in Antwerp; died 1642 or 1643.
Painter.

Christian Koninck the Younger was the son of Christian Koninck the Elder. He was Master of the Guild of St Luke in Antwerp in 1613.

KONINCK, Daniel de
Dutch, 17th century.
Born 1668, in Amsterdam; died c. 1720.
Painter. Portraits, genre scenes.

Daniel de Koninck is known to have been born into a rich family of artists and goldsmiths. From 1687 to 1690 he was the pupil of his uncle Jacob, who at that stage was attached to the Court of Denmark in Copenhagen. He was married on 3 June 1692. At the age of 22 he departed for England, and became a portrait painter in the style of Rembrandt.

AUCTION RECORDS:
LONDON, 17 April 1991, *Bust Portrait of a Man Wearing a Brown Turban* (oil on canvas, 30 3/4 x 24 3/4 ins / 78 x 63 cm) GBP 14,850. NEW YORK, 5 Oct 1995, *Bust Portrait of a Man, Wearing a Turban with a Plume, a Brown Coat and a Chain, the Emblem of his Office* (oil on panel, 34 1/4 x 27 3/4 ins / 87 x 70.5 cm) USD 52,900. LONDON, 12 July 2001, *Head of a Warrior* (oil on panel, 25 x 19 ins / 64 x 47 cm) GBP 7,500. LONDON, 9 Dec 2003, *Portrait of a Man in a Turban and Chain of Office over a Brown Cloak* (oil on panel, 25 x 18 ins / 63 x 46 cm) GBP 7,200.

KONINCK, Edmond de
Belgian, 19th century.
Born 6 February 1839, in Bruges; died 18 March 1883, in Brussels.
Painter. Still-lifes, flowers.

Edmond de Koninck was a student at the academy in Bruges.

KONINCK, J. de
Flemish School, 19th century.
Died 28 December 1863, in Brussels.
Painter. Animals.

J. de Koninck painted *Goats in a Cowshed* and *Cow Lowing*, both in the museum at Ypres. He is almost certainly the same person as the artist J.D. Coninck, who is mentioned in 1842.

KONINCK, Jacob I, or Koningh
Dutch, 17th century.
Born c. 1616, in Amsterdam; died 1 February 1708, probably in Denmark.
Painter, engraver. Historical subjects, figures, genre scenes, landscapes, mountain landscapes, landscapes with figures, urban landscapes, ruins, urban views.
Wall decorations.

Jacob Koninck I married Maria Caterman in 1633. He was living in Amsterdam in 1639, then in The Hague, where he was remarried, to Suzanne Delbeny on 26 July 1648. He returned to Amsterdam in 1659, and in November 1680 left for Denmark. There he painted the queen's bedchamber, and was appointed official painter to the court in 1699. Along with five other painters, Frederick IV offered him the post of director of the union of artists. He resided successively in 1669 in Frederiksstad, in 1705 in Christiania (now Oslo) and in 1708 in Copenhagen.

Paintings by Jacob Koninck I are rare. His engravings, few in number, have often been attributed to Rembrandt.

MUSEUMS AND GALLERIES:
BRUSSELS: *Dutch Landscape* - ROTTERDAM: *Two Houses with Pointed Gables; Landscape with Two Avenues; Farm Surrounded by Trees with a Ruined Tower; Landscape with White Gate; Landscape with Fence; House with Three Chimneys; Landscape with Five Huts; Fisherman in Boat* - ST PETERSBURG (Hermitage): *Old Woman Lending Money.*

AUCTION RECORDS:
LONDON, 13 Dec 1935, *View of Haarlem*, GBP 199. LONDON, 7 June 1974, *Mountainous Landscape*, Gns 2,600. PARIS, 26 June 1992, *Horsemen Resting in a Rocky Landscape* (oil on canvas, 30 1/2 x 24 1/2 ins / 77.5 x 62 cm) FRF 55,000. PARIS, 12 Dec 1995, *View of a Town by an Estuary* (oil on panel, 25 x 31 3/4 ins / 63.5 x 80.5 cm) FRF 55,000. LONDON, 11 Dec 1996, *Wooded Landscape with a Mother and her Child on a Path* (oil on panel, 15 1/2 x 17 3/4 ins / 39.5 x 45 cm) GBP 7,475.

KONINCK, Jacob II
Dutch, 17th - 18th century.
Born between 1647 and 1650, in The Hague; died 16 July 1724, in Copenhagen.
Painter, draughtsman. Portraits, landscapes, animals.

Jacob Koninck II was the pupil of Adrian van de Velde. He lived in Christiania (now Oslo) from 1699 to 1705.

KONINCK, Jacob III, or Koning
Dutch, 18th century.
Died 1734.
Painter.

Jacob Koninck III was a pupil in the painters' guild in Middelburg in 1695.

KONINCK, Jacques de
Flemish School, 18th century.
Born 1703, in Brussels.
Sculptor.

Jacques de Koninck worked for the abbey of Coudenberg in Brussels, and elsewhere.

KONINCK, Philips de, or Koningh
Dutch, 17th century.

Born 5 November 1619, in Amsterdam; died 1688, buried on 4 October in Amsterdam.

Painter, watercolourist, draughtsman. History painting, portraits, still-lifes, genre scenes, landscapes.

Philips de Koninck was one of the most famous pupils of Rembrandt, whose style he adopted, particularly in his drawings. Several of his drawings can easily be confused with those of his master, at least by the untrained eye. De Koninck married Cornelia Furnerini on 1 January 1641. On becoming a widower, he was remarried in Rotterdam on 5 May 1657 to Marguerite van Eyn.

Philips de Koninck painted history paintings, landscapes (some of which have figures painted by Adrien van de Velde) and portraits. In the latter genre, he painted in the style of Rembrandt, but his technique was softened somewhat by the influence of Van Dyck. His landscapes resemble vast panoramas from a horseman's perspective, seen as they are at a distance and from a certain height, with wide tracts of treeless country, often under a threatening sky. His use of colour has a warm clarity and his works have great character. A talented draughtsman, de Koninck also painted religious scenes, using either pen and wash or watercolour.

In 2001 Philips de Koninck was represented at the following group exhibitions: *Twee gouden eeuwen: schilderkunst uit Nederland en Denemarken* (*Two Golden Ages: Masterpieces of Dutch and Danish Painting*) in the Rijksmuseum, Amsterdam, and *Dessins hollandais du Musée Condé à Chantilly* (*Dutch Drawings at the Musée Condé in Chantilly*).

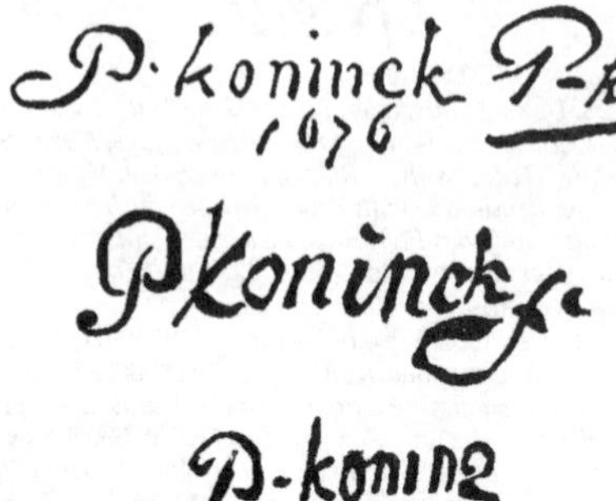

BIBLIOGRAPHY:

Gerson, Horst, *Philips Koninck: ein Beitrag zur Erforschung der holländischen Malerei des XVII. Jahrunderts*, Mann, Berlin, 1936. Mandrella, David, *Dessins hollandais du musée Condé à Chantilly*, exhibition catalogue, Musée Condé, Chantilly, Somogy, Paris, 2001.

MUSEUMS AND GALLERIES:

AMSTERDAM (Rijksmus.): *Landscape with River* (1676); *Entrance to a Forest; Four Portraits of the Poet Joost van den Vondel* - BERLIN: *Flat Landscape* - BRUNSWICK: *Flat Landscape; Young Man in a Plumed Hat* - BRUSSELS: *Impression of the Scheveningen Landscape* - CHANTILLY (Mus. Condé): *Panoramic Landscape with Fishermen* (drawing); *View of a Town in Mist* (drawing) - COLOGNE: *Dutch Landscape* - DRESDEN: *Dutch Landscape* - FLORENCE: *Portrait of the Artist* - FRANKFURT AM MAIN: *Flat Landscape* - HAMBURG: *A Peasant Having an Operation on his Foot* - LONDON: *An Extensive Landscape with a Town in the Middle Distance* (c. 1665-1668, oil on canvas); *An Extensive Landscape with Houses in a Wood and a Distant Town* (c. 1670, oil on canvas, figures and animals probably painted by Adriaen van de Velde); *An Extensive Landscape with a Hawking Party* (after 1670, oil on canvas, on loan at the Mauritshuis in The Hague) - LOS ANGELES (Getty Mus.): *A Panoramic Landscape* (1665, oil on canvas) - OSLO: *A Horseman* - ROTTERDAM: *Flat Landscape* - SCHWERIN: *Happy Boatmen in an Inn* - SIBIU: *Landscape* - ST PETERSBURG (Hermitage): *A Dressmaker* - THE HAGUE: *Mouth of a River, Figures by Joh. Lingelbach.*

AUCTION RECORDS:

PARIS, 1812, *Dutch Landscape*, FRF 2,001. LONDON, 1872, *Bird's-eye View of Holland*, FRF 15,190. PARIS, 27 April 1874, *Still-life*, FRF 8,000. PARIS, 1890, *The Area around Haarlem*, FRF 6,300. LONDON, 1893, *Bird's-eye View of Holland*, FRF 23,600. LONDON, 19 April 1909, *Mountainous Landscape; Landscape with Ruins* (two pen drawings) s 10. LONDON, 11 Feb 1911, *View of Haarlem*, GBP 315. LONDON, 14 July 1911, *Landscape*, GBP 1,155. PARIS, 8-10 June 1920, *Dutch Landscape* (watercolour) FRF 3,200. LONDON, 27 April 1923, *Trumps* (1846) GBP 15. PARIS, 27 May 1924, *The Lady with the Rose*, FRF 6,500. PARIS, 20 Feb 1925, *The Track in the Plain*, FRF 3,200. LONDON, 12 June 1925, *Herdsman in a Landscape*, GBP 1,312. LONDON, 7 May 1926, *Bird's-eye View of Holland*, GBP 7,875. LONDON, 21 Nov 1934, *Wooded Landscape*, GBP 560. GENEVA, 9 June 1935, *Landscape*, CHF 3,100. LONDON, 27 Oct 1943, *River Scene*, GBP 660. LONDON, 4 May 1945, *Three Peasants Playing Cards*, GBP 115. PARIS, 7 Dec 1950, *The Peasant Meal*, FRF 230,000. PARIS, 10 June 1954, *View of the Town of Tiel*, FRF 250,000. LONDON, 27 June 1958, *Extended Landscape*, GBP 367. LUCERNE, 25 Nov 1960, *Landscape with a Town*, CHF 6,000. PARIS, 20 June 1961, *Dutch Landscape* (pen and watercolour heightened with gouache) FRF 6,500. LONDON, 28 Nov 1962, *Landscape with River and Travellers*, GBP 3,400. COLOGNE, 15 April 1964, *Landscape with Cathedral*, DEM 15,000. LONDON, 2 July 1965, *Landscape near Haarlem*, Gns 3,000. NEW YORK, 18 May 1972, *Wooded Landscape*, USD 200,000. LONDON, 29 June 1973, *River Landscape* (1651) Gns 40,000. LONDON, 28 June 1974, *Wooded Landscape with Figures*, Gns 7,000. LONDON, 8 July 1977, *Travellers and Beggars in a Large Wooded Landscape* (oil on canvas, 32 x 43½ ins / 81.2 x 110.5 cm) GBP 120,000. LONDON, 29 June 1979, *Wooded River Landscape with Figures* (oil on canvas, 34 x 43 ins / 86.4 x 109.2 cm) GBP 20,000. AMSTERDAM, 17 Nov 1980, *Wedding Scene* (pen and wash, 7½ x 7 ins / 19.3 x 17.5 cm) NLG 8,000. PARIS, 26 June 1981, *The Dead Christ Mourned by the Women at the Foot of the Cross* (pen and sepia wash, 7 x 8¾ ins / 18 x 22.5 cm) FRF 26,500. LONDON, 15 April 1983, *Shepherd with his Flock and Horseman in a Mountainous Landscape* (oil on canvas, 33½ x 50 ins / 85 x 127 cm) GBP 45,000. AMSTERDAM, 15 Nov 1983, *The Presentation of Christ in the Temple* (pen and wash heightened with white, 5¾ x 5¼ ins / 14.5 x 13.6 cm) NLG 6,400. LONDON, 19 Feb 1987, *Two Men Standing* (pen and brown ink, 6 x 5 ins / 15.4 x 12.5 cm) GBP 6,000. PARIS, 14 April 1988, *Portrait of a Gentleman and his Wife* (1647, oil on panel, 37¾ x 30 ins / 96 x 76 cm) FRF 35,000. AMSTERDAM, 14 Nov 1988, *Extensive Landscape with Windmills* (ink and watercolour, 4½ x 9½ ins / 11.7 x 24 cm) NLG 17,250. NEW YORK, 8 Jan 1991, *Raising of Lazarus* (brown ink, 6¼ x 8½ ins / 16 x 21.5 cm) USD 13,200. AMSTERDAM, 25 Nov 1991, *Left Profile of a Man in a Toga* (ink and wash, 2¾ x 1½ ins / 7.1 x 4.1 cm) NLG 3,220. LONDON, 9 Dec 1992, *Extensive Panorama of a River Landscape* (oil on canvas, 33¾ x 48 ins / 86 x 121 cm) GBP 990,000. AMSTERDAM, 6 May 1993, *Travellers on a Path with a Valley in the Background* (oil on canvas, 43¾ x 52¾ ins / 111 x 134 cm) NLG 97,750. PARIS, 28 Oct 1994, *River Meandering in a Landscape* (watercolour and gouache, 5¼ x 7¾ ins / 13.3 x 20 cm) FRF 1,500,000. LONDON, 3 July 1996, *Extensive Panorama of a Wooded River Landscape* (oil on canvas, 20¾ x 30¼ ins / 52.7 x 77 cm) GBP 925,500. AMSTERDAM, 12 Nov 1996, *View of the Area around Amsterdam with the Westerkerk and Windmills* (pencil, brown ink and wash/black chalk with watercolour and gouache, 5½ x 11½ ins / 13.9 x 29.2 cm) NLG 11,800. LONDON, 3 July 1997, *Extensive Landscape with Figures near a River* (c. 1676, oil on canvas, 49 x 66 ins / 124.5 x 167.5 cm)

GBP 199,500. AMSTERDAM, 8 Nov 1999, *Vanitas, Lady at her Toilet* (1666, oil on canvas, 40 x 32 ins / 101 x 82 cm) NLG 65,000. AMSTERDAM, 9 Nov 1999, *Seated Peasant Holding Jug* (pen and brown ink wash, 7 x 5 ins / 19 x 12 cm) NLG 34,000. NEW YORK, 18 Oct 2000, *Three Men at Dinner with a Servant nearby* (oil on canvas, 22 x 24 ins / 55 x 60 cm) USD 30,000. AMSTERDAM, 8 Nov 2000, *Landscape with Figures Standing by a Fence in the Foreground* (pen and brown ink, 3 x 7 ins / 7 x 19 cm) NLG 7,000. PARIS, 13 June 2001, *The Last Supper and St John* (pen and ink wash heightened with gouache, 7 x 11 ins / 19 x 29 cm) FRF 200,000. LONDON, 12 Dec 2001, *Bleaching Fields near Haarlem with Sportsmen in the Foreground, View of St Bavo beyond* (oil on canvas, 28 x 42 ins / 72 x 106 cm) GBP 120,000. LONDON, 11 April 2002, *Presentation in the Temple* (pen and ink wash heightened with white, 6 x 6 ins / 14 x 14 cm) GBP 8,000. LONDON, 12 Dec 2002, *Landscape with the Goldweigher's field, Haarlem beyond* (oil on panel, 12 x 18 ins / 30 x 45 cm) GBP 60,000. VIENNA, 1 Oct 2003, *Landscape with Pond and Large Tree* (oil on canvas, 34 x 33 ins / 86 x 85 cm) EUR 65,000. NEW YORK, 21 Jan 2004, *Panoramic Landscape with the Mouth of a River* (watercolour and gouache heightened with red chalk, 5 x 11 ins / 13 x 27 cm) USD 42,500. NEW YORK, 22 Jan 2004, *Extensive Landscape with a Lake, Distant Mill and Town* (pen and brown ink wash, 4 x 10 ins / 10 x 25 cm) USD 100,000.

KONINCK, Salomon

Dutch, 17th century.

Born 1609, in Amsterdam; died 1656, in Amsterdam.

Painter, engraver, draughtsman. Religious subjects, portraits, genre scenes.

Salomon Koninck, the nephew of Philips de Koninck, studied under David Colyn, François Venant and Claes Moeyart, and had Bernard van Wollenhove as a pupil. Koninck was a member of the guild in Amsterdam in 1630, and also worked for the King of Denmark.

Koninck is known for his history paintings, scenes from everyday life and particularly for his portraits in the style of Rembrandt. His engravings include: *Portrait of an Old Man, Oriental Man in a Turban, Small Bust of an Old Man, Blind Old Man Seated, Bust of a Man* and *Man Trimming his Pen.*

A Salomon de Coninck, painter of portraits, everyday scenes and history subjects, is recorded as living in Haarlem, and another painter of the same name seems to have been active in Portugal in 1640. It is uncertain whether either of these is identical with this artist.

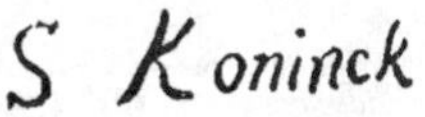

BIBLIOGRAPHY:

Sumowski, Werner, *Gemälde des Rembrandt-Schüler*, PVA, Landau, 1983.

MUSEUMS AND GALLERIES:

AMSTERDAM: *Old Man in a Study; Idolatry of Solomon* - BERLIN: *Calling of St Matthew to the Apostolate; Croesus Showing his Treasures to Solon* (attribution contested by Dr von Wurzbach) - BRUNSWICK: *A Philosopher* - COLOGNE: *Calling of St Matthew* - COPENHAGEN: *Young Lady at her Toilette Reading a Letter; Old Man in his Study* - DRESDEN: *Hermit Reading; Old Man with the Gold Sash* - FRANKFURT AM MAIN: *David Playing the Harp before Saul* (the catalogue and some critics attribute this work to Rembrandt) - GOTHA: *Young Woman in a Green Satin Dress* - HELSINKI: *Old Man and Old Woman* - LEIPZIG: *A Scientist* - LIÈGE: *Rembrandt* - LILLE: *Portrait of a Man* - LYONS: *Sacrifice of Manoah* - MADRID: *Portraits* - MOSCOW (Rumiantsev Mus.): *Old Man* - MUNICH: *Jesus as a Child between the Pharisees and the Teachers* - ROHRAU (Schlossmus., Graf Harrach'sche Familiensammlung): two portraits - ROTTERDAM: *Pontius Pilate; The Weigher of Gold* - SCHWERIN: *Joseph Explains the Dreams to Pharoah* - ST PETERSBURG (Hermitage): *Croesus and Solon; Head of an Old Man; The Work of Wine Growers* - THE HAGUE: *Adoration of the Magi.*

AUCTION RECORDS:

PARIS, 1861, *Young Dutch Woman,* FRF 4,500. PARIS, 1881, *Portrait of an Old Woman,* FRF 2,050. LONDON, 1893, *Interior,* FRF 9,445. PARIS, 1898, *Portrait of a Man,* FRF 3,600. LONDON, 11 May 1908, *Judas Receiving the Price of his Treason in the Temple,* GBP 52. LONDON, 2 July 1909, *Rembrandt's Sister Dressed as Bathsheba,* GBP 52. PARIS, 14 and 15 Dec 1922, *The Baptism of the Eunuch* (pen and wash) FRF 1,000. LONDON, 20 Nov 1925, *Portrait of an Old Lady,* GBP 262. LONDON, 17 Dec 1926, *Rabbi in a Black Robe,* GBP 136. LONDON, 15 June 1928, *The Philosopher,* GBP 126. NEW YORK, 23 Jan 1936, *Portrait of a Polish Nobleman,* GBP 100. LONDON, 15 May 1936, *Rembrandt in a Brown Coat,* GBP 99. LONDON, 23 Dec 1943, *Old Man,* GBP 84. PARIS, 5 Dec 1951, *The Philosopher,* FRF 350,000. LUCERNE, 26-30 June 1962, *The Scientist at his Work Table,* CHF 5,000. LONDON, 3 March 1965, *St Matthew,* GBP 450. LONDON, 29 Nov 1968, *Portrait of a Man Wearing a Turban,* Gns 500. LONDON, 24 April 1970, *View of an Estuary,* Gns 6,500. LONDON, 7 May 1971, *King Solomon at Prayer,* Gns 2,200. NEW YORK, 27 April 1972, *An Ill Matched Couple,* ATS 80,000. NEW YORK, 23 March 1984, *Portrait of an Old Man Holding a Stick* (oil on canvas, 31½ x 27 ins / 80 x 68.5 cm) USD 10,000. LONDON, 3 July 1985, *The Geographer* (oil on canvas, 42½ x 34¼ ins / 108 x 87 cm) GBP 18,500. PARIS, 27 May 1987, *High Priest Meditating on the Scriptures* (oil on panel, 20 x 16¼ ins / 51 x 41.5 cm) FRF 41,000. AMSTERDAM, 18 May 1988, *Study by Candlelight* (1646, oil on panel, 13¼ x 16 ins / 33.5 x 39.7 cm) NLG 92,000. LONDON, 9 July 1993, *The Mocking of Ceres* (1645, oil on panel, 26½ x 21¾ ins / 67 x 55.5 cm) GBP 25,300. LONDON, 8 Dec 1993, *Esther's Banquet* (oil on canvas, 46½ x 48½ ins / 118 x 123 cm) GBP 23,000. NEW YORK, 18 May 1994, *An Old Woman Counting her Money by Candlelight* (oil on canvas, 42¼ x 53¼ ins / 107 x 135 cm) USD 26,450. PARIS, 12 Dec 1995, *The Philosopher's Study* (oil on panel, 7¼ x 9 ins / 18.5 x 23 cm) FRF 60,000. LONDON, 7 July 1999, *Portrait of a Rabbi in a Red Cloak and Skullcap* (oil on canvas, 30 x 31 ins / 77 x 80 cm) GBP 10,000. LONDON, 13 Dec 2000, *Esther Preparing to Meet Ahasuerus* (oil on panel, 33 x 26 ins / 84 x 66 cm) GBP 80,000. LONDON, 11 April 2002, *Susannah and the Elders* (1649, oil on panel, 19 x 15 ins / 47 x 39 cm) GBP 65,000. LONDON, 11 Dec 2002, *Philosopher* (oil on panel, 45 x 33 ins / 114 x 85 cm) GBP 40,000.

KONINCKX, Jacques de. See **CONINCK**

KONING, Arnold Hendrik

Dutch, 19th century.

Born 2 April 1860, in Winschten; died 1945, in Barneveld.

Painter, engraver. Landscapes.

Arnold Hendrik Koning moved at the age of 22 to Amsterdam, where he worked at the academy under the direction of Allebé, Wynveld, Altmann and Keizer. In 1886 he undertook a study trip to France, and on his return lived for two years in The Hague. He discovered a taste for landscape painting during short visits to the provinces of Drenthe, Gelderland and Overijssel, and thereafter settled in the countryside, first in Pyswyle and later, in 1897, in Ede. The museum at Mesdag has a *Study* by him. Koning took part in the *Exposition de Bruxelles* in 1910.

KONING, Cornelis

Dutch, 17th century.

Born c. 1610, in Haarlem; died 4 April 1671.

Engraver (including etching), draughtsman.

Cornelis Koning was deputy burgomaster and burgomaster of Haarlem, and director, from 1642 to 1645, of the Old Person's Hospital. He may be the same artist as the engraver

Cornelis de Koning, who is recorded as having been born in Haarlem around 1624. The list of Koning's engravings is as follows: *Arminius, Founder of the Remonstrants, John Calvin, Laurentius Coster,* after J. van Campen; *Desiderius Erasmus,* after Holbein; *Udabricus, Count of East Friesland,* after A. Andriessen; *Juliana, Countess of East Friesland,* after A. Andriessen; *F. Gomarus, Theologian of Leiden; Wernerus Helmichius; Hadrianus Junius; Martin Luther, Philip Melanchthon, Dierik Philips, Menno Simons, Adrianus Tetrodius,* after F. Grebber; *Arrival of Prince Frederick-Henry of Nassau in The Hague* (1627); *Accurate Representation of the Images outside the Town of Haarlem,* after P. Jaenredam.

KONING, Elisabeth Joanna, Mme Sappert
Dutch, 19th century.
Born 1 March 1816, in Haarlem; died 18 March 1888, in Rotterdam.
Painter, engraver. Flowers, fruit.

Elisabeth Joanna Koning was the pupil of Abb Steenbergen. She married the preacher Strom.

AUCTION RECORDS:

LONDON, 18 June 1980, *Still-life with Flowers* (oil on panel, 12 1/2 x 10 1/4 ins / 32 x 26 cm) GBP 1,600. AMSTERDAM, 7 March 2000, *Still-life with Flowers and Dead Finch* (oil on panel, 12 x 9 ins / 31 x 24 cm) NLG 4,500. AMSTERDAM, 4 July 2000, *Still-life with Orange* (oil on panel, 7 x 9 ins / 18 x 24 cm) NLG 5,000. AMSTERDAM, 7 Dec 2003, *Still-life with Grapes, Peach and Butterfly on a Table* (1830, oil on panel, 15 x 11 ins / 38 x 28 cm) EUR 4,800. AMSTERDAM, 21 April 2004, *Flowers in a Basket with Shells on a Ledge* (1843, oil on panel, 9 x 11 ins / 22 x 29 cm) EUR 5,500.

KONING, Krijn de
Dutch, 20th - 21st century.
Born 1963, in Amsterdam.
Sculptor, installation artist.
Minimal Art.

Krijn de Koning first trained in the department of audiovisual design at the Gerrit Rietveld Academy, Amsterdam (1983 to 1988) then at the Ateliers 63, Haarlem (1988 to 1990). He attended the Institut des Hautes Études en Arts Plastiques, Paris from 1991 to 1993. He lives and works in Amsterdam.

De Koning uses minimal shapes associated with architecture, such as cubes, partitions, right angles, ceilings and apertures, using wood, sometimes painted, or plaster slabs, and creates new spaces designed for the exhibition and the visitor's progression through it. By breaking space into various compartments, he invites the viewer to travel through a shaped, sculpted space.

Collective exhibitions include: Fraïssé Château (1997 with Michel Verjux and Felice Varini). Solo exhibitions include: Palais des Beaux-Arts, Brussels (1994); Brussels, Utrecht, Amsterdam and Galerie Le Sous-Sol, Paris (1995); *Project for the Courtyard of the Hôtel St-Livier, Metz,* Fonds Régional d'Art Contemporain for Lorraine, Metz (2001).

BIBLIOGRAPHY:

Ardenne, Paul, '*Krijn de Koning - Occupation des lieux*' in *Art Press* n° 212, periodical, Paris, April 1996. Koning, Krijn de, *Binnen buiten. Inside outside,* NAi Publ., Rotterdam, 2000 (text in Dutch and English).

MUSEUMS AND GALLERIES:

AMSTERDAM (Stedelijk Mus.) - PARIS (FNAC) - UTRECHT (Centraal Mus.).

KONING, Th.
Dutch, 18th - 19th century.
Born 3 February 1748, in Amsterdam; died after 1825.
Engraver, draughtsman.

Th. Koning specialised in producing engravings after the drawings of J. Buys. His known works include: *A. Walraven, Professor of Oriental Languages,* after G. van Rooyen; *Prof. Voorda,* after H. Pothoven

KONING, Willem
Dutch, 18th century.
Active in Amsterdam c. 1721.
Engraver, print dealer.

Willem Koning is particularly known for a series of 16 plates depicting naval tactics. The print *Portrait of the Countess of Yarmouth,* after Van Hoogh, can almost certainly be attributed to him.

KONINGH, Arie Kelting de, or Ketting
Dutch, 19th century.
Born 3 August 1815, in Dordrecht; died 1867.
Painter. Landscapes.

Arie Kelting de Koningh was the son of Leendert de Koningh the Elder.

AUCTION RECORDS:

AMSTERDAM, 24 March 1980, *Wooded River Landscape with Figures* (oil on panel, 13 1/2 x 17 3/4 ins / 34 x 45 cm) NLG 9,500. AMSTERDAM, 24 Sept 1992, *Sheep and Donkey in a Landscape* (oil on panel, 14 1/4 x 12 1/2 ins / 36 x 32 cm) NLG 4,025. AMSTERDAM, 21 April 1994, *Cows and Sheep near a Pond in a Meadow* (oil on panel, 19 1/2 x 25 1/4 ins / 49.5 x 64 cm) NLG 3,450. AMSTERDAM, 19-20 Feb 1997, *Wooded Landscape with a Peasant Woman in front of her Farm* (1865, oil on panel, 12 3/4 x 17 3/4 ins / 32.5 x 45 cm) NLG 2,537. BRUSSELS, 17 Feb 2003, *Three Hounds Waiting for the Hunt* (oil on panel, 14 x 11 ins / 36 x 29 cm) EUR 2,200.

KONINGH, John de
Dutch, 19th century.
Born 17 October 1808, in London; died 30 June 1845, in Genoa.
Sculptor.

John de Koningh was the son of the painter of seascapes and landscapes Leendert de Koningh the Elder.

KONINGH, Leendert de, the Elder
Dutch, 19th century.
Born 12 April 1777, in Dordrecht; died 8 June 1849, in Dordrecht.
Painter, draughtsman. Landscapes, landscapes with figures, seascapes.

Leendert de Koningh the Elder was the pupil of A. Vermeulen and Versteeg. He travelled to England in 1801, then visited Paris, where he worked under the direction of David. After a period in Holland he returned to England, where he remained until the defeat of Napoleon. De Koningh was a member of the academy of fine art in Amsterdam.

AUCTION RECORDS:

LONDON, 15 May 1908, *River Scene,* GBP 4. LONDON, 28 July 1909, *Wooded Landscape* (1813) GBP 5. LONDON, 29 June 1928, *View of Dordrecht,* GBP 52. NEW YORK, 17 and 18 May 1934, *Milkmaid and her Herd,* USD 45. LONDON, 10 Nov 1936, *River in Holland,* GBP 21. DORDRECHT, 1 Dec 1970, *Landscape,* NLG 3,000. LONDON, 26 Nov 1971, *The Area around a Town with Numerous Figures; Banks of a River in Summer* (two panels in pairs) Gns 2,800. LONDON, 5 July 1978, *Fisherman and Two Cows beside a River* (oil on panel, 13 1/4 x 17 3/4 ins / 33.5 x 45 cm) GBP 1,500. LONDON, 28 Nov 1979, *A Poor Man and his Dog, Begging for Alms* (oil on panel, 23 3/4 x 29 1/2 ins / 60.5 x 75 cm) GBP 4,000. COLOGNE, 20 March 1981, *Livestock at the Watering Place* (oil on wood, 21 1/2 x 30 1/4 ins / 54.5 x 77 cm) DEM 8,500. LONDON, 5 Oct 1983, *Boats Tied up to the Quay* (oil on canvas, 14 1/2 x 17 3/4 ins / 37 x 45 cm) GBP 1,300. NEW YORK, 31 Oct 1985, *Arab and Daughter* (oil on panel, 19 x 14 1/2 ins / 48.2 x 37 cm) USD 5,500. AMSTERDAM, 28 Feb 1989, *Peasants and Cattle Crossing the River on the Ferry, with the Village and Other Boats in the Background* (oil on canvas, 14 1/2 x 22 ins / 37 x 56 cm) NLG 9,200. PARIS, 12 June 1989, *The Grandparent* (1841, oil on panel, 28 x 22 ins / 71 x 56 cm) FRF 45,000. AMSTERDAM, 2 May 1990, *Italian Landscape with Cows in a Meadow* (pencil and watercolour/paper, 11 3/4 x 18 1/2 ins / 30 x 47 cm) NLG 1,380. AMSTERDAM, 6 Nov 1990, *Landscape with Figures and Cattle beside a River* (oil on canvas, 25 1/4 x 32 ins / 64 x 81 cm) NLG 5,750. CALAIS, 14 March 1993, *The Musical Evening* (1844, oil on panel, 28 3/4 x 22 ins / 73 x 56 cm) FRF 29,500. AMSTERDAM, 20 April 1993, *Cows beside a River* (oil on panel, 18 x 21 3/4 ins / 45.5 x 55.5 cm) NLG 2,070. AMSTERDAM, 16 April 1996, *Cows Drinking* (oil on panel, 11 1/2 x 15 1/4 ins / 29.5 x 38.5 cm) NLG 3,068. AMSTERDAM, 27 Oct 1997, *Figures in a Landscape* (oil on panel, 20 3/4 x 29 1/2 ins / 53 x 75 cm) NLG 10,030. PARIS, 17 Dec 1997, *Shepherdess and her Flock near a River* (panel, 19 1/2 x 26 ins / 49.5 x 66 cm) FRF 55,000. AMSTERDAM, 21 Jan 1998, *Milkmaid Filling a Pot on a Jetty* (oil on panel, 18 1/4 x 23 1/2 ins / 46.5 x 60 cm) NLG 4,612. MADRID, 15 April 1999, *River Landscape with Milkmaid and Cattle on Bank* (oil on panel, 13 x 18 ins / 33 x 45 cm) ESP 475,000. LONDON, 19 April 2000, *Shipping Offshore in Breezy Weather* (oil on panel, a pair, 11 x 16 ins / 29 x 41 cm) GBP 4,800. DORCHESTER, 26 Oct 2000, *Milking Time* (oil on panel, 14 x 19 ins / 36 x 48 cm) GBP 1,500. AMSTERDAM, 20 March 2001, *Milkmaid Walking along a Waterway* (oil on panel, 16 x 20 ins / 40 x 51 cm) NLG 8,000. AMSTERDAM, 23 April 2001, *River Landscape with Peasants on their Way to Market* (oil on panel, 15 x 19 ins / 37 x 49 cm) NLG 9,500. AHLDEN, 9 May 2003, *Cows by Water* (oil on panel, 16 x 19 ins / 40 x 47 cm) EUR 4,000. AMSTERDAM, 2 Sept 2003, *Washerwoman at a Riverbank, a Castle Beyond* (oil on panel, 13 x 17 ins / 33 x 43 cm) EUR 2,800.

KONINGH, Leendert de or Leonard de, the Younger

Dutch, 19th century.

Born 29 September 1810, in London; died 17 February 1887, in Dordrecht.

Painter, draughtsman, lithographer. Portraits.

Leendert de Koningh the Younger was the son of Leendert Koningh the Elder

MUSEUMS AND GALLERIES:

DORDRECHT.

AUCTION RECORDS:

AMSTERDAM, 28 May 1986, *Grandfather Playing the Flute* (oil on canvas, 19 1/4 x 23 3/4 ins / 49 x 60.5 cm) NLG 11,000. STOCKHOLM, 29 May 2000, *Card Players* (oil on panel, 22 x 26 ins / 55 x 66 cm) SEK 62,000.

KONINGH, Sophie de

Dutch, 19th century.

Born 16 January 1807, in England; died 5 June 1870, in Dordrecht.

Painter. Flowers.

Sophie de Koningh was the daughter of Leendert de Koningh the Elder.

AUCTION RECORDS:

LONDON, 6 Nov 1973, *The Young Nanny*, Gns 580.

KONINGSBRUGGEN, Ineke van

Dutch, 20th century.

Born 1943, in Hemelen.

Painter, draughtswoman.

Ineke van Koningsbruggen lives and works in Vught. She has shown her work regularly in exhibitions in the Netherlands since 1985. Her painting is gestural and rich in substance.

KONINGSBRUGGEN, Rob van

Dutch, 20th - 21st century.

Born 1948, in The Hague.

Painter.

Minimal Art.

Having initially studied at the Koninklijke Academie van Beeldende Kunsten in 1967, and a private academy in The Hague in 1968, Rob van Koningsbruggen went on to train at Ateliers 63, Haarlem. He lives and works in Amsterdam.

His work, in oil on canvas, relates to the exploitation of primary shapes in American Minimalist art and his paintings are large, almost monochrome areas, sprinkled with a few simple signs.

He has participated in collective exhibitions since 1971 including: Stedelijk Van Abbemueseum, Eindhoven (1973); *11 Dutch Artists*, Edinburgh and Aberdeen (1974); *Fundamentele Schilderkunst* (*Fundamental Painting*), Stedelijk Museum, Amsterdam (1975); *Elementary Forms of Contemporary Painting and Drawing in The Netherlands*, Rheinisches Landesmuseum, Bonn (1975); 9th Paris Biennale (1975). Solo exhibitions include: The Hague (1971); Amsterdam (1972); Amsterdam and The Hague (1973); Stedelijk van Abbemuseum, Eindhoven (1974); retrospective, Stedelijk Museum, Amsterdam (1979); *Rob van Koningsbruggen: peintures et dessins 1971-1988*, Centre d'Art Contemporain, St-Priest (1988).

BIBLIOGRAPHY:

Rob Van Koningsbruggen: peintures et dessins 1971-1988, exhibition catalogue, Centre d'Art contemporain, St-Priest, 1988.

MUSEUMS AND GALLERIES:

AMSTERDAM (Stedelijk Mus.).

AUCTION RECORDS:

AMSTERDAM, 12 Dec 1990, *Om de Hoek* (*Round the Corner*) (oil on canvas, 4 1/4 x 43 1/4 ins / 11 x 110 cm) NLG 5,175. AMSTERDAM, 12 Dec 1991, *Untitled* (1985, acrylic on three joined canvases, 19 3/4 x 47 1/4 ins / 50 x 120 cm) NLG 8,050. AMSTERDAM, 1 Dec 1997, *Untitled* (1982, acrylic/canvas, 39 1/4 x 39 1/4 ins / 100 x 100 cm) NLG 11,800. AMSTERDAM, 30 Nov 2000, *Untitled* (1972, oil on canvas, 24 x 24 ins / 60 x 60 cm) NLG 9,500. AMSTERDAM, 11 June 2001, *Untitled* (1976, oil on canvas, 24 x 24 ins / 60 x 60 cm) NLG 50,000. AMSTERDAM, 3 Dec 2001, *Untitled* (1982, oil on canvas, four attached canvases, 28 x 31 ins / 70 x 80 cm) NLG 37,000. AMSTERDAM, 27 May 2003, *Untitled* (1972, oil on canvas, 55 x 55 ins / 140 x 140 cm) EUR 14,000. AMSTERDAM, 2 Dec 2003, *Untitled* (1988, oil on canvas, 43 x 43 ins / 110 x 110 cm) EUR 9,000. AMSTERDAM, 8 June 2004, *Untitled* (1976, oil on canvas, two separate sheets, 24 x 24 ins / 60 x 60 cm) EUR 10,000. AMSTERDAM, 1 Dec 2004, *Untitled* (1985, oil on canvas, 18 x 18 ins / 45 x 45 cm) EUR 5,500.

KONINGSVELD, Jacobus van

Dutch, 19th century.

Born 1824, in Amsterdam; died 1866, in The Hague.

Painter. Portraits, genre scenes.

Jacobus van Koningsveld was a student at the academy of fine art in Amsterdam and a pupil of J.-A. Kruseman. He visited Paris, but later abandoned painting for photography.

AUCTION RECORDS:

AMSTERDAM, 30 Oct 1990, *Elegant Company on the Beach at Scheveningen* (1859, oil on canvas, 11 1/2 x 30 1/4 ins / 29 x 77 cm) NLG 29,900. AMSTERDAM, 22 April 1992, *Listening at the Door* (1854, oil on panel, 20 x 18 ins / 50.5 x 46 cm) NLG 2,530. AMSTERDAM, 19 April 1994, *Group of Elegant Figures on a Beach* (1859, oil on canvas, 15 1/4 x 30 3/4 ins / 39 x 78 cm) NLG 18,400.

KONINKSLOO. See **CONINXLOO Gillis van III**

KONIONKOFF, Serguei. See **KONENKOV Serguei**

KONITET, Thairans. See **KUNTZE-KONICZ Tadeusz**

KONIUZKO

Polish, 19th century.

Painter.

Koniuzko was a landscape painter.

KONJOVIC, Milan, or Konyovitch
Serb, 20th century.
Born 28 January 1898, in Sombor; died 1983.
Painter, pastellist. Scenes with figures, figures, nudes, portraits, interiors with figures, landscapes, still-lifes. Designs for tapestries.

Milan Konjovic was a pupil of Vlaho Bukovac at the academy of fine arts in Prague in 1919. Having taught himself for a while in Prague, he went to Vienna in 1921, spent periods in Moravská, Sombor and Germany and returned to Prague in 1923. He was in Paris from 1924 to 1932, apart from some travelling, he then returned to Sombor.

At the beginning of his career, Konjovic's work showed the influence of Cézanne, then in 1922, the Cubism of Picasso was evident in about 20 of his canvases; but it was the work of Van Gogh, and the Fauvism and Expressionism of Die Brücke (The Bridge), which influenced the totality of his work and gave him his place in the history of 20th-century Expressionism. From 1924 to 1932, he supported, on principle, the neo-Realist school of Yugoslavia which advocated a return to nature, yet without renouncing the unconventional violence of his personal expression. Konjovic dedicated his powerful temperament, his bold and synthetic drawing, his exuberant colours and his sensuous choice of exciting paint surfaces to celebrating Voivodina, the land of his birth and the countryside extending from the Unna to the Sava, as well as portraying many groups and characters reminiscent of Goya, Van Gogh, and Soutine.

Milan Konjovic was awarded the painting prize of the Republic of Serbia (1950); the art prize for the Executive Council of the Republic of Serbia (1962); and the Gold Plaque of the City of Artists. In his Parisian period, Konjovic took part in the Salons d'Automne, des Indépendants and des Tuileries and held solo shows at the Galerie Bing (1930) and at the Galerie Van Leer (1932). In 1937 he exhibited in Paris, at the Galerie Mouradian-Vallotton, while he featured in the Yugoslav Pavilion at the International Exhibition. From 1945 to 1950 he held seven solo exhibitions including in Belgrade (1947). After 1950, creative freedom was allowed and Konjovic's participation in collective, national and international exhibitions, and in his solo exhibitions, increased, right up to the retrospective, arranged in Paris in 1985 in the context of the Salon d'Automne. In 1966 at Sombor, the Milan Konjovic Gallery was inaugurated.

Bibliography:
Dorderic, Dragoslav (preface), *Milan Konjovic*, exhibition catalogue, Muzej savremene umetnosti, Beograd, 1975 (text in Serbo-Croat). Ambrozic, Katarina, *Konyovitch*, Gal. Milan Konjovic, Sombor, 1985 (extensive documentation).

Museums and Galleries:
Belgrade (Gal. of the Army Mus.) - Belgrade (Muz. savremene umetnotsi) - Belgrade (Narodni Muz.) - Budapest (Szépmuvészeti Múz.) - Dubrovnik (Kulturno Povijesni Muz.) - Grenoble (Mus. de Grenoble) - Ljubljana (Moderna Gal.) - Modena (AG) - Niš (Narodni Muz.) - Novi Sad (various museums) - Prague (Národní Gal.) - Rijeka (Muz. Moderne i Suvremene Umjetnosti) - Sarajevo (Umjetnicka Galerija BiH) - Skopje (Muz. na Sovremena Umetnost) - Sombor (Milan Konjovic Gallery): numerous works - Subotica (Gradski muz.) - Zagreb (Moderna Galerija).

KONNERT, Michel
French, 19th - 20th century.
Born 29 April 1875, in Paris.
Sculptor.

Michel Konnert studied under Augustin Moreau-Vauthier. He exhibited in Paris at the Salon des Artistes Français, of which he became a member.

KONNERTH, Hermann
German, 20th century.
Born 27 February 1881, in Hermannstadt (now Sibiu, Romania).
Painter. Religious subjects, portraits, landscapes.

Konnerth studied in Munich and Paris and was also a writer.

Auction Records:
Berlin, 24 April 1980, *The Country Road* (1929, oil on canvas, 33 1/2 x 42 1/4 ins / 85 x 107 cm) DEM 3,500.

KONNICKI, Stanislav
Polish, 19th century.
Painter. History painting.

Stanislav Konnicki's *Polish Saints* can be seen in the church in Kielce.

KONNIKOV, Piotr
Russian, 20th - 21st century.
Born 1955.
Painter. Figures.

Piotr Konnikov studied at the school of fine arts (Surikov Institute) in Leningrad (St Petersburg) and became a member of the association of Leningrad painters. His style is allusive figuration, the atmosphere of his works having a misty, dream-like feel to them.

Museums and Galleries:
Moscow (Ministry of Culture) - Moscow (State Tretyakov Gal.) - Sotchi (MFA) - Vilnius (Museum of Fine Arts).

KONNO, Masaru
Japanese, 20th century.
Born 1935, in Tokyo.
Painter, print artist.

Konno Masaru won the Tokyo Shell prize in 1960. His work is decorative in nature and based on the repetition of motifs.

KONO, Bairei, real name: Kono Naotoyo, original name: Naotoyo Yasuda, given name: Shi'jun, popular name: Kakusaburo, artist names: Bairei, Choando, Hoppo, Kakurokoen, Kinsen, Charyo, Koun, Koun Shinsho, Kumo no Ie, Musei Shioku, Nyoi Sansho, Omu, Rokuryu, Sansha Kashitsu, Seika Zembo, Seiryukan, Shumpuro, Zaigoan
Japanese, 19th century.
Born 1844; died 1895.
Painter. Landscapes, flowers, birds.

Bairei Kono was a pupil of Nakajima Raisho and of Shiokawa Bunrin of the Shijo School. He taught at his own art school in Kyoto and was a member of the Imperial Art Council.

KONO, Joji
Japanese, 20th century.
Born 1932, in Kyoto.
Painter.

Kono Joji studied letters and aesthetics; his style tends towards geometricism. He was made a member of the Modern Art Association and in 1968 he took part in the third JAFA exhibition, the Contemporary Japanese Art Exhibition in Tokyo, and the International Young Artists Exhibition.

KONO, Michio
Japanese, 20th century.
Born 1938.
Painter.

Kono Michio took part in the seventh International Young Artists Exhibition in Tokyo in 1973 and in the *Japanese Art Today* exhibition held at the Musée d'Art Contemporain, Montréal, in 1974.

KONO, Misao or Micao
Japanese, 20th century.
Born 1900; died 1979.
Active in France.
Painter, watercolourist. Figures, nudes, flowers.

Kono Misao is known within the École de Paris as a painter of women and nudes.

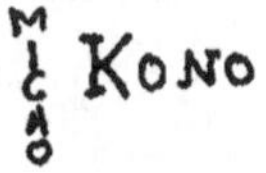

AUCTION RECORDS:
PARIS, 29 Oct 1926, *La Lecture* (*Reading*, FRF 1,400. PARIS, 27 June 1941, *Pivoines* (*Peonies*, FRF 600. PARIS, 2 July 1943, *Nu Assis* (*Seated Nude*, FRF 1,500. GENEVA, 9 June 1976, *Nus* (*Nudes*) (gouache, 13½ x 11 ins / 34 x 28 cm) CHF 500. VERSAILLES, 24 Oct 1976, *Kiki à la Combinaison Noire* (*Kiki in Black Coveralls*) (1927, oil on canvas, 19¾ x 35½ ins / 50 x 90 cm) FRF 4,400. VERSAILLES, 3 Dec 1978, *Nu Étendu* (*Reclining Nude*) (oil on cardboard, 21¼ x 25½ ins / 54 x 65 cm) FRF 6,100. PARIS, 10 Oct 1980, *Femme au Chat Blanc* (*Woman with White Cat*) (oil on canvas against gold background, 36½ x 23½ ins / 93 x 60 cm) FRF 18,500. TOKYO, 15 Feb 1981, *Volupté* (*Voluptuousness*) (colour lithograph, 18¼ x 23¾ ins / 46.6 x 60.5 cm) JPY 280,000. LILLE, 14 March 1981, *Le Bal Masqué* (*Masked Ball*) (1923, oil on canvas, 28¾ x 21¼ ins / 73 x 54 cm) FRF 22,500. PARIS, 3 Dec 1984, *Les Deux Amies* (*Two Friends*) (1927, oil on canvas, 33 x 45¼ ins / 84 x 115 cm) FRF 142,000. PARIS, 8 March 1985, *Les Deux Amies* (*Two Friends*) (1930, oil on canvas, 32 x 46 ins / 81 x 116 cm) FRF 140,000. PARIS, 16 April 1986, *Le Bracelet d'Émeraudes* (*Emerald Bracelet*) (1935, oil on canvas, 16¼ x 11 ins / 41 x 27 cm) FRF 41,000. PARIS, 22 June 1987, *Nu en Buste* (*Nude Bust*) (oil on canvas, 25 x 20¼ ins / 63.5 x 51.5 cm) FRF 40,000. PARIS, 10 Dec 1987, *L'Attente* (*Waiting*) (1927, watercolour, pen and Indian ink, 8½ x 10¾ ins / 21.5 x 27.5 cm) FRF 5,500. PARIS, 24 April 1988, *Nu* (*Nude*) (oil on canvas, 23½ x 19½ ins / 60 x 49.5 cm) FRF 11,000. PARIS, 12 Oct 1988, *Nu à Mi-corps* (*Half-length Nude*) (pencil and watercolour, 19¾ x 15¼ ins / 50 x 39 cm) FRF 7,500. LONDON, 4 April 1989, *Nu Assis* (*Seated Nude*) (oil on canvas, 35¾ x 19¾ ins / 91 x 50 cm) GBP 11,000. PARIS, 21 June 1989, *Fleurs du Japon* (*Japanese Flowers*) (1914, oil on canvas, 32 x 23½ ins / 81 x 60 cm) FRF 33,000. CALAIS, 10 Dec 1989, *Nu Allongé* (*Reclining Nude*) (oil on canvas, 20 x 36¼ ins / 51 x 92 cm) FRF 135,000. PARIS, 26 Feb 1990, *Portrait de Femme* (*Portrait of Woman*) (charcoal, 20¾ x 15¼ ins / 53 x 39 cm) FRF 11,000. CALAIS, 4 March 1990, *Jeune Femme au Bouquet de Fleurs* (*Young Woman with Bouquet of Flowers*) (watercolour, 25¼ x 19 ins / 64 x 48 cm) FRF 35,000. PARIS, 21 March 1990, *Nu* (*Nude*) (1936, oil on canvas, 22 x 18 ins / 56 x 46 cm) FRF 125,000. PARIS, 30 March 1990, *Jeune Femme en Buste* (*Bust of Young Woman*) (oil on canvas, 24 x 19¾ ins / 61 x 50 cm) FRF 130,000. PARIS, 26 April 1990, *Nu Étendu* (*Lying Nude*) (oil on canvas, 16¼ x 13 ins / 41 x 33 cm) FRF 65,000. PARIS, 7 Nov 1990, *Nu Allongé* (*Reclining Nude*) (1974, oil on canvas, 25½ x 35¾ ins / 65 x 91 cm) FRF 55,000. PARIS, 5 Dec 1990, *Bouquet de Roses Blanches* (*Bouquet of White Roses*) (oil on canvas, 15 x 24 ins / 38 x 61 cm) FRF 12,500. FONTAINEBLEAU, 24 Feb 1991, *Colombine* (*Columbine*) (oil on canvas, 19¾ x 25½ ins / 50 x 65 cm) FRF 40,000. NEUILLY, 20 Oct 1991, *Portrait de Jeune Femme* (*Portrait of Young Woman*) (1929, oil on canvas, 7¾ x 5½ ins / 20 x 14 cm) FRF 45,000. PARIS, 5 Feb 1992, *Jeune Fille en Buste* (*Bust of Girl*) (oil on canvas, 18 x 15 ins / 45.5 x 38 cm) FRF 10,000. PARIS, 21 Nov 1995, *Femme au Renard* (*Woman with Fox*) (oil on canvas, 39¼ x 28¾ ins / 100 x 73 cm) FRF 16,000. PARIS, 21 Nov 1997, *Femme aux Bas* (*Woman in Stockings*) (Indian ink drawing, 9 x 4¼ ins / 22 x 11 cm) FRF 1,000. PARIS, 26 March 2000, *Seated Elegant Woman with Cat on Her Lap* (1935, oil on canvas, 36 x 24 ins / 91 x 60 cm) FRF 88,000. PARIS, 10 Dec 2000, *Harlequin and Colombine* (oil on canvas, 46 x 29 ins / 116 x 73 cm) FRF 85,000. GRANVILLE, 27 Jan 2001, *Reclining Woman* (1932, oil on canvas, 16 x 23 ins / 41 x 59 cm) FRF 50,000. VERSAILLES, 7 April 2002, *Seated Female Nude* (oil on canvas, 43 x 28 ins / 110 x 70 cm) EUR 3,300. BERN, 6 Nov 2002, *Woman and Harlequin* (1920-1921, oil on canvas, 36 x 26 ins / 92 x 65 cm) CHF 8,500. PARIS, 21 Oct 2003, *Two Friends* (1930, oil on canvas, 24 x 29 ins / 60 x 73 cm) EUR 7,500. PARIS, 27 Nov 2003, *Young Sleeping Woman* (oil on canvas, 20 x 36 ins / 50 x 92 cm) EUR 11,000.

KONO, Orao
Japanese, 20th century.
Born 1 April 1904, in Nagoya.
Active from 1932, also in France.
Sculptor.

Kono Orao exhibited at the annual Paris exhibitions, the Salon d'Automne, Salon des Indépendants, and Salon de la Jeune Sculpture.

KONO, Yoshio
Japanese, 20th century.
Born 1921, in Osaka.
Painter.

Kono Yoshio graduated from the drawing deparrtment of Kyoto Art School in 1942. Paintings of his were exhibited in the Contemporary Japanese Art Exhibition in Tokyo in 1968 and 1969.

KONOBU. See **SADANOBU II**

KONOK, Tamas
Hungarian, 20th century.
Born 9 January 1930, in Budapest.
Active from 1959 and naturalised in France in 1970.
Painter.
Neo-Constructivism.

While studying the violin at the Budapest conservatoire from 1945 to 1950, Tamas Konok was a pupil of Aurel Bernath and Jeno Barcsay at the school of fine arts from 1948, graduating in 1953. After settling in Paris in 1959, he travelled in Europe and North Africa. In 1963, he received a grant from the Hartford Foundation in California and stayed for a year in the USA. Since 1985 he has been a professor at the University of Budapest.

From his first solo exhibition (Paris, 1960), he showed works that were abstract, treated as wash-drawings picked out with graphic elements and retaining references to exterior reality. He evolved towards a more denuded form of expression, interspersed with coloured graphics. Using acrylic colours on canvas, and on a monochrome background, Tamas Konok traces lines or covers strips in white, black, grey, red; rigorously executed, these lines communicate with each other, cutting across each other, often at right angles, sometimes at a slant, defining and animating at the same time the space on the canvas.

Collective exhibitions include: Budapest; Warsaw; Prague; Bratislava; Berlin; and 4th Paris Biennale (1965). Solo exhibitions include: Galerie Lambert, Paris (1960); Washington and New York (1962); Galerie du Haut-Pavé, Paris; Washington; and Los Angeles (1963); Schiedam-Rotterdam Stedelijk Museum (1964, 1971 and 1977); Cologne and Krefeld (1965); Zurich (1967, 1976, 1976, 1979, 1983, 1986); Rotterdam (1968); Austin Art Museum, and Venice (1969); Galerie Schlegl, Zurich (1972, 1973); Basel (1974, 1984, 1990); The Hague, Geneva, Basel (1977); Paris, Munich, Basel (1978, 1984); Musée des Beaux-Arts, La Chaud-de-Fonds (1979); Xantus Janos Museum, Gyor (1980); Budapest Museum of Fine Arts, and Munich (1981); Tihany Museum, Szentendre Sarspatak (1984); Cologne, Stockholm (1985); Bologna (1986); Paris galerie Franka Berndt (1991). In 1955 he won the prize for Young Artists, in 1957 the Derkovits Prize, in 1959 the Trade Union Prize.

BIBLIOGRAPHY:

Konok, exhibition catalogue, Stedelijk Museum, Rotterdam, 1964. *Tamas Konok*, exhibition catalogue, Gal. Franka Berndt, Paris, 1991. *Geometrische Abstraktion 1910-1990*, exhibition catalogue, Gal. Eremitage, Berlin, 1991.

MUSEUMS AND GALLERIES:

BERN (Kunstmus.) - BUDAPEST (Kassák Múz.) - BUDAPEST (Magyar Nemzeti Gal.) - BUDAPEST (Szépmuvészeti Múz.) - GYÖR (Xantus János Múzeum) - HAMBURG (Städtische Sammlung) - LA CHAUX-DE-FONDS (MBA) - MISKOLC (Herman Ottó Múzeum) - PARIS (BNF) - SCHIEDAM (Stedelijk Mus.) - WINTERTHUR (Kunstmus.).

AUCTION RECORDS:

LUCERNE, 15 May 1993, *Composition* (oil on canvas, 14 1/4 x 17 ins / 36 x 43 cm) CHF 1,900. LUCERNE, 4 June 1994, *Untitled* (1976, oil on canvas, 28 3/4 x 36 1/4 ins / 73 x 92 cm) CHF 2,500. BUDAPEST, 28 April 2004, *Still-life by a Window* (pastel, 20 x 28 ins / 50 x 70 cm) HUF 400,000.

KONOPA, Rudolf

Austrian, 19th - 20th century.

Born 2 February 1864, in Vienna; died 1938.

Painter, pastellist. Genre scenes, portraits, interiors with figures, church interiors, landscapes.

Konopa was taught by Rudolf Carl Huber and Josef Mathias von Trenkwald at the Akademie der Bildenden Künste in Vienna. He exhibited at the Exposition Universelle of 1900 in Paris, receiving a distinction.

AUCTION RECORDS:

ZURICH, 11 May 1978, *At the Bedside of the Sick Man* (oil on canvas, 47 1/2 x 57 ins / 120.5 x 144.5 cm) CHF 2,600. LUCERNE, 12 Nov 1985, *Interior of Stephansdom, Vienna* (1923, watercolour, 18 x 13 1/2 ins / 46 x 34 cm) CHF 2,400. LONDON, 6 Oct 1989, *Rich Interior with Lady Reading near Window* (oil on panel, 12 1/4 x 16 1/4 ins / 31 x 41 cm) GBP 3,850. NEW YORK, 13 March 2001, *Outside the Cathedral* (1927, watercolour over pencil heightened with gouache, 21 x 17 ins / 54 x 42 cm) USD 2,400.

KONOPATZKY, Eugen

Russian, 20th century.

Born in Lutzk.

Painter, engraver.

Eugen Konopatzky exhibited from 1924 in Paris, at the Salon des Indépendants.

KONOVALOV, Vadim

Russian, 20th - 21st century.

Born 1960, in Alapaievsk.

Painter.

Vadim Konovalov attended the school of art in Moscow. He became a member of the union of Soviet artists and settled in Moscow. He has taken part in several national exhibitions since 1984, notably in 1988 at the *1000 Years of Russia* exhibition.

AUCTION RECORDS:

PARIS, 17 Nov 1990, *Red Moscow* (1990, oil on canvas, 78 x 56 3/4 ins / 198 x 144 cm) FRF 5,000.

KONOVALOVA-KOVRIGINA, Tatiana

Russian, 20th century.

Born 1917, in Chita.

Painter. Portraits, scenes with figures, still-lifes, flowers.

During World War II, Tatiana Konovalova-Kovrigina was involved in the propaganda programme of the telegraphic agency in Russia where Rodchenko, Maiakovski and Cheremnykh had also worked. She studied at the Surikov Institute of Fine Arts in Moscow, in D. Korjevski's studio up to 1947. After the war she made decorations for the Metro stations in Moscow and produced compositions on edifying subjects, such as *Arrival of a Man with Decoration, Morning*, which own her a nomination for the Stalin Prize. She was a member of the Union of Painters of the USSR from 1942.

BIBLIOGRAPHY:

Tableaux soviétiques, auction catalogue, Salle Drouot, Paris, 3 October 1990.

AUCTION RECORDS:

PARIS, 3 Oct 1990, *Flowers* (1948, oil on canvas, 31 1/2 x 25 1/2 ins / 80 x 64.5 cm) FRF 11,000. PARIS, 16 June 1991, *Welcome to the Hero* (1948, oil on canvas, 19 3/4 x 29 1/2 ins / 50 x 75 cm) FRF 6,500.

KONOW, Jurgen von

Swedish, 20th century.

Born 1915; died 1959.

Also active in France.

Painter, engraver (including burin/aquatint). Interiors with figures, landscapes with figures, landscapes, waterscapes, gardens.

Jurgen von Konow exhibited at the Salon des Réalités Nouvelles, which paid him homage in 1959. His engraving technique was complex, in that he combined burin, aquatint and soft varnish. His painted or engraved landscapes evince a sensitivity to the regions and seasons, as illustrated by *Finistère, November, The Winter.*

AUCTION RECORDS:

STOCKHOLM, 22 May 1989, *Cactus against the Light* (1948, oil on panel, 9 x 11 ins / 22 x 27 cm) SEK 8,200. STOCKHOLM, 6 Dec 1989, *Nordic Landscape with River* (oil on panel, 9 x 12 1/2 ins / 23 x 32 cm) SEK 4,500. STOCKHOLM, 14 June 1990, *Garden in Summer with Hut and Figures* (oil on canvas, 29 1/4 x 23 1/2 ins / 74 x 60 cm) SEK 10,000. STOCKHOLM, 5-6 Dec 1990, *Soirée at the Theatre of Dramatic Art, Stockholm* (oil on panel, 31 1/2 x 39 1/4 ins / 80 x 100 cm) SEK 15,000. STOCKHOLM, 28 Oct 1991, *Panorama of the Harbour of Halmstads* (1950, oil on panel, 9 x 32 ins / 23 x 81 cm) SEK 4,000. STOCKHOLM, 7 May 2003, *Tegelbacken, Stockholm* (1943, oil on panel, 23 x 25 ins / 58 x 64 cm) SEK 32,000. STOCKHOLM, 27 April 2004, *Stromsborg with Seagulls, Stockholm* (oil on panel, 26 x 21 ins / 65 x 54 cm) SEK 17,000.

KONOW, Karl

Norwegian, 19th century.

Born 4 September 1865, in St Aurdal.

Active in Christiania (now Oslo).

Painter.

Karl Konow received an honourable mention at the Exposition Universelle in Paris in 1900.

KONRAD, called Master or Meester den Figuur Snyder

Flemish School, 16th (?) century.

Active in Mechelen.

Sculptor.

KONRAD, or Koenraad

Dutch, 18th century.

Born 1678, in The Hague; died 1747, in The Hague.

Painter. Flowers.

This artist was the pupil of Netscher.

KONRAD, Bela

Hungarian, 19th century.

Born 15 July 1869, in Sarvar.

Painter, engraver.

The museum in Graz has several works by Bela Konrad, who mainly produced views of public buildings and genre scenes.

KONRAD, Ignace

Hungarian, 20th century.

Born 31 January 1894, in Ketujfalu; died 23 February 1969, in Paris.

Active in France from 1927.
Painter, sculptor, engraver, illustrator. Historical subjects, religious subjects, portraits, equestrian subjects.

Ignace Konrad was a pupil at the academy of fine arts of Budapest, and became a teacher there in 1921, after obtaining a prize for the teaching of drawing at Dresden in 1912. His career as a painter of horses began in 1923. To obtain commissions, he went several times to the USA, travelled in Britain, returned to Hungary in 1936, spent the years from 1944 to 1948 in Austria, and finally went back to Paris in 1948. Konrad painted a good many of the most famous racehorses of his time on behalf of the owners including the American R.B. Strassburger. Apart from the racehorses, he also painted portraits of their owners and of their close relations. He did a large series of 22 pictures to illustrate the epic poem by Zrinyi Miklos *The Peril of Szigetvar*, that commemorated the historic battle of Nicolas Zrinyi against the Turks, during which Suleyman the Magnificent died and which marked the beginning of the decline of Turkish power in central Europe.

In Paris he exhibited at the Salon des Artistes Français, where he showed *The Four Horsemen of the Apocalypse* (1932); a portrait of a horse (1933); *Redemption*, a portrait of a horse, the bust of his son (1950); *Portrait of Madame Morisot* (1951); and the *Equestrian Portrait of the Countess of Wenckheim* (1952). He obtained an honourable mention in 1953 for the picture representing the Regent of Hungary and his brother training racehorses at Alag. He also showed collections of his works at solo exhibitions including the Müterem Gallery, Budapest (1941). Two posthumous exhibitions on the cycle of *The Peril of Szigetvar* took place at Szigetvar (1991) and at Bad-Deutsch-Altenburg near Vienna (1992). In 1994, for the centenary of his birth, the National Army Museum at Budapest and the National Museum of Keszthely presented a collection of his works and, in 1996, about 50 of his works were shown at Villa Strassburger in Deauville. In Budapest in 1926 Konrad had presented *Vision of St Francis of Assisi* in an exhibition on liturgy.

BIBLIOGRAPHY:

Commémoration du 425e anniversaire de la défense de la forteresse de Szigetvar, exhibition catalogue, Altenburg, 1992.

MUSEUMS AND GALLERIES:

DEAUVILLE (Villa Strassburger) - KESZTHELY (Helikon Kastélymúzeum) - SARATOGA SPRINGS (National Mus. of Racing) - WASHINGTON DC (Laurel Race Course): *Worden* (1953); *Master Boing* (1956); *Sailor's Guide* (1958); *Bald Eagle* (1959-1960).

AUCTION RECORDS:

PARIS, 16 Oct 1985, *Portrait of Vikings* (24 3/4 x 31 ins / 63 x 79 cm) FRF 31,000; *Portrait of Asteroid* (38 1/2 x 48 3/4 ins / 98 x 124 cm) FRF 28,000.

KONRAD, Joseph

Hungarian, 20th century.
Born 10 March 1910, in Tolna.
Active in France.
Painter, draughtsman. Portraits, local scenes, landscapes, landscapes with figures, urban landscapes, architectural views.

Joseph Konrad trained at the fine arts academy in Budapest from 1926 to 1928, and continued his studies at the fine arts academy of Greece, thanks to a scholarship. In search of the exotic, he left for Algeria, where he met the writer Claude Meurice Robert. They travelled through Algeria, Morocco, Tunisia and Hoggar, where they were commissioned by the government to research cave paintings in the Blue Mountains. Konrad painted the portraits of various famous people in Algeria and did drawings of African locals. He also worked as an illustrator on *Écho d'Alger* (*Echo of Algiers*).

His work featured in the group exhibition *L'Afrique Française* (*French Africa*) at the Musée des Beaux-Arts, now the Musée d'Art Moderne, in Paris in 1947, as well as in exhibitions at the Union des Artistes de l'Afrique du Nord (Union of North African Artists) in Algiers in 1947, at the Société des Artistes Algériens et Orientalistes (Society of Algerian and Orientalist Artists) in Algiers in 1947, at the Salon des Beaux-Arts in Cannes in 1957, and at the Salon International de Peinture et de Sculpture in Juan-les-Pins in 1977. He exhibited his African people and landscapes at L'Artisan du Home in Algiers in 1945, at the Galerie La Boutique in Algiers in 1946, and at the Galerie Tam in Algiers in 1952.

KONRAD VON WIMPFEN

German, 14th century.
Active in Mainz.
Painter.

He produced decorations for churches in Wimpfen.

KONSÉ, G.

Dutch, 18th - 19th century.
Engraver.

Konsé is remembered for the *Portraits of Bailly, Necker, La Fayette and Louis XVI.*

KONSTANTIN, Frida

Austrian, 20th century.
Born 10 May 1884, in Vienna; died 29 December 1918, in Budapest.
Painter, engraver. Interiors, landscapes, animals.

KONSTANTINOV, Petr Konstantinovich

Russian, 19th century.
Born 1830; died 16 March 1890.
Engraver.

Konstantinov studied under Jordan in St Petersburg. He painted copies of several religious subjects, including a *Way of the Cross*, from a work by Sebastiano del Piombo.

KONTACHY, Joseph

French, 20th century.
Born in the Côte-d'Or.
Painter. Landscapes.

Joseph Kontachy painted views of the Yonne and the Côte-d'Or.

KONTI, Isidore

Austrian, 19th - 20th century.
Born 9 July 1862, in Vienna; died 1938.
Active in the USA from 1892.
Sculptor. Statuettes, groups, busts.

Isidore Konti attended the Akademie der Bildenden Künste in Vienna. In the USA, he became a member of the National Academy in 1901, received a golden medal at St Louis in 1904, and was nominated a member of the academy in 1905. He sculpted commemorative busts, genre subjects and allegorical themes.

AUCTION RECORDS:

NEW YORK, 29 Sept 1977, *Genius of Immortality* (c. 1912, patinated bronze, h. 25 1/2 ins / 64.8 cm) USD 1,300. NEW YORK, 24 Oct 1979, *Genius of Immortality* (1911, bronze, Roman bronze Works N.Y., h. 25 1/2 ins / 65 cm) USD 1,300. NEW YORK, 28 Sept 1989, *Kneeling Men* (bronze, pair of book-presses, h. 6 1/2 ins / 16.5 cm) USD 1,980. NEW YORK, 14 March 1991, *Reverence before the Mirror* (bronze, pair of book-presses, h. 6 1/2 ins / 16.2 cm) USD 3,080. NEW YORK, 4 Dec 1992, *Literature and Drama* (bronze, pair of book-presses, h. 8 3/4 ins / 22.5 cm) USD 3,850. NEW YORK, 11 March 1993, *Group of Girls and an Adolescent* (bronze, h. 16 ins / 40.6 cm) USD 4,600. NEW YORK, 22 Sept 1993, *Allegro, Group of Two Girls and One Boy* (bronze, h. 16 ins / 40.6 cm) USD 3,680. NEW YORK, 27 Sept 1996, *Literature and Theatre* (1911, red-brown patinated bronze, a pair, h. 8 3/4 ins / 22.2 cm) USD 3,220. NEW YORK, 3 Dec 1996, *Men Fighting* (bronze, pair of book-presses, each h. 6¼ ins / 15.8 cm) USD 2,990. NEW YORK, 23 April 1997, *The Pursuit of Happiness, Illusion* (red-brown patinated bronze, allegorical group, h. 20½ ins / 52.1 cm) USD 3,680. NEW YORK, 29 Sept 1999, *Literature and Drama Bookends* (reddish-brown patinated bronze, a pair, h. 9 ins / 22 cm) USD 4,800. MILFORD, 26 Oct 2000, *Poetry and Thought Bookends* (1914, brown patinated bronze, a pair, h. 10 ins / 25 cm) USD 3,750. NEW YORK, 10 Dec 2002, *Pushing Men Bookends* (red-brown patinated bronze, a pair, h. 6 ins / 15 cm) USD 4,000.

KONYOVITCH, Milan. See **KONJOVIC**

KOO, Jeong-a
Korean, 20th - 21st century.
Born 1967, in Seoul.
Active in France.
Installation artist, photographer.

Koo Jeong-a was born in South Korea but settled in France when she was 23. In 2000 she was a member of the Académie de France in Rome. Koo creates installations that range from a clutter of everyday objects such as boxes or chairs to minimalist architectural structures made of white powder. Whichever vocabulary she chooses she uses it methodically, poetically, displaying a gently compulsive strain. There is nothing aggressive in her work except the smell of naphthalene, which she places to discourage spectators from touching it. She plays with slight sensory disturbances, as in '*8/24*', in which thermoplastic packaging, placed on a desk, forms a moving waterlike mass.

Koo took part in 1996 in the group exhibition *Manifesta 1* in Rotterdam; in 1997 in *Cities on the Move*, Secession, Vienna; in 2000 in *Une nouvelle génération: Prodige d'artiste en France* (*A new generation: An Artistic Prodigy in France*) at the Espace Paul Ricard in Paris; in 2002 in the *Hugo Boss Prize Finalists 2002* at the Solomon R. Guggenheim Museum in New York. She showed her work in solo exhibitions in 1997 at the Musée d'Art Moderne, Paris, in 1999 and 2001 at the Galerie Yvon Lambert, Paris, and in 2002 in *121002very* at the CCA Project Gallery in Kitakyushu, Japan.

BIBLIOGRAPHY:

Koo Jeong-A, exhibition catalogue, Musée d'Art moderne de la Ville de Paris, Paris-Musées, Paris, 2000. Herrmann, Matthias/Price, Cedric, *Jeong-A Koo*, exhibition catalogue, Secession, Vienna, 2002 (text in German and French). Koo, Jeong-A, *Frozen with a Smile*, CCA Project Gallery, Kitakyushu, Japan, 2002. Macel, Christine (ed.), *Koo Jeong-A*, Éd. du Centre Georges Pompidou, Paris, 2004.

KOOGEN, Leendert van. See **COOGHEN**

KOOGH, Adrianus van der
Dutch, 19th century.
Born 14 February 1796, in Middelharnis; died 19 September 1831, in Dordrecht.
Painter, lithographer. Landscapes.

Adrianus van der Koogh was the pupil of P. Hofman in Dordrecht. His works are in Rotterdam.

AUCTION RECORDS:

COPENHAGEN, 18 April 1978, *Landscape with Flock* (oil on panel, 12¼ x 16½ ins / 31 x 42 cm) DKK 20,000. AMSTERDAM, 8 June 1983, *Man and Flock near a Farm* (1817, oil on panel, 22 x 29 ins / 56 x 73.5 cm) NLG 6,400. AMSTERDAM, 119 Nov 1985, *Flock at the Watering Place in a Wooded Landscape* (1820, oil on panel, 29½ x 38 ins / 75 x 96.5 cm) NLG 7,500. AMSTERDAM, 7 March 2000, *Travellers on a Sandy Track with Village in a Wooded Landscape* (oil on canvas, 29 x 37 ins / 73 x 95 cm) NLG 25,000. AMSTERDAM, 19 April 2000, *Hilly Landscape with Houses among the Trees* (oil on panel, 17 x 21 ins / 43 x 53 cm) NLG 7,000. COLOGNE, 24 Nov 2001, *Summer River Landscape with Hut and Boats* (oil on panel, 13 x 16 ins / 32 x 41 cm) DEM 8,500. AMSTERDAM, 28 Oct 2003, *Extensive Rolling Landscape with Travellers on a Sandy Track by a Watermill* (c. 1820, oil on canvas, 29 x 40 ins / 73 x 101 cm) EUR 12,000.

KOOGHE, Abraham de, or Cooge
Dutch, 17th century.
Born 1597; died c. 1685.
Active in Delft.
Potter. Landscapes.

De Kooghe was a member of the painters' guild in Delft in 1632.

MUSEUMS AND GALLERIES:

BUDAPEST: *Rocky Landscape*.

KOOI, Willem Bartel van der
Dutch, 18th - 19th century.
Born 13 May 1768, in Augustinusga (Frisia); died 14 July 1836, in Leeuwarden.
Painter. Genre scenes, portraits.

Kooi was the pupil of Herman Wouter Beekkerk in Leeuwarden. He lectured in drawing at the academy in Francker, and was a member of a number of other academies. He executed portraits at the Dutch Court, and in 1808 he won a prize of 2,000 florins at the Amsterdam Exhibition for his painting *Young Woman to whom a Servant is Giving a Letter*. A certain number of Kooi's works are kept in museums, notably at Francker, Leiden and Amsterdam.

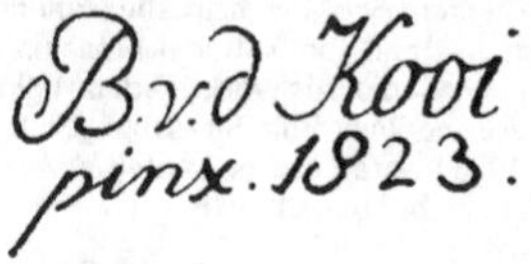

MUSEUMS AND GALLERIES:

AMSTERDAM: *The Love Letter; Interrupted Music; Portrait of Joh. Bapt. Kobell; His Portrait with Dirk-Jacobsz. Ploegsma*.

AUCTION RECORDS:

AMSTERDAM, 14 Nov 1972, *The Joys of Skating*, NLG 32,000. NEW YORK, 19 Sept 1974, *Winter Landscape with Skaters*, USD 6,750.

KOOL, Catharina
Dutch, 19th century.
Born 1860, in Amsterdam.
Painter.

KOOL, Johannes
Dutch, 17th century.
Died 1680, in Amsterdam.
Painter.

Johannes Kool is known to have been active in Amsterdam from 1668 onwards.

KOOL, Rudolph van. See **GROL**

KOOL, Sipke or Spkee
Dutch, 19th century.
Born 27 August 1836, in Leeuwarden; died 1902, in Blaricum.
Painter. Genre scenes.

Sipke Kool was the pupil of C. Bisschof.

MUSEUMS AND GALLERIES:

THE HAGUE (Gemeentemus.): *A Look into the Future; A Refreshment*.

AUCTION RECORDS:
LONDON, 23 Feb 1977, *Baby's Bath Time* (oil on canvas, 13½ x 18½ ins / 34 x 47 cm) GBP 720. AMSTERDAM, 8 March 1978, *Little Girl Helping her Mother to Lay the Table* (oil on canvas, 31 x 23 ins / 78.5 x 58.5 cm) NLG 7,400. AMSTERDAM, 16 Nov 1988, *Peasant Women Chatting at Table with a Servant in Attendance* (oil on canvas, 16¼ x 19¾ ins / 41 x 50 cm) NLG 5,175. NEW YORK, 21 May 1991, *Rocking the Baby to Send it to Sleep* (oil on canvas, 40 x 29 ins / 101.6 x 73.8 cm) USD 825. AMSTERDAM, 19-20 Feb 1997, *Women in Friesian National Costume in an Interior* (oil on panel, 11 x 13¾ ins / 27 x 35 cm) NLG 6,919. NEW YORK, 26 Feb 1997, *Woman and Child near the Hearth* (1881, oil on panel, 7¾ x 9¼ ins / 19.6 x 23.5 cm) USD 2,760.

KOOL, Willem Gillesz., or Koolen
Dutch, 17th century.
Born c. 1608, in Haarlem; died 1666, buried 30 October in Haarlem.
Painter. Genre scenes, landscapes, landscapes with figures, winter landscapes.

Willem Gillesz. Kool was recorded as being a member of the Haarlem painters' guild in 1638, and became its dean in 1656.

MUSEUMS AND GALLERIES:
AACHEN: *Painting* - BORDEAUX: *Fish Market by the Sea* - HAARLEM: *Fish Market* - LEIPZIG: *Winter Landscape* - ST PETERSBURG (Hermitage): *Coastline*.

AUCTION RECORDS:
LONDON, 7 Dec 1960, *Village Market with Numerous Peasants and Carts*, GBP 350. AMSTERDAM, 26 May 1970, *The Return of the Fishermen*, NLG 8,200. LONDON, 19 July 1974, *Fishermen on the Beach*, Gns 3,000. AMSTERDAM, 18 May 1976, *Fishermen on the Beach* (oil on panel, 19 x 25¼ ins / 48 x 64 cm) NLG 32,000. NEW YORK, 16 June 1977, *Winter Landscape with Skaters* (oil on panel, 18¾ x 23½ ins / 47.5 x 59.5 cm) USD 10,500. AMSTERDAM, 24 April 1978, *Seaside Scene* (oil on panel, 15¼ x 21½ ins / 38.5 x 54.5 cm) NLG 19,000. AMSTERDAM, 15 May 1979, *Fishermen Selling their Fish on the Beach* (oil on panel, 15¾ x 19¾ ins / 40 x 50 cm) NLG 21,000. LONDON, 10 April 1981, *Fishermen on the Beach at Scheveningen* (1644, oil on panel, 18½ x 24¼ ins / 47 x 61.6 cm) GBP 10,000. NEW YORK, 18 Jan 1984, *Fishermen Unloading the Results of their Fishing on the Beach* (1648, oil on panel, 16 x 26 ins / 40.5 x 66 cm) USD 9,000. LONDON, 2 July 1986, *Winter Landscape with Skaters* (oil on panel, 23½ x 33 ins / 59.5 x 84 cm) GBP 13,000. NEW YORK, 21 Oct 1988, *Fishermen Pulling in their Catch on the Beach* (1648, oil on panel, 16¼ x 26 ins / 41.2 x 66 cm) USD 16,500. NEW YORK, 7 April 1989, *Landscape with Figures Walking on a Frozen River with a Fortified Town in the Background* (oil on panel, 24 x 33½ ins / 61 x 85 cm) USD 33,000. AMSTERDAM, 13 Nov 1990, *Horsemen Attacking Travellers on a Wooded Track* (oil on panel, 20½ x 27¼ ins / 51.8 x 69.5 cm) NLG 13,800. LONDON, 23 April 1993, *Fishermen Unloading their Catch on the Beach at Egmond-aan-Zee* (oil on panel, 18 x 25 ins / 45.7 x 63.8 cm) GBP 8,970. LONDON, 20 April 1994, *Landscape with a Town beside a River* (oil on panel, 12½ x 16¾ ins / 32 x 42.8 cm) GBP 9,200. AMSTERDAM, 17 Nov 1994, *Fish Merchants on the Beach at Egmond-aan-Zee* (oil on panel, 15½ x 28½ ins / 39.5 x 72.7 cm) NLG 29,900.

KOOLEN, Jacobus, or Kool
Dutch, 17th century.
Died c. 1666.
Active in Haarlem.
Painter.

Koolen painted in the style of Philips Wouwerman and David Teniers.

KOOMBES, Henry
Mauritian, 20th - 21st century.
Born 16 February 1948, in Mauritius.
Painter, pastellist, sculptor, screen printer.

Henry Koombes followed art courses in Cape Town. He lived there for several years, then returned to Mauritius in 1983. He uses acrylic like pastel to show a violently coloured 'lustful imagination'. He has appeared in various exhibitions, among which are: 1992, Gallery Esta Nove, Tokyo; 1995, Fabriks de Marseilles; 1996, Rotterdam; 1997, *Suites Africaines (African Series)* at the Couvent des Cordeliers in Paris.

KOONING, Elaine de
American, 20th century.
Born 1919; died 1989.
Painter (gouache), draughtswoman. Sporting subjects, landscapes, animals.

AUCTION RECORDS:
NEW YORK, 13 Nov 1980, *Squeeze Play* (oil on canvas, 30 x 30 ins / 76 x 76 cm) USD 1,600. NEW YORK, 27 Feb 1981, *Untitled* (1972, oil on canvas, 30 x 24 ins / 76 x 61 cm) USD 1,000. NEW YORK, 23 Feb 1985, *Untitled* (c. 1960, oil/hardboard, 36 x 48 ins / 91.5 x 122 cm) USD 2,600. NEW YORK, 7 May 1990, *Bull Standing* (gouache and ink/paper, 20 x 14½ ins / 50.5 x 36.8 cm) USD 880. NEW YORK, 6 Nov 1990, *A Press* (oil on canvas, 30 x 30 ins / 76.2 x 76.2 cm) USD 7,150. NEW YORK, 27 Feb 1992, *Untittled* (1949, oil/synthetic resin, 10 x 8 ins / 25.4 x 20.2 cm) USD 3,080. NEW YORK, 30 June 1993, *Farmer from the South-West* (1957, oil on card, 48 x 60 ins / 121.9 x 152.4 cm) USD 5,750. NEW YORK, 24 Feb 1995, *Bull* (oil/synthetic resin, 18¼ x 23¾ ins / 46.4 x 60.6 cm) USD 8,050. NEW YORK, 7 May 1996, *Basketball XXX* (1981, acrylic/canvas, 50 x 35 ins / 127 x 88.9 cm) USD 2,300. NEW YORK, 13 Nov 2001, *Portrait of Willem de Kooning* (c. 1952, oil on panel, 39 x 26 ins / 99 x 65 cm) USD 35,000. SAN FRANCISCO, 23 April 2002, *Untitled* (tempera on paper, 11 x 13 ins / 28 x 34 cm) USD 2,250. NEW YORK, 23 May 2002, *Matador* (oil and gouache on canvas, 8 x 10 ins / 20 x 25 cm) USD 3,200. PHILADELPHIA, 27 June 2004, *Redondo* (1960, acrylic on masonite, 18 x 24 ins / 46 x 61 cm) USD 11,000. NEW YORK, 29 June 2004, *Portrait of JFK* (oil on canvas, 31 x 22 ins / 79 x 56 cm) USD 21,000.

KOONING, Willem de
Dutch, 20th century.
Born 24 April 1904, in Rotterdam; died 19 March 1997, in Long Island (New York).
Active in USA from 1926 and naturalised in 1962.
Painter (including gouache/mixed media), watercolourist, pastellist, sculptor, draughtsman.
American Abstract Artists (AAA). New York School.

Willem de Kooning left school in Rotterdam at age 12 as a result of financial pressure, and was apprenticed between 1916 and 1920 as a house painter to a local painting and decorating firm. He was, however, able to attend evening classes at the Academie van Beeldende Kunsten in Rotterdam for eight years, where one of his teachers introduced him to the works of the Neo-Plasticists of the De Stijl Group, under the leadership of Piet Mondrian. In 1924, during a one-year stay in Belgium, he discovered the Flemish Expressionists, including James Ensor. He graduated from the academy in 1925, and in 1926 he left Holland for New York, initially earning his living there by house painting. In 1928 he became familiar with Arshile Gorky, with whom he briefly shared a studio. They were linked by their intention to imbibe the works of the great modern painters before finding their own personal style.

In 1943 he married Elaine Marie Catherine Fried, whom he had met in 1938 and to whom he was to remain attached, despite various vicissitudes. Between 1948 and 1951 he taught at Black Mountain College in North Carolina and then at Yale University. From 1959 to 1960 he was in Italy, and from 1963 he settled in East Hampton, initially in the Springs area. In 1969 he turned his attention to sculpture. After a long alcoholic phase, the painting of his last years was marked by a certain neglect, given that he was somewhat abstracted from the world.

The important retrospectives that were dedicated to him show few works prior to 1934. It would seem that his meeting in 1928 with Arshile Gorky had a determining effect on his development. His first forays into Abstraction date from this time, whereas he later introduced motifs from daily life into his compositions: vases, tables, chairs and windows mixed together in a Post-Cubist spirit in unrealistic spaces. During the Great American Depression, the commissions of mural decorations he undertook (from 1935 to 1936) for the Works Progress Administration (WPA) Federal Art Project (commissions that were perhaps obtained on Arshile Gorky's recommendation) are characteristic of his first abstract period, and they also demonstrate a good knowledge of Picasso's work. In 1937 he won a commission for a huge mural to be painted on the Hall of Pharmacy of the New York World Fair, 1939-1940. He also worked briefly with Fernand Léger, who planned a decoration for the harbour station of the French Line, once again in New York, which was never executed. It is legitimate to think that it was this collaboration that prompted De Kooning to paint his large figures of seated workmen.

Throughout his career he alternated between abstract and figurative works, sometimes even conflating the two, depending on what influence he was exposed to. However, a few key periods in his work can be differentiated, even if they overlap and are disputed by different biographers. Shortly after his arrival in the USA, his first paintings of 1934, forcefully constructed, were still dependant on the general mood of the *De Stijl* Group, rather than on the orthodoxy of Piet Mondrian's Neo-Plasticism. Certain of his ensuing abstract works, inspired by Ashile Gorky's paintings, often consist of vertical streaks, sorts of windows in the painting, with egg-shaped forms looming out of a Cubist space and evocations of hybrid figures. A series of freely-invented abstract works followed, in which the flexible and curvilinear forms and biomorphic shapes bring to mind the three-dimensional idiom of Miró. From 1938 to 1945 he produced self-portraits, the massive 'Classical' figures of men, and then women, such as his *Recumbent Nude* of 1938, which is of an Ingres-like realism, and his *Elegy* of 1939, and then more interpretative versions, such as *Pink Lady*, which dates from around 1944, and his *Pink Angel* of 1945. It should be recognised that in the last figures painted in this period (that is, after 1940), certain parts of the male figures are missing - not as a result of mutilation, but simply absent. His figures of women are, on the contrary, shown in full, but they are distorted so that they appear hideous or monstrous, placing emotional impact above accepted ideas of beauty in the manner of the Expressionists. It was with *Pink Lady* that he perfected the technique that allowed him to express his own contradictory reactions to the female body: for the first time, he used flesh tints - the characteristic 'De Kooning pink'. Such tones are warm-blooded yet repulsive, and very close to decomposition, as evoked in Baudelaire's *Une Charogne* (*A Carcass*).

This process of dissociating organic forms strictly linked to abstract forms, demolishing the classic figure-background relationship, was developed again in a series of black and white paintings - the so-called 'positive-negative' series, executed in a synthetic enamel between 1945 and 1950 (exemplified by his *Study for Guernica* of 1947, which he exhibited at his first one-man exhibition at Egan Gallery in New York in 1948). Between 1950 and 1955, he painted the 'Expressionist' series of women, the most notable being *Woman n° 1*, which he worked on for two years from 1950 to 1952, scraping the surface, repainting, adding extraneous elements, then repainting before scraping them off again, eventually finishing them when he was on the verge of giving up. His recent experience as a draughtsman allowed him to burst through the limits of Cubist drawing, leaving certain parts incomplete (often the arms of individuals that were very figurative). He incorporated elements of Action Painting, aligning himself with the rebellious young American school rather than the established Parisian school.

From 1955 to 1963 (or, more precisely, from 1957 to 1961), De Kooning painted what might be called 'landscape abstractions', exploiting the imagery of water and light, energetically brushed in a manner more related to American Gestural Abstraction. From 1961 to 1965 he resumed the theme of Expressionist women in an appeased psychological climate, and then he abandoned Expressionism in favour of more Gestural Abstraction. The figure of the monstrous goddess-mother - whom he knowingly made the symbol of his work, both in painting and sculpture - reflects his own optical illusions, a contradictory mixture of soft colours and tempestuous brushstrokes or lines traced in charcoal beside the form, reminding the viewer of Balzac's visionary description of the *Chef-d'oeuvre inconnu* (*Unknown Masterpiece*) by the painter Frenhofer.

The early years of De Kooning's painting career were devoted to his early hesitant experiments and it was only around 1944 that his personal style began to evolve and that he participated in national and international group exhibitions, including: in 1943, *XXth Century Painting* at the Bignou Gallery in New York; the *1948 Annual of American Painting* at the Whitney Museum of American Art in New York; at the 1948, 1950, 1952 and 1954 Venice Biennale; in 1951 and 1953 at The Bienal do Museu de Arte Moderna in São Paulo, Brazil; in the 1951 *Abstract Painting and Sculpture in America* exhibit at the Museum of Modern Art in New York; in 1952 in *Considerations on American Painting*; and in 1952, 1955 and 1958 at the Pittsburgh International Exhibition of Contemporary Painting.

He enjoyed an increasing number of one-man exhibitions throughout the world, beginning with his early exhibitions in New York in 1942 and including a one-man show of urban landscapes at the Sydney Janis Gallery in 1953, 1955 and 1956, along with several other exhibitions. In 1965 he had his first retrospective at Smith College in Northampton, Massachusetts. From 1968 to 1969, an itinerant retrospective of his entire output up to that date, which established his international reputation, was held at the Stedelijk Museum in Amsterdam, the Tate Gallery in London, the Museum of Modern Art (MoMA) in New York, the Art Institute of Chicago and the Los Angeles County Museum. Having launched into sculpture in 1969, he showed a collection of his sculptural works for the first time in a one-man exhibition in 1972. Other retrospectives were dedicated to him, including: at the Musée National d'Art Moderne in Paris (1984); Whitney Museum of American Art in New York; the art academies in Berlin; and the Tate Gallery in London (1995). His work has been presented at private galleries world-wide, including, in 1984, in *Peintures et sculptures récentes* (*Recent Paintings and Sculptures*) at the Galerie Daniel Templon in Paris.

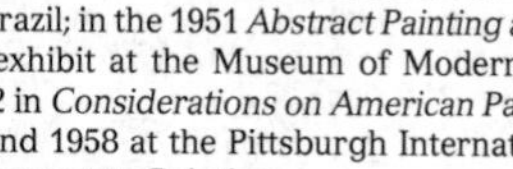

BIBLIOGRAPHY:

Carnduff Ritchie, Andrew, *Abstract Painting and Sculpture in America*, Museum of Modern Art, New York, 1951. De Kooning, Willem, *What abstract art means to me*, New York, 1951. Grossman Janis, Harriet/Blesh, Rudi, *De Kooning*, Grove Press, New York, 1960. Hess, Thomas B./De Kooning, Willem, *Willem de Kooning*, Museum of Modern Art, New York, 1969. O'Doherty, Brian, *American Masters: the voice and the myth. (Chapter entitled: 'De Kooning: notes toward a figure'.)*, Random House, New York, 1973. Rosenberg, Harold, *Willem de Kooning*, Harry N. Abrams Inc., New York, 1974. *Willem de Kooning: The North Atlantic Light*, exhibition catalogue, Stedelijk Museum, Amsterdam, 1983. Gaugh, Harry F., *Willem de Kooning*, Abbeville Press, New York, 1983. *Willem De Kooning*, exhibition catalogue, Musée national d'Art moderne, Paris, 1984 (extensive documentation). Graham, Lanier, *The Prints of Willem de Kooning*, catalogue raisonné, B. Lebon, Paris, 1991 (text in French, German and English). Butler, Cornelia N., et al., *Willem de Kooning - Tracing the Figure*, Princeton University Press, Princeton, 2002.

MUSEUMS AND GALLERIES:

AMSTERDAM (Stedelijk Mus.): *Untitled XVIII* (1977); *North Atlantic Light* (1977); *Untitled V* (1981); *Morning, The Springs* (1983) - BUFFALO (Albright-Knox AG): *Gotham News* (1955, oil on canvas) - CHICAGO (AI): *Excavation* (1950, oil on canvas) - CLEVELAND (MA): *Untitled XIII* (1985) - FORT WORTH (MMA): *Woman* (1965, oil/paper/canvas) - KANSAS CITY (Nelson-Atkins MA): *Woman IV* (1952-1953, oil, varnish and charcoal/canvas) - NEW YORK (Metropolitan Mus. of Art): *Attic* (1949); *Easter Monday* (1956) - NEW YORK (MoMA): *Painting* (1948); *Woman I* (1950-1952); *Woman II* (1952) - NEW YORK (Solomon R. Guggenheim Mus.): *Composition* (1955) - NEW YORK (Whitney Mus. of American Art): *Door to the River* (1960); *Woman Acabonic* (1966) - PARIS (MNAM-CCI): *Woman* (1952, drawing); *Untitled* (1976); *Clam Digger* (1972, sculpture) - PHILADELPHIA (MA): *Seated Woman* (c. 1940) - SEATTLE (AM) - ST LOUIS (GA, Washington University): *Saturday Night* (1956, oil on canvas) - WASHINGTON DC (Hirshhorn Mus. and Sculpture Garden) - WASHINGTON DC (Smithsonian American AM): *The Netherlands, from the United Nation Series* (1944, acrylic/prepared fiberboard); *The Wave* (c. 1942-1944, oil/fiberboard).

AUCTION RECORDS:

NEW YORK, 7 June 1962, *Study for Leaves in Weehawken* USD 1,900. NEW YORK, 30 Oct 1963, *Two Women Standing*, USD 27,000. NEW YORK, 13 Jan 1965, *Merrit Parkway*, USD 40,000. NEW YORK, 25 April 1969, *Abstraction in Pink* (gold and green) USD 8,250. NEW YORK, 14 May 1970, *Two Women Standing*, USD 45,000. NEW YORK, 18 Oct 1973, *Police Gazette*, USD 180,000. MUNICH, 26 Nov 1974, *Composition* (mixed media) DEM 38,000. LONDON, 3 Dec 1974, *Abstraction*, Gns 13,000. NEW YORK, 27 May 1976, *Woman in a Boat* (1964-1965, charcoal/parchment, 56 x 35 1/2 ins / 142 x 90 cm) USD 23,000. NEW YORK, 21 Oct 1976, *Untitled* (1965, oil on paper/canvas, 36 1/2 x 30 ins / 92.5 x 76 cm) USD 20,000. LONDON, 29 June 1977, *Nude* (1969, oil on paper remounted/canvas, 55 1/2 x 42 1/4 ins / 141 x 107.5 cm) GBP 13,500. NEW YORK, 30 March 1978, *Untitled (Figure XII)* (1970, bronze, plaque, 15 x 13 ins / 38 x 33 cm) USD 4,500. NEW YORK, 19 Jan 1979, *Untitled* (1968, pencil and charcoal, 24 x 18 1/4 ins / 61 x 46.5 cm) USD 3,500. NEW YORK, 23 March 1979, *Marshes* (1970, lithograph, 32 x 23 1/2 ins / 81.5 x 59.5 cm) USD 1,400. NEW YORK, 8 Nov 1979, *Tattooed Woman* (1953, pastel and pencil, 15 1/2 x 13 1/2 ins / 39.4 x 34.3 cm) USD 18,000. NEW YORK, 8 Nov 1979, *Untitled* (1978, oil/newspaper remounted/canvas, 22 3/4 x 29 1/4 ins / 57.8 x 74.3 cm) USD 18,000. NEW YORK, 13 May 1981, *Untitled III* (1977, oil on canvas, 80 1/4 x 77 1/4 ins / 204 x 196 cm) USD 220,000. NEW YORK, 5 May 1982, *Floating Figure* (1972, dark-brown patinated bronze, h. 22 3/4 ins / 57.8 cm) USD 4,500. NEW YORK, 9 Nov 1983, *Still-life* (c. 1945, coloured chalks and charcoal/paper, 13 3/4 x 16 3/4 ins / 35 x 42.5 cm) USD 140,000. NEW YORK, 9 Nov 1983, *Untitled* (1959, gouache and sand/paper/canvas, 39 1/4 x 55 1/2 ins / 99.6 x 141 cm) USD 26,000. NEW YORK, 1 Nov 1984, *Two Women* (1953, oil on paper remounted/canvas, 22 x 28 1/4 ins / 55.7 x 72 cm) USD 1,800,000. NEW YORK, 2 May 1985, *Two Women* (c. 1949, card remounted on board, 15 x 20 ins / 38.1 x 50.8 cm) USD 625,000. NEW YORK, 2 May 1985, *Ruth's Zowie* (1957, oil on canvas, 80 ins / 203 cm, 3 1/4 x 70 ins/8 x 178 cm) USD 1,400,000. NEW YORK, 10 Nov 1986, *Head III* (1973, bronze, total height 19 1/2 ins / 49.6 cm) USD 33,000. NEW YORK, 12 Nov 1986, *Woman (Study for Woman I)* (c. 1951-1952, graphite, coloured chalks and pencil/paper, 13 3/4 x 10 3/4 ins / 35 x 27.3 cm) USD 580,000. NEW YORK, 4 May 1987, *Pink Lady* (c. 1944, charcoal and oil on panel, 48 1/4 x 35 1/4 ins / 122.5 x 89.5 cm) USD 3,300,000. NEW YORK, 3 May 1988, *Head III* (bronze, h. 19 1/2 ins / 49.6 cm) USD 99,000; *Woman* (oil and collage/paper, 16 x 12 3/4 ins / 40.5 x 32.4 cm) USD 286,000; *Woman* (oil on paper/canvas, 23 3/4 x 18 3/4 ins / 60.5 x 47.5 cm) USD 132,000. NEW YORK, 8 Oct 1988, *Woman* (pencil/paper, 20 1/4 x 14 ins / 51.4 x 35.5 cm) USD 63,250. NEW YORK, 9 Nov 1988, *Two Women IV* (1952, pencil, coloured chalks, charcoal and gouache/paper, 15 1/2 x 17 3/4 ins / 39.6 x 45.4 cm) USD 1,870,000. NEW YORK, 10 Nov 1988, *Untitled* (1976, oil on paper, newspaper/synthetic resin, 29 1/4 x 23 ins / 74.2 x 58.2 cm) USD 66,000. NEW YORK, 14 Feb 1989, *Two Women* (1959, ink/paper, 23 1/2 x 18 3/4 ins / 59.5 x 47.5 cm) USD 60,500. NEW YORK, 2 May 1989, *Women Collecting Shells (Study)* (oil on paper/synthetic resin, 23 x 28 1/2 ins / 58.3 x 72.3 cm) USD 715,000. NEW YORK, 8 Nov 1989, *Interchange* (1955, oil on canvas, 79 x 69 ins / 200.7 x 175.3 cm) USD 20,680,000. PARIS, 18 Feb 1990, *Study for the Pink Lady* (c. 1945, pencil and pastel, 14 x 16 3/4 ins / 35.3 x 42.6 cm) FRF 800,000. NEW YORK, 7 Nov 1990, *July* (1956, oil on canvas, 68 3/4 x 79 1/4 ins / 174.7 x 201 cm) USD 8,800,000. NEW YORK, 1 May 1991, *Figure with Crossed Legs* (1972, bronze, 24 1/2 x 17 3/4 x 14 ins / 62.2 x 45.1 x 35.5 cm) USD 308,000. STOCKHOLM, 30 May 1991, *Composition* (wash, 22 x 9 ins / 56 x 22 cm) SEK 100,000. NEW YORK, 13 Nov 1991, *Woman* (oil on paper/canvas, 31 x 22 ins / 78.7 x 55.8 cm) USD 3,410,000. NEW YORK, 18 Nov 1992, *Flowers, Mary's Table* (1971, oil on canvas, 80 x 70 ins / 203.2 x 177.8 cm) USD 907,500. LONDON, 3 Dec 1992, *Woman* (1974, oil on paper/canvas, 24 x 19 ins / 61 x 48.3 cm) GBP 25,300. LONDON, 3 May 1993, *Untitled (Black and White Abstraction)* (varnish/double-sided paper, 22 x 30 ins / 55.9 x 76.2 cm) USD 965,000. NEW YORK, 9 Nov 1993, *Woman* (pencil and coloured chalks/paper, 16 1/4 x 11 1/4 ins / 41.2 x 28.5 cm) USD 222,500. LONDON, 2 Dec 1993, *Little Figure* (Indian ink/paper, 17 3/4 x 28 1/4 ins / 45 x 72 cm) GBP 36,700. LOKEREN, 4 Dec 1993, *Tall and Thin* (1970, ink, 8 1/2 x 11 ins / 21.5 x 28 cm) BEF 190,000. PARIS, 10 March 1994, *Woman in Watermill Landscape* (1966, oil on paper, mounted on card, 22 1/2 x 29 1/2 ins / 57 x 75 cm) FRF 460,000. NEW YORK, 3 May 1994, *Untitled XIV* (1982, oil on canvas, 80 x 70 ins / 203.2 x 177.8 cm) USD 882,500. NEW YORK, 4 May 1994, *Figure with Crossed Legs* (1972, bronze, 24 x 18 x 15 ins / 61 x 45.7 x 38.1 cm) USD 365,500. NEW YORK, 9 Nov 1996, *Reflections, to Kermit for our Trip to Japan* (1971, lithograph, 50 1/2 x 34 3/4 ins / 128.5 x 88.5 cm) USD 6,325. NEW YORK, 19 Nov 1996, *Untitled* (c. 1955, pencil and coloured chalks/paper, 16 3/4 x 13 3/4 ins / 42.6 x 34.9 cm) USD 63,000. NEW YORK, 20 Nov 1996, *Woman* (1949, varnish, charcoal and oil on canvas, 60 1/4 x 48 ins / 153.3 x 121.9 cm) USD 15,622,500. NEW YORK, 20 Nov 1996, *Untitled* (1970, oil on paper, newspaper/paper/canvas, 22 1/2 x 29 1/2 ins / 57.2 x 74.9 cm) USD 46,000. PARIS, 29 Nov 1996, *Male Figure* (1964, oil on paper remounted on board, 29 1/2 x 23 1/2 ins / 75 x 60 cm) FRF 620,000.

NEW YORK, 7 May 1997, *Untitled* (c. 1975-1980, pencil/paper, 18 x 24 ins / 45.7 x 61 cm) USD 11,500. NEW YORK, 18-19 Nov 1997, *Two Women Standing* (charcoal, chalk and varnish/card, 30 x 27 ins / 76.2 x 68.6 cm) USD 4,182,500. NEW YORK, 19 Nov 1997, *Untitled XIII* (1977, oil on canvas, 54 1/4 x 60 ins / 137.5 x 152.4 cm) USD 1,597,500. NEW YORK, 19 Nov 1998, *Woman* (1959, brush and Indian ink, 23 x 19 ins / 59 x 47 cm) USD 210,000. NEW YORK, 14 May 1999, *Woman* (1967-1968, paper/canvas, 23 x 19 ins / 58 x 47 cm) USD 260,000. NEW YORK, 15 Nov 2000, *Woman, Blue Eyes* (oil, enamel, charcoal/paper/canvas, 28 x 20 ins / 71 x 51 cm) USD 4,100,000. NEW YORK, 15 Nov 2000, *Monumental Woman* (charcoal, 29 x 22 ins / 73 x 57 cm) USD 2,400,000. NEW YORK, 16 May 2001, *Untitled III* (oil on canvas, 77 x 88 ins / 196 x 223 cm) USD 1,150,000. NEW YORK, 13 Nov 2001, *Woman* (1951, charcoal and pastel, 22 x 17 ins / 55 x 42 cm) USD 1,900,000. NEW YORK, 12 Nov 2002, *Orestes* (1947, enamel, paper and collage/board, 24 x 36 ins / 61 x 92 cm) USD 12,000,000. NEW YORK, 12 Nov 2002, *Woman* (1952, pastel and graphite, 20 x 14 ins / 52 x 36 cm) USD 3,400,000. NEW YORK, 12 Nov 2003, *Spike's Folly I* (1959, oil on canvas, 79 x 69 ins / 200 x 174 cm) USD 10,000,000. NEW YORK, 11 Nov 2003, *Untitled XVII* (1984, oil on canvas, 80 x 70 ins / 203 x 178 cm) USD 3,300,000. NEW YORK, 11 May 2004, *Standing Figure* (1969-1984, brown-patinated bronze, 148 x 252 x 80 ins / 376 x 641 x 203 cm) USD 3,100,000. NEW YORK, 11 May 2004, *Porch in a Landscape* (1977, oil on canvas, 59 x 55 ins / 151 x 140 cm) USD 2,300,000.

KOONS, Jeff

American, 20th - 21st century.
Born 1955, in York (Pennsylvania).
Assemblage and installation artist, photographer, mixed media. Multimedia.
Neo-Conceptual Art (Neo-Geo), Appropriation Art, Neo-Pop Art.

Jeff Koons trained for three years at the Maryland Institute College of Art in Baltimore, and subsequently at the Art Institute of Chicago. He lives and works in New York, Germany and Italy. Before embarking on an artistic career he worked on Wall Street as a commodities broker, and his artwork and his conception of the role of the artist remain suffused with ideas and concepts drawn from this earlier experience: the artist survives by supplying commodities to a specific market, governed by the laws of consumerism, speculation and marketing.

Jeff Koons' output comprises a succession of series of works on various themes, essentially rooted in the use of 'ready-mades' and drawing on the Pop Art tradition. Koons appropriates manufactured objects devoid of their everyday context; his later compositions incorporate ready-mades together with the human body, disassembled and reconstituted, or reproduced using craft techniques. In the Duchampian tradition, selected everyday commercial products are thus accorded the status of artworks, perfectly crafted with extraordinary attention to detail. His earliest pieces (1981-1987) are stainless steel reproductions of banal ornaments, reminiscent of 19th-century genre statuettes - nobles and shepherdesses, dwarves, rabbits. Other works featured vacuum cleaners, floor polishers and other such domestic appliances encased in plexiglass. *Louis XIV* (1986) is a stainless-steel cast of a mass-produced copy of an original bust of Louis XIV. The *Boy with a Sack* (1987), measuring 5 feet 10 in (1.80 metres) in height, is a stainless-steel cast of a mass-produced figurine from the late 19th century. *Bear and Policeman* (1988) is a polychromed wooden sculpture, over 6 feet 7in (2 metres) tall, representing a bear dressed like a child's teddy, its front paws grasping a policeman's shoulders, in a friendly gesture. Koons' work is rooted in craftsmanship and popular imagery; childhood memories are often evoked, using 'recomposed' objects and toys (as in the monumental flower-sculpture *Split-Rocker*, exhibited in 2000 in the Benedict XII cloister of the Palais des Papes in Avignon). For his 1991 exhibition *Made in Heaven* at the Sonnabend Gallery, New York, Koons presented a series of computer-enhanced photographic paintings measuring 6 feet 7 in (2 metres) by 9 feet 8 in (3 metres), together with Murano glass sculptures and one sculpture in painted plaster, showing the artist and his then wife Illona Staller (better known as the Italian porn star-turned politician La Cicciolina), in a variety of sexual encounters, often highly explicit and in graphic anatomical detail. Inevitably, the highly-priced works (a mixture of Koons' trademark kitsch and direct provocation) drew large crowds. A later series of small, beribboned dogs in glass and other materials marked a return to 'pure kitsch', and was inspired by Staller's beloved pet Yorkshire terriers. Koons' highly controversial oeuvre challenges the workings of the commercial art market, and explores the boundaries of popular and elitist taste.

His work has featured in numerous exhibitions since 1980. His solo shows include: *The New* at the New Museum of Contemporary Art, New York in 1980; *Jeff Koons. A Millennium Celebration* at the Deste Foundation, Athens in 2000, *Jeff Koons: Easyfun-Ethereal*, Solomon R. Guggenheim Museum, New York in 2002-2003, and *Jeff Koons: Highlights of 25 Years* at C&M Arts, New York in 2004. His participation in group exhibitions include: *On the Edge: Contemporary Art from the Werner and Elaine Dannheisser Collection* at the Museum of Modern Art, New York in 1997-1998, *The Passions* at the James Cohen Gallery, New York in 2001-2002 and *Animals & Us: The Animal in Contemporary Art* at the Galerie St Etienne, New York in 2004.

BIBLIOGRAPHY:

Jeff Koons, exhibition catalogue, Museum of Modern Art (San Francisco), San Francisco, 1992. Rosenblum, *The Jeff Koons Handbook*, Thames and Hudson, London, 1992. Kellein, Thomas, *Jeff Koons: Pictures 1980-2002*, Distributed Art Publishers, New York, 2002.

MUSEUMS AND GALLERIES:

AMSTERDAM (Stedelijk Mus.) - BORDEAUX (FRAC Aquitaine): New Hoover Convertibles Green, Green, Red... (1981-1987) - BOSTON (MFA): *Balloon Dog* (1991-2004, stainless steel with transparent colour coating) - LONDON (Tate Collection): *Three Ball Total Equilibrium Tank (Two Dr J Silver Series, Spalding NBA Tip-Off)* (1985, mixed media); *Vest with Aqualung* (1985, bronze) - NEW YORK (Solomon R. Guggenheim Mus.): *Blue Poles* (2000, oil on canvas); *Grotto* (2000, oil on canvas); *Hair with Cheese* (2000, oil on canvas); *Mountains* (2000, oil on canvas); *Niagara* (2000, oil on canvas).

AUCTION RECORDS:

NEW YORK, 3 May 1988, *Bob Hope* (1979, stainless steel, 17 x 5 1/2 x 5 1/2 ins / 43 x 14 x 14 cm) USD 27,500. NEW YORK, 30 April 1991, *New Hoover Deluxe Shampoo Polishers, New Hoover Quik-Broom, New Shelton Wet/Dry Tripledeckers* (99 x 53 1/2 x 28 ins / 251.5 x 135.8 x 71.2 cm) USD 137,500. NEW YORK, 13 Nov 1991, *The Empire State of Scotch Dewars* (1986, thick ink/canvas, 44 1/2 x 58 3/4 ins / 113 x 149.2 cm) USD 44,000. NEW YORK, 5 May 1992, *Stacked* (1988, painted wood, 55 x 60 x 25 1/2 ins / 139.6 x 152.4 x 64.7 cm) USD 176,000. NEW YORK, 7 May 1992, *Two Ball 50/50 Tank (spalding Dr J. Silver series, spalding Dr J.241)* (glass and steel support with two basketballs in distilled water, 62 3/4 x 36 3/4 x 13 1/4 ins / 159.4 x 93.4 x 33.6 cm) USD 71,500. NEW YORK, 17 Nov 1992, *Three Ball Total Equilibrium Tank* (glass, iron, water and three basketballs, 60 1/2 x 48 3/4 x 13 1/4 ins / 153.7 x 123.8 x 33.7 cm) USD 148,500. NEW YORK, 19 Nov 1992, *New Shop-vac Wet-dry* (vacuum cleaner and fluorescent tubes in a Plexiglas case, 28 x 22 x 22 ins / 71 x 56 x 56 cm) USD 46,200. NEW YORK, 5 May 1993, *Basketball* (1985, bronze, diam. 9 ins / 22.8 cm) USD 48,300. NEW YORK, 10 Nov 1993, *New Double Shelton Wet Dry* (1980, two vacuum cleaners with fluorescent lighting in a Plexiglas case, 43 x 54 x 28 ins / 109.2 x 137.2 x 71.1 cm) USD 112,500. NEW YORK, 2 Nov 1994, *Louis*

XIV (1986, stainless steel, 48 x 28 x 16 ins / 122 x 71.2 x 40.7 cm) USD 233,500. NEW YORK, 21 Nov 1996, *Speaker* (1979-1980, loud-speaker, two fluorescent lamps and Plexiglas, 54 x 15 1/4 x 17 3/4 ins / 137.2 x 38.7 x 45 cm) USD 46,000. LONDON, 5 Dec 1996, *Wild Boy with Puppy* (1988, painted porcelain, 38 x 39 1/2 x 23 1/2 ins / 96.5 x 100.3 x 59.7 cm) GBP 62,000. NEW YORK, 6-7 May 1997, *Stacked* (1988, polychrome wood, 61 x 53 x 31 ins / 154.9 x 134.6 x 78.7 cm) USD 250,000. NEW YORK, 19 Nov 1997, *Snakes* (1988, painted porcelain, large snake: 23 1/2 x 35 x 10 1/4 ins / 59.7 x 88.9 x 26 cm, small snake: 16 1/2 x 20 x 6 ins/41.9 x 50.8 x 15.2 cm) USD 112,500. NEW YORK, 16 Nov 1999, *Winter Bears* (polychrome wood, two, 48 x 44x15 ins / 122 x 112x39 cm) USD 440,000. NEW YORK, 16 Nov 1999, *Pink Panther* (porcelain, 41 x 20x19 ins / 104 x 52x48 cm) USD 1,650,000. NEW YORK, 17 May 2000, *Wall Relief with Bird* (polychromed wood, 72 x 50x27 ins / 183 x 127x69 cm) USD 550,000. NEW YORK, 16 Nov 2000, *Travel Bar* (stainless steel, 14 x 20x12 ins / 36 x 51x30 cm) USD 420,000. NEW YORK, 15 May 2001, *Michael Jackson and Bubbles* (1988, porcelain-ceramic blend, 42 x 70x33 ins / 107 x 179x83 cm) USD 5,100,000. NEW YORK, 17 May 2001, *Woman in Tub* (1988, porcelain, 24 x 36x27 ins / 62 x 91x69 cm) USD 2,600,000. NEW YORK, 13 May 2002, *Aqualung* (1985, bronze, 27 x 17x17 ins / 69 x 44x44 cm) USD 1,600,000. NEW YORK, 11 Nov 2002, *Self-portrait* (1991, marble, 37 x 20x15 ins / 95 x 52x37 cm) USD 1,850,000. NEW YORK, 11 Nov 2003, *Vase of Flowers* (1988, mirror, 72 x 53x1 ins / 184 x 135x2 cm) USD 750,000. NEW YORK, 11 Nov 2003, *Lifeboat* (1985, bronze, 12 x 80x60 ins / 30 x 203x152 cm) USD 1,800,000. NEW YORK, 11 May 2004, *St Benedict* (2000, oil on canvas, 110 x 80 ins / 279 x 204 cm) USD 1,500,000. NEW YORK, 11 May 2004, *Jim Beam JB Turner Train* (1986, stainless steel, 11 x 114x6 ins / 28 x 289x16 cm) USD 4,900,000.

KOOP, Andreas Ludvig
Danish, 19th century.
Born 12 January 1792, in Copenhagen; died 13 December 1849, in Rome.
Painter.

Andreas Koop executed paintings of historical, Biblical and mythological subjects.

MUSEUMS AND GALLERIES:
COPENHAGEN (Thorvaldsens Mus.): *Portrait of Thorvaldsen* (after Bega).

KOOP, Wanda
Canadian, 20th - 21st century.
Born 1951, in Vancouver.
Painter, video artist.

Wanda Koop is one of Canada's foremost contemporary artists. She graduated from the University of Manitoba School of Art in 1973. Her often monumental works are characterised by her apparently neutral, objective technique, depicting isolated figures of people, birds, submarines, factories, cities and landscapes. These are often subsequently gathered together in environments through which the viewer is free to move. Long recognised for her paintings and drawings, Koop is also increasingly noted for her poetic video creations.

BIBLIOGRAPHY:
Koop, Wanda, *Wanda Koop: Nine Signs*, Glenbow-Alberta Institute, Calgary, 1983. Koop, Wanda, *Airplanes and the Wall*, Winnipeg Art Gallery, Winnipeg, 1986.

KOOPMAN, Augustus B.
American, 19th - 20th century.
Born 2 January 1869, in Charlotte; died 31 January 1914, in Étaples, France.
Painter, engraver, decorative designer. Scenes with figures, landscapes.

Augustus Koopman started his art studies in Philadelphia and completed them in Paris, under William Bouguereau and Tony Robert-Fleury. He twice won the Paris American Art Association prize, along with other awards (Wanamaker in 1898, Clark in 1899). He won two medals at the Paris Exposition universelle in 1900, and one in Buffalo the following year.

AUCTION RECORDS:
NEW YORK, 9 Jan 1902, *Atlantic City*, USD 25. PARIS, 12 May 1919, *Fishermen on the Bank*, FRF 240. LOS ANGELES, 6 June 1978, *Figures on the Beach* (oil on canvas, 34 1/2 x 28 ins / 87.6 x 71.2 cm) USD 1,300.

KOOPMAN, John R.
American, 20th century.
Born 5 June 1881, in Falmouth (Michigan); died 1949.
Painter, watercolourist.

John Koopman studied under William Chase and of Kenneth Hayes Miller. He was a member of the Salmagundi Club.

KOOPMAN, Louis
Dutch, 19th century.
Active in Rotterdam.
Painter. Portraits.

Louis Koopman is known to have painted quite a large number of portraits that were subsequently engraved.

KOOPMAN, W. N.
Dutch, 18th century.
Active in Utrecht during the second half of the 18th century.
Draughtsman, sculptor.

KOOPMANN, Johann Heinrich Carl
German, 19th century.
Born 15 March 1797, in Altona; died 5 April 1894, in Heidelberg.
Painter. History painting, portraits.

Koopmann was a student of Gerdt Hardorff. He studied in Hamburg, Dresden and Rome. He returned to his home town in 1833 and earned a reputation as a professor in Karlsruhe.

KOOREMAN, Dietrich Leonidas
Dutch, 19th century.
Born 9 March 1859, in Leiden.
Painter.

Kooreman was the pupil of Verlat, Portaels and Gérome. He worked in Cologne and Hamburg.

KOORNSTRA, Metten
Dutch, 20th century.
Born 1912; died 1978.
Painter, collage artist. Genre scenes, landscapes, flowers, still-lifes.

AUCTION RECORDS:
AMSTERDAM, 10 April 1989, *Street Girl and Priest* (1967, oil on panel and collage, 11 1/2 x 15 1/4 ins / 29 x 39 cm) NLG 3,680. AMSTERDAM, 24 May 1989, *Still-life of Carnations and Mimosa in Vase* (oil on card, 11 3/4 x 15 3/4 ins / 30 x 40 cm) NLG 1,265. AMSTERDAM, 12 Dec 1990, *Still-life Landscape* (1972, oil on card, 15 1/4 x 11 1/2 ins / 39 x 29 cm) NLG 3,220. AMSTERDAM, 10 Dec 1992, *Beach* (1874, oil on card, 11 x 13 1/2 ins / 27 x 34 cm) NLG 6,325. AMSTERDAM, 6 Dec 1995, *Still-life with Pear* (1970, oil on card, 11 1/2 x 13 3/4 ins / 29 x 35 cm) NLG 3,450. AMSTERDAM, 5 June 1996, *Village on the Banks of the Lys* (1965, oil on card, 11 1/2 x 15 ins / 29 x 38 cm) NLG 6,325. AMSTERDAM, 7 June 2000, *Two Figures on an Empty Road* (1965, oil on board, 12 x 16 ins / 30 x 40 cm) NLG 7,000. AMSTERDAM, 30 Jan 2001, *Still-life with Flowers in a Vase, Cherries and a Pear* (1971, oil on board, 11 x 13 ins / 29 x 32 cm) NLG 5,000. AMSTERDAM, 30 Jan 2001, *14th July* (1964, oil on board, 12 x 16 ins / 30 x 41 cm) NLG 5,500. AMSTERDAM, 3 June 2003, *Still-life with Drawing and Flowers in a Vase* (1971, oil on board, 11 x 15 ins / 29 x 39 cm) EUR 1,700.

Printed and bound in Italy
by G. Canale & C. S.p.A. - Borgaro T. se (Torino)
February 2006